NORTHERN EUROPEAN RUSSIA
pp 124-125
SOUTHERN EUROPEAN RUSSIA
pp 126-127
E BALTIC
TATES &
ELARUS
p 118-119
ROMANIA, MOLDOVA & UKRAINE
pp 116-117
BULGARIA & GREECE
pp 114-115

ASIA pp 148-163
AFGHANISTAN & PAKISTAN
pp148-149
EASTERN CHINA
pp160-161
SOUTHERN INDIA & SRI LANKA
pp154-155
pp152-153

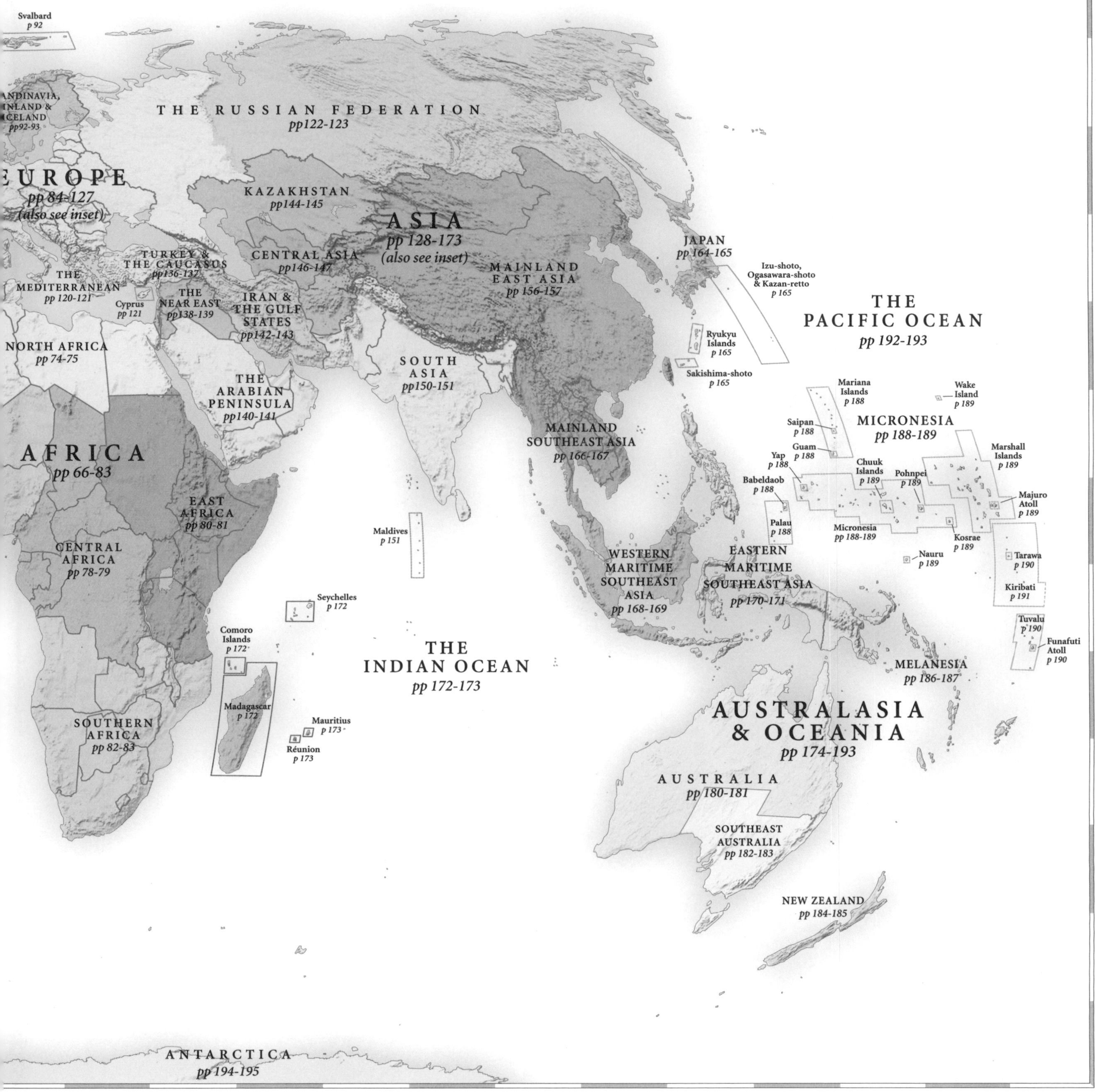
Svalbard
p 92
THE RUSSIAN FEDERATION
pp122-123
KAZAKHSTAN
pp144-145
ASIA
pp 128-173
(also see inset)
CENTRAL ASIA
pp146-147
MAINLAND EAST ASIA
pp 156-157
JAPAN
pp 164-165
Izu-shoto, Ogasawara-shoto & Kazan-retto
p 165
Ryukyu Islands
p 165
Sakishima-shoto
p 165
THE PACIFIC OCEAN
pp 192-193
TURKEY & THE CAUCASUS
pp136-137
THE MEDITERRANEAN
pp 120-121
Cyprus
pp 121
THE NEAR EAST
pp138-139
IRAN & THE GULF STATES
pp142-143
NORTH AFRICA
pp 74-75
THE ARABIAN PENINSULA
pp140-141
SOUTH ASIA
pp150-151
MAINLAND SOUTHEAST ASIA
pp 166-167
AFRICA
pp 66-83
EAST AFRICA
pp 80-81
CENTRAL AFRICA
pp 78-79
Maldives
p 151
Mariana Islands
p 188
Wake Island
p 189
Saipan
p 188
Guam
p 188
MICRONESIA
pp 188-189
Yap
p 188
Marshall Islands
p 189
Chuuk Islands
p 189
Pohnpei
p 189
Babeldaob
p 188
Majuro Atoll
p 189
Palau
p 188
Micronesia
pp 188-189
Kosrae
p 189
Nauru
p 189
Tarawa
p 190
Kiribati
p 191
WESTERN MARITIME SOUTHEAST ASIA
pp 168-169
EASTERN MARITIME SOUTHEAST ASIA
pp 170-171
Seychelles
p 172
Comoro Islands
p 172
THE INDIAN OCEAN
pp 172-173
Tuvalu
p 190
Funafuti Atoll
p 190
MELANESIA
pp 186-187
Madagascar
p 172
Mauritius
p 173
Réunion
p 173
SOUTHERN AFRICA
pp 82-83
AUSTRALASIA & OCEANIA
pp 174-193
AUSTRALIA
pp 180-181
SOUTHEAST AUSTRALIA
pp 182-183
NEW ZEALAND
pp 184-185
ANTARCTICA
pp 194-195

DORLING KINDERSLEY

CONCISE ATLAS *of the* WORLD

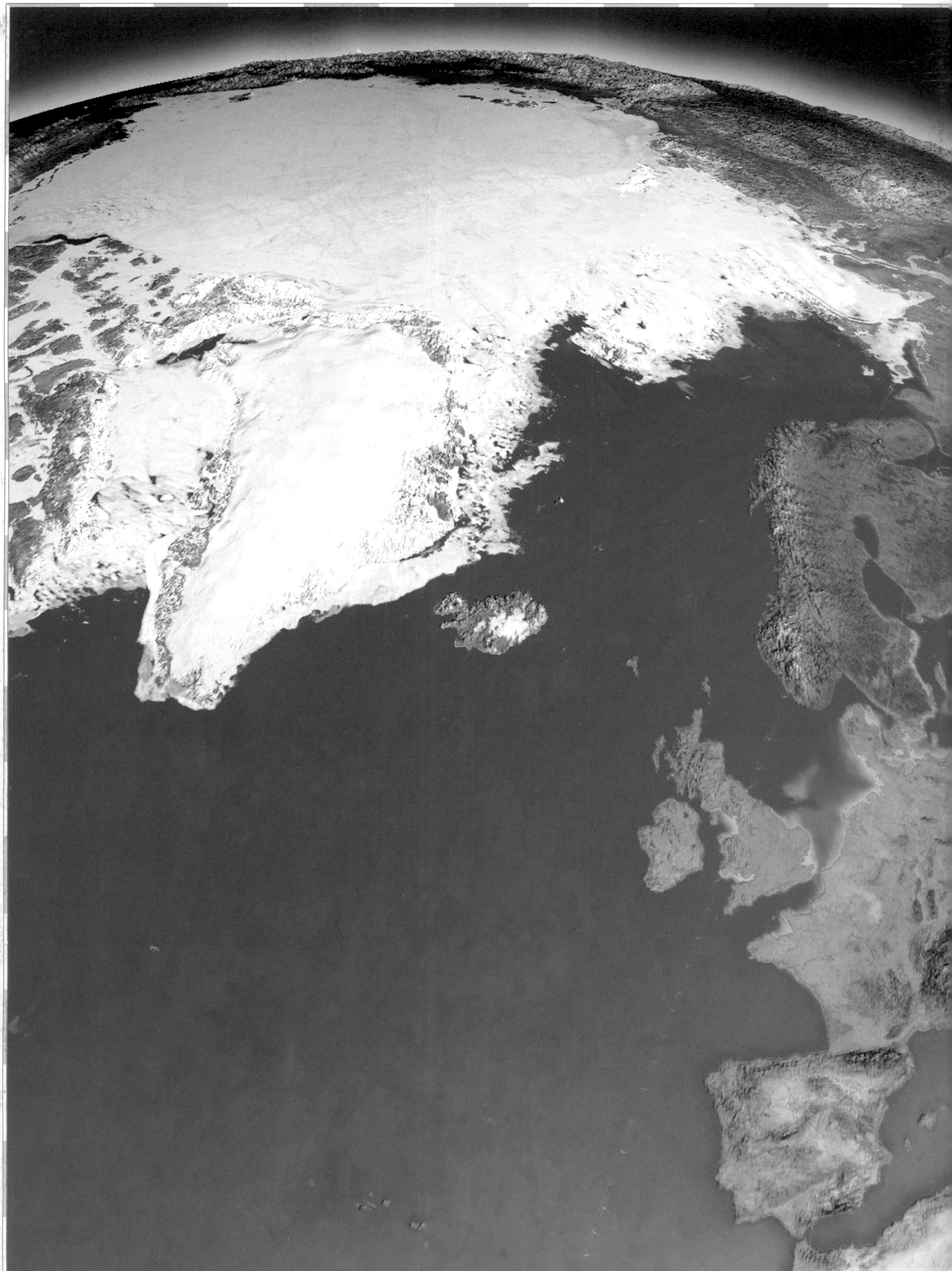

DORLING KINDERSLEY

CONCISE ATLAS *of the* WORLD

A Dorling Kindersley Book

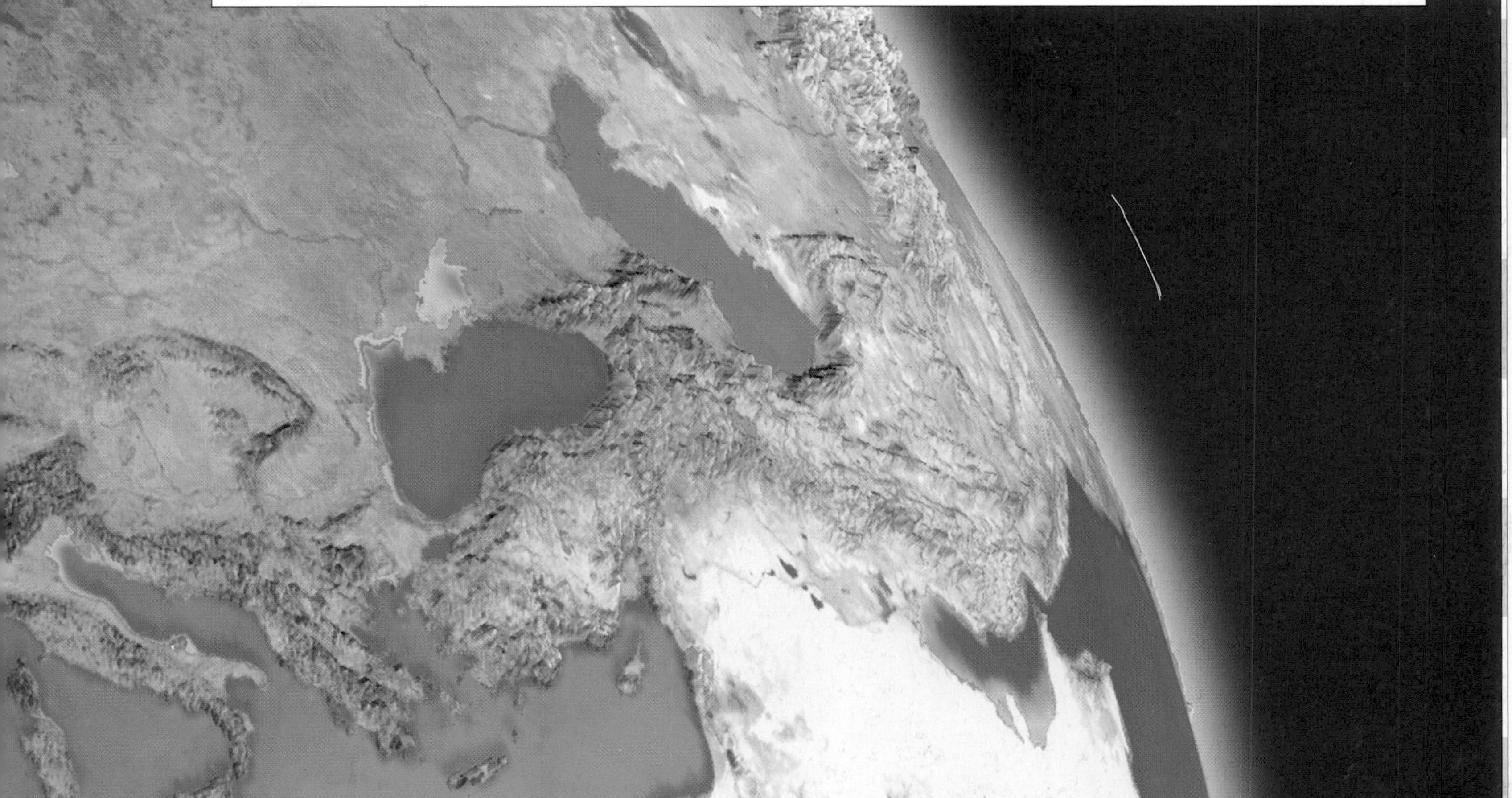

LONDON, NEW YORK, MUNICH, MELBOURNE, DELHI

GENERAL GEOGRAPHICAL CONSULTANTS

PHYSICAL GEOGRAPHY • Denys Brunsden, Emeritus Professor, Department of Geography, King's College, London

HUMAN GEOGRAPHY • Professor J Malcolm Wagstaff, Department of Geography, University of Southampton

PLACE NAMES • Caroline Burgess, Permanent Committee on Geographical Names, London

BOUNDARIES • International Boundaries Research Unit, Mountjoy Research Centre, University of Durham

DIGITAL MAPPING CONSULTANTS

DK Cartopia developed by George Galfalvi and XMap Ltd, London

Professor Jan-Peter Muller, Department of Photogrammetry and Surveying, University College, London

Cover globes, planets and information on the Solar System provided by Philip Eales and Kevin Tildsley, Planetary Visions Ltd, London

REGIONAL CONSULTANTS

NORTH AMERICA • Dr David Green, Department of Geography, King's College, London
Jim Walsh, Head of Reference, Wessell Library, Tufts University, Medford, Massachussetts

SOUTH AMERICA • Dr David Preston, School of Geography, University of Leeds

EUROPE • Dr Edward M Yates, formerly of the Department of Geography, King's College, London

AFRICA • Dr Philip Amis, Development Administration Group, University of Birmingham
Dr Ieuan L Griffiths, Department of Geography, University of Sussex
Dr Tony Binns, Department of Geography, University of Sussex

CENTRAL ASIA • Dr David Turnock, Department of Geography, University of Leicester

SOUTH AND EAST ASIA • Dr Jonathan Rigg, Department of Geography, University of Durham

AUSTRALASIA AND OCEANIA • Dr Robert Allison, Department of Geography, University of Durham

ACKNOWLEDGMENTS

Digital terrain data created by Eros Data Center, Sioux Falls, South Dakota, USA. Processed by GVS Images Inc, California, USA and Planetary Visions Ltd, London, UK • Cambridge International Reference on Current Affairs (CIRCA), Cambridge, UK • Digitization by Robertson Research International, Swanley, UK • Peter Clark

EDITOR-IN-CHIEF
Andrew Heritage

MANAGING EDITOR
Lisa Thomas

SENIOR MANAGING ART EDITOR
Philip Lord

SENIOR CARTOGRAPHIC MANAGER
David Roberts

MANAGING CARTOGRAPHER
Roger Bullen

SENIOR CARTOGRAPHIC EDITOR
Simon Mumford

DATABASE MANAGER
Simon Lewis

CARTOGRAPHERS
Pamela Alford • James Anderson • Caroline Bowie • Dale Buckton • Tony Chambers • Jan Clark • Tom Coulson • Bob Croser • Martin Darlison • Claire Ellam • Sally Gable • Jeremy Hepworth • Geraldine Horner • Chris Jackson • Christine Johnston • Julia Lunn • Michael Martin • James Mills-Hicks • John Plumer • Rob Stokes • John Scott • Ann Stephenson • Julie Turner • Iorwerth Watkins • Sarah Vaughan •Jane Voss • Scott Wallace • Bryony Webb • Alan Whitaker • Peter Winfield

EDITORS
Debra Clapson • Thomas Heath • Wim Jenkins • Jane Oliver
Siobhān Ryan • Elizabeth Wyse

EDITORIAL RESEARCH
Helen Dangerfield • Andrew Rebeiro-Hargrave

ADDITIONAL EDITORIAL ASSISTANCE
Margaret Hynes • Robert Damon • Ailsa Heritage • Constance Novis • Jayne Parsons • Chris Whitwell

EDITORIAL DIRECTION • Louise Cavanagh

DESIGNERS
Scott David • Carol Ann Davis • David Douglas
Rhonda Fisher • Karen Gregory • Nicola Liddiard • Paul Williams

ILLUSTRATIONS
Ciárán Hughes • Advanced Illustration, Congleton, UK

PICTURE RESEARCH
Melissa Albany • James Clarke • Anna Lord • Christine Rista • Sarah Moule • Louise Thomas

ART DIRECTION • Chez Picthall

SYSTEMS COORDINATOR Phil Rowles

PRODUCTION Luca Frassinetti

DIGITAL MAPS CREATED IN DK CARTOPIA BY
Tom Coulson • Thomas Robertshaw
Philip Rowles • Rob Stokes

PLACENAMES DATABASE TEAM
Natalie Clarkson • Ruth Duxbury • Caroline Falce • John Featherstone • Dan Gardiner
Ciárán Hynes • Margaret Hynes • Helen Rudkin • Margaret Stevenson • Annie Wilson

Published in the United States by
Dorling Kindersley Publishing Inc.
375 Hudson Street, New York, New York 10014

First American Edition, 2001
Second Edition 2003, Reprinted with revisions 2004, Third Edition 2005
4 6 8 10 9 7 5

A CIP catalog record for this book is available from the Library of Congress/ ISBN: 0-7566-0966-6

Printed and bound by Star Standard in Singapore.

Introduction

For many, the outstanding legacy of the twentieth century was the way in which the Earth shrank. As we enter the third millennium, it is increasingly important for us to have a clear vision of the World in which we live. The human population has increased fourfold since 1900. The last scraps of *terra incognita* – the polar regions and ocean depths – have been penetrated and mapped. New regions have been colonized, and previously hostile realms claimed for habitation. The advent of aviation technology and mass tourism allows many of us to travel further, faster, and more frequently than ever before. In doing so we are given a bird's-eye view of the Earth's surface denied to our forebears.

At the same time, the amount of information about our World has grown enormously. Telecommunications can span the greatest distances in fractions of a second: our multimedia environment hurls uninterrupted streams of data at us, on the printed page, through the airwaves, and across our television and computer screens; events from all corners of the globe reach us instantaneously, and are witnessed as they unfold. Our sense of stability and certainty has been eroded; instead, we are aware that the World is in a constant state of flux and change. Natural disasters, manmade cataclysms, and conflicts between nations remind us daily of the enormity and fragility of our domain.The events of September 11, 2001 threw into a very stark relief the levels of ignorance and inaccessibility that exist when trying to "know" or "understand" our planet and its many cultures.

The crisis in our current "global" culture has made the need greater than ever before for everyone to possess an atlas. This atlas has been conceived to meet this need. At its core, like all atlases, it seeks to define where places are, to describe their main characteristics, and to locate them in relation to other places. Every attempt has been made to make the information on the maps as clear and accessible as possible. In addition, each page of the atlas provides a wealth of further information, bringing the maps to life. Using photographs, diagrams, "at-a-glance" thematic maps, introductory texts and captions, the atlas builds up a detailed portrait of those features – cultural, political, economics and geomorphological – which make each region unique, and which are also the main agents of change.

This third edition of the *DK Concise Atlas* incorporates thousands of revisions and updates affecting every map and every page, and reflects many of the geopolitical developments which continue to alter the shape of our World. The *DK Concise Atlas* has been created to bring all these benefits to a new audience, in a handy format and at an affordable price.

Andrew Heritage
Editor-in-Chief

Contents

Introduction v

Contents .... vi–vii

How to use this Atlas .... viii–ix

THE WORLD TODAY

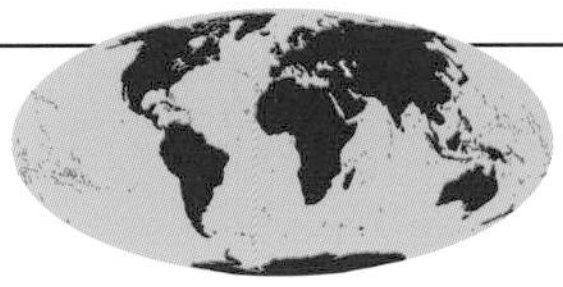

The Solar System .... x–xi

The Physical World .... xii–xiii

Structure of the Earth ...... xiv–xv

Shaping the Landscape ...... xvi–xvii

The World's Oceans .... xviii–xix

The Global Climate .... xx–xxi

Life on Earth .... xxii–xxiii

Population and Settlement .... xxiv–xxv

The Economic System ...... xxvi–xxvii

The Political World ...... xxviii–xxix

States and Boundaries ...... xxx–xxxi

International Disputes xxxii

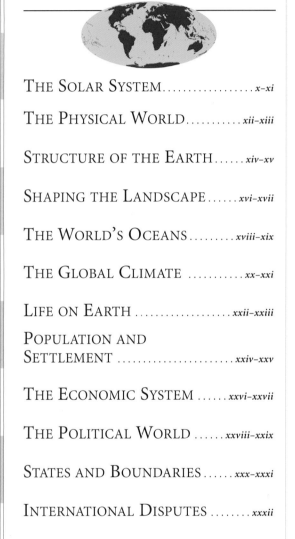

ATLAS OF THE WORLD

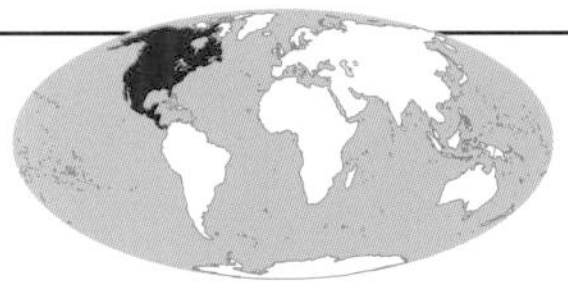

North America

NORTH AMERICA 1

PHYSICAL NORTH AMERICA 2–3

POLITICAL NORTH AMERICA 4–5

NORTH AMERICAN RESOURCES...... 6–7

Canada 8–9

Canada: Western Provinces 10–11
Alberta, British Columbia, Manitoba, Saskatchewan, Yukon

Canada: Eastern Provinces 12–13
New Brunswick, Newfoundland & Labrador, Nova Scotia, Ontario, Prince Edward Island, Québec, St Pierre & Miquelon

Southeastern Canada.............. 14–15
Southern Ontario, Southern Québec

United States of America 16–17

USA: Northeastern States......... 18–19
Connecticut, Maine, Massachussetts, New Hampshire, New Jersey, New York, Pennsylvania, Rhode Island, Vermont

USA: Mid-Eastern States........... 20–21
Delaware, District of Columbia, Kentucky, Maryland, North Carolina, South Carolina, Tennessee, Virginia, West Virginia

USA: Southern States.............. 22–23
Alabama, Florida, Georgia, Louisiana, Mississippi

USA: Texas............................ 24–25

USA: South Midwestern States... 26–27
Arkansas, Kansas, Missouri, Oklahoma

USA: Upper Plains states 28–29
Iowa, Minnesota, Nebraska, North Dakota, South Dakota

USA: Great Lakes States............ 30–31
Illinois, Indiana, Michigan, Ohio, Wisconsin

USA: North Mountain States..... 32–33
Idaho, Montana, Oregon, Washington, Wyoming

USA: California & Nevada......... 34–35

USA: South Mountain States 36–37
Arizona, Colorado, New Mexico, Utah

USA: Hawaii & Alaska............... 38–39

Mexico 40–41

Central America 42–43
Belize, Costa Rica, El Salvador, Guatemala, Honduras, Nicaragua, Panama

The Caribbean 44–45
Anguilla, Antigua & Barbuda, Aruba, Bahamas, Barbados, British Virgin Islands, Cayman Islands, Cuba, Dominica, Dominican Republic, Grenada, Guadeloupe, Haiti, Jamaica, Martinique, Montserrat, Navassa Island, Netherlands Antilles, Puerto Rico, St. Kitts & Nevis, St. Lucia, St. Vincent & the Grenadines, Trinidad & Tobago, Turks & Caicos Islands, Virgin Islands (US)

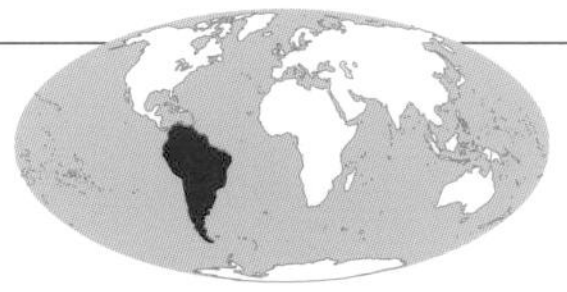

South America

SOUTH AMERICA...................... 46–47

PHYSICAL SOUTH AMERICA 48–49

POLITICAL SOUTH AMERICA 50–51

SOUTH AMERICAN RESOURCES.... 52–53

Northern South America.......... 54–55
Colombia, French Guiana, Guyana, Suriname, Venezuela

Western South America............ 56–57
Bolivia, Ecuador, Peru

Brazil 58–59

Eastern South America............ 60–61
Southeast Brazil, Northeast Argentina, Uruguay

Southern South America 62–63
Argentina, Chile, Paraguay

The Atlantic Ocean................ 64–65

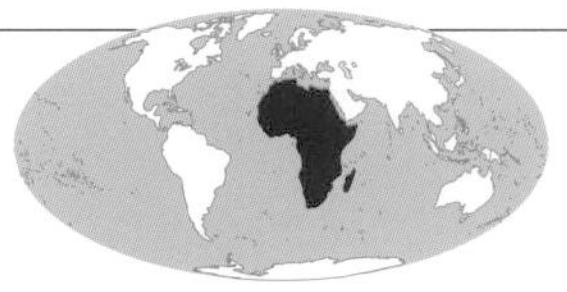

Africa

AFRICA 66–67

PHYSICAL AFRICA.................... 68–69

POLITICAL AFRICA................... 70–71

AFRICAN RESOURCES 72–73

North Africa......................... 74–75
Algeria, Egypt, Libya, Morocco, Tunisia, Western Sahara

West Africa 76–77
Benin, Burkina, Cape Verde, Gambia, Ghana, Guinea, Guinea-Bissau, Ivory Coast, Liberia, Mali, Mauritania, Niger, Nigeria, Senegal, Sierra Leone, Togo

Central Africa 78–79
Cameroon, Central African Republic, Chad, Congo, Dem. Rep. Congo, Equatorial Guinea, Gabon, Sao Tome & Principe

East Africa 80–81
Burundi, Djibouti, Eritrea, Ethiopia, Kenya, Rwanda, Somalia, Sudan, Tanzania, Uganda

Southern Africa 82–83
Angola, Botswana, Lesotho, Malawi, Mozambique, Namibia, South Africa, Swaziland, Zambia, Zimbabwe

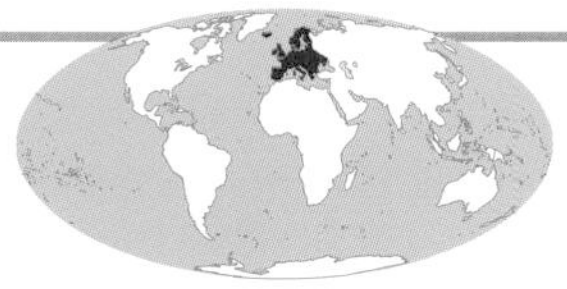

Europe

EUROPE 84–85

PHYSICAL EUROPE 86–87

POLITICAL EUROPE 88–89

EUROPEAN RESOURCES 90–91

SCANDINAVIA, FINLAND & ICELAND .. 92–93
Denmark, Finland, Iceland, Norway, Svalbard, Sweden

SOUTHERN SCANDINAVIA 94–95
Denmark, Faeroe Islands, Southern Norway, Southern Sweden

THE BRITISH ISLES 96–97
Channel Islands, Isle of Man, Ireland, United Kingdom

THE LOW COUNTRIES 98–99
Belgium, Luxembourg, Netherlands

GERMANY 100–101

FRANCE 102–103
France, Monaco

THE IBERIAN PENINSULA 104–105
Andorra, Gibraltar, Portugal, Spain

THE ITALIAN PENINSULA 106–107
Italy, San Marino, Vatican City

THE ALPINE STATES 108–109
Austria, Liechtenstein, Slovenia, Switzerland

CENTRAL EUROPE 110–111
Czech Republic, Hungary, Poland, Slovakia

SOUTHEAST EUROPE 112–113
Albania, Bosnia & Herzegovina, Croatia, Macedonia, Serbia & Montenegro (Yugoslavia)

BULGARIA & GREECE 114–115
(including European Turkey)

ROMANIA, MOLDOVA & UKRAINE 116–117

THE BALTIC STATES & BELARUS 118–119
Belarus, Estonia, Latvia, Lithuania, Kaliningrad

THE MEDITERRANEAN 120–121

THE RUSSIAN FEDERATION 122–123

NORTHERN EUROPEAN RUSSIA 124–125

SOUTHERN EUROPEAN RUSSIA 126–127

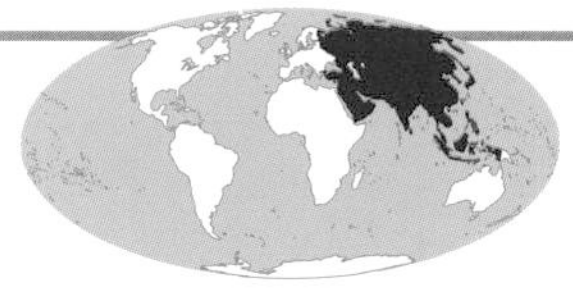

Asia

ASIA 128–129

PHYSICAL ASIA 130–131

POLITICAL ASIA 132–133

ASIAN RESOURCES 134–135

TURKEY & THE CAUCASUS 136–137
Armenia, Azerbaijan, Georgia, Turkey

THE NEAR EAST 138–139
Iraq, Israel, Jordan, Lebanon, Syria

THE ARABIAN PENINSULA 140–141
Bahrain, Kuwait, Oman, Qatar, Saudi Arabia, United Arab Emirates, Yemen

IRAN & THE GULF STATES 142–143
Bahrain, Iran, Kuwait, Qatar, United Arab Emirates

KAZAKHSTAN 144–145

CENTRAL ASIA 146–147
Kyrgyzstan, Tajikistan, Turkmenistan, Uzbekistan

AFGHANISTAN & PAKISTAN 148–149

SOUTH ASIA 150–151
Bangladesh, Bhutan, India, Maldives, Nepal, Pakistan, Sri Lanka

NORTHERN INDIA & THE HIMALAYAN STATES 152–153
Bangladesh, Bhutan, Nepal, Northern India

SOUTHERN INDIA & SRI LANKA 154–155

MAINLAND EAST ASIA 156–157
China, Mongolia, North Korea, South Korea, Taiwan

WESTERN CHINA 158–159

EASTERN CHINA 160–161
Eastern China, Taiwan

NORTHEASTERN CHINA, MONGOLIA & KOREA 162–163
Mongolia, Northeastern China, North Korea, South Korea

JAPAN 164–165

MAINLAND SOUTHEAST ASIA 166–167
Cambodia, Laos, Myanmar, Paracel Islands, Philippines, Spratly Islands, Thailand, Vietnam

WESTERN MARITIME SOUTHEAST ASIA 168–169
Brunei, Indonesia, Malaysia, Singapore

EASTERN MARITIME SOUTHEAST ASIA 170–171
East Timor, Indonesia, Philippines

THE INDIAN OCEAN 172–173

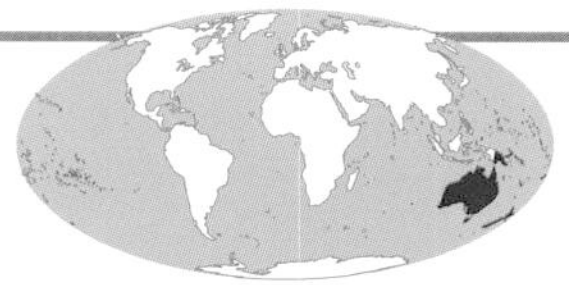

Australasia and Oceania

AUSTRALASIA & OCEANIA 174–175

POLITICAL AUSTRALASIA & OCEANIA 176–177

AUSTRALASIAN & OCEANIAN RESOURCES 178–179

AUSTRALIA 180–181

SOUTHEAST AUSTRALIA 182–183
New South Wales, South Australia, Tasmania, Victoria

NEW ZEALAND 184–185

MELANESIA 186–187
Papua New Guinea, Fiji, Solomon Islands, Vanuatu, New Caledonia

MICRONESIA 188–189
Guam, Marshall Islands, Micronesia, Nauru, Northern Mariana Islands, Palau, Wake Island

POLYNESIA 190–191
Cook Islands, Easter Island, French Polynesia, Kiribati, Niue, Pitcairn Islands, Tokelau, Tuvalu, Wallis & Futuna

THE PACIFIC OCEAN 192–193

ANTARCTICA 194–195

THE ARCTIC 196–197

INDEX-GAZETTEER

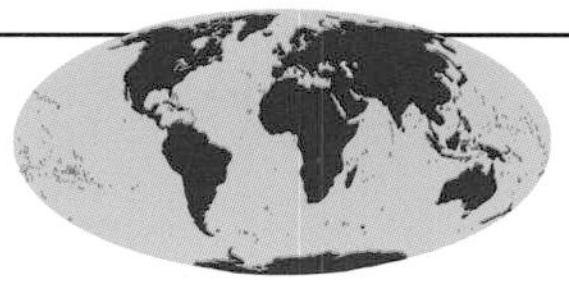

GEOGRAPHICAL COMPARISONS 198–199

COUNTRIES OF THE WORLD
including World Timezones 200–207

GEOGRAPHICAL GLOSSARY 208–210

GEOGRAPHICAL NAMES 211

INDEX 212–349

CREDITS/ACKNOWLEDGEMENTS .. 350

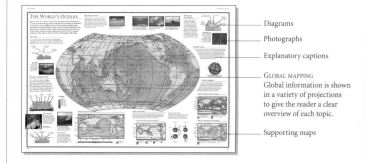

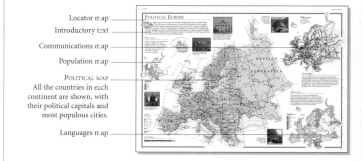

KEY TO REGIONAL MAPS

PHYSICAL FEATURES

elevation

- 6000m / 19,686ft
- 4000m / 13,124ft
- 3000m / 9843ft
- 2000m / 6562ft
- 1000m / 3281ft
- 500m / 1640ft
- 250m / 820ft
- 100m / 328ft
- sea level
- below sea level

- ▲ elevation above sea level (mountain height)
- ▲ volcano
- ✕ pass
- ▼ elevation below sea level (depression depth)

- sand desert
- lava flow
- coastline
- reef
- atoll

sea depth

- sea level
- -250m / -820ft
- -500m / -1640ft
- -1000m / -3281ft
- -2000m / -6562ft
- -3000m / -9843ft

- ▲ seamount / guyot symbol
- ▼ undersea spot depth

DRAINAGE FEATURES

- main river
- secondary river
- tertiary river
- minor river
- main seasonal river
- secondary seasonal river
- canal
- waterfall
- rapids
- dam
- perennial lake
- seasonal lake
- perennial salt lake
- seasonal salt lake
- reservoir
- salt flat / salt pan
- marsh / salt marsh
- mangrove
- wadi
- ○ spring / well / waterhole / oasis

ICE FEATURES

- ice cap / sheet
- ice shelf
- glacier / snowfield
- • • • • summer pack ice limit
- ○ ○ ○ winter pack ice limit

COMMUNICATIONS

- highway
- highway (under construction)
- major road
- minor road
- tunnel (road)
- main line
- minor line
- tunnel (railroad)
- ✈ international airport

BORDERS

- full international border
- undefined international border
- disputed *de facto* border
- disputed territorial claim border
- indication of country extent (Pacific only)
- indication of dependent territory extent (Pacific only)
- demarcation/ cease-fire line
- autonomous / federal region border
- 2nd order internal administrative border
- 3rd order internal administrative border

SETTLEMENTS

- built-up area

settlement population symbols

- ▣ more than 5 million
- ▣ 1 million to 5 million
- ◉ 500,000 to 1 million
- ◎ 100,000 to 500,000
- ⊕ 50,000 to 100.000
- ○ 10,000 to 50,000
- ○ fewer than 10,000

- ■ ● ● country/dependent territory capital city
- ▣ ◉ ◉ autonomous / federal region / 2nd order internal administrative center
- ▣ ◉ ⊕ 3rd order internal administrative center

MISCELLANEOUS FEATURES

- ancient wall
- ◇ site of interest
- • scientific station

GRATICULE FEATURES

- lines of latitude and longitude / Equator
- Tropics / Polar circles
- 45° degrees of longitude / latitude

TYPOGRAPHIC KEY

PHYSICAL FEATURES

landscape features	*Namib Desert* *Massif Central* *ANDES*
headland	*Nordkapp*
elevation / volcano / pass	Mount Meru 4556 m
drainage features	*Lake Geneva*
rivers / canals spring / well / waterhole / oasis / waterfall / rapids / dam	*Mekong*
ice features	*Vatnajökull*
sea features	*Golfe de Lion* *Andaman Sea* *INDIAN OCEAN*
undersea features	*Barracuda Fracture Zone*

REGIONS

country	**ARMENIA**
dependent territory with parent state	NIUE (to NZ)
region outside feature area	ANGOLA
autonomous / federal region	MINAS GERAIS
2nd order internal administrative region	MINSKAYA VOBLASTS'
3rd order internal administrative region	Vaucluse
cultural region	New England

SETTLEMENTS

capital city	**BEIJING**
dependent territory capital city	FORT-DE-FRANCE
other settlements	**Chicago** **Adana** **Tizi Ozou** **Yonezawa** **Farnham**

MISCELLANEOUS

sites of interest / miscellaneous	Valley of the Kings
Tropics / Polar circles	*Antarctic Circle*

HOW TO USE THIS ATLAS

THE ATLAS IS ORGANIZED BY CONTINENT, moving eastward from the International Dateline. The opening section describes the world's structure, systems, and its main features. The Atlas of the World that follows, is a continent-by-continent guide to today's world, starting with a comprehensive insight into the physical, political, and economic structure of each continent, followed by integrated mapping and descriptions of each region or country.

THE WORLD

THE INTRODUCTORY SECTION of the Atlas deals with every aspect of the planet, from physical structure to human geography, providing an overall picture of the world we live in. Complex topics such as the landscape of the Earth, climate, oceans, population, and economic patterns are clearly explained with the aid of maps and diagrams drawn from the latest information.

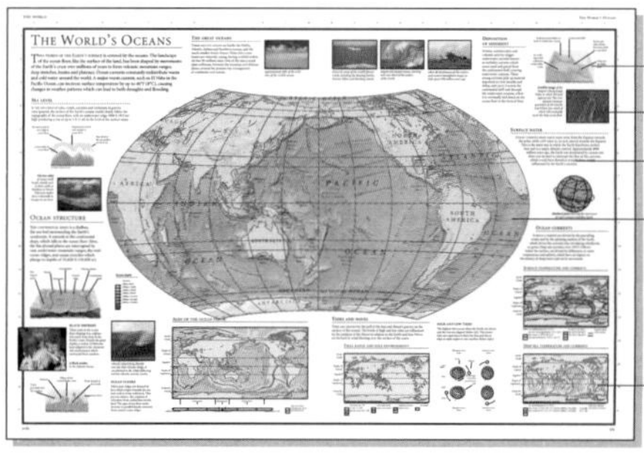

THE WORLD'S OCEANS
Diagrams
Photographs
Explanatory captions
GLOBAL MAPPING
Global information is shown in a variety of projections to give the reader a clear overview of each topic.
Supporting maps

THE POLITICAL CONTINENT

THE POLITICAL PORTRAIT of the continent is a vital reference point for every continental section, showing the position of countries relative to one another, and the relationship between human settlement and geographic location. The complex mosaic of languages spoken in each continent is mapped, as is the effect of communications networks on the pattern of settlement.

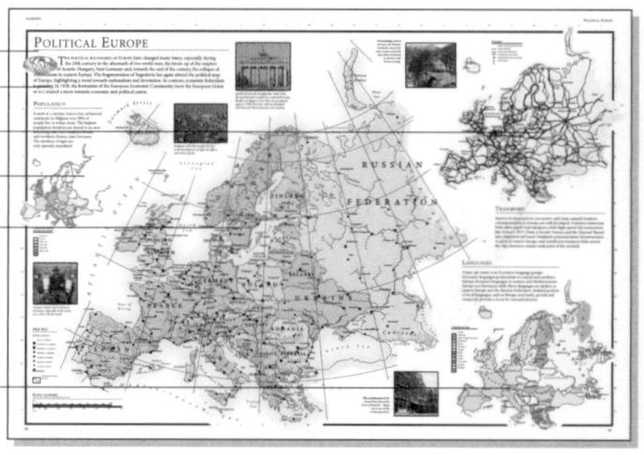

POLITICAL EUROPE
Locator map
Introductory text
Communications map
Population map
POLITICAL MAP
All the countries in each continent are shown, with their political capitals and most populous cities.
Languages map

CONTINENTAL RESOURCES

THE EARTH'S RICH NATURAL RESOURCES, including oil, gas, minerals, and fertile land, have played a key role in the development of society. These pages show the location of minerals and agricultural resources on each continent, and how they have been instrumental in dictating industrial growth and the varieties of economic activity across the continent.

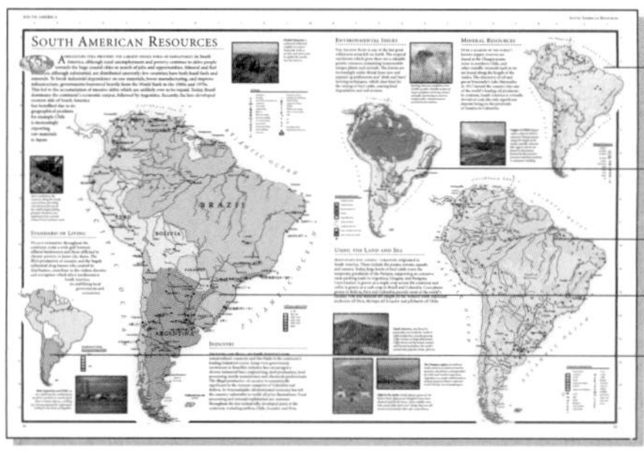

SOUTH AMERICAN RESOURCES
Mineral resources map
Environmental issues map
Land use map
Industry map
Comparative wealth map

The Physical Continent

The astonishing variety of landforms, and the dramatic forces that created and continue to shape the landscape, are explained in the continental physical spread. Cross-sections, illustrations, and terrain maps highlight the different parts of the continent, showing how nature's forces have produced the landscapes we see today.

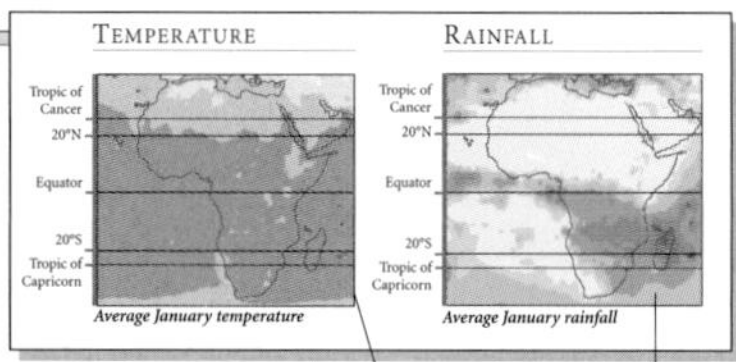

Temperature
Rainfall
Tropic of Cancer
20°N
Equator
20°S
Tropic of Capricorn
Average January temperature
Average January rainfall

Climate charts
Rainfall and temperature charts clearly show the continental patterns of rainfall and temperature.

Climate map
Climatic regions vary across each continent. The map displays the differing climatic regions, as well as daily hours of sunshine at selected weather stations.

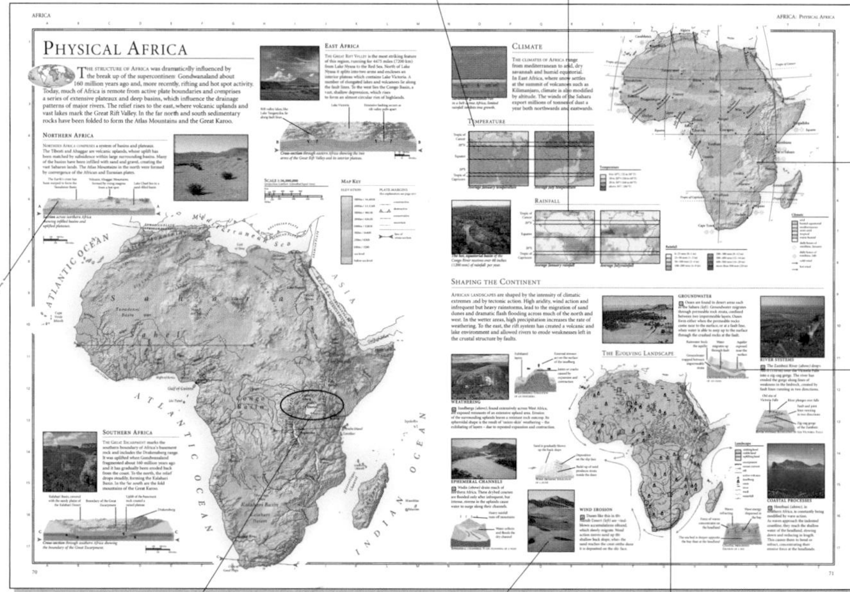

Physical Africa

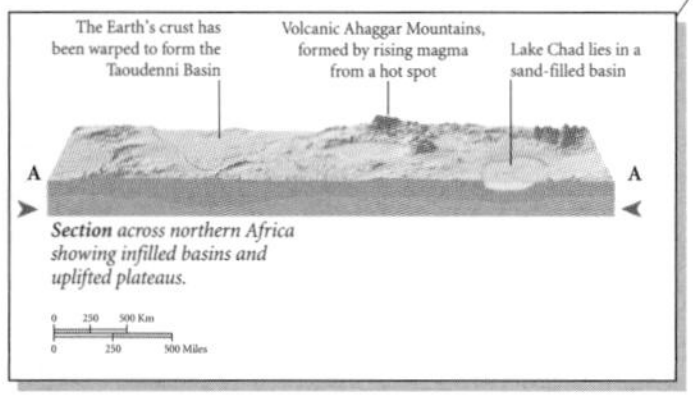

The Earth's crust has been warped to form the Taoudenni Basin
Volcanic Ahaggar Mountains, formed by rising magma from a hot spot
Lake Chad lies in a sand-filled basin
A
A
Section across northern Africa showing infilled basins and uplifted plateaus.

Cross-sections
Detailed cross-sections through selected parts of the continent show the underlying geomorphic structure.

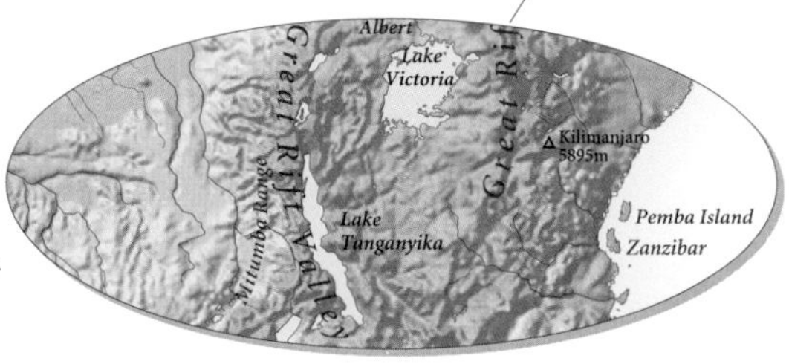

Albert
Lake Victoria
Great Rift Valley
Kilimanjaro 5895m
Lake Tanganyika
Pemba Island
Zanzibar

Main physical map
Detailed satellite data has been used to create an accurate and visually striking picture of the surface of the continent.

Photographs
A wide range of beautiful photographs bring the world's regions to life.

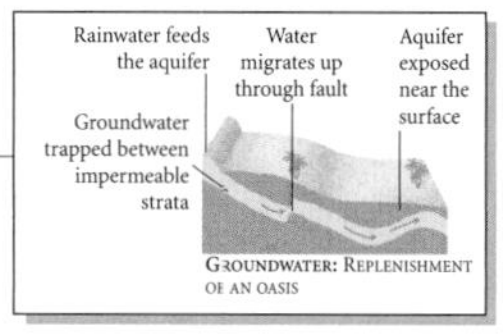

Rainwater feeds the aquifer
Water migrates up through fault
Aquifer exposed near the surface
Groundwater trapped between impermeable strata
Groundwater: Replenishment of an oasis

Landform diagrams
The complex formation of many typical landforms is summarized in these easy-to-understand illustrations.

Landscape evolution map
The physical shape of each continent is affected by a variety of forces which continually sculpt and modify the landscape. This map shows the major processes which affect different parts of the continent.

Regional Mapping

The main body of the Atlas is a unique regional map set, with detailed information on the terrain, the human geography of the region and its infrastructure. Around the edge of the map, additional 'at-a-glance' maps, give an instant picture of regional industry, land use and agriculture. The detailed terrain map (shown in perspective), focuses on the main physical features of the region, and is enhanced by annotated illustrations, and photographs of the physical structure.

Regional locator
This small map shows the location of each country in relation to its continent.

Transportation Network

	340,090 miles (544,144 km)		4813 miles 7700 km
	12,872 miles (20,592 km)		2108 miles (3389 km)

New York's commercial success is tied historically to its transportation connections. The Erie Canal, completed in 1825, opened up the Great Lakes and the interior to New York's markets and carried a stream of immigrants into the Midwest.

Transportation network
The differing extent of the transportation network for each region is shown here, along with key facts about the transportation system.

Key to main map
A key to the population symbols and land heights accompanies the main map.

World locator
This locates the continent in which the region is found on a small world map.

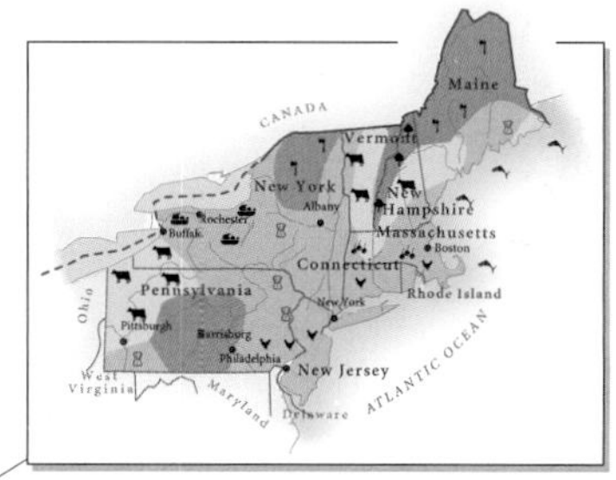

Canada
Maine
Vermont
New Hampshire
Massachusetts
Boston
New York
Connecticut
Rhode Island
Pennsylvania
Philadelphia
New Jersey
West Virginia
Maryland
Delaware
Atlantic Ocean
Ohio

Land use map
This shows the different types of land use which characterize the region, as well as indicating the principal agricultural activities.

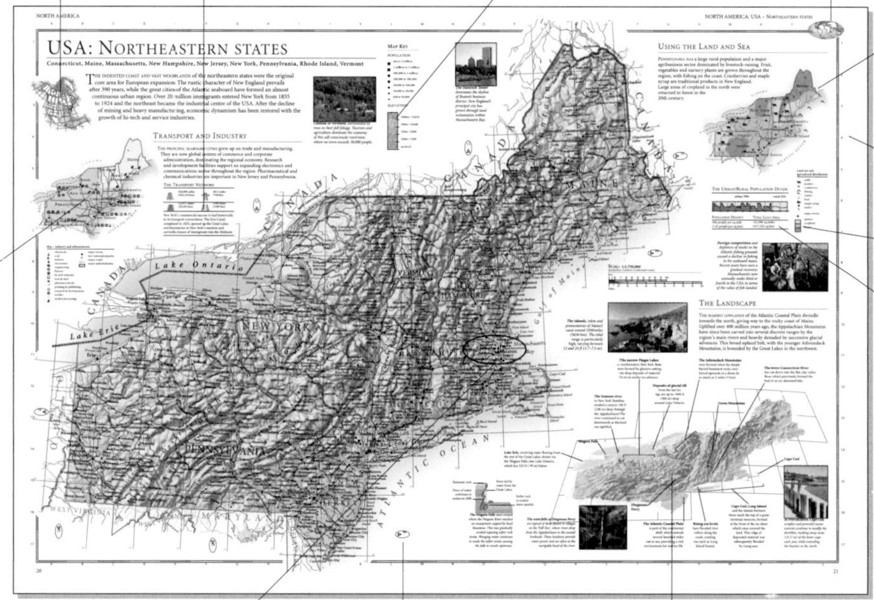

USA: Northeastern States
Connecticut, Maine, Massachusetts, New Hampshire, New Jersey, New York, Pennsylvania, Rhode Island, Vermont

Grid reference
The framing grid provides a location reference for each place listed in the Index.

Map keys
Each supporting map has its own key.

Canada
Maine
Vermont
New Hampshire
Massachusetts
New York
Connecticut
Rhode Island
Pennsylvania
New Jersey
Atlantic Ocean
Ohio
West Virginia
Maryland
Delaware

Transportation and industry map
The main industrial areas are mapped, and the most important industrial and economic activities of the region are shown.

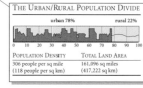

The Urban/Rural Population Divide

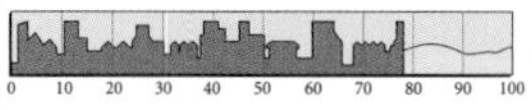

urban 78%
rural 22%
0 10 20 30 40 50 60 70 80 90 100

Population Density	Total Land Area
306 people per sq mile (118 people per sq km)	161,096 sq miles (417,222 sq km)

Urban/rural population divide
The proportion of people in the region who live in urban and rural areas, as well as the overall population density and land area are clearly shown in these simple graphics.

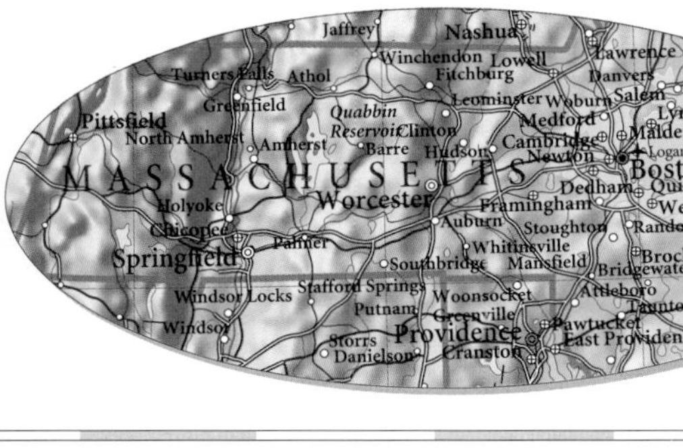

Nashua
Jaffrey
Winchendon
Lowell
Lawrence
Fitchburg
Danvers
Turners Falls
Athol
Leominster
Woburn
Salem
Beverly
Greenfield
Quabbin Reservoir
Clinton
Medford
Lynn
Pittsfield
North Amherst
Amherst
Barre
Hudson
Cambridge
Malden
Logan International
Newton
Boston
Massachusetts
Quincy
Dedham
Weymouth
Holyoke
Worcester
Framingham
Chicopee
Auburn
Stoughton
Randolph
Springfield
Palmer
Whitinsville
Southbridge
Mansfield
Brockton
Bridgewater
Windsor Locks
Stafford Springs
Woonsocket
Attleboro
Putnam
Greenville
Taunton
Windsor
Pawtucket
Storrs
Providence
East Providence
Danielson
Cranston

Continuation symbols
These symbols indicate where adjacent maps can be found.

Main regional map
A wealth of information is displayed on the main map, building up a rich portrait of the interaction between the physical landscape and the human and political geography of each region. The key to the regional maps can be found on page viii.

Landscape map
The computer-generated terrain model accurately portrays an oblique view of the landscape. Annotations highlight the most important geographic features of the region.

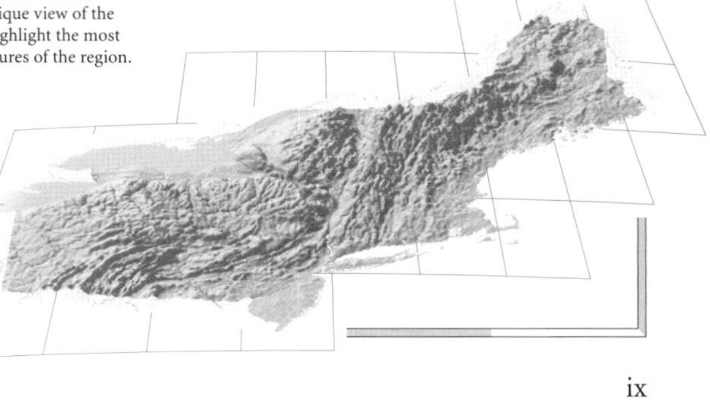

Jupiter

- Diameter: 88,846 miles (142,984 km)
- Mass: 1,900,000 million million million tons
- Temperature: -153°C (extremes not available)
- Distance from Sun: 483 million miles (778 million km)
- Length of day: 9.84 hours
- Length of year: 11.86 earth years
- Surface gravity: 1 kg = 2.53 kg

Mars

- Diameter: 4,217 miles (6,786 km)
- Mass: 642 million million million tons
- Temperature: -137 to 37°C
- Distance from Sun: 142 million miles (228 million km)
- Length of day: 24.623 hours
- Length of year: 1.88 earth years
- Surface gravity: 1 kg = 0.38 kg

Earth

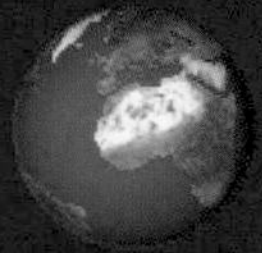

- Diameter: 7,926 miles (12,756 km)
- Mass: 5,976 million million million tons
- Temperature: -70 to 55°C
- Distance from Sun: 93 million miles (150 million km)
- Length of day: 23.92 hours
- Length of year: 365.25 earth days
- Surface gravity: 1 kg = 1 kg

Venus

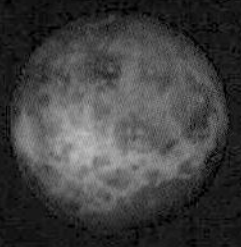

- Diameter: 7,520 miles (12,102 km)
- Mass: 4,870 million million million tons
- Temperature: 457°C (extremes not available)
- Distance from Sun: 67 million miles (108 million km)
- Length of day: 243.01 earth days
- Length of year: 224.7 earth days
- Surface gravity: 1 kg = 0.88 kg

Mercury

- Diameter: 3,031 miles (4,878 km)
- Mass: 330 million million million tons
- Temperature: -173 to 427°C
- Distance from Sun: 36 million miles (58 million km)
- Length of day: 58.65 earth days
- Length of year: 87.97 earth days
- Surface gravity: 1 kg = 0.38 kg

The Solar System

NINE MAJOR PLANETS, their satellites, and countless minor planets (asteroids) orbit the Sun to form the Solar System. The Sun, our nearest star, creates energy from nuclear reactions deep within its interior, providing all the light and heat which make life on Earth possible. The Earth is unique in the Solar System in that it supports life: its size, gravitational pull and distance from the Sun have all created the optimum conditions for the evolution of life. The planetary images seen here are composites derived from actual spacecraft images (not shown to scale).

The Sun

- Diameter: 864,948 miles (1,392,000 km)
- Mass: 1990 million million million million tons

THE SUN was formed when a swirling cloud of dust and gas contracted, pulling matter into its center. When the temperature at the center rose to 1,000,000°C, nuclear fusion – the fusing of hydrogen into helium, creating energy – occurred, releasing a constant stream of heat and light.

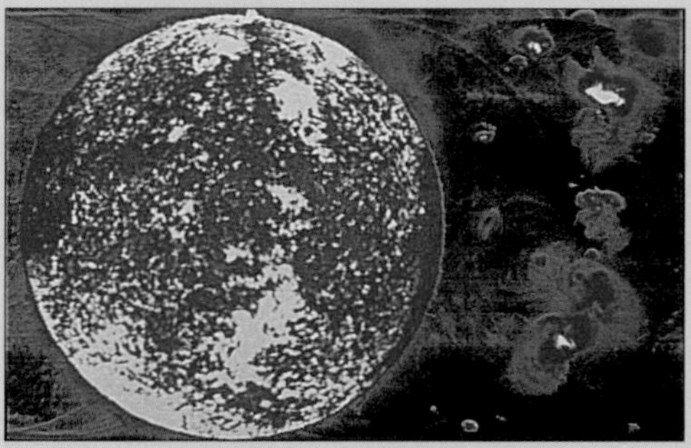

***Solar flares are sudden bursts** of energy from the Sun's surface. They can be 125,000 miles (200,000 km) long.*

The Formation of the Solar System

The cloud of dust and gas thrown out by the Sun during its formation cooled to form the Solar System. The smaller planets nearest the Sun are formed of minerals and metals. The outer planets were formed at lower temperatures, and consist of swirling clouds of gases.

The Milankovitch Cycle

The amount of radiation from the Sun which reaches the Earth is affected by variations in the Earth's orbit and the tilt of the Earth's axis, as well as by "wobbles" in the axis. These variations cause three separate cycles, corresponding with the durations of recent ice ages.

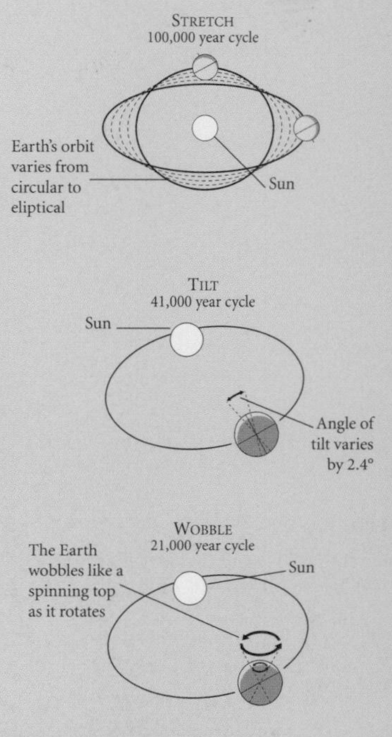
STRETCH
100,000 year cycle
Earth's orbit varies from circular to eliptical
Sun
TILT
41,000 year cycle
Sun
Angle of tilt varies by 2.4°
WOBBLE
21,000 year cycle
The Earth wobbles like a spinning top as it rotates
Sun

SATURN

- Diameter: 74,974 miles (120,660 km)
- Mass: 570,000 million million million tons
- Temperature: -185°C (extremes not available)
- Distance from Sun: 887 million miles (1,427 million km)
- Length of day: 10.23 hours
- Length of year: 29.46 earth years
- Surface gravity: 1 kg = 1.07 kg

URANUS

- Diameter: 31,763 miles (51,118 km)
- Mass: 86,800 million million million tons
- Temperature: -214°C (extremes not available)
- Distance from Sun: 1,783 million miles (2,870 million km)
- Length of day: 17.9 hours
- Length of year: 84.01 earth years
- Surface gravity: 1 kg = 0.92 kg

SPACE DEBRIS

MILLIONS OF OBJECTS, remnants of planetary formation, circle the Sun in a zone lying between Mars and Jupiter: the asteroid belt. Fragments of asteroids break off to form meteoroids, which can reach the Earth's surface. Comets, composed of ice and dust, originated outside our Solar System. Their elliptical orbit brings them close to the Sun and into the inner Solar System.

***Meteor Crater in Arizona** is 4200 ft (1300 m) wide and 660 ft (200 m) deep. It was formed over 10,000 years ago.*

METEOROIDS

Meteoroids are fragments of asteroids which hurtle through space at great velocity. Although millions of meteoroids enter the Earth's atmosphere, the vast majority burn up on entry, and fall to the Earth as a meteor or shooting star. Large meteoroids traveling at speeds of 155,000 mph (250,000 kmph) can sometimes withstand the atmosphere and hit the Earth's surface with tremendous force, creating large craters on impact.

POSSIBLE AND ACTUAL METEORITE CRATERS

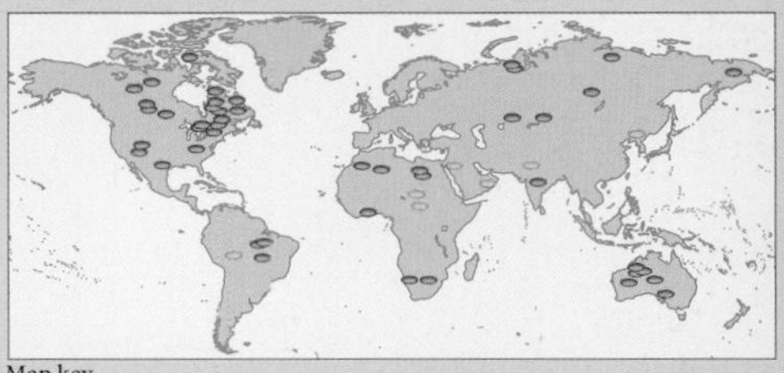

Map key
Possible impact craters — Meteorite impact craters

***The orbit of Halley's Comet** brings it close to the Earth every 76 years. It last visited in 1986.*

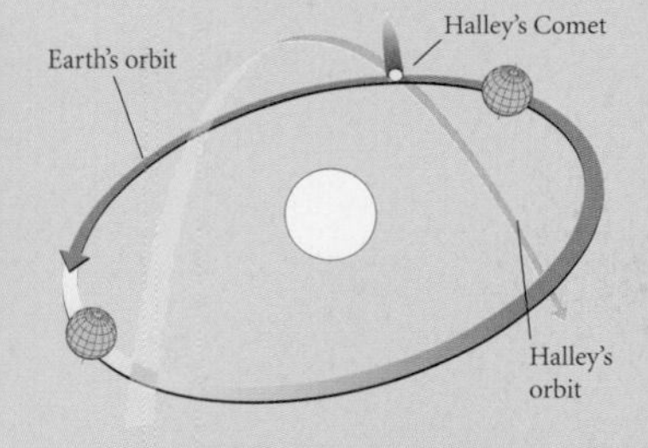
Halley's Comet
Earth's orbit
Halley's orbit

ORBIT OF HALLEY'S COMET AROUND THE SUN

NEPTUNE

- Diameter: 30,775 miles (49,528 km)
- Mass: 102,000 million million million tons
- Temperature: -225°C (extremes not available)
- Distance from Sun: 2794 million miles (4497 million km)
- Length of day: 19.2 hours
- Length of year: 164.79 earth years
- Surface gravity: 1 kg = 1.18 kg

PLUTO

- Diameter: 1,429 miles (2,300 km)
- Mass: 13 million million million tons
- Temperature: -236°C (extremes not available)
- Distance from Sun: 3,666 million miles (5,900 million km)
- Length of day: 6.39 hours
- Length of year: 248.54 earth years
- Surface gravity: 1 kg = 0.30 kg

THE EARTH'S ATMOSPHERE

DURING THE EARLY STAGES of the Earth's formation, ash, lava, carbon dioxide, and water vapor were discharged onto the surface of the planet by constant volcanic eruptions. The water formed the oceans, while carbon dioxide entered the atmosphere or was dissolved in the oceans. Clouds, formed of water droplets, reflected some of the Sun's radiation back into space. The Earth's temperature stabilized and early life forms began to emerge, converting carbon dioxide into life-giving oxygen.

__It is thought__ that the gases that make up the Earth's atmosphere originated deep within the interior, and were released many millions of years ago during intense volcanic activty, similar to this eruption at Mount St. Helens.

ORDER AND RELATIVE DISTANCE FROM THE SUN OF PLANETS

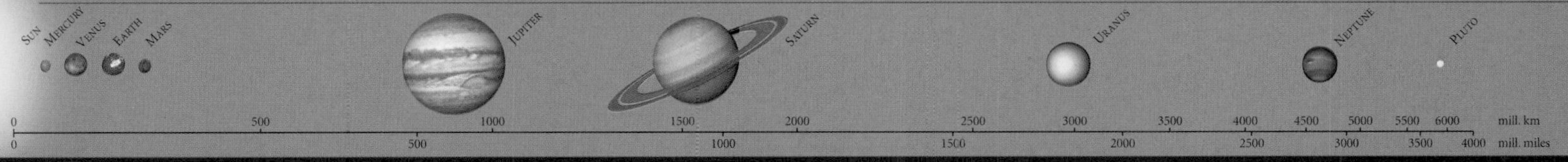
Sun
Mercury
Venus
Earth
Mars
Jupiter
Saturn
Uranus
Neptune
Pluto
0 500 1000 1500 2000 2500 3000 3500 4000 4500 5000 5500 6000 mill. km
0 500 1000 1500 2000 2500 3000 3500 4000 mill. miles

The Physical World

The Earth's surface is constantly being transformed: it is uplifted, folded and faulted by tectonic forces; weathered and eroded by wind, water, and ice. Sometimes change is dramatic, the spectacular results of earthquakes or floods. More often it is a slow process lasting millions of years. A physical map of the world represents a snapshot of the ever-evolving architecture of the Earth. This terrain map shows the whole surface of the Earth, both above and below the sea.

The World in Section

These cross-sections around the Earth, one in the northern hemisphere; one straddling the Equator, reveal the limited areas of land above sea level in comparison with the extent of the sea floor. The greater erosive effects of weathering by wind and water limit the upward elevation of land above sea level, while the deep oceans retain their dramatic mountain and trench profiles.

Aleutian Trench
Pacific Ocean
Rocky Mountains
60°N
30°N
180°
150°W
120°W

Cross-Section: Northern Hemisphere

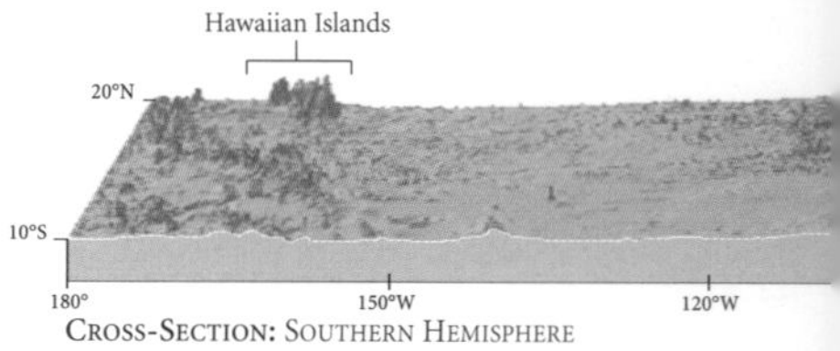
Hawaiian Islands
20°N
10°S
180°
150°W
120°W

Cross-Section: Southern Hemisphere

Map Key

Geographical regions

- ice
- tundra
- needleleaf forest
- broadleaf forest
- cultivated land
- hot desert
- cold desert
- tropical grassland
- tropical rainforest
- mountain
- submarine regions

Scale 1:73,000,000
(projection: Wagner VII)

Km 0 250 500 1,000 1,500 2,000
Miles 0 250 500 1,000 1,500 2,000

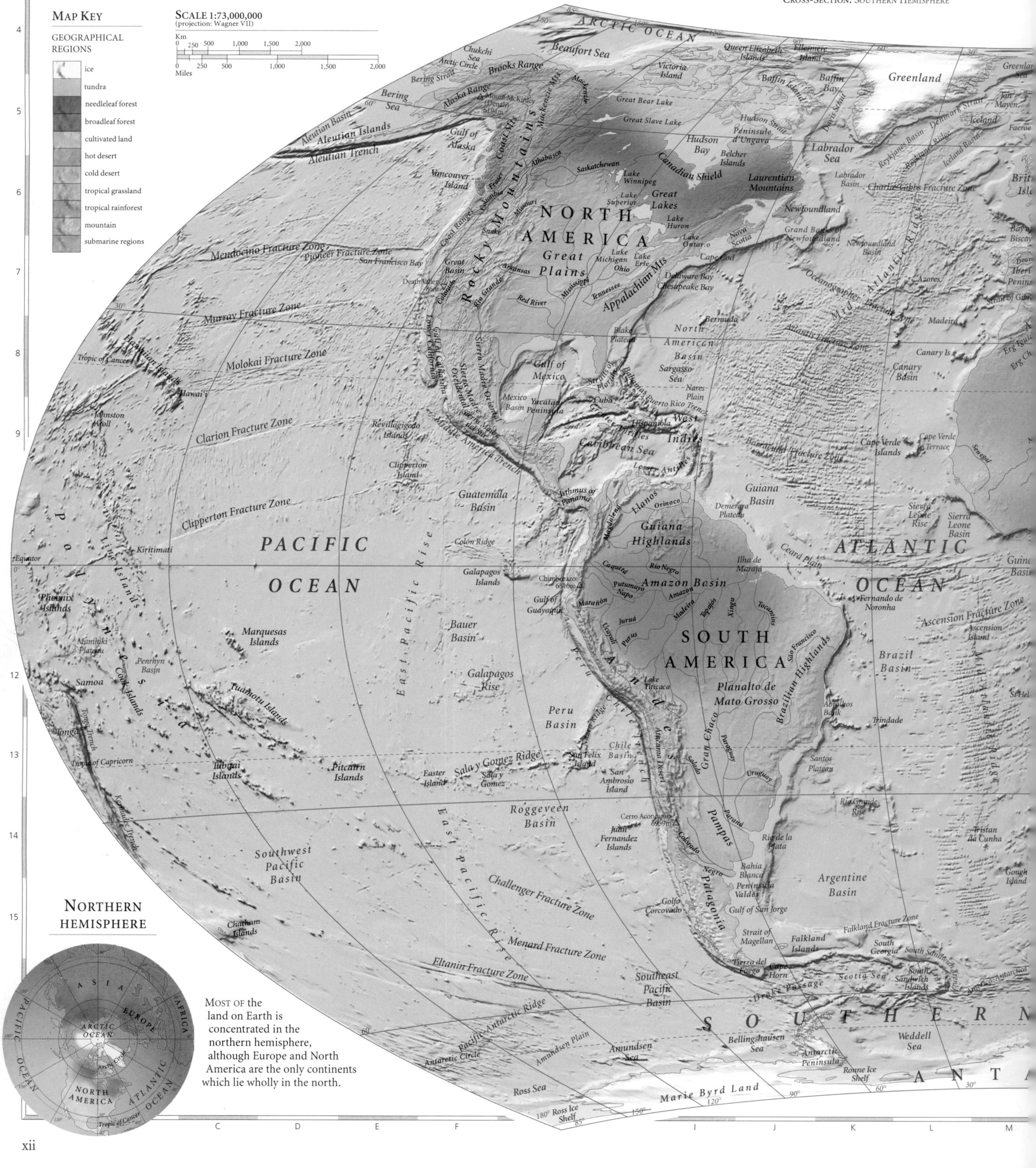
ARCTIC OCEAN
Beaufort Sea
Chukchi Sea
Arctic Circle
Brooks Range
Bering Strait
Bering Sea
Alaska Range
Mount McKinley (Denali) 6194m
Mackenzie Mts
Queen Elizabeth Islands
Ellesmere Island
Victoria Island
Baffin Island
Baffin Bay
Greenland
Great Bear Lake
Great Slave Lake
Hudson Strait
Peninsule d'Ungava
Davis Strait
Denmark Strait
Jan Mayen
Iceland
Aleutian Basin
Aleutian Islands
Aleutian Trench
Gulf of Alaska
Coast Mts
Rocky Mountains
Athabasca
Saskatchewan
Hudson Bay
Belcher Islands
Canadian Shield
Labrador Sea
Labrador Basin
Reykjanes Basin
Reykjanes Ridge
Iceland Basin
Vancouver Island
Fraser
Columbia
Lake Winnipeg
Lake Superior
Great Lakes
Laurentian Mountains
Charlie-Gibbs Fracture Zone
Missouri
Snake
Coast Ranges
NORTH AMERICA
Lake Huron
Lake Ontario
Nova Scotia
Newfoundland
Grand Banks of Newfoundland
Newfoundland Basin
Great Plains
Lake Michigan
Lake Erie
Ohio
Cape Cod
Mendocino Fracture Zone
Pioneer Fracture Zone
San Francisco Bay
Great Basin
Arkansas
Death Valley -86m
Colorado
Rio Grande
Mississippi
Tennessee
Appalachian Mts
Delaware Bay
Chesapeake Bay
Oceanographer Fracture Zone
Mid-Atlantic Ridge
Azores
Red River
Murray Fracture Zone
Bermuda
North American Basin
Blake Plateau
Atlantis Fracture Zone
Madeira
Canary Is
Canary Basin
Hawaiian Islands
Tropic of Cancer
Molokai Fracture Zone
Gulf of California
Sierra Madre Occidental
Sierra Madre Oriental
Gulf of Mexico
Straits of Florida
Bahamas
Sargasso Sea
Nares Plain
Hawai'i
Mexico Basin
Yucatan Peninsula
Cuba
Puerto Rico Trench
Johnston Atoll
Clarion Fracture Zone
Revillagigedo Islands
Hispaniola
West Indies
Antilles
Caribbean Sea
Barracuda Fracture Zone
Cape Verde Islands
Cape Verde Terrace
Middle America Trench
Clipperton Island
Lesser Antilles
Guatemala Basin
Isthmus of Panama
Llanos
Orinoco
Demerara Plateau
Guiana Basin
Sierra Leone Rise
Sierra Leone Basin
Clipperton Fracture Zone
Guiana Highlands
Magdalena
Kiritimati
PACIFIC OCEAN
Colon Ridge
East Pacific Rise
Ceará Plain
ATLANTIC OCEAN
Equator
Line Islands
Caquetá
Rio Negro
Ilha de Marajó
Galapagos Islands
Chimborazo 6310m
Amazon Basin
Putumayo
Napo
Amazon
Phoenix Islands
Polynesia
Gulf of Guayaquil
Marañón
Madeira
Tapajós
Xingu
Tocantins
Fernando de Noronha
Ascension Fracture Zone
Ascension Island
Marquesas Islands
Bauer Basin
Juruá
Purus
Ucayali
SOUTH AMERICA
São Francisco
Brazilian Highlands
Manihiki Plateau
Brazil Basin
Penrhyn Basin
Andes
Cook Islands
Galapagos Rise
Peru
Lake Titicaca
Planalto de Mato Grosso
Samoa
Tuamotu Islands
Abrolhos Bank
St Helena
Tonga Trench
Tonga
Peru Basin
Atacama Desert
Gran Chaco
Paraguay
Trindade
Tropic of Capricorn
Chile Basin
Santos Plateau
Tubuai Islands
Pitcairn Islands
Easter Island
Sala y Gomez Ridge
Sala y Gomez
San Felix Island
San Ambrosio Island
Salado
Uruguay
Kermadec Trench
Roggeveen Basin
Cerro Aconcagua 6959m
Paraná
Rio Grande Rise
Juan Fernandez Islands
Pampas
Tristan da Cunha
Colorado
Río de la Plata
Southwest Pacific Basin
Negro
Bahía Blanca
Península Valdés
Argentine Basin
Gough Island
Challenger Fracture Zone
Golfo Corcovado
Patagonia
Gulf of San Jorge
Chatham Islands
Falkland Fracture Zone
Strait of Magellan
Falkland Islands
South Georgia
Menard Fracture Zone
Eltanin Fracture Zone
Tierra del Fuego
Cape Horn
Scotia Sea
South Sandwich Islands
Southeast Pacific Basin
Drake Passage
Pacific-Antarctic Ridge
SOUTHERN
Amundsen Plain
Antarctic Circle
Amundsen Sea
Bellingshausen Sea
Antarctic Peninsula
Weddell Sea
Ronne Ice Shelf
ANTARCTICA
Ross Sea
Marie Byrd Land
Ross Ice Shelf
180°
150°
120°
90°
60°
30°
85°

Northern Hemisphere

Most of the land on Earth is concentrated in the northern hemisphere, although Europe and North America are the only continents which lie wholly in the north.

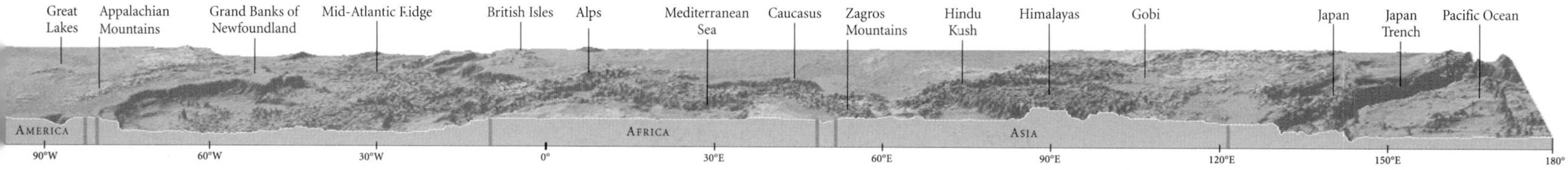
Great Lakes
Appalachian Mountains
Grand Banks of Newfoundland
Mid-Atlantic Ridge
British Isles
Alps
Mediterranean Sea
Caucasus
Zagros Mountains
Hindu Kush
Himalayas
Gobi
Japan
Japan Trench
Pacific Ocean
AMERICA
AFRICA
ASIA
90°W
60°W
30°W
0°
30°E
60°E
90°E
120°E
150°E
180°

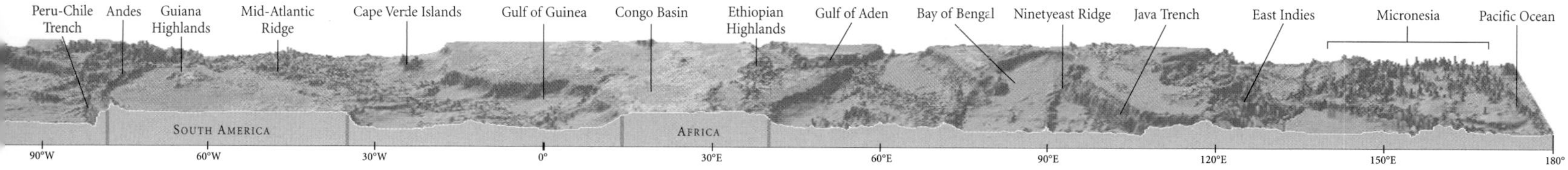
Peru-Chile Trench
Andes
Guiana Highlands
Mid-Atlantic Ridge
Cape Verde Islands
Gulf of Guinea
Congo Basin
Ethiopian Highlands
Gulf of Aden
Bay of Bengal
Ninetyeast Ridge
Java Trench
East Indies
Micronesia
Pacific Ocean
SOUTH AMERICA
AFRICA
90°W
60°W
30°W
0°
30°E
60°E
90°E
120°E
150°E
180°

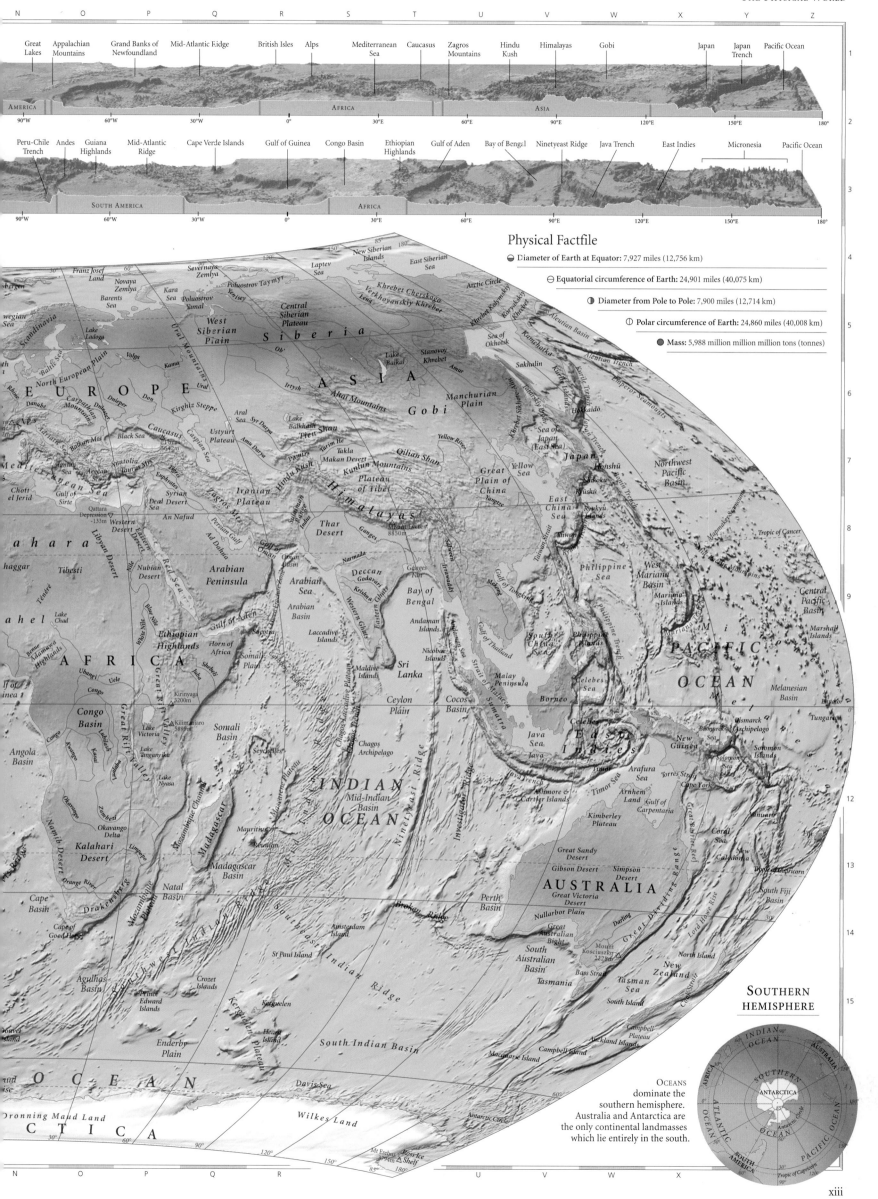

Physical Factfile

- **Diameter of Earth at Equator:** 7,927 miles (12,756 km)
- **Equatorial circumference of Earth:** 24,901 miles (40,075 km)
- **Diameter from Pole to Pole:** 7,900 miles (12,714 km)
- **Polar circumference of Earth:** 24,860 miles (40,008 km)
- **Mass:** 5,988 million million million tons (tonnes)

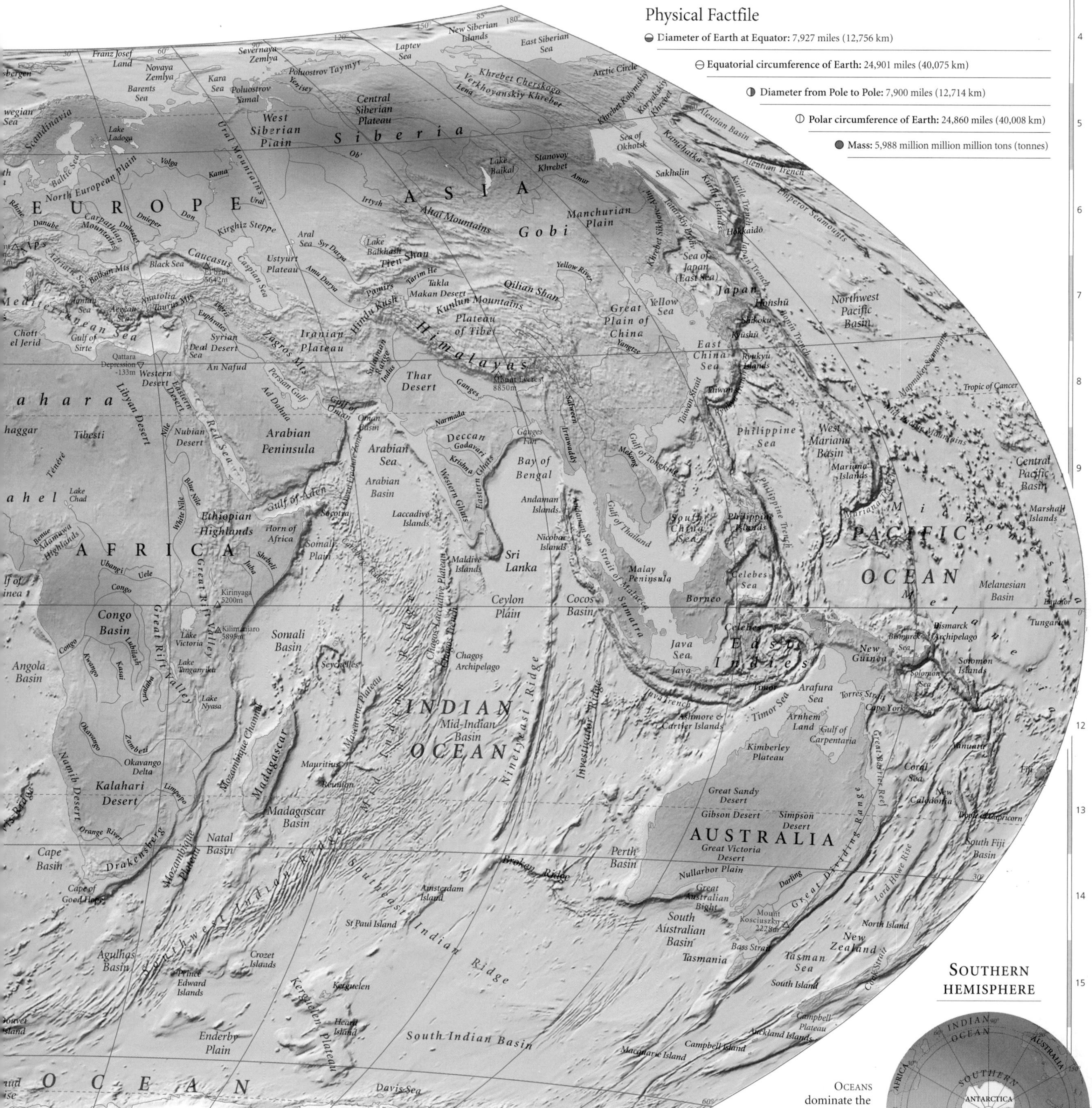
EUROPE
ASIA
AFRICA
AUSTRALIA
INDIAN OCEAN
PACIFIC OCEAN
Siberia
West Siberian Plain
Central Siberian Plateau
Lake Baikal
Gobi
Manchurian Plain
Altai Mountains
Tien Shan
Kunlun Mountains
Plateau of Tibet
Himalayas
Mount Everest 8850m
Thar Desert
Deccan
Arabian Peninsula
Arabian Sea
Bay of Bengal
Sri Lanka
Japan
Philippine Sea
South China Sea
Borneo
Sumatra
Java
Ethiopian Highlands
Congo Basin
Kalahari Desert
Madagascar
Great Rift Valley
Kilimanjaro 5895m
Mid-Indian Basin
Ninetyeast Ridge
Southeast Indian Ridge
Southwest Indian Ridge
Kerguelen Plateau
South Indian Basin
Great Dividing Range
Mount Kosciuszko 2228m
New Zealand
Tasmania
Mt Erebus 3794m
Ross Ice Shelf
Wilkes Land
Dronning Maud Land
Arctic Circle
Tropic of Cancer
Tropic of Capricorn
Antarctic Circle

SOUTHERN HEMISPHERE

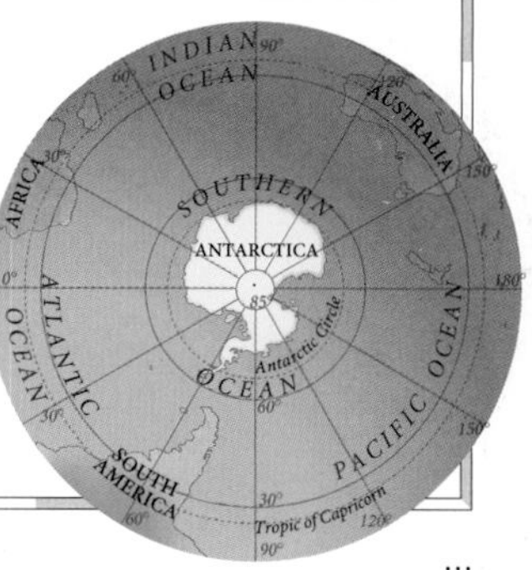
INDIAN OCEAN
AUSTRALIA
AFRICA
SOUTHERN OCEAN
ANTARCTICA
ATLANTIC OCEAN
PACIFIC OCEAN
SOUTH AMERICA
Antarctic Circle
Tropic of Capricorn

OCEANS dominate the southern hemisphere. Australia and Antarctica are the only continental landmasses which lie entirely in the south.

Structure of the Earth

The Earth as it is today is just the latest phase in a constant process of evolution which has occurred over the past 4.5 billion years. The Earth's continents are neither fixed nor stable; over the course of the Earth's history, propelled by currents rising from the intense heat at its center, the great plates on which they lie have moved, collided, joined together, and separated. These processes continue to mold and transform the surface of the Earth, causing earthquakes and volcanic eruptions and creating oceans, mountain ranges, deep ocean trenches, and island chains.

Inside the Earth

The Earth's hot inner core is made up of solid iron, while the outer core is composed of liquid iron and nickel. The mantle nearest the core is viscous, whereas the rocky upper mantle is fairly rigid. The crust is the rocky outer shell of the Earth. Together, the upper mantle and the crust form the lithosphere.

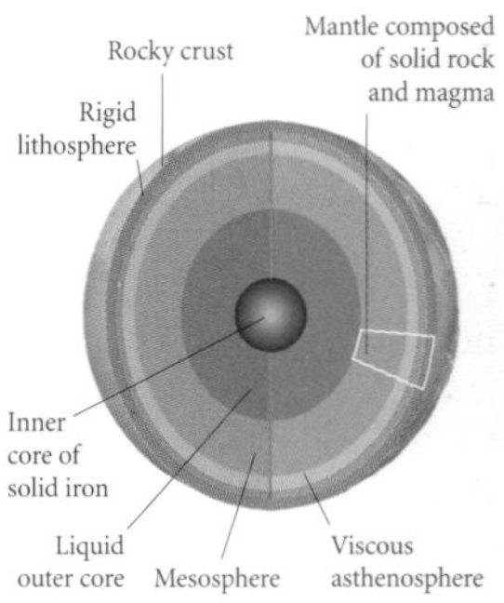
Rocky crust
Mantle composed of solid rock and magma
Rigid lithosphere
Inner core of solid iron
Liquid outer core
Mesosphere
Viscous asthenosphere

The Dynamic Earth

The Earth's crust is made up of eight major (and several minor) rigid continental and oceanic tectonic plates, which fit closely together. The positions of the plates are not static. They are constantly moving relative to one another. The type of movement between plates affects the way in which they alter the structure of the Earth. The oldest parts of the plates, known as shields, are the most stable parts of the Earth and little tectonic activity occurs here.

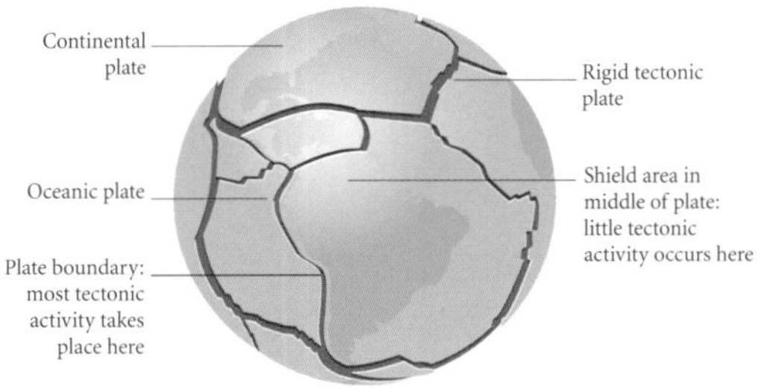
Continental plate
Oceanic plate
Plate boundary: most tectonic activity takes place here
Rigid tectonic plate
Shield area in middle of plate: little tectonic activity occurs here

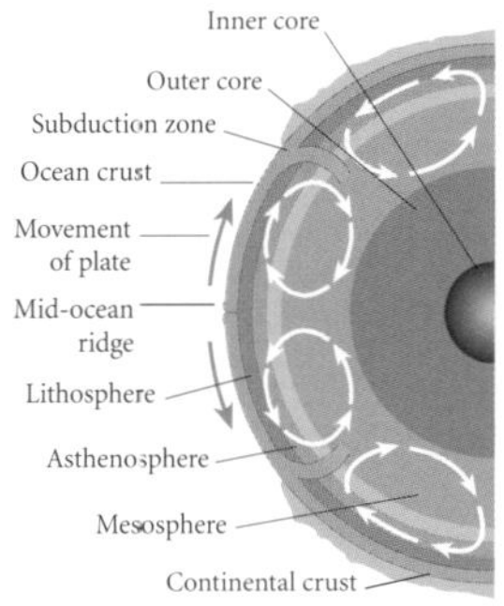
Inner core
Outer core
Subduction zone
Ocean crust
Movement of plate
Mid-ocean ridge
Lithosphere
Asthenosphere
Mesosphere
Continental crust

Convection Currents

Deep within the Earth, at its inner core, temperatures may exceed 8,100°F (4,500°C). This heat warms rocks in the mesosphere which rise through the partially molten mantle, displacing cooler rocks just below the solid crust, which sink, and are warmed again by the heat of the mantle. This process is continuous, creating convection currents which form the moving force beneath the Earth's crust.

Plate Boundaries

The boundaries between the plates are the areas where most tectonic activity takes place. Three types of movement occur at plate boundaries: the plates can either move toward each other, move apart, or slide past each other. The effect this has on the Earth's structure depends on whether the margin is between two continental plates, two oceanic plates, or an oceanic and continental plate.

***The Mid-Atlantic Ridge** rises above sea level in Iceland, producing geysers and volcanoes.*

Mid-Ocean Ridges

—— Mid-ocean ridges are formed when two adjacent oceanic plates pull apart, allowing magma to force its way up to the surface, which then cools to form solid rock. Vast amounts of volcanic material are discharged at these mid-ocean ridges which can reach heights of 10,000 ft (3,000 m).

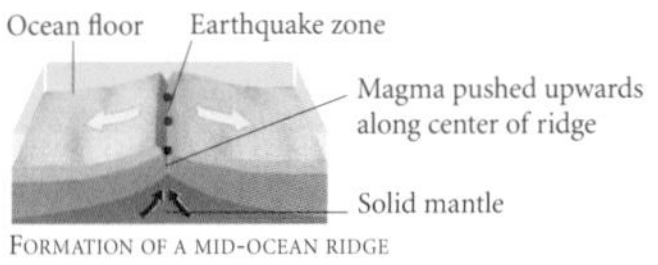
Ocean floor
Earthquake zone
Magma pushed upwards along center of ridge
Solid mantle

Formation of a mid-ocean ridge

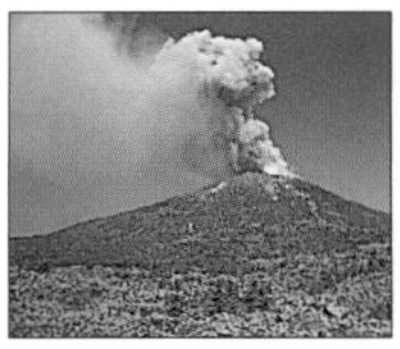

***Mount Pinatubo** is an active volcano, lying on the Pacific "Ring of Fire."*

Ocean Plates Meeting

Oceanic crust is denser and thinner than continental crust; on average it is 3 miles (5 km) thick, while continental crust averages 18–24 miles (30–40 km). When oceanic plates of similar density meet, the crust is contorted as one plate overrides the other, forming deep sea trenches and volcanic island arcs above sea level.

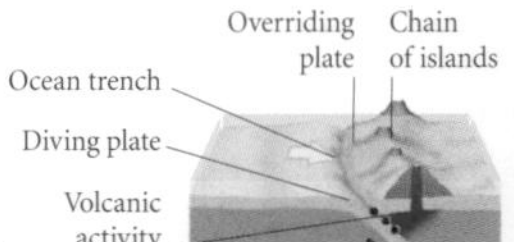
Overriding plate
Chain of islands
Ocean trench
Diving plate
Volcanic activity

Ocean plates meeting to form an island arc

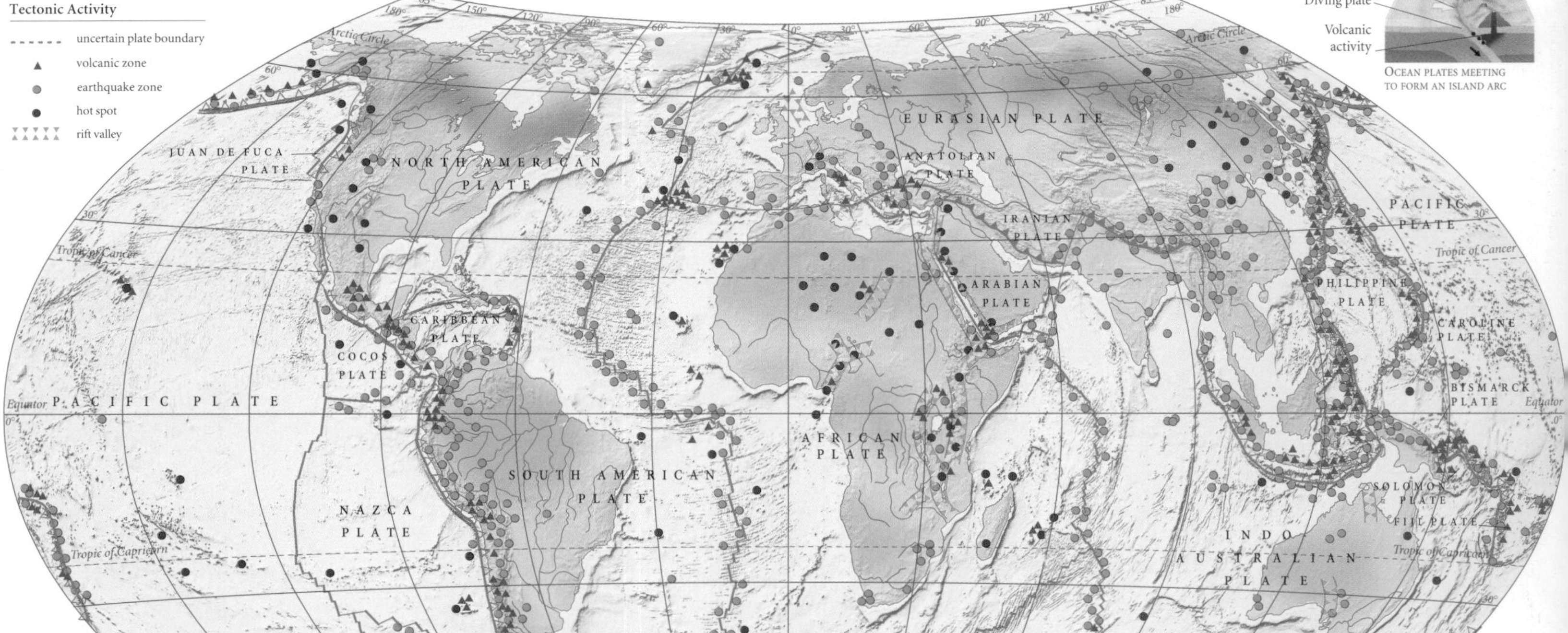
Tectonic Activity
uncertain plate boundary
volcanic zone
earthquake zone
hot spot
rift valley
JUAN DE FUCA PLATE
NORTH AMERICAN PLATE
EURASIAN PLATE
ANATOLIAN PLATE
IRANIAN PLATE
ARABIAN PLATE
PACIFIC PLATE
PHILIPPINE PLATE
CAROLINE PLATE
BISMARCK PLATE
CARIBBEAN PLATE
COCOS PLATE
PACIFIC PLATE
AFRICAN PLATE
SOUTH AMERICAN PLATE
NAZCA PLATE
SOLOMON PLATE
FIJI PLATE
INDO AUSTRALIAN PLATE
SCOTIA PLATE
ANTARCTIC PLATE
Arctic Circle
Tropic of Cancer
Equator
Tropic of Capricorn
Antarctic Circle

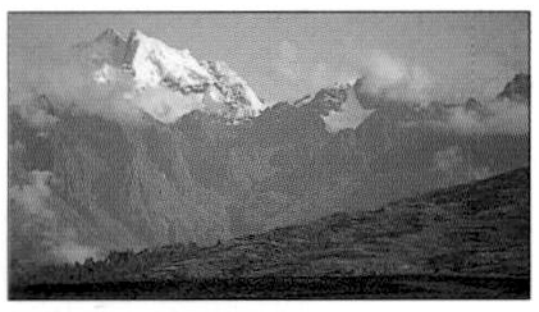

Diving Plates

When an oceanic and a continental plate meet, the denser oceanic plate is driven underneath the continental plate, which is crumpled by the collision to form mountain ranges. As the ocean plate plunges downward, it heats up, and molten rock (magma) is forced up to the surface.

***The Andean mountain** chain is the typical result of the impact of a diving plate.*

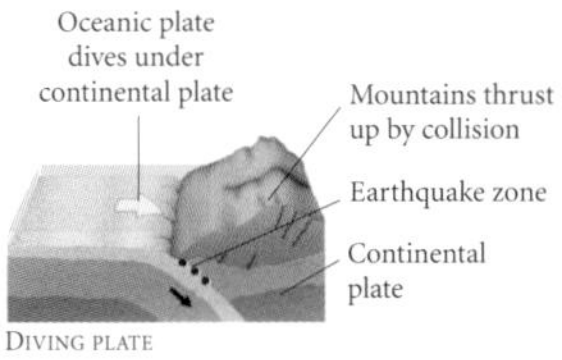
Oceanic plate dives under continental plate
Mountains thrust up by collision
Earthquake zone
Continental plate

Diving plate

***The deep fracture** caused by the sliding plates of the San Andreas Fault can be clearly seen in parts of California.*

Sliding Plates

—— When two plates slide past each other, friction is caused along the fault line which divides them. The plates do not move smoothly, and the uneven movement causes earthquakes.

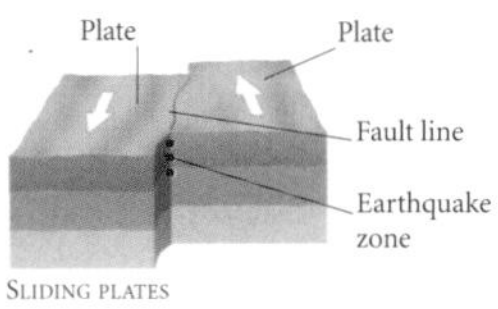
Plate
Plate
Fault line
Earthquake zone

Sliding plates

***The Alps** were formed when the African plate collided with the Eurasian Plate, about 65 million years ago.*

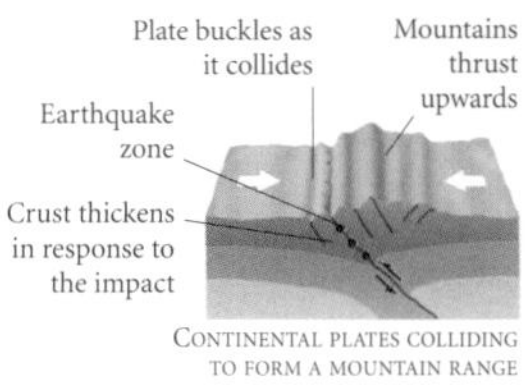
Plate buckles as it collides
Mountains thrust upwards
Earthquake zone
Crust thickens in response to the impact

Continental plates colliding to form a mountain range

Colliding Plates

When two continental plates collide, great mountain chains are thrust upward as the crust buckles and folds under the force of the impact.

CONTINENTAL DRIFT

ALTHOUGH THE PLATES which make up the Earth's crust move only a few inches in a year, over the millions of years of the Earth's history, its continents have moved many thousands of miles, to create new continents, oceans, and mountain chains.

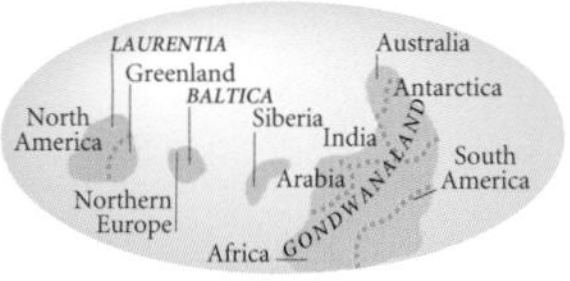
LAURENTIA
Greenland
BALTICA
North America
Siberia
India
Northern Europe
Arabia
Africa
Australia
Antarctica
South America
GONDWANALAND

1: CAMBRIAN PERIOD

570–510 million years ago. *Most continents are in tropical latitudes. The supercontinent of Gondwanaland reaches the South Pole.*

Greenland
SIBERIA
LAURENTIA /BALTICA
North America
Northern Europe
Africa
Arabia
South America
South Asia
Kazakhstania
Australia
India
Antarctica
GONDWANALAND

2: DEVONIAN PERIOD

408–362 million years ago. *The continents of Gondwanaland and Laurentia are drifting northward.*

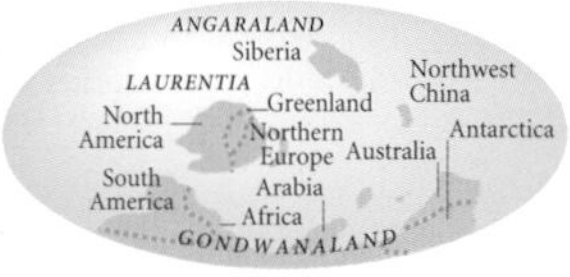
ANGARALAND
Siberia
LAURENTIA
Northwest China
North America
Greenland
Northern Europe
Australia
Antarctica
South America
Arabia
Africa
GONDWANALAND

3: CARBONIFEROUS PERIOD

362–290 million years ago. *The Earth is dominated by three continents; Laurentia, Angaraland, and Gondwanaland.*

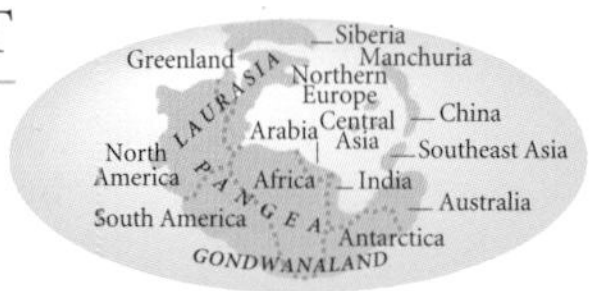
Greenland
Siberia
Manchuria
Northern Europe
Central Asia
China
Southeast Asia
Arabia
North America
LAURASIA
PANGEA
Africa
India
Australia
South America
Antarctica
GONDWANALAND

4: TRIASSIC PERIOD

245–208 million years ago. *All three major continents have joined to form the super-continent of Pangea.*

LAURASIA
North America
Northern Europe
Siberia
Greenland
Manchuria
China
Africa
South America
Arabia
India
Central Asia
Southeast Asia
Australia
Antarctica
GONDWANALAND

5: JURASSIC PERIOD

208–145 million years ago. *The super-continent of Pangea begins to break up, causing an overall rise in sea levels.*

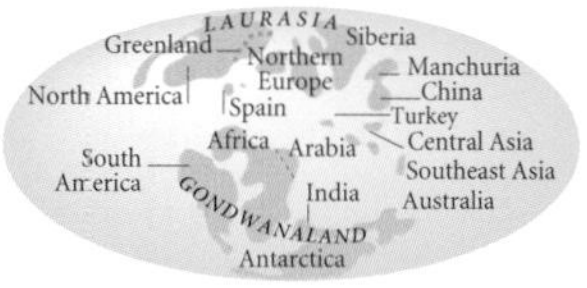
LAURASIA
Greenland
Siberia
Northern Europe
Manchuria
China
North America
Spain
Turkey
Africa
Arabia
Central Asia
Southeast Asia
South America
India
Australia
GONDWANALAND
Antarctica

6: CRETACEOUS PERIOD

145–65 million years ago. *Warm, shallow seas cover much of the land: sea levels are about 80 ft (25 m) above present levels.*

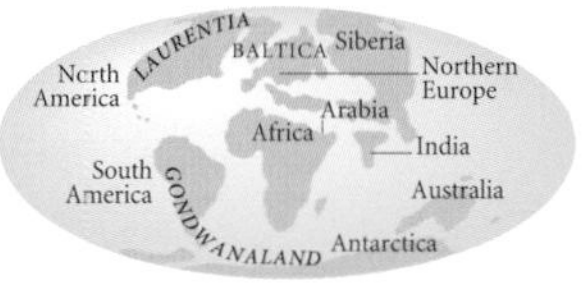
LAURENTIA
BALTICA
Siberia
North America
Northern Europe
Arabia
Africa
India
South America
Australia
GONDWANALAND
Antarctica

7: TERTIARY PERIOD

65–2 million years ago. *Although the world's geography is becoming more recognizable, major events such as the creation of the Himalayan mountain chain, are still to occur during this period.*

CONTINENTAL SHIELDS

THE CENTERS OF THE EARTH'S CONTINENTS, known as shields, were established between 2500 and 500 million years ago; some contain rocks over three billion years old. They were formed by a series of turbulent events: plate movements, earthquakes, and volcanic eruptions. Since the Pre-Cambrian period, over 570 million years ago, they have experienced little tectonic activity, and today, these flat, low-lying slabs of solidified molten rock form the stable centers of the continents. They are bounded or covered by successive belts of younger sedimentary rock.

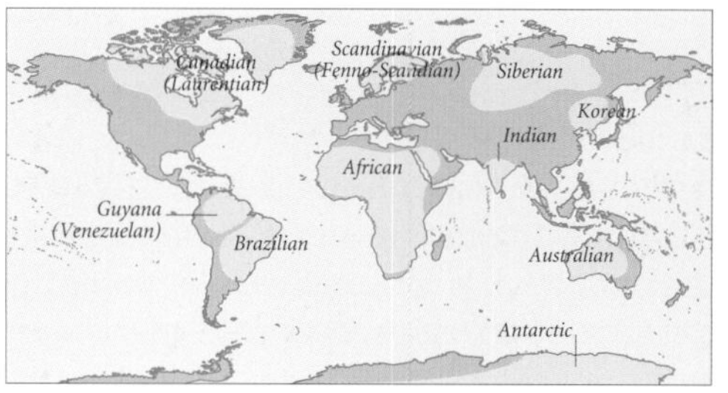
Canadian (Laurentian)
Scandinavian (Fenno-Scandian)
Siberian
Korean
Indian
African
Guyana (Venezuelan)
Brazilian
Australian
Antarctic

CREATION OF THE HIMALAYAS

BETWEEN 10 AND 20 MILLION YEARS AGO, the Indian subcontinent, part of the ancient continent of Gondwanaland, collided with the continent of Asia. The Indo-Australian Plate continued to move northward, displacing continental crust and uplifting the Himalayas, the world's highest mountain chain.

MOVEMENTS OF INDIA

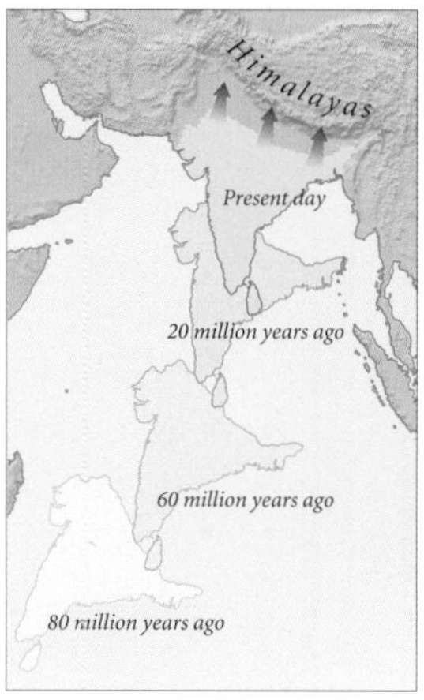
Himalayas
Present day
20 million years ago
60 million years ago
80 million years ago

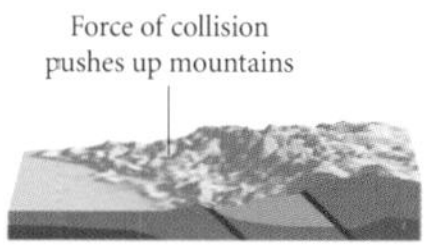
Force of collision pushes up mountains

CROSS-SECTION THROUGH THE HIMALAYAS

The Himalayas *were uplifted when the Indian subcontinent collided with Asia.*

THE HAWAIIAN ISLAND CHAIN

A HOT SPOT lying deep beneath the Pacific Ocean pushes a plume of magma from the Earth's mantle up through the Pacific Plate to form volcanic islands. While the hot spot remains stationary, the plate on which the islands sit is moving slowly. A long chain of islands has been created as the plate passes over the hot spot.

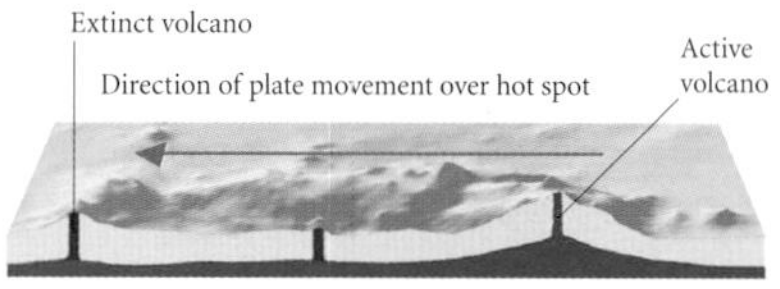
Extinct volcano
Direction of plate movement over hot spot
Active volcano

CROSS-SECTION THROUGH THE HAWAIIAN ISLANDS

EVOLUTION OF THE HAWAIIAN ISLANDS

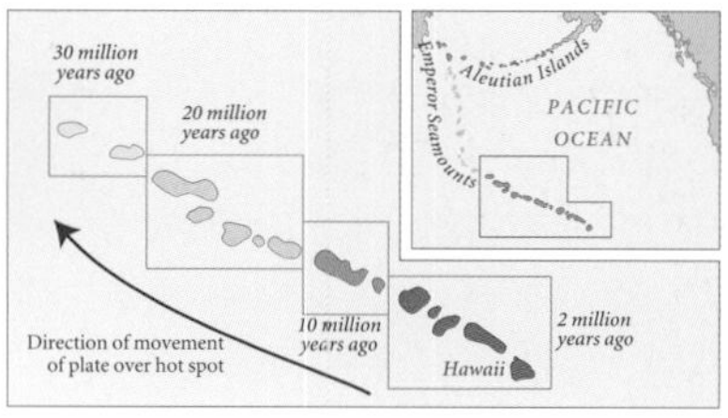
30 million years ago
20 million years ago
10 million years ago
2 million years ago
Hawaii
Direction of movement of plate over hot spot
Emperor Seamounts
Aleutian Islands
PACIFIC OCEAN

THE EARTH'S GEOLOGY

THE EARTH'S ROCKS are created in a continual cycle. Exposed rocks are weathered and eroded by wind, water and chemicals and deposited as sediments. If they pass into the Earth's crust they will be transformed by high temperatures and pressures into metamorphic rocks or they will melt and solidify as igneous rocks.

Gneiss *formations in Norway's Jotunheimen Mountains.*

GNEISS

1 Gneiss is a metamorphic rock made at great depth during the formation of mountain chains, when intense heat and pressure transform sedimentary or igneous rocks.

Basalt *columns at Giant's Causeway, Northern Ireland, UK.*

BASALT

2 Basalt is an igneous rock, formed when small quantities of magma lying close to the Earth's surface cool rapidly.

LIMESTONE

3 Limestone is a sedimentary rock, which is formed mainly from the calcite skeletons of marine animals which have been compressed into rock.

Limestone hills*, Guilin, China.*

SANDSTONE

8 Sandstones are sedimentary rocks formed mainly in deserts, beaches, and deltas. Desert sandstones are formed of grains of quartz which have been well rounded by wind erosion.

Rock stacks *of desert sandstone, at Bryce Canyon National Park, Utah.*

THE WORLD'S MAJOR GEOLOGICAL REGIONS

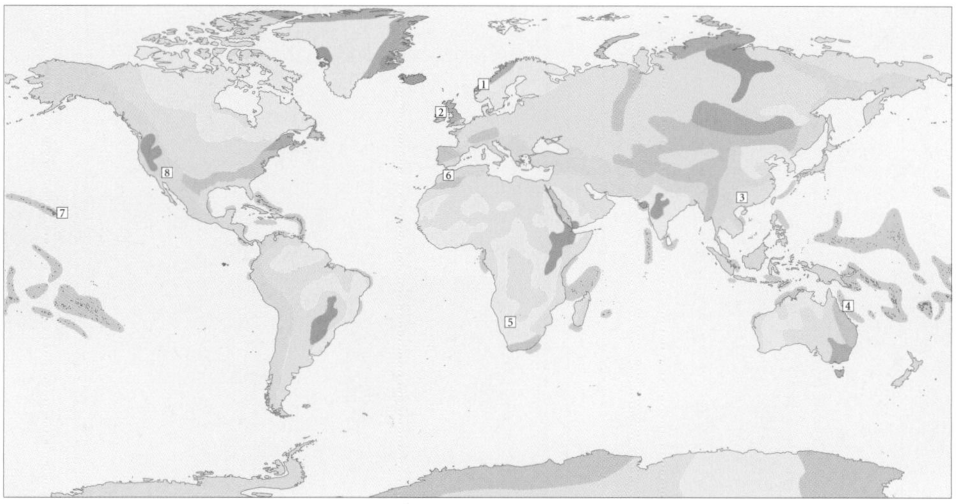
1
2
3
4
5
6
7
8

Geological Regions
- continental shield
- sedimentary cover
- coral formation
- igneous rock types

Mountain Ranges
- Alpine (new)
- Hercynian (old)
- Caledonian (ancient)

CORAL

4 Coral reefs are formed from the skeletons of millions of individual corals.

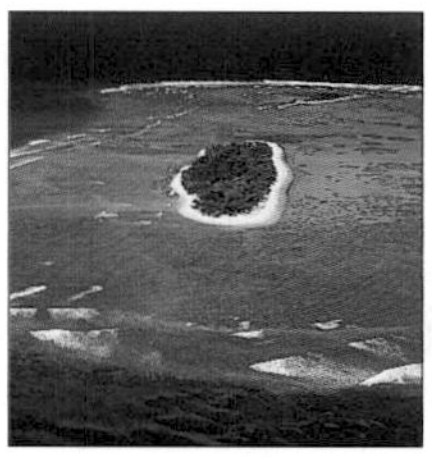

Great Barrier Reef*, Australia.*

Extrusive igneous rocks *are formed during volcanic eruptions, as here in Hawaii.*

ANDESITE

7 Andesite is an extrusive igneous rock formed from magma which has solidified on the Earth's crust after a volcanic eruption.

SCHIST

6 Schist is a metamorphic rock formed during mountain building, when temperature and pressure are comparatively high. Both mudstones and shales reform into schist under these conditions.

Schist formations *in the Atlas Mountains, northwestern Africa.*

GRANITE

5 Granite is an intrusive igneous rock formed from magma which has solidified deep within the Earth's crust. The magma cools slowly, producing a coarse-grained rock.

Namibia's *Namaqualand Plateau is formed of granite.*

SHAPING THE LANDSCAPE

THE BASIC MATERIAL OF THE EARTH'S SURFACE is solid rock: valleys, deserts, soil, and sand are all evidence of the powerful agents of weathering, erosion, and deposition which constantly shape and transform the Earth's landscapes. Water, either flowing continually in rivers or seas, or frozen and compacted into solid sheets of ice, has the most clearly visible impact on the Earth's surface. But wind can transport fragments of rock over huge distances and strip away protective layers of vegetation, exposing rock surfaces to the impact of extreme heat and cold.

WATER

LESS THAN 2% of the world's water is on the land, but it is the most powerful agent of landscape change. Water, as rainfall, groundwater, and rivers, can transform landscapes through both erosion and deposition. Eroded material carried by rivers forms the world's most fertile soils.

***Waterfalls such as the Iguaçu Falls** on the border between Argentina and southern Brazil, erode the underlying rock, causing the falls to retreat.*

COASTAL WATER

THE WORLD'S COASTLINES are constantly changing; every day, tides deposit, sift and sort sand and gravel on the shoreline. Over longer periods, powerful wave action erodes cliffs and headlands and carves out bays.

***A low, wide sandy beach** on South Africa's Cape Peninsula is continually re-shaped by the action of the Atlantic waves.*

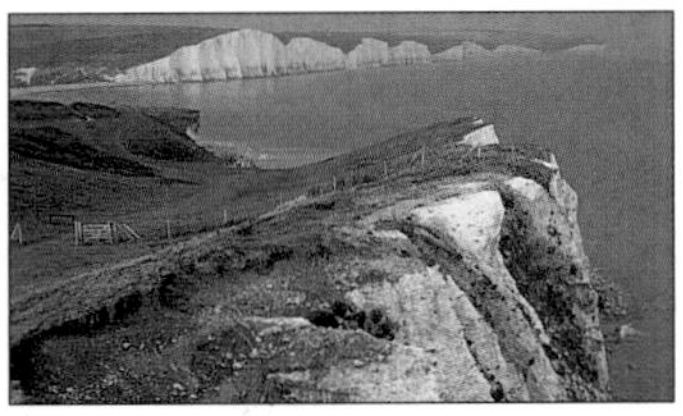

***The sheer chalk cliffs** at Seven Sisters in southern England are constantly under attack from waves.*

GROUNDWATER

IN REGIONS where there are porous rocks such as chalk, water is stored underground in large quantities; these reservoirs of water are known as aquifers. Rain percolates through topsoil into the underlying bedrock, creating an underground store of water. The limit of the saturated zone is called the water table.

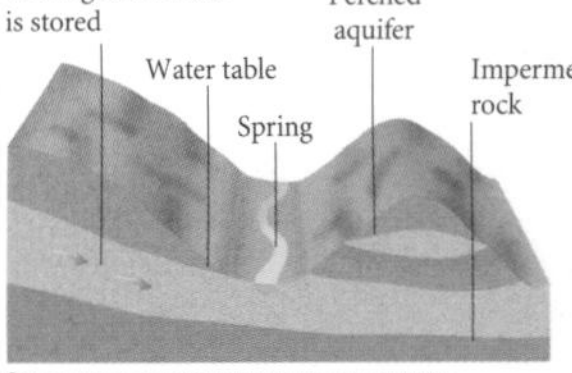

Permeable zone where groundwater is stored
Perched aquifer
Water table
Impermeable rock
Spring

STORAGE OF GROUNDWATER IN AN AQUIFER

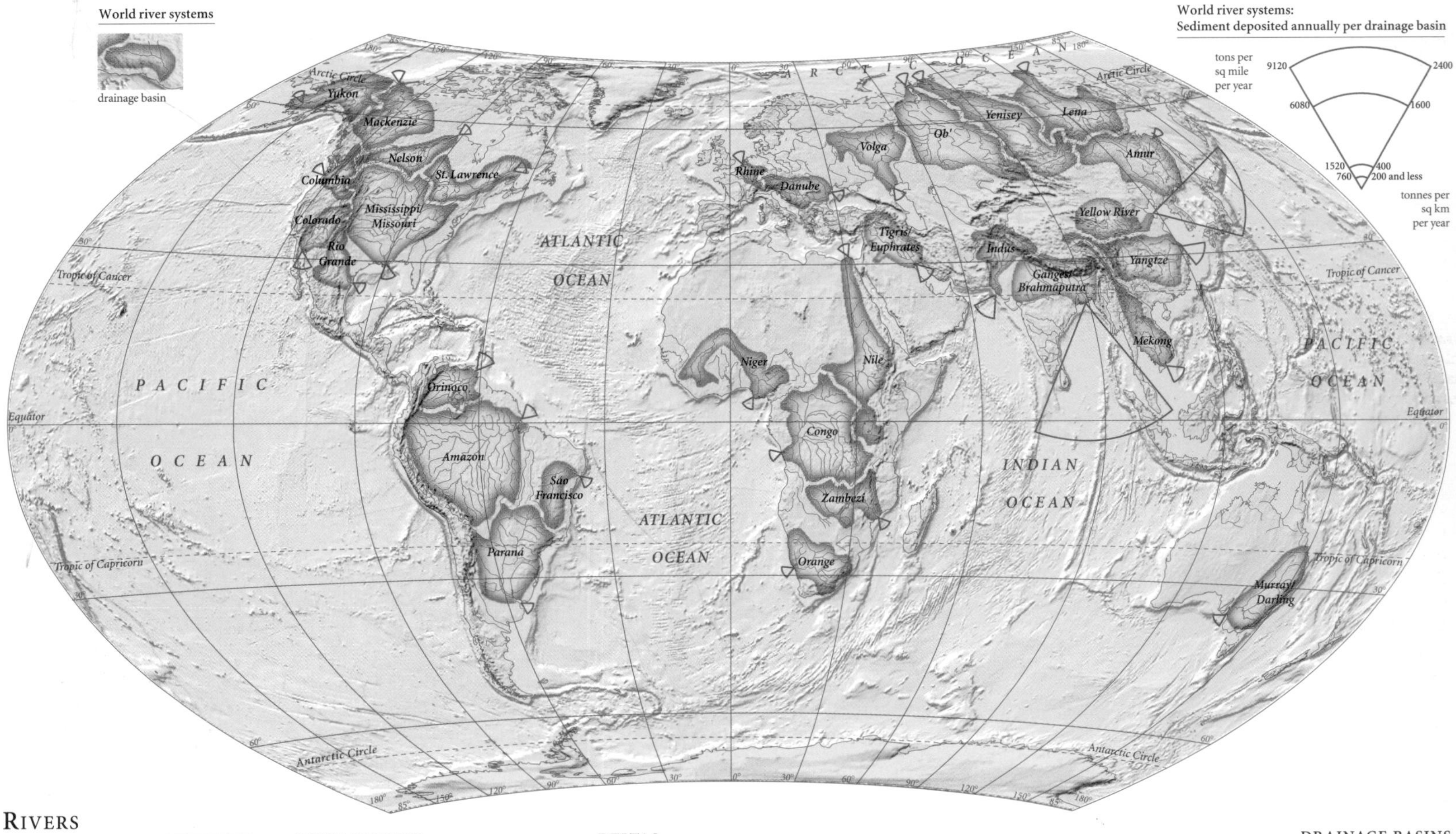

World river systems
drainage basin
World river systems: Sediment deposited annually per drainage basin
tons per sq mile per year
9120
2400
6080
1600
1520
760
400
200 and less
tonnes per sq km per year
Arctic Circle
ARCTIC OCEAN
Yukon
Mackenzie
Nelson
St. Lawrence
Columbia
Mississippi/Missouri
Colorado
Rio Grande
Tropic of Cancer
ATLANTIC OCEAN
PACIFIC OCEAN
Equator
Orinoco
Amazon
São Francisco
Paraná
Tropic of Capricorn
Rhine
Danube
Volga
Ob'
Yenisey
Lena
Amur
Tigris/Euphrates
Indus
Ganges/Brahmaputra
Yellow River
Yangtze
Mekong
Niger
Nile
Congo
Zambezi
Orange
INDIAN OCEAN
Murray/Darling
Antarctic Circle

RIVERS

RIVERS ERODE THE LAND by grinding and dissolving rocks and stones. Most erosion occurs in the river's upper course as it flows through highland areas. Rock fragments are moved along the river bed by fast-flowing water and deposited in areas where the river slows down, such as flat plains, or where the river enters seas or lakes.

RIVER VALLEYS

Over long periods of time rivers erode uplands to form characteristic V-shaped valleys with smooth sides.

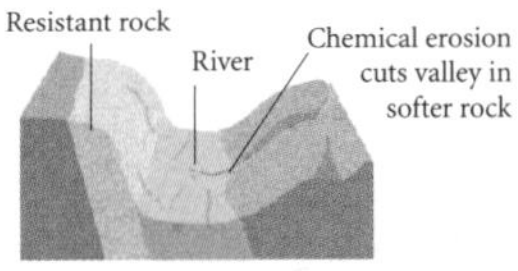

Resistant rock
River
Chemical erosion cuts valley in softer rock

RIVER VALLEY EROSION

DELTAS

When a river deposits its load of silt and sediment (alluvium) on entering the sea, it may form a delta. As this material accumulates, it chokes the mouth of the river, forcing it to create new channels to reach the sea.

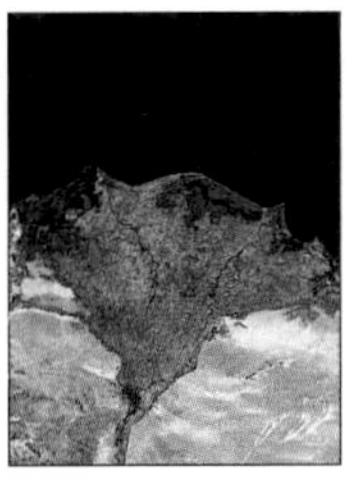

***The Nile** forms a broad delta as it flows into the Mediterranean.*

DRAINAGE BASINS

The drainage basin is the area of land drained by a major trunk river and its smaller branch rivers or tributaries. Drainage basins are separated from one another by natural boundaries known as watersheds.

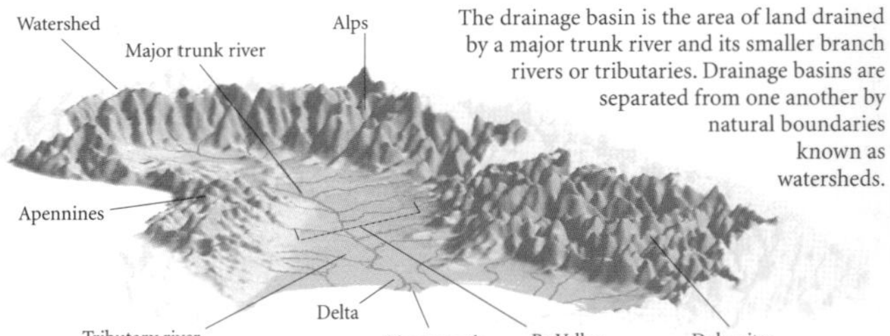

Watershed
Major trunk river
Alps
Apennines
Tributary river
Delta
River mouth
Po Valley
Dolomites

***The drainage basin** of the Po River, northern Italy.*

MEANDERS

In their lower courses, rivers flow slowly. As they flow across the lowlands, they form looping bends called meanders.

***The Mississippi River** forms meanders as it flows across the southern US.*

***The meanders** of Utah's San Juan River have become deeply incised.*

***Mud** is deposited by China's Yellow River in its lower course.*

DEPOSITION

When rivers have deposited large quantities of fertile alluvium, they are forced to find new channels through the alluvium deposits, creating braided river systems.

LANDSLIDES

Heavy rain and associated flooding on slopes can loosen underlying rocks, which crumble, causing the top layers of rock and soil to slip.

***A huge landslide** in the Swiss Alps has left massive piles of rocks and pebbles called scree.*

GULLIES

In areas where soil is thin, rainwater is not effectively absorbed, and may flow overland. The water courses downhill in channels, or gullies, and may lead to rapid erosion of soil.

***A deep gully** in the French Alps caused by the scouring of upper layers of turf.*

Ice

During its long history, the Earth has experienced a number of glacial episodes when temperatures were considerably lower than today. During the last Ice Age, 18,000 years ago, ice covered an area three times larger than it does today. Over these periods, the ice has left a remarkable legacy of transformed landscapes.

Glaciers

Glaciers are formed by the compaction of snow into "rivers" of ice. As they move over the landscape, glaciers pick up and carry a load of rocks and boulders which erode the landscape they pass over, and are eventually deposited at the end of the glacier.

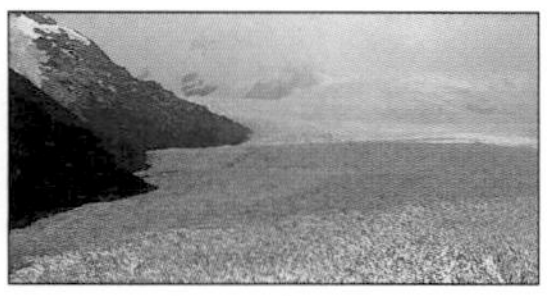

A massive glacier advancing down a valley in southern Argentina.

Glacial valleys

Glaciers can erode much more powerfully than rivers. They form steep-sided, flat-bottomed valleys with a typical U-shaped profile. Valleys created by tributary glaciers, whose floors have not been eroded to the same depth as the main glacial valley floor, are called hanging valleys.

***The U-shaped profile** and piles of morainic debris are characteristic of a valley once filled by a glacier.*

***A series of hanging valleys** high up in the Chilean Andes.*

***The profile** of the Matterhorn has been formed by three cirques lying "back-to-back."*

Cirques

Cirques are basin-shaped hollows which mark the head of a glaciated valley. Where neighboring cirques meet, they are divided by sharp rock ridges called arêtes. It is these arêtes which give the Matterhorn its characteristic profile.

Fjords

Fjords are ancient glacial valleys flooded by the sea following the end of a period of glaciation. Beneath the water, the valley floor can be 4,000 ft (1,300 m) deep.

***A fjord** fills a former glacial valley in southern New Zealand.*

Past and present world ice-cover and glacial features

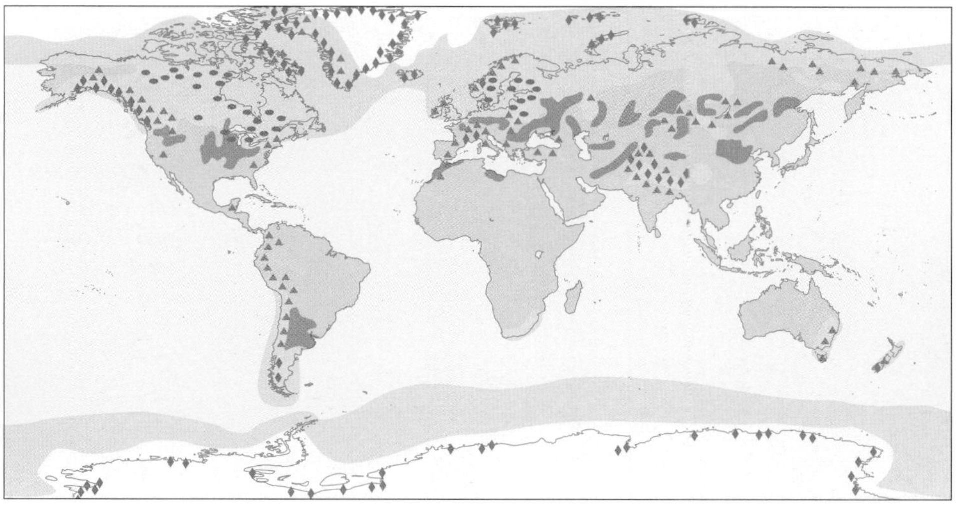
Past and present world ice cover and glacial features
extent of last Ice Age
loess deposits
post-glacial feature
glacial feature
present day ice cover
glacial field

Post-glacial features

When a glacial episode ends, the retreating ice leaves many features. These include depositional ridges called moraines, which may be eroded into low hills known as drumlins; sinuous ridges called eskers; kames, which are rounded hummocks; depressions known as kettle holes; and windblown loess deposits.

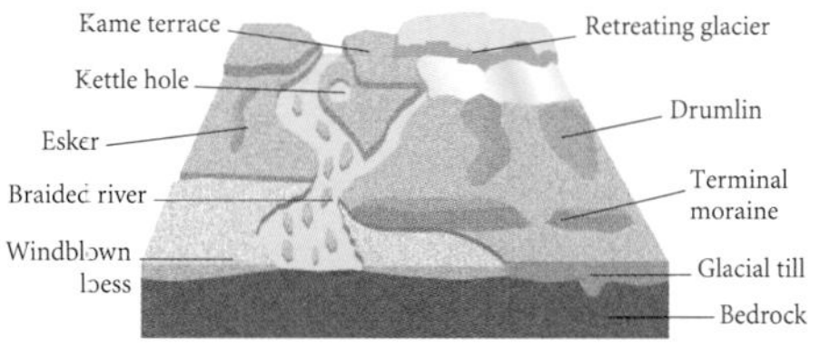
Kame terrace
Kettle hole
Esker
Braided river
Windblown loess
Retreating glacier
Drumlin
Terminal moraine
Glacial till
Bedrock

Post-glacial landscape features

Ice shattering

Water drips into fissures in rocks and freezes, expanding as it does so. The pressure weakens the rock, causing it to crack, and eventually to shatter into polygonal patterns.

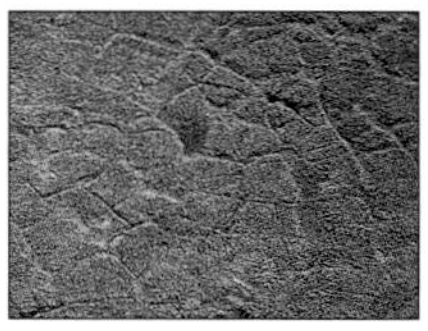

***Irregular polygons** show through the sedge-grass tundra in the Yukon, Canada.*

Periglaciation

Periglacial areas occur near to the edge of ice sheets. A layer of frozen ground lying just beneath the surface of the land is known as permafrost. When the surface melts in the summer, the water is unable to drain into the frozen ground, and so "creeps" downhill, a process known as solifluction

Wind

Strong winds can transport rock fragments great distances, especially where there is little vegetation to protect the rock. In desert areas, wind picks up loose, unprotected sand particles, carrying them over great distances. This powerfully abrasive debris is blasted at the surface by the wind, eroding the landscape into dramatic shapes.

Prevailing winds and dust trajectories

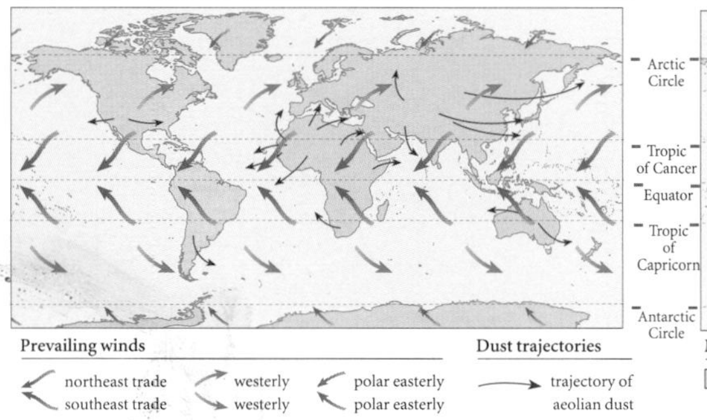
Arctic Circle
Tropic of Cancer
Equator
Tropic of Capricorn
Antarctic Circle
Prevailing winds
northeast trade
southeast trade
westerly
westerly
polar easterly
polar easterly
Dust trajectories
trajectory of aeolian dust

Deposition

The rocky, stony floors of the world's deserts are swept and scoured by strong winds. The smaller, finer particles of sand are shaped into surface ripples, dunes, or sand mountains, which rise to a height of 650 ft (200 m). Dunes usually form single lines, running perpendicular to the direction of the prevailing wind. These long, straight ridges can extend for over 100 miles (160 km).

***Barchan dunes** in the Arabian Desert.*

***Complex dune system** in the Sahara.*

Dunes

Dunes are shaped by wind direction and sand supply. Where sand supply is limited, crescent-shaped barchan dunes are formed.

Types of Dune

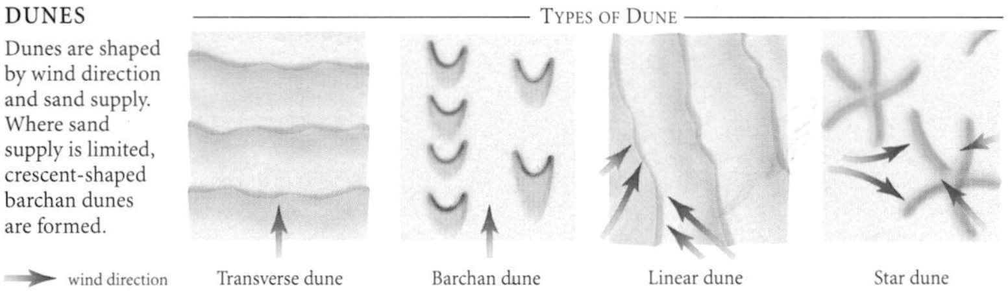
wind direction
Transverse dune
Barchan dune
Linear dune
Star dune

Temperature

Hot and cold deserts

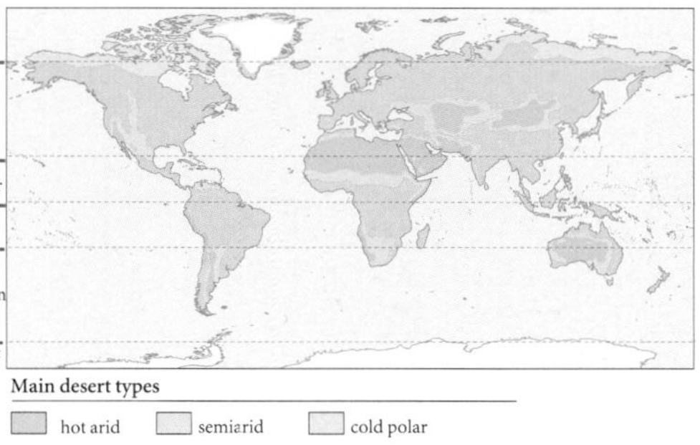
Main desert types
hot arid
semiarid
cold polar

Most of the world's deserts are in the tropics. The cold deserts which occur elsewhere are arid because they are a long way from the rain-giving sea. Rock in deserts is exposed because of lack of vegetation and is susceptible to changes in temperature; extremes of heat and cold can cause both cracks and fissures to appear in the rock.

Heat

Fierce sun can heat the surface of rock, causing it to expand more rapidly than the cooler, underlying layers. This creates tensions which force the rock to crack or break up. In arid regions, the evaporation of water from rock surfaces dissolves certain minerals within the water, causing salt crystals to form in small openings in the rock. The hard crystals force the openings to widen into cracks and fissures.

***The cracked and parched floor** of Death Valley, California. This is one of the hottest deserts on Earth.*

Desert abrasion

Abrasion creates a wide range of desert landforms from faceted pebbles and wind ripples in the sand, to large-scale features such as yardangs (low, streamlined ridges), and scoured desert pavements.

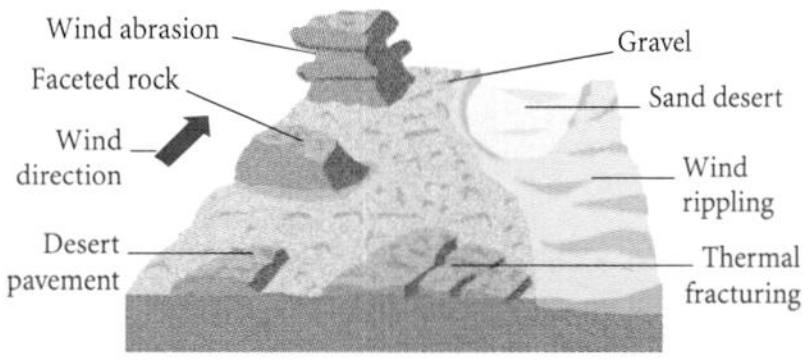
Wind abrasion
Faceted rock
Wind direction
Desert pavement
Gravel
Sand desert
Wind rippling
Thermal fracturing

Features of a desert surface

***This dry valley at Ellesmere Island** in the Canadian Arctic is an example of a cold desert. The cracked floor and scoured slopes are features also found in hot deserts.*

The World's Oceans

Two-thirds of the Earth's surface is covered by the oceans. The landscape of the ocean floor, like the surface of the land, has been shaped by movements of the Earth's crust over millions of years to form volcanic mountain ranges, deep trenches, basins, and plateaus. Ocean currents constantly redistribute warm and cold water around the world. A major warm current, such as El Niño in the Pacific Ocean, can increase surface temperature by up to 46°F (8°C), causing changes in weather patterns which can lead to both droughts and flooding.

The great oceans

There are five oceans on Earth: the Pacific, Atlantic, Indian, and Southern oceans, and the much smaller Arctic Ocean. These five ocean basins are relatively young, having evolved within the last 80 million years. One of the most recent plate collisions, between the Eurasian and African plates, created the present-day arrangement of continents and oceans.

***The Indian Ocean** accounts for approximately 20% of the total area of the world's oceans.*

Sea level

If the influence of tides, winds, currents, and variations in gravity were ignored, the surface of the Earth's oceans would closely follow the topography of the ocean floor, with an underwater ridge 3,000 ft (915 m) high producing a rise of up to 3 ft (1 m) in the level of the surface water.

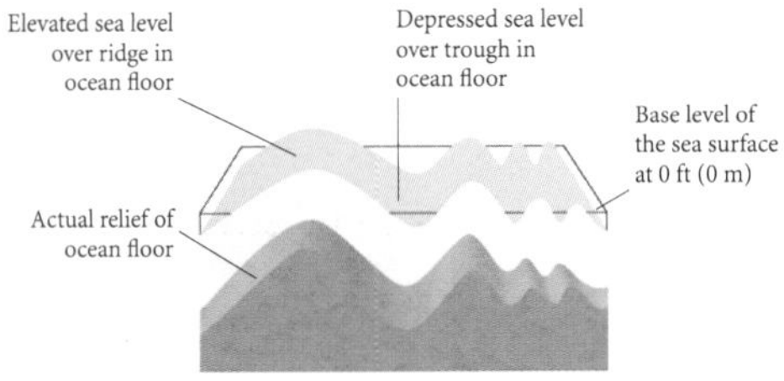
Elevated sea level over ridge in ocean floor
Depressed sea level over trough in ocean floor
Base level of the sea surface at 0 ft (0 m)
Actual relief of ocean floor

How surface waters reflect the relief of the ocean floor

***The low relief** of many small Pacific islands such as these atolls at Huahine in French Polynesia makes them vulnerable to changes in sea level.*

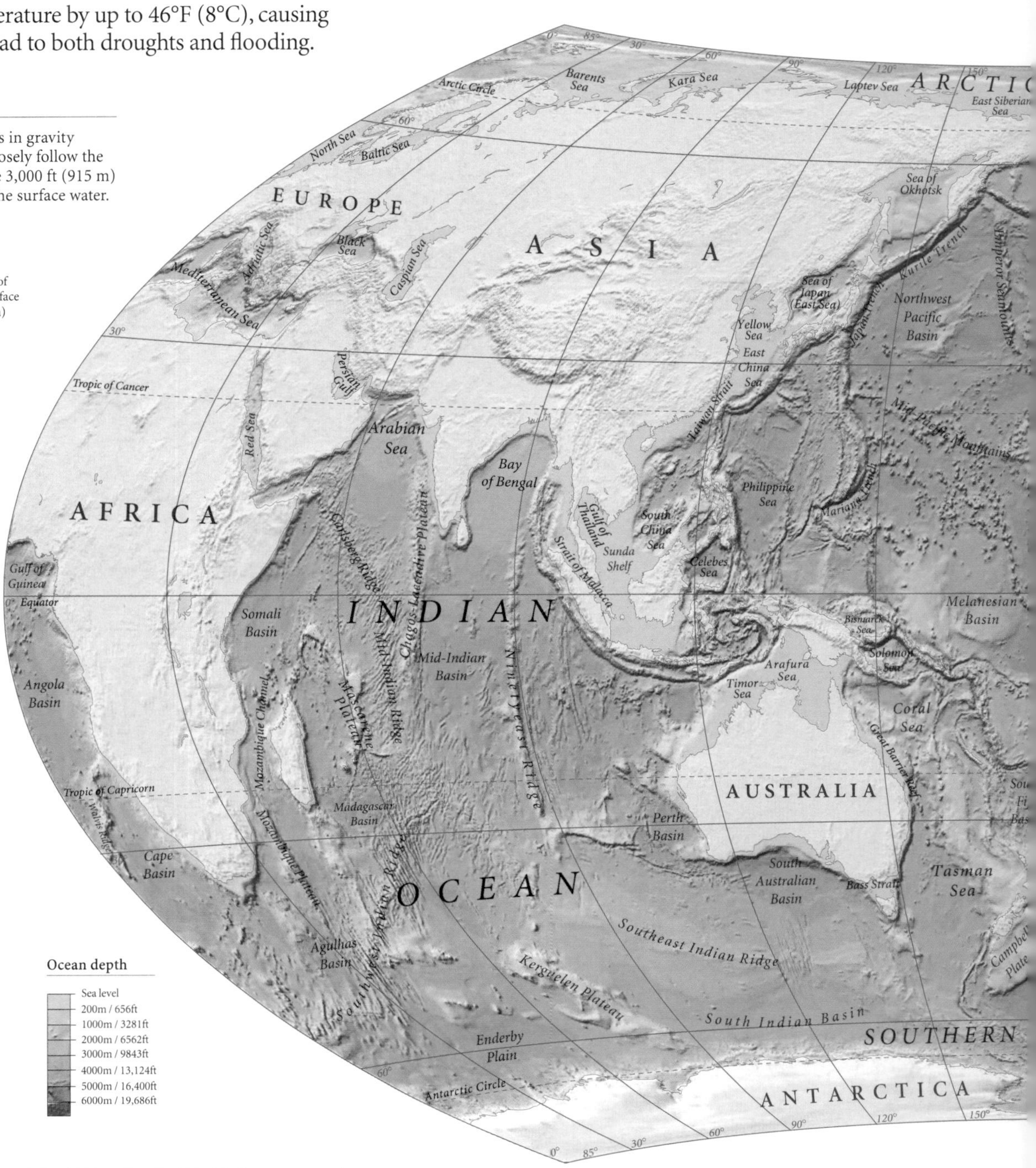
ARCTIC
Arctic Circle
Barents Sea
Kara Sea
Laptev Sea
East Siberian Sea
North Sea
Baltic Sea
EUROPE
Sea of Okhotsk
ASIA
Black Sea
Caspian Sea
Mediterranean Sea
Adriatic Sea
Sea of Japan (East Sea)
Northwest Pacific Basin
Kurile Trench
Yellow Sea
East China Sea
Persian Gulf
Tropic of Cancer
Red Sea
Arabian Sea
Bay of Bengal
Taiwan Strait
Philippine Sea
Mariana Trench
AFRICA
Gulf of Thailand
South China Sea
Sunda Shelf
Celebes Sea
Strait of Malacca
Gulf of Guinea
Equator
Somali Basin
INDIAN
Carlsberg Ridge
Chagos-Laccadive Plateau
Mid-Indian Basin
Ninetyeast Ridge
Melanesian Basin
Bismarck Sea
Solomon Sea
Arafura Sea
Timor Sea
Angola Basin
Coral Sea
Mozambique Channel
Mascarene Plateau
Mid-Indian Ridge
Tropic of Capricorn
Madagascar Basin
AUSTRALIA
Perth Basin
Cape Basin
OCEAN
South Australian Basin
Bass Strait
Tasman Sea
Southeast Indian Ridge
Agulhas Basin
Kerguelen Plateau
South Indian Basin
SOUTHERN
Enderby Plain
Antarctic Circle
ANTARCTICA
Ocean depth
Sea level
200m / 656ft
1000m / 3281ft
2000m / 6562ft
3000m / 9843ft
4000m / 13,124ft
5000m / 16,400ft
6000m / 19,686ft

Ocean structure

The continental shelf is a shallow, flat seabed surrounding the Earth's continents. It extends to the continental slope, which falls to the ocean floor. Here, the flat abyssal plains are interrupted by vast, underwater mountain ranges, the mid-ocean ridges, and ocean trenches which plunge to depths of 35,828 ft (10,920 m).

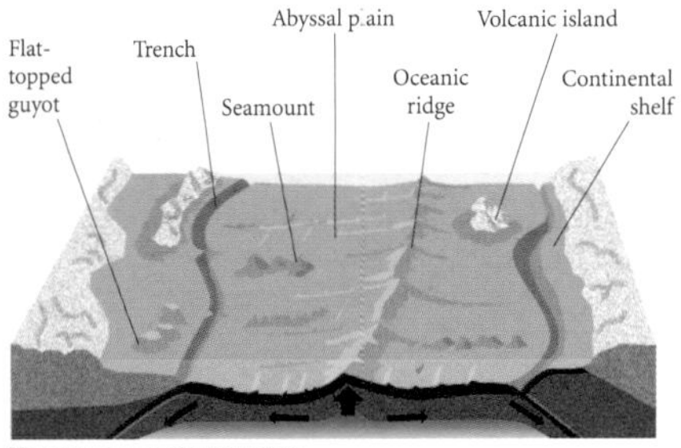
Flat-topped guyot
Trench
Abyssal plain
Seamount
Oceanic ridge
Volcanic island
Continental shelf

Typical sea-floor features

Black smokers

These vents in the ocean floor disgorge hot, sulfur-rich water from deep in the Earth's crust. Despite the great depths, a variety of lifeforms have adapted to the chemical-rich environment which surrounds black smokers.

***A black smoker** in the Atlantic Ocean.*

***Surtsey, near Iceland,** is a volcanic island lying directly over the Mid-Atlantic Ridge. It was formed in the 1960s following intense volcanic activity nearby.*

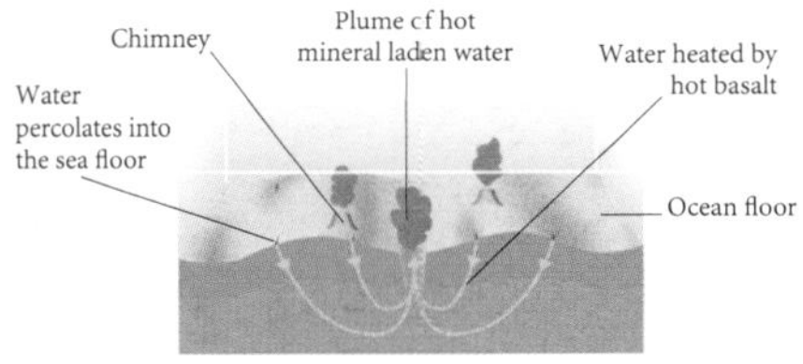
Chimney
Plume of hot mineral laden water
Water heated by hot basalt
Water percolates into the sea floor
Ocean floor

Formation of black smokers

Ocean floors

Mid-ocean ridges are formed by lava which erupts beneath the sea and cools to form solid rock. This process mirrors the creation of volcanoes from cooled lava on the land. The ages of sea floor rocks increase in parallel bands outward from central ocean ridges.

Ages of the ocean floor

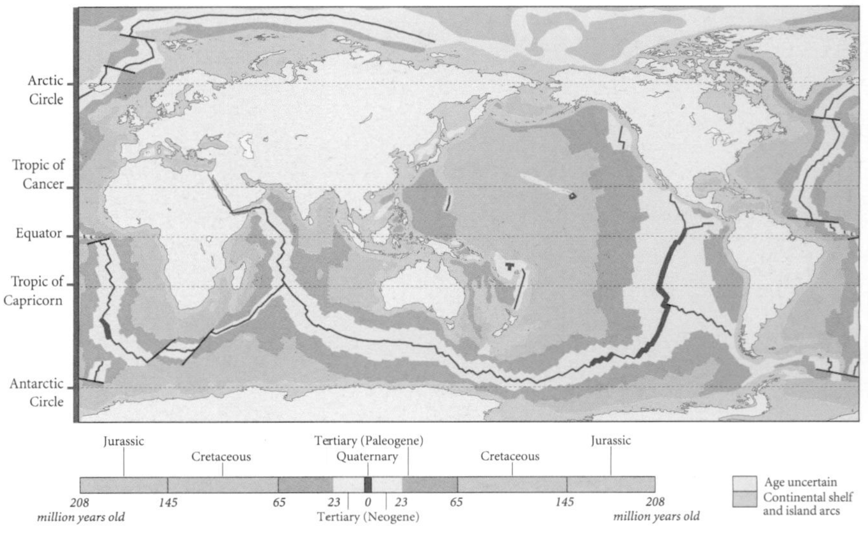
Arctic Circle
Tropic of Cancer
Equator
Tropic of Capricorn
Antarctic Circle
Jurassic
Cretaceous
Tertiary (Paleogene)
Quaternary
Cretaceous
Jurassic
208 million years old
145
65
23
0
23
65
145
208 million years old
Tertiary (Neogene)
Age uncertain
Continental shelf and island arcs

***Currents in the Southern Ocean** are driven by some of the world's fiercest winds, including the Roaring Forties, Furious Fifties, and Shrieking Sixties.*

***The Pacific Ocean** is the world's largest and deepest ocean, covering over one-third of the surface of the Earth.*

***The Atlantic Ocean** was formed when the landmasses of the eastern and western hemispheres began to drift apart 180 million years ago.*

Deposition of sediment

Storms, earthquakes, and volcanic activity trigger underwater currents known as turbidity currents which scour sand and gravel from the continental shelf, creating underwater canyons. These strong currents pick up material deposited at river mouths and deltas, and carry it across the continental shelf and through the underwater canyons, where it is eventually laid down on the ocean floor in the form of fans.

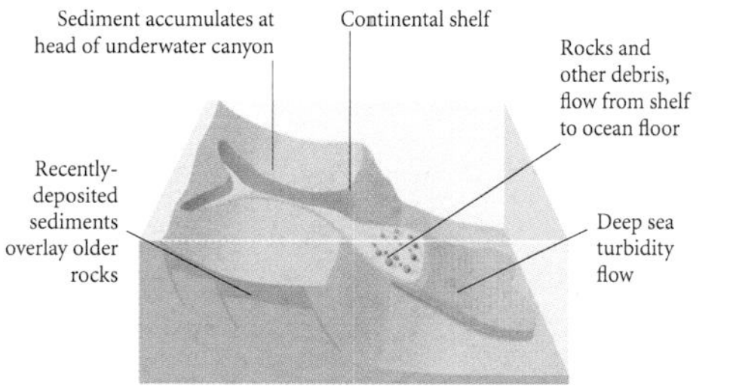

Sediment accumulates at head of underwater canyon
Continental shelf
Rocks and other debris, flow from shelf to ocean floor
Recently-deposited sediments overlay older rocks
Deep sea turbidity flow

How sediment is deposited on the ocean floor

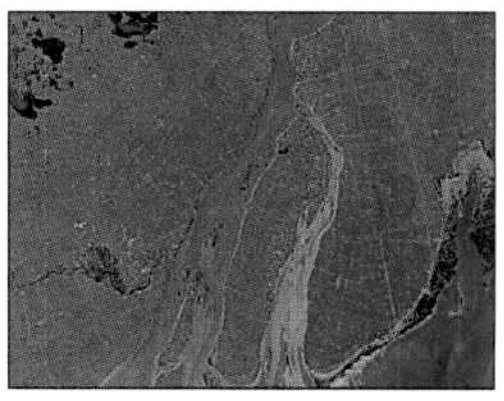

***Satellite image** of the Yangtze (Chang Jiang) Delta, in which the land appears red. The river deposits immense quantities of silt into the East China Sea, much of which will eventually reach the deep ocean floor.*

Greenland Sea
Baffin Bay
Arctic Circle
Davis Strait
Hudson Strait
Beaufort Sea
Hudson Bay
Labrador Sea
Gulf of Alaska
Mid-Atlantic Ridge
Newfoundland Basin
NORTH AMERICA
Mendocino Fracture Zone
Murray Fracture Zone
North American Basin
ATLANTIC
Gulf of Mexico
Sargasso Sea
Canary Basin
Tropic of Cancer
Molokai Fracture Zone
Yucatan Basin
Caribbean Sea
Barracuda Fracture Zone
Clarion Fracture Zone
PACIFIC
Guatemala Basin
Clipperton Fracture Zone
Equator
East Pacific Rise
SOUTH AMERICA
Brazil Basin
Peru Basin
Nazca Ridge
Chile Basin
OCEAN
Tropic of Capricorn
Sala y Gomez Ridge
OCEAN
Southwest Pacific Basin
Rio Grande Rise
Argentine Basin
OCEAN
Scotia Sea
Southeast Pacific Basin
Amundsen Sea
Bellingshausen Sea
Weddell Sea
Antarctic Circle

Surface water

Ocean currents move warm water away from the Equator toward the poles, while cold water is, in turn, moved towards the Equator. This is the main way in which the Earth distributes surface heat and is a major climatic control. Approximately 4,000 million years ago, the Earth was dominated by oceans and there was no land to interrupt the flow of the currents, which would have flowed as straight lines, simply influenced by the Earth's rotation.

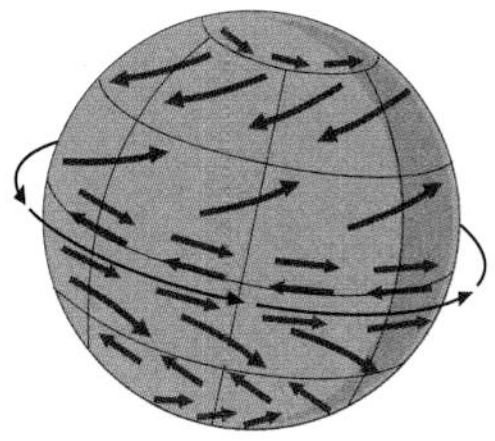

***Idealized globe** showing the movement of water around a landless Earth.*

Ocean currents

Surface currents are driven by the prevailing winds and by the spinning motion of the Earth, which drives the currents into circulating whirlpools, or gyres. Deep sea currents, over 330 ft (100 m) below the surface, are driven by differences in water temperature and salinity, which have an impact on the density of deep water and on its movement.

Surface temperature and currents

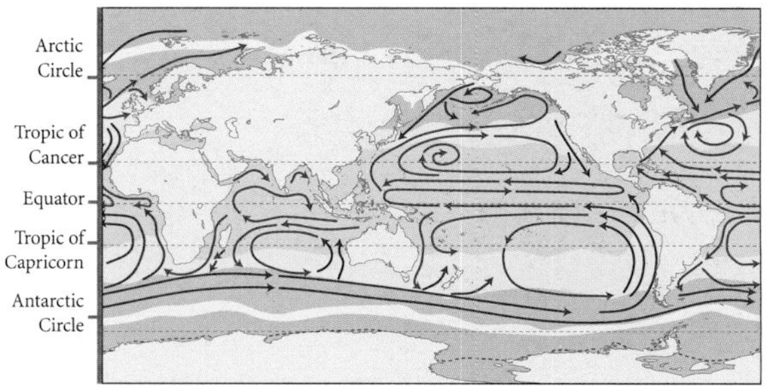

Arctic Circle
Tropic of Cancer
Equator
Tropic of Capricorn
Antarctic Circle

Surface temperature and currents

- Ice-shelf (below 32°F / 0°C)
- Sea-ice* (average) below 28°F / -2°C
- Sea-water 28–32°F / -2–0°C
- 32–50°F / 0–10°C
- 50–68°F / 10–20°C
- 68–86°F / 20–30°C
- warm current
- cold current

* Sea-water freezes at 28.4°F / -1.9°C

Tides and waves

Tides are created by the pull of the Sun and Moon's gravity on the surface of the oceans. The levels of high and low tides are influenced by the position of the Moon in relation to the Earth and Sun. Waves are formed by wind blowing over the surface of the water.

Tidal range and wave environments

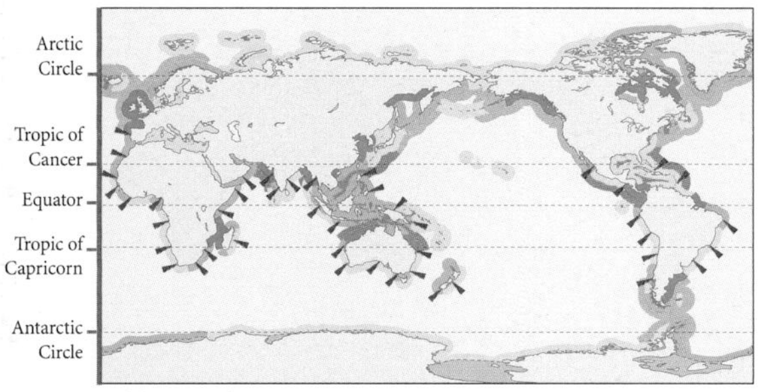

Arctic Circle
Tropic of Cancer
Equator
Tropic of Capricorn
Antarctic Circle

Tidal range and wave environments

- less than 7ft / 2m
- 7–13ft / 2–4m
- greater than 13ft / 4m
- east coast swell
- west coast swell
- tropical cyclone
- storm wave
- ice-shelf

High and low tides

The highest tides occur when the Earth, the Moon and the Sun are aligned *(below left)*. The lowest tides are experienced when the Sun and Moon align at right angles to one another *(below right)*.

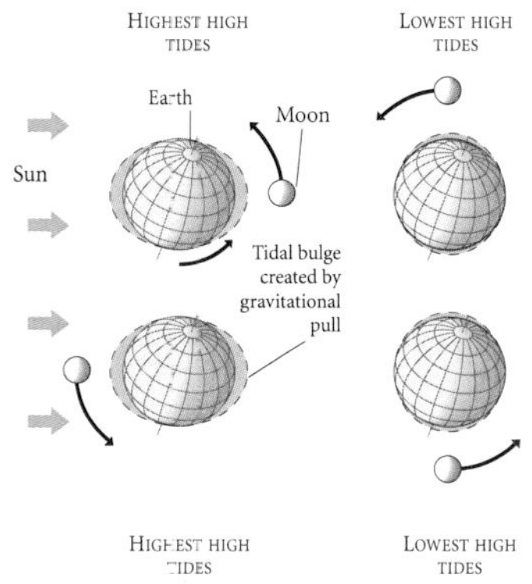

Highest high tides
Lowest high tides
Earth
Moon
Sun
Tidal bulge created by gravitational pull
Highest high tides
Lowest high tides

Deep sea temperature and currents

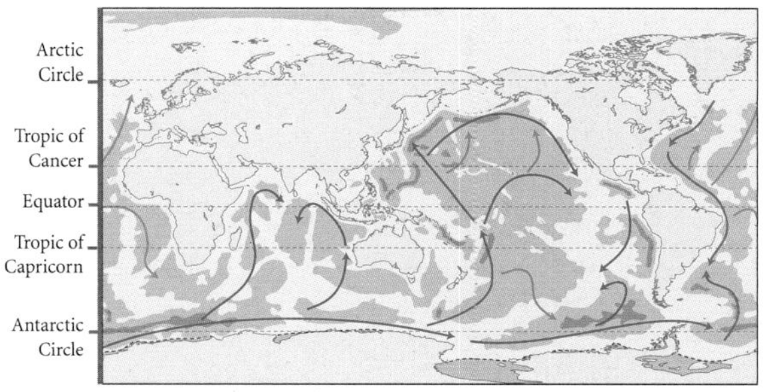

Arctic Circle
Tropic of Cancer
Equator
Tropic of Capricorn
Antarctic Circle

Deep sea temperature and currents

- Ice-shelf (below 32°F/ 0°C)
- Sea-water 28–32°F/-2–0°C (below 16,400ft/ 5000m)
- Sea-water 32–41° F/0–5°C (below 13,120ft/4000m)
- Primary currents
- Secondary currents

THE GLOBAL CLIMATE

THE EARTH'S CLIMATIC TYPES CONSIST of stable patterns of weather conditions averaged out over a long period of time. Different climates are categorized according to particular combinations of temperature and humidity. By contrast, weather consists of short-term fluctuations in wind, temperature, and humidity conditions. Different climates are determined by latitude, altitude, the prevailing wind, and circulation of ocean currents. Longer-term changes in climate, such as global warming or the onset of ice ages, are punctuated by shorter-term events which comprise the day-to-day weather of a region, such as frontal depressions, hurricanes, and blizzards.

GLOBAL AIR CIRCULATION

AIR DOES NOT SIMPLY FLOW FROM THE EQUATOR TO THE POLES, it circulates in giant cells known as Hadley and Ferrel cells. As air warms it expands, becoming less dense and rising; this creates areas of low pressure. As the air rises it cools and condenses, causing heavy rainfall over the tropics and slight snowfall over the poles. This cool air then sinks, forming high pressure belts. At surface level in the tropics these sinking currents are deflected poleward as the westerlies and toward the Equator as the trade winds. At the poles they become the polar easterlies.

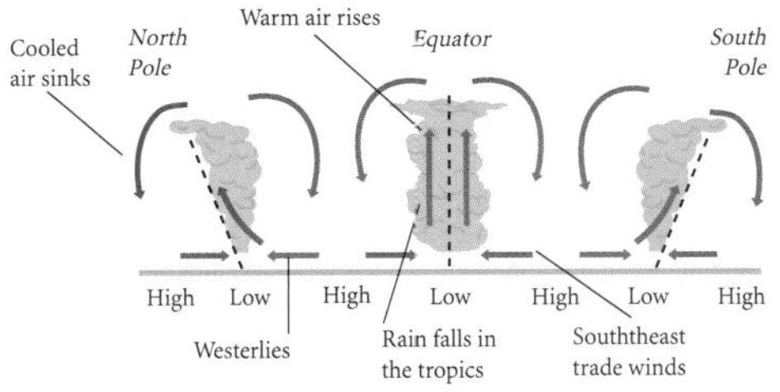
Cooled air sinks
North Pole
Warm air rises
Equator
South Pole
High
Low
High
Low
High
Low
High
Westerlies
Rain falls in the tropics
Southeast trade winds

The Antarctic pack ice expands its area by almost seven times during the winter as temperatures drop and surrounding seas freeze.

THE ATMOSPHERE, WIND, AND WEATHER

THE EARTH'S ATMOSPHERE has been compared to a giant ocean of air which surrounds the planet. Its circulation patterns are similar to the currents in the oceans and are influenced by three factors; the Earth's orbit around the Sun and rotation about its axis, and variations in the amount of heat radiation received from the Sun. If both heat and moisture were not redistributed between the Equator and the poles, large areas of the Earth would be uninhabitable.

Heavy fogs, as here in southern England, form as moisture-laden air passes over cold ground.

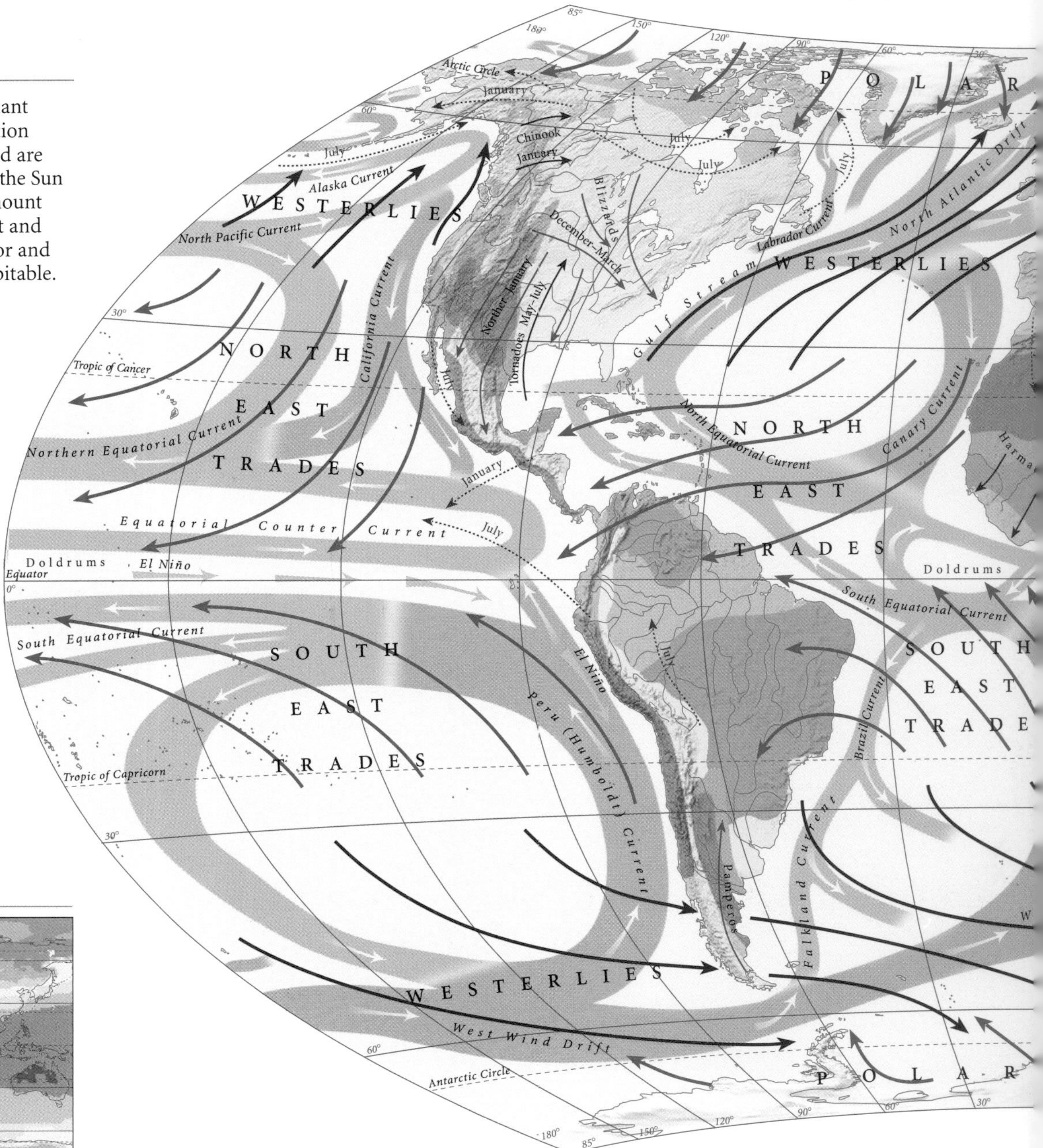
Arctic Circle
January
July
Chinook
January
Alaska Current
WESTERLIES
North Pacific Current
Blizzards
December–March
POLAR
Labrador Current
North Atlantic Drift
Gulf Stream
WESTERLIES
NORTH EAST TRADES
California Current
Northers January
Tornadoes May–July
Tropic of Cancer
Northern Equatorial Current
North Equatorial Current
NORTH EAST TRADES
Canary Current
Harmattan
Equatorial Counter Current
July
Doldrums
El Niño
Equator
Doldrums
South Equatorial Current
SOUTH EAST TRADES
El Niño
Peru (Humboldt) Current
Brazil Current
SOUTH EAST TRADES
Tropic of Capricorn
Falkland Current
Pampero
WESTERLIES
West Wind Drift
Antarctic Circle
POLAR

TEMPERATURE

THE WORLD CAN BE DIVIDED into three major climatic zones, stretching like large belts across the latitudes: the tropics which are warm; the cold polar regions and the temperate zones which lie between them. Temperatures across the Earth range from above 86°F (30°C) in the deserts to as low as -70°F (-55°C) at the poles. Temperature is also controlled by altitude; because air becomes cooler and less dense the higher it gets, mountainous regions are typically colder than those areas which are at, or close to, sea level.

AVERAGE JANUARY TEMPERATURES

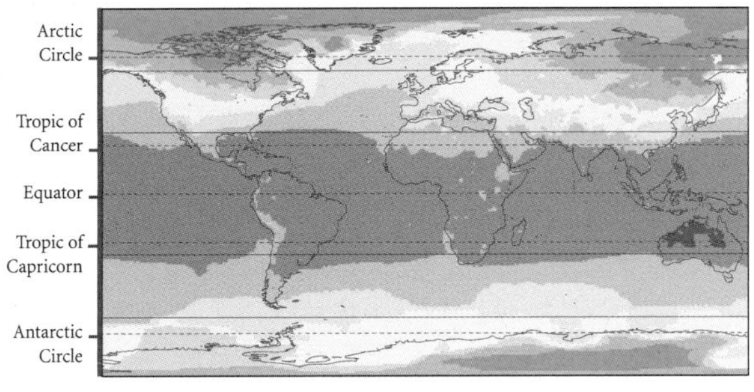
Arctic Circle
Tropic of Cancer
Equator
Tropic of Capricorn
Antarctic Circle

AVERAGE JULY TEMPERATURES

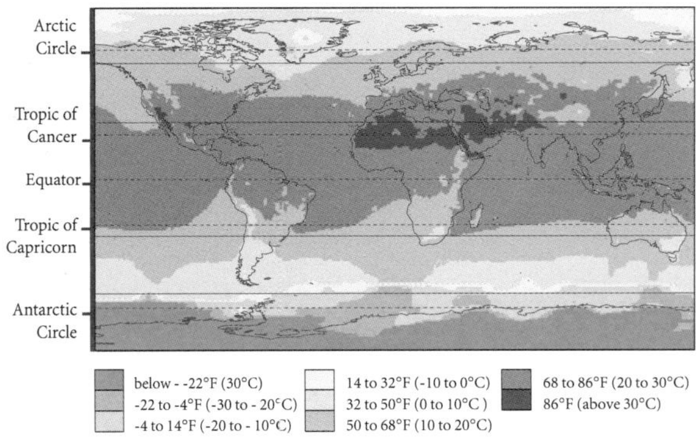
Arctic Circle
Tropic of Cancer
Equator
Tropic of Capricorn
Antarctic Circle
below - -22°F (30°C)
-22 to -4°F (-30 to - 20°C)
-4 to 14°F (-20 to - 10°C)
14 to 32°F (-10 to 0°C)
32 to 50°F (0 to 10°C)
50 to 68°F (10 to 20°C)
68 to 86°F (20 to 30°C)
86°F (above 30°C)

CLIMATIC CHANGE

THE EARTH IS CURRENTLY IN A WARM PHASE between ice ages. Warmer temperatures result in higher sea levels as more of the polar ice caps melt. Most of the world's population lives near coasts, so any changes which might cause sea levels to rise, could have a potentially disastrous impact.

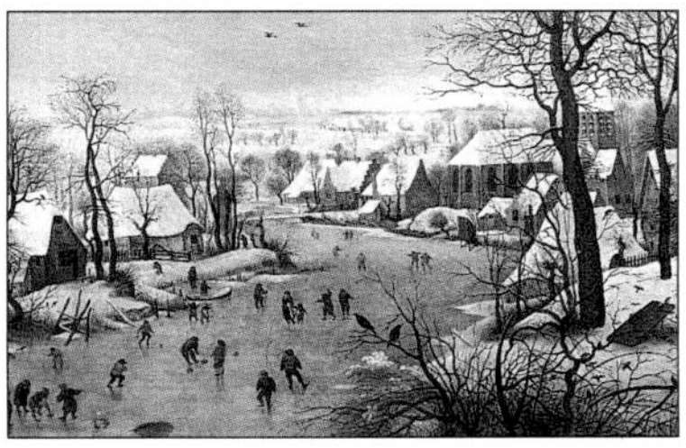

This ice fair, painted by Pieter Brueghel the Younger in the 17th century, shows the Little Ice Age which peaked around 300 years ago.

THE GREENHOUSE EFFECT

Gases such as carbon dioxide are known as "greenhouse gases" because they allow shortwave solar radiation to enter the Earth's atmosphere, but help to stop longwave radiation from escaping. This traps heat, raising the Earth's temperature. An excess of these gases, such as that which results from the burning of fossil fuels, helps trap more heat and can lead to global warming.

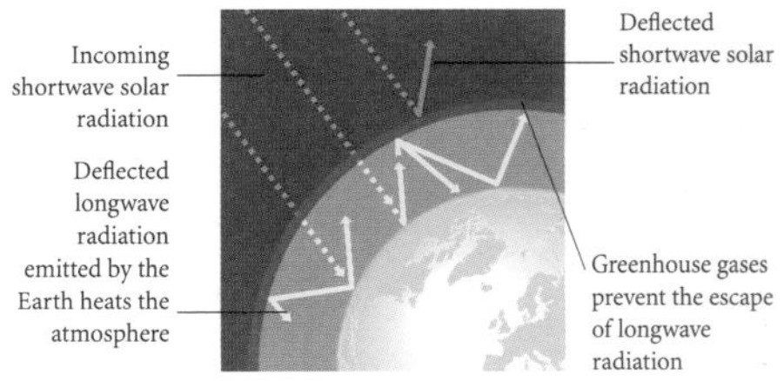
Incoming shortwave solar radiation
Deflected longwave radiation emitted by the Earth heats the atmosphere
Deflected shortwave solar radiation
Greenhouse gases prevent the escape of longwave radiation

The islands of the Caribbean, Mexico's Gulf coast and the southeastern US are often hit by hurricanes formed far out in the Atlantic.

Oceanic water circulation

In general, ocean currents parallel the movement of winds across the Earth's surface. Incoming solar energy is greatest at the Equator and least at the poles. So, water in the oceans heats up most at the Equator and flows poleward, cooling as it moves north or south toward the Arctic or Antarctic. The flow is eventually reversed and cold water currents move back toward the Equator. These ocean currents act as a vast system for moving heat from the Equator toward the poles and are a major influence on the distribution of the Earth's climates.

***In marginal climatic zones** years of drought can completely dry out the land and transform grassland to desert.*

Tilt and rotation

The tilt and rotation of the Earth during its annual orbit largely control the distribution of heat and moisture across its surface, which correspondingly controls its large-scale weather patterns. As the Earth annually rotates around the Sun, half its surface is receiving maximum radiation, creating summer and winter seasons. The angle of the Earth means that on average the tropics receive two and a half times as much heat from the Sun each day as the poles.

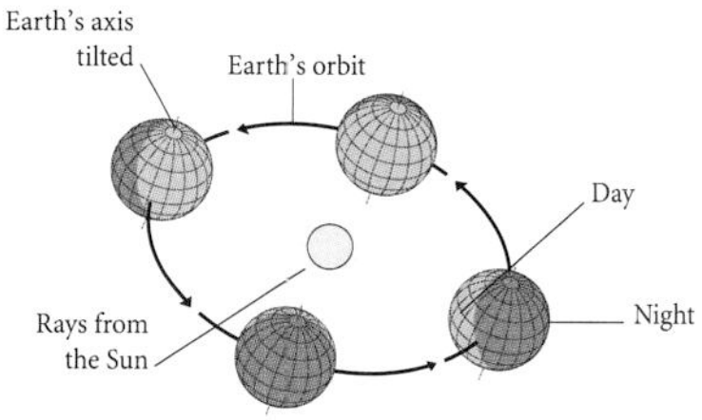
Earth's axis tilted
Earth's orbit
Day
Night
Rays from the Sun

Map Key

Climate zones		Ocean currents	Prevailing winds	Local winds
ice cap	mediterranean	warm	warm	warm
subarctic	semiarid	cold	cold	cold
tundra	arid			seasonal* (June)
continental	hot humid			* (seasonal winds which can either be warm or cold)
temperate	humid equatorial			
warm temperate	tropical			

***The wide range** of environments found in the Andes is strongly related to their altitude, which modifies climatic influences. While the peaks are snow-capped, many protected interior valleys are semitropical.*

The Coriolis effect

The rotation of the Earth influences atmospheric circulation by deflecting winds and ocean currents. Winds blowing in the northern hemisphere are deflected to the right and those in the southern hemisphere are deflected to the left, creating large-scale patterns of wind circulation, such as the northeast and southeast trade winds and the westerlies. This effect is greatest at the poles and least at the Equator.

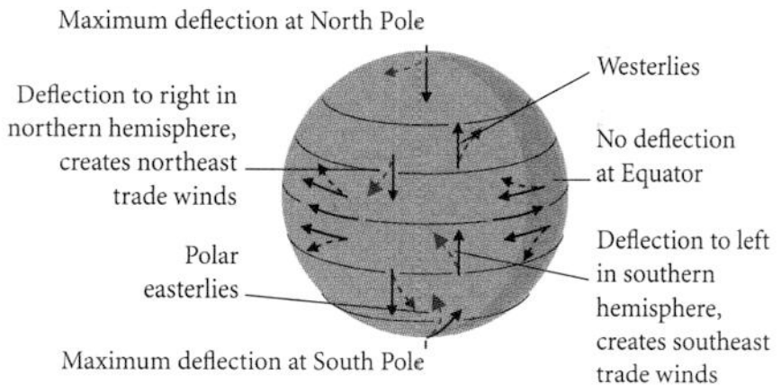
Maximum deflection at North Pole
Deflection to right in northern hemisphere, creates northeast trade winds
Polar easterlies
Maximum deflection at South Pole
Westerlies
No deflection at Equator
Deflection to left in southern hemisphere, creates southeast trade winds

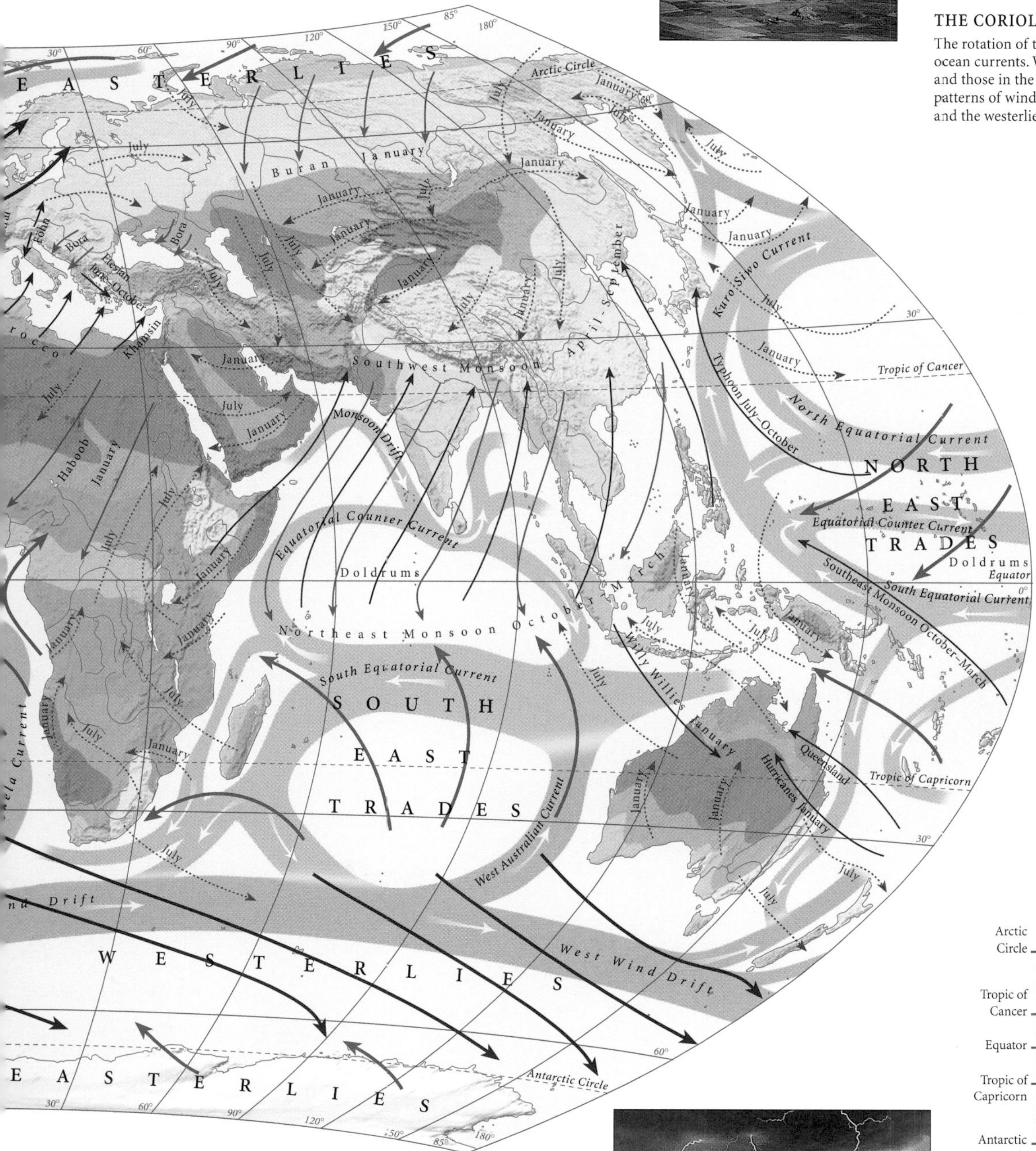
EASTERLIES
Arctic Circle
Buran
Bora
Foehn
Khamsin
Haboob
Southwest Monsoon
Monsoon Drift
Equatorial Counter Current
Doldrums
Northeast Monsoon October–March
South Equatorial Current
SOUTH EAST TRADES
Kuro Siwo Current
Typhoon July–October
Tropic of Cancer
North Equatorial Current
NORTH EAST TRADES
Equator
Southeast Monsoon October–March
Willy Willies
Queensland Hurricanes January
Tropic of Capricorn
West Australian Current
West Wind Drift
WESTERLIES
Antarctic Circle

Precipitation

When warm air expands, it rises and cools, and the water vapor it carries condenses to form clouds. Heavy, regular rainfall is characteristic of the equatorial region, while the poles are cold and receive only slight snowfall. Tropical regions have marked dry and rainy seasons, while in the temperate regions rainfall is relatively unpredictable.

***Monsoon rains**, which affect southern Asia from May to September, are caused by sea winds blowing across the warm land.*

***Heavy tropical rainstorms** occur frequently in Papua New Guinea, often causing soil erosion and landslides in cultivated areas.*

Average January rainfall

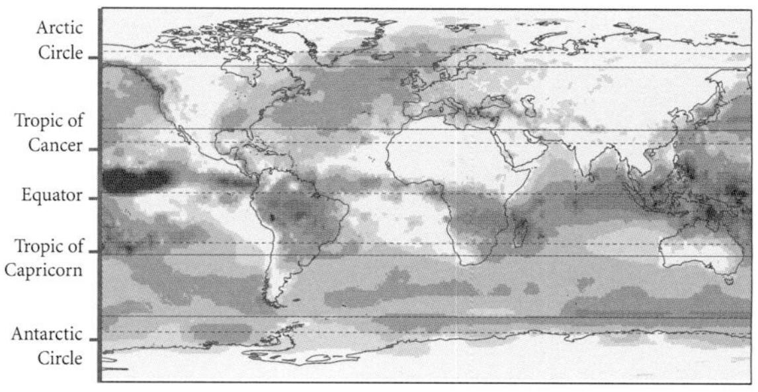
Arctic Circle
Tropic of Cancer
Equator
Tropic of Capricorn
Antarctic Circle

Average July rainfall

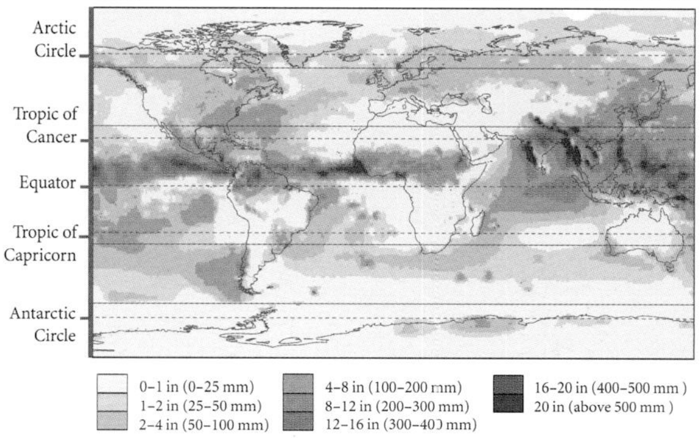
Arctic Circle
Tropic of Cancer
Equator
Tropic of Capricorn
Antarctic Circle
0–1 in (0–25 mm)
1–2 in (25–50 mm)
2–4 in (50–100 mm)
4–8 in (100–200 mm)
8–12 in (200–300 mm)
12–16 in (300–400 mm)
16–20 in (400–500 mm)
20 in (above 500 mm)

***The intensity of some blizzards** in Canada and the northern US can give rise to snowdrifts as high as 10 ft (3 m).*

***The Atacama Desert in Chile** is one of the driest places on Earth, with an average rainfall of less than 2 inches (50 mm) per year.*

***Violent thunderstorms** occur along advancing cold fronts, when cold, dry air masses meet warm, moist air, which rises rapidly, its moisture condensing into thunderclouds. Rain and hail become electrically charged, causing lightning.*

The rainshadow effect

When moist air is forced to rise by mountains, it cools and the water vapor falls as precipitation, either as rain or snow. Only the dry, cold air continues over the mountains, leaving inland areas with little or no rain. This is called the rainshadow effect and is one reason for the existence of the Mojave Desert in California, which lies east of the Coast Ranges.

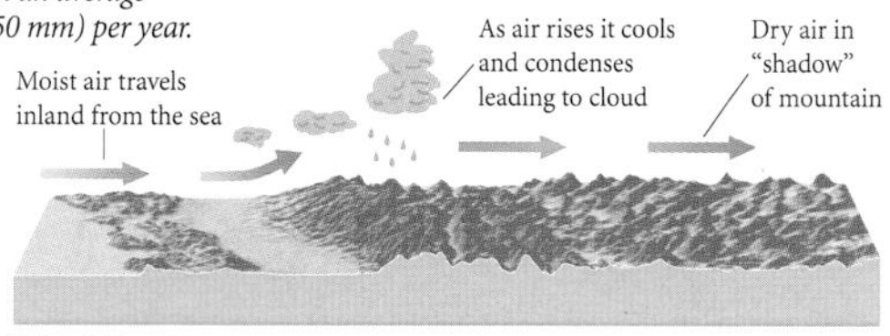
Moist air travels inland from the sea
As air rises it cools and condenses leading to cloud
Dry air in "shadow" of mountain

The rainshadow effect

Life on Earth

A unique combination of an oxygen-rich atmosphere and plentiful water is the key to life on Earth. Apart from the polar ice caps, there are few areas which have not been colonized by animals or plants over the course of the Earth's history. Plants process sunlight to provide them with their energy, and ultimately all the Earth's animals rely on plants for survival. Because of this reliance, plants are known as primary producers, and the availability of nutrients and temperature of an area is defined as its primary productivity, which affects the quantity and type of animals which are able to live there. This index is affected by climatic factors – cold and aridity restrict the quantity of life, whereas warmth and regular rainfall allow a greater diversity of species.

Biogeographical Regions

The Earth can be divided into a series of biogeographical regions, or biomes, ecological communities where certain species of plant and animal coexist within particular climatic conditions. Within these broad classifications, other factors including soil richness, altitude, and human activities such as urbanization, intensive agriculture, and deforestation, affect the local distribution of living species within each biome.

POLAR REGIONS

A layer of permanent ice at the Earth's poles covers both seas and land. Very little plant and animal life can exist in these harsh regions.

TUNDRA

A desolate region, with long, dark freezing winters and short, cold summers. With virtually no soil and large areas of permanently frozen ground known as permafrost, the tundra is largely treeless, though it is briefly clothed by small flowering plants in the summer months.

NEEDLELEAF FORESTS

With milder summers than the tundra and less wind, these areas are able to support large forests of coniferous trees.

BROADLEAF FORESTS

Much of the northern hemisphere was once covered by deciduous forests, which occurred in areas with marked seasonal variations. Most deciduous forests have been cleared for human settlement.

TEMPERATE RAIN FORESTS

In warmer wetter areas, such as southern China, temperate deciduous forests are replaced by evergreen forest.

DESERTS

Deserts are areas with negligible rainfall. Most hot deserts lie within the tropics; cold deserts are dry because of their distance from the moisture-providing sea.

MEDITERRANEAN

Hot, dry summers and short winters typify these areas, which were once covered by evergreen shrubs and woodland, but have now been cleared by humans for agriculture.

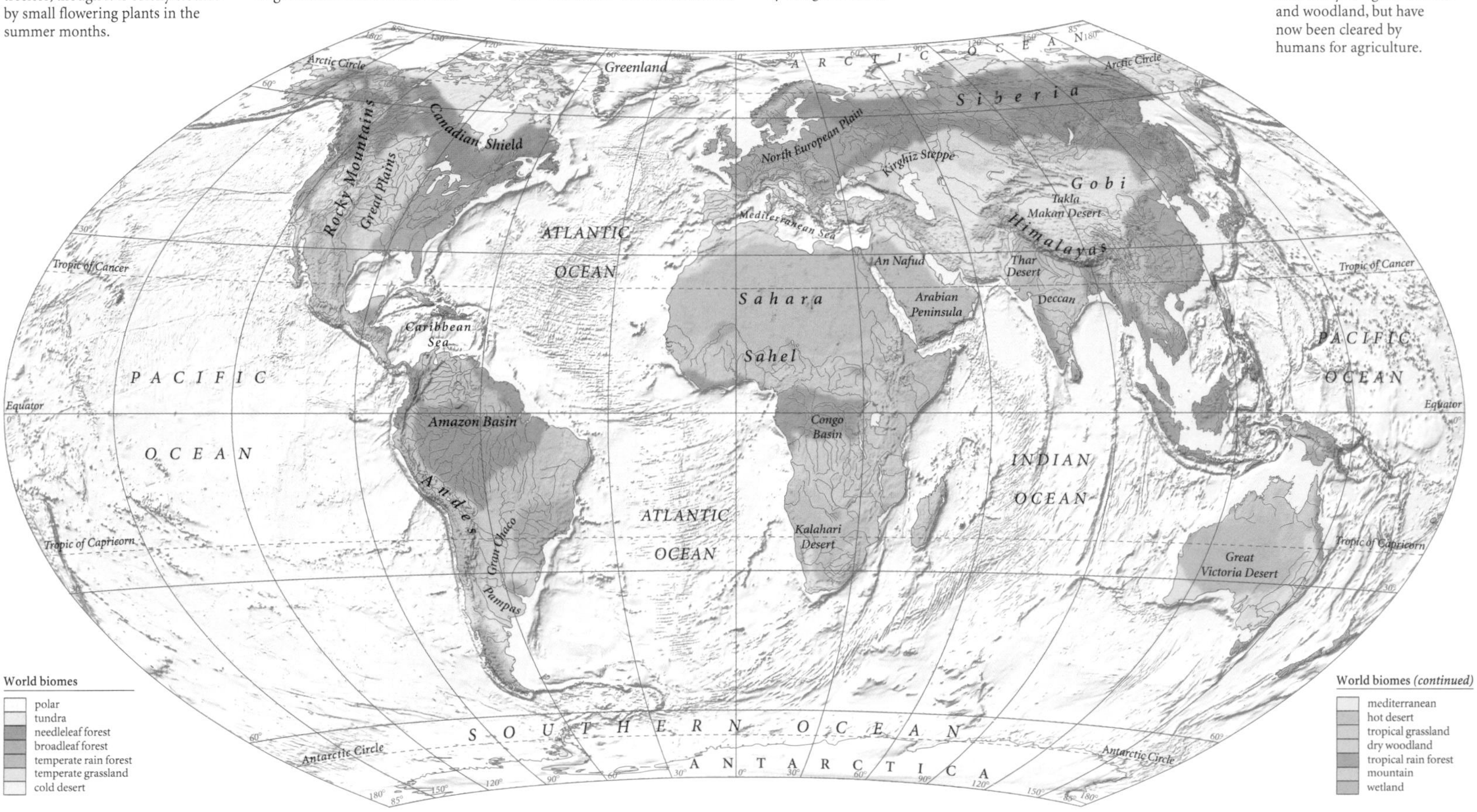
Arctic Circle
Greenland
ARCTIC OCEAN
Siberia
Canadian Shield
Rocky Mountains
Great Plains
North European Plain
Kirghiz Steppe
Gobi
Takla Makan Desert
Himalayas
Mediterranean Sea
ATLANTIC OCEAN
An Nafud
Thar Desert
Tropic of Cancer
Sahara
Arabian Peninsula
Deccan
Caribbean Sea
Sahel
PACIFIC OCEAN
Equator
Amazon Basin
Congo Basin
INDIAN OCEAN
Andes
Gran Chaco
Kalahari Desert
Tropic of Capricorn
Great Victoria Desert
Pampas
SOUTHERN OCEAN
Antarctic Circle
ANTARCTICA
World biomes
polar
tundra
needleleaf forest
broadleaf forest
temperate rain forest
temperate grassland
cold desert
World biomes (continued)
mediterranean
hot desert
tropical grassland
dry woodland
tropical rain forest
mountain
wetland

TROPICAL AND TEMPERATE GRASSLANDS

The major grassland areas are found in the centers of the larger continental landmasses. In Africa's tropical savannah regions, seasonal rainfall alternates with drought. Temperate grasslands, also known as *steppes* and *prairies* are found in the northern hemisphere, and in South America, where they are known as the *pampas*.

DRY WOODLANDS

Trees and shrubs, adapted to dry conditions, grow widely spaced from one another, interspersed by savannah grasslands.

TROPICAL RAIN FORESTS

Characterized by year-round warmth and high rainfall, tropical rain forests contain the highest diversity of plant and animal species on Earth.

MOUNTAINS

Though the lower slopes of mountains may be thickly forested, only ground-hugging shrubs and other vegetation will grow above the tree line which varies according to both altitude and latitude.

WETLANDS

Rarely lying above sea level, wetlands are marshes, swamps and tidal flats. Some, with their moist, fertile soils, are rich feeding grounds for fish and breeding grounds for birds. Others have little soil structure and are too acidic to support much plant and animal life.

BIODIVERSITY

THE NUMBER OF PLANT AND ANIMAL SPECIES, and the range of genetic diversity within the populations of each species, make up the Earth's biodiversity. The plants and animals which are endemic to a region – that is, those which are found nowhere else in the world – are also important in determining levels of biodiversity. Human settlement and intervention have encroached on many areas of the world once rich in endemic plant and animal species. Increasing international efforts are being made to monitor and conserve the biodiversity of the Earth's remaining wild places.

ANIMAL ADAPTATION

THE DEGREE OF AN ANIMAL'S ADAPTABILITY to different climates and conditions is extremely important in ensuring its success as a species. Many animals, particularly the largest mammals, are becoming restricted to ever-smaller regions as human development and modern agricultural practices reduce their natural habitats. In contrast, humans have been responsible – both deliberately and accidentally – for the spread of some of the world's most successful species. Many of these introduced species are now more numerous than the indigenous animal populations.

POLAR ANIMALS

The frozen wastes of the polar regions are able to support only a small range of species which derive their nutritional requirements from the sea. Animals such as the walrus *(left)* have developed insulating fat, stocky limbs, and double-layered coats to enable them to survive in the freezing conditions.

DESERT ANIMALS

Many animals which live in the extreme heat and aridity of the deserts are able to survive for days and even months with very little food or water. Their bodies are adapted to lose heat quickly and to store fat and water. The Gila monster *(above)* stores fat in its tail.

AMAZON RAINFOREST

The vast Amazon Basin is home to the world's greatest variety of animal species. Animals are adapted to live at many different levels from the treetops to the tangled undergrowth which lies beneath the canopy. The sloth *(below)* hangs upside down in the branches. Its fur grows from its stomach to its back to enable water to run off quickly.

DIVERSITY OF ANIMAL SPECIES

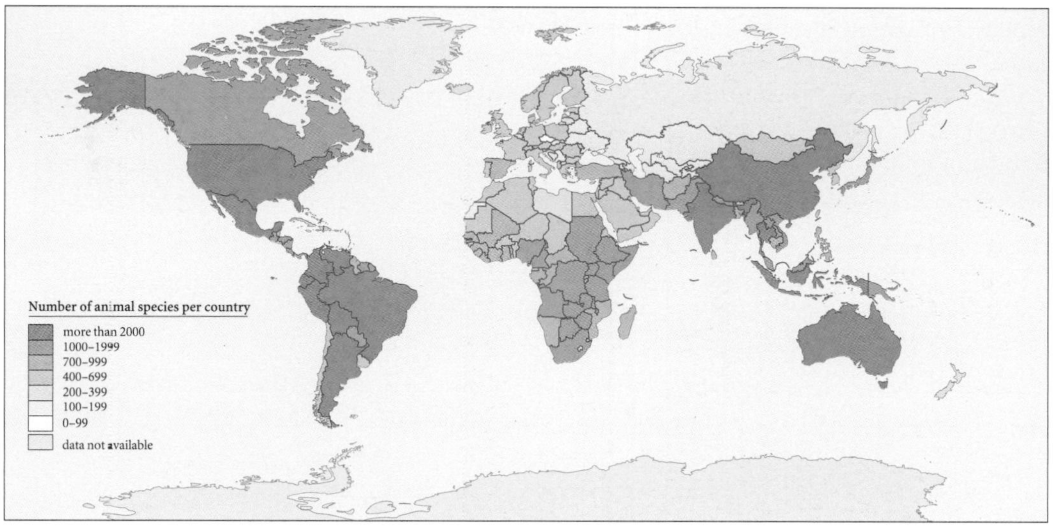
Number of animal species per country
more than 2000
1000–1999
700–999
400–699
200–399
100–199
0–99
data not available

MARINE BIODIVERSITY

The oceans support a huge variety of different species, from the world's largest mammals like whales and dolphins down to the tiniest plankton. The greatest diversities occur in the warmer seas of continental shelves, where plants are easily able to photosynthesize, and around coral reefs, where complex ecosystems are found. On the ocean floor, nematodes can exist at a depth of more than 10,000 ft (3,000 m) below sea level.

HIGH ALTITUDES

Few animals exist in the rarefied atmosphere of the highest mountains. However, birds of prey such as eagles and vultures *(above)*, with their superb eyesight can soar as high as 23,000 ft (7,000 m) to scan for prey below.

URBAN ANIMALS

The growth of cities has reduced the amount of habitat available to many species. A number of animals are now moving closer into urban areas to scavenge from the detritus of the modern city *(left)*. Rodents, particularly rats and mice, have existed in cities for thousands of years, and many insects, especially moths, quickly develop new coloring to provide them with camouflage.

ENDEMIC SPECIES

Isolated areas such as Australia and the island of Madagascar, have the greatest range of endemic species. In Australia, these include marsupials such as the kangaroo *(below)*, which carry their young in pouches on their bodies. Destruction of habitat, pollution, hunting, and predators introduced by humans, are threatening this unique biodiversity.

PLANT ADAPTATION

ENVIRONMENTAL CONDITIONS, particularly climate, soil type, and the extent of competition with other organisms, influence the development of plants into a number of distinctive forms. Similar conditions in quite different parts of the world create similar adaptations in the plants, which may then be modified by other, local, factors specific to the region.

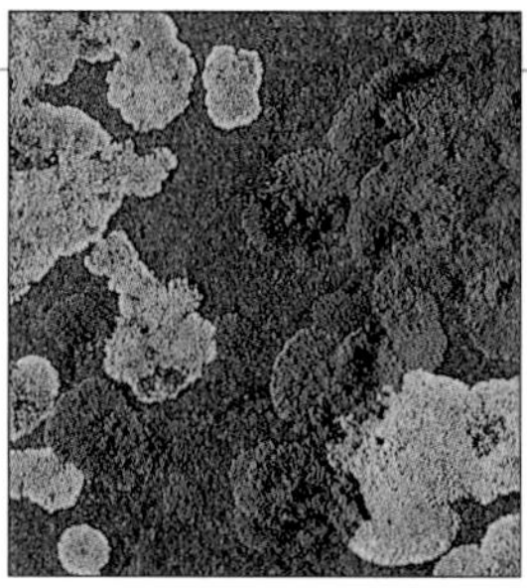

COLD CONDITIONS

In areas where temperatures rarely rise above freezing, plants such as lichens *(left)* and mosses grow densely, close to the ground.

RAIN FORESTS

Most of the world's largest and oldest plants are found in rain forests; warmth and heavy rainfall provide ideal conditions for vast plants like the world's largest flower, the rafflesia *(left)*.

HOT, DRY CONDITIONS

Arid conditions lead to the development of plants whose surface area has been reduced to a minimum to reduce water loss. In cacti *(above)*, which can survive without water for months, leaves are minimal or not present at all.

ANCIENT PLANTS

Some of the world's most primitive plants still exist today, including algae, cycads, and many ferns *(above)*, reflecting the success with which they have adapted to changing conditions.

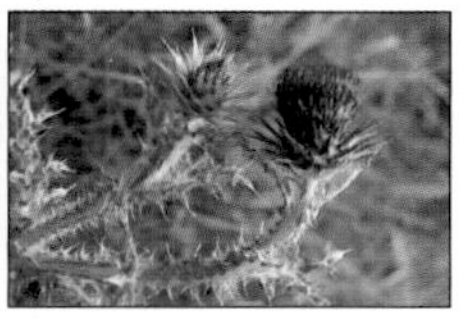

RESISTING PREDATORS

A great variety of plants have developed devices including spines *(above)*, poisons, stinging hairs, and an unpleasant taste or smell to deter animal predators.

DIVERSITY OF PLANT SPECIES

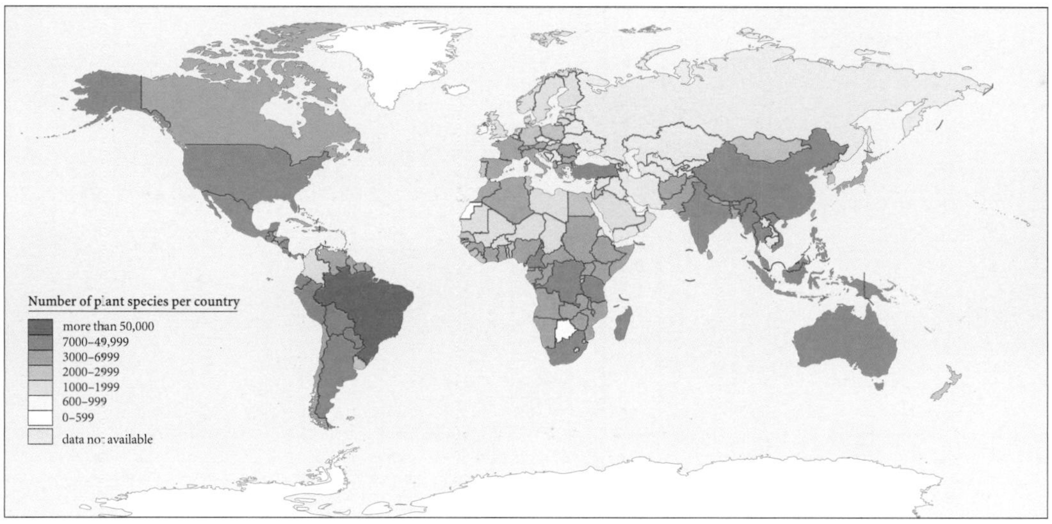
Number of plant species per country
more than 50,000
7000–49,999
3000–6999
2000–2999
1000–1999
600–999
0–599
data not available

WEEDS

Weeds such as bindweed *(above)* are fast-growing, easily dispersed, and tolerant of a number of different environments, enabling them to quickly colonize suitable habitats. They are among the most adaptable of all plants.

Population and Settlement

The Earth's population is projected to rise from its current level of about 6.4 billion to reach some 10 billion by 2025. The global distribution of this rapidly growing population is very uneven, and is dictated by climate, terrain, and natural and economic resources. The great majority of the Earth's people live in coastal zones, and along river valleys. Deserts cover over 20% of the Earth's surface, but support less than 5% of the world's population. It is estimated that over half of the world's population live in cities – most of them in Asia – as a result of mass migration from rural areas in search of jobs. Many of these people live in the so-called "megacities," some with populations as great as 40 million.

Patterns of Settlement

The past 200 years have seen the most radical shift in world population patterns in recorded history.

Nomadic life

All the world's peoples were hunter-gatherers 10,000 years ago. Today nomads, who live by following available food resources, account for less than 0.0001% of the world's population. They are mainly pastoral herders, moving their livestock from place to place in search of grazing land.

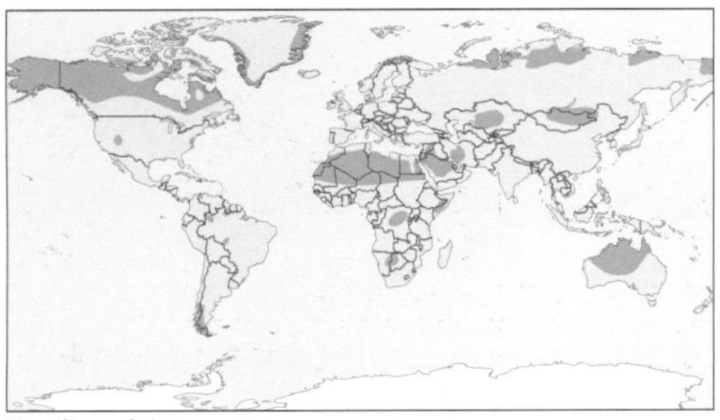

Nomadic population

Nomadic population area

The growth of cities

In 1900 there were only 14 cities in the world with populations of more than a million, mostly in the northern hemisphere. Today, as more and more people in the developing world migrate to towns and cities, there are 29 cities whose population exceeds 5 million, and around 200 "million-cities."

Million-cities in 1900

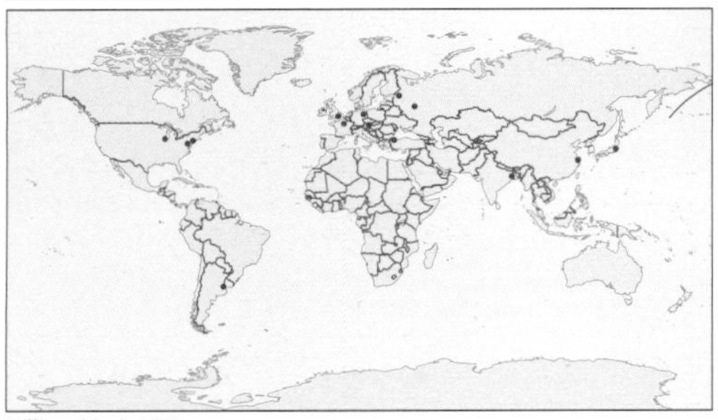

Million-cities in 1900

- Cities over 1 million population

Million-cities in 1995

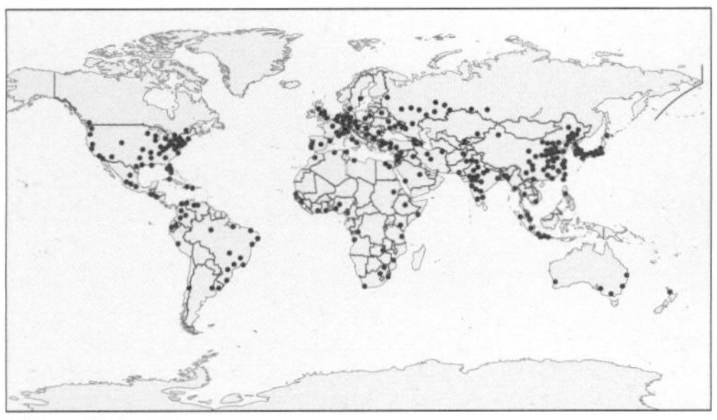

Million-cities in 1995

- Cities over 1 million population

North America

The eastern and western seaboards of the US, with huge expanses of interconnected cities, towns, and suburbs, are vast, densely-populated megalopolises. Central America and the Caribbean also have high population densities. Yet, away from the coasts and in the wildernesses of northern Canada the land is very sparsely settled.

Vancouver on Canada's west coast, grew up as a port city. In recent years it has attracted many Asian immigrants, particularly from the Pacific Rim.

North America's central plains, the continent's agricultural heartland, are thinly populated and highly productive.

Europe

With its temperate climate, and rich mineral and natural resources, Europe is generally very densely settled. The continent acts as a magnet for economic migrants from the developing world, and immigration is now widely restricted. Birthrates in Europe are generally low, and in some countries, such as Germany, the populations have stabilized at zero growth, with a fast-growing elderly population.

Many European cities, like Siena, once reflected the "ideal" size for human settlements. Modern technological advances have enabled them to grow far beyond the original walls.

Within the densely-populated Netherlands the reclamation of coastal wetlands is vital to provide much-needed land for agriculture and settlement.

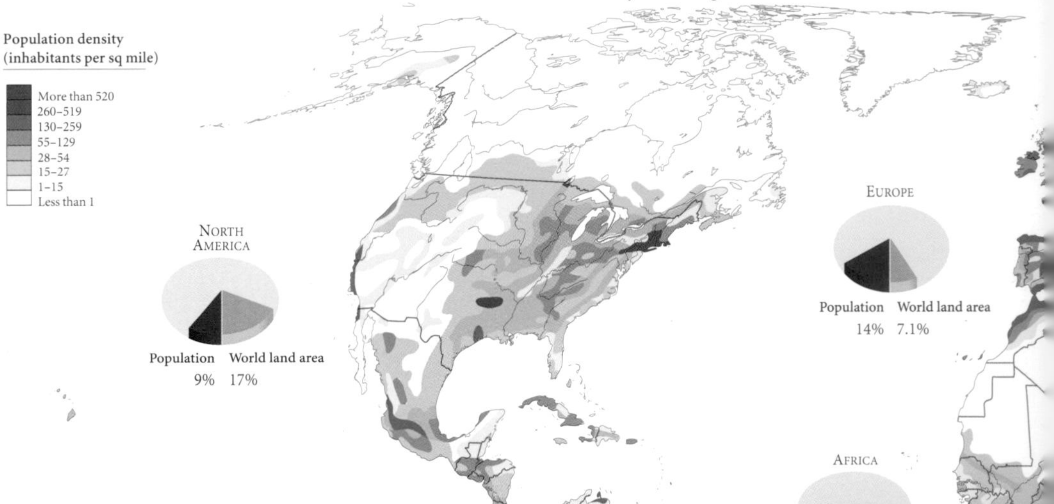
Population density
(inhabitants per sq mile)
More than 520
260–519
130–259
55–129
28–54
15–27
1–15
Less than 1
North America
Population 9%
World land area 17%
Europe
Population 14%
World land area 7.1%
Africa
Population 12%
World land area 20.2%

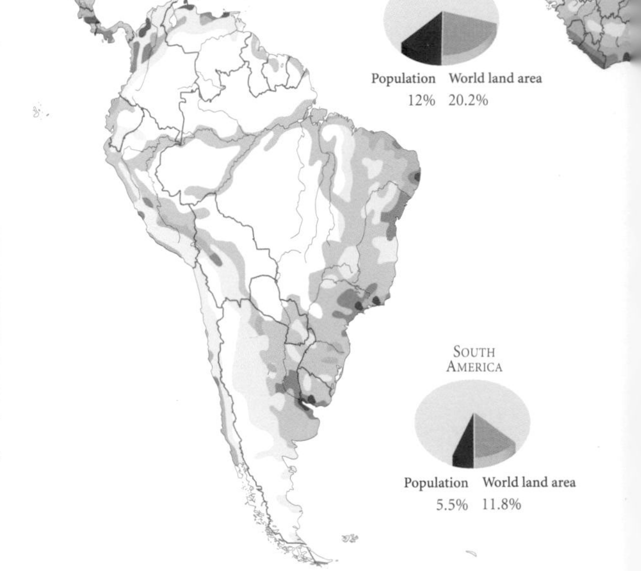
South America
Population 5.5%
World land area 11.8%

South America

Most settlement in South America is clustered in a narrow belt in coastal zones and in the northern Andes. During the 20th century, cities such as São Paulo and Buenos Aires grew enormously, acting as powerful economic magnets to the rural population. Shantytowns have grown up on the outskirts of many major cities to house these immigrants, often lacking basic amenities.

Many people in western South America live at high altitudes in the Andes, both in cities and in villages such as this one in Bolivia.

Venezuela is the most highly urbanized country in South America, with more than 90% of the population living in cities such as Caracas.

Africa

The arid climate of much of Africa means that settlement of the continent is sparse, focusing in coastal areas and fertile regions such as the Nile Valley. Africa still has a high proportion of nomadic agriculturalists, although many are now becoming settled, and the population is predominantly rural.

Cities such as Nairobi (above), Cairo and Johannesburg have grown rapidly in recent years, although only Cairo has a significant population on a global scale.

Traditional lifestyles and homes persist across much of Africa, which has a higher proportion of rural or village-based population than any other continent.

Asia

Most Asian settlement originally centered around the great river valleys such as the Indus, the Ganges, and the Yangtze. Today, almost 60% of the world's population lives in Asia, many in burgeoning cities – particularly in the economically-buoyant Pacific Rim countries. Even rural population densities are high in many countries; practices such as terracing in Southeast Asia making the most of the available land.

Many of China's cities are now vast urban areas with populations of more than 5 million people.

This stilt village in Bangladesh is built to resist the regular flooding. Pressure on land, even in rural areas, forces many people to live in marginal areas.

Population Structures

Population pyramids are an effective means of showing the age structures of different countries, and highlighting changing trends in population growth and decline. The typical pyramid for a country with a growing, youthful population, is broad-based *(left)*, reflecting a high birthrate and a far larger number of young rather than elderly people. In contrast, countries with populations whose numbers are stabilizing have a more balanced distribution of people in each age band, and may even have lower numbers of people in the youngest age ranges, indicating both a high life expectancy, and that the population is now barely replacing itself *(right)*. The Russian Federation *(center)* still bears the scars of World War II, reflected in the dramatically lower numbers of men than women in the 60–80+ age range.

Youthful population (India)

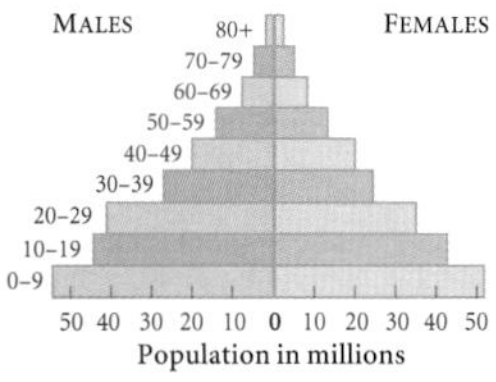
Males
Females
80+
70–79
60–69
50–59
40–49
30–39
20–29
10–19
0–9
50 40 30 20 10 0 10 20 30 40 50
Population in millions

Distorted population (Russian Federation)

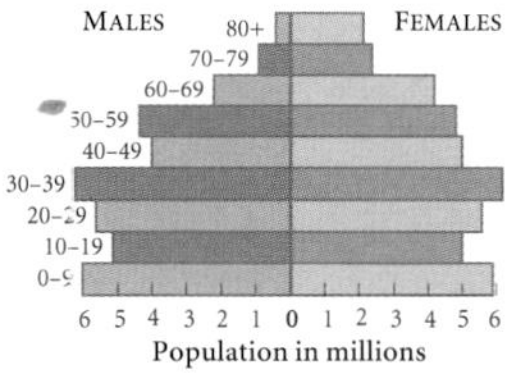
Males
Females
80+
70–79
60–69
50–59
40–49
30–39
20–29
10–19
0–9
6 5 4 3 2 1 0 1 2 3 4 5 6
Population in millions

Aging population (United States of America)

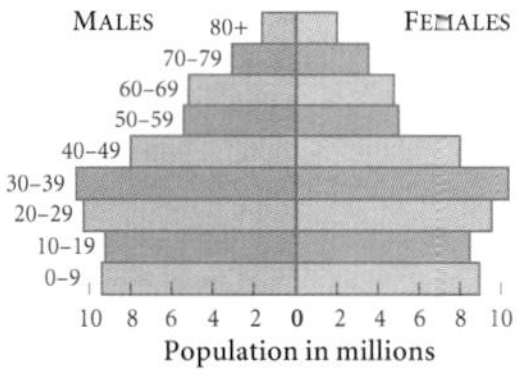
Males
Females
80+
70–79
60–69
50–59
40–49
30–39
20–29
10–19
0–9
10 8 6 4 2 0 2 4 6 8 10
Population in millions

Population Growth

Improvements in food supply and advances in medicine have both played a major role in the remarkable growth in global population, which has increased five-fold over the last 150 years. Food supplies have risen with the mechanization of agriculture and improvements in crop yields. Better nutrition, together with higher standards of public health and sanitation, have led to increased longevity and higher birthrates.

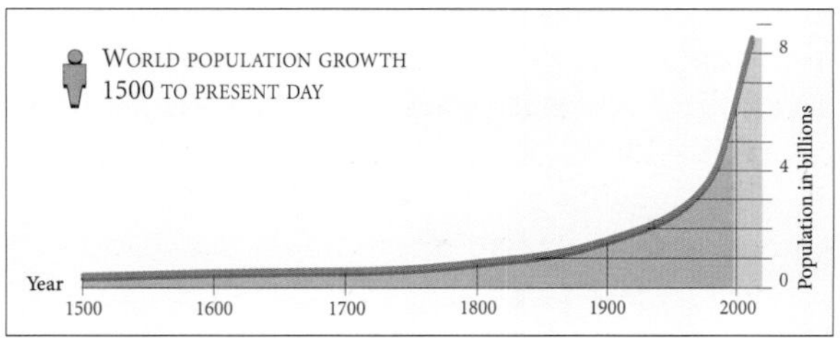
World population growth
1500 to present day
Year
1500
1600
1700
1800
1900
2000
0
4
8
Population in billions

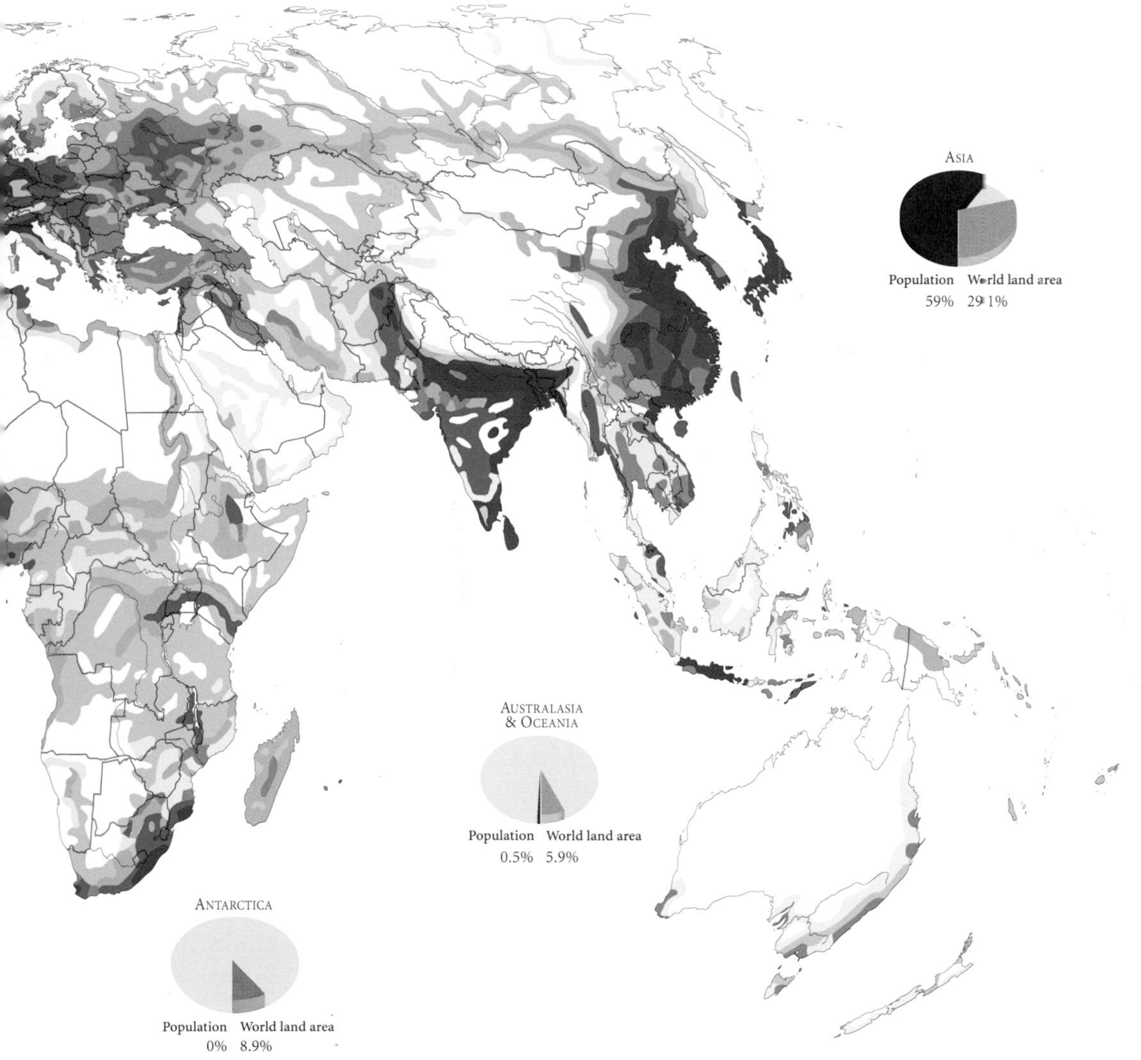
Asia
Population 59%
World land area 29.1%
Australasia & Oceania
Population 0.5%
World land area 5.9%
Antarctica
Population 0%
World land area 8.9%

World nutrition

Two-thirds of the world's food supply is consumed by the industrialized nations, many of which have a daily calorific intake far higher than is necessary for their populations to maintain a healthy body weight. In contrast, in the developing world, about 800 million people do not have enough food to meet their basic nutritional needs.

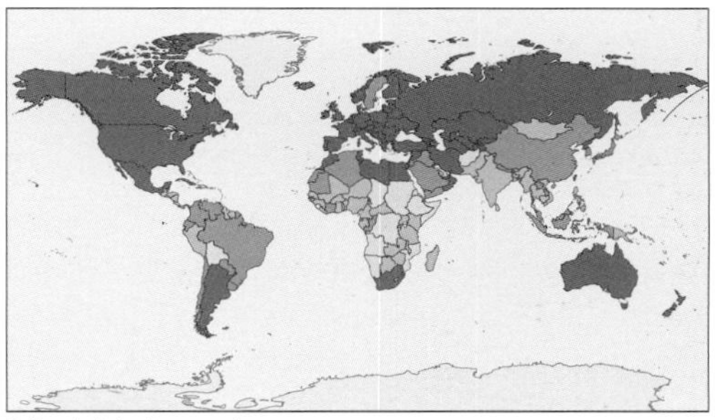

Daily calorie intake per capita

above 3,000 | 2,500–2,999 | 2,000–2,499 | below 2,000 | data not available

World life expectancy

Improved public health and living standards have greatly increased life expectancy in the developed world, where people can now expect to live twice as long as they did 100 years ago. In many of the world's poorest nations, inadequate nutrition and disease, means that the average life expectancy still does not exceed 45 years.

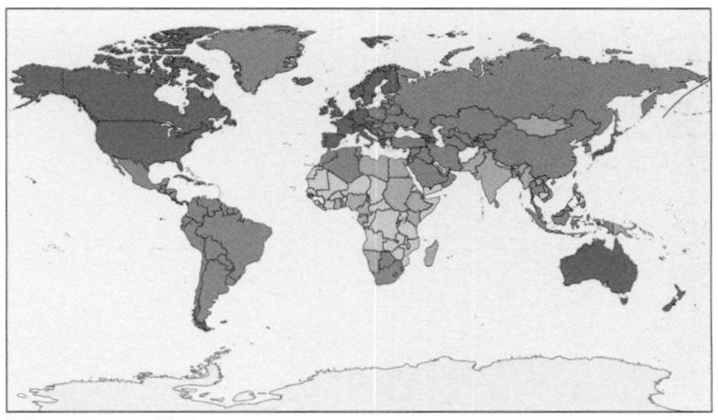

Life expectancy at birth

above 75 years | 65–74 years | 55–64 years | 45–54 years | below 44 years | data not available

Australasia & Oceania

This is the world's most sparsely settled region. The peoples of Australia and New Zealand live mainly in the coastal cities, with only scattered settlements in the arid interior. The Pacific islands can only support limited populations because of their remoteness and lack of resources.

__Brisbane__, on Australia's Gold Coast is the most rapidly expanding city in the country. The great majority of Australia's population lives in cities near the coasts.

__The remote highlands__ of Papua New Guinea are home to a wide variety of peoples, many of whom still subsist by traditional hunting and gathering.

Average world birthrates

Birthrates are much higher in Africa, Asia, and South America than in Europe and North America. Increased affluence and easy access to contraception are both factors which can lead to a significant decline in a country's birthrate.

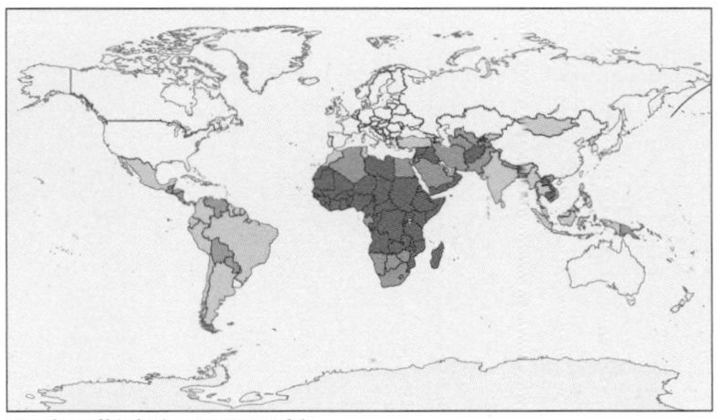

Number of births (per 1,000 people)

above 40 | 30–39 | 20–29 | below 20 | data not available

World infant mortality

In parts of the developing world infant mortality rates are still high; access to medical services such as immunization, adequate nutrition, and the promotion of breast-feeding have been important in combating infant mortality.

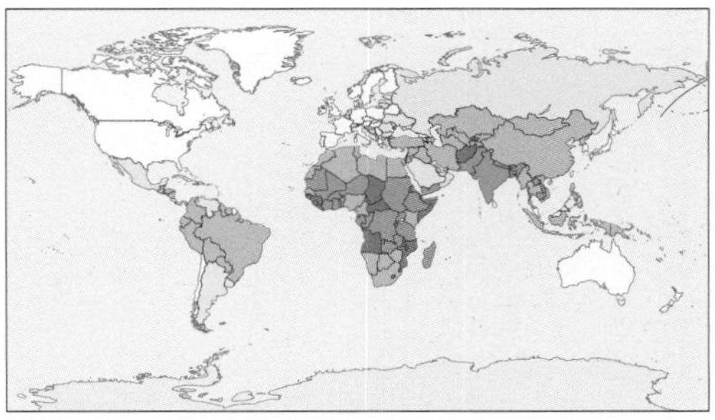

World infant mortality rates (deaths per 1,000 live births)

above 125 | 75–124 | 35–74 | 15–43 | below 15 | data not available

The Economic System

The wealthy countries of the developed world, with their aggressive, market-led economies and their access to productive new technologies and international markets, dominate the world economic system. At the other extreme, many of the countries of the developing world are locked in a cycle of national debt, rising populations, and unemployment. The state-managed economies of the former communist bloc began to be dismantled during the 1990s, and China is emerging as a major economic power following decades of isolation.

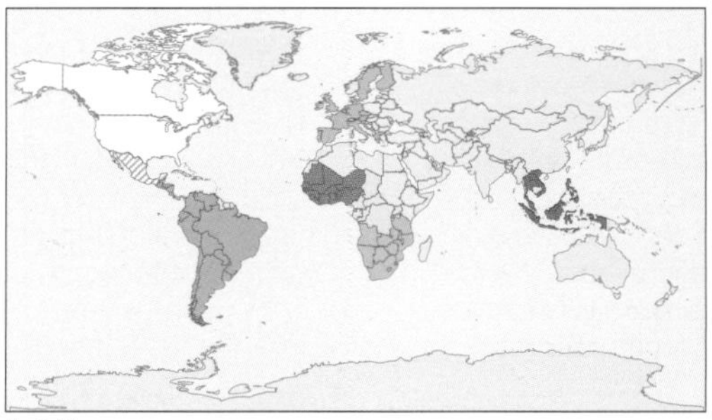

Trade blocs

- EU
- CACM
- NAFTA
- SADC
- ASEAN
- ECOWAS
- LAIA
- CEEAC

Trade Blocs

International trade blocs are formed when groups of countries, often already enjoying close military and political ties, join together to offer mutually preferential terms of trade for both imports and exports. Increasingly, global trade is dominated by three main blocs: the EU, NAFTA, and ASEAN. They are supplanting older trade blocs such as the Commonwealth, a legacy of colonialism.

International Trade Flows

World trade acts as a stimulus to national economies, encouraging growth. Over the last three decades, as heavy industries have declined, services – banking, insurance, tourism, airlines, and shipping – have taken an increasingly large share of world trade. Manufactured articles now account for nearly two-thirds of world trade; raw materials and food make up less than a quarter of the total.

SHIPPING

Ships carry 80% of international cargo, and extensive container ports, where cargo is stored, are vital links in the international transportation network.

Tentulah Coke!
Coke is it!

MULTINATIONALS

Multinational companies are increasingly penetrating inaccessible markets. The reach of many American commodities is now global.

PRIMARY PRODUCTS

Many countries, particularly in the Caribbean and Africa, are still reliant on primary products such as rubber and coffee, which makes them vulnerable to fluctuating prices.

SERVICE INDUSTRIES

Service industries such as banking, tourism and insurance were the fastest-growing industrial sector in the last half of the 20th century. Lloyds of London is the center of the world insurance market.

Countries reliant on a single export

- bananas
- coffee
- oil/petroleum
- copper

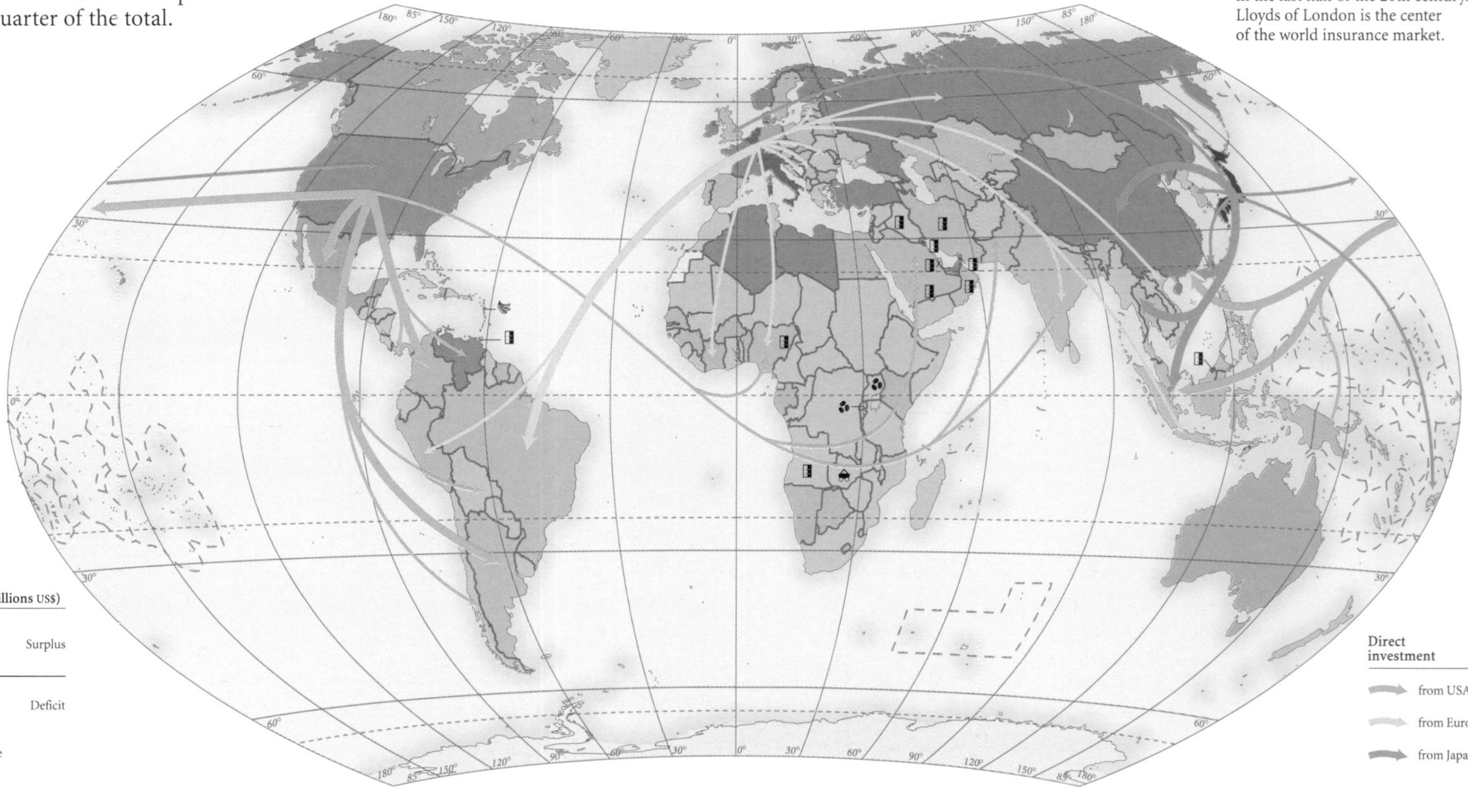

Balance of trade (millions US$)

Surplus:
- over 30,000
- 10,000–29,000
- 1000–9999
- 0–999

Deficit:
- 0–999
- 1000–9999
- 10,000–29,999
- over 30,000

- data unavailable

Direct investment

- from USA
- from Europe
- from Japan

World Money Markets

The financial world has traditionally been dominated by three major centers – Tokyo, New York and London, which house the headquarters of stock exchanges, multinational corporations and international banks. Their geographic location means that, at any one time in a 24-hour day, one major market is open for trading in shares, currencies, and commodities. Since the late 1980s, technological advances have enabled transactions between financial centers to occur at ever-greater speed, and new markets have sprung up throughout the world.

Major Money Markets

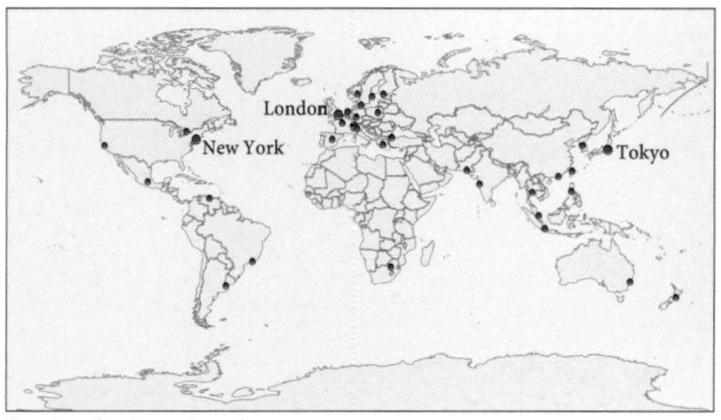
London
New York
Tokyo

Location of major stock markets

- Major stock markets

The Tokyo Stock Market crashed in 1990, leading to a slow-down in the growth of the world's most powerful economy, and a refocusing on economic policy away from export-led growth and toward the domestic market.

New Stock Markets

New stock markets are now opening in many parts of the world, where economies have recently emerged from state controls. In Moscow and Beijing, and several countries in eastern Europe, newly-opened stock exchanges reflect the transition to market-driven economies.

Dealers at the Kolkata Stock Market. *The Indian economy has been opened up to foreign investment and many multinationals now have bases there.*

The Developing World

International trade in capital and currency is dominated by the rich nations of the northern hemisphere. In parts of Africa and Asia, where exports of any sort are extremely limited, home-produced commodities are simply sold in local markets.

Markets have thrived *in communist Vietnam since the introduction of a liberal economic policy.*

WORLD WEALTH DISPARITY

A GLOBAL ASSESSMENT of Gross Domestic Product (GDP) by nation reveals great disparities. The developed world, with only a quarter of the world's population, has 80% of the world's manufacturing income. Civil war, conflict, and political instability further undermine the economic self-sufficiency of many of the world's poorest nations.

***Cities such as Detroit** have been badly hit by the decline in heavy industry.*

URBAN DECAY

ALTHOUGH THE US still dominates the global economy, it faces deficits in both the federal budget and the balance of trade. Vast discrepancies in personal wealth, high levels of unemployment, and the dismantling of welfare provisions throughout the 1980s have led to severe deprivation in several of the inner cities of North America's industrial heartland.

BOOMING CITIES

SINCE THE 1980s the Chinese government has set up special industrial zones, such as Shanghai, where foreign investment is encouraged through tax incentives. Migrants from rural China pour into these regions in search of work, creating "boomtown" economies.

***Foreign investment** has encouraged new infrastructure development in cities like Shanghai.*

URBAN SPRAWL

CITIES ARE EXPANDING all over the developing world, attracting economic migrants in search of work and opportunities. In cities such as Rio de Janeiro, housing has not kept pace with the population explosion, and squalid shanty towns *(favelas)* rub shoulders with middle-class housing.

***The favelas of Rio de Janeiro** sprawl over the hills surrounding the city.*

COMPARATIVE WORLD WEALTH

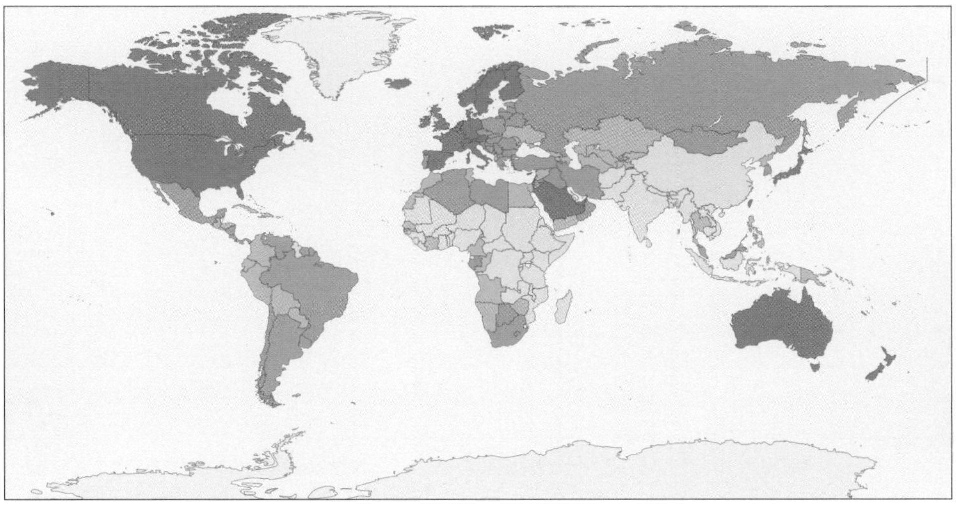

World economies
- high income
- upper-middle income
- lower-middle income
- low income
- data unavailable

ECONOMIC "TIGERS"

THE ECONOMIC "TIGERS" of the Pacific Rim – Taiwan, Singapore, and South Korea – have grown faster than Europe and the US over the last decade. Their export- and service-led economies have benefited from stable government, low labor costs, and foreign investment.

***Hong Kong**, with its fine natural harbor, is one of the most important ports in Asia.*

AGRICULTURAL ECONOMIES

IN PARTS OF THE DEVELOPING WORLD, people survive by subsistence farming – only growing enough food for themselves and their families. With no surplus product, they are unable to exchange goods for currency, the only means of escaping the poverty trap. In other countries, farmers have been encouraged to concentrate on growing a single crop for the export market. This reliance on cash crops leaves farmers vulnerable to crop failure and to changes in the market price of the crop.

***The Ugandan uplands** are fertile, but poor infrastructure hampers the export of cash crops.*

***A shopping arcade** in Paris displays a great profusion of luxury goods.*

THE AFFLUENT WEST

THE CAPITAL CITIES of many countries in the developed world are showcases for consumer goods, reflecting the increasing importance of the service sector, and particularly the retail sector, in the world economy. The idea of shopping as a leisure activity is unique to the western world. Luxury goods and services attract visitors, who in turn generate tourist revenue.

TOURISM

IN 2002, THERE WERE 715 million tourists worldwide. Tourism is now the world's biggest single industry, employing 130 million people, though frequently in low-paid unskilled jobs. While tourists are increasingly exploring inaccessible and less-developed regions of the world, the benefits of the industry are not always felt at a local level. There are also worries about the environmental impact of tourism, as the world's last wildernesses increasingly become tourist attractions.

***Botswana's Okavango Delta** is an area rich in wildlife. Tourists go on safaris to the region, but the impact of tourism is controlled.*

MONEY FLOWS

FOREIGN INVESTMENT in the developing world during the 1970s led to a global financial crisis in the 1980s, when many countries were unable to meet their debt repayments. The International Monetary Fund (IMF) was forced to reschedule the debts and, in some cases, write them off completely. Within the developing world, austerity programs have been initiated to cope with the debt, leading in turn to high unemployment and galloping inflation. In many parts of Africa, stricken economies are now dependent on international aid.

***In rural Southeast Asia**, babies are given medical checks by UNICEF as part of a global aid program sponsored by the UN.*

TOURIST ARRIVALS

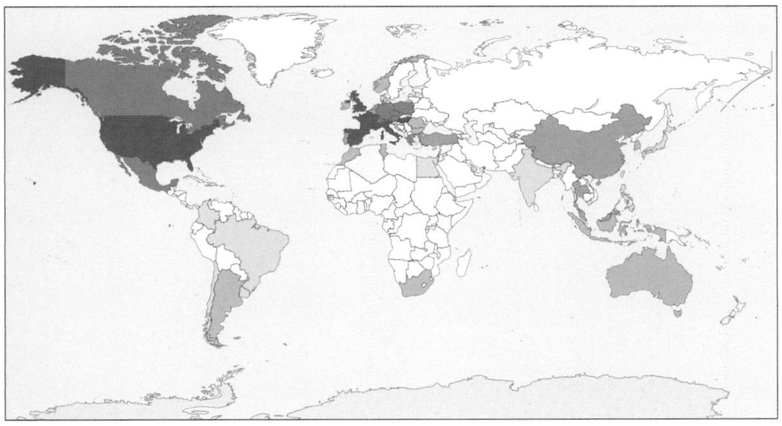

Tourist arrivals
- over 20 million
- 10–20 million
- 5–10 million
- 2.5–5 million
- 1–2.5 million
- 700,000–999,000
- under 700,000
- data unavailable

INTERNATIONAL DEBT: DONORS AND RECEIVERS

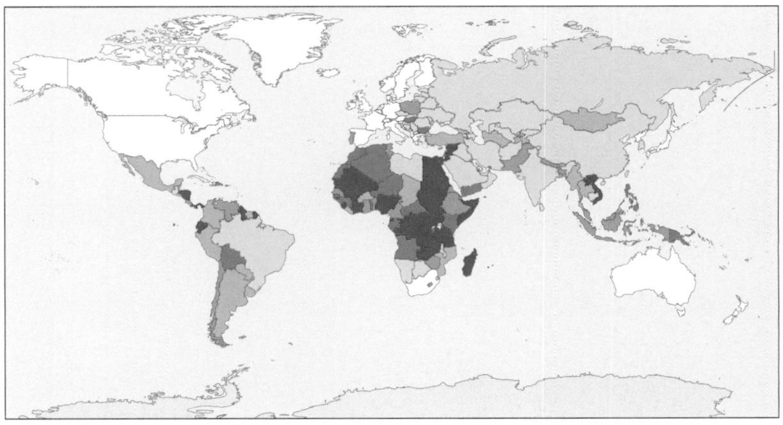

International debt (as percentage of GNP)
- over 100%
- 70–90%
- 50–69%
- 30–49%
- below 30
- negligible
- data unavailable

The Political World

There are 193 independent countries in the world today. With the exception of Antarctica, where territorial claims have been deferred by international treaty, every land area of the Earth's surface either belongs to, or is claimed by, one country or another. The largest country in the world is the Russian Federation, the smallest is Vatican City. Some 60 overseas dependent territories remain, administered variously by France, Australia, Denmark, New Zealand, Norway, Portugal, the UK, the US, and the Netherlands.

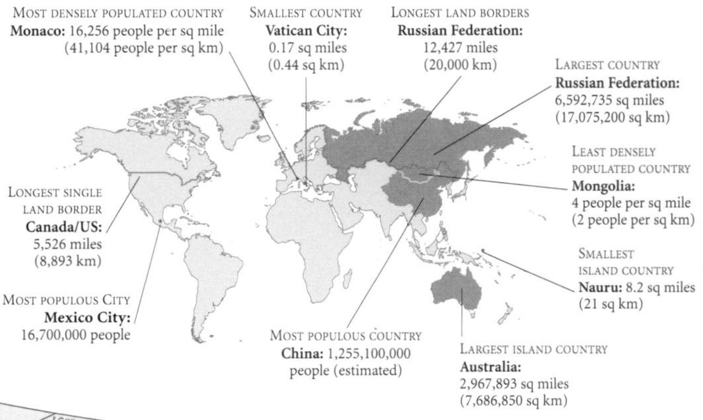

Most densely populated country
Monaco: 16,256 people per sq mile (41,104 people per sq km)
Smallest country
Vatican City: 0.17 sq miles (0.44 sq km)
Longest land borders
Russian Federation: 12,427 miles (20,000 km)
Largest country
Russian Federation: 6,592,735 sq miles (17,075,200 sq km)
Least densely populated country
Mongolia: 4 people per sq mile (2 people per sq km)
Smallest island country
Nauru: 8.2 sq miles (21 sq km)
Largest island country
Australia: 2,967,893 sq miles (7,686,850 sq km)
Most populous country
China: 1,255,100,000 people (estimated)
Most populous City
Mexico City: 16,700,000 people
Longest single land border
Canada/US: 5,526 miles (8,893 km)

International Borders

The map shows three main types of boundary between states. Full borders represent internationally agreed and recognized territorial boundaries. Undefined borders exist where no fixed boundary between states has been demarcated; the boundaries indicated in this way show approximate areas of sovereignty. A disputed border is indicated where a *de facto* territorial boundary exists, which is not agreed or is subject to arbitration.

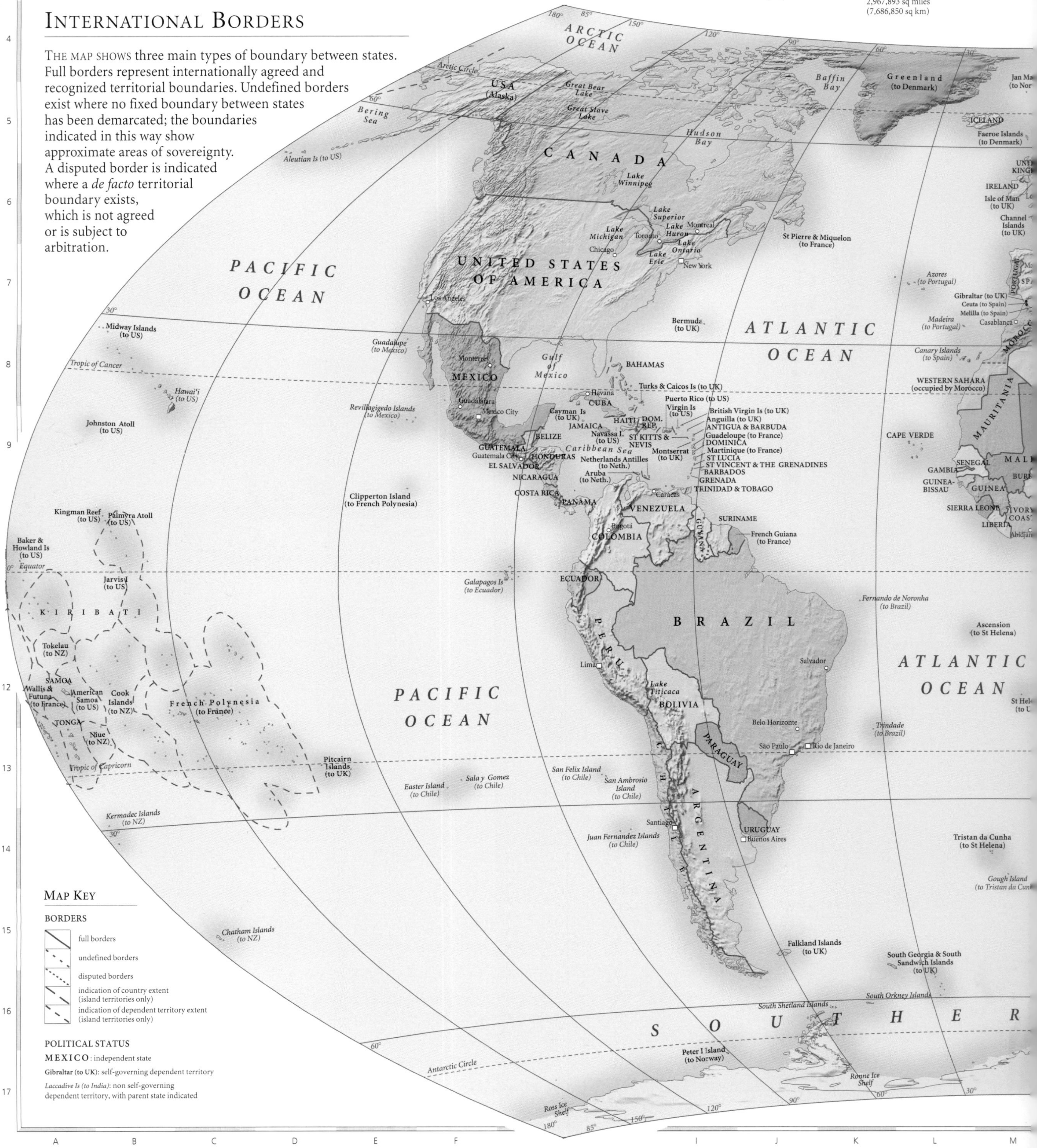

ARCTIC OCEAN
Arctic Circle
USA (Alaska)
Bering Sea
Aleutian Is (to US)
Great Bear Lake
Great Slave Lake
CANADA
Hudson Bay
Baffin Bay
Greenland (to Denmark)
ICELAND
Faeroe Islands (to Denmark)
IRELAND
Isle of Man (to UK)
Channel Islands (to UK)
Lake Winnipeg
Lake Superior
Lake Michigan
Lake Huron
Lake Ontario
Lake Erie
Montreal
Toronto
Chicago
New York
St Pierre & Miquelon (to France)
UNITED STATES OF AMERICA
Los Angeles
PACIFIC OCEAN
Midway Islands (to US)
Tropic of Cancer
Hawai'i (to US)
Johnston Atoll (to US)
Guadalupe (to Mexico)
Revillagigedo Islands (to Mexico)
Monterrey
MEXICO
Guadalajara
Mexico City
Gulf of Mexico
Bermuda (to UK)
BAHAMAS
ATLANTIC OCEAN
Azores (to Portugal)
Madeira (to Portugal)
Gibraltar (to UK)
Ceuta (to Spain)
Melilla (to Spain)
Casablanca
Canary Islands (to Spain)
WESTERN SAHARA (occupied by Morocco)
MAURITANIA
CAPE VERDE
Havana
CUBA
Turks & Caicos Is (to UK)
Cayman Is (to UK)
JAMAICA
HAITI
DOM. REP.
Puerto Rico (to US)
Virgin Is (to US)
British Virgin Is (to UK)
Anguilla (to UK)
ANTIGUA & BARBUDA
Guadeloupe (to France)
DOMINICA
Martinique (to France)
ST LUCIA
ST VINCENT & THE GRENADINES
BARBADOS
GRENADA
TRINIDAD & TOBAGO
Navassa I. (to US)
ST KITTS & NEVIS
Montserrat (to UK)
Caribbean Sea
Netherlands Antilles (to Neth.)
Aruba (to Neth.)
BELIZE
GUATEMALA
Guatemala City
HONDURAS
EL SALVADOR
NICARAGUA
COSTA RICA
PANAMA
Caracas
VENEZUELA
GUYANA
SURINAME
French Guiana (to France)
Bogotá
COLOMBIA
Clipperton Island (to French Polynesia)
Kingman Reef (to US)
Palmyra Atoll (to US)
Baker & Howland Is (to US)
Equator
Jarvis I (to US)
KIRIBATI
Tokelau (to NZ)
SAMOA
Wallis & Futuna (to France)
American Samoa (to US)
Cook Islands (to NZ)
TONGA
Niue (to NZ)
French Polynesia (to France)
Tropic of Capricorn
Pitcairn Islands (to UK)
Kermadec Islands (to NZ)
Galapagos Is (to Ecuador)
ECUADOR
PERU
Lima
BRAZIL
Salvador
Fernando de Noronha (to Brazil)
Ascension (to St Helena)
Lake Titicaca
BOLIVIA
Belo Horizonte
São Paulo
Rio de Janeiro
PARAGUAY
Trindade (to Brazil)
Easter Island (to Chile)
Sala y Gomez (to Chile)
San Felix Island (to Chile)
San Ambrosio Island (to Chile)
Juan Fernandez Islands (to Chile)
Santiago
CHILE
ARGENTINA
URUGUAY
Buenos Aires
Tristan da Cunha (to St Helena)
Gough Island (to Tristan da Cunha)
Chatham Islands (to NZ)
Falkland Islands (to UK)
South Georgia & South Sandwich Islands (to UK)
South Shetland Islands
South Orkney Islands
SOUTHER
Peter I Island (to Norway)
Antarctic Circle
Ronne Ice Shelf
Ross Ice Shelf
GAMBIA
GUINEA-BISSAU
SENEGAL
GUINEA
SIERRA LEONE
LIBERIA

Map Key

Borders

- full borders
- undefined borders
- disputed borders
- indication of country extent (island territories only)
- indication of dependent territory extent (island territories only)

Political Status

MEXICO: independent state

Gibraltar (to UK): self-governing dependent territory

Laccadive Is (to India): non self-governing dependent territory, with parent state indicated

N O P Q R S T U V W X Y Z

The World in 1914

The early years of the 20th century saw the mainly European colonial empires reaching their greatest extents by 1914. Two world wars inaugurated their disintegration, but even in 1950 there were only 82 independent countries. Since then, over 100 have gained their independence, culminating in the breakup of the Soviet Union and former Yugoslavia in the early 1990s.

Percentage of Earth's Land Surface Controlled by Colonial Empires in 1914

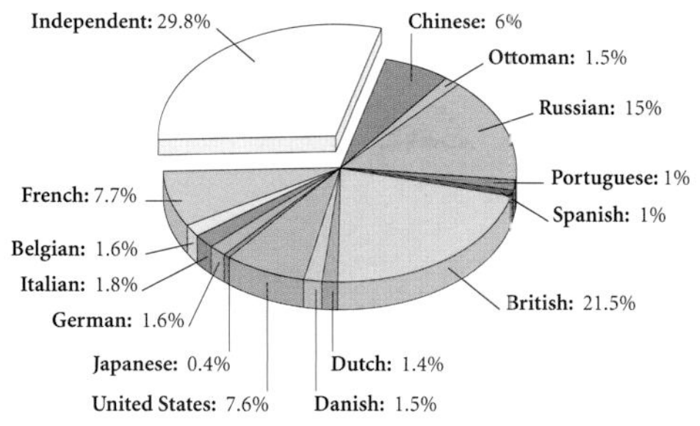
Independent: 29.8%
Chinese: 6%
Ottoman: 1.5%
Russian: 15%
Portuguese: 1%
Spanish: 1%
British: 21.5%
Danish: 1.5%
Dutch: 1.4%
United States: 7.6%
Japanese: 0.4%
German: 1.6%
Italian: 1.8%
Belgian: 1.6%
French: 7.7%

Colonial Empires in 1914

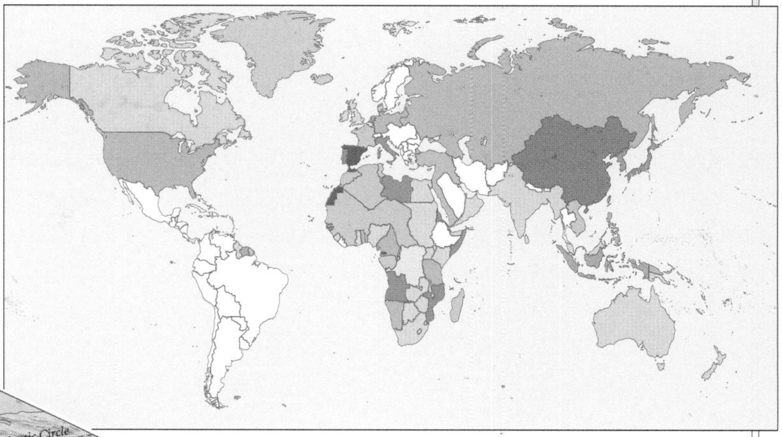
Colonial Empires in 1914
Belgian
British
Chinese
Danish
Dutch
French
German
Italian
Japanese
Ottoman
Portuguese
Russian
Spanish
United States
Independent
Disputed

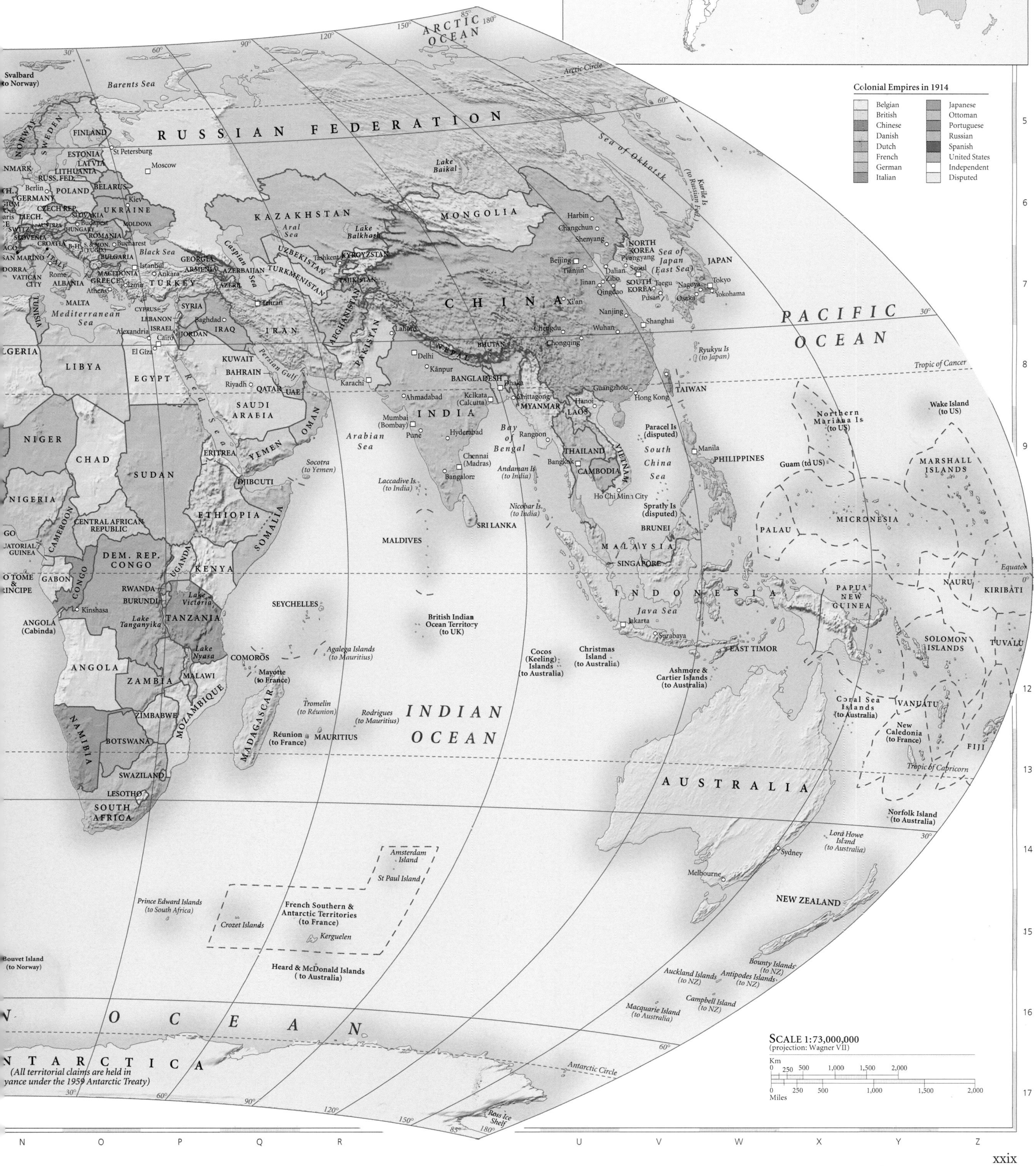
ARCTIC OCEAN
Arctic Circle
Svalbard (to Norway)
Barents Sea
RUSSIAN FEDERATION
Sea of Okhotsk
Kurile Is (to Russian Fed.)
FINLAND
SWEDEN
NORWAY
ESTONIA
LATVIA
LITHUANIA
RUSS. FED.
St Petersburg
Moscow
BELARUS
POLAND
Berlin
GERMANY
CZECH REP.
UKRAINE
Kiev
SLOVAKIA
Budapest
HUNGARY
AUSTRIA
MOLDOVA
ROMANIA
Bucharest
SLOVENIA
CROATIA
B-H
S. & MON. (YUGO.)
BULGARIA
SAN MARINO
ITALY
VATICAN CITY
Rome
ALBANIA
MACEDONIA
GREECE
Athens
Istanbul
Ankara
İzmir
TURKEY
Black Sea
GEORGIA
ARMENIA
AZERBAIJAN
MALTA
Mediterranean Sea
TUNISIA
CYPRUS
LEBANON
SYRIA
ISRAEL
JORDAN
Baghdad
IRAQ
Tehran
IRAN
Alexandria
Cairo
El Giza
EGYPT
LIBYA
KAZAKHSTAN
Aral Sea
Caspian Sea
UZBEKISTAN
TURKMENISTAN
Tashkent
KYRGYZSTAN
TAJIKISTAN
Lake Balkhash
AFGHANISTAN
PAKISTAN
Lahore
Karachi
Delhi
Kanpur
NEPAL
BHUTAN
BANGLADESH
Dhaka
INDIA
Ahmadabad
Kolkata (Calcutta)
Mumbai (Bombay)
Pune
Hyderabad
Chennai (Madras)
Bangalore
Arabian Sea
Bay of Bengal
SRI LANKA
MALDIVES
Laccadive Is (to India)
Andaman Is (to India)
Nicobar Is (to India)
KUWAIT
BAHRAIN
Riyadh
QATAR
UAE
Persian Gulf
SAUDI ARABIA
OMAN
YEMEN
Red Sea
Socotra (to Yemen)
ERITREA
DJIBOUTI
ETHIOPIA
SOMALIA
SUDAN
CHAD
NIGER
NIGERIA
CAMEROON
CENTRAL AFRICAN REPUBLIC
EQUATORIAL GUINEA
SAO TOME & PRINCIPE
GABON
CONGO
DEM. REP. CONGO
Kinshasa
UGANDA
KENYA
RWANDA
BURUNDI
Lake Victoria
Lake Tanganyika
TANZANIA
Lake Nyasa
ANGOLA (Cabinda)
ANGOLA
ZAMBIA
MALAWI
MOZAMBIQUE
ZIMBABWE
NAMIBIA
BOTSWANA
SWAZILAND
LESOTHO
SOUTH AFRICA
MADAGASCAR
COMOROS
Mayotte (to France)
SEYCHELLES
Agalega Islands (to Mauritius)
Tromelin (to Réunion)
Réunion (to France)
MAURITIUS
Rodrigues (to Mauritius)
British Indian Ocean Territory (to UK)
INDIAN OCEAN
Cocos (Keeling) Islands (to Australia)
Christmas Island (to Australia)
Amsterdam Island
St Paul Island
French Southern & Antarctic Territories (to France)
Crozet Islands
Kerguelen
Prince Edward Islands (to South Africa)
Heard & McDonald Islands (to Australia)
Bouvet Island (to Norway)
MONGOLIA
Lake Baikal
CHINA
Harbin
Changchun
Shenyang
Beijing
Tianjin
Jinan
Qingdao
Xi'an
Nanjing
Wuhan
Shanghai
Chengdu
Chongqing
Guangzhou
Hong Kong
NORTH KOREA
Pyongyang
Seoul
SOUTH KOREA
Taegu
Pusan
Dalian
Zibo
Sea of Japan (East Sea)
JAPAN
Tokyo
Yokohama
Nagoya
Osaka
Ryukyu Is (to Japan)
TAIWAN
MYANMAR
Chittagong
Rangoon
LAOS
Hanoi
THAILAND
Bangkok
CAMBODIA
VIETNAM
Ho Chi Minh City
Paracel Is (disputed)
South China Sea
Spratly Is (disputed)
PHILIPPINES
Manila
BRUNEI
MALAYSIA
SINGAPORE
INDONESIA
Java Sea
Jakarta
Surabaya
EAST TIMOR
Ashmore & Cartier Islands (to Australia)
PACIFIC OCEAN
Tropic of Cancer
Northern Mariana Is (to US)
Guam (to US)
Wake Island (to US)
MARSHALL ISLANDS
MICRONESIA
PALAU
PAPUA NEW GUINEA
NAURU
KIRIBATI
Equator
SOLOMON ISLANDS
TUVALU
VANUATU
New Caledonia (to France)
FIJI
Coral Sea Islands (to Australia)
Tropic of Capricorn
AUSTRALIA
Norfolk Island (to Australia)
Lord Howe Island (to Australia)
Sydney
Melbourne
NEW ZEALAND
Bounty Islands (to NZ)
Antipodes Islands (to NZ)
Auckland Islands (to NZ)
Campbell Island (to NZ)
Macquarie Island (to Australia)
OCEAN
Antarctic Circle
ANTARCTICA
(All territorial claims are held in abeyance under the 1959 Antarctic Treaty)
Ross Ice Shelf
SCALE 1:73,000,000
(projection: Wagner VII)
Km 0 250 500 1,000 1,500 2,000
Miles 0 250 500 1,000 1,500 2,000

N O P Q R U V W X Y Z

States and Boundaries

There are over 190 sovereign states in the world today; in 1950 there were only 82. Over the last half-century national self-determination has been a driving force for many states with a history of colonialism and oppression. As more borders are added to the world map, the number of international border disputes increases.

In many cases, where the impetus toward independence has been religious or ethnic, disputes with minority groups have also caused violent internal conflict. While many newly-formed states have moved peacefully toward independence, successfully establishing government by multi-party democracy, dictatorship by military regime or individual despot is often the result of the internal power-struggles which characterize the early stages in the lives of new nations.

The Nature of Politics

Democracy is a broad term: it can range from the ideal of multiparty elections and fair representation to, in countries such as Singapore and Indonesia, a thin disguise for single-party rule. In despotic regimes, on the other hand, a single, often personal authority has total power; institutions such as parliament and the military are mere instruments of the dictator.

The stars and stripes *of the US flag are a potent symbol of the country's status as a federal democracy.*

The Changing World Map

Decolonization

In 1950, large areas of the world remained under the control of a handful of European countries (*page xxviii*). The process of decolonization had begun in Asia, where, following World WarII, much of southern and southeastern Asia sought and achieved self-determination. In the 1960s, a host of African states achieved independence, so that by 1965, most of the larger tracts of the European overseas empires had been substantially eroded. The final major stage in decolonization came with the breakup of the Soviet Union and the Eastern bloc after 1990. The process continues today as the last toeholds of European colonialism, often tiny island nations, press increasingly for independence.

Icons of communism*, including statues of former leaders such as Lenin and Stalin, were destroyed when the Soviet bloc was dismantled in 1989, creating several new nations.*

New nations 1945–1965

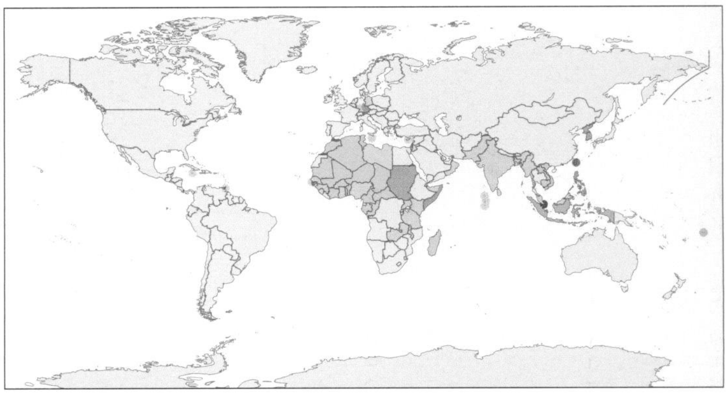

New nations 1965–1996

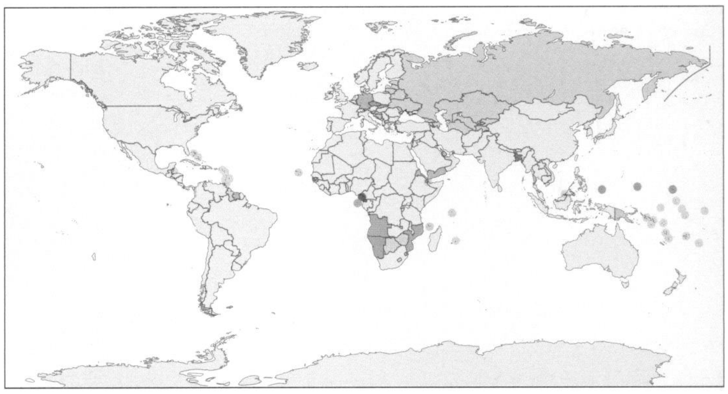

Administration at the time of independence

- Australia
- Aust/NZ/UK
- Belgium
- China
- Czechoslovakia
- Egypt/UK
- Ethiopia
- France
- France/UK
- Italy
- Japan
- Malaysia
- Netherlands
- New Zealand
- Pakistan
- Portugal
- South Africa
- Spain
- UK
- Unified country
- USA
- USSR
- Yugoslavia

Iran *has been one of the modern world's few true theocracies; Islam has an impact on every aspect of political life.*

North Korea is *an independent communist republic. Power is concentrated in the hands of Kim Jong Il.*

Saddam Hussein *former autocratic leader of Iraq, promoted an extreme personality cult for over 20 years. He was ousted by a US-led coalition in 2003.*

South Africa *became a democracy in 1994, when elections ended over a century of white minority rule.*

In Brunei *the Sultan has ruled by decree since 1962; power is closely tied to the royal family. The Sultan's brothers are responsible for finance and foreign affairs.*

Types of government

- Multiparty democracy for more than 10 yrs
- Multiparty/transitional democracy within last 10 yrs
- Single-party government
- Military regime
- Theocracy
- Absolute monarchy
- Current civil unrest

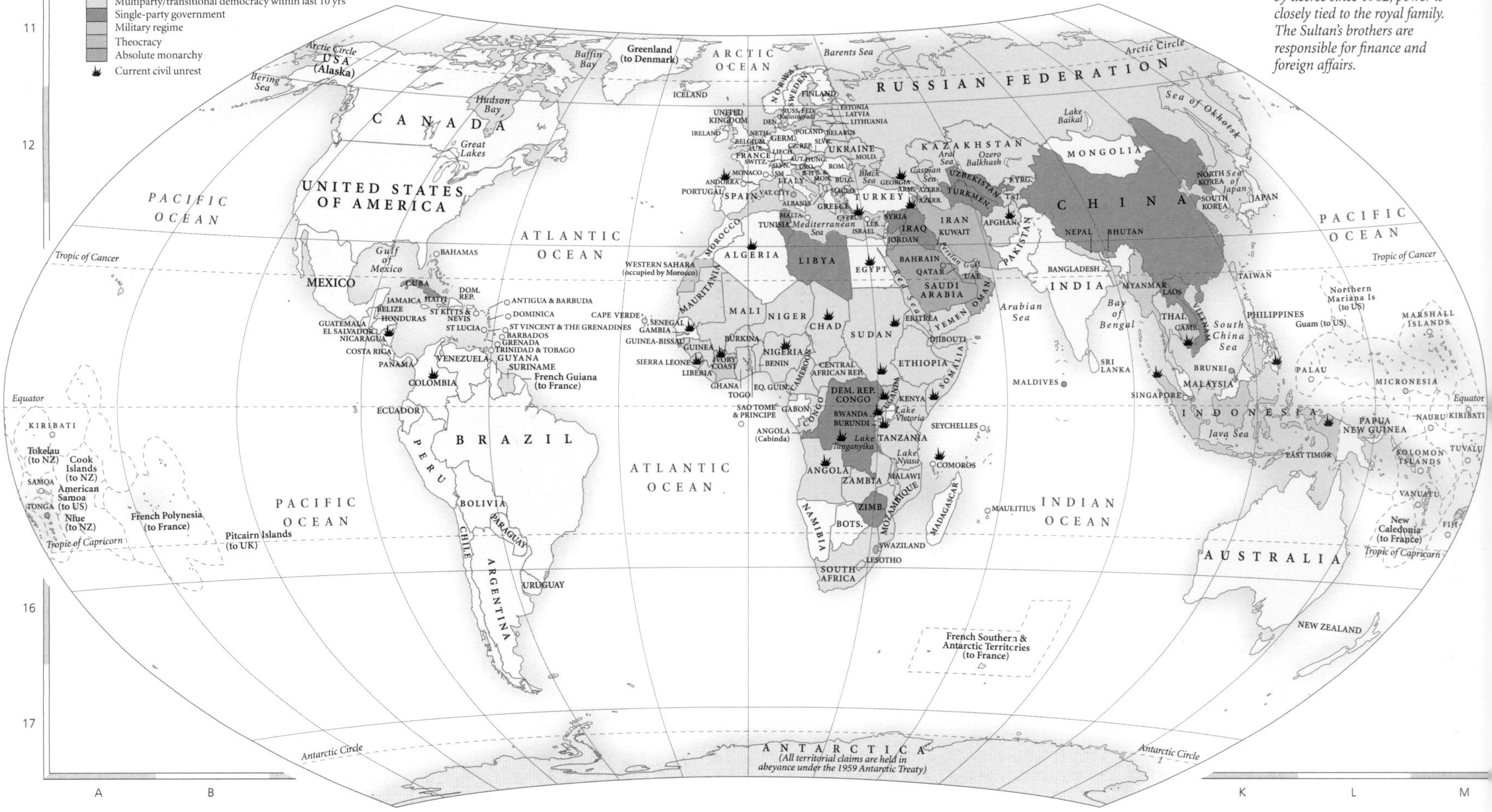
Arctic Circle
USA (Alaska)
Bering Sea
Baffin Bay
Greenland (to Denmark)
ARCTIC OCEAN
Barents Sea
RUSSIAN FEDERATION
Hudson Bay
CANADA
Great Lakes
UNITED STATES OF AMERICA
PACIFIC OCEAN
ATLANTIC OCEAN
Tropic of Cancer
Gulf of Mexico
BAHAMAS
MEXICO
CUBA
DOM. REP.
JAMAICA
HAITI
BELIZE
HONDURAS
ST KITTS & NEVIS
ANTIGUA & BARBUDA
DOMINICA
ST LUCIA
ST VINCENT & THE GRENADINES
BARBADOS
GRENADA
TRINIDAD & TOBAGO
GUATEMALA
EL SALVADOR
NICARAGUA
COSTA RICA
PANAMA
VENEZUELA
GUYANA
SURINAME
French Guiana (to France)
COLOMBIA
ECUADOR
PERU
BRAZIL
BOLIVIA
PARAGUAY
CHILE
ARGENTINA
URUGUAY
Equator
KIRIBATI
Tokelau (to NZ)
Cook Islands (to NZ)
SAMOA
American Samoa (to US)
TONGA
Niue (to NZ)
French Polynesia (to France)
Pitcairn Islands (to UK)
Tropic of Capricorn
ICELAND
UNITED KINGDOM
IRELAND
NORWAY
SWEDEN
FINLAND
ESTONIA
LATVIA
LITHUANIA
DEN.
NETH.
BELGIUM
LUX.
GERM.
POLAND
BELARUS
UKRAINE
MOLD.
FRANCE
SWITZ.
LIECH.
AUST.
HUNG.
ROM.
ANDORRA
MONACO
PORTUGAL
SPAIN
ITALY
VAT. CITY
ALBANIA
GREECE
BULG.
MALTA
TUNISIA
Mediterranean Sea
CYPRUS
LEB.
ISRAEL
SYRIA
JORDAN
IRAQ
TURKEY
GEORGIA
ARM.
AZERB.
Black Sea
Caspian Sea
KAZAKHSTAN
Aral Sea
Ozero Balkhash
UZBEKISTAN
TURKMEN.
KYRG.
TAJ.
AFGHAN.
PAKISTAN
IRAN
KUWAIT
BAHRAIN
QATAR
UAE
SAUDI ARABIA
OMAN
YEMEN
Arabian Sea
MOROCCO
ALGERIA
WESTERN SAHARA (occupied by Morocco)
LIBYA
EGYPT
Red Sea
MAURITANIA
MALI
NIGER
CHAD
SUDAN
ERITREA
DJIBOUTI
ETHIOPIA
SOMALIA
CAPE VERDE
SENEGAL
GAMBIA
GUINEA-BISSAU
GUINEA
SIERRA LEONE
LIBERIA
IVORY COAST
BURKINA
GHANA
TOGO
BENIN
NIGERIA
CAMEROON
CENTRAL AFRICAN REP.
EQ. GUINEA
SAO TOME & PRINCIPE
GABON
CONGO
DEM. REP. CONGO
UGANDA
KENYA
RWANDA
BURUNDI
Lake Victoria
Lake Tanganyika
TANZANIA
SEYCHELLES
ANGOLA
ANGOLA (Cabinda)
ZAMBIA
MALAWI
Lake Nyasa
MOZAMBIQUE
COMOROS
MADAGASCAR
MAURITIUS
ZIMB.
NAMIBIA
BOTS.
SWAZILAND
LESOTHO
SOUTH AFRICA
ATLANTIC OCEAN
INDIAN OCEAN
Lake Baikal
MONGOLIA
Sea of Okhotsk
CHINA
NORTH KOREA
Sea of Japan
SOUTH KOREA
JAPAN
NEPAL
BHUTAN
INDIA
BANGLADESH
MYANMAR
LAOS
Bay of Bengal
THAI.
CAMB.
VIETNAM
SRI LANKA
MALDIVES
TAIWAN
PHILIPPINES
South China Sea
BRUNEI
MALAYSIA
SINGAPORE
INDONESIA
Java Sea
EAST TIMOR
PAPUA NEW GUINEA
Northern Mariana Is (to US)
Guam (to US)
MARSHALL ISLANDS
PALAU
MICRONESIA
NAURU
KIRIBATI
TUVALU
SOLOMON ISLANDS
VANUATU
FIJI
New Caledonia (to France)
AUSTRALIA
NEW ZEALAND
French Southern & Antarctic Territories (to France)
Antarctic Circle
ANTARCTICA
(All territorial claims are held in abeyance under the 1959 Antarctic Treaty)

Lines on the Map

The determination of international boundaries can use a variety of criteria. Many of the borders between older states follow physical boundaries; some mirror religious and ethnic differences; others are the legacy of complex histories of conflict and colonialism, while others have been imposed by international agreements or arbitration.

Post-colonial borders

When the European colonial empires in Africa were dismantled during the second half of the 20th century, the outlines of the new African states mirrored colonial boundaries. These boundaries had been drawn up by colonial administrators, often based on inadequate geographical knowledge. Such arbitrary boundaries were imposed on people of different languages, racial groups, religions, and customs. This confused legacy often led to civil and international war.

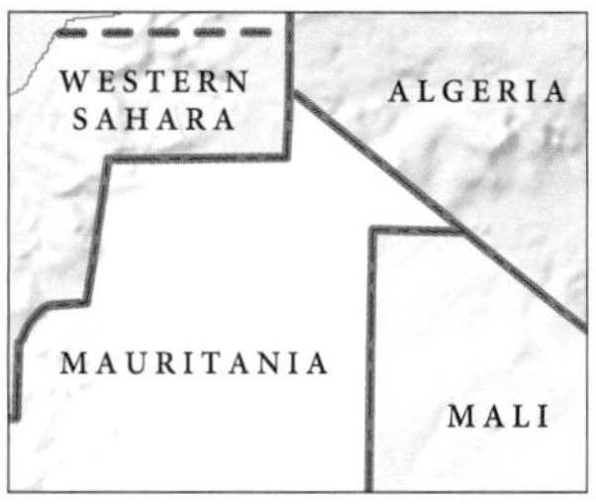
WESTERN SAHARA
ALGERIA
MAURITANIA
MALI

***The conflict** that has plagued many African countries since independence has caused millions of people to become refugees.*

Physical borders

Many of the world's countries are divided by physical borders: lakes, rivers, mountains. The demarcation of such boundaries can, however, lead to disputes. Control of waterways, water supplies, and fisheries are frequent causes of international friction.

Enclaves

The shifting political map over the course of history has frequently led to anomalous situations. Parts of national territories may become isolated by territorial agreement, forming an enclave. The West German part of the city of Berlin, which until 1989 lay several hundred miles within East German territory, was a famous example.

Baltic Sea
ESTONIA
RUSSIAN FEDERATION
LATVIA
LITHUANIA
RUSS. FED. (Kaliningrad)
BELARUS
POLAND

***Since the independence** of Lithuania and Belarus, the peoples of the Russian enclave of Kaliningrad have become physically isolated.*

Antarctica

When Antarctic exploration began a century ago, seven nations, Australia, Argentina, Britain, Chile, France, New Zealand, and Norway, laid claim to the new territory. In 1961 the Antarctic Treaty, signed by 39 nations, agreed to hold all territorial claims in abeyance.

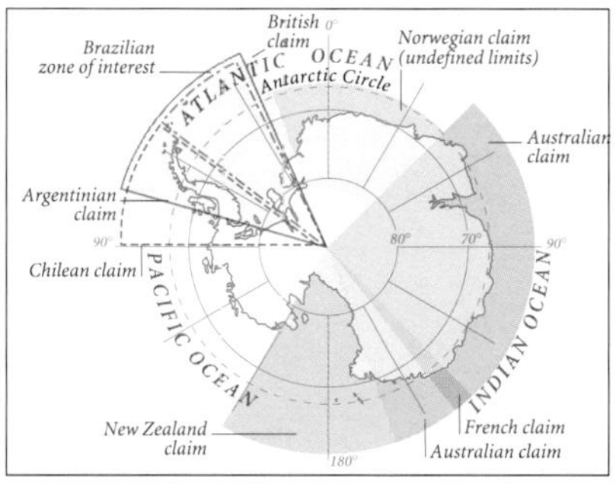
Brazilian zone of interest
British claim
ATLANTIC OCEAN
Antarctic Circle
Norwegian claim (undefined limits)
Australian claim
Argentinian claim
Chilean claim
PACIFIC OCEAN
INDIAN OCEAN
New Zealand claim
French claim
Australian claim

World boundaries

Dates from which current boundaries have existed

- 1990–1993
- 1966–1989
- 1946–1965
- 1915–1945
- 1850–1914
- 1800–1849
- Pre-1800

Geometric borders

Straight lines and lines of longitude and latitude have occasionally been used to determine international boundaries; and indeed the world's longest international boundary, between Canada and the USA follows the 49th Parallel for over one-third of its course. Many Canadian, American and Australian internal administrative boundaries are similarly determined using a geometric solution.

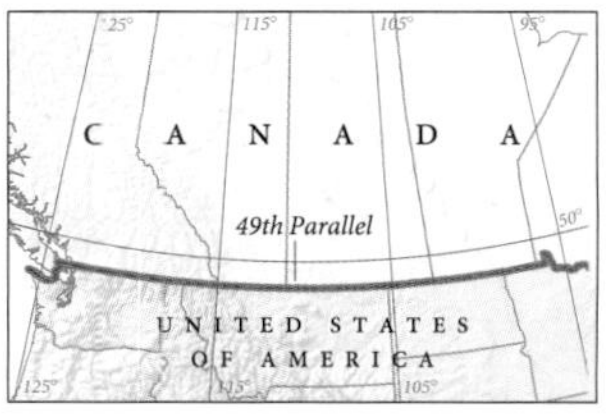
CANADA
49th Parallel
UNITED STATES OF AMERICA

***Different farming techniques** in Canada and the US clearly mark the course of the international boundary in this satellite map.*

Lake borders

Countries which lie next to lakes usually fix their borders in the middle of the lake. Unusually the Lake Nyasa border between Malawi and Tanzania runs along Tanzania's shore.

TANZ.
Lake Nyasa
ZAMBIA
MALAWI
MOZAMBIQUE
MOZAMBIQUE

***Complicated agreements** between colonial powers led to the awkward division of Lake Nyasa.*

River borders

Rivers alone account for one-sixth of the world's borders. Many great rivers form boundaries between a number of countries. Changes in a river's course and interruptions of its natural flow can lead to disputes, particularly in areas where water is scarce. The center of the river's course is the nominal boundary line.

GERMANY
Danube
UKRAINE
SLOVAKIA
AUSTRIA
HUNGARY
ROMANIA
CROATIA
Danube
SERB. & MON. (YUGO.)
BULGARIA

***The Danube** forms all or part of the border between nine European nations.*

Mountain borders

Mountain ranges form natural barriers and are the basis for many major borders, particularly in Europe and Asia. The watershed is the conventional boundary demarcation line, but its accurate determination is often problematic.

FRANCE
Pyrenees
ANDORRA
SPAIN

***The Pyrenees** form a natural mountain border between France and Spain.*

Shifting boundaries – Poland

Borders between countries can change dramatically over time. The nations of eastern Europe have been particularly affected by changing boundaries. Poland is an example of a country whose boundaries have changed so significantly that it has literally moved around Europe. At the start of the 16th century, Poland was the largest nation in Europe. Between 1772 and 1795, it was absorbed into Prussia, Austria, and Russia, and it effectively ceased to exist. After World War I, Poland became an independent country once more, but its borders changed again after World War II following invasions by both Soviet Russia and Nazi Germany.

Moscow
POLAND
Warsaw
Kiev

***In 1634**, Poland was the largest nation in Europe, its eastern boundary reaching toward Moscow.*

Moscow
RUSSIA
PRUSSIA
Warsaw
AUSTRIA
Kiev

***From 1772–1795**, Poland was gradually partitioned between Austria, Russia, and Prussia. Its eastern boundary receded by over 100 miles (160 km).*

Moscow
POLAND
Warsaw
Kiev

***Following World War I**, Poland was reinstated as an independent state, but it was less than half the size it had been in 1634.*

Moscow
POLAND
Warsaw
Kiev

***After World War II**, the Baltic Sea border was extended westward, but much of the eastern territory was annexed by Russia.*

International disputes

There are more than 60 disputed borders or territories in the world today. Although many of these disputes can be settled by peaceful negotiation, some areas have become a focus for international conflict. Ethnic tensions have been a major source of territorial disagreement throughout history, as has the ownership of, and access to, valuable natural resources. The turmoil of the postcolonial era in many parts of Africa is partly a result of the 19th century "carve-up" of the continent, which created potential for conflict by drawing often arbitrary lines through linguistic and cultural areas.

Jammu and Kashmir

Disputes over Jammu and Kashmir have caused three serious wars between India and Pakistan since 1947. Pakistan wishes to annex the largely Muslim territory, while India refuses to cede any territory or to hold a referendum, and also lays claim to the entire territory. Most international maps show the "line of control" agreed in 1972 as the *de facto* border. In addition, both Pakistan and India have territorial disputes with neighboring China. The situation is further complicated by a Kashmiri independence movement, active since the late 1980s.

***Indian army troops** maintain their positions in the mountainous terrain of northern Kashmir.*

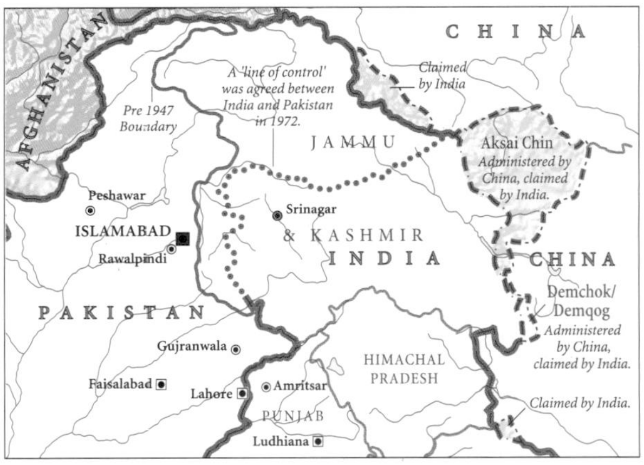
CHINA
AFGHANISTAN
A 'line of control' was agreed between India and Pakistan in 1972.
Claimed by India
Pre 1947 Boundary
JAMMU
& KASHMIR
Aksai Chin
Administered by China, claimed by India.
Peshawar
Srinagar
ISLAMABAD
Rawalpindi
INDIA
CHINA
PAKISTAN
Demchok/Demqog
Administered by China, claimed by India.
Gujranwala
HIMACHAL PRADESH
Faisalabad
Lahore
Amritsar
PUNJAB
Ludhiana
Claimed by India.

North and South Korea

Since 1953, the *de facto* border between North and South Korea has been a ceasefire line which straddles the 38th Parallel and is designated as a demilitarized zone. Both countries have heavy fortifications and troop concentrations behind this zone.

ΛΕΥΤΕΡΙΑ ΣΤΗΝ Κ
FREEDOM FOR CY

***The so-called 'green line'** divides Cyprus into Greek and Turkish sectors.*

Cyprus

Cyprus was partitioned in 1974, following an invasion by Turkish troops. The south is now the Greek Cypriot Republic of Cyprus, while the self-proclaimed Turkish Republic of Northern Cyprus is recognized only by Turkey.

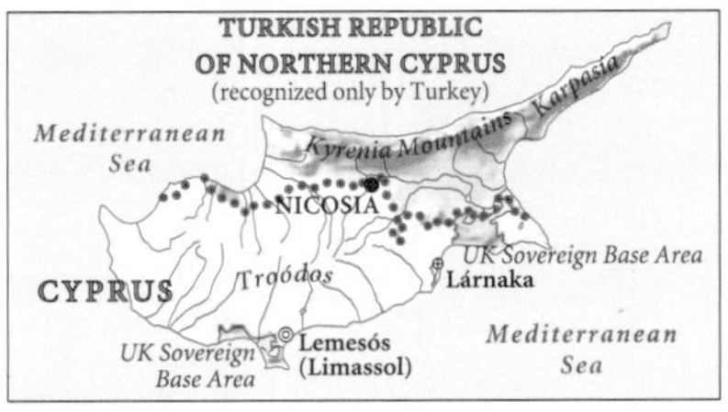
TURKISH REPUBLIC OF NORTHERN CYPRUS
(recognized only by Turkey)
Mediterranean Sea
Kyrenia Mountains
Karpasia
NICOSIA
CYPRUS
Troodos
UK Sovereign Base Area
Lárnaka
UK Sovereign Base Area
Lemesós (Limassol)
Mediterranean Sea

CHINA
Sea of Japan
NORTH KOREA
PYONGYANG
SEOUL
SOUTH KOREA
Yellow Sea

***Heavy fortifications** on the border between North and South Korea.*

Svalbard
ICELAND
Rockall
NORWAY
Northern Ireland
IRELAND
UNITED KINGDOM
RUSSIAN FEDERATION
Kurile Islands
UKRAINE
KAZAKHSTAN
Liancourt Rocks
MOLD.
Chechnya
UNITED STATES OF AMERICA
MACEDONIA
GEORG.
ARM.
AZERB.
UZBEKISTAN
KYRGYSTAN
NORTH KOREA
SPAIN
Gibraltar
Ceuta
Melilla
GREECE
TURKEY
CHINA
SOUTH KOREA
JAPAN
CYPRUS
SYRIA
AFGHANISTAN
Aksai Chin
ISRAEL
IRAQ
IRAN
Jammu and Kashmir
Golan Heights
MOROCCO
ALGERIA
PAKISTAN
NEPAL
Matsu
Senkaku Islands
TAIWAN
CUBA
Guantanamo Bay
HAITI
WESTERN SAHARA
EGYPT
UAE
SAUDI ARABIA
BANGLADESH
INDIA
MYANMAR
LAOS
VIETNAM
Paracel Islands
Wake Island
PHILIPPINES
BELIZE
GUATEMALA
EL SALVADOR
NICARAGUA
SENEGAL
CHAD
ERITREA
SUDAN
Hamish Islands
THAI.
VENEZUELA
GUYANA
SURINAME
French Guiana
NIGERIA
ETHIOPIA
SOMALIA
SRI LANKA
Spratly Islands
SIERRA LEONE
LIBERIA
CAMEROON
COLOMBIA
MALAYSIA
Sipidan and Ligitan
DEM. REP. CONGO
UGANDA
KENYA
SINGAPORE
CONGO
RWANDA
BURUNDI
INDONESIA
SOLOMON ISLANDS
COMOROS
ANGOLA
MADAGASCAR
ZIMBABWE
NAMIBIA
BOTSWANA
MAURITIUS
ARGENTINA
Falkland Islands
Conflicts and international dispute
Countries involved in active external conflict
Active territorial or border disputes
Countries involved in internal conflict

The Falkland Islands

The British Dependent Territory of the Falkland Islands was invaded by Argentina in 1982, sparking a full-scale war with the UK. In 1995, the UK and Argentina reached an agreement on the exploitation of oil reserves around the islands.

***British** warships in Falkland Souna during the 1982 war with Argentina.*

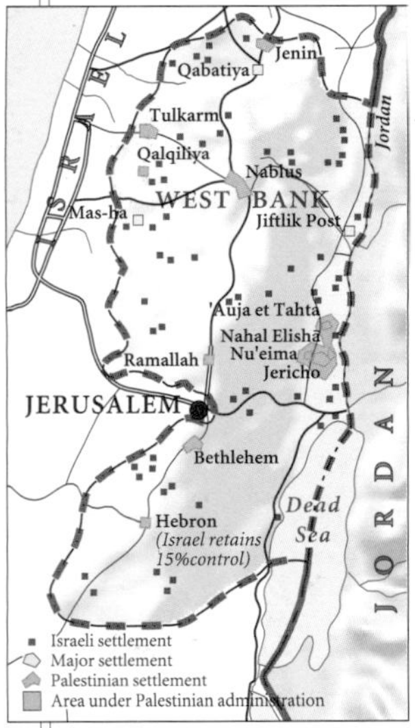
ISRAEL
Jenin
Qabatiya
Tulkarm
Qalqiliya
Nablus
Jordan
Mas-ha
WEST BANK
Jiftlik Post
Auja et Tahta
Nahal Elisha
Nu'eima
Ramallah
Jericho
JERUSALEM
Bethlehem
Dead Sea
Hebron
(Israel retains 15% control)
JORDAN
Israeli settlement
Major settlement
Palestinian settlement
Area under Palestinian administration

Israel

Israel was created in 1948 following the 1947 UN Resolution (147) on Palestine. Until 1979 Israel had no borders, only ceasefire lines from a series of wars in 1948, 1967 and 1973. Treaties with Egypt in 1979 and Jordan in 1994 led to these borders being defined and agreed. Negotiations over Israeli settlements and Palestinian self-government have collapsed into inter-communal warfare since 2000.

LEBANON
Mediterranean Sea
GOLAN HEIGHTS
SYRIA
WEST BANK
GAZA STRIP
ISRAEL
JORDAN
EGYPT

***Barbed-wire fences** surround a settlement in the Golan Heights.*

Former Yugoslavia

Following the disintegration in 1991 of the communist state of Yugoslavia, the breakaway states of Croatia and Bosnia-Herzegovina came into conflict with the "parent" state (consisting of Serbia and Montenegro). Warfare focused on ethnic and territorial ambitions in Bosnia. The tenuous Dayton Accord of 1995 sought to respect the post-1990 borders, whilst providing for ethnic partition and required international peace-keeping troops to maintain the terms of the peace.

CROATIA
Sava
Bihać
Brčko
Banja Luka
Bosna
Tuzla
Jajce
BOSNIA-HERZEGOVINA
Drina
Srebrenica
Gornji Vakuf
Split
SARAJEVO
Goražde
Mostar
Adriatic Sea
SERB. & MON. (YUGOSLAVIA)
Dubrovnik
Republika Srpska
Federacija Bosna i Hercegovina

***Most claimant** states have small military garrisons on the Spratly Islands.*

The Spratly Islands

The site of potential oil and natural gas reserves, the Spratly Islands in the South China Sea have been claimed by China, Vietnam, Taiwan, Malaysia, and the Philippines since the Japanese gave up a wartime claim in 1951.

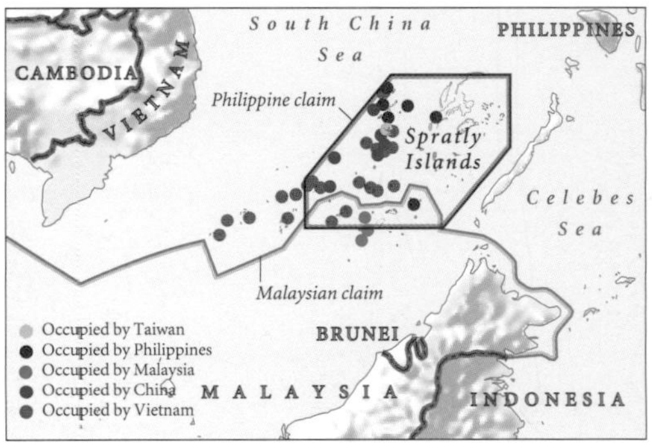
South China Sea
PHILIPPINES
CAMBODIA
VIETNAM
Philippine claim
Spratly Islands
Celebes Sea
Malaysian claim
BRUNEI
MALAYSIA
INDONESIA
Occupied by Taiwan
Occupied by Philippines
Occupied by Malaysia
Occupied by China
Occupied by Vietnam

ATLAS OF THE WORLD

The maps in this atlas are arranged continent by continent, starting from the International Date Line, and moving eastward. The maps provide a unique view of today's world, combining traditional cartographic techniques with the latest remote-sensed and digital technology.

Arctic Circle
NORTH AMERICA
Missouri
Mississippi
EUROPE
ASIA
Ob'
Yenisey
Lena
Amur
Yellow River
Yangtze
Indus
Mekong
Nile
PACIFIC OCEAN
ATLANTIC OCEAN
Tropic of Cancer
Niger
AFRICA
Congo
Zambezi
Equator
Amazon
SOUTH AMERICA
Paraná
ATLANTIC OCEAN
INDIAN OCEAN
AUSTRALASIA & OCEANIA
Darling
Tropic of Capricorn
PACIFIC OCEAN
SOUTHERN OCEAN
Antarctic Circle

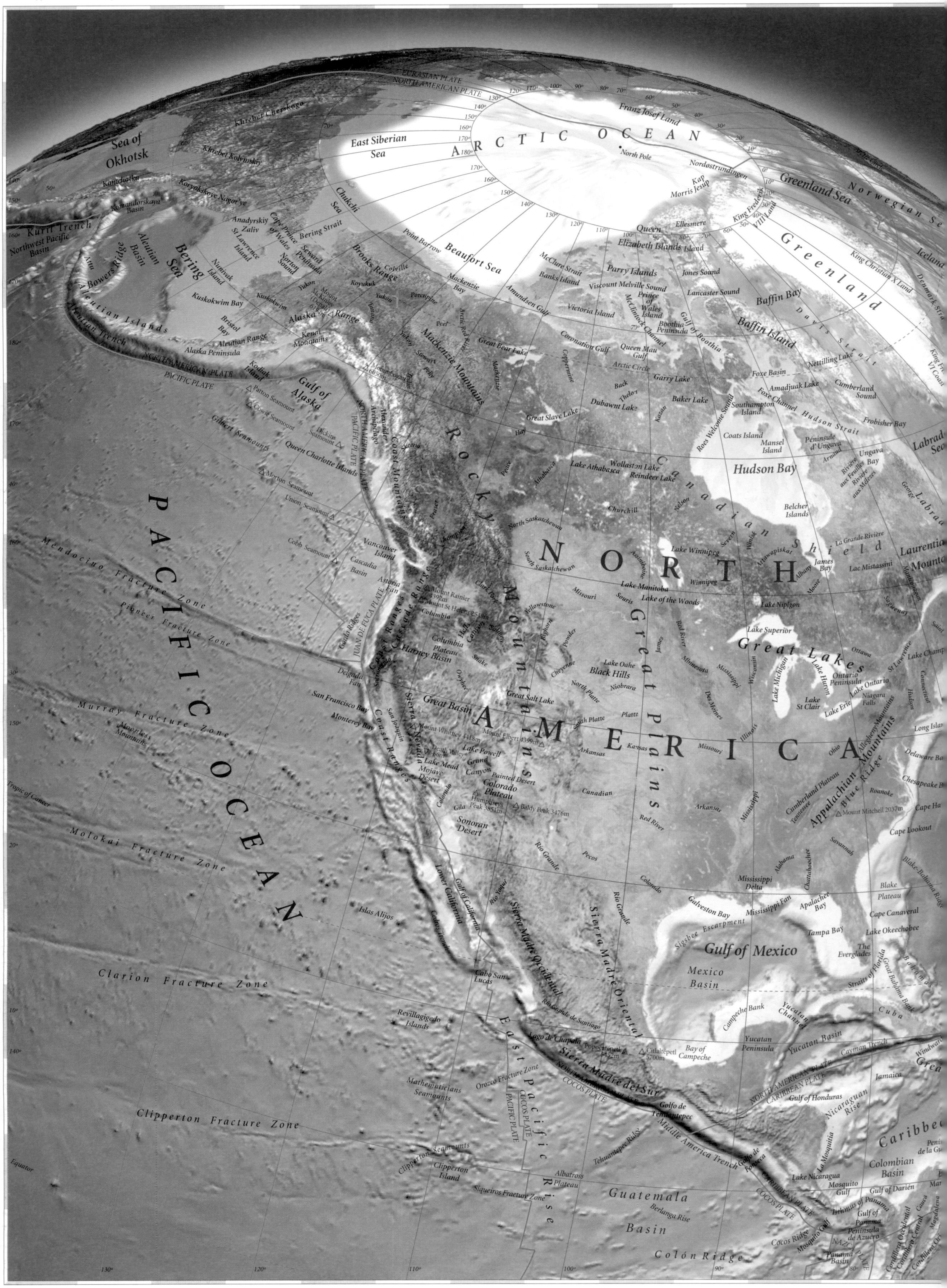

A B C D E F G H I J K L M
1 2 3 4 5 6 7 8 9 10 11 12 13 14 15 16 17
ARCTIC OCEAN
North Pole
EURASIAN PLATE
NORTH AMERICAN PLATE
Franz Josef Land
East Siberian Sea
Khrebet Cherskogo
Khrebet Kolymskiy
Sea of Okhotsk
Kamchatka
Koryakskoye Nagor'ye
Komandorskaya Basin
Kuril Trench
Northwest Pacific Basin
Anadyrskiy Zaliv
Cape Prince of Wales
St Lawrence Island
Chukchi Sea
Bering Strait
Point Barrow
Seward Peninsula
Norton Sound
Aleutian Basin
Bowers Ridge
Bering Sea
Nunivak Island
Kuskokwim Bay
Bristol Bay
Aleutian Islands
Aleutian Trench
Aleutian Range
Alaska Peninsula
NORTH AMERICAN PLATE
PACIFIC PLATE
Kodiak Island
Brooks Range
Colville
Yukon
Koyukuk
Kuskokwim
Alaska Range
Kenai Mountains
Porcupine
Beaufort Sea
Mackenzie Bay
Mackenzie Mountains
Peel
Great Bear Lake
Mackenzie
Gulf of Alaska
Patton Seamount
Cowie Seamount
Gilbert Seamounts
Dickins Seamount
Alexander Archipelago
Queen Charlotte Islands
Morton Seamount
Union Seamount
Coast Mountains
Cobb Seamount
Vancouver Island
Cascadia Basin
Astoria Fan
Mendocino Fracture Zone
Pioneer Fracture Zone
Murray Fracture Zone
Molokai Fracture Zone
Clarion Fracture Zone
Clipperton Fracture Zone
Tropic of Cancer
Equator
PACIFIC OCEAN
JUAN DE FUCA PLATE
Gorda Ridges
Delgada Fan
Coast Ranges
Cascade Range
Mount Rainier
Mount St Helens
Columbia
Columbia Plateau
Harney Basin
Snake
San Francisco Bay
Monterey Bay
Sierra Nevada
San Joaquin
Mount Whitney
Death Valley
Great Basin
Great Salt Lake
Mount Elbert
Lake Powell
Lake Mead
Mojave Desert
Grand Canyon
Painted Desert
Colorado Plateau
Humphreys Peak
Baldy Peak 3476m
Gila
Sonoran Desert
Colorado
Lower California
Gulf of California
Islas Alijos
Cabo San Lucas
Revillagigedo Islands
Mathematicians Seamounts
Orozco Fracture Zone
East Pacific Rise
COCOS PLATE
PACIFIC PLATE
Clipperton Seamounts
Clipperton Island
Albatross Plateau
Siqueiros Fracture Zone
Guatemala Basin
Tehuantepec Ridge
Middle America Trench
Cocos Ridge
Colón Ridge
Sierra Madre Occidental
Sierra Madre Oriental
Sierra Madre del Sur
Lago de Chapala
Popocatépetl
Citlaltépetl 5700m
Golfo de Tehuantepec
Rocky Mountains
Great Plains
NORTH AMERICA
Canadian Shield
Queen Elizabeth Islands
Ellesmere Island
Parry Islands
McClure Strait
Banks Island
Amundsen Gulf
Viscount Melville Sound
Prince of Wales Island
Victoria Island
McClintock Channel
Boothia Peninsula
Gulf of Boothia
Lancaster Sound
Jones Sound
Baffin Bay
Baffin Island
Coronation Gulf
Queen Maud Gulf
Coppermine
Arctic Circle
Back
Thelon
Garry Lake
Baker Lake
Dubawnt Lake
Great Slave Lake
Hay
Peace
Athabasca
Lake Athabasca
Wollaston Lake
Reindeer Lake
Churchill
Nelson
Kazan
Roes Welcome Sound
Southampton Island
Coats Island
Mansel Island
Hudson Bay
Hudson Strait
Foxe Basin
Foxe Channel
Amadjuak Lake
Nettilling Lake
Cumberland Sound
Frobisher Bay
Péninsule d'Ungava
Ungava Bay
Belcher Islands
James Bay
La Grande Rivière
Lac Mistassini
North Saskatchewan
South Saskatchewan
Lake Winnipeg
Lake Manitoba
Lake of the Woods
Winnipeg
Assiniboine
Severn
Albany
Moose
Lake Nipigon
Lake Superior
Great Lakes
Lake Michigan
Lake Huron
Lake Ontario
Lake Erie
Lake St Clair
Niagara Falls
Ontario Peninsula
Ottawa
St Lawrence
Missouri
Souris
Red River
Minnesota
Yellowstone
Bighorn
Powder
Cheyenne
Black Hills
Lake Oahe
North Platte
South Platte
Niobrara
Platte
Kansas
Des Moines
Arkansas
Canadian
Red River
Mississippi
Illinois
Wisconsin
Ohio
Tennessee
Cumberland Plateau
Appalachian Mountains
Allegheny Mountains
Blue Ridge
Mount Mitchell 2037m
Roanoke
Savannah
Chattahoochee
Alabama
Pecos
Rio Grande
Colorado
Mississippi Delta
Mississippi Fan
Galveston Bay
Sigsbee Escarpment
Gulf of Mexico
Mexico Basin
Apalachee Bay
Tampa Bay
Lake Okeechobee
The Everglades
Cape Canaveral
Blake Plateau
Blake-Bahama Ridge
Cape Lookout
Cape Hatteras
Chesapeake Bay
Delaware Bay
Long Island
Hudson
Straits of Florida
Great Bahama Bank
Campeche Bank
Yucatan Channel
Yucatan Peninsula
Yucatan Basin
Bay of Campeche
Cayman Trench
Cuba
Jamaica
NORTH AMERICAN PLATE
CARIBBEAN PLATE
Gulf of Honduras
Nicaraguan Rise
La Mosquitia
Lake Nicaragua
Mosquito Gulf
Colombian Basin
Caribbean
Gulf of Darién
Isthmus of Panama
Gulf of Panama
Península de Azuero
Panama Basin
NAZCA PLATE
Greenland
Greenland Sea
Norwegian Sea
Nordostrundingen
Kap Morris Jesup
King Frederik VIII Land
King Christian X Land
Davis Strait
Denmark Strait
Iceland
Labrador Sea
Labrador
Laurentian Mountains
Saguenay

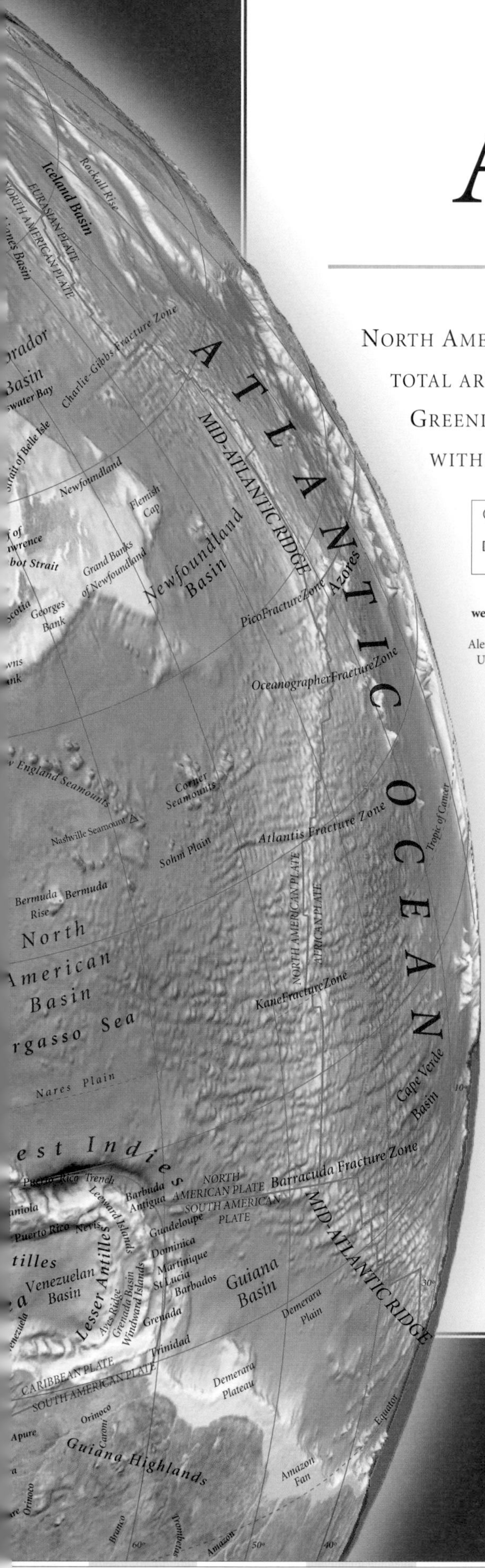

ATLANTIC OCEAN
MID-ATLANTIC RIDGE
Iceland Basin
Rockall Rise
EURASIAN PLATE
NORTH AMERICAN PLATE
Charlie-Gibbs Fracture Zone
Newfoundland
Flemish Cap
Grand Banks of Newfoundland
Newfoundland Basin
Azores
Pico Fracture Zone
Oceanographer Fracture Zone
Corner Seamounts
Nashville Seamount
Sohm Plain
Atlantis Fracture Zone
Tropic of Cancer
Bermuda Rise
Bermuda
North American Basin
Sargasso Sea
NORTH AMERICAN PLATE
AFRICAN PLATE
Kane Fracture Zone
Nares Plain
Cape Verde Basin
Puerto Rico Trench
Barbuda
Antigua
NORTH AMERICAN PLATE
SOUTH AMERICAN PLATE
Barracuda Fracture Zone
Guadeloupe
Dominica
Martinique
St Lucia
Barbados
Leeward Islands
Windward Islands
Lesser Antilles
Aves Ridge
Grenada Basin
Grenada
Venezuelan Basin
Guiana Basin
Demerara Plain
MID-ATLANTIC RIDGE
Trinidad
CARIBBEAN PLATE
SOUTH AMERICAN PLATE
Demerara Plateau
Orinoco
Caroni
Guiana Highlands
Amazon Fan
Equator
Branco
Amazon

North America

North America is the world's third largest continent with a total area of 9,358,340 sq miles (24,238,000 sq km) including Greenland and the Caribbean Islands. It lies wholly within the Northern Hemisphere.

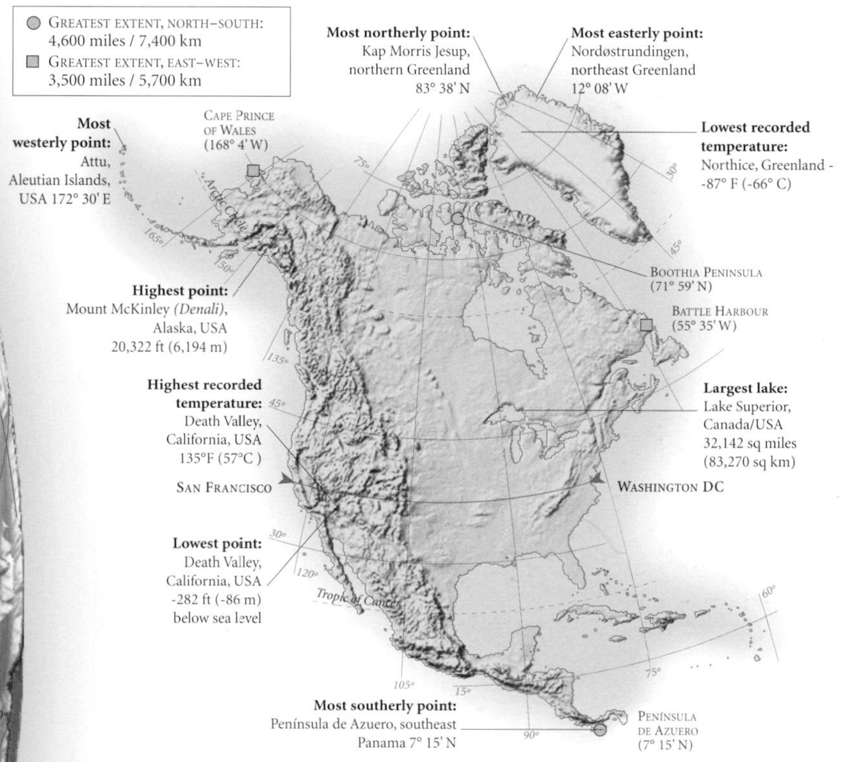

Greatest extent, north–south: 4,600 miles / 7,400 km
Greatest extent, east–west: 3,500 miles / 5,700 km
Most northerly point: Kap Morris Jesup, northern Greenland 83° 38' N
Most easterly point: Nordøstrundingen, northeast Greenland 12° 08' W
Most westerly point: Attu, Aleutian Islands, USA 172° 30' E
Cape Prince of Wales (168° 4' W)
Lowest recorded temperature: Northice, Greenland -87° F (-66° C)
Highest point: Mount McKinley (Denali), Alaska, USA 20,322 ft (6,194 m)
Boothia Peninsula (71° 59' N)
Battle Harbour (55° 35' W)
Highest recorded temperature: Death Valley, California, USA 135°F (57°C)
Largest lake: Lake Superior, Canada/USA 32,142 sq miles (83,270 sq km)
San Francisco
Washington DC
Lowest point: Death Valley, California, USA -282 ft (-86 m) below sea level
Tropic of Cancer
Arctic Circle
Most southerly point: Península de Azuero, southeast Panama 7° 15' N
Península de Azuero (7° 15' N)

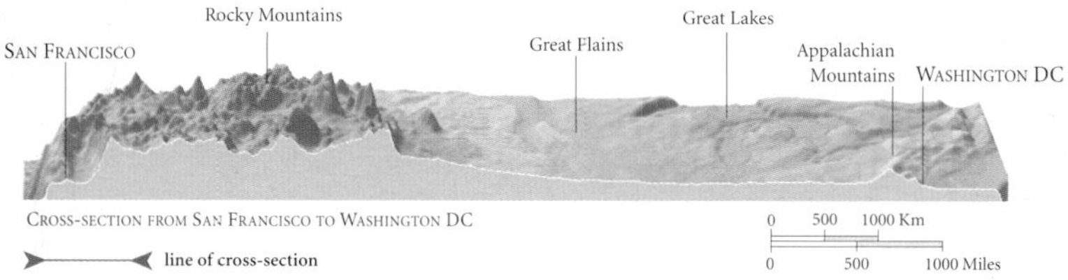

San Francisco
Rocky Mountains
Great Plains
Great Lakes
Appalachian Mountains
Washington DC
0 500 1000 Km
0 500 1000 Miles
line of cross-section

Cross-section from San Francisco to Washington DC

A B C D E F G H I J K L M

Physical North America

The North American continent can be divided into a number of major structural areas: the Western Cordillera, the Canadian Shield, the Great Plains, and Central Lowlands, and the Appalachians. Other smaller regions include the Gulf Atlantic Coastal Plain which borders the southern coast of North America from the southern Appalachians to the Great Plains. This area includes the expanding Mississippi Delta. A chain of volcanic islands, running in an arc around the margin of the Caribbean Plate, lie to the east of the Gulf of Mexico.

The Canadian Shield

Spanning northern Canada and Greenland, this geologically stable plain forms the heart of the continent, containing rocks more than two billion years old. A long history of weathering and repeated glaciation has scoured the region, leaving flat plains, gentle hummocks, numerous small basins and lakes, and the bays and islands of the Arctic.

The hard bedrock of the Canadian Shield is slowly rising
Hudson Bay was depressed by the ice sheet to form North America's largest basin
Once overlain by sedimentary rocks, erosion has reexposed the ancient Laurentian Highlands
A
A

Section across the Canadian Shield showing where the ice sheet has depressed the underlying rock and formed bays and islands.

The Western Cordillera

About 80 million years ago the Pacific and North American plates collided, uplifting the Western Cordillera. This consists of the Aleutian, Coast, Cascade and Sierra Nevada mountains, and the inland Rocky Mountains. These run parallel from the Arctic to Mexico.

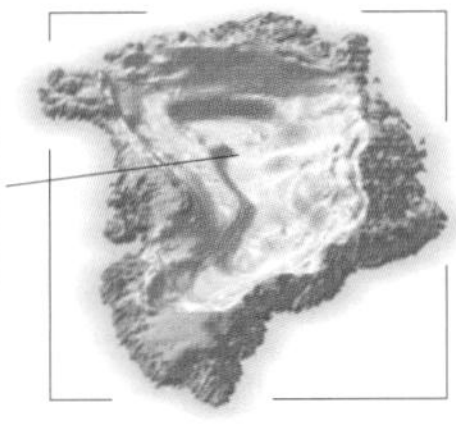
The weight of the ice sheet, 1.8 miles (3 km) thick, has depressed the land to 0.6 miles (1 km) below sea level

***This computer-generated** view shows the ice-covered island of Greenland without its ice cap.*

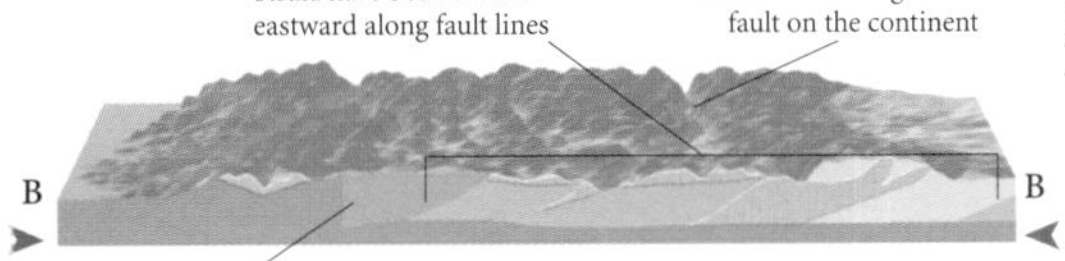
Strata have been thrust eastward along fault lines
The Rocky Mountain Trench is the longest linear fault on the continent
B
B
Volcanic rock

***Cross-section** through the Western Cordillera showing direction of mountain building.* ⟶

Map Key

ELEVATION	PLATE MARGINS (for explanation see page xiv)
3500m / 11,484ft	constructive
3000m / 9843ft	destructive
2500m / 8203ft	conservative
2000m / 6562ft	uncertain
1500m / 4922ft	
1000m / 3281ft	physiographic regions
500m / 1640ft	
250m / 820ft	line of cross-section
100m / 328ft	
sea level	

Scale 1:42,000,000
(projection: Lambert Azimuthal Equal Area)

Km 0 100 200 400 600 800 1000
Miles 0 50 100 200 300 400 500 600 700 800 900 1000

ATLANTIC OCEAN
Greenland
Baffin Bay
Baffin Island
Davis Strait
Foxe Basin
Hudson Strait
Labrador Sea
Labrador
Laurentian Mountains
Newfoundland
Hudson Bay
CANADIAN SHIELD
Beaufort Sea
ASIA
Bering Strait
Bering Sea
Aleutian Islands
Aleutian Range
Alaska Range
Mount McKinley 6194m
Brooks Range
Mackenzie Delta
Mackenzie Mountains
Mackenzie
Great Bear Lake
Great Slave Lake
Lake Athabasca
Reindeer Lake
Gulf of Alaska
NORTH AMERICAN PLATE
PACIFIC PLATE
Coast Mountains
WESTERN CORDILLERA
ROCKY MOUNTAINS
CENTRAL LOWLANDS
GREAT PLAINS
Lake Winnipeg
Lake Manitoba
Lake Superior
Lake Huron
Lake Michigan
Lake Ontario
Lake Erie
Great Lakes
St Lawrence
Nova Scotia
Cape Cod
Appalachian Mountains
APPALACHIANS
Mount Rainier 4392m
Mount St Helens 2549m
Cascade Range
Missouri
Great Basin
Great Salt Lake
Colorado
Colorado Plateau
Grand Canyon
San Andreas Fault
San Joaquin Valley
Sierra Nevada
Death Valley
Mojave Desert
Sonoran Desert
Ohio
Arkansas
Mississippi
GULF ATLANTIC COASTAL PLAIN
Mississippi Delta
Rio Grande
Gulf of California
Lower California
Sierra Madre Occidental
Sierra Madre Oriental
Volcán Pico de Orizaba 5700m
Sierra Madre del Sur
Gulf of Mexico
Yucatan Peninsula
West Indies
Greater Antilles
Lesser Antilles
Caribbean Sea
NORTH AMERICAN PLATE
CARIBBEAN PLATE
Lake Nicaragua
Isthmus of Panama
COCOS PLATE
SOUTH AMERICAN PLATE
SOUTH AMERICA
PACIFIC OCEAN

The Appalachians

The Appalachian Mountains, uplifted about 400 million years ago, are some of the oldest in the world. They have been lowered and rounded by erosion and now slope gently toward the Atlantic across a broad coastal plain.

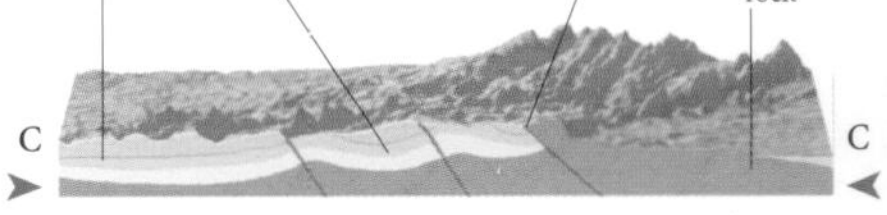
Horizontal strata
Sedimentary strata folded and faulted into ridges and valleys
Softer strata has been crumpled against the harder basement rock
Hard basement rock
C
C

***Cross-section** through the Appalachians showing the numerous folds, which have subsequently been weathered to create a rounded relief.*

The Great Plains & Central Lowlands

Deposits left by retreating glaciers and rivers have made this vast flat area very fertile. In the north this is the result of glaciation, with deposits up to one mile (1.7 km) thick, covering the basement rock. To the south and west, the massive Missouri/Mississippi river system has for centuries deposited silt across the plains, creating broad, flat floodplains and deltas.

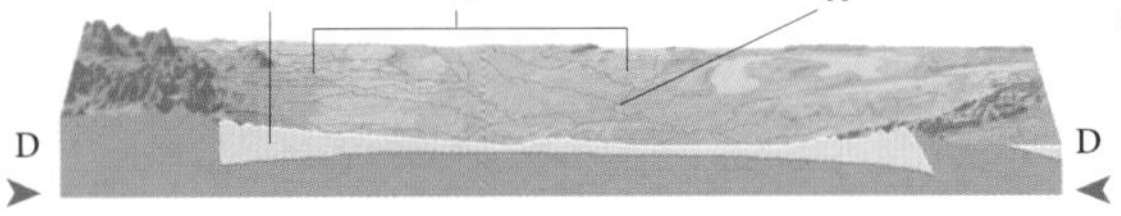
Sedimentary layers overlay domed basement rock
Upland rivers drain south toward the Mississippi Basin
Confluence of the Missouri and Mississippi Rivers
D
D

***Section** across the Great Plains and Central Lowlands showing river systems and structure.*

A B C D E F G K L M

"Tornado alley" in the Mississippi Valley suffers frequent tornadoes.

CLIMATE

NORTH AMERICA'S climate includes extremes ranging from freezing Arctic conditions in Alaska and Greenland, to desert in the southwest, and tropical conditions in southeastern Florida, the Caribbean, and Central America. Central and southern regions are prone to severe storms including tornadoes and hurricanes.

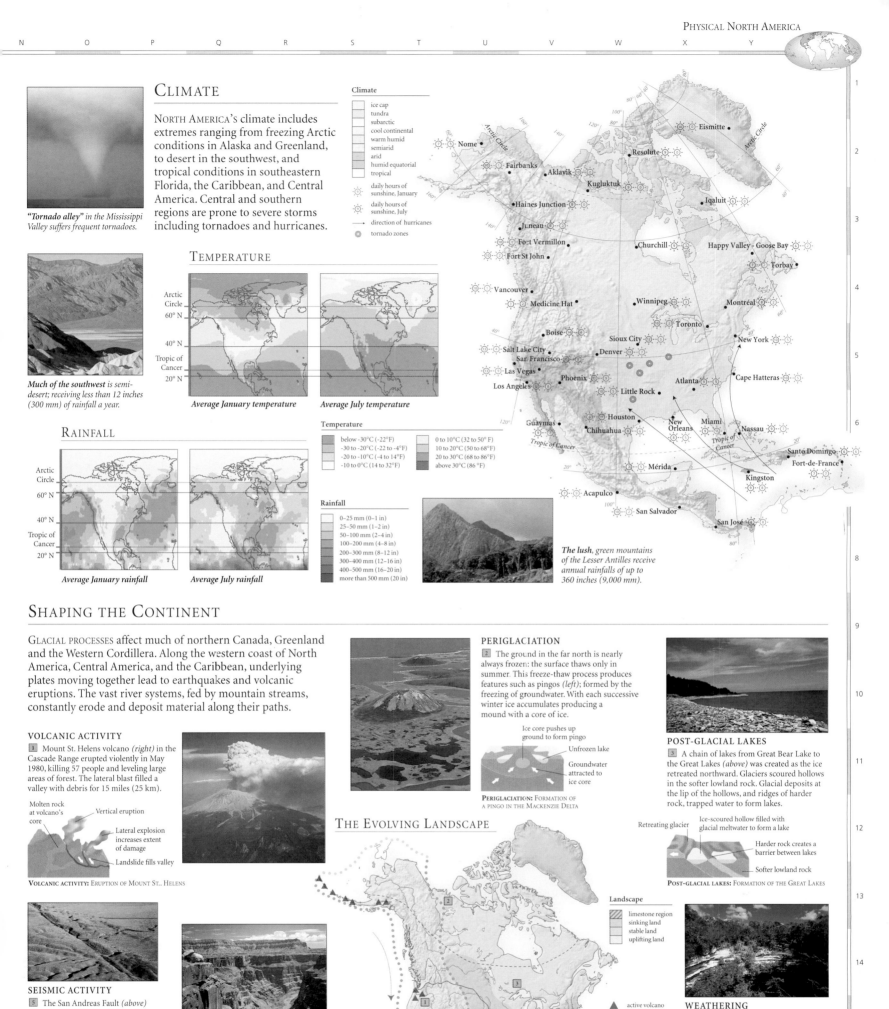

Climate
ice cap
tundra
subarctic
cool continental
warm humid
semiarid
arid
humid equatorial
tropical
daily hours of sunshine, January
daily hours of sunshine, July
direction of hurricanes
tornado zones
Nome
Arctic Circle
Fairbanks
Aklavik
Kugluktuk
Resolute
Eismitte
Iqaluit
Haines Junction
Juneau
Fort Vermillon
Fort St John
Churchill
Happy Valley - Goose Bay
Torbay
Vancouver
Medicine Hat
Winnipeg
Montréal
Toronto
Boise
Sioux City
New York
Salt Lake City
San Francisco
Denver
Las Vegas
Los Angeles
Phoenix
Little Rock
Atlanta
Cape Hatteras
Houston
Guaymas
Chihuahua
New Orleans
Miami
Nassau
Tropic of Cancer
Santo Domingo
Fort-de-France
Mérida
Kingston
Acapulco
San Salvador
San José

Much of the southwest is semi-desert; receiving less than 12 inches (300 mm) of rainfall a year.

TEMPERATURE

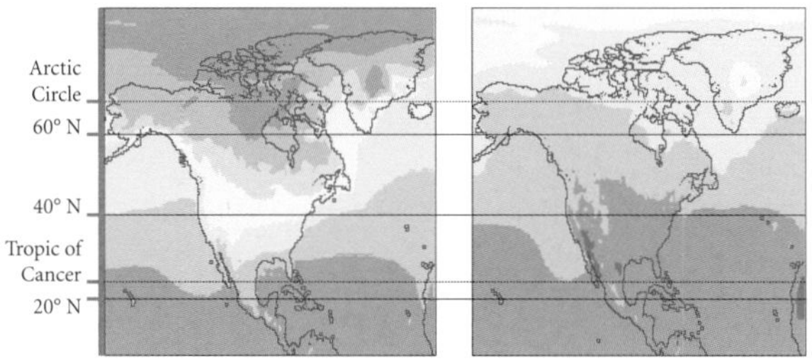
Arctic Circle
60° N
40° N
Tropic of Cancer
20° N

Average January temperature *Average July temperature*

Temperature
below -30°C (-22°F)
-30 to -20°C (-22 to -4°F)
-20 to -10°C (-4 to 14°F)
-10 to 0°C (14 to 32°F)
0 to 10°C (32 to 50° F)
10 to 20°C (50 to 68°F)
20 to 30°C (68 to 86°F)
above 30°C (86 °F)

RAINFALL

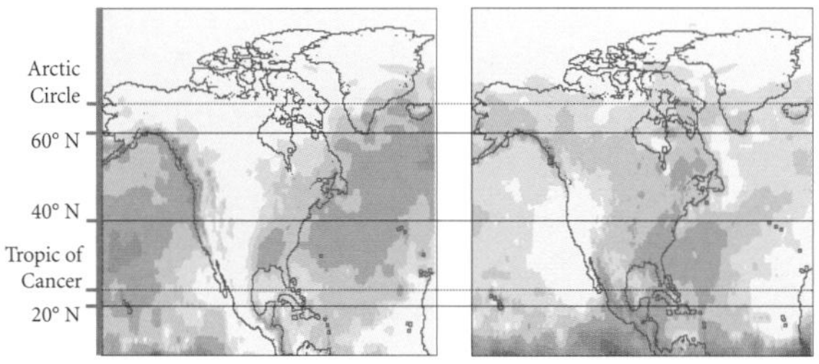
Arctic Circle
60° N
40° N
Tropic of Cancer
20° N

Average January rainfall *Average July rainfall*

Rainfall
0–25 mm (0–1 in)
25–50 mm (1–2 in)
50–100 mm (2–4 in)
100–200 mm (4–8 in)
200–300 mm (8–12 in)
300–400 mm (12–16 in)
400–500 mm (16–20 in)
more than 500 mm (20 in)

The lush, green mountains of the Lesser Antilles receive annual rainfalls of up to 360 inches (9,000 mm).

SHAPING THE CONTINENT

GLACIAL PROCESSES affect much of northern Canada, Greenland and the Western Cordillera. Along the western coast of North America, Central America, and the Caribbean, underlying plates moving together lead to earthquakes and volcanic eruptions. The vast river systems, fed by mountain streams, constantly erode and deposit material along their paths.

VOLCANIC ACTIVITY

1 Mount St. Helens volcano *(right)* in the Cascade Range erupted violently in May 1980, killing 57 people and leveling large areas of forest. The lateral blast filled a valley with debris for 15 miles (25 km).

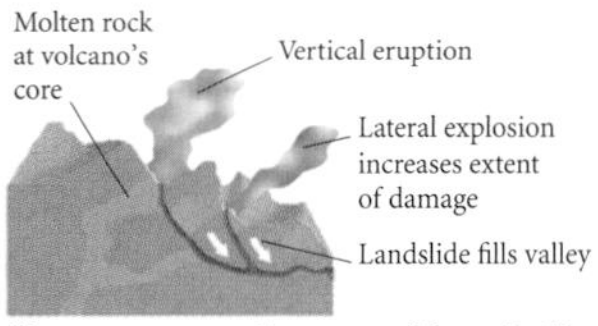
Molten rock at volcano's core
Vertical eruption
Lateral explosion increases extent of damage
Landslide fills valley

VOLCANIC ACTIVITY: ERUPTION OF MOUNT ST. HELENS

PERIGLACIATION

2 The ground in the far north is nearly always frozen: the surface thaws only in summer. This freeze-thaw process produces features such as pingos *(left)*; formed by the freezing of groundwater. With each successive winter ice accumulates producing a mound with a core of ice.

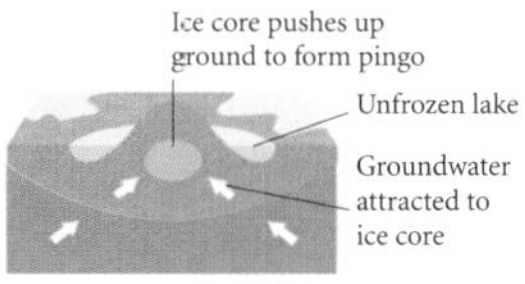
Ice core pushes up ground to form pingo
Unfrozen lake
Groundwater attracted to ice core

PERIGLACIATION: FORMATION OF A PINGO IN THE MACKENZIE DELTA

POST-GLACIAL LAKES

3 A chain of lakes from Great Bear Lake to the Great Lakes *(above)* was created as the ice retreated northward. Glaciers scoured hollows in the softer lowland rock. Glacial deposits at the lip of the hollows, and ridges of harder rock, trapped water to form lakes.

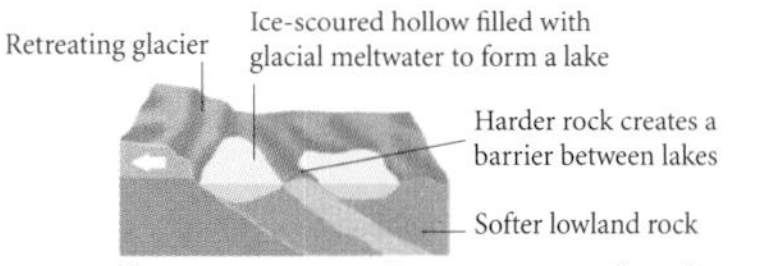
Retreating glacier
Ice-scoured hollow filled with glacial meltwater to form a lake
Harder rock creates a barrier between lakes
Softer lowland rock

POST-GLACIAL LAKES: FORMATION OF THE GREAT LAKES

THE EVOLVING LANDSCAPE

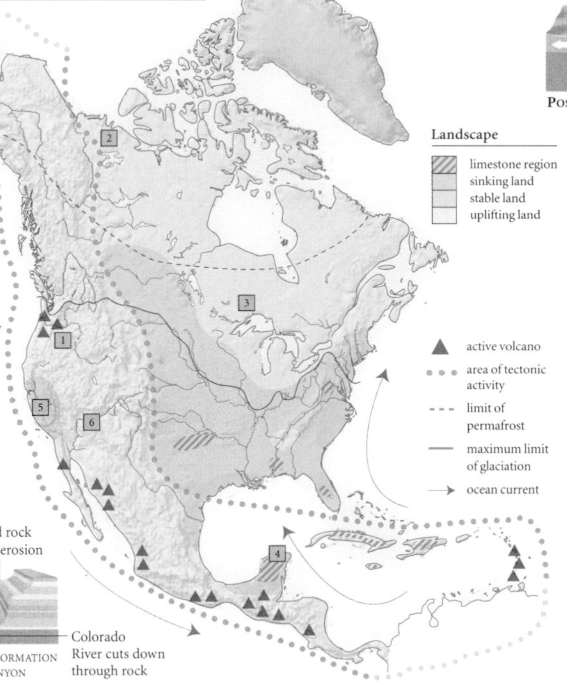
1
2
3
4
5
6
Landscape
limestone region
sinking land
stable land
uplifting land
active volcano
area of tectonic activity
limit of permafrost
maximum limit of glaciation
ocean current

SEISMIC ACTIVITY

5 The San Andreas Fault *(above)* places much of the North America's west coast under constant threat from earthquakes. It is caused by the Pacific Plate grinding past the North American Plate at a faster rate, though in the same direction.

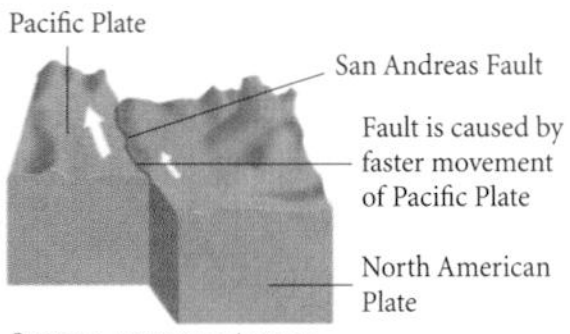
Pacific Plate
San Andreas Fault
Fault is caused by faster movement of Pacific Plate
North American Plate

SEISMIC ACTIVITY: ACTION OF THE SAN ANDREAS FAULT

RIVER EROSION

6 The Grand Canyon *(above)* in the Colorado Plateau was created by the downward erosion of the Colorado River, combined with the gradual uplift of the plateau, over the past 30 million years. The contours of the canyon formed as the softer rock layers eroded into gentle slopes, and the hard rock layers into cliffs. The depth varies from 3,855–6,560 ft (1,175–2,000 m).

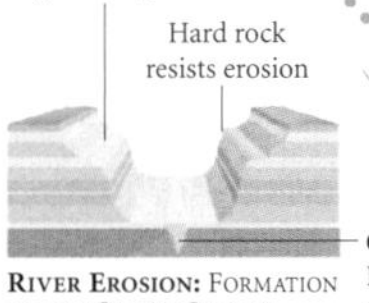
Soft rock is easily eroded into gentle slopes
Hard rock resists erosion
Colorado River cuts down through rock

RIVER EROSION: FORMATION OF THE GRAND CANYON

WEATHERING

4 The Yucatan Peninsula is a vast, flat limestone plateau in southern Mexico. Weathering action from both rainwater and underground streams has enlarged fractures in the rock to form caves and hollows, called sinkholes *(above)*.

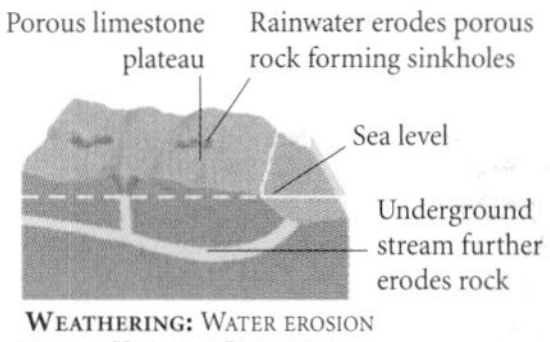
Porous limestone plateau
Rainwater erodes porous rock forming sinkholes
Sea level
Underground stream further erodes rock

WEATHERING: WATER EROSION ON THE YUCATAN PENINSULA

POLITICAL NORTH AMERICA

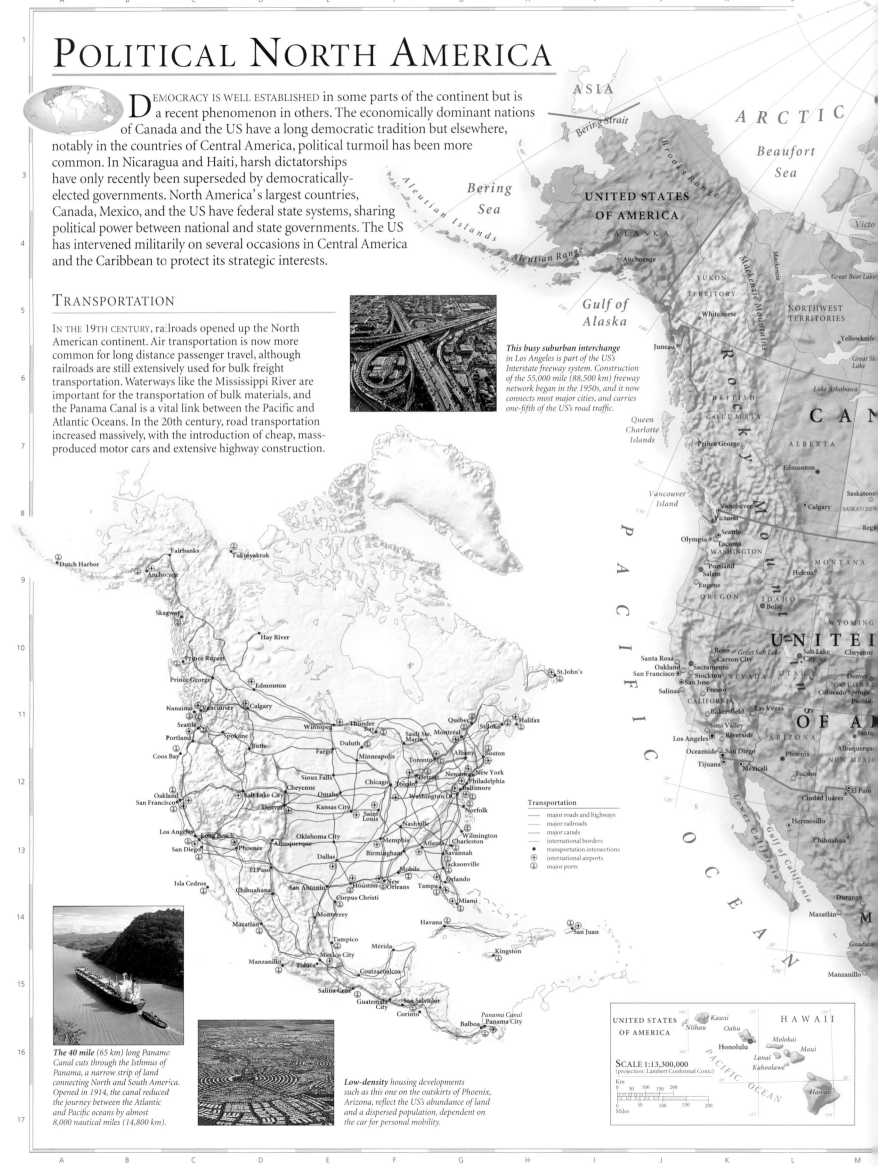

DEMOCRACY IS WELL ESTABLISHED in some parts of the continent but is a recent phenomenon in others. The economically dominant nations of Canada and the US have a long democratic tradition but elsewhere, notably in the countries of Central America, political turmoil has been more common. In Nicaragua and Haiti, harsh dictatorships have only recently been superseded by democratically-elected governments. North America's largest countries, Canada, Mexico, and the US have federal state systems, sharing political power between national and state governments. The US has intervened militarily on several occasions in Central America and the Caribbean to protect its strategic interests.

TRANSPORTATION

IN THE 19TH CENTURY, railroads opened up the North American continent. Air transportation is now more common for long distance passenger travel, although railroads are still extensively used for bulk freight transportation. Waterways like the Mississippi River are important for the transportation of bulk materials, and the Panama Canal is a vital link between the Pacific and Atlantic Oceans. In the 20th century, road transportation increased massively, with the introduction of cheap, mass-produced motor cars and extensive highway construction.

This busy suburban interchange *in Los Angeles is part of the US's Interstate freeway system. Construction of the 55,000 mile (88,500 km) freeway network began in the 1950s, and it now connects most major cities, and carries one-fifth of the US's road traffic.*

ASIA
Bering Strait
ARCTIC
Beaufort Sea
Bering Sea
Aleutian Islands
Aleutian Range
Brooks Range
UNITED STATES OF AMERICA
ALASKA
Anchorage
YUKON TERRITORY
Whitehorse
Mackenzie Mountains
NORTHWEST TERRITORIES
Great Bear Lake
Yellowknife
Gulf of Alaska
Juneau
BRITISH COLUMBIA
Queen Charlotte Islands
Prince George
ALBERTA
Edmonton
Calgary
Lake Athabasca
Vancouver Island
Vancouver
Victoria
Seattle
Olympia
Tacoma
WASHINGTON
Portland
Salem
Eugene
OREGON
IDAHO
Boise
Helena
MONTANA
WYOMING
PACIFIC OCEAN
Rocky Mountains
Reno
Carson City
Great Salt Lake
Salt Lake City
Cheyenne
Santa Rosa
Oakland
San Francisco
Sacramento
Stockton
San Jose
NEVADA
UTAH
Salinas
Fresno
CALIFORNIA
Denver
Colorado Springs
Pueblo
Bakersfield
Las Vegas
Simi Valley
Los Angeles
Riverside
ARIZONA
Oceanside
San Diego
Phoenix
Tijuana
Mexicali
Tucson
Albuquerque
NEW MEXICO
El Paso
Ciudad Juárez
Hermosillo
Chihuahua
Lower California
Gulf of California
Durango
Mazatlán
Manzanillo

Transportation
major roads and highways
major railroads
major canals
international borders
transportation intersections
international airports
major ports
Dutch Harbor
Fairbanks
Anchorage
Tuktoyaktuk
Skagway
Hay River
Prince Rupert
Prince George
Edmonton
Calgary
Nanaimo
Vancouver
Seattle
Portland
Spokane
Butte
Coos Bay
Winnipeg
Thunder Bay
Duluth
Fargo
Minneapolis
Sault Ste. Marie
Toronto
Montréal
Québec
St.John
Halifax
St.John's
Albany
Boston
New York
Newark
Philadelphia
Baltimore
Washington DC
Detroit
Toledo
Chicago
Sioux Falls
Omaha
Cheyenne
Salt Lake City
Denver
Kansas City
Saint Louis
Norfolk
Oakland
San Francisco
Los Angeles
Long Beach
San Diego
Phoenix
Albuquerque
Oklahoma City
Nashville
Memphis
Atlanta
Charleston
Wilmington
Savannah
Birmingham
Dallas
El Paso
Jacksonville
Mobile
New Orleans
Houston
San Antonio
Tampa
Orlando
Miami
Isla Cedros
Chihuahua
Corpus Christi
Monterrey
Mazatlán
Havana
San Juan
Tampico
Mérida
Kingston
Manzanillo
Mexico City
Toluca
Coatzacoalcos
Salina Cruz
Guatemala City
San Salvador
Corinto
Panama Canal
Balboa
Panama City

***The 40 mile** (65 km) long Panama Canal cuts through the Isthmus of Panama, a narrow strip of land connecting North and South America. Opened in 1914, the canal reduced the journey between the Atlantic and Pacific oceans by almost 8,000 nautical miles (14,800 km).*

***Low-density** housing developments such as this one on the outskirts of Phoenix, Arizona, reflect the US's abundance of land and a dispersed population, dependent on the car for personal mobility.*

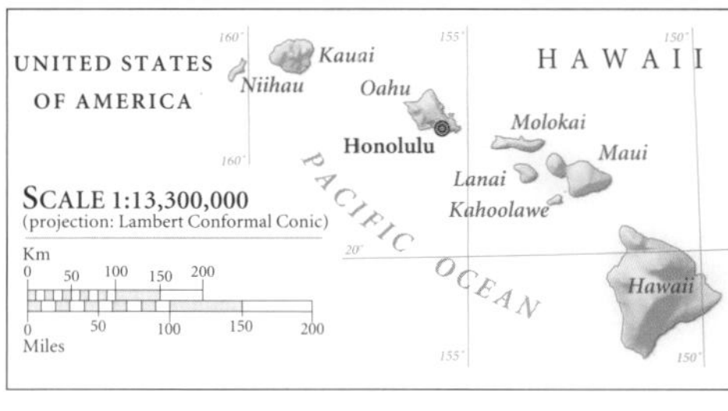
UNITED STATES OF AMERICA
HAWAII
Kauai
Niihau
Oahu
Honolulu
Molokai
Maui
Lanai
Kahoolawe
Hawaii
PACIFIC OCEAN
SCALE 1:13,300,000
(projection: Lambert Conformal Conic)
Km
Miles

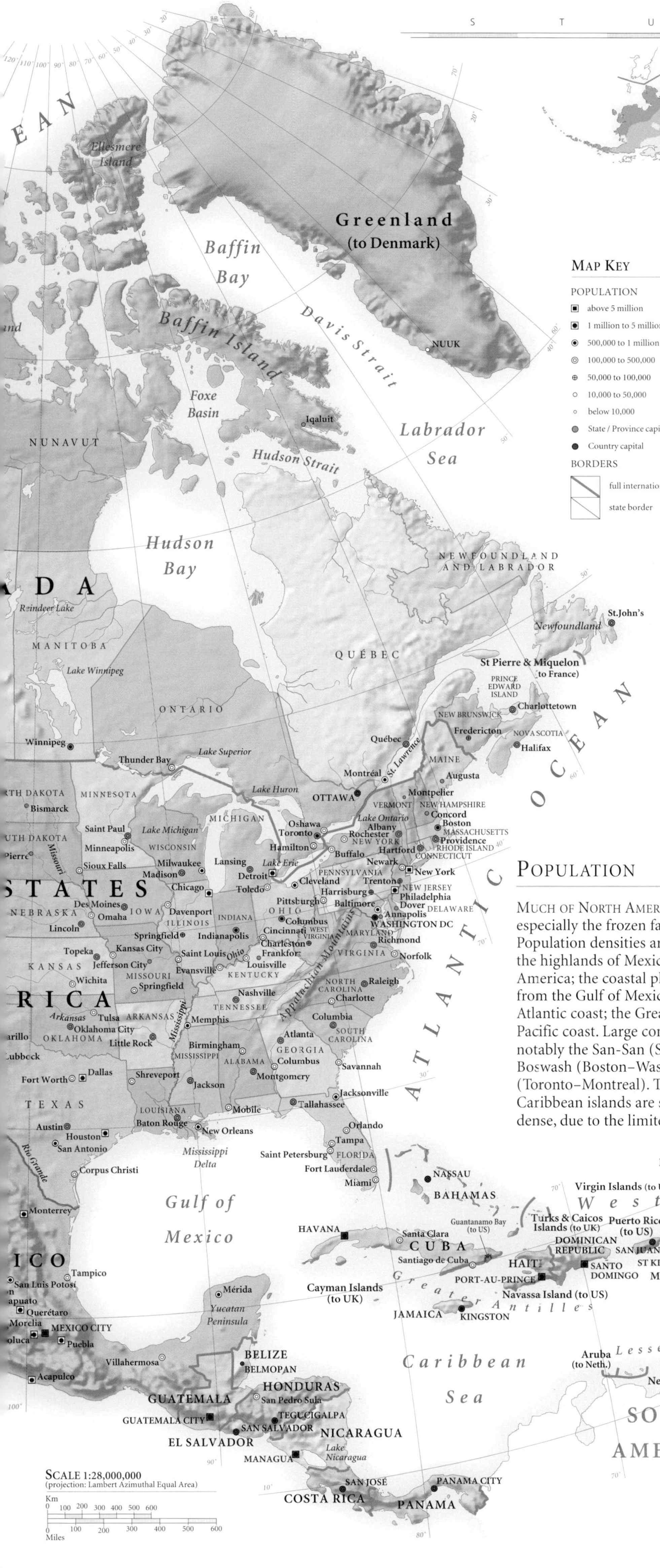
Greenland
(to Denmark)
Baffin Bay
Baffin Island
Davis Strait
NUUK
Ellesmere Island
Foxe Basin
Iqaluit
NUNAVUT
Hudson Strait
Labrador Sea
Hudson Bay
NEWFOUNDLAND AND LABRADOR
Newfoundland
St.John's
QUÉBEC
St Pierre & Miquelon (to France)
PRINCE EDWARD ISLAND
Charlottetown
NEW BRUNSWICK
Fredericton
NOVA SCOTIA
Halifax
Québec
MANITOBA
Lake Winnipeg
ONTARIO
Winnipeg
Thunder Bay
Lake Superior
Lake Huron
Montréal
OTTAWA
MAINE
Augusta
Montpelier
VERMONT
NEW HAMPSHIRE
Concord
Boston
MASSACHUSETTS
Providence
RHODE ISLAND
Hartford
CONNECTICUT
New York
NEW YORK
Albany
Rochester
Buffalo
Lake Ontario
Toronto
Oshawa
Hamilton
Lake Erie
Detroit
Lansing
MICHIGAN
Lake Michigan
WISCONSIN
Milwaukee
Madison
Chicago
MINNESOTA
Saint Paul
Minneapolis
Sioux Falls
Bismarck
STATES
NEBRASKA
IOWA
Des Moines
Omaha
Lincoln
Davenport
ILLINOIS
INDIANA
OHIO
Toledo
Cleveland
Pittsburgh
PENNSYLVANIA
Harrisburg
Newark
Trenton
NEW JERSEY
Philadelphia
Dover
DELAWARE
Baltimore
Annapolis
WASHINGTON DC
MARYLAND
Richmond
VIRGINIA
Norfolk
WEST VIRGINIA
Charleston
Columbus
Cincinnati
Frankfort
Louisville
KENTUCKY
Indianapolis
Springfield
Saint Louis
Kansas City
Topeka
KANSAS
Jefferson City
MISSOURI
Evansville
Wichita
Springfield
Nashville
TENNESSEE
NORTH CAROLINA
Raleigh
Charlotte
Columbia
SOUTH CAROLINA
Atlanta
GEORGIA
Columbus
Savannah
Memphis
Birmingham
ALABAMA
Montgomery
MISSISSIPPI
Jackson
Tulsa
ARKANSAS
Oklahoma City
OKLAHOMA
Little Rock
Dallas
Fort Worth
Shreveport
TEXAS
LOUISIANA
Baton Rouge
New Orleans
Mobile
Tallahassee
Jacksonville
Orlando
Tampa
Saint Petersburg
FLORIDA
Fort Lauderdale
Miami
Austin
Houston
San Antonio
Corpus Christi
Mississippi Delta
Gulf of Mexico
ATLANTIC OCEAN
NASSAU
BAHAMAS
HAVANA
CUBA
Santa Clara
Santiago de Cuba
Guantanamo Bay (to US)
Turks & Caicos Islands (to UK)
DOMINICAN REPUBLIC
SANTO DOMINGO
HAITI
PORT-AU-PRINCE
Puerto Rico (to US)
SAN JUAN
Virgin Islands (to US)
British Virgin Islands (to UK)
Anguilla (to UK)
West Indies
ANTIGUA & BARBUDA
ST KITTS & NEVIS
Montserrat (to UK)
Guadeloupe (to France)
DOMINICA
Martinique (to France)
ST LUCIA
BARBADOS
ST VINCENT & THE GRENADINES
GRENADA
TRINIDAD & TOBAGO
PORT-OF-SPAIN
Lesser Antilles
Greater Antilles
Cayman Islands (to UK)
JAMAICA
KINGSTON
Navassa Island (to US)
Aruba (to Neth.)
Netherlands Antilles (to Neth.)
Caribbean Sea
SOUTH AMERICA
Monterrey
Tampico
San Luis Potosí
Querétaro
MEXICO CITY
Puebla
Acapulco
Mérida
Yucatan Peninsula
Villahermosa
BELIZE
BELMOPAN
GUATEMALA
GUATEMALA CITY
HONDURAS
San Pedro Sula
TEGUCIGALPA
SAN SALVADOR
EL SALVADOR
NICARAGUA
MANAGUA
Lake Nicaragua
SAN JOSÉ
COSTA RICA
PANAMA CITY
PANAMA
SCALE 1:28,000,000
(projection: Lambert Azimuthal Equal Area)

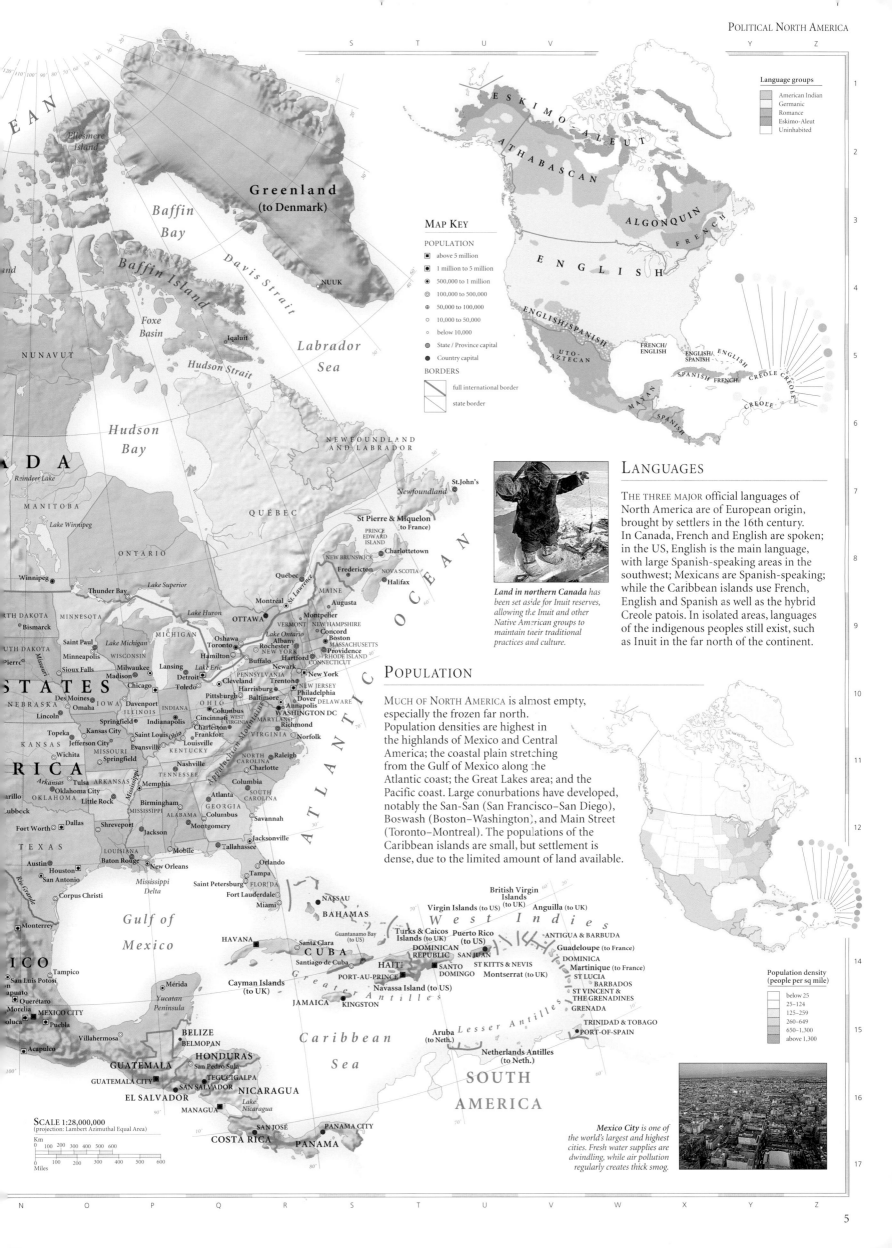

Language groups
American Indian
Germanic
Romance
Eskimo-Aleut
Uninhabited
ESKIMO-ALEUT
ATHABASCAN
ALGONQUIN
FRENCH
ENGLISH
ENGLISH/SPANISH
UTO-AZTECAN
FRENCH/ENGLISH
ENGLISH/SPANISH
ENGLISH
SPANISH
FRENCH
CREOLE
CREOLE
CREOLE
MAYAN
SPANISH

MAP KEY

POPULATION

- above 5 million
- 1 million to 5 million
- 500,000 to 1 million
- 100,000 to 500,000
- 50,000 to 100,000
- 10,000 to 50,000
- below 10,000
- State / Province capital
- Country capital

BORDERS

- full international border
- state border

Land in northern Canada has been set aside for Inuit reserves, allowing the Inuit and other Native American groups to maintain their traditional practices and culture.

LANGUAGES

THE THREE MAJOR official languages of North America are of European origin, brought by settlers in the 16th century. In Canada, French and English are spoken; in the US, English is the main language, with large Spanish-speaking areas in the southwest; Mexicans are Spanish-speaking; while the Caribbean islands use French, English and Spanish as well as the hybrid Creole patois. In isolated areas, languages of the indigenous peoples still exist, such as Inuit in the far north of the continent.

POPULATION

MUCH OF NORTH AMERICA is almost empty, especially the frozen far north. Population densities are highest in the highlands of Mexico and Central America; the coastal plain stretching from the Gulf of Mexico along the Atlantic coast; the Great Lakes area; and the Pacific coast. Large conurbations have developed, notably the San-San (San Francisco–San Diego), Boswash (Boston–Washington), and Main Street (Toronto–Montreal). The populations of the Caribbean islands are small, but settlement is dense, due to the limited amount of land available.

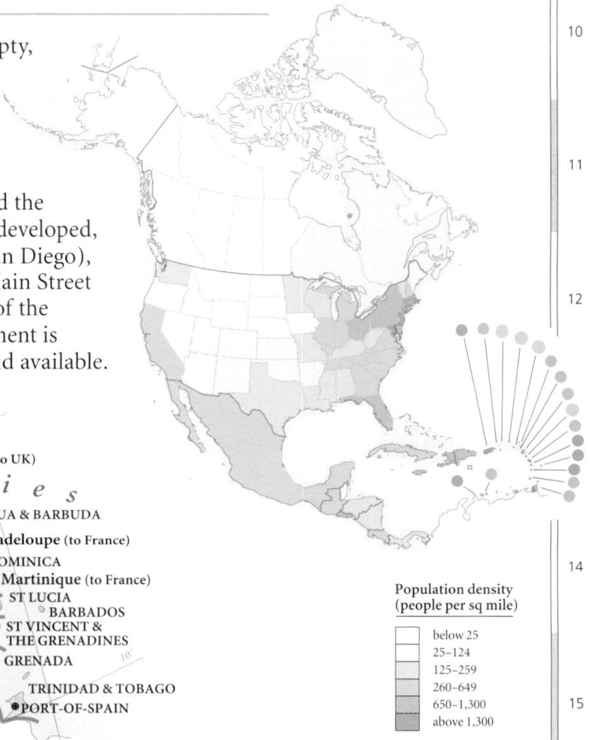
Population density
(people per sq mile)
below 25
25–124
125–259
260–649
650–1,300
above 1,300

***Mexico City** is one of the world's largest and highest cities. Fresh water supplies are dwindling, while air pollution regularly creates thick smog.*

North American Resources

The two northern countries of Canada and the US are richly endowed with natural resources that have helped to fuel economic development. The US is the world's largest economy, although today it is facing stiff competition from the Far East. Mexico has relied on oil revenues but there are hopes that the North American Free Trade Agreement (NAFTA), will encourage trade growth with Canada and the US. The poorer countries of Central America and the Caribbean depend largely on cash crops and tourism.

Standard of Living

The US and Canada have one of the highest overall standards of living in the world. However, many people still live in poverty, especially in urban ghettos and some rural areas. Central America and the Caribbean are markedly poorer than their wealthier northern neighbors. Haiti is the poorest country in the western hemisphere.

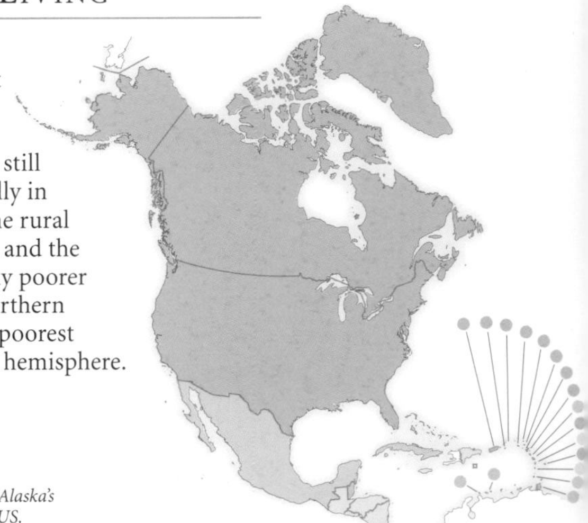

Standard of Living
(UN Human Development Index)
high
low

Industry

The modern, industrialized economies of the US and Canada contrast sharply with those of Mexico, Central America, and the Caribbean. Manufacturing is especially important in the US; vehicle production is concentrated around the Great Lakes, while electronic and hi-tech industries are increasingly found in the western and southern states. Mexico depends on oil exports and assembly work, taking advantage of cheap labor. Many Central American and Caribbean countries rely heavily on agricultural exports.

After its purchase from Russia in 1867, Alaska's frozen lands were largely ignored by the US. Oil reserves similar in magnitude to those in eastern Texas were discovered in Prudhoe Bay, Alaska in 1968. Freezing temperatures and a fragile environment hamper oil extraction.

Fish such as cod, flounder, and plaice are caught in the Grand Banks, off the Newfoundland coast, and processed in many North Atlantic coastal settlements.

South of San Francisco, "Silicon Valley" is both a national and international center for hi-tech industries, electronic industries, and research institutions.

Multinational companies rely on cheap labor and tax benefits to assemble vehicles in Mexican factories.

The health of the Wall Street stock market in New York is the standard measure of the state of the world's economy.

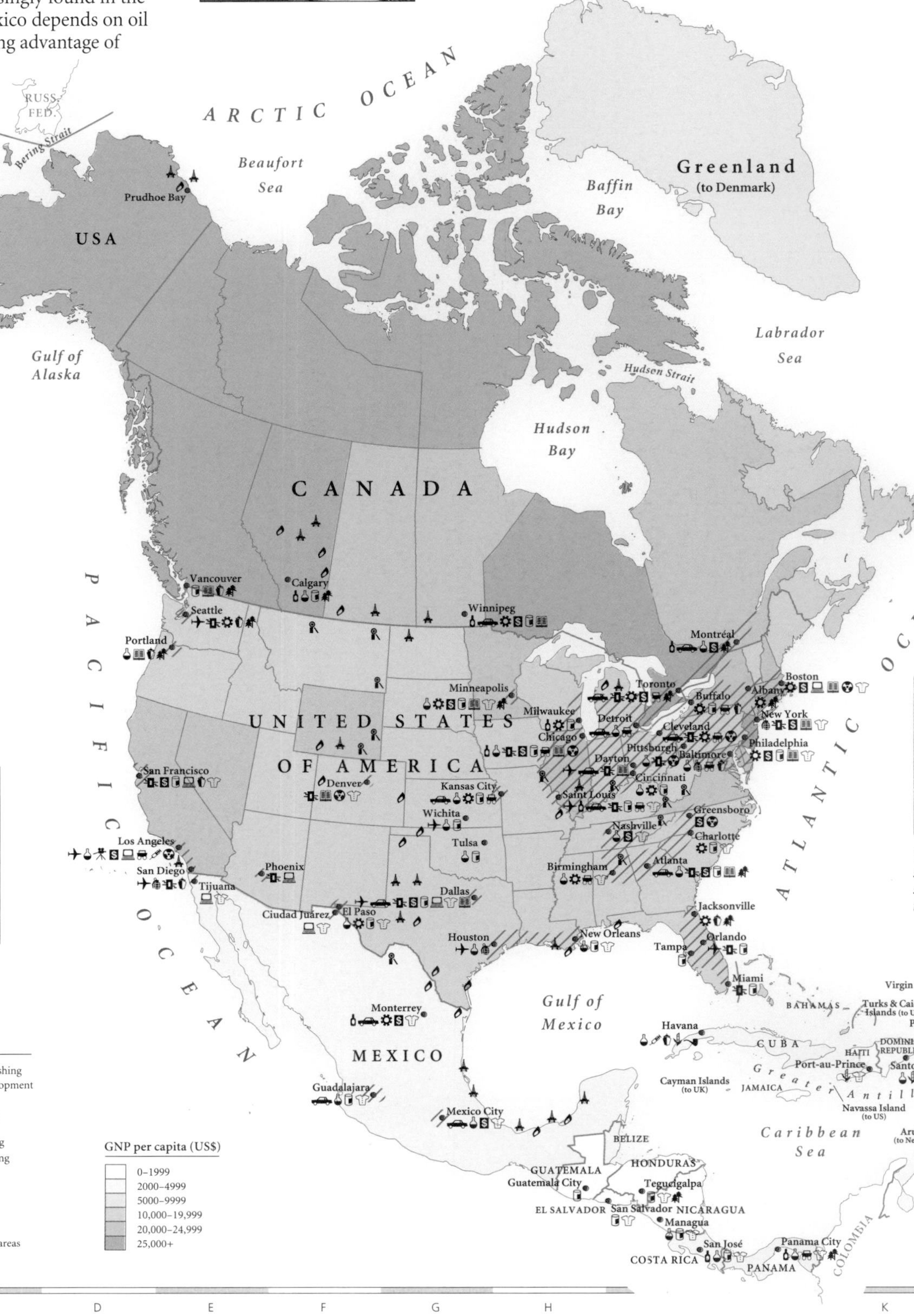

RUSS. FED.
Bering Strait
Bering Sea
ARCTIC OCEAN
Beaufort Sea
Prudhoe Bay
USA
Baffin Bay
Greenland (to Denmark)
Labrador Sea
Gulf of Alaska
Hudson Strait
Hudson Bay
CANADA
PACIFIC OCEAN
ATLANTIC OCEAN
Vancouver
Calgary
Seattle
Winnipeg
Portland
Montréal
Boston
Toronto
Albany
Buffalo
Minneapolis
Milwaukee
Detroit
New York
Chicago
Cleveland
Pittsburgh
Philadelphia
Baltimore
UNITED STATES OF AMERICA
San Francisco
Dayton
Cincinnati
Denver
Kansas City
Saint Louis
Greensboro
Wichita
Nashville
Charlotte
Los Angeles
Tulsa
San Diego
Phoenix
Birmingham
Atlanta
Tijuana
Dallas
Ciudad Juárez
El Paso
Jacksonville
Houston
New Orleans
Orlando
Tampa
Miami
Gulf of Mexico
Monterrey
MEXICO
Guadalajara
Mexico City
West Indies
Virgin Islands (to US)
British Virgin Islands (to UK)
Anguilla (to UK)
Turks & Caicos Islands (to UK)
ST KITTS & NEVIS
ANTIGUA & BARBUDA
Montserrat (to UK)
Guadeloupe (to France)
DOMINICA
Martinique (to France)
ST LUCIA
BARBADOS
ST VINCENT & THE GRENADINES
GRENADA
TRINIDAD & TOBAGO
Port-of-Spain
BAHAMAS
Puerto Rico (to US)
Havana
CUBA
HAITI
DOMINICAN REPUBLIC
San Juan
Port-au-Prince
Santo Domingo
Cayman Islands (to UK)
JAMAICA
Greater Antilles
Navassa Island (to US)
Lesser Antilles
BELIZE
Caribbean Sea
Aruba (to Neth.)
Netherlands Antilles (to Neth.)
VENEZUELA
GUATEMALA
Guatemala City
HONDURAS
Tegucigalpa
EL SALVADOR
San Salvador
NICARAGUA
Managua
San José
COSTA RICA
Panama City
PANAMA
COLOMBIA
Industry
aerospace
brewing
car/vehicle manufacture
chemicals
defense
electronics
engineering
movie industry
finance
food processing
hi-tech industry
iron & steel
pharmaceuticals
printing & publishing
research & development
shipbuilding
sugar processing
textiles
timber processing
tobacco processing
coal
oil
gas
industrial cities
major industrial areas
GNP per capita (US$)
0–1999
2000–4999
5000–9999
10,000–19,999
20,000–24,999
25,000+

N O P Q R S T U V W X Y Z

Environmental Issues

Many fragile environments are under threat throughout the region. In Haiti, all the primary rain forest has been destroyed, while air pollution from factories and cars in Mexico City is among the worst in the world. Elsewhere, industry and mining pose threats, particularly in the delicate arctic environment of Alaska where oil spills have polluted coastlines and decimated fish stocks.

Arctic Ocean
Beaufort Sea
Bering Sea
Baffin Bay
Gulf of Alaska
Labrador Sea
Hudson Bay
Pacific Ocean
Atlantic Ocean
Gulf of Mexico
Caribbean Sea
Environmental Issues
national parks
acid rain
tropical forest
forest destroyed
desert
desertification
polluted rivers
radioactive contamination
marine pollution
heavy marine pollution
poor urban air quality
Vancouver
Sudbury
Montreal
Hamilton
Chicago
New York
Denver
Saint Louis
Los Angeles
San Diego
Phoenix
Houston
Havana
Mexico City
Nelson
Fraser
Columbia
Sacramento
San Joaquin
Platte
Missouri
Arkansas
Ohio
Roanoke
Red River
Rio Grande
Mississippi
Alabama
James
Delaware
Hudson

Wild bison *graze in Yellowstone National Park, the world's first national park. Designated in 1872, geothermal springs and boiling mud are among its natural spectacles, making it a major tourist attraction.*

Mineral Resources

Fossil fuels are exploited in considerable quantities throughout the continent. Coal mining in the Appalachians is declining but vast open pits exist further west in Wyoming. Oil and natural gas are found in Alaska, Texas, the Gulf of Mexico, and the Canadian West. Canada has large quantities of nickel, while Jamaica has considerable deposits of bauxite, and Mexico has large reserves of silver.

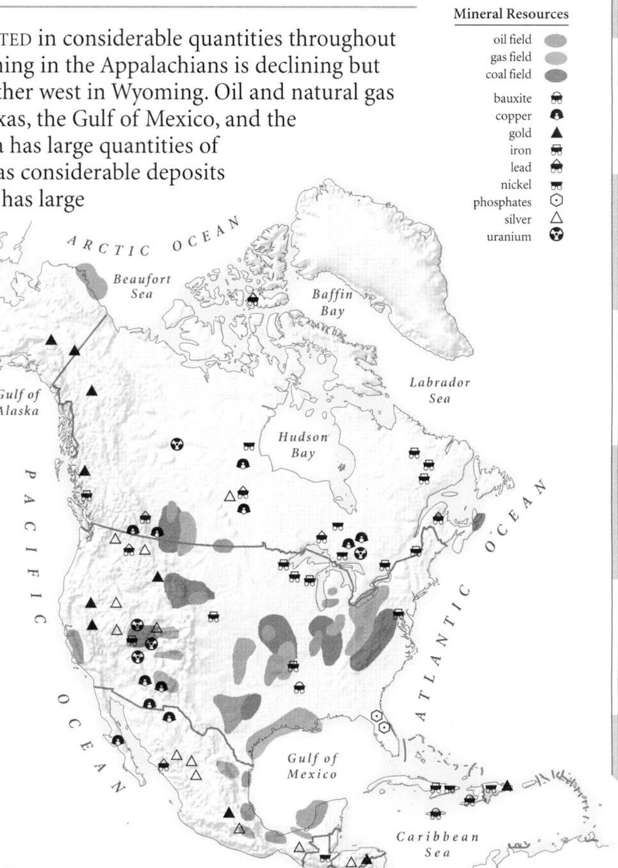

Mineral Resources
oil field
gas field
coal field
bauxite
copper
gold
iron
lead
nickel
phosphates
silver
uranium
Arctic Ocean
Beaufort Sea
Bering Sea
Baffin Bay
Gulf of Alaska
Labrador Sea
Hudson Bay
Pacific Ocean
Atlantic Ocean
Gulf of Mexico
Caribbean Sea

In addition *to fossil fuels, North America is also rich in exploitable metallic ores. This vast, mile-deep (1.6 km) pit is a copper mine in New Mexico.*

Arctic Ocean
Greenland
Bering Strait
Brooks Range
Beaufort Sea
Baffin Bay
Bering Sea
Aleutian Range
Mackenzie Mountains
Mackenzie
Gulf of Alaska
Labrador Sea
Hudson Strait
Hudson Bay
Rocky Mountains
Great Plains
Newfoundland
Edmonton
Calgary
Vancouver
Seattle
Winnipeg
Great Lakes
St Lawrence
Québec
Montréal
Ottawa
Portland
Boston
Cape Cod
Saint Paul
Minneapolis
Milwaukee
Toronto
Buffalo
Detroit
Cleveland
New York
Toledo
Philadelphia
Chicago
Pittsburgh
Baltimore
Washington D.C.
Sacramento
Oakland
San Francisco
San Jose
Colorado
Denver
Missouri
Kansas City
Indianapolis
Columbus
Cincinnati
Louisville
Saint Louis
Ohio
Nashville
Charlotte
Appalachian Mountains
Pacific Ocean
Atlantic Ocean
Los Angeles
San Diego
Phoenix
Albuquerque
Arkansas
Tulsa
Oklahoma City
Memphis
Mississippi
Atlanta
Tucson
Dallas
El Paso
Jacksonville
Austin
Houston
San Antonio
Mississippi Delta
Tampa
Miami
Lower California
Rio Grande
Monterrey
Gulf of Mexico
Havana
San Juan
Santo Domingo
Guadalajara
Yucatan Peninsula
Mexico City
Caribbean Sea
Guatemala City
Managua
Using the Land and Sea
cropland
forest
ice cap
mountain region
pasture
tundra
wetland
desert
major conurbations
cattle
goats
pigs
poultry
reindeer
sheep
bananas
citrus fruits
coffee
corn (maize)
cotton
fishing
fruit
maple syrup
peanuts
rice
shellfish
soybeans
sugar cane
timber
tobacco
vineyards
wheat

In agriculturally *marginal areas where the soil is either too poor, or the climate too dry for crops, cattle ranching proliferates – especially in Mexico and the western reaches of the Great Plains.*

Using the Land and Sea

Abundant land and fertile soils stretch from the Canadian prairies to Texas creating North America's agricultural heartland. Cereals and cattle ranching form the basis of the farming economy, with corn and soybeans also important. Fruit and vegetables are grown in California using irrigation, while Florida is a leading producer of citrus fruits. Caribbean and Central American countries depend on cash crops such as bananas, coffee, and sugar cane, often grown on large plantations. This reliance on a single crop can leave these countries vulnerable to fluctuating world crop prices.

Sugar cane is Cuba's *main agricultural crop, and is grown and processed throughout the Caribbean. Fermented sugar is used to make rum.*

The Great Plains *support large-scale arable farming throughout central North America. Corn is grown in a belt south and west of the Great Lakes, while farther west where the climate is drier, wheat is grown.*

N O P Q R S T U Y Z

CANADA

CANADA IS THE THIRD LARGEST COUNTRY in the world, and with only about one-tenth of its land area inhabited, it is one of the most sparsely populated. Canada became a confederation in 1867, though Newfoundland did not join until 1949. As a founding member of the UN and of the Commonwealth, Canada has played an important role in international affairs. A constitutional crisis, focusing on the French-speaking Québécois, and Inuit and Native American land rights, dominated politics in the 1990s. In 1999, part of the Northwest Territories, Nunavut, became a self-governing homeland for the Inuit.

***The Selwyn Mountains** in northwestern Canada form part of the Rocky Mountains. The highest point, Keele Peak, rises to 9,750 ft (2,972 m).*

TRANSPORTATION & INDUSTRY

ABUNDANT ENERGY in the form of coal, oil, natural gas, and hydroelectric power underpins Canadian industry. Over 75% of manufacturing is concentrated in the Great Lakes–St. Lawrence region, including prospering aerospace, transportation and hi-tech industries. Across Canada as a whole, manufacturing has developed around a diversified, high-quality resource base and a wide range of metallic and nonmetallic minerals.

***Canada** has one of the world's highest rates of energy consumption per person. It is endowed with vast hydroelectric potential from which more than 60% of its electricity requirements are generated.*

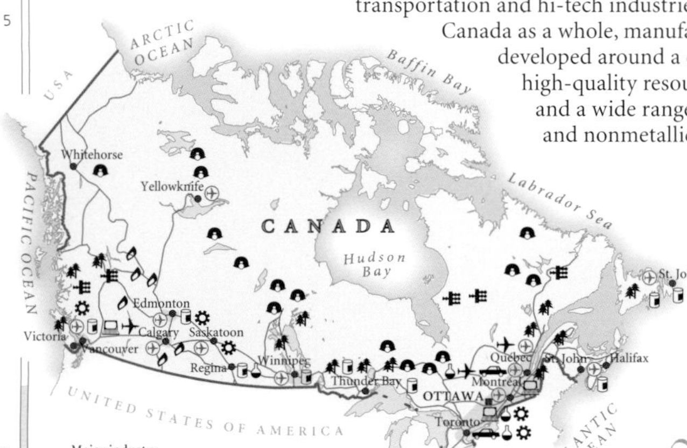

ARCTIC OCEAN
Baffin Bay
Labrador Sea
CANADA
Hudson Bay
PACIFIC OCEAN
ATLANTIC OCEAN
UNITED STATES OF AMERICA
USA
Whitehorse
Yellowknife
Edmonton
Calgary
Saskatoon
Regina
Victoria
Vancouver
Winnipeg
Thunder Bay
OTTAWA
Toronto
Montreal
Quebec
St. John
Halifax
St. John's

Major industry and infrastructure
- aerospace
- car manufacture
- chemicals
- engineering
- food processing
- hi-tech industry
- hydroelectric power
- oil & gas
- mining
- timber processing
- capital cities
- major towns
- international airports
- major roads
- major industrial areas

TRANSPORTATION NETWORK

566,352 miles (912,000 km)	15,189 miles (24,459 km)
8,755 miles (14,098 km)	2,341 miles (3,769 km)

In recent years the road network has been expanded, especially links to remote areas. Meanwhile, for long-distance travel, air transportation now supersedes the declining rail network, which focuses mainly on east–west routes.

USING THE LAND AND SEA

MOST AGRICULTURAL LAND is found in the prairies, which cover 140 million acres (57 million ha) and support wheat and grain-fed cattle. More specialized crops, such as fruit and vegetables, are grown in pockets of land in the east and west. Of Canada's many islands, only Prince Edward Island has notable farmland. Further north, boreal forests, exploited for timber, run in an almost unbroken arc, giving way to uncultivable tundra and ice sheets in the far north.

ARCTIC OCEAN
Baffin Bay
Labrador Sea
CANADA
Hudson Bay
PACIFIC OCEAN
ATLANTIC OCEAN
UNITED STATES OF AMERICA
USA
Whitehorse
Edmonton
Calgary
Saskatoon
Regina
Vancouver
Victoria
Winnipeg
Thunder Bay
OTTAWA
Toronto
Montreal
Québec
St. John
Halifax
Charlottetown
St. John's

THE URBAN/RURAL POPULATION DIVIDE

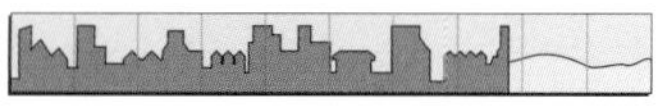

POPULATION DENSITY	TOTAL LAND AREA
8 people per sq mile (3 people per sq km)	3,559,294 sq miles (9,220,970 sq km)

Land use and agricultural distribution
- cattle
- cereals
- fishing
- fruit
- timber
- capital cities
- major towns
- pasture
- cropland
- forest
- wetland
- mountain region
- barren
- tundra

***The climate and topography** of the prairies makes them ideally suited to farming. Long summer days, moderate temperatures, limited rainfall, and flat plains provide excellent conditions for wheat farming.*

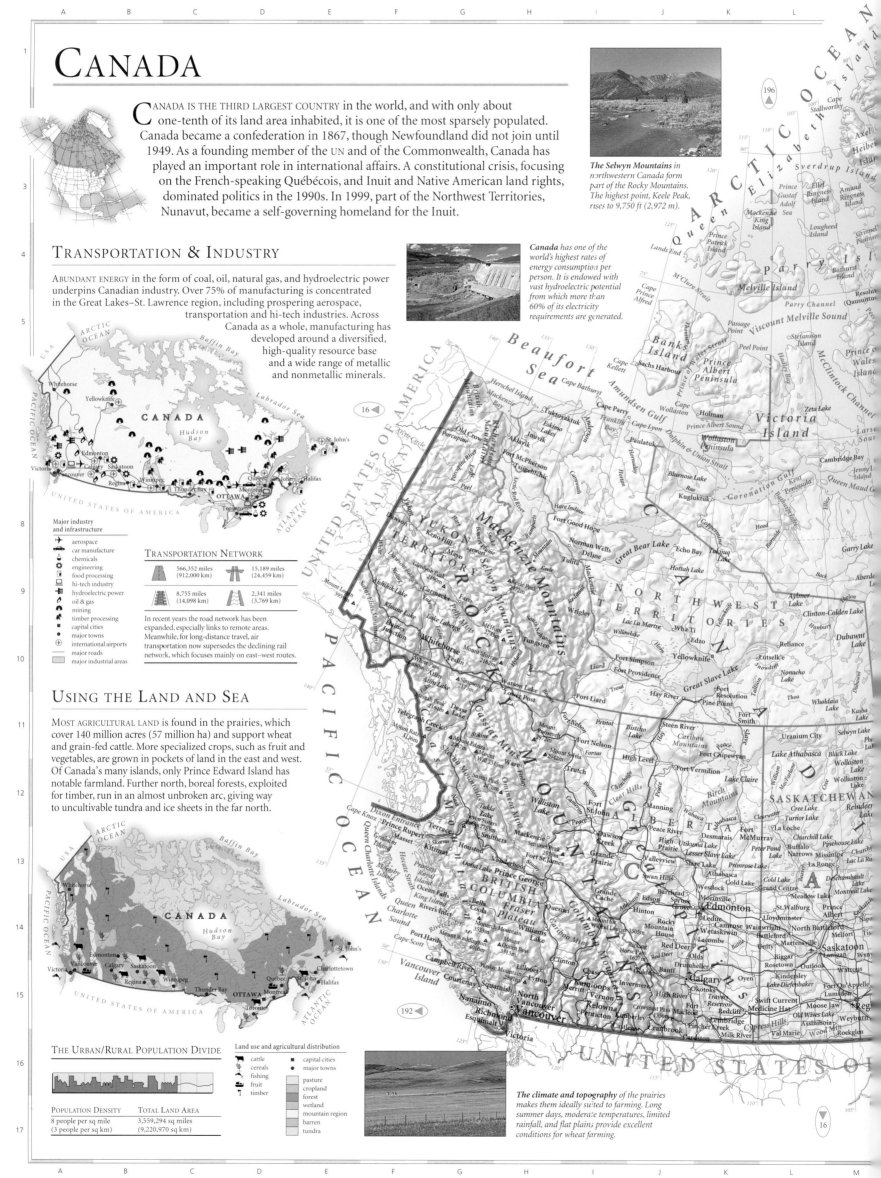

ARCTIC OCEAN
Queen Elizabeth Islands
Sverdrup Islands
Parry Islands
Melville Island
Banks Island
Victoria Island
Beaufort Sea
Amundsen Gulf
UNITED STATES OF AMERICA (ALASKA)
PACIFIC OCEAN
YUKON TERRITORY
NORTHWEST TERRITORIES
NUNAVUT
BRITISH COLUMBIA
ALBERTA
SASKATCHEWAN
ROCKY MOUNTAINS
Mackenzie Mountains
Selwyn Mountains
Great Bear Lake
Great Slave Lake
Lake Athabasca
Whitehorse
Yellowknife
Edmonton
Calgary
Vancouver
Victoria
Saskatoon
Vancouver Island
Queen Charlotte Islands
UNITED STATES OF AMERICA

196
16
192
16

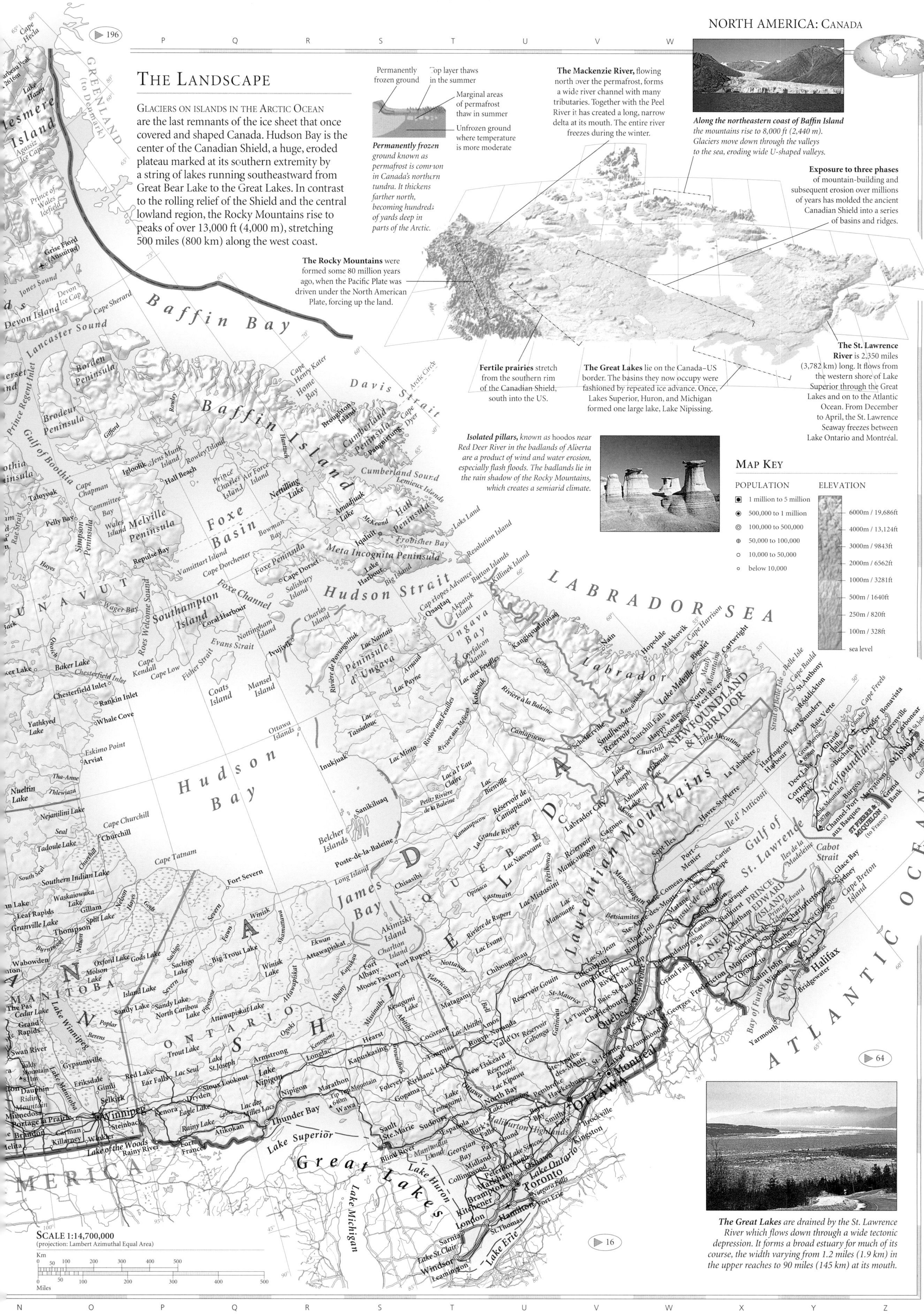
GREENLAND (to Denmark)
Ellesmere Island
Baffin Bay
Baffin Island
Davis Strait
Foxe Basin
Hudson Strait
LABRADOR SEA
Hudson Bay
James Bay
Labrador
NEWFOUNDLAND & LABRADOR
Laurentian Mountains
Gulf of St. Lawrence
ATLANTIC OCEAN
MANITOBA
ONTARIO
Lake Superior
Great Lakes
Lake Michigan
Lake Huron
Lake Ontario
Lake Erie
Winnipeg
Thunder Bay
OTTAWA
Montréal
Québec
Toronto
Halifax
St. John's
NOVA SCOTIA
NEW BRUNSWICK
PRINCE EDWARD ISLAND
Permanently frozen ground
Top layer thaws in the summer
Marginal areas of permafrost thaw in summer
Unfrozen ground where temperature is more moderate

196

The Landscape

Glaciers on islands in the Arctic Ocean are the last remnants of the ice sheet that once covered and shaped Canada. Hudson Bay is the center of the Canadian Shield, a huge, eroded plateau marked at its southern extremity by a string of lakes running southeastward from Great Bear Lake to the Great Lakes. In contrast to the rolling relief of the Shield and the central lowland region, the Rocky Mountains rise to peaks of over 13,000 ft (4,000 m), stretching 500 miles (800 km) along the west coast.

***Permanently frozen** ground known as permafrost is common in Canada's northern tundra. It thickens farther north, becoming hundreds of yards deep in parts of the Arctic.*

The Mackenzie River, flowing north over the permafrost, forms a wide river channel with many tributaries. Together with the Peel River it has created a long, narrow delta at its mouth. The entire river freezes during the winter.

The Rocky Mountains were formed some 80 million years ago, when the Pacific Plate was driven under the North American Plate, forcing up the land.

Fertile prairies stretch from the southern rim of the Canadian Shield, south into the US.

The Great Lakes lie on the Canada–US border. The basins they now occupy were fashioned by repeated ice advance. Once, Lakes Superior, Huron, and Michigan formed one large lake, Lake Nipissing.

Exposure to three phases of mountain-building and subsequent erosion over millions of years has molded the ancient Canadian Shield into a series of basins and ridges.

The St. Lawrence River is 2,350 miles (3,782 km) long. It flows from the western shore of Lake Superior through the Great Lakes and on to the Atlantic Ocean. From December to April, the St. Lawrence Seaway freezes between Lake Ontario and Montréal.

***Along the northeastern coast of Baffin Island** the mountains rise to 8,000 ft (2,440 m). Glaciers move down through the valleys to the sea, eroding wide U-shaped valleys.*

***Isolated pillars,** known as hoodoos near Red Deer River in the badlands of Alberta are a product of wind and water erosion, especially flash floods. The badlands lie in the rain shadow of the Rocky Mountains, which creates a semiarid climate.*

Map Key

POPULATION
- ■ 1 million to 5 million
- ◉ 500,000 to 1 million
- ◎ 100,000 to 500,000
- ⊕ 50,000 to 100,000
- ○ 10,000 to 50,000
- ∘ below 10,000

ELEVATION
- 6000m / 19,686ft
- 4000m / 13,124ft
- 3000m / 9843ft
- 2000m / 6562ft
- 1000m / 3281ft
- 500m / 1640ft
- 250m / 820ft
- 100m / 328ft
- sea level

64

***The Great Lakes** are drained by the St. Lawrence River which flows down through a wide tectonic depression. It forms a broad estuary for much of its course, the width varying from 1.2 miles (1.9 km) in the upper reaches to 90 miles (145 km) at its mouth.*

16

SCALE 1:14,700,000
(projection: Lambert Azimuthal Equal Area)

Km 0 50 100 200 300 400 500
Miles 0 50 100 200 300 400 500

CANADA: WESTERN PROVINCES

Alberta, British Columbia, Manitoba, Saskatchewan, Yukon Territory

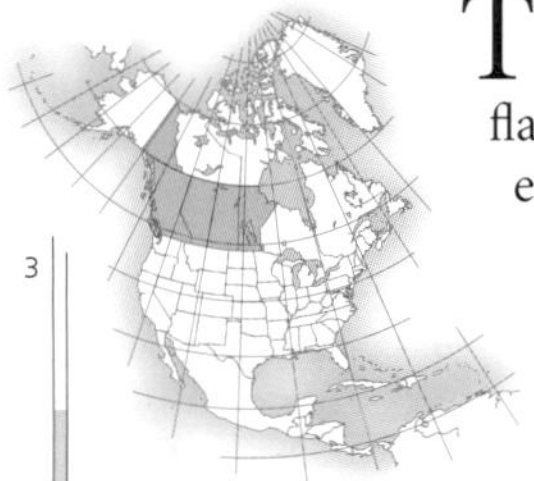

THE MOUNTAINS OF THE WEST COAST, incorporating British Columbia and the Yukon Territory, descend into the vast, flat prairies of Alberta, Saskatchewan, and Manitoba. The empty lands and fertile soils of the prairie provinces attracted migrants, and the descendants of early European immigrants still make up a large proportion of the population. The mechanization of agriculture has reduced the need for labor, and rural population densities remain low. The majority of the people live within 100 miles (160 km) of the southern Canada–US border, and in British Columbia, one of the leading Canadian provinces in terms of economic wealth. The Yukon Territory, in the far north, remains a relatively unspoiled wilderness, containing large, untapped mineral reserves. This province has a significant population of Native Americans people, many of whom maintain a traditional lifestyle.

USING THE LAND AND SEA

WHEAT FARMING IS THE ECONOMIC MAINSTAY of Alberta, Manitoba, and Saskatchewan, which contain 82% of farmland in Canada. Cattle are also raised on the prairies. Forestry and fishing are the most prominent resource-based industries in British Columbia. Despite the mountainous terrain, fruit and specialized grains can be grown in the Okanagan and Fraser valleys.

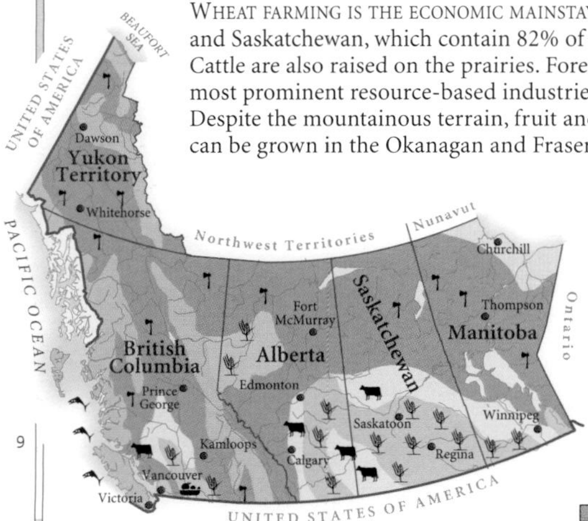
BEAUFORT SEA
UNITED STATES OF AMERICA
PACIFIC OCEAN
Dawson
Yukon Territory
Whitehorse
Northwest Territories
Nunavut
Churchill
Thompson
Manitoba
Ontario
Fort McMurray
Saskatchewan
British Columbia
Alberta
Edmonton
Prince George
Saskatoon
Winnipeg
Kamloops
Calgary
Regina
Vancouver
Victoria
UNITED STATES OF AMERICA
Land use and agricultural distribution
cattle
cereals
fishing
fruit
timber
major towns
pasture
cropland
forest
wetland
barren
tundra

Large, highly-mechanized and often very specialized farms, requiring huge investment but little labor, characterize modern farming in the prairies.

THE URBAN/RURAL POPULATION DIVIDE

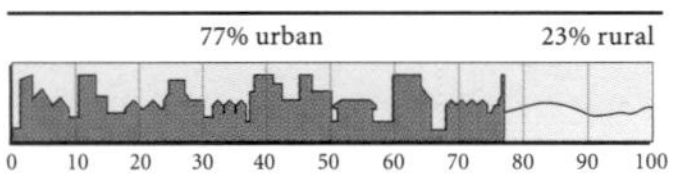
77% urban
23% rural
0 10 20 30 40 50 60 70 80 90 100

POPULATION DENSITY	TOTAL LAND AREA
7 people per sq mile (3 people per sq km)	1,224,449 sq miles (3,172,150 sq km)

TRANSPORTATION & INDUSTRY

THE WESTERN PROVINCES contain a wealth of mineral resources. Alberta holds the bulk of Canada's fossil fuels; the other provinces contain reserves of metallic ores, such as zinc, lead, and silver. Isolation from markets has slowed the development of manufacturing, restricting it to the large cities like Vancouver, Winnipeg, and Calgary. Hydroelectric power is widely exploited, although there is increasing concern about potential ecological damage.

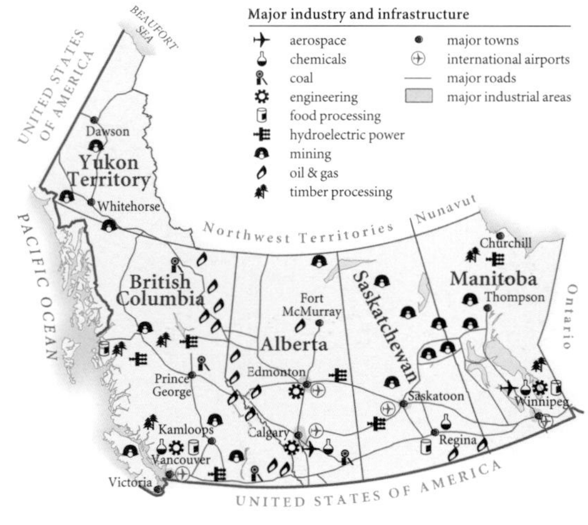
Major industry and infrastructure
aerospace
chemicals
coal
engineering
food processing
hydroelectric power
mining
oil & gas
timber processing
major towns
international airports
major roads
major industrial areas
BEAUFORT SEA
UNITED STATES OF AMERICA
PACIFIC OCEAN
Dawson
Yukon Territory
Whitehorse
Northwest Territories
Nunavut
Churchill
Manitoba
Thompson
Ontario
Fort McMurray
Saskatchewan
British Columbia
Alberta
Edmonton
Prince George
Saskatoon
Winnipeg
Kamloops
Calgary
Regina
Vancouver
Victoria
UNITED STATES OF AMERICA

TRANSPORTATION NETWORK

(roads)	82,438 miles (135,145 km)
(highways)	6,459 miles (10,401 km)
(railways)	10,811 miles (17,410 km)
(waterways)	None

The transportation network of the western provinces is dominated by east–west routes that weave through mountain passes and spread across the plains. Access to some northern areas is restricted to air travel.

Much of the Yukon Territory is uninhabited tundra. Industry is based on the extraction of mineral resources, and to a lesser extent, on the scattered forests of the south.

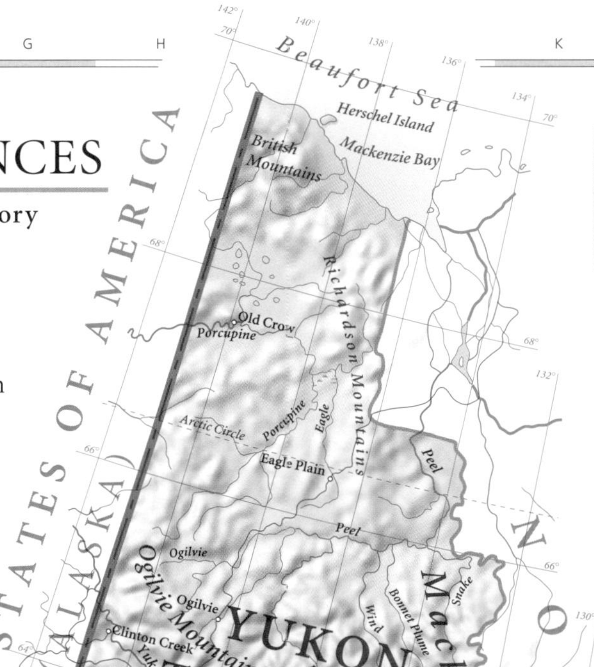

Beaufort Sea
Herschel Island
Mackenzie Bay
British Mountains
UNITED STATES OF AMERICA (ALASKA)
Old Crow
Porcupine
Richardson Mountains
Arctic Circle
Eagle Plain
Peel
Ogilvie
Ogilvie Mountains
Clinton Creek
Dawson
YUKON TERRITORY
Mackenzie Mountains
Glenboyle
Keno Hill
Mayo
Stewart Crossing
Stewart River
Selwyn Mountains
Coffee Creek
Keele Peak 2972m
Beaver Creek
Minto
Koidern
Dawson Range
Carmacks
Glenlyon Peak 2190m
Faro
Ross River
Burwash Landing
Kluane Lake
Aishihik Lake
Pelly Mountains
Mount Logan 5959m
Saint Elias Mountains
Seward Glacier
Haines Junction
Lake Laberge
Champagne
Whitehorse
Johnsons Crossing
Jakes Corner
Carcross
Mount Hunt 2743m
Mount Murray 2162m
Chilkoot Pass 1067m
White Pass 880m
Teslin
Atlin
Atlin Lake
Simpson Peak 2173m
Upper Liard
Lower Post
Watson Lake
Coal River
Liard River
ROCKY MOUNTAINS
Good Hope Lake
Cassiar
Nakina
Cassiar Mountains
Meszah Peak 2164m
Dease Lake
Muncho Lake
Fort Nelson
Telegraph Creek
Glenora
Mount Ratz 3136m
Mount Edziza 2787m
Mount Will 2515m
Bronlund Peak 2594m
Mount Roosevelt 2972m
Mount Sylvia 2942m
Prophet River
Mount Lloyd George 2972m
Ware
Trutch
Skeena Mountains
Mount Pattullo 2729m
Meziadin Junction
Stewart
Sustut Peak 2470m
BRITISH COLUMBIA
Williston Lake
Portland Inlet
Cranberry Junction
Kitwanga
Hazelton
New Hazelton
Seven Sisters Peaks 2755m
Takla Lake
Babine Lake
Granisle
Smithers
Telkwa
Terrace
Houston
Burns Lake
Stuart Lake
Fort St. James
Fraser Lake
Vanderhoof
Dixon Entrance
Prince Rupert
Cape Knox
Masset
Graham Island
Port Clements
Queen Charlotte
Queen Charlotte Islands
Sandspit
Moresby Island
Porcher Island
Port Edward
Kitimat
Douglas Channel
Hecate Strait
Banks Island
Princess Royal Island
Aristazabal Island
Kemano
Ootsa Lake
Eutsuk Lake
PACIFIC OCEAN
Ocean Falls
Bella Bella
Hagensborg
Bella Coola
Nazko
Quesnel
Anahim Lake
Fraser Plateau
Cape St. James
Queen Charlotte Sound
Dawsons Landing
Rivers Inlet
Namu
Mount Saugstad 2908m
Monarch Mountain 3533m
Alexis Creek
Kleena Kleene
Tatla Lake
Williams Lake
Mount Waddington 4016m
Mount Queen Bess 3313m
Mount Gilbert 3109m
Cape Caution
Cape Scott
Port Hardy
Winter Harbour
Port Alice
Cape Cook
Vancouver Island
Gold River
Tahsis
Campbell River
Powell River
Courtenay
Comox
Port Alberni
Tofino
Ucluelet
Nanaimo
Ladysmith
Bamfield
Duncan
Victoria
Vancouver
North Vancouver
Richmond
Burnaby
Squamish
Whistler
Pemberton
Nootka Sound
Barkley Sound
Strait of Juan de Fuca
NORTHWEST TERRITORIES

The Fraser River valley is a major area of settlement in British Columbia. Railroads cross the Rocky Mountains via this valley.

Established in 1907, Jasper National Park lies in the heart of the Rocky Mountains. It is noted for its spectacular alpine scenery and contains part of the large Columbia Icefield.

16

192

N O P Q R S T U V W X Y

THE LANDSCAPE

THE MASSIVE ROCKY MOUNTAINS form a continental divide between rivers flowing eastward and westward. The interior plains lie east of the mountains, stretching from the Arctic Circle south into the US. Covered with glacial deposits from the last Ice Age, these are interspersed with hilly regions and long, steep escarpments.

MAP KEY

POPULATION

- 500,000 to 1 million
- 100,000 to 500,000
- 50,000 to 100,000
- 10,000 to 50,000
- below 10,000

ELEVATION

6000m / 19,686ft
4000m / 13,124ft
3000m / 9843ft
2000m / 6562ft
1000m / 3281ft
500m / 1640ft
250m / 820ft
100m / 328ft
sea level

SCALE 1:8,250,000
(projection: Lambert Conformal Conic)

Km 0 25 50 100 150 200 250
Miles 0 25 50 100 150 200 250

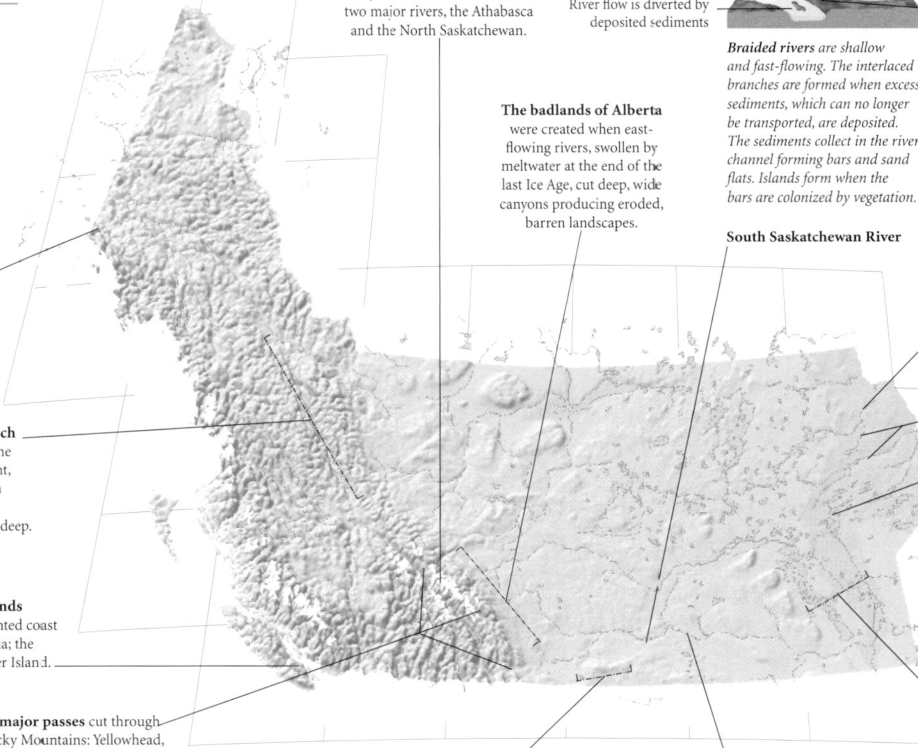

Mount Logan rises 19,551 ft (5,959 m). It is the highest peak in Canada.

The Rocky Mountain Trench is the longest linear fault in the world. It has formed a straight, flat-bottomed valley between 2–9 miles (4–15 km) wide, and up to 3,280 ft (1,000 m) deep.

Hundreds of islands dot the fjord-indented coast of British Columbia; the largest is Vancouver Island.

Three major passes cut through the Rocky Mountains: Yellowhead, Kicking Horse, and Crowsnest. They are all used as transportation routes through the mountains.

The Columbia Icefield in the Rocky Mountains is the source of two major rivers, the Athabasca and the North Saskatchewan.

The badlands of Alberta were created when east-flowing rivers, swollen by meltwater at the end of the last Ice Age, cut deep, wide canyons producing eroded, barren landscapes.

The Cypress Hills rise to 4,806 ft (1,465 m) above the surrounding plain. Having escaped the last glaciation they contain unique plant and animal life. The silvery lupine, bunchberry, and lodgepole pine all grow in the cool, moist climate of the hills.

South Saskatchewan River

The Alberta and Saskatchewan plains bear strong testament to past glaciations. The Assiniboine, Saskatchewan and Qu'Appelle Rivers occupy flat-bottomed, steep-sided valleys eroded during the last Ice Age by glacial meltwater.

Vegetated island
River flow is diverted by deposited sediments
Bar
Sand flat

***Braided rivers** are shallow and fast-flowing. The interlaced branches are formed when excess sediments, which can no longer be transported, are deposited. The sediments collect in the river channel forming bars and sand flats. Islands form when the bars are colonized by vegetation.*

***Across the tundra** of northern Manitoba, widespread permafrost inhibits water from permeating the soil. This causes rivers like the Churchill to flow in many channels, which can be frozen for up to six months during the winter.*

The Nelson and Churchill Rivers drain northward across the Canadian Shield to Hudson Bay. The shield covers three-fifths of Saskatchewan.

Setting Lake

***Ancient granite outcrops**, part of the Canadian Shield, rise above the surface of Setting Lake, which was initially formed by meltwater from the last Ice Age.*

The lowlands of Manitoba are a basin that once held the vast post-glacial Lake Agassiz, remnants of which include Lake Winnipeg, Lake Winnipegosis, and Lake Manitoba.

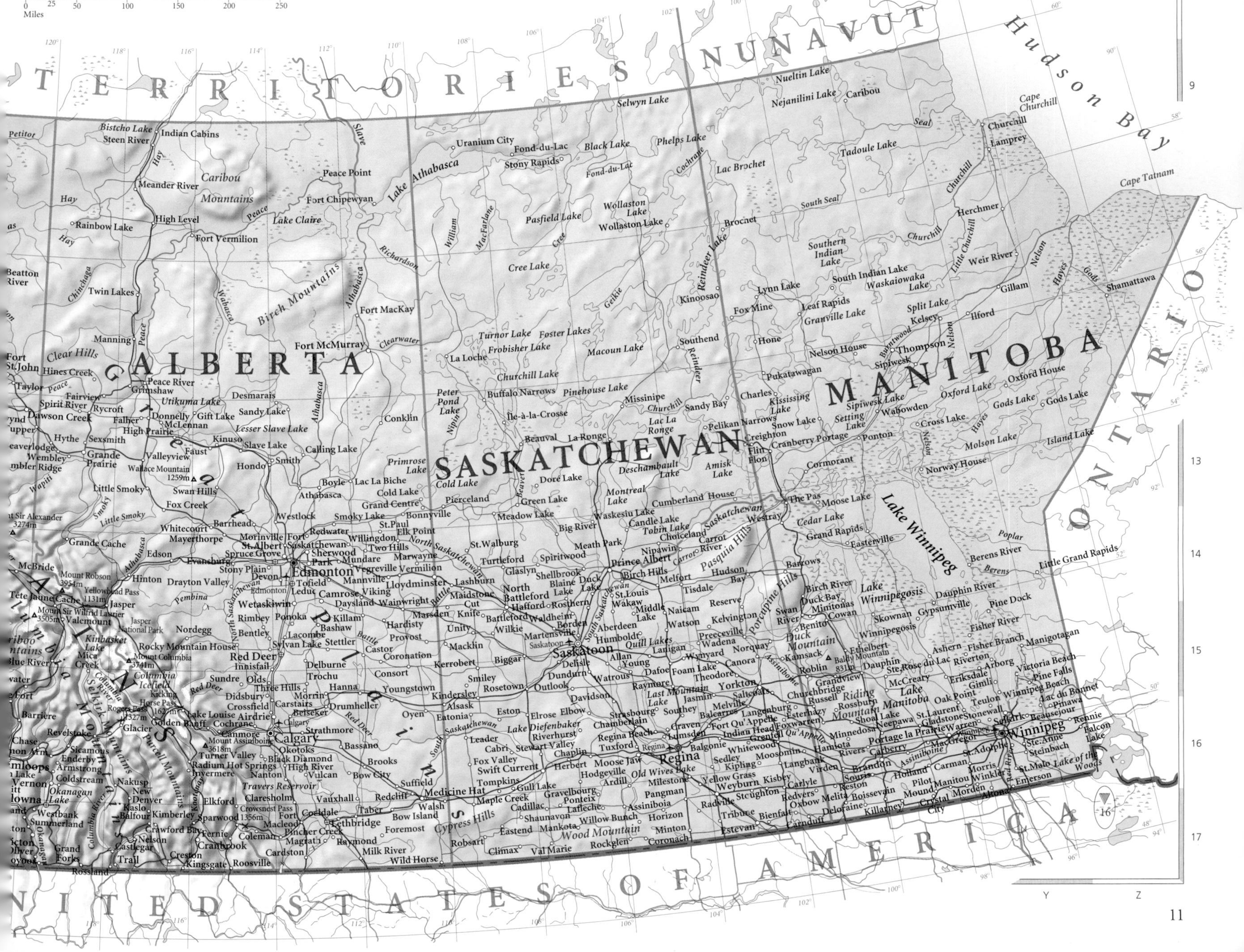

NORTHWEST TERRITORIES
NUNAVUT
Hudson Bay
ALBERTA
SASKATCHEWAN
MANITOBA
ONTARIO
UNITED STATES OF AMERICA
Great Plains
Rocky Mountains
Lake Athabasca
Caribou Mountains
Birch Mountains
Clear Hills
Reindeer Lake
Wollaston Lake
Cree Lake
Lake Winnipeg
Lake Winnipegosis
Lake Manitoba
Cypress Hills
Wood Mountain
Duck Mountain
Riding Mountain
Porcupine Hills
Pasquia Hills
Edmonton
Calgary
Saskatoon
Regina
Winnipeg
Red Deer
Lethbridge
Medicine Hat
Moose Jaw
Prince Albert
Brandon
Fort McMurray
Grande Prairie
Churchill
Thompson
The Pas
Flin Flon
Uranium City
Fort Chipewyan
Peace River
Lloydminster
North Battleford
Yorkton
Swift Current
Estevan
Weyburn
Banff
Jasper
Cape Churchill
Cape Tatnam
Peace
Athabasca
North Saskatchewan
South Saskatchewan
Churchill
Nelson
Assiniboine
Red Deer
Qu'Appelle

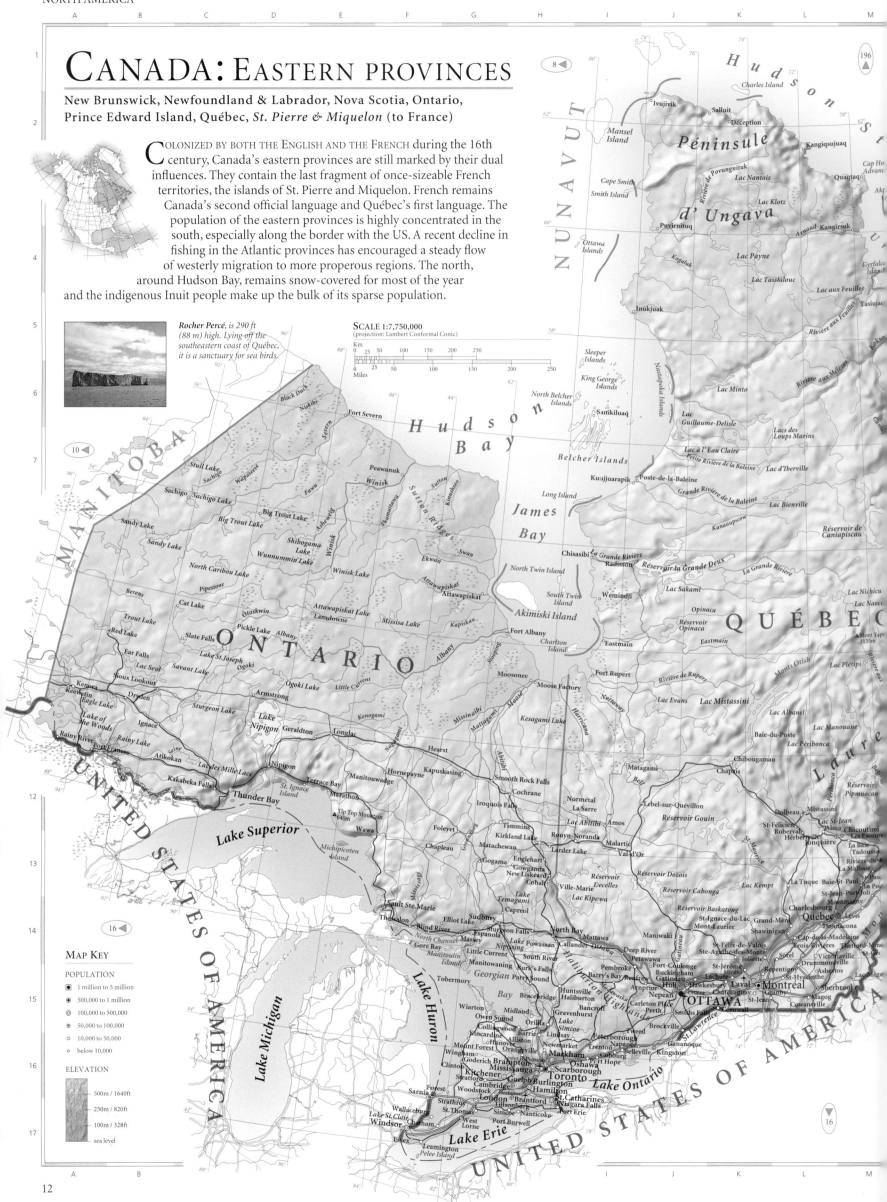

CANADA: EASTERN PROVINCES

New Brunswick, Newfoundland & Labrador, Nova Scotia, Ontario, Prince Edward Island, Québec, *St. Pierre & Miquelon* (to France)

COLONIZED BY BOTH THE ENGLISH AND THE FRENCH during the 16th century, Canada's eastern provinces are still marked by their dual influences. They contain the last fragment of once-sizeable French territories, the islands of St. Pierre and Miquelon. French remains Canada's second official language and Québec's first language. The population of the eastern provinces is highly concentrated in the south, especially along the border with the US. A recent decline in fishing in the Atlantic provinces has encouraged a steady flow of westerly migration to more properous regions. The north, around Hudson Bay, remains snow-covered for most of the year and the indigenous Inuit people make up the bulk of its sparse population.

Rocher Percé, is 290 ft (88 m) high. Lying off the southeastern coast of Québec, it is a sanctuary for sea birds.

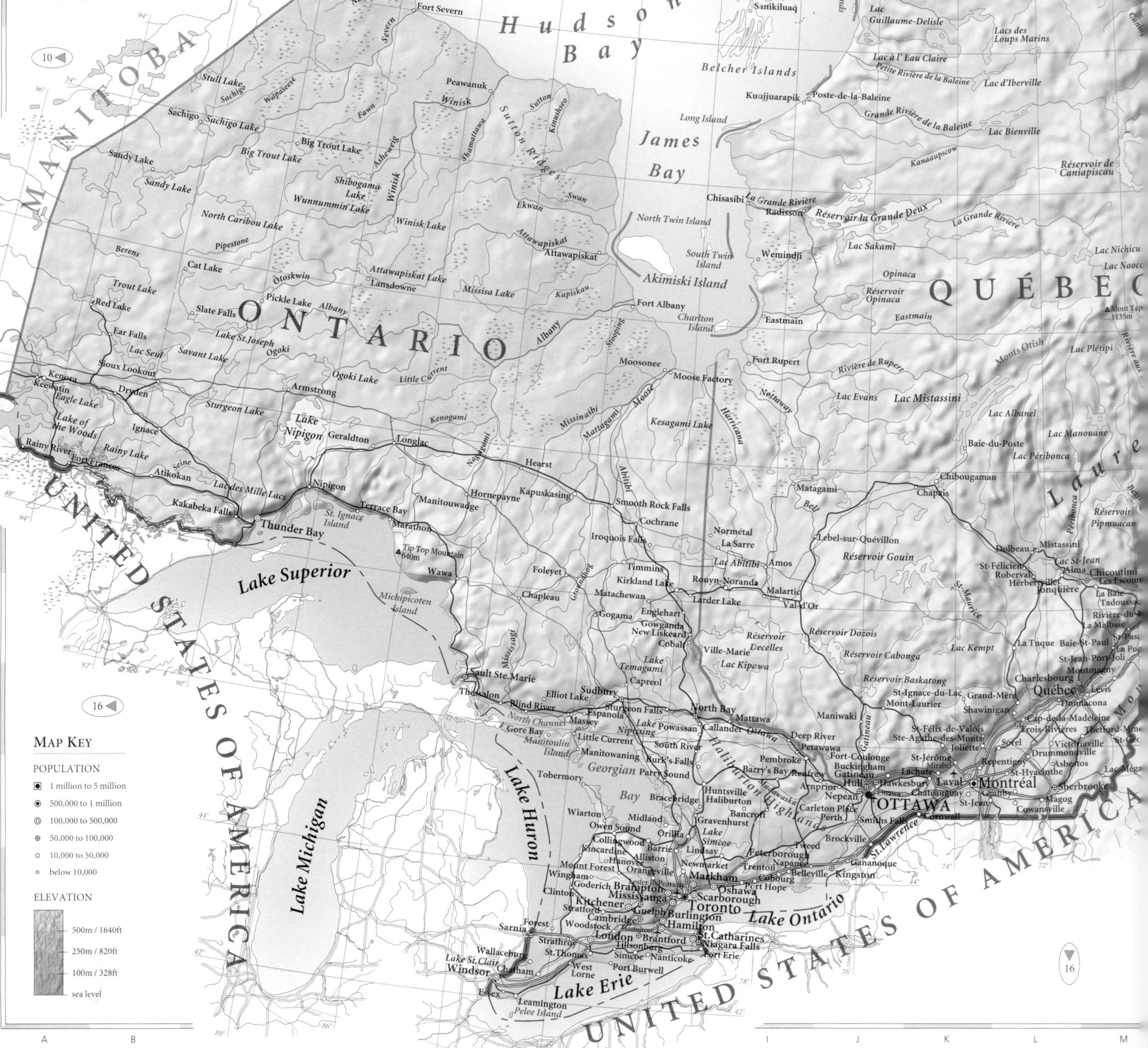
SCALE 1:7,750,000
(projection: Lambert Conformal Conic)
Km 0 25 50 100 150 200 250
Miles 0 25 50 100 150 200 250
MAP KEY
POPULATION
1 million to 5 million
500,000 to 1 million
100,000 to 500,000
50,000 to 100,000
10,000 to 50,000
below 10,000
ELEVATION
500m / 1640ft
250m / 820ft
100m / 328ft
sea level
Hudson Bay
James Bay
NUNAVUT
MANITOBA
ONTARIO
QUÉBEC
UNITED STATES OF AMERICA
Péninsule d' Ungava
Lake Superior
Lake Michigan
Lake Huron
Lake Ontario
Lake Erie
Georgian Bay
OTTAWA
Toronto
Montréal
Québec
Hamilton
London
Windsor
Thunder Bay
Sudbury
Sault Ste.Marie
Kingston
Ottawa
Timmins
Moosonee
Fort Severn
Akimiski Island
Belcher Islands
Mansel Island
Charles Island
Lac Mistassini
Réservoir Gouin
Réservoir de Caniapiscau
Lake Nipigon
Lake of the Woods
Rocher Percé

THE LANDSCAPE

MUCH OF EASTERN CANADA is part of the Canadian Shield. Glaciers have scoured the land leaving deposits that have dammed and diverted streams, to create a rocky landscape strewn with lakes and swamps. Much of the ground is subject to permafrost, which further impedes drainage. The uplands in the far east are the most northerly extension of the Appalachian mountain chain.

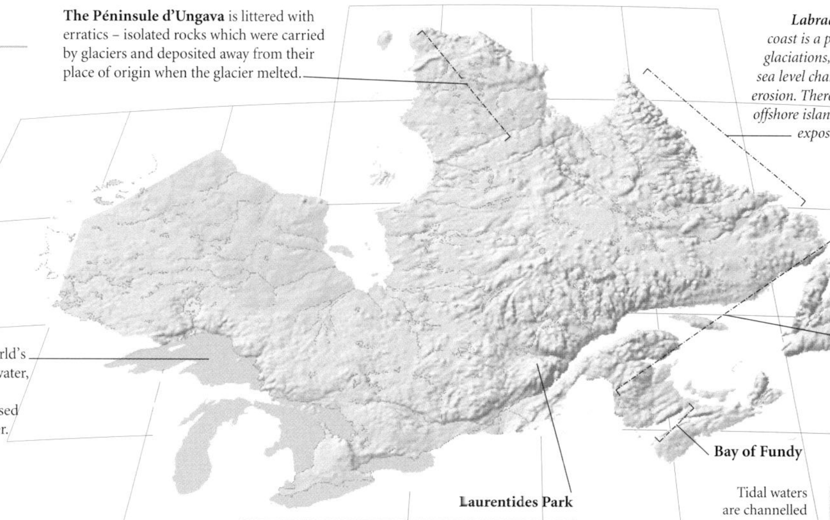

The Péninsule d'Ungava is littered with erratics – isolated rocks which were carried by glaciers and deposited away from their place of origin when the glacier melted.

Lake Superior is the world's largest expanse of fresh water, covering 32,150 sq miles (83,270 sq km). It is crossed by the Canada–US border.

Laurentides Park

Bay of Fundy

The eroded highlands of New Brunswick, Nova Scotia and Newfoundland are part of the Appalachian mountain chain, formed over 400 million years ago.

Labrador's indented coast is a product of past glaciations, which caused sea level change, and wave erosion. There are countless offshore islands, fjords, and exposed headlands.

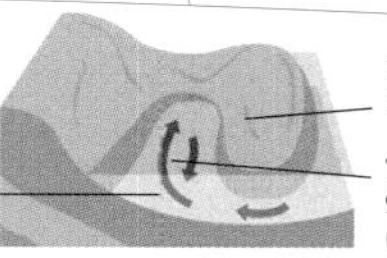
Steep cliffs bound the bay
The bay is 94 miles (151 km) long
Tidal waters are channelled down the bay

***At the Bay of Fundy,** incoming waves are funneled down the long, narrow, steep-sided bay. These topographical features cause fast-flowing tides which can rise 70 ft (21 m).*

***The forested Laurentides Park** incorporates part of the Laurentian Mountains. Within its boundaries are over 1,600 lakes.*

Button Islands
Port Burwell
LABRADOR SEA
Labrador
Saglek Bay
Hebron
Kangiqsualujjuaq
Cod Island
Okak Islands
South Aulatsivik Island
Nain
Tunungayualok Island
Kogaluk
Lac Champdoré
Hopedale
Makkovik
Cape Harrison
Lac aux Goélands
Attikamagen Lake
Schefferville
Petitsikapau Lake
Kanairiktok
Rigolet
Lake Melville
Hamilton Inlet
Mealy Mountains
Cartwright
Smallwood Reservoir
Churchill Falls
North West River
Happy Valley-Goose Bay
NEWFOUNDLAND & LABRADOR
Port Hope Simpson
Shabogamo Lake
Churchill
Lake Joseph
Atikonak Lac
Labrador City
Mont Wright 899m
Ashuanipi Lake
Belle Isle
Cape Bauld
St.Anthony
Red Bay
Forteau
Strait of Belle Isle
Petit Lac Manicouagan
Rivière-St-Paul
St-Augustin
Little Mecatina
Roddickton
Grey Islands
Monts Groulx
Moisie
Natashquan
Romaine
La Tabatière
Port Saunders
White Bay
Réservoir Manicouagan
Laurentian Mountains
Harrington Harbour
Baie Verte
Long Range Mountains
Lac-Allard
Mingan
Havre-St-Pierre
Notre Dame Bay
Fogo Island
Sally's Cove
Gros Morne 808m
Sept-Îles
Longue-Pointe
Moisie
Détroit de Jacques-Cartier
Île d'Anticosti
Gander
Bonavista Bay
Bonavista
Port-Cartier
Port-Menier
Deer Lake
Grand Lake
Grand Falls
Buchans
Red Indian Lake
Honguedo Passage
Corner Brook
Clarenville
Baie-Trinité
Baie-Comeau
Godbout
Mont-Louis
Grande-Vallée
Ste-Anne-des-Monts
Murdochville
Gaspé
Newfoundland
Stephenville
Cape St.George
St. George's Bay
Gulf of St. Lawrence
Trinity Bay
Carbonear
St.John's
Meelpaeg Lake
Cap-Chat
Mont Jacques-Cartier 1268m
Matane
Péninsule de Gaspé
Percé
Rocher Percé
Grande-Rivière
Chandler
Mont-Joli
Amqui
Rimouski
New-Richmond
Dalhousie
Campbellton
Chaleur Bay
Table Mountain 587m
Cape Ray
Channel-Port aux Basques
Burgeo
Harbour Breton
Marystown
Placentia
Placentia Bay
Avalon Peninsula
Cape Race
Îles de la Madeleine
Cabot Strait
Grand Bank
ST PIERRE & MIQUELON (to France)
Caraquet
Shippagan
Tracadie
Bathurst
Kedgwick
Edmundston
St.Léonard
Mount Carleton 820m
Grand Falls
Plaster Rock
Newcastle
Neguac
Chatham
PRINCE EDWARD ISLAND
Prince Edward Island
Tignish
Chéticamp
Cape North
Ingonish Beach
Cape Breton Island
Sydney Mines
Glace Bay
Sydney
Inverness
Richibucto
Souris
Summerside
Kensington
Charlottetown
Shediac
Northumberland Strait
NEW BRUNSWICK
Doaktown
Hartland
Woodstock
Minto
Moncton
Riverview
Sackville
Amherst
Port Hawkesbury
Chedabucto Bay
New Glasgow
Antigonish
Canso
St. John
Fredericton
Oromocto
Sussex
Springhill
Truro
McAdam
St.Stephen
Hampton
Saint John
Minas Basin
NOVA SCOTIA
Kentville
Windsor
Sheet Harbour
Halifax
Dartmouth
Grand Manan Island
Bay of Fundy
Middleton
Digby
Lunenburg
Bridgewater
Lake Rossignol
Liverpool
Sable Island
Yarmouth
Shelburne
Cape Sable
ATLANTIC OCEAN

***The tides** at the Bay of Fundy are among the highest in the world. At low tide the tree-topped rocks have been likened to flowerpots.*

TRANSPORTATION & INDUSTRY

BOTH QUÉBEC AND ONTARIO have a diversified manufacturing sector located in the south. Across the rest of the region, industry is largely based around local resources, which accounts for the large number of fish and timber processing plants and mines. Many of the fast-flowing rivers are also gradually being harnessed for hydroelectric power.

LABRADOR SEA
Hudson Bay
Manitoba
Ontario
Schefferville
Québec
Newfoundland & Labrador
St.John's
Thunder Bay
New Brunswick
Prince Edward Island
Sault Ste. Marie
Québec
Montreal
Nova Scotia
Halifax
OTTAWA
Toronto
ATLANTIC OCEAN
UNITED STATES OF AMERICA
Major industry and infrastructure
aerospace
vehicle manufacture
chemicals
fish processing
food processing
hi-tech industry
hydroelectric power
mining
timber processing
capital cities
major towns
international airports
major roads
major industrial areas

TRANSPORTATION NETWORK

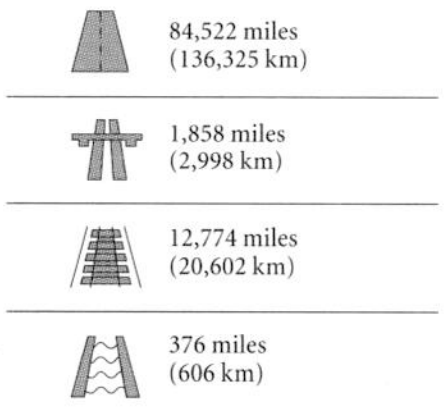
84,522 miles (136,325 km)
1,858 miles (2,998 km)
12,774 miles (20,602 km)
376 miles (606 km)

The majority of Canada's large ports lie in the east. Since the 1960s the region's rail network has been steadily reduced; Newfoundland recently lost its last remaining line, the Long-Cross Island line.

***Fish processing** is a major industry in the Atlantic provinces. Fogo Island, off Newfoundland, has barely a thousand inhabitants but it is able to sustain a number of cod canneries.*

USING THE LAND AND SEA

WITH THIN SOILS restricting farming to the south, the forests that grow in vast unbroken tracts across eastern Canada provide an important source of revenue. Coastal communities rely heavily on the rich fishing grounds of the Atlantic Ocean, although foreign competition and overfishing have resulted in strict policies to conserve stocks.

THE URBAN/RURAL POPULATION DIVIDE

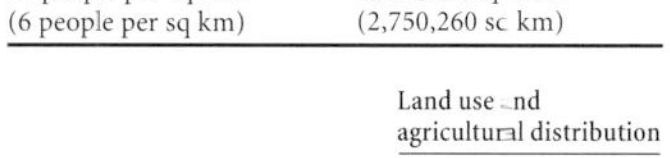
77% urban
23% rural
0 10 20 30 40 50 60 70 80 90 100

POPULATION DENSITY	TOTAL LAND AREA
17 people per sq mile (6 people per sq km)	1,061,600 sq miles (2,750,260 sq km)

LABRADOR SEA
Hudson Bay
Manitoba
Ontario
Québec
Newfoundland & Labrador
St.John's
Thunder Bay
New Brunswick
Prince Edward Island
Québec
Montreal
Nova Scotia
Sault Ste. Marie
OTTAWA
Toronto
Halifax
ATLANTIC OCEAN
UNITED STATES OF AMERICA
Land use and agricultural distribution
cattle
cereals
fishing
fruit
timber
capital cities
major towns
pasture
cropland
forest
tundra

***Prince Edward Island** is the only Atlantic province with notable agricultural land. The island is Canada's leading producer of potatoes.*

▶ 64

SOUTHEASTERN CANADA

Southern Ontario, Southern Québec

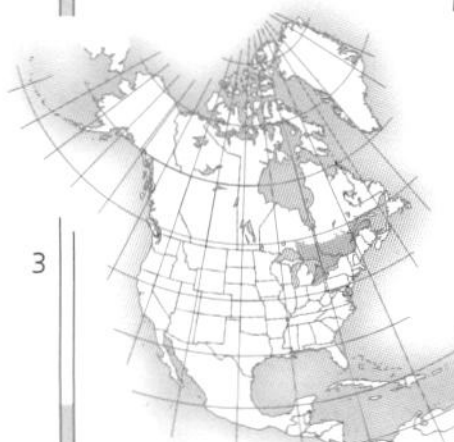

THE SOUTHERN PARTS of Québec and Ontario form the economic heart of Canada. The two provinces are divided by their language and culture; in Québec, French is the main language, whereas English is spoken in Ontario. Separatist sentiment in Québec has led to a provincial referendum on the question of a sovereignty association with Canada. The region contains Canada's capital, Ottawa and its two largest cities: Toronto, the center of commerce and Montréal, the cultural and administrative heart of French Canada.

The port at Montréal is situated on the St. Lawrence Seaway. A network of 16 locks allows sea-going vessels access to routes once plied by fur-trappers and early settlers.

Niagara Falls lies on the border between Canada and the US. It comprises a system of two falls: American Falls, in New York, is separated from Horseshoe Falls, in Ontario, by Goat Island. Horseshoe Falls, seen here, plunges 184 ft (56 m) and is 2,500 ft (762 m) wide.

TRANSPORTATION & INDUSTRY

THE CITIES OF SOUTHERN QUÉBEC AND ONTARIO, and their hinterlands, form the heart of Canadian manufacturing industry. Toronto is Canada's leading financial center, and Ontario's motor and aerospace industries have developed around the city. A major center for nickel mining lies to the north of Toronto. Most of Québec's industry is located in Montréal, the oldest port in North America. Chemicals, paper manufacture, and the construction of transportation equipment are leading industrial activities.

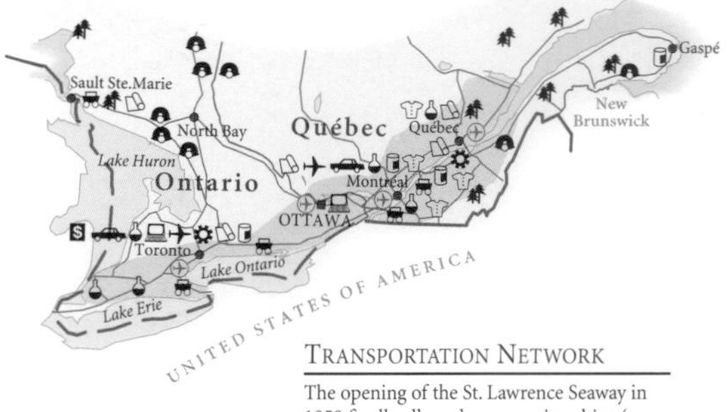

Sault Ste.Marie
North Bay
Lake Huron
Ontario
Québec
Québec
Montréal
OTTAWA
Toronto
Lake Ontario
Lake Erie
Gaspé
New Brunswick
UNITED STATES OF AMERICA

Major industry and infrastructure

- car manufacture
- chemicals
- engineering
- finance
- food processing
- hi-tech industry
- mining
- iron & steel
- textiles
- paper industry
- timber processing
- capital cities
- major towns
- international airports
- major roads
- major industrial areas

TRANSPORTATION NETWORK

The opening of the St. Lawrence Seaway in 1959 finally allowed ocean-going ships (up to 24,000 tons (tonnes)) access to the interior of Canada, creating a vital trading route.

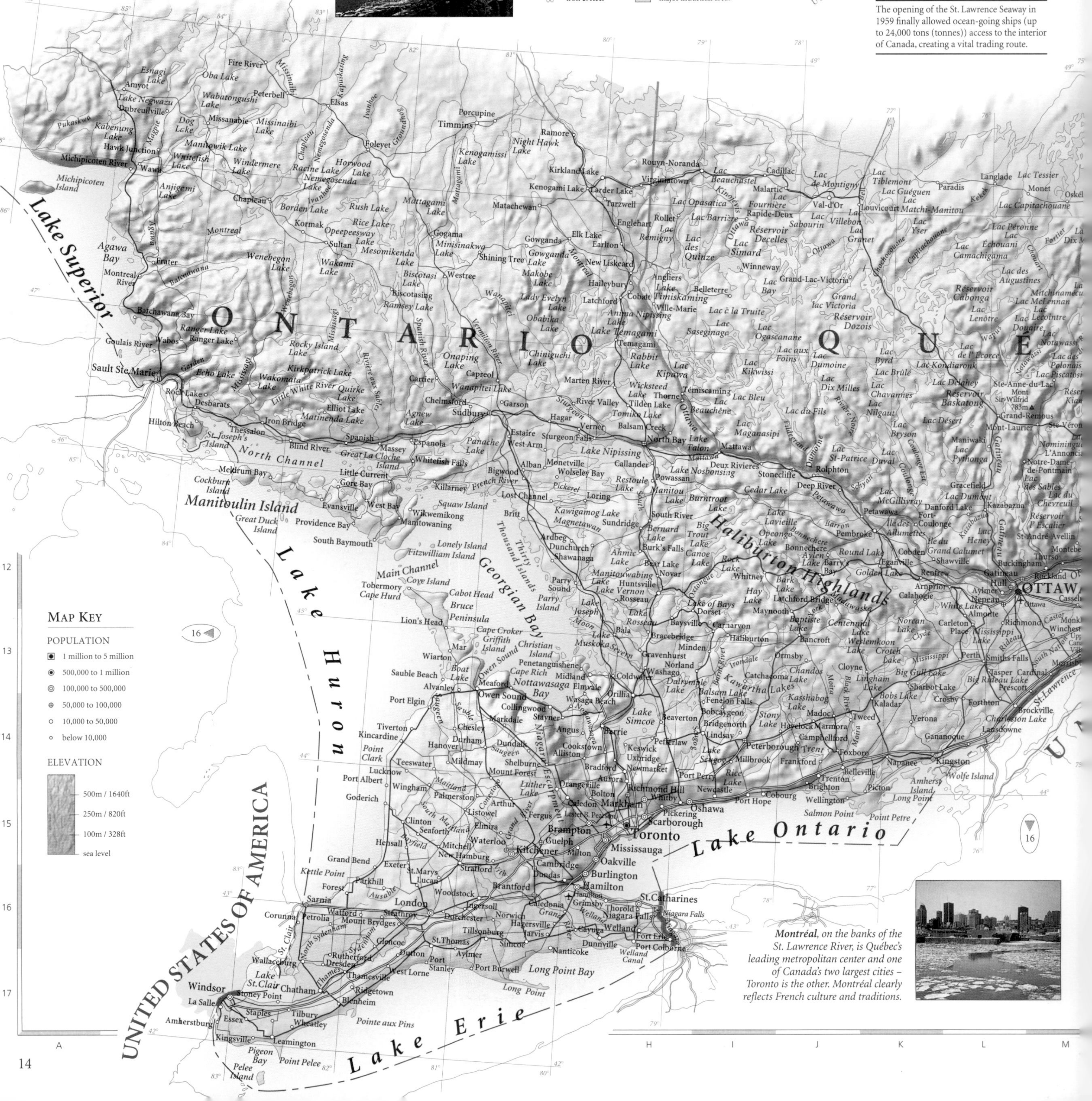

ONTARIO
QUÉ
Lake Superior
Lake Huron
Lake Ontario
Lake Erie
Georgian Bay
North Channel
Manitoulin Island
Haliburton Highlands
UNITED STATES OF AMERICA
OTTAWA
Toronto
Mississauga
Hamilton
London
Windsor
Kitchener
Sudbury
Sault Ste.Marie
Timmins
North Bay
Kingston
Oshawa
Barrie
Peterborough
Rouyn-Noranda
Val-d'Or
Lake Nipissing
Lake Simcoe
Main Channel
Long Point Bay

MAP KEY

POPULATION

- 1 million to 5 million
- 500,000 to 1 million
- 100,000 to 500,000
- 50,000 to 100,000
- 10,000 to 50,000
- below 10,000

ELEVATION

- 500m / 1640ft
- 250m / 820ft
- 100m / 328ft
- sea level

16

16

Montréal, on the banks of the St. Lawrence River, is Québec's leading metropolitan center and one of Canada's two largest cities – Toronto is the other. Montréal clearly reflects French culture and traditions.

USING THE LAND AND SEA

THE PRODUCTIVE NIAGARA "FRUIT BELT" on the shores of Lake Erie and Lake Ontario is a major farming region, although available farmland is being challenged by urban expansion. Québec is Canada's leading producer of maple syrup and dairy products. In the north, farmland gives way to extensive areas of forest, partly used for commercial logging. Fishing occurs in Atlantic waters and in the Great Lakes.

THE URBAN/RURAL POPULATION DIVIDE

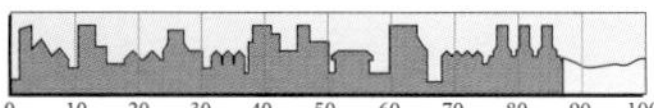

urban 87%
rural 13%
0 10 20 30 40 50 60 70 80 90 100

POPULATION DENSITY	TOTAL LAND AREA
64 people per sq mile (25 people per sq km)	214,230 sq miles (555,000 sq km)

Sault Ste.Marie
Québec
Québec
New Brunswick
Gaspé
Lake Huron
Ontario
Montréal
OTTAWA
Toronto
Lake Ontario
Lake Erie
UNITED STATES OF AMERICA
Land use and agricultural distribution
cattle
fish
cereals
fruit
maple syrup
timber
tobacco
capital cities
major towns
pasture
cropland
forest

Pumpkins are just one of the crops grown in the Niagara "fruit belt." The mild climate, moderated by the lakes, allows the cultivation of a wide range of fruit and vegetables, including cherries, apples, peaches, grapes, and asparagus. Fruit and vegetable growing is confined to southern Canada, due to the colder climate and short growing season of the northern regions.

Laurentian Mountains
Monts Notre-Dame
Péninsule de Gaspé
Monts Chic-Chocs
St. Lawrence
Honguedo Passage
Chaleur Bay
NEW BRUNSWICK
UNITED STATES OF AMERICA
Québec
Montréal
Lac St-Jean
Réservoir Manic Trois
Réservoir Manic Deux
Réservoir Outardes Quatre
Réservoir Pipmuacan
Réservoir Gouin
Sept-Îles
Baie-Comeau
Rimouski
Chicoutimi
Jonquière
Trois-Rivières
Sherbrooke
Tadoussac
Gaspé
Percé
Mont Jacques-Cartier 1268m
Mont Megantic 1105m
Mont Hereford 841m

In contrast to the boreal forest which spans northern Canada, the Gaspé Peninsula (Peninsule de Gaspé) is covered with a band of mixed coniferous-deciduous woodland, including sugar and red maple, cedar, and eastern hemlock.

THE LANDSCAPE

THE HEART OF SOUTHEASTERN CANADA is the lowland area surrounding the St. Lawrence River, the principal outlet for the Great Lakes. The lowlands are bordered to the east by an extension of the Appalachian mountain chain and to the north by the Canadian Shield. The Champlain Sea, which flooded the area during the last glacial period, deposited clay over much of the area.

The wooded Gaspé Peninsula (Peninsule de Gaspé) includes the Notre Dame and Shickshock mountains (Monts Chic-Chocs). These are a northerly outcrop of the Appalachian mountain chain.

SCALE 1:3,250,000
(projection: Lambert Conformal Conic)

Km 0 5 10 20 30 40 50 60 70 80
Miles 0 5 10 20 30 40 50 60 70 80

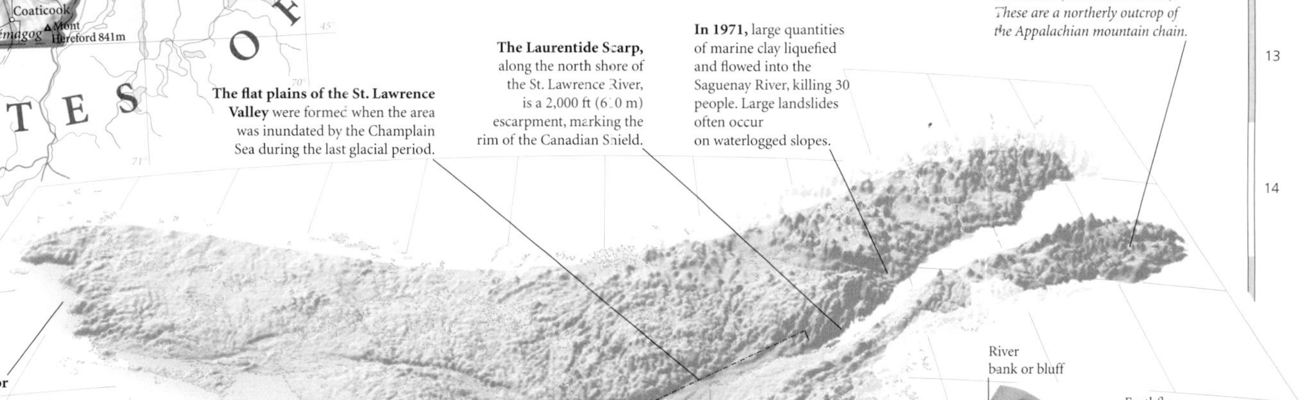

Lake Superior
Lake Huron
Lake Erie
Lake Ontario

The flat plains of the St. Lawrence Valley were formed when the area was inundated by the Champlain Sea during the last glacial period.

The Laurentide Scarp, along the north shore of the St. Lawrence River, is a 2,000 ft (610 m) escarpment, marking the rim of the Canadian Shield.

In 1971, large quantities of marine clay liquefied and flowed into the Saguenay River, killing 30 people. Large landslides often occur on waterlogged slopes.

The Great Lakes moderate the climate of the area surrounding the St. Lawrence River. Their water, which cools more slowly than the land, acts as a reservoir for warmth, extending the growing season into the early autumn.

Mount Royal, around which the city of Montréal has developed, is the result of an igneous intrusion which occurred between 135 and 65 million years ago.

Point Pelee *is a world-famous site for bird migration. Over 250 species of bird have been sighted on the sandspit which forms the southern tip of the Canadian mainland.*

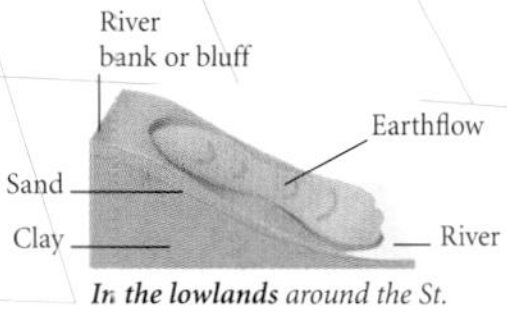

River bank or bluff
Earthflow
Sand
Clay
River

In the lowlands *around the St. Lawrence, earthflows have developed along gentle river banks where sand overlies clay, making the surface layers very unstable. When the slope's natural equilibrium is disturbed, an earthflow can occur.*

THE UNITED STATES OF AMERICA

COTERMINOUS USA (FOR ALASKA AND HAWAII SEE PAGES 38–39)

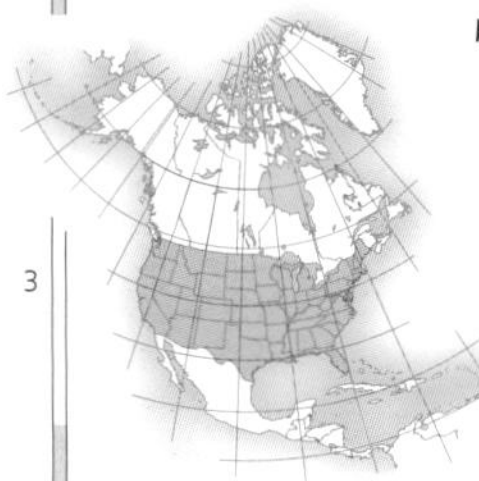

THE US'S PROGRESSION FROM FRONTIER TERRITORY to economic and political superpower has taken less than 200 years. The 48 coterminous states, along with the outlying states of Alaska and Hawaii, are part of a federal union, held together by the guiding principles of the US Constitution, which embodies the ideals of democracy and liberty for all. Abundant fertile land and a rich resource-base fueled and sustained US economic development. With the spread of agriculture and the growth of trade and industry came the need for a larger workforce, which was supplied by millions of immigrants, many seeking an escape from poverty and political or religious persecution. Immigration continues today, particularly from Central America and Asia.

Washington D.C. was established as the nation's capital in 1790. It is home to the seat of national government, on Capitol Hill, as well as the President's official residence, the White House.

Mount Rainier is a dormant volcano in the Cascade Range, Washington. This 14,090 ft (4392 m) peak is flanked by the most extensive glacier outside Alaska.

SCALE 1: 12,700,000
(projection: Lambert Azimuthal Equal Area)

CANADA
UNITED STATES
MEXICO
PACIFIC OCEAN
GULF
WASHINGTON
OREGON
CALIFORNIA
NEVADA
IDAHO
MONTANA
WYOMING
UTAH
ARIZONA
COLORADO
NEW MEXICO
NORTH DAKOTA
SOUTH DAKOTA
NEBRASKA
KANSAS
OKLAHOMA
TEXAS
ROCKY MOUNTAINS
GREAT PLAINS
Seattle
Tacoma
Spokane
Portland
Salem
Eugene
Boise
Sacramento
San Francisco
San Jose
Los Angeles
San Diego
Las Vegas
Reno
Salt Lake City
Phoenix
Tucson
Albuquerque
Santa Fe
Denver
Colorado Springs
Cheyenne
Bismarck
Pierre
Lincoln
Omaha
Topeka
Wichita
Oklahoma City
Tulsa
Dallas
Fort Worth
Austin
Houston
San Antonio
El Paso
Lubbock
Amarillo
Corpus Christi
Laredo
Brownsville
Great Salt Lake
Colorado Plateau
Mount Whitney 4418m
Mount Rainier 4392m
Grand Canyon
Great Basin
Mojave Desert
Sonoran Desert
Snake River Plain

TRANSPORTATION & INDUSTRY

THE US HAS BEEN THE INDUSTRIAL POWERHOUSE of the world since the Second World War, pioneering mass-production and the consumer lifestyle. Initially, heavy engineering and manufacturing in the northeast led the economy. Today, heavy industry has declined and the economy is driven by service and financial industries, with the most important being defense, hi-tech, and electronics.

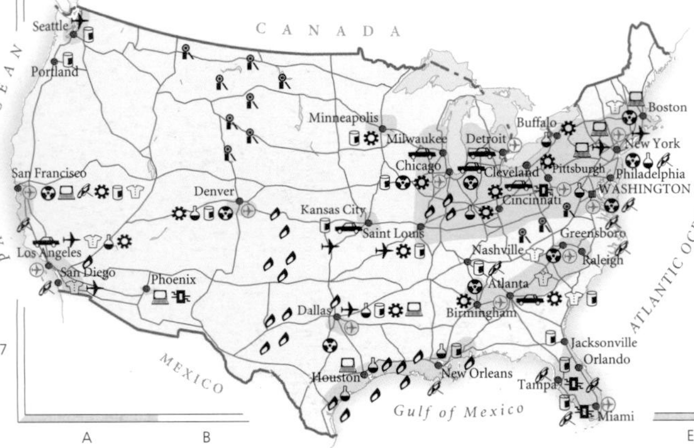

CANADA
PACIFIC OCEAN
ATLANTIC OCEAN
MEXICO
Gulf of Mexico
Seattle
Portland
San Francisco
Los Angeles
San Diego
Phoenix
Denver
Minneapolis
Milwaukee
Chicago
Detroit
Cleveland
Cincinnati
Pittsburgh
Buffalo
Boston
New York
Philadelphia
WASHINGTON DC
Kansas City
Saint Louis
Nashville
Greensboro
Raleigh
Atlanta
Birmingham
Dallas
Houston
New Orleans
Jacksonville
Orlando
Tampa
Miami

TRANSPORTATION NETWORK

3,875,040 miles (6,240,000 km)	52,388 miles (84,361 km)
148,308 miles (235,238 km)	25,467 miles (41,009 km)

Transportation in the US is dominated by the car which, with the extensive Interstate Highway system, allows great personal mobility. Today, internal air flights between major cities provide the most rapid cross-country travel.

Major industry and infrastructure

- aerospace
- car manufacture
- chemicals
- coal
- electronics
- engineering
- food processing
- hi-tech industry
- oil & gas
- research & development
- textiles
- tourism
- capital cities
- major towns
- international airports
- major roads
- major industrial areas

THE LANDSCAPE

THE HIGH, RUGGED MOUNTAIN RANGES of the west are about 80 million years old, geologically young compared to the old, eroded, Appalachian mountain chain, which dates from when North America and Europe were joined together as part of the supercontinent Pangaea, 400 million years ago. In contrast, the Great Plains and Mississippi Basin have a low relief and fertile soils.

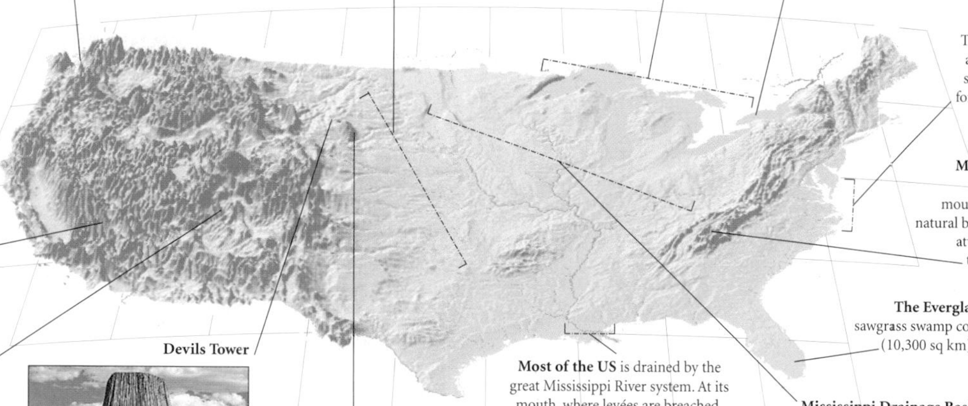

Mount Rainier
Great Plains
The Great Lakes
Niagara Falls

Barrier beaches, bars, and spits are typical of the Atlantic coast. These sand formations around Cape Hatteras stretch along the coast for 200 miles (320 km).

The Great Smoky Mountains, part of the ancient Appalachian mountain chain, formed a natural barrier to early settlers attempting to penetrate the country's interior.

The Everglades are a vast area of sawgrass swamp covering 4,000 sq miles (10,300 sq km) of southern Florida.

Death Valley, California, 282 ft (86 m) below sea level, is the lowest point in the western hemisphere, and one of the hottest places on Earth. Temperatures of 190° F (88° C) have been recorded here.

Monument Valley's striking sandstone spires and pillars *(buttes)* have been formed by the action of wind, water, heat and cold.

Devils Tower

The deep gullies of South Dakota's badlands are created by periodic, torrential rainfall, which erodes the soft soils and rocks. Their form has been greatly affected by changes in land use.

Most of the US is drained by the great Mississippi River system. At its mouth, where levées are breached, floodwaters are carried to the swamps through a series of channels. This region is known as the bayou.

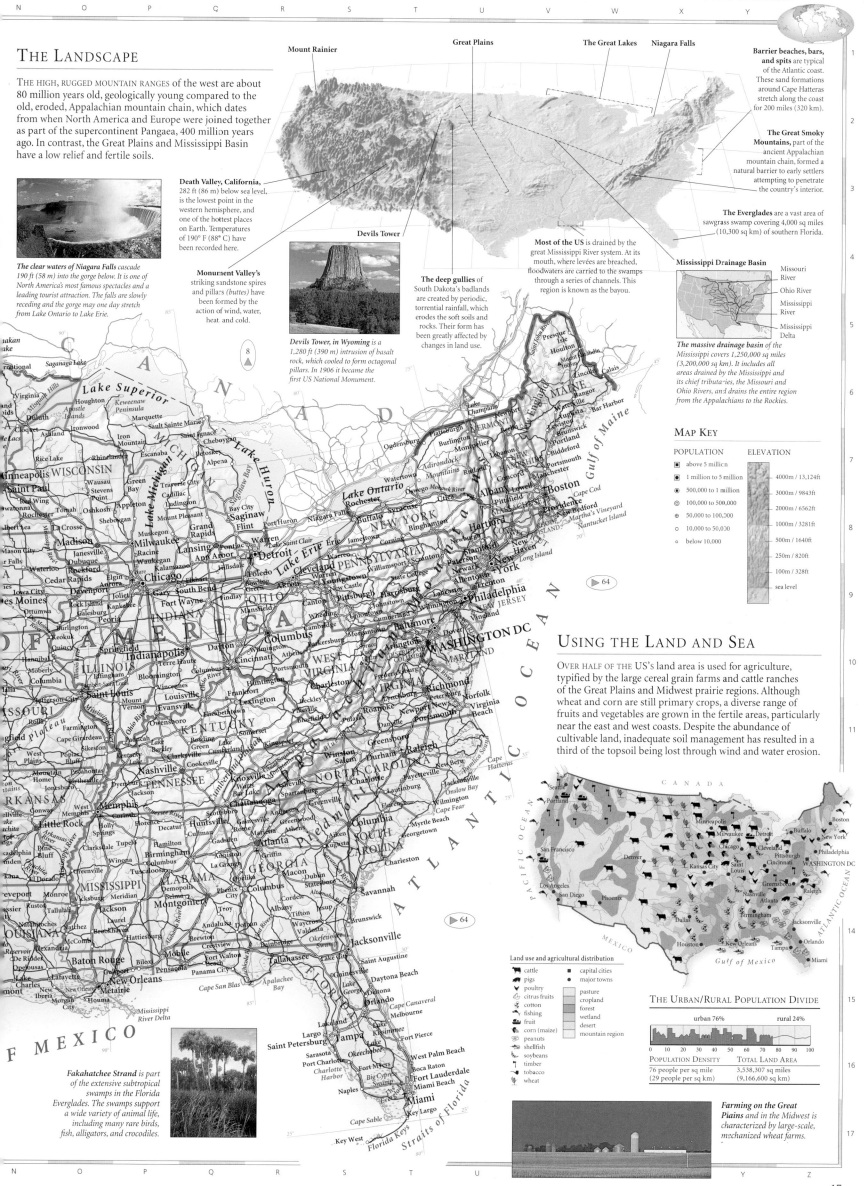

The clear waters of Niagara Falls cascade 190 ft (58 m) into the gorge below. It is one of North America's most famous spectacles and a leading tourist attraction. The falls are slowly receding and the gorge may one day stretch from Lake Ontario to Lake Erie.

***Devils Tower, in Wyoming** is a 1,280 ft (390 m) intrusion of basalt rock, which cooled to form octagonal pillars. In 1906 it became the first US National Monument.*

Mississippi Drainage Basin

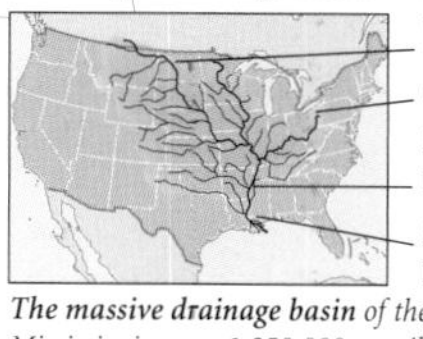

Missouri River
Ohio River
Mississippi River
Mississippi Delta

***The massive drainage basin** of the Mississippi covers 1,250,000 sq miles (3,200,000 sq km). It includes all areas drained by the Mississippi and its chief tributaries, the Missouri and Ohio Rivers, and drains the entire region from the Appalachians to the Rockies.*

CANADA
Lake Superior
Lake Michigan
Lake Huron
Lake Ontario
Lake Erie
UNITED STATES OF AMERICA
ATLANTIC OCEAN
GULF OF MEXICO
Gulf of Maine
Straits of Florida
WISCONSIN
MICHIGAN
ILLINOIS
INDIANA
OHIO
PENNSYLVANIA
NEW YORK
MAINE
VERMONT
NEW HAMPSHIRE
NEW JERSEY
MARYLAND
WEST VIRGINIA
VIRGINIA
KENTUCKY
TENNESSEE
NORTH CAROLINA
SOUTH CAROLINA
GEORGIA
ALABAMA
MISSISSIPPI
FLORIDA
WASHINGTON DC
Chicago
Detroit
Milwaukee
Cleveland
Columbus
Indianapolis
Saint Louis
Nashville
Memphis
Atlanta
Philadelphia
New York
Boston
Baltimore
Richmond
Pittsburgh
Charlotte
Jacksonville
Tampa
Orlando
Miami
New Orleans
Baton Rouge
Birmingham
Montgomery
Tallahassee
Savannah
Charleston
Raleigh
Cincinnati
Louisville
Buffalo
Albany
Hartford

8

64

64

MAP KEY

POPULATION	ELEVATION
above 5 million	4000m / 13,124ft
1 million to 5 million	3000m / 9843ft
500,000 to 1 million	2000m / 6562ft
100,000 to 500,000	1000m / 3281ft
50,000 to 100,000	500m / 1640ft
10,000 to 50,000	250m / 820ft
below 10,000	100m / 328ft
	sea level

USING THE LAND AND SEA

OVER HALF OF THE US's land area is used for agriculture, typified by the large cereal grain farms and cattle ranches of the Great Plains and Midwest prairie regions. Although wheat and corn are still primary crops, a diverse range of fruits and vegetables are grown in the fertile areas, particularly near the east and west coasts. Despite the abundance of cultivable land, inadequate soil management has resulted in a third of the topsoil being lost through wind and water erosion.

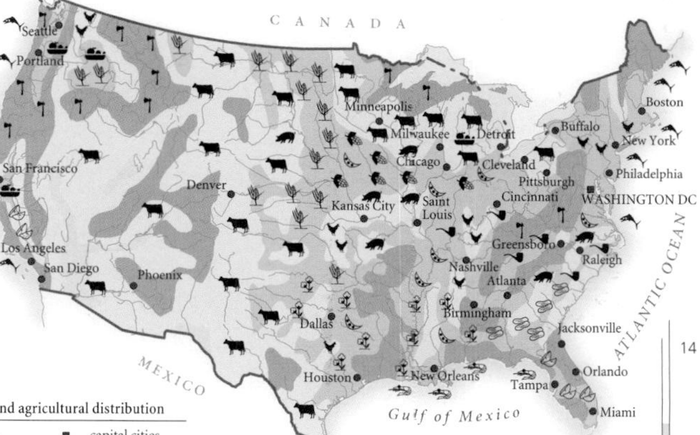

CANADA
PACIFIC OCEAN
ATLANTIC OCEAN
MEXICO
Gulf of Mexico
Seattle
Portland
San Francisco
Los Angeles
San Diego
Phoenix
Denver
Minneapolis
Milwaukee
Detroit
Chicago
Cleveland
Pittsburgh
Cincinnati
Kansas City
Saint Louis
Buffalo
Boston
New York
Philadelphia
WASHINGTON DC
Greensboro
Raleigh
Nashville
Atlanta
Birmingham
Dallas
Houston
New Orleans
Jacksonville
Orlando
Tampa
Miami

Land use and agricultural distribution

cattle	capital cities
pigs	major towns
poultry	pasture
citrus fruits	cropland
cotton	forest
fishing	wetland
fruit	desert
corn (maize)	mountain region
peanuts	
shellfish	
soybeans	
timber	
tobacco	
wheat	

THE URBAN/RURAL POPULATION DIVIDE

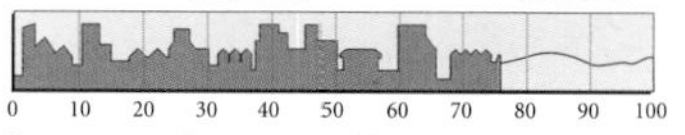

urban 76%
rural 24%
0
10
20
30
40
50
60
70
80
90
100

POPULATION DENSITY	TOTAL LAND AREA
76 people per sq mile (29 people per sq km)	3,538,307 sq miles (9,166,600 sq km)

***Fakahatchee Strand** is part of the extensive subtropical swamps in the Florida Everglades. The swamps support a wide variety of animal life, including many rare birds, fish, alligators, and crocodiles.*

***Farming on the Great Plains** and in the Midwest is characterized by large-scale, mechanized wheat farms.*

USA: Northeastern States

Connecticut, Maine, Massachusetts, New Hampshire, New Jersey, New York, Pennsylvania, Rhode Island, Vermont

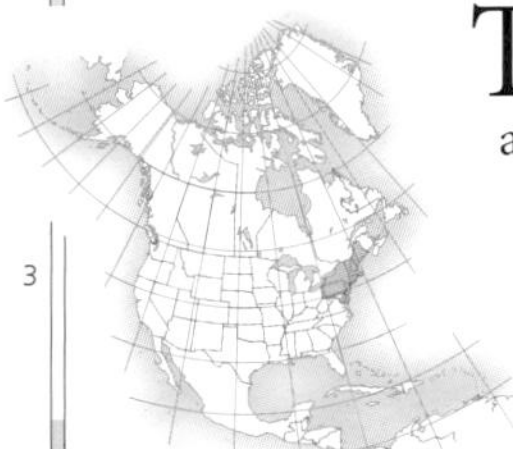

The indented coast and vast woodlands of the northeastern states were the original core area for European expansion. The rustic character of New England prevails after nearly four centuries, while the great cities of the Atlantic seaboard have formed an almost continuous urban region. Over 20 million immigrants entered New York from 1855 to 1924 and the northeast became the industrial center of the US. After the decline of mining and heavy manufacturing, economic dynamism has been restored with the growth of hi-tech and service industries.

Chelsea in Vermont, surrounded by trees in their fall foliage. Tourism and agriculture dominate the economy of this self-consciously rural state, where no town exceeds 30,000 people.

Map Key

POPULATION

- above 5 million
- 1 million to 5 million
- 500,000 to 1 million
- 100,000 to 500,000
- 50,000 to 100,000
- 10,000 to 50,000
- below 10,000

ELEVATION

- 1000m / 3281ft
- 500m / 1640ft
- 250m / 820ft
- 100m / 328ft
- sea level

Transportation & Industry

The principal seaboard cities grew up on trade and manufacturing. They are now global centers of commerce and corporate administration, dominating the regional economy. Research and development facilities support an expanding electronics and communications sector throughout the region. Pharmaceutical and chemical industries are important in New Jersey and Pennsylvania.

Transportation Network

340,090 miles (544,144 km)	4813 miles 7700 km
12,872 miles (20,592 km)	2108 miles (3389 km)

New York's commercial success is tied historically to its transportation connections. The Erie Canal, completed in 1825, opened up the Great Lakes and the interior to New York's markets and carried a stream of immigrants into the Midwest.

CANADA
Maine
Portland
Vermont
New Hampshire
Syracuse
Albany
Rochester
Buffalo
New York
Massachusetts
Boston
Connecticut
Hartford
Providence
Rhode Island
Pennsylvania
Pittsburgh
New York
Harrisburg
Philadelphia
New Jersey
ATLANTIC OCEAN
Ohio
West Virginia
Maryland
Delaware

Major industry and infrastructure

- chemicals
- coal
- defense
- electronics
- engineering
- finance
- hi-tech industry
- iron & steel
- pharmaceuticals
- printing & publishing
- research & development
- textiles
- timber processing
- major towns
- international airports
- major roads
- major industrial area

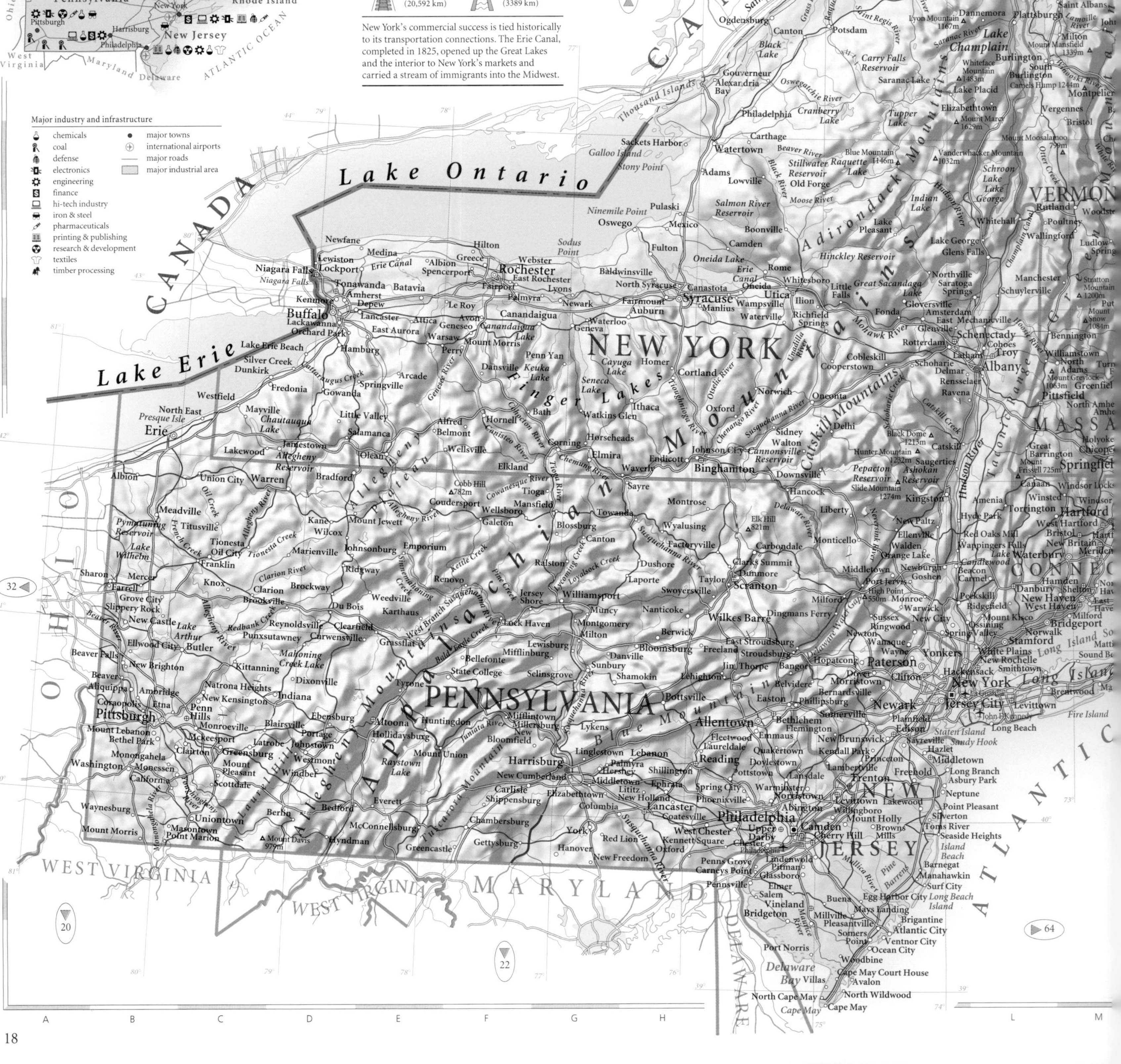
CANADA
Saint Lawrence River
Thousand Islands
Lake Ontario
Lake Erie
NEW YORK
PENNSYLVANIA
NEW JERSEY
VERMONT
MASSA
CONNEC
OHIO
WEST VIRGINIA
MARYLAND
DELAWARE
ATLANTIC
Adirondack Mountains
Catskill Mountains
Finger Lakes
Appalachian Mountains
Allegheny Plateau
Allegheny Mountains
Blue Mountain
Lake Champlain
Long Island
Delaware Bay
Ogdensburg
Massena
Plattsburgh
Burlington
Watertown
Oswego
Rochester
Syracuse
Utica
Schenectady
Albany
Buffalo
Niagara Falls
Ithaca
Binghamton
Erie
Scranton
Wilkes Barre
Williamsport
Allentown
Bethlehem
Reading
Harrisburg
Lancaster
York
Gettysburg
Altoona
State College
Johnstown
Pittsburgh
Philadelphia
Camden
Trenton
Newark
Paterson
Jersey City
New York
Yonkers
Stamford
Bridgeport
Atlantic City
Cape May
Vineland
Mount Marcy 1629m
Mount Davis 979m
14
32
20
22
64

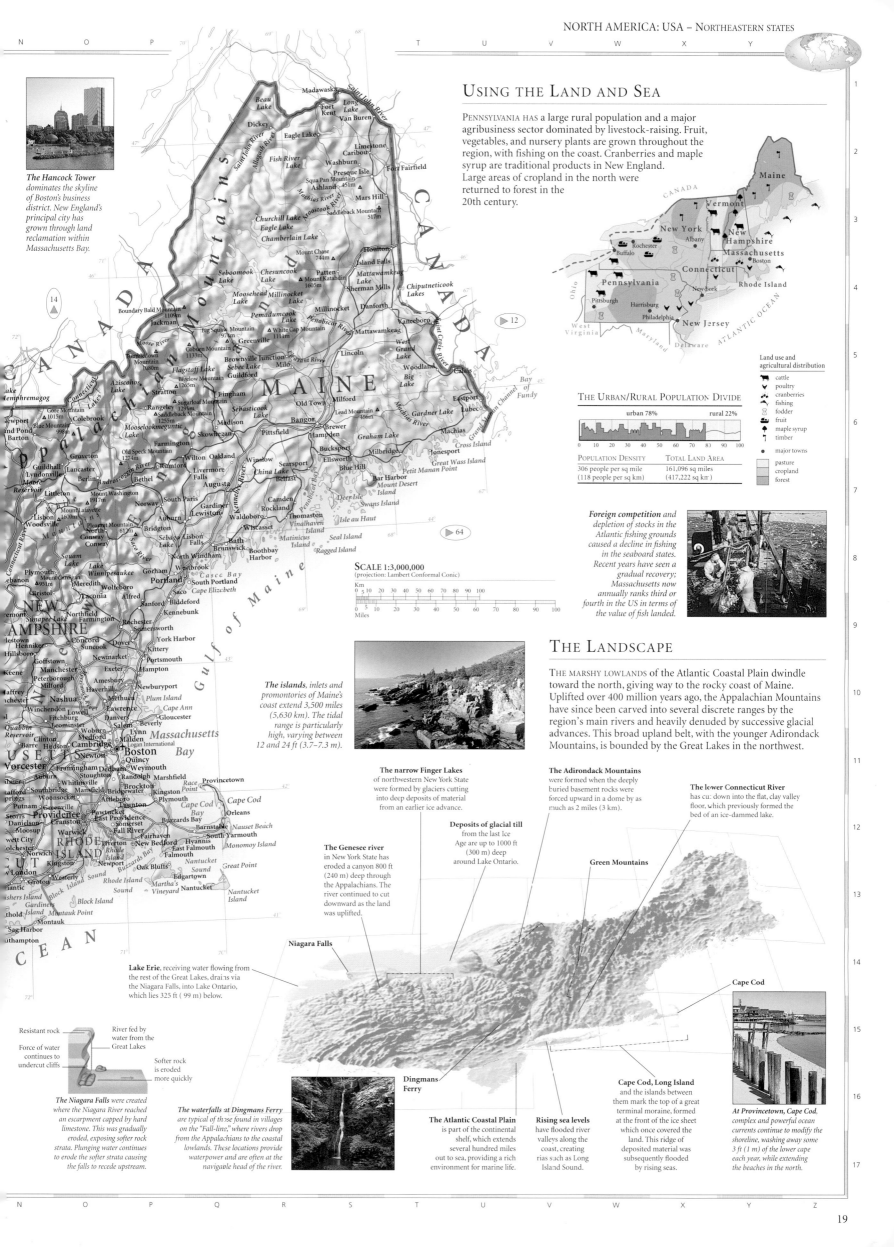

The Hancock Tower dominates the skyline of Boston's business district. New England's principal city has grown through land reclamation within Massachusetts Bay.

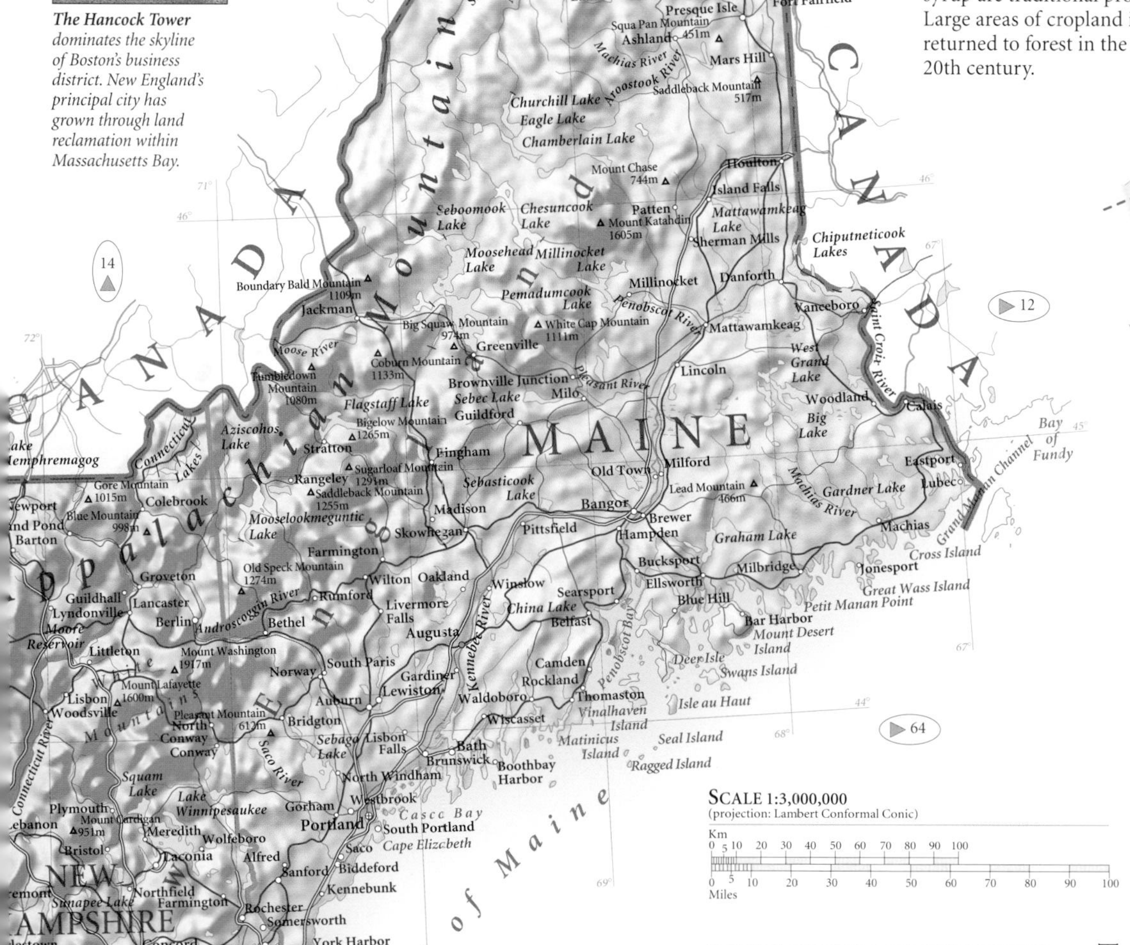

CANADA
MAINE
NEW HAMPSHIRE
Massachusetts
Massachusetts Bay
RHODE ISLAND
Appalachian Mountains
Gulf of Maine
Bay of Fundy
Boston
Portland
Bangor
Augusta
Providence
Cape Cod
Nantucket
Martha's Vineyard
Mount Washington 1917m
Mount Katahdin 1605m
Moosehead Lake
Penobscot Bay
Casco Bay
Cape Cod Bay
Block Island
Rhode Island Sound
Nantucket Sound

14
12
64

SCALE 1:3,000,000
(projection: Lambert Conformal Conic)
Km 0 5 10 20 30 40 50 60 70 80 90 100
Miles 0 5 10 20 30 40 50 60 70 80 90 100

Using the Land and Sea

PENNSYLVANIA HAS a large rural population and a major agribusiness sector dominated by livestock-raising. Fruit, vegetables, and nursery plants are grown throughout the region, with fishing on the coast. Cranberries and maple syrup are traditional products in New England. Large areas of cropland in the north were returned to forest in the 20th century.

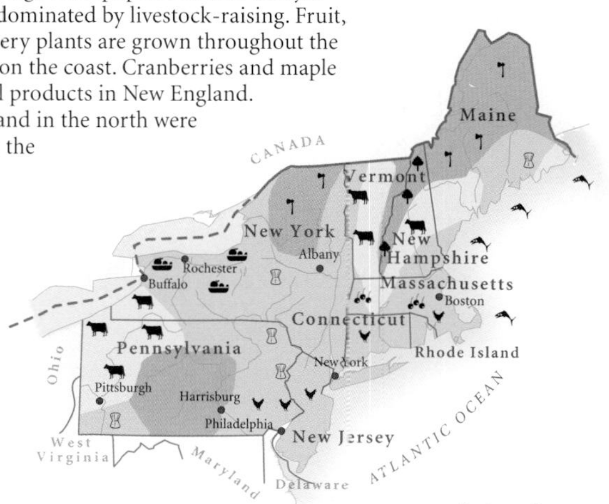

CANADA
Maine
Vermont
New York
New Hampshire
Massachusetts
Connecticut
Rhode Island
Pennsylvania
New Jersey
Ohio
West Virginia
Maryland
Delaware
ATLANTIC OCEAN
Rochester
Buffalo
Albany
Boston
New York
Pittsburgh
Harrisburg
Philadelphia
Land use and agricultural distribution
cattle
poultry
cranberries
fishing
fodder
fruit
maple syrup
timber
major towns
pasture
cropland
forest

The Urban/Rural Population Divide

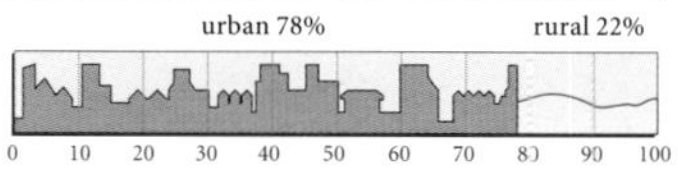

urban 78%
rural 22%
0 10 20 30 40 50 60 70 80 90 100

Population Density	Total Land Area
306 people per sq mile	161,096 sq miles
(118 people per sq km)	(417,222 sq km)

Foreign competition and depletion of stocks in the Atlantic fishing grounds caused a decline in fishing in the seaboard states. Recent years have seen a gradual recovery; Massachusetts now annually ranks third or fourth in the US in terms of the value of fish landed.

The Landscape

THE MARSHY LOWLANDS of the Atlantic Coastal Plain dwindle toward the north, giving way to the rocky coast of Maine. Uplifted over 400 million years ago, the Appalachian Mountains have since been carved into several discrete ranges by the region's main rivers and heavily denuded by successive glacial advances. This broad upland belt, with the younger Adirondack Mountains, is bounded by the Great Lakes in the northwest.

The islands, inlets and promontories of Maine's coast extend 3,500 miles (5,630 km). The tidal range is particularly high, varying between 12 and 24 ft (3.7–7.3 m).

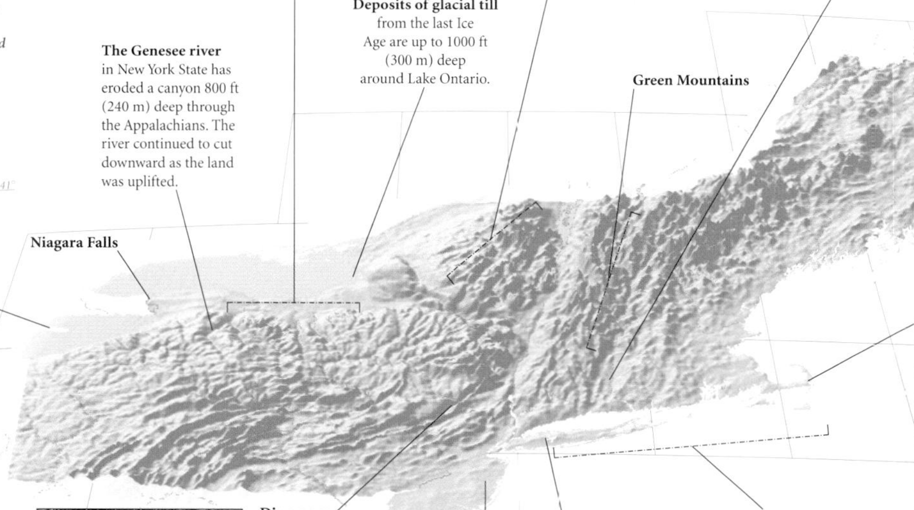

Niagara Falls
Green Mountains
Cape Cod
Dingmans Ferry

The narrow Finger Lakes of northwestern New York State were formed by glaciers cutting into deep deposits of material from an earlier ice advance.

The Adirondack Mountains were formed when the deeply buried basement rocks were forced upward in a dome by as much as 2 miles (3 km).

The lower Connecticut River has cut down into the flat, clay valley floor, which previously formed the bed of an ice-dammed lake.

Deposits of glacial till from the last Ice Age are up to 1000 ft (300 m) deep around Lake Ontario.

The Genesee river in New York State has eroded a canyon 800 ft (240 m) deep through the Appalachians. The river continued to cut downward as the land was uplifted.

Lake Erie, receiving water flowing from the rest of the Great Lakes, drains via the Niagara Falls, into Lake Ontario, which lies 325 ft (99 m) below.

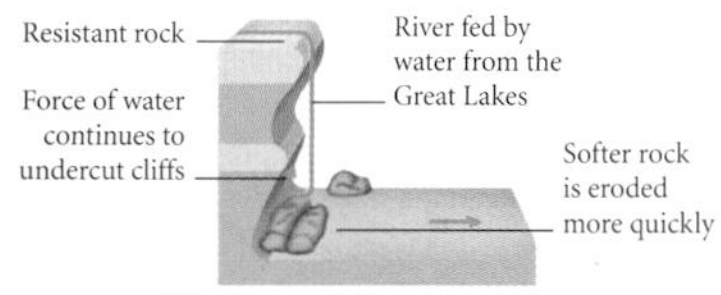

Resistant rock
River fed by water from the Great Lakes
Force of water continues to undercut cliffs
Softer rock is eroded more quickly

The Niagara Falls were created where the Niagara River reached an escarpment capped by hard limestone. This was gradually eroded, exposing softer rock strata. Plunging water continues to erode the softer strata causing the falls to recede upstream.

The waterfalls at Dingmans Ferry are typical of those found in villages on the "Fall-line," where rivers drop from the Appalachians to the coastal lowlands. These locations provide waterpower and are often at the navigable head of the river.

The Atlantic Coastal Plain is part of the continental shelf, which extends several hundred miles out to sea, providing a rich environment for marine life.

Rising sea levels have flooded river valleys along the coast, creating rias such as Long Island Sound.

Cape Cod, Long Island and the islands between them mark the top of a great terminal moraine, formed at the front of the ice sheet which once covered the land. This ridge of deposited material was subsequently flooded by rising seas.

At Provincetown, Cape Cod, complex and powerful ocean currents continue to modify the shoreline, washing away some 3 ft (1 m) of the lower cape each year, while extending the beaches in the north.

USA: Mid-Eastern states

Delaware, District of Columbia, Kentucky, Maryland, North Carolina, South Carolina, Tennessee, Virginia, West Virginia

Key events in American history took place in this diverse region, which became the front line between the North and the South during the Civil War of the 1860s. Strong regional contrasts exist between the fertile coastal plains, the isolated upcountry of the Appalachian Mountains, and the cotton-growing areas of the Mississippi lowlands to the west. While coal mining, a traditional industry in the Appalachians, has declined in recent years leaving much rural poverty, service industries elsewhere have increased, especially in Washington DC, the nation's capital.

Map Key

POPULATION
- 500,000 to 1 million
- 100,000 to 500,000
- 50,000 to 100,000
- 10,000 to 50,000
- below 10,000

ELEVATION
- 6000m / 19,686ft
- 4000m / 13,124ft
- 3000m / 9843ft
- 2000m / 6562ft
- 1000m / 3281ft
- 500m / 1640ft
- 250m / 820ft
- 100m / 328ft
- sea level

SCALE 1:3,250,000
(projection: Lambert Conformal Conic)

Km 0 5 10 20 30 40 50 60 70 80
Miles 0 5 10 20 30 40 50 60 70 80

The Bluegrass region of Kentucky centers on the town of Lexington. This exceptionally fertile rolling plain is well known for its thoroughbred horse-breeding ranches.

INDIANA
ILLINOIS
MISSOURI
ARKANSAS
MISSISSIPPI
ALABAMA
KENTUCKY
TENNESSEE
Ohio River
Mississippi River
Green River
Cumberland River
Tennessee River
Duck River
Kentucky Lake
Lake Barkley
Reelfoot Lake
Louisville
Frankfort
Lexington
Covington
Owensboro
Henderson
Paducah
Bowling Green
Elizabethtown
Hopkinsville
Clarksville
Nashville
Murfreesboro
Jackson
Memphis
Chattanooga
Cookeville
Columbia
Dyersburg
Union City
Springfield
Gallatin
Franklin
Tullahoma
Shelbyville
Lawrenceburg
Glasgow
Danville
Richmond
30
26
22

Transportation & Industry

In the urbanized northeast, manufacturing remains important, alongside a burgeoning service sector. North Carolina is a major center for industrial research and development. Traditional industries include Tennessee whiskey and textiles in South Carolina. The decline of open-cast coal mining in the Appalachians has been hastened by environmental controls, although adventure-tourism is a flourishing new industry.

Major industry and infrastructure
- adventure-tourism
- car manufacture
- coal
- electronics
- engineering
- finance
- food processing
- hi-tech industry
- mining
- research & development
- textiles
- capital cities
- major towns
- international airports
- major roads
- major industrial areas

Pennsylvania
Ohio
Indiana
Illinois
Missouri
Arkansas
Mississippi
Alabama
Georgia
Maryland
Baltimore
WASHINGTON DC
Delaware
Louisville
Charleston
W.Virginia
Virginia
Richmond
Kentucky
Nashville
Memphis
Tennessee
North Carolina
Raleigh
South Carolina
Columbia
ATLANTIC OCEAN

Transportation Network

452,218 miles (723,548 km)	5,737 miles (8,267 km)
18,336 miles (29,503 km)	4,404 miles (7,081 km)

Tennessee's rivers are part of an important inland bulk-transportation network. Memphis connects with New Orleans in the south, and with cities as distant as Minneapolis, Sioux City, Chicago, and Pittsburgh, via the Mississippi and its tributaries.

The Landscape

The eastern tributaries of the Mississippi drain the interior lowlands. The Cumberland Plateau and the parallel ranges of the Appalachians have been successively uplifted and eroded over time, with the eastern side reduced to a series of foothills known as the Piedmont. The broad coastal plain gradually falls away into salt marshes, lagoons, and offshore bars, broken by flooded estuaries along the shores of the Atlantic.

Natural Bridge in eastern Kentucky is an arch 78 ft (26 m) long and 65 ft (20 m) high. It has been shaped from resistant sandstone by gradual weathering processes, which removed the softer rock lying underneath.

The Allegheny Mountains form the northwestern edge of the Appalachian mountain chain. Continuous folding has formed rich seams of bituminous coal.

Farmland on the eastern shores of Chesapeake Bay is sustained by artificial drainage. The area also provides refuge for a variety of waterfowl.

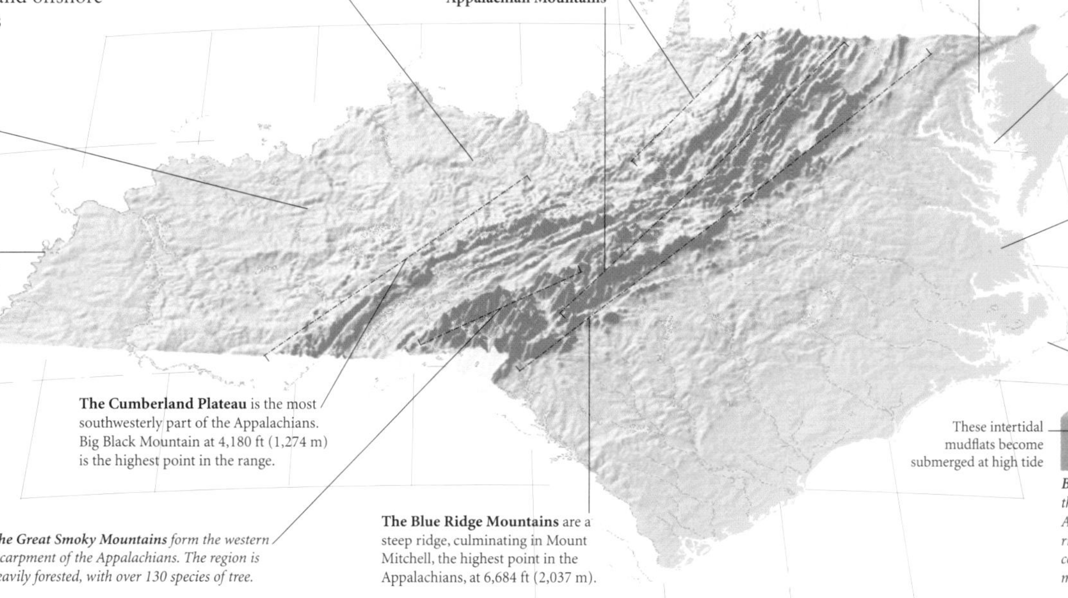

Appalachian Mountains

The many inlets of Chesapeake Bay are the flooded tributaries of the main river valley, which have been inundated by rising sea levels.

The Mammoth Cave is part of an extensive cave system in the limestone region of southwestern Kentucky. It stretches for over 300 miles (485 km) on five different levels and contains three rivers and three lakes.

Salt marshes such as Great Dismal Swamp, develop where the coast is sheltered. Vast areas of such marshland have been reclaimed for farmland and settlement.

The Mississippi River and its tributary the Ohio River form the western border of the region.

Cape Hatteras is the easternmost point of an offshore barrier island; a wave-deposited sandbar which has become permanent, establishing its own vegetation.

Barrier islands

The Cumberland Plateau is the most southwesterly part of the Appalachians. Big Black Mountain at 4,180 ft (1,274 m) is the highest point in the range.

These intertidal mudflats become submerged at high tide

Tidal inlet
Barrier island

Barrier islands are common along the coasts of North and South Carolina. As sea levels rise, wave action builds up ridges of sand and pebbles parallel to the coast, separated by lagoons or intertidal mudflats, which are flooded at high tide.

The Great Smoky Mountains form the western escarpment of the Appalachians. The region is heavily forested, with over 130 species of tree.

The Blue Ridge Mountains are a steep ridge, culminating in Mount Mitchell, the highest point in the Appalachians, at 6,684 ft (2,037 m).

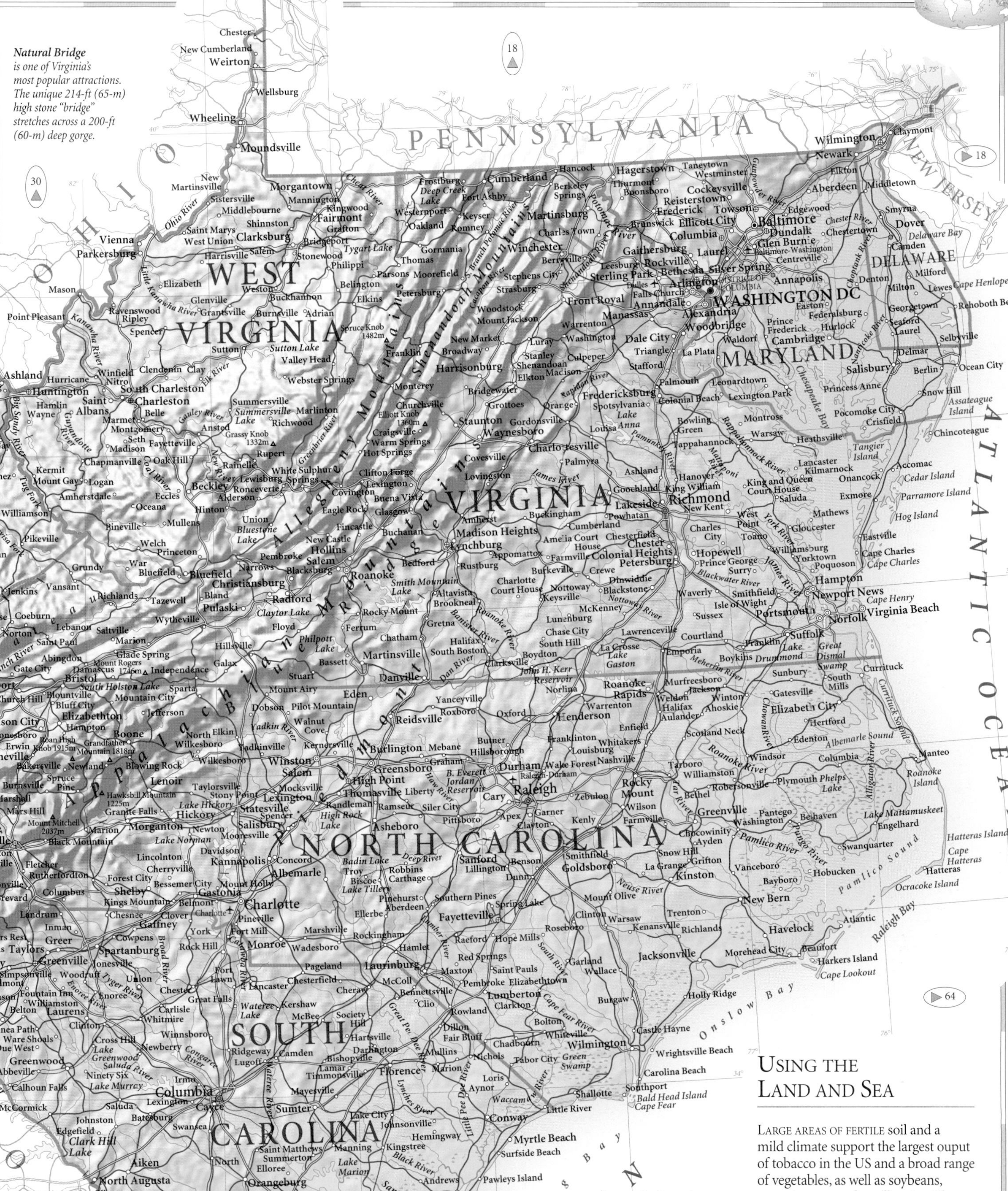
PENNSYLVANIA
OHIO
WEST VIRGINIA
VIRGINIA
MARYLAND
DELAWARE
NEW JERSEY
WASHINGTON DC
NORTH CAROLINA
SOUTH CAROLINA
GEORGIA
ATLANTIC OCEAN
Appalachian Mountains
Blue Ridge
Shenandoah Mountains
Allegheny Mountains
Piedmont
Cumberland Plateau
Great Smoky Mountains
Long Bay
Onslow Bay
Pamlico Sound
Albemarle Sound
Chesapeake Bay
Delaware Bay
Baltimore
Richmond
Raleigh
Charleston
Columbia
Norfolk
Virginia Beach
Charlotte
Greensboro
Winston-Salem
Roanoke
Wilmington
Knoxville
Annapolis
Dover

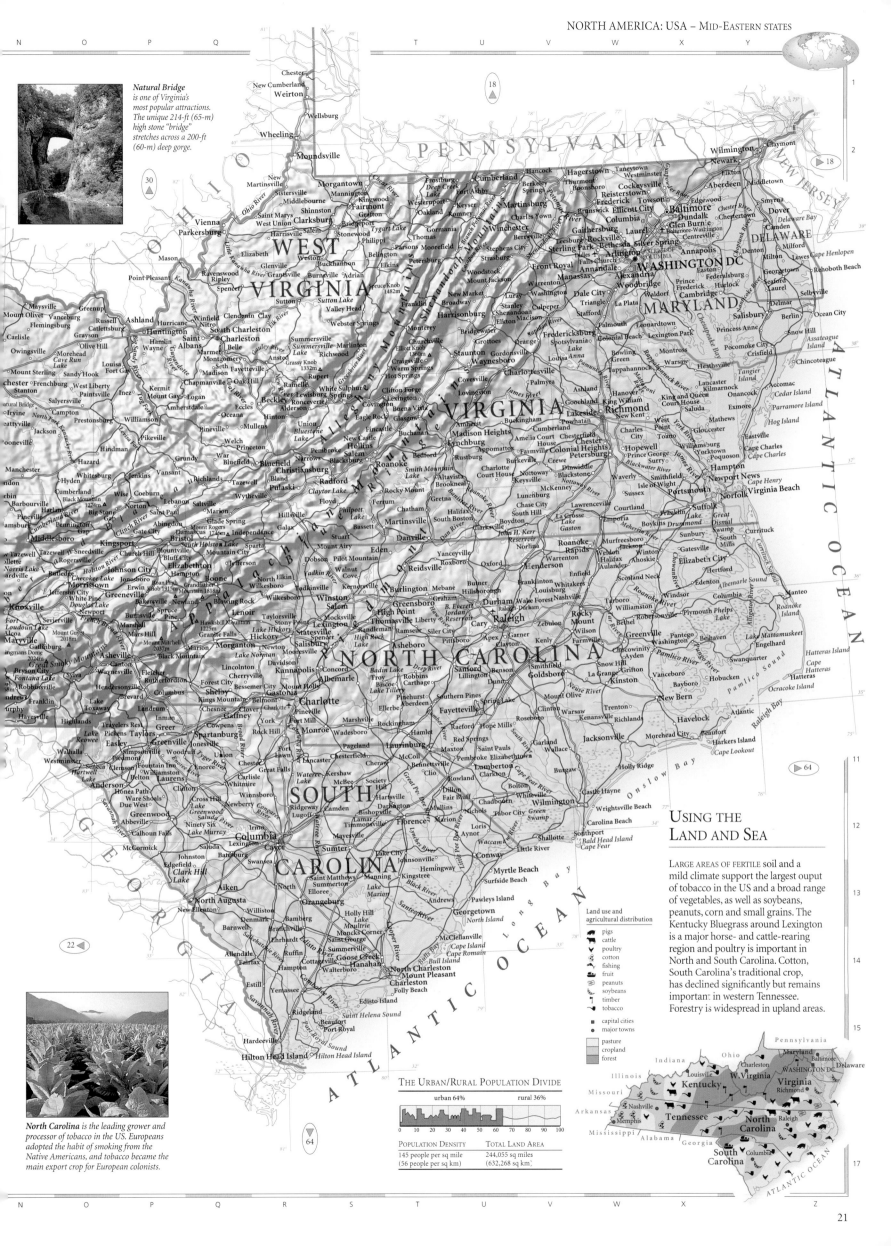

Natural Bridge *is one of Virginia's most popular attractions. The unique 214-ft (65-m) high stone "bridge" stretches across a 200-ft (60-m) deep gorge.*

Using the Land and Sea

Large areas of fertile soil and a mild climate support the largest ouput of tobacco in the US and a broad range of vegetables, as well as soybeans, peanuts, corn and small grains. The Kentucky Bluegrass around Lexington is a major horse- and cattle-rearing region and poultry is important in North and South Carolina. Cotton, South Carolina's traditional crop, has declined significantly but remains important in western Tennessee. Forestry is widespread in upland areas.

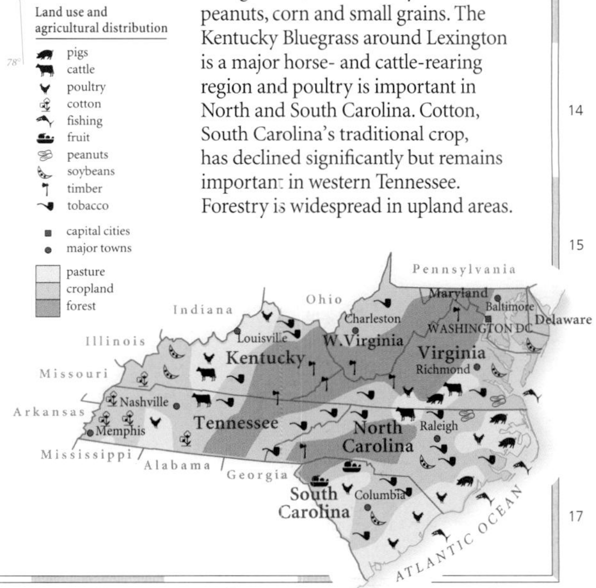
Land use and agricultural distribution
pigs
cattle
poultry
cotton
fishing
fruit
peanuts
soybeans
timber
tobacco
capital cities
major towns
pasture
cropland
forest
Pennsylvania
Ohio
Indiana
Illinois
Missouri
Arkansas
Mississippi
Alabama
Georgia
Kentucky
Tennessee
W. Virginia
Virginia
North Carolina
South Carolina
Maryland
Delaware
WASHINGTON DC
Louisville
Nashville
Memphis
Charleston
Richmond
Raleigh
Columbia
Baltimore
ATLANTIC OCEAN

The Urban/Rural Population Divide

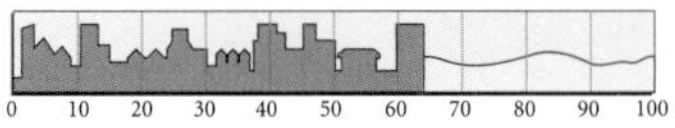
urban 64%
rural 36%
0
10
20
30
40
50
60
70
80
90
100

Population Density	Total Land Area
145 people per sq mile (56 people per sq km)	244,055 sq miles (632,268 sq km)

North Carolina *is the leading grower and processor of tobacco in the US. Europeans adopted the habit of smoking from the Native Americans, and tobacco became the main export crop for European colonists.*

A B C D E F G H I J

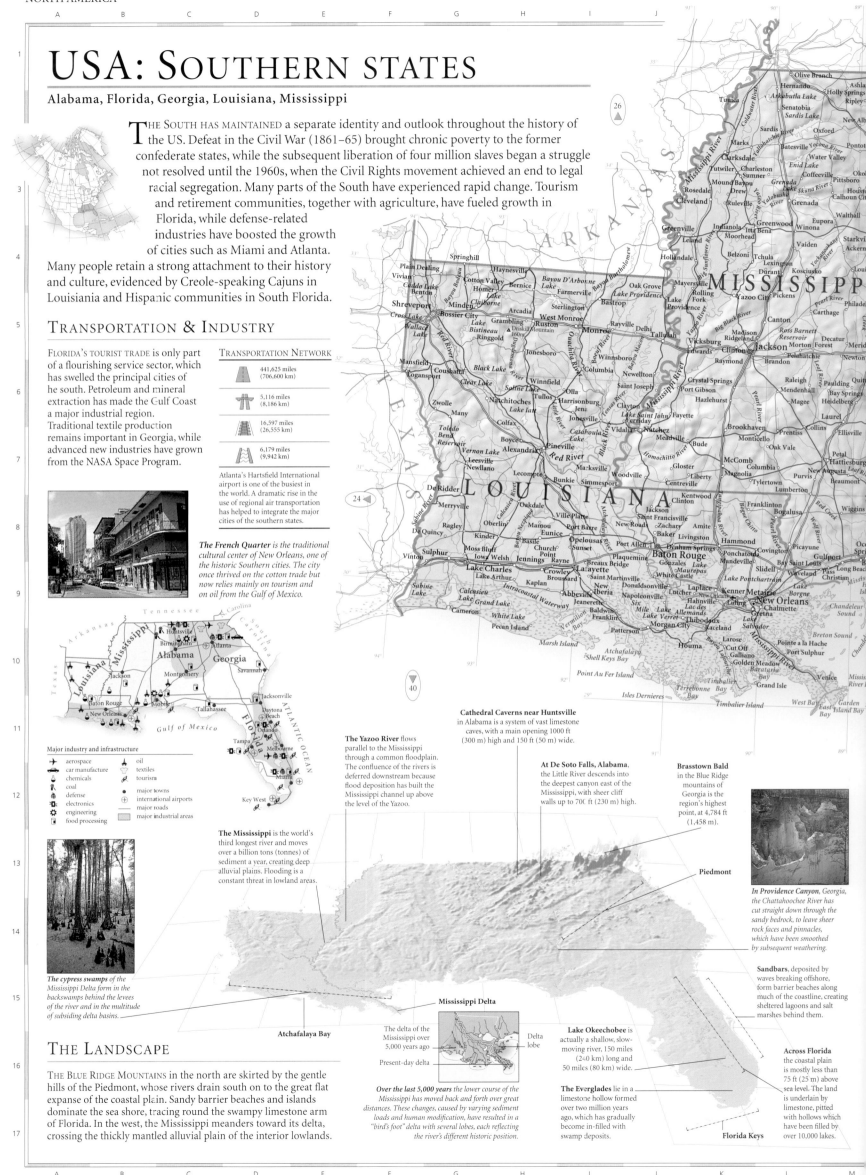

USA: Southern states

Alabama, Florida, Georgia, Louisiana, Mississippi

The South has maintained a separate identity and outlook throughout the history of the US. Defeat in the Civil War (1861–65) brought chronic poverty to the former confederate states, while the subsequent liberation of four million slaves began a struggle not resolved until the 1960s, when the Civil Rights movement achieved an end to legal racial segregation. Many parts of the South have experienced rapid change. Tourism and retirement communities, together with agriculture, have fueled growth in Florida, while defense-related industries have boosted the growth of cities such as Miami and Atlanta. Many people retain a strong attachment to their history and culture, evidenced by Creole-speaking Cajuns in Louisiana and Hispanic communities in South Florida.

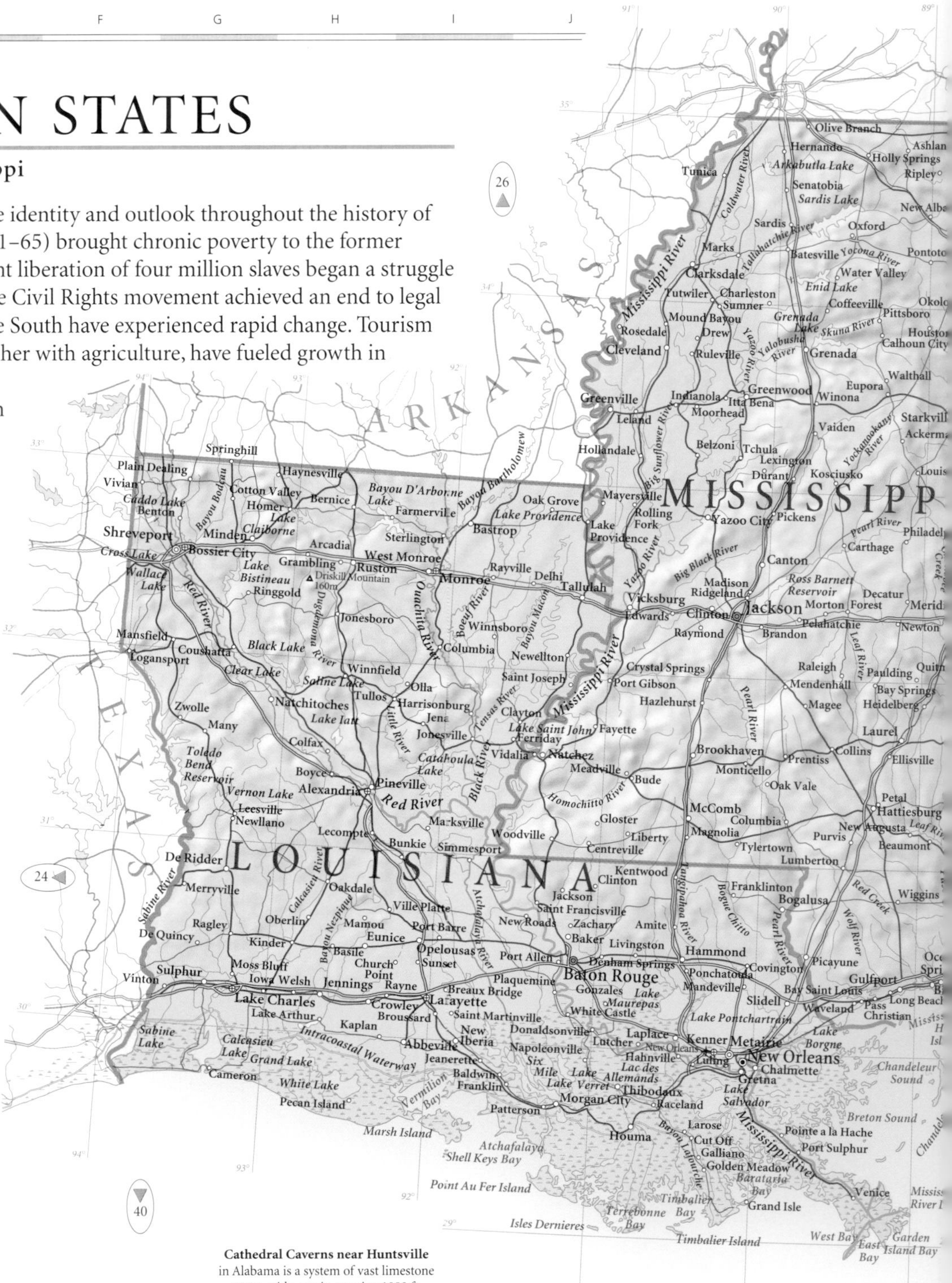

26
24
40
ARKANSAS
MISSISSIPPI
LOUISIANA
TEXAS
Mississippi River
Red River
Shreveport
Bossier City
Monroe
West Monroe
Ruston
Alexandria
Pineville
Natchitoches
Lake Charles
Lafayette
Baton Rouge
New Orleans
Metairie
Kenner
Houma
Jackson
Vicksburg
Natchez
Greenville
Hattiesburg
Gulfport
Biloxi
Meridian
Tunica
Hernando
Olive Branch
Oxford
Clarksdale
Greenwood
McComb
Brookhaven
Laurel
Lake Pontchartrain
Lake Borgne
Chandeleur Sound
Breton Sound
Barataria Bay
Terrebonne Bay
Timbalier Island
Isles Dernieres
Point Au Fer Island
Marsh Island
Atchafalaya Bay
Vermilion Bay
White Lake
Grand Lake
Calcasieu Lake
Sabine Lake
Intracoastal Waterway
Toledo Bend Reservoir
Driskill Mountain 160m
Ross Barnett Reservoir
Sardis Lake
Arkabutla Lake
Yazoo River
Pearl River
Venice
Grand Isle
Morgan City
Thibodaux
Opelousas
Crowley
Jennings
Sulphur
De Ridder
Leesville
Minden
Winnfield
Jonesboro
Bastrop
Lake Providence
Tallulah
Yazoo City
Canton
Columbia
Picayune
Slidell
Covington
Hammond
Bogalusa

Transportation & Industry

Florida's tourist trade is only part of a flourishing service sector, which has swelled the principal cities of he south. Petroleum and mineral extraction has made the Gulf Coast a major industrial region. Traditional textile production remains important in Georgia, while advanced new industries have grown from the NASA Space Program.

Transportation Network

	441,625 miles (706,600 km)
	5,116 miles (8,186 km)
	16,597 miles (26,555 km)
	6,179 miles (9,942 km)

Atlanta's Hartsfield International airport is one of the busiest in the world. A dramatic rise in the use of regional air transportation has helped to integrate the major cities of the southern states.

The French Quarter is the traditional cultural center of New Orleans, one of the historic Southern cities. The city once thrived on the cotton trade but now relies mainly on tourism and on oil from the Gulf of Mexico.

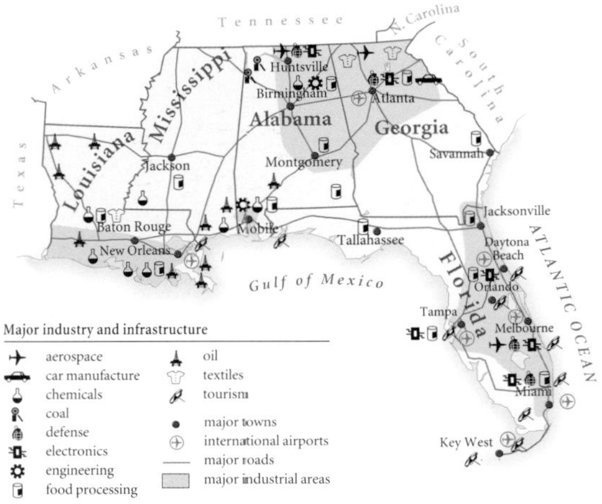

Tennessee
Arkansas
South Carolina
Texas
Mississippi
Louisiana
Alabama
Georgia
Florida
Huntsville
Birmingham
Atlanta
Jackson
Montgomery
Savannah
Baton Rouge
New Orleans
Mobile
Tallahassee
Jacksonville
Daytona Beach
Orlando
Tampa
Melbourne
Miami
Key West
Gulf of Mexico
ATLANTIC OCEAN
Major industry and infrastructure
aerospace
car manufacture
chemicals
coal
defense
electronics
engineering
food processing
oil
textiles
tourism
major towns
international airports
major roads
major industrial areas

The cypress swamps of the Mississippi Delta form in the backswamps behind the levees of the river and in the multitude of subsiding delta basins.

Piedmont
Atchafalaya Bay
Florida Keys

Cathedral Caverns near Huntsville in Alabama is a system of vast limestone caves, with a main opening 1000 ft (300 m) high and 150 ft (50 m) wide.

The Yazoo River flows parallel to the Mississippi through a common floodplain. The confluence of the rivers is deferred downstream because flood deposition has built the Mississippi channel up above the level of the Yazoo.

At De Soto Falls, Alabama, the Little River descends into the deepest canyon east of the Mississippi, with sheer cliff walls up to 700 ft (230 m) high.

Brasstown Bald in the Blue Ridge mountains of Georgia is the region's highest point, at 4,784 ft (1,458 m).

The Mississippi is the world's third longest river and moves over a billion tons (tonnes) of sediment a year, creating deep alluvial plains. Flooding is a constant threat in lowland areas.

In Providence Canyon, Georgia, the Chattahoochee River has cut straight down through the sandy bedrock, to leave sheer rock faces and pinnacles, which have been smoothed by subsequent weathering.

Sandbars, deposited by waves breaking offshore, form barrier beaches along much of the coastline, creating sheltered lagoons and salt marshes behind them.

Mississippi Delta

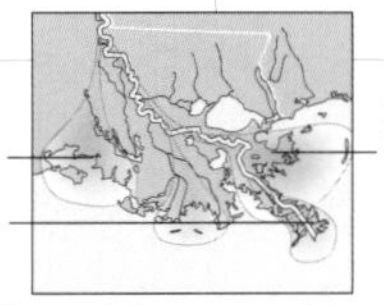

The delta of the Mississippi over 5,000 years ago
Present-day delta
Delta lobe

Over the last 5,000 years the lower course of the Mississippi has moved back and forth over great distances. These changes, caused by varying sediment loads and human modification, have resulted in a "bird's foot" delta with several lobes, each reflecting the river's different historic position.

Lake Okeechobee is actually a shallow, slow-moving river, 150 miles (240 km) long and 50 miles (80 km) wide.

The Everglades lie in a limestone hollow formed over two million years ago, which has gradually become in-filled with swamp deposits.

Across Florida the coastal plain is mostly less than 75 ft (25 m) above sea level. The land is underlain by limestone, pitted with hollows which have been filled by over 10,000 lakes.

The Landscape

The Blue Ridge Mountains in the north are skirted by the gentle hills of the Piedmont, whose rivers drain south on to the great flat expanse of the coastal plain. Sandy barrier beaches and islands dominate the sea shore, tracing round the swampy limestone arm of Florida. In the west, the Mississippi meanders toward its delta, crossing the thickly mantled alluvial plain of the interior lowlands.

A B C D E F G H I J K L M

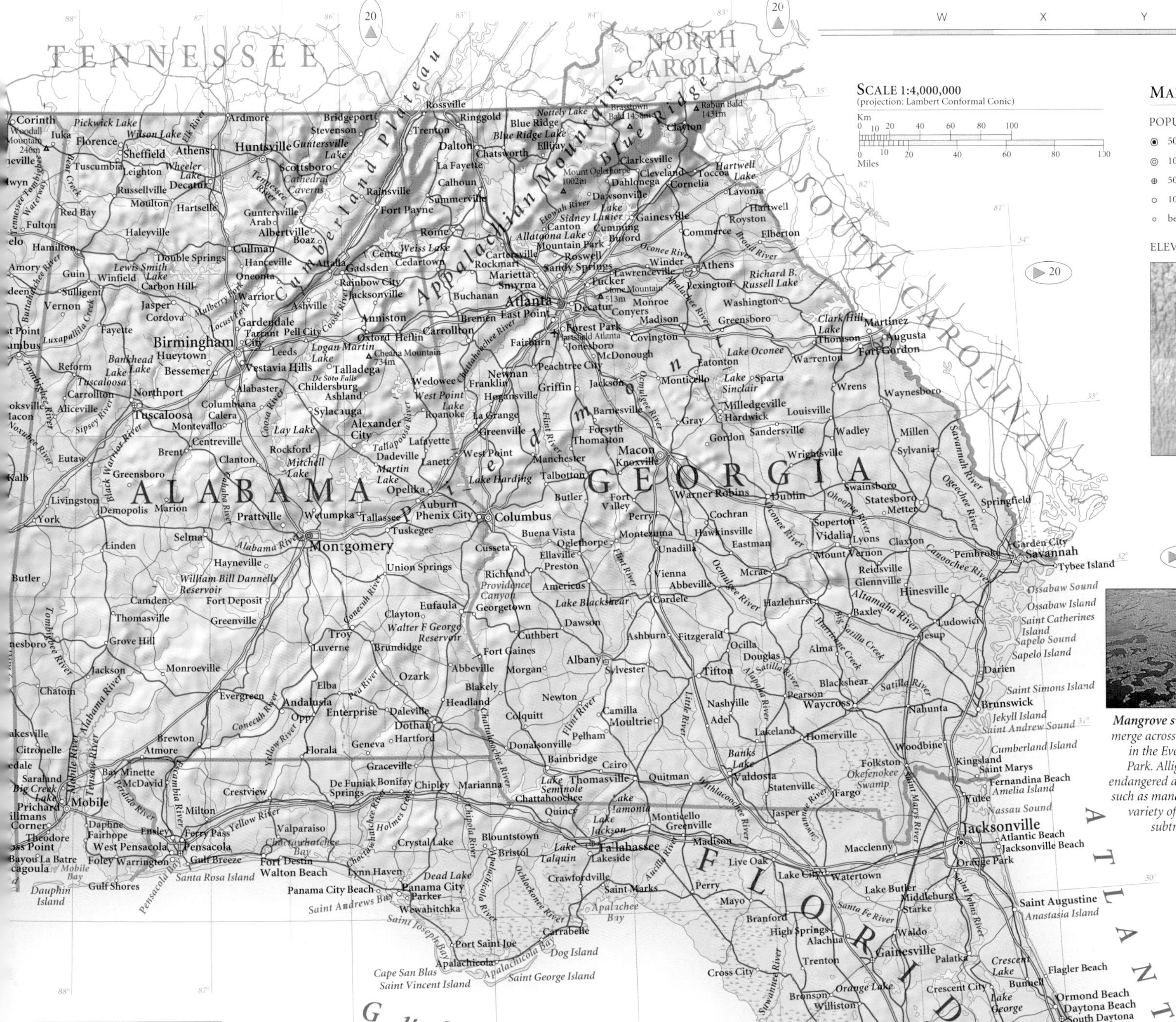

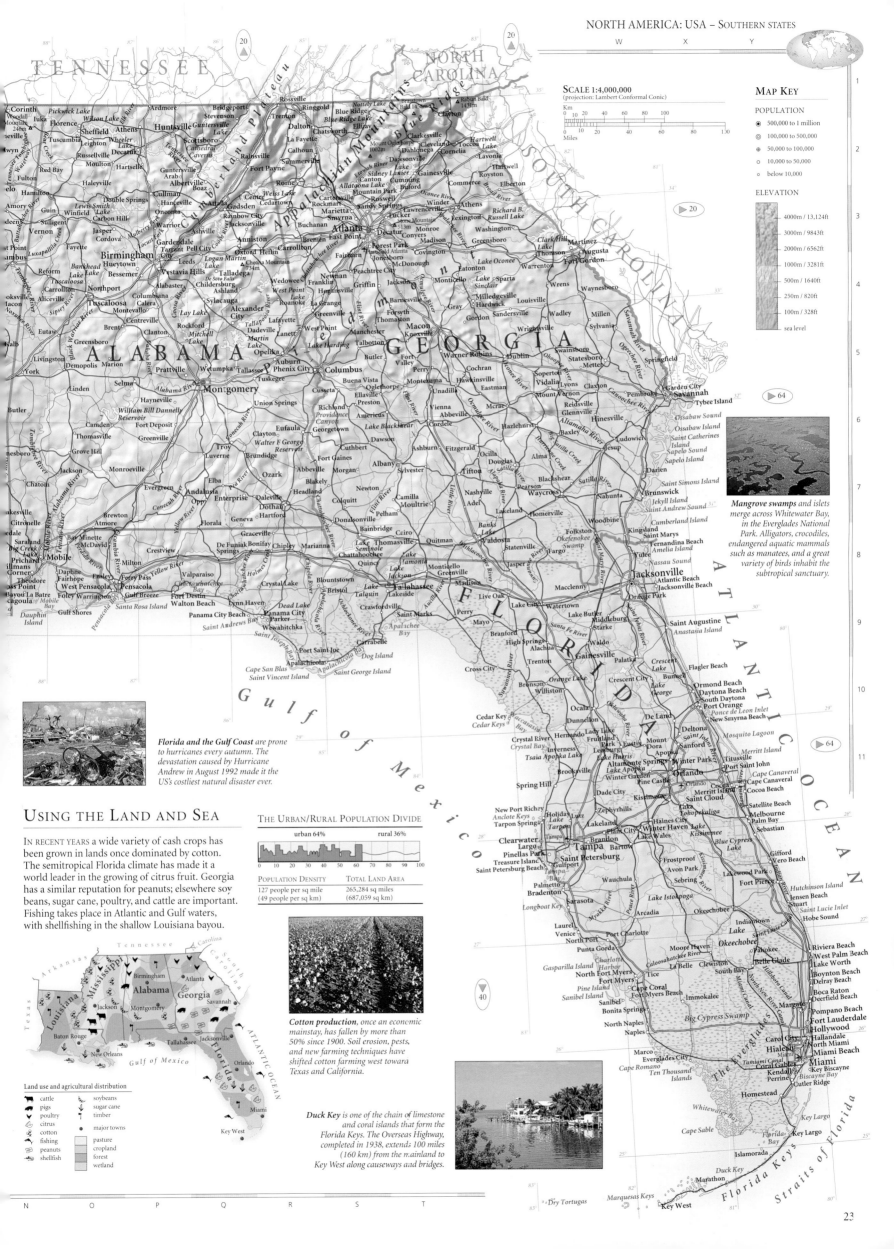

W X Y
SCALE 1:4,000,000
(projection: Lambert Conformal Conic)
Km 0 10 20 40 60 80 100
Miles 0 10 20 40 60 80 130
MAP KEY
POPULATION
500,000 to 1 million
100,000 to 500,000
50,000 to 100,000
10,000 to 50,000
below 10,000
ELEVATION
4000m / 13,124ft
3000m / 9843ft
2000m / 6562ft
1000m / 3281ft
500m / 1640ft
250m / 820ft
100m / 328ft
sea level
TENNESSEE
NORTH CAROLINA
SOUTH CAROLINA
ALABAMA
GEORGIA
FLORIDA
Cumberland Plateau
Appalachian Mountains
Blue Ridge
Piedmont
Gulf of Mexico
ATLANTIC OCEAN
Huntsville
Birmingham
Tuscaloosa
Montgomery
Mobile
Atlanta
Columbus
Macon
Augusta
Savannah
Tallahassee
Jacksonville
Pensacola
Gainesville
Orlando
Tampa
Saint Petersburg
Miami
Key West
Okefenokee Swamp
Lake Okeechobee
The Everglades
Big Cypress Swamp
Florida Keys
Straits of Florida
Dry Tortugas
Marquesas Keys
1 2 3 4 5 6 7 8 9 10 11

Cape Canaveral
Melbourne
Fort Lauderdale
Hollywood
Miami Beach
Key Largo
Islamorada
Marathon
Duck Key
Naples
Fort Myers
Sarasota
Bradenton

Mangrove swamps and islets merge across Whitewater Bay, in the Everglades National Park. Alligators, crocodiles, endangered aquatic mammals such as manatees, and a great variety of birds inhabit the subtropical sanctuary.

***Florida and the Gulf Coast** are prone to hurricanes every autumn. The devastation caused by Hurricane Andrew in August 1992 made it the US's costliest natural disaster ever.*

USING THE LAND AND SEA

IN RECENT YEARS a wide variety of cash crops has been grown in lands once dominated by cotton. The semitropical Florida climate has made it a world leader in the growing of citrus fruit. Georgia has a similar reputation for peanuts; elsewhere soy beans, sugar cane, poultry, and cattle are important. Fishing takes place in Atlantic and Gulf waters, with shellfishing in the shallow Louisiana bayou.

THE URBAN/RURAL POPULATION DIVIDE

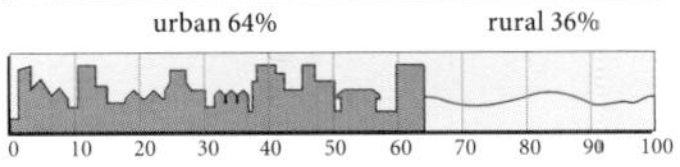

urban 64%
rural 36%
0 10 20 30 40 50 60 70 80 90 100

POPULATION DENSITY	TOTAL LAND AREA
127 people per sq mile (49 people per sq km)	265,284 sq miles (687,059 sq km)

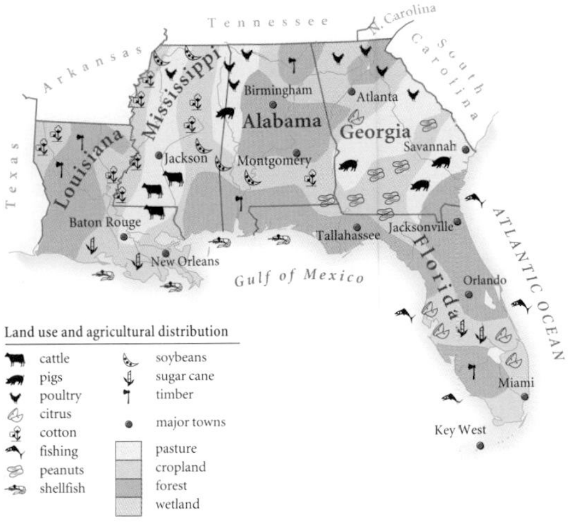

Tennessee
Arkansas
Mississippi
Louisiana
Alabama
Georgia
Florida
South Carolina
Texas
Birmingham
Atlanta
Montgomery
Jackson
Savannah
Baton Rouge
New Orleans
Tallahassee
Jacksonville
Orlando
Miami
Key West
Gulf of Mexico
ATLANTIC OCEAN
Land use and agricultural distribution
cattle
pigs
poultry
citrus
cotton
fishing
peanuts
shellfish
soybeans
sugar cane
timber
major towns
pasture
cropland
forest
wetland

***Cotton production**, once an economic mainstay, has fallen by more than 50% since 1900. Soil erosion, pests, and new farming techniques have shifted cotton farming west toward Texas and California.*

***Duck Key** is one of the chain of limestone and coral islands that form the Florida Keys. The Overseas Highway, completed in 1938, extends 100 miles (160 km) from the mainland to Key West along causeways and bridges.*

USA: Texas

First explored by Spaniards moving north from Mexico in search of gold, Texas was controlled by Spain and then by Mexico, before becoming an independent republic in 1836, and joining the Union of States in 1845. During the 19th century, many migrants who came to Texas raised cattle on the abundant land; in the 20th century, they were joined by prospectors attracted by the promise of oil riches. Today, although natural resources, especially oil, still form the basis of its wealth, the diversified Texan economy includes thriving hi-tech and financial industries. The major urban centers, home to 80% of the population, lie in the south and east, and include Houston, the "oil-city," and Dallas Fort Worth. Hispanic influences remain strong, especially in southern and western Texas.

Dallas was founded in 1841 as a prairie trading post and its development was stimulated by the arrival of railroads. Cotton and then oil funded the town's early growth. Today, the modern, high-rise skyline of Dallas reflects the city's position as a leading center of banking, insurance, and the petroleum industry in the southwest.

Using the Land

Cotton production and livestock-raising, particularly cattle, dominate farming, although crop failures and the demands of local markets have led to some diversification. Following the introduction of modern farming techniques, cotton production spread out from the east to the plains of western Texas. Cattle ranches are widespread, while sheep and goats are raised on the dry Edwards Plateau.

The huge cattle ranches of Texas *developed during the 19th century when land was plentiful and could be acquired cheaply. Today, more cattle and sheep are raised in Texas than in any other state.*

Amarillo
Oklahoma
Arkansas
New Mexico
Dallas
Louisiana
El Paso
Texas
Austin
Houston
San Antonio
MEXICO

Land use and agricultural distribution
- cattle
- goats
- sheep
- cereals
- cotton
- major towns
- pasture
- cropland
- forest
- barren

The Urban/Rural Population Divide

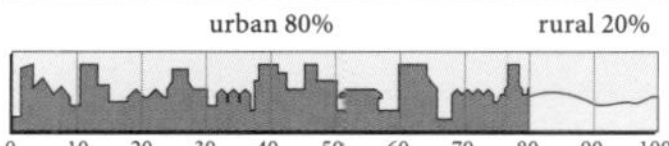
urban 80%
rural 20%
0 10 20 30 40 50 60 70 80 90 100

Population Density	Total Land Area
73 people per sq mile (28 people per sq km)	267,338 sq miles (692,402 sq km)

The Landscape

Texas is made up of a series of massive steps descending from the mountains and high plains of the west and northwest to the coastal lowlands in the southeast. Many of the state's borders are delineated by water. The Rio Grande flows from the Rocky Mountains to the Gulf of Mexico, marking the border with Mexico.

Cap Rock Escarpment *juts out from the plains, running 200 miles (320 km) from north to south. Its height varies from 300 ft (90 m) rising to sheer cliffs up to 1,000 ft (300 m).*

Texline
Dalhart
Hartley
Channing
Canadian River
Adrian
Hereford
Friona
Bovina
Dimmitt
Farwell
Muleshoe
Earth
Springlake
Sudan
Enochs
Morton
Whiteface
Levelland
Plains
Sundown
Tokio
Denver City
Wellman
Seagraves
Seminole
Cedar Lake
Andrews
N E W   M E X I C O

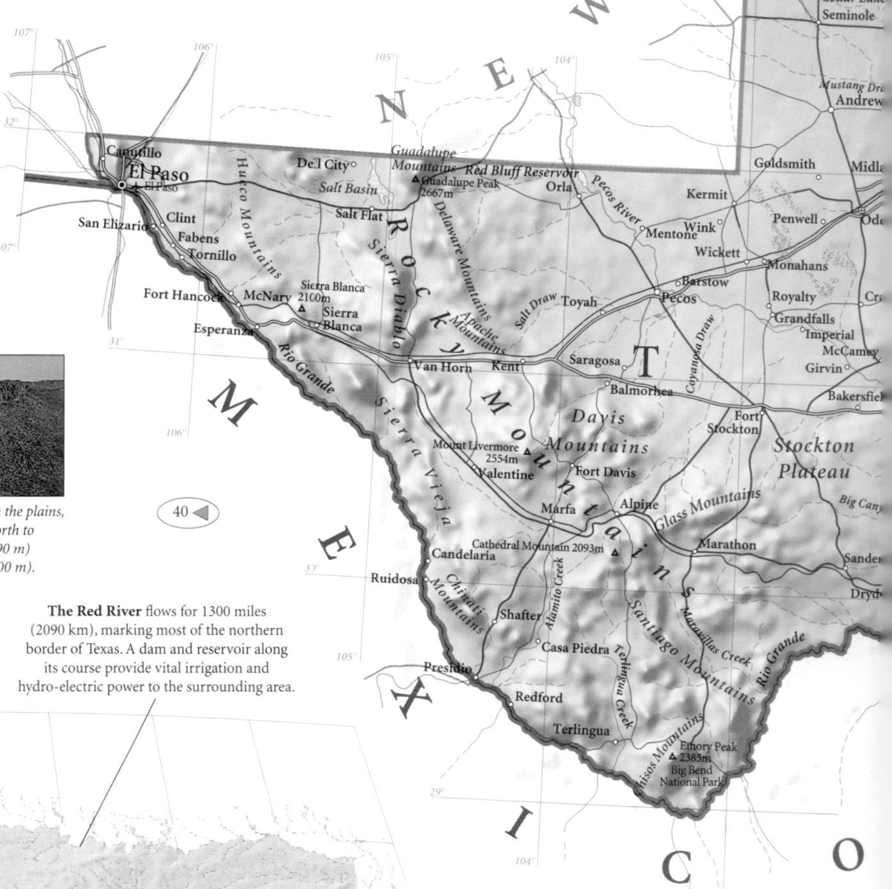
Canutillo
El Paso
San Elizario
Clint
Fabens
Tornillo
Fort Hancock
McNary
Esperanza
Hueco Mountains
Dell City
Salt Basin
Salt Flat
Guadalupe Mountains
Guadalupe Peak 2667m
Red Bluff Reservoir
Orla
Pecos River
Sierra Diablo
Delaware Mountains
Sierra Blanca 2100m
Sierra Blanca
Rocky Mountains
Apache Mountains
Salt Draw
Toyah
Kermit
Wink
Mentone
Wickett
Penwell
Monahans
Barstow
Pecos
Royalty
Grandfalls
Imperial
McCamey
Girvin
Goldsmith
Van Horn
Kent
Saragosa
Balmorhea
Rio Grande
Sierra Vieja
Davis Mountains
Mount Livermore 2554m
Valentine
Fort Davis
Fort Stockton
Stockton Plateau
Marfa
Alpine
Glass Mountains
Marathon
Cathedral Mountain 2093m
Candelaria
Ruidosa
Chinati Mountains
Shafter
Alamito Creek
Casa Piedra
Presidio
Redford
Terlingua
Terlingua Creek
Santiago Mountains
Maravillas Creek
Emory Peak 2385m
Big Bend National Park
Chisos Mountains
T E X A S
M E X I C O

36

40

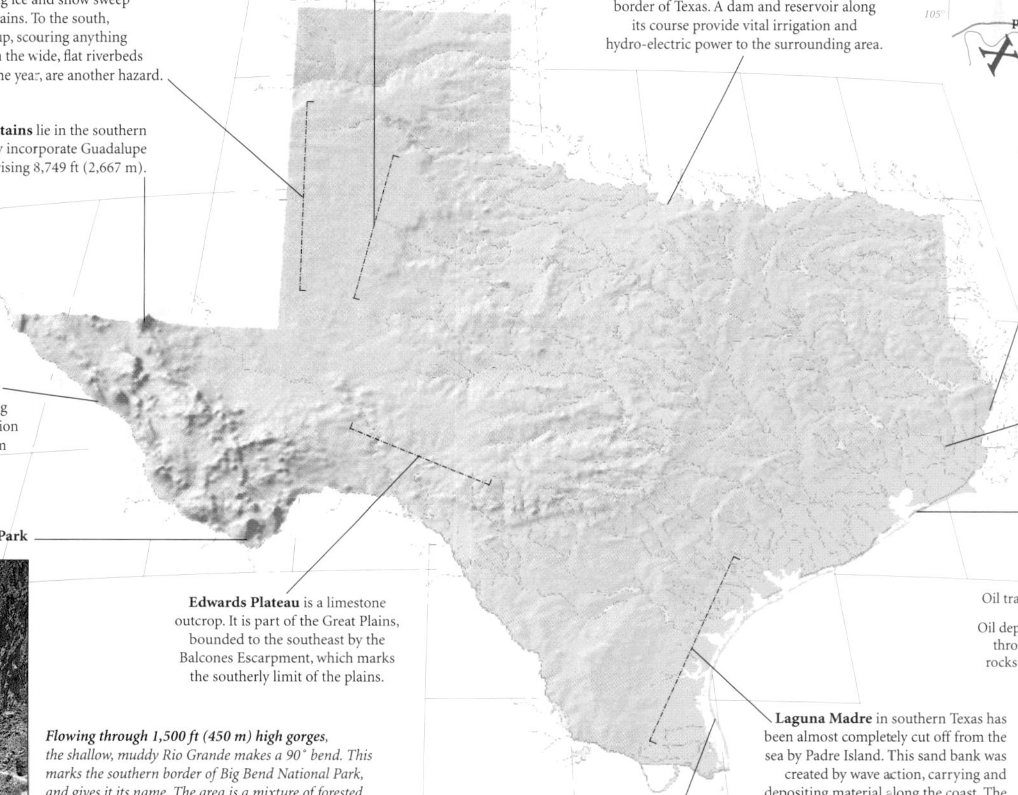

The Llano Estacado or Staked Plain in northern Texas is known for its harsh environment. In the north, freezing winds carrying ice and snow sweep down from the Rocky Mountains. To the south, sandstorms frequently blow up, scouring anything in their paths. Flash floods, in the wide, flat riverbeds that remain dry for most of the year, are another hazard.

The Red River flows for 1300 miles (2090 km), marking most of the northern border of Texas. A dam and reservoir along its course provide vital irrigation and hydro-electric power to the surrounding area.

The Guadalupe Mountains lie in the southern Rocky Mountains. They incorporate Guadalupe Peak, the highest in Texas, rising 8,749 ft (2,667 m).

The Rio Grande flows from the Rocky Mountains through semi-arid land, supporting sparse vegetation. The river actually shrinks along its course, losing more water through evaporation and seepage than it gains from its tributaries and rainfall.

Sabine River

Extensive forests of pine and cypress grow in the eastern corner of the coastal lowlands where the average rainfall is 45 inches (1145 mm) a year. This is higher than the rest of the state and over twice the average in the west.

In the coastal lowlands of southeastern Texas the Earth's crust is warping, causing the land to subside and allowing the sea to invade. Around Galveston, the rate of downward tilting is 6 inches (15 cm) per year. Erosion of the coast is also exacerbated by hurricanes.

Big Bend National Park

Flowing through 1,500 ft (450 m) high gorges, *the shallow, muddy Rio Grande makes a 90° bend. This marks the southern border of Big Bend National Park, and gives it its name. The area is a mixture of forested mountains, deserts, and canyons.*

Edwards Plateau is a limestone outcrop. It is part of the Great Plains, bounded to the southeast by the Balcones Escarpment, which marks the southerly limit of the plains.

Padre Island

Laguna Madre in southern Texas has been almost completely cut off from the sea by Padre Island. This sand bank was created by wave action, carrying and depositing material along the coast. The process is known as longshore drift.

Oil deposits

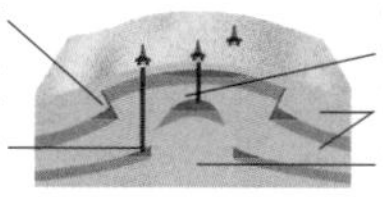
Oil trapped by fault
Oil deposits migrate through reservoir rocks such as shale
Oil accumulates beneath impermeable cap rock
Impermeable rock strata
Salt dome

Oil deposits *are found beneath much of Texas. They collect as oil migrates upward through porous layers of rock until it is trapped, either by a cap of rock above a salt dome, or by a fault line which exposes impermeable rock through which the oil cannot rise.*

TRANSPORTATION & INDUSTRY

INDUSTRY IN THE 20TH CENTURY was largely concentrated on the processing of local raw materials, especially oil – deposits were discovered under 65% of the state's area. The technological demands of the oil industry and defense-related institutions, particularly NASA, have stimulated the development of numerous electronics and hi-tech firms which, alongside many national corporate headquarters, are based in Dallas–Fort Worth and Houston.

Major industry and infrastructure

- chemicals
- defense
- engineering
- finance
- food processing
- gas
- hi-tech industry
- mining
- oil
- textiles
- major towns
- international airports
- major roads
- major industrial areas

TRANSPORTATION NETWORK

293,509 miles (496,614 km)	3,229 miles (5,166 km)
10,681 miles (17,089 km)	845 miles (1,359 km)

The sheer size of Texas promoted the development of an extensive road and rail network. The highway system, although well-developed, is concentrated in the east.

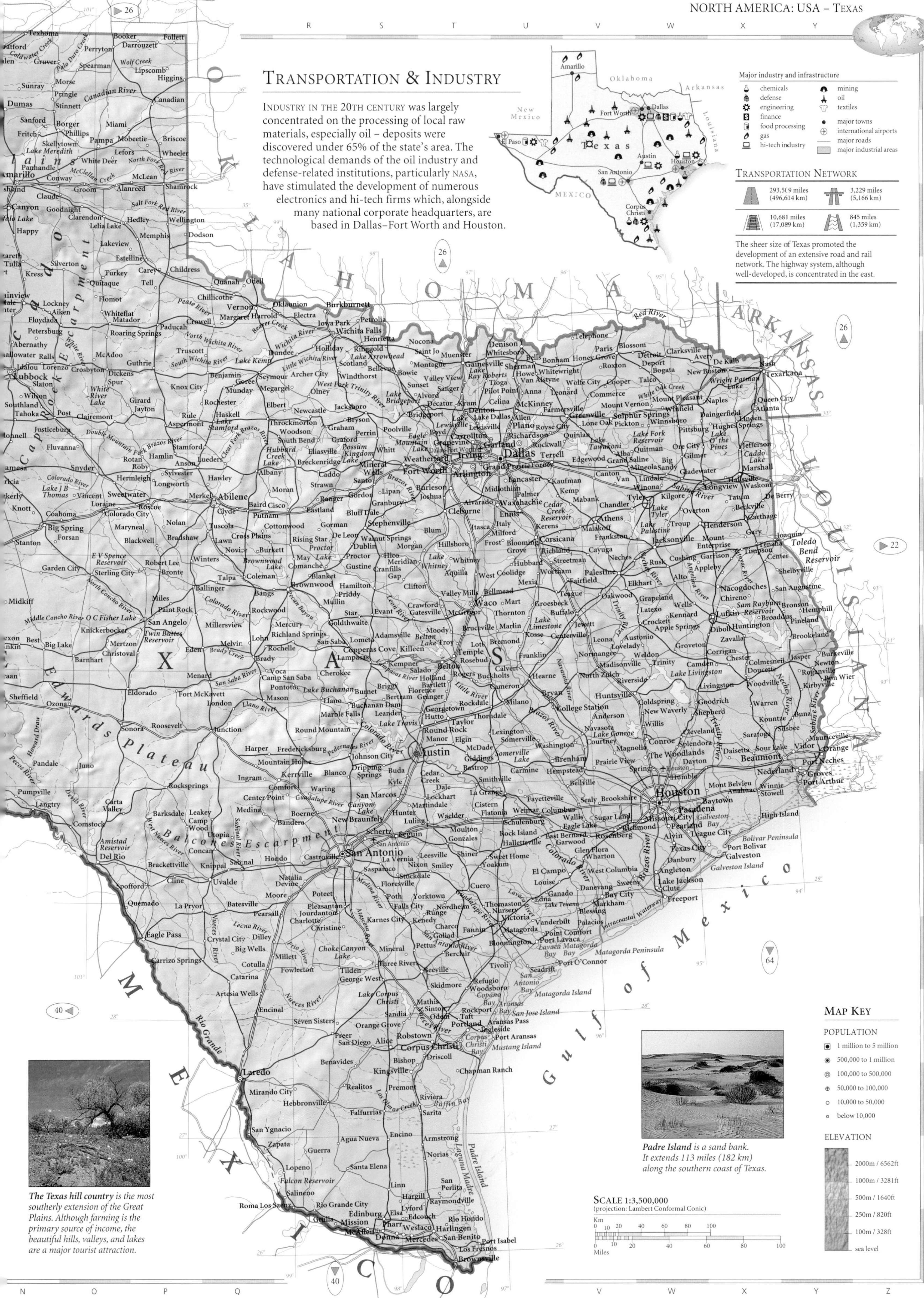

The Texas hill country is the most southerly extension of the Great Plains. Although farming is the primary source of income, the beautiful hills, valleys, and lakes are a major tourist attraction.

Padre Island is a sand bank. It extends 113 miles (182 km) along the southern coast of Texas.

SCALE 1:3,500,000
(projection: Lambert Conformal Conic)

MAP KEY

POPULATION

- 1 million to 5 million
- 500,000 to 1 million
- 100,000 to 500,000
- 50,000 to 100,000
- 10,000 to 50,000
- below 10,000

ELEVATION

- 2000m / 6562ft
- 1000m / 3281ft
- 500m / 1640ft
- 250m / 820ft
- 100m / 328ft
- sea level

USA: South Midwestern States

Arkansas, Kansas, Missouri, Oklahoma

The expansion of the US focused on this region in the mid-19th century. Settlers spread from the confluence of the Missouri and Mississippi Rivers up onto the Great Plains. This treeless expanse, which early explorers had called the Great American Desert was turned into one of the world's richest agricultural regions. But periodic droughts, coupled with overintensive farming, led to the "dustbowl" soil erosion crisis of the 1930s, the abandonment of many farms, and a mass exodus to the west coast. The land has since recovered, although the mechanization of agriculture has led to a decline in the rural population. In recent years, suburban residential development has spread rapidly across the wooded Ozark Plateau in the east of the region.

Transportation & Industry

The processing of agricultural products, such as brewing and meatpacking, has been traditionally important in these states. In Kansas and Oklahoma, diversified manufacturing now supplements income from fossil fuels; Wichita has become a world center for aeronautical engineering, an industry which also employs many people in neighboring Missouri.

Nebraska
Iowa
Illinois
Colorado
Kansas
Topeka
Kansas City
Saint Louis
Wichita
Missouri
Kentucky
New Mexico
Tulsa
Oklahoma
Arkansas
Tennessee
Oklahoma City
Little Rock
Mississippi
Texas
Louisiana
Major industry and infrastructure
aerospace
engineering
finance
food processing
gas
mining
oil
vehicle manufacture
major towns
international airports
major roads
major industrial areas

Agricultural produce from the plains is moved by barges along the Mississippi. The river now carries a far greater tonnage of freight than any other waterway system in the US.

Transportation Network

(road)	380,307 miles (608,491 km)	(highway)	4068 miles (6508 km)
(rail)	16,185 miles (25,896 km)	(waterway)	1994 miles (3208 km)

The Arkansas River and its tributaries allow access to over half of the US's navigable inland waterways. A system of locks and dams along the river provides Tulsa, in Oklahom, with a navigable water route to the Gulf of Mexico.

NEBRASKA
KANSAS
COLORADO
NEW MEXICO
TEXAS
Great Plains
Smoky Hills
Red Hills
Saint Francis
Atwood
Oberlin
Norton
Phillipsburg
Lovewell Reservoir
Mankato
Goodland
Colby
Hoxie
Stockton
Kirwin Reservoir
Smith Center
Osborne
Hill City
Plainville
Mount Sunflower 1231m
Oakley
Wa Keeney
Ellis
Hays
Russell
Wilson Lake
Lincoln
Sharon Springs
Smoky Hill River
Cedar Bluff Reservoir
Ellsworth
Tribune
Leoti
Scott City
Dighton
Ness City
La Crosse
Hoisington
Cheyenne Bottoms
Great Bend
Syracuse
Lakin
Lake McKinney
Garden City
Jetmore
Larned
Kinsley
Saint John
Stafford
Johnson
Ulysses
Cimarron
Dodge City
Greensburg
Pratt
Kingman
Montezuma
Bucklin
Satanta
Sublette
Meade
Minneola
Coldwater
Ashland
Medicine Lodge
Harper
Anthony
Hugoton
Liberal
Elkhart
Black Mesa 1516m
Boise City
Keyes
Guymon
Hooker
Optima Lake
Beaver
Forgan
Buffalo
Kiowa
Alva
Cherokee
Great Salt Plains Lake
Texhoma
Goodwell
Laverne
Elmwood
Fort Supply
Fort Supply Lake
Waynoka
Woodward
Cleo Springs
Shattuck
Arnett
Fairview
Seiling
Canton Lake
Okeene
Canton
Vici
Taloga
Leedey
Watonga
Hammon
Foss Reservoir
Thomas
Geary
Cheyenne
Arapaho
Elk City
Clinton
Weatherford
Sayre
Burns Flat
Cordell
Binger
Hinton
Erick
Fort Cobb Reservoir
Carnegie
Anadarko
Hobart
Altus Lake
Mangum
Mount Scott 751m
Wichita Mountains
Salt Fork Red River
Hollis
Tom Steed Reservoir
Altus
Snyder
Cache
Lawton
Eldorado
Red River
Frederick
Grandfield
Walters
Davidson
Arkansas River
Cimarron River
Canadian River
North Canadian River
Washita River
36
24
28
SCALE 1:3,250,000
(projection: Lambert Conformal Conic)
Km
Miles

Map Key

POPULATION

- 100,000 to 500,000
- 50,000 to 100,000
- 10,000 to 50,000
- below 10,000

ELEVATION

- 1000m / 3281ft
- 500m / 1640ft
- 250m / 820ft
- 100m / 328ft
- sea level

The Landscape

Most of the region consists of high, treeless plains, which gradually descend east from the Rocky Mountains. Drainage follows this slope, with rivers flowing toward the alluvial lowlands of the Mississippi in the southeast. Between the plains and the lowlands lie various ranges of wooded hills, including the deeply incised Ozark Plateau.

The Mississippi, North America's longest river, is joined by the Missouri, its main tributary, on a flood plain which spreads south to the Gulf of Mexico.

The Ozark Plateau is a wooded, hilly region of rivers and narrow, winding lakes. The Lake of the Ozarks was created by the damming of the Osage River in 1930.

Collapsed limestone caverns led to the formation of Big Basin in Kansas; a depression 100 ft (33 m) deep and 1 mile (1.6 km) wide.

Flint Hills is the region's easternmost major escarpment. Steep, grassy uplands are interspersed with rocky, wooded ravines and outcrops of limestone and chert.

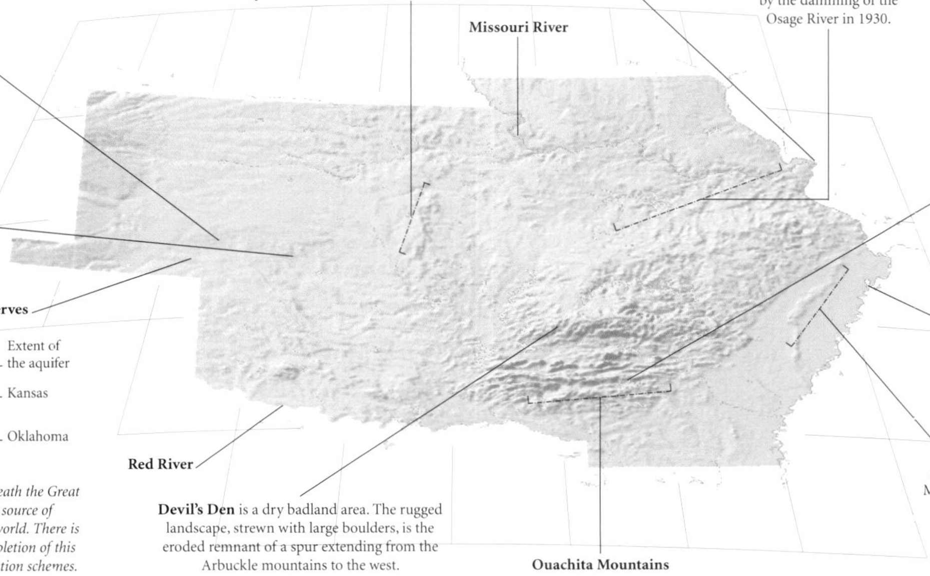

Missouri River
Red River
Ouachita Mountains
Mississippi River

The Great Salt Plains of northern Oklahoma cover 45 sq miles (116 sq km). The arid, white flats were left by the gradual evaporation of an ancient salt lake.

Underground water reserves

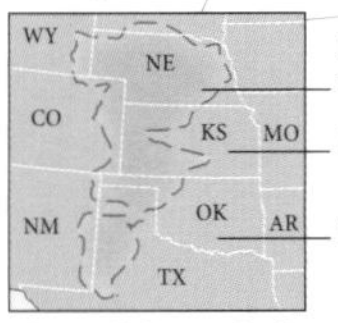

WY
NE
CO
KS
MO
NM
OK
AR
TX
Extent of the aquifer
Kansas
Oklahoma

The Ogallala Aquifer, beneath the Great Plains, is the largest known source of underground water in the world. There is concern about the rapid depletion of this finite water supply by irrigation schemes.

Red River

Devil's Den is a dry badland area. The rugged landscape, strewn with large boulders, is the eroded remnant of a spur extending from the Arbuckle mountains to the west.

Ouachita Mountains

Lake Ouachita, in Arkansas is one of a number of irregularly-shaped lakes found among the ridges of the Ouachita Mountains.

Mississippi River

Crowleys Ridge is a long, sandy ridge, rising from the Mississippi floodplain. It was formed over thousands of years by the deposition of sand blown eastward from the Great Plains.

The landscape of northeast Kansas is interlaced by rivers which have cut broad wooded valleys through the gentle hills. All the rivers in Kansas form part of the massive Missouri/Mississippi drainage basin.

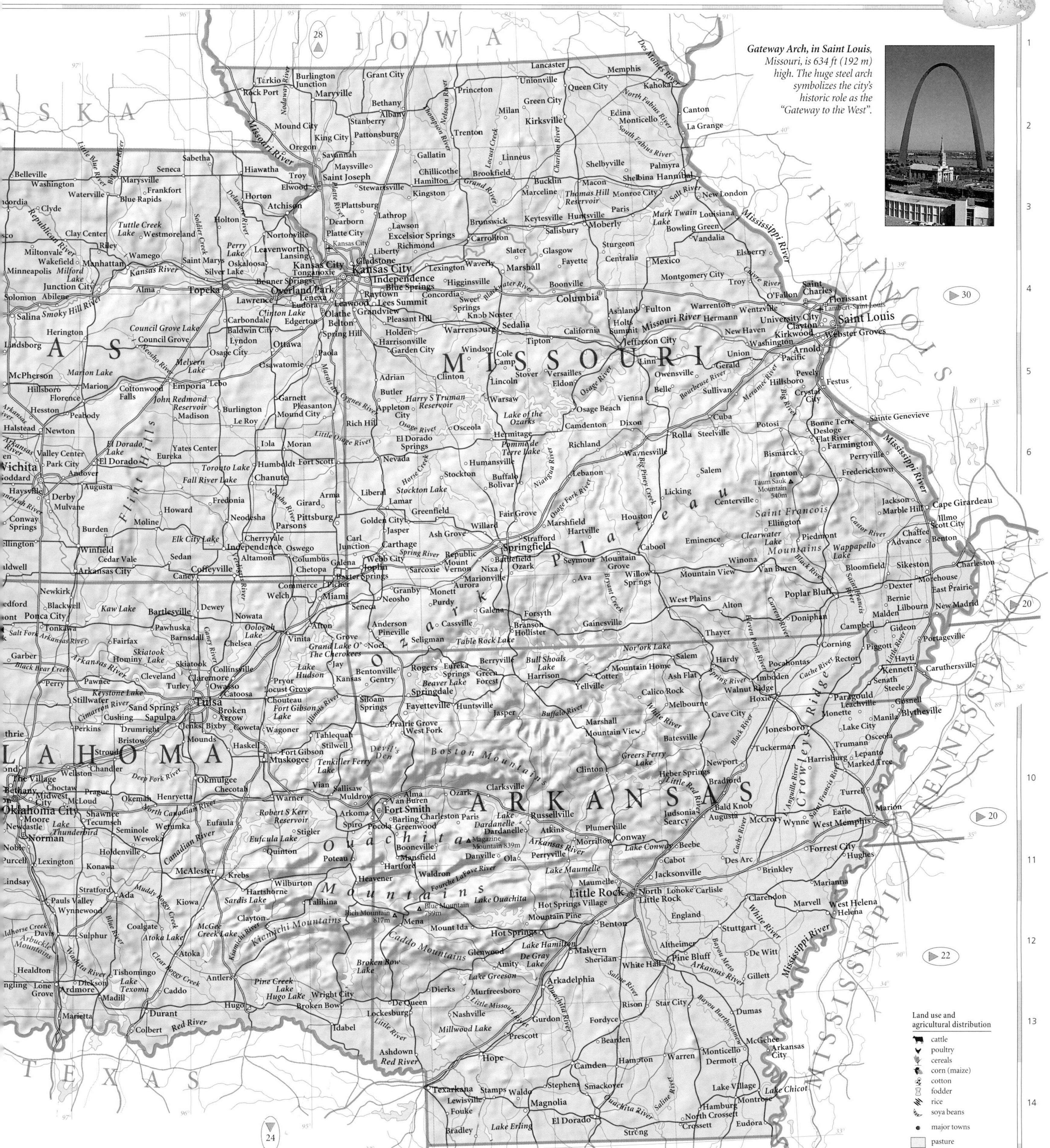
IOWA
KANSAS
MISSOURI
OKLAHOMA
ARKANSAS
TEXAS
LOUISIANA
ILLINOIS
KENTUCKY
TENNESSEE
MISSISSIPPI
Ozark Plateau
Ouachita Mountains
Boston Mountains
Flint Hills
Kansas City
Saint Louis
Springfield
Jefferson City
Columbia
Topeka
Wichita
Tulsa
Oklahoma City
Norman
Fort Smith
Little Rock
Hot Springs
Pine Bluff
Texarkana
Missouri River
Mississippi River
Arkansas River
Red River
Lake of the Ozarks
Taum Sauk Mountain 540m
Magazine Mountain 839m
Rich Mountain 817m
Blue Mountain 799m

Gateway Arch, in Saint Louis, Missouri, is 634 ft (192 m) high. The huge steel arch symbolizes the city's historic role as the "Gateway to the West".

USING THE LAND

THE PROBLEMS of a harsh continental climate, with severe winters and hot, dry summers, are partially offset by the rich soils of the plains. Kansas is a major cereal crop producer, ranking first in US production of wheat and sorghum. Rainfall increases toward the east, favoring the cultivation of soybeans, cotton, and rice, with corn concentrated in Missouri. Huge herds of cattle are raised in Oklahoma, Kansas, and Missouri.

A combine harvester works the land on the great plains. A hundred years ago this region, also known as the prairies – the French word for pasture – was covered with tall, wild grasses.

THE URBAN/RURAL POPULATION DIVIDE

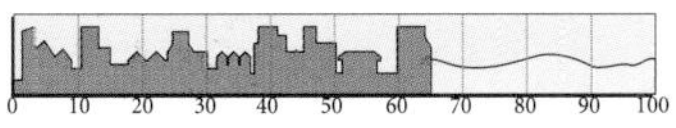
urban 65%
rural 35%
0 10 20 30 40 50 60 70 80 90 100

POPULATION DENSITY	TOTAL LAND AREA
50 people per sq mile (19 people per sq km)	274,900 sq miles (712,177 sq km)

Land use and agricultural distribution

- cattle
- poultry
- cereals
- corn (maize)
- cotton
- fodder
- rice
- soya beans
- major towns
- pasture
- cropland
- forest

Nebraska
Iowa
Illinois
Colorado
Kansas
Missouri
Kentucky
Tennessee
New Mexico
Oklahoma
Arkansas
Texas
Louisiana
Mississippi
Kansas City
Topeka
Wichita
Saint Louis
Tulsa
Oklahoma City
Little Rock

USA: Upper Plains states

Iowa, Minnesota, Nebraska, North Dakota, South Dakota

Lying at the very heart of the North American continent, much of this region was acquired from France as part of the Louisiana Purchase in 1803. The area was largely bypassed by the early waves of westward migrants. When Europeans did settle, during the 19th century, they displaced the Native Americans who lived on the plains. The settlers planted arable crops and raised cattle on the immensely fertile prairie land, founding an agrarian tradition which flourishes today. Most of this region remains rural; of the five states, only in Minnesota has there been significant diversification away from agriculture and resource-based industries into the hi-tech and service sectors.

Using the Land

The popular image of these states as agricultural is entirely justified; prairies stretch uninterrupted across most of the area. Croplands fall into two regions: the wheat belt of the plains, and the corn belt of the central US. Cash crops, such as soybeans, are grown to supplement incomes. Livestock, particularly pigs and cattle, are raised throughout this region.

Dark, fertile prairie soils in the southeast provide Minnesota's most productive farmland. Hot, humid summers create a long growing season for corn cultivation.

CANADA
North Dakota
Bismarck
Minnesota
Lake Superior
Montana
South Dakota
Pierre
Minneapolis
Saint Paul
Wisconsin
Wyoming
Iowa
Cedar Rapids
Des Moines
Illinois
Nebraska
Omaha
Lincoln
Colorado
Missouri
Kansas

Land use and agricultural distribution
- cattle
- pigs
- corn (maize)
- soybeans
- wheat
- major towns
- pasture
- cropland
- forest
- wetland

The Urban/Rural Population Divide

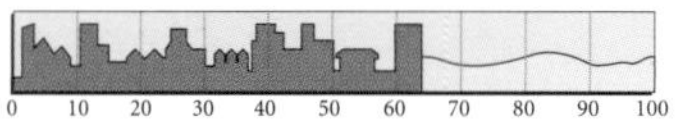
urban 64%
rural 36%
0
10
20
30
40
50
60
70
80
90
100

Population Density	Total Land Area
29 people per sq mile (11 people per sq km)	365,287 sq miles (946,056 sq km)

Transportation & Industry

Water erosion along the Little Missouri River has carried away sedimentary deposits, creating rugged landscapes known as badlands.

Food processing and the production of farm machinery are supported by the large agricultural sector. Mineral exploitation is also an important activity: gold is mined in the ore-rich Black Hills of South Dakota, and both North Dakota and Nebraska are emerging as major petroleum producers.

Transportation Network

504,522 miles (807,235 km)	3,422 miles (5,475 km)
16,940 miles (27,104 km)	683 miles (1,098 km)

Nebraska's central location has made it an important transportation artery for east–west traffic. Minnesota's road network radiates out from the hub of the twin cities, Minneapolis–Saint Paul.

CANADA
North Dakota
Fargo
Bismarck
Minnesota
Duluth
Lake Superior
Montana
South Dakota
Pierre
Minneapolis
Saint Paul
Sioux Falls
Wisconsin
Wyoming
Iowa
Cedar Rapids
Des Moines
Illinois
Nebraska
Omaha
Lincoln
Colorado
Missouri
Kansas

Major industry and infrastructure
- coal
- engineering
- electronics
- finance
- food processing
- oil & gas
- mining
- major towns
- international airports
- major roads
- major industrial areas

The Landscape

These states straddle the Great Plains and the lowlands of the central US, with Minnesota lying in a transition zone between the eastern forests and the prairies. The region was shaped by repeated ice advances and retreats, leaving a flat relief, broken only by the numerous lakes and broad river networks that drain the prairies.

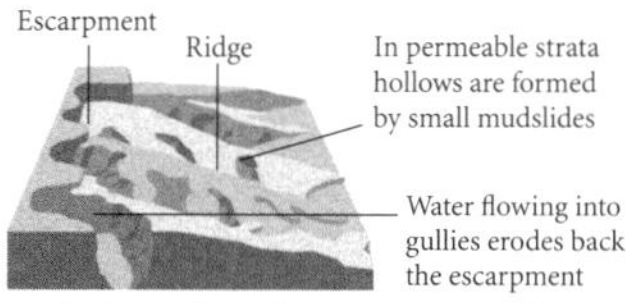
Escarpment
Ridge
In permeable strata hollows are formed by small mudslides
Water flowing into gullies erodes back the escarpment

***Badlands are formed** by stormwater run-off. This flows down the impermeable strata of the escarpment and saturates the permeable strata, leading to mudslides and the formation of gullies.*

The Minnesota landscape contains many post-glacial features, including its numerous lakes, boulder-strewn hills, and mineral-rich deposits.

***In the badlands** of North and South Dakota, horizontal layers of sandstone have been eroded by rivers, leaving a landscape of narrow gullies, sharp crests and pinnacles.*

South Dakota Badlands

***Chimney Rock** is a remnant of an ancient land surface, eroded by the North Platte River. The tip of its spire stands 500 ft (150 m) above the plain.*

North Dakota Badlands

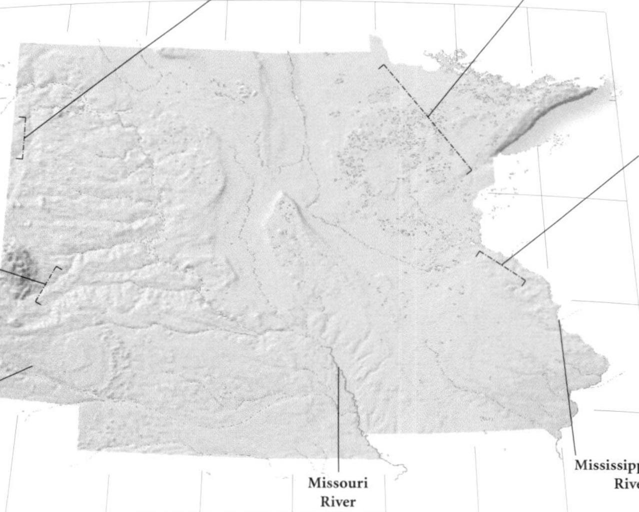
Missouri River
Mississippi River

Although it escaped the last glaciation, the limestone bedrock of southeastern Minnesota has been eroded by surface and subterranean streams, leaving a network of underground caverns and steep-sided valleys.

***In northeastern Iowa**, the Mississippi and its tributaries have deeply incised the underlying bedrock creating a hilly terrain, with bluffs standing 300 ft (90 m) above the valley.*

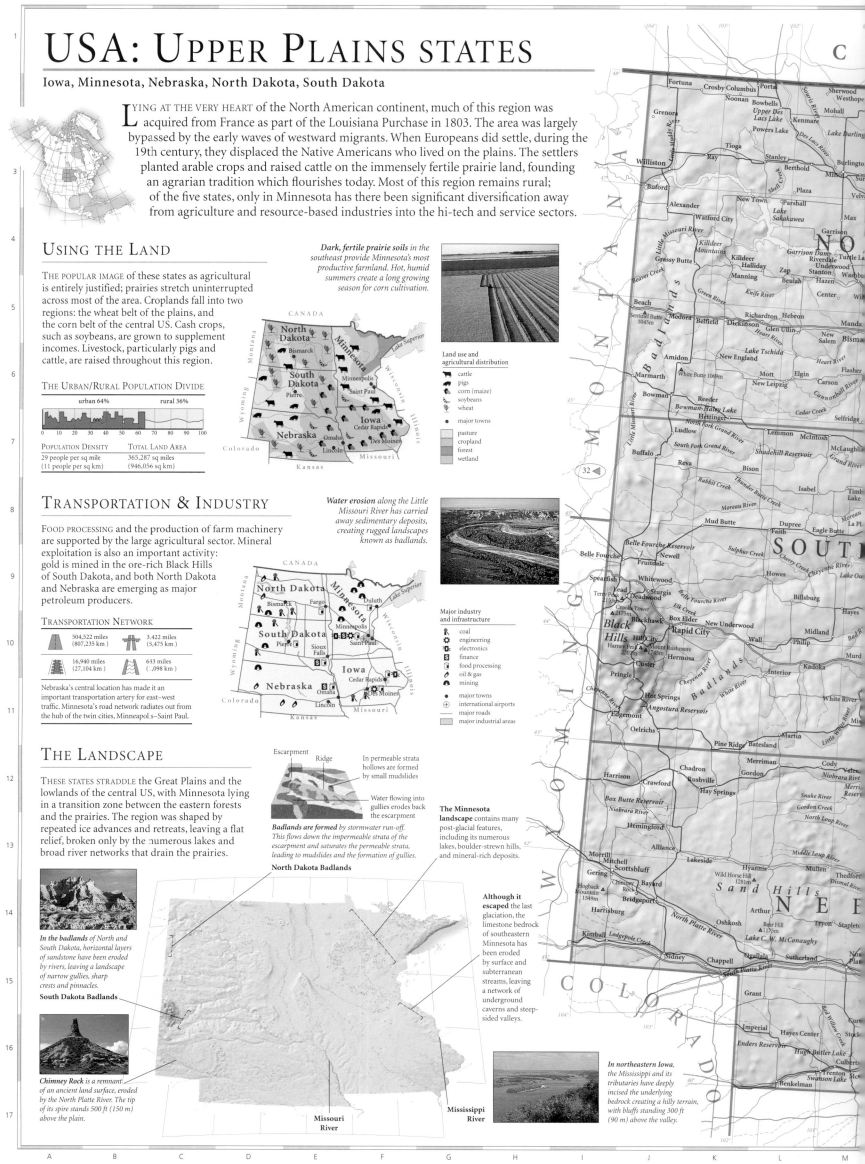

Fortuna
Crosby
Columbus
Portal
Noonan
Bowbells
Upper Des Lacs Lake
Kenmare
Mohall
Grenora
Powers Lake
Tioga
Ray
Stanley
Williston
Buford
New Town
Alexander
Watford City
Lake Sakakawea
Parshall
Killdeer Mountains
Grassy Butte
Killdeer
Halliday
Manning
Beulah
Zap
Hazen
Stanton
Garrison
Knife River
Beach
Medora
Belfield
Dickinson
Richardton
Hebron
Glen Ullin
Heart River
Amidon
New England
Lake Tschida
Marmarth
Mott
New Leipzig
Elgin
Carson
Bowman
Reeder
Bowman-Haley Lake
Hettinger
Lemmon
McIntosh
Ludlow
Buffalo
Reva
Bison
Isabel
Mud Butte
Dupree
Faith
Eagle Butte
Belle Fourche
Belle Fourche Reservoir
Newell
Fruitdale
Spearfish
Whitewood
Sturgis
Lead
Deadwood
Terry Peak 2153m
Crook's Tower 2175m
Blackhawk
Box Elder
Rapid City
New Underwood
Black Hills
Hill City
Harney Peak 2207m
Mount Rushmore 1745m
Hermosa
Custer
Pringle
Wall
Philip
Midland
Interior
Kadoka
Hot Springs
Angostura Reservoir
Badlands
Edgemont
Oelrichs
Martin
Pine Ridge
Batesland
Harrison
Chadron
Crawford
Rushville
Hay Springs
Merriman
Gordon
Cody
Box Butte Reservoir
Niobrara River
Hemingford
Alliance
Lakeside
Hyannis
Mullen
Morrill
Mitchell
Scottsbluff
Gering
Chimney Rock
Bayard
Wild Horse Hill 1281m
Sand Hills
Hogback Mountain 1549m
Bridgeport
Harrisburg
Arthur
Oshkosh
Bear Hill 1175m
Lake C. W. McConaughy
North Platte River
Kimball
Lodgepole Creek
Sidney
Chappell
Ogallala
Sutherland
South Platte River
Grant
Imperial
Hayes Center
Enders Reservoir
Hugh Butler Lake
Trenton
Swanson Lake
Benkelman
MONTANA
WYOMING
COLORADO
NORTH DAKOTA
SOUTH DAKOTA
NEBRASKA
32

N O P Q R S T U V W X Y

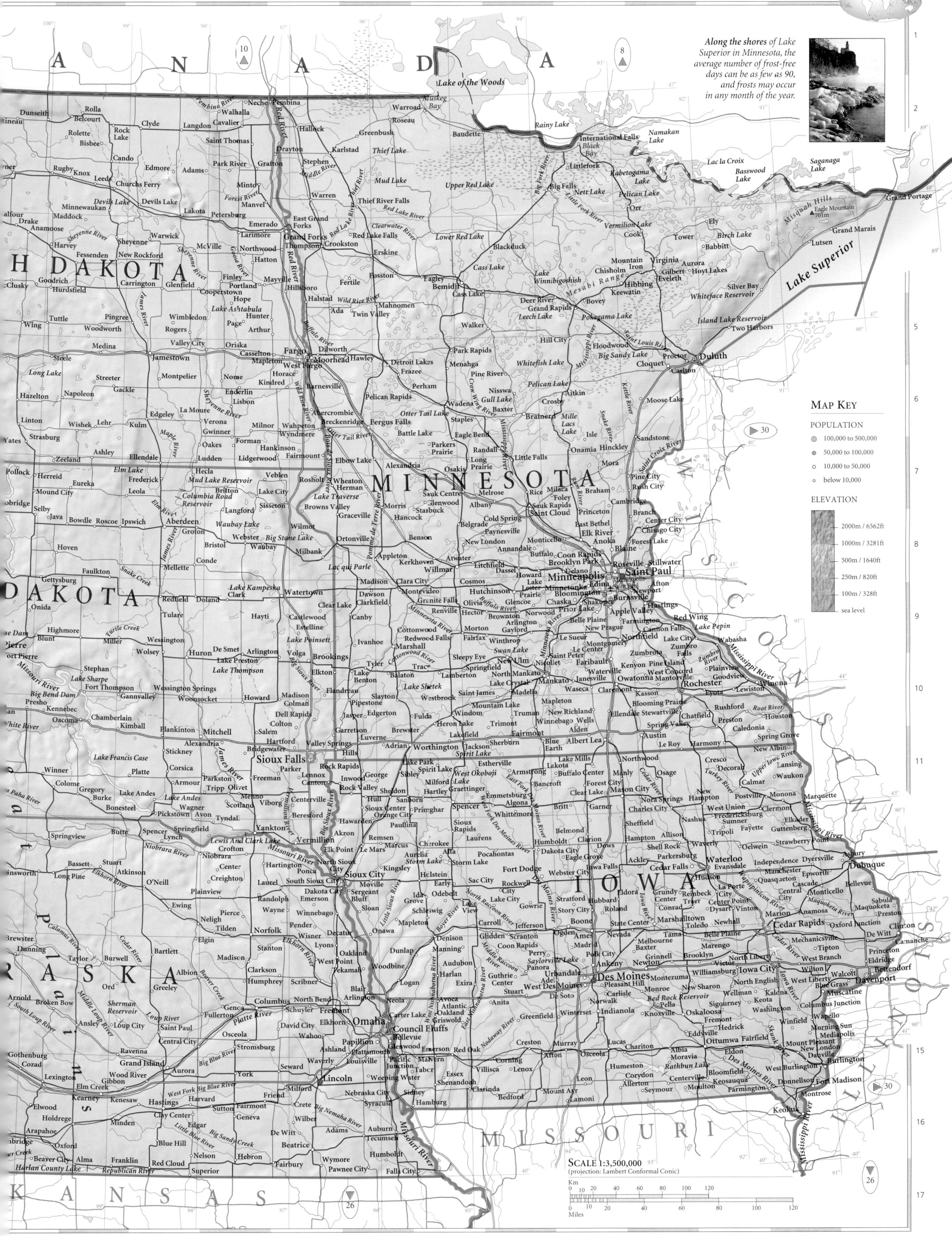
CANADA
NORTH DAKOTA
SOUTH DAKOTA
NEBRASKA
MINNESOTA
IOWA
WISCONSIN
ILLINOIS
MISSOURI
KANSAS
Lake of the Woods
Lake Superior
Rainy Lake
Upper Red Lake
Lower Red Lake
Mille Lacs Lake
Lake Pepin
Red River
Missouri River
Mississippi River
Des Moines River
Fargo
Grand Forks
Duluth
Minneapolis
Saint Paul
Rochester
Sioux Falls
Sioux City
Omaha
Council Bluffs
Lincoln
Des Moines
Cedar Rapids
Waterloo
Dubuque
Davenport
Iowa City
Burlington
Keokuk
Aberdeen
Jamestown
Saint Cloud
Mankato
Grand Portage
Eagle Mountain 701m
MAP KEY
POPULATION
100,000 to 500,000
50,000 to 100,000
10,000 to 50,000
below 10,000
ELEVATION
2000m / 6562ft
1000m / 3281ft
500m / 1640ft
250m / 820ft
100m / 328ft
sea level
SCALE 1:3,500,000
(projection: Lambert Conformal Conic)
Km
Miles

Along the shores of Lake Superior in Minnesota, *the average number of frost-free days can be as few as 90, and frosts may occur in any month of the year.*

N O P Q R S T U V W X Y Z

USA: Great Lakes states

Illinois, Indiana, Michigan, Ohio, Wisconsin

THE STATES BORDERING THE GREAT LAKES developed rapidly in the second half of the 19th century as a result of improvements in communications: railroads to the west and waterways to the south and east. Fertile land and good links with growing eastern seaboard cities encouraged the development of agriculture and food processing. Migrants from Europe and other parts of the US flooded into the region and for much of the 20th century the region's economy boomed. However, in recent years heavy industry has declined, earning the region the unwanted label the "Rustbelt."

Transportation & Industry

Lake Superior
Michigan
Lake Huron
Lake Ontario
Lake Erie
Lake Michigan
CANADA
Minnesota
Iowa
Missouri
Kentucky
West Virginia
Pennsylvania
New York
Wisconsin
Illinois
Indiana
Ohio
Milwaukee
Madison
Chicago
Lansing
Saginaw
Detroit
Toledo
Cleveland
Columbus
Peoria
Springfield
Indianapolis
Cincinnati

Major industry and infrastructure

- car manufacture
- coal
- electronics
- engineering
- finance
- food processing
- iron & steel
- oil
- research & development
- textiles
- major towns
- international airports
- major roads
- major industrial areas

THE GREAT LAKES REGION IS THE CENTER of the US car industry. Since the early part of the 20th century, its prosperity has been closely linked to the fortunes of automobile manufacturing. Iron and steel production has expanded to meet demand from this industry. In the 1970s, nationwide recession, cheaper foreign competition in the automobile sector, pollution in and around the Great Lakes, and the collapse of the meatpacking industry, centered on Chicago, forced these states to diversify their industrial base. New industries have emerged, notably electronics, services, and finance industries.

Transportation Network

540,682 miles (865,091 km)	6,550 miles (10,480 km)
24,928 miles (39,884 km)	2,330 miles (3,748 km)

Few areas of the US have a comparable system. Chicago is a principal transportation terminus with a dense network of roads, railroads, and Interstate freeways that radiates out from the city.

Ever since Ransom Olds and Henry Ford started mass-producing automobiles in Detroit early in the 20th century, the city's name has become synonymous with the American automotive industry.

The Landscape

MUCH OF THIS REGION shows the impact of glaciation which lasted until about 10,000 years ago, and extended as far south as Illinois and Ohio. Although the relief of the region slopes toward the Great Lakes, because the ice sheets blocked northerly drainage, most of the rivers today flow southward, forming part of the massive Mississippi/Missouri drainage basin.

***The dunes** near Sleeping Bear Point rise 400 ft (120 m) from the banks of Lake Michigan. They are constantly being resculpted by wind action.*

Lake Michigan

Lake Erie is the shallowest of the five Great Lakes. Its average depth is about 62 ft (19 m). Storms sweeping across from Canada erode its shores and cause the silting of its harbors.

The many lakes and marshes of Wisconsin and Michigan are the result of glacial erosion and deposition which occurred during the last Ice Age.

Southwestern Wisconsin is known as a "driftless" area. Unlike most of the region, low hills protected it from erosion by the advancing ice sheet.

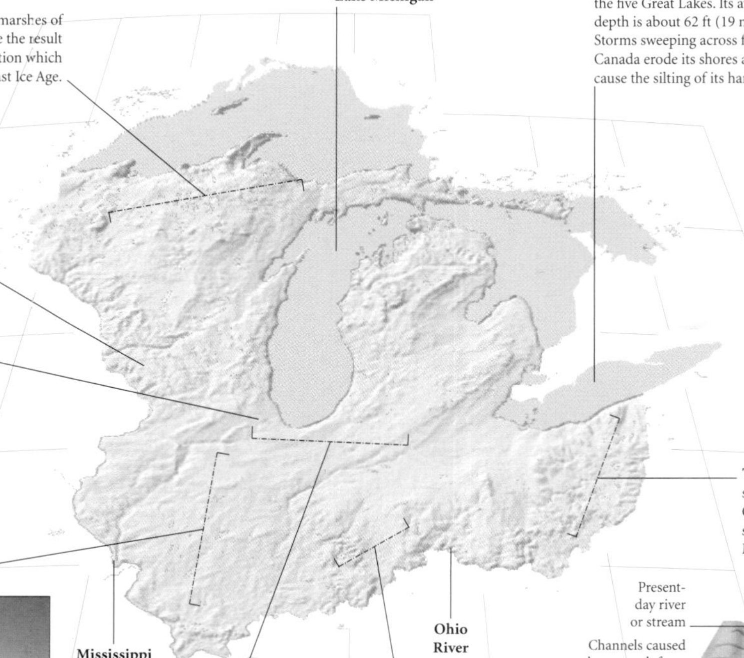

Most of the water used in northern Illinois is pumped from underground reservoirs. Due to increased demand, many areas now face a water shortage. Around Joliet, the water table was lowered by more than 700 ft (210 m) over the last century.

The Appalachian plateau stretches eastward from Ohio. It is dissected by streams flowing west into the Mississippi and Ohio Rivers.

Illinois plains

Mississippi River

Ohio River

The plains of Illinois are characteristic of drift landscapes, scoured and flattened by glacial erosion and covered with fertile glacial deposits.

Relict landforms from the last glaciation, such as shallow basins and ridges, cover all but the south of this region. Ridges, known as moraines, up to 300 ft (100 m) high, lie to the south of Lake Michigan.

Unlike the level prairie to the north, southern Indiana is relatively rugged. Limestone in the hills has been dissolved by water, producing features such as sinkholes and underground caves.

Glacial till

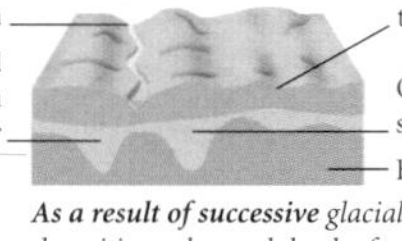

Present-day river or stream
Channels caused by outwash from melting glacier
Most recent till deposits
Older till sheet
Bedrock

***As a result of successive** glacial depositions, the total depth of till along the former southern margin of the Laurentide ice sheet can exceed 1,300 ft (400 m).*

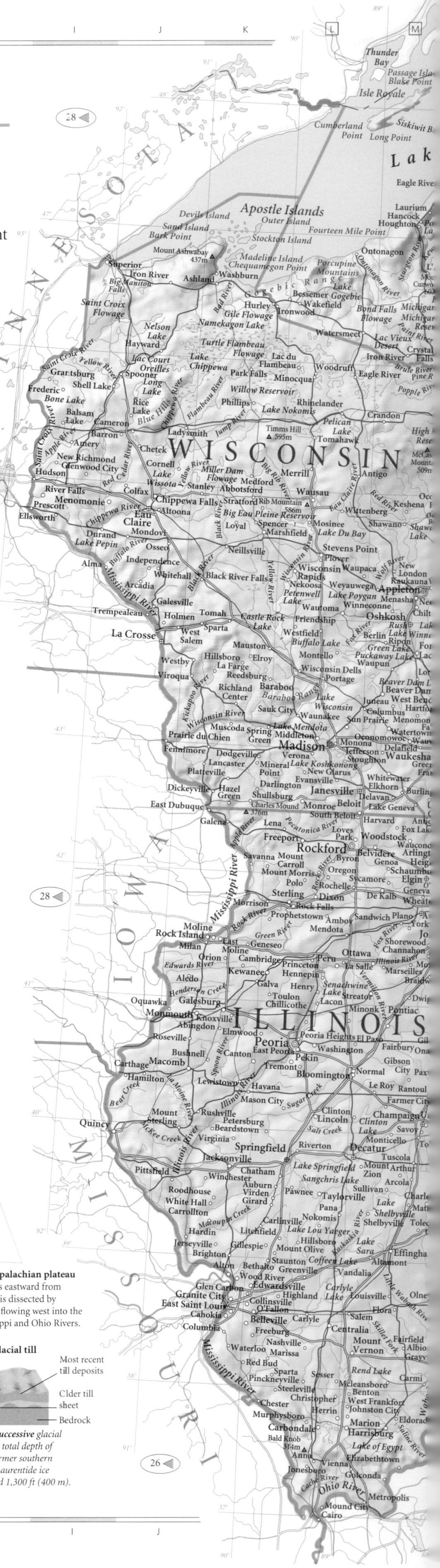

28
26
MINNESOTA
IOWA
MISSOURI
WISCONSIN
ILLINOIS
Lake Superior
Apostle Islands
Isle Royale
Thunder Bay
Superior
Ashland
Eau Claire
La Crosse
Wausau
Green Bay
Appleton
Oshkosh
Madison
Janesville
Beloit
Rockford
Freeport
Dubuque
Moline
Rock Island
Galesburg
Peoria
Bloomington
Normal
Champaign
Decatur
Springfield
Quincy
Jacksonville
East Saint Louis
Belleville
Carbondale
Cairo
Mississippi River
Ohio River
Wisconsin River
Illinois River

CANADA
Lake Superior
Lake Huron
Georgian Bay
Lake Michigan
Lake Erie
Lake Ontario
MICHIGAN
OHIO
INDIANA
NEW YORK
PENNSYLVANIA
WEST VIRGINIA
KENTUCKY
Detroit
Chicago
Toledo
Cleveland
Columbus
Indianapolis
Cincinnati
Grand Rapids
Lansing
Flint
Fort Wayne
South Bend
Dayton
Akron
Youngstown
Evansville
Saginaw
Michipicoten Bay
North Channel
Main Channel
Straits of Mackinac

THE URBAN/RURAL POPULATION DIVIDE

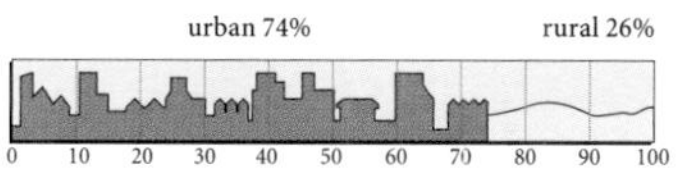
urban 74%
rural 26%
0 10 20 30 40 50 60 70 80 90 100

POPULATION DENSITY	TOTAL LAND AREA
177 people per sq mile (68 people per sq km)	248,283 sq miles (643,028 sq km)

USING THE LAND

THE VARIED SOILS AND CLIMATE of this region have allowed the development of different types of agriculture. Corn and soybeans are the main crops produced, although Michigan is best known for growing fruit, particularly cherries and apples. About 80% of Wisconsin's agricultural income is derived from livestock-rearing and dairying. Pig breeding is important in both Illinois and Indiana.

Lake Superior
CANADA
Minnesota
Michigan
Lake Huron
Lake Michigan
Wisconsin
Milwaukee
Chicago
Detroit
Lake Erie
Lake Ontario
New York
Pennsylvania
Iowa
Illinois
Indiana
Ohio
Cleveland
Springfield
Indianapolis
Columbus
Missouri
Kentucky
West Virginia
Land use and agricultural distribution
cattle
pigs
poultry
corn (maize)
fruit
soybeans
timber
major towns
pasture
cropland
forest

Farms like this one stretch across more than 80% of Illinois, covering 44,800 sq miles (116,000 sq km). The state is the leading US producer of soybeans, which are used for animal feed and oil.

***Lake Superior** is the largest of the Great Lakes and attracts millions of tourists each year. Valuable mineral deposits such as iron and copper are mined close to its shores.*

SCALE 1:4,250,000
(projection: Lambert Conformal Conic)

Km 0 10 20 40 60 80 100
Miles 0 10 20 40 60 80 100

***Although large-scale agribusiness** has mostly replaced family farming in the Midwest, some communities, such as the Amish people in Ohio, retain traditional farming methods, cultivating their smallholdings using limited machinery.*

MAP KEY

POPULATION	ELEVATION
1 million to 5 million	1000m / 3281ft
500,000 to 1 million	500m / 1640ft
100,000 to 500,000	250m / 820ft
50,000 to 100,000	100m / 328ft
10,000 to 50,000	sea level
below 10,000	

USA: North Mountain States

Idaho, Montana, Oregon, Washington, Wyoming

The remoteness of the northwestern states, coupled with the rugged landscape, ensured that this was one of the last areas settled by Europeans in the 19th century. Fur-trappers and gold-prospectors followed the Snake River westward as it wound its way through the Rocky Mountains. The states of the northwest have pioneered many conservationist policies, with the first US National Park opened at Yellowstone in 1872. More recently, the Cascades and Rocky Mountains have become havens for adventure tourism. The mountains still serve to isolate the western seaboard from the rest of the continent. This isolation has encouraged West Coast cities to expand their trade links with countries of the Pacific Rim.

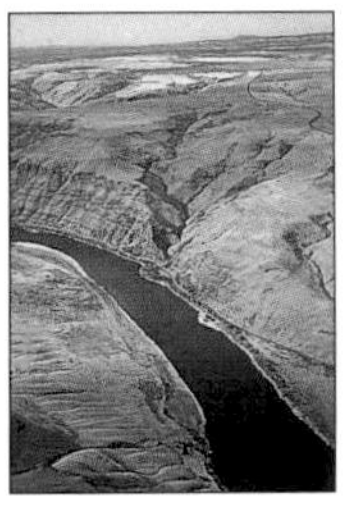

***The Snake River** has cut down into the basalt of the Columbia Basin to form Hells Canyon, the deepest in the US, with cliffs up to 7,900 ft (2,408 m) high.*

Map Key

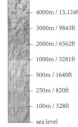

Population
- 500,000 to 1 million
- 100,000 to 500,000
- 50,000 to 100,000
- 10,000 to 50,000
- below 10,000

Elevation
- 4000m / 13,124ft
- 3000m / 9843ft
- 2000m / 6562ft
- 1000m / 3281ft
- 500m / 1640ft
- 250m / 820ft
- 100m / 328ft
- sea level

***Fine-textured, volcanic soils** in the hilly Palouse region of eastern Washington are susceptible to erosion.*

Using the Land

Wheat farming in the east gives way to cattle ranching as rainfall decreases. Irrigated farming in the Snake River valley produces large yields of potatoes and other vegetables. Dairying and fruit-growing take place in the wet western lowlands between the mountain ranges.

The Urban/Rural Population Divide

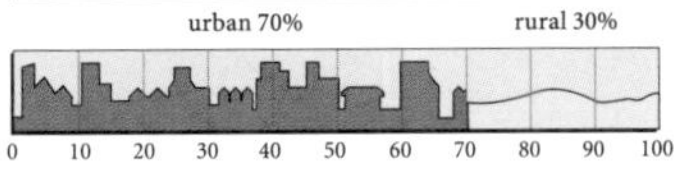

urban 70%
rural 30%
0 10 20 30 40 50 60 70 80 90 100

Population Density	Total Land Area
23 people per sq mile (9 people per sq km)	493,782 sq miles (1,278,846 sq km)

Scale 1:4,250,000 (projection: Lambert Conformal Conic)

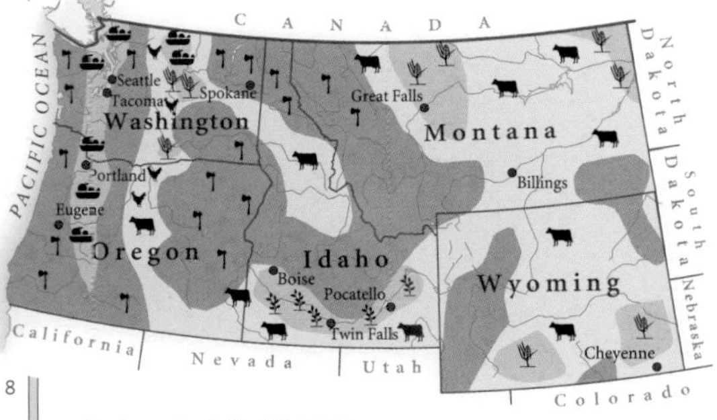

Canada
Pacific Ocean
Seattle
Tacoma
Spokane
Washington
Great Falls
Montana
Portland
Billings
Eugene
Oregon
Idaho
Boise
Pocatello
Twin Falls
Wyoming
Cheyenne
California
Nevada
Utah
Colorado
North Dakota
South Dakota
Nebraska

Land use and agricultural distribution
- cattle
- poultry
- cereals
- fruit
- potatoes
- timber
- major towns
- pasture
- cropland
- forest

Transportation & Industry

Minerals and timber are extremely important in this region. Uranium, precious metals, copper, and coal are all mined, the latter in vast open-cast pits in Wyoming; oil and natural gas are extracted further north. Manufacturing, notably related to the aerospace and electronics industries, is important in western cities.

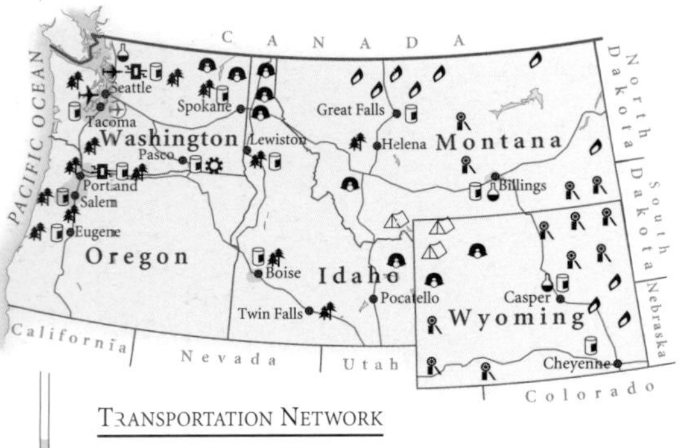

Canada
Pacific Ocean
Seattle
Tacoma
Spokane
Washington
Lewiston
Pasco
Great Falls
Helena
Montana
Billings
Portland
Salem
Eugene
Oregon
Idaho
Boise
Pocatello
Twin Falls
Casper
Wyoming
Cheyenne
California
Nevada
Utah
Colorado
North Dakota
South Dakota
Nebraska

Transportation Network

roads	347,857 miles (556,571 km)
highways	4,200 miles (6,720 km)
railways	12,354 miles (19,766 km)
waterways	1,108 miles (1,782 km)

The Union Pacific Railroad has been in service across Wyoming since 1867. The route through the Rocky Mountains is now shared with the Interstate 80, a major east–west highway.

Major industry and infrastructure
- adventure tourism
- aerospace
- coal
- chemicals
- electronics
- food processing
- mining
- oil & gas
- timber processing
- major towns
- international airports
- major roads
- major industrial areas

Pacific Ocean
Washington
Oregon
California
Nevada
Cascade Range
Coast Ranges
Olympic Mountains
Blue Mountains
Columbia Basin
Harney Basin
Seattle
Tacoma
Olympia
Bellingham
Everett
Spokane
Yakima
Wenatchee
Ellensburg
Richland
Kennewick
Pasco
Walla Walla
Vancouver
Portland
Salem
Eugene
Springfield
Corvallis
Albany
Bend
Medford
Klamath Falls
Roseburg
Coos Bay
Pendleton
La Grande
Baker
Mount Rainier 4392m
Mount Saint Helens 2549m
Mount Adams 3741m
Mount Hood 3424m
Mount Baker 3254m
Mount Olympus 2428m
Mount Jefferson 3199m
Three Sisters 3157m
Columbia River
Snake River
Crater Lake
Cape Flattery
Cape Disappointment
Cape Blanco
Puget Sound
Strait of Juan de Fuca

192
8
34
34

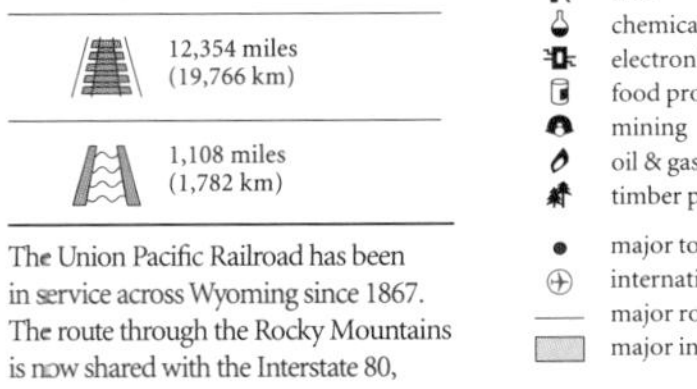

***Seattle lies** in one of Puget Sound's many inlets. The city receives oil and other resources from Alaska, and benefits from expanding trade across the Pacific.*

***Crater Lake, Oregon,** is 6 miles (10 km) wide and 1,800 ft (600 m) deep. It marks the site of a volcanic cone, which collapsed after an eruption within the last 7,000 years.*

THE LANDSCAPE

THE ROCKY MOUNTAINS are flanked by lower parallel ranges, which spread onto the Great Plains in the east and surmount the broad lava plateau which extends westward. The Cascade Range divides the Columbia Basin from the coastlands, where the low areas around Puget Sound are broken by the steep, volcanic Olympic Mountains and the wooded hills of the Coast Ranges.

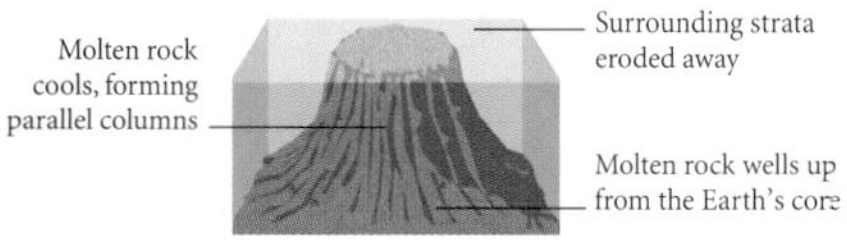
Molten rock cools, forming parallel columns
Surrounding strata eroded away
Molten rock wells up from the Earth's core

***Devil's Tower in Wyoming** is an igneous intrusion, formed below the Earth's surface. Molten rock intruded through cracks in the overlying strata and cooled. Over time, the softer rock layers have been eroded away, leaving only the tower standing.*

Glacial valleys on the seaward side of the Olympic Mountains receive about 142 inches (3,600 mm) of rain per year, supporting the only true rain forest of the northern hemisphere.

The Cascades are glacially scoured volcanic mountains, the highest of which is Mount Rainier, a dormant volcano at 14,409 ft (4,392 m).

Mount St. Helens erupted in 1980, killing 57 people and devastating a huge area.

Puget Sound

Columbia Basin

Grand Coulee and the lesser *coulées* (ravines) were cut by cataclysmic floods, from the release of an ice-dammed lake, at the end of the last ice age.

The Continental Divide, or watershed, crosses the Lewis Range. From here, rivers flow east to Hudson Bay, south to the Gulf of Mexico and west to the Pacific Ocean.

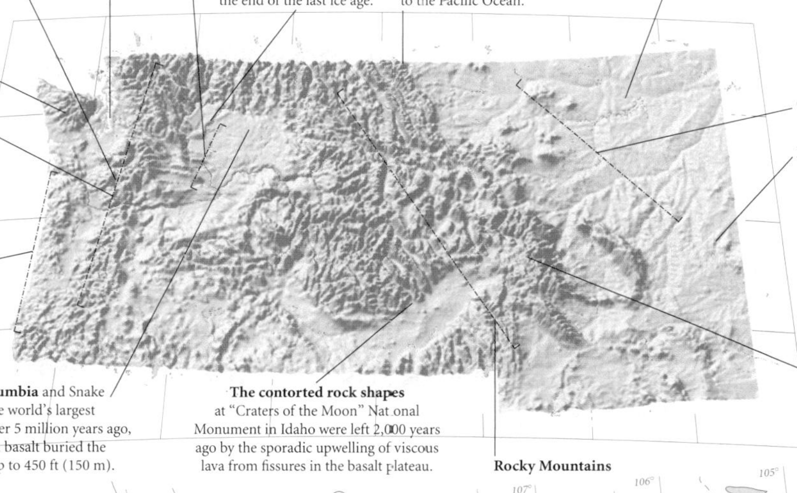

Coast Ranges

Great Plains

Devil's Tower

Rocky Mountains

The plateaus of the Columbia and Snake Rivers represent one of the world's largest accumulations of lava. Over 5 million years ago, successive flows of molten basalt buried the existing land surface by up to 450 ft (150 m).

The contorted rock shapes at "Craters of the Moon" National Monument in Idaho were left 2,000 years ago by the sporadic upwelling of viscous lava from fissures in the basalt plateau.

***Piney Buttes** are the remnants of an older, higher land surface gradually weathered and eroded into isolated outcrops with flat tops and steep sides.*

***Water from the hot springs** in Yellowstone National Park deposits minerals as it cools in rock pools. Long periods of deposition have created these rock terraces.*

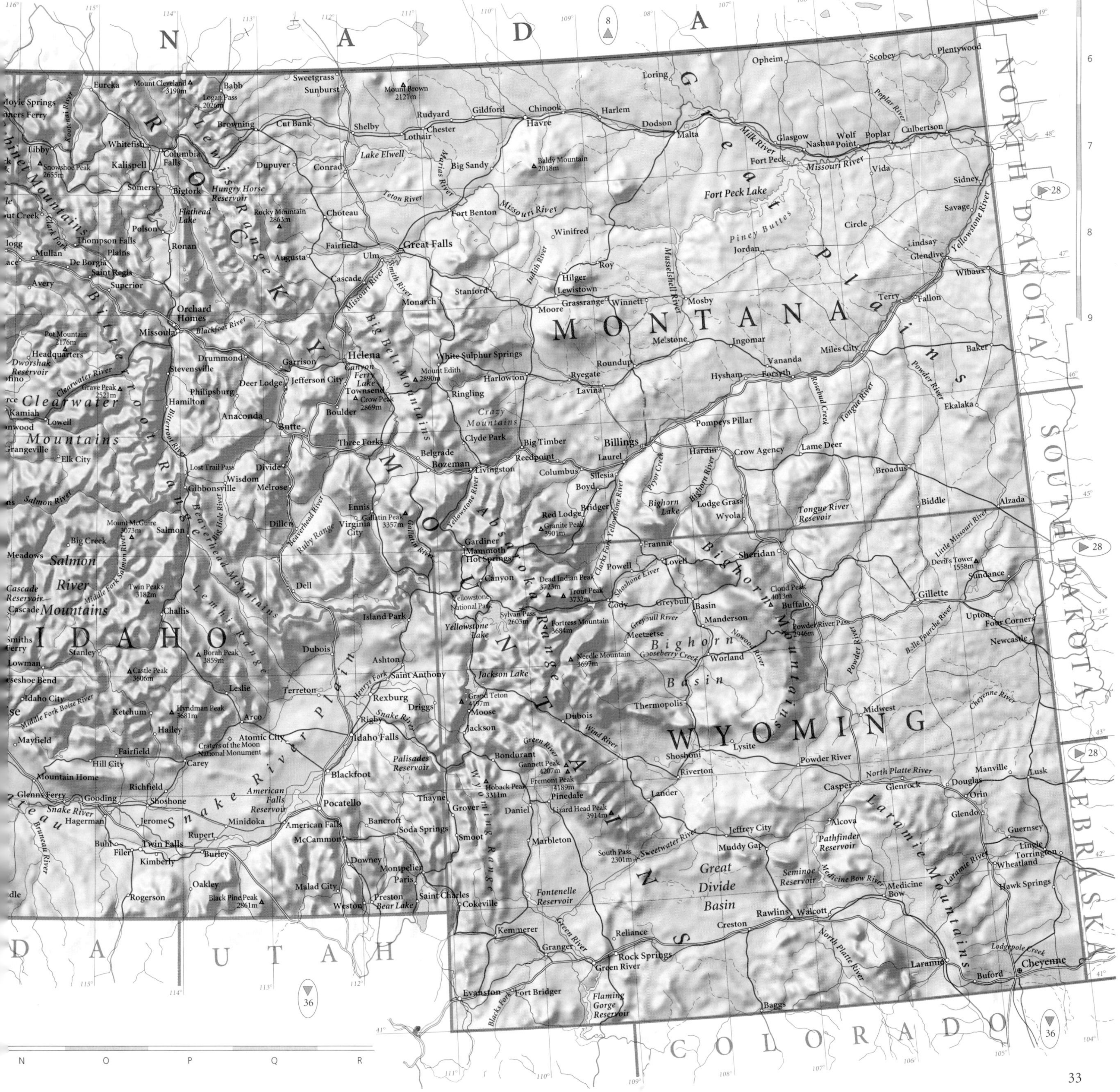
N O P Q R S T U V W X Y
1 2 3 4 5 6 7 8 9
MONTANA
IDAHO
WYOMING
NORTH DAKOTA
SOUTH DAKOTA
NEBRASKA
COLORADO
UTAH
CANADA
ROCKY MOUNTAINS
Great Plains
Bitterroot Range
Lewis Range
Big Belt Mountains
Absaroka Range
Bighorn Mountains
Bighorn Basin
Wind River Range
Laramie Mountains
Great Divide Basin
Snake River Plain
Clearwater Mountains
Salmon River Mountains
Lemhi Range
Beaverhead Mountains
Wyoming Range
Crazy Mountains
Piney Buttes
Fort Peck Lake
Missouri River
Yellowstone River
Snake River
Milk River
Yellowstone Lake
Jackson Lake
Flathead Lake
Helena
Great Falls
Missoula
Butte
Billings
Bozeman
Kalispell
Havre
Glendive
Miles City
Lewistown
Sheridan
Casper
Cheyenne
Laramie
Rock Springs
Rawlins
Gillette
Cody
Idaho Falls
Pocatello
Twin Falls
Devil's Tower 1558m
Grand Teton 4197m
Gannett Peak 4207m
Cloud Peak 4013m
Granite Peak 3901m
Borah Peak 3859m
28
36
8

USA: California & Nevada

THE GOLD RUSH OF 1849 attracted the first major wave of European settlers to the West Coast. The pleasant climate, beautiful scenery and dynamic economy continue to attract immigrants – despite the ever-present danger of earthquakes – and California has become the US's most populous state. The overwhelmingly urban population is concentrated in the vast conurbations of Los Angeles, San Francisco, and San Diego; new immigrants include people from South Korea, the Philippines, Vietnam, and Mexico. Nevada's arid lands were initially exploited for minerals; in recent years, revenue from mining has been superseded by income from the tourist and gambling centers of Las Vegas and Reno.

Map Key

POPULATION
- 1 million to 5 million
- 500,000 to 1 million
- 100,000 to 500,000
- 50,000 to 100,000
- 10,000 to 50 000
- below 10,000

ELEVATION
- 4000m / 13,124ft
- 3000m / 9843ft
- 2000m / 6562ft
- 1000m / 3281ft
- 500m / 1640ft
- 250m / 820ft
- 100m / 328ft
- sea level

SCALE 1:3,250,000
(projection: Lambert Conformal Conic)

Km 0 5 10 20 30 40 50 60 70 80

0 5 10 20 30 40 50 60 70 80 Miles

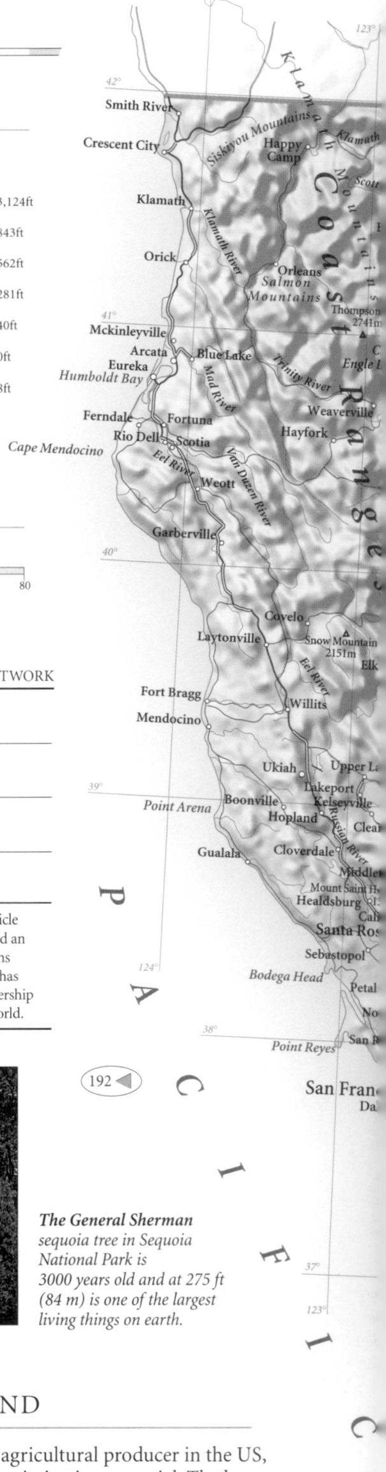

Smith River
Crescent City
Klamath
Orick
Happy Camp
Siskiyou Mountains
Klamath River
Orleans
Salmon Mountains
Coast Ranges
Mckinleyville
Arcata
Eureka
Humboldt Bay
Blue Lake
Trinity River
Mad River
Weaverville
Hayfork
Ferndale
Rio Dell
Fortuna
Scotia
Eel River
Cape Mendocino
Van Duzen River
Weott
Garberville
Covelo
Laytonville
Snow Mountain 2151m
Willits
Fort Bragg
Mendocino
Ukiah
Upper Lake
Lakeport
Boonville
Hopland
Kelseyville
Point Arena
Gualala
Cloverdale
Healdsburg
Santa Rosa
Sebastopol
Bodega Head
Petaluma
Point Reyes
San Francisco
PACIFIC

192

Transportation & Industry

NEVADA'S RICH MINERAL RESERVES ushered in a period of mining wealth which has now been replaced by revenue generated from gambling. California supports a broad set of industries including defense-related industries and research and development facilities. "Silicon Valley," near San Francisco, is a world leading center for microelectronics, while tourism and the Los Angeles film industry also generate large incomes.

DUNES
OASIS
CASINO

Gambling was legalized in Nevada in 1931. Las Vegas has since become the center of this multimillion dollar industry.

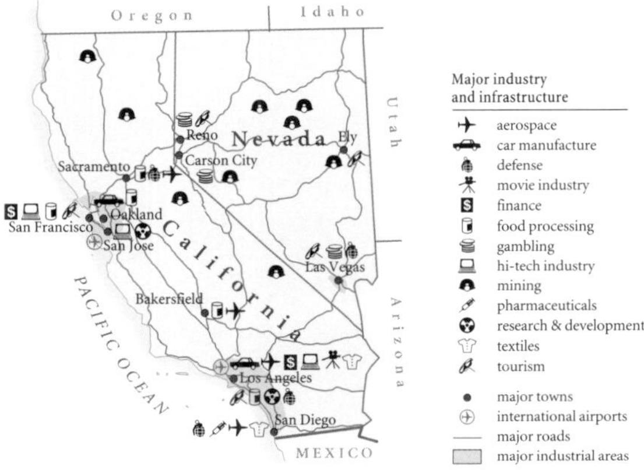

Oregon
Idaho
Utah
Nevada
Reno
Carson City
Ely
Sacramento
San Francisco
Oakland
San Jose
California
Las Vegas
Bakersfield
Los Angeles
San Diego
PACIFIC OCEAN
Arizona
MEXICO
Major industry and infrastructure
aerospace
car manufacture
defense
movie industry
finance
food processing
gambling
hi-tech industry
mining
pharmaceuticals
research & development
textiles
tourism
major towns
international airports
major roads
major industrial areas

Transportation Network

- 211,459 miles (338,334 km)
- 2,944 miles (4,710 km)
- 7,872 miles (12,595 km)
- 190 miles (306 km)

In California, the motor vehicle is a vital part of daily life, and an extensive freeway system runs throughout the state, which has a greater *per capita* car ownership than anywhere else in the world.

The Landscape

THE BROAD CENTRAL VALLEY divides California's coastal mountains from the Sierra Nevada. The San Andreas Fault, running beneath much of the state, is the site of frequent earth tremors and sometimes more serious earthquakes. East of the Sierra Nevada, the landscape is characterized by the basin and range topography with stony deserts and many salt lakes.

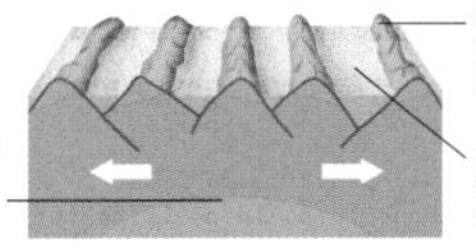

Rising molten rock causes stretching of the Earth's crust
Extensive cracking (faulting) uplifted a series of ridges
As ridges are eroded they fill intervening valleys with sediments

***Molten rock** (magma) welling up to form a dome in the Earth's interior, causes the brittle surface rocks to stretch and crack. Some areas were uplifted to form mountains (ranges), while others sunk to form flat valleys (basins).*

***The General Sherman** sequoia tree in Sequoia National Park is 3000 years old and at 275 ft (84 m) is one of the largest living things on earth.*

Most of California's agriculture is confined to the fertile and extensively irrigated Central Valley, running between the Coast Ranges and the Sierra Nevada. It incorporates the San Joaquin and Sacramento valleys.

The dramatic granitic rock formations of Half Dome and El Capitan, and the verdant coniferous forests, attract millions of visitors annually to Yosemite National Park in the Sierra Nevada.

The Great Basin dominates most of Nevada's topography containing large open basins, punctuated by eroded features such as *buttes* and *mesas*. River flow tends to be seasonal, dependent upon spring showers and winter snow melt.

Sierra Nevada

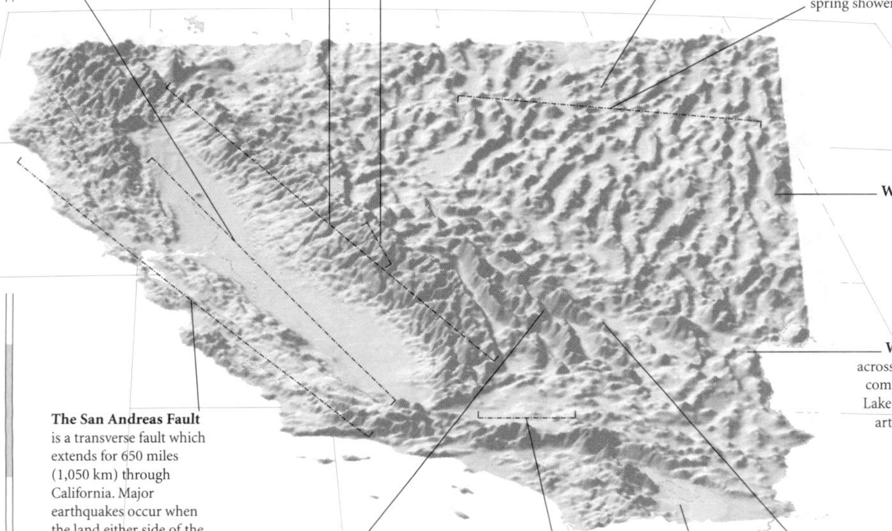

Wheeler Peak is home to some of the world's oldest trees, bristlecone pines, which live for up to 5,000 years.

When the Hoover Dam across the Colorado River was completed in 1936, it created Lake Mead, one of the largest artificial lakes in the world, extending for 115 miles (285 km) upstream.

The San Andreas Fault is a transverse fault which extends for 650 miles (1,050 km) through California. Major earthquakes occur when the land either side of the fault moves at different rates. San Francisco was devastated by an earthquake in 1906.

Death Valley

***Named by migrating settlers** in 1849, Death Valley is the driest, hottest place in North America, as well as being the lowest point on land in the western hemisphere, at 282 ft (86 m) below sea level.*

The sparsely populated Mojave Desert receives less than 8 inches (200 mm) of rainfall a year. It is used extensively for testing weapons and other military purposes.

The Salton Sea was created accidentally between 1905 and 1907 when an irrigation channel from the Colorado River broke out of its banks and formed this salty 300 sq mile (777 sq km), landlocked lake.

Amargosa Desert

***The Sierra Nevada** create a "rainshadow," preventing rain from reaching much of Nevada. Pacific air masses, passing over the mountains, are stripped of their moisture.*

Using the Land

CALIFORNIA is the leading agricultural producer in the US, although low rainfall makes irrigation essential. The long growing season and abundant sunshine allow many crops to be grown in the fertile Central Valley including grapes, citrus fruits, vegetables, and cotton. Almost 17 million acres (6.8 million hectares) of California's forests are used commercially. Nevada's arid climate and poor soil are largely unsuitable for agriculture; 85% of its land is state owned and large areas are used for underground testing of nuclear weapons.

Land use and agricultural distribution
cattle
citrus fruits
fruit
irrigation
timber
vineyards
major towns
pasture
cropland
forest
desert
Oregon
Idaho
Utah
Nevada
Reno
Sacramento
San Francisco
California
Las Vegas
Arizona
PACIFIC OCEAN
Los Angeles
San Diego
MEXICO

***Without considerable** irrigation, this fertile valley at Palm Springs would still be part of the Sonoran Desert. California's farmers account for about 80% of the state's total water usage.*

The Urban/Rural Population Divide

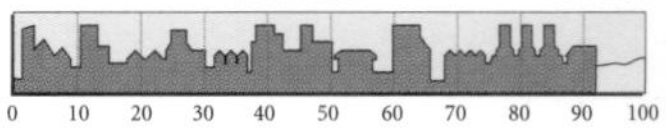

urban 92%
rural 8%
0 10 20 30 40 50 60 70 80 90 100

Population Density	Total Land Area
126 people per sq mile (49 people per sq km)	269,233 sq miles (697,286 sq km)

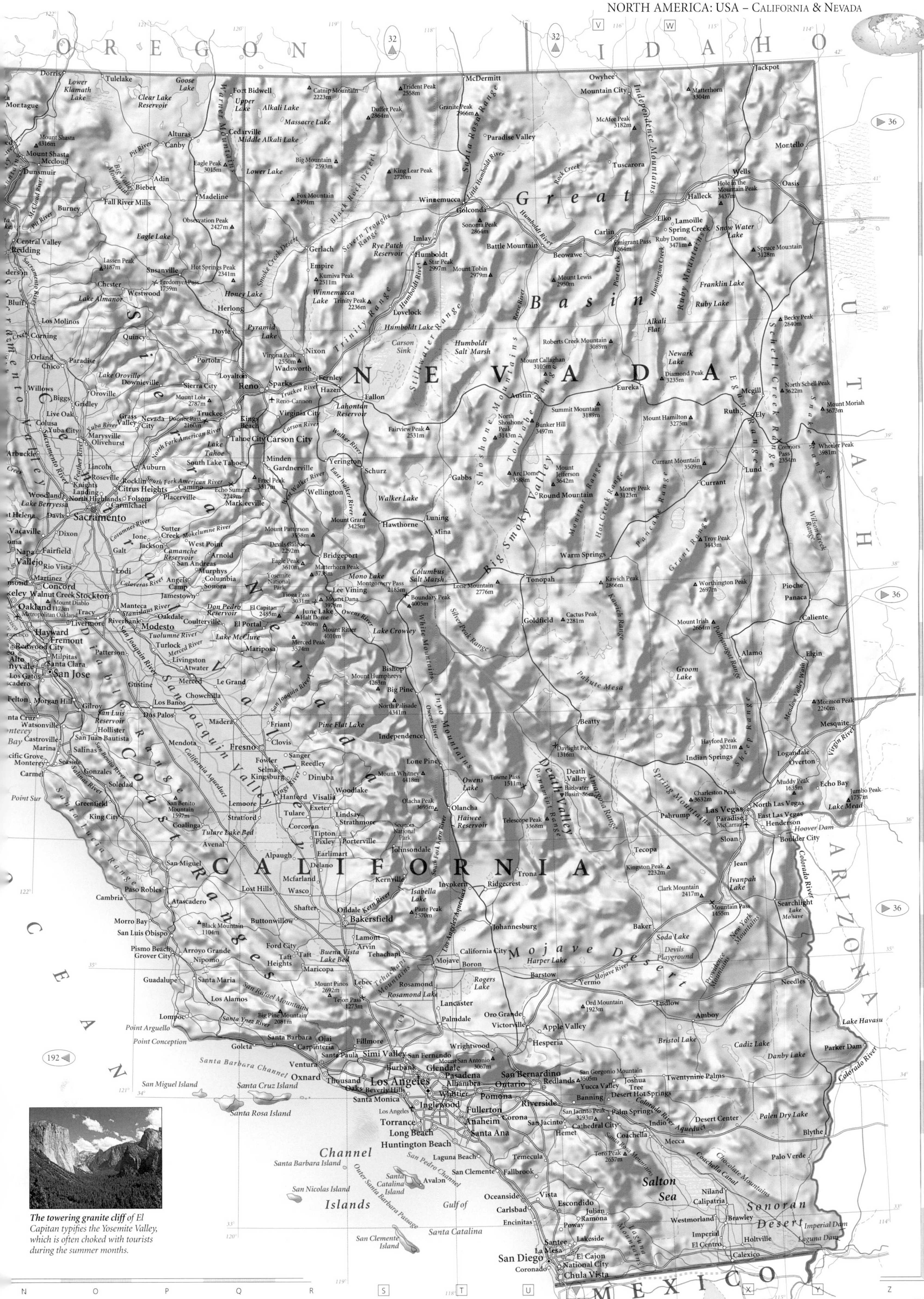
OREGON
IDAHO
UTAH
ARIZONA
MEXICO
NEVADA
CALIFORNIA
OCEAN
Great Basin
Sierra Nevada
Coast Ranges
Diablo Range
Santa Lucia Range
San Joaquin Valley
Sacramento Valley
Mojave Desert
Sonoran Desert
Death Valley
Channel Islands
Salton Sea
Lake Tahoe
Mono Lake
Walker Lake
Pyramid Lake
Lake Mead
Lake Havasu
Colorado River
Humboldt River
Jackpot
Owyhee
Mountain City
McDermitt
Winnemucca
Golconda
Battle Mountain
Elko
Wells
Carlin
Eureka
Ely
McGill
Austin
Fallon
Fernley
Reno
Sparks
Carson City
Virginia City
Yerington
Hawthorne
Tonopah
Goldfield
Beatty
Pioche
Caliente
Mesquite
Las Vegas
North Las Vegas
Henderson
Boulder City
Hoover Dam
Searchlight
Needles
Barstow
Victorville
Lancaster
Palmdale
Bakersfield
Fresno
Modesto
Stockton
Sacramento
Oakland
San Jose
Salinas
Monterey
Santa Maria
San Luis Obispo
Santa Barbara
Ventura
Oxnard
Los Angeles
Glendale
Pasadena
Long Beach
Anaheim
Santa Ana
Riverside
San Bernardino
Palm Springs
Oceanside
Escondido
San Diego
Chula Vista
El Centro
Calexico
Redding
Mount Shasta 4316m
Lassen Peak 3187m
Mount Whitney 4418m
Boundary Peak 4005m
Wheeler Peak 3981m
Point Conception
Point Arguello
Point Sur
Santa Catalina
San Clemente Island
Santa Cruz Island
Santa Rosa Island
San Miguel Island
San Nicolas Island
Santa Barbara Island

The towering granite cliff of El Capitan typifies the Yosemite Valley, which is often choked with tourists during the summer months.

USA: South Mountain states

Arizona, Colorado, New Mexico, Utah

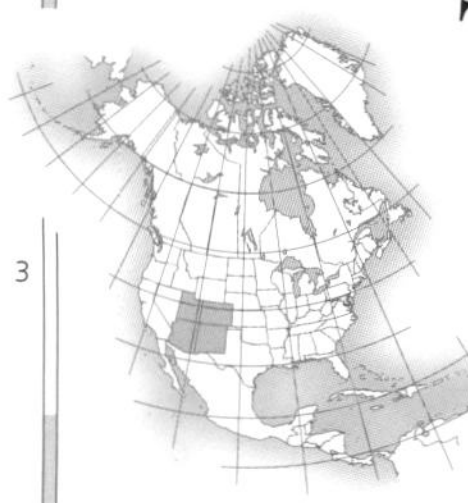

THIS ARID REGION, CHARACTERIZED BY EXPANSIVE PLATEAUS and spectacular canyons is home to several distinct peoples. The ruins of cliff dwellings built a thousand years ago by the Anasazi people still exist today, and native Americans own one-third of the land in Arizona. Spanish and Mexican conquest and settlement left a Hispanic presence which is strongest in New Mexico. The Mormons, who came to the Great Salt Lake seeking religious freedom in 1847, were among the earliest Anglo-American settlers and now make up over 70% of Utah's population. The region's mineral wealth drove rapid development in the 20th century, yet the constraints of a fragile environment, including widespread water shortages, may limit prospects for growth.

When water evaporates it leaves a salt pan
Mudflats
Lake is fed by seasonal snow melt
Water level of lake varies according to quantity of run-off received from snow melt

***The Great Salt Lake** is an ephemeral lake; it can remain dry for extended periods, leaving a pan of evaporated mineral salts in its center.*

The Landscape

THE ARID, ROCKY EXPANSE of the Colorado Plateau is dissected by immense canyons of the Colorado River. Desert lies to the north and south and branches of the Rocky Mountains run east and west. The Great Salt Lake and Desert lie within the Great Basin, a barren region of parallel mountain ranges that extends into Arizona.

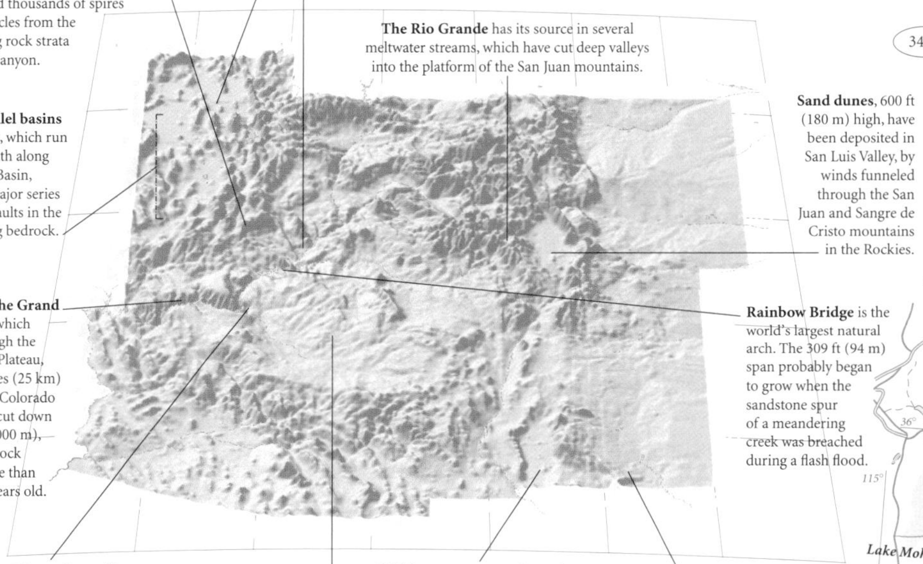

Over 13 million years of weathering has created thousands of spires and pinnacles from the alternating rock strata of Bryce Canyon.

Lake Powell

The Rio Grande has its source in several meltwater streams, which have cut deep valleys into the platform of the San Juan mountains.

Sand dunes, 600 ft (180 m) high, have been deposited in San Luis Valley, by winds funneled through the San Juan and Sangre de Cristo mountains in the Rockies.

The parallel basins and ridges, which run north–south along the Great Basin, reflect a major series of block-faults in the underlying bedrock.

Parts of the Grand Canyon, which cuts through the Colorado Plateau, are 16 miles (25 km) wide. The Colorado River has cut down 6262 ft (2000 m), exposing rock strata more than 2 billion years old.

Rainbow Bridge is the world's largest natural arch. The 309 ft (94 m) span probably began to grow when the sandstone spur of a meandering creek was breached during a flash flood.

The striking colour effects seen in the Painted Desert come from minerals such as gypsum and haematite, combined with ambient heat and dust.

Petrified Forest

Shifting gypsum sands produce a constantly changing land surface, overwhelming plants and any other obstacles in Tularosa Valley.

Carlsbad Caverns

***In the arid landscape** of Petrified Forest National Park in Arizona, the grain of prehistoric trees has been preserved as a fossil imprint in the rocks. The bog-preserved trees were gradually turned to stone by seeping mineral-rich water.*

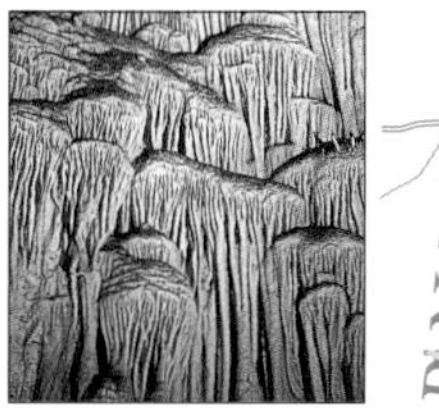

***The intricate stalactites** of Carlsbad Caverns have grown with the seepage of calcium-rich water over the last 100,000 years. The huge caves are home to around 100,000 Mexican freetail bats.*

Transportation & Industry

NEW INDUSTRIES HAVE HELPED reduce the region's dependence on the extraction of minerals and fossil fuels. Precision manufacture has grown rapidly, particularly in Arizona and Colorado. Salt Lake City and Denver are well-established financial centers and New Mexico, the main US producer of uranium, is a prominent region for nuclear research. Colorado is the most important US center for winter sports.

Transportation Network

232,434 miles (373,986 km)	4,059 miles (6,515 km)
8,627 miles (13,881 km)	none

The Colorado Rockies are crossed by 32 mountain passes, some as high as 12,183 ft (3,713 m). The Eisenhower Tunnel west of Denver carries Interstate Highway 70 straight through the Continental Divide.

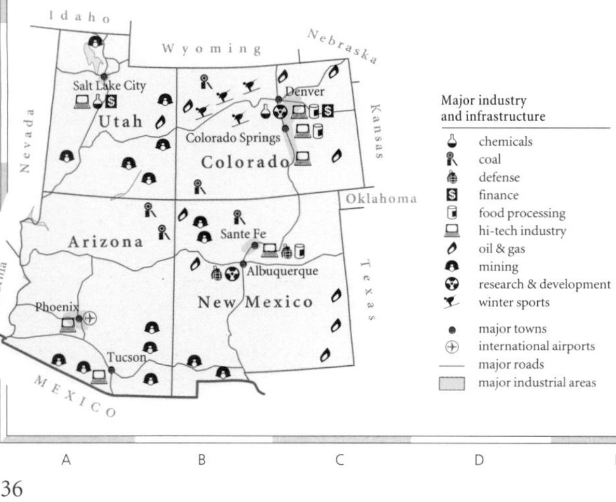

Idaho
Wyoming
Nebraska
Salt Lake City
Utah
Denver
Kansas
Nevada
Colorado Springs
Colorado
Oklahoma
Arizona
Sante Fe
Albuquerque
Texas
California
Phoenix
New Mexico
Tucson
MEXICO
Major industry and infrastructure
chemicals
coal
defense
finance
food processing
hi-tech industry
oil & gas
mining
research & development
winter sports
major towns
international airports
major roads
major industrial areas

***Glen Canyon Dam** on the Colorado river was completed in 1964. it provides hydroelectric power and irrigation water as part of a long-term federal project to harness the river.*

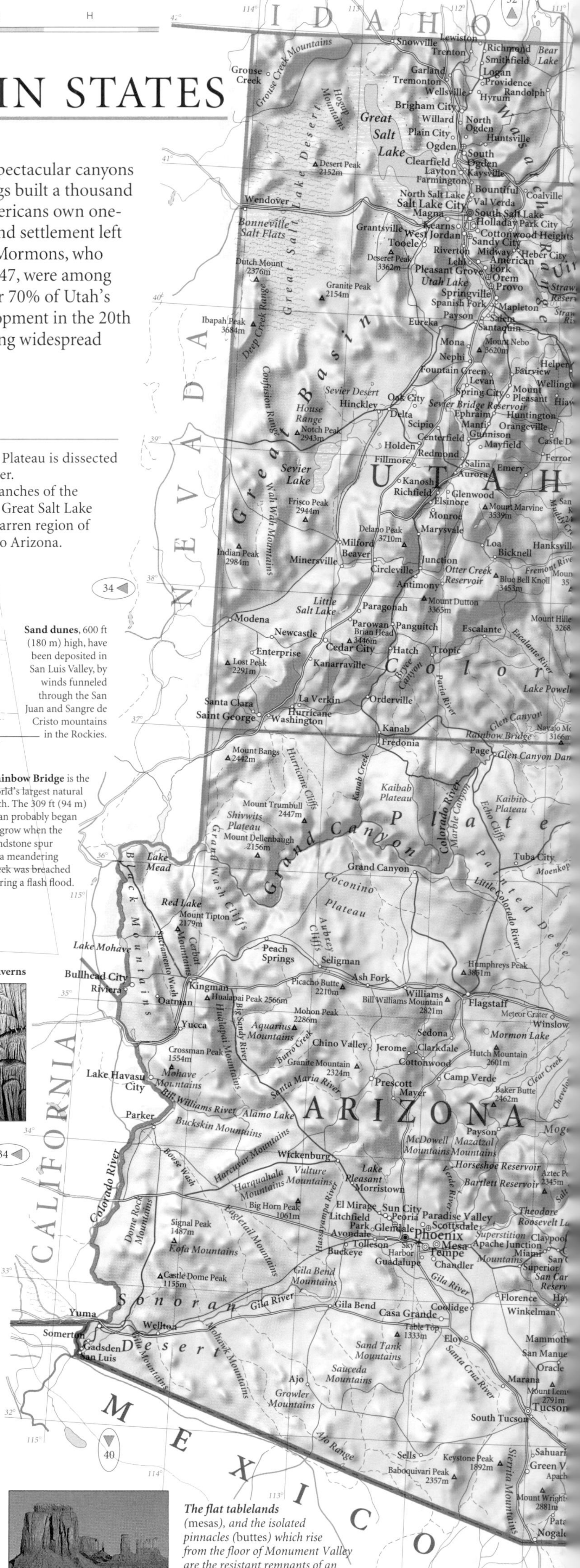

IDAHO
NEVADA
UTAH
ARIZONA
CALIFORNIA
MEXICO
Great Salt Lake
Great Salt Lake Desert
Great Basin
Bonneville Salt Flats
Sevier Lake
Salt Lake City
Ogden
Provo
Logan
Wendover
Sevier Desert
Colorado Plateau
Grand Canyon
Lake Mead
Lake Powell
Lake Mohave
Lake Havasu City
Colorado River
Kingman
Flagstaff
Prescott
Phoenix
Mesa
Tempe
Scottsdale
Glendale
Tucson
South Tucson
Yuma
Sonoran Desert
St George
Cedar City
Kanab
Page
Wickenburg
Bullhead City
Parker
Nogales
34
40
32

***The flat tablelands** (mesas), and the isolated pinnacles (buttes) which rise from the floor of Monument Valley are the resistant remnants of an earlier land surface, gradually cut back by erosion under arid conditions.*

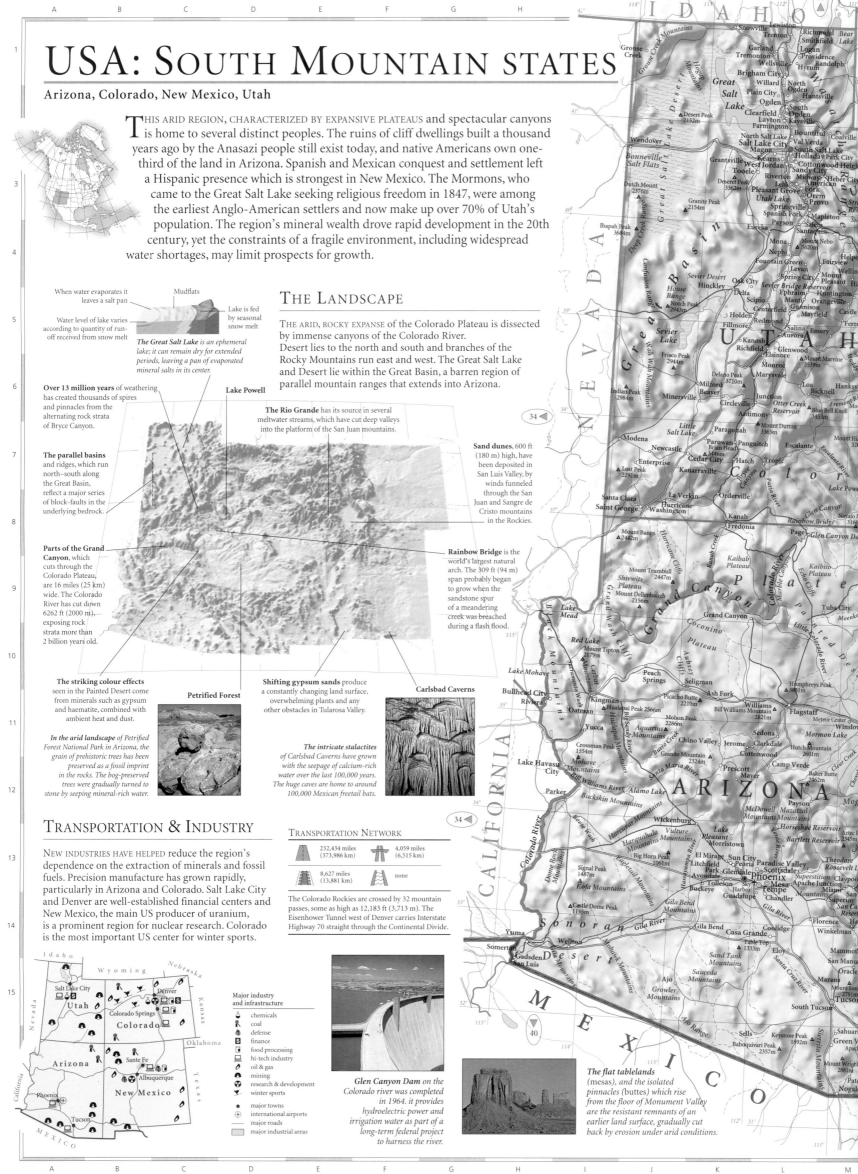

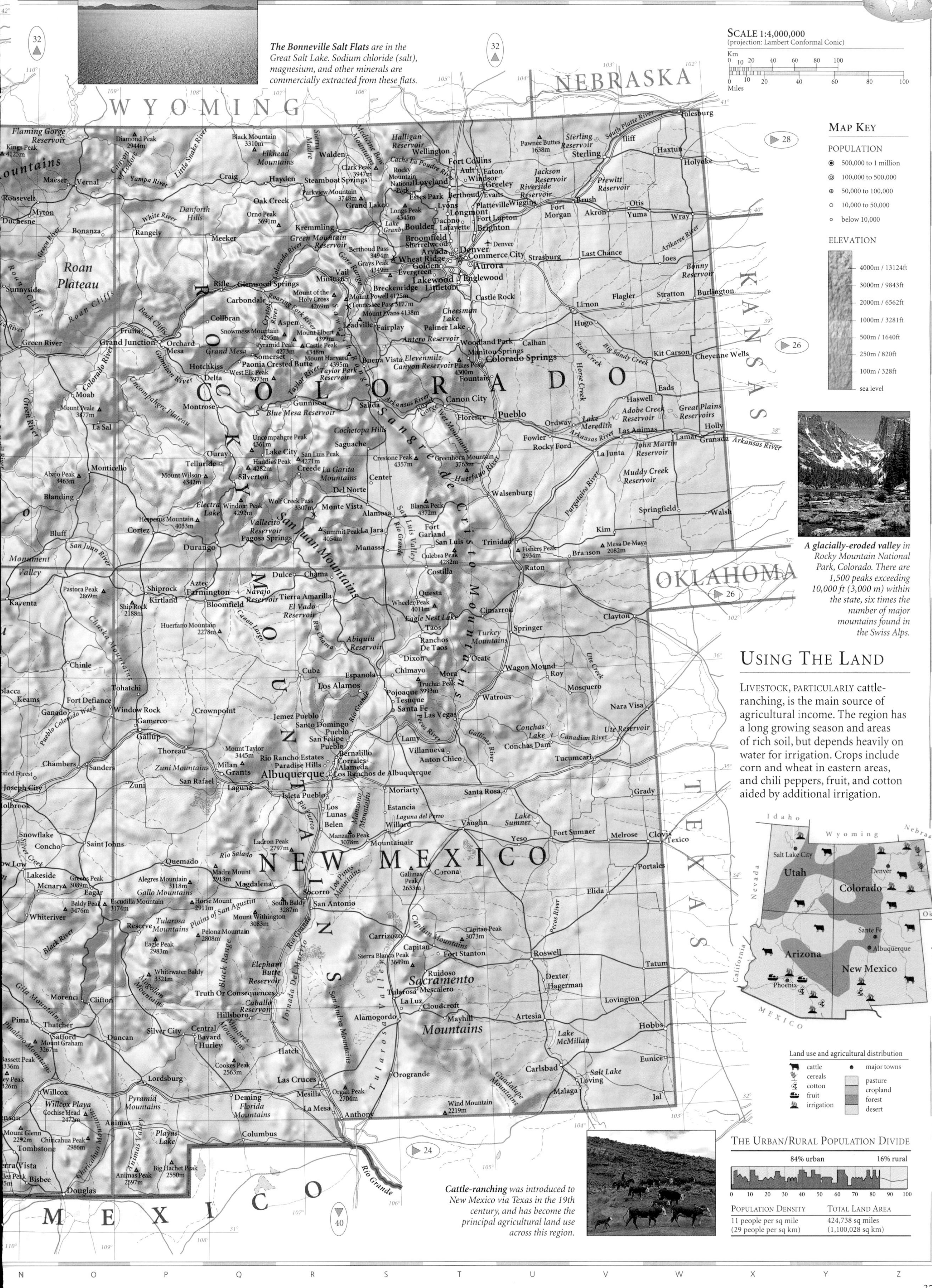
WYOMING
NEBRASKA
KANSAS
OKLAHOMA
TEXAS
COLORADO
NEW MEXICO
MEXICO
ROCKY MOUNTAINS
San Juan Mountains
Sangre de Cristo Mountains
Denver
Aurora
Lakewood
Colorado Springs
Pueblo
Fort Collins
Greeley
Boulder
Grand Junction
Durango
Trinidad
Albuquerque
Santa Fe
Las Cruces
Roswell
Farmington
Gallup
Clovis
Carlsbad
Hobbs
Alamogordo
Taos
Raton
Tucumcari
Santa Rosa
Socorro
Deming
Silver City
Rio Grande
Arkansas River
Pecos River
South Platte River
Roan Plateau
Sacramento Mountains
Mount Elbert 4399m
Pikes Peak 4300m
Wheeler Peak 4011m
Blanca Peak 4372m
Sierra Blanca Peak 3649m
Blue Mesa Reservoir
Elephant Butte Reservoir
Conchas Lake
Ute Reservoir
32
28
26
24
40
Idaho
Utah
Arizona
Nevada
California
Salt Lake City
Sante Fe
Phoenix
84% urban
16% rural
0 10 20 30 40 50 60 70 80 90 100

The Bonneville Salt Flats are in the Great Salt Lake. Sodium chloride (salt), magnesium, and other minerals are commercially extracted from these flats.

SCALE 1:4,000,000
(projection: Lambert Conformal Conic)

Km 0 10 20 40 60 80 100
Miles 0 10 20 40 60 80 100

MAP KEY

POPULATION

- 500,000 to 1 million
- 100,000 to 500,000
- 50,000 to 100,000
- 10,000 to 50,000
- below 10,000

ELEVATION

- 4000m / 13124ft
- 3000m / 9843ft
- 2000m / 6562ft
- 1000m / 3281ft
- 500m / 1640ft
- 250m / 820ft
- 100m / 328ft
- sea level

A glacially-eroded valley in Rocky Mountain National Park, Colorado. There are 1,500 peaks exceeding 10,000 ft (3,000 m) within the state, six times the number of major mountains found in the Swiss Alps.

USING THE LAND

LIVESTOCK, PARTICULARLY cattle-ranching, is the main source of agricultural income. The region has a long growing season and areas of rich soil, but depends heavily on water for irrigation. Crops include corn and wheat in eastern areas, and chili peppers, fruit, and cotton aided by additional irrigation.

Land use and agricultural distribution

- cattle
- cereals
- cotton
- fruit
- irrigation
- major towns
- pasture
- cropland
- forest
- desert

THE URBAN/RURAL POPULATION DIVIDE

POPULATION DENSITY	TOTAL LAND AREA
11 people per sq mile (29 people per sq km)	424,738 sq miles (1,100,028 sq km)

Cattle-ranching was introduced to New Mexico via Texas in the 19th century, and has become the principal agricultural land use across this region.

USA: Hawaiʻi

THE 122 ISLANDS of the Hawaiian archipelago – which are part of Polynesia – are the peaks of the world's largest volcanoes. They rise approximately 6 miles (9.7 km) from the floor of the Pacific Ocean. The largest, the island of Hawaiʻi, remains highly active. Hawaiʻi became the US's 50th state in 1959. A tradition of receiving immigrant workers is reflected in the islands' ethnic diversity, with peoples drawn from around the rim of the Pacific. Only 2% of the current population are native Polynesians.

***The island of Molokaʻi** is formed from volcanic rock. Mature sand dunes cover the rocks in coastal areas.*

Transportation & Industry

TOURISM DOMINATES the economy, with over half of the population employed in services. The naval base at Pearl Harbor is also a major source of employment. Industry is concentrated on the island of Oʻahu and relies mostly on imported materials, while agricultural produce is processed locally.

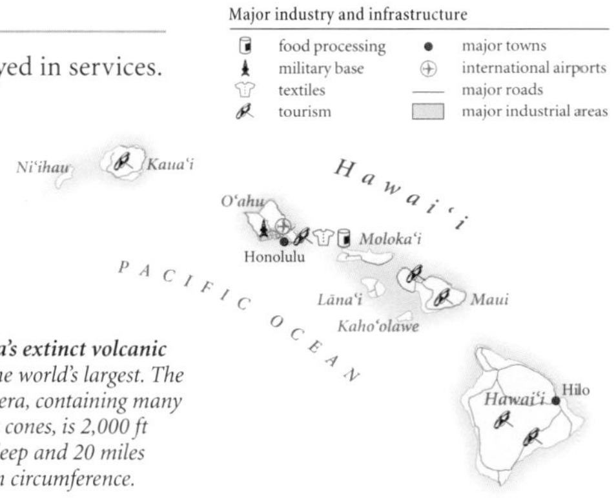
Major industry and infrastructure
food processing
military base
textiles
tourism
major towns
international airports
major roads
major industrial areas
Niʻihau
Kauaʻi
Oʻahu
Honolulu
Molokaʻi
Lānaʻi
Maui
Kahoʻolawe
Hawaiʻi
Hilo
PACIFIC OCEAN

Transportation Network

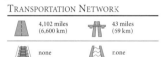

4,102 miles (6,600 km)	43 miles (59 km)
none	none

Hawaiʻi relies on ocean-surface transportation. Honolulu is the main focus of this network, bringing foreign trade and the markets of mainland US to Hawaiʻi's outer islands.

***Haleakala's extinct volcanic crater** is the world's largest. The giant caldera, containing many secondary cones, is 2,000 ft (600 m) deep and 20 miles (32 km) in circumference.*

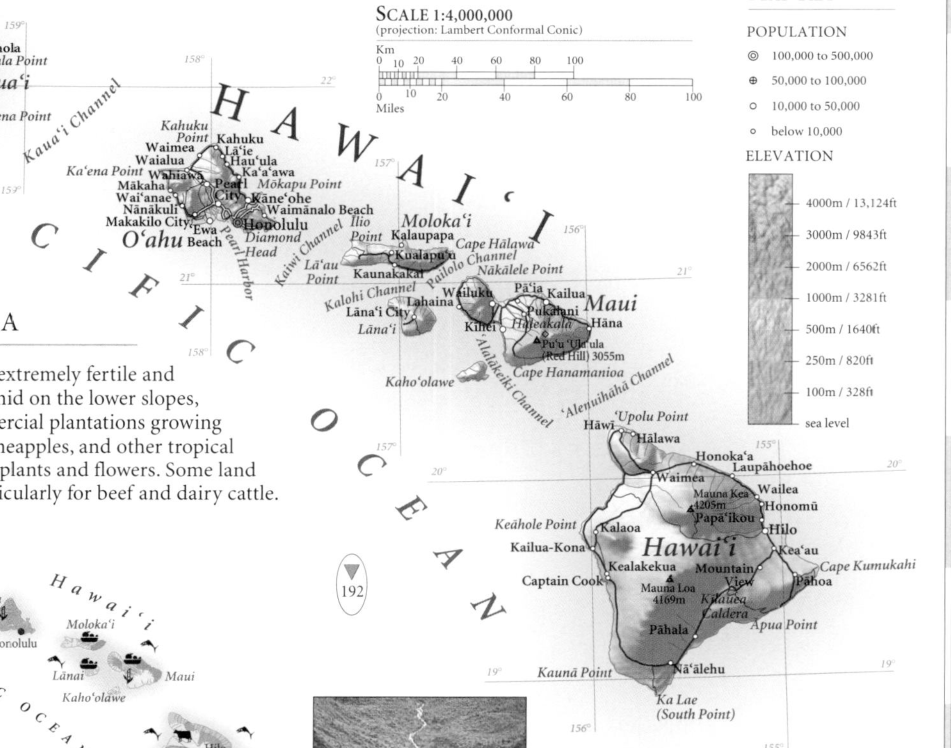
Lehua Island
Kii Landing
Niʻihau
Puʻuwai
Kawaihoa Point
Hanalei
Kīlauea
Anahola
Kahala Point
Nohili Point
Kekaha
Kapaʻa
Līhuʻe
Kauaʻi
Waimea
Kalaheo
Kōloa
ʻEle ʻele
Makahūʻena Point
Kaulakahi Channel
Kauaʻi Channel
Kahuku Point
Kahuku
Lāʻie
Hauʻula
Kaʻaʻawa
Waimea
Waialua
Kaʻena Point
Wahiawā
Mōkapu Point
Mākaha
Pearl City
Kāneʻohe
Waiʻanae
Nānākuli
Waimānalo Beach
Makakilo City
Ewa Beach
Honolulu
Oʻahu
Diamond Head
Pearl Harbor
Kaiwi Channel
Molokaʻi
Ilio Point
Kalaupapa
Cape Hālawa
Kualapuʻu
Pailolo Channel
Lāʻau Point
Kaunakakai
Nākālele Point
Kalohi Channel
Lānaʻi City
Lānaʻi
Lahaina
Wailuku
Pāʻia
Kailua
Maui
Kīhei
Pukalani
Haleakalā
Hāna
Puʻu ʻUlaʻula (Red Hill) 3055m
Kahoʻolawe
Cape Hanamanioa
ʻAlalākeiki Channel
ʻAlenuihāhā Channel
ʻUpolu Point
Hāwī
Hālawa
Honokaʻa
Laupāhoehoe
Waimea
Wailea
Honomū
Mauna Kea 4205m
Pāpaʻikou
Hilo
Keāhole Point
Kalaoa
Kailua-Kona
Hawaiʻi
Keaʻau
Kealakekua
Mountain View
Cape Kumukahi
Captain Cook
Pāhoa
Mauna Loa 4169m
Kīlauea Caldera
Pāhala
Apua Point
Kaunā Point
Nāʻālehu
Ka Lae (South Point)
HAWAIʻI
PACIFIC OCEAN
192
SCALE 1:4,000,000
(projection: Lambert Conformal Conic)

Map Key

POPULATION
- 100,000 to 500,000
- 50,000 to 100,000
- 10,000 to 50,000
- below 10,000

ELEVATION
- 4000m / 13,124ft
- 3000m / 9843ft
- 2000m / 6562ft
- 1000m / 3281ft
- 500m / 1640ft
- 250m / 820ft
- 100m / 328ft
- sea level

Using the Land and Sea

THE VOLCANIC SOILS are extremely fertile and the climate hot and humid on the lower slopes, supporting large commercial plantations growing sugar cane, bananas, pineapples, and other tropical fruit, as well as nursery plants and flowers. Some land is given to pasture, particularly for beef and dairy cattle.

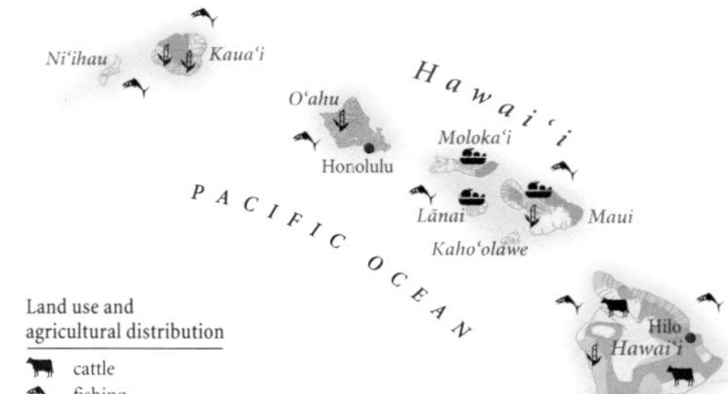
Niʻihau
Kauaʻi
Oʻahu
Honolulu
Molokaʻi
Lānaʻi
Maui
Kahoʻolawe
Hawaiʻi
Hilo
PACIFIC OCEAN
Land use and agricultural distribution
cattle
fishing
fruit
sugar cane
major towns
pasture
cropland
forest
mountain region

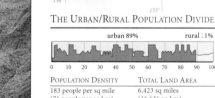

***The island of Kauaʻi** is one of the wettest places in the world, receiving some 450 inches (11,500 mm) of rain a year.*

The Urban/Rural Population Divide

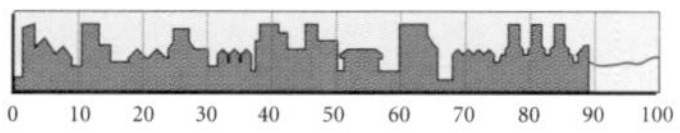
urban 89%
rural 11%
0 10 20 30 40 50 60 70 80 90 100

Population Density	Total Land Area
183 people per sq mile (71 people per sq km)	6,423 sq miles (16,636 sq km)

Using the Land and Sea

THE ICE-FREE COASTLINE of Alaska provides access to salmon fisheries and more than 5.5 million acres (2.2 million ha) of forest. Most of Alaska is uncultivable, and around 90% of food is imported. Barley, hay, and hothouse products are grown around Anchorage, where dairy farming is also concentrated.

The Urban/Rural Population Divide

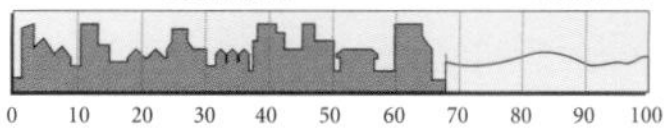
urban 68%
rural 32%
0 10 20 30 40 50 60 70 80 90 100

Population Density	Total Land Area
1 person per sq mile (0.4 people per sq km)	586,412 sq miles (1,518,800 sq km)

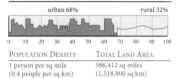

***A raft of timber** from the Tongass forest is hauled by a tug, bound for the pulp mills of the Alaskan coast between Juneau and Ketchikan.*

Cape Lisburne
Wevok
Point Hope
Kivalina
CHUKCHI SEA
Kotzebue Sound
Arctic Circle
RUSSIAN FEDERATION
Shishmaref
Little Diomede Island
Cape Prince of Wales
Wales
Brooks Mountain 883m
Kougarok Mountain 875m
Brevig Mission
Teller
Port Clarence
Cape Douglas
Cape Rodney
Nome
Cape Nome
Bering Strait
122
Northwest Cape
Gambell
Savoonga
Saint Lawrence Island
Southwest Cape
Camp Kulowiye
Northeast Cape
Southeast Cape
BERING SEA
Emmonak
Alakanuk
Sheldons Point
Hamilton
Mountain Village
Scammon Bay
Hooper Bay
Chevak
192
Hall Island
Glory of Russia Cape
Saint Matthew Island
Upright Cape
Pinnacle Island
Cape Mohican
Newtok
Aropuk Lake
Tununak
Toksook Bay
Nightmute
Mekoryuk
Nunivak Island
Roberts Mountain 510m
Chefornak
Kipnuk
Kwigillingok
Cape Mendenhall
Kuskokwim Bay
Saint Paul Island
Saint Paul
Pribilof Islands
Saint George Island
Saint George

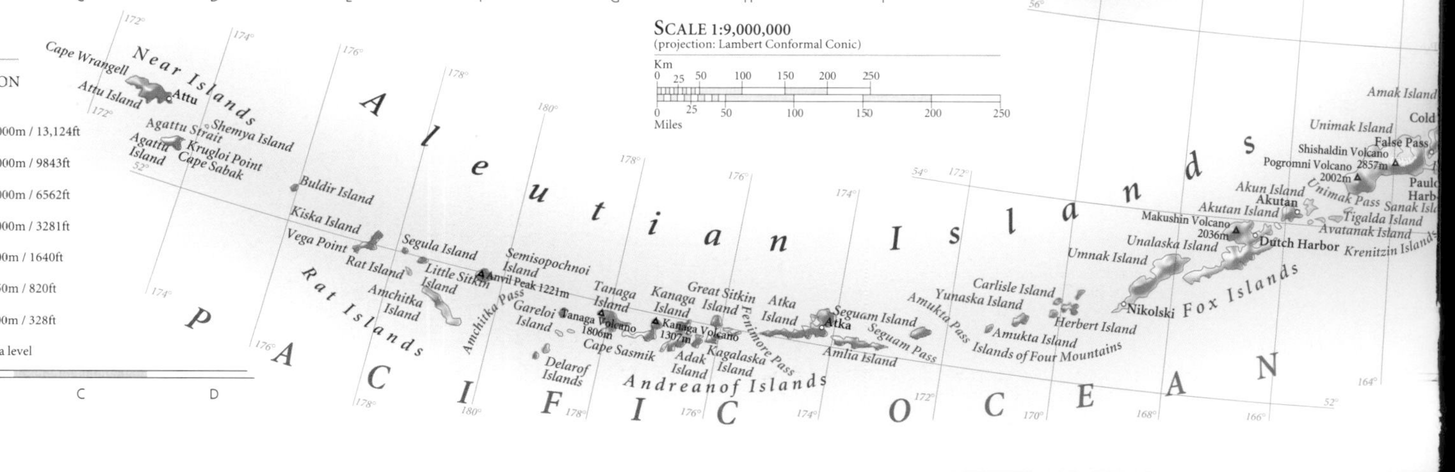
Cape Wrangell
Attu Island
Attu
Near Islands
Shemya Island
Agattu Strait
Agattu Island
Krugloi Point
Cape Sabak
Buldir Island
Kiska Island
Vega Point
Segula Island
Rat Island
Little Sitkin Island
Amchitka Island
Rat Islands
Semisopochnoi Island
Anvil Peak 1221m
Amchitka Pass
Gareloi Island
Tanaga Island
Tanaga Volcano 1806m
Kanaga Island
Kanaga Volcano
Great Sitkin Island
Adak Island
Kagalaska Island
Atka Island
Atka
Cape Sasmik
Delarof Islands
Andreanof Islands
Seguam Island
Seguam Pass
Amlia Island
Amukta Pass
Yunaska Island
Carlisle Island
Herbert Island
Amukta Island
Islands of Four Mountains
Nikolski
Fox Islands
Umnak Island
Unalaska Island
Makushin Volcano 2036m
Dutch Harbor
Akutan Island
Akutan
Akun Island
Unimak Pass
Tigalda Island
Avatanak Island
Krenitzin Islands
Unimak Island
Shishaldin Volcano
Pogromni Volcano 2857m
False Pass
Amak Island
Aleutian Islands
PACIFIC OCEAN
SCALE 1:9,000,000
(projection: Lambert Conformal Conic)

Map Key

POPULATION
- 100,000 to 500,000
- 50,000 to 100,000
- 10,000 to 50,000
- below 10,000

ELEVATION
- 4000m / 13,124ft
- 3000m / 9843ft
- 2000m / 6562ft
- 1000m / 3281ft
- 500m / 1640ft
- 250m / 820ft
- 100m / 328ft
- sea level

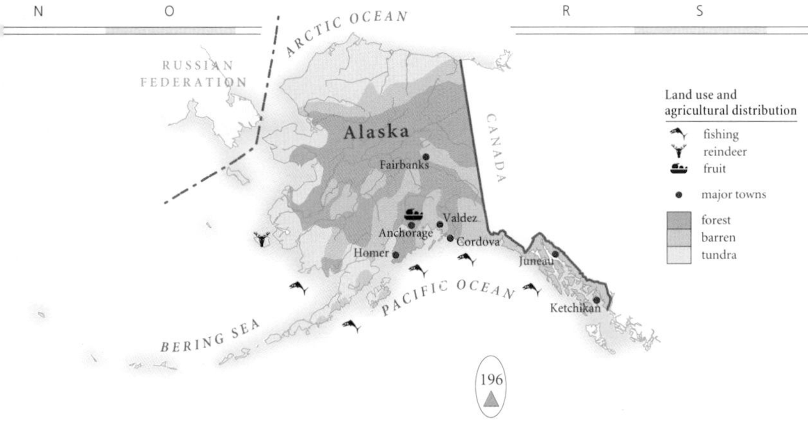

ARCTIC OCEAN
RUSSIAN FEDERATION
Alaska
Fairbanks
Anchorage
Valdez
Cordova
Homer
Juneau
Ketchikan
CANADA
PACIFIC OCEAN
BERING SEA
Land use and agricultural distribution
fishing
reindeer
fruit
major towns
forest
barren
tundra

196

USA: ALASKA

JUST OVER HALF A MILLION people live in Alaska, a wilderness of ice, forest, mountains, and plains, purchased from Russia in 1867 and twice the size of Texas. The discovery of large oil reserves has brought prosperity to the US's "last frontier," while advancing the need to preserve natural habitats and the traditional livelihoods of indigenous peoples, such as the Aleuts and Inupiaq.

ARCTIC OCEAN
BEAUFORT SEA
Brooks Range
ALASKA
CANADA
Yukon Flats
Gulf of Alaska
Alexander Archipelago
Alaska Peninsula
Bristol Bay
Kodiak Island
Anchorage
Fairbanks
Juneau
Prudhoe Bay
Barrow
Valdez
Denali
Kuskokwim Mountains
Saint Elias Mountains
Aleutian Range
Alaska Range

8
192
192

THE LANDSCAPE

THE MOUNTAINS OF THE PACIFIC COAST culminate in the heavily glaciated Alaska Range and extend west, to the Alaska Peninsula and the great volcanic arc of the Aleutian Islands. The interior plains are drained by the Yukon River and bounded by the bare, jagged peaks of the Brooks Range to the north.

The Yukon Delta is a fan of alluvial material eroded by the Yukon River and its tributaries. It is approximately twice the size of the Mississippi Delta.
Brooks Range
West Fork Glacier
The ten highest mountains in the US are all in the Alaska Range, Mount McKinley *(Denali)*, at 20,321 ft (6,194 m) is the highest.
Yukon River
Alaska Range
The arc of the Aleutian Islands marks the boundary between the Eurasian and Pacific tectonic plates.
Fjords are found along the coast where valleys, deeply excavated by large glaciers, were inundated by rising seas.

By August, the Alaska Range is covered with autumnal tundra vegetation.

West Fork Glacier

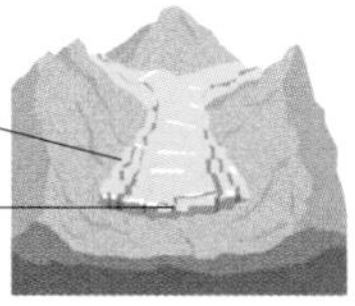

The surging ice mass shears along the glacier margin
Deep crevasses divide the front of the surging glacier into large ice blocks

***Surging glaciers** make rapid and dramatic advances, normally after periods of snow accumulation. West Fork Glacier in the Susitna River Basin traveled 2.5 miles (4 km) in 1987.*

TRANSPORTATION & INDUSTRY

LARGE AREAS OF ALASKA are undeveloped, and much of the existing infrastructure is a legacy of Cold War military investment. Mineral ores, including gold, have been mined for over a century, but the oil business now dominates the economy. Processing industries such as paper-pulp mills supply Japan and other markets on the Pacific Rim.

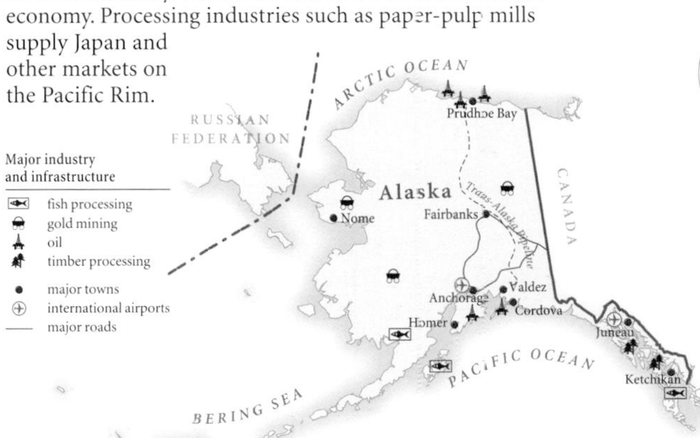

Major industry and infrastructure
fish processing
gold mining
oil
timber processing
major towns
international airports
major roads
ARCTIC OCEAN
RUSSIAN FEDERATION
Prudhoe Bay
Alaska
Nome
Fairbanks
Trans-Alaska Pipeline
Anchorage
Valdez
Cordova
Homer
Juneau
Ketchikan
CANADA
PACIFIC OCEAN
BERING SEA

TRANSPORTATION NETWORK

13,524 miles (21,760 km)		49 miles (78 km)	
482 miles (772 km)		none	

Nearly 80 million gallons of oil are pumped through the Trans-Alaska Pipeline every day. The oil takes six days to travel the 789 miles (1,262 km) from Prudhoe Bay to Valdez.

***The Trans-Alaska Pipeline** has carried crude oil from Prudhoe Bay since 1977. The oilfield is the US's largest and is estimated to be equal in size to the biggest oilfields of the Persian Gulf.*

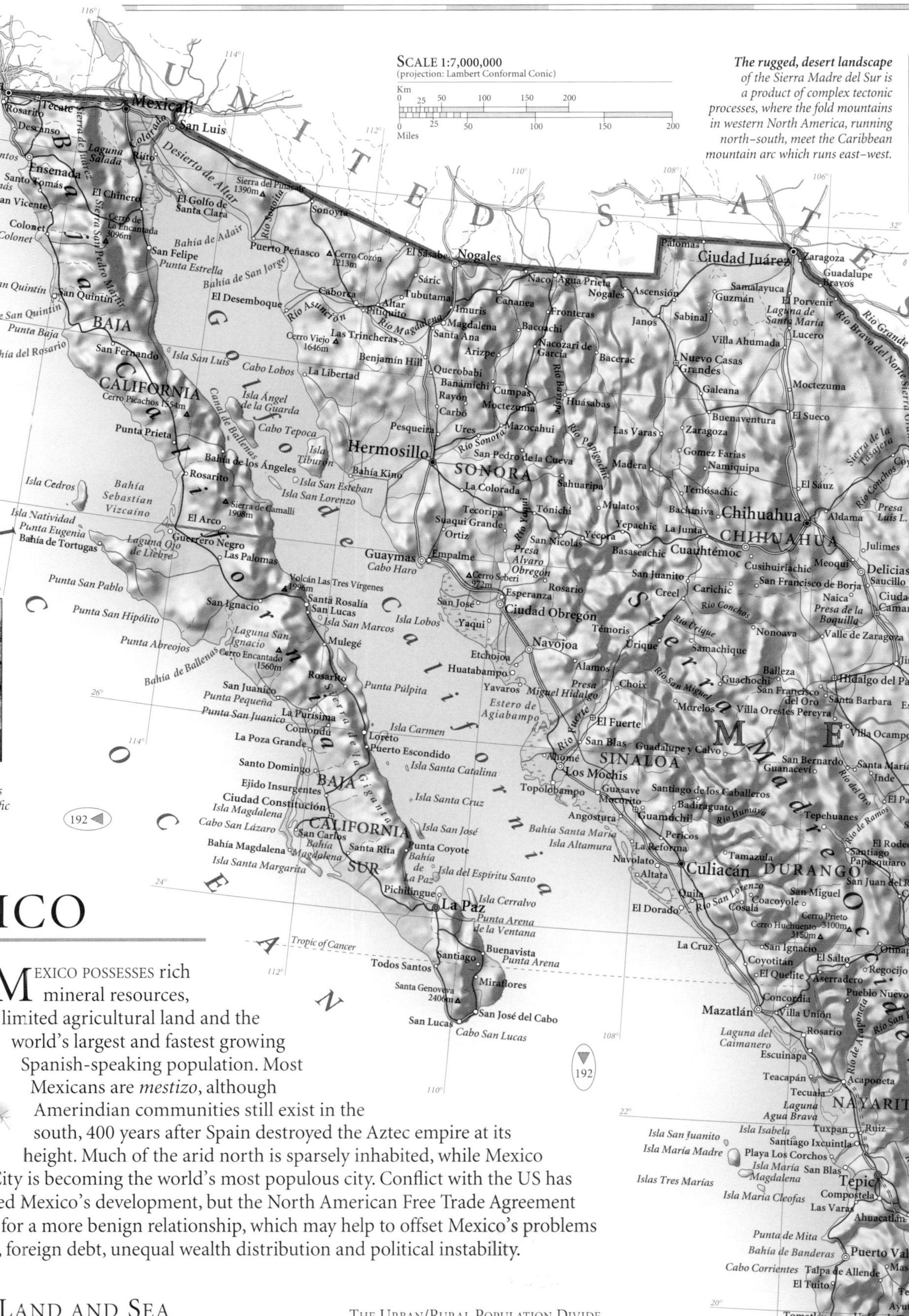
UNITED STATES OF AMERICA
PACIFIC OCEAN
Golfo de California
MEXICO
BAJA CALIFORNIA
BAJA CALIFORNIA SUR
SONORA
CHIHUAHUA
SINALOA
DURANGO
COAHUILA
ZACATECAS
NAYARIT
JALISCO
COLIMA
MICHOACÁN
AGUASCALIENTES
Sierra Madre Occidental
Tijuana
Mexicali
Ensenada
Hermosillo
Ciudad Juárez
Chihuahua
Culiacán
Durango
Mazatlán
La Paz
Guadalajara
Torreón
Zacatecas
Tepic
Colima
Tropic of Cancer
Río Grande
SCALE 1:7,000,000
(projection: Lambert Conformal Conic)

The rugged, desert landscape of the Sierra Madre del Sur is a product of complex tectonic processes, where the fold mountains in western North America, running north–south, meet the Caribbean mountain arc which runs east–west.

Wave action *has cut steep cliffs into the igneous rocks of Isla Cedros, off the Pacific coast of Baja California. The island is home to sea lions, reptiles, and deer.*

MEXICO

MEXICO POSSESSES rich mineral resources, limited agricultural land and the world's largest and fastest growing Spanish-speaking population. Most Mexicans are *mestizo*, although Amerindian communities still exist in the south, 400 years after Spain destroyed the Aztec empire at its height. Much of the arid north is sparsely inhabited, while Mexico City is becoming the world's most populous city. Conflict with the US has long overshadowed Mexico's development, but the North American Free Trade Agreement offers the chance for a more benign relationship, which may help to offset Mexico's problems of hyperinflation, foreign debt, unequal wealth distribution and political instability.

USING THE LAND AND SEA

CORN OCCUPIES much of the cultivated area. Commercial plantations of coffee, sugar, vanilla, and cotton are found along the Gulf coastal plain and in irrigated parts of the arid north, which is otherwise used for extensive ranching. Fishing is important, particularly shellfish for export. A soaring population has created the need for grain imports since 1980.

THE URBAN/RURAL POPULATION DIVIDE

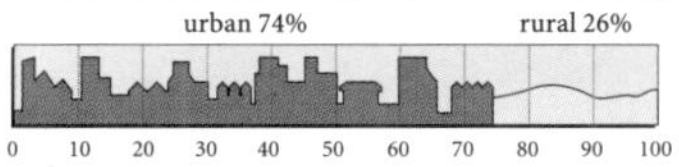
urban 74%
rural 26%
0 10 20 30 40 50 60 70 80 90 100

POPULATION DENSITY	TOTAL LAND AREA
130 people per sq mile (50 people per sq km)	755,865 sq miles (1,958,200 sq km)

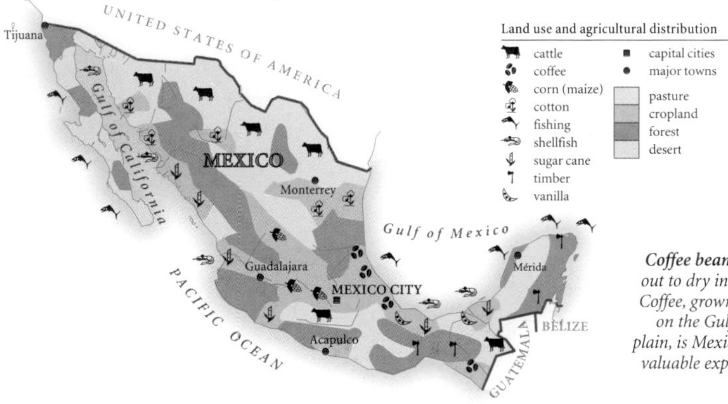
UNITED STATES OF AMERICA
Tijuana
Gulf of California
MEXICO
Monterrey
Gulf of Mexico
Guadalajara
MEXICO CITY
Mérida
Acapulco
PACIFIC OCEAN
BELIZE
GUATEMALA
Land use and agricultural distribution
cattle
coffee
corn (maize)
cotton
fishing
shellfish
sugar cane
timber
vanilla
capital cities
major towns
pasture
cropland
forest
desert

Coffee beans *spread out to dry in the sun. Coffee, grown mainly on the Gulf coastal plain, is Mexico's most valuable export crop.*

MEXICO: ADMINISTRATIVE REGIONS

Ⓓ DISTRITO FEDERAL

MAP KEY

POPULATION

- above 5 million
- 1 million to 5 million
- 500,000 to 1 million
- 100,000 to 500,000
- 50,000 to 100,000
- 10,000 to 50,000
- below 10,000

ELEVATION

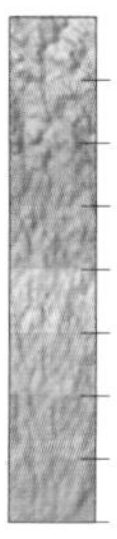
4000m / 13,124ft
3000m / 9843ft
2000m / 6562ft
1000m / 3281ft
500m / 1640ft
250m / 820ft
100m / 328ft
sea level

The Landscape

THE GREAT CENTRAL PLATEAU rises gently southward from the Rio Grande, isolated from the coastal plains by the Sierra Madre Oriental and Occidental. The two ranges converge from east and west respectively, culminating in high volcanic peaks around Mexico City. Further ranges of the Sierra Madre rise to the south of the Balsas Basin, skirted by the low-lying Isthmus of Tehuantepec *(Istmo de Tehuantepec)* and Yucatan Peninsula.

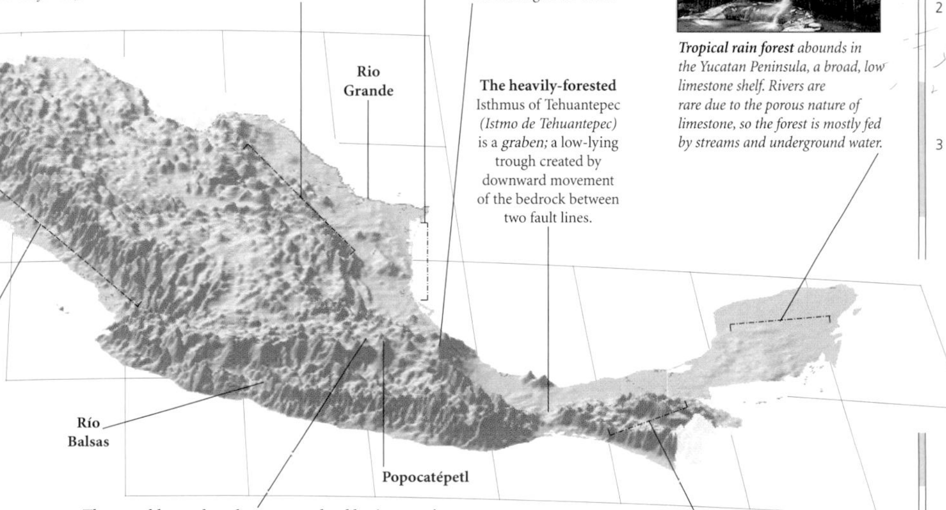

Sierra Madre Oriental
Rio Grande
Sierra Madre Occidental
Río Balsas
Popocatépetl

The long, narrow, extremely arid peninsula of Baja (lower) California is an elongated granite block, separated from the mainland by the flooded rift valley of the Gulf of California *(Golfo de California)*.

Wave action has constructed sand bars which shelter lagoons along the shore of the Gulf coastal plain.

The dormant cone of Volcán Pico de Orizaba is, at 18,700 ft (5,700 m), the highest peak in Mexico. In North America, only Mount McKinley and Mount Logan are taller.

The heavily-forested Isthmus of Tehuantepec *(Istmo de Tehuantepec)* is a *graben*; a low-lying trough created by downward movement of the bedrock between two fault lines.

The unstable, earthquake-prone, upland basin around Mexico City was once a region of shallow lakes. Flood control measures and domestic consumption over the last four centuries have caused the virtual disappearance of this surface water.

The highlands of Chiapas are a series of *horsts*, blocks of land thrust upward between two fault lines. Volcanic cones have developed where lava has flowed out from the faults.

***Tropical rain forest** abounds in the Yucatan Peninsula, a broad, low limestone shelf. Rivers are rare due to the porous nature of limestone, so the forest is mostly fed by streams and underground water.*

Formation of the Gulf of California

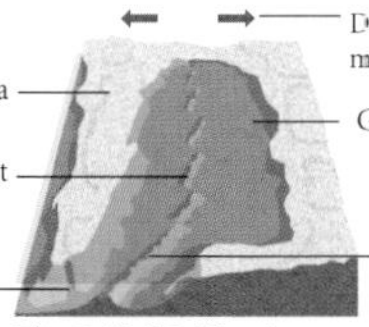

Direction of plate movement
Baja California
Gulf of California
Transform fault
Spreading oceanic ridge
Edge of continental crust

***The Gulf of California** (Golfo de California) began to open out about 4 million years ago as a result of rifting and plate displacement along transform faults.*

***Popocatépetl is a dormant volcano,** part of the Pacific "Rim of Fire." The crater is over half a mile (1 km) wide.*

Transportation & Industry

OIL AND GAS ON THE GULF COAST are Mexico's main sources of export income. Metal mining has declined but the country remains a leading global producer of silver. Manufacturing is heavily concentrated around the metropolitan area of Mexico City, while the duty-free movement of goods in the US border region, under the *Maquiladora* (twin plant) scheme, has created new hi-tech and service growth centers.

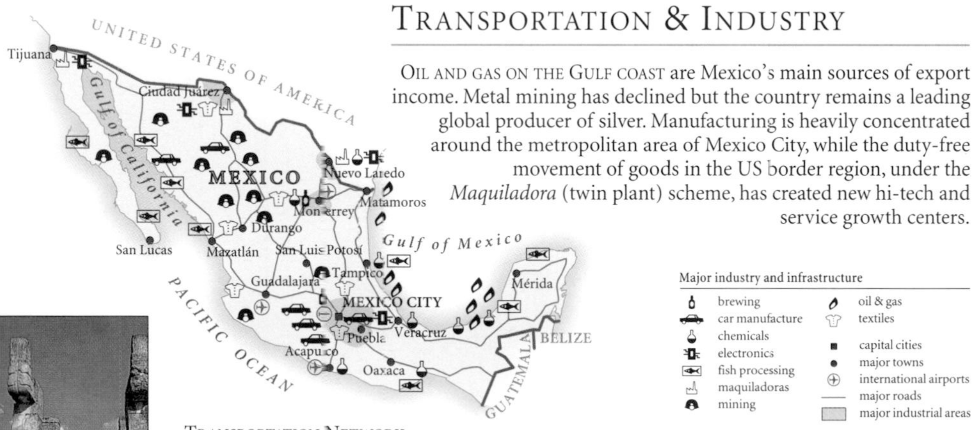

UNITED STATES OF AMERICA
Tijuana
Ciudad Juárez
Gulf of California
MEXICO
Nuevo Laredo
Matamoros
Monterrey
Durango
San Lucas
Mazatlán
San Luis Potosí
Gulf of Mexico
Guadalajara
Tampico
MEXICO CITY
Mérida
Puebla
Veracruz
Acapulco
Oaxaca
PACIFIC OCEAN
BELIZE
GUATEMALA
Major industry and infrastructure
brewing
car manufacture
chemicals
electronics
fish processing
maquiladoras
mining
oil & gas
textiles
capital cities
major towns
international airports
major roads
major industrial areas

***A stone figure** reclines by the Temple of Warriors, within the Mayan city of Chichén-Itzá. The Maya civilization flourished across the Yucatan Peninsula between 200 and 900 AD.*

Transportation Network

	55,021 miles (88,601 km)
	4,186 miles (6,740 km)
	16,422 miles (26,445 km)
	1,801 miles (2,900 km)

Fast, modern highways or *autopistas* now link Mexico City with Toluca, Puebla and other satellite cities, yet distant centers like Chihuahua are still served by narrow roads and an outdated railroad network.

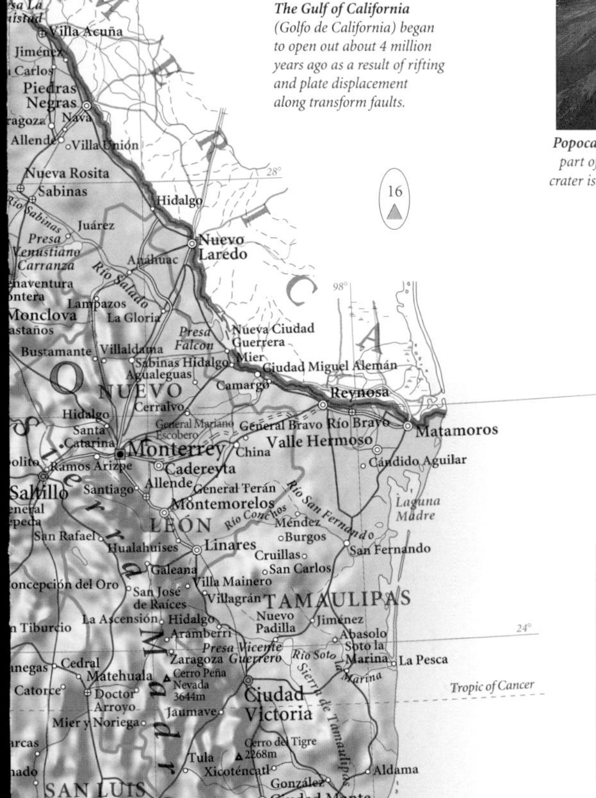

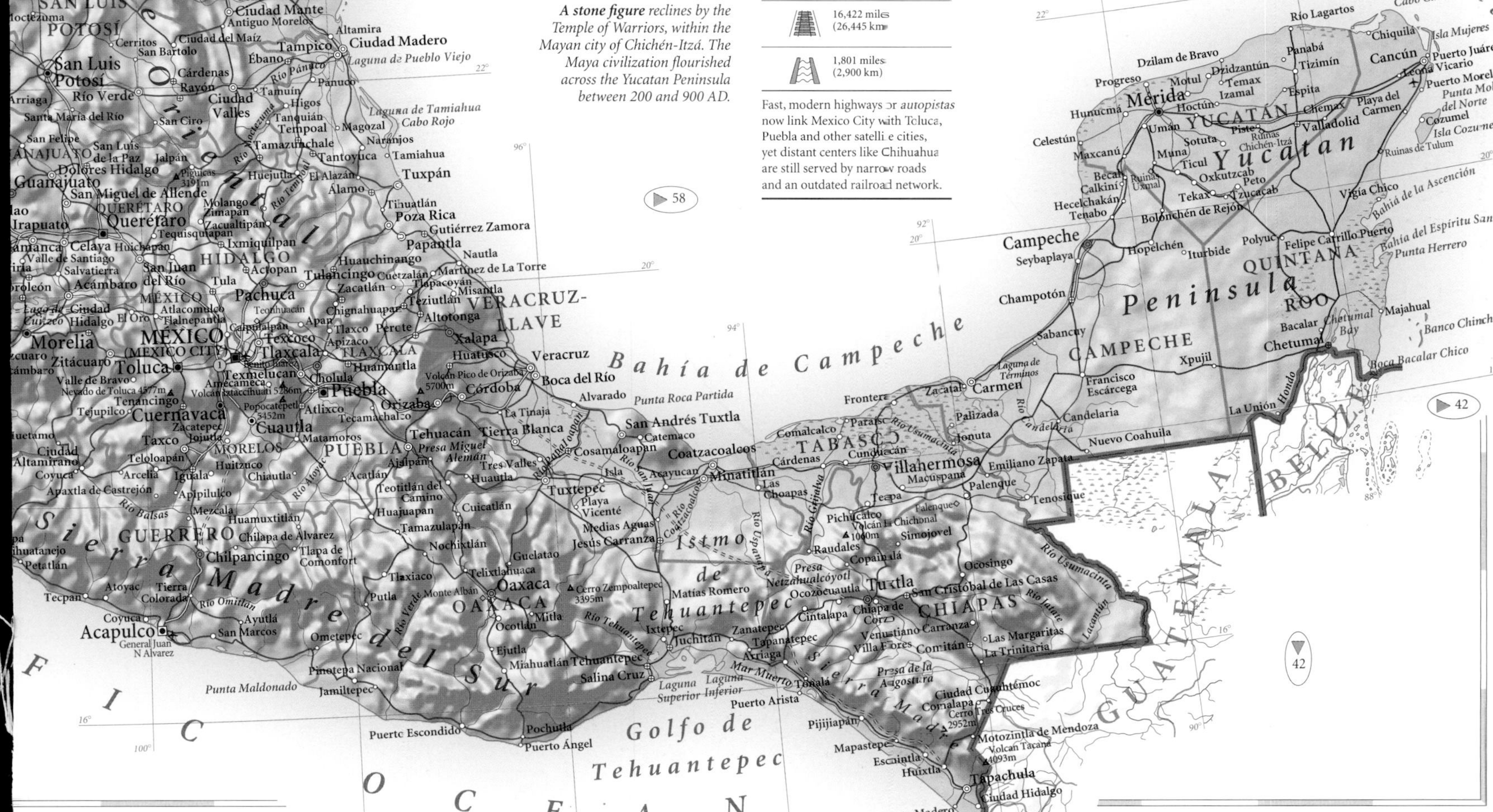

NUEVO LEÓN
TAMAULIPAS
SAN LUIS POTOSÍ
Sierra Madre Oriental
Tropic of Cancer
HIDALGO
QUERÉTARO
MÉXICO
MÉXICO (MEXICO CITY)
TLAXCALA
MORELOS
PUEBLA
VERACRUZ-LLAVE
GUERRERO
OAXACA
Sierra Madre del Sur
Bahía de Campeche
Golfo de Tehuantepec
Istmo de Tehuantepec
TABASCO
CHIAPAS
CAMPECHE
YUCATÁN
Yucatan Peninsula
QUINTANA ROO
Yucatan Channel
GUATEMALA
BELIZE
PACIFIC OCEAN
Monterrey
Ciudad Victoria
Tampico
Ciudad Madero
Querétaro
Pachuca
Morelia
Toluca
Cuernavaca
Puebla
Tlaxcala
Xalapa
Veracruz
Acapulco
Chilpancingo
Oaxaca
Tuxtla
Villahermosa
Campeche
Mérida
Chetumal
Matamoros
Nuevo Laredo
Tapachula

16

58

42

42

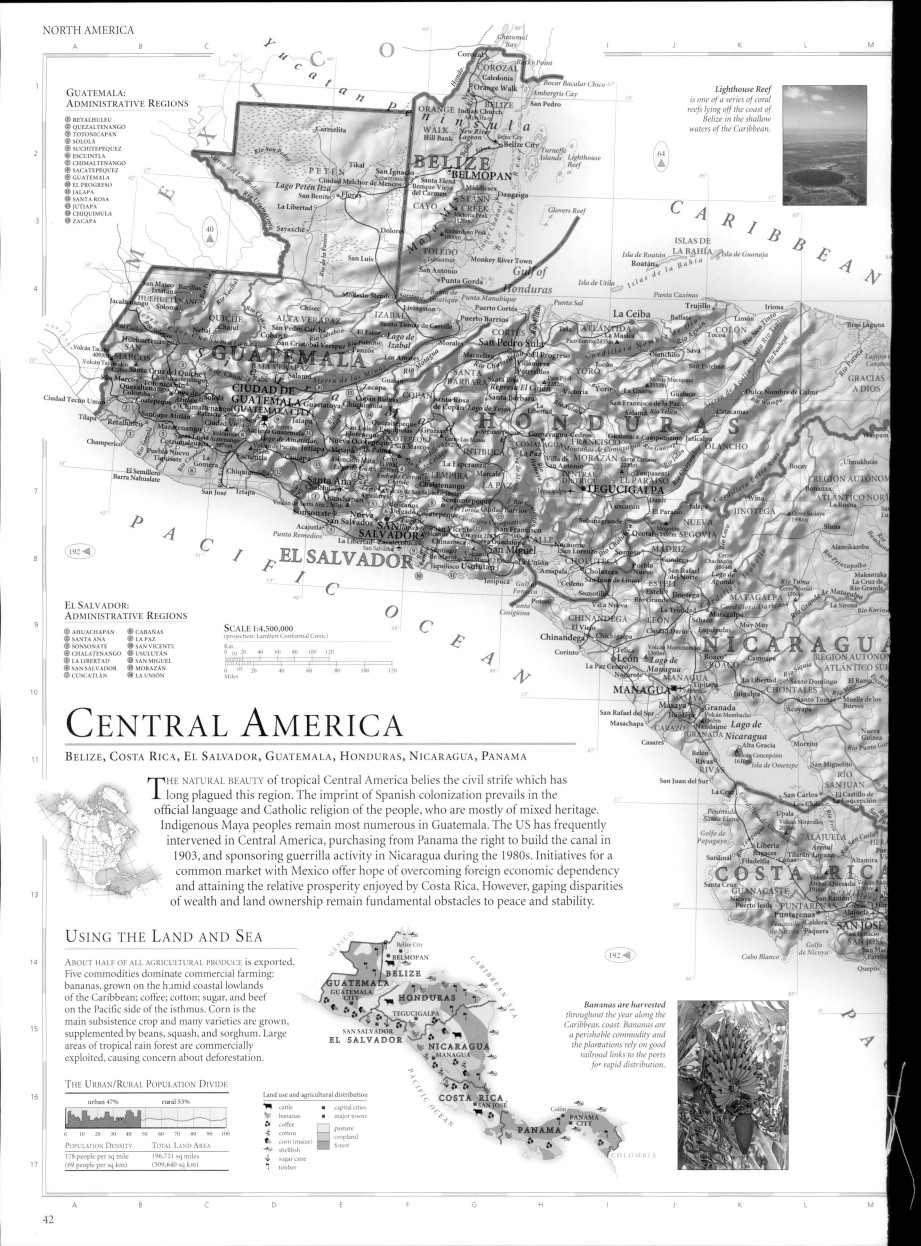

GUATEMALA: ADMINISTRATIVE REGIONS
① RETALHULEU
② QUEZALTENANGO
③ TOTONICAPÁN
④ SOLOLÁ
⑤ SUCHITEPÉQUEZ
⑥ ESCUINTLA
⑦ CHIMALTENANGO
⑧ SACATEPÉQUEZ
⑨ GUATEMALA
⑩ EL PROGRESO
⑪ JALAPA
⑫ SANTA ROSA
⑬ JUTIAPA
⑭ CHIQUIMULA
⑮ ZACAPA
EL SALVADOR: ADMINISTRATIVE REGIONS
① AHUACHAPÁN
② SANTA ANA
③ SONSONATE
④ CHALATENANGO
⑤ LA LIBERTAD
⑥ SAN SALVADOR
⑦ CUSCATLÁN
⑧ CABAÑAS
⑨ LA PAZ
⑩ SAN VICENTE
⑪ USULUTÁN
⑫ SAN MIGUEL
⑬ MORAZÁN
⑭ LA UNIÓN
SCALE 1:4,500,000
(projection: Lambert Conformal Conic)
Yucatan Peninsula
MEXICO
BELIZE
BELMOPAN
Belize City
GUATEMALA
CIUDAD DE GUATEMALA (GUATEMALA CITY)
EL SALVADOR
SAN SALVADOR
HONDURAS
TEGUCIGALPA
NICARAGUA
MANAGUA
COSTA RICA
SAN JOSÉ
CARIBBEAN
PACIFIC OCEAN
Gulf of Honduras
Lago de Nicaragua
Lago de Managua
Lighthouse Reef
Glovers Reef

Lighthouse Reef is one of a series of coral reefs lying off the coast of Belize in the shallow waters of the Caribbean.

Central America

Belize, Costa Rica, El Salvador, Guatemala, Honduras, Nicaragua, Panama

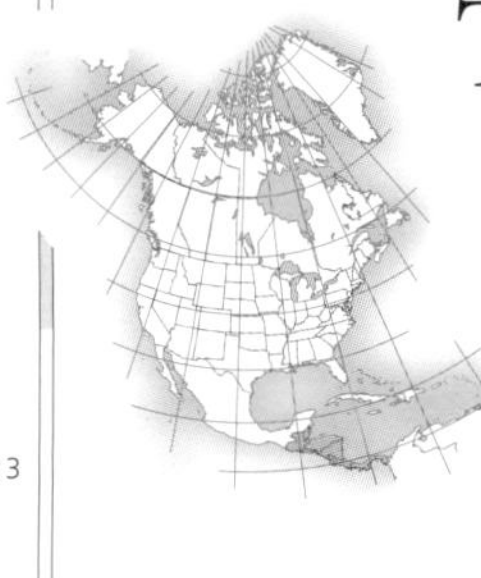

THE NATURAL BEAUTY of tropical Central America belies the civil strife which has long plagued this region. The imprint of Spanish colonization prevails in the official language and Catholic religion of the people, who are mostly of mixed heritage. Indigenous Maya peoples remain most numerous in Guatemala. The US has frequently intervened in Central America, purchasing from Panama the right to build the canal in 1903, and sponsoring guerrilla activity in Nicaragua during the 1980s. Initiatives for a common market with Mexico offer hope of overcoming foreign economic dependency and attaining the relative prosperity enjoyed by Costa Rica. However, gaping disparities of wealth and land ownership remain fundamental obstacles to peace and stability.

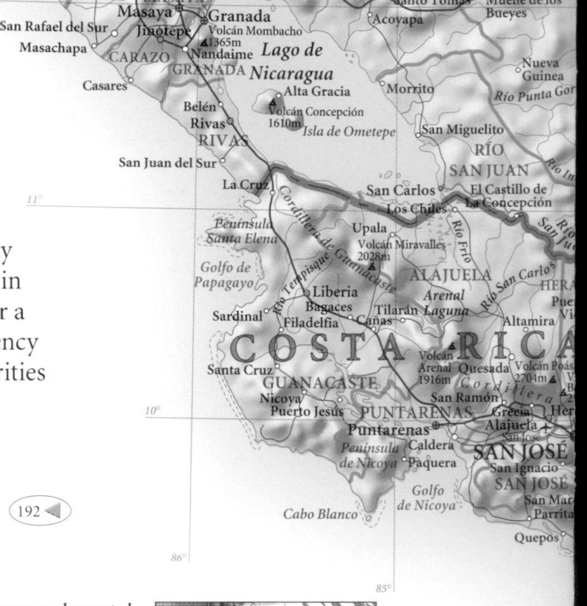

Using the Land and Sea

ABOUT HALF OF ALL AGRICULTURAL PRODUCE is exported. Five commodities dominate commercial farming: bananas, grown on the humid coastal lowlands of the Caribbean; coffee; cotton; sugar, and beef on the Pacific side of the isthmus. Corn is the main subsistence crop and many varieties are grown, supplemented by beans, squash, and sorghum. Large areas of tropical rain forest are commercially exploited, causing concern about deforestation.

The Urban/Rural Population Divide

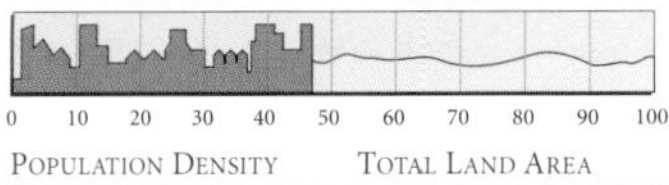

urban 47%
rural 53%
0
10
20
30
40
50
60
70
80
90
100

Population Density	Total Land Area
178 people per sq mile (69 people per sq km)	196,721 sq miles (509,640 sq km)

Land use and agricultural distribution
cattle
bananas
coffee
cotton
corn (maize)
shellfish
sugar cane
timber
capital cities
major towns
pasture
cropland
forest
MEXICO
Belize City
BELMOPAN
BELIZE
GUATEMALA
GUATEMALA CITY
HONDURAS
TEGUCIGALPA
SAN SALVADOR
EL SALVADOR
NICARAGUA
MANAGUA
COSTA RICA
SAN JOSÉ
Colón
PANAMA CITY
PANAMA
CARIBBEAN SEA
PACIFIC OCEAN
COLOMBIA

Bananas are harvested *throughout the year along the Caribbean coast. Bananas are a perishable commodity and the plantations rely on good railroad links to the ports for rapid distribution.*

The Landscape

The Sierra Madre range spreads west from Mexico, between the narrow Pacific coastal plain and the limestone lowland of Petén. Parallel hill ranges sweep across Honduras and extend south, past the Caribbean Mosquito Coast, to lakes Managua and Nicaragua. The Cordillera Central rises to the south, gradually descending to Lake Gatún *(lago Gatún)*. A highly active volcanic belt runs along the Pacific seaboard from Mexico to Costa Rica.

Over 40 active volcanoes line the Pacific coast north of Panama, including Volcán Tajumulco which, at 13,846 ft (4220 m), is the highest point in Central America.

The high plateau of the Sierra de los Cuchumatanes is a *horst*, an upthrusted block of land. The limestone rock is deeply incised with canyons along the plateau edge.

Lake Petén Itzá is typical of the swampy depressions or *bajos* of the Petén region, formed by intense weathering of limestone in the hot and humid climate.

Low, white limestone cliffs, mangrove swamps and coral reefs characterize the coast of Belize, which is part of the Yucatan Peninsula.

***The 990 ft (300 m)** deep crater occupied by Lake Atitlán (Lago de Atitlán) was created after a volcanic explosion caused the original cone to collapse in on itself. On its shores lie other volcanic cones.*

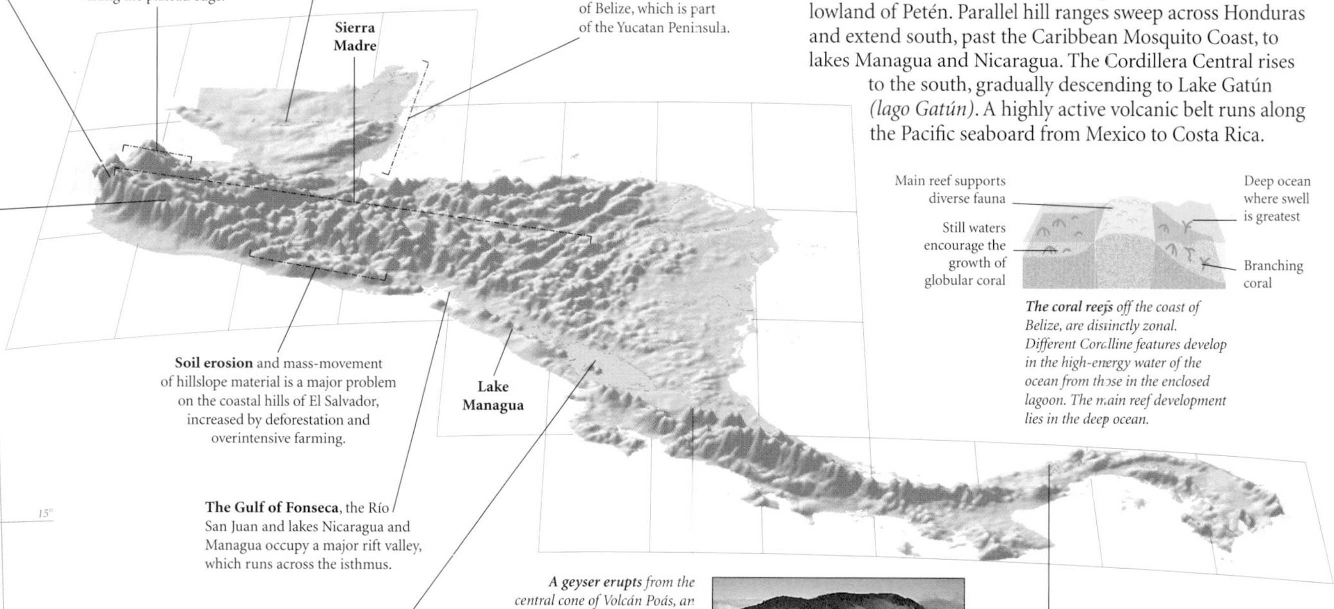
Sierra Madre
Lake Managua
Main reef supports diverse fauna
Still waters encourage the growth of globular coral
Deep ocean where swell is greatest
Branching coral

Soil erosion and mass-movement of hillslope material is a major problem on the coastal hills of El Salvador, increased by deforestation and overintensive farming.

The Gulf of Fonseca, the Río San Juan and lakes Nicaragua and Managua occupy a major rift valley, which runs across the isthmus.

Lake Nicaragua *(Lago de Nicaragua)* contains around 400 islands, some of which are active volcanoes. Unique freshwater species of shark and swordfish have evolved over the long period since the lake was cut off from the Pacific by a belt of volcanic cones.

***The coral reefs** off the coast of Belize, are distinctly zonal. Different Coralline features develop in the high-energy water of the ocean from those in the enclosed lagoon. The main reef development lies in the deep ocean.*

***A geyser erupts** from the central cone of Volcán Poás, an active volcano in the Cordillera Central of Costa Rica, which frequently produces spectacular lava flows.*

Over half of the route of the Panama Canal runs through Lake Gatún *(Lago Gatún)*, the highest stretch of the journey. The freshwater lake also acts as a holding reservoir for the canal, providing water to operate the locks.

Transportation & Industry

Most manufacturing takes the form of cottage industries concentrated in the larger towns, and the production of food, tobacco, furniture, textiles, clothing, and footwear. The region's oil and metallic mineral potential is largely unexploited. The Panamanian economy is dominated by service industries, and the country has one of the world's largest free trade zones at Colón.

***An ox-drawn plough** tills fields of tobacco in the Copán region of Honduras. Only about 25% of the land is cultivated, in this sparsely-populated country.*

MEXICO
Belize City
BELMOPAN
BELIZE
GUATEMALA
GUATEMALA CITY
HONDURAS
TEGUCIGALPA
SAN SALVADOR
EL SALVADOR
NICARAGUA
MANAGUA
CARIBBEAN SEA
PACIFIC OCEAN
COSTA RICA
SAN JOSE
Colón
PANAMA CITY
PANAMA
COLOMBIA

Major industry and infrastructure

- chemicals
- coffee processing
- fish processing
- finance
- food processing
- mining
- textiles
- timber processing
- capital cities
- major towns
- international airports
- major roads
- major industrial areas

Map Key

Population	Elevation
1 million to 5 million	4000m / 13,124ft
500,000 to 1 million	3000m / 9843ft
100,000 to 500,000	2000m / 6562ft
50,000 to 100,000	1000m / 3281ft
10,000 to 50,000	500m / 1640ft
below 10,000	250m / 820ft
	100m / 328ft
	sea level

Transportation Network

12,442 miles (20,035 km)	1,179 miles (1,898 km)
2,226 miles (3,584 km)	3,416 miles (5,500 km)

The completion of a major oil pipeline across Panama in 1982 has reduced crude oil shipments via the Panama Canal, further contributing to a long-term decline in canal traffic.

***Panama's rain forests** are home to many mammals which originated in North America, including jaguars, tapirs, and deer, as well as sloths, anteaters, and armadillos, which long ago migrated from South America.*

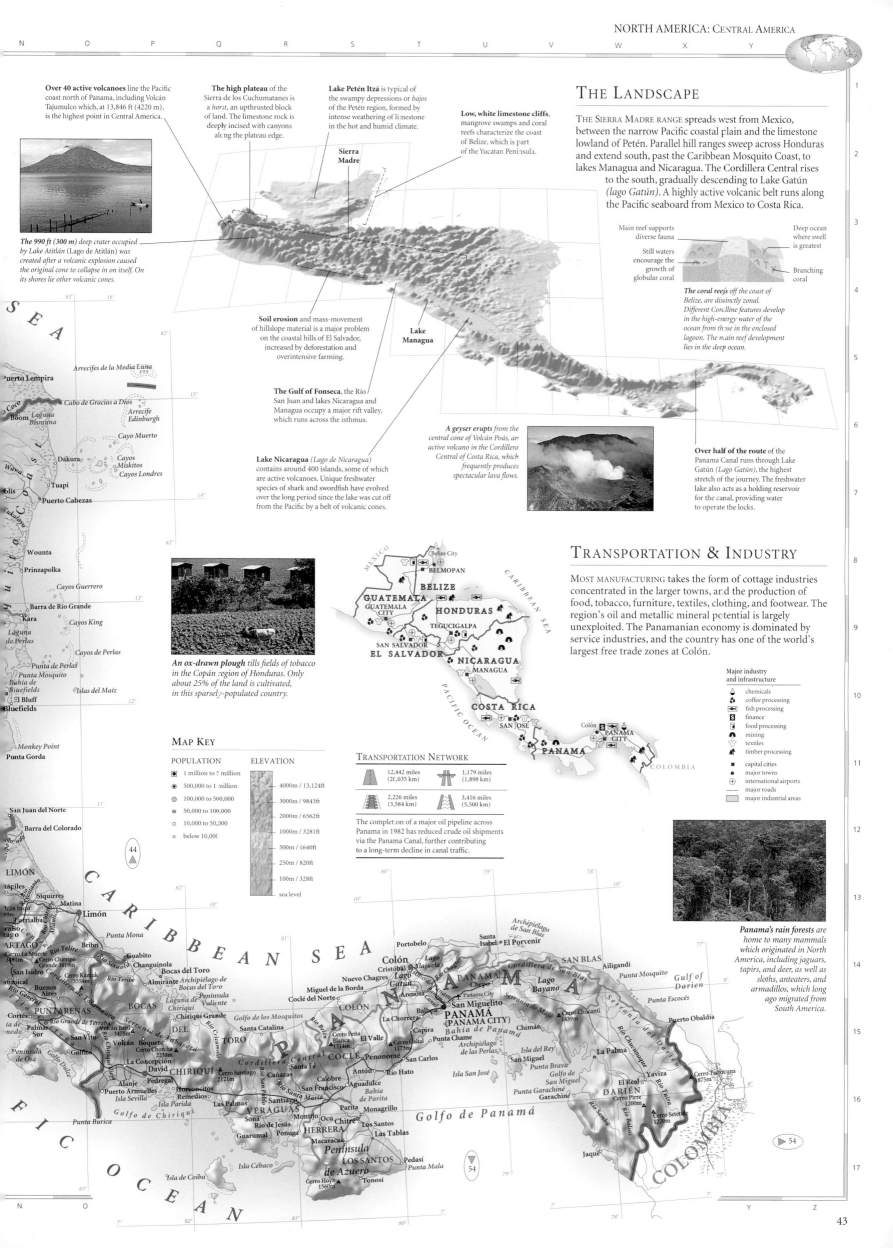

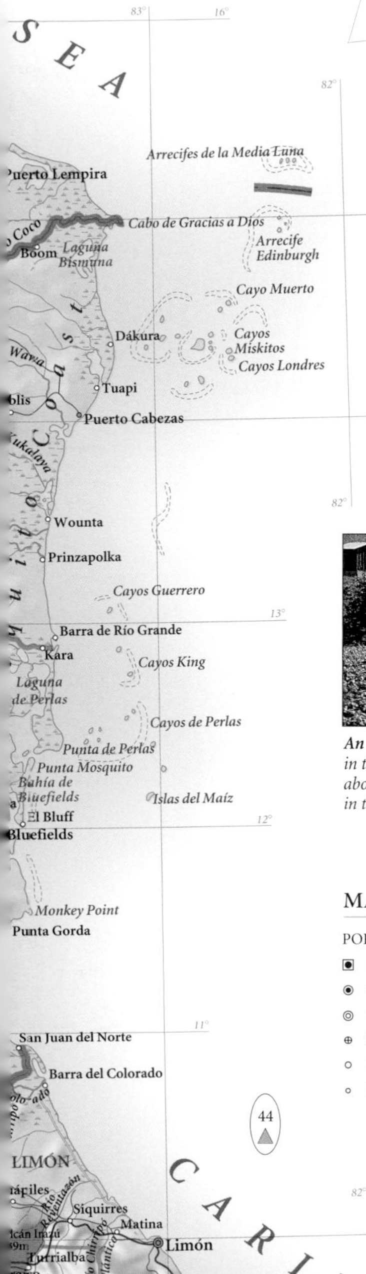
SEA
Arrecifes de la Media Luna
Puerto Lempira
Cabo de Gracias a Dios
Laguna Bismuna
Arrecife Edinburgh
Cayo Muerto
Dákura
Cayos Miskitos
Cayos Londres
Tuapi
Puerto Cabezas
Wounta
Prinzapolka
Cayos Guerrero
Barra de Río Grande
Kara
Cayos King
Laguna de Perlas
Cayos de Perlas
Punta de Perlas
Punta Mosquito
Bahía de Bluefields
Islas del Maíz
El Bluff
Bluefields
Monkey Point
Punta Gorda
San Juan del Norte
Barra del Colorado

CARIBBEAN SEA
PACIFIC OCEAN
LIMÓN
Siquirres
Matina
Limón
Turrialba
Punta Mona
Bribri
Guabito
Changuinola
Bocas del Toro
Almirante
Archipiélago de Bocas del Toro
Península Valiente
Laguna de Chiriquí
BOCAS DEL TORO
PUNTARENAS
Palmar Sur
San Vito
Golfito
Península de Osa
Golfo Dulce
Volcán Barú 3475m
Volcán
Boquete
Cerro Chorcha 2238m
La Concepción
David
CHIRIQUÍ
Alanje
Pedregal
Puerto Armuelles
Isla Sevilla
Horconcitos
Remedios
Isla Parida
Golfo de Chiriquí
Punta Burica
Chiriquí Grande
Golfo de los Mosquitos
Santa Catalina
Cerro Santiago 2121m
Cordillera Central
Cañazas
Santa Fé
Las Palmas
VERAGUAS
Soná
Santiago
Río de Jesús
Guarumal
Ponuga
Montijo
Calobre
San Francisco
Aguadulce
Bahía de Parita
Parita
Monagrillo
Chitré
Ocú
HERRERA
Los Santos
Las Tablas
Macaracas
Península de Azuero
LOS SANTOS
Pedasí
Punta Mala
Tonosí
Cerro Hoya 1560m
Isla Cébaco
Isla de Coiba
Portobelo
Colón
Cristóbal
Lago Gatún
Nuevo Chagres
Miguel de la Borda
Coclé del Norte
COLÓN
Arenosa
La Chorrera
Balboa
Capira
Punta Chame
Cerro Peña Blanca 1314m
El Valle
Cerro Gaital 1173m
COCLÉ
Penonomé
San Carlos
Antón
Río Hato
PANAMÁ
Chepo
Panama City
San Miguelito
PANAMÁ (PANAMA CITY)
Bahía de Panamá
Archipiélago de las Perlas
Isla del Rey
San Miguel
Isla San José
Punta Brava
Golfo de San Miguel
Punta Garachiné
Garachiné
Golfo de Panamá
Archipiélago de San Blas
Santa Isabel
El Porvenir
SAN BLAS
Cordillera de San Blas
Lago Bayano
Ailigandí
Punta Mosquito
Gulf of Darien
Punta Escocés
Serranía de Majé
Cerro Chucanti 1439m
Chimán
Puerto Obaldía
La Palma
Yaviza
DARIÉN
El Real
Cerro Pirre 1200m
Cerro Setetule 1220m
Cerro Tacarcuna 1875m
Jaqué
COLOMBIA
PANAMÁ

44
54
54

GULF OF MEXICO
UNITED STATES OF AMERICA
Straits of Florida
ATLANTIC OCEAN
BAHAMAS
NASSAU
New Providence
Andros Island
Grand Bahama
Freeport
Eleuthera Island
Cat Island
Long Island
Great Exuma Island
Cay Sal
LA HABANA (HAVANA)
Matanzas
Pinar del Río
Isla de la Juventud
Santa Clara
Cienfuegos
Sancti Spíritus
Camagüey
Holguín
Bayamo
Santiago de Cuba
Guantánamo
CUBA
Greater Antilles
CAYMAN ISLANDS (to UK)
GEORGE TOWN
Grand Cayman
Little Cayman
Cayman Brac
JAMAICA
Montego Bay
KINGSTON
Windward Passage
Jamaica Channel
NAVASSA ISLAND (to US)
HAITI
PORT-AU-PRINCE
TURKS & CAICOS ISLANDS (to UK)
Great Inagua
Mayaguana
CARIBBEAN SEA
SCALE 1:6,000,000
(projection: Lambert Conformal Conic)

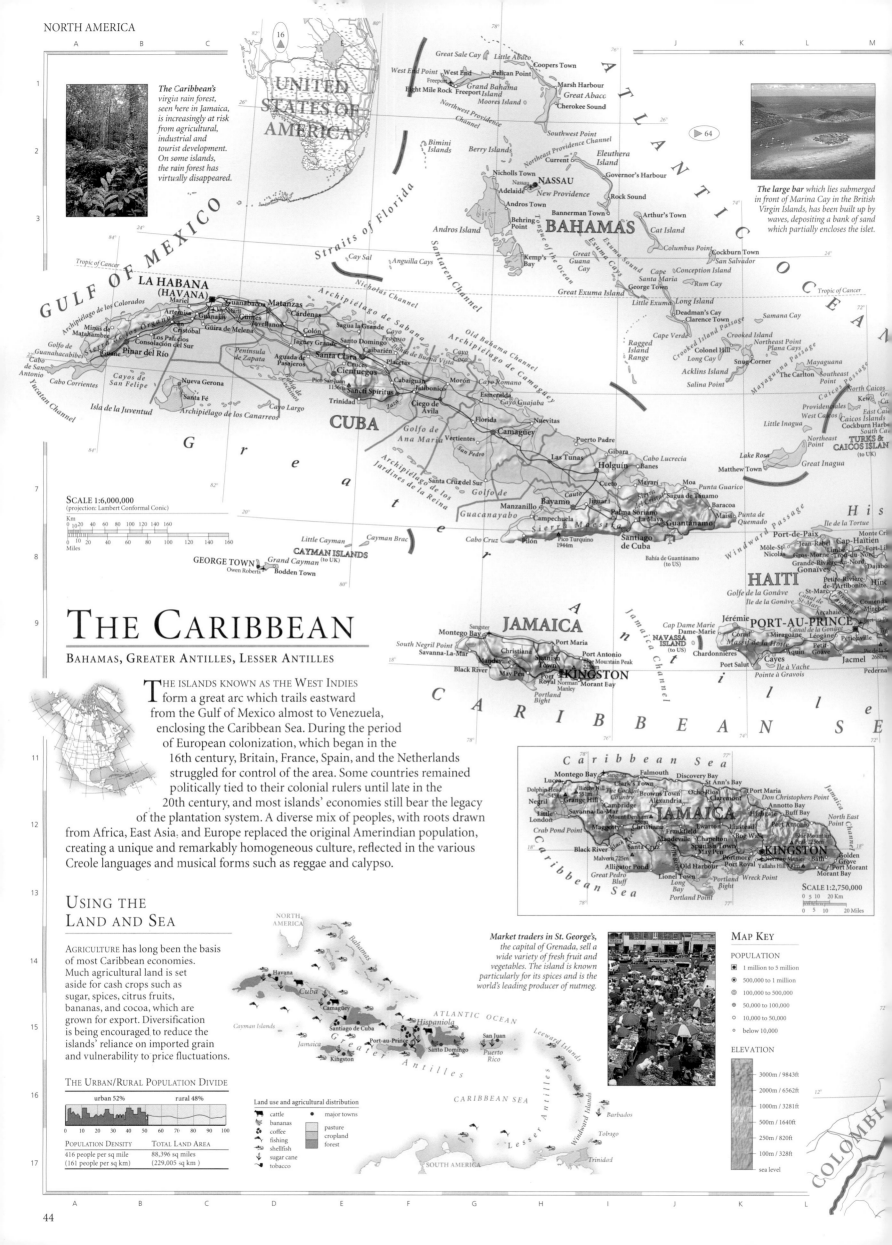

The Caribbean's virgin rain forest, seen here in Jamaica, is increasingly at risk from agricultural, industrial and tourist development. On some islands, the rain forest has virtually disappeared.

***The large bar** which lies submerged in front of Marina Cay in the British Virgin Islands, has been built up by waves, depositing a bank of sand which partially encloses the islet.*

THE CARIBBEAN

BAHAMAS, GREATER ANTILLES, LESSER ANTILLES

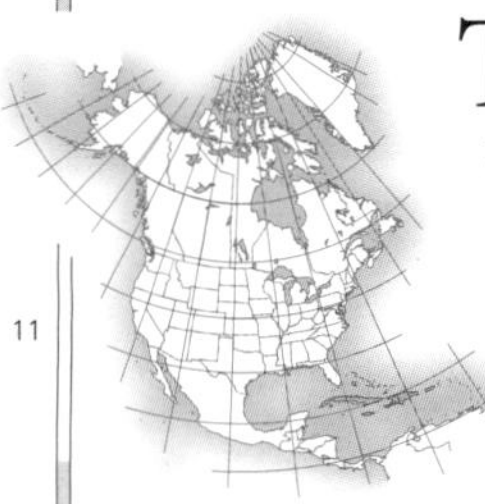

THE ISLANDS KNOWN AS THE WEST INDIES form a great arc which trails eastward from the Gulf of Mexico almost to Venezuela, enclosing the Caribbean Sea. During the period of European colonization, which began in the 16th century, Britain, France, Spain, and the Netherlands struggled for control of the area. Some countries remained politically tied to their colonial rulers until late in the 20th century, and most islands' economies still bear the legacy of the plantation system. A diverse mix of peoples, with roots drawn from Africa, East Asia, and Europe replaced the original Amerindian population, creating a unique and remarkably homogeneous culture, reflected in the various Creole languages and musical forms such as reggae and calypso.

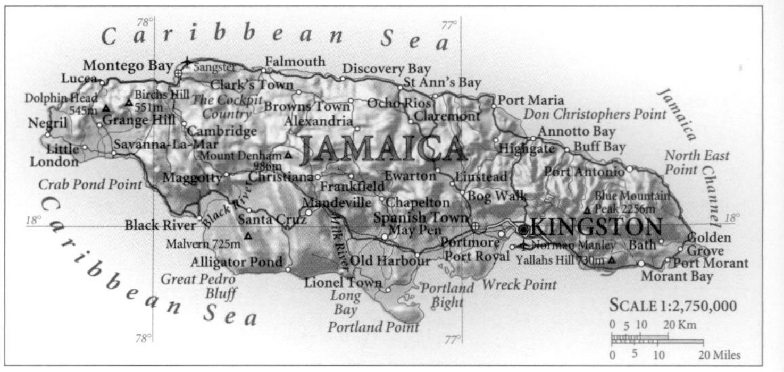

Caribbean Sea
JAMAICA
Montego Bay
KINGSTON
Spanish Town
May Pen
Mandeville
Black River
Port Antonio
Blue Mountain Peak 2256m
SCALE 1:2,750,000

USING THE LAND AND SEA

AGRICULTURE has long been the basis of most Caribbean economies. Much agricultural land is set aside for cash crops such as sugar, spices, citrus fruits, bananas, and cocoa, which are grown for export. Diversification is being encouraged to reduce the islands' reliance on imported grain and vulnerability to price fluctuations.

THE URBAN/RURAL POPULATION DIVIDE

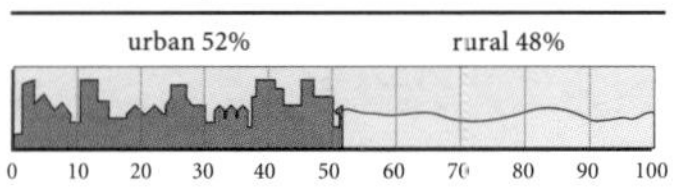

urban 52%
rural 48%
0 10 20 30 40 50 60 70 80 90 100

POPULATION DENSITY	TOTAL LAND AREA
416 people per sq mile (161 people per sq km)	88,396 sq miles (229,005 sq km)

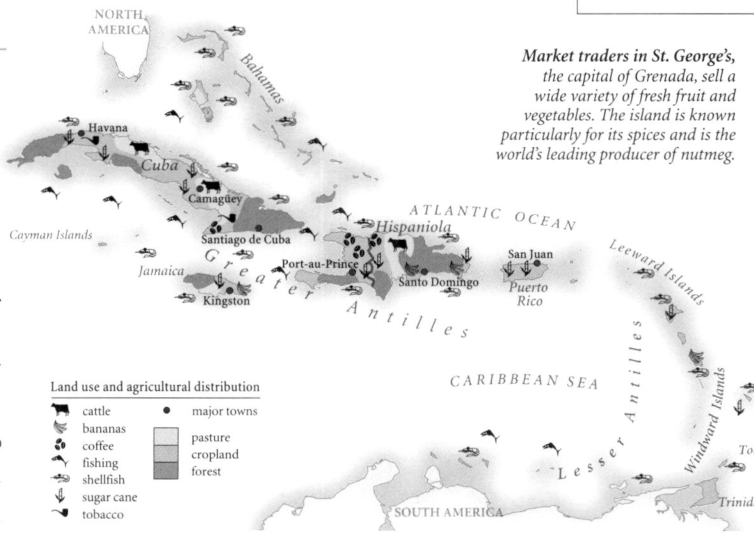

NORTH AMERICA
Bahamas
Havana
Cuba
Camagüey
Cayman Islands
Jamaica
Santiago de Cuba
Kingston
Port-au-Prince
Hispaniola
Santo Domingo
San Juan
Puerto Rico
ATLANTIC OCEAN
Greater Antilles
Leeward Islands
CARIBBEAN SEA
Lesser Antilles
Windward Islands
Barbados
Tobago
Trinidad
SOUTH AMERICA
Land use and agricultural distribution
cattle
bananas
coffee
fishing
shellfish
sugar cane
tobacco
major towns
pasture
cropland
forest

***Market traders in St. George's,** the capital of Grenada, sell a wide variety of fresh fruit and vegetables. The island is known particularly for its spices and is the world's leading producer of nutmeg.*

MAP KEY

POPULATION

- 1 million to 5 million
- 500,000 to 1 million
- 100,000 to 500,000
- 50,000 to 100,000
- 10,000 to 50,000
- below 10,000

ELEVATION

- 3000m / 9843ft
- 2000m / 6562ft
- 1000m / 3281ft
- 500m / 1640ft
- 250m / 820ft
- 100m / 328ft
- sea level

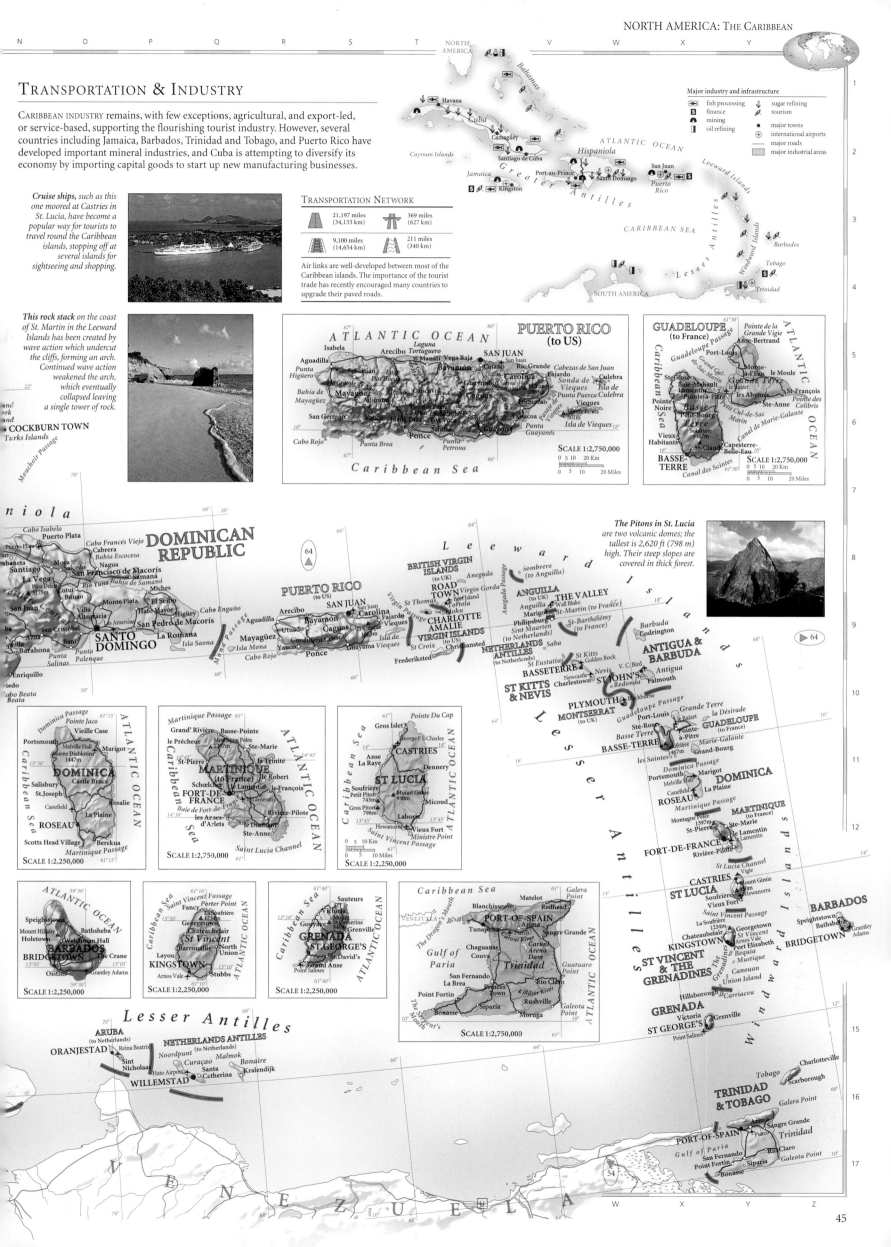

TRANSPORTATION & INDUSTRY

CARIBBEAN INDUSTRY remains, with few exceptions, agricultural, and export-led, or service-based, supporting the flourishing tourist industry. However, several countries including Jamaica, Barbados, Trinidad and Tobago, and Puerto Rico have developed important mineral industries, and Cuba is attempting to diversify its economy by importing capital goods to start up new manufacturing businesses.

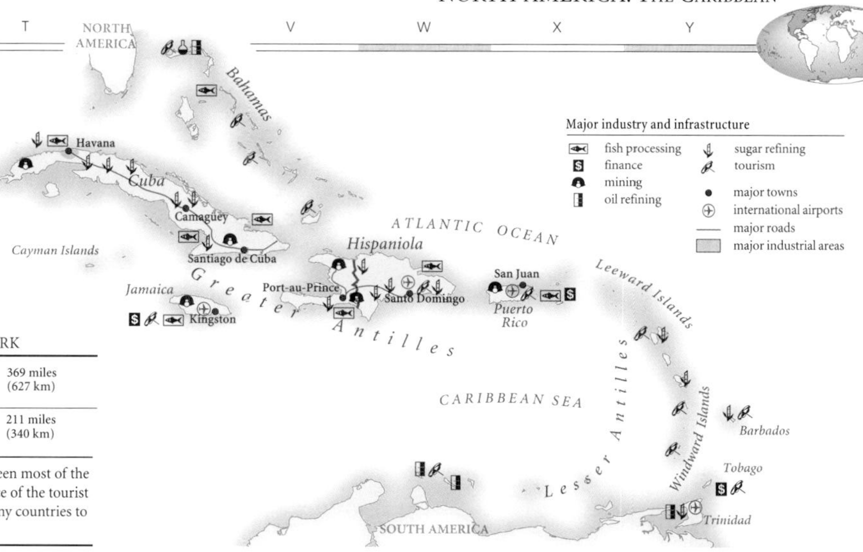
NORTH AMERICA
Bahamas
Havana
Cuba
Camagüey
Santiago de Cuba
Cayman Islands
Jamaica
Kingston
Greater Antilles
Hispaniola
Port-au-Prince
Santo Domingo
ATLANTIC OCEAN
San Juan
Puerto Rico
Leeward Islands
CARIBBEAN SEA
Lesser Antilles
Windward Islands
Barbados
Tobago
Trinidad
SOUTH AMERICA
Major industry and infrastructure
fish processing
finance
mining
oil refining
sugar refining
tourism
major towns
international airports
major roads
major industrial areas

Cruise ships, such as this one moored at Castries in St. Lucia, have become a popular way for tourists to travel round the Caribbean islands, stopping off at several islands for sightseeing and shopping.

TRANSPORTATION NETWORK

21,197 miles (34,133 km)	369 miles (627 km)
9,100 miles (14,654 km)	211 miles (340 km)

Air links are well-developed between most of the Caribbean islands. The importance of the tourist trade has recently encouraged many countries to upgrade their paved roads.

This rock stack on the coast of St. Martin in the Leeward Islands has been created by wave action which undercut the cliffs, forming an arch. Continued wave action weakened the arch, which eventually collapsed leaving a single tower of rock.

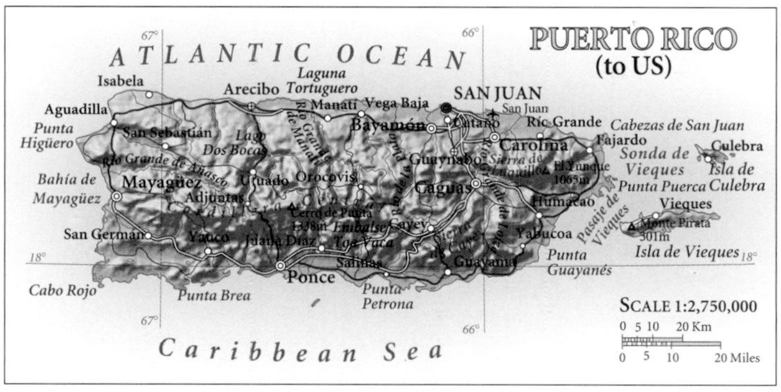
PUERTO RICO
(to US)
ATLANTIC OCEAN
Isabela
Arecibo
Manatí
Vega Baja
SAN JUAN
Aguadilla
Mayagüez
Bayamón
Carolina
Caguas
Ponce
Fajardo
Humacao
Vieques
Isla de Vieques
Culebra
Cabo Rojo
Caribbean Sea
SCALE 1:2,750,000

GUADELOUPE
(to France)
Pointe de la Grande Vigie
Anse-Bertrand
Port-Louis
Grande Terre
le Moule
Pointe-à-Pitre
Basse Terre
Soufrière 1467m
BASSE-TERRE
Marie-Galante
Caribbean Sea
ATLANTIC OCEAN
SCALE 1:2,750,000

The Pitons in St. Lucia are two volcanic domes; the tallest is 2,620 ft (798 m) high. Their steep slopes are covered in thick forest.

COCKBURN TOWN
Turks Islands
Mouchoir Passage
DOMINICAN REPUBLIC
Santiago
La Vega
San Francisco de Macorís
Samaná
SANTO DOMINGO
La Romana
San Pedro de Macorís
Isla Saona
Mona Passage
PUERTO RICO
(to US)
SAN JUAN
Leeward Islands
BRITISH VIRGIN ISLANDS
(to UK)
ROAD TOWN
Anegada
VIRGIN ISLANDS
(to US)
CHARLOTTE AMALIE
ANGUILLA
(to UK)
THE VALLEY
Sint Maarten
(to Netherlands)
NETHERLANDS ANTILLES
(to Netherlands)
St-Barthélémy
(to France)
Saba
ST KITTS & NEVIS
BASSETERRE
Charlestown
ANTIGUA & BARBUDA
ST JOHN'S
Barbuda
Codrington
Antigua
PLYMOUTH
MONTSERRAT
(to UK)
GUADELOUPE
(to France)
BASSE-TERRE
Lesser Antilles
DOMINICA
ROSEAU
MARTINIQUE
(to France)
FORT-DE-FRANCE
ST LUCIA
CASTRIES
ST VINCENT & THE GRENADINES
KINGSTOWN
BARBADOS
BRIDGETOWN
GRENADA
ST GEORGE'S
Windward Islands
TRINIDAD & TOBAGO
PORT-OF-SPAIN
San Fernando
Lesser Antilles
ARUBA
(to Netherlands)
ORANJESTAD
NETHERLANDS ANTILLES
(to Netherlands)
Curaçao
WILLEMSTAD
Bonaire
Kralendijk
VENEZUELA
DOMINICA
Portsmouth
ROSEAU
SCALE 1:2,250,000
MARTINIQUE
(to France)
FORT-DE-FRANCE
SCALE 1:2,750,000
ST LUCIA
CASTRIES
SCALE 1:2,250,000
BARBADOS
BRIDGETOWN
SCALE 1:2,250,000
St Vincent
KINGSTOWN
SCALE 1:2,250,000
GRENADA
ST.GEORGE'S
SCALE 1:2,250,000
PORT-OF-SPAIN
Trinidad
Gulf of Paria
SCALE 1:2,750,000

120°
110°
100°
NORTH
Cedros Trench
Lower California
Gulf of California
Sierra Madre Occidental
Sierra Madre Oriental
Rio Grande
San Lucas Cape
Lago de Chapala
Río Grande de Santiago
Popocatépetl 5452m
East Pacific Rise
Tehuantepec Ridge
Union Reefs
Clipperton Seamounts
Clipperton Island
PACIFIC
COCOS PLATE
NAZCA PLATE
NAZCA PLATE
PACIFIC PLATE

SOUTH AMERICA

REACHING FROM THE HUMID TROPICS DOWN INTO THE COLD SOUTH ATLANTIC, SOUTH AMERICA HAS AN AREA OF 6,886,000 SQ MILES (17,835,000 SQ KM). THERE ARE 12 SEPARATE COUNTRIES, WITH THE LARGEST, BRAZIL, COVERING ALMOST HALF THE CONTINENT.

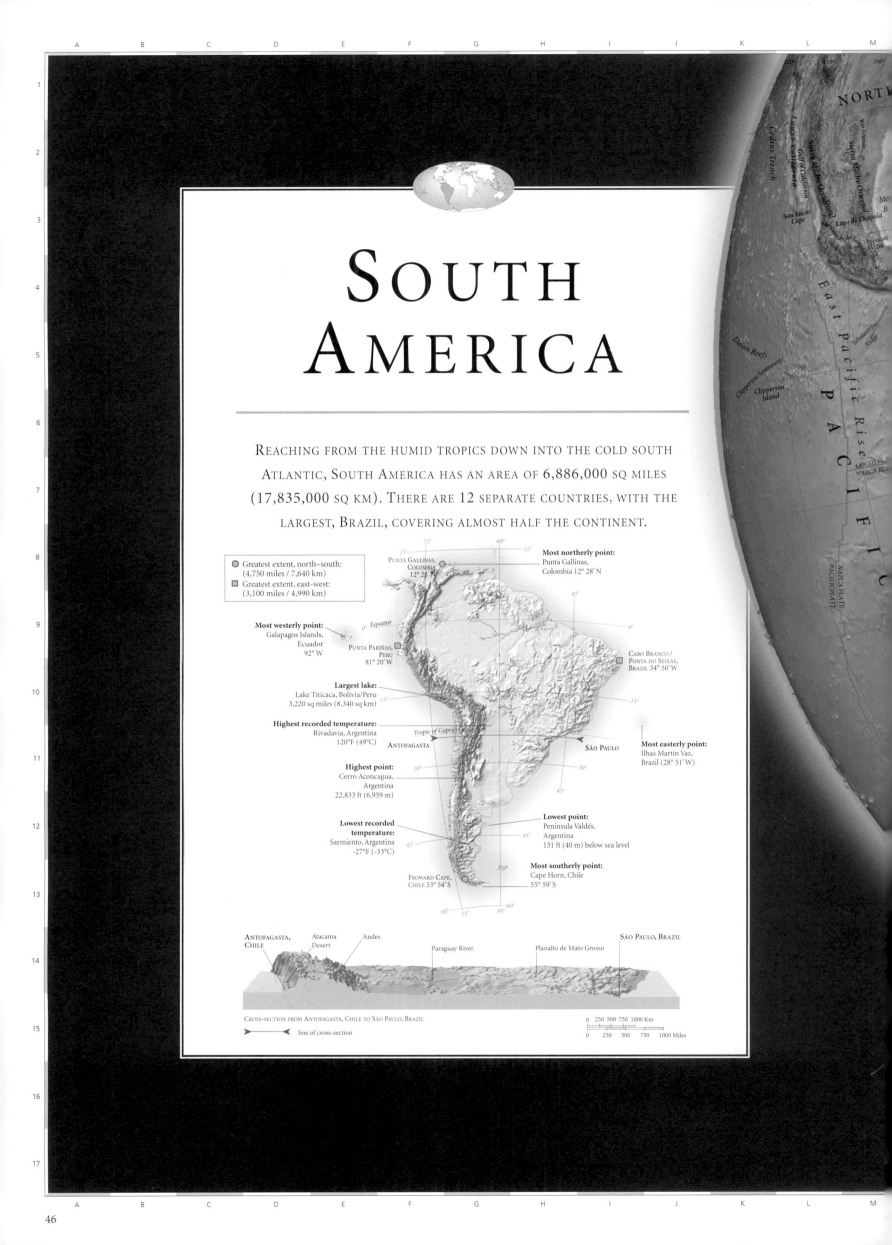

Greatest extent, north–south: (4,750 miles / 7,640 km)
Greatest extent, east-west: (3,100 miles / 4,990 km)
Punta Gallinas, Colombia 12° 28' N
Most northerly point: Punta Gallinas, Colombia 12° 28' N
Most westerly point: Galapagos Islands, Ecuador 92° W
Equator
Punta Pariñas, Peru 81° 20' W
Cabo Branco / Ponta do Seixas, Brazil 34° 50' W
Largest lake: Lake Titicaca, Bolivia/Peru 3,220 sq miles (8,340 sq km)
Highest recorded temperature: Rivadavia, Argentina 120°F (49°C)
Tropic of Capricorn
Antofagasta
São Paulo
Most easterly point: Ilhas Martin Vaz, Brazil (28° 51' W)
Highest point: Cerro Aconcagua, Argentina 22,833 ft (6,959 m)
Lowest point: Peninsula Valdés, Argentina 131 ft (40 m) below sea level
Lowest recorded temperature: Sarmiento, Argentina -27°F (-33°C)
Most southerly point: Cape Horn, Chile 55° 59' S
Froward Cape, Chile 53° 54' S

Antofagasta, Chile
Atacama Desert
Andes
Paraguay River
Planalto de Mato Grosso
São Paulo, Brazil

Cross-section from Antofagasta, Chile to São Paulo, Brazil

line of cross-section

0 250 500 750 1000 Km
0 250 500 750 1000 Miles

AMERICA
Gulf of Mexico
Cape Canaveral
Lake Okeechobee
Apalachee Bay
Mississippi Fan
Straits of Florida
Great Bahama Bank
Bahamas
Hatteras Plain
Sargasso Sea
Nares Plain
Cuba
West Indies
Puerto Rico Trench
Yucatan Basin
Yucatan Peninsula
Cayman Trench
Windward Passage
Hispaniola
Puerto Rico
Leeward Islands
Nevis
Barbuda
Antigua
Guadeloupe
Dominica
Martinique
Saint Lucia
Barbados
Grenada
Tobago
Trinidad
Jamaica
Greater Antilles
Lesser Antilles
Caribbean Sea
Gulf of Honduras
Nicaraguan Rise
Mosquito Coast
Punta Gallinas
Aruba
Bonaire
Curaçao
Isla de Margarita
Peninsula de la Guajira
Gulf of Venezuela
Colombian Basin
Lake Maracaibo
Cordillera de la Costa
Lake Nicaragua
Gulf of Fonseca
Middle America Trench
Guatemala Basin
Mosquito Gulf
Gulf of Darien
Isthmus of Panama
Gulf of Panama
Peninsula de Azuero
Panama Basin
Colón Ridge
CARIBBEAN PLATE
SOUTH AMERICAN PLATE
NORTH AMERICAN PLATE
AFRICAN PLATE
Llanos
Apure
Arauca
Meta
Orinoco
Caura
Caroni
Essequibo
Courantyne
Maroni
Oyapock
Guiana Highlands
Craricoera
Serra Parima
Tumuc-Humac Mountains
Araguari
Trombetas
Pau de Oeste
Paru
Jari
Vichada
Guaviare
Cordillera Occidental
Cordillera Central
Cordillera Oriental
Caquetá
Putumayo
Napo
Uaupés
Rio Negro
Branco
Jauaperi
Represa Balbina
Amazon Basin
Amazon
Japurá
Içá
Jutaí
Purus
Madeira
Canumã
Tapajós
Xingu
Iriri
Chimborazo 6310m
Gulf of Guayaquil
Punta Pariñas
Galapagos Islands
Marañón
Juruá
Tapauá
SOUTH AMERICA
Serra do Cachimbo
Aripuanã
Roosevelt
Ituxi
Acre
Chapada dos Parecis
Guaporé
Madre de Dios
Mamoré
Beni
Planalto de Mato Grosso
Serra Formosa
Serra do Roncador
Araguaia
Ucayali
Urubamba
Apurimac
ANDES
Cordillera Oriental
Cordillera Occidental
Lake Titicaca
Yungas
Lago Poopó
Rio Grande
Altiplano
Peru Basin
Peru-Chile Trench
Mendaña Fracture Zone
Nazca Ridge
Chile Basin
Atacama Desert
Pilcomayo
Gran Chaco
Pantanal
Paraguay
Taquari
Salinas Grandes
Salado
Dulce
Sierras de Córdoba
Laguna Mar Chiquita
Pampas
Mesopotamia
Paraná
Represa de Itaipu
Iguaçu
Uruguay
Islas de los Desventurados
Sala y Gomez Fracture Zone
Easter Island
Roggeveen Basin
Juan Fernández Islands
Río de la Plata
Colorado
Río Negro
Neuquén
Bahía Blanca
Golfo San Matías
Chubut
Limay
Patagonia
Gulf of San Jorge
Lago Buenos Aires
Deseado
Bahía Grande
Golfo Corcovado
Archipiélago de los Chonos
Strait of Magellan
Tierra del Fuego
Cape Horn
East Pacific Rise
NAZCA PLATE
ANTARCTIC PLATE
PACIFIC PLATE
MID-ATLANTIC RIDGE
ATLANTIC OCEAN
Cape Verde Basin
Cape Verde Islands
Gambia Plain
Doldrums Fracture Zone
Demerara Plain
Guiana Basin
Four North Fracture Zone
Saint Paul Fracture Zone
Equator
Amazon Fan
Ceará Plain
Baía de Marajó
Ilha de Marajó
Baía de São Marcos
Atol das Rocas
Fernando de Noronha
Cabo de São Roque
Cabo Branco
Pernambuco Plain
Represa de Tucuruí
Tocantins
Mearim
Itapicuru
Serra Grande
Parnaíba
Planalto da Borborema
Represa de Itaparica
Represa de Sobradinho
Chapada das Mangabeiras
Serra Geral de Goiás
São Francisco
Chapada Diamantina
Brazilian Highlands
Paraguaçu
Baía de Todos os Santos
Brazil Basin
Serra do Espinhaço
Abrolhos Bank
Trindade Spur
Doce
Paranaíba
Aporé
Rio Grande
Serra da Mantiqueira
Serra do Paranapiacaba
Serra do Mar
Ilha de São Sebastião
Santos Plateau
Ilha de São Francisco
Serra Geral
Rio Grande Rise
Lagoa dos Patos
Mirim Lagoon
Embalse de Rio Negro
Cuchilla Grande
Argentine Basin
Argentine Plain
Falkland Escarpment
Maurice Ewing Bank
Falkland Plateau
Falkland Islands
South Sandwich Trench
South Georgia
South Georgia Ridge
South Sandwich Islands
SCOTIA PLATE
Scotia Ridge
Scotia Sea
South Shetland Islands
South Shetland Trough
South Orkney Islands
Weddell Sea
ANTARCTICA

Physical South America

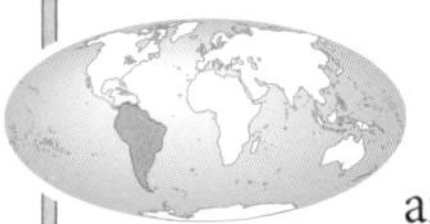

Three major physiographic regions characterize South America. The oldest, the ancient Brazilian Shield and the smaller Guyana and Patagonian shields, form the stable core of the continent. Stretching along the entire west coast are the younger Andean fold mountains with many summits rising to 20,000 ft (6,100 m). These two diverse regions are separated by a number of sedimentary basins carrying South America's large river systems to the sea. These include the massive Amazon Basin and the basin of the Gran Chaco.

Punta Gallinas
Gulf of Venezuela
Lake Maracaibo
Gulf of Darien
Gulf of Panama
COCOS PLATE
NAZCA PLATE
Cauca
Cordillera Occidental
Cordillera Central
Magdalena
Cordillera Oriental
Llanos
Orinoco
Pakaraima Mountains
GUYANA SHIELD
Guiana Highlands
Tumuc-Humac Mountains
Rio Negro
Japurá
Branco
Represa Balbina
Amazon
Ilha de Marajó
Cotopaxi 5897m
Chimborazo 6310m
Cordillera Real
Putumayo
Amazon Basin
Juruá
Purus
Madeira
Tapajós
Xingu
Tocantins
Gulf of Guayaquil
Marañón
Punta Negra
SUB-ANDEAN SYSTEM
Serra dos Carajás
Serra do Cachimbo
Ucayali
Nevado Huascarán 6768m
SOUTH AMERICAN PLATE
NAZCA PLATE
Andes
Madre de Dios
Chapada dos Parecis
Guaporé
Serra Formosa
Araguaia
Tocantins
BRAZILIAN SHIELD
Cabo de São Roque
Planalto da Borborema
Represa de Sobradinho
Planalto de Mato Grosso
Serra do Roncador
Serra Dourada
São Francisco
Brazilian Highlands
PACIFIC OCEAN
Lake Titicaca
Lago Poopó
Altiplano
Pantanal
Serra do Caiapó
Serra do Espinhaço
Serra de Maracaju
Paraná
Pilcomayo
Atacama Desert
Gran Chaco
Paraguay
Serra da Mantiqueira
Serra Geral
Serra do Mar
Cerro Ojos del Salado 6880m
Uruguay
Mesopotamia
Lagoa dos Patos
Mirim Lagoon
Cerro Aconcagua 6959m
Salado
Pampas
Río de la Plata
ATLANTIC OCEAN
NAZCA PLATE
SOUTH AMERICAN PLATE
Colorado
Río Negro
Península Valdés
PATAGONIAN SHIELD
Patagonia
Isla de Chiloé
Lago Colhué Huapí
Chico
Gulf of San Jorge
Deseado
Golfo de Penas
ANTARCTIC PLATE
Bahía Grande
Strait of Magellan
Falkland Islands
Tierra del Fuego
SOUTH AMERICAN PLATE
SCOTIA PLATE
Cape Horn
SCALE 1:30,500,000
(projection: Lambert Azimuthal Equal Area)

The Amazon Basin and Guyana Shield

The River Amazon occupies a large depression in the Earth's crust, formed by the uplift of the Andes. It is covered by thick volcanic deposits and layers of alluvium – these have been laid down by the Amazon's many tributaries. To the north is the smaller Guyana Shield.

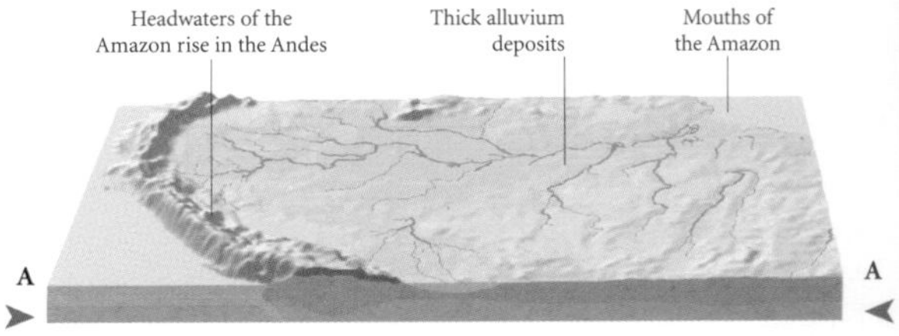

Headwaters of the Amazon rise in the Andes
Thick alluvium deposits
Mouths of the Amazon
A
A
0 500 1000 Km
0 500 1000 Miles

***Section** across northern South America showing Amazon Basin and its drainage pattern.*

The Andean Uplands

The Andean Uplands run along the west coast of South America. They are being uplifted as the Nazca Plate is subducted beneath the South American Plate. They contain some of the world's largest volcanoes, such as Cotopaxi, and Lake Titicaca which occupies a dormant site. The far south has many large ice-sheets and a fragmented coastline.

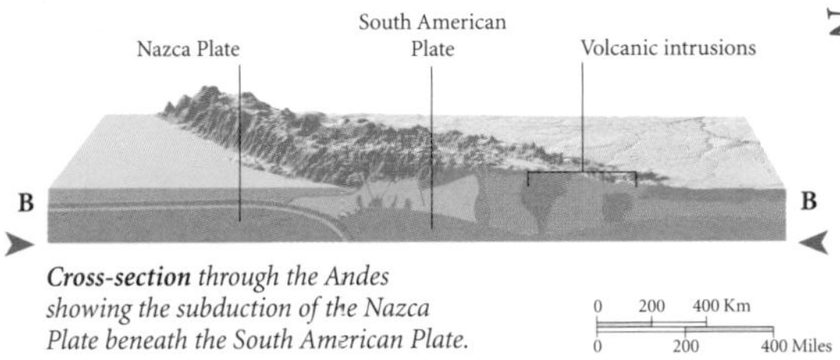

Nazca Plate
South American Plate
Volcanic intrusions
B
B
0 200 400 Km
0 200 400 Miles

***Cross-section** through the Andes showing the subduction of the Nazca Plate beneath the South American Plate.*

Map Key

ELEVATION

- 6000m / 19,686ft
- 4000m / 13,124ft
- 3000m / 9843ft
- 2000m / 6562ft
- 1500m / 4922ft
- 1000m / 3281ft
- 500m / 1640ft
- 250m / 820ft
- 100m / 328ft
- sea level

PLATE MARGINS
(for explanation see page xiv)

- constructive
- destructive
- conservative
- uncertain
- physiographic regions
- line of cross-section

The Brazilian Shield and Gran Chaco

The immense Brazilian Shield underlies more than one-third of South America. It is pitted with numerous volcanic intrusions, and a large basaltic plateau exists between the Paraná River and the Atlantic Ocean. The flat Gran Chaco lies to the west of the shield, covered by sedimentary deposits eroded from the Andes, and transported by South America's mighty rivers.

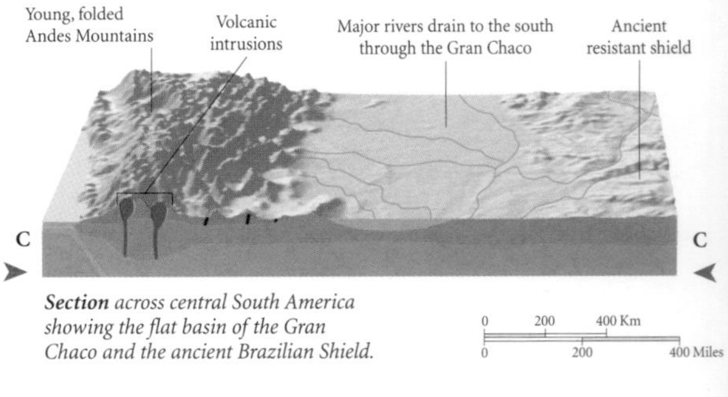

Young, folded Andes Mountains
Volcanic intrusions
Major rivers drain to the south through the Gran Chaco
Ancient resistant shield
C
C
0 200 400 Km
0 200 400 Miles

***Section** across central South America showing the flat basin of the Gran Chaco and the ancient Brazilian Shield.*

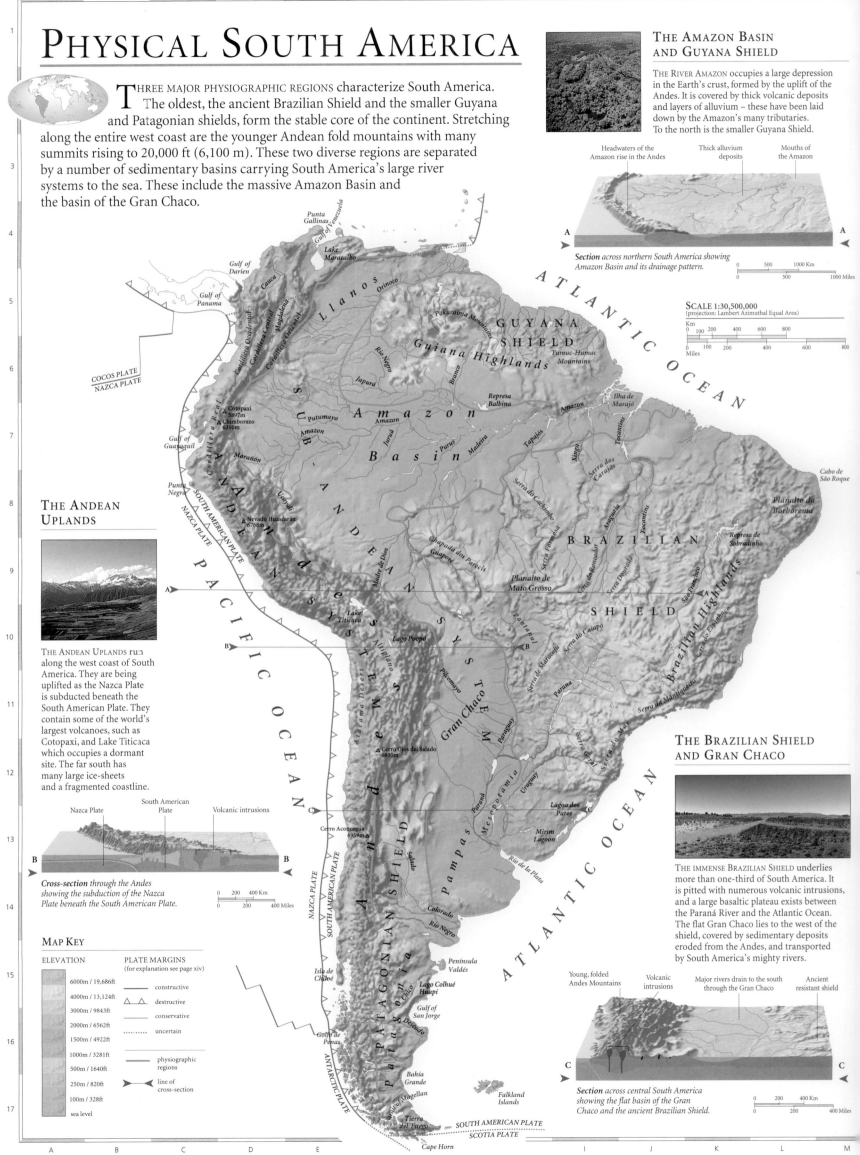

Mild winters and cool summers typify the extensive Pampas grasslands of Argentina.

Chile's hyperarid Atacama Desert is renowned as one of the driest places on Earth.

Climate

The climate of South America is influenced by three principal factors: the seasonal shift of high pressure air masses over the tropics, cold ocean currents along the western coast, affecting temperature and precipitation, and the mountain barrier produced by by the Andes, which creates a rain shadow over much of the south.

Climate

- tundra
- cool continental
- warm humid
- semiarid
- arid
- humid equatorial
- tropical
- daily hours of sunshine, January
- daily hours of sunshine, July
- cold wind

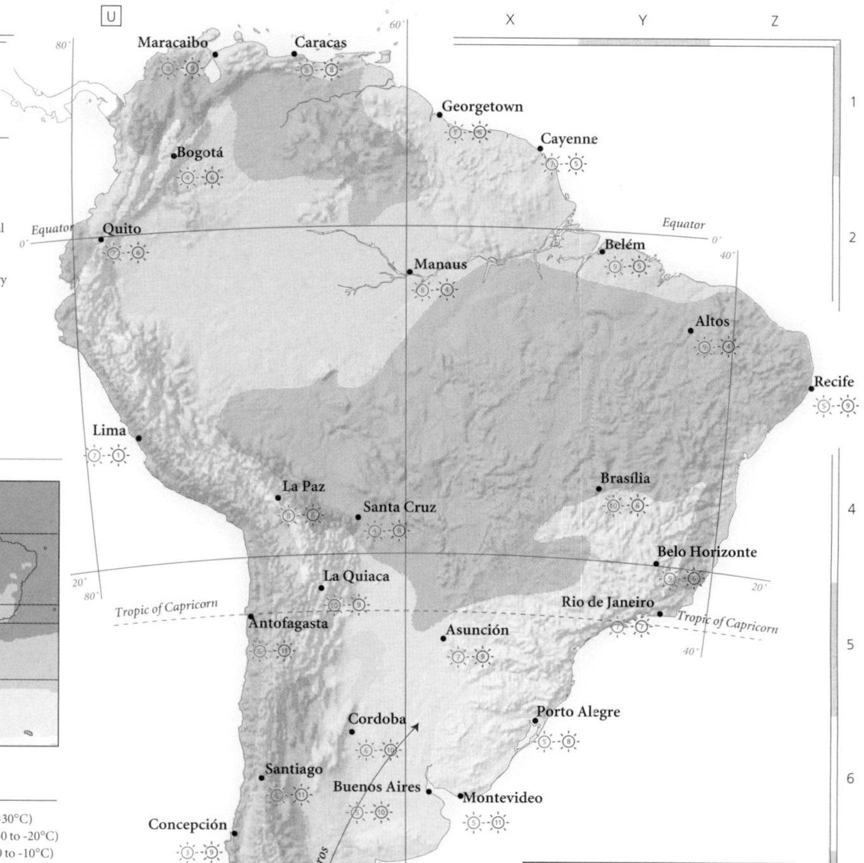

Maracaibo
Caracas
Georgetown
Cayenne
Bogotá
Quito
Equator
Belém
Manaus
Altos
Recife
Lima
La Paz
Santa Cruz
Brasília
Belo Horizonte
La Quiaca
Tropic of Capricorn
Rio de Janeiro
Antofagasta
Asunción
Porto Alegre
Cordoba
Santiago
Buenos Aires
Montevideo
Concepción
Pamperos
Stanley

Temperature

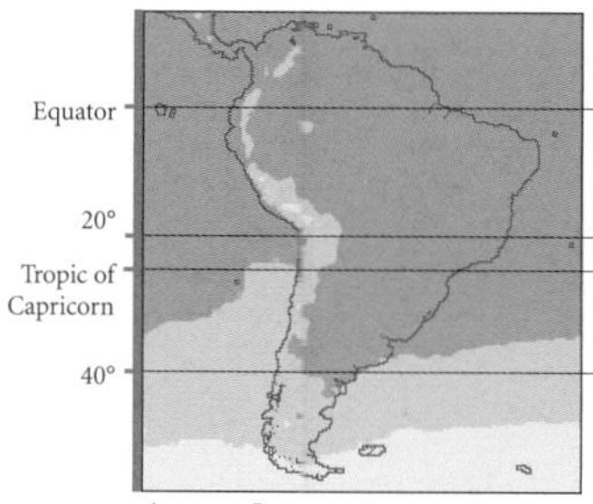

Equator
20°
Tropic of Capricorn
40°

Average January temperature

Average July temperature

Temperature

- below -22°F (-30°C)
- -22 to -4°F (-30 to -20°C)
- -4 to 14°F (-20 to -10°C)
- 14 to 32°F (-10 to 0°C)
- 32 to 50°F (0 to 10°C)
- 50°F (10 to 20°C)
- 68 to 86°F (20 to 30°C)
- above 86°F (30°C)

Rainfall

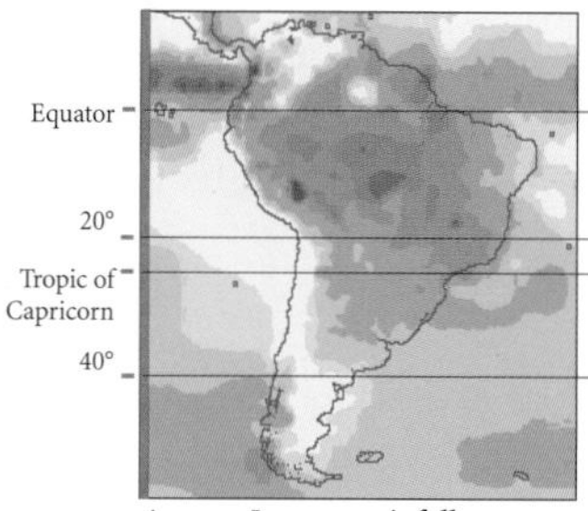

Equator
20°
Tropic of Capricorn
40°

Average January rainfall

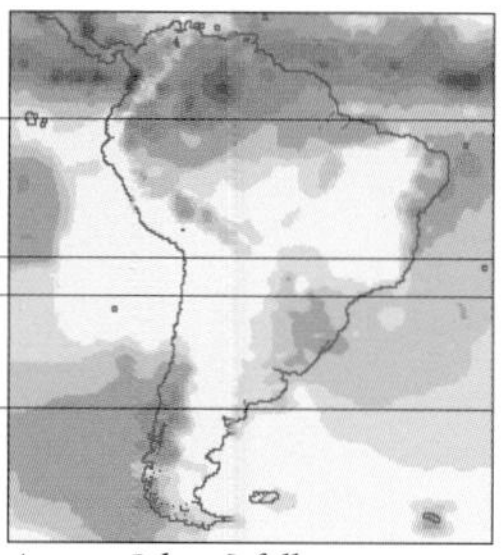

Average July rainfall

Rainfall

- 0–1 in (0–25 mm)
- 1–2 in (25–50 mm)
- 2–4 in (50–100 mm)
- 4–8 in (100–200 mm)
- 8–12 in (200–300 mm)
- 12–16 in (300–400 mm)
- 16–20 in (400–500 mm)
- more than 20 in (500 mm)

Tropical conditions are found across over half of South America. When both rainfall and temperatures are high, hot humid rain forests prevail.

Shaping the Continent

South America's active tectonic belt has been extensively folded over millions of years; landslides are still frequent in the mountains. The large river systems that erode the mountains flow across resistant shield areas, depositing sediment. Present-day glaciation affects the distinctive landscape of the far south.

Mass Movement

6 Debris slides are common in the highlands of South America *(left)*. They occur where soil on a slope is saturated by rainwater and therefore less stable. The actual slides are often triggered by earthquakes.

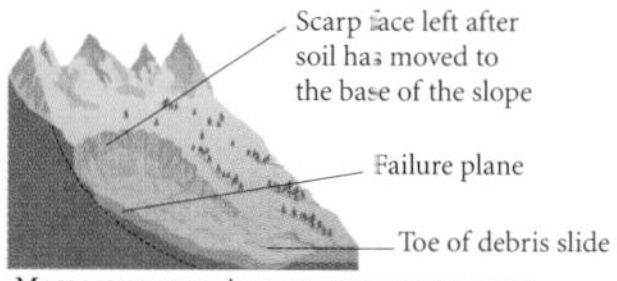

Scarp face left after soil has moved to the base of the slope
Failure plane
Toe of debris slide

Mass movement: A section of a debris slide

Chemical Weathering

1 Table mountains *(left)* are the eroded remnants of an ancient upland. As water percolates along cracks in these high, flat-topped mountains it forms intricate cave systems. Chemical weathering also isolates large blocks which then collapse, accumulating as rockfalls at the foot of scarp slopes.

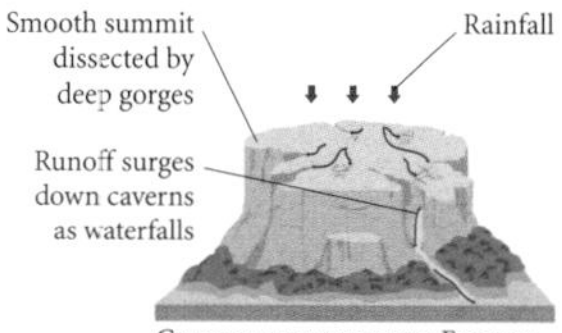

Smooth summit dissected by deep gorges
Rainfall
Runoff surges down caverns as waterfalls

Chemical weathering: Erosion of the Guyana Shield

River Systems

2 Along the Amazon *(above)* there is a great variation in rates of erosion. As the headwaters of the Amazon flow down from the Andes, they erode and transport vast quantities of sediment, and are known as whitewaters. Across the shield areas erosion rates are very low. These rivers, carrying rotting vegetation, are called blackwaters.

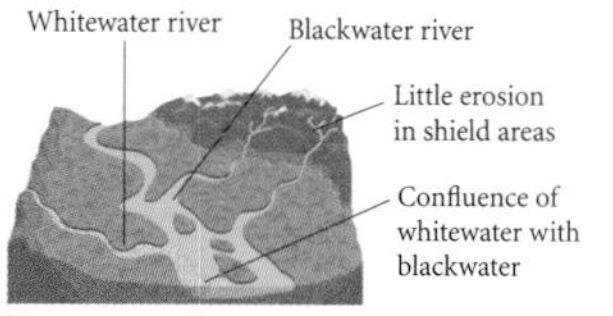

Whitewater river
Blackwater river
Little erosion in shield areas
Confluence of whitewater with blackwater

River systems: Suspended sediments in the Amazon

The Evolving Landscape

1
2
3
4
5
6

Landscape

- uplifting land
- stable land
- sinking land
- glacier
- ocean current
- alluvial fan
- inselberg
- river

Folding

5 Folding occurs beneath the surface under high temperatures and pressures. Rocks become sufficiently malleable to flow and not fracture as tectonic plates collide. In the Valley of the Moon in Chile *(above)*, anticlines (or upfolds) and synclines (or troughs) have been exploited by erosion.

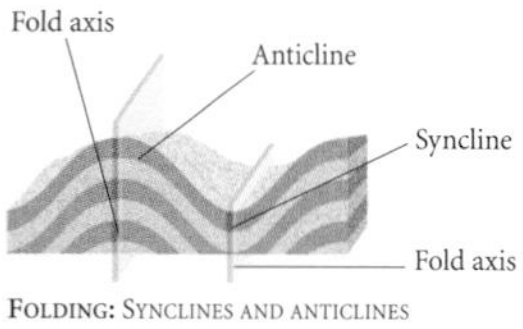

Fold axis
Anticline
Syncline
Fold axis

Folding: Synclines and anticlines

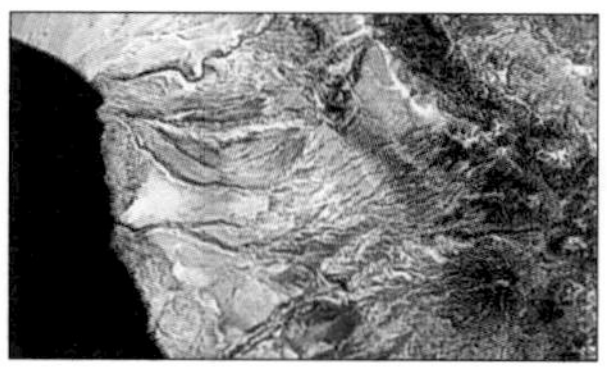

Deposition

4 Large alluvial fans are found extensively across South America *(above)*. Confined mountain rivers, carrying large quantities of eroded material, emerge from a mountain gorge onto the plains, where they deposit their load in huge fans.

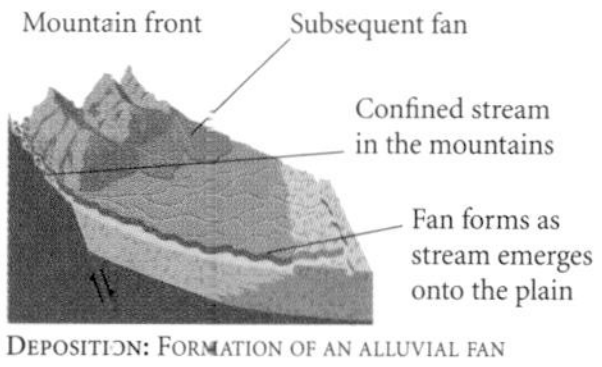

Mountain front
Subsequent fan
Confined stream in the mountains
Fan forms as stream emerges onto the plain

Deposition: Formation of an alluvial fan

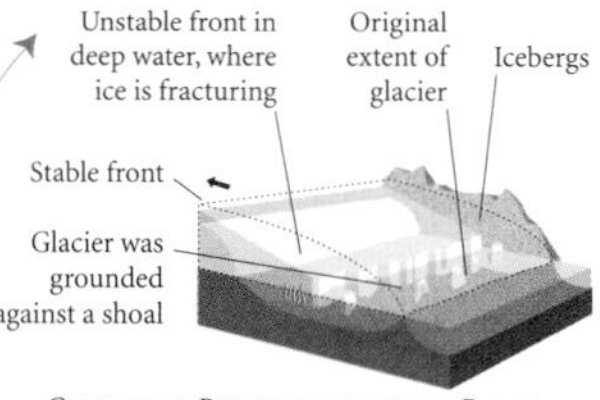

Unstable front in deep water, where ice is fracturing
Original extent of glacier
Icebergs
Stable front
Glacier was grounded against a shoal

Glaciation: Retreating glacier in Patagonia

Glaciation

3 As fjord glaciers in Patagonia *(above)* retreat, they become grounded on shoals. In deeper water the base of the glacier becomes unstable, and icebergs break off (calve) until the glacier snout grounds once more.

Political South America

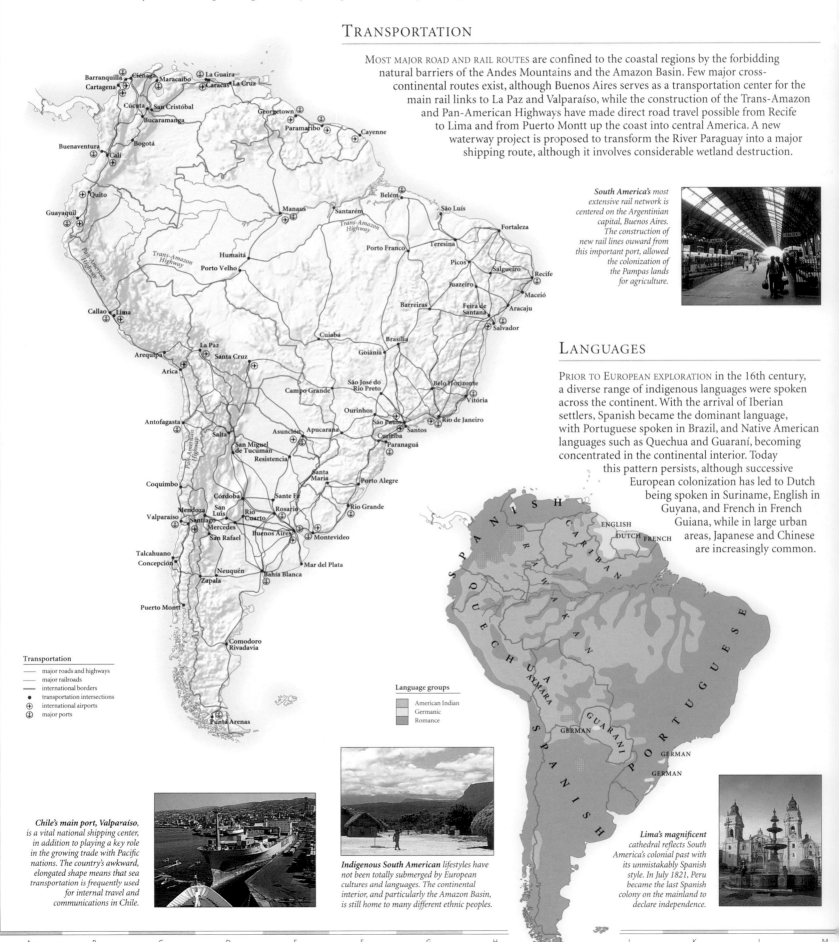

Modern South America's political boundaries have their origins in the territorial endeavors of explorers during the 16th century, who claimed almost the entire continent for Portugal and Spain. The Portuguese land in the east later evolved into the federal state of Brazil, while the Spanish vice-royalties eventually emerged as separate independent nation-states in the early 19th century. South America's growing population has become increasingly urbanized, with the growth of coastal cities into large conurbations like Rio de Janeiro and Buenos Aires. In Brazil, Argentina, Chile and Uruguay, a succession of military dictatorships has given way to fragile, but strengthening, democracies.

***Europe retains** a small foothold in South America. Kourou in French Guiana was the site chosen by the European Space Agency to launch the Ariane rocket. As a result of its status as a French overseas department, French Guiana is actually part of the European Union.*

SCALE 1:24,000,000
(projection: Lambert Azimuthal Equal Area)

Km: 0 50 100 200 300 400 500 600 700 800
Miles: 0 50 100 200 300 400 500 600 700 800

Transportation

Most major road and rail routes are confined to the coastal regions by the forbidding natural barriers of the Andes Mountains and the Amazon Basin. Few major cross-continental routes exist, although Buenos Aires serves as a transportation center for the main rail links to La Paz and Valparaíso, while the construction of the Trans-Amazon and Pan-American Highways have made direct road travel possible from Recife to Lima and from Puerto Montt up the coast into central America. A new waterway project is proposed to transform the River Paraguay into a major shipping route, although it involves considerable wetland destruction.

Barranquilla
Cartagena
Ciénaga
Maracaibo
La Guaira
Caracas
La Cruz
Cúcuta
San Cristóbal
Bucaramanga
Georgetown
Paramaribo
Cayenne
Bogotá
Buenaventura
Cali
Quito
Guayaquil
Belém
São Luís
Manaus
Santarém
Trans-Amazon Highway
Fortaleza
Teresina
Porto Franco
Humaitá
Porto Velho
Trans-Amazon Highway
Pan-American Highway
Picos
Salgueiro
Recife
Juazeiro
Maceió
Barreiras
Feira de Santana
Aracaju
Salvador
Callao
Lima
Cuiabá
Brasília
Goiânia
La Paz
Santa Cruz
Arequipa
Arica
Belo Horizonte
Vitória
São José do Rio Preto
Campo Grande
Ourinhos
São Paulo
Rio de Janeiro
Santos
Antofagasta
Salta
Asunción
Apucarana
Curitiba
Paranaguá
Pan-American Highway
San Miguel de Tucumán
Resistencia
Santa Maria
Coquimbo
Porto Alegre
Córdoba
Sante Fe
San Luis
Rosario
Rio Grande
Mendoza
Valparaíso
Santiago
Rio Cuarto
Mercedes
Buenos Aires
Montevideo
San Rafael
Talcahuano
Concepción
Mar del Plata
Neuquén
Zapala
Bahía Blanca
Puerto Montt
Comodoro Rivadavia
Punta Arenas
Transportation
major roads and highways
major railroads
international borders
transportation intersections
international airports
major ports

***South America's** most extensive rail network is centered on the Argentinian capital, Buenos Aires. The construction of new rail lines ouward from this important port, allowed the colonization of the Pampas lands for agriculture.*

Languages

Prior to European exploration in the 16th century, a diverse range of indigenous languages were spoken across the continent. With the arrival of Iberian settlers, Spanish became the dominant language, with Portuguese spoken in Brazil, and Native American languages such as Quechua and Guaraní, becoming concentrated in the continental interior. Today this pattern persists, although successive European colonization has led to Dutch being spoken in Suriname, English in Guyana, and French in French Guiana, while in large urban areas, Japanese and Chinese are increasingly common.

SPANISH
ARAWAKAN
CARIBAN
ENGLISH
DUTCH
FRENCH
QUECHUA
AYMARA
GUARANI
PORTUGUESE
GERMAN
GERMAN
GERMAN
SPANISH
Language groups
American Indian
Germanic
Romance

***Chile's main port, Valparaíso,** is a vital national shipping center, in addition to playing a key role in the growing trade with Pacific nations. The country's awkward, elongated shape means that sea transportation is frequently used for internal travel and communications in Chile.*

***Indigenous South American** lifestyles have not been totally submerged by European cultures and languages. The continental interior, and particularly the Amazon Basin, is still home to many different ethnic peoples.*

***Lima's magnificent** cathedral reflects South America's colonial past with its unmistakably Spanish style. In July 1821, Peru became the last Spanish colony on the mainland to declare independence.*

Caribbean Sea
ATLANTIC OCEAN
PACIFIC OCEAN
VENEZUELA
CARACAS
Maracaibo
Valencia
Maracay
Barquisimeto
Cumaná
Ciudad Guayana
Barinas
San Cristóbal
Cabimas
Lake Maracaibo
Gulf of Venezuela
Venezuelan territorial claim
TRINIDAD & TOBAGO
GUYANA
GEORGETOWN
Linden
SURINAME
PARAMARIBO
Surinamese territorial claims
French Guiana (to France)
CAYENNE
COLOMBIA
BOGOTÁ
Santa Marta
Barranquilla
Cartagena
Valledupar
Montería
Cúcuta
Bucaramanga
Medellín
Manizales
Pereira
Armenia
Ibagué
Cali
Pasto
Gulf of Darien
Gulf of Panama
PANAMA
Llanos
Guiana Highlands
ECUADOR
QUITO
Esmeraldas
Portoviejo
Ambato
Riobamba
Babahoyo
Guayaquil
Cuenca
Machala
PERU
LIMA
Callao
Piura
Chiclayo
Trujillo
Iquitos
Huancayo
Cusco
Arequipa
Tacna
BOLIVIA
LA PAZ
SUCRE
Cochabamba
Oruro
Santa Cruz
Lake Titicaca
Lago Poopó
BRAZIL
BRASÍLIA
DISTRITO FEDERAL
Amazon Basin
AMAZONAS
Manaus
Boa Vista
RORAIMA
AMAPÁ
Macapá
Belém
Santarém
São Luís
PARÁ
MARANHÃO
Teresina
CEARÁ
Fortaleza
RIO GRANDE DO NORTE
Natal
PARAÍBA
João Pessoa
PIAUÍ
PERNAMBUCO
Jaboatão
Recife
Juazeiro
ALAGOAS
Maceió
SERGIPE
Aracaju
Represa de Sobradinho
BAHIA
Salvador
TOCANTINS
Palmas
ACRE
Rio Branco
RONDÔNIA
Porto Velho
MATO GROSSO
Planalto de Mato Grosso
Cuiabá
Goiânia
GOIÁS
MINAS GERAIS
Belo Horizonte
Brazilian Highlands
MATO GROSSO DO SUL
Campo Grande
Ribeirão Preto
SÃO PAULO
São Paulo
Campinas
Osasco
Sorocaba
Santos
Nova Iguaçu
RIO DE JANEIRO
Rio de Janeiro
Niterói
Juiz de Fora
Vitória
ESPÍRITO SANTO
Londrina
PARANÁ
Curitiba
SANTA CATARINA
Florianópolis
RIO GRANDE DO SUL
Santa Maria
Porto Alegre
Represa Balbina
PARAGUAY
ASUNCIÓN
Ciudad del Este
Villarrica
Gran Chaco
URUGUAY
MONTEVIDEO
Tacuarembó
Melo
ARGENTINA
BUENOS AIRES
La Plata
Río de la Plata
Rosario
Santa Fe
Paraná
Córdoba
Corrientes
Resistencia
Posadas
Formosa
San Miguel de Tucumán
Santiago del Estero
Salta
San Salvador de Jujuy
La Rioja
San Juan
Mendoza
San Luis
Santa Rosa
Bahía Blanca
Mar del Plata
Neuquén
Pampas
Patagonia
Rawson
Gulf of San Jorge
Río Gallegos
Ushuaia
Beagle Channel
Cape Horn
Strait of Magellan
Falkland Islands (to UK)
STANLEY
CHILE
SANTIAGO
Arica
Iquique
Tocopilla
Antofagasta
Atacama Desert
La Serena
Coquimbo
Viña del Mar
Valparaíso
Linares
Concepción
Lota
Temuco
Valdivia
Puerto Montt
Golfo de Penas
Punta Arenas
Andes
Tropic of Capricorn
Equator
MAP KEY
POPULATION
above 5 million
1 million to 5 million
500,000 to 1 million
100,000 to 500,000
50,000 to 100,000
10,000 to 50,000
below 10,000
Country capital
State capital
BORDERS
full international border
disputed de facto border
disputed territorial claim border
state border

***In April 1960**, Brazil's government began the move from Rio de Janeiro to Brasília, a futuristic new city built in the sparsely populated interior. Brasília is now the federal capital of Brazil.*

***Rapid urbanization** was a feature of most South American countries in the latter half of the 20th century. In many cases, this unchecked growth has led to the development of sprawling slums, lacking adequate water and sewerage facilities.*

***Perched high** in the Andes like many of the cities in western South America, La Paz, Bolivia is the world's highest capital city at over 11,500 ft (3,500 m).*

POPULATION

ALMOST HALF OF SOUTH AMERICA'S population lives in Brazil but, due to the large uninhabited expanses of the Amazon Basin, its overall population density is much lower than in other countries. During the 20th century the most important population trend was the movement from rural to urban areas, giving rise to great population concentrations in large cities like São Paulo, Rio de Janeiro, Caracas, Lima, Bogotá, and Buenos Aires.

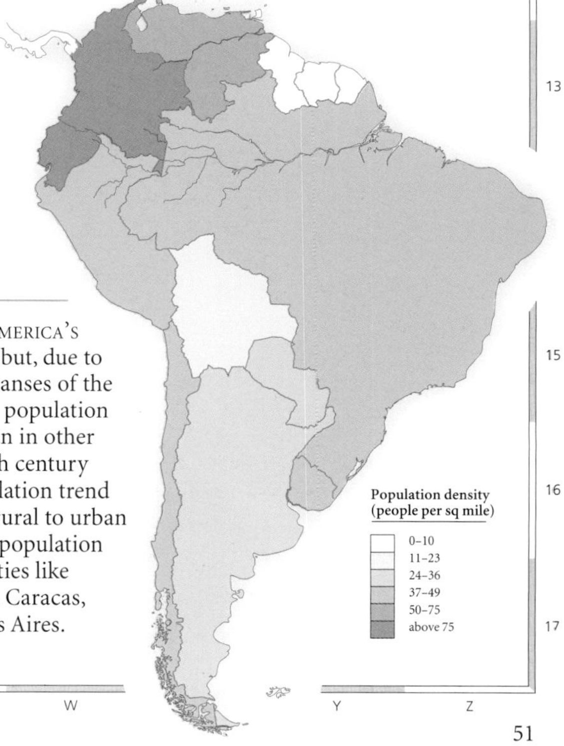
Population density (people per sq mile)
0–10
11–23
24–36
37–49
50–75
above 75

South American Resources

Agriculture still provides the largest single form of employment in South America, although rural unemployment and poverty continue to drive people toward the huge coastal cities in search of jobs and opportunities. Mineral and fuel resources, although substantial, are distributed unevenly; few countries have both fossil fuels and minerals. To break industrial dependence on raw materials, boost manufacturing, and improve infrastructure, governments borrowed heavily from the World Bank in the 1960s and 1970s. This led to the accumulation of massive debts which are unlikely ever to be repaid. Today, Brazil dominates the continent's economic output, followed by Argentina. Recently, the less-developed western side of South America has benefited due to its geographical position; for example Chile is increasingly exporting raw materials to Japan.

***Ciudad Guayana** is a planned industrial complex in eastern Venezuela, built as an iron and steel centre to exploit the nearby iron ore reserves.*

***The cold Peru Current** flows north from the Antarctic along the Pacific coast of Peru, providing rich nutrients for one of the world's largest fishing grounds. Overexploitation has severely reduced Peru's anchovy catch.*

Industry
aerospace
brewing
car/vehicle manufacture
chemicals
electronics
engineering
finance
fish processing
food processing
hi-tech industry
iron & steel
meat processing
metal refining
narcotics
pharmaceuticals
printing & publishing
shipbuilding
sugar processing
textiles
timber processing
tobacco processing
wine
oil
gas
industrial cities
major industrial areas
Caribbean Sea
ATLANTIC OCEAN
PACIFIC OCEAN
PANAMA
Gulf of Panama
VENEZUELA
COLOMBIA
GUYANA
SURINAME
French Guiana (to France)
ECUADOR
PERU
BOLIVIA
BRAZIL
PARAGUAY
CHILE
ARGENTINA
URUGUAY
Amazon Basin
Barranquilla
Cartagena
Maracaibo
Barquisimeto
Caracas
Valencia
Ciudad Guayana
Georgetown
Paramaribo
Medellín
Bogotá
Cali
Quito
Guayaquil
Iquitos
Manaus
Belém
Fortaleza
Natal
Recife
Maceió
Salvador
Brasília
Chiclayo
Chimbote
Lima
Cusco
Arequipa
La Paz
Santa Cruz
Sucre
Arica
Iquique
Chuquicamata
Antofagasta
Belo Horizonte
Rio de Janeiro
São Paulo
Curitiba
Asunción
Ciudad del Este
San Miguel de Tucumán
Corrientes
Porto Alegre
Córdoba
Santa Fe
Rosario
Rio Grande
Valparaíso
Mendoza
Santiago
Buenos Aires
Montevideo
Talca
Concepción
Bahía Blanca
Neuquén
Valdivia
Comodoro Rivadavia
Gulf of San Jorge
Bahía Grande
Falkland Islands (to UK)
Strait of Magellan
Punta Arenas
Cape Horn
GNP per capita (US$)
0–499
500–999
1000–1499
1500–2999
3000–5999
6000+

Standard of Living

Wealth disparities throughout the continent create a wide gulf between affluent landowners and the chronically poor in inner-city slums. The illicit production of cocaine, and the hugely influential drug barons who control its distribution, contribute to the violent disorder and corruption which affect northwestern South America, de-stabilizing local governments and economies.

Standard of Living
(UN Human Development Index)
low
high

***Both Argentina and Chile** are now exploring the southernmost tip of the continent in search of oil. Here in Punta Arenas, a drilling rig is being prepared for exploratory drilling in the Strait of Magellen.*

Industry

Argentina and Brazil are South America's most industrialized countries and São Paulo is the continent's leading industrial center. Long-term government investment in Brazilian industry has encouraged a diverse industrial base; engineering, steel production, food processing, textile manufacture, and chemicals predominate. The illegal production of cocaine is economically significant in the Andean countries of Colombia and Bolivia. In Venezuela, the oil-dominated economy has left the country vulnerable to world oil price fluctuations. Food processing and mineral exploitation are common throughout the less industrially developed parts of the continent, including Bolivia, Chile, Ecuador, and Peru.

Environmental Issues

The Amazon Basin is one of the last great wilderness areas left on Earth. The tropical rain forests which grow there are a valuable genetic resource, containing innumerable unique plants and animals. The forests are increasingly under threat from new and expanding settlements and "slash and burn" farming techniques, which clear land for the raising of beef cattle, causing land degradation and soil erosion.

***Clouds of smoke billow** from the burning Amazon rain forest. Over 25,000 sq miles (60,000 sq km) of virgin rain forest are being cleared annually, destroying an ancient, irreplaceable, natural resource and biodiverse habitat.*

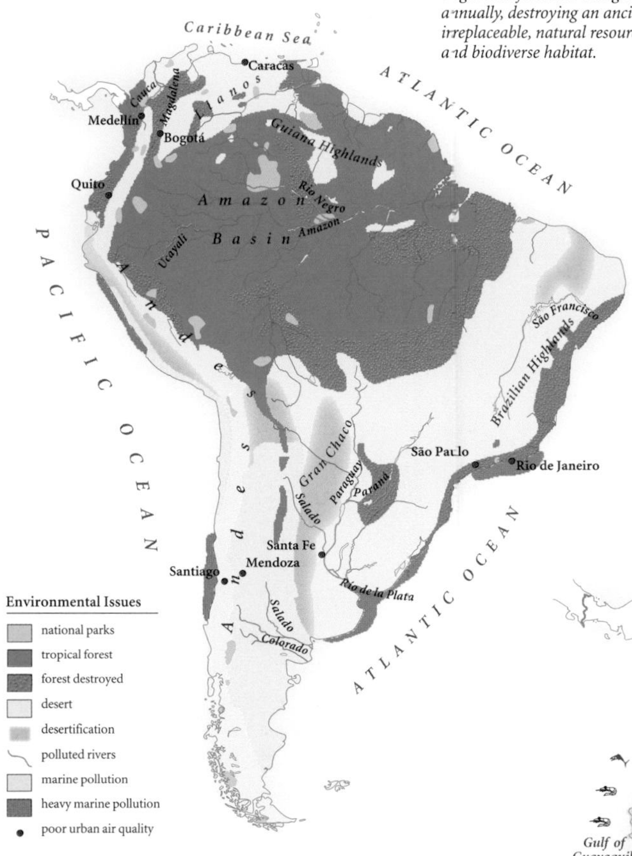

Caribbean Sea
Caracas
Medellín
Bogotá
Quito
Llanos
Guiana Highlands
Amazon Basin
Rio Negro
Amazon
Ucayali
Andes
São Francisco
Brazilian Highlands
Gran Chaco
Paraguay
Paraná
Salado
São Paulo
Rio de Janeiro
Santa Fe
Mendoza
Santiago
Río de la Plata
Colorado
ATLANTIC OCEAN
PACIFIC OCEAN
Environmental Issues
national parks
tropical forest
forest destroyed
desert
desertification
polluted rivers
marine pollution
heavy marine pollution
poor urban air quality

Mineral Resources

Over a quarter of the world's known copper reserves are found at the Chuquicamata mine in northern Chile, and other metallic minerals such as tin are found along the length of the Andes. The discovery of oil and gas at Venezuela's Lake Maracaibo in 1917 turned the country into one of the world's leading oil producers. In contrast, South America is virtually devoid of coal, the only significant deposit being on the peninsula of Guajira in Colombia.

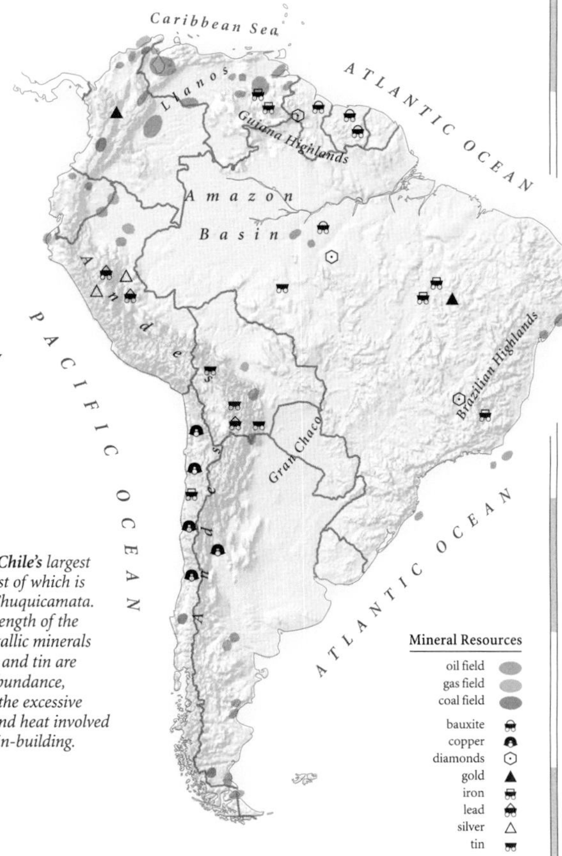

Caribbean Sea
Llanos
Guiana Highlands
Amazon Basin
Andes
Gran Chaco
Brazilian Highlands
ATLANTIC OCEAN
PACIFIC OCEAN
Mineral Resources
oil field
gas field
coal field
bauxite
copper
diamonds
gold
iron
lead
silver
tin

***Copper is Chile's** largest export, most of which is mined at Chuquicamata. Along the length of the Andes, metallic minerals like copper and tin are found in abundance, formed by the excessive pressures and heat involved in mountain-building.*

Using the Land and Sea

Many foods now common worldwide originated in South America. These include the potato, tomato, squash, and cassava. Today, large herds of beef cattle roam the temperate grasslands of the Pampas, supporting an extensive meatpacking trade in Argentina, Uruguay and Paraguay. Corn (maize) is grown as a staple crop across the continent and coffee is grown as a cash crop in Brazil and Colombia. Coca plants grown in Bolivia, Peru, and Colombia provide most of the world's cocaine. Fish and shellfish are caught off the western coast, especially anchovies off Peru, shrimps off Ecuador and pilchards off Chile.

Caribbean Sea
Barranquilla
Maracaibo
Caracas
Gulf of Darien
Gulf of Panama
Medellín
Bogotá
Cali
Llanos
Orinoco
Guiana Highlands
Rio Negro
Amazon
Putumayo
Amazon Basin
Juruá
Manaus
Tapajós
Xingu
Tocantins
Ilha de Marajó
Belém
Fortaleza
Recife
Gulf of Guayaquil
Marañón
Purus
Madeira
Araguaia
Andes
Lima
Planalto de Mato Grosso
Brasília
São Francisco
Brazilian Highlands
Salvador
Belo Horizonte
Rio de Janeiro
São Paulo
Curitiba
Pilcomayo
Gran Chaco
Paraguay
Paraná
Uruguay
Porto Alegre
Córdoba
Rosario
Santiago
Buenos Aires
Montevideo
Pampas
Colorado
Río Negro
Chico
Patagonia
Gulf of San Jorge
Bahía Grande
Tierra del Fuego
Cape Horn
PACIFIC OCEAN
ATLANTIC OCEAN
Using the Land and Sea
barren land
cropland
desert
forest
mountain region
pasture
major conurbations
cattle
pigs
sheep
bananas
corn
citrus fruits
cocoa
cotton
coffee
fishing
oil palms
peanuts
rubber
shellfish
soybeans
sugar cane
vineyards
wheat

***South America,** and Brazil in particular, now leads the world in coffee production, mainly growing Coffea Arabica in large plantations. Coffee beans are harvested, roasted, and brewed to produce the world's second most popular drink, after tea.*

***The Pampas region** of southeast South America is characterized by extensive, flat plains, and populated by cattle and ranchers (gauchos). Argentina is a major world producer of beef, much of which is exported to the US for use in hamburgers.*

***High in the Andes,** hardy alpacas graze on the barren land. Alpacas are thought to have been domesticated by the Incas, whose nobility wore robes made from their wool. Today, they are still reared and prized for their soft, warm fleeces.*

NORTHERN SOUTH AMERICA

COLOMBIA, GUYANA, SURINAME, VENEZUELA, *French Guiana* (to France)

FRINGED BY THE PACIFIC AND ATLANTIC OCEANS and the Caribbean Sea, South America's northern region has a rich range of natural resources, some exploited for centuries by colonial powers including the Spanish, French, Dutch, and British, others still to be fully explored. The prospects for further economic development in Colombia, Guyana and Suriname are blighted by drug-related violence and political instability. Venezuela, despite huge incomes from its oil reserves, remains less developed in other industrial sectors.

French Guiana is an overseas *département* of France, now seeking greater autonomy. Most of the major population centers, such as Bogotá, have grown up in the temperate conditions of the high Andes or, like Caracas, at strategic points along the Caribbean coast.

***Flowers** grown in Colombia are exported all over the world, and include fine carnations and roses. Here, workers are cutting roses which have been grown in plastic greenhouses.*

MAP KEY
POPULATION
1 million to 5 million
500,000 to 1 million
100,000 to 500,000
50,000 to 100,000
10,000 to 50,000
below 10,000
ELEVATION
4000m / 13,124ft
3000m / 9843ft
2000m / 6562ft
1000m / 3281ft
500m / 1640ft
250m / 820ft
100m / 328ft
sea level
SCALE 1:7,250,000
(projection: Lambert Azimuthal Equal Area)
PACIFIC OCEAN
CARIBBEAN
COLOMBIA
VENEZUELA
PANAMA
ECUADOR
PERU
BRAZIL
ARUBA (to Netherlands)
NETHERLANDS ANTILLES (to Netherlands)
ANDES
BOGOTÁ
Medellín
Cali
Barranquilla
Cartagena
Bucaramanga
Cúcuta
Maracaibo
Valencia
Barquisimeto
Gulf of Darien
Golfo de Venezuela
Lago de Maracaibo
Río Meta
Río Caquetá
Río Putumayo
Amazon

***Large open squares** like the Plaza de Bolivar in Bogotá are characteristic of many cities founded by the Spanish.*

***Scattered farms** and villages have grown up on the gentle slopes of this Colombian river valley, utilizing the fertile soils for farming.*

***The River Orinoco** flows from its source in the southern Guiana Highlands to form a broad delta on Venezuela's Atlantic coast. One of its distributary channels opens into a wide bay called the Serpent's Mouth.*

N O P Q R S T U V W X Y

TRANSPORTATION & INDUSTRY

MANY MINERAL RESOURCES are mined in Colombia, including fuels, gold, and precious and semiprecious stones. Revenues from coffee and exports of illegal narcotics are crucial to the economy. Venezuela's major economic activity is the oil industry around Lake Maracaibo *(Lago de Maracaibo)*. Sugar and bauxite are exported from Guyana and Suriname.

TRANSPORTATION NETWORK

(road)	29,185 miles (46,996 km)
(highway)	1,795 miles (2,890 km)
(railroad)	1,729 miles (2,785 km)
(waterways)	17,947 miles (28,900 km)

Rivers are an important means of transportation in Colombia; many are extensively navigable. The Pan-American Highway runs through Colombia. In Venezuela, much infrastructure investment is linked to the oil industry.

Caribbean Sea
ATLANTIC OCEAN
PACIFIC OCEAN
PANAMA
Maracaibo
Barranquilla
Valencia
CARACAS
Cumaná
Ciudad Guayana
GEORGETOWN
PARAMARIBO
Cayenne
VENEZUELA
GUYANA
SURINAME
FRENCH GUIANA
Medellín
BOGOTÁ
Cali
COLOMBIA
ECUADOR
PERU
BRAZIL

Major industry and infrastructure
- chemicals
- finance
- food processing
- iron & steel
- narcotics
- mining
- oil
- oil refining
- pharmaceuticals
- textiles
- timber processing
- capital cities
- major towns
- international airports
- major roads
- major industrial areas

***Vast oil reserves** around Lake Maracaibo (Lago de Maracaibo) form the focus of Venezuelan industry. Incomes from oil are used to invest in other industries and in the development of infrastructure.*

USING THE LAND

THE ANDEAN BASINS support cereals and potatoes. Livestock graze at higher altitudes and on the drier tropical grasslands known as the *llanos*; hardy goats are reared in scrubland areas. Grown at higher elevations, coffee is an important cash crop, as is cotton, sugar cane, bananas, citrus fruits, cocoa, and rice, farmed on the Caribbean lowlands. Coca is the most widely-grown narcotic plant, with heroin poppies grown in Colombia and marijuana in lowland areas throughout the region.

Caribbean Sea
ATLANTIC OCEAN
PACIFIC OCEAN
PANAMA
Maracaibo
CARACAS
VENEZUELA
GEORGETOWN
PARAMARIBO
CAYENNE
GUYANA
SURINAME
FRENCH GUIANA
Medellín
BOGOTÁ
COLOMBIA
ECUADOR
PERU
BRAZIL

Land use and agricultural distribution
- cattle
- goats
- bananas
- cereals
- coffee
- cotton
- sugar cane
- capital cities
- major towns
- pasture
- cropland
- forest
- wetlands
- mountain region

THE URBAN/RURAL POPULATION DIVIDE

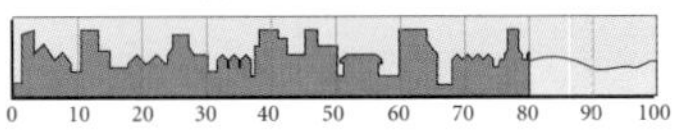

urban 80%
rural 20%
0 10 20 30 40 50 60 70 80 90 100

POPULATION DENSITY	TOTAL LAND AREA
56 people per sq mile (22 people per sq km)	1,111,317 sq miles (2,879,060 sq km)

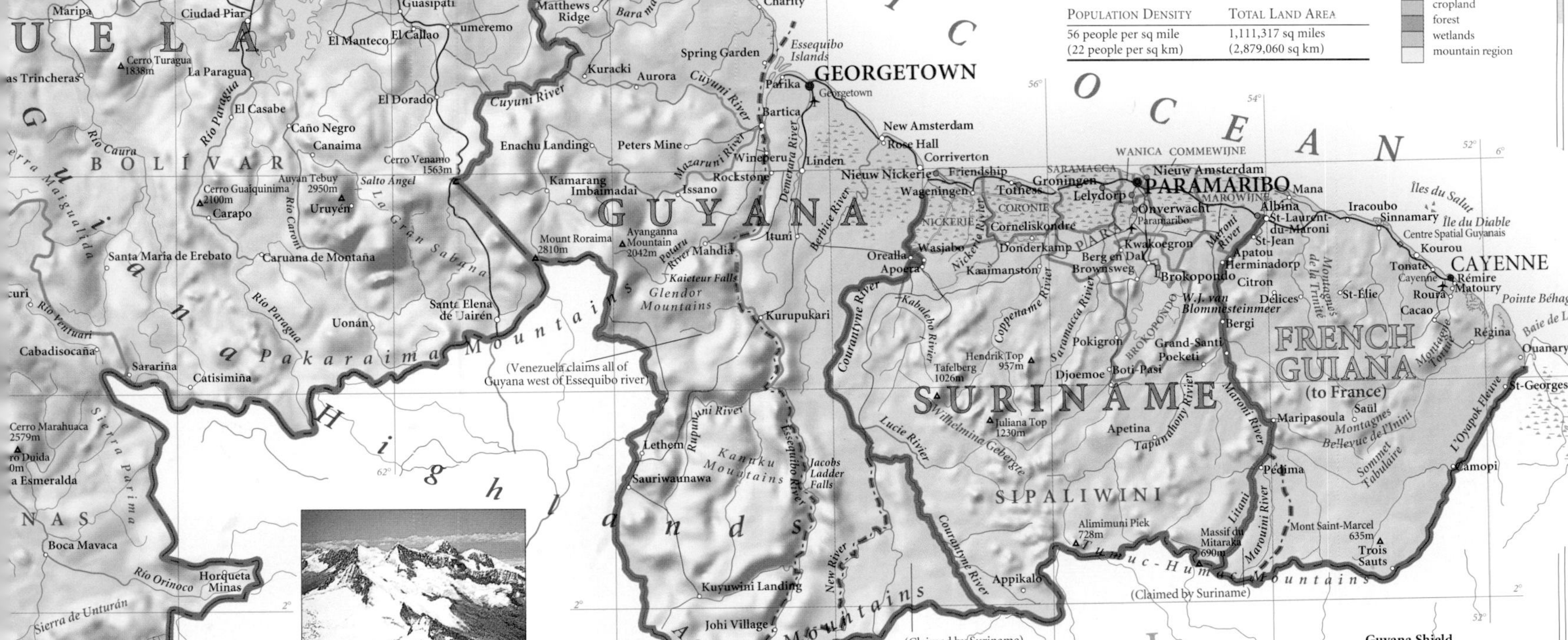

SEA
ATLANTIC OCEAN
TRINIDAD & TOBAGO
64
Isla Blanquilla
Isla de Margarita
Islas Los Testigos
Cumaná
Barcelona
Maturín
MONAGAS
ANZOÁTEGUI
DELTA AMACURO
Ciudad Guayana
Ciudad Bolívar
BOLÍVAR
Salto Angel
Sierra Pacaraima
Pakaraima Mountains
Guiana Highlands
GUYANA
GEORGETOWN
New Amsterdam
Linden
Mount Roraima 2810m
Kaieteur Falls
(Venezuela claims all of Guyana west of Essequibo river)
SURINAME
PARAMARIBO
SIPALIWINI
Juliana Top 1230m
Wilhelmina Gebergte
Tumuc-Humac Mountains
(Claimed by Suriname)
FRENCH GUIANA (to France)
CAYENNE
Kourou
St-Laurent-du-Maroni
Saül
Maripasoula
St-Georges
Acarai Mountains
BRAZIL
58
Equator

The Sierra Nevada de Santa Marta is a granite massif which rises sharply from the Caribbean lowlands to snow-covered peaks, the tallest of which is 18,947 ft (5,775 m) high.

THE LANDSCAPE

AT ITS NORTHERNMOST REACHES, in western Colombia and Venezuela, the great Andean mountain chain splits into three distinct ranges: the Cordillera Oriental, Cordillera Central, and Cordillera Occidental, intercut by a complex series of lesser ranges and basins. The relief becomes lower toward the coast and the interior plains of the northern Amazon Basin, rising again into the tropical hills of the Guiana Highlands.

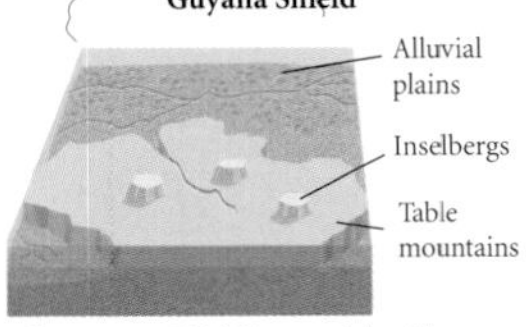

Guyana Shield
Alluvial plains
Inselbergs
Table mountains

***The Guyana Shield** is one of the oldest land surfaces in the world – probably formed more than 4 billion years ago. Chemical weathering over millions of years has created flat-topped table mountains and large numbers of inselbergs.*

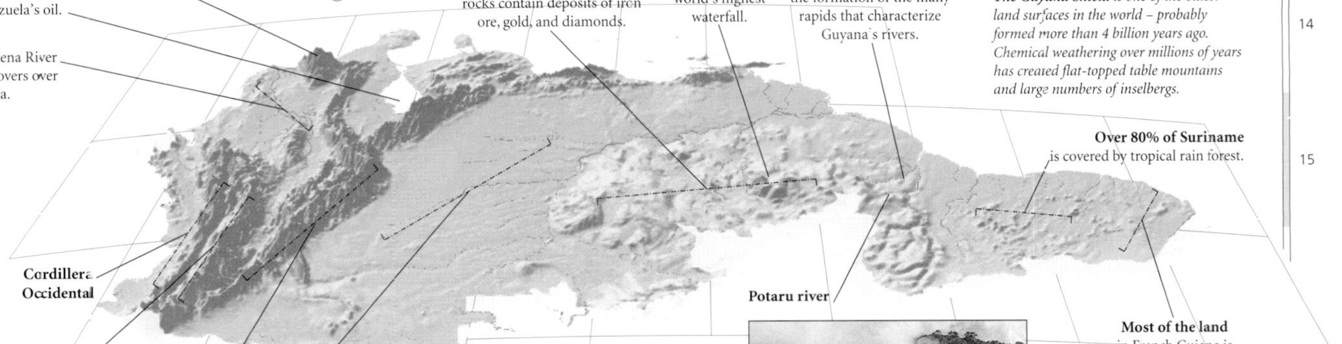

Lake Maracaibo *(Lago de Maracaibo)* is not a true lake but a shallow inlet of the Caribbean Sea. It is the main source of Venezuela's oil.
The drainage basin of the Magdalena River and the Cauca, its main tributary, covers over 20% of Colombia's total surface area.
In the Guiana Highlands, Venezuela's most remote region, the ancient crystalline rocks contain deposits of iron ore, gold, and diamonds.
Angel Falls *(Salto Angel)*, at 3,212 ft (979 m), is the world's highest waterfall.
Igneous intrusions into the crystalline plateau which forms most of central Guyana have led to the formation of the many rapids that characterize Guyana's rivers.
Over 80% of Suriname is covered by tropical rain forest.
Cordillera Occidental
Cordillera Central
Cordillera Oriental
Colombia's eastern lowlands are known locally as *llanos*, meaning grasslands.
Potaru river
Most of the land in French Guiana is low-lying; here, the rocks of the Guiana Highlands have been eroded by rivers flowing toward the sea.

The Potaru River descends 741 ft (226 m) over a sandstone ledge at the Kaieteur Falls in Guyana.

N O P Q R S T U V W X Y Z

Western South America

Bolivia, Ecuador, Peru

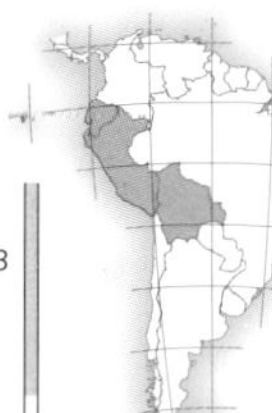

The three states of Western South America share a similar geography and recent history. Dominated by the Inca empire until Spanish conquest in the 16th century, they achieved independence from Spain in the early 19th century. The precipitous terrain of the Andes presents severe difficulties for overland transportation and continues to be a barrier to national unity and stability. Although Ecuador is now a relatively stable democracy, the military is highly influential in Peru and Bolivia, while the drug trade and associated corruption discourages external aid and economic progress. Wealth and power are still largely concentrated in the hands of a small elite of families, who attained their position during the Spanish colonial period. Land rights and political recognition for the indigenous peoples are becoming increasingly important issues, particularly in Ecuador.

Ecuador's capital city, Quito, lies high in the Andes, nestling between snowcapped peaks. At 9,350 ft (2,850 m), Quito is the second highest capital in the world – La Paz in Bolivia is the highest.

COLOMBIA
ECUADOR
PERU
BRAZIL
LORETO
PASTAZA
SUCUMBÍOS
ORELLANA
AMAZONAS
SAN MARTÍN
CAJAMARCA
LAMBAYEQUE
LA LIBERTAD
PIURA
TUMBES
QUITO
Guayaquil
Iquitos
Amazon
Equator

Ecuadorean Administrative Regions

1. CARCHI
2. TUNGURAHUA
3. BOLÍVAR
4. CHIMBORAZO
5. ZAMORA CHINCHIPE

Map Key

POPULATION

- above 5 million
- 1 million to 5 million
- 500,000 to 1 million
- 100,000 to 500,000
- 50,000 to 100,000
- 10,000 to 50,000
- below 10,000

ELEVATION

- 6000m / 19,686ft
- 4000m / 13,124ft
- 3000m / 9843ft
- 2000m / 6562ft
- 1000m / 3281ft
- 500m / 1640ft
- 250m / 820ft
- 100m / 328ft
- sea level

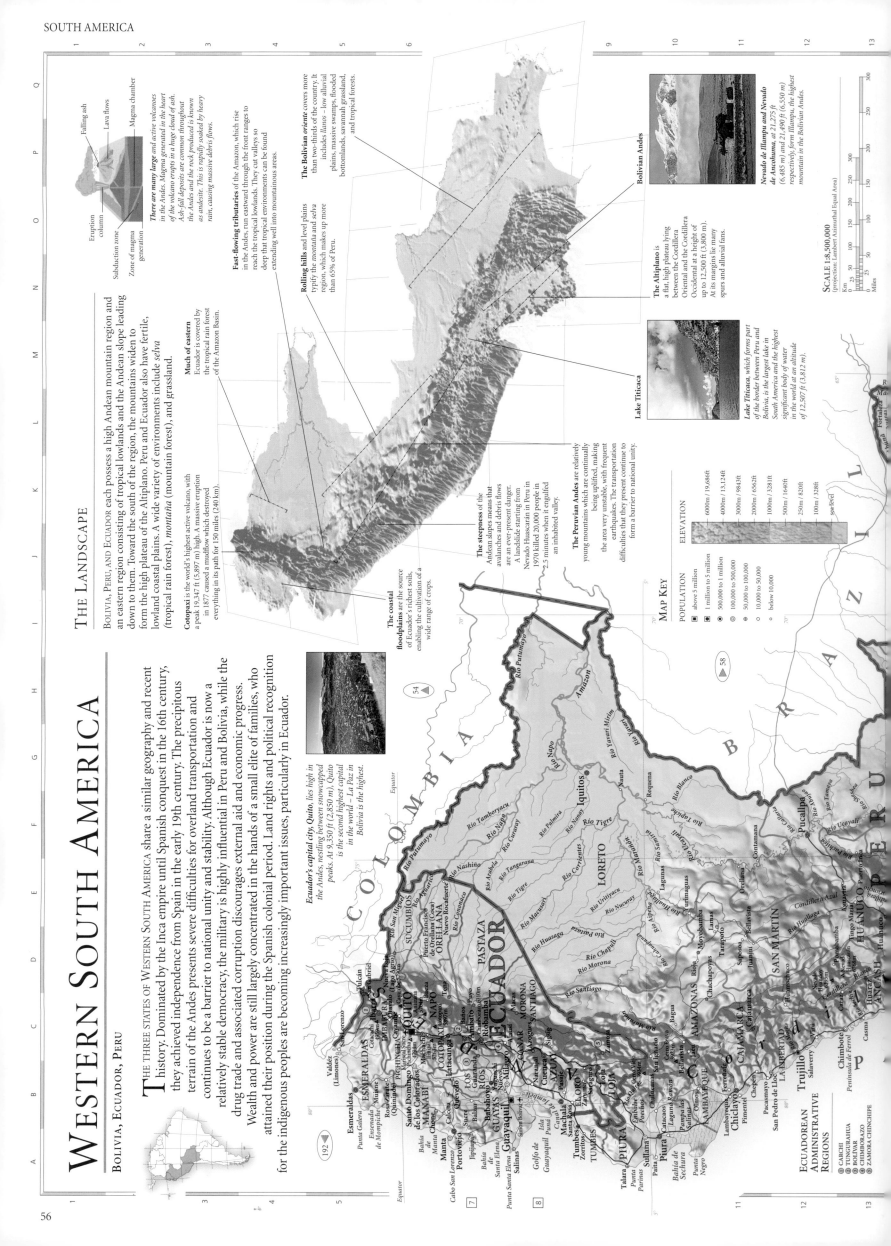

The Landscape

Bolivia, Peru, and Ecuador each possess a high Andean mountain region and an eastern region consisting of tropical lowlands and the Andean slope leading down to them. Toward the south of the region, the mountains widen to form the high plateau of the Altiplano. Peru and Ecuador also have fertile, lowland coastal plains. A wide variety of environments include *selva* (tropical rain forest), *montaña* (mountain forest), and grassland.

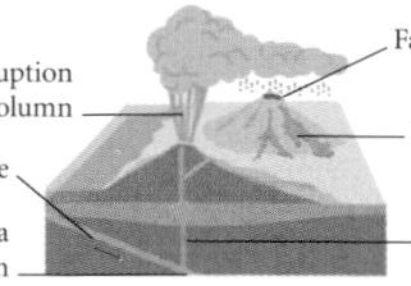

Eruption column
Falling ash
Lava flows
Subduction zone
Zone of magma generation
Magma chamber

***There are many large** and active volcanoes in the Andes. Magma generated in the heart of the volcano erupts in a huge cloud of ash. Ash-fall deposits are common throughout the Andes and the rock produced is known as andesite. This is rapidly soaked by heavy rain, causing massive debris flows.*

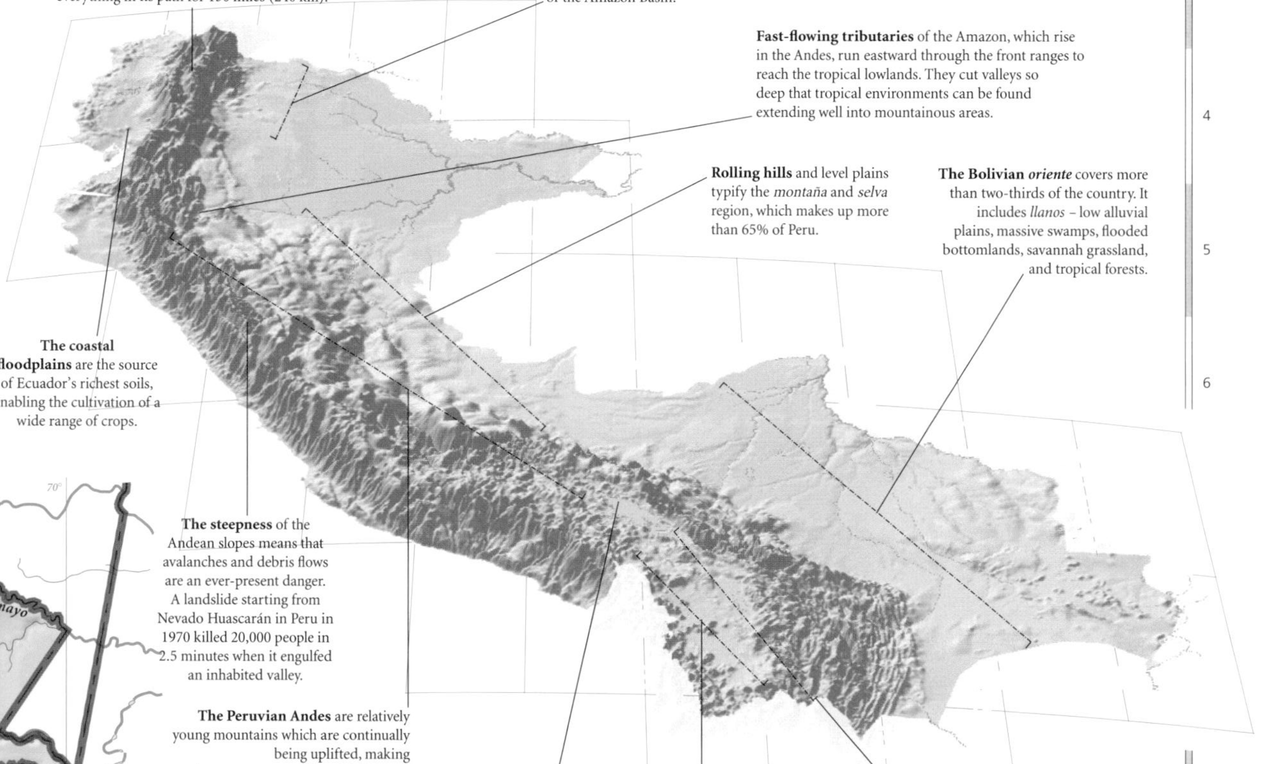

Cotopaxi is the world's highest active volcano, with a peak 19,347 ft (5,897 m) high. A massive eruption in 1877 caused a mudflow which destroyed everything in its path for 150 miles (240 km).

Much of eastern Ecuador is covered by the tropical rain forest of the Amazon Basin.

Fast-flowing tributaries of the Amazon, which rise in the Andes, run eastward through the front ranges to reach the tropical lowlands. They cut valleys so deep that tropical environments can be found extending well into mountainous areas.

Rolling hills and level plains typify the *montaña* and *selva* region, which makes up more than 65% of Peru.

The Bolivian *oriente* covers more than two-thirds of the country. It includes *llanos* – low alluvial plains, massive swamps, flooded bottomlands, savannah grassland, and tropical forests.

The coastal floodplains are the source of Ecuador's richest soils, enabling the cultivation of a wide range of crops.

The steepness of the Andean slopes means that avalanches and debris flows are an ever-present danger. A landslide starting from Nevado Huascarán in Peru in 1970 killed 20,000 people in 2.5 minutes when it engulfed an inhabited valley.

The Peruvian Andes are relatively young mountains which are continually being uplifted, making the area very unstable, with frequent earthquakes. The transportation difficulties that they present continue to form a barrier to national unity.

Lake Titicaca

Lake Titicaca, which forms part of the border between Peru and Bolivia, is the largest lake in South America and the highest significant body of water in the world at an altitude of 12,507 ft (3,812 m).

The Altiplano is a flat, high plateau lying between the Cordillera Oriental and the Cordillera Occidental at a height of up to 12,500 ft (3,800 m). At its margins lie many spurs and alluvial fans.

Bolivian Andes

***Nevado de Illampu and Nevado de Ancohuma**, at 21,275 ft (6,485 m) and 21,490 ft (6,550 m) respectively, form Illampu, the highest mountain in the Bolivian Andes.*

Scale 1:8,500,000
(projection: Lambert Azimuthal Equal Area)

Km 0 25 50 100 150 200 250 300
Miles 0 25 50 100 150 200 250 300

PACIFIC OCEAN
BOLIVIA
PERU
BRAZIL
PARAGUAY
ARGENTINA
CHILE
PANDO
BENI
LA PAZ
COCHABAMBA
SANTA CRUZ
ORURO
POTOSÍ
CHUQUISACA
TARIJA
MADRE DE DIOS
CUSCO
PUNO
AREQUIPA
MOQUEGUA
TACNA
APURÍMAC
AYACUCHO
ICA
HUANCAVELICA
JUNÍN
LIMA
Cordillera Occidental
Altiplano
Cordillera Oriental
Lake Titicaca
Salar de Uyuni
Lago Poopó
LA PAZ
SUCRE
Cochabamba
Santa Cruz
Oruro
Potosí
Trinidad
Cobija
Tarija
Arequipa
Cusco
Tacna
Puno
Ica
Callao
Huancayo
Ayacucho
192
58
62

A colony of marine iguanas basks on the rocks of Isla Fernandina in the Galapagos Islands. Charles Darwin's theory of evolution was inspired by the differences he found between the animal species on neighboring islands in the Galapagos.

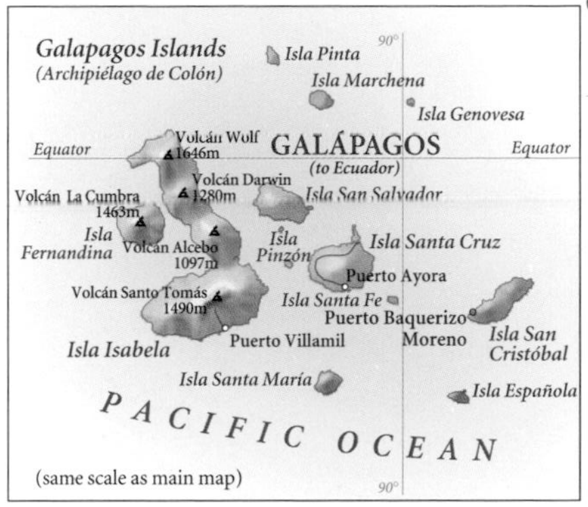
Galapagos Islands
(Archipiélago de Colón)
GALÁPAGOS
(to Ecuador)
Equator
Isla Pinta
Isla Marchena
Isla Genovesa
Volcán Wolf 1646m
Volcán Darwin 1280m
Isla San Salvador
Volcán La Cumbra 1463m
Isla Fernandina
Volcán Alcebo 1097m
Isla Pinzón
Isla Santa Cruz
Puerto Ayora
Isla Santa Fe
Puerto Baquerizo Moreno
Volcán Santo Tomás 1490m
Isla Isabela
Puerto Villamil
Isla San Cristóbal
Isla Santa María
Isla Española
PACIFIC OCEAN
(same scale as main map)

The Galapagos Islands *are mainly composed of lava, with very little vegetation near to the coasts, although the wetter inland slopes are mantled with forest.*

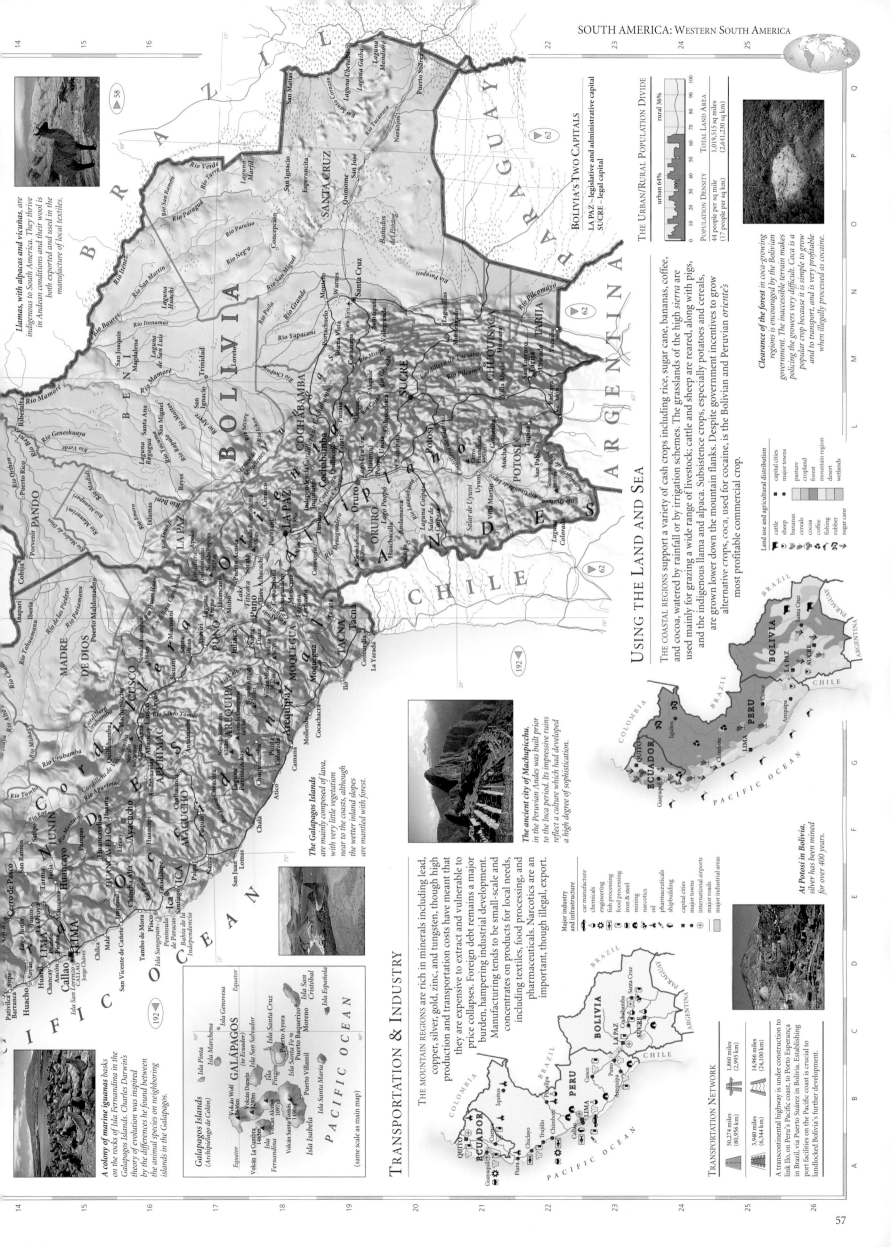

***Llamas, with alpacas and vicuñas,** are indigenous to South America. They thrive in Andean conditions and their wool is both exported and used in the manufacture of local textiles.*

TRANSPORTATION & INDUSTRY

THE MOUNTAIN REGIONS are rich in minerals including lead, copper, silver, gold, zinc, and tungsten, though high production and transportation costs have meant that they are expensive to extract and vulnerable to price collapses. Foreign debt remains a major burden, hampering industrial development. Manufacturing tends to be small-scale and concentrates on products for local needs, including textiles, food processing, and pharmaceuticals. Narcotics are an important, though illegal, export.

COLOMBIA
QUITO
ECUADOR
Guayaquil
Cuenca
Iquitos
Piura
Chiclayo
Trujillo
Chimbote
Pucallpa
PERU
Callao
LIMA
Cusco
Puno
Arequipa
BOLIVIA
LA PAZ
Cochabamba
SUCRE
Santa Cruz
BRAZIL
PARAGUAY
ARGENTINA
CHILE
PACIFIC OCEAN
Major industry and infrastructure
car manufacture
chemicals
engineering
fish processing
food processing
iron & steel
mining
narcotics
oil
pharmaceuticals
shipbuilding
capital cities
major towns
international airports
major roads
major industrial areas

***The ancient city of Machupicchu,** in the Peruvian Andes was built prior to the Inca period. Its impressive ruins reflect a culture which had developed a high degree of sophistication.*

TRANSPORTATION NETWORK

50,274 miles (80,956 km)	1,860 miles (2,995 km)
3,940 miles (6,344 km)	14,966 miles (24,100 km)

A transcontinental highway is under construction to link Ilo, on Peru's Pacific coast, to Porto Esperança in Brazil, via Puerto Suárez in Bolivia. Establishing port facilities on the Pacific coast is crucial to landlocked Bolivia's further development.

***At Potosí in Bolivia,** silver has been mined for over 400 years.*

BOLIVIA'S TWO CAPITALS

LA PAZ – legislative and administrative capital
SUCRE – legal capital

USING THE LAND AND SEA

THE COASTAL REGIONS support a variety of cash crops including rice, sugar cane, bananas, coffee, and cocoa, watered by rainfall or by irrigation schemes. The grasslands of the high *sierra* are used mainly for grazing a wide range of livestock; cattle and sheep are reared, along with pigs, and the indigenous llama and alpaca. Subsistence crops, especially potatoes and cereals, are grown lower down the mountain flanks. Despite government incentives to grow alternative crops, coca, used for cocaine, is the Bolivian and Peruvian *oriente's* most profitable commercial crop.

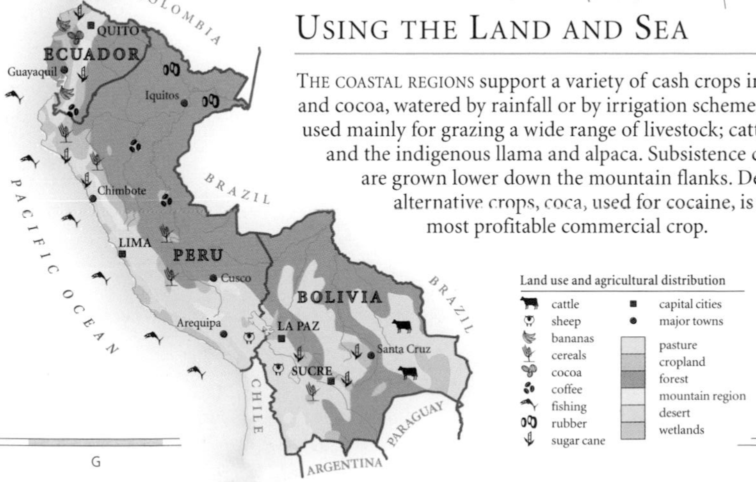
COLOMBIA
QUITO
ECUADOR
Guayaquil
Iquitos
Chimbote
LIMA
PERU
Cusco
Arequipa
BOLIVIA
LA PAZ
SUCRE
Santa Cruz
BRAZIL
PARAGUAY
ARGENTINA
CHILE
PACIFIC OCEAN
Land use and agricultural distribution
cattle
sheep
bananas
cereals
cocoa
coffee
fishing
rubber
sugar cane
capital cities
major towns
pasture
cropland
forest
mountain region
desert
wetlands

THE URBAN/RURAL POPULATION DIVIDE

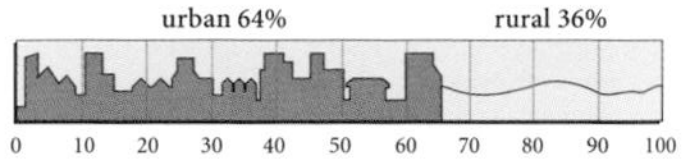
urban 64%
rural 36%
0
10
20
30
40
50
60
70
80
90
100

POPULATION DENSITY	TOTAL LAND AREA
44 people per sq mile (17 people per sq km)	1,019,515 sq miles (2,611,230 sq km)

***Clearance of the forest** in coca-growing regions is encouraged by the Bolivian government. The inaccessible terrain makes policing the growers very difficult. Coca is a popular crop because it is simple to grow and to transport, and is very profitable when illegally processed as cocaine.*

BRAZIL

BRAZIL IS THE LARGEST COUNTRY in South America, with a population of 175 million – greater than the combined total for the whole of the rest of the continent. The 26 states which make up the federal republic of Brazil are administered from the purpose-built capital, Brasília. Tropical rain forest, covering more than one-third of the country, contains rich natural resources, but great tracts are sacrificed to agriculture, industry and urban expansion on a daily basis. Most of Brazil's multiethnic population now live in cities, some of which are vast areas of urban sprawl; São Paulo is one of the world's biggest conurbations, with more than 17 million inhabitants. Although prosperity is a reality for some, many people still live in great poverty, and mounting foreign debts continue to damage Brazil's prospects of economic advancement.

USING THE LAND

BRAZIL HAS IMMENSE NATURAL RESOURCES, including minerals and hardwoods, many of which are found in the fragile rain forest. Brazil is the world's leading coffee grower and a major producer of livestock, sugar, and orange juice concentrate. Soybeans for animal feed, particularly for poultry feed, have become the country's most significant crop.

COLOMBIA
VENEZUELA
GUYANA
SURINAME
FRENCH GUIANA
ATLANTIC OCEAN
PERU
BOLIVIA
PARAGUAY
ARGENTINA
URUGUAY
BRAZIL
Manaus
Belém
Carajás
Fortaleza
Recife
Salvador
BRASÍLIA
Belo Horizonte
Rio de Janeiro
São Paulo
Curitiba
Porto Alegre
Land use and agricultural distribution
cattle
pigs
sheep
citrus fruits
coffee
cotton
soya beans
sugar cane
timber
capital cities
major towns
pasture
cropland
forest

THE URBAN/RURAL POPULATION DIVIDE

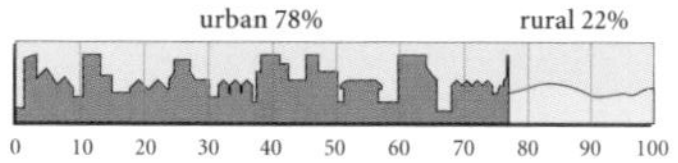
urban 78%
rural 22%
0
10
20
30
40
50
60
70
80
90
100

POPULATION DENSITY	TOTAL LAND AREA
50 people per sq mile (19 people per sq km)	3,286,472 sq miles (8,511,970 sq km)

The fecundity of parts of Brazil's rain forest results from exceptionally high levels of rainfall and the quantities of silt deposited by the Amazon River system.

THE LANDSCAPE

THE AMAZON BASIN, containing the largest area of tropical rain forest on Earth, covers nearly half of Brazil. It is bordered by two shield areas: in the south by the Brazilian Highlands, and in the north by the Guiana Highlands. The east coast is dominated by a great escarpment which runs for 1,600 miles (2,565 km).

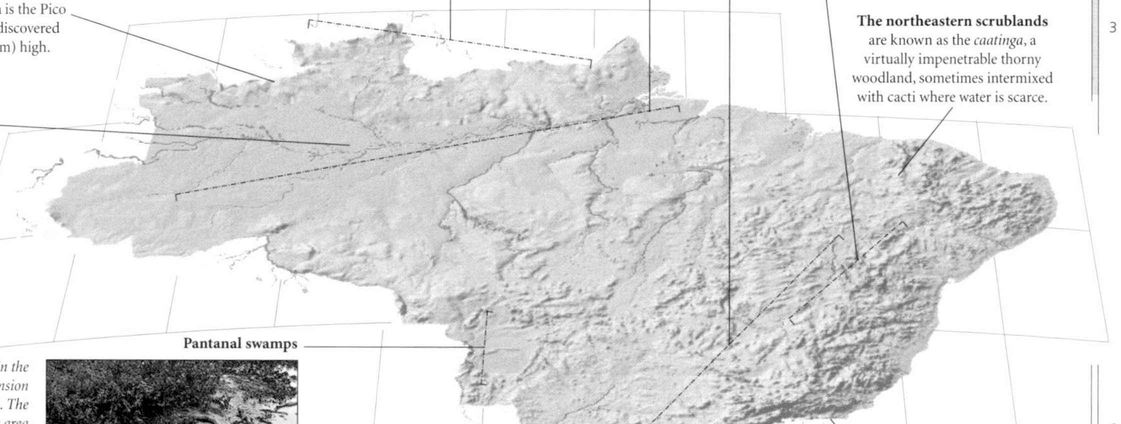
Guiana Highlands
Pantanal swamps

The Amazon Basin is the largest river basin in the world. The Amazon River and over a thousand tributaries drain an area of 2,375,000 sq miles (6,150,000 sq km) and carry one-fifth of the world's fresh water out to sea.

The ancient Brazilian Highlands have a varied topography. Their plateaus, hills, and deep valleys are bordered by highly-eroded mountains containing important mineral deposits. They are drained by three great river systems, the Amazon, the Paraguay–Paraná, and the São Francisco.

The São Francisco Basin has a climate unique in Brazil. Known as the "drought polygon," it has almost no rain during the dry season, leading to regular disastrous droughts.

The northeastern scrublands are known as the *caatinga*, a virtually impenetrable thorny woodland, sometimes intermixed with cacti where water is scarce.

Brazil's highest mountain is the Pico da Neblina which was only discovered in 1962. It is 9,888 ft (3,014 m) high.

The floodplains which border the Amazon River are made up of a variety of different features including shallow lakes and swamps, mangrove forests in the tidal delta area, and fertile levées on river banks and point bars.

*The **Pantanal region** in the south of Brazil is an extension of the Gran Chaco plain. The swamps and marshes of this area are renowned for their beauty, and abundant and unique wildlife, including wildfowl and these caimans, a type of crocodile.*

The famous Sugar Loaf Mountain (*Pão de Açúcar*) which overlooks Rio de Janeiro is a fine example of a volcanic plug a domed core of solidified lava left after the slopes of the original volcano have eroded away.

*The **Iguaçu River** surges over the spectacular Iguaçu Falls (Saltos do Iguaçu) toward the Paraná River. Falls like these are increasingly under pressure from large-scale hydroelectric projects such as that at Itaipú.*

Hillslope gullying

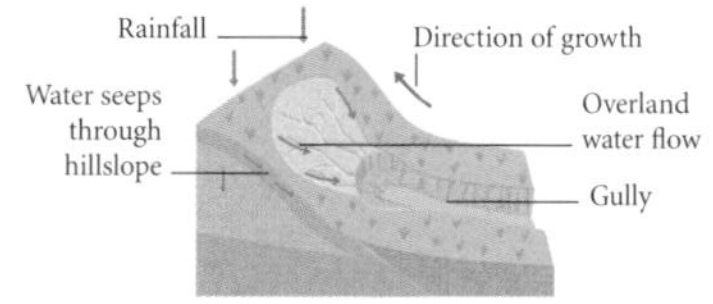
Rainfall
Direction of growth
Water seeps through hillslope
Overland water flow
Gully

***Large-scale** gullies are common in Brazil, particularly on hillslopes from which vegetation has been removed. Gullies grow headwards (up the slope), aided by a combination of erosion through water seepage and rainwater runoff.*

Deep natural harbors such as Baia de Guanabara were created where the steep slopes of the Serra da Mantiqueira plunge directly into the ocean.

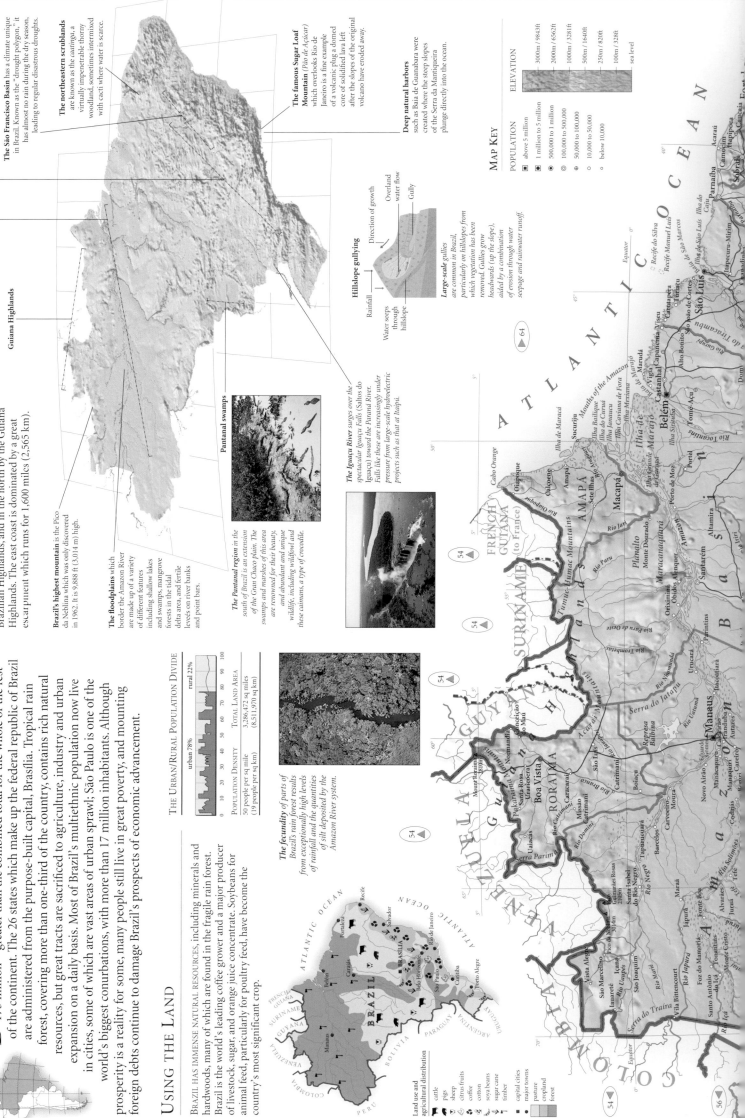

MAP KEY
POPULATION
above 5 million
1 million to 5 million
500,000 to 1 million
100,000 to 500,000
50,000 to 100,000
10,000 to 50,000
below 10,000
ELEVATION
3000m / 9843ft
2000m / 6562ft
1000m / 3281ft
500m / 1640ft
250m / 820ft
100m / 328ft
sea level
54
64
56
VENEZUELA
GUYANA
SURINAME
FRENCH GUIANA (to France)
COLOMBIA
ATLANTIC OCEAN
Guiana Highlands
Pakaraima Mountains
Tumuc-Humac Mountains
Acaraí Mountains
Serra Parima
Serra do Tatrá
Serra do Jatapu
Mount Roraima 2810m
Pico da Neblina 3014m
Guimarães Rosas 2105m
RORAIMA
AMAPÁ
Boa Vista
Macapá
Belém
Manaus
São Luís
Santarém
Cabo Orange
Oiapoque
Calçoene
Amapá
Sucuriju
Ilha de Maracá
Ilha de Marajó
Mouths of the Amazon
Planalto
Maracanaquará
Equator

SCALE 1:14,250,000
(projection: Lambert Azimuthal Equal Area)

Km 0 25 50 100 150 200 250 300 350 400
Miles 0 25 50 100 150 200 250 300 350 400

TRANSPORTATION & INDUSTRY

BRAZILIAN INDUSTRY is diverse and well developed, in part as a result of past government incentives, including the prohibition of imports. Industries which have benefited include car manufacture, petrochemicals, and microelectronics. Textiles, clothing, and footwear are among Brazil's most successful exports. The country's services and tourism sectors are also expanding rapidly.

BRAZIL
ATLANTIC OCEAN
COLOMBIA
VENEZUELA
GUYANA
SURINAME
FRENCH GUIANA
PERU
BOLIVIA
PARAGUAY
ARGENTINA
URUGUAY
Manaus
Belém
Fortaleza
Recife
Salvador
BRASÍLIA
Belo Horizonte
Rio de Janeiro
São Paulo
Curitiba
Porto Alegre

Major industry and infrastructure

car manufacture	mining	capital cities
chemicals	oil	major towns
electronics	printing & publishing	international airports
finance	textiles	major roads
food processing	timber processing	major industrial areas
iron & steel	tourism	

TRANSPORTATION NETWORK

- 139,351 miles (224,397 km)
- 3,105 miles (5,000 km)
- 18,865 miles (30,379 km)
- 31,050 miles (50,000 km)

An extensive new road network is being built to link Brazil's main centers. Investment is needed to update the antiquated railroad system. In São Paulo, the subway system is being extended to accommodate the expanding population.

***Brazil's urban population** has grown by over 6% per year since the mid-1970s – at current population levels a rate of nearly 6 million people annually. In Rio de Janeiro prosperous neighborhoods exist alongside over 450 shantytowns or favelas, some of which house as many as 250,000 people.*

***A gaucho** in traditional costume herds beef cattle on the grasslands of the Rio Grande do Sul in southern Brazil.*

***Picinguaba Beach** lies in Serra do Mar State Park in São Paulo state. São Paulo's beaches stretch for 386 miles (622 km) along the Atlantic coast.*

Eastern South America

Uruguay, Northeast Argentina, Southeast Brazil

The vast conurbations of Rio de Janeiro, São Paulo, and Buenos Aires form the core of South America's highly-urbanized eastern region. São Paulo state, with almost 35 million inhabitants, is among the world's 20 most powerful economies, and São Paulo is the fastest growing city on the continent. Rio de Janeiro and Buenos Aires, transformed in the last hundred years from port cities to great metropolitan areas each with more than 10 million inhabitants, typify the unstructured growth and wealth disparities of South America's great cities. In Uruguay, over half of the population lives in the capital, Montevideo, which faces Buenos Aires across the Plate River *(Río de la Plata)*. Immigration from the countryside has created severe pressure on the urban infrastructure, particularly on available housing, leading to a profusion of crowded shanty settlements *(favelas or barrios)*.

Using the Land

Most of Uruguay and the Pampas of northern Argentina are devoted to the rearing of livestock, especially cattle and sheep, which are central to both countries' economies. Soybeans, first produced in Brazil's Rio Grande do Sul, are now more widely grown for large-scale export, as are cereals, sugar cane, and grapes. Subsistence crops, including potatoes, corn and sugar beets, are grown on the remaining arable land.

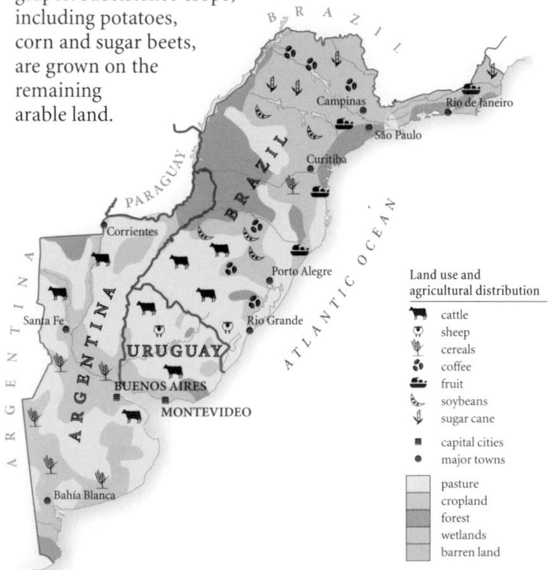

BRAZIL
ARGENTINA
URUGUAY
PARAGUAY
ATLANTIC OCEAN
Campinas
Rio de Janeiro
São Paulo
Curitiba
Corrientes
Porto Alegre
Santa Fe
Rio Grande
BUENOS AIRES
MONTEVIDEO
Bahía Blanca
Land use and agricultural distribution
cattle
sheep
cereals
coffee
fruit
soybeans
sugar cane
capital cities
major towns
pasture
cropland
forest
wetlands
barren land

The rolling grasslands of Uruguay are ideally suited to the rearing of cattle, which are concentrated in great herds throughout the region.

Scale 1: 7,000,000
(projection: Lambert Azimuthal Equal Area)

Km 0 25 50 100 150 200
Miles 0 25 50 100 150 200

Soybeans are harvested, *pressed, and processed into soycake, which is used as animal feed. The cake is fed mainly to chickens on large-scale factory farms, and the growth in soy production has been an important factor in the expansion of the Brazilian poultry trade.*

Transportation & Industry

Southeast Brazil is home to much of the important motor and capital goods industry, largely based around São Paulo; iron and steel production is also concentrated in this region. Uruguay's economy continues to be based mainly on the export of livestock products including meat and leather goods. Buenos Aires is Argentina's chief port, and the region has a varied and sophisticated economic base including service-based industries such as finance and publishing, as well as primary processing.

Map Key

Population	Elevation
above 5 million	2000m / 6562ft
1 million to 5 million	1000m / 3281ft
500,000 to 1 million	500m / 1640ft
100,000 to 500,000	250m / 820ft
50,000 to 100,000	100m / 328ft
10,000 to 50,000	sea level
below 10,000	

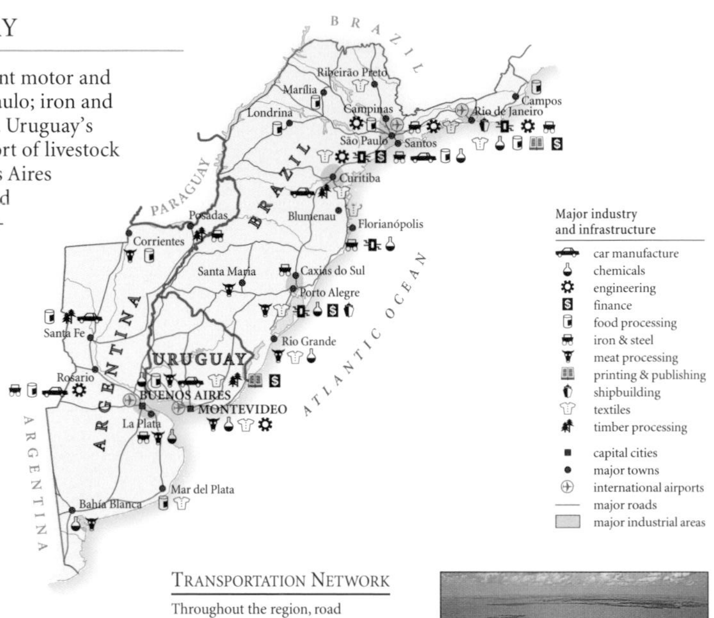

BRAZIL
ARGENTINA
URUGUAY
PARAGUAY
ATLANTIC OCEAN
Ribeirão Preto
Marília
Londrina
Campinas
São Paulo
Santos
Rio de Janeiro
Campos
Curitiba
Posadas
Corrientes
Blumenau
Florianópolis
Santa Maria
Caxias do Sul
Porto Alegre
Santa Fe
Rio Grande
Rosario
BUENOS AIRES
MONTEVIDEO
La Plata
Mar del Plata
Bahía Blanca
Major industry and infrastructure
car manufacture
chemicals
engineering
finance
food processing
iron & steel
meat processing
printing & publishing
shipbuilding
textiles
timber processing
capital cities
major towns
international airports
major roads
major industrial areas

Transportation Network

Throughout the region, road networks need to be expanded to cope with urban development. Plans are underway to build a bridge over the Plate River *(Río de la Plata)* to link Colonia and Buenos Aires.

The Itaipú dam *on the Paraná River is one of the largest hydroelectric projects in the world, jointly financed by Brazil and Paraguay.*

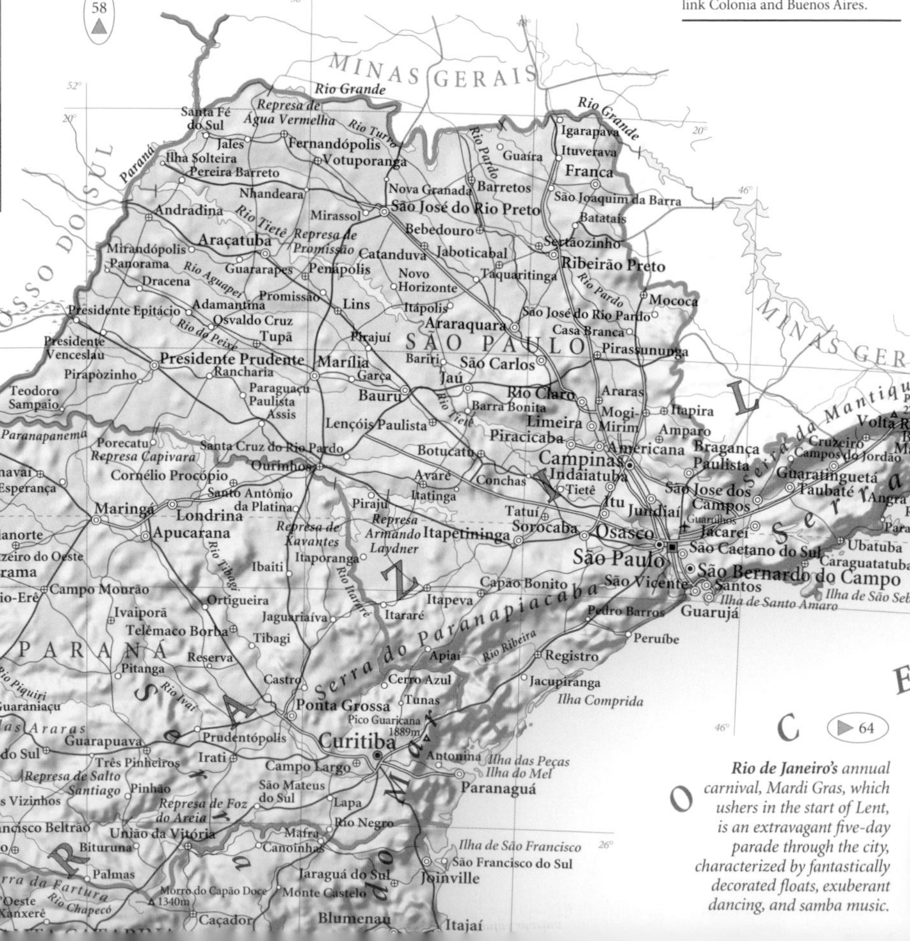

MINAS GERAIS
SÃO PAULO
PARANÁ
RIO DE JANEIRO
ESPÍRITO SANTO
MATO GROSSO DO SUL
PARAGUAY
OCEAN
Serra do Mar
Serra da Mantiqueira
São Paulo
Rio de Janeiro
Curitiba
Campinas
Santos
Ribeirão Preto
Londrina
Maringá
Tropic of Capricorn

58
62
64

Rio de Janeiro's *annual carnival, Mardi Gras, which ushers in the start of Lent, is an extravagant five-day parade through the city, characterized by fantastically decorated floats, exuberant dancing, and samba music.*

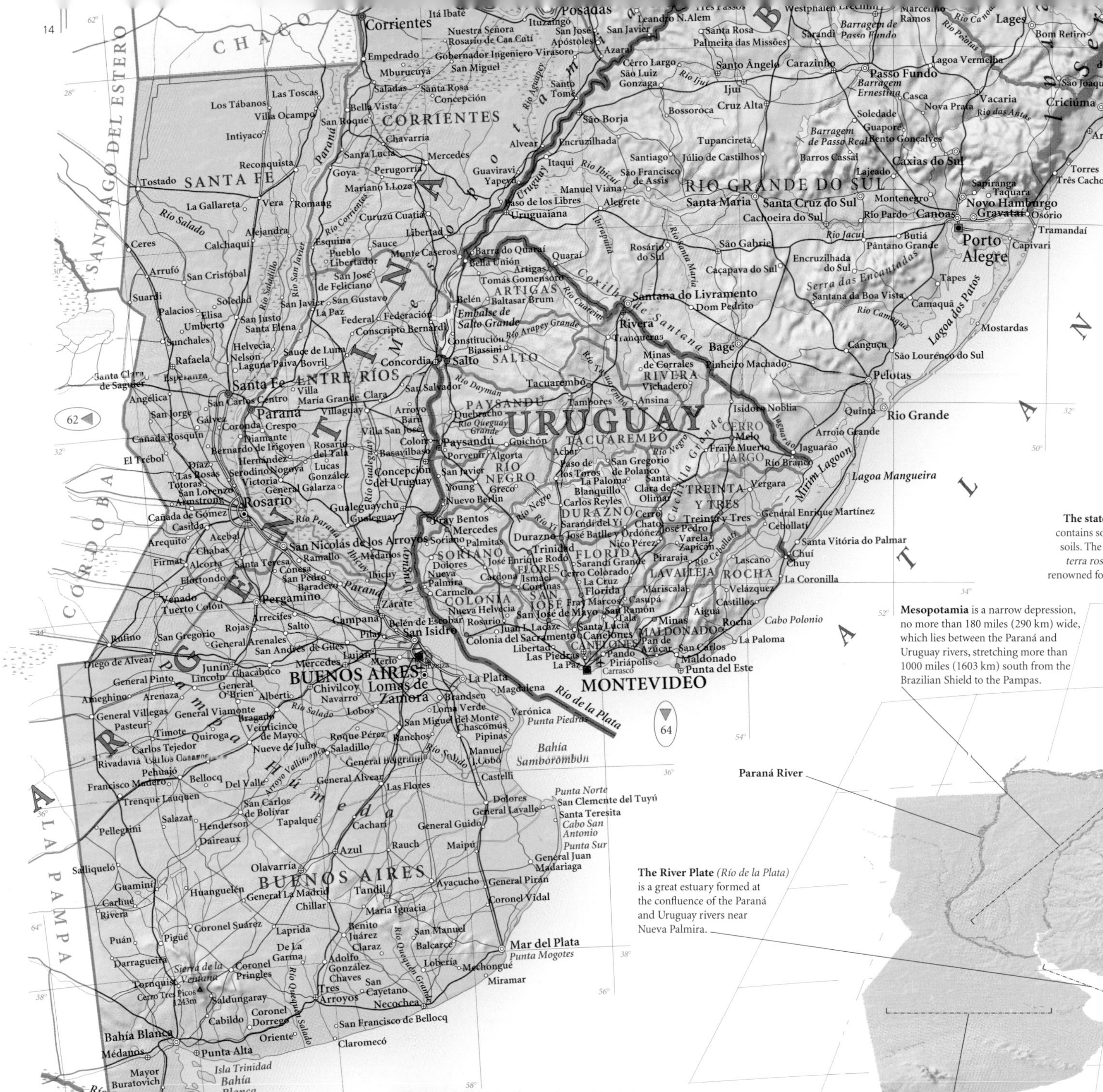

The Landscape

The southern reaches of the Brazilian Highlands follow the Atlantic coast to form low, rolling hills in the northeast of Uruguay. Much of South America's mid-eastern region and all of Uruguay has a gentle relief with land rarely rising above 300 ft (100 m). Argentina's northeast comprises two main regions: a long, narrow lowland known as Mesopotamia; and part of the Pampas grasslands.

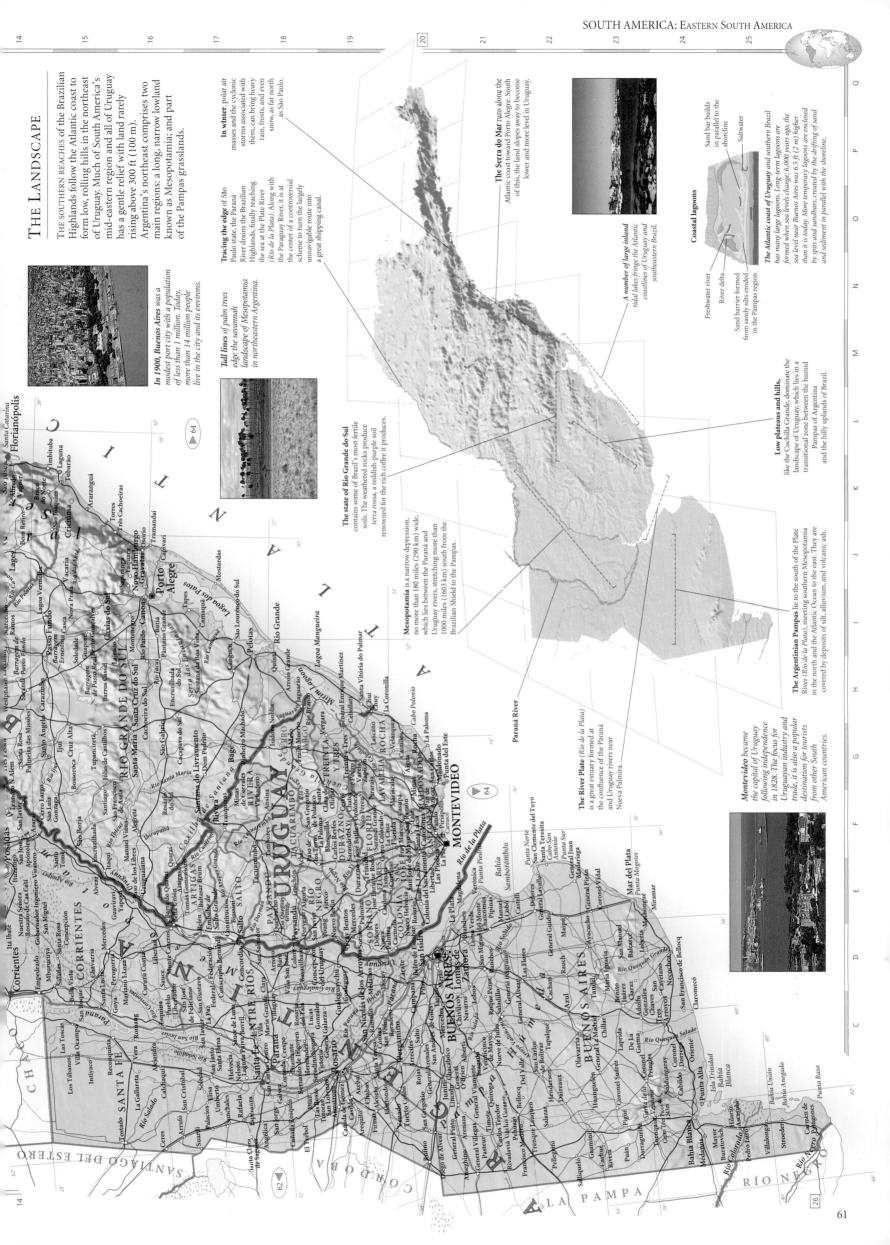

*In 1900, **Buenos Aires** was a modest port city with a population of less than 1 million. Today, more than 14 million people live in the city and its environs.*

***Tall lines** of palm trees edge the savannah landscape of Mesopotamia in northeastern Argentina.*

Tracing the edge of São Paulo state, the Paraná River drains the Brazilian Highlands, finally reaching the sea at the Plate River (*Río de la Plata*). Along with the Paraguay River, it is at the center of a controversial scheme to turn the largely unnavigable route into a great shipping canal.

In winter, polar air masses and the cyclonic storms associated with them, can bring heavy rain, frosts, and even snow, as far north as São Paulo.

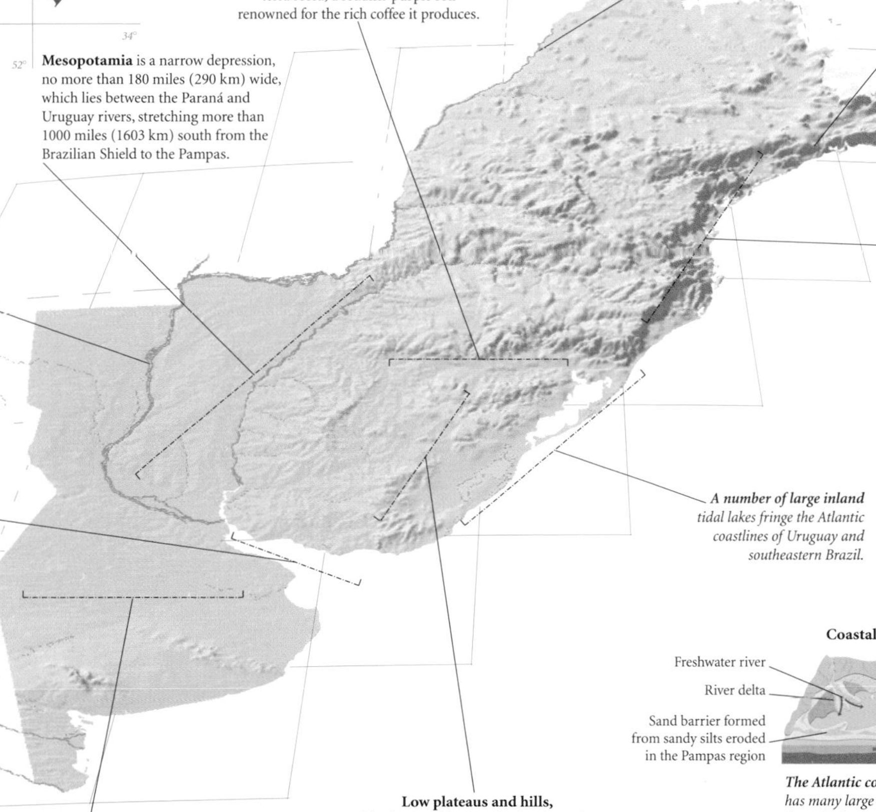

The state of Rio Grande do Sul contains some of Brazil's most fertile soils. The weathered rocks produce *terra rossa*, a reddish-purple soil renowned for the rich coffee it produces.

Mesopotamia is a narrow depression, no more than 180 miles (290 km) wide, which lies between the Paraná and Uruguay rivers, stretching more than 1000 miles (1603 km) south from the Brazilian Shield to the Pampas.

The Serra do Mar runs along the Atlantic coast toward Porto Alegre. South of this, the land slopes away to become lower and more level in Uruguay.

Paraná River

The River Plate (*Río de la Plata*) is a great estuary formed at the confluence of the Paraná and Uruguay rivers near Nueva Palmira.

***A number of large inland** tidal lakes fringe the Atlantic coastlines of Uruguay and southeastern Brazil.*

Montevideo became the capital of Uruguay following independence in 1828. The focus for Uruguayan industry and trade, it is also a popular destination for tourists from other South American countries.

The Argentinian Pampas lie to the south of the Plate River (*Río de la Plata*), meeting southern Mesopotamia in the north and the Atlantic Ocean to the east. They are covered by deposits of silt, alluvium, and volcanic ash.

Low plateaus and hills, like the Cuchilla Grande, dominate the landscape of Uruguay, which lies in a transitional zone between the humid Pampas of Argentina and the hilly uplands of Brazil.

Coastal lagoons

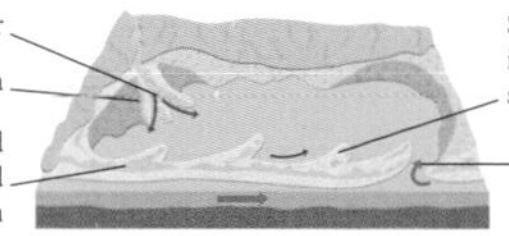
Freshwater river
River delta
Sand barrier formed from sandy silts eroded in the Pampas region
Sand bar builds in parallel to the shoreline
Saltwater

***The Atlantic coast of Uruguay** and southern Brazil has many large lagoons. Long-term lagoons are formed when sea levels change; 6,000 years ago, the sea level near Buenos Aires was 6.5 ft (2 m) higher than it is today. More temporary lagoons are enclosed by spits and sandbars, created by the drifting of sand and sediment in parallel with the shoreline.*

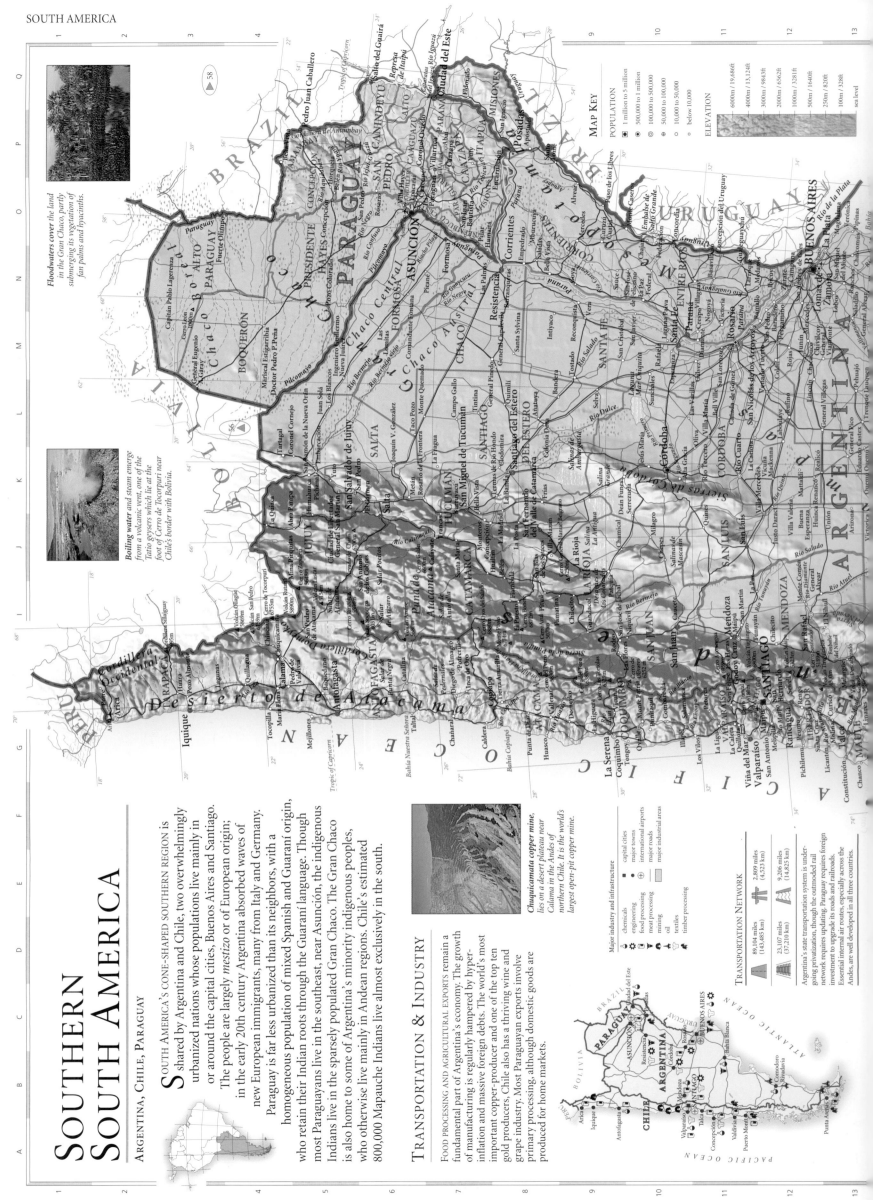

Southern South America

Argentina, Chile, Paraguay

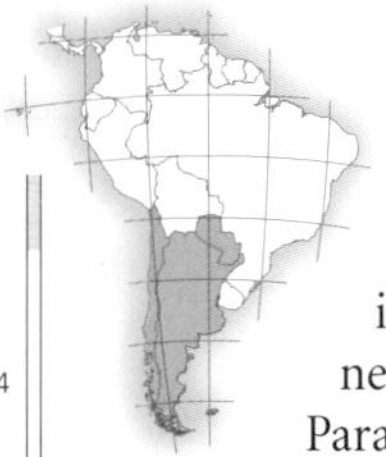

South America's cone-shaped southern region is shared by Argentina and Chile, two overwhelmingly urbanized nations whose populations live mainly in or around the capital cities, Buenos Aires and Santiago. The people are largely *mestizo* or of European origin; in the early 20th century Argentina absorbed waves of new European immigrants, many from Italy and Germany. Paraguay is far less urbanized than its neighbors, with a homogeneous population of mixed Spanish and Guaraní origin, who retain their Indian roots through the Guaraní language. Though most Paraguayans live in the southeast, near Asunción, the indigenous Indians live in the sparsely populated Gran Chaco. The Gran Chaco is also home to some of Argentina's minority indigenous peoples, who otherwise live mainly in Andean regions. Chile's estimated 800,000 Mapauche Indians live almost exclusively in the south.

Transportation & Industry

Food processing and agricultural exports remain a fundamental part of Argentina's economy. The growth of manufacturing is regularly hampered by hyper-inflation and massive foreign debts. The world's most important copper-producer and one of the top ten gold producers, Chile also has a thriving wine and grape industry. Most Paraguayan exports involve primary processing, although domestic goods are produced for home markets.

Chuquicamata copper mine, *lies on a desert plateau near Calama in the Andes of northern Chile. It is the world's largest open-pit copper mine.*

PERU
BOLIVIA
BRAZIL
PARAGUAY
URUGUAY
CHILE
ARGENTINA
ASUNCIÓN
Ciudad del Este
Posadas
Resistencia
Córdoba
Rosario
BUENOS AIRES
Mendoza
SANTIAGO
Valparaíso
Talca
Concepción
Valdivia
Puerto Montt
Punta Arenas
Arica
Iquique
Antofagasta
Bahía Blanca
Comodoro Rivadavia
PACIFIC OCEAN
ATLANTIC OCEAN

Major industry and infrastructure

- chemicals
- engineering
- food processing
- meat processing
- mining
- oil
- textiles
- timber processing
- capital cities
- major towns
- international airports
- major roads
- major industrial areas

Transportation Network

89,104 miles (143,485 km)		2,809 miles (4,523 km)	
23,107 miles (37,210 km)		9,206 miles (14,825 km)	

Argentina's state transportation system is undergoing privatization, though the outmoded rail network requires updating. Paraguay requires foreign investment to upgrade its roads and railroads. Essential internal air routes, especially across the Andes, are well developed in all three countries.

Boiling water *and steam emerge from a volcanic vent, one of the Tatio geysers which lie at the foot of Cerro de Tocorpuri near Chile's border with Bolivia.*

Floodwaters cover *the land in the Gran Chaco, partly submerging its vegetation of fan palms and hyacinths.*

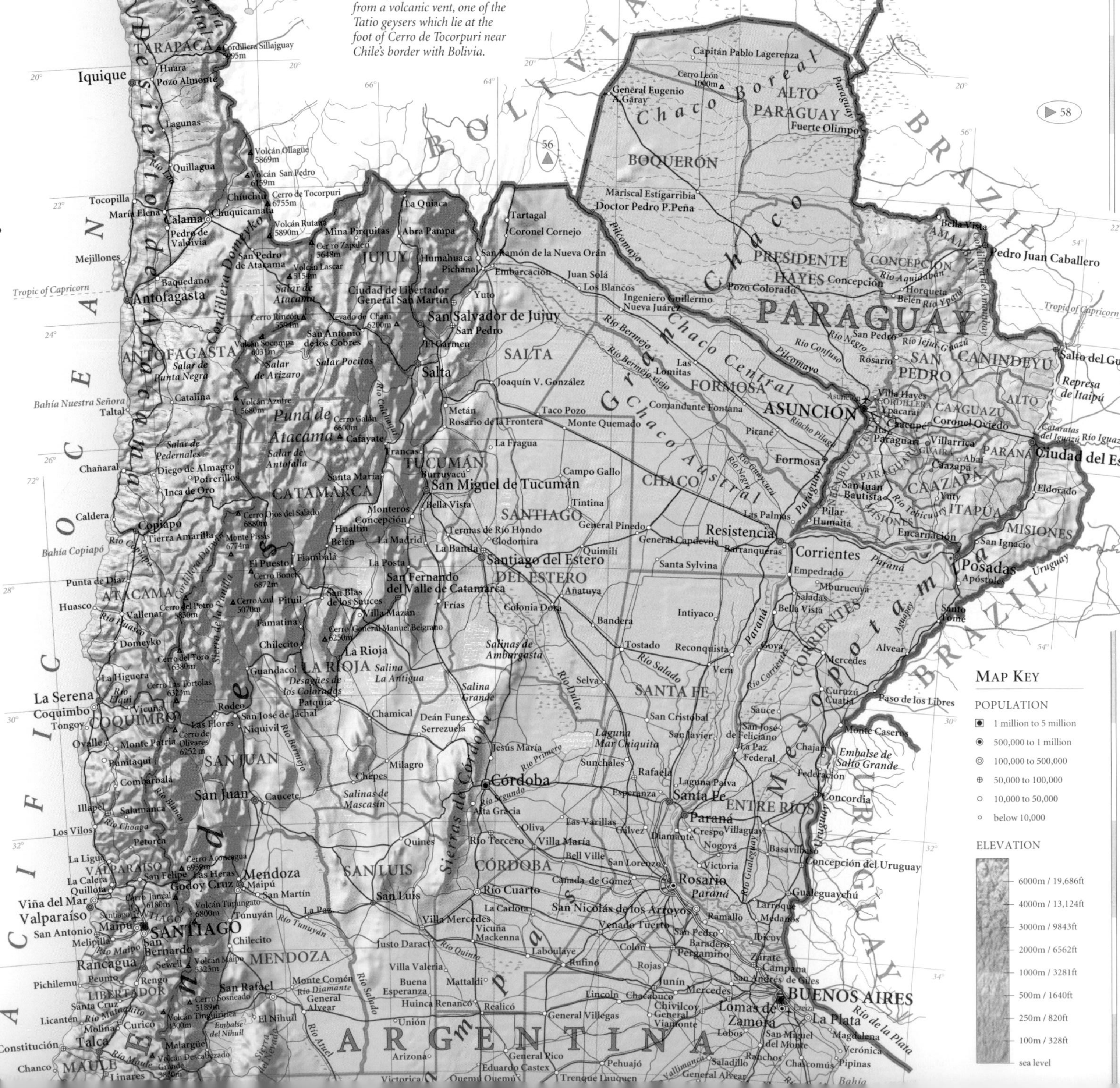

PERU
BOLIVIA
BRAZIL
PARAGUAY
URUGUAY
ARGENTINA
PACIFIC OCEAN
Desierto de Atacama
Gran Chaco
Chaco Boreal
Chaco Central
Chaco Austral
Mesopotamia
Pampas
Andes
Sierras de Córdoba
Arica
Iquique
Antofagasta
Calama
Copiapó
La Serena
Coquimbo
Viña del Mar
Valparaíso
SANTIAGO
Rancagua
Talca
Constitución
ASUNCIÓN
Ciudad del Este
Pedro Juan Caballero
Encarnación
Posadas
Corrientes
Resistencia
Formosa
Salta
San Salvador de Jujuy
San Miguel de Tucumán
Santiago del Estero
Córdoba
Santa Fe
Paraná
Rosario
Mendoza
San Juan
San Luis
Río Cuarto
La Rioja
BUENOS AIRES
La Plata
▶ 58
▲ 56
MAP KEY
POPULATION
1 million to 5 million
500,000 to 1 million
100,000 to 500,000
50,000 to 100,000
10,000 to 50,000
below 10,000
ELEVATION
6000m / 19,686ft
4000m / 13,124ft
3000m / 9843ft
2000m / 6562ft
1000m / 3281ft
500m / 1640ft
250m / 820ft
100m / 328ft
sea level

THE LANDSCAPE

THE ANDES RUN FROM NORTH TO SOUTH, forming a precipitous natural border between Chile and Argentina. East of the Andes are the scrublands of the Gran Chaco and the plains of the Pampas, which extend northward toward Paraguay. In the far southwest, Chile's indented Pacific coastline has many features typical of areas which have been affected by glaciation.

The Atacama Desert (Desierto de Atacama) *in Chile is one of the driest places on Earth where some areas have never recorded any rain. It contains a number of salt lakes.*

Landlocked Paraguay relies on its river system for access to the sea and to produce hydroelectric power. The most important river system is the Paraguay–Paraná which provides links into neighboring countries including Brazil, Uruguay, and Argentina.

The Gran Chaco combines poor drainage, extremely hot temperatures and thorn-infested scrub to make it one of South America's most inhospitable regions.

Most of the highest mountains in Chile's northern Andes are volcanoes like Volcán Lascar and Volcán Rutana.

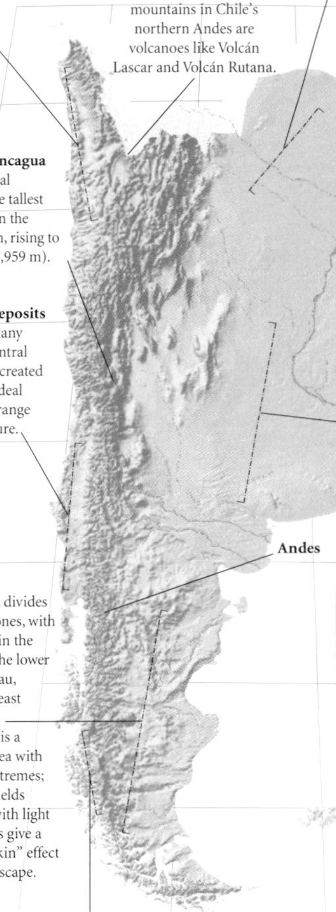
Andes

Cerro Aconcagua in the central Andes is the tallest mountain in the whole chain, rising to 22,834 ft (6,959 m).

Alluvial deposits from the many rivers in central Chile have created rich soils, ideal for a wide range of agriculture.

The Pampas derive their name from an Indian word meaning flat surface. The dry western region is largely desert, whereas the east is well-watered, supporting temperate grasses.

Patagonia divides into two zones, with the Andes in the west, and the lower main plateau, extending east toward the Atlantic. It is a desolate area with climatic extremes; dark lava fields scattered with light bunchgrass give a "leopard skin" effect to the landscape.

The Andean mountain system, *which forms Argentina's western border, was created by folding and faulting, following the convergence of the Nazca and South American tectonic plates.*

Argentinian Pampas

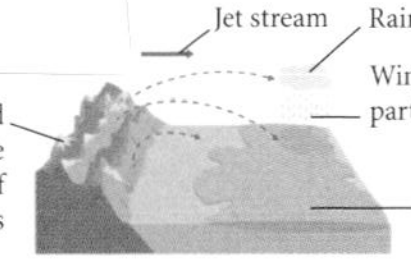
Jet stream
Rainfall
Windblown particles
Ice-capped Andes are source of loess
Thick layer of loess sediments

A thick, fertile layer *of loess lies in the basin underlying the Argentinian Pampas. It has been laid down following successive periods of glaciation. The minute loess particles are transported as dust and deposited by a downward air motion, or following rainfall.*

The Patagonian ice sheet is the world's third largest ice field, covering 6,560 sq miles (17,000 sq km). Patagonia also contains many typical features from past glaciations. These include glacial lakes, U-shaped valleys, fjords, and deep-cut channels.

Cape Horn is the most southerly point of South America. The severity of the "Roaring Forties" winds makes the Horn one of the world's most treacherous shipping regions.

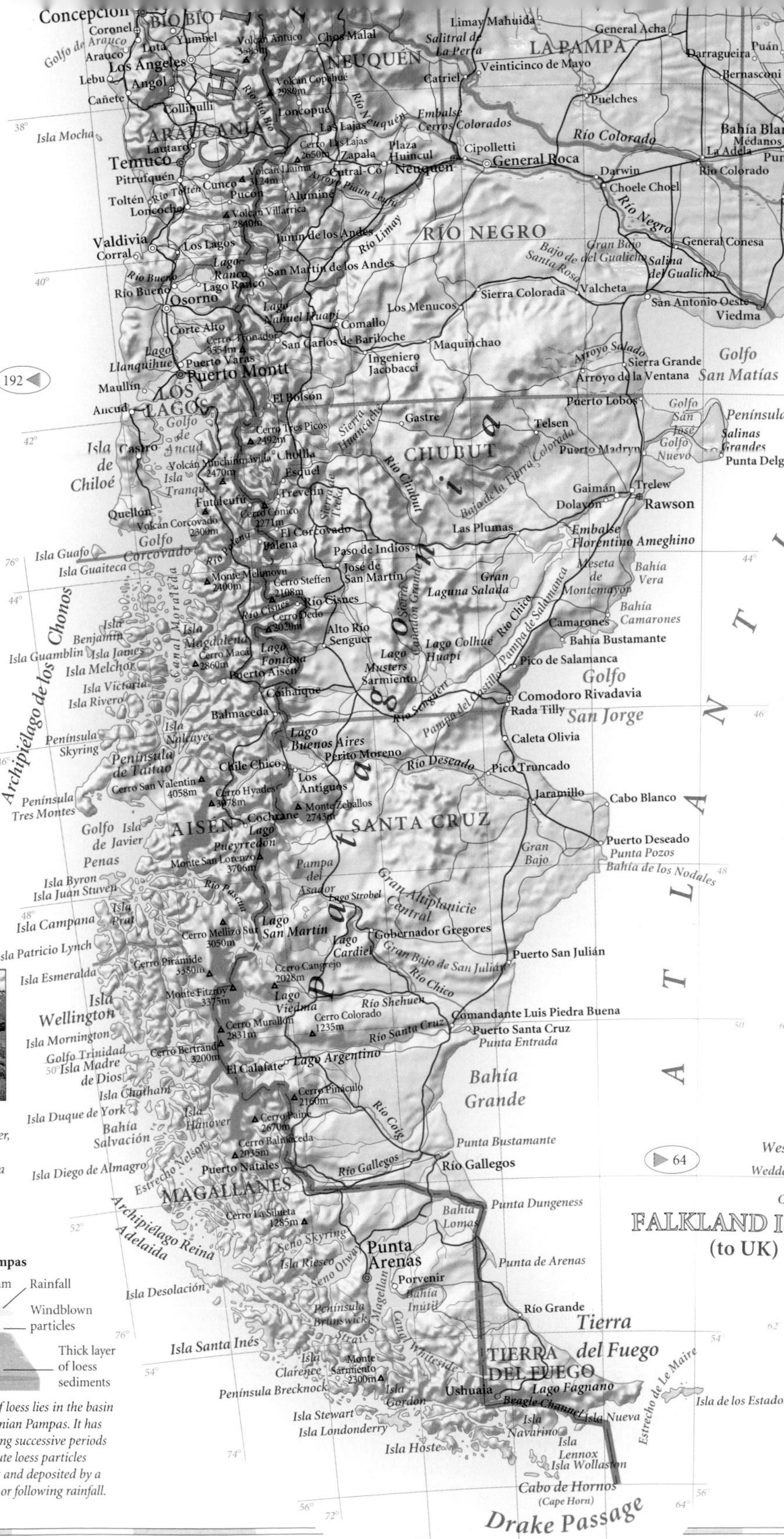
LA PAMPA
NEUQUÉN
RÍO NEGRO
CHUBUT
SANTA CRUZ
ARAUCANÍA
LOS LAGOS
AISÉN
MAGALLANES
TIERRA DEL FUEGO
Patagonia
ATLANTIC OCEAN
Mar del Plata
Bahía Blanca
Golfo San Matías
Península Valdés
Golfo San Jorge
Comodoro Rivadavia
Puerto Montt
Temuco
Valdivia
Concepción
Isla de Chiloé
Archipiélago de los Chonos
Punta Arenas
Río Gallegos
Ushuaia
Drake Passage
Cabo de Hornos (Cape Horn)
FALKLAND ISLANDS (to UK)
West Falkland
East Falkland
STANLEY
192
64
SCALE 1:9,750,000
(projection: Lambert Azimuthal Equal Area)

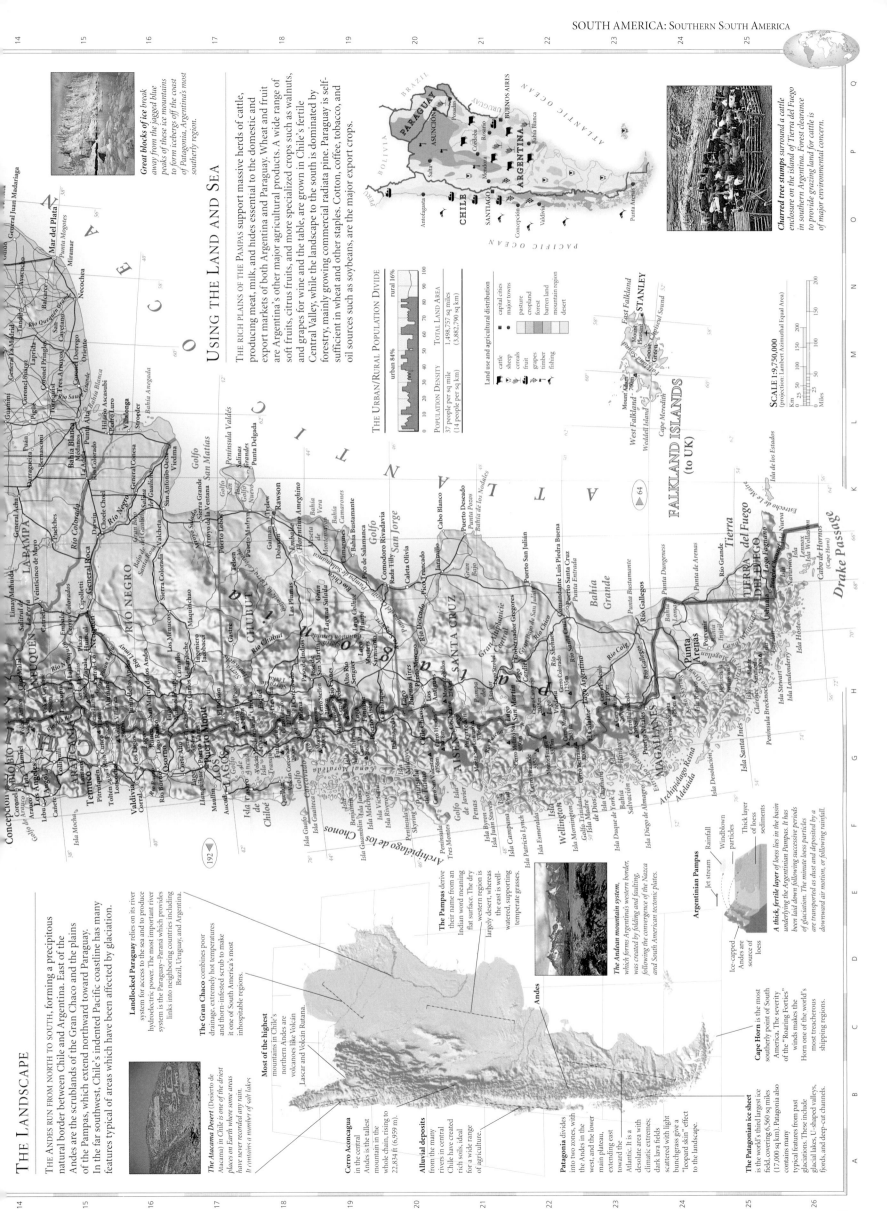

Great blocks of ice *break away from the jagged blue peaks of these ice mountains to form icebergs off the coast of Patagonia, Argentina's most southerly region.*

USING THE LAND AND SEA

THE RICH PLAINS OF THE PAMPAS support massive herds of cattle, producing meat, milk, and hides essential to the domestic and export markets of both Argentina and Paraguay. Wheat and fruit are Argentina's other major agricultural products. A wide range of soft fruits, citrus fruits, and more specialized crops such as walnuts, and grapes for wine and the table, are grown in Chile's fertile Central Valley, while the landscape to the south is dominated by forestry, mainly growing commercial radiata pine. Paraguay is self-sufficient in wheat and other staples. Cotton, coffee, tobacco, and oil sources such as soybeans, are the major export crops.

THE URBAN/RURAL POPULATION DIVIDE

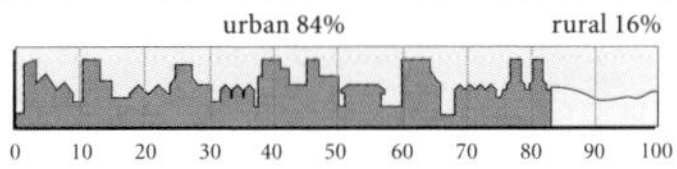
urban 84%
rural 16%
0 10 20 30 40 50 60 70 80 90 100

POPULATION DENSITY	TOTAL LAND AREA
37 people per sq mile (14 people per sq km)	1,498,757 sq miles (3,882,790 sq km)

Land use and agricultural distribution
cattle
sheep
cereals
fruit
grapes
timber
fishing
capital cities
major towns
pasture
cropland
forest
barren land
mountain region
desert
PACIFIC OCEAN
ATLANTIC OCEAN
BOLIVIA
BRAZIL
PERU
PARAGUAY
ASUNCIÓN
URUGUAY
CHILE
ARGENTINA
SANTIAGO
BUENOS AIRES
Antofagasta
Salta
Posadas
Córdoba
Rosario
Mendoza
Concepción
Valdivia
Bahía Blanca
Punta Arenas

Charred tree stumps *surround a cattle enclosure on the island of Tierra del Fuego in southern Argentina. Forest clearance to provide grazing land for cattle is of major environmental concern.*

THE ATLANTIC OCEAN

THE ATLANTIC IS THE YOUNGEST OF THE WORLD'S OCEANS, formed about 180 million years ago when the landmasses of the eastern and western hemispheres separated. Its underwater topography is dominated by the Mid-Atlantic Ridge, a huge mountain system running north to south along the center of the ocean. Although most of the ridge's peaks lie below the sea, some emerge as volcanic islands, like Iceland and the Azores. The Atlantic contains a wealth of resources, including substantial oil and gas reserves and rich fishing grounds. Until the 1950s, the north Atlantic was the world's busiest shipping route; cheaper air transportation and alternative routes have shifted patterns of world trade.

Surtsey near Iceland, *lies on the Mid-Atlantic Ridge. The island was formed in 1963 following a volcanic eruption caused by sea-floor spreading.*

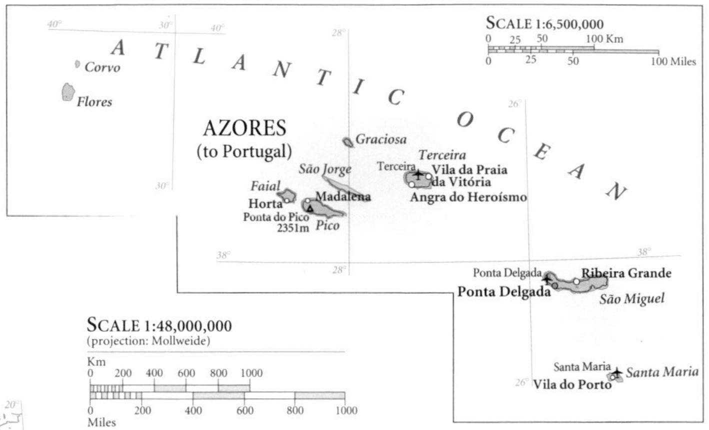
SCALE 1:6,500,000
AZORES
(to Portugal)
ATLANTIC OCEAN
Corvo
Flores
Graciosa
São Jorge
Terceira
Vila da Praia da Vitória
Angra do Heroísmo
Faial
Horta
Madalena
Ponta do Pico 2351m
Pico
Ponta Delgada
Ribeira Grande
São Miguel
Santa Maria
Vila do Porto

RESOURCES

DEVELOPMENT OF THE OIL AND GAS RESERVES in the Atlantic began in the 1940s around the Gulf of Mexico. Since then other areas have been exploited, including the North Sea, the west coast of Africa and the area east of Newfoundland and Nova Scotia. There is also extensive mining of sand, gravel, and shell deposits by the US and UK. For centuries, the north Atlantic's fishing grounds have been utilized more heavily than other oceans, leading to a serious decline in many fish stocks.

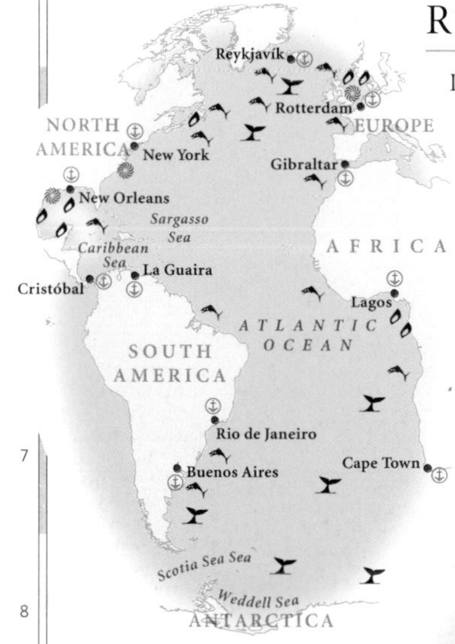
NORTH AMERICA
EUROPE
AFRICA
SOUTH AMERICA
ANTARCTICA
ATLANTIC OCEAN
Reykjavík
Rotterdam
New York
Gibraltar
New Orleans
Sargasso Sea
Caribbean Sea
La Guaira
Cristóbal
Lagos
Rio de Janeiro
Buenos Aires
Cape Town
Scotia Sea
Weddell Sea
Resources (including wildlife)
fish
whales
aggregates
oil & gas
major towns
major ports

SCALE 1:48,000,000
(projection: Mollweide)
NORTH AMERICA
CANADA
UNITED STATES OF AMERICA
Greenland
(to Denmark)
ICELAND
EUROPE
AFRICA
ATLANTIC
Baffin Bay
Baffin Basin
Davis Strait
Labrador Sea
Labrador Basin
Denmark Strait
Iceland Basin
Reykjanes Ridge
Charlie-Gibbs Fracture Zone
Northwest Atlantic Mid-Ocean Canyon
Newfoundland Basin
Mid-Atlantic Ridge
Sargasso Sea
Sohm Plain
Hatteras Plain
Nares Plain
Gulf of Mexico
Caribbean Sea
Cape Verde Basin
Gambia Plain
East Azores Fracture Zone
Atlantis Fracture Zone
Kane Fracture Zone
Vema Fracture Zone
Doldrums Fracture Zone
Four North Fracture Zone
Barracuda Fracture Zone
Demerara Plain
North Sea
British Isles
UNITED KINGDOM
REPUBLIC OF IRELAND
FRANCE
SPAIN
PORTUGAL
MOROCCO
ALGERIA
MAURITANIA
SENEGAL
MEXICO
CUBA
BAHAMAS
VENEZUELA
SOUTH
MADEIRA
(to Portugal)
SCALE 1:2,500,000
Porto Santo
Madeira
Funchal
Ilhas Desertas
ISLAS CANARIAS
(CANARY ISLANDS)
(to Spain)
SCALE 1:6,500,000
La Palma
Santa Cruz de la Palma
Santa Cruz de Tenerife
Tenerife
Pico del Teide 3718m
Gomera
Hierro
Las Palmas de Gran Canaria
Gran Canaria
Fuerteventura
Lanzarote
Arrecife
Puerto del Rosario

On January 5 1993, *the oil tanker Braer ran aground in the Shetland Islands, spilling 83,660 tons (85,000 tonnes) of light crude oil into the ocean, devastating the local marine ecosystem.*

Fishing *in the seas around northwestern Europe dates back over 1,500 years. The high nutrient content of the seas makes them ideal breeding grounds for many species of fish.*

SCALE 1:500,000
BERMUDA
(to UK)
St George's Island
St George
St David's Island
HAMILTON
ATLANTIC OCEAN

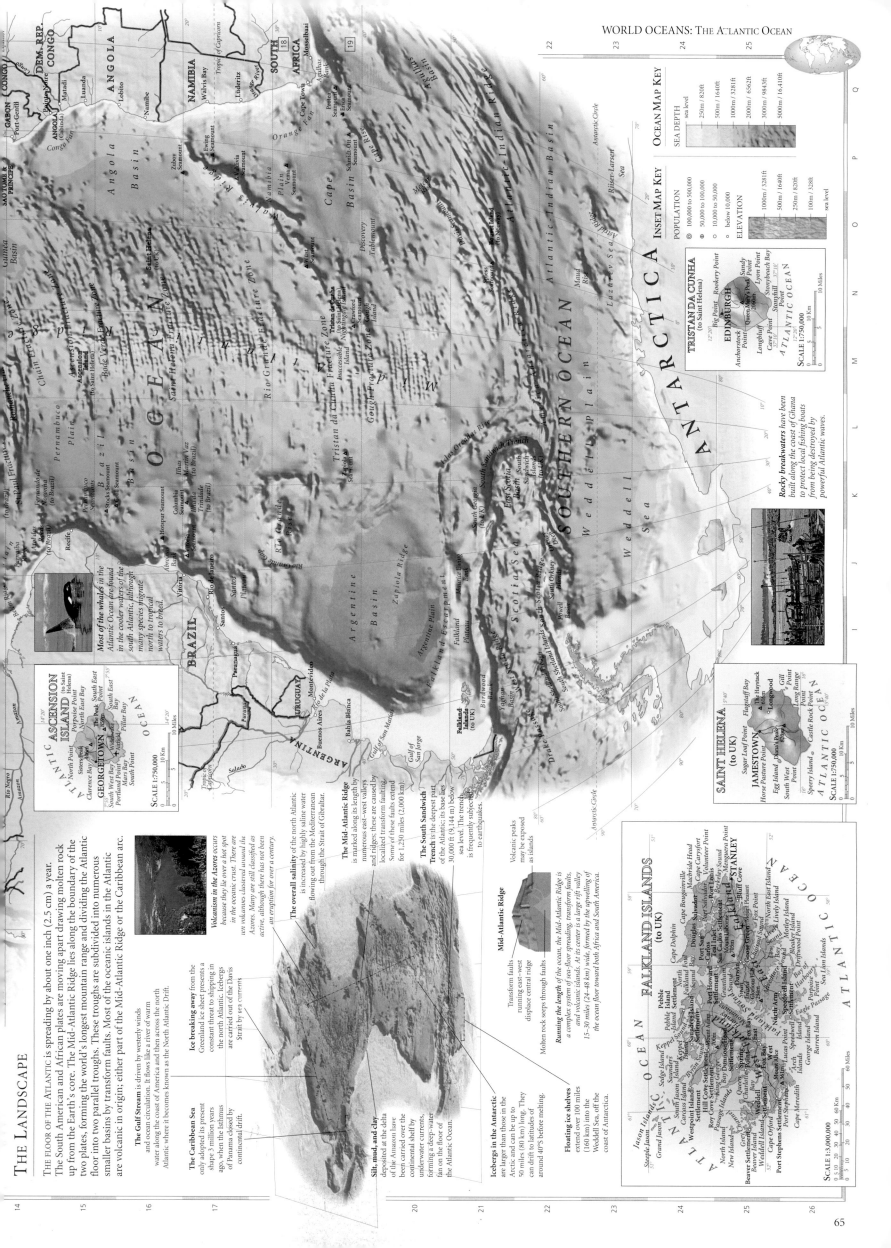

THE LANDSCAPE

THE FLOOR OF THE ATLANTIC is spreading by about one inch (2.5 cm) a year. The South American and African plates are moving apart drawing molten rock up from the Earth's core. The Mid-Atlantic Ridge lies along the boundary of the two plates, forming the world's longest mountain range and dividing the Atlantic floor into two parallel troughs. These troughs are subdivided into numerous smaller basins by transform faults. Most of the oceanic islands in the Atlantic are volcanic in origin; either part of the Mid-Atlantic Ridge or the Caribbean arc.

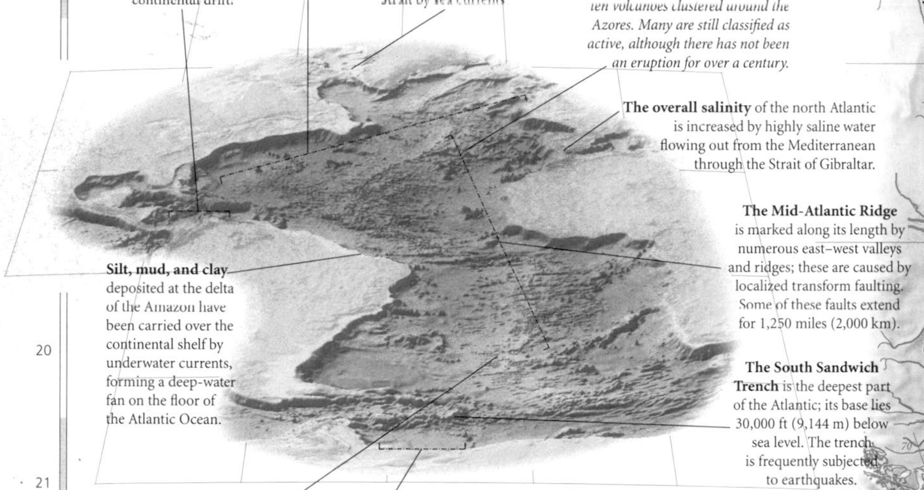

The Gulf Stream is driven by westerly winds and ocean circulation. It flows like a river of warm water along the coast of America and then across the north Atlantic where it becomes known as the North Atlantic Drift.
The Caribbean Sea only adopted its present shape 3 million years ago, when the Isthmus of Panama closed by continental drift.
Ice breaking away from the Greenland ice sheet presents a constant threat to shipping in the north Atlantic. Icebergs are carried out of the Davis Strait by sea currents
The overall salinity of the north Atlantic is increased by highly saline water flowing out from the Mediterranean through the Strait of Gibraltar.
The Mid-Atlantic Ridge is marked along its length by numerous east–west valleys and ridges; these are caused by localized transform faulting. Some of these faults extend for 1,250 miles (2,000 km).
The South Sandwich Trench is the deepest part of the Atlantic; its base lies 30,000 ft (9,144 m) below sea level. The trench is frequently subjected to earthquakes.
Silt, mud, and clay deposited at the delta of the Amazon have been carried over the continental shelf by underwater currents, forming a deep-water fan on the floor of the Atlantic Ocean.
Icebergs in the Antarctic are larger than those in the Arctic and can be up to 50 miles (80 km) long. They can drift to latitudes of around 40°S before melting.
Floating ice shelves extend over 100 miles (160 km) into the Weddell Sea, off the coast of Antarctica.

Volcanism in the Azores occurs because they lie over a hot spot in the oceanic crust. There are ten volcanoes clustered around the Azores. Many are still classified as active, although there has not been an eruption for over a century.

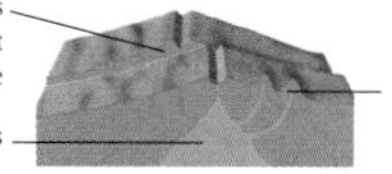

Mid-Atlantic Ridge
Transform faults running east–west displace central ridge
Volcanic peaks may be exposed as islands
Molten rock seeps through faults

Running the length of the ocean, the Mid-Atlantic Ridge is a complex system of sea-floor spreading, transform faults, and volcanic islands. At its center is a large rift valley 15–30 miles (24–48 km) wide, formed by the upwelling of the ocean floor toward both Africa and South America.

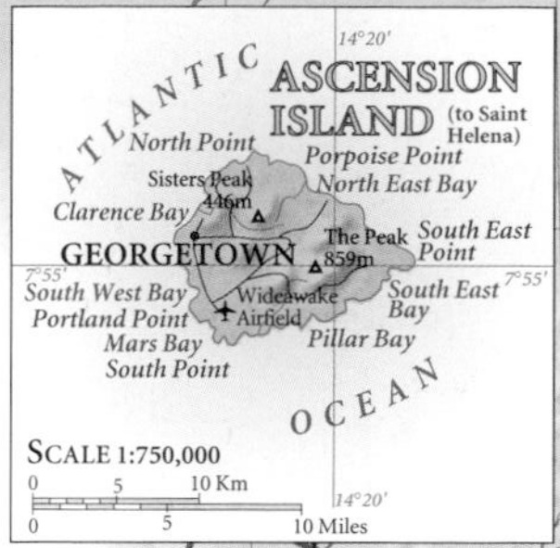

ASCENSION ISLAND (to Saint Helena)
ATLANTIC OCEAN
North Point
Porpoise Point
North East Bay
Sisters Peak 446m
Clarence Bay
GEORGETOWN
The Peak 859m
South East Point
South West Bay
Wideawake Airfield
South East Bay
Portland Point
Mars Bay
Pillar Bay
South Point
SCALE 1:750,000
0 5 10 Km
0 5 10 Miles

Most of the whales *in the Atlantic Ocean are found in the cooler waters of the south Atlantic, although many species migrate north to tropical waters to breed.*

OCEAN
BRAZIL
URUGUAY
ARGENTINA
NAMIBIA
ANGOLA
SOUTH AFRICA
DEM. REP. CONGO
GABON
CONGO
SAO TOME & PRINCIPE
Rio de Janeiro
Buenos Aires
Montevideo
Cape Town
Walvis Bay
Luanda
Recife
Argentine Basin
Brazil Basin
Angola Basin
Cape Basin
Mid-Atlantic Ridge
Walvis Ridge
Rio Grande Rise
Scotia Sea
SOUTHERN OCEAN
Weddell Plain
Weddell Sea
Atlantic-Indian Ridge
Atlantic-Indian Basin
South Sandwich Trench
ANTARCTICA
Antarctic Circle
Tropic of Capricorn
INSET MAP KEY
POPULATION
100,000 to 500,000
50,000 to 100,000
10,000 to 50,000
below 10,000
ELEVATION
1000m / 3281ft
500m / 1640ft
250m / 820ft
100m / 328ft
sea level
OCEAN MAP KEY
SEA DEPTH
sea level
250m / 820ft
500m / 1640ft
1000m / 3281ft
2000m / 6562ft
3000m / 9843ft
5000m / 16,410ft

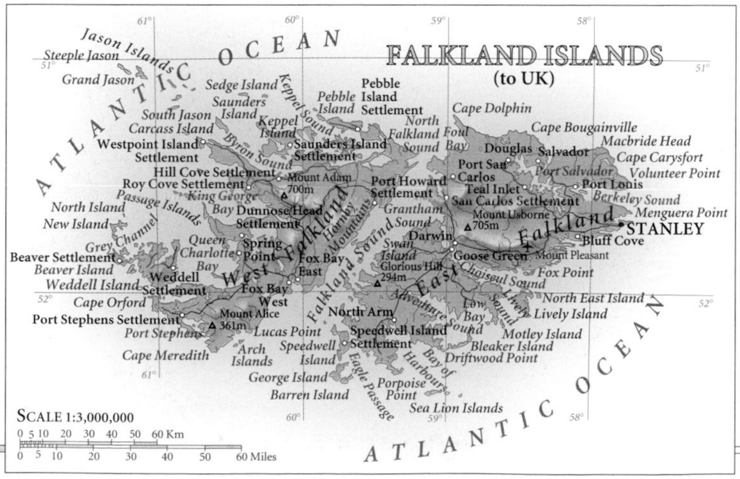

FALKLAND ISLANDS (to UK)
ATLANTIC OCEAN
Jason Islands
Steeple Jason
Grand Jason
Pebble Island
Cape Dolphin
Cape Bougainville
Macbride Head
West Falkland
East Falkland
Falkland Sound
STANLEY
Port Howard
San Carlos Settlement
Darwin
Goose Green
Mount Usborne 705m
Mount Adam 700m
Port Stephens Settlement
Beaver Settlement
Sea Lion Islands
SCALE 1:3,000,000
0 10 20 30 40 50 60 Km
0 10 20 30 40 50 60 Miles

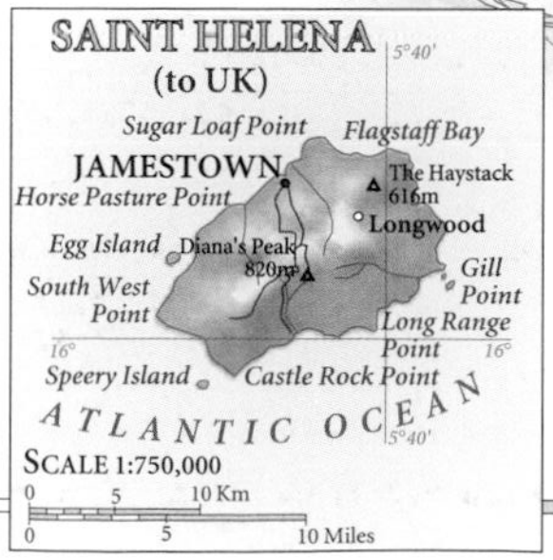

SAINT HELENA (to UK)
JAMESTOWN
Sugar Loaf Point
Flagstaff Bay
The Haystack 616m
Longwood
Horse Pasture Point
Egg Island
Diana's Peak 820m
Gill Point
South West Point
Long Range Point
Speery Island
Castle Rock Point
ATLANTIC OCEAN
SCALE 1:750,000
0 5 10 Km
0 5 10 Miles

Rocky breakwaters *have been built along the coast of Ghana to protect local fishing boats from being destroyed by powerful Atlantic waves.*

TRISTAN DA CUNHA (to Saint Helena)
Big Point
Rookery Point
EDINBURGH
Anchorstock Point
Queen Mary's Peak 2060m
Sandy Point
Lyon Point
Longbluff
Stonybeach Bay
Cave Point
Stonyhill Point
ATLANTIC OCEAN
SCALE 1:750,000
0 5 10 Km
0 5 10 Miles

Azores
Horseshoe Seamounts
East Azores Fracture Zone
Madeira
Canary Basin
Canary Islands
Cape Verde Plain
Santo Antão
Cape Verde Terrace
Cape Verde Basin
Cape Verde Islands
Senegal
Aoukâr
Pointe des Almadies
Guinea Fracture Zone
Sierra Leone Fracture Zone
Saint Paul Fracture Zone
Sierra Leone Basin

AFRICA

THE WORLD'S SECOND LARGEST CONTINENT, AFRICA COVERS AN AREA OF 11,712,434 SQ MILES (30,335,000 SQ KM). IT HAS 53 SEPARATE COUNTRIES, INCLUDING MADAGASCAR IN THE INDIAN OCEAN – THE HIGHEST NUMBER OF ANY CONTINENT.

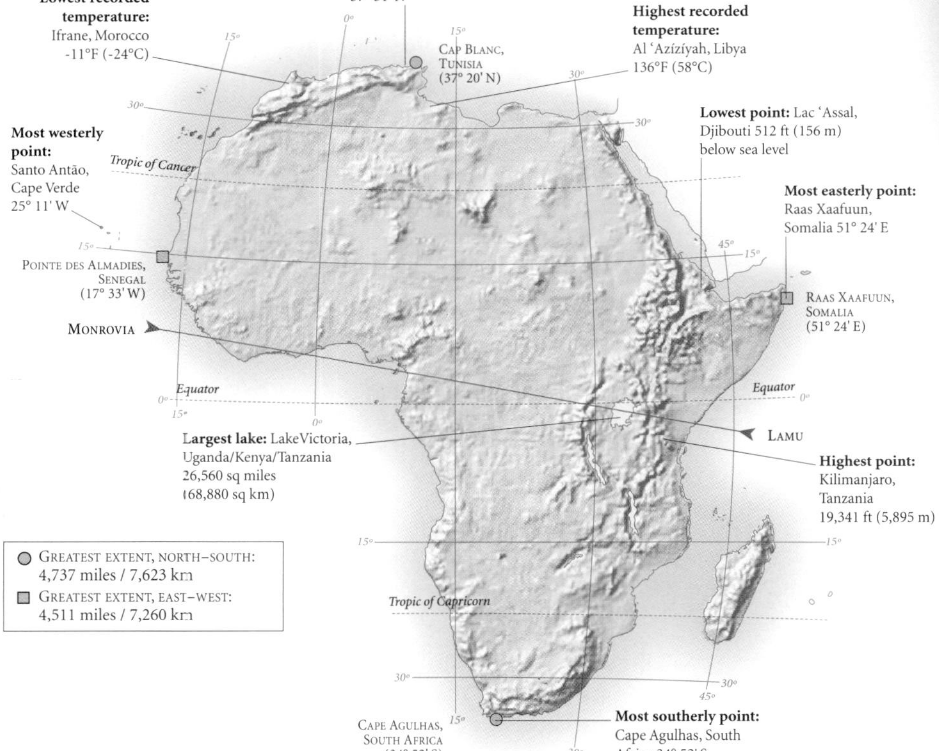

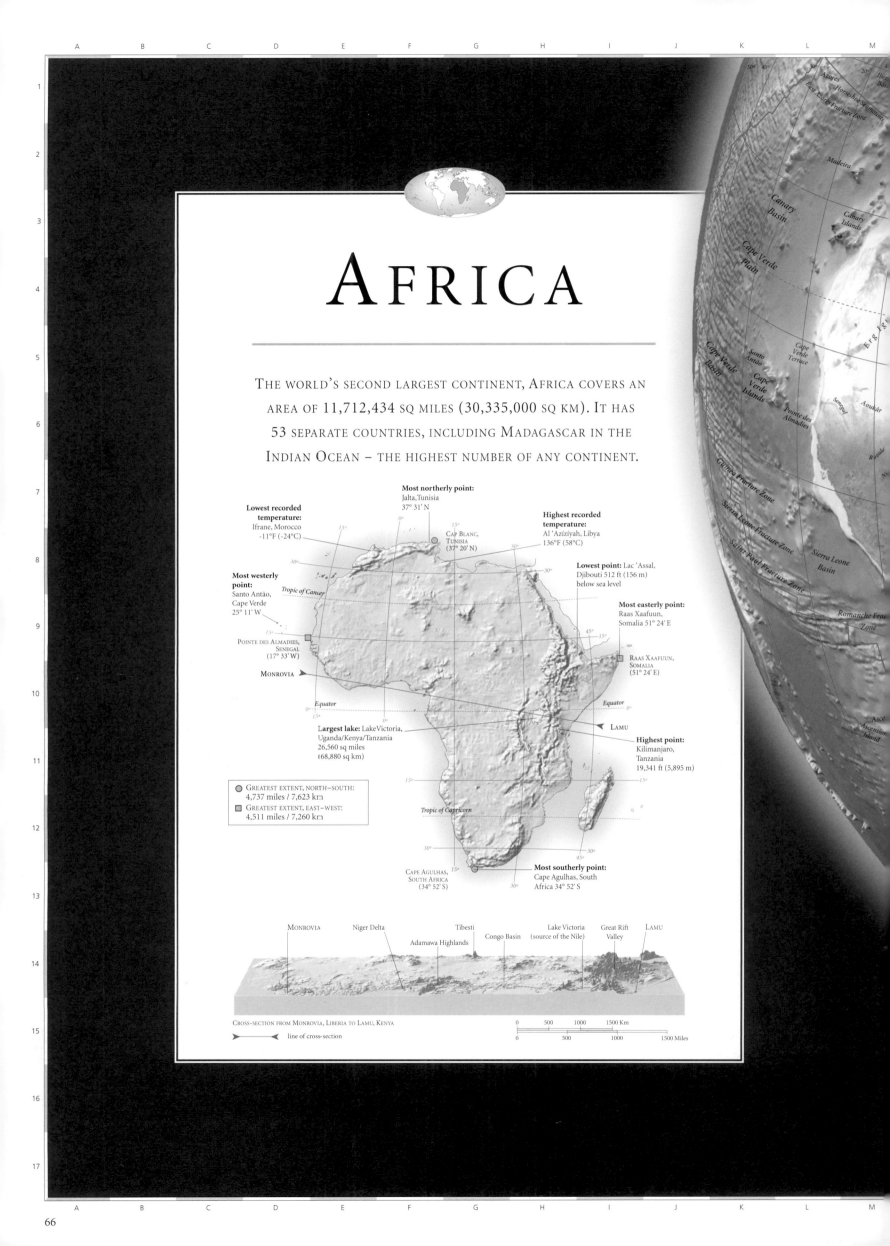

Most northerly point: Jalta, Tunisia 37° 31' N
Lowest recorded temperature: Ifrane, Morocco -11°F (-24°C)
Highest recorded temperature: Al 'Azīzīyah, Libya 136°F (58°C)
CAP BLANC, TUNISIA (37° 20' N)
Lowest point: Lac 'Assal, Djibouti 512 ft (156 m) below sea level
Most westerly point: Santo Antão, Cape Verde 25° 11' W
Tropic of Cancer
Most easterly point: Raas Xaafuun, Somalia 51° 24' E
POINTE DES ALMADIES, SENEGAL (17° 33' W)
RAAS XAAFUUN, SOMALIA (51° 24' E)
MONROVIA
Equator
LAMU
Largest lake: Lake Victoria, Uganda/Kenya/Tanzania 26,560 sq miles (68,880 sq km)
Highest point: Kilimanjaro, Tanzania 19,341 ft (5,895 m)
Tropic of Capricorn
CAPE AGULHAS, SOUTH AFRICA (34° 52' S)
Most southerly point: Cape Agulhas, South Africa 34° 52' S

● GREATEST EXTENT, NORTH–SOUTH: 4,737 miles / 7,623 km
■ GREATEST EXTENT, EAST–WEST: 4,511 miles / 7,260 km

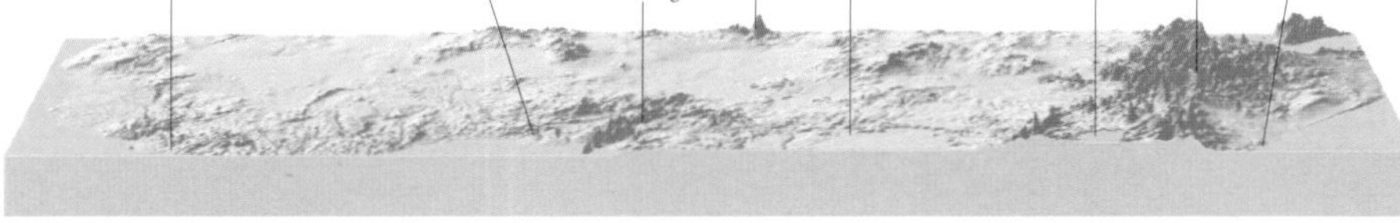

MONROVIA
Niger Delta
Adamawa Highlands
Tibesti
Congo Basin
Lake Victoria (source of the Nile)
Great Rift Valley
LAMU

CROSS-SECTION FROM MONROVIA, LIBERIA TO LAMU, KENYA

line of cross-section

0 500 1000 1500 Km
0 500 1000 1500 Miles

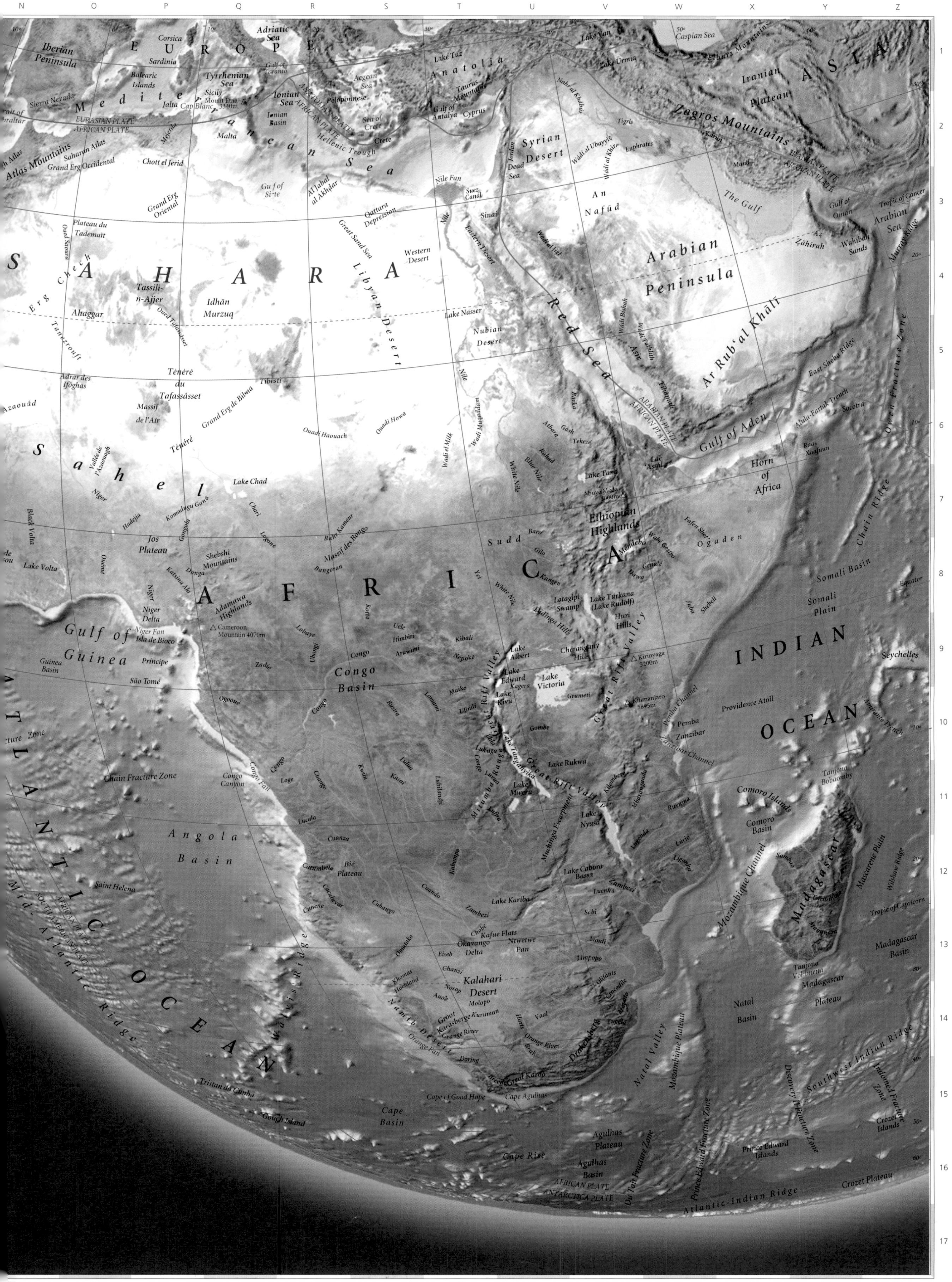
N
O
P
Q
R
S
T
U
V
W
X
Y
Z
1
2
3
4
5
6
7
8
9
10
11
12
13
14
15
16
17
Iberian Peninsula
EUROPE
Corsica
Sardinia
Adriatic Sea
Balearic Islands
Tyrrhenian Sea
Sicily
Mount Etna 3340m
Gulf of Taranto
Ionian Sea
Ionian Basin
Malta
Sierra Nevada
Mediterranean Sea
EURASIAN PLATE
AFRICAN PLATE
Saharan Atlas
Atlas Mountains
Grand Erg Occidental
Chott el Jerid
Aegean Sea
Peloponnese
Sea of Crete
Crete
Hellenic Trough
ANATOLIAN PLATE
AFRICAN PLATE
Lake Tuz
Anatolia
Taurus Mountains
Gulf of Antalya
Cyprus
Lake Van
Lake Urmia
Caspian Sea
Elburz Mountains
Iranian Plateau
ASIA
Zagros Mountains
Tigris
Euphrates
Syrian Desert
Jordan
Dead Sea
Nahr al Khabur
Wadi al Ubayyid
Wadi al Khirr
IRANIAN PLATE
ARABIAN PLATE
The Gulf
Gulf of Oman
Tropic of Cancer
Arabian Sea
Az Zahirah
Wahibah Sands
Murray Ridge
An Nafud
Arabian Peninsula
Ar Rub' al Khali
Nile Fan
Suez Canal
Sinai
Nile
Eastern Desert
Gulf of Sirte
Al Jabal al Akhdar
Qattara Depression
Great Sand Sea
Western Desert
Libyan Desert
Grand Erg Oriental
Plateau du Tademaït
Oued Saoura
Erg Chech
SAHARA
Tassili-n-Ajjer
Idhān Murzuq
Ahaggar
Oued Tafassasset
Tanezrouft
Lake Nasser
Nubian Desert
Red Sea
Adrar des Ifôghas
Ténéré du Tafassâsset
Tibesti
Azaouâd
Massif de l'Aïr
Grand Erg de Bilma
Ténéré
Ouadi Haouach
Ouadi Howa
Wadi al Milk
Wadi Muqaddam
Atbara
Gash
Tekezē
Barka
ARABIAN PLATE
AFRICAN PLATE
Gulf of Aden
Socotra
East Sheba Ridge
Alula-Fartak Trench
Owen Fracture Zone
Lac Assal
Ras Xaafuun
Horn of Africa
Sahel
Vallée de l'Azaouagh
Niger
Lake Chad
Komadugu Gana
Chari
Rahad
Blue Nile
White Nile
Lake Tana
Abuye Meda
Ethiopian Highlands
Black Volta
Hadejia
Jos Plateau
Gongola
Logone
Bahr Kameur
Massif des Bongo
Sudd
Baro
Gilo
Mendebo
Wabē Gestro
Fafen Shet'
Ogaden
Chain Ridge
Lake Volta
Ouémé
Shebshi Mountains
Donga
Katsina Ala
Bangoran
AFRICA
Kangen
White Nile
Yei
Genalē
Dawa
Somali Basin
Equator
Niger
Niger Delta
Adamawa Highlands
Kotto
Lotagipi Swamp
Lake Turkana (Lake Rudolf)
Dodinga Hills
Huri Hills
Juba
Shebeli
Somali Plain
Gulf of Guinea
Niger Fan
Isla de Bioco
Cameroon Mountain 4070m
Lobaye
Uele
Itimbiri
Kibali
Aruwimi
Nepoko
Lake Albert
Cherangany Hills
Kirinyaga 5200m
INDIAN OCEAN
Seychelles
Guinea Basin
Príncipe
São Tomé
Zadié
Ubangi
Congo
Congo Basin
Lake Edward
Kagera
Lake Victoria
Lake Kivu
Maiko
Ulindi
Lomami
Tshuapa
Western Rift Valley
Grumeti
Great Rift Valley
Kilimanjaro 5895m
Pemba Channel
Pemba
Zanzibar
Providence Atoll
Amirante Trench
Ogooué
Congo
Gombe
Zanzibar Channel
Chain Fracture Zone
Congo Canyon
Congo Fan
Cengo
Loge
Cuango
Kwilu
Lulua
Kasai
Lubilanji
Lukuga
Lake Tanganyika
Lake Rukwa
Great Rift Valley
Lake Mweru
Mitumba Range
Luapula
Kilombero
Rovuma
Comoro Islands
Tanjona Bobaomby
Comoro Basin
Lucala
Cuanza
Angola Basin
Lake Nyasa
Muchinga Escarpment
Lugenda
Lurio
Ligonha
Mozambique Channel
Madagascar
Mascarene Plain
Wilshaw Ridge
Saint Helena
Catumbela
Bié Plateau
Kabompo
Cuando
Lake Cabora Bassa
Zambezi
Luenha
Lake Kariba
Tropic of Capricorn
Madagascar Basin
ATLANTIC OCEAN
SOUTH AMERICAN PLATE
AFRICAN PLATE
Mid-Atlantic Ridge
Cunene
Cubango
Save
Chobe
Kafue Flats
Okavango Delta
Nxwetwe Pan
Runde
Omatako
Eiseb
Limpopo
Tanjona Vohimena
Madagascar Plateau
Walvis Ridge
Khomas Hochland
Chanzi
Kalahari Desert
Molopo
Olifants
Crocodile
Nosop
Auob
Groot Karasberge
Kuruman
Vaal
Harts
Tugela
Natal Basin
Namib Desert
Orange River
Orange Fan
Orange
Drakensberg
Doring
Great Karoo
Natal Valley
Mozambique Plateau
Southwest Indian Ridge
Indomed Fracture Zone
Discovery II Fracture Zone
Tristan da Cunha
Cape of Good Hope
Cape Agulhas
Cape Basin
Gough Island
Agulhas Plateau
Prince Edward Fracture Zone
Crozet Islands
Cape Rise
Agulhas Basin
Du Toit Fracture Zone
Prince Edward Islands
AFRICAN PLATE
ANTARCTICA PLATE
Atlantic-Indian Ridge
Crozet Plateau

Physical Africa

The structure of Africa was dramatically influenced by the break up of the supercontinent Gondwanaland about 160 million years ago and, more recently, rifting and hot spot activity. Today, much of Africa is remote from active plate boundaries and comprises a series of extensive plateaus and deep basins, which influence the drainage patterns of major rivers. The relief rises to the east, where volcanic uplands and vast lakes mark the Great Rift Valley. In the far north and south sedimentary rocks have been folded to form the Atlas Mountains and the Great Karoo.

Northern Africa

Northern Africa comprises a system of basins and plateaus. The Tibesti and Ahaggar are volcanic uplands, whose uplift has been matched by subsidence within large surrounding basins. Many of the basins have been infilled with sand and gravel, creating the vast Saharan lands. The Atlas Mountains in the north were formed by convergence of the African and Eurasian plates.

The Earth's crust has been warped to form the Taoudenni Basin
Volcanic Ahaggar Mountains, formed by rising magma from a hot spot
Lake Chad lies in a sand-filled basin
A
A

Section across northern Africa showing infilled basins and uplifted plateaus.

East Africa

The Great Rift Valley is the most striking feature of this region, running for 4,475 miles (7,200 km) from Lake Nyasa to the Red Sea. North of Lake Nyasa it splits into two arms and encloses an interior plateau which contains Lake Victoria. A number of elongated lakes and volcanoes lie along the fault lines. To the west lies the Congo Basin, a vast, shallow depression, which rises to form an almost circular rim of highlands.

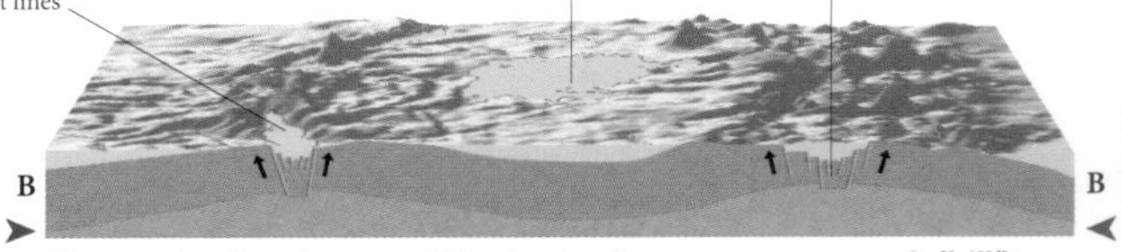
Rift valley lakes, like Lake Tanganyika, lie along fault lines
Lake Victoria
Extensive faulting occurs as rift valley pulls apart
B
B

Cross-section through eastern Africa showing the two arms of the Great Rift Valley and its interior plateau.

Scale 1:40,000,000
(projection: Lambert Azimuthal Equal Area)

Map Key

Elevation	Plate margins (for explanation see page xiv)
5000m / 16,405ft	constructive
4000m / 13,124ft	destructive
3000m / 9843ft	conservative
2000m / 6562ft	uncertain
1000m / 3281ft	line of cross-section
500m / 1640ft	
250m / 820ft	
100m / 328ft	
sea level	
below sea level	

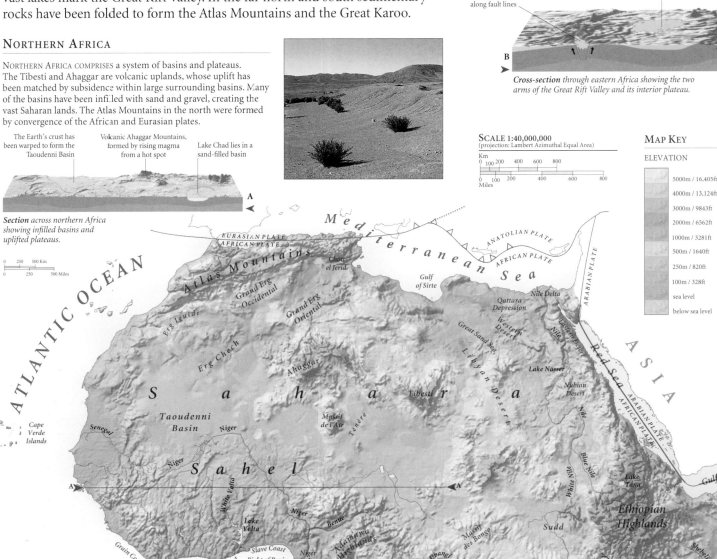

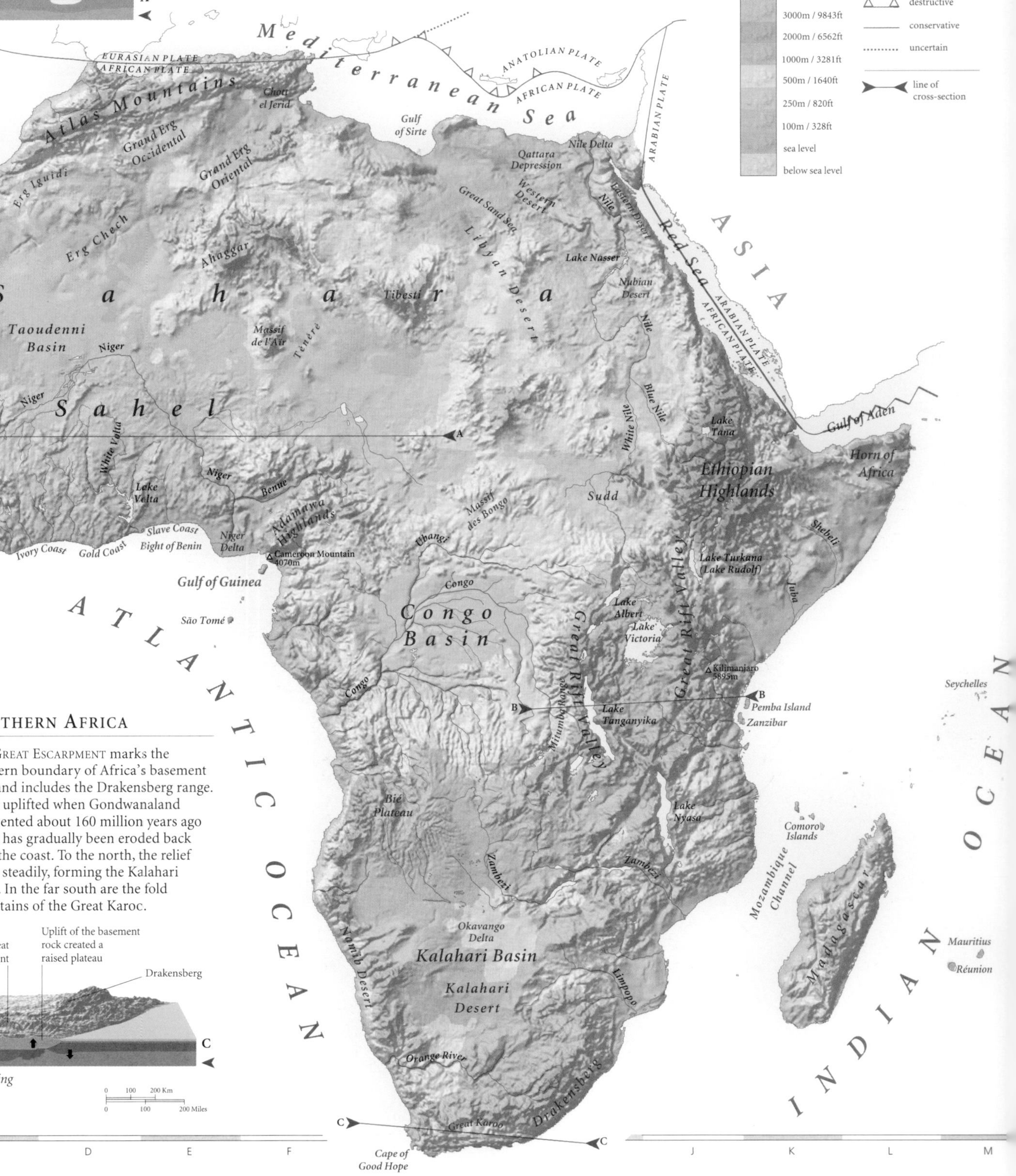
ATLANTIC OCEAN
Mediterranean Sea
EURASIAN PLATE
AFRICAN PLATE
ANATOLIAN PLATE
ARABIAN PLATE
Atlas Mountains
Chott el Jerid
Gulf of Sirte
Grand Erg Occidental
Grand Erg Oriental
Erg Iguidi
Erg Chech
Nile Delta
Qattara Depression
Western Desert
Great Sand Sea
Libyan Desert
Eastern Desert
Nile
ASIA
Red Sea
Lake Nasser
Nubian Desert
ARABIAN PLATE
AFRICAN PLATE
Ahaggar
Sahara
Tibesti
Taoudenni Basin
Massif de l'Aïr
Ténéré
Cape Verde Islands
Senegal
Niger
Sahel
Blue Nile
White Nile
Lake Tana
Gulf of Aden
Horn of Africa
Ethiopian Highlands
White Volta
Lake Volta
Benue
Adamawa Highlands
Massif des Bongo
Sudd
Grain Coast
Ivory Coast
Gold Coast
Slave Coast
Bight of Benin
Niger Delta
Cameroon Mountain 4070m
Ubangi
Shebeli
Lake Turkana (Lake Rudolf)
Juba
Gulf of Guinea
São Tomé
Congo
Congo Basin
Lake Albert
Lake Victoria
Great Rift Valley
Kilimanjaro 5895m
Seychelles
Mitumba Range
Lake Tanganyika
Pemba Island
Zanzibar
Bié Plateau
Lake Nyasa
Comoro Islands
Mozambique Channel
Madagascar
Zambezi
Okavango Delta
Kalahari Basin
Kalahari Desert
Namib Desert
Limpopo
Mauritius
Réunion
Orange River
Drakensberg
Great Karoo
Cape of Good Hope
INDIAN OCEAN
A
A
B
B
C
C

Southern Africa

The Great Escarpment marks the southern boundary of Africa's basement rock and includes the Drakensberg range. It was uplifted when Gondwanaland fragmented about 160 million years ago and it has gradually been eroded back from the coast. To the north, the relief drops steadily, forming the Kalahari Basin. In the far south are the fold mountains of the Great Karoo.

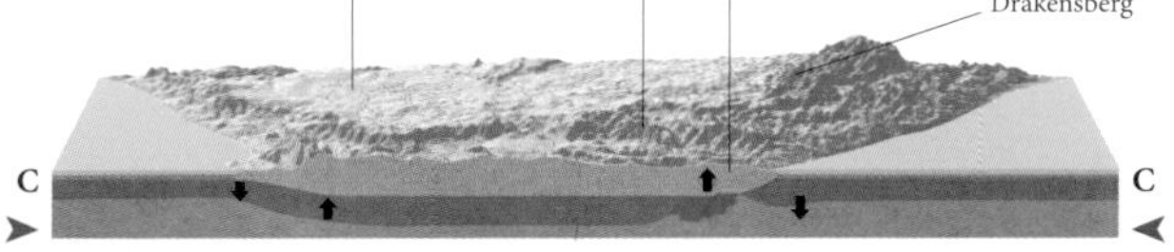
Kalahari Basin, covered with the sandy plains of the Kalahari Desert
Boundary of the Great Escarpment
Uplift of the basement rock created a raised plateau
Drakensberg
C
C

Cross-section through southern Africa showing the boundary of the Great Escarpment.

Climate

Savannah grasslands run in a belt across Africa; limited rainfall inhibits tree growth.

THE CLIMATES OF AFRICA range from mediterranean to arid, dry savannah and humid equatorial. In East Africa, where snow settles at the summit of volcanoes such as Kilimanjaro, climate is also modified by altitude. The winds of the Sahara export millions of tonnes of dust a year both northward and eastward.

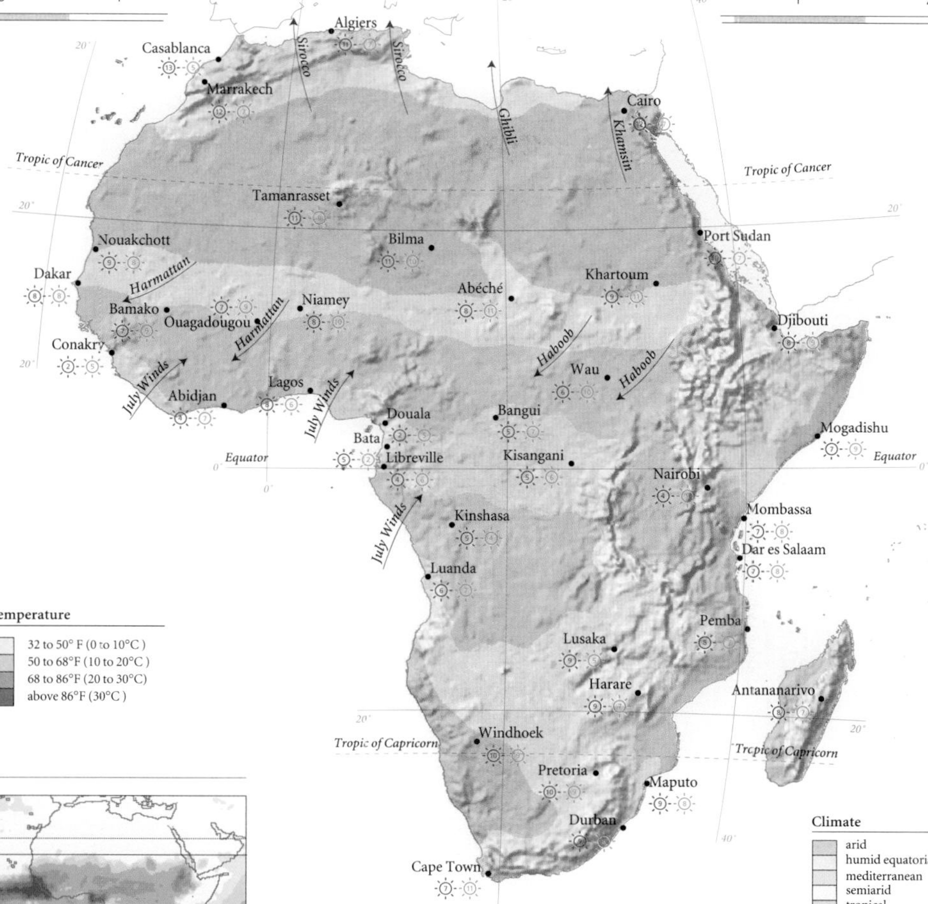
Algiers
Casablanca
Marrakech
Sirocco
Sirocco
Ghibli
Cairo
Khamsin
Tropic of Cancer
Tropic of Cancer
Tamanrasset
Nouakchott
Bilma
Port Sudan
Dakar
Harmattan
Bamako
Ouagadougou
Niamey
Abéché
Khartoum
Harmattan
Djibouti
Conakry
Haboob
Haboob
Wau
July Winds
Abidjan
Lagos
July Winds
Douala
Bangui
Mogadishu
Bata
Libreville
Kisangani
Equator
Equator
Nairobi
July Winds
Kinshasa
Mombasa
Dar es Salaam
Luanda
Pemba
Lusaka
Harare
Antananarivo
Tropic of Capricorn
Windhoek
Tropic of Capricorn
Pretoria
Maputo
Durban
Cape Town

Climate
- arid
- humid equatorial
- mediterranean
- semiarid
- tropical
- warm humid
- daily hours of sunshine, January
- daily hours of sunshine, July
- cold wind
- hot wind

Temperature

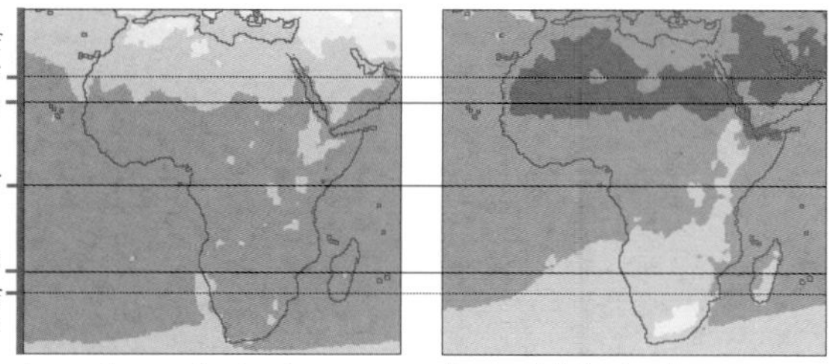
Tropic of Cancer
20°N
Equator
20°S
Tropic of Capricorn

Average January temperature

Average July temperature

Temperature
- 32 to 50° F (0 to 10°C)
- 50 to 68°F (10 to 20°C)
- 68 to 86°F (20 to 30°C)
- above 86°F (30°C)

The hot, equatorial basin of the Congo River receives over 48 inches (1,200 mm) of rainfall per year.

Rainfall

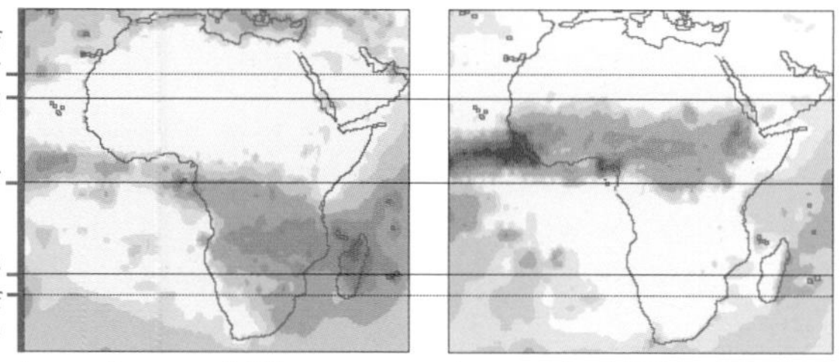
Tropic of Cancer
20°N
Equator
20°S
Tropic of Capricorn

Average January rainfall

Average July rainfall

Rainfall
- 0–1 in (0–25 mm)
- 1–2 in (25–50 mm)
- 2–4 in (50–100 mm)
- 4–8 in (100–200 mm)
- 8–12 in (200–300 mm)
- 12–16 in (300–400 mm)
- 16–20 in (400–500 mm)
- more than 20 in (500 mm)

Shaping the Continent

AFRICAN LANDSCAPES are shaped by the intensity of climatic extremes and by tectonic action. High aridity, wind action, and infrequent but heavy rainstorms, lead to the migration of sand dunes and dramatic flash flooding across much of the north and west. In the wetter areas, high precipitation increases the rate of weathering. To the east, the rift system has created a volcanic and lake environment and allowed rivers to erode weaknesses left in the crustal structure by faults.

Groundwater

1 Oases are found in desert areas such as the Sahara *(left)*. Groundwater migrates through permeable rock strata, confined between two impermeable layers. Oases form either when the permeable rocks come near to the surface, or at a fault line, when water is able to seep up to the surface through the crushed rocks at the fault.

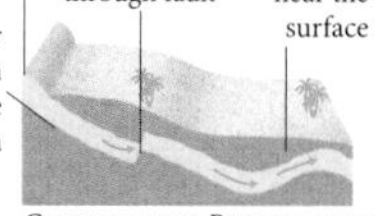
Rainwater feeds the aquifer
Water migrates up through fault
Aquifer exposed near the surface
Groundwater trapped between impermeable strata

GROUNDWATER: REPLENISHMENT OF AN OASIS

River Systems

2 The Zambezi River *(above)* drops 360 ft (110 m) over the Victoria Falls into a zigzag gorge. The river has eroded the gorge along lines of weakness in the bedrock, created by fault lines running in two directions.

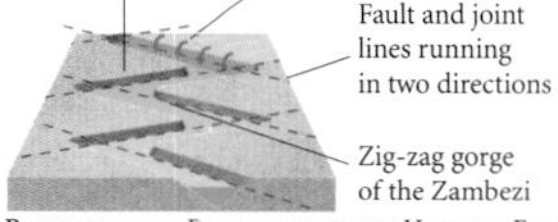
Old site of Victoria Falls
River plunges over falls
Fault and joint lines running in two directions
Zig-zag gorge of the Zambezi

RIVER SYSTEMS: RETREATING OF THE VICTORIA FALLS

The Evolving Landscape

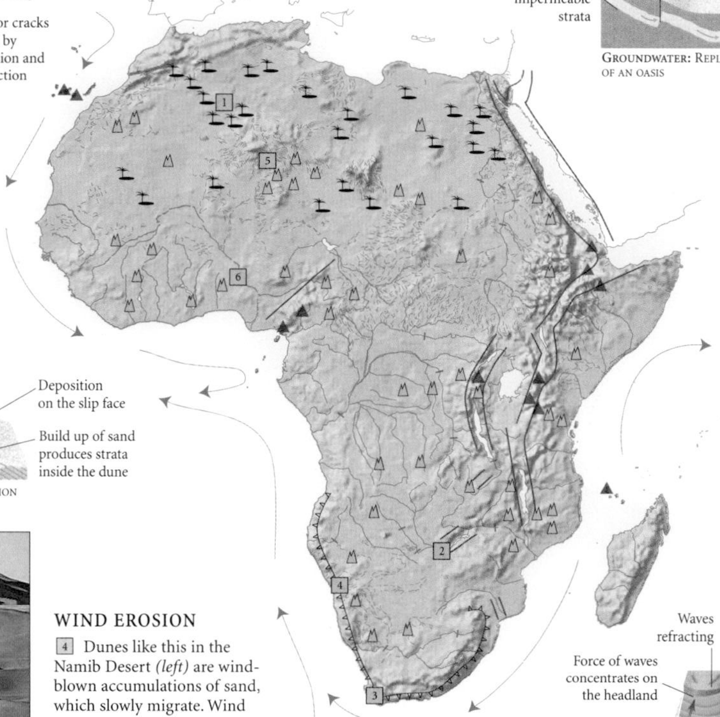
1
2
3
4
5
6

Landscape
- sinking land
- stable land
- uplifting land
- escarpment
- ocean current
- rift
- active volcano
- inselberg
- oasis
- river
- wadi
- waterfall

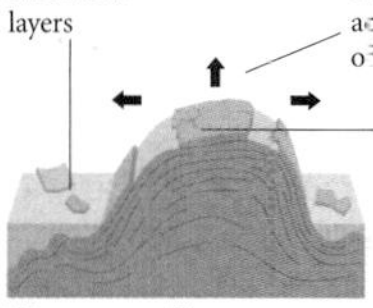
Exfoliated layers
External stresses act on the surface of the inselberg
Joints or cracks caused by expansion and contraction

WEATHERING: FORMATION OF AN INSELBERG

Weathering

6 Inselbergs *(above)*, found extensively across West Africa, are exposed remnants of an extensive upland area. Erosion of the surrounding uplands leaves a resistant rock outcrop. Its spheroidal shape is the result of "onion-skin" weathering – the exfoliating of layers – due to repeated expansion and contraction.

Ephemeral Channels

5 Wadis *(above)* drain much of northern Africa. These drybed courses are flooded only after infrequent, but intense, storms in the uplands cause water to surge along their channels.

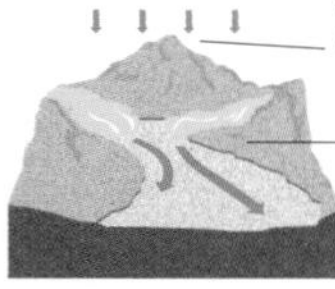
Heavy rainfall runs off mountains
Water collects and floods the dry channel

EPHEMERAL CHANNELS: FLASH FLOODING OF A WADI

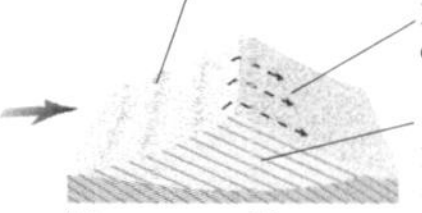
Sand is gradually blown up the back slope
Deposition on the slip face
Build up of sand produces strata inside the dune

WIND EROSION: MIGRATION OF A DUNE

Wind Erosion

4 Dunes like this in the Namib Desert *(left)* are wind-blown accumulations of sand, which slowly migrate. Wind action moves sand up the shallow back slope; when the sand reaches the crest of the dune it is deposited on the slip face.

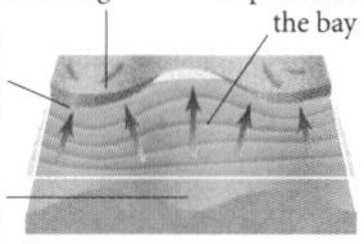
Waves refracting
Wave energy dispersed in the bay
Force of waves concentrates on the headland
The sea bed is deeper opposite the bay than at the headland

COASTAL PROCESSES: EROSION OF A BAY

Coastal Processes

3 Houtbaai *(above)*, in southern Africa, is constantly being modified by wave action. As waves approach the indented coastline, they reach the shallow water of the headland, slowing down and reducing in length. This causes them to bend or refract, concentrating their erosive force at the headlands.

Political Africa

The political map of modern Africa only emerged following the end of the Second World War. Over the next half-century, all of the countries formerly controlled by European powers gained independence from their colonial rulers – only Liberia and Ethiopia were never colonized. The postcolonial era has not been an easy period for many countries, but there have been moves toward multiparty democracy in much of West Africa, and in Zambia, Tanzania, and Kenya. In South Africa, democratic elections replaced the internationally-condemned apartheid system only in 1994. Other countries have still to find political stability; corruption in government, and ethnic tensions are serious problems. National infrastructures, based on the colonial transportation systems built to exploit Africa's resources, are often inappropriate for independent economic development.

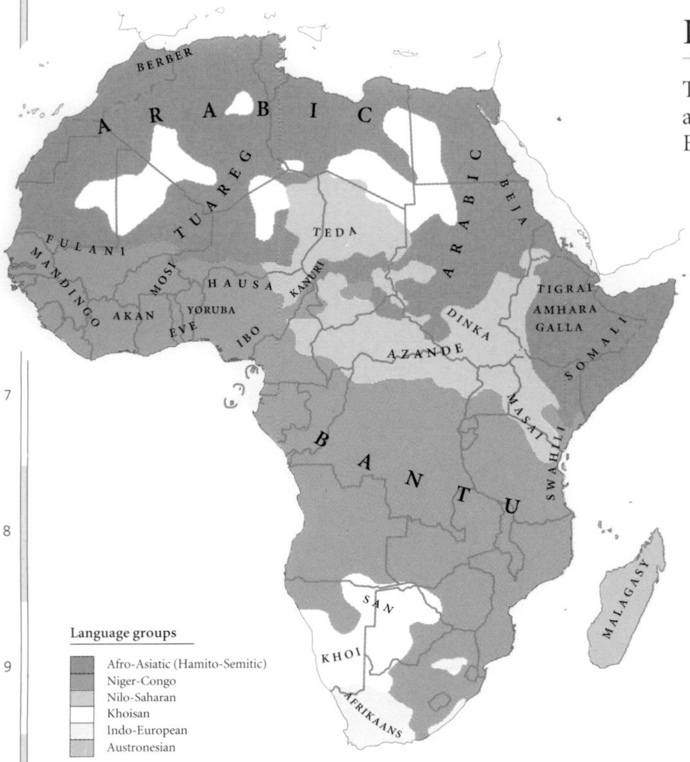

BERBER
ARABIC
TUAREG
TEDA
FULANI
MANDINGO
MOSI
HAUSA
KANURI
YORUBA
AKAN
EVE
IBO
DINKA
AZANDE
BEJA
TIGRAI
AMHARA
GALLA
SOMALI
MASAI
SWAHILI
BANTU
SAN
KHOI
AFRIKAANS
MALAGASY
Language groups
Afro-Asiatic (Hamito-Semitic)
Niger-Congo
Nilo-Saharan
Khoisan
Indo-European
Austronesian

Languages

Three major world languages act as *lingua francas* across the African continent: Arabic in North Africa; English in southern and eastern Africa and Nigeria; and French in Central and West Africa, and in Madagascar. A huge number of African languages are spoken as well – over 2,000 have been recorded, with more than 400 in Nigeria alone – reflecting the continuing importance of traditional cultures and values. In the north of the continent, the extensive use of Arabic reflects Middle Eastern influences while Bantu is widely-spoken across much of southern Africa.

Official African languages

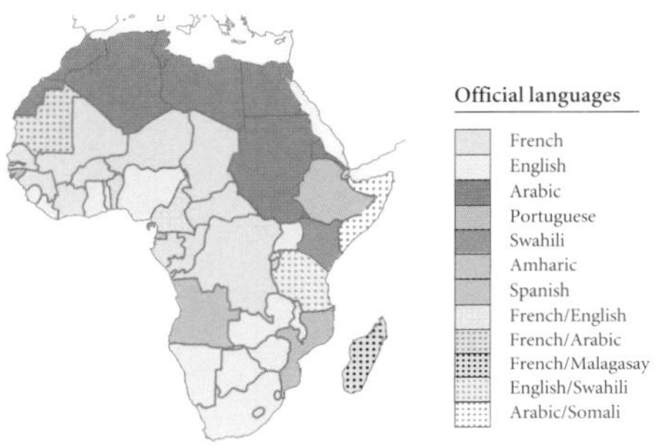

Official languages
French
English
Arabic
Portuguese
Swahili
Amharic
Spanish
French/English
French/Arabic
French/Malagasy
English/Swahili
Arabic/Somali

Islamic influences *are evident throughout North Africa. The Great Mosque at Kairouan, Tunisia, is Africa's holiest Islamic place.*

In northeastern Nigeria, *people speak Kanuri – a dialect of the Saharan language group.*

Transportation

African railroads were built to aid the exploitation of natural resources, and most offer passage only from the interior to the coastal cities, leaving large parts of the continent untouched – five landlocked countries have no railroads at all. The Congo, Nile, and Niger River networks offer limited access to land within the continental interior, but have a number of waterfalls and cataracts which prevent navigation from the sea. Many roads were developed in the 1960s and 1970s, but economic difficulties are making the maintenance and expansion of the networks difficult.

South Africa *has the largest concentration of railroads in Africa. Over 20,000 miles (32,000 km) of routes have been built since 1870.*

Traditional means of transportation, *such as the camel, are still widely used across the less accessible parts of Africa.*

The Congo River, *though not suitable for river transportation along its entire length, forms a vital link for people and goods in its navigable inland reaches.*

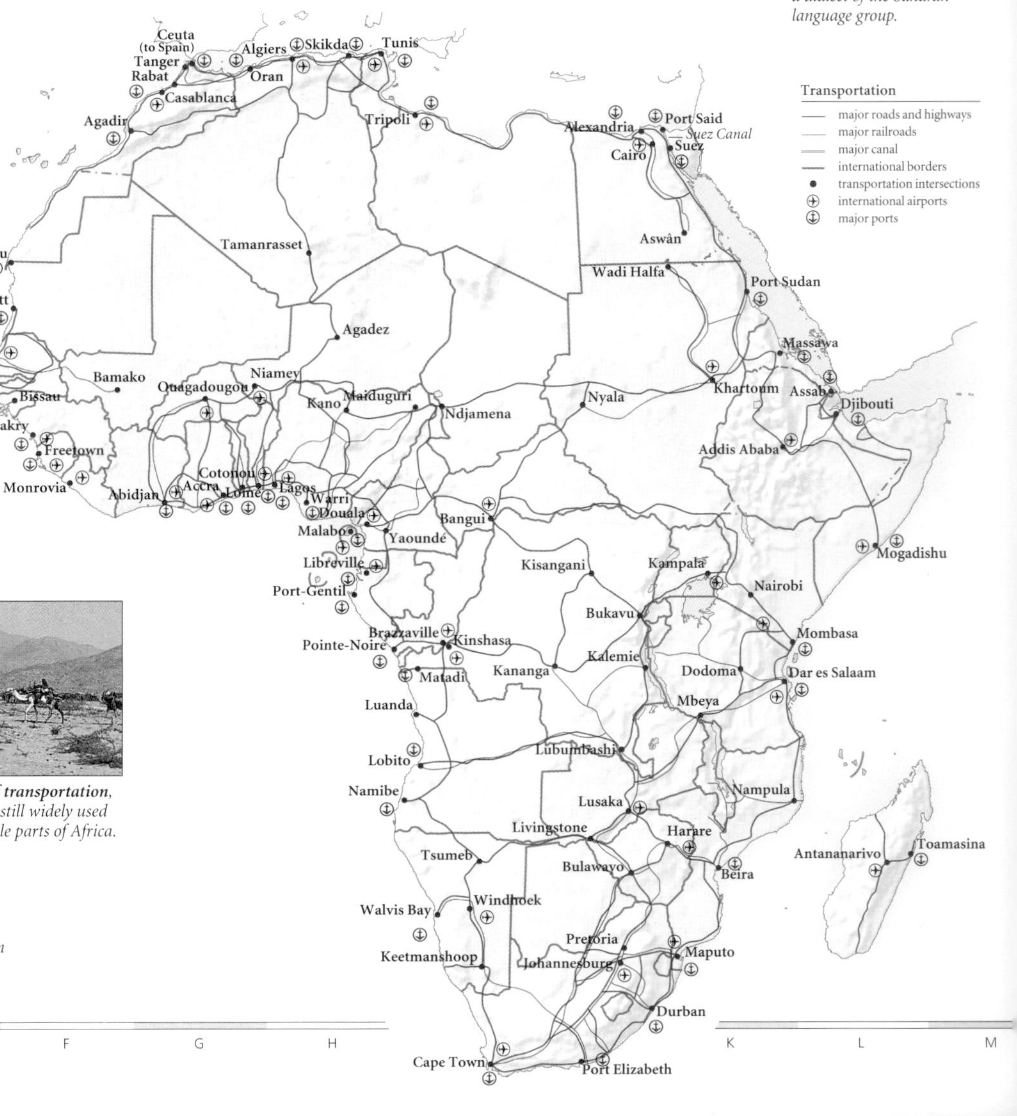

Ceuta (to Spain)
Tanger
Rabat
Casablanca
Algiers
Oran
Skikda
Tunis
Tripoli
Agadir
Alexandria
Port Said
Suez Canal
Cairo
Suez
Aswân
Wadi Halfa
Port Sudan
Tamanrasset
Nouâdhibou
Nouakchott
Dakar
Banjul
Bissau
Conakry
Freetown
Monrovia
Bamako
Ouagadougou
Niamey
Agadez
Kano
Maiduguri
Ndjamena
Nyala
Khartoum
Massawa
Assab
Djibouti
Addis Ababa
Abidjan
Accra
Cotonou
Lomé
Lagos
Warri
Douala
Malabo
Yaoundé
Bangui
Libreville
Port-Gentil
Kisangani
Kampala
Nairobi
Mogadishu
Bukavu
Brazzaville
Kinshasa
Pointe-Noire
Matadi
Kananga
Kalemie
Dodoma
Mombasa
Dar es Salaam
Luanda
Mbeya
Lobito
Lubumbashi
Namibe
Lusaka
Nampula
Livingstone
Harare
Tsumeb
Bulawayo
Beira
Antananarivo
Toamasina
Walvis Bay
Windhoek
Keetmanshoop
Pretoria
Johannesburg
Maputo
Durban
Cape Town
Port Elizabeth
Transportation
major roads and highways
major railroads
major canal
international borders
transportation intersections
international airports
major ports

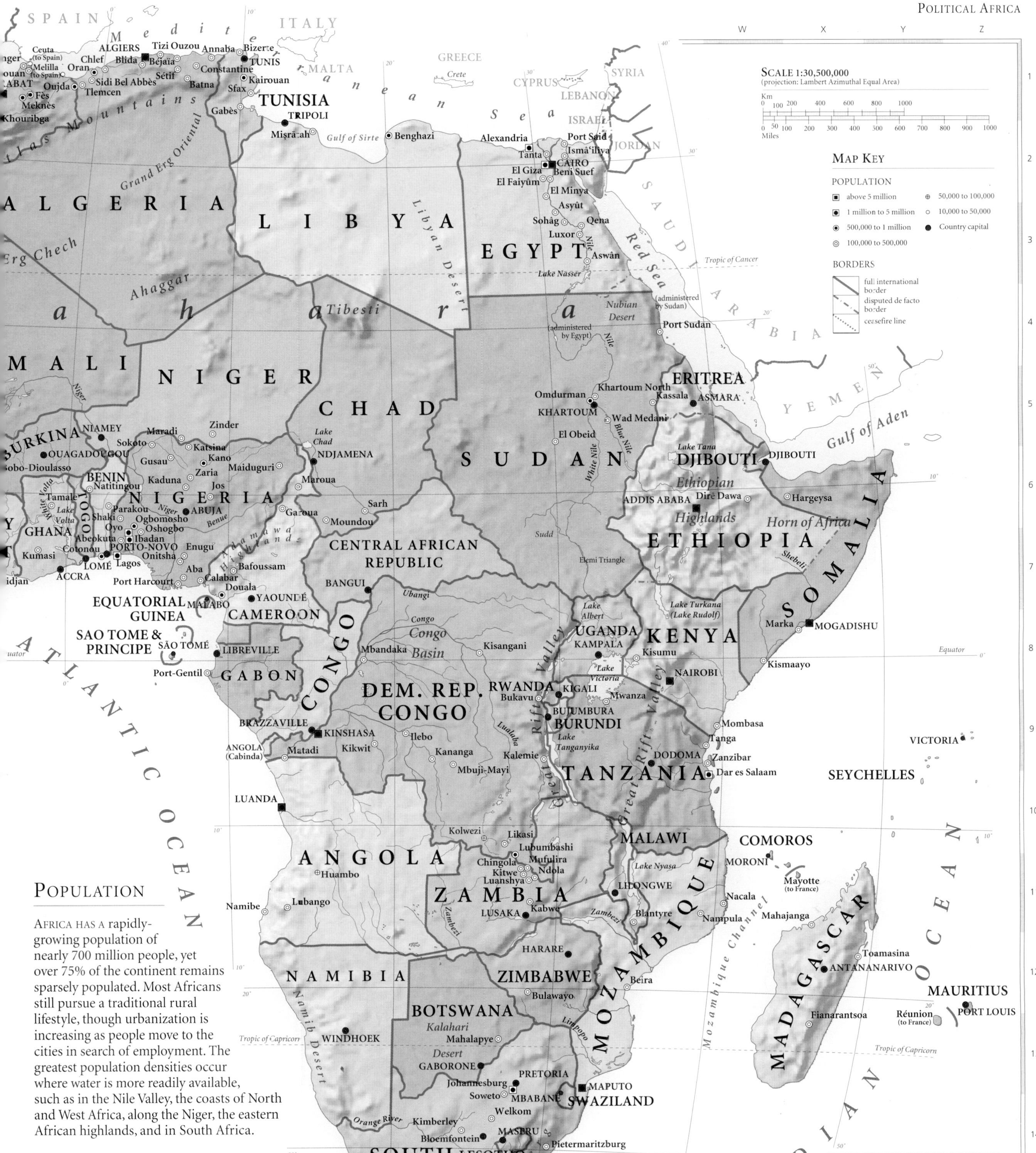
SCALE 1:30,500,000
(projection: Lambert Azimuthal Equal Area)
Km 0 100 200 400 600 800 1000
Miles 0 50 100 200 300 400 500 600 700 800 900 1000
MAP KEY
POPULATION
above 5 million
1 million to 5 million
500,000 to 1 million
100,000 to 500,000
50,000 to 100,000
10,000 to 50,000
Country capital
BORDERS
full international border
disputed de facto border
ceasefire line
ALGERIA
LIBYA
EGYPT
TUNISIA
MALI
NIGER
CHAD
SUDAN
ERITREA
DJIBOUTI
ETHIOPIA
SOMALIA
BURKINA
BENIN
TOGO
GHANA
NIGERIA
CENTRAL AFRICAN REPUBLIC
CAMEROON
EQUATORIAL GUINEA
SAO TOME & PRINCIPE
GABON
CONGO
DEM. REP. CONGO
UGANDA
KENYA
RWANDA
BURUNDI
TANZANIA
ANGOLA
ZAMBIA
MALAWI
MOZAMBIQUE
ZIMBABWE
NAMIBIA
BOTSWANA
SOUTH AFRICA
LESOTHO
SWAZILAND
MADAGASCAR
COMOROS
SEYCHELLES
MAURITIUS
SPAIN
ITALY
GREECE
CYPRUS
SYRIA
LEBANON
ISRAEL
JORDAN
SAUDI ARABIA
YEMEN
Mediterranean Sea
ATLANTIC OCEAN
INDIAN OCEAN
Red Sea
Gulf of Aden
Mozambique Channel
Tropic of Cancer
Equator
Tropic of Capricorn
Sahara
Libyan Desert
Nubian Desert
Namib Desert
Kalahari Desert
Congo Basin
Ethiopian Highlands
Horn of Africa
Great Rift Valley
Drakensberg
Cape of Good Hope
ALGIERS
TUNIS
TRIPOLI
CAIRO
KHARTOUM
ASMARA
DJIBOUTI
ADDIS ABABA
MOGADISHU
NAIROBI
KAMPALA
KIGALI
BUJUMBURA
DODOMA
LILONGWE
LUSAKA
HARARE
MAPUTO
MBABANE
MASERU
PRETORIA
GABORONE
WINDHOEK
LUANDA
KINSHASA
BRAZZAVILLE
LIBREVILLE
MALABO
SÃO TOMÉ
YAOUNDÉ
BANGUI
NDJAMENA
NIAMEY
OUAGADOUGOU
ABUJA
PORTO-NOVO
LOMÉ
ACCRA
MORONI
ANTANANARIVO
VICTORIA
PORT LOUIS

POPULATION

AFRICA HAS A rapidly-growing population of nearly 700 million people, yet over 75% of the continent remains sparsely populated. Most Africans still pursue a traditional rural lifestyle, though urbanization is increasing as people move to the cities in search of employment. The greatest population densities occur where water is more readily available, such as in the Nile Valley, the coasts of North and West Africa, along the Niger, the eastern African highlands, and in South Africa.

Population density (people per sq mile)

- below 130
- 130–259
- 260–379
- 380–519
- 520–780
- above 780

***A thin layer of smog** blankets the dusty streets of Cairo, Africa's most populous city and home to over six million people. In the 1990s Cairo grew at a rate of about 1,500 people per day.*

***Thriving street markets** in Gambia's capital, Banjul, trade a variety of locally-grown produce. Africa's population is still predominantly rural.*

African Resources

The economies of most African countries are dominated by subsistence and cash crop agriculture, with limited industrialization. Manufacturing is largely confined to South Africa. Many countries depend on a single resource, such as copper or gold, or a cash crop, such as coffee, for export income, which can leave them vulnerable to fluctuations in world commodity prices. In order to diversify their economies and develop a wider industrial base, investment from overseas is being actively sought by many African governments.

Industry

Many African industries concentrate on the extraction and processing of raw materials. These include the oil industry, food processing, mining, and textile production. South Africa accounts for over half of the continent's industrial output with much of the remainder coming from the countries along the northern coast. Over 60% of Africa's workforce is employed in agriculture.

***The unspoiled natural splendor** of wildlife reserves, like the Serengeti National Park in Tanzania, attract tourists to Africa from around the globe. The tourist industry in Kenya and Tanzania is particularly well developed, where it accounts for almost 10% of GNP.*

Standard of Living

Since the 1960s most countries in Africa have seen significant improvements in life expectancy, healthcare and education. However, 18 of the 20 most deprived countries in the world are African, and the continent as a whole lies well behind the rest of the world in terms of meeting many basic human needs.

Standard of Living
(UN Human Development Index)
high
low

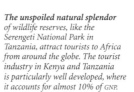

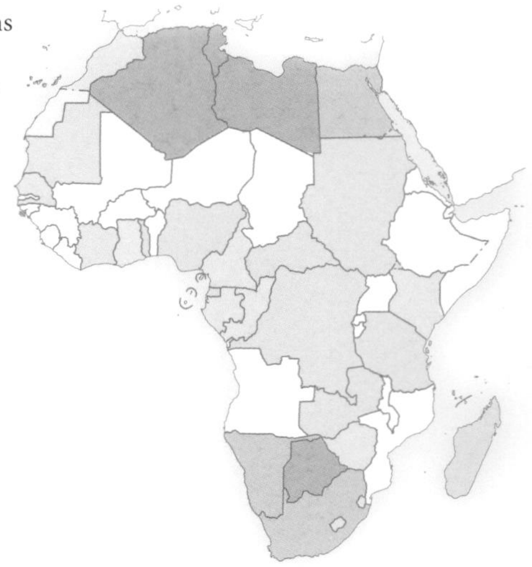

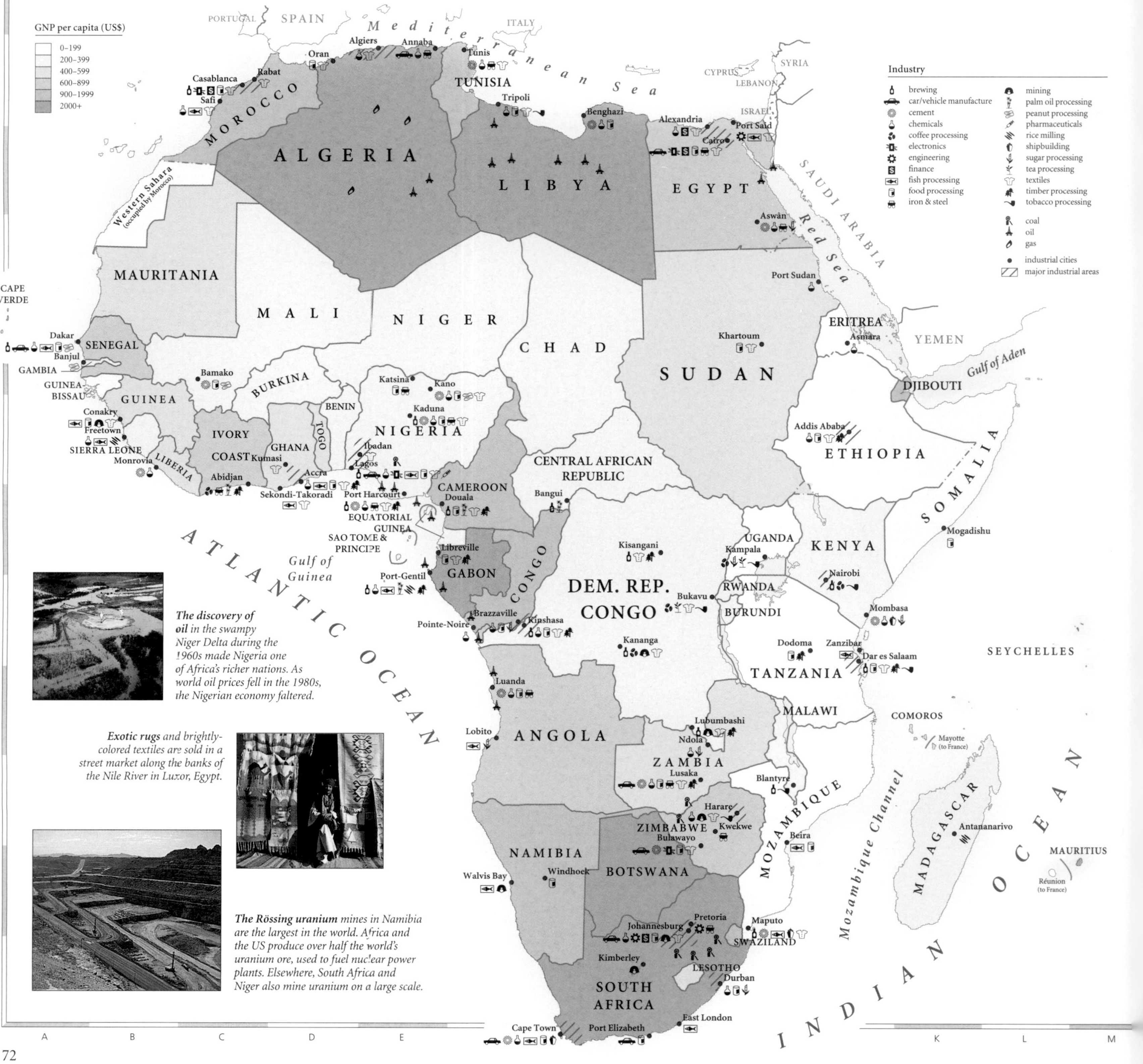
GNP per capita (US$)
0–199
200–399
400–599
600–899
900–1999
2000+
Industry
brewing
car/vehicle manufacture
cement
chemicals
coffee processing
electronics
engineering
finance
fish processing
food processing
iron & steel
mining
palm oil processing
peanut processing
pharmaceuticals
rice milling
shipbuilding
sugar processing
tea processing
textiles
timber processing
tobacco processing
coal
oil
gas
industrial cities
major industrial areas
PORTUGAL
SPAIN
ITALY
Mediterranean Sea
CYPRUS
SYRIA
LEBANON
ISRAEL
SAUDI ARABIA
Red Sea
YEMEN
Gulf of Aden
Casablanca
Rabat
Safi
Oran
Algiers
Annaba
Tunis
Tripoli
Benghazi
Alexandria
Cairo
Port Said
Aswân
Port Sudan
Khartoum
Asmara
Addis Ababa
Mogadishu
MOROCCO
ALGERIA
TUNISIA
LIBYA
EGYPT
Western Sahara (occupied by Morocco)
MAURITANIA
MALI
NIGER
CHAD
SUDAN
ERITREA
DJIBOUTI
ETHIOPIA
SOMALIA
CAPE VERDE
Dakar
SENEGAL
Banjul
GAMBIA
GUINEA-BISSAU
GUINEA
Conakry
Freetown
SIERRA LEONE
Monrovia
LIBERIA
Bamako
BURKINA
IVORY COAST
Abidjan
GHANA
Kumasi
Accra
Sekondi-Takoradi
TOGO
BENIN
NIGERIA
Katsina
Kano
Kaduna
Ibadan
Lagos
Port Harcourt
CAMEROON
Douala
EQUATORIAL GUINEA
SAO TOME & PRINCIPE
Gulf of Guinea
Libreville
GABON
Port-Gentil
CONGO
Pointe-Noire
Brazzaville
Kinshasa
CENTRAL AFRICAN REPUBLIC
Bangui
DEM. REP. CONGO
Kisangani
Kananga
Bukavu
UGANDA
Kampala
KENYA
Nairobi
RWANDA
BURUNDI
Mombasa
Dodoma
Zanzibar
Dar es Salaam
TANZANIA
SEYCHELLES
ATLANTIC OCEAN
Luanda
ANGOLA
Lobito
Lubumbashi
Ndola
ZAMBIA
Lusaka
MALAWI
Blantyre
COMOROS
Mayotte (to France)
Harare
Kwekwe
ZIMBABWE
Bulawayo
Beira
MOZAMBIQUE
Mozambique Channel
MADAGASCAR
Antananarivo
MAURITIUS
Réunion (to France)
NAMIBIA
Walvis Bay
Windhoek
BOTSWANA
Pretoria
Johannesburg
Maputo
SWAZILAND
Kimberley
LESOTHO
Durban
SOUTH AFRICA
Cape Town
Port Elizabeth
East London
INDIAN OCEAN

***The discovery of oil** in the swampy Niger Delta during the 1960s made Nigeria one of Africa's richer nations. As world oil prices fell in the 1980s, the Nigerian economy faltered.*

***Exotic rugs** and brightly-colored textiles are sold in a street market along the banks of the Nile River in Luxor, Egypt.*

***The Rössing uranium** mines in Namibia are the largest in the world. Africa and the US produce over half the world's uranium ore, used to fuel nuclear power plants. Elsewhere, South Africa and Niger also mine uranium on a large scale.*

N O P Q R S T U V W X Y Z

Environmental Issues

One of Africa's most serious environmental problems occurs in marginal areas such as the Sahel where scrub and forest clearance, often for cooking fuel, combined with overgrazing, are causing desertification. Game reserves in southern and eastern Africa have helped to preserve many endangered animals, although the needs of growing populations have led to conflict over land use, and poaching is a serious problem.

Environmental Issues

- national parks
- tropical forest
- forest destroyed
- desert
- desertification
- polluted rivers
- radioactive contamination
- marine pollution
- heavy marine pollution
- poor urban air quality

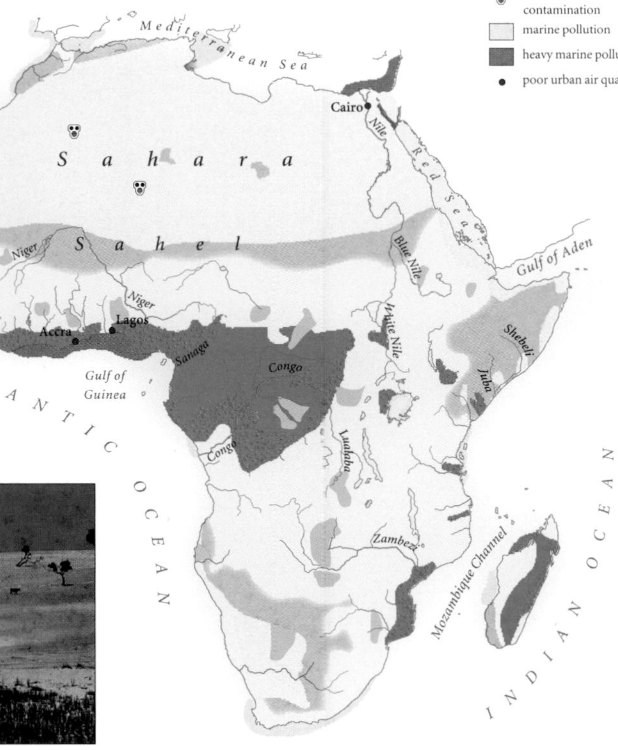

Mediterranean Sea
Cairo
Nile
Red Sea
Sahara
Sahel
Niger
Blue Nile
White Nile
Gulf of Aden
Accra
Lagos
Sanaga
Congo
Gulf of Guinea
Shebelle
Juba
Lualaba
ATLANTIC OCEAN
Zambezi
Mozambique Channel
INDIAN OCEAN

The Sahel's delicate natural equilibrium is easily destroyed by the clearing of vegetation, drought, and overgrazing. This causes the Sahara to advance south, engulfing the savannah grasslands.

Mineral Resources

Africa's ancient plateaus contain some of the world's most substantial reserves of precious stones and metals. About 30% of the world's gold is mined in South Africa; Zambia has great copper deposits; and diamonds are mined in Botswana, Dem. Rep. Congo, and South Africa. Oil has brought great economic benefits to Algeria, Libya, and Nigeria.

Mineral Resources

- oil field
- gas field
- coal field
- bauxite
- copper
- diamonds
- gold
- iron
- phosphates
- tin
- uranium

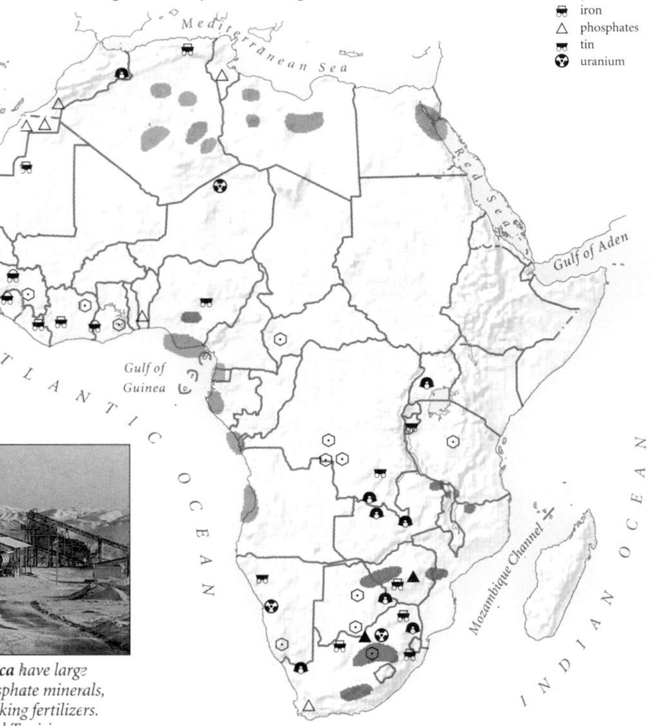

Mediterranean Sea
Red Sea
Gulf of Aden
Gulf of Guinea
ATLANTIC OCEAN
Mozambique Channel
INDIAN OCEAN

***North and West Africa** have large deposits of white phosphate minerals, which are used in making fertilizers. Morocco, Senegal, and Tunisia are the continent's leading producers.*

***Workers on a tea plantation** gather one of Africa's most important cash crops, providing a valuable source of income. Coffee, rubber, bananas, cotton, and cocoa are also widely grown as cash crops.*

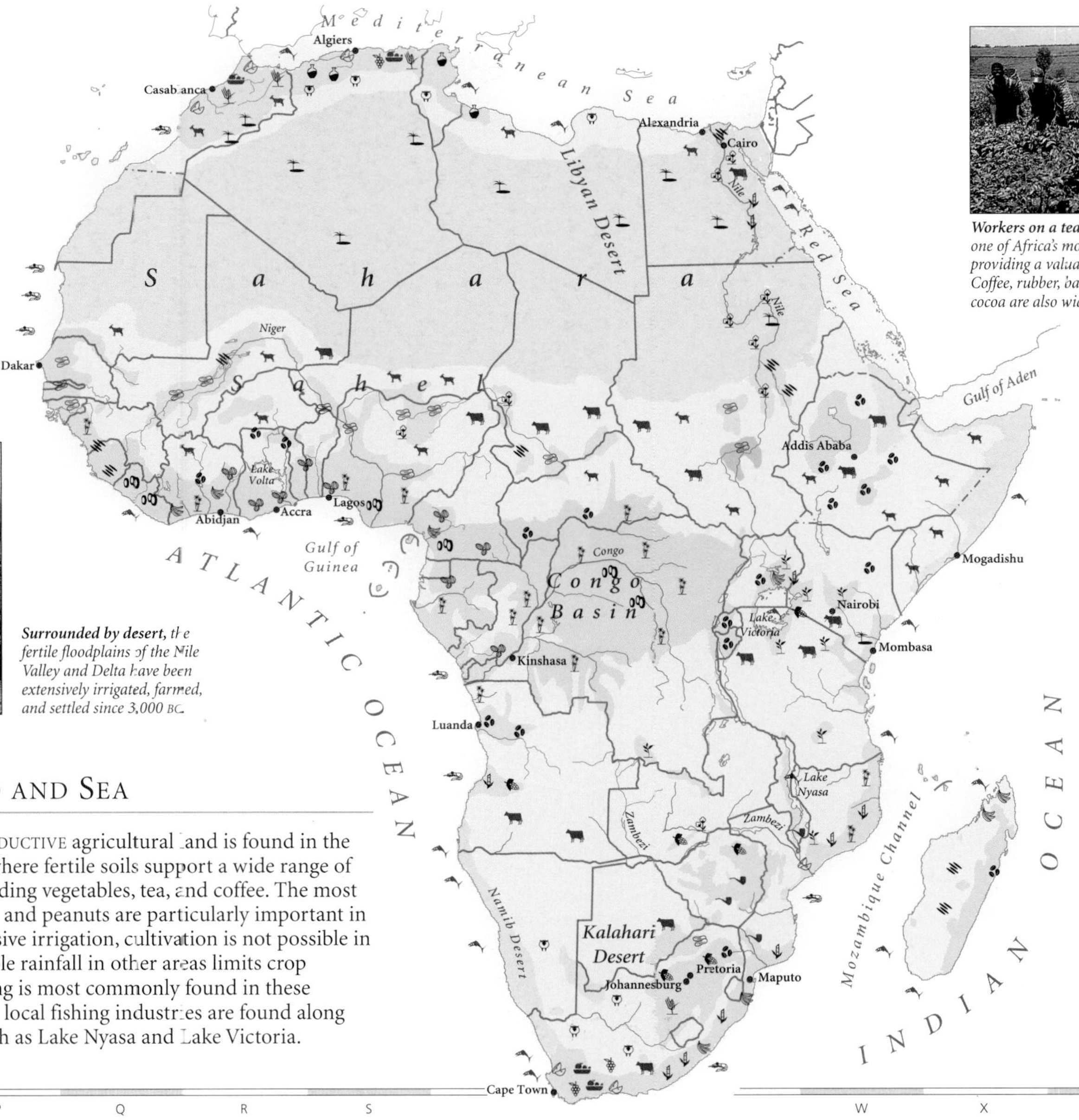

Mediterranean Sea
Algiers
Casablanca
Alexandria
Cairo
Libyan Desert
Nile
Red Sea
Sahara
Niger
Dakar
Sahel
Gulf of Aden
Addis Ababa
Lake Volta
Abidjan
Accra
Lagos
Gulf of Guinea
Congo
Congo Basin
Mogadishu
Nairobi
Lake Victoria
Mombasa
Kinshasa
ATLANTIC OCEAN
Luanda
Lake Nyasa
Zambezi
Namib Desert
Kalahari Desert
Pretoria
Johannesburg
Maputo
Mozambique Channel
INDIAN OCEAN
Cape Town

***Surrounded by desert,** the fertile floodplains of the Nile Valley and Delta have been extensively irrigated, farmed, and settled since 3,000 BC.*

Using the Land and Sea

- cropland
- desert
- forest
- pasture
- wetland
- major conurbations
- cattle
- goats
- cereals
- sheep
- bananas
- corn (maize)
- citrus fruits
- cocoa
- cotton
- coffee
- dates
- fishing
- fruit
- oil palms
- olives
- peanuts
- rice
- rubber
- shellfish
- sugar cane
- tea
- tobacco
- vineyards
- wheat

Using the Land and Sea

Some of Africa's most productive agricultural land is found in the eastern volcanic uplands, where fertile soils support a wide range of valuable export crops including vegetables, tea, and coffee. The most widely-grown grain is corn and peanuts are particularly important in West Africa. Without intensive irrigation, cultivation is not possible in desert regions and unreliable rainfall in other areas limits crop production. Pastoral herding is most commonly found in these marginal lands. Substantial local fishing industries are found along coasts and in vast lakes such as Lake Nyasa and Lake Victoria.

N O P Q R S W X Y Z

A B C D E F G H I J K L M

North Africa

Algeria, Egypt, Libya, Morocco, Tunisia, Western Sahara

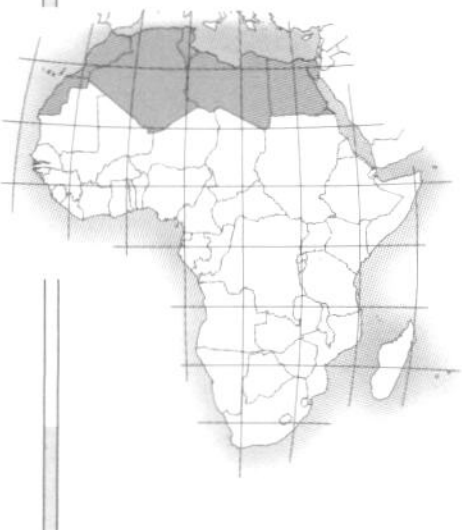

Fringed by the Mediterranean along the northern coast and by the arid Sahara in the south, North Africa reflects the influence of many invaders, both European and, most importantly, Arab, giving the region an almost universal Islamic flavor and a common Arabic language. The countries lying to the west of Egypt are often referred to as the Maghreb, an Arabic term for "west." Today, Morocco and Tunisia exploit their culture and landscape for tourism, while rich oil and gas deposits aid development in Libya and Algeria, despite political turmoil. Egypt, with its fertile, Nile-watered agricultural land and varied industrial base, is the most populous nation.

These rock piles in Algeria's Ahaggar Mountains are the result of weathering caused by extremes of temperature. Great cracks or joints appear in the rocks, which are then worn and smoothed by the wind.

The Landscape

The Atlas Mountains, which extend across much of Morocco, northern Algeria, and Tunisia, are part of the fold mountain system which also runs through much of southern Europe. They recede to the south and east, becoming a steppe landscape before meeting the Sahara desert which covers more than 90% of the region. The sediments of the Sahara overlie an ancient plateau of crystalline rock, some of which is more than four billion years old.

Map Key

Population	Elevation
above 5 million	4000m / 13,124ft
1 million to 5 million	3000m / 9843ft
500,000 to 1 million	2000m / 6562ft
100,000 to 500,000	1000m / 3281ft
50,000 to 100,000	500m / 1640ft
10,000 to 50,000	250m / 820ft
below 10,000	100m / 328ft
	sea level

Scale 1:12,250,000
(projection: Lambert Azimuthal Equal Area)

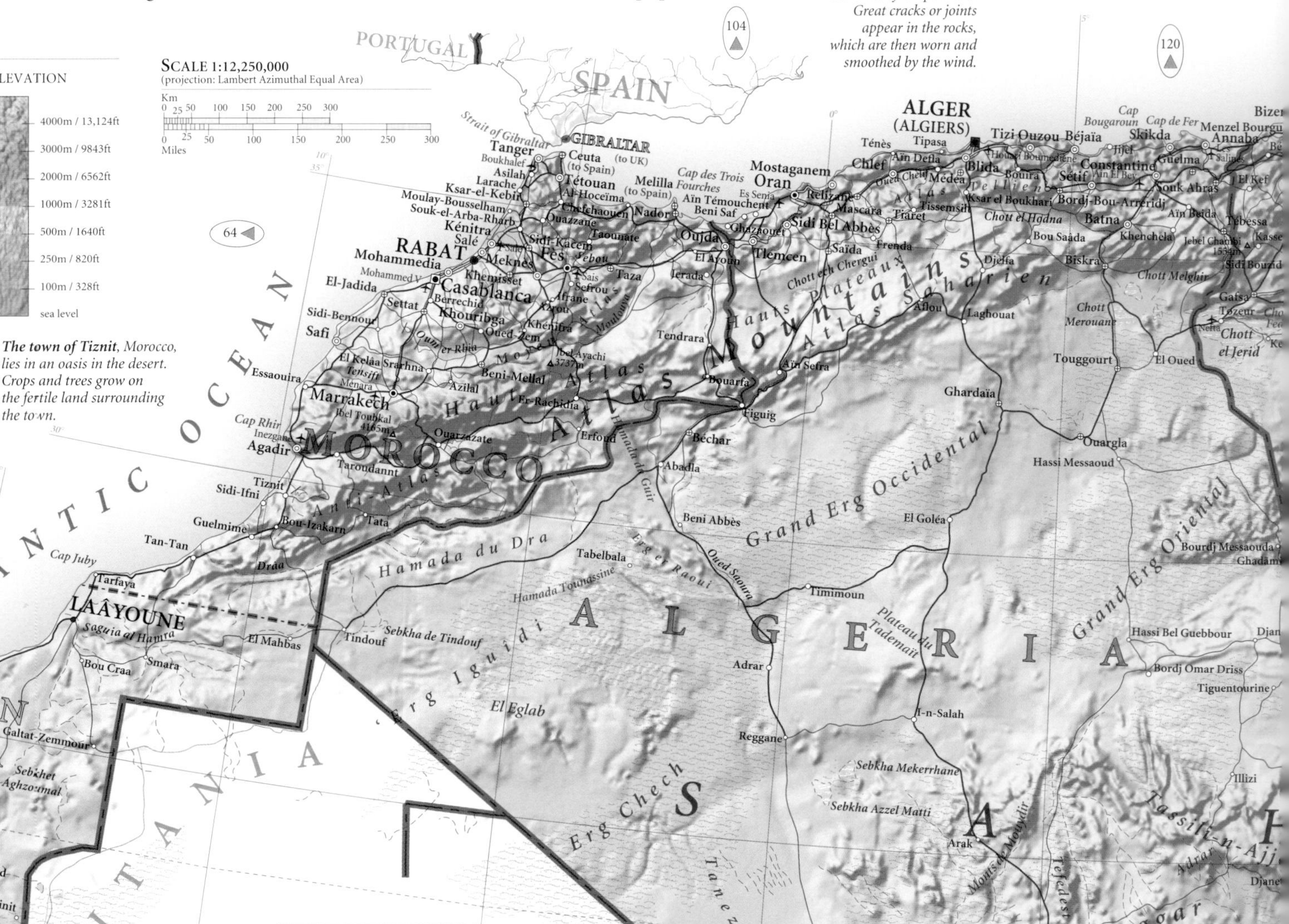

PORTUGAL
SPAIN
GIBRALTAR (to UK)
Strait of Gibraltar
Tanger
Ceuta (to Spain)
Tétouan
Melilla (to Spain)
RABAT
Casablanca
Marrakech
Agadir
MOROCCO
ATLANTIC OCEAN
ALGER (ALGIERS)
Oran
Constantine
Annaba
Grand Erg Occidental
Grand Erg Oriental
ALGERIA
LAÂYOUNE
WESTERN SAHARA (occupied by Morocco)
Tropic of Cancer
MAURITANIA
MALI
Tamanrasset
Ahaggar
Haut Atlas
Anti Atlas

104
120
64
76
76

The town of Tiznit, Morocco, lies in an oasis in the desert. Crops and trees grow on the fertile land surrounding the town.

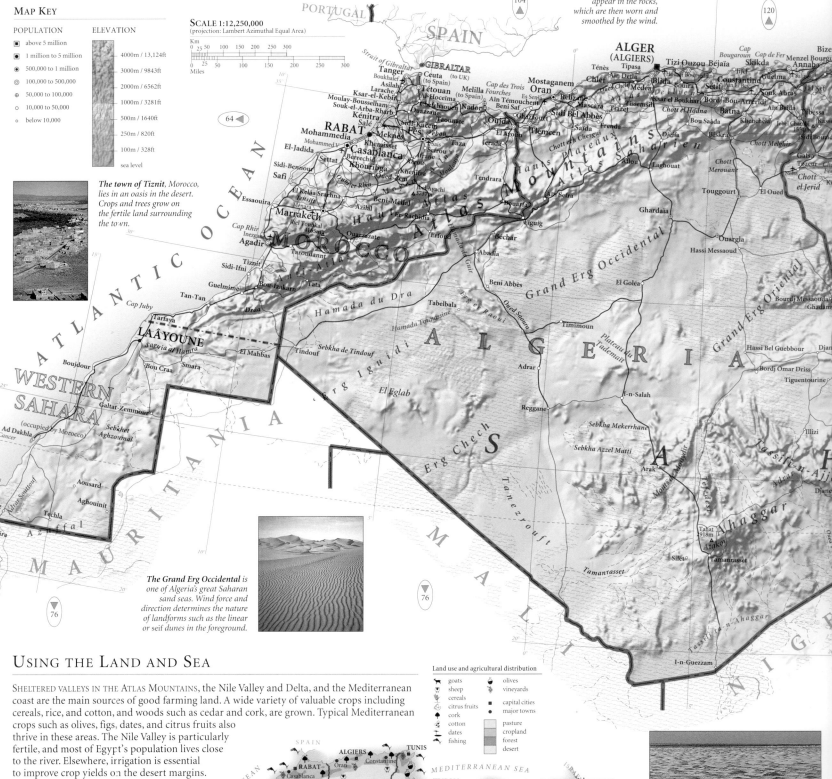

***The Grand Erg Occidental** is one of Algeria's great Saharan sand seas. Wind force and direction determines the nature of landforms such as the linear or seif dunes in the foreground.*

Using the Land and Sea

Sheltered valleys in the Atlas Mountains, the Nile Valley and Delta, and the Mediterranean coast are the main sources of good farming land. A wide variety of valuable crops including cereals, rice, and cotton, and woods such as cedar and cork, are grown. Typical Mediterranean crops such as olives, figs, dates, and citrus fruits also thrive in these areas. The Nile Valley is particularly fertile, and most of Egypt's population lives close to the river. Elsewhere, irrigation is essential to improve crop yields on the desert margins.

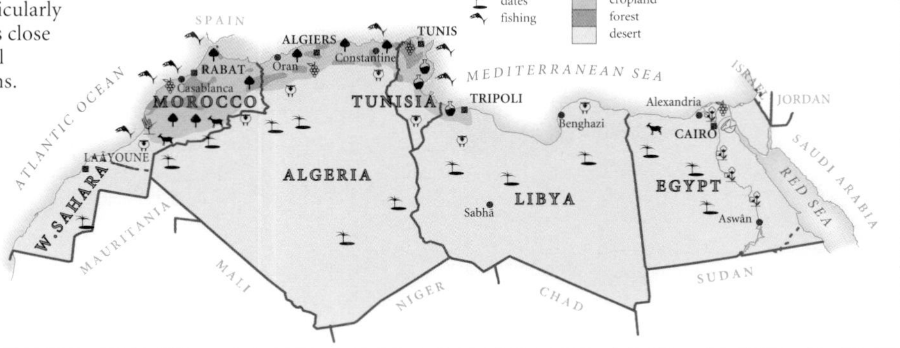

Land use and agricultural distribution
goats
sheep
cereals
citrus fruits
cork
cotton
dates
fishing
olives
vineyards
capital cities
major towns
pasture
cropland
forest
desert
SPAIN
ALGIERS
TUNIS
RABAT
Casablanca
Oran
Constantine
MOROCCO
TUNISIA
TRIPOLI
MEDITERRANEAN SEA
Alexandria
CAIRO
JORDAN
ISRAEL
SAUDI ARABIA
RED SEA
Benghazi
ATLANTIC OCEAN
LAÂYOUNE
ALGERIA
LIBYA
EGYPT
Sabhā
Aswân
W. SAHARA
MAURITANIA
MALI
NIGER
CHAD
SUDAN

Many North African nomads, such as the Bedouin, maintain a traditional pastoral lifestyle on the desert fringes, moving their herds of sheep, goats, and camels from place to place – crossing country borders in order to find sufficient grazing land.

The Urban/Rural Population Divide

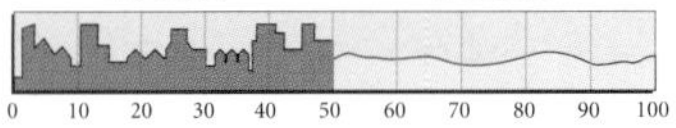

urban 50%
rural 50%
0 10 20 30 40 50 60 70 80 90 100

Population Density	Total Land Area
62 people per sq mile (24 people per sq km)	2,215,020 sq miles (5,738,394 sq km)

A B C D E F G H I J K L M

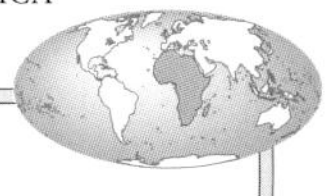

N O P Q R S T U V W X Y

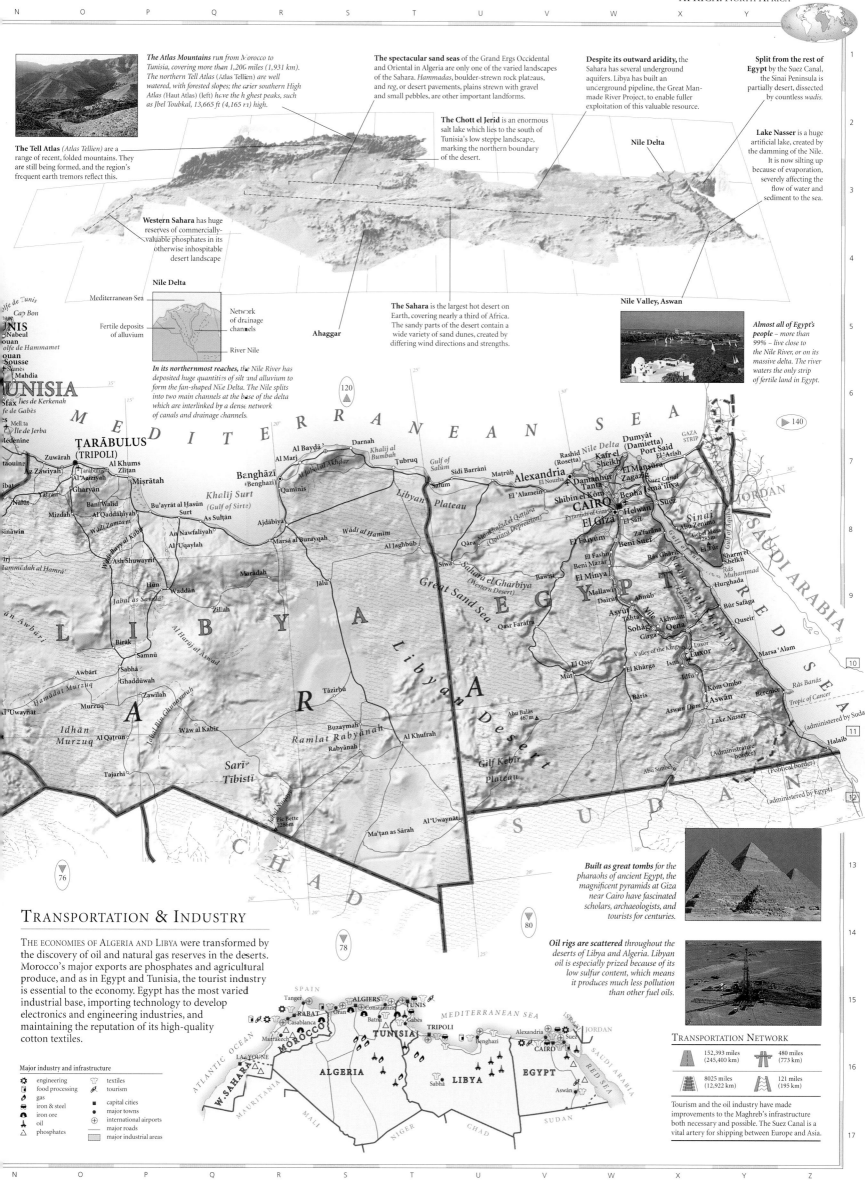

The Atlas Mountains run from Morocco to Tunisia, covering more than 1,200 miles (1,931 km). The northern Tell Atlas (Atlas Tellien) are well watered, with forested slopes; the drier southern High Atlas (Haut Atlas) (left) have the highest peaks, such as Jbel Toubkal, 13,665 ft (4,165 m) high.

The spectacular sand seas of the Grand Ergs Occidental and Oriental in Algeria are only one of the varied landscapes of the Sahara. *Hammadas*, boulder-strewn rock plateaus, and *reg*, or desert pavements, plains strewn with gravel and small pebbles, are other important landforms.

Despite its outward aridity, the Sahara has several underground aquifers. Libya has built an underground pipeline, the Great Man-made River Project, to enable fuller exploitation of this valuable resource.

Split from the rest of Egypt by the Suez Canal, the Sinai Peninsula is partially desert, dissected by countless *wadis*.

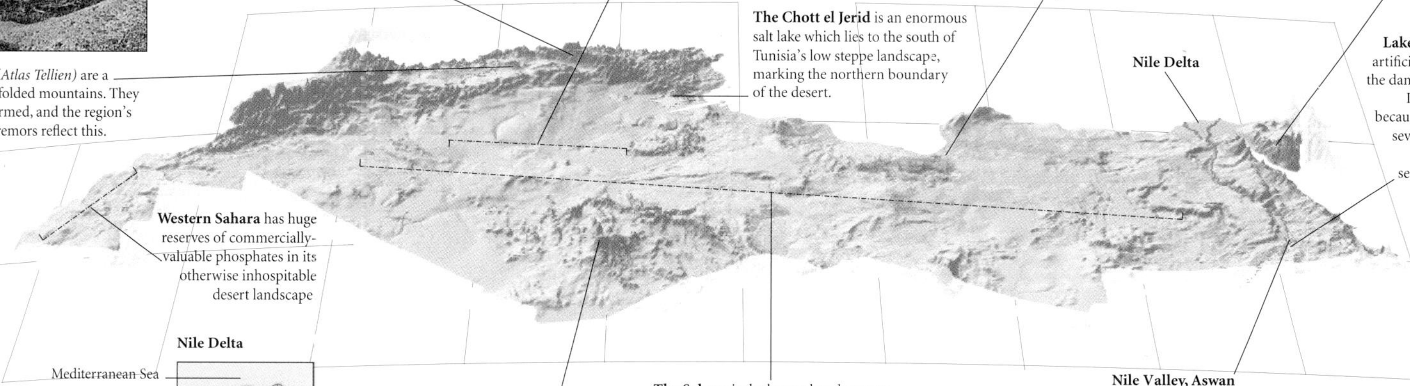

Nile Delta
Nile Valley, Aswan
Ahaggar

The Tell Atlas *(Atlas Tellien)* are a range of recent, folded mountains. They are still being formed, and the region's frequent earth tremors reflect this.

The Chott el Jerid is an enormous salt lake which lies to the south of Tunisia's low steppe landscape, marking the northern boundary of the desert.

Lake Nasser is a huge artificial lake, created by the damming of the Nile. It is now silting up because of evaporation, severely affecting the flow of water and sediment to the sea.

Western Sahara has huge reserves of commercially-valuable phosphates in its otherwise inhospitable desert landscape

Nile Delta

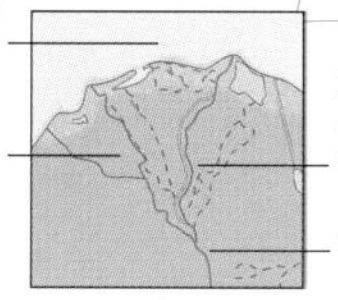

Mediterranean Sea
Fertile deposits of alluvium
Network of drainage channels
River Nile

In its northernmost reaches, the Nile River has deposited huge quantities of silt and alluvium to form the fan-shaped Nile Delta. The Nile splits into two main channels at the base of the delta which are interlinked by a dense network of canals and drainage channels.

The Sahara is the largest hot desert on Earth, covering nearly a third of Africa. The sandy parts of the desert contain a wide variety of sand dunes, created by differing wind directions and strengths.

***Almost all of Egypt's people** – more than 99% – live close to the Nile River, or on its massive delta. The river waters the only strip of fertile land in Egypt.*

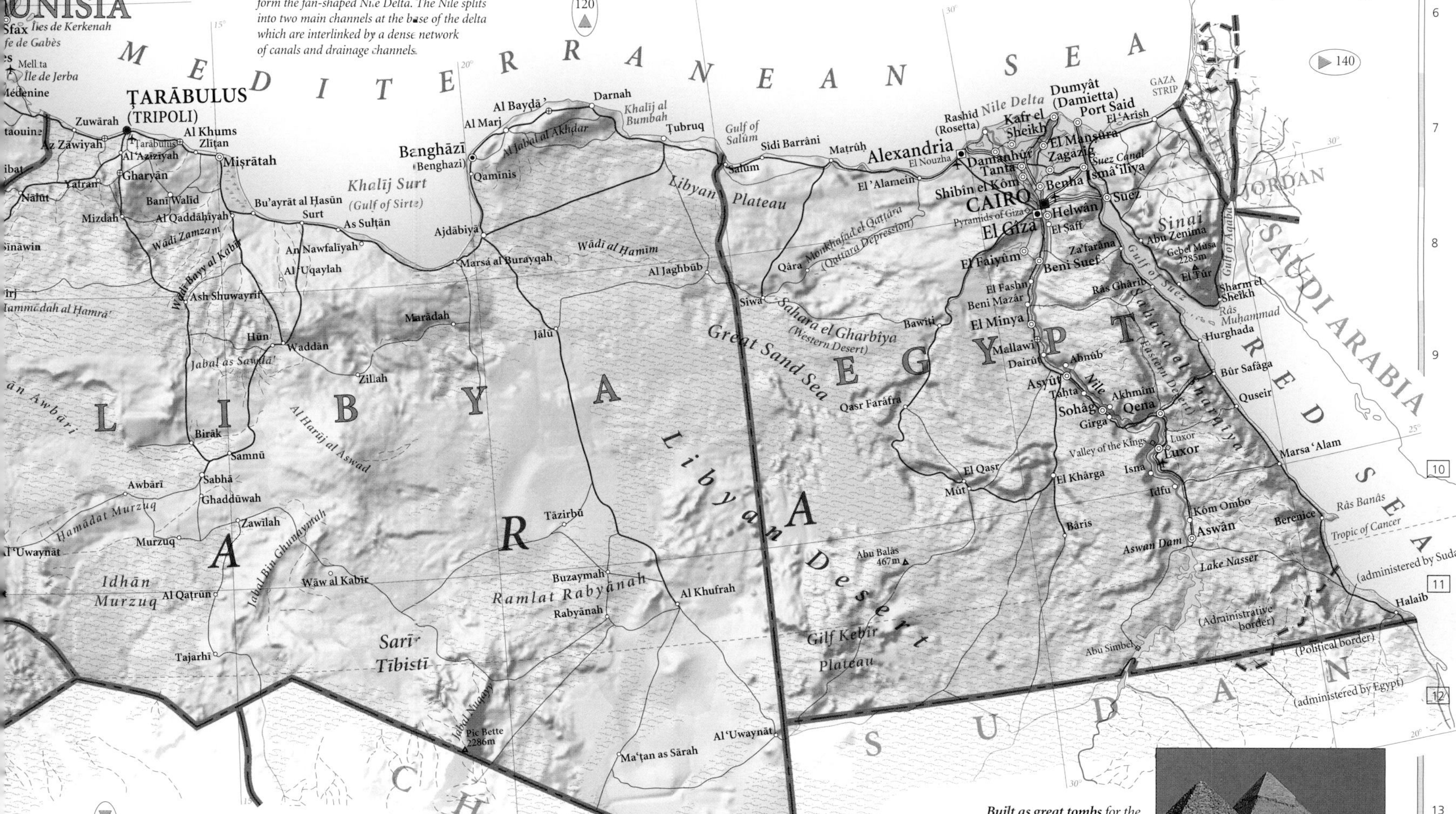

TUNISIA
Sfax
Mahdia
Sousse
Nabeul
Cap Bon
Golfe de Hammamet
Îles de Kerkenah
Golfe de Gabès
Île de Jerba
Médenine
MEDITERRANEAN SEA
ṬARĀBULUS (TRIPOLI)
Zuwārah
Az Zāwiyah
Al Khums
Zliṭan
Miṣrātah
Gharyān
Nālūt
Yafran
Mizdah
Bani Walīd
Al Qaddāḥīyah
Wādī Zamzam
Bu'ayrāt al Ḥasūn
Surt
Khalīj Surt (Gulf of Sirtz)
As Sulṭān
An Nawfalīyah
Al 'Uqaylah
Ash Shuwayrif
Hūn
Waddān
Jabal as Sawdā'
Zillah
Birāk
Samnū
Sabhā
Awbārī
Ghaddūwah
Zawilah
Murzuq
Hamādat Murzuq
Idhān Murzuq
Al Qaṭrūn
Tajarhī
Al 'Uwaynāt
Wāw al Kabīr
Al Harūj al Aswad
LIBYA
Banghāzī (Benghazi)
Al Bayḍā'
Darnah
Al Marj
Al Jabal al Akhḍar
Khalīj al Bumbah
Ṭubruq
Qaminis
Ajdābiyā
Marsá al Burayqah
Wādī al Hamim
Al Jaghbūb
Mārādah
Jālū
Tāzirbū
Buzaymah
Rabyānah
Ramlat Rabyānah
Al Khufrah
Sarīr Tībistī
Pic Bette 2286m
Ma'ṭan as Sārah
Al 'Uwaynāt
Gulf of Salûm
Salûm
Sîdi Barrâni
Matrûh
Libyan Plateau
Alexandria
El Nouzha
El 'Alamein
Qâra
Siwa
Munkhafad el Qaṭṭâra (Qattara Depression)
Sahara el Gharbîya (Western Desert)
Great Sand Sea
Libyan Desert
Qasr Farâfra
Bawiti
EGYPT
El Qasr
Mût
El Khârga
Bâris
Abu Ballâs 467m
Gilf Kebir Plateau
Abu Simbel
Rashîd (Rosetta)
Nile Delta
Dumyât (Damietta)
Port Said
El 'Arîsh
Kafr el Sheikh
Damanhûr
Tanta
El Mansûra
Zagazig
Suez Canal
Ismâ'ilîya
Shibîn el Kôm
Benha
CAIRO
Helwân
Pyramids of Giza
El Gîza
Suez
El Faiyûm
El Saff
Beni Suef
Za'farâna
Sinai
Gebel Mûsa 2285m
Gulf of Suez
Gulf of Aqaba
El Ṭûr
Râs Ghârib
Sharm el Sheikh
Râs Muhammad
El Fashn
Beni Mazâr
El Minya
Mallawi
Dairût
Abnûb
Asyût
Tahta
Akhmîm
Sohâg
Girga
Qena
Eastern Desert
Hurghada
Bûr Safâga
Quseir
Valley of the Kings
Luxor
Isna
Idfu
Kôm Ombo
Aswân
Aswan Dam
Lake Nasser
Marsa 'Alam
Berenice
Râs Banâs
Tropic of Cancer
Halaib
(administered by Sudan)
(Administrative border)
(Political border)
(administered by Egypt)
GAZA STRIP
JORDAN
SAUDI ARABIA
RED SEA
SUDAN
CHAD
120
140
76
78
80

***Built as great tombs** for the pharaohs of ancient Egypt, the magnificent pyramids at Giza near Cairo have fascinated scholars, archaeologists, and tourists for centuries.*

***Oil rigs are scattered** throughout the deserts of Libya and Algeria. Libyan oil is especially prized because of its low sulfur content, which means it produces much less pollution than other fuel oils.*

TRANSPORTATION & INDUSTRY

THE ECONOMIES OF ALGERIA AND LIBYA were transformed by the discovery of oil and natural gas reserves in the deserts. Morocco's major exports are phosphates and agricultural produce, and as in Egypt and Tunisia, the tourist industry is essential to the economy. Egypt has the most varied industrial base, importing technology to develop electronics and engineering industries, and maintaining the reputation of its high-quality cotton textiles.

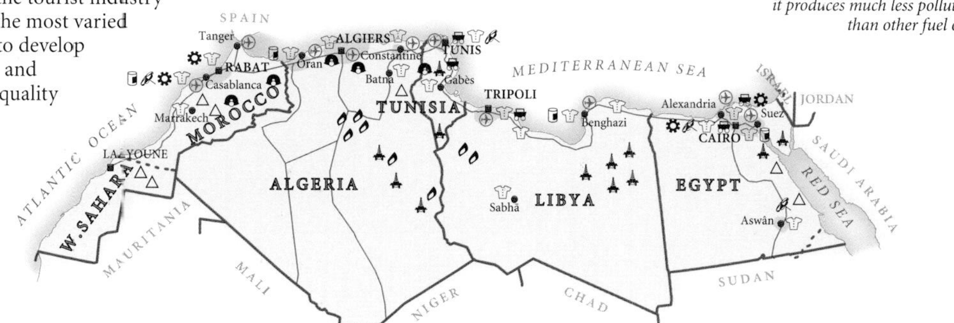

SPAIN
Tanger
RABAT
Casablanca
Marrakech
MOROCCO
LAÂYOUNE
W. SAHARA
ATLANTIC OCEAN
MAURITANIA
ALGIERS
Oran
Constantine
Batna
ALGERIA
TUNIS
Gabès
TUNISIA
MEDITERRANEAN SEA
TRIPOLI
Benghazi
Sabhā
LIBYA
Alexandria
CAIRO
Suez
Aswân
EGYPT
ISRAEL
JORDAN
SAUDI ARABIA
RED SEA
MALI
NIGER
CHAD
SUDAN

Major industry and infrastructure

- engineering
- food processing
- gas
- iron & steel
- iron ore
- oil
- phosphates
- textiles
- tourism
- capital cities
- major towns
- international airports
- major roads
- major industrial areas

TRANSPORTATION NETWORK

152,393 miles (245,400 km)	480 miles (773 km)
8025 miles (12,922 km)	121 miles (195 km)

Tourism and the oil industry have made improvements to the Maghreb's infrastructure both necessary and possible. The Suez Canal is a vital artery for shipping between Europe and Asia.

N O P Q R S T U V W X Y Z

West Africa

Benin, Burkina, Cape Verde, Gambia, Ghana, Guinea, Guinea-Bissau, Ivory Coast, Liberia, Mali, Mauritania, Niger, Nigeria, Senegal, Sierra Leone, Togo

West Africa is an immensely diverse region, encompassing the desert landscapes and mainly Muslim populations of the southern Saharan countries, and the tropical rain forests of the more humid south, with a great variety of local languages and cultures. The rich natural resources and accessibility of the area were quickly exploited by Europeans; most of the Africans taken by slave traders came from this region, causing serious depopulation. The very different influences of West Africa's leading colonial powers, Britain and France, remain today, reflected in the languages and institutions of the countries they once governed.

The dry scrub of the Sahel is only suitable for grazing herd animals like these cattle in Mali.

SCALE 1:10,000,000
(projection: Lambert Azimuth Equal Area)

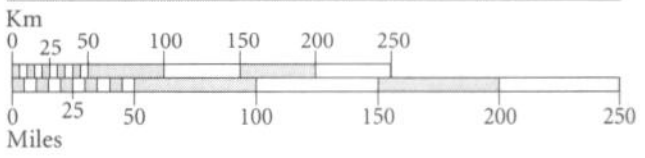
Km
0 25 50 100 150 200 250
0 25 50 100 150 200 250
Miles

Transportation & Industry

Abundant natural resources including oil and metallic minerals are found in much of West Africa, although investment is required for their further exploitation. Nigeria experienced an oil boom during the 1970s but subsequent growth has been sporadic. Most industry in other countries has a primary basis, including mining, logging, and food processing.

Transportation Network

163,769 miles (263,719 km)	1,554 miles (2,502 km)
6,819 miles (10,980 km)	9,470 miles (15,250 km)

The road and rail systems are most developed near the coasts. Some of the landlocked countries remain disadvantaged by the difficulty of access to ports, and their poor road networks.

MOROCCO
W. SAHARA
ALGERIA
LIBYA
CHAD
MAURITANIA
NOUAKCHOTT
MALI
NIGER
DAKAR
SENEGAL
BANJUL
GAMBIA
BISSAU
GUINEA-BISSAU
CONAKRY
GUINEA
BAMAKO
NIAMEY
BURKINA
OUAGADOUGOU
FREETOWN
SIERRA LEONE
MONROVIA
LIBERIA
IVORY COAST
YAMOUSSOUKRO
GHANA
ACCRA
TOGO
LOMÉ
BENIN
PORTO-NOVO
NIGERIA
ABUJA
Kano
Ibadan
Lagos
Port Harcourt
CAMEROON
ATLANTIC OCEAN

Major industry and infrastructure

- chemicals
- cotton spinning
- food processing
- mining
- oil
- palm oil processing
- peanut processing
- textiles
- vehicle manufacture
- capital cities
- major towns
- international airports
- major roads
- major industrial areas

Map Key

POPULATION

- 1 million to 5 million
- 500,000 to 1 million
- 100,000 to 500,000
- 50,000 to 100,000
- 10,000 to 50,000
- below 10,000

ELEVATION

- 2000m / 6562ft
- 1000m / 3281ft
- 500m / 1640ft
- 250m / 820ft
- 100m / 328ft
- sea level

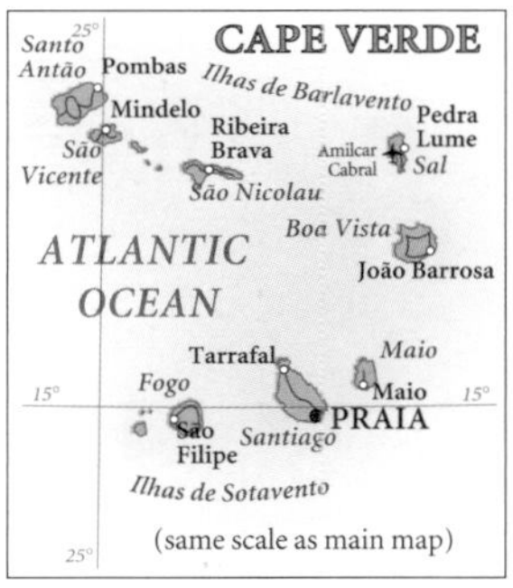
CAPE VERDE
Santo Antão
Pombas
Ilhas de Barlavento
Mindelo
São Vicente
Ribeira Brava
Amílcar Cabral
Pedra Lume
Sal
São Nicolau
Boa Vista
João Barrosa
ATLANTIC OCEAN
Tarrafal
Maio
Fogo
São Filipe
Santiago
PRAIA
Ilhas de Sotavento
(same scale as main map)

The southern regions of West Africa still contain great swaths of tropical rain forest, including some of the world's most prized hardwood trees, such as mahogany and iroko.

Using the Land and Sea

The humid southern regions are most suitable for cultivation; in these areas, cash crops such as coffee, cotton, cocoa, and rubber are grown in large quantities. Peanuts are grown throughout West Africa. In the north, advancing desertification has made the Sahel increasingly uncultivable, and pastoral farming is more common. Great herds of sheep, cattle, and goats are grazed on the savannah grasses. Fishing is important in coastal and delta areas.

The Gambia, mainland Africa's smallest country, produces great quantities of peanuts. Winnowing is used to separate the nuts from their stalks.

MOROCCO
W. SAHARA
ALGERIA
SAHARA
LIBYA
CHAD
MAURITANIA
NOUAKCHOTT
MALI
NIGER
DAKAR
SENEGAL
BANJUL
GAMBIA
BISSAU
GUINEA-BISSAU
CONAKRY
GUINEA
BAMAKO
NIAMEY
BURKINA
OUAGADOUGOU
FREETOWN
SIERRA LEONE
MONROVIA
LIBERIA
IVORY COAST
YAMOUSSOUKRO
GHANA
ACCRA
TOGO
LOMÉ
BENIN
PORTO-NOVO
NIGERIA
ABUJA
Lagos
CAMEROON
ATLANTIC OCEAN

Land use and agricultural distribution

- goats
- sheep
- cocoa
- coffee
- cotton
- oil palms
- peanuts
- rubber
- shellfish
- capital cities
- major towns
- pasture
- cropland
- forest
- desert

The Urban/Rural Population Divide

urban 36% rural 64%

Population Density	Total Land Area
98 people per sq mile (38 people per sq km)	2,337,137 sq miles (6,054,760 sq km)

WESTERN SAHARA
(occupied by Morocco)
Tropic of Cancer
Aïn Ben Tili
Bir Mogreïn
Yetti
'Ayoûn 'Abd el Mâlek
TIRIS ZEMMOUR
Kâghet
El Mreiti
Zouérat
Fdérik
El Hammâmi
Tourine
Touâjîl
Maqteïr
Erg
El Mrâyer
Râs Nouâdhibou
Boû Lanouâr
Nouâdhibou
Dakhlet Nouâdhibou
DAKHLET NOUÂDHIBOU
Azeffâl
Choum
Ouadâne
Ouarâne
Akchâr
Atâr
Chinguetti
ADRAR
INCHIRI
Et Tidra
Akjoujt
Oujeft
Râs Timirist
Bennichchâb
Nouâmghâr
El Mreyyé
ATLANTIC OCEAN
MAURITANIA
Rachîd
Tidjikja
TAGANT
Tîchît
Sebkhet Te-n-Dghâmcha
TRARZA
NOUAKCHOTT
Aoukâr
HODH ECH CHARGUI
Boutilimit
Moudjéria
Mâgta' Lahjar
BRAKNA
Aleg
Boûmdeïd
Tîguent
Rkîz
Mederdra
Tâmchekket
Oualâta
Rosso
Bogué
Guérou
Kiffa
HODH EL GHARBI
Ayoûn el 'Atroûs
Néma
Richard Toll
Podor
Dagana
Lac de Guier
Saint Louis
Babâbé
Kaédi
Mbout
ASSABA
Kankossa
Kobenni
Tîmbedgha
Amourj
GORGOL
Sélibabi
GUIDIMAKA
Ould Yenjé
Louga
Kébémer
Linguère
Matam
Ranérou
Mékhé
Tivaouane
DAKAR
Thiès
Rufisque
Touba
Mbaké
Bambey
Diourbel
Fatick
Kaolack
SENEGAL
Mbour
Joal-Fadiout
Sokone
Kaffrine
Koungheul
Saloum
Nioro du Rip
BANJUL
GAMBIA
Brikama
Georgetown
Basse Santa Su
Tambacounda
Dialakoto
Bakel
Kidira
Goudiri
Ambidédi
Kayes
Yélimané
Nioro
Nara
Diéma
Mourdiah
KAYES
KOULIKORO
Diouloulou
Ziguinchor
Bignona
Kolda
Vélingara
Médina Gounas
Sédhiou
Bafoulabé
Diamou
Sadiola
Toukoto
Kita
Kolokani
Banamba
GUINEA-BISSAU
Bissau
BISSAU
Quinhámel
Farim
Cacheu
Bissorã
Mansôa
Bafatá
Gabú
Fulacunda
Bolama
Buba
Catió
Arquipélago dos Bijagós
Koundara
Kédougou
Mali
Labé
Pita
Fouta Djallon
Tougué
MOYENNE-GUINÉE
Kéniéba
Satadougou
Kokofata
Niagassola
BAMAKO
Ouéléssébougou
Boké
GUINÉE-MARITIME
Kamsar
Télimélé
Dalaba
Kindia
Fria
Boffa
Mamou
HAUTE-GUINÉE
Dabola
Dinguiraye
Siguiri
Kouroussa
Kangaba
Doko
Yanfolila
Bougouni
SIKASSO
Cap Verga
GUINEA
Kankan
Faranah
Dubréka
Coyah
Forécariah
CONAKRY
Kabala
Tokounou
Kérouané
Mandiana
Manankoro
Kambia
Makeni
Port Loko
Lungi
Pepel
Lunsar
Magburaka
Koidu
FREETOWN
SIERRA LEONE
Moyamba
Shenge
Bo
Kenema
Sherbro Island
Bonthe
Pujehun
Kailahun
Macenta
Guéckédou
GUINÉE FORESTIÈRE
Nzérékoré
Yomou
Lola
Beyla
Boola
Sulima
Robertsport
Tubmanburg
Kakata
Gbanga
Ganta
Sanniquellie
Danané
MONROVIA
Monrovia
Marshall
Harbel
LIBERIA
Buchanan
Zwedru
River Cess
Greenville
Grand Cess
Harper
Tabou
Cape Palmas
ATLANTIC OCEAN
IVOR

N O P Q R S T U V W X Y

The Landscape

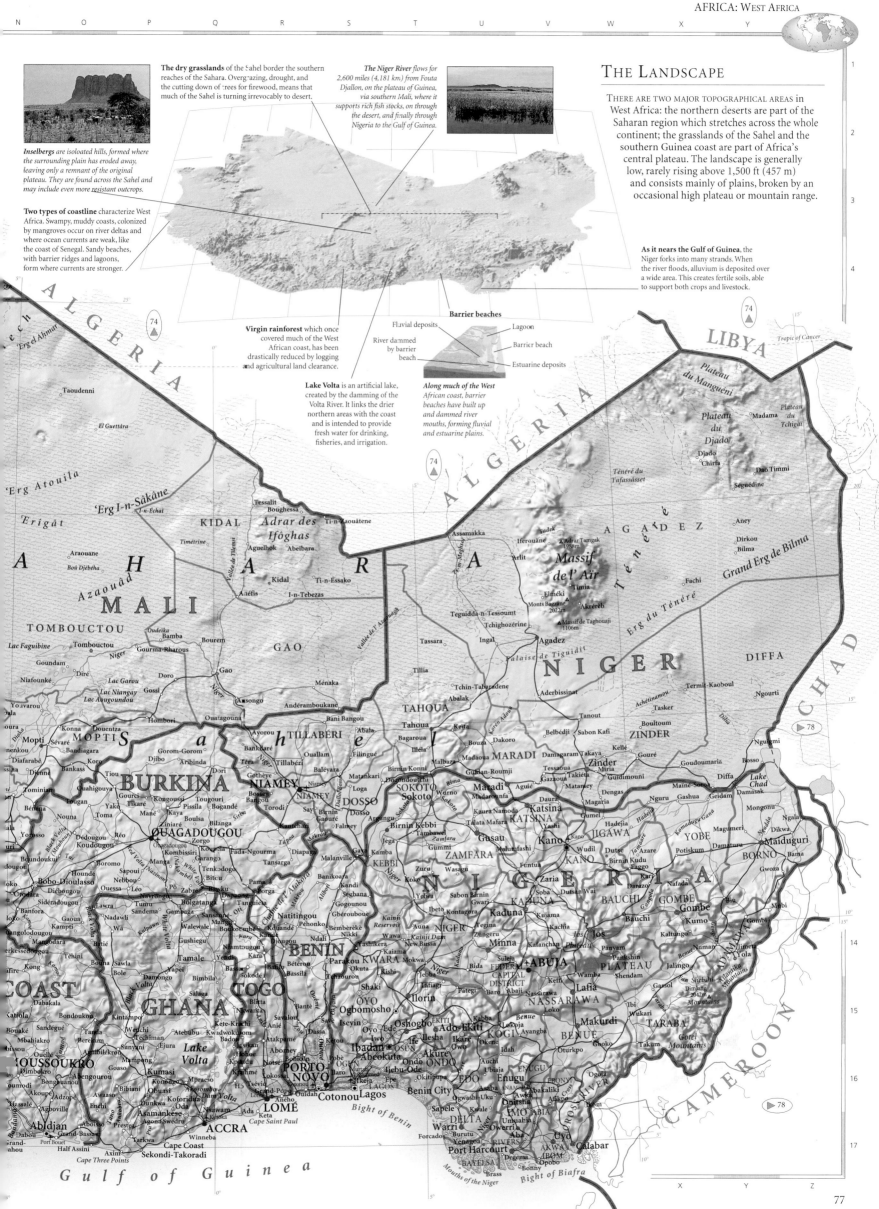

There are two major topographical areas in West Africa: the northern deserts are part of the Saharan region which stretches across the whole continent; the grasslands of the Sahel and the southern Guinea coast are part of Africa's central plateau. The landscape is generally low, rarely rising above 1,500 ft (457 m) and consists mainly of plains, broken by an occasional high plateau or mountain range.

***Inselbergs** are isoloated hills, formed where the surrounding plain has eroded away, leaving only a remnant of the original plateau. They are found across the Sahel and may include even more resistant outcrops.*

The dry grasslands of the Sahel border the southern reaches of the Sahara. Overgrazing, drought, and the cutting down of trees for firewood, means that much of the Sahel is turning irrevocably to desert.

***The Niger River** flows for 2,600 miles (4,181 km) from Fouta Djallon, on the plateau of Guinea, via southern Mali, where it supports rich fish stocks, on through the desert, and finally through Nigeria to the Gulf of Guinea.*

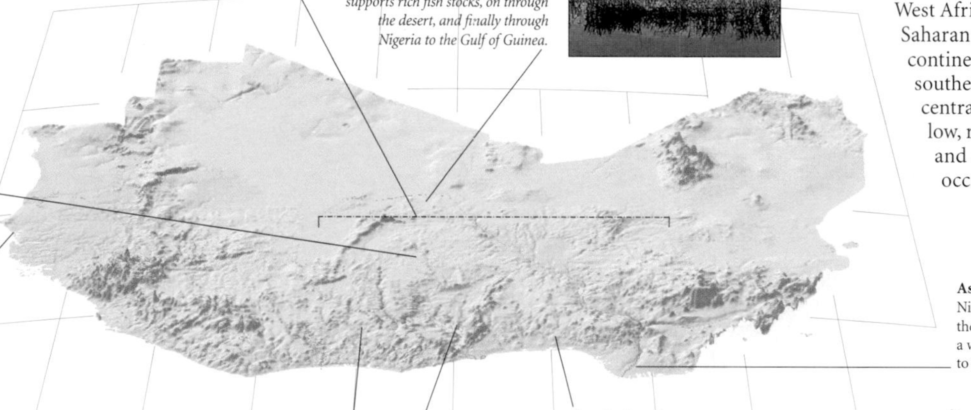

Two types of coastline characterize West Africa. Swampy, muddy coasts, colonized by mangroves occur on river deltas and where ocean currents are weak, like the coast of Senegal. Sandy beaches, with barrier ridges and lagoons, form where currents are stronger.

As it nears the Gulf of Guinea, the Niger forks into many strands. When the river floods, alluvium is deposited over a wide area. This creates fertile soils, able to support both crops and livestock.

Virgin rainforest which once covered much of the West African coast, has been drastically reduced by logging and agricultural land clearance.

Lake Volta is an artificial lake, created by the damming of the Volta River. It links the drier northern areas with the coast and is intended to provide fresh water for drinking, fisheries, and irrigation.

Barrier beaches

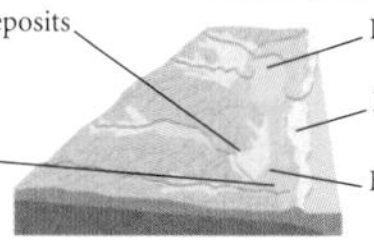
Fluvial deposits
River dammed by barrier beach
Lagoon
Barrier beach
Estuarine deposits

***Along much of the West** African coast, barrier beaches have built up and dammed river mouths, forming fluvial and estuarine plains.*

ALGERIA
LIBYA
CHAD
CAMEROON
MALI
NIGER
NIGERIA
BURKINA
BENIN
TOGO
GHANA
COAST
Tropic of Cancer
Plateau du Manguéni
Plateau du Djado
Ténéré du Tafassâsset
AGADEZ
Massif de l'Aïr
Ténéré
Grand Erg de Bilma
Erg du Ténéré
DIFFA
ZINDER
MARADI
TAHOUA
TILLABÉRI
NIAMEY
DOSSO
Adrar des Ifôghas
KIDAL
GAO
TOMBOUCTOU
MOPTI
Azaouâd
'Erg Atouila
'Erg I-n-Sâkâne
Taoudenni
Tombouctou
Gao
Kidal
Agadez
Zinder
Maradi
Tahoua
Niamey
OUAGADOUGOU
Bobo-Dioulasso
Sokoto
Katsina
Kano
Maiduguri
Kaduna
Zaria
Jos
Bauchi
Gombe
ABUJA
Ilorin
Ogbomosho
Oshogbo
Ibadan
Abeokuta
Lagos
PORTO NOVO
Cotonou
LOMÉ
ACCRA
Kumasi
Tamale
Lake Volta
Abidjan
Sekondi-Takoradi
Cape Coast
Benin City
Enugu
Onitsha
Port Harcourt
Calabar
Makurdi
Lake Chad
Kainji Reservoir
Jos Plateau
Bight of Benin
Bight of Biafra
Mouths of the Niger
Gulf of Guinea
Cape Three Points
Cape Saint Paul

74
78

Central Africa

Cameroon, Central African Republic, Chad, Congo, Dem. Rep. Congo, Equatorial Guinea, Gabon, Sao Tome & Principe

The great rain forest basin of the Congo River embraces most of remote Central Africa. The interior was largely unknown to Europeans until late in the 19th century, when its tribal kingdoms were split – principally between France and Belgium – with Sao Tome and Principe the lone Portuguese territory, and Equatorial Guinea controlled by Spain. Open democracy and regional economic integration are important goals for these nations – several of which have only recently emerged from restrictive regimes – and investment is needed to improve transportation infrastructures. Many of the small, but fast-growing and increasingly urban population, speak French, the regional *lingua franca*, along with several hundred Pygmy, Bantu, and Sudanic dialects.

The Landscape

Lake Chad lies in a desert basin bounded by the volcanic Tibesti Mountains in the north, plateaus in the east and, in the south, the broad watershed of the Congo Basin. The vast circular depression of the Congo is isolated from the coastal plain by the granite Massif du Chaillu. To the northwest, the volcanoes and fold mountains of the Cameroon Ridge *(Dorsale Camerounaise)* extend as islands into the Gulf of Guinea. The high fold mountains fringing the east of the Congo Basin fall steeply to the lakes of the Great Rift Valley.

A plug of resistant lava, at the southwestern end of the Cameroon Ridge (Dorsale Camerounaise), is all that remains of an eroded volcano.

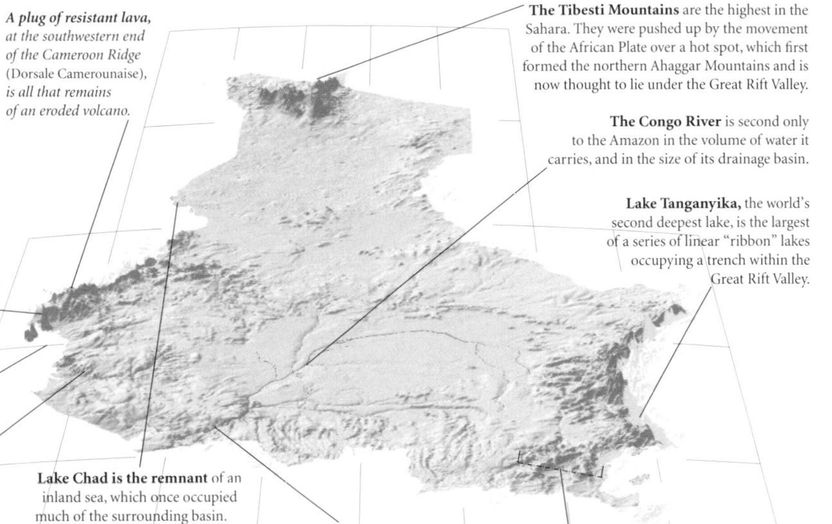

The Tibesti Mountains are the highest in the Sahara. They were pushed up by the movement of the African Plate over a hot spot, which first formed the northern Ahaggar Mountains and is now thought to lie under the Great Rift Valley.
The Congo River is second only to the Amazon in the volume of water it carries, and in the size of its drainage basin.
Lake Tanganyika, the world's second deepest lake, is the largest of a series of linear "ribbon" lakes occupying a trench within the Great Rift Valley.
The volcanic massif of Cameroon Mountain occupies an area which remains volcanically active.
Gulf of Guinea
Massif du Chaillu
Lake Chad is the remnant of an inland sea, which once occupied much of the surrounding basin. A series of droughts since the 1970s has reduced the area of this shallow freshwater lake to about 1,000 sq miles (2,599 sq km).
The lake-like expansion of the Congo River at Stanley Pool is the lowest point of the interior basin, although the river still descends more than 1,000 ft (300 m) to reach the sea.
Rich mineral deposits in the "Copper Belt" of Dem. Rep. Congo were formed under intense heat and pressure when the ancient African Shield was uplifted to form the region's mountains.

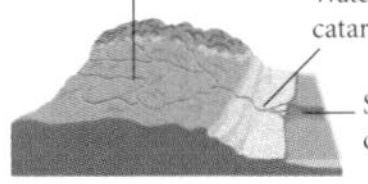

Broad, shallow basin
Waterfalls and cataracts
Submarine canyon

The Congo River flows sluggishly through the rain forest of the interior basin. Toward the coast, the river drops steeply in a series of waterfalls and cataracts. At this point, the erosional power of the river becomes so great that it has formed a deep submarine canyon offshore.

***Virgin tropical rain forest** covers the Ruwenzori range on the borders of Dem. Rep. Congo and Uganda.*

Transportation & Industry

Large reserves of valuable minerals are found in Central Africa: copper, cobalt, zinc, and tin are mined in Dem. Rep. Congo and Cameroon; diamonds in the Central African Republic, and manganese in Gabon. Congo, Cameroon, Gabon, and Dem. Rep. Congo have oil deposits and oil has also been recently discovered in Chad. Goods such as palm oil and rubber are processed for export.

***The ancient rocks** of Dem. Rep. Congo hold immense and varied mineral reserves. This open pit copper mine is at Kolwezi in the far south.*

LIBYA
NIGER
SUDAN
CHAD
NDJAMENA
NIGERIA
CAMEROON
CENTRAL AFRICAN REPUBLIC
BANGUI
Douala
YAOUNDÉ
MALABO
EQ. GUINEA
SAO TOME & PRINCIPE
LIBREVILLE
Port-Gentil
GABON
CONGO
BRAZZAVILLE
KINSHASA
DEM. REP. CONGO
Kisangani
Bukavu
Kananga
UGANDA
RWANDA
BURUNDI
TANZANIA
ANGOLA (CABINDA)
ANGOLA
Kolwezi
Lubumbashi
ZAMBIA
ATLANTIC OCEAN

Major industry and infrastructure
- brewing
- chemicals
- cobalt
- copper
- diamonds
- food processing
- manganese
- oil
- palm oil processing
- textiles
- tin
- capital cities
- major towns
- international airports
- major roads
- major industrial areas

Transportation Network

124,349 miles (200,240 km)	342 miles (550 km)
3,830 miles (6,167 km)	15,261 miles (24,575 km)

The Trans-Gabon railroad, which began operating in 1987, has opened up new sources of timber and manganese. Elsewhere, much investment is needed to update and improve road, rail, and water transportation.

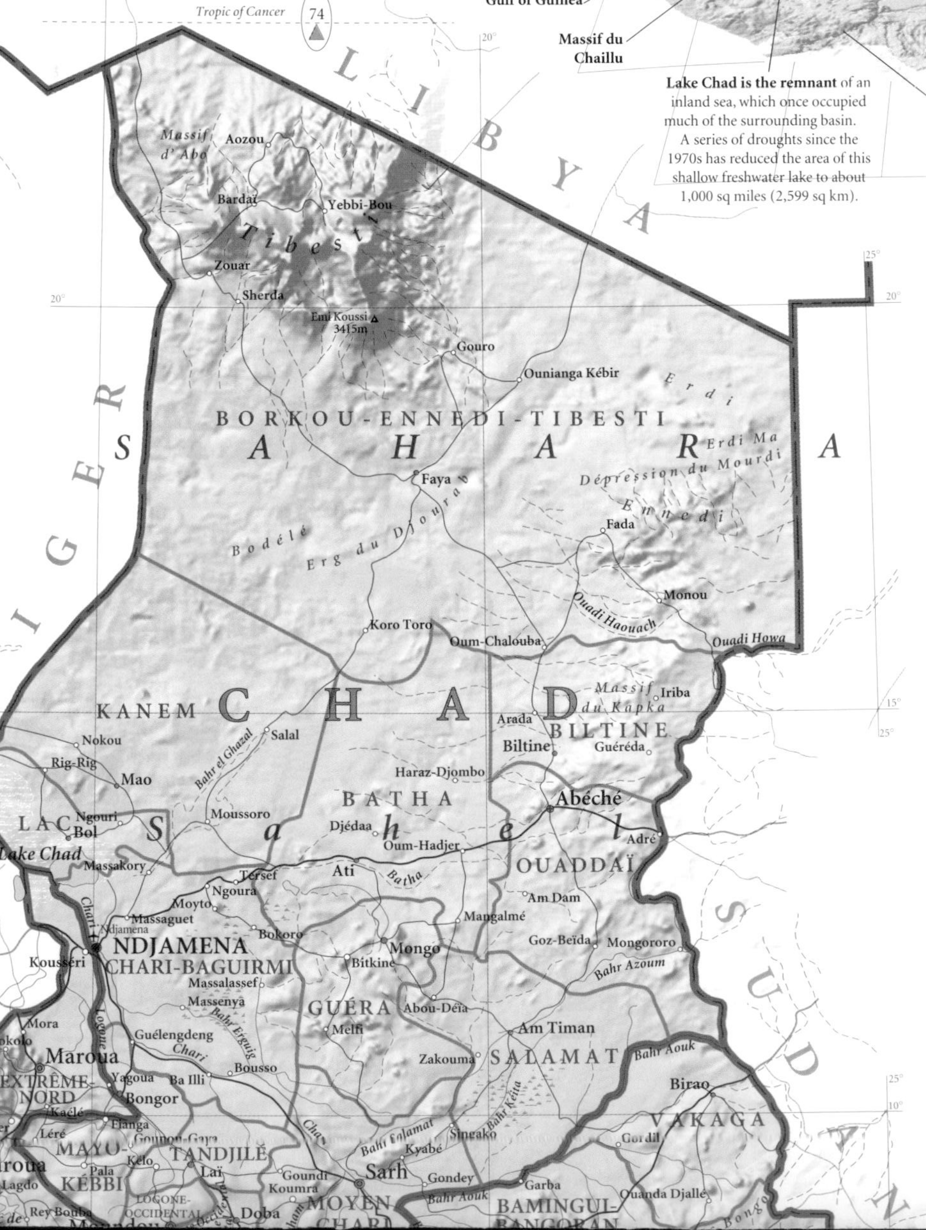

Tropic of Cancer
74
LIBYA
NIGER
SUDAN
CHAD
SAHARA
Sahel
Massif d'Abo
Aozou
Bardaï
Yebbi-Bou
Tibesti
Zouar
Sherda
Emi Koussi 3415m
Gouro
Ounianga Kébir
BORKOU-ENNEDI-TIBESTI
Erdi
Erdi Ma
Dépression du Mourdi
Ennedi
Faya
Fada
Bodélé
Erg du Djourab
Monou
Koro Toro
Oum-Chalouba
Ouadi Haouach
Ouadi Howa
KANEM
Nokou
Salal
Rig-Rig
Mao
Massif du Kapka
Iriba
Arada
Biltine
BILTINE
Guéréda
Haraz-Djombo
BATHA
Abéché
LAC
Ngouri
Bol
Lake Chad
Moussoro
Djédaa
Oum-Hadjer
Adré
OUADDAÏ
Massakory
Ati
Am Dam
Tersef
Ngoura
Moyto
Massaguet
Mangalmé
Bokoro
Goz-Beïda
Mongororo
Kousséri
NDJAMENA
CHARI-BAGUIRMI
Bitkine
Mongo
Massalassef
Massenya
GUÉRA
Abou-Déïa
Am Timan
Mora
Mokolo
Maroua
Guélengdeng
Melfi
Zakouma
SALAMAT
EXTRÊME-NORD
Yagoua
Ba Illi
Bousso
Bongor
Birao
Guider
Garoua
Lagdo
Poli
MAYO-KEBBI
TANDJILÉ
Laï
Kélo
Goundi
Koumra
Sarh
Gondey
Kyabé
VAKAGA
Doba
MOYEN-CHARI
BAMINGUI-BANGORAN
Garba
Ouanda Djallé
76

***The vast sandflats** surrounding Lake Chad were once covered by water. Changing climatic patterns caused the lake to shrink, and desert now covers much of its previous area.*

Map Key

Population
- 1 million to 5 million
- 500,000 to 1 million
- 100,000 to 500,000
- 50,000 to 100,000
- 10,000 to 50,000
- below 10,000

Elevation
- 4000m / 13,124ft
- 3000m / 9843ft
- 2000m / 6562ft
- 1000m / 3281ft
- 500m / 1640ft
- 250m / 820ft
- 100m / 328ft
- sea level

Scale 1:10,500,000
(projection: Lambert Azimuthal Equal Area)

Km 0 25 50 100 150 200 250
Miles 0 25 50 100 150 200 250

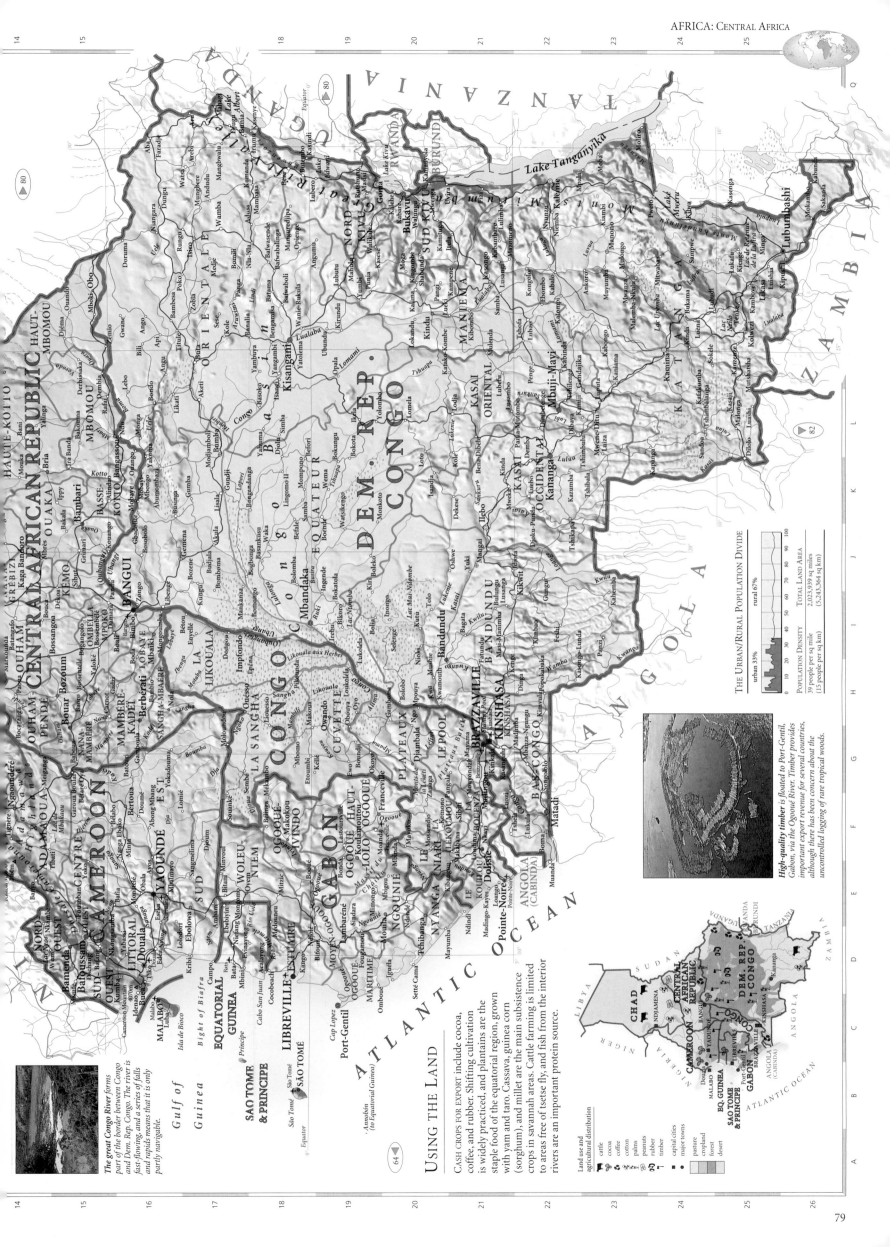

The great Congo River forms part of the border between Congo and Dem. Rep. Congo. The river is fast-flowing, and a series of falls and rapids means that it is only partly navigable.

CENTRAL AFRICAN REPUBLIC
CAMEROON
EQUATORIAL GUINEA
SAO TOME & PRINCIPE
GABON
CONGO
DEM. REP. CONGO
ANGOLA (CABINDA)
ANGOLA
ZAMBIA
TANZANIA
UGANDA
RWANDA
BURUNDI
ATLANTIC OCEAN
Gulf of Guinea
Bight of Biafra
BANGUI
YAOUNDÉ
MALABO
LIBREVILLE
SÃO TOMÉ
BRAZZAVILLE
KINSHASA
Douala
Port-Gentil
Pointe-Noire
Matadi
Mbandaka
Kisangani
Kananga
Mbuji-Mayi
Lubumbashi
Lake Tanganyika
Lake Kivu
Lake Albert
Lake Edward
Lake Mweru
Equator
64
80
82

USING THE LAND

CASH CROPS FOR EXPORT include cocoa, coffee, and rubber. Shifting cultivation is widely practiced, and plantains are the staple food of the equatorial region, grown with yam and taro. Cassava, guinea corn (sorghum), and millet are the main subsistence crops in savannah areas. Cattle farming is limited to areas free of tsetse fly, and fish from the interior rivers are an important protein source.

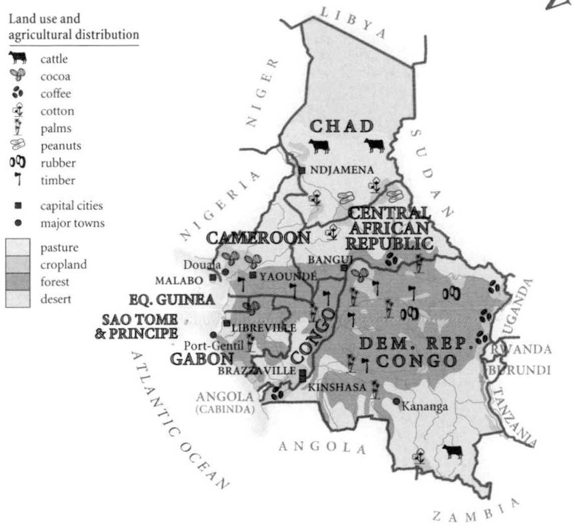

Land use and agricultural distribution
cattle
cocoa
coffee
cotton
palms
peanuts
rubber
timber
capital cities
major towns
pasture
cropland
forest
desert
CHAD
NDJAMENA
CAMEROON
CENTRAL AFRICAN REPUBLIC
BANGUI
YAOUNDÉ
Douala
MALABO
EQ. GUINEA
SAO TOME & PRINCIPE
LIBREVILLE
Port-Gentil
GABON
CONGO
BRAZZAVILLE
KINSHASA
DEM. REP. CONGO
Kananga
ANGOLA (CABINDA)
ANGOLA
ZAMBIA
TANZANIA
UGANDA
RWANDA
BURUNDI
LIBYA
NIGER
NIGERIA
SUDAN
ATLANTIC OCEAN

High-quality timber is floated to Port-Gentil, Gabon, via the Ogooué River. Timber provides important export revenue for several countries, although there has been concern about the uncontrolled logging of rare tropical woods.

THE URBAN/RURAL POPULATION DIVIDE

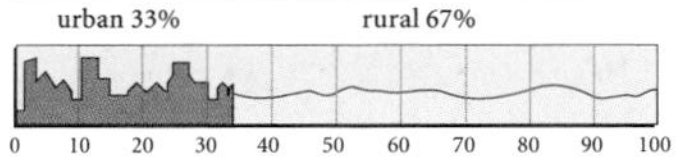

urban 33%
rural 67%
0
10
20
30
40
50
60
70
80
90
100

POPULATION DENSITY	TOTAL LAND AREA
39 people per sq mile (15 people per sq km)	2,023,939 sq miles (5,243,364 sq km)

East Africa

Burundi, Djibouti, Eritrea, Ethiopia, Kenya, Rwanda, Somalia, Sudan, Tanzania, Uganda

The countries of East Africa divide into two distinct cultural regions. Sudan and the "Horn" nations have been influenced by the Middle East; Ethiopia was the home of one of the earliest Christian civilizations, and Sudan reflects both Muslim and Christian influences. The southern countries share a closer cultural affinity with other sub-Saharan nations. Some of Africa's most densely populated countries lie in this region, and the needs of a growing number of people have put pressure on marginal lands and fragile environments. Although most East African economies remain strongly agricultural, Kenya has developed a varied industrial base.

The Landscape

East Africa's most significant landscape feature is the Great Rift Valley, which formed during the most recent phase of continental movement when the rigid basement rocks cracked and buckled. Great blocks of land were raised and lowered, creating huge flat-bottomed valleys and steep escarpments, sometimes covered by volcanic extrusions in highland areas.

This dome at Gonder, in Ethiopia, is a volcanic intrusion, formed when molten rock pushed up the surface of the Earth and then solidified, leaving an outcrop of igneous rock.

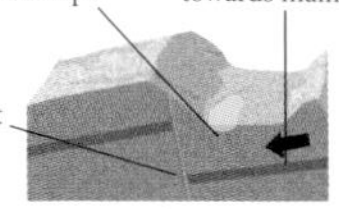
Ephemeral lake forms at far edge of slope
Central block slopes towards main fault
Boundary fault

The eastern arm of the Great Rift Valley is gradually being pulled apart; however the forces on one side are greater than the other causing the land to slope. This affects regional drainage which migrates down the slope.

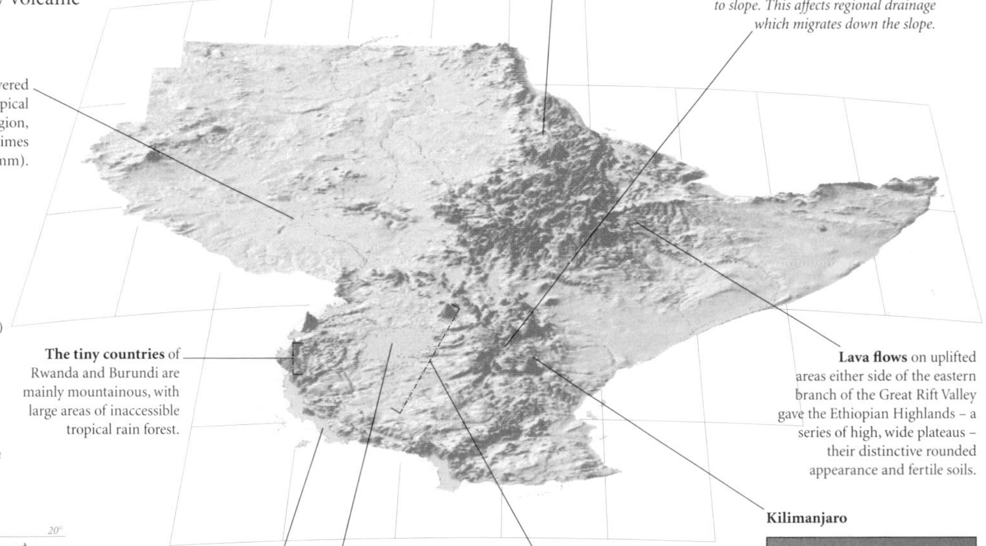

Much of northern Sudan is covered by desert. However, in the tropical wetlands of the southern Sudd region, annual rainfall can sometimes exceed 40 inches (1,000 mm).

The tiny countries of Rwanda and Burundi are mainly mountainous, with large areas of inaccessible tropical rain forest.

Lava flows on uplifted areas either side of the eastern branch of the Great Rift Valley gave the Ethiopian Highlands – a series of high, wide plateaus – their distinctive rounded appearance and fertile soils.

Lake Tanganyika lies 8,202 ft (2,500 m) above sea level. It has a depth of nearly 4,700 ft (1,435 m). The lake traces the valley floor for some 400 miles (644 km) of the western arm of the Great Rift Valley.

Lake Victoria occupies a vast basin between the two arms of the Great Rift Valley. It is the world's second largest lake in terms of surface area, extending 26,560 sq miles (68,880 sq km). The lake contains numerous islands and coral reefs.

A vast plateau lies between the eastern and western rift valleys in Kenya, Uganda, and western Tanzania. It has been leveled by long periods of erosion to form a peneplain, but is dotted with inselbergs – outcrops of more resistant rocks.

Kilimanjaro

An extinct volcano, Kilimanjaro is Africa's highest mountain, rising 19,340 ft (5,895 m). It is one of the few places in Africa where snow settles, allowing glacier ice to form.

The Kassala region in eastern Sudan is watered by the Atbara River, an important tributary of the Nile. Most of the population is engaged in agriculture, growing cotton and cereals.

EGYPT
LIBYA
CHAD
SUDAN
ERITREA
ETHIOPIA
DJIBOUTI
YEMEN
RED SEA
Gulf of Aden
Libyan Desert
Nubian Desert
Lake Nasser
Wadi Halfa
KHARTOUM
Omdurman
Khartoum North
Port Sudan
Suakin
Kassala
ASMARA
Massawa
Atbara
Wad Medani
El Obeid
Gedaref
Gonder
Bahir Dar
Dire Dawa
Harer
Hargeysa
Berbera
Burco
ADIS ABEBA
Nyala
El Fasher
El Geneina
Malakal
Dahlak Archipelago
(administered by Egypt)
(administered by Sudan)
(Administrative border)
(Political border)
74
78
140

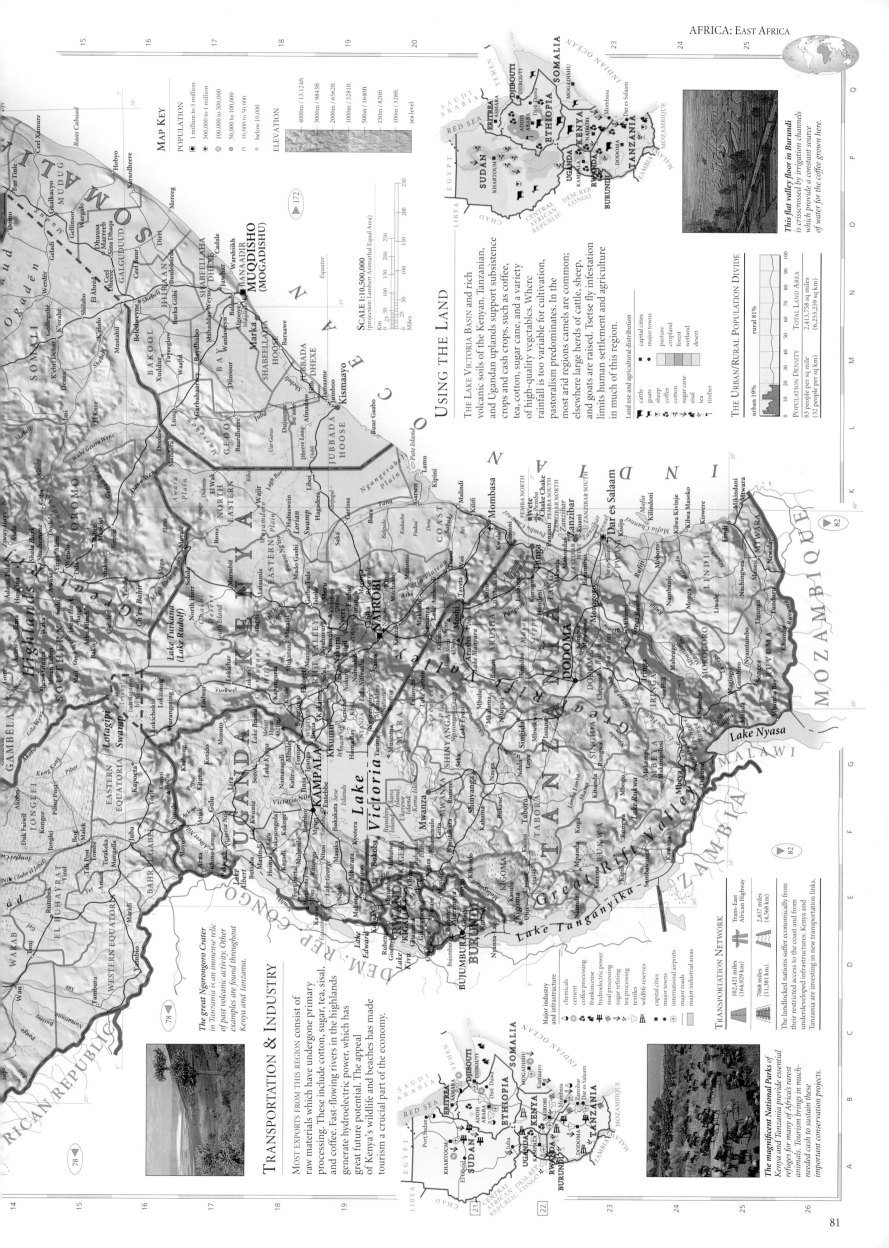

UGANDA
KENYA
TANZANIA
SOMALIA
DEM. REP. CONGO
ZAMBIA
MOZAMBIQUE
MALAWI
Lake Victoria
Lake Turkana (Lake Rudolf)
Lake Tanganyika
Lake Nyasa
Great Rift Valley
INDIAN OCEAN
KAMPALA
NAIROBI
DODOMA
MUQDISHO (MOGADISHU)
BUJUMBURA
KIGALI
Mombasa
Dar es Salaam
Zanzibar
Kismaayo
Equator
SCALE 1:10,500,000
(projection: Lambert Azimuthal Equal Area)
MAP KEY
POPULATION
1 million to 5 million
500,000 to 1 million
100,000 to 500,000
50,000 to 100,000
10,000 to 50,000
below 10,000
ELEVATION
4000m / 13,124ft
3000m / 9843ft
2000m / 6562ft
1000m / 3281ft
500m / 1640ft
250m / 820ft
100m / 328ft
sea level

78

The great Ngorongoro Crater in Tanzania is an immense relic of past volcanic activity. Other examples are found throughout Kenya and Tanzania.

Transportation & Industry

Most exports from this region consist of raw materials which have undergone primary processing. These include cotton, sugar, tea, sisal, and coffee. Fast-flowing rivers in the highlands generate hydroelectric power, which has great future potential. The appeal of Kenya's wildlife and beaches has made tourism a crucial part of the economy.

SUDAN
ERITREA
DJIBOUTI
ETHIOPIA
SOMALIA
UGANDA
KENYA
RWANDA
BURUNDI
TANZANIA
INDIAN OCEAN

Major industry and infrastructure
- chemicals
- cement
- coffee processing
- frankincense
- hydroelectric power
- sisal processing
- sugar refining
- tea processing
- textiles
- wildlife reserves
- capital cities
- major towns
- international airports
- major roads
- major industrial areas

The magnificent National Parks of Kenya and Tanzania provide essential refuges for many of Africa's rarest animals. Tourism brings in much-needed cash to sustain these important conservation projects.

Transportation Network

102,421 miles (164,929 km)	Trans-East African Highway
7068 miles (11,381 km)	2,837 miles (4,568 km)

The landlocked nations suffer economically from their restricted access to the coast and from underdeveloped infrastructures. Kenya and Tanzania are investing in new transportation links.

82

Using the Land

The Lake Victoria Basin and rich volcanic soils of the Kenyan, Tanzanian, and Ugandan uplands support subsistence crops and cash crops, such as coffee, tea, cotton, sugar cane, and a variety of high-quality vegetables. Where rainfall is too variable for cultivation, pastoralism predominates. In the most arid regions camels are common; elsewhere large herds of cattle, sheep, and goats are raised. Tsetse fly infestation limits human settlement and agriculture in much of this region.

Land use and agricultural distribution
- cattle
- goats
- sheep
- coffee
- cotton
- sugar cane
- sisal
- tea
- timber
- capital cities
- major towns
- pasture
- cropland
- forest
- wetland
- desert

SUDAN
ERITREA
DJIBOUTI
ETHIOPIA
SOMALIA
UGANDA
KENYA
RWANDA
BURUNDI
TANZANIA
INDIAN OCEAN

The Urban/Rural Population Divide

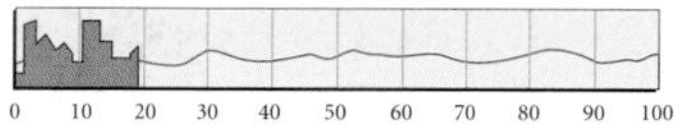
urban 19%
rural 81%

Population Density	Total Land Area
83 people per sq mile (32 people per sq km)	2,413,758 sq miles (6,253,259 sq km)

This flat valley floor in Burundi is crisscrossed by irrigation channels which provide a constant source of water for the coffee grown here.

172
82

Southern Africa

Angola, Botswana, Lesotho, Malawi, Mozambique, Namibia, South Africa, Swaziland, Zambia, Zimbabwe

Africa's vast southern plateau has been a contested homeland for disparate peoples for many centuries. The European incursion began with the slave trade and quickened in the 19th century, when the discovery of enormous mineral wealth secured South Africa's regional economic dominance. The struggle against white minority rule led to strife in Namibia, Zimbabwe, and the former Portuguese territories of Angola and Mozambique. South Africa's notorious apartheid laws, which denied basic human rights to more than 75% of the people, led to the state being internationally ostracized until 1994, when the first fully democratic elections inaugurated a new era of racial justice.

Transportation & Industry

South Africa, the world's largest exporter of gold, has a varied economy which generates about 75% of the region's income and draws migrant labor from neighboring states. Angola exports petroleum; Botswana and Namibia rely on diamond mining; and Zambia is seeking to diversify its economy to compensate for declining copper reserves.

Almost all new mining ventures in Zimbabwe are now subject to government control. This mine at Bindura in northeastern Zimbabwe produces nickel, one of the country's top three minerals in terms of economic value.

DEM. REP. CONGO
TANZANIA
LUANDA
Lobito
ANGOLA
ZAMBIA
Ndola
LUSAKA
MALAWI
LILONGWE
Blantyre
HARARE
MOZAMBIQUE
ZIMBABWE
Bulawayo
Beira
NAMIBIA
WINDHOEK
Walvis Bay
BOTSWANA
GABORONE
PRETORIA
MAPUTO
Johannesburg
MBABANE
SWAZILAND
MASERU
LESOTHO
Durban
S. AFRICA
CAPE TOWN
Port Elizabeth
ATLANTIC OCEAN
INDIAN OCEAN

Major industry and infrastructure

car manufacture	gold	capital cities
coal	oil	major towns
copper	textiles	international airports
diamonds	uranium	major roads
food processing	wildlife reserves	major industrial areas

Transportation Network

84,213 miles (135,609 km)	746 miles (1,202 km)
23,208 miles (37,372 km)	3,815 miles (6,144 km)

Southern Africa's Cape-gauge rail network is by far the largest in the continent. About two-thirds of the 20,000 mile (32,000 km) system lies within South Africa. Lines such as the Harare–Bulawayo route have become corridors for industrial growth.

The Landscape

Most of southern Africa rests on a concave plateau comprising the Kalahari basin and a mountainous fringe, skirted by a coastal plain which widens out in Mozambique. The plateau extends north, toward the Planalto de Bié in Angola, the Congo Basin and the lake-filled troughs of the Great Rift Valley. The eastern region is drained by the Zambezi and Limpopo Rivers, and the Orange is the major western river.

Thousands of years of evaporating water have produced the Etosha Pan, one of the largest salt flats in the world. Lake and river sediments in the area indicate that the region was once less arid.

***Finger Rock, near Khorixas, Namibia** is a remnant of a former land surface, which has been denuded by erosion over the last 5 million years. These occasional stacks of partially weathered rocks interrupt the plains of the dry southern interior.*

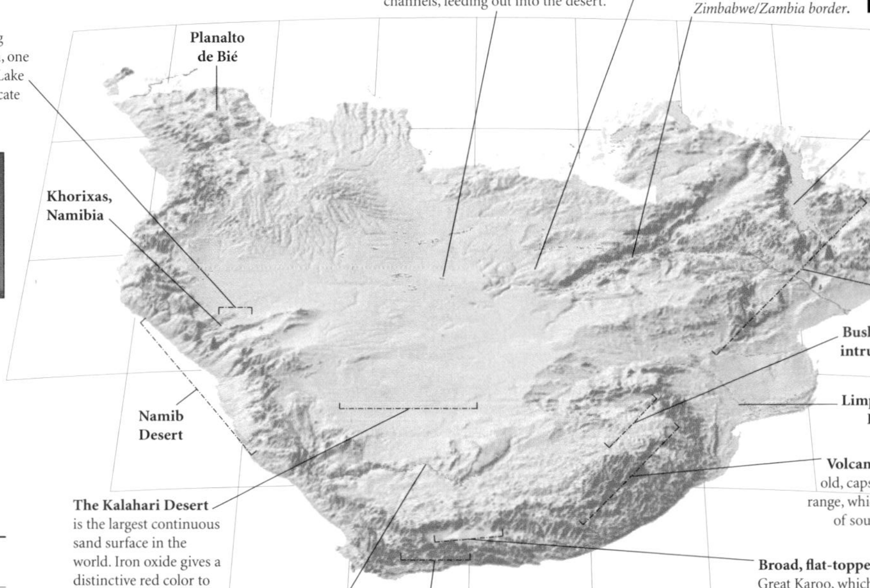

Planalto de Bié
Khorixas, Namibia
Namib Desert
Great Rift Valley
Bushveld intrusion
Limpopo River

The Okavango/Cubango River flows from the Planalto de Bié to the swamplands of the Okavango Delta, one of the world's largest inland deltas, where it divides into countless distributary channels, feeding out into the desert.

At Victoria Falls, the Zambezi River has cut a spectacular gorge taking advantage of large joints in the basalt, which were first formed as the lava cooled and contracted.

The fast-flowing Zambezi River cuts a deep, wide channel as it flows along the Zimbabwe/Zambia border.

Lake Nyasa occupies one of the deep troughs of the Great Rift Valley, where the land has been displaced downward by as much as 3,000 ft (920 m).

Volcanic lava, over 250 million years old, caps the peaks of the Drakensberg range, which lie on the mountainous rim of southern Africa's interior plateau.

Broad, flat-topped mountains characterize the Great Karoo, which have been cut from level rock strata under extremely arid conditions.

The Kalahari Desert is the largest continuous sand surface in the world. Iron oxide gives a distinctive red color to the windblown sand, which, in eastern areas covers the bedrock by over 200 ft (60 m).

The Orange River, one of the longest in Africa, rises in Lesotho and is the only major river in the south which flows westward, rather than to the east coast.

The mountains of the Little Karoo are composed of sedimentary rocks which have been substantially folded and faulted.

Bushveld intrusion

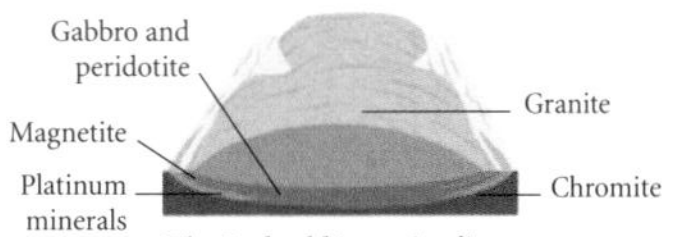

Gabbro and peridotite
Granite
Magnetite
Chromite
Platinum minerals

***The Bushveld intrusion** lies on South Africa's high "veld." Molten magma intruded into the Earth's crust creating a saucer-shaped feature, more than 180 miles (300 km) across, containing regular layers of precious minerals, overlain by a dome of granite.*

***Following a series of droughts,** this baobab tree in Zimbabwe now stands alone in a field once filled by sugar cane. The thick trunk and small leaves of the baobab help it to conserve water, enabling it to survive even in drought conditions.*

Scale 1:10,500,000
(projection: Lambert Azimuthal Equal Area)

Km 0 25 50 100 150 200 250 300
Miles 0 25 50 100 150 200 250 300

South Africa's Three Capitals

PRETORIA – administrative capital
CAPE TOWN – legislative capital
BLOEMFONTEIN – judicial capital

Map Key

POPULATION
- 1 million to 5 million
- 500,000 to 1 million
- 100,000 to 500,000
- 50,000 to 100,000
- 10,000 to 50,000
- below 10,000

ELEVATION
- 3000m / 9843ft
- 2000m / 6562ft
- 1000m / 3281ft
- 500m / 1640ft
- 250m / 820ft
- 100m / 328ft
- sea level

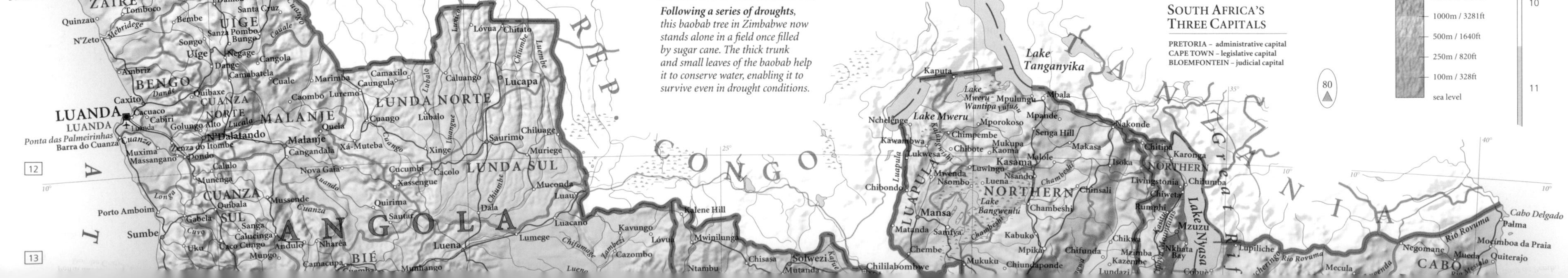

CONGO
CABINDA (To Angola)
DEM. REP. CONGO
ANGOLA
LUANDA
ZAIRE
UIGE
BENGO
CUANZA NORTE
MALANJE
LUNDA NORTE
LUNDA SUL
CUANZA SUL
BIÉ
Lake Tanganyika
Lake Mweru
NORTHERN
TANZANIA
Lake Nyasa

78
78
80

ZAMBIA
MALAWI
MOZAMBIQUE
ZIMBABWE
BOTSWANA
NAMIBIA
SOUTH AFRICA
SWAZILAND
LESOTHO
LUSAKA
LILONGWE
HARARE
WINDHOEK
GABORONE
PRETORIA
MAPUTO
MBABANE
MASERU
CAPE TOWN
BLOEMFONTEIN
Kalahari Desert
Namib Desert
Mozambique Channel
INDIAN OCEAN
ATLANTIC OCEAN
Tropic of Capricorn

172

A wide range of crops are grown in South Africa, aided in many areas by irrigation schemes, such as the Orange River Project, which supplement irregular rainfall.

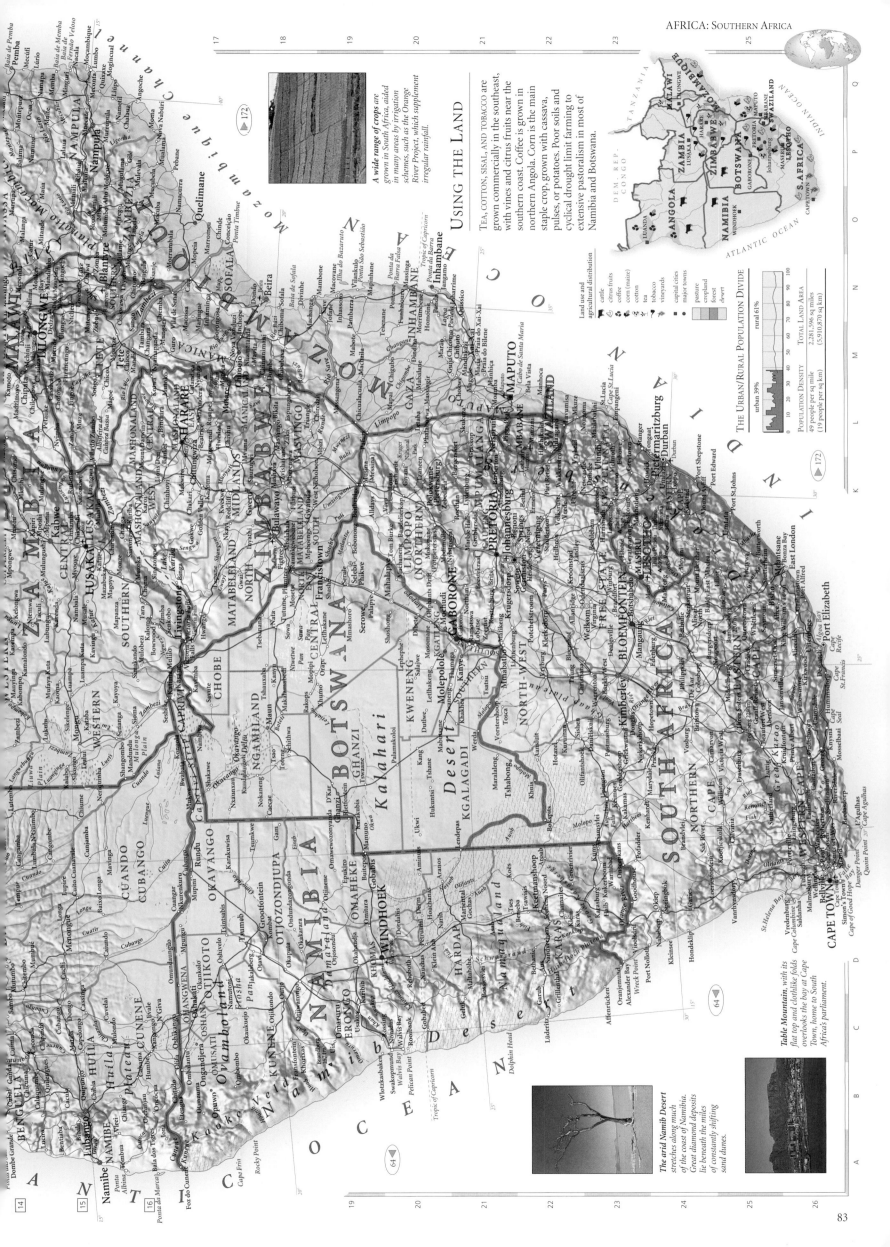

USING THE LAND

TEA, COTTON, SISAL, AND TOBACCO are grown commercially in the southeast, with vines and citrus fruits near the southern coast. Coffee is grown in northern Angola. Corn is the main staple crop, grown with cassava, pulses, or potatoes. Poor soils and cyclical drought limit farming to extensive pastoralism in most of Namibia and Botswana.

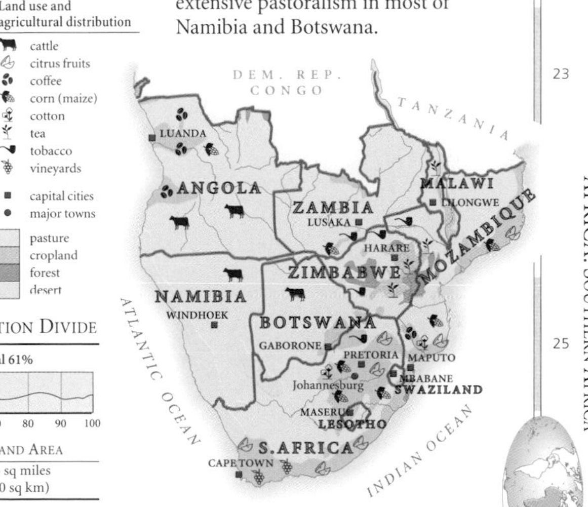
Land use and agricultural distribution
cattle
citrus fruits
coffee
corn (maize)
cotton
tea
tobacco
vineyards
capital cities
major towns
pasture
cropland
forest
desert
DEM. REP. CONGO
TANZANIA
ANGOLA
ZAMBIA
MALAWI
MOZAMBIQUE
ZIMBABWE
NAMIBIA
BOTSWANA
SWAZILAND
LESOTHO
S. AFRICA
ATLANTIC OCEAN
INDIAN OCEAN

THE URBAN/RURAL POPULATION DIVIDE

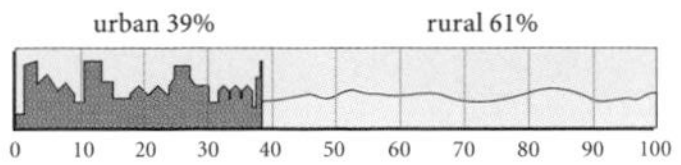
urban 39%
rural 61%
0 10 20 30 40 50 60 70 80 90 100

POPULATION DENSITY	TOTAL LAND AREA
49 people per sq mile (19 people per sq km)	2,281,596 sq miles (5,910,870 sq km)

64

The arid Namib Desert stretches along much of the coast of Namibia. Great diamond deposits lie beneath the miles of constantly shifting sand dunes.

64

***Table Mountain**, with its flat top and clothlike folds overlooks the bay at Cape Town, home to South Africa's parliament.*

172

ARCTIC OCEAN
North Pole
Ellesmere Island
Greenland
King Frederik VIII Land
King Christian X Land
Greenland Sea
Laptev Sea
Severnaya Zemlya
Ostrov Rudol'fa
Franz Josef Land
Poluostrov Taymyr
Kara Sea
Mys Flissingskiy
Spitsbergen
NORTH AMERICAN PLATE
EURASIAN PLATE
Barents Sea
Novaya Zemlya
Poluostrov Yamal
Baydaratskaya Guba
Gulf of Ob
Yenisey
Bjørnøya
Barents Trough
North Cape
Nordkinn
Kara Strait
Tromsøflaket
Fugløya Bank
Murmansk Rise
Ostrov Kolguyev
Poluostrov Kanin
Pechora
West Siberian Plain
ASIA
Ural Mountains
Jan Mayen Fracture Zone
Jan Mayen
Jan Mayen Ridge
Norwegian Sea
Norwegian Basin
Kolbeinsey Ridge
Denmark Strait
Arctic Circle
Iceland Plateau
Bjargtangar
Iceland
Vatnajökull
Reykjanes Ridge
Faeroe-Iceland Ridge
Voring Plateau
Vesterålen
Lofoten
Inarijärvi
Kebnekaise 2117m
Torneälven
Kola Peninsula
Ozero Imandra
Timanskiy Kryazh
Mezen'
White Sea
Onega Bay
Ozero Vygozero
Northern Dvina
Traena Bank
Kölen
Scandinavia
Umeälven
Oulujoki
Gulf of Bothnia
Lake Ladoga
Lake Onega
Iceland Basin
ATLANTIC OCEAN
Faeroe Islands
Bill Baileys Bank
Faeroe-Shetland Trough
Shetland Islands
Hatton Ridge
Galdhøpiggen 2469m
Ljungan
Viking Bank
Åland
Gulf of Finland
Rybinsk Reservoir
Rockall Rise
Orkney Islands
Outer Hebrides
Ben Nevis 1343m
Grampian Mountains
Norwegian Trench
Skagerrak
Vänern
Vättern
Lake Peipus
Lake Il'men
Gulf of Riga
Lake Pskov
Gotland
Feni Ridge
Rockall Trough
North Channel
North Sea
Jutland Bank
Kattegat
Great Fisher Bank
Jylland
Sjælland
Baltic Sea
North European Plain
Western Dvina
Volga Upland
British Isles
Ireland
Irish Sea
Pennines
Snowdon 1085m
Dogger Bank
Shannon
Trent
Britain
Frisian Islands
Neman
Central Russian Upland
Porcupine Plain
Celtic Sea
Celtic Shelf
St. George's Channel
Bristol Channel
Severn
The Fens
Thames
Strait of Dover
Elbe
Oder
Warta
Vistula
Bug
Pripet Marshes
Desna
Dnieper Lowlands
EUROPE
Harz
Land's End
English Channel
Channel Islands
Ardennes
Rhine
Kiev Reservoir
Kremenchuk Reservoir
Tsimlyansk Reservoir
Kirghiz Steppe
Seine
Marne
Moselle
Danube
Dniester
Podil's'ka Vysochina
Pivdennyy Buh
Carpathian Mountains
Vosges
Black Forest
Lake Constance
Tisza
Loire
Vienne
Cher
Bay of Biscay
Charcot Seamounts
Biscay Plain
Azores-Biscay Rise
Massif Central
Lake Geneva
Alps
Mont Blanc 4807m
Lake Balaton
Bakony
Great Hungarian Plain
Transylvanian Alps
Black Sea Lowland
Sea of Azov
Crimea
Kerch Strait
Black Sea
Dordogne
Lot
Garonne
Cévennes
Lake Garda
Po
Adriatic Sea
Dinaric Alps
Drava
Sava
Theta Cap
Galicia Bank
Iberian Plain
Miño
Cordillera Cantábrica
Iberian Peninsula
Aragón
Pyrenees
Aneto 3404m
Gulf of Lion
Ligurian Sea
Apennines
Corno Grande 2912m
Balkan Mountains
Maritsa
Rhodope Mountains
Bosporus
Douro
Duero
Ebro
Sistema Central
Sistema Ibérico
Corsica
Strait of Bonifacio
Adriatic Basin
Lake Scutari
Lake Ohrid
Lake Prespa
Sea of Marmara
EURASIAN PLATE
ANATOLIAN PLATE
Anatolia
Tagus
Cabo da Roca
Guadiana
Júcar
Gulf of Valencia
Balearic Islands
Algerian Basin
Sardinia
Tyrrhenian Sea
Tyrrhenian Basin
Gulf of Taranto
Strait of Otranto
Pindus Mountains
Aegean Sea
Tagus Plain
Sierra Morena
Guadalquivir
Segura
Gorringe Ridge
Cape Saint Vincent
Sistemas Béticos
Sierra Nevada
Mediterranean Sea
Strait of Sicily
Strait of Messina
Mount Etna 3340m
Ionian Sea
Peloponnese
Mirtóan Sea
Sea of Crete
Rhodes Basin
Gulf of Antalya
Taurus Mountains
Horseshoe Seamounts
Ampere Seamount
Punta de Tarifa
Strait of Gibraltar
Alboran Sea
Oued Chelif
EURASIAN PLATE
AFRICAN PLATE
Sicily
Malta
Ionian Basin
Crete
Gávdos
Cyprus
Cyprus Basin
ARABIAN PLATE
AFRICAN PLATE
Seine Plain
Seine Seamount
Madeira
Rif
Sebou
Tell Atlas
Atlas Mountains
Middle Atlas
Oum er Rbia
Mediterranean Ridge
Levantine Basin
Dacia Seamount
Agadir Canyon
High Atlas
Saharan Atlas
Chott el Jerid
Gulf of Sirte
Nile Fan
Canary Islands
Grand Erg Occidental
Grand Erg Oriental
Qattara Depression -133m
Western Desert
Libyan Desert
Suez Canal
Nile
'Erg Iguidi
Erg Chech
AFRICA
SAHARA

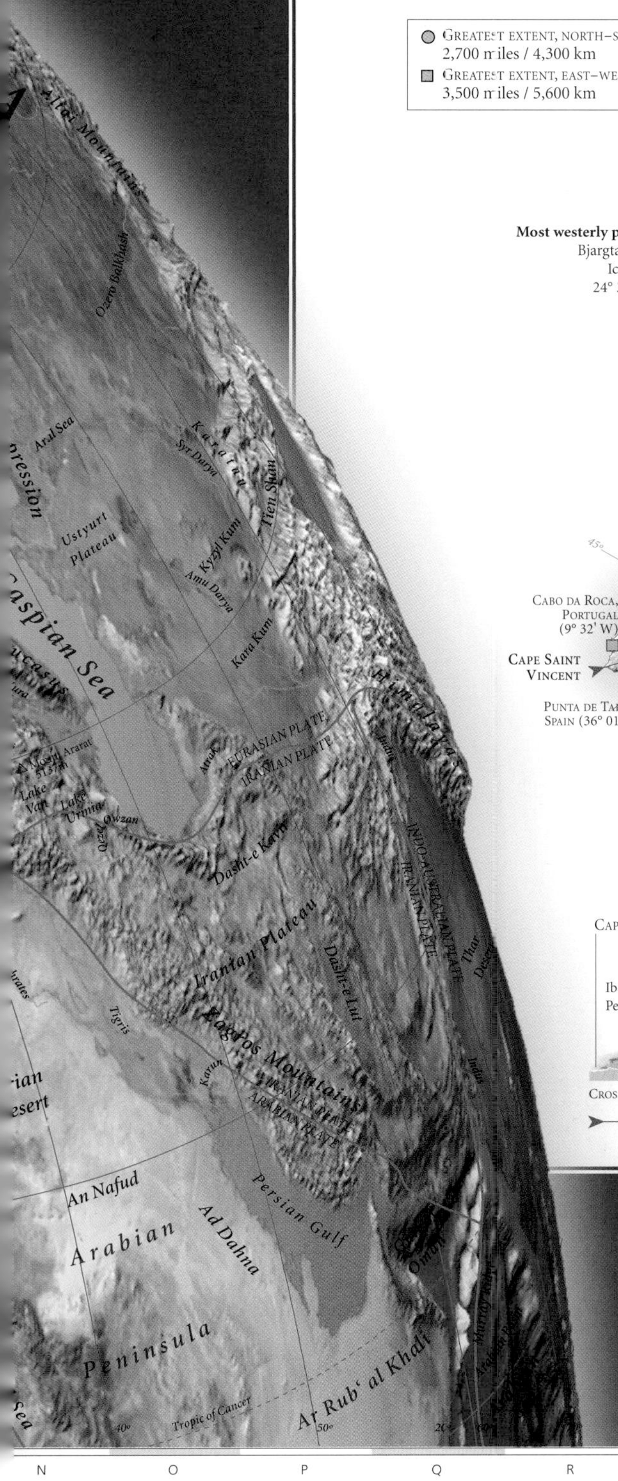

Aral Sea
Ustyurt Plateau
Caspian Sea
Syr Darya
Kyzyl Kum
Amu Darya
Kara Kum
Tien Shan
Eurasian Plate
Iranian Plateau
Dasht-e Kavir
Dasht-e Lut
Zagros Mountains
Tigris
Karun
Persian Gulf
An Nafud
Arabian Peninsula
Ad Dahna
Ar Rub' al Khali
Tropic of Cancer

EUROPE

EUROPE IS THE WORLD'S SECOND SMALLEST CONTINENT, COVERING 4,053,309 SQ MILES (10,498,000 SQ KM). IT COMPRISES 44 SEPARATE COUNTRIES, INCLUDING TURKEY AND THE RUSSIAN FEDERATION, ALTHOUGH THE GREATER PARTS OF THESE NATIONS LIE IN ASIA.

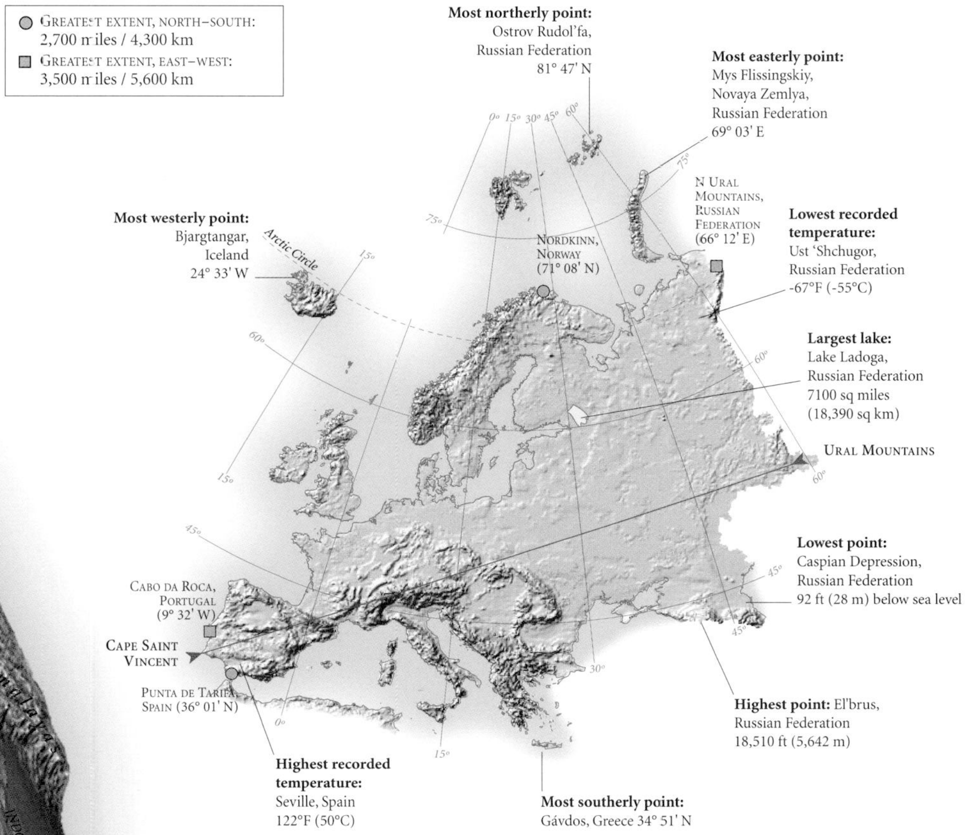

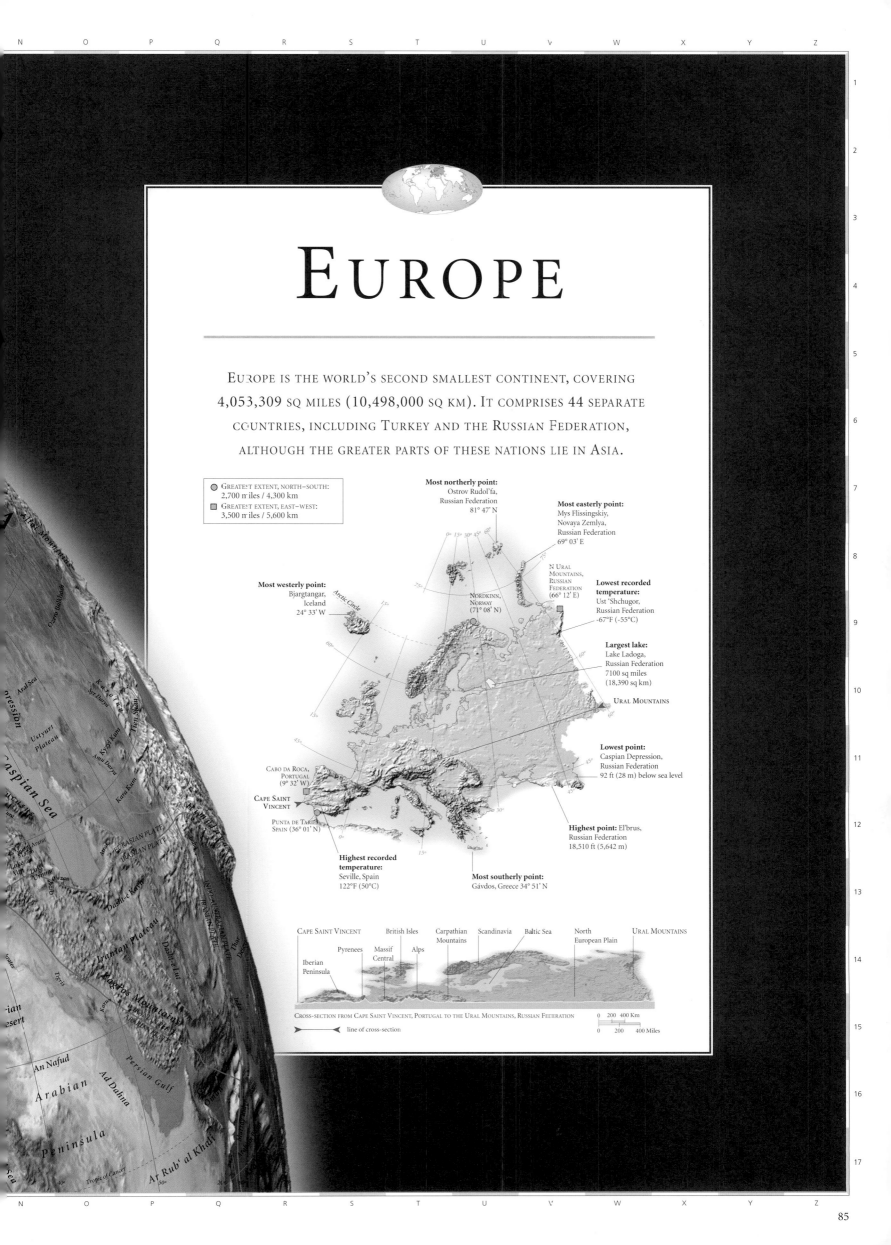

● GREATEST EXTENT, NORTH–SOUTH: 2,700 miles / 4,300 km
■ GREATEST EXTENT, EAST–WEST: 3,500 miles / 5,600 km
Most northerly point: Ostrov Rudol'fa, Russian Federation 81° 47' N
Most easterly point: Mys Flissingskiy, Novaya Zemlya, Russian Federation 69° 03' E
N URAL MOUNTAINS, RUSSIAN FEDERATION (66° 12' E)
Most westerly point: Bjargtangar, Iceland 24° 33' W
Arctic Circle
NORDKINN, NORWAY (71° 08' N)
Lowest recorded temperature: Ust 'Shchugor, Russian Federation -67°F (-55°C)
Largest lake: Lake Ladoga, Russian Federation 7100 sq miles (18,390 sq km)
URAL MOUNTAINS
Lowest point: Caspian Depression, Russian Federation 92 ft (28 m) below sea level
CABO DA ROCA, PORTUGAL (9° 32' W)
CAPE SAINT VINCENT
PUNTA DE TARIFA, SPAIN (36° 01' N)
Highest point: El'brus, Russian Federation 18,510 ft (5,642 m)
Highest recorded temperature: Seville, Spain 122°F (50°C)
Most southerly point: Gávdos, Greece 34° 51' N

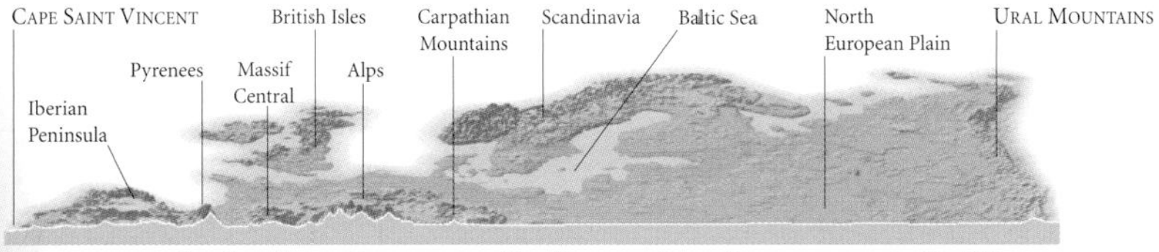

CAPE SAINT VINCENT
British Isles
Carpathian Mountains
Scandinavia
Baltic Sea
North European Plain
URAL MOUNTAINS
Pyrenees
Massif Central
Alps
Iberian Peninsula

CROSS-SECTION FROM CAPE SAINT VINCENT, PORTUGAL TO THE URAL MOUNTAINS, RUSSIAN FEDERATION

line of cross-section

0 200 400 Km
0 200 400 Miles

Physical Europe

THE PHYSICAL DIVERSITY of Europe belies its relatively small size. To the northwest and south it is enclosed by mountains. The older, rounded Atlantic Highlands of Scandinavia and the British Isles lie to the north and the younger, rugged peaks of the Alpine Uplands to the south. In between lies the North European Plain, stretching 2,485 miles (4,000 km) from The Fens in England to the Ural Mountains in Russia. South of the plain lies a series of gently folded sedimentary rocks separated by ancient plateaus, known as massifs.

The North European Plain

RISING LESS THAN 1,000 ft (300 m)above sea level, the North European Plain strongly reflects past glaciation. Ridges of both coarse moraine and finer, wind-blown deposits have accumulated over much of the region. The ice sheet also diverted a number of river channels from their original courses.

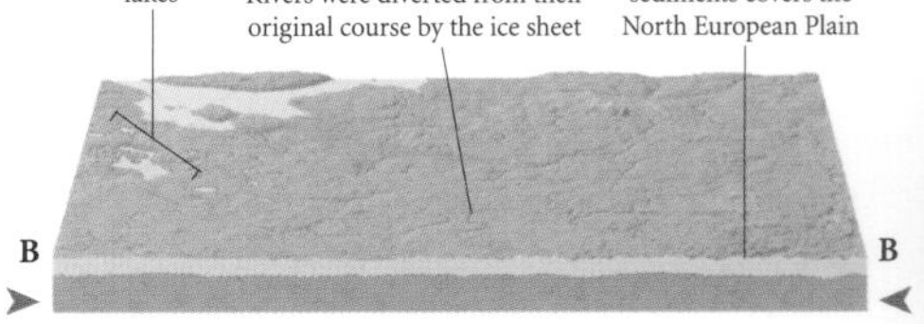
Glacial lakes
Rivers were diverted from their original course by the ice sheet
A layer of glacial sediments covers the North European Plain
B
B
0 100 200 Km
0 100 200 Miles

Section across the North European Plain showing its low relief and drainage.

The Atlantic Highlands

THE ATLANTIC HIGHLANDS were formed by compression against the Scandinavian Shield during the Caledonian mountain-building period over 500 million years ago. The highlands were once part of a continuous mountain chain, now divided by the North Sea and a submerged rift valley.

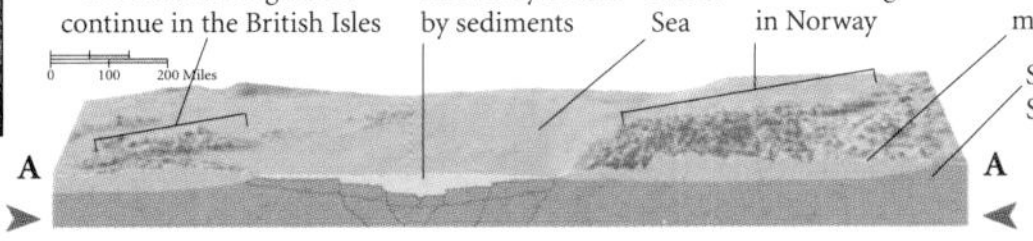
The Atlantic Highlands continue in the British Isles
Rift valley buried by sediments
North Sea
Atlantic Highlands in Norway
Rocks affected by ancient mountain-building
Scandinavian Shield
A
A
0 100 200 Km
0 100 200 Miles

***Cross-section** through northeastern Europe showing the continuous mountain chain and rift valley system.*

SCALE 1:25,500,000
(projection: Lambert Azimuthal Equal Area)
Km 0 100 200 400 600
Miles 0 50 100 200 300 400 500 600
MAP KEY
ELEVATION
4000m / 13,124ft
3000m / 9843ft
2000m / 6562ft
1000m / 3281ft
500m / 1640ft
250m / 820ft
100m / 328ft
sea level
PLATE MARGINS
(for explanation see page xiv)
constructive
destructive
conservative
uncertain
physiographic regions
line of cross-section
Novaya Zemlya
Kara Sea
Ostrov Kolguyev
Barents Sea
Kola Peninsula
White Sea
Ural Mountains
Northern Dvina
Norwegian Sea
ATLANTIC HIGHLANDS
Kölen
SCANDINAVIAN SHIELD
Faeroe Islands
Shetland Islands
Outer Hebrides
ATLANTIC OCEAN
NORTH AMERICAN PLATE
EURASIAN PLATE
Iceland
Gulf of Bothnia
Lake Onega
Lake Ladoga
British Isles
Ireland
Shannon
Britain
The Fens
Thames
Vänern
Vättern
North Sea
Jylland
Baltic Sea
Gulf of Riga
Western Dvina
NORTH EUROPEAN PLAIN
Central Russian Upland
Volga Uplands
Volga
English Channel
Rhine
Elbe
Oder
Vistula
Harz
Ardennes
Seine
Loire
PLATEAUX AND LOWLANDS
Dnieper
Don
Bay of Biscay
Massif Central
Rhône
Garonne
Douro
Iberian Peninsula
Pyrenees
Ebro
Guadalquivir
ALPS
Mt Blanc 4807m
Po
Danube
Carpathian Mountains
Great Hungarian Plain
Dniester
Sea of Azov
Crimea
Caspian Sea
Caucasus
Elbrus 5642m
Black Sea
ASIA
Balkan Mountains
Dinaric Alps
Apennines
ALPINE UPLANDS
Corsica
Sardinia
Balearic Islands
Adriatic Sea
Tyrrhenian Sea
Vesuvius 1171m
Sicily
Etna 3263m
Malta
Ionian Sea
Peloponnese
Aegean Sea
Crete
Mediterranean Sea
EURASIAN PLATE
AFRICAN PLATE
ANATOLIAN PLATE

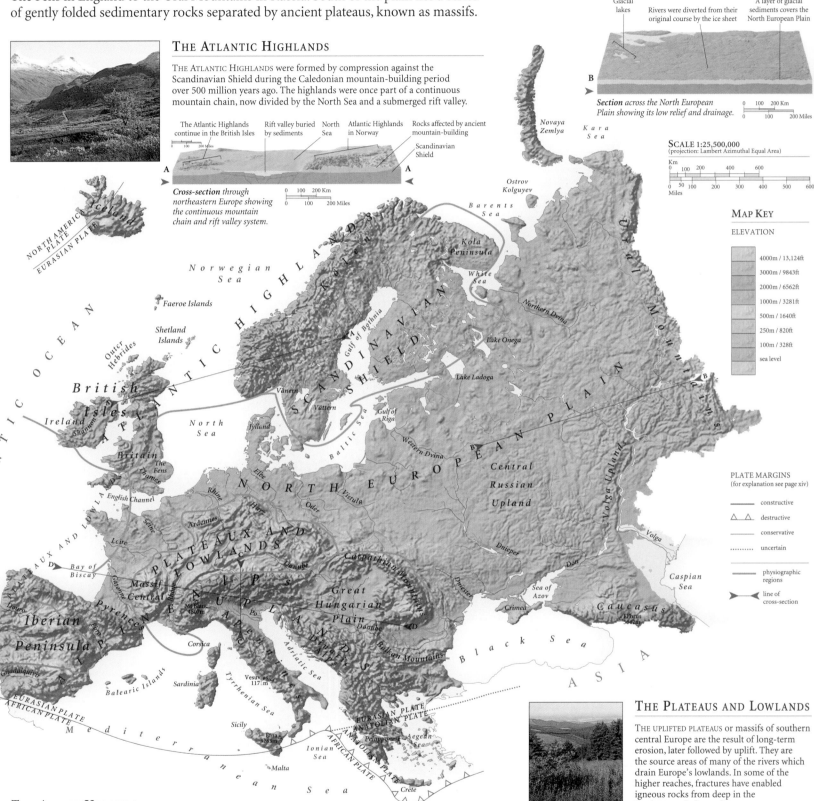

The Plateaus and Lowlands

THE UPLIFTED PLATEAUS or massifs of southern central Europe are the result of long-term erosion, later followed by uplift. They are the source areas of many of the rivers which drain Europe's lowlands. In some of the higher reaches, fractures have enabled igneous rocks from deep in the Earth to reach the surface.

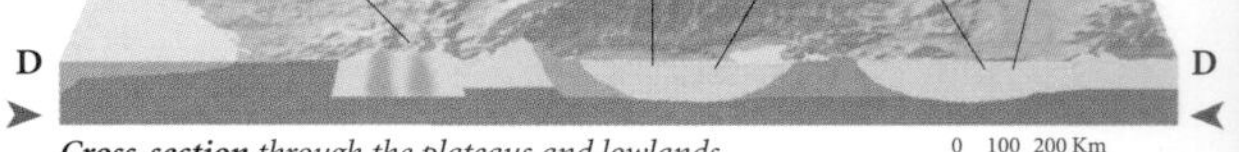
Igneous rocks have intruded into the Massif Central
Older, eroded massifs lie behind the arc of the Alps
Tectonically formed basins
Po Valley
Great Hungarian Plain
D
D
0 100 200 Km
0 100 200 Miles

***Cross-section** through the plateaus and lowlands showing the lower elevation of the ancient massifs.*

The Alpine Uplands

THE COLLISION OF the African and European continents, which began about 65 million years ago, folded and then uplifted a series of mountain ranges running across southern Europe and into Asia. Two major lines of folding can be traced: one includes the Pyrenees, the Alps, and the Carpathian Mountains; the other incorporates the Apennines and the Dinaric Alps.

European basement rock
Alps
Weak sedimentary strata have been folded
African Plate moved northward
The Apennines
C
C
0 50 100 Km
0 50 100 Miles

***Cross-section** through the Alps showing folding and faulting caused by plate tectonics.*

N O P Q R S T U V W X Y Z

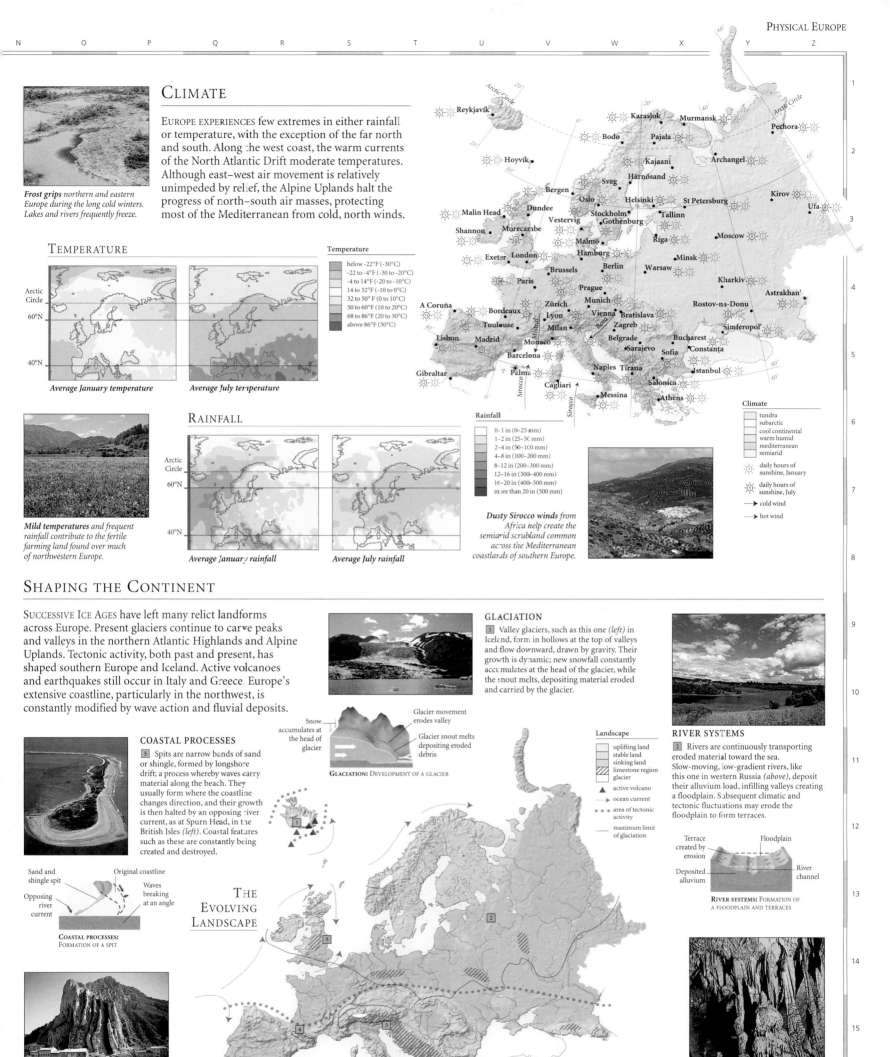

Frost grips northern and eastern Europe during the long cold winters. Lakes and rivers frequently freeze.

CLIMATE

EUROPE EXPERIENCES few extremes in either rainfall or temperature, with the exception of the far north and south. Along the west coast, the warm currents of the North Atlantic Drift moderate temperatures. Although east–west air movement is relatively unimpeded by relief, the Alpine Uplands halt the progress of north–south air masses, protecting most of the Mediterranean from cold, north winds.

TEMPERATURE

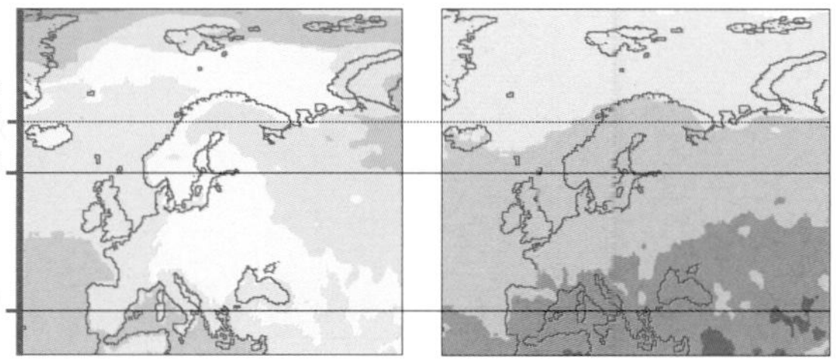
Arctic Circle
60°N
40°N
Temperature
below -22°F (-30°C)
-22 to -4°F (-30 to -20°C)
-4 to 14°F (-20 to -10°C)
14 to 32°F (-10 to 0°C)
32 to 50°F (0 to 10°C)
50 to 60°F (10 to 20°C)
68 to 86°F (20 to 30°C)
above 86°F (30°C)

Average January temperature *Average July temperature*

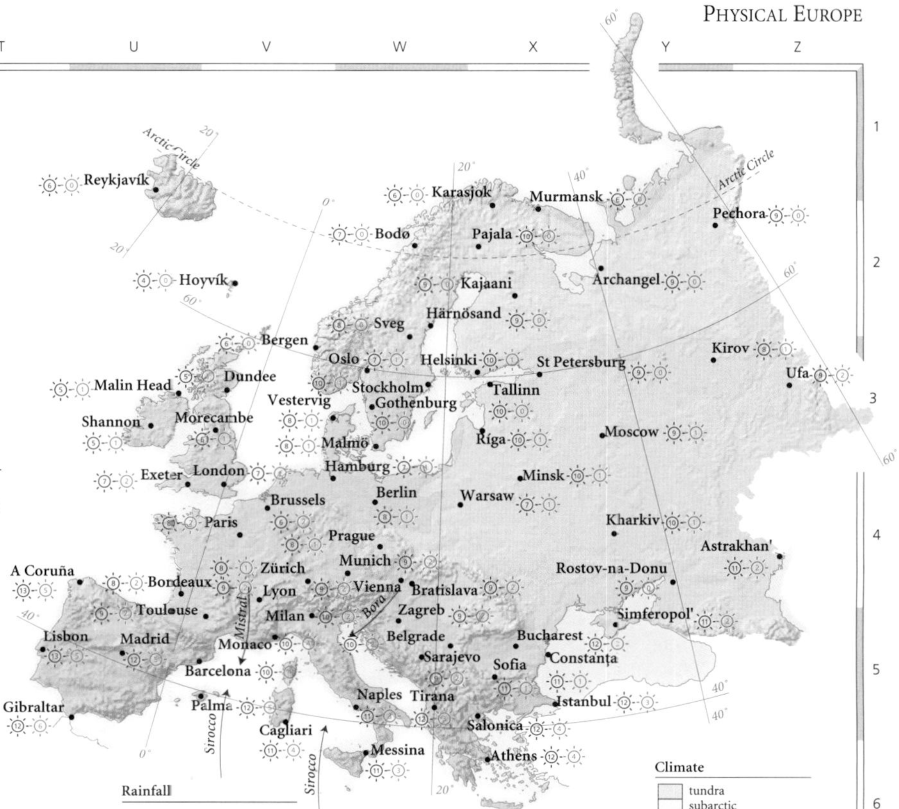
Arctic Circle
Reykjavík
Karasjok
Murmansk
Pechora
Bodø
Pajala
Hoyvík
Kajaani
Archangel
Härnösand
Sveg
Bergen
Oslo
Helsinki
St Petersburg
Kirov
Malin Head
Dundee
Stockholm
Tallinn
Ufa
Vestervig
Gothenburg
Shannon
Morecambe
Moscow
Riga
Malmö
Hamburg
Exeter
London
Minsk
Berlin
Warsaw
Brussels
Paris
Prague
Kharkiv
Munich
Astrakhan'
A Coruña
Zürich
Rostov-na-Donu
Bordeaux
Lyon
Vienna
Bratislava
Mistral
Bora
Toulouse
Milan
Zagreb
Simferopol'
Lisbon
Madrid
Monaco
Belgrade
Bucharest
Sarajevo
Sofia
Constanța
Barcelona
Gibraltar
Palma
Naples
Tirana
Istanbul
Sirocco
Cagliari
Salonica
Messina
Athens
Climate
tundra
subarctic
cool continental
warm humid
mediterranean
semiarid
daily hours of sunshine, January
daily hours of sunshine, July
cold wind
hot wind

***Mild temperatures** and frequent rainfall contribute to the fertile farming land found over much of northwestern Europe.*

RAINFALL

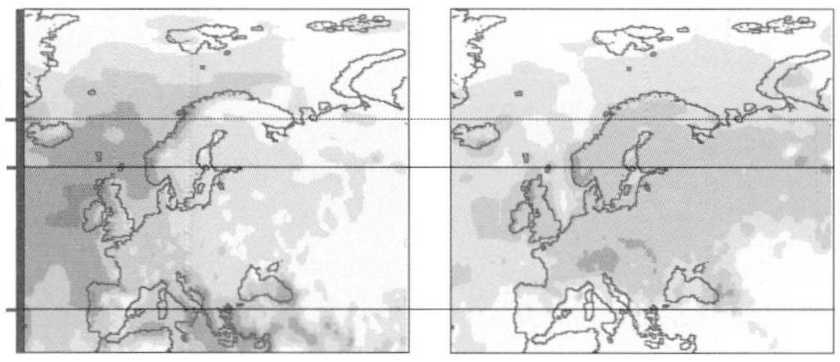
Arctic Circle
60°N
40°N
Rainfall
0–1 in (0–25 mm)
1–2 in (25–50 mm)
2–4 in (50–100 mm)
4–8 in (100–200 mm)
8–12 in (200–300 mm)
12–16 in (300–400 mm)
16–20 in (400–500 mm)
more than 20 in (500 mm)

Average January rainfall *Average July rainfall*

***Dusty Sirocco winds** from Africa help create the semiarid scrubland common across the Mediterranean coastlands of southern Europe.*

SHAPING THE CONTINENT

SUCCESSIVE ICE AGES have left many relict landforms across Europe. Present glaciers continue to carve peaks and valleys in the northern Atlantic Highlands and Alpine Uplands. Tectonic activity, both past and present, has shaped southern Europe and Iceland. Active volcanoes and earthquakes still occur in Italy and Greece. Europe's extensive coastline, particularly in the northwest, is constantly modified by wave action and fluvial deposits.

GLACIATION

1 Valley glaciers, such as this one *(left)* in Iceland, form in hollows at the top of valleys and flow downward, drawn by gravity. Their growth is dynamic; new snowfall constantly accumulates at the head of the glacier, while the snout melts, depositing material eroded and carried by the glacier.

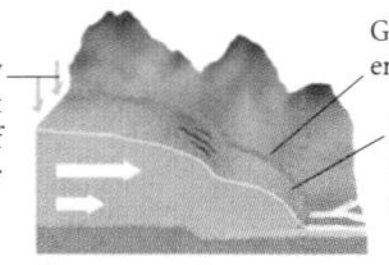
Snow accumulates at the head of glacier
Glacier movement erodes valley
Glacier snout melts depositing eroded debris

GLACIATION: DEVELOPMENT OF A GLACIER

RIVER SYSTEMS

2 Rivers are continuously transporting eroded material toward the sea. Slow-moving, low-gradient rivers, like this one in western Russia *(above)*, deposit their alluvium load, infilling valleys creating a floodplain. Subsequent climatic and tectonic fluctuations may erode the floodplain to form terraces.

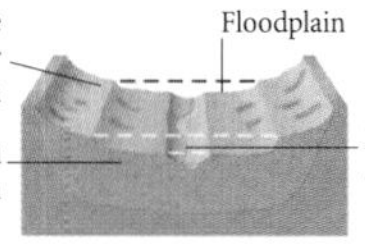
Terrace created by erosion
Floodplain
Deposited alluvium
River channel

RIVER SYSTEMS: FORMATION OF A FLOODPLAIN AND TERRACES

COASTAL PROCESSES

5 Spits are narrow bands of sand or shingle, formed by longshore drift; a process whereby waves carry material along the beach. They usually form where the coastline changes direction, and their growth is then halted by an opposing river current, as at Spurn Head, in the British Isles *(left)*. Coastal features such as these are constantly being created and destroyed.

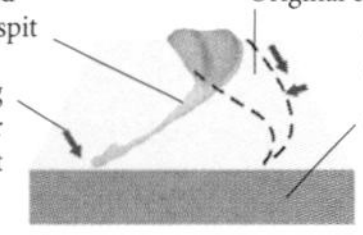
Sand and shingle spit
Original coastline
Waves breaking at an angle
Opposing river current

COASTAL PROCESSES: FORMATION OF A SPIT

THE EVOLVING LANDSCAPE

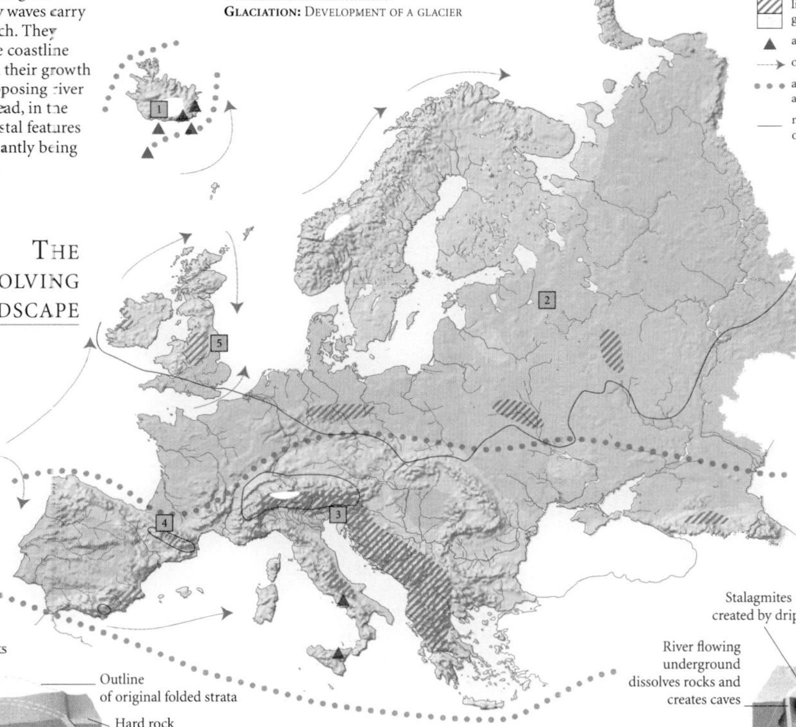
1
2
3
4
5
Landscape
uplifting land
stable land
sinking land
limestone region
glacier
active volcano
ocean current
area of tectonic activity
maximum limit of glaciation

EROSION AND WEATHERING

4 Much of Europe was once subjected to folding and faulting, exposing hard and soft rock layers. Subsequent erosion and weathering has worn away the softer strata, leaving up-ended layers of hard rock as in the French Pyrenees *(above)*.

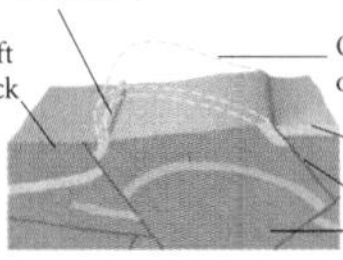
Exposed up-ended rocks
Soft rock
Outline of original folded strata
Hard rock
Fault line
Folded rock strata

EROSION AND WEATHERING: MODIFICATION OF A FOLD

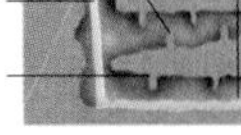
Stalagmites created by drips
Underground cavern
River flowing underground dissolves rocks and creates caves
Stalactites formed by seeping water

WEATHERING: FORMATION OF A CAVE

WEATHERING

3 As surface water filters through permeable limestone, the rock dissolves to form underground caves, like Postojna in the Karst region of Slovenia *(above)*. Stalactites grow downward as lime-enriched water seeps from roof fractures; stalagmites grow upward where drips splash down.

N O P Q R S T U V W X Y Z

POLITICAL EUROPE

THE POLITICAL BOUNDARIES OF EUROPE have changed many times, especially during the 20th century in the aftermath of two world wars, the breakup of the empires of Austria-Hungary, Nazi Germany and, toward the end of the century, the collapse of communism in eastern Europe. The fragmentation of Yugoslavia has again altered the political map of Europe, highlighting a trend toward nationalism and devolution. In contrast, economic federalism is growing. In 1958, the formation of the European Economic Community (now the European Union or EU) started a move toward economic and political union and increasing internal migration.

***The Brandenburg Gate in Berlin** is a potent symbol of German reunification. From 1961, the road beneath it ended in a wall, built to stop the flow of refugees to the West. It was opened again in 1989 when the wall was destroyed and East and West Germany were reunited.*

POPULATION

EUROPE IS A DENSELY POPULATED, urbanized continent; in Belgium over 90% of people live in urban areas. The highest population densities are found in an area stretching east from southern Britain and northern France, into Germany. The northern fringes are only sparsely populated.

Population density (people per sq mile)

- below 130
- 130–259
- 260–379
- 380–519
- 520–780
- above 780

***Traditional lifestyles** still persist in many remote and rural parts of Europe, especially in the south, east, and in the far north.*

***Demand for space** in densely populated European cities like London has led to the development of high-rise offices and urban sprawl.*

Denmark Strait
REYKJAVÍK
ICELAND
Norwegian Sea
Faeroe Islands (to Denmark)
ATLANTIC OCEAN
Shetland Islands
Orkney Islands
Outer Hebrides
NORWAY
SWEDEN
FINLAND
Gulf of Bothnia
Trondheim
Bergen
Stavanger
OSLO
Kristiansand
Uppsala
Örebro
STOCKHOLM
Vänern
Vättern
Jönköping
Gothenburg
Tampere
Turku
HELSINKI
Åland
TALLINN
ESTONIA
St Petersburg
Gotland
Ventspils
LATVIA
RIGA
Liepāja
Baltic Sea
North Sea
DENMARK
Ålborg
COPENHAGEN
Odense
Helsingborg
Malmö
SCOTLAND
Aberdeen
Dundee
Glasgow
Edinburgh
NORTHERN IRELAND
Belfast
IRELAND
DUBLIN
Isle of Man (to UK)
Newcastle upon Tyne
UNITED KINGDOM
Leeds
Liverpool
Manchester
Sheffield
WALES
Birmingham
ENGLAND
Cardiff
Thames
LONDON
Southampton
Channel Islands (to UK)
English Channel
LITHUANIA
Kaunas
VILNIUS
RUSS. FED. (Kaliningrad)
Kaliningrad
Gdańsk
Vitsyebsk
MINSK
Babruysk
BELARUS
Homyel'
Brest
AMSTERDAM
THE HAGUE
Rotterdam
NETH.
Groningen
Bremen
Hamburg
Elbe
Hannover
BERLIN
Oder
Bydgoszcz
Vistula
Poznań
Łódź
WARSAW
POLAND
Wrocław
Antwerp
BELGIUM
BRUSSELS
Nijmegen
Düsseldorf
Bonn
Liège
GERMANY
Leipzig
Dresden
Rhine
LUXEMBOURG
Frankfurt am Main
PRAGUE
CZECH REPUBLIC
Kraków
L'viv
UKRAINE
Le Havre
Seine
Rennes
PARIS
Nantes
St-Nazaire
Loire
Orléans
Strasbourg
Nuremberg
Stuttgart
Munich
Salzburg
Danube
VIENNA
BRATISLAVA
SLOVAKIA
Győr
Miskolc
Chernivtsi
Dniester
MOLDOVA
CHIȘINĂU
Bay of Biscay
FRANCE
Limoges
Zürich
BERN
SWITZERLAND
Alps
Innsbruck
AUSTRIA
LIECHTENSTEIN
BUDAPEST
HUNGARY
Cluj-Napoca
ROMANIA
Brașov
A Coruña
Bordeaux
Geneva
Lyon
Milan
LJUBLJANA
SLOVENIA
Trieste
ZAGREB
CROATIA
Bilbao
Toulouse
Rhône
Turin
Verona
Venice
Genoa
Po
Bologna
Porto
Duero
Valladolid
Ebro
PORTUGAL
Tagus
LISBON
Setúbal
MADRID
SPAIN
Zaragoza
ANDORRA LA VELLA
ANDORRA
Pyrenees
Marseille
Nice
MONACO
Florence
Pisa
SAN MARINO
BOS. & HERZ.
SARAJEVO
Mostar
BELGRADE
BUCHAREST
Constanța
Ruse
Corsica
Barcelona
Valencia
Adriatic Sea
SERBIA & MONTENEGRO (YUGOSLAVIA)
BULGARIA
SOFIA
Stara Zagora
Burgas
Varna
Seville
Córdoba
Cádiz
Málaga
Murcia
Mallorca
Menorca
Eivissa
Palma
Balearic Islands
Sardinia
VATICAN CITY
ROME
ITALY
Tyrrhenian Sea
Naples
Bari
TIRANA
ALBANIA
SKOPJE
MACEDONIA
Salonica
Istanbul
Gibraltar (to UK)
Ceuta (to Spain)
Melilla (to Spain)
Cagliari
Cosenza
Lárisa
Aegean Sea
GREECE
Mediterranean Sea
Palermo
Sicily
Messina
Catania
Ionian Sea
Piraeus
ATHENS
MALTA
VALLETTA
Iráklejo
Crete
Arctic Circle
Murmansk

MAP KEY

POPULATION

- ▣ above 5 million
- ◙ 1 million to 5 million
- ◉ 500,000 to 1 million
- ◎ 100,000 to 500,000
- ⊕ 50,000 to 100,000
- ○ 10,000 to 50,000
- ● Country capital

BORDERS

- full international border

SCALE 1:17,250,000
(projection: Lambert Azimuthal Equal Area)

Km: 0 50 100 200 300 400 500 600 700 800 900 1000
Miles: 0 50 100 200 300 400 500 600 700

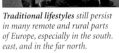

Novaya Zemlya
Kara Sea
Barents Sea
White Sea
Vorkuta
Arctic Circle
Ural Mountains
RUSSIAN FEDERATION
Arkhangel'sk
Northern Dvina
Lake Onega
Perm'
Kirov
Vologda
Ufa
Yaroslavl'
Kazan'
Nizhniy Novgorod
MOSCOW
Ul'yanovsk
Tol'yatti
Samara
Orenburg
Kazakhstan
Tula
Saratov
Voronezh
Volgograd
Kharkiv
Volga
INE
Dnipropetrovs'k
Donets'k
Astrakhan'
Rostov-na-Donu
Caspian Sea
Dnieper
Sea of Azov
Stavropol'
Groznyy
Simferopol'
Novorossiysk
Caucasus
Georgia
Azerbaijan
Black Sea

Overcoming natural barriers, the Brenner Autobahn, one of the main routes across the Alps, links Innsbruck in Austria with Verona in Italy.

Transportation
major roads and highways
major railroads
international borders
transportation intersections
major international airports
major ports
Reykjavík
Murmansk
Vorkuta
Archangel
Trondheim
Perm'
Bergen
Oslo
Helsinki
St Petersburg
Vologda
Kirov
Aberdeen
Grangemouth
Stockholm
Tallinn
Gothenburg
Nizhniy Novgorod
Newcastle upon Tyne
Middlesbrough
Dublin
Riga
Copenhagen
Helsingborg
Moscow
Samara
Liverpool
Birmingham
Gdańsk
Kaliningrad
Vilnius
Minsk
London
Amsterdam
Hamburg
Southampton
Rotterdam
Antwerp
Brussels
Berlin
Warsaw
Poznań
le Havre
Frankfurt am Main
Brest
Paris
Prague
Kharkiv
Volgograd
St-Nazaire
Kiev
Strasbourg
Nuremberg
Vienna
Bratislava
Rostov-na-Donu
Astrakhan'
A Coruña
Bern
Munich
Budapest
Bordeaux
Bilbao
Innsbruck
Lyon
Milan
Trieste
Ljubljana
Odesa
Genoa
Zagreb
Verona
Bologna
Novorossiysk
Lisbon
Marseille
Belgrade
Bucharest
Constanța
Madrid
Barcelona
Varna
Sofia
Valencia
Rome
Istanbul
Cádiz
Naples
Gibraltar
Salonica
Piraeus
Athens
Valletta

TRANSPORTATION

DESPITE ITS FRAGMENTED GEOGRAPHY and many natural frontiers, communications in Europe are well developed. Extensive highway links allow rapid road transportation. High-speed rail connections like France's TGV *(Train à Grande Vitesse)*, and the Channel Tunnel have improved rail travel. Outdated communication infrastructures in parts of eastern Europe, and insufficient transportation links across the Alps, however, remain weak parts of the network.

LANGUAGES

THERE ARE THREE MAIN EUROPEAN language groups: Germanic languages predominate in central and northern Europe; Romance languages in western and Mediterranean Europe and Romania; while Slavic languages are spoken in eastern Europe and the Russian Federation. Isolated pockets of local languages, such as Basque and Gaelic, persist and frequently provide a focus for national identity.

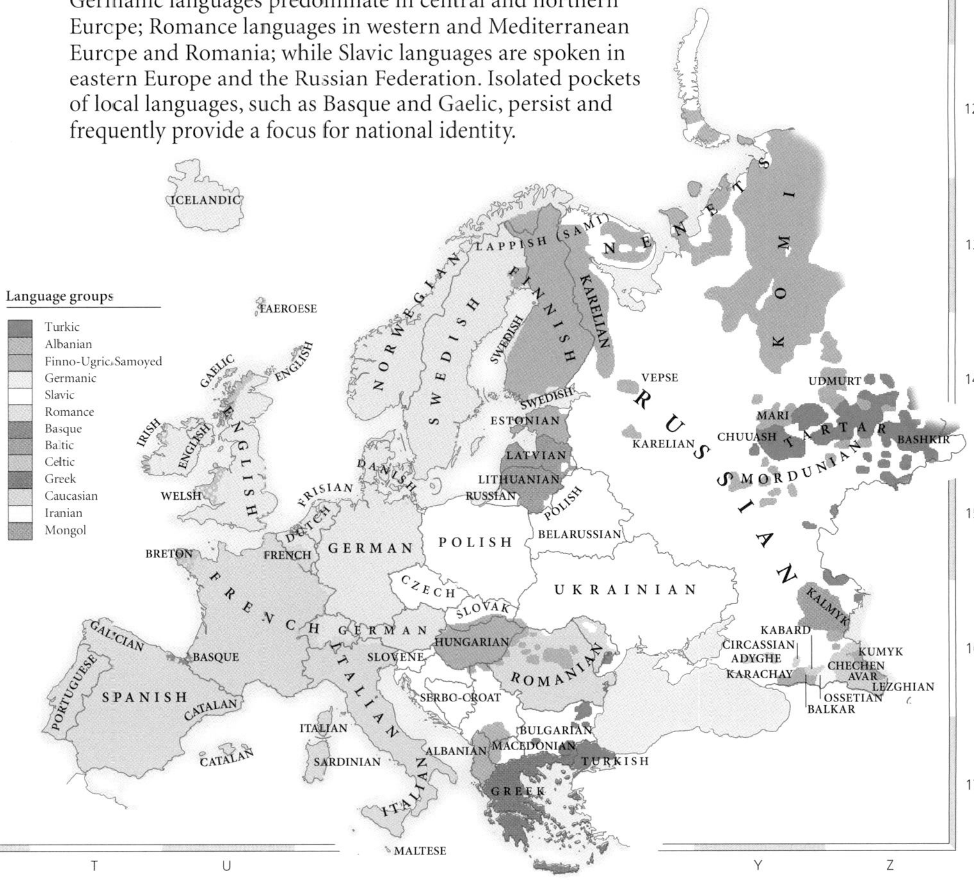
Language groups
Turkic
Albanian
Finno-Ugric/Samoyed
Germanic
Slavic
Romance
Basque
Baltic
Celtic
Greek
Caucasian
Iranian
Mongol
ICELANDIC
FAEROESE
LAPPISH (SAMI)
NENETS
KOMI
NORWEGIAN
SWEDISH
FINNISH
KARELIAN
GAELIC
ENGLISH
IRISH
ESTONIAN
VEPSE
UDMURT
MARI
TARTAR
BASHKIR
CHUVASH
KARELIAN
RUSSIAN
LATVIAN
LITHUANIAN
MORDUNIAN
WELSH
FRISIAN
DANISH
POLISH
BELARUSSIAN
BRETON
DUTCH
FRENCH
GERMAN
CZECH
SLOVAK
UKRAINIAN
KALMYK
HUNGARIAN
ROMANIAN
KABARD
CIRCASSIAN
ADYGHE
KARACHAY
KUMYK
CHECHEN
AVAR
LEZGHIAN
OSSETIAN
BALKAR
GALICIAN
BASQUE
SLOVENE
PORTUGUESE
SPANISH
CATALAN
ITALIAN
SERBO-CROAT
BULGARIAN
MACEDONIAN
ALBANIAN
TURKISH
SARDINIAN
GREEK
MALTESE

The architecture of the Grand Place lies at the heart of Brussels – home city to one of the EU headquarters.

European Resources

Europe's large tracts of fertile, accessible land, combined with its generally temperate climate, have allowed a greater percentage of land to be used for agricultural purposes than in any other continent. Extensive coal and iron ore deposits were used to create steel and manufacturing industries during the 19th and 20th centuries. Today, although natural resources have been widely exploited, and heavy industry is of declining importance, the growth of hi-tech and service industries has enabled Europe to maintain its wealth.

Industry

Europe's wealth was generated by the rise of industry and colonial exploitation during the 19th century. The mining of abundant natural resources made Europe the industrial center of the world. Adaptation has been essential in the changing world economy, and a move to service-based industries has been widespread except in eastern Europe, where heavy industry still dominates.

Other power sources are becoming more attractive as fossil fuels run out; 16% of Europe's electricity is now provided by hydroelectric power.

***Countries like Hungary** are still struggling to modernize inefficient factories left over from extensive, centrally-planned industrialization during the communist era.*

***Frankfurt am Main** is an example of a modern service-based city. The skyline is dominated by headquarters from the worlds of banking and commerce.*

Standard of Living

Living standards in western Europe are among the highest in the world, although there is a growing sector of homeless, jobless people. Eastern Europeans have lower overall standards of living – a legacy of stagnated economies.

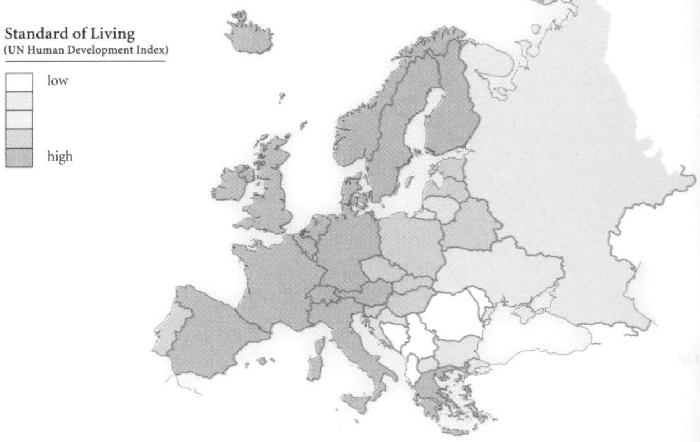
Standard of Living
(UN Human Development Index)
low
high

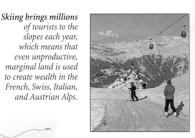

***Skiing brings millions** of tourists to the slopes each year, which means that even unproductive, marginal land is used to create wealth in the French, Swiss, Italian, and Austrian Alps.*

Novaya Zemlya
Ostrov Kolguyev
Barents Sea
Norwegian Sea
Faeroe Islands (to Denmark)
ATLANTIC OCEAN
ICELAND
Reykjavík
IRELAND
Dublin
Belfast
Isle of Man (to UK)
UNITED KINGDOM
Glasgow
Newcastle upon Tyne
Liverpool
Manchester
Birmingham
Cardiff
London
Channel Islands (to UK)
North Sea
NORWAY
Trondheim
Bergen
Oslo
SWEDEN
Stockholm
Gothenburg
Malmö
Gulf of Bothnia
FINLAND
Turku
Helsinki
Tallinn
ESTONIA
LATVIA
Riga
LITHUANIA
Vilnius
RUSS. FED. (Kaliningrad)
Baltic Sea
DENMARK
Copenhagen
NETH.
Amsterdam
Rotterdam
BELG.
Antwerp
Brussels
Liège
LUX.
Essen
Cologne
Hamburg
Berlin
GERMANY
Leipzig
Dresden
Frankfurt am Main
Stuttgart
Munich
Metz
Strasbourg
Lille
Rouen
Paris
Nantes
FRANCE
Bay of Biscay
Bordeaux
Lyon
Toulouse
Marseille
MONACO
ANDORRA
Corsica
A Coruña
Bilbao
Porto
PORTUGAL
Lisbon
SPAIN
Madrid
Barcelona
Seville
Gibraltar (to UK)
Ceuta (to Spain)
Melilla (to Spain)
MOROCCO
Balearic Islands
Mediterranean Sea
Sardinia
SWITZ.
Zürich
LIECH.
AUSTRIA
Linz
Vienna
Turin
Milan
Genoa
Venice
Bologna
SAN MARINO
ITALY
VATICAN CITY
Rome
Naples
Taranto
Tyrrhenian Sea
Adriatic Sea
Sicily
Palermo
MALTA
SLVN.
Zagreb
CROATIA
BOSNIA & HERZ.
Belgrade
SERBIA & MONTENEGRO (YUGOSLAVIA)
ALBANIA
MACED.
GREECE
Salonica
Piraeus
Athens
Ionian Sea
Aegean Sea
Crete
POLAND
Gdańsk
Poznań
Łódź
Warsaw
Katowice
Kraków
CZECH REP.
Prague
SLOVAKIA
Bratislava
HUNGARY
Budapest
ROMANIA
Ploești
Bucharest
Constanța
BULGARIA
Sofia
Varna
Istanbul
TURKEY
MOLDOVA
Odesa
BELARUS
Minsk
UKRAINE
Kiev
Kharkiv
Dnipropetrovs'k
Donets'k
Kryvyy Rih
Black Sea
GEORGIA
AZERBAIJAN
RUSSIAN FEDERATION
Murmansk
Archangel
St Petersburg
Cherepovets
Yaroslavl'
Ivanovo
Nizhniy Novgorod
Moscow
Ryazan'
Tula
Kursk
Voronezh
Perm'
Kazan'
Ufa
Tol'yatti
Samara
Saratov
Volgograd
Rostov-na-Donu
KAZAKHSTAN
Caspian Sea
GNP per capita (US$)
below 1999
2000–4999
5000–9999
10,000–19,999
20,000–24,999
above 25,000
Industry
aerospace
brewing
car/vehicle manufacture
chemicals
defense
electronics
engineering
finance
food processing
hi-tech industry
iron & steel
pharmaceuticals
printing & publishing
shipbuilding
textiles
timber processing
wine
coal
oil
gas
industrial cities
major industrial areas

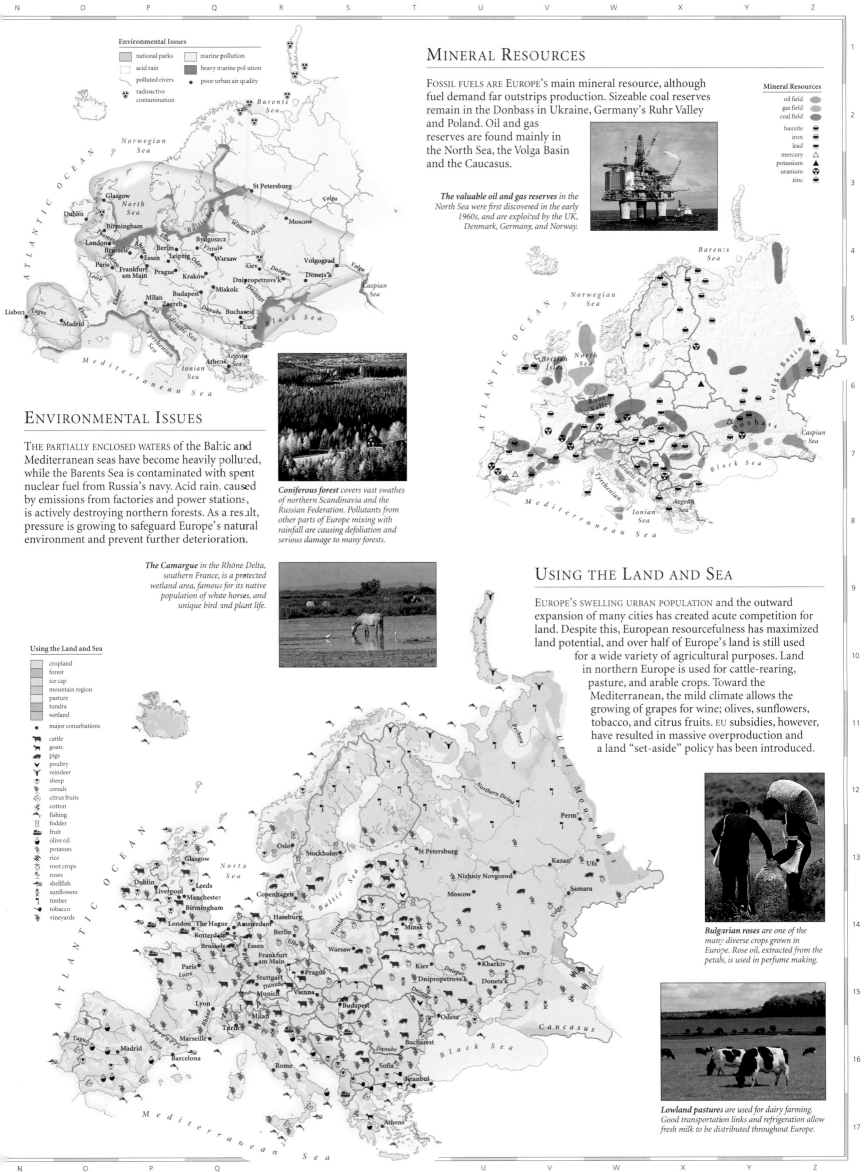

Environmental Issues
national parks
acid rain
polluted rivers
radioactive contamination
marine pollution
heavy marine pollution
poor urban air quality
Barents Sea
Norwegian Sea
ATLANTIC OCEAN
North Sea
Baltic Sea
Black Sea
Caspian Sea
Mediterranean Sea
Ionian Sea
Aegean Sea
Adriatic Sea
Tyrrhenian Sea
Dublin
Glasgow
Birmingham
London
Brussels
Paris
Essen
Frankfurt am Main
Berlin
Leipzig
Prague
Bydgoszcz
Warsaw
Kraków
Kiev
Dnipropetrovs'k
Donets'k
Volgograd
Moscow
St Petersburg
Miskolc
Budapest
Zagreb
Milan
Bucharest
Euxe
Athens
Lisbon
Madrid

ENVIRONMENTAL ISSUES

THE PARTIALLY ENCLOSED WATERS of the Baltic and Mediterranean seas have become heavily polluted, while the Barents Sea is contaminated with spent nuclear fuel from Russia's navy. Acid rain, caused by emissions from factories and power stations, is actively destroying northern forests. As a result, pressure is growing to safeguard Europe's natural environment and prevent further deterioration.

***Coniferous forest** covers vast swathes of northern Scandinavia and the Russian Federation. Pollutants from other parts of Europe mixing with rainfall are causing defoliation and serious damage to many forests.*

***The Camargue** in the Rhône Delta, southern France, is a protected wetland area, famous for its native population of white horses, and unique bird and plant life.*

MINERAL RESOURCES

FOSSIL FUELS ARE EUROPE'S main mineral resource, although fuel demand far outstrips production. Sizeable coal reserves remain in the Donbass in Ukraine, Germany's Ruhr Valley and Poland. Oil and gas reserves are found mainly in the North Sea, the Volga Basin and the Caucasus.

***The valuable oil and gas reserves** in the North Sea were first discovered in the early 1960s, and are exploited by the UK, Denmark, Germany, and Norway.*

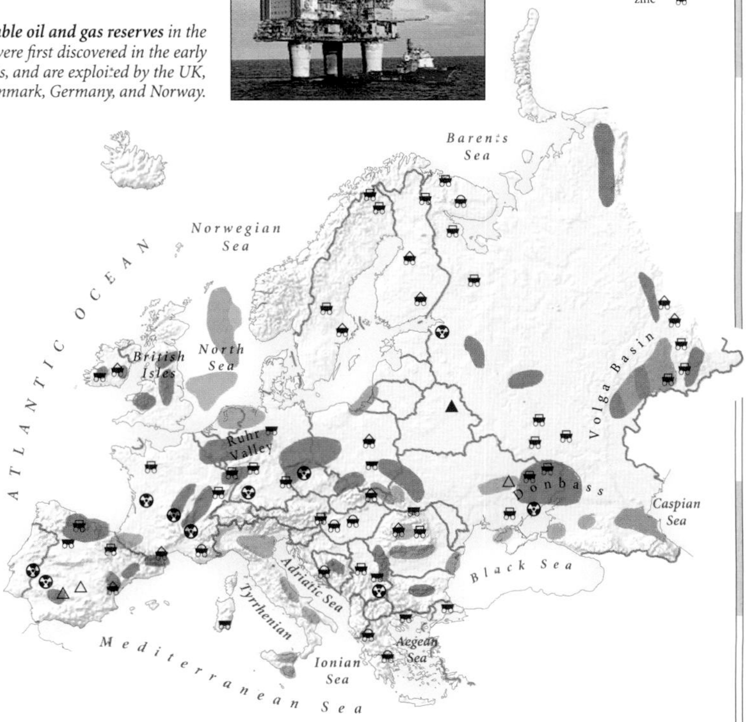
Mineral Resources
oil field
gas field
coal field
bauxite
iron
lead
mercury
potassium
uranium
zinc
Barents Sea
Norwegian Sea
ATLANTIC OCEAN
British Isles
North Sea
Ruhr Valley
Volga Basin
Donbass
Caspian Sea
Black Sea
Adriatic Sea
Tyrrhenian Sea
Ionian Sea
Aegean Sea
Mediterranean Sea

USING THE LAND AND SEA

EUROPE'S SWELLING URBAN POPULATION and the outward expansion of many cities has created acute competition for land. Despite this, European resourcefulness has maximized land potential, and over half of Europe's land is still used for a wide variety of agricultural purposes. Land in northern Europe is used for cattle-rearing, pasture, and arable crops. Toward the Mediterranean, the mild climate allows the growing of grapes for wine; olives, sunflowers, tobacco, and citrus fruits. EU subsidies, however, have resulted in massive overproduction and a land "set-aside" policy has been introduced.

Using the Land and Sea
cropland
forest
ice cap
mountain region
pasture
tundra
wetland
major conurbations
cattle
goats
pigs
poultry
reindeer
sheep
cereals
citrus fruits
cotton
fishing
fodder
fruit
olive oil
potatoes
rice
root crops
roses
shellfish
sunflowers
timber
tobacco
vineyards
ATLANTIC OCEAN
North Sea
Baltic Sea
Black Sea
Mediterranean Sea
Ural Mountains
Caucasus
Pechora
Northern Dvina
Volga
Don
Dnieper
Dniester
Danube
Vistula
Elbe
Rhine
Seine
Loire
Rhône
Po
Ebro
Tagus
Pyrenees
Oslo
Stockholm
St Petersburg
Perm'
Kazan'
Ufa
Samara
Nizhniy Novgorod
Moscow
Glasgow
Dublin
Leeds
Liverpool
Manchester
Birmingham
London
The Hague
Amsterdam
Rotterdam
Brussels
Essen
Copenhagen
Hamburg
Berlin
Minsk
Warsaw
Kiev
Kharkiv
Dnipropetrovs'k
Donets'k
Paris
Frankfurt am Main
Prague
Stuttgart
Munich
Vienna
Budapest
Odesa
Lyon
Milan
Turin
Marseille
Madrid
Barcelona
Bucharest
Sofia
Rome
Istanbul
Athens

***Bulgarian roses** are one of the many diverse crops grown in Europe. Rose oil, extracted from the petals, is used in perfume making.*

***Lowland pastures** are used for dairy farming. Good transportation links and refrigeration allow fresh milk to be distributed throughout Europe.*

Scandinavia, Finland & Iceland

Denmark, Norway, Sweden, Finland, Iceland

Jutting into the Arctic Circle, this northern swath of Europe has some of the continent's harshest environments, but benefits from great reserves of oil, gas, and natural evergreen forests. While most early settlers came from the south, migrants to Finland came from the east, giving it a distinct language and culture. Since the late 19th century, the Scandinavian states have developed strong egalitarian traditions. Today, their welfare benefits systems are among the most extensive in the world, and standards of living are high. The Lapps, or Sami, maintain their traditional lifestyle in the northern regions of Norway, Sweden, and Finland.

GREENLAND SEA
Denmark Strait
ICELAND
ATLANTIC OCEAN
REYKJAVÍK
Vatnajökull
NORDHURLAND EYSTRA
NORDHURLAND VESTRA
VESTURLAND
VESTFIRDHIR
AUSTURLAND
SUDHURLAND
Arctic Circle

(same scale as main map)

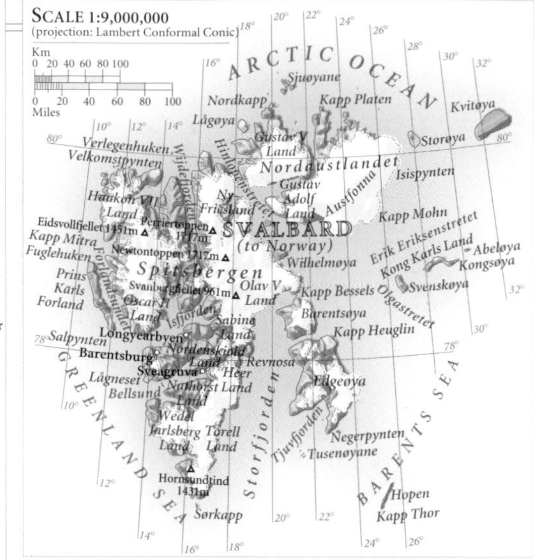
SCALE 1:9,000,000
(projection: Lambert Conformal Conic)
ARCTIC OCEAN
SVALBARD (to Norway)
Nordaustlandet
Spitsbergen
BARENTS SEA
GREENLAND SEA
Storfjorden

The Landscape

Glaciers up to 10,000 ft (3,000 m) deep covered most of Scandinavia and Finland during the last Ice Age. The effects of glaciation mark the entire landscape, from the mountains to the lowlands, across the tundra landscape of Lapland, and the lake districts of Sweden and Finland.

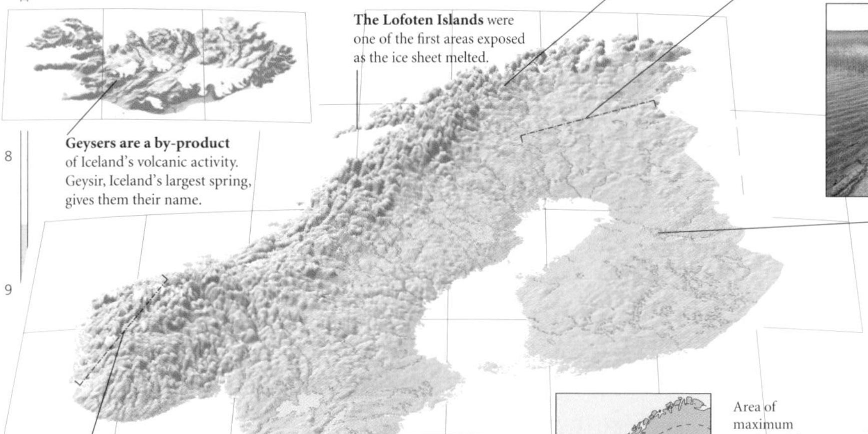
Oulujärvi

Halti Mountain is Finland's highest point, at 4,356 ft (1,328 m).

Lapland, north of the Arctic Circle, is an area of undulating fells and plains known as tundra. The subsoil is permanently frozen and therefore impermeable. There are many peat bogs. Pools reappear in the summer when the surface thaws.

The Lofoten Islands were one of the first areas exposed as the ice sheet melted.

Geysers are a by-product of Iceland's volcanic activity. Geysir, Iceland's largest spring, gives them their name.

Oulujärvi

Finland's landscape was fashioned by ice action. Glaciers gouged out its distinctive shallow lake basins, such as Oulujärvi, and left debris called moraines in their wake.

Fjords

***The fjords** on the western coast of Norway were once gentle river valleys. Their deep floors and steep sides were carved out by glaciers during the last Ice Age, and they were later flooded by the sea.*

Sjælland coast

***On the coast of Sjælland,** these cliffs have been eroded by the sea, exposing layers of chalk and limestone.*

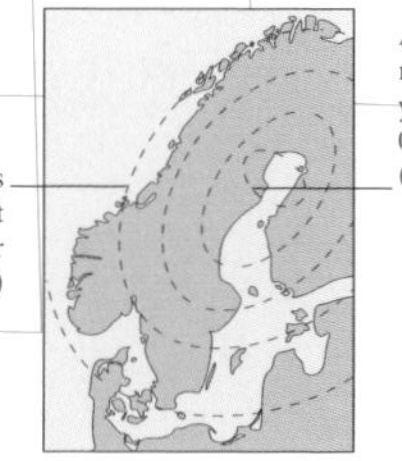
Area of maximum yearly uplift 0.3 in/yr (9 mm/yr)
Slower rates of uplift 0.1 in/yr (3 mm/yr)

***Scandinavia** is still recovering from the last Ice Age, when ice depressed the land by 2,000 ft (600 m). This gradual uplift is known as isostatic rebound.*

Scale 1:5,500,000
(projection: Lambert Conformal Conic)

ARCTIC OCEAN
BARENTS SEA
FINNMARK
TROMS
NORDLAND
NORRBOTTEN
LAPPI
Lapland

▶ 122

Using the Land and Sea

The cold climate, short growing season, poorly developed soil, steep slopes, and exposure to high winds across northern regions means that most agriculture is concentrated, with the population, in the south. Most of Finland and much of Norway and Sweden are covered by dense forests of pine, spruce and birch, which supply the timber industries.

GREENLAND SEA
ICELAND
REYKJAVÍK
ATLANTIC OCEAN
ARCTIC OCEAN
RUSSIAN FEDERATION
NORWEGIAN SEA
NORTH SEA
BALTIC SEA
GERMANY
NORWAY
SWEDEN
FINLAND
DENMARK
OSLO
STOCKHOLM
HELSINKI
COPENHAGEN
Trondheim
Bergen
Uppsala
Linköping
Gothenburg
Malmö
Tampere
Turku
Land use and agricultural distribution
fishing
pigs
reindeer
sheep
cereals
timber
capital cities
major towns
pasture
cropland
forest
mountain region
tundra

The Urban/Rural Population Divide

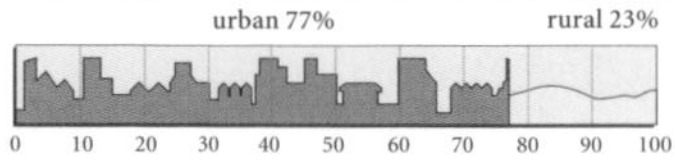
urban 77%
rural 23%
0 10 20 30 40 50 60 70 80 90 100

Population Density	Total Land Area
51 people per sq mile (20 people per sq km)	473,970 sq miles (1,227,610 sq km)

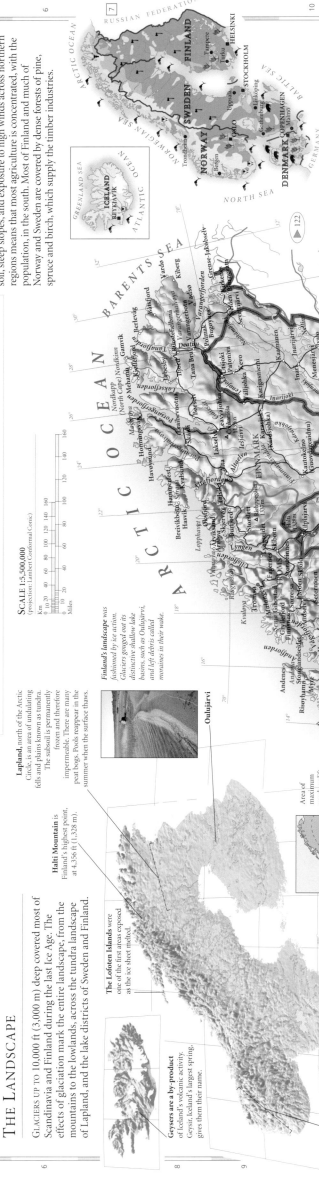

NORWEGIAN SEA
NORWAY
SWEDEN
FINLAND
DENMARK
Gulf of Bothnia
Gulf of Finland
BALTIC SEA
NORTH SEA
Skagerrak
Kattegat
OSLO
STOCKHOLM
HELSINKI
KØBENHAVN (COPENHAGEN)

Many Lappish people, *in addition to traditional reindeer herding, now also make their living from fishing and farming, or working in cities. Tourism provides some with an extra source of income.*

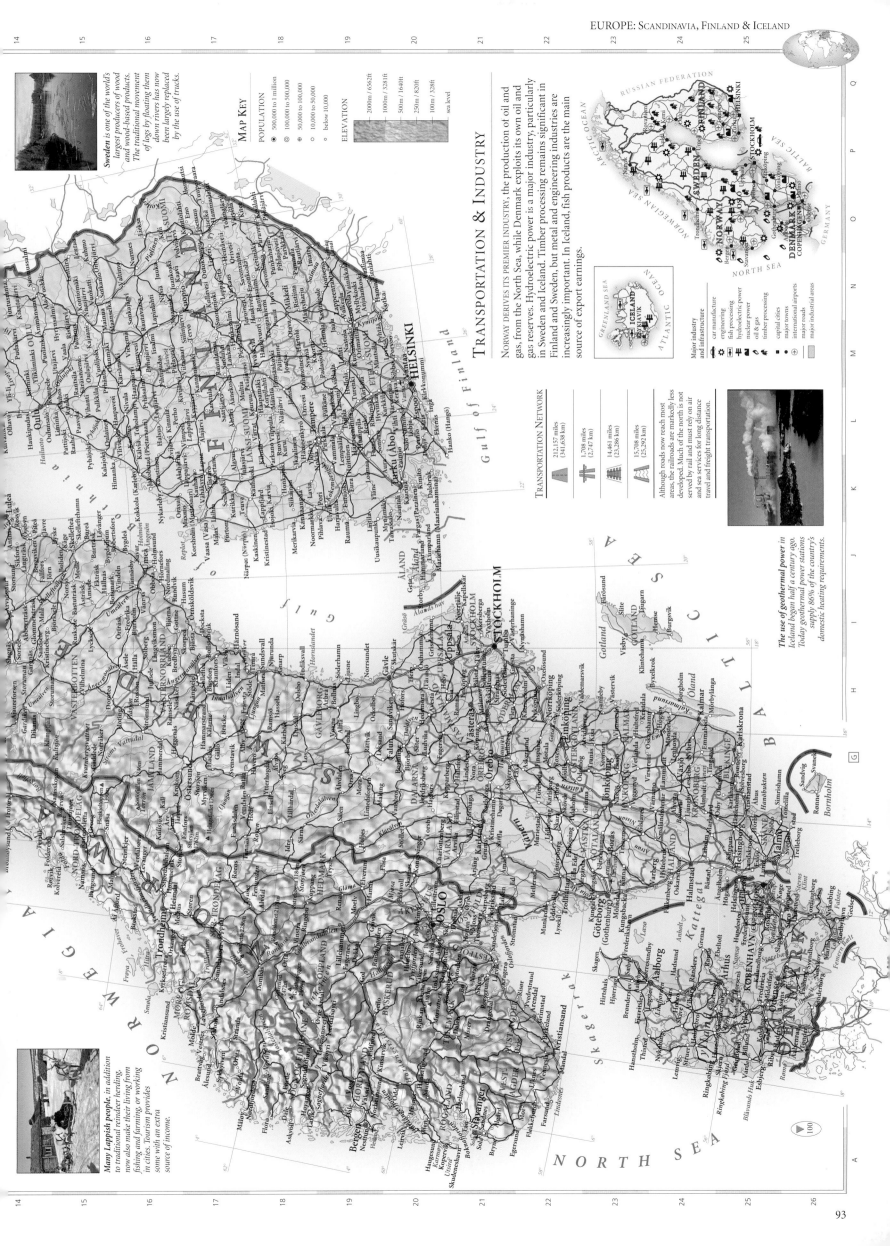

***Sweden** is one of the world's largest producers of wood and wood-based products. The traditional movement of logs by floating them down rivers has now been largely replaced by the use of trucks.*

Map Key

POPULATION

- 500,000 to 1 million
- 100,000 to 500,000
- 50,000 to 100,000
- 10,000 to 50,000
- below 10,000

ELEVATION

- 2000m / 6562ft
- 1000m / 3281ft
- 500m / 1640ft
- 250m / 820ft
- 100m / 328ft
- sea level

Transportation & Industry

NORWAY DERIVES ITS PREMIER INDUSTRY, the production of oil and gas, from the North Sea, while Denmark exploits its own oil and gas reserves. Hydroelectric power is a major industry, particularly in Sweden and Iceland. Timber processing remains significant in Finland and Sweden, but metal and engineering industries are increasingly important. In Iceland, fish products are the main source of export earnings.

Transportation Network

Roads	212,157 miles (341,638 km)
Motorways	1,708 miles (2,747 km)
Railways	14,461 miles (23,286 km)
Waterways	15,708 miles (25,292 km)

Although roads now reach most areas, the railroads are markedly less developed. Much of the north is not served by rail and must rely on air and sea services for long distance travel and freight transportation.

***The use of geothermal power** in Iceland began half a century ago. Today geothermal power stations supply 86% of the country's domestic heating requirements.*

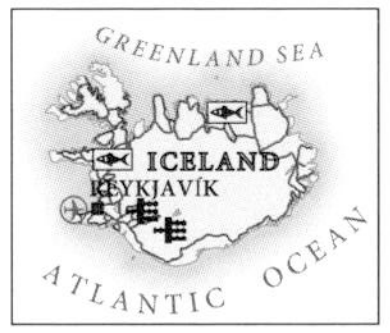
GREENLAND SEA
ICELAND
REYKJAVIK
ATLANTIC OCEAN

ARCTIC OCEAN
NORWEGIAN SEA
RUSSIAN FEDERATION
NORWAY
SWEDEN
FINLAND
DENMARK
OSLO
STOCKHOLM
HELSINKI
COPENHAGEN
NORTH SEA
BALTIC SEA
GERMANY

Major industry and infrastructure

- car manufacture
- engineering
- fish processing
- hydroelectric power
- nuclear power
- oil & gas
- timber processing
- capital cities
- major towns
- international airports
- major roads
- major industrial areas

100

Southern Scandinavia

Southern Norway, Southern Sweden, Denmark

Scandinavia's economic and political hub is the more habitable and accessible southern region. Many of the area's major cities are on the southern coasts, including Oslo and Stockholm, the capitals of Norway and Sweden. In Denmark, most of the population and the capital, Copenhagen, are located on its many islands. A cultural unity links the three Scandinavian countries. Their main languages, Danish, Swedish, and Norwegian, are mutually intelligible, and they all retain their monarchies, although the parliaments have legislative control.

Using the Land

Agriculture in southern Scandinavia is highly mechanized although farms are small. Denmark is the most intensively farmed country and its western pastureland is used mainly for pig farming. Cereal crops including wheat, barley, and oats, predominate in eastern Denmark and in the far south of Sweden. Southern Norway, and Sweden have large tracts of forest which are exploited for logging.

The Urban/Rural Population Divide

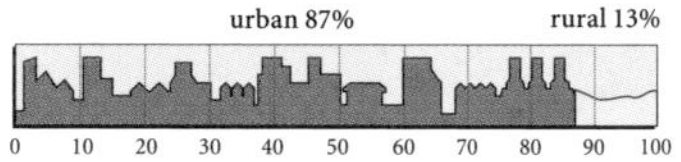
urban 87%
rural 13%
0 10 20 30 40 50 60 70 80 90 100

Population Density	Total Land Area
152 people per sq mile (61 people per sq km)	173,487 sq miles (456,564 sq km)

Land use and agricultural distribution
cattle
pigs
sheep
cereals
fodder
root crops
timber
capital cities
major towns
pasture
cropland
forest
mountain region
NORWEGIAN SEA
Trondheim
NORWAY
Bergen
OSLO
SWEDEN
Uppsala
Örebro
STOCKHOLM
Linköping
Gothenburg
Aalborg
DENMARK
COPENHAGEN
Odense
Malmö
NORTH SEA
BALTIC SEA
GERMANY

In Norway winters are longer and colder inland than in coastal areas, where the warm current of the North Atlantic Drift moderates the climate.

The Landscape

Southern Scandinavia, with the exception of Norway, has a flatter terrain than the rest of the region. Denmark and southern Sweden are both extensions of the North European Plain. In this area, because of glacial deposition rather than erosion, the soils are deeper and more fertile.

In the past, glaciers such as this one in Olden, Norway, were much larger. Today, many are retreating to yield the spectacular glacial scenery.

Limestone pillars eroded by the sea dot the coast of Gotland and surrounding islands.

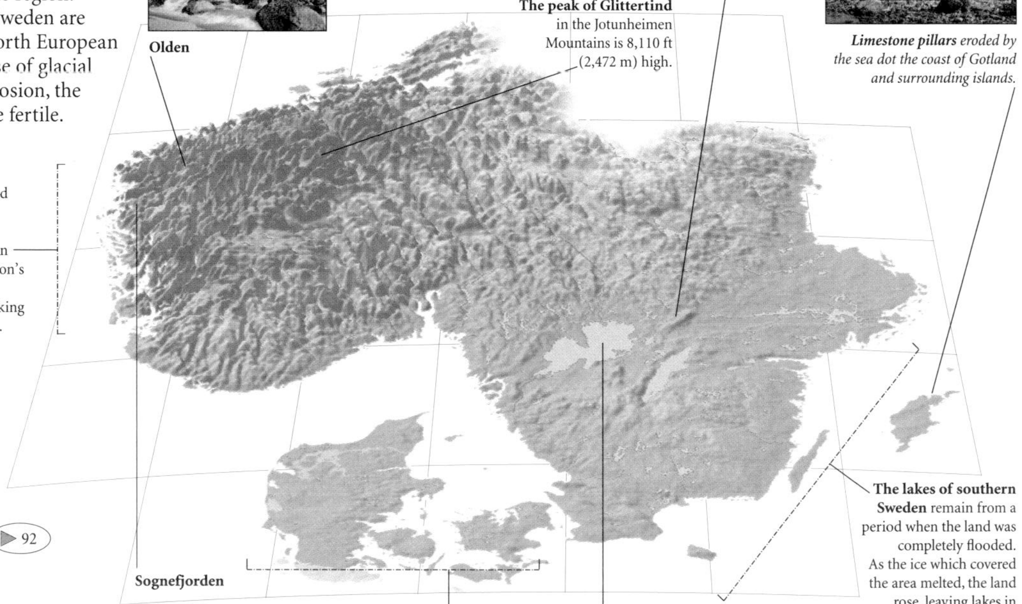
Olden
The peak of Glittertind in the Jotunheimen Mountains is 8,110 ft (2,472 m) high.
Distinctive low ridges, called eskers, are found across southern Sweden. They are formed from sand and gravel deposits left by retreating glaciers.
Acid rain, caused by industrial pollution carried north from elsewhere in Europe, harms plant and animal life in Scandinavian forests and lakes. The region's surface rocks lack lime to neutralize the acid, so making the problem more serious.
The lakes of southern Sweden remain from a period when the land was completely flooded. As the ice which covered the area melted, the land rose, leaving lakes in shallow, ice-scoured depressions. Sweden has over 90,000 lakes.
Vänern in Sweden is the largest lake in Scandinavia. It covers an area of 2,080 sq miles (5,390 sq km).
Denmark's flat and fertile soils are formed on glacial deposits between 100–160 ft (30–50 m) deep.
Sognefjorden

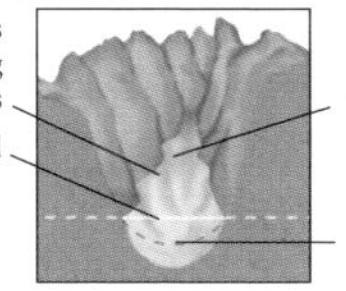
Erosion by glaciers deepened existing river valleys
Sea level
When the ice retreated the valley was flooded by the sea
Old valley floor

Sognefjorden is the deepest of Norway's many fjords. It drops to 4,291 ft (1,308 m) below sea level.

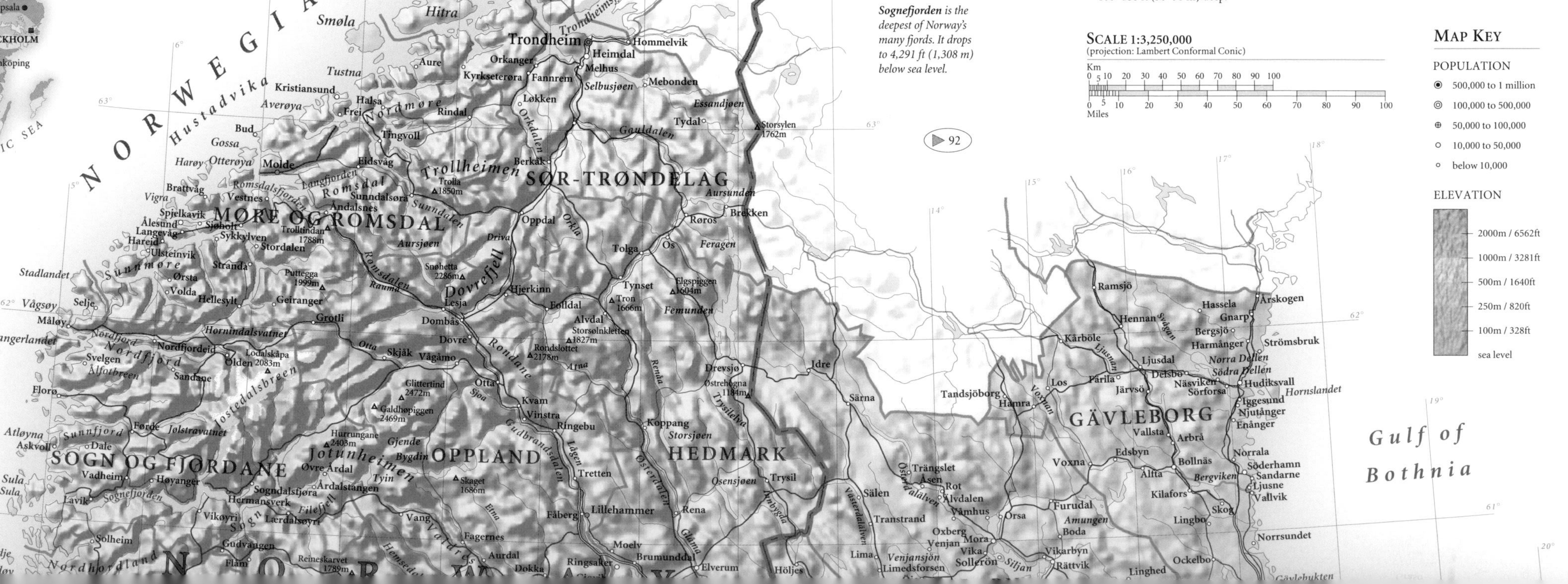
NORWEGIAN SEA
Frohavet
Hustadvika
Trondheim
Trondheimsfjorden
SØR-TRØNDELAG
MØRE OG ROMSDAL
SOGN OG FJORDANE
OPPLAND
HEDMARK
GÄVLEBORG
Jotunheimen
Dovrefjell
Trollheimen
Gulf of Bothnia
Storsylen 1762m
Glittertind 2472m
Galdhøpiggen 2469m
Snøhetta 2286m
92
96

Scale 1:3,250,000
(projection: Lambert Conformal Conic)

Map Key

Population
- 500,000 to 1 million
- 100,000 to 500,000
- 50,000 to 100,000
- 10,000 to 50,000
- below 10,000

Elevation
- 2000m / 6562ft
- 1000m / 3281ft
- 500m / 1640ft
- 250m / 820ft
- 100m / 328ft
- sea level

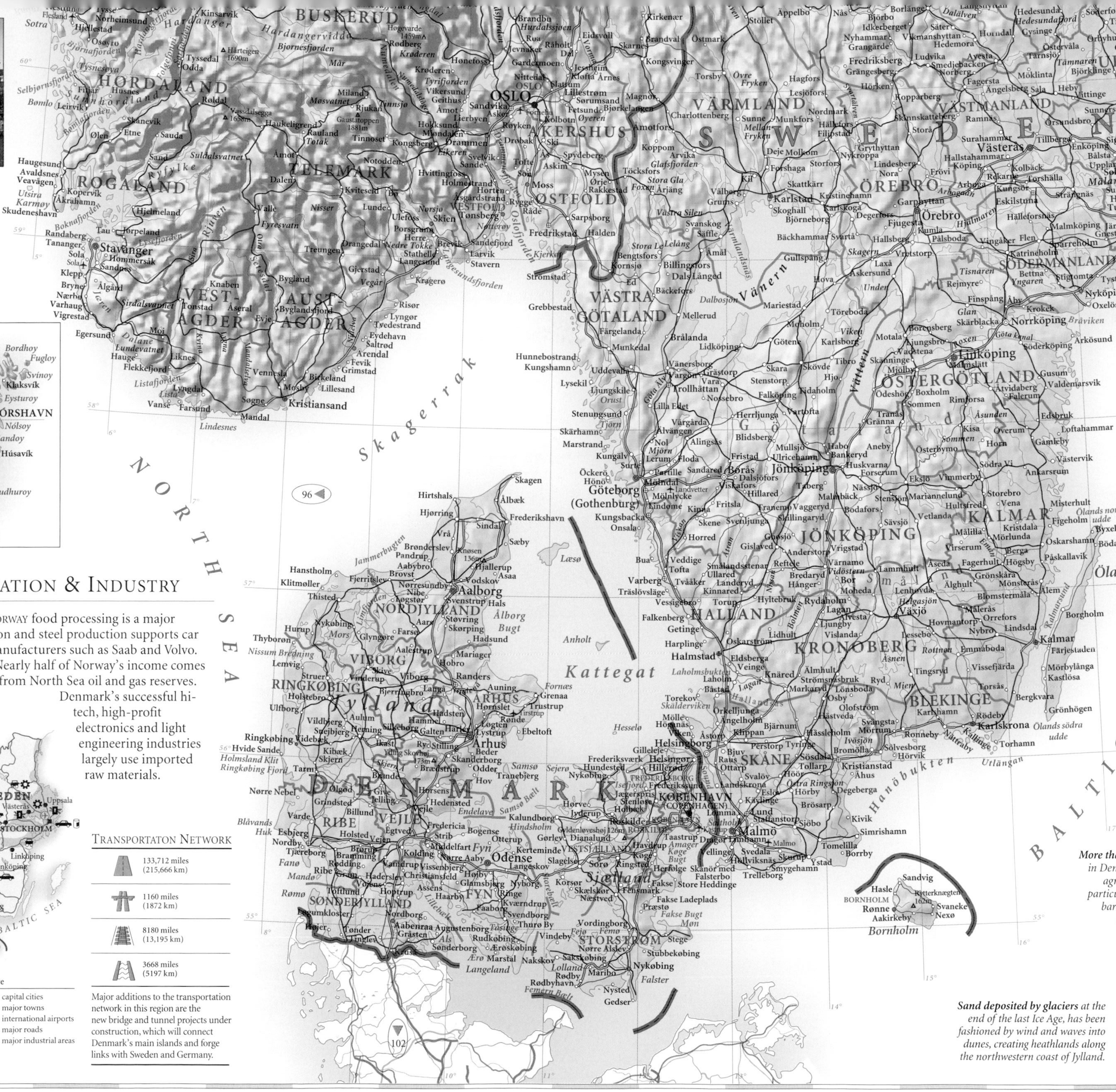

NORTH SEA
Skagerrak
Kattegat
BALTIC SEA
Ålands Hav
Hanöbukten
SWEDEN
DENMARK
BUSKERUD
HORDALAND
ROGALAND
TELEMARK
VEST-AGDER
AUST-AGDER
AKERSHUS
ØSTFOLD
VESTFOLD
VÄRMLAND
VÄSTMANLAND
UPPSALA
STOCKHOLM
ÖREBRO
SÖDERMANLAND
ÖSTERGÖTLAND
VÄSTRA GÖTALAND
JÖNKÖPING
KALMAR
HALLAND
KRONOBERG
BLEKINGE
SKÅNE
GOTLAND
NORDJYLLAND
VIBORG
ÅRHUS
RINGKØBING
VEJLE
RIBE
SØNDERJYLLAND
FYN
VESTSJÆLLAND
STORSTRØM
KØBENHAVN
FREDERIKSBORG
Jylland
Sjælland
Götaland
Småland
Vänern
Vättern
Mälaren
Öland
Gotland
Bornholm
Langeland
Falster
Lolland
Anholt
Læsø
OSLO
STOCKHOLM
KØBENHAVN (COPENHAGEN)
Göteborg (Gothenburg)
Malmö
Stavanger
Kristiansand
Uppsala
Västerås
Örebro
Norrköping
Linköping
Jönköping
Karlstad
Aalborg
Århus
Odense
Helsingborg
Kalmar
Karlskrona
Visby

Shipbuilding in Gothenburg *has declined in recent years as manufacturers in other sectors have come to the fore. One of these is the car firm, Volvo, a major employer in Gothenburg.*

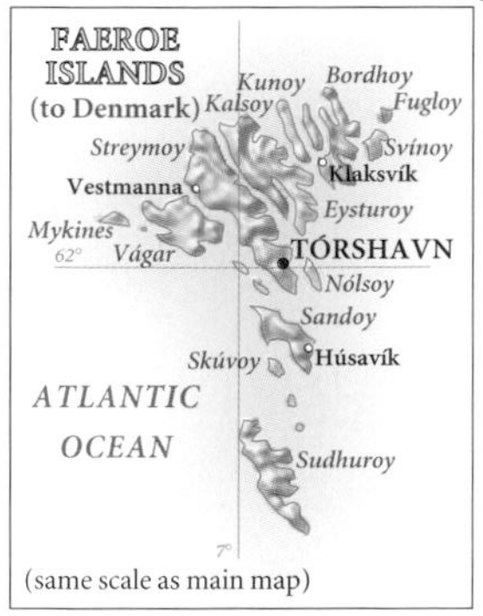

FAEROE ISLANDS
(to Denmark)
Kunoy
Bordhoy
Kalsoy
Fugloy
Svínoy
Streymoy
Klaksvík
Eysturoy
Vestmanna
Mykines
Vágar
TÓRSHAVN
Nólsoy
Sandoy
Skúvoy
Húsavík
Sudhuroy
ATLANTIC OCEAN
(same scale as main map)

Transportation & Industry

In Denmark and Norway food processing is a major industry. Swedish iron and steel production supports car manufacturers such as Saab and Volvo. Nearly half of Norway's income comes from North Sea oil and gas reserves. Denmark's successful hi-tech, high-profit electronics and light engineering industries largely use imported raw materials.

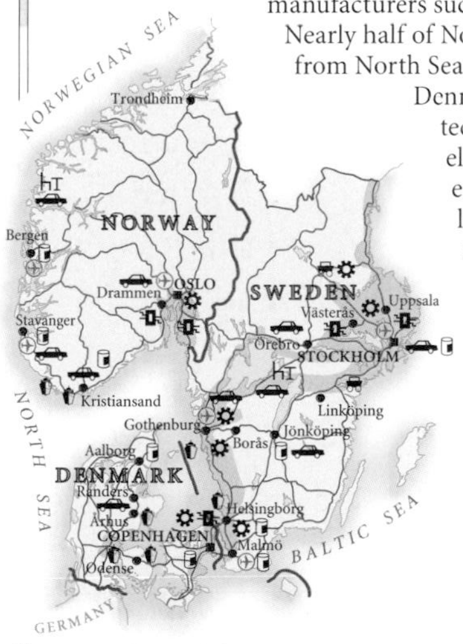

NORWEGIAN SEA
Trondheim
NORWAY
Bergen
OSLO
Drammen
Stavanger
Kristiansand
SWEDEN
Uppsala
Västerås
Örebro
STOCKHOLM
Linköping
Jönköping
Gothenburg
Borås
Aalborg
Randers
Århus
DENMARK
Helsingborg
Malmö
COPENHAGEN
Odense
NORTH SEA
BALTIC SEA
GERMANY

Major industry and infrastructure

- car manufacture
- electronics
- engineering
- furniture industry
- iron & steel
- shipbuilding
- food processing
- capital cities
- major towns
- international airports
- major roads
- major industrial areas

Transportaton Network

- 133,712 miles (215,666 km)
- 1160 miles (1872 km)
- 8180 miles (13,195 km)
- 3668 miles (5197 km)

Major additions to the transportation network in this region are the new bridge and tunnel projects under construction, which will connect Denmark's main islands and forge links with Sweden and Germany.

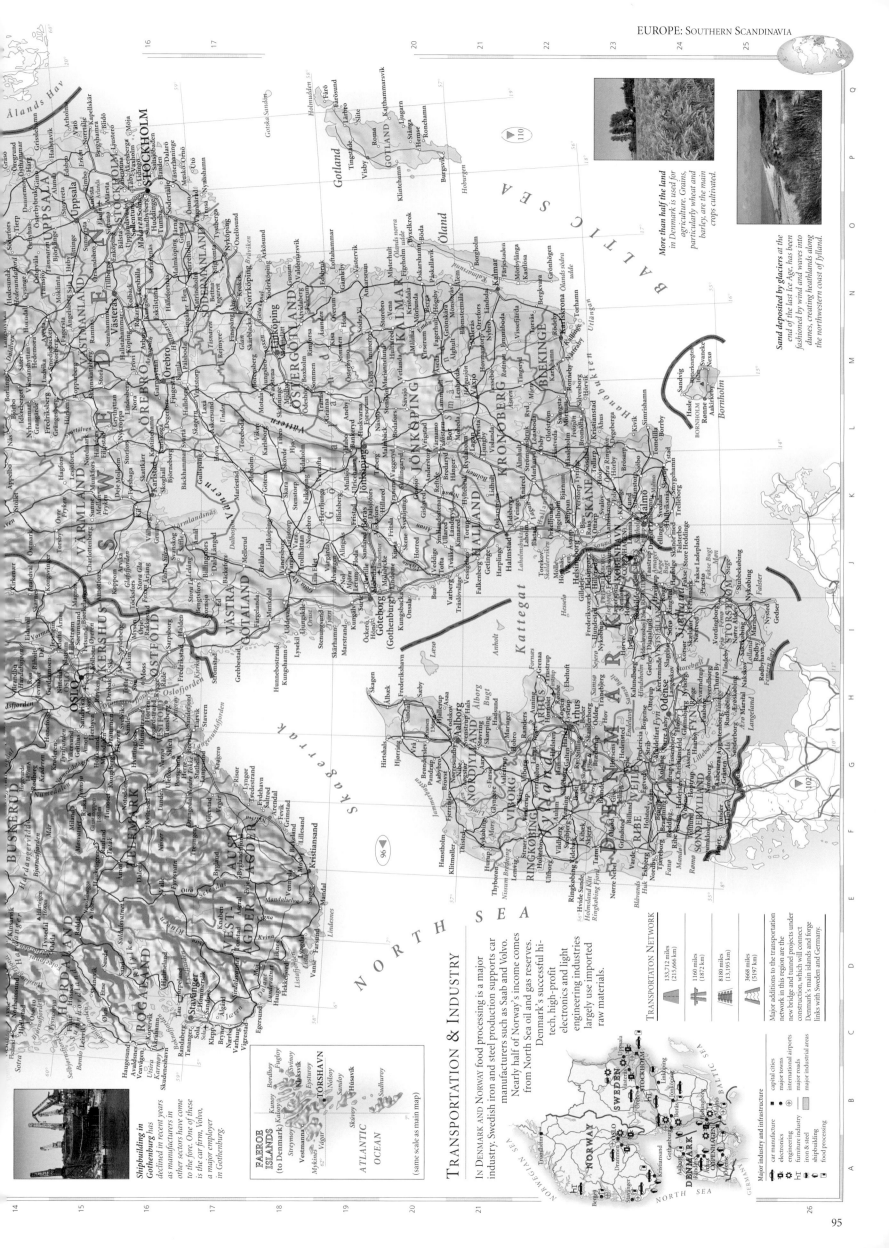

More than half the land *in Denmark is used for agriculture. Grains, particularly wheat and barley, are the main crops cultivated.*

Sand deposited by glaciers *at the end of the last Ice Age, has been fashioned by wind and waves into dunes, creating heathlands along the northwestern coast of Jylland.*

The British Isles

United Kingdom, Ireland

The British Isles have for centuries played a central role in European and world history. England, Wales, Scotland, and Northern Ireland together form the United Kingdom (UK), while the southern portion of Ireland is an independent country, self-governing since 1921. Although England has tended to be the politically and economically dominant partner in the UK, the Scots, Welsh and Irish maintain independent cultures, distinct national identities and languages. Southeastern England is the most densely populated part of this crowded region, with over nine million people living in and around the London area.

Transportation and Industry

The British Isles' industrial base was founded primarily on coal, iron and textiles, based largely in the north. Today, the most productive sectors include hi-tech industries clustered mainly in southeastern England, chemicals, finance and the service sector, particularly tourism.

Major industry and infrastructure
car manufacture
chemicals
engineering
hi-tech industry
iron & steel
tourism
capital cities
major towns
international airports
major roads
major industrial areas
ATLANTIC OCEAN
NORTH SEA
English Channel
Aberdeen
Dundee
Edinburgh
Glasgow
UNITED KINGDOM
Newcastle upon Tyne
Belfast
Leeds
Liverpool
Manchester
DUBLIN
IRELAND
Nottingham
Birmingham
Norwich
Cork
Cardiff
Oxford
Bristol
LONDON

Transportation Network

288,330 miles (464,300 km)		2,046 miles (3,295 km)	
11,874 miles (19,121 km)		3,806 miles (6,129 km)	

The UK's congested roads have become a major focus of environmental concern in recent years. No longer an island, the UK was finally linked to continental Europe by the Channel Tunnel in 1994.

Clew Bay in western Ireland, is characteristic of the heavily indented west coast, where deep wide-mouthed bays separate the mountains of Mayo, Donegal, and Kerry as they thrust out into the Atlantic Ocean.

The valley of Glen Coe in the Scottish Highlands is a U-shaped valley, typical of the north and west of the British Isles, where glaciers shaped much of the landscape.

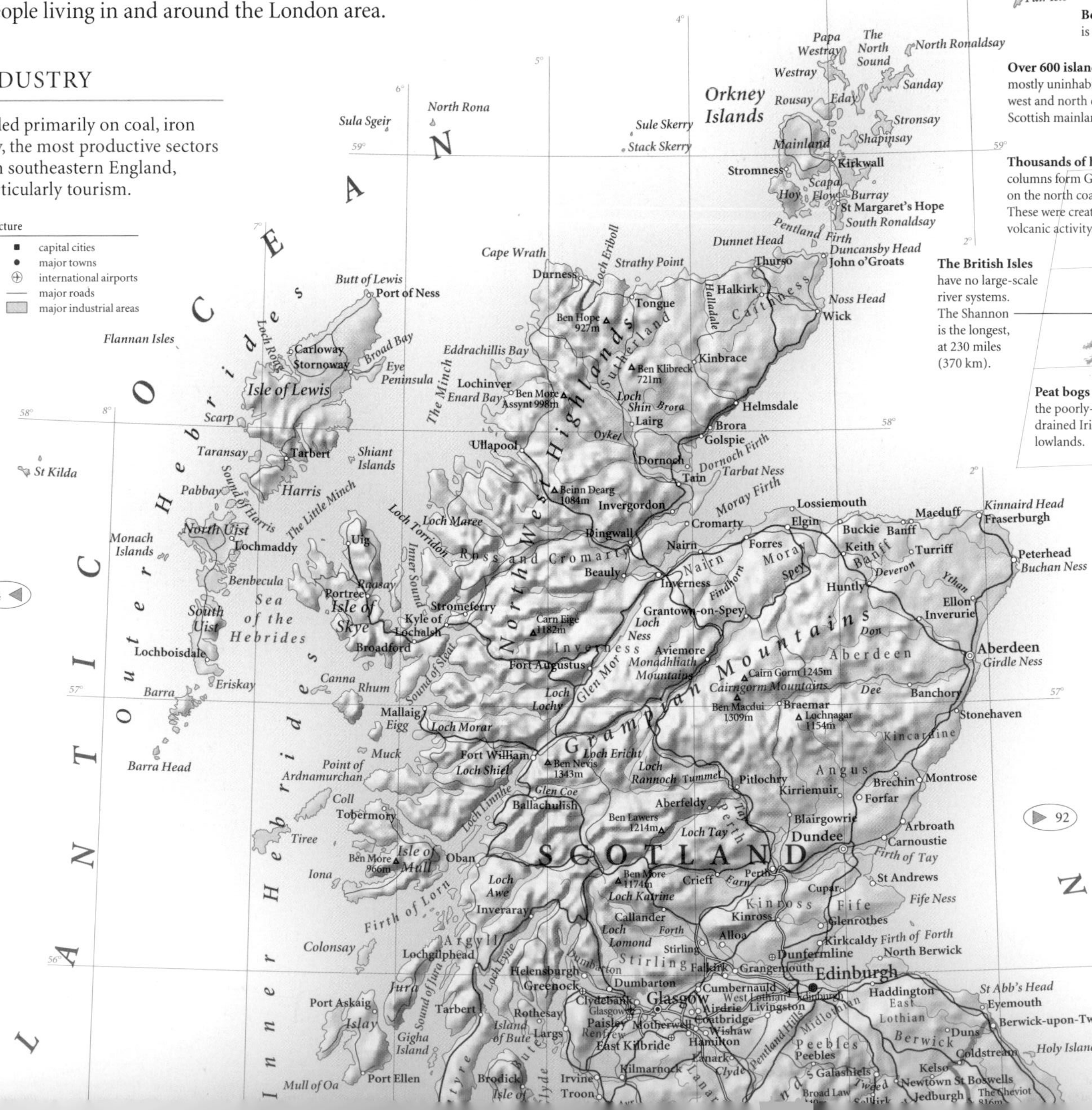
ATLANTIC OCEAN
NORTH SEA
SCOTLAND
Shetland Islands
Orkney Islands
Outer Hebrides
Inner Hebrides
Sea of the Hebrides
North West Highlands
Grampian Mountains
Isle of Lewis
Isle of Skye
Aberdeen
Dundee
Edinburgh
Glasgow
Inverness
Fort William
Ben Nevis 1343m
St Kilda
Cape Wrath
Dunnet Head
John o'Groats
Firth of Forth
Firth of Lorn
Moray Firth
64
92

64 ◀ ▶ 92

The Landscape

Rugged uplands dominate the landscape of Scotland, Wales, and northern England. All the peaks in the British Isles over 4,000 ft (1,219 m) lie in highland Scotland. Lowland England rises into several ranges of rolling hills, including the older Mendips, and the Cotswolds and the Chilterns, which were formed at the same time as the Alps in southern Europe.

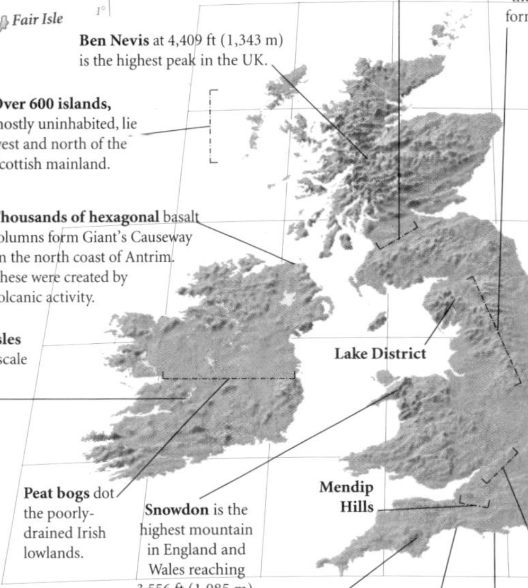
Lake District
Mendip Hills
Chiltern Hills
Black Ven, Lyme Regis
Durdle Door

The lowlands of Scotland, drained by the Tay, Forth, and Clyde Rivers, are centred on a rift valley. The region contains valuable coal reserves.

Ben Nevis at 4,409 ft (1,343 m) is the highest peak in the UK.

Over 600 islands, mostly uninhabited, lie west and north of the Scottish mainland.

Thousands of hexagonal basalt columns form Giant's Causeway on the north coast of Antrim. These were created by volcanic activity.

The British Isles have no large-scale river systems. The Shannon is the longest, at 230 miles (370 km).

Peat bogs dot the poorly-drained Irish lowlands.

Snowdon is the highest mountain in England and Wales reaching 3,556 ft (1,085 m).

The Pennines, sometimes called "the backbone of England," are formed of limestones and grits.

Ullswater in the Lake District fills a deep valley formed by glacial erosion.

The Fens are a low-lying area reclaimed from the sea.

The Cotswold Hills are characterized by a series of limestone ridges overlooking clay vales.

***Dartmoor,** studded with tors, is an exposed part of a vast granite dome, formed when molten rock intruded into the Earth's crust.*

Coastal erosion around the British Isles forms striking features such as this limestone arch, Durdle Door in Dorset.

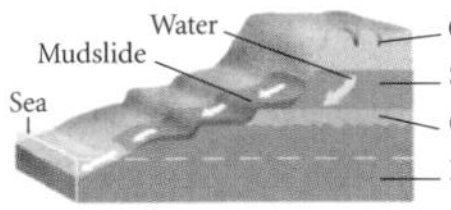
Water
Mudslide
Sea
Cracks
Sandstone
Clay
Limestone

***Much of the south coast** is subject to landslides. Following rain, porous sandstones feed water into the underlying, less permeable clays which then crumble and slide into the sea.*

Map Key

Population	Elevation
above 5 million	1000m / 3281ft
1 million to 5 million	500m / 1640ft
500,000 to 1 million	250m / 820ft
100,000 to 500,000	100m / 328ft
50,000 to 100,000	sea level
10,000 to 50,000	
below 10,000	

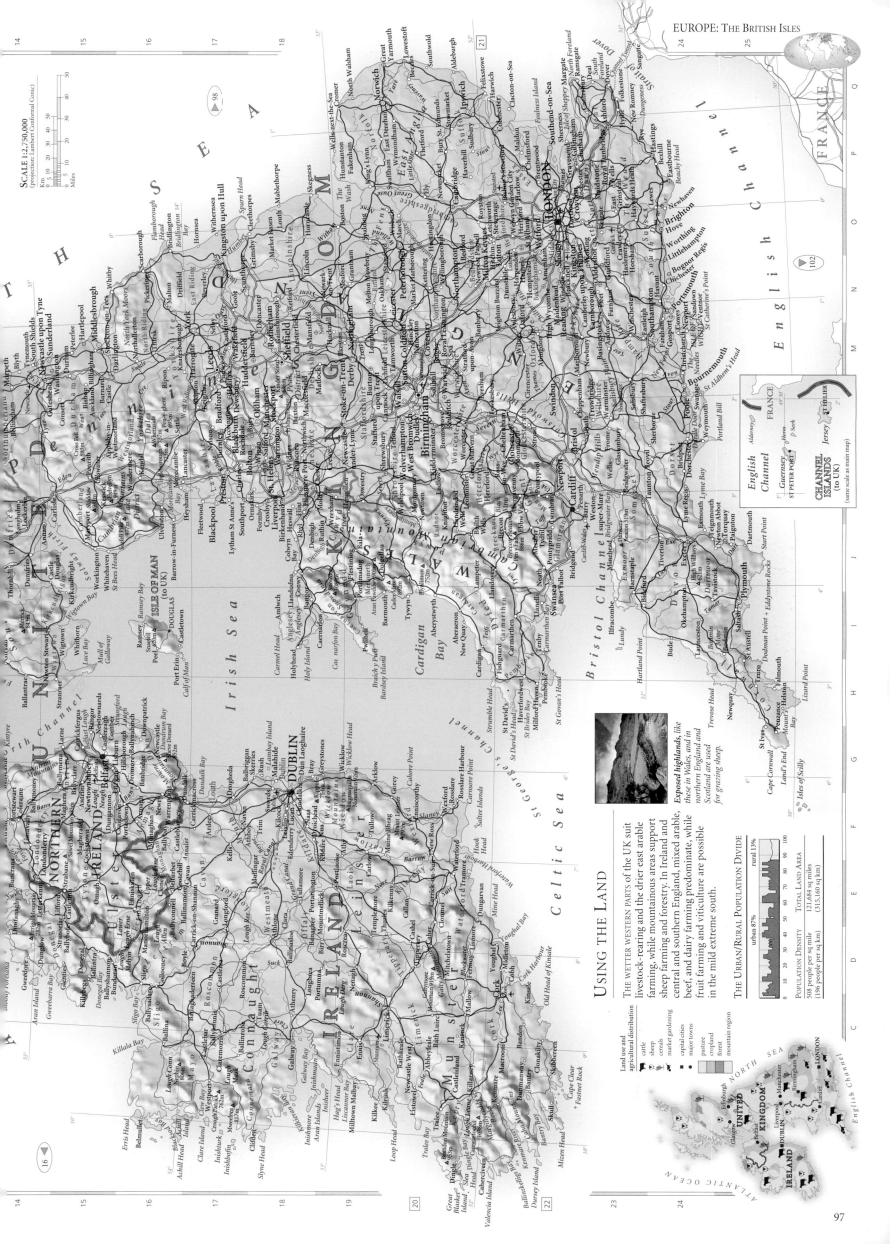

SCALE 1:2,750,000
(projection: Lambert Conformal Conic)
Km
Miles
UNITED KINGDOM
NORTHERN IRELAND
IRELAND
WALES
ENGLAND
Irish Sea
Celtic Sea
Cardigan Bay
Bristol Channel
English Channel
NORTH SEA
St George's Channel
North Channel
ISLE OF MAN (to UK)
DUBLIN
LONDON
Belfast
Cardiff
Birmingham
Manchester
Liverpool
Leeds
Sheffield
Bristol
Newcastle upon Tyne
Kingston upon Hull
Cork
Limerick
Galway
Plymouth
Southampton
Norwich
Ulster
Connaught
Leinster
Munster
English Channel
CHANNEL ISLANDS (to UK)
(same scale as main map)
Guernsey
Jersey
Alderney
Sark
Herm
ST PETER PORT
ST HELIER
FRANCE

USING THE LAND

THE WETTER WESTERN PARTS of the UK suit livestock-rearing and the drier east arable farming, while mountainous areas support sheep farming and forestry. In Ireland and central and southern England, mixed arable, beef, and dairy farming predominate, while fruit farming and viticulture are possible in the mild extreme south.

Exposed highlands, *like these in Wales, and in northern England and Scotland are used for grazing sheep.*

THE URBAN/RURAL POPULATION DIVIDE

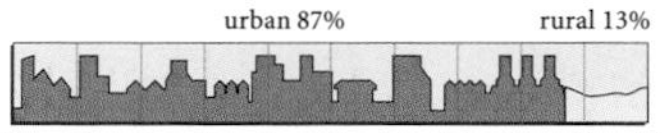
urban 87%
rural 13%
0
10
20
30
40
50
60
70
80
90
100

POPULATION DENSITY	TOTAL LAND AREA
508 people per sq mile (196 people per sq km)	121,684 sq miles (315,160 sq km)

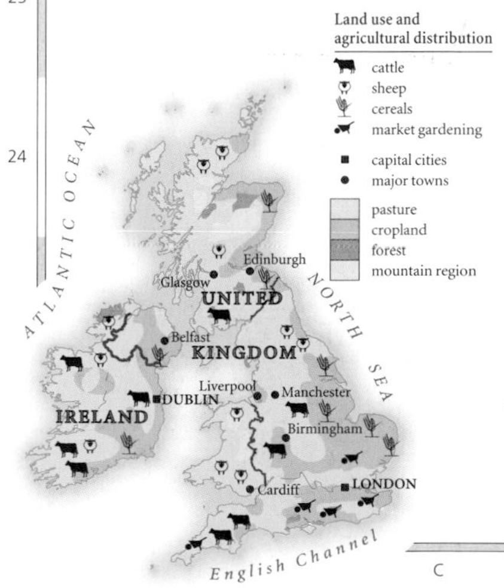
Land use and agricultural distribution
cattle
sheep
cereals
market gardening
capital cities
major towns
pasture
cropland
forest
mountain region
ATLANTIC OCEAN
NORTH SEA
English Channel
UNITED KINGDOM
IRELAND
Edinburgh
Glasgow
Belfast
DUBLIN
Liverpool
Manchester
Birmingham
Cardiff
LONDON

The Low Countries

Belgium, Luxembourg, Netherlands

One of northwestern Europe's strategic crossroads, the Low Countries are united by a common history in which they have often been a battleground in European wars. For over a thousand years they were ruled by foreign powers. Even after they achieved independence, the three countries maintained close links, later forming the world's first totally free labor and goods market, the Benelux Economic Union, which became the core of the European Community (now the European Union or EU). These states have remained at the forefront of wider European cooperation; Brussels, The Hague, and Luxembourg are hosts to major institutions of the EU.

NETHERLANDS
AMSTERDAM
THE HAGUE
Groningen
Enschede
Utrecht
Rotterdam
Breda
Nijmegen
Eindhoven
Bruges
Ghent
Kortrijk
Antwerp
BRUSSELS
Maastricht
BELGIUM
Liège
Charleroi
LUXEMBOURG
LUXEMBOURG
Differdange
NORTH SEA
GERMANY
FRANCE

Major industry and infrastructure
- aerospace
- finance
- engineering
- hi-tech industry
- pharmaceuticals
- textiles
- capital cities
- major towns
- international airports
- major roads
- major industrial areas

Transportation & Industry

In the western Netherlands, a massive, sprawling industrialized zone encompasses many new hi-tech and service industries. Belgium's central region has emerged as the country's light manufacturing and services center. Luxembourg city is home to more than 160 banks and the European headquarters of many international companies.

Transportation Network

280,630 miles (451,900 km)	2,536 miles (4,083 km)
4,037 miles (6,501 km)	4,366 miles (7,031 km)

The Low Countries hold a key position on the North Sea, containing Europe's two largest ports, Rotterdam and Antwerp, which are connected to a comprehensive system of inland waterways.

The Landscape

The main geographical regions of the Netherlands are the northern glacial heathlands, the low-lying lands of the Rhine and Maas/Meuse, the reclaimed polders, and the dune coast and islands. Belgium includes part of the Ardennes, together with the coalfields on its northern flanks, and the fertile Flanders Plain.

Schoorl

Heathlands, like these at Schoorl, are found along the coast of the Netherlands. Much of the coast was breached by the sea in the 5th century, creating its distinctive inlets and islands.

***One-third of the Netherlands** lies below sea level and flooding is a constant threat. Barrages have been built across the mouths of many rivers to contain floodwaters.*

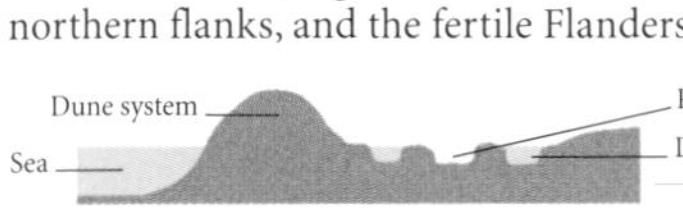

Dune system
Sea
Polder
Drainage ditch

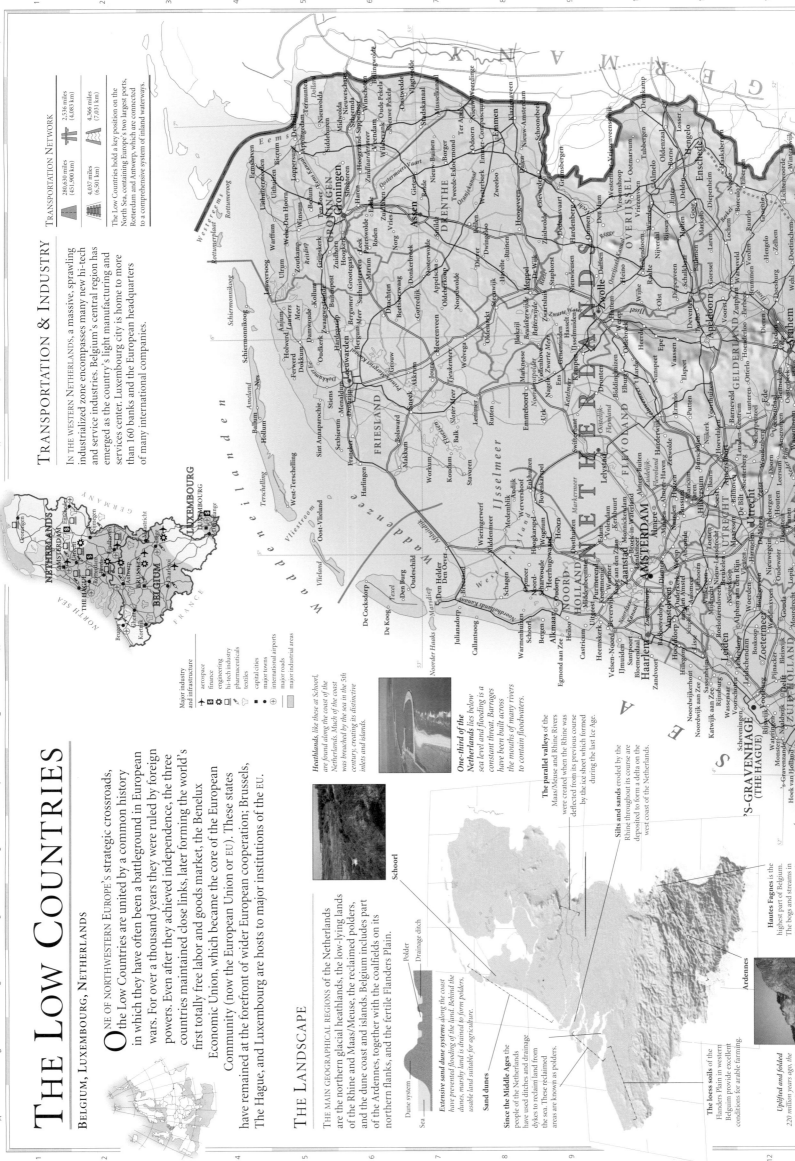

***Extensive sand dune systems** along the coast have prevented flooding of the land. Behind the dunes, marshy land is drained to form polders, usable land suitable for agriculture.*

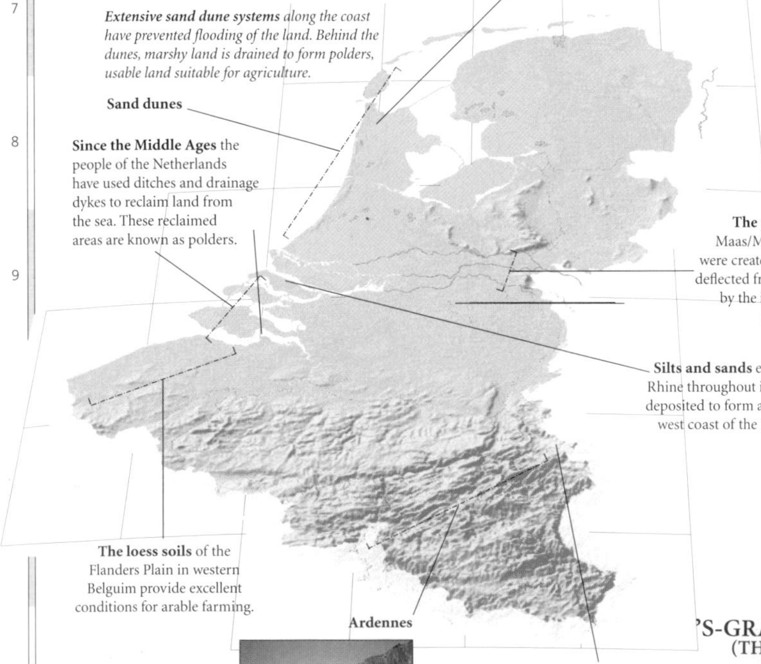

Sand dunes

Since the Middle Ages the people of the Netherlands have used ditches and drainage dykes to reclaim land from the sea. These reclaimed areas are known as polders.

The parallel valleys of the Maas/Meuse and Rhine Rivers were created when the Rhine was deflected from its previous course by the ice sheet which formed during the last Ice Age.

Silts and sands eroded by the Rhine throughout its course are deposited to form a delta on the west coast of the Netherlands.

The loess soils of the Flanders Plain in western Belgium provide excellent conditions for arable farming.

Ardennes

***Uplifted and folded** 220 million years ago, the Ardennes have since been reduced to relatively level plateaus, then sharply incised by rivers such as the Maas/Meuse.*

Hautes Fagnes is the highest part of Belgium. The bogs and streams in this upland region result from high rainfall and low temperatures.

Waddenzee
Waddeneilanden
Westereems
NETHERLANDS
FRIESLAND
GRONINGEN
DRENTHE
OVERIJSSEL
FLEVOLAND
GELDERLAND
UTRECHT
NOORD HOLLAND
ZUID HOLLAND
IJsselmeer
Markermeer
AMSTERDAM
'S-GRAVENHAGE (THE HAGUE)
Rotterdam
Utrecht
Haarlem
Leiden
Zoetermeer
Groningen
Leeuwarden
Assen
Zwolle
Lelystad
Apeldoorn
Arnhem
Nijmegen
Enschede
Hengelo
Almere
Amersfoort
Hilversum
Zaanstad
Alkmaar
Den Helder
Emmen
Delfzijl
Texel
Vlieland
Terschelling
Ameland
Schiermonnikoog
NORTH SEA
GERMANY

▶ 100

The Dutch city of Rotterdam lies within one of the most densely populated and highly industrialized regions in the world, known as "Randstad Holland."

Scale 1:1,100,000
(projection: Lambert Conformal Conic)
Km 0 5 10 20 30 40
Miles 0 5 10 20 30 40
Map Key
Population
500,000 to 1 million
100,000 to 500,000
50,000 to 100,000
10,000 to 50,000
below 10,000
Elevation
500m / 1640ft
250m / 820ft
100m / 328ft
sea level
BELGIUM
GERMANY
FRANCE
LUXEMBOURG
BRUSSEL/BRUXELLES (BRUSSELS)
WEST-VLAANDEREN
OOST-VLAANDEREN
ANTWERPEN
LIMBURG
NOORD-BRABANT
ZEELAND
VLAAMS BRABANT
BRABANT WALLON
HAINAUT
NAMUR
LIÈGE
LUXEMBOURG
DIEKIRCH
GREVENMACHER
Ardennes
Famenne
Flanders
100
102

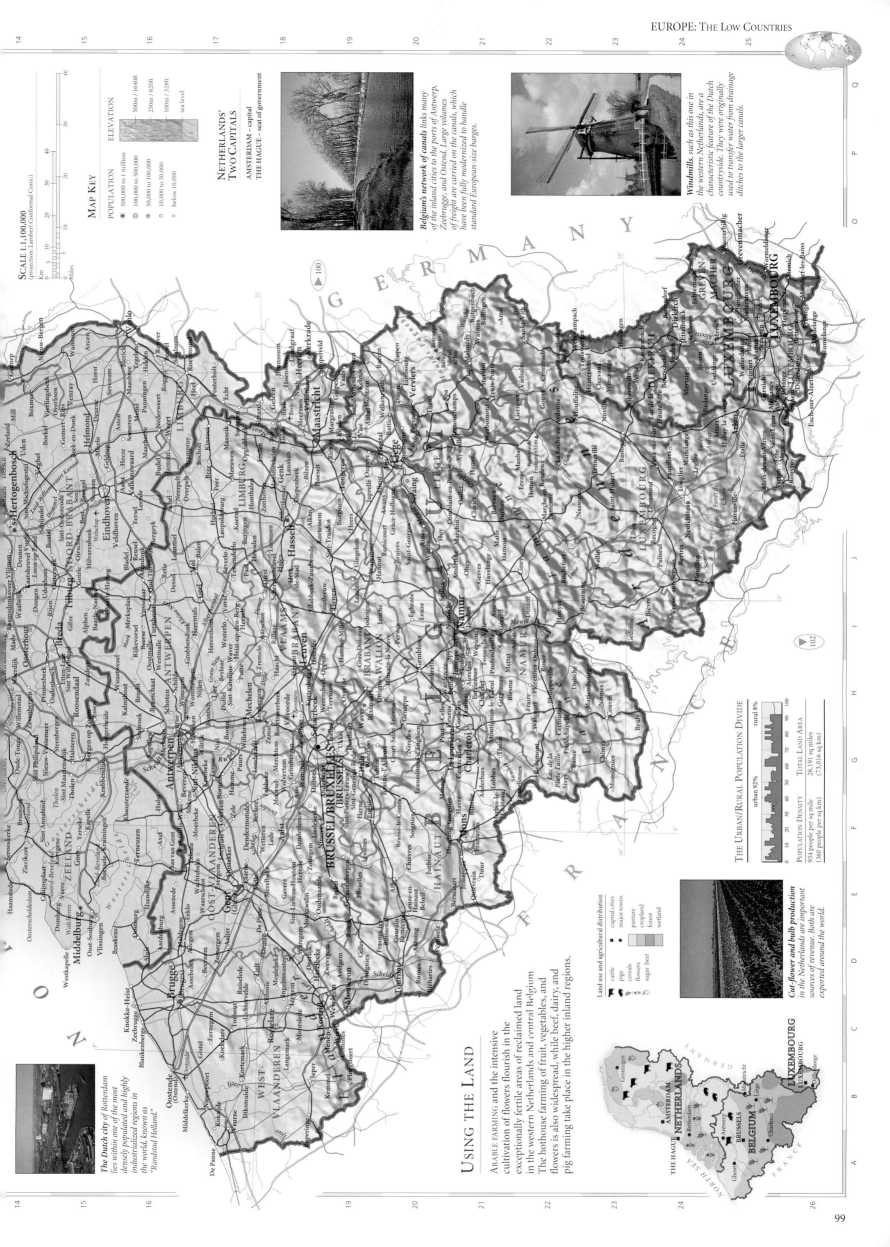

Netherlands' Two Capitals

AMSTERDAM – capital
THE HAGUE – seat of government

Belgium's network of canals links many of the inland cities to the ports of Antwerp, Zeebrugge, and Ostend. Large volumes of freight are carried on the canals, which have been fully modernized to handle standard European-size barges.

Windmills, such as this one in the western Netherlands, are a characteristic feature of the Dutch countryside. They were originally used to transfer water from drainage ditches to the larger canals.

Using the Land

Arable farming and the intensive cultivation of flowers flourish in the exceptionally fertile areas of reclaimed land in the western Netherlands and central Belgium. The hothouse farming of fruit, vegetables, and flowers is also widespread, while beef, dairy, and pig farming take place in the higher inland regions.

Land use and agricultural distribution
cattle
pigs
cereals
flowers
sugar beet
capital cities
major towns
pasture
cropland
forest
wetland
THE HAGUE
AMSTERDAM
NETHERLANDS
Groningen
Rotterdam
Antwerp
Ghent
BRUSSELS
BELGIUM
Maastricht
Liège
Charleroi
LUXEMBOURG
Differdange
NORTH SEA
GERMANY
FRANCE

Cut-flower and bulb production in the Netherlands are important sources of revenue. Both are exported around the world.

The Urban/Rural Population Divide

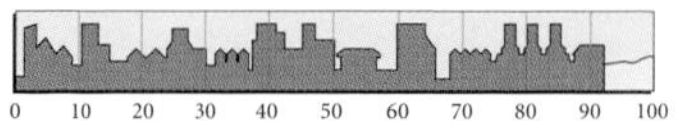
urban 92%
rural 8%
0 10 20 30 40 50 60 70 80 90 100

Population Density	Total Land Area
934 people per sq mile (360 people per sq km)	28,191 sq miles (73,016 sq km)

GERMANY

DESPITE THE DEVASTATION of its industry and infrastructure during the Second World War and its separation from eastern Germany during the Cold War, West Germany made a rapid recovery in the following generation to become Europe's most formidable economic power. When the Berlin Wall was dismantled in 1989, the two halves of Germany were politically united for the first time in 40 years. Complete social and economic unity remain a longer term goal, as East German industry and society adapt to a free market. Germany has been a key player in the creation of the European Union (EU) and in moves toward a single European currency.

USING THE LAND

GERMANY has a large, efficient agricultural sector, and produces more than three-quarters of its own food. The major crops grown are cereals and sugar beet on the more fertile soils, and root crops, rye, oats, and fodder on the poorer soils of the northern plains and central uplands. Southern Germany is also a principal producer of high quality wines. Vineyards cover the slopes surrounding the Rhine and its tributaries.

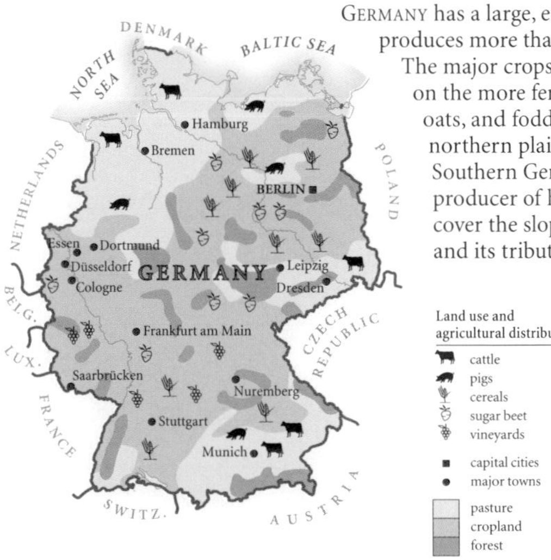
DENMARK
BALTIC SEA
NORTH SEA
POLAND
NETHERLANDS
BELG.
LUX.
FRANCE
SWITZ.
AUSTRIA
CZECH REPUBLIC
GERMANY
Hamburg
Bremen
BERLIN
Essen
Dortmund
Düsseldorf
Cologne
Leipzig
Dresden
Frankfurt am Main
Saarbrücken
Nuremberg
Stuttgart
Munich
Land use and agricultural distribution
cattle
pigs
cereals
sugar beet
vineyards
capital cities
major towns
pasture
cropland
forest

THE URBAN/RURAL POPULATION DIVIDE

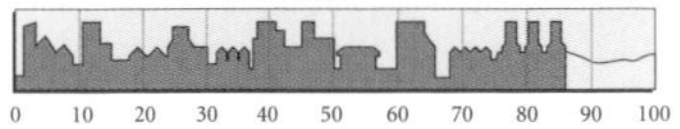
urban 87%
rural 13%
0 10 20 30 40 50 60 70 80 90 100

POPULATION DENSITY	TOTAL LAND AREA
598 people per sq mile (231 people per sq km)	13,804 sq miles (356,910 sq km)

The Moselle River flows through the Rhine State Uplands (Rheinisches Schiefergebirge). *During a period of uplift, preexisting river meanders were deeply incised, to form its present dramatic contours.*

***The heathlands** of northern Germany are covered by glacial deposits of sandy outwash soil which makes them largely infertile. They support only sheep and solitary trees.*

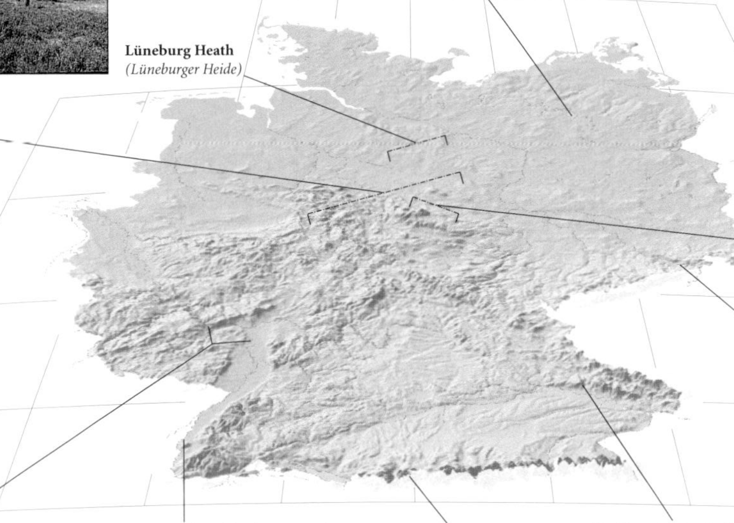
Lüneburg Heath (Lüneburger Heide)
Elbe River
Rhine Rift Valley

Much of the landscape of northern Germany has been shaped by glaciation. During the last Ice Age, the ice sheet advanced as far the northern slopes of the central uplands.

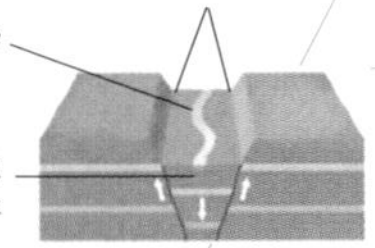
Fault lines
Rhine
Downfaulted block

***Part of the floor** of the Rhine Rift Valley was let down between two parallel faults in the Earth's crust.*

Müritz lake covers 45 sq miles (117 sq km), but is only 1,08 ft (33 m) deep. It lies in a shallow valley formed by meltwater flowing out from a retreating ice sheet. These valleys are known as *Urstromtäler*.

The Harz Mountains were formed 300 million years ago. They are block-faulted mountains, formed when a section of the Earth's crust was thrust up between two faults.

The Rhine is Germany's principal waterway and one of Europe's longest rivers, flowing 820 miles (1,320 km).

Zugspitze, the highest peak in Germany at 9,719 ft (2,962 m), was formed during the Alpine mountain-building period, 30 million years ago.

The Danube rises in the Black Forest *(Schwarzwald)* and flows east, across a wide valley, on its course to the Black Sea.

THE LANDSCAPE

THE PLAINS OF NORTHERN GERMANY, the volcanic plateaus and mountains of the central uplands, and the Bavarian Alps are the three principal geographic regions in Germany. North to south the land rises steadily from barely 300 ft (90 m) in the plains to 6,500 ft (2,000 m) in the Bavarian Alps, which are a small but distinct region in the far south.

***The Elbe flows** in wide meanders across the north German plain to the North Sea. At its mouth it is 10 miles (16 km) wide.*

SCALE 1:2,500,000
(projection: Lambert Conformal Conic)

BALTIC SEA
NORTH SEA
DENMARK
POLAND
NETHERLANDS
SCHLESWIG-HOLSTEIN
MECKLENBURG-VORPOMMERN
NIEDERSACHSEN
BRANDENBURG
BREMEN
HAMBURG
BERLIN
Hamburg
Bremen
Hannover
Kiel
Rostock
Lübeck
Schwerin
Potsdam
Kieler Bucht
Mecklenburger Bucht
Pomeranian Bay
Helgoländer Bucht
Ostfriesische Inseln
North Frisian Islands (Nordfriesische Inseln)
92
96
98
110

Map Key

Population

- 1 million to 5 million
- 500,000 to 1 million
- 100,000 to 500,000
- 50,000 to 100,000
- 10,000 to 50,000
- below 10,000

Elevation

- 2000m / 6562ft
- 1000m / 3281ft
- 500m / 1640ft
- 250m / 820ft
- 100m / 328ft
- sea level

Transportation Network

Roads	393,093 miles (633,000 km)
Motorways	6949 miles (11,190 km)
Railways	23,877 miles (38,450 km)
Waterways	4,595 miles (7,400 km)

Germany has a complex network of inland waterways. The Rhine and Danube are at the center of a vast canal system which links central and eastern Europe to the north.

GERMANY
NORDRHEIN-WESTFALEN
HESSEN
THÜRINGEN
SACHSEN
RHEINLAND-PFALZ
SAARLAND
BADEN-WÜRTTEMBERG
BAYERN
CZECH REPUBLIC
AUSTRIA
SWITZERLAND
FRANCE
LUXEMBOURG
BELGIUM
Erzgebirge
Thüringer Wald
Bohemian Forest
Schwäbische Alb
Schwarzwald
Bavarian Alps
Lake Constance
Danube (Donau)
Rhine (Rhein)
Köln (Cologne)
Düsseldorf
Dortmund
Essen
Frankfurt am Main
Wiesbaden
Mainz
Stuttgart
Mannheim
Nürnberg (Nuremberg)
München (Munich)
Augsburg
Regensburg
Würzburg
Dresden
Leipzig
Chemnitz
Halle
Erfurt
Saarbrücken
Karlsruhe
Freiburg im Breisgau
98
102
108
108
110

***The Bavarian Alps** straddle the country's southern border at an average height of 6,500 ft (2,000 m).*

***In the Black Forest** (Schwarzwald), in southwestern Germany, woodland cloaks sandstone and granite hills, which contain rich mineral springs.*

Transportation & Industry

Today, the main industries which contribute to Germany's economic power are industrial machine building, electronics, chemicals, and car manufacture, including the famous Mercedes and BMW firms. While the introduction of a free market in the east has forced the closure of many less efficient companies there, west German manufacturers have moved in to set up new plants and businesses.

DENMARK
BALTIC SEA
NORTH SEA
NETHERLANDS
POLAND
CZECH REPUBLIC
AUSTRIA
SWITZ.
FRANCE
LUX.
BELG.
GERMANY
Kiel
Rostock
Hamburg
Bremen
BERLIN
Osnabrück
Hannover
Dortmund
Essen
Düsseldorf
Cologne
Leipzig
Dresden
Frankfurt am Main
Saarbrücken
Heidelberg
Nuremberg
Stuttgart
Ingolstadt
Augsburg
Munich

Major industry and infrastructure

- car manufacture
- chemicals
- hi-tech industry
- iron & steel
- mining
- precision engineering
- research & development
- shipbuilding
- capital cities
- major towns
- international airports
- major roads
- major industrial areas

A B C D E F G H I J

France

France, Monaco

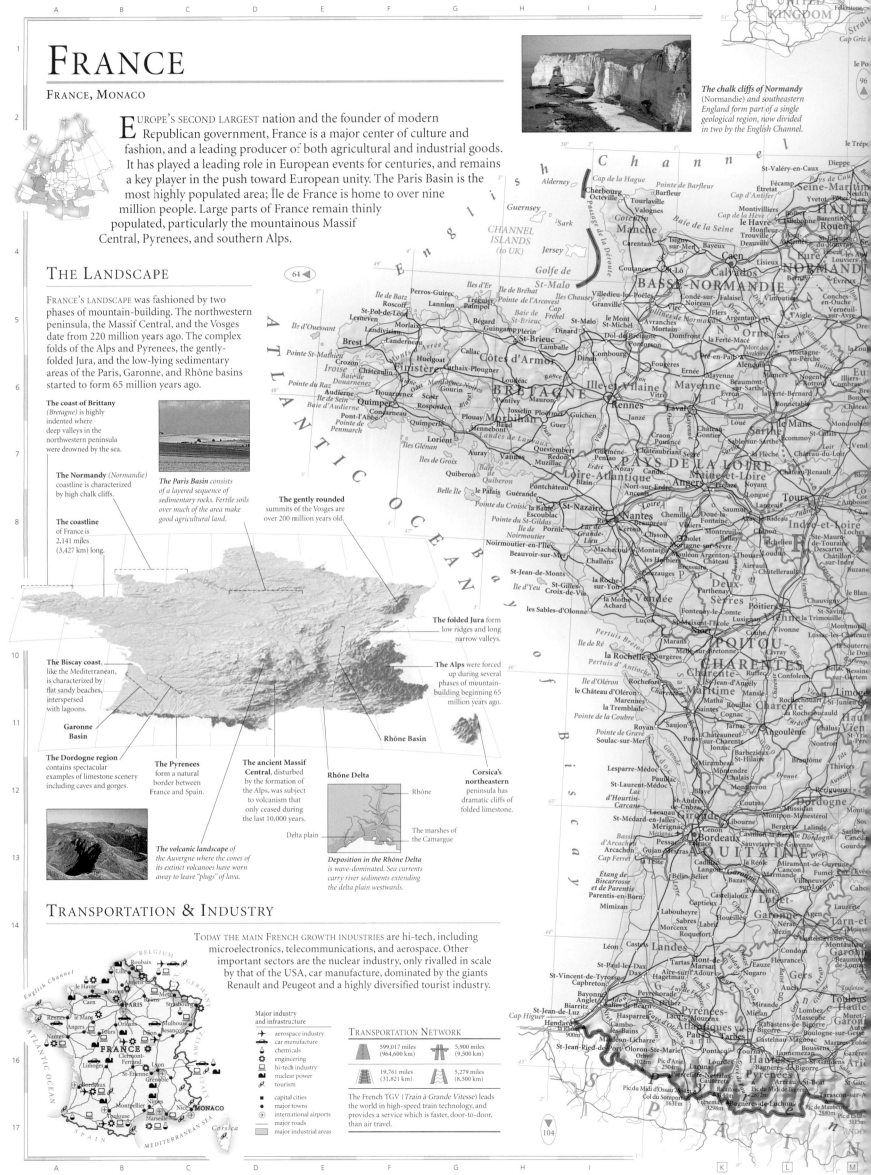

Europe's second largest nation and the founder of modern Republican government, France is a major center of culture and fashion, and a leading producer of both agricultural and industrial goods. It has played a leading role in European events for centuries, and remains a key player in the push toward European unity. The Paris Basin is the most highly populated area; Île de France is home to over nine million people. Large parts of France remain thinly populated, particularly the mountainous Massif Central, Pyrenees, and southern Alps.

The chalk cliffs of Normandy (Normandie) *and southeastern England form part of a single geological region, now divided in two by the English Channel.*

The Landscape

France's landscape was fashioned by two phases of mountain-building. The northwestern peninsula, the Massif Central, and the Vosges date from 220 million years ago. The complex folds of the Alps and Pyrenees, the gently-folded Jura, and the low-lying sedimentary areas of the Paris, Garonne, and Rhône basins started to form 65 million years ago.

The coast of Brittany *(Bretagne)* is highly indented where deep valleys in the northwestern peninsula were drowned by the sea.

The Paris Basin consists of a layered sequence of sedimentary rocks. Fertile soils over much of the area make good agricultural land.

The Normandy *(Normandie)* coastline is characterized by high chalk cliffs.

The coastline of France is 2,141 miles (3,427 km) long.

The gently rounded summits of the Vosges are over 200 million years old.

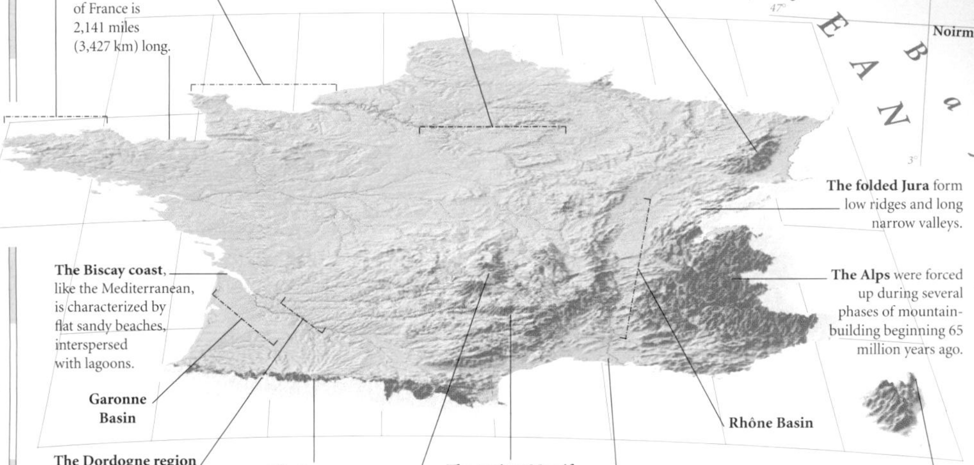

The folded Jura form low ridges and long narrow valleys.

The Biscay coast, like the Mediterranean, is characterized by flat sandy beaches, interspersed with lagoons.

The Alps were forced up during several phases of mountain-building beginning 65 million years ago.

Garonne Basin

Rhône Basin

The Dordogne region contains spectacular examples of limestone scenery including caves and gorges.

The Pyrenees form a natural border between France and Spain.

The ancient Massif Central, disturbed by the formation of the Alps, was subject to volcanism that only ceased during the last 10,000 years.

Rhône Delta

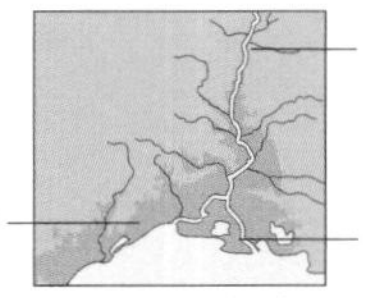

Rhône
Delta plain
The marshes of the Camargue

Deposition in the Rhône Delta is wave-dominated. Sea currents carry river sediments extending the delta plain westwards.

Corsica's northeastern peninsula has dramatic cliffs of folded limestone.

The volcanic landscape of the Auvergne where the cones of its extinct volcanoes have worn away to leave "plugs" of lava.

Transportation & Industry

Today the main French growth industries are hi-tech, including microelectronics, telecommunications, and aerospace. Other important sectors are the nuclear industry, only rivalled in scale by that of the USA, car manufacture, dominated by the giants Renault and Peugeot and a highly diversified tourist industry.

BELGIUM
English Channel
GERMANY
SWITZERLAND
ITALY
ATLANTIC OCEAN
MEDITERRANEAN SEA
SPAIN
FRANCE
Roubaix
Lille
Amiens
le Havre
Rouen
Caen
PARIS
Reims
Metz
Strasbourg
Rennes
le Mans
Orléans
Angers
Tours
Dijon
Mulhouse
Besançon
Nantes
Clermont-Ferrand
Limoges
Lyon
St-Étienne
Grenoble
Bordeaux
Montpellier
Nîmes
Toulouse
Marseille
Nice
MONACO
Corsica

Major industry and infrastructure

- aerospace industry
- car manufacture
- chemicals
- engineering
- hi-tech industry
- nuclear power
- tourism
- capital cities
- major towns
- international airports
- major roads
- major industrial areas

Transportation Network

599,017 miles (964,600 km)	5,900 miles (9,500 km)
19,761 miles (31,821 km)	5,279 miles (8,500 km)

The French TGV (*Train à Grande Vitesse*) leads the world in high-speed train technology, and provides a service which is faster, door-to-door, than air travel.

UNITED KINGDOM
English Channel
CHANNEL ISLANDS (to UK)
Alderney
Guernsey
Sark
Jersey
Golfe de St-Malo
ATLANTIC OCEAN
Bay of Biscay
BASSE-NORMANDIE
HAUTE-NORMANDIE
BRETAGNE
PAYS DE LA LOIRE
POITOU-CHARENTES
AQUITAINE
SPAIN
Cherbourg
Caen
Rouen
le Havre
Brest
Rennes
Nantes
St-Nazaire
Angers
le Mans
Tours
Poitiers
la Rochelle
Niort
Angoulême
Bordeaux
Bayonne
Biarritz
Pau
Tarbes
Lourdes
Agen
Quimper
Lorient
Vannes
St-Brieuc
St-Malo
Laval
Saumur
Cognac
Périgueux

64

96

104

A B C D E F G H I K L M

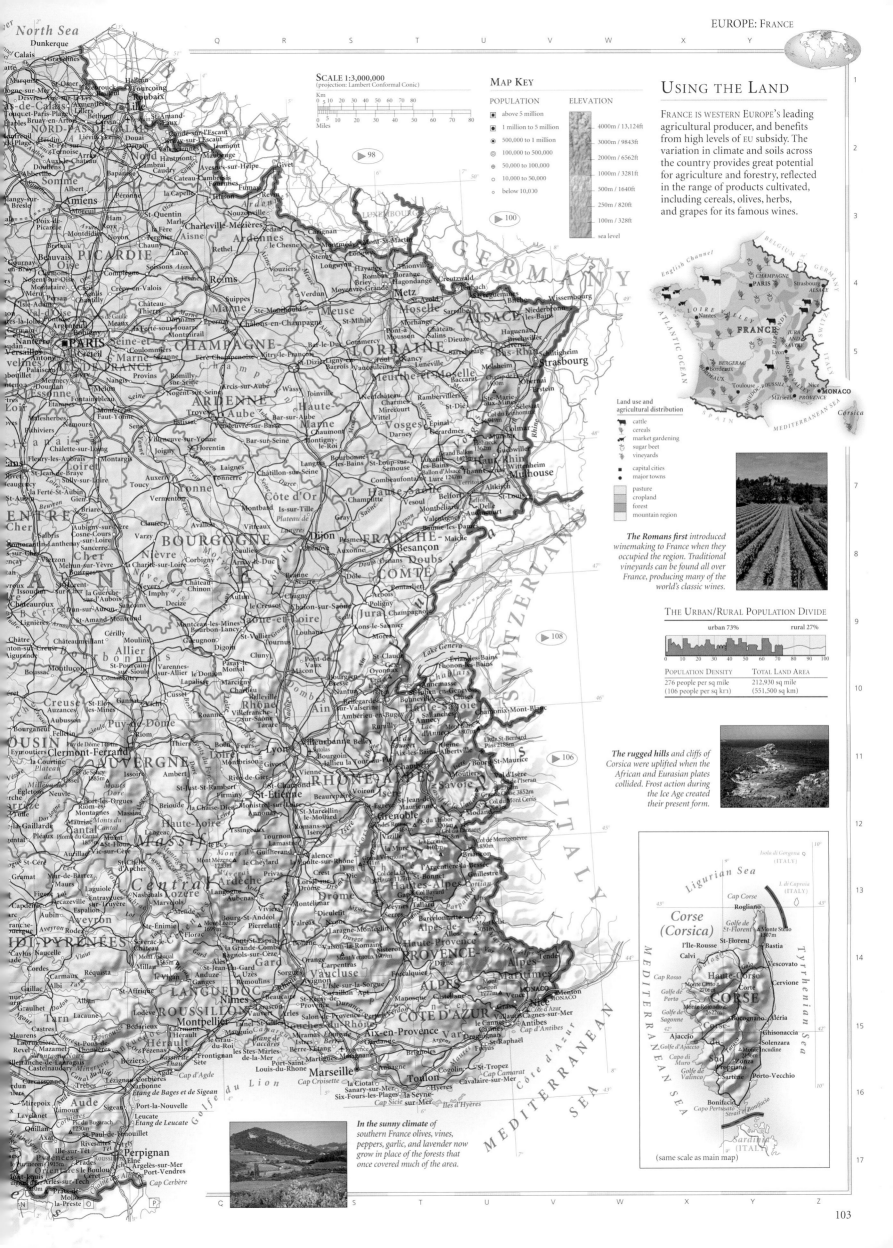

North Sea
SCALE 1:3,000,000
(projection: Lambert Conformal Conic)
MAP KEY
POPULATION
above 5 million
1 million to 5 million
500,000 to 1 million
100,000 to 500,000
50,000 to 100,000
10,000 to 50,000
below 10,000
ELEVATION
4000m / 13,124ft
3000m / 9843ft
2000m / 6562ft
1000m / 3281ft
500m / 1640ft
250m / 820ft
100m / 328ft
sea level
LUXEMBOURG
GERMANY
SWITZERLAND
ITALY
MONACO
PARIS
CHAMPAGNE-ARDENNE
LORRAINE
ALSACE
BOURGOGNE
FRANCHE-COMTÉ
RHÔNE-ALPES
AUVERGNE
PICARDIE
PROVENCE-ALPES-CÔTE D'AZUR
LANGUEDOC-ROUSSILLON
Massif Central
Golfe du Lion
MEDITERRANEAN SEA
Marseille
Lyon
Strasbourg
Toulon
Nice
Montpellier
Perpignan
Dijon
Grenoble

USING THE LAND

FRANCE IS WESTERN EUROPE'S leading agricultural producer, and benefits from high levels of EU subsidy. The variation in climate and soils across the country provides great potential for agriculture and forestry, reflected in the range of products cultivated, including cereals, olives, herbs, and grapes for its famous wines.

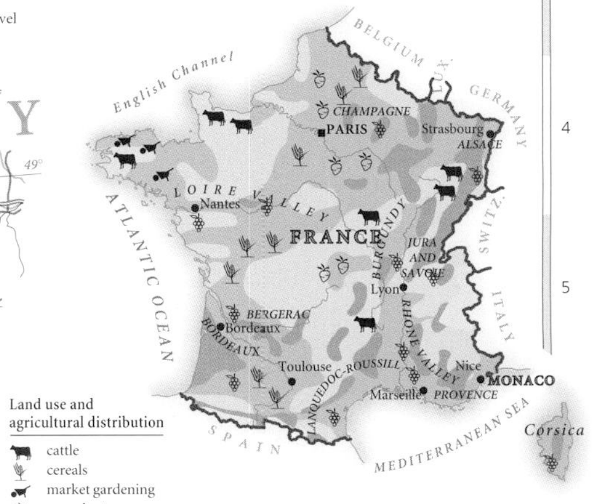
English Channel
ATLANTIC OCEAN
BELGIUM
GERMANY
SWITZERLAND
ITALY
SPAIN
MEDITERRANEAN SEA
CHAMPAGNE
PARIS
Strasbourg
ALSACE
LOIRE VALLEY
Nantes
FRANCE
JURA AND SAVOIE
Lyon
BERGERAC
Bordeaux
BORDEAUX
RHÔNE VALLEY
Toulouse
LANGUEDOC-ROUSSILLON
Marseille
PROVENCE
Nice
MONACO
Corsica
Land use and agricultural distribution
cattle
cereals
market gardening
sugar beet
vineyards
capital cities
major towns
pasture
cropland
forest
mountain region

The Romans first introduced winemaking to France when they occupied the region. Traditional vineyards can be found all over France, producing many of the world's classic wines.

THE URBAN/RURAL POPULATION DIVIDE

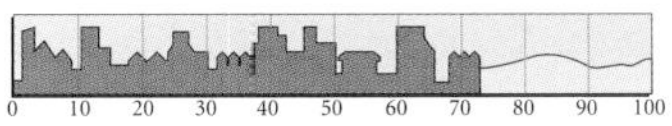
urban 73%
rural 27%
0 10 20 30 40 50 60 70 80 90 100

POPULATION DENSITY	TOTAL LAND AREA
276 people per sq mile (106 people per sq km)	212,930 sq mile (551,500 sq km)

The rugged hills and cliffs of Corsica were uplifted when the African and Eurasian plates collided. Frost action during the Ice Age created their present form.

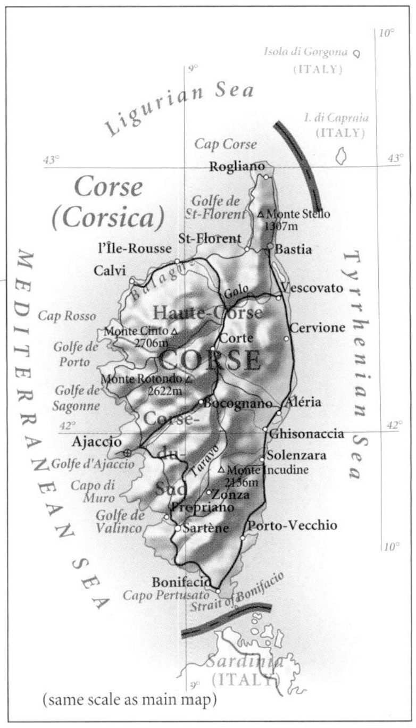
Ligurian Sea
Corse (Corsica)
Tyrrhenian Sea
MEDITERRANEAN SEA
Cap Corse
Bastia
Calvi
Ajaccio
Porto-Vecchio
Bonifacio
Strait of Bonifacio
Sardinia (ITALY)
(same scale as main map)

In the sunny climate of southern France olives, vines, peppers, garlic, and lavender now grow in place of the forests that once covered much of the area.

The Iberian peninsula

Andorra, Gibraltar, Portugal, Spain *(Azores, Canary Islands, Madeira on p.64)*

The Iberian peninsula is separated from the rest of Europe by the Pyrenees, and at its most southerly point is only 5 miles (8 km) from North Africa. The location of Iberia has been central to its diverse history. The Greeks, Carthaginians, Romans, Visigoths, and most recently the Moors, invaded Iberia at various times. For much of the 20th century, both Spain and Portugal were governed by right-wing dictators. Since the establishment of democratic governments in the mid-1970s, modernization has been rapid and both countries are now among the most popular of European holiday destinations.

Using the Land

The principal crops grown in Iberia are cereals, especially wheat and barley. Both countries are major wine producers, most notably of Rioja, sherry, and port. Sheep are kept throughout the region, and citrus fruits thrive on the Mediterranean coast. The successful forest industry in Iberia produces two-thirds of the world's cork.

***The steep, terraced slopes** of the Douro Valley in northern Portugal, are used to cultivate vines. The grapes harvested produce Portugal's famous port wine.*

Bay of Biscay
FRANCE
ANDORRA
Braga
Oporto
Barcelona
SPAIN
MADRID
PORTUGAL
LISBON
Setúbal
Valencia
Islas Baleares
Seville
ATLANTIC OCEAN
MEDITERRANEAN SEA

Land use and agricultural distribution
- sheep
- cereals
- citrus fruit
- olives
- vineyards
- cork
- capital cities
- major towns
- pasture
- cropland
- forest
- mountain region

The Urban/Rural Population Divide

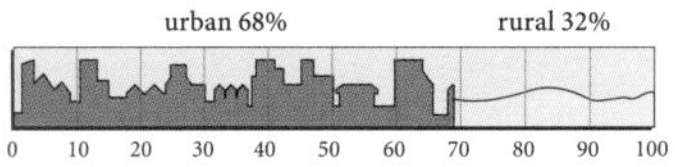
urban 68%
rural 32%
0 10 20 30 40 50 60 70 80 90 100

Population Density	Total Land Area
215 people per sq mile (83 people per sq km)	230,569 sq miles (597,170 sq km)

Transportation & Industry

Since the 1970s, the economies of Spain and Portugal have expanded and diversified. In both countries, tourism has outstripped agriculture in economic importance. Spain's resource base is varied, including coal, iron, and the world's largest reserves of mercury. Portugal is a leading producer of tungsten ore.

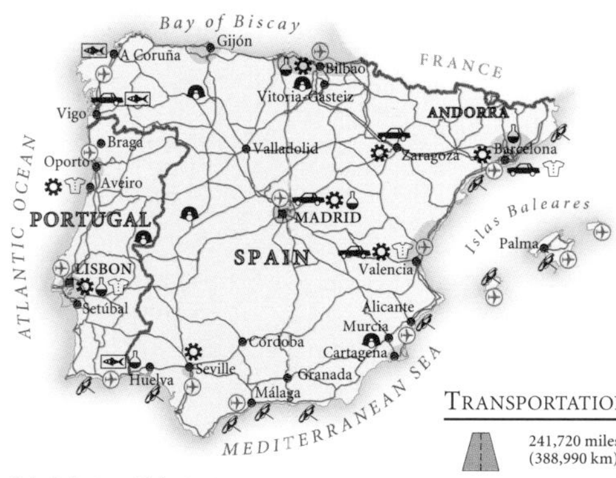
Bay of Biscay
Gijón
A Coruña
Bilbao
Vitoria-Gasteiz
FRANCE
ANDORRA
Vigo
Braga
Valladolid
Zaragoza
Barcelona
Oporto
Aveiro
PORTUGAL
MADRID
Islas Baleares
Palma
LISBON
Setúbal
SPAIN
Valencia
Alicante
Murcia
Córdoba
Cartagena
Seville
Granada
Huelva
Málaga
ATLANTIC OCEAN
MEDITERRANEAN SEA

Major industry and infrastructure
- car manufacture
- chemicals
- engineering
- fish processing
- mining
- textiles
- tourism
- capital cities
- major towns
- international airports
- major roads
- major industrial areas

Transportation Network

241,720 miles (388,990 km)	1,552 miles (2,529 km)
11,793 miles (18,979 km)	1,159 miles (1,865 km)

Radiating from Madrid, the road network in Spain dates from the 18th century, but now includes many highways. Portugal's road system has been completely modernized in recent years.

***The eroded cliffs** of the Algarve in southern Portugal were carved by Atlantic waves. The numerous rocky bays and beaches, and the region's pleasant climate, have made it a popular tourist destination.*

Bay of
Cabo Ortegal
Punta da Estaca de Bares
A Coruña (La Coruña)
Ferrol
Santiago de Compostela
GALICIA
Lugo
Oviedo
ASTURIAS
Gijón (Xixón)
Cordillera Cantábrica
Pontevedra
Vigo
Ourense
León
VIANA DO CASTELO
BRAGA
BRAGANÇA
Zamora
Valladolid
PORTO
Porto (Oporto)
VILA REAL
AVEIRO
VISEU
GUARDA
Salamanca
Ávila
COIMBRA
Coimbra
CASTELO BRANCO
PORTUGAL
LEIRIA
SANTARÉM
PORTALEGRE
Cáceres
EXTREMADURA
LISBOA (LISBON)
Setúbal
SETÚBAL
ÉVORA
Badajoz
BEJA
Huelva
Sevilla (Seville)
FARO
Faro
Golfo de Cádiz
Cádiz
Córdoba
Málaga
Costa de la Luz
GIBRALTAR (to UK)
Strait of Gibraltar
Ceuta (to Spain)
MOROCCO
ATLANTIC OCEAN
64
74

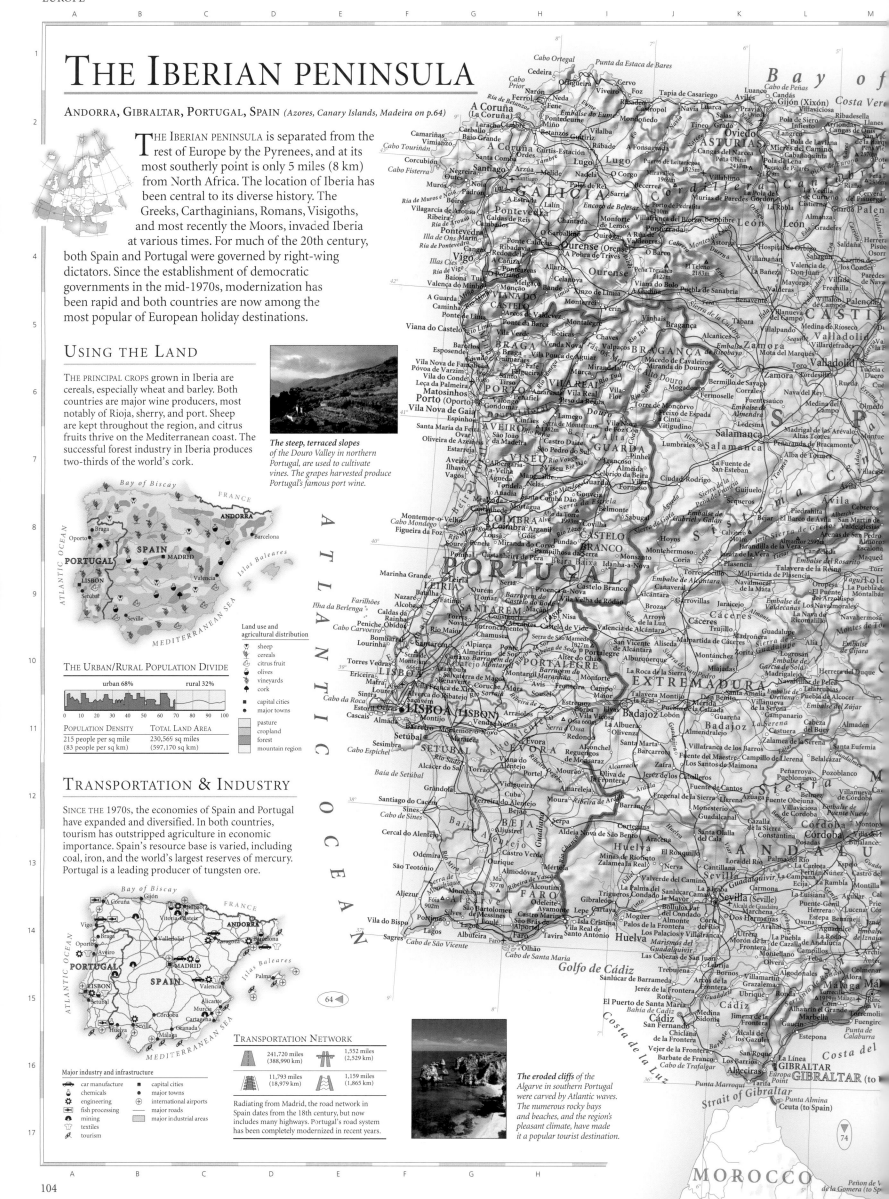

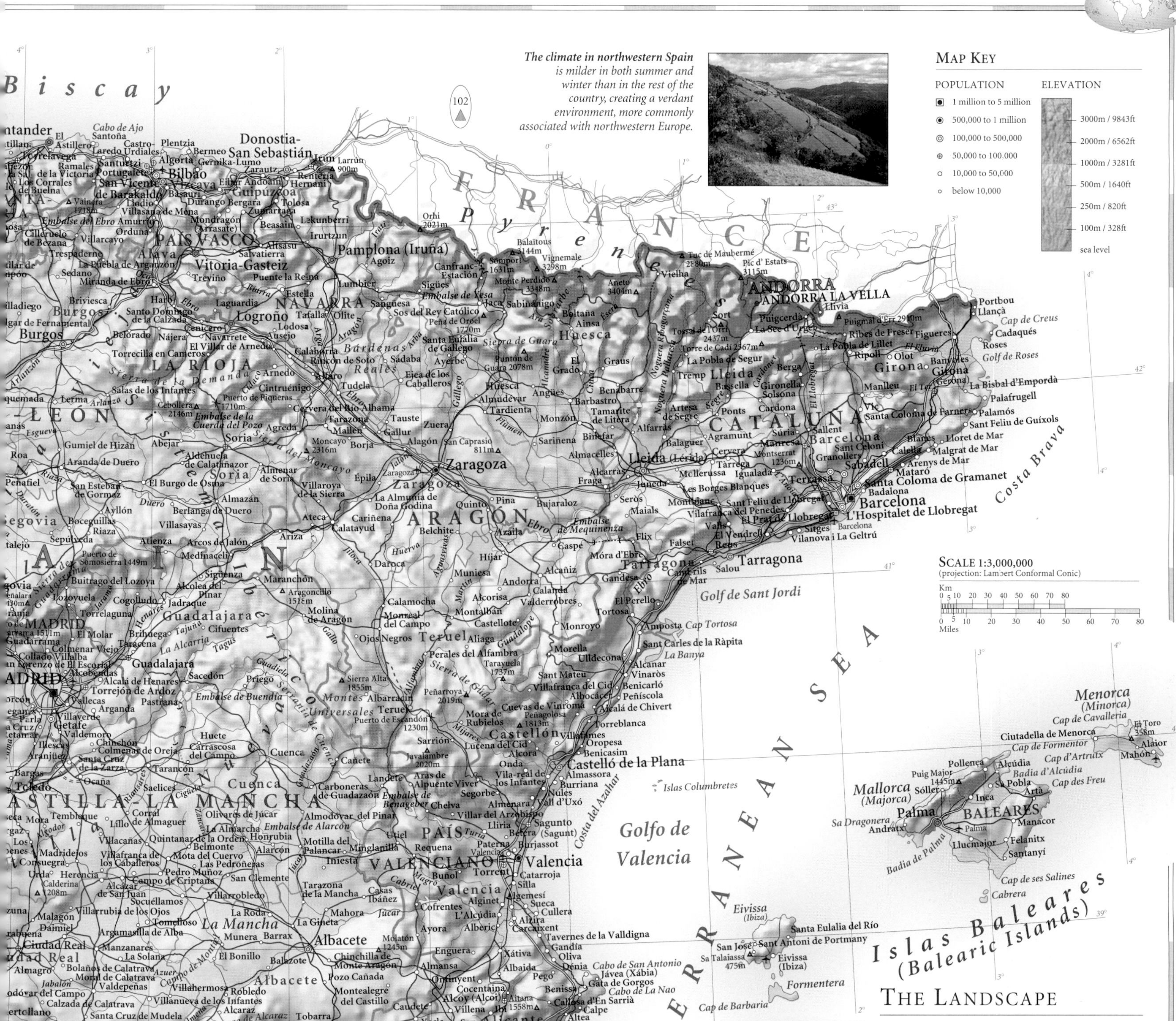
N O P Q R S T U V W X Y
Bay of Biscay
FRANCE
Pyrenees
ANDORRA
ANDORRA LA VELLA
PAÍS VASCO
NAVARRA
LA RIOJA
ARAGÓN
CATALUÑA
CASTILLA-LA MANCHA
PAÍS VALENCIANO
MURCIA
MADRID
Donostia-San Sebastián
Bilbao
Vitoria-Gasteiz
Pamplona (Iruña)
Logroño
Zaragoza
Lleida (Lérida)
Barcelona
L'Hospitalet de Llobregat
Santa Coloma de Gramanet
Tarragona
Castelló de la Plana
Valencia
Alicante (Alacant)
Murcia
Cartagena
Albacete
Cuenca
Teruel
Guadalajara
Granada
Almería
Costa Brava
Costa del Azahar
Costa Blanca
Costa del Sol
Golf de Sant Jordi
Golfo de Valencia
MEDITERRANEAN SEA
Islas Baleares (Balearic Islands)
Mallorca (Majorca)
Menorca (Minorca)
Eivissa (Ibiza)
Formentera
Palma
Islas Columbretes
Alboran Sea
Isla de Alborán
Melilla (to Spain)
Peñon de Alhucemas (to Spain)
Islas Chafarinas (to Spain)
MAP KEY
POPULATION
1 million to 5 million
500,000 to 1 million
100,000 to 500,000
50,000 to 100,000
10,000 to 50,000
below 10,000
ELEVATION
3000m / 9843ft
2000m / 6562ft
1000m / 3281ft
500m / 1640ft
250m / 820ft
100m / 328ft
sea level
SCALE 1:3,000,000
(projection: Lambert Conformal Conic)
Km
Miles
R S T U V W X Y Z

The climate in northwestern Spain is milder in both summer and winter than in the rest of the country, creating a verdant environment, more commonly associated with northwestern Europe.

THE LANDSCAPE

A VAST PLATEAU, the Meseta dominates the centre of the peninsula, enclosed by the Cordillera Cantábrica to the north and the Sierra Morena to the south. It is drained by three major rivers, the Douro/Duero, the Tagus, and the Guadalquivir. The peninsula experiences great variations in climate and rainfall, both regionally and locally.

The Pyrenees form Iberia's northeastern boundary, running for 270 miles (440 km), dividing the peninsula from the rest of Europe.

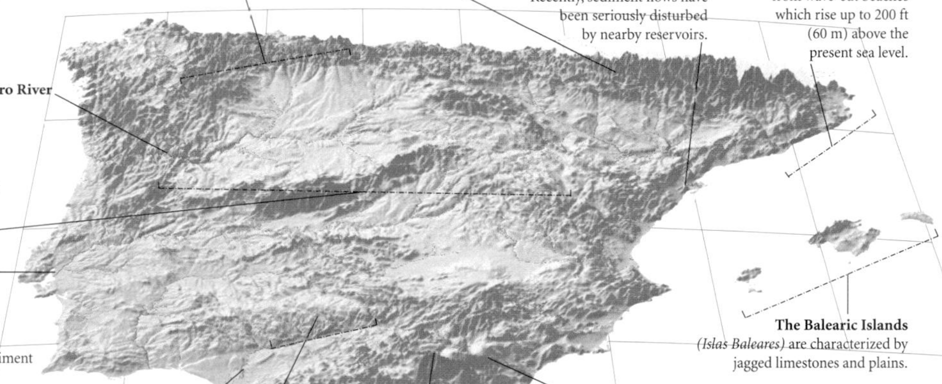
Cordillera Cantábrica
Douro/Duero River
Tagus River
Sierra Morena

The Ebro River has formed the peninsula's largest delta. Recently, sediment flows have been seriously disturbed by nearby reservoirs.

On the northeastern coast sea level changes are evident from wave-cut beaches which rise up to 200 ft (60 m) above the present sea level.

The Meseta plateau averages 1,970 ft (600 m) in height and is now largely dry and treeless.

The Balearic Islands (*Islas Baleares*) are characterized by jagged limestones and plains.

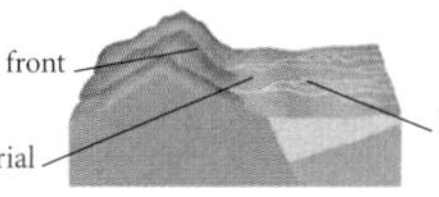
Mountain front
Weathered material
Pediment

Pediments are characteristic of semi-arid lands across Iberia. A pediment is a flat, low-lying, eroded platform, cut into the bedrock. Weathered material is transported by streams and deposited in broad fan shapes on the pediment.

The Guadalquivir River brings vital irrigation water to the plains, and like many of Iberia's rivers, is prone to flooding.

The Sierra Nevada in southern Spain contain Iberia's highest peak, Mulhacén, which rises 11,418 ft (3,481 m).

In the Sierra de los Filabres deforestation and overgrazing, which cause soil erosion, have created semidesert badlands.

The Italian Peninsula

Italy, San Marino, Vatican City

The Italian peninsula is a land of great contrasts. Until unification in 1861, Italy was a collection of independent states, whose competitiveness during the Renaissance resulted in the architectural and artistic magnificence of cities such as Rome, Florence, and Venice. The majority of Italy's population and economic activity is concentrated in the north, centered on the sophisticated industrial city of Milan. Southern Italy, the *Mezzogiorno*, has a harsh terrain, and remains far less developed than the north. Attempts to attract industry and investment in the south are frequently deterred by the entrenched network of organized crime and corruption.

The Landscape

The mainly mountainous and hilly Italian peninsula took its present form following a collision between the African and Eurasian tectonic plates. The Alps in the northwest rise to a high point of 15,772 ft (4,807 m) at Mont Blanc *(Monte Bianco)* on the French border, while the Apennines *(Appennino)* form a rugged backbone, running along the entire length of the country.

The island of Sardinia is an ancient land mass; an uplifted section of very old igneous rocks. Its rugged mountainous regions provide pasture for sheep and goats, while its valleys support some agriculture.

Costa Smeralda

The Dolomites (Alpi Dolomitiche) *are formed of thick limestones, overlying weaker marine strata. They have distinctive serrated peaks and many massive landslides occur.*

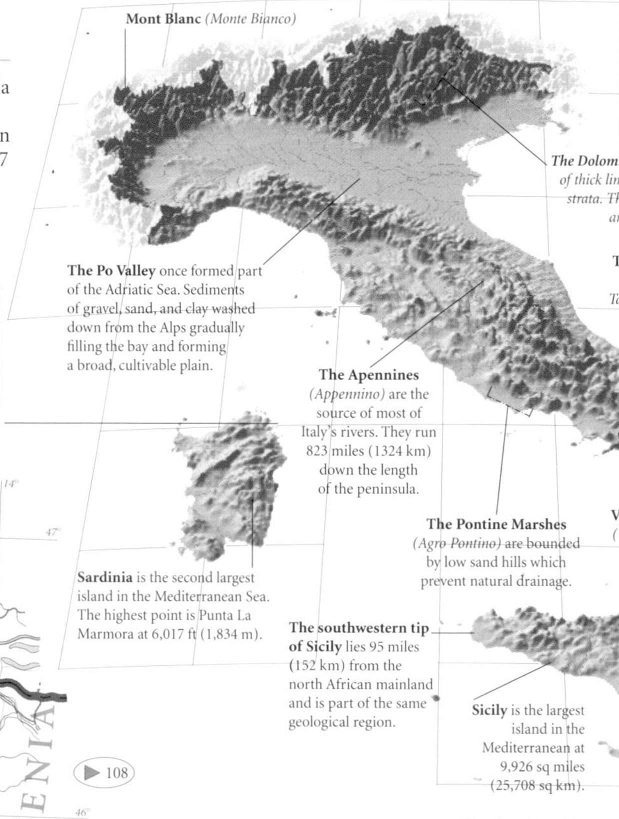
Mont Blanc (Monte Bianco)
The Po Valley once formed part of the Adriatic Sea. Sediments of gravel, sand, and clay washed down from the Alps gradually filling the bay and forming a broad, cultivable plain.
The distinctive square shape of the Gulf of Taranto (Golfo di Taranto) was defined by numerous block faults. Earthquakes are common in this region.
The Apennines (Appennino) are the source of most of Italy's rivers. They run 823 miles (1324 km) down the length of the peninsula.
Sardinia is the second largest island in the Mediterranean Sea. The highest point is Punta La Marmora at 6,017 ft (1,834 m).
The Pontine Marshes (Agro Pontino) are bounded by low sand hills which prevent natural drainage.
Vesuvius (Vesuvio)
The southwestern tip of Sicily lies 95 miles (152 km) from the north African mainland and is part of the same geological region.
Sicily is the largest island in the Mediterranean at 9,926 sq miles (25,708 sq km).
The Strait of Messina (Stretto di Messina) is between 2 and 12 miles (3–19 km) wide, and is a rich fishing ground.

Vesuvius *(Vesuvio)*

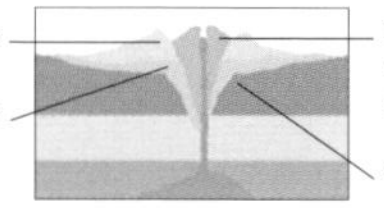
Monte Somma
Old crater
Present-day crater has developed within the old crater of Monte Somma
Old crater

There have been four volcanoes on the site of Vesuvius since volcanic activity began here more than 10,000 years ago.

SWITZERLAND
AUSTRIA
SLOVENIA
CROATIA
FRANCE
MONACO
SAN MARINO
Gulf of Venice
Golfo di Genova
Ligurian Sea
LOMBARDIA
PIEMONTE
VALLE D'AOSTA
TRENTINO ALTO ADIGE
VENETO
FRIULI-VENEZIA GIULIA
EMILIA-ROMAGNA
LIGURIA
TOSCANA
MARCHE
UMBRIA
Milano (Milan)
Torino (Turin)
Genova (Genoa)
Venezia (Venice)
Bologna
Firenze (Florence)
Trieste
Verona
Padova (Padua)
Ancona
Perugia
Livorno
Pisa
La Spezia
Rimini
Ravenna
Ferrara
Modena
Parma
Brescia
Bergamo
Trento
Bolzano

108
108
108
112
120
102

SCALE 1:2,750,000
(projection: Lambert Conformal Conic)

Using the Land

Italy produces 95% of its own food. The best farming land is in the Po Valley in northern Italy, where soft wheat and rice are grown. Irrigation is essential to agriculture in much of the south. Italy is a major producer and exporter of citrus fruits, olives, tomatoes, and wine.

The Urban/Rural Population Divide

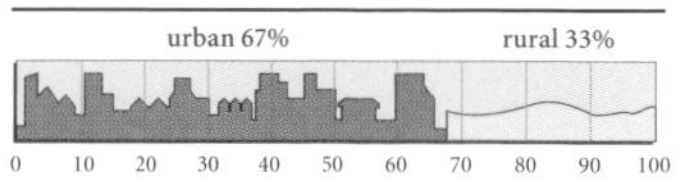
urban 67%
rural 33%
0 10 20 30 40 50 60 70 80 90 100

Population Density	Total Land Area
492 people per sq mile (190 people per sq km)	116,320 sq miles (301,270 sq km)

SWITZERLAND
AUSTRIA
SLOVENIA
CROATIA
FRANCE
Milan
Turin
Genoa
Bologna
SAN MARINO
Florence
ITALY
ROME
Naples
Bari
Sassari
Sardinia
Cagliari
Palermo
Sicily
Catania
Adriatic Sea
Tyrrhenian Sea
Ionian Sea
MEDITERRANEAN SEA
Land use and agricultural distribution
cattle
cereals
citrus fruits
olive oil
rice
vineyards
capital cities
major towns
pasture
cropland
forest
mountain region

Tyrrhenian Sea
Ionian Sea
Mediterranean Sea
Malta Channel
Strait of Sicily
Strait of Otranto
Strait of Bonifacio
Adriatic Sea
Golfo di Taranto
Sardegna (Sardinia)
Corse (Corsica)
Sicilia (Sicily)
Isole Eolie
Isole Egadi
ROMA (ROME)
VATICAN CITY
Napoli
Palermo
Bari
Taranto
Cagliari
Catanzaro
Messina
Catania
Siracusa
Lecce
Foggia
LAZIO
ABRUZZO
MOLISE
CAMPANIA
PUGLIA
BASILICATA
CALABRIA
SICILIA
SARDEGNA

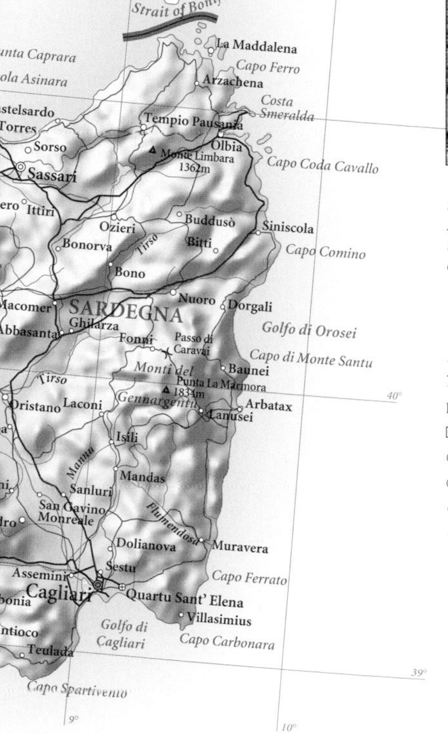

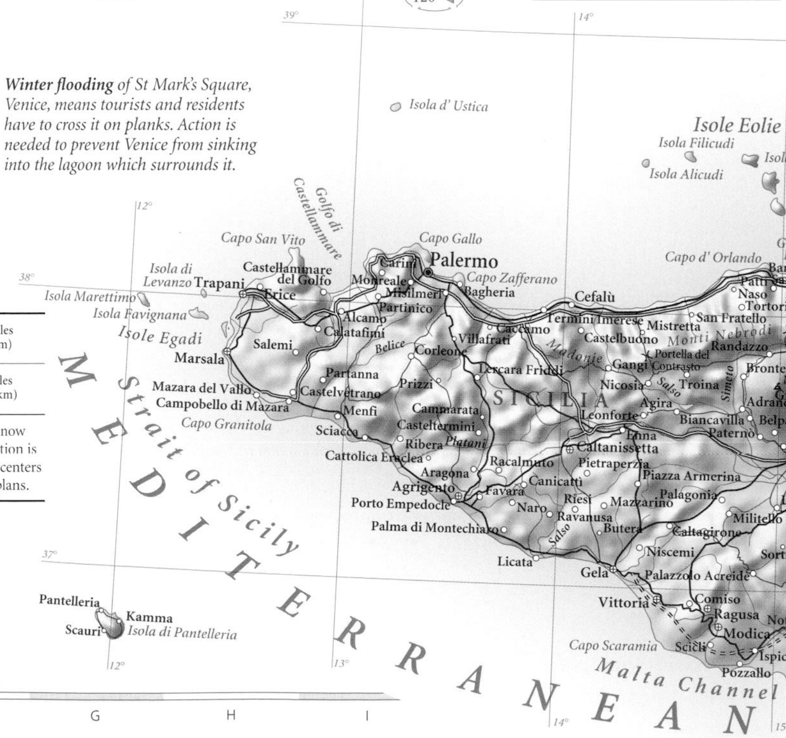

Tuscany (Toscana) has long produced grapes and olives. Sandstones form its higher reaches, while clays and alluvial soils fill its fertile valleys.

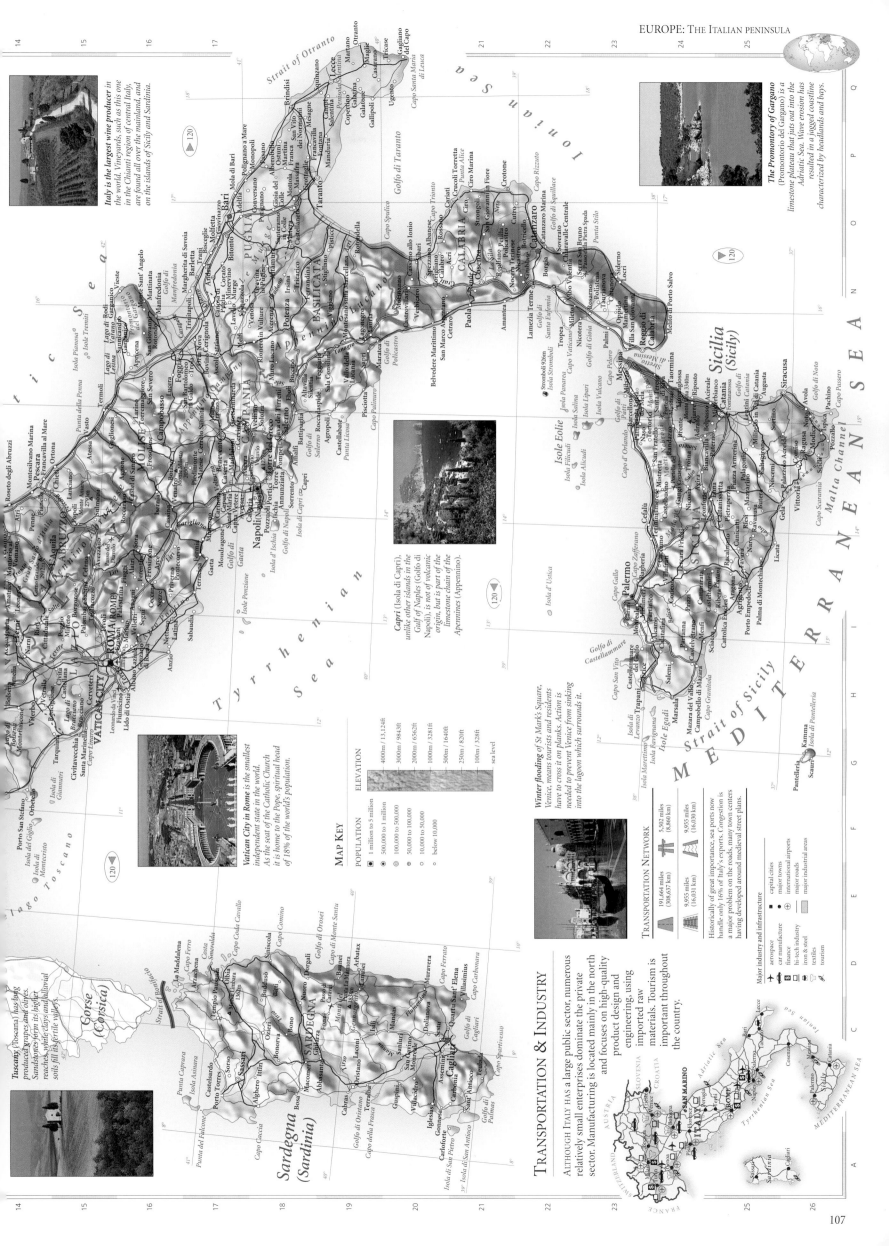

Italy is the largest wine producer in the world. Vineyards, such as this one in the Chianti region of central Italy, are found all over the mainland, and on the islands of Sicily and Sardinia.

Vatican City in Rome is the smallest independent state in the world. As the seat of the Catholic Church it is home to the Pope, spiritual head of 18% of the world's population.

Map Key

POPULATION	ELEVATION
1 million to 5 million	4000m / 13,124ft
500,000 to 1 million	3000m / 9843ft
100,000 to 500,000	2000m / 6562ft
50,000 to 100,000	1000m / 3281ft
10,000 to 50,000	500m / 1640ft
below 10,000	250m / 820ft
	100m / 328ft
	sea level

Capri (Isola di Capri), unlike other islands in the Gulf of Naples (Golfo di Napoli), is not of volcanic origin, but is part of the limestone chain of the Apennines (Appennino).

Transportation & Industry

ALTHOUGH ITALY HAS a large public sector, numerous relatively small enterprises dominate the private sector. Manufacturing is located mainly in the north and focuses on high-quality product design and engineering, using imported raw materials. Tourism is important throughout the country.

Winter flooding of St Mark's Square, Venice, means tourists and residents have to cross it on planks. Action is needed to prevent Venice from sinking into the lagoon which surrounds it.

Transportation Network

191,664 miles (308,637 km)	5,502 miles (8,860 km)
9,955 miles (16,031 km)	9,955 miles (16,030 km)

Historically of great importance, sea ports now handle only 16% of Italy's exports. Congestion is a major problem on the roads, many town centers having developed around medieval street plans.

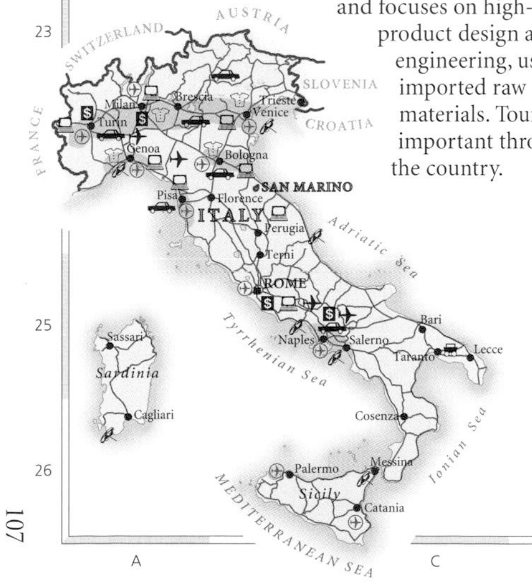
AUSTRIA
SWITZERLAND
SLOVENIA
CROATIA
FRANCE
SAN MARINO
ITALY
ROME
Adriatic Sea
Tyrrhenian Sea
Ionian Sea
MEDITERRANEAN SEA
Sardinia
Sicily

Major industry and infrastructure

aerospace	capital cities
car manufacture	major towns
finance	international airports
hi-tech industry	major roads
iron & steel	major industrial areas
textiles	
tourism	

The Promontory of Gargano (Promontorio del Gargano) is a limestone plateau that juts out into the Adriatic Sea. Wave erosion has resulted in a jagged coastline characterized by headlands and bays.

The Alpine States

Austria, Liechtenstein, Slovenia, Switzerland

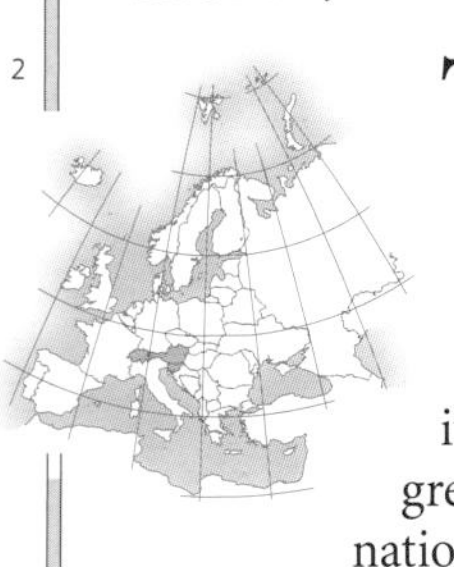

The Alpine countries of Austria, Switzerland, Liechtenstein, and Slovenia form a narrow strip across western Europe's geographical core, lying on the main north–south trading routes across the Alps. Switzerland, politically neutral since 1815, is an important international meeting place and houses one of the headquarters of the United Nations, which it joined in 2002. Austria, once at the heart of the great Habsburg Empire has been a fully independent nation since 1955, and maintains a deserved reputation as an international center of culture. Slovenia declared independence from the former Yugoslavia in 1991 and despite initial economic hardship, is now starting to achieve the prosperity enjoyed by its Alpine neighbors.

Using the Land

The Alpine region's mountainous terrain discourages cultivation over much of the land area. The primary agricultural activity is the raising of dairy and beef cattle on the pasture land of the lower mountain slopes. Austria is self-supporting in grains, and crops such as wheat, barley, and grapes are grown on the east Austrian lowlands. Woodlands are more prevalent in the eastern Alps; both Austria and Slovenia have large tracts of forest.

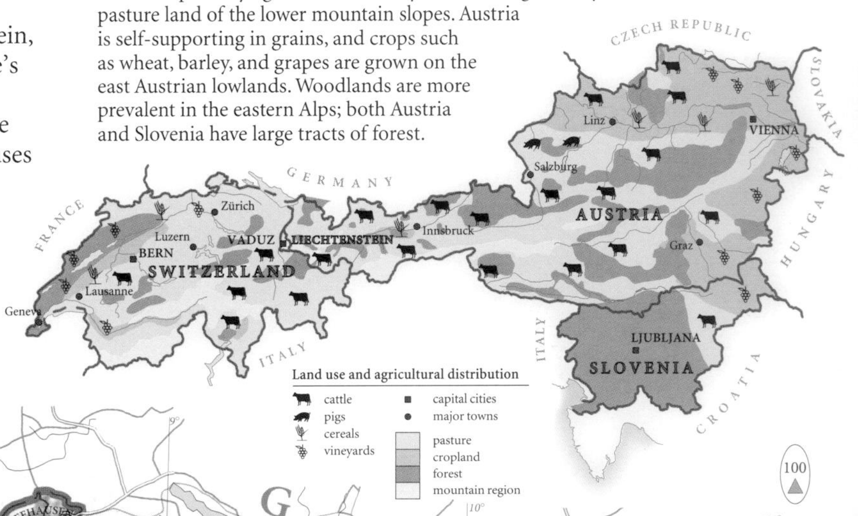

CZECH REPUBLIC
SLOVAKIA
GERMANY
FRANCE
ITALY
HUNGARY
CROATIA
VIENNA
Linz
Salzburg
AUSTRIA
Innsbruck
Graz
Zürich
Luzern
BERN
VADUZ
LIECHTENSTEIN
SWITZERLAND
Lausanne
LJUBLJANA
SLOVENIA
Land use and agricultural distribution
cattle
pigs
cereals
vineyards
capital cities
major towns
pasture
cropland
forest
mountain region

The Matterhorn, on the Swiss-Italian border, is one of the highest mountains in the Alps, at 14,692 ft (4,478 m). The term "horn" refers to its distinctive peak, formed by three glaciers eroding hollows, known as cirques, in each of its sides.

100
102
106
SWITZERLAND
LIECHTENSTEIN
BERN
VADUZ
Lausanne
Genève (Geneva)
Lake Geneva (Lac Léman)
Lake Constance
Zürich
Basel
Luzern
Berner Alpen
Glarner Alpen
Pennine Alps
Rhaetian Alps
Lepontine Alps
Lake Maggiore
Lugano
Matterhorn 4478m
Dufour Spitze 4634m

The Landscape

The Alps occupy three-fifths of Switzerland, most of southern Austria and the northwest of Slovenia. They were formed by the collision of the African and Eurasian tectonic plates, which began 65 million years ago. Their complex geology is reflected in the differing heights and rock types of the various ranges. The Rhine flows along Liechtenstein's border with Switzerland, creating a broad floodplain in the north and west of Liechtenstein. In the far northeast and east are a number of lowland regions, including the Vienna Basin, Burgenland, and the plain of the Danube. Slovenia's major rivers flow across the lower eastern regions; in the west, the rivers flow underground through the limestone Karst region.

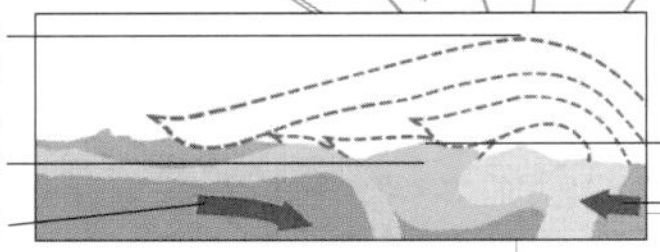

Original height after uplift and folding
Folded strata are overturned creating a *nappe*
Eurasian Plate
Present-day height of Alps
African Plate

***The convergence of the African and Eurasian plates** compressed and folded huge masses of rock strata. As the plates continued to move together, the folded strata were overturned, creating complex nappes. Much of the rock strata has since been eroded, resulting in the current topography of the Alps.*

***Constricted as it cuts through** ridges in the Alps, the Danube meanders across the lowlands, where uplift combined with river erosion has deepened meanders.*

The Vienna Basin lies mainly below 390 ft (120 m). It gradually subsided and filled with sediment as the Alps were uplifted.

Neusiedler See straddles the border of Austria and Hungary; the area around it provides some of the best wine-growing land in Austria.

The mountains of the Jura form a natural border between Switzerland and France. Their marine limestones date from over 200 million years ago. When the Alps were formed the Jura were folded into a series of parallel ridges and troughs.

Tectonic activity has resulted in dramatic changes in land height over very short distances. Lake Geneva, lying at 1,221 ft (372 m) is only 43 miles (70 km) away from the 15,772 ft (4,807 m) peak of Mont Blanc, on the France–Italy border.

The Bernese Alps (*Berner Alpen*) contain the Aletsch, which at 15 miles (24 km) is the longest Alpine glacier.

The Rhine, like other major Alpine rivers, follows a broad, flat trough between the mountains. Along part of its course, the Rhine forms the boundary between Switzerland and Liechtenstein.

The first road through the Brenner Pass was built in 1772, although it has been used as a mountain route since Roman times. It is the lowest of the main Alpine passes at 4,298 ft (1374 m).

Karst region

The deep, blue lakes of the Karst region are part of a drainage network which runs largely underground through this limestone area.

The limestone cave system at Postojna extends for more than 10 miles (16 km) and includes caverns reaching 125 ft (40 m) in height and width.

The Austrian Alps comprise three distinct mountain ranges, separated by deep trenches. The northern and southern ranges are rugged limestones, while the Tauern range is formed of crystalline rocks.

The Tauern range in the central Austrian Alps contains the highest mountain in Austria, the towering Grossglockner, rising 12,461 ft (3,798 m).

CZECH REPUBLIC
SLOVAKIA
HUNGARY
AUSTRIA
SLOVENIA
CROATIA
ITALY
GERMANY
OBERÖSTERREICH
NIEDERÖSTERREICH
STEIERMARK
SALZBURG
TIROL
KÄRNTEN
BURGENLAND
WIEN (VIENNA)
Linz
Salzburg
Graz
Innsbruck
Klagenfurt
Sankt Pölten
Villach
Maribor
LJUBLJANA
Danube (Donau)
Hohe Tauern
Niedere Tauern
Karawanken
Gulf of Trieste
Grossglockner 3798m
Triglav 2864m
100
106
110
112

The Urban/Rural Population Divide

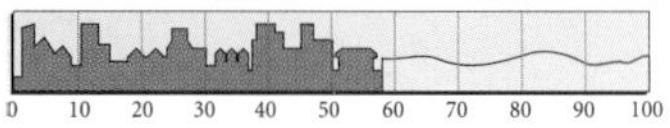
58% urban
42% rural
0 10 20 30 40 50 60 70 80 90 100

Population Density	Total Land Area
310 people per sq mile (120 people per sq km)	56,135 sq miles (145,390 sq km)

In this mountainous region, the flatter, more accessible areas are often used for both cattle grazing and recreation.

These converging glaciers are marked by dark lines of moraine. This eroded material is carried by glaciers, and deposited as the ice melts.

SCALE 1:2,000,000
(projection: Lambert Conformal Conic)

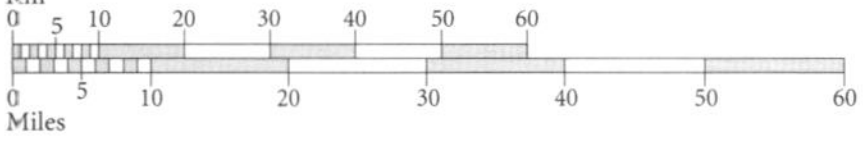
Km
0 5 10 20 30 40 50 60
0 5 10 20 30 40 50 60
Miles

The Austrian Tirol contains some of the most spectacular Alpine scenery. Snow cover is a permanent feature in the highest reaches.

Map Key

POPULATION
- 1 million to 5 million
- 500,000 to 1 million
- 100,000 to 500,000
- 50,000 to 100,000
- 10,000 to 50,000
- below 10,000

ELEVATION

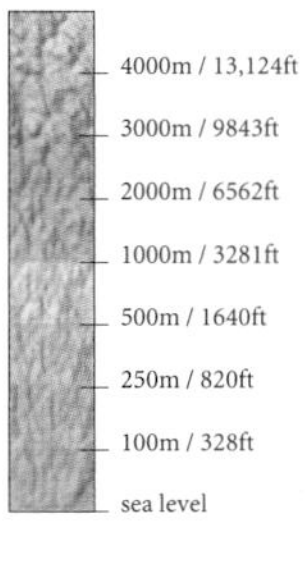
4000m / 13,124ft
3000m / 9843ft
2000m / 6562ft
1000m / 3281ft
500m / 1640ft
250m / 820ft
100m / 328ft
sea level

Transportation & Industry

ALL FOUR NATIONS concentrate on high-quality manufacturing and services. Austrian iron and steel production is complemented by construction industries; and Slovenia, traditionally the industrial powerhouse of the western Balkans has increasingly diversified industries. Liechtenstein and Switzerland, lacking raw materials, produce pharmaceuticals and precision instruments, such as watches, and act as international banking centers. The spectacular scenery of the region encourages tourism all year round.

Transportation Network

119,805 miles (192,923 km)	2044 miles (3292 km)
6227 miles (10,028 km)	984 miles (1584 km)

Tunnels and passes through the Alps are an important feature of this region. The NEAT project, providing two new high-speed rail links between Basel and Milan, was given approval in 1992.

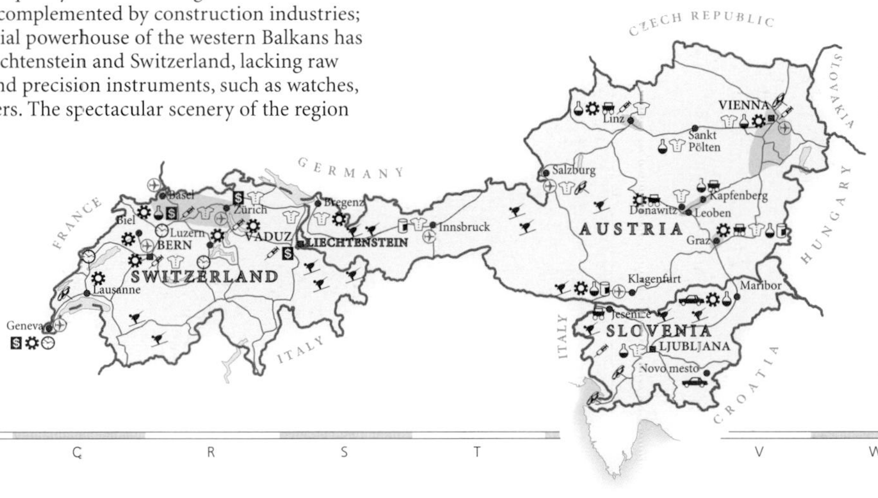
CZECH REPUBLIC
SLOVAKIA
HUNGARY
CROATIA
ITALY
FRANCE
GERMANY
AUSTRIA
SWITZERLAND
SLOVENIA
LIECHTENSTEIN
VADUZ
BERN
LJUBLJANA
VIENNA
Linz
Sankt Pölten
Salzburg
Kapfenberg
Donawitz
Leoben
Graz
Innsbruck
Klagenfurt
Maribor
Jesenice
Novo mesto
Basel
Zürich
Luzern
Biel
Lausanne
Geneva
Bregenz
Major industry and infrastructure
car manufacture
chemicals
engineering
finance
food processing
iron & steel
pharmaceuticals
textiles
tourism
watch making
winter sports
capital cities
major towns
international airports
major roads
major industrial areas

The Schönbrunn Palace in Vienna was the summer residence of the Habsburg monarchy. Today, it is a major tourist attraction.

Central Europe

Czech Republic, Hungary, Poland, Slovakia

When Slovakia and the Czech Republic became separate countries in 1993, they joined Hungary and Poland in a new role as independent nation states, following centuries of shifting boundaries and imperial strife. This turbulent history bequeathed the region a rich cultural heritage, shared through the works of its many great writers and composers, and celebrated in the vibrant historic capitals of Prague, Budapest, and Warsaw. Having shaken off years of Soviet domination in 1989, these states are confronting the challenge of winning commercial investment to modernize outmoded industries as they integrate their economies with those of the European Union.

The Landscape

The forested Carpathian Mountains, uplifted with the Alps, lie southeast of the older Bohemian massif, which contains the Sudeten and Krušné Hory *(Erzgebirge)* ranges. They divide the fertile plains of the Danube to the south and the Vistula *(Wisła)*, which flows north across vast expanses of glacial deposits into the Baltic Sea.

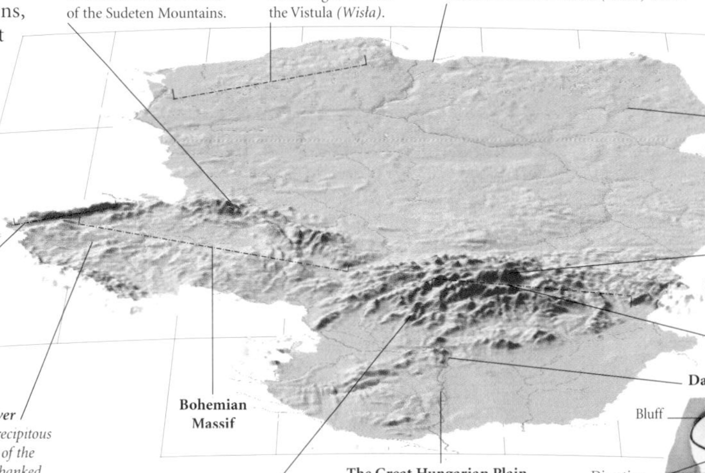

Hot mineral springs occur where geothermally heated water wells up through faults and fractures in the rocks of the Sudeten Mountains.
Pomerania is a sandy coastal region of glacially-formed lakes stretching west from the Vistula *(Wisła)*.
Longshore currents moving east along the Baltic coast have built a 40 mile (65 km) spit composed of material from the Vistula *(Wisła)* River.
Krušné Hory *(Erzgebirge)*
Bohemian Massif
Gerlachovský štít, in the Tatra Mountains, is Slovakia's highest mountain, at 8,711ft (2,655 m).
Carpathian Mountains
Danube River
The Slovak Ore Mountains *(Slovenské Rudohorie)* are noted for their mineral resources, including high-grade iron ore.
The Great Hungarian Plain formed by the floodplain of the Danube is a mixture of steppe and cultivated land, covering nearly half of Hungary's total area.

The Biebrza River has left meanders and oxbow lakes as it flows across low-lying ground.

The Berounka River cuts through the precipitous wooded landscape of the Bohemian massif, banked by a broad floodplain.

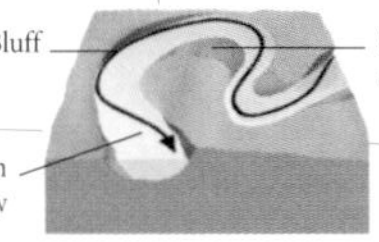

Bluff
Slip-off slope
Direction of flow

***Meanders** form as rivers flow across plains at a low gradient. A steep cliff or bluff, forms on the outside curve, and a gentler slip-off slope on the inside bend.*

Transportation & Industry

Heavy industry has dominated postwar life in Central Europe. Poland has large coal reserves, having inherited the Silesian coalfield from Germany after the Second World War, allowing the export of large quantities of coal, along with other minerals. Hungary specializes in consumer goods and services, while Slovakia's industrial base is still relatively small. The Czech Republic's traditional glassworks and breweries bring some stability to its precarious Soviet-built manufacturing sector.

BALTIC SEA
RUSSIAN FED. (Kaliningrad)
LITHUANIA
BELARUS
UKRAINE
ROMANIA
GERMANY
AUSTRIA
SLOVENIA
CROATIA
S. & MON.
Gdańsk
Szczecin
Białystok
WARSAW
Poznań
Łódź
POLAND
Wrocław
Katowice
Kraków
PRAGUE
Ostrava
CZECH REPUBLIC
Brno
SLOVAKIA
BRATISLAVA
Miskolc
Győr
BUDAPEST
HUNGARY
Szeged

Major industry and infrastructure

- car manufacture
- chemicals
- engineering
- food processing
- mining
- shipbuilding
- tourism
- capital cities
- major towns
- international airports
- major roads
- major industrial areas

Transportation Network

213,997 miles (344,600 km)	817 miles (1,315 km)
27,479 miles (44,249 km)	3,784 miles (6,094 km)

The huge growth of tourism and business has prompted major investment in the transportation infrastructure, with new roadbuilding schemes within and between the main cities of the region.

***Budapest, the capital of Hungary,** straddles the Danube. It comprises the historic towns of Buda, on the west bank, and Pest, which contains the Parliament Building, seen here on the far bank.*

BALTIC SEA
Gulf of Danzig
Pomeranian Bay
RUSSIAN FEDERATION (Kaliningrad)
LITHUANIA
BELARUS
POLAND
POMORSKIE
WARMIŃSKO-MAZURSKIE
PODLASKIE
ZACHODNIO-POMORSKIE
KUJAWSKO-POMORSKIE
MAZOWIECKIE
WIELKOPOLSKIE
LUBUSKIE
ŁÓDZKIE
LUBELSKIE
Pomerania
Mazury
Gdańsk
Gdynia
Sopot
Elbląg
Olsztyn
Szczecin
Koszalin
Słupsk
Bydgoszcz
Toruń
Białystok
WARSZAWA (WARSAW)
Poznań
Łódź
Płock
Włocławek
Gorzów Wielkopolski
Kalisz
118

CZECH REPUBLIC
SLOVAKIA
HUNGARY
AUSTRIA
UKRAINE
ROMANIA
CROATIA
SLOVENIA
SERB. & MON. (YUGOSLAVIA)
PRAHA (PRAGUE)
BRATISLAVA
BUDAPEST
Wrocław
Kraków
Bohemian Forest
Carpathian Mountains
Tatra Mountains
Slovenské rudohorie
Little Alföld
Great Hungarian Plain
MAP KEY
POPULATION
1 million to 5 million
500,000 to 1 million
100,000 to 500,000
50,000 to 100,000
10,000 to 50,000
below 10,000
ELEVATION
2000m / 6562ft
1000m / 3281ft
500m / 1640ft
250m / 820ft
100m / 328ft
sea level
SCALE 1:2,750,000
(projection: Lambert Conformal Conic)

USING THE LAND

CEREALS, SUGAR BEET, AND POTATOES are Central Europe's main crops, along with hops for the Czech breweries, sweet peppers for paprika, sunflowers and vines in milder areas. The plains of Poland and Hungary are well-suited to livestock-rearing, while forestry is important in the mountains of Slovakia.

BALTIC SEA
Gdańsk
Białystok
WARSAW
Poznań
POLAND
Wrocław
Katowice
PRAGUE
CZECH REPUBLIC
SLOVAKIA
BRATISLAVA
BUDAPEST
HUNGARY
GERMANY
AUSTRIA
SLOVENIA
CROATIA
S. & MON.
ROMANIA
UKRAINE
BELARUS
Land use and agricultural distribution
cattle
pigs
cereals
potatoes
root crops
timber
vineyards
capital cities
major towns
pasture
cropland
forest

Hay, used to feed livestock, *is one of the major crops grown on the fertile foothills of Slovakia's Tatra Mountains.*

THE URBAN/RURAL POPULATION DIVIDE

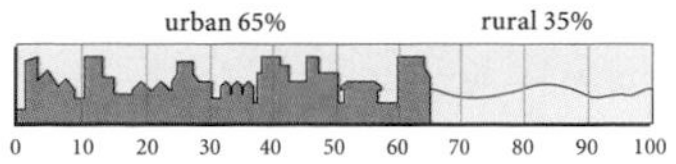
urban 65%
rural 35%
0 10 20 30 40 50 60 70 80 90 100

POPULATION DENSITY	TOTAL LAND AREA
312 people per sq mile (120 people per sq km)	201,561 sq miles (522,180 sq km)

The upper Dunajec River *of Poland and eastern Slovakia forms a gorge through the Pieniny range of the Carpathian Mountains.*

Southeast Europe

Albania, Bosnia & Herzegovina, Croatia, Macedonia, Serbia & Montenegro (Yugoslavia)

For 46 years the federation of Yugoslavia held together the most diverse ethnic region in Europe, along the picturesque mountain hinterland of the Dalmatian coast. Economic collapse resulted in internal tensions. In the early 1990s, civil war broke out in both Croatia and Bosnia as the ethnic populations struggled to establish their own exclusive territories. Peace was only restored by the UN after NATO launched air strikes in 1995. In the province of Kosovo, attempts to gain autonomy from Yugoslavia in 1998 were crushed by the Serbian government. The slaughter of ethnic Albanians in Kosovo provoked the West to launch NATO air strikes yet again in the region, and Yugoslav forces withdrew. The flood of refugees from Kosovo has severely strained Albania.

Hot, dry summers and mild winters *offer excellent conditions for viticulture in Montenegro. The precipitous Dinaric Alps have kept this region relatively isolated for centuries.*

SCALE 1:2,750,000
(projection: Lambert Conformal Conic)

Km 0 5 10 20 30 40 50 60 70
Miles 0 5 10 20 30 40 50 60 70

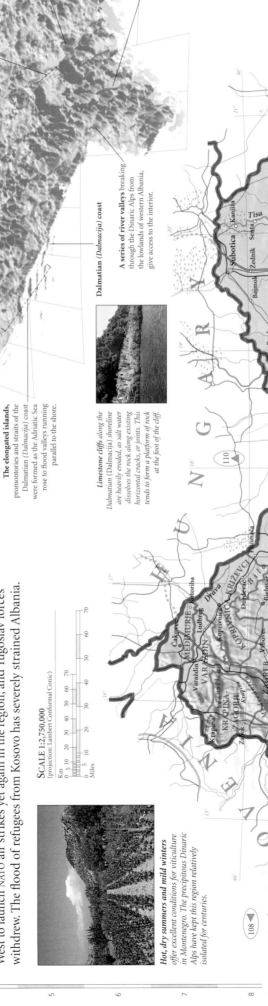

The Landscape

The Tisza, Sava, and Drava Rivers drain the broad northern lowland, meeting the Danube after it crosses the Hungarian border. In the west, the Dinaric Alps divide the Adriatic Sea from the interior. Mainland valleys and elongated islands run parallel to the steep Dalmatian *(Dalmacija)* coastline, following alternating bands of resistant limestone.

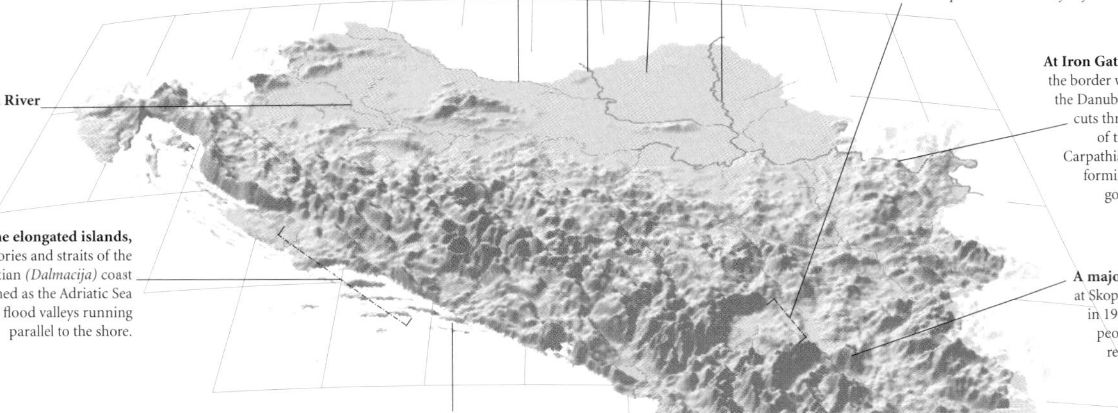
At least 70% of the fresh water in the Western Balkans drains eastward into the Black Sea, mostly via the Danube *(Dunav)*.
The river floodplains of the Pannonian Basin are flanked by terraces of gravel and wind-blown glacial deposits known as loess.
Drava River
Tisza River
Sava River
At Iron Gate *(derdap)*, on the border with Romania, the Danube narrows and cuts through foothills of the Balkan and Carpathian mountains, forming the deepest gorge in Europe.
The elongated islands, promontories and straits of the Dalmatian *(Dalmacija)* coast were formed as the Adriatic Sea rose to flood valleys running parallel to the shore.
A major earthquake at Skopje, Macedonia, in 1963 killed 1,000 people. The whole region lies on an active crustal plate margin.
Dalmatian *(Dalmacija)* coast
A series of river valleys breaking through the Dinaric Alps from the lowlands of western Albania, give access to the interior.
Lake Ohrid

Poljes in the Kosovo region

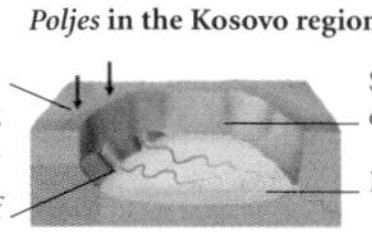
Underground drainage along joints in the rock
Sheer limestone walls enclose all sides
Flat polje floor
Spring at foot of cliff

Rain and underground water *dissolve limestone along massive vertical joints (cracks). This creates poljes: depressions several miles across with steep walls and broad, flat floors.*

Limestone cliffs *along the Dalmatian (Dalmacija) shoreline are heavily eroded, as salt water dissolves the rock along existing horizontal cracks, or joints. This tends to form a platform of rock at the foot of the cliff.*

Lake Ohrid *borders Albania and Macedonia. Ohrid is the deepest lake in the Western Balkans, reaching depths of 938 ft (286 m).*

SLOVENIA
HUNGARY
ROMANIA
CROATIA
BOSNIA & HERZEGOVINA
SERBIA
ZAGREB
BEOGRAD (BELGRADE)
VOJVODINA
Gulf of Trieste
Novi Sad
Osijek
Subotica
Rijeka

108
110
116

The historic center of Mostar in southern Bosnia, with its famous 16th-century Turkish bridge, was destroyed by shelling during 1993. The town was formerly the capital of Herzegovina.

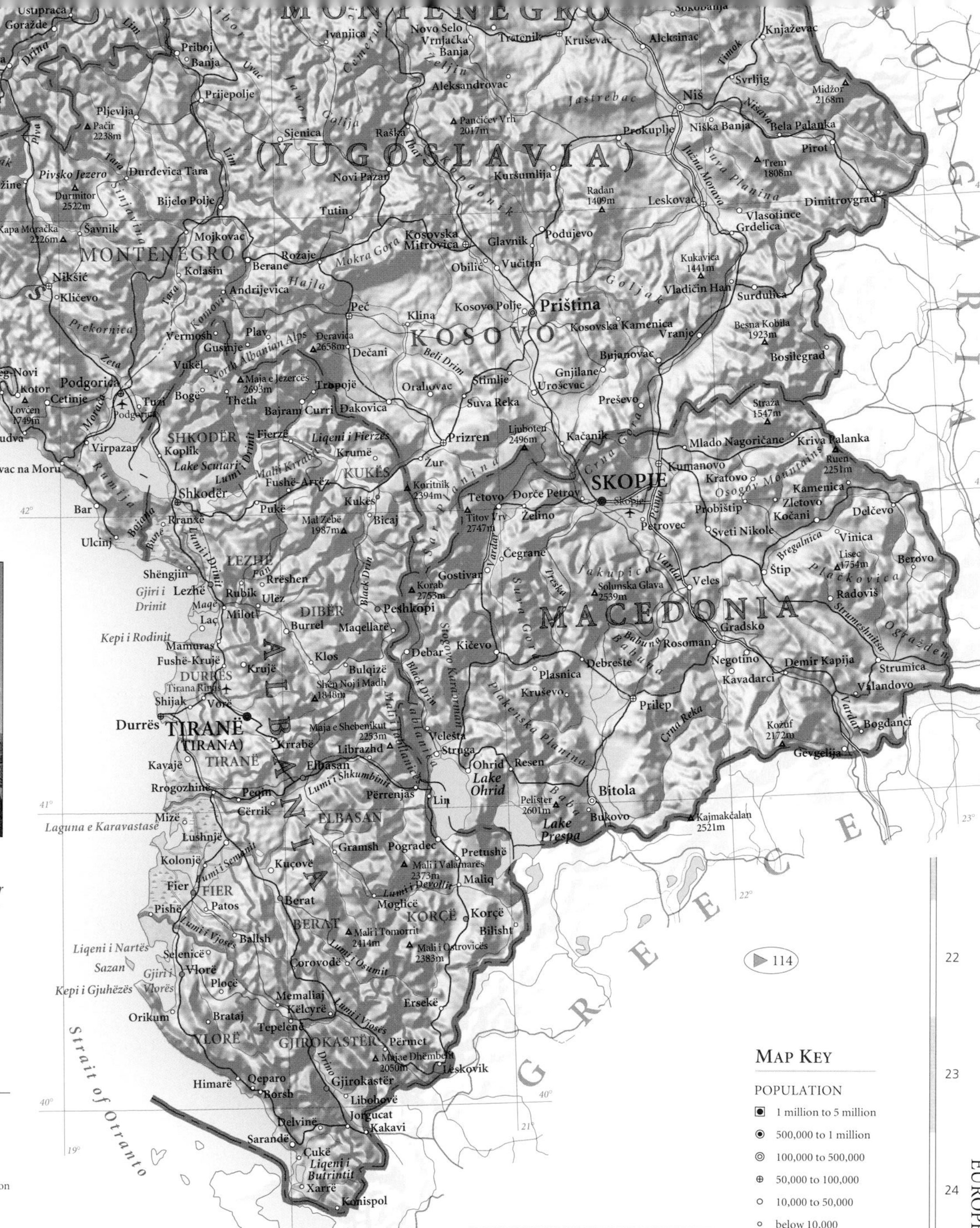

MONTENEGRO
(YUGOSLAVIA)
KOSOVO
MACEDONIA
ALBANIA
GREECE
BULGARIA
Adriatic Sea
Strait of Otranto
SKOPJE
TIRANË (TIRANA)
Priština
Podgorica
Split
Dubrovnik
DUBROVNIK-NERETVA
SPLIT-DALMACIJA
Lake Ohrid
Lake Prespa
Bitola
Durrës
Shkodër
Niš

114

Transportation & Industry

Processing industries based on the region's wealth of mineral reserves predominate in Albania and Macedonia. In other regions, industrial plants have been commandeered, if not destroyed in the war and mineral extraction has severely declined. The fast-flowing rivers found throughout the Dinaric Alps are exploited to generate hydroelectric power.

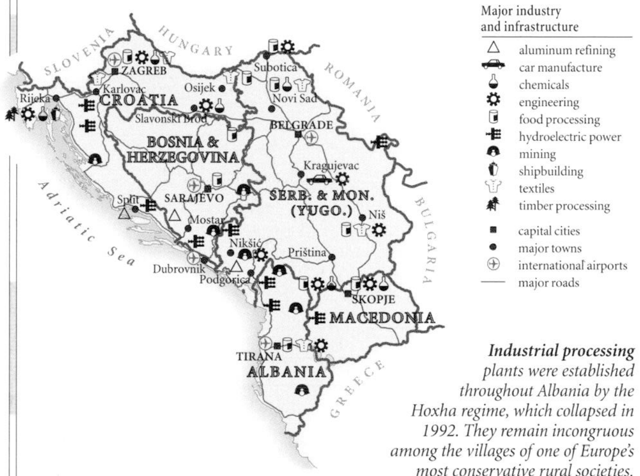

HUNGARY
ROMANIA
BULGARIA
GREECE
SLOVENIA
Adriatic Sea
ZAGREB
CROATIA
BOSNIA & HERZEGOVINA
BELGRADE
SERB. & MON. (YUGO.)
SKOPJE
MACEDONIA
TIRANA
ALBANIA
Major industry and infrastructure
aluminum refining
car manufacture
chemicals
engineering
food processing
hydroelectric power
mining
shipbuilding
textiles
timber processing
capital cities
major towns
international airports
major roads

Transportation Network

72,719 miles (117,100 km)	415 miles (668 km)
4,808 miles (7,743 km)	1,911 miles (3,078 km)

The war has resulted in the destruction or disintegration of infrastructure for transportation, communications, and power supply, with essential provisions moved under armed UN convoy.

Industrial processing plants were established throughout Albania by the Hoxha regime, which collapsed in 1992. They remain incongruous among the villages of one of Europe's most conservative rural societies.

The ancient Croatian port of Dubrovnik was one of the former Yugoslavia's most popular tourist resorts and an important point of access to the sea along the Dalmatian (Dalmacija) coast. Shelling of the old city by Serb forces in 1991 provoked international condemnation.

Using the Land

Crops of wheat, maize, sugar beet, vegetables, and fruit are widely grown. The hilly terrain is suited to forestry and livestock farming. The mild, Mediterranean climate of the coastal regions provides ideal conditions for growing vines and olives. Albania's largely agricultural economy has been adversely affected by the recent dismantling of state farms.

SLOVENIA
HUNGARY
ROMANIA
BULGARIA
GREECE
Adriatic Sea
ZAGREB
CROATIA
BOSNIA & HERZEGOVINA
BELGRADE
SERB. & MON. (YUGO.)
SKOPJE
MACEDONIA
TIRANA
ALBANIA
Land use and agricultural distribution
pigs
sheep
cereals
fruit
olives
sugar beet
timber
tobacco
vineyards
capital cities
major towns
pasture
cropland
forest
mountain region

Sweet red peppers are dried in the sun, ready to make paprika. Macedonia's economy is mainly agricultural and its fertile soils support a broad range of crops.

The Urban/Rural Population Divide

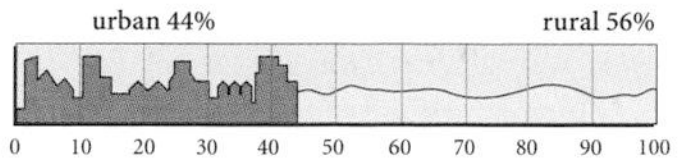

urban 44%
rural 56%
0 10 20 30 40 50 60 70 80 90 100

Population Density	Total Land Area
256 people per sq mile (99 people per sq km)	95,038 sq miles (246,278 sq km)

The Tara River is one of Montenegro's major rivers. It flows into the Danube via the Drina and Sava Rivers. Along its course the Tara has eroded spectacular gorges up to 3,280 ft (1,000 m) deep.

Map Key

Population

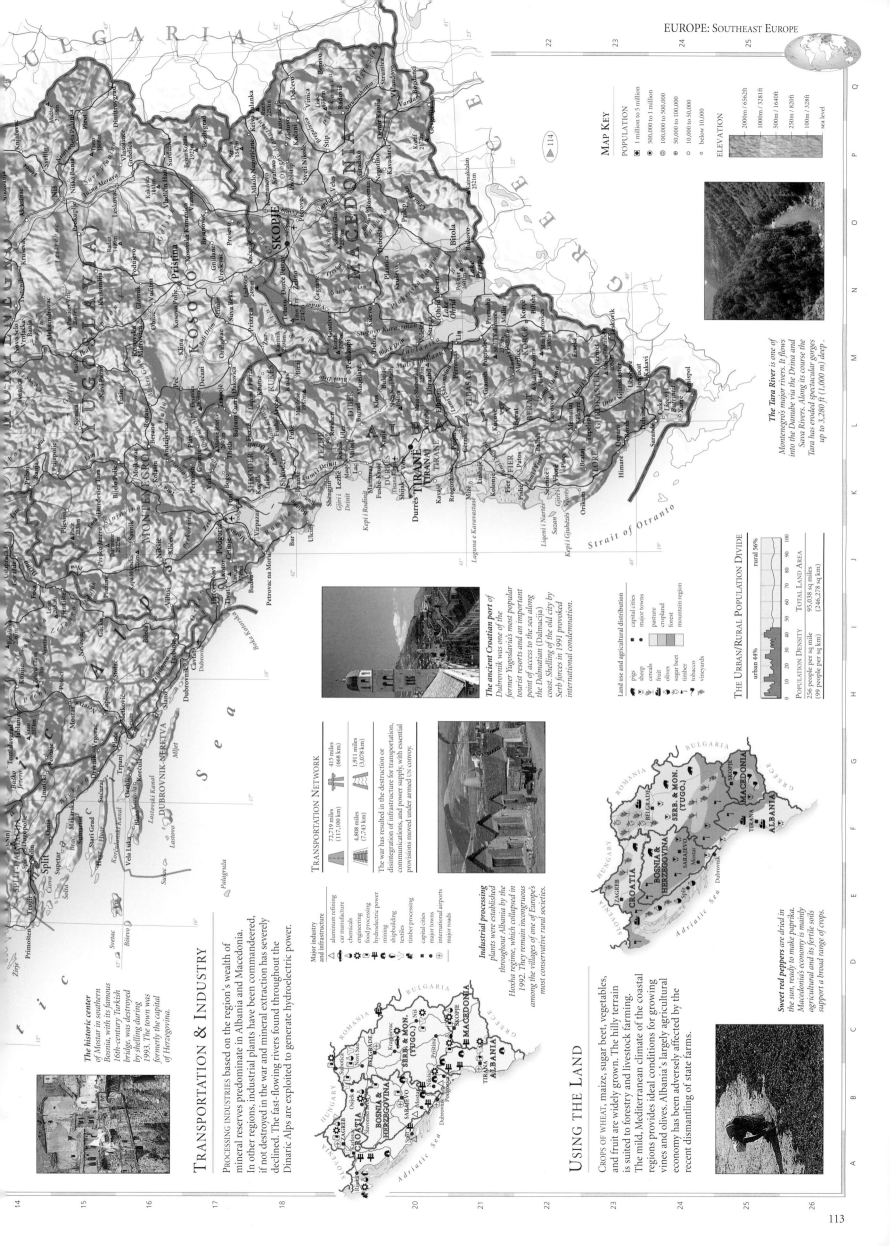

- 1 million to 5 million
- 500,000 to 1 million
- 100,000 to 500,000
- 50,000 to 100,000
- 10,000 to 50,000
- below 10,000

Elevation

- 2000m / 6562ft
- 1000m / 3281ft
- 500m / 1640ft
- 250m / 820ft
- 100m / 328ft
- sea level

Bulgaria & Greece

Including European Turkey

GREECE IS RENOWNED as the original hearth of Western civilization. The rugged terrain and numerous islands have profoundly affected its development, creating a strong agricultural and maritime tradition. In the past 50 years, this formerly rural society has rapidly urbanized, with more than half the population now living in the capital, Athens, and in the northern city of Salonica. Bulgaria, dominated for centuries by the Ottoman Turks, became part of the eastern bloc after the Second World War, only slowly emerging from Soviet influence in 1989. Moves toward democracy led to some instability in Bulgaria and Greece, now outweighed by the challenge of integration with the European Union.

Transportation & Industry

SOVIET INVESTMENT introduced heavy industry into Bulgaria, and the processing of agricultural produce, such as tobacco, is important throughout the country. Both countries have substantial shipyards and Greece has one of the world's largest merchant fleets. Many small craft workshops, producing textiles and processed foods, are clustered around Greek cities. The service and construction sectors have profited from the successful tourist industry.

ROMANIA
BULGARIA
SOFIA
Pleven
Ruse
Varna
Stara Zagora
Burgas
Plovdiv
BLACK SEA
SERB. & MON. (YUGO.)
MACEDONIA
ALBANIA
TURKEY
Istanbul
GREECE
Salonica
Larisa
Volos
Aegean Sea
Patra
Corinth
ATHENS
Ionian Sea
Irakleio
MEDITERRANEAN SEA
Major industry and infrastructure
chemicals
engineering
food processing
shipbuilding
textiles
tourism
capital cities
major towns
international airports
major roads
major industrial areas

Transportation Network

	103,930 miles (167,630 km)
	345 miles (557 km)
	4,346 miles (6,995 km)
	294 miles (474 km)

Bulgaria's railroads require investment to revive an outdated infrastructure. In Greece, despite a developing road network, ferry-boats remain the most effective form of transportation in many areas.

***A towering pinnacle** at Metéora in central Greece is home to the monastery of Roussanou. The 24 rock towers which dominate the plain of Thessaly (Thessalía) are remnants of an old plateau. Long-term weathering along fissures in the rock has worn away the rest of the plateau.*

The Landscape

BULGARIA'S BALKAN MOUNTAINS divide the Danubian Plain *(Dunavska Ravnina)* and Maritsa Basin, meeting the Black Sea in the east along sandy beaches. The steep Rhodope Mountains form a natural barrier with Greece, while the younger Pindus form a rugged central spine which descends into the Aegean Sea to give a vast archipelago of over 2000 islands, the largest of which is Crete.

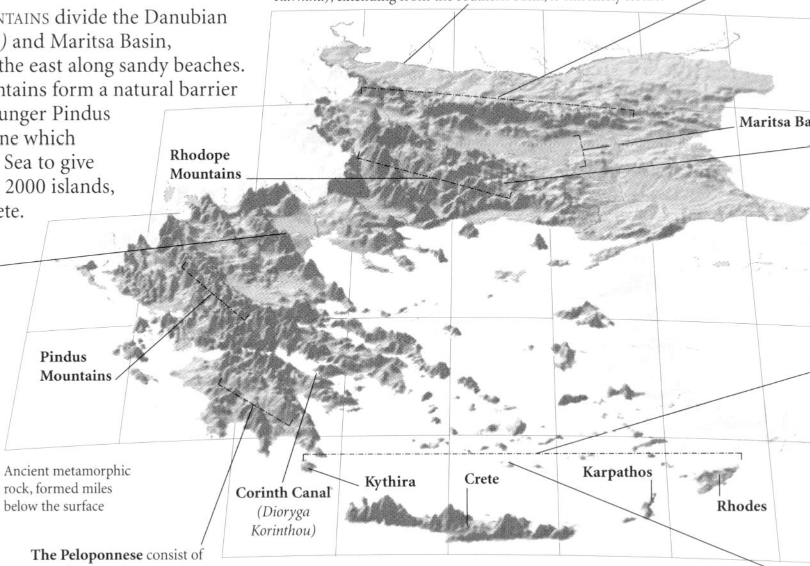
Balkan Mountains
Maritsa Basin
Rhodope Mountains
Pindus Mountains
Corinth Canal (Dioryga Korinthou)
Kythira
Crete
Karpathos
Rhodes

The Danube, Europe's second longest river, forms most of Bulgaria's northern border. The Danubian Plain *(Dunavska Ravnina)*, extending from the southern bank, is extremely fertile.

Mount Olympus is the mythical home of the Greek Gods and, at 9,570 ft (2,917 m), is the highest mountain in Greece.

The islands of Crete, Kythira, Karpathos, and Rhodes are part of an arc which bends southeastward from the Peloponnese, forming the southern boundary of the Aegean.

The Peloponnese consist of several mountainous peninsulas, linked to the mainland by the Isthmus of Corinth. The Corinth Canal *(Dioryga Korinthou)*, built in 1893, cuts through the isthmus, linking the Aegean and Ionian Seas.

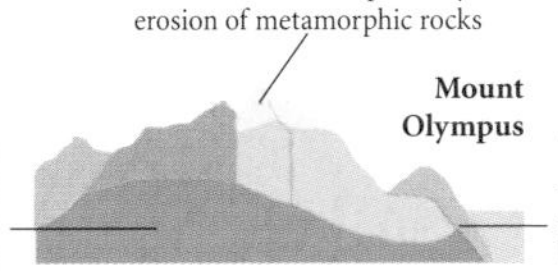
Limestone rocks exposed by erosion of metamorphic rocks
Mount Olympus
Younger limestones created in shallow seas
Ancient metamorphic rock, formed miles below the surface

Mount Olympus is a composite of rocks formed by two major tectonic events. First the older metamorphic rocks were thrust over the limestones, then two million years ago regional warping and subsequent erosion, reexposed the limestone.

*The **Arda river** cuts through the Rhodope mountains in rugged, rocky gorges.*

***Layers of black volcanic ash** still cover the island of Thira. This volcano last erupted 3,500 years ago, but still shows signs of volcanic activity.*

ROMANIA
SERBIA & MONTENEGRO (YUGOSLAVIA)
MACEDONIA
BULGARIA
TURKEY
BLACK SEA
Dunavska Ravnina
Stara Planina
Rhodope Mountains
Sofiya
Plovdiv
Varna
Burgas
Ruse
Pleven
Stara Zagora
Shumen
Dobrich
Sliven
Yambol
Haskovo
Edirne
Istanbul
Tekirdağ
Kırklareli
SCALE 1:2,750,000
(projection: Lambert Conformal Conic)
Km
Miles
112
116

112 ◀
116 ▲

ALBANIA
GREECE
TURKEY
Aegean Sea
VÓREION AIGAÍON
NÓTION AIGAÍON
Ionian Sea
Ióni Nísoi (Ionian Islands)
IÓNIOI NÍSOI
Píndos (Pindus Mountains)
DYTIKÍ MAKEDONÍA
KENTRIKÍ MAKEDONÍA
THESSALÍA
ÍPEIROS
STEREÁ ELLÁS
DYTIKÍ ELLÁS
PELOPÓNNISOS
ATTIKÍ
ÁGION ÓROS
Thessaloníki (Salonica)
Chalkidikí
Lárisa
Vólos
Pátra
ATHÍNA (ATHENS)
Peiraías (Piraeus)
Évvoia (Euboea)
Vóreioi Sporádes
Kykládes (Cyclades)
Dodekánisos (Dodecanese)
Kríti (Crete)
Irákleio
Chaniá
Ródos (Rhodes)
Lésvos (Lesbos)
Chíos
Sámos
Kárpathos
Kritikó Pélagos (Sea of Crete)
Mirtóo Pelagos
Karpáthio Pélagos
MEDITERRANEAN SEA
ÇANAKKALE
(Sea of Marmara)
112
136
120

Map Key

Population

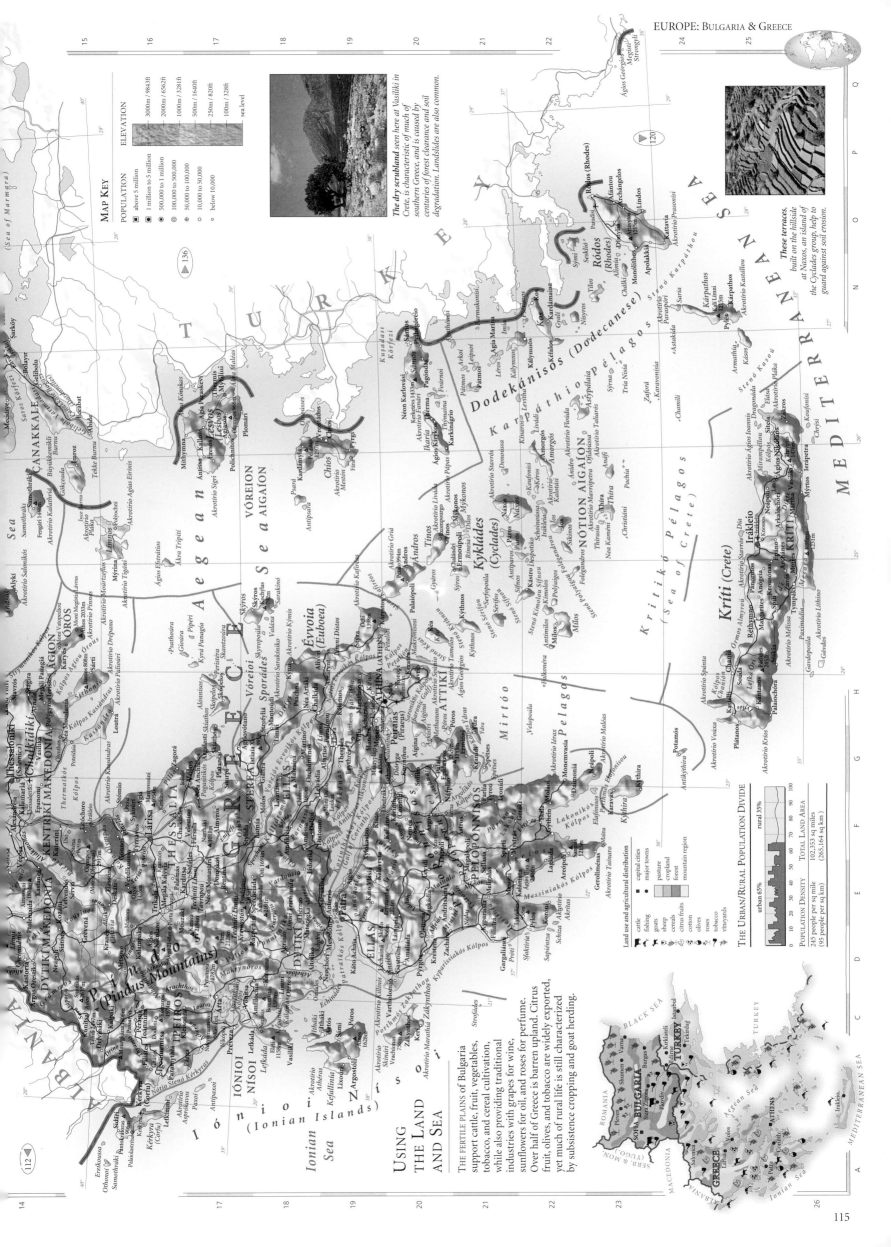

- ▣ above 5 million
- ◙ 1 million to 5 million
- ◉ 500,000 to 1 million
- ◎ 100,000 to 500,000
- ⊕ 50,000 to 100,000
- ○ 10,000 to 50,000
- ◦ below 10,000

Elevation

- 3000m / 9843ft
- 2000m / 6562ft
- 1000m / 3281ft
- 500m / 1640ft
- 250m / 820ft
- 100m / 328ft
- sea level

***The dry scrubland** seen here at Vasiliki in Crete, is characteristic of much of southern Greece, and is caused by centuries of forest clearance and soil degradation. Landslides are also common.*

Using the Land and Sea

The fertile plains of Bulgaria support cattle, fruit, vegetables, tobacco, and cereal cultivation, while also providing traditional industries with grapes for wine, sunflowers for oil, and roses for perfume. Over half of Greece is barren upland. Citrus fruit, olives, and tobacco are widely exported, yet much of rural life is still characterized by subsistence cropping and goat herding.

ROMANIA
BLACK SEA
SERB. & MON. (YUGO.)
MACEDONIA
ALBANIA
BULGARIA
SOFIA
Pleven
Shumen
Varna
Stara Zagora
Burgas
Plovdiv
Kirklareli
Edirne
Istanbul
TURKEY
Tekirdağ
GREECE
Salonica
Larisa
Volos
Patra
Corinth
ATHENS
Aegean Sea
Ionian Sea
Irakleio
MEDITERRANEAN SEA

Land use and agricultural distribution

- cattle
- fishing
- goats
- sheep
- cereals
- citrus fruits
- cotton
- olives
- roses
- tobacco
- vineyards
- capital cities
- major towns
- pasture
- cropland
- forest
- mountain region

The Urban/Rural Population Divide

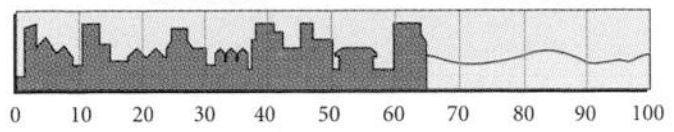
urban 65%
rural 35%
0
10
20
30
40
50
60
70
80
90
100

Population Density	Total Land Area
245 people per sq mile (95 people per sq km)	102,353 sq miles (265,164 sq km)

These terraces, built on the hillside at Naxos, an island of the Cyclades group, help to guard against soil erosion.

Romania, Moldova & Ukraine

The industrial, social, and cultural make-up of Romania and the former Soviet states of Moldova and Ukraine still bear the imprint of their communist past. As part of the USSR, Ukraine was a leading agricultural, industrial, and energy producer. These industries, like those in Moldova and Romania, are now being reoriented more firmly toward Western markets. As a result of shifting borders, and Soviet policy actively encouraging Russian immigration into other Soviet states like Ukraine and Moldova, all three countries now contain large numbers of foreign nationals. Moldovans and Romanians are still close in terms of language and culture, although Moldova is striving to remain an independent nation.

ROMANIA
POLAND
SLOVAKIA
HUNGARY
SERBIA & MONTENEGRO (YUGOSLAVIA)
BULGARIA

Using the Land

The fertile black soils of Ukraine, often called "the breadbasket of Europe," have enabled the cultivation of a variety of cereals and vegetables, which are widely exported. Romania and Moldova also grow cereals, sunflowers, and vegetables, and are noted for the quality of their wines.

The fertile lands and tolerant climate of Moldova are ideally suited to growing grapes for wine.

BELARUS
RUSSIAN FEDERATION
POLAND
SLOVAKIA
HUNGARY
SERB. & MON. (YUGOSLAVIA)
BULGARIA
BLACK SEA
UKRAINE
MOLDOVA
ROMANIA
L'viv
KIEV
Dnipropetrovs'k
Chernivtsi
CHIŞINĂU
Odesa
Timişoara
Braşov
BUCHAREST
Land use and agricultural distribution
cattle
pigs
poultry
sheep
cereals
cotton
sugar beet
sunflowers
vineyards
capital cities
major towns
pasture
cropland
forest
wetland

The Urban/Rural Population Divide

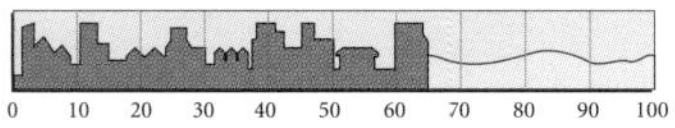

urban 65%
rural 35%
0 10 20 30 40 50 60 70 80 90 100

Population Density	Total Land Area
232 people per sq mile (89 people per sq km)	334,947 sq miles (867,740 sq km)

Glacial lakes are found throughout the Transylvanian Alps (Carpaţii Meridionali), although the mountains no longer have any permanent snow cover.

Transportation & Industry

Heavy industry using local raw materials characterizes much of this region. The industrial heartland of Ukraine, specializing in metal and machine-building industries, is based around its vast mineral reserves in the Donbass region. In Moldova, food processing draws on produce from its agricultural sector. Romanian industry relies both on local raw materials and imported iron, steel, and oil.

BELARUS
RUSSIAN FEDERATION
POLAND
SLOVAKIA
HUNGARY
SERB. & MON. (YUGOSLAVIA)
BULGARIA
BLACK SEA
UKRAINE
MOLDOVA
ROMANIA
Luts'k
L'viv
KIEV
Kharkiv
Kremenchuk
Dnipropetrovs'k
Donbass
Donets'k
Kryvyy Rih
Chernivtsi
Bălţi
CHIŞINĂU
Odesa
Simferopol'
Cluj-Napoca
Timişoara
Braşov
Galaţi
BUCHAREST
Major industry and infrastructure
car manufacture
chemicals
coal
engineering
food processing
mining
oil & gas
textiles
tourism
capital cities
major towns
international airports
major roads
major industrial areas

Transportation Network

151,089 miles (243,300 km)	70 miles (113 km)
21,889 miles (35,248 km)	3803 miles (6124 km)

Increased industrialization has necessitated the upgrading of road and rail networks in all three countries. Modernization has tended to focus only on major cities and industrial areas.

During the 1960s and 1970s, many industries, like this carbon factory, developed using the mineral resources on the flanks of the Transylvanian Alps (Carpaţii Meridionali).

110 ◀ 110 ◀ 112 ◀ 114

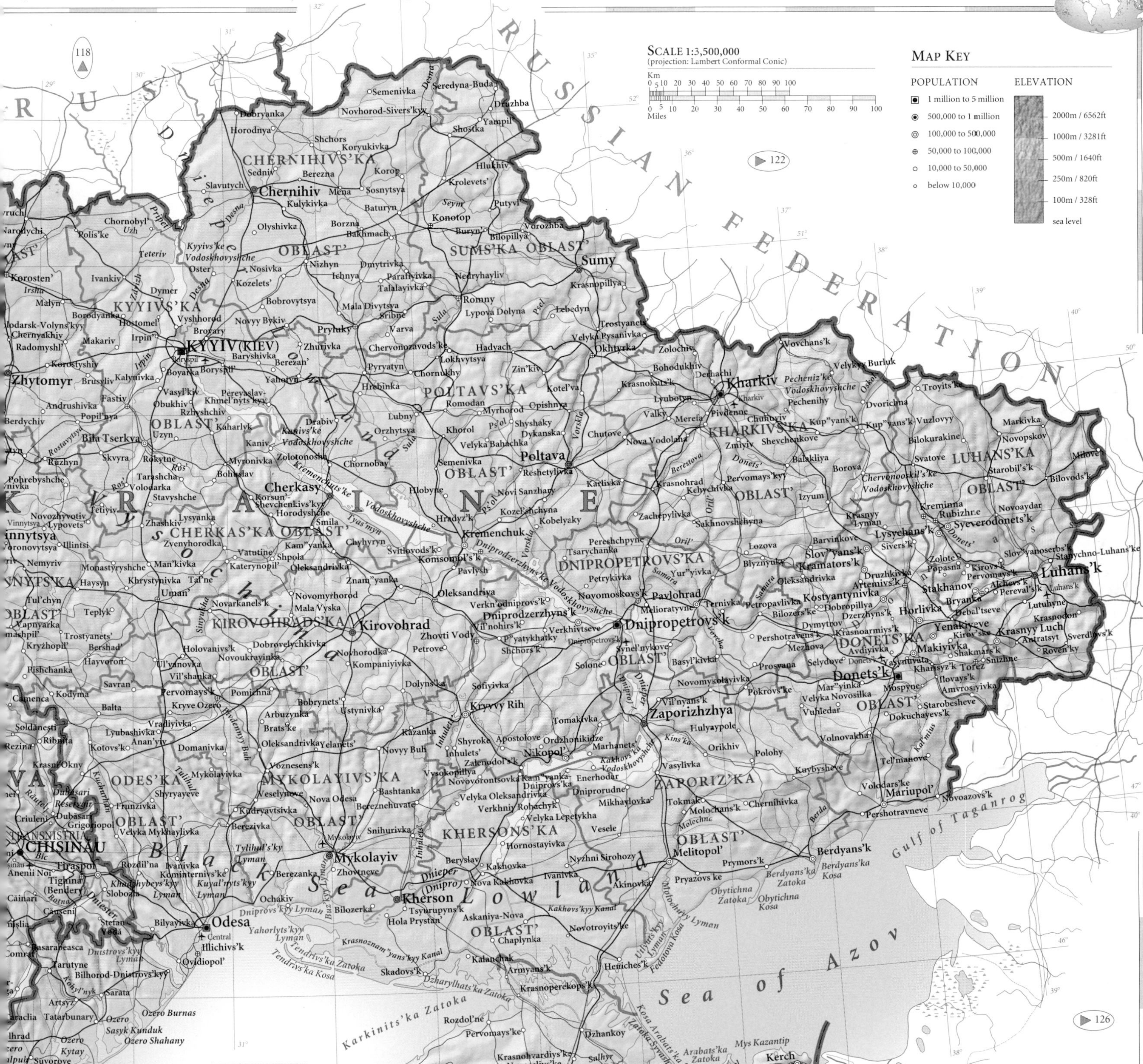
SCALE 1:3,500,000
(projection: Lambert Conformal Conic)
MAP KEY
POPULATION
1 million to 5 million
500,000 to 1 million
100,000 to 500,000
50,000 to 100,000
10,000 to 50,000
below 10,000
ELEVATION
2000m / 6562ft
1000m / 3281ft
500m / 1640ft
250m / 820ft
100m / 328ft
sea level
RUSSIAN FEDERATION
UKRAINE
KYYIV (KIEV)
CHISINAU
Sea of Azov
BLACK SEA
Black Sea Lowland
Gulf of Taganrog
RESPUBLIKA KRYM
118
122
126
120

The Swallow's Nest *castle at Yalta is one of many tourist resorts on the Crimean (Krym) coast, dubbed the "Russian Riviera."*

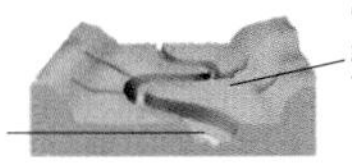
Old glaciated valley
Water has eroded a new post-glacial valley

Balkas are common throughout Ukraine. They are large U-shaped valleys, formed during the last Ice Age, which contain narrower, deep valleys. These were incised by a sudden flow of water, following an ice melt.

THE LANDSCAPE

VAST FLAT LOWLANDS and gently rolling hills cover most of southeastern Europe. In the southwest, the Carpathian Mountains form a gentle arc. To the south of the Carpathian Mountains lies the Danube Plain, across which the Danube River flows to the Black Sea. To the north and east, the hills of Moldova level out into low plains, running east to the steppes of Ukraine.

Divided into crystalline massifs, the southern arm of the Carpathian Mountains, the Transylvanian Alps (Carpații Meridionali), extend 170 miles (274 km) across southwestern Romania.

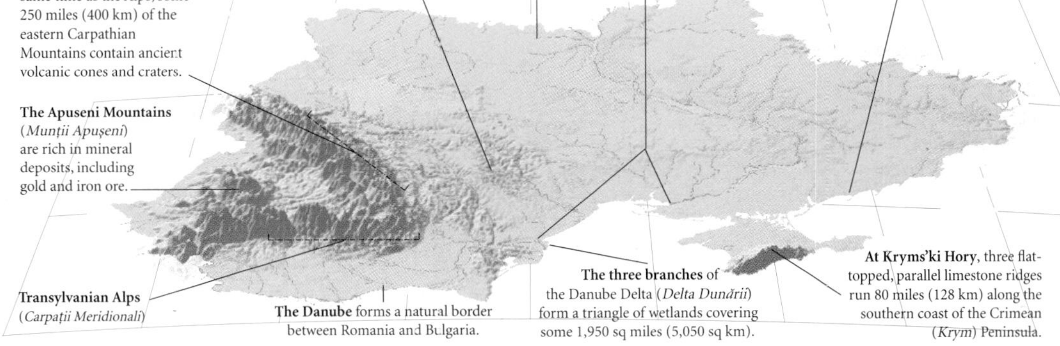
Uplifted and folded at the same time as the Alps, some 250 miles (400 km) of the eastern Carpathian Mountains contain ancient volcanic cones and craters.
The Apuseni Mountains (*Munții Apuseni*) are rich in mineral deposits, including gold and iron ore.
Transylvanian Alps (*Carpații Meridionali*)
The Codrii Hills dominate the landscape of central Moldova; they are intersected by deep, flat valleys and ravines.
Steppe landscape covers two-thirds of Ukraine. These flat, treeless grasslands extend from central Europe to central Asia.
Most of the major rivers in southeastern Europe, like the Danube, the Dniester and Dnieper flow south and east to the Black Sea.
Counterclockwise currents have created the sandspits which fringe the Sea of Azov.
The Danube forms a natural border between Romania and Bulgaria.
The three branches of the Danube Delta (*Delta Dunării*) form a triangle of wetlands covering some 1,950 sq miles (5,050 sq km).
At Kryms'ki Hory, three flat-topped, parallel limestone ridges run 80 miles (128 km) along the southern coast of the Crimean (*Krym*) Peninsula.

The Baltic States & Belarus

Belarus, Estonia, Latvia, Lithuania, Kaliningrad

Occupying Europe's main corridor to Russia, the four distinct cultures of Estonia, Latvia, Lithuania, and Belarus share a history of struggle for nationhood against the interests of more powerful neighbors. As the first republics to declare their independence from the Soviet Union in 1990–91, the Baltic states of Estonia, Latvia, and Lithuania sought an economic role in the EU, while reaffirming their European cultural roots through the church and a strong musical tradition. Meanwhile, Belarus has shown economic and political allegiance to Russia by joining the Commonwealth of Independent States.

The seaport of Riga is Latvia's capital and the center of economic and cultural life. With a 34% Russian minority in Latvia, language and the right to national citizenship are key issues.

Gulf of Finland
Narva Bay
Gulf of Riga
Irbe Strait
BALTIC SEA
RUSSIAN FEDERATION
ESTONIA
LATVIA
LITHUANIA
TALLINN
RĪGA
Lake Peipus
Lake Pskov
Saaremaa
Hiiumaa
Tartu
Pärnu
Ventspils
Liepāja
Klaipėda
Šiauliai
Panevėžys
Daugavpils
Vitsyebsk
Western Dvina (Daugava)

▶ 122

Using The Land

Across the four nations cattle and pig farming are widespread, together with diverse arable crops, including flax for making linen, potatoes used to produce vodka, cereals, and other vegetables. Almost a third of the land is forested; demand for timber has increased the importance of forest management.

Land use and agricultural distribution
cattle
pigs
cereals
flax
potatoes
timber
capital cities
major towns
pasture
cropland
forest
wetland
TALLINN
ESTONIA
LATVIA
RIGA
LITHUANIA
VILNIUS
BELARUS
MINSK
RUSS.FED.
Kaliningrad
BALTIC SEA
RUSSIAN FEDERATION
POLAND
UKRAINE

The Urban/Rural Population Divide

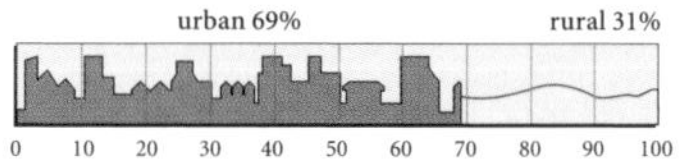

urban 69%
rural 31%
0 10 20 30 40 50 60 70 80 90 100

Population Density	Total Land Area
122 people per sq mile (47 people per sq km)	145,006 sq miles (375,656 sq km)

A pine forest in northern Belarus. *Conifers in the north give way to hardwood forest farther south. Timber mills are supplied with logs floated along the country's many navigable waterways.*

The Western Dvina River *provides hydro-electric power and, during the summer months, access to the Baltic Sea. The lower course of the river freezes from December to April.*

Map Key

POPULATION
- 1 million to 5 million
- 500,000 to 1 million
- 100,000 to 500,000
- 50,000 to 100,000
- 10,000 to 50,000
- below 10,000

ELEVATION
- 250m / 820ft
- 100m / 328ft
- sea level

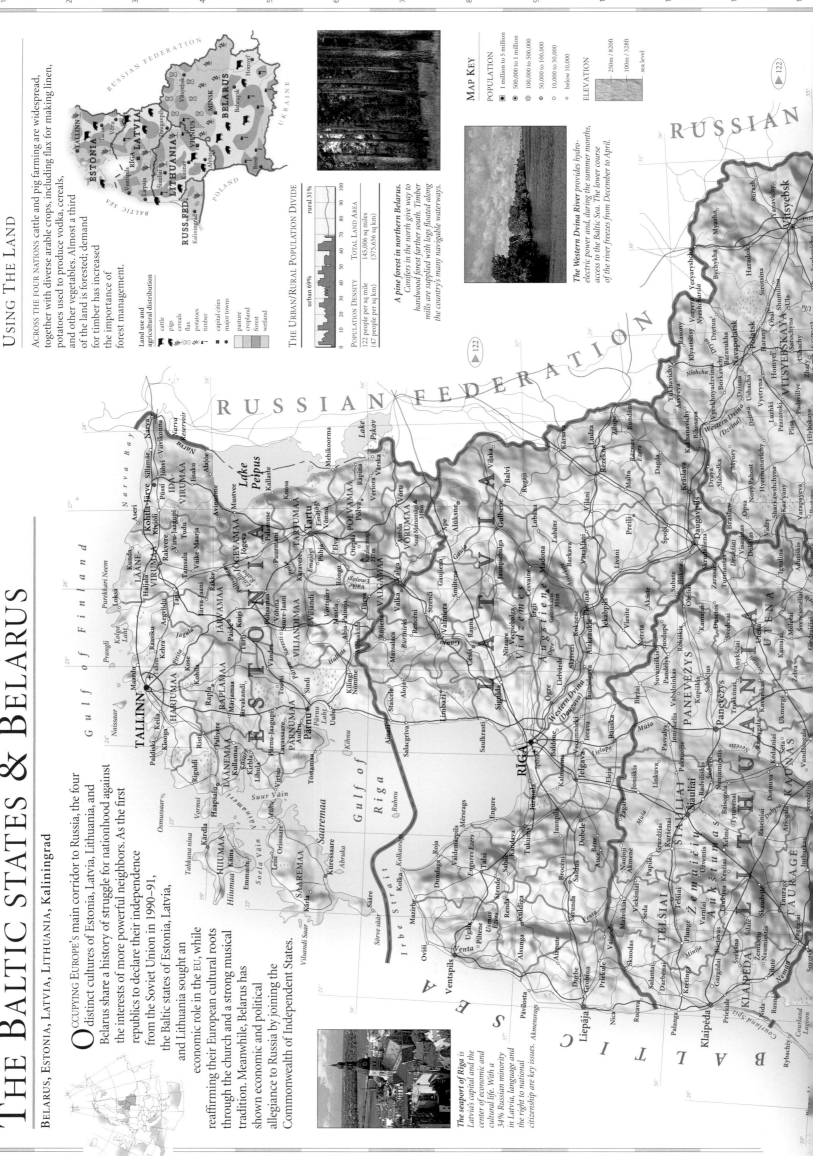

▶ 122

RUSSIAN FEDERATION
Kaliningrad
KALININGRADSKAYA OBLAST'
POLAND
VILNIUS
MINSK
BELARUS
HRODZYENSKAYA VOBLASTS'
MINSKAYA VOBLASTS'
MAHILYOWSKAYA VOBLASTS'
BRESTSKAYA VOBLASTS'
HOMYEL'SKAYA VOBLASTS'
UKRAINE
Hrodna
Brest
Babruysk
Mahilyow
Homyel'
Orsha
Pinsk
Pripet Marshes
Dnieper (Dnyapro)
116
110

SCALE 1:2,750,000
(projection: Lambert Conformal Conic)

Km 0 5 10 20 30 40 50 60 70 80 90 100
Miles 0 5 10 20 30 40 50 60 70 80 90 100

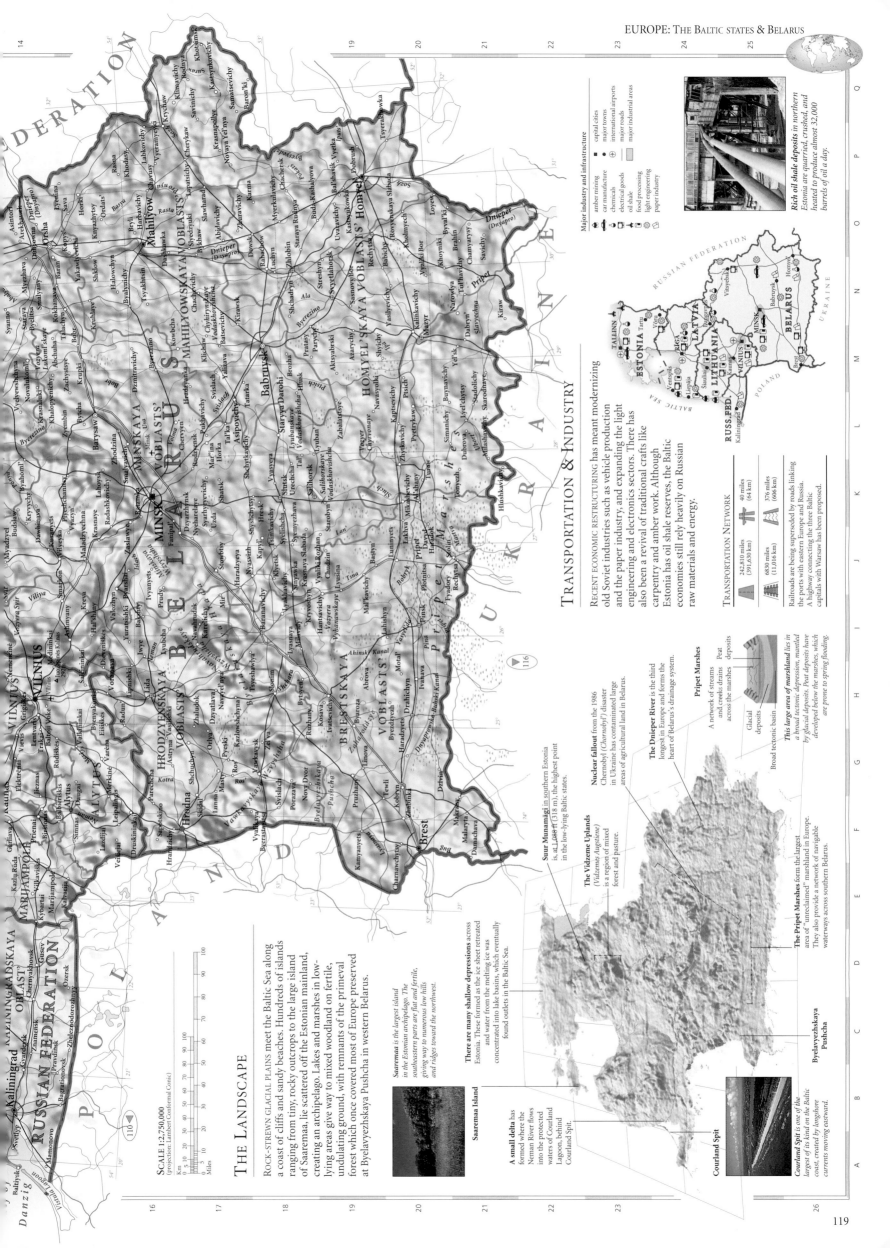

THE LANDSCAPE

ROCK-STREWN GLACIAL PLAINS meet the Baltic Sea along a coast of cliffs and sandy beaches. Hundreds of islands ranging from tiny, rocky outcrops to the large island of Saaremaa, lie scattered off the Estonian mainland, creating an archipelago. Lakes and marshes in low-lying areas give way to mixed woodland on fertile, undulating ground, with remnants of the primeval forest which once covered most of Europe preserved at Byelavyezhskaya Pushcha in western Belarus.

Saaremaa is the largest island in the Estonian archipelago. The southeastern parts are flat and fertile, giving way to numerous low hills and ridges toward the northwest.

Saaremaa Island

There are many shallow depressions across Estonia. These formed as the ice sheet retreated and water from the melting ice was concentrated into lake basins, which eventually found outlets in the Baltic Sea.

A small delta has formed where the Neman River flows into the protected waters of Courland Lagoon, behind Courland Spit.

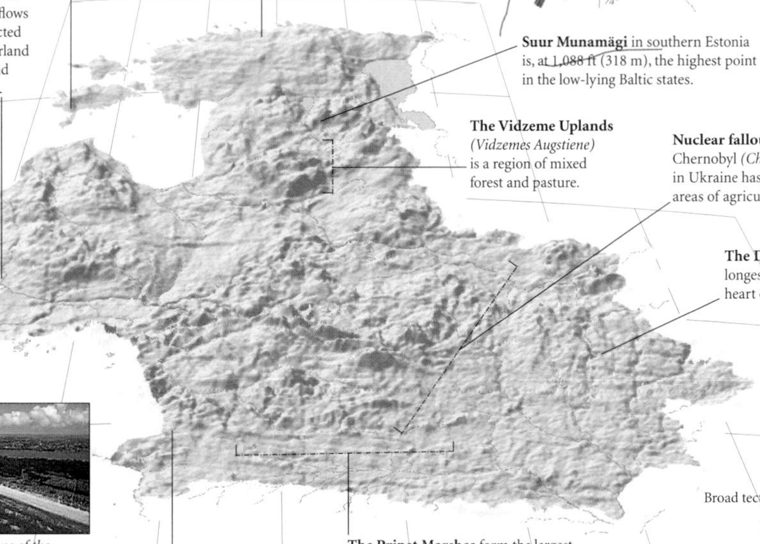

Suur Munamägi in southern Estonia is, at 1,088 ft (318 m), the highest point in the low-lying Baltic states.

The Vidzeme Uplands *(Vidzemes Augstiene)* is a region of mixed forest and pasture.

Nuclear fallout from the 1986 Chernobyl *(Chornobyl')* disaster in Ukraine has contaminated large areas of agricultural land in Belarus.

The Dnieper River is the third longest in Europe and forms the heart of Belarus's drainage system.

Pripet Marshes

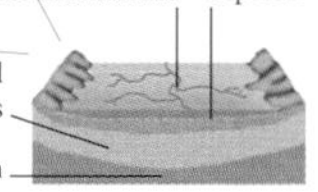
A network of streams and creeks drains across the marshes
Peat deposits
Glacial deposits
Broad tectonic basin

***This large area of marshland** lies in a broad tectonic depression, mantled by glacial deposits. Peat deposits have developed below the marshes, which are prone to spring flooding.*

The Pripet Marshes form the largest area of "unreclaimed" marshland in Europe. They also provide a network of navigable waterways across southern Belarus.

Courland Spit

***Courland Spit** is one of the largest of its kind on the Baltic coast, created by longshore currents moving eastward.*

Byelavyezhskaya Pushcha

TRANSPORTATION & INDUSTRY

RECENT ECONOMIC RESTRUCTURING has meant modernizing old Soviet industries such as vehicle production and the paper industry, and expanding the light engineering and electronics sectors. There has also been a revival of traditional crafts like carpentry and amber work. Although Estonia has oil shale reserves, the Baltic economies still rely heavily on Russian raw materials and energy.

TRANSPORTATION NETWORK

242,810 miles (391,630 km)	40 miles (64 km)
6830 miles (11,016 km)	376 miles (606 km)

Railroads are being superseded by roads linking the ports with eastern Europe and Russia. A highway connecting the three Baltic capitals with Warsaw has been proposed.

TALLINN
ESTONIA
Tartu
Võru
RIGA
LATVIA
Ventspils
Liepāja
Daugavpils
Šiauliai
LITHUANIA
Kaunas
VILNIUS
RUSS.FED.
Kaliningrad
MINSK
Vitsyebsk
Babruysk
Homyel'
Brest
BELARUS
BALTIC SEA
RUSSIAN FEDERATION
POLAND
UKRAINE

Major industry and infrastructure

- amber mining
- car manufacture
- chemicals
- electrical goods
- oil shale
- food processing
- light engineering
- paper industry
- capital cities
- major towns
- international airports
- major roads
- major industrial areas

***Rich oil shale deposits** in northern Estonia are quarried, crushed, and heated to produce almost 32,000 barrels of oil a day.*

THE MEDITERRANEAN

THE MEDITERRANEAN SEA stretches over 2,500 miles (4,000 km) east to west, separating Europe from Africa. At its westernmost point it is connected to the Atlantic Ocean through the Strait of Gibraltar. In the east, the Suez Canal, opened in 1869, gives passage to the Indian Ocean. In the northeast, linked by the Sea of Marmara, lies the Black Sea. Throughout history the Mediterranean has been a focal area for many great empires and civilizations, reflected in the variety of cultures found in the 28 states and territories that border its shores. Since the 1960s, development along the southern coast of Europe has expanded rapidly to accommodate increasing numbers of tourists and to enable the exploitation of oil and gas reserves. This has resulted in rising levels of pollution, threatening the future of the sea.

Monte Carlo in Monaco is just one of the luxurious resorts scattered along the Riviera, which stretches along the coast from Cannes in France to La Spezia in Italy. The region's mild winters and hot summers have attracted wealthy tourists since the early 19th century.

ATLANTIC OCEAN
Bay of Biscay
FRANCE
SPAIN
PORTUGAL
ANDORRA
MONACO
ITALY
SWITZERLAND
SAN MARINO
VATICAN CITY
MOROCCO
ALGERIA
TUNISIA
MALTA
MEDITERRANEAN
A Coruña
Gijón (Xixón)
Oviedo
Santander
Bilbao
Donostia-San Sebastián
Bordeaux
Toulouse
Montpellier
Nîmes
Marseille
Toulon
Nice
Cannes
Torino (Turin)
Milano (Milan)
Genova (Genoa)
Bologna
Firenze (Florence)
Pisa
Livorno
Ravenna
Rimini
Ancona
Venezia (Venice)
ROMA (ROME)
Napoli (Naples)
Salerno
Porto
Vigo
Ourense
León
Valladolid
Salamanca
Burgos
Logroño
Zaragoza
Lleida
Barcelona
Tarragona
Perpignan
LISBOA (LISBON)
Setúbal
Badajoz
MADRID
Getafe
Valencia
Castelló de la Plana
Albacete
Alicante
Elche
Murcia
Cartagena
Córdoba
Sevilla (Seville)
Jaén
Granada
Málaga
Almería
Huelva
Cádiz
Algeciras
GIBRALTAR (to UK)
Strait of Gibraltar
Tanger
Ceuta (part of Spain)
Tétouan
Melilla (part of Spain)
Alboran Sea
Kénitra
RABAT
Salé
Casablanca
Mohammedia
Meknès
Fès
Oujda
Safi
Marrakech
Beni-Mellal
Haut Atlas
Moyen Atlas
Oran
Mostaganem
Chlef
Tlemcen
Sidi Bel Abbès
ALGER (ALGIERS)
Blida
Tizi Ouzou
Béjaïa
Skikda
Constantine
Sétif
Annaba
Batna
Atlas Tellien
Hauts Plateaux
Atlas Saharien
Massif de l'Aurès
Bizerte
TUNIS
Sousse
Sfax
Gabès
Médenine
ṬARĀBULUS (TRIPOLI)
Mişrātah
Gharyān
Islas Baleares (Balearic Islands)
Mallorca (Majorca)
Menorca (Minorca)
Palma
Eivissa (Ibiza)
Formentera
Algerian Basin
Golfe du Lion
Ligurian Sea
Corse (Corsica) (to France)
Ajaccio
Sardegna (Sardinia) (to Italy)
Sassari
Cagliari
Tyrrhenian Sea
Tyrrhenian Basin
Sicilia (Sicily)
Palermo
Agrigento
Catania
Strait of Sicily
VALLETTA
Isole Pelagie (to Italy)
Golfe de Hammamet
Golfe de Gabès

THE LANDSCAPE

THE MEDITERRANEAN SEA IS ALMOST TOTALLY LANDLOCKED, joined to the Atlantic Ocean through the Strait of Gibraltar, which is only 8 miles (13 km) wide. Lying on an active plate margin, sea floor movements have formed a variety of basins, troughs, and ridges. A submarine ridge running from Tunisia to Sicily divides the sea into two distinct basins. The western basin is characterized by broad, smooth abyssal (or ocean) plains. In contrast, the eastern basin is dominated by a large ridge system, running east to west.

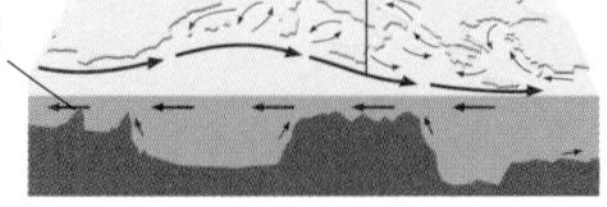
Denser, more saline currents flow back to Atlantic
Main surface current

Atlantic surface water enters the Mediterranean Sea via the Straits of Gibraltar and generally flows eastward, becoming progressively more saline and dense as water evaporates. This denser water sinks and at depths below 280 ft (80 m), flows back to the Atlantic Ocean.

Industrial pollution flowing from the Dnieper and Danube Rivers has destroyed a large proportion of the fish population that used to inhabit the upper layers of the Black Sea.

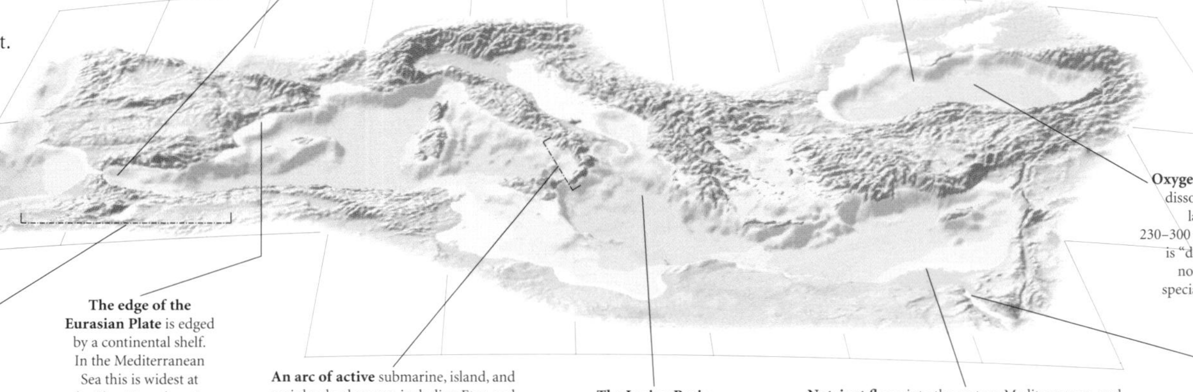

***The Atlas Mountains** are a range of fold mountains that lie in Morocco and Algeria. They run parallel to the Mediterranean, forming a topographical and climatic divide between the Mediterranean coast and the western Sahara.*

The edge of the Eurasian Plate is edged by a continental shelf. In the Mediterranean Sea this is widest at he Ebro Fan where it extends 60 miles (96 km).

An arc of active submarine, island, and mainland volcanoes, including Etna and Vesuvius, lie in and around southern Italy. The area is also susceptible to earthquakes and landslides.

The Ionian Basin is the deepest in the Mediterranean, reaching depths of 16,800 ft (5,121 m).

Nutrient flows into the eastern Mediterranean, and sediment flows to the Nile Delta have been severely lowered by the building of the Aswan Dam across the Nile in Egypt. This is causing the delta to shrink.

Oxygen in the Black Sea is dissolved only in its upper layers; at depths below 230–300 ft (70–100 m) the sea is "dead" and can support no life-forms other than specially-adapted bacteria.

The Suez Canal, opened in 1869, extends 100 miles (160 km) from Port Said to the Gulf of Suez.

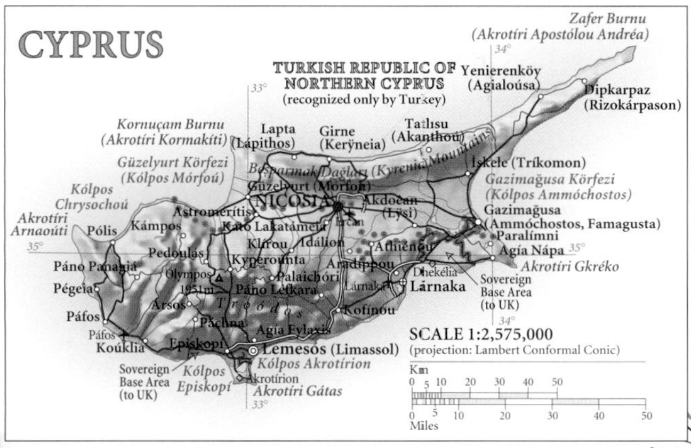
CYPRUS
TURKISH REPUBLIC OF NORTHERN CYPRUS (recognized only by Turkey)
Zafer Burnu (Akrotíri Apostólou Andréa)
Yenierenköy (Agialoúsa)
Dipkarpaz (Rizokárpason)
Kornuçam Burnu (Akrotíri Kormakíti)
Lapta (Lápithos)
Girne (Kerýneia)
Tatlısu (Akanthoú)
Güzelyurt Körfezi (Kólpos Mórfou)
Kólpos Chrysochoú
Akrotíri Arnaoúti
Pólis
NICOSIA
İskele (Tríkomon)
Gazimağusa Körfezi (Kólpos Ammóchostos)
Gazimağusa (Ammóchostos, Famagusta)
Paralímni
Agía Nápa
Akrotíri Gkréko
Lárnaka
Sovereign Base Area (to UK)
Páfos
Lemesós (Limassol)
Kólpos Akrotíriou
Kólpos Episkopí
Akrotíri Gátas
SCALE 1:2,575,000
(projection: Lambert Conformal Conic)

IN 1974 TURKEY OCCUPIED the northern part of Cyprus while Greek Cypriots remained in control of the south. Cyprus was effectively partitioned and a UN buffer zone currently divides the two areas. In 1983 the north of the island proclaimed itself the Turkish Republic of North Cyprus. It was only recognized by Turkey.

The city of Venice is built on an archipelago of islands and mud-flats in the middle of a lagoon at the head of the Adriatic Sea. The city's numerous canals follow water routes between the original 118 islands.

Cyprus is the third largest Mediterranean island after Sardinia and Sicily. The island is mountainous; containing two main ranges, the Troodos and the Kyrenia mountains.

UKRAINE
RUSSIAN FEDERATION
MOLDOVA
ROMANIA
BULGARIA
GEORGIA
TURKEY
GREECE
ALBANIA
MACEDONIA
SERB. & MON. (YUGOSLAVIA)
BOSNIA & HERZEGOVINA
CROATIA
SYRIA
LEBANON
ISRAEL
JORDAN
SAUDI ARABIA
EGYPT
LIBYA
CYPRUS
BLACK SEA
Sea of Azov
Aegean Sea
Adriatic Sea
Ionian Sea
MEDITERRANEAN SEA
Red Sea
Odesa
BUCUREŞTI (BUCHAREST)
SOFIYA (SOFIA)
SKOPJE
TIRANË (TIRANA)
SARAJEVO
ATHÍNA (ATHENS)
ANKARA
İstanbul
İzmir
NICOSIA
BEYROUTH (BEIRUT)
DIMASHQ (DAMASCUS)
JERUSALEM
'AMMĀN
CAIRO
Alexandria
Banghāzī (Benghazi)
SCALE 1:10,100,000
(projection: Lambert Conformal Conic)

Beirut is Lebanon's largest city. In the 1960s and 70s it was the chief financial, commercial, and transportation center for the Arab states. In 1975 civil war broke out and although rebuilding is under way, many buildings bear the scars of the war, that finally ended in 1990.

MAP KEY

POPULATION
- above 5 million
- 1 million to 5 million
- 500,000 to 1 million
- 100,000 to 500,000
- 50,000 to 100,000
- 10,000 to 50,000
- below 10,000

ELEVATION
- 4000m / 13,124ft
- 3000m / 9843ft
- 2000m / 6562ft
- 1000m / 3281ft
- 500m / 1640ft
- 250m / 820ft
- 100m / 328ft
- sea level

SEA DEPTH
- sea level
- 250m / 820ft
- 500m / 1640ft
- 1000m / 3281ft
- 2000m / 6562ft
- 3000m / 9843ft

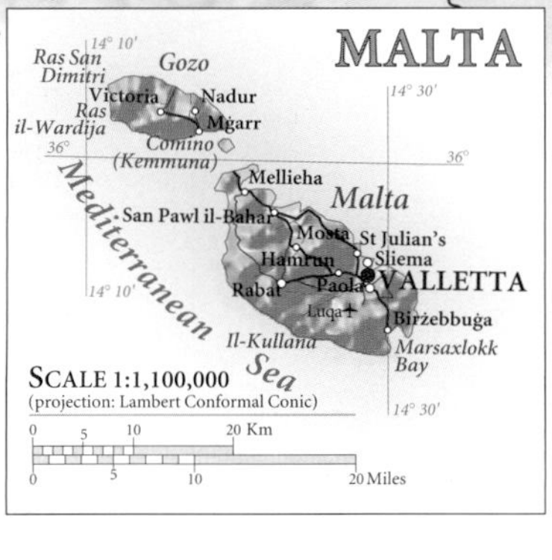
MALTA
Gozo
Victoria
Nadur
Mġarr
Comino (Kemmuna)
Mellieħa
San Pawl il-Baħar
Malta
St Julian's
Sliema
VALLETTA
Rabat
Birżebbuġa
Marsaxlokk Bay
Mediterranean Sea
SCALE 1:1,100,000
(projection: Lambert Conformal Conic)

Commercial fisheries are found throughout the Mediterranean. Operations have traditionally been small-scale. As elsewhere, high demand has caused a decline in fish stocks.

The Suez Canal links the Mediterranean with the Red Sea providing an important shipping route between Europe and Asia.

The Russian Federation

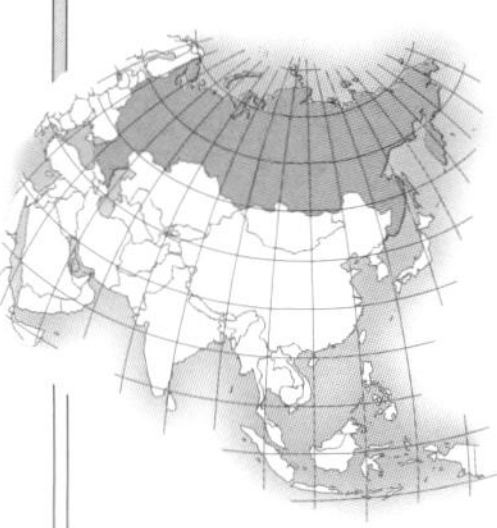

The Cold War era of global relations was concluded in 1991 with the formal dissolution of the Soviet Union. The Russian Federation declared its separate sovereignty from the foundering communist empire following independence declarations from a number of former Soviet republics. As the leading member of the Commonwealth of Independent States, the Russian Federation has a central role in the development of post-Soviet Eurasia. Crossing 11 time zones, the Russian Federation is almost twice the size of the US, and with more than 150 ethnic minorities and 21 autonomous republics, regionalist dissent within its own territory remains a danger.

***Summer beds of moss and lichen** scatter a 90% surface cover of ice across the islands of Franz Josef Land (Zemlya Frantsa-Iosifa), the northernmost land in the eastern hemisphere.*

The Russian Federation: Administrative Regions

124-125
126-127
The administrative area names in European Russia have been omitted west of the Ural Mountains. Please refer to pages 124–125 and 126–127 where these areas are shown at a larger scale.
BARENTS SEA
ARCTIC
Karskoye More
Novaya Zemlya
Zemlya Frantsa-Iosifa
Beloye More
Caspian Sea
BLACK SEA
Sea of Azov
KAZAKHSTAN
Moskva (Moscow)
Sankt-Peterburg
Arkhangel'sk (Archangel)
Murmansk
Nizhniy Novgorod
Yekaterinburg
Chelyabinsk
Omsk
Novosibirsk
Tomsk
Krasnoyarsk
Kemerovo
Barnaul
Novokuznetsk
Orenburg
Samara
Saratov
Volgograd
Astrakhan'
Rostov-na-Donu
Voronezh
Kazan'
Perm'
Ufa
Tyumen'
Kurgan
Noril'sk
Vorkuta
Surgut
Irkutsk
Abakan
Kyzyl
Poluostrov Yamal
Zapadno-Sibirskaya Ravnina
Srednesibirskoye Ploskogor'ye
Severo-Sibirskaya
TAYMYRSKIY (DOLGANO-NENETSKIY) AVTONOMNYY OKRUG
YAMALO-NENETSKIY AVTONOMNYY OKRUG
KHANTY-MANSIYSKIY AVTONOMNYY OKRUG
EVENKIYSKIY AVTONOMNYY OKRUG
92
118
110
116
136
144
162

The North European Plain is marked by huge moraine ridges left by the Scandinavian Ice Sheet and by long intermoraine drainage channels, known as *Urstromtäler*.

***The Khatanga River** meanders slowly across the Poluostrov Taymyr, a low-lying tundra landscape which floods in the spring thaw, until the water can escape to the sea.*

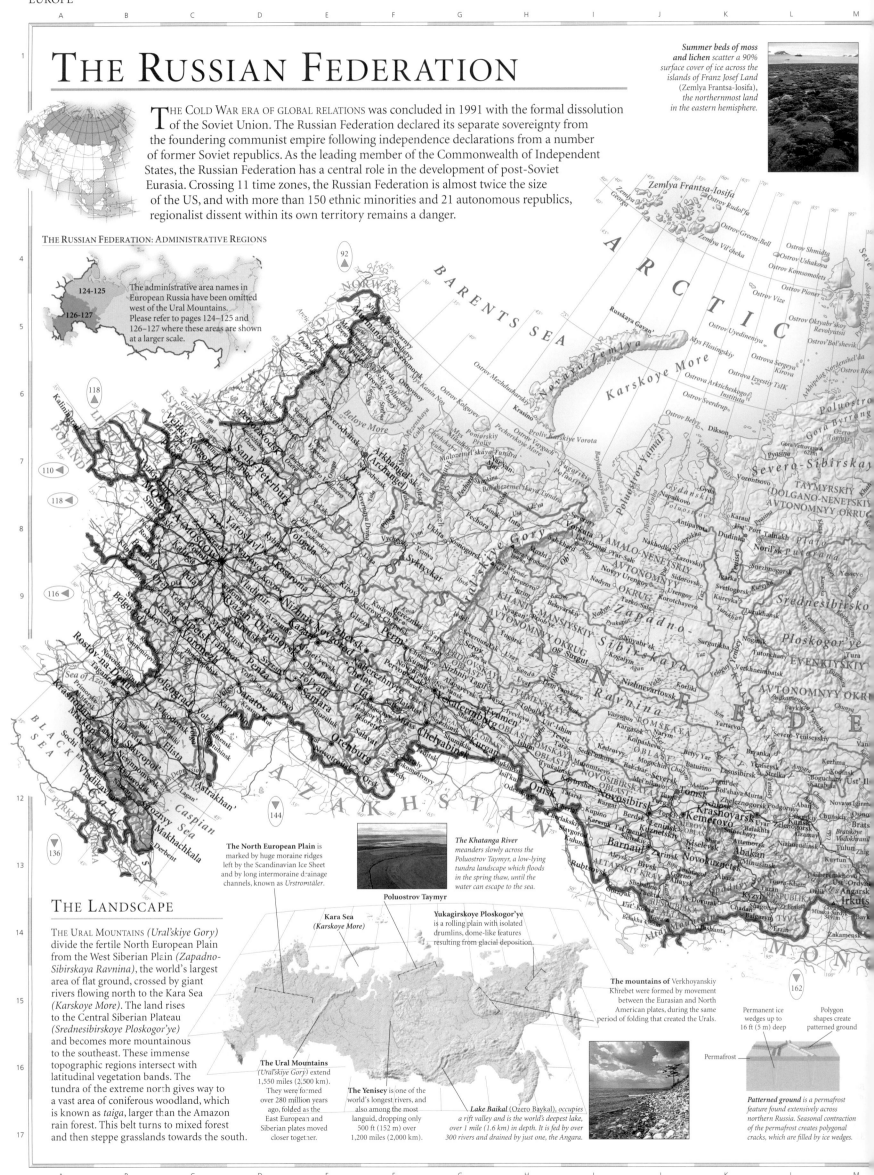

The Landscape

The Ural Mountains *(Ural'skiye Gory)* divide the fertile North European Plain from the West Siberian Plain *(Zapadno-Sibirskaya Ravnina)*, the world's largest area of flat ground, crossed by giant rivers flowing north to the Kara Sea *(Karskoye More)*. The land rises to the Central Siberian Plateau *(Srednesibirskoye Ploskogor'ye)* and becomes more mountainous to the southeast. These immense topographic regions intersect with latitudinal vegetation bands. The tundra of the extreme north gives way to a vast area of coniferous woodland, which is known as *taiga*, larger than the Amazon rain forest. This belt turns to mixed forest and then steppe grasslands towards the south.

Poluostrov Taymyr

Kara Sea *(Karskoye More)*

Yukagirskoye Ploskogor'ye is a rolling plain with isolated drumlins, dome-like features resulting from glacial deposition.

The mountains of Verkhoyanskiy Khrebet were formed by movement between the Eurasian and North American plates, during the same period of folding that created the Urals.

The Ural Mountains *(Ural'skiye Gory)* extend 1,550 miles (2,500 km). They were formed over 280 million years ago, folded as the East European and Siberian plates moved closer together.

The Yenisey is one of the world's longest rivers, and also among the most languid, dropping only 500 ft (152 m) over 1,200 miles (2,000 km).

***Lake Baikal** (Ozero Baykal), occupies a rift valley and is the world's deepest lake, over 1 mile (1.6 km) in depth. It is fed by over 300 rivers and drained by just one, the Angara.*

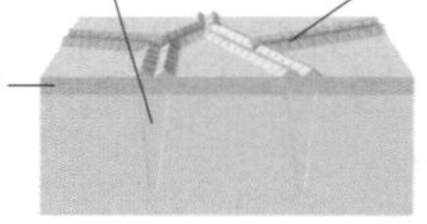
Permanent ice wedges up to 16 ft (5 m) deep
Polygon shapes create patterned ground
Permafrost

***Patterned ground** is a permafrost feature found extensively across northern Russia. Seasonal contraction of the permafrost creates polygonal cracks, which are filled by ice wedges.*

ARCTIC OCEAN
Barents Sea
Murmansk
Archangel
St. Petersburg
MOSCOW
Nizhniy Novgorod
RUSSIAN FEDERATION
Siberia
Magadan
Yakutsk
Bering Sea
Sea of Okhotsk
Volgograd
Novosibirsk
Irkutsk
Yuzhno-Sakhalinsk
Sea of Japan (East Sea)
Vladivostok
KAZAKHSTAN
MONGOLIA
CHINA
Caspian Sea
Black Sea
BELA.
UKR.

The Urban/Rural Population Divide

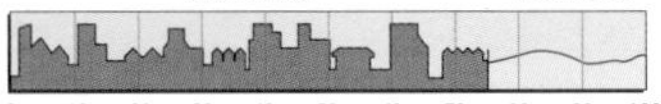
urban 76%
rural 24%
0 10 20 30 40 50 60 70 80 90 100

Population Density	Total Land Area
22 people per sq mile (9 people per sq km)	65,592,800 sq miles (17,075,400 sq km)

Land use and agricultural distribution

cattle · cereals · root crops · timber · capital cities · major towns · pasture · cropland · forest · desert · mountain region · barren

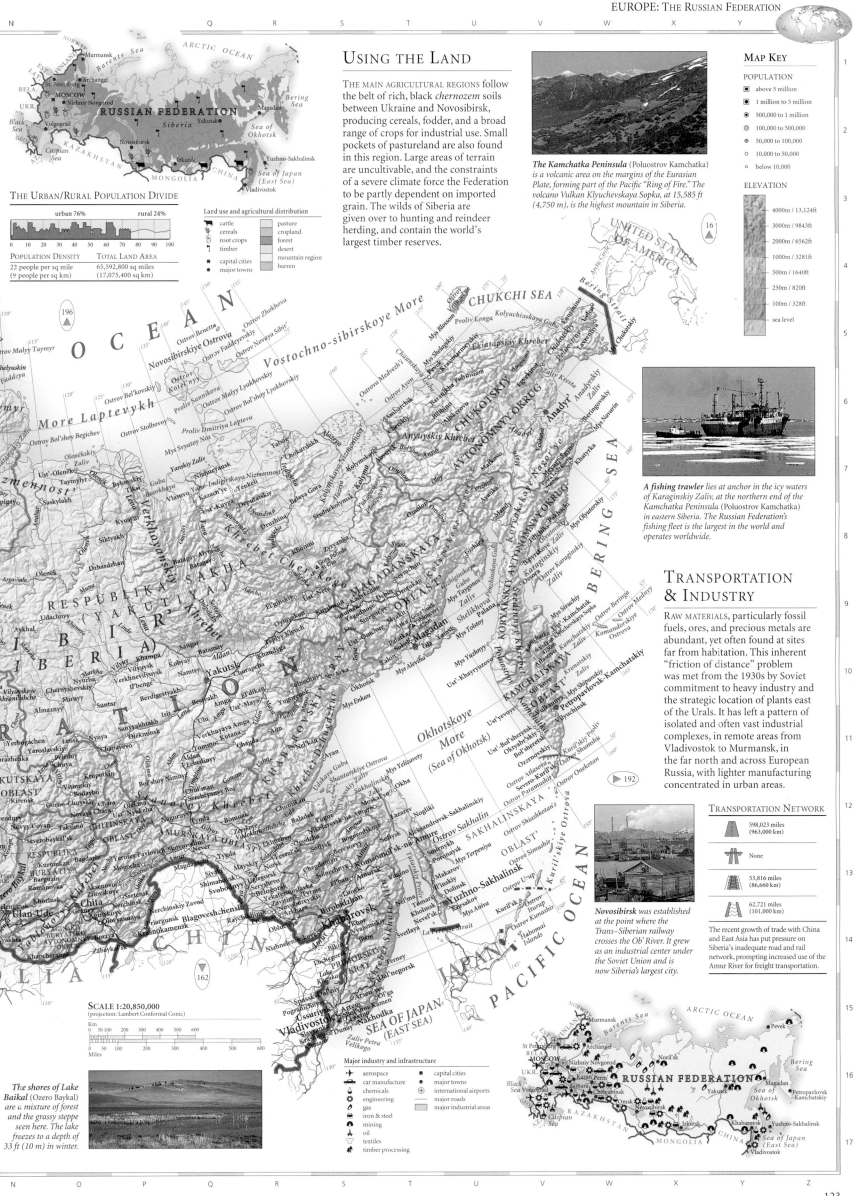

Using the Land

The main agricultural regions follow the belt of rich, black *chernozem* soils between Ukraine and Novosibirsk, producing cereals, fodder, and a broad range of crops for industrial use. Small pockets of pastureland are also found in this region. Large areas of terrain are uncultivable, and the constraints of a severe climate force the Federation to be partly dependent on imported grain. The wilds of Siberia are given over to hunting and reindeer herding, and contain the world's largest timber reserves.

The Kamchatka Peninsula *(Poluostrov Kamchatka) is a volcanic area on the margins of the Eurasian Plate, forming part of the Pacific "Ring of Fire." The volcano Vulkan Klyuchevskaya Sopka, at 15,585 ft (4,750 m), is the highest mountain in Siberia.*

Map Key

Population

- above 5 million
- 1 million to 5 million
- 500,000 to 1 million
- 100,000 to 500,000
- 50,000 to 100,000
- 10,000 to 50,000
- below 10,000

Elevation

- 4000m / 13,124ft
- 3000m / 9843ft
- 2000m / 6562ft
- 1000m / 3281ft
- 500m / 1640ft
- 250m / 820ft
- 100m / 328ft
- sea level

OCEAN
CHUKCHI SEA
Bering Strait
UNITED STATES OF AMERICA
Vostochno-sibirskoye More
More Laptevykh
Novosibirskiye Ostrova
CHUKOTSKIY AVTONOMNYY OKRUG
Anadyr'
BERING SEA
MAGADANSKAYA OBLAST'
Magadan
KORYAKSKIY AVTONOMNYY OKRUG
KAMCHATSKAYA OBLAST'
Petropavlovsk-Kamchatskiy
RESPUBLIKA SAKHA (YAKUTIYA)
Yakutsk
SIBERIA
FEDERATION
Okhotskoye More (Sea of Okhotsk)
KHABAROVSKIY KRAY
SAKHALINSKAYA OBLAST'
Yuzhno-Sakhalinsk
Khabarovsk
Blagoveshchensk
Chita
Ulan-Ude
PRIMORSKIY KRAY
Vladivostok
Nakhodka
SEA OF JAPAN (EAST SEA)
JAPAN
PACIFIC OCEAN
CHINA
MONGOLIA
SCALE 1:20,850,000
(projection: Lambert Conformal Conic)

16
196
192
162

A fishing trawler *lies at anchor in the icy waters of Karaginskiy Zaliv, at the northern end of the Kamchatka Peninsula (Poluostrov Kamchatka) in eastern Siberia. The Russian Federation's fishing fleet is the largest in the world and operates worldwide.*

Transportation & Industry

Raw materials, particularly fossil fuels, ores, and precious metals are abundant, yet often found at sites far from habitation. This inherent "friction of distance" problem was met from the 1930s by Soviet commitment to heavy industry and the strategic location of plants east of the Urals. It has left a pattern of isolated and often vast industrial complexes, in remote areas from Vladivostok to Murmansk, in the far north and across European Russia, with lighter manufacturing concentrated in urban areas.

Novosibirsk *was established at the point where the Trans-Siberian railway crosses the Ob' River. It grew as an industrial center under the Soviet Union and is now Siberia's largest city.*

Transportation Network

Roads	598,023 miles (963,000 km)
Motorways	None
Railways	53,816 miles (86,660 km)
Waterways	62,721 miles (101,000 km)

The recent growth of trade with China and East Asia has put pressure on Siberia's inadequate road and rail network, prompting increased use of the Amur River for freight transportation.

The shores of Lake Baikal (Ozero Baykal) *are a mixture of forest and the grassy steppe seen here. The lake freezes to a depth of 33 ft (10 m) in winter.*

Major industry and infrastructure

aerospace · car manufacture · chemicals · engineering · gas · iron & steel · mining · oil · textiles · timber processing · capital cities · major towns · international airports · major roads · major industrial areas

ARCTIC OCEAN
Barents Sea
Murmansk
Archangel
St Petersburg
MOSCOW
Nizhniy Novgorod
Kazan
Perm'
Samara
Chelyabinsk
Noril'sk
Pevek
RUSSIAN FEDERATION
Bering Sea
Magadan
Yakutsk
Sea of Okhotsk
Petropavlovsk-Kamchatskiy
Omsk
Novosibirsk
Irkutsk
Khabarovsk
Yuzhno-Sakhalinsk
Sea of Japan (East Sea)
Vladivostok
Volgograd
Caspian Sea
Black Sea
KAZAKHSTAN
MONGOLIA
CHINA

Northern European Russia

Reaching into the Arctic Circle, this region of lakeland, forest, and tundra is historically bound to Europe by St. Petersburg, the old imperial capital of Tsarist Russia and home to a third of the region's population. Communist rule from Moscow left the north politically marginalized, contributing to the present problems of outmoded industry, poor infrastructure, and serious environmental neglect. However, with borders embracing Finland, Norway, the Baltic, and the northern sea route to the Atlantic, the region's success in foreign trade is now of prime importance to the Russian economy.

St. Peter and Paul Fortress *is the oldest building in St. Petersburg, founded by Peter the Great in 1703 as a modern, European capital for Russia.*

The Landscape

The ancient bedrock of the Scandinavian Shield lies exposed across the glacially scoured Khibiny Mountains of the Kola Peninsula *(Kol'skiy Poluostrov)*, becoming mantled with till toward the North European Plain. The Valdai Hills *(Valdayskaya Vozvyshennost')* form an important watershed for the plain's rivers, while thick forest veils a complicated topography of moraines, lakes, and ground disturbed by frost action. The Ural Mountains *(Ural'skiye Gory)* form a border with Asia in the east.

The Khibiny Mountains *were formed by volcanic intrusions into the Scandinavian Shield, over 570 million years ago.*

Kola Peninsula *(Kol'skiy Poluostrov)*

The Kola Peninsula (Kol'skiy Poluostrov) *is part of the Scandinavian Shield, an area of ancient bedrock underlying Scandinavia. Rocks in excess of 2,500 million years old are exposed across the peninsula.*

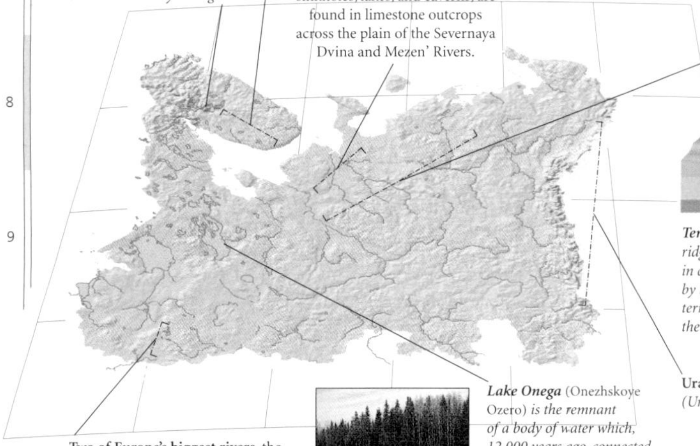

Karst features, including sinkholes, lakes, and caverns, are found in limestone outcrops across the plain of the Severnaya Dvina and Mezen' Rivers.

The low-lying plains of the Pechora, Mezen', and Severnaya Dvina Rivers were flooded by the sea while the land was still isostatically depressed following the last Ice Age, a process which has hidden the landforms created by glacial deposition.

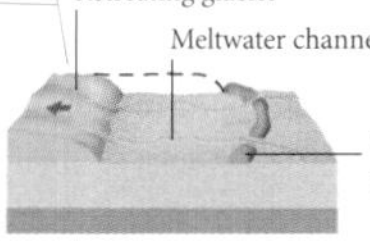
Retreating glacier
Meltwater channels
Terminal moraine

Terminal moraines *are crescent-shaped ridges of glacial deposits, widely found in central Russia. Detritus is carried by the glacier and deposited at its terminus (snout) as it melts, marking the limit of the ice advance.*

Ural Mountains *(Ural'skiye Gory)*

Two of Europe's biggest rivers, the Volga and Western Dvina, rise in the swampy uplands of the Valdai Hills *(Valdayskaya Vozvyshennost').*

Lake Onega *(Onezhskoye Ozero) is the remnant of a body of water which, 12,000 years ago, connected the White Sea (Beloye More) with the Gulf of Finland and the Baltic Sea.*

Using the Land and Sea

The cold climate confines agriculture mainly to southern and western provinces, where dairy farming predominates and arable land is given over to fodder crops as well as flax, potatoes, oats, and rye. Areas beyond the northern margins of cultivation are used for forestry, hunting, herding, and fishing, with some vegetables grown in hothouses around urban areas.

Land use and agricultural distribution
cattle
fishing
reindeer
timber
fodder
major towns
pasture
cropland
forest
mountain region
wetland
tundra
barren
ice
BARENTS SEA
White Sea
RUSSIAN FEDERATION
FINLAND
EST.
LAT.
LITH.
BELA.
Murmansk
Apatity
Amderma
Archangel
Pechora
Petrozavodsk
St Petersburg
Velikiy Novgorod
Cherepovets
Vologda
Pskov
Kotlas
Kirov
Yaroslavl'

The Urban/Rural Population Divide

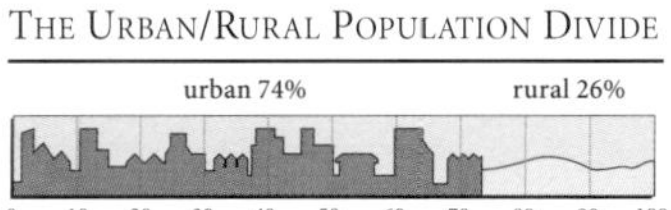
urban 74%
rural 26%
0 10 20 30 40 50 60 70 80 90 100

Population Density	Total Land Area
26 people per sq mile	829,398 sq miles
10 people per sq km	(2,148,700 sq km)

Many rapids *are found along the 175 mile (280 km) course of the Suna River.*

NORWAY
FINLAND
ESTONIA
LATVIA
BELARUS
Barents Sea
Beloye More (White Sea)
Gulf of Finland
Kol'skiy Poluostrov
Kandalakshskiy Zaliv
Onezhskaya Guba
Dvinskaya Guba
Murmansk
MURMANSKAYA OBLAST'
Monchegorsk
Apatity
Kirovsk
Kandalaksha
Kem'
Belomorsk
Severodvinsk
Arkhangel'sk
ARKHANGEL'SKAYA
RESPUBLIKA KARELIYA
Petrozavodsk
Onezhskoye Ozero
Ladozhskoye Ozero
Vyborg
Sankt-Peterburg (Saint Petersburg)
LENINGRADSKAYA OBLAST'
Kronshtadt
Kolpino
Tikhvin
Vologda
VOLOGODSKAYA
Cherepovets
NOVGORODSKAYA OBLAST'
Velikiy Novgorod
Pskov
PSKOVSKAYA OBLAST'
Lake Peipus
Velikiye Luki
TVERSKAYA OBLAST'
Tver'
Valdayskaya Vozvyshennost'
YAROSLAVSKAYA OBLAST'
Yaroslavl'
Rybinsk
Kostroma
Ivanovo
IVANOVSKAYA
VLADIMIRSKAYA OBLAST'
MOSKOVSKAYA OBLAST'
SMOLENSKAYA OBLAST'
Arctic Circle
92
118

A B C D E F G H I J K L M

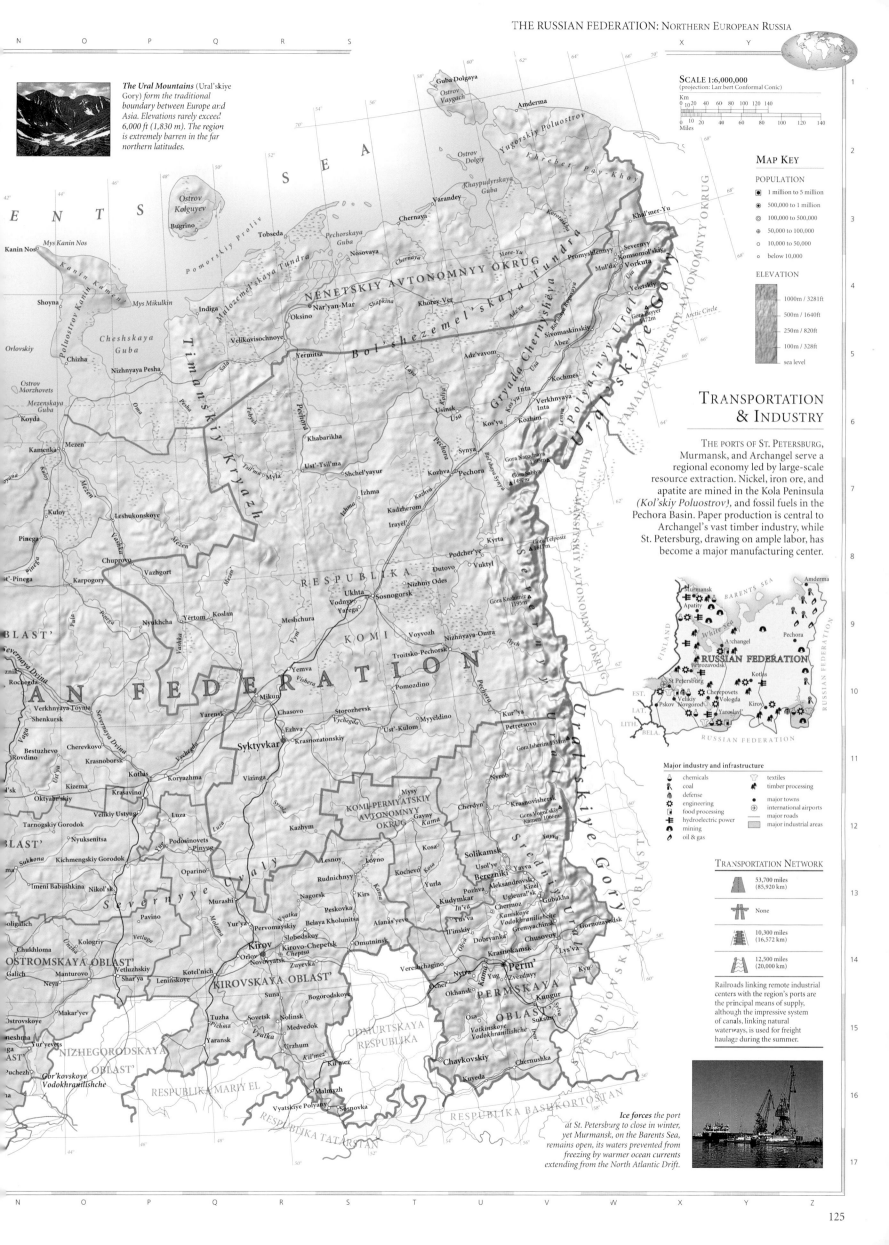

The Ural Mountains (Ural'skiye Gory) *form the traditional boundary between Europe and Asia. Elevations rarely exceed 6,000 ft (1,830 m). The region is extremely barren in the far northern latitudes.*

BARENTS SEA
Kanin Nos
Mys Kanin Nos
Ostrov Kolguyev
Bugrino
Pomorskiy Proliv
Tobseda
Pechorskaya Guba
Nosovaya
Chernaya
Varandey
Khaypudyrskaya Guba
Ostrov Dolgiy
Guba Dolgaya
Ostrov Vaygach
Amderma
Yugorskiy Poluostrov
Khrebet Pay-Khoy
Khal'mer-Yu
Severnyy
Komsomol'skiy
Vorkuta
Mul'da
Promyshlennyy
Yeletskiy
Gora Payyer 1472m
Arctic Circle
Sivomaskinskiy
Abez'
Kochmes
Inta
Verkhnyaya Inta
Kozhim
Usinsk
Usa
Kos'yu
Gora Narodnaya 1895m
Gora Sablya 1497m
Synya
Pechora
Kozhva
Izhma
Kadzherom
Irayel'
Kyrta
Gora Telpos-iz 1617m
Podcher'ye
Vuktyl
Dutovo
Nizhniy Odes
Ukhta
Sosnogorsk
Vodnyy
Yarega
Gora Kozhim-iz 1195m
Voyvozh
Nizhnyaya Omra
Troitsko-Pechorsk
Pomozdino
Kur'ya
Petretsovo
Gora Isherim 1331m
Nyrob
Cherdyn'
Krasnovishersk
Gora Vogul'skiy Kamen' 1066m
Solikamsk
Usol'ye
Yayva
Berezniki
Aleksandrovsk
Kizel
Ugleural'sk
Gubakha
Gornozavodsk
Chusovoy
Lys'va
Krasnokamsk
Perm'
Kungur
Suksun
Chaykovskiy
Kuyeda
Chernushka
NENETSKIY AVTONOMNYY OKRUG
Nar'yan-Mar
Oksino
Shapkina
Khorey-Ver
Bol'shezemel'skaya Tundra
Gryada Chernysheva
Polyarnyy Ural
Ural'skiye Gory
YAMALO-NENETSKIY AVTONOMNYY OKRUG
KHANTY-MANSIYSKIY AVTONOMNYY OKRUG
Severnyy Ural
Sredniy Ural
SVERDLOVSKAYA OBLAST'
Shoyna
Mys Mikulkin
Kanin Kamen'
Poluostrov Kanin
Cheshskaya Guba
Indiga
Malozemel'skaya Tundra
Velikovisochnoye
Yermitsa
Chizha
Nizhnyaya Pesha
Orlovskiy
Ostrov Morzhovets
Mezenskaya Guba
Koyda
Mezen'
Kamenka
Timanskiy Kryazh
Khabarikha
Ust'-Tsil'ma
Shchel'yayur
Myla
Kuloy
Leshukonskoye
Pinega
Chuprovo
Vazhgort
Karpogory
RESPUBLIKA KOMI
Nyukhcha
Yertom
Koslan
Meshchura
Yemva
RUSSIAN FEDERATION
Rochegda
Verkhnyaya Toyma
Shenkursk
Yarensk
Mikun'
Chasovo
Storozhevsk
Myyeldino
Ust'-Kulom
Ezhva
Syktyvkar
Krasnozatonskiy
Bestuzhevo
Cherevkovo
Rovdino
Krasnoborsk
Kotlas
Koryazhma
Vizinga
Kizema
Krasavino
Oktyabr'skiy
Velikiy Ustyug
Luza
Tarnogskiy Gorodok
Nyuksenitsa
Podosinovets
Pinyug
Kichmengskiy Gorodok
Oparino
Imeni Babushkina
Nikol'sk
Severnyye Uvaly
Murashi
Pavino
Kologriv
Chukhloma
KOSTROMSKAYA OBLAST'
Galich
Vetluzhskiy
Shar'ya
Manturovo
Neya
Leninskoye
Kotel'nich
KIROVSKAYA OBLAST'
Kirov
Orlov
Novovyatsk
Slobodskoy
Kirovo-Chepetsk
Zuyevka
Pervomayskiy
Yur'ya
Belaya Kholunitsa
Omutninsk
Afanas'yevo
Peskovka
Nagorsk
Kirs
Rudnichnyy
Lesnoy
Loyno
Kazhym
KOMI-PERMYATSKIY AVTONOMNYY OKRUG
Mysy
Gayny
Kosa
Kochevo
Yurla
Kudymkar
Pozhva
In'va
Yus'va
Il'inskiy
Dobryanka
Chermoz
Kamskoye Vodokhranilishche
Gremyachinsk
Vereshchagino
Nytva
Ocher
Okhansk
Yug
Zvezdnyy
PERMSKAYA OBLAST'
Osa
Votkinskoye Vodokhranilishche
Suna
Bogorodskoye
Tuzha
Sovetsk
Nolinsk
Medvedok
Yaransk
Urzhum
Kil'mez'
Makar'yev
Yur'yevets
NIZHEGORODSKAYA OBLAST'
Gor'kovskoye Vodokhranilishche
Puchezh
RESPUBLIKA MARIY EL
Malmyzh
Vyatskiye Polyany
Sosnovka
RESPUBLIKA TATARSTAN
UDMURTSKAYA RESPUBLIKA
RESPUBLIKA BASHKORTOSTAN

SCALE 1:6,000,000
(projection: Lambert Conformal Conic)

Km 0 10 20 40 60 80 100 120 140
Miles 0 10 20 40 60 80 100 120 140

MAP KEY

POPULATION

- 1 million to 5 million
- 500,000 to 1 million
- 100,000 to 500,000
- 50,000 to 100,000
- 10,000 to 50,000
- below 10,000

ELEVATION

- 1000m / 3281ft
- 500m / 1640ft
- 250m / 820ft
- 100m / 328ft
- sea level

TRANSPORTATION & INDUSTRY

THE PORTS OF ST. PETERSBURG, Murmansk, and Archangel serve a regional economy led by large-scale resource extraction. Nickel, iron ore, and apatite are mined in the Kola Peninsula *(Kol'skiy Poluostrov)*, and fossil fuels in the Pechora Basin. Paper production is central to Archangel's vast timber industry, while St. Petersburg, drawing on ample labor, has become a major manufacturing center.

BARENTS SEA
Amderma
Murmansk
Apatity
White Sea
Archangel
Pechora
FINLAND
RUSSIAN FEDERATION
Petrozavodsk
Kotlas
St Petersburg
EST.
Cherepovets
Vologda
Velikiy Novgorod
Pskov
Yaroslavl'
Kirov
LAT.
LITH.
BELA.

Major industry and infrastructure

- chemicals
- coal
- defense
- engineering
- food processing
- hydroelectric power
- mining
- oil & gas
- textiles
- timber processing
- major towns
- international airports
- major roads
- major industrial areas

TRANSPORTATION NETWORK

- 53,700 miles (85,920 km)
- None
- 10,300 miles (16,572 km)
- 12,500 miles (20,000 km)

Railroads linking remote industrial centers with the region's ports are the principal means of supply, although the impressive system of canals, linking natural waterways, is used for freight haulage during the summer.

Ice forces *the port at St. Petersburg to close in winter, yet Murmansk, on the Barents Sea, remains open, its waters prevented from freezing by warmer ocean currents extending from the North Atlantic Drift.*

BALTIC SEA
LITHUANIA
POLAND
BELARUS
UKRAINE
RUSSIA
KALININGRADSKAYA OBLAST'
Kaliningrad
SMOLENSKAYA OBLAST'
Smolensk
MOSKVA (MOSCOW)
KALUZHSKAYA OBLAST'
Kaluga
Tula
BRYANSKAYA OBLAST'
Bryansk
ORLOVSKAYA OBLAST'
Orel
KURSKAYA OBLAST'
Kursk
BELGORODSKAYA OBLAST'
Belgorod
VORONEZHSKAYA OBLAST'
Voronezh
LIPETSKAYA OBLAST'
Lipetsk
RYAZANSKAYA OBLAST'
Ryazan'
ROSTOVSKAYA OBLAST'
Rostov-na-Donu
KRASNODARSKIY KRAY
Krasnodar
Sea of Azov
Gulf of Taganrog
BLACK SEA
Sochi
Novorossiysk
Smolensko-Moskovskaya Vozvyshennost'
Srednerusskaya Vozvyshennost'
118
110
116

Kaliningrad has been a Russian enclave since 1945. The port is an important center for the Russian Federation's Baltic fishing fleet.

***St Basil's Cathedral**, completed in 1561, stands in Moscow's Red Square next to the Kremlin; the original fortified stronghold of the city.*

SOUTHERN EUROPEAN RUSSIA

THIS REGION, DIVIDED FROM ASIA by desert, seas, and mountains, has exerted a powerful influence both east and west since the 13th century. Over 70 years of Communist rule produced a highly urbanized, industrial society dominated by Moscow, which was the capital of the Soviet Union until 1991. Almost two-thirds of the Russian Federation's population live in this core area, with a relatively high *per capita* share of its wealth. However, the rapid growth of a market economy has caused great social upheaval, with rising crime and political instability.

THE LANDSCAPE

ANCIENT FOLDS in the deep sedimentary strata of the North European Plain have created a sequence of high and low regions. The Central Russian Upland *(Srednerusskaya Vozvyshennost')* in the west is deeply incised by rivers draining into the lowland of the Oka and Don Rivers. In the east the Volga, Europe's longest river flows south to the Caspian Sea, dividing the Volga Uplands *(Privolzhskaya Vozvyshennost')* from the foothills of the Ural Mountains *(Ural'skiye Gory)*. The Caucasus Mountains and the Black Sea form a natural border to the southwest.

***A plantation of Scots pine** helps consolidate the loose sandy soils of the Meshchera Lowland* (Meshcherskaya Nizina)*, which lies on the bed of an old glacial lake.*

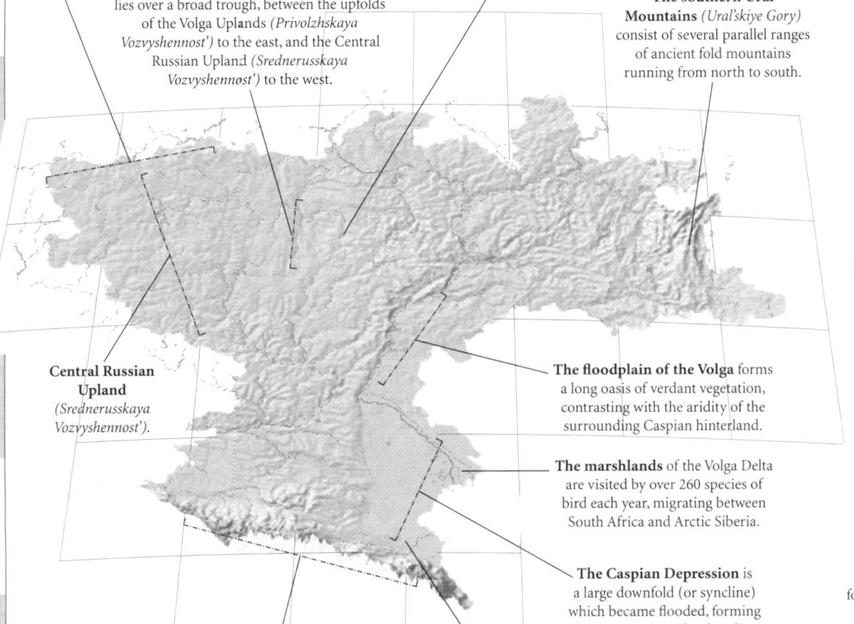

The Smolensk-Moscow Upland *(Smolensko-Moskovskaya Vozvyshennost')* is a series of terminal moraine ridges marking the southern extent of the last glaciation.

Glacial till covers the bedrock to the north of the North European Plain, giving a gentle surface relief.

The lowland of the Oka and Don Rivers lies over a broad trough, between the upfolds of the Volga Uplands *(Privolzhskaya Vozvyshennost')* to the east, and the Central Russian Upland *(Srednerusskaya Vozvyshennost')* to the west.

The southern Ural Mountains *(Ural'skiye Gory)* consist of several parallel ranges of ancient fold mountains running from north to south.

Central Russian Upland *(Srednerusskaya Vozvyshennost').*

The floodplain of the Volga forms a long oasis of verdant vegetation, contrasting with the aridity of the surrounding Caspian hinterland.

The marshlands of the Volga Delta are visited by over 260 species of bird each year, migrating between South Africa and Arctic Siberia.

The Caspian Depression is a large downfold (or syncline) which became flooded, forming the Caspian Sea. The shoreline is 98 ft (30 m) below sea level.

Drifting sand occupies large areas of the south, forming dunes up to 50 ft (15 m) high.

***The Caucasus Mountains** run from the Black Sea to the Caspian Sea. They include El'brus which, at 18,511 ft (5,642 m), is the highest point in Europe. It is still uplifting at a rate of 0.4 inches (10 mm/yr).*

Salt dome

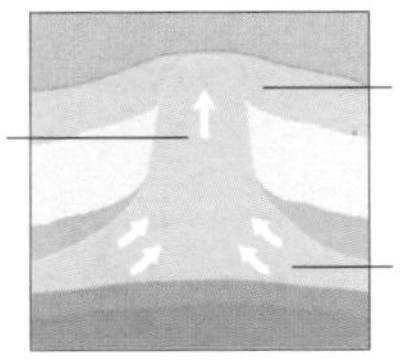
Salt dome is forced up and through the rock strata
Sedimentary strata
Salts are forced upwards by denser overlying strata

***Salt domes**, rounded hills up to 500 ft (150 m) high, are produced as less dense rock salts are displaced under the extreme pressure of denser, overlying strata and forced up toward the surface creating domes. They are widespread in the Caspian Depression.*

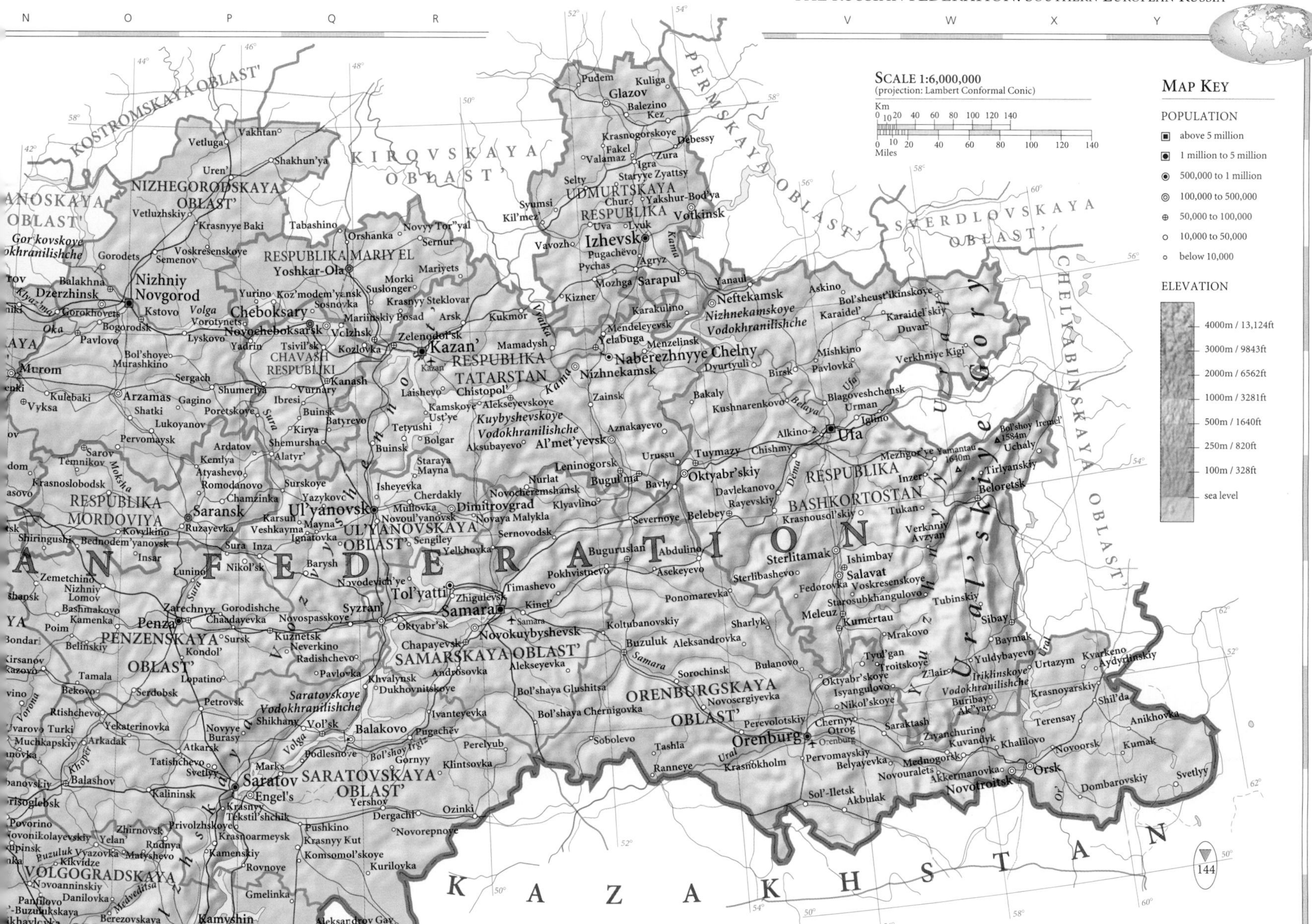
N O P Q R
V W X Y
KOSTROMSKAYA OBLAST'
KIROVSKAYA OBLAST'
PERMSKAYA OBLAST'
SVERDLOVSKAYA OBLAST'
CHELYABINSKAYA OBLAST'
NIZHEGORODSKAYA OBLAST'
UDMURTSKAYA RESPUBLIKA
RESPUBLIKA MARIY EL
Nizhniy Novgorod
Cheboksary
CHAVASH RESPUBLIKI
Kazan'
RESPUBLIKA TATARSTAN
Izhevsk
Naberezhnyye Chelny
Ufa
RESPUBLIKA BASHKORTOSTAN
Ural'skiye Gory
RESPUBLIKA MORDOVIYA
Saransk
Ul'yanovsk
UL'YANOVSKAYA OBLAST'
PENZENSKAYA OBLAST'
Penza
Tol'yatti
Samara
SAMARSKAYA OBLAST'
ORENBURGSKAYA OBLAST'
Orenburg
Orsk
Saratov
SARATOVSKAYA OBLAST'
VOLGOGRADSKAYA OBLAST'
Volgograd
ASTRAKHANSKAYA OBLAST'
Astrakhan'
RESPUBLIKA KALMYKIYA
Elista
Caspian Depression
Caspian Sea
STAVROPOL'SKIY KRAY
CHECHENSKAYA RESPUBLIKA
Groznyy
Nal'chik
Vladikavkaz
Makhachkala
RESPUBLIKA DAGESTAN
Derbent
KAZAKHSTAN
AZERBAIJAN
GEORGIA
RUSSIAN FEDERATION
144
136
N O S T U V W X Z

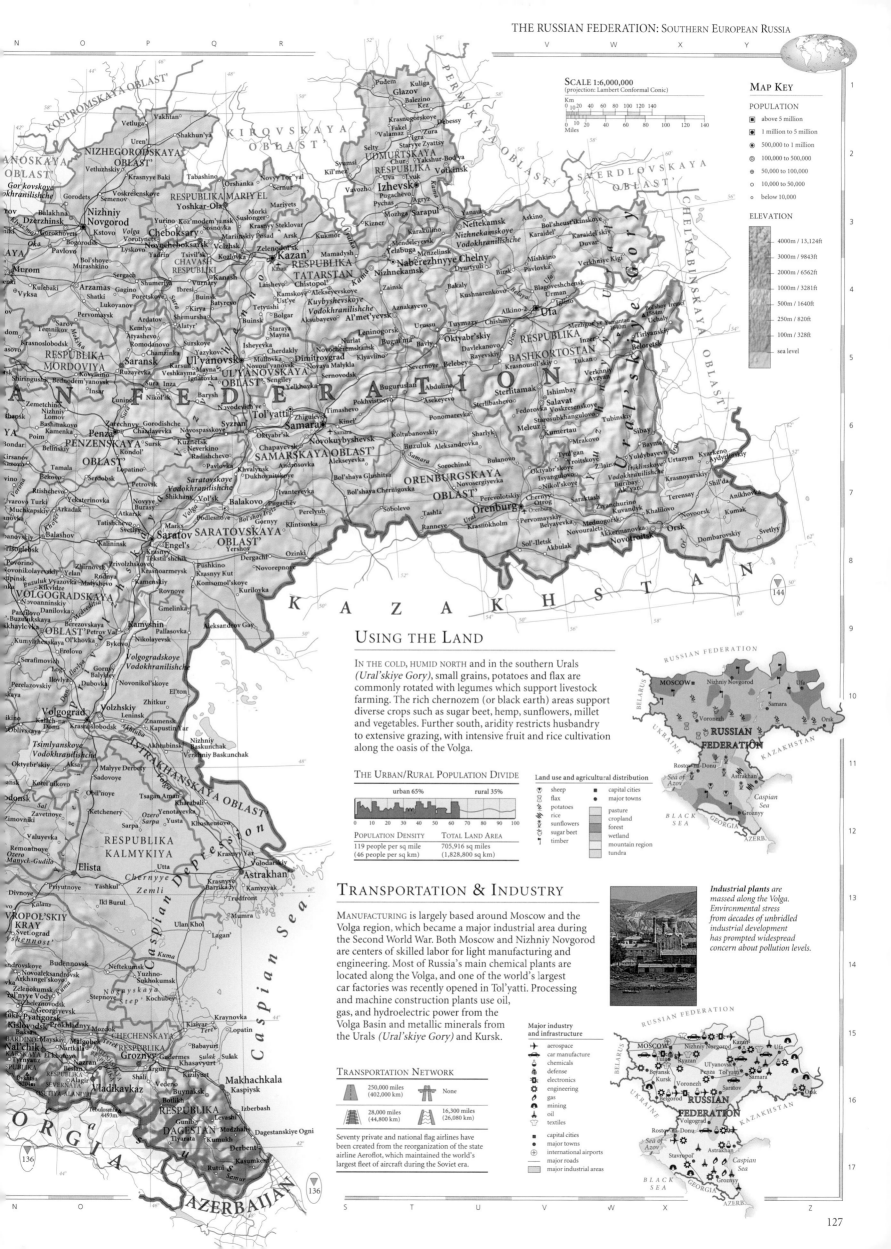

SCALE 1:6,000,000
(projection: Lambert Conformal Conic)

Km 0 10 20 40 60 80 100 120 140
Miles 0 10 20 40 60 80 100 120 140

MAP KEY

POPULATION

- above 5 million
- 1 million to 5 million
- 500,000 to 1 million
- 100,000 to 500,000
- 50,000 to 100,000
- 10,000 to 50,000
- below 10,000

ELEVATION

- 4000m / 13,124ft
- 3000m / 9843ft
- 2000m / 6562ft
- 1000m / 3281ft
- 500m / 1640ft
- 250m / 820ft
- 100m / 328ft
- sea level

USING THE LAND

IN THE COLD, HUMID NORTH and in the southern Urals *(Ural'skiye Gory)*, small grains, potatoes and flax are commonly rotated with legumes which support livestock farming. The rich chernozem (or black earth) areas support diverse crops such as sugar beet, hemp, sunflowers, millet and vegetables. Further south, aridity restricts husbandry to extensive grazing, with intensive fruit and rice cultivation along the oasis of the Volga.

RUSSIAN FEDERATION
MOSCOW
Nizhniy Novgorod
Ufa
Samara
Voronezh
Orsk
BELARUS
UKRAINE
RUSSIAN FEDERATION
KAZAKHSTAN
Rostov-na-Donu
Sea of Azov
Astrakhan'
Caspian Sea
Groznyy
BLACK SEA
GEORGIA
AZERB.

THE URBAN/RURAL POPULATION DIVIDE

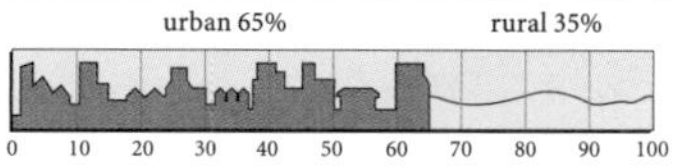
urban 65%
rural 35%
0 10 20 30 40 50 60 70 80 90 100

POPULATION DENSITY	TOTAL LAND AREA
119 people per sq mile (46 people per sq km)	705,916 sq miles (1,828,800 sq km)

Land use and agricultural distribution

- sheep
- flax
- potatoes
- rice
- sunflowers
- sugar beet
- timber
- capital cities
- major towns
- pasture
- cropland
- forest
- wetland
- mountain region
- tundra

TRANSPORTATION & INDUSTRY

MANUFACTURING is largely based around Moscow and the Volga region, which became a major industrial area during the Second World War. Both Moscow and Nizhniy Novgorod are centers of skilled labor for light manufacturing and engineering. Most of Russia's main chemical plants are located along the Volga, and one of the world's largest car factories was recently opened in Tol'yatti. Processing and machine construction plants use oil, gas, and hydroelectric power from the Volga Basin and metallic minerals from the Urals *(Ural'skiye Gory)* and Kursk.

Industrial plants are massed along the Volga. Environmental stress from decades of unbridled industrial development has prompted widespread concern about pollution levels.

Major industry and infrastructure

- aerospace
- car manufacture
- chemicals
- defense
- electronics
- engineering
- gas
- mining
- oil
- textiles
- capital cities
- major towns
- international airports
- major roads
- major industrial areas

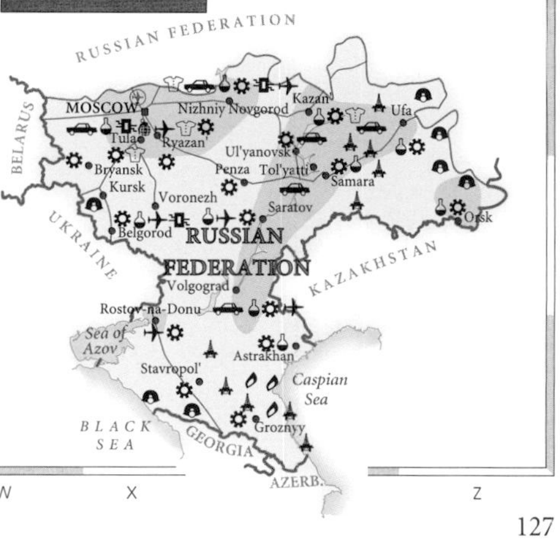
RUSSIAN FEDERATION
MOSCOW
Nizhniy Novgorod
Kazan'
Ufa
Tula
Ryazan'
Ul'yanovsk
Bryansk
Penza
Tol'yatti
Samara
Kursk
Voronezh
Saratov
Belgorod
RUSSIAN FEDERATION
Orsk
BELARUS
UKRAINE
KAZAKHSTAN
Volgograd
Rostov-na-Donu
Sea of Azov
Astrakhan'
Stavropol'
Caspian Sea
Groznyy
BLACK SEA
GEORGIA
AZERB.

TRANSPORTATION NETWORK

250,000 miles (402,000 km)	None
28,000 miles (44,800 km)	16,300 miles (26,080 km)

Seventy private and national flag airlines have been created from the reorganization of the state airline Aeroflot, which maintained the world's largest fleet of aircraft during the Soviet era.

ASIA

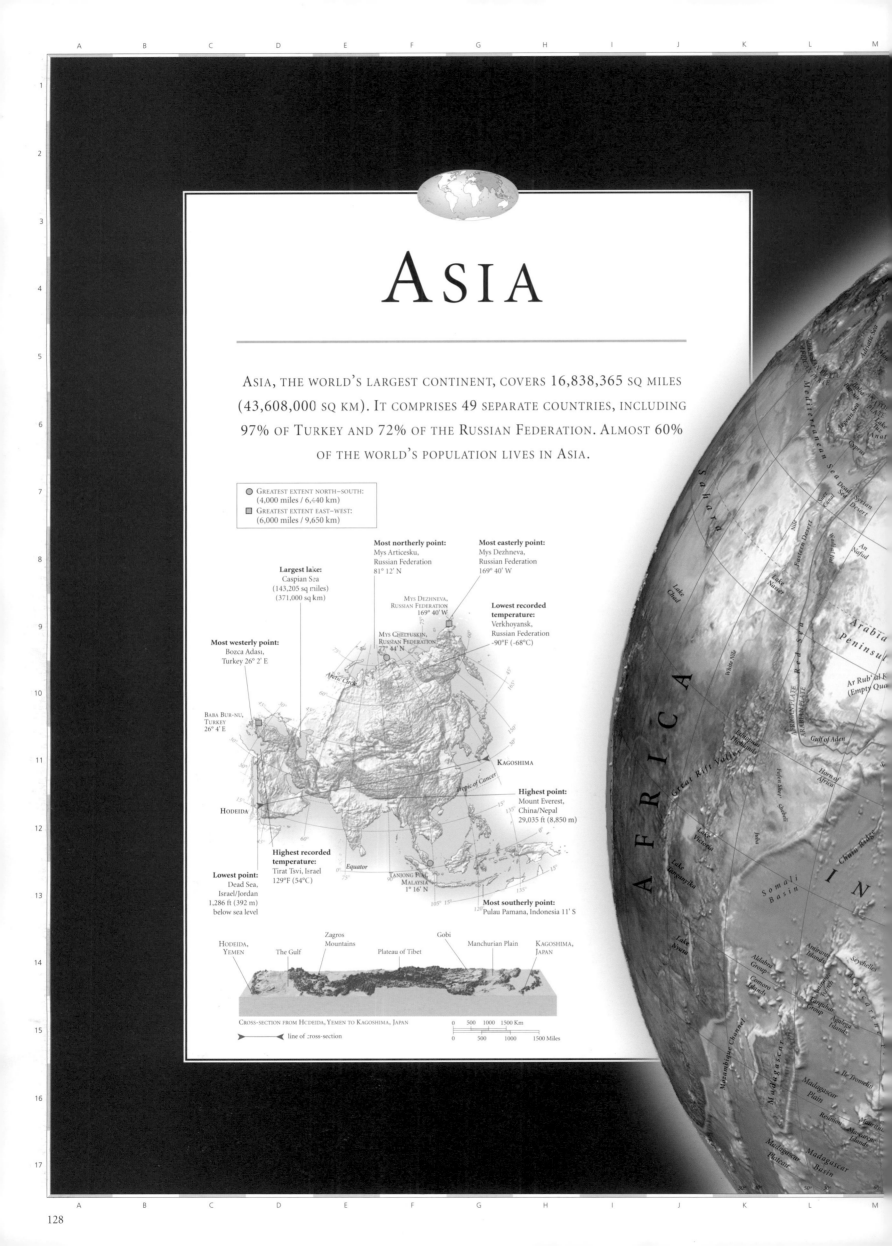

ASIA, THE WORLD'S LARGEST CONTINENT, COVERS 16,838,365 SQ MILES (43,608,000 SQ KM). IT COMPRISES 49 SEPARATE COUNTRIES, INCLUDING 97% OF TURKEY AND 72% OF THE RUSSIAN FEDERATION. ALMOST 60% OF THE WORLD'S POPULATION LIVES IN ASIA.

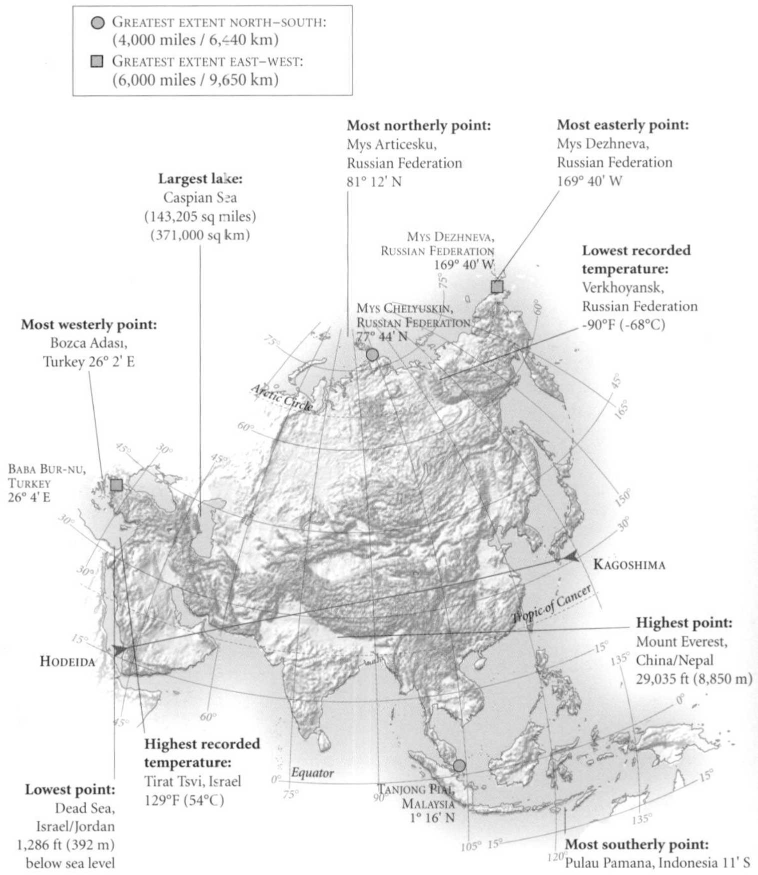

GREATEST EXTENT NORTH–SOUTH: (4,000 miles / 6,440 km)
GREATEST EXTENT EAST–WEST: (6,000 miles / 9,650 km)
Most northerly point: Mys Articesku, Russian Federation 81° 12' N
Most easterly point: Mys Dezhneva, Russian Federation 169° 40' W
Largest lake: Caspian Sea (143,205 sq miles) (371,000 sq km)
MYS DEZHNEVA, RUSSIAN FEDERATION 169° 40' W
Lowest recorded temperature: Verkhoyansk, Russian Federation -90°F (-68°C)
MYS CHELYUSKIN, RUSSIAN FEDERATION 77° 44' N
Most westerly point: Bozca Adası, Turkey 26° 2' E
Arctic Circle
BABA BUR-NU, TURKEY 26° 4' E
KAGOSHIMA
Tropic of Cancer
Highest point: Mount Everest, China/Nepal 29,035 ft (8,850 m)
HODEIDA
Highest recorded temperature: Tirat Tsvi, Israel 129°F (54°C)
Equator
TANJONG PIAI, MALAYSIA 1° 16' N
Lowest point: Dead Sea, Israel/Jordan 1,286 ft (392 m) below sea level
Most southerly point: Pulau Pamana, Indonesia 11' S

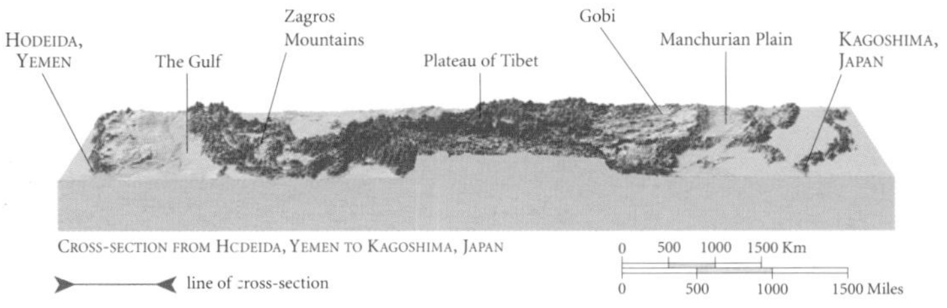

HODEIDA, YEMEN
The Gulf
Zagros Mountains
Plateau of Tibet
Gobi
Manchurian Plain
KAGOSHIMA, JAPAN

CROSS-SECTION FROM HODEIDA, YEMEN TO KAGOSHIMA, JAPAN

line of cross-section

0 500 1000 1500 Km
0 500 1000 1500 Miles

AFRICA
Mediterranean Sea
Sahara
Lake Chad
Nile
Eastern Desert
Lake Nasser
Red Sea
Arabian Peninsula
Ar Rub' al Khali (Empty Quarter)
An Nafud
Syrian Desert
Dead Sea
Suez Canal
Cyprus
Aegean Sea
Adriatic Sea
Gulf of Aden
Horn of Africa
Ethiopian Highlands
White Nile
Great Rift Valley
Lake Victoria
Lake Tanganyika
Lake Nyasa
Juba
Somali Basin
Chain Ridge
Seychelles
Amirante Islands
Aldabra Group
Comoro Islands
Farquhar Group
Agalega Islands
Mozambique Channel
Madagascar
Madagascar Plain
Madagascar Basin
Madagascar Plateau
Réunion
Ile Tromelin
AFRICAN PLATE
ARABIAN PLATE

N O P Q R S T U V W X Y Z
1 2 3 4 5 6 7 8 9 10 11 12 13 14 15 16 17
ARCTIC OCEAN
North Pole
NORTH AMERICAN PLATE
EURASIAN PLATE
Franz Josef Land
Norwegian Sea
Scandinavia
North Sea
Gulf of Bothnia
Barents Sea
North Cape
Kola Peninsula
White Sea
Novaya Zemlya
Kara Sea
Severnaya Zemlya
Mys Chelyuskin
Laptev Sea
New Siberian Islands
East Siberian Sea
Long Strait
Bering Strait
Chukot Range
Bering Sea
Baltic Sea
Gulf of Finland
Lake Ladoga
Lake Onega
North European Plain
Central Russian Upland
EUROPE
Poluostrov Taymyr
North Siberian Lowland
Putorana Mountains
Ural Mountains
West Siberian Plain
Central Siberian Plateau
Siberia
Verkhoyanskiy Khrebet
Khrebet Cherskogo
Kolyma
Sea of Okhotsk
Kamchatka
Aleutian Basin
Black Sea
Sea of Azov
Caspian Depression
Caspian Sea
Caucasus
Kirghiz Steppe
Ustyurt Plateau
Aral Sea
Lake Balkhash
Lake Zaysan
Altai Mountains
Sayanskiy Khrebet
Lake Baikal
Yablonovyy Khrebet
Stanovoy Khrebet
Zeya Reservoir
Turan Lowland
Kara Kum
Ozero Issyk-Kul'
Dzungaria
Tien Shan
ASIA
Plateau of Mongolia
Gobi
Great Khingan Range
Manchurian Plain
Hulun Nur
Elburz Mountains
Great Salt Desert
EURASIAN PLATE
IRANIAN PLATE
Zagros Mountains
Iranian Plateau
Kuh-e Fuladi 5143m
Pamirs
Hindu Kush
Karakoram Range
Tarim Basin
Takla Makan Desert
Lop Nur
Qilian Shan
Nan Shan
Ordos Desert
Sea of Japan (East Sea)
Korea Bay
Bo Hai
Yellow Sea
Kunlun Mountains
Plateau of Tibet
Qinghai Hu
Great Plain of China
Strait of Hormuz
Gulf of Oman
Rigestan
Sulaiman Range
Punjab Plains
Himalayas
Thar Desert
Annapurna 8091m
Mount Everest 8850m
Yellow River
Yangtze
East China Sea
Korea Strait
Japan
PACIFIC OCEAN
Arabian Sea
Arabian Basin
Gulf of Kachchh
Gulf of Khambhat
Vindhya Range
Satpura Range
Ajanta Range
Deccan
Western Ghats
Eastern Ghats
Malabar Coast
Coromandel Coast
Mouths of the Ganges
Bay of Bengal
Ryukyu Islands
Taiwan
Taiwan Strait
Hainan Strait
Gulf of Tongking
Hainan
Luzon Strait
Philippine Sea
Laccadive Islands
Cape Comorin
Gulf of Mannar
Sri Lanka
Gulf of Martaban
Andaman Islands
Andaman Sea
Gulf of Thailand
Tonle Sap
South China Sea
Philippine Basin
Mindoro
Maldives
Nicobar Islands
Mouths of the Mekong
South China Basin
Palawan
Sulu Sea
INDIAN OCEAN
Ceylon Plain
Chagos-Laccadive Plateau
Malay Peninsula
Strait of Malacca
Anambas Islands
Natuna Islands
Sunda Shelf
Gunung Kinabalu 4094m
Celebes Sea
Chagos Bank
Nikitin Seamount
Chagos Trench
Tanjong Piai
Greater Sunda Islands
Borneo
Molucca Sea
Gunung Kerinci 3805m
Pulau Bangka
Sumatra
Celebes
Moluccas
Mid-Indian Basin
Cocos Basin
Ninetyeast Ridge
East Indies
Java Sea
Banda Sea
Java
Sunda Trough
Lesser Sunda Islands
Timor
Arafura Sea
Java Trench
Timor Trough
Cocos Islands
Christmas Island
AUSTRALIA

PHYSICAL ASIA

THE NATURAL LANDSCAPE of Asia can be divided into two distinct physical regions; one covers the north, while the other spans the south. Northern Asia consists of old mountain chains like the Ural Mountains, plateaus, including the vast Plateau of Tibet, shields, and basins. In contrast, the landscapes of the south are much younger, formed by tectonic activity beginning c. 65 million years ago, leading to an almost continuous mountain chain running from Europe, across much of Asia, and culminating in the mighty Himalayan mountains. North of the mountains lies a belt of deserts. In the far south, tectonic activity has formed narrow island arcs. To the west lies the Arabian Shield, once part of the African Plate. As it was rifted apart from Africa, the Arabian Plate collided with the Eurasian Plate, uplifting the Zagros Mountains.

THE ARABIAN SHIELD AND IRANIAN PLATEAU

APPROXIMATELY FIVE MILLION YEARS AGO, rifting of the continental crust split the Arabian Plate from the African Plate and flooded the Red Sea. As this rift spread, the Arabian Plate collided with the Eurasian Plate, transforming part of the Tethys seabed into the Zagros Mountains which run northwest-southeast across western Iran.

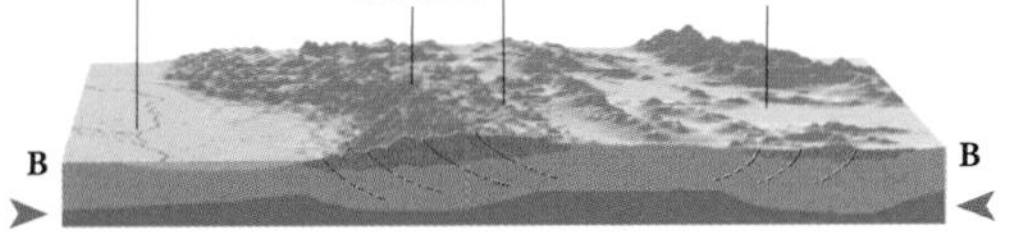
The confluence of the Tigris and Euphrates on the Mesopotamian Depression
Folded sedimentary rock strata
Zagros Mountains
Iranian Plateau
B
B
0 50 100 Km
0 50 100 Miles

Cross-section through southwestern Asia, showing the Mesopotamian Depression, the folded Zagros Mountains and the Iranian Plateau.

COASTAL LOWLANDS AND ISLAND ARCS

THE COASTAL PLAINS that fringe Southeast Asia contain many large delta systems, caused by high levels of rainfall and erosion of the Himalayas, the Plateau of Tibet, and relict loess deposits. To the south is an extensive island archipelago, lying on the drowned Sunda Shelf. Most of these islands are volcanic in origin, caused by the subduction of the Indo-Australian Plate beneath the Eurasian Plate.

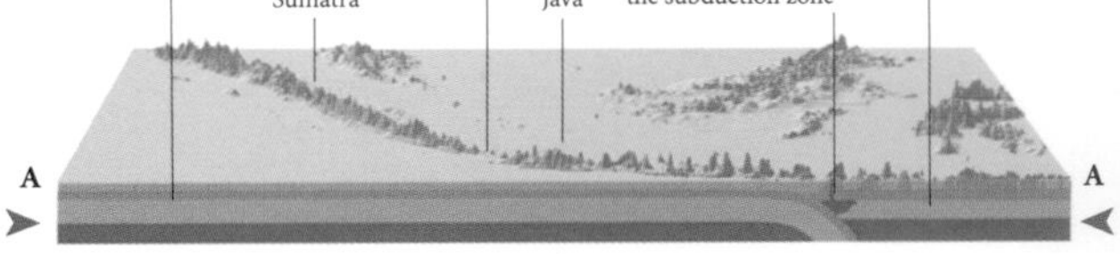
Indo-Australian Plate
Island arc caused by subduction
Sumatra
Java
Volcanoes occur at the subduction zone
Eurasian Plate
A
A
0 200 400 Km
0 200 400 Miles

Cross-section through Southeast Asia showing the subduction zone between the Indo-Australian and Eurasian plates and the island arc.

EAST ASIAN PLAINS AND UPLANDS

SEVERAL, SMALL, ISOLATED shield areas, such as the Shandong Peninsula, are found in east Asia. Between these stable shield areas, large river systems like the Yangtze and the Yellow River have deposited thick layers of sediment, forming extensive alluvial plains. The largest of these is the Great Plain of China, the relief of which does not rise above 300 ft (100 m).

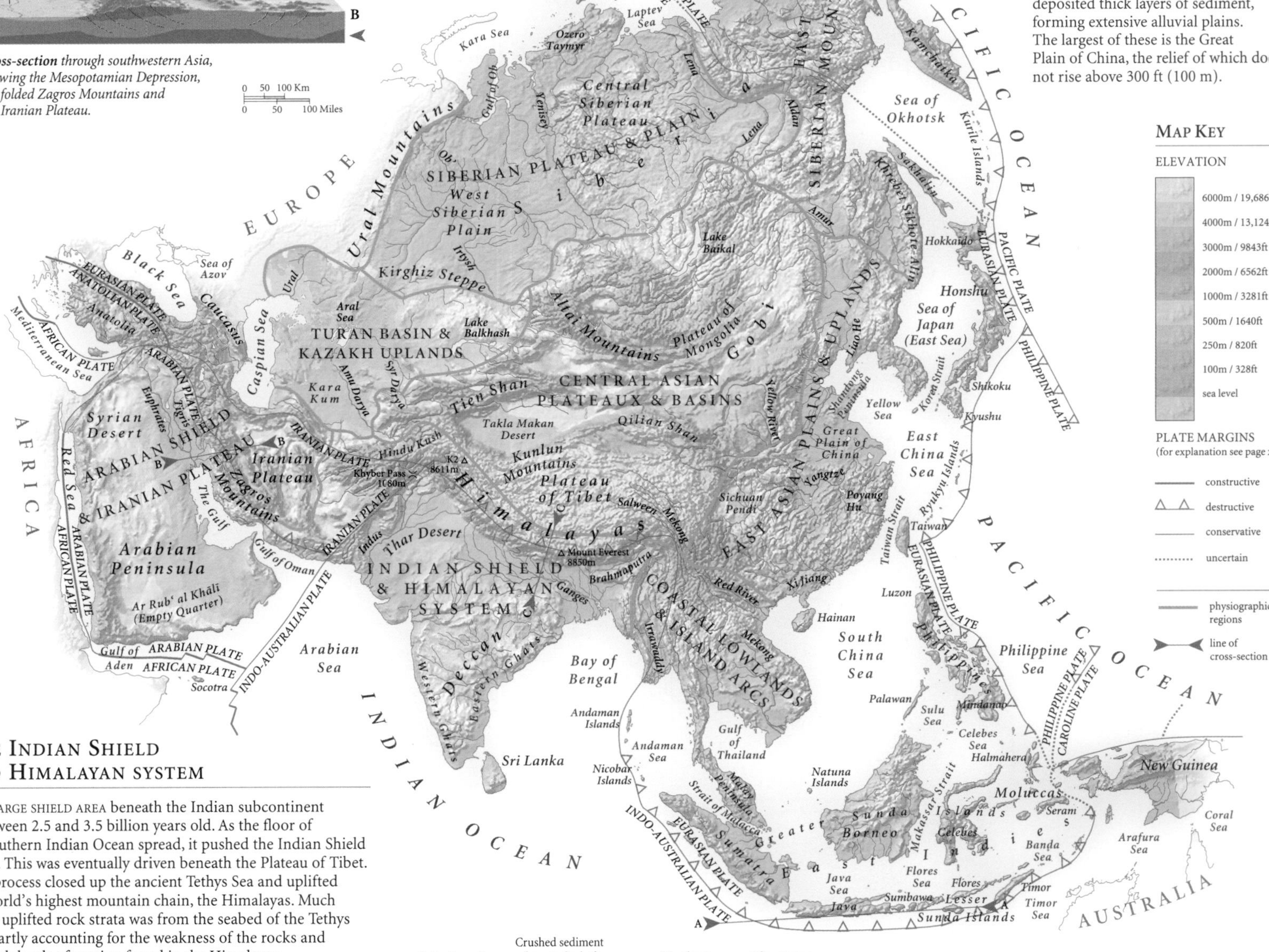
ARCTIC OCEAN
PACIFIC OCEAN
INDIAN OCEAN
EUROPE
AFRICA
AUSTRALIA
Chukchi Sea
Bering Sea
Gulf of Anadyr
Wrangel Island
East Siberian Sea
NORTH AMERICAN PLATE
EURASIAN PLATE
Severnaya Zemlya
Laptev Sea
Kara Sea
Ozero Taymyr
Central Siberian Plateau
SIBERIAN PLATEAU & PLAIN
West Siberian Plain
Siberia
EAST SIBERIAN MOUNTAINS
Kamchatka
Sea of Okhotsk
Kurile Islands
Sakhalin
Khrebet Sikhote Alin
Hokkaido
PACIFIC PLATE
Honshu
Sea of Japan (East Sea)
PHILIPPINE PLATE
Shikoku
Kyushu
Ural Mountains
Gulf of Ob
Ob
Yenisey
Lena
Aldan
Amur
Lake Baikal
Irtysh
Kirghiz Steppe
Ural
Aral Sea
Lake Balkhash
TURAN BASIN & KAZAKH UPLANDS
Altai Mountains
Plateau of Mongolia
Gobi
EAST ASIAN PLAINS & UPLANDS
Liao He
Black Sea
Sea of Azov
EURASIAN PLATE
ANATOLIAN PLATE
Anatolia
Caucasus
Caspian Sea
Mediterranean Sea
AFRICAN PLATE
ARABIAN PLATE
Kara Kum
Amu Darya
Syr Darya
Tien Shan
CENTRAL ASIAN PLATEAUX & BASINS
Takla Makan Desert
Qilian Shan
Yellow River
Shandong Peninsula
Yellow Sea
Korea Strait
Great Plain of China
East China Sea
Syrian Desert
Euphrates
Tigris
ARABIAN SHIELD
IRANIAN PLATE
Iranian Plateau
Hindu Kush
Khyber Pass 1080m
K2 8611m
Kunlun Mountains
Plateau of Tibet
Yangtze
Poyang Hu
Ryukyu Islands
Sichuan Pendi
Salween
Mekong
Taiwan Strait
Taiwan
Red Sea
& IRANIAN PLATEAU
Zagros Mountains
The Gulf
Himalayas
Mount Everest 8850m
Thar Desert
Indus
Arabian Peninsula
Gulf of Oman
INDIAN SHIELD & HIMALAYAN SYSTEM
Brahmaputra
Ganges
Red River
Xi Jiang
Luzon
Ar Rub' al Khali (Empty Quarter)
ARABIAN PLATE
AFRICAN PLATE
INDO-AUSTRALIAN PLATE
COASTAL LOWLANDS & ISLAND ARCS
Irrawaddy
Hainan
South China Sea
Philippines
Philippine Sea
Gulf of Aden
Socotra
Arabian Sea
Deccan
Western Ghats
Eastern Ghats
Bay of Bengal
Palawan
Mindanao
Andaman Islands
Andaman Sea
Gulf of Thailand
Sulu Sea
Celebes Sea
Halmahera
CAROLINE PLATE
Sri Lanka
Nicobar Islands
Natuna Islands
New Guinea
Malay Peninsula
Strait of Malacca
Sumatra
Borneo
Makassar Strait
Moluccas
Seram
Celebes
Greater Sunda Islands
East Indies
Banda Sea
Coral Sea
Arafura Sea
Java
Java Sea
Flores Sea
Flores
Sumbawa
Lesser Sunda Islands
Timor
Timor Sea

MAP KEY

ELEVATION

- 6000m / 19,686ft
- 4000m / 13,124ft
- 3000m / 9843ft
- 2000m / 6562ft
- 1000m / 3281ft
- 500m / 1640ft
- 250m / 820ft
- 100m / 328ft
- sea level

PLATE MARGINS
(for explanation see page xiv)

- constructive
- destructive
- conservative
- uncertain
- physiographic regions
- line of cross-section

THE INDIAN SHIELD AND HIMALAYAN SYSTEM

THE LARGE SHIELD AREA beneath the Indian subcontinent is between 2.5 and 3.5 billion years old. As the floor of the southern Indian Ocean spread, it pushed the Indian Shield north. This was eventually driven beneath the Plateau of Tibet. This process closed up the ancient Tethys Sea and uplifted the world's highest mountain chain, the Himalayas. Much of the uplifted rock strata was from the seabed of the Tethys Sea, partly accounting for the weakness of the rocks and the high levels of erosion found in the Himalayas.

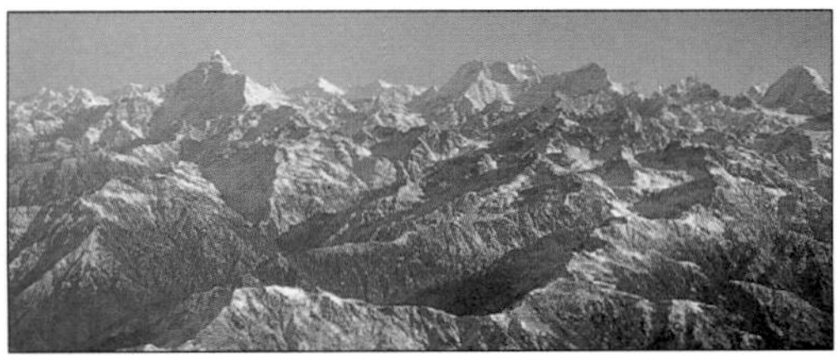

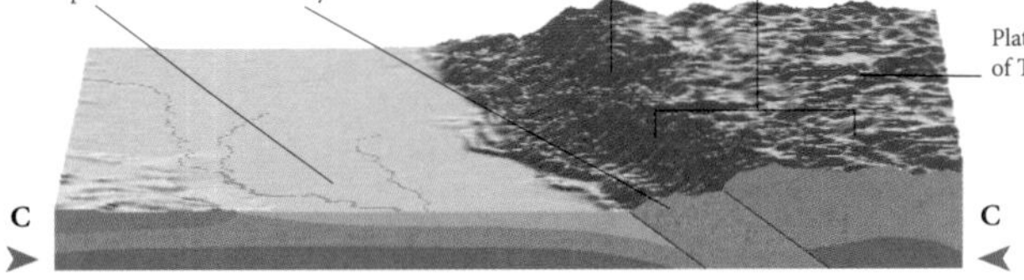
Indo-Gangetic Depression
Crushed sediment from seabed of the Tethys Sea
Himalayas
Thrust zone
Plateau of Tibet
C
C
0 50 100 Km
0 50 100 Miles

Cross-section through the Himalayas showing thrust faulting of the rock strata.

SCALE 1:63,000,000
(projection: Lambert Azimuthal Equal Area)

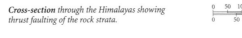

Km 0 250 500 1000 1500
Miles 0 250 500 1000 1500

Climate

The Gobi desert experiences major extremes in climate, with winter temperatures sometimes falling below -40°C (-40°F) and summer temperatures exceeding 45°C (113°F).

ASIA'S CLIMATE exhibits marked differences from region to region, with polar conditions in the north, hot and cold deserts in central regions and subtropical conditions in the south. Monsoon winds cause alternate wet and dry seasons across the south. These air masses moving north from the ocean are stripped of their moisture over the Himalayas causing arid conditions across the Plateau of Tibet. Both the south and east are susceptible to cyclones or typhoons.

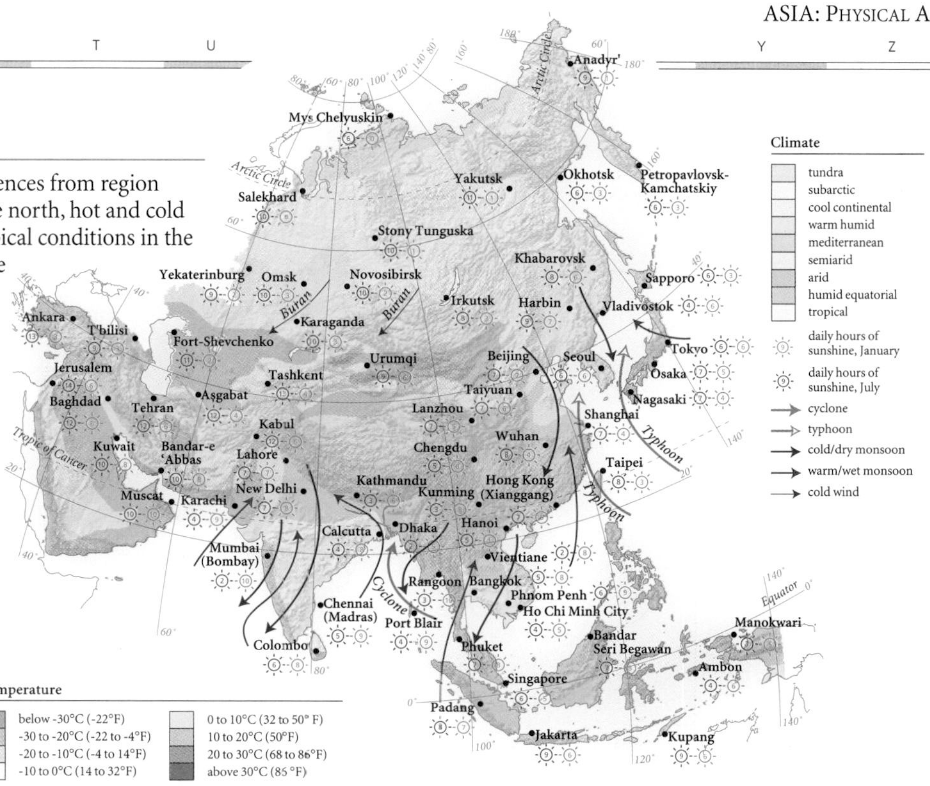
Anadyr'
Mys Chelyuskin
Arctic Circle
Salekhard
Yakutsk
Okhotsk
Petropavlovsk-Kamchatskiy
Stony Tunguska
Khabarovsk
Yekaterinburg
Omsk
Novosibirsk
Irkutsk
Harbin
Sapporo
Vladivostok
Buran
Karaganda
Ankara
T'bilisi
Fort-Shevchenko
Urumqi
Beijing
Seoul
Tokyo
Jerusalem
Tashkent
Taiyuan
Osaka
Baghdad
Tehran
Asgabat
Lanzhou
Nagasaki
Shanghai
Kabul
Wuhan
Typhoon
Kuwait
Bandar-e 'Abbas
Lahore
Chengdu
Taipei
Tropic of Cancer
Muscat
Karachi
New Delhi
Kathmandu
Kunming
Hong Kong (Xianggang)
Mumbai (Bombay)
Calcutta
Dhaka
Hanoi
Vientiane
Rangoon
Bangkok
Phnom Penh
Ho Chi Minh City
Chennai (Madras)
Cyclone
Port Blair
Colombo
Phuket
Bandar Seri Begawan
Manokwari
Equator
Ambon
Singapore
Padang
Jakarta
Kupang
Climate
tundra
subarctic
cool continental
warm humid
mediterranean
semiarid
arid
humid equatorial
tropical
daily hours of sunshine, January
daily hours of sunshine, July
cyclone
typhoon
cold/dry monsoon
warm/wet monsoon
cold wind

Temperature

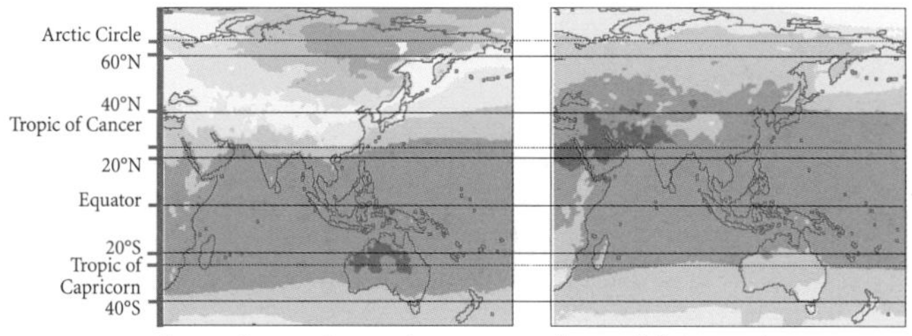
Arctic Circle
60°N
40°N
Tropic of Cancer
20°N
Equator
20°S
Tropic of Capricorn
40°S

Average January temperature *Average July temperature*

Temperature

- below -30°C (-22°F)
- -30 to -20°C (-22 to -4°F)
- -20 to -10°C (-4 to 14°F)
- -10 to 0°C (14 to 32°F)
- 0 to 10°C (32 to 50° F)
- 10 to 20°C (50°F)
- 20 to 30°C (68 to 86°F)
- above 30°C (85 °F)

Tropical cyclones occur principally during late summer and early autumn. The intense winds and heavy rainfall can devastate entire villages.

Rainfall

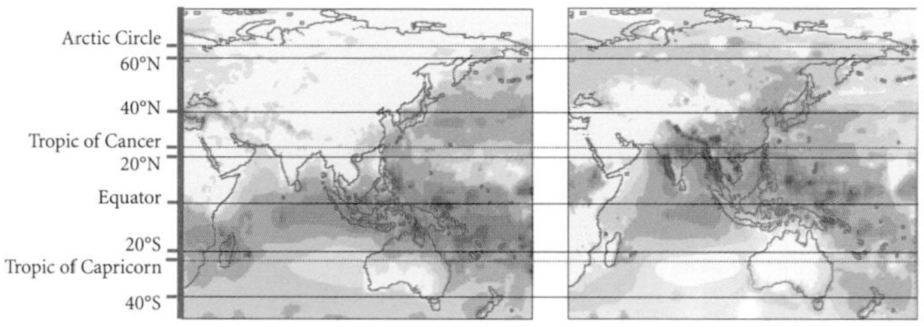
Arctic Circle
60°N
40°N
Tropic of Cancer
20°N
Equator
20°S
Tropic of Capricorn
40°S

Average January rainfall *Average July rainfall*

Rainfall

- 0–25 mm (0–1 in)
- 25–50 mm (1–2 in)
- 50–100 mm (2–4 in)
- 100–200 mm (4–8 in)
- 200–300 mm (8–12 in)
- 300–400 mm (12–16 in)
- 400–500 mm (16–20 in)
- more than 500 mm (20 in)

Through India, the southwest monsoon, which brings heavy rainfall from May to September, accounts for 80% of annual precipitation.

Shaping the Landscape

IN THE NORTH, melting of extensive permafrost leads to typical periglacial features such as thermokarst. In the arid areas wind action transports sand creating extensive dune systems. An active tectonic margin in the south causes continued uplift, and volcanic and seismic activity, but also high rates of weathering and erosion. Across the continent, huge rivers erode and transport vast quantities of sediment depositing it on the plains or forming large deltas.

River Systems

1 Vast river systems flow across Asia, many originating in the Himalayas and the Plateau of Tibet. Seasonal melting of snow and monsoon rains swell the river flow leading to flooding and erosion. The Yellow River *(left)* gets its color from the high level of eroded material from the loess plateau.

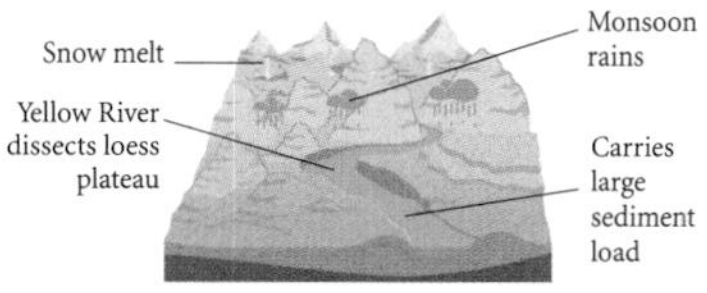
Snow melt
Monsoon rains
Yellow River dissects loess plateau
Carries large sediment load

RIVER SYSTEMS: EROSION OF THE LOESS PLATEAU BY THE YELLOW RIVER

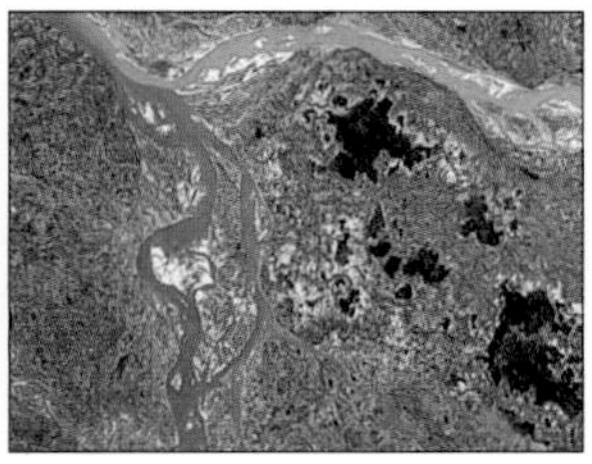

Sedimentation

4 The Ganges/Brahmaputra is a tide-dominated delta *(left)*. The two rivers transport huge quantities of mountain sediment, which is deposited on the delta plain. This debris is then redistributed by tidal currents, to form extensions to the bars, beach ridges, and deltaic deposits.

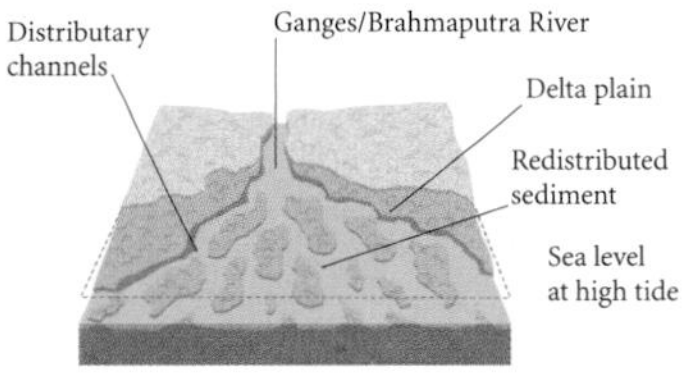
Distributary channels
Ganges/Brahmaputra River
Delta plain
Redistributed sediment
Sea level at high tide

SEDIMENTATION: THE DESTRUCTION OF A DELTA

The Evolving Landscape

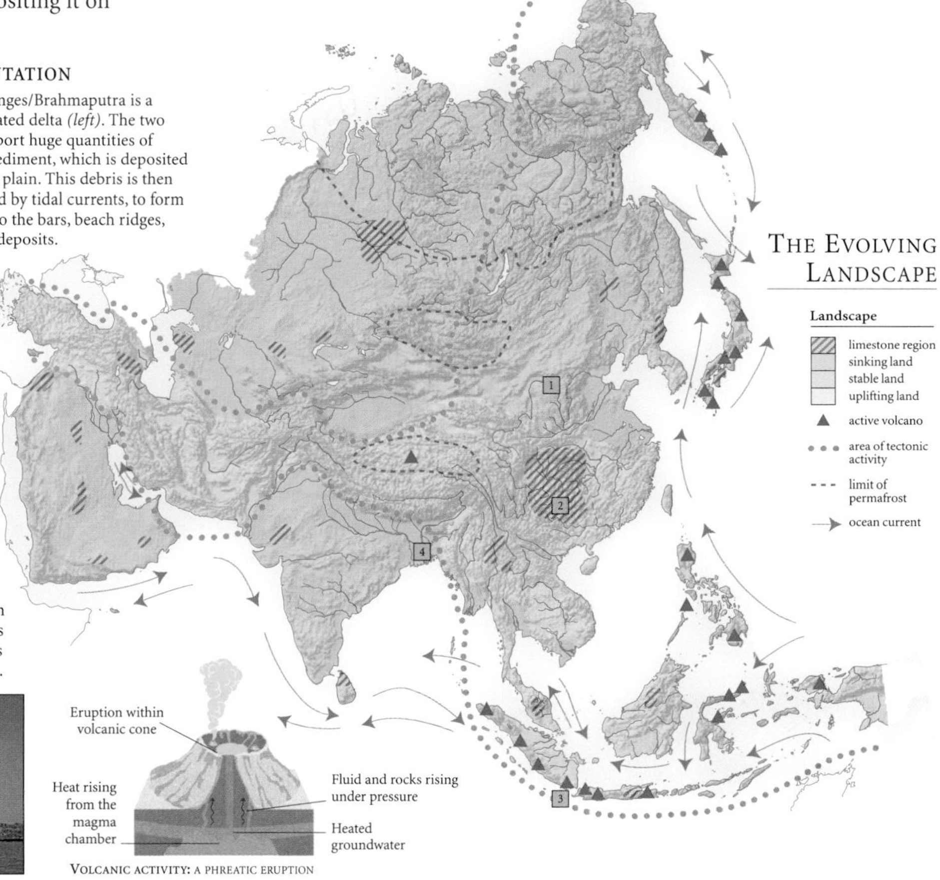
1
2
3
4
Landscape
limestone region
sinking land
stable land
uplifting land
active volcano
area of tectonic activity
limit of permafrost
ocean current
Eruption within volcanic cone
Heat rising from the magma chamber
Fluid and rocks rising under pressure
Heated groundwater

Chemical Weathering

2 Tower karsts are widespread across south China *(above)* and Vietnam. It is thought the karstic towers were formed under a soil cover, where small depressions in the limestone bedrock began to be weathered by soil water acids, eventually creating larger hollows. This process continued over millions of years, deepening the hollows and leaving steep-sided limestone hills.

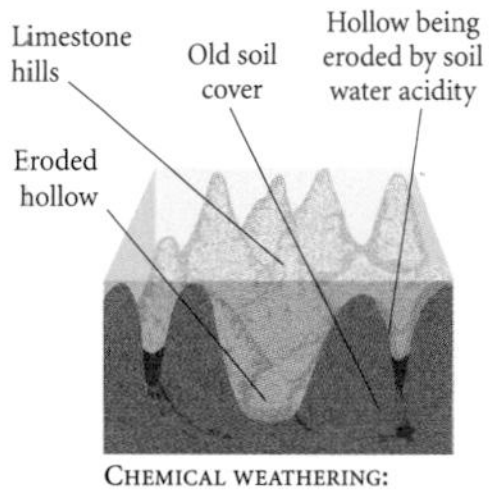
Limestone hills
Old soil cover
Hollow being eroded by soil water acidity
Eroded hollow

CHEMICAL WEATHERING: FORMATION OF TOWER KARST

Volcanic Activity

3 Volcanic eruptions occur frequently across Southeast Asia's island arcs *(below)*. Low-level eruptions occur when groundwater, superheated by underlying magma, becomes pressurized, forcing hot fluid and rocks up through cracks in the volcanic cone. This is known as a phreatic eruption.

VOLCANIC ACTIVITY: A PHREATIC ERUPTION

Political Asia

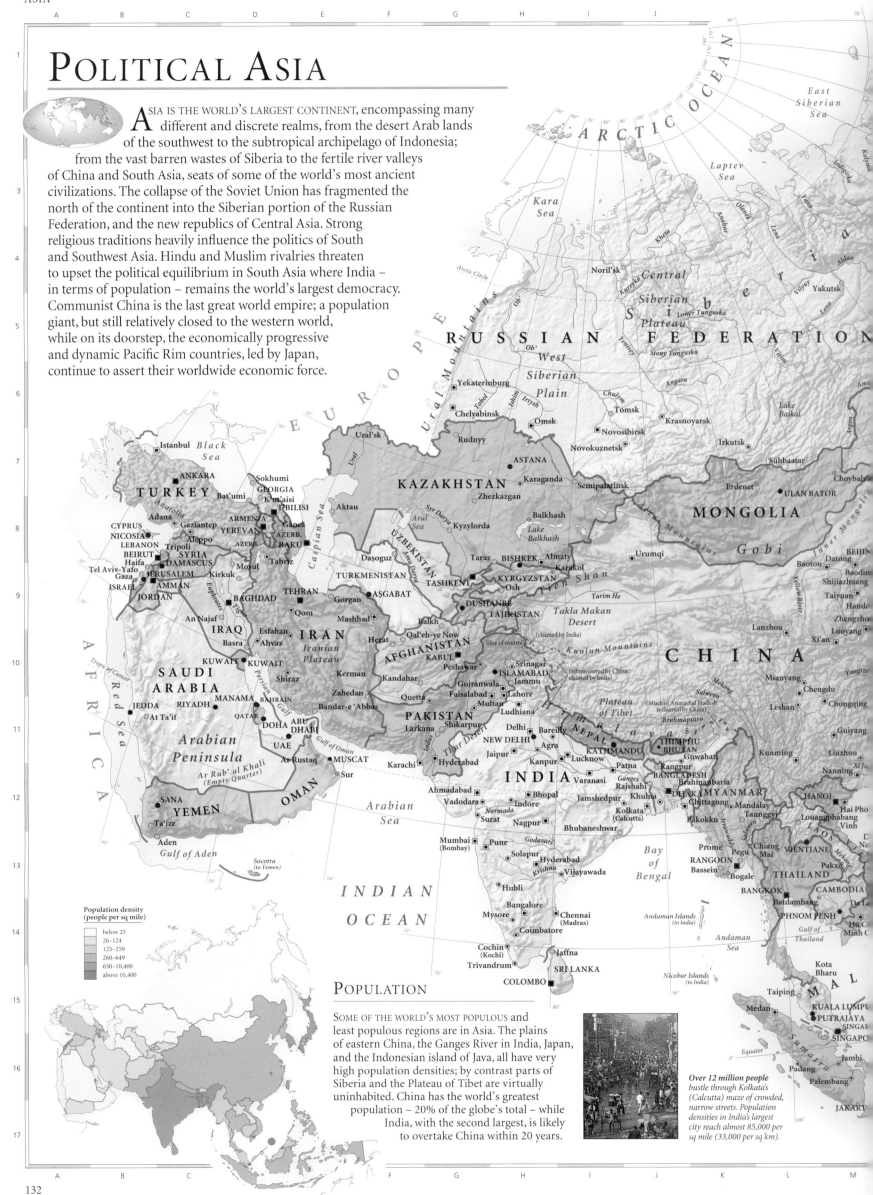

ASIA IS THE WORLD'S LARGEST CONTINENT, encompassing many different and discrete realms, from the desert Arab lands of the southwest to the subtropical archipelago of Indonesia; from the vast barren wastes of Siberia to the fertile river valleys of China and South Asia, seats of some of the world's most ancient civilizations. The collapse of the Soviet Union has fragmented the north of the continent into the Siberian portion of the Russian Federation, and the new republics of Central Asia. Strong religious traditions heavily influence the politics of South and Southwest Asia. Hindu and Muslim rivalries threaten to upset the political equilibrium in South Asia where India – in terms of population – remains the world's largest democracy. Communist China is the last great world empire; a population giant, but still relatively closed to the western world, while on its doorstep, the economically progressive and dynamic Pacific Rim countries, led by Japan, continue to assert their worldwide economic force.

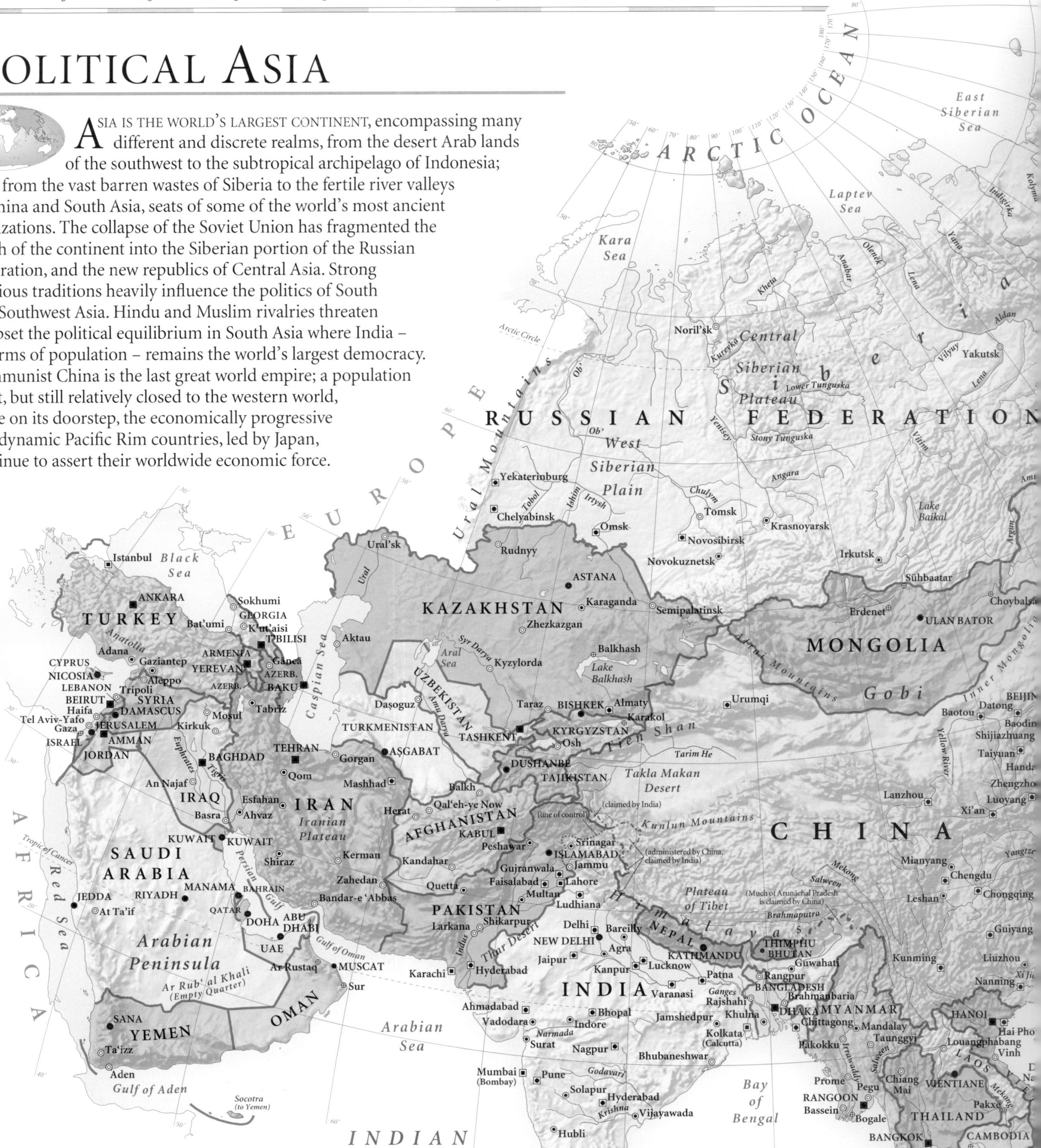
ARCTIC OCEAN
East Siberian Sea
Laptev Sea
Kara Sea
Arctic Circle
RUSSIAN FEDERATION
Siberia
Central Siberian Plateau
West Siberian Plain
Noril'sk
Yakutsk
Lower Tunguska
Stony Tunguska
Yekaterinburg
Chelyabinsk
Omsk
Tomsk
Novosibirsk
Krasnoyarsk
Novokuznetsk
Irkutsk
Lake Baikal
Ural Mountains
EUROPE
Ural'sk
Rudnyy
ASTANA
Karaganda
Semipalatinsk
KAZAKHSTAN
Zhezkazgan
Balkhash
Lake Balkhash
Aral Sea
Kyzylorda
Süхbaatar
Erdenet
ULAN BATOR
MONGOLIA
Altai Mountains
Gobi
Choybalsan
Istanbul
Black Sea
ANKARA
TURKEY
Anatolia
Sokhumi
GEORGIA
Bat'umi
K'ut'aisi
TBILISI
ARMENIA
YEREVAN
AZERB.
Gəncə
BAKU
Aktau
Caspian Sea
Adana
Gaziantep
CYPRUS
NICOSIA
Aleppo
LEBANON
Tripoli
SYRIA
BEIRUT
Haifa
DAMASCUS
Tel Aviv-Yafo
Gaza
JERUSALEM
ISRAEL
AMMAN
JORDAN
Mosul
Tabriz
Kirkuk
BAGHDAD
IRAQ
An Najaf
Basra
TEHRAN
Qom
Gorgan
AŞGABAT
TURKMENISTAN
Daşoguz
UZBEKISTAN
TASHKENT
BISHKEK
Almaty
Karakol
KYRGYZSTAN
Osh
DUSHANBE
TAJIKISTAN
Tien Shan
Taraz
Urumqi
Tarim He
Takla Makan Desert
Mashhad
Balkh
Qal'eh-ye Now
Herat
AFGHANISTAN
KABUL
Kandahar
Esfahan
Ahvaz
IRAN
Iranian Plateau
Kerman
Zahedan
Bandar-e 'Abbas
KUWAIT
Shiraz
SAUDI ARABIA
Persian Gulf
MANAMA
BAHRAIN
QATAR
DOHA
ABU DHABI
UAE
RIYADH
JEDDA
At Ta'if
Red Sea
Arabian Peninsula
Ar Rub' al Khali (Empty Quarter)
Gulf of Oman
Ar Rustaq
MUSCAT
Sur
OMAN
SANA
YEMEN
Ta'izz
Aden
Gulf of Aden
Socotra (to Yemen)
AFRICA
Tropic of Cancer
Peshawar
ISLAMABAD
Srinagar
Jammu
(line of control)
(claimed by India)
(administered by China, claimed by India)
Kunlun Mountains
Gujranwala
Faisalabad
Lahore
Quetta
Multan
Ludhiana
PAKISTAN
Larkana
Shikarpur
Thar Desert
Indus
Karachi
Hyderabad
Delhi
NEW DELHI
Bareilly
Agra
Jaipur
Kanpur
Lucknow
NEPAL
KATHMANDU
Himalayas
THIMPHU
BHUTAN
Guwahati
Plateau of Tibet
(Much of Arunachal Pradesh is claimed by China)
Brahmaputra
CHINA
Lanzhou
Xi'an
Mianyang
Chengdu
Leshan
Chongqing
Kunming
Guiyang
Liuzhou
Nanning
BEIJING
Datong
Baotou
Baoding
Shijiazhuang
Taiyuan
Handan
Zhengzhou
Luoyang
Inner Mongolia
Yellow River
Yangtze
Mekong
Salween
INDIA
Varanasi
Patna
Ganges
Rajshahi
Rangpur
BANGLADESH
Brahmanbaria
DHAKA
Khulna
Chittagong
Jamshedpur
Kolkata (Calcutta)
Ahmadabad
Vadodara
Bhopal
Indore
Narmada
Surat
Nagpur
Bhubaneshwar
Mumbai (Bombay)
Pune
Godavari
Solapur
Hyderabad
Krishna
Vijayawada
Hubli
Bangalore
Mysore
Chennai (Madras)
Coimbatore
Cochin (Kochi)
Trivandrum
Jaffna
SRI LANKA
COLOMBO
Arabian Sea
INDIAN OCEAN
Bay of Bengal
Andaman Islands (to India)
Andaman Sea
Nicobar Islands (to India)
MYANMAR
Mandalay
Taunggyi
Pakokku
Irrawaddy
Prome
Pegu
RANGOON
Bassein
Bogale
HANOI
Hai Phong
Louangphabang
Vinh
LAOS
Chiang Mai
VIENTIANE
Pakxe
THAILAND
BANGKOK
Batdambang
CAMBODIA
PHNOM PENH
Gulf of Thailand
Ho Chi Minh City
Kota Bharu
Taiping
Medan
KUALA LUMPUR
PUTRAJAYA
SINGAPORE
Sumatra
Equator
Jambi
Padang
Palembang
JAKARTA
Yenisey
Ob'
Irtysh
Ishim
Tobol
Chulym
Angara
Kheta
Kureyka
Anabar
Olenek
Lena
Vilyuy
Vitim
Aldan
Yana
Indigirka
Kolyma
Argun
Syr Darya
Amu Darya
Euphrates
Tigris

Population

SOME OF THE WORLD'S MOST POPULOUS and least populous regions are in Asia. The plains of eastern China, the Ganges River in India, Japan, and the Indonesian island of Java, all have very high population densities; by contrast parts of Siberia and the Plateau of Tibet are virtually uninhabited. China has the world's greatest population – 20% of the globe's total – while India, with the second largest, is likely to overtake China within 20 years.

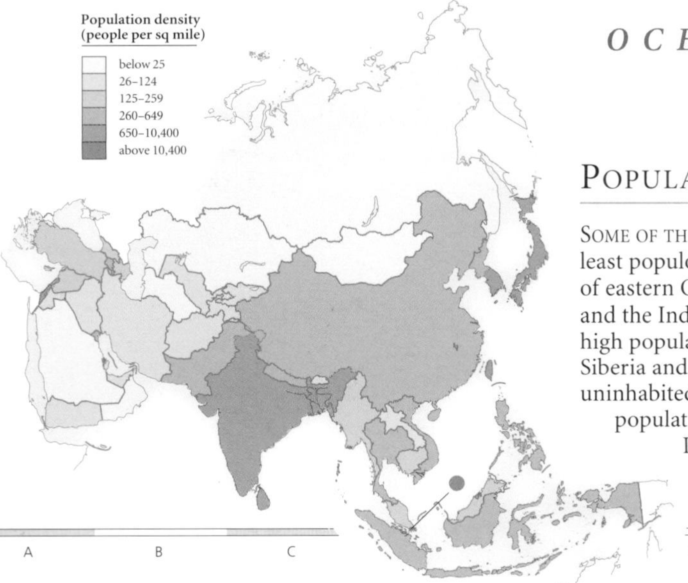
Population density (people per sq mile)
below 25
26–124
125–259
260–649
650–10,400
above 10,400

Over 12 million people bustle through Kolkata's (Calcutta) maze of crowded, narrow streets. Population densities in India's largest city reach almost 85,000 per sq mile (33,000 per sq km).

Bering Sea
PACIFIC OCEAN
Anadyr'
Arctic Circle
Kolyma Range
Kamchatka
Magadan
Petropavlovsk-Kamchatskiy
Sea of Okhotsk
Kurile Islands
Sakhalin
Amur
Yuzhno-Sakhalinsk
Khabarovsk
Hokkaido
Sapporo
Qiqihar
Harbin
Jilin
Vladivostok
Chongjin
Sea of Japan (East Sea)
JAPAN
Sendai
NORTH KOREA
Shenyang
Hamhung
Wonsan
PYONGYANG
TOKYO
Yokohama
Dalian
SEOUL
Inch'on
SOUTH KOREA
Taegu
Pusan
Kyoto
Nagoya
Kobe
Osaka
Hiroshima
Kitakyushu
Kumamoto
Fukuoka
Kagoshima
Honshu
Qingdao
Yellow Sea
Xuzhou
Nanjing
Shanghai
East China Sea
Hangzhou
Ningbo
Jinhua
Ryukyu Islands
Tropic of Cancer
Nanchang
Fuzhou
Taiwan Strait
TAIPEI
T'aichung
TAIWAN
T'ainan
Kaohsiung
Shantou
Guangzhou
Hong Kong (Xianggang)
Philippine Sea
Tuguegarao
Luzon
Baguio
South China Sea
MANILA
Legaspi
PHILIPPINES
Bacolod
Cebu
Mindanao
Davao
Zamboanga
General Santos
Equator
Jayapura
BANDAR SERI BEGAWAN
BRUNEI
Manado
New Guinea
Papua (Irian Jaya)
Moluccas
Borneo
Balikpapan
Celebes
Ambon
Pontianak
INDONESIA
Banjarmasin
Makassar
Java Sea
Flores Sea
Flores
DILI
EAST TIMOR
Timor
Timor Sea
Semarang
Surabaya
Java
Malang

MAP KEY

POPULATION

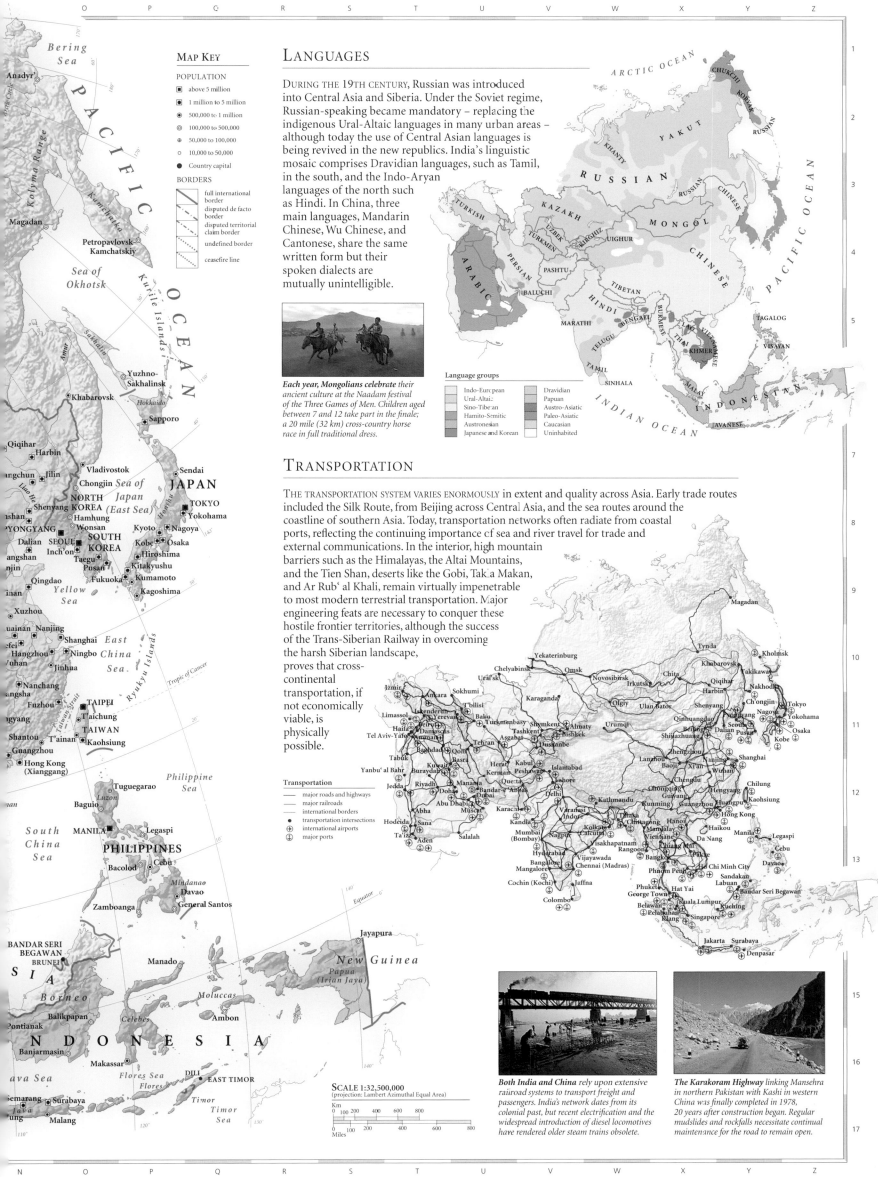

- above 5 million
- 1 million to 5 million
- 500,000 to 1 million
- 100,000 to 500,000
- 50,000 to 100,000
- 10,000 to 50,000
- Country capital

BORDERS

- full international border
- disputed de facto border
- disputed territorial claim border
- undefined border
- ceasefire line

LANGUAGES

DURING THE 19TH CENTURY, Russian was introduced into Central Asia and Siberia. Under the Soviet regime, Russian-speaking became mandatory – replacing the indigenous Ural-Altaic languages in many urban areas – although today the use of Central Asian languages is being revived in the new republics. India's linguistic mosaic comprises Dravidian languages, such as Tamil, in the south, and the Indo-Aryan languages of the north such as Hindi. In China, three main languages, Mandarin Chinese, Wu Chinese, and Cantonese, share the same written form but their spoken dialects are mutually unintelligible.

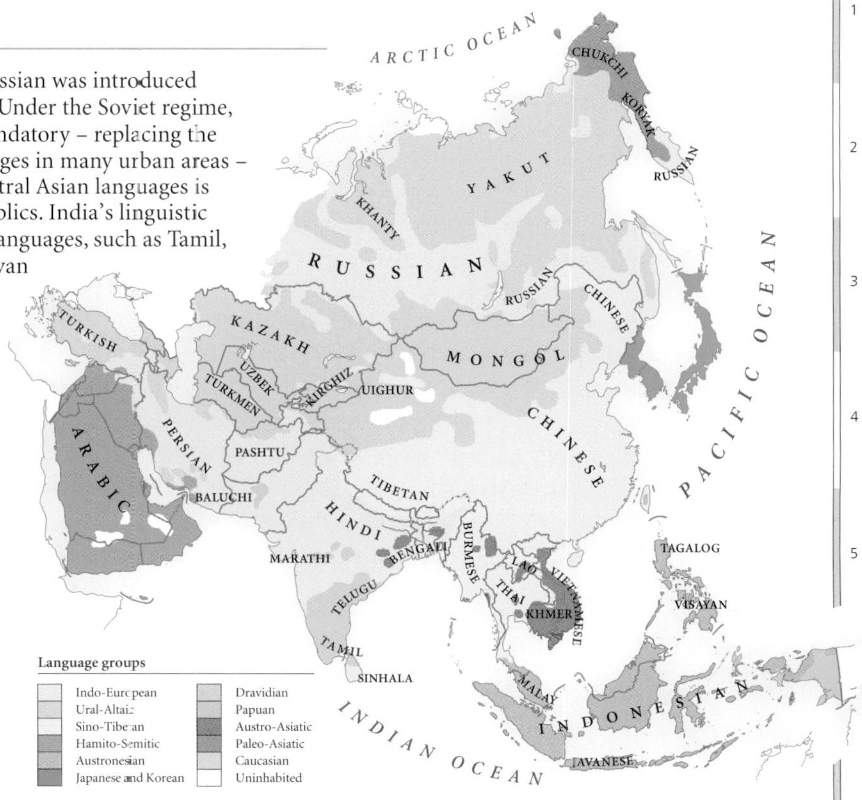

ARCTIC OCEAN
CHUKCHI
KORYAK
RUSSIAN
YAKUT
KHANTY
RUSSIAN
TURKISH
KAZAKH
CHINESE
MONGOL
UZBEK
TURKMEN
KIRGHIZ
UIGHUR
ARABIC
PERSIAN
PASHTU
CHINESE
BALUCHI
TIBETAN
HINDI
BENGALI
BURMESE
MARATHI
TELUGU
TAMIL
SINHALA
LAO
THAI
VIETNAMESE
KHMER
TAGALOG
VISAYAN
MALAY
INDONESIAN
JAVANESE
PACIFIC OCEAN
INDIAN OCEAN
Language groups
Indo-European
Ural-Altaic
Sino-Tibetan
Hamito-Semitic
Austronesian
Japanese and Korean
Dravidian
Papuan
Austro-Asiatic
Paleo-Asiatic
Caucasian
Uninhabited

***Each year, Mongolians celebrate** their ancient culture at the Naadam festival of the Three Games of Men. Children aged between 7 and 12 take part in the finale; a 20 mile (32 km) cross-country horse race in full traditional dress.*

TRANSPORTATION

THE TRANSPORTATION SYSTEM VARIES ENORMOUSLY in extent and quality across Asia. Early trade routes included the Silk Route, from Beijing across Central Asia, and the sea routes around the coastline of southern Asia. Today, transportation networks often radiate from coastal ports, reflecting the continuing importance of sea and river travel for trade and external communications. In the interior, high mountain barriers such as the Himalayas, the Altai Mountains, and the Tien Shan, deserts like the Gobi, Takla Makan, and Ar Rubʿ al Khali, remain virtually impenetrable to most modern terrestrial transportation. Major engineering feats are necessary to conquer these hostile frontier territories, although the success of the Trans-Siberian Railway in overcoming the harsh Siberian landscape, proves that cross-continental transportation, if not economically viable, is physically possible.

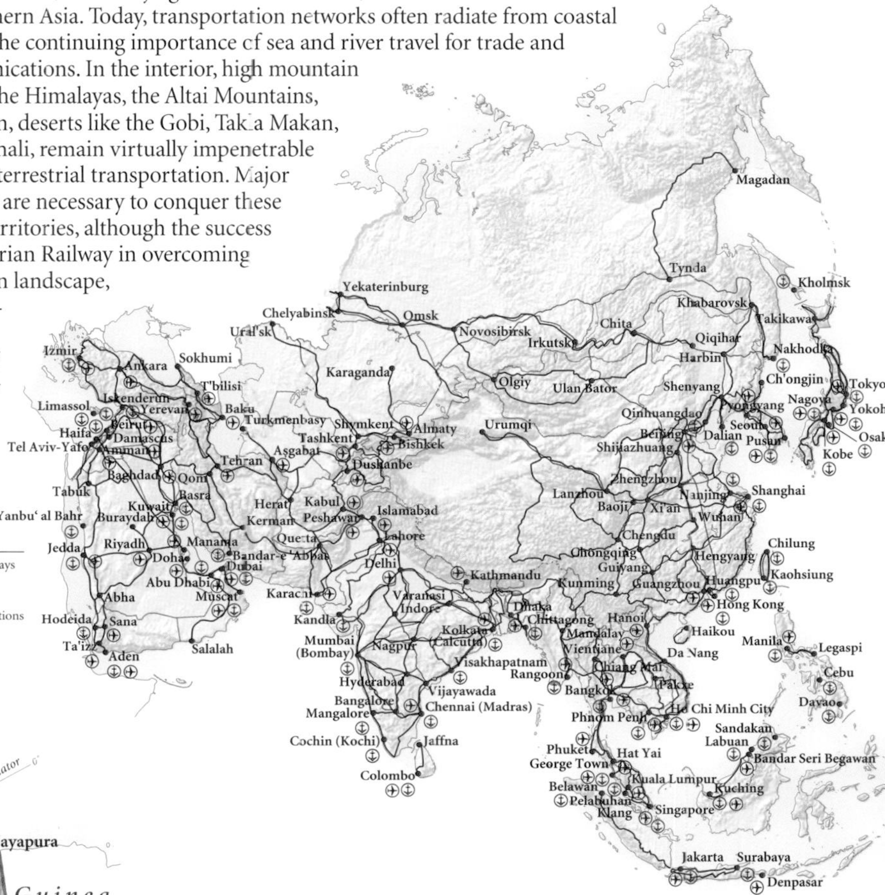

Transportation
major roads and highways
major railroads
international borders
transportation intersections
international airports
major ports
Magadan
Tynda
Kholmsk
Khabarovsk
Takikawa
Yekaterinburg
Chelyabinsk
Omsk
Novosibirsk
Irkutsk
Chita
Qiqihar
Nakhodka
Harbin
Ural'sk
Karaganda
Ch'ongjin
Tokyo
Izmir
Ankara
Sokhumi
Olgiy
Ulan Bator
Shenyang
Yokohama
Limassol
Iskenderun
T'bilisi
Nagoya
Osaka
Yerevan
Baku
Shymkent
Almaty
Urumqi
Qinhuangdao
Seoul
Kobe
Haifa
Beirut
Turkmenbasy
Bishkek
Beijing
Dalian
Pusan
Tel Aviv-Yafo
Damascus
Tashkent
Shijiazhuang
Amman
Asgabat
Dushanbe
Baghdad
Tehran
Zhengzhou
Tabuk
Qom
Lanzhou
Nanjing
Shanghai
Basra
Herat
Kabul
Baoji
Xi'an
Wuhan
Yanbu' al Bahr
Kuwait
Kerman
Peshawar
Islamabad
Buraydah
Quetta
Lahore
Chengdu
Jedda
Riyadh
Manama
Bandar-e-'Abbas
Chilung
Doha
Dubai
Delhi
Chongqing
Hengyang
Kaohsiung
Abu Dhabi
Kathmandu
Guiyang
Muscat
Karachi
Kunming
Guangzhou
Huangpu
Abha
Varanasi
Hong Kong
Kandla
Indore
Dhaka
Hanoi
Hodeida
Sana
Kolkata (Calcutta)
Chittagong
Haikou
Manila
Legaspi
Ta'izz
Mumbai (Bombay)
Nagpur
Mandalay
Vientiane
Da Nang
Aden
Salalah
Visakhapatnam
Rangoon
Chiang Mai
Cebu
Hyderabad
Bangkok
Pattaya
Davao
Bangalore
Vijayawada
Ho Chi Minh City
Mangalore
Chennai (Madras)
Phnom Penh
Sandakan
Cochin (Kochi)
Jaffna
Labuan
Phuket
Hat Yai
Bandar Seri Begawan
George Town
Colombo
Kuala Lumpur
Kuching
Belawan
Pelabuhan Klang
Singapore
Jakarta
Surabaya
Denpasar

***Both India and China** rely upon extensive railroad systems to transport freight and passengers. India's network dates from its colonial past, but recent electrification and the widespread introduction of diesel locomotives have rendered older steam trains obsolete.*

***The Karakoram Highway** linking Mansehra in northern Pakistan with Kashi in western China was finally completed in 1978, 20 years after construction began. Regular mudslides and rockfalls necessitate continual maintenance for the road to remain open.*

SCALE 1:32,500,000
(projection: Lambert Azimuthal Equal Area)

Km 0 100 200 400 600 800

Miles 0 100 200 400 600 800

A B C D E F G H I J K L M

Asian Resources

Although agriculture remains the economic mainstay of most Asian countries, the number of people employed in agriculture has steadily declined, as new industries have been developed during the past 30 years. China, Indonesia, Malaysia, Thailand, and Turkey have all experienced far-reaching structural change in their economies, while the breakup of the Soviet Union has created a new economic challenge in the Central Asian republics. The countries of the Persian Gulf illustrate the rapid transformation from rural nomadism to modern, urban society which oil wealth has brought to parts of the continent. Asia's most economically dynamic countries, Japan, Singapore, South Korea, and Taiwan, fringe the Pacific Ocean and are known as the Pacific Rim. In contrast, other Southeast Asian countries like Laos and Cambodia remain both economically and industrially underdeveloped.

Standard of Living

Despite Japan's high standards of living, and Southwest Asia's oil-derived wealth, immense disparities exist across the continent. Afghanistan remains one of the world's most underdeveloped nations, as do the mountain states of Nepal and Bhutan. Further rapid population growth is exacerbating poverty and overcrowding in many parts of India and Bangladesh.

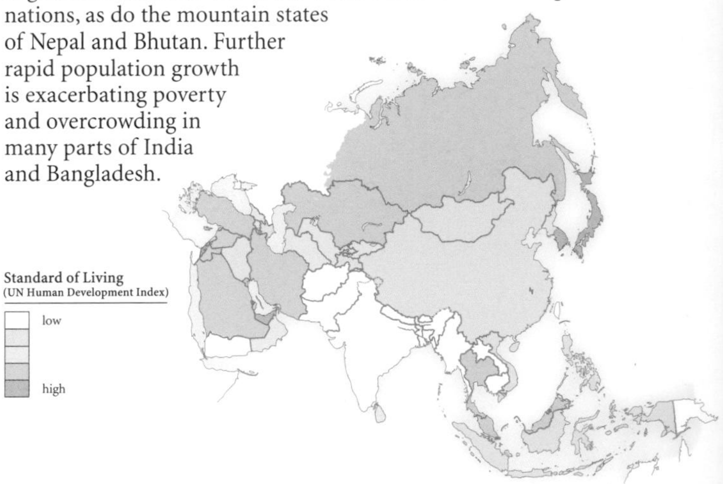
Standard of Living
(UN Human Development Index)
low
high

Industry

Japanese industry leads the continent in both productivity and efficiency; electronics, hi-tech industries, car manufacture and shipbuilding are important. In recent years, the so-called economic "tigers" of the Pacific Rim such as Taiwan and South Korea are now challenging Japan's economic dominance. Heavy industries such as engineering, chemicals, and steel typify the industrial complexes along the corridor created by the Trans-Siberian Railway, the Fergana Valley in Central Asia, and also much of the huge industrial plain of east China. The discovery of oil in the Persian Gulf brought immense wealth and international pressure to countries that previously relied on subsistence agriculture.

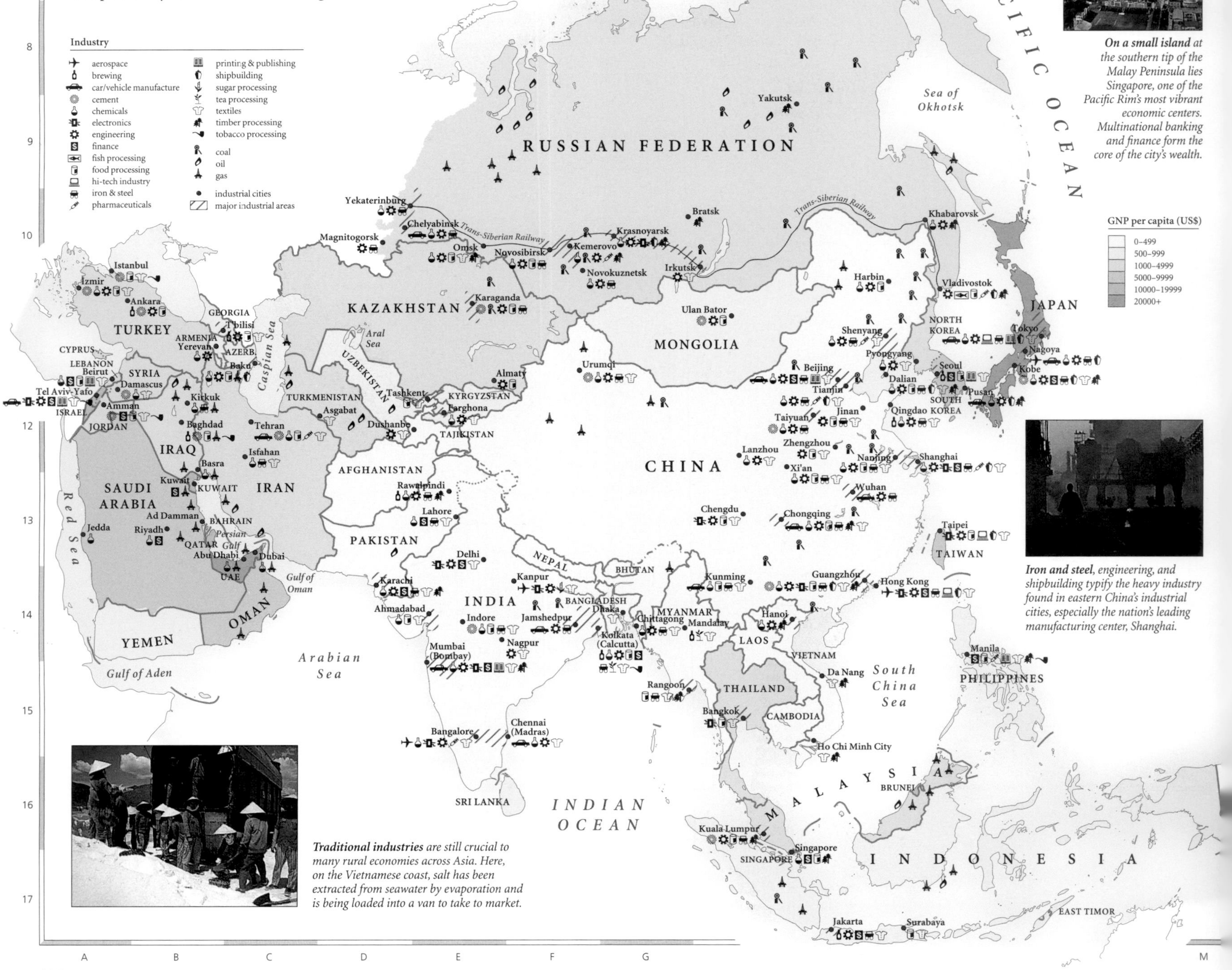
Industry
aerospace
brewing
car/vehicle manufacture
cement
chemicals
electronics
engineering
finance
fish processing
food processing
hi-tech industry
iron & steel
pharmaceuticals
printing & publishing
shipbuilding
sugar processing
tea processing
textiles
timber processing
tobacco processing
coal
oil
gas
industrial cities
major industrial areas
GNP per capita (US$)
0–499
500–999
1000–4999
5000–9999
10000–19999
20000+
ARCTIC OCEAN
PACIFIC OCEAN
INDIAN OCEAN
Sea of Okhotsk
Arabian Sea
South China Sea
Gulf of Aden
Gulf of Oman
Persian Gulf
Red Sea
Caspian Sea
Aral Sea
RUSSIAN FEDERATION
KAZAKHSTAN
MONGOLIA
CHINA
JAPAN
NORTH KOREA
SOUTH KOREA
TAIWAN
PHILIPPINES
INDONESIA
MALAYSIA
BRUNEI
SINGAPORE
EAST TIMOR
VIETNAM
CAMBODIA
LAOS
THAILAND
MYANMAR
BANGLADESH
BHUTAN
NEPAL
INDIA
SRI LANKA
PAKISTAN
AFGHANISTAN
IRAN
IRAQ
TURKEY
SYRIA
LEBANON
CYPRUS
ISRAEL
JORDAN
SAUDI ARABIA
KUWAIT
BAHRAIN
QATAR
UAE
OMAN
YEMEN
GEORGIA
ARMENIA
AZERB.
TURKMENISTAN
UZBEKISTAN
KYRGYZSTAN
TAJIKISTAN
Trans-Siberian Railway
Yekaterinburg
Chelyabinsk
Magnitogorsk
Omsk
Novosibirsk
Kemerovo
Novokuznetsk
Krasnoyarsk
Bratsk
Irkutsk
Yakutsk
Khabarovsk
Vladivostok
Karaganda
Almaty
Tashkent
Farghona
Dushanbe
Asgabat
Istanbul
Izmir
Ankara
Tbilisi
Yerevan
Baku
Beirut
Damascus
Tel Aviv-Yafo
Amman
Kirkuk
Baghdad
Basra
Tehran
Isfahan
Kuwait
Ad Damman
Riyadh
Jedda
Abu Dhabi
Dubai
Rawalpindi
Lahore
Karachi
Delhi
Kanpur
Ahmadabad
Indore
Jamshedpur
Nagpur
Mumbai (Bombay)
Kolkata (Calcutta)
Dhaka
Chittagong
Bangalore
Chennai (Madras)
Mandalay
Rangoon
Bangkok
Hanoi
Da Nang
Ho Chi Minh City
Kuala Lumpur
Singapore
Jakarta
Surabaya
Manila
Ulan Bator
Urumqi
Harbin
Shenyang
Beijing
Tianjin
Dalian
Pyongyang
Seoul
Pusan
Qingdao
Jinan
Taiyuan
Zhengzhou
Xi'an
Lanzhou
Nanjing
Shanghai
Wuhan
Chengdu
Chongqing
Kunming
Guangzhou
Hong Kong
Taipei
Tokyo
Nagoya
Kobe

On a small island at the southern tip of the Malay Peninsula lies Singapore, one of the Pacific Rim's most vibrant economic centers. Multinational banking and finance form the core of the city's wealth.

Iron and steel, engineering, and shipbuilding typify the heavy industry found in eastern China's industrial cities, especially the nation's leading manufacturing center, Shanghai.

***Traditional industries** are still crucial to many rural economies across Asia. Here, on the Vietnamese coast, salt has been extracted from seawater by evaporation and is being loaded into a van to take to market.*

A B C D E F G M

ENVIRONMENTAL ISSUES

THE TRANSFORMATION OF UZBEKISTAN by the former Soviet Union into the world's second largest producer of cotton led to the diversion of several major rivers for irrigation. Starved of this water, the Aral Sea diminished in volume by over 50% in 30 years, irreversibly altering the ecology of the area. Heavy industries in eastern China have polluted coastal waters, rivers, and urban air, while in Myanmar, Malaysia, and Indonesia, ancient hardwood rain forests are felled faster than they can regenerate.

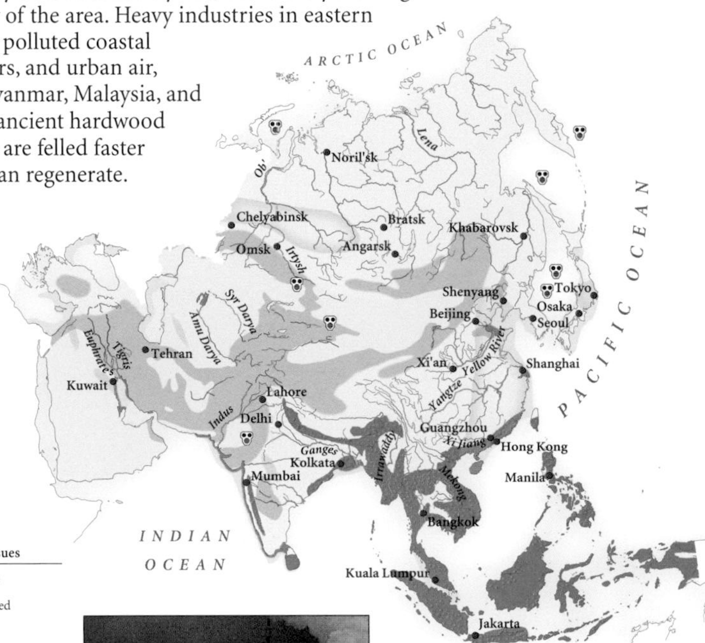
ARCTIC OCEAN
PACIFIC OCEAN
INDIAN OCEAN
Noril'sk
Lena
Ob'
Chelyabinsk
Bratsk
Khabarovsk
Omsk
Irtysh
Angarsk
Syr Darya
Amu Darya
Shenyang
Tokyo
Osaka
Beijing
Seoul
Tigris
Euphrates
Tehran
Xi'an
Yellow River
Shanghai
Kuwait
Yangtze
Lahore
Indus
Delhi
Guangzhou
Xi Jiang
Hong Kong
Ganges
Kolkata
Irrawaddy
Mekong
Mumbai
Manila
Bangkok
Kuala Lumpur
Jakarta
Environmental Issues
tropical forest
forest destroyed
desert
desertification
acid rain
polluted rivers
marine pollution
heavy marine pollution
radioactive contamination
poor urban air quality

The long-term environmental impact of the Gulf War (1991) is still uncertain. As Iraqi troops left Kuwait, equipment was abandoned to rust and thousands of oil wells were set alight, pouring crude oil into the Persian Gulf.

***Although Siberia** remains a quintessentially frozen, inhospitable wasteland, vast untapped mineral reserves – especially the oil and gas of the West Siberian Plain – have lured industrial development to the area since the 1950s and 1960s.*

MINERAL RESOURCES

AT LEAST 60% OF THE WORLD'S known oil and gas deposits are found in Asia; notably the vast oil fields of the Persian Gulf, and the less-exploited oil and gas fields of the Ob' Basin in west Siberia. Immense coal reserves in Siberia and China have been utilized to support large steel industries. Southeast Asia has some of the world's largest deposits of tin, found in a belt running down the Malay Peninsula to Indonesia.

Mineral Resources
oil field
gas field
coal field
chromite
copper
gold
iron
lead
nickel
platinum
tin
wolfram
ARCTIC OCEAN
PACIFIC OCEAN
INDIAN OCEAN
Himalayas

USING THE LAND AND SEA

VAST AREAS OF ASIA REMAIN UNCULTIVATED as a result of unsuitable climatic and soil conditions. In favorable areas such as river deltas, farming is intensive. Rice is the staple crop of most Asian countries, grown in paddy fields on waterlogged alluvial plains and terraced hillsides, and often irrigated for higher yields. Across the black earth region of the Eurasian steppe in southern Siberia and Kazakhstan, wheat farming is the dominant activity. Cash crops, like tea in Sri Lanka and dates in the Arabian Peninsula, are grown for export, and provide valuable income. The sovereignty of the rich fishing grounds in the South China Sea is disputed by China, Malaysia, Taiwan, the Philippines, and Vietnam, because of potential oil reserves.

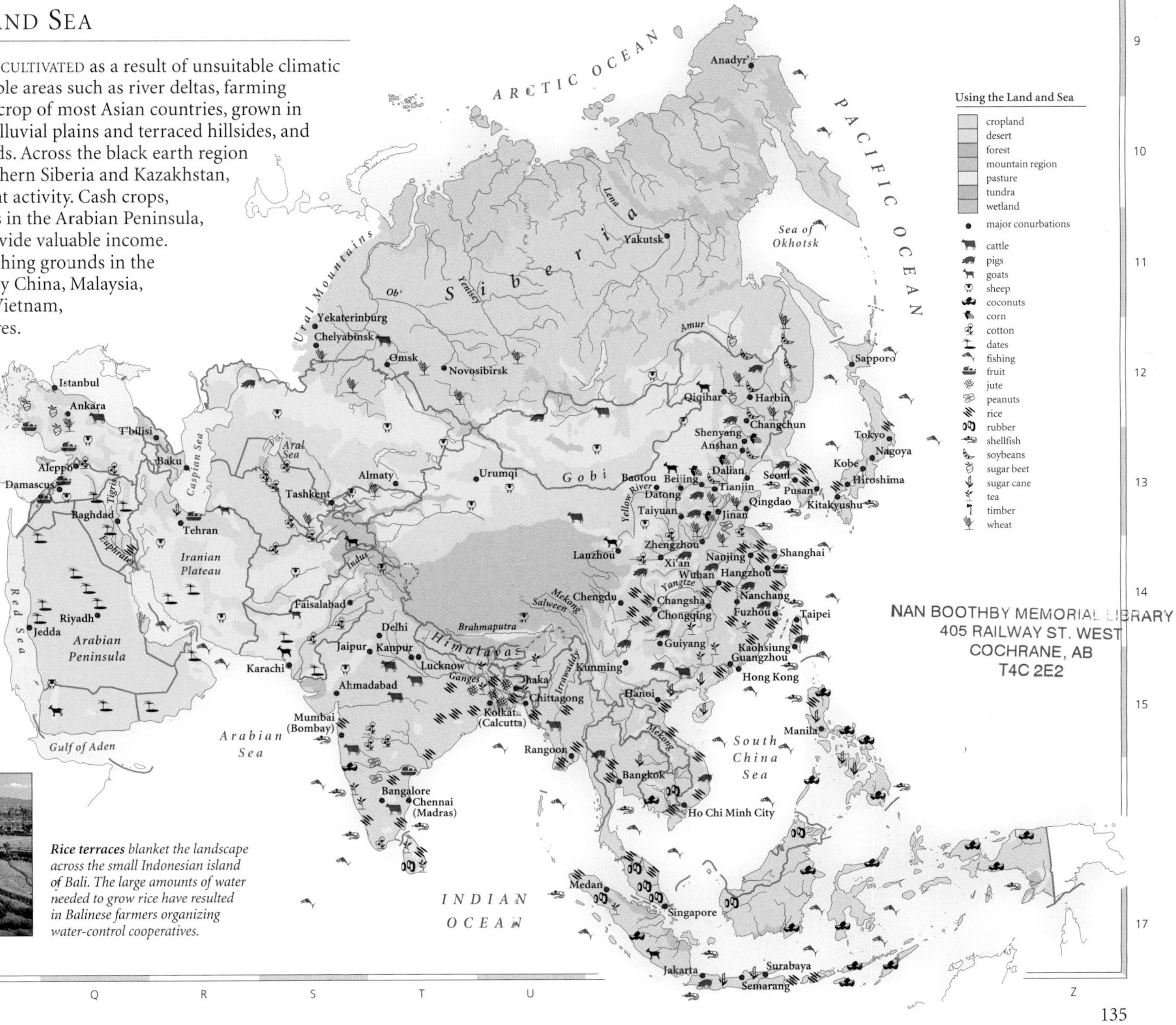
ARCTIC OCEAN
PACIFIC OCEAN
INDIAN OCEAN
Anadyr'
Sea of Okhotsk
Lena
Siberia
Yakutsk
Ural Mountains
Ob'
Yenisey
Amur
Yekaterinburg
Chelyabinsk
Omsk
Novosibirsk
Sapporo
Istanbul
Ankara
T'bilisi
Baku
Caspian Sea
Aral Sea
Qiqihar
Harbin
Changchun
Shenyang
Anshan
Tokyo
Nagoya
Aleppo
Damascus
Tashkent
Almaty
Urumqi
Gobi
Baotou
Beijing
Datong
Dalian
Tianjin
Seoul
Kobe
Hiroshima
Pusan
Kitakyushu
Qingdao
Taiyuan
Jinan
Baghdad
Tigris
Euphrates
Tehran
Iranian Plateau
Lanzhou
Zhengzhou
Xi'an
Nanjing
Wuhan
Hangzhou
Shanghai
Indus
Red Sea
Riyadh
Jedda
Arabian Peninsula
Faisalabad
Mekong
Salween
Chengdu
Changsha
Chongqing
Nanchang
Fuzhou
Taipei
Brahmaputra
Delhi
Jaipur
Kanpur
Himalayas
Lucknow
Karachi
Guiyang
Kaohsiung
Guangzhou
Hong Kong
Kunming
Dhaka
Chittagong
Ganges
Ahmadabad
Hanoi
Kolkata (Calcutta)
Gulf of Aden
Mumbai (Bombay)
Arabian Sea
Rangoon
Irrawaddy
Manila
South China Sea
Bangkok
Bangalore
Chennai (Madras)
Ho Chi Minh City
Medan
Singapore
Jakarta
Surabaya
Semarang
Using the Land and Sea
cropland
desert
forest
mountain region
pasture
tundra
wetland
major conurbations
cattle
pigs
goats
sheep
coconuts
corn
cotton
dates
fishing
fruit
jute
peanuts
rice
rubber
shellfish
soybeans
sugar beet
sugar cane
tea
timber
wheat

***Date palms** have been cultivated in oases throughout the Arabian Peninsula since antiquity. In addition to the fruit, palms are used for timber, fuel, rope, and for making vinegar, syrup, and a liquor known as arrack.*

***Rice terraces** blanket the landscape across the small Indonesian island of Bali. The large amounts of water needed to grow rice have resulted in Balinese farmers organizing water-control cooperatives.*

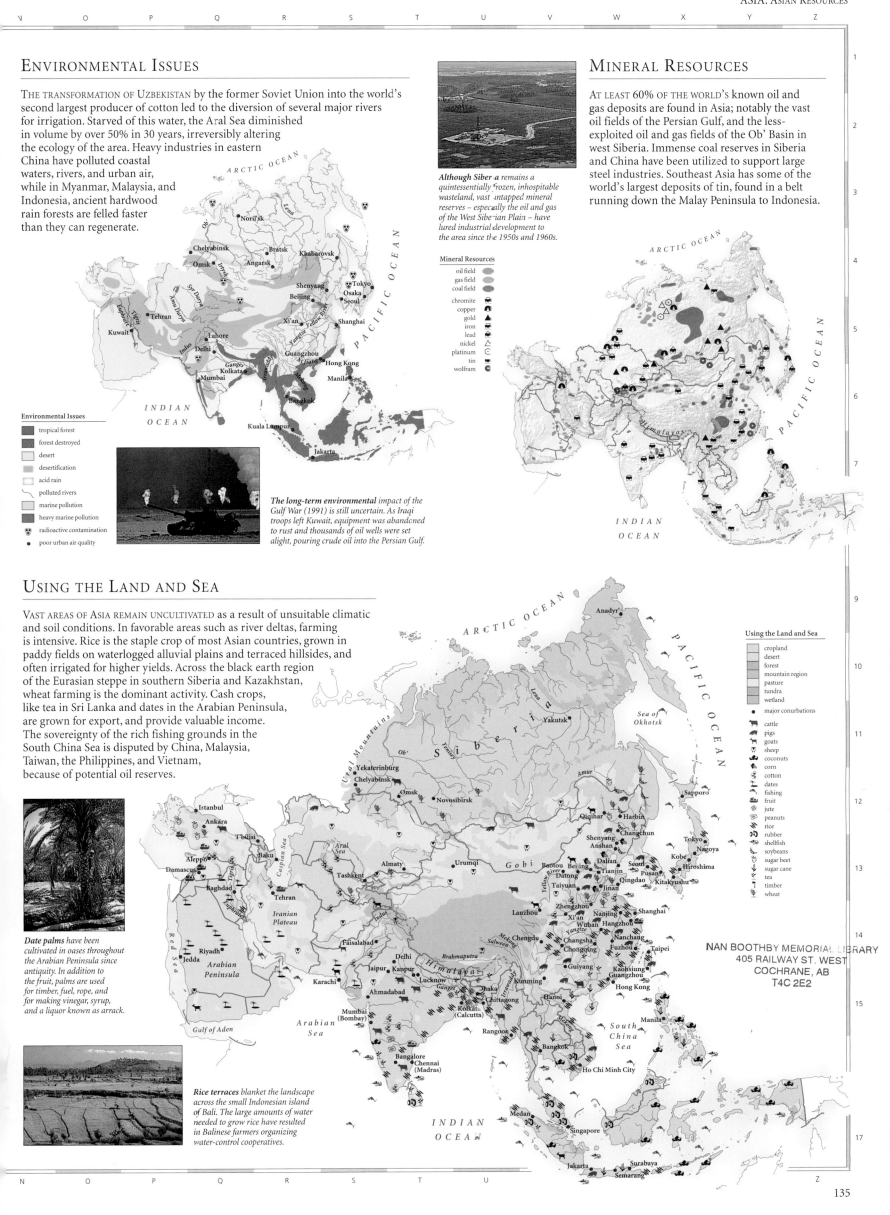

TURKEY & THE CAUCASUS

ARMENIA, AZERBAIJAN, GEORGIA, TURKEY

THIS REGION OCCUPIES THE FRAGMENTED JUNCTION between Europe, Asia, and the Russian Federation. Sunni Islam provides a common identity for the secular state of Turkey, which the revered leader Kemal Atatürk established from the remnants of the Ottoman Empire after the First World War. Turkey has a broad resource base and expanding trade links with Europe, but the east is relatively undeveloped and strife between the state and a large Kurdish minority has yet to be resolved. Georgia is similarly challenged by ethnic separatism, while the Christian state of Armenia and the mainly Muslim and oil-rich Azerbaijan are locked in conflict over the territory of Nagornyy Karabakh.

USING THE LAND AND SEA

TURKEY IS LARGELY SELF-SUFFICIENT in food. The irrigated Black Sea coastlands have the world's highest yields of hazelnuts. Tobacco, cotton, sultanas, tea, and figs are the region's main cash crops and a great range of fruit and vegetables are grown. Wine grapes are among the labor-intensive crops which allow full use of limited agricultural land in the Caucasus. Sturgeon fishing is particularly important in Azerbaijan.

RUSSIAN FEDERATION
CASPIAN SEA
BULGARIA
GREECE
BLACK SEA
Istanbul
Samsun
GEORGIA
T'BILISI
BAKU
ARMENIA
YEREVAN
AZERBAIJAN
ANKARA
Izmir
TURKEY
Konya
Diyarbakir
IRAN
Antalya
Adana
MEDITERRANEAN SEA
SYRIA
IRAQ

Land use and agricultural distribution

- cattle
- goats
- cotton
- fishing
- fruit
- hazelnuts
- olives
- sugar beet
- tobacco
- vineyards
- capital cities
- major towns
- pasture
- cropland
- forest

THE URBAN/RURAL POPULATION DIVIDE

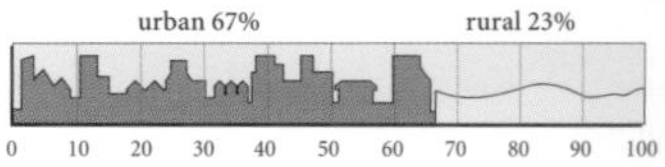

urban 67%
rural 23%
0
10
20
30
40
50
60
70
80
90
100

POPULATION DENSITY	TOTAL LAND AREA
218 people per sq mile (84 people per sq km)	368,912 sq miles (955,730 sq km)

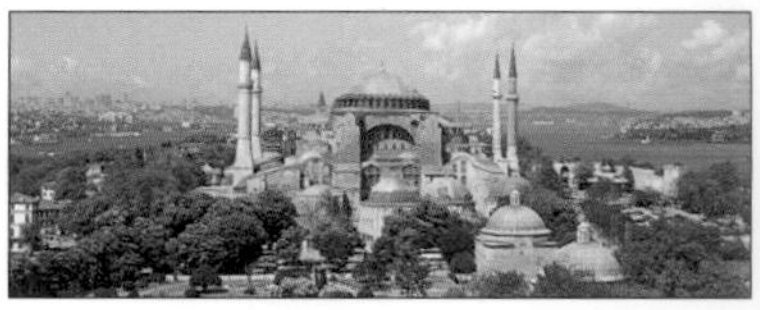

For many centuries, Istanbul has held tremendous strategic importance as a crucial gateway between Europe and Asia. Founded by the Greeks as Byzantium, the city became the center of the East Roman Empire and was known as Constantinople to the Romans. From the 15th century onward the city became the center of the great Ottoman Empire.

TRANSPORTATION & INDUSTRY

TURKEY LEADS THE REGION'S well-diversified economy. Petrochemicals, textiles, engineering, and food processing are the main industries. Azerbaijan is able to export oil, while the other states rely heavily on hydro-electric power and imported fuel. Georgia produces precision machinery. War and earthquake damage have devastated Armenia's infrastructure.

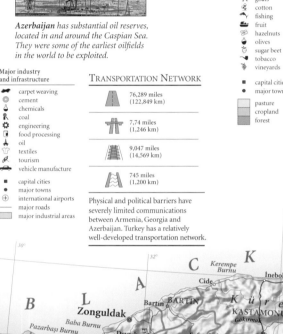

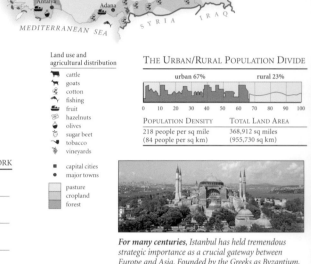

***Azerbaijan** has substantial oil reserves, located in and around the Caspian Sea. They were some of the earliest oilfields in the world to be exploited.*

RUSSIAN FEDERATION
CASPIAN SEA
BULGARIA
GREECE
BLACK SEA
K'ut'aisi
GEORGIA
T'BILISI
Bat'umi
Istanbul
Izmit
Samsun
BAKU
ARMENIA
YEREVAN
AZERBAIJAN
Bursa
ANKARA
Sivas
Erzurum
Izmir
TURKEY
Kayseri
Konya
Diyarbakir
IRAN
Antalya
Adana
Gaziantep
Iskenderun
MEDITERRANEAN SEA
SYRIA
IRAQ

Major industry and infrastructure

- carpet weaving
- cement
- chemicals
- coal
- engineering
- food processing
- oil
- textiles
- tourism
- vehicle manufacture
- capital cities
- major towns
- international airports
- major roads
- major industrial areas

TRANSPORTATION NETWORK

Roads	76,289 miles (122,849 km)
Motorways	7,74 miles (1,246 km)
Railways	9,047 miles (14,569 km)
Waterways	745 miles (1,200 km)

Physical and political barriers have severely limited communications between Armenia, Georgia and Azerbaijan. Turkey has a relatively well-developed transportation network.

114
BULGARIA
GREECE
BLACK SEA
Edirne
Kırklareli
KIRKLARELİ
Igneada Burnu
Kıyıköy
Uzunköprü
Lüleburgaz
Çorlu
İSTANBUL
İstanbul
İstanbul Boğazı (Bosporus)
Beykoz
TEKİRDAĞ
Tekirdağ
EDİRNE
Silivri
Küçük Çekmece
Zonguldak
ZONGULDAK
Bartın
BARTIN
Karabük
KARABÜK
Safranbolu
Kastamonu
KASTAMONU
İnebolu
Cide
Kerempe Burnu
İnce Burnu
Sinop
SİNOP
Ayancık
Gerze
Boyabat
Bafra
Bafra Burnu
Samsun
SAMSUN
Civa Burnu
Çarşamba
Terme
Ünye
Marmara Denizi (Sea of Marmara)
Marmara
Gelibolu
Çanakkale Boğazı (Dardanelles)
Saros Körfezi
İmroz
Gökçeada
Çanakkale
ÇANAKKALE
Bozcaada
Ezine
Erdek
Bandırma
Mudanya
Gemlik
Yalova
YALOVA
İzmit
KOCAELİ
Gebze
Adapazarı
SAKARYA
Düzce
Bolu
BOLU
Gerede
Bursa
BURSA
İnegöl
Uludağ 2543m
Bilecik
BİLECİK
Köroğlu Dağları
Balıkesir
BALIKESİR
Edremit
Edremit Körfezi
Ayvalık
Bergama
Soma
Dikili
Aegean Sea
Eskişehir
ESKİŞEHİR
Kütahya
KÜTAHYA
Sivrihisar
Polatlı
ANKARA
Çankırı
ÇANKIRI
Çorum
ÇORUM
Amasya
AMASYA
Merzifon
Tokat
TOKAT
Kırıkkale
KIRIKKALE
Yozgat
YOZGAT
Sivas
Manisa
MANİSA
Akhisar
İzmir
Çeşme
Uşak
UŞAK
Afyon
AFYON
Kula
Aydın
AYDIN
Kuşadası
Kuşadası Körfezi
Denizli
DENİZLİ
Nazilli
Tuz Gölü
Kırşehir
KIRŞEHİR
Nevşehir
NEVŞEHİR
Kayseri
KAYSERİ
Erciyes Dağı 3917m
Aksaray
AKSARAY
Konya
KONYA
Beyşehir Gölü
Eğirdir Gölü
Isparta
ISPARTA
Burdur
BURDUR
Niğde
NİĞDE
Hasan Dağı 3268m
Muğla
MUĞLA
Bodrum
Gökova Körfezi
Marmaris
Dalaman
Fethiye
Antalya
ANTALYA
Antalya Körfezi
Alanya
Karaman
KARAMAN
Karadağ 2271m
Ereğli
Mersin
İÇEL
Tarsus
Adana
ADANA
Osmaniye
OSMANİYE
Kahramanmaraş
KAHRAMANMARAŞ
Gaziantep
GAZİANTEP
Kilis
KİLİS
İskenderun
İskenderun Körfezi
Antakya
HATAY
Samandağı
Yayladağı
Anamur
Anamur Burnu
Silifke
İncekum Burnu
Toros Dağları
Taurus
ANATOLIA
TURKEY
MEDITERRANEAN SEA
120
114

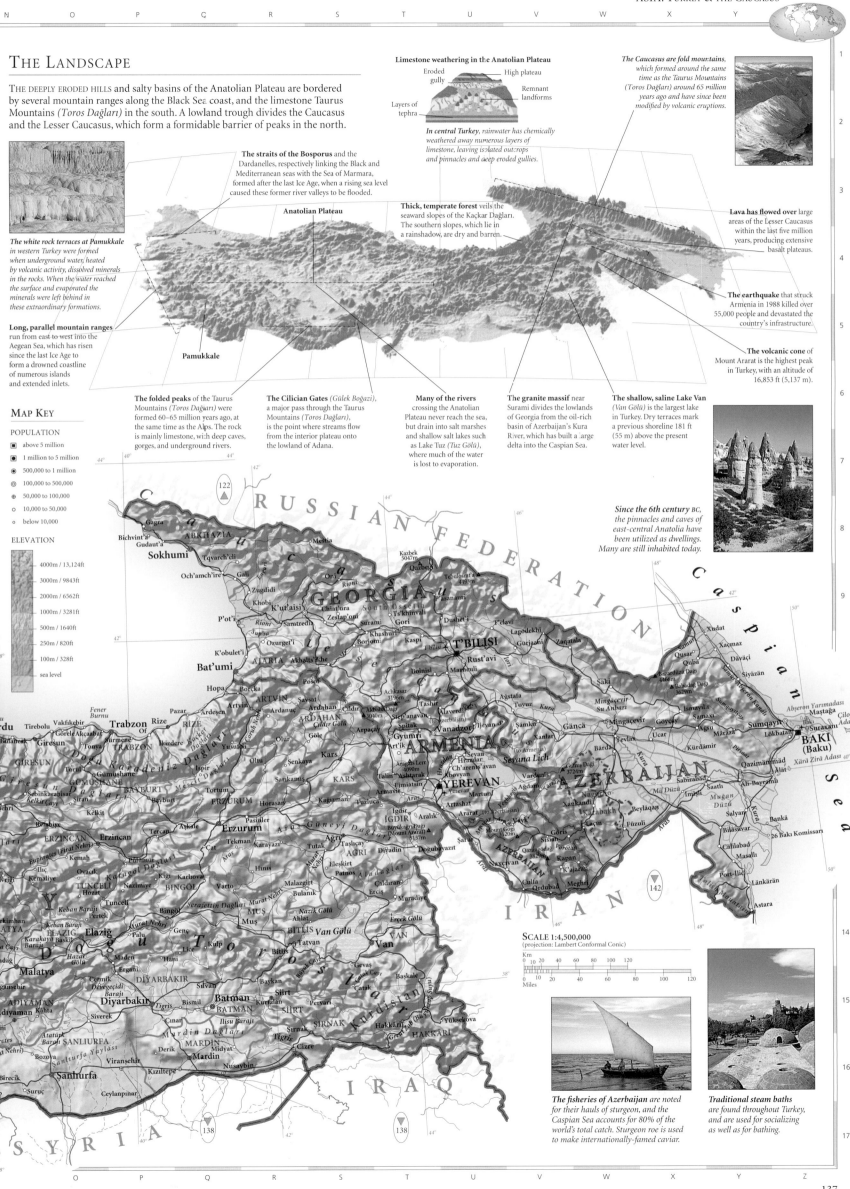

THE LANDSCAPE

THE DEEPLY ERODED HILLS and salty basins of the Anatolian Plateau are bordered by several mountain ranges along the Black Sea coast, and the limestone Taurus Mountains *(Toros Dağları)* in the south. A lowland trough divides the Caucasus and the Lesser Caucasus, which form a formidable barrier of peaks in the north.

Limestone weathering in the Anatolian Plateau

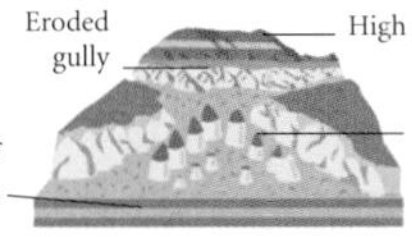
Eroded gully
High plateau
Remnant landforms
Layers of tephra

***In central Turkey**, rainwater has chemically weathered away numerous layers of limestone, leaving isolated outcrops and pinnacles and deep eroded gullies.*

***The Caucasus are fold mountains**, which formed around the same time as the Taurus Mountains (Toros Dağları) around 65 million years ago and have since been modified by volcanic eruptions.*

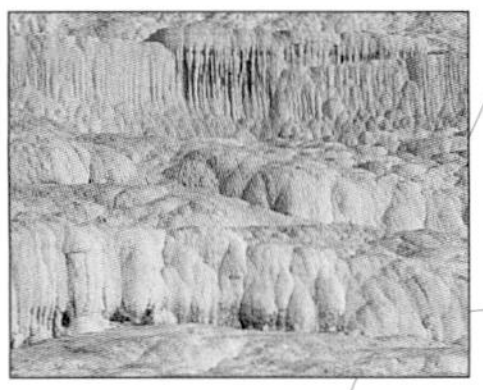

***The white rock terraces at Pamukkale** in western Turkey were formed when underground water, heated by volcanic activity, dissolved minerals in the rocks. When the water reached the surface and evaporated the minerals were left behind in these extraordinary formations.*

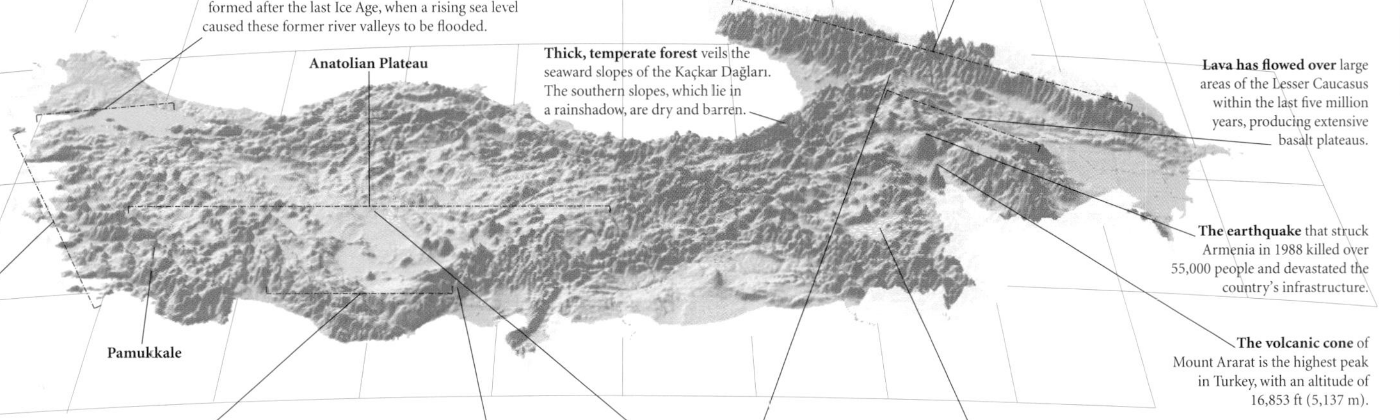
Anatolian Plateau
Pamukkale

The straits of the Bosporus and the Dardanelles, respectively linking the Black and Mediterranean seas with the Sea of Marmara, formed after the last Ice Age, when a rising sea level caused these former river valleys to be flooded.

Thick, temperate forest veils the seaward slopes of the Kaçkar Dağları. The southern slopes, which lie in a rainshadow, are dry and barren.

Lava has flowed over large areas of the Lesser Caucasus within the last five million years, producing extensive basalt plateaus.

Long, parallel mountain ranges run from east to west into the Aegean Sea, which has risen since the last Ice Age to form a drowned coastline of numerous islands and extended inlets.

The earthquake that struck Armenia in 1988 killed over 55,000 people and devastated the country's infrastructure.

The volcanic cone of Mount Ararat is the highest peak in Turkey, with an altitude of 16,853 ft (5,137 m).

The folded peaks of the Taurus Mountains *(Toros Dağları)* were formed 60–65 million years ago, at the same time as the Alps. The rock is mainly limestone, with deep caves, gorges, and underground rivers.

The Cilician Gates *(Gülek Boğazi)*, a major pass through the Taurus Mountains *(Toros Dağları)*, is the point where streams flow from the interior plateau onto the lowland of Adana.

Many of the rivers crossing the Anatolian Plateau never reach the sea, but drain into salt marshes and shallow salt lakes such as Lake Tuz *(Tuz Gölü)*, where much of the water is lost to evaporation.

The granite massif near Surami divides the lowlands of Georgia from the oil-rich basin of Azerbaijan's Kura River, which has built a large delta into the Caspian Sea.

The shallow, saline Lake Van *(Van Gölü)* is the largest lake in Turkey. Dry terraces mark a previous shoreline 181 ft (55 m) above the present water level.

***Since the 6th century BC**, the pinnacles and caves of east-central Anatolia have been utilized as dwellings. Many are still inhabited today.*

MAP KEY

POPULATION

- above 5 million
- 1 million to 5 million
- 500,000 to 1 million
- 100,000 to 500,000
- 50,000 to 100,000
- 10,000 to 50,000
- below 10,000

ELEVATION

- 4000m / 13,124ft
- 3000m / 9843ft
- 2000m / 6562ft
- 1000m / 3281ft
- 500m / 1640ft
- 250m / 820ft
- 100m / 328ft
- sea level

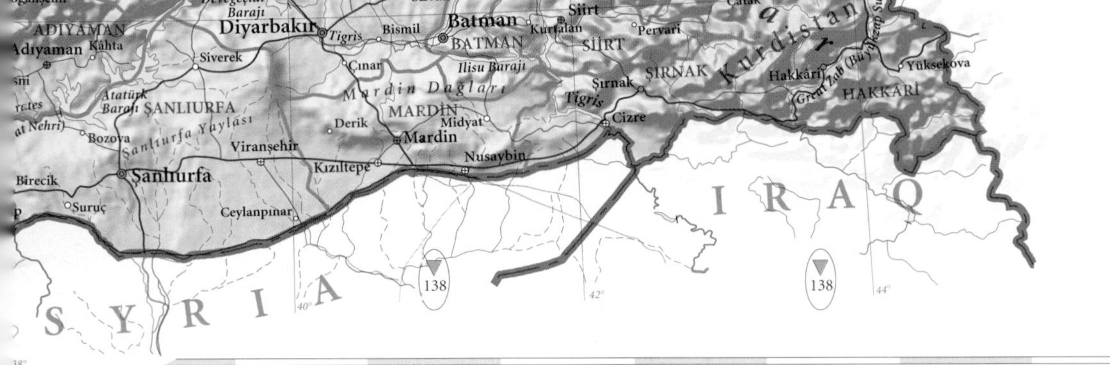
RUSSIAN FEDERATION
Caucasus
GEORGIA
ARMENIA
AZERBAIJAN
IRAN
IRAQ
SYRIA
Caspian Sea
T'BILISI
YEREVAN
BAKI (Baku)
Sokhumi
Bat'umi
K'ut'aisi
Rust'avi
Gyumri
Vanadzor
Gäncä
Sumqayıt
Mingäçevir
Trabzon
Erzurum
Kars
Van
Van Gölü
Batman
Diyarbakır
Malatya
Elazığ
Şanlıurfa
Mardin
Sevana Lich
Kazbek 5047m
Ağrı
Bingöl
Muş
Bitlis
Tatvan
Hakkâri
Abşeron Yarımadası
Länkäran
Astara
Naxçıvan
122
142
138
138

SCALE 1:4,500,000
(projection: Lambert Conformal Conic)

Km 0 10 20 40 60 80 100 120
Miles 0 10 20 40 60 80 100 120

***The fisheries of Azerbaijan** are noted for their hauls of sturgeon, and the Caspian Sea accounts for 80% of the world's total catch. Sturgeon roe is used to make internationally-famed caviar.*

***Traditional steam baths** are found throughout Turkey, and are used for socializing as well as for bathing.*

The Near East

Iraq, Israel, Jordan, Lebanon, Syria

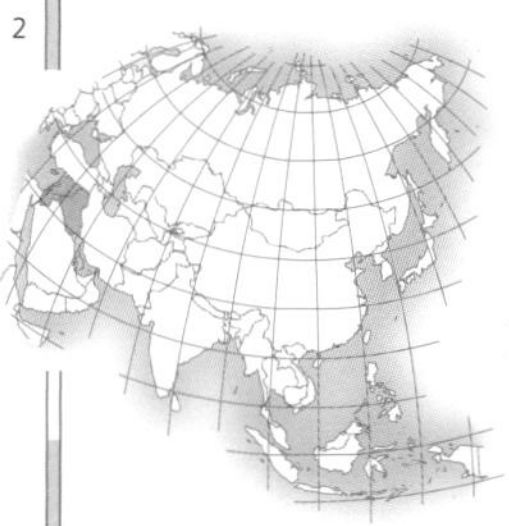

Some of the world's oldest civilizations developed in this region – the Fertile Crescent – which is venerated by Jews, Muslims, and Christians, but torn by competing religious, ethnic, and national claims to the land. Turkish Ottoman rule ended with World War I and the region was divided into areas administered by Britain and France. The UN endorsed calls for a Jewish homeland in what was then Palestine and in 1948 the state of Israel was declared. Hostility toward the Jewish state led to a series of wars with its Arab neighbors. After 2000, attempts to broker peaceful resolutions with both the Palestinian population and with adjacent Arab states were hampered by a revival of Islamic militarism and conflicting international interests in the oil-rich region. This led to an Israeli retrenchment and culminated in a US-led invasion of Iraq in 2003, which toppled the Ba'athist regime of Saddam Hussein in the name of a "war on terror."

TURKEY
Maydān Ikbiz
Halab (Aleppo)
HALAB
Ar Raqqah
Idlib
IDLIB
Al Lādhiqīyah (Latakia)
AL LĀDHIQĪYAH
Ḥamāh
ḤAMĀH
Ṭarṭūs
Ḥimṣ (Homs)
SYRIA
Tudmur (Palmyra)
ḤIMṢ
LEBANON
BEYROUTH (BEIRUT)
DIMASHQ (DAMASCUS)
DIMASHQ
DAR'Ā
AS SUWAYDĀ'
Syrian Desert
Ḥefa (Haifa)
Tel Aviv-Yafo
JERUSALEM
'AMMĀN
Az Zarqā'
AL MAFRAQ
AZ ZARQĀ'
AL 'ĀṢIMAH
Dead Sea
Be'ér Sheva
ISRAEL
AL KARAK
AṬ ṬAFĪLAH
JORDAN
MA'ĀN
Gaza Strip
Khān Yūnis
MEDITERRANEAN SEA
EGYPT
Elat
Al 'Aqabah
Gulf of Aqaba

136

120

140

Using the Land and Sea

Water scarcity limits cropland to the north and to areas watered principally by the Tigris, Euphrates, and Jordan Rivers. In Israel, new irrigation techniques are allowing cultivation in the arid Negev. Wheat is the chief grain and large areas of scrub support livestock herding. Commercial produce includes dates, tobacco, citrus fruits, olives, grapes, and cotton, which is Syria's main export crop. Fishing is still important in the Mediterranean.

The Urban/Rural Population Divide

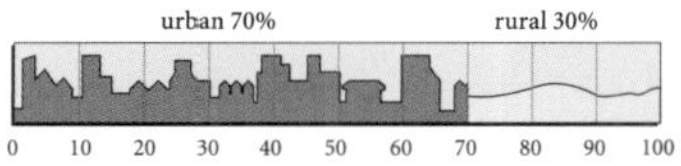

urban 70%
rural 30%
0 10 20 30 40 50 60 70 80 90 100

Population Density	Total Land Area
163 people per sq mile (63 people per sq km)	325,460 sq miles (843,160 sq km)

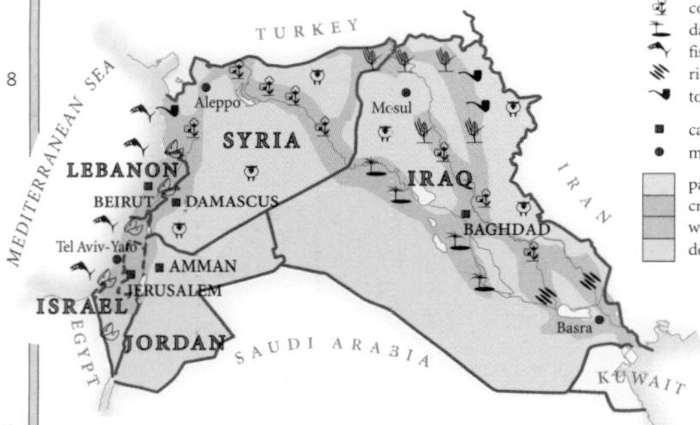

TURKEY
MEDITERRANEAN SEA
Aleppo
SYRIA
Mosul
IRAQ
IRAN
LEBANON
BEIRUT
DAMASCUS
BAGHDAD
Tel Aviv-Yafo
AMMAN
JERUSALEM
ISRAEL
JORDAN
EGYPT
SAUDI ARABIA
Basra
KUWAIT
Land use and agricultural distribution
sheep
cereals
citrus fruits
cotton
dates
fishing
rice
tobacco
capital cities
major towns
pasture
cropland
wetland
desert

Transportation & Industry

The petrochemical industry is well established, and central to the economies of Syria and Iraq, which was the world's second largest oil exporter before the war with Iran which began in 1980. Lebanon has traditionally been a center for commerce, while Israel has a well-diversified economy with an expanding tourist industry, despite few natural resources.

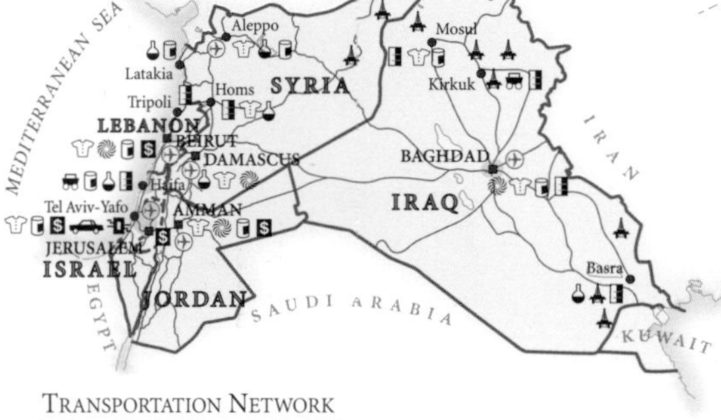

TURKEY
MEDITERRANEAN SEA
Aleppo
Mosul
Latakia
Homs
SYRIA
Kirkuk
Tripoli
LEBANON
BEIRUT
DAMASCUS
BAGHDAD
IRAQ
IRAN
Haifa
Tel Aviv-Yafo
AMMAN
JERUSALEM
ISRAEL
JORDAN
EGYPT
SAUDI ARABIA
Basra
KUWAIT
Major industry and infrastructure
car manufacture
cement
chemicals
electronics
finance
food processing
iron & steel
oil
oil refining
textiles
capital cities
major towns
international airports
major roads
major industrial areas

Transportation Network

- 75,427 miles (121,461 km)
- 1,468 miles (2,364 km)
- 3,271 miles (5,267 km)
- 498 miles (802 km)

Jordan's seaport of Al 'Aqabah is connected to Damascus in Syria by road and rail. This route to the Red Sea provides for large exports of phosphate and trade with states in The Persian Gulf.

The Dome of the Rock in Jerusalem is a magnificent mosque, revered by Muslims. Close by is the Wailing Wall, the city's most sacred Jewish landmark and the Church of the Holy Sepulchre, a famous Christian place of worship.

The city of Petra, carved from spectacular rose-colored limestone, lies deep within a canyon in southern Jordan. Revenues from the spice trade funded the construction of the city which was built by the Nabatean people in about 400 BC.

Water and wind erosion over thousands of years have created the Canyon of the Oasis at En 'Avedat in the Negev Desert (HaNegev). Extreme diurnal temperature fluctuations, coupled with wind erosion, have caused layers of rock to crack and peel away.

The Landscape

The Al Jazirah plateau divides the Euphrates and Tigris Rivers, which cross the Mesopotamian plain to reach their confluence in the southeast. The rocky Syrian Desert extends west to the northern extremity of the Great Rift Valley, which runs from the mountains of Lebanon to the Gulf of Aqaba. The River Jordan flows south along this trough into the Dead Sea, divided from the Mediterranean coastal plain by a steep-sided plateau.

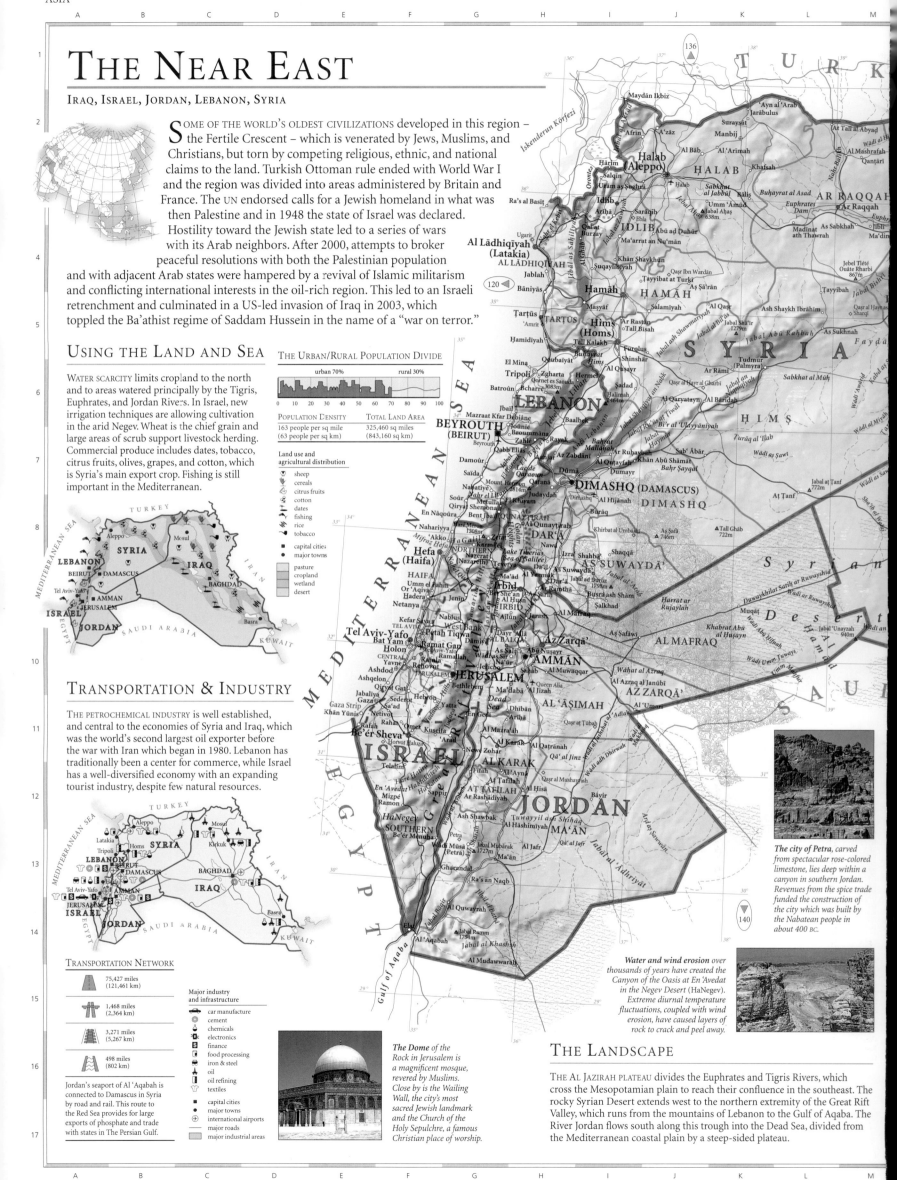

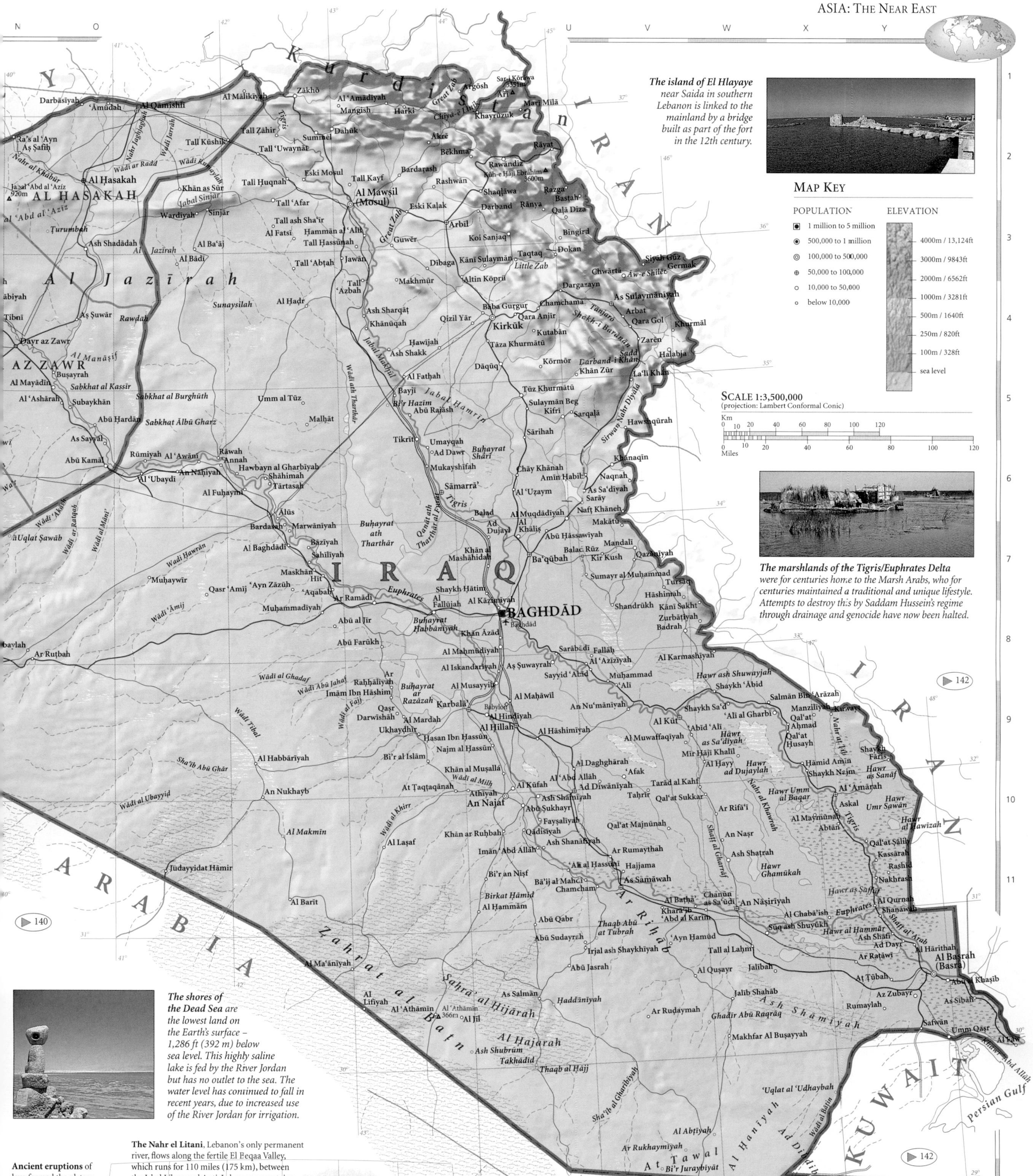
N O P Q R S T U V W X Y Z
1 2 3 4 5 6 7 8 9 10 11 15 16 17
Kurdistan
IRAN
IRAQ
BAGHDĀD
ARABIA
KUWAIT
Al Jazīrah
AL ḤASAKAH
AZ ZAWR
Al Mawṣil (Mosul)
Arbīl
Kirkūk
As Sulaymānīyah
Tikrīt
Sāmarrā'
Ba'qūbah
Al Fallūjah
Ar Ramādī
Karbalā'
Al Ḥillah
An Najaf
Ad Dīwānīyah
Al Kūt
Al 'Amārah
An Nāṣirīyah
Al Baṣrah (Basra)
Umm Qaṣr
Al Fāw
Ar Rutbah
Euphrates
Tigris
Great Zab
Little Zab
Persian Gulf
Zahrat al Baṭn
Ash Shāmīyah
Al Hajārah
Buḥayrat ath Tharthār
Hawr al Ḥammār
Ar Rimāh
Al Ḥaniyah
Ad Dibdibah
At Tawal
140
142

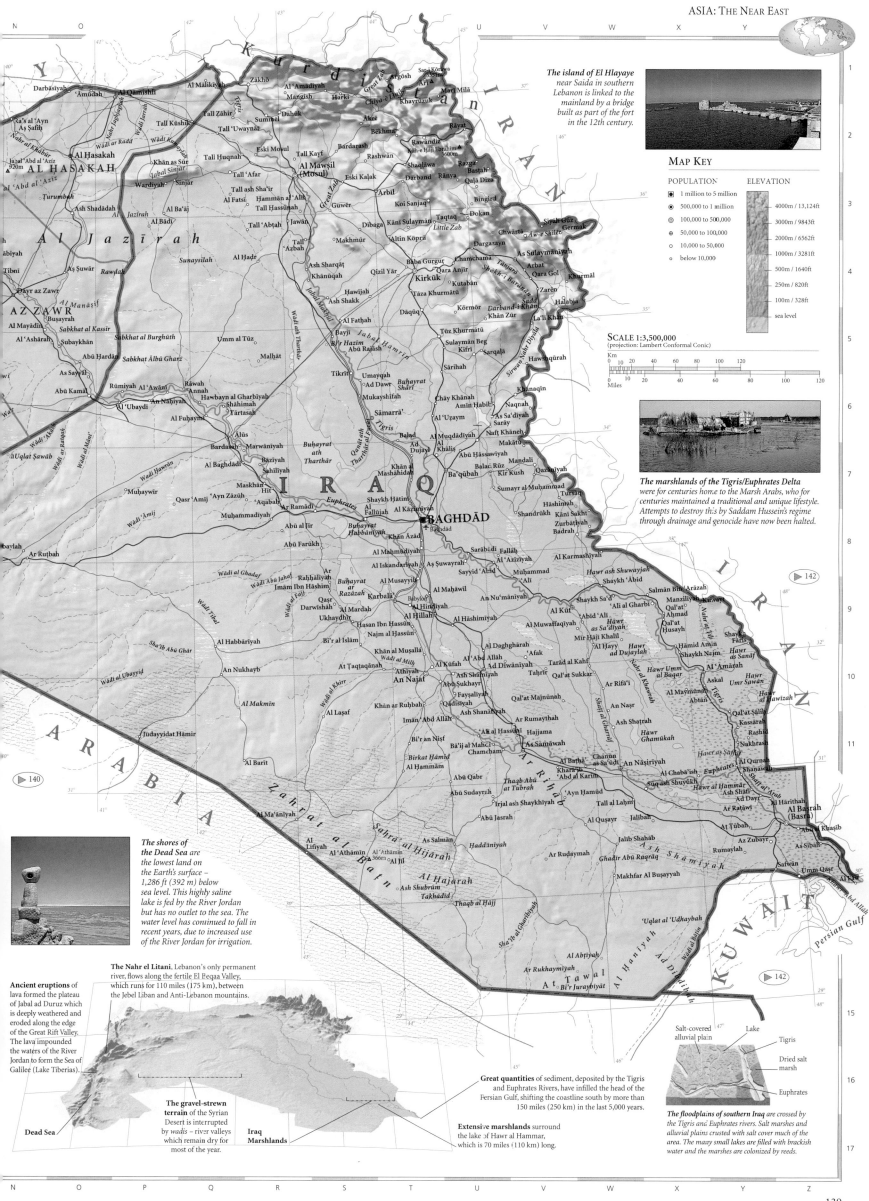

The island of El Hlayaye near Saida in southern Lebanon is linked to the mainland by a bridge built as part of the fort in the 12th century.

MAP KEY

POPULATION

- ■ 1 million to 5 million
- ◉ 500,000 to 1 million
- ◎ 100,000 to 500,000
- ⊕ 50,000 to 100,000
- ○ 10,000 to 50,000
- ∘ below 10,000

ELEVATION

- 4000m / 13,124ft
- 3000m / 9843ft
- 2000m / 6562ft
- 1000m / 3281ft
- 500m / 1640ft
- 250m / 820ft
- 100m / 328ft
- sea level

SCALE 1:3,500,000
(projection: Lambert Conformal Conic)

Km 0 10 20 40 60 80 100 120

Miles 0 10 20 40 60 80 100 120

The marshlands of the Tigris/Euphrates Delta were for centuries home to the Marsh Arabs, who for centuries maintained a traditional and unique lifestyle. Attempts to destroy this by Saddam Hussein's regime through drainage and genocide have now been halted.

The shores of the Dead Sea are the lowest land on the Earth's surface – 1,286 ft (392 m) below sea level. This highly saline lake is fed by the River Jordan but has no outlet to the sea. The water level has continued to fall in recent years, due to increased use of the River Jordan for irrigation.

Ancient eruptions of lava formed the plateau of Jabal ad Duruz which is deeply weathered and eroded along the edge of the Great Rift Valley. The lava impounded the waters of the River Jordan to form the Sea of Galilee (Lake Tiberias).

The Nahr el Litani, Lebanon's only permanent river, flows along the fertile El Beqaa Valley, which runs for 110 miles (175 km), between the Jebel Liban and Anti-Lebanon mountains.

Dead Sea

The gravel-strewn terrain of the Syrian Desert is interrupted by *wadis* – river valleys which remain dry for most of the year.

Iraq Marshlands

Extensive marshlands surround the lake of Hawr al Hammar, which is 70 miles (110 km) long.

Great quantities of sediment, deposited by the Tigris and Euphrates Rivers, have infilled the head of the Persian Gulf, shifting the coastline south by more than 150 miles (250 km) in the last 5,000 years.

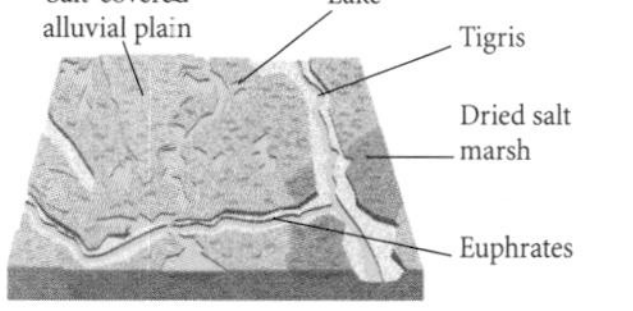
Salt-covered alluvial plain
Lake
Tigris
Dried salt marsh
Euphrates

The floodplains of southern Iraq are crossed by the Tigris and Euphrates rivers. Salt marshes and alluvial plains crusted with salt cover much of the area. The many small lakes are filled with brackish water and the marshes are colonized by reeds.

The Arabian Peninsula

Bahrain, Kuwait, Oman, Qatar, Saudi Arabia, United Arab Emirates (UAE), Yemen

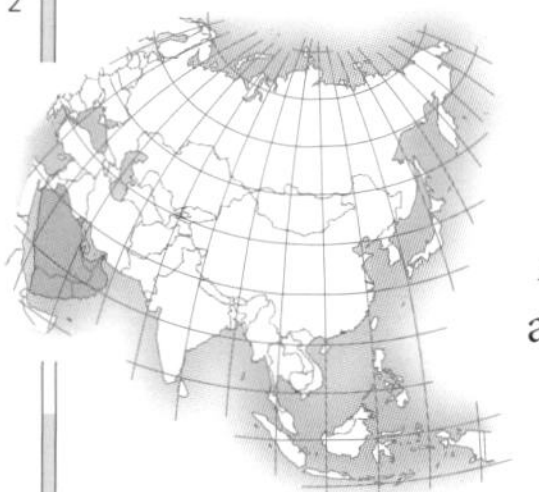

Huge expanses of desert cover much of the Arabian Peninsula, limiting settlement to oases, the mountains along the Red Sea and coastal belts. The most populous area is the fertile highlands of Yemen. The Islamic faith and Arabic language give the region a cultural and religious unity, and the Saudi city of Mecca *(Makkah)* is Islam's most holy place, visited by over two million pilgrims each year. More than half the world's oil reserves are contained in this region, and the exploitation of oil and gas has brought great wealth, particularly to Saudi Arabia. Yemen and Oman are the least developed of the Arabian states, with large rural populations. Within Saudi Arabia over two-thirds of the people live in urban areas.

Using the Land

Most of the Arabian Peninsula is unsuited to settled agriculture, making irrigation and land reclamation projects essential. The narrow coastal plain and isolated oases, commonly amounting to less than 1% of the land area, are used to cultivate grains, coffee, and exotic fruits. Goats, sheep, and camels are widespread throughout the region.

The Urban/Rural Population Divide

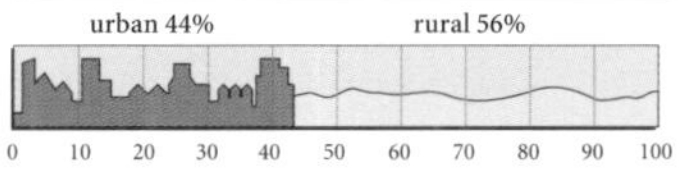

urban 44%
rural 56%
0 10 20 30 40 50 60 70 80 90 100

Population Density	Total Land Area
37 people per sq mile	1,147,856 sq miles
(14 people per sq km)	(2,973,720 sq km)

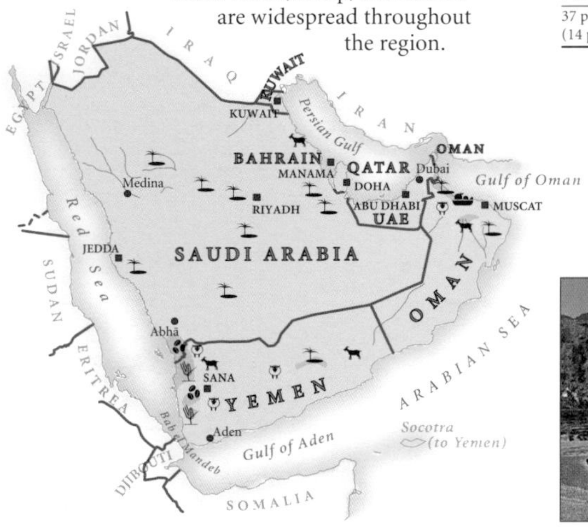

ISRAEL
JORDAN
IRAQ
KUWAIT
KUWAIT
IRAN
Persian Gulf
EGYPT
BAHRAIN
MANAMA
QATAR
DOHA
Dubai
ABU DHABI
UAE
OMAN
MUSCAT
Gulf of Oman
Medina
RIYADH
JEDDA
SAUDI ARABIA
Red Sea
SUDAN
OMAN
Abha
SANA
YEMEN
ARABIAN SEA
ERITREA
Aden
Bab el Mandeb
Gulf of Aden
Socotra (to Yemen)
DJIBOUTI
SOMALIA
Land use and agricultural distribution
goats
sheep
cereals
coffee
dates
fruit
capital cities
major towns
pasture
cropland
desert

The fertile soils of Yemen have encouraged settlement of almost all of the land from sea level up to the mountains at 10,000 ft (3,050 m). In the higher reaches elaborate terraces have been constructed to facilitate crop cultivation.

The Landscape

A plateau more than 2,500 ft (760 m) high extends across much of the Arabian Peninsula. The plateau slopes eastward from the massive, rifted escarpment along the coast of the Red Sea, to the shallow waters of the Persian Gulf. The interior is characterized by *cuestas* and valleys, drained by a system of *wadis*. A crescent of sand and gravel deserts lies to the east.

The An Nafud Desert is covered with *barchan* dunes varying between 30–100 ft (10–30 m) high. The "horns" of the crescent-shaped dunes reflect the direction in which they are being moved by the wind.

Inselbergs are dotted over a wide area of the Najd Plateau. These resistant remnants of the ancient basement rock are left standing when the softer weathered rock has been worn away.

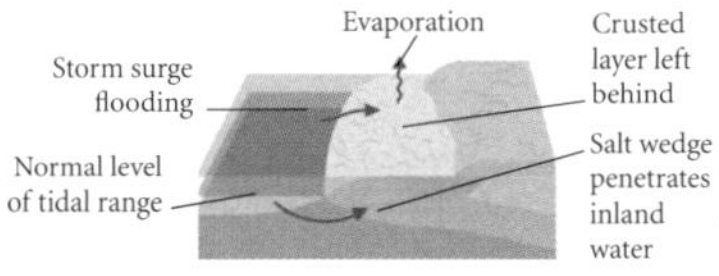

Evaporation
Storm surge flooding
Crusted layer left behind
Normal level of tidal range
Salt wedge penetrates inland water

A sabkha is a flat, salt-encrusted plain which occurs near the coast just above the high water mark. Flooding by sea water leads to saturation of the land with saline-rich groundwater. As this evaporates, a cracked layer of sand, cemented together with salt, gypsum, and calcium carbonate is left behind.

Few areas in the Arabian Peninsula have rivers flowing through them. Most are drained by ephemeral watercourses called *wadis*.

Across the Najd Plateau the flat relief is broken by *mesas;* steep-sided rock plateaus and *cuestas;* ridges with one steep and one gentle slope.

The Hejaz *(Al Ḥijāz)* and Asir Mountains form part of the same geological region as the highlands of Sudan and Eritrea, to which they were once joined. They were separated when faulting opened the Red Sea, over 50 million years ago.

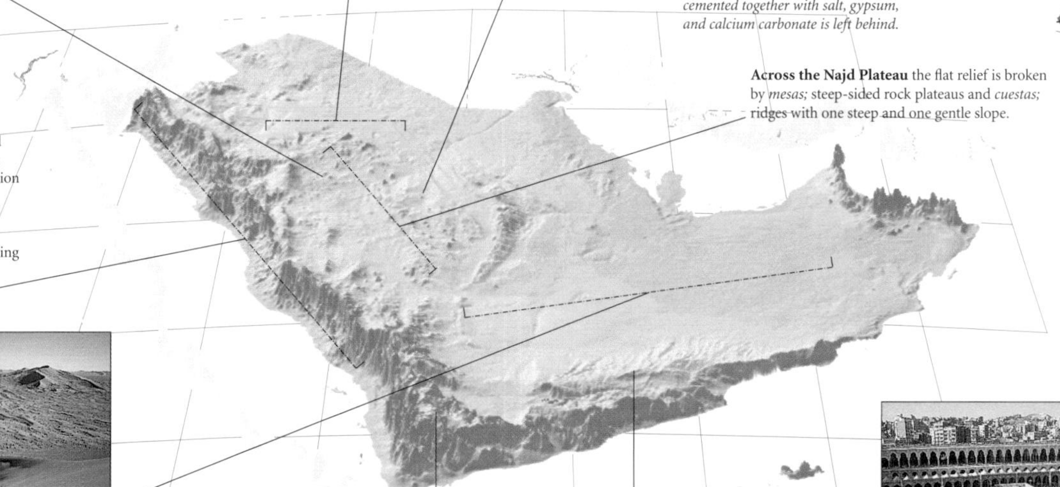

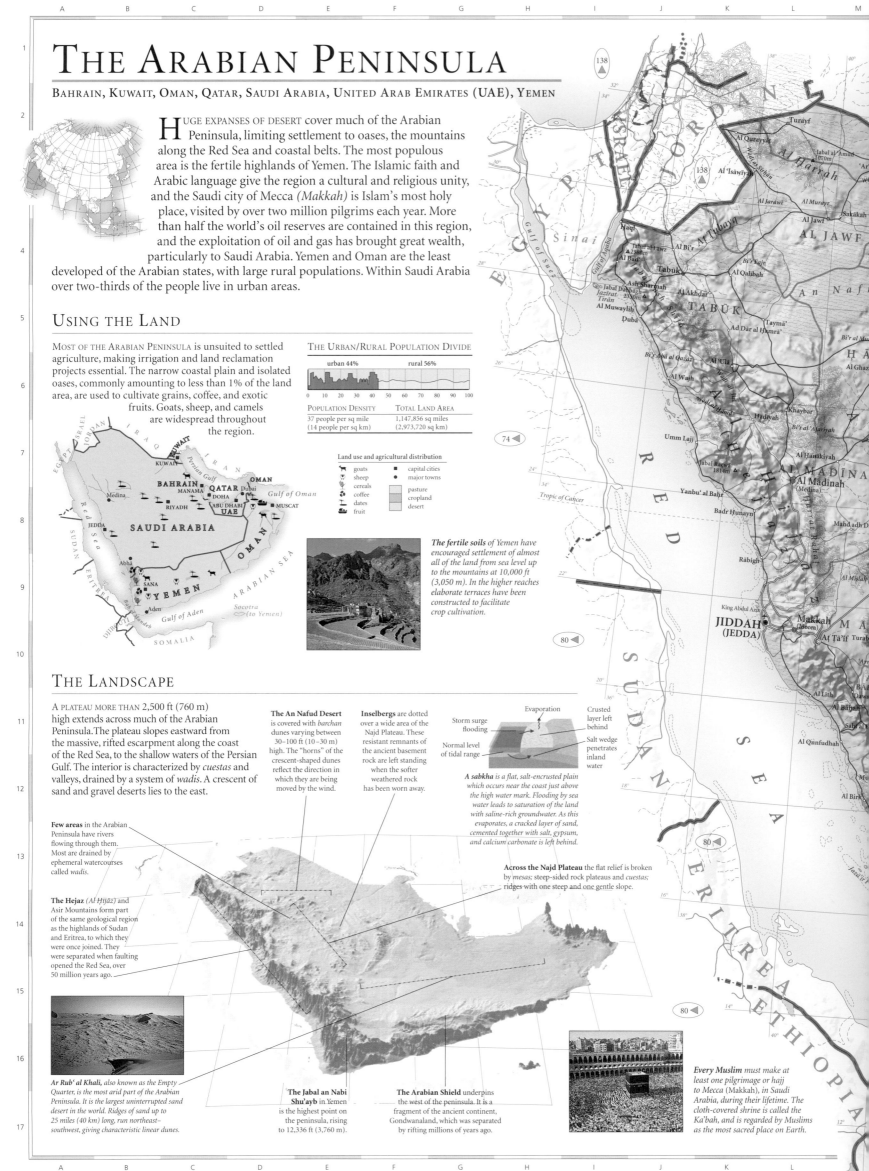

Ar Rub' al Khali, also known as the Empty Quarter, is the most arid part of the Arabian Peninsula. It is the largest uninterrupted sand desert in the world. Ridges of sand up to 25 miles (40 km) long, run northeast–southwest, giving characteristic linear dunes.

The Jabal an Nabi Shu'ayb in Yemen is the highest point on the peninsula, rising to 12,336 ft (3,760 m).

The Arabian Shield underpins the west of the peninsula. It is a fragment of the ancient continent, Gondwanaland, which was separated by rifting millions of years ago.

Every Muslim must make at least one pilgrimage or hajj to Mecca (Makkah), in Saudi Arabia, during their lifetime. The cloth-covered shrine is called the Ka'bah, and is regarded by Muslims as the most sacred place on Earth.

138
ISRAEL
JORDAN
EGYPT
Sinai
Gulf of Suez
Gulf of Aqaba
Turayf
Al Qurayyat
Al Harrah
Al 'Isawiyah
Al Jarawi
Al Murayr
Sakakah
Al Jawf
AL JAWF
Haql
Al Bi'r
Al Tubayq
Al Bad'
Tabuk
Bi'r Fajr
Al Qalibah
Ash Sharmah
Jazirat Tiran
Al Akhdar
An Nafud
Al Muwaylih
TABUK
Tayma'
Duba
Ad Dar al Hamra'
Bi'r Aba al Qazaz
Al 'Ula
Al Wajh
74
Umm Lajj
Khaybar
Hadiyah
Al Hanakiyah
Jabal Radwa 1814m
Yanbu' al Bahr
AL MADINA
Al Madinah (Medina)
Tropic of Cancer
Badr Hunayn
Mahd adh Dh
RED SEA
Rabigh
King Abdul Aziz
JIDDAH (JEDDA)
Makkah (Mecca)
At Ta'if
80
Al Lith
Al Qunfudhah
SUDAN
ERITREA
ETHIOPIA

***Saudi Arabia** contains the world's largest oil reserves, lying mainly along the Persian Gulf coast. Each day the region produces 8.3 million barrels of oil. Here, in the desert, excess oil is being burnt off.*

TRANSPORTATION & INDUSTRY

THE EXTRACTION AND REFINING OF OIL AND GAS are the major industrial activities in the Arabian Peninsula. The region also has an active construction sector, with many Arab cities reflecting the wealth generated by the oil industry. The service sector is dominated by financial and technical institutions, which, like the construction sector, mainly serve the oil industry. Traditional handicrafts such as carpet-weaving are found in rural areas.

TRANSPORTATION NETWORK

Roads	65,239 miles (105,054 km)	Air	2,071 miles (3,333 km)
Railways	864 miles (1,392 km)	Waterways	none

Internal surface transportation is poorly developed across the peninsula. Along the coast, commercial routes have developed, but connections between bordering states rely on major airports.

KUWAIT
BAHRAIN
QATAR
OMAN
UAE
SAUDI ARABIA
YEMEN
IRAQ
IRAN
JORDAN
ISRAEL
EGYPT
SUDAN
ERITREA
DJIBOUTI
SOMALIA
Red Sea
Persian Gulf
Gulf of Oman
Gulf of Aden
ARABIAN SEA
KUWAIT
Al Jubayl
Ad Dammam
MANAMA
DOHA
ABU DHABI
Dubai
MUSCAT
Yanbu' al Bahr
RIYADH
JEDDAH
SANA
Aden
Al Mukalla
Socotra (to Yemen)
Bab el Mandeb

Major industry and infrastructure
- cement
- chemicals
- iron & steel
- oil
- oil refining
- food processing
- capital cities
- major towns
- international airports
- major roads
- major industrial areas

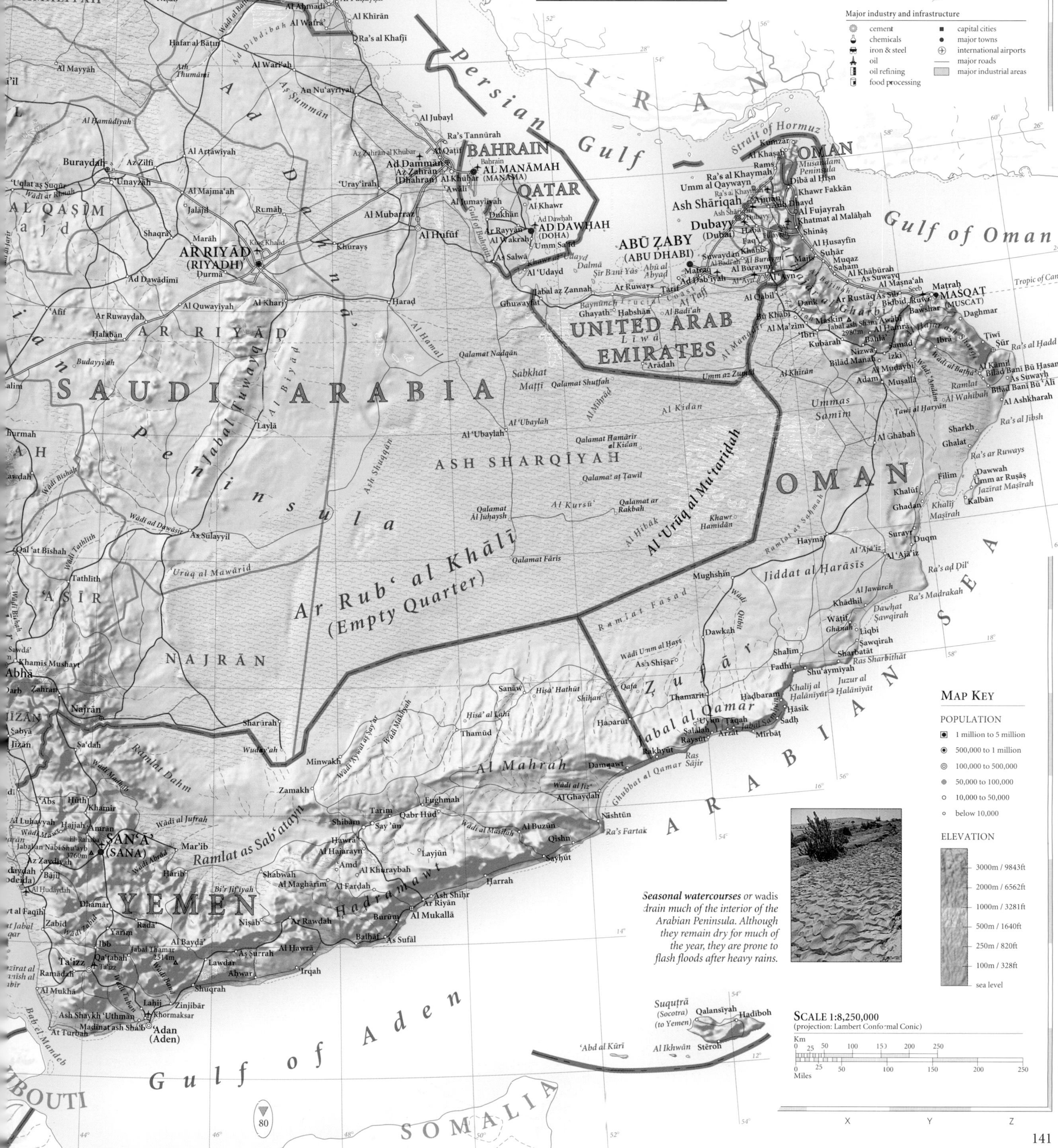
IRAQ
IRAN
KUWAIT
AL KUWAYT (KUWAIT)
BAHRAIN
AL MANĀMAH (MANAMA)
QATAR
AD DAWḤAH (DOHA)
UNITED ARAB EMIRATES
ABŪ ẒABY (ABU DHABI)
Dubayy (Dubai)
OMAN
MASQAṬ (MUSCAT)
SAUDI ARABIA
AR RIYĀḌ (RIYADH)
YEMEN
ṢAN'Ā' (SANA)
'Adan (Aden)
Persian Gulf
Gulf of Oman
Strait of Hormuz
Tropic of Cancer
ARABIAN SEA
Gulf of Aden
Bab el Mandeb
DJIBOUTI
SOMALIA
Ar Rub' al Khālī (Empty Quarter)
Ad Dahnā'
Arabian Peninsula
ASH SHARQĪYAH
NAJRĀN
AR RIYĀḌ
AL QAṢĪM
ḤAḌRAMAWT
Al Mahrah
Ramlat as Sab'atayn
Jiddat al Ḥarāsīs
Al 'Urūq al Mu'tariḍah
Ẓufār
Suquṭrā (Socotra) (to Yemen)
Hadiboh
Al Mukallā
Ṣalālah
Ta'izz
Al Ḥudaydah
Jiddah
Buraydah
Al Hufūf
Ad Dammām
Al Jubayl
Ra's al Khaymah
Ash Shāriqah
Ṣuḥār
Ṣūr
Nizwá
Ma'rib
Shabwah
Najrān
Abhā

***Seasonal watercourses** or wadis drain much of the interior of the Arabian Peninsula. Although they remain dry for much of the year, they are prone to flash floods after heavy rains.*

MAP KEY

POPULATION
- 1 million to 5 million
- 500,000 to 1 million
- 100,000 to 500,000
- 50,000 to 100,000
- 10,000 to 50,000
- below 10,000

ELEVATION
- 3000m / 9843ft
- 2000m / 6562ft
- 1000m / 3281ft
- 500m / 1640ft
- 250m / 820ft
- 100m / 328ft
- sea level

SCALE 1:8,250,000
(projection: Lambert Conformal Conic)

Km 0 25 50 100 150 200 250
Miles 0 25 50 100 150 200 250

138
142
80

Iran & the Gulf States

Bahrain, Iran, Kuwait, Qatar, United Arab Emirates (UAE)

The discovery of oil in the Persian Gulf in the 1930s brought great wealth to the surrounding states. The revenue was largely used to modernize industry and infrastructure, initiating great social change in these formerly agrarian countries. Today, over 80% of the people in the Gulf states live in urban areas, and foreign nationals make up a sizeable proportion of the population in Kuwait, Qatar, and the United Arab Emirates. The importance of control of the oil reserves has led to a number of territorial disputes, including most recently the Iran–Iraq War (1980-88) and the First Gulf War (1991). Islam is practiced almost exclusively throughout the region and two distinct strands are found; Sunni Muslims in Qatar, Kuwait, and UAE, and Shi'a Muslims in Iran and Bahrain. In 1979 Iran became the world's largest theocracy.

The Landscape

The land rises steeply from the fragmented coastal lowlands bordering the Persian Gulf, to reach Iran's interior plateau, bounded by heavily-eroded mountain chains. An unstable plate boundary runs northwest to southeast across Iran causing frequent earthquakes. On the sandy west coast of the Persian Gulf, the relief is generally flat, with patches of salt marsh. Bahrain consists of two groups of islands, which are mostly small and rocky.

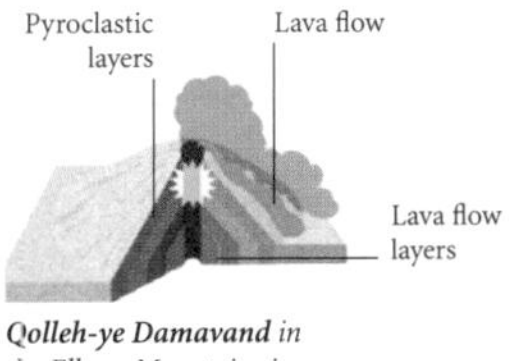
Pyroclastic layers
Lava flow
Lava flow layers

Qolleh-ye Damavand in the Elburz Mountains is a composite volcano. It comprises layers of lava and pyroclasts fragmentary rocks which accumulate on the slopes of the volcano after being ejected into the air.

***Marine sediments** from deep beneath the ancient Tethys Sea have been uplifted to form the Elburz Mountains, which stretch along the shores of the Caspian Sea, northern Iran.*

Lava and ash from previous volcanic activity covers a 200-mile (320-km) stretch from the border with Azerbaijan to the Caspian Sea.

Iran's two mountain chains, the Zagros and Elburz, were uplifted at the same time as the Alps in Europe, when the African Plate collided with the Eurasian Plate.

Caspian Sea

Qolleh-ye Damavand

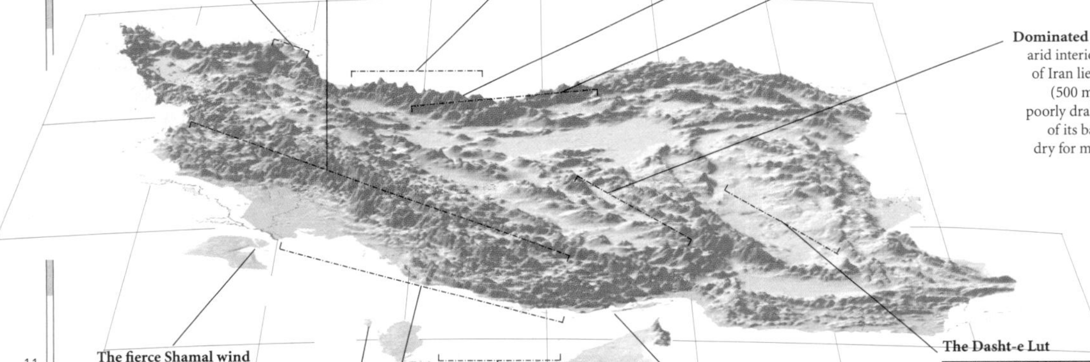

Dominated by a vast, semi-arid interior plateau, most of Iran lies above 1,640 ft (500 m). The region is poorly drained with many of its basins remaining dry for months at a time.

The fierce Shamal wind affects much of this region. Every summer it blows dust south from the flood plains of the Tigris and Euphrates, reducing visibility to such an extent that Kuwait International Airport is frequently forced to close.

The oilfields of The Gulf are formed from marine shale deposits lying in sedimentary basins at the margins of the Zagros Mountains.

Autumn winds blowing across The Gulf can reach speeds of up to 95 mph (150 kmph) causing severe storms, squalls, and waterspouts.

The Dasht-e Lut

***The Dasht-e Lut** covers a large portion of eastern Iran with its dry, wind-eroded plain of scattered sandstone pillars and salty depressions. During the summer, temperatures soar, making it one of the world's hottest, driest places.*

Prolific springs tapping artesian water make cultivation possible across the north of Bahrain's main island. This provides a sharp contrast to the sandy plains in the south and west.

Numerous islands lie along the southern coast of the Persian Gulf. Some of these are salt domes, created when less dense salts were displaced and forced up to the surface by denser, overlying strata.

Using the Land and Sea

ARMENIA
AZERBAIJAN
TURKEY
Tabriz
Caspian Sea
TURKMENISTAN
Mashhad
TEHRAN
IRAQ
IRAN
Esfahan
AFGHANISTAN
Abadan
KUWAIT
KUWAIT
Shiraz
Kerman
PAKISTAN
SAUDI ARABIA
Persian Gulf
Bandar-e 'Abbas
BAHRAIN
MANAMA
QATAR
DOHA
ABU DHABI
Gulf of Oman
U.A.E.
OMAN

Along the coast of the Caspian Sea, desalinated water allows fruits and vegetables to be produced, although water shortages and desert soils still limit farming. Sheep are the most important livestock raised in Iran and commercial forests cover the northwest of the country. Shrimp stocks were decimated by pollution during the Gulf War, but fishing remains important for domestic and export markets.

Land use and agricultural distribution

- goats
- sheep
- cereals
- citrus fruits
- cotton
- dates
- fishing
- timber
- capital cities
- major towns
- pasture
- cropland
- forest
- desert
- wetland

***All of the Gulf states** have commercial fishing fleets. Before the discovery of oil, fishing was the region's leading industry.*

The Urban/Rural Population Divide

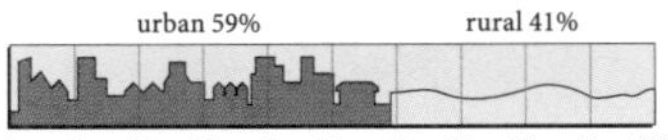
urban 59%
rural 41%
0 10 20 30 40 50 60 70 80 90 100

Population Density	Total Land Area
118 people per sq mile (46 people per sq km)	642,883 sq miles (1,665,500 sq km)

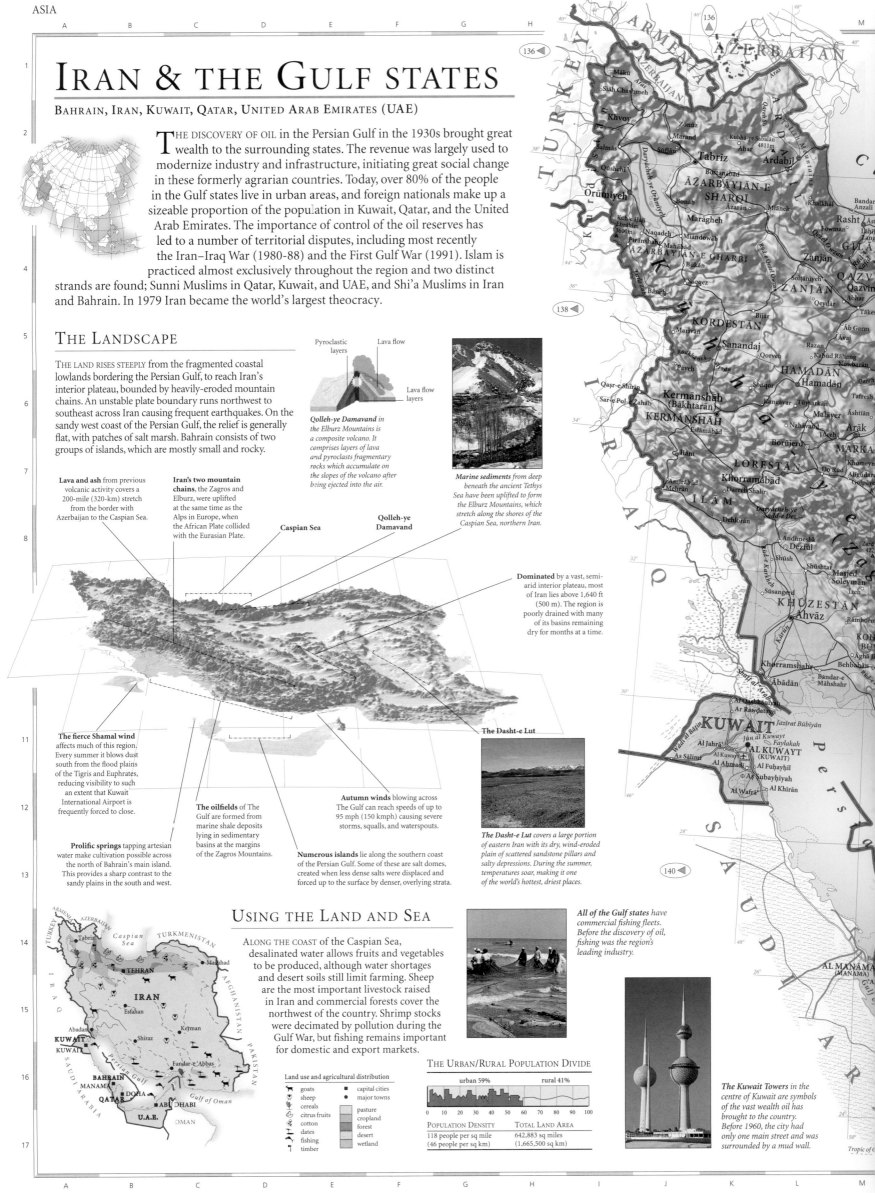

***The Kuwait Towers** in the centre of Kuwait are symbols of the vast wealth of the city has brought to the country. Before 1960, the city had only one main street and was surrounded by a mud wall.*

ARMENIA
AZERBAIJAN
TURKEY
Mākū
Siāh Chashmeh
Khvoy
Salmās
Qūshchī
Orūmīyeh
Marand
Tabrīz
Ahar
Ardabīl
ĀZARBĀYJĀN-E SHARQĪ
Bonāb
Marāgheh
Mīāneh
Naqadeh
Mahābād
Mīāndowāb
ĀZARBĀYJĀN-E GHARBĪ
Bukān
Saqqez
Bāneh
Zanjān
ZANJĀN
Qazvīn
Rasht
KORDESTĀN
Marīvān
Sanandaj
Bījār
HAMADĀN
Hamadān
Qasr-e Shīrīn
Kermānshāh (Bākhtarān)
KERMĀNSHĀH
Eslāmābād
Īlām
LORESTĀN
Khorramābād
Borūjerd
Malāyer
Arāk
ĪLĀM
Dehlorān
Dezfūl
Shūsh
Shūshtar
KHŪZESTĀN
Ahvāz
Khorramshahr
Ābādān
Bandar-e Māhshahr
Behbahān
IRAQ
KUWAIT
Al Jahrā'
AL KUWAYT (KUWAIT)
Al Ahmadī
Al Fuhayhīl
Aş Şubayhīyah
Al Wafrā'
Al Khīrān
Jazīrat Būbīyān
SAUDI ARABIA
AL MANĀMA (MANAMA)
Tropic of Cancer

136
138
140

Many volcanoes lie in Iran's 1,200 mile (1930 km) volcanic belt, including the country's highest peak, the now-extinct Qolleh-ye Damavand at 18,600 ft (5,671 m).

146

Extensive oil and gas exploitation in the Gulf region has allowed the economic transformation of the Gulf states. Kuwait and the United Arab Emirates today have the highest per capita incomes in the world.

TURKMENISTAN
AFGHANISTAN
PAKISTAN
IRAN
Caspian Sea
GOLESTĀN
MĀZANDARĀN
SEMNĀN
KHORĀSĀN
EṢFAHĀN
YAZD
KERMĀN
FĀRS
HORMOZGĀN
SĪSTĀN VA BALŪCHESTĀN
TEHRĀN
QOM
Mashhad
Eṣfahān
Yazd
Kermān
Shīrāz
Zāhedān
Bandar-e 'Abbās
Dasht-e Kavīr
Dasht-e Lūt
Iranian Plateau
Zagros Mountains
Kūhhā-ye Alborz (Elburz Mountains)
Strait of Hormuz
Gulf of Oman
Makran Coast
QATAR
AD DAWḤAH (DOHA)
BAHRAIN
UNITED ARAB EMIRATES
ABŪ ẒABY (ABU DHABI)
Dubayy (Dubai)
OMAN
Tropic of Cancer

148

148

TRANSPORTATION & INDUSTRY

BOTH ONSHORE AND OFFSHORE oil reserves are exploited throughout the region. Kuwait not only extracts but also refines 80% of its oil. Bahrain has diversified its economy to become the main commercial and financial center in the Persian Gulf. Iran produces a wide range of products: textile mills are widespread and carpet weaving is an important export industry.

Caspian Sea
TURKMENISTAN
IRAN
TEHRAN
Tabriz
Rasht
Gorgan
Mashhad
Qom
Kermanshah
Esfahan
Birjand
Ahvaz
Abadan
KUWAIT
Shiraz
Kerman
Zahedan
Bandar-e Bushehr
Bandar-e 'Abbas
BAHRAIN
MANAMA
DOHA
QATAR
Dubai
ABU DHABI
U.A.E.
OMAN
Gulf of Oman
Persian Gulf
SAUDI ARABIA
IRAQ
AFGHANISTAN
PAKISTAN

Major industry and infrastructure

	carpet manufacture		capital city
	chemicals		major towns
	finance		international airports
	food processing		major roads
	oil		major industrial areas
	oil refining		
	textiles		

TRANSPORTATION NETWORK

50,340 miles (81,063 km)	466 miles (750 km)
3723 miles (5995 km)	81 miles (130 km)

Major towns and neighboring countries are linked by adequate road networks, although rural areas are less well served. Bahrain is linked to the mainland by a 15 mile (25 km) long causeway.

MAP KEY

POPULATION	ELEVATION
above 5 million	4000m / 13,124ft
1 million to 5 million	3000m / 9843ft
500,000 to 1 million	2000m / 6562ft
100,000 to 500,000	1000m / 3281ft
50,000 to 100,000	500m / 1640ft
10,000 to 50,000	250m / 820ft
below 10,000	100m / 328ft
	sea level

SCALE 1:6,000,000
(projection: Lambert Conformal Conic)

Km 0 10 20 40 60 80 100 120 140 160 180 200
Miles 0 10 20 40 60 80 100 120 140 160 180 200

KAZAKHSTAN

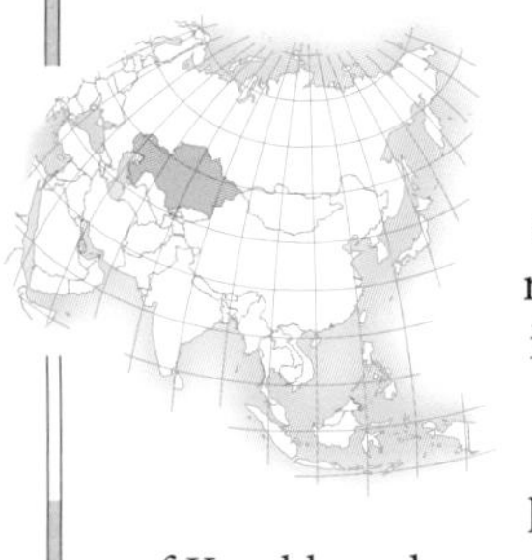

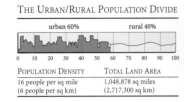

ABUNDANT NATURAL RESOURCES lie in the immense steppe grasslands, deserts, and central plateau of the former Soviet republic of Kazakhstan. An intensive program of industrial and agricultural development to exploit these resources during the Soviet era resulted in catastrophic industrial pollution, including fallout from nuclear testing and the shrinkage of the Aral Sea. Since independence, the government has encouraged foreign investment and liberalized the economy to promote growth. The adoption of Kazakh as the national language is intended to encourage a new sense of national identity in a state where living conditions for the majority remain harsh, both in cramped urban centers and impoverished rural areas.

TRANSPORTATION & INDUSTRY

THE SINGLE MOST IMPORTANT INDUSTRY in Kazakhstan is mining, based around extensive oil deposits near the Caspian Sea, the world's largest chromium mine, and vast reserves of iron ore. Recent foreign investment has helped to develop industries including food processing and steel manufacture, and to expand the exploitation of mineral resources. The Russian space program is still based at Baykonur, near Zhezkazgan in central Kazakhstan.

RUSSIAN FEDERATION
Petropavlovsk
Pavlodar
Rudnyy
Ural'sk
Aktobe
ASTANA
Temirtau
Karaganda
Semipalatinsk
Ust'-Kamenogorsk
Atyrau
KAZAKHSTAN
Zhezkazgan
Caspian Sea
Aktau
Aral Sea
Kyzylorda
Taldykorgan
Almaty
Taraz
Shymkent
UZBEKISTAN
KYRGYZSTAN
CHINA
TURKMENISTAN

Major industry and infrastructure

chemicals	capital cities
engineering	major towns
fish processing	international airports
food processing	major roads
iron & steel	major industrial areas
metallurgy	
mining	
oil	

TRANSPORTATION NETWORK

Roads	87,561 miles (141,000 km)
Highways	none
Railways	8,483 miles (13,660 km)
Waterways	none

Industrial areas in the north and east are well-connected to Russia. Air and rail links with Germany and China have been established through foreign investment. Better access to Baltic ports is being sought.

An open-cast coal mine in Kazakhstan. Foreign investment is being actively sought by the Kazakh government in order to fully exploit the potential of the country's rich mineral reserves.

USING THE LAND AND SEA

THE REARING OF LARGE HERDS of sheep and goats on the steppe grasslands forms the core of Kazakh agriculture. Arable cultivation and cotton-growing in pasture and desert areas was encouraged during the Soviet era, but relative yields are low. The heavy use of fertilizers and the diversion of natural water sources for irrigation has degraded much of the land.

THE URBAN/RURAL POPULATION DIVIDE

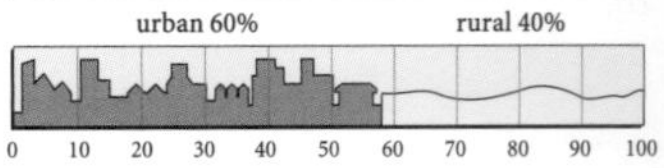
urban 60%
rural 40%
0 10 20 30 40 50 60 70 80 90 100

POPULATION DENSITY	TOTAL LAND AREA
16 people per sq mile (6 people per sq km)	1,048,878 sq miles (2,717,300 sq km)

Land use and agricultural distribution
cattle
goats
sheep
cotton
fishing
wheat
capital cities
major towns
pasture
cropland
forest
mountain region
desert
RUSSIAN FEDERATION
Ural'sk
Rudnyy
ASTANA
Semipalatinsk
Ust'-Kamenogorsk
Karaganda
Atyrau
KAZAKHSTAN
Caspian Sea
Aktau
Aral Sea
Kyzylorda
Taldykorgan
Almaty
Shymkent
UZBEKISTAN
KYRGYZSTAN
CHINA
TURKMENISTAN

The nomadic peoples who moved their herds around the steppe grasslands are now largely settled, although echoes of their traditional lifestyle, in particular their superb riding skills, remain.

RUSSIAN
Ural'sk
Kamenka
Zachagansk
Fedorovka
Burlin
Aksay
Chingirlau
Algabas
Chapayev
ZAPADNYY KAZAKHSTAN
Yesensay
Zhympity
Lubenka
Kaztalovka
Zhalpaktal
Dzhanibek
Urda
Novaya Kazanka
Kaldygayty
Martuk
Aktobe (Aktyubinsk)
Khobda
Akzhar
Khromtau
Alga
Kandyagash
Komsomol'skoye
Karabutak
Uil
Miyaly
Ryn-Peski
Kulagino
Inderborskiy
Karabau
Shubarkuduk
Zhuryn
Emba
Caspian Depression
ATYRAU
AKTYUBINSK
Gory Mugodzhary
Sagiz
Makhambet
Makat
Dossor
Akkystau
Atyrau
Ganyushkino
Komsomol'skiy
Kul'sary
Koschagyl
Zharkamys
Irgiz
Shalkar
Karaton
Boranbul
Sarykamys
Caspian Sea
Zaliv Komsomolets
Ostrov Kulaly
Mys Tyub-Karagan
Fort-Shevchenko
Shebir
Sor Mertvyy Kultuk
Beyneu
Turush
Severnyy Chink Ustyurta
Plato Shagyray
Peski Bol'shiye Barsuki
Saksaul'skiy
Aral'sk
Tauchik
Shetpe
Zharmysh
Say-Utes
Aktau
Plato Mangyshlak
MANGISTAU
Zhetybay
Zhanaozen
Kuryk
Ustyurt Plateau
Ostrov Vozrozhdeniya
Aral Sea
Uyaly
Ayteke Bi
Kazalinsk
Maylybas
Syr Darya
Baykonyr
Dzhusaly
KYZYLORDA
Kostanay
Rudnyy
Tobol
Lisakovsk
Oktyabr'sk
Denisovka
Zhitikara
KOSTANAY
Turgayskaya Stolovaya Strana
Zhailma
Karabalyk
Nadezhdinka
Fedorovka
Ozërnoye
Ozero Kyzylkol'
UZBEKISTAN
TURKMENISTAN
SCALE 1:7,000,000
(projection: Lambert Conformal Conic)
Km 0 25 50 100 150 200 250
Miles 0 25 50 100 150 200 250

MAP KEY

POPULATION	ELEVATION
1 million to 5 million	4000m / 13,124ft
500,000 to 1 million	3000m / 9843ft
100,000 to 500,000	2000m / 6562ft
50,000 to 100,000	1000m / 3281ft
10,000 to 50,000	500m / 1640ft
below 10,000	250m / 820ft
	100m / 328ft
	sea level

122
146

N O P Q R S T U V W X Y

THE LANDSCAPE

STRETCHING MORE THAN 1,250 MILES (2,000 km) from the Caspian Sea in the west to China in the east, more than 40% of Kazakhstan is covered by steppe grasslands which give way to barren desert in the south. The land rises eastward towards the mineral-rich central plateau, to form the Altai Mountains.

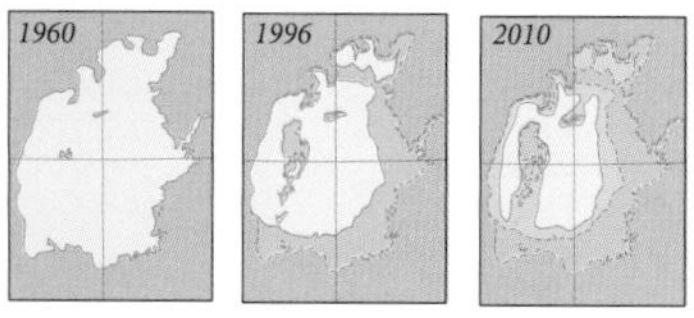

1960
1996
2010

Since 1960, the Aral Sea has shrunk by 40%, become extremely saline, and lost all but five of its once-abundant fish species. Factors in this ecological disaster include the excessive use of fertilizers, defoliants and the diversion of its main source rivers for the irrigation of desert lands.

The Caspian Sea is the largest body of inland water in the world.

The desert of Peski Bol'shiye Barsuki is mainly sandy, displaying a number of classic dune formations. Groundwater supports a small amount of vegetation.

A large number of salt lakes fill depressions in the rolling uplands of central Kazakhstan.

***The Altai Mountains** lie on Kazakhstan's eastern borders with China and the Russian Federation. Cold and largely barren, they are the source of many of the rivers which flow across the steppe.*

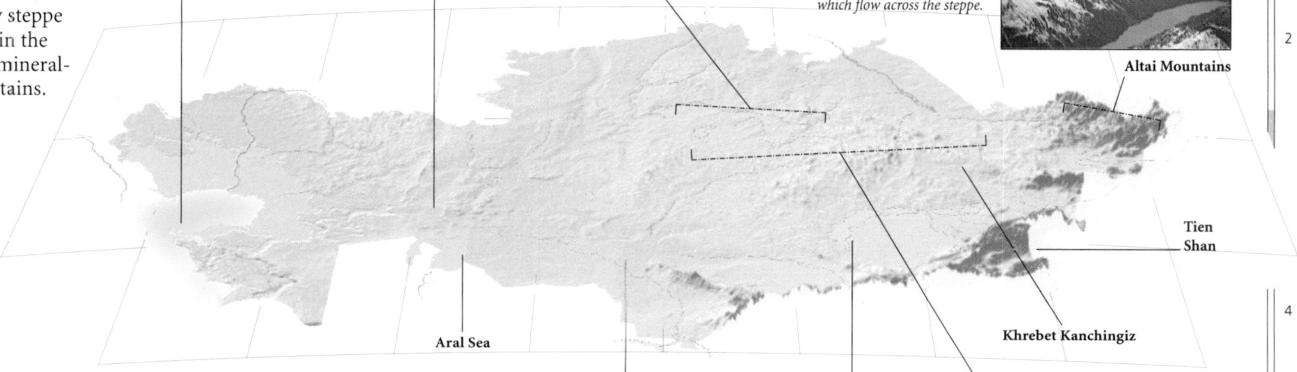

Altai Mountains
Tien Shan
Khrebet Kanchingiz
Aral Sea

Its waters taken for industry and irrigation, the Syr Darya, one of Kazakhstan's major rivers, now barely reaches the Aral Sea which it used to fill. Like many Kazakh rivers it has been heavily polluted with chemicals and its flow has been restricted by up to 60%.

The waters of Lake Balkhash (*Ozero Balkhash*), unlike those of the Aral Sea, are still able to support a fishing industry.

The central Kazakh Uplands (*Kazakhskiy Melkosopochnik*) contain much of the country's mineral riches. The landscape is largely flat with occasional rocky outcrops and hillocks.

***Immense stretches of steppe grasslands** characterize much of the Kazakh landscape. These lowland areas have been used for arable cultivation in recent years, although problems with irrigation have meant that much of the land is being allowed to revert to its natural vegetation and pastoral usage.*

FEDERATION
CHINA
KYRGYZSTAN
SEVERNYY KAZAKHSTAN
AKMOLA
PAVLODAR
KARAGANDA
VOSTOCHNYY KAZAKHSTAN
ALMATY
ZHAMBYL
YUZHNYY KAZAKHSTAN
Kazakhskiy Melkosopochnik
Betpak-Dala
Peski Moyynkum
Kyzyl Kum
Ozero Balkhash
Kulunda Steppe
Altai Mountains
Tien Shan
Kirghiz Range
Dzhungarskiy Alatau
Khrebet Karatau
Khrebet Tarbagatay
Kalbinskiy Khrebet
Narymskiy Khrebet
Khrebet Kanchingiz
Gory Ulytau
Gory Yermentau
Peski Saryyesik-Atyrau
Peski Taukum
Gora Belukha 4506m
Gora Vysokaya Belak 2776m
Pik Khan Tengri 6995m
Gory Agat 464m
Nuclear Testing Ground
Petropavlovsk
Kokshetau
ASTANA
Pavlodar
Semipalatinsk
Ust'-Kamenogorsk
Karaganda
Zhezkazgan
Kyzylorda
Shymkent
Taraz
Almaty (Alma-Ata)
Taldykorgan
Ekibastuz
Temirtau
Balkhash
Leninogorsk
Turkestan
Baykonur
Satpayev
Arkalyk
Ozero Zaysan
Ozero Alakol'
Ozero Tengiz
Ozero Sasykkol'
Ozero Karakoyyn
Kapchagayskoye Vodokhranilishche
Chardarinskoye Vodokhranilishche
Irtysh
Ishim
Syr Darya
Chu
Ili
Sarysu
Nura
Tobol
Ozero Shubar-Tengiz
Ozero Kushmurun
122
146
156

Rows of pine trees edge this valley near Almaty. The snow-covered slopes in the background are used for skiing.

R S T U V W X Y Z

Central Asia

Kyrgyzstan, Tajikistan, Turkmenistan, Uzbekistan

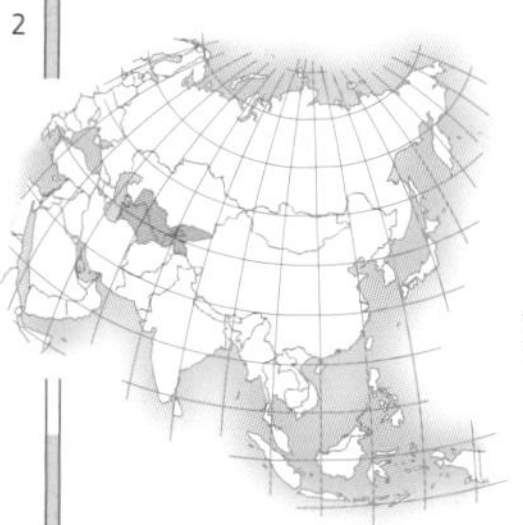

The four republics that declared independence in 1991 were created in the early years of the Soviet Union, promoting ethnic divisions in a region whose common focus, since the 8th century, has been Islam. Traditional rural, nomadic ways of life have survived the Soviet era, while the benefits of modern industry and grand irrigation schemes have resulted in severe pollution in the delicate, arid environment of the steppe, particularly in Uzbekistan. Many ethnic minority groups are scattered among the four republics, with isolated communities in the mountains of Kyrgyzstan. The current Islamic revival has brought hope of greater regional unity, in spite of religious factionalism which, in 1992, plunged Tajikistan into civil war.

The desert of the Kara Kum (Garagum) *occupies over 70% of Turkmenistan; its wind-scoured surface of dune ridges and depressions severely limits human settlement.*

The southern shoreline *of the Aral Sea has retreated over 30 miles (48 km) since 1960. A major cause is the diversion of water from the Amu Darya River for irrigation via the Kara Kum Canal* (Garagum Kanaly).

Map Key
POPULATION
1 million to 5 million
500,000 to 1 million
100,000 to 500,000
50,000 to 100,000
10,000 to 50,000
below 10,000
ELEVATION
6000m / 19,686ft
4000m / 13,124ft
3000m / 9843ft
2000m / 6562ft
1000m / 3281ft
500m / 1640ft
250m / 820ft
100m / 328ft
sea level
KAZAKHSTAN
UZBEKISTAN
TURKMENISTAN
IRAN
AFGHANISTAN
Aral Sea
Caspian Sea
Ostrov Vozrozhdeniya
Ustyurt Plateau
QORAQALPOG'ISTON RESPUBLIKASI
Turan Lowland
Kyzyl Kum
Tosquduq Qumlari
NAVOIY VILOYATI
BUXORO VILOYATI
XORAZM VILOYATI
DAŞOGUZ WELAÝATY
BALKAN WELAÝATY
AHAL WELAÝATY
LEBAP WELAÝATY
MARY WELAÝATY
Garagum
Merkezi Garagumy
Üngüz Angyrsyndaky Garagum
Krasnovodskoye Plato
Garabogaz Aylagy
Köpetdag Gershi
Garabil Belentligi
Nukus
Urganch
Daşoguz
Buxoro
Navoiy
Türkmenabat
Mary
Aşgabat
Türkmenbaşy
Balkanabat
Tejen
Serdar
Gazojak
Xiva
Qo'ng'irot
Zarafshon
Kagan
Kerki
Serhetabat
144
142
148

Transportation & Industry

Fossil fuels are extracted and processed in all four states, with scope for further exploitation. Agriculture provides raw materials for many industries, including food and textiles processing, and the manufacture of leather goods, clothing, and carpets. Farm machinery is also produced.

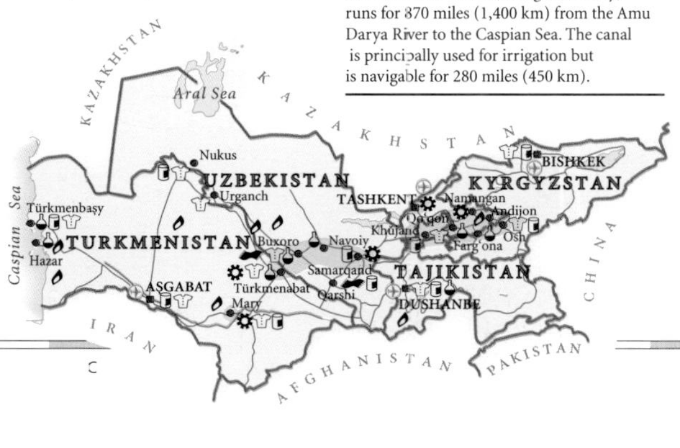

Major industry and infrastructure
carpet weaving
chemicals
engineering
food processing
oil & gas
textiles
capital cities
major towns
international airports
major roads
major industrial areas
KAZAKHSTAN
UZBEKISTAN
TURKMENISTAN
KYRGYZSTAN
TAJIKISTAN
BISHKEK
TASHKENT
DUSHANBE
AŞGABAT
Aral Sea
Caspian Sea
Nukus
Urganch
Türkmenbaşy
Hazar
Buxoro
Navoiy
Samarqand
Qarshi
Türkmenabat
Mary
Namangan
Andijon
Farg'ona
Osh
Khujand
IRAN
AFGHANISTAN
PAKISTAN
CHINA

Transportation Network

road	85,574 miles (137,800 km)	motorway	None
rail	4,184 miles (6,738 km)	waterway	1,180 miles (1,900 km)

The Kara Kum Canal *(Garagum Kanaly)* runs for 870 miles (1,400 km) from the Amu Darya River to the Caspian Sea. The canal is principally used for irrigation but is navigable for 280 miles (450 km).

N O P Q R S T U V W X Y

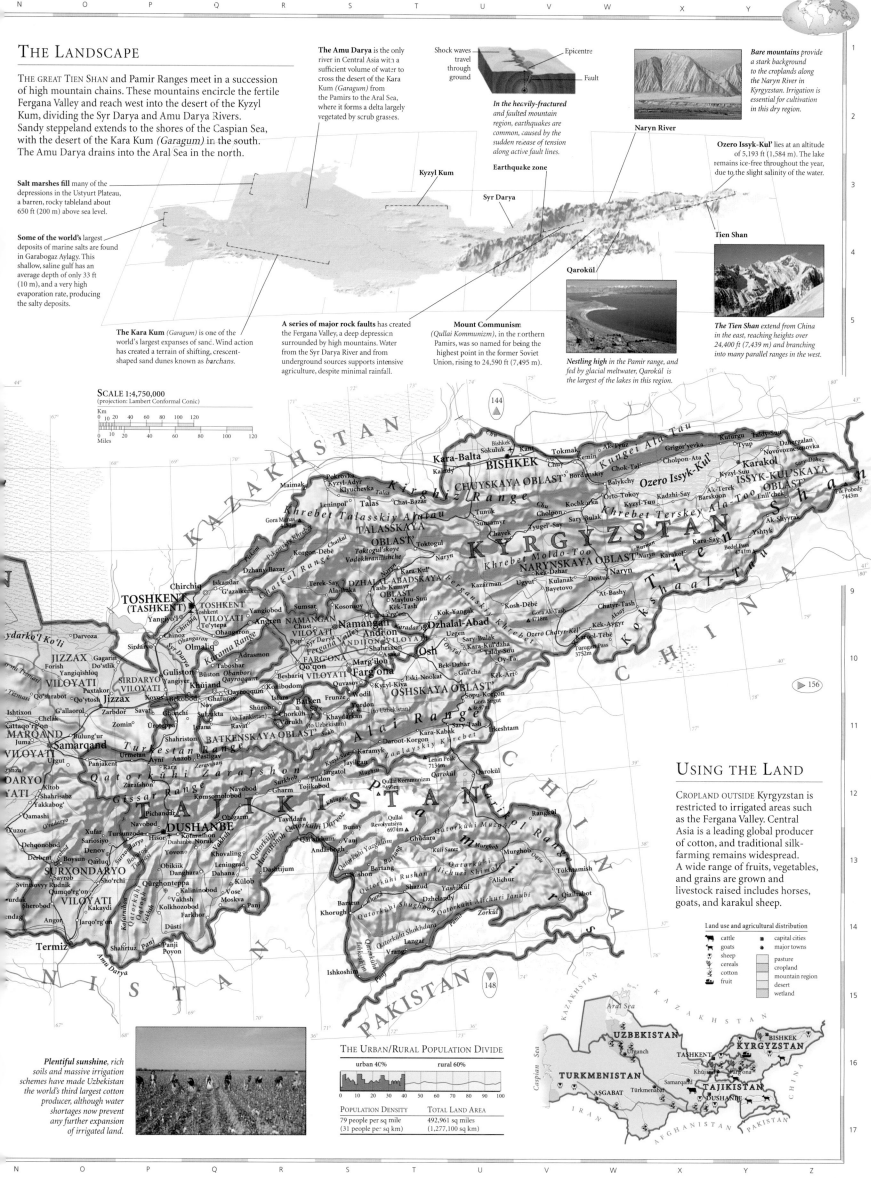

THE LANDSCAPE

THE GREAT TIEN SHAN and Pamir Ranges meet in a succession of high mountain chains. These mountains encircle the fertile Fergana Valley and reach west into the desert of the Kyzyl Kum, dividing the Syr Darya and Amu Darya Rivers. Sandy steppeland extends to the shores of the Caspian Sea, with the desert of the Kara Kum *(Garagum)* in the south. The Amu Darya drains into the Aral Sea in the north.

The Amu Darya is the only river in Central Asia with a sufficient volume of water to cross the desert of the Kara Kum *(Garagum)* from the Pamirs to the Aral Sea, where it forms a delta largely vegetated by scrub grasses.

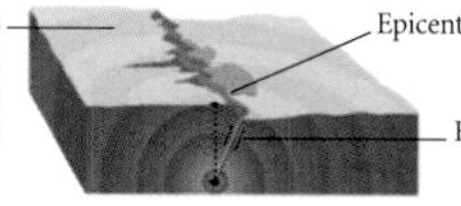

Shock waves travel through ground
Epicentre
Fault

***In the heavily-fractured** and faulted mountain region, earthquakes are common, caused by the sudden release of tension along active fault lines.*

***Bare mountains** provide a stark background to the croplands along the Naryn River in Kyrgyzstan. Irrigation is essential for cultivation in this dry region.*

Kyzyl Kum
Syr Darya
Earthquake zone
Naryn River
Tien Shan
Qarokŭl

Salt marshes fill many of the depressions in the Ustyurt Plateau, a barren, rocky tableland about 650 ft (200 m) above sea level.

Some of the world's largest deposits of marine salts are found in Garabogaz Aylagy. This shallow, saline gulf has an average depth of only 33 ft (10 m), and a very high evaporation rate, producing the salty deposits.

Ozero Issyk-Kul' lies at an altitude of 5,193 ft (1,584 m). The lake remains ice-free throughout the year, due to the slight salinity of the water.

***The Tien Shan** extend from China in the east, reaching heights over 24,400 ft (7,439 m) and branching into many parallel ranges in the west.*

***Nestling high** in the Pamir range, and fed by glacial meltwater, Qarokŭl is the largest of the lakes in this region.*

The Kara Kum *(Garagum)* is one of the world's largest expanses of sand. Wind action has created a terrain of shifting, crescent-shaped sand dunes known as *barchans*.

A series of major rock faults has created the Fergana Valley, a deep depression surrounded by high mountains. Water from the Syr Darya River and from underground sources supports intensive agriculture, despite minimal rainfall.

Mount Communism *(Qullai Kommunizm)*, in the northern Pamirs, was so named for being the highest point in the former Soviet Union, rising to 24,590 ft (7,495 m).

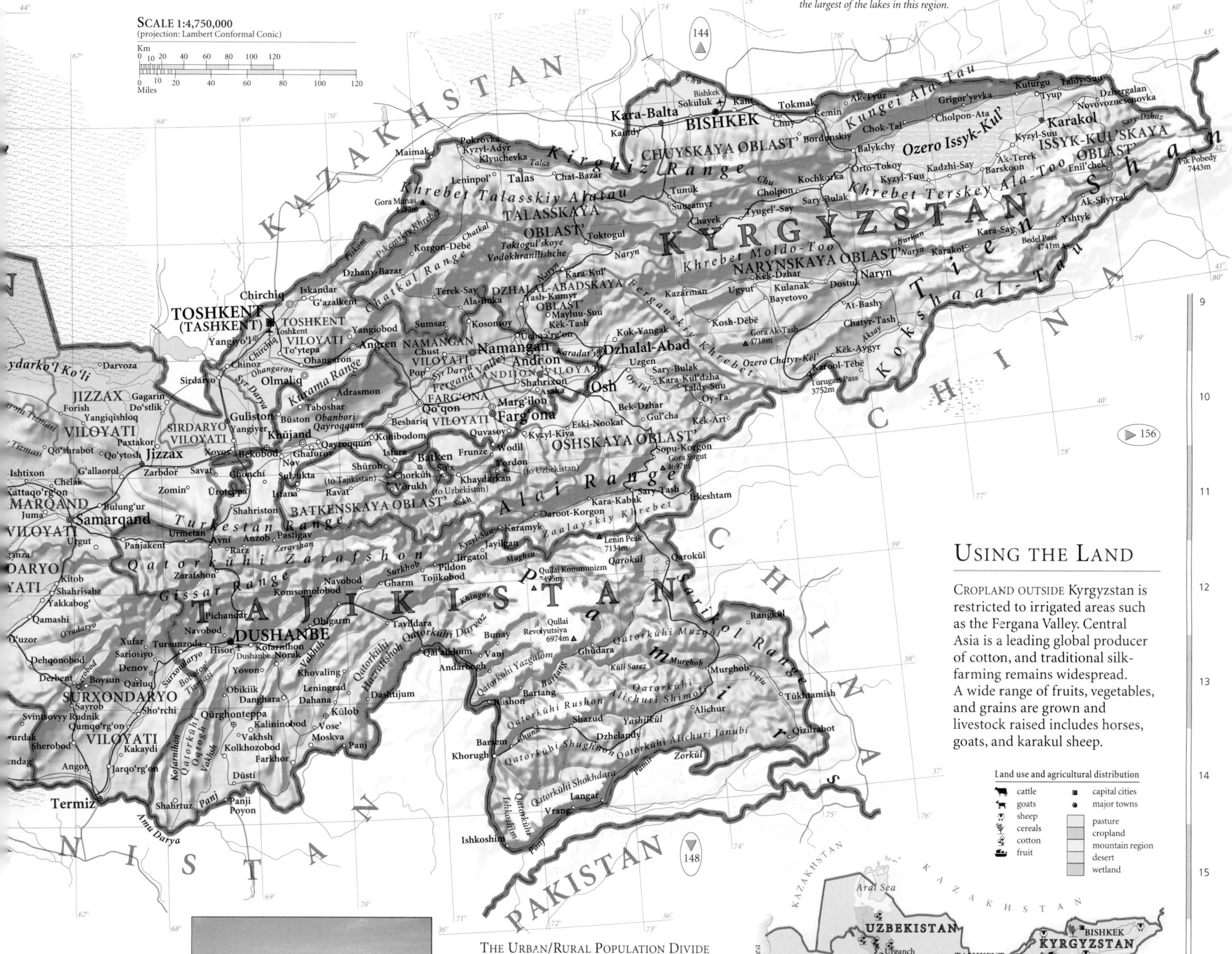

SCALE 1:4,750,000
(projection: Lambert Conformal Conic)
Km 0 10 20 40 60 80 100 120
Miles 0 10 20 40 60 80 100 120
144
156
148
KAZAKHSTAN
KYRGYZSTAN
TAJIKISTAN
CHINA
PAKISTAN
BISHKEK
TOSHKENT (TASHKENT)
DUSHANBE
CHUYSKAYA OBLAST'
TALASSKAYA OBLAST'
NARYNSKAYA OBLAST'
ISSYK-KUL'SKAYA OBLAST'
DZHALAL-ABADSKAYA OBLAST'
OSHSKAYA OBLAST'
BATKENSKAYA OBLAST'
TOSHKENT VILOYATI
NAMANGAN VILOYATI
FARG'ONA VILOYATI
ANDIJON VILOYATI
SIRDARYO VILOYATI
JIZZAX VILOYATI
SURXONDARYO VILOYATI
Ozero Issyk-Kul'
Kirghiz Range
Talasskiy Alatau
Fergana Valley
Fergana Range
Chatkal Range
Kurama Range
Turkestan Range
Alai Range
Zaalayskiy Khrebet
Gissar Range
Zarafshon Range
Tien Shan
Kokshaal-Tau
Pamir
Sarikol Range
Pik Pobedy 7443m
Lenin Peak 7134m
Qullai Kommunizm 7495m
Qullai Revolyutsiya 6974m
Karakol
Naryn
Osh
Dzhalal-Abad
Namangan
Andijon
Farg'ona
Qo'qon
Khŭjand
Jizzax
Samarqand
Termiz
Khorugh
Qarokŭl
Amu Darya
Syr Darya

Land use and agricultural distribution
cattle
goats
sheep
cereals
cotton
fruit
capital cities
major towns
pasture
cropland
mountain region
desert
wetland
Aral Sea
KAZAKHSTAN
UZBEKISTAN
TURKMENISTAN
KYRGYZSTAN
TAJIKISTAN
BISHKEK
TASHKENT
DUSHANBE
AŞGABAT
Urganch
Türkmenabat
Samarqand
Khŭjand
Farg'ona
Caspian Sea
IRAN
AFGHANISTAN
PAKISTAN
CHINA

USING THE LAND

CROPLAND OUTSIDE Kyrgyzstan is restricted to irrigated areas such as the Fergana Valley. Central Asia is a leading global producer of cotton, and traditional silk-farming remains widespread. A wide range of fruits, vegetables, and grains are grown and livestock raised includes horses, goats, and karakul sheep.

***Plentiful sunshine,** rich soils and massive irrigation schemes have made Uzbekistan the world's third largest cotton producer, although water shortages now prevent any further expansion of irrigated land.*

THE URBAN/RURAL POPULATION DIVIDE

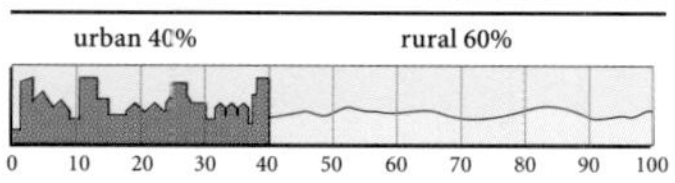

urban 40%
rural 60%
0 10 20 30 40 50 60 70 80 90 100

POPULATION DENSITY	TOTAL LAND AREA
79 people per sq mile (31 people per sq km)	492,961 sq miles (1,277,100 sq km)

N O P Q R S T U V W X Y Z

Afghanistan & Pakistan

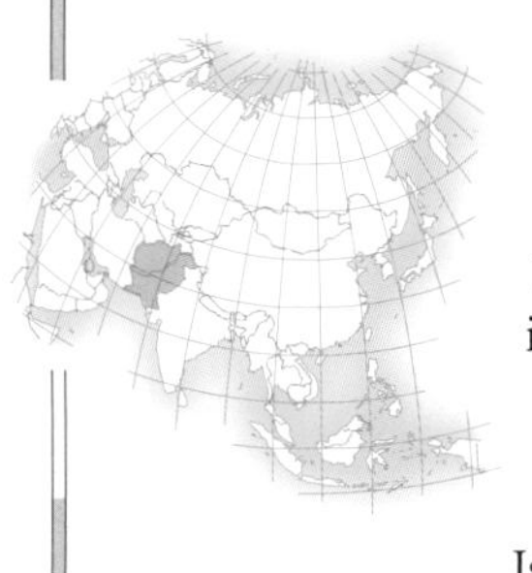

Pakistan was created by the partition of British India in 1947, becoming the western arm of a new Islamic state for Indian Muslims; the eastern sector, in Bengal, seceded to become the separate country of Bangladesh in 1971. Over half of Pakistan's 149 million people live in the Punjab, at the fertile head of the great Indus Basin. The river sustains a national economy based on irrigated agriculture, including cotton for the vital textiles industry. Afghanistan, a mountainous, landlocked country, with an ancient and independent culture, has been wracked by war since 1979. Factional strife escalated into an international conflict in late 2001, as US-led troops ousted the miltant and fundamentally Islamist *taliban* regime as part of their "war on terror."

The town of Bamian lies high in the Hindu Kush west of Kabul. Between the 2nd and 5th centuries two huge statues of Buddha were carved into the nearby rock, the largest of which stood 125ft (38m) high. The statues were destroyed by the taliban regime in March 2001.

Transportation & Industry

Pakistan is highly dependent on the cotton textiles industry, although diversified manufacture is expanding around cities such as Karachi and Lahore. Afghanistan's limited industry is based mainly on the processing of agricultural raw materials and includes traditional crafts such as carpet weaving.

UZBEKISTAN
TAJIKISTAN
TURKMENISTAN
CHINA
IRAN
INDIA
ARABIAN SEA
AFGHANISTAN
PAKISTAN
Mazar-e Sharif
Herat
KABUL
Peshawar
ISLAMABAD
Rawalpindi
Kandahar
Lahore
Faisalabad
Quetta
Multan
Bahawalpur
Sukkur
Karachi
Hyderabad
Major industry and infrastructure
carpet weaving
chemicals
engineering
finance
food processing
iron & steel
oil & gas
textiles
capital cities
major towns
international airports
major roads
major industrial areas

Transportation Network

- 141,340 miles (227,600 km)
- 211 miles (340 km)
- 4,852 miles (7,814 km)
- 745 miles (1,200 km)

The Karakoram Highway was completed after 20 years of construction in 1978. It breaches the Himalayan mountain barrier providing a commercial motor route linking lowland Pakistan and China.

The Karakoram Highway is one of the highest major roads in the world. It took over 24,000 workers almost 20 years to complete.

The Landscape

Afghanistan's topography is dominated by the mountains of the Hindu Kush, which spread south and west into numerous mountain spurs. The dry plateau of southwestern Afghanistan extends into Pakistan and the hills which overlook the great Indus Basin. In northern Pakistan the Hindu Kush, Himalayan and Karakoram ranges meet to form one of the world's highest mountain regions.

The Hunza River rises in the northern Karakoram Range, running for 120 miles (193 km) before joining the Gilgit River.

The arid Hindu Kush makes much of Afghanistan uninhabitable, with over 50% of the land lying above 6,500 ft (2,000 m).

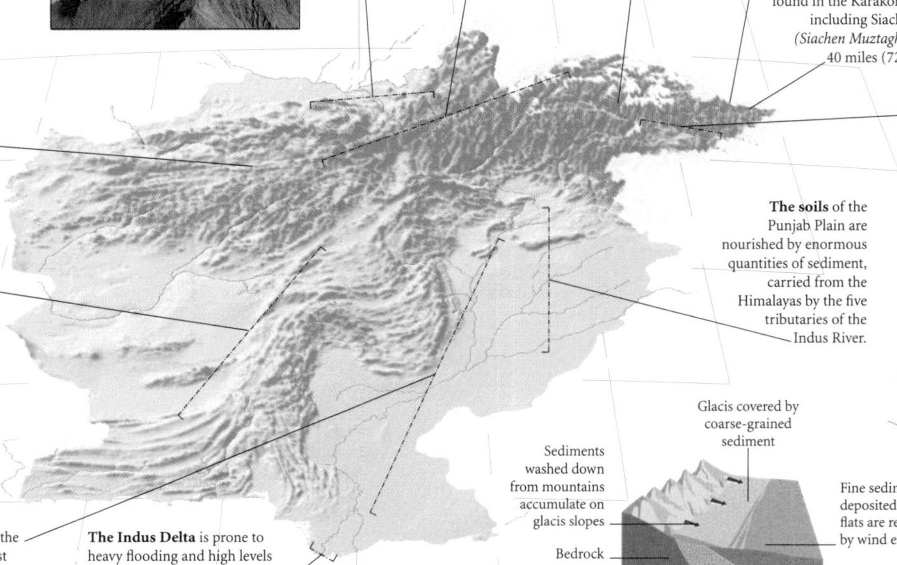
Hunza River
Hindu Kush
Himalayas

The plains and foothills which extend from the northern slopes of the Hindu Kush are part of the great grassy steppe lands of Central Asia.

K2 (Mount Godwin Austen), in the Karakoram Range, is the second highest mountain in the world, at an altitude of 28,251 ft (8,611 m).

Some of the largest glaciers outside the polar regions are found in the Karakoram Range, including Siachen Glacier *(Siachen Muztagh)*, which is 40 miles (72 km) long.

Frequent earthquakes mean that mountain-building processes are continuing in this region, as the Indo-Australian Plate drifts northward, colliding with the Eurasian Plate.

Mountain chains running southwest from the Hindu Kush into Pakistan form a barrier to the humid winds which blow from the Indian Ocean, creating arid conditions across southern Afghanistan.

The soils of the Punjab Plain are nourished by enormous quantities of sediment, carried from the Himalayas by the five tributaries of the Indus River.

The Indus Basin is part of the Indus-Ganges lowland, a vast depression which has been filled with layers of sediment over the last 50 million years. These deposits are estimated to be over 16,400 ft (5,000 m) deep.

The Indus Delta is prone to heavy flooding and high levels of salinity. It remains a largely uncultivated wilderness area.

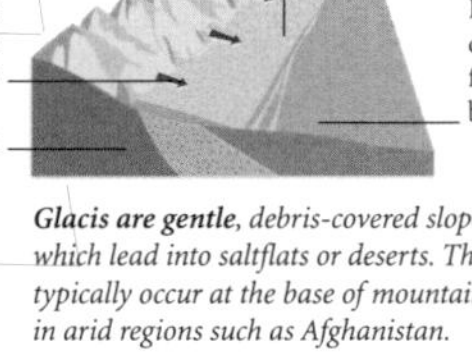
Glacis covered by coarse-grained sediment
Sediments washed down from mountains accumulate on glacis slopes
Bedrock
Fine sediments deposited on salt flats are removed by wind erosion.

Glacis are gentle, debris-covered slopes which lead into saltflats or deserts. They typically occur at the base of mountains in arid regions such as Afghanistan.

TURKMEN
IRAN
AFGHA
ARABIAN
146
142
142
Kārīz-e Elyās
Towraghoudi
Qarah Bāgh
Kūshk
BĀDGHĪS
Bālā Morghāb
Qal'eh-ye Now
Qādes
Eslām Qal'eh
Kūhestān
Dasht-e Hamdam Āb
Zendeh Jān
Ghūriān
Herāt
Selseleh-ye Sefīd Kūh
HERĀT
GHOWR
Namakzar
Shīndand
Dak
Dasht-e Bābūs
FARĀH
Anār Darreh
Farāh Rud
Farāh
Delārām
Now Zād
Hāmūn-e Şāberī
Dasht-e Khāsh
Hāmūn-e Pūzak
NĪMRŪZ
Chakhānsūr
Zaranj
Dasht-e Mārgow
Darvīshān
Lashkar Gāh
Gereshk
Kūchnay Darweyshān
HELMAND
Deh Shū
Daryā-ye Helmand
Dasht-e Gowd-e Zereh
Chāgai Hills
Hāmūn-i Lora
Nok Kundi
Yakmach
Dālbandin
Dasht-i Tāhlāb
Tāhlāb
Hāmūn-i Māshkel
BA
Kamarod
Siāhān Range
Panjgūr
Central Makrān
Ispikān
Nihing
Mand
Nasirābād
Kech
Hoshāb
Turbat
Kolwa
Dasht
Suntsar
Khor Kalmat
Jiwani
Gwādar
Gwadar West Bay
Gwadar East Bay
Pasni
Astola Island
Ormāra

SCALE 1:5,000,000
(projection: Lambert Conformal Conic)

Km 0 10 20 40 60 80 100 120 140 160 180 200
Miles 0 10 20 40 60 80 100 120 140 160 180 200

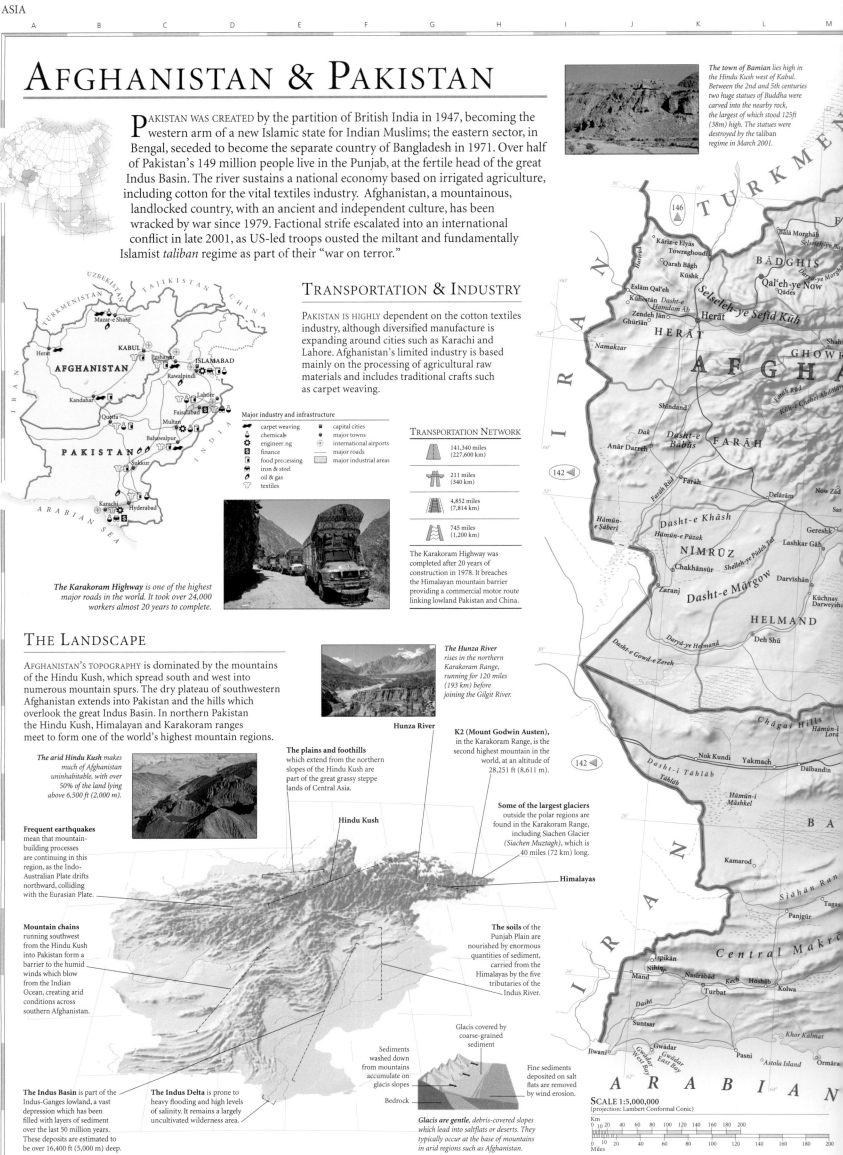

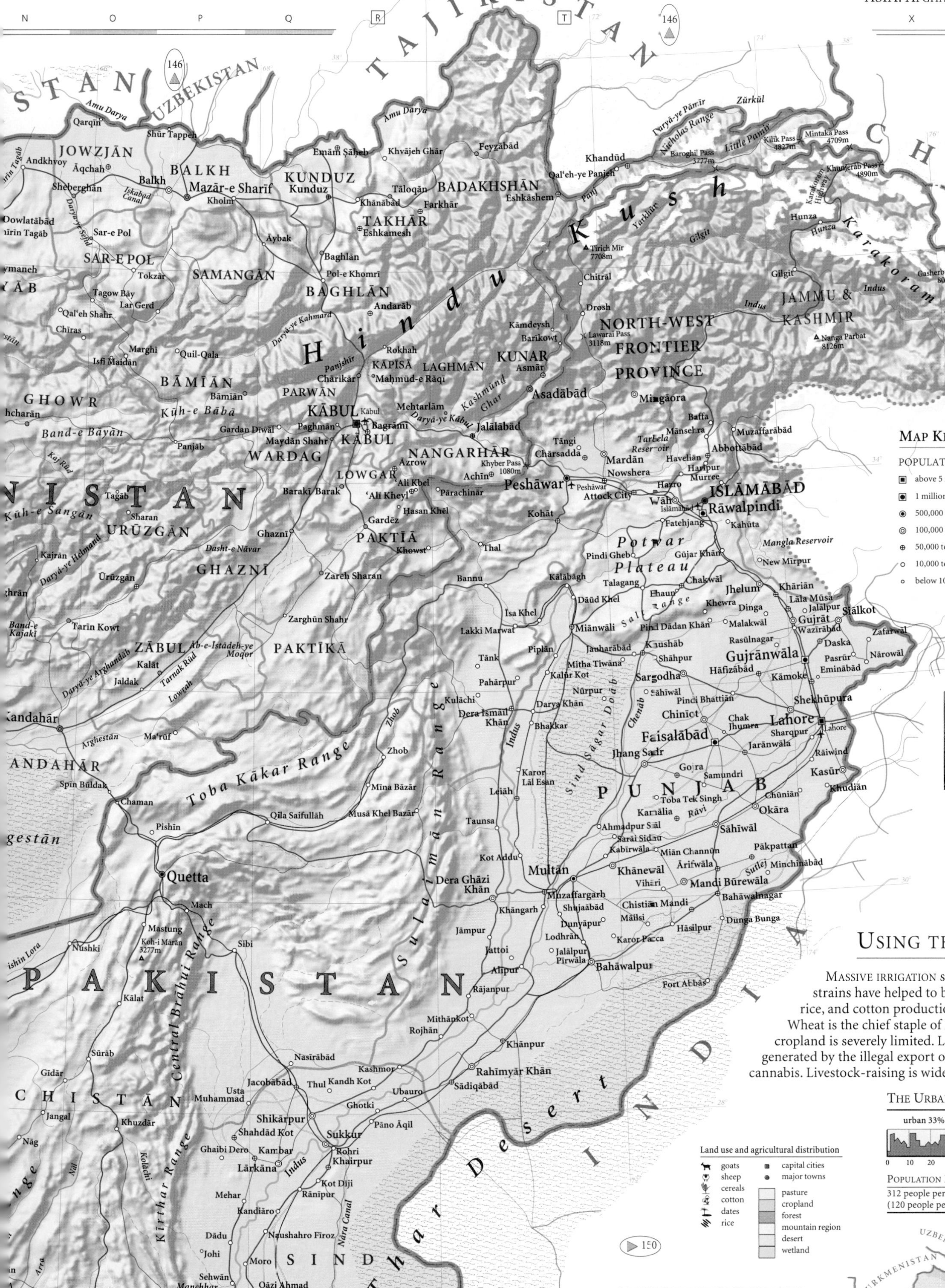
N O P Q R S T
X Y
1 2 3 4 5 6 7 8 9 10 11 12 13 14 15 16 17
146
156
150
172
TAJIKISTAN
UZBEKISTAN
CHINA
(claimed by India)
INDIA
PAKISTAN
Hindu Kush
Karakoram Range
Thar Desert
Rann of Kachchh
Mouths of the Indus
SEA
JOWZJĀN
BALKH
KUNDUZ
BADAKHSHĀN
TAKHĀR
SAMANGĀN
SAR-E POL
BAGHLĀN
BĀMĪĀN
PARWĀN
KĀPĪSĀ
LAGHMĀN
KUNAR
KĀBUL
WARDAK
LOWGAR
NANGARHĀR
PAKTĪĀ
GHAZNĪ
URŪZGĀN
ZĀBUL
PAKTĪKĀ
GHOWR
NORTH-WEST FRONTIER PROVINCE
JAMMU & KASHMIR
PUNJAB
SIND
Potwar Plateau
Salt Range
Sind Sāgar Doāb
Sulaimān Range
Toba Kākar Range
Central Brāhui Range
Kīrthar Range
Amu Darya
Indus
Jhelum
Chenāb
Rāvi
Sutlej
Zhob
Panj
Mazār-e Sharīf
Kābul
Qandahār
Quetta
Peshāwar
Islāmābād
Rāwalpindi
Lahore
Faisalābād
Multān
Gujrānwāla
Hyderābād
Karāchi
Sukkur
Bahāwalpur
Sargodha
Sialkot
Jalālābād
Gilgit
Hunza
Chitrāl
Tirich Mīr 7708m
K2 8611m
Gasherbrum 8068m
Nanga Parbat 8126m
Khyber Pass 1080m
Lowarai Pass 3118m
Karakoram Pass 5568m
Khunjerāb Pass 4890m
Mintaka Pass 4709m
Kilik Pass 4827m
Baroghil Pass 3777m
Koh-i Mārān 3277m
Tarbela Reservoir
Mangla Reservoir
Manchhar Lake
Sonmiāni Bay
Hawkes Bay
MAP KEY
POPULATION
above 5 million
1 million to 5 million
500,000 to 1 million
100,000 to 500,000
50,000 to 100,000
10,000 to 50,000
below 10,000
ELEVATION
6000m / 19,686ft
4000m / 13,124ft
3000m / 9843ft
2000m / 6562ft
1000m / 3281ft
500m / 1640ft
250m / 820ft
100m / 328ft
sea level

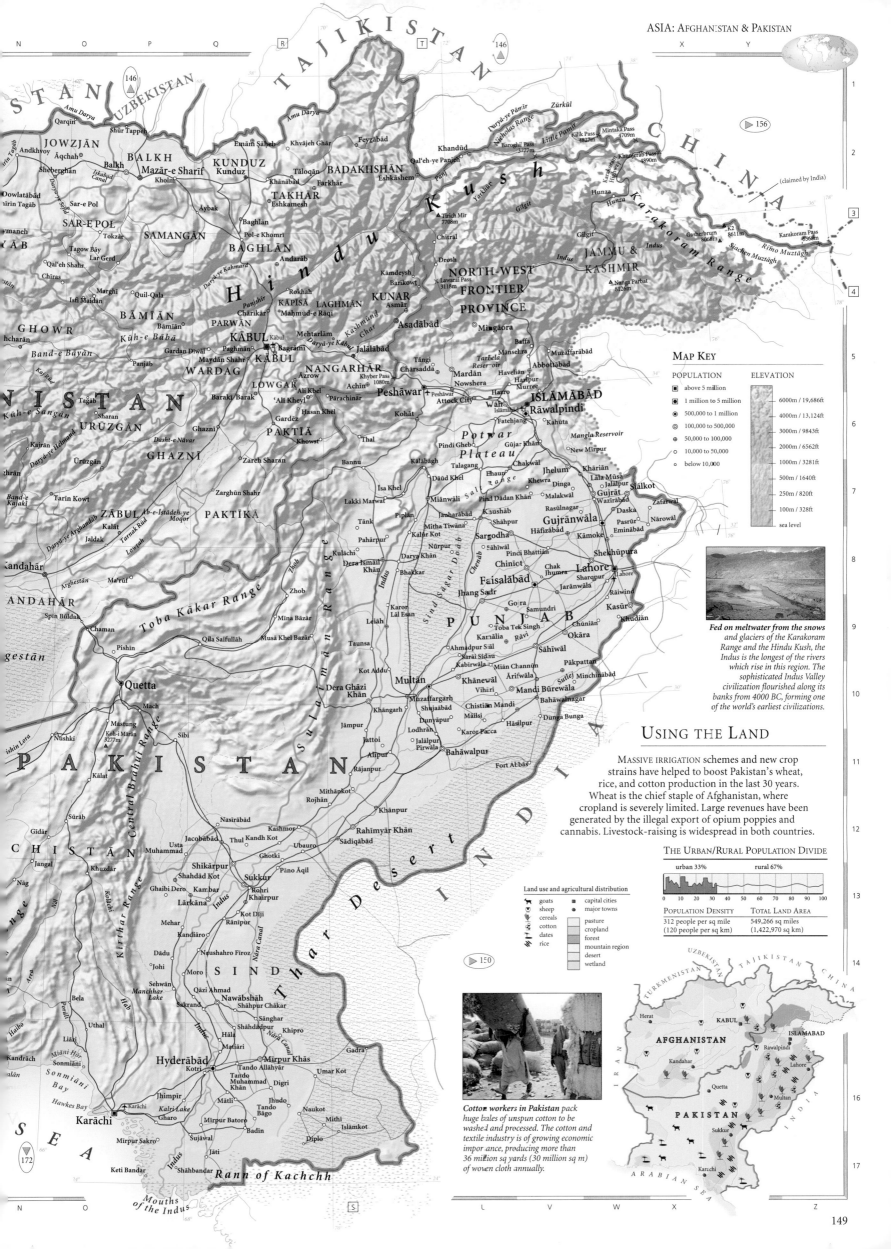

Fed on meltwater from the snows and glaciers of the Karakoram Range and the Hindu Kush, the Indus is the longest of the rivers which rise in this region. The sophisticated Indus Valley civilization flourished along its banks from 4000 BC, forming one of the world's earliest civilizations.

USING THE LAND

MASSIVE IRRIGATION schemes and new crop strains have helped to boost Pakistan's wheat, rice, and cotton production in the last 30 years. Wheat is the chief staple of Afghanistan, where cropland is severely limited. Large revenues have been generated by the illegal export of opium poppies and cannabis. Livestock-raising is widespread in both countries.

THE URBAN/RURAL POPULATION DIVIDE

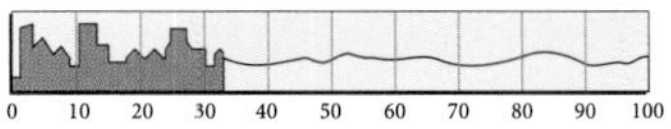
urban 33%
rural 67%
0 10 20 30 40 50 60 70 80 90 100

POPULATION DENSITY	TOTAL LAND AREA
312 people per sq mile (120 people per sq km)	549,266 sq miles (1,422,970 sq km)

Cotton workers in Pakistan pack huge bales of unspun cotton to be washed and processed. The cotton and textile industry is of growing economic importance, producing more than 36 million sq yards (30 million sq m) of woven cloth annually.

Land use and agricultural distribution
goats
sheep
cereals
cotton
dates
rice
capital cities
major towns
pasture
cropland
forest
mountain region
desert
wetland
UZBEKISTAN
TAJIKISTAN
TURKMENISTAN
CHINA
IRAN
INDIA
ARABIAN SEA
AFGHANISTAN
PAKISTAN
Herat
KABUL
ISLAMABAD
Rawalpindi
Lahore
Kandahar
Quetta
Multan
Sukkur
Karachi

South Asia

Bangladesh, Bhutan, India, Maldives, Nepal, Pakistan, Sri Lanka

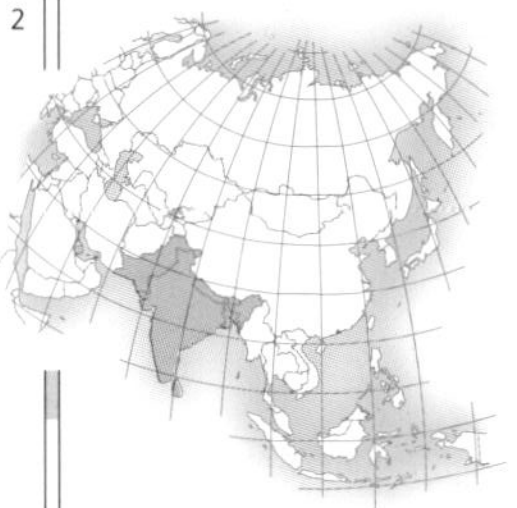

More than one-fifth of the world's population lives in the south Asian subcontinent. Great cultural diversity has come from a long succession of foreign invaders, including Hindu Aryans, Islamic Moguls, and the British, whose empire incorporated the princely states of the Maharajas and extended to the borders of Nepal and Bhutan in the Himalayas. Half a century after independence, India is the world's largest democracy, and at the current rate of growth, may overtake China as the world's most populous country within the next century. There are points of tension in the region over claims for independence by the Sikhs in the Indian Punjab and the Tamil separatists in Sri Lanka, and the long-standing dispute with Pakistan over Jammu and Kashmir in the north.

The Landscape

South Asia is effectively isolated from the rest of Asia by desert along the western flank of Pakistan, and a continuous wall of mountains, dominated by the Himalayas, to the north and east. The great basins of the Indus and Ganges separate this mountain fringe from the rolling plateau of the Indian peninsula, which is bordered by a line of coastal hills, the Eastern and Western Ghats.

The Indus Valley near Skardu in northern Pakistan has been partially infilled by great quantities of eroded sediment. Most of this is carried from the region's bare slopes by swollen rivers during the spring thaw and mass movement activity.

The Himalayas are the highest and most extensive mountain system in the world. They were formed when the Indo-Australian Plate collided with the Eurasian Plate about 40 million years ago, thrusting up huge masses of land and creating a "ripple" effect, which formed lesser mountain ranges in Tibet and Southeast Asia. Mount Everest is the world's tallest mountain at 29,035 ft (8,850 m).

Almost all of Bangladesh lies in the immense delta formed by the Ganges and the Brahmaputra which merge and flow out into the Bay of Bengal.

The Indus River flows more than 1,970 miles (3,180 km) from southwestern Tibet to its mouth on the Arabian Sea. It has an estimated catchment area of 450,000 sq miles (1,165,500 sq km).

The coast of western Pakistan is a staircase of folded rock strata caused by successive periods of rapid uplift.

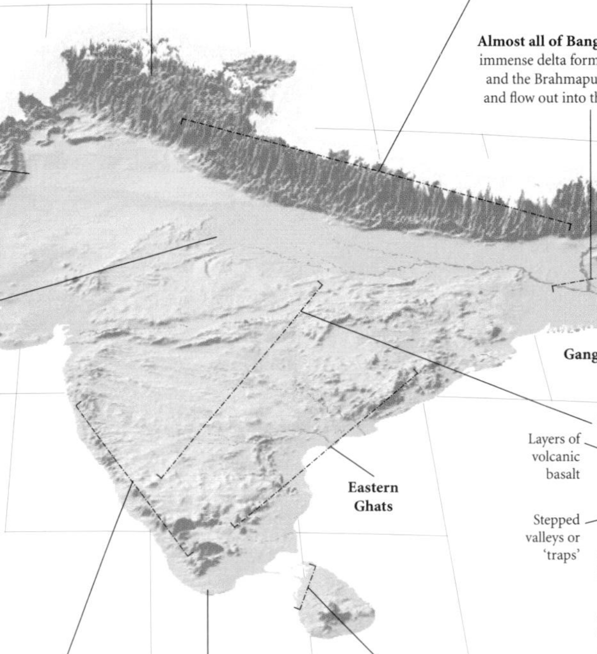

Bharatpur
Ganges Delta
Deccan Plateau
Eastern Ghats

Rivers flowing from the Himalayas into a broad depression in northern India have formed marshes around Bharatpur. They are now a sanctuary for numerous bird species.

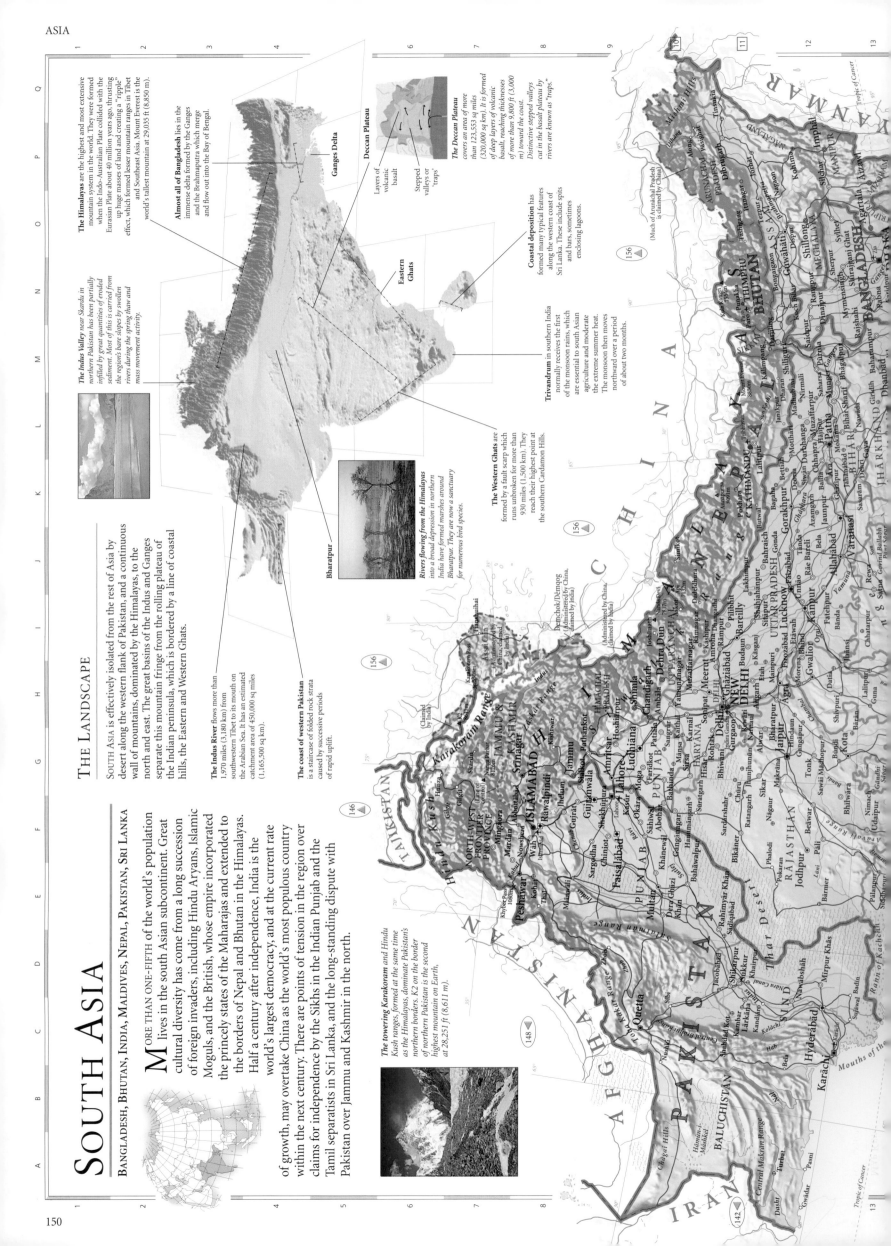

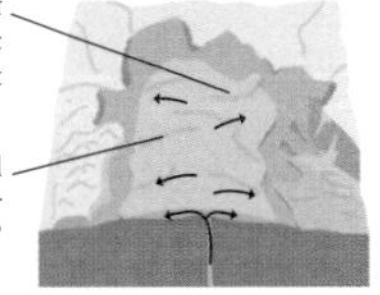

Layers of volcanic basalt
Stepped valleys or 'traps'

The Deccan Plateau covers an area of more than 123,553 sq miles (320,000 sq km). It is formed of deep layers of volcanic basalt, reaching thicknesses of more than 9,800 ft (3,000 m) toward the coast. Distinctive stepped valleys cut in the basalt plateau by rivers are known as "traps."

The Western Ghats are formed by a fault scarp which runs unbroken for more than 930 miles (1,500 km). They reach their highest point at the southern Cardamon Hills.

Trivandrum in southern India normally receives the first of the monsoon rains, which are essential to south Asian agriculture and moderate the extreme summer heat. The monsoon then moves northward over a period of about two months.

Coastal deposition has formed many typical features along the western coast of Sri Lanka. These include spits and bars, sometimes enclosing lagoons.

The towering Karakoram and Hindu Kush ranges, formed at the same time as the Himalayas, dominate Pakistan's northern borders. K2 on the border of northern Pakistan is the second highest mountain on Earth, at 28,251 ft (8,611 m).

AFGHANISTAN
TAJIKISTAN
PAKISTAN
IRAN
CHINA
NEPAL
BHUTAN
BANGLADESH
INDIA
MYANMAR
BALUCHISTAN
NORTH-WEST FRONTIER PROVINCE
JAMMU & KASHMIR
PUNJAB
HIMACHAL PRADESH
UTTARANCHAL
HARYANA
UTTAR PRADESH
RAJASTHAN
SIND
BIHAR
JHARKHAND
SIKKIM
ASSAM
ARUNACHAL PRADESH
MEGHALAYA
MANIPUR
NAGALAND
ISLĀMĀBĀD
NEW DELHI
KATHMANDU
THIMPHU
Karāchi
Quetta
Peshāwar
Lahore
Delhi
Lucknow
Kānpur
Jaipur
Hyderābād
Multān
Faisalābād
Rāwalpindi
Srinagar
Hindu Kush
Karakoram Range
Thar Desert
Central Makrān Range
Chāgai Hills
Toba Kakar Range
Sulaimān Range
Rann of Kachchh
Mouths of the Indus
Tropic of Cancer
(Much of Arunāchal Pradesh is claimed by China)
Aksai Chin (Administered by China, claimed by India)
Demchok/Dêmqog (Administered by China, claimed by India)
K2 8611m
Nanga Parbat 8126m
Mount Everest 8850m
Annapurna 8091m
Nanda Devi 7817m
Kula Kangri 7554m
146
148
156
142

Map Key

POPULATION

- ■ above 5 million
- ▣ 1 million to 5 million
- ◉ 500,000 to 1 million
- ◎ 100,000 to 500,000
- ⊕ 50,000 to 100,000
- ○ 10,000 to 50,000
- ○ below 10,000

ELEVATION

- 6000m / 19,686ft
- 4000m / 13,124ft
- 3000m / 9843ft
- 2000m / 6562ft
- 1000m / 3281ft
- 500m / 1640ft
- 250m / 820ft
- 100m / 328ft
- sea level

INDIA
Arabian Sea
Bay of Bengal
INDIAN OCEAN
Coromandel Coast
Malabar Coast
Western Ghats
Eastern Ghats
Deccan
MAHĀRĀSHTRA
KARNATAKA
ANDHRA PRADESH
TAMIL NADU
KERALA
ORISSA
CHHATTISGARH
GUJARAT
Mumbai (Bombay)
Kolkata (Calcutta)
Chennai (Madras)
Hyderābād
Bangalore
Nāgpur
Pune
Ahmadābād
Vadodara
Indore
Bhopāl
Jabalpur
Visākhapatnam
Bhubaneshwar
Cochin (Kochi)
Trivandrum
Madurai
Coimbatore
Mysore
Pondicherry
Gulf of Mannar
Gulf of Khambhāt
Palk Strait
Mouths of the Ganges
Chittagong
LAKSHADWEEP
Lakshadweep (Laccadive Islands)
Kavaratti
Nine Degree Channel
Eight Degree Channel
Minicoy Island
SRI LANKA
COLOMBO
Sri Jayawardanapura
Kandy
Jaffna
Trincomalee
Galle
Andaman Sea
Andaman Islands
Nicobar Islands
ANDAMAN & NICOBAR ISLANDS
Port Blair
Ten Degree Channel
Great Channel
Indira Point
SCALE 1:11,000,000
(projection: Lambert Conformal Conic)

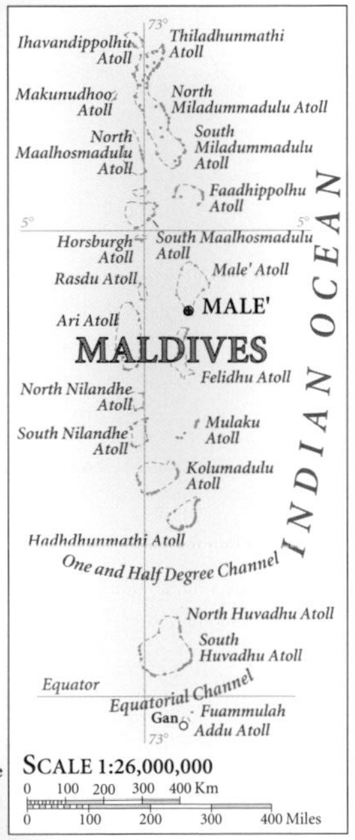

INDIAN OCEAN
MALDIVES
MALE'
Equator
One and Half Degree Channel
SCALE 1:26,000,000

Transportation & Industry

Most industrial workers across South Asia are involved in small-scale production serving local markets. Large-scale industry remains concentrated around great cities such as Kolkata (Calcutta) and Mumbai (Bombay). India has a broad industrial base and manufacturing growth has accelerated under a recently liberalized economy. Textiles and clothing, leather, and jewelry are among South Asia's leading exports.

PAKISTAN
INDIA
NEPAL
BHUTAN
BANGLADESH
SRI LANKA
CHINA
Arabian Sea
Bay of Bengal
INDIAN OCEAN

Major industry and infrastructure

- aerospace
- car manufacture
- chemicals
- electronics
- engineering
- finance
- food processing
- iron & steel
- textiles
- capital cities
- major towns
- international airports
- major roads
- major industrial areas

Transportation Network

335,154 miles (539,701 km)		21,015 miles (33,840 km)	
44,166 miles (71,120 km)		17,225 miles (27,738 km)	

India's railroad network, established under British colonial rule, is the sixth most extensive in the world and continues to play a unique role in integrating the country's disparate regions.

***Religion and commerce** sit side by side in the Nepalese capital, Kathmandu. Nepal is a Hindu state and these small, highly decorated shrines are commonplace. As in India, cows are venerated, and allowed free rein throughout the city.*

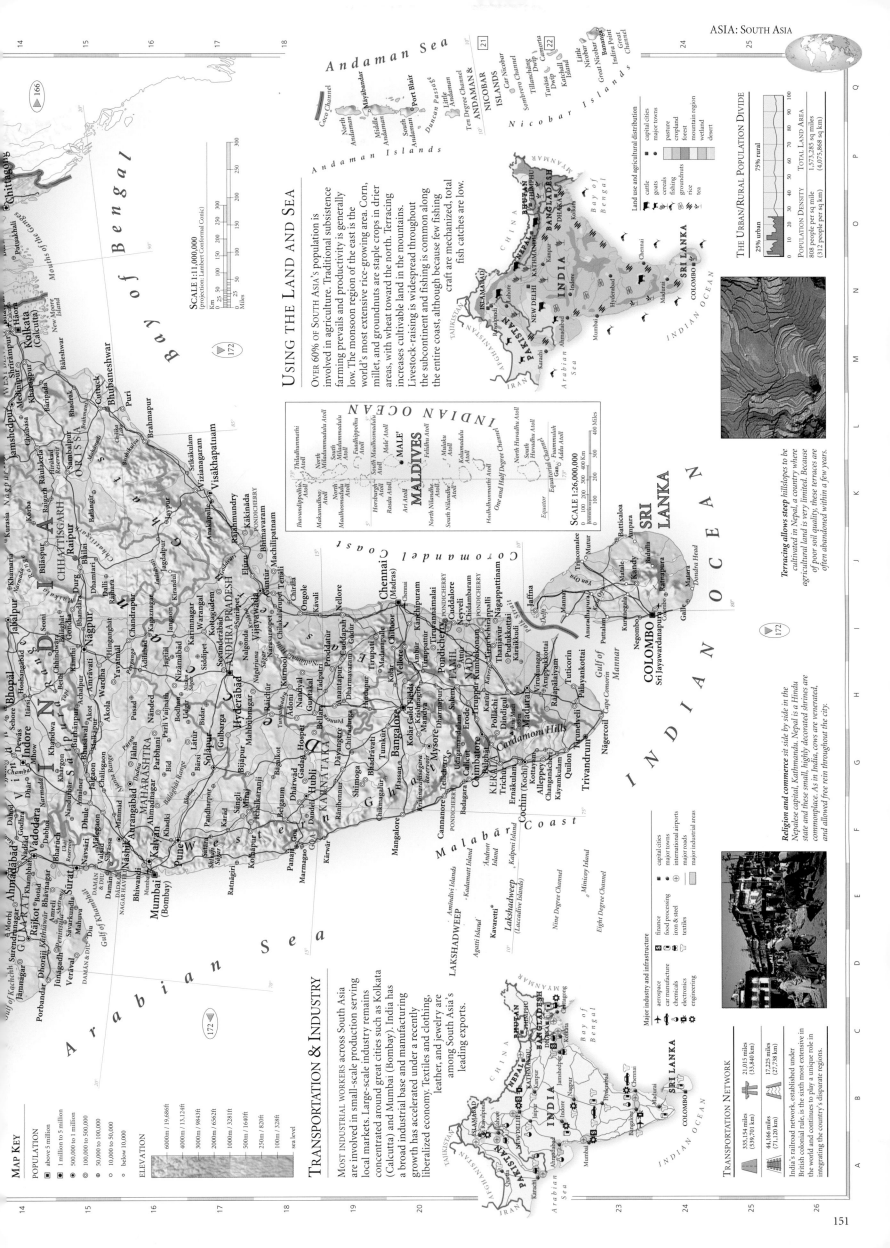

Using the Land and Sea

Over 60% of South Asia's population is involved in agriculture. Traditional subsistence farming prevails and productivity is generally low. The monsoon region of the east is the world's most extensive rice-growing area. Corn, millet, and groundnuts are staple crops in drier areas, with wheat toward the north. Terracing increases cultivable land in the mountains. Livestock-raising is widespread throughout the subcontinent and fishing is common along the entire coast, although because few fishing craft are mechanized, total fish catches are low.

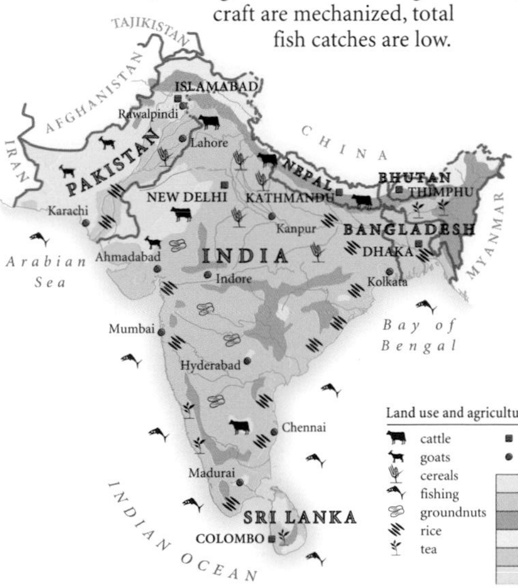

PAKISTAN
INDIA
NEPAL
BHUTAN
BANGLADESH
SRI LANKA
CHINA
Arabian Sea
Bay of Bengal
INDIAN OCEAN

Land use and agricultural distribution

- cattle
- goats
- cereals
- fishing
- groundnuts
- rice
- tea
- capital cities
- major towns
- pasture
- cropland
- forest
- mountain region
- wetland
- desert

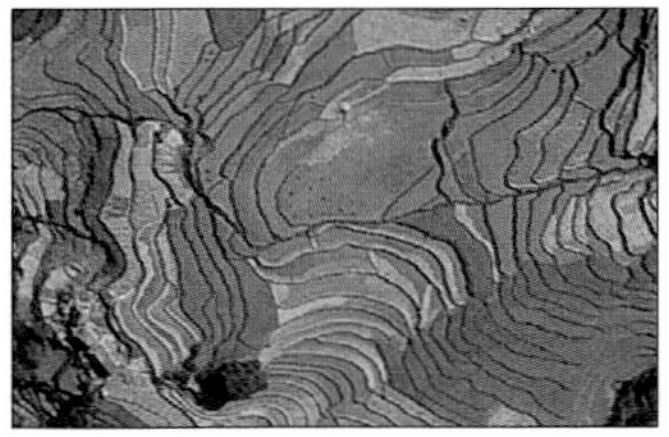

***Terracing allows steep** hillslopes to be cultivated in Nepal, a country where agricultural land is very limited. Because of poor soil quality, these terraces are often abandoned within a few years.*

The Urban/Rural Population Divide

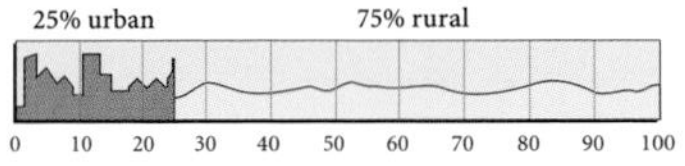

25% urban
75% rural
0 10 20 30 40 50 60 70 80 90 100

Population Density	Total Land Area
808 people per sq mile (312 people per sq km)	1,573,285 sq miles (4,075,868 sq km)

NORTHERN INDIA & THE HIMALAYAN STATES

BANGLADESH, BHUTAN, NEPAL, Arunachal Pradesh, Assam, Bihar, Chandigarh, Delhi, Haryana, Himachal Pradesh, Jammu & Kashmir, Jhārkand, Manipur, Meghalaya, Mizoram, Nagaland, Punjab, Rajasthan, Sikkim, Tripura, Uttar Pradesh, Uttaranchal, West Bengal

THE GANGES AND BRAHMAPUTRA river basins and the massive mountain barrier of the Himalayas define this region's landscape and have served to reinforce potent cultural and religious differences among its people. Hinduism pervades most aspects of national life and is a growing political force within India, a secular country which also encompasses the center of Sikhism at Amritsar and the world's largest Muslim minority. Nepal is a crowded mountain state, which faces severe ecological problems from deforestation, while the tiny Himalayan Buddhist kingdom of Bhutan is emerging from long-term isolation, to welcome selected visitors. The Muslim state of Bangladesh, formerly East Pakistan, is one of the world's most densely populated countries and one of the poorest, with more than 120 million people living largely on the massive Ganges/Brahmaputra Delta. Many Bangladeshis live under threat of repeated, catastrophic floods.

The Golden Temple in Amritsar, the most sacred shrine of the Sikh religion, was the scene of violent clashes between Sikh separatists and government forces in 1984.

SCALE 1:6,500,000
(projection: Lambert Conformal Conic)
AFGHANISTAN
CHINA
PAKISTAN
INDIA
JAMMU AND KASHMIR
HIMACHAL PRADESH
PUNJAB
HARYANA
UTTARANCHAL
RĀJASTHAN
UTTAR PRADESH
GUJARAT
MADHYA PRADESH
Thar Desert
Karakoram Range
Ladakh Range
Zāskār Range
Pīr Panjal Range
Aksai Chin (Administered by China, claimed by India)
(Claimed by India)
(Line of control)
K2 8611m
Nanga Parbat 8126m
Srīnagar
Jammu
Amritsar
Ludhiāna
Chandigarh
Shimla
Dehra Dūn
DELHI
NEW DELHI
Jaipur
Jodhpur
Bīkāner
Ajmer
Udaipur
Kota
Āgra
Lucknow
Kānpur
Allahābād
Jhānsi
Bareilly
Meerut
Tropic of Cancer

MAP KEY

POPULATION
- 1 million to 5 million
- 500,000 to 1 million
- 100,000 to 500,000
- 50,000 to 100,000
- 10,000 to 50,000
- below 10,000

ELEVATION
- 6000m / 19,686ft
- 4000m / 13,124ft
- 3000m / 9843ft
- 2000m / 6562ft
- 1000m / 3281ft
- 500m / 1640ft
- 250m / 820ft
- 100m / 328ft
- sea level

156
148
154

TRANSPORTATION & INDUSTRY

TEXTILES, ENGINEERING, chemicals, and electronics are leading industries in north India. The plateau of Chota Nagpur provides ore for iron and steel production in the major industrial region northeast of Calcutta. Bangladesh processes jute and Nepal has a small manufacturing sector based on agricultural produce, while Bhutan's limited industry is concentrated in the southern lowland area.

Srinagar
Amritsar
Ludhiana
Chandigarh
Delhi
NEW DELHI
NEPAL
KATHMANDU
BHUTAN
THIMPHU
INDIA
Lucknow
Kanpur
Jaipur
Jodhpur
Kota
Dibrugarh
Guwahati
BANGLADESH
DHAKA
Dhanbad
Ranchi
Jamshedpur
Kolkata
Chittagong
BAY OF BENGAL
PAKISTAN
CHINA
MYANMAR

Major industry and infrastructure
- adventure tourism
- car manufacture
- chemicals
- coal
- electronics
- engineering
- finance
- food processing
- iron & steel
- jute processing
- oil
- tea processing
- textiles
- capital cities
- major towns
- international airports
- major roads
- major industrial areas

TRANSPORTATION NETWORK

Over 60% of Bangladesh's internal trade is carried by boat. The country has a very disjointed land transportation network, with no bridges over the Brahmaputra and few road crossings on the Ganges River.

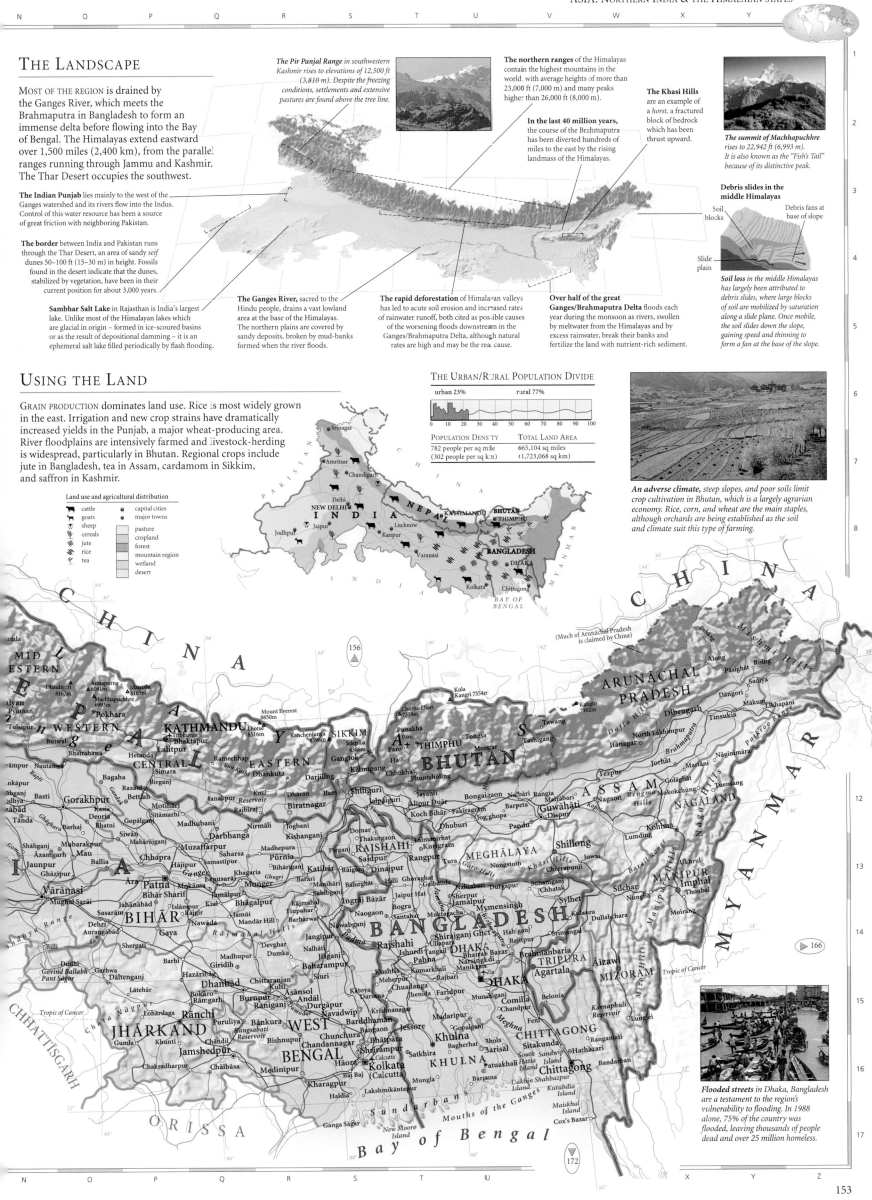

The Landscape

Most of the region is drained by the Ganges River, which meets the Brahmaputra in Bangladesh to form an immense delta before flowing into the Bay of Bengal. The Himalayas extend eastward over 1,500 miles (2,400 km), from the parallel ranges running through Jammu and Kashmir. The Thar Desert occupies the southwest.

The Pir Panjal Range *in southwestern Kashmir rises to elevations of 12,500 ft (3,810 m). Despite the freezing conditions, settlements and extensive pastures are found above the tree line.*

The northern ranges of the Himalayas contain the highest mountains in the world, with average heights of more than 23,000 ft (7,000 m) and many peaks higher than 26,000 ft (8,000 m).

In the last 40 million years, the course of the Brahmaputra has been diverted hundreds of miles to the east by the rising landmass of the Himalayas.

The Khasi Hills are an example of a *horst*, a fractured block of bedrock which has been thrust upward.

The summit of Machhapuchhre *rises to 22,942 ft (6,993 m). It is also known as the "Fish's Tail" because of its distinctive peak.*

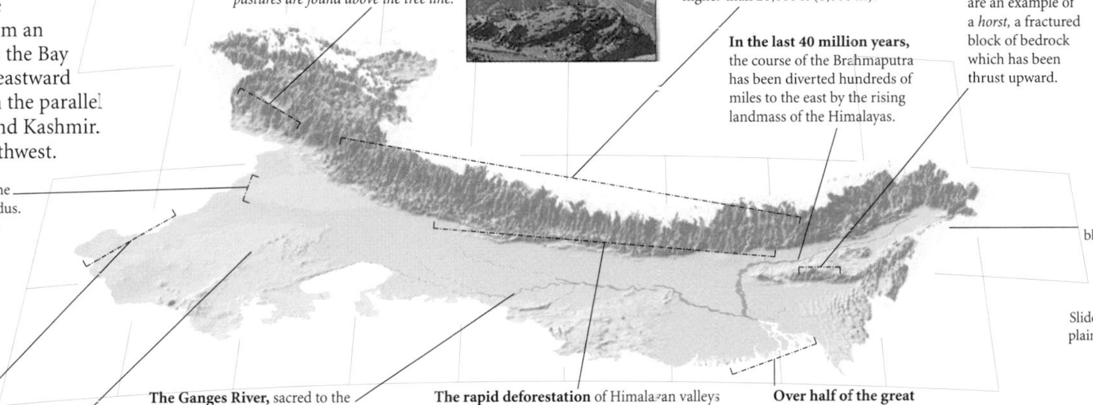

The Indian Punjab lies mainly to the west of the Ganges watershed and its rivers flow into the Indus. Control of this water resource has been a source of great friction with neighboring Pakistan.

The border between India and Pakistan runs through the Thar Desert, an area of sandy *seif* dunes 50–100 ft (15–30 m) in height. Fossils found in the desert indicate that the dunes, stabilized by vegetation, have been in their current position for about 3,000 years.

Sambhar Salt Lake in Rajasthan is India's largest lake. Unlike most of the Himalayan lakes which are glacial in origin – formed in ice-scoured basins or as the result of depositional damming – it is an ephemeral salt lake filled periodically by flash flooding.

The Ganges River, sacred to the Hindu people, drains a vast lowland area at the base of the Himalayas. The northern plains are covered by sandy deposits, broken by mud-banks formed when the river floods.

The rapid deforestation of Himalayan valleys has led to acute soil erosion and increased rates of rainwater runoff, both cited as possible causes of the worsening floods downstream in the Ganges/Brahmaputra Delta, although natural rates are high and may be the real cause.

Over half of the great Ganges/Brahmaputra Delta floods each year during the monsoon as rivers, swollen by meltwater from the Himalayas and by excess rainwater, break their banks and fertilize the land with nutrient-rich sediment.

Debris slides in the middle Himalayas

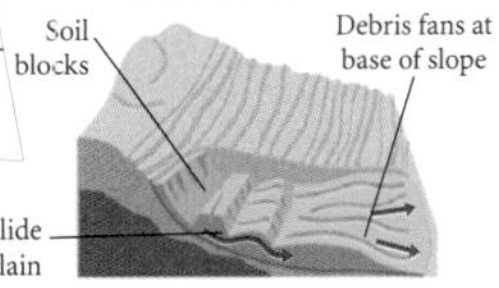
Soil blocks
Debris fans at base of slope
Slide plain

Soil loss *in the middle Himalayas has largely been attributed to debris slides, where large blocks of soil are mobilized by saturation along a slide plane. Once mobile, the soil slides down the slope, gaining speed and thinning to form a fan at the base of the slope.*

Using the Land

Grain production dominates land use. Rice is most widely grown in the east. Irrigation and new crop strains have dramatically increased yields in the Punjab, a major wheat-producing area. River floodplains are intensively farmed and livestock-herding is widespread, particularly in Bhutan. Regional crops include jute in Bangladesh, tea in Assam, cardamom in Sikkim, and saffron in Kashmir.

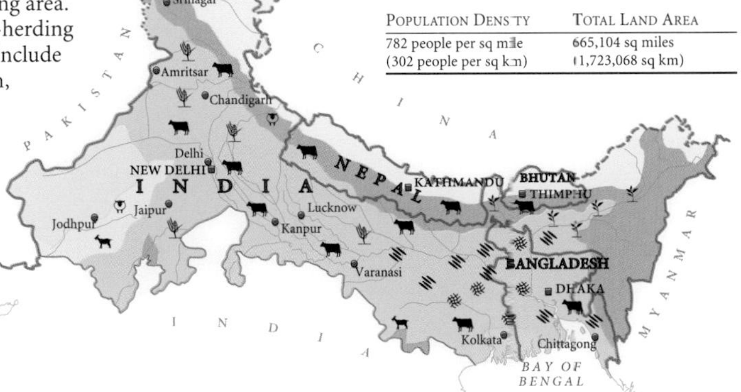
Land use and agricultural distribution
cattle
goats
sheep
cereals
jute
rice
tea
capital cities
major towns
pasture
cropland
forest
mountain region
wetland
desert
Srinagar
Amritsar
Chandigarh
Delhi
NEW DELHI
INDIA
Jodhpur
Jaipur
Lucknow
Kanpur
Varanasi
Kolkata
NEPAL
KATHMANDU
BHUTAN
THIMPHU
BANGLADESH
DHAKA
Chittagong
BAY OF BENGAL
PAKISTAN
CHINA
MYANMAR

The Urban/Rural Population Divide

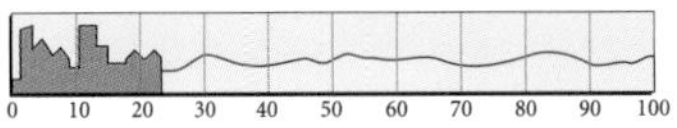
urban 23%
rural 77%
0 10 20 30 40 50 60 70 80 90 100

Population Density	Total Land Area
782 people per sq mile (302 people per sq km)	665,104 sq miles (1,723,068 sq km)

An adverse climate, *steep slopes, and poor soils limit crop cultivation in Bhutan, which is a largely agrarian economy. Rice, corn, and wheat are the main staples, although orchards are being established as the soil and climate suit this type of farming.*

CHINA
NEPAL
BHUTAN
BANGLADESH
INDIA
MYANMAR
(Much of Arunāchal Pradesh is claimed by China)
ARUNĀCHAL PRADESH
ASSAM
MEGHĀLAYA
NĀGĀLAND
MANIPUR
MIZORAM
TRIPURA
SIKKIM
BIHĀR
JHĀRKAND
WEST BENGAL
CHHATTISGARH
ORISSA
KATHMANDU
THIMPHU
DHAKA
Kolkata (Calcutta)
Chittagong
Mount Everest 8850m
Kanchenjunga 8598m
Annapurna 8091m
Dhaulāgiri 8167m
Manaslu 8163m
Machhapuchhre 6993m
Kula Kangri 7554m
Chomo Lhari 7314m
Kangto 7102m
Bay of Bengal
Mouths of the Ganges
Sundarbans
Tropic of Cancer
156
166
172

Flooded streets *in Dhaka, Bangladesh are a testament to the region's vulnerability to flooding. In 1988 alone, 75% of the country was flooded, leaving thousands of people dead and over 25 million homeless.*

Southern India & Sri Lanka

Sri Lanka, Andhra Pradesh, Chhattīsgarh, Dadra & Nagar Haveli, Daman & Diu, Goa, Gujarat, Karnataka, Kerala, Lakshadweep, Madhya Pradesh, Maharashtra, Orissa, Pondicherry, Tamil Nadu

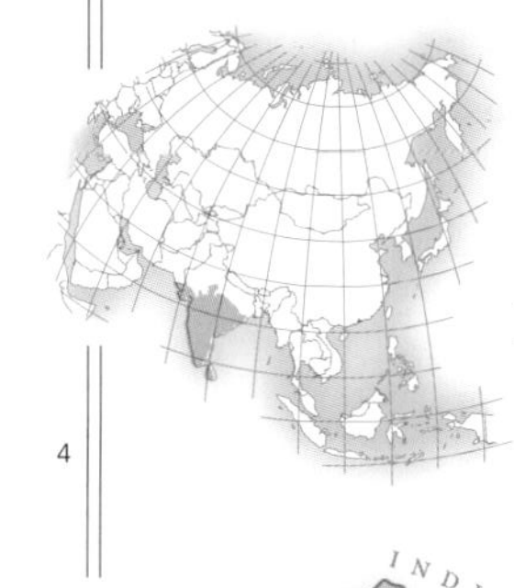

The unique and highly independent southern states reflect the diverse and decentralized nature of India, which has fourteen official languages. The southern half of the peninsula lay beyond the reach of early invaders from the north and retained the distinct and ancient culture of Dravidian peoples such as the Tamils, whose language is spoken in preference to Hindi throughout southern India. The interior plateau of southern India is less densely populated than the coastal lowlands, where the European colonial imprint is strongest. Urban and industrial growth is accelerating, but southern India's vast population remains predominantly rural. The island of Sri Lanka has two distinct cultural groups; the mainly Buddhist Sinhalese majority, and the Tamil minority whose struggle for a homeland in the northeast has led to prolonged civil war.

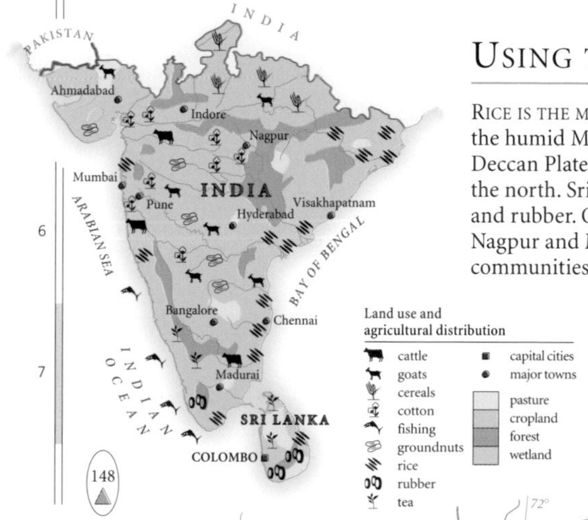

PAKISTAN
INDIA
Ahmadabad
Indore
Nagpur
Mumbai
Pune
INDIA
Hyderabad
Visakhapatnam
ARABIAN SEA
BAY OF BENGAL
Bangalore
Chennai
Madurai
INDIAN OCEAN
SRI LANKA
COLOMBO
Land use and agricultural distribution
cattle
goats
cereals
cotton
fishing
groundnuts
rice
rubber
tea
capital cities
major towns
pasture
cropland
forest
wetland

Using the Land and Sea

Rice is the main staple in the east, in Sri Lanka and along the humid Malabar Coast. Peanuts are grown on the Deccan Plateau, with wheat, corn, and chickpeas, toward the north. Sri Lanka is a leading exporter of tea, coconuts and rubber. Cotton plantations supply local mills around Nagpur and Mumbai (Bombay). Fishing supports many communities in Kerala and the Laccadive Islands.

The Urban/Rural Population Divide

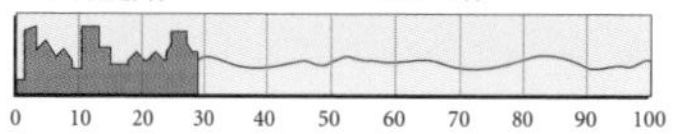

urban 29%
rural 71%
0 10 20 30 40 50 60 70 80 90 100

Population Density	Total Land Area
715 people per sq mile (276 people per sq km)	698,295 sq miles (1,809,054 sq km)

Commercial plantations, growing tea, (seen here), cardamom, coffee, coconuts, and rubber, occupy about half the agricultural land in Kerala, necessitating food imports for local consumption.

The Landscape

The undulating Deccan Plateau underlies most of southern India; it slopes gently down toward the east and is largely enclosed by the Ghats coastal hill ranges. The Western Ghats run continuously along the Arabian Sea coast, while the Eastern Ghats are interrupted by rivers which follow the slope of the plateau and flow across broad lowlands into the Bay of Bengal. The plateaus and basins of Sri Lanka's central highlands are surrounded by a broad plain.

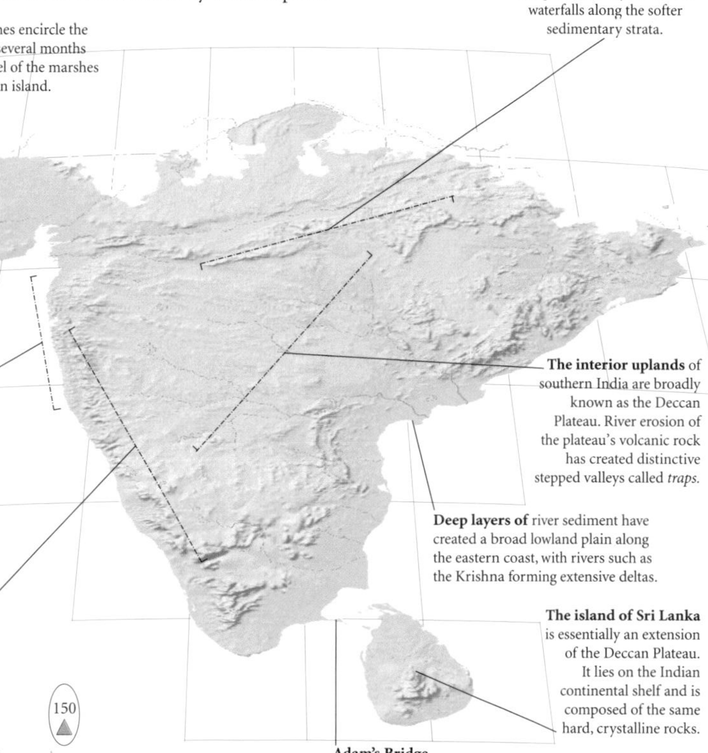

The Rann of Kachchh tidal marshes encircle the low-lying Kachchh Peninsula. For several months during the rainy season the water level of the marshes rises and Kachchh becomes an island.

Along the northern boundary of the Deccan Plateau, old basement rocks are interspersed with younger sedimentary strata. This creates spectacular scarplands, cut by numerous waterfalls along the softer sedimentary strata.

The Konkan coast, which runs between Daman and Goa, is characterized by rocky headlands, and bays with crescent-shaped beaches. Flooded river valleys known as *rias* extend inland.

The interior uplands of southern India are broadly known as the Deccan Plateau. River erosion of the plateau's volcanic rock has created distinctive stepped valleys called *traps.*

The Western Ghats run north–south marking the western boundary of the Deccan Plateau. Their height rises to the south where their summits reach altitudes of 8,000 ft (2,500 m).

Deep layers of river sediment have created a broad lowland plain along the eastern coast, with rivers such as the Krishna forming extensive deltas.

The island of Sri Lanka is essentially an extension of the Deccan Plateau. It lies on the Indian continental shelf and is composed of the same hard, crystalline rocks.

Adam's Bridge

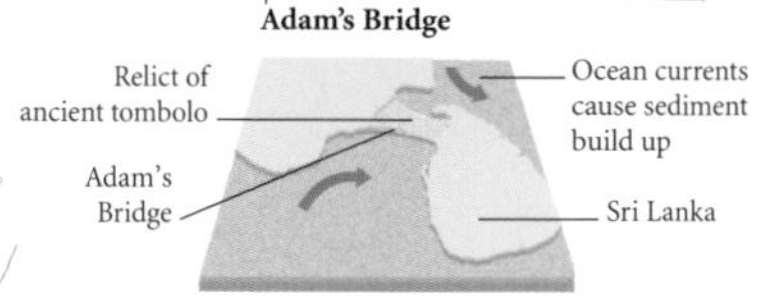

Relict of ancient tombolo
Adam's Bridge
Ocean currents cause sediment build up
Sri Lanka

Adam's Bridge (Rama's Bridge) is a chain of sandy shoals lying about 4 ft (1.2 m) under the sea between India and Sri Lanka. They once formed the world's longest tombolo, or land bridge, before the sea level began to rise several thousand years ago.

PAKISTAN
RĀJASTHĀN
UTTAR PRADESH
GUJARĀT
MADHYA PRADESH
MAHĀRĀSHTRA
CHHATTĪSGARH
JHĀRKAND
WEST BENGAL
ORISSA
Rann of Kachchh
Gulf of Kachchh
Gulf of Khambhāt
Kāthiāwār Peninsula
Ahmadābād
Vadodara
Sūrat
Rājkot
Bhopāl
Indore
Gwalior
Jabalpur
Nāgpur
Raipur
Bhubaneshwar
Cuttack
Nāshik
Aurangābād

148
150
172

Map Key

POPULATION
- above 5 million
- 1 million to 5 million
- 500,000 to 1 million
- 100,000 to 500,000
- 50,000 to 100,000
- 10,000 to 50,000
- below 10,000

ELEVATION
- 2000m / 6562ft
- 1000m / 3281ft
- 500m / 1640ft
- 250m / 820ft
- 100m / 328ft
- sea level

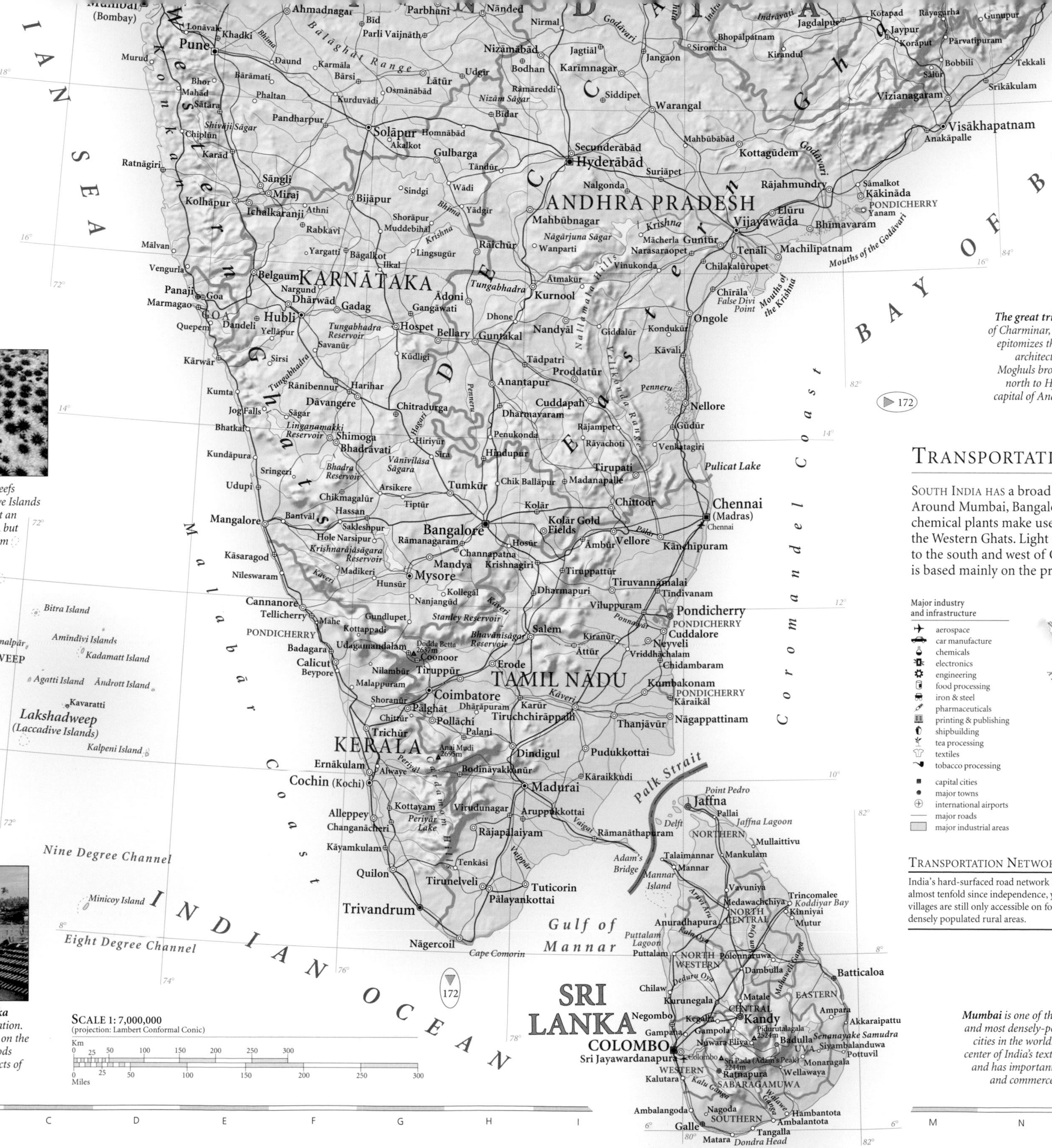

ARABIAN SEA
BAY OF BENGAL
INDIAN OCEAN
Konkan
Western Ghats
Deccan
Eastern Ghats
Malabar Coast
Coromandel Coast
Gulf of Mannar
Palk Strait
Nine Degree Channel
Eight Degree Channel
LAKSHADWEEP
Lakshadweep (Laccadive Islands)
KARNĀTAKA
ANDHRA PRADESH
TAMIL NĀDU
KERALA
GOA
PONDICHERRY
SRI LANKA
COLOMBO
Sri Jayawardanapura
Mumbai (Bombay)
Pune
Hyderābād
Secunderābād
Bangalore
Chennai (Madras)
Mysore
Coimbatore
Madurai
Cochin (Kochi)
Trivandrum
Visākhapatnam
Vijayawāda
Pondicherry
Jaffna
Kandy
Cape Comorin
SCALE 1: 7,000,000
(projection: Lambert Conformal Conic)
Km
Miles

***Sea pencils** thrive on the coral reefs around the coast of the Laccadive Islands and Sri Lanka. The reefs support an amazing diversity of marine life, but are increasingly under threat from growing coastal populations.*

***Local fisheries around Sri Lanka** afford great potential for exploitation. However, many fishermen living on the coastal fringes saw their livelihoods destroyed by the devastating effects of the Asian tsunami in 2004.*

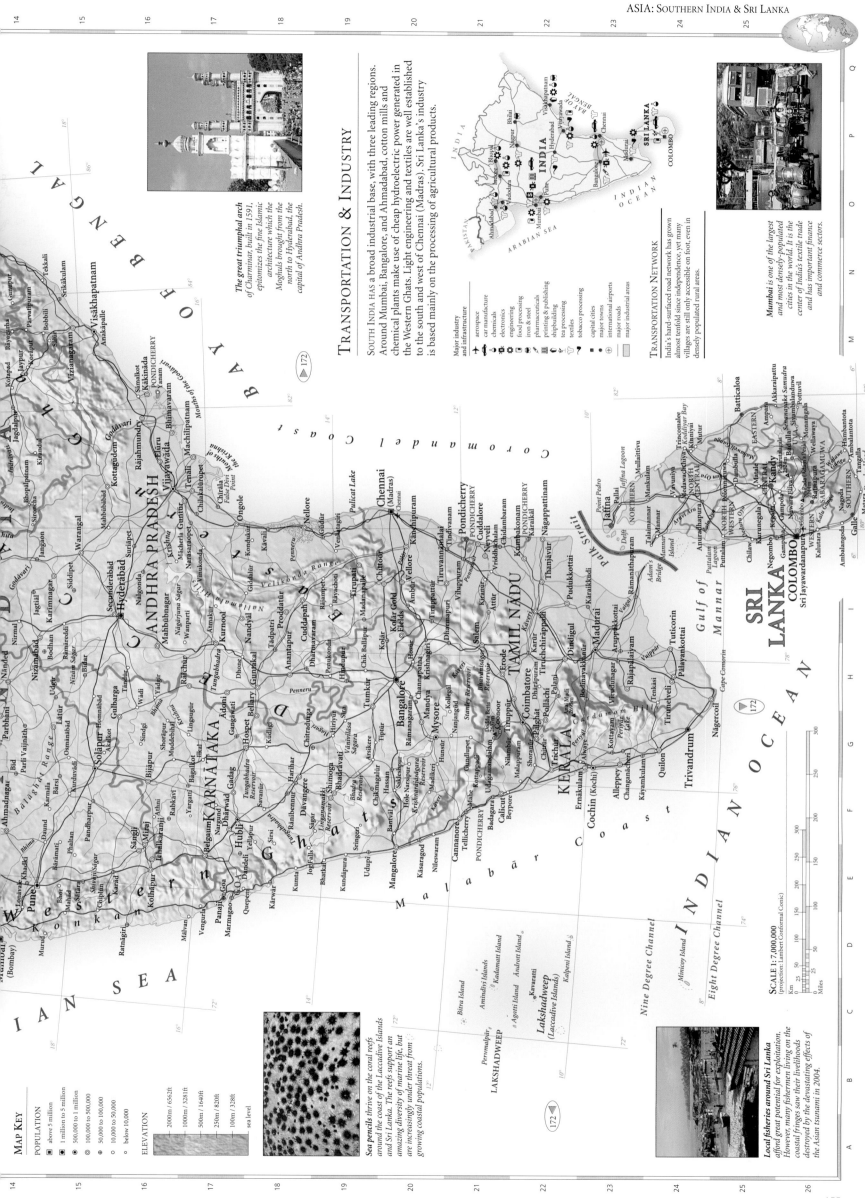

***The great triumphal arch** of Charminar, built in 1591, epitomizes the fine Islamic architecture which the Moghuls brought from the north to Hyderabad, the capital of Andhra Pradesh.*

▶ 172

Transportation & Industry

South India has a broad industrial base, with three leading regions. Around Mumbai, Bangalore, and Ahmadabad, cotton mills and chemical plants make use of cheap hydroelectric power generated in the Western Ghats. Light engineering and textiles are well established to the south and west of Chennai (Madras). Sri Lanka's industry is based mainly on the processing of agricultural products.

Major industry and infrastructure
aerospace
car manufacture
chemicals
electronics
engineering
food processing
iron & steel
pharmaceuticals
printing & publishing
shipbuilding
tea processing
textiles
tobacco processing
capital cities
major towns
international airports
major roads
major industrial areas
PAKISTAN
INDIA
ARABIAN SEA
BAY OF BENGAL
INDIAN OCEAN
Ahmadabad
Vadodara
Indore
Bhopal
Nagpur
Bhilai
Mumbai
Pune
Hyderabad
Visakhapatnam
Vijayawada
Bangalore
Chennai
Madurai
SRI LANKA
COLOMBO

Transportation Network

India's hard-surfaced road network has grown almost tenfold since independence, yet many villages are still only accessible on foot, even in densely populated rural areas.

***Mumbai** is one of the largest and most densely-populated cities in the world. It is the center of India's textile trade and has important finance and commerce sectors.*

172 ◀

▼ 172

Mainland East Asia

China, Mongolia, North Korea, South Korea, Taiwan

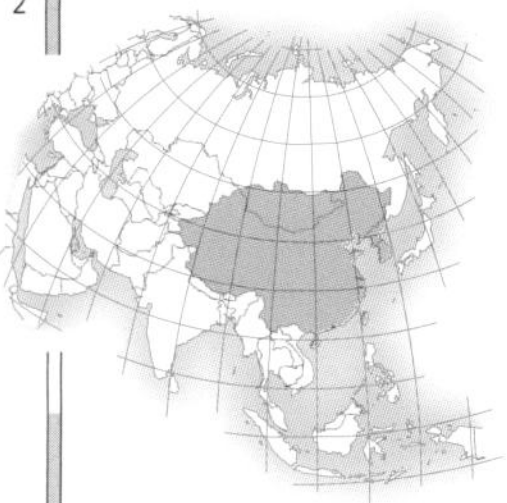

China, the world's most populous nation, has an unbroken cultural history, longer than that of any other country, and is rapidly emerging as a leading world power. When Mao Zedong established Communist rule in 1949, China had become a backward feudal empire, stricken by civil war and over a century of European and Japanese incursions. The closed regime withstood the traumas of rapid industrialization, communal farming, and the brutal purges of the Cultural Revolution. Since the 1980s has introduced economic reforms, led by expanded foreign trade. China's population is heavily concentrated in the east and, despite accelerating urban growth, remains predominantly rural. One cultural group, the Han, make up over 90% of the people, while five "Autonomous Regions" have been established in the south and west for the main ethnic minorities.

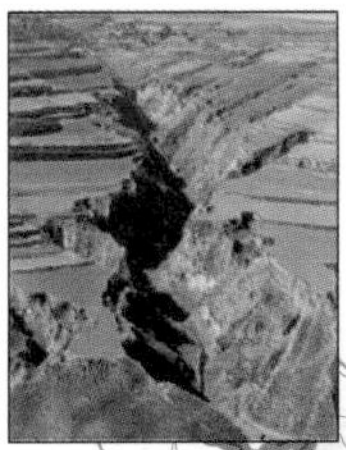

Gansu province, through which the ancient Silk Route passes on its way to the west, is characterized by extensive loess deposits which are terraced and used for crop cultivation.

KAZAKHSTAN
KYRGYZSTAN
TAJIKISTAN
AFGHANISTAN
XINJIANG UYGUR ZIZHIQU
Tarim Pendi
Taklimakan Shamo
Tien Shan
Altai Mountains
Junggar Pendi
Ürümqi
Kashi
Aksu
Kuqa
Hami
Turpan
Karamay
Shihezi
Korla
Yecheng
Hotan
Qiemo
Ruoqiang
Kunlun Shan
Altun Shan
Qaidam Pendi
QINGHAI
Golmud
Qingzang Gaoyuan (Plateau of Tibet)
Tanggula Shan
XIZANG ZIZHIQU (TIBET)
Lhasa
Xigazê
Nyainqêntanglha Shan
Gangdisê Shan
Karakoram Range
HIMALAYAS
INDIA
NEPAL
BHUTAN
MYANMAR
Mount Everest 8850m
K2 8611m
Muz Tag 6973m
Aksai Chin (Administered by China, claimed by India)
Demchok/Dêmqog (Administered by China, claimed by India)
Lop Nur
Dunhuang
HOVD
UVS
BAYAN-ÖLGIY
GOVI-ALTAY
Tropic of Cancer

144 146 146 150 150 150 150 166

Transportation & Industry

Large-scale industrial growth has always been a priority of the Communist government. Metals and machine production, chemicals, and engineering are among the leading industries, concentrated in the major cities of the east coast. Textiles and clothing manufacture, the main consumer goods sector, is relatively well dispersed, with a few significant centers such as Shanghai, Beijing, and Hong Kong.

RUSSIAN FEDERATION
KAZAKH.
KYRG.
TAJIK.
PAK.
INDIA
NEPAL
BHUTAN
MYANMAR
LAOS
VIET.
ULAN BATOR
MONGOLIA
CHINA
NORTH KOREA
PYONGYANG
SOUTH KOREA
SEOUL
BEIJING
Shenyang
Taiyuan
Lanzhou
Nanjing
Shanghai
Wuhan
Chongqing
Kunming
Guangzhou
Hong Kong
TAIPEI
TAIWAN
(claimed by India)

Major industry and infrastructure

- car manufacture
- chemicals
- electronics
- engineering
- finance
- food processing
- iron & steel
- shipbuilding
- textiles
- capital cities
- major towns
- international airports
- major roads
- major industrial areas

Transportation Network

	734,473 miles (1,182,727 km)		1,182 miles (1,904 km)
	41,798 miles (67,308 km)		70,495 miles (113,519 km)

Steam trains use China's abundant coal and are still the main form of passenger and goods transportation. The railroad network is now struggling to meet an ever-growing demand.

Coal is China's most abundant mineral resource. This mine at Fuxin in Liaoning province is used to provide coal for a nearby power station.

The Landscape

The East Asian landmass is arranged in three distinct levels, the highest of which is the Plateau of Tibet in the southwest. The arid uplands of northwestern China form a barren middle step. The main rivers flow eastward from these two platforms to the East China and South China sea coasts, across a broad region of alluvial lowlands and low hills.

Paektu-san, at 9,023 ft (2,750 m), is North Korea's highest peak; an extinct volcanic cone now filled by a crater lake.

The Plateau of Tibet occupies about a quarter of China's total area. The Yangtze, Mekong, Indus, and Brahmaputra Rivers all originate in the south and east of the plateau.

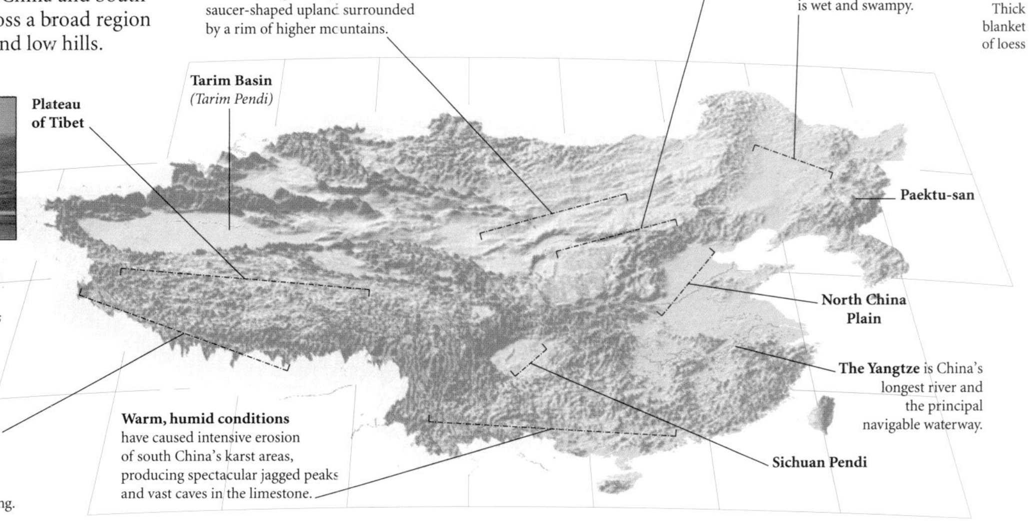

Plateau of Tibet
Tarim Basin (Tarim Pendi)
Paektu-san
North China Plain
Sichuan Pendi

The Gobi Desert extends across the Nei Mongol Gaoyuan; a vast saucer-shaped upland surrounded by a rim of higher mountains.

The loess plateau of northern China is the world's greatest expanse of loess, a loose soil made up of wind-blown material. The plateau has been heavily eroded by tributaries of the Yellow River.

Shifting sand dunes are found in the arid west of the northeast China Plain, while the eastern part of this great expanse is wet and swampy.

The Himalayas extend along the southwestern edge of the Plateau of Tibet, forming a continuous mountain barrier over 1,500 miles (2,500 km) long.

Warm, humid conditions have caused intensive erosion of south China's karst areas, producing spectacular jagged peaks and vast caves in the limestone.

The Yangtze is China's longest river and the principal navigable waterway.

River-eroded fine soils
Thick blanket of loess

Because of its very small grain-size, loess has been easily transported and deposited by winds which scour the plains, and in northern China, deposits of loess can be up to 3,000 ft (1,000 m) thick. Loess-based soils are very fertile, but clearing land for agriculture quickly destabilizes the soil and allows it to be eroded.

Although it is over 20 years since his death, the legacy of Chairman Mao Zedong, architect of the Great Proletarian Cultural Revolution, is still very much in evidence across China's landscape. In 1959 Mao launched a 20-year period of industrialization and socioeconomic realignment, rejecting western ideals and social codes.

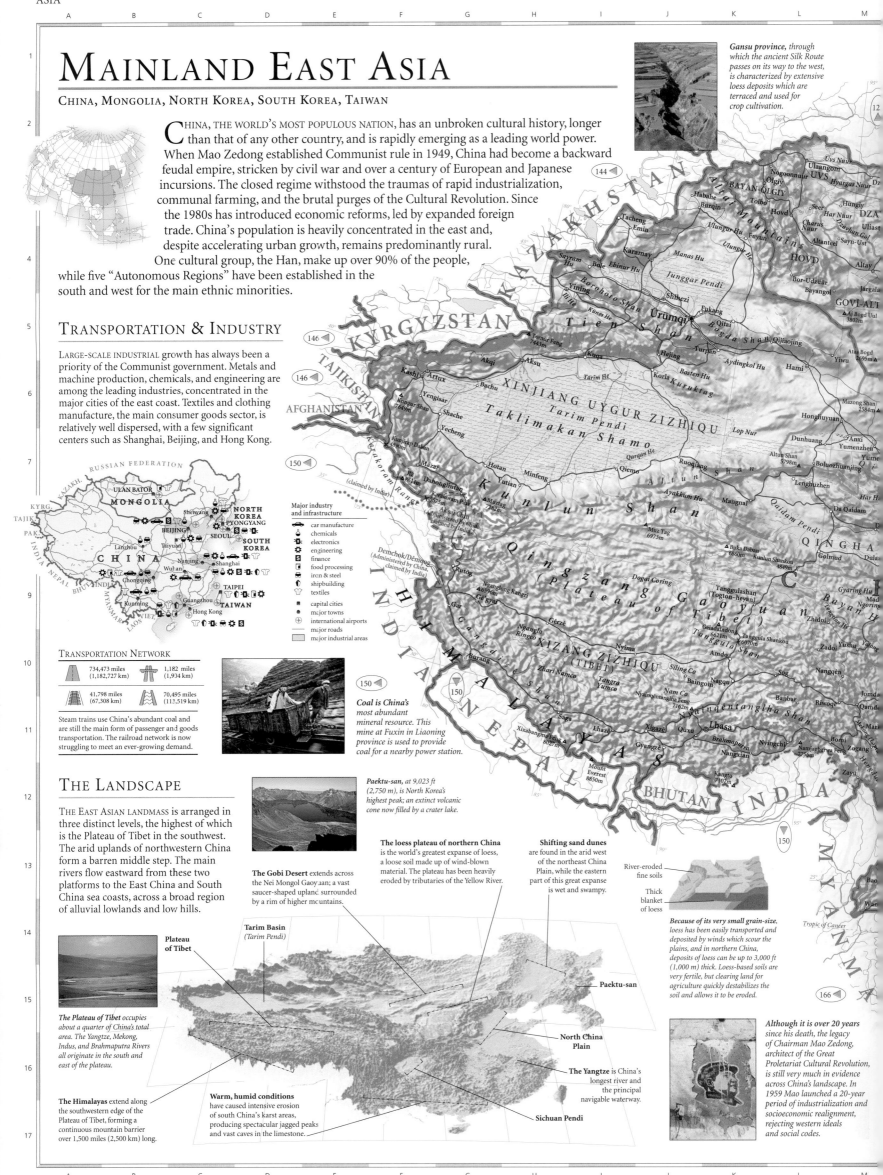

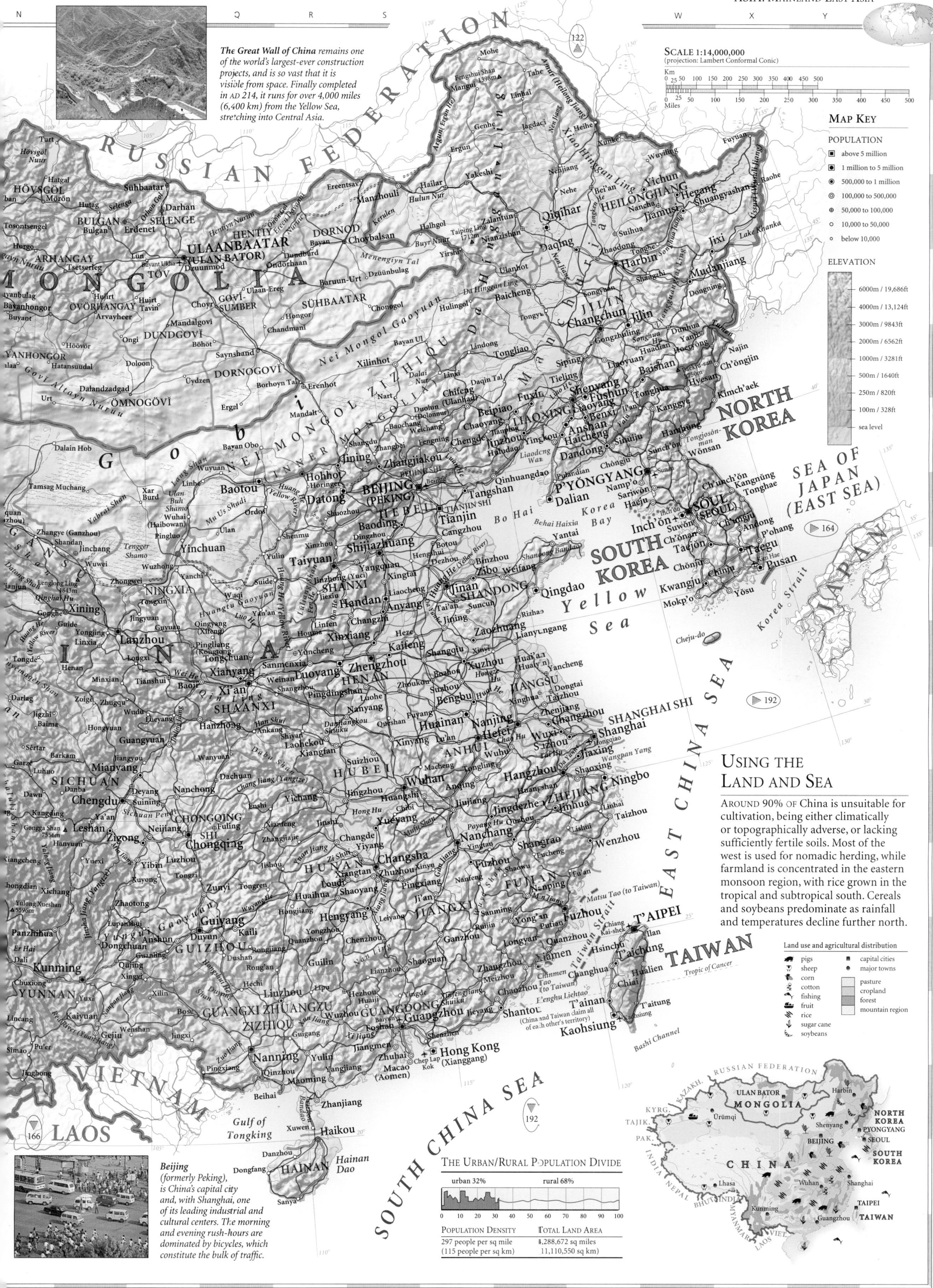
RUSSIAN FEDERATION
MONGOLIA
CHINA
NORTH KOREA
SOUTH KOREA
JAPAN
TAIWAN
VIETNAM
LAOS
SEA OF JAPAN (EAST SEA)
EAST CHINA SEA
SOUTH CHINA SEA
Yellow Sea
Bo Hai
Korea Bay
Gulf of Tongking
Gobi
INNER MONGOLIA
NEI MONGOL ZIZHIQU
HEILONGJIANG
JILIN
LIAONING
HEBEI
SHANXI
SHANDONG
HENAN
SHAANXI
NINGXIA
GANSU
SICHUAN
CHONGQING SHI
HUBEI
ANHUI
JIANGSU
ZHEJIANG
JIANGXI
HUNAN
FUJIAN
GUIZHOU
YUNNAN
GUANGXI ZHUANGZU ZIZHIQU
GUANGDONG
HAINAN
SHANGHAI SHI
ULAANBAATAR (ULAN BATOR)
BEIJING (PEKING)
P'YŎNGYANG
SŎUL (SEOUL)
T'AIPEI
Harbin
Shenyang
Tianjin
Shanghai
Wuhan
Chongqing
Chengdu
Guangzhou
Hong Kong (Xianggang)
Macao (Aomen)
Nanjing
Xi'an
Lanzhou
Kunming
Busan
Dalian
Qingdao
Taiyuan
Shijiazhuang
Zhengzhou
Changsha
Nanchang
Fuzhou
Hangzhou
Hefei
Jinan
Guiyang
Nanning
Haikou
Kaohsiung
Taegu
Inch'ŏn
Baotou
Hohhot
Yinchuan
Xining
Changchun
Qiqihar
Dandong
Korea Strait
Taiwan Strait
Bashi Channel
Tropic of Cancer
(China and Taiwan claim all of each other's territory)
122
164
192
166
pigs
sheep
corn
cotton
fishing
fruit
rice
sugar cane
soybeans
capital cities
major towns
pasture
cropland
forest
mountain region
urban 32%
rural 68%

***The Great Wall of China** remains one of the world's largest-ever construction projects, and is so vast that it is visible from space. Finally completed in AD 214, it runs for over 4,000 miles (6,400 km) from the Yellow Sea, stretching into Central Asia.*

Scale 1:14,000,000
(projection: Lambert Conformal Conic)

Km 0 25 50 100 150 200 250 300 350 400 450 500
Miles 0 25 50 100 150 200 250 300 350 400 450 500

Map Key

Population

- above 5 million
- 1 million to 5 million
- 500,000 to 1 million
- 100,000 to 500,000
- 50,000 to 100,000
- 10,000 to 50,000
- below 10,000

Elevation

- 6000m / 19,686ft
- 4000m / 13,124ft
- 3000m / 9843ft
- 2000m / 6562ft
- 1000m / 3281ft
- 500m / 1640ft
- 250m / 820ft
- 100m / 328ft
- sea level

Using the Land and Sea

Around 90% of China is unsuitable for cultivation, being either climatically or topographically adverse, or lacking sufficiently fertile soils. Most of the west is used for nomadic herding, while farmland is concentrated in the eastern monsoon region, with rice grown in the tropical and subtropical south. Cereals and soybeans predominate as rainfall and temperatures decline further north.

Land use and agricultural distribution

***Beijing** (formerly Peking), is China's capital city and, with Shanghai, one of its leading industrial and cultural centers. The morning and evening rush-hours are dominated by bicycles, which constitute the bulk of traffic.*

The Urban/Rural Population Divide

Population Density	Total Land Area
297 people per sq mile (115 people per sq km)	4,288,672 sq miles (11,110,550 sq km)

Western China

Gansu, Ningxia, Qinghai, Tibet, Xinjiang

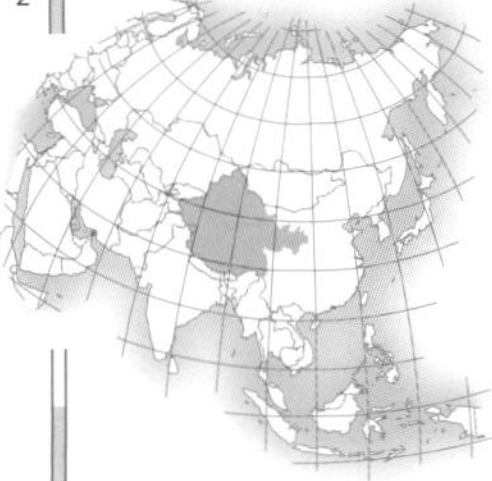

The plateaus and basins of China's dry, desolate western domain are sparsely populated and largely undeveloped, although they have rich mineral reserves; they also form a critical buffer zone for China, in a geographically important and culturally sensitive part of the Asian continent. Across most of the west, the Han Chinese are outnumbered by a range of cultural groups, including the Uygur, the largest group of the various seminomadic Muslim peoples from Central Asia. The remote, inhospitable Plateau of Tibet is the world's coldest and highest plateau. It has been occupied by the Chinese since 1950. Tibet is one of western China's five "Autonomous Regions," but its reclusive Buddhist culture has been systematically undermined by the Chinese government.

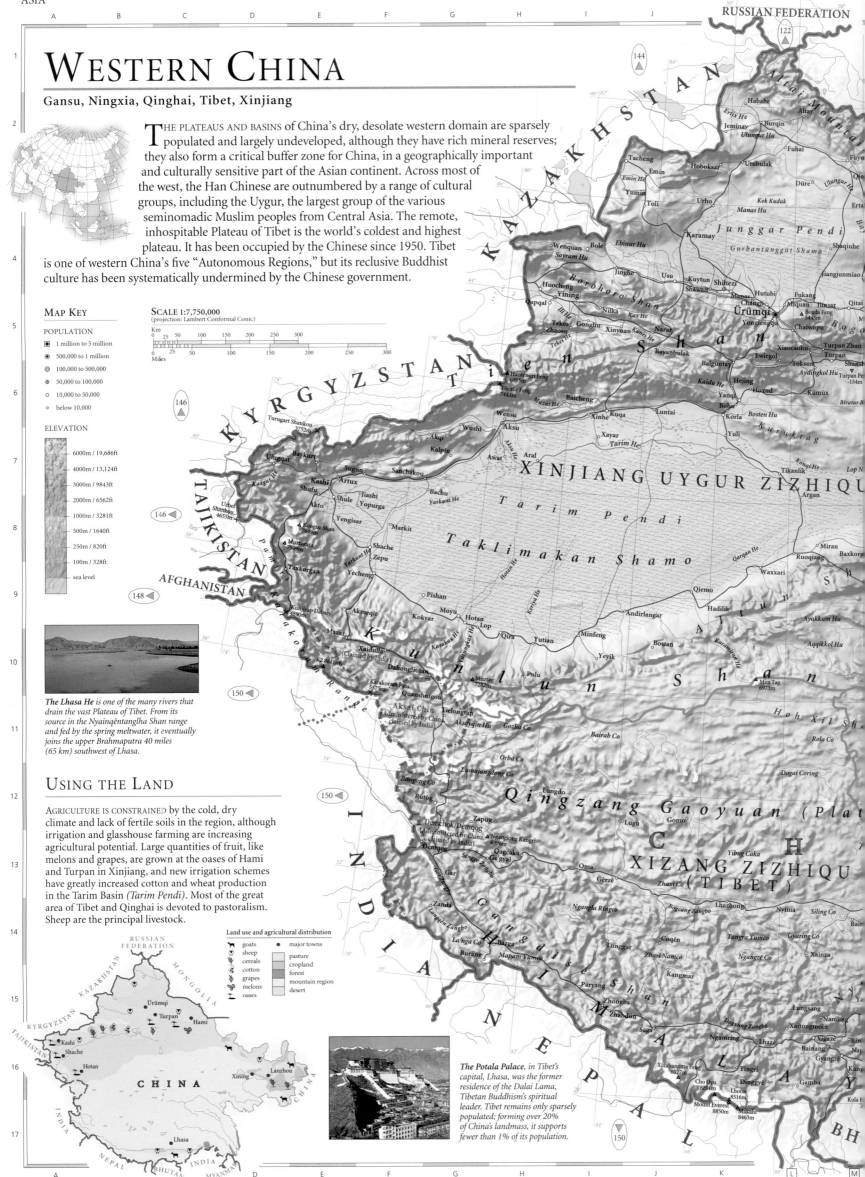

Map Key

POPULATION

- 1 million to 5 million
- 500,000 to 1 million
- 100,000 to 500,000
- 50,000 to 100,000
- 10,000 to 50,000
- below 10,000

ELEVATION

- 6000m / 19,686ft
- 4000m / 13,124ft
- 3000m / 9843ft
- 2000m / 6562ft
- 1000m / 3281ft
- 500m / 1640ft
- 250m / 820ft
- 100m / 328ft
- sea level

Scale 1:7,750,000
(projection: Lambert Conformal Conic)

Km 0 25 50 100 150 200 250 300
Miles 0 25 50 100 150 200 250 300

RUSSIAN FEDERATION
KAZAKHSTAN
KYRGYZSTAN
TAJIKISTAN
AFGHANISTAN
INDIA
NEPAL
XINJIANG UYGUR ZIZHIQU
XIZANG ZIZHIQU (TIBET)
Tarim Pendi
Taklimakan Shamo
Junggar Pendi
Tien Shan
Kunlun Shan
Altun Shan
Qingzang Gaoyuan (Plat
Gangdisê Shan
Himalaya
Ürümqi
Kashi
Hotan
Aksu
Turpan

The Lhasa He is one of the many rivers that drain the vast Plateau of Tibet. From its source in the Nyainqêntanglha Shan range and fed by the spring meltwater, it eventually joins the upper Brahmaputra 40 miles (65 km) southwest of Lhasa.

Using the Land

Agriculture is constrained by the cold, dry climate and lack of fertile soils in the region, although irrigation and glasshouse farming are increasing agricultural potential. Large quantities of fruit, like melons and grapes, are grown at the oases of Hami and Turpan in Xinjiang, and new irrigation schemes have greatly increased cotton and wheat production in the Tarim Basin *(Tarim Pendi)*. Most of the great area of Tibet and Qinghai is devoted to pastoralism. Sheep are the principal livestock.

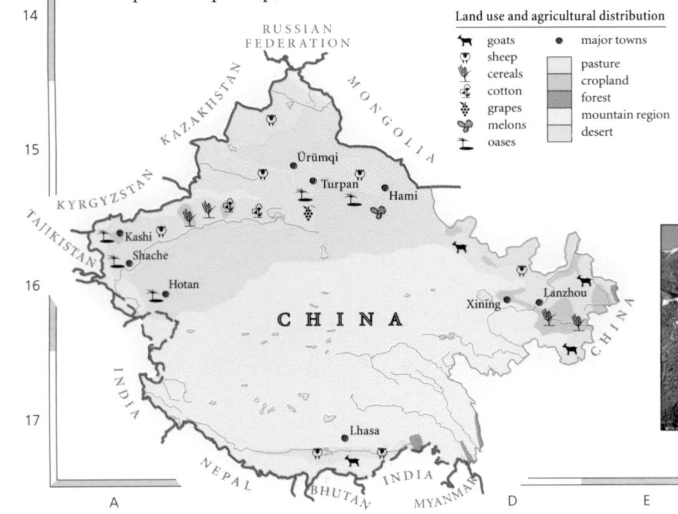

Land use and agricultural distribution
goats
sheep
cereals
cotton
grapes
melons
oases
major towns
pasture
cropland
forest
mountain region
desert
RUSSIAN FEDERATION
MONGOLIA
KAZAKHSTAN
KYRGYZSTAN
TAJIKISTAN
CHINA
INDIA
NEPAL
BHUTAN
MYANMAR
Ürümqi
Turpan
Hami
Kashi
Shache
Hotan
Xining
Lanzhou
Lhasa

The Potala Palace, in Tibet's capital, Lhasa, was the former residence of the Dalai Lama, Tibetan Buddhism's spiritual leader. Tibet remains only sparsely populated; forming over 20% of China's landmass, it supports fewer than 1% of its population.

THE LANDSCAPE

THE HIMALAYAS MARK the southwestern edge of the Plateau of Tibet, an extreme mountain wilderness which occupies nearly a quarter of China's total area. A large structural depression, the Qaidam Pendi, lies at its northeastern edge. The Kunlun mountain chain isolates the plateau from the desert to the north, where the Tien Shan range forms a spur between the Tarim Basin *(Tarim Pendi)* and Dzungarian Basin *(Junggar Pendi)*.

The Tien Shan reach elevations of over 24,419 ft (7443 m) and have permanent ice fields, from which large glaciers extend.
Dzungarian Basin *(Junggar Pendi)*
Northwestern China is largely a region of internal drainage. The Tarim He flows only as far as Lop Nur, where its water is lost by evapotranspiration from the lake and land surface.
A vast glacial lake filled much of the Tarim Basin *(Tarim Pendi)* during the last Ice Age. This area is now occupied by the Takla Makan Desert *(Taklimakan Shamo)*. A remnant of the lake, Lop Nur, forms the eastern margin, where it is fed by the Tarim He.
The Turpan Depression *(Turpan Pendi)* is the lowest and hottest place in China. Temperatures can exceed 117°F (47°C) around the lake of Aydingkol Hu, which lies 505 ft (154 m) below sea level.
Sand dunes cover western parts of the basin of Qaidam Pendi. Strong winds frequently carry the sands east, threatening the agricultural areas around the lake of Qinghai Hu.
Mount Everest is the world's highest peak, at 29,035 ft (8,850 m). The summit marks the border between China and Nepal.

The Bogda Shan, an eastward arm of the Tien Shan range, rise high above the Turpan Depression (Turpan Pendi).

The terrain of the Plateau of Tibet consists of mountain peaks and open plateaus, dotted with brackish lakes. These are probably remnants of the Tethys Sea, which covered the area before it was uplifted following the collision of the Indo-Australian and Eurasian plates.

Tarim Basin *(Tarim Pendi)*

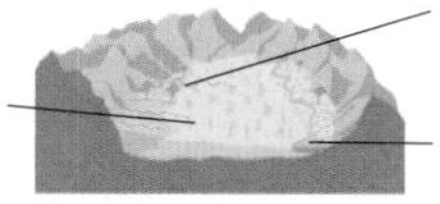
Barchan sand dunes in Takla Makan Desert *(Taklimakan Shamo)*
Oases at edge of basin
Lop Nur

The Tarim Basin *(Tarim Pendi) has no permanent rivers. Rainfall from the surrounding Plateau of Tibet and Tien Shan ranges drains into the basin's sand and gravel floor.*

From its source, *high in eastern Qinghai, the Yellow River starts on a 3,395 mile (5,464 km) journey to the Yellow Sea.*

MONGOLIA
NEI MONGOL ZIZHIQU
GANSU
NINGXIA
QINGHAI
SHAANXI
SICHUAN
YUNNAN
INDIA
MYANMAR
Plateau of Tibet
Qaidam Pendi
Qilian Shan
Burhan Budai Shan
Bayan Har Shan
Anyemaqen Shan
Tanggula Shan
Nyainqêntanglha Shan
Hengduan Shan
Hami
Barkol Hu
Dunhuang
Anxi
Yumen
Jiayuguan
Jiuquan (Suzhou)
Zhangye (Ganzhou)
Jinchang
Wuwei
Yinchuan
Shizuishan
Wuzhong
Lanzhou
Xining
Qinghai Hu
Golmud
Delhi
Dulan
Huang He (Yellow River)
Tianshui
Pingliang (Kongtong)
Qingyang (Xifeng)
Guyuan
Linxia
Hezuo
Wudu
Yushu
Qamdo
Nyingchi
Mainling
Zayü
Altun Shan 5798m
Mazong Shan 2584m
Maqên Kangri 6282m
Namjagbarwa Feng 7756m
Kangto 7102m

162
162
160
160
160
150
166

TRANSPORTATION & INDUSTRY

OIL EXTRACTION AT Yumen and in the Dzungarian and Qaidam basins has led to the growth of the petrochemical industry and a range of heavy manufacturing plants in the cities of Lanzhou and Urumqi. Tibet, and most of Xinjiang, have little industry beyond traditional handicrafts, especially textiles at Hotan and Kashi, located along the ancient Silk Route. Nuclear and space-research testing are carried out at Lop Nur in Xinjiang.

TRANSPORTATION NETWORK

The construction of roads connecting Lhasa in Tibet with Sichuan, Qinghai, and Xinjiang was achieved in the 1950s, in spite of the extreme physical conditions of the Plateau of Tibet.

RUSSIAN FEDERATION
KAZAKHSTAN
MONGOLIA
KYRGYZSTAN
TAJIKISTAN
CHINA
INDIA
NEPAL
BHUTAN
MYANMAR
Karamay
Shihezi
Ürümqi
Turpan
Hami
Kashi
Shache
Hotan
Yumen
Jiuquan
Yinchuan
Xining
Lanzhou
Lhasa
Major industry and infrastructure
agribusiness
chemicals
coal
engineering
food processing
iron & steel
nuclear testing
oil
textiles
major towns
major roads
major industrial areas

Eastern China

Taiwan, Anhui, Beijing, Fujian, Guangdong, Guangxi, Guizhou, Hainan, Hebei, Henan, Hubei, Hunan, Jiangsu, Jiangxi, Shaanxi, Shandong, Shanghai, Shanxi, Sichuan, Tianjin, Yunnan, Zhejiang

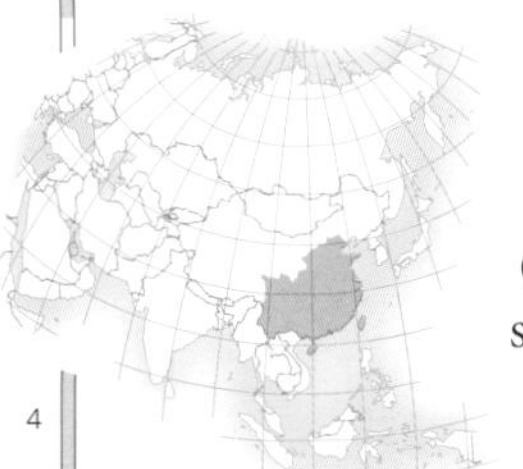

The east is China's heartland. Massive industrial development since 1949 has transformed much of the densely populated rural landscape, in a region still prone to flooding and drought. Over 20 cities have populations of over a million, including the giant metropolis of Shanghai and the capital Beijing, which has been China's cultural and political center since the 13th century. The ethnically diverse southwest and the oil-rich interior provinces of Sichuan and Shaanxi have largely missed out on the remarkable economic growth occurring in designated free-trade areas along the coasts of the South and East China seas. The republic of Taiwan was established in 1949 by Chinese nationalists ousted from the mainland by the victorious Communist forces. Taiwan now has one of the strongest economies in the world but its sovereignty is not recognized by China. Hong Kong provides a major international trade link for China; a 99-year "lease" period of British control was concluded in 1997.

North of the Qin Ling range in Shaanxi province, is an agriculturally fertile region covered with fine, wind-blown deposits and known as the loess plateau. The loose sediments are vulnerable to water erosion.

Using the Land and Sea

This is a region of intensive cultivation. Wheat, millet, sorghum, and cotton are the main crops of the Yellow River basin. South from Sichuan, rice becomes the principal crop, grown with wheat, corn, and cotton along the Yangtze River. Tea is produced in the hills and sugar cane along the coast of the southeast, where flat land is limited. Pigs and poultry are raised in great numbers.

CHINA
BEIJING
Tianjin
Bo Hai
Taiyuan
Qingdao
Yellow Sea
CHINA
Xi'an
Shanghai
Hangzhou
East China Sea
Chengdu
Wuhan
CHINA
INDIA
MYANMAR
Fuzhou
TAIPEI
TAIWAN
Kunming
Guangzhou
Hong Kong
VIETNAM
LAOS
Hainan Dao
South China Sea

Land use and agricultural distribution

- cattle
- pigs
- cereals
- corn (maize)
- cotton
- fishing
- peanuts
- rice
- sugar cane
- tea
- capital cities
- major towns
- pasture
- cropland
- forest
- mountain region

On the hills above the North China Plain, slopes are terraced to utilize the rich loess soils of the Taihang Shan range.

Map Key

POPULATION

- above 5 million
- 1 million to 5 million
- 500,000 to 1 million
- 100,000 to 500,000
- 50,000 to 100,000
- 10,000 to 50,000
- below 10,000

ELEVATION

- 6000m / 19,686ft
- 4000m / 13,124ft
- 3000m / 9843ft
- 2000m / 6562ft
- 1000m / 3281ft
- 500m / 1640ft
- 250m / 820ft
- 100m / 328ft
- sea level

SCALE 1:8,500,000
(projection: Lambert Conformal Conic)

Km 0 25 50 100 150 200 250 300
Miles 0 25 50 100 150 200 250 300

QINGHAI
GANSU
NINGXIA
NEI MONGOL
SHAANXI
SICHUAN
CHONGQING SHI
GUIZHOU
YUNNAN
GUANGXI ZHUANGZU ZIZHIQU
XIZANG ZIZHIQU (TIBET)
MYANMAR
LAOS
VIETNAM
Gulf of Tongking
Hainan Dao
HAINAN
Qin Ling
Taibai Shan 3767m
Xianyang
Xi'an
Baoji
Hanzhong
Yan'an
Tongchuan
Yulin
Shenmu
Zoigê
Aba
Barkam
Songpan
Mianyang
Deyang
Chengdu
Dujiangyan
Kangding
Gongga Shan 7556m
Emei Shan 3099m
Leshan
Zigong
Neijiang
Yibin
Luzhou
Chongqing
Nanchong
Dazhou
Wanzhou
Fuling
Sichuan Pendi
Daxue Shan
Qionglai Shan
Shaluli Shan
Batang
Litang
Zhongdian
Lijiang
Dali
Er Hai
Yulong Xueshan 5596m
Panzhihua
Dongchuan
Kunming
Dian Chi
Qujing
Yuxi
Gejiu
Kaiyuan
Simao
Jinghong
Mengla
Baoshan
Ruili
Tropic of Cancer
Zhaotong
Zunyi
Guiyang
Anshun
Duyun
Kaili
Liuzhou
Guilin
Wuzhou
Nanning
Yulin
Qinzhou
Beihai
Zhanjiang
Haikou
Sanya
Wuzhi Shan 1867m
Yichang
Three Gorges Dam
Chang Jiang (Yangtze)
Jinsha Jiang (Yangtze)
Red River (Yuan Jiang)
Mekong (Lancang Jiang)
Nu Shan
Hengduan Shan
Yunnan Gaoyuan
Dian Chi
Shiping
Weizhou Dao
Leizhou Bandao
Qiongzhou Haixia

The former Portuguese territory of Macao, with its colonial architecture, bars and casinos, reverted to Chinese rule in 1999.

Beijing (Peking)
Tianjin
Bo Hai
Hebei
Shandong
Jiangsu
Anhui
Shanghai
Shanghai Shi
Yellow Sea
East China Sea
Zhejiang
Jiangxi
Fujian
Guangdong
Taiwan
Taipei
Taiwan Strait
Hong Kong (Xianggang)
Kowloon (Jiulong)
Macao (Aomen)
South China Sea
Tropic of Cancer

The Landscape

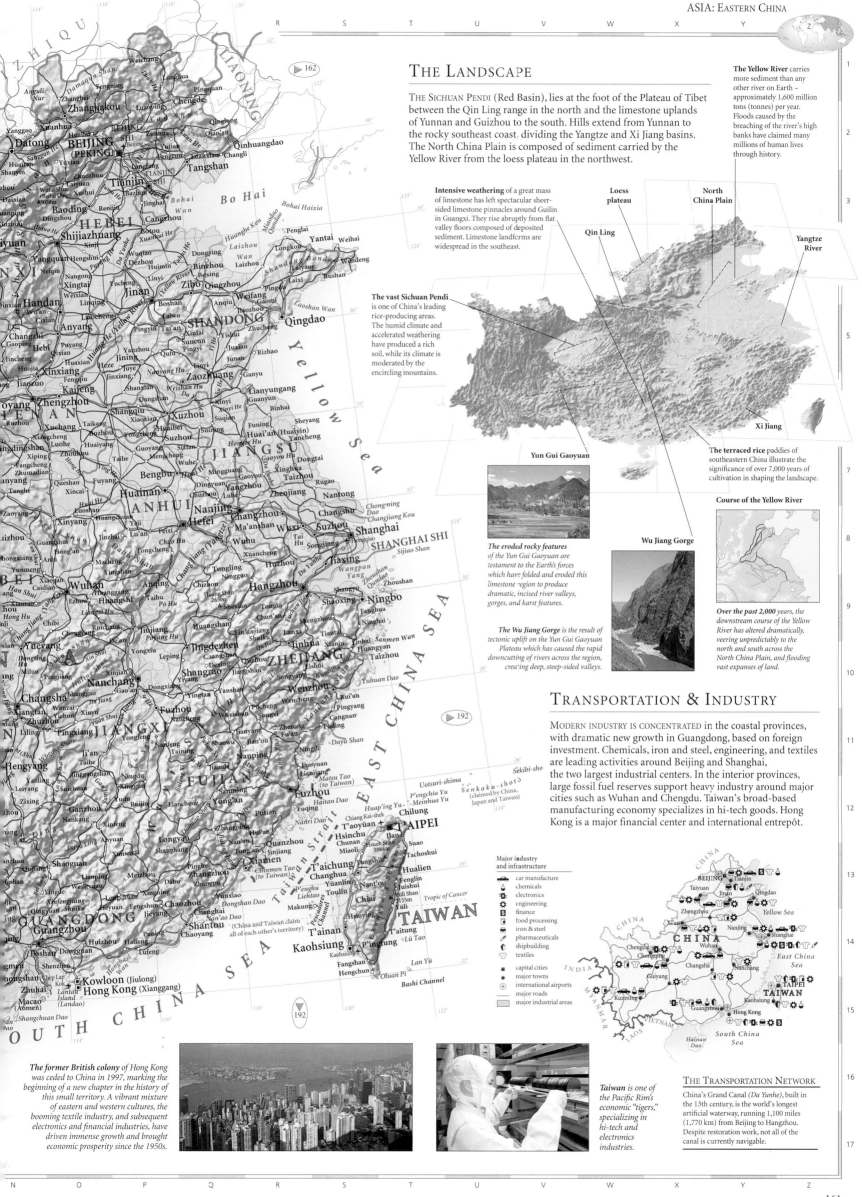

The Sichuan Pendi (Red Basin), lies at the foot of the Plateau of Tibet between the Qin Ling range in the north and the limestone uplands of Yunnan and Guizhou to the south. Hills extend from Yunnan to the rocky southeast coast, dividing the Yangtze and Xi Jiang basins. The North China Plain is composed of sediment carried by the Yellow River from the loess plateau in the northwest.

The Yellow River carries more sediment than any other river on Earth – approximately 1,600 million tons (tonnes) per year. Floods caused by the breaching of the river's high banks have claimed many millions of human lives through history.

Intensive weathering of a great mass of limestone has left spectacular sheer-sided limestone pinnacles around Guilin in Guangxi. They rise abruptly from flat valley floors composed of deposited sediment. Limestone landforms are widespread in the southeast.

The vast Sichuan Pendi is one of China's leading rice-producing areas. The humid climate and accelerated weathering have produced a rich soil, while its climate is moderated by the encircling mountains.

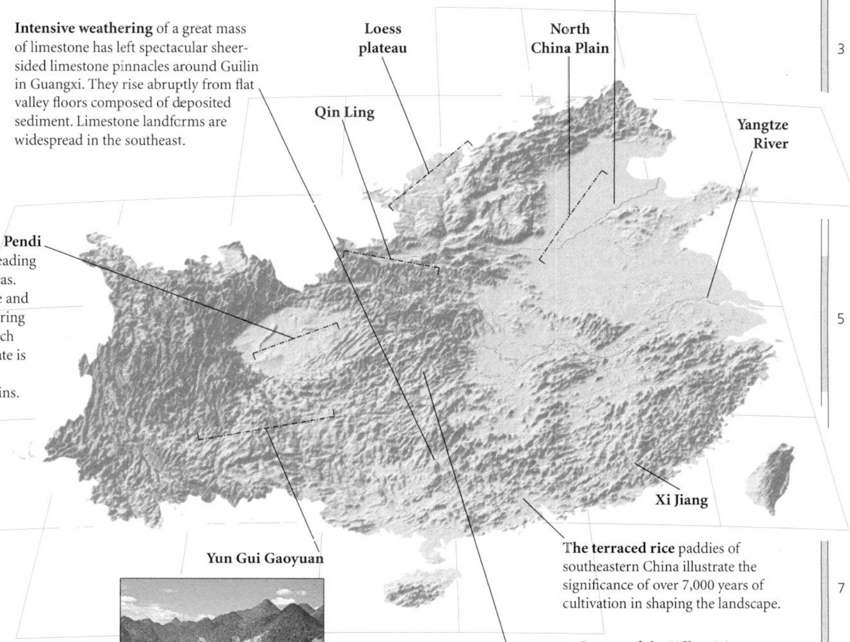

Loess plateau
North China Plain
Qin Ling
Yangtze River
Xi Jiang
Yun Gui Gaoyuan
Wu Jiang Gorge

The terraced rice paddies of southeastern China illustrate the significance of over 7,000 years of cultivation in shaping the landscape.

The eroded rocky features of the Yun Gui Gaoyuan are testament to the Earth's forces which have folded and eroded this limestone region to produce dramatic, incised river valleys, gorges, and karst features.

__The Wu Jiang Gorge__ is the result of tectonic uplift on the Yun Gui Gaoyuan Plateau which has caused the rapid downcutting of rivers across the region, creating deep, steep-sided valleys.

Course of the Yellow River

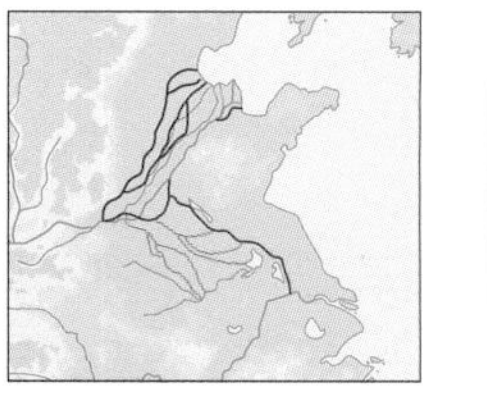

__Over the past 2,000__ years, the downstream course of the Yellow River has altered dramatically, veering unpredictably to the north and south across the North China Plain, and flooding vast expanses of land.

Transportation & Industry

Modern industry is concentrated in the coastal provinces, with dramatic new growth in Guangdong, based on foreign investment. Chemicals, iron and steel, engineering, and textiles are leading activities around Beijing and Shanghai, the two largest industrial centers. In the interior provinces, large fossil fuel reserves support heavy industry around major cities such as Wuhan and Chengdu. Taiwan's broad-based manufacturing economy specializes in hi-tech goods. Hong Kong is a major financial center and international entrepôt.

Major industry and infrastructure
car manufacture
chemicals
electronics
engineering
finance
food processing
iron & steel
pharmaceuticals
shipbuilding
textiles
capital cities
major towns
international airports
major roads
major industrial areas
CHINA
Beijing
Tianjin
Taiyuan
Jinan
Qingdao
Zhengzhou
Xi'an
Nanjing
Shanghai
Wuhan
Chengdu
Chongqing
Changsha
Nanchang
Guiyang
Kunming
Guangzhou
Hong Kong
Kaohsiung
Taipei
TAIWAN
Yellow Sea
East China Sea
South China Sea
Hainan Dao
India
Myanmar
Laos
Vietnam

__The former British colony__ of Hong Kong was ceded to China in 1997, marking the beginning of a new chapter in the history of this small territory. A vibrant mixture of eastern and western cultures, the booming textile industry, and subsequent electronics and financial industries, have driven immense growth and brought economic prosperity since the 1950s.

__Taiwan__ is one of the Pacific Rim's economic "tigers," specializing in hi-tech and electronics industries.

The Transportation Network

China's Grand Canal (*Da Yunhe*), built in the 13th century, is the world's longest artificial waterway, running 1,100 miles (1,770 km) from Beijing to Hangzhou. Despite restoration work, not all of the canal is currently navigable.

Northeastern China, Mongolia & Korea

Mongolia, North Korea, South Korea, Heilongjiang, Inner Mongolia, Jilin, Liaoning

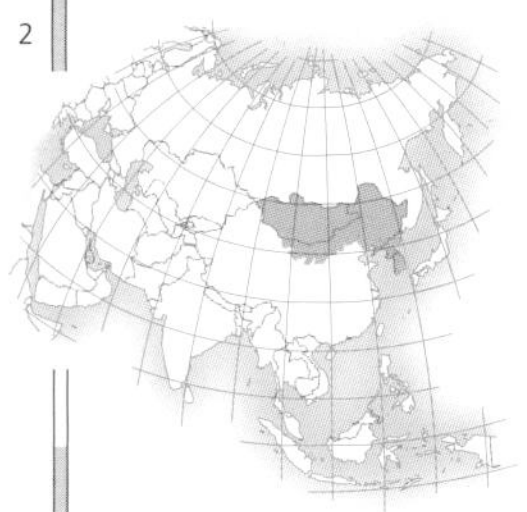

This northerly region has been a domain of shifting borders and competing colonial powers for centuries. Mongolia was the heartland of Chinghiz Khan's vast Mongol empire in the 13th century, while northeastern China was home to the Manchus, China's last ruling dynasty (1644–1911). The mineral and forest wealth of the northeast helped make this China's principal region of heavy industry, although the outdated state factories now face decline. South Korea's state-led market economy has grown dramatically and Seoul is now one of the world's largest cities. The austere communist regime of North Korea has isolated itself from the expanding markets of the Pacific Rim and faces continuing economic stagnation.

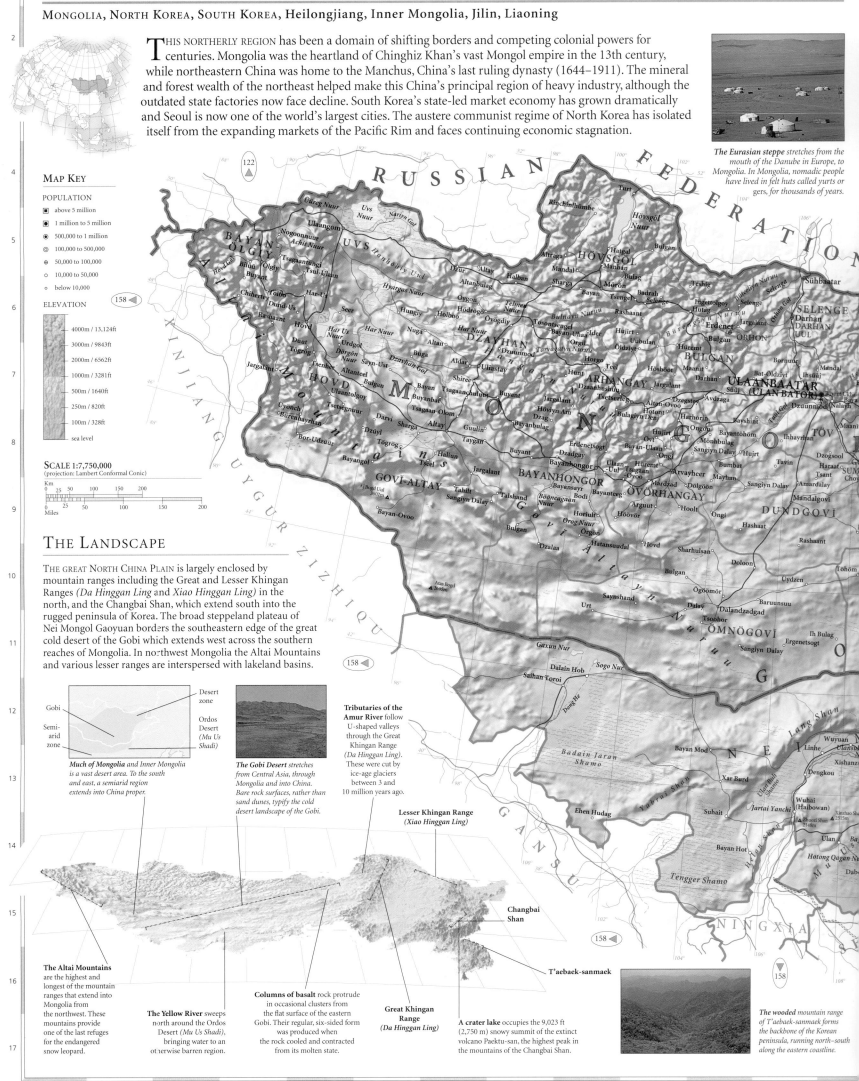

***The Eurasian steppe** stretches from the mouth of the Danube in Europe, to Mongolia. In Mongolia, nomadic people have lived in felt huts called yurts or gers, for thousands of years.*

Map Key

POPULATION

- above 5 million
- 1 million to 5 million
- 500,000 to 1 million
- 100,000 to 500,000
- 50,000 to 100,000
- 10,000 to 50,000
- below 10,000

ELEVATION

- 4000m / 13,124ft
- 3000m / 9843ft
- 2000m / 6562ft
- 1000m / 3281ft
- 500m / 1640ft
- 250m / 820ft
- 100m / 328ft
- sea level

SCALE 1:7,750,000
(projection: Lambert Conformal Conic)

Km 0 25 50 100 150 200
Miles 0 25 50 100 150 200

RUSSIAN FEDERATION
MONGOLIA
XINJIANG UYGUR ZIZHIQU
GANSU
NINGXIA
NEI
Altai Mountains
Govi Altayn Nuruu
UVS
BAYAN-ÖLGIY
HOVD
HÖVSGÖL
DZAVHAN
ARHANGAY
BULGAN
SELENGE
DARHAN UUL
ULAANBAATAR (ULAN BATOR)
TÖV
BAYANHONGOR
ÖVÖRHANGAY
DUNDGOVĬ
ÖMNÖGOVĬ
GOVĬ-ALTAY
Uvs Nuur
Üüreg Nuur
Ulaangom
Hövsgöl Nuur
Hyargas Nuur
Har Us Nuur
Har Nuur
Mörön
Erdenet
Darhan
Sühbaatar
Uliastay
Altay
Hovd
Tsetserleg
Harhorin
Arvayheer
Bayanhongor
Mandalgovi
Dalandzadgad
Saynshand
Badain Jaran Shamo
Tengger Shamo
Gaxun Nur
Sogo Nur
Dalain Hob
Saihan Toroi
Wuhai (Haibowan)
Bayan Hot
158
122

The Landscape

The great North China Plain is largely enclosed by mountain ranges including the Great and Lesser Khingan Ranges (*Da Hinggan Ling* and *Xiao Hinggan Ling*) in the north, and the Changbai Shan, which extend south into the rugged peninsula of Korea. The broad steppeland plateau of Nei Mongol Gaoyuan borders the southeastern edge of the great cold desert of the Gobi which extends west across the southern reaches of Mongolia. In northwest Mongolia the Altai Mountains and various lesser ranges are interspersed with lakeland basins.

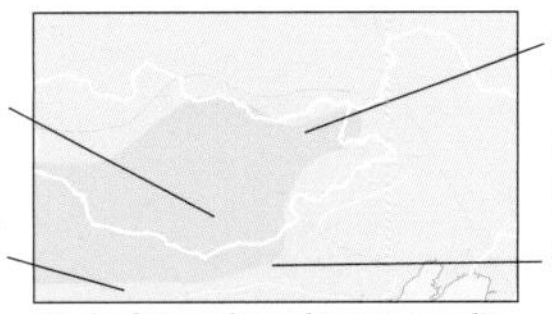

Gobi
Semi-arid zone
Desert zone
Ordos Desert (Mu Us Shadi)

***Much of Mongolia** and Inner Mongolia is a vast desert area. To the south and east, a semiarid region extends into China proper.*

***The Gobi Desert** stretches from Central Asia, through Mongolia and into China. Bare rock surfaces, rather than sand dunes, typify the cold desert landscape of the Gobi.*

Tributaries of the Amur River follow U-shaped valleys through the Great Khingan Range (*Da Hinggan Ling*). These were cut by ice-age glaciers between 3 and 10 million years ago.

Lesser Khingan Range (*Xiao Hinggan Ling*)

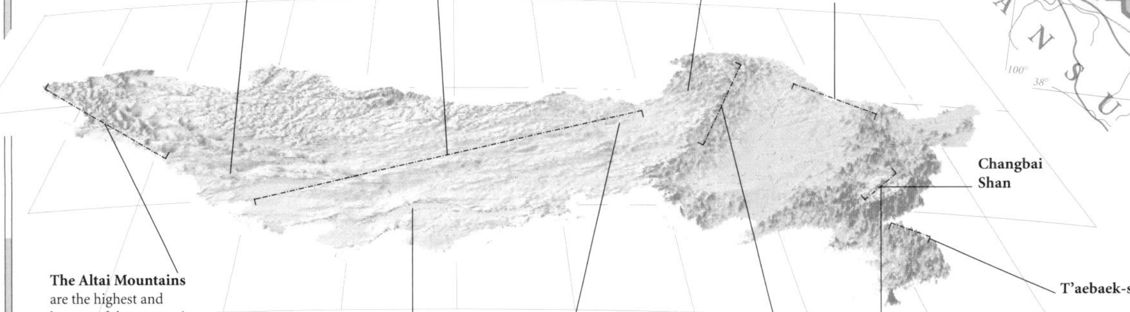

Changbai Shan

T'aebaek-sanmaek

The Altai Mountains are the highest and longest of the mountain ranges that extend into Mongolia from the northwest. These mountains provide one of the last refuges for the endangered snow leopard.

The Yellow River sweeps north around the Ordos Desert (*Mu Us Shadi*), bringing water to an otherwise barren region.

Columns of basalt rock protrude in occasional clusters from the flat surface of the eastern Gobi. Their regular, six-sided form was produced when the rock cooled and contracted from its molten state.

Great Khingan Range (*Da Hinggan Ling*)

A crater lake occupies the 9,023 ft (2,750 m) snowy summit of the extinct volcano Paektu-san, the highest peak in the mountains of the Changbai Shan.

***The wooded** mountain range of T'aebaek-sanmaek forms the backbone of the Korean peninsula, running north–south along the eastern coastline.*

N O P Q R S T U V W X Y

Transportation & Industry

North Korea's centrally-planned economy is strongly oriented toward heavy industry, while South Korea has a broad manufacturing base which includes textiles, steel, electronics, and one of the world's largest shipbuilding industries. Mongolia and Inner Mongolia's great mineral resource potential is largely undeveloped. The heavy industrial region around Shenyang produces iron, steel, chemicals, and cement on a massive scale.

Ulan Bator, the Mongolian capital bears many of the hallmarks of Soviet-style central planning, the result of economic and industrial assistance from the Soviet Union following Mongolian independence in 1921.

Transportation Network

Liaoning has China's most comprehensive railroad network, the legacy of the Japanese occupation of Manchuria in the 20th century. The railroads are used primarily for freight transportation.

Major industry and infrastructure
car manufacture
chemicals
coal
electronics
engineering
finance
food processing
iron & steel
pharmaceuticals
shipbuilding
textiles
capital cities
major towns
international airports
major roads
major industrial areas
RUSSIAN FEDERATION
ULAN BATOR
MONGOLIA
CHINA
Qiqihar
Harbin
Changchun
Jilin
Shenyang
Anshan
Baotou
Dalian
SEA OF JAPAN (EAST SEA)
NORTH KOREA
PYONGYANG
SEOUL
Inch'on
Yellow Sea
SOUTH KOREA
Kwangju
Pusan
Cheju-do

While North Korea has remained politically and economically isolated from the rest of the world, South Korea has enjoyed immense economic growth. It has benefited considerably from US economic aid in the aftermath of the Korean war of 1950–1953.

RUSSIAN FEDERATION
HEILONGJIANG
JILIN
LIAONING
CHINA
NEI MONGOL ZIZHIQU (INNER MONGOLIA)
HEBEI
SHANXI
DORNOD
HENTIY
SÜHBAATAR
NORTH KOREA
SOUTH KOREA
JAPAN
Bo Hai
Liaodong Wan
Korea Bay
Yellow Sea
Sea of Japan (East Sea)
Korea Strait
Cheju Strait
P'YŎNGYANG
SEOUL
Harbin
Changchun
Shenyang
Qiqihar
Dalian
Hohhot
Baotou
Pusan
122
160

Using the Land and Sea

Mongolia and Inner Mongolia rely heavily on livestock farming, with only about 1% of the land area cultivated. Northeastern China produces wheat, corn, soybeans, and sugar beet. The cool climate limits the range of crops and large upland areas of the northeast remain forested. Rice is the staple food of North and South Korea. The latter has become a leading ocean-fishing nation.

Land use and agricultural distribution
goats
pigs
sheep
corn
fishing
rice
soybeans
sugar beet
wheat
capital cities
major towns
pasture
cropland
forest
mountain region
desert
RUSSIAN FEDERATION
ULAN BATOR
MONGOLIA
CHINA
Harbin
Shenyang
Baotou
Bo Hai
SEA OF JAPAN (EAST SEA)
NORTH KOREA
PYONGYANG
SEOUL
Yellow Sea
SOUTH KOREA
Pusan
Cheju-do
Korea Strait

JAPAN

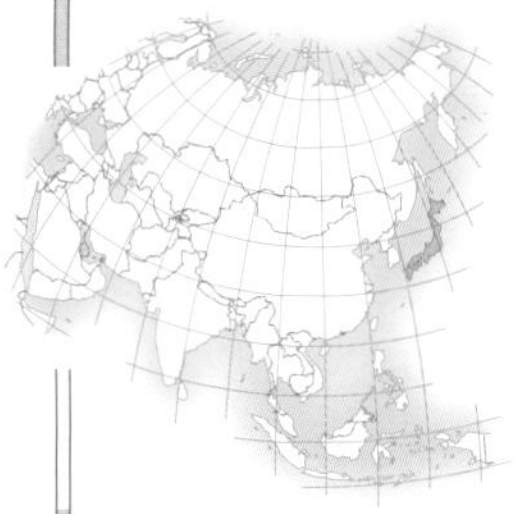

In the years since the end of the Second World War, Japan has become the world's most dynamic industrial nation. The country comprises a string of over 4,000 islands which lie in a great northeast to southwest arc in the northwest Pacific. Four major islands: Hokkaido, Honshu, Shikoku, and Kyushu are home to the great majority of Japan's population of 128 million people, although the mountainous terrain of the central region means that most cities are situated on the coast. A densely populated industrial belt stretches along much of Honshu's southern coast, including Japan's crowded capital, Tokyo. Alongside its spectacular economic growth and the increasing westernization of its cities, Japan still maintains a most singular culture, reflected in its traditional food, formal behavioural codes, unique Shinto religion, and deep reverence for the emperor.

Transportation & Industry

Japan is the world's second largest market economy, outranked only by the US. Technological development, particularly of computers, electronic goods, cars, and motorcycles is second to none. Japanese industry invests in its workforce, and in long-term research and development to maintain the high standard of its products, and a reputation for innovation. Japanese businesses are now global both in their manufacturing bases and in the distribution of goods.

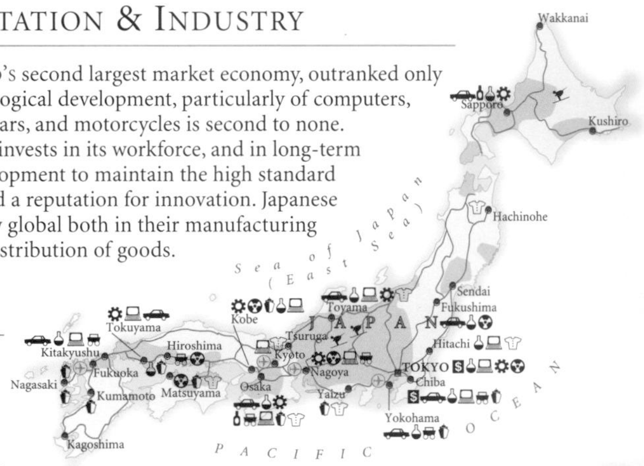

Wakkanai
Sapporo
Kushiro
Hachinohe
Sea of Japan (East Sea)
Sendai
Fukushima
Toyama
Kobe
Tokuyama
Kitakyushu
Hiroshima
Tsuruga
Kyoto
Nagoya
Hitachi
TOKYO
Chiba
Nagasaki
Fukuoka
Kumamoto
Matsuyama
Osaka
Yaizu
Yokohama
Kagoshima
JAPAN
PACIFIC OCEAN

Major industry and infrastructure
- brewing
- car manufacture
- chemicals
- hi-tech industry
- engineering
- finance
- iron & steel
- research & development
- shipbuilding
- textiles
- winter sports
- capital cities
- major towns
- international airports
- major roads
- major industrial areas

Transportation Network

720,360 miles (1,160,000 km)	6,070 miles (12,529 km)
12,529 miles (20,175 km)	1,099 miles (1,770 km)

Japanese road construction traditionally lagged behind that of its extensive and technologically advanced railroad network. The road network's relative lack of development has led to severe urban congestion, although expressways have now been built in some cities.

Known in the west as the "bullet train," the Shinkansen is the second-fastest train in the world. It speeds past the snow-capped peak of Mount Fuji between the cities of Tokyo and Osaka.

The Landscape

The islands of Japan lie on the Pacific "Ring of Fire," and form a series of clearly defined arcs. The largely mountainous landscape was formed very recently in geological terms. Volcanic eruptions and earthquakes continue to reshape the terrain and to shake the country's complex infrastructure. There is no one continuous mountain range; the mountains divide into many small land blocks separated by lowlands and dissected by numerous river valleys.

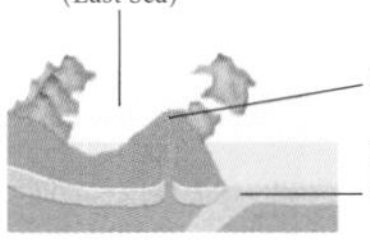

Sea of Japan (East Sea)
Active volcanic island
Japan Trench (subduction zone)

***Japan is part of** an arc of volcanic islands, formed by the Pacific Plate diving under the Eurasian Plate. This process generates intense stress which is periodically released as earthquakes.*

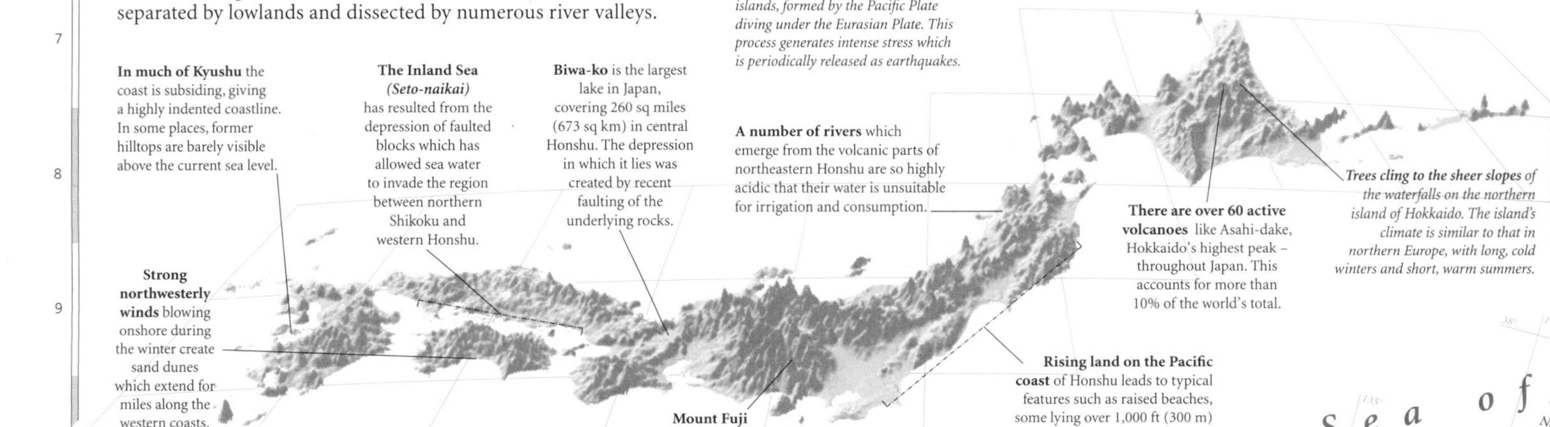

Mount Fuji

In much of Kyushu the coast is subsiding, giving a highly indented coastline. In some places, former hilltops are barely visible above the current sea level.

The Inland Sea (*Seto-naikai*) has resulted from the depression of faulted blocks which has allowed sea water to invade the region between northern Shikoku and western Honshu.

Biwa-ko is the largest lake in Japan, covering 260 sq miles (673 sq km) in central Honshu. The depression in which it lies was created by recent faulting of the underlying rocks.

A number of rivers which emerge from the volcanic parts of northeastern Honshu are so highly acidic that their water is unsuitable for irrigation and consumption.

There are over 60 active volcanoes like Asahi-dake, Hokkaido's highest peak – throughout Japan. This accounts for more than 10% of the world's total.

Strong northwesterly winds blowing onshore during the winter create sand dunes which extend for miles along the western coasts.

Rising land on the Pacific coast of Honshu leads to typical features such as raised beaches, some lying over 1,000 ft (300 m) above sea level.

***Trees cling to the sheer slopes** of the waterfalls on the northern island of Hokkaido. The island's climate is similar to that in northern Europe, with long, cold winters and short, warm summers.*

***Mount Fuji** is Japan's highest mountain, rising 12,388 ft (3,776 m) above the Kanto Plain in the central region of Honshu. The flat land below is suitable for growing crops such as tea. Like many Japanese mountains, it is revered as a sacred site.*

Sea of Japan
JAPAN
HONSHU
Korea Strait
Tsushima
Kitakyūshū
Fukuoka
Nagasaki
Kumamoto
Kyūshū
Kagoshima
Miyazaki
Ōita
Hiroshima
Okayama
Matsuyama
Shikoku
Kōchi
Takamatsu
Tokushima
Kobe
Osaka
Kyoto
Nara
Wakayama
Nagoya
Gifu
Kanazawa
Toyama
Fukui
Hamamatsu
Shizuoka
Matsue
Tottori
Shimonoseki
Yamaguchi
Seto-naikai
Kii-suidō
Ōsumi-kaikyō
Tanega-shima
Yaku-shima
East China Sea
Philippine Sea

157

***Autumnal trees** near Gifu, on central Honshu, create a spectacular display. Native trees on this island include camphor, pasania, Japanese evergreen oak, camellia, and holly.*

***The 1995 Kobe earthquake** highlighted Japan's vulnerability to earthquakes, despite technological advances. It shattered much of the infrastructure of this important port. More than 5,000 people died as buildings and overhead highways collapsed and fires broke out.*

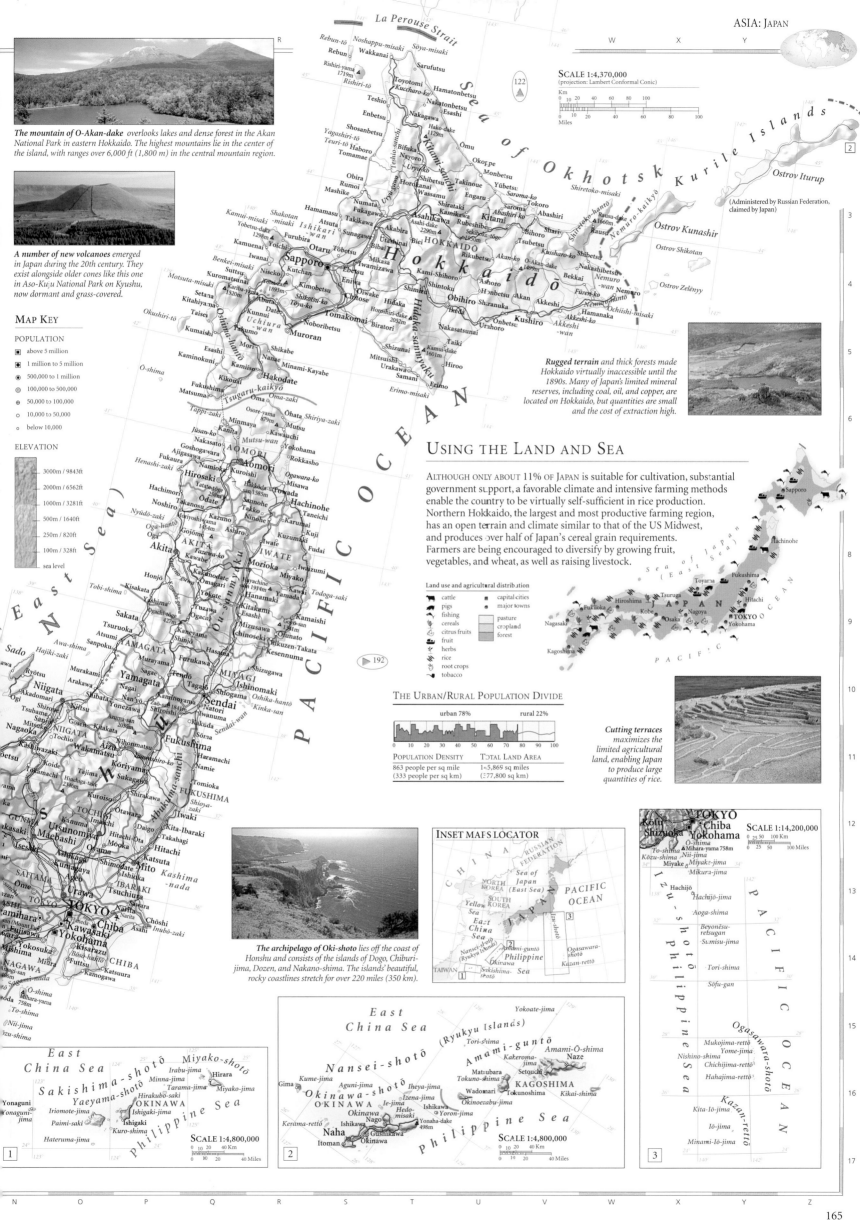

The mountain of O-Akan-dake *overlooks lakes and dense forest in the Akan National Park in eastern Hokkaido. The highest mountains lie in the center of the island, with ranges over 6,000 ft (1,800 m) in the central mountain region.*

A number of new volcanoes *emerged in Japan during the 20th century. They exist alongside older cones like this one in Aso-Kuju National Park on Kyushu, now dormant and grass-covered.*

MAP KEY

POPULATION

- above 5 million
- 1 million to 5 million
- 500,000 to 1 million
- 100,000 to 500,000
- 50,000 to 100,000
- 10,000 to 50,000
- below 10,000

ELEVATION

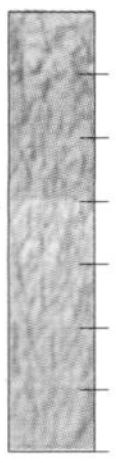

- 3000m / 9843ft
- 2000m / 6562ft
- 1000m / 3281ft
- 500m / 1640ft
- 250m / 820ft
- 100m / 328ft
- sea level

SCALE 1:4,370,000
(projection: Lambert Conformal Conic)
La Perouse Strait
Sea of Okhotsk
Kurile Islands
Ostrov Iturup
(Administered by Russian Federation, claimed by Japan)
Ostrov Kunashir
Ostrov Shikotan
Ostrov Zelënyy
Hokkaidō
Sapporo
Asahikawa
Hakodate
Aomori
Akita
Morioka
Sendai
Yamagata
Niigata
Fukushima
TOKYO
Yokohama
Chiba
Kawasaki
PACIFIC OCEAN
East Sea
Tsugaru-kaikyō

Rugged terrain *and thick forests made Hokkaido virtually inaccessible until the 1890s. Many of Japan's limited mineral reserves, including coal, oil, and copper, are located on Hokkaido, but quantities are small and the cost of extraction high.*

122

192

USING THE LAND AND SEA

ALTHOUGH ONLY ABOUT 11% OF JAPAN is suitable for cultivation, substantial government support, a favorable climate and intensive farming methods enable the country to be virtually self-sufficient in rice production. Northern Hokkaido, the largest and most productive farming region, has an open terrain and climate similar to that of the US Midwest, and produces over half of Japan's cereal grain requirements. Farmers are being encouraged to diversify by growing fruit, vegetables, and wheat, as well as raising livestock.

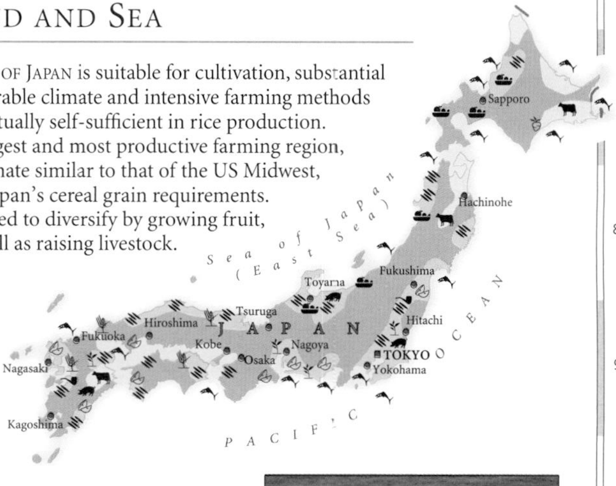

Land use and agricultural distribution
cattle
pigs
fishing
cereals
citrus fruits
fruit
herbs
rice
root crops
tobacco
capital cities
major towns
pasture
cropland
forest
Sapporo
Hachinohe
Sea of Japan (East Sea)
Fukushima
Toyama
Tsuruga
Hiroshima
Fukuoka
JAPAN
Kobe
Nagoya
Osaka
Hitachi
TOKYO
Yokohama
Nagasaki
Kagoshima
PACIFIC OCEAN

Cutting terraces *maximizes the limited agricultural land, enabling Japan to produce large quantities of rice.*

THE URBAN/RURAL POPULATION DIVIDE

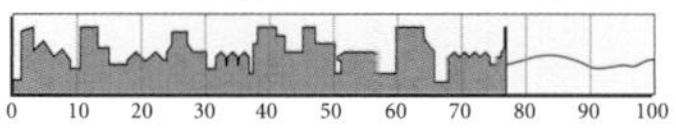

urban 78%
rural 22%
0 10 20 30 40 50 60 70 80 90 100

POPULATION DENSITY	TOTAL LAND AREA
863 people per sq mile (333 people per sq km)	145,869 sq miles (377,800 sq km)

The archipelago of Oki-shoto *lies off the coast of Honshu and consists of the islands of Dogo, Chiburi-jima, Dozen, and Nakano-shima. The islands' beautiful, rocky coastlines stretch for over 220 miles (350 km).*

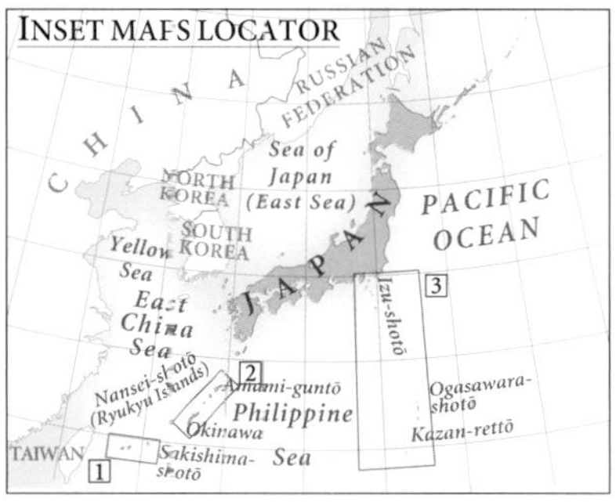

INSET MAPS LOCATOR
CHINA
RUSSIAN FEDERATION
NORTH KOREA
SOUTH KOREA
Sea of Japan (East Sea)
PACIFIC OCEAN
Yellow Sea
East China Sea
JAPAN
Philippine Sea
TAIWAN

TŌKYŌ
Chiba
Yokohama
SCALE 1:14,200,000
Izu-shotō
Hachijō-jima
Aoga-shima
Tori-shima
Sōfu-gan
Ogasawara-shotō
Kazan-rettō
PACIFIC OCEAN
Philippine Sea
3

East China Sea
Sakishima-shotō
Miyako-shotō
Yaeyama-shotō
OKINAWA
Ishigaki
Philippine Sea
SCALE 1:4,800,000
1

East China Sea
Nansei-shotō (Ryukyu Islands)
Amami-guntō
Okinawa-shotō
OKINAWA
KAGOSHIMA
Naha
Philippine Sea
SCALE 1:4,800,000
2

Mainland Southeast Asia

Cambodia, Laos, Myanmar, Thailand, Vietnam

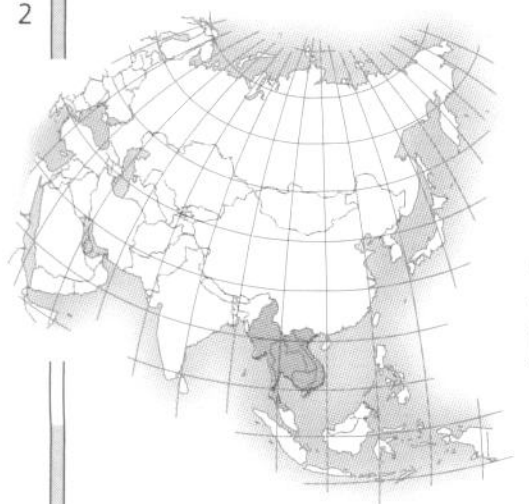

THICKLY FORESTED MOUNTAINS, intercut by the broad valleys of five great rivers characterize the landscape of Southeast Asia's mainland countries. Agriculture remains the main activity for much of the population, which is concentrated in the river flood plains and deltas. Linked ethnic and cultural roots give the region a distinct identity. Most people on the mainland are Theravada Buddhists. Foreign intervention began in the 16th century with the opening of the spice trade; Cambodia, Laos, and Vietnam were French colonies until the end of the Second World War, Myanmar was under British control. Only Thailand was never colonized. Today, Thailand is poised to play a leading role in the economic development of the Pacific Rim, and Laos and Vietnam have begun to mend the devastation of the Vietnam War, and to develop their economies. With continuing political instability and a shattered infrastructure, Cambodia faces an uncertain future, while Myanmar is seeking investment and the ending of its 42-year isolation from the world community.

The Irrawaddy River is Myanmar's vital central artery, watering the ricefields and providing a rich source of fish, as well as an important transportation link, particularly for local traffic.

The coastline of the Isthmus of Kra

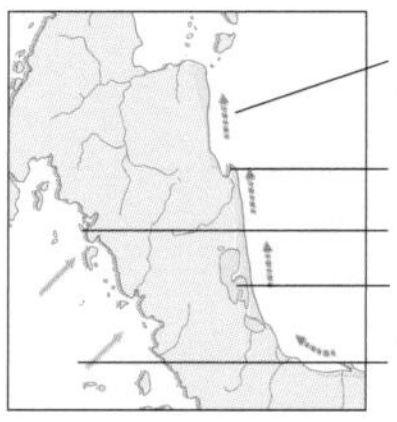
Longshore drift
Spit
Eroded coastline
Lagoon
Wave attack

The east and west coasts of the Isthmus of Kra differ greatly. The tectonically uplifting west coast is exposed to the harsh south-westerly monsoon and is heavily eroded. On the east coast, longshore currents produce depositional features such as spits and lagoons.

The Landscape

A SERIES OF MOUNTAIN RANGES runs north–south through the mainland, formed as the result of the collision between the Eurasian Plate and the Indian subcontinent, which created the Himalayas. They are interspersed by the valleys of a number of great rivers. On their passage to the sea these rivers have deposited sediment, forming huge, fertile floodplains and deltas.

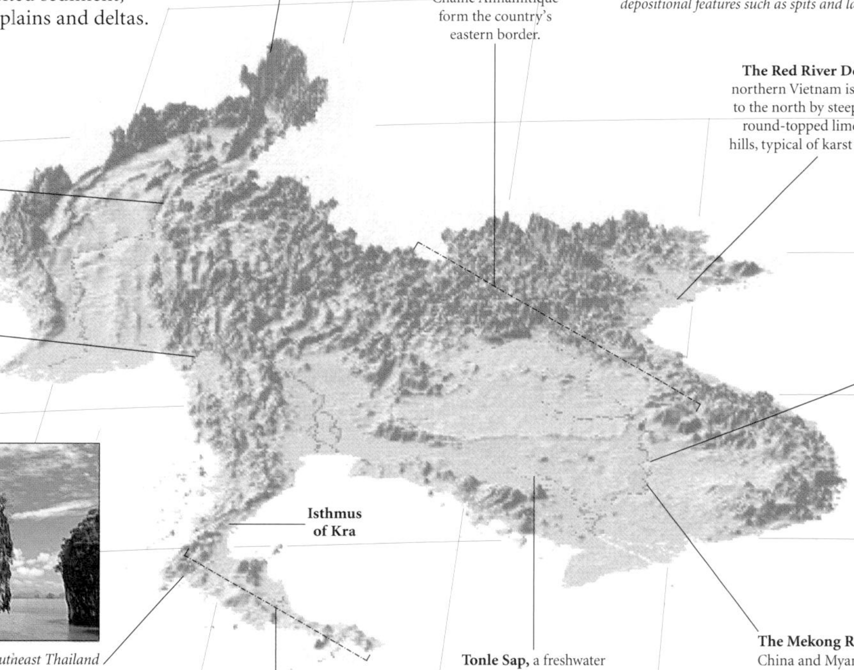

Hkakabo Razi is the highest point in mainland Southeast Asia. It rises 19,300 ft (5,885 m) at the border between China and Myanmar.

Mountains dominate the Laotian landscape with more than 90% of the land lying more than 600 ft (180 m) above sea level. The mountains of the Chaine Annamitique form the country's eastern border.

The Irrawaddy River runs virtually north–south, draining Myanmar. The Irrawaddy Delta is the country's main rice-growing area.

The Red River Delta in northern Vietnam is fringed to the north by steep-sided, round-topped limestone hills, typical of karst scenery.

Salween River

Mekong River

Isthmus of Kra

Malay Peninsula

Tonle Sap, a freshwater lake, drains into the Mekong Delta via the Mekong River. It is the largest lake in Southeast Asia.

The Mekong River flows through southern China and Myanmar, then for much of its length forms the border between Laos and Thailand, flowing through Cambodia before terminating in a vast delta on the southern Vietnamese coast.

The coast of the Isthmus of Kra, in southeast Thailand has many small, precipitous islands like these, formed by chemical erosion on limestone, which is weathered along vertical cracks. The humidity of the climate in Southeast Asia increases the rate of weathering.

The fast-flowing waters of the Mekong River cascade over this waterfall in Champasak province in Laos. The force of the water erodes rocks at the base of the fall.

Using the Land and Sea

THE FERTILE FLOODPLAINS of rivers such as the Mekong and Salween, and the humid climate, enable the production of rice throughout the region. Cambodia, Myanmar, and Laos still have substantial forests, producing hardwoods such as teak and rosewood. Cash crops include tropical fruits such as coconuts, bananas, and pineapples, rubber, oil palm, sugar cane and the jute substitute, kenaf. Pigs and cattle are the main livestock raised. Large quantities of marine and freshwater fish are caught throughout the region.

Commercial logging – still widespread in Myanmar – has now been stopped in Thailand because of overexploitation of the tropical rain forest.

The Urban/Rural Population Divide

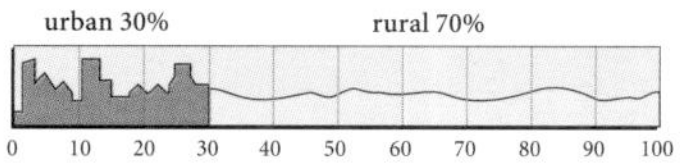
urban 30%
rural 70%
0 10 20 30 40 50 60 70 80 90 100

Population Density	Total Land Area
322 people per sq mile (124 people per sq km)	733,828 sq miles (1,901,110 sq km)

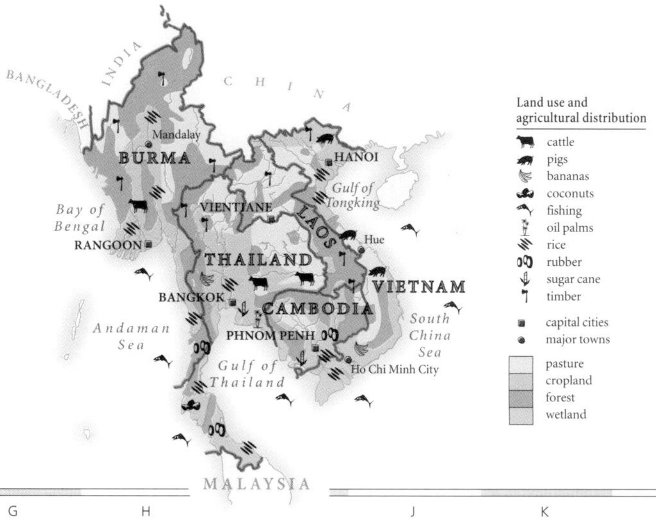
INDIA
CHINA
BANGLADESH
BURMA
Mandalay
HANOI
Gulf of Tongking
VIENTIANE
LAOS
Hue
Bay of Bengal
RANGOON
THAILAND
VIETNAM
BANGKOK
CAMBODIA
PHNOM PENH
Andaman Sea
South China Sea
Gulf of Thailand
Ho Chi Minh City
MALAYSIA
Land use and agricultural distribution
cattle
pigs
bananas
coconuts
fishing
oil palms
rice
rubber
sugar cane
timber
capital cities
major towns
pasture
cropland
forest
wetland

152
BANGLADESH
Tropic of Cancer
SAGAING
Thaungdut
Tamu
Pinlebu
Kindat
Mawlaik
Kawlin
Kalewa
Kanbalu
Falam
Kalemyo
Mingin
Haka
Kani
Monywa
Yinmabin
Budalin
Shwebo
Mandalay
Sagaing
Paletwa
CHIN STATE
Mount Victoria
Sinchaingbyin
Buthidaung
Pauk
Myingyan
Pakokku
Rathedaung
Sittwe
Myohaung
Chauk
Salin
MAGWE
Minbu
Magwe
Minhla
Kyaukpyu
Ramree Island
Cheduba Island
Letpan
Taungup
Allanmyo
Thayetmyo
Sandoway
Prome
PEGU
Shwedaung
Paungde
Myanaung
Nattalin
Gyobingauk
Mezaligon
Letpadan
Henzada
Lemyethna
Ngathainggyaung
Kyaunggon
Danubyu
IRRAWADDY
Bassein
Maubin
Myaungmya
Wakema
Kyaiklat
Moulmeingyun
Bogale
Labutta
Pyapon
YANGON (RANGOON)
Pegu
Mouths of the Irrawaddy
Bay of Bengal
Preparis Island
Great Coco Island
Little Coco Island
Gulf of Martaban
172
Andaman Sea
Mergui Archipelago
Ban Kam Phu
Ko Phra Thong
Takua Pa
Phuket
Thalang
Ko Phuket
Strait of Malacca

TRANSPORTATION & INDUSTRY

INDUSTRIAL MANUFACTURING has become increasingly important in Thailand and Vietnam in recent years. The assembling of component-based electrical and electronic goods is becoming more common throughout this region, with foreign companies benefiting from low labor costs and the upgrading of technology. The economies of Myanmar and Cambodia are still based on agricultural produce and the processing of raw materials. Tin is the region's most important metal, and nickel, copper, and chromite are also mined, although the quantities produced are not significant on a global scale. Thailand's successful tourist industry is the country's highest earner of foreign exchange.

Major industry and infrastructure

- chemicals
- electronics
- engineering
- food processing
- iron & steel
- oil & gas
- mining
- shipbuilding
- textiles
- timber processing
- capital cities
- major towns
- international airports
- major roads
- major industrial areas

BANGLADESH
INDIA
CHINA
Mandalay
BURMA
HANOI
Hai Phong
Gulf of Tongking
Bay of Bengal
Chiang Mai
VIENTIANE
LAOS
RANGOON
Moulmein
THAILAND
Hue
Da Nang
VIETNAM
Andaman Sea
BANGKOK
CAMBODIA
South China Sea
PHNOM PENH
Gulf of Thailand
Ho Chi Minh City
Hat Yai
MALAYSIA

TRANSPORTATION NETWORK

131,566 miles (211,845 km)	
267 miles (430 km)	
7,785 miles (12,536 km)	
28,393 miles (45,722 km)	

Transportation development has concentrated on the building of road networks. Water and sea transportation remain important, although air links have improved, particularly in Thailand.

***Opium poppies** are destroyed under army supervision in Thailand. This action is part of a government-sponsored initiative to reduce the trade in drugs such as heroin, which is derived from these plants. Drug trafficking is a major problem throughout the region; the area is known as the "Golden Triangle," and Laos is the third-largest producer of opium poppies in the world.*

CHINA
KACHIN STATE
SHAN STATE
Shan Plateau
THAILAND
LAOS
VIETNAM
CAMBODIA
HÀ NỘI
Hai Phong
VIANGCHAN (VIENTIANE)
KRUNG THEP (BANGKOK)
PHNUM PENH (PHNOM PENH)
Hô Chi Minh
Đa Năng
Huê
Gulf of Tongking
Gulf of Thailand
SOUTH CHINA SEA
PARACEL ISLANDS (disputed)
Amphitrite Group
Lincoln Island
Crescent Group
Passu Keah
Triton Island
Tropic of Cancer
Mouths of the Mekong
Côn Đao

160
160
170
168
168

SCALE 1:8,611,000
(projection Lambert Conformal Conic)

Km 0 25 50 100 150 200
Miles 0 25 50 100 150 200

MAP KEY

POPULATION

- above 5 million
- 1 million to 5 million
- 500,000 to 1 million
- 100,000 to 500,000
- 50,000 to 100,000
- 10,000 to 50,000
- below 10,000

ELEVATION

- 4000m / 13,124ft
- 3000m / 9843ft
- 2000m / 6562ft
- 1000m / 3281ft
- 500m / 1640ft
- 250m / 820ft
- 100m / 328ft
- sea level

***The city of Hue** in central Vietnam was the country's capital under the 13 emperors of the Nguyen dynasty from 1802 to 1945. It is the site of a number of religious monuments, including the Thien-Mu Pagoda.*

A B C D E F G H I J K L M

Western Maritime Southeast Asia

Indonesia, Malaysia, Brunei, Singapore

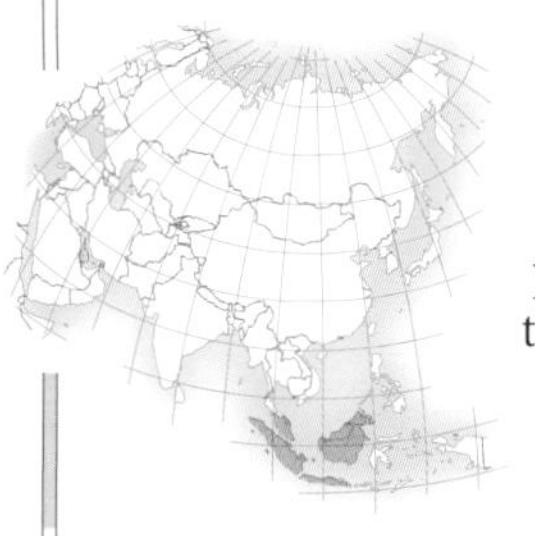

The world's largest archipelago, Indonesia's myriad islands stretch 3,100 miles (5,000 km) eastwards across the Pacific, from the Malay Peninsula to western New Guinea. Only about 1,500 of the 13,677 islands are inhabited and the huge, predominently Muslim population is unevenly distributed, with some two-thirds crowded onto the western islands of Java, Madura, and Bali. The national government is trying to resettle large numbers of people from these islands to other parts of the country to reduce population pressure there. Malaysia, split between the mainland and the east Malaysian states of Sabah and Sarawak on Borneo, has a diverse population, as well as a fast-growing economy, although the pace of its development is still far outstripped by that of Singapore. This small island nation is the financial and commercial capital of Southeast Asia. The Sultanate of Brunei in northern Borneo, one of the world's last princely states, has an extremely high standard of living, based on its oil revenues.

Ranks of gleaming skyscrapers, *new highways, and infrastructure construction reflect the investment that is pouring into Southeast Asian cities like the Malaysian capital, Kuala Lumpur. Many of the city's inhabitants subsist at a level far removed from the prosperity implied by its outward modernity.*

Transportation Network

- 160,350 miles (258,213 km)
- 188 miles (302 km)
- 5,482 miles (8,828 km)
- 8,827 miles (14,207,075 km)

Singapore's subway system is among the most efficient in the world. Malaysia has several fast, modern highways and most roads are paved. Java, Madura, and Sumatra have by far the most developed land transportation networks in Indonesia.

Major industry and infrastructure

- aerospace
- copra processing
- chemicals
- electronics
- engineering
- finance
- food processing
- iron & steel
- oil
- ship building
- timber processing
- textiles
- capital cities
- major towns
- international airports
- major roads
- major industrial areas

SCALE 1:8,750,000
(projection: Mercator)

Km 0 25 50 100 150 200
0 25 50 100 150 200 Miles

The Landscape

Indonesia's western islands are characterized by rugged volcanic mountains cloaked with dense tropical forest, which slope down to coastal plains covered by thick alluvial swamps. The Sunda Shelf, an extension of the Eurasian Plate, lies between Java, Bali, Sumatra, and Borneo. These islands' mountains rise from a base below the sea, and they were once joined together by dry land, which has since been submerged by rising sea levels.

Danau (lake) Toba in Sumatra *fills an enormous caldera 18 miles (30 km) wide and 62 miles (100 km) long – the largest in the world. It was formed through a combination of volcanic action and tectonic activity.*

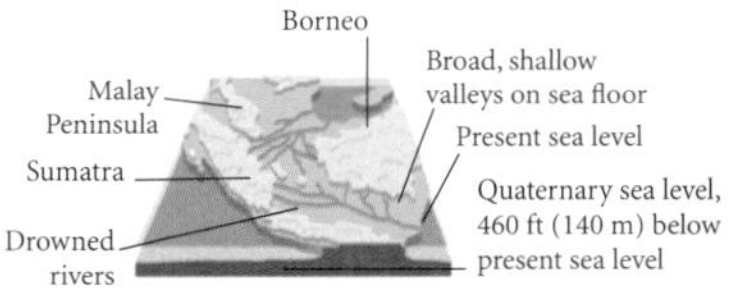

Borneo
Malay Peninsula
Sumatra
Drowned rivers
Broad, shallow valleys on sea floor
Present sea level
Quaternary sea level, 460 ft (140 m) below present sea level

The Sunda Shelf underlies this whole region. *It is one of the largest submarine shelves in the world, covering an area of 714,285 sq miles (1,850,000 sq km). During the early Quaternary period, when sea levels were lower, the shelf was exposed.*

Malay Peninsula has a rugged east coast, but the west coast, fronting the Strait of Malacca, has many sheltered beaches and bays. The two coasts are divided by the Banjaran Titiwangsa, which run the length of the peninsula.

The third largest island in the world, Borneo has a total area of 292,222 sq miles (757,050 sq km). Although mountainous, it is one of the most stable of the Indonesian islands, with little volcanic activity.

Gunung Kinabalu is the highest peak in Malaysia, rising 13,455 ft (4,101 m)

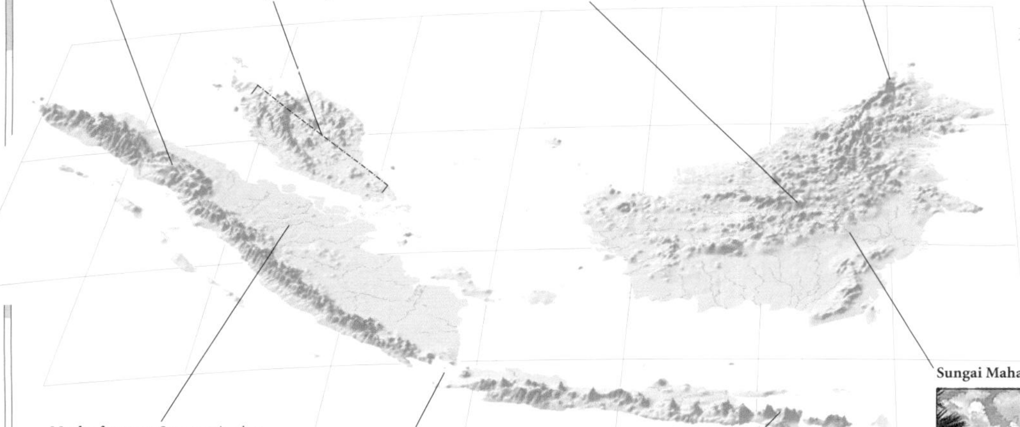

Much of eastern Sumatra is a low-lying swampy forest that is difficult to penetrate, seriously impeding the development of the inland area.

The island of Krakatau (Palau Rakata), lying between Sumatra and Java, was all but destroyed in 1883, when the volcano erupted. The release of gas and dust into the atmosphere disrupted cloud cover and global weather patterns for several years.

Indonesia has around 220 active volcanoes and hundreds more that are considered extinct. They are strung out along the island arc from Sumatra and Java, then through the Lesser Sunda Islands and into the Moluccas and Sulawesi (see pages 170–171).

Sungai Mahakam River

A large part of Borneo *is drained by navigable rivers, the main, and often the only, lifelines of trade and commerce. The river of Sungai Mahakam cuts through the island's central highlands.*

THAILAND
Strait of Malacca
INDIAN OCEAN
Kota Bharu
Kuala Terengganu
George Town
Alor Setar
Kangar
PERLIS
KEDAH
Pulau Langkawi
Pulau Pinang
PINANG
Ipoh
Taiping
KELANTAN
TERENGGANU
PERAK
PAHANG
Kuantan
SELANGOR
KUALA LUMPUR
PUTRAJAYA
Shah Alam
Klang
Seremban
NEGERI SEMBILAN
MELAKA
Melaka
JOHOR
Johor Bahru
SINGAPORE
Tanjungpinang
RIAU
Pekanbaru
Dumai
Bandaaceh
Sigli
Lhoksukon
Langsa
ACEH
Meulaboh
Calang
Pulau Weh
Pulau Brueuh
Medan
Binjai
Belawan
Tebingtinggi
Pematangsiantar
Tanjungbalai
Labuhanbilik
SUMATERA UTARA
Pulau Simeulue
Sinabang
Pulau Rabi
Kepulauan Banyak
Pulau Nias
Gunungsitoli
Telukdalam
Kepulauan Batu
Padangsidempuan
Sibolga
Danau Toba
Pulau Samosir
Padang
Bukittinggi
Padangpanjang
Danau Singkarak
Danau Maninjau
SUMATERA BARAT
Pulau Siberut
Kepulauan Mentawai
Selat Mentawai
Pulau Sipura
Pulau Pagai Utara
Pulau Pagai Selatan
JAMBI
Jambi
Muarabungo
Gunung Kerinci 3804m
Sungaipenuh
BENGKULU
Bengkulu
Palembang
SUMATERA SELATAN
Pulau Enggano
Lahat
Kotabumi
LAMPUNG
Equator
166
172

172

A B C D E F G H I J K L M

N O P Q R S T U V W X Y

TRANSPORTATION & INDUSTRY

SINGAPORE HAS a thriving economy based on international trade and finance. Annual trade through the port is among the highest of any in the world. Indonesia's western islands still depend on natural resources, particularly petroleum, gas, and wood, although the economy is rapidly diversifying with manufactured exports including garments, consumer electronics, and footwear. A high-profile aircraft industry has developed in Bandung on Java. Malaysia has a fast-growing and varied manufacturing sector, although oil, gas, and timber remain important resource-based industries.

THAILAND
South China Sea
BANDAR SERI BEGAWAN
BRUNEI
George Town
Medan
KUALA LUMPUR
PUTRAJAYA
MALAYSIA
Celebes Sea
Kuching
SINGAPORE
Borneo
Pontianak
Balikpapan
Sumatra
Padang
Palembang
INDIAN OCEAN
Java Sea
INDONESIA
JAKARTA
Semarang
Bandung
Surabaya
Java
Denpasar

166

USING THE LAND AND SEA

Rice is the most important arable crop in Indonesia and Malaysia, and both countries manage to meet almost all of their domestic demand. Malaysian rubber accounts for 25% of world production and is the main cash crop, grown on plantations and small farms, along with oil palms and copra. Timber is exported from both Malaysia and Indonesia. Modern agricultural techniques enable Singapore to produce fruits and vegetables despite a shortage of suitable land.

Land use and agricultural distribution
- coconuts
- fishing
- oil palms
- rice
- rubber
- shellfish
- sugar cane
- timber
- capital cities
- major towns
- pasture
- cropland
- forest
- wetland

THAILAND
South China Sea
BRUNEI
BANDAR SERI BEGAWAN
Celebes Sea
Medan
KUALA LUMPUR
PUTRAJAYA
MALAYSIA
Kuching
SINGAPORE
Pontianak
Borneo
Balikpapan
Padang
Sumatra
Palembang
INDIAN OCEAN
Java Sea
INDONESIA
JAKARTA
Bandung
Semarang
Java
Surabaya
Denpasar

Spiral cuts *in the bark of this rubber palm show where it has been tapped. Sophisticated cloning techniques mean that trees that produce consistently high quantities of rubber can be easily reproduced.*

170

THE URBAN/RURAL POPULATION DIVIDE

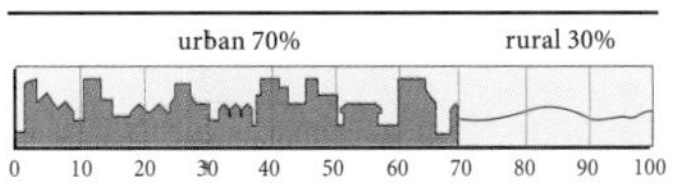
urban 70%
rural 30%
0 10 20 30 40 50 60 70 80 90 100

POPULATION DENSITY	TOTAL LAND AREA
196 people per sq mile (122 people per sq km)	922,807 sq miles (1,485,118 sq km)

SOUTH CHINA SEA
Sulu Sea
PHILIPPINES
Celebes Sea
Natuna Sea
MALAYSIA
INDONESIA
Java Sea
Bali Sea
Makassar Strait
Balabac Strait
BRUNEI
BANDAR SERI BEGAWAN
SABAH
SARAWAK
Borneo
Kalimantan
KALIMANTAN BARAT
KALIMANTAN TENGAH
KALIMANTAN TIMUR
KALIMANTAN SELATAN
KEPULAUAN RIAU
BANGKA-BELITUNG
Kota Kinabalu
Gunung Kinabalu 4101m
Kudat
Sandakan
Labuan
Tawau
Kuala Belait
Miri
Bintulu
Sibu
Kuching
Pontianak
Singkawang
Samarinda
Balikpapan
Tarakan
Banjarmasin
Palangkaraya
Pangkalpinang
Tanjungpandan
Pulau Bangka
Pulau Belitung
Bukit Raya 2278m
Gunung Menyapa 2000m
Equator
SULAWESI TENGAH
SULAWESI SELATAN
JAKARTA
Bogor
Bandung
Cirebon
Semarang
JAWA BARAT
JAWA TENGAH
JAWA TIMUR
Surabaya
Yogyakarta
YOGYAKARTA
Surakarta
Madiun
Kediri
Malang
Probolinggo
Jember
BALI
Denpasar
NUSA TENGGARA BARAT
Pulau Madura
Pulau Bawean
Pulau Karimunjawa
Kepulauan Seribu
ndarlampung

170

This tiny island near Kota Kinabulu, *in Sabah, eastern Malaysia, is part of a designated national park. Thickly forested, it is surrounded by broad, sandy beaches and shallow inland seas.*

MAP KEY

POPULATION
- above 5 million
- 1 million to 5 million
- 500,000 to 1 million
- 100,000 to 500,000
- 50,000 to 100,000
- 10,000 to 50,000
- below 10,000

ELEVATION

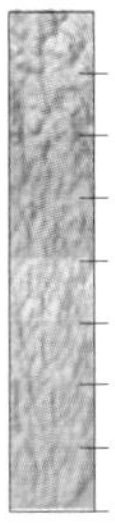
4000m / 13,124ft
3000m / 9843ft
2000m / 6562ft
1000m / 3281ft
500m / 1640ft
250m / 820ft
100m / 328ft
sea level

170

The volcano of *Gunung Semeru in eastern Java lies on the Pacific "Ring of Fire." It is part of the ancient Tennegger volcano and remains highly active.*

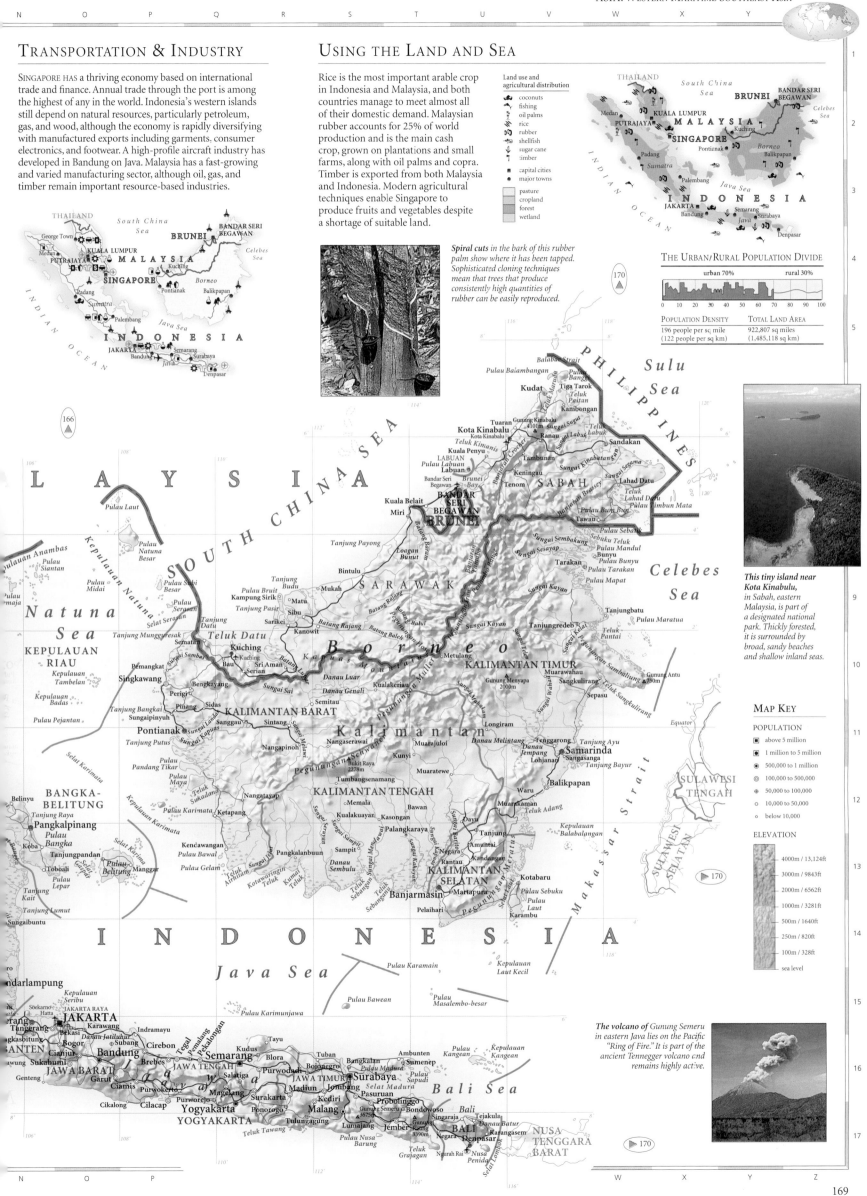

170

N O P W X Y Z

Eastern Maritime Southeast Asia

Indonesia, East Timor, Philippines

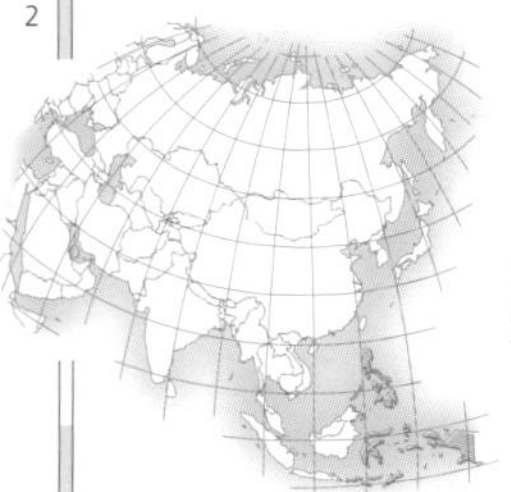

The Philippines takes its name from Philip II of Spain who was king when the islands were colonized during the 16th century. Almost 400 years of Spanish, and later US, rule have left their mark on the country's culture; English is widely spoken and over 90% of the population is Christian. The Philippines' economy is agriculturally based – inadequate infrastructure and electrical power shortages have so far hampered faster industrial growth. Indonesia's eastern islands are less economically developed than the rest of the country. Papua (Irian Jaya), which constitutes the western portion of New Guinea, is one of the world's last great wildernesses. It accounts for more than 20% of Indonesia's total area but less than 1% of its population.

***The traditional** boat-shaped houses of the Toraja people in Sulawesi. Although now Christian, the Toraja still practice the animist traditions and rituals of their ancestors. They are famous for their elaborate funeral ceremonies and burial sites in cliffside caves.*

The Landscape

Located on the Pacific "Ring of Fire" the Philippines' 7,100 islands are subject to frequent earthquakes and volcanic activity. Their terrain is largely mountainous, with narrow coastal plains and interior valleys and plains. Luzon and Mindanao are by far the largest islands and comprise roughly 66% of the country's area. Indonesia's eastern islands are mountainous and dotted with volcanoes, both active and dormant.

***Lake Taal** on the Philippines island of Luzon lies within the crater of an immense volcano that erupted twice in the 20th century, first in 1911 and again in 1965, causing the deaths of more than 3200 people.*

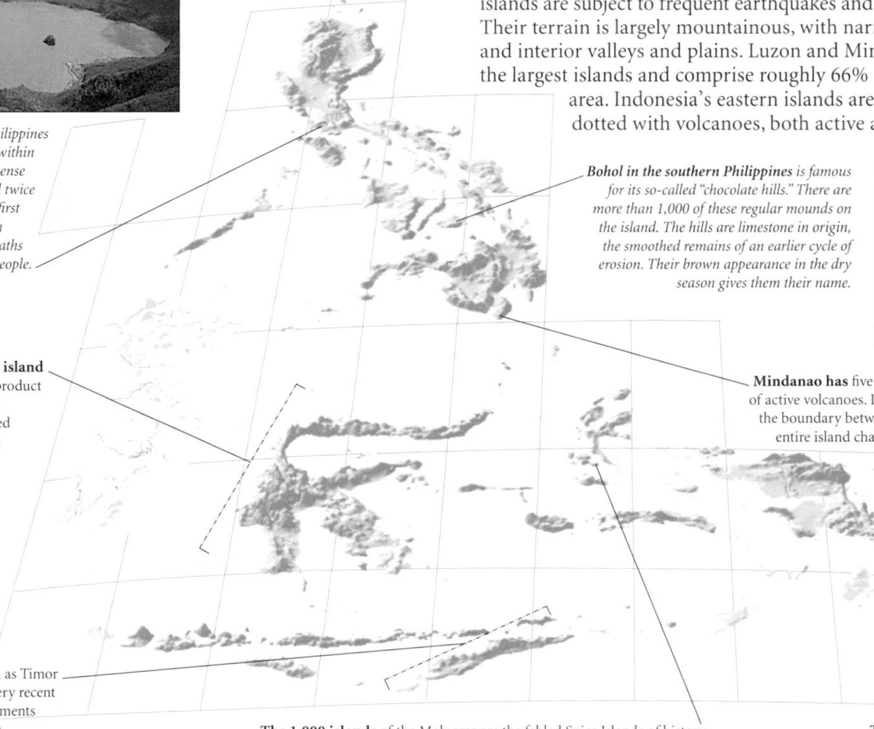

***Bohol in the southern Philippines** is famous for its so-called "chocolate hills." There are more than 1,000 of these regular mounds on the island. The hills are limestone in origin, the smoothed remains of an earlier cycle of erosion. Their brown appearance in the dry season gives them their name.*

The four-pronged island of Sulawesi is the product of complex tectonic activity that ruptured and then reattached small fragments of the Earth's crust to form the island's many peninsulas.

Mindanao has five mountain ranges many of which have large numbers of active volcanoes. Lying just west of the Philippines Trench, which forms the boundary between the colliding Philippine and Eurasian plates, the entire island chain is subject to earthquakes and volcanic activity.

Coral islands such as Timor show evidence of very recent and dramatic movements of the Earth's plates. Reefs in Timor have risen by as much as 4,000 ft (1,300 m) in the last million years.

The 1,000 islands of the Moluccas are the fabled Spice Islands of history, whose produce attracted traders from around the globe. Most of the northern and central Moluccas have dense vegetation and rugged mountainous interiors where elevations often exceed 3,000 feet (9,144 m).

The Pegunungan Maoke range in central Papua (Irian Jaya) contains the world's highest range of limestone mountains, some with peaks more than 16,400 ft (5,000 m) in height. Heavy rainfall and high temperatures, which promote rapid weathering, have led to the creation of large underground caves and river systems such as the river of Sungai Baliem.

Transportation & Industry

The Philippines' economy is primarily a mixture of agriculture and light industry. The manufacturing sector is still developing; many factories are licensees of foreign companies producing finished goods for export. Mining is also important – the country's chromite, nickel, and copper deposits are among the largest in the world. Agriculture is the main activity in eastern Indonesia. Most industry has a primary basis, including logging, food-processing, and mining. Nickel, the most important metal, is produced on Sulawesi, in Irian Jaya, and in the Moluccas.

Luzon Strait
Luzon
MANILA
Philippine Sea
South China Sea
PHILIPPINES
Cebu
Sulu Sea
Zamboanga
Mindanao
Davao
MALAYSIA
PACIFIC OCEAN
Celebes Sea
Manado
Halmahera
Maluku (Moluccas)
Celebes
Ceram
Jayapura
Makassar
Banda Sea
New Guinea
PAPUA NEW GUINEA
INDONESIA
Arafura Sea
Lombok
Sumbawa
Flores
DILI
EAST TIMOR
Sumba
Timor
Kupang
Timor Sea
INDIAN OCEAN
Major industry and infrastructure
copra processing
chemicals
finance
food processing
mining
oil
timber processing
textiles
capital cities
major towns
international airports
major roads
major industrial areas

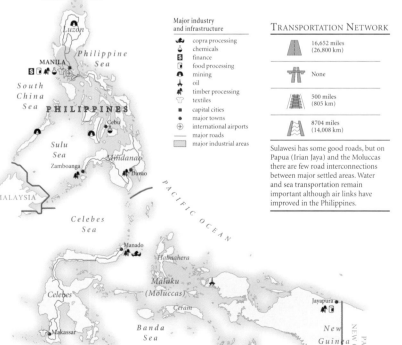

Transportation Network

Roads	16,652 miles (26,800 km)
Motorways	None
Railways	500 miles (805 km)
Waterways	8704 miles (14,008 km)

Sulawesi has some good roads, but on Papua (Irian Jaya) and the Moluccas there are few road interconnections between major settled areas. Water and sea transportation remain important although air links have improved in the Philippines.

***Manila is** the Philippines' chief port and transportation center, and the focus of the country's commercial, industrial, and cultural activities. Much of the city lies below sea level, and it suffers from floods during the rainy summer season.*

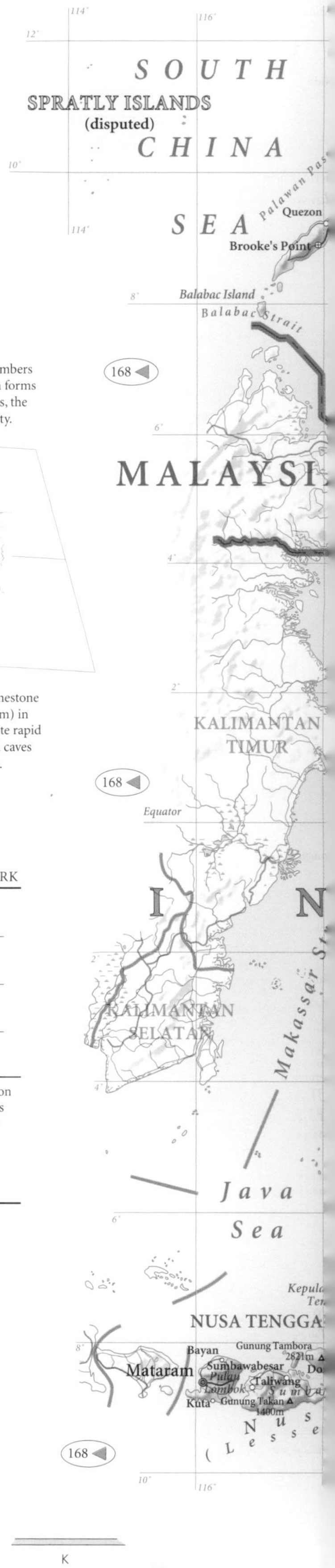
SOUTH CHINA SEA
SPRATLY ISLANDS
(disputed)
Quezon
Brooke's Point
Balabac Island
Balabac Strait
168
MALAYSIA
KALIMANTAN TIMUR
Equator
KALIMANTAN SELATAN
Makassar Strait
Java Sea
NUSA TENGGARA
Gunung Tambora 2821m
Bayan
Mataram
Sumbawabesar
Lombok
Kuta
Gunung Takan 1400m

Luzon Strait
Batan Islands
Balintang Channel
Babuyan Island
Babuyan Channel
Luzon
MANILA
Mindoro Strait
Sibuyan Sea
Philippine Sea
PHILIPPINES
Panay Island
Cebu
Bohol Sea
Mindanao
Davao
Zamboanga
Moro Gulf
Sulu Sea
Sulu Archipelago
Celebes Sea
SULAWESI UTARA
Manado
Gulf of Tomini
Molucca Sea
MALUKU UTARA
Halmahera
Halmahera Sea
Ceram Sea
Sulawesi (Celebes)
SULAWESI TENGAH
SULAWESI TENGGARA
Makassar
MALUKU
Banda Sea
Flores Sea
NUSA TENGGARA TIMUR
Savu Sea
DILI
EAST TIMOR
Kupang
Timor Sea
Ambon
Arafura Sea
PAPUA (IRIAN JAYA)
Jayapura
New Guinea
PAPUA NEW GUINEA
Torres Strait
PACIFIC OCEAN
INDONESIA

192

USING THE LAND AND SEA

INDONESIA'S EASTERN ISLANDS are less intensively cultivated than those in the west. Coconuts, coffee, and spices such as cloves and nutmeg are the major commercial crops while rice, corn, and soybeans are grown for local consumption. The Philippines' rich, fertile soils support year-round production of a wide range of crops. The country is one of the world's largest producers of coconuts and a major exporter of coconut products, including one-third of the world's copra. Although much of the arable land is given over to rice and corn, the main staple food crops, tropical fruits such as bananas, pineapples, and mangos, and sugar cane are also grown for export.

The terracing of land to restrict soil erosion and create flat surfaces for agriculture is a common practice throughout Southeast Asia, particularly where land is scarce. These terraces are on Luzon in the Philippines.

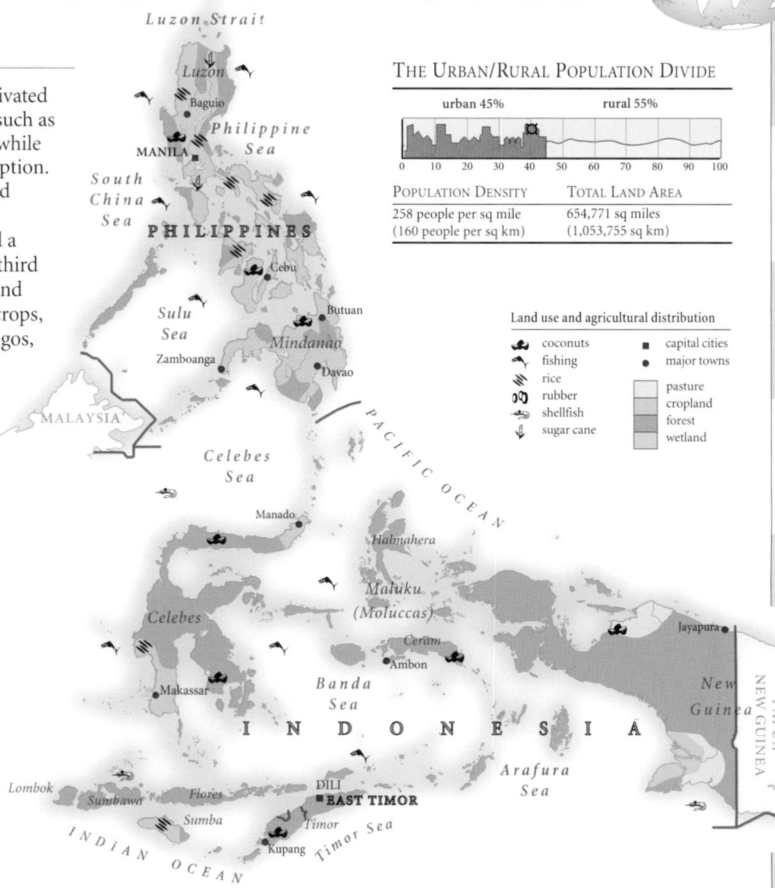
Luzon Strait
Luzon
Baguio
MANILA
Philippine Sea
South China Sea
PHILIPPINES
Cebu
Sulu Sea
Zamboanga
Butuan
Mindanao
Davao
MALAYSIA
PACIFIC OCEAN
Celebes Sea
Manado
Halmahera
Maluku (Moluccas)
Celebes
Ceram
Ambon
Jayapura
New Guinea
PAPUA NEW GUINEA
Makassar
Banda Sea
INDONESIA
Lombok
Sumbawa
Flores
Sumba
DILI
EAST TIMOR
Timor
Kupang
Timor Sea
Arafura Sea
INDIAN OCEAN
Land use and agricultural distribution
coconuts
fishing
rice
rubber
shellfish
sugar cane
capital cities
major towns
pasture
cropland
forest
wetland

THE URBAN/RURAL POPULATION DIVIDE

urban 45% rural 55%

0 10 20 30 40 50 60 70 80 90 100

POPULATION DENSITY	TOTAL LAND AREA
258 people per sq mile (160 people per sq km)	654,771 sq miles (1,053,755 sq km)

MAP KEY

POPULATION	ELEVATION
▣ 1 million to 5 million	4000m / 13,124ft
◉ 500,000 to 1 million	3000m / 9843ft
◎ 100,000 to 500,000	2000m / 6562ft
⊕ 50,000 to 100,000	1000m / 3281ft
○ 10,000 to 50,000	500m / 1640ft
○ below 10,000	250m / 820ft
	100m / 328ft
	sea level

More than two-thirds of Papua's (Irian Jaya) land area is heavily forested and the population of around 1.5 million live mainly in isolated tribal groups using more than 80 distinct languages.

SCALE 1:11,800,000
(projection: Lambert Azimuthal Equal Area)

Km 0 50 100 200 300 400
Miles 0 50 100 200 300 400

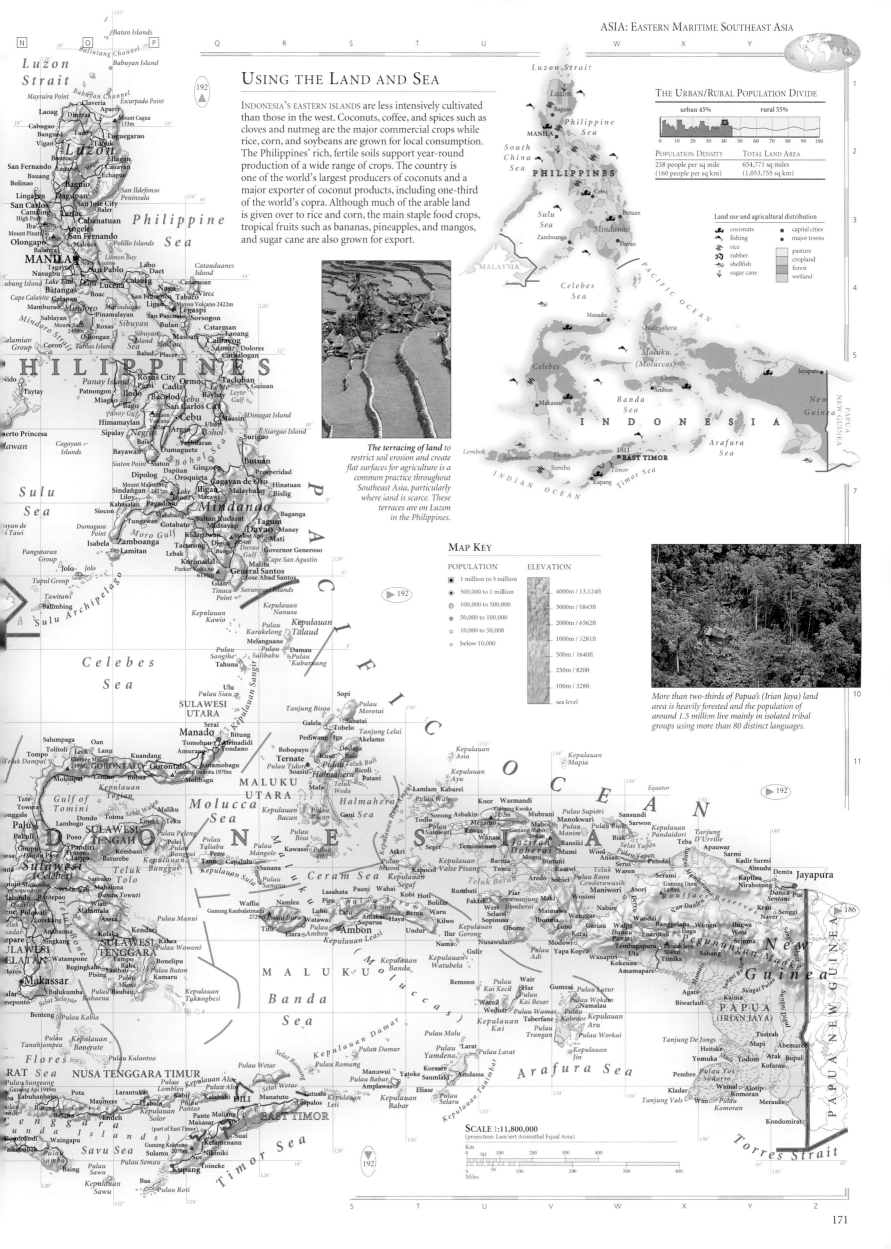

192
186

THE INDIAN OCEAN

DESPITE BEING THE SMALLEST of the three major oceans, the evolution of the Indian Ocean was the most complex. The ocean basin was formed during the breakup of the supercontinent Gondwanaland, when the Indian subcontinent moved northeast, Africa moved west and Australia separated from Antarctica. Like the Pacific Ocean, the warm waters of the Indian Ocean are punctuated by coral atolls and islands. About one-fifth of the world's population – over a billion people – live on its shores. In 2004, 290,000 died and millions more were left homeless after a tsunami devastated large stretches of the ocean's coastline.

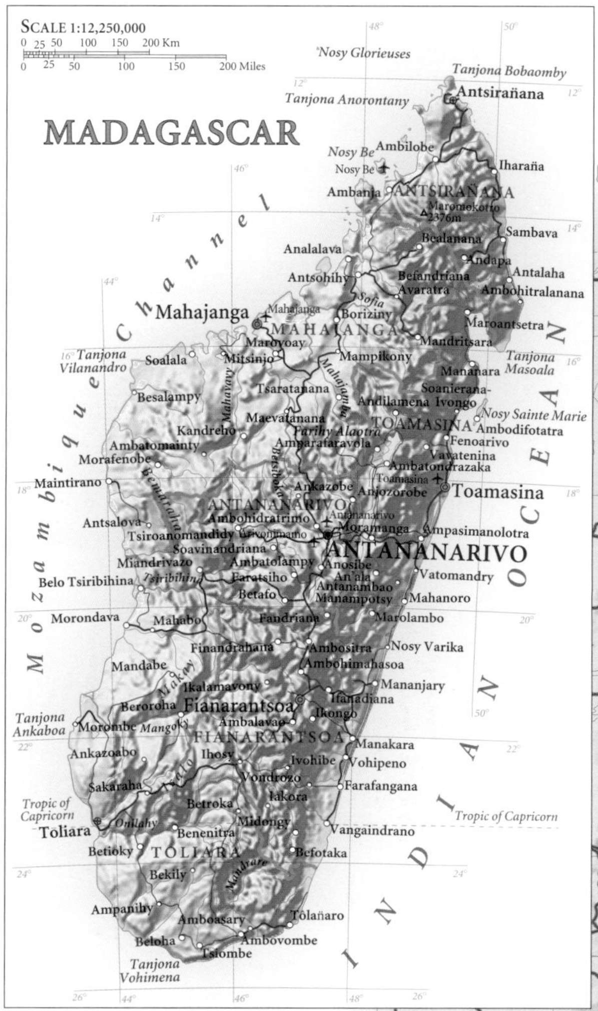
SCALE 1:12,250,000
MADAGASCAR
Mozambique Channel
INDIAN OCEAN
Antsirañana
Mahajanga
Toamasina
ANTANANARIVO
Fianarantsoa
Toliara
Tropic of Capricorn

EGYPT
SAUDI
SUDAN
ERITREA
DJIBOUTI
ETHIOPIA
KENYA
TANZANIA
MOZAMBIQUE
SOUTH AFRICA
SWAZILAND
LESOTHO
COMOROS
Natal Basin
Agulhas Plateau
Agulhas Basin
Atlantic-Indian Ridge
Atlantic-Indian Basin
Antarctic Circle

THE LANDSCAPE

THE INDIAN OCEAN BEGAN FORMING about 150 million years ago, but in its present form it is relatively young, only about 36 million years old. Along the three subterranean mountain chains of its mid-ocean ridge the seafloor is still spreading. The Indian Ocean has fewer trenches than other oceans and only a narrow continental shelf around most of its surrounding land.

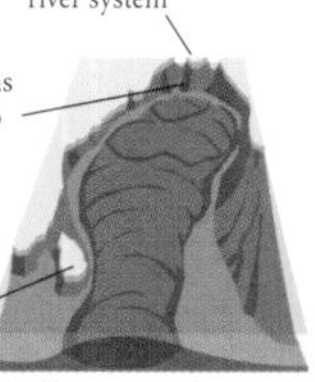

Sediments come from Ganges/Brahmaputra river system

Submarine canyons transport sediment to fan – some of these are more than 1,500 miles (2,500 km) long

Sri Lanka

The mid-oceanic ridge runs from the Arabian Sea. It diverges east of Madagascar. One arm runs southwest to join the Mid-Atlantic Ridge, the other branches southeast, joining the Pacific-Antarctic Ridge, southeast of Tasmania.

The Ninetyeast Ridge takes its name from the line of longitude it follows. It is the world's longest and straightest under-sea ridge.

Two of the world's largest rivers flow into the Indian Ocean; the Indus and the Ganges/Brahmaputra. Both have deposited enormous fans of sediment.

The Ganges Fan *is one of the world's largest submarine accumulations of sediment, extending far beyond Sri Lanka. It is fed by the Ganges/Brahmaputra River system, whose sediment is carried through a network of underwater canyons at the edge of the continental shelf.*

Indus River

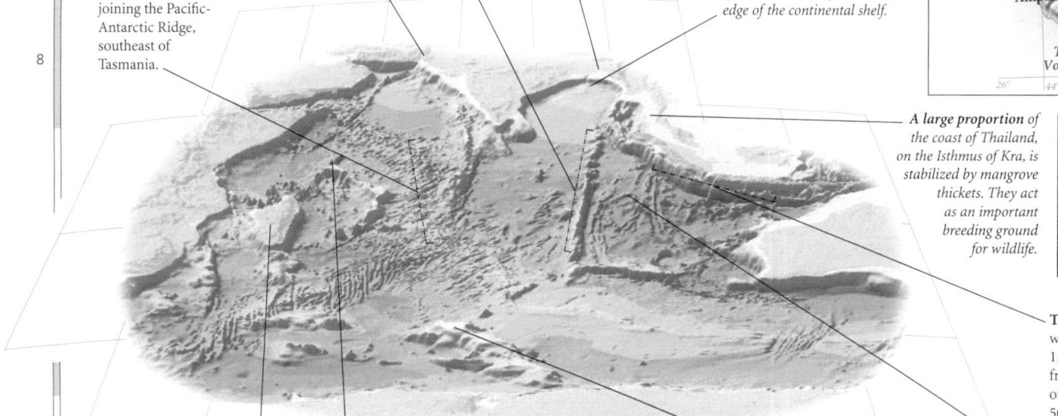

A large proportion *of the coast of Thailand, on the Isthmus of Kra, is stabilized by mangrove thickets. They act as an important breeding ground for wildlife.*

The Java Trench is the world's longest, it runs 1,600 miles (2,570 km) from the southwest of Java, but is only 50 miles (80 km) wide.

The relief of Madagascar rises from a low-lying coastal strip in the east, to the central plateau. The plateau is also a major watershed separating Madagascar's three main river basins.

The central group *of the Seychelles are mountainous, granite islands. They have a narrow coastal belt and lush, tropical vegetation cloaks the highlands.*

The Kerguelen Islands in the Southern Ocean were created by a hot spot in the Earth's crust. The islands were formed in succession as the Antarctic Plate moved slowly over the hot spot.

The circulation in the northern Indian Ocean is controlled by the monsoon winds. Biannually these winds reverse their pattern, causing a reversal in the surface currents and alternative high and low pressure conditions over Asia and Australia.

RESOURCES

MANY OF THE SMALL ISLANDS in the Indian Ocean rely exclusively on tuna-fishing and tourism to maintain their economies. Most fisheries are artisanal, although large-scale tuna-fishing does take place in the Seychelles, Mauritius and the western Indian Ocean. Nonliving resources include oil in the Persian Gulf, pearls in the Red Sea, and tin from deposits off the shores of Myanmar, Thailand, and Indonesia.

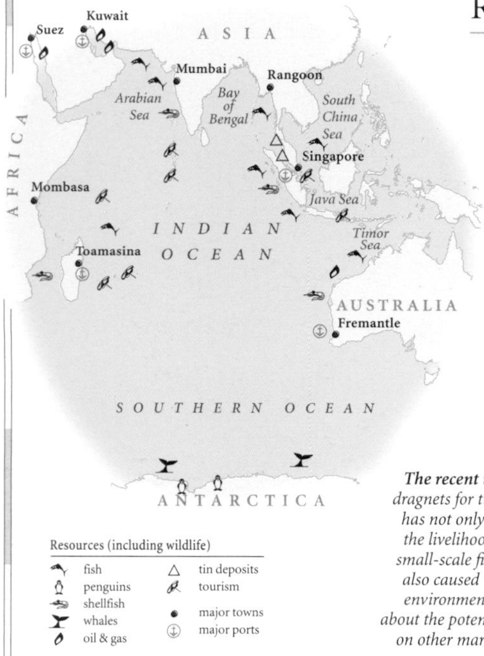
ASIA
AFRICA
INDIAN OCEAN
AUSTRALIA
SOUTHERN OCEAN
ANTARCTICA
Suez
Kuwait
Mumbai
Rangoon
Singapore
Mombasa
Toamasina
Fremantle
Arabian Sea
Bay of Bengal
South China Sea
Java Sea
Timor Sea
Resources (including wildlife)
fish
penguins
shellfish
whales
oil & gas
tin deposits
tourism
major towns
major ports

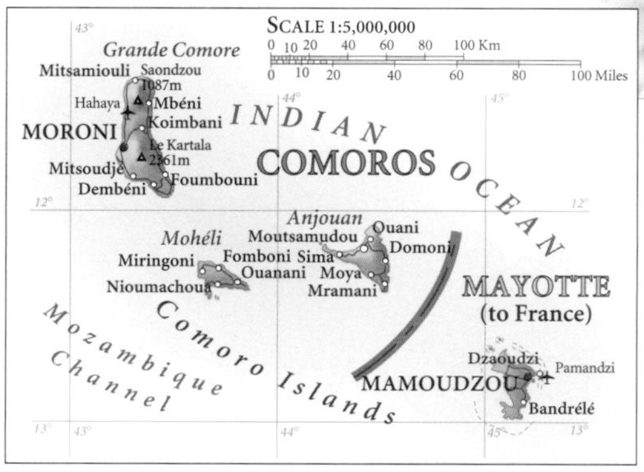
SCALE 1:5,000,000
Grande Comore
MORONI
COMOROS
INDIAN OCEAN
Mohéli
Anjouan
MAYOTTE (to France)
MAMOUDZOU
Comoro Islands
Mozambique Channel

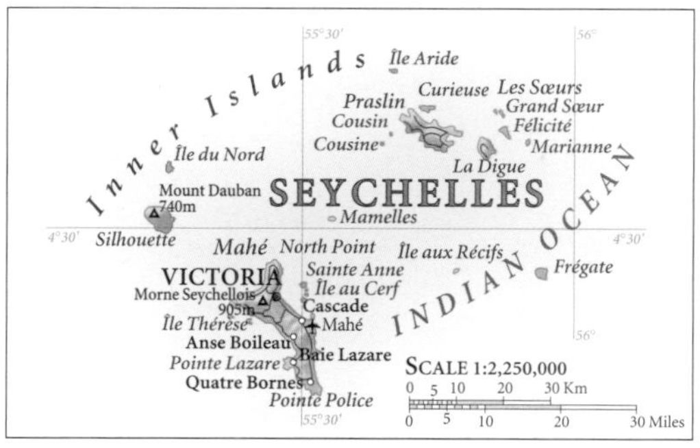
Inner Islands
SEYCHELLES
INDIAN OCEAN
Praslin
La Digue
Mahé
VICTORIA
Silhouette
SCALE 1:2,250,000

The recent use *of large dragnets for tuna-fishing has not only threatened the livelihoods of many small-scale fisheries, but also caused widespread environmental concern about the potential impact on other marine species.*

Coral reefs *support an enormous diversity of animal and plant life. Many species of tiny tropical fish, like these squirrel fish, live and feed around the profusion of reefs and atolls in the Indian Ocean.*

N O P Q R S T U V W X Y Z
1 2 3 9 10 12 13 14 15 16 17
SCALE 1:47,000,000
(projection Mollweide)
Km 0 200 400 600 800 1000
0 200 400 600 800 1000 Miles
IRAN
PAKISTAN
ASIA
INDIA
CHINA
BANGLADESH
MYANMAR
LAOS
THAILAND
VIETNAM
CAMBODIA
PHILIPPINES
TAIWAN
MALAYSIA
INDONESIA
EAST TIMOR
MALDIVES
SRI LANKA
MAURITIUS
AUSTRALIA
New Guinea
Borneo
Java Sea
South China Sea
East China Sea
Philippine Sea
Bay of Bengal
Arabian Sea
Andaman Sea
Gulf of Thailand
Sulu Sea
Celebes Sea
Banda Sea
Timor Sea
Arafura Sea
Gulf of Carpentaria
Great Australian Bight
INDIAN OCEAN
SOUTHERN OCEAN
ANTARCTICA
Ninetyeast Ridge
Mid-Indian Ridge
Southeast Indian Ridge
Carlsberg Ridge
Chagos-Laccadive Plateau
Mid-Indian Basin
Arabian Basin
Cocos Basin
Wharton Basin
Perth Basin
Crozet Basin
Kerguelen Plateau
South Australian Basin
South Indian Basin
Java Trench
Broken Ridge
Ceylon Plain
British Indian Ocean Territory (to UK)
Cocos Islands (to Australia)
Christmas Island (to Australia)
Ashmore & Cartier Islands (to Australia)
French Southern & Antarctic Territories (to France)
Heard & McDonald Islands (to Australia)
Réunion (to France)
Tropic of Cancer
Equator
Tropic of Capricorn
Antarctic Circle

The steeper eastern side of Madagascar is drained by numerous short, fast-flowing rivers. In contrast, larger, more languid rivers flow across the west. Both erode huge quantities of Madagascar's reddish soil.

There are over 1,300 small coral islands in the Maldives, but only about 200 are inhabited. They are based around an ancient submerged volcanic mountain range and all the islands are low-lying, none rising more than 6 ft (1.8 m) above sea level.

The island of Mauritius is volcanic in origin. Its central plateau is bounded by mountains which may once have formed the rim of a volcanic crater.

RÉUNION (to France)
SCALE 1:2,250,000
0 5 10 20 30 Km
0 5 10 20 30 Miles
ST-DENIS
Ste-Marie
Le Port
Ste-Suzanne
St-André
St-Paul
Salazie
St-Benoît
St-Gilles-les-Bains
Piton des Neiges 3070m
Trois-Bassins
Cilaos
La Plaine-des-Palmistes
St-Leu
Ste-Rose
Pointe au Sel
Le Tampon
Piton de la Fournaise 2632m
St-Louis
St-Pierre
Point de la Rivière
St-Etienne
St-Joseph
St-Philippe
Pointe de la Table
INDIAN OCEAN

Inset Map Key

POPULATION

- 500,000 to 1 million
- 100,000 to 500,000
- 50,000 to 100,000
- 10,000 to 50,000
- below 10,000

ELEVATION

- 3000m / 9843ft
- 2000m / 6562ft
- 1000m / 3281ft
- 500m / 1640ft
- 250m / 820ft
- 100m / 328ft
- sea level

Ocean Map Key

SEA DEPTH

- sea level
- 250m / 820ft
- 500m / 1640ft
- 1000m / 3281ft
- 2000m / 6562ft
- 3000m / 9843ft

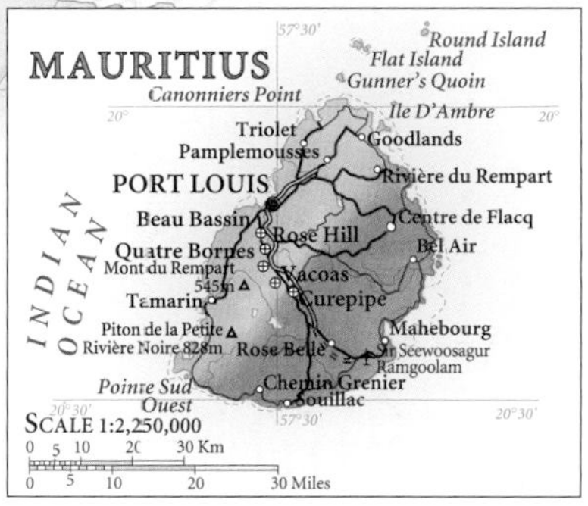

MAURITIUS
Round Island
Flat Island
Gunner's Quoin
Canonniers Point
Ile D'Ambre
Triolet
Pamplemousses
Goodlands
PORT LOUIS
Rivière du Rempart
Beau Bassin
Rose Hill
Centre de Flacq
Quatre Bornes
Bel Air
Mont du Rempart
Vacoas
Tamarin
Curepipe
Piton de la Petite Rivière Noire 828m
Mahebourg
Rose Belle
Plaisance
Pointe Sud Ouest
Chemin Grenier
Souillac
INDIAN OCEAN
SCALE 1:2,250,000
0 5 10 20 30 Km
0 5 10 20 30 Miles

AUSTRALASIA AND OCEANIA

AUSTRALASIA AND OCEANIA, COVERING A LAND AREA OF 3,285,048 SQ MILES (8,508,238 SQ KM), TAKES IN 14 COUNTRIES INCLUDING THE CONTINENT OF AUSTRALIA, NEW ZEALAND, PAPUA NEW GUINEA, AND MANY ISLAND GROUPS SCATTERED ACROSS THE PACIFIC OCEAN.

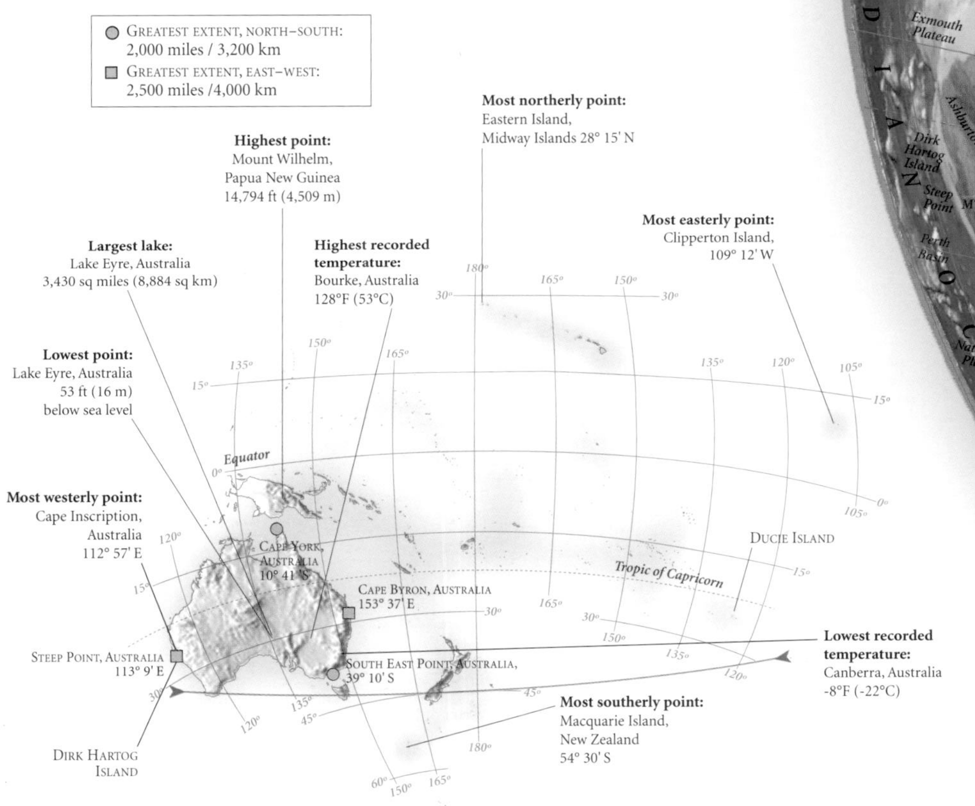

● GREATEST EXTENT, NORTH–SOUTH: 2,000 miles / 3,200 km
■ GREATEST EXTENT, EAST–WEST: 2,500 miles /4,000 km
Most northerly point: Eastern Island, Midway Islands 28° 15′ N
Highest point: Mount Wilhelm, Papua New Guinea 14,794 ft (4,509 m)
Most easterly point: Clipperton Island, 109° 12′ W
Largest lake: Lake Eyre, Australia 3,430 sq miles (8,884 sq km)
Highest recorded temperature: Bourke, Australia 128°F (53°C)
Lowest point: Lake Eyre, Australia 53 ft (16 m) below sea level
Most westerly point: Cape Inscription, Australia 112° 57′ E
Equator
Tropic of Capricorn
CAPE YORK, AUSTRALIA 10° 41′ S
CAPE BYRON, AUSTRALIA 153° 37′ E
DUCIE ISLAND
STEEP POINT, AUSTRALIA 113° 9′ E
SOUTH EAST POINT, AUSTRALIA, 39° 10′ S
Lowest recorded temperature: Canberra, Australia -8°F (-22°C)
Most southerly point: Macquarie Island, New Zealand 54° 30′ S
DIRK HARTOG ISLAND

DIRK HARTOG ISLAND, AUSTRALIA
Great Dividing Range
New Caledonia
New Zealand
Tonga
Tuamoto Islands
DUCIE ISLAND, PITCAIRN ISLANDS

CROSS-SECTION FROM DIRK HARTOG ISLAND, AUSTRALIA TO DUCIE ISLAND, PITCAIRN ISLANDS

line of cross-section

0 500 1000 1500 Km
0 500 1000 1500 Miles

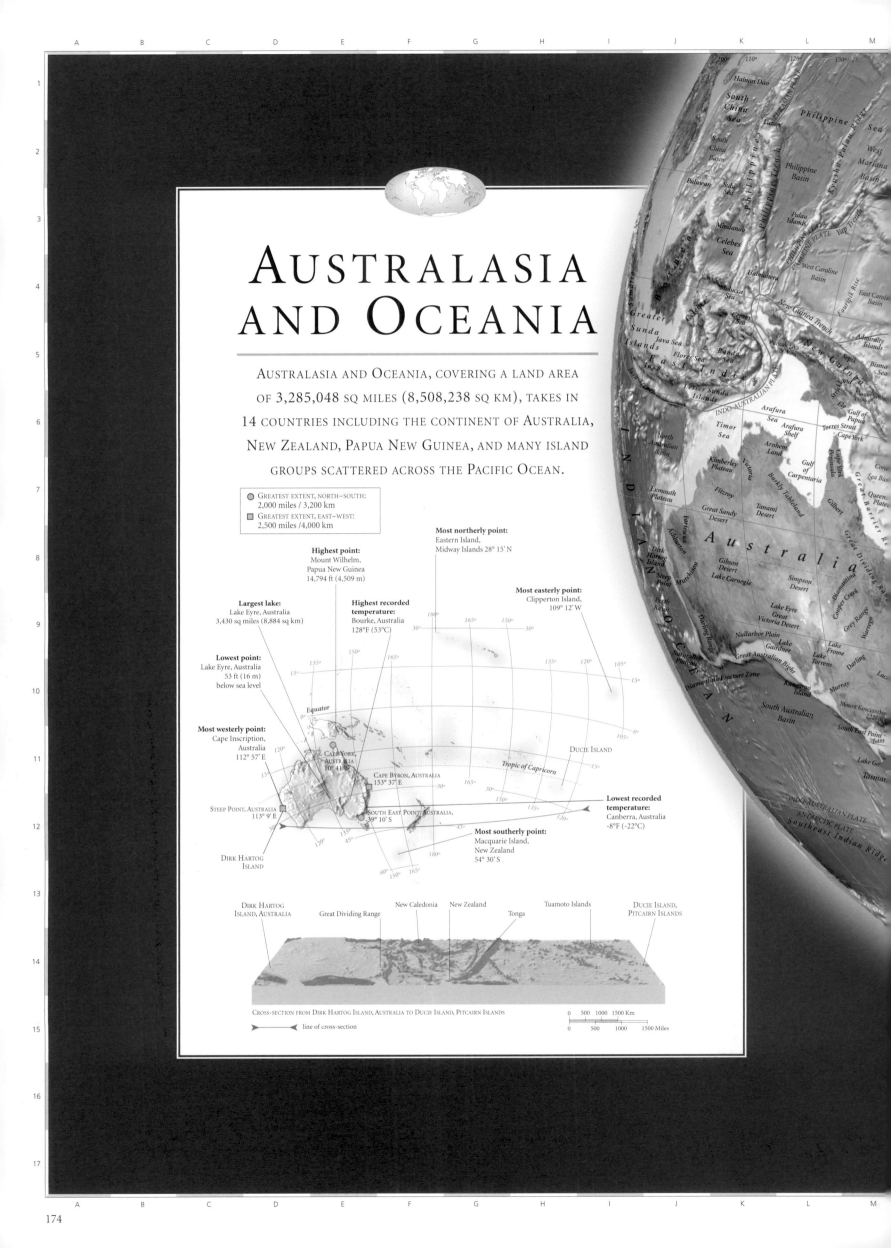

South China Sea
Philippine Sea
Philippine Basin
Celebes Sea
Java Sea
Banda Sea
Timor Sea
Arafura Sea
INDO-AUSTRALIAN PLATE
North Australian Basin
Kimberley Plateau
Arnhem Land
Gulf of Carpentaria
Exmouth Plateau
Great Sandy Desert
Tanami Desert
Australia
Gibson Desert
Simpson Desert
Lake Eyre
Great Victoria Desert
Nullarbor Plain
Great Australian Bight
South Australian Basin
INDIAN OCEAN
Diamantina Fracture Zone
New Guinea
Torres Strait
Cape York

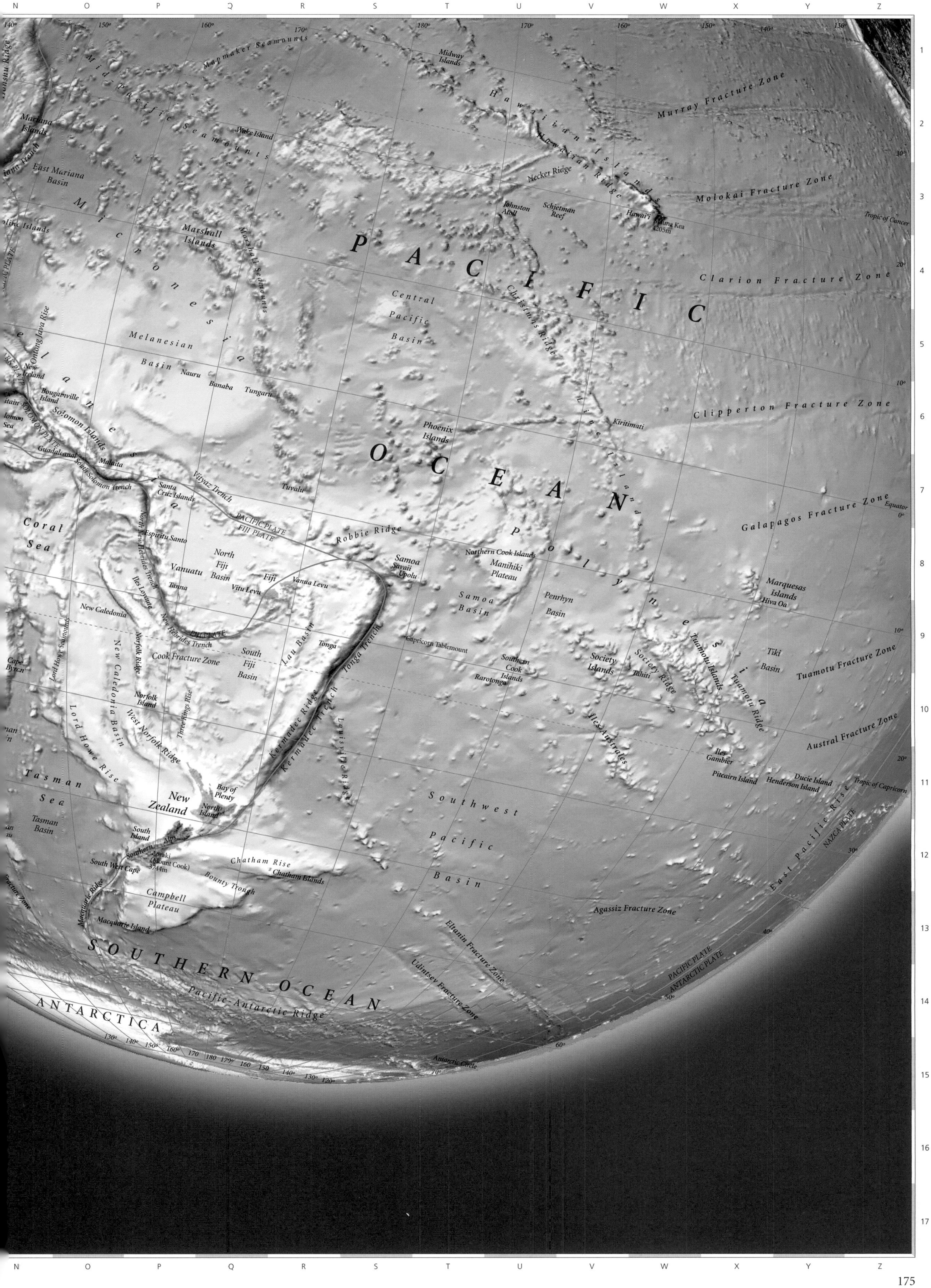

N O P Q R S T U V W X Y Z
1 2 3 4 5 6 7 8 9 10 11 12 13 14 15 16 17
PACIFIC OCEAN
SOUTHERN OCEAN
ANTARCTICA
Micronesia
Melanesia
Polynesia
Mapmaker Seamounts
Mid-Pacific Seamounts
Midway Islands
Hawaiian Islands
Hawaiian Ridge
Murray Fracture Zone
Molokai Fracture Zone
Clarion Fracture Zone
Clipperton Fracture Zone
Galapagos Fracture Zone
Tuamotu Fracture Zone
Austral Fracture Zone
Agassiz Fracture Zone
Eltanin Fracture Zone
Udintsev Fracture Zone
Mariana Islands
East Mariana Basin
Wake Island
Necker Ridge
Johnston Atoll
Schjetman Reef
Hawai'i
Mauna Kea 4205m
Tropic of Cancer
Marshall Islands
Marshall Seamounts
Christmas Ridge
Central Pacific Basin
Ontong Java Rise
Melanesian Basin
New Ireland
Nauru
Banaba
Tungaru
Bougainville Island
Solomon Islands
Solomon Sea
Guadalcanal
Malaita
South Solomon Trench
Vityaz Trench
Santa Cruz Islands
Tuvalu
Phoenix Islands
Kiritimati
Line Islands
Coral Sea
PACIFIC PLATE
FIJI PLATE
Robbie Ridge
Espiritu Santo
North New Hebrides Trench
Vanuatu
Tanna
North Fiji Basin
Fiji
Vitu Levu
Vanua Levu
Samoa
Savaii
Upolu
Northern Cook Islands
Manihiki Plateau
Samoa Basin
Penrhyn Basin
Marquesas Islands
Hiva Oa
Iles Loyauté
New Caledonia
New Hebrides Trench
Lau Basin
Tonga
Tonga Trench
Capricorn Tablemount
Southern Cook Islands
Rarotonga
Society Islands
Tahiti
Society Ridge
Tuamotu Islands
Tuamotu Ridge
Tiki Basin
Cape Byron
Lord Howe Seamounts
Norfolk Ridge
New Caledonia Basin
Cook Fracture Zone
South Fiji Basin
Norfolk Island
West Norfolk Ridge
Three Kings Rise
Kermadec Ridge
Kermadec Trench
Louisville Ridge
Iles Australes
Iles Gambier
Pitcairn Island
Ducie Island
Henderson Island
Tropic of Capricorn
Lord Howe Rise
Tasman Sea
Tasman Basin
New Zealand
North Island
Bay of Plenty
South Island
Southern Alps
Aoraki (Mount Cook) 3744m
South West Cape
Southwest Pacific Basin
Chatham Rise
Chatham Islands
Bounty Trough
Campbell Plateau
Macquarie Ridge
Macquarie Island
East Pacific Rise
NAZCA PLATE
PACIFIC PLATE
ANTARCTIC PLATE
Pacific-Antarctic Ridge
Antarctic Circle
Equator

POLITICAL AUSTRALASIA AND OCEANIA

VAST EXPANSES OF OCEAN separate this geographically fragmented realm, characterized more by each country's isolation than by any political unity. Australia's and New Zealand's traditional ties with the United Kingdom, as members of the Commonwealth, are now being called into question as Australasian and Oceanian nations are increasingly looking to forge new relationships with neighboring Asian countries like Japan. External influences have featured strongly in the politics of the Pacific Islands; the various territories of Micronesia were largely under US control until the late 1980s, and France, New Zealand, the US, and the UK still have territories under colonial rule in Polynesia. Nuclear weapons-testing by Western superpowers was widespread during the Cold War period, but has now been discontinued.

Western Australia's mineral wealth has transformed its state capital, Perth, into one of Australia's major cities. Perth is one of the world's most isolated cities – over 2,500 miles (4,000 km) from the population centers of the eastern seaboard.

POPULATION

DENSITY OF SETTLEMENT in the region is generally low. Australia is one of the least densely populated countries on Earth with over 80% of its population living within 25 miles (40 km) of the coast – mostly in the southeast of the country. New Zealand, and the island groups of Melanesia, Micronesia, and Polynesia, are much more densely populated, although many of the smaller islands remain uninhabited.

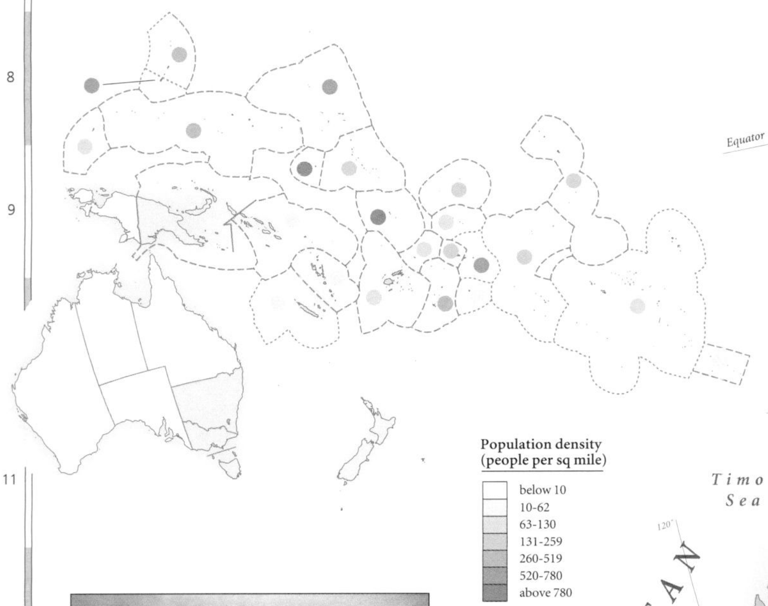
Population density
(people per sq mile)
below 10
10-62
63-130
131-259
260-519
520-780
above 780

***The myriad of small coral islands** that are scattered across the Pacific Ocean are often uninhabited, as they offer little shelter from the weather, often no fresh water, and only limited food supplies.*

***The planes** of the Australian Royal Flying Doctor Service are able to cover large expanses of barren land quickly, bringing medical treatment to the most inaccessible and far-flung places.*

Philippine Sea
Northern Mariana Islands (to US)
Mariana Islands
Saipan
Guam (to US)
HAGÅTNA
Micronesia
Bikini Atoll
Ralik C
Wake Island (to US)
KOROR (OREOR)
Babeldaob
Yap
PALAU
Caroline Islands
Chuuk
Pohnpei
PALIKIR
Kosrae
MICRONESIA
Melanesia
NAURU
PAPUA NEW GUINEA
Bismarck Sea
New Ireland
Wewak
New Britain
Rabaul
New Guinea
Madang
Mount Hagen
Lae
Ubai
Arawa
Bougainville Island
Solomon Islands
Solomon Sea
Tapini
PORT MORESBY
New Georgia Islands
HONIARA
Guadalcanal
SOLOMON ISLANDS
Santa Cruz Islands
Equator
Arafura Sea
Torres Strait
Cape York Peninsula
Coral Sea
Coral Sea Islands (to Australia)
VANUATU
Espiritu Santo
Malekula
PORT-VILA
New Caledonia (to France)
NOUMÉA
Timor Sea
Darwin
Arnhem Land
Joseph Bonaparte Gulf
Katherine
Gulf of Carpentaria
Cairns
Great Barrier Reef
Normanton
Townsville
Wyndham
Kimberley Plateau
NORTHERN TERRITORY
Hughenden
Mackay
Derby
Tennant Creek
Tanami Desert
Mount Isa
QUEENSLAND
Rockhampton
Broome
Barcaldine
INDIAN OCEAN
Great Sandy Desert
Alice Springs
Simpson Desert
Charleville
Miles
Brisbane
Port Hedland
AUSTRALIA
Toowoomba
Great Dividing Range
Cunnamulla
Grafton
Norfolk I (to Aust)
Hamersley Range
Gibson Desert
Lake Eyre North
Bourke
Barwon
Grey Range
Darling
Lord Howe Island (to Australia)
WESTERN AUSTRALIA
SOUTH AUSTRALIA
Flinders Ranges
Lake Torrens
Wilcannia
NEW SOUTH WALES
Dubbo
Newcastle
Tropic of Capricorn
Carnarvon
Great Victoria Desert
Lake Everard
Lake Gairdner
Port Augusta
Murray
Campbelltown
Sydney
Wollongong
CANBERRA
AUSTRALIAN CAPITAL TERRITORY
Mount Magnet
Ceduna
Whyalla
Wagga Wagga
Kalgoorlie
Nullarbor Plain
Great Australian Bight
Adelaide
Kangaroo Island
Bendigo
VICTORIA
Horsham
Ballarat
Melbourne
Geelong
Geraldton
Mount Gambier
Tasman Sea
Perth
Esperance
Bass Strait
Launceston
TASMANIA
Tasmania
Hobart
Albany
SOUTHERN

LANGUAGES

ENGLISH IS SPOKEN THROUGHOUT Australia and New Zealand. In Australia, English has been superimposed on a mosaic of Aboriginal languages. In New Zealand, the indigenous language, Maori, is the official language besides Polynesian. In Papua New Guinea, Melanesian Pidgin has become a *lingua franca* alongside several hundred indigenous languages. Across the region, the indigenous languages can be grouped into (1) the Aboriginal languages of Australia, (2) the Papuan languages spoken mostly inland in Papua New Guinea, and (3) the widely dispersed Austronesian, which includes coastal languages of Papua New Guinea, New Zealand Maori and languages of Oceania.

Language groups
Australian
Papuan
Indo-European
Austronesian
CHAMORRO
MARSHALLESE
GILBERTESE
EASTERN AUSTRONESIAN
TOK PISIN (PIDGIN)
PAPUAN
PIDGIN
ENGLISH
PIDGIN ENGLISH
FRENCH
HINDI
FIJIAN
TONGAN
SAMOAN
TAHITIAN FRENCH
ENGLISH
MAORI
ENGLISH

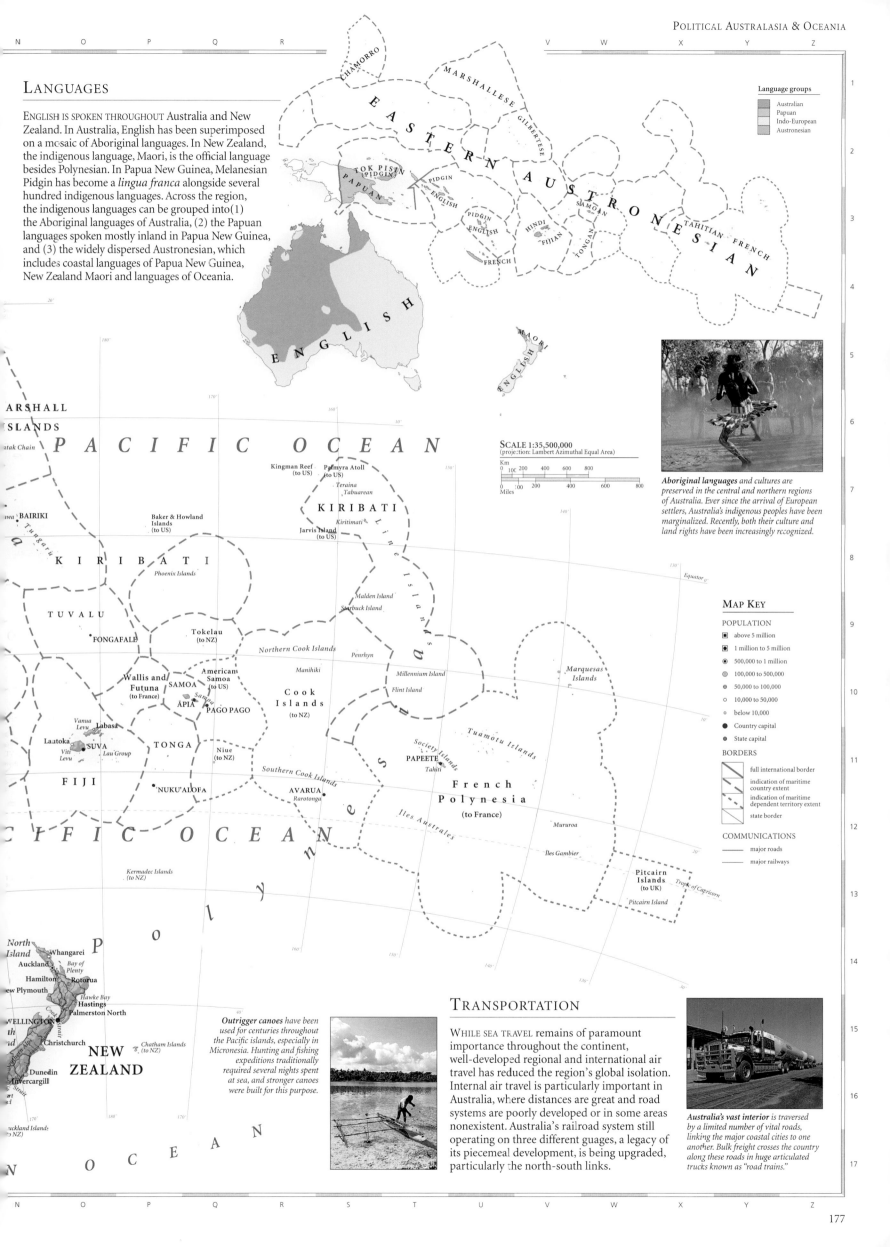

Aboriginal languages and cultures are preserved in the central and northern regions of Australia. Ever since the arrival of European settlers, Australia's indigenous peoples have been marginalized. Recently, both their culture and land rights have been increasingly recognized.

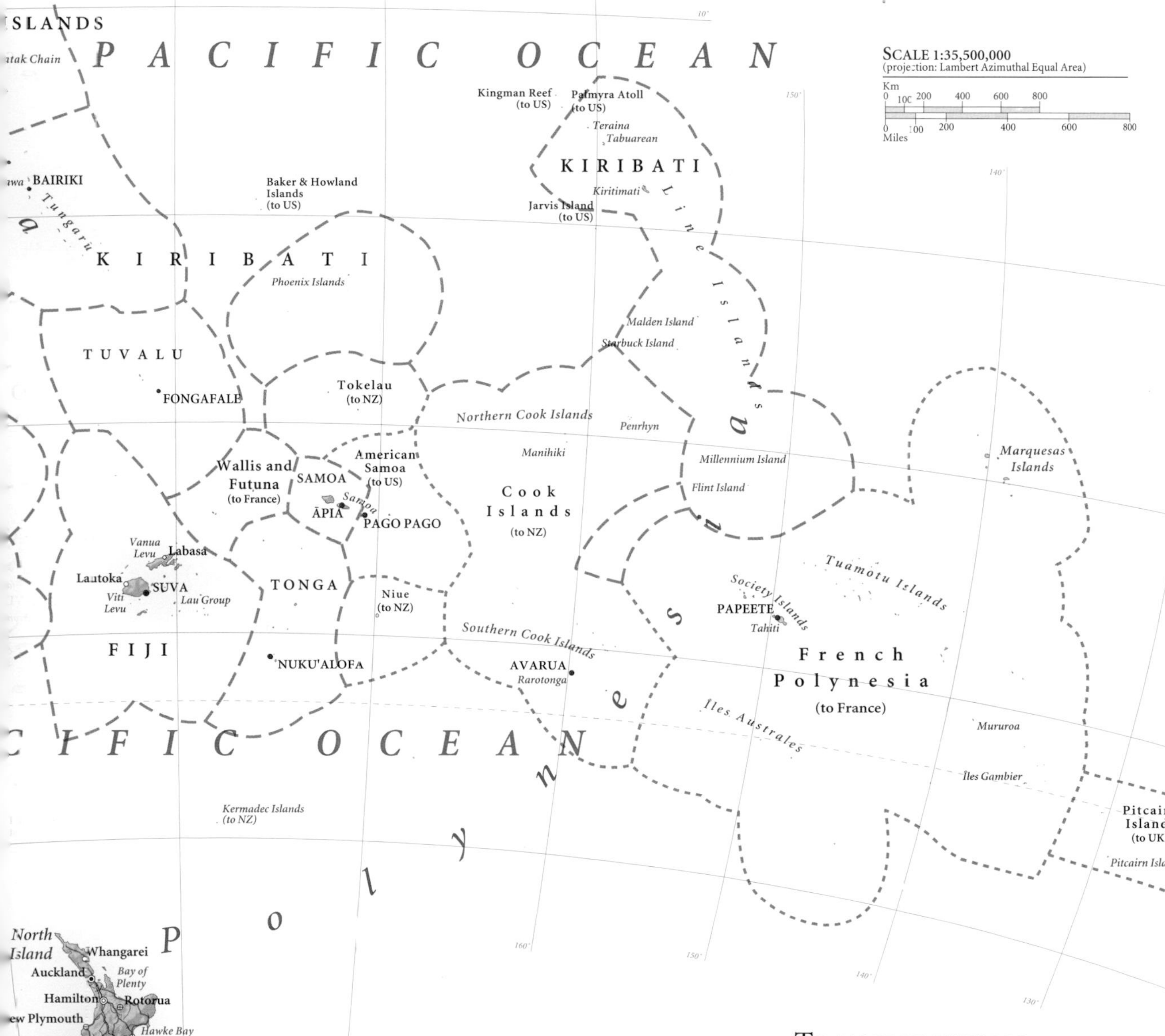
PACIFIC OCEAN
MARSHALL ISLANDS
Ratak Chain
BAIRIKI
Tungaru
KIRIBATI
Baker & Howland Islands (to US)
Phoenix Islands
Kingman Reef (to US)
Palmyra Atoll (to US)
Teraina
Tabuaerean
KIRIBATI
Kiritimati
Jarvis Island (to US)
Line Islands
Malden Island
Starbuck Island
TUVALU
FONGAFALE
Tokelau (to NZ)
Northern Cook Islands
Penrhyn
Manihiki
Millennium Island
Flint Island
Wallis and Futuna (to France)
SAMOA
APIA
Samoa
American Samoa (to US)
PAGO PAGO
Cook Islands (to NZ)
Marquesas Islands
Vanua Levu
Labasa
Lautoka
SUVA
Viti Levu
Lau Group
TONGA
Niue (to NZ)
Tuamotu Islands
Society Islands
PAPEETE
Tahiti
FIJI
NUKU'ALOFA
Southern Cook Islands
AVARUA
Rarotonga
French Polynesia (to France)
Îles Australes
Mururoa
Îles Gambier
PACIFIC OCEAN
Polynesia
Pitcairn Islands (to UK)
Pitcairn Island
Kermadec Islands (to NZ)
Equator
Tropic of Capricorn
North Island
Whangarei
Auckland
Bay of Plenty
Hamilton
Rotorua
New Plymouth
Hawke Bay
Hastings
Palmerston North
WELLINGTON
Cook Strait
Christchurch
Southern Alps
NEW ZEALAND
Chatham Islands (to NZ)
Dunedin
Invercargill
Foveaux Strait
Auckland Islands (to NZ)
OCEAN

SCALE 1:35,500,000
(projection: Lambert Azimuthal Equal Area)

Km 0 100 200 400 600 800
Miles 0 100 200 400 600 800

MAP KEY

POPULATION
- above 5 million
- 1 million to 5 million
- 500,000 to 1 million
- 100,000 to 500,000
- 50,000 to 100,000
- 10,000 to 50,000
- below 10,000
- Country capital
- State capital

BORDERS
- full international border
- indication of maritime country extent
- indication of maritime dependent territory extent
- state border

COMMUNICATIONS
- major roads
- major railways

Outrigger canoes have been used for centuries throughout the Pacific islands, especially in Micronesia. Hunting and fishing expeditions traditionally required several nights spent at sea, and stronger canoes were built for this purpose.

TRANSPORTATION

WHILE SEA TRAVEL remains of paramount importance throughout the continent, well-developed regional and international air travel has reduced the region's global isolation. Internal air travel is particularly important in Australia, where distances are great and road systems are poorly developed or in some areas nonexistent. Australia's railroad system still operating on three different guages, a legacy of its piecemeal development, is being upgraded, particularly the north-south links.

***Australia's vast interior** is traversed by a limited number of vital roads, linking the major coastal cities to one another. Bulk freight crosses the country along these roads in huge articulated trucks known as "road trains."*

Australasian and Oceanian Resources

Natural resources are of major economic importance throughout Australasia and Oceania. Australia in particular is a major world exporter of raw materials such as coal, iron ore, and bauxite, while New Zealand's agricultural economy is dominated by sheep-raising. Trade with western Europe has declined significantly in the last 20 years, and the Pacific Rim countries of Southeast Asia are now the main trading partners, as well as a source of new settlers to the region. Australasia and Oceania's greatest resources are its climate and environment; tourism increasingly provides a vital source of income for the whole continent.

The largely unpolluted *waters of the Pacific Ocean support rich and varied marine life, much of which is farmed commercially. Here, oysters are gathered for market off the coast of New Zealand's South Island.*

Huge flocks of sheep *are a common sight in New Zealand, where they outnumber people by 20 to 1. New Zealand is one of the world's largest exporters of wool and frozen lamb.*

Standard of Living

In marked contrast to its neighbor, Australia, with one of the world's highest life expectancies and standards of living, Papua New Guinea is one of the world's least developed countries. In addition, high population growth and urbanization rates throughout the Pacific islands contribute to overcrowding. In Australia and New Zealand, the Aboriginal and Maori people have been isolated, although recently their traditional land ownership rights have begun to be legally recognized in an effort to ease their social and economic isolation, and to improve living standards.

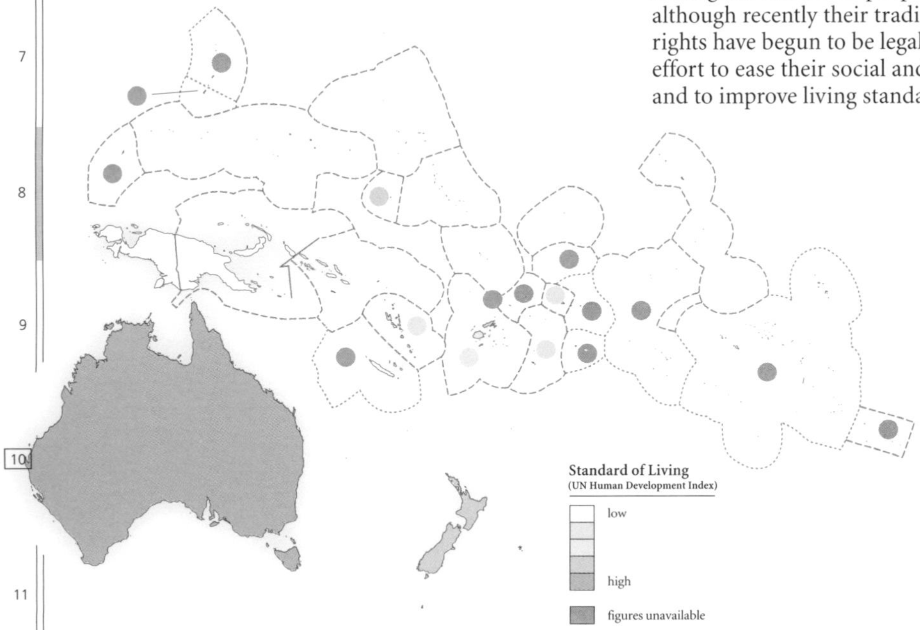

Standard of Living
(UN Human Development Index)
low
high
figures unavailable

Northern Mariana Islands
(to US)
Saipan
Guam
(to US)
MICRO
PALAU
PAPUA NEW GUINEA
New Guinea
Port Mores
Arafura Sea
Torres Strait
Timor Sea
Darwin
Gulf of Carpentaria
Great Barrier
Townsville
AUSTRALIA
INDIAN OCEAN
Adelaide
Perth
SOUTHER

Environmental Issues

The prospect of rising sea levels poses a threat to many low-lying islands in the Pacific. The testing of nuclear weapons, once common throughout the region, was finally discontinued in 1996. Australia's ecological balance has been irreversibly altered by the introduction of alien species. Although it has the world's largest underground water reserve, the Great Artesian Basin, the availability of fresh water in Australia remains critical. Periodic droughts combined with overgrazing lead to desertification and increase the risk of devastating bush fires, and occasional flash floods.

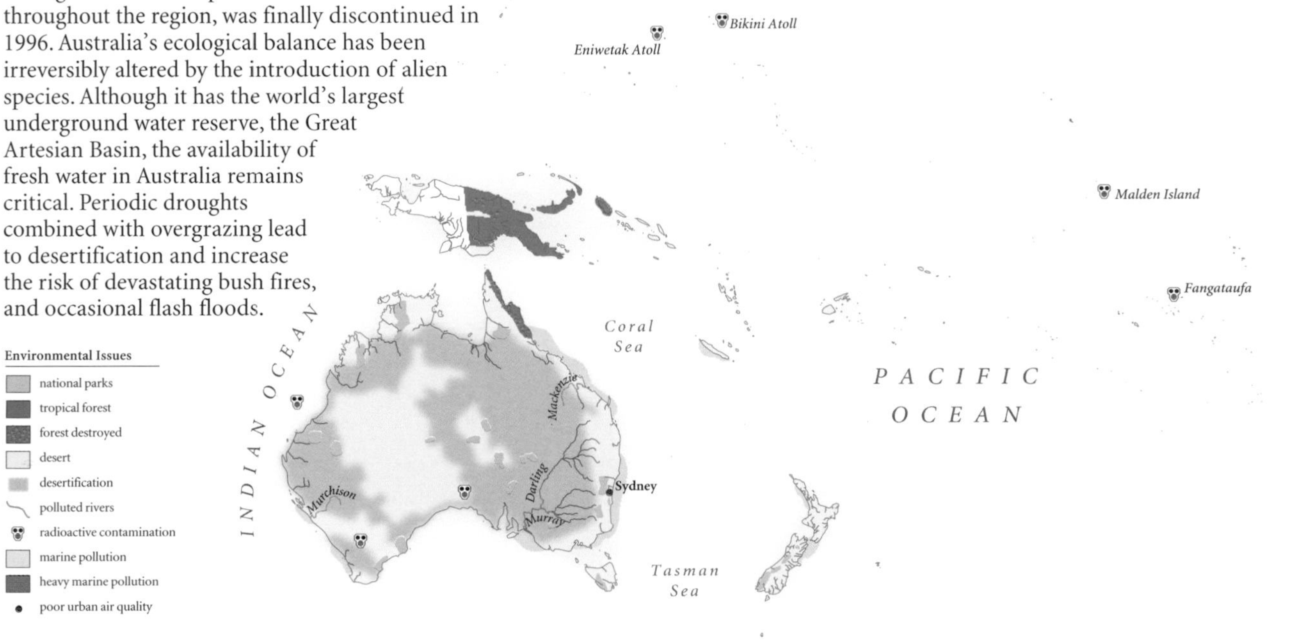

Environmental Issues
national parks
tropical forest
forest destroyed
desert
desertification
polluted rivers
radioactive contamination
marine pollution
heavy marine pollution
poor urban air quality
Eniwetak Atoll
Bikini Atoll
Malden Island
Fangataufa
INDIAN OCEAN
Coral Sea
PACIFIC OCEAN
Tasman Sea
Mackenzie
Darling
Murray
Murchison
Sydney

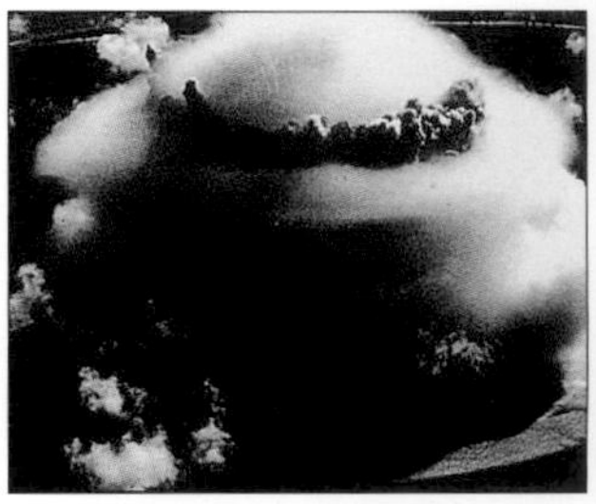

In 1946 Bikini Atoll, *in the Marshall Islands, was chosen as the site for Operation Crossroads – investigating the effects of atomic bombs upon naval vessels. Further nuclear tests continued until the early 1990s. The long-term environmental effects are unknown.*

The massive Ok Tedi copper mine was opened in 1988. It is situated in the midst of remote tropical jungle in Papua New Guinea.

AGRICULTURE, INDUSTRY, AND MINERALS

MUCH OF THE REGION'S INDUSTRY IS RESOURCE-BASED: sheep farming for wool and meat in Australia and New Zealand; mining in Australia and Papua New Guinea and fishing throughout the Pacific islands. Manufacturing is mainly limited to the large coastal cities in Australia and New Zealand, like Sydney, Adelaide, Melbourne, Brisbane, Perth, and Auckland, although small-scale enterprises operate in the Pacific islands, concentrating on processing of fish and foods. Tourism continues to provide revenue to the area – in Fiji it accounts for 15% of GNP.

Plumes of steam rise from the electricity turbines on New Zealand's North Island. New Zealand is one of the few countries in the world where geothermal energy makes a significant contribution to national energy production.

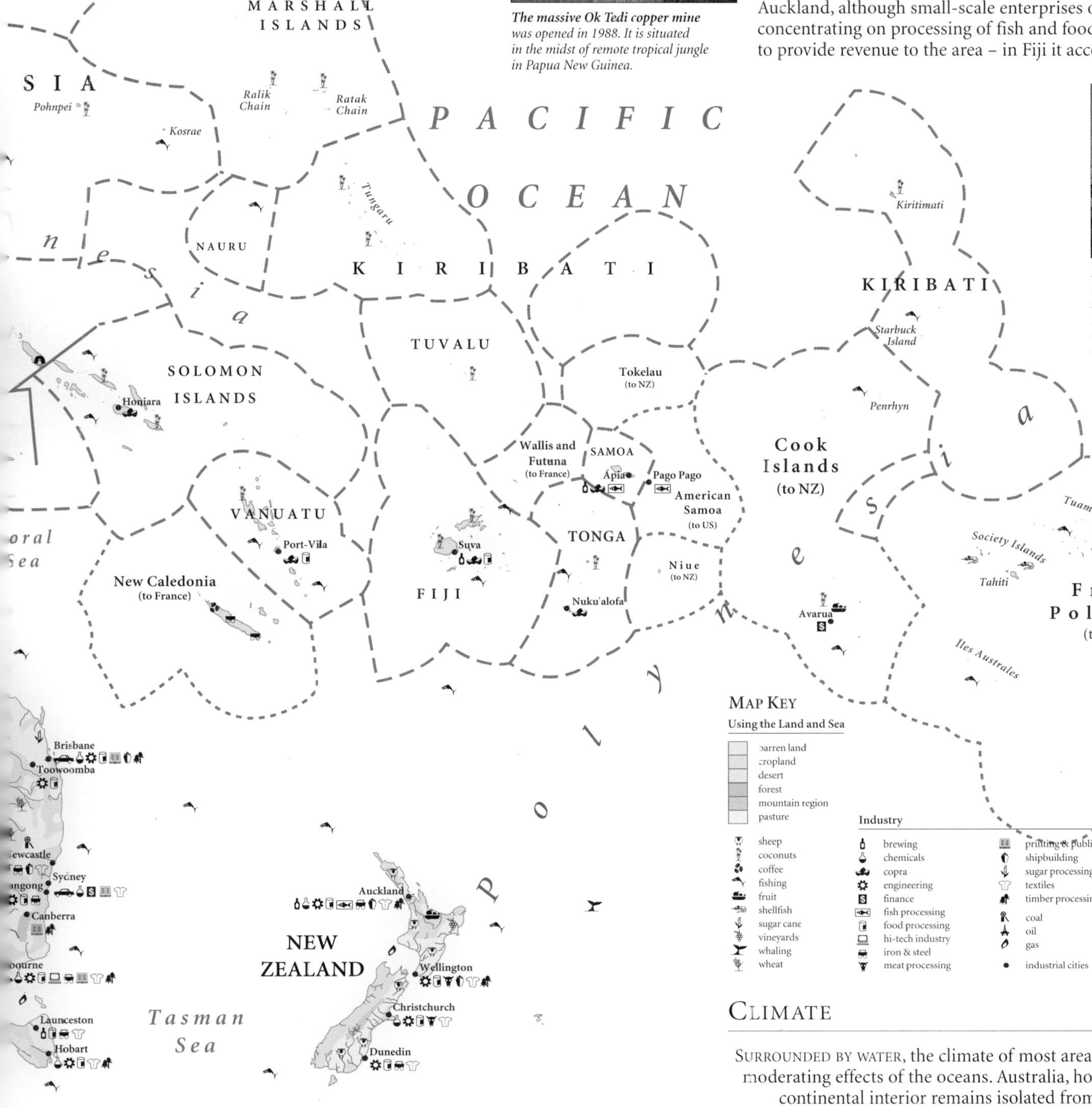

MARSHALL ISLANDS
Ralik Chain
Ratak Chain
Pohnpei
Kosrae
PACIFIC OCEAN
Tungaru
NAURU
KIRIBATI
Kiritimati
Starbuck Island
Penrhyn
TUVALU
SOLOMON ISLANDS
Honiara
Tokelau (to NZ)
Wallis and Futuna (to France)
SAMOA
Apia
Pago Pago
American Samoa (to US)
Cook Islands (to NZ)
Marquesas Islands
Tuamotu Islands
Society Islands
Tahiti
French Polynesia (to France)
VANUATU
Port-Vila
New Caledonia (to France)
FIJI
Suva
TONGA
Nuku'alofa
Niue (to NZ)
Avarua
Iles Australes
Iles Gambier
Pitcairn Islands (to UK)
Polynesia
Brisbane
Toowoomba
Newcastle
Sydney
Canberra
Launceston
Hobart
Tasman Sea
NEW ZEALAND
Auckland
Wellington
Christchurch
Dunedin
MAP KEY
Using the Land and Sea
barren land
cropland
desert
forest
mountain region
pasture
sheep
coconuts
coffee
fishing
fruit
shellfish
sugar cane
vineyards
whaling
wheat
Industry
brewing
chemicals
copra
engineering
finance
fish processing
food processing
hi-tech industry
iron & steel
meat processing
printing & publishing
shipbuilding
sugar processing
textiles
timber processing
coal
oil
gas
industrial cities
Mineral Resources
bauxite
copper
gold
iron
lead
nickel

CLIMATE

SURROUNDED BY WATER, the climate of most areas is profoundly affected by the moderating effects of the oceans. Australia, however, is the exception. Its dry continental interior remains isolated from the ocean; temperatures soar during the day, and droughts are common. The coastal regions, where most people live, are cooler and wetter. The numerous islands scattered across the Pacific are generally hot and humid, subject to the different air circulation patterns and ocean currents that affect the area, including the El Niño ocean current anomaly, which produces extreme aridity.

The tourist trade continues to bring valuable income to the region. Fiji, Guam, and the Cook Islands are favored destinations for Japanese, American, and Australian tourists. Surfers Paradise near Brisbane, Australia, is part of the fastest growing tourist area in the country; 40 years ago, the area was wild bushland.

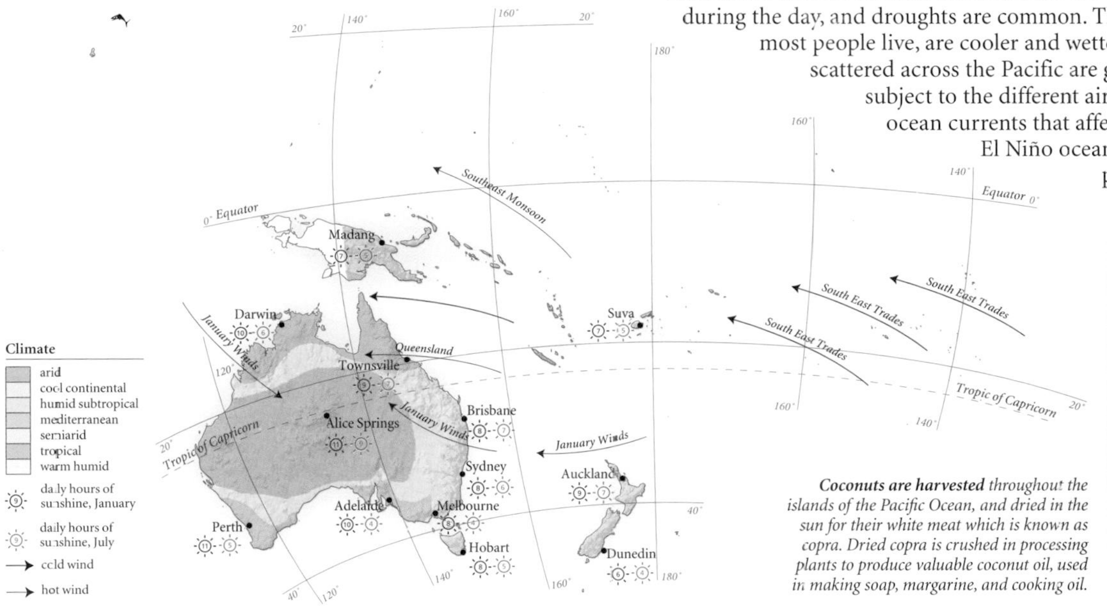

Climate
arid
cool continental
humid subtropical
mediterranean
semiarid
tropical
warm humid
daily hours of sunshine, January
daily hours of sunshine, July
cold wind
hot wind
Equator
Southeast Monsoon
Madang
Darwin
January Winds
Queensland
Townsville
Alice Springs
Tropic of Capricorn
Brisbane
Sydney
Adelaide
Melbourne
Perth
Hobart
Suva
Auckland
Dunedin
South East Trades

Coconuts are harvested throughout the islands of the Pacific Ocean, and dried in the sun for their white meat which is known as copra. Dried copra is crushed in processing plants to produce valuable coconut oil, used in making soap, margarine, and cooking oil.

Australia

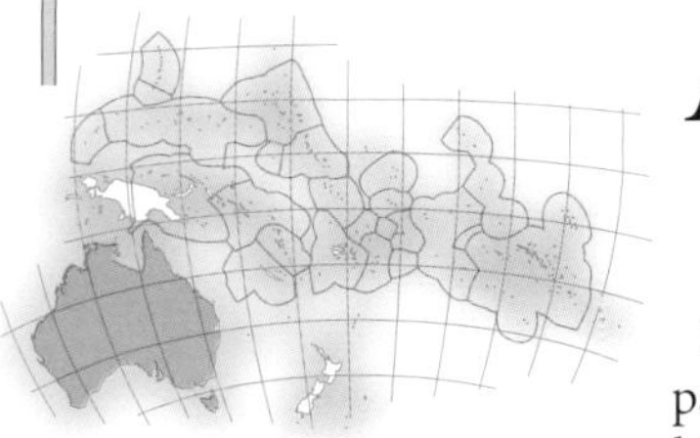

AUSTRALIA IS THE WORLD'S smallest continent, a stable landmass lying between the Indian and Pacific oceans. Previously home to its aboriginal peoples only, since the end of the 18th century immigration has transformed the face of the country. Initially settlers came mainly from western Europe, particularly the UK, and for years Australia remained wedded to its British colonial past. More recent immigrants have come from eastern Europe, and from Asian countries such as Japan, South Korea, and Indonesia. Australia is now forging strong trading links with these "Pacific Rim" countries and its economic future seems to lie with Asia and the Americas, rather than Europe, its traditional partner.

***Uluru (Ayers Rock)**, the world's largest free-standing rock, is a massive outcrop of red sandstone in Australia's desert center. Wind and sandstorms have ground the rock into the smooth curves seen here. Uluru is revered as a sacred site by many aboriginal peoples.*

Using the Land

OVER 165 MILLION SHEEP are dispersed in vast herds around the country, contributing to a major export industry. Cattle-ranching is important, particularly in the west. Wheat, and grapes for Australia's wine industry, are grown mainly in the south. Much of the country is desert, unsuitable for agriculture unless irrigation is used.

The Urban/Rural Population Divide

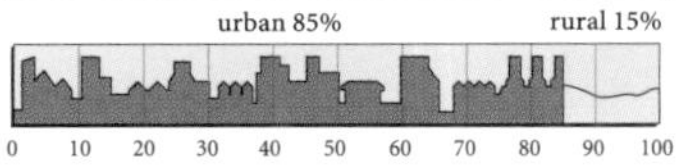

urban 85%
rural 15%
0 10 20 30 40 50 60 70 80 90 100

Population Density	Total Land Area
6 people per sq mile (2 people per sq km)	2,967,893 sq miles (7,686,850 sq km)

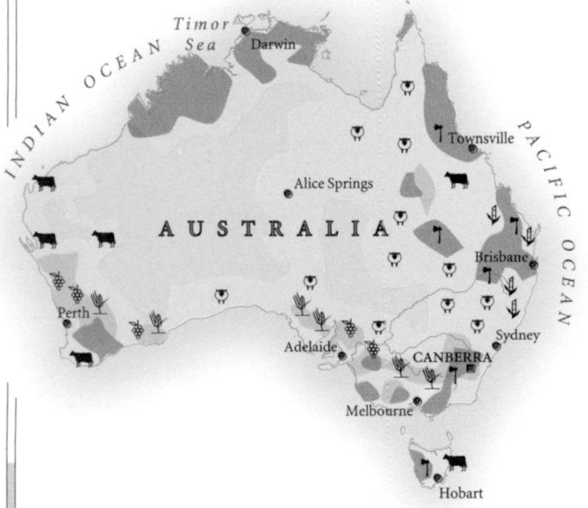

Timor Sea
INDIAN OCEAN
PACIFIC OCEAN
AUSTRALIA
Darwin
Townsville
Alice Springs
Brisbane
Perth
Adelaide
Sydney
CANBERRA
Melbourne
Hobart

Land use and agricultural distribution

- cattle
- sheep
- cereals
- sugar cane
- timber
- vineyards
- capital cities
- major towns
- pasture
- cropland
- forest
- desert
- mountain region

Lines of ripening vines stretch for miles in Barossa Valley, a major wine-growing region near Adelaide.

The Landscape

AUSTRALIA CONSISTS OF MANY ERODED PLATEAUS, lying firmly in the middle of the Indo-Australian Plate. It is the world's flattest continent, and the driest, after Antarctica. The coasts tend to be more hilly and fertile, especially in the east. The mountains of the Great Dividing Range form a natural barrier between the eastern coastal areas and the flat, dry plains and desert regions of the Australian "outback."

***The Great Barrier Reef** is the world's largest area of coral islands and reefs. It runs for about 1,240 miles (2,000 km) along the Queensland coast.*

***The Pinnacles** are a series of rugged sandstone pillars. Their strange shapes have been formed by water and wind erosion.*

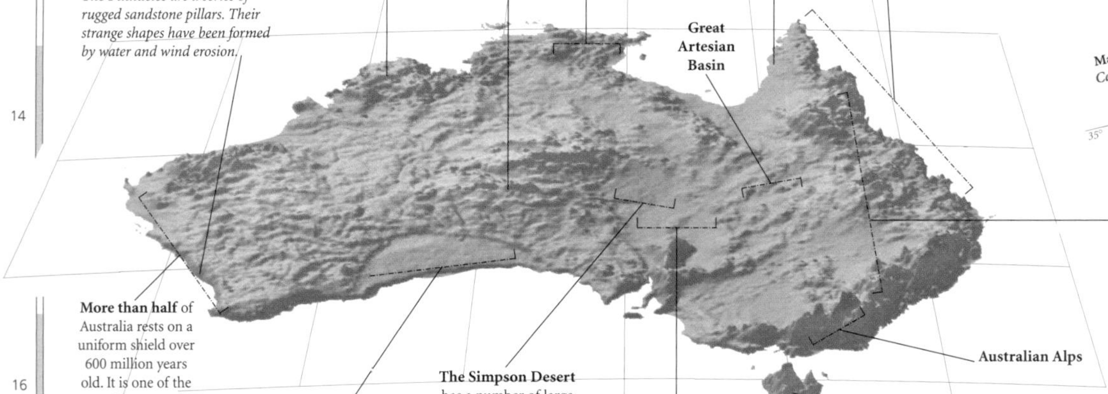

The ancient Kimberley Plateau is the source of some of Australia's richest mineral deposits, including diamonds.

Arnhem Land

The tropical rainforest of the Cape York Peninsula contains more than 600 different varieties of tree.

Uluru (Ayers Rock)

Great Artesian Basin

The Great Dividing Range forms a watershed between east- and west-flowing rivers. Erosion has created deep valleys, gorges, and waterfalls where rivers tumble over escarpments on their way to the sea.

More than half of Australia rests on a uniform shield over 600 million years old. It is one of the Earth's original geological plates.

The Nullarbor Plain is a low-lying limestone plateau which is so flat that the Trans-Australian Railway runs through it in a straight line for more than 300 miles (483 km).

The Simpson Desert has a number of large salt pans, created by the evaporation of past rivers and now sourced by seasonal rains. Some are crusted with gypsum, but most are covered by common salt crystals.

Australian Alps

The Lake Eyre basin, lying 51 ft (16 m) below sea level, is one of the largest inland drainage systems in the world, covering an area of more than 500,000 sq miles (1,300,000 sq km).

Tasmania has the same geological structure as the Australian Alps. During the last period of glaciation, 18,000 years ago, sea levels were some 300 ft (100 m) lower and it was joined to the mainland.

SCALE 1:11,500,000
(projection: Lambert Conformal Conic)

Km 0 25 50 100 150 200 250 300 350
Miles 0 25 50 100 150 200 250 300 350

Map Key

POPULATION
- 1 million to 5 million
- 500,000 to 1 million
- 100,000 to 500,000
- 50,000 to 100,000
- 10,000 to 50,000
- below 10,000

ELEVATION
- 2000m / 6562ft
- 1000m / 3281ft
- 500m / 1640ft
- 250m / 820ft
- 100m / 328ft
- sea level

154
INDIAN OCEAN
Cape Londonderry
Cape Bougainville
Kalumburu
Bigge Island
Bonaparte Archipelago
Heywood Islands
Adele Island
Mount Hann 779m
Collier Bay
Kimberley Plateau
King Leopold Ranges
King Sound
Lombadina
Derby
Kuping
Broome
Fitzroy Crossing
Fitzroy River
Eighty Mile Beach
Great Sandy Desert
Dampier Archipelago
Port Hedland
Wickham
Dampier
Karratha
Roebourne
Whim Creek
De Grey River
Marble Bar
Barrow Island
Fortescue River
Percival Lakes
Lake Dora
Lake Auld
Wittenoom
Onslow
Exmouth Gulf
North West Cape
Exmouth
Learmonth
Hamersley Range
Ashburton River
Tom Price
Mount Meharry 1251m
Paraburdoo
Newman
Little Sandy Desert
Lake Disappointment
Gibson Desert
Coral Bay
Kenneth Range
Barlee Range
WESTERN AUSTRALIA
Minilya
Tropic of Capricorn
Mount Augustus 1105m
Kumarina Roadhouse
Lake Macleod
Waldburg Range
Carnarvon Range
Gascoyne River
Gascoyne Junction
Robinson Range
Lake Gregory
Lake Carnegie
Bernier Island
Carnarvon
Dorre Island
Shark Bay
Wiluna
Lake Way
Lake Wells
Denham
Meekatharra
Dirk Hartog Island
Murchison River
Lake Annean
Lake Austin
Lake Throssell
Lake Yeo
Kalbarri
Mount Magnet
Leonora
Lake Carey
Yalgoo
Lake Ballard
Lake Barlee
Geraldton
Mongers Lake
Menzies
Lake Rebecca
Lake Moore
Rawlinna
Kitchener
Moora
Wubin
Pithara
Kalgoorlie
Coolgardie
Kambalda
Lake Lefroy
The Pinnacles
Southern Cross
Lake Cowan
Balladonia
Merredin
Northam
Lake Johnston
Norseman
Gingin
York
Lake Dundas
Wanneroo
Perth
Kondinin
Fremantle
Rockingham
Brookton
Lake Hope
Lake King
Tower Peak 594m
Mandurah
Narrogin
Ravensthorpe
Esperance
Wagin
Bunbury
Collie
Katanning
Busselton
Bridgetown
Manjimup
Stirling Range
Margaret River
Cape Leeuwin
Augusta
Pemberton
Mount Barker
Albany

Great Artesian Basin

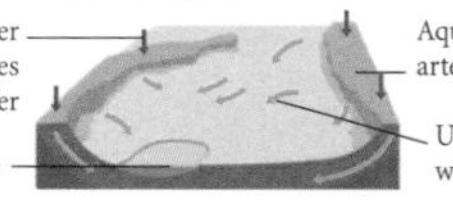

Rainwater replenishes aquifer
Aquifers from which artesian water is obtained
Lake Eyre
Underground water movements

***The Great Artesian Basin** underlies nearly 20% of the total area of Australia, providing a valuable store of underground water, essential to Australian agriculture. The ephemeral rivers which drain the northern part of the basin have highly braided courses and, in consequence, the area is known as "channel country."*

N
Q
T
U
W
X
Y
Z
1
2
3
4
5
6
8
13
14
15
16
17
Torres Strait
Badu Island
Moa Island
Prince of Wales Island
Cape York
Endeavour Strait
Arafura Sea
Croker Island
Cobourg Peninsula
Marchinbar Island
Wessel Islands
Elcho Island
South Goulburn Island
Bathurst Island
Melville Island
Van Diemen Gulf
Beagle Gulf
Darwin
Timor Sea
Noonamah
Jabiru
Cooinda
Adelaide River
Arnhem Land
Mount Evelyn 366m
Bulman
Pine Creek
Nhulunbuy
Groote Eylandt
Gulf of Carpentaria
Joseph Bonaparte Gulf
Daly River
Katherine
Mataranka
Roper Bar
Larrimah
Victoria River
Wyndham
Timber Creek
Kununurra
Victoria River Roadhouse
Daly Waters
Sir Edward Pellew Group
Borroloola
Barkly Tableland
Lake Argyle
Turkey Creek
Bungle Bungle Range
Top Springs Roadhouse
Sturt Plain
Cape Crawford Roadhouse
Wellesley Islands
Mornington Island
Bentinck Island
Newcastle Waters
Kalkarindji
Lake Woods
Renner Springs Roadhouse
Halls Creek
Burketown
Karumba
Normanton
Tanami Desert
Tennant Creek
Camooweal
NORTHERN TERRITORY
Mount Isa
Cloncurry
Selwyn Range
Julia Creek
Barrow Creek Roadhouse
Lake Mackay
Yuendumu
AUSTRALIA
Lake Macdonald
Mount Liebig 1274m
Mount Zeil 1531m
Macdonnell Ranges
Ross River
Alice Springs
Glen Helen
Hermannsburg
Hopkins Lake
Lake Neale
Lake Amadeus
James Ranges
Simpson Desert
Erldunda Roadhouse
Yulara
Kata Tjuta (Mount Olga) 1069m
Uluru (Ayers Rock) 867m
Kulgera Roadhouse
Finke
Tomkinson Ranges
Musgrave Ranges
Chandler
Great Victoria Desert
Lake Eyre Basin
Sturt Stony Desert
Diamantina River
Cooper Creek
Lake Yamma Yamma
Warburton Creek
Tirari Desert
Lake Eyre North
Pootnoura
Coober Pedy
SOUTH AUSTRALIA
Lake Gregory
Lake Blanche
Lake Eyre South
Marree
Lake Maurice
Lake Callabonna
Nullarbor Plain
Wynbring
Roxby Downs
Lyndhurst
Watson
Tarcoola
Glendambo
Lake Torrens
Lake Frome
Reid
Woomera
Lake Everard
Lake Gairdner
Flinders Ranges
Saint Mary Peak 1180m
Bockabie
Eucla
Madura
Ceduna
Gawler Ranges
Great Australian Bight
Port Augusta
Mount Remarkable 960m
Whyalla
Port Pirie
Crystal Brook
Wudinna
Elliston
Eyre Peninsula
Peterborough
Jamestown
Mount Bryan 932m
Burra
Spencer Gulf
Wallaroo
Clare
Maitland
Gawler
Elizabeth
Tumby Bay
Port Lincoln
Adelaide
Barossa Valley
Investigator Strait
Kingscote
Kangaroo Island
Tailem Bend
Murray River
Renmark
Mildura
Loxton
Keith
Naracoorte
Mount Gambier
Portland
Warrnambool
Hamilton
Horsham
Dimboola
Lake Corangamite
Geelong
Cape Otway
Ballarat
Bacchus Marsh
Werribee
Sunbury
VICTORIA
Melbourne
Dandenong
Moe
Morwell
Traralgon
Sale
Bairnsdale
Orbost
Bendigo
Shepparton
Echuca
Wangaratta
Mount Buller
Mount Bogong 1986m
Mount Kosciuszko 2228m
Australian Alps
Snowy River
Cooma
Bega
Narooma
Albury
Wodonga
Wagga Wagga
CANBERRA
AUSTRALIAN CAPITAL TERRITORY
JERVIS BAY TERRITORY
Nowra-Bomaderry
Wollongong
Sydney
Kingsford Smith
Parramatta
Penrith
Campbelltown
Gosford
Newcastle
Cessnock
Lithgow
Bathurst
Orange
Cowra
Young
Griffith
Hay
Balranald
Deniliquin
Swan Hill
Kerang
Sea Lake
Ouyen
Birchip
Murrumbidgee River
Lachlan River
Hillston
Lake Garnpung
Ivanhoe
Forbes
Parkes
Burrendong Reservoir
Lake Windamere
Dubbo
Gilgandra
Mudgee
Muswellbrook
NEW SOUTH WALES
Cobar
Nyngan
Coonabarabran
Gunnedah
Tamworth
Armidale
Round Mountain 1583m
Coffs Harbour
Port Macquarie
Taree
Grafton
Lismore
Cape Byron
Murwillumbah
Gold Coast
Brisbane
Surfers Paradise
Ipswich
Toowoomba
Warwick
Stanthorpe
Goondiwindi
Darling Downs
Dalby
Caboolture
Sunshine Coast
Caloundra
Maroochydore-Mooloolaba
Nambour
Gympie
Maryborough
Hervey Bay
Fraser Island
Gayndah
Murgon
Miles
Bundaberg
Biloela
Banana
Moura
Gladstone
Curtis Island
Rockhampton
Tropic of Capricorn
Yeppoon
Marlborough
Northumberland Isles
Sarina
Mackay
Mount Dalrymple 1259m
Bloomsbury
Whitsunday Group
Bowen
Townsville
Mount Elliot 1234m
Charters Towers
Ingham
Hinchinbrook Island
Cardwell
Tully
Innisfail
Bartle Frere 1622m
Cairns
Atherton
Mareeba
Ravenshoe
Mount Garnet
Port Douglas
Mossman
Cape Tribulation
Cooktown
Laura
Lakeland Downs
Ayton
Princess Charlotte Bay
Cape York Peninsula
Coen
Weipa
Mitchell River
Gilbert River
Norman River
Flinders River
Georgetown
Forsayth
Gregory Range
Bambaroo
Mount Stewart 997m
Great Dividing Range
Great Barrier Reef
Coral Sea
Tasman Sea
Hughenden
QUEENSLAND
Winton
Boulia
Lake Galilee
Dalrymple Lake
Clarke Range
Moranbah
Clermont
Mackenzie River
Longreach
Barcaldine
Alpha
Emerald
Blackwater
Fairbairn Reservoir
Springsure
Rolleston
Blackall
Consuelo Peak 1219m
Great Artesian Basin
Windorah
Augathella
Charleville
Mitchell
Roma
Dawson River
Quilpie
Thargomindah
Grey Range
Cunnamulla
Warrego River
Bollon
Balonne River
Saint George
Dirranbandi
Moonie
Wanaaring
Milparinka
Barrier Range
Bourke
Darling River
Barwon River
Walgett
Namoi River
Narrabri
Moree
Coolabah
Wilcannia
Broken Hill
Menindee Lake
King Island
Bass Strait
Hunter Island
Flinders Island
Furneaux Group
Cape Barren Island
Banks Strait
Marrawah
Burnie
Devonport
George Town
Launceston
Mount Ossa 1617m
Saint Marys
TASMANIA
Lake Gordon
Lake Pedder
Hobart
Kingston
Maria Island
South Bruny Island
South East Point

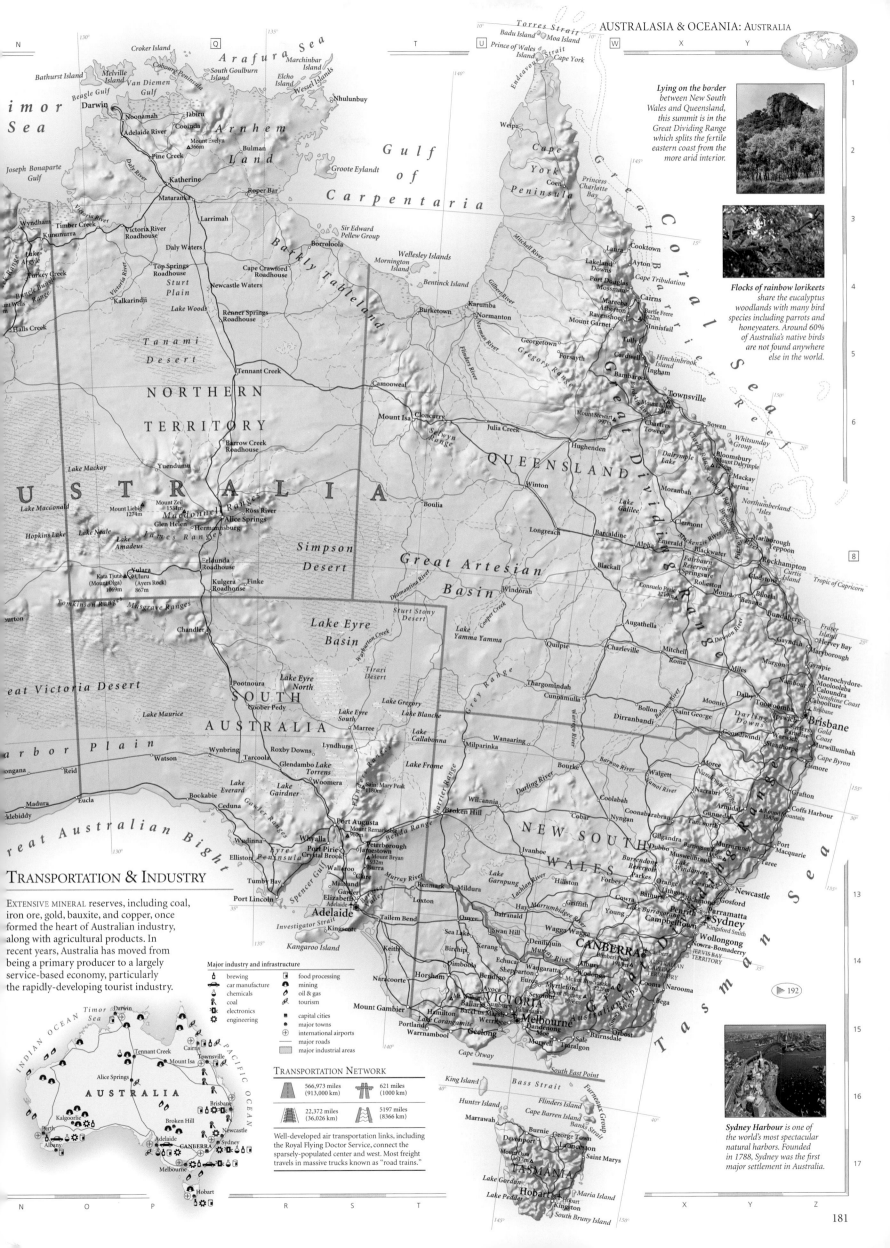

Lying on the border between New South Wales and Queensland, this summit is in the Great Dividing Range which splits the fertile eastern coast from the more arid interior.

Flocks of rainbow lorikeets share the eucalyptus woodlands with many bird species including parrots and honeyeaters. Around 60% of Australia's native birds are not found anywhere else in the world.

▶ 192

Sydney Harbour is one of the world's most spectacular natural harbors. Founded in 1788, Sydney was the first major settlement in Australia.

TRANSPORTATION & INDUSTRY

EXTENSIVE MINERAL reserves, including coal, iron ore, gold, bauxite, and copper, once formed the heart of Australian industry, along with agricultural products. In recent years, Australia has moved from being a primary producer to a largely service-based economy, particularly the rapidly-developing tourist industry.

Major industry and infrastructure

- brewing
- car manufacture
- chemicals
- coal
- electronics
- engineering
- food processing
- mining
- oil & gas
- tourism
- capital cities
- major towns
- international airports
- major roads
- major industrial areas

TRANSPORTATION NETWORK

566,973 miles (913,000 km)	621 miles (1000 km)
22,372 miles (36,026 km)	5197 miles (8366 km)

Well-developed air transportation links, including the Royal Flying Doctor Service, connect the sparsely-populated center and west. Most freight travels in massive trucks known as "road trains."

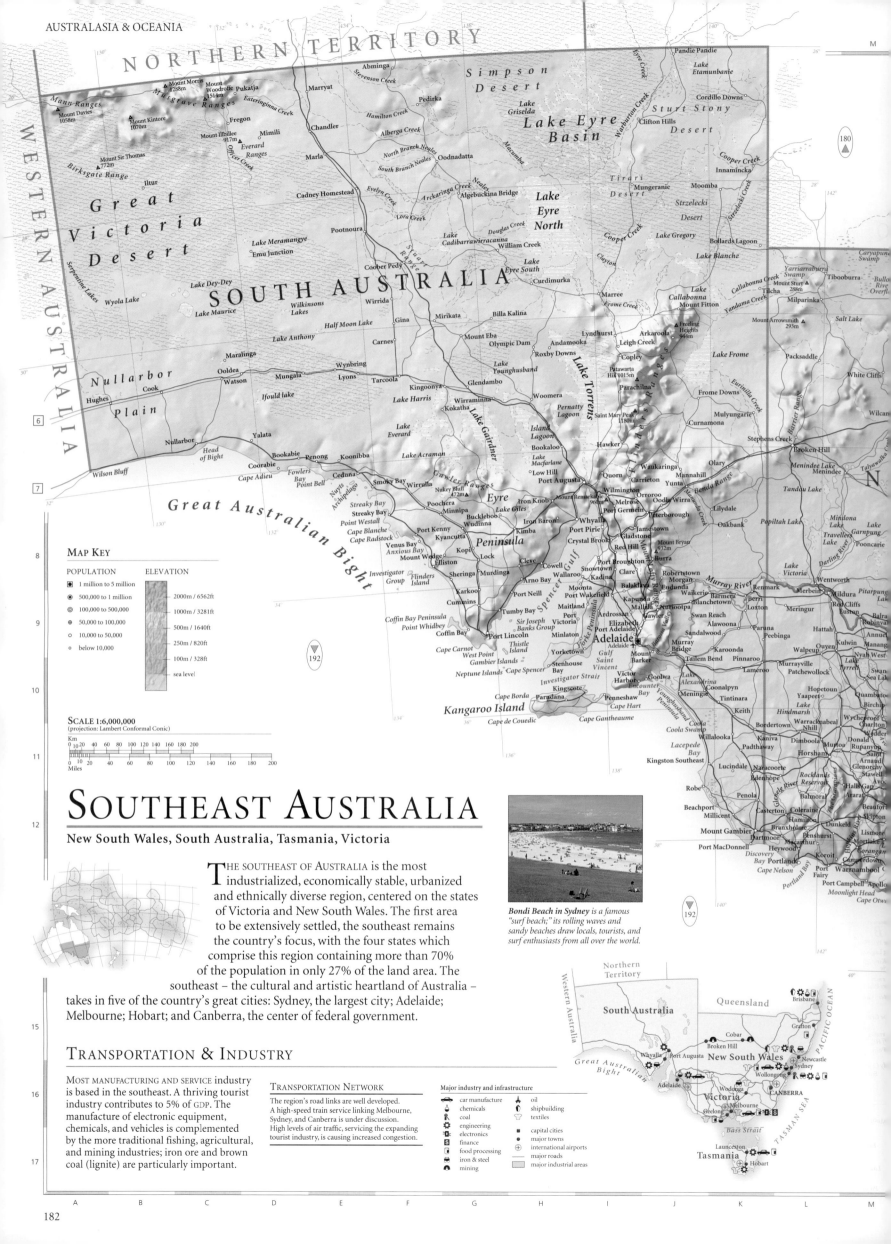

NORTHERN TERRITORY
WESTERN AUSTRALIA
SOUTH AUSTRALIA
Simpson Desert
Lake Eyre Basin
Sturt Stony Desert
Great Victoria Desert
Nullarbor Plain
Great Australian Bight
Lake Eyre North
Lake Eyre South
Lake Torrens
Lake Gairdner
Lake Frome
Flinders Ranges
Musgrave Ranges
Mann Ranges
Everard Ranges
Gawler Ranges
Eyre Peninsula
Yorke Peninsula
Spencer Gulf
Gulf Saint Vincent
Investigator Strait
Kangaroo Island
Murray River
Darling River
Cooper Creek
Strzelecki Desert
Tirari Desert
Adelaide
Port Augusta
Port Pirie
Whyalla
Port Lincoln
Ceduna
Coober Pedy
Woomera
Broken Hill
Mildura
Mount Gambier
Mount Woodroffe 1514m
Mount Morris 1288m
Mount Davies 1058m
Mount Kintore 1070m
Mount Illbillee 917m
Mount Sir Thomas 772m
Saint Mary Peak 1180m
Freeling Heights 944m
Mount Remarkable 960m
Mount Bryan 932m
Nukey Bluff 472m
Mount Arrowsmith 293m
Mount Sturt 288m
Pandie Pandie
Lake Etamunbanie
Cordillo Downs
Innamincka
Moomba
Oodnadatta
Marla
Marryat
Abminga
Pedirka
Chandler
Mimili
Fregon
Pukatja
Iltur
Cadney Homestead
Pootnoura
Emu Junction
Maralinga
Ooldea
Watson
Cook
Hughes
Nullarbor
Wilson Bluff
Head of Bight
Yalata
Penong
Koonibba
Streaky Bay
Elliston
Tumby Bay
Cowell
Wallaroo
Kadina
Moonta
Port Wakefield
Clare
Burra
Peterborough
Gladstone
Jamestown
Morgan
Renmark
Berri
Loxton
Murray Bridge
Victor Harbor
Goolwa
Kingscote
Penneshaw
Cape Borda
Cape de Couedic
Cape Gantheaume
Lake Alexandrina
The Coorong
Tintinara
Keith
Bordertown
Kingston Southeast
Robe
Beachport
Millicent
Naracoorte
Penola
Port MacDonnell
Dartmoor
Casterton
Hamilton
Portland
Warrnambool
Port Campbell
Horsham
Lake Victoria
Wentworth
Tibooburra
Milparinka
Packsaddle
Menindee Lake
Menindee
Tandou Lake
Lake Blanche
Lake Callabonna
Lake Gregory
Arkaroola
Leigh Creek
Lyndhurst
Olympic Dam
Roxby Downs
Andamooka
Glendambo
Kingoonya
Tarcoola
Lake Everard
Lake Harris
Lake Acraman
Iron Knob
Iron Baron
Kimba
Wudinna
Minnipa
Poochera
Wirrulla
Cummins
Coffin Bay
Point Whidbey
Neptune Islands
Gambier Islands
Thistle Island
Sir Joseph Banks Group
Investigator Group
Flinders Island
Nuyts Archipelago
Cape Adieu
Fowlers Bay
Point Bell
Pacific Ocean
MAP KEY
POPULATION
1 million to 5 million
500,000 to 1 million
100,000 to 500,000
50,000 to 100,000
10,000 to 50,000
below 10,000
ELEVATION
2000m / 6562ft
1000m / 3281ft
500m / 1640ft
250m / 820ft
100m / 328ft
sea level
SCALE 1:6,000,000
(projection: Lambert Conformal Conic)
Km
Miles
180
192

SOUTHEAST AUSTRALIA

New South Wales, South Australia, Tasmania, Victoria

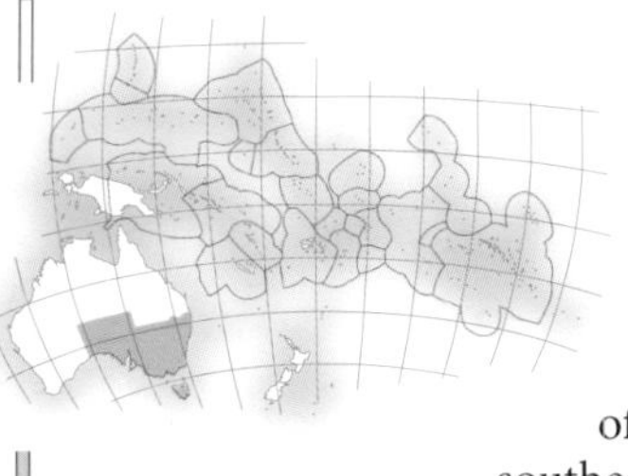

THE SOUTHEAST OF AUSTRALIA is the most industrialized, economically stable, urbanized and ethnically diverse region, centered on the states of Victoria and New South Wales. The first area to be extensively settled, the southeast remains the country's focus, with the four states which comprise this region containing more than 70% of the population in only 27% of the land area. The southeast – the cultural and artistic heartland of Australia – takes in five of the country's great cities: Sydney, the largest city; Adelaide; Melbourne; Hobart; and Canberra, the center of federal government.

***Bondi Beach in Sydney** is a famous "surf beach;" its rolling waves and sandy beaches draw locals, tourists, and surf enthusiasts from all over the world.*

192

TRANSPORTATION & INDUSTRY

MOST MANUFACTURING AND SERVICE industry is based in the southeast. A thriving tourist industry contributes to 5% of GDP. The manufacture of electronic equipment, chemicals, and vehicles is complemented by the more traditional fishing, agricultural, and mining industries; iron ore and brown coal (lignite) are particularly important.

TRANSPORTATION NETWORK

The region's road links are well developed. A high-speed train service linking Melbourne, Sydney, and Canberra is under discussion. High levels of air traffic, servicing the expanding tourist industry, is causing increased congestion.

Major industry and infrastructure

- car manufacture
- chemicals
- coal
- engineering
- electronics
- finance
- food processing
- iron & steel
- mining
- oil
- shipbuilding
- textiles
- capital cities
- major towns
- international airports
- major roads
- major industrial areas

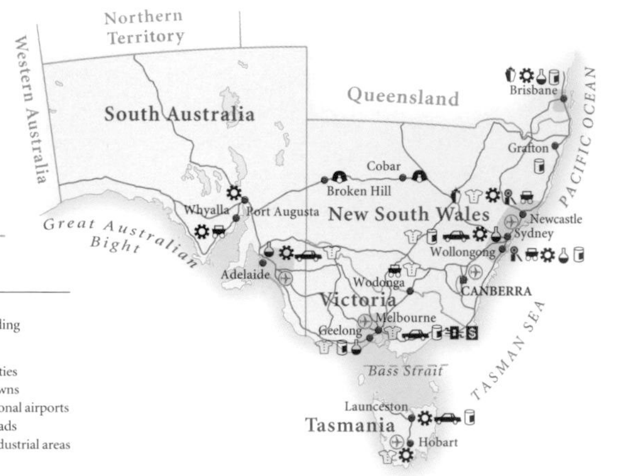
Northern Territory
Western Australia
South Australia
Queensland
New South Wales
Victoria
Tasmania
Great Australian Bight
Bass Strait
TASMAN SEA
PACIFIC OCEAN
Brisbane
Grafton
Cobar
Broken Hill
Whyalla
Port Augusta
Newcastle
Sydney
Wollongong
CANBERRA
Adelaide
Wodonga
Melbourne
Geelong
Launceston
Hobart

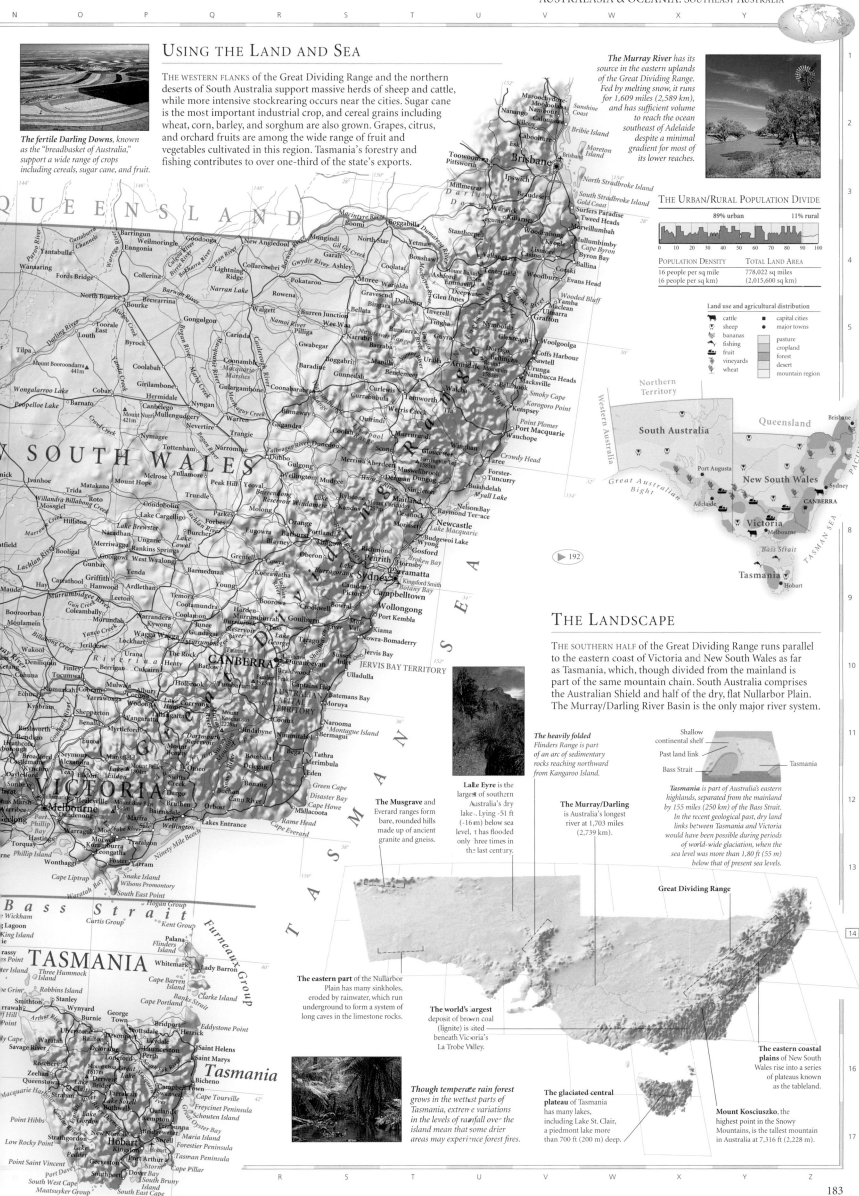

USING THE LAND AND SEA

The fertile Darling Downs, known as the "breadbasket of Australia," support a wide range of crops including cereals, sugar cane, and fruit.

THE WESTERN FLANKS of the Great Dividing Range and the northern deserts of South Australia support massive herds of sheep and cattle, while more intensive stockrearing occurs near the cities. Sugar cane is the most important industrial crop, and cereal grains including wheat, corn, barley, and sorghum are also grown. Grapes, citrus, and orchard fruits are among the wide range of fruit and vegetables cultivated in this region. Tasmania's forestry and fishing contributes to over one-third of the state's exports.

***The Murray River** has its source in the eastern uplands of the Great Dividing Range. Fed by melting snow, it runs for 1,609 miles (2,589 km), and has sufficient volume to reach the ocean southeast of Adelaide despite a minimal gradient for most of its lower reaches.*

QUEENSLAND
NEW SOUTH WALES
VICTORIA
TASMANIA
Brisbane
Sydney
CANBERRA
Melbourne
Hobart
Newcastle
Wollongong
Tasman Sea
Great Dividing Range
Bass Strait
Furneaux Group
JERVIS BAY TERRITORY
AUSTRALIAN CAPITAL TERRITORY

▶ 192

THE URBAN/RURAL POPULATION DIVIDE

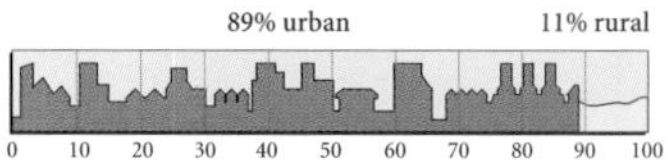
89% urban
11% rural
0
10
20
30
40
50
60
70
80
90
100

POPULATION DENSITY	TOTAL LAND AREA
16 people per sq mile (6 people per sq km)	778,022 sq miles (2,015,600 sq km)

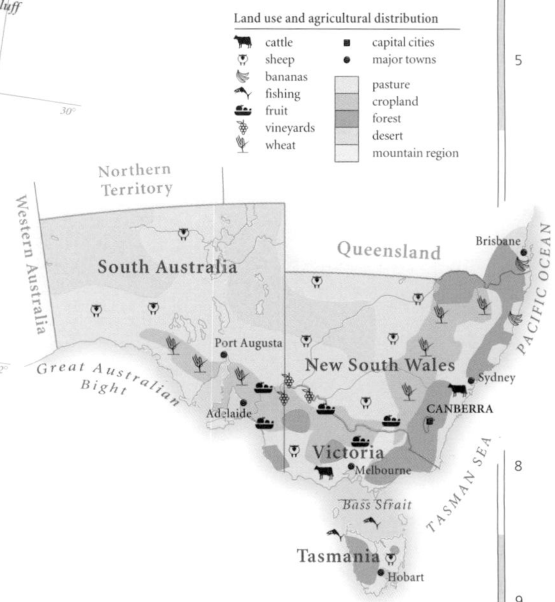
Land use and agricultural distribution
cattle
sheep
bananas
fishing
fruit
vineyards
wheat
capital cities
major towns
pasture
cropland
forest
desert
mountain region
Northern Territory
Western Australia
South Australia
Queensland
New South Wales
Victoria
Tasmania
Brisbane
Port Augusta
Adelaide
Sydney
CANBERRA
Melbourne
Hobart
Great Australian Bight
Bass Strait
TASMAN SEA
PACIFIC OCEAN

THE LANDSCAPE

THE SOUTHERN HALF of the Great Dividing Range runs parallel to the eastern coast of Victoria and New South Wales as far as Tasmania, which, though divided from the mainland is part of the same mountain chain. South Australia comprises the Australian Shield and half of the dry, flat Nullarbor Plain. The Murray/Darling River Basin is the only major river system.

***The heavily folded** Flinders Range is part of an arc of sedimentary rocks reaching northward from Kangaroo Island.*

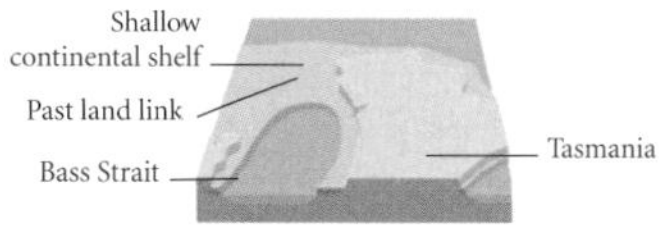
Shallow continental shelf
Past land link
Bass Strait
Tasmania

***Tasmania** is part of Australia's eastern highlands, separated from the mainland by 155 miles (250 km) of the Bass Strait. In the recent geological past, dry land links between Tasmania and Victoria would have been possible during periods of world-wide glaciation, when the sea level was more than 1,80 ft (55 m) below that of present sea levels.*

The Musgrave and Everard ranges form bare, rounded hills made up of ancient granite and gneiss.

Lake Eyre is the largest of southern Australia's dry lakes. Lying -51 ft (-16 m) below sea level, it has flooded only three times in the last century.

The Murray/Darling is Australia's longest river at 1,703 miles (2,739 km).

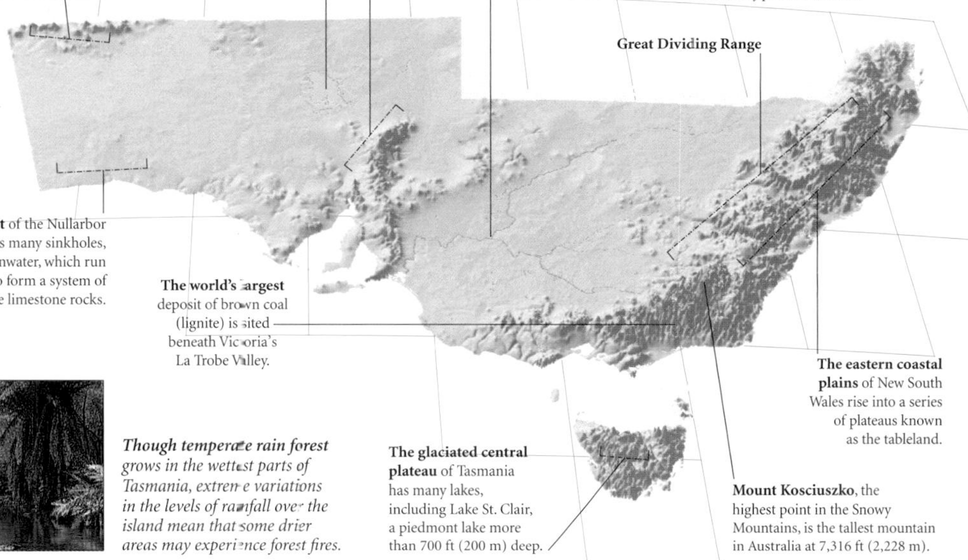
Great Dividing Range

The eastern part of the Nullarbor Plain has many sinkholes, eroded by rainwater, which run underground to form a system of long caves in the limestone rocks.

The world's largest deposit of brown coal (lignite) is sited beneath Victoria's La Trobe Valley.

The eastern coastal plains of New South Wales rise into a series of plateaus known as the tableland.

***Though temperate rain forest** grows in the wettest parts of Tasmania, extreme variations in the levels of rainfall over the island mean that some drier areas may experience forest fires.*

The glaciated central plateau of Tasmania has many lakes, including Lake St. Clair, a piedmont lake more than 700 ft (200 m) deep.

Mount Kosciuszko, the highest point in the Snowy Mountains, is the tallest mountain in Australia at 7,316 ft (2,228 m).

New Zealand

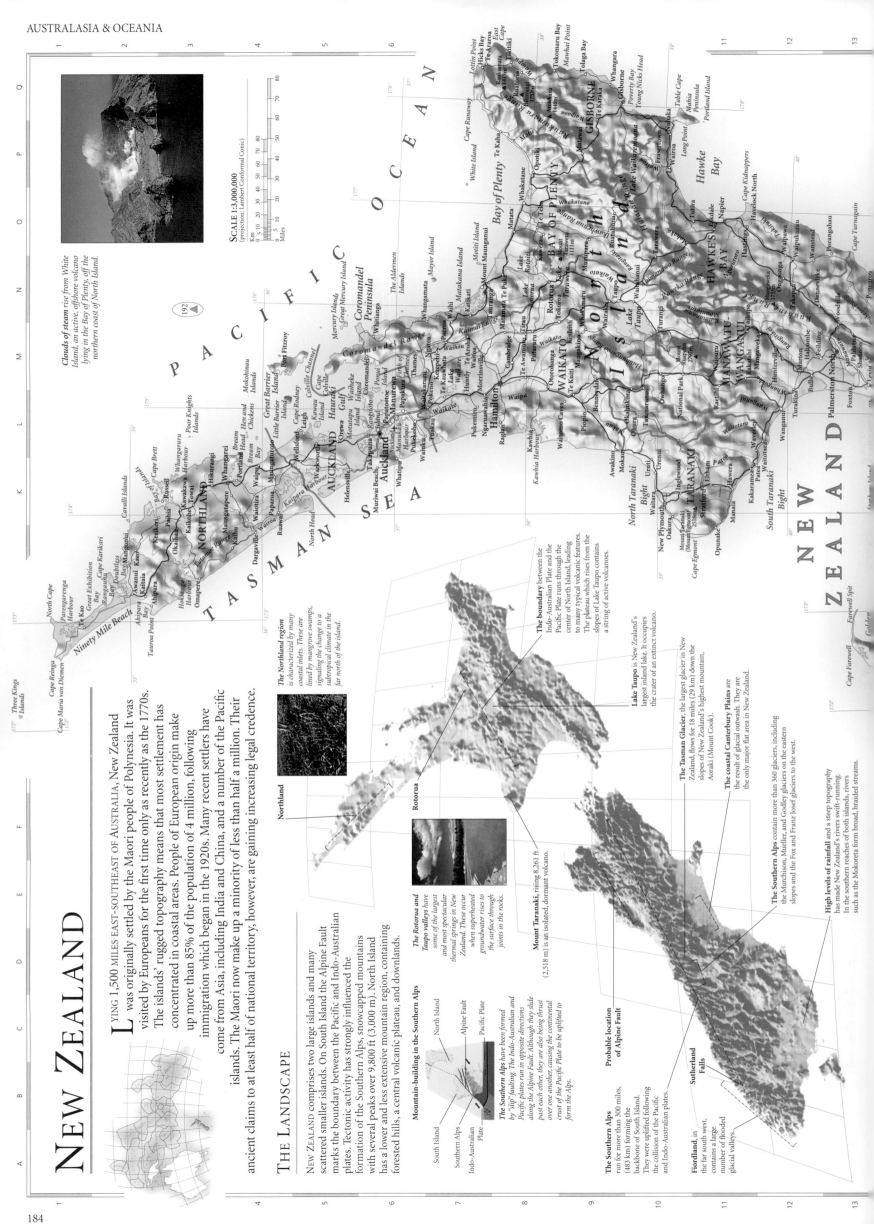

Lying 1,500 miles east-southeast of Australia, New Zealand was originally settled by the Maori people of Polynesia. It was visited by Europeans for the first time only as recently as the 1770s. The islands' rugged topography means that most settlement has concentrated in coastal areas. People of European origin make up more than 85% of the population of 4 million, following immigration which began in the 1920s. Many recent settlers have come from Asia, including India and China, and a number of the Pacific islands. The Maori now make up a minority of less than half a million. Their ancient claims to at least half of national territory, however, are gaining increasing legal credence.

The Landscape

New Zealand comprises two large islands and many scattered smaller islands. On South Island the Alpine Fault marks the boundary between the Pacific and Indo-Australian plates. Tectonic activity has strongly influenced the formation of the Southern Alps, snowcapped mountains with several peaks over 9,800 ft (3,000 m). North Island has a lower and less extensive mountain region, containing forested hills, a central volcanic plateau, and downlands.

Mountain-building in the Southern Alps

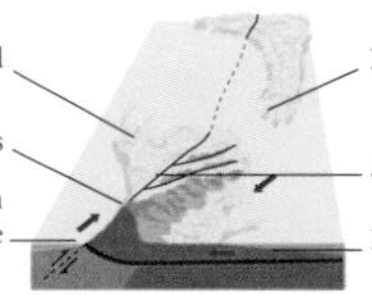
South Island
North Island
Southern Alps
Alpine Fault
Indo-Australian Plate
Pacific Plate

***The Southern Alps** have been formed by "slip" faulting. The Indo-Australian and Pacific plates run in opposite directions along the Alpine Fault. Although they slide past each other, they are also being thrust over one another, causing the continental crust of the Pacific Plate to be uplifted to form the Alps.*

***The Rotorua and Taupo valleys** have some of the largest and most spectacular thermal springs in New Zealand. These occur when superheated groundwater rises to the surface through joints in the rocks.*

***The Northland region** is characterized by many coastal inlets. These are lined by mangrove swamps, signaling the change to a subtropical climate in the far north of the island.*

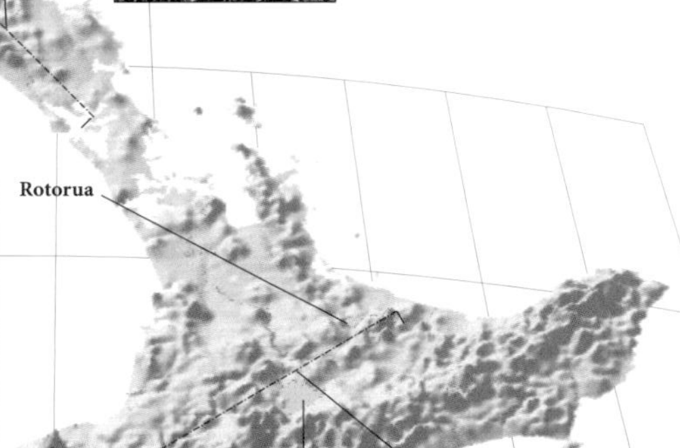
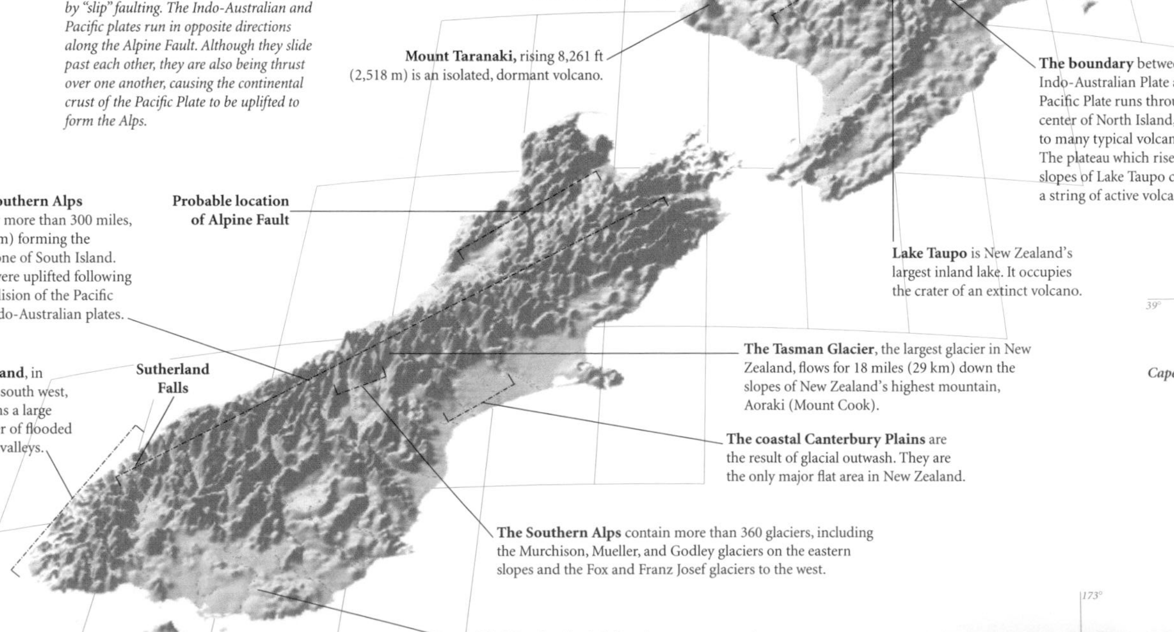

Northland

Rotorua

Mount Taranaki, rising 8,261 ft (2,518 m) is an isolated, dormant volcano.

The boundary between the Indo-Australian Plate and the Pacific Plate runs through the center of North Island, leading to many typical volcanic features. The plateau which rises from the slopes of Lake Taupo contains a string of active volcanoes.

Lake Taupo is New Zealand's largest inland lake. It occupies the crater of an extinct volcano.

The Southern Alps run for more than 300 miles, (483 km) forming the backbone of South Island. They were uplifted following the collision of the Pacific and Indo-Australian plates.

Probable location of Alpine Fault

Fiordland, in the far south west, contains a large number of flooded glacial valleys.

Sutherland Falls

The Tasman Glacier, the largest glacier in New Zealand, flows for 18 miles (29 km) down the slopes of New Zealand's highest mountain, Aoraki (Mount Cook).

The coastal Canterbury Plains are the result of glacial outwash. They are the only major flat area in New Zealand.

The Southern Alps contain more than 360 glaciers, including the Murchison, Mueller, and Godley glaciers on the eastern slopes and the Fox and Franz Josef glaciers to the west.

High levels of rainfall and a steep topography has made New Zealand's rivers swift-running. In the southern reaches of both islands, rivers such as the Mokoreta form broad, braided streams.

***Clouds of steam** rise from White Island, an active, offshore volcano lying in the Bay of Plenty, off the northern coast of North Island.*

SCALE 1:3,000,000
(projection: Lambert Conformal Conic)

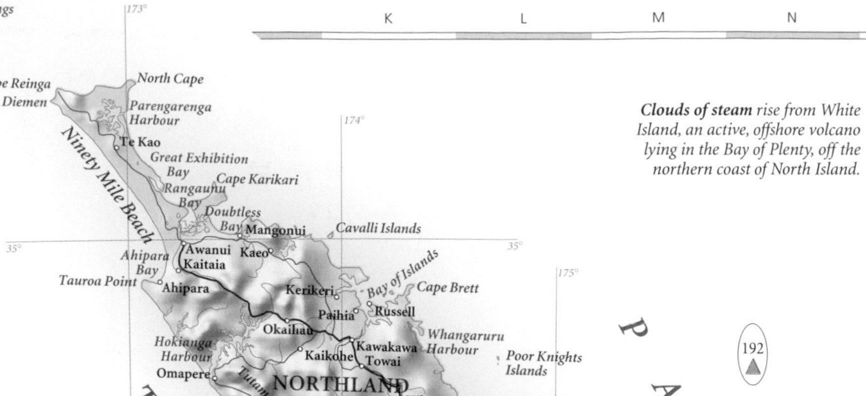

Km 0 5 10 20 30 40 50 60 70 80
Miles 0 5 10 20 30 40 50 60 70 80
192
PACIFIC OCEAN
TASMAN SEA
NEW ZEALAND
North Island
Three Kings Islands
Cape Reinga
Cape Maria van Diemen
North Cape
Parengarenga Harbour
Te Kao
Ninety Mile Beach
Great Exhibition Bay
Cape Karikari
Rangaunu Bay
Doubtless Bay
Mangonui
Cavalli Islands
Ahipara Bay
Awanui
Kaitaia
Kaeo
Tauroa Point
Ahipara
Kerikeri
Bay of Islands
Cape Brett
Paihia
Russell
Okaihau
Kawakawa
Kaikohe
Towai
Whangaruru Harbour
Poor Knights Islands
Hokianga Harbour
Omapere
NORTHLAND
Hikurangi
Maungatapere
Whangarei
Kaihu
Portland
Bream Head
Bream Bay
Hen and Chickens
Mokohinau Islands
Dargaville
Waiotira
Waipu
Paparoa
Maungaturoto
Great Barrier Island
Little Barrier Island
Port Fitzroy
Ruawai
Wellsford
Cape Rodney
Leigh
North Head
Kaipara Harbour
Warkworth
Kawau Island
Colville Channel
Cape Colville
AUCKLAND
Hauraki Gulf
Helensville
Orewa
Motutapu Island
Waiheke Island
Mercury Islands
Great Mercury Island
Coromandel
Coromandel Peninsula
Whitianga
Muriwai Beach
Takapuna
Rangitoto Island
Ponui Island
Auckland
Papatoetoe
Manurewa
Whatipu
Manukau Harbour
Papakura
Firth of Thames
Thames
The Aldermen Islands
Pukekohe
Waiuku
Waitakaruru
Ngatea
Whangamata
Mayor Island
Tuakau
Pokeno
Kerepehi
Te Kauwhata
Paeroa
Waihi
Matakana Island
Huntly
Te Aroha
Waitoa
Katikati
Pukemiro
Ngaruawahia
Morrinsville
Motiti Island
Mount Maunganui
Tauranga
White Island
Cape Runaway
Lottin Point
Hicks Bay
Te Araroa
East Cape
Hamilton
Raglan
Matamata
Te Puke
Bay of Plenty
Te Kaha
Raukumara 1413m
Cambridge
Matata
Whakatane
Ruatoria
Hikurangi 1752m
Tikitiki
Te Awamutu
Tirau
Putaruru
Lake Rotorua
Lake Rotoiti
Kawhia Harbour
Kawhia
Kawerau
Te Teko
Opotiki
Otorohanga
Rotorua
Tokoroa
BAY OF PLENTY
Mount Tarawera 1111m
Arowhana 1440m
Tokomaru Bay
Mawhai Point
Waitomo Caves
WAIKATO
Te Kuiti
Kinleith
Mangakino
Whakamaru
Murupara
Matawai
GISBORNE
Tolaga Bay
Piopio
Benneydale
Te Karaka
Awakino
Mokau
Wairakei
Taupo
Ruatahuna
Whangara
Gisborne
Poverty Bay
Young Nicks Head
North Taranaki Bight
Okahukura
Ohura
Lake Taupo
Waitahanui
Lake Waikaremoana
Waitara
Uruti
Taumarunui
Tarawera
New Plymouth
Oakura
Urenui
Owhango
Turangi
Frasertown
Nuhaka
Wairoa
Table Cape
Long Point
Mahia Peninsula
Portland Island
Mount Taranaki (Mount Egmont) 2518m
Cape Egmont
Inglewood
TARANAKI
Stratford
Eltham
National Park
Mount Ruapehu 2797m
Tutira
Hawke Bay
Opunake
Raetihi
Waiouru
HAWKE'S BAY
Eskdale
Napier
Manaia
Hawera
MANAWATU-WANGANUI
Kakatahi
Mangaweka
Taihape
Hastings
Cape Kidnappers
Havelock North
Kakaramea
Patea
Waverley
Waitotara
South Taranaki Bight
Hunterville
Mangaweka 1733m
Ongaonga
Waipawa
Wanganui
Takapau
Waipukurau
Turakina
Marton
Bulls
Halcombe
Feilding
Dannevirke
Wanstead
Porangahau
Palmerston North
Foxton
Woodville
Shannon
Pahiatua
Pongaroa
Cape Turnagain
Cape Farewell
Farewell Spit

Map Key

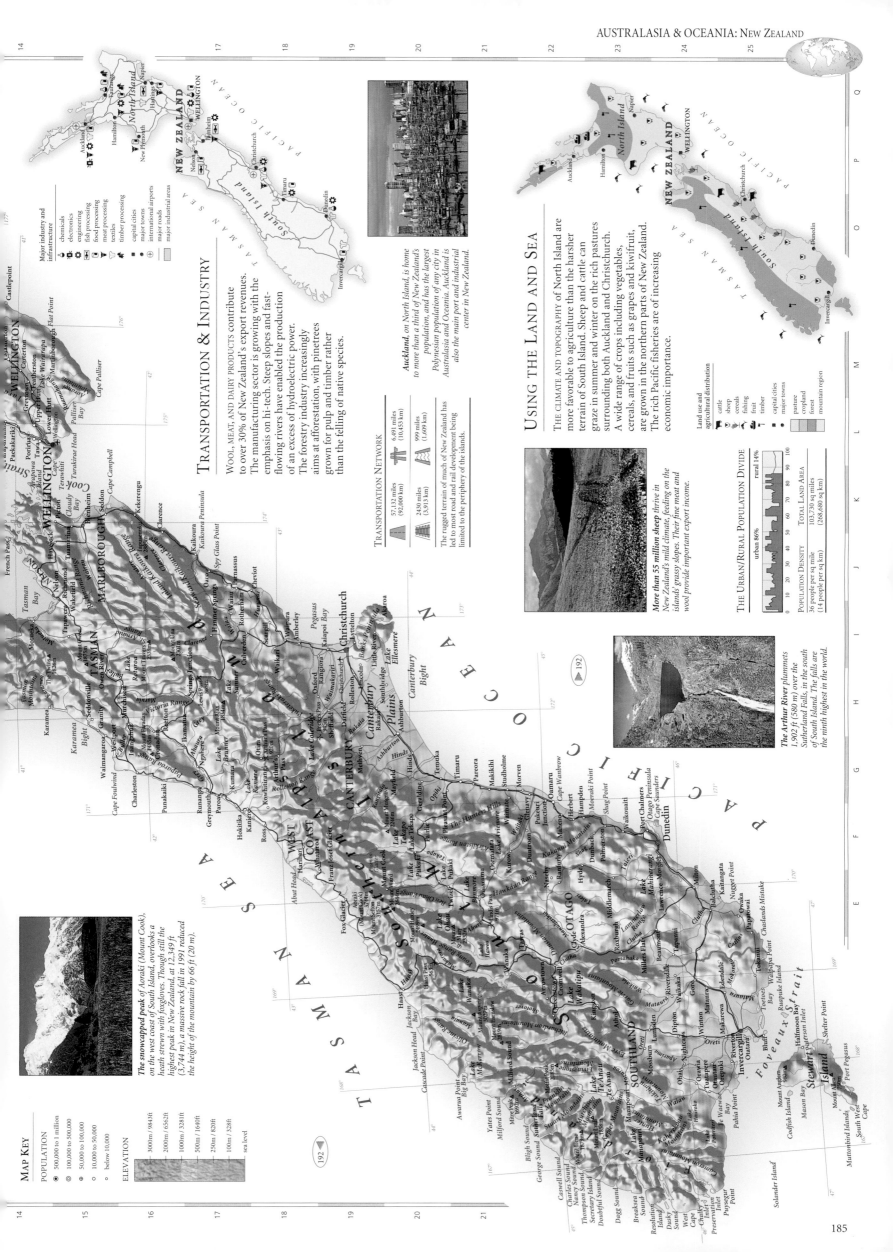

POPULATION
- 500,000 to 1 million
- 100,000 to 500,000
- 50,000 to 100,000
- 10,000 to 50,000
- below 10,000

ELEVATION
- 3000m / 9843ft
- 2000m / 6562ft
- 1000m / 3281ft
- 500m / 1640ft
- 250m / 820ft
- 100m / 328ft
- sea level

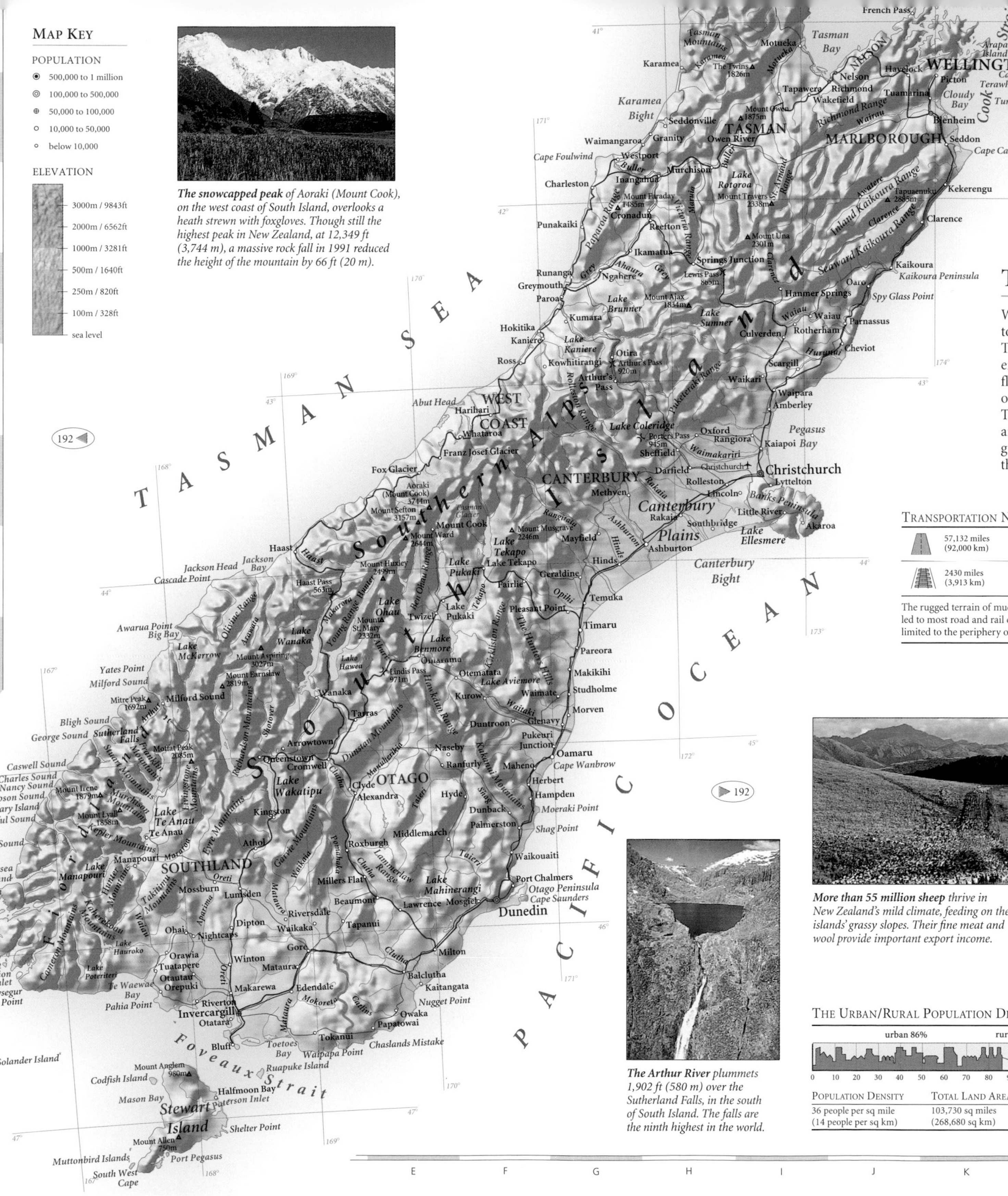
TASMAN SEA
PACIFIC OCEAN
Southern Alps
South Island
WELLINGTON
Christchurch
Dunedin
Invercargill
Foveaux Strait
Stewart Island
CANTERBURY
OTAGO
SOUTHLAND
WEST COAST
TASMAN
MARLBOROUGH
NELSON
Canterbury Plains
Canterbury Bight
Cook Strait
Tasman Bay
Karamea Bight
Pegasus Bay
Lake Wakatipu
Lake Te Anau
Lake Manapouri
Lake Ellesmere
Lake Tekapo
Lake Pukaki
Lake Ohau
Lake Wanaka
Lake Hawea
Nelson
Blenheim
Greymouth
Hokitika
Westport
Timaru
Oamaru
Queenstown
Gore
Kaikoura
192
192

***The snowcapped peak** of Aoraki (Mount Cook), on the west coast of South Island, overlooks a heath strewn with foxgloves. Though still the highest peak in New Zealand, at 12,349 ft (3,744 m), a massive rock fall in 1991 reduced the height of the mountain by 66 ft (20 m).*

Transportation & Industry

WOOL, MEAT, AND DAIRY PRODUCTS contribute to over 30% of New Zealand's export revenues. The manufacturing sector is growing with the emphasis on hi-tech. Steep slopes and fast-flowing rivers have enabled the production of an excess of hydroelectric power. The forestry industry increasingly aims at afforestation, with pinetrees grown for pulp and timber rather than the felling of native species.

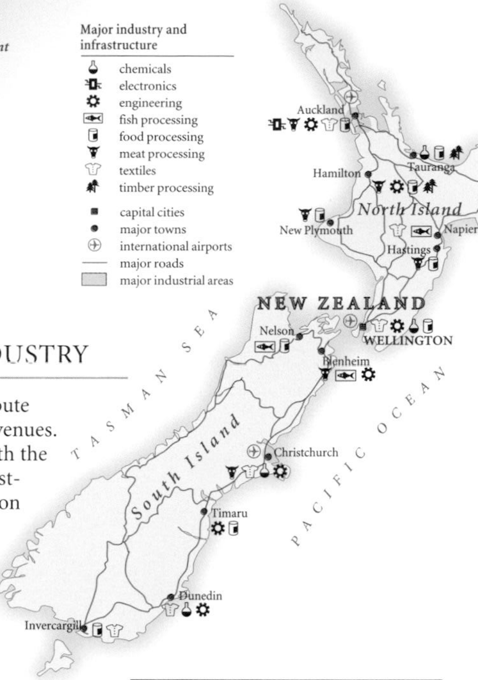
Major industry and infrastructure
chemicals
electronics
engineering
fish processing
food processing
meat processing
textiles
timber processing
capital cities
major towns
international airports
major roads
major industrial areas
NEW ZEALAND
North Island
South Island
TASMAN SEA
PACIFIC OCEAN
Auckland
Hamilton
Tauranga
New Plymouth
Napier
Hastings
WELLINGTON
Nelson
Blenheim
Christchurch
Timaru
Dunedin
Invercargill

Transportation Network

57,132 miles (92,000 km)	6,491 miles (10,453 km)
2430 miles (3,913 km)	999 miles (1,609 km)

The rugged terrain of much of New Zealand has led to most road and rail development being limited to the periphery of the islands.

***Auckland**, on North Island, is home to more than a third of New Zealand's population, and has the largest Polynesian population of any city in Australasia and Oceania. Auckland is also the main port and industrial center in New Zealand.*

Using the Land and Sea

THE CLIMATE AND TOPOGRAPHY of North Island are more favorable to agriculture than the harsher terrain of South Island. Sheep and cattle can graze in summer and winter on the rich pastures surrounding both Auckland and Christchurch. A wide range of crops including vegetables, cereals, and fruits such as grapes and kiwifruit, are grown in the northern parts of New Zealand. The rich Pacific fisheries are of increasing economic importance.

***More than 55 million sheep** thrive in New Zealand's mild climate, feeding on the islands' grassy slopes. Their fine meat and wool provide important export income.*

***The Arthur River** plummets 1,902 ft (580 m) over the Sutherland Falls, in the south of South Island. The falls are the ninth highest in the world.*

Land use and agricultural distribution
cattle
sheep
cereals
fishing
fruit
timber
capital cities
major towns
pasture
cropland
forest
mountain region
NEW ZEALAND
North Island
South Island
TASMAN SEA
PACIFIC OCEAN
Auckland
Hamilton
Napier
WELLINGTON
Christchurch
Dunedin
Invercargill

The Urban/Rural Population Divide

urban 86% rural 14%

Population Density	Total Land Area
36 people per sq mile (14 people per sq km)	103,730 sq miles (268,680 sq km)

MELANESIA

PAPUA NEW GUINEA, FIJI, SOLOMON ISLANDS, VANUATU, *New Caledonia* (to France)

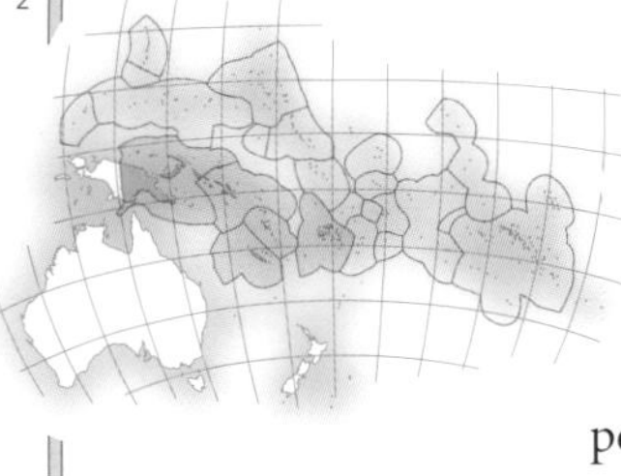

LYING IN THE SOUTHWEST PACIFIC OCEAN, northeast of Australia and south of the Equator, the islands of Melanesia form one of the three geographic divisions (along with Polynesia and Micronesia) of Oceania. Melanesia's name derives from the Greek *melas*, "black," and *nesoi*, "islands." Most of the larger islands are volcanic in origin. The smaller islands tend to be coral atolls and are mainly uninhabited. Rugged mountains, covered by dense rain forest, take up most of the land area. Melanesian's cultivate yams, taro, and sweet potatoes for local consumption and live in small, usually dispersed, homesteads.

***Huli tribesmen** from Southern Highlands Province in Papua New Guinea parade in ceremonial dress, their powdered wigs decorated with exotic plumage and their faces and bodies painted with coloured pigments.*

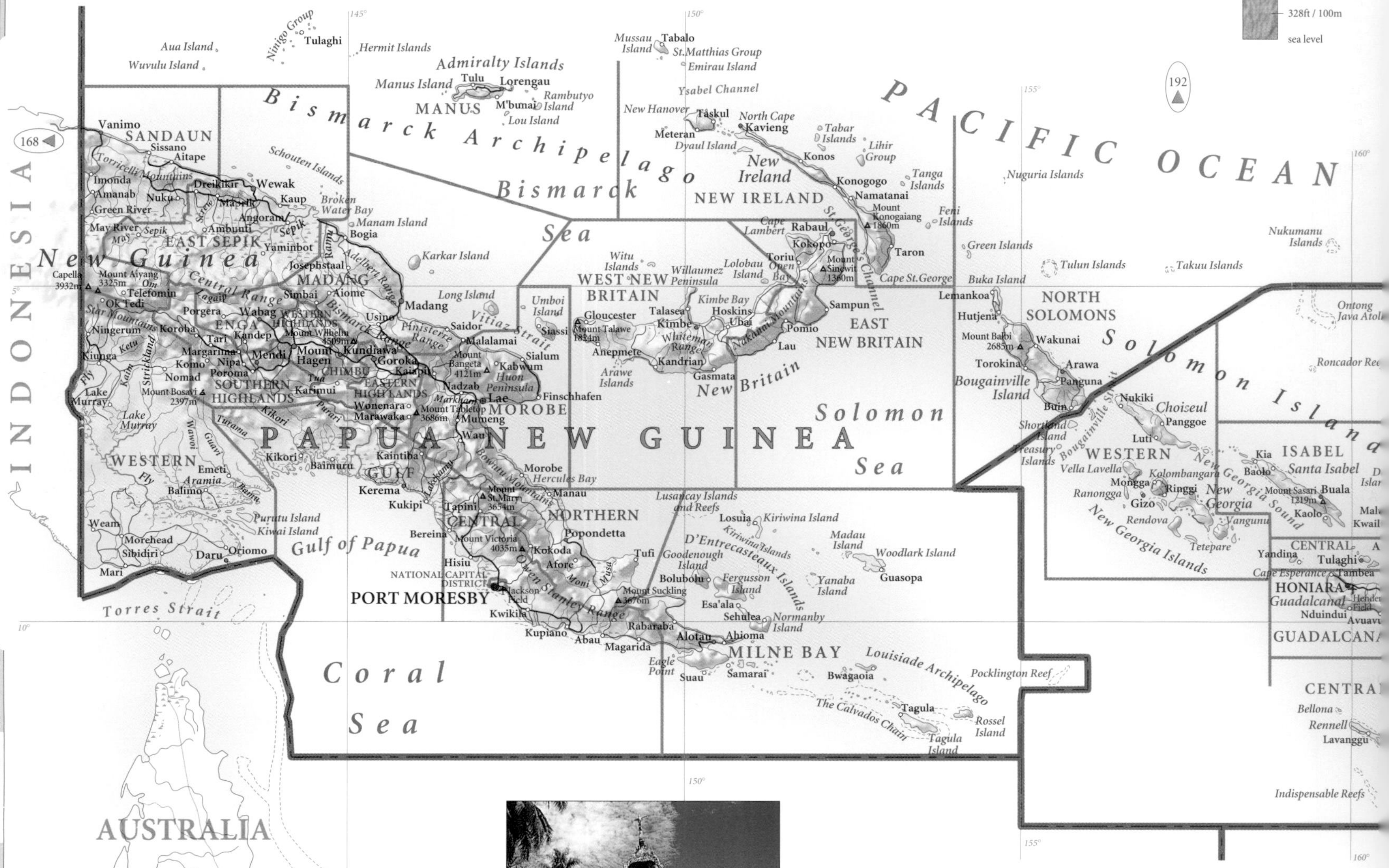
MAP KEY
POPULATION
100,000 to 500,000
50,000 to 100,000
10,000 to 50,000
below 10,000
ELEVATION
13,124ft / 4000m
9843ft / 3000m
6562ft / 2000m
3281ft / 1000m
1640ft / 500m
820ft / 250m
328ft / 100m
sea level
PACIFIC OCEAN
Bismarck Archipelago
Bismarck Sea
Admiralty Islands
MANUS
NEW IRELAND
WEST NEW BRITAIN
EAST NEW BRITAIN
New Britain
NORTH SOLOMONS
Solomon Sea
Solomon Islands
WESTERN
ISABEL
CENTRAL
GUADALCANAL
HONIARA
INDONESIA
New Guinea
SANDAUN
EAST SEPIK
MADANG
ENGA
WESTERN HIGHLANDS
SOUTHERN HIGHLANDS
CHIMBU
EASTERN HIGHLANDS
MOROBE
PAPUA NEW GUINEA
WESTERN
GULF
CENTRAL
NORTHERN
NATIONAL CAPITAL DISTRICT
PORT MORESBY
MILNE BAY
Gulf of Papua
Torres Strait
Coral Sea
AUSTRALIA
Louisiade Archipelago
D'Entrecasteaux Islands
Bougainville Island
Choiseul
New Georgia Islands
168
192
180

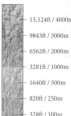

***Lying close to the banks** of the Sepik River in northern Papua New Guinea, this building is known as the Spirit House. It is constructed from leaves and twigs, ornately woven and trimmed into geometric patterns. The house is decorated with a mask and topped by a carved statue.*

***On one of Vanuatu's many islands**, simple beach houses stand at the water's edge, surrounded by coconut palms and other tropical vegetation. The unspoilt beaches and tranquillity of its islands are drawing ever-larger numbers of tourists to Vanuatu.*

TRANSPORTATION & INDUSTRY

The processing of natural resources generates significant export revenue for the countries of Melanesia. The region relies mainly on copra, tuna, and timber exports, with some production of cocoa and palm oil. The islands have substantial mineral resources including the world's largest copper reserves on Bougainville Island; gold, and potential oil and natural gas. Tourism has become the fastest growing sector in most of the countries' economies.

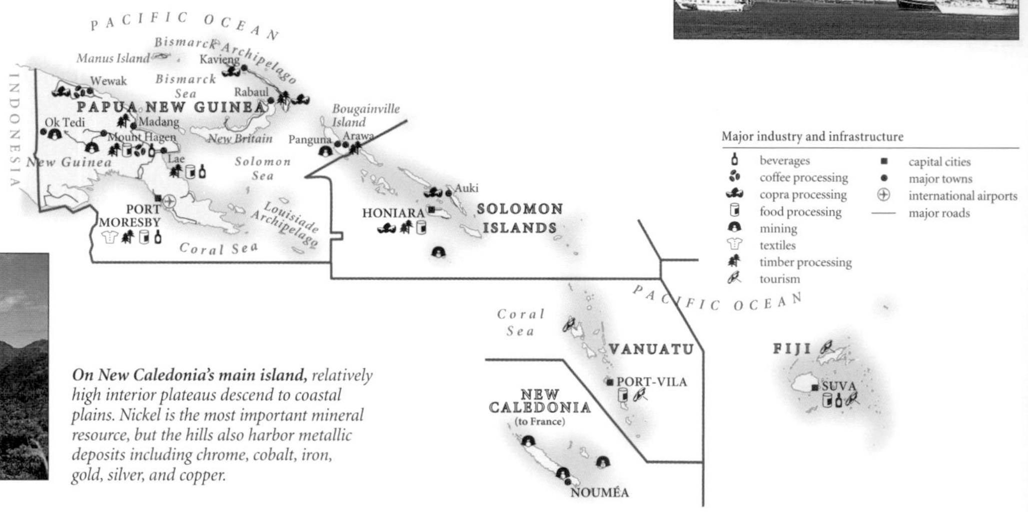
PACIFIC OCEAN
Bismarck Archipelago
Manus Island
Kavieng
Bismarck Sea
Wewak
Rabaul
PAPUA NEW GUINEA
Ok Tedi
Madang
Mount Hagen
New Britain
Bougainville Island
Panguna
Arawa
INDONESIA
New Guinea
Lae
Solomon Sea
PORT MORESBY
Louisiade Archipelago
Coral Sea
Auki
HONIARA
SOLOMON ISLANDS
Coral Sea
PACIFIC OCEAN
VANUATU
PORT-VILA
FIJI
SUVA
NEW CALEDONIA (to France)
NOUMÉA
Major industry and infrastructure
beverages
coffee processing
copra processing
food processing
mining
textiles
timber processing
tourism
capital cities
major towns
international airports
major roads

TRANSPORTATION NETWORK

1,236 miles (1,990 km)	None
370 miles (595 km)	6,924 miles (11,143 km)

As most of the islands of Melanesia lie off the major sea and air routes, services to and from the rest of the world are infrequent. Transportation by road on rugged terrain is difficult and expensive.

***On New Caledonia's main island,** relatively high interior plateaus descend to coastal plains. Nickel is the most important mineral resource, but the hills also harbor metallic deposits including chrome, cobalt, iron, gold, silver, and copper.*

THE LANDSCAPE

MELANESIA COMPRISES HIGH, VOLCANIC ISLANDS, low coral islands and continental islands. New Guinea is part of the Australian continental platform, and is separated from it only by the shallow flooding of the Torres Strait. The plate margin of the Pacific and Indo-Australian plates cuts through mainland Papua New Guinea. Volcanic activity, resulting from the collision of these plates, has sculpted much of Melanesia's landscape.

The slopes of this extinct volcano near Talasea on the island of New Britain have been almost entirely colonized by rain forest vegetation.

***A series of coral reefs** can be seen in the clear waters off Cape Esperance on the island of Guadalcanal in the Solomons.*

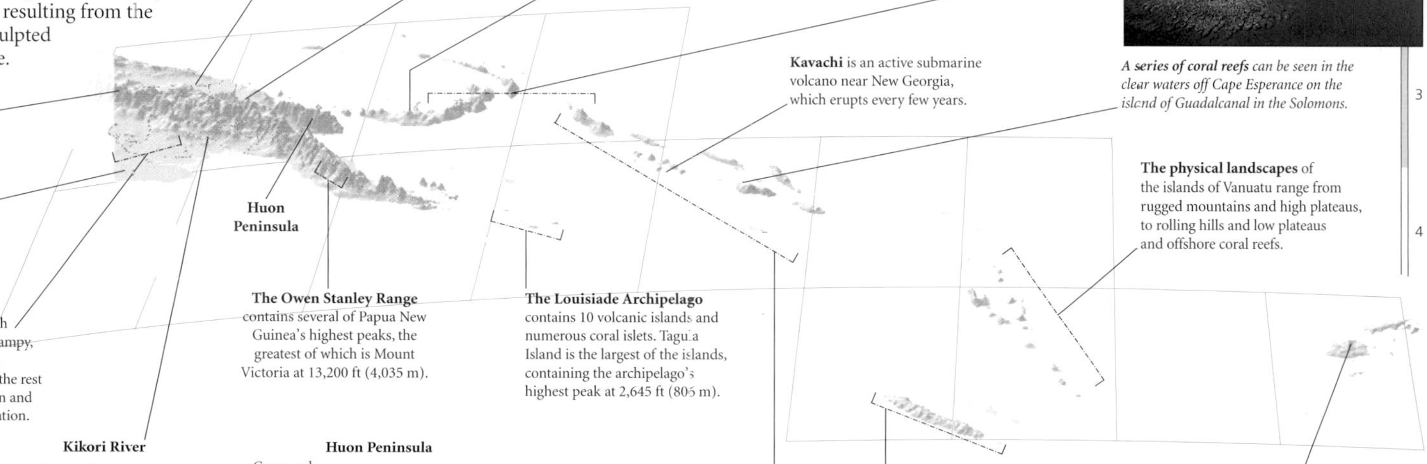

The Sepik River drains the lowlands north of the Central Range, flowing eastward into the Bismarck Sea.

The Bismarck Range is precipitous, rugged and covered in dense vegetation, rising to 14,793 ft (4,509 m) at Mount Wilhelm in central Papua New Guinea.

Most of Papua New Guinea's outlying islands, including New Britain, Bougainville Island and New Ireland, are precipitous and of volcanic origin.

The Star Mountains include some of the most remote terrain on Earth. The area is rich in gold and copper.

Kavachi is an active submarine volcano near New Georgia, which erupts every few years.

Southern Papua New Guinea is part of the Indo-Australian Plate. New Guinea only became separated physically from Australia about 8,000 years ago following the flooding of the Torres Strait.

Huon Peninsula

The physical landscapes of the islands of Vanuatu range from rugged mountains and high plateaus, to rolling hills and low plateaus and offshore coral reefs.

The lowland plains in the south and north of Papua New Guinea's main island are swampy, and contain some fertile alluvial soils. This contrasts with the mountainous islands in the rest of the country where soils are generally thin and nutrients are retained in the existing vegetation.

The Owen Stanley Range contains several of Papua New Guinea's highest peaks, the greatest of which is Mount Victoria at 13,200 ft (4,035 m).

The Louisiade Archipelago contains 10 volcanic islands and numerous coral islets. Tagula Island is the largest of the islands, containing the archipelago's highest peak at 2,645 ft (805 m).

Kikori River

The Solomon Islands are mountainous continental-type islands with largely andesitic volcanoes.

New Caledonia's main island is surrounded by coral reef that extends from the Huon island group in the north, to Île des Pins in the south.

Viti Levu, the largest of Fiji's islands, contains the country's highest mountain, Mount Victoria at 4,339 ft (1,323 m).

***Papua New Guinea's rivers,** though fairly short, carry extremely high sediment loads, largely due to soil erosion. This is caused by a combination of very steep slopes and heavy rainfall, and is made worse by forest clearance, particularly 'slash and burn' techniques and road or mine operations.*

Huon Peninsula

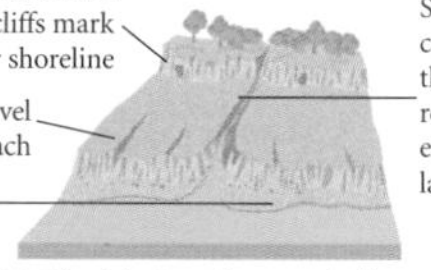
Caves and undercut cliffs mark former shoreline
Former level of beach
Current beach
Stream cuts down through recently exposed land

***Uplift of the land** in tectonically active regions can lead to former coastlines being lifted beyond the reach of the sea. New cliffs and caves are formed at a lower level, and rivers cut down through the lower land to reach sea level once more.*

USING THE LAND AND SEA

Almost 60% of the population of Melanesia is engaged in agriculture and animal husbandry at a subsistence level. Coconuts and cocoa are grown for export revenue. Over 80% of the land area is cloaked by tropical forest and woodlands, which have proved to be a rich timber source. In coastal areas, fishing, mainly for tuna, is a staple industry.

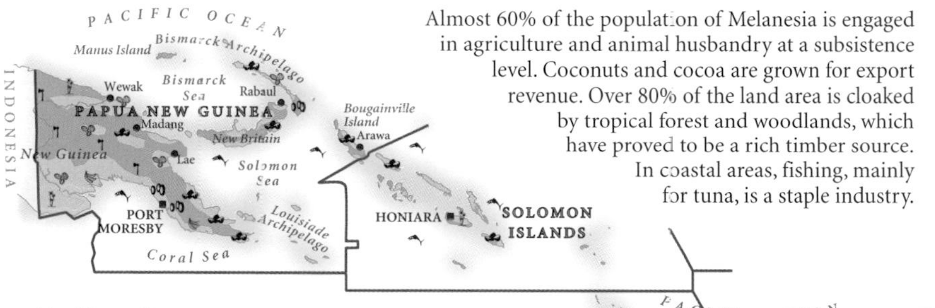
PACIFIC OCEAN
Manus Island
Bismarck Archipelago
Wewak
Bismarck Sea
Rabaul
PAPUA NEW GUINEA
Madang
INDONESIA
New Guinea
New Britain
Lae
Bougainville Island
Arawa
Solomon Sea
PORT MORESBY
Louisiade Archipelago
Coral Sea
HONIARA
SOLOMON ISLANDS
PACIFIC OCEAN
Coral Sea
VANUATU
PORT-VILA
FIJI
SUVA
NEW CALEDONIA (to France)
NOUMÉA
Land use and agricultural distribution
bananas
cocoa
coconuts
fishing
oil palms
rubber
timber
capital cities
major towns
cropland
forest
wetland

THE URBAN/RURAL POPULATION DIVIDE

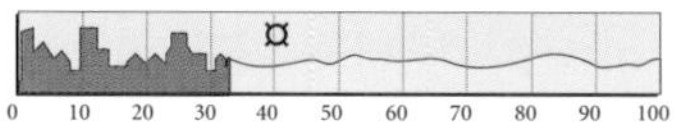
urban 32%
rural 68%
0
10
20
30
40
50
60
70
80
90
100

POPULATION DENSITY	TOTAL LAND AREA
32 people per sq mile (12 people per sq km)	205,354 sq miles (532,006 sq km)

***Abaca Eco-tourist Park** near Lautoka on the island of Viti Levu in western Fiji is one of a number of projects aimed at combining tourism with awareness about the environment. The government and people of Fiji are keen to protect the unique ecology of the islands and prevent further damage to the coral reefs. Until the recent ending of nuclear testing in the Pacific by Western nations, Fiji lay downwind of some of the main testing sites.*

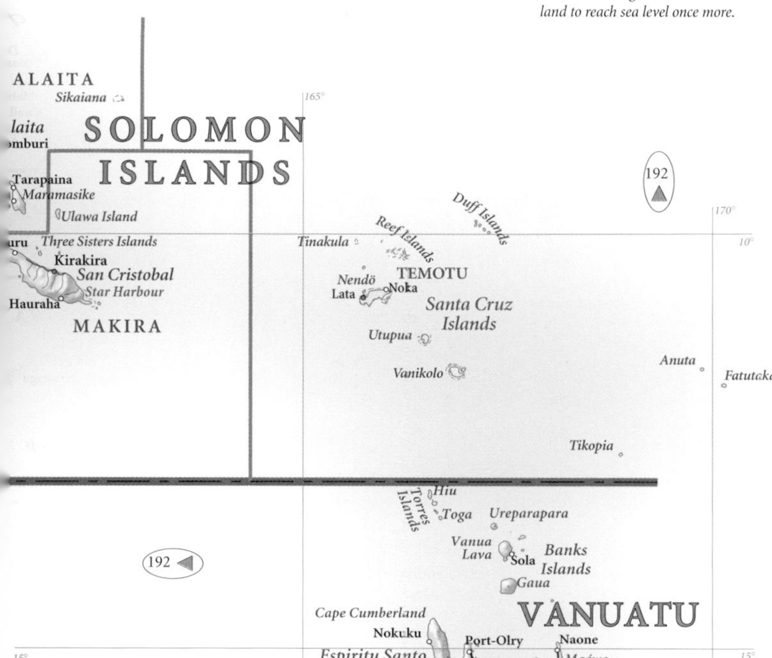
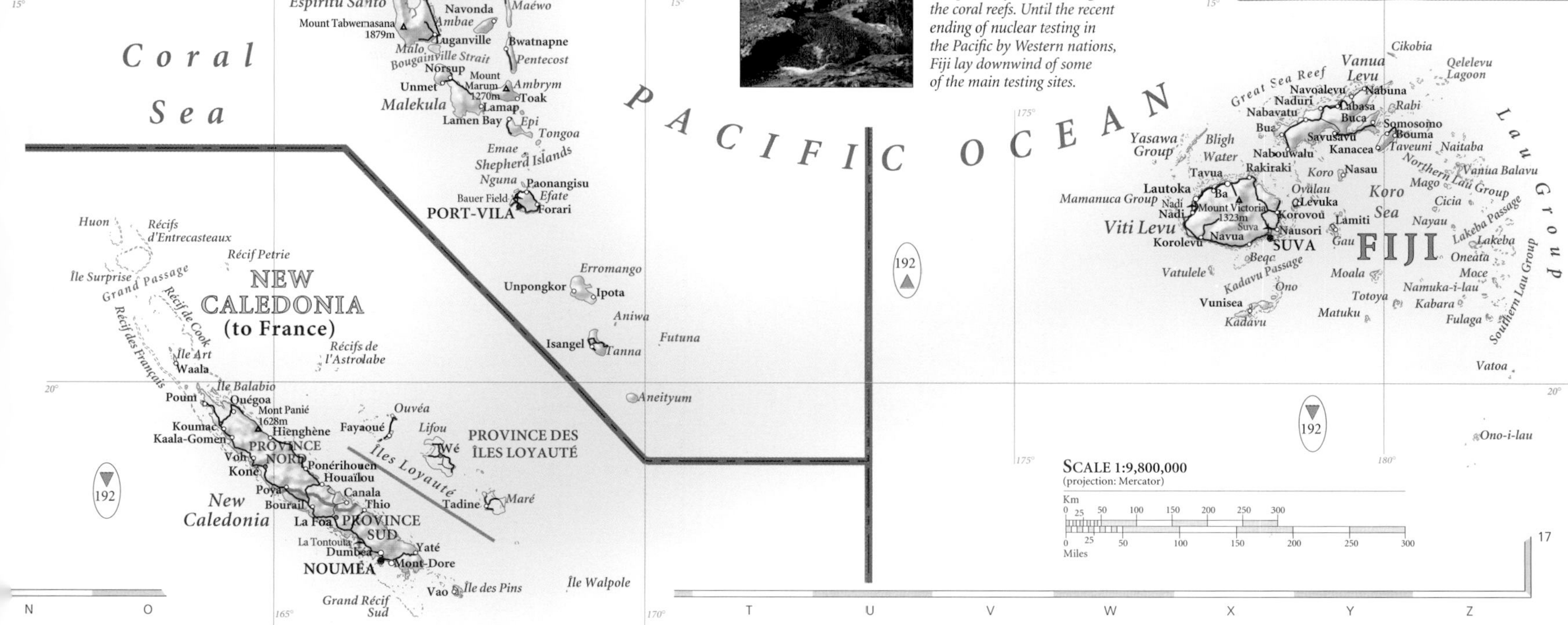
N
O
P
Q
R
S
T
W
X
Y
ALAITA
Sikaiana
SOLOMON ISLANDS
Ulawa Island
Three Sisters Islands
Kirakira
San Cristobal
Star Harbour
Hauraha
MAKIRA
Reef Islands
Duff Islands
Tinakula
Nendö
Lata
Noka
TEMOTU
Santa Cruz Islands
Utupua
Vanikolo
Anuta
Fatutaka
Tikopia
192
Torres Islands
Hiu
Toga
Ureparapara
Vanua Lava
Sola
Banks Islands
Gaua
VANUATU
Cape Cumberland
Nokuku
Port-Olry
Naone
Espiritu Santo
Navonda
Maéwo
Ambae
Mount Tabwemasana 1879m
Luganville
Bwatnapne
Malo
Bougainville Strait
Pentecost
Norsup
Unmet
Mount Marum 1270m
Ambrym
Toak
Malekula
Lamap
Lamen Bay
Epi
Tongoa
Emae
Shepherd Islands
Nguna
Paonangisu
Bauer Field
Efate
Forari
PORT-VILA
Coral Sea
PACIFIC OCEAN
Erromango
Unpongkor
Ipota
Aniwa
Futuna
Isangel
Tanna
Aneityum
Huon
Récifs d'Entrecasteaux
Récif Petrie
Île Surprise
Grand Passage
Récif de Cook
NEW CALEDONIA (to France)
Récifs de l'Astrolabe
Récif des Français
Île Art
Waala
Île Balabio
Poum
Ouégoa
Mont Panié 1628m
Hienghène
Koumac
Kaala-Gomen
PROVINCE NORD
Voh
Koné
Ponérihouen
Houaïlou
Fayaoué
Ouvéa
Lifou
Wé
PROVINCE DES ÎLES LOYAUTÉ
Îles Loyauté
Tadine
Maré
Poya
Bourail
Canala
Thio
New Caledonia
La Foa
PROVINCE SUD
La Tontouta
Dumbéa
Yaté
Mont-Dore
NOUMÉA
Vao
Île des Pins
Île Walpole
Grand Récif Sud
Cikobia
Vanua Levu
Qelelevu Lagoon
Great Sea Reef
Navoalevu
Nabuna
Naduri
Labasa
Rabi
Nabavatu
Buca
Somosomo
Bua
Savusavu
Bouma
Taveuni
Naitaba
Yasawa Group
Bligh Water
Nabouwalu
Kanacea
Tavua
Rakiraki
Koro
Nasau
Northern Lau Group
Vanua Balavu
Lau Group
Ba
Ovalau
Mago
Mamanuca Group
Lautoka
Nadi
Mount Victoria 1323m
Levuka
Cicia
Koro Sea
Viti Levu
Korovou
Lamiti
Nayau
Lakeba Passage
Suva
Navua
Nausori
Korolevu
SUVA
Gau
Lakeba
FIJI
Oneata
Beqa
Vatulele
Kadavu Passage
Moala
Mace
Ono
Namuka-i-lau
Vunisea
Totoya
Kabara
Kadavu
Matuku
Fulaga
Southern Lau Group
Vatoa
Ono-i-lau
SCALE 1:9,800,000
(projection: Mercator)
Km
0
25
50
100
150
200
250
300
Miles
U
V
Z

Micronesia

Marshall Islands, Micronesia, Nauru, Palau,
Guam, Northern Mariana Islands, Wake Island

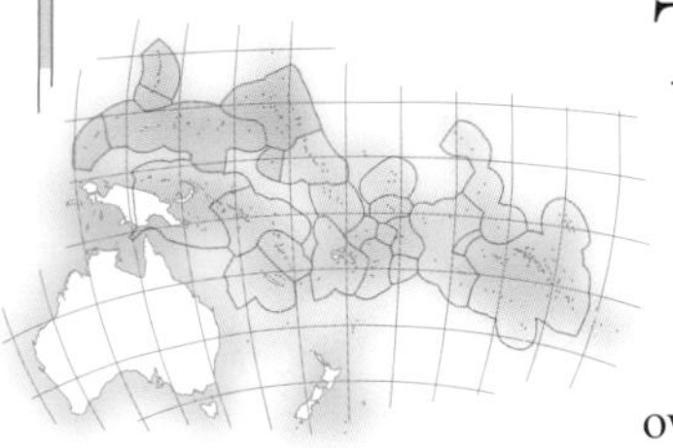

The Micronesian islands lie in the western reaches of the Pacific Ocean and are all part of the same volcanic zone. The Federated States of Micronesia is the largest group, with more than 600 atolls and forested volcanic islands in an area of more than 1,120 sq miles (2,900 sq km). Micronesia is a mixture of former colonies, overseas territories, and dependencies. Most of the region still relies on aid and subsidies to sustain economies limited by resources, isolation, and an emigrating population, drawn to New Zealand and Australia by the attractions of a western lifestyle.

Palau

Palau is an archipelago of over 200 islands, only eight of which are inhabited. It was the last remaining UN trust territory in the Pacific, controlled by the US until 1994, when it became independent. The economy operates on a subsistence level, with coconuts and cassava the principal crops. Fishing licenses and tourism provide foreign currency.

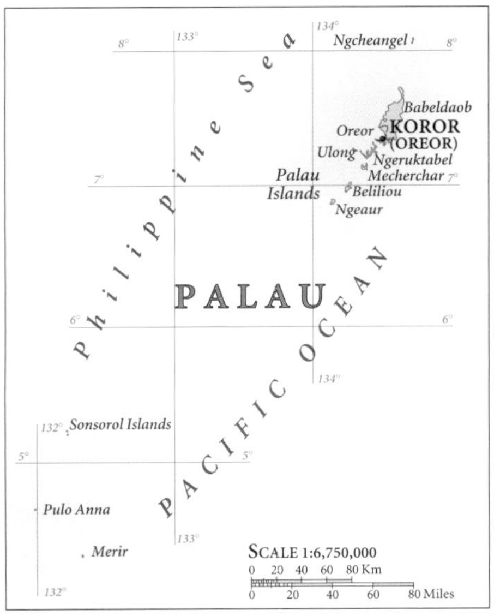
Philippine Sea
PALAU
PACIFIC OCEAN
Ngcheangel
Babeldaob
Oreor
KOROR (OREOR)
Ulong
Ngeruktabel
Mecherchar
Palau Islands
Beliliou
Ngeaur
Sonsorol Islands
Pulo Anna
Merir
SCALE 1:6,750,000
0 20 40 60 80 Km
0 20 40 60 80 Miles

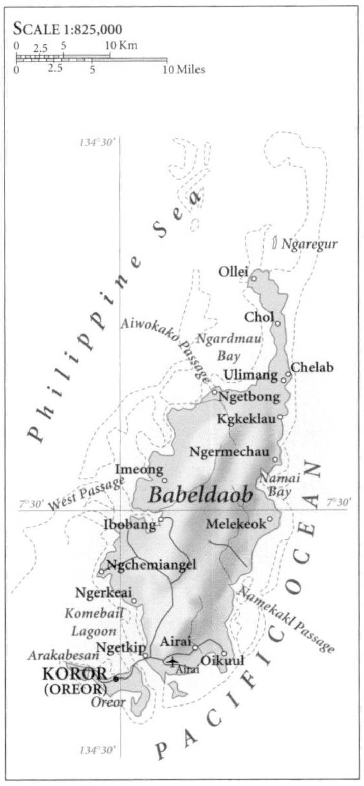
SCALE 1:825,000
0 2.5 5 10 Km
0 2.5 5 10 Miles
Philippine Sea
Ngaregur
Ollei
Aiwokako Passage
Chol
Ngardmau Bay
Chelab
Ulimang
Ngetbong
Kgkeklau
Ngermechau
Imeong
West Passage
Babeldaob
Namai Bay
Ibobang
Melekeok
Ngchemiangel
Ngerkeai
Komebail Lagoon
Namekakl Passage
Arakabesan
Ngetkip
Airai
KOROR (OREOR)
Oreor
Oikuul
PACIFIC OCEAN

Guam (to US)

Lying at the southern end of the Mariana Islands, Guam is an important US military base and tourist destination. Social and political life is dominated by the indigenous Chamorro, who make up just under half the population, although the increasing prevalence of western culture threatens Guam's traditional social stability.

***The tranquillity** of these coastal lagoons, at Inarajan in southern Guam, belies the fact that the island lies in a region where typhoons are common.*

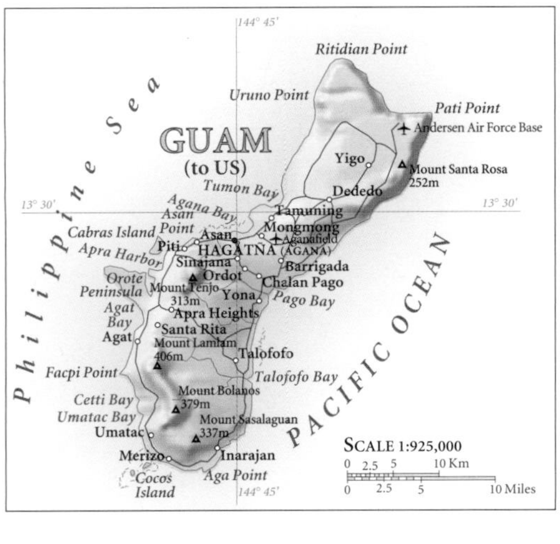
Philippine Sea
GUAM (to US)
PACIFIC OCEAN
Ritidian Point
Uruno Point
Pati Point
Andersen Air Force Base
Yigo
Mount Santa Rosa 252m
Tumon Bay
Dededo
Agana Bay
Tamuning
Cabras Island
Asan Point
Asan
Mongmong
Apra Harbor
Piti
HAGÅTÑA (AGANA)
Sinajana
Barrigada
Orote Peninsula
Mount Tenjo 313m
Ordot
Chalan Pago
Yona
Pago Bay
Agat Bay
Agat
Santa Rita
Apra Heights
Mount Lamlam 406m
Talofofo
Facpi Point
Talofofo Bay
Cetti Bay
Mount Bolanos 379m
Umatac Bay
Umatac
Mount Sasalaguan 337m
Merizo
Inarajan
Cocos Island
Aga Point
SCALE 1:925,000
0 2.5 5 10 Km
0 2.5 5 10 Miles

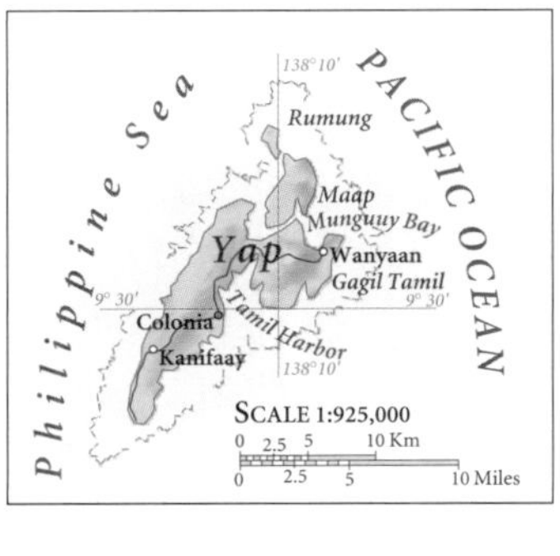
Philippine Sea
PACIFIC OCEAN
Rumung
Maap
Munguuy Bay
Yap
Wanyaan
Gagil Tamil
Tamil Harbor
Colonia
Kanifaay
SCALE 1:925,000
0 2.5 5 10 Km
0 2.5 5 10 Miles

Northern Mariana Islands (to US)

A US Commonwealth territory, the Northern Marianas comprise the whole of the Mariana archipelago except for Guam. The islands retain their close links with the US and continue to receive American aid. Tourism, though bringing in much-needed revenue, has speeded the decline of the traditional subsistence economy. Most of the population lives on Saipan.

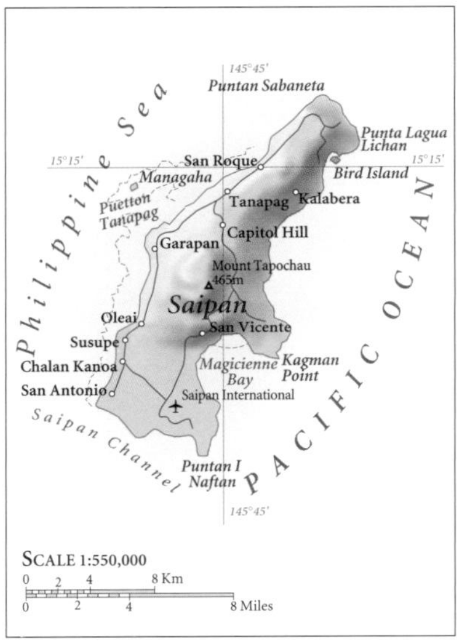
Philippine Sea
Puntan Sabaneta
Punta Lagua Lichan
San Roque
Managaha
Bird Island
Puetton Tanapag
Tanapag
Kalabera
Capitol Hill
Garapan
Mount Tapochau 465m
Saipan
Oleai
San Vicente
Susupe
Chalan Kanoa
Magicienne Bay
Kagman Point
San Antonio
Saipan International
Saipan Channel
Puntan I Naftan
PACIFIC OCEAN
SCALE 1:550,000
0 2 4 8 Km
0 2 4 8 Miles

***The Palau Islands** have numerous hidden lakes and lagoons. These sustain their own ecosystems which have developed in isolation. This has produced adaptations in the animals and plants that are often unique to each lake.*

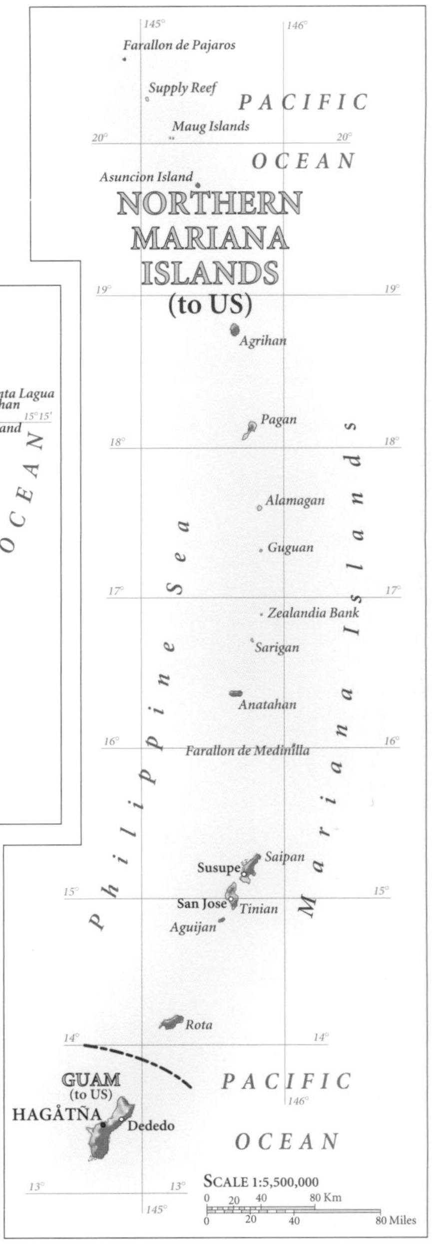
Farallon de Pajaros
Supply Reef
PACIFIC OCEAN
Maug Islands
Asuncion Island
NORTHERN MARIANA ISLANDS (to US)
Agrihan
Pagan
Alamagan
Guguan
Zealandia Bank
Sarigan
Anatahan
Farallon de Medinilla
Philippine Sea
Mariana Islands
Saipan
Susupe
San Jose
Tinian
Aguijan
Rota
GUAM (to US)
HAGÅTÑA
Dededo
PACIFIC OCEAN
SCALE 1:5,500,000
0 20 40 80 Km
0 20 40 80 Miles

Micronesia

A mixture of high volcanic islands and low-lying coral atolls, the Federated States of Micronesia include all the Caroline Islands except Palau. Pohnpei, Kosrae, Chuuk, and Yap are the four main island cluster states, each of which has its own language, with English remaining the official language. Nearly half the population is concentrated on Pohnpei, the largest island. Independent since 1986, the islands continue to receive considerable aid from the US which supplements an economy based primarily on fishing and copra processing.

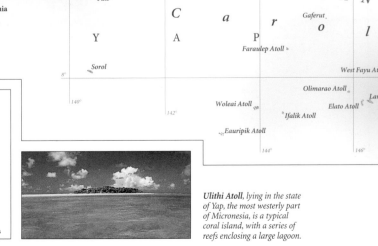

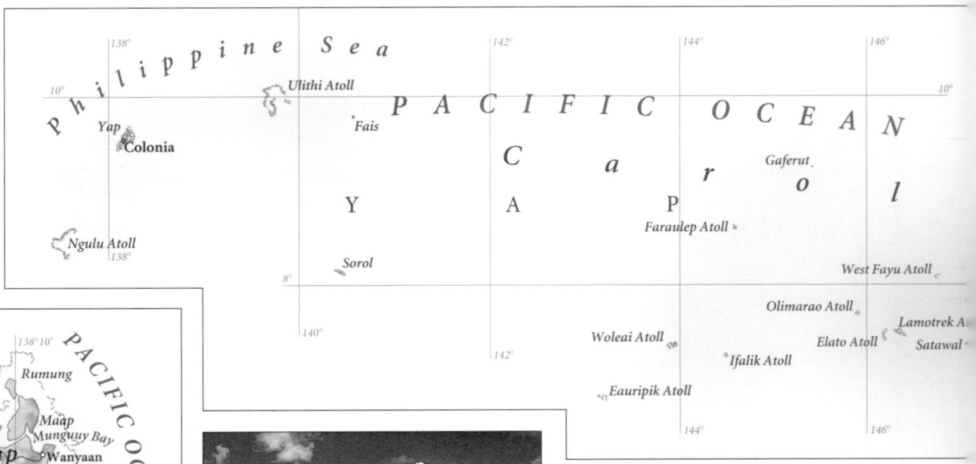
Philippine Sea
Ulithi Atoll
PACIFIC OCEAN
Yap
Colonia
Fais
Caroline
YAP
Gaferut
Ngulu Atoll
Faraulep Atoll
Sorol
West Fayu Atoll
Olimarao Atoll
Lamotrek A
Woleai Atoll
Elato Atoll
Satawal
Ifalik Atoll
Eauripik Atoll

***Ulithi Atoll**, lying in the state of Yap, the most westerly part of Micronesia, is a typical coral island, with a series of reefs enclosing a large lagoon.*

MARSHALL ISLANDS

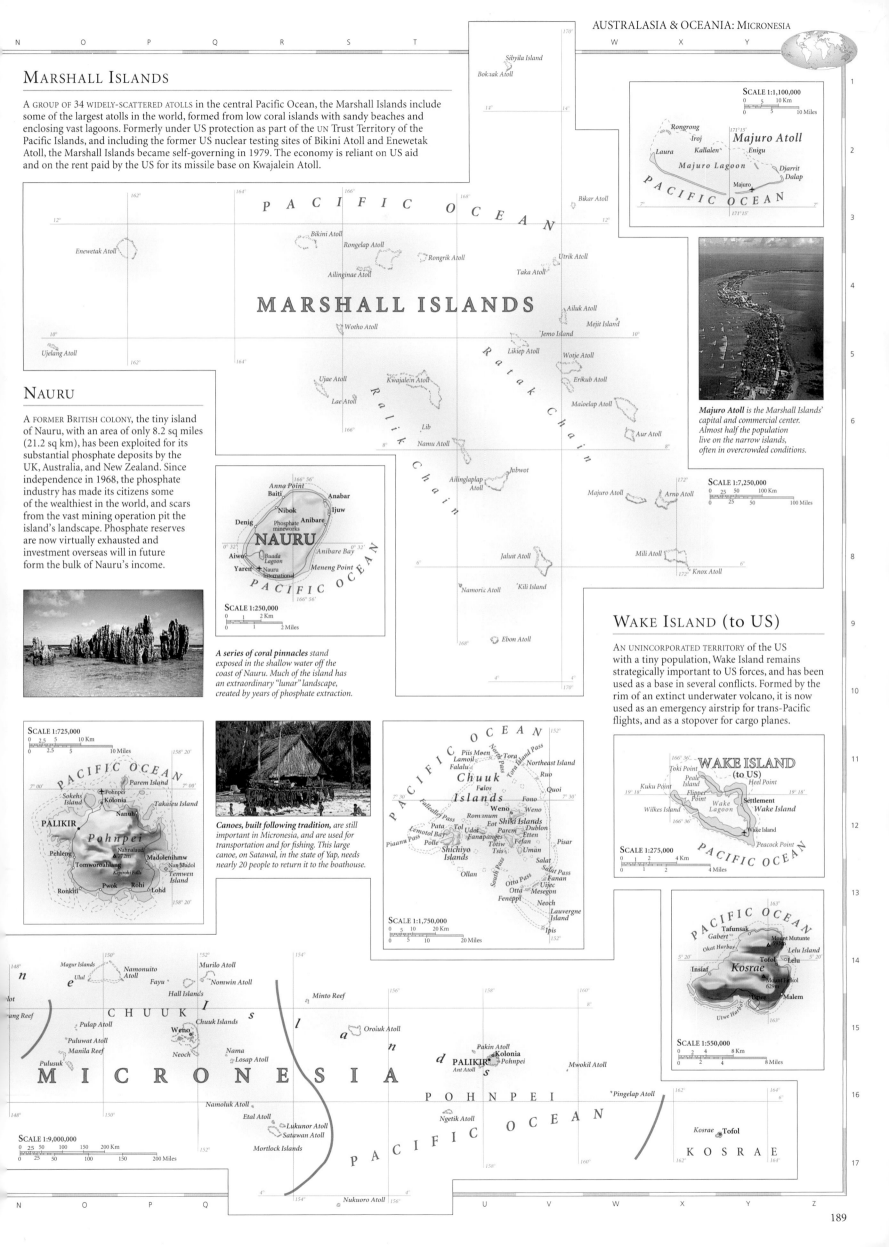

A GROUP OF 34 WIDELY-SCATTERED ATOLLS in the central Pacific Ocean, the Marshall Islands include some of the largest atolls in the world, formed from low coral islands with sandy beaches and enclosing vast lagoons. Formerly under US protection as part of the UN Trust Territory of the Pacific Islands, and including the former US nuclear testing sites of Bikini Atoll and Enewetak Atoll, the Marshall Islands became self-governing in 1979. The economy is reliant on US aid and on the rent paid by the US for its missile base on Kwajalein Atoll.

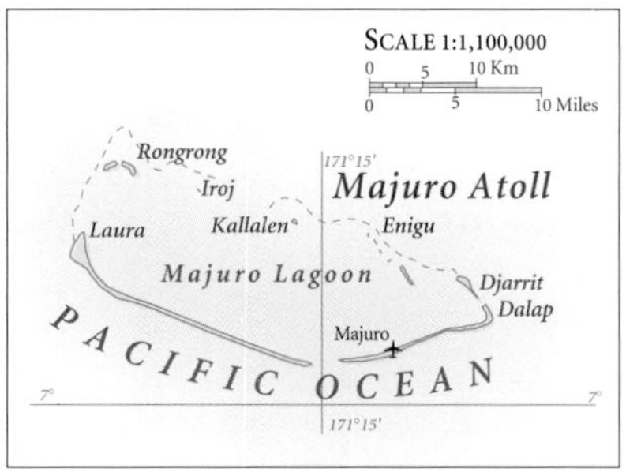
SCALE 1:1,100,000
Majuro Atoll
Rongrong
Iroj
Laura
Kallalen
Enigu
Majuro Lagoon
Djarrit
Dalap
Majuro
PACIFIC OCEAN

Majuro Atoll is the Marshall Islands' capital and commercial center. Almost half the population live on the narrow islands, often in overcrowded conditions.

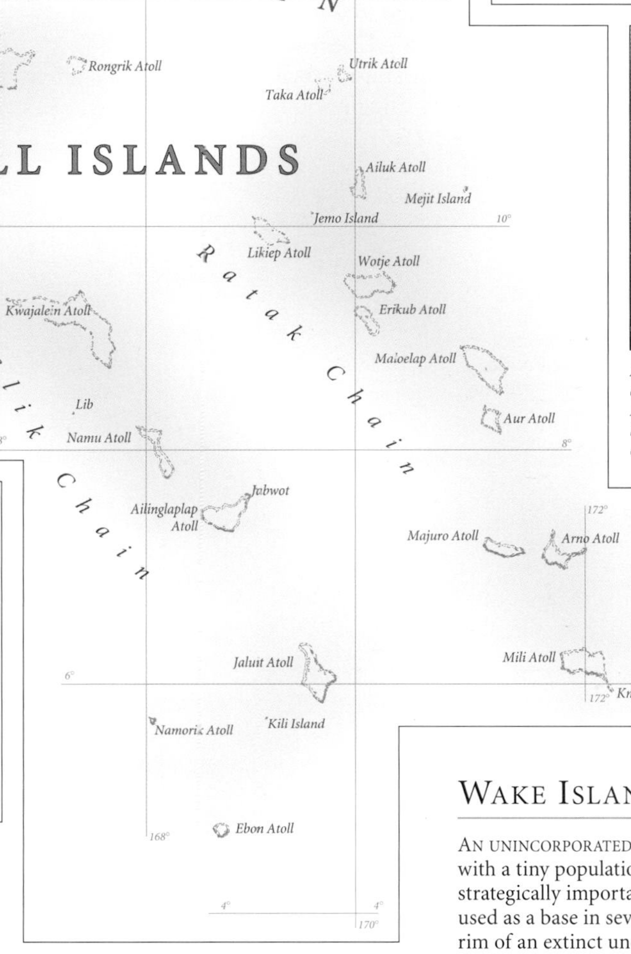
PACIFIC OCEAN
MARSHALL ISLANDS
Sibyila Island
Bokaak Atoll
Bikar Atoll
Enewetak Atoll
Bikini Atoll
Rongelap Atoll
Rongrik Atoll
Ailinginae Atoll
Utrik Atoll
Taka Atoll
Ailuk Atoll
Mejit Island
Wotho Atoll
Jemo Island
Ujelang Atoll
Likiep Atoll
Wotje Atoll
Ratak Chain
Ujae Atoll
Kwajalein Atoll
Erikub Atoll
Lae Atoll
Maloelap Atoll
Ralik Chain
Lib
Aur Atoll
Namu Atoll
Jabwot
Ailinglaplap Atoll
Majuro Atoll
Arno Atoll
SCALE 1:7,250,000
Jaluit Atoll
Mili Atoll
Knox Atoll
Namorik Atoll
Kili Island
Ebon Atoll

NAURU

A FORMER BRITISH COLONY, the tiny island of Nauru, with an area of only 8.2 sq miles (21.2 sq km), has been exploited for its substantial phosphate deposits by the UK, Australia, and New Zealand. Since independence in 1968, the phosphate industry has made its citizens some of the wealthiest in the world, and scars from the vast mining operation pit the island's landscape. Phosphate reserves are now virtually exhausted and investment overseas will in future form the bulk of Nauru's income.

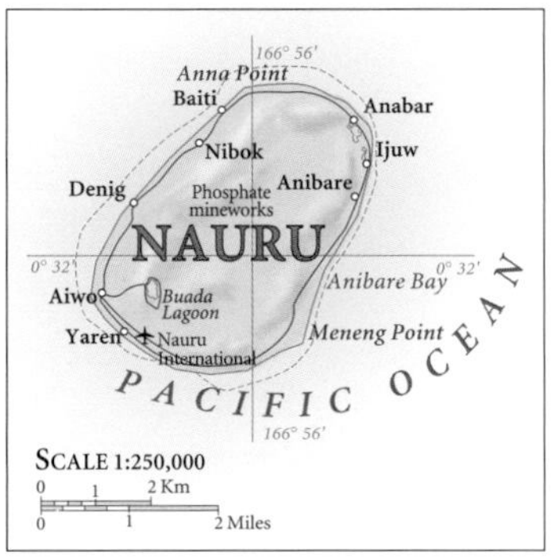
Anna Point
Baiti
Anabar
Nibok
Ijuw
Denig
Phosphate mineworks
Anibare
NAURU
Anibare Bay
Aiwo
Buada Lagoon
Yaren
Nauru International
Meneng Point
PACIFIC OCEAN
SCALE 1:250,000

A series of coral pinnacles stand exposed in the shallow water off the coast of Nauru. Much of the island has an extraordinary "lunar" landscape, created by years of phosphate extraction.

WAKE ISLAND (to US)

AN UNINCORPORATED TERRITORY of the US with a tiny population, Wake Island remains strategically important to US forces, and has been used as a base in several conflicts. Formed by the rim of an extinct underwater volcano, it is now used as an emergency airstrip for trans-Pacific flights, and as a stopover for cargo planes.

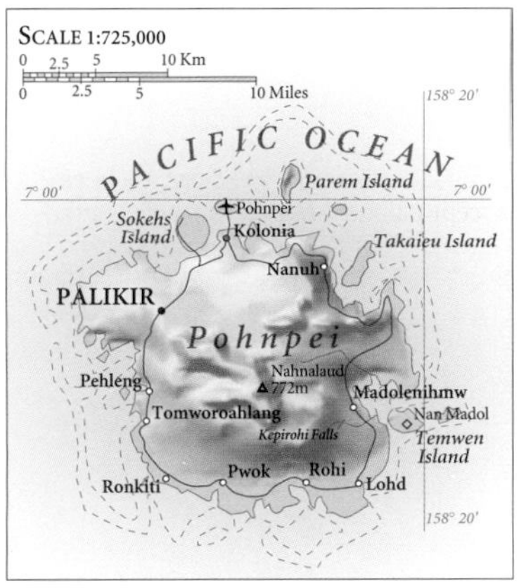
SCALE 1:725,000
PACIFIC OCEAN
Parem Island
Pohnpei
Sokehs Island
Kolonia
Takatieu Island
PALIKIR
Nanuh
Pohnpei
Nahnalaud 772m
Pehleng
Madolenihmw
Tomworoahlang
Nan Madol
Kepirohi Falls
Temwen Island
Ronkiti
Pwok
Rohi
Lohd

Canoes, built following tradition, are still important in Micronesia, and are used for transportation and for fishing. This large canoe, on Satawal, in the state of Yap, needs nearly 20 people to return it to the boathouse.

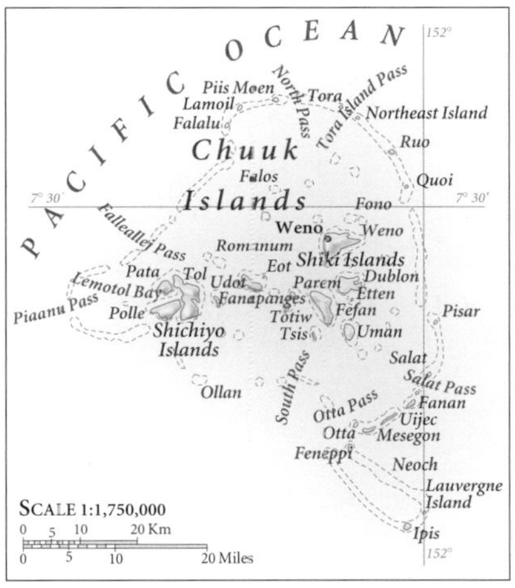
PACIFIC OCEAN
Piis Moen
Lamoil
Falalu
North Pass
Tora
Tora Island Pass
Northeast Island
Ruo
Chuuk Islands
Falos
Quoi
Fono
Weno
Falleallej Pass
Romanum
Eot
Shiki Islands
Dublon
Pata
Tol
Udot
Fanapanges
Parem
Etten
Piaanu Pass
Polle
Totiw
Fefan
Pisar
Shichiyo Islands
Tsis
Uman
Salat
Salat Pass
Ollan
South Pass
Otta Pass
Fanan
Otta
Uijec
Mesegon
Feneppi
Neoch
Lauvergne Island
Ipis
SCALE 1:1,750,000

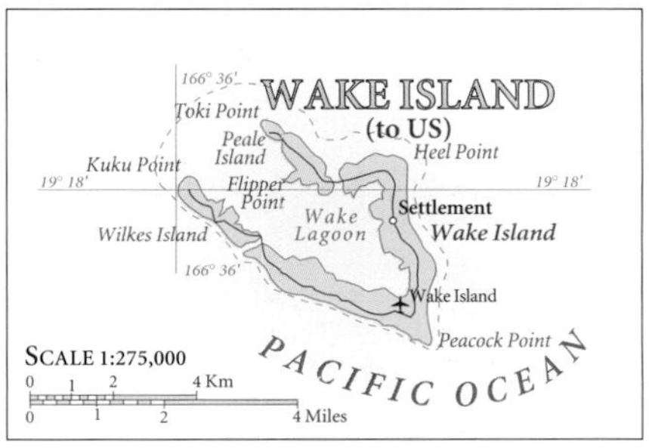
WAKE ISLAND (to US)
Toki Point
Peale Island
Kuku Point
Heel Point
Flipper Point
Wake Lagoon
Settlement
Wilkes Island
Wake Island
Peacock Point
PACIFIC OCEAN
SCALE 1:275,000

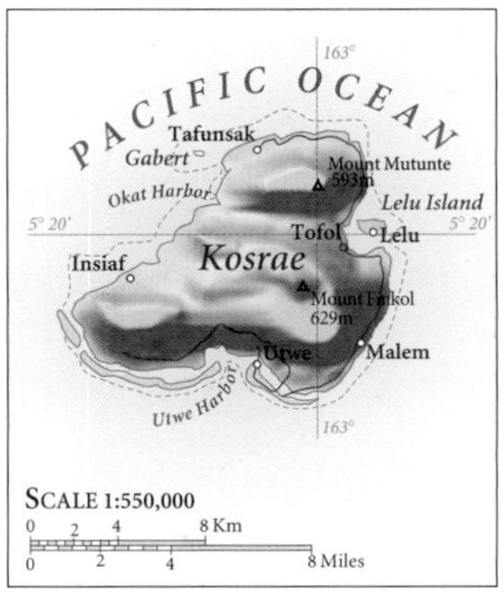
PACIFIC OCEAN
Tafunsak
Gabert
Mount Mutunte 593m
Okat Harbor
Lelu Island
Tofol
Lelu
Insiaf
Kosrae
Mount Finkol 629m
Utwe
Malem
Utwe Harbor
SCALE 1:550,000

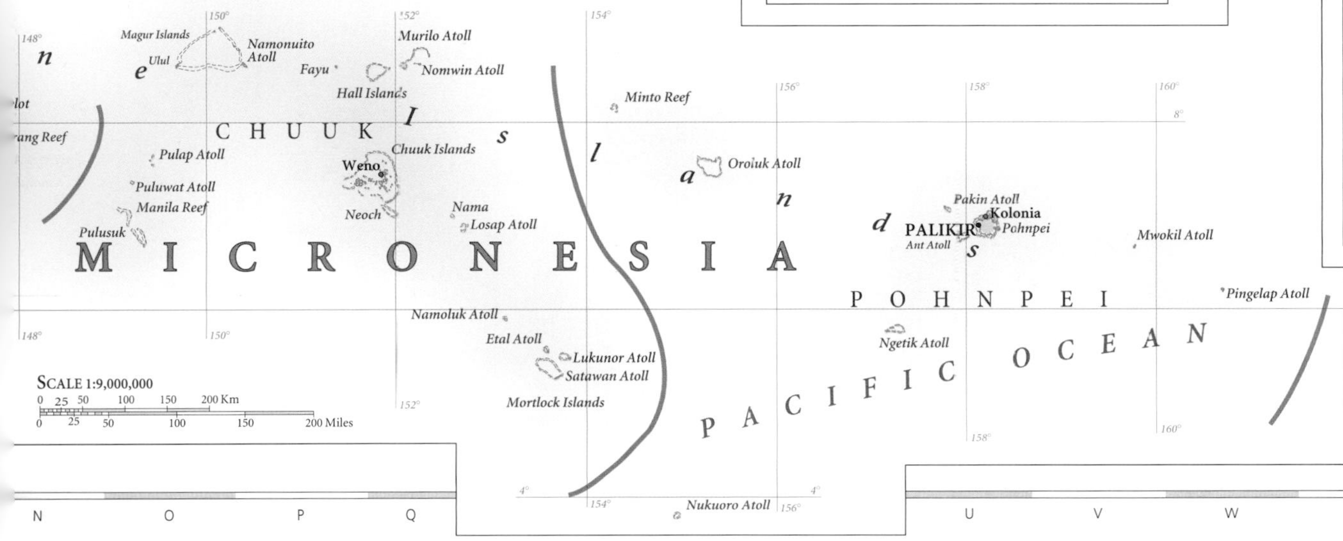
Magur Islands
Namonuito Atoll
Murilo Atoll
Ulul
Fayu
Nomwin Atoll
Hall Islands
Minto Reef
CHUUK
Weno
Chuuk Islands
Oroluk Atoll
Pulap Atoll
Puluwat Atoll
Manila Reef
Neoch
Nama
Losap Atoll
Pakin Atoll
Kolonia
Pulusuk
PALIKIR
Pohnpei
Ant Atoll
Mwokil Atoll
MICRONESIA
Federated States of Micronesia
POHNPEI
Pingelap Atoll
Namoluk Atoll
Etal Atoll
Ngetik Atoll
Lukunor Atoll
Satawan Atoll
Mortlock Islands
Kosrae
Tofol
KOSRAE
PACIFIC OCEAN
Nukuoro Atoll
SCALE 1:9,000,000

POLYNESIA

KIRIBATI, TUVALU, *Cook Islands, Easter Island, French Polynesia, Niue, Pitcairn Islands, Tokelau, Wallis & Futuna*

THE NUMEROUS ISLAND GROUPS OF POLYNESIA lie to the east of Australia, scattered over a vast area in the south Pacific. The islands are a mixture of low-lying coral atolls, some of which enclose lagoons, and the tips of great underwater volcanoes. The populations on the islands are small, and most people are of Polynesian origin, as are the Maori of New Zealand. Local economies remain simple, relying mainly on subsistence crops, mineral deposits, many now exhausted, fishing, and tourism.

KIRIBATI

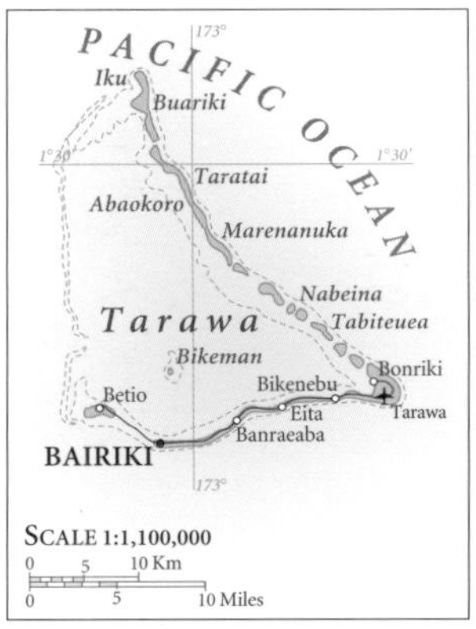

PACIFIC OCEAN
Iku
Buariki
Taratai
Abaokoro
Marenanuka
Nabeina
Tarawa
Tabiteuea
Bikeman
Bonriki
Betio
Bikenebu
Eita
Tarawa
Banraeaba
BAIRIKI
SCALE 1:1,100,000
0 5 10 Km
0 5 10 Miles

A FORMER BRITISH COLONY, Kiribati became independent in 1979. Banaba's phosphate deposits ran out in 1980, following decades of exploitation by the British. Economic development remains slow and most agriculture is at a subsistence level, though coconuts provide export income, and underwater agriculture is being developed.

***With the exception of Banaba** all the islands in Kiribati's three groups are low-lying, coral atolls. This aerial view shows the sparsely vegetated islands, intercut by many small lagoons.*

TUVALU

A CHAIN of nine coral atolls, 360 miles (579 km) long with a land area of just over 9 sq miles (23 sq km), Tuvalu is one of the world's smallest and most isolated states. As the Ellice Islands, Tuvalu was linked to the Gilbert Islands (now part of Kiribati) as a British colony until independence in 1978. Politically and socially conservative, Tuvaluans live by fishing and subsistence farming.

***Funafuti Atoll** contains more than 40% of Tuvalu's people, giving it an extremely high population density.*

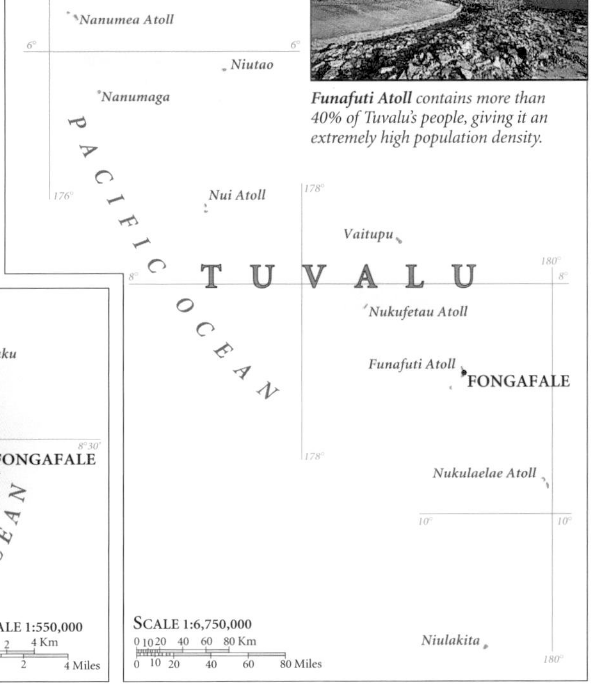

Nanumea Atoll
Niutao
Nanumaga
PACIFIC OCEAN
Nui Atoll
Vaitupu
TUVALU
Nukufetau Atoll
Funafuti Atoll
FONGAFALE
Nukulaelae Atoll
Niulakita
SCALE 1:6,750,000
0 10 20 40 60 80 Km
0 10 20 40 60 80 Miles

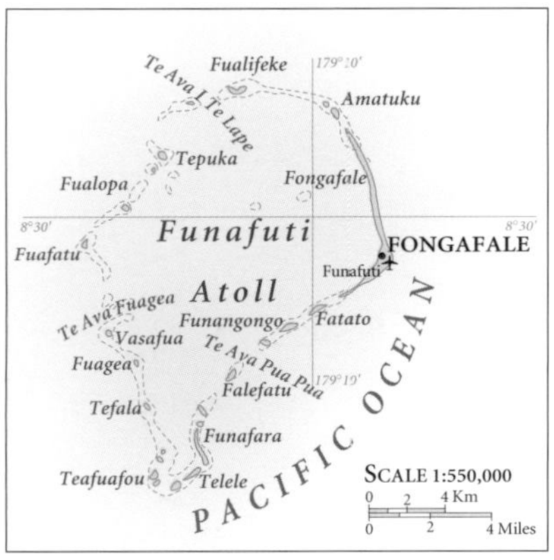

Fualifeke
Te Ava I Te Lape
Amatuku
Tepuka
Fualopa
Fongafale
Funafuti Atoll
Fuafatu
FONGAFALE
Funafuti
Te Ava Fuagea
Funangongo
Fatato
Vasafua
Te Ava Pua Pua
Fuagea
Falefatu
Tefala
Funafara
Teafuafou
Telele
PACIFIC OCEAN
SCALE 1:550,000
0 2 4 Km
0 2 4 Miles

TOKELAU (to New Zealand)

A LOW-LYING CORAL ATOLL, Tokelau is a dependent territory of New Zealand with few natural resources. Although a 1990 cyclone destroyed crops and infrastructure, a tuna cannery and the sale of fishing licenses have raised revenue and a catamaran link between the islands has increased their tourism potential. Tokelau's small size and economic weakness makes independence from New Zealand unlikely.

***Fishermen cast their nets** to catch small fish in the shallow waters off Atafu Atoll, the most westerly island in Tokelau.*

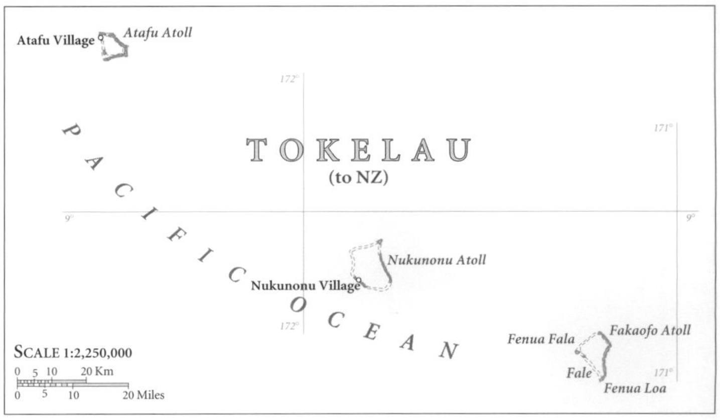

Atafu Village
Atafu Atoll
TOKELAU
(to NZ)
PACIFIC OCEAN
Nukunonu Atoll
Nukunonu Village
Fenua Fala
Fakaofo Atoll
Fale
Fenua Loa
SCALE 1:2,250,000
0 5 10 20 Km
0 5 10 20 Miles

WALLIS & FUTUNA (to France)

IN CONTRAST TO OTHER FRENCH overseas territories in the south Pacific, the inhabitants of Wallis and Futuna have shown little desire for greater autonomy. A subsistence economy produces a variety of tropical crops, while foreign currency remittances come from expatriates and from the sale of licenses to Japanese and Korean fishing fleets.

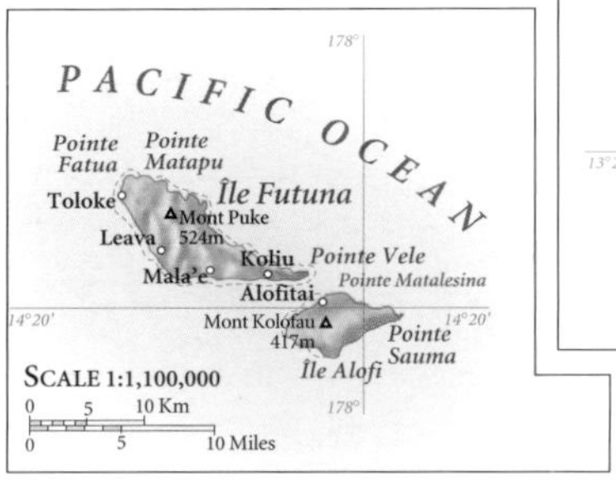

PACIFIC OCEAN
Pointe Fatua
Pointe Matapu
Toloke
Île Futuna
Mont Puke 524m
Leava
Koliu
Pointe Vele
Mala'e
Pointe Matalesina
Alofitai
Mont Kolofau 417m
Pointe Sauma
Île Alofi
SCALE 1:1,100,000
0 5 10 Km
0 5 10 Miles

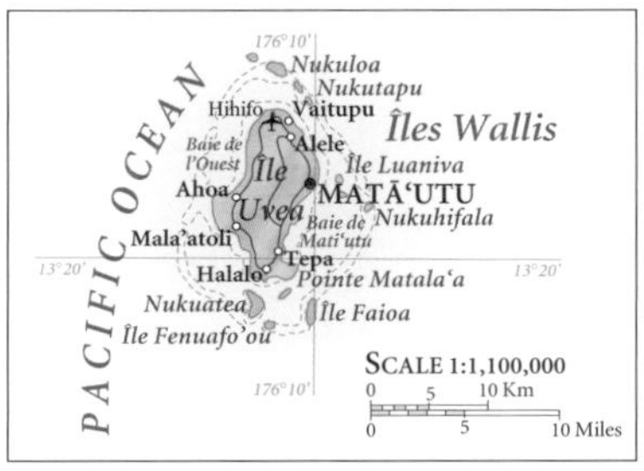

Nukuloa
Nukutapu
Hihifo
Vaitupu
Îles Wallis
Baie de l'Ouest
Alele
Île Luaniva
Ahoa
Île Uvea
MATĀ'UTU
Baie de Matā'utu
Nukuhifala
Mala'atoli
Tepa
Halalo
Pointe Matala'a
Nukuatea
Île Faioa
Île Fenuafo'ou
PACIFIC OCEAN
SCALE 1:1,100,000
0 5 10 Km
0 5 10 Miles

NIUE (to New Zealand)

NIUE, the world's largest coral island, is self-governing but exists in free association with New Zealand. Tropical fruits are grown for local consumption; tourism and the sale of postage stamps provide foreign currency. The lack of local job prospects has led more than 10,000 Niueans to emigrate to New Zealand, which has now invested heavily in Niue's economy in the hope of reversing this trend.

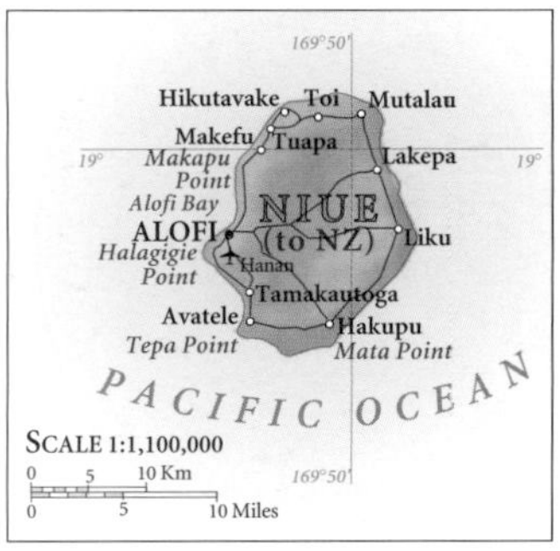

Hikutavake
Toi
Mutalau
Makefu
Tuapa
Makapu Point
Lakepa
Alofi Bay
NIUE (to NZ)
ALOFI
Liku
Halagigie Point
Hanan
Tamakautoga
Avatele
Hakupu
Tepa Point
Mata Point
PACIFIC OCEAN
SCALE 1:1,100,000
0 5 10 Km
0 5 10 Miles

***Waves have cut back** the original coastline, exposing a sandy beach, near Mutalau in the northeast corner of Niue.*

***Palm trees fringe** the white sands of a beach on Aitutaki in the Southern Cook Islands, where tourism is of increasing economic importance.*

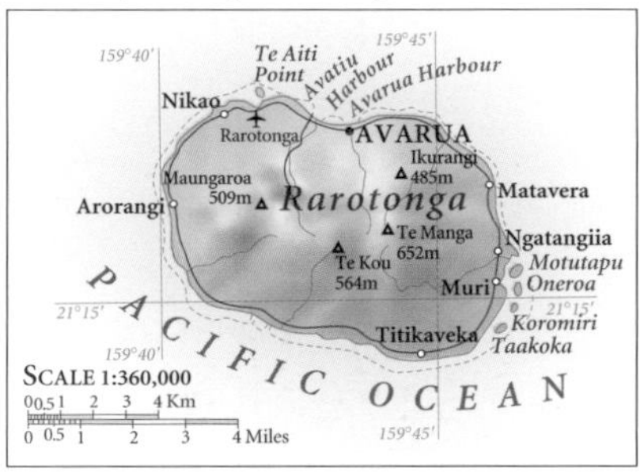

Te Aiti Point
Avatiu Harbour
Avarua Harbour
Nikao
Rarotonga
AVARUA
Ikurangi 485m
Matavera
Maungaroa 509m
Rarotonga
Arorangi
Te Manga 652m
Ngatangiia
Te Kou 564m
Motutapu
Muri
Oneroa
Titikaveka
Koromiri
Taakoka
PACIFIC OCEAN
SCALE 1:360,000
0 0.5 1 2 3 4 Km
0 0.5 1 2 3 4 Miles

COOK ISLANDS (to New Zealand)

A MIXTURE OF CORAL ATOLLS and volcanic peaks, the Cook Islands achieved self-government in 1965 but exist in free association with New Zealand. A diverse economy includes pearl and giant clam farming, and an ostrich farm, plus tourism and banking. A 1991 friendship treaty with France provides for French surveillance of territorial waters.

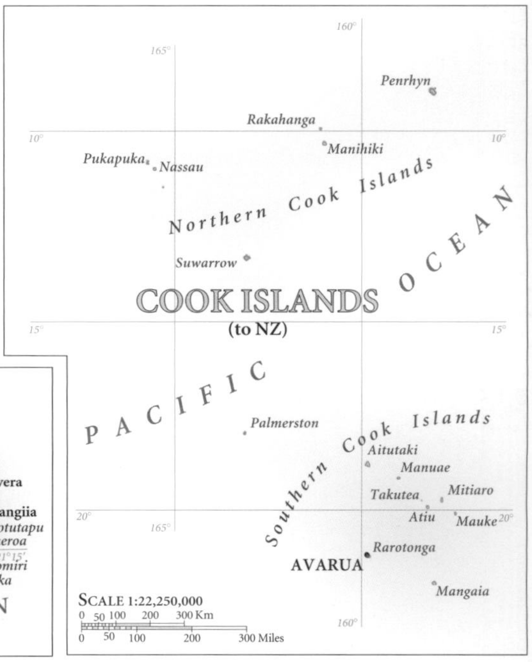

Penrhyn
Rakahanga
Manihiki
Pukapuka
Nassau
Northern Cook Islands
Suwarrow
COOK ISLANDS
(to NZ)
PACIFIC OCEAN
Palmerston
Southern Cook Islands
Aitutaki
Manuae
Takutea
Mitiaro
Atiu
Mauke
Rarotonga
AVARUA
Mangaia
SCALE 1:22,250,000
0 50 100 200 300 Km
0 50 100 200 300 Miles

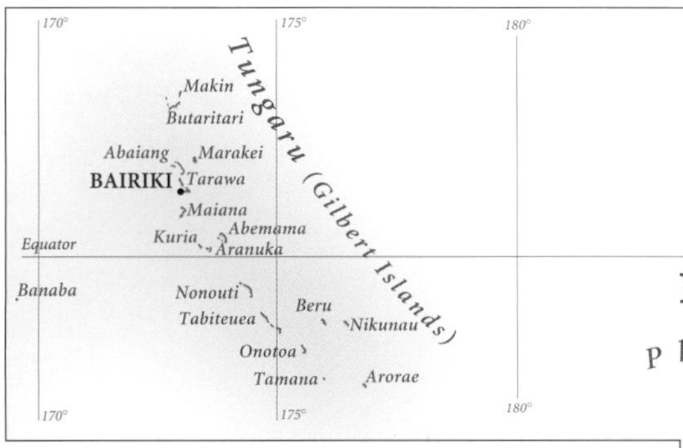
Tungaru (Gilbert Islands)
Makin
Butaritari
Abaiang
Marakei
BAIRIKI
Tarawa
Maiana
Abemama
Kuria
Aranuka
Equator
Banaba
Nonouti
Tabiteuea
Beru
Nikunau
Onotoa
Tamana
Arorae

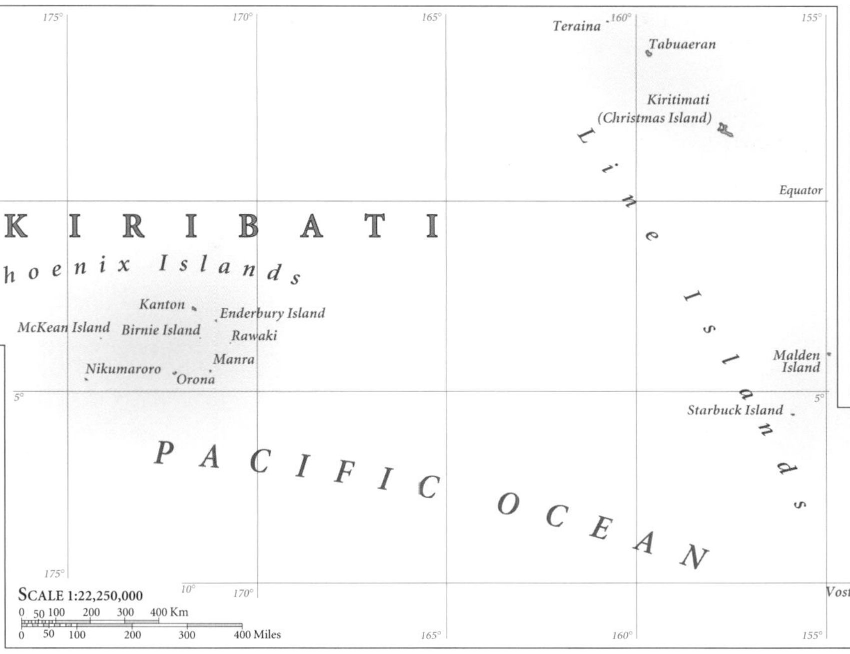
Teraina
Tabuaeran
Kiritimati
(Christmas Island)
Line Islands
KIRIBATI
Phoenix Islands
Equator
Kanton
Enderbury Island
McKean Island
Birnie Island
Rawaki
Manra
Nikumaroro
Orona
Malden Island
Starbuck Island
PACIFIC OCEAN
Millennium Island
Vostok Island
Flint Island
SCALE 1:22,250,000

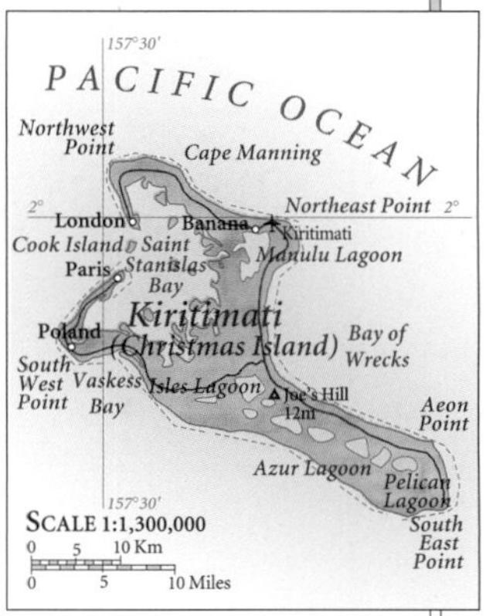
PACIFIC OCEAN
Northwest Point
Cape Manning
Northeast Point
London
Banana
Kiritimati
Cook Island
Saint Stanislas Bay
Manulu Lagoon
Paris
Poland
Kiritimati (Christmas Island)
Bay of Wrecks
South West Point
Vaskess Bay
Isles Lagoon
Joe's Hill 12m
Aeon Point
Azur Lagoon
Pelican Lagoon
South East Point
SCALE 1:1,300,000

FRENCH POLYNESIA (to France)

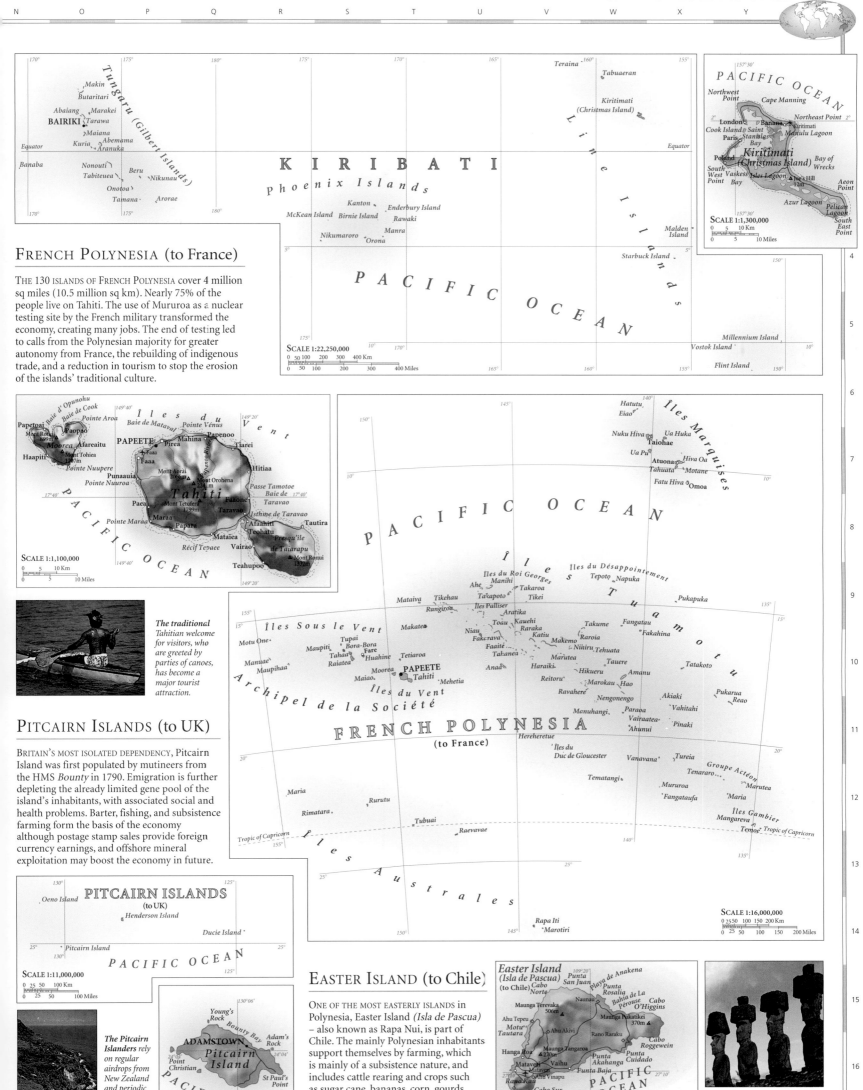

THE 130 ISLANDS OF FRENCH POLYNESIA cover 4 million sq miles (10.5 million sq km). Nearly 75% of the people live on Tahiti. The use of Mururoa as a nuclear testing site by the French military transformed the economy, creating many jobs. The end of testing led to calls from the Polynesian majority for greater autonomy from France, the rebuilding of indigenous trade, and a reduction in tourism to stop the erosion of the islands' traditional culture.

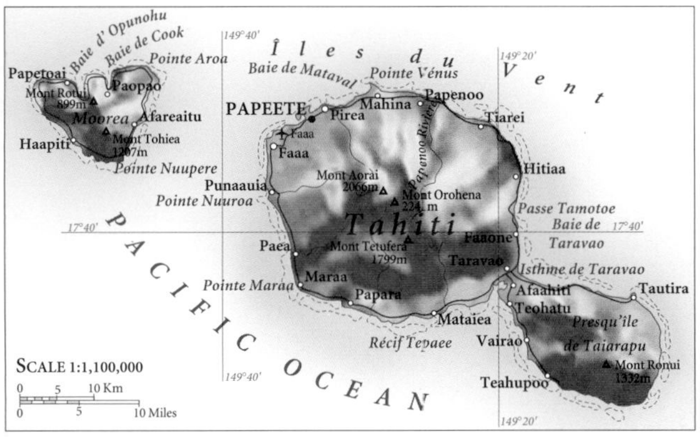
Îles du Vent
Baie d'Opunohu
Baie de Cook
Pointe Aroa
Baie de Matavai
Pointe Vénus
Papetoai
Paopao
Mont Rotui 899m
Moorea
Afareaitu
Mont Tohiea 1207m
Haapiti
Pointe Nuupere
PAPEETE
Pirea
Mahina
Papenoo
Tiarei
Faaa
Hitiaa
Punaauia
Pointe Nuuroa
Mont Aorai 2066m
Mont Orohena 2241m
Tahiti
Passe Tamotoe
Baie de Taravao
Paea
Mont Tetufera 1799m
Faaone
Taravao
Isthme de Taravao
Pointe Maraa
Maraa
Afaahiti
Teohatu
Tautira
Papara
Mataiea
Presqu'île de Taiarapu
Récif Tepaee
Vairao
Mont Ronui 1332m
Teahupoo
PACIFIC OCEAN
SCALE 1:1,100,000

The traditional Tahitian welcome for visitors, who are greeted by parties of canoes, has become a major tourist attraction.

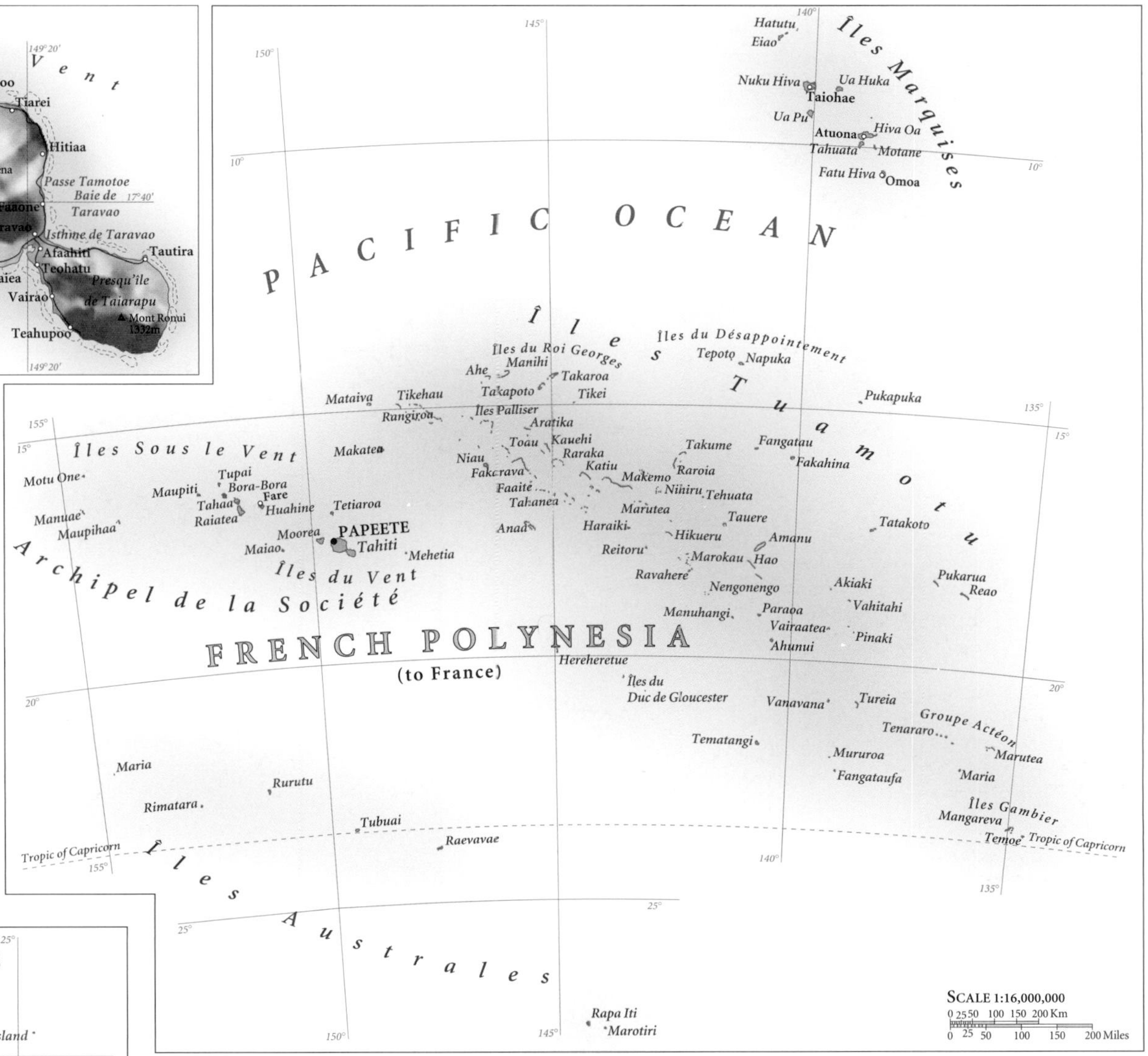
Hatutu
Eiao
Îles Marquises
Nuku Hiva
Ua Huka
Taiohae
Ua Pu
Atuona
Hiva Oa
Tahuata
Motane
Fatu Hiva
Omoa
PACIFIC OCEAN
Îles du Roi Georges
Îles du Désappointement
Tepoto
Napuka
Manihi
Ahe
Takaroa
Takapoto
Tikei
Îles Palliser
Pukapuka
Mataiva
Tikehau
Rangiroa
Arutua
Îles Tuamotu
Îles Sous le Vent
Makatea
Toau
Kauehi
Raraka
Takume
Fangatau
Fakahina
Niau
Katiu
Fakarava
Makemo
Raroia
Faaite
Niihiru
Tehuata
Motu One
Tupai
Bora-Bora
Maupiti
Fare
Tahaa
Huahine
Tetiaroa
Raiatea
Tahanea
Marutea
Manuae
Maupihaa
Anaa
Haraiki
Tauere
Moorea
PAPEETE
Tahiti
Hikueru
Amanu
Tatakoto
Maiao
Mehetia
Reitoru
Marokau
Hao
Îles du Vent
Ravahere
Akiaki
Pukarua
Reao
Archipel de la Société
Nengonengo
Vahitahi
Manuhangi
Paraoa
Vairaatea
Pinaki
Ahunui
FRENCH POLYNESIA
(to France)
Hereheretue
Îles du Duc de Gloucester
Vanavana
Tureia
Groupe Actéon
Tenararo
Tematangi
Marutea
Maria
Mururoa
Fangataufa
Maria
Rurutu
Rimatara
Îles Gambier
Mangareva
Tubuai
Temoe
Tropic of Capricorn
Raevavae
Îles Australes
Rapa Iti
Marotiri
SCALE 1:16,000,000

PITCAIRN ISLANDS (to UK)

BRITAIN'S MOST ISOLATED DEPENDENCY, Pitcairn Island was first populated by mutineers from the HMS *Bounty* in 1790. Emigration is further depleting the already limited gene pool of the island's inhabitants, with associated social and health problems. Barter, fishing, and subsistence farming form the basis of the economy although postage stamp sales provide foreign currency earnings, and offshore mineral exploitation may boost the economy in future.

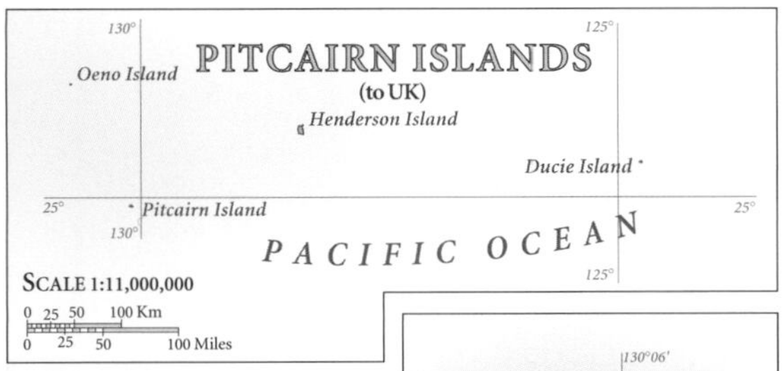
PITCAIRN ISLANDS
(to UK)
Oeno Island
Henderson Island
Ducie Island
Pitcairn Island
PACIFIC OCEAN
SCALE 1:11,000,000

The Pitcairn Islanders *rely on regular airdrops from New Zealand and periodic visits by supply vessels to provide them with basic commodities.*

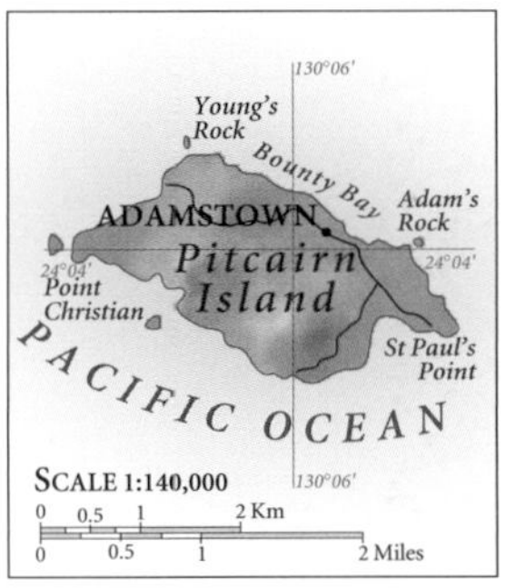
Young's Rock
Bounty Bay
ADAMSTOWN
Adam's Rock
Pitcairn Island
Point Christian
St Paul's Point
PACIFIC OCEAN
SCALE 1:140,000

EASTER ISLAND (to Chile)

ONE OF THE MOST EASTERLY ISLANDS in Polynesia, Easter Island *(Isla de Pascua)* – also known as Rapa Nui, is part of Chile. The mainly Polynesian inhabitants support themselves by farming, which is mainly of a subsistence nature, and includes cattle rearing and crops such as sugar cane, bananas, corn, gourds, and potatoes. In recent years, tourism has become the most important source of income and the island sustains a small commercial airport.

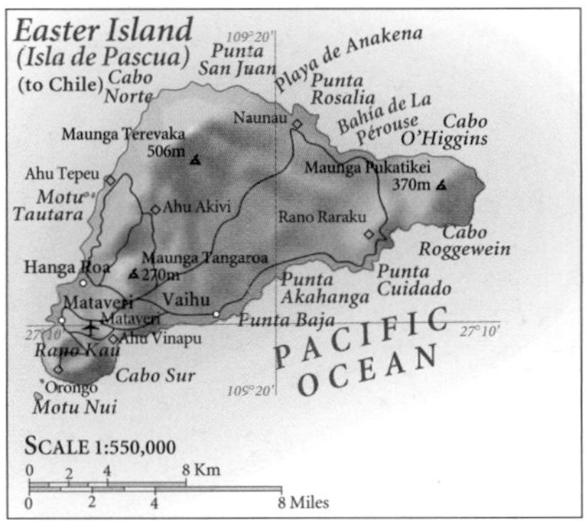
Easter Island
(Isla de Pascua)
(to Chile)
Cabo Norte
Punta San Juan
Playa de Anakena
Punta Rosalia
Bahía de La Pérouse
Cabo O'Higgins
Naunau
Maunga Terevaka 500m
Ahu Tepeu
Maunga Pukatikei 370m
Motu Tautara
Ahu Akivi
Rano Raraku
Cabo Roggewein
Hanga Roa
Maunga Tangaroa 270m
Vaihu
Punta Akahanga
Punta Cuidado
Mataveri
Ahu Vinapu
Punta Baja
Rano Kau
Cabo Sur
Orongo
Motu Nui
PACIFIC OCEAN
SCALE 1:550,000

The Naunau, *a series of huge stone statues overlook Playa de Anakena, on Easter Island. Carved from a soft volcanic rock, they were erected between 400 and 900 years ago.*

Pacific Ocean

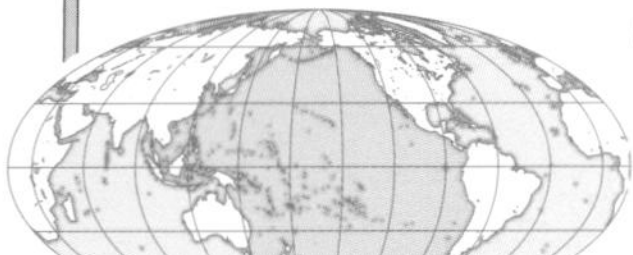

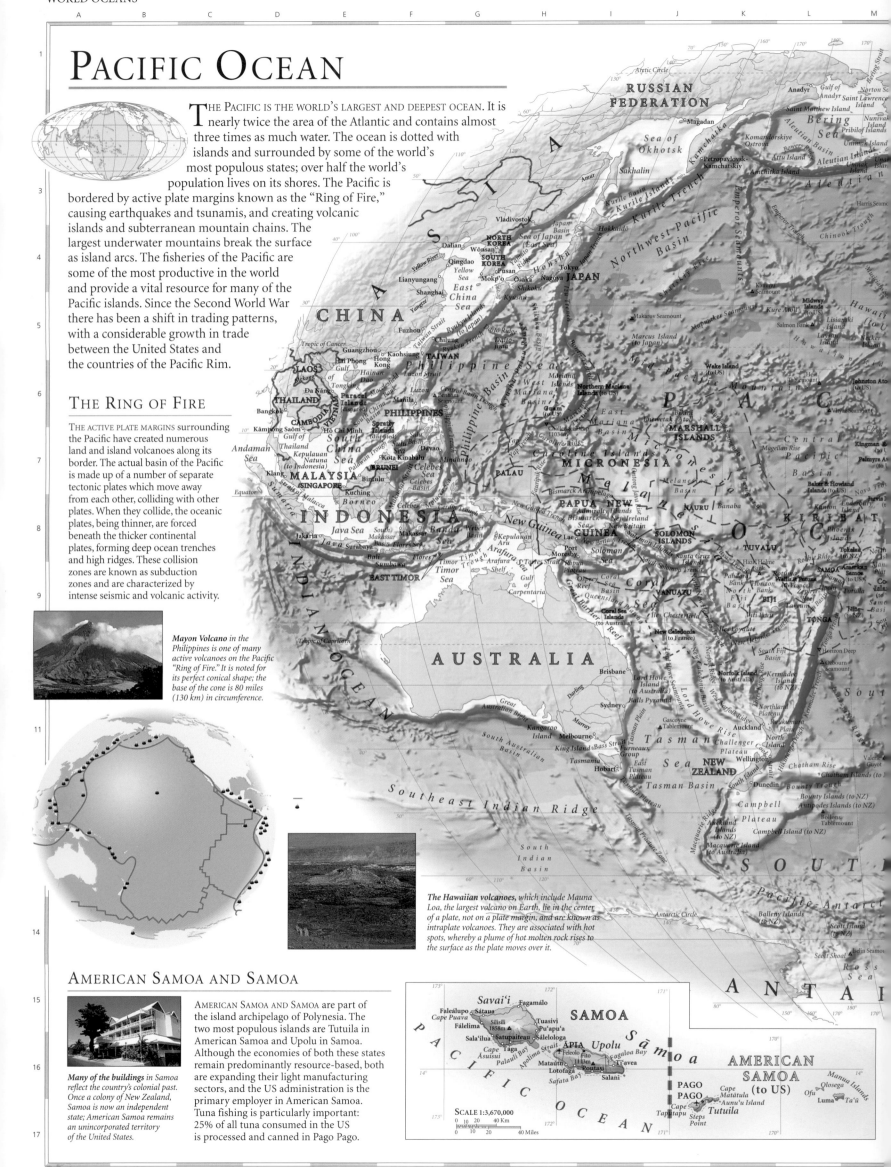

The Pacific is the world's largest and deepest ocean. It is nearly twice the area of the Atlantic and contains almost three times as much water. The ocean is dotted with islands and surrounded by some of the world's most populous states; over half the world's population lives on its shores. The Pacific is bordered by active plate margins known as the "Ring of Fire," causing earthquakes and tsunamis, and creating volcanic islands and subterranean mountain chains. The largest underwater mountains break the surface as island arcs. The fisheries of the Pacific are some of the most productive in the world and provide a vital resource for many of the Pacific islands. Since the Second World War there has been a shift in trading patterns, with a considerable growth in trade between the United States and the countries of the Pacific Rim.

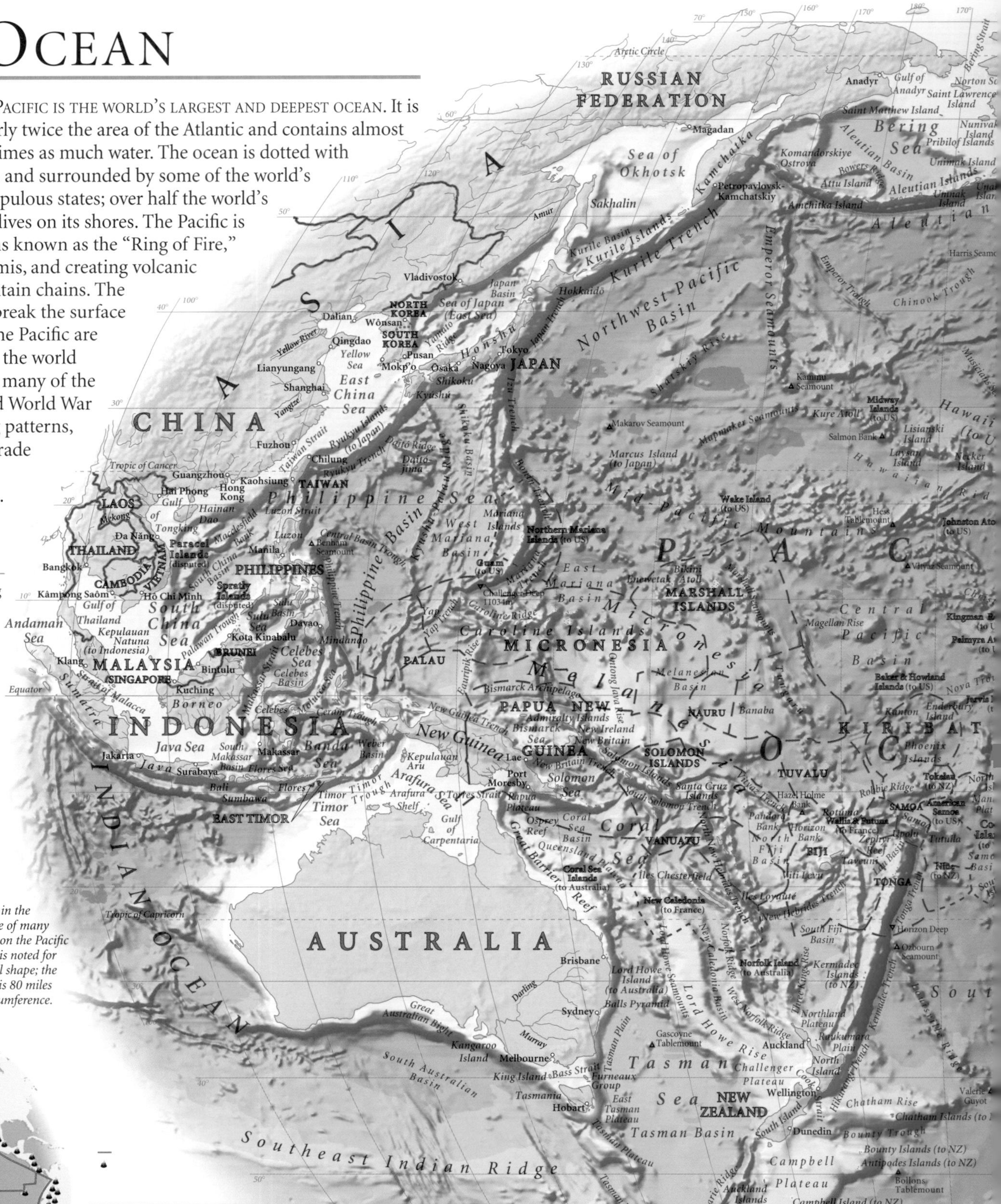
RUSSIAN FEDERATION
ASIA
CHINA
JAPAN
NORTH KOREA
SOUTH KOREA
TAIWAN
PHILIPPINES
MALAYSIA
INDONESIA
AUSTRALIA
NEW ZEALAND
PAPUA NEW GUINEA
MICRONESIA
MARSHALL ISLANDS
SOLOMON ISLANDS
NAURU
KIRIBATI
TUVALU
VANUATU
FIJI
TONGA
SAMOA
PALAU
EAST TIMOR
BRUNEI
SINGAPORE
THAILAND
LAOS
CAMBODIA
VIETNAM
PACIFIC OCEAN
INDIAN OCEAN
SOUTHERN OCEAN
ANTARCTICA
Sea of Okhotsk
Bering Sea
Sea of Japan (East Sea)
East China Sea
Yellow Sea
South China Sea
Philippine Sea
Coral Sea
Tasman Sea
Arafura Sea
Timor Sea
Java Sea
Celebes Sea
Banda Sea
Northwest Pacific Basin
Mid-Pacific Mountains
Central Pacific Basin
Southeast Indian Ridge
South Indian Basin
Tasman Basin
Campbell Plateau
Kurile Trench
Emperor Seamounts
Aleutian Trench
Kermadec Trench
Tonga Trench
Great Barrier Reef

The Ring of Fire

The active plate margins surrounding the Pacific have created numerous land and island volcanoes along its border. The actual basin of the Pacific is made up of a number of separate tectonic plates which move away from each other, colliding with other plates. When they collide, the oceanic plates, being thinner, are forced beneath the thicker continental plates, forming deep ocean trenches and high ridges. These collision zones are known as subduction zones and are characterized by intense seismic and volcanic activity.

***Mayon Volcano** in the Philippines is one of many active volcanoes on the Pacific "Ring of Fire." It is noted for its perfect conical shape; the base of the cone is 80 miles (130 km) in circumference.*

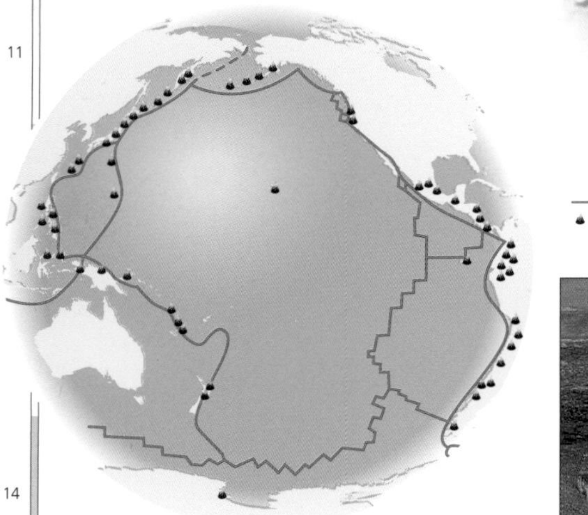

***The Hawaiian volcanoes,** which include Mauna Loa, the largest volcano on Earth, lie in the center of a plate, not on a plate margin, and are known as intraplate volcanoes. They are associated with hot spots, whereby a plume of hot molten rock rises to the surface as the plate moves over it.*

American Samoa and Samoa

***Many of the buildings** in Samoa reflect the country's colonial past. Once a colony of New Zealand, Samoa is now an independent state; American Samoa remains an unincorporated territory of the United States.*

American Samoa and Samoa are part of the island archipelago of Polynesia. The two most populous islands are Tutuila in American Samoa and Upolu in Samoa. Although the economies of both these states remain predominantly resource-based, both are expanding their light manufacturing sectors, and the US administration is the primary employer in American Samoa. Tuna fishing is particularly important: 25% of all tuna consumed in the US is processed and canned in Pago Pago.

SAMOA
AMERICAN SAMOA (to US)
Savai'i
Upolu
Tutuila
Samoa
PACIFIC OCEAN
ĀPIA
PAGO PAGO
Falealupo
Cape Puava
Fálelima
Sala'ilua
Fagamálo
Tuasivi
Pu'apu'a
Sálelologa
Satupaiteau
Silisili 1858m
Cape Āsuisui
Palauli Bay
Apolima Strait
Mataūtu
Lotofagā
Safata Bay
Salani
Fagaloa Bay
Ti'avea
Ofu
Olosega
Manua Islands
Ta'ū
Luma
Aunu'u Island
Cape Matātula
Cape Taputapu
Steps Point
SCALE 1:3,670,000
0 10 20 40 Km
0 10 20 40 Miles

THE LANDSCAPE

ALTHOUGH IT IS STILL THE LARGEST OCEAN, the basin of the Pacific has been gradually decreasing in size due to the movement of the Indo-Australian Plate. The oldest parts are about 135 million years old. The eastern border of the Pacific is characterized by a continuous mountain chain running the length of the North and South American continents. The eastern basin has a low, uninterrupted relief, at depths averaging 15,000 ft (4,570 m). In contrast, the western Pacific is scattered with island arcs and bounded by a series of deep ocean trenches. An almost continuous chain of volcanoes surrounds the ocean and an active mid-ocean ridge runs northeast–southwest.

UNITED STATES OF AMERICA (ALASKA)
NORTH AMERICA
CANADA
UNITED STATES OF AMERICA
MEXICO
Gulf of Mexico
Gulf of Alaska
Anchorage
Kodiak Island
Vancouver
Seattle
San Francisco
Long Beach
Puerto Vallarta
BELIZE
GUATEMALA
HONDURAS
EL SALVADOR
NICARAGUA
COSTA RICA
PANAMA
Panama City
Caribbean Sea
COLOMBIA
Buenaventura
Tumaco
Esmeraldas
ECUADOR
Guayaquil
Paita
PERU
Callao
Antofagasta
Valparaíso
Talcahuano
Punta Arenas
CHILE
SOUTH AMERICA
Tropic of Cancer
Tropic of Capricorn
Equator
Arctic Circle
Antarctic Circle
Honolulu
Hawai'i
Kiritimati
French Polynesia (to France)
Marquesas Islands
Nuku Hiva
Hiva Oa
Tahiti
Bora-Bora
Society Islands
Rangiroa
Tuamotu Islands
Îles Gambier
Îles Australes
Pitcairn Island
Pitcairn Islands (to UK)
Henderson Island
Ducie Island
Easter Island (to Chile)
Sala y Gomez (to Chile)
Islas Juan Fernández (to Chile)
Isla Alejandro Selkirk
Isla Róbinson Crusoe
Islas de los Desventurados (to Chile)
Isla San Ambrosio
Isla San Félix
Clipperton Island (to France)
Revillagigedo Islands (to Mexico)
Guadalupe (to Mexico)
Galapagos Islands (to Ecuador)
Isla Isabela
Isla San Cristóbal
Peter I Island (to Norway)
Mendocino Fracture Zone
Murray Fracture Zone
Molokai Fracture Zone
Clarion Fracture Zone
Clipperton Fracture Zone
Galapagos Fracture Zone
Marquesas Fracture Zone
Tuamotu Fracture Zone
Austral Fracture Zone
Easter Fracture Zone
Challenger Fracture Zone
Agassiz Fracture Zone
Menard Fracture Zone
Eltanin Fracture Zone
Udintsev Fracture Zone
Mendaña Fracture Zone
Mocha Fracture Zone
Guafo Fracture Zone
East Pacific Rise
Middle America Trench
Peru–Chile Trench
Guatemala Basin
Panama Basin
Peru Basin
Chile Basin
Bauer Basin
Yupanqui Basin
Roggeveen Basin
Tiki Basin
Galapagos Rise
Gallego Rise
Chile Rise
Nazca Ridge
Sala y Gomez Ridge
Carnegie Ridge
Cocos Ridge
Colón Ridge
Mornington Abyssal Plain
Bellingshausen Plain
Amundsen Plain
Southeast Pacific Basin
Tufts Plain
Cascadia Basin
Gilbert Seamounts
Pratt Seamount
Welker Seamount
Patton Seamount
Comstock Seamount
Endeavour Seamount
President Thiers Seamount
Moonless Mountains
De Gerlache Seamounts
Marie Byrd Seamount
Drake Passage
Amundsen Sea
Bellingshausen Sea
SOUTHERN OCEAN
ANTARCTICA
PACIFIC OCEAN

The Mariana Trench marks a subduction zone between the Pacific Plate and the Philippine Plate. It is the world's deepest trench, reaching depths of 36,201 ft (11,034 m).

Micronesia consists of numerous small, oceanic islands in the western Pacific. The Micronesian islands are all oceanic in origin, rising directly up from the ocean floor.

The Peru–Chile Trench is the longest trench in the Pacific, extending 3660 miles (5900 km), and following the line of the Andes mountain range down the west coast of South America.

The Tonga Trench lies north of New Zealand's North Island. The trench reaches average depths of 34,448 ft (10,500 m), which is more than twice the average depth of the ocean.

Bora-Bora's twin mountain peaks are the remnants of an ancient volcano, now surrounded by a large lagoon, fringed with coral.

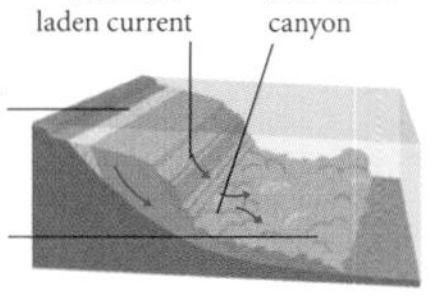

Sediment-laden current
Submarine canyon
Continental shelf
Ocean floor

***Turbidity currents** are sinking masses of sediment-laden water. Their erosive force creates deep, narrow submarine canyons along the continental shelf to the ocean floor, where the sediments are deposited.*

INSET MAP KEY

POPULATION

○ below 10,000

ELEVATION

1000m / 3281ft
500m / 1640ft
250m / 820ft
100m / 328ft
sea level

OCEAN MAP KEY

SEA DEPTH

sea level
250m / 820ft
500m / 1640ft
1000m / 3281ft
2000m / 6562ft
3000m / 9843ft
5000m / 16,410ft

SCALE 1:67,500,000
(projection: Mollweide)

Km 0 200 400 600 800 1000
Miles 0 200 400 600 800 1000

TONGA

THE KINGDOM OF TONGA lies in the southwest Pacific, about 2000 miles (3000 km) off the east coast of Australia. It comprises 169 islands of which only 36 are permanently inhabited. The majority of the population live on the largest island, Tongatapu. There are only three sizeable towns and the main commercial centre is the capital Nuku'alofa. Tonga's economy is based mainly on agriculture; coconuts, bananas and vanilla are grown as cash crops for export. Although there is some light manufacturing, growing land shortages have forced increased migration to New Zealand and Australia.

***Coral reefs and atolls** are found throughout the warm waters of the south Pacific. Reefs build up from the skeletons of millions of coral polyps – tiny sea creatures that cling to the reef and secrete calcium carbonate around their bodies, forming a hard protective skeleton.*

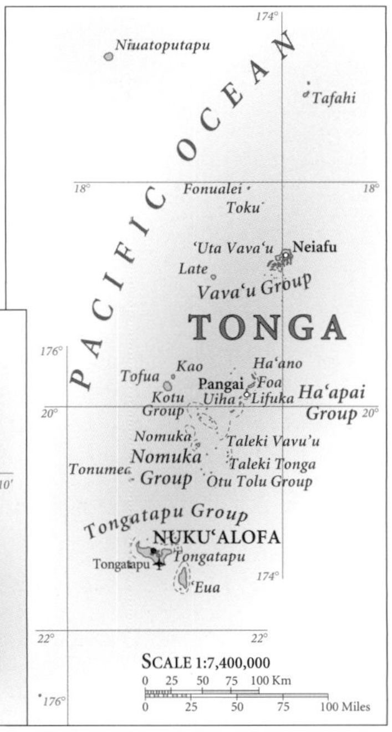

Niuatoputapu
Tafahi
PACIFIC OCEAN
Fonualei
Toku
'Uta Vava'u
Neiafu
Late
Vava'u Group
TONGA
Kao
Tofua
Ha'ano
Foa
Pangai
Lifuka
Uiha
Kotu
Ha'apai Group
Nomuka
Nomuka Group
Tonumea
Taleki Vavu'u
Taleki Tonga
Otu Tolu Group
Tongatapu Group
NUKU'ALOFA
Tongatapu
'Eua
SCALE 1:7,400,000

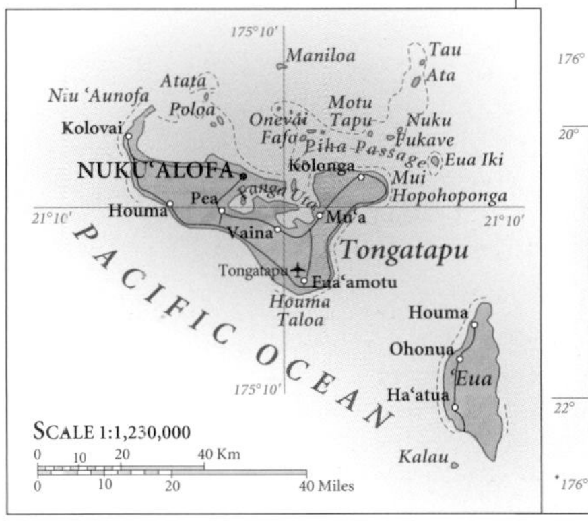

Niu 'Aunofa
Atata
Manilona
Tau
Ata
Kolovai
Poloa
Onevai
Motu Tapu
Nuku
Fafa
Pika Passage
Fukave
NUKU'ALOFA
Kolonga
Eua Iki
Mui Hopohoponga
Houma
Pea
Mu'a
Vaini
Tongatapu
Fua'amotu
Houma Taloa
PACIFIC OCEAN
Houma
Ohonua
'Eua
Ha'atua
Kalau
SCALE 1:1,230,000

***The islands of Tonga** fall into two belts; those in the east are low, coral islands, while those in the west are high and volcanic. Four of the islands still contain active volcanoes. The mountainous, western islands are covered with verdant tropical vegetation.*

***Wave action** has eroded this shoreline near Port Campbell in southeastern Australia leaving isolated pinnacles of rock cut off from the main coastline. They are known as the 'Twelve Apostles'.*

Antarctica

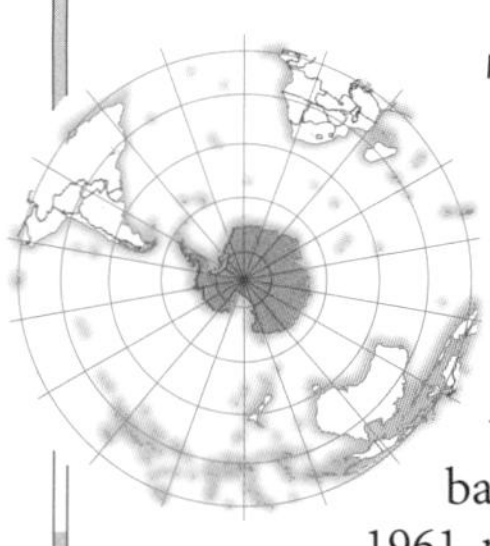

The ice-covered continent of Antarctica, which is the Earth's most southerly region, has drawn explorers and entrepreneurs seeking challenge and riches in its wintry lands for over 200 years. The extreme climate has deterred any large-scale settlement of the continent, and though commercial hunters built outposts in the past, habitation is now limited to scientific bases. The Antarctic Treaty, which came into force in 1961, provides for international governance and scientific cooperation in place of potential territorial conflict.

Territorial Claims

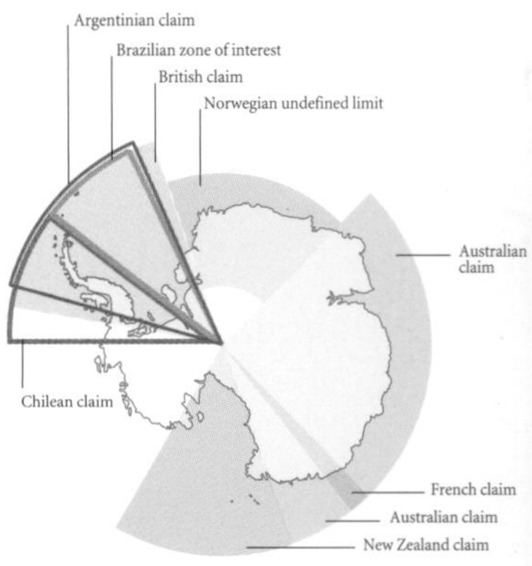

Argentinian claim
Brazilian zone of interest
British claim
Norwegian undefined limit
Australian claim
Chilean claim
French claim
Australian claim
New Zealand claim

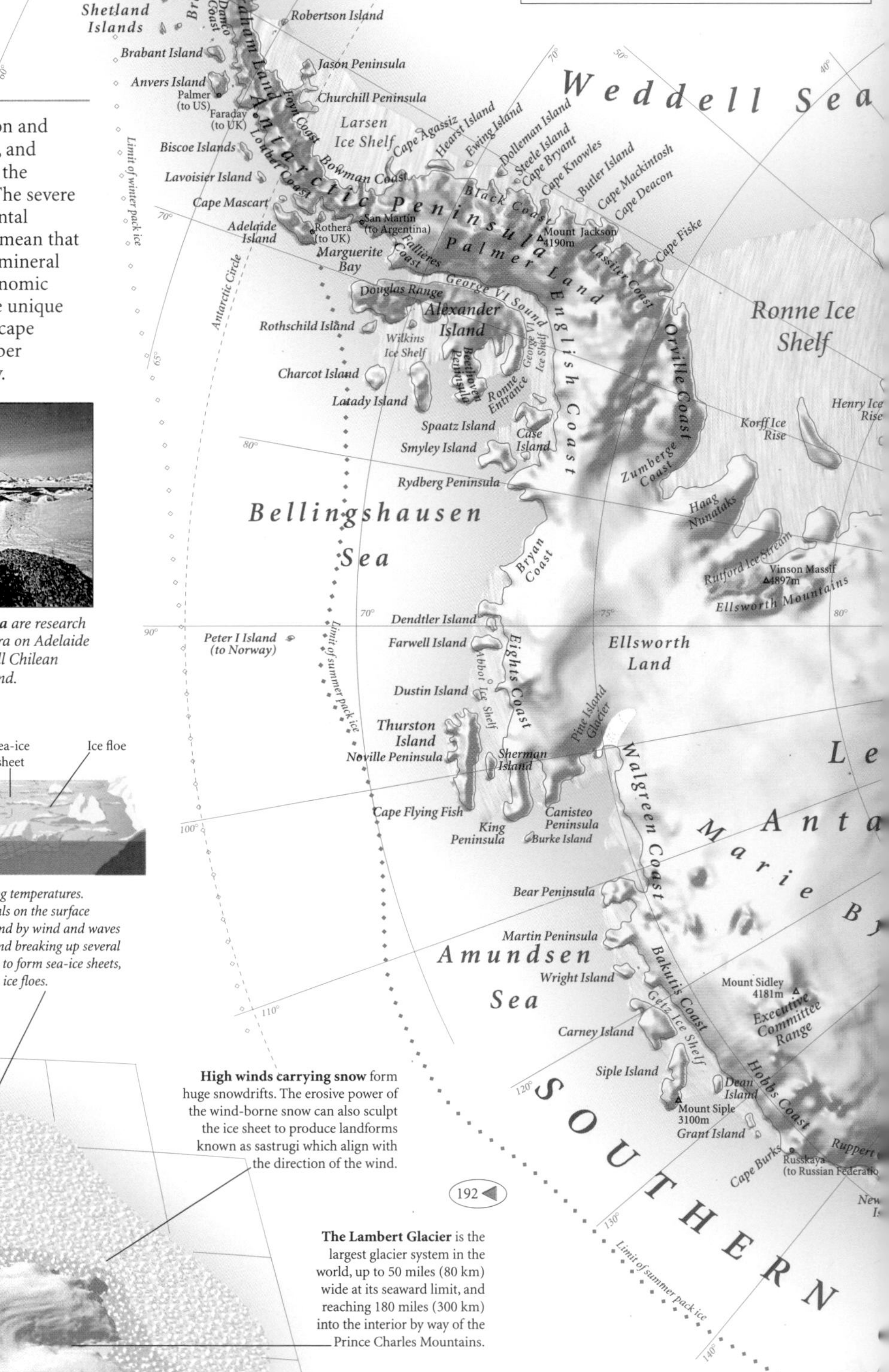

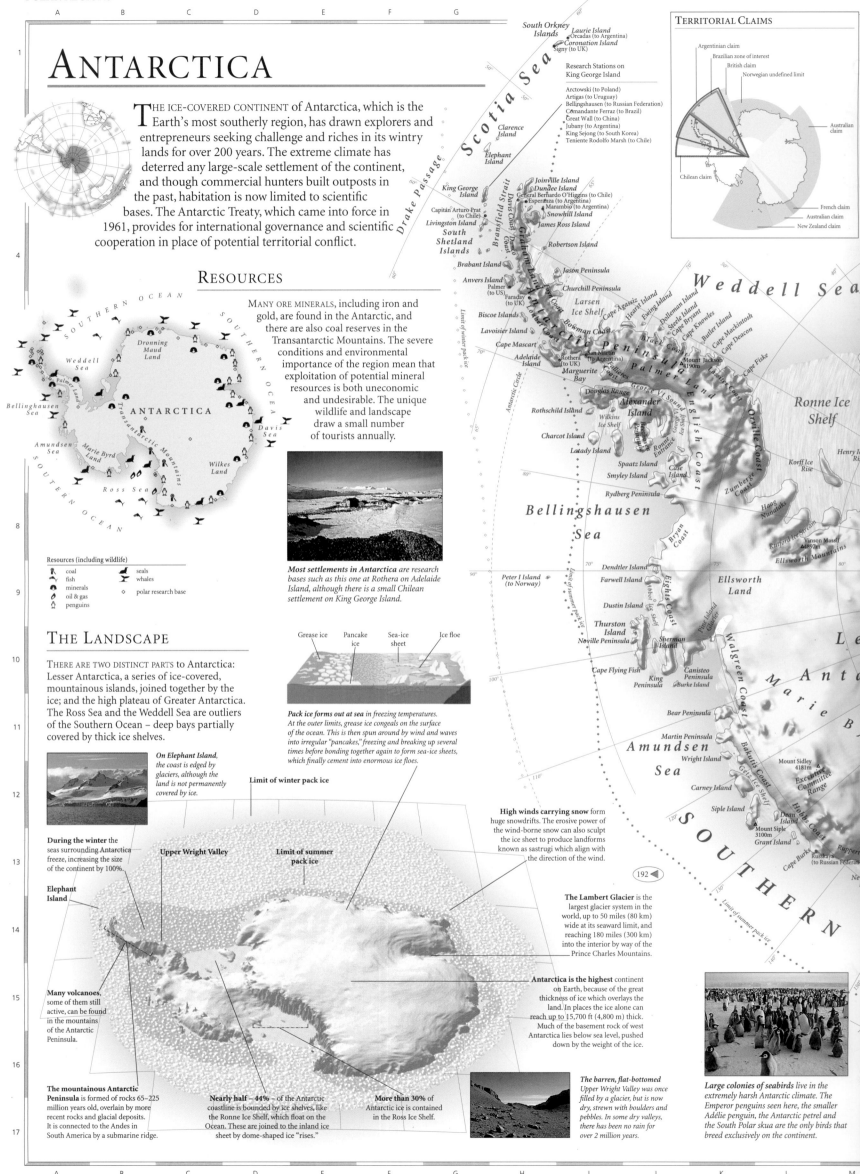

South Orkney Islands
Laurie Island
Orcadas (to Argentina)
Coronation Island
Signy (to UK)
Research Stations on King George Island
Arctowski (to Poland)
Artigas (to Uruguay)
Bellingshausen (to Russian Federation)
Comandante Ferraz (to Brazil)
Great Wall (to China)
Jubany (to Argentina)
King Sejong (to South Korea)
Teniente Rodolfo Marsh (to Chile)
Scotia Sea
Drake Passage
Clarence Island
Elephant Island
King George Island
Capitán Arturo Prat (to Chile)
Livingston Island
South Shetland Islands
Bransfield Strait
Davis Coast
Danco Coast
Joinville Island
Dundee Island
General Bernardo O'Higgins (to Chile)
Esperanza (to Argentina)
Marambio (to Argentina)
Snowhill Island
James Ross Island
Robertson Island
Brabant Island
Anvers Island
Palmer (to US)
Faraday (to UK)
Graham Land
Jason Peninsula
Churchill Peninsula
Larsen Ice Shelf
Biscoe Islands
Lavoisier Island
Cape Mascart
Adelaide Island
Rothera (to UK)
San Martin (to Argentina)
Marguerite Bay
Antarctic Peninsula
Bowman Coast
Black Coast
Palmer Land
Mount Jackson 4190m
Lassiter Coast
Cape Agassiz
Hearst Island
Ewing Island
Dolleman Island
Steele Island
Cape Bryant
Cape Knowles
Butler Island
Cape Mackintosh
Cape Deacon
Cape Fiske
Weddell Sea
Limit of winter pack ice
Antarctic Circle
Douglas Range
George VI Sound
Alexander Island
Rothschild Island
Wilkins Ice Shelf
Beethoven Peninsula
Charcot Island
Latady Island
Ronne Entrance
English Coast
Orville Coast
Ronne Ice Shelf
Henry Ice Rise
Korff Ice Rise
Spaatz Island
Smyley Island
Case Island
Zumberge Coast
Rydberg Peninsula
Bellingshausen Sea
Hag Nunataks
Rutford Ice Stream
Vinson Massif 4897m
Ellsworth Mountains
Bryan Coast
Peter I Island (to Norway)
Dendtler Island
Farwell Island
Dustin Island
Eights Coast
Abbot Ice Shelf
Ellsworth Land
Thurston Island
Noville Peninsula
Pine Island Glacier
Sherman Island
Cape Flying Fish
King Peninsula
Canisteo Peninsula
Burke Island
Walgreen Coast
Marie Byrd Land
Lesser Antarctica
Limit of summer pack ice
Bear Peninsula
Martin Peninsula
Amundsen Sea
Wright Island
Bakutis Coast
Mount Sidley 4181m
Executive Committee Range
Getz Ice Shelf
Carney Island
Siple Island
Hobbs Coast
Dean Island
Mount Siple 3100m
Grant Island
Cape Burks
Ruppert Coast
Russkaya (to Russian Federation)
Southern Ocean

192

Resources

Many ore minerals, including iron and gold, are found in the Antarctic, and there are also coal reserves in the Transantarctic Mountains. The severe conditions and environmental importance of the region mean that exploitation of potential mineral resources is both uneconomic and undesirable. The unique wildlife and landscape draw a small number of tourists annually.

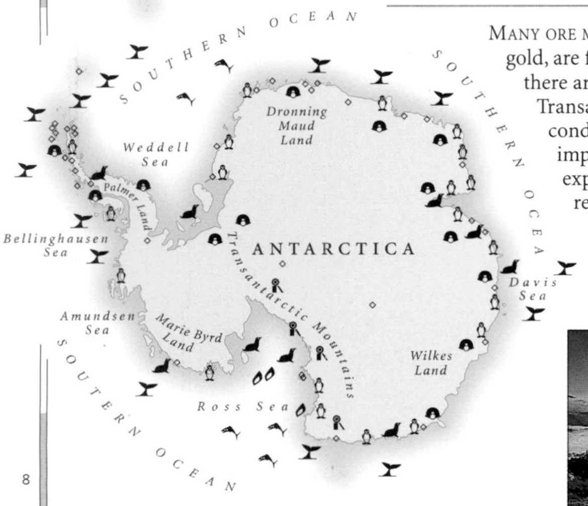

Southern Ocean
Dronning Maud Land
Weddell Sea
Palmer Land
Bellinghausen Sea
Antarctica
Transantarctic Mountains
Davis Sea
Amundsen Sea
Marie Byrd Land
Wilkes Land
Ross Sea
Southern Ocean

Resources (including wildlife)

- coal
- fish
- minerals
- oil & gas
- penguins
- seals
- whales
- polar research base

***Most settlements in Antarctica** are research bases such as this one at Rothera on Adelaide Island, although there is a small Chilean settlement on King George Island.*

The Landscape

There are two distinct parts to Antarctica: Lesser Antarctica, a series of ice-covered, mountainous islands, joined together by the ice; and the high plateau of Greater Antarctica. The Ross Sea and the Weddell Sea are outliers of the Southern Ocean – deep bays partially covered by thick ice shelves.

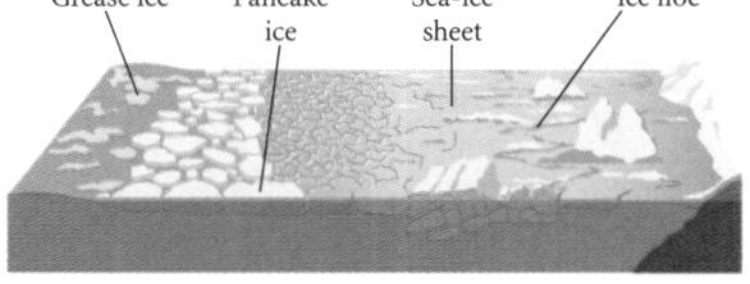

Grease ice
Pancake ice
Sea-ice sheet
Ice floe

***Pack ice forms out at sea** in freezing temperatures. At the outer limits, grease ice congeals on the surface of the ocean. This is then spun around by wind and waves into irregular "pancakes," freezing and breaking up several times before bonding together again to form sea-ice sheets, which finally cement into enormous ice floes.*

***On Elephant Island,** the coast is edged by glaciers, although the land is not permanently covered by ice.*

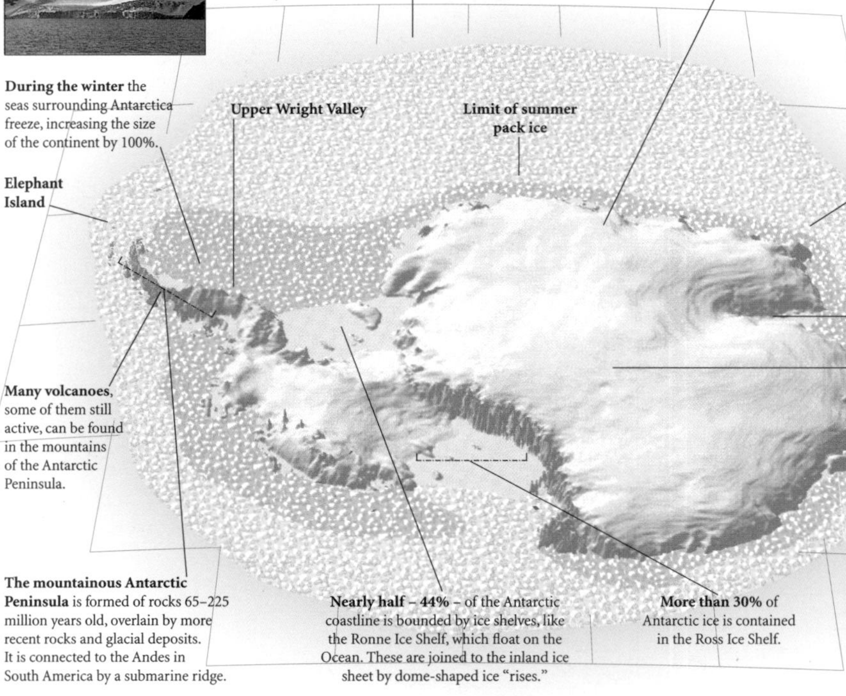

Limit of winter pack ice
Upper Wright Valley
Limit of summer pack ice
Elephant Island

During the winter the seas surrounding Antarctica freeze, increasing the size of the continent by 100%.

High winds carrying snow form huge snowdrifts. The erosive power of the wind-borne snow can also sculpt the ice sheet to produce landforms known as sastrugi which align with the direction of the wind.

The Lambert Glacier is the largest glacier system in the world, up to 50 miles (80 km) wide at its seaward limit, and reaching 180 miles (300 km) into the interior by way of the Prince Charles Mountains.

Antarctica is the highest continent on Earth, because of the great thickness of ice which overlays the land. In places the ice alone can reach up to 15,700 ft (4,800 m) thick. Much of the basement rock of west Antarctica lies below sea level, pushed down by the weight of the ice.

Many volcanoes, some of them still active, can be found in the mountains of the Antarctic Peninsula.

The mountainous Antarctic Peninsula is formed of rocks 65–225 million years old, overlain by more recent rocks and glacial deposits. It is connected to the Andes in South America by a submarine ridge.

Nearly half – 44% – of the Antarctic coastline is bounded by ice shelves, like the Ronne Ice Shelf, which float on the Ocean. These are joined to the inland ice sheet by dome-shaped ice "rises."

More than 30% of Antarctic ice is contained in the Ross Ice Shelf.

***The barren, flat-bottomed** Upper Wright Valley was once filled by a glacier, but is now dry, strewn with boulders and pebbles. In some dry valleys, there has been no rain for over 2 million years.*

***Large colonies of seabirds** live in the extremely harsh Antarctic climate. The Emperor penguins seen here, the smaller Adélie penguin, the Antarctic petrel and the South Polar skua are the only birds that breed exclusively on the continent.*

SOUTHERN OCEAN
SOUTHERN OCEAN
ANTARCTICA
Dronning Maud Land
Fimbulheimen
Thorshavnheiane
Prinsesse Astrid Kyst
Prinsesse Ragnhild Kyst
Kronprinsesse Märtha Kyst
Prins Harald Kyst
Kronprins Olav Kyst
Enderby Land
Kemp Land
Mac. Robertson Land
Princess Elizabeth Land
Greater Antarctica
Wilhelm II Land
Wilkes Land
Terre Adélie
George V Land
Oates Land
Victoria Land
Transantarctic Mountains
Queen Maud Mountains
Ross Ice Shelf
Ross Sea
Roosevelt Island
Ross Island
Coats Land
Filchner Ice Shelf
Recovery Glacier
Support Force Glacier
Pensacola Mountains
Foundation Ice Stream
Amundsen-Scott (to US)
South Pole
Vostok (to Russian Federation)
South Geomagnetic Pole
Mount Kirkpatrick 4528m
Mount Markham 4351m
Mount McClintock 3492m
Mount Lister 4026m
Mount Erebus 3794m
Mount Minto 4163m
Mount Menzies 3355m
Mount Victor 2588m
Mount Elkins 2300m
Scott Base (to NZ)
McMurdo Base (to US)
Prince Charles Mountains
Lambert Glacier
Amery Ice Shelf
Mackenzie Bay
Davis Sea
Dumont d'Urville Sea
Mawson (to Australia)
Davis (to Australia)
Casey (to Australia)
Mirny (to Russian Federation)
Dumont d'Urville (to France)
Leningradskaya (to Russian Federation)
Halley (to UK)
Belgrano II (to Argentina)
Sanae (to South Africa)
Georg von Neumayer (to Germany)
Maitri (to India)
Novolazarevskaya (to Russian Federation)
Asuka (to Japan)
Syowa (to Japan)
Molodezhnaya (to Russian Federation)
Zhongshan (to China)
Antarctic Circle
Limit of summer pack ice
MAP KEY
ELEVATION
ice cap
ice shelf
exposed land
SCALE 1:16,500,000
(projection: Lambert Azimuthal Equal Area)
Km
Miles

The sun sets over the Antarctic Peninsula for more than six months during the winter. However, there are more hours of sunshine during the brief Antarctic summer than most equatorial countries experience in a whole year.

Immense, flat-topped icebergs are formed when blocks of ice break away from the main ice sheet. Though the exposed area is enormous, the volume of ice concealed beneath the water may be many times greater.

The Arctic

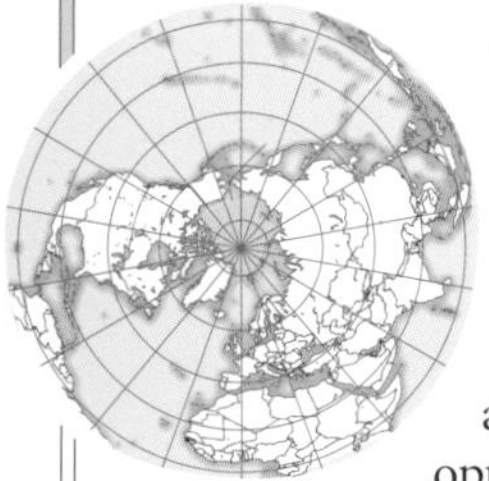

THREE CONTINENTS, ASIA, NORTH AMERICA, AND EUROPE, reach into the Arctic Circle at their northernmost limits, almost entirely encircling the Arctic Ocean. Despite the region's extraordinarily harsh climate, it has been inhabited for thousands of years by peoples such as the European Lapps, the Russian Nenet, and the North American Inuit, who draw a living from fishing, herding, and hunting. More recently, particularly in the Russian Arctic, opportunities to exploit oil and other mineral reserves have encouraged immigration. Pollution of the Arctic's unique ecology and damage to the traditional lifestyles of many native peoples have been the unfortunate results of this activity, and international cooperation is needed to safeguard the future of the region.

Map Key

POPULATION

- above 5 million
- 1 million to 5 million
- 500,000 to 1 million
- 100,000 to 500,000
- 50,000 to 100,000
- 10,000 to 50,000
- below 10,000

SEA DEPTH

- sea level
- 250m / 820ft
- 500m / 1640ft
- 1000m / 3281ft
- 2000m / 6562ft
- 3000m / 9843ft

SCALE 1:23,500,000
(projection: Lambert Azimuthal Equal Area)

Km 0 100 200 300 400 500 600
Miles 0 100 200 300 400 500 600

***Windblown snow** etches deep patterns in the ice sheet known as sastrugi. They align with the direction of the wind*

Resources

LARGE QUANTITIES of coal, oil, and natural gas are to be found in the basins of the Arctic Ocean, and in northern Canada, Alaska and the Russian Federation. The cost and difficulty of extraction and, more recently, awareness of damage to the environment, have limited exploitation to coastal regions. The unfrozen waters have stocks of fish including cod, flounder, and haddock. Quotas have now been put in place to restrict the number of fish caught annually. Reindeer are herded in large numbers by many of the native Arctic peoples. Most grain and vegetables are imported from elsewhere.

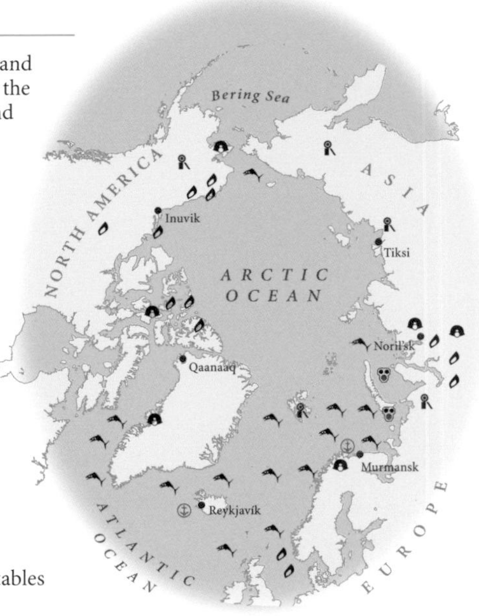

Bering Sea
NORTH AMERICA
ASIA
ARCTIC OCEAN
Inuvik
Tiksi
Noril'sk
Qaanaaq
Murmansk
Reykjavík
ATLANTIC OCEAN
EUROPE

***Icebreakers** are ships with specially strengthened hulls, designed to break a path through the ice. They are used to keep important routes open during the winter, when falling temperatures cause much of the Arctic Ocean to freeze over.*

Resources

- coal
- fish
- mining
- oil & gas
- radioactive contamination
- major towns
- major ports

The Landscape

THE ARCTIC OCEAN comprises two large ocean basins divided by three submarine ridges, the greatest of which, the Lomonosov Ridge, is a huge underwater mountain range which has an average height of more than 10,000 ft (3,000 m). The lands which encircle the Arctic Ocean are underlain by great shield areas of ancient rocks, which were heavily glaciated during the last Ice Age.

***Icebergs** are constantly broken up and reshaped by wind and the oceans. This flat-topped iceberg has been undercut, leaving a craggy ice cliff.*

A complex and ancient mountain system, extending from the Queen Elizabeth Islands to eastern Greenland was formed more than 245 million years ago.

The Canadian Shield underlies almost all of the Canadian Arctic. It is a very stable plateau of ancient rock, now covered by glacial lakes and sediment, which supports tundra vegetation.

The Arctic Ocean is the world's smallest ocean with a total area of 5,440,000 sq miles (15,100,000 sq km).

At a latitude of more than 75° N, the Arctic Ocean is almost permanently covered by pack-ice, though high winds and the movement of the seas may cause the ice to crack and break up.

In the more southerly reaches of the Arctic, like Siberia, much of the land is covered by permafrost. In the summer, higher temperatures warm the frozen ground, causing a number of typical phenomena. These include solifluction, the fast downhill movement of top soil layers; freeze/thaw activity, which patterns the ground into regular polygonal shapes, and the formation of large domes with a frozen ice core, known as pingos.

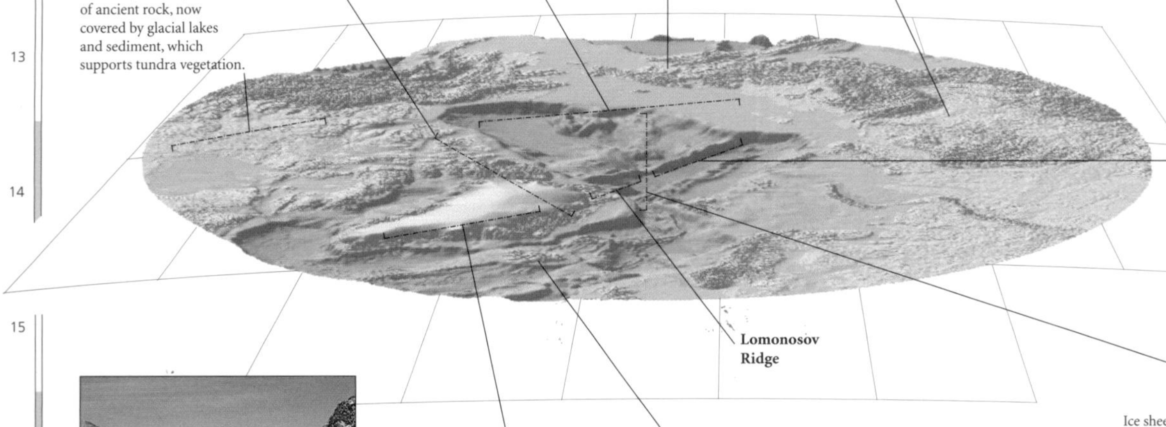

Lomonosov Ridge
Lomonosov Ridge
Arctic ice shelf

***Much of Greenland** is covered by a massive ice sheet more than 650,000 sq miles (1,683,400 sq km) in extent. The weight of the ice has depressed the central land area to form a basin lying more than 1,000 ft (300 m) below sea level. Only at the edges of the island is bare rock visible.*

Iceland has five major glaciers, sustained by heavy snowfall. Parts of the ice cap cover active volcanoes, such as Bárdharbunga, which periodically erupt causing the melted ice to form a great lake at the glacier margins.

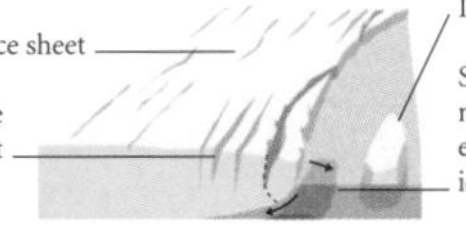

Ice sheet
Iceberg
Crevasses occur at the edge of the ice sheet
Sea water melts the edge of the ice sheet

***At the boundary** of the Arctic ice shelves, sea water flows under the ice causing melting and forming crevasses on the surface. This eventually weakens blocks of ice which break away as icebergs. This process is known as calving.*

192
8
8
64
CANADA
NORTH AMERICA
Great Bear Lake
Great Slave Lake
Kugluktuk
Bathurst Inlet
Cambridge Bay
Churchill
Hudson Bay
Southampton Island
Coats Island
Repulse Bay
Melville Peninsula
Mansel Island
Ivujivik
Inukjuak
Foxe Basin
Prince Charles Island
Hudson Strait
Lake Harbour
Baffin Island
Ungava Bay
Cape Chidley
Davis Strait
Nain
Labrador Sea
Labrador Basin
Maniitsoq
NUUK
Paamiut
Ivittuut
Qaqortoq
Nanortalik
Nunap Isua (Kap Farvel)
Eirik Ridge
ATLANTIC

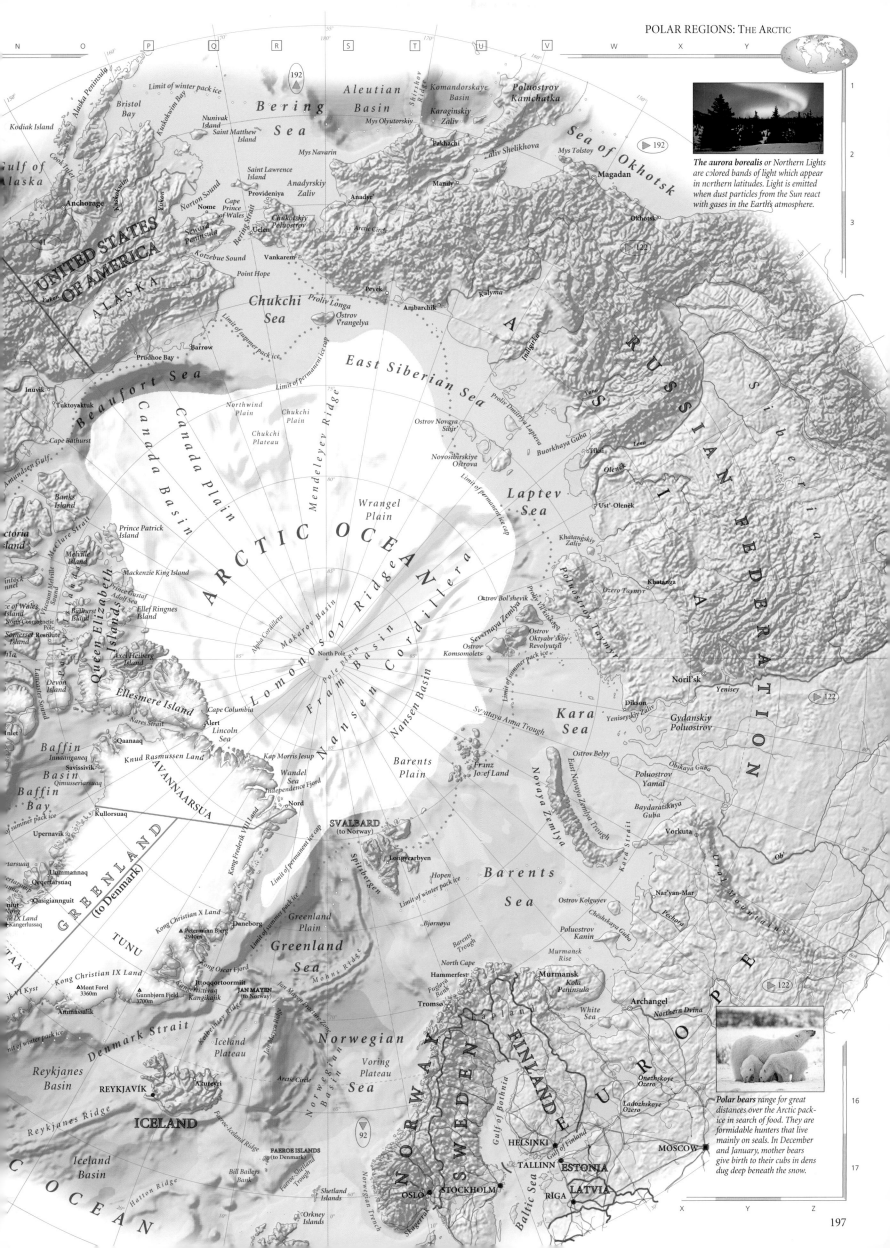

N O P Q R S T U V W X Y
Bering Sea
Aleutian Basin
Shirshov Ridge
Komandorskaye Basin
Poluostrov Kamchatka
Karaginskiy Zaliv
Mys Olyutorskiy
Limit of winter pack ice
Bristol Bay
Alaska Peninsula
Kuskokwim Bay
Nunivak Island
Saint Matthew Island
Kodiak Island
Gulf of Alaska
Cook Inlet
Anchorage
Kuskokwim
Yukon
Norton Sound
Nome
Cape Prince of Wales
Seward Peninsula
Bering Strait
Saint Lawrence Island
Provideniya
Anadyrskiy Zaliv
Mys Navarin
Anadyr'
Chukotskiy Poluostrov
Uelen
Arctic Circle
Pakhachi
Zaliv Shelikhova
Manily
Mys Tolstoy
Sea of Okhotsk
Magadan
Okhotsk
UNITED STATES OF AMERICA
ALASKA
Kotzebue Sound
Point Hope
Vankarem
Pevek
Ambarchik
Kolyma
Chukchi Sea
Proliv Longa
Ostrov Vrangelya
Limit of summer pack ice
Limit of permanent ice cap
Barrow
Prudhoe Bay
Beaufort Sea
Inuvik
Tuktoyaktuk
Cape Bathurst
Amundsen Gulf
Banks Island
Victoria Island
McClure Strait
Prince Patrick Island
Melville Island
Mackenzie King Island
Viscount Melville Sound
Prince Gustaf Adolf Sea
Ellef Ringnes Island
Bathurst Island
North Geomagnetic Pole
Somerset Island
Resolute
Queen Elizabeth Islands
Axel Heiberg Island
Devon Island
Lancaster Sound
Ellesmere Island
Nares Strait
Cape Columbia
Alert
Lincoln Sea
Qaanaaq
Baffin Bay
Baffin Basin
Innaanganeq
Savissivik
Qimusseriarsuaq
Knud Rasmussen Land
AVANNAARSUA
Kullorsuaq
Upernavik
Uummannaq
Qeqertarsuaq
Qasigiannguit
Kangerlussuaq
GREENLAND (to Denmark)
TUNU
Kap Morris Jesup
Wandel Sea
Independence Fjord
Nord
Kong Frederik VIII Land
Kong Christian X Land
Daneborg
Petermann Bjerg 2940m
Kong Oscar Fjord
Ittoqqortoormiit
Kangertittivaq
Kangikajik
Kong Christian IX Land
Mont Forel 3360m
Gunnbjørn Fjeld 3700m
Ammassalik
Denmark Strait
Canada Basin
Canada Plain
Northwind Plain
Chukchi Plain
Chukchi Plateau
Mendeleyev Ridge
East Siberian Sea
Wrangel Plain
ARCTIC OCEAN
Alpha Cordillera
Makarov Basin
Lomonosov Ridge
North Pole
Pole Plain
Fram Basin
Nansen Cordillera
Nansen Basin
Barents Plain
Ostrov Novaya Sibir'
Proliv Dmitriya Lapteva
Novosibirskiye Ostrova
Buorkhaya Guba
Tiksi
Lena
Yana
Indigirka
Olenëk
Ust'-Olenëk
Laptev Sea
Khatangskiy Zaliv
Khatanga
Ozero Taymyr
Poluostrov Taymyr
Ostrov Bol'shevik
Proliv Vil'kitskogo
Severnaya Zemlya
Ostrov Oktyabr'skoy Revolyutsii
Ostrov Komsomolets
Noril'sk
Yenisey
Dikson
Yeniseyskiy Zaliv
Gydanskiy Poluostrov
RUSSIAN FEDERATION
Siberia
Svyataya Anna Trough
Kara Sea
Frnz Jozef Land
Ostrov Belyy
Obskaya Guba
Poluostrov Yamal
Baydaratskaya Guba
Vorkuta
Ob'
Ural Mountains
Novaya Zemlya
East Novaya Zemlya Trough
Kara Strait
SVALBARD (to Norway)
Spitsbergen
Longyearbyen
Hopen
Limit of winter pack ice
Barents Sea
Ostrov Kolguyev
Nar'yan-Mar
Pechora
Cheshskaya Guba
Poluostrov Kanin
Bjørnøya
Barents Trough
Greenland Plain
Greenland Sea
Mohns Ridge
Jan Mayen Fracture Zone
JAN MAYEN (to Norway)
Jan Mayen Ridge
Kolbeinsey Ridge
North Cape
Hammerfest
Fugløya Bank
Murmansk Rise
Murmansk
Kola Peninsula
Tromsø
Lapland
White Sea
Archangel
Northern Dvina
EUROPE
Norwegian Sea
Iceland Plateau
Voring Plateau
Norwegian Basin
Arctic Circle
Reykjanes Basin
REYKJAVÍK
Akureyri
ICELAND
Reykjanes Ridge
Faeroe-Iceland Ridge
FAEROE ISLANDS (to Denmark)
Faeroe-Shetland Trough
Bill Baileys Bank
Iceland Basin
Hatton Ridge
ATLANTIC OCEAN
Shetland Islands
Orkney Islands
Norwegian Trench
Skagerrak
NORWAY
SWEDEN
FINLAND
Gulf of Bothnia
Gulf of Finland
HELSINKI
TALLINN
ESTONIA
LATVIA
RIGA
Baltic Sea
OSLO
STOCKHOLM
Onezhskoye Ozero
Ladozhskoye Ozero
MOSCOW
192
122
92
41
1 2 3 16 17
X Y Z

The aurora borealis *or Northern Lights are colored bands of light which appear in northern latitudes. Light is emitted when dust particles from the Sun react with gases in the Earth's atmosphere.*

Polar bears *range for great distances over the Arctic pack-ice in search of food. They are formidable hunters that live mainly on seals. In December and January, mother bears give birth to their cubs in dens dug deep beneath the snow.*

Geographical Comparisons

Largest Countries

Russian Federation	6,592,735 sq miles	(17,075,200 sq km)
Canada	3,855,171 sq miles	(9,984,670 sq km)
USA	3,717,792 sq miles	(9,629,091 sq km)
China	3,705,386 sq miles	(9,596,960 sq km)
Brazil	3,286,470 sq miles	(8,511,965 sq km)
Australia	2,967,893 sq miles	(7,686,850 sq km)
India	1,269,339 sq miles	(3,287,590 sq km)
Argentina	1,068,296 sq miles	(2,766,890 sq km)
Kazakhstan	1,049,150 sq miles	(2,717,300 sq km)
Sudan	967,493 sq miles	(2,505,810 sq km)

Smallest Countries

Vatican City	0.17 sq miles	(0.44 sq km)
Monaco	0.75 sq miles	(1.95 sq km)
Nauru	8 sq miles	(21 sq km)
Tuvalu	10 sq miles	(26 sq km)
San Marino	24 sq miles	(61 sq km)
Liechtenstein	62 sq miles	(160 sq km)
Marshall Islands	70 sq miles	(181 sq km)
St. Kitts & Nevis	101 sq miles	(261 sq km)
Maldives	116 sq miles	(300 sq km)
Malta	122 sq miles	(316 sq km)

Largest Islands

(to the nearest 1000 - or 100,000 for the largest)

Greenland	849,400 sq miles	(2,200,000 sq km)
New Guinea	312,000 sq miles	(808,000 sq km)
Borneo	292,222 sq miles	(757,050 sq km)
Madagascar	229,300 sq miles	(594,000 sq km)
Sumatra	202,300 sq miles	(524,000 sq km)
Baffin Island	183,800 sq miles	(476,000 sq km)
Honshu	88,800 sq miles	(230,000 sq km)
Britain	88,700 sq miles	(229,800 sq km)
Victoria Island	81,900 sq miles	(212,000 sq km)
Ellesmere Island	75,700 sq miles	(196,000 sq km)

Richest Countries

(GNP per capita, in US$)

Liechtenstein	50,000
Luxembourg	39,470
Norway	38,730
Switzerland	36,170
USA	35,400
Japan	34,010
Denmark	30,260
Iceland	27,960
Monaco	27,500
Sweden	25,970

Poorest Countries

(GNP per capita, in US$)

Burundi	100
Congo, Dem. Rep.	100
Ethiopia	100
Somalia	120
Guinea-Bissau	130
Liberia	140
Sierra Leone	140
Malawi	160
Tajikistan	180
Niger	180
Eritrea	190
Mozambique	200

Most Populous Countries

China	1,304,200,000
India	1,065,500,000
USA	294,000,000
Indonesia	219,900,000
Brazil	178,500,000
Pakistan	153,600,000
Bangladesh	146,700,000
Russian Federation	143,200,000
Japan	127,700,000
Nigeria	124,000,000

Least Populous Countries

Vatican City	921
Tuvalu	11,305
Nauru	12,570
Palau	19,717
San Marino	28,119
Monaco	32,130
Liechtenstein	33,145
St Kitts & Nevis	38,763
Marshall Islands	56,429
Antigua & Barbuda	67,897
Andorra	69,150
Dominica	69,655

Most Densely Populated Countries

Monaco	42,840 people per sq mile	(16,477 per sq km)
Singapore	18,220 people per sq mile	(7,049 per sq km)
Vatican City	5,359 people per sq mile	(2,070 per sq km)
Malta	3,177 people per sq mile	(1,231 per sq km)
Bangladesh	2,837 people per sq mile	(1,096 per sq km)
Maldives	2,741 people per sq mile	(1,060 per sq km)
Bahrain	2,652 people per sq mile	(1,025 per sq km)
Taiwan	1,815 people per sq mile	(701 per sq km)
Mauritius	1,671 people per sq mile	(645 per sq km)
Barbados	1,627 people per sq mile	(628 per sq km)

Most Sparsely Populated Countries

Mongolia	4 people per sq mile	(2 per sq km)
Namibia	6 people per sq mile	(2 per sq km)
Australia	7 people per sq mile	(3 per sq km)
Iceland	7 people per sq mile	(3 per sq km)
Mauritania	7 people per sq mile	(3 per sq km)
Suriname	7 people per sq mile	(3 per sq km)
Botswana	8 people per sq mile	(3 per sq km)
Libya	8 people per sq mile	(3 per sq km)
Canada	9 people per sq mile	(3 per sq km)
Guyana	10 people per sq mile	(4 per sq km)

Most Widely Spoken Languages

1. Chinese (Mandarin)	**6. Arabic**
2. English	**7. Bengali**
3. Hindi	**8. Portuguese**
4. Spanish	**9. Malay-Indonesian**
5. Russian	**10. French**

Countries With The Most Land Borders

14: China *(Afghanistan, Bhutan, India, Kazakhstan, Kyrgyzstan, Laos, Mongolia, Myanmar, Nepal, North Korea, Pakistan, Russian Federation, Tajikistan, Vietnam)*

14: Russian Federation *(Azerbaijan, Belarus, China, Estonia, Finland, Georgia, Kazakhstan, Latvia, Lithuania, Mongolia, North Korea, Norway, Poland, Ukraine)*

10: Brazil *(Argentina, Bolivia, Colombia, French Guiana, Guyana, Paraguay, Peru, Suriname, Uruguay, Venezuela)*

9: Congo, Dem. Rep. *(Angola, Burundi, Central African Republic, Congo, Rwanda, Sudan, Tanzania, Uganda, Zambia)*

9: Germany *(Austria, Belgium, Czech Republic, Denmark, France, Luxembourg, Netherlands, Poland, Switzerland)*

9: Sudan *(Central African Republic, Chad, Congo, Dem. Rep., Egypt, Eritrea, Ethiopia, Kenya, Libya, Uganda)*

8: Austria *(Czech Republic, Germany, Hungary, Italy, Liechtenstein, Slovakia, Slovenia, Switzerland)*
8: France *(Andorra, Belgium, Germany, Italy, Luxembourg, Monaco, Spain, Switzerland)*
8: Tanzania *(Burundi, Congo, Dem. Rep., Kenya, Malawi, Mozambique, Rwanda, Uganda, Zambia)*
8: Turkey *(Armenia, Azerbaijan, Bulgaria, Georgia, Greece, Iran, Iraq, Syria)*
8: Zambia *(Angola, Botswana, Congo, Dem. Rep., Malawi, Mozambique, Namibia, Tanzania, Zimbabwe)*

Longest Rivers

Nile (NE Africa)	4,160 miles	(6,695 km)
Amazon (South America)	4,049 miles	(6,516 km)
Yangtze (China)	3,915 miles	(6,299 km)
Mississippi/Missouri (USA)	3,710 miles	(5,969 km)
Ob'-Irtysh (Russian Federation)	3,461 miles	(5,570 km)
Yellow River (China)	3,395 miles	(5,464 km)
Congo (Central Africa)	2,900 miles	(4,667 km)
Mekong (Southeast Asia)	2,749 miles	(4,425 km)
Lena (Russian Federation)	2,734 miles	(4,400 km)
Mackenzie (Canada)	2,640 miles	(4,250 km)
Yenisey (Russian Federation)	2,541 miles	(4,090 km)

Highest Mountains

(height above sea level)

Everest	29,035 ft	(8,850 m)
K2	28,253 ft	(8,611 m)
Kanchenjunga I	28,210 ft	(8,598 m)
Makalu I	27,767 ft	(8,463 m)
Cho Oyu	26,907 ft	(8,201 m)
Dhaulagiri I	26,796 ft	(8,167 m)
Manaslu I	26,783 ft	(8,163 m)
Nanga Parbat I	26,661 ft	(8,126 m)
Annapurna I	26,547 ft	(8,091 m)
Gasherbrum I	26,471 ft	(8,068 m)

Largest Bodies of Inland Water

(with area and depth)

Caspian Sea	143,243 sq miles (371,000 sq km)	3,215 ft (980 m)
Lake Superior	31,151 sq miles (83,270 sq km)	1,289 ft (393 m)
Lake Victoria	26,560 sq miles (68,880 sq km)	328 ft (100 m)
Lake Huron	23,436 sq miles (60,700 sq km)	751 ft (229 m)
Lake Michigan	22,402 sq miles (58,020 sq km)	922 ft (281 m)
Lake Tanganyika	12,703 sq miles (32,900 sq km)	4,700 ft (1,435 m)
Great Bear Lake	12,274 sq miles (31,790 sq km)	1,047 ft (319 m)
Lake Baikal	11,776 sq miles (30,500 sq km)	5,712 ft (1,741 m)
Great Slave Lake	10,981 sq miles (28,440 sq km)	459 ft (140 m)
Lake Erie	9,915 sq miles (25,680 sq km)	197 ft (60 m)

Deepest Ocean Features

Challenger Deep, Marianas Trench (Pacific)	36,201 ft	(11,034 m)
Vityaz III Depth, Tonga Trench (Pacific)	35,704 ft	(10,882 m)
Vityaz Depth, Kurile-Kamchatka Trench (Pacific)	34,588 ft	(10,542 m)
Cape Johnson Deep, Philippine Trench (Pacific)	34,441 ft	(10,497 m)
Kermadec Trench (Pacific)	32,964 ft	(10,047 m)
Ramapo Deep, Japan Trench (Pacific)	32,758 ft	(9,984 m)
Milwaukee Deep, Puerto Rico Trench (Atlantic)	30,185 ft	(9,200 m)
Argo Deep, Torres Trench (Pacific)	30,070 ft	(9,165 m)
Meteor Depth, South Sandwich Trench (Atlantic)	30,000 ft	(9,144 m)
Planet Deep, New Britain Trench (Pacific)	29,988 ft	(9,140 m)

Greatest Waterfalls

(mean flow of water)

Boyoma (Congo, Dem. Rep.)	600,400 cu. ft/sec	(17,000 cu.m/sec)
Khône (Laos/Cambodia)	410,000 cu. ft/sec	(11,600 cu.m/sec)
Niagara (USA/Canada)	195,000 cu. ft/sec	(5,500 cu.m/sec)
Grande (Uruguay)	160,000 cu. ft/sec	(4,500 cu.m/sec)
Paulo Afonso (Brazil)	100,000 cu. ft/sec	(2,800 cu.m/sec)
Urubupunga (Brazil)	97,000 cu. ft/sec	(2,750 cu.m/sec)
Iguaçu (Argentina/Brazil)	62,000 cu. ft/sec	(1,700 cu.m/sec)
Maribondo (Brazil)	53,000 cu. ft/sec	(1,500 cu.m/sec)
Kabalega (Uganda)	42,000 cu. ft/sec	(1,200 cu.m/sec)
Victoria (Zimbabwe)	39,000 cu. ft/sec	(1,100 cu.m/sec)
Churchill (Canada)	35,000 cu. ft/sec	(1,000 cu.m/sec)
Cauvery (India)	33,000 cu. ft/sec	(900 cu.m/sec)

Highest Waterfalls

Angel (Venezuela)	3,212 ft	(979 m)
Tugela (South Africa)	3,110 ft	(948 m)
Utigard (Norway)	2,625 ft	(800 m)
Mongefossen (Norway)	2,539 ft	(774 m)
Mtarazi (Zimbabwe)	2,500 ft	(762 m)
Yosemite (USA)	2,425 ft	(739 m)
Ostre Mardola Foss (Norway)	2,156 ft	(657 m)
Tyssestrengane (Norway)	2,119 ft	(646 m)
***Cuquenan** (Venezuela)	2,001 ft	(610 m)
Sutherland (New Zealand)	1,903 ft	(580 m)
***Kjellfossen** (Norway)	1,841 ft	(561 m)

** indicates that the total height is a single leap*

Largest Deserts

Sahara	3,450,000 sq miles	(9,065,000 sq km)
Gobi	500,000 sq miles	(1,295,000 sq km)
Ar Rub al Khali	289,600 sq miles	(750,000 sq km)
Great Victorian	249,800 sq miles	(647,000 sq km)
Sonoran	120,000 sq miles	(311,000 sq km)
Kalahari	120,000 sq miles	(310,800 sq km)
Kara Kum	115,800 sq miles	(300,000 sq km)
Takla Makan	100,400 sq miles	(260,000 sq km)
Namib	52,100 sq miles	(135,000 sq km)
Thar	33,670 sq miles	(130,000 sq km)

NB – Most of Antarctica is a polar desert, with only 50 mm of precipitation annually

Hottest Inhabited Places

Djibouti (Djibouti)	86° F	(30 °C)
Timbouctou (Mali)	84.7° F	(29.3 °C)
Tirunelveli (India)		
Tuticorin (India)		
Nellore (India)	84.5° F	(29.2 °C)
Santa Marta (Colombia)		
Aden (Yemen)	84° F	(28.9 °C)
Madurai (India)		
Niamey (Niger)		
Hodeida (Yemen)	83.8° F	(28.8 °C)
Ouagadougou (Burkina)		
Thanjavur (India)		
Tiruchchirappalli (India)		

Driest Inhabited Places

Aswân (Egypt)	0.02 in	(0.5 mm)
Luxor (Egypt)	0.03 in	(0.7 mm)
Arica (Chile)	0.04 in	(1.1 mm)
Ica (Peru)	0.1 in	(2.3 mm)
Antofagasta (Chile)	0.2 in	(4.9 mm)
El Minya (Egypt)	0.2 in	(5.1 mm)
Asyût (Egypt)	0.2 in	(5.2 mm)
Callao (Peru)	0.5 in	(12.0 mm)
Trujillo (Peru)	0.55 in	(14.0 mm)
El Faiyûm (Egypt)	0.8 in	(19.0 mm)

Wettest Inhabited Places

Buenaventura (Colombia)	265 in	(6,743 mm)
Monrovia (Liberia)	202 in	(5,131 mm)
Pago Pago (American Samoa)	196 in	(4,990 mm)
Moulmein (Myanmar)	191 in	(4,852 mm)
Lae (Papua New Guinea)	183 in	(4,645 mm)
Baguio (Luzon Island, Philippines)	180 in	(4,573 mm)
Sylhet (Bangladesh)	176 in	(4,457 mm)
Bogor (Java, Indonesia)	166 in	(4,225 mm)
Padang (Sumatra, Indonesia)	166 in	(4,225 mm)
Conakry (Guinea)	171 in	(4,341 mm)

THE TIME ZONES

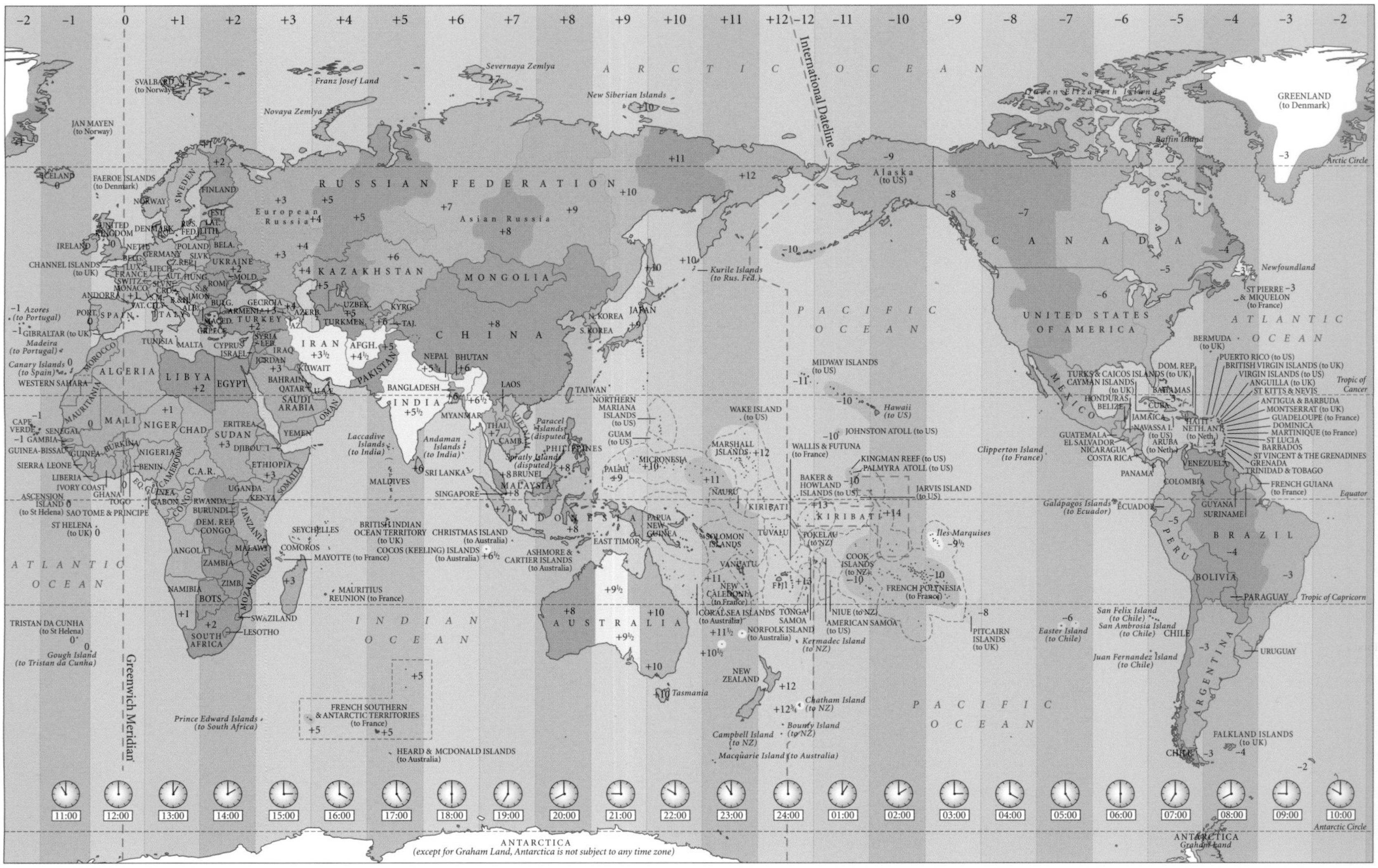
-2 -1 0 +1 +2 +3 +4 +5 +6 +7 +8 +9 +10 +11 +12 -12 -11 -10 -9 -8 -7 -6 -5 -4 -3 -2
A R C T I C O C E A N
International Dateline
Greenwich Meridian
RUSSIAN FEDERATION
CANADA
UNITED STATES OF AMERICA
GREENLAND (to Denmark)
KAZAKHSTAN
MONGOLIA
CHINA
INDIA
IRAN
LIBYA
ALGERIA
EGYPT
SUDAN
BRAZIL
AUSTRALIA
NEW ZEALAND
P A C I F I C O C E A N
A T L A N T I C O C E A N
I N D I A N O C E A N
Arctic Circle
Tropic of Cancer
Equator
Tropic of Capricorn
Antarctic Circle
ANTARCTICA
(except for Graham Land, Antarctica is not subject to any time zone)
11:00 12:00 13:00 14:00 15:00 16:00 17:00 18:00 19:00 20:00 21:00 22:00 23:00 24:00 01:00 02:00 03:00 04:00 05:00 06:00 07:00 08:00 09:00 10:00

The numbers at the top of the map indicate the number of hours each time zone is ahead or behind Greenwich Mean Time (GMT). The clocks and 24-hour times given at the bottom of the map show the time in each time zone when it is 12:00 hours noon GMT.

TIME ZONES

The present system of international timekeeping divides the world into 24 time zones by means of 24 standard meridians of longitude, each 15° apart. Time is measured in each zone as so many hours ahead or behind the time at the Greenwich Meridian (GMT). Countries, or parts of countries, falling in the vicinity of each zone, adopt its time as shown on the map above. Therefore, using the map, when it is 12:00 noon GMT, it will be 2:00 pm in Zambia; similarly, when it is 4:30 pm. GMT, it will be 11:30 am in Peru.

GREENWICH MEAN TIME (GMT)

Greenwich Mean Time (or Universal Time, as it is more correctly called) has been the internationally accepted basis for calculating solar time – measured in relation to the Earth's rotation around the Sun – since 1884. Greenwich Mean Time is specifically the solar time at the site of the former Royal Observatory in the London Borough of Greenwich, United Kingdom. The Greenwich Meridian is an imaginary line around the world that runs through the North and South poles. It corresponds to 0° of longitude, which lies on this site at Greenwich. Time is measured around the world in relation to the official time along the Meridian.

STANDARD TIME

Standard time is the official time, designated by law, in any specific country or region. Standard time was initiated in 1884, after it became apparent that the practice of keeping various systems of local time was causing confusion – particularly in the USA and Canada, where several railroad routes passed through scores of areas which calculated local time by different rules. The standard time of a particular region is calculated in reference to the longitudinal time zone in which it falls. In practice, these zones do not always match their longitudinal position; in some places the area of the zone has been altered in shape for the convenience of inhabitants, as can be seen in the map. For example, while Greenland occupies three time zones, the majority of the territory uses a standard time of -3 hours GMT. Similarly China, which spans five time zones, is standardized at +8 hours GMT.

THE INTERNATIONAL DATELINE

The International Dateline is an imaginary line that extends from pole to pole, and roughly corresponds to a line of 180° longitude for much of its length. This line is the arbitrary marker between calendar days. By moving from east to west across the line, a traveller will need to set their calendar back one day, while those travelling in the opposite direction will need to add a day. This is to compensate for the use of standard time around the world, which is based on the time at noon along the Greenwich Meridian, approximately halfway around the world. Wide deviations from 180° longitude occur through the Bering Strait – to avoid dividing Siberia into two separate calendar days – and in the Pacific Ocean – to allow certain Pacific islands the same calendar day as New Zealand. Changes were made to the International Dateline in 1995 that made Millennium Island (formerly Caroline Island) in Kiribati the first land area to witness the beginning of the year 2000.

DAYLIGHT SAVING TIME

Also known as summer time, daylight saving is a system of advancing clocks in order to extend the waking day during periods of later daylight hours. This normally means advancing clocks by one hour in early spring, and reverting back to standard time in early autumn. The system of daylight saving is used throughout much of Europe, the USA, Australia, and many other countries worldwide, although there are no standardized dates for the changeover to summer time due to the differences in hours of daylight at different latitudes. Daylight saving was first introduced in certain countries during the First World War, to decrease the need for artificial light and heat – the system stayed in place after the war, as it proved practical. During the Second World War, some countries went so far as to keep their clocks an hour ahead of standard time continuously, and the UK temporarily introduced 'double summer time', which advanced clocks two hours ahead of standard time during the summer months.

COUNTRIES OF THE WORLD

THERE ARE CURRENTLY 193 independent countries in the world – more than at any previous time – and 59 dependencies. Antarctica is the only land area on Earth that is not officially part of, and does not belong to, any single country.

In 1950, the world comprised 82 countries. In the decades following, many more states came into being as they achieved independence from their former colonial rulers. Most recent additions were caused by the breakup of the former Soviet Union in 1991, and the former Yugoslavia in 1992, which swelled the ranks of independent states. In 2002 East Timor became the latest country to gain independence.

COUNTRY FACTFILE KEY

Formation Date of independence / date current borders were established
Population Total population / population density – based on total *land* area / percentage of urban-based population
Languages An asterisk (*) denotes the official language(s)
Calorie consumption Average number of calories consumed daily per person

AFGHANISTAN
Central Asia

Official name Islamic State of Afghanistan
Formation 1919 / 1919
Capital Kabul
Population 23.9 million / 95 people per sq mile (37 people per sq km) / 22%
Total area 250,000 sq miles (647,500 sq km)
Languages Pashtu*, Dari, Farsi, Tajik, Turkmen, Uzbek,
Religions Sunni Muslim 84%, Shi'a Muslim 15%, other 1%
Ethnic mix Pashtun 38%, Tajik 25%, Hazara 19%, Uzbek and Turkmen 15%, other 3%
Government Transitional regime
Currency New afghani = 100 puls
Literacy rate 36%
Calorie consumption 1,539 calories

ALBANIA
Southeast Europe

Official name Republic of Albania
Formation 1912 / 1921
Capital Tirana
Population 3.2 million / 302 people per sq mile (117 people per sq km) / 42%
Total area 11,100 sq miles (28,748 sq km)
Languages Albanian*, Greek
Religions Sunni Muslim 70%, Orthodox Christian 20%, Roman Catholic 10%
Ethnic mix Albanian 86%, Greek 12%, other 2%
Government Parliamentary system
Currency Lek = 100 qindarka (qintars)
Literacy rate 99%
Calorie consumption 2,900 calories

ALGERIA
North Africa

Official name People's Democratic Republic of Algeria
Formation 1962 / 1962
Capital Algiers
Population 31.8 million / 35 people per sq mile (13 people per sq km) / 60%
Total area 919,590 sq miles (2,381,740 sq km)
Languages Arabic*, French, Tamazight
Religions Sunni Muslim 99%, Christian and Jewish 1%
Ethnic mix Arab 75%, Berber 24%, other 1%
Government Presidential system
Currency Algerian dinar = 100 centimes
Literacy rate 69%
Calorie consumption 2,987 calories

ANDORRA
Southwest Europe

Official name Principality of Andorra
Formation 1278 / 1278
Capital Andorra la Vella
Population 69,150 / 384 people per sq mile (149 people per sq km) / 63%
Total area 181 sq miles (468 sq km)
Languages Catalan*, French, Portuguese, Spanish
Religions Roman Catholic 94%, other 6%
Ethnic mix Spanish 46%, Andorran 28%, French 8%, other 18%
Government Parliamentary system
Currency Euro = 100 cents
Literacy rate 99%
Calorie consumption Not available

ANGOLA
Southern Africa

Official name Republic of Angola
Formation 1975 / 1975
Capital Luanda
Population 13.6 million / 28 people per sq mile (11 people per sq km) / 34%
Total area 481,351 sq miles (1,246,700 sq km)
Languages Portuguese*, Kikongo, Kimbundu, Umbundu
Religions Roman Catholic 50%, Protestant 20%, other 30%
Ethnic mix Ovimbundu 37%, Kimbundu 25%, Bakongo 13%, other 25%
Government Presidential system
Currency Readjusted kwanza = 100 lwei
Literacy rate 40%
Calorie consumption 1,953 calories

ANTIGUA & BARBUDA
West Indies

Official name Antigua and Barbuda
Formation 1981 / 1981
Capital St. John's
Population 67,897 / 399 people per sq mile (154 people per sq km) / 37%
Total area 170 sq miles (442 sq km)
Languages English*, English patois
Religions Anglican 45%, other Protestant 42%, Roman Catholic 10%, Rastafarian 1%, other 2%
Ethnic mix Black African 95%, other 5%
Government Parliamentary system
Currency Eastern Caribbean dollar = 100 cents
Literacy rate 87%
Calorie consumption 2,381 calories

ARGENTINA
South America

Official name Republic of Argentina
Formation 1816 / 1816
Capital Buenos Aires
Population 38.4 million / 36 people per sq mile (14 people per sq km) / 90%
Total area 1,068,296 sq miles (2,766,890 sq km)
Languages Spanish*, Amerindian languages, Italian
Religions Roman Catholic 90%, Protestant 2%, Jewish 2%, other 6%
Ethnic mix Indo-European 83%, Mestizo 14%, Jewish 2%, Amerindian 1%
Government Presidential system
Currency Argentine peso = 100 centavos
Literacy rate 97%
Calorie consumption 3,171 calories

ARMENIA
Southwest Asia

Official name Republic of Armenia
Formation 1991 / 1991
Capital Yerevan
Population 3.1 million / 269 people per sq mile (104 people per sq km) / 70%
Total area 11,506 sq miles (29,800 sq km)
Languages Armenian*, Azeri, Russian
Religions Armenian Apostolic Church 94%, other Christian and Muslim 6%
Ethnic mix Armenian 93%, Azeri 3%, Russian 2%, other 2%
Government Presidential system
Currency Dram = 100 luma
Literacy rate 99%
Calorie consumption 1991 calories

AUSTRALIA
Australasia & Oceania

Official name Commonwealth of Australia
Formation 1901 / 1901
Capital Canberra
Population 19.7 million / 7 people per sq mile (3 people per sq km) / 85%
Total area 2,967,893 sq miles (7,686,850 sq km)
Languages English*, Aboriginal languages, Arabic, Cantonese, Greek, Italian, Vietnamese,
Religions Christian 64%, other 36%
Ethnic mix European 92%, Asian 5%, Aboriginal and other 3%
Government Parliamentary system
Currency Australian dollar = 100 cents
Literacy rate 99%
Calorie consumption 3,126 calories

AUSTRIA
Central Europe

Official name Republic of Austria
Formation 1918 / 1919
Capital Vienna
Population 8.1 million / 254 people per sq mile (98 people per sq km) / 65%
Total area 32,378 sq miles (83,858 sq km)
Languages German*, Croatian, Hungarian (Magyar), Slovenian
Religions Roman Catholic 78%, non-religious 9%, Protestant 5%, other 8%
Ethnic mix Austrian 93%, Croat, Slovene, and Hungarian 6%, other 1%
Government Parliamentary system
Currency Euro = 100 cents
Literacy rate 99%
Calorie consumption 3,799 calories

AZERBAIJAN
Southwest Asia

Official name Republic of Azerbaijan
Formation 1991 / 1991
Capital Baku
Population 8.4 million / 251 people per sq mile (97 people per sq km) / 57%
Total area 33,436 sq miles (86,600 sq km)
Languages Azeri, Russian
Religions Shi'a Muslim 68%, Sunni Muslim 26%, Russian Orthodox 3%, Armenian Apostolic Church (Orthodox) 2%, other 1%
Ethnic mix Azeri 90%, Dagestani 3%, Russian 3% Armenian 2%, other 2%,
Government Presidential system
Currency Manat = 100 gopik
Literacy rate 97%
Calorie consumption 2,474 calories

BAHAMAS
West Indies

Official name Commonwealth of the Bahamas
Formation 1973 / 1973
Capital Nassau
Population 314,000 / 81 people per sq mile (31 people per sq km) / 89%
Total area 5,382 sq miles (13,940 sq km)
Languages English*, English Creole, French Creole
Religions Baptist 32%, Anglican 20%, Roman Catholic 19%, Methodist 6%, Church of God 6%, other 17%
Ethnic mix Black African 85%, other 15%
Government Parliamentary system
Currency Bahamian dollar = 100 cents
Literacy rate 96%
Calorie consumption 2,777 calories

BAHRAIN
Southwest Asia

Official name Kingdom of Bahrain
Formation 1971 / 1971
Capital Manama
Population 724,000 / 2,652 people per sq mile (1025 people per sq km) / 97%
Total area 239 sq miles (620 sq km)
Languages Arabic*
Religions Muslim (mainly Shi'a) 99%, other 1%
Ethnic mix Bahraini 70%, Iranian, Indian, and Pakistani 24%, other Arab 4%, European 2%
Government Monarchy
Currency Bahraini dinar = 1,000 fils
Literacy rate 89%
Calorie consumption Not available

BANGLADESH
South Asia

Official name People's Republic of Bangladesh
Formation 1971 / 1971
Capital Dhaka
Population 147 million / 2,837 people per sq mile (1,096 people per sq km) / 25%
Total area 55,598 sq miles (144,000 sq km)
Languages Bengali*, Chakma, Garo, Khasi, Marma (Magh), Mro, Santhali, Tripuri, Urdu
Religions Muslim (mainly Sunni) 87%, Hindu 12%, other 1%
Ethnic mix Bengali 98%, other 2%
Government Parliamentary system
Currency Taka = 100 poisha
Literacy rate 41%
Calorie consumption 2,187 calories

BARBADOS
West Indies

Official name Barbados
Formation 1966 / 1966
Capital Bridgetown
Population 270,000 / 1,627 people per sq mile (628 people per sq km) / 50%
Total area 166 sq miles (430 sq km)
Languages English*, Bajan (Barbadian English)
Religions Anglican 40%, non-religious 17%, Pentecostal 8%, Methodist 7%, Roman Catholic 4%, other 24%
Ethnic mix Black African 90%, other 10%
Government Parliamentary system
Currency Barbados dollar = 100 cents
Literacy rate 99%
Calorie consumption 2,992 calories

BELARUS
Eastern Europe

Official name Republic of Belarus
Formation 1991 / 1991
Capital Minsk
Population 9.9 million / 124 people per sq mile (48 people per sq km) / 71%
Total area 80,154 sq miles (207,600 sq km)
Languages Belarussian*, Russian
Religions Orthodox Christian 60%, other (including Muslim, Jews and Protestant) 32%, Roman Catholic 8%
Ethnic mix Belarussian 78%, Russian 13%, Polish 4%, Ukrainian 3%, other 2%
Government Presidential system
Currency Belarussian rouble = 100 kopeks
Literacy rate 99%
Calorie consumption 2,925 calories

BELGIUM
Northwest Europe

Official name Kingdom of Belgium
Formation 1830 / 1919
Capital Brussels
Population 10.3 million / 813 people per sq mile (314 people per sq km) / 97%
Total area 11,780 sq miles (30,510 sq km)
Languages Dutch (Flemish)*, French*, German
Religions Roman Catholic 88%, Muslim 2%, other 10%
Ethnic mix Fleming 58%, Walloon 33%, Italian 2%, Moroccan 1%, other 6%
Government Parliamentary system
Currency Euro = 100 cents
Literacy rate 99%
Calorie consumption 3,682 calories

BELIZE
Central America

Official name Belize
Formation 1981 / 1981
Capital Belmopan
Population 256,000 / 29 people per sq mile (11 people per sq km) / 54%
Total area 8,867 sq miles (22,966 sq km)
Languages English*, English Creole, Garifuna (Carib), Mayan, Spanish
Religions Roman Catholic 62%, Anglican 12%, Methodist 6%, Mennonite 4%, other 16%
Ethnic mix Mestizo 44%, Creole 30%, Maya 11%, Garifuna 7%, Asian Indian 4%, other 4%
Government Parliamentary system
Currency Belizean dollar = 100 cents
Literacy rate 77%
Calorie consumption 2,886 calories

BENIN
West Africa

Official name Republic of Benin
Formation 1960 / 1960
Capital Porto-Novo
Population 6.7 million / 157 people per sq mile (61 people per sq km) / 42%
Total area 43,483 sq miles (112,620 sq km)
Languages French*, Adja, Bariba, Fon, Houeda, Somba, Yoruba
Religions Voodoo 50%, Muslim 30%, Christian 20%
Ethnic mix Fon 47%, Adja 12%, Bariba 10%, other 31%
Government Presidential system
Currency CFA franc = 100 centimes
Literacy rate 40%
Calorie consumption 2,455 calories

BHUTAN
South Asia

Official name Kingdom of Bhutan
Formation 1656 / 1865
Capital Thimphu
Population 2.3 million / 127 people per sq mile (49 people per sq km) / 7%
Total area 18,147 sq miles (47,000 sq km)
Languages Dzongkha*, Nepali, Assamese
Religions Mahayana Buddhist 70%, Hindu 24%, other 6%
Ethnic mix Bhute 50%, Nepalese 25%, other 25%
Government Monarchy
Currency Ngultrum = 100 chetrum
Literacy rate 47%
Calorie consumption Not available

BOLIVIA
South America

Official name Republic of Bolivia
Formation 1825 / 1938
Capital La Paz (administrative) / Sucre (judicial)
Population 8.8 million / 21 people per sq mile (8 people per sq km) / 63%
Total area 424,162 sq miles (1,098,580 sq km)
Languages Aymara*, Quechua*, Spanish*
Religions Roman Catholic 93%, other 7%
Ethnic mix Quechua 37%, Aymara 32%, mixed race 13%, European 10%, other 8%
Government Presidential system
Currency Boliviano = 100 centavos
Literacy rate 87%
Calorie consumption 2,267 calories

BOSNIA & HERZEGOVINA
Southeast Europe

Official name Bosnia and Herzegovina
Formation 1992 / 1992
Capital Sarajevo
Population 4.2 million / 213 people per sq mile (82 people per sq km) / 43%
Total area 19,741 sq miles (51,129 sq km)
Languages Serbo-Croat*
Religions Muslim (mainly Sunni) 40%, Orthodox Christian 31%, Roman Catholic 15%, Protestant 4%, other 10%
Ethnic mix Bosniak 48%, Serb 38%, Croat 14%
Government Parliamentary system
Currency Marka = 100 pfeninga
Literacy rate 95%
Calorie consumption 2,845 calories

BOTSWANA
Southern Africa

Official name Republic of Botswana
Formation 1966 / 1966
Capital Gaborone
Population 1.8 million / 8 people per sq mile (3 people per sq km) / 50%
Total area 231,803 sq miles (600,370 sq km)
Languages English*, isiNdebele, Khoikhoi, San, Setswana, Shona
Religions Traditional beliefs 50%, Christian (mainly Protestant) 30%, other (including Muslim) 20%
Ethnic mix Tswana 98%, other 2%
Government Presidential system
Currency Pula = 100 thebe
Literacy rate 79%
Calorie consumption 2,292 calories

BRAZIL
South America

Official name Federative Republic of Brazil
Formation 1822 / 1828
Capital Brasília
Population 179 million / 55 people per sq mile (21 people per sq km) / 81%
Total area 3,286,470 sq miles (8,511,965 sq km)
Languages Portuguese*, Amerindian languages, German, Italian, Japanese, Polish, Spanish
Religions Roman Catholic 74%, Protestant 15%, Atheist 7%, other 4%
Ethnic mix Black 53%, mixed race 40%, White 6%, other 1%
Government Presidential system
Currency Real = 100 centavos
Literacy rate 86%
Calorie consumption 3,002 calories

BRUNEI
Southeast Asia

Official name Sultanate of Brunei
Formation 1984 / 1984
Capital Bandar Seri Begawan
Population 358,000 / 176 people per sq mile (68 people per sq km) / 72%
Total area 2,228 sq miles (5,770 sq km)
Languages Malay*, Chinese, English
Religions Muslim (mainly Sunni) 66%, Buddhist 14%, Christian 10%, other 10%
Ethnic mix Malay 67%, Chinese 16%, Indigenous 6%, other 11%
Government Monarchy
Currency Brunei dollar = 100 cents
Literacy rate 94%
Calorie consumption 2,814 calories

BULGARIA
Southeast Europe

Official name Republic of Bulgaria
Formation 1908 / 1947
Capital Sofia
Population 7.9 million / 185 people per sq mile (71 people per sq km) / 70%
Total area 42,822 sq miles (110,910 sq km)
Languages Bulgarian*, Romani, Turkish
Religions Orthodox Christian 83%, Muslim 12%, Roman Catholic 1%, other 4%
Ethnic mix Bulgarian 84%, Turkish 9%, Roma 5%, other 2%
Government Parliamentary system
Currency Lev = 100 stotinki
Literacy rate 99%
Calorie consumption 2,626 calories

BURKINA
West Africa

Official name Burkina Faso
Formation 1960 / 1960
Capital Ouagadougou
Population 13 million / 123 people per sq mile (47 people per sq km) / 19%
Total area 105,869 sq miles (274,200 sq km)
Languages French*, Dyula, Fulani, Mossi, Songhai, Tuareg
Religions Muslim 55%, Traditional beliefs 35%, Roman Catholic 9%, other Christian 1%
Ethnic mix Mossi 50%, other 50%
Government Presidential system
Currency CFA franc = 100 centimes
Literacy rate 25%
Calorie consumption 2,485 calories

BURUNDI
Central Africa

Official name Republic of Burundi
Formation 1962 / 1962
Capital Bujumbura
Population 6.8 million / 687 people per sq mile (265 people per sq km) / 9%
Total area 10,745 sq miles (27,830 sq km)
Languages French*, Kirundi*, Kiswahili
Religions Christian (mainly Roman Catholic) 60%, Traditional beliefs 39%, Muslim 1%
Ethnic mix Hutu 85%, Tutsi 14%, Twa 1%
Government Transitional regime
Currency Burundi franc = 100 centimes
Literacy rate 50%
Calorie consumption 1,612 calories

CAMBODIA
Southeast Asia

Official name Kingdom of Cambodia
Formation 1953 / 1953
Capital Phnom Penh
Population 14.1 million / 207 people per sq mile (80 people per sq km) / 16%
Total area 69,900 sq miles (181,040 sq km)
Languages Khmer*, Cham, Chinese, French, Vietnamese
Religions Buddhist 93%, Muslim 6%, Christian 1%
Ethnic mix Khmer 90%, Vietnamese 4%, Chinese 1%, other 5%
Government Parliamentary system
Currency Riel = 100 sen
Literacy rate 69%
Calorie consumption 1,967 calories

CAMEROON
Central Africa

Official name Republic of Cameroon
Formation 1960 / 1961
Capital Yaoundé
Population 16 million / 89 people per sq mile (34 people per sq km) / 49%
Total area 183,567 sq miles (475,400 sq km)
Languages English*, French*, Bamileke, Fang, Fulani
Religions Roman Catholic 35%, Traditional beliefs 25%, Muslim 22%, Protestant 18%
Ethnic mix Cameroon highlanders 31%, Equatorial Bantu 19%, Kirdi 11%, other 39%
Government Presidential system
Currency CFA franc = 100 centimes
Literacy rate 68%
Calorie consumption 2,242 calories

CANADA
North America

Official name Canada
Formation 1867 / 1949
Capital Ottawa
Population 31.5 million / 9 people per sq mile (3 people per sq km) / 77%
Total area 3,717,792 sq miles (9,984,670 sq km)
Languages English*, French*, Chinese, Cree, German, Inuktitut, Italian, Portuguese, Ukrainian
Religions Roman Catholic 44%, Protestant 29%, other and non-religious 27%
Ethnic mix British origin 44%, French origin 25%, other European 20%, other 11%
Government Parliamentary system
Currency Canadian dollar = 100 cents
Literacy rate 99%
Calorie consumption 3,176 calories

CAPE VERDE
Atlantic Ocean

Official name Republic of Cape Verde
Formation 1975 / 1975
Capital Praia
Population 463,000 / 298 people per sq mile (115 people per sq km) / 62%
Total area 1,557 sq miles (4,033 sq km)
Languages Portuguese*, Portuguese Creole
Religions Roman Catholic 97%, Protestant (Church of the Nazarene) 1%, other 2%
Ethnic mix Mestiço 60%, African 30%, other 10%
Government Mixed presidential–parliamentary system
Currency Cape Verde escudo = 100 centavos
Literacy rate 76%
Calorie consumption 3,308 calories

CENTRAL AFRICAN REPUBLIC
Central Africa

Official name Central African Republic
Formation 1960 / 1960
Capital Bangui
Population 3.9 million / 16 people per sq mile (6 people per sq km) / 41%
Total area 240,534 sq miles (622,984 sq km)
Languages French*, Banda, Gbaya, Sango
Religions Traditional beliefs 60%, Christian (mainly Roman Catholic) 35%, Muslim 5%
Ethnic mix Baya 34%, Banda 27%, Mandjia 21%, Sara 10%, other 8%
Government Transitional regime
Currency CFA franc = 100 centimes
Literacy rate 49%
Calorie consumption 1,949 calories

CHAD
Central Africa

Official name Republic of Chad
Formation 1960 / 1960
Capital N'Djamena
Population 8.6 million / 18 people per sq mile (7 people per sq km) / 24%
Total area 495,752 sq miles (1,284,000 sq km)
Languages Arabic*, French*, Maba, Sara
Religions Muslim 55%, Traditional beliefs 35%, Christian 10%
Ethnic mix Nomads (Tuareg and Toubou) 38%, Sara 30%, Arab 15%, other 17%
Government Presidential system
Currency CFA franc = 100 centimes
Literacy rate 46%
Calorie consumption 2,245 calories

CHILE
South America

Official name Republic of Chile
Formation 1818 / 1883
Capital Santiago
Population 15.8 million / 55 people per sq mile (21 people per sq km) / 86%
Total area 292,258 sq miles (756,950 sq km)
Languages Spanish*, Amerindian languages
Religions Roman Catholic 80%, other and non-religious 20%
Ethnic mix Mixed race and European 90%, Amerindian 10%
Government Presidential system
Currency Chilean peso = 100 centavos
Literacy rate 96%
Calorie consumption 2,868 calories

CHINA
East Asia

Official name People's Republic of China
Formation 960 / 1999
Capital Beijing
Population 1.3 billion / 362 people per sq mile (140 people per sq km) / 32%
Total area 3,705,386 sq miles (9,596,960 sq km)
Languages Mandarin*, Cantonese, Hakka, Hsiang, Kan, Min, Wu
Religions Non-religious 59%, Traditional beliefs 20%, Buddhist 6%, Muslim 2%, other 13%
Ethnic mix Han 92%, Zhuang 1%, Hui 1%, other 6%
Government One-party state
Currency Renminbi (Yuan) = 10 jiao
Literacy rate 91%
Calorie consumption 2,963 calories

COLOMBIA
South America

Official name Republic of Colombia
Formation 1819 / 1903
Capital Bogotá
Population 44.2 million / 110 people per sq mile (43 people per sq km) / 74%
Total area 439,733 sq miles (1,138,910 sq km)
Languages Spanish*, Wayuu, Páez, and other Amerindian languages
Religions Roman Catholic 95%, other 5%
Ethnic mix Mestizo 58%, White 20%, European–African 14%, African 4%, African–Amerindian 3%, Amerindian 1%
Government Presidential system
Currency Colombian peso = 100 centavos
Literacy rate 92%
Calorie consumption 2,580 calories

COMOROS
Indian Ocean

Official name Union of the Comoros
Formation 1975 / 1975
Capital Moroni
Population 768,000 / 892 people per sq mile (344 people per sq km) / 33%
Total area 838 sq miles (2,170 sq km)
Languages Arabic*, French*, Comoran
Religions Muslim (mainly Sunni) 98%, Roman Catholic 1%, other 1%
Ethnic mix Comoran 97%, other 3%
Government Presidential system
Currency Comoros franc = 100 centimes
Literacy rate 56%
Calorie consumption 1,735 calories

CONGO
Central Africa

Official name Republic of the Congo
Formation 1960 / 1960
Capital Brazzaville
Population 3.7 million / 28 people per sq mile (11 people per sq km) / 63%
Total area 132,046 sq miles (342,000 sq km)
Languages French*, Kongo, Lingala, Teke
Religions Traditional beliefs 50%, Roman Catholic 25%, Protestant 23%, Muslim 2%
Ethnic mix Bakongo 48%, Sangha 20%, Teke 17%, Mbochi 12%, other 3%
Government Presidential system
Currency CFA franc = 100 centimes
Literacy rate 83%
Calorie consumption 2,221 calories

CONGO, DEM. REP.
Central Africa

Official name Democratic Republic of the Congo
Formation 1960/ 1960
Capital Kinshasa
Population 52.8 million / 60 people per sq mile (23 people per sq km) / 30%
Total area 905,563 sq miles (2,345,410 sq km)
Languages French*, Kiswahili, Tshiluba, Kikongo, Lingala
Religions Roman Catholic 50%, Protestant 20%, Traditional beliefs and other 10%, Muslim 10%, Kimbanguist 10%
Ethnic mix Bantu and Hamitic 45%, other 55%
Government Transitional regime
Currency Congolese franc = 100 centimes
Literacy rate 63%
Calorie consumption 1,535 calories

COSTA RICA
Central America

Official name Republic of Costa Rica
Formation 1838 / 1838
Capital San José
Population 4.2 million / 213 people per sq mile (82 people per sq km) / 52%
Total area 19,730 sq miles (51,100 sq km)
Languages Spanish*, Bribri, Cabecar, English Creole
Religions Roman Catholic 76%, other (including Protestant) 24%
Ethnic mix Mestizo and European 96%, Black 2%, Chinese 1%, Amerindian 1%
Government Presidential system
Currency Costa Rican colón = 100 centimos
Literacy rate 96%
Calorie consumption 2,761 calories

CROATIA
Southeast Europe

Official name Republic of Croatia
Formation 1991 / 1991
Capital Zagreb
Population 4.4 million / 202 people per sq mile (78 people per sq km) / 58%
Total area 21,831 sq miles (56,542 sq km)
Languages Croatian*
Religions Roman Catholic 88%, Orthodox Christian 4%, Muslim 1%, other 7%
Ethnic mix Croat 90%, Serb 4%, Bosniak 1%, other 5%
Government Parliamentary system
Currency Kuna = 100 lipas
Literacy rate 98%
Calorie consumption 2,678 calories

CUBA
West Indies

Official name Republic of Cuba
Formation 1902 / 1902
Capital Havana
Population 11.3 million / 264 people per sq mile (102 people per sq km) / 75%
Total area 42,803 sq miles (110,860 sq km)
Languages Spanish*
Religions non-religious 49%, Roman Catholic 40%, Atheist 6%, Protestant 1%, other 4%
Ethnic mix White 66%, European–African 22%, Black 12%
Government One-party state
Currency Cuban peso = 100 centavos
Literacy rate 97%
Calorie consumption 2,643 calories

CYPRUS
Southeast Europe

Official name Republic of Cyprus
Formation 1960 / 1960
Capital Nicosia
Population 802,000 / 225 people per sq mile (87 people per sq km) / 57%
Total area 3,571 sq miles (9,250 sq km)
Languages Greek, Turkish
Religions Orthodox Christian 78%, Muslim 18%, other 4%
Ethnic mix Greek 85%, Turkish 12%, other 3%
Government Presidential system
Currency Cyprus pound (Turkish lira in TRNC) = 100 cents (Cyprus pound); 100 kurus (Turkish lira)
Literacy rate 97%
Calorie consumption 3,302 calories

CZECH REPUBLIC
Central Europe

Official name Czech Republic
Formation 1993 / 1993
Capital Prague
Population 10.2 million / 335 people per sq mile (129 people per sq km) / 75%
Total area 30,450 sq miles (78,866 sq km)
Languages Czech*, Hungarian (Magyar), Slovak,
Religions Roman Catholic 39%, Atheist 38%, Protestant 3%, Hussite 2%, other 18%
Ethnic mix Czech 81%, Moravian 13%, Slovak 6%
Government Parliamentary system
Currency Czech koruna = 100 haleru
Literacy rate 99%
Calorie consumption 3,097 calories

DENMARK
Northern Europe

Official name Kingdom of Denmark
Formation 950 / 1944
Capital Copenhagen
Population 5.4 million / 330 people per sq mile (127 people per sq km) / 85%
Total area 16,639 sq miles (43,094 sq km)
Languages Danish*
Religions Evangelical Lutheran 89%, Roman Catholic 1%, other 10%
Ethnic mix Danish 96%, Faeroese and Inuit 1%, other (including Scandinavian and Turkish) 3%
Government Parliamentary system
Currency Danish krone = 100 øre
Literacy rate 99%
Calorie consumption 3,454 calories

DJIBOUTI
East Africa

Official name Republic of Djibouti
Formation 1977 / 1977
Capital Djibouti
Population 703,000 / 79 people per sq mile (30 people per sq km) / 83%
Total area 8,494 sq miles (22,000 sq km)
Languages Arabic*, French*, Afar, Somali
Religions Muslim (mainly Sunni) 94%, Christian 6%
Ethnic mix Issa 60%, Afar 35%, other 5%
Government Presidential system
Currency Djibouti franc = 100 centimes
Literacy rate 66%
Calorie consumption 2,218 calories

DOMINICA
West Indies

Official name Commonwealth of Dominica
Formation 1978 / 1978
Capital Roseau
Population 69,655 / 240 people per sq mile (93 people per sq km) / 71%
Total area 291 sq miles (754 sq km)
Languages English*, French Creole
Religions Roman Catholic 77%, Protestant 15%, other 8%
Ethnic mix Black 91%, mixed race 6%, Carib 2%, other 1%
Government Parliamentary system
Currency Eastern Caribbean dollar = 100 cents
Literacy rate 76%
Calorie consumption 2,995 calories

DOMINICAN REPUBLIC
West Indies

Official name Dominican Republic
Formation 1865 / 1865
Capital Santo Domingo
Population 8.7 million / 466 people per sq mile (180 people per sq km) / 65%
Total area 18,679 sq miles (48,380 sq km)
Languages Spanish*, French Creole
Religions Roman Catholic 92%, other and non-religious 8%
Ethnic mix Mixed race 75%, White 15%, Black 10%
Government Presidential system
Currency Dominican Republic peso = 100 centavos
Literacy rate 84%
Calorie consumption 2,333 calories

EAST TIMOR
Southeast Asia

Official name Democratic Republic of Timor-Leste
Formation 2002 / 2002
Capital Dili
Population 778,000 / 138 people per sq mile (53 people per sq km) / 8%
Total area 5,756 sq miles (14,874 sq km)
Languages Portuguese*, Tetum (Portuguese/Austronesian)*, Bahasa Indonesia
Religions Roman Catholic 95%, other 5%
Ethnic mix Papuan groups 85%, Indonesian 13%, Chinese 2%
Government Parliamentary system
Currency US dollar = 100 cents
Literacy rate 59%
Calorie consumption Not available

ECUADOR
South America

Official name Republic of Ecuador
Formation 1830 / 1941
Capital Quito
Population 13 million / 122 people per sq mile (47 people per sq km) / 65%
Total area 109,483 sq miles (283,560 sq km)
Languages Quechua*, Spanish*, other Amerindian languages
Religions Roman Catholic 93%, Protestant, Jewish, and other 7%
Ethnic mix Mestizo 55%, Amerindian 25%, Black 10%, White 10%
Government Presidential system
Currency US dollar = 100 cents
Literacy rate 91%
Calorie consumption 2,792 calories

EGYPT
North Africa

Official name Arab Republic of Egypt
Formation 1936 / 1982
Capital Cairo
Population 71.9 million / 187 people per sq mile (72 people per sq km) / 45%
Total area 386,660 sq miles (1,001,450 sq km)
Languages Arabic*, Berber, English, French
Religions Muslim (mainly Sunni) 94%, Coptic Christian and other 6%
Ethnic mix Eastern Hamitic 90%, Nubian, Armenian, and Greek 10%
Government Presidential system
Currency Egyptian pound = 100 piastres
Literacy rate 56%
Calorie consumption 3,385 calories

EL SALVADOR
Central America

Official name Republic of El Salvador
Formation 1841 / 1841
Capital San Salvador
Population 6.5 million / 812 people per sq mile (314 people per sq km) / 47%
Total area 8,124 sq miles (21,040 sq km)
Languages Spanish*
Religions Roman Catholic 80%, Evangelical 18%, other 2%
Ethnic mix Mestizo 94%, Amerindian 5%, White 1%
Government Presidential system
Currency Salvadorean colón & US dollar = 100 centavos (colón); 100 cents (US dollar)
Literacy rate 80%
Calorie consumption 2,512 calories

EQUATORIAL GUINEA
Central Africa

Official name Republic of Equatorial Guinea
Formation 1968 / 1968
Capital Malabo
Population 494,000 / 46 people per sq mile (18 people per sq km) / 48%
Total area 10,830 sq miles (28,051 sq km)
Languages Spanish*, Bubi, Fang
Religions Roman Catholic 90%, other 10%
Ethnic mix Fang 85%, Bubi 4%, other 11%
Government Presidential system
Currency CFA franc = 100 centimes
Literacy rate 84%
Calorie consumption Not available

ERITREA
East Africa

Official name State of Eritrea
Formation 1993 / 2002
Capital Asmara
Population 4.1 million / 90 people per sq mile (35 people per sq km) / 19%
Total area 46,842 sq miles (121,320 sq km)
Languages Arabic*, Tigrinya*, Afar, Bilen,English, Hadareb, Kunama, Nara, Saho, Tigre
Religions Christian 45%, Muslim 45%, other 10%
Ethnic mix Tigray 50%, Tigray and Kunama 40%, Afar 4%, Saho 3%, other 3%
Government Transitional regime
Currency Nakfa = 100 cents
Literacy rate 57%
Calorie consumption 1,690 calories

Estonia
Northeast Europe

Official name Republic of Estonia
Formation 1991 / 1991
Capital Tallinn
Population 1.3 million / 75 people per sq mile (29 people per sq km) / 69%
Total area 17,462 sq miles (45,226 sq km)
Languages Estonian*, Russian
Religions Evangelical Lutheran 56%, Orthodox Christian 25%, other 19%
Ethnic mix Estonian 62%, Russian 30%, other 8%
Government Parliamentary system
Currency Kroon = 100 senti
Literacy rate 99%
Calorie consumption 3,048 calories

Ethiopia
East Africa

Official name Federal Democratic Republic of Ethiopia
Formation 1896 / 2002
Capital Addis Ababa
Population 70.7 million / 165 people per sq mile (64 people per sq km) / 18%
Total area 435,184 sq miles (1,127,127 sq km)
Languages Amharic*, Tigrinya, Galla
Religions Muslim 40%, Orthodox Christian 40%, Traditional beliefs 15%, other 5%
Ethnic mix Oromo 40%, Amhara 25%, Sidamo 9%, Berta 6%, Somali 6%, other 14%
Government Parliamentary system
Currency Ethiopian birr = 100 cents
Literacy rate 42%
Calorie consumption 2,037 calories

Fiji
Australasia & Oceania

Official name Republic of the Fiji Islands
Formation 1970 / 1970
Capital Suva
Population 839,000 / 119 people per sq mile (46 people per sq km) / 49%
Total area 7,054 sq miles (18,270 sq km)
Languages English*, Fijian*, Hindi, Tamil, Telugu, Urdu
Religions Hindu 38%, Methodist 37%, Roman Catholic 9%, Muslim 8%, other 8%
Ethnic mix Melanesian 48%, Indian 46%, other 6%
Government Parliamentary system
Currency Fiji dollar = 100 cents
Literacy rate 93%
Calorie consumption 2,789 calories

Finland
Northern Europe

Official name Republic of Finland
Formation 1917 / 1947
Capital Helsinki
Population 5.2 million / 44 people per sq mile (17 people per sq km) / 67%
Total area 130,127 sq miles (337,030 sq km)
Languages Finnish*, Swedish*, Sámi
Religions Evangelical Lutheran 89%, Orthodox Christian 1%, Roman Catholic 1%, other 9%
Ethnic mix Finnish 93%, other (including Sámi) 7%
Government Parliamentary system
Currency Euro = 100 cents
Literacy rate 99%
Calorie consumption 3,202 calories

France
Western Europe

Official name French Republic
Formation 987 / 1919
Capital Paris
Population 60.1 million / 283 people per sq mile (109 people per sq km) / 76%
Total area 211,208 sq miles (547,030 sq km)
Languages French*, Basque, Breton, Catalan, German, Provençal
Religions Roman Catholic 88%, Muslim 8%, Protestant 2%, Jewish 1%, Buddhist 1%
Ethnic mix French 90%, North African 6%, German 2%, other 2%
Government Presidential–parliamentary system
Currency Euro = 100 cents
Literacy rate 99%
Calorie consumption 3,629 calories

Gabon
Central Africa

Official name Gabonese Republic
Formation 1960 / 1960
Capital Libreville
Population 1.3 million / 13 people per sq mile (5 people per sq km) / 81%
Total area 103,346 sq miles (267,667 sq km)
Languages French*, Fang, Mpongwe, Nzebi, Punu, Sira,
Religions Christian 55%, Traditional beliefs 40%, Muslim 1%, other 4%
Ethnic mix Fang 35%, other Bantu 29%, Eshira 25%, European and other African 9%, French 2%
Government Presidential system
Currency CFA franc = 100 centimes
Literacy rate 71%
Calorie consumption 2,602 calories

Gambia
West Africa

Official name Republic of the Gambia
Formation 1965 / 1965
Capital Banjul
Population 1.4 million / 363 people per sq mile (140 people per sq km) / 33%
Total area 4,363 sq, miles (11,300 sq km)
Languages English*, Fulani, Jola, Mandinka, Soninke, Wolof
Religions Sunni Muslim 90%, Christian 9%, Traditional beliefs 1%
Ethnic mix Mandinka 42%, Fulani 18%, Wolof 16%, Jola 10%, Serahuli 9%, other 5%
Government Presidential system
Currency Dalasi = 100 butut
Literacy rate 38%
Calorie consumption 2,300 calories

Georgia
Southwest Asia

Official name Georgia
Formation 1991 / 1991
Capital Tbilisi
Population 5.1 million / 190 people per sq mile (73 people per sq km) / 61%
Total area 26,911 sq miles (69,700 sq km)
Languages Georgian*, Russian
Religions Georgian Orthodox 65%, Muslim 11%, Russian Orthodox 10%, Armenian Orthodox 8%, other 6%
Ethnic mix Georgian 70%, Armenian 8%, Russian 6%, Azeri 6%, Ossetian 3%, other 7%
Government Presidential system
Currency Lari = 100 tetri
Literacy rate 99%
Calorie consumption 2,247 calories

Germany
Northern Europe

Official name Federal Republic of Germany
Formation 1871 / 1990
Capital Berlin
Population 82.5 million / 611 people per sq mile (236 people per sq km) /88%
Total area 137,846 sq miles (357,021 sq km)
Languages German*, Turkish
Religions Protestant 34%, Roman Catholic 33%, Muslim 3%, other 30%
Ethnic mix German 92%, other European 3%, Turkish 2%, other 3%
Government Parliamentary system
Currency Euro = 100 cents
Literacy rate 99%
Calorie consumption 3,567 calories

Ghana
West Africa

Official name Republic of Ghana
Formation 1957 / 1957
Capital Accra
Population 20.9 million / 235 people per sq mile (91 people per sq km) / 38%
Total area 92,100 sq miles (238,540 sq km)
Languages English*, Adangbe, Dagomba (Dagbani), Ewe, Fanti, Ga, Gurma, Twi
Religions Christian 69%, Muslim 16%, Traditional beliefs 9%, other 6%
Ethnic mix Ashanti and Fanti 52%, Moshi-Dagomba 16%, Ewe 12%, Ga 8%, other 12%
Government Presidential system
Currency Cedi = 100 psewas
Literacy rate 74%
Calorie consumption 2,670 calories

Greece
Southeast Europe

Official name Hellenic Republic
Formation 1829 / 1947
Capital Athens
Population 11 million / 218 people per sq mile (84 people per sq km) / 60%
Total area 50,942 sq miles (131,940 sq km)
Languages Greek*, Albanian, Macedonian, Turkish
Religions Orthodox Christian 98%, Muslim 1%, other 1%
Ethnic mix Greek 98%, other 2%
Government Parliamentary system
Currency Euro = 100 cents
Literacy rate 97%
Calorie consumption 3,754 calories

Grenada
West Indies

Official name Grenada
Formation 1974 / 1974
Capital St. George's
Population 89,258 / 681 people per sq mile (263 people per sq km) / 38%
Total area 131 sq miles (340 sq km)
Languages English*, English Creole
Religions Roman Catholic 68%, Anglican 17%, other 15%
Ethnic mix Black African 82%, Mulatto (mixed race) 13%, East Indian 3%, other 2%
Government Parliamentary system
Currency Eastern Caribbean dollar = 100 cents
Literacy rate 94%
Calorie consumption 2,749 calories

Guatemala
Central America

Official name Republic of Guatemala
Formation 1838 / 1838
Capital Guatemala City
Population 12.3 million / 294 people per sq mile (113 people per sq km) / 40%
Total area 42,042 sq miles (108,890 sq km)
Languages Spanish*, Cakchiquel, Kekchí, Mam, Quiché,
Religions Roman Catholic 65%, Protestant 33%, other and non-religious 2%
Ethnic mix Amerindian 60%, Mestizo 30%, other 10%
Government Presidential system
Currency Quetzal = 100 centavos
Literacy rate 70%
Calorie consumption 2,203 calories

Guinea
West Africa

Official name Republic of Guinea
Formation 1958 / 1958
Capital Conakry
Population 8.5 million / 90 people per sq mile (35 people per sq km) / 33%
Total area 94,925 sq miles (245,857 sq km)
Languages French*, Fulani, Malinke, Soussou
Religions Muslim 65%, Traditional beliefs 33%, Christian 2%
Ethnic mix Fulani 30%, Malinke 30%, Soussou 15%, Kissi 10%, other tribes 10%, other 5%
Government Presidential system
Currency Guinea franc = 100 centimes
Literacy rate 41%
Calorie consumption 2,362 calories

Guinea-Bissau
West Africa

Official name Republic of Guinea-Bissau
Formation 1974 / 1974
Capital Bissau
Population 1.5 million / 138 people per sq mile (53 people per sq km) / 24%
Total area 13,946 sq miles (36,120 sq km)
Languages Portuguese*, Balante, Fulani, Malinke, Portuguese Creole,
Religions Traditional beliefs 52%, Muslim 40%, Christian 8%
Ethnic mix Other tribes 31%, Balante 25%, Fula 20%, Mandinka 12%, Mandyako 11%, other 1%
Government Transitional regime
Currency CFA franc = 100 centimes
Literacy rate 40%
Calorie consumption 2,481 calories

Guyana
South America

Official name Cooperative Republic of Guyana
Formation 1966 / 1966
Capital Georgetown
Population 765,000 / 10 people per sq mile (4 people per sq km) / 38%
Total area 83,000 sq miles (214,970 sq km)
Languages English*, Amerindian languages, English Creole, Hindi, Tamil
Religions Christian 57%, Hindu 33%, Muslim 9%, other 1%
Ethnic mix East Indian 52%, Black African 38%, other 10%
Government Presidential system
Currency Guyana dollar = 100 cents
Literacy rate 97%
Calorie consumption 2,515 calories

Haiti
West Indies

Official name Republic of Haiti
Formation 1804 / 1844
Capital Port-au-Prince
Population 8.3 million / 780 people per sq mile (301 people per sq km) / 36%
Total area 10,714 sq miles (27,750 sq km)
Languages French*, French Creole*
Religions Roman Catholic 80%, Protestant 16%, non-religious 1%, other (including Voodoo) 3%
Ethnic mix Black African 95%, Mulatto (mixed race) and European 5%
Government Transitional regime
Currency Gourde = 100 centimes
Literacy rate 52%
Calorie consumption 2,045 calories

Honduras
Central America

Official name Republic of Honduras
Formation 1838 / 1838
Capital Tegucigalpa
Population 6.9 million / 160 people per sq mile (62 people per sq km) / 53%
Total area 43,278 sq miles (112,090 sq km)
Languages Spanish*, English Creole, Garífuna (Carib)
Religions Roman Catholic 97%, Protestant 3%
Ethnic mix Mestizo 90%, Black African 5%, Amerindian 4%, White 1%
Government Presidential system
Currency Lempira = 100 centavos
Literacy rate 80%
Calorie consumption 2,406 calories

Hungary
Central Europe

Official name Republic of Hungary
Formation 1918 / 1947
Capital Budapest
Population 9.9 million / 278 people per sq mile (107 people per sq km) / 64%
Total area 35,919 sq miles (93,030 sq km)
Languages Hungarian (Magyar)*
Religions Roman Catholic 52%, Calvinist 16%, non-religious 14%, Lutheran 3%, other 15%
Ethnic mix Magyar 90%, Roma 2%, German 1%, other 7%
Government Parliamentary system
Currency Forint = 100 fillér
Literacy rate 99%
Calorie consumption 3,520 calories

Iceland
Northwest Europe

Official name Republic of Iceland
Formation 1944 / 1944
Capital Reykjavík
Population 290,000 / 7 people per sq mile (3 people per sq km) / 93%
Total area 39,768 sq miles (103,000 sq km)
Languages Icelandic*
Religions Evangelical Lutheran 93%, non-religious 6%, other (mostly Christian) 1%
Ethnic mix Icelandic 94%, Danish 1%, other 5%
Government Parliamentary system
Currency Icelandic króna = 100 aurar
Literacy rate 99%
Calorie consumption 3,231 calories

India
South Asia

Official name Republic of India
Formation 1947 / 1947
Capital New Delhi
Population 1.07 billion / 928 people per sq mile (358 people per sq km) / 28%
Total area 1,269,338 sq miles (3,287,590 sq km)
Languages English*, Hindi*, Bengali, Bihari, Gujarati, Kanarese, Marathi, Tamil, Telugu, Urdu,
Religions Hindu 83%, Muslim 11%, Christian 2%, Sikh 2%, Buddhist 1%, other 1%
Ethnic mix Indo-Aryan 72%, Dravidian 25%, Mongoloid and other 3%
Government Parliamentary system
Currency Indian rupee = 100 paise
Literacy rate 61%
Calorie consumption 2,487 calories

Indonesia
Southeast Asia

Official name Republic of Indonesia
Formation 1949 / 1999
Capital Jakarta
Population 220 million / 317 people per sq mile (122 people per sq km) / 41%
Total area 741,096 sq miles (1,919,440 sq km)
Languages Bahasa Indonesia*, Dutch, Javanese, Madurese, Sundanese
Religions Sunni Muslim 87%, Protestant 6%, Roman Catholic 3%, Hindu 2%, Buddhist 1%, other 1%
Ethnic mix Javanese 45%, Sundanese 14%, Coastal Malays 8%, Madurese 8%, other 25%
Government Presidential system
Currency Rupiah = 100 sen
Literacy rate 88%
Calorie consumption 2,904 calories

Iran
Southwest Asia

Official name Islamic Republic of Iran
Formation 1502 / 1990
Capital Tehran
Population 68.9 million / 109 people per sq mile (42 people per sq km) / 62%
Total area 636,293 sq miles (1,648,000 sq km)
Languages Farsi*, Arabic, Azeri, Baluchi, Gilaki, Kurdish, Luri, Mazanderani, Turkmen
Religions Shi'a Muslim 93%, Sunni Muslim 6%, other 1%
Ethnic mix Persian 50%, Azari 24%, Kurdish 8%, Lur and Bakhtiari 8%, other 10%
Government Islamic theocracy
Currency Iranian rial = 100 dinars
Literacy rate 77%
Calorie consumption 2,931 calories

Iraq
Southwest Asia

Official name Republic of Iraq
Formation 1932 / 1990
Capital Baghdad
Population 25.2 million / 149 people per sq mile (58 people per sq km) / 77%
Total area 168,753 sq miles (437,072 sq km)
Languages Arabic*, Armenian, Assyrian, Kurdish, Turkic languages
Religions Shi'a Muslim 62%, Sunni Muslim 33%, other (including Christian) 5%
Ethnic mix Arab 79%, Kurdish 16%, Persian 3%, Turkmen 2%
Government Transitional regime
Currency New Iraqi dinar = 1,000 fils
Literacy rate 40%
Calorie consumption 2,197 calories

Ireland
Northwest Europe

Official name Ireland
Formation 1922 / 1922
Capital Dublin
Population 4 million / 150 people per sq mile (58 people per sq km) / 59%
Total area 27,135 sq miles (70,280 sq km)
Languages English*, Irish Gaelic*
Religions Roman Catholic 88%, Anglican 3%, other and non-religious 9%
Ethnic mix Irish 93%, British 3%, other 4%
Government Parliamentary system
Currency Euro = 100 cents
Literacy rate 99%
Calorie consumption 3,666 calories

Israel
Southwest Asia

Official name State of Israel
Formation 1948 / 1994
Capital Jerusalem
Population 6.4 million / 815 people per sq mile (315 people per sq km) / 91%
Total area 8,019 sq miles (20,770 sq km)
Languages Hebrew*, Arabic, German, Persian, Polish, Romanian, Russian, Yiddish
Religions Jewish 80%, Muslim (mainly Sunni) 16%, Druze and other 2%, Christian 2%
Ethnic mix Jewish 80%, other (mostly Arab) 20%
Government Parliamentary system
Currency Shekel = 100 agorat
Literacy rate 95%
Calorie consumption 3,512 calories

Italy
Southern Europe

Official name Italian Republic
Formation 1861 / 1947
Capital Rome
Population 57.4 million / 506 people per sq mile (195 people per sq km) / 67%
Total area 116,305 sq miles (301,230 sq km)
Languages Italian*, French, German, Rhaeto-Romanic, Sardinian
Religions Roman Catholic 85%, Muslim 2%, other and non-religious 13%
Ethnic mix Italian 94%, Sardinian 2%, other 4%
Government Parliamentary system
Currency Euro = 100 cents
Literacy rate 99%
Calorie consumption 3,680 calories

Ivory Coast
West Africa

Official name Republic of Côte d'Ivoire
Formation 1960 / 1960
Capital Yamoussoukro
Population 16.6 million / 135 people per sq mile (52 people per sq km) / 46%
Total area 124,502 sq miles (322,460 sq km)
Languages French*, Akan, Kru, Voltaic
Religions Muslim 38%, Roman Catholic 25%, Traditional beliefs 25%, Protestant 6%, other 6%
Ethnic mix Baoulé 23%, Bété 18%, Senufo 15%, Agni-Ashanti 14%, Mandinka 11%, other 19%
Government Presidential system
Currency CFA franc = 100 centimes
Literacy rate 50%
Calorie consumption 2,594 calories

Jamaica
West Indies

Official name Jamaica
Formation 1962 /1962
Capital Kingston
Population 2.7 million / 646 people per sq mile (249 people per sq km) / 56%
Total area 4,243 sq miles (10,990 sq km)
Languages English*, English Creole
Religions Christian 55%, other and non-religious 45%
Ethnic mix Black African 75%, Mulatto (mixed race) 13%, European and Chinese 11%, East Indian 1%
Government Parliamentary system
Currency Jamaican dollar = 100 cents
Literacy rate 88%
Calorie consumption 2,705 calories

Japan
East Asia

Official name Japan
Formation 1590 / 1972
Capital Tokyo
Population 128 million / 878 people per sq mile (339 people per sq km) / 79%
Total area 145,882 sq miles (377,835 sq km)
Languages Japanese, Korean, Chinese
Religions Shinto and Buddhist 76%, Buddhist 16%, other (including Christian) 8%
Ethnic mix Japanese 99%, other (mainly Korean) 1%
Government Parliamentary system
Currency Yen = 100 sen
Literacy rate 99%
Calorie consumption 2,746 calories

Jordan
Southwest Asia

Official name Hashemite Kingdom of Jordan
Formation 1946 / 1967
Capital Amman
Population 5.5 million / 160 people per sq mile (62 people per sq km) / 74%
Total area 35,637 sq miles (92,300 sq km)
Languages Arabic*
Religions Muslim (mainly Sunni) 92%, other (mostly Christian) 8%
Ethnic mix Arab 98%, Circassian 1%, Armenian 1%
Government Monarchy
Currency Jordanian dinar = 1,000 fils
Literacy rate 91%
Calorie consumption 2,769 calories

Kazakhstan
Central Asia

Official name Republic of Kazakhstan
Formation 1991 / 1991
Capital Astana
Population 15.4 million / 15 people per sq mile (6 people per sq km) / 56%
Total area 1,049,150 sq miles (2,717,300 sq km)
Languages Kazakh*, Russian*, German, Tatar, Uighur, Ukrainian, Uzbek
Religions Muslim (mainly Sunni) 47%, Orthodox Christian 44%, other 9%
Ethnic mix Kazakh 53%, Russian 30%, Ukrainian 4%, German 2%, Tatar 2%, other 9%
Government Presidential system
Currency Tenge = 100 tiyn
Literacy rate 99%
Calorie consumption 2,477 calories

Kenya
East Africa

Official name Republic of Kenya
Formation 1963 / 1963
Capital Nairobi
Population 32 million / 146 people per sq mile (56 people per sq km) / 33%
Total area 224,961 sq miles (582,650 sq km)
Languages Kiswahili*, English*, Kalenjin, Kamba, Kikuyu, Luo
Religions Christian 60%, Traditional beliefs 25%, Muslim 6%, other 9%
Ethnic mix Kikuyu 21%, Luhya 14%, Luo 13%, Kalenjin 11%, Kamba 11%, other 30%
Government Presidential system
Currency Kenya shilling = 100 cents
Literacy rate 84%
Calorie consumption 2058 calories

Kiribati
Australasia & Oceania

Official name Republic of Kiribati
Formation 1979 / 1979
Capital Bairiki (Tarawa Atoll)
Population 98,549 / 360 people per sq mile (139 people per sq km) / 36%
Total area 277 sq miles (717 sq km)
Languages English*, Kiribati
Religions Roman Catholic 53%, Kiribati Protestant Church 39%, other 8%
Ethnic mix Micronesian 96%, other 4%
Government Non-party system
Currency Australian dollar = 100 cents
Literacy rate 99%
Calorie consumption 2,922 calories

Kuwait
Southwest Asia

Official name State of Kuwait
Formation 1961 / 1961
Capital Kuwait City
Population 2.5 million / 363 people per sq mile (140 people per sq km) / 98%
Total area 6,880 sq miles (17,820 sq km)
Languages Arabic*, English
Religions Sunni Muslim 45%, Shi'a Muslim 40%, Christian, Hindu, and other 15%
Ethnic mix Kuwaiti 45%, other Arab 35%, South Asian 9%, Iranian 4%, other 7%
Government Monarchy
Currency Kuwaiti dinar = 1,000 fils
Literacy rate 83%
Calorie consumption 3,170 calories

Kyrgyzstan
Central Asia

Official name Kyrgyz Republic
Formation 1991 / 1991
Capital Bishkek
Population 5.1 million / 67 people per sq mile (26 people per sq km) / 33%
Total area 76,641 sq miles (198,500 sq km)
Languages Kyrgyz*, Russian*, Tatar, Ukrainian, Uzbek
Religions Muslim (mainly Sunni) 70%, Orthodox Christian 30%
Ethnic mix Kyrgyz 57%, Russian 19%, Uzbek 13%, Tatar 2%, Ukrainian 2%, other 7%
Government Presidential system
Currency Som = 100 tyyn
Literacy rate 97%
Calorie consumption 2,882 calories

Laos
Southeast Asia

Official name Lao People's Democratic Republic
Formation 1953 / 1953
Capital Vientiane
Population 5.7 million / 64 people per sq mile (25 people per sq km) / 24%
Total area 91,428 sq miles (236,800 sq km)
Languages Lao*, Chinese, French, Mon-Khmer, Vietnamese, Yao
Religions Buddhist 85%, other (including Animist) 15%
Ethnic mix Lao Loum 66%, Lao Theung 30%, Lao Soung 2%, other 2%
Government One-party state
Currency New kip = 100 at
Literacy rate 66%
Calorie consumption 2309 calories

Latvia
Northeast Europe

Official name Republic of Latvia
Formation 1991 / 1991
Capital Riga
Population 2.3 million / 92 people per sq mile (36 people per sq km) / 69%
Total area 24,938 sq miles (64,589 sq km)
Languages Latvian*, Russian
Religions Lutheran 55%, Roman Catholic 24%, Orthodox Christian 9%, other 12%
Ethnic mix Latvian 57%, Russian 32%, Belarussian 4%, Ukrainian 3%, other 4%
Government Parliamentary system
Currency Lats = 100 santims
Literacy rate 99%
Calorie consumption 2,809 calories

Lebanon
Southwest Asia

Official name Republic of Lebanon
Formation 1941 / 1941
Capital Beirut
Population 3.7 million / 937 people per sq mile (362 people per sq km) / 90%
Total area 4,015 sq miles (10,400 sq km)
Languages Arabic*, Armenian, Assyrian, French
Religions Muslim 70%, Christian 30%
Ethnic mix Arab 94%, Armenian 4%, other 2%
Government Parliamentary system
Currency Lebanese pound = 100 piastres
Literacy rate 87%
Calorie consumption 3,184 calories

Lesotho
Southern Africa

Official name Kingdom of Lesotho
Formation 1966 / 1966
Capital Maseru
Population 1.8 million / 154 people per sq mile (59 people per sq km) / 28%
Total area 11,720 sq miles (30,355 sq km)
Languages English*, Sesotho*, isiZulu
Religions Christian 90%, Traditional beliefs 10%
Ethnic mix Sotho 97%, European and Asian 3%
Government Parliamentary system
Currency Loti = 100 lisente
Literacy rate 81%
Calorie consumption 2,320 calories

Liberia
West Africa

Official name Republic of Liberia
Formation 1847 / 1847
Capital Monrovia
Population 3.4 million / 91 people per sq mile (35 people per sq km) / 45%
Total area 43,000 sq miles (111,370 sq km)
Languages English*, Bassa, Gola, Grebo, Kissi, Kpelle, Kru, Loma, Vai
Religions Christian 68%, Traditional beliefs 18%, Muslim 14%
Ethnic mix Indigenous tribes (16 main groups) 95%, Americo-Liberians 5%
Government Transitional regime
Currency Liberian dollar = 100 cents
Literacy rate 56%
Calorie consumption 1,946 calories

Libya
North Africa

Official name Great Socialist People's Libyan Arab Jamahariyah
Formation 1951 / 1951
Capital Tripoli
Population 5.6 million / 8 people per sq mile (3 people per sq km) / 88%
Total area 679,358 sq miles (1,759,540 sq km)
Languages Arabic*, Tuareg
Religions Muslim (mainly Sunni) 97%, other 3%
Ethnic mix Arab and Berber 95%, other 5%
Government One-party state
Currency Libyan dinar = 1,000 dirhams
Literacy rate 82%
Calorie consumption 3,333 calories

Liechtenstein
Central Europe

Official name Principality of Liechtenstein
Formation 1719 / 1719
Capital Vaduz
Population 33,145 / 535 people per sq mile (207 people per sq km) / 21%
Total area 62 sq miles (160 sq. km)
Languages German*, Alemannish dialect, Italian
Religions Roman Catholic 81%, Protestant 7%, other 12%
Ethnic mix Liechtensteiner 62%, Foreign residents 38%
Government Parliamentary system
Currency Swiss franc = 100 rappen/centimes
Literacy rate 99%
Calorie consumption Not available

Lithuania
Northeast Europe

Official name Republic of Lithuania
Formation 1991 / 1991
Capital Vilnius
Population 3.4 million / 135 people per sq mile (52 people per sq km) / 68%
Total area 25,174 sq miles (65,200 sq km)
Languages Lithuanian*, Russian
Religions Roman Catholic 83%, Protestant 5%, other 12%
Ethnic mix Lithuanian 80%, Russian 9%, Polish 7%, Belarussian 2%, other 2%
Government Parliamentary system
Currency Litas = 100 centu (euro is also legal tender)
Literacy rate 99%
Calorie consumption 3,384 calories

Luxembourg
Northwest Europe

Official name Grand Duchy of Luxembourg
Formation 1867 / 1867
Capital Luxembourg
Population 453,000 / 454 people per sq mile (175 people per sq km) / 92%
Total area 998 sq miles (2,586 sq km)
Languages French*, German*, Luxembourgish*
Religions Roman Catholic 97%, Protestant, Orthodox Christian, and Jewish 3%
Ethnic mix Luxembourger 73%, Foreign residents 27%
Government Parliamentary system
Currency Euro = 100 cents
Literacy rate 99%
Calorie consumption 3,701 calories

Macedonia
Southeast Europe

Official name Republic of Macedonia
Formation 1991 / 1991
Capital Skopje
Population 2.02 million / 204 people per sq mile (79 people per sq km) / 62%
Total area 9,781 sq miles (25,333 sq km)
Languages Macedonian, Albanian, Serbo-Croat
Religions Orthodox Christian 59%, Muslim 26%, Roman Catholic 4%, Protestant 1%, other 10%
Ethnic mix Macedonian 64%, Albanian 25%, Turkish 4%, Roma 3%, Serb 2%, other 2%
Government Mixed presidential–parliamentary system
Currency Macedonian denar = 100 deni
Literacy rate 94%
Calorie consumption 2,552 calories

Madagascar
Indian Ocean

Official name Republic of Madagascar
Formation 1960 / 1960
Capital Antananarivo
Population 17.4 million / 77 people per sq mile (30 people per sq km) / 30%
Total area 226,656 sq miles (587,040 sq km)
Languages Malagasy*, French*
Religions Traditional beliefs 52%, Christian (mainly Roman Catholic) 41%, Muslim 7%
Ethnic mix Other Malay 46%, Merina 26%, Betsimisaraka 15%, Betsileo 12%, other 1%
Government Presidential system
Currency Ariary = 5 iraimbilanja
Literacy rate 67%
Calorie consumption 2,072 calories

Malawi
Southern Africa

Official name Republic of Malawi
Formation 1964 / 1964
Capital Lilongwe
Population 12.1 million / 333 people per sq mile (129 people per sq km) / 25%
Total area 45,745 sq miles (118,480 sq km)
Languages English*, Chewa*, Lomwe, Ngoni, Yao
Religions Protestant 55%, Roman Catholic 20%, Muslim 20%, Traditional beliefs 5%
Ethnic mix Bantu 99%, other 1%
Government Presidential system
Currency Malawi kwacha = 100 tambala
Literacy rate 62%
Calorie consumption 2,168 calories

Malaysia
Southeast Asia

Official name Federation of Malaysia
Formation 1963 / 1965
Capital Kuala Lumpur; Putrajaya (administrative)
Population 24.4 million / 192 people per sq mile (74 people per sq km) / 57%
Total area 127,316 sq. miles (329,750 sq. km)
Languages Malay*, Chinese*, Bahasa Malaysia, Tamil, English
Religions Muslim 53%, Buddhist 19%, Chinese faiths 12%, Christian 7%, other 9%
Ethnic mix Malay 48%, Chinese 29%, Indigenous tribes 12%, Indian 6%, other 5%
Government Parliamentary system
Currency Ringgit = 100 sen
Literacy rate 89%
Calorie consumption 2,927 calories

Maldives
Indian Ocean

Official name Republic of Maldives
Formation 1965 / 1965
Capital Male'
Population 318,000 / 2,741 people per sq mile (1,060 people per sq km) / 30%
Total area 116 sq miles (300 sq km)
Languages Dhivehi (Maldivian)*, Arabic, Sinhala, Tamil
Religions Sunni Muslim 100%
Ethnic mix Arab–Sinhalese–Malay 100%
Government Non-party system
Currency Rufiyaa = 100 lari
Literacy rate 97%
Calorie consumption 2,587 calories

Mali
West Africa

Official name Republic of Mali
Formation 1960 / 1960
Capital Bamako
Population 13 million / 28 people per sq mile (11 people per sq km) / 30%
Total area 478,764 sq miles (1,240,000 sq km)
Languages French*, Bambara, Fulani, Senufo, Soninke
Religions Muslim (mainly Sunni) 80%, Traditional beliefs 18%, Christian 1%, other 1%
Ethnic mix Bambara 32%, Fulani 14%, Senufu 12%, Soninka 9%, Tuareg 7%, other 26%
Government Presidential system
Currency CFA franc = 100 centimes
Literacy rate 26%
Calorie consumption 2,376 calories

Malta
Southern Europe

Official name Republic of Malta
Formation 1964 / 1964
Capital Valletta
Population 394,000 / 3,177 people per sq mile (1,231 people per sq km) / 91%
Total area 122 sq miles (316 sq km)
Languages Maltese*, English
Religions Roman Catholic 98%, other and non-religious 2%
Ethnic mix Maltese 96%, other 4%
Government Parliamentary system
Currency Maltese lira = 100 cents
Literacy rate 93%
Calorie consumption 3,496 calories

Marshall Islands
Australasia & Oceania

Official name Republic of the Marshall Islands
Formation 1986 / 1986
Capital Majuro
Population 56,429 / 806 people per sq mile (312 people per sq km) / 69%
Total area 70 sq miles (181 sq km)
Languages Marshallese*, English*, German, Japanese
Religions Protestant 90%, Roman Catholic 8%, other 2%
Ethnic mix Micronesian 97%, other 3%
Government Presidential system
Currency US dollar = 100 cents
Literacy rate 91%
Calorie consumption Not available

Mauritania
West Africa

Official name Islamic Republic of Mauritania
Formation 1960 / 1960
Capital Nouakchott
Population 2.9 million / 7 people per sq mile (3 people per sq km) / 58%
Total area 397,953 sq miles (1,030,700 sq km)
Languages French*, Hassaniyah Arabic, Wolof
Religions Sunni Muslim 100%
Ethnic mix Maure 81%, Wolof 7%, Tukolor 5%, Soninka 3%, other 4%
Government Presidential system
Currency Ouguiya = 5 khoums
Literacy rate 41%
Calorie consumption 2,764 calories

Mauritius
Indian Ocean

Official name Republic of Mauritius
Formation 1968 / 1968
Capital Port Louis
Population 1.2 million / 1,671 people per sq mile (645 people per sq km) / 41%
Total area 718 sq miles (1,860 sq km)
Languages English*, Chinese, French, French Creole, Hindi, Tamil, Urdu
Religions Hindu 52%, Roman Catholic 26%, Muslim 17%, Protestant 2%, other 3%
Ethnic mix Indo-Mauritian 68%, Creole 27%, Sino-Mauritian 3%, Franco-Mauritian 2%
Government Parliamentary system
Currency Mauritian rupee = 100 cents
Literacy rate 84%
Calorie consumption 2,995 calories

Mexico
North America

Official name United Mexican States
Formation 1836 / 1848
Capital Mexico City
Population 104 million / 140 people per sq mile (54 people per sq km) / 74%
Total area 761,602 sq miles (1,972,550 sq km)
Languages Spanish*, Mayan, Mixtec, Nahuatl, Otomi, Totonac, Tzeltal, Tzotzil, Zapotec
Religions Roman Catholic 88%, Protestant 5%, other 7%
Ethnic mix Mestizo 60%, Amerindian 30%, European 9%, other 1%
Government Presidential system
Currency Mexican peso = 100 centavos
Literacy rate 91%
Calorie consumption 3,160 calories

Micronesia
Australasia & Oceania

Official name Federated States of Micronesia
Formation 1986 / 1986
Capital Palikir (Pohnpei Island)
Population 108,143 / 399 people per sq mile (154 people per sq km) / 28%
Total area 271 sq miles (702 sq km)
Languages English, Kosraean, Mortlockese, Pohnpeian, Trukese
Religions Roman Catholic 50%, Protestant 48%, other 2%
Ethnic mix Micronesian 100%
Government Non-party system
Currency US dollar = 100 cents
Literacy rate 81%
Calorie consumption Not available

Moldova
Southeast Europe

Official name Republic of Moldova
Formation 1991 / 1991
Capital Chisinau
Population 4.3 million / 330 people per sq mile (128 people per sq km) / 46%
Total area 13,067 sq miles (33,843 sq km)
Languages Moldovan*, Russian, Ukrainian
Religions Orthodox Christian 98%, Jewish 2%
Ethnic mix Moldovan 65%, Ukrainian 14%, Russian 13%, Gagauz 4%, other 4%
Government Parliamentary system
Currency Moldovan leu = 100 bani
Literacy rate 99%
Calorie consumption 2,712 calories

Monaco
Southern Europe

Official name Principality of Monaco
Formation 1861 / 1861
Capital Monaco-Ville
Population 32,130 / 42,840 people per sq mile (16,477 people per sq km) / 100%
Total area 0.75 sq miles (1.95 sq km)
Languages French*, Italian, Monégasque, English
Religions Roman Catholic 89%, Protestant 6%, other 5%
Ethnic mix French 47%, Monégasque 17%, Italian 16%, other 20%
Government Monarchy
Currency Euro = 100 cents
Literacy rate 99%
Calorie consumption Not available

Mongolia
East Asia

Official name Mongolia
Formation 1924 / 1924
Capital Ulan Bator
Population 2.6 million / 4 people per sq mile (2 people per sq km) / 64%
Total area 604,247 sq miles (1,565,000 sq km)
Languages Khalkha Mongolian*, Kazakh, Chinese, Russian
Religions Tibetan Buddhist 96%, Muslim 4%
Ethnic mix Mongol 90%, Kazakh 4%, Chinese 2%, Russian 2%, other 2%
Government Mixed presidential–parliamentary system
Currency Tugrik (tögrög) = 100 möngö
Literacy rate 98%
Calorie consumption 1,974 calories

MOROCCO
North Africa

Official name Kingdom of Morocco
Formation 1956 / 1956
Capital Rabat
Population 30.6 million / 178 people per sq mile (69 people per sq km) / 56%
Total area 172,316 sq. miles (446,300 sq. km)
Languages Arabic*, French, Spanish, Tamazight (Berber)
Religions Muslim (mainly Sunni) 99%, other (mostly Christian) 1%
Ethnic mix Arab 70%, Berber 29%, European 1%
Government Monarchy
Currency Moroccan dirham = 100 centimes
Literacy rate 51%
Calorie consumption 3,046 calories

MOZAMBIQUE
Southern Africa

Official name Republic of Mozambique
Formation 1975 / 1975
Capital Maputo
Population 18.9 million / 62 people per sq mile (24 people per sq km) / 40%
Total area 309,494 sq miles (801,590 sq km)
Languages Portuguese*, Lomwe, Makua, Sena, Xitsonga
Religions Traditional beliefs 56%, Christian 30%, Muslim 14%
Ethnic mix Makua Lomwe 47%, Tsonga 23%, Malawi 12%, Shona 11%, Yao 4%, other 3%
Government Presidential system
Currency Metical = 100 centavos
Literacy rate 47%
Calorie consumption 1,980 calories

MYANMAR
Southeast Asia

Official name Union of Myanmar
Formation 1948 /1948
Capital Rangoon (Yangon)
Population 49.5 million / 195 people per sq mile (75 people per sq km) / 28%
Total area 261,969 sq miles (678,500 sq km)
Languages Burmese*, Chin, Kachin, Karen, Mon, Rakhine, Shan, Yangbye
Religions Buddhist 87%, Christian 6%, Muslim 4%, Hindu 1%, other 2%
Ethnic mix Burman (Bamah) 68%, Shan 9%, Karen 6%, Rakhine 4%, other 13%
Government Military-based regime
Currency Kyat = 100 pyas
Literacy rate 85%
Calorie consumption 2,822 calories

NAMIBIA
Southern Africa

Official name Republic of Namibia
Formation 1990 / 1994
Capital Windhoek
Population 2 million / 6 people per sq mile (2 people per sq km) / 31%
Total area 318,694 sq miles (825,418 sq km)
Languages English*, Afrikaans, Bergdama, German, Kavango, Ovambo
Religions Christian 90%, Traditional beliefs 10%
Ethnic mix Ovambo 50%, other tribes 16%, Kavango 9%, Damara 8%, Herero 8%, other 9%
Government Presidential system
Currency Namibian dollar = 100 cents
Literacy rate 83%
Calorie consumption 2,745 calories

NAURU
Australasia & Oceania

Official name Republic of Nauru
Formation 1968 / 1968
Capital None
Population 12,570 / 1,552 people per sq mile (599 people per sq km) / 100%
Total area 8.1 sq miles (21 sq km)
Languages Nauruan*, Chinese, English, Kiribati, Tuvaluan
Religions Nauruan Congregational Church 60%, Roman Catholic 35%, other 5%
Ethnic mix Nauruan 62%, other Pacific islanders 25%, Chinese and Vietnamese 8%, European 5%
Government Parliamentary system
Currency Australian dollar = 100 cents
Literacy rate 95%
Calorie consumption Not available

NEPAL
South Asia

Official name Kingdom of Nepal
Formation 1769 / 1769
Capital Kathmandu
Population 25.2 million / 477 people per sq mile (184 people per sq km) / 12%
Total area 54,363 sq miles (140,800 sq km)
Languages Nepali*, Bhojpuri, Maithili
Religions Hindu 90%, Buddhist 5%, Muslim 3%, other (including Christian) 2%
Ethnic mix Nepalese 52%, Maithili 11%, Tibeto-Burmese 10%, Bhojpuri 8%, other 19%
Government Monarchy
Currency Nepalese rupee = 100 paise
Literacy rate 44%
Calorie consumption 2,459 calories

NETHERLANDS
Northwest Europe

Official name Kingdom of the Netherlands
Formation 1648 / 1839
Capital Amsterdam; The Hague (administrative)
Population 16.1 million / 1,229 people per sq mile (475 people per sq km) / 89%
Total area 16,033 sq miles (41,526 sq km)
Languages Dutch*, Frisian
Religions Roman Catholic 36%, Protestant 27%, Muslim 3%, other 34%
Ethnic mix Dutch 82%, Moroccan 2%, Surinamese 2%, Turkish 2%, other 12%
Government Parliamentary system
Currency Euro = 100 cents
Literacy rate 97%
Calorie consumption 3,282 calories

NEW ZEALAND
Australasia & Oceania

Official name New Zealand
Formation 1947 / 1947
Capital Wellington
Population 3.9 million / 38 people per sq mile (15 people per sq km) / 86%
Total area 103,737 sq miles (268,680 sq km)
Languages English*, Maori
Religions Anglican 24%, Presbyterian 18%, non-religious 16%, Roman Catholic 15%, Methodist 5%, other 22%
Ethnic mix European 77%, Maori 12%, other immigrant 6%, Pacific islanders 5%
Government Parliamentary system
Currency New Zealand dollar = 100 cents
Literacy rate 99%
Calorie consumption 3,235 calories

NICARAGUA
Central America

Official name Republic of Nicaragua
Formation 1838 / 1838
Capital Managua
Population 5.5 million / 120 people per sq mile (46 people per sq km) / 65%
Total area 49,998 sq miles (129,494 sq km)
Languages Spanish*, English Creole, Miskito
Religions Roman Catholic 80%, Protestant Evangelical 17%, other 3%
Ethnic mix Mestizo 69%, White 14%, Black 8%, Amerindian 5%, Zambo 4%
Government Presidential system
Currency Córdoba oro = 100 centavos
Literacy rate 77%
Calorie consumption 2,256 calories

NIGER
West Africa

Official name Republic of Niger
Formation 1960 / 1960
Capital Niamey
Population 12 million / 25 people per sq mile (9 people per sq km) / 21%
Total area 489,188 sq miles (1,267,000 sq km)
Languages French*, Djerma, Fulani, Hausa, Teda, Tuareg
Religions Muslim 85%, Traditional beliefs 14%, other (including Christian) 1%
Ethnic mix Hausa 54%, Djerma and Songhai 21%, Fulani 10%, Tuareg 9%, other 6%
Government Presidential system
Currency CFA franc = 100 centimes
Literacy rate 17%
Calorie consumption 2,118 calories

NIGERIA
West Africa

Official name Federal Republic of Nigeria
Formation 1960 / 1961
Capital Abuja
Population 124 million / 353 people per sq mile (136 people per sq km) / 44%
Total area 356,667 sq miles (923,768 sq km)
Languages English*, Hausa, Ibo, Yoruba
Religions Muslim 50%, Christian 40%, Traditional beliefs 10%
Ethnic mix Hausa 21%, Yoruba 21%, Ibo 18%, Fulani 11%, other 29%
Government Presidential system
Currency Naira = 100 kobo
Literacy rate 67%
Calorie consumption 2,747 calories

NORTH KOREA
East Asia

Official name Democratic People's Republic of Korea
Formation 1948 / 1953
Capital Pyongyang
Population 22.7 million / 488 people per sq mile (189 people per sq km) / 60%
Total area 46,540 sq miles (120,540 sq km)
Languages Korean*, Chinese
Religions Atheist 100%
Ethnic mix Korean 100%
Government One-party state
Currency North Korean won = 100 chon
Literacy rate 99%
Calorie consumption 2,201 calories

NORWAY
Northern Europe

Official name Kingdom of Norway
Formation 1905 / 1905
Capital Oslo
Population 4.5 million / 38 people per sq mile (15 people per sq km) / 76%
Total area 125,181 sq miles (324,220 sq km)
Languages Norwegian* (Bokmål and Nynorsk), Sámi
Religions Evangelical Lutheran 89%, Roman Catholic 1%, other and non-religious 10%
Ethnic mix Norwegian 93%, Sámi 1%, other 6%
Government Parliamentary system
Currency Norwegian krone = 100 øre
Literacy rate 99%
Calorie consumption 3,382 calories

OMAN
Southwest Asia

Official name Sultanate of Oman
Formation 1951 / 1951
Capital Muscat
Population 2.9 million / 35 people per sq mile (14 people per sq km) / 84%
Total area 82,031 sq miles (212,460 sq km)
Languages Arabic*, Baluchi, Farsi, Hindi, Punjabi
Religions Ibadi Muslim 75%, other Muslim and Hindu 25%
Ethnic mix Arab 88%, Baluchi 4%, Persian 3%, Indian and Pakistani 3%, African 2%
Government Monarchy
Currency Omani rial = 1,000 baizas
Literacy rate 74%
Calorie consumption Not available

PAKISTAN
South Asia

Official name Islamic Republic of Pakistan
Formation 1947 / 1971
Capital Islamabad
Population 154 million / 516 people per sq mile (199 people per sq km) / 37%
Total area 310,401 sq miles (803,940 sq km)
Languages Urdu*, Baluchi, Brahui, Pashtu, Punjabi, Sindhi
Religions Sunni Muslim 77%, Shi'a Muslim 20%, Hindu 2%, Christian 1%
Ethnic mix Punjabi 56%, Pathan (Pashtun) 15%, Sindhi 14%, Mohajir 7%, Baluchi 4%, other 4%
Government Presidential system
Currency Pakistani rupee = 100 paisa
Literacy rate 44%
Calorie consumption 2,457 calories

PALAU
Australasia & Oceania

Official name Republic of Palau
Formation 1994 / 1994
Capital Koror
Population 19,717 / 101 people per sq mile (39 people per sq km) / 70%
Total area 177 sq miles (458 sq km)
Languages Angaur, English, Japanese, Palauan, Sonsorolese, Tobi
Religions Christian 66%, Modekngei 34%
Ethnic mix Micronesian 87%, Filipino 8%, Chinese and other Asian 5%
Government Non-party system
Currency US dollar = 100 cents
Literacy rate 98%
Calorie consumption Not available

PANAMA
Central America

Official name Republic of Panama
Formation 1903 / 1903
Capital Panama City
Population 3.1 million / 106 people per sq mile (41 people per sq km) / 56%
Total area 30,193 sq miles (78,200 sq km)
Languages Spanish*, Amerindian languages, Chibchan languages, English Creole
Religions Roman Catholic 86%, Protestant 6%, other 8%
Ethnic mix Mestizo 60%, White 14%, Black 12%, Amerindian 8%, Asian 4%, other 2%
Government Presidential system
Currency Balboa = 100 centesimos
Literacy rate 92%
Calorie consumption 2,386 calories

PAPUA NEW GUINEA
Australasia & Oceania

Official name Independent State of Papua New Guinea
Formation 1975 / 1975
Capital Port Moresby
Population 5.7 million / 33 people per sq mile (13 people per sq km) / 17%
Total area 178,703 sq miles (462,840 sq km)
Languages Papuan*, Pidgin English*, English, Motu, 750 (est.) native languages
Religions Protestant 60%, Roman Catholic 37%, other 3%
Ethnic mix Melanesian and mixed race 100%
Government Parliamentary system
Currency Kina = 100 toeas
Literacy rate 65%
Calorie consumption 2,193 calories

PARAGUAY
South America

Official name Republic of Paraguay
Formation 1811 / 1938
Capital Asunción
Population 5.9 million / 38 people per sq mile (15 people per sq km) / 56%
Total area 157,046 sq miles (406,750 sq km)
Languages Guaraní*, Spanish*, German
Religions Roman Catholic 96%, Protestant (including Mennonite) 4%
Ethnic mix Mestizo 90%, Amerindian 2%, other 8%
Government Presidential system
Currency Guaraní = 100 centimos
Literacy rate 92%
Calorie consumption 2,576 calories

PERU
South America

Official name Republic of Peru
Formation 1824 / 1941
Capital Lima
Population 27.2 million / 55 people per sq mile (21 people per sq km) / 73%
Total area 496,223 sq miles (1,285,200 sq km)
Languages Spanish*, Quechua*, Aymara*
Religions Roman Catholic 95%, other 5%
Ethnic mix Amerindian 50%, Mestizo 40%, White 7%, other 3%
Government Presidential system
Currency New sol = 100 centimos
Literacy rate 85%
Calorie consumption 2,610 calories

PHILIPPINES
Southeast Asia

Official name Republic of the Philippines
Formation 1946 / 1946
Capital Manila
Population 80 million / 695 people per sq mile (268 people per sq km) / 59%
Total area 115,830 sq miles (300,000 sq km)
Languages Filipino*, English*, Bicolano, Cebuano, Hiligaynon, Ilocano, Samaran, Tagalog
Religions Roman Catholic 83%, Protestant 9%, Muslim 5%, other (including Buddhist) 3%
Ethnic mix Malay 95%, Chinese 2%, other 3%
Government Presidential system
Currency Philippine peso = 100 centavos
Literacy rate 93%
Calorie consumption 2,372 calories

POLAND
Northern Europe

Official name Republic of Poland
Formation 1918 / 1945
Capital Warsaw
Population 38.6 million / 328 people per sq mile (127 people per sq km) / 66%
Total area 120,728 sq miles (312,685 sq km)
Languages Polish*
Religions Roman Catholic 93%, Orthodox Christian 2%, other and non-religious 5%
Ethnic mix Polish 97%, Silesian 1%, other 2%
Government Parliamentary system
Currency Zloty = 100 groszy
Literacy rate 99%
Calorie consumption 3,397 calories

PORTUGAL
Southwest Europe

Official name Republic of Portugal
Formation 1139 / 1640
Capital Lisbon
Population 10.1 million / 284 people per sq mile (110 people per sq km) / 64%
Total area 35,672 sq miles (92,391 sq km)
Languages Portuguese*
Religions Roman Catholic 97%, Protestant 1%, other 2%
Ethnic mix Portuguese 98%, African and other 2%
Government Parliamentary system
Currency Euro = 100 cents
Literacy rate 93%
Calorie consumption 3,751 calories

QATAR
Southwest Asia

Official name State of Qatar
Formation 1971 / 1971
Capital Doha
Population 610,000 / 144 people per sq mile (55 people per sq km) / 93%
Total area 4,416 sq miles (11,437 sq km)
Languages Arabic*
Religions Muslim (mainly Sunni) 95%, other 5%
Ethnic mix Arab 40%, Indian 18%, Pakistani 18%, Iranian 10%, other 14%
Government Monarchy
Currency Qatar riyal = 100 dirhams
Literacy rate 82%
Calorie consumption Not available

ROMANIA
Southeast Europe

Official name Romania
Formation 1878 / 1947
Capital Bucharest
Population 22.3 million / 251 people per sq mile (97 people per sq km) / 56%
Total area 91,699 sq miles (237,500 sq km)
Languages Romanian*, Hungarian (Magyar), Romani, German
Religions Romanian Orthodox 87%, Roman Catholic 5%, other 8%
Ethnic mix Romanian 89%, Magyar 7%, Roma 3%, other 1%
Government Presidential system
Currency Romanian leu = 100 bani
Literacy rate 97%
Calorie consumption 3,407 calories

RUSSIAN FEDERATION
Europe / Asia

Official name Russian Federation
Formation 1480 / 1991
Capital Moscow
Population 143 million / 22 people per sq mile (8 people per sq km) / 78%
Total area 6,592,735 sq miles (17,075,200 sq km)
Languages Russian*, Chavash, Tatar, Ukrainian, various other national languages
Religions Orthodox Christian 75%, Muslim 10%, other 15%
Ethnic mix Russian 82%, Tatar 4%, Ukrainian 3%, Chavash 1%, other 10%
Government Presidential system
Currency Russian rouble = 100 kopeks
Literacy rate 99%
Calorie consumption 3,014 calories

RWANDA
Central Africa

Official name Republic of Rwanda
Formation 1962 / 1962
Capital Kigali
Population 8.4 million / 872 people per sq mile (337 people per sq km) / 6%
Total area 10,169 sq miles (26,338 sq km)
Languages French*, Kinyarwanda*, Kiswahili, English
Religions Roman Catholic 56%, Traditional beliefs 25%, Muslim 10%, Protestant 9%
Ethnic mix Hutu 90%, Tutsi 9%, other (including Twa) 1%
Government Presidential system
Currency Rwanda franc = 100 centimes
Literacy rate 69%
Calorie consumption 2,086 calories

SAINT KITTS & NEVIS
West Indies

Official name Federation of Saint Christopher and Nevis
Formation 1983 / 1983
Capital Basseterre
Population 38,763 / 279 people per sq mile (108 people per sq km) / 34%
Total area 101 sq miles (261 sq km)
Languages English*, English Creole
Religions Anglican 33%, Methodist 29%, other 22%, Moravian 9%, Roman Catholic 7%
Ethnic mix Black 94%, Mixed race 3%, White 1%, other and Amerindian 2%
Government Parliamentary system
Currency Eastern Caribbean dollar = 100 cents
Literacy rate 98%
Calorie consumption 2,997 calories

SAINT LUCIA
West Indies

Official name Saint Lucia
Formation 1979 / 1979
Capital Castries
Population 162,157 / 687 people per sq mile (266 people per sq km) / 38%
Total area 239 sq miles (620 sq km)
Languages English*, French Creole
Religions Roman Catholic 90%, other 10%
Ethnic mix Black 90%, Mulatto (mixed race) 6%, Asian 3%, White 1%
Government Parliamentary system
Currency Eastern Caribbean dollar = 100 cents
Literacy rate 95%
Calorie consumption 2,849 calories

SAINT VINCENT & THE GRENADINES *West Indies*

Official name Saint Vincent and the Grenadines
Formation 1979 / 1979
Capital Kingstown
Population 116,812 / 892 people per sq mile (344 people per sq km) / 55%
Total area 150 sq miles (389 sq km)
Languages English*, English Creole
Religions Anglican 47%, Methodist 28%, Roman Catholic 13%, other 12%
Ethnic mix Black 66%, Mulatto (mixed race) 19%, Asian 6%, White 4%, other 5%
Government Parliamentary system
Currency Eastern Caribbean dollar = 100 cents
Literacy rate 83%
Calorie consumption 2,609 calories

SAMOA
Australasia & Oceania

Official name Independent State of Samoa
Formation 1962 / 1962
Capital Apia
Population 178,000 / 163 people per sq mile (63 people per sq km) / 22%
Total area 1,104 sq miles (2,860 sq km)
Languages Samoan*, English*
Religions Christian 99%, other 1%
Ethnic mix Polynesian 90%, Euronesian 9%, other 1%
Government Parliamentary system
Currency Tala = 100 sene
Literacy rate 99%
Calorie consumption Not available

SAN MARINO
Southern Europe

Official name Republic of San Marino
Formation 1631 / 1631
Capital San Marino
Population 28,119 / 1,172 people per sq mile (461 people per sq km) / 94%
Total area 23.6 sq miles (61 sq km)
Languages Italian*
Religions Roman Catholic 93%, other and non-religious 7%
Ethnic mix Sammarinese 80%, Italian 19%, other 1%
Government Parliamentary system
Currency Euro = 100 cents
Literacy rate 99%
Calorie consumption Not available

SAO TOME & PRINCIPE
West Africa

Official name Democratic Republic of São Tomé and Príncipe
Formation 1975 / 1975
Capital São Tomé
Population 175,883 / 474 people per sq mile (183 people per sq km) / 47%
Total area 386 sq. miles (1,001 sq. km)
Languages Portuguese*, Portuguese Creole
Religions Roman Catholic 84%, other 16%
Ethnic mix Black 90%, Portuguese and Creole 10%
Government Presidential system
Currency Dobra = 100 centimos
Literacy rate 83%
Calorie consumption 2,567 calories

SAUDI ARABIA
Southwest Asia

Official name Kingdom of Saudi Arabia
Formation 1932 / 1932
Capital Riyadh; Jedda (administrative)
Population 24.2 million / 30 people per sq mile (11 people per sq km) / 86%
Total area 756,981 sq miles (1,960,582 sq km)
Languages Arabic*
Religions Sunni Muslim 85%, Shi'a Muslim 15%
Ethnic mix Arab 90%, Afro-Asian 10%
Government Monarchy
Currency Saudi riyal = 100 halalat
Literacy rate 78%
Calorie consumption 2,841 calories

SENEGAL
West Africa

Official name Republic of Senegal
Formation 1960 / 1960
Capital Dakar
Population 10.1 million / 136 people per sq mile (52 people per sq km) / 47%
Total area 75,749 sq miles (196,190 sq km)
Languages French*, Diola, Malinke, Mandinka, Pulaar, Serer, Soninke, Wolof
Religions Sunni Muslim 90%, Christian (mainly Roman Catholic) 5%, Traditional beliefs 5%
Ethnic mix Wolof 43%, Toucouleur 24%, Serer 15%, Diola 4%, Malinke 3%, other 11%
Government Presidential system
Currency CFA franc = 100 centimes
Literacy rate 39%
Calorie consumption 2,277 calories

SERBIA & MONTENEGRO (YUGOSLAVIA)
SE Europe

Official name Serbia and Montenegro
Formation 1992 / 1992
Capital Belgrade
Population 10.5 million / 266 people per sq mile (103 people per sq km) / 52%
Total area 39,517 sq miles (102,350 sq km)
Languages Serbo-Croat*, Albanian, Hungarian
Religions Orthodox Christian 65%, Muslim 19%, Roman Catholic 4%, Protestant 1%, other 11%
Ethnic mix Serb 62%, Albanian 17%, Montenegrin 5%, Magyar 3%, Bosniak 3%, other 10%
Government Parliamentary system
Currency Dinar (Serbia); euro (Montenegro) = 100 para (dinar); 100 cents (euro)
Literacy rate 98%
Calorie consumption 2,778 calories

SEYCHELLES
Indian Ocean

Official name Republic of Seychelles
Formation 1976 / 1976
Capital Victoria
Population 80,469 / 774 people per sq mile (298 people per sq km) / 64%
Total area 176 sq miles (455 sq km)
Languages French Creole*, English, French
Religions Roman Catholic 90%, Anglican 8%, other (including Muslim) 2%
Ethnic mix Creole 89%, Indian 5%, Chinese 2%, other 4%
Government Presidential system
Currency Seychelles rupee = 100 cents
Literacy rate 92%
Calorie consumption 2,461 calories

SIERRA LEONE
West Africa

Official name Republic of Sierra Leone
Formation 1961 / 1961
Capital Freetown
Population 5 million / 181 people per sq mile (70 people per sq km) / 37%
Total area 27,698 sq miles (71,740 sq km)
Languages English*, Mende, Temne, Krio
Religions Muslim 30%, Traditional beliefs 30%, Christian 10%, other 30%
Ethnic mix Mende 35%, Temne 32%, Limba 8%, Kuranko 4%, other 21%
Government Presidential system
Currency Leone = 100 cents
Literacy rate 36%
Calorie consumption 1,913 calories

SINGAPORE
Southeast Asia

Official name Republic of Singapore
Formation 1965 / 1965
Capital Singapore
Population 4.3 million / 18,220 people per sq mile (7,049 people per sq km) / 100%
Total area 250 sq miles (648 sq km)
Languages English*, Malay*, Mandarin*, Tamil*
Religions Buddhist 55%, Taoist 22%, Muslim 16%, Hindu, Christian, and Sikh 7%
Ethnic mix Chinese 77%, Malay 14%, Indian 8%, other 1%
Government Parliamentary system
Currency Singapore dollar = 100 cents
Literacy rate 93%
Calorie consumption Not available

SLOVAKIA
Central Europe

Official name Slovak Republic
Formation 1993 / 1993
Capital Bratislava
Population 5.4 million / 285 people per sq mile (110 people per sq km) / 57%
Total area 18,859 sq miles (48,845 sq km)
Languages Slovak*, Hungarian (Magyar), Czech
Religions Roman Catholic 60%, Atheist 10%, Protestant 8%, Orthodox Christian 4%, other 18%
Ethnic mix Slovak 85%, Magyar 11%, Czech 1%, Roma 1%, other 2%
Government Parliamentary system
Currency Slovak koruna = 100 halierov
Literacy rate 99%
Calorie consumption 2,894 calories

SLOVENIA
Central Europe

Official name Republic of Slovenia
Formation 1991 / 1991
Capital Ljubljana
Population 2 million / 256 people per sq mile (99 people per sq km) / 50%
Total area 7,820 sq miles (20,253 sq km)
Languages Slovene*, Serbo-Croat
Religions Roman Catholic 96%, Muslim 1%, other 3%
Ethnic mix Slovene 83%, Serb 2%, Croat 2%, Bosniak 1%, other 12%
Government Parliamentary system
Currency Tolar = 100 stotinov
Literacy rate 99%
Calorie consumption 2,935 calories

SOLOMON ISLANDS
Australasia & Oceania

Official name Solomon Islands
Formation 1978 / 1978
Capital Honiara
Population 477,000 / 44 people per sq mile (17 people per sq km) / 20%
Total area 10,985 sq miles (28,450 sq km)
Languages English*, Melanesian Pidgin, Pidgin English
Religions Anglican 34%, Roman Catholic 19%, South Seas Evangelical Church 17%, Methodist 11%, Seventh-day Adventist 10%, other 9%
Ethnic mix Melanesian 94%, other 6%
Government Parliamentary system
Currency Solomon Islands dollar = 100 cents
Literacy rate 77%
Calorie consumption 2,272 calories

SOMALIA
East Africa

Official name Somalia
Formation 1960 / 1960
Capital Mogadishu
Population 9.9 million / 41 people per sq mile (16 people per sq km) / 28%
Total area 246,199 sq miles (637,657 sq km)
Languages Somali*, Arabic*, English, Italian
Religions Sunni Muslim 98%, Christian 2%
Ethnic mix Somali 85%, other 15%
Government Transitional regime
Currency Somali shilling = 100 centesimi
Literacy rate 24%
Calorie consumption 1,628 calories

SOUTH AFRICA
Southern Africa

Official name Republic of South Africa
Formation 1934 / 1994
Capital Pretoria; Cape Town; Bloemfontein
Population 45 million / 95 people per sq mile (37 people per sq km) / 55%
Total area 471,008 sq miles (1,219,912 sq km)
Languages Afrikaans, English, 9 other African languages
Religions Christian 68%, Traditional beliefs and animist 29%, Muslim 2%, Hindu 1%
Ethnic mix Black 79%, White 10%, Coloured 9%, Asian 2%
Government Presidential system
Currency Rand = 100 cents
Literacy rate 86%
Calorie consumption 2,921 calories

SOUTH KOREA
East Asia

Official name Republic of Korea
Formation 1948 / 1953
Capital Seoul
Population 47.7 million / 1,251 people per sq mile (483 people per sq km) / 82%
Total area 38,023 sq miles (98,480 sq km)
Languages Korean*, Chinese
Religions Mahayana Buddhist 47%, Protestant 38%, Roman Catholic 11%, Confucianist 3%, other 1%
Ethnic mix Korean 100%
Government Presidential system
Currency South Korean won = 100 chon
Literacy rate 98%
Calorie consumption 3,055 calories

SPAIN
Southwest Europe

Official name Kingdom of Spain
Formation 1492 / 1713
Capital Madrid
Population 41.1 million / 213 people per sq mile (82 people per sq km) / 78%
Total area 194,896 sq miles (504,782 sq km)
Languages Spanish*, Catalan*, Galician*, Basque*
Religions Roman Catholic 96%, other 4%
Ethnic mix Castilian Spanish 72%, Catalan 17%, Galician 6%, Basque 2%, Roma 1%, other 2%
Government Parliamentary system
Currency Euro = 100 cents
Literacy rate 98%
Calorie consumption 3,422 calories

SRI LANKA
South Asia

Official name Democratic Socialist Republic of Sri Lanka
Formation 1948 / 1948
Capital Colombo
Population 19.1 million / 764 people per sq mile (295 people per sq km) / 24%
Total area 25,332 sq miles (65,610 sq km)
Languages Sinhala, Tamil, Sinhala-Tamil, English
Religions Buddhist 69%, Hindu 15%, Muslim 8%, Christian 8%
Ethnic mix Sinhalese 74%, Tamil 18%, Moor 7%, Burgher, Malay, and Veddha 1%
Government Mixed presidential–parliamentary system
Currency Sri Lanka rupee = 100 cents
Literacy rate 92%
Calorie consumption 2,274 calories

SUDAN
East Africa

Official name Republic of the Sudan
Formation 1956 / 1956
Capital Khartoum
Population 33.6 million / 35 people per sq mile (13 people per sq km) / 36%
Total area 967,493 sq miles (2,505,810 sq km)
Languages Arabic*, Bari, Beja, Dinka, Fur, Lotuko, Nubian, Nuer, Shilluk, Zande
Religions Muslim (mainly Sunni) 70%, Traditional beliefs 20%, Christian 9%, other 1%
Ethnic mix Other Black 52%, Arab 40%, Dinka and Beja 7%, other 1%
Government Presidential system
Currency Sudanese pound or dinar = 100 piastres
Literacy rate 60%
Calorie consumption 2,288 calories

SURINAME
South America

Official name Republic of Suriname
Formation 1975 / 1975
Capital Paramaribo
Population 436,000 / 7 people per sq mile (3 people per sq km) / 74%
Total area 63,039 sq miles (163,270 sq km)
Languages Dutch*, Chinese, Carib, Javanese, Saramaccan, Sarnami Hindi, Sranan (Creole)
Religions Hindu 27%, Protestant 25%, Roman Catholic 23%, Muslim 20%, Traditional beliefs 5%
Ethnic mix Creole 34%, South Asian 34%, Javanese 18%, Black 9%, other 5%
Government Parliamentary system
Currency Surinam dollar (guilder until 2004) = 100 cents
Literacy rate 94%
Calorie consumption 2,643 calories

SWAZILAND
Southern Africa

Official name Kingdom of Swaziland
Formation 1968 / 1968
Capital Mbabane
Population 1.1 million / 166 people per sq mile (64 people per sq km) / 26%
Total area 6,704 sq miles (17,363 sq km)
Languages English*, siSwati*, isiZulu, Xitsonga
Religions Christian 60%, Traditional beliefs 40%
Ethnic mix Swazi 97%, other 3%
Government Monarchy
Currency Lilangeni = 100 cents
Literacy rate 81%
Calorie consumption 2,593 calories

SWEDEN
Northern Europe

Official name Kingdom of Sweden
Formation 1523 / 1905
Capital Stockholm
Population 8.9 million / 56 people per sq mile (22 people per sq km) / 83%
Total area 173,731 sq miles (449,964 sq km)
Languages Swedish*, Finnish, Sámi
Religions Evangelical Lutheran 82%, Roman Catholic 2%, Muslim 2%, Orthodox Christian 1%, other 13%
Ethnic mix Swedish 88%, Foreign-born or first-generation immigrant 10%, Finnish and Sámi 2%
Government Parliamentary system
Currency Swedish krona = 100 öre
Literacy rate 99%
Calorie consumption 3,164 calories

SWITZERLAND
Central Europe

Official name Swiss Confederation
Formation 1291 / 1857
Capital Bern
Population 7.2 million / 469 people per sq mile (181 people per sq km) / 68%
Total area 15,942 sq miles (41,290 sq km)
Languages French*, German*, Italian*, Romansch*, Swiss-German
Religions Roman Catholic 46%, Protestant 40%, Muslim 2%, other and non-religious 12%
Ethnic mix German 65%, French 18%, Italian 10%, Romansch 1%, other 6%
Government Parliamentary system
Currency Swiss franc = 100 rappen/centimes
Literacy rate 99%
Calorie consumption 3,440 calories

SYRIA
Southwest Asia

Official name Syrian Arab Republic
Formation 1941 / 1967
Capital Damascus
Population 17.8 million / 250 people per sq mile (97 people per sq km) / 55%
Total area 71,498 sq miles (184,180 sq km)
Languages Arabic*, Armenian, Circassian, French, Kurdish, Turkic languages, Assyrian, Aramaic
Religions Sunni Muslim 74%, Other Muslim 16%, Christian 10%
Ethnic mix Arab 89%, Kurdish 6%, Armenian, Turkmen, and Circassian 2%, other 3%
Government One-party state
Currency Syrian pound = 100 piasters
Literacy rate 83%
Calorie consumption 3,038 calories

TAIWAN
East Asia

Official name Republic of China (ROC)
Formation 1949 / 1949
Capital Taipei
Population 22.6 million / 1,815 people per sq mile (701 people per sq km) / 69%
Total area 13,892 sq miles (35,980 sq km)
Languages Mandarin*, Amoy, Hakka
Religions Buddhist, Confucianist, and Taoist 93%, Christian 5%, other 2%
Ethnic mix Indigenous Chinese 84%, Mainland Chinese 14%, Aboriginal 2%
Government Presidential system
Currency Taiwan dollar = 100 cents
Literacy rate 96%
Calorie consumption Not available

TAJIKISTAN
Central Asia

Official name Republic of Tajikistan
Formation 1991 / 1991
Capital Dushanbe
Population 6.2 million / 112 people per sq mile (43 people per sq km) / 28%
Total area 55,251 sq miles (143,100 sq km)
Languages Tajik*, Russian, Uzbek
Religions Sunni Muslim 80%, Shi'a Muslim 5%, other 15%
Ethnic mix Tajik 62%, Uzbek 24%, Russian 8%, Tatar 1%, Kyrgyz 1%, other 4%
Government Presidential system
Currency Somoni = 100 diram
Literacy rate 99%
Calorie consumption 1,662 calories

TANZANIA
East Africa

Official name United Republic of Tanzania
Formation 1964 / 1964
Capital Dodoma
Population 37 million / 108 people per sq mile (42 people per sq km) / 33%
Total area 364,898 sq miles (945,087 sq km)
Languages English*, Kiswahili*, Chagga, Hehe, Makonde, Nyamwezi, Sandawe, Sukuma, Yao
Religions Muslim 33%, Christian 33%, Traditional beliefs 30%, other 4%
Ethnic mix Native African (over 120 tribes) 99%, European and Asian 1%
Government Presidential system
Currency Tanzanian shilling = 100 cents
Literacy rate 77%
Calorie consumption 1,997 calories

THAILAND
Southeast Asia

Official name Kingdom of Thailand
Formation 1238 / 1907
Capital Bangkok
Population 62.8 million / 318 people per sq mile (123 people per sq km) / 22%
Total area 198,455 sq miles (514,000 sq km)
Languages Thai*, Chinese, Karen, Khmer, Malay, Miao, Mon
Religions Buddhist 95%, Muslim 4%, other (including Christian) 1%
Ethnic mix Thai 83%, Chinese 12%, Malay 3%, Khmer and other 2%
Government Parliamentary system
Currency Baht = 100 stang
Literacy rate 93%
Calorie consumption 2,486 calories

TOGO
West Africa

Official name Republic of Togo
Formation 1960 / 1960
Capital Lomé
Population 4.9 million / 233 people per sq mile (90 people per sq km) / 33%
Total area 21,924 sq miles (56,785 sq km)
Languages French*, Ewe, Gurma, Kabye
Religions Traditional beliefs 50%, Christian 35%, Muslim 15%
Ethnic mix Ewe 46%, Kabye 27%, other African 26%, European 1%
Government Presidential system
Currency CFA franc = 100 centimes
Literacy rate 60%
Calorie consumption 2,287 calories

TONGA
Australasia & Oceania

Official name Kingdom of Tonga
Formation 1970 / 1970
Capital Nuku'alofa
Population 108,141 / 389 people per sq mile (150 people per sq km) / 43%
Total area 289 sq miles (748 sq km)
Languages Tongan*, English
Religions Free Wesleyan 41%, Roman Catholic 16%, Church of Jesus Christ of Latter-day Saints 14%, Free Church of Tonga 12%, other 17%
Ethnic mix Polynesian 99%, other 1%
Government Monarchy
Currency Pa'anga (Tongan dollar) = 100 seniti
Literacy rate 99%
Calorie consumption Not available

TRINIDAD & TOBAGO
West Indies

Official name Republic of Trinidad and Tobago
Formation 1962 / 1962
Capital Port-of-Spain
Population 1.3 million / 656 people per sq mile (253 people per sq km) / 74%
Total area 1,980 sq miles (5,128 sq km)
Languages English*, English Creole, French, Hindi, Spanish
Religions Christian 60%, Hindu 24%, Muslim 7%, other and non-religious 9%
Ethnic mix East Indian 40%, Black 40%, mixed race 19%, White and Chinese 1%
Government Parliamentary system
Currency Trinidad and Tobago dollar = 100 cents
Literacy rate 99%
Calorie consumption 2,756 calories

TUNISIA
North Africa

Official name Republic of Tunisia
Formation 1956 / 1956
Capital Tunis
Population 9.8 million / 163 people per sq mile (63 people per sq km) / 68%
Total area 63,169 sq miles (163,610 sq km)
Languages Arabic*, French
Religions Muslim (mainly Sunni) 98%, Christian 1%, Jewish 1%
Ethnic mix Arab and Berber 98%, Jewish 1%, European 1%
Government Presidential system
Currency Tunisian dinar = 1,000 millimes
Literacy rate 73%
Calorie consumption 3,293 calories

TURKEY
Asia / Europe

Official name Republic of Turkey
Formation 1923 / 1939
Capital Ankara
Population 71.3 million / 240 people per sq mile (93 people per sq km) / 75%
Total area 301,382 sq miles (780,580 sq km)
Languages Turkish*, Arabic, Armenian, Circassian, Georgian, Greek, Kurdish, Ladino
Religions Muslim (mainly Sunni) 99%, other 1%
Ethnic mix Turkish 70%, Kurdish 20%, Arab 2%, other 8%
Government Parliamentary system
Currency Turkish lira = 100 kurus
Literacy rate 87%
Calorie consumption 3,343 calories

TURKMENISTAN
Central Asia

Official name Turkmenistan
Formation 1991 / 1991
Capital Asgabat
Population 4.9 million / 26 people per sq mile (10 people per sq km) / 45%
Total area 188,455 sq miles (488,100 sq km)
Languages Turkmen*, Kazakh, Russian, Tatar, Uzbek
Religions Sunni Muslim 87%, Orthodox Christian 11%, other 2%
Ethnic mix Turkmen 77%, Uzbek 9%, Russian 7%, Kazakh 2%, Tatar 1%, other 4%
Government One-party state
Currency Manat = 100 tenga
Literacy rate 98%
Calorie consumption 2,738 calories

TUVALU
Australasia & Oceania

Official name Tuvalu
Formation 1978 / 1978
Capital Fongafale
Population 11,305 / 1,130 people per sq mile (435 people per sq km) / 45%
Total area 10 sq miles (26 sq km)
Languages English, Kiribati, Tuvaluan
Religions Church of Tuvalu 97%, Baha'i 1%, Seventh-day Adventist 1%, other 1%
Ethnic mix Polynesian 96%, other 4%
Government Non-party system
Currency Australian dollar and Tuvaluan dollar = 100 cents
Literacy rate 98%
Calorie consumption Not available

UGANDA
East Africa

Official name Republic of Uganda
Formation 1962 / 1962
Capital Kampala
Population 25.8 million / 335 people per sq mile (129 people per sq km) / 14%
Total area 91,135 sq miles (236,040 sq km)
Languages English*, Acholi, Chiga, Lango, Luganda, Lugbara, Nkole, Teso
Religions Roman Catholic 38%, Protestant 33%, Traditional beliefs 13%, Muslim (mainly Sunni) 8%, other 8%
Ethnic mix Bantu tribes 50%, other 50%
Government Non-party system
Currency New Uganda shilling = 100 cents
Literacy rate 69%
Calorie consumption 2,398 calories

UKRAINE
Eastern Europe

Official name Ukraine
Formation 1991 / 1991
Capital Kiev
Population 47.7 million / 205 people per sq mile (79 people per sq km) / 68%
Total area 223,089 sq miles (603,700 sq km)
Languages Ukrainian*, Russian, Tatar
Religions Christian (mainly Orthodox) 95%, Jewish 1%, other 4%
Ethnic mix Ukrainian 73%, Russian 22%, Jewish 1%, other 4%
Government Presidential system
Currency Hryvna = 100 kopiykas
Literacy rate 99%
Calorie consumption 3,008 calories

UNITED ARAB EMIRATES
Southwest Asia

Official name United Arab Emirates
Formation 1971 / 1972
Capital Abu Dhabi
Population 3 million / 93 people per sq mile (36 people per sq km) / 86%
Total area 32,000 sq miles (82,880 sq km)
Languages Arabic*, English, Farsi, Indian and Pakistani languages
Religions Muslim (mainly Sunni) 96%, Christian, Hindu, and other 4%
Ethnic mix Asian 60%, Emirian 25%, other Arab 12%, European 3%
Government Monarchy
Currency UAE dirham = 100 fils
Literacy rate 77%
Calorie consumption 3,340 calories

UNITED KINGDOM
Northwest Europe

Official name United Kingdom of Great Britain and Northern Ireland
Formation 1707 / 1922
Capital London
Population 59.3 million / 636 people per sq mile (245 people per sq km) / 90%
Total area 94,525 sq miles (244,820 sq km)
Languages English*, Gaelic, Scottish, Welsh
Religions Anglican 45%, Roman Catholic 9%, Presbyterian 4%, other and non-religious 42%
Ethnic mix English 80%, Scottish 9%, West Indian, Asian, and other 5%, Northern Irish 3%, Welsh 3%
Government Parliamentary system
Currency Pound sterling = 100 pence
Literacy rate 99%
Calorie consumption 3,368 calories

UNITED STATES
North America

Official name United States of America
Formation 1776 / 1959
Capital Washington DC
Population 294 million / 83 people per sq mile (32 people per sq km) / 77%
Total area 3,717,792 sq miles (9,626,091 sq km)
Languages English*, Spanish, Chinese, French, German, Italian, Polish
Religions Protestant 52%, Roman Catholic 25%, Jewish 2%, other and non-religious 21%
Ethnic mix White 69%, Hispanic 13%, Black American/African 13%, Asian 4%, Native American 1%
Government Presidential system
Currency US dollar = 100 cents
Literacy rate 99%
Calorie consumption 3,766 calories

URUGUAY
South America

Official name Eastern Republic of Uruguay
Formation 1828 / 1828
Capital Montevideo
Population 3.4 million / 50 people per sq mile (19 people per sq km) / 91%
Total area 68,039 sq miles (176,220 sq km)
Languages Spanish*
Religions Roman Catholic 66%, Jewish 2%, Protestant 2%, other and non-religious 30%
Ethnic mix White 90%, Mestizo 6%, Black 4%
Government Presidential system
Currency Uruguayan peso = 100 centésimos
Literacy rate 98%
Calorie consumption 2,848 calories

UZBEKISTAN
Central Asia

Official name Republic of Uzbekistan
Formation 1991 / 1991
Capital Tashkent
Population 26.1 million / 151 people per sq mile (58 people per sq km) / 37%
Total area 172,741 sq miles (447,400 sq km)
Languages Uzbek*, Kazakh, Russian, Tajik
Religions Sunni Muslim 88%, Orthodox Christian 9%, other 3%
Ethnic mix Uzbek 71%, Russian 8%, Tajik 5%, Kazakh 4%, other 12%
Government Presidential system
Currency Som = 100 tiyin
Literacy rate 99%
Calorie consumption 2,197 calories

VANUATU
Australasia & Oceania

Official name Republic of Vanuatu
Formation 1980 / 1980
Capital Port Vila
Population 212,000 / 45 people per sq mile (17 people per sq km) / 20%
Total area 4,710 sq miles (12,200 sq km)
Languages Bislama*, English*, French*, other indigenous languages
Religions Presbyterian 37%, Anglican 15%, Roman Catholic 15%, Traditional beliefs 8%, Seventh-day Adventist 6%, other 19%
Ethnic mix Melanesian 94%, Polynesian 3%, other 3%
Government Parliamentary system
Currency Vatu = 100 centimes
Literacy rate 34%
Calorie consumption 2,565 calories

VATICAN CITY
Southern Europe

Official name State of the Vatican City
Formation 1929 / 1929
Capital Vatican City
Population 911 / 5,359 people per sq mile (2,070 people per sq km) / 100%
Total area 0.17 sq miles (0.44 sq km)
Languages Italian*, Latin*
Religions Roman Catholic 100%
Ethnic mix The current pope is Polish, Cardinals are from many nationalities, most of the resident lay persons are Italian.
Government Papal state
Currency Euro = 100 cents
Literacy rate 99%
Calorie consumption Not available

VENEZUELA
South America

Official name Bolivarian Republic of Venezuela
Formation 1830 / 1830
Capital Caracas
Population 25.7 million / 75 people per sq mile (29 people per sq km) / 87%
Total area 352,143 sq miles (912,050 sq km)
Languages Spanish*, Amerindian languages
Religions Roman Catholic 89%, Protestant and other 11%
Ethnic mix Mestizo 69%, White 20%, Black 9%, Amerindian 2%
Government Presidential system
Currency Bolívar = 100 centimos
Literacy rate 93%
Calorie consumption 2,376 calories

VIETNAM
Southeast Asia

Official name Socialist Republic of Vietnam
Formation 1976 / 1976
Capital Hanoi
Population 81.4 million / 648 people per sq mile (250 people per sq km) / 20%
Total area 127,243 sq miles (329,560 sq km)
Languages Vietnamese*, Chinese, Jarai, Khmer, Miao, Muong, Nung, Thai, Yao
Religions Buddhist 55%, Christian 7%, other and non-religious 38%
Ethnic mix Vietnamese 88%, Chinese 4%, Thai 2%, other 6%
Government One-party state
Currency Dông = 10 hao = 100 xu
Literacy rate 93%
Calorie consumption 2,533 calories

YEMEN
Southwest Asia

Official name Republic of Yemen
Formation 1990 / 1990
Capital Sana
Population 20 million / 92 people per sq mile (36 people per sq km) / 25%
Total area 203,849 sq miles (527,970 sq km)
Languages Arabic*
Religions Sunni Muslim 55%, Shi'a Muslim 42%, Christian, Hindu, and Jewish 3%
Ethnic mix Arab 95%, Afro-Arab 3%, Indian, Somali, and European 2%
Government Presidential system
Currency Yemeni rial = 100 sene
Literacy rate 49%
Calorie consumption 2,050 calories

ZAMBIA
Southern Africa

Official name Republic of Zambia
Formation 1964 / 1964
Capital Lusaka
Population 10.8 million / 38 people per sq mile (15 people per sq km) / 45%
Total area 290,584 sq miles (752,614 sq km)
Languages English*, Bemba, Lala-Bisa, Lozi, Nsenga, Nyanja, Tonga
Religions Christian 63%, Traditional beliefs 36%, Muslim and Hindu 1%
Ethnic mix Bemba 34%, other African 26%, Tonga 16%, Nyanja 14%, Lozi 9%, European 1%
Government Presidential system
Currency Zambian kwacha = 100 ngwee
Literacy rate 80%
Calorie consumption 1,885 calories

ZIMBABWE
Southern Africa

Official name Republic of Zimbabwe
Formation 1980 / 1980
Capital Harare
Population 12.9 million / 86 people per sq mile (33 people per sq km) / 35%
Total area 150,803 sq miles (390,580 sq km)
Languages English*, isiNdebele, Shona
Religions Syncretic (Christian/traditional beliefs) 50%, Christian 25%, Traditional beliefs 24%, other (including Muslim) 1%
Ethnic mix Shona 71%, Ndebele 16%, other African 11%, White 1%, Asian 1%
Government Presidential system
Currency Zimbabwe dollar = 100 cents
Literacy rate 90%
Calorie consumption 2,133 calories

GLOSSARY

THIS GLOSSARY lists all geographical, technical, and foreign language terms that appear in the text, followed by a brief definition of the term. Any acronyms used in the text are also listed in full. Terms in italics are for cross-reference and indicate that the word is separately defined in the glossary.

A

Aboriginal The original (*indigenous*) inhabitants of a country or continent. Especially used with reference to Australia.

Abyssal plain A broad *plain* found in the depths of the ocean, more than 10,000 ft (3,000 m) below sea level.

Acid rain Rain, sleet, snow, or mist which has absorbed waste gases from fossil-fueled power stations and vehicle exhausts, becoming more acid. It causes severe environmental damage.

Adaptation The gradual evolution of plants and animals so that they become better suited to survive and reproduce in their *environment*.

Afforestation The planting of new forest in areas that were once forested but have been cleared.

Agribusiness A term applied to activities such as the growing of crops, rearing of animals, or the manufacture of farm machinery, which eventually leads to the supply of agricultural produce at market.

Air mass A huge, homogeneous mass of air, within which horizontal patterns of temperature and *humidity* are consistent. Air masses are separated by *fronts*.

Alliance An agreement between two or more states, to work together to achieve common purposes.

Alluvial fan A large fan-shaped deposit of fine sediments deposited by a river as it emerges from a narrow, mountain valley onto a broad, open *plain*.

Alluvium Material deposited by rivers. Nowadays usually only applied to finer particles of silt and clay.

Alpine Mountain *environment*, between the *treeline* and the level of permanent snow cover.

Alpine mountains Ranges of mountains formed between 30 and 65 million years ago, by *folding*, in western and central Europe.

Amerindian A term applied to people *indigenous* to North, Central, and South America.

Animal husbandry The business of rearing animals.

Antarctic circle The parallel which lies at *latitude* of 66° 32′ S.

Anticline A geological *fold* that forms an arch shape, curving upward in the rock *strata*.

Anticyclone An area of relatively high atmospheric pressure.

Aquaculture Collective term for the farming of produce derived from the sea, including fish-farming, the cultivation of shellfish, and plants such as seaweed.

Aquifer A body of rock that can absorb water. Also applied to any rock strata that have sufficient porosity to yield *groundwater* through wells or springs.

Arable Land which has been plowed and is being used, or is suitable, for growing crops.

Archipelago A group or chain of islands.

Arctic Circle The parallel that lies at a *latitude* of 66° 32′ N.

Arête A thin, jagged mountain ridge that divides two adjacent *cirques*, found in regions where *glaciation* has occurred.

Arid Dry. An area of low rainfall, where the rate of *evaporation* may be greater than that of *precipitation*. Often defined as those areas that receive less than one inch (25 mm) of rain a year. In these areas only drought-resistant plants can survive.

Artesian well A naturally occurring source of underground water, stored in an *aquifer*.

Artisanal Small-scale, manual operation, such as fishing, using little or no machinery.

ASEAN Association of Southeast Asian Nations. Established in 1967 to promote economic, social, and cultural cooperation. Its members include Brunei, Indonesia, Malaysia, Philippines, Singapore, and Thailand.

Aseismic A region where *earthquake* activity has ceased.

Asteroid A minor planet circling the Sun, mainly between the orbits of Mars and Jupiter.

Asthenosphere A zone of hot, partially melted rock, which underlies the *lithosphere*, within the Earth's *crust*.

Atmosphere The envelope of odorless, colorless and tasteless gases surrounding the Earth, consisting of *oxygen* (23%), *nitrogen* (75%), argon (1%), *carbon dioxide* (0.03%), as well as tiny proportions of other gases.

Atmospheric pressure The pressure created by the action of gravity on the gases surrounding the Earth.

Atoll A ring-shaped island or *coral reef* often enclosing a *lagoon* of sea water.

Avalanche The rapid movement of a mass of snow and ice down a steep slope. Similar movements of other materials are described as *rock avalanches* or *landslides* and *sand avalanches*.

B

Badlands A landscape that has been heavily eroded and dissected by rainwater, and which has little or no vegetation.

Back slope The gentler windward slope of a sand *dune* or gentler slope of a *cuesta*.

Bajos An *alluvial fan* deposited by a river at the base of mountains and hills that encircle *desert* areas.

Bar, coastal An offshore strip of sand or shingle, either above or below the water. Usually parallel to the shore but sometimes crescent-shaped or at an oblique angle.

Barchan A crescent-shaped sand *dune*, formed where wind direction is very consistent. The horns of the crescent point downwind and where there is enough sand the barchan is mobile.

Barrio A Spanish term for the shantytowns – settlements of shacks – that are clustered around many South and Central American cities (*see also Favela*).

Basalt Dark, fine-grained *igneous rock* that is formed near the Earth's surface from fast-cooling *lava*.

Base level The level below which flowing water cannot erode the land.

Basement rock A mass of ancient rock often of *PreCambrian age*, covered by a layer of more recent *sedimentary rocks*. Commonly associated with *shield* areas.

Beach Lake or sea shore where waves break and there is an accumulation of loose sand, mud, gravel, or pebbles.

Bedrock Solid, consolidated and relatively unweathered rock, found on the surface of the land or just below a layer of soil or *weathered* rock.

Biodiversity The quantity of animal or plant species in a given area.

Biomass The total mass of organic matter – plants and animals – in a given area. It is usually measured in kilogrammes per square meter. Plant biomass is proportionally greater than that of animals, except in cities.

Biosphere The zone just above and below the Earth's surface, where all plants and animals live.

Blizzard A severe windstorm with snow and sleet. Visibility is often severely restricted.

Bluff The steep bank of a *meander*, formed by the erosive action of a river.

Boreal forest Tracts of mainly coniferous forest found in northern *latitudes*.

Breccia A type of rock composed of sharp fragments, cemented by a fine-grained material such as clay.

Butte An isolated, flat-topped hill with steep or vertical sides, buttes are the eroded remnants of a former land surface.

C

Caatinga Portuguese (Brazilian) term for thorny woodland growing in areas of pale granitic soils.

CACM Central American Common Market. Established in 1960 to further economic ties between its members, which are Costa Rica, El Salvador, Guatemala, Honduras, and Nicaragua.

Calcite Hexagonal crystals of calcium carbonate.

Caldera A huge volcanic vent, often containing a number of smaller vents, and sometimes a crater lake.

Carbon cycle The transfer of carbon to and from the *atmosphere*. This occurs on land through *photosynthesis*. In the sea, *carbon dioxide* is absorbed, some returning to the air and some taken up into the bodies of sea creatures.

Carbon dioxide A colorless, odorless gas (CO_2) that makes up 0.03% of the *atmosphere*.

Carbonation The process whereby rocks are broken down by carbonic acid. Carbon dioxide in the air dissolves in rainwater, forming carbonic acid. *Limestone* terrain can be rapidly eaten away.

Cash crop A single crop grown specifically for export sale, rather than for local use. Typical examples include coffee, tea, and citrus fruits.

Cassava A type of grain meal, used to produce tapioca. A staple crop in many parts of Africa.

Castle kopje Hill or rock outcrop, especially in southern Africa, where steep sides, and a summit composed of blocks, give a castle-like appearance.

Cataracts A series of stepped waterfalls created as a river flows over a band of hard, resistant rock.

Causeway A raised route through marshland or a body of water.

CEEAC Economic Community of Central African States. Established in 1983 to promote regional cooperation and if possible, establish a common market between 16 Central African nations.

Chemical weathering The chemical reactions leading to the decomposition of rocks. Types of chemical weathering include *carbonation*, *hydrolysis*, and *oxidation*.

Chernozem A fertile soil, also known as "black earth" consisting of a layer of dark topsoil, rich in decaying vegetation, overlying a lighter chalky layer.

Cirque Armchair-shaped basin, found in mountain regions, with a steep back, or rear, wall and a raised rock lip, often containing a lake (or *tarn*). The cirque floor has been eroded by a *glacier*, while the back wall is eroded both by the *glacier* and by *weathering*.

Climate The average weather conditions in a given area over a period of years, sometimes defined as 30 years or more.

Cold War A period of hostile relations between the US and the Soviet Union and their allies after the Second World War.

Composite volcano Also known as a strato-volcano, the volcanic cone is composed of alternating deposits of *lava* and *pyroclastic* material.

Compound A substance made up of *elements* chemically combined in a consistent way.

Condensation The process whereby a gas changes into a liquid. For example, water vapor in the *atmosphere* condenses around tiny airborne particles to form droplets of water.

Confluence The point at which two rivers meet.

Conglomerate Rock composed of large, water-worn or rounded pebbles, held together by a natural cement.

Coniferous forest A forest type containing trees which are generally, but not necessarily, *evergreen* and have slender, needlelike leaves. Coniferous trees reproduce by means of seeds contained in a cone.

Continental drift The theory that the continents of today are fragments of one or more prehistoric *supercontinents* which have moved across the Earth's surface, creating ocean basins. The theory has been superseded by a more sophisticated one – *plate tectonics*.

Continental shelf An area of the continental crust, below sea level, which slopes gently. It is separated from the deep ocean by a much more steeply inclined *continental slope*.

Continental slope A steep slope running from the edge of the *continental shelf* to the ocean floor.

Conurbation A vast metropolitan area created by the expansion of towns and cities into a virtually continuous urban area.

Cool continental A rainy *climate* with warm summers [warmest month below 76°F (22°C)] and often severe winters [coldest month below 32°F (0°C)].

Copra The dried, white kernel of a coconut, from which coconut oil is extracted.

Coral reef An underwater barrier created by colonies of the coral polyp. Polyps secrete a protective skeleton of calcium carbonate, and reefs develop as live polyps build on the skeletons of dead generations.

Core The center of the Earth, consisting of a dense mass of iron and nickel. It is thought that the outer core is molten or liquid, and that the hot inner core is solid due to extremely high pressures.

Coriolis effect A deflecting force caused by the rotation of the Earth. In the northern hemisphere a body, such as an *air mass* or ocean current, is deflected to the right, and in the southern hemisphere to the left. This prevents winds from blowing straight from areas of high to low pressure.

Coulées A US / Canadian term for a ravine formed by river *erosion*.

Craton A large block of the Earth's *crust* which has remained stable for a long period of *geological time*. It is made up of ancient *shield* rocks.

Cretaceous A period of *geological time* beginning about 145 million years ago and lasting until about 65 million years ago.

Crevasse A deep crack in a *glacier*.

Crust The hard, thin outer shell of the Earth. The crust floats on the *mantle*, which is softer and more dense. Under the oceans (oceanic crust) the crust is 3.7–6.8 miles (6–11 km) thick. Continental crust averages 18–24 miles (30–40 km).

Crystalline rock Rocks formed when molten *magma* crystallizes (*igneous rocks*) or when heat or pressure cause re-crystallization (*metamorphic rocks*). Crystalline rocks are distinct from *sedimentary rocks*.

Cuesta A hill which rises into a steep slope on one side but has a gentler gradient on its other slope.

Cyclone An area of low *atmospheric pressure*, occurring where the air is warm and relatively low in density, causing low level winds to spiral. *Hurricanes* and *typhoons* are tropical cyclones.

D

De facto
1 Government or other activity that takes place, or exists in actuality if not by right.
2 A border, which exists in practice, but which is not officially recognized by all the countries it adjoins.

Deciduous forest A forest of trees that shed their leaves annually at a particular time or season. In *temperate* climates the fall of leaves occurs in the autumn. Some *coniferous* trees, such as the larch, are deciduous. Deciduous vegetation contrasts with *evergreen*, which keeps its leaves for more than a year.

Defoliant Chemical spray used to remove foliage (leaves) from trees.

Deforestation The act of cutting down and clearing large areas of forest for human activities, such as agricultural land or urban development.

Delta Low-lying, fan-shaped area at a river mouth, formed by the *deposition* of successive layers of *sediment*. Slowing as it enters the sea, a river deposits sediment and may, as a result, split into numerous smaller channels, known as *distributaries*.

Denudation The combined effect of *weathering*, *erosion*, and *mass movement*, which, over long periods, exposes underlying rocks.

Deposition The laying down of material that has accumulated:
(*1*) after being *eroded* and then transported by physical forces such as wind, ice, or water;
(*2*) as organic remains, such as coal and coral;
(*3*) as the result of *evaporation* and chemical *precipitation*.

Depression
1 In climatic terms it is a large low pressure system.
2 A complex *fold*, producing a large valley, which incorporates both a *syncline* and an *anticline*.

Desert An *arid* region of low rainfall, with little vegetation or animal life, which is adapted to the dry conditions. The term is now applied not only to hot tropical and subtropical regions, but to arid areas of the continental interiors and to the ice deserts of the *Arctic* and *Antarctic*.

Desertification The gradual extension of *desert* conditions in *arid* or *semiarid* regions, as a result of climatic change or human activity, such as over-grazing and *deforestation*.

Despot A ruler with absolute power. Despots are often associated with oppressive regimes.

Detritus Piles of rock deposited by an erosive agent such as a river or *glacier*.

Distributary A minor branch of a river, which does not rejoin the main stream, common at *deltas*.

Diurnal Daily, something that occurs each day. Diurnal temperature refers to the variation in temperature over the course of a full day and night.

Divide A US term describing the area of high ground separating two *drainage basins*.

Donga A steep-sided *gully*, resulting from *erosion* by a river or by floods.

Dormant A term used to describe a *volcano* which is not currently erupting. They differ from extinct volcanoes as dormant volcanoes are still considered likely to erupt in the future.

Drainage basin The area drained by a single river system, its boundary is marked by a *watershed* or *divide*.

Drought A long period of continuously low rainfall.

Drumlin A long, streamlined hillock composed of material deposited by a *glacier*. They often occur in groups known as swarms.

Dune A mound or ridge of sand, shaped, and often moved, by the wind. They are found in hot *deserts* and on low-lying coasts where onshore winds blow across sandy beaches.

Dyke A wall constructed in low-lying areas to contain floodwaters or protect from high tides.

E

Earthflow The rapid movement of soil and other loose surface material down a slope, when saturated by water. Similar to a mudflow but not as fast-flowing, due to a lower percentage of water.

Earthquake Sudden movements of the Earth's *crust*, causing the ground to shake. Frequently occurring at *tectonic plate* margins. The shock, or series of shocks, spreads out from an *epicenter*.

EC The European Community (*see* EU).

Ecosystem A system of living organisms – plants and animals – interacting with their *environment*.

ECOWAS Economic Community of West African States. Established in 1975, it incorporates 16 West African states and aims to promote closer regional and economic cooperation.

Element
1 A constituent of the *climate* – *precipitation*, *humidity*, temperature, *atmospheric pressure*, or wind.
2 A substance that cannot be separated into simpler substances by chemical means.

El Niño A climatic phenomenon, the El Niño effect occurs about 14 times each century and leads to major shifts in global air circulation. It is associated with unusually warm currents off the coasts of Peru, Ecuador and Chile. The anomaly can last for up to two years.

Environment The conditions created by the surroundings (both natural and artificial) within which an organism lives. In human geography the word includes the surrounding economic, cultural, and social conditions.

Eon (aeon) Traditionally a long, but indefinite, period of *geological time*.

Ephemeral A nonpermanent feature, often used in connection with seasonal rivers or lakes in dry areas.

Epicenter The point on the Earth's surface directly above the underground origin – or focus – of an *earthquake*.

Equator The line of *latitude* which lies equidistant between the North and South Poles.

Erg An extensive area of sand *dunes*, particularly in the Sahara Desert.

Erosion The processes which wear away the surface of the land. *Glaciers*, wind, rivers, waves, and currents all carry debris which causes *erosion*. Some definitions also include *mass movement* due to gravity as an agent of erosion.

Escarpment A steep slope at the margin of a level, upland surface. In a landscape created by *folding*, escarpments (or scarps) frequently lie behind a more gentle backward slope.

Esker A narrow, winding ridge of sand and gravel deposited by streams of water flowing beneath or at the edge of a *glacier*.

Erratic A rock transported by a *glacier* and deposited some distance from its place of origin.

Eustacy A world-wide fall or rise in ocean levels.

EU The European Union. Established in 1965, it was formerly known as the EEC (European Economic Community) and then the EC (European Community). Its members are Austria, Belgium, Denmark, Finland, France, Germany, Greece, Ireland, Italy, Luxembourg, Netherlands, Portugal, Spain, Sweden, and UK. It seeks to establish an integrated European common market and eventual federation.

Evaporation The process whereby a liquid or solid is turned into a gas or vapor. Also refers to the diffusion of water vapor into the *atmosphere* from exposed water surfaces such as lakes and seas.

Evapotranspiration The loss of moisture from the Earth's surface through a combination of *evaporation*, and *transpiration* from the leaves of plants.

Evergreen Plants with long-lasting leaves, which are not shed annually or seasonally.

Exfoliation A kind of *weathering* whereby scalelike flakes of rock are peeled or broken off by the development of salt crystals in water within the rocks. *Groundwater*, which contains dissolved salts, seeps to the surface and evaporates, precipitating a film of salt crystals, which expands causing fine cracks. As these grow, flakes of rock break off.

Extrusive rock *Igneous* rock formed when molten material (*magma*) pours forth at the Earth's surface and cools rapidly. It usually has a glassy texture.

F

Factionalism The actions of one or more minority political group acting against the interests of the majority government.

Fault A fracture or crack in rock, where strains (*tectonic* movement) have caused blocks to move, vertically or laterally, relative to each other.

Fauna Collective name for the animals of a particular period of time, or region.

Favela Brazilian term for the shantytowns or temporary huts that have grown up around the edge of many South and Central American cities.

Ferrel cell A component in the global pattern of air circulation, which rises in the colder *latitudes* (60° N and S) and descends in warmer *latitudes* (30° N and S). The Ferrel cell forms part of the world's three-cell air circulation pattern, with the *Hadley* and Polar cells.

Fissure A deep crack in a rock or a *glacier*.

Fjord A deep, narrow inlet, created when the sea inundates the *U-shaped valley* created by a *glacier*.

Flash flood A sudden, short-lived rise in the water level of a river or stream, or surge of water down a dry river channel, or *wadi*, caused by heavy rainfall.

Flax A plant used to make linen.

Floodplain The broad, flat part of a river valley, adjacent to the river itself, formed by *sediment* deposited during flooding.

Flora The collective name for the plants of a particular period of time or region.

Flow The movement of a river within its banks, particularly in terms of the speed and volume of water.

Fold A bend in the rock *strata* of the Earth's *crust*, resulting from compression.

Fossil The remains, or traces, of a dead organism preserved in the Earth's *crust*.

Fossil dune A *dune* formed in a once-*arid* region which is now wetter. *Dunes* normally move with the wind, but in these cases vegetation makes them stable.

Fossil fuel Fuel – coal, natural gas or oil – composed of the fossilized remains of plants and animals.

Front The boundary between two *air masses*, which contrast sharply in temperature and *humidity*.

Frontal depression An area of low pressure caused by rising warm air. They are generally 600–1,200 miles (1,000–2,000 km) in diameter. Within *depressions* there are both warm and cold fronts.

Frost shattering A form of *weathering* where water freezes in cracks, causing expansion. As temperatures fluctuate and the ice melts and refreezes, it eventually causes the rocks to shatter and fragments of rock to break off.

G

Gaucho South American term for a stock herder or cowboy who works on the grassy *plains* of Paraguay, Uruguay, and Argentina.

Geological timescale The chronology of the Earth's history as revealed in its rocks. Geological time is divided into a number of periods: *eon*, era, period, epoch, age, and chron (the shortest). These units are not of uniform length.

Geosyncline A concave fold (*syncline*) or large depression in the Earth's *crust*, extending hundreds of miles. This basin contains a deep layer of sediment, especially at its center, from the land masses around it.

Geothermal energy Heat derived from hot rocks within the Earth's *crust* and resulting in hot springs, steam, or hot rocks at the surface. The energy is generated by rock movements, and from the breakdown of radioactive elements occurring under intense pressure.

GDP Gross Domestic Product. The total value of goods and services produced by a country excluding income from foreign countries.

Geyser A jet of steam and hot water that intermittently erupts from vents in the ground in areas that are, or were, *volcanic*. Some geysers occasionally reach heights of 196 ft (60 m).

Ghetto An area of a city or region occupied by an overwhelming majority of people from one racial or religious group, who may be subject to persecution or containment.

Glaciation The growth of *glaciers* and *ice sheets*, and their impact on the landscape.

Glacier A body of ice moving downslope under the influence of gravity and consisting of compacted and frozen snow. A glacier is distinct from an *ice sheet*, which is wider and less confined by features of the landscape.

Glacio-eustacy A world-wide change in the level of the oceans, caused when the formation of *ice sheets* takes up water or when their melting returns water to the ocean. The formation of ice sheets in the *Pleistocene* epoch, for example, caused sea level to drop by about 320 ft (100 m).

Glaciofluvial To do with glacial *meltwater*, the landforms it creates and its processes; *erosion*, transportation, and *deposition*. Glaciofluvial effects are more powerful and rapid where they occur within or beneath the *glacier*, rather than beyond its edge.

Glacis A gentle slope or *pediment*.

Global warming An increase in the average temperature of the Earth. At present the *greenhouse effect* is thought to contribute to this.

GNP Gross National Product. The total value of goods and services produced by a country.

Gondwanaland The *supercontinent* thought to have existed over 200 million years ago in the southern hemisphere. Gondwanaland is believed to have comprised today's Africa, Madagascar, Australia, parts of South America, *Antarctica*, and the Indian subcontinent.

Graben A block of rock let down between two parallel *faults*. Where the graben occurs within a valley, the structure is known as a *rift valley*.

Grease ice Slicks of ice which form in *Antarctic* seas, when ice crystals are bonded together by wind and wave action.

Greenhouse effect A change in the temperature of the *atmosphere*. Short-wave solar radiation travels through the *atmosphere* unimpeded to the Earth's surface, whereas outgoing, long-wave terrestrial radiation is absorbed by materials that reradiate it back to the Earth. Radiation trapped in this way, by water vapor, carbon dioxide, and other "greenhouse gases," keeps the Earth warm. As more *carbon dioxide* is released into the atmosphere by the burning of *fossil fuels*, the greenhouse effect may cause a global increase in temperature.

Groundwater Water that has seeped into the pores, cavities, and cracks of rocks or into soil and water held in an *aquifer*.

Gully A deep, narrow channel eroded in the landscape by *ephemeral* streams.

Guyot A small, flat-topped submarine mountain, formed as a result of subsidence which occurs during *sea-floor spreading*.

Gypsum A soft mineral *compound* (hydrated calcium sulphate), used as the basis of many forms of plaster, including plaster of Paris.

H

Hadley cell A large-scale component in the global pattern of air circulation. Warm air rises over the *Equator* and blows at high altitude toward the poles, sinking in subtropical regions (30° N and 30° S) and creating high pressure. The air then flows at the surface toward the *Equator* in the form of trade winds. There is one cell in each hemisphere. Named after G. Hadley, who published his theory in 1735.

Hamada An Arabic word for a plateau of bare rock in a *desert*.

Hanging valley A tributary valley that ends suddenly, high above the bed of the main valley. The effect is found where the main valley has been more deeply eroded by a *glacier*, than has the tributary valley. A stream in a hanging valley will descend to the floor of the main valley as a waterfall or *cataract*.

Headwards The action of a river eroding back upstream, as opposed to the normal process of downstream *erosion*. Headwards erosion is often associated with *gullying*.

Hoodos Pinnacles of rock that have been worn away by *weathering* in *semiarid* regions.

Horst A block of the Earth's *crust* which has been left upstanding by the sinking of adjoining blocks along fault lines.

Hot spot A region of the Earth's *crust* where high thermal activity occurs, often leading to volcanic eruptions. Hot spots often occur far from plate boundaries, but their movement is associated with *plate tectonics*.

Humid equatorial Rainy *climate* with no winter, where the coolest month is generally above 64°F (18°C).

Humidity The relative amount of moisture held in the Earth's *atmosphere*.

Hurricane
1 A tropical *cyclone* occurring in the Caribbean and western North Atlantic.
2 A wind of more than 65 knots (75 kmph).

Hydroelectric power Energy produced by harnessing the rapid movement of water down steep mountain slopes to drive turbines to generate electricity.

Hydrolysis The chemical breakdown of rocks in reaction with water, forming new compounds.

I

Ice Age A period in the Earth's history when surface temperatures in the temperate *latitudes* were much lower and *ice sheets* expanded considerably. There have been *ice ages* from *Pre-Cambrian* times onward. The most recent began two million years ago and ended 10,000 years ago.

Ice cap A permanent dome of ice in highland areas. The term ice cap is often seen as distinct from *ice sheet*, which denotes a much wider covering of ice; and is also used refer to the very extensive polar and Greenland ice caps.

Ice floe A large, flat mass of ice floating free on the ocean surface. It is usually formed after the break-up of winter ice by heavy storms.

Ice sheet A continuous, very thick layer of ice and snow. The term is usually used of ice masses which are continental in extent.

Ice shelf A floating mass of ice attached to the edge of a coast. The seaward edge is usually a sheer cliff up to 100 ft (30 m) high.

Ice wedge Massive blocks of ice up to 6.5 ft (2 m) wide at the top and extending 32 ft (10 m) deep. They are found in cracks in *polygonally-patterned* ground in *periglacial* regions.

Iceberg A large mass of ice in a lake or a sea, which has broken off from a floating *ice sheet* (an *ice shelf*) or from a *glacier*.

Igneous rock Rock formed when molten material, *magma*, from the hot, lower layers of the Earth's *crust*, cools, solidifies, and crystallizes, either within the Earth's *crust* (*intrusive*) or on the surface (*extrusive*).

IMF International Monetary Fund. Established in 1944 as a UN agency, it contains 182 members around the world and is concerned with world monetary stability and economic development.

Incised meander A *meander* where the river, following its original course, cuts deeply into *bedrock*. This may occur when a mature, meandering river begins to erode its bed much more vigorously after the surrounding land has been uplifted.

Indigenous People, plants, or animals native to a particular region.

Infrastructure The communications and services – roads, railroads, and telecommunications – necessary for the functioning of a country or region.

Inselberg An isolated, steep-sided hill, rising from a low *plain* in *semiarid* and *savannah* landscapes. Inselbergs are usually composed of a rock, such as granite, which resists *erosion*.

Interglacial A period of global *climate*, between two *ice ages*, when temperatures rise and *ice sheets* and *glaciers* retreat.

Intraplate volcano A *volcano* which lies in the centre of one of the Earth's *tectonic plates*, rather than, as is more common, at its edge. They are thought to have been formed by a *hot spot*.

Intrusion (intrusive igneous rock) Rock formed when molten material, *magma*, penetrates existing rocks below the Earth's surface before cooling and solidifying. These rocks cool more slowly than extrusive rock and therefore tend to have coarser grains.

Irrigation The artificial supply of agricultural water to dry areas, often involving the creation of canals and the diversion of natural watercourses.

Island arc A curved chain of islands. Typically, such an arc fringes an ocean trench, formed at the margin between two *tectonic plates*. As one plate overrides another, *earthquakes* and volcanic activity are common and the islands themselves are often volcanic cones.

Isostasy The state of equilibrium that the Earth's *crust* maintains as its lighter and heavier parts float on the denser underlying mantle.

Isthmus A narrow strip of land connecting two larger landmasses or islands.

J

Jet stream A narrow belt of westerly winds in the *troposphere*, at altitudes above 39,000 ft (12,000 m). Jet streams tend to blow more strongly in winter and include: the subtropical jet stream; the *polar* front jet stream in mid-*latitudes*; the *Arctic* jet stream; and the polar-night jet stream.

Joint A crack in a rock, formed where blocks of rock have not shifted relative to each other, as is the case with a *fault*. Joints are created by *folding*; by shrinkage in *igneous rock* as it cools or *sedimentary rock* as it dries out; and by the release of pressure in a rock mass when overlying materials are removed by *erosion*.

Jute A plant fiber used to make coarse ropes, sacks, and matting.

K

Kame A mound of stratified sand and gravel with steep sides, deposited in a *crevasse* by *meltwater* running over a *glacier*. When the ice retreats, this forms an undulating terrain of hummocks.

Karst A barren *limestone* landscape created by carbonic acid in streams and rainwater, in areas where *limestone* is close to the surface. Typical features include caverns, towerlike hills, *sinkholes*, and flat limestone pavements.

Kettle hole A round hollow formed in a glacial deposit by a detached block of glacial ice, which later melted. They can fill with water to form kettle-lakes.

L

Lagoon A shallow stretch of coastal salt-water behind a partial barrier such as a sandbank or *coral reef*. Lagoon is also used to describe the water encircled by an *atoll*.

LAIA Latin American Integration Association. Established in 1980, its members are Argentina, Bolivia, Brazil, Chile, Colombia, Ecuador, Mexico, Paraguay, Peru, Uruguay, and Venezuela. It aims to promote economic cooperation between member states.

Landslide The sudden downslope movement of a mass of rock or earth on a slope, caused either by heavy rain; the impact of waves; an *earthquake* or human activity.

Laterite A hard red deposit left by *chemical weathering* in tropical conditions, and consisting mainly of oxides of iron and aluminium.

Latitude The angular distance from the *Equator*, to a given point on the Earth's surface. Imaginary lines of *latitude* running parallel to the Equator encircle the Earth, and are measured in degrees north or south of the Equator. The Equator is 0°, the poles 90° South and North respectively. Also called parallels.

Laurasia In the theory of *continental drift*, the northern part of the great *supercontinent* of *Pangaea*. Laurasia is said to consist of N America, Greenland and all of Eurasia north of the Indian subcontinent.

Lava The molten rock, *magma*, which erupts onto the Earth's surface through a *volcano*, or through a *fault* or crack in the Earth's *crust*. Lava refers to the rock both in its molten and in its later, solidified form.

Leaching The process whereby water dissolves minerals and moves them down through layers of soil or rock.

Levée A raised bank alongside the channel of a river. Levées are either human-made or formed in times of flood when the river overflows its channel, slows and deposits much of its *sediment* load.

Lichen An organism which is the symbiotic product of an algae and a fungus. Lichens form in tight crusts on stones and trees, and are resistant to extreme cold. They are often found in tundra regions.

Lignite Low-grade coal, also known as brown coal. Found in large deposits in eastern Europe.

Limestone A porous *sedimentary* rock formed from carbonate materials.

Lingua franca The language adopted as the common language between speakers whose native languages are different. This is common in former colonial states.

Lithosphere The rigid upper layer of the Earth, comprising the *crust* and the upper part of the *mantle*.

Llanos Vast grassland *plains* of northern South America.

Loess Fine-grained, yellow deposits of unstratified silts and sands. Loess is believed to be wind-carried *sediment* created in the last *Ice Age*. Some deposits may later have been redistributed by rivers. Loess-derived soils are of high quality, fertile, and easy to work.

Longitude A division of the Earth which pinpoints how far east or west a given place is from the Prime Meridian (0°) which runs through the Royal Observatory at Greenwich, England (UK). Imaginary lines of longitude are drawn around the world from pole to pole. The world is divided into 360 degrees.

Longshore drift The movement of sand and silt along the coast, carried by waves hitting the beach at an angle.

M

Magma Underground, molten rock, which is very hot and highly charged with gas. It is generated at great pressure, at depths 10 miles (16 km) or more below the Earth's surface. It can issue as *lava* at the Earth's surface or, more often, solidify below the surface as *intrusive igneous rock*.

Mantle The layer of the Earth between the *crust* and the *core*. It is about 1,800 miles (2,900 km) thick. The uppermost layer of the mantle is the soft, 125-mile (200 km) thick *asthenosphere* on which the more rigid *lithosphere* floats.

Maquiladoras Factories on the Mexico side of the Mexico/US border, that are allowed to import raw materials and components duty-free and use low-cost labor to assemble the goods, finally exporting them for sale in the US.

Market gardening The intensive growing of fruit and vegetables close to large local markets.

Mass movement Downslope movement of weathered materials such as rock, often helped by rainfall or glacial *meltwater*. Mass movement may be a gradual process or rapid, as in a *landslide* or rockfall.

Massif A single very large mountain or an area of mountains with uniform characteristics and clearly-defined boundaries.

Meander A looplike bend in a river, which is found typically in the lower, mature reaches of a river but can form wherever the valley is wide and the slope gentle.

Mediterranean climate A temperate *climate* of hot, dry summers and warm, damp winters. This is typical of the western fringes of the world's continents in the warm temperate regions between *latitudes* of 30° and 40° (north and south).

Meltwater Water resulting from the melting of a *glacier* or *ice sheet*.

Mesa A broad, flat-topped hill, characteristic of *arid* regions.

Mesosphere A layer of the Earth's *atmosphere*, between the *stratosphere* and the *thermosphere*. Extending from about 25–50 miles (40–80 km) above the surface of the Earth.

Mestizo A person of mixed *Amerindian* and European origin.

Metallurgy The refining and working of metals.

Metamorphic rocks Rocks that have been altered from their original form, in terms of texture, composition, and structure by intense heat, pressure, or by the introduction of new chemical substances – or a combination of more than one of these.

Meteor A body of rock, metal or other material, that travels through space at great speeds. Meteors are visible as they enter the Earth's *atmosphere* as shooting stars and fireballs.

Meteorite The remains of a *meteor* that has fallen to Earth.

Meteoroid A *meteor* that is still traveling in space, outside the Earth's *atmosphere*.

Mezzogiorno A term applied to the southern portion of Italy.

Milankovitch hypothesis A theory suggesting that there are a series of cycles that slightly alter the Earth's position when rotating about the Sun. The cycles identified all affect the amount of *radiation* the Earth receives at different *latitudes*. The theory is seen as a key factor in the cause of *ice ages*.

Millet A grain-crop, forming part of the staple diet in much of Africa.

Mistral A strong, dry, cold northerly or north-westerly wind, which blows from the Massif Central of France to the Mediterranean Sea. It is common in winter and its cold blasts can cause crop damage in the Rhône Delta, in France.

Mohorovičić discontinuity (Moho) The structural divide at the margin between the Earth's *crust* and the *mantle*. On average it is 20 miles (35 km) below the continents and 6 miles (10 km) below the oceans. The different densities of the *crust* and the mantle cause *earthquake* waves to accelerate at this point.

Monarchy A form of government in which the head of state is a single hereditary monarch. The monarch may be a mere figurehead, or may retain significant authority.

Monsoon A wind that changes direction biannually. The change is caused by the reversal of pressure over landmasses and the adjacent oceans. Because the inflowing moist winds bring rain, the term monsoon is also used to refer to the rains themselves. The term is derived from and most commonly refers to the seasonal winds of south and east Asia.

Montaña Mountain areas along the west coast of South America.

Moraine Debris, transported and deposited by a *glacier* or *ice sheet* in unstratified, mixed, piles of rock, boulders, pebbles, and clay.

Mountain-building The formation of *fold* mountains by tectonic activity. Also known as orogeny, mountain-building often occurs on the margin where two *tectonic plates* collide. The periods when most mountain-building occurred are known as orogenic phases and lasted many millions of years.

Mudflow An *avalanche* of mud that occurs when a mass of soil is drenched by rain or melting snow. It is a type of *mass movement*, faster than an *earthflow* because it is lubricated by water.

N

Nappe A mass of rocks which has been overfolded by repeated thrust *faulting*.

NAFTA The North American Free Trade Association. Established in 1994 between Canada, Mexico, and the US to set up a free-trade zone.

NASA The North American Space Agency. It is a government body, established in 1958 to develop manned and unmanned space programs.

NATO The North Atlantic Treaty Organization. Established in 1949 to promote mutual defense and cooperation between its members, which are Belgium, Canada, Czech Republic, Denmark, France, Germany, Greece, Iceland, Italy, Luxembourg, the Netherlands, Norway, Portugal, Poland, Spain, Turkey, UK, and US.

Nitrogen The odorless, colorless gas that makes up 78% of the atmosphere. Within the soil, it is a vital nutrient for plants.

Nomads (nomadic) Wandering communities that move around in search of suitable pasture for their herds of animals.

Nuclear fusion A technique used to create a new nucleus by the merging of two lighter ones, resulting in the release of large quantities of energy.

O

Oasis A fertile area in the midst of a *desert*, usually watered by an underground *aquifer*.

Oceanic ridge A mid-ocean ridge formed, according to the theory of *plate tectonics*, when plates drift apart and hot *magma* pours through to form new oceanic *crust*.

Oligarchy The government of a state by a small, exclusive group of people – such as an elite class or a family group.

Onion-skin weathering The *weathering* away or *exfoliation* of a rock or outcrop by the peeling off of surface layers.

Oriente A flatter region lying to the east of the Andes in South America.

Outwash plain *Glaciofluvial* material (typically clay, sand, and gravel) carried beyond an ice sheet by *meltwater* streams, forming a broad, flat deposit.

Oxbow lake A crescent-shaped lake formed on a river *floodplain* when a river erodes the outside bend of a *meander*, making the neck of the *meander* narrow until the river cuts across the neck. The meander is cut off and is dammed off with sediment, creating an oxbow lake. Also known as a cut-off or mortlake.

Oxidation A form of *chemical weathering* where *oxygen* dissolved in water reacts with minerals in rocks – particularly iron – to form oxides. Oxidation causes brown or yellow staining on rocks, and eventually leads to the break down of the rock.

Oxygen A colorless, odorless gas which is one of the main constituents of the Earth's *atmosphere* and is essential to life on Earth.

Ozone layer A layer of enriched *oxygen* (O_3) within the stratosphere, mostly between 18–50 miles (30–80 km) above the Earth's surface. It is vital to the existence of life on Earth because it absorbs harmful shortwave ultraviolet radiation, while allowing beneficial longer wave ultraviolet radiation to penetrate to the Earth's surface.

P

Pacific Rim The name given to the economically-dynamic countries bordering the Pacific Ocean.

Pack ice Ice masses more than 10 ft (3 m) thick that form on the sea surface and are not attached to a landmass.

Pancake ice Thin discs of ice, up to 8 ft (2.4 m) wide which form when slicks of *grease ice* are tossed together by winds and stormy seas.

Pangaea In the theory of continental drift, Pangaea is the original great land mass which, about 190 million years ago, began to split into Gondwanaland in the south and Laurasia in the north, separated by the Tethys Sea.

Pastoralism Grazing of livestock– usually sheep, goats, or cattle. Pastoralists in many drier areas have traditionally been *nomadic*.

Parallel *see Latitude.*

Peat Ancient, partially-decomposed vegetation found in wet, boggy conditions where there is little *oxygen*. It is the first stage in the development of coal and is often dried for use as fuel. It is also used to improve soil quality.

Pediment A gently-sloping ramp of *bedrock* below a steeper slope, often found at mountain edges in *desert* areas, but also in other climatic zones. Pediments may include depositional elements such as *alluvial fans*.

Peninsula A thin strip of land surrounded on three of its sides by water. Large examples include Florida and Korea.

Per capita Latin term meaning "for each person."

Periglacial Regions on the edges of *ice sheets* or *glaciers* or, more commonly, cold regions experiencing intense frost action, *permafrost* or both. Periglacial climates bring long, freezing winters and short, mild summers.

Permafrost Permanently frozen ground, typical of *Arctic* regions. Although a layer of soil above the permafrost melts in summer, the melted water does not drain through the permafrost.

Permeable rocks Rocks through which water can seep, because they are either porous or cracked.

Pharmaceuticals The manufacture of medicinal drugs.

Phreatic eruption A volcanic eruption which occurs when *lava* combines with *groundwater,* superheating the water and causing a sudden emission of steam at the surface.

Physical weathering (mechanical weathering) The breakdown of rocks by physical, as opposed to chemical, processes. Examples include: changes in pressure or temperature; the effect of windblown sand; the pressure of growing salt crystals in cracks within rock; and the expansion and contraction of water within rock as it freezes and thaws.

Pingo A dome of earth with a core of ice, found in *tundra* regions. Pingos are formed either when *groundwater* freezes and expands, pushing up the land surface, or when trapped, freezing water in a lake expands and pushes up lake *sediments* to form the pingo dome.

Placer A belt of mineral-bearing rock *strata* lying at or close to the Earth's surface, from which minerals can be easily extracted.

Plain A flat, level region of land, often relatively low-lying.

Plateau A highland tract of flat land.

Plate *see Tectonic plates.*

Plate tectonics The study of *tectonic plates,* that helps to explain *continental drift*, mountain formation and volcanic activity. The movement of tectonic plates may be explained by the currents of rock rising and falling from within the Earth's *mantle,* as it heats up and then cools. The boundaries of the plates are known as plate margins and most mountains, *earthquakes,* and *volcanoes* occur at these margins. Constructive margins are moving apart; destructive margins are crunching together and conservative margins are sliding past one another.

Pleistocene A period of *geological time* spanning from about 5.2 million years ago to 1.6 million years ago.

Plutonic rock *Igneous* rocks found deep below the surface. They are coarse-grained because they cooled and solidified slowly.

Polar The zones within the *Arctic* and *Antarctic* circles.

Polje A long, broad *depression* found in *karst* (*limestone*) regions.

Polygonal patterning Typical ground patterning, found in areas where the soil is subject to severe frost action, often in *periglacial* regions.

Porosity A measure of how much water can be held within a rock or a soil. Porosity is measured as the percentage of holes or pores in a material, compared to its total volume. For example, the porosity of slate is less than 1%, whereas that of gravel is 25–35%.

Prairies Originally a French word for grassy *plains* with few or no trees.

Pre-Cambrian The earliest period of *geological time* dating from over 570 million years ago.

Precipitation The fall of moisture from the *atmosphere* onto the surface of the Earth, whether as dew, hail, rain, sleet, or snow.

Pyramidal peak A steep, isolated mountain summit, formed when the back walls of three or more *cirques* are cut back and move toward each other. The cliffs around such a horned peak, or horn, are divided by sharp *arêtes.* The Matterhorn in the Swiss Alps is an example.

Pyroclasts Fragments of rock ejected during volcanic eruptions.

Q

Quaternary The current period of *geological time,* which started about 1.6 million years ago.

R

Radiation The emission of energy in the form of particles or waves. Radiation from the sun includes heat, light, ultraviolet rays, gamma rays, and X-rays. Only some of the solar energy radiated into space reaches the Earth.

Rainforest Dense forests in tropical zones with high rainfall, temperature and *humidity*. Strictly, the term applies to the equatorial rain forest in tropical lowlands with constant rainfall and no seasonal change. The Congo and Amazon basins are examples. The term is applied more loosely to lush forest in other climates. Within rain forests organic life is dense and varied: at least 40% of all plant and animal species are found here and there may be as many as 100 tree species per hectare.

Rainshadow An area which experiences low rainfall, because of its position on the leeward side of a mountain range.

Reg A large area of stony *desert*, where tightly-packed gravel lies on top of clayey sand. A reg is formed where the wind blows away the finer sand.

Remote-sensing Method of obtaining information about the *environment* using unmanned equipment, such as a satellite, that relays the information to a point where it is collected and used.

Resistance The capacity of a rock to resist *denudation,* by processes such as *weathering* and *erosion.*

Ria A flooded *V-shaped river valley* or estuary, flooded by a rise in sea level (*eustacy*) or sinking land. It is shorter than a *fjord* and gets deeper as it meets the sea.

Rift valley A long, narrow depression in the Earth's *crust*, formed by the sinking of rocks between two *faults*.

River channel The trough which contains a river and is molded by the flow of water within it.

Roche moutonée A rock found in a glaciated valley. The side facing the flow of the *glacier* has been smoothed and rounded, while the other side has been left more rugged because the *glacier*, as it flows over it, has plucked out frozen fragments and carried them away.

Runoff Water draining from a land surface by flowing across it.

S

Sabkha The floor of an isolated *depression* that occurs in an *arid environment* – usually covered by salt deposits and devoid of vegetation.

SADC Southern African Development Community. Established in 1992 to promote economic integration between its member states, which are Angola, Botswana, Lesotho, Malawi, Mauritius, Mozambique, Namibia, South Africa, Swaziland, Tanzania, Zambia, and Zimbabwe.

Salt plug A rounded hill produced by the upward doming of rock *strata* caused by the movement of salt or other evaporite deposits under intense pressure.

Sastrugi Ice ridges formed by wind action. They lie parallel to the direction of the wind.

Savannah Open grassland found between the zone of *deserts*, and that of tropical *rain forests* in the tropics and subtropics. Scattered trees and shrubs are found in some kinds of savannah. A savannah *climate* usually has wet and dry seasons.

Scarp *see Escarpment.*

Scree Piles of rock fragments beneath a cliff or rock face, caused by mechanical *weathering*, especially *frost shattering*, where the expansion and contraction of freezing and thawing water within the rock, gradually breaks it up.

Sea-floor spreading The process whereby *tectonic plates* move apart, allowing hot *magma* to erupt and solidify. This forms a new sea floor and, ultimately, widens the ocean.

Seamount An isolated, submarine mountain or hill, probably of volcanic origin.

Season A period of time linked to regular changes in the weather, especially the intensity of solar *radiation.*

Sediment Grains of rock transported and deposited by rivers, sea, ice, or wind.

Sedimentary rocks Rocks formed from the debris of preexisting rocks or of organic material. They are found in many *environments* – on the ocean floor, on beaches, rivers, and *deserts*. Organically-formed sedimentary rocks include coal and chalk. Other sedimentary rocks, such as flint, are formed by chemical processes. Most of these rocks contain *fossils*, which can be used to date them.

Seif A sand *dune* which lies parallel to the direction of the prevailing wind. Seifs form steep-sided ridges, sometimes extending for miles.

Seismic activity Movement within the Earth, such as an *earthquake* or *tremor.*

Selva A region of wet forest found in the Amazon Basin.

Semiarid, semidesert The *climate* and landscape which lies between *savannah* and *desert* or between savannah and a *mediterranean* climate. In semiarid conditions there is a little more moisture than in a true *desert*; and more patches of drought-resistant vegetation can survive.

Shale (marine shale) A compacted *sedimentary rock*, with fine-grained particles. Marine shale is formed on the seabed. Fuel such as oil may be extracted from it.

Sheetwash Water that runs downhill in thin sheets without forming channels. It can cause *sheet erosion*.

Sheet erosion The washing away of soil by a thin film or sheet of water, known as *sheetwash*.

Shield A vast stable block of the Earth's *crust*, which has experienced little or no *mountain-building*.

Sierra The Spanish word for mountains.

Sinkhole A circular *depression* in a *limestone* region. They are formed by the collapse of an underground cave system or the *chemical weathering* of the *limestone.*

Sisal A plant-fiber used to make matting.

Slash and burn A farming technique involving the cutting down and burning of scrub forest, to create agricultural land. After a number of seasons this land is abandoned and the process is repeated. This practice is common in Africa and South America.

Slip face The steep leeward side of a sand *dune* or slope. Opposite side to a *back slope.*

Soil A thin layer of rock particles mixed with the remains of dead plants and animals. This occurs naturally on the surface of the Earth and provides a medium for plants to grow.

Soil creep The very gradual downslope movement of rock debris and soil, under the influence of gravity. This is a type of *mass movement.*

Soil erosion The wearing away of soil more quickly than it is replaced by natural processes. Soil can be carried away by wind as well as by water. Human activities, such as overgrazing and the clearing of land for farming, accelerate the process in many areas.

Solar energy Energy derived from the Sun. Solar energy is converted into other forms of energy. For example, the wind and waves, as well as the creation of plant material in photosynthesis, depend on solar energy.

Solifluction A kind of *soil creep,* where water in the surface layer has saturated the soil and rock debris which slips slowly downhill. It often happens where frozen top-layer deposits thaw, leaving frozen layers below them.

Sorghum A type of grass found in South America, similar to sugar cane. When refined it is used to make molasses.

Spit A thin linear deposit of sand or shingle extending from the sea shore. Spits are formed as angled waves shift sand along the beach, eventually extending a ridge of sand beyond a change in the angle of the coast. Spits are common where the coastline bends, especially at estuaries.

Squash A type of edible gourd.

Stack A tall, isolated pillar of rock near a coastline, created as wave action erodes away the adjacent rock.

Stalactite A tapering cylinder of mineral deposit, hanging from the roof of a cave in a *karst* area. It is formed by calcium carbonate, dissolved in water, which drips through the roof of a *limestone* cavern.

Stalagmite A cone of calcium carbonate, similar to a *stalactite,* rising from the floor of a *limestone* cavern and formed when drops of water fall from the roof of a *limestone* cave. If the water has dripped from a *stalactite* above the stalagmite, the two may join to form a continuous pillar.

Staple crop The main crop on which a country is economically and or physically reliant. For example, the major crop grown for large-scale local consumption in South Asia is rice.

Steppe Large areas of dry grassland in the northern hemisphere – particularly found in southeast Europe and central Asia.

Strata The plural of stratum, a distinct, virtually horizontal layer of deposited material, lying parallel to other layers.

Stratosphere A layer of the *atmosphere,* above the *troposphere,* extending from about 7–30 miles (11–50 km) above the Earth's surface. In the lower part of the stratosphere, the temperature is relatively stable and there is little moisture.

Strike-slip fault Occurs where plates move sideways past each other and blocks of rocks move horizontally in relation to each other, not up or down as in normal *faults.*

Subduction zone A region where two *tectonic plates* collide, forcing one beneath the other. Typically, a dense oceanic plate dips below a lighter continental plate, melting in the heat of the *asthenosphere.* This is why the zone is also called a destructive margins (*see Plate tectonics*). These zones are characterized by *earthquakes,* volcanoes, *mountain-building,* and the development of oceanic trenches and *island arcs.*

Submarine canyon A steep-sided valley, that extends along the *continental shelf* to the ocean floor. Often formed by *turbidity currents.*

Submarine fan Deposits of silt and *alluvium*, carried by large rivers forming great fan-shaped deposits on the ocean floor.

Subsistence agriculture An agricultural practice in which enough food is produced to support the farmer and his dependents, but not providing any surplus to generate an income.

Subtropical A term applied loosely to *climates* which are nearly tropical or tropical for a part of the year – areas north or south of the *tropics* but outside the *temperate zone.*

Supercontinent A large continent that breaks up to form smaller continents or that forms when smaller continents merge. In the theory of *continental drift*, the supercontinents are *Pangaea, Gondwanaland,* and *Laurasia.*

Sustainable development An approach to development, especially applied to economies across the world which exploit natural resources without destroying them or the *environment.*

Syncline A basin-shaped downfold in rock *strata*, created when the *strata* are compressed, for example where *tectonic plates* collide.

T

Tableland A highland area with a flat or gently undulating surface.

Taiga The belt of *coniferous* forest found in the north of Asia and North America. The conifers are adapted to survive low temperatures and long periods of snowfall.

Tarn A Scottish term for a small mountain lake, usually found at the head of a *glacier*.

Tectonic plates Plates, or tectonic plates, are the rigid slabs which form the Earth's outer shell, the *lithosphere.* Eight big plates and several smaller ones have been identified.

Temperate A moderate *climate* without extremes of temperature, typical of the mid-*latitudes* between the *tropics* and the *polar* circles.

Theocracy A state governed by religious laws – today Iran is the world's largest theocracy.

Thermokarst Subsidence created by the thawing of ground ice in *periglacial* areas, creating depressions.

Thermosphere A layer of the Earth's *atmosphere* which lies above the *mesophere,* about 60–300 miles (100–500 km) above the Earth

Terraces Steps cut into steep slopes to create flat surfaces for cultivating crops. They also help reduce soil *erosion* on unconsolidated slopes. They are most common in heavily-populated parts of Southeast Asia.

Till Unstratified glacial deposits or drift left by a *glacier* or *ice sheet.* Till includes mixtures of clay, sand, gravel, and boulders.

Topography The typical shape and features of a given area such as land height and terrain.

Tombolo A large sand *spit* which attaches part of the mainland to an island.

Tornado A violent, spiraling windstorm, with a center of very low pressure. Wind speeds reach 200 mph (320 kmph) and there is often thunder and heavy rain.

Transform fault In *plate tectonics,* a *fault* of continental scale, occurring where two plates slide past each other, staying close together for example, the San Andreas Fault, USA. The jerky, uneven movement creates *earthquakes* but does not destroy or add to the Earth's *crust*

Transpiration The loss of water vapor through the pores (or stomata) of plants. The process helps to return moisture to the *atmosphere.*

Trap An area of fine-grained *igneous rock* that has been extruded and cooled on the Earth's surface in stages, forming a series of steps or terraces.

Treeline The line beyond which trees cannot grow, dependent on *latitude* and altitude, as well as local factors such as soil.

Tremor A slight *earthquake.*

Trench (oceanic trench) A long, deep trough in the ocean floor, formed, according to the theory of *plate tectonics*, when two plates collide and one dives under the other, creating a *subduction zone.*

Tropics The zone between the *Tropic of Cancer* and the *Tropic of Capricorn* where the *climate* is hot. Tropical climate is also applied to areas rather further north and south of the *Equator* where the climate is similar to that of the true tropics.

Tropic of Cancer A line of *latitude* or imaginary circle round the Earth, lying at 23° 28' N.

Tropic of Capricorn A line of *latitude* or imaginary circle round the Earth, lying at 23° 28' S.

Troposphere The lowest layer of the Earth's *atmosphere.* From the surface, it reaches a height of between 4–10 miles (7–16 km). It is the most turbulent zone of the atmosphere and accounts for the generation of most of the world's weather. The layer above it is called the *stratosphere.*

Tsunami A huge wave created by shock waves from an *earthquake* under the sea. Reaching speeds of up to 600 mph (960 kmph), the wave may increase to heights of 50 ft (15 m) on entering coastal waters; and it can cause great damage.

Tundra The treeless *plains* of the *Arctic Circle*, found south of the *polar* region of permanent ice and snow, and north of the belt of *coniferous* forests known as *taiga.* In this region of long, very cold winters, vegetation is usually limited to mosses, *lichens,* sedges, and rushes, although flowers and dwarf shrubs blossom in the brief summer.

Turbidity current An oceanic feature. A turbidity current is a mass of *sediment*-laden water that has substantial erosive power. Turbidity currents are thought to contribute to the formation of *submarine canyons.*

Typhoon A kind of *hurricane* (or tropical cyclone) bringing violent winds and heavy rain, a typhoon can do great damage. They occur in the South China Sea, especially around the Philippines.

U

U-shaped valley A river valley that has been deepened and widened by a *glacier*. They are characteristically flat-bottomed and steep-sided and generally much deeper than river valleys.

UN United Nations. Established in 1945, it contains 188 nations and aims to maintain international peace and security, and promote cooperation over economic, social, cultural, and humanitarian problems.

UNICEF United Nations Children's Fund. A UN organization set up to promote family and child related programs.

Urstromtäler A German word used to describe *meltwater* channels that flowed along the front edge of the advancing *ice sheet* during the last Ice Age, 18,000–20,000 years ago.

V

V-shaped valley A typical valley eroded by a river in its upper course.

Virgin rain forest Tropical *rain-forest* in its original state, untouched by human activity such as logging, clearance for agriculture, settlement, or roadbuilding.

Viticulture The cultivation of grapes for wine.

Volcano An opening or vent in the Earth's *crust* where molten rock, *magma*, erupts. Volcanoes tend to be conical but may also be a crack in the Earth's surface or a hole blasted through a mountain. The magma is accompanied by other materials such as gas, steam, and fragments of rock, or *pyroclasts.* They tend to occur on destructive or constructive tectonicplate margins.

W–Z

Wadi The dry bed left by a torrent of water. Also classified as a *ephemeral* stream, found in *arid* and *semiarid* regions, which are subject to sudden and often severe flash flooding.

Warm humid climate A rainy climate with warm summers and mild winters.

Water cycle The continuous circulation of water between the Earth's surface and the *atmosphere.* The processes include *evaporation* and *transpiration* of moisture into the atmosphere, and its return as *precipitation,* some of which flows into lakes and oceans.

Water table The upper level of *groundwater* saturation in permeable rock *strata.*

Watershed The dividing line between one *drainage basin* – an area where all streams flow into a single river system – and another. In the US, watershed also means the whole drainage basin of a single river system – its catchment area.

Waterspout A rotating column of water in the form of cloud, mist, and spray which form on open water. Often has the appearance of a small *tornado.*

Weathering The decay and breakup of rocks at or near the Earth's surface, caused by water, wind, heat or ice, organic material, or the *atmosphere. Physical weathering* includes the effects of frost and temperature changes. Biological weathering includes the effects of plant roots, burrowing animals and the acids produced by animals, especially as they decay after death. *Carbonation* and *hydrolysis* are among many kinds of *chemical weathering.*

Geographical Names

The following glossary lists all geographical terms occurring on the maps and in main-entry names in the Index-Gazetteer. These terms may precede, follow or be run together with the proper element of the name; where they precede it the term is reversed for indexing purposes – thus Poluostrov Yamal is indexed as Yamal, Poluostrov.

Key
Geographical term *Language,* Term

A

Å *Danish, Norwegian,* River
Āb *Persian,* River
Adrar *Berber,* Mountains
Agía, Ágios *Greek,* Saint
Air *Indonesian,* River
Ákra *Greek,* Cape, point
Alpen *German,* Alps
Alt- *German,* Old
Altiplanicie *Spanish,* Plateau
Älve(en) *Swedish,* River
-ån *Swedish,* River
Anse *French,* Bay
'Aqabat *Arabic,* Pass
Archipiélago *Spanish,* Archipelago
Arcipelago *Italian,* Archipelago
Arquipélago *Portuguese,* Archipelago
Arrecife(s) *Spanish,* Reef(s)
Aru *Tamil,* River
Augstiene *Latvian,* Upland
Aukštuma *Lithuanian,* Upland
Aust- *Norwegian,* Eastern
Avtonomnyy Okrug *Russian,* Autonomous district
Āw *Kurdish,* River
'Ayn *Arabic,* Spring, well
'Ayoûn *Arabic,* Wells

B

Baelt *Danish,* Strait
Bahía *Spanish,* Bay
Baḥr *Arabic,* River
Baía *Portuguese,* Bay
Baie *French,* Bay
Bañado *Spanish,* Marshy land
Bandao *Chinese,* Peninsula
Banjaran *Malay,* Mountain range
Barajı *Turkish,* Dam
Barragem *Portuguese,* Reservoir
Bassin *French,* Basin
Batang *Malay,* Stream
Beinn, Ben *Gaelic,* Mountain
-berg *Afrikaans, Norwegian,* Mountain
Besar *Indonesian, Malay,* Big
Birkat, Birket *Arabic,* Lake, well, cistern
Boğazi *Turkish,* Lake
Boka *Serbo-Croatian,* Bay
Bol'sh-aya, -iye, -oy, -oye *Russian,* Big
Botigh(i) *Uzbek,* Depression basin
-bre(en) *Norwegian,* Glacier
Bredning *Danish,* Bay
Bucht *German,* Bay
Bugt(en) *Danish,* Bay
Buḥayrat *Arabic,* Lake, reservoir
Buḥeiret *Arabic,* Lake
Bukit *Malay,* Mountain
-bukta *Norwegian,* Bay
bukten *Swedish,* Bay
Bulag *Mongolian,* Spring
Bulak *Uighur,* Spring
Burnu *Turkish,* Cape, point
Buuraha *Somali,* Mountains

C

Cabo *Portuguese,* Cape
Caka *Tibetan,* Salt lake
Canal *Spanish,* Channel
Cap *French,* Cape
Capo *Italian,* Cape, headland
Cascada *Portuguese,* Waterfall
Cayo(s) *Spanish,* Islet(s), rock(s)
Cerro *Spanish,* Mountain
Chaîne *French,* Mountain range
Chapada *Portuguese,* Hills, upland
Chau *Cantonese,* Island
Chay *Turkish,* River
Chhâk *Cambodian,* Bay
Chhu *Tibetan,* River
-chŏsuji *Korean,* Reservoir
Chott *Arabic,* Depression, salt lake
Chŭli *Uzbek,* Grassland, steppe
Ch'ün-tao *Chinese,* Island group
Chuŏr Phnum *Cambodian,* Mountains
Ciudad *Spanish,* City, town
Co *Tibetan,* Lake
Colline(s) *French,* Hill(s)
Cordillera *Spanish,* Mountain range
Costa *Spanish,* Coast
Côte *French,* Coast
Coxilha *Portuguese,* Mountains
Cuchilla *Spanish,* Mountains

D

Daban *Mongolian, Uighur,* Pass
Daği *Azerbaijani, Turkish,* Mountain
Dağlari *Azerbaijani, Turkish,* Mountains
-dake *Japanese,* Peak
-dal(en) *Norwegian,* Valley
Danau *Indonesian,* Lake
Dao *Chinese,* Island
Đao *Vietnamese,* Island
Daryā *Persian,* River
Daryācheh *Persian,* Lake
Dasht *Persian,* Desert, plain
Dawḥat *Arabic,* Bay
Denizi *Turkish,* Sea
Dere *Turkish,* Stream
Desierto *Spanish,* Desert
Dili *Azerbaijani,* Spit
-do *Korean,* Island
Dooxo *Somali,* Valley
Düzü *Azerbaijani,* Steppe
-dwīp *Bengali,* Island

E

-eilanden *Dutch,* Islands
Embalse *Spanish,* Reservoir
Ensenada *Spanish,* Bay
Erg *Arabic,* Dunes
Estany *Catalan,* Lake
Estero *Spanish,* Inlet
Estrecho *Spanish,* Strait
Étang *French,* Lagoon, lake
-ey *Icelandic,* Island
Ezero *Bulgarian, Macedonian,* Lake
Ezers *Latvian,* Lake

F

Feng *Chinese,* Peak
Fjord *Danish,* Fjord
-fjord(en) *Danish, Norwegian, Swedish,* fjord
-fjørdhur *Faeroese,* Fjord
Fleuve *French,* River
Fliegu *Maltese,* Channel
-fljór *Icelandic,* River
-flói *Icelandic,* Bay
Forêt *French,* Forest

G

-gan *Japanese,* Rock
-gang *Korean,* River
Ganga *Hindi, Nepali, Sinhala,* River
Gaoyuan *Chinese,* Plateau
Garagumy *Turkmen,* Sands
-gawa *Japanese,* River
Gebel *Arabic,* Mountain
-gebirge *German,* Mountain range
Ghadīr *Arabic,* Well
Ghubbat *Arabic,* Bay
Gjiri *Albanian,* Bay
Gol *Mongolian,* River
Golfe *French,* Gulf
Golfo *Italian, Spanish,* Gulf
Göl(ü) *Turkish,* Lake
Golyam, -a *Bulgarian,* Big
Gora *Russian, Serbo-Croatian,* Mountain
Góra *Polish,* Mountain
Gory *Russian,* Mountain
Gryada *Russian,* Ridge
Guba *Russian,* Bay
-gundo *Korean,* Island group
Gunung *Malay,* Mountain

H

Ḥadd *Arabic,* Spit
-haehyŏp *Korean,* Strait
Haff *German,* Lagoon
Hai *Chinese,* Bay, lake, sea
Haixia *Chinese,* Strait
Hamada *Arabic,* Plateau
Ḥammādat *Arabic,* Plateau
Hāmūn *Persian,* Lake
-hantō *Japanese,* Peninsula
Har, Haré *Hebrew,* Mountain
Ḥarrat *Arabic,* Lava-field
Hav(et) *Danish, Swedish,* Sea
Hawr *Arabic,* Lake
Hāyk' *Amharic,* Lake
He *Chinese,* River
-hegység *Hungarian,* Mountain range
Heide *German,* Heath, moorland
Helodrano *Malagasy,* Bay
Higashi- *Japanese,* East(ern)
Ḥiṣā' *Arabic,* Well
Hka *Burmese,* River
-ho *Korean,* Lake
Hô *Korean,* Reservoir
Ḥolot *Hebrew,* Dunes
Hora *Belorussian, Czech,* Mountain
Hrada *Belorussian,* Mountain, ridge
Hsi *Chinese,* River
Hu *Chinese,* Lake
Huk *Danish,* Point

I

Île(s) *French,* Island(s)
Ilha(s) *Portuguese,* Island(s)
Ilhéu(s) *Portuguese,* Islet(s)
Imeni *Russian,* In the name of
Inish- *Gaelic,* Island
Insel(n) *German,* Island(s)
Irmağı, Irmak *Turkish,* River
Isla(s) *Spanish,* Island(s)
Isola (Isole) *Italian,* Island(s)

J

Jabal *Arabic,* Mountain
Jāl *Arabic,* Ridge
-järv *Estonian,* Lake
-järvi *Finnish,* Lake
Jazā'ir *Arabic,* Islands
Jazīrat *Arabic,* Island
Jazīreh *Persian,* Island
Jebel *Arabic,* Mountain
Jezero *Serbo-Croatian,* Lake
Jezioro *Polish,* Lake
Jiang *Chinese,* River
-jima *Japanese,* Island
Jižní *Czech,* Southern
-jõgi *Estonian,* River
-joki *Finnish,* River
-jökull *Icelandic,* Glacier
Jūn *Arabic,* Bay
Juzur *Arabic,* Islands

K

Kaikyō *Japanese,* Strait
-kaise *Lappish,* Mountain
Kali *Nepali,* River
Kalnas *Lithuanian,* Mountain
Kalns *Latvian,* Mountain
Kang *Chinese,* Harbor
Kangri *Tibetan,* Mountain(s)
Kaôh *Cambodian,* Island
Kapp *Norwegian,* Cape
Káto *Greek,* Lower
Kavīr *Persian,* Desert
K'edi *Georgian,* Mountain range
Kediet *Arabic,* Mountain
Kepi *Albanian,* Cape, point
Kepulauan *Indonesian, Malay,* Island group
Khalig, Khalīj *Arabic,* Gulf
Khawr *Arabic,* Inlet
Khola *Nepali,* River
Khrebet *Russian,* Mountain range
Ko *Thai,* Island
-ko *Japanese,* Inlet, lake
Kólpos *Greek,* Bay
-kopf *German,* Peak
Körfäzi *Azerbaijani,* Bay
Körfezi *Turkish,* Bay
Kõrgustik *Estonian,* Upland
Kosa *Russian, Ukrainian,* Spit
Koshi *Nepali,* River
Kou *Chinese,* River-mouth
Kowtal *Persian,* Pass
Kray *Russian,* Region, territory
Kryazh *Russian,* Ridge
Kuduk *Uighur,* Well
Kūh(hā) *Persian,* Mountain(s)
-kul' *Russian,* Lake
Kŭl(i) *Tajik, Uzbek,* Lake
-kundo *Korean,* Island group
-kysten *Norwegian,* Coast
Kyun *Burmese,* Island

L

Laaq *Somali,* Watercourse
Lac *French,* Lake
Lacul *Romanian,* Lake
Lagh *Somali,* Stream
Lago *Italian, Portuguese, Spanish,* Lake
Lagoa *Portuguese,* Lagoon
Laguna *Italian, Spanish,* Lagoon, lake
Laht *Estonian,* Bay
Laut *Indonesian,* Bay
Lembalemba *Malagasy,* Plateau
Lerr *Armenian,* Mountain
Lerrnashght'a *Armenian,* Mountain range
Les *Czech,* Forest
Lich *Armenian,* Lake
Liehtao *Chinese,* Island group
Liqeni *Albanian,* Lake
Límni *Greek,* Lake
Ling *Chinese,* Mountain range
Llano *Spanish,* Plain, prairie
Lumi *Albanian,* River
Lyman *Ukrainian,* Estuary

M

Madīnat *Arabic,* City, town
Mae Nam *Thai,* River
-mägi *Estonian,* Hill
Maja *Albanian,* Mountain
Mal *Albanian,* Mountains
Mal-aya, -oye, -yy, *Russian,* Small
-man *Korean,* Bay
Mar *Spanish,* Lake
Marios *Lithuanian,* Lake
Massif *French,* Mountains
Meer *German,* Lake
-meer *Dutch,* Lake
Melkosopochnik *Russian,* Plain
-meri *Estonian,* Sea
Mifraz *Hebrew,* Bay
Minami- *Japanese,* South(ern)
-misaki *Japanese,* Cape, point
Monkhafad *Arabic,* Depression
Montagne(s) *French,* Mountain(s)
Montañas *Spanish,* Mountains
Mont(s) *French,* Mountain(s)
Monte *Italian, Portuguese,* Mountain
More *Russian,* Sea
Mörön *Mongolian,* River
Mys *Russian,* Cape, point

N

-nada *Japanese,* Open stretch of water
Nagor'ye *Russian,* Upland
Naḥal *Hebrew,* River
Nahr *Arabic,* River
Nam *Laotian,* River
Namakzār *Persian,* Salt desert
Né-a, -on, -os *Greek,* New
Nedre- *Norwegian,* Lower
-neem *Estonian,* Cape, point
Nehri *Turkish,* River
-nes *Norwegian,* Cape, point
Nevado *Spanish,* Mountain (snow-capped)
Nieder- *German,* Lower
Nishi- *Japanese,* West(ern)
-nísi *Greek,* Island
Nisoi *Greek,* Islands
Nizhn-eye, -iy, -iye, -yaya *Russian,* Lower
Nizmennost' *Russian,* Lowland, plain
Nord *Danish, French, German,* North
Norte *Portuguese, Spanish,* North
Nos *Bulgarian,* Point, spit
Nosy *Malagasy,* Island
Nov-a, -i, *Bulgarian, Serbo-Croatian,* New
Nov-aya, -o, -oye, -yy, -yye *Russian,* New
Now-a, -e, -y *Polish,* New
Nur *Mongolian,* Lake
Nuruu *Mongolian,* Mountains
Nuur *Mongolian,* Lake
Nyzovyna *Ukrainian,* Lowland, plain

O

-ø *Danish,* Island
Ober- *German,* Upper
Oblast' *Russian,* Province
Órmos *Greek,* Bay
Orol(i) *Uzbek,* Island
Øster- *Norwegian,* Eastern
Ostrov(a) *Russian,* Island(s)
Otok *Serbo-Croatian,* Island
Oued *Arabic,* Watercourse
-oy *Faeroese,* Island
-øy(a) *Norwegian,* Island
Oya *Sinhala,* River
Ozero *Russian, Ukrainian,* Lake

P

Passo *Italian,* Pass
Pegunungan *Indonesian, Malay,* Mountain range
Pélagos *Greek,* Sea
Pendi *Chinese,* Basin
Penisola *Italian,* Peninsula
Pertuis *French,* Strait
Peski *Russian,* Sands
Phanom *Thai,* Mountain
Phou *Laotian,* Mountain
Pi *Chinese,* Point
Pic *Catalan, French,* Peak
Pico *Portuguese, Spanish,* Peak
-piggen *Danish,* Peak
Pik *Russian,* Peak
Pivostriv *Ukrainian,* Peninsula
Planalto *Portuguese,* Plateau
Planina, Planini *Bulgarian, Macedonian, Serbo-Croatian,* Mountain range
Plato *Russian,* Plateau
Ploskogor'ye *Russian,* Upland
Poluostrov *Russian,* Peninsula
Ponta *Portuguese,* Point
Porthmós *Greek,* Strait
Pótamos *Greek,* River
Presa *Spanish,* Dam
Prokhod *Bulgarian,* Pass
Proliv *Russian,* Strait
Pulau *Indonesian, Malay,* Island
Pulu *Malay,* Island
Punta *Spanish,* Point
Pushcha *Belarussian,* Forest
Puszcza *Polish,* Forest

Q

Qā' *Arabic,* Depression
Qalamat *Arabic,* Well
Qatorkŭh(i) *Tajik,* Mountain
Qiuling *Chinese,* Hills
Qolleh *Persian,* Mountain
Qu *Tibetan,* Stream
Quan *Chinese,* Well
Qulla(i) *Tajik,* Peak
Qundao *Chinese,* Island group

R

Raas *Somali,* Cape
-rags *Latvian,* Cape
Ramlat *Arabic,* Sands
Ra's *Arabic,* Cape, headland, point
Ravnina *Bulgarian, Russian,* Plain
Récif *French,* Reef
Recife *Portuguese,* Reef
Reka *Bulgarian,* River
Represa (Rep.) *Portuguese, Spanish,* Reservoir
Reshteh *Persian,* Mountain range
Respublika *Russian,* Republic, first-order administrative division
Respublika(si) *Uzbek,* Republic, first-order administrative division
-retsugan *Japanese,* Chain of rocks
-rettō *Japanese,* Island chain
Riacho *Spanish,* Stream
Riban' *Malagasy,* Mountains
Rio *Portuguese,* River
Río *Spanish,* River
Riu *Catalan,* River
Rivier *Dutch,* River
Rivière *French,* River
Rowd *Pashtu,* River
Rt *Serbo-Croatian,* Point
Rūd *Persian,* River
Rūdkhāneh *Persian,* River
Rudohorie *Slovak,* Mountains
Ruisseau *French,* Stream

S

-saar *Estonian,* Island
-saari *Finnish,* Island
Sabkhat *Arabic,* Salt marsh
Sāgar(a) *Hindi,* Lake, reservoir
Ṣaḥrā' *Arabic,* Desert
Saint, Sainte *French,* Saint
Salar *Spanish,* Salt-pan
Salto *Portuguese, Spanish,* Waterfall
Samudra *Sinhala,* Reservoir
-san *Japanese, Korean,* Mountain
-sanchi *Japanese,* Mountains
-sandur *Icelandic,* Beach
Sankt *German, Swedish,* Saint
-sanmaek *Korean,* Mountain range
-sanmyaku *Japanese,* Mountain range
San, Santa, Santo *Italian, Portuguese, Spanish,* Saint
São *Portuguese,* Saint
Sarīr *Arabic,* Desert
Sebkha, Sebkhet *Arabic,* Depression, salt marsh
Sedlo *Czech,* Pass
See *German,* Lake
Selat *Indonesian,* Strait
Selatan *Indonesian,* Southern
-selkä *Finnish,* Lake, ridge
Selseleh *Persian,* Mountain range
Serra *Portuguese,* Mountain
Serranía *Spanish,* Mountain
-seto *Japanese,* Channel, strait
Sever-naya, -noye, -nyy, -o *Russian,* Northern
Sha'īb *Arabic,* Watercourse
Shākh *Kurdish,* Mountain
Shamo *Chinese,* Desert
Shan *Chinese,* Mountain(s)
Shankou *Chinese,* Pass
Shanmo *Chinese,* Mountain range
Shaṭṭ *Arabic,* Distributary
Shet' *Amharic,* River
Shi *Chinese,* Municipality
-shima *Japanese,* Island
Shiqqat *Arabic,* Depression
-shotō *Japanese,* Group of islands
Shuiku *Chinese,* Reservoir
Shūrkhog(i) *Uzbek,* Salt marsh
Sierra *Spanish,* Mountains
Sint *Dutch,* Saint
-sjø(en) *Norwegian,* Lake
-sjön *Swedish,* Lake
Solonchak *Russian,* Salt lake
Solonchakovyye Vpadiny *Russian,* Salt basin, wetlands
Son *Vietnamese,* Mountain
Sông *Vietnamese,* River
Sør- *Norwegian,* Southern
-spitze *German,* Peak
Star-á, -é *Czech,* Old
Star-aya, -oye, -yy, -yye *Russian,* Old
Stenó *Greek,* Strait
Step' *Russian,* Steppe
Štít *Slovak,* Peak
Stœng *Cambodian,* River
Stolovaya Strana *Russian,* Plateau
Stredné *Slovak,* Middle
Střední *Czech,* Middle
Stretto *Italian,* Strait
Su Anbari *Azerbaijani,* Reservoir
-suidō *Japanese,* Channel, strait
Sund *Swedish,* Sound, strait
Sungai *Indonesian, Malay,* River
Suu *Turkish,* River

T

Tal *Mongolian,* Plain
Tandavan' *Malagasy,* Mountain range
Tangorombohitr' *Malagasy,* Mountain massif
Tanjung *Indonesian, Malay,* Cape, point
Tao *Chinese,* Island
Ṭaraq *Arabic,* Hills
Tassili *Berber,* Mountain, plateau
Tau *Russian,* Mountain(s)
Taungdan *Burmese,* Mountain range
Techníti Límni *Greek,* Reservoir
Tekojärvi *Finnish,* Reservoir
Teluk *Indonesian, Malay,* Bay
Tengah *Indonesian,* Middle
Terara *Amharic,* Mountain
Timur *Indonesian,* Eastern
-tind(an) *Norwegian,* Peak
Tizma(si) *Uzbek,* Mountain range, ridge
-tō *Japanese,* Island
Tog *Somali,* Valley
-tōge *Japanese,* Pass
Togh(i) *Uzbek,* Mountain
Tônlé *Cambodian,* Lake
Top *Dutch,* Peak
-tunturi *Finnish,* Mountain
Ṭurāq *Arabic,* Hills
Tur'at *Arabic,* Channel

U

Udde(n) *Swedish,* Cape, point
'Uqlat *Arabic,* Well
Utara *Indonesian,* Northern
Uul *Mongolian,* Mountains

V

Väin *Estonian,* Strait
Vallée *French,* Valley
-vatn *Icelandic,* Lake
-vatnet *Norwegian,* Lake
Velayat *Turkmen,* Province
-vesi *Finnish,* Lake
Vestre- *Norwegian,* Western
-vidda *Norwegian,* Plateau
-vík *Icelandic,* Bay
-viken *Swedish,* Bay, inlet
Vinh *Vietnamese,* Bay
Víztárloló *Hungarian,* Reservoir
Vodaskhovishcha *Belarussian,* Reservoir
Vodokhranilishche (Vdkhr.) *Russian,* Reservoir
Vodoskhovyshche (Vdskh.) *Ukrainian,* Reservoir
Volcán *Spanish,* Volcano
Vostochn-o, yy *Russian,* Eastern
Vozvyshennost' *Russian,* Upland, plateau
Vozyera *Belarussian,* Lake
Vpadina *Russian,* Depression
Vrchovina *Czech,* Mountains
Vrha *Macedonian,* Peak
Vychodné *Slovak,* Eastern
Vysochyna *Ukrainian,* Upland
Vysočina *Czech,* Upland

W

Waadi *Somali,* Watercourse
Wādī *Arabic* Watercourse
Wāḥat, Wâhat *Arabic,* Oasis
Wald *German,* Forest
Wan *Chinese,* Bay
Way *Indonesian,* River
Webi *Somali,* River
Wenz *Amharic,* River
Wiloyat(i) *Uzbek,* Province
Wyżyna *Polish,* Upland
Wzgórza *Polish,* Upland
Wzvyshsha *Belarussian,* Upland

X

Xé *Laotian,* River
Xi *Chinese,* Stream

Y

-yama *Japanese,* Mountain
Yanchi *Chinese,* Salt lake
Yang *Chinese,* Bay
Yanhu *Chinese,* Salt lake
Yarımadası *Azerbaijani, Turkish,* Peninsula
Yaylası *Turkish,* Plateau
Yazovir *Bulgarian,* Reservoir
Yoma *Burmese,* Mountains
Ytre- *Norwegian,* Outer
Yü *Chinese,* Island
Yunhe *Chinese,* Canal
Yuzhn-o, -yy *Russian,* Southern

Z

-zaki *Japanese,* Cape, point
Zaliv *Bulgarian, Russian,* Bay
-zan *Japanese,* Mountain
Zangbo *Tibetan,* River
Zapadn-aya, -o, -yy *Russian,* Western
Západné *Slovak,* Western
Západní *Czech,* Western
Zatoka *Polish, Ukrainian,* Bay
-zee *Dutch,* Sea
Zemlya *Russian,* Earth, land
Zizhiqu *Chinese,* Autonomous region

Index

Glossary of Abbreviations

This glossary provides a comprehensive guide to the abbreviations used in this Atlas, and in the Index.

A

abbrev. abbreviated
AD Anno Domini
Afr. Afrikaans
Alb. Albanian
Amh. Amharic
anc. ancient
approx. approximately
Ar. Arabic
Arm. Armenian
ASEAN Association of South East Asian Nations
ASSR Autonomous Soviet Socialist Republic
Aust. Australian
Az. Azerbaijani
Azerb. Azerbaijan

B

Basq. Basque
BC before Christ
Bel. Belarussian
Ben. Bengali
Ber. Berber
B-H Bosnia-Herzegovina
bn billion (one thousand million)
BP British Petroleum
Bret. Breton
Brit. British
Bul. Bulgarian
Bur. Burmese

C

C central
C. Cape
°C degrees Centigrade
CACM Central America Common Market
Cam. Cambodian
Cant. Cantonese
CAR Central African Republic
Cast. Castilian
Cat. Catalan
CEEAC Central America Common Market
Chin. Chinese
CIS Commonwealth of Independent States
cm centimetre(s)
Cro. Croat
Cz. Czech
Czech Rep. Czech Republic

D

Dan. Danish
Div. Divehi
Dom. Rep. Dominican Republic
Dut. Dutch

E

E east
EC *see* EU
EEC *see* EU
ECOWAS Economic Community of West African States
ECU European Currency Unit
EMS European Monetary System
Eng. English
est estimated
Est. Estonian
EU European Union (previously European Community [EC], European Economic Community [EEC])

F

°F degrees Fahrenheit
Faer. Faeroese
Fij. Fijian
Fin. Finnish
Fr. French
Fris. Frisian
ft foot/feet
FYROM Former Yugoslav Republic of Macedonia

G

g gram(s)
Gael. Gaelic
Gal. Galician
GDP Gross Domestic Product (the total value of goods and services produced by a country excluding income from foreign countries)
Geor. Georgian
Ger. German
Gk Greek
GNP Gross National Product (the total value of goods and services produced by a country)

H

Heb. Hebrew
HEP hydro-electric power
Hind. Hindi
hist. historical
Hung. Hungarian

I

I. Island
Icel. Icelandic
in inch(es)
In. Inuit (Eskimo)
Ind. Indonesian
Intl International
Ir. Irish
Is Islands
It. Italian

J

Jap. Japanese

K

Kaz. Kazakh
kg kilogram(s)
Kir. Kirghiz
km kilometre(s)
km² square kilometre (singular)
Kor. Korean
Kurd. Kurdish

L

L. Lake
LAIA Latin American Integration Association
Lao. Laotian
Lapp. Lappish
Lat. Latin
Latv. Latvian
Liech. Liechtenstein
Lith. Lithuanian
Lus. Lusatian
Lux. Luxembourg

M

m million/metre(s)
Mac. Macedonian
Maced. Macedonia
Mal. Malay
Malg. Malagasy
Malt. Maltese
mi. mile(s)
Mong. Mongolian
Mt. Mountain
Mts Mountains

N

N north
NAFTA North American Free Trade Agreement
Nep. Nepali
Neth. Netherlands
Nic. Nicaraguan
Nor. Norwegian
NZ New Zealand

P

Pash. Pashtu
PNG Papua New Guinea
Pol. Polish
Poly. Polynesian
Port. Portuguese
prev. previously

R

Rep. Republic
Res. Reservoir
Rmsch Romansch
Rom. Romanian
Rus. Russian
Russ. Fed. Russian Federation

S

S south
SADC Southern Africa Development Community
SCr. Serbian/Croatian
Sinh. Sinhala
Slvk Slovak
Slvn. Slovene
Som. Somali
Sp. Spanish
St., St Saint
Strs Straits
Swa. Swahili
Swe. Swedish
Switz. Switzerland

T

Taj. Tajik
Th. Thai
Thai. Thailand
Tib. Tibetan
Turk. Turkish
Turkm. Turkmenistan

U

UAE United Arab Emirates
Uigh. Uighur
UK United Kingdom
Ukr. Ukrainian
UN United Nations
Urd. Urdu
US/USA United States of America
USSR Union of Soviet Socialist Republics
Uzb. Uzbek

V

var. variant
Vdkhr. Vodokhranilishche (Russian for reservoir)
Vdskh. Vodoskhovyshche (Ukrainian for reservoir)
Vtn. Vietnamese

W

W west
Wel. Welsh

Y

Yugo. Yugoslavia

This index lists all the placenames and features shown on the regional and continental maps in this Atlas. Placenames are referenced to the largest scale map on which they appear. The policy followed throughout the Atlas is to use the local spelling or local name at regional level; commonly-used English language names may occasionally be added (in parentheses) where this is an aid to identification e.g. Firenze (Florence). English names, where they exist, have been used for all international features e.g. oceans and country names; they are also used on the continental maps and in the introductory World Today section; these are then fully cross-referenced to the local names found on the regional maps. The index also contains commonly-found alternative names and variant spellings, which are also fully cross-referenced.

All main entry names are those of settlements unless otherwise indicated by the use of italicized definitions or representative symbols, which are keyed at the foot of each page.

1

25 de Mayo *see* Veinticinco de Mayo
137 *Y13* **26 Bakı Komissarı** ***Rus.*** Imeni 26 Bakinskikh Komissarov. SE Azerbaijan
26 Baku Komissarlary Adyndaky *see* Uzboý
10 *M16* **100 Mile House** ***var.*** Hundred Mile House. British Columbia, SW Canada

A

Aa *see* Gauja
95 *G24* **Aabenraa** ***var.*** Åbenrå, ***Ger.*** Apenrade. Sønderjylland, SW Denmark
95 *G20* **Aabybro** ***var.*** Åbybro. Nordjylland, N Denmark
101 *C16* **Aachen** ***Dut.*** Aken, ***Fr.*** Aix-la-Chapelle; ***anc.*** Aquae Grani, Aquisgranum. Nordrhein-Westfalen, W Germany
Aaiún *see* Laâyoune
95 *M24* **Aakirkeby** ***var.*** Åkirkeby. Bornholm, E Denmark
Ãak Nông *see* Gia Nghia
95 *G20* **Aalborg** ***var.*** Ålborg, Ålborg-Nørresundby; ***anc.*** Alburgum. Nordjylland, N Denmark
Aalborg Bugt *see* Ålborg Bugt
101 *J21* **Aalen** Baden-Württemberg, S Germany
95 *G21* **Aalestrup** ***var.*** Ålestrup. Viborg, NW Denmark
98 *I11* **Aalsmeer** Noord-Holland, C Netherlands
99 *F18* **Aalst** ***Fr.*** Alost. Oost-Vlaanderen, C Belgium
99 *K18* **Aalst** Noord-Brabant, S Netherlands
98 *O12* **Aalten** Gelderland, E Netherlands
99 *D17* **Aalter** Oost-Vlaanderen, NW Belgium
Aanaar *see* Inari
Aanaarjävri *see* Inarijärvi
93 *M17* **Äänekoski** Länsi-Suomi, W Finland
138 *H7* **Aanjar** ***var.*** 'Anjar. C Lebanon
83 *G21* **Aansluit** Northern Cape, N South Africa
Aar *see* Aare
108 *F7* **Aarau** Aargau, N Switzerland
108 *D8* **Aarberg** Bern, W Switzerland
99 *D16* **Aardenburg** Zeeland, SW Netherlands
108 *D8* **Aare** ***var.*** Aar. ≈ W Switzerland
108 *F7* **Aargau** ***Fr.*** Argovie. ◈ *canton* N Switzerland
Aarhus *see* Århus
Aarlen *see* Arlon
95 *G21* **Aars** ***var.*** Års. Nordjylland, N Denmark
99 *I17* **Aarschot** Vlaams Brabant, C Belgium
Aassi, Nahr el *see* Orontes
Aat *see* Ath
160 *G7* **Aba** ***prev.*** Ngawa. Sichuan, C China
77 *V17* **Aba** Abia, S Nigeria
79 *P16* **Aba** Orientale, NE Dem. Rep. Congo
140 *J6* **Abā al Qazāz, Bi'r** *well* NW Saudi Arabia
Abā as Su'ūd *see* Najrān
59 *G14* **Abacaxis, Rio** ≈ NW Brazil
Abaco Island *see* Great Abaco/Little Abaco
Abaco Island *see* Great Abaco, N Bahamas
142 *K10* **Ābādān** Khūzestān, SW Iran
143 *O10* **Ābādeh** Fārs, C Iran
74 *H8* **Abadla** W Algeria
59 *M20* **Abaeté** Minas Gerais, SE Brazil
Abag Qi *see* Xin Hot
62 *P7* **Abaí** Caazapá, S Paraguay
191 *O2* **Abaiang** ***var.*** Apia; ***prev.*** Charlotte Island. *atoll* Tungaru, W Kiribati
Abaj *see* Abay
77 *U15* **Abaji** Federal Capital District, C Nigeria
37 *O7* **Abajo Peak** ▲ Utah, W USA
77 *V16* **Abakaliki** Ebonyi, SE Nigeria
122 *K13* **Abakan** Respublika Khakasiya, S Russian Federation
77 *S11* **Abala** Tillabéri, SW Niger
77 *U11* **Abalak** Tahoua, C Niger
119 *N14* **Abalyanka** ***Rus.*** Obolyanka. ≈ N Belarus
122 *L12* **Aban** Krasnoyarskiy Kray, S Russian Federation
143 *P9* **Āb Anbār-e Kān Sorkh** Yazd, C Iran
57 *G16* **Abancay** Apurímac, SE Peru
190 *H2* **Abaokoro** *atoll* Tungaru, W Kiribati
Abariringa *see* Kanton
143 *P10* **Abarkū** Yazd, C Iran
165 *V3* **Abashiri** ***var.*** Abasiri. Hokkaidō, NE Japan
165 *U3* **Abashiri-ko** ◎ Hokkaidō, NE Japan
Abasiri *see* Abashiri
41 *P10* **Abasolo** Tamaulipas, C Mexico
186 *F9* **Abau** Central, S PNG
145 *R10* **Abay** ***var.*** Abaj. Karaganda, C Kazakhstan
81 *I15* **Ābaya Hāyk'** ***Eng.*** Lake Margherita, ***It.*** Abbaia. ◎ SW Ethiopia
Ābay Wenz *see* Blue Nile
122 *K13* **Abaza** Respublika Khakasiya, S Russian Federation
Abbaia *see* Ābaya Hāyk'
143 *Q13* **Āb Bārīk** Fārs, S Iran
107 *C18* **Abbasanta** Sardegna, Italy, C Mediterranean Sea
Abbatis Villa *see* Abbeville
30 *M3* **Abbaye, Point** *headland* Michigan, N USA
Abbazia *see* Opatija
Abbé, Lake *see* Abhe, Lake
103 *N2* **Abbeville** ***anc.*** Abbatis Villa. Somme, N France
23 *R7* **Abbeville** Alabama, S USA
23 *U6* **Abbeville** Georgia, SE USA
22 *I9* **Abbeville** Louisiana, S USA
21 *P12* **Abbeville** South Carolina, SE USA
97 *B20* **Abbeyfeale** ***Ir.*** Mainistir na Féile. SW Ireland
106 *D8* **Abbiategrasso** Lombardia, NW Italy
93 *I14* **Abborrträsk** Norrbotten, N Sweden
194 *J9* **Abbot Ice Shelf** *ice shelf* Antarctica
10 *M17* **Abbotsford** British Columbia, SW Canada
30 *K6* **Abbotsford** Wisconsin, N USA
149 *U5* **Abbottābād** North-West Frontier Province, NW Pakistan
119 *M14* **Abchuha** ***Rus.*** Obchuga. Minskaya Voblasts', NW Belarus
98 *I10* **Abcoude** Utrecht, C Netherlands
139 *N2* **'Abd al 'Azīz, Jabal** ⛰ NE Syria
141 *U17* **'Abd al Kūrī** *island* SE Yemen
139 *Z13* **'Abd Allāh, Khawr** *bay* Iraq/Kuwait
127 *U6* **Abdulino** Orenburgskaya Oblast', W Russian Federation
78 *J10* **Abéché** ***var.*** Abécher, Abeshr. Ouaddaï, SE Chad
Abécher *see* Abéché
143 *S8* **Āb-e Garm va Sard** Yazd, E Iran
77 *R8* **Abeïbara** Kidal, NE Mali
105 *P5* **Abejar** Castilla-León, N Spain
54 *E9* **Abejorral** Antioquia, W Colombia
Abela *see* Ávila
Abellinum *see* Avellino
92 *Q2* **Abeløya** *island* Kong Karls Land, E Svalbard
80 *I13* **Ābeltī** Oromo, C Ethiopia
191 *O2* **Abemama** ***var.*** Apamama; ***prev.*** Roger Simpson Island. *atoll* Tungaru, W Kiribati
171 *Y15* **Abemaree** ***var.*** Abemarre. Papua, E Indonesia
77 *O16* **Abengourou** E Ivory Coast
Åbenrå *see* Aabenraa
101 *L22* **Abens** ≈ SE Germany
77 *S16* **Abeokuta** Ogun, SW Nigeria
97 *I20* **Aberaeron** SW Wales, UK
Aberbrothock *see* Arbroath
Abercorn *see* Mbala
29 *R6* **Abercrombie** North Dakota, N USA
183 *T7* **Aberdeen** New South Wales, SE Australia
11 *T15* **Aberdeen** Saskatchewan, S Canada
83 *H25* **Aberdeen** Eastern Cape, S South Africa
96 *L9* **Aberdeen** ***anc.*** Devana. NE Scotland, UK
21 *X2* **Aberdeen** Maryland, NE USA
23 *N3* **Aberdeen** Mississippi, S USA
21 *T10* **Aberdeen** North Carolina, SE USA
29 *P8* **Aberdeen** South Dakota, N USA
32 *F8* **Aberdeen** Washington, NW USA
96 *K9* **Aberdeen** *cultural region* NE Scotland, UK
8 *L8* **Aberdeen Lake** ◎ Nunavut, NE Canada
96 *J10* **Aberfeldy** C Scotland, UK
97 *K21* **Abergavenny** ***anc.*** Gobannium. SE Wales, UK
Abergwaun *see* Fishguard
Abermarre *see* Abemaree
25 *N5* **Abernathy** Texas, SW USA
Abersee *see* Wolfgangsee
Abertawe *see* Swansea
Aberteifi *see* Cardigan
32 *I15* **Abert, Lake** ◎ Oregon, NW USA
97 *I20* **Aberystwyth** W Wales, UK
Abeshr *see* Abéché
Ábeskovvu *see* Abisko
106 *F10* **Abetone** Toscana, C Italy
125 *V5* **Abez'** Respublika Komi, NW Russian Federation
142 *M5* **Āb Garm** Qazvin, N Iran
141 *N12* **Abhā** 'Asīr, SW Saudi Arabia
142 *M5* **Abhar** Zanjān, NW Iran
Abhé Bad/Ābhē Bid Hāyk' *see* Abhe, Lake
80 *K12* **Abhe, Lake** ***var.*** Lake Abbé, ***Amh.*** Ābhē Bid Hāyk', ***Som.*** Abhé Bad. ◎ Djibouti/Ethiopia
77 *V17* **Abia** ◈ *state* SE Nigeria
139 *V9* **'Abīd 'Alī** E Iraq
119 *O17* **Abidavichy** ***Rus.*** Obidovichi. Mahilyowskaya Voblasts', E Belarus
115 *L15* **Abide** Çanakkale, NW Turkey
77 *N17* **Abidjan** S Ivory Coast
Āb-i-Istāda *see* Īstādeh-ye Moqor, Āb-e-
27 *N4* **Abilene** Kansas, C USA
25 *Q7* **Abilene** Texas, SW USA
Abindonia *see* Abingdon
97 *M21* **Abingdon** ***anc.*** Abindonia. S England, UK
30 *K12* **Abingdon** Illinois, N USA
21 *P8* **Abingdon** Virginia, NE USA
Abingdon *see* Pinta, Isla
18 *J15* **Abington** Pennsylvania, NE USA
126 *K14* **Abinsk** Krasnodarskiy Kray, SW Russian Federation
37 *R9* **Abiquiu Reservoir** ▣ New Mexico, SW USA
92 *I10* **Abisko** ***Lapp.*** Ábeskovvu. Norrbotten, N Sweden
12 *G12* **Abitibi** ≈ Ontario, S Canada
12 *H12* **Abitibi, Lac** ◎ Ontario /Québec, S Canada
80 *J10* **Ābīy Ādī** Tigray, N Ethiopia
118 *H6* **Abja-Paluoja** Viljandimaa, S Estonia
137 *Q8* **Abkhazia** ◈ *autonomous republic* NW Georgia
182 *F1* **Abminga** South Australia
75 *W9* **Abnûb** C Egypt
Åbo *see* Turku
152 *G9* **Abohar** Punjab, N India
77 *O17* **Aboisso** SE Ivory Coast
78 *H5* **Abo, Massif d'** ⛰ NW Chad
77 *R16* **Abomey** S Benin
79 *F16* **Abong Mbang** Est, SE Cameroon
111 *L23* **Abony** Pest, C Hungary
78 *J11* **Abou-Déïa** Salamat, SE Chad
Aboudouhour *see* Abū aḑ Ḑuhūr
Abou Kémal *see* Abū Kamāl
Abou Simbel *see* Abu Simbel
137 *T12* **Abovyan** C Armenia
171 *O2* **Abra** ≈ Luzon, N Philippines
141 *P15* **Abrād, Wādī** *seasonal river* W Yemen
Abraham Bay *see* The Carlton
104 *G10* **Abrantes** ***var.*** Abrántes. Santarém, C Portugal
62 *J4* **Abra Pampa** Jujuy, N Argentina
Abrashlare *see* Brezovo
54 *G7* **Abrego** Norte de Santander, N Colombia
Abrene *see* Pytalovo
40 *C7* **Abreojos, Punta** *headland* W Mexico
65 *J16* **Abrolhos Bank** *undersea feature* W Atlantic Ocean
119 *H19* **Abrova** ***Rus.*** Obrovo. Brestskaya Voblasts', SW Belarus
116 *G11* **Abrud** ***Ger.*** Gross-Schlatten, ***Hung.*** Abrudbánya. Alba, SW Romania
Abrudbánya *see* Abrud
118 *E6* **Abruka** *island* SW Estonia
107 *J15* **Abruzzese, Appennino** ⛰ C Italy
107 *J14* **Abruzzo** ◈ *region* C Italy
141 *N14* **'Abs** ***var.*** Sūq 'Abs. W Yemen
33 *T12* **Absaroka Range** ⛰ Montana/Wyoming, NW USA
137 *Z11* **Abşeron Yarımadası** ***Rus.*** Apsheronskiy Poluostrov. *peninsula* E Azerbaijan
143 *N6* **Āb Shīrīn** Eşfahān, C Iran
139 *X10* **Abtān** SE Iraq
109 *R6* **Abtenau** Salzburg, NW Austria
164 *E12* **Abu** Yamaguchi, Honshū, SW Japan
152 *E14* **Ābu** Rājasthān, N India
138 *I4* **Abū aḑ Ḑuhūr** ***Fr.*** Aboudouhour. Idlib, NW Syria
143 *P17* **Abū al Abyaḑ** *island* C UAE
138 *K10* **Abū al Ḩuşayn, Khabrat** ◎ N Jordan
139 *R8* **Abū al Jīr** C Iraq
139 *Y12* **Abū al Khaşīb** ***var.*** Abul Khasib. SE Iraq
139 *U12* **Abū at Tubrah, Thaqb** *well* S Iraq
75 *V11* **Abu Balâs** ▲ SW Egypt
Abu Dhabi *see* Abū Z̧aby
139 *R8* **Abū Farūkh** C Iraq
80 *C12* **Abu Gabra** Southern Darfur, W Sudan
139 *P10* **Abū Ghār, Sha'īb** *dry watercourse* S Iraq
80 *G7* **Abu Hamed** River Nile, N Sudan
139 *O5* **Abū Ḩardān** ***var.*** Hajîne. Dayr az Zawr, E Syria
139 *T7* **Abū Ḩāssawīyah** E Iraq
138 *K10* **Abū Ḩifnah, Wādī** *dry watercourse* N Jordan
77 *V15* **Abuja** ● (Nigeria) Federal Capital District, C Nigeria
139 *R9* **Abū Jahaf, Wādī** *dry watercourse* C Iraq
56 *F12* **Abujao, Río** ≈ E Peru
139 *U12* **Abū Jasrah** S Iraq
139 *O6* **Abū Kamāl** ***Fr.*** Abou Kémal. Dayr az Zawr, E Syria
165 *P12* **Abukuma-sanchi** ⛰ Honshū, C Japan
Abula *see* Ávila
Abul Khasib *see* Abū al Khaşīb
79 *K16* **Abumombazi** ***var.*** Abumonbazi. Equateur, N Dem. Rep. Congo
Abumonbazi *see* Abumombazi
59 *D15* **Abunã** Rondônia, W Brazil
56 *K13* **Abunã, Rio** ***var.*** Río Abuná. ≈ Bolivia/Brazil
138 *G10* **Abū Nuşayr** ***var.*** Abu Nuseir. 'Al Āşimah, W Jordan

◆ Country ● Country Capital ◇ Dependent Territory ○ Dependent Territory Capital ◈ Administrative Region ✕ International Airport ▲ Mountain ⛰ Mountain Range Volcano ≈ River ◎ Lake ▣ Reservoir

Abu Nuseir *see* Abū Nuşayr
139 *T12* **Abū Qabr** S Iraq
138 *K5* **Abū Raḩbah, Jabal** ⛰ C Syria
139 *S5* **Abū Rajāsh** N Iraq
139 *W13* **Abū Raqrāq, Ghadīr** *well* S Iraq
152 *E14* **Ābu Road** Rājasthān, N India
80 *I6* **Abu Shagara, Ras** *headland* NE Sudan
75 *W12* **Abu Simbel** ***var.*** Abou Simbel, Abū Sunbul. *ancient monument* S Egypt
139 *U12* **Abū Sudayrah** S Iraq
139 *T10* **Abū Şukhayr** S Iraq
Abū Sunbul *see* Abu Simbel
165 *R4* **Abuta** Hokkaidō, NE Japan
185 *E18* **Abut Head** *headland* South Island, NZ
80 *E9* **Abu 'Urug** Northern Kordofan, C Sudan
80 *K12* **Ābuyē Mēda** ▲ C Ethiopia
80 *D11* **Abu Zabad** Western Kordofan, C Sudan
Abū Ẓabī *see* Abū Ẓaby
143 *P16* **Abū Ẓaby** ***var.*** Abū Ẓabī, ***Eng.*** Abu Dhabi. ● (UAE) Abū Ẓaby, C UAE
75 *X8* **Abu Zenîma** E Egypt
95 *N17* **Åby** Östergötland, S Sweden
Abyaḑ, Al Baḩr al *see* White Nile
Åbybro *see* Aabybro
80 *D13* **Abyei** Western Kordofan, S Sudan
Abyla *see* Ávila
Abymes *see* les Abymes
Abyssinia *see* Ethiopia
Açâba *see* Assaba
54 *F11* **Acacias** Meta, C Colombia
58 *L13* **Açailandia** Maranhão, E Brazil
Acaill *see* Achill Island
42 *E8* **Acajutla** Sonsonate, W El Salvador
79 *D17* **Acalayong** SW Equatorial Guinea
41 *N13* **Acámbaro** Guanajuato, C Mexico
54 *C6* **Acandí** Chocó, NW Colombia
104 *H4* **A Cañiza** ***var.*** La Cañiza. Galicia, NW Spain
40 *J11* **Acaponeta** Nayarit, C Mexico
40 *J11* **Acaponeta, Río de** ≈ C Mexico
41 *O16* **Acapulco** ***var.*** Acapulco de Juárez. Guerrero, S Mexico
Acapulco de Juárez *see* Acapulco
55 *T13* **Acarai Mountains** ***Sp.*** Serra Acaraí. ⛰ Brazil/Guyana
Acaraí, Serra *see* Acarai Mountains
58 *O13* **Acaraú** Ceará, NE Brazil
54 *J6* **Acarigua** Portuguesa, N Venezuela
42 *C6* **Acatenango, Volcán de** ※ S Guatemala
41 *Q15* **Acatlán** ***var.*** Acatlán de Osorio. Puebla, S Mexico
Acatlán de Osorio *see* Acatlán
41 *S15* **Acayucan** ***var.*** Acayucán. Veracruz-Llave, E Mexico
Accho *see* 'Akko
21 *Y5* **Accomac** Virginia, NE USA
77 *Q17* **Accra** ● (Ghana) SE Ghana
97 *L17* **Accrington** NW England, UK
61 *B19* **Acebal** Santa Fe, C Argentina
168 *H8* **Aceh** ***off.*** Daerah Istimewa Aceh, ***var.*** Acheen, Achin, Atchin, Atjeh. ◈ *autonomous district* NW Indonesia
107 *M18* **Acerenza** Basilicata, S Italy
107 *K17* **Acerra** ***anc.*** Acerrae. Campania, S Italy
Acerrae *see* Acerra
Ach'asar Lerr *see* Achkasar
57 *J17* **Achacachi** La Paz, W Bolivia
54 *K7* **Achaguas** Apure, C Venezuela
154 *H12* **Achalpur** ***prev.*** Elichpur, Ellichpur. Mahārāshtra, C India
61 *F18* **Achar** Tacuarembó, C Uruguay
115 *H19* **Acharnés** ***var.*** Aharnes; ***prev.*** Akharnaí. Attikí, C Greece
Acheen *see* Aceh
99 *K16* **Achel** Limburg, NE Belgium
115 *D16* **Achelóos** ***var.*** Akhelóös, Aspropótamos; ***anc.*** Achelous. ≈ W Greece
Achelous *see* Achelóos
163 *W8* **Acheng** Heilongjiang, NE China
109 *N6* **Achenkirch** Tirol, W Austria
101 *L24* **Achenpass** *pass* Austria/Germany
109 *N7* **Achensee** ◎ W Austria
101 *F22* **Achern** Baden-Württemberg, SW Germany
115 *C16* **Acherón** ≈ W Greece
77 *W11* **Achétinamou** ≈ S Niger
152 *J12* **Achhnera** Uttar Pradesh, N India
42 *C7* **Achiguate, Río** ≈ S Guatemala
97 *A16* **Achill Head** ***Ir.*** Ceann Acla. *headland* W Ireland
97 *A16* **Achill Island** ***Ir.*** Acaill. *island* W Ireland
100 *H11* **Achim** Niedersachsen, NW Germany
149 *S5* **Achīn** Nangarhār, E Afghanistan
Achin *see* Aceh
122 *K12* **Achinsk** Krasnoyarskiy Kray, S Russian Federation
162 *E5* **Achit Nuur** ◎ NW Mongolia
137 *T11* **Achkasar** ***Arm.*** Ach'asar Lerr. ▲ Armenia/Georgia
126 *K13* **Achuyevo** Krasnodarskiy Kray, SW Russian Federation
81 *F16* **Achwa** ***var.*** Aswa. ≈ N Uganda
136 *E15* **Acıgöl** *salt lake* SW Turkey
107 *L24* **Acireale** Sicilia, Italy, C Mediterranean Sea
Aciris *see* Agri
25 *N7* **Ackerly** Texas, SW USA
22 *M4* **Ackerman** Mississippi, S USA
29 *W13* **Ackley** Iowa, C USA
44 *J5* **Acklins Island** *island* SE Bahamas
Acla, Ceann *see* Achill Head
62 *H11* **Aconcagua, Cerro** ▲ W Argentina
Açores/Açores, Arquipélago dos/Açores, Ilhas dos *see* Azores
104 *G2* **A Coruña** ***Cast.*** La Coruña ◈ *province* Galicia, NW Spain
104 *H2* **A Coruña** ***Cast.*** La Coruña, ***Eng.*** Corunna; ***anc.*** Caronium. Galicia, NW Spain
42 *L10* **Acoyapa** Chontales, S Nicaragua
106 *H13* **Acquapendente** Lazio, C Italy
106 *J13* **Acquasanta Terme** Marche, C Italy
106 *I13* **Acquasparta** Lazio, C Italy
106 *C9* **Acqui Terme** Piemonte, NW Italy
Acrae *see* Palazzolo Acreide
182 *F7* **Acraman, Lake** *salt lake* South Australia
59 *A15* **Acre** ***off.*** Estado do Acre. ◈ *state* W Brazil
Acre *see* 'Akko
59 *C16* **Acre, Rio** ≈ W Brazil
107 *N20* **Acri** Calabria, SW Italy
Acte *see* Ágion Óros
191 *Y12* **Actéon, Groupe** *island group* Îles Tuamotu, SE French Polynesia
15 *P12* **Acton-Vale** Québec, SE Canada
41 *P13* **Actopan** ***var.*** Actopán. Hidalgo, C Mexico
59 *P14* **Açu** ***var.*** Assu. Rio Grande do Norte, E Brazil
Acunum Acusio *see* Montélimar
77 *Q17* **Ada** SE Ghana
29 *R5* **Ada** Minnesota, N USA
31 *R12* **Ada** Ohio, N USA
27 *O12* **Ada** Oklahoma, C USA
112 *L8* **Ada** Serbia, N Serbia and Montenegro (Yugo.)
Ada Bazar *see* Adapazarı
40 *D3* **Adair, Bahía de** *bay* NW Mexico
104 *M7* **Adaja** ≈ N Spain
38 *H17* **Adak Island** *island* Aleutian Islands, Alaska, USA
Adalia *see* Antalya
Adalia, Gulf of *see* Antalya Körfezi
141 *X9* **Adam** N Oman
Adama *see* Nazrēt
60 *I8* **Adamantina** São Paulo, S Brazil
79 *E14* **Adamaoua** ***Eng.*** Adamawa. ◈ *province* N Cameroon
68 *F11* **Adamaoua, Massif d'** ***Eng.*** Adamawa Highlands. *plateau* NW Cameroon
77 *Y14* **Adamawa** ◈ *state* E Nigeria
Adamawa *see* Adamaoua
Adamawa Highlands *see* Adamaoua, Massif d'
106 *F6* **Adamello** ▲ N Italy
81 *J14* **Ādamī Tulu** Oromo, C Ethiopia
63 *M23* **Adam, Mount** ***var.*** Monte Independencia. ▲ West Falkland, Falkland Islands
29 *R16* **Adams** Nebraska, C USA
18 *H8* **Adams** New York, NE USA
29 *Q3* **Adams** North Dakota, N USA
155 *I23* **Adam's Bridge** *chain of shoals* NW Sri Lanka
32 *H10* **Adams, Mount** ▲ Washington, NW USA
Adam's Peak *see* Sri Pada
191 *R16* **Adam's Rock** *island* Pitcairn Island, Pitcairn Islands
191 *P16* **Adamstown** ○ (Pitcairn Islands) Pitcairn Island, Pitcairn Islands
20 *G10* **Adamsville** Tennessee, S USA
25 *S9* **Adamsville** Texas, SW USA
141 *O17* **'Adan** ***Eng.*** Aden. SW Yemen
136 *K16* **Adana** ***var.*** Seyhan. Adana, S Turkey
136 *K16* **Adana** ***var.*** Seyhan. ◈ *province* S Turkey
Adâncata *see* Horlivka
169 *V12* **Adang, Teluk** *bay* Borneo, C Indonesia
136 *F11* **Adapazarı** ***prev.*** Ada Bazar. Sakarya, NW Turkey
80 *H8* **Adarama** River Nile, NE Sudan
195 *Q16* **Adare, Cape** *headland* Antarctica
106 *E6* **Adda** ***anc.*** Addua. ≈ N Italy
80 *A13* **Adda** ≈ W Sudan
143 *Q17* **Aḑ Ḑab'īyah** Abū Ẓaby, C UAE
143 *O18* **Aḑ Ḑafrah** *desert* S UAE
141 *Q6* **Ad Dahnā'** *desert* E Saudi Arabia
74 *A11* **Ad Dakhla** ***var.*** Dakhla. SW Western Sahara
Ad Dalanj *see* Dilling
Ad Damar *see* Ed Damer
Ad Damazīn *see* Ed Damazin
Ad Dāmir *see* Ed Damer
173 *N2* **Ad Dammām** *desert* NE Saudi Arabia
141 *R6* **Ad Dammān** ***var.*** Dammām. Ash Sharqīyah, NE Saudi Arabia
Ad Dāmūr *see* Damoûr
140 *K5* **Ad Dār al Ḩamrā'** Tabūk, NW Saudi Arabia
140 *M13* **Ad Darb** Jīzān, SW Saudi Arabia
141 *O8* **Ad Dawādimī** Ar Riyāḑ, C Saudi Arabia
143 *N16* **Ad Dawḩah** ***Eng.*** Doha. ● (Qatar) C Qatar
143 *N16* **Ad Dawḩah** ***Eng.*** Doha. ✕ C Qatar
139 *S6* **Ad Dawr** N Iraq
139 *Y12* **Ad Dayr** ***var.*** Dayr, Shahbān. E Iraq
Addi Arkay *see* Ādī Ārk'ay
139 *X15* **Ad Dibdibah** *physical region* Iraq/Kuwait
Aḑ Ḑiffah *see* Libyan Plateau
Addis Ababa *see* Ādīs Ābeba
Addison *see* Webster Springs
139 *U10* **Ad Dīwānīyah** ***var.*** Diwaniyah. C Iraq
Addua *see* Adda
151 *K22* **Addu Atoll** *atoll* S Maldives
Ad Dujail *see* Ad Dujayl
139 *T7* **Ad Dujayl** ***var.*** Ad Dujail. N Iraq
Ad Duwaym/Ad Duwēm *see* Ed Dueim
99 *D16* **Adegem** Oost-Vlaanderen, NW Belgium
23 *U7* **Adel** Georgia, SE USA
29 *U14* **Adel** Iowa, C USA
182 *I9* **Adelaide** *state capital* South Australia
44 *H2* **Adelaide** New Providence, N Bahamas
182 *I9* **Adelaide** ✕ South Australia
194 *H6* **Adelaide Island** *island* Antarctica
181 *P2* **Adelaide River** Northern Territory, N Australia
76 *M10* **'Adel Bagrou** Hodh ech Chargui, SE Mauritania
186 *D6* **Adelbert Range** ⛰ N PNG
180 *K3* **Adele Island** *island* Western Australia
107 *O17* **Adelfia** Puglia, SE Italy
195 *V16* **Adélie Coast** *physical region* Antarctica
195 *V14* **Adélie, Terre** *physical region* Antarctica
Adelnau *see* Odolanów
Adelsberg *see* Postojna
Aden *see* 'Adan
141 *Q17* **Aden, Gulf of** *gulf* SW Arabian Sea
77 *V10* **Aderbissinat** Agadez, C Niger
Adhaim *see* Al 'Uẓaym
143 *R16* **Adh Dhayd** ***var.*** Al Dhaid. Ash Shāriqah, NE UAE
140 *M4* **'Adhfā'** *spring/well* NW Saudi Arabia
138 *I13* **'Ādhriyāt, Jabāl al** ⛰ S Jordan
80 *I10* **Ādī Ārk'ay** ***var.*** Addi Arkay. Amhara, N Ethiopia
182 *C7* **Adieu, Cape** *headland* South Australia
106 *H8* **Adige** ***Ger.*** Etsch. ≈ N Italy
80 *J10* **Ādīgrat** Tigray, N Ethiopia
154 *I13* **Ādilabād** ***var.*** Ādilābād. Andhra Pradesh, C India
35 *P2* **Adin** California, W USA
171 *V14* **Adi, Pulau** *island* E Indonesia
18 *K8* **Adirondack Mountains** ⛰ New York, NE USA
80 *J13* **Ādīs Ābeba** ***Eng.*** Addis Ababa. ● (Ethiopia) Ādīs Ābeba, C Ethiopia
80 *J13* **Ādīs Ābeba** ✕ Ādīs Ābeba, C Ethiopia
80 *I11* **Ādīs Zemen** Amhara, N Ethiopia
Adi Ugri *see* Mendefera
137 *N15* **Adıyaman** Adıyaman, SE Turkey
137 *N15* **Adıyaman** ◈ *province* S Turkey
116 *L11* **Adjud** Vrancea, E Romania
45 *T6* **Adjuntas** C Puerto Rico
Adjuntas, Presa de las *see* Vicente Guerrero, Presa
Ādkup *see* Erikub Atoll
126 *L15* **Adler** Krasnodarskiy Kray, SW Russian Federation
Adler *see* Orlice
108 *G7* **Adliswil** Zürich, NW Switzerland
32 *G7* **Admiralty Inlet** *inlet* Washington, NW USA
39 *X13* **Admiralty Island** *island* Alexander Archipelago, Alaska, USA
186 *E5* **Admiralty Islands** *island group* N PNG
136 *B14* **Adnan Menderes** ✕ (İzmir) İzmir, W Turkey
37 *V6* **Adobe Creek Reservoir** ⊡ Colorado, C USA
77 *T16* **Ado-Ekiti** Ekiti, SW Nigeria
Adola *see* Kibre Mengist
61 *C23* **Adolfo González Chaues** Buenos Aires, E Argentina
155 *H17* **Ādoni** Andhra Pradesh, C India
102 *K15* **Adour** ***anc.*** Aturus. ≈ SW France
Adowa *see* Ādwa
105 *O15* **Adra** Andalucía, S Spain
107 *L24* **Adrano** Sicilia, Italy, C Mediterranean Sea
74 *I9* **Adrar** C Algeria
76 *K7* **Adrar** ◈ *region* C Mauritania
74 *L11* **Adrar** ⛰ SE Algeria
74 *A12* **Adrar Souttouf** ⛰ SW Western Sahara
Adrasman *see* Adrasmon
147 *Q10* **Adrasmon** ***Rus.*** Adrasman. NW Tajikistan
78 *K10* **Adré** Ouaddaï, E Chad
106 *H9* **Adria** ***anc.*** Atria, Hadria, Hatria. Veneto, NE Italy
31 *R10* **Adrian** Michigan, N USA
29 *S11* **Adrian** Minnesota, N USA
27 *R5* **Adrian** Missouri, C USA
24 *M2* **Adrian** Texas, SW USA
21 *S4* **Adrian** West Virginia, NE USA
Adrianople/Adrianopolis *see* Edirne
121 *P7* **Adriatic Basin** *undersea feature* Adriatic Sea, N Mediterranean Sea
Adriatico, Mare *see* Adriatic Sea
106 *L13* **Adriatic Sea** ***Alb.*** Deti Adriatik, ***It.*** Mare Adriatico, ***SCr.*** Jadransko More, ***Slvn.*** Jadransko Morje. *sea* N Mediterranean Sea
Adriatik, Deti *see* Adriatic Sea
Adua *see* Ādwa
Aduana del Sásabe *see* El Sásabe
79 *O17* **Adusa** Orientale, NE Dem. Rep. Congo
118 *J13* **Adutiškis** Vilnius, E Lithuania
27 *Y7* **Advance** Missouri, USA
65 *D25* **Adventure Sound** *bay* East Falkland, Falkland Islands
80 *J10* **Ādwa** ***var.*** Adowa, ***It.*** Adua. Tigray, N Ethiopia
123 *Q8* **Adycha** ≈ NE Russian Federation
126 *L14* **Adygeya, Respublika** ◈ *autonomous republic* SW Russian Federation
Adzhikui *see* Ajyguýy
77 *N17* **Adzopé** SE Ivory Coast
127 *U4* **Adz'va** ≈ NW Russian Federation
125 *U5* **Adz'vavom** Respublika Komi, NW Russian Federation
Ædua *see* Autun
115 *K19* **Aegean Islands** *island group* Greece/Turkey
Aegean North *see* Vóreion Aigaíon
115 *I17* **Aegean Sea** ***Gk.*** Aigaíon Pélagos, Aigaío Pélagos, ***Turk.*** Ege Denizi. *sea* NE Mediterranean Sea
Aegean South *see* Nótion Aigaíon
118 *H3* **Aegviidu** ***Ger.*** Charlottenhof. Harjumaa, NW Estonia
Aegyptus *see* Egypt
Aelana *see* Al 'Aqabah
Aelok *see* Ailuk Atoll
Aelōninae *see* Ailinginae Atoll
Aeļōnļapļap *see* Ailinglaplap Atoll
Æmilia *see* Emilia-Romagna
Æmilianum *see* Millau
Aemona *see* Ljubljana
Aenaria *see* Ischia
Aeolian Islands *see* Eolie, Isole
191 *Z3* **Aeon Point** *headland* Kiritimati, NE Kiribati
95 *G24* **Ærø** ***Ger.*** Arrö. *island* C Denmark
95 *H24* **Ærøskøbing** Fyn, C Denmark
Æsernia *see* Isernia
104 *G3* **A Estrada** Galicia, NW Spain
115 *C18* **Aetós** Itháki, Iónioi Nísoi, Greece, C Mediterranean Sea
191 *Q8* **Afaahiti** Tahiti, W French Polynesia
139 *U10* **'Afak** C Iraq
Afanasjevo *see* Afanas'yevo
125 *T14* **Afanas'yevo** ***var.*** Afanasjevo. Kirovskaya Oblast', NW Russian Federation
Afándou *see* Afántou
115 *O23* **Afántou** ***var.*** Afándou. Ródos, Dodekánisos, Greece, Aegean Sea
Afar Depression *see* Danakil Desert
80 *K11* **Afar** ◈ *region* NE Ethiopia
191 *O7* **Afareaitu** Moorea, W French Polynesia
140 *L7* **'Afariyah, Bi'r al** *well* NW Saudi Arabia
Afars et des Issas, Territoire Français des *see* Djibouti
83 *D22* **Affenrücken** Karas, SW Namibia
Afghānestān, Dowlat-e Eslāmī-ye *see* Afghanistan
148 *M6* **Afghanistan** ***off.*** Islamic State of Afghanistan, ***Per.*** Dowlat-e Eslāmī-ye Afghānestān; ***prev.*** Republic of Afghanistan. ◆ *Islamic state* C Asia
Afgoi *see* Afgooye
81 *N17* **Afgooye** ***It.*** Afgoi. Shabeellaha Hoose, S Somalia
141 *N8* **'Afīf** Ar Riyāḑ, C Saudi Arabia
77 *V17* **Afikpo** Ebonyi, SE Nigeria
Afiun Karahissar *see* Afyon
Åfjord *see* Åi Åfjord
109 *V6* **Aflenz Kurort** Steiermark, E Austria
74 *J6* **Aflou** N Algeria
81 *L18* **Afmadow** Jubbada Hoose, S Somalia
39 *Q14* **Afognak Island** *island* Alaska, USA
104 *J2* **A Fonsagrada** Galicia, NW Spain
186 *E9* **Afore** Northern, S PNG
59 *O15* **Afrânio** Pernambuco, E Brazil
68-69 **Africa** *continent*
68 *L11* **Africa, Horn of** *physical region* Ethiopia/Somalia
172 *K11* **Africana Seamount** *undersea feature* SW Indian Ocean
86 *A14* **African Plate** *tectonic feature*
138 *I2* **'Afrīn** Ḩalab, N Syria
136 *M15* **Afşin** Kahramanmaraş, C Turkey
98 *J7* **Afsluitdijk** *dam* N Netherlands
29 *U15* **Afton** Iowa, C USA
29 *W9* **Afton** Minnesota, N USA
27 *R8* **Afton** Oklahoma, C USA
136 *F14* **Afyon** ***prev.*** Afyonkarahisar. Afyon, W Turkey
136 *F14* **Afyon** ***var.*** Afiun Karahissar, Afyonkarahisar. ◈ *province* W Turkey
Afyonkarahisar *see* Afyon
Agadès *see* Agadez
77 *V10* **Agadez** ***prev.*** Agadès. Agadez, C Niger
77 *W8* **Agadez** ◈ *department* N Niger
74 *E8* **Agadir** SW Morocco
64 *M9* **Agadir Canyon** *undersea feature* SE Atlantic Ocean
145 *R12* **Agadyr'** Karaganda, C Kazakhstan
173 *O7* **Agalega Islands** *island group* N Mauritius
42 *K6* **Agalta, Sierra de** ⛰ E Honduras
122 *I10* **Agan** ≈ C Russian Federation
Agana/Agaña *see* Hagåtña
188 *B15* **Agana Bay** *bay* NW Guam
188 *C16* **Agana Field** ✕ (Agana) C Guam
171 *Kk13* **Agano-gawa** ≈ Honshū, C Japan
188 *B17* **Aga Point** *headland* S Guam
154 *G9* **Agar** Madhya Pradesh, C India
81 *I14* **Āgaro** Oromo, C Ethiopia
153 *V15* **Agartala** Tripura, NE India
194 *I5* **Agassiz, Cape** *headland* Antarctica
9 *N2* **Agassiz Ice Cap** *ice feature* Nunavut, N Canada
175 *V13* **Agassiz Fracture Zone** *tectonic feature* S Pacific Ocean
188 *B16* **Agat** W Guam
188 *B16* **Agat Bay** *bay* W Guam
145 *P13* **Agat, Gory** *hill* C Kazakhstan
Agatha *see* Agde
115 *M20* **Agathónisi** *island* Dodekánisos, Greece, Aegean Sea
171 *X14* **Agats** Papua, E Indonesia
155 *C21* **Agatti Island** *island* Lakshadweep, India, N Indian Ocean
38 *D16* **Agattu Island** *island* Aleutian Islands, Alaska, USA
38 *D16* **Agattu Strait** *strait* Aleutian Islands, Alaska, USA
14 *B8* **Agawa** ≈ Ontario, S Canada
14 *B8* **Agawa Bay** *lake bay* Ontario, S Canada
77 *N17* **Agboville** SE Ivory Coast
137 *V12* **Ağdam** ***Rus.*** Agdam. SW Azerbaijan
103 *P16* **Agde** ***anc.*** Agatha. Hérault, S France
103 *P16* **Agde, Cap d'** *headland* S France
Agedabia *see* Ajdābiyā
102 *L14* **Agen** ***anc.*** Aginnum. Lot-et-Garonne, SW France
Agendicum *see* Sens
165 *O13* **Ageo** Saitama, Honshū, S Japan
109 *R5* **Ager** ≈ N Austria
Agere Hiywet *see* Hägere Hiywet
108 *G8* **Ägerisee** ◎ W Switzerland
142 *M10* **Āghā Jārī** Khūzestān, SW Iran
39 *P15* **Aghiyuk Island** *island* Alaska, USA
74 *B12* **Aghouinit** SE Western Sahara
Aghri Dagh *see* Büyükağrı Dağı
74 *B10* **Aghzoumal, Sebkhet** ***var.*** Sebjet Agsumal. *salt lake* E Western Sahara
115 *F15* **Agiá** ***var.*** Ayiá. Thessalía, C Greece
40 *G7* **Agiabampo, Estero de** *estuary* NW Mexico
121 *P3* **Agía Fýlaxis** ***var.*** Ayia Phyla. S Cyprus
Agialoúsa *see* Yenierenköy
115 *M21* **Agía Marína** Léros, Dodekánisos, Greece, Aegean Sea
121 *Q2* **Agía Nápa** ***var.*** Ayia Napa. E Cyprus
115 *L16* **Agía Paraskeví** Lésvos, E Greece
115 *J15* **Agías Eirínis, Akrotírio** *headland* Límnos, E Greece
115 *L17* **Agiasós** ***var.*** Ayiásos, Ayiássos. Lésvos, E Greece
Aginnum *see* Agen
123 *O14* **Aginskiy Buryatskiy Avtonomnyy Okrug** ◈ *autonomous district* S Russian Federation
123 *O14* **Aginskoye** Aginskiy Buryatskiy Avtonomnyy Okrug, S Russian Federation
115 *I14* **Ágion Óros** ***Eng.*** Mount Athos. ◈ *monastic republic* NE Greece
115 *H14* **Ágion Óros** ***var.*** Akte, Aktí; ***anc.*** Acte. *peninsula* NE Greece
114 *D13* **Ágios Achílleios** *religious building* Dytikí Makedonía, N Greece
115 *J16* **Ágios Efstrátios** ***var.*** Áyios Evstrátios, Hagios Evstrátios. *island* E Greece
115 *H20* **Ágios Geórgios** *island* Kykládes, Greece, Aegean Sea
115 *Q23* **Ágios Geórgios** *island* SE Greece
115 *E21* **Ágios Ilías** ▲ S Greece
115 *K25* **Ágios Ioannis, Akrotírio** *headland* Kríti, Greece, E Mediterranean Sea
115 *L20* **Ágios Kírykos** ***var.*** Áyios Kírikos. Ikaría, Dodekánisos, Greece, Aegean Sea
115 *D16* **Ágios Nikolaos** Thessalía, C Greece
115 *K25* **Ágios Nikólaos** ***var.*** Áyios Nikólaos. Kríti, Greece, E Mediterranean Sea
115 *H14* **Agíou Órous, Kólpos** *gulf* N Greece
107 *K24* **Agira** ***anc.*** Agyrium. Sicilia, Italy, C Mediterranean Sea
115 *G20* **Agkístri** *island* S Greece
114 *G12* **Ágkistro** ***var.*** Angistro. ▲ NE Greece
103 *O17* **Agly** ≈ S France
Agnetheln *see* Agnita
14 *E10* **Agnew Lake** ◎ Ontario, S Canada
77 *O16* **Agnibilékrou** E Ivory Coast
116 *I11* **Agnita** ***Ger.*** Agnetheln, ***Hung.*** Szentágota. Sibiu, SW Romania
107 *K15* **Agnone** Molise, C Italy
164 *K14* **Ago** Mie, Honshū, SW Japan
106 *C8* **Agogna** ≈ N Italy
Agoitz *see* Agoiz
105 *R3* **Agoiz** ***var.*** Agoitz, Aoiz. Navarra, N Spain
77 *P17* **Agona Swedru** ***var.*** Swedru. SE Ghana
Agordat *see* Akurdet
Agosta *see* Augusta
103 *N15* **Agout** ≈ S France
152 *J12* **Āgra** Uttar Pradesh, N India
Agra and Oudh, United Provinces of *see* Uttar Pradesh
Agram *see* Zagreb
105 *U5* **Agramunt** Cataluña, NE Spain
105 *Q5* **Agreda** Castilla-León, N Spain
137 *S13* **Ağrı** ***var.*** Karaköse; ***prev.*** Karakılısse. Ağrı, NE Turkey
137 *S13* **Ağrı** ◈ *province* NE Turkey
107 *N19* **Agri** ***anc.*** Aciris. ≈ S Italy
Agri Dagi *see* Büyükağrı Dağı
107 *J24* **Agrigento** ***Gk.*** Akragas; ***prev.*** Girgenti. Sicilia, Italy, C Mediterranean Sea
188 *K4* **Agrihan** *island* N Northern Mariana Islands
115 *D18* **Agrínio** ***prev.*** Agrinion. Dytikí Ellás, W Greece
Agrinion *see* Agrínio
115 *G17* **Agriovótano** Évvoia, C Greece
107 *L18* **Agropoli** Campania, S Italy
127 *T3* **Agryz** Udmurtskaya Respublika, NW Russian Federation
137 *U11* **Ağstafa** ***Rus.*** Akstafa. NW Azerbaijan
137 *X11* **Ağsu** ***Rus.*** Akhsu. C Azerbaijan
Agsumal, Sebjet *see* Aghzoumal, Sebkhet
40 *J11* **Agua Brava, Laguna** *lagoon* W Mexico
54 *F7* **Aguachica** Cesar, N Colombia
59 *J20* **Água Clara** Mato Grosso do Sul, SW Brazil
44 *D5* **Aguada de Pasajeros** Cienfuegos, C Cuba
54 *J5* **Aguada Grande** Lara, N Venezuela
45 *S5* **Aguadilla** W Puerto Rico
43 *S16* **Aguadulce** Coclé, S Panama
104 *L14* **Aguadulce** Andalucía, S Spain
41 *O8* **Agualeguas** Nuevo León, NE Mexico
40 *L9* **Aguanaval, Río** ≈ C Mexico
42 *J5* **Aguán, Río** ≈ N Honduras
25 *R16* **Agua Nueva** Texas, SW USA
60 *J8* **Aguapeí, Rio** ≈ S Brazil
61 *E14* **Aguapey, Río** ≈ NE Argentina
40 *G3* **Agua Prieta** Sonora, NW Mexico
104 *G5* **A Guarda** ***var.*** A Guardia, Laguardia, La Guardia. Galicia, NW Spain
A Guardia *see* A Guarda
56 *E6* **Aguarico, Río** ≈ Ecuador/Peru
55 *O6* **Aguasay** Monagas, NE Venezuela
40 *M12* **Aguascalientes** Aguascalientes, C Mexico
40 *L12* **Aguascalientes** ◈ *state* C Mexico
57 *I18* **Aguas Calientes, Río** ≈ S Peru
105 *R7* **Aguasvivas** ≈ NE Spain
60 *J7* **Água Vermelha, Represa de** ⊡ S Brazil
56 *E12* **Aguaytía** Ucayali, C Peru
104 *I5* **A Gudiña** ***var.*** La Gudiña. Galicia, NW Spain
104 *G7* **Águeda** Aveiro, N Portugal
104 *J8* **Águeda** ≈ Portugal/Spain
77 *Q8* **Aguelhok** Kidal, NE Mali
77 *V12* **Aguié** Maradi, S Niger
188 *K8* **Aguijan** *island* S Northern Mariana Islands
104 *M14* **Aguilar** ***var.*** Aguilar de la Frontera. Andalucía, S Spain
104 *M3* **Aguilar de Campóo** Castilla-León, N Spain
Aguilar de la Frontera *see* Aguilar
42 *F7* **Aguilares** San Salvador, C El Salvador
105 *Q14* **Aguilas** Murcia, SE Spain
40 *L15* **Aguililla** Michoacán de Ocampo, SW Mexico
Agulhas *see* L'Agulhas
172 *J11* **Agulhas Bank** *undersea feature* SW Indian Ocean
172 *K11* **Agulhas Basin** *undersea feature* SW Indian Ocean
83 *F26* **Agulhas, Cape** ***Afr.*** Kaap Agulhas. *headland* SW South Africa
Agulhas, Kaap *see* Agulhas, Cape
60 *O9* **Agulhas Negras, Pico das** ▲ SE Brazil
172 *K11* **Agulhas Plateau** *undersea feature* SW Indian Ocean
165 *S16* **Aguni-jima** *island* Nansei-shotō, SW Japan
Agurain *see* Salvatierra
54 *G5* **Agustín Codazzi** ***var.*** Codazzi. Cesar, N Colombia
Agyrium *see* Agira
74 *L12* **Ahaggar** *high plateau region* SE Algeria
146 *E12* **Ahal Welaýaty** ***Rus.*** Akhalskiy Velayat. ◈ *province* C Turkmenistan
142 *K2* **Ahar** Āžarbāyjān-e Khāvarī, NW Iran
Aharnes *see* Acharnés
138 *J3* **Aḩaş, Jabal** ▲ NW Syria
138 *J3* **Aḩaş, Jebal** ⛰ W Syria
185 *G16* **Ahaura** ≈ South Island, NZ
100 *E13* **Ahaus** Nordrhein-Westfalen, NW Germany
191 *U9* **Ahe** *atoll* Îles Tuamotu, C French Polynesia
184 *N10* **Ahimanawa Range** ⛰ North Island, NZ
119 *I19* **Ahinski Kanal** ***Rus.*** Oginskiy Kanal. *canal* SW Belarus
186 *G10* **Ahioma** SE PNG
184 *I2* **Ahipara** Northland, North Island, NZ
184 *I2* **Ahipara Bay** *bay* SE Tasman Sea
Áhkká *see* Akka
39 *N13* **Ahklun Mountains** ⛰ Alaska, USA
137 *R14* **Ahlat** Bitlis, E Turkey
101 *F14* **Ahlen** Nordrhein-Westfalen, W Germany
154 *D10* **Ahmadābād** ***var.*** Ahmedabad. Gujarāt, W India
143 *R10* **Ahmadābād** Kermān, C Iran
Ahmadi *see* Al Aḩmadī
Ahmad Khel *see* Ḩasan Khēl
155 *F14* **Ahmadnagar** ***var.*** Ahmednagar. Mahārāshtra, W India
149 *T9* **Ahmadpur Siāl** Punjab, E Pakistan
77 *N5* **Aḩmar, 'Erg el** *desert* N Mali
80 *K13* **Ahmar Mountains** ⛰ C Ethiopia
Ahmedabad *see* Ahmadābād
Ahmednagar *see* Ahmadnagar
114 *N12* **Ahmetbey** Kırklareli, NW Turkey
14 *H12* **Ahmic Lake** ◎ Ontario, S Canada
190 *G12* **Ahoa** Île Uvea, E Wallis and Futuna
40 *G8* **Ahomé** Sinaloa, C Mexico
21 *X8* **Ahoskie** North Carolina, SE USA
101 *D17* **Ahr** ≈ W Germany
143 *N12* **Ahram** ***var.*** Ahrom. Būshehr, S Iran
100 *J9* **Ahrensburg** Schleswig-Holstein, N Germany
Ahrom *see* Ahram
93 *L17* **Ähtäri** Länsi-Suomi, W Finland
40 *K12* **Ahuacatlán** Nayarit, C Mexico
42 *E7* **Ahuachapán** Ahuachapán, W El Salvador
42 *A9* **Ahuachapán** ◈ *department* W El Salvador

◆ COUNTRY
● COUNTRY CAPITAL
◇ DEPENDENT TERRITORY
○ DEPENDENT TERRITORY CAPITAL
◈ ADMINISTRATIVE REGION
✕ INTERNATIONAL AIRPORT
▲ MOUNTAIN
⛰ MOUNTAIN RANGE
※ VOLCANO
≈ RIVER
◎ LAKE
⊡ RESERVOIR

191 V16 **Ahu Akivi** *var.* Siete Moai. *ancient monument* Easter Island, Chile, E Pacific Ocean
191 W11 **Ahunui** *atoll* Îles Tuamotu, C French Polynesia
185 E20 **Ahuriri** ≈ South Island, NZ
95 L22 **Åhus** Skåne, S Sweden
Ahu Tahira *see* Ahu Vinapu
191 V16 **Ahu Tepeu** *ancient monument* Easter Island, Chile, E Pacific Ocean
191 V17 **Ahu Vinapu** *var.* Ahu Tahira. *ancient monument* Easter Island, Chile, E Pacific Ocean
142 L9 **Ahvāz** *var.* Ahwāz; *prev.* Nāsiri. Khūzestān, SW Iran
Ahvenanmaa *see* Åland
141 Q16 **Aḥwar** SW Yemen
Ahwāz *see* Ahvāz
94 H7 **Åi Åfjord** *var.* Åfjord, Årnes. Sør-Trondelag, C Norway
Aibak *see* Āybak
101 K22 **Aichach** Bayern, SE Germany
164 L14 **Aichi** *off.* Aichi-ken, *var.* Aiti. ◆ *prefecture* Honshū, SW Japan
Aïdin *see* Aydın
Aidussina *see* Ajdovščina
Aifir, Clochán an *see* Giant's Causeway
Aigaíon Pélagos/Aigaío Pélagos *see* Aegean Sea
109 S3 **Aigen im Mülkreis** Oberösterreich, N Austria
115 G20 **Aígina** *var.* Aíyina, Egina. Aígina, C Greece
115 G20 **Aígina** *island* S Greece
115 E18 **Aígio** *var.* Egio; *prev.* Aíyion. Dytikí Ellás, S Greece
108 C10 **Aigle** Vaud, SW Switzerland
103 P14 **Aigoual, Mont** ▲ S France
173 O16 **Aigrettes, Pointe des** *headland* W Réunion
61 G19 **Aiguá** *var.* Aigua. Maldonado, S Uruguay
103 S13 **Aigues** ≈ SE France
103 N10 **Aigurande** Indre, C France
Ai-hun *see* Heihe
165 N10 **Aikawa** Niigata, Sado, C Japan
21 Q13 **Aiken** South Carolina, SE USA
25 N4 **Aiken** Texas, SW USA
160 F13 **Ailao Shan** ▲ SW China
43 W14 **Ailigandí** San Blas, NE Panama
189 R4 **Ailinginae Atoll** *var.* Aelōninae. *atoll* Ralik Chain, SW Marshall Islands
189 T7 **Ailinglaplap Atoll** *var.* Aelōnlaplap. *atoll* Ralik Chain, S Marshall Islands
Aillionn, Loch *see* Allen, Lough
96 H13 **Ailsa Craig** *island* SW Scotland, UK
189 V5 **Ailuk Atoll** *var.* Aelok. *atoll* Ratak Chain, NE Marshall Islands
123 R11 **Aim** Khabarovskiy Kray, E Russian Federation
103 R11 **Ain** ◆ *department* E France
103 S10 **Ain** ≈ E France
118 G7 **Ainaži** *Est.* Heinaste, *Ger.* Hainasch. Limbaži, N Latvia
74 L6 **Aïn Beida** NE Algeria
76 K4 **'Aïn Ben Tili** Tiris Zemmour, N Mauritania
74 J5 **Aïn Defla** *var.* Aïn Eddefla. N Algeria
Aïn Eddefla *see* Aïn Defla
74 L5 **Aïn El Bey** ✕ (Constantine) NE Algeria
115 C19 **Aínos** ▲ Kefallinía, Iónioi Nísoi, Greece, C Mediterranean Sea
105 T4 **Ainsa** Aragón, NE Spain
74 I7 **Aïn Sefra** NW Algeria
29 N13 **Ainsworth** Nebraska, C USA
Aintab *see* Gaziantep
74 H5 **Aïn Témouchent** N Algeria
186 C6 **Aiome** Madang, N PNG
Aïoun el Atrous/Aïoun el Atroûss *see* 'Ayoûn el 'Atroûs
54 E11 **Aipe** Huila, C Colombia
56 D9 **Aipena, Río** ≈ N Peru
57 L19 **Aiquile** Cochabamba, C Bolivia
Aïr *see* Aïr, Massif de l'
188 E10 **Airai** Babeldaob, C Palau
188 E10 **Airai** ✕ (Oreor) Babeldaob, N Palau
168 I11 **Airbangis** Sumatera, NW Indonesia
11 Q16 **Airdrie** Alberta, SW Canada
96 I12 **Airdrie** S Scotland, UK
Air du Azbine *see* Aïr, Massif de l'
97 M17 **Aire** ≈ N England, UK
102 K15 **Aire-sur-l'Adour** Landes, SW France
103 O1 **Aire-sur-la-Lys** Pas-de-Calais, N France
9 Q6 **Air Force Island** *island* Baffin Island, Nunavut, NE Canada
169 Q13 **Airhitam, Teluk** *bay* Borneo, C Indonesia
171 Q11 **Airmadidi** Sulawesi, N Indonesia
77 V8 **Aïr, Massif de l'** *var.* Aïr, Air du Azbine, Asben. ▲ N Niger
108 G10 **Airolo** Ticino, S Switzerland
102 K9 **Airvault** Deux-Sèvres, W France
101 K19 **Aisch** ≈ S Germany
63 G20 **Aisén** *off.* Región Aisén del General Carlos Ibañez del Campo, *var.* Aysen. ◆ *region* S Chile
10 H7 **Aishihik Lake** ◎ Yukon Territory, W Canada
103 P3 **Aisne** ◆ *department* N France
103 R4 **Aisne** ≈ NE France
109 T4 **Aist** ≈ N Austria
114 K13 **Aisými** Anatolikí Makedonía kai Thráki, NE Greece
105 S11 **Aitana** ▲ E Spain
186 B5 **Aitape** *var.* Eitape. Sandaun, NW PNG
Aiti *see* Aichi
29 V6 **Aitkin** Minnesota, N USA
115 D18 **Aitolikó** *var.* Etoliko; *prev.* Aitolikón. Dytikí Ellás, C Greece
Aitolikón *see* Aitolikó
190 L15 **Aitutaki** *island* S Cook Islands
116 H11 **Aiud** *Ger.* Strassburg, *Hung.* Nagyenyed; *prev.* Engeten. Alba, SW Romania
118 I9 **Aiviekste** ≈ C Latvia
189 Q8 **Aiwo** SW Nauru
188 E8 **Aiwokako Passage** *passage* Babeldaob, N Palau
Aix *see* Aix-en-Provence
103 S15 **Aix-en-Provence** *var.* Aix; *anc.* Aquae Sextiae. Bouches-du-Rhône, SE France
Aix-la-Chapelle *see* Aachen
103 T11 **Aix-les-Bains** Savoie, E France
186 A6 **Aiyang, Mount** ▲ NW PNG
Aíyina *see* Aígina
Aíyion *see* Aígio
153 W15 **Āīzawl** Mizoram, NE India
118 H9 **Aizkraukle** Aizkraukle, S Latvia
118 C9 **Aizpute** Liepāja, W Latvia
165 O11 **Aizu-Wakamatsu** *var.* Aizuwakamatu. Fukushima, Honshū, C Japan
Aizuwakamatu *see* Aizu-Wakamatsu
103 X15 **Ajaccio** Corse, France, C Mediterranean Sea
103 X15 **Ajaccio, Golfe d'** *gulf* Corse, France, C Mediterranean Sea
41 Q15 **Ajalpán** Puebla, S Mexico
154 F13 **Ajanta Range** ▲ C India
137 R10 **Ajaria** ◆ *autonomous republic* SW Georgia
Ajastan *see* Armenia
93 G14 **Ajaureforsen** Västerbotten, N Sweden
185 H17 **Ajax, Mount** ▲ South Island, NZ
162 F9 **Aj Bogd Uul** ▲ SW Mongolia
75 R8 **Ajdābiyā** *var.* Agedabia, Ajdābiyah. NE Libya
Ajdābiyah *see* Ajdābiyā
109 S12 **Ajdovščina** *Ger.* Haidenschaft, *It.* Aidussina. W Slovenia
165 Q7 **Ajigasawa** Aomori, Honshū, C Japan
Ajjinena *see* El Geneina
111 H23 **Ajka** Veszprém, W Hungary
138 G9 **'Ajlūn** Irbid, N Jordan
138 H9 **'Ajlūn, Jabal** ▲ W Jordan
Ajluokta *see* Drag
143 R15 **'Ajmān** *var.* Ajman, 'Ujmān. 'Ajmān, NE UAE
152 G12 **Ajmer** *var.* Ajmere. Rājasthān, N India
36 J15 **Ajo** Arizona, SW USA
105 N2 **Ajo, Cabo de** *headland* N Spain
36 J16 **Ajo Range** ▲ Arizona, SW USA
146 C14 **Ajyguyy** *Rus.* Adzhikui. Balkan Welaýaty, W Turkmenistan
Akaba *see* Al 'Aqabah
165 T3 **Akabira** Hokkaidō, NE Japan
165 N10 **Akadomari** Niigata, Sado, C Japan
81 E20 **Akagera** *var.* Kagera. ≈ Rwanda/Tanzania *see also* Kagera
191 W16 **Akahanga, Punta** *headland* Easter Island, Chile, E Pacific Ocean
80 J13 **Āk'ak'i** Oromo, C Ethiopia
155 G15 **Akalkot** Mahārāshtra, W India
Akamagaseki *see* Shimonoseki
165 U4 **Akan** Hokkaidō, NE Japan
165 U4 **Akan-ko** ◎ Hokkaidō, NE Japan
Akanthoú *see* Tatlısu
185 I19 **Akaroa** Canterbury, South Island, NZ
80 E6 **Akasha** Northern, N Sudan
164 I13 **Akashi** *var.* Akasi. Hyōgo, Honshū, SW Japan
139 N7 **'Akāsh, Wādī** *var.* Wādī 'Ukash. *dry watercourse* W Iraq
Akasi *see* Akashi
92 K11 **Äkäsjokisuu** Lappi, N Finland
137 S11 **Akbaba Dağı** ▲ Armenia/Turkey
Akbük Limanı *see* Güllük Körfezi
127 V8 **Akbulak** Orenburgskaya Oblast', W Russian Federation
137 O11 **Akçaabat** Trabzon, NE Turkey
137 N15 **Akçadağ** Malatya, C Turkey
136 G11 **Akçakoca** Bolu, NW Turkey
Akchakaya, Vpadina *see* Akdzhakaya, Vpadina
76 H7 **Akchâr** *desert* W Mauritania
145 S12 **Akchatau** *Kaz.* Aqshataū. Karaganda, C Kazakhstan
136 L13 **Akdağlar** ▲ C Turkey
136 E17 **Ak Dağları** ▲ SW Turkey
136 K13 **Akdağmadeni** Yozgat, C Turkey
146 G8 **Akdepe** *prev.* Ak-Tepe, Leninsk, *Turkm.* Lenin. Daşoguz Welaýaty, N Turkmenistan
Ak-Dere *see* Byala
121 P2 **Akdoğan** *Gk.* Lýsi. C Cyprus
122 J14 **Ak-Dovurak** Respublika Tyva, S Russian Federation
146 F9 **Akdzhakaya, Vpadina** *var.* Vpadina Akchakaya. *depression* N Turkmenistan
171 S11 **Akelamo** Pulau Halmahera, E Indonesia
Aken *see* Aachen
Akermanceaster *see* Bath
95 P15 **Åkersberga** Stockholm, C Sweden
95 H15 **Akershus** ◆ *county* S Norway
79 L16 **Aketi** Orientale, N Dem. Rep. Congo
146 C10 **Akgyr Erezi** *Rus.* Gryada Akkyr. *hill range* NW Turkmenistan
Akhalskiy Velayat *see* Ahal Welaýaty
137 S10 **Akhalts'ikhe** SW Georgia
Akhangaran *see* Ohangaron
Akharnaí *see* Acharnés
75 R7 **Akhḍar, Al Jabal al** *hill range* NE Libya
Akhelóös *see* Achelóos
39 Q15 **Akhiok** Kodiak Island, Alaska, USA
136 C13 **Akhisar** Manisa, W Turkey
75 X10 **Akhmīm** *anc.* Panopolis. C Egypt
152 H6 **Akhnūr** Jammu and Kashmir, NW India
Akhsu *see* Ağsu
127 P11 **Akhtuba** ≈ SW Russian Federation
127 P11 **Akhtubinsk** Astrakhanskaya Oblast', SW Russian Federation
Akhtyrka *see* Okhtyrka
164 H14 **Aki** Kōchi, Shikoku, SW Japan
39 N12 **Akiachak** Alaska, USA
39 N12 **Akiak** Alaska, USA
191 X11 **Akiaki** *atoll* Îles Tuamotu, E French Polynesia
12 H9 **Akimiski Island** *island* Nunavut, C Canada
136 K17 **Akıncı Burnu** *headland* S Turkey
Akıncılar *see* Selçuk
117 U10 **Akinovka** Zaporiz'ka Oblast', S Ukraine
Åkirkeby *see* Aakirkeby
165 P8 **Akita** Akita, Honshū, C Japan
165 Q8 **Akita** *off.* Akita-ken. ◆ *prefecture* Honshū, C Japan
76 H8 **Akjoujt** *prev.* Fort-Repoux. Inchiri, W Mauritania
92 H11 **Akka** ▲ *Lapp.* Áhkká. N Sweden
92 H11 **Akkajaure** ◎ N Sweden
Akkala *see* Oqqal'a
155 L25 **Akkaraipattu** Eastern Province, E Sri Lanka
145 P13 **Akkense** Karaganda, C Kazakhstan
Akkerman *see* Bilhorod-Dnistrovs'kyy
127 W8 **Akkermanovka** Orenburgskaya Oblast', W Russian Federation
165 V4 **Akkeshi** Hokkaidō, NE Japan
165 V4 **Akkeshi-ko** ◎ Hokkaidō, NE Japan
165 V5 **Akkeshi-wan** *bay* NW Pacific Ocean
138 F8 **'Akko** *Eng.* Acre, *Fr.* Saint-Jean-d'Acre; *Bibl.* Accho, Ptolemaïs. Northern, N Israel
145 Q8 **Akkol'** *Kaz.* Aqköl; *prev.* Alekseyevka, *Kaz.* Alekseevka. Akmola, C Kazakhstan
145 T14 **Akkol'** *Kaz.* Aqköl. Almaty, SE Kazakhstan
145 Q16 **Akkol'** *Kaz.* Aqköl. Zhambyl, S Kazakhstan
144 M11 **Akkol', Ozero** *prev.* Ozero Zhaman-Akkol'. ◎ C Kazakhstan
98 L6 **Akkrum** Friesland, N Netherlands
145 U8 **Akku** *prev.* Lebyazh'ye. Pavlodar, NE Kazakhstan
144 F12 **Akkystau** *Kaz.* Aqqystaū. Atyrau, SW Kazakhstan
8 G6 **Aklavik** Northwest Territories, NW Canada
Akmenrags *see* Akmensrags
118 B9 **Akmensrags** *prev.* Akmeņrags. *headland* W Latvia
158 E9 **Akmeqit** Xinjiang Uygur Zizhiqu, NW China
146 J14 **Akmeydan** Mary Welaýaty, C Turkmenistan
Akmola *see* Astana
145 P9 **Akmola** *off.* Akmolinskaya Oblast', *Kaz.* Aqmola Oblysy; *prev.* Tselinogradskaya Oblast. ◆ *province* C Kazakhstan
Akmolinsk *see* Astana
Akmolinskaya Oblast' *see* Akmola
Aknavásár *see* Târgu Ocna
118 I11 **Aknīste** Jēkabpils, S Latvia
81 G14 **Akobo** Jonglei, SE Sudan
81 G14 **Akobo** *var.* Åkobowenz. ≈ Ethiopia/Sudan
Åkobowenz *see* Akobo
154 H12 **Akola** Mahārāshtra, C India
Akordat *see* Akurdet
77 Q16 **Akosombo Dam** *dam* SE Ghana
154 H12 **Akot** Mahārāshtra, C India
77 N16 **Akoupé** SE Ivory Coast
12 M3 **Akpatok Island** *island* Nunavut, E Canada
158 G7 **Akqi** Xinjiang Uygur Zizhiqu, NW China
138 I2 **Akrād, Jabal al** ▲ N Syria
Akragas *see* Agrigento
92 H3 **Akranes** Vesturland, W Iceland
139 S2 **Ākrē** *Ar.* 'Aqrah. N Iraq
95 C16 **Åkrahamn** Rogaland, S Norway
77 V9 **Akréréb** Agadez, C Niger
115 D22 **Akrítas, Akrotírio** *headland* S Greece
37 V3 **Akron** Colorado, C USA
29 R12 **Akron** Iowa, C USA
31 U12 **Akron** Ohio, N USA
Akrotiri *see* Akrotírion
Akrotiri Bay *see* Akrotírion, Kólpos
121 P3 **Akrotírion** *var.* Akrotiri. *UK air base* S Cyprus
121 P3 **Akrotírion, Kólpos** *var.* Akrotiri Bay. *bay* S Cyprus
121 O3 **Akrotiri Sovereign Base Area** *UK military installation* S Cyprus
158 F11 **Aksai Chin** *Chin.* Aksayqin. *disputed region* China/India
Aksaj *see* Aksay
136 I15 **Aksaray** Aksaray, C Turkey
136 I15 **Aksaray** ◆ *province* C Turkey
144 G8 **Aksay** *var.* Aksaj, *Kaz.* Aqsay. Zapadnyy Kazakhstan, NW Kazakhstan
127 O11 **Aksay** Volgogradskaya Oblast', SW Russian Federation
147 W10 **Aksay** *var.* Toxkan He. ≈ China/Kyrgyzstan
Aksay/Aksay Kazakzu Zizhixian *see* Boluozhuanjing/Hongliuwan
Aksayqin *see* Aksai Chin
158 G11 **Aksayqin Hu** ◎ NW China
136 G14 **Akşehir** Konya, W Turkey
136 G14 **Akşehir Gölü** ◎ C Turkey
136 G16 **Akseki** Antalya, SW Turkey
123 P13 **Aksenovo-Zilovskoye** Chitinskaya Oblast', S Russian Federation
145 V11 **Akshatau, Khrebet** ▲ E Kazakhstan
147 Y8 **Ak-Shyyrak** Issyk-Kul'skaya Oblast', E Kyrgyzstan
Akstafa *see* Ağstafa
158 H7 **Aksu** Xinjiang Uygur Zizhiqu, NW China
145 R8 **Aksu** *Kaz.* Aqsū. Akmola, N Kazakhstan
145 T8 **Aksu** *var.* Jermak, *Kaz.* Ermak; *prev.* Yermak. Pavlodar, NE Kazakhstan
145 W13 **Aksu** *Kaz.* Aqsū. Almaty, SE Kazakhstan
145 V13 **Aksu** *Kaz.* Aqsū. ≈ SE Kazakhstan
145 X11 **Aksuat** *Kaz.* Aqsūat. Vostochnyy Kazakhstan, E Kazakhstan
145 Y11 **Aksuat** *Kaz.* Aqsūat. Vostochnyy Kazakhstan, SE Kazakhstan
127 S4 **Aksubayevo** Respublika Tatarstan, W Russian Federation
158 H7 **Aksu He** *Rus.* Sary-Dzhaz. ≈ China/Kyrgyzstan *see also* Sary-Dzhaz
80 J10 **Āksum** Tigray, N Ethiopia
145 O12 **Aktas** *Kaz.* Aqtas. Karaganda, C Kazakhstan
Aktash *see* Oqtosh
147 V9 **Ak-Tash, Gora** ▲ C Kyrgyzstan
145 R10 **Aktau** *Kaz.* Aqtaū. Karaganda, C Kazakhstan
144 E11 **Aktau** *Kaz.* Aqtaū; *prev.* Shevchenko. Mangistau, W Kazakhstan
Aktau, Khrebet *see* Oqtogh, SW Tajikistan
Aktau, Khrebet *see* Oqtow Tizmasi, C Uzbekistan
Akte *see* Ágion Óros
Ak-Tepe *see* Akdepe
147 X7 **Ak-Terek** Issyk-Kul'skaya Oblast', E Kyrgyzstan
Aktí *see* Ágion Óros
158 E8 **Akto** Xinjiang Uygur Zizhiqu, NW China
144 I10 **Aktobe** *Kaz.* Aqtöbe. *prev.* Aktyubinsk. Aktyubinsk, NW Kazakhstan
145 V12 **Aktogay** *Kaz.* Aqtoghay. Vostochnyy Kazakhstan, E Kazakhstan
119 M18 **Aktsyabrski** *Rus.* Oktyabr'skiy; *prev.* Karpilovka. Homyel'skaya Voblasts', SE Belarus
Aktyubinsk *see* Aktobe
144 H11 **Aktyubinsk** *off.* Aktyubinskaya Oblast', *Kaz.* Aqtöbe Oblysy. ◆ *province* W Kazakhstan
Aktyubinsk *see* Aktobe
147 W7 **Ak-Tyuz** *var.* Aktyuz. Chuyskaya Oblast', N Kyrgyzstan
79 J17 **Akula** Equateur, NW Dem. Rep. Congo
164 C15 **Akune** Kagoshima, Kyūshū, SW Japan
38 L16 **Akun Island** *island* Aleutian Islands, Alaska, USA
80 J9 **Akurdet** *var.* Agordat, Akordat. C Eritrea
77 T16 **Akure** Ondo, SW Nigeria
92 J2 **Akureyri** Nordhurland Eystra, N Iceland
38 L17 **Akutan** Akutan Island, Alaska, USA
38 K17 **Akutan Island** *island* Aleutian Islands, Alaska, USA
77 V17 **Akwa Ibom** ◆ *state* SE Nigeria
Akyab *see* Sittwe
127 W7 **Ak"yar** Respublika Bashkortostan, W Russian Federation
144 J10 **Akzhar** *prev.* Novorossiyskiy, Novorossiyskoye. Aktyubinsk, NW Kazakhstan
145 Y11 **Akzhar** *Kaz.* Aqzhar. Vostochnyy Kazakhstan, E Kazakhstan
94 F13 **Ål** Buskerud, S Norway
119 N18 **Ala** *Rus.* Ola. ≈ SE Belarus
20 H11 **Alabama** *off.* State of Alabama; also known as Camellia State, Heart of Dixie, The Cotton State, Yellowhammer State. ◆ *state* S USA
23 P6 **Alabama River** ≈ Alabama, S USA
23 P4 **Alabaster** Alabama, S USA
139 U10 **Al 'Abd Allāh** *var.* Al Abdullah. S Iraq
Al Abdullah *see* Al 'Abd Allāh
139 W14 **Al Abṭīyah** *well* S Iraq
147 S9 **Ala-Buka** Dzhalal-Abadskaya Oblast', W Kyrgyzstan
136 J12 **Alaca** Çorum, N Turkey
136 K10 **Alaçam** Samsun, N Turkey
Alacant *see* Alicante
23 V9 **Alachua** Florida, SE USA
137 S13 **Aladağlar** ▲ W Turkey
136 K15 **Ala Dağları** ▲ C Turkey
127 O16 **Alagir** Respublika Severnaya Osetiya, SW Russian Federation
106 B6 **Alagna Valsesia** Valle d'Aosta, NW Italy
103 P12 **Alagnon** ≈ C France
59 P16 **Alagoas** *off.* Estado de Alagoas. ◆ *state* E Brazil
59 P17 **Alagoinhas** Bahia, E Brazil
105 R5 **Alagón** Aragón, NE Spain
104 J9 **Alagón** ≈ W Spain
93 K16 **Alahärmä** Länsi-Suomi, W Finland
al Ahdar *see* Al Akhḍar
Álaheaieatnu *see* Altaelva
142 K12 **Al Aḥmadī** *var.* Ahmadi. E Kuwait
Al Ain *see* Al 'Ayn
105 Z8 **Alaior** *prev.* Alayor. Menorca, Spain, W Mediterranean Sea
147 T11 **Alai Range** *Rus.* Alayskiy Khrebet. ▲ Kyrgyzstan/Tajikistan
Alais *see* Alès
141 X11 **Al 'Ajā'iz** E Oman
141 X11 **Al 'Ajā'iz** *oasis* SE Oman
93 L16 **Alajärvi** Länsi-Suomi, W Finland
118 K4 **Alajõe** Ida-Virumaa, NE Estonia
42 M13 **Alajuela** Alajuela, C Costa Rica
42 L12 **Alajuela** *off.* Provincia de Alajuela. ◆ *province* N Costa Rica
43 T14 **Alajuela, Lago** ◎ C Panama
38 M11 **Alakanuk** Alaska, USA
140 K5 **Al Akhḍar** *var.* al Ahdar. Tabūk, NW Saudi Arabia
Alakol' *see* Alakol', Ozero
145 X13 **Alakol', Ozero** *Kaz.* Alakōl. ◎ SE Kazakhstan
124 I5 **Alakurtti** Murmanskaya Oblast', NW Russian Federation
38 F10 **'Alalākeiki Channel** *var.* Alalakeiki Channel *channel* Hawai'i, USA, C Pacific Ocean
Al 'Alamayn *see* El 'Alamein
139 R1 **Al 'Amādīyah** N Iraq
188 K5 **Alamagan** *island* C Northern Mariana Islands
139 X10 **Al 'Amārah** *var.* Amara. E Iraq
80 J11 **Ālamat'ā** Tigray, N Ethiopia
37 R11 **Alameda** New Mexico, SW USA
121 T13 **'Alam el Rûm, Râs** *headland* N Egypt
Alamícamba *see* Alamikamba
42 M8 **Alamikamba** *var.* Alamícamba. Región Autónoma Atlántico Norte, NE Nicaragua
24 K11 **Alamito Creek** ≈ Texas, SW USA
40 M8 **Alamitos, Sierra de los** ▲ NE Mexico
35 X9 **Alamo** Nevada, W USA
20 F9 **Alamo** Tennessee, S USA
41 Q12 **Álamo** Veracruz-Llave, C Mexico
37 S14 **Alamogordo** New Mexico, SW USA
36 J12 **Alamo Lake** ▣ Arizona, SW USA
40 H7 **Alamos** Sonora, NW Mexico
37 S7 **Alamosa** Colorado, C USA
93 J20 **Åland** *var.* Aland Islands, *Fin.* Ahvenanmaa. ◆ *province* SW Finland
93 J19 **Åland** *Fin.* Ahvenanmaa. *island* SW Finland
88 K9 **Åland** *var.* Aland Islands, *Fin.* Ahvenanmaa. *island group* SW Finland
Aland Islands *see* Åland
Aland Sea *see* Ålands Hav
95 Q14 **Ålands Hav** *var.* Aland Sea. *strait* Baltic Sea/Gulf of Bothnia
43 P16 **Alanje** Chiriquí, SW Panama
25 O2 **Alanreed** Texas, SW USA
136 G17 **Alanya** Antalya, S Turkey
23 U7 **Alapaha River** ≈ Florida/Georgia, SE USA
122 G10 **Alapayevsk** Sverdlovskaya Oblast', C Russian Federation
Alappuzha *see* Alleppey
138 F14 **Al 'Aqabah** *var.* Akaba, Aqaba, 'Aqaba; *anc.* Aelana, Elath. Ma'ān, SW Jordan
Al 'Arabīyah as Su'ūdīyah *see* Saudi Arabia
al Araïch *see* Larache
105 Q10 **Alarcón** Castilla-La Mancha, C Spain
105 Q9 **Alarcón, Embalse de** ▣ C Spain
138 J2 **Al 'Arīmah** *Fr.* Arime. Ḥalab, N Syria
Al 'Arīsh *see* El 'Arîsh
141 P6 **Al Arṭāwīyah** Ar Riyāḍ, N Saudi Arabia
Alasca, Golfo de *see* Alaska, Gulf of
136 D14 **Alaşehir** Manisa, W Turkey
139 N5 **Al 'Ashārah** *var.* Ashara. Dayr az Zawr, E Syria
138 H10 **'Al Āṣimah** *off.* Muḥāfaẓat 'Al Āṣimah. *prev.* 'Ammān ◆ *governorate* NW Jordan
Al Ashkhara *see* Al Ashkharah
141 Z9 **Al Ashkharah** *var.* Al Ashkhara. NE Oman
39 P8 **Alaska** *off.* State of Alaska; also known as Land of the Midnight Sun, The Last Frontier, Seward's Folly; *prev.* Russian America. ◆ *state* NW USA
39 T13 **Alaska, Gulf of** *var.* Golfo de Alasca. *gulf* Canada/USA
39 O15 **Alaska Peninsula** *peninsula* Alaska, USA
39 Q11 **Alaska Range** ▲ Alaska, USA
Al-Asnam *see* Chlef
106 B10 **Alassio** Liguria, NW Italy
Alat *see* Olot
137 Y12 **Älät** *Rus.* Alyat; *prev.* Alyaty-Pristan'. SE Azerbaijan
139 S13 **Al 'Athāmīn** S Iraq
39 P7 **Alatna River** ≈ Alaska, USA
107 J15 **Alatri** Lazio, C Italy
Alattio *see* Alta
127 P5 **Alatyr'** Chuvashskaya Respublika, W Russian Federation
56 C7 **Alausí** Chimborazo, C Ecuador
105 O3 **Álava** *Basq.* Araba. ◆ *province* País Vasco, N Spain
137 T11 **Alaverdi** N Armenia
Alavo *see* Alavus
93 N14 **Ala-Vuokki** Oulu, E Finland
93 K17 **Alavus** *Swe.* Alavo. Länsi-Suomi, W Finland
Al 'Awābī *see* Awābī
139 P6 **Al 'Awānī** W Iraq
Al Awaynāt *see* Al 'Uwaynāt
182 K9 **Alawoona** South Australia
Alaykel'/Alay-Kuu *see* Kök-Art
143 R17 **Al 'Ayn** *var.* Al Ain. Abū Ẓaby, E UAE
143 R17 **Al 'Ayn** *var.* Al Ain. ✕ Abū Ẓaby, E UAE
138 G12 **Al 'Aynā** Al Karak, W Jordan
Alayor *see* Alaior
Alayskiy Khrebet *see* Alai Range
123 S6 **Alazeya** ≈ NE Russian Federation
139 U8 **Al 'Azīzīyah** *var.* Aziziya. E Iraq
120 M12 **Al 'Azīzīyah** NW Libya
138 I10 **Al Azraq al Janūbī** Az Zarqā', N Jordan
106 B9 **Alba** *anc.* Alba Pompeia. Piemonte, NW Italy
25 V6 **Alba** Texas, SW USA
116 G11 **Alba** ◆ *county* W Romania
139 P3 **Al Ba'āj** N Iraq
138 J2 **Al Bāb** Ḥalab, N Syria
116 G10 **Albac** *Hung.* Fehérvölgy; *prev.* Álbák. Alba, SW Romania
105 Q11 **Albacete** Castilla-La Mancha, C Spain
105 P11 **Albacete** ◆ *province* Castilla-La Mancha, C Spain
140 I4 **Al Bad'** Tabūk, NW Saudi Arabia
104 L7 **Alba de Tormes** Castilla-León, N Spain
139 P3 **Al Bādī** N Iraq
141 V8 **Al Badī'ah** ✕ (Abū Ẓaby) Abū Ẓaby, C UAE
143 P17 **Al Badī'ah** *var.* Al Bedei'ah. *spring/well* C UAE
139 Q7 **Al Baghdādī** *var.* Khān al Baghdādī. SW Iraq
Al Bāha *see* Al Bāḥah
140 M11 **Al Bāḥah** *var.* Al Bāha. Al Bāḥah, SW Saudi Arabia
140 M11 **Al Bāḥah** *off.* Minṭaqat al Bāḥah. ◆ *province* W Saudi Arabia
Al Baḥrayn *see* Bahrain
105 S11 **Albaida** País Valenciano, E Spain
116 H11 **Alba Iulia** *Ger.* Weissenburg, *Hung.* Gyulafehérvár; *prev.* Bălgrad, Karlsburg, Károly-Fehérvár. Alba, W Romania
Álbák *see* Albac
138 G10 **Al Balqā'** *off.* Muḥāfaẓat al Balqā', *var.* Balqā'. ◆ *governorate* NW Jordan
14 F11 **Alban** Ontario, S Canada
103 O15 **Alban** Tarn, S France
12 K11 **Albanel, Lac** ◎ Québec, SE Canada
113 L20 **Albania** *off.* Republic of Albania, *Alb.* Republika e Shqipërisë, Shqipëria; *prev.* People's Socialist Republic of Albania. ◆ *republic* SE Europe
Albania *see* Aubagne
107 H15 **Albano Laziale** Lazio, C Italy
180 J14 **Albany** Western Australia
23 S7 **Albany** Georgia, SE USA
31 P13 **Albany** Indiana, N USA
20 L8 **Albany** Kentucky, S USA
29 U7 **Albany** Minnesota, N USA
27 R2 **Albany** Missouri, C USA
18 L10 **Albany** *state capital* New York, NE USA
32 G12 **Albany** Oregon, NW USA
25 Q6 **Albany** Texas, SW USA
12 F10 **Albany** ≈ Ontario, S Canada
Alba Pompeia *see* Alba
Alba Regia *see* Székesfehérvár
138 J6 **Al Bāridah** *var.* Bāridah. Ḥimş, C Syria
139 Q11 **Al Barīt** S Iraq
105 R8 **Albarracín** Aragón, NE Spain
139 Y12 **Al Baṣrah** *Eng.* Basra; *hist.* Busra, Bussora. SE Iraq
139 V11 **Al Baṭḥā'** SE Iraq
141 X8 **Al Bāṭinah** *var.* Batinah. *coastal region* N Oman
(0) H16 **Albatross Plateau** *undersea feature* E Pacific Ocean
Al Batrūn *see* Batroûn
121 Q12 **Al Bayḍā'** *var.* Beida. NE Libya
141 P16 **Al Bayḍā'** *var.* Al Beida. SW Yemen
Al Bedei'ah *see* Al Badī'ah
Al Beida *see* Al Bayḍā'
21 S10 **Albemarle** *var.* Albermarle. North Carolina, SE USA
Albemarle Island *see* Isabela, Isla
21 N8 **Albemarle Sound** *inlet* W Atlantic Ocean
106 B10 **Albenga** Liguria, NW Italy
104 L8 **Alberche** ≈ C Spain
103 O17 **Albères, Chaîne des** *var.* les Albères, Montes Albères. ▲ France/Spain
Albères, Montes *see* Albères, Chaîne des
182 F2 **Alberga Creek** *seasonal river* South Australia
104 G7 **Albergaria-a-Velha** Aveiro, N Portugal
105 S10 **Alberic** País Valenciano, E Spain
Albermarle *see* Albemarle
107 P18 **Alberobello** Puglia, SE Italy
108 J7 **Alberschwende** Vorarlberg, W Austria
103 O3 **Albert** Somme, N France
11 O12 **Alberta** ◆ *province* SW Canada
Albert Edward Nyanza *see* Edward, Lake
61 C20 **Alberti** Buenos Aires, E Argentina
111 K23 **Albertirsa** Pest, C Hungary
99 I16 **Albertkanaal** *canal* N Belgium
79 P17 **Albert, Lake** *var.* Albert Nyanza, Lac Mobutu Sese Seko. ◎ Uganda/Dem. Rep. Congo
29 V11 **Albert Lea** Minnesota, N USA
81 F16 **Albert Nile** ≈ NW Uganda
Albert Nyanza *see* Albert, Lake
103 T11 **Albertville** Savoie, E France
23 Q2 **Albertville** Alabama, S USA
Albertville *see* Kalemie
103 N15 **Albi** *anc.* Albiga. Tarn, S France
29 W15 **Albia** Iowa, C USA
Albiga *see* Albi
55 X9 **Albina** Marowijne, NE Suriname
83 A15 **Albina, Ponta** *headland* SW Angola
30 M16 **Albion** Illinois, N USA
31 P11 **Albion** Indiana, N USA

◆ Country ◇ Dependent Territory ◆ Administrative Region ▲ Mountain ⚠ Volcano ◎ Lake
● Country Capital ○ Dependent Territory Capital ✕ International Airport ▲ Mountain Range ≈ River ▣ Reservoir

29 P14 **Albion** Nebraska, C USA
18 E9 **Albion** New York, NE USA
18 B12 **Albion** Pennsylvania, NE USA
Al Biqā' *see* El Beqaa
140 J4 **Al Bi'r** *var.* Bi'r Ibn Hirmās. Tabūk, NW Saudi Arabia
140 M12 **Al Birk** Makkah, SW Saudi Arabia
141 Q9 **Al Biyāḍ** *desert* C Saudi Arabia
98 H13 **Alblasserdam** Zuid-Holland, SW Netherlands
105 T8 **Albocácer** *var.* Albocasser. País Valenciano, E Spain
Albocasser *see* Albocácer
95 H19 **Ålbæk** Nordjylland, N Denmark
Albona *see* Labin
105 O17 **Alborán, Isla de** *island* S Spain
Alborán, Mar de *see* Alboran Sea
105 N17 **Alboran Sea** *Sp.* Mar de Alborán. *sea* SW Mediterranean Sea
Ålborg *see* Aalborg
95 H21 **Ålborg Bugt** *var.* Aalborg Bugt. *bay* N Denmark
Ålborg-Nørresundby *see* Aalborg
143 O5 **Alborz, Reshteh-ye Kūhhā-ye** *Eng.* Elburz Mountains. ▲ N Iran
105 Q14 **Albox** Andalucía, S Spain
101 H23 **Albstadt** Baden-Württemberg, SW Germany
104 G14 **Albufeira** Beja, S Portugal
139 P5 **Ālbū Gharz, Sabkhat** ◎ W Iraq
105 O15 **Albuñol** Andalucía, S Spain
37 Q11 **Albuquerque** New Mexico, SW USA
141 W8 **Al Buraymī** *var.* Buraimi. N Oman
143 R17 **Al Buraymī** *var.* Buraimi. *spring/well* Oman/UAE
Al Burayqah *see* Marsá al Burayqah
Alburgum *see* Aalborg
104 I10 **Alburquerque** Extremadura, W Spain
181 V14 **Albury** New South Wales, SE Australia
141 T14 **Al Buzūn** SE Yemen
93 G17 **Alby** Västernorrland, C Sweden
Albyn, Glen *see* Mor, Glen
104 G12 **Alcácer do Sal** Setúbal, W Portugal
Alcalá de Chisvert *see* Alcalà de Chivert
105 T8 **Alcalà de Chivert** *var.* Alcalá de Chisvert. País Valenciano, E Spain
104 K14 **Alcalá de Guadaira** Andalucía, S Spain
105 O8 **Alcalá de Henares** *Ar.* Alkal'a; *anc.* Complutum. Madrid, C Spain
104 K16 **Alcalá de los Gazules** Andalucía, S Spain
105 N14 **Alcalá La Real** Andalucía, S Spain
107 I23 **Alcamo** Sicilia, Italy, C Mediterranean Sea
105 T4 **Alcanadre** ≈ NE Spain
105 T8 **Alcanar** Cataluña, NE Spain
104 J5 **Alcañices** Castilla-León, N Spain
105 T7 **Alcañiz** Aragón, NE Spain
104 I9 **Alcántara** Extremadura, W Spain
104 J9 **Alcántara, Embalse de** ⊠ W Spain
105 R13 **Alcantarilla** Murcia, SE Spain
105 P11 **Alcaraz** Castilla-La Mancha, C Spain
105 P12 **Alcaraz, Sierra de** ▲ C Spain
104 I12 **Alcarrache** ≈ SW Spain
105 T6 **Alcarràs** Cataluña, NE Spain
105 N14 **Alcaudete** Andalucía, S Spain
Alcázar *see* Ksar-el-Kebir
105 O10 **Alcázar de San Juan** *anc.* Alce. Castilla-La Mancha, C Spain
Alcazarquivir *see* Ksar-el-Kebir
Alce *see* Alcázar de San Juan
57 B17 **Alcebo, Volcán** ☢ Galapagos Islands, Ecuador, E Pacific Ocean
139 X12 **Al Chabā'ish** *var.* Al Kaba'ish. SE Iraq
117 Y7 **Alchevs'k** *prev.* Kommunarsk, Voroshilovsk. Luhans'ka Oblast', E Ukraine
Alcira *see* Alzira
21 N9 **Alcoa** Tennessee, S USA
104 F9 **Alcobaça** Leiria, C Portugal
105 N8 **Alcobendas** Madrid, C Spain
Alcoi *see* Alcoy
105 P7 **Alcolea del Pinar** Castilla-La Mancha, C Spain
104 I11 **Alconchel** Extremadura, W Spain
105 S9 **Alcora** País Valenciano, E Spain
105 N8 **Alcorcón** Madrid, C Spain
105 S7 **Alcorisa** Aragón, NE Spain
61 B19 **Alcorta** Santa Fe, C Argentina
104 H14 **Alcoutim** Faro, S Portugal
33 W15 **Alcova** Wyoming, C USA
105 S11 **Alcoy** *Cat.* Alcoi. País Valenciano, E Spain
105 Y9 **Alcúdia, Badia d'** *bay* Mallorca, Spain, W Mediterranean Sea
172 M7 **Aldabra Group** *island group* SW Seychelles
139 U10 **Al Daghghārah** C Iraq
40 J5 **Aldama** Chihuahua, N Mexico
41 P11 **Aldama** Tamaulipas, C Mexico
123 Q11 **Aldan** Respublika Sakha (Yakutiya), NE Russian Federation
123 Q10 **Aldan** ≈ NE Russian Federation
162 G7 **Aldar** Dzavhan, W Mongolia
al Dar al Baida *see* Rabat
97 Q20 **Aldeburgh** E England, UK
105 P5 **Aldehuela de Calatañazor** Castilla-León, N Spain
Aldeia Nova *see* Aldeia Nova de São Bento
104 H13 **Aldeia Nova de São Bento** *var.* Aldeia Nova. Beja, S Portugal
29 V11 **Alden** Minnesota, N USA
184 N6 **Aldermen Islands, The** *island group* N NZ
97 L25 **Alderney** *island* Channel Islands
97 N22 **Aldershot** S England, UK
21 R6 **Alderson** West Virginia, NE USA
Al Dhaid *see* Adh Dhayd
30 J11 **Aledo** Illinois, N USA
76 H9 **Aleg** Brakna, SW Mauritania
64 Q10 **Alegranza** *island* Islas Canarias, Spain, NE Atlantic Ocean
37 P12 **Alegres Mountain** ▲ New Mexico, SW USA
61 F15 **Alegrete** Rio Grande do Sul, S Brazil
61 C16 **Alejandra** Santa Fe, C Argentina
193 T11 **Alejandro Selkirk, Isla** *island* Islas Juan Fernández, Chile, E Pacific Ocean
124 I12 **Alekhovshchina** Leningradskaya Oblast', NW Russian Federation
39 O13 **Aleknagik** Alaska, USA
Aleksandriya *see* Oleksandriya
Aleksandropol' *see* Gyumri
126 L3 **Aleksandrov** Vladimirskaya Oblast', W Russian Federation
113 N14 **Aleksandrovac** Serbia, C Serbia and Montenegro (Yugo.)
127 R9 **Aleksandrov Gay** Saratovskaya Oblast', W Russian Federation
127 U6 **Aleksandrovka** Orenburgskaya Oblast', W Russian Federation
Aleksandrovka *see* Oleksandrivka
114 J8 **Aleksandrovo** Lovech, N Bulgaria
125 V13 **Aleksandrovsk** Permskaya Oblast', NW Russian Federation
Aleksandrovsk *see* Zaporizhzhya
127 N14 **Aleksandrovskoye** Stavropol'skiy Kray, SW Russian Federation
123 T12 **Aleksandrovsk-Sakhalinskiy** Ostrov Sakhalin, Sakhalinskaya Oblast', SE Russian Federation
110 J10 **Aleksandrów Kujawski** Kujawsko-pomorskie, C Poland
110 K12 **Aleksandrów Łódzki** Łódzkie, C Poland
Alekseevka *see* Terekty
126 L9 **Alekseyevka** Belgorodskaya Oblast', W Russian Federation
145 P7 **Alekseyevka** *Kaz.* Alekseevka. Akmola, N Kazakhstan
127 S7 **Alekseyevka** Samarskaya Oblast', W Russian Federation
Alekseyevka *see* Akkol', Akmola, Kazakhstan
Alekseyevka *see* Terekty, Vostochnyy Kazakhstan, Kazakhstan
127 R4 **Alekseyevskoye** Respublika Tatarstan, W Russian Federation
126 K5 **Aleksin** Tul'skaya Oblast', W Russian Federation
113 O14 **Aleksinac** Serbia, SE Serbia and Montenegro (Yugo.)
190 G11 **Alele** Île Uvea, E Wallis and Futuna
95 N20 **Älem** Kalmar, S Sweden
102 L6 **Alençon** Orne, N France
58 I12 **Alenquer** Pará, NE Brazil
38 G10 **'Alenuihāhā Channel** *var.* Alenuihaha Channel. *channel* Hawai'i, USA, C Pacific Ocean
Alep/Aleppo *see* Ḥalab
103 Y15 **Aléria** Corse, France, C Mediterranean Sea
197 Q11 **Alert** Ellesmere Island, Nunavut, N Canada
103 Q14 **Alès** *prev.* Alais. Gard, S France
116 G9 **Aleşd** *Hung.* Élesd. Bihor, SW Romania
106 C9 **Alessandria** *Fr.* Alexandrie. Piemonte, N Italy
Ålestrup *see* Aalestrup
94 D9 **Ålesund** Møre og Romsdal, S Norway
108 E10 **Aletschhorn** ▲ SW Switzerland
197 S1 **Aleutian Basin** *undersea feature* Bering Sea
38 H17 **Aleutian Islands** *island group* Alaska, USA
39 P14 **Aleutian Range** ▲ Alaska, USA
(0) B5 **Aleutian Trench** *undersea feature* S Bering Sea
123 T10 **Alevina, Mys** *headland* E Russian Federation
15 Q6 **Alex** ≈ Québec, SE Canada
28 J3 **Alexander** North Dakota, N USA
39 W14 **Alexander Archipelago** *island group* Alaska, USA
Alexanderbaai *see* Alexander Bay
83 D23 **Alexander Bay** *Afr.* Alexanderbaai. Northern Cape, W South Africa
23 Q5 **Alexander City** Alabama, S USA
194 J6 **Alexander Island** *island* Antarctica
Alexander Range *see* Kirghiz Range
183 O12 **Alexandra** Victoria, SE Australia
185 D22 **Alexandra** Otago, South Island, NZ
115 F14 **Alexándreia** *var.* Alexándria. Kentrikí Makedonía, N Greece
Alexandretta *see* İskenderun
Alexandretta, Gulf of *see* İskenderun Körfezi
15 N13 **Alexandria** Ontario, SE Canada
121 U13 **Alexandria** *Ar.* Al Iskandarīyah. N Egypt
44 J12 **Alexandria** C Jamaica
116 J15 **Alexandria** Teleorman, S Romania
31 P13 **Alexandria** Indiana, N USA
20 M4 **Alexandria** Kentucky, S USA
22 H7 **Alexandria** Louisiana, S USA
29 T7 **Alexandria** Minnesota, N USA
29 Q11 **Alexandria** South Dakota, N USA
21 W4 **Alexandria** Virginia, NE USA
Alexándria *see* Alexándreia
18 I7 **Alexandria Bay** New York, NE USA
Alexandrie *see* Alessandria
182 J10 **Alexandrina, Lake** ◎ South Australia
114 K13 **Alexandroúpoli** *var.* Alexandroúpolis, *Turk.* Dedeagaç, Dedeagach. Anatolikí Makedonía kai Thráki, NE Greece
Alexandroúpolis *see* Alexandroúpoli
10 L15 **Alexis Creek** British Columbia, SW Canada
122 I13 **Aleysk** Altayskiy Kray, S Russian Federation
10 L15 **Alexis Creek** British Columbia, SW Canada
122 I13 **Aleysk** Altayskiy Kray, S Russian Federation
139 S8 **Al Fallūjah** *var.* Falluja. C Iraq
105 R8 **Alfambra** ≈ E Spain
Al Faqa *see* Faq'
141 R15 **Al Farḍah** C Yemen
105 Q4 **Alfaro** La Rioja, N Spain
105 U5 **Alfarràs** Cataluña, NE Spain
Al Fāshir *see* El Fasher
Al Fashn *see* El Fashn
114 M7 **Alfatar** Silistra, NE Bulgaria
139 S5 **Al Fatḥah** C Iraq
139 P2 **Al Fatsī** N Iraq
139 Z13 **Al Fāw** *var.* Fao. SE Iraq
Al Fayyūm *see* El Faiyûm
115 D20 **Alfeiós** *prev.* Alfiós, *anc.* Alpheius, Alpheus. ≈ S Greece
100 I13 **Alfeld** Niedersachsen, C Germany
Alfiós *see* Alfeiós
Alföld *see* Great Hungarian Plain
94 C11 **Ålfotbreen** *glacier* S Norway
19 P9 **Alfred** Maine, NE USA
18 F11 **Alfred** New York, NE USA
61 K14 **Alfredo Vagner** Santa Catarina, S Brazil
94 M12 **Alfta** Gävleborg, C Sweden
140 K12 **Al Fuḥayḥīl** *var.* Fahaheel. SE Kuwait
139 Q6 **Al Fuḥaymī** C Iraq
143 S16 **Al Fujayrah** *Eng.* Fujairah. Al Fujayrah, NE UAE
143 S16 **Al Fujayrah** *Eng.* Fujairah. ✕ Al Fujayrah, NE UAE
Al Furāt *see* Euphrates
144 I10 **Alga** *Kaz.* Algha. Aktyubinsk, NW Kazakhstan
144 G9 **Algabas** Zapadnyy Kazakhstan, NW Kazakhstan
95 C17 **Ålgård** Rogaland, S Norway
104 G14 **Algarve** *cultural region* S Portugal
182 G3 **Algebuckina Bridge** South Australia
104 K16 **Algeciras** Andalucía, SW Spain
105 S10 **Algemesí** País Valenciano, E Spain
Al-Genain *see* El Geneina
120 F9 **Alger** *var.* Algiers, El Djazaïr, Al Jazair. ● (Algeria) N Algeria
74 H9 **Algeria** *off.* Democratic and Popular Republic of Algeria. ◆ *republic* N Africa
120 J8 **Algerian Basin** *var.* Balearic Plain *undersea feature* W Mediterranean Sea
Algha *see* Alga
138 I4 **Al Ghāb** ◎ NW Syria
141 X10 **Al Ghābah** *var.* Ghaba. C Oman
141 U14 **Al Ghayḍah** E Yemen
140 M6 **Al Ghazālah** Ḥā'il, NW Saudi Arabia
107 B17 **Alghero** Sardegna, Italy, C Mediterranean Sea
95 M20 **Älghult** Kronoberg, S Sweden
Al Ghurdaqah *see* Hurghada
Algiers *see* Alger
105 S10 **Alginet** País Valenciano, E Spain
83 I26 **Algoa Bay** *bay* S South Africa
104 L15 **Algodonales** Andalucía, S Spain
105 N9 **Algodor** ≈ C Spain
Al Golea *see* El Goléa
31 N6 **Algoma** Wisconsin, N USA
29 U12 **Algona** Iowa, C USA
20 L8 **Algood** Tennessee, S USA
105 O2 **Algorta** País Vasco, N Spain
61 E18 **Algorta** Río Negro, W Uruguay
Al Haba *see* Haba
139 Q10 **Al Habbārīyah** S Iraq
Al Hadhar *see* Al Ḥaḍr
139 Q4 **Al Ḥaḍr** *var.* Al Hadhar; *anc.* Hatra. NW Iraq
139 T13 **Al Ḥajarah** *desert* S Iraq
141 W8 **Al Ḥajar al Gharbī** ▲ N Oman
141 Y8 **Al Ḥajar ash Sharqī** ▲ NE Oman
141 R15 **Al Ḥajarayn** C Yemen
138 L10 **Al Ḥamād** *desert* Jordan/Saudi Arabia
Al Hamad *see* Syrian Desert
75 N9 **Al Ḥamādah al Ḥamrā'** *var.* Al Ḥamrā'. *desert* NW Libya
105 N15 **Alhama de Granada** Andalucía, S Spain
105 R13 **Alhama de Murcia** Murcia, SE Spain
35 T15 **Alhambra** California, W USA
139 T12 **Al Ḥammām** S Iraq
141 X8 **Al Ḥamrā'** NE Oman
Al Ḥamrā' *see* Al Ḥamādah al Ḥamrā'
141 O6 **Al Ḥamūdīyah** *spring/well* N Saudi Arabia
140 M7 **Al Ḥanākīyah** Al Madīnah, W Saudi Arabia
139 W14 **Al Ḥanīyah** *escarpment* Iraq/Saudi Arabia
139 Y12 **Al Hārithah** SE Iraq
140 L3 **Al Ḥarrah** *desert* NW Saudi Arabia
75 Q10 **Al Harūj al Aswad** *desert* C Libya
Al Hasaifin *see* Al Ḥusayfin
139 N2 **Al Ḥasakah** *var.* Al Hasijah, El Haseke, *Fr.* Hassetché. Al Ḥasakah, NE Syria
139 O2 **Al Ḥasakah** *off.* Muḥāfaẓat al Ḥasakah, *var.* Al Hasakah, Āl Hasakah, Ḥasakah, Hassakeh. ◆ *governorate* NE Syria
139 T9 **Al Hāshimīyah** C Iraq
138 G13 **Al Hāshimīyah** Ma'ān, S Jordan
Al Hasijah *see* Al Ḥasakah
104 M15 **Alhaurín el Grande** Andalucía, S Spain
141 Q16 **Al Ḥawrā** S Yemen
139 V10 **Al Ḥayy** *var.* Kut al Hai, Kūt al Ḥayy. E Iraq
141 U11 **Al Ḥibāk** *desert* E Saudi Arabia
138 H8 **Al Hījānah** *var.* Hejanah, Hijanah. Dimashq, W Syria
140 K7 **Al Ḥijāz** *Eng.* Hejaz. *physical region* NW Saudi Arabia
Al Hilbeh *see* 'Ulayyānīyah, Bi'r al
139 T9 **Al Ḥillah** *var.* Hilla. C Iraq
139 T9 **Al Hindīyah** *var.* Hindiya. C Iraq
138 G12 **Al Ḥisā** Aṭ Ṭafīlah, W Jordan
74 G5 **Al-Hoceïma** *var.* al Hoceima, Al-Hoceima, Alhucemas; *prev.* Villa Sanjurjo. N Morocco
Alhucemas *see* Al-Hoceïma
105 N17 **Alhucemas, Peñon de** *island group* S Spain
141 N15 **Al Ḥudaydah** *Eng.* Hodeida. W Yemen
141 N15 **Al Ḥudaydah** *Eng.* Hodeida. ✕ W Yemen
140 M4 **Al Ḥudūd ash Shamālīyah** *var.* Minṭaqat al Ḥudūd ash Shamālīyah, *Eng.* Northern Border Region. ◆ *province* N Saudi Arabia
141 S7 **Al Hufūf** *var.* Hofuf. Ash Sharqīyah, NE Saudi Arabia
al-Hurma *see* Al Khurmah
141 X7 **Al Ḥusayfin** *var.* Al Hasaifin. N Oman
138 G9 **Al Ḥuṣn** *var.* Husn. Irbid, N Jordan
139 U9 **'Alī** E Iraq
105 O10 **Alia** Extremadura, W Spain
143 P9 **'Alīābād** Yazd, C Iran
'Aliabad *see* Qā'emshahr
105 S7 **Aliaga** Aragón, NE Spain
136 B13 **Aliağa** İzmir, W Turkey
Aliákmon *see* Aliákmonas
115 F14 **Aliákmonas** *prev.* Aliákmon, *anc.* Haliacmon. ≈ N Greece
139 W9 **'Alī al Gharbī** E Iraq
139 U11 **'Alī al Ḥassūnī** S Iraq
115 G18 **Alíartos** Stereá Ellás, C Greece
137 Y12 **Äli-Bayramlı** *Rus.* Ali-Bayramly. SE Azerbaijan
Ali-Bayramly *see* Äli-Bayramlı
114 F12 **Alibey Barajı** ⊠ NW Turkey
77 S13 **Alibori** ≈ N Benin
112 M10 **Alibunar** Serbia, NE Serbia and Montenegro (Yugo.)
105 S12 **Alicante** *Cat.* Alacant; *Lat.* Lucentum. País Valenciano, SE Spain
105 S12 **Alicante** ◆ *province* País Valenciano, SE Spain
105 S12 **Alicante** ✕ Murcia, E Spain
83 I25 **Alice** Eastern Cape, S South Africa
25 S14 **Alice** Texas, SW USA
83 I25 **Alicedale** Eastern Cape, S South Africa
65 E25 **Alice, Mount** *hill* West Falkland, Falkland Islands
107 P20 **Alice, Punta** *headland* S Italy
181 Q7 **Alice Springs** Northern Territory, C Australia
23 N4 **Aliceville** Alabama, S USA
147 U13 **Alichur** SE Tajikistan
147 U14 **Alichuri Janubí, Qatorkŭhi** *Rus.* Yuzhno-Alichurskiy Khrebet. ▲ SE Tajikistan
147 U13 **Alichuri Shimolí, Qatorkŭhi** *Rus.* Severo-Alichurskiy Khrebet. ▲ SE Tajikistan
107 K22 **Alicudi, Isola** *island* Isole Eolie, S Italy
152 J11 **Aligarh** Uttar Pradesh, N India
142 M7 **Alīgūdarz** Lorestān, W Iran
163 U5 **Alihe** *var.* Oroqen Zizhiqi. Nei Mongol Zizhiqu, N China
(0) F12 **Alijos, Islas** *island group* California, SW USA
149 R6 **'Alī Kbel** *Pash.* 'Alī Khēl. Paktīkā, E Afghanistan
Ali Khel *see* 'Alī Kheyl, Paktīā, Afghanistan
'Alī Khēl *see* 'Alī Kbel, Paktīkā, Afghanistan
149 R6 **'Alī Kheyl** *var.* Ali Khel, Jajı. Paktīā, SE Afghanistan
141 V17 **Al Ikhwān** *island group* SE Yemen
Aliki *see* Alykí
79 H19 **Alima** ≈ C Congo
Al Imārāt al 'Arabīyah al Muttaḥidah *see* United Arab Emirates
115 N23 **Alimía** *island* Dodekánisos, Greece, Aegean Sea
55 V12 **Alimimuni Piek** ▲ S Suriname
79 K15 **Alindao** Basse-Kotto, S Central African Republic
95 J18 **Alingsås** Västra Götaland, S Sweden
81 K18 **Alinjugul** *spring/well* E Kenya
149 S11 **Alīpur** Punjab, E Pakistan
153 T12 **Alīpur Duār** West Bengal, NE India
18 B14 **Aliquippa** Pennsylvania, NE USA
80 L12 **'Ali Sabieh** *var.* 'Alī Sabīḥ. S Djibouti
'Alī Sabīḥ *see* 'Ali Sabieh
140 K3 **Al 'Īsāwīyah** Al Jawf, NW Saudi Arabia
104 J10 **Aliseda** Extremadura, W Spain
139 T8 **Al Iskandarīyah** C Iraq
Al Iskandarīyah *see* Alexandria
123 T6 **Aliskerovo** Chukotskiy Avtonomnyy Okrug, NE Russian Federation
114 H13 **Alistráti** Kentrikí Makedonía, NE Greece
39 P15 **Alitak Bay** *bay* Kodiak Island, Alaska, USA
Al Ittiḥād *see* Madīnat ash Sha'b
115 H18 **Alivéri** *var.* Alivérion. Évvoia, C Greece
Alivérion *see* Alivéri
Aliwal-Noord *see* Aliwal North
83 I24 **Aliwal North** *Afr.* Aliwal-Noord. Eastern Cape, SE South Africa
121 Q13 **Al Jabal al Akhḍar** ▲ NE Libya
138 H13 **Al Jafr** Ma'ān, S Jordan
75 T8 **Al Jaghbūb** NE Libya
142 K11 **Al Jahrā'** *var.* Al Jahrah, Jahra. C Kuwait
Al Jahrah *see* Al Jahrā'
Al Jamāhīrīyah al 'Arabīyah al Lībīyah ash Sha'bīyah al Ishtirākī *see* Libya
140 K3 **Al Jarāwī** *spring/well* NW Saudi Arabia
141 X11 **Al Jawārah** *oasis* SE Oman
140 L3 **Al Jawf** *var.* Jauf. Al Jawf, NW Saudi Arabia
140 L4 **Al Jawf** *off.* Minṭaqat al Jawf. ◆ *province* N Saudi Arabia
Al Jawlān *see* Golan Heights
Al Jazair *see* Alger
139 N4 **Al Jazīrah** *physical region* Iraq/Syria
104 F14 **Aljezur** Faro, S Portugal
139 S13 **Al Jīl** S Iraq
138 G11 **Al Jīzah** *var.* Jiza. 'Al Āṣimah, N Jordan
Al Jīzah *see* El Gîza
Al Jubail *see* Al Jubayl
141 S6 **Al Jubayl** *var.* Al Jubail. Ash Sharqīyah, NE Saudi Arabia
141 T10 **Al Juḥaysh, Qalamat** *well* SE Saudi Arabia
143 N15 **Al Jumaylīyah** N Qatar
Al Junaynah *see* El Geneina
104 G13 **Aljustrel** Beja, S Portugal
Al Kaba'ish *see* Al Chabā'ish
Al-Kadhimain *see* Al Kāẓimīyah
Al Kāf *see* El Kef
Alkal'a *see* Alcalá de Henares
35 W4 **Alkali Flat** *salt flat* Nevada, W USA
35 Q1 **Alkali Lake** ◎ Nevada, W USA
141 Z9 **Al Kāmil** NE Oman
138 G11 **Al Karak** *var.* El Kerak, Karak, Kerak; *anc.* Kir Moab, Kir of Moab. Al Karak, W Jordan
138 G12 **Al Karak** *off.* Muḥāfaẓat al Karak. ◆ *governorate* W Jordan
139 W8 **Al Karmashīyah** E Iraq
Al-Kashaniya *see* Al Qash'ānīyah
Al-Kasr al-Kebir *see* Ksar-el-Kebir
139 T8 **Al Kāẓimīyah** *var.* Al-Kadhimain, Kadhimain. C Iraq
99 J18 **Alken** Limburg, NE Belgium
141 X8 **Al Khābūrah** *var.* Khabura. N Oman
Al Khalīl *see* Hebron
139 T7 **Al Khāliṣ** C Iraq
Al Khaluf *see* Khalūf
Al Khārijah *see* El Khârga
141 Q8 **Al Kharj** Ar Riyāḍ, C Saudi Arabia
141 W6 **Al Khaṣab** *var.* Khasab. N Oman
Al Khaur *see* Al Khawr
143 N15 **Al Khawr** *var.* Al Khaur, Al Khor. N Qatar
142 K12 **Al Khīrān** *var.* Al Khiran. SE Kuwait
141 W9 **Al Khīrān** *spring/well* NW Oman
Al Khiyām *see* El Khiyam
Al-Khobar *see* Al Khubar
Al Khor *see* Al Khawr
141 S6 **Al Khubar** *var.* Al-Khobar. Ash Sharqīyah, NE Saudi Arabia
75 T11 **Al Khufrah** SE Libya
120 M12 **Al Khums** *var.* Homs, Khoms, Khums. NW Libya
141 R15 **Al Khuraybah** C Yemen
140 M9 **Al Khurmah** *var.* al-Hurma. Makkah, W Saudi Arabia
141 V9 **Al Kidan** *desert* NE Saudi Arabia
127 V4 **Alkino-2** Respublika Bashkortostan, W Russian Federation
98 H9 **Alkmaar** Noord-Holland, NW Netherlands
139 T10 **Al Kūfah** *var.* Kufa. S Iraq
141 T10 **Al Kursū'** *desert* E Saudi Arabia
139 V9 **Al Kūt** *var.* Kūt al 'Amārah, Kut al Imara. E Iraq
Al-Kuwait *see* Al Kuwayt
Al Kuwayr *see* Guwēr
142 K11 **Al Kuwayt** *var.* Al-Kuwait, *Eng.* Kuwait, Kuwait City; *prev.* Qurein. ● (Kuwait) E Kuwait
142 K11 **Al Kuwayt** ✕ C Kuwait
115 G19 **Alkyonidón, Kólpos** *gulf* C Greece
141 N4 **Al Labbah** *physical region* N Saudi Arabia
138 G4 **Al Lādhiqīyah** *Eng.* Latakia, *Fr.* Lattaquié; *anc.* Laodicea, Laodicea ad Mare. Al Lādhiqīyah, W Syria
138 H4 **Al Lādhiqīyah** *off.* Muḥāfaẓat al Lādhiqīyah, *var.* Al Lathqiyah, Latakia, Lattakia. ◆ *governorate* W Syria
19 R2 **Allagash River** ≈ Maine, NE USA
152 M13 **Allahābād** Uttar Pradesh, N India
143 S3 **Allāh Dāgh, Reshteh-ye** ▲ NE Iran
39 Q8 **Allakaket** Alaska, USA
11 T15 **Allan** Saskatchewan, S Canada
166 L6 **Allanmyo** Magwe, C Myanmar
83 I22 **Allanridge** Free State, C South Africa
104 H4 **Allariz** Galicia, NW Spain
139 R11 **Al Laṣaf** *var.* Al Lussuf. S Iraq
Al Lathqiyah *see* Al Lādhiqīyah
23 S2 **Allatoona Lake** ◎ Georgia, SE USA
83 J19 **Alldays** Limpopo, NE South Africa
Alle *see* Łyna
31 P10 **Allegan** Michigan, N USA
18 E14 **Allegheny Mountains** ▲ NE USA
18 E12 **Allegheny Plateau** ▲ New York/Pennsylvania, NE USA
18 D11 **Allegheny Reservoir** ⊠ New York/Pennsylvania, NE USA
18 E12 **Allegheny River** ≈ New York/Pennsylvania, NE USA
22 K9 **Allemands, Lac des** ◎ Louisiana, S USA
25 U6 **Allen** Texas, SW USA
21 R14 **Allendale** South Carolina, SE USA
41 N6 **Allende** Coahuila de Zaragoza, NE Mexico
41 O9 **Allende** Nuevo León, NE Mexico
97 D16 **Allen, Lough** *Ir.* Loch Aillionn. ◎ NW Ireland
185 B26 **Allen, Mount** ▲ Stewart Island, Southland, SW NZ
109 V2 **Allensteig** Niederösterreich, N Austria
Allenstein *see* Olsztyn
18 I14 **Allentown** Pennsylvania, NE USA
155 G23 **Alleppey** *var.* Alappuzha; *prev.* Alleppi. Kerala, SW India
Alleppi *see* Alleppey
100 J12 **Aller** ≈ NW Germany
29 V16 **Allerton** Iowa, C USA
99 K19 **Alleur** Liège, E Belgium
101 J25 **Allgäuer Alpen** ▲ Austria/Germany
28 J13 **Alliance** Nebraska, C USA
31 U12 **Alliance** Ohio, N USA
103 O10 **Allier** ◆ *department* N France
139 R13 **Al Līfīyah** S Iraq
44 J13 **Alligator Pond** C Jamaica
21 Y9 **Alligator River** ≈ North Carolina, SE USA
29 W12 **Allison** Iowa, C USA
14 G14 **Alliston** Ontario, S Canada
140 L11 **Al Līth** Makkah, SW Saudi Arabia
Al Liwā' *see* Līwā
96 J12 **Alloa** C Scotland, UK
103 U14 **Allos** Alpes-de-Haute-Provence, SE France
108 D6 **Allschwil** Basel-Land, NW Switzerland
Al Lubnān *see* Lebanon
141 N14 **Al Luḥayyah** W Yemen
14 K12 **Allumettes, Île des** *island* Québec, SE Canada
Al Lussuf *see* Al Laṣaf
109 S5 **Alm** ≈ N Austria
15 Q7 **Alma** Québec, SE Canada
27 S10 **Alma** Arkansas, C USA
23 V7 **Alma** Georgia, SE USA
27 P4 **Alma** Kansas, C USA
31 Q8 **Alma** Michigan, N USA
29 O17 **Alma** Nebraska, C USA
30 I7 **Alma** Wisconsin, N USA
139 R12 **Al Ma'ānīyah** S Iraq
Alma-Ata *see* Almaty
Alma-Atinskaya Oblast' *see* Almaty
Almacellas *see* Almacelles
105 T5 **Almacelles** *var.* Almacellas. Cataluña, NE Spain
104 F11 **Almada** Setúbal, W Portugal
104 L11 **Almadén** Castilla-La Mancha, C Spain
66 L6 **Almadies, Pointe des** *headland* W Senegal
140 L7 **Al Madīnah** *Eng.* Medina. Al Madīnah, W Saudi Arabia
140 L7 **Al Madīnah** *off.* Minṭaqat al Madīnah. ◆ *province* W Saudi Arabia
138 H9 **Al Mafraq** *var.* Mafraq. Al Mafraq, N Jordan
138 J10 **Al Mafraq** *off.* Muḥāfaẓat al Mafraq. ◆ *governorate* NW Jordan
141 R15 **Al Maghārim** C Yemen
105 N11 **Almagro** Castilla-La Mancha, C Spain
Al Maḥallah al Kubrá *see* El Maḥalla el Kubra
139 T9 **Al Maḥāwīl** *var.* Khān al Maḥāwīl. C Iraq
Al Mahdīyah *see* Mahdia
139 T8 **Al Maḥmūdīyah** *var.* Mahmudiya. C Iraq
141 T14 **Al Mahrah** ▲ E Yemen
141 P7 **Al Majma'ah** Ar Riyāḍ, C Saudi Arabia
139 Q1 **Al Makmīn** *well* S Iraq
139 Q1 **Al Mālikīyah** *var.* Malkiye. Al Ḥasakah, N Syria
Almalyk *see* Olmaliq
Al Mamlakah al Urdunīyah al Hāshimīyah *see* Jordan
Al Mamlakah *see* Morocco
143 Q18 **Al Manādir** *var.* Al Manadir. *desert* Oman/UAE
142 L15 **Al Manāmah** *Eng.* Manama. ● (Bahrain) N Bahrain
139 O5 **Al Manāṣif** ▲ E Syria
35 O4 **Almanor, Lake** ◎ California, W USA
105 R11 **Almansa** Castilla-La Mancha, C Spain
Al Manṣūrah *see* El Manṣûra
104 L3 **Almanza** Castilla-León, N Spain
104 L8 **Almanzor** ▲ W Spain
105 P14 **Almanzora** ≈ SE Spain
139 S9 **Al Mardah** C Iraq
Al-Mariyya *see* Almería
75 R7 **Al Marj** *var.* Barka, *It.* Barce. NE Libya
138 L2 **Al Mashrafah** Ar Raqqah, N Syria
141 X8 **Al Maṣna'ah** *var.* Al Muṣana'a. NE Oman
105 T9 **Almassora** País Valenciano, E Spain
Almatinskaya Oblast' *see* Almaty
145 U15 **Almaty** *var.* Alma-Ata. Almaty, SE Kazakhstan

● Country ● Country Capital ◇ Dependent Territory ○ Dependent Territory Capital ◆ Administrative Region ✕ International Airport ▲ Mountain ▲ Mountain Range ☢ Volcano ≈ River ◎ Lake ⊠ Reservoir

145 S14 **Almaty** *off.* Almatinskaya Oblast', *Kaz.* Almaty Oblysy; *prev.* Alma-Atinskaya Oblast'. ◐ *province* SE Kazakhstan
145 U15 **Almaty** × Almaty, SE Kazakhstan
Almaty Oblysy *see* Almaty
al-Mawailih *see* Al Muwaylih
139 R3 **Al Mawṣil** *Eng.* Mosul. N Iraq
139 N5 **Al Mayādīn** *var.* Mayadin, *Fr.* Meyadine. Dayr az Zawr, E Syria
139 X10 **Al Maymūnah** *var.* Maimuna. SE Iraq
141 N5 **Al Mayyāh** Ḥā'il, N Saudi Arabia
Al Ma'zam *see* Al Ma'zim
105 P6 **Almazán** Castilla-León, N Spain
141 W8 **Al Ma'zim** *var.* Al Ma'zam. NW Oman
123 N11 **Almaznyy** Respublika Sakha (Yakutiya), NE Russian Federation
Al Mazra' *see* Al Mazra'ah
138 G11 **Al Mazra'ah** *var.* Al Mazra', Mazra'a. Al Karak, W Jordan
101 G15 **Alme** ≈ W Germany
104 I7 **Almeida** Guarda, N Portugal
104 G10 **Almeirim** Santarém, C Portugal
98 O10 **Almelo** Overijssel, E Netherlands
105 S9 **Almenara** País Valenciano, E Spain
105 P12 **Almenaras** ▲ S Spain
105 P5 **Almenar de Soria** Castilla-León, N Spain
104 J6 **Almendra, Embalse de** ⊡ Castilla-León, NW Spain
104 J11 **Almendralejo** Extremadura, W Spain
98 J10 **Almere** *var.* Almere-stad. Flevoland, C Netherlands
98 J10 **Almere-Buiten** Flevoland, C Netherlands
98 J10 **Almere-Haven** Flevoland, C Netherlands
Almere-stad *see* Almere
105 P15 **Almería** *Ar.* Al-Mariyya; *anc.* Unci, *Lat.* Portus Magnus. Andalucía, S Spain
105 P14 **Almería** ◐ *province* Andalucía, S Spain
105 P15 **Almería, Golfo de** *gulf* S Spain
127 S5 **Al'met'yevsk** Respublika Tatarstan, W Russian Federation
95 L21 **Älmhult** Kronoberg, S Sweden
141 U9 **Al Miḥrāḍ** *desert* NE Saudi Arabia
Al Mīnā' *see* El Mina
104 L17 **Almina, Punta** *headland* Ceuta, Spain, N Africa
Al Minyā *see* El Minya
Al Miqdādīyah *see* Al Muqdādīyah
43 P14 **Almirante** Bocas del Toro, NW Panama
Almirós *see* Almyrós
140 M9 **Al Mislaḥ** *spring/well* W Saudi Arabia
Almissa *see* Omiš
104 G13 **Almodôvar** *var.* Almodóvar. Beja, S Portugal
104 M11 **Almodóvar del Campo** Castilla-La Mancha, C Spain
105 Q9 **Almodóvar del Pinar** Castilla-La Mancha, C Spain
31 S9 **Almont** Michigan, N USA
14 L13 **Almonte** Ontario, SE Canada
104 J14 **Almonte** Andalucía, S Spain
104 K9 **Almonte** ≈ W Spain
152 K9 **Almora** Uttaranchal, N India
104 M8 **Almorox** Castilla-La Mancha, C Spain
141 S7 **Al Mubarraz** Ash Sharqīyah, E Saudi Arabia
Al Muḍaibī *see* Al Muḍaybī
138 G15 **Al Mudawwarah** Ma'ān, SW Jordan
141 Y9 **Al Muḍaybī** *var.* Al Muḍaibī. NE Oman
Almudébar *see* Almudévar
105 S5 **Almudévar** *var.* Almudébar. Aragón, NE Spain
141 S15 **Al Mukallā** *var.* Mukalla. SE Yemen
141 N16 **Al Mukhā** *Eng.* Mocha. SW Yemen
105 N15 **Almuñécar** Andalucía, S Spain
139 U7 **Al Muqdādīyah** *var.* Al Miqdādīyah. C Iraq
140 L3 **Al Murayr** *spring/well* NW Saudi Arabia
136 M12 **Almus** Tokat, N Turkey
Al Muṣana'a *see* Al Maṣna'ah
139 T9 **Al Musayyib** *var.* Musaiyib. C Iraq
139 V9 **Al Muwaffaqīyah** S Iraq
138 H10 **Al Muwaqqar** *var.* El Muwaqqar. 'Al Āṣimah, W Jordan
140 J5 **Al Muwayliḥ** *var.* al-Mawailih. Tabūk, NW Saudi Arabia
115 F17 **Almyrós** *var.* Almirós. Thessalía, C Greece
115 I24 **Almyroú, Órmos** *bay* Kriti, Greece, E Mediterranean Sea
Al Nūwfalīyah *see* An Nawfalīyah
96 L13 **Alnwick** N England, UK
Al Obayyid *see* El Obeid
Al Odaid *see* Al 'Udayd
190 B16 **Alofi** ○ (Niue) W Niue
190 A16 **Alofi Bay** *bay* W Niue, C Pacific Ocean
190 E13 **Alofi, Île** *island* S Wallis and Futuna
190 E13 **Alofitai** Île Alofi, W Wallis and Futuna
Aloha State *see* Hawaii
118 G7 **Aloja** Limbaži, N Latvia
153 X10 **Along** Arunāchal Pradesh, NE India
115 H16 **Alónnisos** *island* Vóreioi Sporádes, Greece, Aegean Sea
104 M15 **Álora** Andalucía, S Spain
171 Q16 **Alor, Kepulauan** *island group* E Indonesia
171 Q16 **Alor, Pulau** *prev.* Ombai. *island* Kepulauan Alor, E Indonesia
168 I7 **Alor Setar** *var.* Alor Star, Alur Setar. Kedah, Peninsular Malaysia
Alost *see* Aalst
154 F9 **Ālot** Madhya Pradesh, C India
186 G10 **Alotau** Milne Bay, SE PNG
171 Y16 **Alotip** Papua, E Indonesia
Al Oued *see* El Oued
35 R12 **Alpaugh** California, W USA
Alpen *see* Alps
31 R6 **Alpena** Michigan, N USA
Alpes *see* Alps
103 S14 **Alpes-de-Haute-Provence** ◐ *department* SE France
103 U14 **Alpes-Maritimes** ◐ *department* SE France
181 W8 **Alpha** Queensland, E Australia
197 R9 **Alpha Cordillera** *var.* Alpha Ridge. *undersea feature* Arctic Ocean
Alpha Ridge *see* Alpha Cordillera
Alpheius *see* Alfeiós
99 I15 **Alphen** Noord-Brabant, S Netherlands
98 H11 **Alphen aan den Rijn** *var.* Alphen. Zuid-Holland, C Netherlands
Alpheus *see* Alfeiós
Alpi *see* Alps
104 G10 **Alpiarça** Santarém, C Portugal
24 K10 **Alpine** Texas, SW USA
108 F8 **Alpnach** Unterwalden, W Switzerland
108 D11 **Alps** *Fr.* Alpes, *Ger.* Alpen, *It.* Alpi. ▲▲ C Europe
141 W8 **Al Qābil** *var.* Qabil. N Oman
Al Qaḍārif *see* Gedaref
75 P8 **Al Qaddāḥīyah** N Libya
Al Qāhirah *see* Cairo
140 K4 **Al Qalībah** Tabūk, NW Saudi Arabia
139 O1 **Al Qāmishlī** *var.* Kamishli, Qamishly. Al Ḥasakah, NE Syria
138 I6 **Al Qaryatayn** *var.* Qaryatayn, *Fr.* Qariateïne. Ḥimṣ, C Syria
142 K11 **Al Qash'ānīyah** *var.* Al-Kashaniya. NE Kuwait
141 N7 **Al Qaṣīm** *off.* Minṭaqat Qaṣīm, Qassim. ◐ *province* C Saudi Arabia
138 J5 **Al Qaṣr** Ḥimṣ, C Syria
Al Qaṣr *see* El Qaṣr
Al Qaṣrayn *see* Kasserine
141 S6 **Al Qaṭīf** Ash Sharqīyah, NE Saudi Arabia
138 G11 **Al Qaṭrānah** *var.* El Qatrani, Qatrana. Al Karak, W Jordan
75 P11 **Al Qaṭrūn** SW Libya
Al Qayrawān *see* Kairouan
Al-Qsar al-Kbir *see* Ksar-el-Kebir
Al Qubayyāt *see* Qoubaïyât
Al Quds/Al Quds ash Sharīf *see* Jerusalem
104 H12 **Alqueva, Barragem do** ⊡ Portugal/Spain
138 G8 **Al Qunayṭirah** *var.* El Kuneitra, El Quneitra, Kuneitra, Qunaytra. Al Qunayṭirah, SW Syria
138 G8 **Al Qunayṭirah** *off.* Muḥāfaẓat al Qunayṭirah, *var.* El Q'unaytirah, Qunaytirah, *Fr.* Kuneitra. ◐ *governorate* SW Syria
140 M11 **Al Qunfudhah** Makkah, SW Saudi Arabia
140 K2 **Al Qurayyāt** Al Jawf, NW Saudi Arabia
139 Y11 **Al Qurnah** *var.* Kurna. SE Iraq
139 V12 **Al Quṣayr** S Iraq
138 I6 **Al Quṣayr** *var.* El Quseir, Quṣayr, *Fr.* Kousseir. Ḥimṣ, W Syria
Al Quṣayr *see* Quseir
138 H7 **Al Quṭayfah** *var.* Quṭayfah, Qutayfe, Quteife, *Fr.* Kouteifé. Dimashq, W Syria
141 P8 **Al Quwayʻīyah** Ar Riyāḍ, C Saudi Arabia
Al Quwayr *see* Guwēr
138 F14 **Al Quwayrah** *var.* El Quweira. Ma'ān, SW Jordan
Al Rayyan *see* Ar Rayyān
Al Ruweis *see* Ar Ruways
95 G24 **Als** *Ger.* Alsen. *island* SW Denmark
103 U5 **Alsace** *Ger.* Elsass; *anc.* Alsatia. ◐ *region* NE France
11 R16 **Alsask** Saskatchewan, S Canada
Alsasua *see* Altsasu
Alsatia *see* Alsace
101 C16 **Alsdorf** Nordrhein-Westfalen, W Germany
10 G8 **Alsek** ≈ Canada/USA
Alsen *see* Als
101 F19 **Alsenz** ≈ W Germany
101 H17 **Alsfeld** Hessen, C Germany
119 K20 **Al'shany** *Rus.* Ol'shany. Brestskaya Voblasts', SW Belarus
Alsókubin *see* Dolný Kubín
118 C9 **Alsunga** Kuldīga, W Latvia
Alt *see* Olt
92 K9 **Alta** *Fin.* Alattio. Finnmark, N Norway
29 T12 **Alta** Iowa, C USA
108 I7 **Altach** Vorarlberg, W Austria
92 K9 **Altaelva** *Lapp.* Álaheaieatnu. ≈ N Norway
92 J8 **Altafjorden** *fjord* NE Norwegian Sea
62 K10 **Alta Gracia** Córdoba, C Argentina
42 K11 **Alta Gracia** Rivas, SW Nicaragua
54 H4 **Altagracia** Zulia, NW Venezuela
54 M5 **Altagracia de Orituco** Guárico, N Venezuela
Altai *see* Altai Mountains
130 G10 **Altai Mountains** *var.* Altai, *Chin.* Altay Shan, *Rus.* Altay. ▲▲ Asia/Europe
23 V6 **Altamaha River** ≈ Georgia, SE USA
58 J13 **Altamira** Pará, NE Brazil
54 D12 **Altamira** Huila, S Colombia
42 M13 **Altamira** Alajuela, N Costa Rica
41 Q11 **Altamira** Tamaulipas, C Mexico
30 L15 **Altamont** Illinois, N USA
27 Q7 **Altamont** Kansas, C USA
32 H16 **Altamont** Oregon, NW USA
20 K10 **Altamont** Tennessee, S USA
23 X11 **Altamonte Springs** Florida, SE USA
107 O17 **Altamura** *anc.* Lupatia. Puglia, SE Italy
40 H9 **Altamura, Isla** *island* C Mexico
162 G7 **Altan** Dzavhan, W Mongolia
162 G6 **Altanbulag** Dzavhan, N Mongolia
163 Q7 **Altan Emel** *var.* Xin Barag Youqi. Nei Mongol Zizhiqu, N China
162 J8 **Altan-Ovoo** Arhangay, C Mongolia
162 E7 **Altanteel** Hovd, W Mongolia
40 F3 **Altar** Sonora, NW Mexico
40 D2 **Altar, Desierto de** *var.* Sonoran Desert. *desert* Mexico/USA *see also* Sonoran Desert
105 Q8 **Alta, Sierra** ▲ N Spain
40 H9 **Altata** Sinaloa, C Mexico
42 D4 **Alta Verapaz** *off.* Departamento de Alta Verapaz. ◐ *department* C Guatemala
107 L18 **Altavilla Silentia** Campania, S Italy
21 T7 **Altavista** Virginia, NE USA
158 L2 **Altay** Xinjiang Uygur Zizhiqu, NW China
162 G5 **Altay** Dzavhan, N Mongolia
162 G8 **Altay** *prev.* Yösönbulag. Govĭ-Altay, W Mongolia
Altay *see* Altai Mountains
122 J14 **Altay, Respublika** *var.* Gornyy Altay; *prev.* Gorno-Altayskaya Respublika. ◐ *autonomous republic* S Russian Federation
Altay Shan *see* Altai Mountains
123 I13 **Altayskiy Kray** ◐ *territory* S Russian Federation
Altbetsche *see* Bečej
101 L20 **Altdorf** Bayern, SE Germany
108 G8 **Altdorf** *var.* Altorf. Uri, C Switzerland
105 T11 **Altea** País Valenciano, E Spain
100 L10 **Alte Elde** ≈ N Germany
101 M16 **Altenburg** Thüringen, E Germany
Altenburg *see* București, Romania
Altenburg *see* Baia de Criș, Romania
100 P12 **Alte Oder** ≈ NE Germany
104 H10 **Alter do Chão** Portalegre, C Portugal
92 I10 **Altevatnet** *Lapp.* Álttesjávri. ◎ N Norway
27 V12 **Altheimer** Arkansas, C USA
109 T9 **Althofen** Kärnten, S Austria
114 H7 **Altimir** Vratsa, NW Bulgaria
136 K11 **Altınkaya Barajı** ⊡ N Turkey
139 S3 **Altin Köprü** *var.* Altun Kupri. N Iraq
136 E13 **Altıntaş** Kütahya, W Turkey
57 K18 **Altiplano** *physical region* W South America
Altkanischa *see* Kanjiža
103 U7 **Altkirch** Haut-Rhin, NE France
Altlublau *see* Stará L'ubovňa
100 L12 **Altmark** *cultural region* N Germany
Altmoldowa *see* Moldova Veche
25 W8 **Alto** Texas, SW USA
104 H11 **Alto Alentejo** *physical region* S Portugal
59 I19 **Alto Araguaia** Mato Grosso, C Brazil
58 L12 **Alto Bonito** Pará, NE Brazil
83 O15 **Alto Molócuè** Zambézia, NE Mozambique
30 K15 **Alton** Illinois, N USA
27 W8 **Alton** Missouri, C USA
11 X17 **Altona** Manitoba, S Canada
18 E14 **Altoona** Pennsylvania, NE USA
30 J6 **Altoona** Wisconsin, N USA
62 N3 **Alto Paraguay** *off.* Departamento del Alto Paraguay. ◐ *department* N Paraguay
59 L17 **Alto Paraíso de Goiás** Goiás, S Brazil
62 P6 **Alto Paraná** *off.* Departamento del Alto Paraná. ◐ *department* E Paraguay
Alto Paraná *see* Paraná
59 L15 **Alto Parnaíba** Maranhão, E Brazil
56 H13 **Alto Purús, Río** ≈ E Peru
Altorf *see* Altdorf
63 H19 **Alto Río Senguer** *var.* Alto Río Senguerr. Chubut, S Argentina
41 Q13 **Altotonga** Veracruz-Llave, E Mexico
101 N23 **Altötting** Bayern, SE Germany
Altpasua *see* Stara Pazova
162 I5 **Altraga** Hövsgöl, N Mongolia
Alt-Schwanenburg *see* Gulbene
105 P3 **Altsasu** *Cast.* Alsasua. Navarra, N Spain
Altsohl *see* Zvolen
108 I7 **Altstätten** Sankt Gallen, NE Switzerland
Álttesjávri *see* Altevatnet
42 G1 **Altun Ha** *ruins* Belize, N Belize
Altun Kupri *see* Altin Köprü
158 D8 **Altun Shan** ▲ C China
158 L9 **Altun Shan** *var.* Altyn Tagh. ▲▲ NW China
35 P2 **Alturas** California, W USA
26 K12 **Altus** Oklahoma, C USA
26 K11 **Altus Lake** ⊡ Oklahoma, C USA
Altvater *see* Praděd
Altyn Tagh *see* Altun Shan
Alu *see* Shortland Island
al-'Ubaila *see* Al 'Ubaylah
139 O6 **Al 'Ubaydī** W Iraq
141 T9 **Al 'Ubaylah** *var.* al-'Ubaila. Ash Sharqīyah, E Saudi Arabia
141 T9 **Al 'Ubaylah** *spring/well* E Saudi Arabia
Al Ubayyiḍ *see* El Obeid
141 T7 **Al 'Udayd** *var.* Al Odaid. Abū Ẓaby, W UAE
118 J8 **Alūksne** *Ger.* Marienburg. Alūksne, NE Latvia
140 K6 **Al 'Ulā** Al Madīnah, NW Saudi Arabia
173 N4 **Alula-Fartak Trench** *var.* Illaue Fartak Trench. *undersea feature* W Indian Ocean
138 I11 **Al 'Umarī** 'Al Āṣimah, E Jordan
31 S13 **Alum Creek Lake** ⊡ Ohio, N USA
63 H15 **Aluminé** Neuquén, C Argentina
95 O14 **Alunda** Uppsala, C Sweden
117 T14 **Alupka** Respublika Krym, S Ukraine
75 P8 **Al 'Uqaylah** N Libya
Al Uqṣur *see* Luxor
Al Urdunn *see* Jordan
168 J9 **Alur Panal** *bay* Sumatera, W Indonesia
141 V10 **Al 'Urūq al Mu'tariḍah** *salt lake* SE Saudi Arabia
139 Q7 **Ālūs** C Iraq
117 T13 **Alushta** Respublika Krym, S Ukraine
75 U12 **Al 'Uwaynāt** SE Libya
75 N11 **Al 'Uwaynāt** *var.* Al Awaynāt. SW Libya
139 T6 **Al 'Uẓaym** *var.* Adhaim. E Iraq
26 L8 **Alva** Oklahoma, C USA
104 H8 **Alva** ≈ N Portugal
95 J18 **Älvängen** Västra Götaland, S Sweden
14 F14 **Alvanley** Ontario, S Canada
41 S14 **Alvarado** Veracruz-Llave, E Mexico
25 T7 **Alvarado** Texas, SW USA
58 D13 **Alvarães** Amazonas, NW Brazil
40 G6 **Alvaro Obregón, Presa** ⊡ W Mexico
94 H10 **Alvdal** Hedmark, S Norway
94 K12 **Älvdalen** Dalarna, C Sweden
61 E15 **Alvear** Corrientes, NE Argentina
104 F10 **Alverca do Ribatejo** Lisboa, C Portugal
95 L20 **Alvesta** Kronoberg, S Sweden
25 W12 **Alvin** Texas, SW USA
94 O13 **Älvkarleby** Uppsala, C Sweden
25 S5 **Alvord** Texas, SW USA
93 G18 **Älvros** Jämtland, C Sweden
92 J13 **Älvsbyn** Norrbotten, N Sweden
142 K12 **Al Wafrā'** SE Kuwait
140 J6 **Al Wajh** Tabūk, NW Saudi Arabia
143 N16 **Al Wakrah** *var.* Wakra. C Qatar
138 M8 **al Walaj, Sha'īb** *dry watercourse* W Iraq
152 I11 **Alwar** Rājasthān, N India
141 Q5 **Al Wari'ah** Ash Sharqīyah, N Saudi Arabia
155 G22 **Alwaye** Kerala, SW India
Alxa Zuoqi *see* Bayan Hot
Alx Youqi *see* Ehen Hudag
Al Yaman *see* Yemen
138 G9 **Al Yarmūk** Irbid, N Jordan
Alyat/Alyaty-Pristan' *see* Ālāt
115 I14 **Alykí** *var.* Aliki. Thásos, N Greece
119 F14 **Alytus** *Pol.* Olita. Alytus, S Lithuania
119 F15 **Alytus** ◐ *province* S Lithuania
101 N23 **Alz** ≈ SE Germany
33 Y11 **Alzada** Montana, NW USA
122 L12 **Alzamay** Irkutskaya Oblast', S Russian Federation
99 M25 **Alzette** ≈ S Luxembourg
105 S10 **Alzira** *var.* Alcira ; *anc.* Saetabicula, Suero. País Valenciano, E Spain
Al Zubair *see* Az Zubayr
181 O8 **Amadeus, Lake** *seasonal lake* Northern Territory, C Australia
81 E15 **Amadi** Western Equatoria, SW Sudan
9 R7 **Amadjuak Lake** ◎ Baffin Island, Nunavut, N Canada
95 J23 **Amager** *island* E Denmark
165 N14 **Amagi-san** ▲ Honshū, S Japan
171 S13 **Amahai** *var.* Masohi. Pulau Seram, E Indonesia
38 M16 **Amak Island** *island* Alaska, USA
164 B14 **Amakusa-nada** *gulf* Kyūshū, SW Japan
95 J16 **Åmål** Västra Götaland, S Sweden
54 E8 **Amalfi** Antioquia, N Colombia
107 L18 **Amalfi** Campania, S Italy
115 D19 **Amaliáda** *var.* Amaliás. Dytikí Ellás, S Greece
Amaliás *see* Amaliáda
154 F12 **Amalner** Mahārāshtra, C India
171 W14 **Amamapare** Papua, E Indonesia
59 H21 **Amambaí, Serra de** *var.* Cordillera de Amambay, Serra de Amambay. ▲▲ Brazil/Paraguay *see also* Amambay, Cordillera de
62 P4 **Amambay** *off.* Departamento del Amambay. ◐ *department* E Paraguay
62 P5 **Amambay, Cordillera de** *var.* Serra de Amambaí, Serra de Amambay. ▲▲ Brazil/Paraguay *see also* Amambaí, Serra de
Amambay, Serra de *see* Amambaí, Serra de/Amambay, Cordillera de
165 U16 **Amami-guntō** *island group* SW Japan
165 V15 **Amami-Ō-shima** *island* S Japan
186 A5 **Amanab** Sandaun, NW PNG
106 J13 **Amandola** Marche, C Italy
107 N21 **Amantea** Calabria, SW Italy
191 W10 **Amanu** *island* Îles Tuamotu, C French Polynesia
58 J10 **Amapá** Amapá, NE Brazil
58 J11 **Amapá** *off.* Estado de Amapá; *prev.* Território de Amapá. ◐ *state* NE Brazil
42 H8 **Amapala** Valle, S Honduras
Amara *see* Al 'Amārah
104 H6 **Amarante** Porto, N Portugal
166 M5 **Amarapura** Mandalay, C Myanmar
162 L9 **Amardalay** Dundgovĭ, C Mongolia
104 I12 **Amareleja** Beja, S Portugal
35 V11 **Amargosa Range** ▲▲ California, W USA
25 N2 **Amarillo** Texas, SW USA
Amarinthos *see* Amárynthos
107 K15 **Amaro, Monte** ▲ C Italy
115 H18 **Amárynthos** *var.* Amarinthos. Évvoia, C Greece
Amasia *see* Amasya
136 K12 **Amasya** *anc.* Amasia. Amasya, N Turkey
136 K11 **Amasya** ◐ *province* N Turkey
42 F4 **Amatique, Bahía de** *bay* Gulf of Honduras, W Caribbean Sea
42 D6 **Amatitlán, Lago de** ◎ S Guatemala
107 J14 **Amatrice** Lazio, C Italy
190 C8 **Amatuku** *atoll* C Tuvalu
99 J20 **Amay** Liège, E Belgium
48 F7 **Amazon** *Sp.* Amazonas. ≈ Brazil/Peru
59 C14 **Amazonas** *off.* Estado do Amazonas. ◐ *state* N Brazil
54 G15 **Amazonas** *off.* Comisaria del Amazonas. ◐ *province* SE Colombia
56 C10 **Amazonas** *off.* Departamento de Amazonas. ◐ *department* N Peru
54 M12 **Amazonas** *off.* Territorio Amazonas. ◐ *federal territory* S Venezuela
Amazonas *see* Amazon
48 F7 **Amazon Basin** *basin* N South America
47 V5 **Amazon Fan** *undersea feature* W Atlantic Ocean
58 K11 **Amazon, Mouths of the** *delta* NE Brazil
187 R13 **Ambae** *var.* Aoba, Omba. *island* C Vanuatu
152 I9 **Ambāla** Haryāna, NW India
155 J26 **Ambalangoda** Southern Province, SW Sri Lanka
155 K26 **Ambalantota** Southern Province, S Sri Lanka
172 I6 **Ambalavao** Fianarantsoa, C Madagascar
54 E10 **Ambalema** Tolima, C Colombia
79 E17 **Ambam** Sud, S Cameroon
172 J2 **Ambanja** Antsirañana, N Madagascar
123 T6 **Ambarchik** Respublika Sakha (Yakutiya), NE Russian Federation
62 K9 **Ambargasta, Salinas de** *salt lake* C Argentina
124 J6 **Ambarnyy** Respublika Kareliya, NW Russian Federation
56 C7 **Ambato** Tungurahua, C Ecuador
172 I5 **Ambatolampy** Antananarivo, C Madagascar
172 H4 **Ambatomainty** Mahajanga, W Madagascar
172 J4 **Ambatondrazaka** Toamasina, C Madagascar
101 L20 **Amberg** *var.* Amberg in der Oberpfalz. Bayern, SE Germany
Amberg in der Oberpfalz *see* Amberg
42 H1 **Ambergris Cay** *island* NE Belize
103 S11 **Ambérieu-en-Bugey** Ain, E France
185 I18 **Amberley** Canterbury, South Island, NZ
103 P11 **Ambert** Puy-de-Dôme, C France
Ambianum *see* Amiens
76 J11 **Ambidédi** Kayes, SW Mali
154 M10 **Ambikāpur** Chhattīsgarh, C India
172 J2 **Ambilobe** Antsirañana, N Madagascar
39 O7 **Ambler** Alaska, USA
Amblève *see* Amel
Ambo *see* Hägere Hiywet
172 I8 **Amboasary** Toliara, S Madagascar
172 J4 **Ambodifotatra** *var.* Ambodifototra. Toamasina, E Madagascar
Amboenten *see* Ambunten
172 I5 **Ambohidratrimo** Antananarivo, C Madagascar
172 I6 **Ambohimahasoa** Fianarantsoa, SE Madagascar
172 K3 **Ambohitralanana** Antsirañana, NE Madagascar
Amboina *see* Ambon
102 M8 **Amboise** Indre-et-Loire, C France
171 S13 **Ambon** *prev.* Amboina, Amboyna. Pulau Ambon, E Indonesia
171 S13 **Ambon, Pulau** *island* E Indonesia
81 I20 **Amboseli, Lake** ◎ Kenya/Tanzania
172 I6 **Ambositra** Fianarantsoa, SE Madagascar
172 I8 **Ambovombe** Toliara, S Madagascar
35 W14 **Amboy** California, W USA
30 L11 **Amboy** Illinois, N USA
Amboyna *see* Ambon
Ambracia *see* Árta
18 B14 **Ambridge** Pennsylvania, NE USA
Ambrim *see* Ambrym
Ambrizete *see* N'Zeto
187 R13 **Ambrym** *var.* Ambrim. *island* C Vanuatu
8 K3 **Amund Ringnes Island** *island Nunavut, N Canada*
169 T16 **Ambunten** *prev.* Amboenten. Pulau Madura, E Indonesia
186 B6 **Ambunti** East Sepik, NW PNG
155 I20 **Āmbūr** Tamil Nādu, SE India
38 E17 **Amchitka Island** *island* Aleutian Islands, Alaska, USA
38 F17 **Amchitka Pass** *strait* Aleutian Islands, Alaska, USA
141 R15 **'Amd** C Yemen
78 J10 **Am Dam** Ouaddaï, E Chad
171 U16 **Amdassa** Pulau Yamdena, E Indonesia
125 U1 **Amderma** Nenetskiy Avtonomnyy Okrug, NW Russian Federation
159 N14 **Amdo** Xizang Zizhiqu, W China
40 K13 **Ameca** Jalisco, SW Mexico
41 P14 **Amecameca** *var.* Amecameca de Juárez. México, C Mexico
Amecameca de Juárez *see* Amecameca
61 A20 **Ameghino** Buenos Aires, E Argentina
99 M21 **Amel** *Fr.* Amblève. Liège, E Belgium
98 K4 **Ameland** *Fris.* It Amelân. *island* Waddeneilanden, N Netherlands
Amelân, It *see* Ameland
107 H14 **Amelia** Umbria, C Italy
21 V6 **Amelia Court House** Virginia, NE USA
23 W8 **Amelia Island** *island* Florida, SE USA
18 L12 **Amenia** New York, NE USA
America *see* United States of America
65 M21 **America-Antarctica Ridge** *undersea feature* S Atlantic Ocean
America in Miniature *see* Maryland
60 L9 **Americana** São Paulo, S Brazil
33 Q15 **American Falls** Idaho, NW USA
33 Q15 **American Falls Reservoir** ⊡ Idaho, NW USA
36 L3 **American Fork** Utah, W USA
192 K16 **American Samoa** ◇ *US unincorporated territory* W Polynesia
23 S6 **Americus** Georgia, SE USA
98 K12 **Amerongen** Utrecht, C Netherlands
98 K11 **Amersfoort** Utrecht, C Netherlands
97 N21 **Amersham** SE England, UK
30 I5 **Amery** Wisconsin, N USA
195 W6 **Amery Ice Shelf** *ice shelf* Antarctica
29 V13 **Ames** Iowa, C USA
19 P10 **Amesbury** Massachusetts, NE USA
Amestratus *see* Mistretta
115 F18 **Amfíkleia** *var.* Amfíklia. Stereá Ellás, C Greece
Amfíklia *see* Amfíkleia
115 D17 **Amfilochía** *var.* Amfilokhía. Dytikí Ellás, C Greece
Amfilokhía *see* Amfilochía
114 H13 **Amfípoli** *anc.* Amphipolis. *site of ancient city* Kentrikí Makedonía, NE Greece
115 F18 **Ámfissa** Stereá Ellás, C Greece
123 Q10 **Amga** Respublika Sakha (Yakutiya), NE Russian Federation
123 Q11 **Amga** ≈ NE Russian Federation
163 R7 **Amgalang** *var.* Xin Barag Zuoqi. Nei Mongol Zizhiqu, N China
123 V5 **Amguema** ≈ NE Russian Federation
123 S12 **Amgun'** ≈ SE Russian Federation
80 J12 **Amhara** ◐ *region* N Ethiopia
13 P15 **Amherst** Nova Scotia, SE Canada
18 M11 **Amherst** Massachusetts, NE USA
18 D10 **Amherst** New York, NE USA
24 M4 **Amherst** Texas, SW USA
21 U6 **Amherst** Virginia, NE USA
Amherst *see* Kyaikkami
14 C18 **Amherstburg** Ontario, S Canada
21 Q6 **Amherstdale** West Virginia, NE USA
14 K15 **Amherst Island** *island* Ontario, SE Canada
Amida *see* Diyarbakır
28 J6 **Amidon** North Dakota, N USA
103 O3 **Amiens** *anc.* Ambianum, Samarobriva. Somme, N France
139 P8 **'Āmij, Wādī** *var.* Wadi 'Amīq. *dry watercourse* W Iraq
136 L17 **Amik Ovası** ◎ S Turkey
76 E9 **Amilcar Cabral** × Sal, NE Cape Verde
Amilḥayt, Wādī *see* Umm al Ḥayt, Wādī
Amíndaion/Amindeo *see* Amýntaio
155 C21 **Amīndīvi Islands** *island group* Lakshadweep, India, N Indian Ocean
139 U6 **Āmin Ḥabīb** E Iraq
83 E20 **Aminuis** Omaheke, E Namibia
'Amīq, Wadi *see* 'Āmij, Wādī
142 J7 **Amīrābād** Īlām, NW Iran
Amirante Bank *see* Amirante Ridge
173 N6 **Amirante Basin** *undersea feature* W Indian Ocean
173 N6 **Amirante Islands** *var.* Amirantes Group. *island group* C Seychelles
173 N7 **Amirante Ridge** *var.* Amirante Bank. *undersea feature* W Indian Ocean
Amirantes Group *see* Amirante Islands
173 N7 **Amirante Trench** *undersea feature* W Indian Ocean
11 U13 **Amisk Lake** ◎ Saskatchewan, C Canada
Amistad, Presa de la *see* Amistad Reservoir
25 O12 **Amistad Reservoir** *var.* Presa de la Amistad. ⊡ Mexico/USA
Amisus *see* Samsun
22 K8 **Amite** *var.* Amite City. Louisiana, S USA
Amite City *see* Amite
27 T12 **Amity** Arkansas, C USA

◆ Country ● Country Capital ◇ Dependent Territory ○ Dependent Territory Capital ◐ Administrative Region × International Airport ▲ Mountain ▲▲ Mountain Range Volcano ≈ River ◎ Lake ⊡ Reservoir

154 H11 **Amla** prev. Amulla. Madhya Pradesh, C India
38 I17 **Amlia Island** island Aleutian Islands, Alaska, USA
97 I18 **Amlwch** NW Wales, UK
Ammaia see Portalegre
138 H10 **'Ammān** var. Amman; anc. Philadelphia, Bibl. Rabbah Ammon, Rabbath Ammon. ● (Jordan) 'Al Āşimah, NW Jordan
'Ammān see 'Al Āşimah
93 N14 **Ämmänsaari** Oulu, E Finland
92 H13 **Ammarnäs** Västerbotten, N Sweden
197 O15 **Ammassalik** var. Angmagssalik. Tunu, S Greenland
101 K24 **Ammer** ≈ SE Germany
101 K24 **Ammersee** ◎ SE Germany
98 J13 **Ammerzoden** Gelderland, C Netherlands
Ammóchostos see Gazimağusa
Ammóchostos, Kólpos see Gazimağusa Körfezi
Amnok-kang see Yalu
Amoea see Portalegre
Amoentai see Amuntai
Amoerang see Amurang
143 O4 **Āmol** var. Amul. Māzandarān, N Iran
115 K21 **Amorgós** Amorgós, Kykládes, Greece, Aegean Sea
115 K22 **Amorgós** island Kykládes, Greece, Aegean Sea
23 N3 **Amory** Mississippi, S USA
12 I13 **Amos** Québec, SE Canada
95 G15 **Åmot** Buskerud, S Norway
95 E15 **Åmot** Telemark, S Norway
95 J15 **Åmotfors** Värmland, C Sweden
76 L10 **Amourj** Hodh ech Chargui, SE Mauritania
Amoy see Xiamen
172 H7 **Ampanihy** Toliara, SW Madagascar
155 L25 **Ampara** var. Amparai. Eastern Province, E Sri Lanka
172 J4 **Amparafaravola** Toamasina, E Madagascar
Amparai see Ampara
60 M9 **Amparo** São Paulo, S Brazil
172 J5 **Ampasimanolotra** Toamasina, E Madagascar
57 H17 **Ampato, Nevado** ▲ S Peru
101 L23 **Amper** ≈ SE Germany
64 M9 **Ampère Seamount** undersea feature E Atlantic Ocean
Amphipolis see Amfípoli
167 X10 **Amphitrite Group** island group N Paracel Islands
171 T16 **Amplawas** var. Emplawas. Pulau Babar, E Indonesia
105 U7 **Amposta** Cataluña, NE Spain
15 V7 **Amqui** Québec, SE Canada
141 O14 **'Amrān** W Yemen
Amraoti see Amrāvati
154 H12 **Amrāvati** prev. Amraoti. Mahārāshtra, C India
154 C11 **Amreli** Gujarāt, W India
108 H6 **Amriswil** Thurgau, NE Switzerland
138 H5 **'Amrīt** ruins Ṭarṭūs, W Syria
152 H7 **Amritsar** Punjab, N India
152 J10 **Amroha** Uttar Pradesh, N India
100 G7 **Amrum** island NW Germany
93 I15 **Åmsele** Västerbotten, N Sweden
98 I10 **Amstelveen** Noord-Holland, C Netherlands
98 I10 **Amsterdam** ● (Netherlands) Noord-Holland, C Netherlands
18 K10 **Amsterdam** New York, NE USA
173 Q11 **Amsterdam Fracture Zone** tectonic feature S Indian Ocean
173 R11 **Amsterdam Island** island NE French Southern and Antarctic Territories
109 U4 **Amstetten** Niederösterreich, N Austria
78 J11 **Am Timan** Salamat, SE Chad
146 L12 **Amu-Buxoro Kanali** var. Aral-Bukhorskiy Kanal. canal C Uzbekistan
139 O1 **'Āmūdah** var. Amude. Al Ḩasakah, N Syria
147 O15 **Amu Darya** Rus. Amudar'ya, Taj. Dar"yoi Amu, Turkm. Amyderya, Uzb. Amudaryo; anc. Oxus. ≈ C Asia
Amu-Dar'ya see Amyderýa
Amudar'ya/Amudaryo/Amu, Dar"yoi see Amu Darya
Amude see 'Āmūdah
140 L3 **'Amūd, Jabal al** ▲ NW Saudi Arabia
38 J17 **Amukta Island** island Aleutian Islands, Alaska, USA
38 I17 **Amukta Pass** strait Aleutian Islands, Alaska, USA
Amul see Āmol
Amulla see Amla
Amundsen Basin see Fram Basin
195 X3 **Amundsen Bay** bay Antarctica
195 P10 **Amundsen Coast** physical region Antarctica
8 I6 **Amundsen Gulf** gulf Northwest Territories, N Canada
193 O14 **Amundsen Plain** undersea feature S Pacific Ocean
195 Q9 **Amundsen-Scott** US research station Antarctica
194 J11 **Amundsen Sea** sea S Pacific Ocean
94 M12 **Amungen** ◎ C Sweden
169 U13 **Amuntai** prev. Amoentai. Borneo, C Indonesia
130 I9 **Amur** Chin. Heilong Jiang. ≈ China/Russian Federation
171 Q11 **Amurang** prev. Amoerang. Sulawesi, C Indonesia
105 O3 **Amurrio** País Vasco, N Spain
123 S13 **Amursk** Khabarovskiy Kray, SE Russian Federation
123 Q12 **Amurskaya Oblast'** ◆ province SE Russian Federation
80 G7 **'Amur, Wadi** ≈ NE Sudan
115 C17 **Amvrakikós Kólpos** gulf W Greece
Amvrosiyevka see Amvrosiyivka
117 X8 **Amvrosiyivka** Rus. Amvrosiyevka. Donets'ka Oblast', SE Ukraine
146 M14 **Amyderýa** Rus. Amu-Dar'ya. Lebap Welaýaty, NE Turkmenistan
Amyderya see Amu Darya
114 E13 **Amýntaio** var. Amindeo; prev. Amíndaion. Dytikí Makedonía, N Greece
14 B6 **Amyot** Ontario, S Canada
191 U10 **Anaa** atoll Îles Tuamotu, C French Polynesia
Anabanoea see Anabanua
171 N14 **Anabanua** prev. Anabanoea. Sulawesi, C Indonesia
189 R8 **Anabar** NE Nauru
123 N8 **Anabar** ≈ NE Russian Federation
An Abhainn Mhór see Blackwater
55 O6 **Anaco** Anzoátegui, NE Venezuela
33 Q10 **Anaconda** Montana, NW USA
32 H7 **Anacortes** Washington, NW USA
26 M11 **Anadarko** Oklahoma, C USA
114 N12 **Ana Dere** ≈ NW Turkey
104 G8 **Anadia** Aveiro, N Portugal
Anadolu Dağları see Doğu Karadeniz Dağları
123 V6 **Anadyr'** Chukotskiy Avtonomnyy Okrug, NE Russian Federation
123 V6 **Anadyr'** ≈ NE Russian Federation
Anadyr, Gulf of see Anadyrskiy Zaliv
131 X4 **Anadyrskiy Khrebet** var. Chukot Range. ▲▲ NE Russian Federation
123 W6 **Anadyrskiy Zaliv** Eng. Gulf of Anadyr. gulf NE Russian Federation
115 K22 **Anáfi** anc. Anaphe. island Kykládes, Greece, Aegean Sea
107 J15 **Anagni** Lazio, C Italy
'Ānah see 'Annah
35 T15 **Anaheim** California, W USA
10 L15 **Anahim Lake** British Columbia, SW Canada
38 B8 **Anahola** Kaua'i, Hawai'i, USA, C Pacific Ocean
25 X11 **Anahuac** Texas, SW USA
41 O7 **Anáhuac** Nuevo León, NE Mexico
155 G22 **Anai Mudi** ▲ S India
Anaiza see 'Unayzah
155 M15 **Anakāpalle** Andhra Pradesh, E India
191 W15 **Anakena, Playa de** beach Easter Island, Chile, E Pacific Ocean
39 Q7 **Anaktuvuk Pass** Alaska, USA
39 Q6 **Anaktuvuk River** ≈ Alaska, USA
172 J3 **Analalava** Mahajanga, NW Madagascar
44 F6 **Ana María, Golfo de** gulf C Cuba
Anambas Islands see Anambas, Kepulauan
169 N8 **Anambas, Kepulauan** var. Anambas Islands. island group W Indonesia
77 U17 **Anambra** ◆ state SE Nigeria
29 N4 **Anamoose** North Dakota, N USA
29 Y13 **Anamosa** Iowa, C USA
136 H17 **Anamur** İçel, S Turkey
136 H17 **Anamur Burnu** headland S Turkey
154 O12 **Ānandadur** Orissa, E India
155 H18 **Anantapur** Andhra Pradesh, S India
152 H5 **Anantnāg** var. Islamabad. Jammu and Kashmir, NW India
Ananyev see Anan'yiv
117 O9 **Anan'yiv** Rus. Ananyev. Odes'ka Oblast', SW Ukraine
126 J14 **Anapa** Krasnodarskiy Kray, SW Russian Federation
Anaphe see Anáfi
59 K18 **Anápolis** Goiás, C Brazil
143 R10 **Anār** Kermān, C Iran
Anár see Inari
143 P7 **Anārak** Eşfahān, C Iran
Anar Dara see Anār Darreh
148 J7 **Anār Darreh** var. Anar Dara. Farāh, W Afghanistan
Anárjohka see Inarijoki
23 X9 **Anastasia Island** island Florida, SE USA
188 K7 **Anatahan** island C Northern Mariana Islands
130 M6 **Anatolia** plateau C Turkey
86 F14 **Anatolian Plate** tectonic feature Asia/Europe
114 H13 **Anatolikí Makedonía kai Thráki** Eng. Macedonia East and Thrace. ◆ region NE Greece
Anatom see Aneityum
62 L8 **Añatuya** Santiago del Estero, N Argentina
An Baile Meánach see Ballymena
An Bhearú see Barrow
An Bhóinn see Boyne
An Blascaod Mór see Great Blasket Island
An Cabhán see Cavan
An Caisleán Nua see Newcastle
An Caisleán Riabhach see Castlereagh, Northern Ireland, UK
An Caisleán Riabhach see Castlerea, Ireland
56 C13 **Ancash** off. Departamento de Ancash. ◆ department W Peru
An Cathair see Caher
102 J8 **Ancenis** Loire-Atlantique, NW France
An Chanáil Ríoga see Royal Canal
An Cheacha see Caha Mountains
39 R11 **Anchorage** Alaska, USA
39 R12 **Anchorage** × Alaska, USA
39 Q13 **Anchor Point** Alaska, USA
An Chorr Chríochach see Cookstown
65 M24 **Anchorstack Point** headland W Tristan da Cunha
An Clár see Clare
An Clochán see Clifden
An Clochán Liath see Dunglow
23 U12 **Anclote Keys** island group Florida, SE USA
An Cóbh see Cobh
57 J17 **Ancohuma, Nevado de** ▲ W Bolivia
An Comar see Comber
57 D14 **Ancón** Lima, W Peru
106 J12 **Ancona** Marche, C Italy
Ancuabe see Ancuabi
82 Q13 **Ancuabi** var. Ancuabe. Cabo Delgado, NE Mozambique
63 F17 **Ancud** prev. San Carlos de Ancud. Los Lagos, S Chile
63 G17 **Ancud, Golfo de** gulf S Chile
Ancyra see Ankara
163 V8 **Anda** Heilongjiang, NE China
57 G16 **Andahuaylas** Apurímac, S Peru
An Daingean see Dingle
153 R15 **Āndāl** West Bengal, NE India
94 E9 **Åndalsnes** Møre og Romsdal, S Norway
104 K13 **Andalucía** Eng. Andalusia. ◆ autonomous community S Spain
23 P7 **Andalusia** Alabama, S USA
Andalusia see Andalucía
151 Q21 **Andaman and Nicobar Islands** var. Andamans and Nicobars. ◆ union territory India, NE Indian Ocean
173 T4 **Andaman Basin** undersea feature NE Indian Ocean
151 P19 **Andaman Islands** island group India, NE Indian Ocean
173 T4 **Andaman Sea** sea NE Indian Ocean
57 K19 **Andamarca** Oruro, C Bolivia
182 H5 **Andamooka** South Australia
141 Y9 **'Andām, Wādī** seasonal river NE Oman
172 J3 **Andapa** Antsiranana, NE Madagascar
149 R4 **Andarāb** var. Banow. Baghlān, NE Afghanistan
Andarbag see Andarbogh
147 S13 **Andarbogh** Rus. Andarbag, Anderbak. S Tajikistan
109 Z5 **Andau** Burgenland, E Austria
108 I10 **Andeer** Graubünden, S Switzerland
92 H9 **Andenes** Nordland, C Norway
99 J20 **Andenne** Namur, SE Belgium
77 S11 **Andéramboukane** Gao, E Mali
Anderbak see Andarbogh
99 G18 **Anderlecht** Brussels, C Belgium
99 G21 **Anderlues** Hainaut, S Belgium
108 G9 **Andermatt** Uri, C Switzerland
101 E17 **Andernach** anc. Antunnacum. Rheinland-Pfalz, SW Germany
188 D15 **Andersen Air Force Base** air base NE Guam
39 R9 **Anderson** Alaska, USA
35 N4 **Anderson** California, W USA
31 P13 **Anderson** Indiana, N USA
27 R8 **Anderson** Missouri, C USA
21 P11 **Anderson** South Carolina, SE USA
25 V10 **Anderson** Texas, SW USA
95 K20 **Anderstorp** Jönköping, S Sweden
54 D9 **Andes** Antioquia, W Colombia
47 P7 **Andes** ▲▲ W South America
29 P12 **Andes, Lake** ◎ South Dakota, N USA
92 H9 **Andfjorden** fjord E Norwegian Sea
155 H16 **Andhra Pradesh** ◆ state E India
98 J8 **Andijk** Noord-Holland, NW Netherlands
147 S10 **Andijon** Rus. Andizhan. Andijon Viloyati, E Uzbekistan
147 S10 **Andijon Viloyati** Rus. Andizhanskaya Oblast'. ◆ province E Uzbekistan
Andikíthira see Antikýthira
172 J4 **Andilamena** Toamasina, C Madagascar
142 L8 **Andīmeshk** var. Andimishk; prev. Salehābād. Khūzestān, SW Iran
Andimishk see Andīmeshk
Andipáros see Antíparos
Andipaxi see Antípaxoi
Andípsara see Antípsara
136 L16 **Andırın** Kahramanmaraş, S Turkey
158 J8 **Andirlangar** Xinjiang Uygur Zizhiqu, NW China
Andírrion see Antírrio
Ándissa see Ántissa
Andizhan see Andijon
Andizhanskaya Oblast' see Andijon Viloyati
149 N2 **Andkhvoy** Fāryāb, N Afghanistan
105 Q2 **Andoain** País Vasco, N Spain
163 Y15 **Andong** Jap. Antō. E South Korea
109 R4 **Andorf** Oberösterreich, N Austria
105 S7 **Andorra** Aragón, NE Spain
105 V4 **Andorra** off. Principality of Andorra, Cat. Valls d'Andorra, Fr. Vallée d'Andorre. ◆ monarchy SW Europe
Andorra see Andorra la Vella
105 V4 **Andorra la Vella** var. Andorra, Fr. Andorre la Vielle, Sp. Andorra la Vieja. ● (Andorra) C Andorra
Andorra la Vieja see Andorra la Vella
Andorra, Valls d'/Andorre, Vallée d' see Andorra
Andorre la Vielle see Andorra la Vella
97 M22 **Andover** S England, UK
27 N6 **Andover** Kansas, C USA
92 G10 **Andøya** island C Norway
60 I8 **Andradina** São Paulo, S Brazil
39 N10 **Andreafsky River** ≈ Alaska, USA
38 H17 **Andreanof Islands** island group Aleutian Islands, Alaska, USA
124 H16 **Andreapol'** Tverskaya Oblast', W Russian Federation
Andreas, Cape see Zafer Burnu
Andreevka see Kabanbay
21 N10 **Andrews** North Carolina, SE USA
21 T13 **Andrews** South Carolina, SE USA
24 M7 **Andrews** Texas, SW USA
173 N5 **Andrew Tablemount** var. Gora Andryu. undersea feature W Indian Ocean
Andreyevka see Kabanbay
107 N17 **Andria** Puglia, SE Italy
113 K16 **Andrijevica** Montenegro, SW Serbia and Montenegro (Yugo.)
115 E20 **Andrítsaina** Pelopónnisos, S Greece
An Droichead Nua see Newbridge
Andropov see Rybinsk
115 J19 **Ándros** Ándros, Kykládes, Greece, Aegean Sea
115 J20 **Ándros** island Kykládes, Greece, Aegean Sea
19 O7 **Androscoggin River** ≈ Maine/New Hampshire, NE USA
44 F3 **Andros Island** island NW Bahamas
127 R7 **Androsovka** Samarskaya Oblast', W Russian Federation
44 G3 **Andros Town** Andros Island, NW Bahamas
155 D21 **Āndrott Island** island Lakshadweep, India, N Indian Ocean
117 N5 **Andrushivka** Zhytomyrs'ka Oblast', N Ukraine
111 K17 **Andrychów** Małopolskie, S Poland
Andryu, Gora see Andrew Tablemount
92 I10 **Andselv** Troms, N Norway
79 O17 **Andudu** Orientale, NE Dem. Rep. Congo
105 N13 **Andújar** anc. Illiturgis. Andalucía, SW Spain
82 C12 **Andulo** Bié, W Angola
103 Q14 **Anduze** Gard, S France
An Earagail see Errigal Mountain
95 L19 **Aneby** Jönköping, S Sweden
Anécho see Aného
77 Q9 **Anéfis** Kidal, NE Mali
45 U8 **Anegada** island NE British Virgin Islands
61 E25 **Anegada, Bahía** bay E Argentina
45 U9 **Anegada Passage** passage Anguilla/British Virgin Islands
77 R17 **Aného** var. Anécho; prev. Petit-Popo. S Togo
197 D17 **Aneityum** var. Anatom; prev. Kéamu. island S Vanuatu
117 N10 **Anenii Noi** Rus. Novyye Aneny. C Moldova
186 F7 **Anepmete** New Britain, E PNG
105 U4 **Aneto** ▲ NE Spain
146 F13 **Änew** Rus. Annau. Ahal Welaýaty, C Turkmenistan
Änewetak see Enewetak Atoll
77 Y8 **Aney** Agadez, NE Niger
An Fheoir see Nore
122 L12 **Angara** ≈ C Russian Federation
122 M13 **Angarsk** Irkutskaya Oblast', S Russian Federation
93 G17 **Ånge** Västernorrland, C Sweden
Angel see Úhlava
40 D4 **Ángel de la Guarda, Isla** island NW Mexico
171 O3 **Angeles** off. Angeles City. Luzon, N Philippines
Angeles City see Angeles
Angel Falls see Ángel, Salto
95 J22 **Ängelholm** Skåne, S Sweden
61 A17 **Angélica** Santa Fe, C Argentina
25 W8 **Angelina River** ≈ Texas, SW USA
55 Q9 **Ángel, Salto** Eng. Angel Falls. waterfall E Venezuela
95 M15 **Ängelsberg** Västmanland, C Sweden
35 P8 **Angels Camp** California, W USA
109 W7 **Anger** Steiermark, SE Austria
Angerapp see Ozersk
Angerburg see Węgorzewo
93 H15 **Ångermanälven** ≈ N Sweden
100 P11 **Angermünde** Brandenburg, NE Germany
102 K7 **Angers** anc. Juliomagus. Maine-et-Loire, NW France
15 W7 **Angers** ≈ Québec, SE Canada
93 J16 **Ängesön** island N Sweden
Angistro see Ágkistro
114 H13 **Angítis** ≈ NE Greece
167 R13 **Ângk Tasaôm** prev. Angtassom. Takêv, S Cambodia
185 C25 **Anglem, Mount** ▲ Stewart Island, Southland, SW NZ
97 I18 **Anglesey** cultural region NW Wales, UK
97 I18 **Anglesey** island NW Wales, UK
102 I15 **Anglet** Pyrénées-Atlantiques, SW France
25 W12 **Angleton** Texas, SW USA
Anglia see England
14 H9 **Angliers** Québec, SE Canada
Anglo-Egyptian Sudan see Sudan
Angmagssalik see Ammassalik
167 Q7 **Ang Nam Ngum** ◎ C Laos
79 N16 **Ango** Orientale, N Dem. Rep. Congo
83 Q15 **Angoche** Nampula, E Mozambique
63 G14 **Angol** Araucanía, C Chile
31 Q11 **Angola** Indiana, N USA
82 A9 **Angola** off. Republic of Angola; prev. People's Republic of Angola, Portuguese West Africa. ◆ republic SW Africa
65 P15 **Angola Basin** undersea feature E Atlantic Ocean
39 X13 **Angoon** Admiralty Island, Alaska, USA
147 O14 **Angor** Surkhondaryo Wiloyati, S Uzbekistan
Angora see Ankara
186 C6 **Angoram** East Sepik, NW PNG
40 H8 **Angostura** Sinaloa, C Mexico
Angostura see Ciudad Bolívar
41 U17 **Angostura, Presa de la** ⊡ SE Mexico
28 J11 **Angostura Reservoir** ⊡ South Dakota, N USA
102 L11 **Angoulême** anc. Iculisma. Charente, W France
102 K11 **Angoumois** cultural region W France
64 O2 **Angra do Heroísmo** Terceira, Azores, Portugal, NE Atlantic Ocean
60 O10 **Angra dos Reis** Rio de Janeiro, SE Brazil
Angra Pequena see Lüderitz
147 Q10 **Angren** Toshkent Viloyati, E Uzbekistan
Angtassom see Ângk Tasaôm
167 O10 **Ang Thong** var. Angthong. Ang Thong, C Thailand
79 M16 **Angu** Orientale, N Dem. Rep. Congo
105 S5 **Angües** Aragón, NE Spain
45 U9 **Anguilla** ◇ UK dependent territory E West Indies
45 V9 **Anguilla** island E West Indies
44 F4 **Anguilla Cays** islets SW Bahamas
Angul see Anugul
161 N1 **Anguli Nur** ◎ E China
79 O18 **Angumu** Orientale, E Dem. Rep. Congo
14 G14 **Angus** Ontario, S Canada
96 J10 **Angus** cultural region E Scotland, UK
59 K19 **Anhangüera** Goiás, S Brazil
99 I21 **Anhée** Namur, S Belgium
95 I21 **Anholt** island C Denmark
160 M11 **Anhua** var. Dongping. Hunan, S China
161 P8 **Anhui** var. Anhui Sheng, Anhwei, Wan. ◆ province E China
Anhui Sheng/Anhwei see Anhui
39 O11 **Aniak** Alaska, USA
39 O12 **Aniak River** ≈ Alaska, USA
An Iarmhí see Westmeath
189 R8 **Anibare** E Nauru
189 R8 **Anibare Bay** bay E Nauru, W Pacific Ocean
Anicium see le Puy
115 K22 **Ánidro** island Kykládes, Greece, Aegean Sea
77 R15 **Anié** C Togo
77 Q15 **Anié** ≈ C Togo
102 J16 **Anie, Pic d'** ▲ SW France
127 Y7 **Anikhovka** Orenburgskaya Oblast', W Russian Federation
14 G9 **Anima Nipissing Lake** ◎ Ontario, S Canada
37 O16 **Animas** New Mexico, SW USA
37 P16 **Animas Peak** ▲ New Mexico, SW USA
37 P16 **Animas Valley** valley New Mexico, SW USA
116 F13 **Anina** Ger. Steierdorf, Hung. Stájerlakanina; prev. Ştaierdorf-Anina, Steierdorf-Anina, Steyerlak-Anina. Caraş-Severin, SW Romania
29 U14 **Anita** Iowa, C USA
123 U14 **Aniva, Mys** headland Ostrov Sakhalin, SE Russian Federation
187 S15 **Aniwa** island S Vanuatu
93 M19 **Anjalankoski** Etelä-Suomi, S Finland
'Anjar see Aanjar
Anjiangying see Luanping
14 B8 **Anjigami Lake** ◎ Ontario, S Canada
164 K14 **Anjō** var. Anzyô. Aichi, Honshū, SW Japan
102 J8 **Anjou** cultural region NW France
172 I13 **Anjouan** var. Nzwani, Johanna Island. island SE Comoros
172 J4 **Anjozorobe** Antananarivo, C Madagascar
163 W13 **Anju** W North Korea
98 M5 **Anjum** Fris. Eanjum. Friesland, N Netherlands
172 G6 **Ankaboa, Tanjona** headland W Madagascar
160 L7 **Ankang** prev. Xing'an. Shaanxi, C China
136 I12 **Ankara** prev. Angora, anc. Ancyra. ● (Turkey) Ankara, C Turkey
136 H12 **Ankara** ◆ province C Turkey
95 N19 **Ankarsrum** Kalmar, S Sweden
172 H6 **Ankazoabo** Toliara, SW Madagascar
172 I4 **Ankazobe** Antananarivo, C Madagascar
29 V14 **Ankeny** Iowa, C USA
167 UU **An Khê** Gia Lai, C Vietnam
100 O9 **Anklam** Mecklenburg-Vorpommern, NE Germany
80 K13 **Ānkober** Amhara, N Ethiopia
77 O17 **Ankobra** ≈ S Ghana
79 N22 **Ankoro** Katanga, SE Dem. Rep. Congo
99 L24 **Anlier, Forêt d'** forest SE Belgium
160 I13 **Anlong** Guizhou, S China
An Longfort see Longford
167 R11 **Ânlong Vêng** Siĕmréab, NW Cambodia
An Lorgain see Lurgan
161 N8 **Anlu** Hubei, C China
An Mhí see Meath
An Mhuir Cheilteach see Celtic Sea
An Muileann gCearr see Mullingar
93 F16 **Ånn** Jämtland, C Sweden
126 M8 **Anna** Voronezhskaya Oblast', W Russian Federation
30 L17 **Anna** Illinois, N USA
25 U5 **Anna** Texas, SW USA
74 L5 **Annaba** prev. Bône. NE Algeria
An Nabatīyah at Taḥtā see Nabatîyé
101 N17 **Annaberg-Buchholz** Sachsen, E Germany
109 T9 **Annabichl** × (Klagenfurt) Kärnten, S Austria
140 M5 **An Nafūd** desert NW Saudi Arabia
139 P6 **'Annah** var. 'Ānah. NW Iraq
139 P6 **An Nāḩiyah** W Iraq
139 T10 **An Najaf** var. Najaf. S Iraq
21 V5 **Anna, Lake** ⊡ Virginia, NE USA
97 F16 **Annalee** ≈ N Ireland
167 S9 **Annamitique, Chaîne** ▲▲ C Laos
97 J14 **Annan** S Scotland, UK
29 U8 **Annandale** Minnesota, N USA
21 W4 **Annandale** Virginia, NE USA
189 Q7 **Anna Point** headland N Nauru
21 X3 **Annapolis** state capital Maryland, NE USA
188 A10 **Anna, Pulo** island S Palau
153 O10 **Annapurna** ▲ C Nepal
An Nāqūrah see En Nâqoûra
31 R10 **Ann Arbor** Michigan, N USA
An Nás see Naas
139 W12 **An Nāşirīyah** var. Nasiriya. SE Iraq
139 W11 **An Naşr** E Iraq
Annau see Änew
121 O13 **An Nawfalīyah** var. Al Nūwfalīyah. N Libya
19 P10 **Ann, Cape** headland Massachusetts, NE USA
180 I10 **Annean, Lake** ◎ Western Australia
Anneciacum see Annecy
103 T11 **Annecy** anc. Anneciacum. Haute-Savoie, E France
103 T11 **Annecy, Lac d'** ◎ E France
103 T10 **Annemasse** Haute-Savoie, E France
39 Z14 **Annette Island** island Alexander Archipelago, Alaska, USA
An Nhon see Binh Đinh
An Nīl al Abyaḍ see White Nile
An Nīl al Azraq see Blue Nile
23 Q3 **Anniston** Alabama, S USA
79 A19 **Annobón** island W Equatorial Guinea
103 R12 **Annonay** Ardèche, E France
44 K12 **Annotto Bay** C Jamaica
141 R5 **An Nu'ayrīyah** var. Nariya. Ash Sharqīyah, NE Saudi Arabia
182 M9 **Annuello** Victoria, SE Australia
139 Q10 **An Nukhayb** S Iraq
139 U9 **An Nu'mānīyah** E Iraq
Áno Arkhánai see Epáno Archánes
115 J25 **Anógeia** var. Anogia, Anóyia. Kríti, Greece, E Mediterranean Sea
Anogia see Anógeia
29 V8 **Anoka** Minnesota, N USA
An Ómaigh see Omagh
172 I1 **Anorontany, Tanjona** headland N Madagascar
172 J5 **Anosibe An'Ala** Toamasina, E Madagascar
Anóyia see Anógeia
An Pointe see Warrenpoint
161 P9 **Anqing** Anhui, E China
161 Q5 **Anqiu** Shandong, E China
An Ráth see Ráth Luirc
An Ribhéar see Kenmare River
An Ros see Rush
99 K19 **Ans** Liège, E Belgium
Ansāb see Nişāb
171 W12 **Ansas** Papua, E Indonesia
101 J20 **Ansbach** Bayern, SE Germany
An Sciobairín see Skibbereen
An Scoil see Skull
An Seancheann see Old Head of Kinsale
45 Y5 **Anse-Bertrand** Grande Terre, N Guadeloupe
172 H17 **Anse Boileau** Mahé, NE Seychelles
45 S11 **Anse La Raye** NW Saint Lucia
54 D9 **Anserma** Caldas, W Colombia
109 T4 **Ansfelden** Oberösterreich, N Austria
163 U12 **Anshan** Liaoning, NE China
160 J12 **Anshun** Guizhou, S China
61 F17 **Ansina** Tacuarembó, C Uruguay
29 O15 **Ansley** Nebraska, C USA
25 P6 **Anson** Texas, SW USA
77 Q10 **Ansongo** Gao, E Mali
An Srath Bán see Strabane
21 R5 **Ansted** West Virginia, NE USA
171 Y13 **Ansudu** Papua, E Indonesia
57 G15 **Anta** Cusco, S Peru
57 G16 **Antabamba** Apurímac, C Peru
Antafalva see Kovačica
136 L17 **Antakya** anc. Antioch, Antiochia. Hatay, S Turkey
172 K3 **Antalaha** Antsiranana, NE Madagascar
136 F17 **Antalya** prev. Adalia, anc. Attaleia, Bibl. Attalia. Antalya, SW Turkey
136 F17 **Antalya** ◆ province SW Turkey
136 F16 **Antalya** × Antalya, SW Turkey
121 U10 **Antalya Basin** undersea feature E Mediterranean Sea
Antalya, Gulf of see Antalya Körfezi
136 F16 **Antalya Körfezi** var. Gulf of Adalia, Eng. Gulf of Antalya. gulf SW Turkey

● Country ● Country Capital ◇ Dependent Territory ○ Dependent Territory Capital ◆ Administrative Region × International Airport ▲ Mountain ▲▲ Mountain Range Volcano ≈ River ◎ Lake ⊡ Reservoir

172 J5 **Antanambao Manampotsy** Toamasina, E Madagascar
172 I5 **Antananarivo** *prev.* Tananarive. ● (Madagascar) Antananarivo, C Madagascar
172 I4 **Antananarivo** ◐ *province* C Madagascar
172 J5 **Antananarivo** ✕ Antananarivo, C Madagascar
An tAonach *see* Nenagh
204-205 **Antarctica** *continent*
194 I5 **Antarctic Peninsula** *peninsula* Antarctica
61 J15 **Antas, Rio das** ≈ S Brazil
189 U16 **Ant Atoll** *atoll* Caroline Islands, E Micronesia
An Teampall Mór *see* Templemore
Antep *see* Gaziantep
104 M15 **Antequera** *anc.* Anticaria, Antiquaria. Andalucía, S Spain
Antequera *see* Oaxaca
37 S5 **Antero Reservoir** ▣ Colorado, C USA
26 M7 **Anthony** Kansas, C USA
37 R16 **Anthony** New Mexico, SW USA
182 D5 **Anthony, Lake** *salt lake* South Australia
74 E8 **Anti-Atlas** ⛰ SW Morocco
103 U15 **Antibes** *anc.* Antipolis. Alpes-Maritimes, SE France
103 U15 **Antibes, Cap d'** *headland* SE France
Anticaria *see* Antequera
13 Q11 **Anticosti, Île d'** *Eng.* Anticosti Island. *island* Québec, E Canada
Anticosti Island *see* Anticosti, Île d'
102 K3 **Antifer, Cap d'** *headland* N France
30 L6 **Antigo** Wisconsin, N USA
13 Q15 **Antigonish** Nova Scotia, SE Canada
64 P11 **Antigua** Fuerteventura, Islas Canarias, NE Atlantic Ocean
45 X10 **Antigua** *island* S Antigua and Barbuda, Leeward Islands
Antigua *see* Antigua Guatemala
45 W9 **Antigua and Barbuda** ◆ *commonwealth republic* E West Indies
42 C6 **Antigua Guatemala** *var.* Antigua. Sacatepéquez, SW Guatemala
41 P11 **Antiguo Morelos** *var.* Antiguo-Morelos. Tamaulipas, C Mexico
115 F19 **Antíkyras, Kólpos** *gulf* C Greece
115 G24 **Antikýthira** *var.* Andikíthira. *island* S Greece
138 I7 **Anti-Lebanon** *var.* Jebel esh Sharqi, *Ar.* Al Jabal ash Sharqī, *Fr.* Anti-Liban. ⛰ Lebanon/Syria
Anti-Liban *see* Anti-Lebanon
115 I22 **Antímilos** *island* Kykládes, Greece, Aegean Sea
36 L6 **Antimony** Utah, W USA
An tInbhear Mór *see* Arklow
30 M10 **Antioch** Illinois, N USA
Antioch *see* Antakya
102 I10 **Antioche, Pertuis d'** *inlet* W France
Antiochia *see* Antakya
54 D8 **Antioquia** Antioquia, C Colombia
54 E8 **Antioquia** *off.* Departamento de Antioquia. ◐ *province* C Colombia
115 J21 **Antíparos** *var.* Andipáros. *island* Kykládes, Greece, Aegean Sea
115 B17 **Antípaxoi** *var.* Andipaxi. *island* Iónioi Nísoi, Greece, C Mediterranean Sea
122 J8 **Antipayuta** Yamalo-Nenetskiy Avtonomnyy Okrug, N Russian Federation
192 L12 **Antipodes Islands** *island group* S NZ
Antipolis *see* Antibes
115 J18 **Antípsara** *var.* Andípsara. *island* E Greece
Antiquaria *see* Antequera
15 N10 **Antique, Lac** ◎ Québec, SE Canada
115 E18 **Antírrio** *var.* Andírrion. Dytikí Elláda, C Greece
115 K16 **Ántissa** *var.* Ándissa. Lésvos, E Greece
An tIúr *see* Newry
Antivari *see* Bar
56 C6 **Antizana** ▲ N Ecuador
27 Q13 **Antlers** Oklahoma, C USA
93 J14 **Antnäs** Norrbotten, N Sweden
Antō *see* Andong
62 G5 **Antofagasta** Antofagasta, N Chile
62 G6 **Antofagasta** *off.* Región de Antofagasta. ◐ *region* N Chile
62 I7 **Antofalla, Salar de** *salt lake* NW Argentina
99 D20 **Antoing** Hainaut, SW Belgium
24 M5 **Anton** Texas, SW USA
43 S16 **Antón** Coclé, C Panama
37 T11 **Anton Chico** New Mexico, SW USA
60 K12 **Antonina** Paraná, S Brazil
103 O5 **Antony** Hauts-de-Seine, N France
Antratsit *see* Antratsyt
117 Y8 **Antratsyt** *Rus.* Antratsit. Luhans'ka Oblast', E Ukraine
97 G15 **Antrim** *Ir.* Aontroim. NE Northern Ireland, UK
97 G14 **Antrim** *Ir.* Aontroim. *cultural region* NE Northern Ireland, UK
97 G14 **Antrim Mountains** ⛰ NE Northern Ireland, UK
172 H5 **Antsalova** Mahajanga, W Madagascar
Antserana *see* Antsirañana
An tSionainn *see* Shannon
172 J2 **Antsirañana** *var.* Antserana; *prev.* Antsirane, Diégo-Suarez. Antsirañana, N Madagascar
172 J2 **Antsirañana** ◐ *province* N Madagascar
Antsirane *see* Antsirañana
An tSiúir *see* Suir
118 I7 **Antsla** *Ger.* Anzen. Võrumaa, SE Estonia
An tSláine *see* Slaney
172 J3 **Antsohihy** Mahajanga, NW Madagascar
63 G14 **Antuco, Volcán** ▲ C Chile
169 W10 **Antu, Gunung** ▲ Borneo, N Indonesia
An Tullach *see* Tullow
An-tung *see* Dandong
Antunnacum *see* Andernach
Antwerp *see* Antwerpen
99 G16 **Antwerpen** *Eng.* Antwerp, *Fr.* Anvers. Antwerpen, N Belgium
99 H16 **Antwerpen** *Eng.* Antwerp. ◐ *province* N Belgium
An Uaimh *see* Navan
154 N12 **Anugul** *var.* Angul. Orissa, E India
152 F9 **Anūpgarh** Rājasthān, NW India
154 K10 **Anūppur** Madhya Pradesh, C India
155 K24 **Anuradhapura** North Central Province, C Sri Lanka
187 S11 **Anuta** *island*, E Solomon Islands
Anvers *see* Antwerpen
194 G4 **Anvers Island** *island* Antarctica
39 N11 **Anvik** Alaska, USA
39 N10 **Anvik River** ≈ Alaska, USA
38 F17 **Anvil Peak** ▲ Semisopochnoi Island, Alaska, USA
159 P7 **Anxi** *var.* Yuanquan. Gansu, N China
182 F8 **Anxious Bay** *bay* South Australia
161 O5 **Anyang** Henan, C China
159 S11 **A'nyêmaqên Shan** ⛰ C China
118 H12 **Anykščiai** Utena, E Lithuania
161 P13 **Anyuan** *var.* Xinshan. Jiangxi, S China
123 T7 **Anyuysk** Chukotskiy Avtonomnyy Okrug, NE Russian Federation
123 T7 **Anyuyskiy Khrebet** ⛰ NE Russian Federation
54 D8 **Anza** Antioquia, C Colombia
Anzen *see* Antsla
107 I16 **Anzio** Lazio, C Italy
55 O6 **Anzoátegui** *off.* Estado Anzoátegui. ◐ *state* NE Venezuela
147 P12 **Anzob** W Tajikistan
Anzyō *see* Anjō
165 X13 **Aoga-shima** *island* Izu-shotō, SE Japan
Aohan Qi *see* Xinhui
Aoiz *see* Agoiz
186 M9 **Aola** *var.* Tenaghau. Guadalcanal, C Solomon Islands
166 M15 **Ao Luk Nua** Krabi, SW Thailand
Aomen *see* Macao
172 N8 **Aomori** Aomori, Honshū, C Japan
165 Q6 **Aomori** *off.* Aomori-ken. ◐ *prefecture* Honshū, C Japan
Aontroim *see* Antrim
117 C15 **Aóos** *var.* Vijosa, Vijosë, *Alb.* Lumi i Vjosës,. ≈ Albania/Greece ***see also*** Vjosës, Lumi i
191 Q7 **Aorai, Mont** ⩕ Tahiti, W French Polynesia
185 E19 **Aoraki** *prev.* Aorangi, Mount Cook. ▲ South Island, NZ
167 R13 **Aôral, Phnum** *prev.* Phnom Aural. ▲ W Cambodia
Aorangi *see* Aoraki
185 L15 **Aorangi Mountains** ⛰ North Island, NZ
184 H13 **Aorere** ≈ South Island, NZ
106 A7 **Aosta** *anc.* Augusta Praetoria. Valle d'Aosta, NW Italy
77 O11 **Aougoundou, Lac** ◎ S Mali
76 K9 **Aoukâr** *var.* Aouker. *plateau* C Mauritania
78 J13 **Aouk, Bahr** ≈ Central African Republic/Chad
Aouker *see* Aoukâr
74 B11 **Aousard** SE Western Sahara
164 H12 **Aoya** Tottori, Honshū, SW Japan
Aoyang *see* Shanggao
78 H5 **Aozou** Borkou-Ennedi-Tibesti, N Chad
26 M11 **Apache** Oklahoma, C USA
36 L14 **Apache Junction** Arizona, SW USA
24 J9 **Apache Mountains** ⛰ Texas, SW USA
36 M16 **Apache Peak** ▲ Arizona, SW USA
116 H10 **Apahida** Cluj, NW Romania
23 T9 **Apalachee Bay** *bay* Florida, SE USA
23 T3 **Apalachee River** ≈ Georgia, SE USA
23 S10 **Apalachicola** Florida, SE USA
23 S10 **Apalachicola Bay** *bay* Florida, SE USA
23 R9 **Apalachicola River** ≈ Florida, SE USA
Apam *see* Apan
Apamama *see* Abemama
41 P14 **Apan** *var.* Apam. Hidalgo, C Mexico
42 J8 **Apanás, Lago de** ◎ NW Nicaragua
54 H14 **Apaporis, Río** ≈ Brazil/Colombia
185 C23 **Aparima** ≈ South Island, NZ
171 O1 **Aparri** Luzon, N Philippines
112 J9 **Apatin** Serbia, NW Serbia and Montenegro (Yugo.)
124 J4 **Apatity** Murmanskaya Oblast', NW Russian Federation
55 X9 **Apatou** NW French Guiana
40 M14 **Apatzingán** *var.* Apatzingán de la Constitución. Michoacán de Ocampo, SW Mexico
171 X12 **Apauwar** Papua, E Indonesia
Apaxtla *see* Apaxtla de Castrejón
41 O15 **Apaxtla de Castrejón** *var.* Apaxtla. Guerrero, S Mexico
118 J7 **Ape** Alūksne, NE Latvia
98 L11 **Apeldoorn** Gelderland, E Netherlands
Apennines *see* Appennino
Apenrade *see* Aabenraa
57 L17 **Apere, Río** ≈ C Bolivia
55 W11 **Apetina** Sipaliwini, SE Suriname
21 U9 **Apex** North Carolina, SE USA
79 M16 **Api** Orientale, N Dem. Rep. Congo
152 M9 **Api** ▲ NW Nepal
Apia *see* Abaiang
192 H16 **Āpia** ● (Samoa) Upolu, SE Samoa
60 K11 **Apiaí** São Paulo, S Brazil
170 M16 **Api, Gunung** ▲ Pulau Sangeang, S Indonesia
187 N9 **Apio** Maramasike Island, N Solomon Islands
41 O15 **Apipilulco** Guerrero, S Mexico
41 P14 **Apizaco** Tlaxcala, S Mexico
104 I4 **A Pobla de Trives** *Cast.* Puebla de Trives. Galicia, NW Spain
55 U9 **Apoera** Sipaliwini, NW Suriname
115 O23 **Apolakkiá** Ródos, Dodekánisos, Greece, Aegean Sea
101 L16 **Apolda** Thüringen, C Germany
192 H16 **Apolima Strait** *strait* C Pacific Ocean
182 M13 **Apollo Bay** Victoria, SE Australia
Apollonia *see* Sozopol
57 J16 **Apolo** La Paz, W Bolivia
57 J16 **Apolobamba, Cordillera** ⛰ Bolivia/Peru
171 Q8 **Apo, Mount** ⩕ Mindanao, S Philippines
23 W11 **Apopka** Florida, SE USA
23 W11 **Apopka, Lake** ◎ Florida, SE USA
59 J19 **Aporé, Rio** ≈ SW Brazil
30 K2 **Apostle Islands** *island group* Wisconsin, N USA
Apostolas Andreas, Cape *see* Zafer Burnu
61 F14 **Apóstoles** Misiones, NE Argentina
Apostólou Andréa, Akrotíri *see* Zafer Burnu
117 S9 **Apostolove** *Rus.* Apostolovo. Dnipropetrovs'ka Oblast', E Ukraine
Apostolovo *see* Apostolove
17 S10 **Appalachian Mountains** ⛰ E USA
95 K14 **Äppelbo** Dalarna, C Sweden
98 N7 **Appelscha** *Fris.* Appelskea. Friesland, N Netherlands
Appelskea *see* Appelscha
106 G11 **Appennino** *Eng.* Apennines. ⛰ Italy/San Marino
107 L17 **Appennino Campano** ⛰ C Italy
108 I7 **Appenzell** Appenzell, NW Switzerland
108 H7 **Appenzell** ◐ *canton* NE Switzerland
55 V12 **Appikalo** Sipaliwini, S Suriname
98 O5 **Appingedam** Groningen, NE Netherlands
25 X8 **Appleby** Texas, SW USA
97 L15 **Appleby-in-Westmorland** NW England, UK
30 K10 **Apple River** ≈ Illinois, N USA
30 I5 **Apple River** ≈ Wisconsin, N USA
25 W9 **Apple Springs** Texas, SW USA
29 S8 **Appleton** Minnesota, N USA
30 M7 **Appleton** Wisconsin, N USA
27 S5 **Appleton City** Missouri, C USA
35 U14 **Apple Valley** California, W USA
29 V9 **Apple Valley** Minnesota, N USA
21 U6 **Appomattox** Virginia, NE USA
188 B16 **Apra Harbour** *harbour* W Guam
188 B16 **Apra Heights** W Guam
106 F6 **Aprica, Passo dell'** *pass* N Italy
107 M15 **Apricena** *anc.* Hadria Picena. Puglia, SE Italy
126 L14 **Apsheronsk** Krasnodarskiy Kray, SW Russian Federation
Apsheronskiy Poluostrov *see* Abşeron Yarımadası
103 S15 **Apt** *anc.* Apta Julia. Vaucluse, SE France
Apta Julia *see* Apt
38 H12 **'Apua Point** *var.* Apua Point *headland* Hawai'i, USA, C Pacific Ocean
60 I10 **Apucarana** Paraná, S Brazil
Apulia *see* Puglia
54 K8 **Apure** *off.* Estado Apure. ◐ *state* C Venezuela
54 J7 **Apure, Río** ≈ W Venezuela
57 F16 **Apurímac** *off.* Departamento de Apurímac. ◐ *department* C Peru
57 F15 **Apurímac, Río** ≈ S Peru
116 G10 **Apuseni, Munții** ⛰ W Romania
Aqaba/'Aqaba *see* Al 'Aqabah
138 F15 **Aqaba, Gulf of** *var.* Gulf of Elat, *Ar.* Khalīj al 'Aqabah; *anc.* Sinus Aelaniticus. *gulf* NE Red Sea
139 R7 **'Aqabah** C Iraq
'Aqabah, Khalīj al *see* Aqaba, Gulf of
149 O2 **Āqchah** *var.* Āqcheh. Jowzjān, N Afghanistan
Āqcheh *see* Āqchah
Aqköl *see* Akkol'
Aqmola *see* Astana
Aqmola Oblysy *see* Akmola
158 L10 **Aqqikkol Hu** ◎ NW China
Aqqystaū *see* Akkystau
'Aqrah *see* Ākrē
Aqsay *see* Aksay
Aqshataū *see* Akchatau
Aqsū *see* Aksu
Aqsūat *see* Aksuat
Aqtas *see* Aktas
Aqtaū *see* Aktau
Aqtöbe/Aqtöbe Oblysy *see* Aktobe
Aqtoghay *see* Aktogay
Aquae Augustae *see* Dax
Aquae Calidae *see* Bath
Aquae Flaviae *see* Chaves
Aquae Grani *see* Aachen
Aquae Panoniae *see* Baden
Aquae Sextiae *see* Aix-en-Provence
Aquae Solis *see* Bath
Aquae Tarbelicae *see* Dax
36 J11 **Aquarius Mountains** ⛰ Arizona, SW USA
62 O5 **Aquidabán, Río** ≈ E Paraguay
59 H20 **Aquidauana** Mato Grosso do Sul, S Brazil
40 L15 **Aquila** Michoacán de Ocampo, S Mexico
Aquila/Aquila degli Abruzzi *see* L'Aquila
25 T8 **Aquilla** Texas, SW USA
44 L9 **Aquin** S Haiti
Aquisgranum *see* Aachen
102 J13 **Aquitaine** ◐ *region* SW France
Aqzhar *see* Akzhar
153 P13 **Āra** *prev.* Arrah. Bihār, N India
105 S4 **Ara** ≈ NE Spain
23 P2 **Arab** Alabama, S USA
Araba *see* Álava
138 G12 **'Arabah, Wādī al** *Heb.* Ha'Arava. *dry watercourse* Israel/Jordan
117 U12 **Arabats'ka Strilka, Kosa** *spit* S Ukraine
117 U12 **Arabats'ka Zatoka** *gulf* S Ukraine
'Arab, Baḥr al *see* Arab, Bahr el
80 C12 **Arab, Bahr el** *var.* Baḥr al 'Arab. ≈ S Sudan
56 E7 **Arabela, Río** ≈ N Peru
173 O4 **Arabian Basin** *undersea feature* N Arabian Sea
Arabian Desert *see* Sahara el Sharqīya
141 N9 **Arabian Peninsula** *peninsula* SW Asia
85 P15 **Arabian Plate** *tectonic feature* Africa/Asia/Europe
141 W14 **Arabian Sea** *sea* NW Indian Ocean
Arabicus, Sinus *see* Red Sea
'Arabī, Khalīj al *see* Persian Gulf
Arabistan *see* Khūzestān
'Arabīyah as Su'ūdīyah, Al Mamlakah al *see* Saudi Arabia
'Arabīyah Jumhūrīyah, Miṣr al *see* Egypt
138 I9 **'Arab, Jabal al** ▲ S Syria
Arab Republic of Egypt *see* Egypt
Arabs Gulf *see* 'Arab, Khalīg el
139 Y12 **'Arab, Shaṭṭ al** *Eng.* Shatt al Arab, *Per.* Arvand Rūd. ≈ Iran/Iraq
136 I11 **Araç** Kastamonu, N Turkey
59 P16 **Aracaju** *state capital* Sergipe, E Brazil
54 F5 **Aracataca** Magdalena, N Colombia
58 P13 **Aracati** Ceará, E Brazil
60 J8 **Araçatuba** São Paulo, S Brazil
104 J13 **Aracena** Andalucía, S Spain
115 F20 **Arachnaío** ⛰ S Greece
115 D16 **Árachthos** *var.* Arta; *prev.* Árakhthos, *anc.* Arachthus. ≈ W Greece
Arachthus *see* Árachthos
59 N19 **Araçuai** Minas Gerais, SE Brazil
136 I11 **Araç Çayı** ≈ N Turkey
138 F11 **'Arad** Southern, S Israel
116 F11 **Arad** Arad, W Romania
116 F11 **Arad** ◐ *county* W Romania
78 J9 **Arada** Biltine, NE Chad
143 P18 **'Arādah** Abū Ẓaby, S UAE
Aradhippou *see* Aradíppou
121 Q3 **Aradíppou** *var.* Aradhippou. SE Cyprus
174 K6 **Arafura Sea** *Ind.* Laut Arafuru. *sea* W Pacific Ocean
174 L6 **Arafura Shelf** *undersea feature* C Arafura Sea
Arafuru, Laut *see* Arafura Sea
59 J18 **Aragarças** Goiás, C Brazil
Aragats, Gora *see* Aragats Lerr
137 T12 **Aragats Lerr** *Rus.* Gora Aragats. ▲ W Armenia
32 E14 **Arago, Cape** *headland* Oregon, NW USA
105 R6 **Aragón** ◐ *autonomous community* E Spain
105 Q4 **Aragón** ≈ NE Spain
107 J24 **Aragona** Sicilia, Italy, C Mediterranean Sea
105 Q7 **Aragoncillo** ▲ C Spain
54 L5 **Aragua** *off.* Estado Aragua. ◐ *state* N Venezuela
55 N6 **Aragua de Barcelona** Anzoátegui, NE Venezuela
55 O5 **Aragua de Maturín** Monagas, NE Venezuela
59 K15 **Araguaia, Río** *var.* Araguaya. ≈ C Brazil
59 K19 **Araguari** Minas Gerais, SE Brazil
58 J11 **Araguari** ≈ SW Brazil
Araguaya *see* Araguaia, Río
104 K14 **Arahal** Andalucía, S Spain
165 N11 **Arai** Niigata, Honshū, C Japan
Árainn *see* Inishmore
Árainn Mhór *see* Aran Island
Ara Jovis *see* Aranjuez
74 J11 **Arak** C Algeria
171 Y15 **Arak** Papua, E Indonesia
142 M7 **Arāk** *prev.* Sultānābād. Markazī, W Iran
188 D10 **Arakabesan** *island* Palau Islands, N Palau
55 S7 **Arakaka** NW Guyana
166 K6 **Arakan State** *var.* Rakhine State. ◐ *state* W Myanmar
166 K5 **Arakan Yoma** ⛰ W Myanmar
165 O10 **Arakawa** Niigata, Honshū, C Japan
Árakhthos *see* Árachthos
Araks/Arak's *see* Aras
158 H7 **Aral** Xinjiang Uygur Zizhiqu, NW China
Aral *see* Aral'sk, Kazakhstan
Aral *see* Vose', Tajikistan
Aral-Bukhorskiy Kanal *see* Amu-Buxoro Kanali
137 T12 **Aralik** Iğdır, E Turkey
146 H5 **Aral Sea** *Kaz.* Aral Tengizi, *Rus.* Aral'skoye More, *Uzb.* Orol Dengizi. *inland sea* Kazakhstan/Uzbekistan
144 L13 **Aral'sk** *Kaz.* Aral. Kzylorda, SW Kazakhstan
Aral'skoye More/Aral Tengizi *see* Aral Sea
41 O10 **Aramberri** Nuevo León, NE Mexico
186 B8 **Aramia** ≈ SW PNG
143 N6 **Ārān** *var.* Golārā. Eşfahān, C Iran
105 N5 **Aranda de Duero** Castilla-León, N Spain
112 M12 **Aranđelovac** *prev.* Arandjelovac. Serbia, C Serbia and Montenegro (Yugo.)
Arandjelovac *see* Aranđelovac
97 J19 **Aran Fawddwy** ▲ NW Wales, UK
97 C14 **Aran Island** *Ir.* Árainn Mhór. *island* NW Ireland
97 A18 **Aran Islands** *island group* W Ireland
105 N9 **Aranjuez** *anc.* Ara Jovis. Madrid, C Spain
83 E20 **Aranos** Hardap, SE Namibia
25 U14 **Aransas Bay** *inlet* Texas, SW USA
25 T14 **Aransas Pass** Texas, SW USA
191 O3 **Aranuka** *prev.* Nanouki. *atoll* Tungaru, W Kiribati
167 Q11 **Aranyaprathet** Prachin Buri, S Thailand
Aranyosasztal *see* Zlatý Stôl
Aranyosgyéres *see* Câmpia Turzii
Aranyosmarót *see* Zlaté Moravce
164 C14 **Arao** Kumamoto, Kyūshū, SW Japan
77 O8 **Araouane** Tombouctou, N Mali
26 L10 **Arapaho** Oklahoma, C USA
29 N16 **Arapahoe** Nebraska, C USA
57 I16 **Arapa, Laguna** ◎ SE Peru
185 K14 **Arapawa Island** *island* C NZ
61 E17 **Arapey Grande, Río** ≈ N Uruguay
59 P16 **Arapiraca** Alagoas, E Brazil
140 M3 **'Ar'ar** Al Ḥudūd ash Shamālīyah, NW Saudi Arabia
54 G15 **Araracuara** Caquetá, S Colombia
61 K15 **Araranguá** Santa Catarina, S Brazil
60 L8 **Araraquara** São Paulo, S Brazil
59 O13 **Araras** Ceará, E Brazil
58 I14 **Araras** Pará, N Brazil
60 L9 **Araras** São Paulo, S Brazil
60 H11 **Araras, Serra das** ⛰ S Brazil
137 U12 **Ararat** S Armenia
182 M12 **Ararat** Victoria, SE Australia
Ararat, Mount *see* Büyükağrı Dağı
140 M3 **'Ar'ar, Wādī** *dry watercourse* Iraq/Saudi Arabia
131 N7 **Aras** *Arm.* Arak's, *Az.* Araz Nehri, *Per.* Rūd-e Aras, *Rus.* Araks; *prev.* Araxes. ≈ SW Asia
105 R9 **Aras de Alpuente** País Valenciano, E Spain
137 S13 **Aras Güneyi Dağları** ⛰ NE Turkey
Aras, Rūd-e *see* Aras
191 U9 **Aratika** *atoll* Îles Tuamotu, C French Polynesia
Aratürük *see* Yiwu
54 I8 **Arauca** Arauca, NE Colombia
54 I8 **Arauca** *off.* Intendencia de Arauca. ◐ *province* NE Colombia
63 G15 **Araucanía** *off.* Región de la Araucanía. ◐ *region* C Chile
54 L7 **Arauca, Río** ≈ Colombia/Venezuela
63 F14 **Arauco** Bío Bío, C Chile
63 F14 **Arauco, Golfo de** *gulf* S Chile
54 H8 **Arauquita** Arauca, C Colombia
Arausio *see* Orange
152 F13 **Arāvali Range** ⛰ N India
186 J7 **Arawa** Bougainville Island, NE PNG
185 C20 **Arawata** ≈ South Island, NZ
186 F7 **Arawe Islands** *island group* E PNG
59 L20 **Araxá** Minas Gerais, SE Brazil
Araxes *see* Aras
55 O5 **Araya** Sucre, N Venezuela
105 R4 **Arba** ≈ N Spain
81 I15 **Ārba Minch'** Southern, S Ethiopia
139 U4 **Arbat** NE Iraq
107 D19 **Arbatax** Sardegna, Italy, C Mediterranean Sea
Arbe *see* Rab
Arbela *see* Arbīl
139 S3 **Arbīl** *var.* Erbil, Irbīl, *Kurd.* Hawlēr; *anc.* Arbela. N Iraq
95 M16 **Arboga** Västmanland, C Sweden
95 M16 **Arbogaån** ≈ C Sweden
103 S9 **Arbois** Jura, E France
54 D6 **Arboletes** Antioquia, NW Colombia
11 X15 **Arborg** Manitoba, S Canada
94 N12 **Arbrå** Gävleborg, C Sweden
96 K10 **Arbroath** *anc.* Aberbrothock. E Scotland, UK
35 N6 **Arbuckle** California, W USA
27 N12 **Arbuckle Mountains** ⛰ Oklahoma, C USA
Arbuzinka *see* Arbyzynka
117 Q8 **Arbyzynka** *Rus.* Arbuzinka. Mykolayivs'ka Oblast', S Ukraine
103 U12 **Arc** ≈ E France
102 J13 **Arcachon** Gironde, SW France
102 J13 **Arcachon, Bassin d'** *inlet* SW France
18 E10 **Arcade** New York, NE USA
23 W14 **Arcadia** Florida, SE USA
22 H5 **Arcadia** Louisiana, S USA
30 J7 **Arcadia** Wisconsin, N USA
Arcae Remorum *see* Châlons-en-Champagne
44 L9 **Arcahaie** C Haiti
34 K3 **Arcata** California, W USA
35 U6 **Arc Dome** ▲ Nevada, W USA
107 J16 **Arce** Lazio, C Italy
41 O15 **Arcelia** Guerrero, S Mexico
99 M15 **Arcen** Limburg, SE Netherlands
Archangel *see* Arkhangel'sk
Archangel Bay *see* Chëshskaya Guba
115 O23 **Archángelos** *var.* Arhangelos, Arkhángelos. Ródos, Dodekánisos, Greece, Aegean Sea
114 F7 **Archar** ≈ NW Bulgaria
31 R11 **Archbold** Ohio, N USA
105 R12 **Archena** Murcia, SE Spain
25 R5 **Archer City** Texas, SW USA
104 M14 **Archidona** Andalucía, S Spain
65 B25 **Arch Islands** *island group* SW Falkland Islands
106 G13 **Arcidosso** Toscana, C Italy
103 Q5 **Arcis-sur-Aube** Aube, N France
182 F3 **Arckaringa Creek** *seasonal river* South Australia
106 G7 **Arco** Trentino-Alto Adige, N Italy
33 Q14 **Arco** Idaho, NW USA
30 M14 **Arcola** Illinois, N USA
105 P6 **Arcos de Jalón** Castilla-León, N Spain
104 K15 **Arcos de la Frontera** Andalucía, S Spain
104 G5 **Arcos de Valdevez** Viana do Castelo, N Portugal
59 P15 **Arcoverde** Pernambuco, E Brazil
102 H5 **Arcovest, Pointe de l'** *headland* NW France
Arctic-Mid Oceanic Ridge *see* Nansen Cordillera
197 R8 **Arctic Ocean** *ocean*
8 G7 **Arctic Red River** ≈ Northwest Territories /Yukon Territory, NW Canada
Arctic Red River *see* Tsiigehtchic
39 S6 **Arctic Village** Alaska, USA
194 H1 **Arctowski** *Polish research station* South Shetland Islands, Antarctica
114 I12 **Arda** *var.* Ardhas, *Gk.* Ardas. ≈ Bulgaria/Greece ***see also*** Ardas
142 L2 **Ardabīl** *var.* Ardebil. Ardabīl, NW Iran
142 L2 **Ardabīl** *off.* Ostān-e Ardabīl. ◐ *province* NW Iran
137 R11 **Ardahan** Ardahan, NE Turkey
137 S11 **Ardahan** ◐ *province* NE Turkey
143 P8 **Ardakān** Yazd, C Iran
94 E12 **Årdalstangen** Sogn og Fjordane, S Norway
137 R11 **Ardanuç** Artvin, NE Turkey
114 L12 **Ardas** *var.* Ardhas, *Bul.* Arda. ≈ Bulgaria/Greece ***see also*** Arda
138 I13 **Arḍ aş Ṣawwān** *var.* Ardh es Suwwān. *plain* S Jordan
127 P5 **Ardatov** Respublika Mordoviya, W Russian Federation
14 G12 **Ardbeg** Ontario, S Canada
Ardeal *see* Transylvania
Ardebil *see* Ardabīl
103 Q13 **Ardèche** ≈ C France
103 Q13 **Ardèche** ◐ *department* E France
97 F17 **Ardee** *Ir.* Baile Átha Fhirdhia. NE Ireland
103 Q3 **Ardennes** ◐ *department* NE France
99 J23 **Ardennes** *physical region* Belgium/France
137 Q11 **Ardeşen** Rize, NE Turkey
143 O7 **Ardestān** *var.* Ardistan. Eşfahān, C Iran
108 J9 **Ardez** Graubünden, SE Switzerland
Ardhas *see* Arda/Ardas
Ardh es Suwwān *see* Arḍ aş Ṣawwān
104 I12 **Ardila, Ribeira de** *Sp.* Ardilla. ≈ Portugal/Spain ***see also*** Ardilla
11 T17 **Ardill** Saskatchewan, S Canada
104 I12 **Ardilla** *Port.* Ribeira de Ardila. ≈ Portugal/Spain ***see also*** Ardila, Ribeira de
40 M11 **Ardilla, Cerro la** ▲ C Mexico
114 J12 **Ardino** Kŭrdzhali, S Bulgaria
Ardistan *see* Ardestān
183 P9 **Ardlethan** New South Wales, SE Australia
Ard Mhacha *see* Armagh
23 P1 **Ardmore** Alabama, S USA
27 N13 **Ardmore** Oklahoma, C USA
20 J10 **Ardmore** Tennessee, S USA
96 G10 **Ardnamurchan, Point of** *headland* N Scotland, UK
Árdni *see* Arnøya
99 C17 **Ardooie** West-Vlaanderen, W Belgium
182 I9 **Ardrossan** South Australia
116 H9 **Ardusat** *Hung.* Erdőszáda. Maramureş, N Romania
93 F16 **Åre** Jämtland, C Sweden
79 P16 **Arebi** Orientale, NE Dem. Rep. Congo
45 T5 **Arecibo** C Puerto Rico
171 V13 **Aredo** Papua, E Indonesia
59 P14 **Areia Branca** Rio Grande do Norte, E Brazil
119 O14 **Arekhawsk** *Rus.* Orekhovsk. Vitsyebskaya Voblasts', N Belarus
Arel *see* Arlon
Arelas/Arelate *see* Arles
Arenal, Embalse de *see* Arenal Laguna
42 L12 **Arenal Laguna** *var.* Embalse de Arenal. ◎ NW Costa Rica
42 L13 **Arenal, Volcán** ⩕ NW Costa Rica
34 K6 **Arena, Point** *headland* California, W USA
59 H17 **Arenápolis** Mato Grosso, W Brazil

◆ Country ● Country Capital ◇ Dependent Territory ○ Dependent Territory Capital ◐ Administrative Region ✕ International Airport ▲ Mountain ⛰ Mountain Range ⩕ Volcano ≈ River ◎ Lake ▣ Reservoir

40 G10 **Arena, Punta** *headland* W Mexico
104 L8 **Arenas de San Pedro** Castilla-León, N Spain
63 I24 **Arenas, Punta de** *headland* S Argentina
61 B20 **Arenaza** Buenos Aires, E Argentina
95 F17 **Arendal** Aust-Agder, S Norway
99 J16 **Arendonk** Antwerpen, N Belgium
43 T15 **Arenosa** Panamá, N Panama
Arensburg *see* Kuressaare
105 W5 **Arenys de Mar** Cataluña, NE Spain
106 C9 **Arenzano** Liguria, NW Italy
115 F22 **Areópoli** *prev.* Areópolis. Pelopónnisos, S Greece
Areópolis *see* Areópoli
57 H18 **Arequipa** Arequipa, SE Peru
57 G17 **Arequipa** *off.* Departamento de Arequipa. ◈ *department* SW Peru
61 B19 **Arequito** Santa Fe, C Argentina
104 M7 **Arévalo** Castilla-León, N Spain
106 H12 **Arezzo** *anc.* Arretium. Toscana, C Italy
105 Q4 **Arga** ⁓ N Spain
Argaeus *see* Erciyes Dağı
115 G17 **Argalastí** Thessalía, C Greece
105 O10 **Argamasilla de Alba** Castilla-La Mancha, C Spain
158 L8 **Argan** Xinjiang Uygur Zizhiqu, NW China
105 O8 **Arganda** Madrid, C Spain
104 H8 **Arganil** Coimbra, N Portugal
171 P6 **Argao** Cebu, C Philippines
153 V15 **Argartala** Tripura, NE India
123 N9 **Arga-Sala** ⁓ NE Russian Federation
103 P17 **Argelès-sur-Mer** Pyrénées-Orientales, S France
103 T15 **Argens** ⁓ SE France
106 H9 **Argenta** Emilia-Romagna, N Italy
102 K5 **Argentan** Orne, N France
103 N12 **Argentat** Corrèze, C France
106 A9 **Argentera** Piemonte, NE Italy
103 N5 **Argenteuil** Val-d'Oise, N France
62 K13 **Argentina** *off.* Republic of Argentina. ◆ *republic* S South America
Argentina Basin *see* Argentine Basin
Argentine Abyssal Plain *see* Argentine Plain
65 I19 **Argentine Basin** *var.* Argentina Basin. *undersea feature* SW Atlantic Ocean
65 I20 **Argentine Plain** *var.* Argentine Abyssal Plain. *undersea feature* SW Atlantic Ocean
Argentine Rise *see* Falkland Plateau
63 H22 **Argentino, Lago** ◎ S Argentina
102 K8 **Argenton-Château** Deux-Sèvres, W France
102 M9 **Argenton-sur-Creuse** Indre, C France
Argentoratum *see* Strasbourg
116 I12 **Argeş** ◈ *county* S Romania
116 K14 **Argeş** ⁓ S Romania
149 O8 **Arghandāb, Daryā-ye** ⁓ SE Afghanistan
Arghastān *see* Arghestān
149 O8 **Arghestān** *Pash.* Arghastān. ⁓ SE Afghanistan
Argirocastro *see* Gjirokastër
80 E7 **Argo** Northern, N Sudan
173 P7 **Argo Fracture Zone** *tectonic feature* C Indian Ocean
115 F20 **Argolikós Kólpos** *gulf* S Greece
103 R4 **Argonne** *physical region* NE France
115 F20 **Árgos** Pelopónnisos, S Greece
139 S1 **Argōsh** N Iraq
115 D14 **Árgos Orestikó** Dytikí Makedonía, N Greece
115 B19 **Argostóli** *var.* Argostólion. Kefallinía, Iónioi Nísoi, Greece, C Mediterranean Sea
Argostólion *see* Argostóli
Argovie *see* Aargau
35 O14 **Arguello, Point** *headland* California, W USA
127 P16 **Argun** Chechenskaya Respublika, SW Russian Federation
157 T2 **Argun** *Chin.* Ergun He, *Rus.* Argun'. ⁓ China/Russian Federation
77 T12 **Argungu** Kebbi, NW Nigeria
162 J9 **Arguut** Övörhangay, C Mongolia
181 N3 **Argyle, Lake** *salt lake* Western Australia
96 G12 **Argyll** *cultural region* W Scotland, UK
Argyrokastron *see* Gjirokastër
162 I7 **Arhangay** ◈ *province* C Mongolia
Arhangelos *see* Archángelos
95 P14 **Arholma** Stockholm, C Sweden
95 G22 **Århus** *var.* Aarhus. Århus, C Denmark
95 G22 **Århus** ◈ *county* C Denmark
139 T1 **Āri** E Iraq
Aria *see* Herāt
83 F22 **Ariamsvlei** Karas, SE Namibia
107 L17 **Ariano Irpino** Campania, S Italy
54 F11 **Ariari, Río** ⁓ C Colombia
151 K19 **Ari Atoll** *atoll* C Maldives
77 P11 **Aribinda** N Burkina
62 G2 **Arica** *hist.* San Marcos de Arica. Tarapacá, N Chile
54 H16 **Arica** Amazonas, S Colombia
62 G2 **Arica** ✕ Tarapacá, N Chile
114 E13 **Aridaía** *var.* Aridea, Aridhaía. Dytikí Makedonía, N Greece
Aridea *see* Aridaía
172 I15 **Aride, Île** *island* Inner Islands, NE Seychelles
Aridhaía *see* Aridaía
103 N17 **Ariège** ◈ *department* S France
102 M16 **Ariège** *var.* la Riege. ⁓ Andorra/France
116 H11 **Arieş** ⁓ W Romania
149 U10 **Ārifwāla** Punjab, E Pakistan
Ariguaní *see* El Difícil
138 G11 **Arīḥā** Al Karak, W Jordan
138 I3 **Arīḥā** *var.* Arīhā. Idlib, W Syria
Arīḥā *see* Jericho
37 W4 **Arikaree River** ⁓ Colorado/Nebraska, C USA
164 B14 **Arikawa** Nagasaki, Nakadōri-jima, SW Japan
112 L13 **Arilje** Serbia, W Serbia and Montenegro (Yugo.)
45 U14 **Arima** Trinidad, Trinidad and Tobago
Arime *see* Al 'Arīmah
Ariminum *see* Rimini
59 H16 **Arinos, Rio** ⁓ W Brazil
40 M14 **Ario de Rosales** *var.* Ario de Rosáles. Michoacán de Ocampo, SW Mexico
118 F12 **Ariogala** Kaunas, C Lithuania
47 T7 **Aripuanã** ⁓ W Brazil
59 E15 **Ariquemes** Rondônia, W Brazil
121 W13 **'Arīsh, Wādi el** ⁓ NE Egypt
54 K6 **Arismendi** Barinas, C Venezuela
10 J14 **Aristazabal Island** *island* SW Canada
60 F13 **Aristóbulo del Valle** Misiones, NE Argentina
172 I5 **Arivonimamo** ✕ (Antananarivo) Antananarivo, C Madagascar
Arixang *see* Wenquan
105 Q6 **Ariza** Aragón, NE Spain
62 I6 **Arizaro, Salar de** *salt lake* NW Argentina
62 K13 **Arizona** San Luis, C Argentina
36 J12 **Arizona** *off.* State of Arizona; *also known as* Copper State, Grand Canyon State. ◈ *state* SW USA
40 G4 **Arizpe** Sonora, NW Mexico
95 J16 **Årjäng** Värmland, C Sweden
143 P8 **Arjenān** Yazd, C Iran
92 I13 **Arjeplog** Norrbotten, N Sweden
54 E5 **Arjona** Bolívar, N Colombia
105 N13 **Arjona** Andalucía, S Spain
123 S10 **Arka** Khabarovskiy Kray, E Russian Federation
22 L2 **Arkabutla Lake** ⊡ Mississippi, S USA
127 O7 **Arkadak** Saratovskaya Oblast', W Russian Federation
27 T13 **Arkadelphia** Arkansas, C USA
115 J25 **Arkalochóri** *prev.* Arkalohori, Arkalokhórion. Kríti, Greece, E Mediterranean Sea
Arkalohori/Arkalokhórion *see* Arkalochóri
145 O10 **Arkalyk** *Kaz.* Arqalyq. Kostanay, N Kazakhstan
27 U10 **Arkansas** *off.* State of Arkansas; *also known as* The Land of Opportunity. ◈ *state* S USA
27 W14 **Arkansas City** Arkansas, C USA
27 O7 **Arkansas City** Kansas, C USA
16 K11 **Arkansas River** ⁓ C USA
182 J5 **Arkaroola** South Australia
Arkhángelos *see* Archángelos
124 L8 **Arkhangel'sk** *Eng.* Archangel. Arkhangel'skaya Oblast', NW Russian Federation
124 L9 **Arkhangel'skaya Oblast'** ◈ *province* NW Russian Federation
127 O14 **Arkhangel'skoye** Stavropol'skiy Kray, SW Russian Federation
123 R14 **Arkhara** Amurskaya Oblast', S Russian Federation
97 G19 **Arklow** *Ir.* An tInbhear Mór. SE Ireland
115 M20 **Arkoí** *island* Dodekánisos, Greece, Aegean Sea
27 R11 **Arkoma** Oklahoma, C USA
100 O7 **Arkona, Kap** *headland* NE Germany
95 N17 **Arkösund** Östergötland, S Sweden
122 J6 **Arkticheskogo Instituta, Ostrova** *island* N Russian Federation
95 O15 **Arlanda** ✕ (Stockholm) Stockholm, C Sweden
146 C11 **Arlandag** *Rus.* Gora Arlan. ▲ W Turkmenistan
Arlan, Gora *see* Arlandag
105 O5 **Arlanza** ⁓ N Spain
105 N5 **Arlanzón** ⁓ N Spain
103 R15 **Arles** *var.* Arles-sur-Rhône; *anc.* Arelas, Arelate. Bouches-du-Rhône, SE France
Arles-sur-Rhône *see* Arles
103 O17 **Arles-sur-Tech** Pyrénées-Orientales, S France
29 U9 **Arlington** Minnesota, N USA
29 R15 **Arlington** Nebraska, C USA
32 J11 **Arlington** Oregon, NW USA
29 R10 **Arlington** South Dakota, N USA
20 E10 **Arlington** Tennessee, S USA
25 T6 **Arlington** Texas, SW USA
21 W4 **Arlington** Virginia, NE USA
32 H7 **Arlington** Washington, NW USA
30 M10 **Arlington Heights** Illinois, N USA
77 U8 **Arlit** Agadez, C Niger
99 L24 **Arlon** *Dut.* Aarlen, *Ger.* Arel; *Lat.* Orolaunum. Luxembourg, SE Belgium
27 R7 **Arma** Kansas, C USA
97 F16 **Armagh** *Ir.* Ard Mhacha. S Northern Ireland, UK
97 F16 **Armagh** *cultural region* S Northern Ireland, UK
102 K15 **Armagnac** *cultural region* S France
103 Q7 **Armançon** ⁓ C France
60 K10 **Armando Laydner, Represa** ⊡ S Brazil
115 M24 **Armathía** *island* SE Greece
126 M14 **Armavir** Krasnodarskiy Kray, SW Russian Federation
137 T12 **Armavir** *Rus.* Oktemberyan. *prev.* Hoktemberyan. SW Armenia
54 E10 **Armenia** Quindío, W Colombia
137 T12 **Armenia** *off.* Republic of Armenia, *var.* Ajastan, *Arm.* Hayastani Hanrapetut'yun; *prev.* Armenian Soviet Socialist Republic. ◆ *republic* SW Asia
Armenierstadt *see* Gherla
103 O1 **Armentières** Nord, N France
40 K14 **Armería** Colima, SW Mexico
183 T5 **Armidale** New South Wales, SE Australia
29 P11 **Armour** South Dakota, N USA
61 B18 **Armstrong** Santa Fe, C Argentina
11 N16 **Armstrong** British Columbia, SW Canada
12 D11 **Armstrong** Ontario, S Canada
29 U11 **Armstrong** Iowa, C USA
25 S16 **Armstrong** Texas, SW USA
117 S11 **Armyans'k** *Rus.* Armyansk. Respublika Krym, S Ukraine
115 H14 **Arnaía** *var.* Arnea. Kentrikí Makedonía, N Greece
121 N2 **Arnaoúti, Akrotíri** *var.* Arnaoútis, Cape Arnaouti. *headland* W Cyprus
Arnaouti, Cape/Arnaoútis *see* Arnaoúti, Akrotíri
12 L4 **Arnaud** ⁓ Québec, E Canada
103 Q8 **Arnay-le-Duc** Côte d'Or, C France
Arnea *see* Arnaía
105 Q4 **Arnedo** La Rioja, N Spain
95 I14 **Årnes** Akershus, S Norway
Årnes *see* Åi Åfjord
26 K9 **Arnett** Oklahoma, C USA
98 L12 **Arnhem** Gelderland, SE Netherlands
181 Q2 **Arnhem Land** *physical region* Northern Territory, N Australia
106 F11 **Arno** ⁓ C Italy
Arno *see* Arno Atoll
189 W7 **Arno Atoll** *var.* Arno. *atoll* Ratak Chain, NE Marshall Islands
182 H8 **Arno Bay** South Australia
35 Q8 **Arnold** California, W USA
27 X5 **Arnold** Missouri, C USA
29 N15 **Arnold** Nebraska, C USA
109 R10 **Arnoldstein** *Slvn.* Pod Klošter. Kärnten, S Austria
103 N9 **Arnon** ⁓ C France
45 P14 **Arnos Vale** ✕ (Kingstown) Saint Vincent, SE Saint Vincent and the Grenadines
92 I8 **Arnøya** *Lapp.* Árdni *island* N Norway
14 L12 **Arnprior** Ontario, SE Canada
101 G15 **Arnsberg** Nordrhein-Westfalen, W Germany
101 K16 **Arnstadt** Thüringen, C Germany
Arnswalde *see* Choszczno
54 K5 **Aroa** Yaracuy, N Venezuela
83 E21 **Aroab** Karas, SE Namibia
115 E19 **Ároania** ▲▲ S Greece
191 O6 **Aroa, Pointe** *headland* Moorea, W French Polynesia
Aroe Islands *see* Aru, Kepulauan
101 H15 **Arolsen** Niedersachsen, C Germany
106 C7 **Arona** Piemonte, NE Italy
19 R3 **Aroostook River** ⁓ Canada/USA
Arop Island *see* Long Island
38 M12 **Aropuk Lake** ◎ Alaska, USA
191 P4 **Arorae** *atoll* Tungaru, W Kiribati
190 G16 **Arorangi** Rarotonga, S Cook Islands
108 I9 **Arosa** Graubünden, S Switzerland
104 F4 **Arousa, Ría de** *estuary* E Atlantic Ocean
184 P8 **Arowhana** ▲ North Island, NZ
137 V12 **Arp'a** *Az.* Arpaçay. ⁓ Armenia/Azerbaijan
137 S11 **Arpaçay** Kars, NE Turkey
Arpaçay *see* Arp'a
Arqalyq *see* Arkalyk
149 N14 **Arra** ⁓ SW Pakistan
Arrabona *see* Győr
Arrah *see* Āra
Ar Rahad *see* Er Rahad
139 R9 **Ar Raḥḥālīyah** C Iraq
60 Q10 **Arraial do Cabo** Rio de Janeiro, SE Brazil
104 H11 **Arraiolos** Évora, S Portugal
139 R8 **Ar Ramādī** *var.* Ramadi, Rumadiya. SW Iraq
138 J6 **Ar Rāmī** Ḥimş, C Syria
Ar Rams *see* Rams
138 H9 **Ar Ramthā** *var.* Ramtha. Irbid, N Jordan
96 H13 **Arran, Isle of** *island* SW Scotland, UK
138 L3 **Ar Raqqah** *var.* Rakka; *anc.* Nicephorium. Ar Raqqah, N Syria
138 L3 **Ar Raqqah** *off.* Muḥāfaẓat al Raqqah, *var.* Raqqah, *Fr.* Rakka. ◈ *governorate* N Syria
103 O2 **Arras** *anc.* Nemetocenna. Pas-de-Calais, N France
Arrasate *see* Mondragón
138 G12 **Ar Rashādīyah** Aṭ Ṭafīlah, W Jordan
138 I5 **Ar Rastān** *var.* Rastâne. Ḥimş, W Syria
139 X12 **Ar Raṭāwī** E Iraq
102 L15 **Arrats** ⁓ S France
141 N10 **Ar Rawḍah** Makkah, S Saudi Arabia
141 Q15 **Ar Rawḍah** S Yemen
142 K11 **Ar Rawdatayn** *var.* Raudhatain. N Kuwait
143 N16 **Ar Rayyān** *var.* Al Rayyan. C Qatar
102 L17 **Arreau** Hautes-Pyrénées, S France
64 Q11 **Arrecife** *var.* Arrecife de Lanzarote, Puerto Arrecife. Lanzarote, Islas Canarias, NE Atlantic Ocean
Arrecife de Lanzarote *see* Arrecife
43 P6 **Arrecife Edinburgh** *reef* NE Nicaragua
61 C19 **Arrecifes** Buenos Aires, E Argentina
102 F6 **Arrée, Monts d'** ▲▲ NW France
Ar Refā'ī *see* Ar Rifā'ī
Arretium *see* Arezzo
Arriaca *see* Guadalajara
109 S9 **Arriach** Kärnten, S Austria
41 T16 **Arriaga** Chiapas, SE Mexico
41 N12 **Arriaga** San Luis Potosí, C Mexico
139 W10 **Ar Rifā'ī** *var.* Ar Refā'ī. SE Iraq
139 V12 **Ar Riḥāb** *salt flat* S Iraq
104 L2 **Arriondas** Asturias, N Spain
141 Q7 **Ar Riyāḍ** *Eng.* Riyadh. ● (Saudi Arabia) Ar Riyāḍ, C Saudi Arabia
141 O8 **Ar Riyāḍ** *off.* Minṭaqat ar Riyāḍ. ◈ *province* C Saudi Arabia
141 S15 **Ar Riyān** S Yemen
Arrö *see* Ærø
61 H18 **Arroio Grande** Rio Grande do Sul, S Brazil
102 K15 **Arros** ⁓ S France
103 Q9 **Arroux** ⁓ C France
25 R5 **Arrowhead, Lake** ⊡ Texas, SW USA
182 L5 **Arrowsmith, Mount** *hill* New South Wales, SE Australia
185 D21 **Arrowtown** Otago, South Island, NZ
61 D17 **Arroyo Barú** Entre Ríos E Argentina
104 J10 **Arroyo de la Luz** Extremadura, W Spain
63 J16 **Arroyo de la Ventana** Río Negro, SE Argentina
35 P13 **Arroyo Grande** California, W USA
Ar Ru'ays *see* Ar Ruways
141 R11 **Ar Rub' al Khālī** *Eng.* Empty Quarter, Great Sandy Desert. *desert* SW Asia
139 V13 **Ar Ruḍaymah** S Iraq
61 A16 **Arrufó** Santa Fe, C Argentina
138 I7 **Ar Ruḥaybah** *var.* Ruhaybeh, *Fr.* Rouhaïbé. Dimashq, W Syria
139 V15 **Ar Rukhaymīyah** *well* S Iraq
139 U11 **Ar Rumaythah** *var.* Rumaitha. S Iraq
141 X8 **Ar Rustāq** *var.* Rostak, Rustaq. N Oman
139 N8 **Ar Ruṭbah** *var.* Rutba. SW Iraq
140 M3 **Ar Rūthīyah** *spring/well* NW Saudi Arabia
ar-Ruwaida *see* Ar Ruwayḍah
141 O8 **Ar Ruwayḍah** *var.* ar-Ruwaida. Jīzān, C Saudi Arabia
143 N15 **Ar Ruways** *var.* Al Ruweis, Ar Ru'ays, Ruwais. N Qatar
143 O17 **Ar Ruways** *var.* Ar Ru'ays, Ruwaisv. Abū Ẓaby, W UAE
Års *see* Aars
Arsanias *see* Murat Nehri
123 S15 **Arsen'yev** Primorskiy Kray, SE Russian Federation
155 G19 **Arsikere** Karnātaka, W India
127 R3 **Arsk** Respublika Tatarstan, W Russian Federation
94 N10 **Årskogen** Gävleborg, C Sweden
121 O3 **Ársos** C Cyprus
94 N13 **Årsunda** Gävleborg, C Sweden
Arta *see* Árachthos
115 C17 **Árta** *anc.* Ambracia. Ípeiros, W Greece
137 T12 **Artashat** S Armenia
40 M15 **Arteaga** Michoacán de Ocampo, SW Mexico
123 S15 **Artem** Primorskiy Kray, SE Russian Federation
44 C4 **Artemisa** La Habana, W Cuba
117 W7 **Artemivs'k** Donets'ka Oblast', E Ukraine
122 K13 **Artemovsk** Krasnoyarskiy Kray, S Russian Federation
105 U5 **Artesa de Segre** Cataluña, NE Spain
37 U14 **Artesia** New Mexico, SW USA
25 Q14 **Artesia Wells** Texas, SW USA
108 G8 **Arth** Schwyz, C Switzerland
14 F15 **Arthur** Ontario, S Canada
30 M14 **Arthur** Illinois, N USA
28 L14 **Arthur** Nebraska, C USA
29 Q5 **Arthur** North Dakota, N USA
185 B21 **Arthur** ⁓ South Island, NZ
18 B13 **Arthur, Lake** ⊡ Pennsylvania, NE USA
183 N15 **Arthur River** ⁓ Tasmania, SE Australia
185 G18 **Arthur's Pass** Canterbury, South Island, NZ
185 G17 **Arthur's Pass** *pass* South Island, NZ
44 I3 **Arthur's Town** Cat Island, C Bahamas
44 M9 **Artibonite, Rivière de l'** ⁓ C Haiti
61 E16 **Artigas** *prev.* San Eugenio, San Eugenio del Cuareim. Artigas, N Uruguay
61 E16 **Artigas** ◈ *department* N Uruguay
194 H1 **Artigas** *Uruguayan research station* Antarctica
137 T11 **Art'ik** W Armenia
187 O16 **Art, Île** *island* Îles Belep, W New Caledonia
103 O2 **Artois** *cultural region* N France
136 L12 **Artova** Tokat, N Turkey
105 Y9 **Artrutx, Cap d'** *var.* Cabo Dartuch. *headland* Menorca, Spain, W Mediterranean Sea
Artsiz *see* Artsyz
117 N11 **Artsyz** *Rus.* Artsiz. Odes'ka Oblast', SW Ukraine
158 E7 **Artux** Xinjiang Uygur Zizhiqu, NW China
137 R11 **Artvin** Artvin, NE Turkey
137 R11 **Artvin** ◈ *province* NE Turkey
146 G14 **Artyk** Ahal Welaýaty, C Turkmenistan
79 Q16 **Aru** Orientale, NE Dem. Rep. Congo
81 E17 **Arua** NW Uganda
104 I4 **A Rúa de Valdeorras** *var.* La Rúa. Galicia, NW Spain
Aruângua *see* Luangwa
45 O15 **Aruba** *var.* Oruba. ◇ *Dutch autonomous region* S West Indies
47 Q4 **Aruba** *island* Aruba, Lesser Antilles
Aru Islands *see* Aru, Kepulauan
171 W15 **Aru, Kepulauan** *Eng.* Aru Islands; *prev.* Aroe Islands. *island group* E Indonesia
153 W10 **Arunāchal Pradesh** *prev.* North East Frontier Agency, North East Frontier Agency of Assam. ◈ *state* NE India
Arun Qi *see* Naji
155 H23 **Aruppukkottai** Tamil Nādu, SE India
81 I20 **Arusha** Arusha, N Tanzania
81 I21 **Arusha** ◈ *region* E Tanzania
81 I20 **Arusha** ✕ Arusha, N Tanzania
54 C9 **Arusí, Punta** *headland* NW Colombia
155 J23 **Aruvi Aru** ⁓ NW Sri Lanka
79 M17 **Aruwimi** *var.* Ituri (upper course). ⁓ NE Dem.Rep. Congo
Árva *see* Orava
37 T4 **Arvada** Colorado, C USA
Arvand Rūd *see* 'Arab, Shaṭṭ al
162 J8 **Arvayheer** Övörhangay, C Mongolia
9 O10 **Arviat** *prev.* Eskimo Point. Nunavut, C Canada
93 I14 **Arvidsjaur** Norrbotten, N Sweden
95 J15 **Arvika** Värmland, C Sweden
92 J8 **Årviksand** Troms, N Norway
35 S13 **Arvin** California, W USA
163 S8 **Arxan** Nei Mongol Zizhiqu, N China
145 P7 **Arykbalyk** *Kaz.* Aryqbalyq. Severnyy Kazakhstan, N Kazakhstan
Aryqbalyq *see* Arykbalyk
145 P17 **Arys'** *Kaz.* Arys. Yuzhnyy Kazakhstan, S Kazakhstan
Arys *see* Orzysz
Arys Köli *see* Arys, Ozero
145 O14 **Arys, Ozero** *Kaz.* Arys Köli. ◎ C Kazakhstan
107 D16 **Arzachena** Sardegna, Italy, C Mediterranean Sea
127 O4 **Arzamas** Nizhegorodskaya Oblast', W Russian Federation
141 V13 **Arzāt** S Oman
104 H3 **Arzúa** Galicia, NW Spain
111 A16 **Aš** *Ger.* Asch. Karlovarský Kraj, W Czech Republic
95 H15 **Ås** Akershus, S Norway
95 H20 **Asaa** *prev.* Åsa. Nordjylland, N Denmark
Aså *see* Asaa
83 E21 **Asab** Karas, S Namibia
77 U16 **Asaba** Delta, S Nigeria
149 S4 **Asadābād** *var.* Asadābād; *prev.* Chaghasarāy. Kunar, E Afghanistan
138 K3 **Asad, Buḥayrat al** ◎ N Syria
63 H20 **Asador, Pampa del** *plain* S Argentina
165 P14 **Asahi** Chiba, Honshū, S Japan
164 M11 **Asahi** Toyama, Honshū, SW Japan
165 T3 **Asahi-dake** ▲ Hokkaidō, N Japan
165 T3 **Asahikawa** Hokkaidō, N Japan
147 S10 **Asaka** *Rus.* Assake; *prev.* Leninsk. Andijon Viloyati, E Uzbekistan
77 P17 **Asamankese** SE Ghana
188 B15 **Asan** W Guam
188 B15 **Asan Point** *headland* W Guam
153 R15 **Āsānsol** West Bengal, NE India
80 K12 **Āsayita** Afar, NE Ethiopia
171 T12 **Asbakin** Papua, E Indonesia
Asben *see* Aïr, Massif de l'
15 Q12 **Asbestos** Québec, SE Canada
29 Y13 **Asbury** Iowa, C USA
18 K15 **Asbury Park** New Jersey, NE USA
41 Z12 **Ascención, Bahiá de la** *bay* NW Caribbean Sea
40 I3 **Ascensión** Chihuahua, N Mexico
65 M14 **Ascension Fracture Zone** *tectonic feature* C Atlantic Ocean
65 G14 **Ascension Island** ◇ *dependency of St. Helena* C Atlantic Ocean
65 N16 **Ascension Island** *island* C Atlantic Ocean
Asch *see* Aš
109 S3 **Aschach an der Donau** Oberösterreich, N Austria
101 H18 **Aschaffenburg** Bayern, SW Germany
101 F14 **Ascheberg** Nordrhein-Westfalen, W Germany
101 L14 **Aschersleben** Sachsen-Anhalt, C Germany
106 G12 **Asciano** Toscana, C Italy
106 J13 **Ascoli Piceno** *anc.* Asculum Picenum. Marche, C Italy
107 M17 **Ascoli Satriano** *anc.* Asculub, Asculum Apulum. Puglia, SE Italy
108 G11 **Ascona** Ticino, S Switzerland
Asculub *see* Ascoli Satriano
Asculum Picenum *see* Ascoli Piceno
80 L11 **Aseb** *var.* Assab, *Amh.* Āseb. SE Eritrea
95 M20 **Åseda** Kronoberg, S Sweden
127 T6 **Asekeyevo** Orenburgskaya Oblast', W Russian Federation
81 J14 **Āsela** *var.* Asella, Aselle, Asselle. Oromo, C Ethiopia
93 H15 **Åsele** Västerbotten, N Sweden
Asella/Aselle *see* Āsela
94 K12 **Åsen** Dalarna, C Sweden
114 J11 **Asenovgrad** *prev.* Stanimaka. Plovdiv, C Bulgaria
171 O13 **Asera** Sulawesi, C Indonesia
95 E17 **Åseral** Vest-Agder, S Norway
118 J3 **Aseri** *var.* Asserien, *Ger.* Asserin. Ida-Virumaa, NE Estonia
40 J10 **Aserradero** Durango, W Mexico
146 F13 **Aşgabat** *prev.* Ashgabat, Ashkhabad, Poltoratsk. ● (Turkmenistan) Ahal Welaýaty, C Turkmenistan
146 F13 **Aşgabat** ✕ Ahal Welaýaty, C Turkmenistan
95 H16 **Åsgårdstrand** Vestfold, S Norway
Ashara *see* Al 'Ashārah
23 T6 **Ashburn** Georgia, SE USA
185 G19 **Ashburton** Canterbury, South Island, NZ
185 G19 **Ashburton** ⁓ South Island, NZ
180 H8 **Ashburton River** ⁓ Western Australia
145 V10 **Ashchysu** ⁓ E Kazakhstan
10 M16 **Ashcroft** British Columbia, SW Canada
138 E10 **Ashdod** *anc.* Azotos, *Lat.* Azotus. Central, W Israel
27 S14 **Ashdown** Arkansas, C USA
21 T9 **Asheboro** North Carolina, SE USA
11 X15 **Ashern** Manitoba, S Canada
21 P10 **Asheville** North Carolina, SE USA
12 E8 **Asheweig** ⁓ Ontario, C Canada
27 V9 **Ash Flat** Arkansas, C USA
183 T4 **Ashford** New South Wales, SE Australia
97 P22 **Ashford** SE England, UK
36 K11 **Ash Fork** Arizona, SW USA
Ashgabat *see* Aşgabat
27 T7 **Ash Grove** Missouri, C USA
165 O12 **Ashikaga** *var.* Asikaga. Tochigi, Honshū, S Japan
165 Q8 **Ashiro** Iwate, Honshū, C Japan
164 F15 **Ashizuri-misaki** *headland* Shikoku, SW Japan
Ashkelon *see* Ashqelon
Ashkhabad *see* Aşgabat
23 Q4 **Ashland** Alabama, S USA
26 K7 **Ashland** Kansas, C USA
21 P5 **Ashland** Kentucky, S USA
19 S2 **Ashland** Maine, NE USA
22 M1 **Ashland** Mississippi, S USA
27 U4 **Ashland** Missouri, C USA
29 S15 **Ashland** Nebraska, C USA
31 T12 **Ashland** Ohio, N USA
32 G15 **Ashland** Oregon, NW USA
21 W6 **Ashland** Virginia, NE USA
30 K3 **Ashland** Wisconsin, N USA
20 I8 **Ashland City** Tennessee, S USA
183 S4 **Ashley** New South Wales, SE Australia
29 O7 **Ashley** North Dakota, N USA
173 W7 **Ashmore and Cartier Islands** ◇ *Australian external territory* E Indian Ocean
119 I14 **Ashmyany** *Rus.* Oshmyany. Hrodzyenskaya Voblasts', W Belarus
18 K12 **Ashokan Reservoir** ⊡ New York, NE USA
165 U4 **Ashoro** Hokkaidō, N Japan
138 E10 **Ashqelon** *var.* Ashkelon. Southern, C Israel
Ashraf *see* Behshahr
139 O3 **Ash Shadādah** *var.* Ash Shaddādah, Jisr ash Shadadi, Shaddādī, Shedadi, Tell Shedadi. Al Ḥasakah, NE Syria
Ash Shaddādah *see* Ash Shadādah
139 Y12 **Ash Shāfi** E Iraq
139 R4 **Ash Shakk** *var.* Shaykh. C Iraq
Ash Sham/Ash Shām *see* Dimashq
139 T10 **Ash Shāmīyah** *var.* Shamiya. C Iraq
139 Y13 **Ash Shāmīyah** *var.* Al Bādiyah al Janūbīyah. *desert* S Iraq
139 T11 **Ash Shanāfīyah** *var.* Ash Shināfīyah. S Iraq
138 G13 **Ash Sharāh** *var.* Esh Sharā. ▲▲ W Jordan
143 R16 **Ash Shāriqah** *Eng.* Sharjah. Ash Shāriqah, NE UAE
143 R16 **Ash Shāriqah** *var.* Sharjah. ✕ Ash Shāriqah, NE UAE
140 I4 **Ash Sharmah** *var.* Šarma. Tabūk, NW Saudi Arabia
139 R4 **Ash Sharqāṭ** NW Iraq
141 S10 **Ash Sharqīyah** *off.* Al Minṭaqah ash Sharqīyah, *Eng.* Eastern Region. ◈ *province* E Saudi Arabia
139 W11 **Ash Shaṭrah** *var.* Shatra. SE Iraq
138 G13 **Ash Shawbak** Ma'ān, W Jordan
138 L5 **Ash Shaykh Ibrāhīm** Ḥimş, C Syria
141 O17 **Ash Shaykh 'Uthmān** SW Yemen
141 S15 **Ash Shiḥr** SE Yemen
Ash Shināfīyah *see* Ash Shanāfīyah
141 V12 **Ash Shişar** *var.* Shisur. SW Oman
139 S13 **Ash Shubrūm** *well* S Iraq
141 R10 **Ash Shuqqān** *desert* E Saudi Arabia
75 O9 **Ash Shuwayrif** *var.* Ash Shwayrif. N Libya
Ash Shwayrif *see* Ash Shuwayrif
31 U10 **Ashtabula** Ohio, N USA
29 Q5 **Ashtabula, Lake** ⊡ North Dakota, N USA
137 T12 **Ashtarak** W Armenia
142 M6 **Āshtīān** *var.* Āshtiyān. Markazī, W Iran
Āshtiyān *see* Āshtīān
33 R13 **Ashton** Idaho, NW USA
13 O10 **Ashuanipi Lake** ◎ Newfoundland and Labrador, E Canada
15 P6 **Ashuapmushuan** ⁓ Québec, SE Canada
23 Q3 **Ashville** Alabama, S USA
31 S14 **Ashville** Ohio, N USA

◆ Country ● Country Capital ◇ Dependent Territory ○ Dependent Territory Capital ◈ Administrative Region ✕ International Airport ▲ Mountain ▲▲ Mountain Range ⩕ Volcano ⁓ River ◎ Lake ⊡ Reservoir

30 K3 **Ashwabay, Mount** *hill* Wisconsin, N USA
171 T11 **Asia, Kepulauan** *island group* E Indonesia
154 N13 **Āsika** Orissa, E India
Asikaga *see* Ashikaga
93 M18 **Asikkala** *var.* Vääksy. Etelä-Suomi, S Finland
74 G5 **Asilah** N Morocco
'Aṣī, Nahr al *see* Orontes
107 B16 **Asinara, Isola** *island* W Italy
122 J12 **Asino** Tomskaya Oblast', C Russian Federation
119 O14 **Asintorf** *Rus.* Osintorf. Vitsyebskaya Voblasts', N Belarus
119 L17 **Asipovichy** *Rus.* Osipovichi. Mahilyowskaya Voblasts', C Belarus
141 N12 **'Asīr** *off.* Minṭaqat 'Asīr. ◈ *province* SW Saudi Arabia
140 M11 **'Asīr** *Eng.* Asir. ▲▲ SW Saudi Arabia
139 X10 **Askal** E Iraq
137 P13 **Aşkale** Erzurum, NE Turkey
117 T11 **Askaniya-Nova** Khersons'ka Oblast', S Ukraine
95 H15 **Asker** Akershus, S Norway
95 L17 **Askersund** Örebro, C Sweden
Askī Kalak *see* Eski Kaļak
95 I15 **Askim** Østfold, S Norway
127 V3 **Askino** Respublika Bashkortostan, W Russian Federation
115 D14 **Áskio** ▲ N Greece
152 L9 **Askot** Uttaranchal, N India
94 C12 **Askvoll** Sogn og Fjordane, S Norway
136 A13 **Aslan Burnu** *headland* W Turkey
136 L16 **Aslantaş Barajı** ⊡ S Turkey
149 S4 **Asmār** *var.* Bar Kunar. Kunar, E Afghanistan
80 I9 **Asmara** *Amh.* Āsmera. ● (Eritrea) C Eritrea
Āsmera *see* Asmara
95 L21 **Åsnen** ◎ S Sweden
115 F19 **Asopós** ≈ S Greece
171 W13 **Asori** Papua, E Indonesia
80 G12 **Āsosa** Benishangul, W Ethiopia
32 M10 **Asotin** Washington, NW USA
Aspadana *see* Eşfahān
Aspang *see* Aspang Markt
109 X6 **Aspang Markt** *var.* Aspang. Niederösterreich, E Austria
105 S12 **Aspe** País Valenciano, E Spain
37 R5 **Aspen** Colorado, C USA
25 P6 **Aspermont** Texas, SW USA
Asphaltites, Lacus *see* Dead Sea
Aspinwall *see* Colón
185 C20 **Aspiring, Mount** ▲ South Island, NZ
115 B16 **Asprókavos, Akrotírio** *headland* Kérkyra, Iónioi Nísoi, Greece, C Mediterranean Sea
Aspropótamos *see* Achelóos
Assab *see* Aseb
76 J10 **Assaba** *var.* Açâba. ◈ *region* S Mauritania
138 L4 **As Sabkhah** *var.* Sabkha. Ar Raqqah, NE Syria
139 U6 **As Sa'dīyah** E Iraq
Assad, Lake *see* Asad, Buḩayrat al
138 I8 **Aş Şafā** ▲ S Syria
138 I10 **Aş Şafāwī** Al Mafraq, N Jordan
Aş Şaff *see* El Şaff
139 N2 **Aş Şafīḩ** Al Ḩasakah, N Syria
Aş Şaḩrā' al Gharbīyah *see* Sahara el Gharbîya
Aş Şaḩrā' ash Sharqīyah *see* Sahara el Sharqîya
Assake *see* Asaka
As Salamīyah *see* Salamīyah
141 Q4 **As Sālimī** *var.* Salemy. SW Kuwait
67 W7 **'Assal, Lac** ◎ C Djibouti
As Sallūm *see* Salûm
139 T13 **As Salmān** S Iraq
138 G10 **As Salṭ** *var.* Salt. Al Balqā', NW Jordan
142 M16 **As Salwā** *var.* Salwa, Salwah. S Qatar
153 V12 **Assam** ◈ *state* NE India
Assamaka *see* Assamakka
77 T8 **Assamakka** *var.* Assamaka. Agadez, NW Niger
139 U11 **As Samāwah** *var.* Samawa. S Iraq
As Saqia al Hamra *see* Saguia al Hamra
138 J4 **Aş Şā'rān** Ḩamāh, C Syria
138 G9 **Aş Şarīḩ** Irbid, N Jordan
21 Z5 **Assateague Island** *island* Maryland, NE USA
139 O6 **As Sayyāl** *var.* Sayyāl. Dayr az Zawr, E Syria
99 G18 **Asse** Vlaams Brabant, C Belgium
99 D16 **Assebroek** West-Vlaanderen, NW Belgium
Asselle *see* Āsela
107 C20 **Assemini** Sardegna, Italy, C Mediterranean Sea
98 N7 **Assen** Drenthe, NE Netherlands
99 E16 **Assenede** Oost-Vlaanderen, NW Belgium
95 G24 **Assens** Fyn, C Denmark
Asserien/Asserin *see* Aseri
99 I21 **Assesse** Namur, SE Belgium
141 Y8 **As Sīb** *var.* Seeb. NE Oman
139 Z13 **As Sībah** *var.* Sibah. SE Iraq
11 T17 **Assiniboia** Saskatchewan, S Canada
11 V15 **Assiniboine** ≈ Manitoba, S Canada
11 P16 **Assiniboine, Mount** ▲ Alberta/British Columbia, SW Canada
Assiout *see* Asyût
60 J9 **Assis** São Paulo, S Brazil
106 I13 **Assisi** Umbria, C Italy
Assiut *see* Asyût
Assling *see* Jesenice
Assouan *see* Aswân
Assu *see* Açu
Assuan *see* Aswân
142 K12 **Aş Şubayḩīyah** *var.* Subiyah. S Kuwait
141 R16 **As Sufāl** S Yemen
138 L5 **As Sukhnah** *var.* Sukhne, *Fr.* Soukhné. Ḩimş, C Syria
139 U4 **As Sulaymānīyah** *var.* Sulaimaniya, *Kurd.* Slēmānī. NE Iraq
141 P11 **As Sulayyil** Ar Riyāḑ, S Saudi Arabia
121 O13 **As Sulṭān** N Libya
141 Q5 **Aş Şummān** *desert* N Saudi Arabia
141 Q16 **Aş Şurrah** SW Yemen
139 N4 **Aş Şuwār** *var.* Şuwār. Dayr az Zawr, E Syria
138 H9 **As Suwaydā'** *var.* El Suweida, Es Suweida, Suweida, *Fr.* Soueida. As Suwaydā', SW Syria
138 H9 **As Suwaydā'** *off.* Muḩāfaẓat as Suwaydā', *var.* As Suwaydā, Suwaydá, Suweida, *Fr.* Soueida. ◈ *governorate* S Syria
141 Z9 **As Suwayḩ** NE Oman
141 X8 **As Suwayq** *var.* Suwaik. N Oman
139 T8 **Aş Şuwayrah** *var.* Suwaira. E Iraq
As Suways *see* Suez
Asta Colonia *see* Asti
Astacus *see* İzmit
115 M23 **Astakída** *island* SE Greece
145 Q9 **Astana** *prev.* Akmola, Akmolinsk, Tselinograd, Aqmola. ● (Kazakhstan) Akmola, N Kazakhstan
142 M3 **Āstāneh** Gīlān, NW Iran
Asta Pompeia *see* Asti
137 Y14 **Astara** S Azerbaijan
Astarabad *see* Gorgān
99 L15 **Asten** Noord-Brabant, SE Netherlands
Asterābād *see* Gorgān
106 C8 **Asti** *anc.* Asta Colonia, Asta Pompeia, Hasta Colonia, Hasta Pompeia. Piemonte, NW Italy
Astigi *see* Ecija
Astipálaia *see* Astypálaia
148 L16 **Astola Island** *island* SW Pakistan
152 H4 **Astor** Jammu and Kashmir, NW India
104 K4 **Astorga** *anc.* Asturica Augusta. Castilla-León, N Spain
32 F10 **Astoria** Oregon, NW USA
(0) F8 **Astoria Fan** *undersea feature* E Pacific Ocean
95 J22 **Åstorp** Skåne, S Sweden
Astrabad *see* Gorgān
127 Q13 **Astrakhan'** Astrakhanskaya Oblast', SW Russian Federation
Astrakhan-Bazar *see* Cälilabad
127 Q11 **Astrakhanskaya Oblast'** ◈ *province* SW Russian Federation
93 J15 **Åsträsk** Västerbotten, N Sweden
Astrida *see* Butare
65 O22 **Astrid Ridge** *undersea feature* S Atlantic Ocean
187 P15 **Astrolabe, Récifs de l'** *reef* C New Caledonia
121 P2 **Astromerítis** N Cyprus
115 F20 **Ástros** Pelopónnisos, S Greece
119 G16 **Astryna** *Rus.* Ostryna. Hrodzyenskaya Voblasts', W Belarus
104 J2 **Asturias** ◈ *autonomous community* NW Spain
Asturias *see* Oviedo
Asturica Augusta *see* Astorga
115 L22 **Astypálaia** *var.* Astipálaia, *It.* Stampalia. *island* Kykládes, Greece, Aegean Sea
192 G16 **Āsuisui, Cape** *headland* Savai'i, W Samoa
195 S2 **Asuka** *Japanese research station* Antarctica
62 O6 **Asunción** ● (Paraguay) Central, S Paraguay
62 O6 **Asunción** × Central, S Paraguay
188 K3 **Asuncion Island** *island* N Northern Mariana Islands
42 E6 **Asunción Mita** Jutiapa, SE Guatemala
Asunción Nochixtlán *see* Nochixtlán
40 E3 **Asunción, Río** ≈ NW Mexico
95 M18 **Åsunden** ◎ S Sweden
118 K11 **Asvyeya** *Rus.* Osveya. Vitsyebskaya Voblasts', N Belarus
Aswa *see* Achwa
75 X11 **Aswân** *var.* Assouan, Assuan; *anc.* Syene. SE Egypt
75 X11 **Aswan High Dam** *dam* SE Egypt
75 W9 **Asyût** *var.* Assiout, Assiut, Siut; *anc.* Lycopolis. C Egypt
193 W15 **Ata** *island* Tongatapu Group, SW Tonga
62 G8 **Atacama** *off.* Región de Atacama. ◈ *region* C Chile
Atacama Desert *see* Atacama, Desierto de
62 H4 **Atacama, Desierto de** *Eng.* Atacama Desert. *desert* N Chile
62 I6 **Atacama, Puna de** ▲▲ NW Argentina
62 I5 **Atacama, Salar de** *salt lake* N Chile
54 E11 **Ataco** Tolima, C Colombia
190 H8 **Atafu Atoll** *island* NW Tokelau
190 H8 **Atafu Village** Atafu Atoll, NW Tokelau
74 K12 **Atakor** ▲▲ SE Algeria
77 R14 **Atakora, Chaîne de l'** *var.* Atakora Mountains. ▲▲ N Benin
Atakora Mountains *see* Atakora, Chaîne de l'
77 R16 **Atakpamé** C Togo
146 F11 **Atakui** Ahal Welaýaty, C Turkmenistan
58 B13 **Atalaia do Norte** Amazonas, N Brazil
146 M14 **Atamyrat** *prev.* Kerki. Lebap Welaýaty, E Turkmenistan
76 I7 **Aṭâr** Adrar, W Mauritania
162 G10 **Atas Bogd** ▲ SW Mongolia
35 P12 **Atascadero** California, W USA
25 S13 **Atascosa River** ≈ Texas, SW USA
145 R11 **Atasu** Karaganda, C Kazakhstan
145 R12 **Atasu** ≈ C Kazakhstan
193 V15 **Atata** *island* Tongatapu Group, S Tonga
136 H10 **Atatürk** × (İstanbul) İstanbul, NW Turkey
137 N16 **Atatürk Barajı** ⊡ S Turkey
Atax *see* Aude
80 G8 **Atbara** *var.* 'Aṭbārah. River Nile, NE Sudan
80 H8 **Atbara** *var.* Nahr 'Aṭbarah. ≈ Eritrea/Sudan
'Aṭbārah/'Aṭbarah, Nahr *see* Atbara
145 P9 **Atbasar** Akmola, N Kazakhstan
At-Bashi *see* At-Bashy
147 W9 **At-Bashy** *var.* At-Bashi. Narynskaya Oblast', C Kyrgyzstan
22 I10 **Atchafalaya Bay** *bay* Louisiana, S USA
22 I8 **Atchafalaya River** ≈ Louisiana, S USA
Atchin *see* Aceh
27 Q3 **Atchison** Kansas, C USA
77 P16 **Atebubu** C Ghana
105 Q6 **Ateca** Aragón, NE Spain
40 K11 **Atengo, Río** ≈ C Mexico
Aternum *see* Pescara
107 K15 **Atessa** Abruzzo, C Italy
Ateste *see* Este
99 E19 **Ath** *var.* Aat. Hainaut, SW Belgium
11 Q13 **Athabasca** Alberta, SW Canada
11 Q12 **Athabasca** *var.* Athabaska. ≈ Alberta, SW Canada
11 R10 **Athabasca, Lake** ◎ Alberta/Saskatchewan, SW Canada
Athabaska *see* Athabasca
115 C16 **Athamánon** ▲▲ C Greece
97 F17 **Athboy** *Ir.* Baile Átha Buí. E Ireland
Athenae *see* Athína
97 C18 **Athenry** *Ir.* Baile Átha an Rí. W Ireland
23 P2 **Athens** Alabama, S USA
23 T3 **Athens** Georgia, SE USA
31 T14 **Athens** Ohio, N USA
20 M10 **Athens** Tennessee, S USA
25 V7 **Athens** Texas, SW USA
Athens *see* Athína
115 B18 **Athéras, Akrotírio** *headland* Kefallinía, Iónioi Nísoi, Greece, C Mediterranean Sea
181 W4 **Atherton** Queensland, NE Australia
81 I19 **Athi** ≈ S Kenya
121 Q2 **Athíenou** SE Cyprus
115 H19 **Athína** *Eng.* Athens; *prev.* Athínai, *anc.* Athenae. ● (Greece) Attikí, C Greece
Athínai *see* Athína
139 S10 **Athīyah** C Iraq
97 D18 **Athlone** *Ir.* Baile Átha Luain. C Ireland
155 F16 **Athni** Karnātaka, W India
185 C23 **Athol** Southland, South Island, NZ
19 N11 **Athol** Massachusetts, NE USA
115 I15 **Áthos** ▲ NE Greece
Athos, Mount *see* Ágion Óros
Ath Thawrah *see* Madīnat ath Thawrah
141 P5 **Ath Thumāmī** *spring/well* N Saudi Arabia
99 L25 **Athus** Luxembourg, SE Belgium
97 E19 **Athy** *Ir.* Baile Átha Í. C Ireland
78 I10 **Ati** Batha, C Chad
81 F16 **Atiak** NW Uganda
57 G17 **Atico** Arequipa, SW Peru
105 O6 **Atienza** Castilla-La Mancha, C Spain
39 Q6 **Atigun Pass** *pass* Alaska, USA
12 B12 **Atikokan** Ontario, S Canada
13 O9 **Atikonak Lac** ◎ Newfoundland and Labrador, E Canada
42 C6 **Atitlán, Lago de** ◎ W Guatemala
190 L16 **Atiu** *island* S Cook Islands
Atjeh *see* Aceh
123 T9 **Atka** Magadanskaya Oblast', E Russian Federation
38 H17 **Atka** Atka Island, Alaska, USA
38 H17 **Atka Island** *island* Aleutian Islands, Alaska, USA
127 O7 **Atkarsk** Saratovskaya Oblast', W Russian Federation
27 U11 **Atkins** Arkansas, C USA
29 O13 **Atkinson** Nebraska, C USA
171 T12 **Atkri** Papua, E Indonesia
41 O13 **Atlacomulco** *var.* Atlacomulco de Fabela. México, C Mexico
Atlacomulco de Fabela *see* Atlacomulco
23 S3 **Atlanta** *state capital* Georgia, SE USA
31 R6 **Atlanta** Michigan, N USA
25 X6 **Atlanta** Texas, SW USA
29 T15 **Atlantic** Iowa, C USA
21 Y10 **Atlantic** North Carolina, SE USA
23 W8 **Atlantic Beach** Florida, SE USA
18 J17 **Atlantic City** New Jersey, NE USA
172 L14 **Atlantic-Indian Basin** *undersea feature* SW Indian Ocean
172 K13 **Atlantic-Indian Ridge** *undersea feature* SW Indian Ocean
54 E4 **Atlántico** *off.* Departamento del Atlántico. ◈ *province* NW Colombia
66-67 **Atlantic Ocean** *ocean*
42 K7 **Atlántico Norte, Región Autónoma** *prev.* Zelaya Norte. ◈ *autonomous region* NE Nicaragua
42 L10 **Atlántico Sur, Región Autónoma** *prev.* Zelaya Sur. ◈ *autonomous region* SE Nicaragua
42 I5 **Atlántida** ◈ *department* N Honduras
77 Y15 **Atlantika Mountains** ▲▲ E Nigeria
64 J10 **Atlantis Fracture Zone** *tectonic feature* NW Atlantic Ocean
74 H7 **Atlas Mountains** ▲▲ NW Africa
123 V11 **Atlasova, Ostrov** *island* SE Russian Federation
123 V10 **Atlasovo** Kamchatskaya Oblast', E Russian Federation
120 G11 **Atlas Saharien** *var.* Saharan Atlas. ▲▲ Algeria/Morocco
Atlas, Tell *see* Atlas Tellien
120 H10 **Atlas Tellien** *Eng.* Tell Atlas. ▲▲ N Algeria
10 I9 **Atlin** British Columbia, W Canada
10 I9 **Atlin Lake** ◎ British Columbia, W Canada
41 P14 **Atlixco** Puebla, S Mexico
94 B11 **Atløyna** *island* S Norway
155 I17 **Ātmakūr** Andhra Pradesh, C India
23 O8 **Atmore** Alabama, S USA
101 J20 **Atmühl** ≈ S Germany
94 H11 **Atna** ≈ S Norway
164 E13 **Atō** Yamaguchi, Honshū, SW Japan
57 L21 **Atocha** Potosí, S Bolivia
27 P12 **Atoka** Oklahoma, C USA
27 O12 **Atoka Lake** *var.* Atoka Reservoir. ⊡ Oklahoma, C USA
Atoka Reservoir *see* Atoka Lake
33 Q14 **Atomic City** Idaho, NW USA
40 L10 **Atotonilco** Zacatecas, C Mexico
40 M13 **Atotonilco el Alto** *var.* Atotonilco. Jalisco, SW Mexico
77 N7 **Atouila, 'Erg** *desert* N Mali
41 N16 **Atoyac** *var.* Atoyac de Alvarez. Guerrero, S Mexico
Atoyac de Alvarez *see* Atoyac
41 P15 **Atoyac, Río** ≈ S Mexico
39 O5 **Atqasuk** Alaska, USA
Atrak/Atrak, Rūd-e *see* Etrek
95 J20 **Ätran** ≈ S Sweden
54 C7 **Atrato, Río** ≈ NW Colombia
Atrek *see* Etrek
107 K14 **Atri** Abruzzo, C Italy
Atria *see* Adria
165 P9 **Atsumi** Yamagata, Honshū, C Japan
165 S3 **Atsuta** Hokkaidō, NE Japan
143 Q17 **Aṭ Ṭaff** *desert* C UAE
138 G12 **Aṭ Ṭafīlah** *var.* Et Tafila, Tafila. Aṭ Ṭafīlah, W Jordan
138 G12 **Aṭ Ṭafīlah** *off.* Muḩāfaẓat aṭ Ṭafīlah. ◈ *governorate* W Jordan
140 L10 **Aṭ Ṭā'if** Makkah, W Saudi Arabia
Attaleia/Attalia *see* Antalya
23 Q3 **Attalla** Alabama, S USA
138 L2 **At Tall al Abyaḑ** *var.* Tall al Abyaḑ, Tell Abyad, *Fr.* Tell Abiad. Ar Raqqah, N Syria
138 L7 **Aṭ Ṭanf** Ḩimş, S Syria
Attapu *see* Samakhixai
139 S10 **At Taqtaqānah** C Iraq
115 O23 **Attávytos** ▲ Ródos, Dodekánisos, Greece, Aegean Sea
139 V15 **At Tawal** *desert* Iraq/Saudi Arabia
12 G9 **Attawapiskat** Ontario, C Canada
12 F9 **Attawapiskat** ≈ Ontario, S Canada
12 D9 **Attawapiskat Lake** ◎ Ontario, C Canada
At Taybé *see* Ţayyibah
101 F16 **Attendorn** Nordrhein-Westfalen, W Germany
109 R5 **Attersee** Salzburg, NW Austria
109 R5 **Attersee** ◎ N Austria
99 L24 **Attert** Luxembourg, SE Belgium
138 M4 **At Tibnī** *var.* Tibnī. Dayr az Zawr, NE Syria
31 N13 **Attica** Indiana, N USA
18 E10 **Attica** New York, NE USA
Attica *see* Attikí
13 N7 **Attikamagen Lake** ◎ Newfoundland and Labrador, E Canada
115 H20 **Attikí** *Eng.* Attica. ◈ *region* C Greece
19 O12 **Attleboro** Massachusetts, NE USA
109 R5 **Attnang** Oberösterreich, N Austria
149 U6 **Attock City** Punjab, E Pakistan
Attopeu *see* Samakhixai
25 X8 **Attoyac River** ≈ Texas, SW USA
38 D16 **Attu** Attu Island, Alaska, USA
139 Y12 **Aṭ Ṭūbah** E Iraq
140 K4 **Aṭ Ṭubayq** *plain* Jordan/Saudi Arabia
38 C16 **Attu Island** *island* Aleutian Islands, Alaska, USA
Aṭ Ṭūr *see* El Ṭûr
155 I21 **Āttūr** Tamil Nādu, SE India
141 N17 **At Turbah** SW Yemen
62 I12 **Atuel, Río** ≈ C Argentina
Atugi *see* Atsugi
191 X7 **Atuona** Hiva Oa, NE French Polynesia
Aturus *see* Adour
95 M18 **Åtvidaberg** Östergötland, S Sweden
35 P9 **Atwater** California, W USA
29 T8 **Atwater** Minnesota, N USA
26 I2 **Atwood** Kansas, C USA
31 U12 **Atwood Lake** ⊡ Ohio, N USA
127 P5 **Atyashevo** Respublika Mordoviya, W Russian Federation
144 F12 **Atyrau** *prev.* Gur'yev. Atyrau, W Kazakhstan
144 E11 **Atyrau** *off.* Atyrauskaya Oblast', *var. Kaz.* Atyraū Oblysy; *prev.* Gur'yevskaya Oblast'. ◈ *province* W Kazakhstan
Atyraū Oblysy/Atyrauskaya Oblast' *see* Atyrau
108 I7 **Au** Vorarlberg, NW Austria
186 B4 **Aua Island** *island* NW PNG
103 S16 **Aubagne** *anc.* Albania. Bouches-du-Rhône, SE France
99 L25 **Aubange** Luxembourg, SE Belgium
103 Q6 **Aube** ◈ *department* N France
103 R6 **Aube** ≈ N France
99 L19 **Aubel** Liège, E Belgium
103 Q13 **Aubenas** Ardèche, E France
103 O8 **Aubigny-sur-Nère** Cher, C France
103 O13 **Aubin** Aveyron, S France
103 O13 **Aubrac, Monts d'** ▲▲ S France
36 J10 **Aubrey Cliffs** *cliff* Arizona, SW USA
23 R5 **Auburn** Alabama, S USA
35 P6 **Auburn** California, W USA
30 K14 **Auburn** Illinois, N USA
31 Q11 **Auburn** Indiana, N USA
20 J7 **Auburn** Kentucky, S USA
19 P8 **Auburn** Maine, NE USA
19 N11 **Auburn** Massachusetts, NE USA
29 S16 **Auburn** Nebraska, C USA
18 H10 **Auburn** New York, NE USA
32 H8 **Auburn** Washington, NW USA
103 N11 **Aubusson** Creuse, C France
118 E10 **Auce** *Ger.* Autz. Dobele, SW Latvia
102 L15 **Auch** *Lat.* Augusta Auscorum, Elimberrum. Gers, S France
77 U16 **Auchi** Edo, S Nigeria
23 T9 **Aucilla River** ≈ Florida/Georgia, SE USA
184 L6 **Auckland** Auckland, North Island, NZ
184 K5 **Auckland** *off.* Auckland Region. ◈ *region* North Island, NZ
184 L6 **Auckland** × Auckland, North Island, NZ
192 J12 **Auckland Islands** *island group* S NZ
103 O16 **Aude** ◈ *department* S France
103 N16 **Aude** *anc.* Atax. ≈ S France
Audenarde *see* Oudenaarde
Audern *see* Audru
102 E6 **Audierne** Finistère, NW France
102 E6 **Audierne, Baie d'** *bay* NW France
103 U7 **Audincourt** Doubs, E France
118 G5 **Audru** *Ger.* Audern. Pärnumaa, SW Estonia
29 T14 **Audubon** Iowa, C USA
101 N17 **Aue** Sachsen, E Germany
100 H12 **Aue** ≈ NW Germany
100 L9 **Auerbach** Bayern, SE Germany
101 M17 **Auerbach** Sachsen, E Germany
108 I10 **Auererrhein** ≈ SW Switzerland
101 N17 **Auersberg** ▲ E Germany
181 W9 **Augathella** Queensland, E Australia
31 Q12 **Auglaize River** ≈ Ohio, N USA
83 F22 **Augrabies Falls** *waterfall* W South Africa
31 R7 **Au Gres River** ≈ Michigan, N USA
Augsbourg *see* Augsburg
101 K22 **Augsburg** *Fr.* Augsbourg; *anc.* Augusta Vindelicorum. Bayern, S Germany
180 I14 **Augusta** Western Australia
107 L25 **Augusta** *It.* Agosta. Sicilia, Italy, C Mediterranean Sea
27 W11 **Augusta** Arkansas, C USA
23 V3 **Augusta** Georgia, SE USA
27 O6 **Augusta** Kansas, C USA
19 Q7 **Augusta** *state capital* Maine, NE USA
33 Q8 **Augusta** Montana, NW USA
Augusta *see* London
Augusta Auscorum *see* Auch
Augusta Emerita *see* Mérida
Augusta Praetoria *see* Aosta
Augusta Suessionum *see* Soissons
Augusta Trajana *see* Stara Zagora
Augusta Treverorum *see* Trier
Augusta Vangionum *see* Worms
Augusta Vindelicorum *see* Augsburg
95 G24 **Augustenborg** *Ger.* Augustenburg. Sønderjylland, SW Denmark
Augustenburg *see* Augustenborg
39 Q13 **Augustine Island** *island* Alaska, USA
14 L9 **Augustines, Lac des** ◎ Québec, SE Canada
Augustobona Tricassium *see* Troyes
Augustodunum *see* Autun
Augustodurum *see* Bayeux
Augustoritum Lemovicensium *see* Limoges
110 O8 **Augustów** *Rus.* Avgustov. Podlaskie, NE Poland
Augustow Canal *see* Augustowski, Kanał
110 O8 **Augustowski, Kanał** *Eng.* Augustow Canal, *Rus.* Avgustovskiy Kanal. *canal* NE Poland
180 I9 **Augustus, Mount** ▲ Western Australia
186 M9 **Auki** Malaita, N Solomon Islands
21 W8 **Aulander** North Carolina, SE USA
180 L7 **Auld, Lake** *salt lake* Western Australia
Aulie Ata/Auliye-Ata *see* Taraz
144 M8 **Auliyekol'** *prev.* Semiozernoye. Kostanay, N Kazakhstan
106 E10 **Aulla** Toscana, C Italy
102 F6 **Aulne** ≈ NW France
Aulong *see* Ulong
37 T3 **Ault** Colorado, C USA
Avlum *see* Aulum
103 N3 **Aumale** Seine-Maritime, N France
Auminzatau, Gory *see* Owminzatovo-Toshi
77 T14 **Auna** Niger, W Nigeria
95 H21 **Auning** Århus, C Denmark
192 K17 **Aunu'u Island** *island* W American Samoa
83 E20 **Auob** *var.* Oup. ≈ Namibia/South Africa
93 K19 **Aura** Länsi-Suomi, W Finland
109 R5 **Aurach** ≈ N Austria
Aural, Phnom *see* Aôral, Phnum
153 O14 **Aurangābād** Bihār, N India
154 F13 **Aurangābād** Mahārāshtra, C India
189 V7 **Aur Atoll** *atoll* E Marshall Islands
102 G7 **Auray** Morbihan, NW France
94 G13 **Aurdal** Oppland, S Norway
94 F8 **Aure** Møre og Romsdal, S Norway
29 T12 **Aurelia** Iowa, C USA
Aurelia Aquensis *see* Baden-Baden
Aurelianum *see* Orléans
120 J10 **Aurès, Massif de l'** ▲▲ NE Algeria
100 F10 **Aurich** Niedersachsen, NW Germany
103 O13 **Aurillac** Cantal, C France
Aurine, Alpi *see* Zillertaler Alpen
Aurium *see* Ourense
14 H15 **Aurora** Ontario, S Canada
55 S8 **Aurora** NW Guyana
37 T4 **Aurora** Colorado, C USA
30 M11 **Aurora** Illinois, N USA
31 Q15 **Aurora** Indiana, N USA
29 W4 **Aurora** Minnesota, N USA
27 S8 **Aurora** Missouri, C USA
29 P16 **Aurora** Nebraska, C USA
36 J5 **Aurora** Utah, W USA
Aurora *see* Maéwo, Vanuatu
Aurora *see* San Francisco, Philippines
94 F10 **Aursjøen** ◎ S Norway
94 I9 **Aursunden** ◎ S Norway
83 D21 **Aus** Karas, SW Namibia
Ausa *see* Vic
14 E16 **Ausable** ≈ Ontario, S Canada
31 O3 **Au Sable Point** *headland* Michigan, N USA
31 S7 **Au Sable Point** *headland* Michigan, N USA
31 R6 **Au Sable River** ≈ Michigan, N USA
57 H16 **Ausangate, Nevado** ▲ C Peru
Auschwitz *see* Oświęcim
Ausculum Apulum *see* Ascoli Satriano
105 Q4 **Ausejo** La Rioja, N Spain
Aussig *see* Ústí nad Labem
95 F17 **Aust-Agder** ◈ *county* S Norway
92 P2 **Austfonna** *glacier* NE Svalbard
31 P15 **Austin** Indiana, N USA
29 W11 **Austin** Minnesota, N USA
35 U5 **Austin** Nevada, W USA
25 S10 **Austin** *state capital* Texas, S USA
180 J10 **Austin, Lake** *salt lake* Western Australia
31 V11 **Austintown** Ohio, N USA
25 V9 **Austonio** Texas, SW USA
Australes, Archipel des *see* Australes, Îles
Australes et Antarctiques Françaises, Terres *see* French Southern and Antarctic Territories
191 T14 **Australes, Îles** *var.* Archipel des Australes, Îles Tubuai, Tubuai Islands, *Eng.* Austral Islands. *island group* SW French Polynesia
175 Y11 **Austral Fracture Zone** *tectonic feature* S Pacific Ocean
181 O7 **Australia** *off.* Commonwealth of Australia. ◆ *commonwealth republic*
174 M8 **Australia** *continent*
183 Q12 **Australian Alps** ▲▲ SE Australia
183 R11 **Australian Capital Territory** *prev.* Federal Capital Territory. ◈ *territory* SE Australia
Australie, Bassin Nord de l' *see* North Australian Basin
Austral Islands *see* Australes, Îles
Austrava *see* Ostrov
109 T6 **Austria** *off.* Republic of Austria, *Ger.* Österreich. ◆ *republic* C Europe
92 K3 **Austurland** ◈ *region* SE Iceland
92 G10 **Austvågøya** *island* C Norway
Ausuituq *see* Grise Fiord
58 G13 **Autazes** Amazonas, N Brazil
102 M16 **Auterive** Haute-Garonne, S France
Autesiodorum *see* Auxerre
103 N2 **Authie** ≈ N France
Autissiodorum *see* Auxerre
40 K14 **Autlán** *var.* Autlán de Navarro. Jalisco, SW Mexico
Autlán de Navarro *see* Autlán
Autricum *see* Chartres
103 Q9 **Autun** *anc.* Ædua, Augustodunum. Saône-et-Loire, C France
Autz *see* Auce
99 H20 **Auvelais** Namur, S Belgium
103 P11 **Auvergne** ◈ *region* C France
102 M12 **Auvézère** ≈ W France
103 P7 **Auxerre** *anc.* Autesiodorum, Autissiodorum. Yonne, C France
103 N2 **Auxi-le-Château** Pas-de-Calais, N France
103 S8 **Auxonne** Côte d'Or, C France
55 P9 **Auyan Tebuy** ▲ SE Venezuela
103 O10 **Auzances** Creuse, C France
27 U8 **Ava** Missouri, C USA
142 M5 **Āvaj** Qazvin, N Iran
95 C15 **Avaldsnes** Rogaland, S Norway
103 Q8 **Avallon** Yonne, C France
102 K6 **Avaloirs, Mont des** ▲ NW France
35 S16 **Avalon** Santa Catalina Island, California, W USA
18 J17 **Avalon** New Jersey, NE USA
13 V13 **Avalon Peninsula** *peninsula* Newfoundland and Labrador, E Canada
197 Q11 **Avannaarsua** ◈ *province* N Greenland
60 K10 **Avaré** São Paulo, S Brazil
Avaricum *see* Bourges
190 H16 **Avarua** ○ (Cook Islands) Rarotonga, S Cook Islands
190 H16 **Avarua Harbour** *harbour* Rarotonga, S Cook Islands
Avasfelsőfalu *see* Negreşti-Oaş
38 L17 **Avatanak Island** *island* Aleutian Islands, Alaska, USA
190 B16 **Avatele** S Niue

◆ Country ● Country Capital ◇ Dependent Territory ○ Dependent Territory Capital ◈ Administrative Region × International Airport ▲ Mountain ▲▲ Mountain Range Ѫ Volcano ≈ River ◎ Lake ⊡ Reservoir

190 H16 **Avatiu** Rarotonga, S Cook Islands
190 H15 **Avatiu Harbour** *harbour* Rarotonga, S Cook Islands
Avdeyevka *see* Avdiyivka
114 J13 **Ávdira** Anatolikí Makedonía kai Thráki, NE Greece
117 X8 **Avdiyivka** *Rus.* Avdeyevka. Donets'ka Oblast', SE Ukraine
162 K7 **Avdzaga** C Mongolia
104 G6 **Ave** ∽ N Portugal
104 G7 **Aveiro** *anc.* Talabriga. Aveiro, W Portugal
104 G7 **Aveiro** ⬖ *district* N Portugal
Avela *see* Ávila
99 D18 **Avelgem** West-Vlaanderen, W Belgium
61 D20 **Avellaneda** Buenos Aires, E Argentina
107 L17 **Avellino** *anc.* Abellinum. Campania, S Italy
35 Q12 **Avenal** California, W USA
Avenio *see* Avignon
94 E8 **Averoya** *island* S Norway
107 K17 **Aversa** Campania, S Italy
33 N9 **Avery** Idaho, NW USA
25 W5 **Avery** Texas, SW USA
Aves, Islas de *see* Las Aves, Islas
Avesnes *see* Avesnes-sur-Helpe
103 Q2 **Avesnes-sur-Helpe** *var.* Avesnes. Nord, N France
64 G12 **Aves Ridge** *undersea feature* SE Caribbean Sea
95 M14 **Avesta** Dalarna, C Sweden
103 O14 **Aveyron** ⬖ *department* S France
103 N14 **Aveyron** ∽ S France
107 J15 **Avezzano** Abruzzo, C Italy
115 D16 **Avgó** ▲ C Greece
Avgustov *see* Augustów
Avgustovskiy Kanal *see* Augustowski, Kanał
96 J9 **Aviemore** N Scotland, UK
185 F21 **Aviemore, Lake** ◎ South Island, NZ
103 R15 **Avignon** *anc.* Avenio. Vaucluse, SE France
104 M7 **Ávila** *var.* Avila; *anc.* Abela, Abula, Abyla, Avela. Castilla-León, C Spain
104 L8 **Ávila** ⬖ *province* Castilla-León, C Spain
104 K2 **Avilés** Asturias, NW Spain
118 J4 **Avinurme** *Ger.* Awwinorm. Ida-Virumaa, NE Estonia
104 H10 **Avis** Portalegre, C Portugal
95 F22 **Avlum** Ringkøbing, C Denmark
182 M11 **Avoca** Victoria, SE Australia
29 T14 **Avoca** Iowa, C USA
182 M11 **Avoca River** ∽ Victoria, SE Australia
107 L25 **Avola** Sicilia, Italy, C Mediterranean Sea
18 F10 **Avon** New York, NE USA
29 P12 **Avon** South Dakota, N USA
97 M23 **Avon** ∽ S England, UK
97 L20 **Avon** ∽ C England, UK
66 K13 **Avondale** Arizona, SW USA
23 X13 **Avon Park** Florida, SE USA
102 J5 **Avranches** Manche, N France
103 O3 **Avre** ∽ N France
186 M6 **Avuavu** *var.* Kolotambu. Guadalcanal, C Solomon Islands
Avveel *see* Ivalo, Finland
Avveel *see* Ivalojoki, Finland
Avvil *see* Ivalo
77 O17 **Awaaso** *var.* Awaso. SW Ghana
141 X8 **Awābī** *var.* Al 'Awābī. NE Oman
184 L9 **Awakino** Waikato, North Island, NZ
142 M15 **'Awālī** C Bahrain
99 K19 **Awans** Liège, E Belgium
184 I2 **Awanui** Northland, North Island, NZ
148 M14 **Awārān** Baluchistān, SW Pakistan
81 K16 **Awara Plain** *plain* NE Kenya
81 M13 **Āwarē** Somali, E Ethiopia
138 M6 **'Awāriḍ, Wādī** *dry watercourse* E Syria
185 B20 **Awarua Point** *headland* South Island, NZ
81 J14 **Āwasa** Southern, S Ethiopia
80 K13 **Āwash** Afar, NE Ethiopia
80 K12 **Āwash** *var.* Hawash. ∽ C Ethiopia
Awaso *see* Awaaso
158 H7 **Awat** Xinjiang Uygur Zizhiqu, NW China
185 J15 **Awatere** ∽ South Island, NZ
75 O10 **Awbārī** SW Libya
75 N9 **Awbārī, Idhān** *var.* Edeyen d'Oubari. *desert* Algeria/Libya
80 C13 **Aweil** Northern Bahr el Ghazal, SW Sudan
96 H11 **Awe, Loch** ◎ W Scotland, UK
77 U16 **Awka** Anambra, SW Nigeria
39 O6 **Awuna River** ∽ Alaska, USA
Awwinorm *see* Avinurme
Ax *see* Dax
Axarfjördhur *see* Öxarfjördhur
103 N17 **Axat** Aude, S France
99 F16 **Axel** Zeeland, SW Netherlands
8 M2 **Axel Heiberg Island** *var.* Axel Heiburg. *island* Nunavut, N Canada
Axel Heiburg *see* Axel Heiberg Island
77 O17 **Axim** S Ghana
114 F13 **Axiós** *var.* Vardar. ∽ Greece/FYR Macedonia *see also* Vardar
103 N17 **Ax-les-Thermes** Ariège, S France
120 D11 **Ayachi, Jbel** ▲ C Morocco
61 D22 **Ayacucho** Buenos Aires, E Argentina
57 F15 **Ayacucho** Ayacucho, S Peru
57 E16 **Ayacucho** *off.* Departamento de Ayacucho. ⬖ *department* SW Peru
145 W11 **Ayagoz** *var.* Ayaguz, *Kaz.* Ayaköz; *prev.* Sergiopol. Vostochnyy Kazakhstan, E Kazakhstan
145 V12 **Ayagoz** *var.* Ayaguz, *Kaz.* Ayaköz. ∽ E Kazakhstan
Ayaguz *see* Ayagoz
Ayakagytma *see* Oyoqig'itma
Ayakkuduk *see* Oyoqquduq
158 L10 **Ayakkum Hu** ◎ NW China
Ayaköz *see* Ayagoz
104 H14 **Ayamonte** Andalucía, S Spain
123 S11 **Ayan** Khabarovskiy Kray, E Russian Federation
136 J10 **Ayancık** Sinop, N Turkey
55 S9 **Ayanganna Mountain** ▲ C Guyana
77 U16 **Ayangba** Kogi, C Nigeria
123 U7 **Ayanka** Koryakskiy Avtonomnyy Okrug, E Russian Federation
54 E7 **Ayapel** Córdoba, NW Colombia
136 H12 **Ayaş** Ankara, N Turkey
57 I16 **Ayaviri** Puno, S Peru
149 P3 **Āybak** *var.* Aibak, Haibak; *prev.* Samangān. Samangān, NE Afghanistan
147 N10 **Aydarko'l Ko'li** *Rus.* Ozero Aydarkul'. ◎ C Uzbekistan
Aydarkul', Ozero *see* Aydarko'l Ko'li
21 W10 **Ayden** North Carolina, SE USA
136 C15 **Aydın** *var.* Aidin; *anc.* Tralles. Aydın, SW Turkey
136 C15 **Aydın** *var.* Aïdin. ⬖ *province* SW Turkey
136 I17 **Aydıncık** İçel, S Turkey
136 C15 **Aydın Dağları** ▲▲ W Turkey
158 L6 **Aydingkol Hu** ◎ NW China
127 X7 **Aydyrlinskiy** Orenburgskaya Oblast', W Russian Federation
105 S4 **Ayerbe** Aragón, NE Spain
Ayers Rock *see* Uluru
Ayeyarwady *see* Irrawaddy
Ayiá *see* Agiá
Ayia Napa *see* Agía Nápa
Ayia Phyla *see* Agía Fýlaxis
Ayiásos/Ayiássos *see* Agiasós
Áyios Evstrátios *see* Ágios Efstrátios
Áyios Kírikos *see* Ágios Kírykos
Áyios Nikólaos *see* Ágios Nikólaos
Ayios Seryios *see* Yeniboğaziçi
80 I11 **Āykel** Amhara, N Ethiopia
123 N9 **Aykhal** Respublika Sakha (Yakutiya), NE Russian Federation
14 J12 **Aylen Lake** ◎ Ontario, SE Canada
97 N21 **Aylesbury** SE England, UK
105 O6 **Ayllón** Castilla-León, N Spain
14 F17 **Aylmer** Ontario, S Canada
14 L12 **Aylmer** Québec, SE Canada
15 R12 **Aylmer, Lac** ◎ Québec, SE Canada
8 L9 **Aylmer Lake** ◎ Northwest Territories, NW Canada
145 V14 **Aynabulak** Almaty, SE Kazakhstan
138 K2 **'Ayn al 'Arab** Ḥalab, N Syria
Aynayn *see* 'Aynīn
139 V12 **'Ayn Ḥamūd** S Iraq
147 P12 **Ayní** *prev. Rus.* Varzimanor Ayni. W Tajikistan
140 M10 **'Aynīn** *var.* Aynayn. *spring/well* SW Saudi Arabia
21 U12 **Aynor** South Carolina, SE USA
139 Q7 **'Ayn Zāzūh** C Iraq
153 N12 **Ayodhya** Uttar Pradesh, N India
123 S6 **Ayon, Ostrov** *island* NE Russian Federation
105 R11 **Ayora** País Valenciano, E Spain
77 Q11 **Ayorou** Tillabéri, W Niger
79 E16 **Ayos** Centre, S Cameroon
76 L5 **'Ayoûn 'Abd el Mâlek** *well* N Mauritania
76 K10 **'Ayoûn el 'Atroûs** *var.* Aïoun el Atrous, Aïoun el Atroûss. Hodh el Gharbi, SE Mauritania
96 I13 **Ayr** W Scotland, UK
96 I13 **Ayr** ∽ W Scotland, UK
96 I13 **Ayrshire** *cultural region* SW Scotland, UK
Aysen *see* Aisén
80 L12 **Āysha** Somali, E Ethiopia
144 L14 **Ayteke Bi** *Kaz.* Zhangaqazaly *prev.* Novokazalinsk. Kyzylorda, SW Kazakhstan
146 K8 **Aytim** Navoiy Viloyati, N Uzbekistan
181 W4 **Ayton** Queensland, NE Australia
114 M9 **Aytos** Burgas, E Bulgaria
171 T11 **Ayu, Kepulauan** *island group* E Indonesia
A Yun Pa *see* Cheo Reo
169 V11 **Ayu, Tanjung** *headland* Borneo, N Indonesia
40 K13 **Ayutla** Jalisco, C Mexico
41 P16 **Ayutlá** *var.* Ayutla de los Libres. Guerrero, S Mexico
Ayutla de los Libres *see* Ayutlá
167 O11 **Ayutthaya** *var.* Phra Nakhon Si Ayutthaya. Phra Nakhon Si Ayutthaya, C Thailand
136 B13 **Ayvalık** Balıkesir, W Turkey
99 L20 **Aywaille** Liège, E Belgium
141 R13 **'Aywat aş Şay'ar, Wādī** *seasonal river* N Yemen
Azaffal *see* Azeffâl
105 T9 **Azahar, Costa del** *coastal region* E Spain
105 S6 **Azaila** Aragón, NE Spain
104 F10 **Azambuja** Lisboa, C Portugal
153 N13 **Āzamgarh** Uttar Pradesh, N India
77 O9 **Azaouâd** *desert* C Mali
77 S10 **Azaouagh, Vallée de l'** *var.* Azaouak. ∽ W Niger
Azaouak *see* Azaouagh, Vallée de l'
61 F14 **Azara** Misiones, NE Argentina
142 K3 **Āzarān** Āzarbāyjān-e Khāvarī, N Iran
Azärbaycan/Azärbaycan Respublikası *see* Azerbaijan
Āzarbāyjān-e Bākhtarī *see* Āzarbāyjān-e Gharbī
142 I4 **Āzarbāyjān-e Gharbī** *off.* Ostān-e Āzarbāyjān-e Gharbī; *Eng.* West Azerbaijan *prev.* Āzarbāyjān-e Bākhtarī. ⬖ *province* NW Iran
Āzarbāyjān-e Khāvarī *see* Āzarbāyjān-e Sharqī
142 J3 **Āzarbāyjān-e Sharqī** *off.* Ostān-e Āzarbāyjān-e Sharqī, *Eng.* East Azerbaijan; *prev.* Āzarbāyjān-e Sharqī. ⬖ *province* NW Iran
77 W13 **Azare** Bauchi, N Nigeria
119 M19 **Azarychy** *Rus.* Ozarichi. Homyel'skaya Voblasts', SE Belarus
102 L8 **Azay-le-Rideau** Indre-et-Loire, C France
138 I2 **A'zāz** Ḥalab, NW Syria
76 H7 **Azeffâl** *var.* Azaffal. *desert* Mauritania/Western Sahara
137 V12 **Azerbaijan** *off.* Azerbaijani Republic, *Az.* Azärbaycan, Azärbaycan Respublikası; *prev.* Azerbaijan SSR. ◆ *republic* SE Asia
145 T7 **Azhbulat, Ozero** ◎ NE Kazakhstan
74 F7 **Azilal** C Morocco
Azimabad *see* Patna
19 O6 **Aziscohos Lake** ⊡ Maine, NE USA
Azizbekov *see* Vayk'
Azizie *see* Telish
Aziziya *see* Al 'Azīzīyah
127 T4 **Aznakayevo** Respublika Tatarstan, W Russian Federation
56 C8 **Azogues** Cañar, S Ecuador
64 N2 **Azores** *var.* Açores, Ilhas dos Açores, *Port.* Arquipélago dos Açores. *island group* Portugal, NE Atlantic Ocean
64 L8 **Azores-Biscay Rise** *undersea feature* E Atlantic Ocean
Azotos/Azotus *see* Ashdod
78 K11 **Azoum, Bahr** *seasonal river* SE Chad
126 L12 **Azov** Rostovskaya Oblast', SW Russian Federation
126 J13 **Azov, Sea of** *Rus.* Azovskoye More, *Ukr.* Azovs'ke More. *sea* NE Black Sea
Azovs'ke More/Azovskoye More *see* Azov, Sea of
138 I10 **Azraq, Wāḥat al** *oasis* N Jordan
Āzro *see* Āzrow
74 G6 **Azrou** C Morocco
149 R5 **Āzrow** *var.* Āzro. Lowgar, E Afghanistan
37 P8 **Aztec** New Mexico, SW USA
36 M13 **Aztec Peak** ▲ Arizona, SW USA
45 N9 **Azua** *var.* Azua de Compostela. S Dominican Republic
Azua de Compostela *see* Azua
104 K12 **Azuaga** Extremadura, W Spain
56 B8 **Azuay** ⬖ *province* W Ecuador
164 C13 **Azuchi-Ō-shima** *island* SW Japan
105 O11 **Azuer** ∽ C Spain
43 S17 **Azuero, Península de** *peninsula* S Panama
62 I6 **Azufre, Volcán** *var.* Volcán Lastarria. ▲ N Chile
116 J12 **Azuga** Prahova, SE Romania
61 C22 **Azul** Buenos Aires, E Argentina
62 I8 **Azul, Cerro** ▲ NW Argentina
56 E12 **Azul, Cordillera** ▲▲ C Peru
165 P11 **Azuma-san** ▲ Honshū, C Japan
103 V15 **Azur, Côte d'** *coastal region* SE France
191 Z3 **Azur Lagoon** ◎ Kiritimati, E Kiribati
'Azza *see* Gaza
Az Zāb al Kabīr *see* Great Zab
138 H7 **Az Zabdānī** *var.* Zabadani. Dimashq, W Syria
141 W8 **Az Zāhirah** *desert* NW Oman
141 S6 **Az Zahrān** *Eng.* Dhahran. Ash Sharqīyah, NE Saudi Arabia
141 R6 **Az Zahrān al Khubar** *var.* Dhahran Al Khobar. ✕ Ash Sharqīyah, NE Saudi Arabia
Az Zaqāzīq *see* Zagazig
138 H10 **Az Zarqā'** *var.* Zarqa. Az Zarqā', NW Jordan
138 I11 **Az Zarqā'** *off.* Muḥāfaẓat az Zarqā', *var.* Zarqa. ⬖ *governorate* N Jordan
75 O7 **Az Zāwiyah** *var.* Zawia. NW Libya
141 N15 **Az Zaydīyah** W Yemen
74 I11 **Azzel Matti, Sebkha** *var.* Sebkra Azz el Matti. *salt flat* C Algeria
141 P6 **Az Zilfī** Ar Riyāḍ, N Saudi Arabia
139 Y13 **Az Zubayr** *var.* Al Zubair. SE Iraq
Az Zuqur *see* Jabal Zuuqar, Jazīrat

B

187 X15 **Ba** *prev.* Mba. Viti Levu, W Fiji
Ba *see* Đa Răng
171 P17 **Baa** Pulau Rote, C Indonesia
138 H7 **Baalbek** *var.* Ba'labakk; *anc.* Heliopolis. E Lebanon
108 G8 **Baar** Zug, N Switzerland
81 L17 **Baardheere** *var.* Bardere, *It.* Bardera. Gedo, SW Somalia
80 Q12 **Baargaal** Bari, NE Somalia
99 I15 **Baarle-Hertog** Antwerpen, N Belgium
99 I15 **Baarle-Nassau** Noord-Brabant, S Netherlands
98 J11 **Baarn** Utrecht, C Netherlands
114 D13 **Baba** *var.* Buševa, *Gk.* Varnoús. ▲▲ FYR Macedonia/Greece
76 H10 **Bababé** Brakna, W Mauritania
136 G10 **Baba Burnu** *headland* NW Turkey
117 N13 **Babadag** Tulcea, SE Romania
137 X10 **Babadağ Dağı** ▲ NE Azerbaijan
146 H14 **Babadaýhan** *Rus.* Babadaykhan; *prev.* Kirovsk. Ahal Welaýaty, C Turkmenistan
Babadaykhan *see* Babadaýhan
146 G14 **Babadurmaz** Ahal Welaýaty, C Turkmenistan
114 M12 **Babaeski** Kırklareli, NW Turkey
139 T4 **Bāba Gurgur** N Iraq
56 B7 **Babahoyo** *prev.* Bodegas. Los Ríos, C Ecuador
149 P5 **Bābā, Kūh-e** ▲▲ C Afghanistan
171 N12 **Babana** Sulawesi, C Indonesia
Babao *see* Qilian
171 Q12 **Babar, Kepulauan** *island group* E Indonesia
171 T12 **Babar, Pulau** *island* Kepulauan Babar, E Indonesia
152 G4 **Bābāsar Pass** *pass* India/Pakistan
Babashy, Gory *see* Babaşy
146 C9 **Babaşy** *Rus.* Gory Babashy. ▲▲ W Turkmenistan
168 M13 **Babat** Sumatera, W Indonesia
Babatag, Khrebet *see* Bobotogh, Qatorkŭhi
81 H21 **Babati** Arusha, NE Tanzania
124 J13 **Babayevo** Vologodskaya Oblast', NW Russian Federation
127 Q15 **Babayurt** Respublika Dagestan, SW Russian Federation
33 P6 **Babb** Montana, NW USA
29 X4 **Babbitt** Minnesota, N USA
188 E9 **Babeldaob** *var.* Babeldaop, Babelthuap. *island* N Palau
Babeldaop *see* Babeldaob
141 N17 **Bab el Mandeb** *strait* Gulf of Aden/Red Sea
Babelthuap *see* Babeldaob
111 K17 **Babia Góra** *var.* Babia Hora. ▲ Slovakia/Poland
Babia Hora *see* Babia Góra
Babian Jiang *see* Black River
Babichi *see* Babichy
119 N19 **Babichy** *Rus.* Babichi. Homyel'skaya Voblasts', SE Belarus
112 I10 **Babina Greda** Vukovar-Srijem, E Croatia
10 K13 **Babine Lake** ◎ British Columbia, SW Canada
143 O4 **Bābol** *var.* Babul, Balfrush, Barfrush; *prev.* Barfurush. Māzandarān, N Iran
143 O4 **Bābolsar** *var.* Babulsar; *prev.* Meshed-i-Sar. Māzandarān, N Iran
36 L16 **Baboquivari Peak** ▲ Arizona, SW USA
79 G15 **Baboua** Nana-Mambéré, W Central African Republic
119 M17 **Babruysk** *Rus.* Bobruysk. Mahilyowskaya Voblasts', E Belarus
Babu *see* Hezhou
Babul *see* Bābol
Babulsar *see* Bābolsar
113 O19 **Babuna** ∽ C FYR Macedonia
113 O19 **Babuna** ▲▲ C FYR Macedonia
148 K7 **Bābūs, Dasht-e** *Pash.* Bebas, Dasht-i. ▲▲ W Afghanistan
171 O1 **Babuyan Channel** *channel* N Philippines
171 O1 **Babuyan Island** *island* N Philippines
139 T9 **Babylon** *site of ancient city* C Iraq
112 J9 **Bač** *Ger.* Batsch. Serbia, NW Serbia and Montenegro (Yugo.)
58 M13 **Bacabal** Maranhão, E Brazil
41 Y14 **Bacalar** Quintana Roo, SE Mexico
41 Y14 **Bacalar Chico, Boca** *strait* SE Mexico
171 Q12 **Bacan, Kepulauan** *island group* E Indonesia
171 S12 **Bacan, Pulau** *prev.* Batjan. *island* Maluku, E Indonesia
116 L10 **Bacău** *Hung.* Bákó. Bacău, NE Romania
116 K11 **Bacău** ⬖ *county* E Romania
Bắc Bộ, Vịnh *see* Tongking, Gulf of
167 T5 **Bắc Can** Bắc Thai, N Vietnam
103 T5 **Baccarat** Meurthe-et-Moselle, NE France
183 N12 **Bacchus Marsh** Victoria, SE Australia
40 H4 **Bacerac** Sonora, NW Mexico
116 L10 **Băceşti** Vaslui, E Romania
167 T6 **Bắc Giang** Ha Bắc, N Vietnam
54 I5 **Bachaquero** Zulia, NW Venezuela
Bacher *see* Pohorje
118 M13 **Bacheykava** *Rus.* Bocheykovo. Vitsyebskaya Voblasts', N Belarus
40 I5 **Bachíniva** Chihuahua, N Mexico
158 G8 **Bachu** Xinjiang Uygur Zizhiqu, NW China
9 N8 **Back** ∽ Nunavut, N Canada
112 K10 **Bačka Palanka** *prev.* Palanka. Serbia, NW Serbia and Montenegro (Yugo.)
112 K8 **Bačka Topola** *Hung.* Topolya; *prev. Hung.* Bácstopolya. Serbia, N Serbia and Montenegro (Yugo.)
95 J17 **Bäckefors** Västra Götaland, S Sweden
Bäckermühle Schulzenmühle *see* Żywiec
95 L16 **Bäckhammar** Värmland, C Sweden
112 K9 **Bački Petrovac** *Hung.* Petrőcz; *prev.* Petrovac, Petrovácz. Serbia, NW Serbia and Montenegro (Yugo.)
101 I21 **Backnang** Baden-Württemberg, SW Germany
167 S15 **Bac Liêu** *var.* Vinh Loi. Minh Hai, S Vietnam
167 T6 **Bắc Ninh** Ha Bắc, N Vietnam
40 G4 **Bacoachi** Sonora, NW Mexico
171 P6 **Bacolod** *off.* Bacolod City. Negros, C Philippines
171 O4 **Baco, Mount** ▲ Mindoro, N Philippines
111 K25 **Bácsalmás** Bács-Kiskun, S Hungary
Bácsjózseffalva *see* Žednik
111 J24 **Bács-Kiskun** *off.* Bács-Kiskun Megye. ⬖ *county* S Hungary
Bácsszenttamás *see* Srbobran
Bácstopolya *see* Bačka Topola
Bactra *see* Balkh
Bada *see* Xilin
155 F21 **Badagara** Kerala, SW India
101 M24 **Bad Aibling** Bayern, SE Germany
162 I13 **Badain Jaran Shamo** *desert* N China
104 J11 **Badajoz** *anc.* Pax Augusta. Extremadura, W Spain
104 J11 **Badajoz** ⬖ *province* Extremadura, W Spain
149 S2 **Badakhshān** ⬖ *province* NE Afghanistan
105 W6 **Badalona** *anc.* Baetulo. Cataluña, E Spain
154 O11 **Bādāmapāhārh** Orissa, E India
152 K8 **Badarīnāth** ▲ N India
169 O10 **Badas, Kepulauan** *island group* W Indonesia
109 S6 **Bad Aussee** Salzburg, E Austria
31 S8 **Bad Axe** Michigan, N USA
101 G16 **Bad Berleburg** Nordrhein-Westfalen, W Germany
101 L17 **Bad Blankenburg** Thüringen, C Germany
Bad Borseck *see* Borsec
101 G18 **Bad Camberg** Hessen, W Germany
100 L8 **Bad Doberan** Mecklenburg-Vorpommern, N Germany
101 N14 **Bad Düben** Sachsen, E Germany
109 X4 **Baden** *var.* Baden bei Wien; *anc.* Aquae Panoniae, Thermae Pannonicae. Niederösterreich, NE Austria
108 F9 **Baden** Aargau, N Switzerland
101 G21 **Baden-Baden** *anc.* Aurelia Aquensis. Baden-Württemberg, SW Germany
Baden bei Wien *see* Baden
101 G22 **Baden-Württemberg** *Fr.* Bade-Wurtemberg. ⬖ *state* SW Germany
112 A10 **Baderna** Istra, NW Croatia
Bade-Wurtemberg *see* Baden-Württemberg
101 H20 **Bad Fredrichshall** Baden-Württemberg, S Germany
100 P11 **Bad Freienwalde** Brandenburg, NE Germany
109 Q8 **Badgastein** *var.* Gastein. Salzburg, NW Austria
Badger State *see* Wisconsin
148 L4 **Bādghīs** ⬖ *province* NW Afghanistan
109 T5 **Bad Hall** Oberösterreich, N Austria
101 J14 **Bad Harzburg** Niedersachsen, C Germany
101 I16 **Bad Hersfeld** Hessen, C Germany
98 I10 **Badhoevedorp** Noord-Holland, C Netherlands
109 Q8 **Bad Hofgastein** Salzburg, NW Austria
Bad Homburg *see* Bad Homburg vor der Höhe
101 G18 **Bad Homburg vor der Höhe** *var.* Bad Homburg. Hessen, W Germany
101 E17 **Bad Honnef** Nordrhein-Westfalen, W Germany
149 Q17 **Badīn** Sind, SE Pakistan
21 S10 **Badin Lake** ⊡ North Carolina, SE USA
40 I8 **Badiraguato** Sinaloa, C Mexico
109 R6 **Bad Ischl** Oberösterreich, N Austria
Badjawa *see* Bajawa
Badje-Sohppar *see* Övre Soppero
101 J18 **Bad Kissingen** Bayern, SE Germany
Bad Königswart *see* Lázně Kynžvart
101 F19 **Bad Kreuznach** Rheinland-Pfalz, SW Germany
101 F24 **Bad Krozingen** Baden-Württemberg, SW Germany
101 G16 **Bad Laasphe** Nordrhein-Westfalen, W Germany
28 J6 **Badlands** *physical region* North Dakota, N USA
101 K16 **Bad Langensalza** Thüringen, C Germany
109 T3 **Bad Leonfelden** Oberösterreich, N Austria
101 I20 **Bad Mergentheim** Baden-Württemberg, SW Germany
101 H17 **Bad Nauheim** Hessen, W Germany
101 E17 **Bad Neuenahr-Ahrweiler** Rheinland-Pfalz, W Germany
Bad Neustadt *see* Bad Neustadt an der Saale
101 J18 **Bad Neustadt an der Saale** *var.* Bad Neustadt. Berlin, C Germany
Badnur *see* Betūl
100 H13 **Bad Oeynhausen** Nordrhein-Westfalen, NW Germany
100 J9 **Bad Oldesloe** Schleswig-Holstein, N Germany
77 Q16 **Badou** C Togo
Bad Polzin *see* Połczyn-Zdrój
100 H13 **Bad Pyrmont** Niedersachsen, C Germany
109 X9 **Bad Radkersburg** Steiermark, SE Austria
139 V8 **Badrah** E Iraq
162 J6 **Badrah** Hövsgöl, N Mongolia
101 N24 **Bad Reichenhall** Bayern, SE Germany
140 K8 **Badr Ḥunayn** Al Madīnah, W Saudi Arabia
28 M10 **Bad River** ∽ South Dakota, N USA
30 K4 **Bad River** ∽ Wisconsin, N USA
100 H13 **Bad Salzuflen** Nordrhein-Westfalen, NW Germany
101 J16 **Bad Salzungen** Thüringen, C Germany
109 V8 **Bad Sankt Leonhard im Lavanttal** Kärnten, S Austria
100 K9 **Bad Schwartau** Schleswig-Holstein, N Germany
101 L24 **Bad Tölz** Bayern, SE Germany
181 U1 **Badu Island** *island* Queensland, NE Australia
155 K25 **Badulla** Uva Province, C Sri Lanka
109 X5 **Bad Vöslau** Niederösterreich, NE Austria
101 I24 **Bad Waldsee** Baden-Württemberg, S Germany
35 U11 **Badwater Basin** *depression* California, W USA
101 J20 **Bad Windsheim** Bayern, C Germany
101 J23 **Bad Wörishofen** Bayern, S Germany
100 G10 **Bad Zwischenahn** Niedersachsen, NW Germany
104 M13 **Baena** Andalucía, S Spain
Baeterrae/Baeterrae Septimanorum *see* Béziers
Baetic Cordillera/Baetic Mountains *see* Béticos, Sistemas
Baetulo *see* Badalona
57 K18 **Baeza** Napo, NE Ecuador
105 N13 **Baeza** Andalucía, S Spain
79 D15 **Bafang** Ouest, W Cameroon
76 H12 **Bafatá** C Guinea-Bissau
149 U5 **Baffa** North-West Frontier Province, NW Pakistan
197 O11 **Baffin Basin** *undersea feature* N Labrador Sea
197 N12 **Baffin Bay** *bay* Canada/Greenland
25 T15 **Baffin Bay** *inlet* Texas, SW USA
196 M12 **Baffin Island** *island* Nunavut, NE Canada
79 E15 **Bafia** Centre, C Cameroon
77 R14 **Bafilo** NE Togo
76 J12 **Bafing** ∽ W Africa
76 J12 **Bafoulabé** Kayes, W Mali
79 D15 **Bafoussam** Ouest, W Cameroon
143 R9 **Bāfq** Yazd, C Iran
136 L10 **Bafra** Samsun, N Turkey
136 L10 **Bafra Burnu** *headland* N Turkey
143 S12 **Bāft** Kermān, S Iran
79 N18 **Bafwabalinga** Orientale, NE Dem. Rep. Congo
79 N18 **Bafwaboli** Orientale, NE Dem. Rep. Congo
79 N17 **Bafwasende** Orientale, NE Dem. Rep. Congo
42 K13 **Bagaces** Guanacaste, NW Costa Rica
153 O12 **Bagaha** Bihār, N India
155 F16 **Bāgalkot** Karnātaka, W India
81 J22 **Bagamoyo** Pwani, E Tanzania
168 J8 **Bagan Datuk** *var.* Bagan Datok. Perak, Peninsular Malaysia
171 R7 **Baganga** Mindanao, S Philippines
168 J9 **Bagansiapiapi** *var.* Pasirpangarayan. Sumatera, W Indonesia
162 M8 **Baga Nuur** *var.* Nüürst. Töv, C Mongolia
Bagaria *see* Bagheria
77 T11 **Bagaroua** Tahoua, W Niger
79 I20 **Bagata** Bandundu, W Dem. Rep. Congo
Bagdad *see* Baghdād
123 O13 **Bagdarin** Respublika Buryatiya, S Russian Federation
61 G17 **Bagé** Rio Grande do Sul, S Brazil
Bagenalstown *see* Muine Bheag
Bagerhat *see* Bagherhat
103 P16 **Bages et de Sigean, Étang de** ◎ S France
33 W17 **Baggs** Wyoming, C USA
154 F11 **Bāgh** Madhya Pradesh, C India
139 T8 **Baghdād** *var.* Bagdad, *Eng.* Baghdad. ● (Iraq) C Iraq
139 T8 **Baghdād** ✕ C Iraq
153 T16 **Bagherhat** *var.* Bagerhat. Khulna, S Bangladesh
107 J23 **Bagheria** *var.* Bagaria. Sicilia, Italy, C Mediterranean Sea
143 S10 **Bāghīn** Kermān, C Iran
149 Q3 **Baghlān** Baghlān, NE Afghanistan
149 Q3 **Baghlān** *var.* Bāghlān. ⬖ *province* NE Afghanistan
148 M7 **Bāghrān** Helmand, S Afghanistan
29 T4 **Bagley** Minnesota, N USA
106 H10 **Bagnacavallo** Emilia-Romagna, C Italy
102 K16 **Bagnères-de-Bigorre** Hautes-Pyrénées, S France
102 L17 **Bagnères-de-Luchon** Hautes-Pyrénées, S France
106 F11 **Bagni di Lucca** Toscana, C Italy
106 H11 **Bagno di Romagna** Emilia-Romagna, C Italy
103 R14 **Bagnols-sur-Cèze** Gard, S France
162 M14 **Bag Nur** ◎ N China
171 P6 **Bago** *off.* Bago City. Negros, C Philippines
Bago *see* Pegu
76 M13 **Bagoé** ∽ Ivory Coast/Mali
Bagrāmē *see* Bagrāmī
149 R5 **Bagrāmī** *var.* Bagrāmē. Kābul, E Afghanistan
119 B14 **Bagrationovsk** *Ger.* Preussisch Eylau. Kaliningradskaya Oblast', W Russian Federation
Bagrax *see* Bohu
Bagrax Hu *see* Bosten Hu
56 C10 **Bagua** Amazonas, NE Peru
171 O2 **Baguio** *off.* Baguio City. Luzon, N Philippines
77 V9 **Bagzane, Monts** ▲ N Niger
Bāḥah, Minṭaqat al *see* Al Bāḥah
Bahama Islands *see* Bahamas

◆ Country ● Country Capital ◇ Dependent Territory ○ Dependent Territory Capital ⬖ Administrative Region ✕ International Airport ▲ Mountain ▲▲ Mountain Range Ж Volcano ∽ River ◎ Lake ⊡ Reservoir

44 H3 **Bahamas** off. Commonwealth of the Bahamas. ◆ commonwealth republic N West Indies
(0) L13 **Bahamas** var. Bahama Islands. island group N West Indies
153 S15 **Baharampur** prev. Berhampore. West Bengal, NE India
146 E12 **Baharly** var. Bäherden, Rus. Bakharden; prev. Bakherden. Ahal Welaýaty, C Turkmenistan
149 U10 **Bahāwalnagar** Punjab, E Pakistan
149 T11 **Bahāwalpur** Punjab, E Pakistan
136 L16 **Bahçe** Osmaniye, S Turkey
160 J8 **Ba He** ≈ C China
Bäherden see Baharly
59 N16 **Bahia** off. Estado da Bahia. ◈ state E Brazil
61 B24 **Bahía Blanca** Buenos Aires, E Argentina
40 L15 **Bahía Bufadero** Michoacán de Ocampo, SW Mexico
63 J19 **Bahía Bustamante** Chubut, SE Argentina
40 D5 **Bahía de los Ángeles** Baja California, NW Mexico
40 C6 **Bahía de Tortugas** Baja California Sur, W Mexico
42 J4 **Bahía, Islas de la** Eng. Bay Islands. island group N Honduras
40 E5 **Bahía Kino** Sonora, NW Mexico
40 E9 **Bahía Magdalena** var. Puerto Magdalena. Baja California Sur, W Mexico
54 C8 **Bahía Solano** var. Ciudad Mutis, Solano. Chocó, W Colombia
80 I11 **Bahir Dar** var. Bahr Dar, Bahrdar Giyorgis. Amhara, N Ethiopia
141 X8 **Bahlā'** var. Bahlah, Bahlat. NW Oman
Bāhla see Bālān
Bahlah/Bahlat see Bahlā'
152 M11 **Bahraich** Uttar Pradesh, N India
143 M14 **Bahrain** off. State of Bahrain, Dawlat al Bahrayn, Ar. Al Baḥrayn; prev. Bahrein, anc. Tylos or Tyros. ◆ monarchy SW Asia
142 M14 **Bahrain** ✕ C Bahrain
142 M15 **Bahrain, Gulf of** gulf Persian Gulf, NW Arabian Sea
138 I7 **Baḥrat Mallāḥah** ◎ W Syria
Bahrayn, Dawlat al see Bahrain
Bahr Dar/Bahrdar Giyorgis see Bahir Dar
Bahrein see Bahrain
81 E16 **Bahr el Gabel** ◈ state S Sudan
80 E13 **Bahr ez Zaref** ≈ C Sudan
67 R8 **Bahr Kameur** ≈ N Central African Republic
Bahr Tabariya, Sea of see Tiberias, Lake
143 W15 **Bāhū Kalāt** Sīstān va Balūchestān, SE Iran
118 N13 **Bahushewsk** Rus. Bogushëvsk. Vitsyebskaya Voblasts', NE Belarus
Bai see Tagow Bāy
116 G13 **Baia de Aramă** Mehedinți, SW Romania
116 G11 **Baia de Criș** Ger. Altenburg, Hung. Körösbánya. Hunedoara, SW Romania
83 A16 **Baia dos Tigres** Namibe, SW Angola
82 A13 **Baia Farta** Benguela, W Angola
116 H9 **Baia Mare** Ger. Frauenbach, Hung. Nagybánya; prev. Neustadt. Maramureș, NW Romania
116 H8 **Baia Sprie** Ger. Mittelstadt, Hung. Felsőbánya. Maramureș, NW Romania
78 G13 **Baïbokoum** Logone-Oriental, SW Chad
160 F12 **Baicao Ling** ▲ SW China
163 U9 **Baicheng** var. Pai-ch'eng; prev. T'aon-an. Jilin, NE China
158 I6 **Baicheng** var. Bay. Xinjiang Uygur Zizhiqu, NW China
116 J13 **Băicoi** Prahova, SE Romania
Baidoa see Baydhabo
15 U6 **Baie-Comeau** Québec, SE Canada
15 T7 **Baie-des-Bacon** Québec, SE Canada
15 S8 **Baie-des-Rochers** Québec, SE Canada
15 U6 **Baie-des-Sables** Québec, SE Canada
12 K11 **Baie-du-Poste** Québec, SE Canada
172 H17 **Baie Lazare** Mahé, NE Seychelles
45 Y5 **Baie-Mahault** Basse Terre, C Guadeloupe
15 R9 **Baie-St-Paul** Québec, SE Canada
15 V5 **Baie-Trinité** Québec, SE Canada
13 T11 **Baie Verte** Newfoundland and Labrador, SE Canada
163 X11 **Baihe** prev. Erdaobaihe. Jilin, NE China
Baiguan see Shangyu
139 U11 **Bā'ij al Mahdī** S Iraq
Baiji see Bayjī
Baikal, Lake see Baykal, Ozero
Bailādila see Kirandul
Baile an Chaistil see Ballycastle
Baile an Róba see Ballinrobe
Baile an tSratha see Ballintra
Baile Átha an Rí see Athenry
Baile Átha Buí see Athboy
Baile Átha Cliath see Dublin
Baile Átha Fhirdhia see Ardee
Baile Átha Í see Athy
Baile Átha Luain see Athlone
Baile Átha Troim see Trim
Baile Brigín see Balbriggan
Baile Easa Dara see Ballysadare
116 I13 **Băile Govora** Vâlcea, SW Romania
116 F13 **Băile Herculane** Ger. Herkulesbad, Hung. Herkulesfürdő. Caraș-Severin, SW Romania
Baile Locha Riach see Loughrea
Baile Mhistéala see Mitchelstown
Baile Monaidh see Ballymoney
105 N12 **Bailén** Andalucía, S Spain
Baile na hInse see Ballynahinch
Baile na Lorgan see Castleblayney
Baile na Mainistreach see Newtownabbey
Baile Nua na hArda see Newtownards
116 I12 **Băile Olănești** Vâlcea, SW Romania
116 H14 **Băilești** Dolj, SW Romania
163 N12 **Bailingmiao** var. Darhan Muminggan Lianheqi. Nei Mongol Zizhiqu, N China
58 K11 **Bailique, Ilha** island NE Brazil
103 O1 **Bailleul** Nord, N France
78 H12 **Ba Illi** Chari-Baguirmi, SW Chad
159 V12 **Bailong Jiang** ≈ C China
82 C13 **Bailundo** Port. Vila Teixeira da Silva. Huambo, C Angola
159 T13 **Baima** var. Sêraitang. Qinghai, C China
Baima see Baxoi
186 C8 **Baimuru** Gulf, S PNG
158 M16 **Bainang** Xizang Zizhiqu, W China
23 S8 **Bainbridge** Georgia, SE USA
171 O17 **Baing** Pulau Sumba, SE Indonesia
158 M14 **Baingoin** Xizang Zizhiqu, W China
104 G2 **Baio Grande** Galicia, NW Spain
104 G4 **Baiona** Galicia, NW Spain
163 V7 **Baiquan** Heilongjiang, NE China
Bā'ir see Bāyir
158 I11 **Bairab Co** ◎ W China
25 Q7 **Baird** Texas, SW USA
39 N7 **Baird Mountains** ▲▲ Alaska, USA
Baireuth see Bayreuth
190 H3 **Bairiki** ● (Kiribati) Tarawa, NW Kiribati
Bairin Youqi see Daban
Bairin Zuoqi see Lindong
145 P17 **Bairkum** Kaz. Bayyrqum. Yuzhnyy Kazakhstan, S Kazakhstan
183 P12 **Bairnsdale** Victoria, SE Australia
171 P6 **Bais** Negros, S Philippines
102 L15 **Baïse** var. Baise. ≈ S France
163 W11 **Baishan** prev. Hunjiang. Jilin, NE China
Baishan see Mashan
118 F12 **Baisogala** Šiauliai, C Lithuania
189 Q7 **Baiti** N Nauru
104 G13 **Baixo Alentejo** physical region S Portugal
64 P5 **Baixo, Ilhéu de** island Madeira, Portugal, NE Atlantic Ocean
83 E15 **Baixo Longa** Cuando Cubango, SE Angola
159 V10 **Baiyin** Gansu, C China
160 E8 **Baiyü** var. Jianshe. Sichuan, C China
161 N14 **Baiyun** ✕ (Guangzhou) Guangdong, S China
160 K4 **Baiyu Shan** ▲ C China
111 J25 **Baja** Bács-Kiskun, S Hungary
40 C4 **Baja California** ◈ state NW Mexico
40 C4 **Baja California** Eng. Lower California. peninsula NW Mexico
40 E9 **Baja California Sur** ◈ state W Mexico
Bājah see Béja
Bajan see Bayan
191 V16 **Baja, Punta** headland Easter Island, Chile, E Pacific Ocean
40 B4 **Baja, Punta** headland NW Mexico
55 R5 **Baja, Punta** headland NE Venezuela
42 D5 **Baja Verapaz** off. Departamento de Baja Verapaz. ◈ department C Guatemala
171 N16 **Bajawa** prev. Badjawa. Flores, S Indonesia
153 S16 **Baj Baj** prev. Budge-Budge. West Bengal, E India
141 N15 **Bājil** W Yemen
183 U4 **Bajimba, Mount** ▲ New South Wales, SE Australia
112 K13 **Bajina Bašta** Serbia, W Serbia and Montenegro (Yugo.)
153 U14 **Bajitpur** Dhaka, E Bangladesh
112 K8 **Bajmok** Serbia, NW Serbia and Montenegro (Yugo.)
Bajo Boquete see Boquete
113 L17 **Bajram Curri** Kukës, N Albania
79 J14 **Bakala** Ouaka, C Central African Republic
127 T4 **Bakaly** Respublika Bashkortostan, W Russian Federation
Bakan see Shimonoseki
145 U14 **Bakanas** Kaz. Baqanas. Almaty, SE Kazakhstan
145 V12 **Bakanas** Kaz. Baqanas. ≈ E Kazakhstan
145 U14 **Bakbakty** Kaz. Baqbaqty. Almaty, SE Kazakhstan
122 J12 **Bakchar** Tomskaya Oblast', C Russian Federation
76 I11 **Bakel** E Senegal
35 W13 **Baker** California, W USA
22 J8 **Baker** Louisiana, S USA
33 Y9 **Baker** Montana, NW USA
32 L12 **Baker** Oregon, NW USA
192 L7 **Baker and Howland Islands** ◇ US unincorporated territory W Polynesia
36 L12 **Baker Butte** ▲ Arizona, SW USA
39 X15 **Baker Island** island Alexander Archipelago, Alaska, USA
9 N9 **Baker Lake** Nunavut, N Canada
9 N9 **Baker Lake** ◎ Nunavut, N Canada
32 H6 **Baker, Mount** ▲ Washington, NW USA
35 R13 **Bakersfield** California, W USA
24 M9 **Bakersfield** Texas, SW USA
21 P9 **Bakersville** North Carolina, SE USA
Bakhābī see Bū Khābī
Bakharden see Baharly
Bakhardok see Bokurdak
143 U5 **Bākharz, Kuhhā-ye** ▲▲ NE Iran
152 D13 **Bākhāsar** Rājasthān, NW India
Bakhchisaray see Bakhchysaray
117 T13 **Bakhchysaray** Rus. Bakhchisaray. Respublika Krym, S Ukraine
Bakherden see Baharly
117 R3 **Bakhmach** Chernihivs'ka Oblast', N Ukraine
Bākhtarān see Kermānshāh
143 Q11 **Bakhtegān, Daryācheh-ye** ◎ C Iran
145 X12 **Bakhty** Vostochnyy Kazakhstan, E Kazakhstan
137 Z11 **Bakı** Eng. Baku. ● (Azerbaijan) E Azerbaijan
137 Z11 **Bakı** ✕ E Azerbaijan
136 C13 **Bakır Çayı** ≈ W Turkey
92 L1 **Bakkafjördhur** Austurland, NE Iceland
92 L1 **Bakkaflói** sea area W Norwegian Sea
81 I15 **Bako** Southern, S Ethiopia
76 L15 **Bako** NW Ivory Coast
Bákó see Bacău
111 H23 **Bakony** Eng. Bakony Mountains, Ger. Bakonywald. ▲▲ W Hungary
Bakony Mountains/Bakonywald see Bakony
81 M16 **Bakool** off. Gobolka Bakool. ◈ region W Somalia
79 L15 **Bakouma** Mbomou, SE Central African Republic
127 N15 **Baksan** Kabardino-Balkarskaya Respublika, SW Russian Federation
119 I16 **Bakshty** Hrodzyenskaya Voblasts', W Belarus
Baku see Bakı
194 K12 **Bakutis Coast** physical region Antarctica
Bakwanga see Mbuji-Mayi
145 O15 **Bakyrly** Yuzhnyy Kazakhstan, S Kazakhstan
14 H13 **Bala** Ontario, S Canada
97 J19 **Bala** NW Wales, UK
136 I13 **Balâ** Ankara, C Turkey
170 L7 **Balabac Island** island W Philippines
Balabac, Selat see Balabac Strait
169 V5 **Balabac Strait** var. Selat Balabac. strait Malaysia/Philippines
Ba'labakk see Baalbek
187 P16 **Balabio, Île** island Province Nord, W New Caledonia
116 I14 **Balaci** Teleorman, S Romania
139 S7 **Balad** N Iraq
123 R12 **Baladek** Khabarovskiy Kray, SE Russian Federation
139 U7 **Balad Rūz** E Iraq
154 J11 **Bālāghāt** Madhya Pradesh, C India
155 F14 **Bālāghāt Range** ▲▲ W India
103 X14 **Balagne** physical region Corse, France, C Mediterranean Sea
105 U5 **Balaguer** Cataluña, NE Spain
105 S3 **Balaïtous** var. Pic de Balaïtous, Pic de Balaïtous. ▲ France/Spain
Balaïtous, Pic de see Balaïtous
Balák see Ballangen
127 O3 **Balakhna** Nizhegorodskaya Oblast', W Russian Federation
122 L12 **Balakhta** Krasnoyarskiy Kray, S Russian Federation
182 I9 **Balaklava** South Australia
Balakleya see Balakliya
117 V6 **Balakliya** Rus. Balakleya. Kharkivs'ka Oblast', E Ukraine
127 Q7 **Balakovo** Saratovskaya Oblast', W Russian Federation
83 P14 **Balama** Cabo Delgado, N Mozambique
169 U6 **Balambangan, Pulau** island East Malaysia
148 L3 **Bālā Morghāb** Laghmān, NW Afghanistan
152 E11 **Bālān** prev. Bāhla. Rājasthān, NW India
116 J10 **Bălan** Hung. Balánbánya. Harghita, C Romania
Balánbánya see Bălan
171 O3 **Balanga** Luzon, N Philippines
154 M12 **Balāngīr** prev. Bolangir. Orissa, E India
127 N8 **Balashov** Saratovskaya Oblast', W Russian Federation
Balasore see Bāleshwar
111 K21 **Balassagyarmat** Nógrád, N Hungary
29 S10 **Balaton** Minnesota, N USA
111 H24 **Balaton** var. Lake Balaton, Ger. Plattensee. ◎ W Hungary
111 I23 **Balatonfüred** var. Füred. Veszprém, W Hungary
Balaton, Lake see Balaton
116 I11 **Bălăușeri** Ger. Bladenmarkt, Hung. Balavásár. Mureș, C Romania
Balavásár see Bălăușeri
105 Q11 **Balazote** Castilla-La Mancha, C Spain
Balázsfalva see Blaj
119 F14 **Balbieriškis** Kaunas, S Lithuania
186 J7 **Balbi, Mount** ▲ Bougainville Island, NE PNG
58 F11 **Balbina, Represa** ⊞ NW Brazil
43 T15 **Balboa** Panamá, C Panama
97 G17 **Balbriggan** Ir. Baile Brigín. E Ireland
Balbunar see Kubrat
81 N17 **Balcad** Shabeellaha Dhexe, C Somalia
61 D23 **Balcarce** Buenos Aires, E Argentina
11 U16 **Balcarres** Saskatchewan, S Canada
114 O8 **Balchik** Dobrich, NE Bulgaria
185 E24 **Balclutha** Otago, South Island, NZ
25 Q12 **Balcones Escarpment** escarpment Texas, SW USA
18 F14 **Bald Eagle Creek** ≈ Pennsylvania, NE USA
Baldenburg see Biały Bór
21 V12 **Bald Head Island** island North Carolina, SE USA
27 W10 **Bald Knob** Arkansas, C USA
30 K17 **Bald Knob** hill Illinois, N USA
Baldohn see Baldone
118 G9 **Baldone** Ger. Baldohn. Rīga, W Latvia
22 I9 **Baldwin** Louisiana, S USA
31 P7 **Baldwin** Michigan, N USA
27 Q4 **Baldwin City** Kansas, C USA
39 N8 **Baldwin Peninsula** headland Alaska, USA
18 H9 **Baldwinsville** New York, NE USA
23 N2 **Baldwyn** Mississippi, S USA
11 W15 **Baldy Mountain** ▲ Manitoba, S Canada
33 T7 **Baldy Mountain** ▲ Montana, NW USA
37 O13 **Baldy Peak** ▲ Arizona, SW USA
Bâle see Basel
105 X9 **Baleares** ◈ autonomous community E Spain
105 X11 **Baleares, Islas** Eng. Balearic Islands. island group Spain, W Mediterranean Sea
Baleares Major see Mallorca
Balearic Islands see Baleares, Islas
Balearic Plain see Algerian Basin
Balearis Minor see Menorca
169 S9 **Baleh, Batang** ≈ East Malaysia
12 J8 **Baleine, Grande Rivière de la** ≈ Québec, E Canada
12 K7 **Baleine, Petite Rivière de la** ≈ Québec, SE Canada
13 N6 **Baleine, Rivière à la** ≈ Québec, E Canada
99 J16 **Balen** Antwerpen, N Belgium
171 O3 **Baler** Luzon, N Philippines
154 P11 **Bāleshwar** prev. Balasore. Orissa, E India
77 S12 **Baléyara** Tillabéri, W Niger
127 T1 **Balezino** Udmurtskaya Respublika, NW Russian Federation
42 J4 **Balfate** Colón, N Honduras
11 O17 **Balfour** British Columbia, SW Canada
29 N3 **Balfour** North Dakota, N USA
Balfrush see Bābol
122 L14 **Balgazyn** Respublika Tyva, S Russian Federation
11 U16 **Balgonie** Saskatchewan, S Canada
Bālgrad see Alba Iulia
81 J19 **Balguda** spring/well S Kenya
158 K6 **Balguntay** Xinjiang Uygur Zizhiqu, NW China
141 R16 **Balḥāf** S Yemen
152 F13 **Bāli** Rājasthān, N India
169 U17 **Bali** ◈ province S Indonesia
169 T17 **Bali** island C Indonesia
111 K16 **Balice** ✕ (Kraków) Małopolskie, S Poland
171 Y14 **Baliem, Sungai** ≈ Papua, E Indonesia
136 C12 **Balıkesir** Balıkesir, W Turkey
136 C12 **Balıkesir** ◈ province NW Turkey
138 L3 **Balīkh, Nahr** ≈ N Syria
169 V12 **Balikpapan** Borneo, C Indonesia
Bali, Laut see Bali Sea
171 N9 **Balimbing** Tawitawi, SW Philippines
186 B8 **Balimo** Western, SW PNG
Bálinc see Balinț
101 H23 **Balingen** Baden-Württemberg, SW Germany
116 F11 **Balinț** Hung. Bálinc. Timiș, W Romania
171 O1 **Balintang Channel** channel N Philippines
138 K3 **Bālis** Ḥalab, N Syria
169 T16 **Bali Sea** Ind. Laut Bali. sea C Indonesia
98 K7 **Balk** Friesland, N Netherlands
146 B11 **Balkanabat** Rus. Nebitdag. Balkan Welaýaty, W Turkmenistan
121 R6 **Balkan Mountains** Bul./SCr. Stara Planina. ▲▲ Bulgaria/Serbia and Montenegro (Yugo.)
Balkanskiy Velayat see Balkan Welaýaty
146 B9 **Balkan Welaýaty** Rus. Balkanskiy Velayat. ◈ province W Turkmenistan
145 P8 **Balkashino** Akmola, N Kazakhstan
149 O2 **Balkh** anc. Bactra. Balkh, N Afghanistan
149 P2 **Balkh** ◈ province N Afghanistan
145 T13 **Balkhash** Kaz. Balqash. Karaganda, SE Kazakhstan
Balkhash, Lake see Balkhash, Ozero
145 T13 **Balkhash, Ozero** Eng. Lake Balkhash, Kaz. Balqash. ◎ SE Kazakhstan
Balla Balla see Mbalabala
96 H10 **Ballachulish** N Scotland, UK
180 M12 **Balladonia** Western Australia
97 C16 **Ballaghaderreen** Ir. Bealach an Doirín. C Ireland
92 H10 **Ballangen** Lapp. Bálák. Nordland, NW Norway
97 H14 **Ballantrae** W Scotland, UK
183 N12 **Ballarat** Victoria, SE Australia
180 K11 **Ballard, Lake** salt lake Western Australia
Ballari see Bellary
76 L11 **Ballé** Koulikoro, W Mali
40 D7 **Ballenas, Bahía de** bay W Mexico
40 D5 **Ballenas, Canal de** channel NW Mexico
195 R17 **Balleny Islands** island group Antarctica
40 J7 **Balleza** var. San Pablo Balleza. Chihuahua, N Mexico
114 M13 **Ballı** Tekirdağ, NW Turkey
153 O13 **Ballia** Uttar Pradesh, N India
183 V4 **Ballina** New South Wales, SE Australia
97 C16 **Ballina** Ir. Béal an Átha. W Ireland
97 D16 **Ballinamore** Ir. Béal an Átha Móir. NW Ireland
97 D18 **Ballinasloe** Ir. Béal Átha na Sluaighe. W Ireland
25 P8 **Ballinger** Texas, SW USA
97 C17 **Ballinrobe** Ir. Baile an Róba. W Ireland
97 A21 **Ballinskelligs Bay** Ir. Bá na Scealg. inlet SW Ireland
97 D15 **Ballintra** Ir. Baile an tSratha. NW Ireland
103 T7 **Ballon d'Alsace** ▲ NE France
Ballon de Guebwiller see Grand Ballon
113 K21 **Ballsh** var. Ballshi. Fier, SW Albania
Ballshi see Ballsh
98 K4 **Ballum** Friesland, N Netherlands
97 F16 **Ballybay** Ir. Béal Átha Beithe. N Ireland
97 E14 **Ballybofey** Ir. Bealach Féich. NW Ireland
97 G14 **Ballycastle** Ir. Baile an Chaistil. N Northern Ireland, UK
97 G15 **Ballyclare** Ir. Bealach Cláir. E Northern Ireland, UK
97 E16 **Ballyconnell** Ir. Béal Átha Conaill. N Ireland
97 C17 **Ballyhaunis** Ir. Beál Átha hAmhnais. W Ireland
97 G14 **Ballymena** Ir. An Baile Meánach. NE Northern Ireland, UK
97 F14 **Ballymoney** Ir. Baile Monaidh. NE Northern Ireland, UK
97 G15 **Ballynahinch** Ir. Baile na hInse. SE Northern Ireland, UK
97 D16 **Ballysadare** Ir. Baile Easa Dara. NW Ireland
97 D15 **Ballyshannon** Ir. Béal Átha Seanaidh. NW Ireland
63 H19 **Balmaceda** Aisén, S Chile
63 G23 **Balmaceda, Cerro** ▲ S Chile
111 N22 **Balmazújváros** Hajdú-Bihar, E Hungary
108 E10 **Balmhorn** ▲ SW Switzerland
182 L12 **Balmoral** Victoria, SE Australia
24 K9 **Balmorhea** Texas, SW USA
Balneario Claromecó see Claromecó
Balochistān see Baluchistān
82 B13 **Balombo** Port. Norton de Matos, Vila Norton de Matos. Benguela, W Angola
82 B13 **Balombo** ≈ W Angola
181 X10 **Balonne River** ≈ Queensland, E Australia
152 E13 **Bālotra** Rājasthān, N India
145 V14 **Balpyk Bi** prev. Kirovskiy Kaz. Kīrov. Almaty, SE Kazakhstan
Balqā'/Balqā', Muḥāfaẓat al see Al Balqā'
Balqash see Balkhash/Balkhash, Ozero
152 M12 **Balrāmpur** Uttar Pradesh, N India
182 M9 **Balranald** New South Wales, SE Australia
116 H14 **Balș** Olt, S Romania
14 H11 **Balsam Creek** Ontario, S Canada
30 I5 **Balsam Lake** Wisconsin, N USA
14 I14 **Balsam Lake** ◎ Ontario, SE Canada
59 M15 **Balsas** Maranhão, E Brazil
41 O15 **Balsas, Río** var. Río Mexcala. ≈ S Mexico
43 W16 **Balsas, Río** ≈ SE Panama
119 O18 **Bal'shavik** Rus. Bol'shevik. Homyel'skaya Voblasts', SE Belarus
95 O15 **Bålsta** Uppsala, C Sweden
108 E7 **Balsthal** Solothurn, NW Switzerland
117 O8 **Balta** Odes'ka Oblast', SW Ukraine
105 N5 **Baltanás** Castilla-León, N Spain
61 E16 **Baltasar Brum** Artigas, N Uruguay
116 M9 **Bălți** Rus. Bel'tsy. N Moldova
Baltic Port see Paldiski
118 B10 **Baltic Sea** Ger. Ostee, Rus. Baltiskoye More. sea N Europe
21 X3 **Baltimore** Maryland, NE USA
31 T13 **Baltimore** Ohio, N USA
21 X3 **Baltimore-Washington** ✕ Maryland, E USA
Baltischport/Baltiski see Paldiski
Baltiskoye More see Baltic Sea
119 A14 **Baltiysk** Ger. Pillau. Kaliningradskaya Oblast', W Russian Federation
Baltkrievija see Belarus
119 H14 **Baltoji Vokė** Vilnius, SE Lithuania
Balūchestān va Sīstān see Sīstān va Balūchestān
148 M12 **Baluchistān** var. Balochistān, Beluchistan. ◈ province SW Pakistan
171 P5 **Balud** Masbate, N Philippines
169 T9 **Balui, Batang** ≈ East Malaysia
153 S13 **Bālurghat** West Bengal, NE India
118 J8 **Balvi** Balvi, NE Latvia
147 W7 **Balykchy** Kir. Ysyk-Köl; prev. Issyk-Kul', Rybach'ye. Issyk-Kul'skaya Oblast', NE Kyrgyzstan
56 B7 **Balzar** Guayas, W Ecuador
108 I8 **Balzers** S Liechtenstein
143 T12 **Bam** Kermān, SE Iran
77 Y13 **Bama** Borno, NE Nigeria
76 L12 **Bamako** ● (Mali) Capital District, SW Mali
77 P10 **Bamba** Gao, C Mali
42 M8 **Bambana, Río** ≈ NE Nicaragua
79 J15 **Bambari** Ouaka, C Central African Republic
181 W5 **Bambaroo** Queensland, NE Australia
101 K19 **Bamberg** Bayern, SE Germany
21 R14 **Bamberg** South Carolina, SE USA
79 M16 **Bambesa** Orientale, N Dem. Rep. Congo
76 G11 **Bambey** W Senegal
79 H16 **Bambio** Sangha-Mbaéré, SW Central African Republic
83 I24 **Bamboesberge** ▲ S South Africa
79 D14 **Bamenda** Nord-Ouest, W Cameroon
10 K17 **Bamfield** Vancouver Island, British Columbia, SW Canada
Bami see Bamy
149 P4 **Bāmīān** var. Bāmiān. Bāmīān, NE Afghanistan
149 O4 **Bāmīān** ◈ province C Afghanistan
79 J14 **Bamingui** Bamingui-Bangoran, C Central African Republic
78 J13 **Bamingui** ≈ N Central African Republic
78 J13 **Bamingui-Bangoran** ◈ prefecture N Central African Republic
143 V13 **Bampūr** Sīstān va Balūchestān, SE Iran
186 C8 **Bamu** ≈ SW PNG
146 E12 **Bamy** Rus. Bami. Ahal Welaýaty, C Turkmenistan
Bán see Bánovce nad Bebravou
81 N17 **Banaadir** off. Gobolka Banaadir. ◈ region S Somalia
191 N3 **Banaba** var. Ocean Island. island Tungaru, W Kiribati
59 O14 **Banabuiú, Açude** ⊞ NE Brazil
57 O19 **Bañados del Izozog** salt lake SE Bolivia
97 D18 **Banagher** Ir. Beannchar. C Ireland
79 M17 **Banalia** Orientale, N Dem. Rep. Congo
76 L12 **Banamba** Koulikoro, W Mali
40 G4 **Banámichi** Sonora, NW Mexico
181 Y9 **Banana** Queensland, E Australia
191 Z2 **Banana** prev. Main Camp. Kiritimati, E Kiribati
59 K16 **Bananal, Ilha do** island C Brazil
23 Y12 **Banana River** lagoon Florida, SE USA
151 Q22 **Bananga** Andaman and Nicobar Islands, India, NE Indian Ocean
Banaras see Vārānasi
114 N13 **Banarlı** Tekirdağ, NW Turkey
152 H12 **Banās** ≈ N India
75 Z11 **Banâs, Râs** headland E Egypt
112 N10 **Banatski Karlovac** Serbia, NE Serbia and Montenegro (Yugo.)
141 P16 **Banā, Wādī** dry watercourse SW Yemen
136 E14 **Banaz** Uşak, W Turkey
136 E14 **Banaz Çayı** ≈ W Turkey
159 P14 **Banbar** var. Coka. Xizang Zizhiqu, W China
97 G15 **Banbridge** Ir. Droichead na Banna. SE Northern Ireland, UK
Ban Bua Yai see Bua Yai
97 M21 **Banbury** S England, UK
167 O7 **Ban Chiang Dao** Chiang Mai, NW Thailand
96 K9 **Banchory** NE Scotland, UK
14 J13 **Bancroft** Ontario, SE Canada
33 R15 **Bancroft** Idaho, NW USA
29 U11 **Bancroft** Iowa, C USA
154 I9 **Banda** Madhya Pradesh, C India
152 L13 **Bānda** Uttar Pradesh, N India
168 F7 **Bandaaceh** var. Banda Atjeh; prev. Koetaradja, Kutaradja, Kutaraja. Sumatera, W Indonesia
Banda Atjeh see Bandaaceh
171 S14 **Banda, Kepulauan** island group E Indonesia
Banda, Laut see Banda Sea
77 N17 **Bandama** var. Bandama Fleuve. ≈ S Ivory Coast
77 N15 **Bandama Blanc** ≈ C Ivory Coast
Bandama Fleuve see Bandama
Bandar 'Abbās see Bandar-e 'Abbās
153 W16 **Bandarban** Chittagong, SE Bangladesh
80 Q13 **Bandarbeyla** var. Bender Beila, Bender Beyla. Bari, NE Somalia
143 R14 **Bandar-e 'Abbās** var. Bandar 'Abbās; prev. Gombroon. Hormozgān, S Iran
142 M3 **Bandar-e Anzalī** Gīlān, NW Iran
143 N12 **Bandar-e Būshehr** var. Būshehr, Eng. Bushire. Būshehr, S Iran
142 M11 **Bandar-e Gonāveh** var. Ganāveh; prev. Gonāveh. Būshehr, SW Iran
143 R14 **Bandar-e Khamīr** Hormozgān, S Iran
143 Q14 **Bandar-e Langeh** var. Bandar-e Lengeh, Lingeh. Hormozgān, S Iran
Bandar-e Lengeh see Bandar-e Langeh
142 L10 **Bandar-e Māhshahr** var. Māh-Shahr; prev. Bandar-e Ma'shūr. Khūzestān, SW Iran
Bandar-e Ma'shūr see Bandar-e Māhshahr
143 O14 **Bandar-e Nakhīlū** Hormozgān, S Iran
Bandar-e Shāh see Bandar-e Torkaman
143 P4 **Bandar-e Torkaman** var. Bandar-e Torkeman, Bandar-e Torkman; prev. Bandar-e Shāh. Golestān, N Iran
Bandar-e Torkeman/Bandar-e Torkman see Bandar-e Torkaman

◆ Country ● Country Capital ◇ Dependent Territory ○ Dependent Territory Capital ◈ Administrative Region ✕ International Airport ▲ Mountain ▲▲ Mountain Range Volcano ≈ River ◎ Lake ⊞ Reservoir

Bandar Kassim *see* Boosaaso
168 *M15* **Bandarlampung** *prev.* Tanjungkarang, Teloekbetoeng, Telukbetung. Sumatera, W Indonesia
Bandar Maharani *see* Muar
Bandar Masulipatnam *see* Machilipatnam
Bandar Penggaram *see* Batu Pahat
169 *T7* **Bandar Seri Begawan** *prev.* Brunei Town. ● (Brunei) N Brunei
169 *T7* **Bandar Seri Begawan** × N Brunei
171 *R15* **Banda Sea** *var.* Laut Banda. *sea* E Indonesia
104 *H5* **Bande** Galicia, NW Spain
59 *G15* **Bandeirantes** Mato Grosso, W Brazil
59 *N20* **Bandeira, Pico da** ▲ SE Brazil
83 *K19* **Bandelierkop** Limpopo, NE South Africa
62 *L8* **Bandera** Santiago del Estero, N Argentina
25 *Q11* **Bandera** Texas, SW USA
40 *J13* **Banderas, Bahía de** *bay* W Mexico
77 *O11* **Bandiagara** Mopti, C Mali
152 *I12* **Bāndīkūi** Rājasthān, N India
136 *C11* **Bandırma** *var.* Penderma. Balıkesir, NW Turkey
Bandjarmasin *see* Banjarmasin
Bandoeng *see* Bandung
97 *C21* **Bandon** *Ir.* Droicheadna Bandan. SW Ireland
32 *E14* **Bandon** Oregon, NW USA
167 *R8* **Ban Dong Bang** Nong Khai, E Thailand
167 *Q6* **Ban Donkon** Oudômxai, N Laos
172 *J14* **Bandrélé** SE Mayotte
79 *H20* **Bandundu** *prev.* Banningville. Bandundu, W Dem. Rep. Congo
79 *I21* **Bandundu** *off.* Région de Bandundu. ◈ *region* W Dem. Rep. Congo
169 *O16* **Bandung** *prev.* Bandoeng. Jawa, C Indonesia
116 *L15* **Băneasa** Constanţa, SW Romania
142 *J4* **Bāneh** Kordestān, N Iran
44 *I7* **Banes** Holguín, E Cuba
11 *P16* **Banff** Alberta, SW Canada
96 *K8* **Banff** NE Scotland, UK
96 *K8* **Banff** *cultural region* NE Scotland, UK
Bánffyhunyad *see* Huedin
77 *N14* **Banfora** SW Burkina
155 *H19* **Bangalore** Karnātaka, S India
153 *S16* **Bangaon** West Bengal, NE India
79 *L15* **Bangassou** Mbomou, SE Central African Republic
186 *D7* **Bangeta, Mount** ▲ C PNG
171 *P12* **Banggai, Kepulauan** *island group* C Indonesia
171 *Q12* **Banggai, Pulau** *island* Kepulauan Banggai, N Indonesia
171 *X13* **Banggelapa** Papua, E Indonesia
Banggi *see* Banggi, Pulau
169 *V6* **Banggi, Pulau** *var.* Banggi. *island* East Malaysia
121 *P13* **Banghāzī** *Eng.* Bengazi, Benghazi, *It.* Bengasi. NE Libya
Bang Hieng *see* Xé Banghiang
169 *O13* **Bangka-Belitung** *off.* Propinsi Bangka-Belitung. ◈ *province* W Indonesia
169 *P11* **Bangkai, Tanjung** *var.* Bankai. *headland* Borneo, N Indonesia
169 *S16* **Bangkalan** Pulau Madura, C Indonesia
169 *N12* **Bangka, Pulau** *island* W Indonesia
169 *N13* **Bangka, Selat** *strait* Sumatera, W Indonesia
168 *J11* **Bangkinang** Sumatera, W Indonesia
168 *K12* **Bangko** Sumatera, W Indonesia
Bangkok *see* Krung Thep
Bangkok, Bight of *see* Krung Thep, Ao
153 *T14* **Bangladesh** *off.* People's Republic of Bangladesh; *prev.* East Pakistan. ◆ *republic* S Asia
167 *V13* **Ba Ngoi** Khanh Hoa, S Vietnam
152 *K5* **Bangong Co** *var.* Pangong Tso. ◎ China/India *see also* Pangong Tso
97 *G15* **Bangor** *Ir.* Beannchar. E Northern Ireland, UK
97 *I18* **Bangor** NW Wales, UK
19 *R6* **Bangor** Maine, NE USA
18 *I14* **Bangor** Pennsylvania, NE USA
67 *R8* **Bangoran** ≈ S Central African Republic
Bang Phra *see* Trat
Bang Pla Soi *see* Chon Buri
25 *Q8* **Bangs** Texas, SW USA
167 *N13* **Bang Saphan** *var.* Bang Saphan Yai. Prachuap Khiri Khan, SW Thailand
Bang Saphan Yai *see* Bang Saphan
36 *I8* **Bangs, Mount** ▲ Arizona, SW USA
93 *E15* **Bangsund** Nord-Trøndelag, C Norway
171 *O2* **Bangued** Luzon, N Philippines
79 *I15* **Bangui** ● (Central African Republic) Ombella-Mpoko, SW Central African Republic
79 *I15* **Bangui** × Ombella-Mpoko, SW Central African Republic
83 *N16* **Bangula** Southern, S Malawi
Bangwaketse *see* Southern
82 *K12* **Bangweulu, Lake** *var.* Lake Bengweulu. ◎ N Zambia
Banhā *see* Benha
Ban Hat Yai *see* Hat Yai
167 *Q7* **Ban Hin Heup** Viangchan, C Laos
Ban Houayxay/Ban Houei Sai *see* Houayxay
167 *O12* **Ban Hua Hin** *var.* Hua Hin. Prachuap Khiri Khan, SW Thailand
79 *L14* **Bani** Haute-Kotto, E Central African Republic
77 *N12* **Bani** ≈ S Mali
45 *O9* **Baní** S Dominican Republic
Banias *see* Bāniyās
77 *S11* **Bani Bangou** Tillabéri, SW Niger
76 *M12* **Banifing** *var.* Ngorolaka. ≈ Burkina/Mali
77 *R13* **Banikoara** N Benin
Banī Mazār *see* Beni Mazâr
114 *K8* **Baniski Lom** ≈ N Bulgaria
21 *U7* **Banister River** ≈ Virginia, NE USA
Banī Suwayf *see* Beni Suef
75 *O8* **Banī Walīd** NW Libya
138 *H5* **Bāniyās** *var.* Banias, Baniyas, Paneas. Ṭarṭūs, W Syria
113 *K14* **Banja** Serbia, W Serbia and Montenegro (Yugo.)
Banjak, Kepulauan *see* Banyak, Kepulauan
112 *J12* **Banja Koviljača** Serbia, W Serbia and Montenegro (Yugo.)
112 *G11* **Banja Luka** Republika Srpska, NW Bosnia and Herzegovina
169 *T13* **Banjarmasin** *prev.* Bandjarmasin. Borneo, C Indonesia
76 *F11* **Banjul** *prev.* Bathurst. ● (Gambia) W Gambia
76 *F11* **Banjul** × W Gambia
Bank *see* Bankä
137 *Y13* **Bankä** *Rus.* Bank. SE Azerbaijan
167 *S11* **Ban Kadian** *var.* Ban Kadiene. Champasak, S Laos
Ban Kadiene *see* Ban Kadian
Bankai *see* Bangkai, Tanjung
166 *M14* **Ban Kam Phuam** Phangnga, SW Thailand
Ban Kantang *see* Kantang
77 *O11* **Bankass** Mopti, S Mali
95 *L19* **Bankeryd** Jönköping, S Sweden
83 *K16* **Banket** Mashonaland West, N Zimbabwe
167 *T11* **Ban Khamphô** Attapu, S Laos
23 *O4* **Bankhead Lake** ▣ Alabama, S USA
77 *Q11* **Bankilaré** Tillabéri, SW Niger
Banks, Îles *see* Banks Islands
10 *I14* **Banks Island** *island* British Columbia, SW Canada
187 *R12* **Banks Islands** *Fr.* Îles Banks. *island group* N Vanuatu
23 *U8* **Banks Lake** ◎ Georgia, SE USA
32 *K8* **Banks Lake** ▣ Washington, NW USA
185 *I19* **Banks Peninsula** *peninsula* South Island, NZ
183 *Q15* **Banks Strait** *strait* SW Tasman Sea
Ban Kui Nua *see* Kui Buri
153 *R16* **Bānkura** West Bengal, NE India
167 *S8* **Ban Lakxao** *var.* Lak Sao. Bolikhamxai, C Laos
167 *O16* **Ban Lam Phai** Songkhla, SW Thailand
Ban Mae Sot *see* Mae Sot
Ban Mae Suai *see* Mae Suai
Ban Mak Khaeng *see* Udon Thani
166 *M3* **Banmauk** Sagaing, N Myanmar
Banmo *see* Bhamo
167 *T10* **Ban Mun-Houamuang** S Laos
97 *F14* **Bann** *var.* Lower Bann, Upper Bann. ≈ N Northern Ireland, UK
167 *S10* **Ban Nadou** Salavan, S Laos
167 *S9* **Ban Nakala** Savannakhét, S Laos
167 *Q8* **Ban Nakha** Viangchan, C Laos
167 *S9* **Ban Nakham** Khammouan, S Laos
167 *P7* **Ban Namoun** Xaignabouli, N Laos
167 *O17* **Ban Nang Sata** Yala, SW Thailand
167 *N15* **Ban Na San** Surat Thani, SW Thailand
167 *R7* **Ban Nasi** Xiangkhoang, N Laos
44 *I3* **Bannerman Town** Eleuthera Island, C Bahamas
35 *V15* **Banning** California, W USA
Banningville *see* Bandundu
167 *S11* **Ban Nongsim** Champasak, S Laos
149 *S7* **Bannu** *prev.* Edwardesabad. North-West Frontier Province, NW Pakistan
Bañolas *see* Banyoles
56 *C7* **Baños** Tungurahua, C Ecuador
Bánovce *see* Bánovce nad Bebravou
111 *I19* **Bánovce nad Bebravou** *var.* Bánovce, *Hung.* Bán. Trenčiansky Kraj, W Slovakia
112 *I12* **Banovići** Federacija Bosna I Hercegovina, E Bosnia and Herzegovina
Banow *see* Andarāb
Ban Pak Phanang *see* Pak Phanang
167 *O7* **Ban Pan Nua** Lampang, NW Thailand
167 *Q9* **Ban Phai** Khon Kaen, E Thailand
167 *T9* **Ban Phou A Douk** Khammouan, C Laos
167 *Q8* **Ban Phu** Uthai Thani, W Thailand
167 *O11* **Ban Pong** Ratchaburi, W Thailand
190 *I3* **Banraeaba** Tarawa, W Kiribati
167 *N10* **Ban Sai Yok** Kanchanaburi, W Thailand
Ban Sattahip/Ban Sattahipp *see* Sattahip
Ban Sichon *see* Sichon
Ban Si Racha *see* Siracha
111 *J19* **Banská Bystrica** *Ger.* Neusohl, *Hung.* Besztercebánya. Banskobystrický Kraj, C Slovakia
111 *K20* **Banskobystrický Kraj** ◈ *region* C Slovakia
167 *R8* **Ban Sôppheung** Bolikhamxai, C Laos
Ban Sop Prap *see* Sop Prap
152 *G15* **Bānswāra** Rājasthān, N India
167 *N15* **Ban Ta Khun** Surat Thani, SW Thailand
Ban Takua Pa *see* Takua Pa
167 *S8* **Ban Talak** Khammouan, C Laos
77 *R15* **Bantè** W Benin
169 *N16* **Banten** *off.* Propinsi Banten. ◈ *province* W Indonesia
167 *Q8* **Ban Thabôk** Bolikhamxai, C Laos
167 *T9* **Ban Tôp** Savannakhét, S Laos
97 *B21* **Bantry** *Ir.* Beanntraí. SW Ireland
97 *A21* **Bantry Bay** *Ir.* Bá Bheanntraí. *bay* SW Ireland
155 *F19* **Bantvāl** *var.* Bantwāl. Karnātaka, E India
Bantwāl *see* Bantvāl
114 *N9* **Banya** Burgas, E Bulgaria
168 *G10* **Banyak, Kepulauan** *prev.* Kepulauan Banjak. *island group* NW Indonesia
105 *U8* **Banya, La** *headland* E Spain
79 *E14* **Banyo** Adamaoua, NW Cameroon
105 *X4* **Banyoles** *var.* Bañolas. Cataluña, NE Spain
167 *N16* **Ban Yong Sata** Trang, SW Thailand
195 *X14* **Banzare Coast** *physical region* Antarctica
173 *Q14* **Banzare Seamounts** *undersea feature* S Indian Ocean
Banzart *see* Bizerte
163 *Q12* **Baochang** *var.* Taibus Qi. Nei Mongol Zizhiqu, N China
161 *O3* **Baoding** *var.* Pao-ting; *prev.* Tsingyuan. Hebei, E China
Baoebaoe *see* Baubau
Baoi, Oileán *see* Dursey Island
160 *J6* **Baoji** *var.* Pao-chi, Paoki. Shaanxi, C China
163 *U9* **Baokang** *var.* Hoqin Zuoyi Zhongji. Nei Mongol Zizhiqu, N China
186 *L8* **Baolo** Santa Isabel, N Solomon Islands
167 *U13* **Bao Lôc** Lâm Đông, S Vietnam
163 *Z7* **Baoqing** Heilongjiang, NE China
Baoqing *see* Shaoyang
79 *H15* **Baoro** Nana-Mambéré, W Central African Republic
160 *E12* **Baoshan** *var.* Pao-shan. Yunnan, SW China
163 *N13* **Baotou** *var.* Pao-t'ou, Paotow. Nei Mongol Zizhiqu, N China
76 *L14* **Baoulé** ≈ S Mali
76 *K12* **Baoulé** ≈ W Mali
103 *O2* **Bapaume** Pas-de-Calais, N France
14 *J13* **Baptiste Lake** ◎ Ontario, SE Canada
Bapu *see* Meigu
Baqanas *see* Bakanas
Baqbaqty *see* Bakbakty
159 *P14* **Baqên** *var.* Dartang. Xizang Zizhiqu, W China
138 *F14* **Bāqir, Jabal** ▲▲ S Jordan
139 *T7* **Ba'qūbah** *var.* Qubba. C Iraq
62 *H5* **Baquedano** Antofagasta, N Chile
116 *M6* **Bar** Vinnyts'ka Oblast', C Ukraine
113 *J18* **Bar** *It.* Antivari. Montenegro, SW Serbia and Montenegro (Yugo.)
80 *E10* **Bara** Northern Kordofan, C Sudan
81 *M18* **Baraawe** *It.* Brava. Shabeellaha Hoose, S Somalia
152 *M12* **Bāra Banki** Uttar Pradesh, N India
30 *L8* **Baraboo** Wisconsin, N USA
30 *K8* **Baraboo Range** *hill range* Wisconsin, N USA
Baracaldo *see* San Vicente de Barakaldo
15 *Y6* **Barachois** Québec, SE Canada
44 *J7* **Baracoa** Guantánamo, E Cuba
61 *C19* **Baradero** Buenos Aires, E Argentina
183 *R6* **Baradine** New South Wales, SE Australia
Baraf Daja Islands *see* Damar, Kepulauan
154 *M12* **Baragarh** Orissa, E India
81 *I17* **Baragoi** Rift Valley, W Kenya
45 *N9* **Barahona** SW Dominican Republic
153 *W13* **Barail Range** ▲▲ NE India
80 *I9* **Baraka** *var.* Barka, *Ar.* Khawr Barakah. *seasonal river* Eritrea/Sudan
80 *G10* **Barakat** Gezira, C Sudan
Barakī *see* Barakī Barak
149 *Q6* **Barakī Barak** *var.* Barakī, Baraki Rajan. Lowgar, E Afghanistan
Baraki Rajan *see* Barakī Barak
154 *N11* **Bārākot** Orissa, E India
55 *S7* **Barama River** ≈ N Guyana
155 *E14* **Bārāmati** Mahārāshtra, W India
152 *H5* **Bāramūla** Jammu and Kashmir, NW India
119 *N14* **Baran'** Vitsyebskaya Voblasts', NE Belarus
152 *I14* **Bārān** Rājasthān, N India
139 *U4* **Barānān, Shākh-i** ▲▲ E Iraq
119 *I17* **Baranavichy** *Pol.* Baranowicze, *Rus.* Baranovichi. Brestskaya Voblasts', SW Belarus
123 *T6* **Baranikha** Chukotskiy Avtonomnyy Okrug, NE Russian Federation
116 *M4* **Baranivka** Zhytomyrs'ka Oblast', N Ukraine
39 *W14* **Baranof Island** *island* Alexander Archipelago, Alaska, USA
Baranovichi/ Baranowicze *see* Baranavichy
111 *N15* **Baranów Sandomierski** Podkarpackie, SE Poland
111 *I26* **Baranya** *off.* Baranya Megye. ◈ *county* S Hungary
153 *R13* **Barāri** Bihār, NE India
22 *L10* **Barataria Bay** *bay* Louisiana, S USA
Barat Daya, Kepulauan *see* Damar, Kepulauan
118 *L12* **Baravukha** *Rus.* Borovukha. Vitsyebskaya Voblasts', N Belarus
54 *E11* **Baraya** Huila, C Colombia
59 *M21* **Barbacena** Minas Gerais, SE Brazil
54 *B13* **Barbacoas** Nariño, SW Colombia
54 *L6* **Barbacoas** Aragua, N Venezuela
45 *Z13* **Barbados** ◆ *commonwealth republic* SE West Indies
47 *S3* **Barbados** *island* Barbados
105 *U11* **Barbaria, Cap de** *var.* Cabo de Berberia. *headland* Formentera, E Spain
114 *N13* **Barbaros** Tekirdağ, NW Turkey
74 *A11* **Barbas, Cap** *headland* S Western Sahara
105 *T5* **Barbastro** Aragón, NE Spain
104 *K16* **Barbate** ≈ SW Spain
104 *K16* **Barbate de Franco** Andalucía, S Spain
9 *N1* **Barbeau Peak** ▲ Nunavut, N Canada
83 *K21* **Barberton** Mpumalanga, NE South Africa
31 *U12* **Barberton** Ohio, N USA
102 *K12* **Barbezieux-St-Hilaire** Charente, W France
54 *G9* **Barbosa** Boyacá, C Colombia
21 *N7* **Barbourville** Kentucky, S USA
45 *W9* **Barbuda** *island* N Antigua and Barbuda
181 *W8* **Barcaldine** Queensland, E Australia
Barcarozsnyó *see* Râşnov
104 *I11* **Barcarrota** Extremadura, W Spain
Barcău *see* Berettyó
Barce *see* Al Marj
107 *L23* **Barcellona** *It.* Barcellona Pozzo di Gotto. Sicilia, Italy, C Mediterranean Sea
Barcellona Pozzo di Gotto *see* Barcellona
105 *W6* **Barcelona** *anc.* Barcino, Barcinona. Cataluña, E Spain
55 *N5* **Barcelona** Anzoátegui, NE Venezuela
105 *S5* **Barcelona** ◈ *province* Cataluña, NE Spain
105 *W6* **Barcelona** × Cataluña, E Spain
103 *U14* **Barcelonnette** Alpes-de-Haute-Provence, SE France
58 *E12* **Barcelos** Amazonas, N Brazil
104 *G5* **Barcelos** Braga, N Portugal
110 *I19* **Barcin** *Ger.* Bartschin. Kujawski-pomorskie, C Poland
Barcino/Barcinona *see* Barcelona
Barcoo *see* Cooper Creek
111 *H26* **Barcs** Somogy, SW Hungary
137 *W11* **Bärdä** *Rus.* Barda. C Azerbaijan
78 *H5* **Bardaï** Borkou-Ennedi-Tibesti, N Chad
139 *R2* **Bardaṛash** N Iraq
139 *Q7* **Bardasah** SW Iraq
153 *S15* **Barddhamān** West Bengal, NE India
111 *N18* **Bardejov** *Ger.* Bartfeld, *Hung.* Bártfa. Prešovský Kraj, E Slovakia
105 *R4* **Bárdenas Reales** *physical region* N Spain
Bardera/Bardere *see* Baardheere
Bardesīr *see* Bardsīr
92 *K3* **Bárdharbunga** ▲ C Iceland
Bardhë, Drini i *see* Beli Drim
106 *E9* **Bardi** Emilia-Romagna, C Italy
106 *A8* **Bardonecchia** Piemonte, W Italy
97 *H19* **Bardsey Island** *island* NW Wales, UK
143 *S11* **Bardsīr** *var.* Bardesīr, Mashīz. Kermān, C Iran
20 *L6* **Bardstown** Kentucky, S USA
Barduli *see* Barletta
20 *G7* **Bardwell** Kentucky, S USA
152 *K11* **Bareilly** *var.* Bareli. Uttar Pradesh, N India
Bareli *see* Bareilly
98 *H13* **Barendrecht** Zuid-Holland, SW Netherlands
102 *M3* **Barentin** Seine-Maritime, N France
92 *N3* **Barentsburg** Spitsbergen, W Svalbard
Barentsevo More/Barents Havet *see* Barents Sea
92 *O3* **Barentsøya** *island* E Svalbard
197 *T11* **Barents Plain** *undersea feature* N Barents Sea
127 *P3* **Barents Sea** *Nor.* Barents Havet, *Rus.* Barentsevo More. *sea* Arctic Ocean
197 *U14* **Barents Trough** *undersea feature* SW Barents Sea
80 *I9* **Barentu** W Eritrea
102 *J3* **Barfleur** Manche, N France
102 *J3* **Barfleur, Pointe de** *headland* N France
Barfrush/Barfurush *see* Bābol
158 *H14* **Barga** Xizang Zizhiqu, W China
105 *N9* **Bargas** Castilla-La Mancha, C Spain
81 *I15* **Bargē** Southern, S Ethiopia
106 *A9* **Barge** Piemonte, NE Italy
153 *U16* **Barguna** Khulna, S Bangladesh
Bärguşad *see* Vorotan
123 *N13* **Barguzin** Respublika Buryatiya, S Russian Federation
153 *O13* **Barhaj** Uttar Pradesh, N India
183 *N10* **Barham** New South Wales, SE Australia
152 *J12* **Barhan** Uttar Pradesh, N India
19 *S7* **Bar Harbor** Mount Desert Island, Maine, NE USA
153 *R14* **Barharwa** Jhārkhand, NE India
153 *P15* **Barhi** Jhārkhand, N India
107 *O17* **Bari** *var.* Bari delle Puglie; *anc.* Barium. Puglia, SE Italy
80 *P12* **Bari** *off.* Gobolka Bari. ◈ *region* NE Somalia
167 *T14* **Ba Ria** Ba Ria-Vung Tau, S Vietnam
Bāridah *see* Al Bāridah
Bari delle Puglie *see* Bari
Barikot *see* Barīkowṭ
149 *T4* **Barīkowṭ** *var.* Barikot. Kunar, NE Afghanistan
42 *C4* **Barillas** *var.* Santa Cruz Barillas. Huehuetenango, NW Guatemala
54 *J6* **Barinas** Barinas, W Venezuela
54 *I7* **Barinas** *off.* Estado Barinas; *prev.* Zamora. ◈ *state* C Venezuela
54 *I6* **Barinitas** Barinas, NW Venezuela
154 *P11* **Bāripada** Orissa, E India
60 *K9* **Bariri** São Paulo, S Brazil
75 *W11* **Bârîs** S Egypt
152 *G14* **Bari Sādri** Rājasthān, N India
153 *U16* **Barisal** Khulna, S Bangladesh
168 *I10* **Barisan, Pegunungan** ▲▲ Sumatera, W Indonesia
169 *T12* **Barito, Sungai** ≈ Borneo, C Indonesia
Barium *see* Bari
Bārjās *see* Porjus
Barka *see* Baraka
Barka *see* Al Marj
160 *H8* **Barkam** Sichuan, C China
118 *J9* **Barkava** Madona, C Latvia
10 *M15* **Barkerville** British Columbia, SW Canada
14 *J12* **Bark Lake** ◎ Ontario, SE Canada
20 *H7* **Barkley, Lake** ▣ Kentucky/Tennessee, S USA
10 *K17* **Barkley Sound** *inlet* British Columbia, W Canada
83 *J24* **Barkly East** *Afr.* Barkly-Oos. Eastern Cape, SE South Africa
Barkly-Oos *see* Barkly East
181 *S4* **Barkly Tableland** *plateau* Northern Territory/Queensland, N Australia
Barkly-Wes *see* Barkly West
83 *H22* **Barkly West** *Afr.* Barkly-Wes. Northern Cape, N South Africa
159 *O5* **Barkol** *var.* Barkol Kazak Zizhixian. Xinjiang Uygur Zizhiqu, NW China
159 *O5* **Barkol Hu** ◎ NW China
Barkol Kazak Zizhixian *see* Barkol
30 *J3* **Bark Point** *headland* Wisconsin, N USA
25 *P11* **Barksdale** Texas, SW USA
Bar Kunar *see* Asmār
116 *L11* **Bârlad** *prev.* Bîrlad. Vaslui, E Romania
116 *M11* **Bârlad** *prev.* Bîrlad. ≈ E Romania
76 *D9* **Barlavento, Ilhas de** *var.* Windward Islands. *island group* N Cape Verde
103 *R5* **Bar-le-Duc** *var.* Bar-sur-Ornain. Meuse, NE France
180 *K11* **Barlee, Lake** ◎ Western Australia
180 *H8* **Barlee Range** ▲▲ Western Australia
107 *N16* **Barletta** *anc.* Barduli. Puglia, SE Italy
110 *E10* **Barlinek** *Ger.* Berlinchen. Zachodnio-pomorskie, NW Poland
27 *S11* **Barling** Arkansas, C USA
171 *U12* **Barma** Papua, E Indonesia
183 *Q9* **Barmedman** New South Wales, SE Australia
Barmen-Elberfeld *see* Wuppertal
152 *D12* **Bārmer** Rājasthān, NW India
182 *K9* **Barmera** South Australia
97 *I19* **Barmouth** NW Wales, UK
154 *F10* **Barnagar** Madhya Pradesh, C India
152 *H9* **Barnāla** Punjab, NW India
97 *L15* **Barnard Castle** N England, UK
183 *O6* **Barnato** New South Wales, SE Australia
122 *I13* **Barnaul** Altayskiy Kray, C Russian Federation
109 *V8* **Bärnbach** Steiermark, SE Austria
18 *K16* **Barnegat** New Jersey, NE USA
23 *S4* **Barnesville** Georgia, SE USA
29 *R6* **Barnesville** Minnesota, N USA
31 *U13* **Barnesville** Ohio, N USA
98 *K11* **Barneveld** *var.* Barnveld. Gelderland, C Netherlands
25 *O9* **Barnhart** Texas, SW USA
27 *P8* **Barnsdall** Oklahoma, C USA
97 *M17* **Barnsley** N England, UK
19 *Q12* **Barnstable** Massachusetts, NE USA
97 *I23* **Barnstaple** SW England, UK
Barnveld *see* Barneveld
21 *Q14* **Barnwell** South Carolina, SE USA
67 *U8* **Baro** *var.* Baro Wenz. ≈ Ethiopia/Sudan
77 *U15* **Baro** Niger, C Nigeria
Baro *see* Baro Wenz
Baroda *see* Vadodara
149 *U2* **Baroghil Pass** *var.* Kowtal-e Barowghīl. *pass* Afghanistan/Pakistan
119 *Q17* **Baron'ki** *Rus.* Boron'ki. Mahilyowskaya Voblasts', E Belarus
182 *J9* **Barossa Valley** *valley* South Australia
Baroui *see* Salisbury
81 *H14* **Baro Wenz** *var.* Baro, Nahr Barū. ≈ Ethiopia/Sudan
153 *U12* **Barpeta** Assam, NE India
31 *S7* **Barques, Pointe Aux** *headland* Michigan, N USA
54 *J5* **Barquisimeto** Lara, NW Venezuela
59 *N16* **Barra** Bahia, E Brazil
96 *E9* **Barra** *island* NW Scotland, UK
183 *T5* **Barraba** New South Wales, SE Australia
60 *L9* **Barra Bonita** São Paulo, S Brazil
64 *J12* **Barracuda Fracture Zone** *var.* Fifteen Twenty Fracture Zone. *tectonic feature* SW Atlantic Ocean
64 *G11* **Barracuda Ridge** *undersea feature* N Atlantic Ocean
43 *N12* **Barra del Colorado** Limón, NE Costa Rica
43 *N9* **Barra de Río Grande** Región Autónoma Atlántico Sur, E Nicaragua
82 *A11* **Barra do Cuanza** Luanda, NW Angola
60 *O9* **Barra do Piraí** Rio de Janeiro, SE Brazil
61 *D16* **Barra do Quaraí** Rio Grande do Sul, SE Brazil
59 *G14* **Barra do São Manuel** Pará, N Brazil
83 *N19* **Barra Falsa, Ponta da** *headland* S Mozambique
96 *E10* **Barra Head** *headland* NW Scotland, UK
Barram *see* Baram, Batang
60 *O9* **Barra Mansa** Rio de Janeiro, SE Brazil
57 *D14* **Barranca** Lima, W Peru
54 *F8* **Barrancabermeja** Santander, N Colombia
54 *H4* **Barrancas** La Guajira, N Colombia
54 *J6* **Barrancas** Barinas, NW Venezuela
55 *Q6* **Barrancas** Monagas, NE Venezuela
54 *F6* **Barranco de Loba** Bolívar, N Colombia
104 *I12* **Barrancos** Beja, S Portugal
62 *N7* **Barranqueras** Chaco, N Argentina
54 *E4* **Barranquilla** Atlántico, N Colombia
83 *N20* **Barra, Ponta da** *headland* S Mozambique
105 *P11* **Barrax** Castilla-La Mancha, C Spain
19 *N11* **Barre** Massachusetts, NE USA
18 *M7* **Barre** Vermont, NE USA
59 *M17* **Barreiras** Bahia, E Brazil
104 *F11* **Barreiro** Setúbal, W Portugal
65 *C26* **Barren Island** *island* S Falkland Islands
20 *K7* **Barren River Lake** ▣ Kentucky, S USA
60 *L7* **Barretos** São Paulo, S Brazil
11 *P14* **Barrhead** Alberta, SW Canada
14 *G14* **Barrie** Ontario, S Canada
11 *N16* **Barrière** British Columbia, SW Canada
14 *H8* **Barrière, Lac** ◎ Québec, SE Canada
182 *L6* **Barrier Range** *hill range* New South Wales, SE Australia
42 *G3* **Barrier Reef** *reef* E Belize
188 *C16* **Barrigada** C Guam
Barrington Island *see* Santa Fe, Isla
183 *T7* **Barrington Tops** ▲ New South Wales, SE Australia
183 *O4* **Barringun** New South Wales, SE Australia
59 *K18* **Barro Alto** Goiás, S Brazil
59 *N14* **Barro Duro** Piauí, NE Brazil
30 *I5* **Barron** Wisconsin, N USA
14 *J12* **Barron** ≈ Ontario, SE Canada
61 *H15* **Barros Cassal** Rio Grande do Sul, S Brazil
45 *P14* **Barrouallie** Saint Vincent, W Saint Vincent and the Grenadines
39 *O4* **Barrow** Alaska, USA
97 *E20* **Barrow** *Ir.* An Bhearú. ≈ SE Ireland
181 *Q6* **Barrow Creek Roadhouse** Northern Territory, N Australia
97 *J16* **Barrow-in-Furness** NW England, UK
180 *G7* **Barrow Island** *island* Western Australia
39 *O4* **Barrow, Point** *headland* Alaska, USA
11 *V14* **Barrows** Manitoba, S Canada
97 *J22* **Barry** S Wales, UK
14 *J12* **Barry's Bay** Ontario, SE Canada
144 *K14* **Barsakel'mes, Ostrov** *island* SW Kazakhstan
Baršć Łužyca *see* Forst
147 *S14* **Barsem** S Tajikistan
145 *V11* **Barshatas** Vostochnyy Kazakhstan, E Kazakhstan
155 *F14* **Bārsi** Mahārāshtra, W India
100 *I13* **Barsinghausen** Niedersachsen, C Germany
147 *X8* **Barskoon** Issyk-Kul'skaya Oblast', E Kyrgyzstan
100 *F10* **Barssel** Niedersachsen, NW Germany
35 *U14* **Barstow** California, W USA
24 *L8* **Barstow** Texas, SW USA
103 *R6* **Bar-sur-Aube** Aube, NE France
Bar-sur-Ornain *see* Bar-le-Duc
103 *Q6* **Bar-sur-Seine** Aube, N France
147 *S13* **Bartang** S Tajikistan
147 *T13* **Bartang** ≈ SE Tajikistan
Bartenstein *see* Bartoszyce
Bártfa/Bartfeld *see* Bardejov
100 *N7* **Barth** Mecklenburg-Vorpommern, NE Germany
27 *W13* **Bartholomew, Bayou** ≈ Arkansas/Louisiana, S USA
55 *T8* **Bartica** N Guyana
136 *H10* **Bartın** Bartin, NW Turkey
136 *H10* **Bartın** ◈ *province* NW Turkey
181 *W4* **Bartle Frere** ▲ Queensland, E Australia
27 *P8* **Bartlesville** Oklahoma, C USA
29 *P14* **Bartlett** Nebraska, C USA
20 *E10* **Bartlett** Tennessee, S USA
25 *T9* **Bartlett** Texas, SW USA
36 *L13* **Bartlett Reservoir** ▣ Arizona, SW USA
19 *N6* **Barton** Vermont, NE USA
110 *L7* **Bartoszyce** *Ger.* Bartenstein. Warmińsko-Mazurskie, NE Poland,
23 *W12* **Bartow** Florida, SE USA
Bartschin *see* Barcin

◆ Country ◇ Dependent Territory ◈ Administrative Region ▲ Mountain ☒ Volcano ◎ Lake
● Country Capital ○ Dependent Territory Capital × International Airport ▲▲ Mountain Range ≈ River ▣ Reservoir

168 J10 **Barumun, Sungai** ≈ Sumatera, W Indonesia
Barū, Nahr *see* Baro Wenz
169 S17 **Barung, Nusa** *island* S Indonesia
168 H9 **Barus** Sumatera, NW Indonesia
162 L10 **Baruunsuu** Ömnögovĭ, S Mongolia
163 P8 **Baruun-Urt** Sühbaatar, E Mongolia
43 P15 **Barú, Volcán** *var.* Volcán de Chiriquí. ✶ W Panama
99 K21 **Barvaux** Luxembourg, SE Belgium
42 M13 **Barva, Volcán** ✶ NW Costa Rica
117 W6 **Barvinkove** Kharkivs'ka Oblast', E Ukraine
154 G11 **Barwāh** Madhya Pradesh, C India
Bärwalde Neumark *see* Mieszkowice
154 F11 **Barwāni** Madhya Pradesh, C India
183 P5 **Barwon River** ≈ New South Wales, SE Australia
119 L15 **Barysaw** *Rus.* Borisov. Minskaya Voblasts', NE Belarus
127 Q6 **Barysh** Ul'yanovskaya Oblast', W Russian Federation
117 Q4 **Baryshivka** Kyyivs'ka Oblast', N Ukraine
79 J17 **Basankusu** Equateur, NW Dem. Rep. Congo
117 N11 **Basarabeasca** *Rus.* Bessarabka. SE Moldova
116 M14 **Basarabi** Constanța, SW Romania
40 H6 **Basaseachic** Chihuahua, NW Mexico
105 O2 **Basauri** País Vasco, N Spain
61 D18 **Basavilbaso** Entre Ríos, E Argentina
79 F21 **Bas-Congo** *off.* Région du Bas-Congo; *prev.* Bas-Zaïre. ◈ *region* SW Dem. Rep. Congo
108 E6 **Basel** *Eng.* Basle, *Fr.* Bâle. Basel-Stadt, NW Switzerland
108 E7 **Basel** *Eng.* Basle, *Fr.* Bâle. ◈ *canton* NW Switzerland
143 T14 **Bashākerd, Kūhhā-ye** ⛰ SE Iran
11 Q15 **Bashaw** Alberta, SW Canada
146 K16 **Bashbedeng** Mary Welaýaty, S Turkmenistan
161 T15 **Bashi Channel** *Chin.* Pa-shih Hai-hsia. *channel* Philippines/Taiwan
Bashkiria *see* Bashkortostan, Respublika
122 F11 **Bashkortostan, Respublika** *prev.* Bashkiria. ◈ *autonomous republic* W Russian Federation
127 N6 **Bashmakovo** Penzenskaya Oblast', W Russian Federation
146 J10 **Bashsakarba** Lebap Welaýaty, NE Turkmenistan
117 R9 **Bashtanka** Mykolayivs'ka Oblast', S Ukraine
22 H8 **Basile** Louisiana, S USA
107 M18 **Basilicata** ◈ *region* S Italy
33 V13 **Basin** Wyoming, C USA
97 N22 **Basingstoke** S England, UK
143 U8 **Başīrān** Khorāsān, E Iran
112 B10 **Baška** *It.* Bescanuova. Primorje-Gorski Kotar, NW Croatia
137 T15 **Başkale** Van, SE Turkey
14 L10 **Baskatong, Réservoir** ⊠ Québec, SE Canada
137 O14 **Baskil** Elaziğ, E Turkey
Basle *see* Basel
154 H9 **Bāsoda** Madhya Pradesh, C India
79 L17 **Basoko** Orientale, N Dem. Rep. Congo
Basque Country, The *see* País Vasco
Basra *see* Al Başrah
103 U5 **Bas-Rhin** ◈ *department* NE France
Bassam *see* Grand-Bassam
11 Q16 **Bassano** Alberta, SW Canada
106 H7 **Bassano del Grappa** Veneto, NE Italy
77 Q15 **Bassar** *var.* Bassari. NW Togo
Bassari *see* Bassar
172 L9 **Bassas da India** *island group* W Madagascar
108 D7 **Bassecourt** Jura, W Switzerland
166 K8 **Bassein** *var.* Pathein. Irrawaddy, SW Myanmar
79 J15 **Basse-Kotto** ◈ *prefecture* S Central African Republic
105 V5 **Bassella** Cataluña, NE Spain
102 J5 **Basse-Normandie** *Eng.* Lower Normandy. ◈ *region* N France
45 Q11 **Basse-Pointe** N Martinique
76 H12 **Basse Santa Su** E Gambia
Basse-Saxe *see* Niedersachsen
45 X6 **Basse-Terre** ○ (Guadeloupe) Basse Terre, SW Guadeloupe
45 X6 **Basse Terre** *island* W Guadeloupe
45 V10 **Basseterre** ● (Saint Kitts and Nevis) Saint Kitts, Saint Kitts and Nevis
29 O13 **Bassett** Nebraska, C USA
21 S7 **Bassett** Virginia, NE USA
37 N15 **Bassett Peak** ▲ Arizona, SW USA
76 M10 **Bassikounou** Hodh ech Chargui, SE Mauritania
77 R15 **Bassila** W Benin
Bass, Îlots de *see* Marotiri
31 O11 **Bass Lake** Indiana, N USA
183 O14 **Bass Strait** *strait* SE Australia
100 H11 **Bassum** Niedersachsen, NW Germany
29 X3 **Basswood Lake** ◎ Canada/USA
95 J21 **Båstad** Skåne, S Sweden
139 U2 **Baştah** E Iraq
153 N12 **Basti** Uttar Pradesh, N India
103 X14 **Bastia** Corse, France, C Mediterranean Sea
99 L23 **Bastogne** Luxembourg, SE Belgium
22 I5 **Bastrop** Louisiana, S USA
25 T11 **Bastrop** Texas, SW USA
93 J15 **Bastuträsk** Västerbotten, N Sweden
119 J19 **Bastyn'** *Rus.* Bostyn'. Brestskaya Voblasts', SW Belarus
Basuo *see* Dongfang
Basutoland *see* Lesotho
119 O15 **Basya** ≈ E Belarus
117 V8 **Basyl'kivka** Dnipropetrovs'ka Oblast', E Ukraine
79 D17 **Bata** NW Equatorial Guinea
79 D17 **Bata** ✕ S Equatorial Guinea
Batae Coritanorum *see* Leicester
123 Q8 **Batagay** Respublika Sakha (Yakutiya), NE Russian Federation
123 P8 **Batagay-Alyta** Respublika Sakha (Yakutiya), NE Russian Federation
112 L10 **Batajnica** Serbia, N Serbia and Montenegro (Yugo.)
136 H15 **Bataklık Gölü** ◎ S Turkey
114 H11 **Batak, Yazovir** ⊠ SW Bulgaria
152 H7 **Batāla** Punjab, N India
104 F9 **Batalha** Leiria, C Portugal
79 N17 **Batama** Orientale, NE Dem. Rep. Congo
123 Q10 **Batamay** Respublika Sakha (Yakutiya), NE Russian Federation
160 F9 **Batang** *var.* Bazhong. Sichuan, C China
79 I14 **Batangafo** Ouham, NW Central African Republic
171 P8 **Batangas** *off.* Batangas City. Luzon, N Philippines
Bătania *see* Battonya
171 Q10 **Batan Islands** *island group* N Philippines
60 L8 **Batatais** São Paulo, S Brazil
18 E10 **Batavia** New York, NE USA
Batavia *see* Jakarta
173 T9 **Batavia Seamount** *undersea feature* E Indian Ocean
126 L12 **Bataysk** Rostovskaya Oblast', SW Russian Federation
14 B9 **Batchawana** ≈ Ontario, S Canada
14 B9 **Batchawana Bay** Ontario, S Canada
167 Q12 **Bătdâmbâng** *prev.* Battambang. Bătdâmbâng, NW Cambodia
79 G20 **Batéké, Plateaux** *plateau* S Congo
183 S11 **Batemans Bay** New South Wales, SE Australia
21 Q13 **Batesburg** South Carolina, SE USA
28 K12 **Batesland** South Dakota, N USA
27 V10 **Batesville** Arkansas, C USA
31 Q14 **Batesville** Indiana, N USA
22 L2 **Batesville** Mississippi, S USA
25 Q13 **Batesville** Texas, SW USA
44 L13 **Bath** E Jamaica
97 L22 **Bath** *hist.* Akermanceaster, *anc.* Aquae Calidae, Aquae Solis. SW England, UK
19 Q8 **Bath** Maine, NE USA
18 F11 **Bath** New York, NE USA
Bath *see* Berkeley Springs
78 I10 **Batha** *off.* Préfecture du Batha. ◈ *prefecture* C Chad
78 I10 **Batha** *seasonal river* C Chad
141 Y8 **Baṭḥā', Wādī al** *dry watercourse* NE Oman
152 H9 **Bathinda** Punjab, NW India
98 M11 **Bathmen** Overijssel, E Netherlands
45 Z14 **Bathsheba** E Barbados
183 R8 **Bathurst** New South Wales, SE Australia
13 O13 **Bathurst** New Brunswick, SE Canada
Bathurst *see* Banjul
8 H6 **Bathurst, Cape** *headland* Northwest Territories, NW Canada
196 L8 **Bathurst Inlet** Nunavut, N Canada
8 M4 **Bathurst Inlet** *inlet* Nunavut, N Canada
181 O1 **Bathurst Island** *island* Northern Territory, N Australia
197 O9 **Bathurst Island** *island* Parry Islands, Nunavut, N Canada
77 G14 **Batié** SW Burkina
Batinah *see* Al Bāṭinah
141 Y9 **Bāṭin, Wādī al** *dry watercourse* SW Asia
15 P9 **Batiscan** ≈ Québec, SE Canada
136 F16 **Batı Toroslar** ⛰ SW Turkey
Batjan *see* Bacan, Pulau
147 R11 **Batken** Batkenskaya Oblast', SW Kyrgyzstan
Batken Oblasty *see* Batkenskaya Oblast'
147 Q11 **Batkenskaya Oblast'** *Kir.* Batken Oblasty. ◈ *province* SW Kyrgyzstan
Batlle y Ordóñez *see* José Batlle y Ordóñez
183 Q10 **Batlow** New South Wales, SE Australia
137 Q15 **Batman** *var.* Iluh. Batman, SE Turkey
137 Q15 **Batman** ◈ *province* SE Turkey
74 L6 **Batna** NE Algeria
Batoe *see* Batu, Kepulauan
162 K7 **Bat-Öldziyt** Töv, C Mongolia
22 J8 **Baton Rouge** *state capital* Louisiana, S USA
79 G15 **Batouri** Est, E Cameroon
138 G14 **Batrā', Jibāl al** ⛰ S Jordan
138 G6 **Batroûn** *var.* Al Batrūn. N Lebanon
Batsch *see* Bač
Batsevichi *see* Batsevichy
119 M17 **Batsevichy** *Rus.* Batsevichi. Mahilyowskaya Voblasts', E Belarus
92 M7 **Båtsfjord** Finnmark, N Norway
Battambang *see* Bătdâmbâng
195 X3 **Batterbee, Cape** *headland* Antarctica
155 L24 **Batticaloa** Eastern Province, E Sri Lanka
99 L19 **Battice** Liège, E Belgium
107 L18 **Battipaglia** Campania, S Italy
11 R15 **Battle** ≈ Alberta /Saskatchewan, SW Canada
Battle Born State *see* Nevada
31 Q10 **Battle Creek** Michigan, N USA
27 T7 **Battlefield** Missouri, C USA
11 S15 **Battleford** Saskatchewan, S Canada
29 S6 **Battle Lake** Minnesota, N USA
35 U3 **Battle Mountain** Nevada, W USA
111 M25 **Battonya** *Rom.* Bătania. Békés, SE Hungary
168 D11 **Batu, Kepulauan** *prev.* Batoe. *island group* W Indonesia
137 Q10 **Bat'umi** W Georgia
168 K10 **Batu Pahat** *prev.* Bandar Penggaram. Johor, Peninsular Malaysia
171 O12 **Baturebe** Sulawesi, N Indonesia
122 J12 **Baturino** Tomskaya Oblast', C Russian Federation
117 R3 **Baturyn** Chernihivs'ka Oblast', N Ukraine
138 F10 **Bat Yam** Tel Aviv, C Israel
127 Q4 **Batyrevo** Chuvashskaya Respublika, W Russian Federation
Batys Qazaqstan Oblysy *see* Zapadnyy Kazakhstan
102 F5 **Batz, Île de** *island* NW France
169 Q10 **Bau** Sarawak, East Malaysia
171 N2 **Bauang** Luzon, N Philippines
171 P14 **Baubau** *var.* Baoebaoe. Pulau Buton, C Indonesia
77 W14 **Bauchi** Bauchi, NE Nigeria
77 W14 **Bauchi** ◈ *state* C Nigeria
102 H7 **Baud** Morbihan, NW France
29 T2 **Baudette** Minnesota, N USA
193 S9 **Bauer Basin** *undersea feature* E Pacific Ocean
187 R14 **Bauer Field** *var.* Port Vila. ✕ (Port-Vila) Éfaté, C Vanuatu
13 T9 **Bauld, Cape** *headland* Newfoundland and Labrador, E Canada
103 T8 **Baume-les-Dames** Doubs, E France
101 I15 **Baunatal** Hessen, C Germany
107 D18 **Baunei** Sardegna, Italy, C Mediterranean Sea
57 M15 **Baures, Río** ≈ N Bolivia
60 K9 **Bauru** São Paulo, S Brazil
Baushar *see* Bawshar
118 G10 **Bauska** *Ger.* Bauske. Bauska, S Latvia
Bauske *see* Bauska
101 Q15 **Bautzen** *Lus.* Budyšin. Sachsen, E Germany
145 Q16 **Bauyrzhan Momyshuly** *Kaz.* Baūyrzhan Momyshuly; *prev.* Burnoye. Zhambyl, S Kazakhstan
Bauzanum *see* Bolzano
Bavaria *see* Bayern
109 N7 **Bavarian Alps** *Ger.* Bayrische Alpen. ⛰ Austria/Germany
Bavière *see* Bayern
40 H4 **Bavispe, Río** ≈ NW Mexico
127 T5 **Bavly** Respublika Tatarstan, W Russian Federation
169 P13 **Bawal, Pulau** *island* N Indonesia
169 T12 **Bawan** Borneo, C Indonesia
183 O12 **Baw Baw, Mount** ▲ Victoria, SE Australia
169 S15 **Bawean, Pulau** *island* S Indonesia
75 V9 **Bawīṭī** N Egypt
77 Q13 **Bawku** N Ghana
167 N7 **Bawlakè** Kayah State, C Myanmar
169 H11 **Bawo Ofuloa** Pulau Tanahmasa, W Indonesia
141 Y8 **Bawshar** *var.* Baushar. NE Oman
Ba Xian *see* Bazhou
158 M8 **Baxkorgan** Xinjiang Uygur Zizhiqu, W China
23 V6 **Baxley** Georgia, SE USA
159 R15 **Baxoi** *var.* Baima. Xizang Zizhiqu, W China
29 W14 **Baxter** Iowa, C USA
29 U6 **Baxter** Minnesota, N USA
27 R8 **Baxter Springs** Kansas, C USA
81 M17 **Bay** *off.* Gobolka Bay. ◈ *region* SW Somalia
Bay *see* Baicheng
44 H7 **Bayamo** Granma, E Cuba
45 U5 **Bayamón** E Puerto Rico
163 W8 **Bayan** Heilongjiang, NE China
170 L16 **Bayan** *prev.* Bajan. Pulau Lombok, C Indonesia
162 I6 **Bayan** Arhangay, C Mongolia
163 P7 **Bayan** Dornod, E Mongolia
163 N9 **Bayan** Dornogovĭ, SE Mongolia
162 F7 **Bayan** Govĭ-Altay, W Mongolia
163 O8 **Bayan** Hentiy, C Mongolia
152 I12 **Bayāna** Rājasthān, N India
149 N5 **Bāyān, Band-e** ⛰ C Afghanistan
162 H8 **Bayanbulag** Bayanhongor, C Mongolia
163 N7 **Bayanbulag** Hentiy, C Mongolia
158 J5 **Bayanbulak** Xinjiang Uygur Zizhiqu, W China
Bayan Gol *see* Dengkou
162 F8 **Bayangol** Govĭ-Altay, SW Mongolia
159 R12 **Bayan Har Shan** *var.* Bayan Khar. ⛰ C China
162 I8 **Bayanhongor** Bayanhongor, C Mongolia
162 H9 **Bayanhongor** ◈ *province* C Mongolia
162 K14 **Bayan Hot** *var.* Alxa Zuoqi. Nei Mongol Zizhiqu, N China
163 T9 **Bayan Huxu** *var.* Horqin Zuoyi Zhongji. Nei Mongol Zizhiqu, N China
Bayan Khar *see* Bayan Har Shan
168 J7 **Bayan Lepas** ✕ (George Town) Pinang, Peninsular Malaysia
162 K13 **Bayan Mod** Nei Mongol Zizhiqu, N China
Bayan Nuru *see* Xar Burd
163 N12 **Bayan Obo** Nei Mongol Zizhiqu, N China
43 V15 **Bayano, Lago** ◎ E Panama
162 C5 **Bayan-Ölgiy** ◈ *province* NW Mongolia
162 F9 **Bayan-Ovoo** Govĭ-Altay, SW Mongolia
162 H9 **Bayansayr** Bayanhongor, C Mongolia
159 Q9 **Bayan Shan** ▲ C China
162 J9 **Bayanteeg** Övörhangay, C Mongolia
162 L8 **Bayantöhöm** Töv, C Mongolia
Bayan Tumen *see* Choybalsan
162 H6 **Bayan-Uhaa** Dzavhan, C Mongolia
163 R10 **Bayan Ul** *var.* Xi Ujimqin Qi. Nei Mongol Zizhiqu, N China
162 J8 **Bayan-Ulaan** Övörhangay, C Mongolia
28 J14 **Bayard** Nebraska, C USA
37 P15 **Bayard** New Mexico, SW USA
103 T13 **Bayard, Col** *pass* SE France
163 O8 **Bayasgalant** Sühbaatar, E Mongolia
136 J12 **Bayat** Çorum, N Turkey
171 P6 **Bayawan** Negros, C Philippines
143 R10 **Bayāz** Kermān, C Iran
171 Q6 **Baybay** Leyte, C Philippines
21 X10 **Bayboro** North Carolina, SE USA
137 P12 **Bayburt** Bayburt, NE Turkey
137 P12 **Bayburt** ◈ *province* NE Turkey
31 R8 **Bay City** Michigan, N USA
25 V12 **Bay City** Texas, SW USA
122 I7 **Baydaratskaya Guba** *var.* Baydarata Bay. *bay* N Russian Federation
81 M16 **Baydhabo** *var.* Baydhowa, Isha Baydhabo, *It.* Baidoa. Bay, SW Somalia
Baydhowa *see* Baydhabo
101 N21 **Bayerischer Wald** ⛰ SE Germany
101 K21 **Bayern** *Eng.* Bavaria, *Fr.* Bavière. ◈ *state* SE Germany
147 V9 **Bayetovo** Narynskaya Oblast', C Kyrgyzstan
102 K4 **Bayeux** *anc.* Augustodurum. Calvados, N France
14 E15 **Bayfield** ≈ Ontario, S Canada
145 O15 **Baygekum** *Kaz.* Bäygequm. Kzylorda, S Kazakhstan
Bäygequm *see* Baygekum
136 C14 **Bayındır** İzmir, SW Turkey
138 H12 **Bāyir** *var.* Bā'ir. Ma'ān, S Jordan
Bay Islands *see* Bahía, Islas de la
139 R5 **Bayjī** *var.* Baiji. N Iraq
Baykadam *see* Saudakent
123 N13 **Baykal, Ozero** *Eng.* Lake Baikal. ◎ S Russian Federation
123 M14 **Baykal'sk** Irkutskaya Oblast', S Russian Federation
137 R15 **Baykan** Siirt, SE Turkey
123 L11 **Baykit** Evenkiyskiy Avtonomnyy Okrug, C Russian Federation
145 N12 **Baykonur** *var.* Baykonyr. Karaganda, C Kazakhstan
144 M14 **Baykonyr** *var.* Baykonur *Kaz.* Bayqongyr; *prev.* Leninsk. Kyzylorda, S Kazakhstan
Baykonyr *see* Baykonur
158 E7 **Baykurt** Xinjiang Uygur Zizhiqu, W China
14 I9 **Bay, Lac** ◎ Québec, SE Canada
127 W6 **Baymak** Respublika Bashkortostan, W Russian Federation
23 O8 **Bay Minette** Alabama, S USA
143 O17 **Baynūnah** *desert* W UAE
184 O8 **Bay of Plenty** *off.* Bay of Plenty Region. ◈ *region* North Island, NZ
191 Z3 **Bay of Wrecks** *bay* Kiritimati, E Kiribati
102 I15 **Bayonne** *anc.* Lapurdum. Pyrénées-Atlantiques, SW France
22 H4 **Bayou D'Arbonne Lake** ⊠ Louisiana, S USA
23 N9 **Bayou La Batre** Alabama, S USA
Bayou State *see* Mississippi
Bayqadam *see* Saudakent
Bayqongyr *see* Baykonyr
Bayram-Ali *see* Baýramaly
146 J14 **Baýramaly** *var.* Bayramaly; *prev.* Bayram-Ali. Mary Welaýaty, S Turkmenistan
101 L19 **Bayreuth** *var.* Baireuth. Bayern, SE Germany
Bayrische Alpen *see* Bavarian Alps
Bayrūt *see* Beyrouth
22 L9 **Bay Saint Louis** Mississippi, S USA
Baysān *see* Bet She'an
162 L8 **Bayshint** Töv, C Mongolia
14 H13 **Bays, Lake of** ◎ Ontario, S Canada
22 M6 **Bay Springs** Mississippi, S USA
Bay State *see* Massachusetts
Baysun *see* Boysun
14 H13 **Baysville** Ontario, S Canada
141 N15 **Bayt al Faqīh** W Yemen
158 M4 **Baytik Shan** ⛰ China/Mongolia
Bayt Laḥm *see* Bethlehem
25 W11 **Baytown** Texas, SW USA
169 V11 **Bayur, Tanjung** *headland* Borneo, N Indonesia
121 N14 **Bayy al Kabīr, Wādī** *dry watercourse* NW Libya
Bayyrqum *see* Bairkum
105 P14 **Baza** Andalucía, S Spain
137 X10 **Bazardüzü Dağı** *Rus.* Gora Bazardyuzyu. ▲ N Azerbaijan
Bazardyuzyu, Gora *see* Bazardüzü Dağı
Bazargic *see* Dobrich
83 N18 **Bazaruto, Ilha do** *island* SE Mozambique
102 K14 **Bazas** Gironde, SW France
105 O14 **Baza, Sierra de** ⛰ S Spain
160 J8 **Bazhong** Sichuan, C China
Bazhong *see* Batang
161 P3 **Bazhou** *prev.* Baxian, Ba Xian. Hebei, E China
14 M9 **Bazin** ≈ Québec, SE Canada
Bazin *see* Pezinok
139 Q7 **Bāzīyah** C Iraq
138 H6 **Bcharré** *var.* Bcharreh, Bsharrī, Bsherri. NE Lebanon
Bcharreh *see* Bcharré
28 J5 **Beach** North Dakota, N USA
182 K12 **Beachport** South Australia
97 O23 **Beachy Head** *headland* SE England, UK
18 K13 **Beacon** New York, NE USA
63 J25 **Beagle Channel** *channel* Argentina/Chile
181 O1 **Beagle Gulf** *gulf* Northern Territory, N Australia
Bealach an Doirín *see* Ballaghaderreen
Bealach Cláir *see* Ballyclare
Bealach Féich *see* Ballybofey
172 J3 **Bealanana** Mahajanga, NE Madagascar
Béal an Átha *see* Ballina
Béal an Átha Móir *see* Ballinamore
Béal an Mhuirhead *see* Belmullet
Béal Átha Beithe *see* Ballybay
Béal Átha Conaill *see* Ballyconnell
Beál Átha hAmhnais *see* Ballyhaunis
Béal Átha na Sluaighe *see* Ballinasloe
Béal Átha Seanaidh *see* Ballyshannon
Bealdovuopmi *see* Peltovuoma
Béal Feirste *see* Belfast
Béal Tairbirt *see* Belturbet
Beanna Boirche *see* Mourne Mountains
Beannchar *see* Banagher, Ireland
Beannchar *see* Bangor, Northern Ireland, UK
Beanntraí *see* Bantry
Bearalváhki *see* Berlevåg
23 N2 **Bear Creek** ≈ Alabama/Mississippi, S USA
30 J13 **Bear Creek** ≈ Illinois, N USA
27 U13 **Bearden** Arkansas, C USA
195 Q10 **Beardmore Glacier** *glacier* Antarctica
30 K13 **Beardstown** Illinois, N USA
28 L14 **Bear Hill** ▲ Nebraska, C USA
Bear Island *see* Bjørnøya
14 H12 **Bear Lake** Ontario, S Canada
36 M1 **Bear Lake** ◎ Idaho/Utah, NW USA
39 U11 **Bear, Mount** ▲ Alaska, USA
102 J16 **Béarn** *cultural region* SW France
194 J11 **Bear Peninsula** *peninsula* Antarctica
152 I7 **Beās** ≈ India/Pakistan
105 P3 **Beasain** País Vasco, N Spain
105 O12 **Beas de Segura** Andalucía, S Spain
45 N10 **Beata, Cabo** *headland* SW Dominican Republic
45 N10 **Beata, Isla** *island* SW Dominican Republic
64 F11 **Beata Ridge** *undersea feature* N Caribbean Sea
29 R17 **Beatrice** Nebraska, C USA
83 L16 **Beatrice** Mashonaland East, NE Zimbabwe
11 N11 **Beatton** ≈ British Columbia, W Canada
11 N11 **Beatton River** British Columbia, W Canada
35 V10 **Beatty** Nevada, W USA
21 N6 **Beattyville** Kentucky, S USA
173 X16 **Beau Bassin** W Mauritius
103 R15 **Beaucaire** Gard, S France
14 I8 **Beauchastel, Lac** ◎ Québec, SE Canada
14 I10 **Beauchêne, Lac** ◎ Québec, SE Canada
183 V3 **Beaudesert** Queensland, E Australia
182 M12 **Beaufort** Victoria, SE Australia
21 X11 **Beaufort** North Carolina, SE USA
21 R15 **Beaufort** South Carolina, SE USA
38 M11 **Beaufort Sea** *sea* Arctic Ocean
Beaufort-Wes *see* Beaufort West
83 G25 **Beaufort West** *Afr.* Beaufort-Wes. Western Cape, SW South Africa
103 N7 **Beaugency** Loiret, C France
19 R2 **Beau Lake** ⊠ Maine, NE USA
96 I8 **Beauly** N Scotland, UK
99 G21 **Beaumont** Hainaut, S Belgium
185 E23 **Beaumont** Otago, South Island, NZ
22 M7 **Beaumont** Mississippi, S USA
25 X10 **Beaumont** Texas, SW USA
102 M15 **Beaumont-de-Lomagne** Tarn-et-Garonne, S France
102 L6 **Beaumont-sur-Sarthe** Sarthe, NW France
103 R8 **Beaune** Côte d'Or, C France
15 R9 **Beaupré** Québec, SE Canada
102 J8 **Beaupréau** Maine-et-Loire, NW France
99 I22 **Beauraing** Namur, SE Belgium
103 R12 **Beaurepaire** Isère, E France
11 Y16 **Beausejour** Manitoba, S Canada
103 N4 **Beauvais** *anc.* Bellovacum, Caesaromagus. Oise, N France
11 S13 **Beauval** Saskatchewan, C Canada
102 I9 **Beauvoir-sur-Mer** Vendée, NW France
39 R8 **Beaver** Alaska, USA
26 J8 **Beaver** Oklahoma, C USA
18 B14 **Beaver** Pennsylvania, NE USA
36 K6 **Beaver** Utah, W USA
10 L9 **Beaver** ≈ British Columbia/Yukon Territory, W Canada
11 S13 **Beaver** ≈ Saskatchewan, C Canada
29 N17 **Beaver City** Nebraska, C USA
10 G6 **Beaver Creek** Yukon Territory, W Canada
31 R14 **Beavercreek** Ohio, N USA
39 S8 **Beaver Creek** ≈ Alaska, USA
26 H3 **Beaver Creek** ≈ Kansas/Nebraska, C USA
28 J5 **Beaver Creek** ≈ Montana/North Dakota, N USA
29 Q14 **Beaver Creek** ≈ Nebraska, C USA
25 Q4 **Beaver Creek** ≈ Texas, SW USA
30 M8 **Beaver Dam** Wisconsin, N USA
30 M8 **Beaver Dam Lake** ◎ Wisconsin, N USA
18 B14 **Beaver Falls** Pennsylvania, NE USA
33 P12 **Beaverhead Mountains** ⛰ Idaho/Montana, NW USA
33 Q12 **Beaverhead River** ≈ Montana, NW USA
65 A25 **Beaver Island** *island* W Falkland Islands
31 P5 **Beaver Island** *island* Michigan, N USA
27 S9 **Beaver Lake** ⊠ Arkansas, C USA
11 N13 **Beaverlodge** Alberta, W Canada
18 I8 **Beaver River** ≈ New York, NE USA
26 J8 **Beaver River** ≈ Oklahoma, C USA
18 B13 **Beaver River** ≈ Pennsylvania, NE USA
65 A25 **Beaver Settlement** Beaver Island, W Falkland Islands
Beaver State *see* Oregon
14 H14 **Beaverton** Ontario, S Canada
32 G11 **Beaverton** Oregon, NW USA
152 G12 **Beāwar** Rājasthān, N India
Bebas, Dasht-i *see* Bābūs, Dasht-e
60 L8 **Bebedouro** São Paulo, S Brazil
101 I16 **Bebra** Hessen, C Germany
41 W12 **Becal** Campeche, SE Mexico
15 Q11 **Bécancour** ≈ Québec, SE Canada
97 Q19 **Beccles** E England, UK
112 L9 **Bečej** *Ger.* Altbetsche, *Hung.* Óbecse, Rácz-Becse; *prev.* Magyar-Becse, Stari Bečej. Serbia, N Serbia and Montenegro (Yugo.)
104 I3 **Becerreá** Galicia, NW Spain
74 H7 **Béchar** *prev.* Colomb-Béchar. W Algeria
39 O14 **Becharof Lake** ◎ Alaska, USA
116 H15 **Bechet** *var.* Bechetu. Dolj, SW Romania
Bechetu *see* Bechet
21 R6 **Beckley** West Virginia, NE USA
101 G14 **Beckum** Nordrhein-Westfalen, W Germany
25 X7 **Beckville** Texas, SW USA
35 X4 **Becky Peak** ▲ Nevada, W USA
116 I9 **Beclean** *Hung.* Bethlen; *prev.* Betlen. Bistrița-Năsăud, N Romania
Bécs *see* Wien
111 H18 **Bečva** *Ger.* Betschau, *Pol.* Beczwa. ≈ E Czech Republic
Beczwa *see* Bečva
103 P15 **Bédarieux** Hérault, S France
120 B10 **Beddouza, Cap** *headland* W Morocco
80 I13 **Bedelē** Oromo, C Ethiopia
147 Y8 **Bedel Pass** *Rus.* Pereval Bedel. *pass* China/Kyrgyzstan
Bedel, Pereval *see* Bedel Pass
95 H22 **Beder** Århus, C Denmark
97 N20 **Bedford** E England, UK
31 O15 **Bedford** Indiana, N USA
29 U16 **Bedford** Iowa, C USA
20 L4 **Bedford** Kentucky, S USA
18 D15 **Bedford** Pennsylvania, NE USA
21 T6 **Bedford** Virginia, NE USA
97 N20 **Bedfordshire** *cultural region* E England, UK
127 N5 **Bednodem'yanovsk** Penzenskaya Oblast', W Russian Federation
98 N5 **Bedum** Groningen, NE Netherlands
27 V11 **Beebe** Arkansas, C USA
45 T9 **Beef Island** ✕ (Road Town) Tortola, E British Virgin Islands
Beehive State *see* Utah
99 L18 **Beek** Limburg, SE Netherlands
99 L18 **Beek** ✕ (Maastricht) Limburg, SE Netherlands
99 K14 **Beek-en-Donk** Noord-Brabant, S Netherlands
138 F13 **Be'ér Menuḥa** *var.* Be'er Menukha. Southern, S Israel
Be'er Menukha *see* Be'ér Menuḥa
99 D16 **Beernem** West-Vlaanderen, NW Belgium
99 I16 **Beerse** Antwerpen, N Belgium
Beersheba *see* Be'ér Sheva'
138 E11 **Be'ér Sheva'** *var.* Beersheba, *Ar.* Bir es Saba. Southern, S Israel
98 J13 **Beesd** Gelderland, C Netherlands
99 M16 **Beesel** Limburg, SE Netherlands
83 J21 **Beestekraal** North-West, N South Africa
194 J7 **Beethoven Peninsula** *peninsula* Alexander Island, Antarctica
Beetstersweach *see* Beetsterzwaag
98 M6 **Beetsterzwaag** *Fris.* Beetstersweach. Friesland, N Netherlands
25 S13 **Beeville** Texas, SW USA
79 J18 **Befale** Equateur, NW Dem. Rep. Congo
Befandriana *see* Befandriana Avaratra
172 J3 **Befandriana Avaratra** *var.* Befandriana, Befandriana Nord. Mahajanga, NW Madagascar
Befandriana Nord *see* Befandriana Avaratra
79 K18 **Befori** Equateur, N Dem. Rep. Congo

◆ Country ● Country Capital ◇ Dependent Territory ○ Dependent Territory Capital ◈ Administrative Region ✕ International Airport ▲ Mountain ⛰ Mountain Range ✶ Volcano ≈ River ◎ Lake ⊠ Reservoir

172 *I7* **Befotaka** Fianarantsoa, S Madagascar
183 *R11* **Bega** New South Wales, SE Australia
102 *G5* **Bégard** Côtes d'Armor, NW France
112 *M9* **Begejski Kanal** *canal* NE Serbia and Montenegro (Yugo.)
94 *G13* **Begna** ≈ S Norway
Begoml' *see* Byahoml'
Begovat *see* Bekobod
153 *Q13* **Begusarāi** Bihār, NE India
143 *R9* **Behābād** Yazd, C Iran
Behagle *see* Laï
55 *Z10* **Béhague, Pointe** *headland* E French Guiana
Behar *see* Bihār
142 *M10* **Behbahān** *var.* Behbehān. Khūzestān, SW Iran
Behbehān *see* Behbahān
44 *G3* **Behring Point** Andros Island, W Bahamas
143 *P4* **Behshahr** *prev.* Ashraf. Māzandarān, N Iran
163 *V6* **Bei'an** Heilongjiang, NE China
Beibunar *see* Sredishte
Beibu Wan *see* Tongking, Gulf of
Beida *see* Al Bayḍā'
80 *H13* **Beigi** Oromo, C Ethiopia
160 *L16* **Beihai** Guangxi Zhuangzu Zizhiqu, S China
159 *Q10* **Bei Hulsan Hu** ◎ C China
161 *N13* **Bei Jiang** ≈ S China
161 *O2* **Beijing** *var.* Pei-ching, *Eng.* Peking; *prev.* Pei-p'ing. *country/municipality capital* (China) Beijing Shi, E China
161 *P2* **Beijing** ✈ Beijing Shi, E China
Beijing *see* Beijing Shi
161 *O2* **Beijing Shi** *var.* Beijing, Jing, Pei-ching, *Eng.* Peking; *prev.* Pei-p'ing. ◈ *municipality* E China
76 *G8* **Beïla** Trarza, W Mauritania
98 *N7* **Beilen** Drenthe, NE Netherlands
160 *L15* **Beiliu** Guangxi Zhuangzu Zizhiqu, S China
159 *O12* **Beilu He** ≈ W China
Beilul *see* Beylul
163 *U12* **Beining** *prev.* Beizhen. Liaoning, NE China
96 *H8* **Beinn Dearg** ▲ N Scotland, UK
Beinn MacDuibh *see* Ben Macdui
160 *I12* **Beipan Jiang** ≈ S China
163 *T12* **Beipiao** Liaoning, NE China
83 *N17* **Beira** Sofala, C Mozambique
83 *N17* **Beira** ✈ Sofala, C Mozambique
104 *I7* **Beira Alta** *former province* N Portugal
104 *H9* **Beira Baixa** *former province* C Portugal
104 *G8* **Beira Litoral** *former province* N Portugal
Beirut *see* Beyrouth
Beisān *see* Bet She'an
11 *Q16* **Beiseker** Alberta, SW Canada
Beitai Ding *see* Wutai Shan
83 *K19* **Beitbridge** Matabeleland South, S Zimbabwe
116 *G10* **Beiuş** *Hung.* Belényes. Bihor, NW Romania
Beizhen *see* Beining
104 *H12* **Beja** *anc.* Pax Julia. Beja, SE Portugal
104 *G13* **Beja** ◈ *district* S Portugal
74 *M5* **Béja** *var.* Bājah. N Tunisia
120 *I9* **Béjaïa** *var.* Bejaïa, *Fr.* Bougie; *anc.* Saldae. NE Algeria
104 *K8* **Béjar** Castilla-León, N Spain
Bejraburi *see* Phetchaburi
Bekaa Valley *see* El Beqaa
Bekabad *see* Bekobod
Békás *see* Bicaz
169 *O15* **Bekasi** Jawa, C Indonesia
Bek-Budi *see* Qarshi
146 *A8* **Bekdaş** *Rus.* Bekdash. Balkan Welaýaty, NW Turkmenistan
Bekdash *see* Bekdaş
147 *T10* **Bek-Dzhar** Oshskaya Oblast', SW Kyrgyzstan
111 *N24* **Békés** *Rom.* Bichiş. Békés, SE Hungary
111 *M24* **Békés** *off.* Békés Megye. ◈ *county* SE Hungary
111 *M24* **Békéscsaba** *Rom.* Bichiş-Ciaba. Békés, SE Hungary
139 *S2* **Bēkhma** E Iraq
172 *H7* **Bekily** Toliara, S Madagascar
165 *W4* **Bekkai** Hokkaidō, NE Japan
147 *Q11* **Bekobod** *Rus.* Bekabad; *prev.* Begovat. Toshkent Viloyati, E Uzbekistan
127 *O7* **Bekovo** Penzenskaya Oblast', W Russian Federation
Bél *see* Beliu
152 *M13* **Bela** Uttar Pradesh, N India
149 *N15* **Bela** Baluchistān, SW Pakistan
79 *F15* **Bélabo** Est, C Cameroon
112 *N10* **Bela Crkva** *Ger.* Weisskirchen, *Hung.* Fehértemplom. Serbia, W Serbia and Montenegro (Yugo.)
173 *Y16* **Bel Air** *var.* Rivière Sèche. E Mauritius
104 *L12* **Belalcázar** Andalucía, S Spain
113 *P15* **Bela Palanka** Serbia, SE Serbia and Montenegro (Yugo.)
119 *H16* **Belarus** *off.* Republic of Belarus, *var.* Belorussia, *Latv.* Baltkrievija; *prev.* Belorussian SSR, *Rus.* Belorusskaya SSR. ◆ *republic* E Europe
Belau *see* Palau
59 *H21* **Bela Vista** Mato Grosso do Sul, SW Brazil
83 *L21* **Bela Vista** Maputo, S Mozambique
168 *I8* **Belawan** Sumatera, W Indonesia
Bělá Woda *see* Weisswasser
127 *U4* **Belaya** ≈ W Russian Federation
123 *R7* **Belaya Gora** Respublika Sakha (Yakutiya), NE Russian Federation
126 *M11* **Belaya Kalitva** Rostovskaya Oblast', SW Russian Federation
125 *R14* **Belaya Kholunitsa** Kirovskaya Oblast', NW Russian Federation
Belaya Tserkov' *see* Bila Tserkva
77 *V11* **Belbédji** Zinder, S Niger
110 *K13* **Bełchatów** *var.* Belchatow. Łodzkie, C Poland
Belcher, Îles *see* Belcher Islands
12 *H7* **Belcher Islands** *Fr.* Îles Belcher. *island group* Nunavut, SE Canada
105 *S6* **Belchite** Aragón, NE Spain
29 *O2* **Belcourt** North Dakota, N USA
31 *P9* **Belding** Michigan, N USA
127 *U5* **Belebey** Respublika Bashkortostan, W Russian Federation
81 *N16* **Beledweyne** *var.* Belet Huen, *It.* Belet Uen. Hiiraan, C Somalia
146 *B10* **Belek** Balkan Welaýaty, W Turkmenistan
58 *L12* **Belém** *var.* Pará. *state capital* Pará, N Brazil
65 *I14* **Belém Ridge** *undersea feature* C Atlantic Ocean
37 *R12* **Belen** New Mexico, SW USA
62 *I7* **Belén** Catamarca, NW Argentina
54 *G9* **Belén** Boyacá, C Colombia
42 *J11* **Belén** Rivas, SW Nicaragua
62 *O5* **Belén** Concepción, C Paraguay
61 *D16* **Belén** Salto, N Uruguay
61 *D20* **Belén de Escobar** Buenos Aires, E Argentina
114 *J7* **Belene** Pleven, N Bulgaria
114 *J7* **Belene, Ostrov** *island* N Bulgaria
43 *R15* **Belén, Río** ≈ C Panama
Belényes *see* Beiuş
Belesar, Embalse de *see* Belesar, Encoro de
104 *H3* **Belesar, Encoro de** *Sp.* Embalse de Belesar. ⊠ NW Spain
Belet Huen/Belet Uen *see* Beledweyne
126 *J5* **Belëv** Tul'skaya Oblast', W Russian Federation
97 *G15* **Belfast** *Ir.* Béal Feirste. ◈ E Northern Ireland, UK
19 *R7* **Belfast** Maine, NE USA
97 *G15* **Belfast** ✈ E Northern Ireland, UK
97 *G15* **Belfast Lough** *Ir.* Loch Lao *inlet* E Northern Ireland, UK
28 *K5* **Belfield** North Dakota, N USA
103 *U7* **Belfort** Territoire-de-Belfort, E France
Belgard *see* Białogard
155 *E17* **Belgaum** Karnātaka, W India
Belgian Congo *see* Congo (Democratic Republic of)
195 *T3* **Belgica Mountains** ▲ Antarctica
België/Belgique *see* Belgium
99 *F20* **Belgium** *off.* Kingdom of Belgium, *Dut.* België, *Fr.* Belgique. ◆ *monarchy* NW Europe
126 *J8* **Belgorod** Belgorodskaya Oblast', W Russian Federation
Belgorod-Dnestrovskiy *see* Bilhorod-Dnistrovs'kyy
126 *J8* **Belgorodskaya Oblast'** ◈ *province* W Russian Federation
Belgrad *see* Beograd
29 *T8* **Belgrade** Minnesota, N USA
33 *S11* **Belgrade** Montana, NW USA
Belgrade *see* Beograd
195 *N5* **Belgrano II** *Argentinian research station* Antarctica
Belgrano, Cabo *see* Meredith, Cape
21 *X9* **Belhaven** North Carolina, SE USA
107 *I23* **Belice** *anc.* Hypsas. ≈ Sicilia, Italy, C Mediterranean Sea
Belice *see* Belize/Belize City
113 *M16* **Beli Drim** *Alb.* Drini i Bardhë. ≈ Albania/Serbia and Montenegro (Yugo.)
Beligrad *see* Berat
188 *C8* **Beliliou** *prev.* Peleliu. *island* S Palau
114 *L8* **Beli Lom, Yazovir** ⊠ NE Bulgaria
112 *I8* **Beli Manastir** *Hung.* Pélmonostor; *prev.* Monostor. Osijek-Baranja, NE Croatia
102 *J13* **Bélin-Béliet** Gironde, SW France
79 *F17* **Bélinga** Ogooué-Ivindo, NE Gabon
21 *S4* **Belington** West Virginia, NE USA
127 *O6* **Belinskiy** Penzenskaya Oblast', W Russian Federation
169 *N12* **Belinyu** Pulau Bangka, W Indonesia
169 *O13* **Belitung, Pulau** *island* W Indonesia
116 *F10* **Beliu** *Hung.* Bél. Arad, W Romania
114 *I9* **Beli Vit** ≈ NW Bulgaria
42 *G2* **Belize** *Sp.* Belice; *prev.* British Honduras, Colony of Belize. ◆ *commonwealth republic* Central America
42 *F2* **Belize** *Sp.* Belice. ◈ *district* NE Belize
42 *G2* **Belize** ≈ Belize/Guatemala
Belize *see* Belize City
42 *G2* **Belize City** *var.* Belize, *Sp.* Belice. Belize, NE Belize
42 *G2* **Belize City** ✈ Belize, NE Belize
Beljak *see* Villach
39 *N16* **Belkofski** Alaska, USA
123 *O6* **Bel'kovskiy, Ostrov** *island* Novosibirskiye Ostrova, NE Russian Federation
14 *J8* **Bell** ≈ Québec, SE Canada
10 *J15* **Bella Bella** British Columbia, SW Canada
102 *M10* **Bellac** Haute-Vienne, C France
10 *K15* **Bella Coola** British Columbia, SW Canada
106 *D6* **Bellagio** Lombardia, N Italy
31 *P6* **Bellaire** Michigan, N USA
106 *D6* **Bellano** Lombardia, N Italy
155 *G17* **Bellary** *var.* Ballari. Karnātaka, S India
183 *S5* **Bellata** New South Wales, SE Australia
61 *D16* **Bella Unión** Artigas, N Uruguay
61 *C14* **Bella Vista** Corrientes, NE Argentina
62 *J7* **Bella Vista** Tucumán, N Argentina
62 *P4* **Bella Vista** Amambay, C Paraguay
56 *B10* **Bellavista** Cajamarca, N Peru
56 *D11* **Bellavista** San Martín, N Peru
183 *U6* **Bellbrook** New South Wales, SE Australia
27 *V5* **Belle** Missouri, C USA
21 *Q5* **Belle** West Virginia, NE USA
31 *R13* **Bellefontaine** Ohio, N USA
18 *F14* **Bellefonte** Pennsylvania, NE USA
28 *J9* **Belle Fourche** South Dakota, N USA
28 *J9* **Belle Fourche Reservoir** ⊠ South Dakota, N USA
28 *K9* **Belle Fourche River** ≈ South Dakota/Wyoming, N USA
103 *S10* **Bellegarde-sur-Valserine** Ain, E France
23 *Y14* **Belle Glade** Florida, SE USA
102 *G8* **Belle Île** *island* NW France
13 *T9* **Belle Isle** *island* Belle Isle, Newfoundland and Labrador, E Canada
13 *S10* **Belle Isle, Strait of** *strait* Newfoundland and Labrador, E Canada
Bellenz *see* Bellinzona
29 *W14* **Belle Plaine** Iowa, C USA
29 *V9* **Belle Plaine** Minnesota, N USA
14 *I9* **Belleterre** Québec, SE Canada
14 *J15* **Belleville** Ontario, SE Canada
103 *R10* **Belleville** Rhône, E France
30 *K15* **Belleville** Illinois, N USA
27 *N3* **Belleville** Kansas, C USA
29 *Z13* **Bellevue** Iowa, C USA
29 *S15* **Bellevue** Nebraska, C USA
31 *S11* **Bellevue** Ohio, N USA
25 *S5* **Bellevue** Texas, SW USA
32 *H8* **Bellevue** Washington, NW USA
55 *Y11* **Bellevue de l'Inini, Montagnes** ▲ S French Guiana
103 *S11* **Belley** Ain, E France
Bellin *see* Kangirsuk
183 *V6* **Bellingen** New South Wales, SE Australia
97 *L14* **Bellingham** N England, UK
32 *H6* **Bellingham** Washington, NW USA
Belling Hausen Mulde *see* Southeast Pacific Basin
194 *H2* **Bellingshausen** *Russian research station* South Shetland Islands, Antarctica
Bellingshausen *see* Motu One
Bellingshausen Abyssal Plain *see* Bellingshausen Plain
196 *R14* **Bellingshausen Plain** *var.* Bellingshausen Abyssal Plain. *undersea feature* SE Pacific Ocean
194 *I8* **Bellingshausen Sea** *sea* Antarctica
93 *P6* **Bellingwolde** Groningen, NE Netherlands
108 *H11* **Bellinzona** *Ger.* Bellenz. Ticino, S Switzerland
25 *T8* **Bellmead** Texas, SW USA
54 *E8* **Bello** Antioquia, W Colombia
61 *B21* **Bellocq** Buenos Aires, E Argentina
Bello Horizonte *see* Belo Horizonte
186 *L10* **Bellona** *var.* Mungiki. *island* S Solomon Islands
Bellovacum *see* Beauvais
182 *D7* **Bell, Point** *headland* South Australia
20 *F9* **Bells** Tennessee, S USA
25 *U5* **Bells** Texas, SW USA
92 *N3* **Bellsund** *inlet* SW Svalbard
106 *H6* **Belluno** Veneto, NE Italy
62 *L11* **Bell Ville** Córdoba, C Argentina
83 *E26* **Bellville** Western Cape, SW South Africa
25 *U11* **Bellville** Texas, SW USA
104 *L12* **Belmez** Andalucía, S Spain
29 *V12* **Belmond** Iowa, C USA
18 *E11* **Belmont** New York, NE USA
21 *R10* **Belmont** North Carolina, SE USA
59 *O18* **Belmonte** Bahia, E Brazil
104 *I8* **Belmonte** Castelo Branco, C Portugal
105 *P10* **Belmonte** Castilla-La Mancha, C Spain
42 *G2* **Belmopan** ● (Belize) Cayo, C Belize
97 *B16* **Belmullet** *Ir.* Béal an Mhuirhead. W Ireland
123 *R13* **Belogorsk** Amurskaya Oblast', SE Russian Federation
Belogorsk *see* Bilohirs'k
114 *F7* **Belogradchik** Vidin, NW Bulgaria
172 *H8* **Beloha** Toliara, S Madagascar
59 *M20* **Belo Horizonte** *prev.* Bello Horizonte. *state capital* Minas Gerais, SE Brazil
26 *M3* **Beloit** Kansas, C USA
30 *L9* **Beloit** Wisconsin, N USA
Belokorovichi *see* Bilokorovychi
126 *J8* **Belomorsk** Respublika Kareliya, NW Russian Federation
126 *J8* **Belomorsko-Baltiyskiy Kanal** *Eng.* White Sea-Baltic Canal, White Sea Canal. *canal* NW Russian Federation
153 *V15* **Belonia** Tripura, NE India
Belopol'ye *see* Bilopillya
105 *O4* **Belorado** Castilla-León, N Spain
126 *L14* **Belorechensk** Krasnodarskiy Kray, SW Russian Federation
127 *W5* **Beloretsk** Respublika Bashkortostan, W Russian Federation
Belorussia/Belorussian SSR *see* Belarus
Belorusskaya Gryada *see* Byelaruskaya Hrada
Belorusskaya SSR *see* Belarus
Beloshchel'ye *see* Nar'yan-Mar
114 *N8* **Beloslav** Varna, E Bulgaria
Belostok *see* Białystok
172 *H5* **Belo Tsiribihina** *var.* Belo-sur-Tsiribihina. Toliara, W Madagascar
Belovár *see* Bjelovar
Belovezhskaya Pushcha *see* Białowieska, Puszcza/Byelavyezhskaya Pushcha
114 *H10* **Belovo** Pazardzhik, C Bulgaria
Belovodsk *see* Bilovods'k
122 *H9* **Beloyarskiy** Khanty-Mansiyskiy Avtonomnyy Okrug, N Russian Federation
124 *K7* **Beloye More** *Eng.* White Sea. *sea* NW Russian Federation
124 *K13* **Beloye, Ozero** ◎ NW Russian Federation
114 *J10* **Belozem** Plovdiv, C Bulgaria
124 *K13* **Belozërsk** Vologodskaya Oblast', NW Russian Federation
99 *E20* **Belœil** Hainaut, SW Belgium
108 *D8* **Belp** Bern, W Switzerland
108 *D8* **Belp** ✈ (Bern) Bern, C Switzerland
107 *L24* **Belpasso** Sicilia, Italy, C Mediterranean Sea
31 *U14* **Belpre** Ohio, N USA
98 *M8* **Belterwijde** ◎ N Netherlands
27 *R4* **Belton** Missouri, C USA
21 *P11* **Belton** South Carolina, SE USA
25 *T9* **Belton** Texas, SW USA
25 *S9* **Belton Lake** ⊠ Texas, SW USA
Bel'tsy *see* Bălţi
97 *E16* **Belturbet** *Ir.* Béal Tairbirt. N Ireland
Beluchistan *see* Baluchistān
145 *Z9* **Belukha, Gora** ▲ Kazakhstan/Russian Federation
107 *M20* **Belvedere Marittimo** Calabria, SW Italy
30 *L10* **Belvidere** Illinois, N USA
18 *J14* **Belvidere** New Jersey, NE USA
Bely *see* Belyy
127 *V8* **Belyayevka** Orenburgskaya Oblast', W Russian Federation
Belynichi *see* Byalynichy
124 *H17* **Belyy** *var.* Bely, Beyj. Tverskaya Oblast', W Russian Federation
126 *I6* **Belyye Berega** Bryanskaya Oblast', W Russian Federation
122 *J6* **Belyy, Ostrov** *island* N Russian Federation
122 *J11* **Belyy Yar** Tomskaya Oblast', C Russian Federation
100 *N13* **Belzig** Brandenburg, NE Germany
22 *K4* **Belzoni** Mississippi, S USA
172 *H4* **Bemaraha** *var.* Plateau du Bemaraha. ▲ W Madagascar
82 *B10* **Bembe** Uíge, NW Angola
77 *S14* **Bembèrèkè** *var.* Bimbéréké. N Benin
104 *K12* **Bembézar** ≈ SW Spain
104 *J3* **Bembibre** Castilla-León, N Spain
29 *T4* **Bemidji** Minnesota, N USA
98 *L12* **Bemmel** Gelderland, SE Netherlands
171 *T13* **Bemu** Pulau Seram, E Indonesia
Benāb *see* Bonāb
105 *T5* **Benabarre** *var.* Benavarn. Aragón, NE Spain
Benaco *see* Garda, Lago di
79 *L20* **Bena-Dibele** Kasai Oriental, C Dem. Rep. Congo
105 *R9* **Benageber, Embalse de** ⊠ E Spain
183 *O11* **Benalla** Victoria, SE Australia
104 *M14* **Benamejí** Andalucía, S Spain
Benares *see* Vārānasi
Benavarn *see* Benabarre
104 *F10* **Benavente** Santarém, C Portugal
104 *K5* **Benavente** Castilla-León, N Spain
25 *S15* **Benavides** Texas, SW USA
96 *F8* **Benbecula** *island* NW Scotland, UK
Bencovazzo *see* Benkovac
32 *H13* **Bend** Oregon, NW USA
182 *K7* **Benda Range** ▲ South Australia
183 *T6* **Bendemeer** New South Wales, SE Australia
Bender *see* Tighina
Bender Beila/Bender Beyla *see* Bandarbeyla
Bender Cassim/Bender Qaasim *see* Boosaaso
Bendery *see* Tighina
183 *N11* **Bendigo** Victoria, SE Australia
118 *E10* **Bēne** Dobele, SW Latvia
98 *K13* **Beneden-Leeuwen** Gelderland, C Netherlands
101 *L24* **Benediktenwand** ▲ S Germany
Benemérita de San Cristóbal *see* San Cristóbal
77 *N12* **Bénéna** Ségou, S Mali
172 *I7* **Benenitra** Toliara, S Madagascar
Beneschau *see* Benešov
Beneški Zaliv *see* Venice, Gulf of
111 *D17* **Benešov** *Ger.* Beneschau. Středočeský Kraj, W Czech Republic
123 *Q5* **Benetta, Ostrov** *island* Novosibirskiye Ostrova, NE Russian Federation
107 *L17* **Benevento** *anc.* Beneventum, Malventum. Campania, S Italy
Beneventum *see* Benevento
173 *S3* **Bengal, Bay of** *bay* N Indian Ocean
79 *M17* **Bengamisa** Orientale, N Dem. Rep. Congo
Bengasi *see* Banghāzī
Bengazi *see* Banghāzī
161 *P7* **Bengbu** *var.* Peng-pu. Anhui, E China
32 *L9* **Benge** Washington, NW USA
Benghazi *see* Banghāzī
168 *K10* **Bengkalis** Pulau Bengkalis, W Indonesia
168 *K10* **Bengkalis, Pulau** *island* W Indonesia
169 *Q10* **Bengkayang** Borneo, C Indonesia
Bengkoelen/Bengkoeloe *see* Bengkulu
168 *K14* **Bengkulu** *prev.* Bengkoeloe, Benkoelen, Benkulen. Sumatera, W Indonesia
168 *J13* **Bengkulu** *off.* Propinsi Bengkulu; *prev.* Bengkoelen, Benkoelen, Benkulen. ◈ *province* W Indonesia
82 *A11* **Bengo** ◈ *province* W Angola
95 *J16* **Bengtsfors** Västra Götaland, S Sweden
82 *B13* **Benguela** *var.* Benguella. Benguela, W Angola
83 *A14* **Benguela** ◈ *province* W Angola
Benguella *see* Benguela
Bengweulu, Lake *see* Bangweulu, Lake
121 *V13* **Benha** *var.* Banhā. N Egypt
192 *F5* **Benham Seamount** *undersea feature* W Philippine Sea
96 *H6* **Ben Hope** ▲ N Scotland, UK
79 *P18* **Beni** Nord Kivu, NE Dem. Rep. Congo
57 *L15* **Beni** *var.* El Beni. ◈ *department* N Bolivia
74 *H8* **Beni Abbès** W Algeria
105 *T8* **Benicarló** País Valenciano, E Spain
105 *T9* **Benicasim** País Valenciano, E Spain
105 *T12* **Benidorm** País Valenciano, SE Spain
75 *W9* **Beni Mazâr** *var.* Banī Mazār. C Egypt
120 *C11* **Beni-Mellal** C Morocco
77 *R14* **Benin** *off.* Republic of Benin; *prev.* Dahomey. ◆ *republic* W Africa
77 *S17* **Benin, Bight of** *gulf* W Africa
77 *U16* **Benin City** Edo, SW Nigeria
57 *K16* **Beni, Río** ≈ N Bolivia
120 *F10* **Beni Saf** *var.* Beni-Saf. NW Algeria
80 *H12* **Benishangul** ◈ *region* W Ethiopia
105 *T11* **Benissa** País Valenciano, E Spain
121 *V14* **Beni Suef** *var.* Banī Suwayf. N Egypt
11 *V15* **Benito** Manitoba, S Canada
Benito *see* Uolo, Río
61 *C23* **Benito Juárez** Buenos Aires, E Argentina
41 *P14* **Benito Juaréz Internacional** ✈ (México) México, S Mexico
25 *P5* **Benjamin** Texas, SW USA
58 *B13* **Benjamin Constant** Amazonas, N Brazil
40 *F4* **Benjamín Hill** Sonora, NW Mexico
63 *F19* **Benjamín, Isla** *island* Archipiélago de los Chonos, S Chile
165 *Q4* **Benkei-misaki** *headland* Hokkaidō, NE Japan
28 *L17* **Benkelman** Nebraska, C USA
96 *I7* **Ben Klibreck** ▲ N Scotland, UK
Benkoelen *see* Bengkulu
112 *D13* **Benkovac** *It.* Bencovazzo. Zadar, SW Croatia
Benkulen *see* Bengkulu
96 *I11* **Ben Lawers** ▲ C Scotland, UK
96 *J9* **Ben Macdui** *var.* Beinn MacDuibh. ▲ C Scotland, UK
96 *G11* **Ben More** ▲ W Scotland, UK
96 *I11* **Ben More** ▲ C Scotland, UK
96 *H7* **Ben More Assynt** ▲ N Scotland, UK
185 *E20* **Benmore, Lake** ◎ South Island, NZ
98 *L12* **Bennekom** Gelderland, SE Netherlands
21 *T11* **Bennettsville** South Carolina, SE USA
96 *H10* **Ben Nevis** ▲ N Scotland, UK
184 *M9* **Benneydale** Waikato, North Island, NZ
Bennichab *see* Bennichchâb
76 *H8* **Bennichchâb** *var.* Bennichab. Inchiri, W Mauritania
18 *L10* **Bennington** Vermont, NE USA
185 *E20* **Ben Ohau Range** ▲ South Island, NZ
83 *J21* **Benoni** Gauteng, NE South Africa
172 *J2* **Be, Nosy** *var.* Nossi-Bé. *island* NW Madagascar
Bénoué *see* Benue
42 *F2* **Benque Viejo del Carmen** Cayo, W Belize
101 *G19* **Bensheim** Hessen, W Germany
37 *N16* **Benson** Arizona, SW USA
29 *S8* **Benson** Minnesota, N USA
21 *U10* **Benson** North Carolina, SE USA
171 *N15* **Benteng** Pulau Selayar, C Indonesia
83 *A14* **Bentiaba** Namibe, SW Angola
181 *T4* **Bentinck Island** *island* Wellesley Islands, Queensland, N Australia
80 *E13* **Bentiu** Wahda, S Sudan
138 *G8* **Bent Jbaïl** *var.* Bint Jubayl. S Lebanon
11 *Q15* **Bentley** Alberta, SW Canada
61 *I15* **Bento Gonçalves** Rio Grande do Sul, S Brazil
27 *U12* **Benton** Arkansas, C USA
30 *L16* **Benton** Illinois, N USA
20 *H7* **Benton** Kentucky, S USA
22 *G5* **Benton** Louisiana, S USA
27 *Y7* **Benton** Missouri, C USA
20 *M10* **Benton** Tennessee, S USA
31 *O10* **Benton Harbor** Michigan, N USA
27 *S9* **Bentonville** Arkansas, C USA
77 *V16* **Benue** ◈ *state* SE Nigeria
78 *F13* **Benue** *Fr.* Bénoué. ≈ Cameroon/Nigeria
163 *V12* **Benxi** *prev.* Pen-ch'i, Penhsihu, Penki. Liaoning, NE China
Benyakoni *see* Byenyakoni
112 *K10* **Beočin** Serbia, N Serbia and Montenegro (Yugo.)
Beodericsworth *see* Bury St Edmunds
112 *M11* **Beograd** *Eng.* Belgrade, *Ger.* Belgrad; *anc.* Singidunum. ● (Serbia and Montenegro (Yugo.)) Serbia, N Serbia and Montenegro (Yugo.)
112 *L11* **Beograd** *Eng.* Belgrade. ✈ Serbia, N Serbia and Montenegro (Yugo.)
76 *M16* **Béoumi** C Ivory Coast
35 *V3* **Beowawe** Nevada, W USA
164 *E14* **Beppu** Ōita, Kyūshū, SW Japan
187 *X15* **Beqa** *prev.* Mbengga. *island* W Fiji
Beqa Barrier Reef *see* Kavukavu Reef
45 *Y14* **Bequia** *island* C Saint Vincent and the Grenadines
113 *L16* **Berane** *prev.* Ivangrad. Montenegro, SW Serbia and Montenegro (Yugo.)
113 *L21* **Berat** *var.* Berati, *SCr.* Beligrad. Berat, C Albania
113 *L21* **Berat** ◈ *district* C Albania
Berătău *see* Berettyó
Berati *see* Berat
Beraun *see* Berounka, Czech Republic
Beraun *see* Beroun, Czech Republic
171 *U13* **Berau, Teluk** *var.* MacCluer Gulf. *bay* Papua, E Indonesia
80 *G8* **Berber** River Nile, NE Sudan
80 *N12* **Berbera** Woqooyi Galbeed, NW Somalia
79 *H16* **Berbérati** Mambéré-Kadéï, SW Central African Republic
Berberia, Cabo de *see* Barbaria, Cap de
55 *T9* **Berbice River** ≈ NE Guyana
Berchid *see* Berrechid
103 *N2* **Berck-Plage** Pas-de-Calais, N France
25 *T13* **Berclair** Texas, SW USA
117 *W10* **Berda** ≈ SE Ukraine
Berdichev *see* Berdychiv
123 *P10* **Berdigestyakh** Respublika Sakha (Yakutiya), NE Russian Federation
122 *J12* **Berdsk** Novosibirskaya Oblast', C Russian Federation
117 *W10* **Berdyans'k** *Rus.* Berdyansk; *prev.* Osipenko. Zaporiz'ka Oblast', SE Ukraine
117 *W10* **Berdyans'ka Kosa** *spit* SE Ukraine
117 *V10* **Berdyans'ka Zatoka** *gulf* S Ukraine
117 *N5* **Berdychiv** *Rus.* Berdichev. Zhytomyrs'ka Oblast', N Ukraine
20 *M6* **Berea** Kentucky, S USA
Beregovo/Beregszász *see* Berehove
116 *G8* **Berehove** *Cz.* Berehovo, *Hung.* Beregszász, *Rus.* Beregovo. Zakarpats'ka Oblast', W Ukraine
Berehovo *see* Berehove
186 *D9* **Bereina** Central, S PNG
146 *C11* **Bereket** *prev. Rus.* Gazandzhyk, Kazandzhik, *Turkm.* Gazanjyk. Balkan Welaýaty, W Turkmenistan
45 *O12* **Berekua** S Dominica
77 *O16* **Berekum** W Ghana
75 *Y11* **Berenice** *var.* Minâ Baranîs. SE Egypt
9 *O14* **Berens** ≈ Manitoba/Ontario, C Canada
11 *X14* **Berens River** Manitoba, C Canada
29 *R12* **Beresford** South Dakota, N USA
116 *J4* **Berestechko** Volyns'ka Oblast', NW Ukraine
116 *M11* **Bereşti** Galaţi, E Romania
117 *U6* **Berestova** ≈ E Ukraine
Beretău *see* Berettyó
111 *N23* **Berettyó** *Rom.* Barcău; *prev.* Berătău, Beretău. ≈ Hungary/Romania
111 *N23* **Berettyóújfalu** Hajdú-Bihar, E Hungary
Berëza/Bereza Kartuska *see* Byaroza
117 *Q4* **Berezan'** Kyyivs'ka Oblast', N Ukraine
117 *Q10* **Berezanka** Mykolayivs'ka Oblast', S Ukraine
116 *J6* **Berezhany** *Pol.* Brzeżany. Ternopil's'ka Oblast', W Ukraine
Berezina *see* Byerezino
Berezino *see* Byerazino
117 *P10* **Berezivka** *Rus.* Berezovka. Odes'ka Oblast', SW Ukraine
117 *Q2* **Berezna** Chernihivs'ka Oblast', NE Ukraine
116 *L3* **Berezne** Rivnens'ka Oblast', NW Ukraine
117 *R9* **Bereznehuvate** Mykolayivs'ka Oblast', S Ukraine
125 *N10* **Bereznik** Arkhangel'skaya Oblast', NW Russian Federation
125 *U13* **Berezniki** Permskaya Oblast', NW Russian Federation
Berezovka *see* Berezivka
122 *H9* **Berezovo** Khanty-Mansiyskiy Avtonomnyy Okrug, N Russian Federation
127 *O9* **Berezovskaya** Volgogradskaya Oblast', SW Russian Federation
123 *S13* **Berezovyy** Khabarovskiy Kray, E Russian Federation
83 *E25* **Berg** ≈ W South Africa
Berg *see* Berg bei Rohrbach
105 *V4* **Berga** Cataluña, NE Spain
95 *N20* **Berga** Kalmar, S Sweden
136 *B13* **Bergama** İzmir, W Turkey

◆ Country ● Country Capital ◇ Dependent Territory ○ Dependent Territory Capital ◈ Administrative Region ✈ International Airport ▲ Mountain ▲ Mountain Range Volcano ≈ River ◎ Lake ⊠ Reservoir

106 E7 **Bergamo** anc. Bergomum. Lombardia, N Italy
105 P3 **Bergara** País Vasco, N Spain
109 S3 **Berg bei Rohrbach** var. Berg. Oberösterreich, N Austria
100 O6 **Bergen** Mecklenburg-Vorpommern, NE Germany
101 I11 **Bergen** Niedersachsen, NW Germany
98 H8 **Bergen** Noord-Holland, NW Netherlands
94 C13 **Bergen** Hordaland, S Norway
Bergen see Mons
55 W9 **Berg en Dal** Brokopondo, C Suriname
99 G15 **Bergen op Zoom** Noord-Brabant, S Netherlands
102 L13 **Bergerac** Dordogne, SW France
99 J16 **Bergeyk** Noord-Brabant, S Netherlands
101 D16 **Bergheim** Nordrhein-Westfalen, W Germany
55 X10 **Bergi** Sipaliwini, E Suriname
101 E16 **Bergisch Gladbach** Nordrhein-Westfalen, W Germany
101 F14 **Bergkamen** Nordrhein-Westfalen, W Germany
95 N21 **Bergkvara** Kalmar, S Sweden
Bergomum see Bergamo
98 K13 **Bergse Maas** ≈ S Netherlands
95 P15 **Bergshamra** Stockholm, C Sweden
94 N10 **Bergsjö** Gävleborg, C Sweden
93 J14 **Bergsviken** Norrbotten, N Sweden
98 L6 **Bergum** Fris. Burgum. Friesland, N Netherlands
98 M6 **Bergumer Meer** ◎ N Netherlands
94 N12 **Bergviken** ◎ C Sweden
168 M11 **Berhala, Selat** strait Sumatera, W Indonesia
Berhampore see Baharampur
123 W9 **Beringa, Ostrov** island E Russian Federation
99 J17 **Beringen** Limburg, NE Belgium
39 T12 **Bering Glacier** glacier Alaska, USA
Beringov Proliv see Bering Strait
123 W6 **Beringovskiy** Chukotskiy Avtonomnyy Okrug, NE Russian Federation
192 L2 **Bering Sea** sea N Pacific Ocean
38 L9 **Bering Strait** Rus. Beringov Proliv. strait Bering Sea/Chukchi Sea
Berislav see Beryslav
105 O15 **Berja** Andalucía, S Spain
94 H9 **Berkåk** Sør-Trøndelag, S Norway
98 N11 **Berkel** ≈ Germany/Netherlands
35 N8 **Berkeley** California, W USA
65 E24 **Berkeley Sound** sound NE Falkland Islands
21 V2 **Berkeley Springs** var. Bath. West Virginia, NE USA
195 N6 **Berkner Island** island Antarctica
114 G8 **Berkovitsa** Montana, NW Bulgaria
97 M22 **Berkshire** cultural region S England, UK
99 H17 **Berlaar** Antwerpen, N Belgium
Berlanga see Berlanga de Duero
105 P6 **Berlanga de Duero** var. Berlanga. Castilla-León, N Spain
(0) I16 **Berlanga Rise** undersea feature E Pacific Ocean
99 F17 **Berlare** Oost-Vlaanderen, NW Belgium
104 E9 **Berlenga, Ilha da** island C Portugal
92 M7 **Berlevåg** Lapp. Bearalváhki. Finnmark, N Norway
100 O12 **Berlin** ● (Germany) Berlin, NE Germany
21 Z4 **Berlin** Maryland, NE USA
19 O7 **Berlin** New Hampshire, NE USA
18 D16 **Berlin** Pennsylvania, NE USA
30 L7 **Berlin** Wisconsin, N USA
100 O12 **Berlin** ◈ state NE Germany
Berlinchen see Barlinek
31 U12 **Berlin Lake** ⊞ Ohio, N USA
183 R11 **Bermagui** New South Wales, SE Australia
40 L8 **Bermejillo** Durango, C Mexico
62 M6 **Bermejo (viejo), Río** ≈ N Argentina
62 L5 **Bermejo, Río** ≈ N Argentina
62 I10 **Bermejo, Río** ≈ W Argentina
105 P2 **Bermeo** País Vasco, N Spain
104 K6 **Bermillo de Sayago** Castilla-León, N Spain
106 E6 **Bermina, Pizzo** Rmsch. Piz Bernina. ▲ Italy/Switzerland see also Bernina, Piz
64 A12 **Bermuda** var. Bermuda Islands, Bermudas; prev. Somers Islands. ◇ UK crown colony NW Atlantic Ocean
1 N11 **Bermuda** var. Great Bermuda, Long Island, Main Island. island Bermuda
Bermuda Islands see Bermuda
Bermuda-New England Seamount Arc see New England Seamounts
1 N11 **Bermuda Rise** undersea feature C Sargasso Sea
Bermudas see Bermuda
108 D8 **Bern** Fr. Berne. ● (Switzerland) Bern, W Switzerland
108 D9 **Bern** Fr. Berne. ◈ canton W Switzerland
37 R11 **Bernalillo** New Mexico, SW USA
14 H12 **Bernard Lake** ◎ Ontario, S Canada
61 B18 **Bernardo de Irigoyen** Santa Fe, NE Argentina
18 J14 **Bernardsville** New Jersey, NE USA
63 K14 **Bernasconi** La Pampa, C Argentina
100 O12 **Bernau** Brandenburg, NE Germany
102 L4 **Bernay** Eure, N France
101 L14 **Bernburg** Sachsen-Anhalt, C Germany
109 X5 **Berndorf** Niederösterreich, NE Austria
31 Q12 **Berne** Indiana, N USA
Berne see Bern
108 D10 **Berner Alpen** var. Berner Oberland, Eng. Bernese Oberland. ⛰ SW Switzerland
Berner Oberland/Bernese Oberland see Berner Alpen
109 Y2 **Bernhardsthal** Niederösterreich, N Austria
22 H4 **Bernice** Louisiana, S USA
27 Y8 **Bernie** Missouri, C USA
180 G9 **Bernier Island** island Western Australia
Bernina Pass see Bernina, Passo del
108 J10 **Bernina, Passo del** Eng. Bernina Pass. pass SE Switzerland
108 J10 **Bernina, Piz** It. Pizzo Bermina. ▲ Italy/Switzerland see also Bermina, Pizzo
99 E20 **Bérnissart** Hainaut, SW Belgium
101 E18 **Bernkastel-Kues** Rheinland-Pfalz, W Germany
Beroea see Ḩalab
172 H6 **Beroroha** Toliara, SW Madagascar
Béroubouay see Gbéroubouè
111 C17 **Beroun** Ger. Beraun. Středočeský Kraj, W Czech Republic
111 C16 **Berounka** Ger. Beraun. ≈ W Czech Republic
113 Q18 **Berovo** E FYR Macedonia
74 F6 **Berrechid** var. Berchid. W Morocco
103 R15 **Berre, Étang de** ◎ SE France
103 S15 **Berre-l'Étang** Bouches-du-Rhône, SE France
182 K9 **Berri** South Australia
31 O10 **Berrien Springs** Michigan, N USA
183 O10 **Berrigan** New South Wales, SE Australia
103 N9 **Berry** cultural region C France
35 N7 **Berryessa, Lake** ◎ California, W USA
44 G2 **Berry Islands** island group N Bahamas
27 T9 **Berryville** Arkansas, C USA
21 V3 **Berryville** Virginia, NE USA
83 D21 **Berseba** Karas, S Namibia
117 O8 **Bershad'** Vinnyts'ka Oblast', C Ukraine
28 L3 **Berthold** North Dakota, N USA
37 T3 **Berthoud** Colorado, C USA
37 S4 **Berthoud Pass** pass Colorado, C USA
79 F15 **Bertoua** Est, E Cameroon
25 S10 **Bertram** Texas, SW USA
63 G22 **Bertrand, Cerro** ▲ S Argentina
99 J23 **Bertrix** Luxembourg, SE Belgium
191 P3 **Beru** var. Peru. atoll Tungaru, W Kiribati
Beruni see Beruniy
146 I9 **Beruniy** var. Biruni, Rus. Beruni. Qoraqalpog'iston Respublikasi, W Uzbekistan
58 F13 **Beruri** Amazonas, NW Brazil
18 H14 **Berwick** Pennsylvania, NE USA
96 K12 **Berwick** cultural region SE Scotland, UK
96 L12 **Berwick-upon-Tweed** N England, UK
117 S10 **Beryslav** Rus. Berislav. Khersons'ka Oblast', S Ukraine
Berytus see Beyrouth
172 H4 **Besalampy** Mahajanga, W Madagascar
103 T8 **Besançon** anc. Besontium, Vesontio. Doubs, E France
103 P10 **Besbre** ≈ C France
Bescanuova see Baška
Besdan see Bezdan
Besed' see Byesyedz'
147 R10 **Beshariq** Rus. Besharyk; prev. Kirovo. Farg'ona Viloyati, E Uzbekistan
Besharyk see Beshariq
146 L9 **Beshbuloq** Rus. Beshulak. Navoiy Viloyati, N Uzbekistan
Beshenkovichi see Byeshankovichy
146 M13 **Beshkent** Qashqadaryo Viloyati, S Uzbekistan
Beshulak see Beshbuloq
112 L10 **Beška** Serbia, N Serbia and Montenegro (Yugo.)
Beskra see Biskra
127 O16 **Beslan** Respublika Severnaya Osetiya, SW Russian Federation
113 P16 **Besna Kobila** ▲ SE Serbia and Montenegro (Yugo.)
137 N16 **Besni** Adıyaman, S Turkey
Besontium see Besançon
121 Q2 **Beşparmak Dağları** Eng. Kyrenia Mountains. ⛰ N Cyprus
Bessarabka see Basarabeasca
92 O2 **Bessels, Kapp** headland C Svalbard
23 P4 **Bessemer** Alabama, S USA
30 K3 **Bessemer** Michigan, N USA
21 Q10 **Bessemer City** North Carolina, SE USA
102 M10 **Bessines-sur-Gartempe** Haute-Vienne, C France
99 K15 **Best** Noord-Brabant, S Netherlands
25 N9 **Best** Texas, SW USA
125 O11 **Bestuzhevo** Arkhangel'skaya Oblast', NW Russian Federation
123 M11 **Bestyakh** Respublika Sakha (Yakutiya), NE Russian Federation
Beszterce see Bistriţa
Besztercebánya see Banská Bystrica
172 I5 **Betafo** Antananarivo, C Madagascar
104 H2 **Betanzos** Galicia, NW Spain
104 G2 **Betanzos, Ría de** estuary NW Spain
79 G15 **Bétaré Oya** Est, E Cameroon
105 S9 **Bétera** País Valenciano, E Spain
77 R15 **Bétérou** C Benin
83 K21 **Bethal** Mpumalanga, NE South Africa
30 K15 **Bethalto** Illinois, N USA
83 D21 **Bethanie** var. Bethanien, Bethany. Karas, S Namibia
Bethanien see Bethanie
27 S2 **Bethany** Missouri, C USA
27 N10 **Bethany** Oklahoma, C USA
Bethany see Bethanie
39 N12 **Bethel** Alaska, USA
19 P7 **Bethel** Maine, NE USA
21 W9 **Bethel** North Carolina, SE USA
18 B15 **Bethel Park** Pennsylvania, NE USA
21 W3 **Bethesda** Maryland, NE USA
83 J22 **Bethlehem** Free State, C South Africa
18 I14 **Bethlehem** Pennsylvania, NE USA
138 F10 **Bethlehem** Ar. Bayt Laḩm, Heb. Bet Leḥem. C West Bank
Bethlen see Beclean
83 I24 **Bethulie** Free State, C South Africa
103 O1 **Béthune** Pas-de-Calais, N France
102 M3 **Béthune** ≈ N France
104 M14 **Béticos, Sistemas** var. Sistema Penibético, Eng. Baetic Cordillera, Baetic Mountains. ⛰ S Spain
54 I6 **Betijoque** Trujillo, NW Venezuela
59 M20 **Betim** Minas Gerais, SE Brazil
190 H3 **Betio** Tarawa, W Kiribati
172 H7 **Betioky** Toliara, S Madagascar
Bet Leḥem see Bethlehem
Betlen see Beclean
167 O17 **Betong** Yala, SW Thailand
79 I16 **Bétou** La Likouala, N Congo
145 P14 **Betpak-Dala** Kaz. Betpaqdala. plateau S Kazakhstan
Betpaqdala see Betpak-Dala
172 H7 **Betroka** Toliara, S Madagascar
Betschau see Bečva
138 G9 **Bet She'an** Ar. Baysān, Beisān; anc. Scythopolis. Northern, N Israel
15 T6 **Betsiamites** Québec, SE Canada
15 T6 **Betsiamites** ≈ Québec, SE Canada
172 I4 **Betsiboka** ≈ N Madagascar
99 M25 **Bettembourg** Luxembourg, S Luxembourg
99 M23 **Bettendorf** Diekirch, NE Luxembourg
29 Z14 **Bettendorf** Iowa, C USA
75 R13 **Bette, Pic** var. Bikkū Bīttī, It. Picco Bette. ▲ S Libya
Bette, Picco see Bette, Pic
153 P12 **Bettiah** Bihār, N India
39 Q7 **Bettles** Alaska, USA
95 N17 **Bettna** Södermanland, C Sweden
154 H11 **Betūl** prev. Badnur. Madhya Pradesh, C India
154 H9 **Betwa** ≈ C India
101 F16 **Betzdorf** Rheinland-Pfalz, W Germany
82 C9 **Béu** Uíge, NW Angola
35 P8 **Beulah** Michigan, N USA
28 L5 **Beulah** North Dakota, N USA
98 M8 **Beulakerwijde** ◎ N Netherlands
98 L13 **Beuningen** Gelderland, SE Netherlands
Beuthen see Bytom
103 N7 **Beuvron** ≈ C France
99 F16 **Beveren** Oost-Vlaanderen, N Belgium
21 T9 **B.Everett Jordan Reservoir** var. Jordan Lake. ⊞ North Carolina, SE USA
97 N17 **Beverley** E England, UK
Beverley see Beverly
99 J17 **Beverlo** Limburg, NE Belgium
19 P11 **Beverly** Massachusetts, NE USA
32 J9 **Beverly** var. Beverley. Washington, NW USA
35 S15 **Beverly Hills** California, W USA
101 I14 **Beverungen** Nordrhein-Westfalen, C Germany
98 H9 **Beverwijk** Noord-Holland, W Netherlands
108 C10 **Bex** Vaud, W Switzerland
97 P23 **Bexhill** var. Bexhill-on-Sea. SE England, UK
Bexhill-on-Sea see Bexhill
136 E17 **Bey Dağları** ⛰ SW Turkey
Beyj see Belyy
136 E10 **Beykoz** İstanbul, NW Turkey
76 K15 **Beyla** Guinée-Forestière, SE Guinea
137 X12 **Beyläqan** prev. Zhdanov. SW Azerbaijan
80 L10 **Beylul** var. Beilul. SE Eritrea
144 H14 **Beyneu** Kaz. Beyneū. Mangistau, SW Kazakhstan
Beyneū see Beyneu
165 X14 **Beyonēsu-retsugan** Eng. Bayonnaise Rocks. island group SE Japan
136 G12 **Beypazarı** Ankara, NW Turkey
155 F21 **Beypore** Kerala, SW India
138 G7 **Beyrouth** var. Bayrūt, Eng. Beirut; anc. Berytus. ● (Lebanon) W Lebanon
138 G7 **Beyrouth** ✈ W Lebanon
136 G15 **Beyşehir** Konya, SW Turkey
136 G15 **Beyşehir Gölü** ◎ C Turkey
108 J7 **Bezau** Vorarlberg, NW Austria
112 J8 **Bezdan** Ger. Besdan, Hung. Bezdán. Serbia, NW Serbia and Montenegro (Yugo.)
Bezdezh see Byezdzyezh
124 G15 **Bezhanitsy** Pskovskaya Oblast', W Russian Federation
124 K15 **Bezhetsk** Tverskaya Oblast', W Russian Federation
103 P16 **Béziers** anc. Baeterrae, Baeterrae Septimanorum, Julia Beterrae. Hérault, S France
Bezmein see Büzmeýin
Bezwada see Vijayawāda
154 P12 **Bhadrak** var. Bhadrakh. Orissa, E India
Bhadrakh see Bhadrak
155 F19 **Bhadra Reservoir** ⊞ SW India
155 F18 **Bhadrāvati** Karnātaka, SW India
153 R14 **Bhāgalpur** Bihār, NE India
Bhairab see Bhairab Bazar
153 U14 **Bhairab Bazar** var. Bhairab. Dhaka, C Bangladesh
153 O11 **Bhairahawa** Western, S Nepal
149 S8 **Bhakkar** Punjab, E Pakistan
153 P11 **Bhaktapur** Central, C Nepal
167 N3 **Bhamo** var. Banmo. Kachin State, N Myanmar
Bhāmragad see Bhāmragarh
154 K13 **Bhāmragarh** var. Bhāmragad. Mahārāshtra, C India
154 J12 **Bhandāra** Mahārāshtra, C India
Bhārat see India
152 J12 **Bharatpur** prev. Bhurtpore. Rājasthān, N India
154 D11 **Bharūch** Gujarāt, W India
155 E18 **Bhatkal** Karnātaka, W India
153 O13 **Bhatni** var. Bhatni Junction. Uttar Pradesh, N India
Bhatni Junction see Bhatni
153 S16 **Bhātpāra** West Bengal, NE India
149 U7 **Bhaun** Punjab, E Pakistan
Bhaunagar see Bhāvnagar
154 M13 **Bhavānīpātna** Orissa, E India
155 H21 **Bhavānīsāgar Reservoir** ⊞ S India
154 D11 **Bhāvnagar** prev. Bhaunagar. Gujarāt, W India
Bheanntraí, Bá see Bantry Bay
Bheara, Béal an see Gweebarra Bay
154 K12 **Bhilai** Chhattīsgarh, C India
152 G13 **Bhīlwāra** Rājasthān, N India
155 E14 **Bhīma** ≈ S India
155 K16 **Bhīmavaram** Andhra Pradesh, E India
154 I7 **Bhind** Madhya Pradesh, C India
152 E13 **Bhīnmāl** Rājasthān, N India
Bhir see Bīd
154 D13 **Bhiwandi** Mahārāshtra, W India
152 H10 **Bhiwāni** Haryāna, N India
152 L13 **Bhognīpur** Uttar Pradesh, N India
153 U16 **Bhola** Khulna, S Bangladesh
154 H10 **Bhopāl** Madhya Pradesh, C India
155 J14 **Bhopālpatnam** Chhattīsgarh, C India
155 E14 **Bhor** Mahārāshtra, W India
154 O12 **Bhubaneshwar** prev. Bhubaneswar, Bhuvaneshwar. Orissa, E India
Bhubaneswar see Bhubaneshwar
154 B9 **Bhuj** Gujarāt, W India
Bhuket see Phuket
Bhurtpore see Bharatpur
Bhusaval see Bhusāwal
154 G12 **Bhusāwal** prev. Bhusaval. Mahārāshtra, C India
153 T12 **Bhutan** off. Kingdom of Bhutan, var. Druk-yul. ◆ monarchy S Asia
Bhuvaneshwar see Bhubaneshwar
143 T15 **Biābān, Kūh-e** ⛰ S Iran
77 V18 **Biafra, Bight of** var. Bight of Bonny. bay W Africa
171 W12 **Biak** Papua, E Indonesia
171 W12 **Biak, Pulau** island E Indonesia
110 P12 **Biała Podlaska** Lubelskie, E Poland
110 F7 **Białogard** Ger. Belgard. Zachodnio-pomorskie, NW Poland
110 P10 **Białowieska, Puszcza** Bel. Byelavyezhskaya Pushcha, Rus. Belovezhskaya Pushcha. physical region Belarus/Poland see also Byelavyezhskaya Pushcha
110 G8 **Biały Bór** Ger. Baldenburg. Zachodnio-pomorskie, NW Poland
110 P9 **Białystok** Rus. Belostok, Bielostok. Podlaskie, NE Poland
107 L24 **Biancavilla** prev. Inessa. Sicilia, Italy, C Mediterranean Sea
Bianco, Monte see Blanc, Mont
76 L15 **Biankouma** W Ivory Coast
167 R7 **Bia, Phou** var. Pou Bia. ▲ C Laos
Bia, Pou see Bia, Phou
143 R5 **Bīārjmand** Semnān, N Iran
105 P4 **Biarra** ≈ NE Spain
102 I15 **Biarritz** Pyrénées-Atlantiques, SW France
108 H10 **Biasca** Ticino, S Switzerland
61 E17 **Biassini** Salto, N Uruguay
165 S3 **Bibai** Hokkaidō, NE Japan
83 B15 **Bibala** Port. Vila Arriaga. Namibe, SW Angola
104 I4 **Bibéi** ≈ NW Spain
Biberach see Biberach an der Riss
101 I23 **Biberach an der Riss** var. Biberach, Ger. Biberach an der Riß. Baden-Württemberg, S Germany
108 E7 **Biberist** Solothurn, NW Switzerland
77 O16 **Bibiani** SW Ghana
112 C13 **Bibinje** Zadar, SW Croatia
Biblical Gebal see Jbaïl
116 I5 **Bibrka** Pol. Bóbrka, Rus. Bobrka. L'vivs'ka Oblast', NW Ukraine
117 N10 **Bic** ≈ S Moldova
113 M18 **Bicaj** Kukës, NE Albania
116 K10 **Bicaz** Hung. Békás. Neamţ, NE Romania
183 Q16 **Bicheno** Tasmania, SE Australia
Bichiș see Békés
Bichiș-Ciaba see Békéscsaba
Bichitra see Phichit
137 P8 **Bichvint'a** Rus. Pitsunda. NW Georgia
15 T7 **Bic, Île du** island Québec, SE Canada
32 J10 **Bickleton** Washington, NW USA
36 L6 **Bicknell** Utah, W USA
171 S11 **Bicoli** Pulau Halmahera, E Indonesia
111 J22 **Bicske** Fejér, C Hungary
155 F14 **Bīd** prev. Bhir. Mahārāshtra, W India
77 U15 **Bida** Niger, C Nigeria
155 H15 **Bīdar** Karnātaka, C India
141 Y8 **Bidbid** NE Oman
19 P9 **Biddeford** Maine, NE USA
98 L9 **Biddinghuizen** Flevoland, C Netherlands
33 X11 **Biddle** Montana, NW USA
97 J23 **Bideford** SW England, UK
82 D13 **Bié** ◈ province C Angola
35 O2 **Bieber** California, W USA
110 O9 **Biebrza** ≈ NE Poland
165 T3 **Biei** Hokkaidō, NE Japan
108 D8 **Biel** Fr. Bienne. Bern, W Switzerland
100 G13 **Bielefeld** Nordrhein-Westfalen, NW Germany
108 D8 **Bieler See** Fr. Lac de Bienne. ◎ W Switzerland
Bielitz/Bielitz-Biala see Bielsko-Biała
106 C7 **Biella** Piemonte, N Italy
Bielostok see Białystok
111 J17 **Bielsko-Biała** Ger. Bielitz, Bielitz-Biala. Śląskie, S Poland
110 P10 **Bielsk Podlaski** Białystok, E Poland
Bien Bien see Điên Biên
Biên Đông see South China Sea
11 V17 **Bienfait** Saskatchewan, S Canada
167 T14 **Biên Hoa** Đông Nai, S Vietnam
Bienne see Biel
Bienne, Lac de see Bieler See
12 K8 **Bienville, Lac** ◎ Québec, C Canada
82 D13 **Bié, Planalto do** var. Bié Plateau. plateau C Angola
Bié Plateau see Bié, Planalto do
108 B9 **Bière** Vaud, W Switzerland
98 O4 **Bierum** Groningen, NE Netherlands
98 I13 **Biesbos** var. Biesbosch. wetland S Netherlands
Biesbosch see Biesbos
99 H21 **Biesme** Namur, S Belgium
101 H21 **Bietigheim-Bissingen** Baden-Württemberg, SW Germany
99 I23 **Bièvre** Namur, SE Belgium
79 D18 **Bifoun** Moyen-Ogooué, NW Gabon
165 T2 **Bifuka** Hokkaidō, NE Japan
136 C11 **Biga** Çanakkale, NW Turkey
136 C13 **Bigadiç** Balıkesir, W Turkey
26 J7 **Big Basin** basin Kansas, C USA
185 B20 **Big Bay** bay South Island, NZ
31 O5 **Big Bay de Noc** ◎ Michigan, N USA
31 N3 **Big Bay Point** headland Michigan, N USA
33 R10 **Big Belt Mountains** ⛰ Montana, NW USA
29 N10 **Big Bend Dam** dam South Dakota, N USA
24 K12 **Big Bend National Park** national park Texas, S USA
22 K5 **Big Black River** ≈ Mississippi, S USA
27 O3 **Big Blue River** ≈ Kansas/Nebraska, C USA
24 M10 **Big Canyon** ≈ Texas, SW USA
33 N12 **Big Creek** Idaho, NW USA
23 N8 **Big Creek Lake** ⊞ Alabama, S USA
23 X15 **Big Cypress Swamp** wetland Florida, SE USA
39 S9 **Big Delta** Alaska, USA
30 K6 **Big Eau Pleine Reservoir** ⊞ Wisconsin, N USA
19 P5 **Bigelow Mountain** ▲ Maine, NE USA
29 U3 **Big Falls** Minnesota, N USA
33 P8 **Bigfork** Montana, NW USA
29 U3 **Big Fork River** ≈ Minnesota, N USA
11 S15 **Biggar** Saskatchewan, S Canada
180 L3 **Bigge Island** island Western Australia
35 O5 **Biggs** California, W USA
32 I11 **Biggs** Oregon, NW USA
14 K13 **Big Gull Lake** ◎ Ontario, SE Canada
37 P16 **Big Hachet Peak** ▲ New Mexico, SW USA
33 P11 **Big Hole River** ≈ Montana, NW USA
33 V13 **Bighorn Basin** basin Wyoming, C USA
33 U11 **Bighorn Lake** ◎ Montana /Wyoming, N USA
33 W13 **Bighorn Mountains** ⛰ Wyoming, C USA
36 J13 **Big Horn Peak** ▲ Arizona, SW USA
33 V11 **Bighorn River** ≈ Montana/Wyoming, NW USA
9 S7 **Big Island** island Nunavut, NE Canada
39 O16 **Big Koniuji Island** island Shumagin Islands, Alaska, USA
25 N9 **Big Lake** Texas, SW USA
19 T5 **Big Lake** ◎ Maine, NE USA
30 I3 **Big Manitou Falls** waterfall Wisconsin, N USA
35 R2 **Big Mountain** ▲ Nevada, W USA
108 G10 **Bignasco** Ticino, S Switzerland
29 R16 **Big Nemaha River** ≈ Nebraska, C USA
76 G12 **Bignona** SW Senegal
Bigorra see Tarbes
Bigosovo see Bihosava
35 S10 **Big Pine** California, W USA
35 Q14 **Big Pine Mountain** ▲ California, W USA
27 V6 **Big Piney Creek** ≈ Missouri, C USA
65 M24 **Big Point** headland N Tristan da Cunha
31 P8 **Big Rapids** Michigan, N USA
30 K6 **Big Rib River** ≈ Wisconsin, N USA
14 L14 **Big Rideau Lake** ◎ Ontario, SE Canada
11 T14 **Big River** Saskatchewan, C Canada
27 X5 **Big River** ≈ Missouri, C USA
31 N7 **Big Sable Point** headland Michigan, N USA
33 S7 **Big Sandy** Montana, NW USA
25 W6 **Big Sandy** Texas, SW USA
37 V5 **Big Sandy Creek** ≈ Colorado, C USA
29 Q16 **Big Sandy Creek** ≈ Nebraska, C USA
29 V5 **Big Sandy Lake** ◎ Minnesota, N USA
36 J11 **Big Sandy River** ≈ Arizona, SW USA
21 P5 **Big Sandy River** ≈ S USA
23 V6 **Big Satilla Creek** ≈ Georgia, SE USA
29 R12 **Big Sioux River** ≈ Iowa/South Dakota, N USA
35 U7 **Big Smoky Valley** valley Nevada, W USA
25 N7 **Big Spring** Texas, SW USA
19 Q5 **Big Squaw Mountain** ▲ Maine, NE USA
21 O7 **Big Stone Gap** Virginia, NE USA
29 Q8 **Big Stone Lake** ◎ Minnesota/South Dakota, N USA
22 K4 **Big Sunflower River** ≈ Mississippi, S USA
33 T11 **Big Timber** Montana, NW USA
12 D8 **Big Trout Lake** Ontario, C Canada
14 I12 **Big Trout Lake** ◎ Ontario, SE Canada
35 O2 **Big Valley Mountains** ⛰ California, W USA
25 Q13 **Big Wells** Texas, SW USA
14 F11 **Bigwood** Ontario, S Canada
112 D11 **Bihać** Federacija Bosna I Hercegovina, NW Bosnia and Herzegovina
153 P13 **Bihār** prev. Behar. ◈ state N India
Bihār see Bihār Sharīf
81 F20 **Biharamulo** Kagera, NW Tanzania
153 R13 **Bihārīganj** Bihār, NE India
153 P14 **Bihār Sharīf** var. Bihār. Bihār, N India
116 F10 **Bihor** ◈ county NW Romania
165 V3 **Bihoro** Hokkaidō, NE Japan
118 K11 **Bihosava** Rus. Bigosovo. Vitsyebskaya Voblasts', NW Belarus
Bijagos Archipelago see Bijagós, Arquipélago dos
76 G13 **Bijagós, Arquipélago dos** var. Bijagos Archipelago. island group W Guinea-Bissau
155 F16 **Bijāpur** Karnātaka, C India
142 K5 **Bījār** Kordestān, W Iran
112 J11 **Bijeljina** Republika Srpska, NE Bosnia and Herzegovina
113 K15 **Bijelo Polje** Montenegro, SW Serbia and Montenegro (Yugo.)
160 I11 **Bijie** Guizhou, S China
152 J10 **Bijnor** Uttar Pradesh, N India
152 F11 **Bīkāner** Rājasthān, NW India
189 V3 **Bikar Atoll** var. Pikaar. atoll Ratak Chain, N Marshall Islands
190 H3 **Bikeman** atoll Tungaru, W Kiribati
190 I3 **Bikenebu** Tarawa, W Kiribati
123 S14 **Bikin** Khabarovskiy Kray, SE Russian Federation
123 S14 **Bikin** ≈ SE Russian Federation
189 R3 **Bikini Atoll** var. Pikinni. atoll Ralik Chain, NW Marshall Islands
83 L17 **Bikita** Masvingo, E Zimbabwe
Bikkū Bīttī see Bette, Pic
79 I19 **Bikoro** Equateur, W Dem. Rep. Congo
141 Z9 **Bilād Banī Bū 'Alī** NE Oman
141 Z9 **Bilād Banī Bū Ḩasan** NE Oman
141 X9 **Bilād Manaḩ** var. Manaḩ. NE Oman
77 Q12 **Bilanga** C Burkina
152 F12 **Bilāra** Rājasthān, N India
152 K10 **Bilāri** Uttar Pradesh, N India
138 J5 **Bil'ās, Jabal al** ⛰ C Syria
154 L11 **Bilāspur** Chhattīsgarh, C India
152 I8 **Bilāspur** Himāchal Pradesh, N India
168 J9 **Bila, Sungai** ≈ Sumatera, W Indonesia
137 Y13 **Biläsuvar** Rus. Bilyasuvar; prev. Pushkino. SE Azerbaijan
117 O5 **Bila Tserkva** Rus. Belaya Tserkov'. Kyyivs'ka Oblast', N Ukraine
167 N11 **Bilauktaung Range** var. Thanintari Taungdan. ⛰ Myanmar/Thailand
105 O2 **Bilbao** Basq. Bilbo. País Vasco, N Spain
Bilbo see Bilbao
92 H2 **Bíldudalur** Vestfirdhir, NW Iceland
113 I16 **Bileća** Republika Srpska, S Bosnia and Herzegovina
136 E12 **Bilecik** Bilecik, NW Turkey
136 F12 **Bilecik** ◈ province NW Turkey
116 E11 **Biled** Ger. Billed, Hung. Billéd. Timiş, W Romania
111 O15 **Biłgoraj** Lubelskie, E Poland
117 P11 **Bilhorod-Dnistrovs'kyy** Rus. Belgorod-Dnestrovskiy, Rom. Cetatea Albă; prev. Akkerman, anc. Tyras. Odes'ka Oblast', SW Ukraine

◆ Country ● Country Capital ◇ Dependent Territory ○ Dependent Territory Capital ◈ Administrative Region ✈ International Airport ▲ Mountain ⛰ Mountain Range Volcano ≈ River ◎ Lake ⊞ Reservoir

79 M16 **Bili** Orientale, N Dem. Rep. Congo
123 T6 **Bilibino** Chukotskiy Avtonomnyy Okrug, NE Russian Federation
166 M8 **Bilin** Mon State, S Myanmar
113 N21 **Bilisht** var. Bilishti. Korçë, SE Albania
Bilishti see Bilisht
183 N10 **Billabong Creek** var. Moulamein Creek. seasonal river New South Wales, SE Australia
182 G4 **Billa Kalina** South Australia
197 Q17 **Bill Baileys Bank** undersea feature N Atlantic Ocean
Billed/Billed see Biled
153 N14 **Billi** Uttar Pradesh, N India
97 M15 **Billingham** N England, UK
33 U11 **Billings** Montana, NW USA
95 J16 **Billingsfors** Västra Götaland, S Sweden
Bill of Cape Clear, The see Clear, Cape
28 L9 **Billsburg** South Dakota, N USA
95 F23 **Billund** Ribe, W Denmark
36 L11 **Bill Williams Mountain** ▲ Arizona, SW USA
36 I12 **Bill Williams River** ≈ Arizona, SW USA
77 Y8 **Bilma** Agadez, NE Niger
77 Y8 **Bilma, Grand Erg de** desert NE Niger
181 Y9 **Biloela** Queensland, E Australia
112 G8 **Bilo Gora** ▲▲ N Croatia
117 U13 **Bilohirs'k** Rus. Belogorsk; prev. Karasubazar. Respublika Krym, S Ukraine
116 M3 **Bilokorovychi** Rus. Belokorovichi. Zhytomyrs'ka Oblast', N Ukraine
117 X5 **Bilokurakine** Luhans'ka Oblast', E Ukraine
117 T3 **Bilopillya** Rus. Belopol'ye. Sums'ka Oblast', NE Ukraine
117 Y6 **Bilovods'k** Rus. Belovodsk. Luhans'ka Oblast', E Ukraine
22 M9 **Biloxi** Mississippi, S USA
117 R10 **Bilozerka** Khersons'ka Oblast', S Ukraine
117 W7 **Bilozers'ke** Donets'ka Oblast', E Ukraine
98 J11 **Bilthoven** Utrecht, C Netherlands
78 K9 **Biltine** Biltine, E Chad
78 J9 **Biltine** off. Préfecture de Biltine. ◈ prefecture E Chad
162 D5 **Bilüü** Bayan-Ölgiy, W Mongolia
Bilwi see Puerto Cabezas
Bilyasuvar see Biläsuvar
117 O11 **Bilyayivka** Odes'ka Oblast', SW Ukraine
99 K18 **Bilzen** Limburg, NE Belgium
Bimbéréké see Bembèrèkè
183 R10 **Bimberi Peak** ▲ New South Wales, SE Australia
77 Q15 **Bimbila** E Ghana
79 I15 **Bimbo** Ombella-Mpoko, SW Central African Republic
44 F2 **Bimini Islands** island group W Bahamas
154 I9 **Bīna** Madhya Pradesh, C India
143 T4 **Bīnālūd, Kūh-e** ▲▲ NE Iran
99 F20 **Binche** Hainaut, S Belgium
Bindloe Island see Marchena, Isla
83 L16 **Bindura** Mashonaland Central, NE Zimbabwe
105 T5 **Binefar** Aragón, NE Spain
83 J16 **Binga** Matabeleland North, W Zimbabwe
183 T5 **Bingara** New South Wales, SE Australia
101 F18 **Bingen am Rhein** Rheinland-Pfalz, SW Germany
26 M11 **Binger** Oklahoma, C USA
Bingerau see Węgrów
Bin Ghalfān, Jazā'ir see Ḥalāniyāt, Juzur al
19 Q6 **Bingham** Maine, NE USA
18 H11 **Binghamton** New York, NE USA
Bin Ghanīmah, Jabal see Bin Ghunaymah, Jabal
75 P11 **Bin Ghunaymah, Jabal** var. Jabal Bin Ghanīmah. ▲▲ C Libya
139 U3 **Bingird** NE Iraq
Bingmei see Congjiang
137 P14 **Bingöl** Bingöl, E Turkey
137 P14 **Bingöl** ◈ province E Turkey
161 R6 **Binhai** var. Binhai Xian. Dongkan. Jiangsu, E China
Binhai Xian see Binhai
167 V11 **Binh Đinh** var. An Nhon. Binh Đinh, C Vietnam
167 U10 **Binh Sơn** var. Châu Ô. Quang Ngai, C Vietnam
Binimani see Bintimani
168 I8 **Binjai** Sumatera, W Indonesia
183 R6 **Binnaway** New South Wales, SE Australia
108 E6 **Binningen** Basel-Land, NW Switzerland
168 J8 **Bintang, Banjaran** ▲▲ Peninsular Malaysia
168 M10 **Bintan, Pulau** island Kepulauan Riau, W Indonesia
76 J14 **Bintimani** var. Binimani. ▲ NE Sierra Leone
Bint Jubayl see Bent Jbaïl
169 S9 **Bintulu** Sarawak, East Malaysia
171 V12 **Bintuni** prev. Steenkool. Papua, E Indonesia
163 W8 **Binxian** Heilongjiang, NE China
160 K14 **Binyang** var. Binzhou. Guangxi Zhuangzu Zizhiqu, S China
161 Q4 **Binzhou** Shandong, E China
Binzhou see Binyang
63 G14 **Bío Bío** off. Región del Bío Bío. ◈ region C Chile
63 G14 **Bío Bío, Río** ≈ C Chile
79 C16 **Bioco, Isla de** var. Bioko, Eng. Fernando Po, Sp. Fernando Póo; prev. Macías Nguema Biyogo. island NW Equatorial Guinea
112 D13 **Biograd na Moru** It. Zaravecchia. Zadar, SW Croatia
Bioko see Bioco, Isla de
113 F14 **Biokovo** ▲▲ S Croatia
Biorra see Birr
Bipontium see Zweibrücken
143 W13 **Bīrag, Kūh-e** ▲▲ SE Iran
75 O10 **Birāk** var. Brak. C Libya
139 S10 **Bi'r al Islām** C Iraq
154 N11 **Biramitrapur** Orissa, E India
139 T11 **Bi'r an Niṣf** S Iraq
78 L12 **Birao** Vakaga, NE Central African Republic
146 J10 **Birata** Rus. Darganata, Dargan-Ata. Lebap Welaýaty, NE Turkmenistan
158 M6 **Biratar Bulak** well NW China
153 R12 **Biratnagar** Eastern, SE Nepal
165 R5 **Biratori** Hokkaidō, NE Japan
39 S8 **Birch Creek** Alaska, USA
38 M11 **Birch Creek** ≈ Alaska, USA
11 T14 **Birch Hills** Saskatchewan, S Canada
182 M10 **Birchip** Victoria, SE Australia
29 X4 **Birch Lake** ⊚ Minnesota, N USA
11 Q11 **Birch Mountains** ▲ Alberta, W Canada
11 V15 **Birch River** Manitoba, S Canada
44 H12 **Birchs Hill** hill W Jamaica
39 R11 **Birchwood** Alaska, USA
188 I5 **Bird Island** island S Northern Mariana Islands
137 N16 **Birecik** Şanlıurfa, S Turkey
152 M10 **Birendranagar** var. Surkhet. Mid Western, W Nepal
Bir es Saba see Be'ér Sheva'
74 A12 **Bir-Gandouz** SW Western Sahara
153 P12 **Birganj** Central, C Nepal
81 B14 **Biri** ≈ W Sudan
Bi'r Ibn Hirmās see Al Bi'r
143 U8 **Bīrjand** Khorāsān, E Iran
139 T11 **Birkat Ḥāmid** well S Iraq
95 F18 **Birkeland** Aust-Agder, S Norway
101 E19 **Birkenfeld** Rheinland-Pfalz, SW Germany
97 K18 **Birkenhead** NW England, UK
109 W7 **Birkfeld** Steiermark, SE Austria
182 A2 **Birksgate Range** ▲▲ South Australia
Birlad see Bârlad
97 K20 **Birmingham** C England, UK
23 P4 **Birmingham** Alabama, S USA
97 M20 **Birmingham** ✕ C England, UK
Bir Moghrein see Bîr Mogreïn
76 J4 **Bîr Mogreïn** var. Bir Moghrein; prev. Fort-Trinquet. Tiris Zemmour, N Mauritania
191 S4 **Birnie Island** atoll Phoenix Islands, C Kiribati
Birni-Ngaouré see Birnin Gaouré
77 S12 **Birnin Gaouré** var. Birni-Ngaouré. Dosso, SW Niger
77 S12 **Birnin Kebbi** Kebbi, NW Nigeria
Birni-Nkonni see Birnin Konni
77 T12 **Birnin Konni** var. Birni-Nkonni. Tahoua, SW Niger
77 W13 **Birnin Kudu** Jigawa, N Nigeria
123 S16 **Birobidzhan** Yevreyskaya Avtonomnaya Oblast', SE Russian Federation
97 D18 **Birr** var. Parsonstown, Ir. Biorra. C Ireland
183 P4 **Birrie River** ≈ New South Wales/Queensland, SE Australia
108 D7 **Birse** ≈ NW Switzerland
Birsen see Biržai
108 E6 **Birsfelden** Basel-Land, NW Switzerland
127 U4 **Birsk** Respublika Bashkortostan, W Russian Federation
119 F14 **Birštonas** Kaunas, C Lithuania
159 P14 **Biru** Xinjiang Uygur Zizhiqu, W China
Biruni see Beruniy
122 L12 **Biryusa** ≈ C Russian Federation
122 L12 **Biryusinsk** Irkutskaya Oblast', C Russian Federation
118 G10 **Biržai** Ger. Birsen. Panevėžys, NE Lithuania
121 P16 **Birżebbuġa** SE Malta
Bisanthe see Tekirdağ
171 R12 **Bisa, Pulau** island Maluku, E Indonesia
37 N17 **Bisbee** Arizona, SW USA
29 O2 **Bisbee** North Dakota, N USA
Biscaia, Baía de see Biscay, Bay of
102 I13 **Biscarrosse et de Parentis, Étang de** ⊚ SW France
104 M1 **Biscay, Bay of** Sp. Golfo de Vizcaya, Port. Baía de Biscaia. bay France/Spain
23 Z16 **Biscayne Bay** bay Florida, SE USA
64 M7 **Biscay Plain** undersea feature SE Bay of Biscay
107 N17 **Bisceglie** Puglia, SE Italy
Bischoflack see Škofja Loka
Bischofsburg see Biskupiec
109 Q7 **Bischofshofen** Salzburg, NW Austria
101 P15 **Bischofswerda** Sachsen, E Germany
103 V5 **Bischwiller** Bas-Rhin, NE France
21 T10 **Biscoe** North Carolina, SE USA
194 G5 **Biscoe Islands** island group Antarctica
14 E9 **Biscotasi Lake** ⊚ Ontario, S Canada
14 E9 **Biscotasing** Ontario, S Canada
54 J6 **Biscucuy** Portuguesa, NW Venezuela
114 K11 **Biser** Khaskovo, S Bulgaria
113 D15 **Biševo** It. Busi. island SW Croatia
141 N12 **Bishah, Wādī** dry watercourse C Saudi Arabia
147 U7 **Bishkek** var. Pishpek; prev. Frunze. ● (Kyrgyzstan) Chuyskaya Oblast', N Kyrgyzstan
147 U7 **Bishkek** ✕ Chuyskaya Oblast', N Kyrgyzstan
153 R16 **Bishnupur** West Bengal, NE India
83 J25 **Bisho** Eastern Cape, S South Africa
35 S9 **Bishop** California, W USA
25 S15 **Bishop** Texas, SW USA
97 L15 **Bishop Auckland** N England, UK
Bishop's Lynn see King's Lynn
97 O21 **Bishop's Stortford** E England, UK
21 S12 **Bishopville** South Carolina, SE USA
138 M5 **Bishrī, Jabal** ▲ E Syria
163 U4 **Bishui** Heilongjiang, NE China
81 G17 **Bisina, Lake** prev. Lake Salisbury. ⊚ E Uganda
Biskara see Biskra
74 L6 **Biskra** var. Beskra, Biskara. NE Algeria
110 M8 **Biskupiec** Ger. Bischofsburg. Warmińsko-Mazurskie, NE Poland
171 R7 **Bislig** Mindanao, S Philippines
27 X6 **Bismarck** Missouri, C USA
28 M5 **Bismarck** state capital North Dakota, N USA
186 D5 **Bismarck Archipelago** island group NE PNG
131 Z16 **Bismarck Plate** tectonic feature W Pacific Ocean
186 D7 **Bismarck Range** ▲▲ N PNG
186 E6 **Bismarck Sea** sea W Pacific Ocean
137 P15 **Bismil** Diyarbakır, SE Turkey
43 N6 **Bismuna, Laguna** lagoon NE Nicaragua
Bisnulok see Phitsanulok
171 R10 **Bisoa, Tanjung** headland Pulau Halmahera, N Indonesia
28 K7 **Bison** South Dakota, N USA
93 H17 **Bispfors** Jämtland, C Sweden
76 G13 **Bissau** ● (Guinea-Bissau) W Guinea-Bissau
76 G13 **Bissau** ✕ W Guinea-Bissau
99 M24 **Bissen** Luxembourg, C Luxembourg
Bissojohka see Børselv
76 G12 **Bissorã** W Guinea-Bissau
11 O10 **Bistcho Lake** ⊚ Alberta, W Canada
22 G5 **Bistineau, Lake** ▣ Louisiana, S USA
Bistrica see Ilirska Bistrica
116 I9 **Bistrița** Ger. Bistritz, Hung. Beszterce; prev. Nösen. Bistrița-Năsăud, N Romania
116 K10 **Bistrița** Ger. Bistritz. ≈ NE Romania
116 I9 **Bistrița-Năsăud** ◈ county N Romania
Bistritz see Bistrița
Bistritz ober Pernstein see Bystřice nad Pernštejnem
152 L11 **Biswān** Uttar Pradesh, N India
110 M7 **Bisztynek** Warmińsko-Mazurskie, NE Poland
79 E17 **Bitam** Woleu-Ntem, N Gabon
101 D18 **Bitburg** Rheinland-Pfalz, SW Germany
103 U4 **Bitche** Moselle, NE France
78 I11 **Bitkine** Guéra, C Chad
137 R15 **Bitlis** Bitlis, SE Turkey
137 R14 **Bitlis** ◈ province E Turkey
Bitoeng see Bitung
113 N20 **Bitola** Turk. Monastir; prev. Bitolj. S FYR Macedonia
Bitolj see Bitola
107 O17 **Bitonto** anc. Butuntum. Puglia, SE Italy
77 Q13 **Bitou** var. Bittou. SE Burkina
155 C20 **Bitra Island** island Lakshadweep, India, N Indian Ocean
101 M14 **Bitterfeld** Sachsen-Anhalt, E Germany
32 O9 **Bitterroot Range** ▲▲ Idaho/Montana, NW USA
33 P10 **Bitterroot River** ≈ Montana, NW USA
107 D18 **Bitti** Sardegna, Italy, C Mediterranean Sea
Bittou see Bitou
171 Q11 **Bitung** prev. Bitoeng. Sulawesi, C Indonesia
60 I12 **Bituruna** Paraná, S Brazil
77 Y13 **Biu** Borno, E Nigeria
Biumba see Byumba
164 J13 **Biwa-ko** ⊚ Honshū, SW Japan
171 X14 **Biwarlaut** Papua, E Indonesia
27 P10 **Bixby** Oklahoma, C USA
122 J13 **Biya** ≈ S Russian Federation
Biy-Khem see Bol'shoy Yenisey
122 J13 **Biysk** Altayskiy Kray, S Russian Federation
164 H13 **Bizen** Okayama, Honshū, SW Japan
Bizerta see Bizerte
120 K10 **Bizerte** Ar. Banzart, Eng. Bizerta. N Tunisia
Bizkaia see Vizcaya
92 G2 **Bjargtangar** headland W Iceland
Bjärnå see Perniö
95 K22 **Bjärnum** Skåne, S Sweden
93 I16 **Bjästa** Västernorrland, C Sweden
113 I14 **Bjelašnica** ▲ SE Bosnia and Herzegovina
112 C10 **Bjelolasica** ▲ NW Croatia
112 F8 **Bjelovar** Hung. Belovár. Bjelovar-Bilogora, N Croatia
112 F8 **Bjelovar-Bilogora** off. Bjelovarsko-Bilogorska Županija. ◈ province NE Croatia
Bjelovarsko-Bilogorska Županija see Bjelovar-Bilogora
92 H10 **Bjerkvik** Nordland, C Norway
95 G21 **Bjerringbro** Viborg, NW Denmark
Bjeshkët e Namuna see North Albanian Alps
95 L14 **Björbo** Dalarna, C Sweden
95 I15 **Bjørkelangen** Akershus, S Norway
95 O14 **Björklinge** Uppsala, C Sweden
93 I14 **Björksele** Västerbotten, N Sweden
93 I16 **Björna** Västernorrland, C Sweden
95 C14 **Bjørnafjorden** fjord S Norway
95 L16 **Björneborg** Värmland, C Sweden
Björneborg see Pori
95 E14 **Bjornesfjorden** ⊚ S Norway
92 M9 **Bjørnevatn** Finnmark, N Norway
197 T13 **Bjørnøya** Eng. Bear Island. island N Norway
93 I15 **Bjurholm** Västerbotten, N Sweden
95 J22 **Bjuv** Skåne, S Sweden
76 M12 **Bla** Ségou, W Mali
181 W8 **Blackall** Queensland, E Australia
29 V2 **Black Bay** lake bay Minnesota, N USA
27 N9 **Black Bear Creek** ≈ Oklahoma, C USA
97 K17 **Blackburn** NW England, UK
45 W10 **Blackburne** ✕ (Plymouth) E Montserrat
39 T11 **Blackburn, Mount** ▲ Alaska, USA
35 N5 **Black Butte Lake** ▣ California, W USA
194 J5 **Black Coast** physical region Antarctica
11 Q16 **Black Diamond** Alberta, SW Canada
18 K11 **Black Dome** ▲ New York, NE USA
113 L18 **Black Drin** Alb. Lumi i Drinit të Zi, SCr. Crni Drim. ≈ Albania/FYR Macedonia
12 D6 **Black Duck** ≈ Ontario, C Canada
29 U4 **Blackduck** Minnesota, N USA
33 R14 **Blackfoot** Idaho, NW USA
33 P9 **Blackfoot River** ≈ Montana, NW USA
Black Forest see Schwarzwald
28 J10 **Blackhawk** South Dakota, N USA
28 I10 **Black Hills** ▲▲ South Dakota/Wyoming, N USA
11 T10 **Black Lake** ⊚ Saskatchewan, C Canada
31 Q5 **Black Lake** ⊚ Michigan, N USA
18 I7 **Black Lake** ⊚ New York, NE USA
22 G6 **Black Lake** ▣ Louisiana, S USA
26 F7 **Black Mesa** ▲ Oklahoma, C USA
21 P10 **Black Mountain** North Carolina, SE USA
35 P13 **Black Mountain** ▲ California, W USA
37 Q2 **Black Mountain** ▲ Colorado, C USA
21 O7 **Black Mountain** ▲ Kentucky, E USA
96 K1 **Black Mountains** ▲▲ SE Wales, UK
36 H10 **Black Mountains** ▲▲ Arizona, SW USA
33 Q16 **Black Pine Peak** ▲ Idaho, NW USA
97 K17 **Blackpool** NW England, UK
37 Q14 **Black Range** ▲▲ New Mexico, SW USA
44 I12 **Black River** W Jamaica
14 J14 **Black River** ≈ Ontario, SE Canada
131 U12 **Black River** Chin. Babian Jiang, Lixian Jiang, Fr. Rivière Noire, Vtn. Sông Đa. ≈ China/Vietnam
44 I12 **Black River** ≈ W Jamaica
39 T7 **Black River** ≈ Alaska, USA
37 N13 **Black River** ≈ Arizona, SW USA
27 X7 **Black River** ≈ Arkansas/Missouri, C USA
22 I7 **Black River** ≈ Louisiana, S USA
31 S8 **Black River** ≈ Michigan, N USA
31 Q5 **Black River** ≈ Michigan, N USA
18 I8 **Black River** ≈ New York, NE USA
21 T13 **Black River** ≈ South Carolina, SE USA
30 J7 **Black River** ≈ Wisconsin, N USA
30 J7 **Black River Falls** Wisconsin, N USA
35 R3 **Black Rock Desert** desert Nevada, W USA
Black Sand Desert see Garagum
21 S7 **Blacksburg** Virginia, NE USA
136 H10 **Black Sea** var. Euxine Sea, Bul. Cherno More, Rom. Marea Neagră, Rus. Chernoye More, Turk. Karadeniz, Ukr. Chorne More. sea Asia/Europe
117 Q10 **Black Sea Lowland** Ukr. Prychornomors'ka Nyzovyna. depression SE Europe
33 S17 **Blacks Fork** ≈ Wyoming, C USA
23 V7 **Blackshear** Georgia, SE USA
23 S6 **Blackshear, Lake** ▣ Georgia, SE USA
97 A16 **Blacksod Bay** Ir. Cuan an Fhóid Duibh. inlet W Ireland
21 V7 **Blackstone** Virginia, NE USA
77 O14 **Black Volta** var. Borongo, Mouhoun, Moun Hou, Fr. Volta Noire. ≈ W Africa
23 O5 **Black Warrior River** ≈ Alabama, S USA
181 X8 **Blackwater** Queensland, E Australia
97 D20 **Blackwater** Ir. An Abhainn Mhór. ≈ S Ireland
27 T4 **Blackwater River** ≈ Missouri, C USA
21 W7 **Blackwater River** ≈ Virginia, NE USA
Blackwater State see Nebraska
27 N8 **Blackwell** Oklahoma, C USA
25 P7 **Blackwell** Texas, SW USA
99 J15 **Bladel** Noord-Brabant, S Netherlands
Bladenmarkt see Bălăuşeri
114 G11 **Blagoevgrad** prev. Gorna Dzhumaya. Blagoevgrad, SW Bulgaria
114 G11 **Blagoevgrad** ◈ province SW Bulgaria
123 Q14 **Blagoveshchensk** Amurskaya Oblast', SE Russian Federation
127 V4 **Blagoveshchensk** Respublika Bashkortostan, W Russian Federation
102 I7 **Blain** Loire-Atlantique, NW France
29 V8 **Blaine** Minnesota, N USA
32 H6 **Blaine** Washington, NW USA
11 T15 **Blaine Lake** Saskatchewan, S Canada
29 S14 **Blair** Nebraska, C USA
96 J10 **Blairgowrie** C Scotland, UK
18 C15 **Blairsville** Pennsylvania, NE USA
116 H11 **Blaj** Ger. Blasendorf, Hung. Balázsfalva. Alba, SW Romania
64 F9 **Blake-Bahama Ridge** undersea feature W Atlantic Ocean
23 S7 **Blakely** Georgia, SE USA
64 E10 **Blake Plateau** var. Blake Terrace. undersea feature W Atlantic Ocean
30 M1 **Blake Point** headland Michigan, N USA
Blake Terrace see Blake Plateau
61 B24 **Blanca, Bahía** bay E Argentina
56 C12 **Blanca, Cordillera** ▲▲ W Peru
105 T12 **Blanca, Costa** physical region SE Spain
37 S7 **Blanca Peak** ▲ Colorado, C USA
24 I9 **Blanca, Sierra** ▲ Texas, SW USA
120 K9 **Blanc, Cap** headland N Tunisia
Blanc, Cap see Nouâdhibou, Râs
31 R12 **Blanchard River** ≈ Ohio, N USA
182 E8 **Blanche, Cape** headland South Australia
182 J4 **Blanche, Lake** ⊚ South Australia
31 R14 **Blanchester** Ohio, N USA
182 J9 **Blanchetown** South Australia
45 U13 **Blanchisseuse** Trinidad, Trinidad and Tobago
103 T11 **Blanc, Mont** It. Monte Bianco. ▲ France/Italy
25 R11 **Blanco** Texas, SW USA
42 K14 **Blanco, Cabo** headland NW Costa Rica
32 D14 **Blanco, Cape** headland Oregon, NW USA
62 H10 **Blanco, Río** ≈ W Argentina
56 F10 **Blanco, Río** ≈ NE Peru
15 O9 **Blanc, Réservoir** ▣ Québec, SE Canada
21 R7 **Bland** Virginia, NE USA
92 I2 **Blanda** ≈ N Iceland
37 O7 **Blanding** Utah, W USA
105 X5 **Blanes** Cataluña, NE Spain
103 N3 **Blangy-sur-Bresle** Seine-Maritime, N France
111 C18 **Blanice** Ger. Blanitz. ≈ SE Czech Republic
Blanitz see Blanice
99 C16 **Blankenberge** West-Vlaanderen, NW Belgium
101 D17 **Blankenheim** Nordrhein-Westfalen, W Germany
25 R8 **Blanket** Texas, SW USA
55 O3 **Blanquilla, Isla** var. La Blanquilla. island N Venezuela
Blanquilla, La see Blanquilla, Isla
61 F18 **Blanquillo** Durazno, C Uruguay
111 G18 **Blansko** Ger. Blanz. Jihomoravský Kraj, SE Czech Republic
83 N15 **Blantyre** var. Blantyre-Limbe. Southern, S Malawi
83 N15 **Blantyre** ✕ Southern, S Malawi
Blantyre-Limbe see Blantyre
Blanz see Blansko
98 J10 **Blaricum** Noord-Holland, C Netherlands
Blasendorf see Blaj
Blatnitsa see Durankulak
113 F15 **Blato** It. Blatta. Dubrovnik-Neretva, S Croatia
Blatta see Blato
108 E10 **Blatten** Valais, SW Switzerland
101 J20 **Blaufelden** Baden-Württemberg, SW Germany
95 E23 **Blåvands Huk** headland W Denmark
102 G6 **Blavet** ≈ NW France
102 J12 **Blaye** Gironde, SW France
183 R8 **Blayney** New South Wales, SE Australia
65 D25 **Bleaker Island** island SE Falkland Islands
109 T10 **Bled** Ger. Veldes. NW Slovenia
99 D20 **Bléharies** Hainaut, SW Belgium
109 U9 **Bleiburg** Slvn. Pliberk. Kärnten, S Austria
101 L17 **Bleiloch-Stausee** ▣ C Germany
98 H12 **Bleiswijk** Zuid-Holland, W Netherlands
95 L22 **Blekinge** ◈ county S Sweden
14 D17 **Blenheim** Ontario, S Canada
185 K15 **Blenheim** Marlborough, South Island, NZ
99 M15 **Blerick** Limburg, SE Netherlands
Blesae see Blois
25 V13 **Blessing** Texas, SW USA
14 I10 **Bleu, Lac** ⊚ Québec, SE Canada
Blibba see Blitta
120 H10 **Blida** var. El Boulaida, El Boulaïda. N Algeria
95 P15 **Blidö** Stockholm, C Sweden
95 K18 **Blidsberg** Västra Götaland, S Sweden
185 A21 **Bligh Sound** sound South Island, NZ
187 X14 **Bligh Water** strait NW Fiji
14 D11 **Blind River** Ontario, S Canada
31 R11 **Blissfield** Michigan, N USA
77 R15 **Blitta** prev. Blibba. C Togo
19 O13 **Block Island** island Rhode Island, NE USA
19 O13 **Block Island Sound** sound Rhode Island, NE USA
98 H10 **Bloemendaal** Noord-Holland, W Netherlands
83 H23 **Bloemfontein** var. Mangaung. ● (South Africa-judicial capital) Free State, C South Africa
83 I22 **Bloemhof** North-West, NW South Africa
102 M7 **Blois** anc. Blesae. Loir-et-Cher, C France
98 L8 **Blokzijl** Overijssel, N Netherlands
95 N20 **Blomstermåla** Kalmar, S Sweden
92 I2 **Blönduós** Nordhurland Vestra, N Iceland
110 L11 **Błonie** Mazowieckie, C Poland
97 C14 **Bloody Foreland** Ir. Cnoc Fola. headland NW Ireland
31 N15 **Bloomfield** Indiana, N USA
29 X16 **Bloomfield** Iowa, C USA
27 Y8 **Bloomfield** Missouri, C USA
37 P9 **Bloomfield** New Mexico, SW USA
25 U7 **Blooming Grove** Texas, SW USA
29 W10 **Blooming Prairie** Minnesota, N USA
30 L13 **Bloomington** Illinois, N USA
31 O15 **Bloomington** Indiana, N USA
29 V9 **Bloomington** Minnesota, N USA
25 U13 **Bloomington** Texas, SW USA
18 H14 **Bloomsburg** Pennsylvania, NE USA
181 X7 **Bloomsbury** Queensland, NE Australia
169 R16 **Blora** Jawa, C Indonesia
18 G12 **Blossburg** Pennsylvania, NE USA
25 V5 **Blossom** Texas, SW USA
123 T5 **Blossom, Mys** headland Ostrov Vrangelya, NE Russian Federation
23 R8 **Blountstown** Florida, SE USA
21 P8 **Blountville** Tennessee, S USA
21 Q9 **Blowing Rock** North Carolina, SE USA
108 J8 **Bludenz** Vorarlberg, W Austria
36 L6 **Blue Bell Knoll** ▲ Utah, W USA
23 Y12 **Blue Cypress Lake** ⊚ Florida, SE USA
29 U11 **Blue Earth** Minnesota, N USA
21 Q7 **Bluefield** Virginia, NE USA
21 R7 **Bluefield** West Virginia, NE USA
43 N10 **Bluefields** Región Autónoma Atlántico Sur, SE Nicaragua
43 N10 **Bluefields, Bahía de** bay W Caribbean Sea
29 Z14 **Blue Grass** Iowa, C USA
Bluegrass State see Kentucky
Blue Hen State see Delaware
19 S7 **Blue Hill** Maine, NE USA
29 P16 **Blue Hill** Nebraska, C USA
30 J5 **Blue Hills** hill range Wisconsin, N USA
34 L3 **Blue Lake** California, W USA
Blue Law State see Connecticut
37 Q6 **Blue Mesa Reservoir** ▣ Colorado, C USA
27 S12 **Blue Mountain** ▲ Arkansas, C USA
19 O6 **Blue Mountain** ▲ New Hampshire, NE USA
18 K8 **Blue Mountain** ▲ New York, NE USA
18 H15 **Blue Mountain** ridge Pennsylvania, NE USA
44 H10 **Blue Mountain Peak** ▲ E Jamaica
183 S8 **Blue Mountains** ▲▲ New South Wales, SE Australia
32 L11 **Blue Mountains** ▲▲ Oregon/Washington, NW USA
80 G12 **Blue Nile** ◈ state E Sudan
80 H12 **Blue Nile** var. Abai, Bahr el Azraq, Amh. Ābay Wenz, Ar. An Nil al Azraq. ≈ Ethiopia/Sudan
8 J7 **Bluenose Lake** ⊚ Nunavut, NW Canada
27 O3 **Blue Rapids** Kansas, C USA
23 S1 **Blue Ridge** Georgia, SE USA
17 S11 **Blue Ridge** var. Blue Ridge Mountains. ▲▲ North Carolina/Virginia, E USA
23 S1 **Blue Ridge Lake** ▣ Georgia, SE USA
Blue Ridge Mountains see Blue Ridge
11 N15 **Blue River** British Columbia, SW Canada
27 O12 **Blue River** ≈ Oklahoma, C USA
27 R4 **Blue Springs** Missouri, C USA
21 R6 **Bluestone Lake** ▣ West Virginia, NE USA
185 C25 **Bluff** Southland, South Island, NZ
37 O8 **Bluff** Utah, W USA
21 P8 **Bluff City** Tennessee, S USA
65 E24 **Bluff Cove** East Falkland, Falkland Islands
25 S7 **Bluff Dale** Texas, SW USA
183 N15 **Bluff Hill Point** headland Tasmania, SE Australia
31 Q12 **Bluffton** Indiana, N USA
31 R12 **Bluffton** Ohio, N USA
25 T7 **Blum** Texas, SW USA
101 G24 **Blumberg** Baden-Württemberg, SW Germany
60 K13 **Blumenau** Santa Catarina, S Brazil
29 N9 **Blunt** South Dakota, N USA
32 H15 **Bly** Oregon, NW USA
39 R13 **Blying Sound** sound Alaska, USA
97 M14 **Blyth** N England, UK
35 Y16 **Blythe** California, W USA
27 Y9 **Blytheville** Arkansas, C USA

◆ Country
● Country Capital
◇ Dependent Territory
○ Dependent Territory Capital
◈ Administrative Region
✕ International Airport
▲ Mountain
▲▲ Mountain Range
Volcano
≈ River
⊚ Lake
▣ Reservoir

117 V7 **Blyznyuky** Kharkivs'ka Oblast', E Ukraine
76 I15 **Bo** S Sierra Leone
95 G16 **Bø** Telemark, S Norway
171 O4 **Boac** Marinduque, N Philippines
42 K10 **Boaco** Boaco, S Nicaragua
42 J10 **Boaco** ◈ *department* C Nicaragua
79 I15 **Boali** Ombella-Mpoko, SW Central African Republic
Boalsert *see* Bolsward
31 V12 **Boardman** Ohio, N USA
32 J11 **Boardman** Oregon, NW USA
14 F13 **Boat Lake** ◎ Ontario, S Canada
58 F10 **Boa Vista** *state capital* Roraima, NW Brazil
76 D9 **Boa Vista** *island* Ilhas de Barlavento, E Cape Verde
23 Q2 **Boaz** Alabama, S USA
160 L15 **Bobai** Guangxi Zhuangzu Zizhiqu, S China
172 J1 **Bobaomby, Tanjona** *Fr.* Cap d'Ambre. *headland* N Madagascar
155 M14 **Bobbili** Andhra Pradesh, E India
106 D9 **Bobbio** Emilia-Romagna, C Italy
14 I14 **Bobcaygeon** Ontario, SE Canada
Bober *see* Bóbr
103 O5 **Bobigny** Seine-St-Denis, N France
77 N13 **Bobo-Dioulasso** SW Burkina
110 G8 **Bobolice** *Ger.* Bublitz. Zachodnio-pomorskie, NW Poland
83 J19 **Bobonong** Central, E Botswana
171 R11 **Bobopayo** Pulau Halmahera, E Indonesia
147 P13 **Bobotogh, Qatorkŭhi** *Rus.* Khrebet Babatag. ▲▲ Tajikistan/Uzbekistan
114 G10 **Bobovdol** Kyustendil, W Bulgaria
119 M15 **Bobr** Minskaya Voblasts', NW Belarus
119 M15 **Bobr** ≈ C Belarus
111 E14 **Bóbr** *Eng.* Bobrawa, *Ger.* Bober. ≈ SW Poland
Bobrawa *see* Bóbr
Bobrik *see* Bobryk
Bobrinets *see* Bobrynets'
Bobrka/Bóbrka *see* Bibrka
126 L8 **Bobrov** Voronezhskaya Oblast', W Russian Federation
117 Q4 **Bobrovytsya** Chernihivs'ka Oblast', N Ukraine
Bobruysk *see* Babruysk
119 J19 **Bobryk** *Rus.* Bobrik. ≈ SW Belarus
117 Q8 **Bobrynets'** *Rus.* Bobrinets. Kirovohrads'ka Oblast', C Ukraine
14 K14 **Bobs Lake** ◎ Ontario, SE Canada
54 I6 **Bobures** Zulia, NW Venezuela
42 H1 **Boca Bacalar Chico** *headland* N Belize
112 G11 **Bočac** Republika Srpska, NW Bosnia and Herzegovina
41 R14 **Boca del Río** Veracruz-Llave, S Mexico
55 O4 **Boca de Pozo** Nueva Esparta, NE Venezuela
59 C15 **Boca do Acre** Amazonas, N Brazil
55 N12 **Boca Mavaca** Amazonas, S Venezuela
79 G14 **Bocaranga** Ouham-Pendé, W Central African Republic
23 Z15 **Boca Raton** Florida, SE USA
43 P14 **Bocas del Toro** Bocas del Toro, NW Panama
43 P15 **Bocas del Toro** *off.* Provincia de Bocas del Toro. ◈ *province* NW Panama
43 P15 **Bocas del Toro, Archipiélago de** *island group* NW Panama
42 L7 **Bocay** Jinotega, N Nicaragua
105 N6 **Boceguillas** Castilla-León, N Spain
Bocheykovo *see* Bacheykava
111 L17 **Bochnia** Małopolskie, SE Poland
99 K16 **Bocholt** Limburg, NE Belgium
101 D14 **Bocholt** Nordrhein-Westfalen, W Germany
101 E15 **Bochum** Nordrhein-Westfalen, W Germany
103 Y15 **Bocognano** Corse, France, C Mediterranean Sea
54 I6 **Boconó** Trujillo, NW Venezuela
116 F12 **Bocşa** *Ger.* Bokschen, *Hung.* Boksánbánya. Caraş-Severin, SW Romania
79 H15 **Boda** Lobaye, SW Central African Republic
94 L12 **Boda** Dalarna, C Sweden
95 O20 **Böda** Kalmar, S Sweden
95 L19 **Bodafors** Jönköping, S Sweden
123 O12 **Bodaybo** Irkutskaya Oblast', E Russian Federation
22 G5 **Bodcau, Bayou** *var.* Bodcau Creek. ≈ Louisiana, S USA
Bodcau Creek *see* Bodcau, Bayou
44 D8 **Bodden Town** *var.* Boddentown. Grand Cayman, SW Cayman Islands
101 K14 **Bode** ≈ C Germany
34 L7 **Bodega Head** *headland* California, W USA
Bodegas *see* Babahoyo
98 H11 **Bodegraven** Zuid-Holland, C Netherlands
78 H8 **Bodélé** *depression* W Chad
92 J13 **Boden** Norrbotten, N Sweden
Bodensee *see* Constance, Lake, C Europe
65 M15 **Bode Verde Fracture Zone** *tectonic feature* E Atlantic Ocean
155 H14 **Bodhan** Andhra Pradesh, C India
162 I9 **Bodĭ** Bayanhongor, C Mongolia
155 H22 **Bodināyakkanūr** Tamil Nādu, SE India
108 H10 **Bodio** Ticino, S Switzerland
97 I24 **Bodmin** SW England, UK
97 I24 **Bodmin Moor** *moorland* SW England, UK
92 G12 **Bodø** Nordland, C Norway
59 H20 **Bodoquena, Serra da** ▲▲ SW Brazil
136 B16 **Bodrum** Muğla, SW Turkey
Bodzafordulő *see* Întorsura Buzăului
99 L14 **Boekel** Noord-Brabant, SE Netherlands
Boeloekoemba *see* Bulukumba
103 Q11 **Boën** Loire, E France
79 K18 **Boende** Equateur, C Dem. Rep. Congo
25 R11 **Boerne** Texas, SW USA
Boeroe *see* Buru, Pulau
Boetoeng *see* Buton, Pulau
22 I5 **Boeuf River** ≈ Arkansas/Louisiana, S USA
76 H14 **Boffa** Guinée-Maritime, W Guinea
Bó Finne, Inis *see* Inishbofin
Boga *see* Bogë
166 L9 **Bogale** Irrawaddy, SW Myanmar
22 L8 **Bogalusa** Louisiana, S USA
77 Q12 **Bogandé** C Burkina
79 I15 **Bogangolo** Ombella-Mpoko, C Central African Republic
183 Q7 **Bogan River** ≈ New South Wales, SE Australia
25 W5 **Bogata** Texas, SW USA
111 D14 **Bogatynia** *Ger.* Reichenau. Dolnośląskie, SW Poland
136 K13 **Boğazlıyan** Yozgat, C Turkey
79 J17 **Bogbonga** Equateur, NW Dem. Rep. Congo
158 J14 **Bogcang Zangbo** ≈ W China
158 L5 **Bogda Feng** ▲ NW China
114 I9 **Bogdan** ▲ C Bulgaria
113 Q20 **Bogdanci** SE FYR Macedonia
158 M5 **Bogda Shan** *var.* Po-ko-to Shan. ▲▲ NW China
113 K17 **Bogë** *var.* Boga. Shkodër, N Albania
Bogendorf *see* Łuków
95 G23 **Bogense** Fyn, C Denmark
183 T3 **Boggabilla** New South Wales, SE Australia
183 S6 **Boggabri** New South Wales, SE Australia
186 D6 **Bogia** Madang, N PNG
97 N23 **Bognor Regis** SE England, UK
Bogodukhov *see* Bohodukhiv
181 V15 **Bogong, Mount** ▲ Victoria, SE Australia
169 O16 **Bogor** *Dut.* Buitenzorg. Jawa, C Indonesia
126 L5 **Bogoroditsk** Tul'skaya Oblast', W Russian Federation
127 O3 **Bogorodsk** Nizhegorodskaya Oblast', W Russian Federation
Bogorodskoje *see* Bogorodskoye
123 S12 **Bogorodskoye** Khabarovskiy Kray, SE Russian Federation
125 R15 **Bogorodskoye** *var.* Bogorodskoje. Kirovskaya Oblast', NW Russian Federation
54 F10 **Bogotá** *prev.* Santa Fe, Santa Fe de Bogotá. ● (Colombia) Cundinamarca, C Colombia
153 T14 **Bogra** Rajshahi, N Bangladesh
Bogschan *see* Boldu
122 L12 **Boguchany** Krasnoyarskiy Kray, C Russian Federation
126 M9 **Boguchar** Voronezhskaya Oblast', W Russian Federation
76 H10 **Bogué** Brakna, SW Mauritania
22 K8 **Bogue Chitto** ≈ Louisiana/Mississippi, S USA
Bogushëvsk *see* Bahushewsk
Boguslav *see* Bohuslav
44 K12 **Bog Walk** C Jamaica
161 Q3 **Bo Hai** *var.* Gulf of Chihli. *gulf* NE China
161 R3 **Bohai Haixia** *strait* NE China
161 Q3 **Bohai Wan** *bay* NE China
111 C17 **Bohemia** *Cz.* Čechy, *Ger.* Böhmen. *cultural and historical region* W Czech Republic
111 B18 **Bohemian Forest** *Cz.* Ceský Les, Šumava, *Ger.* Böhmerwald. ▲▲ C Europe
Bohemian-Moravian Highlands *see* Českomoravská Vrchovina
77 R16 **Bohicon** S Benin
109 S11 **Bohinjska Bistrica** *Ger.* Wocheiner Feistritz. NW Slovenia
Bohkká *see* Pokka
Böhmen *see* Bohemia
Böhmerwald *see* Bohemian Forest
Böhmisch-Krumau *see* Český Krumlov
Böhmisch-Leipa *see* Česká Lípa
Böhmisch-Mährische Höhe *see* Českomoravská Vrchovina
Böhmisch-Trübau *see* Česká Třebová
117 U5 **Bohodukhiv** *Rus.* Bogodukhov. Kharkivs'ka Oblast', E Ukraine
171 Q6 **Bohol** *island* C Philippines
171 Q7 **Bohol Sea** *var.* Mindanao Sea. *sea* S Philippines
116 I7 **Bohorodchany** Ivano-Frankivs'ka Oblast', W Ukraine
162 M9 **Böhöt** Dundgovĭ, C Mongolia
158 K6 **Bohu** *var.* Bagrax. Xinjiang Uygur Zizhiqu, NW China
111 I17 **Bohumín** *Ger.* Oderberg; *prev.* Neuoderberg, Nový Bohumín. Moravskoslezský Kraj, E Czech Republic
117 P6 **Bohuslav** *Rus.* Boguslav. Kyyivs'ka Oblast', N Ukraine
58 F11 **Boiaçu** Roraima, N Brazil
107 K16 **Boiano** Molise, C Italy
15 R8 **Boilleau** Québec, SE Canada
59 O17 **Boipeba, Ilha de** *island* SE Brazil
104 G3 **Boiro** Galicia, NW Spain
31 Q5 **Bois Blanc Island** *island* Michigan, N USA
29 R7 **Bois de Sioux River** ≈ Minnesota, N USA
33 N14 **Boise** *var.* Boise City. *state capital* Idaho, NW USA
26 G8 **Boise City** Oklahoma, C USA
33 N14 **Boise River, Middle Fork** ≈ Idaho, NW USA
Bois, Lac des *see* Woods, Lake of the
Bois-le-Duc *see* 's-Hertogenbosch
11 W17 **Boissevain** Manitoba, S Canada
15 T7 **Boisvert, Pointe au** *headland* Québec, SE Canada
100 K10 **Boizenburg** Mecklenburg-Vorpommern, N Germany
Bojador *see* Boujdour
113 K18 **Bojana** *Alb.* Bunë. ≈ Albania/Serbia and Montenegro (Yugo.) *see also* Bunë
143 S3 **Bojnūrd** *var.* Bujnurd. Khorāsān, N Iran
169 R16 **Bojonegoro** *prev.* Bodjonegoro. Jawa, C Indonesia
189 T1 **Bokaak Atoll** *var.* Bokak, Taongi. *atoll* Ratak Chain, NE Marshall Islands
Bokak *see* Bokaak Atoll
146 K8 **Bo'kantov-Tog'lari** *Rus.* Gory Bukantau. ▲ N Uzbekistan
153 Q15 **Bokāro** Jhārkhand, N India
79 I18 **Bokatola** Equateur, NW Dem. Rep. Congo
76 H13 **Boké** Guinée-Maritime, W Guinea
Bokhara *see* Buxoro
183 Q4 **Bokhara River** ≈ New South Wales/Queensland, SE Australia
95 C16 **Boknafjorden** *fjord* S Norway
78 H11 **Bokoro** Chari-Baguirmi, W Chad
79 K19 **Bokota** Equateur, NW Dem. Rep. Congo
167 N13 **Bokpyin** Tenasserim, S Myanmar
Boksánbánya/Bokschen *see* Bocşa
83 F21 **Bokspits** Kgalagadi, SW Botswana
79 K18 **Bokungu** Equateur, C Dem. Rep. Congo
146 F12 **Bokurdak** *Rus.* Bakhardok. Ahal Welaýaty, C Turkmenistan
78 G10 **Bol** Lac, W Chad
76 G13 **Bolama** SW Guinea-Bissau
Bolangir *see* Balāngīr
Bolanos *see* Bolaños, Mount, Guam
Bolaños *see* Bolaños de Calatrava, Spain
105 N11 **Bolaños de Calatrava** *var.* Bolaños. Castilla-La Mancha, C Spain
188 B17 **Bolanos, Mount** *var.* Bolaños. ▲ S Guam
40 L12 **Bolaños, Río** ≈ C Mexico
114 M12 **Bolayır** Çanakkale, NW Turkey
102 L3 **Bolbec** Seine-Maritime, N France
116 L13 **Boldu** *var.* Bogschan. Buzău, SE Romania
146 H8 **Boldumsaz** *prev.* Kalinin, Kalininsk, Porsy. Daşoguz Welaýaty, N Turkmenistan
158 I4 **Bole** *var.* Bortala. Xinjiang Uygur Zizhiqu, NW China
77 O15 **Bole** NW Ghana
79 J19 **Boleko** Equateur, W Dem. Rep. Congo
111 E14 **Bolesławiec** *Ger.* Bunzlau. Dolnośląskie, SW Poland
127 R4 **Bolgar** *prev.* Kuybyshev. Respublika Tatarstan, W Russian Federation
77 P14 **Bolgatanga** N Ghana
Bolgrad *see* Bolhrad
117 N12 **Bolhrad** *Rus.* Bolgrad. Odes'ka Oblast', SW Ukraine
163 Y8 **Boli** Heilongjiang, NE China
79 I19 **Bolia** Bandundu, W Dem. Rep. Congo
93 J14 **Boliden** Västerbotten, N Sweden
171 T13 **Bolifar** Pulau Seram, E Indonesia
171 N2 **Bolinao** Luzon, N Philippines
27 T6 **Bolivar** Missouri, C USA
20 F10 **Bolivar** Tennessee, S USA
54 C12 **Bolívar** Cauca, SW Colombia
54 F7 **Bolívar** *off.* Departmento de Bolívar. ◈ *province* N Colombia
56 A13 **Bolívar** ◈ *province* C Ecuador
55 N9 **Bolívar** *off.* Estado Bolívar. ◈ *state* SE Venezuela
25 X12 **Bolivar Peninsula** *headland* Texas, SW USA
54 I6 **Bolívar, Pico** ▲ W Venezuela
57 K17 **Bolivia** *off.* Republic of Bolivia. ◆ *republic* W South America
112 O13 **Boljevac** Serbia, E Serbia and Montenegro (Yugo.)
Bolkenhain *see* Bolków
126 J5 **Bolkhov** Orlovskaya Oblast', W Russian Federation
111 F14 **Bolków** *Ger.* Bolkenhain. Dolnośląskie, SW Poland
182 K3 **Bollards Lagoon** South Australia
103 R14 **Bollène** Vaucluse, SE France
94 N12 **Bollnäs** Gävleborg, C Sweden
181 W10 **Bollon** Queensland, C Australia
192 L12 **Bollons Tablemount** *undersea feature* S Pacific Ocean
93 H17 **Bollstabruk** Västernorrland, C Sweden
Bolluilos de Par del Condado *see* Bollullos Par del Condado
104 J14 **Bollullos Par del Condado** *var.* Bolluilos de Par del Condado. Andalucía, S Spain
95 K21 **Bolmen** ◎ S Sweden
137 T10 **Bolnisi** S Georgia
79 H19 **Bolobo** Bandundu, W Dem. Rep. Congo
106 G10 **Bologna** Emilia-Romagna, N Italy
124 I15 **Bologoye** Tverskaya Oblast', W Russian Federation
79 J18 **Bolomba** Equateur, NW Dem. Rep. Congo
41 X13 **Bolónchén de Rejón** *var.* Bolonchén de Rejón. Campeche, SE Mexico
114 J13 **Boloústra, Akrotírio** *headland* NE Greece
167 L8 **Bolovens, Plateau des** *plateau* S Laos
106 H13 **Bolsena** Lazio, C Italy
107 G14 **Bolsena, Lago di** ◎ C Italy
126 B3 **Bol'shakovo** *Ger.* Kreuzingen; *prev.* Gross-Skaisgirren. Kaliningradskaya Oblast', W Russian Federation
Bol'shaya Berëstovitsa *see* Vyalikaya Byerastavitsa
127 S7 **Bol'shaya Chernigovka** Samarskaya Oblast', W Russian Federation
127 S7 **Bol'shaya Glushitsa** Samarskaya Oblast', W Russian Federation
144 H9 **Bol'shaya Khobda** *Kaz.* Ülkenqobda. ≈ Kazakhstan/Russian Federation
126 M12 **Bol'shaya Martynovka** Rostovskaya Oblast', SW Russian Federation
122 K12 **Bol'shaya Murta** Krasnoyarskiy Kray, C Russian Federation
127 V4 **Bol'shaya Rogovaya** ≈ NW Russian Federation
127 U7 **Bol'shaya Synya** ≈ NW Russian Federation
145 V9 **Bol'shaya Vladimirovka** Vostochnyy Kazakhstan, E Kazakhstan
123 V11 **Bol'sheretsk** Kamchatskaya Oblast', E Russian Federation
127 W3 **Bol'sheust'ikinskoye** Respublika Bashkortostan, W Russian Federation
Bol'shevik *see* Bal'shavik
122 L5 **Bol'shevik, Ostrov** *island* Severnaya Zemlya, N Russian Federation
127 U4 **Bol'shezemel'skaya Tundra** *physical region* NW Russian Federation
144 J13 **Bol'shiye Barsuki, Peski** *desert* SW Kazakhstan
123 T7 **Bol'shoy Anyuy** ≈ NE Russian Federation
123 N7 **Bol'shoy Begichev, Ostrov** *island* NE Russian Federation
123 S15 **Bol'shoy Kamen'** Primorskiy Kray, SE Russian Federation
127 O4 **Bol'shoye Murashkino** Nizhegorodskaya Oblast', W Russian Federation
127 W4 **Bol'shoy Iremel'** ▲ W Russian Federation
127 R7 **Bol'shoy Irgiz** ≈ W Russian Federation
123 Q6 **Bol'shoy Lyakhovskiy, Ostrov** *island* NE Russian Federation
123 Q11 **Bol'shoy Nimnyr** Respublika Sakha (Yakutiya), NE Russian Federation
Bol'shoy Rozhan *see* Vyaliki Rozhan
144 E10 **Bol'shoy Uzen'** *Kaz.* Ülkenözen. ≈ Kazakhstan/Russian Federation
40 K6 **Bolson de Mapimi** ▲▲ NW Mexico
98 K6 **Bolsward** *Fris.* Boalsert. Friesland, N Netherlands
105 T4 **Boltaña** Aragón, NE Spain
14 G15 **Bolton** Ontario, S Canada
97 K17 **Bolton** *prev.* Bolton-le-Moors. NW England, UK
21 V12 **Bolton** North Carolina, SE USA
Bolton-le-Moors *see* Bolton
136 G11 **Bolu** Bolu, NW Turkey
136 G11 **Bolu** ◈ *province* NW Turkey
186 G9 **Bolubolu** Goodenough Island, S PNG
92 H1 **Bolungarvík** Vestfirdhir, NW Iceland
159 O10 **Boluntay** Qinghai, W China
159 P8 **Boluozhuanjing** *var.* Aksay, Aksay Kazakzu Zizhixian. Gansu, N China
136 F14 **Bolvadin** Afyon, W Turkey
114 M10 **Bolyarovo** *prev.* Pashkeni. Yambol, E Bulgaria
106 G6 **Bolzano** *Ger.* Bozen; *anc.* Bauzanum. Trentino-Alto Adige, N Italy
79 F22 **Boma** Bas-Congo, W Dem. Rep. Congo
183 R12 **Bombala** New South Wales, SE Australia
104 F10 **Bombarral** Leiria, C Portugal
Bombay *see* Mumbai
171 U13 **Bomberai, Semenanjung** *headland* Papua, E Indonesia
81 F18 **Bombo** S Uganda
79 I17 **Bomboma** Equateur, NW Dem. Rep. Congo
59 I14 **Bom Futuro** Pará, N Brazil
159 Q15 **Bomi** *var.* Bowo, Zhamo. Xizang Zizhiqu, W China
79 N17 **Bomili** Orientale, NE Dem. Rep. Congo
59 N17 **Bom Jesus da Lapa** Bahia, E Brazil
60 Q8 **Bom Jesus do Itabapoana** Rio de Janeiro, SE Brazil
95 C15 **Bømlafjorden** *fjord* S Norway
95 B15 **Bømlo** *island* S Norway
123 Q12 **Bomnak** Amurskaya Oblast', SE Russian Federation
79 I17 **Bomongo** Equateur, NW Dem. Rep. Congo
61 K14 **Bom Retiro** Santa Catarina, S Brazil
79 L15 **Bomu** *var.* Mbomou, Mbomu, M'Bomu. ≈ Central African Republic/Dem. Rep. Congo
142 J3 **Bonāb** *var.* Benāb, Bunab. Āzarbāyjān-e Khāvarī, N Iran
45 Q16 **Bonaire** *island* E Netherlands Antilles
39 U11 **Bona, Mount** ▲ Alaska, USA
183 Q12 **Bonang** Victoria, SE Australia
42 L7 **Bonanza** Región Autónoma Atlántico Norte, NE Nicaragua
37 O4 **Bonanza** Utah, W USA
45 O9 **Bonao** C Dominican Republic
180 L3 **Bonaparte Archipelago** *island group* Western Australia
32 K6 **Bonaparte, Mount** ▲ Washington, NW USA
39 N11 **Bonasila Dome** ▲ Alaska, USA
92 H11 **Bonåsjøen** Nordland, C Norway
45 T15 **Bonasse** Trinidad, Trinidad and Tobago
15 X7 **Bonaventure** Québec, SE Canada
15 X7 **Bonaventure** ≈ Québec, SE Canada
13 V11 **Bonavista** Newfoundland and Labrador, SE Canada
13 U11 **Bonavista Bay** *inlet* NW Atlantic Ocean
79 E19 **Bonda** Ogooué-Lolo, C Gabon
127 N6 **Bondari** Tambovskaya Oblast', W Russian Federation
106 G9 **Bondeno** Emilia-Romagna, C Italy
30 L4 **Bond Falls Flowage** ▣ Michigan, N USA
79 L16 **Bondo** Orientale, N Dem. Rep. Congo
171 N17 **Bondokodi** Pulau Sumba, S Indonesia
77 O15 **Bondoukou** E Ivory Coast
Bondoukui/Bondoukuy *see* Boundoukui
169 T17 **Bondowoso** Jawa, C Indonesia
33 S14 **Bondurant** Wyoming, C USA
Bone *see* Watampone, Indonesia
Bône *see* Annaba, Algeria
30 I5 **Bone Lake** ◎ Wisconsin, N USA
171 P14 **Bonelipu** Pulau Buton, C Indonesia
171 O15 **Bonerate, Kepulauan** *var.* Macan. *island group* C Indonesia
29 O12 **Bonesteel** South Dakota, N USA
62 I8 **Bonete, Cerro** ▲ N Argentina
171 O14 **Bone, Teluk** *bay* Sulawesi, C Indonesia
108 D6 **Bonfol** Jura, NW Switzerland
153 U12 **Bongaigaon** Assam, NE India
79 K17 **Bongandanga** Equateur, NW Dem. Rep. Congo
78 L13 **Bongo, Massif des** *var.* Chaîne des Mongos. ▲▲ NE Central African Republic
78 G12 **Bongor** Mayo-Kébbi, SW Chad
77 N16 **Bongouanou** E Ivory Coast
167 V11 **Bông Sơn** *var.* Hoai Nhơn. Binh Đinh, C Vietnam
25 U5 **Bonham** Texas, SW USA
Bonhard *see* Bonyhád
103 U6 **Bonhomme, Col du** *pass* NE France
103 Y16 **Bonifacio** Corse, France, C Mediterranean Sea
Bonifacio, Bocche de/Bonifacio, Bouches de *see* Bonifacio, Strait of
103 Y16 **Bonifacio, Strait of** *Fr.* Bouches de Bonifacio, *It.* Bocche de Bonifacio. *strait* C Mediterranean Sea
23 Q8 **Bonifay** Florida, SE USA
Bonin Islands *see* Ogasawara-shotō
192 H5 **Bonin Trench** *undersea feature* NW Pacific Ocean
23 W15 **Bonita Springs** Florida, SE USA
42 I5 **Bonito, Pico** ▲ N Honduras
101 E17 **Bonn** Nordrhein-Westfalen, W Germany
14 J12 **Bonnechere** Ontario, SE Canada
14 J12 **Bonnechere** ≈ Ontario, SE Canada
33 N7 **Bonners Ferry** Idaho, NW USA
27 R4 **Bonner Springs** Kansas, C USA
102 L6 **Bonnétable** Sarthe, NW France
27 X6 **Bonne Terre** Missouri, C USA
10 J5 **Bonnet Plume** ≈ Yukon Territory, NW Canada
102 M6 **Bonneval** Eure-et-Loir, C France
103 T10 **Bonneville** Haute-Savoie, E France
36 J3 **Bonneville Salt Flats** *salt flat* Utah, W USA
77 U18 **Bonny** Rivers, S Nigeria
Bonny, Bight of *see* Biafra, Bight of
37 W4 **Bonny Reservoir** ▣ Colorado, C USA
11 R14 **Bonnyville** Alberta, SW Canada
107 C18 **Bono** Sardegna, Italy, C Mediterranean Sea
Bononia *see* Vidin, Bulgaria
Bononia *see* Boulogne-sur-Mer, France
107 B18 **Bonorva** Sardegna, Italy, C Mediterranean Sea
30 M15 **Bonpas Creek** ≈ Illinois, N USA
190 I3 **Bonriki** Tarawa, W Kiribati
183 T4 **Bonshaw** New South Wales, SE Australia
76 I16 **Bonthe** SW Sierra Leone
171 N2 **Bontoc** Luzon, N Philippines
25 Y9 **Bon Wier** Texas, SW USA
111 J25 **Bonyhád** *Ger.* Bonhard. Tolna, S Hungary
Bonzabaai *see* Bonza Bay
83 J25 **Bonza Bay** *Afr.* Bonzabaai. Eastern Cape, S South Africa
182 D7 **Bookabie** South Australia
182 H6 **Bookaloo** South Australia
37 P5 **Book Cliffs** *cliff* Colorado/Utah, W USA
25 P1 **Booker** Texas, SW USA
76 K15 **Boola** Guinée-Forestière, SE Guinea
183 O8 **Booligal** New South Wales, SE Australia
99 G17 **Boom** Antwerpen, N Belgium
43 N6 **Boom** *var.* Boon. Región Autónoma Atlántico Norte, NE Nicaragua
183 S3 **Boomi** New South Wales, SE Australia
Boon *see* Boom
29 V13 **Boone** Iowa, C USA
21 Q8 **Boone** North Carolina, SE USA
27 S11 **Booneville** Arkansas, C USA
21 N6 **Booneville** Kentucky, S USA
23 N2 **Booneville** Mississippi, S USA
21 V3 **Boonsboro** Maryland, NE USA
162 H9 **Böön Tsagaan Nuur** ◎ S Mongolia
34 L6 **Boonville** California, W USA
31 N16 **Boonville** Indiana, N USA
27 U4 **Boonville** Missouri, C USA
18 I9 **Boonville** New York, NE USA
80 M12 **Boorama** Woqooyi Galbeed, NW Somalia
183 O6 **Booroondarra, Mount** *hill* New South Wales, SE Australia
183 N9 **Booroorban** New South Wales, SE Australia
183 R9 **Boorowa** New South Wales, SE Australia
99 H17 **Boortmeerbeek** Vlaams Brabant, C Belgium
80 P11 **Boosaaso** *var.* Bandar Kassim, Bender Qaasim, Bosaso, *It.* Bender Cassim. Bari, N Somalia
19 Q8 **Boothbay Harbor** Maine, NE USA
Boothia Felix *see* Boothia Peninsula
9 N6 **Boothia, Gulf of** *gulf* Nunavut, NE Canada
8 M6 **Boothia Peninsula** *prev.* Boothia Felix. *peninsula* Nunavut, NE Canada
79 E18 **Booué** Ogooué-Ivindo, NE Gabon
101 J21 **Bopfingen** Baden-Württemberg, S Germany
101 F18 **Boppard** Rheinland-Pfalz, W Germany
62 M4 **Boquerón** *off.* Departamento de Boquerón. ◈ *department* W Paraguay
43 P15 **Boquete** *var.* Bajo Boquete. Chiriquí, W Panama
40 J6 **Boquilla, Presa de la** ▣ N Mexico
40 L5 **Boquillas** *var.* Boquillas del Carmen. Coahuila de Zaragoza, NE Mexico
Boquillas del Carmen *see* Boquillas
81 F15 **Bor** Jonglei, S Sudan
95 L20 **Bor** Jönköping, S Sweden
136 J15 **Bor** Niğde, S Turkey
112 P12 **Bor** Serbia, E Serbia and Montenegro (Yugo.)
191 S10 **Bora-Bora** *island* Îles Sous le Vent, W French Polynesia
167 Q9 **Borabu** Maha Sarakham, E Thailand
33 P13 **Borah Peak** ▲ Idaho, NW USA
145 G13 **Boralday** *prev.* Burunday. Almaty SE Kazakhstan
144 G13 **Borankul** *prev.* Opornyy. Mangistau, SW Kazakhstan
95 J19 **Borås** Västra Götaland, S Sweden
145 U15 **Boralday** *prev.* Burunday. Almaty, SE Kazakhstan
143 N11 **Borāzjān** *var.* Borazjān. Būshehr, S Iran
Borazjān *see* Borāzjān
58 G13 **Borba** Amazonas, N Brazil
104 H11 **Borba** Évora, S Portugal
Borbetomagus *see* Worms
55 O7 **Borbón** Bolívar, E Venezuela
59 Q15 **Borborema, Planalto da** *plateau* NE Brazil
116 M14 **Borcea, Braţul** ≈ S Romania
Borchalo *see* Marneuli
195 R15 **Borchgrevink Coast** *physical region* Antarctica
137 Q11 **Borçka** Artvin, NE Turkey
98 N11 **Borculo** Gelderland, E Netherlands
182 G10 **Borda, Cape** *headland* South Australia
102 K13 **Bordeaux** *anc.* Burdigala. Gironde, SW France
11 T15 **Borden** Saskatchewan, S Canada
14 D8 **Borden Lake** ◎ Ontario, S Canada
9 N4 **Borden Peninsula** *peninsula* Baffin Island, Nunavut, NE Canada
182 K11 **Bordertown** South Australia
92 H2 **Bordheyri** Vestfirdhir, NW Iceland
95 B18 **Bordhoy** *Dan.* Bordø *Island* Faeroe Islands
106 B11 **Bordighera** Liguria, NW Italy
74 K5 **Bordj-Bou-Arreridj** *var.* Bordj Bou Arreridj, Bordj Bou Arréridj. N Algeria
74 L10 **Bordj Omar Driss** E Algeria
143 N13 **Bord Khūn** Hormozgān, S Iran
147 V7 **Bordunskiy** Chuyskaya Oblast', N Kyrgyzstan
95 M17 **Borensberg** Östergötland, S Sweden
Borgå *see* Porvoo
92 L2 **Borgarfjördhur** Austurland, NE Iceland
92 H3 **Borgarnes** Vesturland, W Iceland
93 G14 **Børgefjell** ▲▲ C Norway
98 O7 **Borger** Drenthe, NE Netherlands
25 N2 **Borger** Texas, SW USA
95 N20 **Borgholm** Kalmar, S Sweden
107 N22 **Borgia** Calabria, SW Italy

◆ Country ● Country Capital ◇ Dependent Territory ○ Dependent Territory Capital ◈ Administrative Region ✈ International Airport ▲ Mountain ▲▲ Mountain Range ⚶ Volcano ≈ River ◎ Lake ▣ Reservoir

99 J18 Borgloon Limburg, NE Belgium
195 P2 Borg Massif ▲ Antarctica
22 L9 Borgne, Lake ◎ Louisiana, S USA
106 C7 Borgomanero Piemonte, NE Italy
106 G10 Borgo Panigale ✕ (Bologna) Emilia-Romagna, N Italy
107 J15 Borgorose Lazio, C Italy
106 A9 Borgo San Dalmazzo Piemonte, N Italy
106 G11 Borgo San Lorenzo Toscana, C Italy
106 C7 Borgosesia Piemonte, NE Italy
106 E9 Borgo Val di Taro Emilia-Romagna, C Italy
106 G6 Borgo Valsugana Trentino-Alto Adige, N Italy
163 O11 Borhoyn Tal Dornogovĭ, SE Mongolia
167 R8 Borikhan var. Borikhane. Bolikhamxai, C Laos
Borikhane see Borikhan
Borislav see Boryslav
127 N8 Borisoglebsk Voronezhskaya Oblast', W Russian Federation
Borisov see Barysaw
Borisovgrad see Pŭrvomay
Borispol' see Boryspil'
172 I3 Boriziny Mahajanga, NW Madagascar
105 Q5 Borja Aragón, NE Spain
Borjas Blancas see Les Borges Blanques
137 S10 Borjomi Rus. Borzhomi. C Georgia
118 L12 Borkavichy Rus. Borkovichi. Vitsyebskaya Voblasts', N Belarus
101 H16 Borken Hessen, C Germany
101 E14 Borken Nordrhein-Westfalen, W Germany
92 H10 Borkenes Troms, N Norway
78 H7 Borkou-Ennedi-Tibesti off. Préfecture du Borkou-Ennedi-Tibesti. ◐ prefecture N Chad
Borkovichi see Borkavichy
100 E9 Borkum island NW Germany
81 K17 Bor, Lagh var. Lak Bor. dry watercourse NE Kenya
Bor, Lak see Bor, Lagh
95 M14 Borlänge Dalarna, C Sweden
106 C9 Bormida ∼ NW Italy
106 F6 Bormio Lombardia, N Italy
101 M16 Borna Sachsen, E Germany
98 O10 Borne Overijssel, E Netherlands
99 F17 Bornem Antwerpen, N Belgium
169 S10 Borneo island Brunei/Indonesia/Malaysia
101 E16 Bornheim Nordrhein-Westfalen, W Germany
95 L24 Bornholm ◐ county E Denmark
95 L24 Bornholm island E Denmark
77 Y13 Borno ◐ state NE Nigeria
104 K15 Bornos Andalucía, S Spain
162 L7 Bornuur Töv, C Mongolia
117 O4 Borodyanka Kyyivs'ka Oblast', N Ukraine
158 I5 Borohoro Shan ▲▲ NW China
77 O13 Boromo SW Burkina
35 T13 Boron California, W USA
Borongo see Black Volta
Boron'ki see Baron'ki
Borosjenő see Ineu
Borossebes see Sebiș
76 L15 Borotou NW Ivory Coast
117 W6 Borova Kharkivs'ka Oblast', E Ukraine
114 H8 Borovan Vratsa, NW Bulgaria
124 I14 Borovichi Novgorodskaya Oblast', W Russian Federation
Borovlje see Ferlach
112 J9 Borovo Vukovar-Srijem, NE Croatia
145 Q7 Borovoye Kaz. Būrabay. Akmola, N Kazakhstan
126 K4 Borovsk Kaluzhskaya Oblast', W Russian Federation
145 N7 Borovskoy Kostanay, N Kazakhstan
Borovukha see Baravukha
95 L23 Borrby Skåne, S Sweden
181 R3 Borroloola Northern Territory, N Australia
116 F9 Borș Bihor, NW Romania
116 I9 Borșa Hung. Borsa. Maramureș, N Romania
116 J10 Borsec Ger. Bad Borseck, Hung. Borszék. Harghita, C Romania
92 K8 Børselv Lapp. Bissojohka. Finnmark, N Norway
113 L23 Borsh var. Borshi. Vlorë, S Albania
Borshchev see Borshchiv
116 K7 Borshchiv Pol. Borszczów, Rus. Borshchev. Ternopil's'ka Oblast', W Ukraine
Borshi see Borsh
111 L20 Borsod-Abaúj-Zemplén off. Borsod-Abaúj-Zemplén Megye. ◐ county NE Hungary
99 E15 Borssele Zeeland, SW Netherlands
Borszczów see Borshchiv
Borszék see Borsec
Bortala see Bole
103 O12 Bort-les-Orgues Corrèze, C France
Bor u České Lípy see Nový Bor
162 E8 Bor-Udzüür Hovd, W Mongolia
143 N9 Borūjen Chahār Maḩall va Bakhtīārī, C Iran
142 L7 Borūjerd var. Burujird. Lorestān, W Iran
116 H6 Boryslav Pol. Borysław, Rus. Borislav. L'vivs'ka Oblast', NW Ukraine
Borysław see Boryslav
117 P4 Boryspil' Rus. Borispol'. Kyyivs'ka Oblast', N Ukraine
117 P4 Boryspil' Rus. Borispol'. ✕ (Kyyiv) Kyyivs'ka Oblast', N Ukraine
Borzhomi see Borjomi
117 R3 Borzna Chernihivs'ka Oblast', NE Ukraine
123 O14 Borzya Chitinskaya Oblast', S Russian Federation
107 B18 Bosa Sardegna, Italy, C Mediterranean Sea
112 F10 Bosanska Dubica var. Kozarska Dubica. Republika Srpska, NW Bosnia and Herzegovina
112 G10 Bosanska Gradiška var. Gradiška. Republika Srpska, N Bosnia and Herzegovina
112 F10 Bosanska Kostajnica var. Srpska Kostajnica. Republika Srpska, NW Bosnia and Herzegovina
112 E11 Bosanska Krupa var. Krupa, Krupa na Uni. Federacija Bosna I Hercegovina, NW Bosnia and Herzegovina
112 H10 Bosanski Brod var. Srpski Brod. Republika Srpska, N Bosnia and Herzegovina
112 E10 Bosanski Novi var. Novi Grad. Republika Srpska, NW Bosnia and Herzegovina
112 E11 Bosanski Petrovac var. Petrovac. Federacija Bosna I Hercegovina, NW Bosnia and Herzegovina
112 N12 Bosanski Petrovac Serbia, E Serbia and Montenegro (Yugo.)
112 I10 Bosanski Šamac var. Šamac. Republika Srpska, N Bosnia and Herzegovina
112 E12 Bosansko Grahovo var. Grahovo, Hrvatsko Grahovo. Federacija Bosna I Hercegovina, W Bosnia and Herzegovina
Bosaso see Boosaaso
186 B7 Bosavi, Mount ☒ W PNG
160 J14 Bose Guangxi Zhuangzu Zizhiqu, S China
161 Q5 Boshan Shandong, E China
113 P16 Bosilegrad prev. Bosiljgrad. Serbia, SE Serbia and Montenegro (Yugo.)
Bosiljgrad see Bosilegrad
Bösing see Pezinok
98 H12 Boskoop Zuid-Holland, C Netherlands
111 G18 Boskovice Ger. Boskowitz. Jihomoravský Kraj, SE Czech Republic
Boskowitz see Boskovice
112 I10 Bosna ∼ N Bosnia and Herzegovina
113 G14 Bosna I Hercegovina, Federacija ◐ republic Bosnia and Herzegovina
112 H12 Bosnia and Herzegovina off. Republic of Bosnia and Herzegovina. ◆ republic SE Europe
79 J16 Bosobolo Equateur, NW Dem. Rep. Congo
165 O14 Bōsō-hantō peninsula Honshū, S Japan
Bosora see Buşrá ash Shām
Bosphorus/Bosporus see İstanbul Boğazı
Bosporus Cimmerius see Kerch Strait
Bosporus Thracius see İstanbul Boğazı
Bosra see Buşrá ash Shām
79 H14 Bossangoa Ouham, C Central African Republic
Bossé Bangou see Bossey Bangou
79 I15 Bossembélé Ombella-Mpoko, C Central African Republic
79 H15 Bossentélé Ouham-Pendé, W Central African Republic
77 R12 Bossey Bangou var. Bossé Bangou. Tillabéri, SW Niger
22 G5 Bossier City Louisiana, S USA
83 D20 Bossiesvlei Hardap, S Namibia
77 Y11 Bosso Diffa, SE Niger
61 F15 Bossoroca Rio Grande do Sul, S Brazil
158 J10 Bostan Xinjiang Uygur Zizhiqu, W China
142 K3 Bostānābād Āz̄arbāyjān-e Khāvarī, N Iran
158 K6 Bosten Hu var. Bagrax Hu. ◎ NW China
97 O18 Boston prev. St.Botolph's Town. E England, UK
19 O11 Boston state capital Massachusetts, NE USA
146 I9 Bo'ston Rus. Bustan. Qoraqalpog'iston Respublikasi, W Uzbekistan
10 M17 Boston Bar British Columbia, SW Canada
27 T10 Boston Mountains ▲▲ Arkansas, C USA
15 P8 Bostonnais ∼ Québec, SE Canada
Bostyn' see Bastyn'
112 J10 Bosut ∼ E Croatia
154 C11 Botād Gujarāt, W India
183 T9 Botany Bay inlet New South Wales, SE Australia
83 G18 Boteti var. Botletle. ∼ N Botswana
114 J9 Botev ▲ C Bulgaria
114 H9 Botevgrad prev. Orkhaniye. Sofiya, W Bulgaria
93 J16 Bothnia, Gulf of Fin. Pohjanlahti, Swe. Bottniska Viken. gulf N Baltic Sea
183 P17 Bothwell Tasmania, SE Australia
104 H5 Boticas Vila Real, N Portugal
55 W10 Boti-Pasi Sipaliwini, C Suriname
Botletle see Boteti
127 P16 Botlikh Chechenskaya Respublika, SW Russian Federation
117 N10 Botna ∼ E Moldova
116 I9 Botoșani Hung. Botosány. Botoșani, NE Romania
116 K8 Botoșani ◐ county NE Romania
Botosány see Botoșani
161 P4 Botou prev. Bozhen. Hebei, E China
99 M20 Botrange ▲ E Belgium
107 O21 Botricello Calabria, SW Italy
83 I23 Botshabelo Free State, C South Africa
93 J15 Botsmark Västerbotten, N Sweden
83 G19 Botswana off. Republic of Botswana. ◆ republic S Africa
29 N2 Bottineau North Dakota, N USA
Bottniska Viken see Bothnia, Gulf of
60 L9 Botucatu São Paulo, S Brazil
76 M16 Bouaflé C Ivory Coast
77 N16 Bouaké var. Bwake. C Ivory Coast
79 G14 Bouar Nana-Mambéré, W Central African Republic
74 H7 Bouarfa NE Morocco
111 B19 Boubín ▲ SW Czech Republic
79 I14 Bouca Ouham, W Central African Republic
15 T5 Boucher ∼ Québec, SE Canada
103 R15 Bouches-du-Rhône ◐ department SE France
74 C9 Bou Craa var. Bu Craa. NW Western Sahara
77 O9 Boû Djébéha oasis C Mali
108 C8 Boudry Neuchâtel, W Switzerland
180 L2 Bougainville, Cape headland Western Australia
65 E24 Bougainville, Cape headland East Falkland, Falkland Islands
Bougainville, Détroit de see Bougainville Strait, Vanuatu
186 J7 Bougainville Island island NE PNG
186 I8 Bougainville Strait strait N Solomon Islands
187 Q13 Bougainville Strait Fr. Détroit de Bougainville. strait C Vanuatu
120 I9 Bougaroun, Cap headland NE Algeria
77 R8 Boughessa Kidal, NE Mali
Bougie see Béjaïa
76 L13 Bougouni Sikasso, SW Mali
99 J24 Bouillon Luxembourg, SE Belgium
74 K5 Bouira var. Bouïra. N Algeria
74 D8 Bou-Izakarn SW Morocco
74 B9 Boujdour var. Bojador. W Western Sahara
74 G5 Boukhalef ✕ (Tanger) N Morocco
Boukombé see Boukoumbé
77 R14 Boukoumbé var. Boukombé. C Benin
76 G6 Boû Lanouâr Dakhlet Nouâdhibou, W Mauritania
37 T4 Boulder Colorado, C USA
33 R10 Boulder Montana, NW USA
35 X12 Boulder City Nevada, W USA
181 T7 Boulia Queensland, C Australia
15 N10 Boullé ∼ Québec, SE Canada
102 J9 Boulogne ∼ NW France
Boulogne see Boulogne-sur-Mer
102 L16 Boulogne-sur-Gesse Haute-Garonne, S France
103 N1 Boulogne-sur-Mer var. Boulogne; anc. Bononia, Gesoriacum, Gessoriacum. Pas-de-Calais, N France
77 Q12 Boulsa C Burkina
77 W11 Boultoum Zinder, C Niger
187 Y14 Bouma Taveuni, N Fiji
79 G16 Boumba ∼ SE Cameroon
76 J9 Boûmdeïd var. Boumdeït. Assaba, S Mauritania
Boumdeït see Boûmdeïd
115 C17 Boumistós ▲ W Greece
77 O15 Bouna NE Ivory Coast
19 P4 Boundary Bald Mountain ▲ Maine, NE USA
35 S8 Boundary Peak ▲ Nevada, W USA
76 M14 Boundiali N Ivory Coast
79 G19 Boundji Cuvette, C Congo
77 O13 Boundoukui var. Bondoukui, Bondoukuy. W Burkina
36 L2 Bountiful Utah, W USA
Bounty Basin see Bounty Trough
191 Q16 Bounty Bay bay Pitcairn Island, C Pacific Ocean
192 L12 Bounty Islands island group S NZ
175 Q13 Bounty Trough var. Bounty Basin. undersea feature S Pacific Ocean
187 P17 Bourail Province Sud, C New Caledonia
27 V5 Bourbeuse River ∼ Missouri, C USA
103 Q9 Bourbon-Lancy Saône-et-Loire, C France
31 N11 Bourbonnais Illinois, N USA
103 O10 Bourbonnais cultural region C France
103 S7 Bourbonne-les-Bains Haute-Marne, N France
Bourbon Vendée see la Roche-sur-Yon
74 M8 Bourdj Messaouda E Algeria
77 Q10 Bourem Gao, C Mali
Bourg see Bourg-en-Bresse
133 N11 Bourganeuf Creuse, C France
Bourgas see Burgas
Bourge-en-Bresse see Bourg-en-Bresse
103 S10 Bourg-en-Bresse var. Bourg, Bourge-en-Bresse. Ain, E France
103 O8 Bourges anc. Avaricum. Cher, C France
103 T11 Bourget, Lac du ◎ E France
103 P8 Bourgogne Eng. Burgundy. ◐ region E France
103 S11 Bourgoin-Jallieu Isère, E France
103 R14 Bourg-St-Andéol Ardèche, E France
103 U11 Bourg-St-Maurice Savoie, E France
108 C11 Bourg St.Pierre Valais, SW Switzerland
76 H8 Boû Rjeimât well W Mauritania
183 P5 Bourke New South Wales, SE Australia
97 M24 Bournemouth S England, UK
99 M23 Bourscheid Diekirch, NE Luxembourg
74 K6 Bou Saâda var. Bou Saada. N Algeria
36 I13 Bouse Wash ∼ Arizona, SW USA
103 N10 Boussac Creuse, C France
102 M16 Boussens Haute-Garonne, S France
78 H12 Bousso prev. Fort-Bretonnet. Chari-Baguirmi, S Chad
76 H9 Boutilimit Trarza, SW Mauritania
65 D21 Bouvet Island ◇ Norwegian dependency S Atlantic Ocean
77 U11 Bouza Tahoua, SW Niger
109 R10 Bovec Ger. Flitsch, It. Plezzo. NW Slovenia
98 J8 Bovenkarspel Noord-Holland, NW Netherlands
29 V5 Bovey Minnesota, N USA
32 M9 Bovill Idaho, NW USA
24 L4 Bovina Texas, SW USA
107 M17 Bovino Puglia, SE Italy
61 C17 Bovril Entre Ríos, E Argentina
28 L2 Bowbells North Dakota, N USA
11 Q16 Bow City Alberta, SW Canada
29 O8 Bowdle South Dakota, N USA
181 X6 Bowen Queensland, NE Australia
152 L2 Bowers Ridge undersea feature S Bering Sea
25 S5 Bowie Texas, SW USA
11 R17 Bow Island Alberta, SW Canada
Bowkān see Būkān
20 J7 Bowling Green Kentucky, S USA
27 V3 Bowling Green Missouri, C USA
31 R11 Bowling Green Ohio, N USA
21 W5 Bowling Green Virginia, NE USA
28 J6 Bowman North Dakota, N USA
9 Q7 Bowman Bay bay NW Atlantic Ocean
194 I5 Bowman Coast physical region Antarctica
28 J7 Bowman-Haley Lake ⊠ North Dakota, N USA
195 Z11 Bowman Island island Antarctica
Bowo see Bomi
183 S9 Bowral New South Wales, SE Australia
186 E8 Bowutu Mountains ▲▲ C PNG
83 I16 Bowwood Southern, S Zambia
28 I12 Box Butte Reservoir ⊠ Nebraska, C USA
28 J10 Box Elder South Dakota, N USA
95 M18 Boxholm Östergötland, S Sweden
Bo Xian/Boxian see Bozhou
161 Q4 Boxing Shandong, E China
99 L14 Boxmeer Noord-Brabant, SE Netherlands
99 J14 Boxtel Noord-Brabant, S Netherlands
136 J10 Boyabat Sinop, N Turkey
54 F9 Boyacá off. Departamento de Boyacá. ◐ province C Colombia
117 O4 Boyarka Kyyivs'ka Oblast', N Ukraine
22 H7 Boyce Louisiana, S USA
33 U11 Boyd Montana, NW USA
25 S6 Boyd Texas, SW USA
21 V8 Boydton Virginia, NE USA
Boyer Ahmadī va Kohkīlūyeh see Kohgīlūyeh va Būyer Aḩmad
29 T13 Boyer River ∼ Iowa, C USA
21 W8 Boykins Virginia, NE USA
11 Q13 Boyle Alberta, SW Canada
97 D16 Boyle Ir. Mainistirna Búille. C Ireland
97 F17 Boyne Ir. An Bhóinn. ∼ E Ireland
31 Q5 Boyne City Michigan, N USA
23 Z14 Boynton Beach Florida, SE USA
147 O13 Boysun Rus. Baysun. Surkhondaryo Wiloyati, S Uzbekistan
Bozau see Întorsura Buzăului
136 B12 Bozcaada island Çanakkale, NW Turkey
136 C14 Boz Dağları ▲▲ W Turkey
33 S11 Bozeman Montana, NW USA
Bozen see Bolzano
79 J16 Bozene Equateur, NW Dem. Rep. Congo
161 P7 Bozhou var. Boxian, Bo Xian. Anhui, E China
136 H16 Bozkır Konya, S Turkey
136 K13 Bozok Yaylası plateau C Turkey
79 H14 Bozoum Ouham-Pendé, W Central African Republic
137 N16 Bozova Sanlıurfa, S Turkey
Bozrah see Buşrá ash Shām
136 E12 Bozüyük Bilecik, NW Turkey
106 B9 Bra Piemonte, NW Italy
194 G4 Brabant Island island Antarctica
99 I20 Brabant Wallon ◐ province C Belgium
113 F15 Brač var. Brach, It. Brazza; anc. Brattia. island S Croatia
Bracara Augusta see Braga
107 H15 Bracciano Lazio, C Italy
107 H14 Bracciano, Lago di ◎ C Italy
14 H13 Bracebridge Ontario, S Canada
Brach see Brač
93 G17 Bräcke Jämtland, C Sweden
25 P12 Brackettville Texas, SW USA
97 N22 Bracknell S England, UK
61 K14 Braço do Norte Santa Catarina, S Brazil
116 G11 Brad Hung. Brád. Hunedoara, SW Romania
107 N18 Bradano ∼ S Italy
23 V13 Bradenton Florida, SE USA
14 H14 Bradford Ontario, S Canada
97 L17 Bradford N England, UK
27 W10 Bradford Arkansas, C USA
18 D12 Bradford Pennsylvania, NE USA
27 T15 Bradley Arkansas, C USA
25 P7 Bradshaw Texas, SW USA
25 Q9 Brady Texas, SW USA
25 Q9 Brady Creek ∼ Texas, SW USA
96 J10 Braemar NE Scotland, UK
116 K8 Brăești Botoșani, NW Romania
104 G5 Braga anc. Bracara Augusta. Braga, NW Portugal
104 G5 Braga ◐ district N Portugal
116 J15 Bragadiru Teleorman, S Romania
61 C20 Bragado Buenos Aires, E Argentina
104 J5 Bragança Eng. Braganza; anc. Julio Briga. Bragança, NE Portugal
104 I5 Bragança ◐ district N Portugal
60 N9 Bragança Paulista São Paulo, S Brazil
Braganza see Bragança
Bragin see Brahin
Brahe see Brda
Brahestad see Raahe
119 O20 Brahin Rus. Bragin. Homyel'skaya Voblasts', SE Belarus
153 U15 Brahmanbaria Chittagong, E Bangladesh
154 O12 Brāhmani ∼ E India
154 N13 Brahmapur Orissa, E India
131 S10 Brahmaputra var. Padma, Tsangpo, Ben. Jamuna, Chin. Yarlung Zangbo Jiang, Ind. Bramaputra, Dihang, Siang. ∼ S Asia
97 H19 Braich y Pwll headland NW Wales, UK
183 R10 Braidwood New South Wales, SE Australia
30 M11 Braidwood Illinois, N USA
116 M13 Brăila Brăila, E Romania
116 L13 Brăila ◐ county SE Romania
99 G19 Braine-l'Alleud Brabant Wallon, C Belgium
99 F19 Braine-le-Comte Hainaut, SW Belgium
29 U6 Brainerd Minnesota, N USA
99 J19 Braives Liège, E Belgium
83 H23 Brak ∼ C South Africa
Brak see Birāk
99 E18 Brakel Oost-Vlaanderen, SW Belgium
98 J13 Brakel Gelderland, C Netherlands
76 H9 Brakna ◐ region S Mauritania
95 J17 Brålanda Västra Götaland, S Sweden
Bramaputra see Brahmaputra
95 F23 Bramming Ribe, W Denmark
14 G15 Brampton Ontario, S Canada
100 F12 Bramsche Niedersachsen, NW Germany
116 J12 Bran Ger. Törzburg, Hung. Törcsvár. Brașov, S Romania
29 W8 Branch Minnesota, N USA
21 R14 Branchville South Carolina, SE USA
47 Y6 Branco, Cabo headland E Brazil
58 F11 Branco, Rio ∼ N Brazil
108 J8 Brand Vorarlberg, W Austria
83 B18 Brandberg ▲ NW Namibia
95 H14 Brandbu Oppland, S Norway
95 F22 Brande Ringkøbing, W Denmark
Brandebourg see Brandenburg
100 M12 Brandenburg var. Brandenburg an der Havel. Brandenburg, NE Germany
20 K5 Brandenburg Kentucky, S USA
100 N12 Brandenburg off. Freie und Hansestadt Hamburg, Fr. Brandebourg. ◐ state NE Germany
Brandenburg an der Havel see Brandenburg
83 I23 Brandfort Free State, C South Africa
11 W16 Brandon Manitoba, S Canada
23 V12 Brandon Florida, SE USA
22 L6 Brandon Mississippi, S USA
97 A20 Brandon Mountain Ir. Cnoc Bréanainn. ▲ SW Ireland
Brandsen see Coronel Brandsen
95 I14 Brandval Hedmark, S Norway
83 F24 Brandvlei Northern Cape, W South Africa
23 U9 Branford Florida, SE USA
110 K7 Braniewo Ger. Braunsberg. Warmińsko-Mazurskie, NE Poland
194 H3 Bransfield Strait strait Antarctica
37 U8 Branson Colorado, C USA
27 T8 Branson Missouri, C USA
14 G16 Brantford Ontario, S Canada
102 L12 Brantôme Dordogne, SW France
182 L12 Branxholme Victoria, SE Australia
Brasil see Brazil
59 C16 Brasiléia Acre, W Brazil
59 K18 Brasília ● (Brazil) Distrito Federal, C Brazil
Braslav see Braslaw
118 J12 Braslaw Pol. Brasław, Rus. Braslav. Vitsyebskaya Voblasts', N Belarus
116 J12 Brașov Ger. Kronstadt, Hung. Brassó; prev. Orașul Stalin. Brașov, C Romania
116 I12 Brașov ◐ county C Romania
77 U18 Brass Bayelsa, S Nigeria
99 H16 Brasschaat var. Brasschaet. Antwerpen, N Belgium
Brasschaet see Brasschaat
169 V8 Brassey, Banjaran var. Brassey Range. ▲▲ East Malaysia
Brassey Range see Brassey, Banjaran
Brassó see Brașov
23 T1 Brasstown Bald ▲ Georgia, SE USA
113 K22 Brataj Vlorë, SW Albania
114 J10 Bratan var. Morozov. ▲ C Bulgaria
111 F21 Bratislava Ger. Pressburg, Hung. Pozsony. ● (Slovakia) Bratislavský Kraj, W Slovakia
111 H21 Bratislavský Kraj ◐ region W Slovakia
114 H10 Bratiya ▲ C Bulgaria
122 M12 Bratsk Irkutskaya Oblast', C Russian Federation
117 Q8 Brats'ke Mykolayivs'ka Oblast', S Ukraine
122 M13 Bratskoye Vodokhranilishche Eng. Bratsk Reservoir. ⊠ S Russian Federation
Bratsk Reservoir see Bratskoye Vodokhranilishche
Brattia see Brač
94 D9 Brattvåg Møre og Romsdal, S Norway
112 K12 Bratunac Republika Srpska, E Bosnia and Herzegovina
114 J10 Bratya Daskalovi prev. Grozdovo. Stara Zagora, C Bulgaria
109 U2 Braunau ∼ N Austria
Braunau see Braunau am Inn
109 Q4 Braunau am Inn var. Braunau. Oberösterreich, N Austria
Braunsberg see Braniewo
100 J13 Braunschweig Eng./Fr. Brunswick. Niedersachsen, N Germany
Brava see Baraawe
105 Y6 Brava, Costa coastal region NE Spain
43 V16 Brava, Punta headland E Panama
95 N17 Bråviken inlet S Sweden
56 B10 Bravo, Cerro ▲ N Peru
Bravo del Norte, Río/Bravo, Río see Grande, Rio
35 X17 Brawley California, W USA
97 G18 Bray Ir. Bré. E Ireland
59 G16 Brazil off. Federative Republic of Brazil, Port. República Federativa do Brasil, Sp. Brasil; prev. United States of Brazil. ◆ federal republic South America
65 K15 Brazil Basin var. Brazilian Basin, Brazil'skaya Kotlovina. undersea feature W Atlantic Ocean
Brazilian Basin see Brazil Basin
Brazilian Highlands see Central, Planalto
Brazil'skaya Kotlovina see Brazil Basin
25 U10 Brazos River ∼ Texas, SW USA
Brazza see Brač
79 G21 Brazzaville ● (Congo) Capital District, S Congo
79 G21 Brazzaville ✕ Le Pool, S Congo
112 J11 Brčko Republika Srpska, NE Bosnia and Herzegovina
110 H8 Brda Ger. Brahe. ∼ N Poland
Bré see Bray
185 A23 Breaksea Sound sound South Island, NZ
184 L4 Bream Bay bay North Island, NZ
184 L4 Bream Head headland North Island, NZ
Bréanainn, Cnoc see Brandon Mountain
45 S6 Brea, Punta headland W Puerto Rico
22 I9 Breaux Bridge Louisiana, S USA
116 J13 Breaza Prahova, SE Romania
169 P16 Brebes Jawa, C Indonesia
96 K10 Brechin E Scotland, UK
99 H15 Brecht Antwerpen, N Belgium
37 S4 Breckenridge Colorado, C USA
29 R6 Breckenridge Minnesota, N USA
25 R6 Breckenridge Texas, SW USA
97 J21 Brecknock cultural region SE Wales, UK
63 G25 Brecknock, Península headland S Chile
111 G19 Břeclav Ger. Lundenburg. Jihomoravský Kraj, SE Czech Republic
97 J21 Brecon E Wales, UK
97 J21 Brecon Beacons ▲▲ S Wales, UK
99 I14 Breda Noord-Brabant, S Netherlands
95 K20 Bredaryd Jönköping, S Sweden
83 F26 Bredasdorp Western Cape, SW South Africa
93 H16 Bredbyn Västernorrland, N Sweden
122 F11 Bredy Chelyabinskaya Oblast', C Russian Federation
99 K17 Bree Limburg, NE Belgium
67 T15 Breede ∼ S South Africa
98 I7 Breezand Noord-Holland, NW Netherlands
113 P18 Bregalnica ∼ E FYR Macedonia
108 I6 Bregenz anc. Brigantium. Vorarlberg, W Austria
108 J7 Bregenzer Wald ▲▲ W Austria
114 F6 Bregovo Vidin, NW Bulgaria
102 H5 Bréhat, Île de island NW France
92 H2 Breiðhafjörður bay W Iceland
92 L3 Breiðdalsvík Austurland, E Iceland
108 H9 Breil Ger. Brigels. Graubünden, S Switzerland
92 J8 Breivikbotn Finnmark, N Norway
94 I9 Brekken Sør-Trøndelag, S Norway
94 G7 Brekstad Sør-Trøndelag, S Norway
94 B10 Bremangerlandet island S Norway
Brême see Bremen
100 H11 Bremen Fr. Brême. Bremen, NW Germany
23 R3 Bremen Georgia, SE USA
31 O11 Bremen Indiana, N USA
100 H10 Bremen off. Freie Hansestadt Bremen, Fr. Brême. ◐ state N Germany
100 G9 Bremerhaven Bremen, NW Germany
Bremersdorp see Manzini
32 G8 Bremerton Washington, NW USA
100 H10 Bremervörde Niedersachsen, NW Germany
25 U9 Bremond Texas, SW USA

◆ Country ● Country Capital ◇ Dependent Territory ○ Dependent Territory Capital ◐ Administrative Region ✕ International Airport ▲ Mountain ▲▲ Mountain Range ☒ Volcano ∼ River ◎ Lake ⊠ Reservoir

25 U10 **Brenham** Texas, SW USA
108 M8 **Brenner** Tirol, W Austria
Brenner, Col du/Brennero, Passo del *see* Brenner Pass
108 M8 **Brenner Pass** *var.* Brenner Sattel, *Fr.* Col du Brenner, *Ger.* Brennerpass, *It.* Passo del Brennero. *pass* Austria/Italy
Brenner Sattel *see* Brenner Pass
108 G10 **Brenno** ∼ SW Switzerland
106 F7 **Breno** Lombardia, N Italy
23 O5 **Brent** Alabama, S USA
106 H7 **Brenta** ∼ NE Italy
97 P21 **Brentwood** E England, UK
18 L14 **Brentwood** Long Island, New York, NE USA
106 F7 **Brescia** *anc.* Brixia. Lombardia, N Italy
99 D15 **Breskens** Zeeland, SW Netherlands
Breslau *see* Dolnośląskie
106 H5 **Bressanone** *Ger.* Brixen. Trentino-Alto Adige, N Italy
96 M2 **Bressay** *island* NE Scotland, UK
102 K9 **Bressuire** Deux-Sèvres, W France
119 F20 **Brest** *Pol.* Brześć nad Bugiem, *Rus.* Brest-Litovsk; *prev.* Brześć Litewski. Brestskaya Voblasts', SW Belarus
102 F5 **Brest** Finistère, NW France
Brest-Litovsk *see* Brest
112 A10 **Brestova** Istra, NW Croatia
Brestskaya Oblast' *see* Brestskaya Voblasts'
119 G19 **Brestskaya Voblasts'** *prev. Rus.* Brestskaya Oblast'. ⬖ *province* SW Belarus
102 G6 **Bretagne** *Eng.* Brittany; *Lat.* Britannia Minor. ⬖ *region* NW France
116 G12 **Bretea-Română** *Hung.* Oláhbrettye; *prev.* Bretea-Romînă. Hunedoara, W Romania
Bretea-Romînă *see* Bretea-Română
103 O3 **Breteuil** Oise, N France
102 I10 **Breton, Pertuis** *inlet* W France
22 L10 **Breton Sound** *sound* Louisiana, S USA
184 K2 **Brett, Cape** *headland* North Island, NZ
101 G21 **Bretten** Baden-Württemberg, SW Germany
99 K15 **Breugel** Noord-Brabant, S Netherlands
106 B6 **Breuil-Cervinia** *It.* Cervinia. Valle d'Aosta, NW Italy
98 I11 **Breukelen** Utrecht, C Netherlands
21 P10 **Brevard** North Carolina, SE USA
38 L9 **Brevig Mission** Alaska, USA
95 G16 **Brevik** Telemark, S Norway
183 P5 **Brewarrina** New South Wales, SE Australia
19 R6 **Brewer** Maine, NE USA
29 T11 **Brewster** Minnesota, N USA
29 N14 **Brewster** Nebraska, C USA
31 U12 **Brewster** Ohio, N USA
183 O8 **Brewster, Lake** ◎ New South Wales, SE Australia
23 P7 **Brewton** Alabama, S USA
Brezhnev *see* Naberezhnyye Chelny
109 W12 **Brežice** *Ger.* Rann. E Slovenia
114 G9 **Breznik** Pernik, W Bulgaria
111 K19 **Brezno** *Ger.* Bries, Briesen, *Hung.* Breznóbánya; *prev.* Brezno nad Hronom. Banskobystrický Kraj, C Slovakia
Breznóbánya/Brezno nad Hronom *see* Brezno
116 I12 **Brezoi** Vâlcea, SW Romania
114 J10 **Brezovo** *prev.* Abrashlare. Plovdiv, C Bulgaria
79 K14 **Bria** Haute-Kotto, C Central African Republic
103 U13 **Briançon** *anc.* Brigantio. Hautes-Alpes, SE France
36 K7 **Brian Head** ▲ Utah, W USA
103 O7 **Briare** Loiret, C France
183 V2 **Bribie Island** *island* Queensland, E Australia
43 O14 **Bribrí** Limón, E Costa Rica
116 L8 **Briceni** *var.* Brinceni, *Rus.* Brichany. N Moldova
Bricgstow *see* Bristol
Brichany *see* Briceni
99 M24 **Bridel** Luxembourg, C Luxembourg
97 J22 **Bridgend** S Wales, UK
14 I14 **Bridgenorth** Ontario, SE Canada
23 Q1 **Bridgeport** Alabama, S USA
35 R8 **Bridgeport** California, W USA
18 L13 **Bridgeport** Connecticut, NE USA
31 N15 **Bridgeport** Illinois, N USA
28 J14 **Bridgeport** Nebraska, C USA
25 S6 **Bridgeport** Texas, SW USA
21 S3 **Bridgeport** West Virginia, NE USA
25 S5 **Bridgeport, Lake** ⊞ Texas, SW USA
33 U11 **Bridger** Montana, NW USA
18 I17 **Bridgeton** New Jersey, NE USA
180 J14 **Bridgetown** Western Australia
45 Y14 **Bridgetown** ● (Barbados) SW Barbados
183 P17 **Bridgewater** Tasmania, SE Australia
13 P16 **Bridgewater** Nova Scotia, SE Canada
19 P12 **Bridgewater** Massachusetts, NE USA
29 Q11 **Bridgewater** South Dakota, N USA
21 U5 **Bridgewater** Virginia, NE USA
19 P8 **Bridgton** Maine, NE USA
97 K23 **Bridgwater** SW England, UK
97 K22 **Bridgwater Bay** *bay* SW England, UK
97 O16 **Bridlington** E England, UK
97 O16 **Bridlington Bay** *bay* E England, UK
183 P15 **Bridport** Tasmania, SE Australia
97 K24 **Bridport** S England, UK
103 O5 **Brie** *cultural region* N France
Brieg *see* Brzeg
Briel *see* Brielle
98 G12 **Brielle** *var.* Briel, Bril, *Eng.* The Brill. Zuid-Holland, SW Netherlands
108 E9 **Brienz** Bern, C Switzerland
108 E9 **Brienzer See** ◎ SW Switzerland
Bries/Briesen *see* Brezno
Brietzig *see* Brzesko
103 S4 **Briey** Meurthe-et-Moselle, NE France
108 E10 **Brig** *Fr.* Brigue, *It.* Briga. Valais, SW Switzerland
Briga *see* Brig
101 G24 **Brigach** ∼ S Germany
18 K17 **Brigantine** New Jersey, NE USA
Brigantio *see* Briançon
Brigantium *see* Bregenz
Brigels *see* Breil
25 S9 **Briggs** Texas, SW USA
36 L1 **Brigham City** Utah, W USA
14 J15 **Brighton** Ontario, SE Canada
97 O23 **Brighton** SE England, UK
37 T4 **Brighton** Colorado, C USA
30 K15 **Brighton** Illinois, N USA
103 T16 **Brignoles** Var, SE France
Brigue *see* Brig
105 O7 **Brihuega** Castilla-La Mancha, C Spain
112 A10 **Brijuni** *It.* Brioni. *island group* NW Croatia
76 G12 **Brikama** W Gambia
Bril *see* Brielle
Brill, The *see* Brielle
101 G15 **Brilon** Nordrhein-Westfalen, W Germany
Brinceni *see* Briceni
107 Q18 **Brindisi** *anc.* Brundisium, Brundusium. Puglia, SE Italy
27 W11 **Brinkley** Arkansas, C USA
Brioni *see* Brijuni
103 P12 **Brioude** *anc.* Brivas. Haute-Loire, C France
Briovera *see* St-Lô
183 U2 **Brisbane** *state capital* Queensland, E Australia
183 V2 **Brisbane** ✕ Queensland, E Australia
25 P2 **Briscoe** Texas, SW USA
106 H10 **Brisighella** Emilia-Romagna, C Italy
108 G11 **Brissago** Ticino, S Switzerland
97 K22 **Bristol** *anc.* Bricgstow. SW England, UK
18 M12 **Bristol** Connecticut, NE USA
23 R9 **Bristol** Florida, SE USA
19 N9 **Bristol** New Hampshire, NE USA
29 Q8 **Bristol** South Dakota, N USA
21 P8 **Bristol** Tennessee, S USA
18 M8 **Bristol** Vermont, NE USA
39 N14 **Bristol Bay** *bay* Alaska, USA
97 I22 **Bristol Channel** *inlet* England/Wales, UK
35 W14 **Bristol Lake** ◎ California, W USA
27 P10 **Bristow** Oklahoma, C USA
86 C10 **Britain** *var.* Great Britain. *island* UK
Britannia Minor *see* Bretagne
10 L12 **British Columbia** *Fr.* Colombie-Britannique. ⬖ *province* SW Canada
British Guiana *see* Guyana
British Honduras *see* Belize
173 Q7 **British Indian Ocean Territory** ◇ *UK dependent territory* C Indian Ocean
86 B9 **British Isles** *island group* NW Europe
10 I1 **British Mountains** ▲ Yukon Territory, NW Canada
British North Borneo *see* Sabah
British Solomon Islands Protectorate *see* Solomon Islands
45 S8 **British Virgin Islands** *var.* Virgin Islands. ◇ *UK dependent territory* E West Indies
83 J21 **Brits** North-West, N South Africa
83 H24 **Britstown** Northern Cape, W South Africa
14 F12 **Britt** Ontario, S Canada
29 V12 **Britt** Iowa, C USA
Brittany *see* Bretagne
29 Q7 **Britton** South Dakota, N USA
Briva Curretia *see* Brive-la-Gaillarde
Briva Isarae *see* Pontoise
Brivas *see* Brioude
Brive *see* Brive-la-Gaillarde
102 M12 **Brive-la-Gaillarde** *prev.* Brive, *anc.* Briva Curretia. Corrèze, C France
105 O4 **Briviesca** Castilla-León, N Spain
Brixen *see* Bressanone
Brixia *see* Brescia
145 S15 **Brlik** *prev.* Novotroickoje, Novotroitskoye. Zhambyl, SE Kazakhstan
Brněnský Kraj *see* Jihomoravský Kraj
111 G18 **Brno** *Ger.* Brünn. Jihomoravský Kraj, SE Czech Republic
96 G7 **Broad Bay** *bay* NW Scotland, UK
25 X8 **Broaddus** Texas, SW USA
183 O12 **Broadford** Victoria, SE Australia
96 G9 **Broadford** N Scotland, UK
96 J13 **Broad Law** ▲ S Scotland, UK
23 U3 **Broad River** ∼ Georgia, SE USA
21 N8 **Broad River** ∼ North Carolina/South Carolina, SE USA
181 Y8 **Broadsound Range** ▲ Queensland, E Australia
33 X11 **Broadus** Montana, NW USA
21 U4 **Broadway** Virginia, NE USA
118 E9 **Brocēni** Saldus, SW Latvia
11 U11 **Brochet** Manitoba, C Canada
11 U10 **Brochet, Lac** ◎ Manitoba, C Canada
15 S5 **Brochet, Lac au** ◎ Québec, SE Canada
101 K14 **Brocken** ▲ C Germany
19 O12 **Brockton** Massachusetts, NE USA
14 L14 **Brockville** Ontario, SE Canada
18 D13 **Brockway** Pennsylvania, NE USA
Brod/Bród *see* Slavonski Brod
9 N5 **Brodeur Peninsula** *peninsula* Baffin Island, Nunavut, NE Canada
96 H13 **Brodick** W Scotland, UK
Brod na Savi *see* Slavonski Brod
110 K9 **Brodnica** *Ger.* Buddenbrock. Kujawski-pomorskie, C Poland
112 G10 **Brod-Posavina** *off.* Brodsko-Posavska Županija. ⬖ *province* NE Croatia
116 J5 **Brody** L'vivs'ka Oblast', NW Ukraine
95 G22 **Brædstrup** Vejle, C Denmark
98 I10 **Broek-in-Waterland** Noord-Holland, C Netherlands
32 L13 **Brogan** Oregon, NW USA
110 N10 **Brok** Mazowieckie, C Poland
27 P9 **Broken Arrow** Oklahoma, C USA
183 T9 **Broken Bay** *bay* New South Wales, SE Australia
29 N15 **Broken Bow** Nebraska, C USA
27 R13 **Broken Bow** Oklahoma, C USA
27 R12 **Broken Bow Lake** ⊞ Oklahoma, C USA
182 L6 **Broken Hill** New South Wales, SE Australia
173 S10 **Broken Ridge** *undersea feature* S Indian Ocean
186 C6 **Broken Water Bay** *bay* W Bismarck Sea
55 W10 **Brokopondo** Brokopondo, NE Suriname
55 W10 **Brokopondo** ⬖ *district* C Suriname
Bromberg *see* Bydgoszcz
95 L22 **Bromölla** Skåne, S Sweden
97 L20 **Bromsgrove** W England, UK
95 G20 **Brønderslev** Nordjylland, N Denmark
106 D8 **Broni** Lombardia, N Italy
10 K11 **Bronlund Peak** ▲ British Columbia, W Canada
93 F14 **Brønnøysund** Nordland, C Norway
23 V10 **Bronson** Florida, SE USA
31 Q11 **Bronson** Michigan, N USA
25 X8 **Bronson** Texas, SW USA
107 L24 **Bronte** Sicilia, Italy, C Mediterranean Sea
25 P8 **Bronte** Texas, SW USA
25 Y9 **Brookeland** Texas, SW USA
170 M7 **Brooke's Point** Palawan, W Philippines
27 T3 **Brookfield** Missouri, C USA
22 K7 **Brookhaven** Mississippi, S USA
32 E16 **Brookings** Oregon, NW USA
29 R10 **Brookings** South Dakota, N USA
29 W14 **Brooklyn** Iowa, C USA
29 U8 **Brooklyn Park** Minnesota, N USA
21 U7 **Brookneal** Virginia, NE USA
11 R16 **Brooks** Alberta, SW Canada
25 V11 **Brookshire** Texas, SW USA
38 L8 **Brooks Mountain** ▲ Alaska, USA
38 M11 **Brooks Range** ▲ Alaska, USA
31 O12 **Brookston** Indiana, N USA
23 V11 **Brooksville** Florida, SE USA
23 N4 **Brooksville** Mississippi, S USA
180 J13 **Brookton** Western Australia
31 Q14 **Brookville** Indiana, N USA
18 D13 **Brookville** Pennsylvania, NE USA
31 Q14 **Brookville Lake** ⊞ Indiana, N USA
180 K5 **Broome** Western Australia
37 S4 **Broomfield** Colorado, C USA
Broos *see* Orăştie
96 J7 **Brora** N Scotland, UK
96 J7 **Brora** ∼ N Scotland, UK
95 F23 **Brørup** Ribe, W Denmark
95 L23 **Brösarp** Skåne, S Sweden
116 J9 **Broşteni** Suceava, NE Romania
102 M6 **Brou** Eure-et-Loir, C France
Broucsella *see* Brussel/Bruxelles
Broughton Bay *see* Tongjosŏn-man
9 R5 **Broughton Island** Nunavut, NE Canada
138 G7 **Broummâna** C Lebanon
22 I9 **Broussard** Louisiana, S USA
98 E13 **Brouwersdam** *dam* SW Netherlands
98 E13 **Brouwershaven** Zeeland, SW Netherlands
117 P4 **Brovary** Kyyivs'ka Oblast', N Ukraine
95 G20 **Brovst** Nordjylland, N Denmark
31 S8 **Brown City** Michigan, N USA
24 M6 **Brownfield** Texas, SW USA
33 Q7 **Browning** Montana, NW USA
33 R6 **Brown, Mount** ▲ Montana, NW USA
(0) M9 **Browns Bank** *undersea feature* NW Atlantic Ocean
31 O14 **Brownsburg** Indiana, N USA
18 J16 **Browns Mills** New Jersey, NE USA
44 J12 **Browns Town** C Jamaica
31 P15 **Brownstown** Indiana, N USA
29 R8 **Browns Valley** Minnesota, N USA
20 K7 **Brownsville** Kentucky, S USA
20 F9 **Brownsville** Tennessee, S USA
25 T17 **Brownsville** Texas, SW USA
55 W10 **Brownsweg** Brokopondo, C Suriname
29 U9 **Brownton** Minnesota, N USA
19 R5 **Brownville Junction** Maine, NE USA
25 R8 **Brownwood** Texas, SW USA
25 R8 **Brownwood Lake** ⊞ Texas, SW USA
104 I9 **Brozas** Extremadura, W Spain
119 M18 **Brozha** Mahilyowskaya Voblasts', E Belarus
103 O2 **Bruay-en-Artois** Pas-de-Calais, N France
103 P2 **Bruay-sur-l'Escaut** Nord, N France
14 F13 **Bruce Peninsula** *peninsula* Ontario, S Canada
20 H9 **Bruceton** Tennessee, S USA
25 T9 **Bruceville** Texas, SW USA
101 G21 **Bruchsal** Baden-Württemberg, SW Germany
109 Q7 **Bruck** Salzburg, NW Austria
Bruck *see* Bruck an der Mur
109 Y4 **Bruck an der Leitha** Niederösterreich, NE Austria
109 V7 **Bruck an der Mur** *var.* Bruck. Steiermark, C Austria
101 M24 **Bruckmühl** Bayern, SE Germany
168 E7 **Brueuh, Pulau** *island* NW Indonesia
Bruges *see* Brugge
108 F6 **Brugg** Aargau, NW Switzerland
99 C16 **Brugge** *Fr.* Bruges. West-Vlaanderen, NW Belgium
109 R9 **Bruggen** Kärnten, S Austria
101 E16 **Brühl** Nordrhein-Westfalen, W Germany
99 F14 **Bruinisse** Zeeland, SW Netherlands
169 R9 **Bruit, Pulau** *island* East Malaysia
14 K10 **Brûlé, Lac** ◎ Québec, SE Canada
30 M4 **Brule River** ∼ Michigan/Wisconsin, N USA
99 H23 **Brûly** Namur, S Belgium
59 N17 **Brumado** Bahia, E Brazil
98 M11 **Brummen** Gelderland, E Netherlands
94 H13 **Brumunddal** Hedmark, S Norway
23 Q6 **Brundidge** Alabama, S USA
Brundisium/Brundusium *see* Brindisi
33 N15 **Bruneau River** ∼ Idaho, NW USA
Bruneck *see* Brunico
169 T8 **Brunei** *off.* Sultanate of Brunei, *Mal.* Negara Brunei Darussalam. ◆ *monarchy* SE Asia
169 T7 **Brunei Bay** *var.* Teluk Brunei. *bay* N Brunei
Brunei, Teluk *see* Brunei Bay
Brunei Town *see* Bandar Seri Begawan
106 H5 **Brunico** *Ger.* Bruneck. Trentino-Alto Adige, N Italy
Brünn *see* Brno
185 G17 **Brunner, Lake** ◎ South Island, NZ
99 M18 **Brunssum** Limburg, SE Netherlands
23 W7 **Brunswick** Georgia, SE USA
19 Q8 **Brunswick** Maine, NE USA
21 V3 **Brunswick** Maryland, NE USA
27 T3 **Brunswick** Missouri, C USA
31 T11 **Brunswick** Ohio, N USA
Brunswick *see* Braunschweig
63 H24 **Brunswick, Península** *headland* S Chile
111 H17 **Bruntál** *Ger.* Freudenthal. Moravskoslezský Kraj, E Czech Republic
195 N3 **Brunt Ice Shelf** *ice shelf* Antarctica
Brusa *see* Bursa
37 U3 **Brush** Colorado, C USA
42 M5 **Brus Laguna** Gracias a Dios, E Honduras
60 K13 **Brusque** Santa Catarina, S Brazil
Brussa *see* Bursa
99 E18 **Brussel** *var.* Brussels, *Fr.* Bruxelles, *Ger.* Brüssel; *anc.* Broucsella. ● (Belgium) Brussels, C Belgium *see also* Bruxelles
Brüssel/Brussels *see* Brussel/Bruxelles
117 O5 **Brusyliv** Zhytomyrs'ka Oblast', N Ukraine
183 Q12 **Bruthen** Victoria, SE Australia
Bruttium *see* Calabria
Brüx *see* Most
99 E18 **Bruxelles** *var.* Brussels, *Dut.* Brussel, *Ger.* Brüssel; *anc.* Broucsella. ● (Belgium) Brussels, C Belgium *see also* Brussel
54 J7 **Bruzual** Apure, W Venezuela
31 Q11 **Bryan** Ohio, N USA
25 U10 **Bryan** Texas, SW USA
194 J4 **Bryan Coast** *physical region* Antarctica
122 L11 **Bryanka** Krasnoyarskiy Kray, C Russian Federation
117 Y7 **Bryanka** Luhans'ka Oblast', E Ukraine
182 J8 **Bryan, Mount** ▲ South Australia
126 I6 **Bryansk** Bryanskaya Oblast', W Russian Federation
126 H6 **Bryanskaya Oblast'** ⬖ *province* W Russian Federation
194 J5 **Bryant, Cape** *headland* Antarctica
27 U8 **Bryant Creek** ∼ Missouri, C USA
36 K8 **Bryce Canyon** *canyon* Utah, W USA
119 O15 **Bryli** *Rus.* Bryli. Mahilyowskaya Voblasts', E Belarus
95 C17 **Bryne** Rogaland, S Norway
25 R6 **Bryson** Texas, SW USA
21 N10 **Bryson City** North Carolina, SE USA
14 K11 **Bryson, Lac** ◎ Québec, SE Canada
126 K13 **Bryukhovetskaya** Krasnodarskiy Kray, SW Russian Federation
111 H15 **Brzeg** *Ger.* Brieg; *anc.* Civitas Altae Ripae. Opolskie, S Poland
111 G14 **Brzeg Dolny** *Ger.* Dyhernfurth. Dolnośląskie, SW Poland
Brześć Litewski/Brześć nad Bugiem *see* Brest
111 L17 **Brzesko** *Ger.* Brietzig. Małopolskie, S Poland
Brzeżany *see* Berezhany
110 K12 **Brzeziny** Łódzkie, C Poland
Brzostowica Wielka *see* Vyalikaya Byerastavitsa
111 O17 **Brzozów** Podkarpackie, SE Poland
Bsharrī/Bsherri *see* Bcharré
187 X14 **Bua** Vanua Levu, N Fiji
95 J20 **Bua** Halland, S Sweden
82 M13 **Bua** ∼ C Malawi
Bua *see* Čiovo
81 L18 **Bu'aale** *It.* Buale. Jubbada Dhexe, SW Somalia
189 Q8 **Buada Lagoon** *lagoon* Nauru, C Pacific Ocean
186 M8 **Buala** Santa Isabel, E Solomon Islands
Buale *see* Bu'aale
190 H1 **Buariki** *atoll* Tungaru, W Kiribati
167 Q10 **Bua Yai** *var.* Ban Bua Yai. Nakhon Ratchasima, E Thailand
75 P8 **Bu'ayrāt al Ḥasūn** *var.* Buwayrāt al Ḥasūn. C Libya
76 H13 **Buba** S Guinea-Bissau
171 P11 **Bubaa** Sulawesi, N Indonesia
81 D20 **Bubanza** NW Burundi
83 K18 **Bubi** *prev.* Bubye. ∼ S Zimbabwe
142 L11 **Būbīyan, Jazīrat** *island* E Kuwait
Bublitz *see* Bobolice
Bubye *see* Bubi
187 Y13 **Buca** *prev.* Mbutha. Vanua Levu, N Fiji
136 F16 **Bucak** Burdur, SW Turkey
54 G8 **Bucaramanga** Santander, N Colombia
107 M18 **Buccino** Campania, S Italy
116 K9 **Bucecea** Botoşani, NE Romania
116 J6 **Buchach** *Pol.* Buczacz. Ternopil's'ka Oblast', W Ukraine
183 Q12 **Buchan** Victoria, SE Australia
76 J17 **Buchanan** *prev.* Grand Bassa. SW Liberia
23 R3 **Buchanan** Georgia, SE USA
31 O11 **Buchanan** Michigan, N USA
21 T6 **Buchanan** Virginia, NE USA
25 R10 **Buchanan Dam** Texas, SW USA
25 R10 **Buchanan, Lake** ⊞ Texas, SW USA
96 L8 **Buchan Ness** *headland* NE Scotland, UK
13 T12 **Buchans** Newfoundland and Labrador, SE Canada
Bucharest *see* Bucureşti
101 H20 **Buchen** Baden-Württemberg, SW Germany
100 I10 **Buchholz in der Nordheide** Niedersachsen, NW Germany
108 F7 **Buchs** Aargau, N Switzerland
108 I8 **Buchs** Sankt Gallen, NE Switzerland
100 H13 **Bückeburg** Niedersachsen, NW Germany
36 K14 **Buckeye** Arizona, SW USA
Buckeye State *see* Ohio
21 S4 **Buckhannon** West Virginia, NE USA
25 T9 **Buckholts** Texas, SW USA
96 K8 **Buckie** NE Scotland, UK
14 M12 **Buckingham** Québec, SE Canada
21 U6 **Buckingham** Virginia, NE USA
97 N21 **Buckinghamshire** *cultural region* SE England, UK
39 N8 **Buckland** Alaska, USA
182 G7 **Buckleboo** South Australia
26 K7 **Bucklin** Kansas, C USA
27 T3 **Bucklin** Missouri, C USA
36 I12 **Buckskin Mountains** ▲ Arizona, SW USA
19 R7 **Bucksport** Maine, NE USA
82 A9 **Buco Zau** Cabinda, NW Angola
Bu Craa *see* Bou Craa
116 K14 **Bucureşti** *Eng.* Bucharest, *Ger.* Bukarest; *prev.* Altenburg, *anc.* Cetatea Damboviţei. ● (Romania) Bucureşti, S Romania
31 S12 **Bucyrus** Ohio, N USA
Buczacz *see* Buchach
94 E9 **Bud** Møre og Romsdal, S Norway
25 S11 **Buda** Texas, SW USA
119 O18 **Buda-Kashalyova** *Rus.* Buda-Koshelëvo. Homyel'skaya Voblasts', SE Belarus
Buda-Koshelëvo *see* Buda-Kashalyova
166 L4 **Budalin** Sagaing, C Myanmar
111 J22 **Budapest** *off.* Budapest Főváros, *SCr.* Budimpešta. ● (Hungary) Pest, N Hungary
152 K11 **Budaun** Uttar Pradesh, N India
141 O9 **Budayyi'ah** *oasis* C Saudi Arabia
195 Y12 **Budd Coast** *physical region* Antarctica
Buddenbrock *see* Brodnica
107 C17 **Buddusò** Sardegna, Italy, C Mediterranean Sea
97 I23 **Bude** SW England, UK
22 J7 **Bude** Mississippi, S USA
Budějovický Kraj *see* Jihočeský Kraj
99 K16 **Budel** Noord-Brabant, SE Netherlands
100 I8 **Büdelsdorf** Schleswig-Holstein, N Germany
127 O14 **Budënnovsk** Stavropol'skiy Kray, SW Russian Federation
116 K14 **Budeşti** Călăraşi, SE Romania
Budgewoi *see* Budgewoi Lake
183 T8 **Budgewoi Lake** *var.* Budgewoi. New South Wales, SE Australia
92 I2 **Búdhardalur** Vesturland, W Iceland
Budimpešta *see* Budapest
79 J16 **Budjala** Equateur, NW Dem. Rep. Congo
106 G10 **Budrio** Emilia-Romagna, C Italy
Budslav *see* Budslaw
119 K14 **Budslaw** *Rus.* Budslav. Minskaya Voblasts', N Belarus
Budua *see* Budva
169 R9 **Budu, Tanjung** *headland* East Malaysia
113 J17 **Budva** *It.* Budua. Montenegro, SW Serbia and Montenegro (Yugo.)
Budweis *see* České Budějovice
Budyšin *see* Bautzen
79 D16 **Buea** Sud-Ouest, SW Cameroon
103 S13 **Buëch** ∼ SE France
18 J17 **Buena** New Jersey, NE USA
62 K12 **Buena Esperanza** San Luis, C Argentina
54 C11 **Buenaventura** Valle del Cauca, W Colombia
40 I4 **Buenaventura** Chihuahua, N Mexico
57 M18 **Buena Vista** Santa Cruz, C Bolivia
40 G10 **Buenavista** Baja California Sur, W Mexico
37 S5 **Buena Vista** Colorado, C USA
23 S5 **Buena Vista** Georgia, SE USA
21 T6 **Buena Vista** Virginia, NE USA
44 F5 **Buena Vista, Bahia de** *bay* N Cuba
35 R13 **Buena Vista Lake Bed** ◎ California, W USA
105 P8 **Buendía, Embalse de** ⊞ C Spain
63 F16 **Bueno, Río** ∼ S Chile
62 N12 **Buenos Aires** *hist.* Santa Maria del Buen Aire. ● (Argentina) Buenos Aires, E Argentina
43 O15 **Buenos Aires** Puntarenas, SE Costa Rica
61 C20 **Buenos Aires** *off.* Provincia de Buenos Aires. ⬖ *province* E Argentina
63 H19 **Buenos Aires, Lago** *var.* Lago General Carrera. ◎ Argentina/Chile
54 C13 **Buesaco** Nariño, SW Colombia
29 U8 **Buffalo** Minnesota, N USA
26 T6 **Buffalo** Missouri, C USA
18 D10 **Buffalo** New York, NE USA
27 K8 **Buffalo** Oklahoma, C USA
28 J7 **Buffalo** South Dakota, N USA
25 V8 **Buffalo** Texas, SW USA
33 W12 **Buffalo** Wyoming, C USA
29 U11 **Buffalo Center** Iowa, C USA
24 M3 **Buffalo Lake** ⊞ Texas, SW USA
30 K7 **Buffalo Lake** ⊞ Wisconsin, N USA
11 S12 **Buffalo Narrows** Saskatchewan, C Canada
27 U9 **Buffalo River** ∼ Arkansas, C USA
29 R5 **Buffalo River** ∼ Minnesota, N USA
20 I10 **Buffalo River** ∼ Tennessee, S USA
30 J6 **Buffalo River** ∼ Wisconsin, N USA
44 L12 **Buff Bay** E Jamaica
23 T3 **Buford** Georgia, SE USA
28 J3 **Buford** North Dakota, N USA
33 Y17 **Buford** Wyoming, C USA
116 J14 **Buftea** Bucureşti, S Romania
84 I9 **Bug** *Bel.* Zakhodni Buh, *Eng.* Western Bug, *Rus.* Zapadnyy Bug, *Ukr.* Zakhidnyy Buh. ∼ E Europe
54 D11 **Buga** Valle del Cauca, W Colombia
162 F7 **Buga** Dzavhan, W Mongolia
103 O17 **Bugarach, Pic du** ▲ S France
146 B12 **Bugdaýly** *Rus.* Bugdayly. Balkan Welaýaty, W Turkmenistan
Buggs Island Lake *see* John H.Kerr Reservoir
Bughotu *see* Santa Isabel
171 O14 **Bugingkalo** Sulawesi, C Indonesia
64 P6 **Bugio** *island* Madeira, Portugal, NE Atlantic Ocean
92 M8 **Bugøynes** Finnmark, N Norway
125 Q3 **Bugrino** Nenetskiy Avtonomnyy Okrug, NW Russian Federation
127 T5 **Bugul'ma** Respublika Tatarstan, W Russian Federation
Bügür *see* Luntai
127 T6 **Buguruslan** Orenburgskaya Oblast', W Russian Federation
159 R9 **Buh He** ∼ C China
33 O15 **Buhl** Idaho, NW USA
101 F22 **Bühl** Baden-Württemberg, SW Germany
116 K10 **Buhuşi** Bacău, E Romania
Buie d'Istria *see* Buje
97 J20 **Builth Wells** E Wales, UK
186 J8 **Buin** Bougainville Island, NE PNG
108 J9 **Buin, Piz** ▲ Austria/Switzerland
127 Q4 **Buinsk** Chuvashskaya Respublika, W Russian Federation
127 Q4 **Buinsk** Respublika Tatarstan, W Russian Federation
163 R8 **Buir Nur** *Mong.* Buyr Nuur. ◎ China/Mongolia *see also* Buyr Nuur
98 M5 **Buitenpost** *Fris.* Bûtenpost. Friesland, N Netherlands

◆ Country ● Country Capital ◇ Dependent Territory ○ Dependent Territory Capital ⬖ Administrative Region ✕ International Airport ▲ Mountain ▲ Mountain Range ⚲ Volcano ∼ River ◎ Lake ⊞ Reservoir

Buitenzorg see Bogor
83 F19 **Buitepos** Omaheke, E Namibia
105 N7 **Buitrago del Lozoya** Madrid, C Spain
Buj see Buy
104 M13 **Bujalance** Andalucía, S Spain
113 O17 **Bujanovac** Serbia, SE Serbia and Montenegro (Yugo.)
105 S6 **Bujaraloz** Aragón, NE Spain
112 A9 **Buje** *It.* Buie d'Istria. Istra, NW Croatia
Bujnurd see Bojnūrd
81 D21 **Bujumbura** *prev.* Usumbura. ● (Burundi) W Burundi
81 D20 **Bujumbura** ✕ W Burundi
159 N11 **Buka Daban** *var.* Bkadaban Feng. ▲ C China
Bukadaban Feng see Buka Daban
186 J6 **Buka Island** *island* NE PNG
81 F18 **Bukakata** S Uganda
79 N24 **Bukama** Katanga, SE Dem. Rep. Congo
142 J4 **Būkān** *var.* Bowkān. Āžarbāyjān-e Bākhtarī, NW Iran
Bukantau, Gory see Bo'kantov Tog'lari
Bukarest see Bucureşti
79 O19 **Bukavu** *prev.* Costermansville. Sud Kivu, E Dem. Rep. Congo
81 F21 **Bukene** Tabora, NW Tanzania
141 W8 **Bū Khābī** *var.* Bakhābī. NW Oman
Bukhara see Buxoro
Bukharskaya Oblast' see Buxoro Viloyati
146 J11 **Buxoro Viloyati** *Rus.* Bukharskaya Oblast'. ◈ *province* C Uzbekistan
168 M14 **Bukitkemuning** Sumatera, W Indonesia
168 I11 **Bukittinggi** *prev.* Fort de Kock. Sumatera, W Indonesia
111 L21 **Bükk** ⛰ NE Hungary
81 F19 **Bukoba** Kagera, NW Tanzania
113 N20 **Bukovo** S FYR Macedonia
108 G6 **Bülach** Zürich, NW Switzerland
Būlaevo see Bulayevo
162 I6 **Bulag** Hövsgöl, N Mongolia
162 M7 **Bulag** Töv, C Mongolia
162 I8 **Bulagiyn Denj** Arhangay, C Mongolia
183 U7 **Bulahdelah** New South Wales, SE Australia
171 P4 **Bulan** Luzon, N Philippines
137 N11 **Bulancak** Giresun, N Turkey
152 J10 **Bulandshahr** Uttar Pradesh, N India
137 R14 **Bulanık** Muş, E Turkey
127 V7 **Bulanovo** Orenburgskaya Oblast', W Russian Federation
83 J17 **Bulawayo** *var.* Buluwayo. Matabeleland North, SW Zimbabwe
83 J17 **Bulawayo** ✕ Matabeleland North, SW Zimbabwe
145 Q6 **Bulayevo** *Kaz.* Būlaevo. Severnyy Kazakhstan, N Kazakhstan
136 D15 **Buldan** Denizli, SW Turkey
154 G12 **Buldāna** Mahārāshtra, C India
38 E16 **Buldir Island** *island* Aleutian Islands, Alaska, USA
Buldur see Burdur
162 H9 **Bulgan** Bayanhongor, C Mongolia
162 K6 **Bulgan** Bulgan, N Mongolia
162 F7 **Bulgan** Hovd, W Mongolia
162 J5 **Bulgan** Hövsgöl, N Mongolia
162 J10 **Bulgan** Ömnögovĭ, S Mongolia
162 J7 **Bulgan** ◈ *province* N Mongolia
114 H10 **Bulgaria** *off.* Republic of Bulgaria, *Bul.* Bŭlgariya; *prev.* People's Republic of Bulgaria. ◆ *republic* SE Europe
Bŭlgariya see Bulgaria
114 L9 **Bŭlgarka** ▲ E Bulgaria
171 S11 **Buli** Pulau Halmahera, E Indonesia
171 S11 **Buli, Teluk** *bay* Pulau Halmahera, E Indonesia
160 J13 **Buliu He** ≈ S China
Bullange see Büllingen
Bulla, Ostrov see Xärä Zirä Adası
104 M11 **Bullaque** ≈ C Spain
105 Q13 **Bullas** Murcia, SE Spain
80 M12 **Bullaxaar** Woqooyi Galbeed, NW Somalia
108 C9 **Bulle** Fribourg, SW Switzerland
185 G15 **Buller** ≈ South Island, NZ
183 P12 **Buller, Mount** ▲ Victoria, SE Australia
36 H11 **Bullhead City** Arizona, SW USA
99 N21 **Büllingen** *Fr.* Bullange. Liège, E Belgium
Bullion State see Missouri
21 T14 **Bull Island** *island* South Carolina, SE USA
182 M4 **Bulloo River Overflow** *wetland* New South Wales, SE Australia
184 M12 **Bulls** Manawatu-Wanganui, North Island, NZ
21 T14 **Bulls Bay** *bay* South Carolina, SE USA
27 U9 **Bull Shoals Lake** ⊡ Arkansas/Missouri, C USA
181 Q2 **Bulman** Northern Territory, N Australia
162 I6 **Bulnayn Nuruu** ⛰ N Mongolia
171 O11 **Bulowa, Gunung** ▲ Sulawesi, N Indonesia
Bulqiza see Bulqizë
113 L19 **Bulqizë** *var.* Bulqiza. Dibër, C Albania
Bulsar see Valsād
171 N14 **Bulukumba** *prev.* Boeloekoemba. Sulawesi, C Indonesia
79 I21 **Bulungu** Bandundu, SW Dem. Rep. Congo
Bulungur see Bulung'ur
147 O11 **Bulung'ur** *Rus.* Bulungur; *prev.* Krasnogvardeysk. Samarqand Viloyati, C Uzbekistan
Buluwayo see Bulawayo
79 K17 **Bumba** Equateur, N Dem. Rep. Congo
121 R12 **Bumbah, Khalīj al** *gulf* N Libya
162 K8 **Bumbat** Övörhangay, C Mongolia
81 F19 **Bumbire Island** *island* N Tanzania
169 V8 **Bum Bun, Pulau** *island* East Malaysia
81 J17 **Buna** North Eastern, NE Kenya
25 Y10 **Buna** Texas, SW USA
Bunab see Bonāb
Bunai see M'bunai
147 S13 **Bunay** S Tajikistan
180 I13 **Bunbury** Western Australia
97 E14 **Buncrana** *Ir.* Bun Cranncha. NW Ireland
Bun Cranncha see Buncrana
181 Z9 **Bundaberg** Queensland, E Australia
183 T5 **Bundarra** New South Wales, SE Australia
100 G13 **Bünde** Nordrhein-Westfalen, NW Germany
152 H13 **Būndi** Rājasthān, N India
Bun Dobhráin see Bundoran
97 D15 **Bundoran** *Ir.* Bun Dobhráin. NW Ireland
113 K18 **Bunë** *SCr.* Bojana. ≈ Albania/Serbia and Montenegro (Yugo.) **see also** Bojana
171 Q8 **Bunga** ≈ Mindanao, S Philippines
168 I12 **Bungalaut, Selat** *strait* W Indonesia
167 R8 **Bung Kan** Nong Khai, E Thailand
181 N4 **Bungle Bungle Range** ⛰ Western Australia
82 C10 **Bungo** Uíge, NW Angola
81 G18 **Bungoma** Western, W Kenya
164 F15 **Bungo-suidō** *strait* SW Japan
164 E14 **Bungo-Takada** Ōita, Kyūshū, SW Japan
100 K8 **Bungsberg** *hill* N Germany
Bungur see Bunyu
79 P17 **Bunia** Orientale, NE Dem. Rep. Congo
35 U6 **Bunker Hill** ▲ Nevada, W USA
22 I7 **Bunkie** Louisiana, S USA
23 X10 **Bunnell** Florida, SE USA
105 S10 **Buñol** País Valenciano, E Spain
98 K11 **Bunschoten** Utrecht, C Netherlands
136 K14 **Bünyan** Kayseri, C Turkey
169 W8 **Bunyu** *var.* Bungur. Borneo, N Indonesia
169 W8 **Bunyu, Pulau** *island* N Indonesia
Bunzlau see Bolesławiec
Buoddobohki see Patoniva
123 P7 **Buorkhaya Guba** *bay* N Russian Federation
171 Z15 **Bupul** Papua, E Indonesia
81 K19 **Bura** Coast, SE Kenya
80 P12 **Buraan** Sanaag, N Somalia
Būrabay see Borovoye
Buraida see Buraydah
Buraimi see Al Buraymī
145 Y11 **Buran** Vostochnyy Kazakhstan, E Kazakhstan
158 G15 **Burang** Xizang Zizhiqu, W China
Burao see Burco
138 H8 **Burāq** Dar'ā, S Syria
141 O6 **Buraydah** *var.* Buraida. Al Qaşīm, N Saudi Arabia
35 S15 **Burbank** California, W USA
31 N11 **Burbank** Illinois, N USA
183 Q8 **Burcher** New South Wales, SE Australia
80 N13 **Burco** *var.* Burao, Bur'o. Togdheer, NW Somalia
146 L13 **Burdalyk** Lebap Welaýaty, E Turkmenistan
181 W6 **Burdekin River** ≈ Queensland, NE Australia
27 O7 **Burden** Kansas, C USA
Burdigala see Bordeaux
136 E15 **Burdur** *var.* Buldur. Burdur, SW Turkey
136 E15 **Burdur** *var.* Buldur. ◈ *province* SW Turkey
136 E15 **Burdur Gölü** *salt lake* SW Turkey
65 H21 **Burdwood Bank** *undersea feature* SW Atlantic Ocean
80 I12 **Burē** Amhara, N Ethiopia
80 H13 **Burē** Oromo, C Ethiopia
93 J15 **Bureå** Västerbotten, N Sweden
101 G14 **Büren** Nordrhein-Westfalen, W Germany
162 K6 **Bürengiyn Nuruu** ⛰ N Mongolia
162 E8 **Bürenhayrhan** Hovd, W Mongolia
Būrewāla see Mandi Būrewāla
92 J9 **Burfjord** Troms, N Norway
100 L13 **Burg** *var.* Burg an der Ihle, Burg bei Magdeburg. Sachsen-Anhalt, C Germany
Burg an der Ihle see Burg
114 N10 **Burgas** *var.* Bourgas. Burgas, E Bulgaria
114 N9 **Burgas** ✕ Burgas, E Bulgaria
114 M10 **Burgas** ◈ *province* E Bulgaria
114 N10 **Burgaski Zaliv** *gulf* E Bulgaria
114 M10 **Burgasko Ezero** *lagoon* E Bulgaria
21 V11 **Burgaw** North Carolina, SE USA
Burg bei Magdeburg see Burg
108 E8 **Burgdorf** Bern, NW Switzerland
109 Y7 **Burgenland** *off.* Land Burgenland. ◈ *state* SE Austria
13 S13 **Burgeo** Newfoundland and Labrador, SE Canada
83 I24 **Burgersdorp** Eastern Cape, SE South Africa
83 K20 **Burgersfort** Mpumalanga, NE South Africa
101 N23 **Burghausen** Bayern, SE Germany
139 O5 **Burghūth, Sabkhat al** ◎ E Syria
101 M20 **Burglengenfeld** Bayern, SE Germany
41 P9 **Burgos** Tamaulipas, C Mexico
105 N4 **Burgos** Castilla-León, N Spain
105 N4 **Burgos** ◈ *province* Castilla-León, N Spain
Burgstadlberg see Hradiště
95 P20 **Burgsvik** Gotland, SE Sweden
Burgum see Bergum
Burgundy see Bourgogne
159 Q11 **Burhan Budai Shan** ⛰ C China
136 B12 **Burhaniye** Balıkesir, W Turkey
154 G12 **Burhānpur** Madhya Pradesh, C India
127 W7 **Buribay** Respublika Bashkortostan, W Russian Federation
43 O17 **Burica, Punta** *headland* Costa Rica/Panama
167 Q10 **Buriram** *var.* Buri Ram, Puriramya. Buri Ram, E Thailand
105 S10 **Burjassot** País Valenciano, E Spain
81 N16 **Burka Giibi** Hiiraan, C Somalia
147 X8 **Burkan** ≈ E Kyrgyzstan
25 R4 **Burkburnett** Texas, SW USA
29 O12 **Burke** South Dakota, N USA
10 K15 **Burke Channel** *channel* British Columbia, W Canada
194 J10 **Burke Island** *island* Antarctica
20 L7 **Burkesville** Kentucky, S USA
181 T4 **Burketown** Queensland, NE Australia
25 Q8 **Burkett** Texas, SW USA
25 Y9 **Burkeville** Texas, SW USA
21 V7 **Burkeville** Virginia, NE USA
77 O12 **Burkina** *off.* Burkina Faso; *prev.* Upper Volta. ◆ *republic* W Africa
Burkina Faso see Burkina
194 L13 **Burks, Cape** *headland* Antarctica
14 H12 **Burk's Falls** Ontario, S Canada
101 H23 **Burladingen** Baden-Württemberg, S Germany
25 T7 **Burleson** Texas, SW USA
33 P15 **Burley** Idaho, NW USA
144 G8 **Burlin** Zapadnyy Kazakhstan, NW Kazakhstan
14 G16 **Burlington** Ontario, S Canada
37 W4 **Burlington** Colorado, C USA
29 Y15 **Burlington** Iowa, C USA
27 P5 **Burlington** Kansas, C USA
21 T9 **Burlington** North Carolina, SE USA
28 M3 **Burlington** North Dakota, N USA
18 L7 **Burlington** Vermont, NE USA
30 M9 **Burlington** Wisconsin, N USA
27 Q1 **Burlington Junction** Missouri, C USA
Burma see Myanmar
10 L17 **Burnaby** British Columbia, SW Canada
117 O12 **Burnas, Ozero** ◎ SW Ukraine
25 S10 **Burnet** Texas, SW USA
35 O3 **Burney** California, W USA
183 O16 **Burnie** Tasmania, SE Australia
97 L17 **Burnley** NW England, UK
Burnoye see Bauyrzhan Momyshuly
153 R15 **Burnpur** West Bengal, NE India
32 K14 **Burns** Oregon, NW USA
26 K11 **Burns Flat** Oklahoma, C USA
20 M7 **Burnside** Kentucky, S USA
8 K8 **Burnside** ≈ Nunavut, NW Canada
32 L15 **Burns Junction** Oregon, NW USA
10 L13 **Burns Lake** British Columbia, SW Canada
29 V9 **Burnsville** Minnesota, N USA
21 P9 **Burnsville** North Carolina, SE USA
21 R4 **Burnsville** West Virginia, NE USA
14 I13 **Burnt River** ≈ Ontario, SE Canada
14 I11 **Burntroot Lake** ◎ Ontario, SE Canada
11 W12 **Burntwood** ≈ Manitoba, C Canada
Bur'o see Burco
158 L2 **Burqin** Xinjiang Uygur Zizhiqu, NW China
182 J8 **Burra** South Australia
183 S9 **Burragorang, Lake** ⊡ New South Wales, SE Australia
96 K5 **Burray** *island* NE Scotland, UK
113 L19 **Burrel** *var.* Burreli. Dibër, C Albania
Burreli see Burrel
183 R8 **Burrendong Reservoir** ⊡ New South Wales, SE Australia
183 R5 **Burren Junction** New South Wales, SE Australia
105 T9 **Burriana** País Valenciano, E Spain
183 R10 **Burrinjuck Reservoir** ⊡ New South Wales, SE Australia
35 J12 **Burro Creek** ≈ Arizona, SW USA
40 M5 **Burro, Serranías del** ⛰ NW Mexico
62 K7 **Burruyacú** Tucumán, N Argentina
136 E12 **Bursa** *var.* Brussa; *prev.* Brusa, *anc.* Prusa. Bursa, NW Turkey
136 D12 **Bursa** *var.* Brusa, Brussa. ◈ *province* NW Turkey
75 Y9 **Būr Safāga** *var.* Būr Safājah. E Egypt
Būr Safājah see Būr Safāga
Būr Sa'īd see Port Said
81 O14 **Bur Tinle** Mudug, C Somalia
31 Q5 **Burt Lake** ◎ Michigan, N USA
118 H7 **Burtnieks** *var.* Burtnieks Ezers. ◎ N Latvia
Burtnieku Ezers see Burtnieks
31 Q9 **Burton** Michigan, N USA
Burton on Trent see Burton upon Trent
97 M19 **Burton upon Trent** *var.* Burton on Trent, Burton-upon-Trent. C England, UK
93 J15 **Burträsk** Västerbotten, N Sweden
145 S14 **Burubaytal** *prev.* Burylbaytal. Zhambyl, SE Kazakhstan
Burujird see Borūjerd
Burultokay see Fuhai
141 R15 **Burūm** SE Yemen
Burunday see Boralday
81 D21 **Burundi** *off.* Republic of Burundi; *prev.* Kingdom of Burundi, Urundi. ◆ *republic* C Africa
171 R13 **Buru, Pulau** *prev.* Boeroe. *island* E Indonesia
77 T17 **Burutu** Delta, S Nigeria
10 G7 **Burwash Landing** Yukon Territory, W Canada
29 O14 **Burwell** Nebraska, C USA
97 L17 **Bury** NW England, UK
123 N13 **Buryatiya, Respublika** *prev.* Buryatskaya ASSR. ◈ *autonomous republic* S Russian Federation
Buryatskaya ASSR see Buryatiya, Respublika
Burylbaytal see Burubaytal
117 S3 **Buryn'** Sums'ka Oblast', NE Ukraine
97 P20 **Bury St Edmunds** *hist.* Beodericsworth. E England, UK
114 G8 **Bŭrziya** ≈ NW Bulgaria
106 D9 **Busalla** Liguria, NW Italy
Busan see Pusan
139 N5 **Buşayrah** Dayr az Zawr, E Syria
Busayyah see Baba
143 N12 **Būshehr** *off.* Ostān-e Būshehr. ◈ *province* SW Iran
Būshehr/Bushire see Bandar-e Būshehr
25 N2 **Bushland** Texas, SW USA
30 J12 **Bushnell** Illinois, N USA
Busi see Biševo
81 G18 **Busia** SE Uganda
Busiasch see Buziaş
79 K16 **Businga** Equateur, NW Dem. Rep. Congo
79 J18 **Busira** ≈ NW Dem. Rep. Congo
116 I5 **Bus'k** *Rus.* Busk. L'vivs'ka Oblast', W Ukraine
95 E14 **Buskerud** ◈ *county* S Norway
113 F14 **Buško Jezero** ⊡ SW Bosnia and Herzegovina
111 M15 **Busko-Zdrój** Świętokrzyskie, C Poland
Busra see Al Başrah, Iraq
Buşrá see Buşrá ash Shām, Syria
138 H9 **Buşrá ash Shām** *var.* Bosora, Bosra, Bozrah, Buşrá. Dar'ā, S Syria
180 I13 **Busselton** Western Australia
81 C14 **Busseri** ≈ W Sudan
106 E9 **Busseto** Emilia-Romagna, C Italy
106 A8 **Bussoleno** Piemonte, NE Italy
Bussora see Al Başrah
98 J10 **Bussum** Noord-Holland, C Netherlands
41 N7 **Bustamante** Nuevo León, NE Mexico
63 I23 **Bustamante, Punta** *headland* S Argentina
Bustan see Bŭston
116 J12 **Buşteni** Prahova, SE Romania
106 D7 **Busto Arsizio** Lombardia, N Italy
147 Q10 **Bŭston** *Rus.* Buston. NW Tajikistan
100 H8 **Büsum** Schleswig-Holstein, N Germany
79 M16 **Buta** Orientale, N Dem. Rep. Congo
81 E20 **Butare** *prev.* Astrida. S Rwanda
191 O2 **Butaritari** *atoll* Tungaru, W Kiribati
Butawal see Butwal
96 H13 **Bute** *cultural region* SW Scotland, UK
162 K6 **Büteeliyn Nuruu** ⛰ N Mongolia
10 L16 **Bute Inlet** *fjord* British Columbia, W Canada
96 H12 **Bute, Island of** *island* SW Scotland, UK
79 P18 **Butembo** Nord Kivu, NE Dem. Rep. Congo
Butenpost see Bûtenpost
107 K25 **Butera** Sicilia, Italy, C Mediterranean Sea
99 M20 **Bütgenbach** Liège, E Belgium
Butha Qi see Zalantun
166 J5 **Buthidaung** Arakan State, W Myanmar
61 I16 **Butiá** Rio Grande do Sul, S Brazil
81 F17 **Butiaba** NW Uganda
23 N6 **Butler** Alabama, S USA
23 S5 **Butler** Georgia, SE USA
31 Q11 **Butler** Indiana, N USA
27 R5 **Butler** Missouri, C USA
18 B14 **Butler** Pennsylvania, NE USA
194 K5 **Butler Island** *island* Antarctica
21 U8 **Butner** North Carolina, SE USA
171 F14 **Buton, Pulau** *var.* Pulau Butung; *prev.* Boetoeng. *island* C Indonesia
Bütow see Bytów
113 L23 **Butrintit, Liqeni i** ◎ S Albania
23 N3 **Buttahatchee River** ≈ Alabama/Mississippi, S USA
33 Q10 **Butte** Montana, NW USA
29 O12 **Butte** Nebraska, C USA
168 J7 **Butterworth** Pinang, Peninsular Malaysia
83 J25 **Butterworth** *var.* Gcuwa. Eastern Cape, SE South Africa
13 O3 **Button Islands** *island group* Nunavut, NE Canada
35 R13 **Buttonwillow** California, W USA
171 Q7 **Butuan** *off.* Butuan City. Mindanao, S Philippines
Butung, Pulau see Buton, Pulau
Butuntum see Bitonto
126 M8 **Buturlinovka** Voronezhskaya Oblast', W Russian Federation
153 O11 **Butwal** *var.* Butawal. Western, C Nepal
101 G17 **Butzbach** Hessen, W Germany
100 L9 **Bützow** Mecklenburg-Vorpommern, N Germany
80 N13 **Buuhoodle** Togdheer, N Somalia
81 N16 **Buulobarde** *var.* Buulo Berde. Hiiraan, C Somalia
Buulo Berde see Buulobarde
80 P12 **Buuraha Cal Miskaat** ⛰ NE Somalia
81 L19 **Buur Gaabo** Jubbada Hoose, S Somalia
99 M22 **Buurgplaatz** ▲ N Luxembourg
Buwayrāt al Hasūn see Bu'ayrāt al Ḩasūn
146 L11 **Buxoro** *var.* Bokhara, *Rus.* Bukhara. Buxoro Viloyati, C Uzbekistan
100 I10 **Buxtehude** Niedersachsen, NW Germany
97 L18 **Buxton** C England, UK
124 M14 **Buy** *var.* Buj. Kostromskaya Oblast', NW Russian Federation
162 G7 **Buyanbat** Govĭ-Altay, W Mongolia
162 H8 **Buyant** Bayanhongor, C Mongolia
162 D6 **Buyant** Bayan-Ölgiy, W Mongolia
162 H7 **Buyant** Dzavhan, C Mongolia
163 N9 **Buyant** Hentiy, C Mongolia
163 N10 **Buyant-Uhaa** Dornogovĭ, SE Mongolia
162 M7 **Buyant Ukha** ✕ (Ulaanbaatar) Töv, N Mongolia
127 Q16 **Buynaksk** Respublika Dagestan, SW Russian Federation
119 L20 **Buynavichy** *Rus.* Buynovichi. Homyel'skaya Voblasts', SE Belarus
Buynovichi see Buynavichy
76 L16 **Buyo** SW Ivory Coast
76 L16 **Buyo, Lac de** ⊡ W Ivory Coast
163 R7 **Buyr Nuur** *var.* Buir Nur. ◎ China/Mongolia **see also** Buir Nur
137 T13 **Büyükağrı Dağı** *var.* Aghri Dagh, Agri Dagi, Koh I Noh, Masis, *Eng.* Great Ararat, Mount Ararat. ▲ E Turkey
137 R15 **Büyük Çayı** ≈ NE Turkey
114 O13 **Büyük Çekmece** İstanbul, NW Turkey
114 N12 **Büyükkarıştıran** Kırklareli, NW Turkey
115 L14 **Büyükkemikli Burnu** *headland* NW Turkey
136 E15 **Büyükmenderes Nehri** ≈ SW Turkey
Büyükzap Suyu see Great Zab
102 M9 **Buzançais** Indre, C France
116 K13 **Buzău** Buzău, SE Romania
116 K13 **Buzău** ◈ *county* SE Romania
116 L12 **Buzău** ≈ E Romania
75 S11 **Buzaymah** *var.* Bzīmah. SE Libya
164 E13 **Buzen** Fukuoka, Kyūshū, SW Japan
116 F12 **Buziaş** *Ger.* Busiasch, *Hung.* Buziásfürdő; *prev.* Buziás. Timiş, W Romania
Buziásfürdő see Buziaş
83 M18 **Búzi, Rio** ≈ C Mozambique
117 Q10 **Buz'kyy Lyman** *bay* S Ukraine
146 F13 **Büzmeyin** Byuzmeyin; *prev.* Bezmein. Ahal Welaýaty, C Turkmenistan
145 O8 **Buzuluk** Akmola, C Kazakhstan
127 T6 **Buzuluk** Orenburgskaya Oblast', W Russian Federation
127 N8 **Buzuluk** ≈ SW Russian Federation
19 P12 **Buzzards Bay** Massachusetts, NE USA
19 P13 **Buzzards Bay** *bay* Massachusetts, NE USA
83 G16 **Bwabata** Caprivi, NE Namibia
186 H10 **Bwagaoia** Misima Island, SE PNG
Bwake see Bouaké
187 R13 **Bwatnapne** Pentecost, C Vanuatu
119 K14 **Byahoml'** *Rus.* Begoml'. Vitsyebskaya Voblasts', N Belarus
114 J8 **Byala** Ruse, N Bulgaria
114 N9 **Byala** *prev.* Ak-Dere. Varna, E Bulgaria
Byala Reka see Erydropótamos
114 H8 **Byala Slatina** Vratsa, NW Bulgaria
119 N15 **Byalynichy** *Rus.* Belynichi. Mahilyowskaya Voblasts', E Belarus
119 G19 **Byaroza** *Pol.* Bereza Kartuska, *Rus.* Berëza. Brestskaya Voblasts', SW Belarus
Bybles see Jbaïl
111 O14 **Bychawa** Lubelskie, SE Poland
Bychikha see Bychykha
118 N11 **Bychykha** *Rus.* Bychikha. Vitsyebskaya Voblasts', NE Belarus
111 I14 **Byczyna** *Ger.* Pitschen. Opolskie, S Poland
110 I10 **Bydgoszcz** *Ger.* Bromberg. Kujawski-pomorskie, C Poland
119 I17 **Byelaruskaya Hrada** *Rus.* Belorusskaya Gryada. *ridge* N Belarus
119 G18 **Byelavyezhskaya Pushcha** *Pol.* Puszcza Białowieska, *Rus.* Belovezhskaya Pushcha. *forest* Belarus/Poland **see also** Białowieska, Puszcza
119 H15 **Byenyakoni** *Rus.* Benyakoni. Hrodzyenskaya Voblasts', W Belarus
119 M16 **Byerazino** *Rus.* Berezino. Minskaya Voblasts', C Belarus
118 L13 **Byerazino** *Rus.* Berezino. Vitsyebskaya Voblasts', N Belarus
119 L14 **Byerezino** *Rus.* Berezina. ≈ C Belarus
118 M13 **Byeshankovichy** *Rus.* Beshenkovichi. Vitsyebskaya Voblasts', N Belarus
31 U13 **Byesville** Ohio, N USA
119 P18 **Byesyedz'** *Rus.* Besed'. ≈ SE Belarus
119 H19 **Byezdzyezh** *Rus.* Bezdezh. Brestskaya Voblasts', SW Belarus
93 J15 **Bygdeå** Västerbotten, N Sweden
94 F12 **Bygdin** ◎ S Norway
93 J15 **Bygdsiljum** Västerbotten, N Sweden
95 E17 **Bygland** Aust-Agder, S Norway
95 E17 **Byglandsfjord** Aust-Agder, S Norway
119 N16 **Bykhaw** *Rus.* Bykhov. Mahilyowskaya Voblasts', E Belarus
Bykhov see Bykhaw
127 P9 **Bykovo** Volgogradskaya Oblast', SW Russian Federation
123 P7 **Bykovskiy** Respublika Sakha (Yakutiya), NE Russian Federation
195 R12 **Byrd Glacier** *glacier* Antarctica
14 K10 **Byrd, Lac** ◎ Québec, SE Canada
183 P5 **Byrock** New South Wales, SE Australia
30 L10 **Byron** Illinois, N USA
183 V4 **Byron Bay** New South Wales, SE Australia
183 V4 **Byron, Cape** *headland* New South Wales, E Australia
63 F21 **Byron, Isla** *island* S Chile
Byron Island see Nikunau
65 B24 **Byron Sound** *sound* NW Falkland Islands
122 M6 **Byrranga, Gora** ⛰ N Russian Federation
93 J14 **Byske** Västerbotten, N Sweden
111 K18 **Bystrá** ▲ N Slovakia
111 F18 **Bystřice nad Pernštejnem** *Ger.* Bistritz ober Pernstein. Vysočina, C Czech Republic
Bystrovka see Kemin
111 G16 **Bystrzyca Kłodzka** *Ger.* Habelschwerdt. Wałbrzych, SW Poland
111 I18 **Bytča** Žilinský Kraj, N Slovakia
119 L15 **Bytcha** *Rus.* Bytcha. Minskaya Voblasts', NE Belarus
Byteń/Byten' see Bytsyen'
111 J16 **Bytom** *Ger.* Beuthen. Śląskie, S Poland
110 H7 **Bytów** *Ger.* Bütow. Pomorskie, N Poland
119 H18 **Bytsyen'** *Pol.* Byteń, *Rus.* Byten'. Brestskaya Voblasts', SW Belarus
81 E19 **Byumba** *var.* Biumba. N Rwanda
Byuzmeyin see Büzmeyin
119 O20 **Byval'ki** Homyel'skaya Voblasts', SE Belarus
95 O20 **Byxelkrok** Kalmar, S Sweden
Byzantium see İstanbul
Bzīmah see Buzaymah

C

62 O6 **Caacupé** Cordillera, S Paraguay
62 P6 **Caaguazú** *off.* Departamento de Caaguazú. ◈ *department* C Paraguay
82 C13 **Caála** *var.* Kaala, *Port.* Vila Robert Williams. Huambo, C Angola
62 P7 **Caazapá** Caazapá, S Paraguay
62 P7 **Caazapá** *off.* Departamento de Caazapá. ◈ *department* SE Paraguay
81 P15 **Cabaad, Raas** *headland* C Somalia
55 N10 **Cabadisocaña** Amazonas, S Venezuela
44 F5 **Cabaiguán** Sancti Spíritus, C Cuba
Caballeria, Cabo see Cavalleria, Cap de
37 Q14 **Caballo Reservoir** ⊡ New Mexico, SW USA
40 L6 **Caballos Mesteños, Llano de los** *plain* N Mexico
104 L2 **Cabañaquinta** Asturias, N Spain
42 B9 **Cabañas** ◈ *department* E El Salvador
171 O3 **Cabanatuan** *off.* Cabanatuan City. Luzon, N Philippines
15 T8 **Cabano** Québec, SE Canada
104 L11 **Cabeza del Buey** Extremadura, W Spain
45 V5 **Cabezas de San Juan** *headland* E Puerto Rico
105 N2 **Cabezón de la Sal** Cantabria, N Spain
Cabhán see Cavan
61 B23 **Cabildo** Buenos Aires, E Argentina
Cabillonum see Chalon-sur-Saône
54 H5 **Cabimas** Zulia, NW Venezuela
82 A9 **Cabinda** *var.* Kabinda. Cabinda, NW Angola
82 A9 **Cabinda** *var.* Kabinda. ◈ *province* NW Angola
33 N7 **Cabinet Mountains** ⛰ Idaho/Montana, NW USA
82 B11 **Cabiri** Bengo, NW Angola
63 J20 **Cabo Blanco** Santa Cruz, SE Argentina
82 P13 **Cabo Delgado** *off.* Província de Capo Delgado. ◈ *province* NE Mozambique
14 L9 **Cabonga, Réservoir** ⊡ Québec, SE Canada
27 V7 **Cabool** Missouri, C USA
183 V2 **Caboolture** Queensland, E Australia
Cabora Bassa, Lake see Cahora Bassa, Albufeira de

◆ Country ● Country Capital ◇ Dependent Territory ○ Dependent Territory Capital ◈ Administrative Region ✕ International Airport ▲ Mountain ⛰ Mountain Range ⊼ Volcano ≈ River ◎ Lake ⊡ Reservoir

40 F3 **Caborca** Sonora, NW Mexico
Cabo San Lucas see San Lucas
27 V11 **Cabot** Arkansas, C USA
14 F12 **Cabot Head** headland Ontario, S Canada
13 R13 **Cabot Strait** strait E Canada
Cabo Verde, Ilhas do see Cape Verde
104 M14 **Cabra** Andalucía, S Spain
107 B19 **Cabras** Sardegna, Italy, C Mediterranean Sea
188 A15 **Cabras Island** island W Guam
45 O8 **Cabrera** N Dominican Republic
105 X10 **Cabrera** anc. Capraria. island Islas Baleares, Spain, W Mediterranean Sea
104 J4 **Cabrera** ≈ NW Spain
105 Q15 **Cabrera, Sierra** ▲ S Spain
11 S16 **Cabri** Saskatchewan, S Canada
105 R10 **Cabriel** ≈ E Spain
54 M7 **Cabruta** Guárico, C Venezuela
171 N2 **Cabugao** Luzon, N Philippines
59 G10 **Cabuyaro** Meta, C Colombia
60 I13 **Caçador** Santa Catarina, S Brazil
42 G8 **Cacaguatique, Cordillera** var. Cordillera. ▲ NE El Salvador
112 L13 **Čačak** Serbia, C Serbia and Montenegro (Yugo.)
55 Y10 **Cacao** NE French Guiana
61 H16 **Caçapava do Sul** Rio Grande do Sul, S Brazil
21 U3 **Cacapon River** ≈ West Virginia, NE USA
107 J23 **Caccamo** Sicilia, Italy, C Mediterranean Sea
107 A17 **Caccia, Capo** headland Sardegna, Italy, C Mediterranean Sea
146 H15 **Çäçe** var. Chäche, Rus. Chaacha. Ahal Welaýaty, S Turkmenistan
59 G18 **Cáceres** Mato Grosso, W Brazil
104 J10 **Cáceres** Ar. Qazris. Extremadura, W Spain
104 J9 **Cáceres** ◈ province Extremadura, W Spain
Cachacrou see Scotts Head Village
61 C21 **Cacharí** Buenos Aires, E Argentina
26 L12 **Cache** Oklahoma, C USA
10 M16 **Cache Creek** British Columbia, SW Canada
35 N6 **Cache Creek** ≈ California, W USA
37 S3 **Cache La Poudre River** ≈ Colorado, C USA
Cacheo see Cacheu
27 W11 **Cache River** ≈ Arkansas, C USA
30 L17 **Cache River** ≈ Illinois, N USA
76 G12 **Cacheu** var. Cacheo. W Guinea-Bissau
59 I15 **Cachimbo** Pará, NE Brazil
59 H15 **Cachimbo, Serra do** ▲ C Brazil
82 D13 **Cachingues** Bié, C Angola
54 G7 **Cáchira** Norte de Santander, N Colombia
61 H16 **Cachoeira do Sul** Rio Grande do Sul, S Brazil
59 O20 **Cachoeiro de Itapemirim** Espírito Santo, SE Brazil
82 E12 **Cacolo** Lunda Sul, NE Angola
83 C14 **Caconda** Huíla, C Angola
82 A9 **Cacongo** Cabinda, NW Angola
35 U9 **Cactus Peak** ▲ Nevada, W USA
82 A11 **Cacuaco** Luanda, NW Angola
83 B14 **Cacula** Huíla, SW Angola
67 R12 **Caculuvar** ≈ SW Angola
59 O19 **Caçumba, Ilha** island SE Brazil
55 N10 **Cacuri** Amazonas, S Venezuela
81 N17 **Cadale** Shabeellaha Dhexe, E Somalia
105 X4 **Cadaqués** Cataluña, NE Spain
111 J18 **Čadca** Hung. Csaca. Žilinský Kraj, N Slovakia
27 P13 **Caddo** Oklahoma, C USA
25 R6 **Caddo** Texas, SW USA
25 X6 **Caddo Lake** ▣ Louisiana/Texas, SW USA
27 S12 **Caddo Mountains** ▲ Arkansas, C USA
41 O8 **Cadereyta** Nuevo León, NE Mexico
97 J19 **Cader Idris** ▲ NW Wales, United Kingdom
182 F3 **Cadibarrawirracanna, Lake** salt lake South Australia
14 I7 **Cadillac** Québec, SE Canada
11 T17 **Cadillac** Saskatchewan, S Canada
102 K13 **Cadillac** Gironde, SW France
31 P7 **Cadillac** Michigan, N USA
105 V4 **Cadí, Torre de** ▲ NE Spain
171 P5 **Cadiz** off. Cadiz City. Negros, C Philippines
20 H7 **Cadiz** Kentucky, S USA
31 U13 **Cadiz** Ohio, N USA
104 J15 **Cádiz** anc. Gades, Gadier, Gadir, Gadire. Andalucía, SW Spain
104 K15 **Cádiz** ◈ province Andalucía, SW Spain
104 I15 **Cadiz, Bahía de** bay SW Spain
Cadiz City see Cadiz
104 H15 **Cádiz, Golfo de** Eng. Gulf of Cadiz. gulf Portugal/Spain
Cadiz, Gulf of see Cádiz, Golfo de
35 X14 **Cadiz Lake** ◎ California, W USA
182 E2 **Cadney Homestead** South Australia
Cadurcum see Cahors
83 F17 **Caecae** Ngamiland, NW Botswana
102 K4 **Caen** Calvados, N France
Caene/Caenepolis see Qena
Caerdydd see Cardiff
Caer Glou see Gloucester
Caer Gybi see Holyhead
Caerleon see Chester
Caer Luel see Carlisle
97 I18 **Caernarfon** var. Caernarvon, Carnarvon. NW Wales, UK
97 H18 **Caernarfon Bay** bay NW Wales, UK
97 I19 **Caernarvon** cultural region NW Wales, UK
Caernarvon see Caernarfon
Caesaraugusta see Zaragoza
Caesarea Mazaca see Kayseri
Caesarobriga see Talavera de la Reina
Caesarodunum see Tours
Caesaromagus see Beauvais
Caesena see Cesena
59 N17 **Caetité** Bahia, E Brazil
62 J6 **Cafayate** Salta, N Argentina
171 O2 **Cagayan** ≈ Luzon, N Philippines
171 Q7 **Cagayan de Oro** off. Cagayan de Oro City. Mindanao, S Philippines
170 M8 **Cagayan de Tawi Tawi** island S Philippines
171 N6 **Cagayan Islands** island group C Philippines
31 O14 **Cagles Mill Lake** ▣ Indiana, N USA
106 I12 **Cagli** Marche, C Italy
107 C20 **Cagliari** anc. Caralis. Sardegna, Italy, C Mediterranean Sea
107 C20 **Cagliari, Golfo di** gulf Sardegna, Italy, C Mediterranean Sea
103 U15 **Cagnes-sur-Mer** Alpes-Maritimes, SE France
54 L5 **Cagua** Aragua, N Venezuela
171 O1 **Cagua, Mount** ▲ Luzon, N Philippines
54 F13 **Caguán, Río** ≈ SW Colombia
45 U6 **Caguas** E Puerto Rico
146 C9 **Çagyl** Rus. Chagyl. Balkan Welaýaty, NW Turkmenistan
23 P5 **Cahaba River** ≈ Alabama, S USA
42 E5 **Cahabón, Río** ≈ C Guatemala
83 B15 **Cahama** Cunene, SW Angola
97 B21 **Caha Mountains** Ir. An Cheacha. ▲ SW Ireland
97 D20 **Caher** Ir. An Cathair. S Ireland
97 A21 **Cahersiveen** Ir. Cathair Saidhbhín. SW Ireland
30 K15 **Cahokia** Illinois, N USA
83 L15 **Cahora Bassa, Albufeira de** var. Lake Cabora Bassa. ▣ NW Mozambique
97 G20 **Cahore Point** Ir. Rinn Chathóir. headland SE Ireland
102 M14 **Cahors** anc. Cadurcum. Lot, S France
56 D9 **Cahuapanas, Río** ≈ N Peru
116 M12 **Cahul** Rus. Kagul. S Moldova
Cahul, Lacul see Kahul, Ozero
83 N16 **Caia** Sofala, C Mozambique
59 J19 **Caiapó, Serra do** ▲ C Brazil
44 F5 **Caibarién** Villa Clara, C Cuba
55 O5 **Caicara** Monagas, NE Venezuela
54 L5 **Caicara del Orinoco** Bolívar, C Venezuela
59 P14 **Caicó** Rio Grande do Norte, E Brazil
44 M6 **Caicos Islands** island group W Turks and Caicos Islands
44 L5 **Caicos Passage** strait Bahamas/Turks and Caicos Islands
161 O9 **Caidian** prev. Hanyang. Hubei, C China
Caiffa see Hefa
180 M12 **Caiguna** Western Australia
Caillí, Ceann see Hag's Head
40 J11 **Caimanero, Laguna del** var. Laguna del Camaronero. lagoon E Pacific Ocean
117 N10 **Căinari** Rus. Kaynary. C Moldova
57 L19 **Caine, Río** ≈ C Bolivia
Caiphas see Hefa
195 N4 **Caird Coast** physical region Antarctica
96 J9 **Cairn Gorm** ▲ C Scotland, UK
96 J9 **Cairngorm Mountains** ▲ C Scotland, UK
39 P12 **Cairn Mountain** ▲ Alaska, USA
181 W4 **Cairns** Queensland, NE Australia
121 V13 **Cairo** Ar. Al Qāhirah, var. El Qâhira. ● (Egypt) N Egypt
23 T8 **Cairo** Georgia, SE USA
30 L17 **Cairo** Illinois, N USA
75 V8 **Cairo** ✕ C Egypt
Caiseal see Cashel
Caisleán an Bharraigh see Castlebar
Caisleán na Finne see Castlefinn
96 J6 **Caithness** cultural region N Scotland, UK
83 D15 **Caiundo** Cuando Cubango, S Angola
56 C11 **Cajamarca** prev. Caxamarca. Cajamarca, NW Peru
56 B11 **Cajamarca** off. Departamento de Cajamarca. ◈ department N Peru
103 N14 **Cajarc** Lot, S France
42 G6 **Cajón, Represa El** ▣ NW Honduras
58 N12 **Caju, Ilha do** island NE Brazil
Cakaubalavu Reef see Kavukavu Reef
159 R10 **Caka Yanhu** ◎ C China
112 E7 **Čakovec** Ger. Csakathurn, Hung. Csáktornya; prev. Ger. Tschakathurn. Međimurje, N Croatia
77 V17 **Calabar** Cross River, S Nigeria
14 K13 **Calabogie** Ontario, SE Canada
54 L6 **Calabozo** Guárico, C Venezuela
107 N20 **Calabria** anc. Bruttium. ◈ region SW Italy
104 M16 **Calaburra, Punta de** headland S Spain
116 G14 **Calafat** Dolj, SW Romania
Calafate see El Calafate
105 Q4 **Calahorra** La Rioja, N Spain
103 N1 **Calais** Pas-de-Calais, N France
19 T5 **Calais** Maine, NE USA
Calais, Pas de see Dover, Strait of
Calalen see Kallalen
62 H4 **Calama** Antofagasta, N Chile
Calamianes see Calamian Group
170 M5 **Calamian Group** var. Calamianes. island group W Philippines
105 R7 **Calamocha** Aragón, NE Spain
29 N14 **Calamus River** ≈ Nebraska, C USA
116 G12 **Călan** Ger. Kalan, Hung. Pusztakalán. Hunedoara, SW Romania
105 S7 **Calanda** Aragón, NE Spain
168 F9 **Calang** Sumatera, W Indonesia
171 N4 **Calapan** Mindoro, N Philippines
Călăras see Călărași
116 M9 **Călărași** var. Călăras, Rus. Kalarash. C Moldova
116 L14 **Călărași** Călărași, SE Romania
116 K14 **Călărași** ◈ county SE Romania
54 E10 **Calarca** Quindío, W Colombia
105 Q12 **Calasparra** Murcia, SE Spain
107 I23 **Calatafimi** Sicilia, Italy, C Mediterranean Sea
105 Q6 **Calatayud** Aragón, NE Spain
171 O4 **Calauag** Luzon, N Philippines
35 P8 **Calaveras River** ≈ California, W USA
171 N4 **Calavite, Cape** headland Mindoro, N Philippines
171 Q8 **Calbayog** off. Calbayog City. Samar, C Philippines
22 G9 **Calcasieu Lake** ◎ Louisiana, S USA
22 H8 **Calcasieu River** ≈ Louisiana, S USA
56 B6 **Calceta** Manabí, W Ecuador
61 B16 **Calchaquí** Santa Fe, C Argentina
62 J6 **Calchaquí, Río** ≈ NW Argentina
58 J10 **Calçoene** Amapá, NE Brazil
153 S16 **Calcutta** West Bengal, NE India
153 S16 **Calcutta** ✕ West Bengal, N India
54 E9 **Caldas** off. Departamento de Caldas. ◈ province W Colombia
104 F10 **Caldas da Rainha** Leiria, W Portugal
104 G3 **Caldas de Reis** var. Caldas de Reyes. Galicia, NW Spain
Caldas de Reyes see Caldas de Reis
58 F13 **Caldeirão** Amazonas, NW Brazil
62 G7 **Caldera** Atacama, N Chile
42 L14 **Caldera** Puntarenas, W Costa Rica
105 N10 **Calderina** ▲ C Spain
137 T13 **Çaldıran** Van, E Turkey
32 M14 **Caldwell** Idaho, NW USA
27 N8 **Caldwell** Kansas, C USA
14 G15 **Caledon** Ontario, S Canada
83 I23 **Caledon** var. Mohokare. ≈ Lesotho/South Africa
42 G1 **Caledonia** Corozal, N Belize
14 G16 **Caledonia** Ontario, S Canada
29 X11 **Caledonia** Minnesota, N USA
105 X5 **Calella** var. Calella de la Costa. Cataluña, NE Spain
Calella de la Costa see Calella
23 P4 **Calera** Alabama, S USA
63 I19 **Caleta Olivia** Santa Cruz, SE Argentina
35 X17 **Calexico** California, W USA
97 H16 **Calf of Man** island SW Isle of Man
11 Q16 **Calgary** Alberta, SW Canada
11 Q16 **Calgary** ✕ Alberta, SW Canada
37 U5 **Calhan** Colorado, C USA
64 O5 **Calheta** Madeira, Portugal, NE Atlantic Ocean
23 R2 **Calhoun** Georgia, SE USA
20 I6 **Calhoun** Kentucky, S USA
22 M3 **Calhoun City** Mississippi, S USA
21 P12 **Calhoun Falls** South Carolina, SE USA
54 D11 **Cali** Valle del Cauca, W Colombia
27 V9 **Calico Rock** Arkansas, C USA
155 F21 **Calicut** var. Kozhikode. Kerala, SW India
35 Y9 **Caliente** Nevada, W USA
27 U5 **California** Missouri, C USA
18 B15 **California** Pennsylvania, NE USA
35 Q12 **California** off. State of California; also known as El Dorado, The Golden State. ◈ state W USA
35 P11 **California Aqueduct** aqueduct California, W USA
35 T13 **California City** California, W USA
40 F6 **California, Golfo de** Eng. Gulf of California; prev. Sea of Cortez. gulf W Mexico
California, Gulf of see California, Golfo de
137 Y13 **Cälilabad** Rus. Dzhalilabad; prev. Astrakhan-Bazar. S Azerbaijan
116 I12 **Călimănești** Vâlcea, SW Romania
116 J9 **Călimani, Munții** ▲ N Romania
Calinisc see Cupcina
35 X17 **Calipatria** California, W USA
Calisia see Kalisz
34 M7 **Calistoga** California, W USA
83 G25 **Calitzdorp** Western Cape, SW South Africa
41 W12 **Calkiní** Campeche, E Mexico
182 K4 **Callabonna Creek** var. Tilcha Creek. seasonal river New South Wales/South Australia
182 J4 **Callabonna, Lake** ◎ South Australia
102 G5 **Callac** Côtes d'Armor, NW France
35 U5 **Callaghan, Mount** ▲ Nevada, W USA
Callain see Callan
97 E19 **Callan** Ir. Callain. S Ireland
14 H11 **Callander** Ontario, S Canada
96 I11 **Callander** C Scotland, UK
98 H7 **Callantsoog** Noord-Holland, NW Netherlands
57 D14 **Callao** Callao, W Peru
57 D15 **Callao** off. Departamento del Callao. ◈ constitutional province W Peru
56 F11 **Callaria, Río** ≈ E Peru
Callatis see Mangalia
11 Q13 **Calling Lake** Alberta, W Canada
Callosa de Ensarriá see Callosa d'En Sarrià
105 T11 **Callosa d'En Sarrià** var. Callosa de Ensarriá. País Valenciano, E Spain
105 S12 **Callosa de Segura** País Valenciano, E Spain
29 X11 **Calmar** Iowa, C USA
Calmar see Kalmar
43 R16 **Calobre** Veraguas, C Panama
23 X14 **Caloosahatchee River** ≈ Florida, SE USA
183 V2 **Caloundra** Queensland, E Australia
Calp see Calpe
105 T11 **Calpe** Cat. Calp. País Valenciano, E Spain
41 P14 **Calpulalpan** Tlaxcala, S Mexico
107 K25 **Caltagirone** Sicilia, Italy, C Mediterranean Sea
107 J24 **Caltanissetta** Sicilia, Italy, C Mediterranean Sea
82 E11 **Caluango** Lunda Norte, NE Angola
82 C12 **Calucinga** Bié, W Angola
82 B12 **Calulo** Cuanza Sul, NW Angola
83 B14 **Caluquembe** Huíla, W Angola
80 Q11 **Caluula** Bari, NE Somalia
102 K4 **Calvados** ◈ department N France
186 I10 **Calvados Chain, The** island group SE PNG
25 U9 **Calvert** Texas, SW USA
20 H7 **Calvert City** Kentucky, S USA
103 X14 **Calvi** Corse, France, C Mediterranean Sea
40 L12 **Calvillo** Aguascalientes, C Mexico
83 F24 **Calvinia** Northern Cape, W South Africa
104 K8 **Calvitero** ▲ W Spain
101 G22 **Calw** Baden-Württemberg, SW Germany
Calydon see Kalydón
105 N11 **Calzada de Calatrava** Castilla-La Mancha, C Spain
Cama see Kama
82 C11 **Camabatela** Cuanza Norte, NW Angola
64 Q5 **Camacha** Porto Santo, Madeira, Portugal, NE Atlantic Ocean
14 L8 **Camachigama, Lac** ◎ Québec, SE Canada
40 M9 **Camacho** Zacatecas, C Mexico
82 D13 **Camacupa** var. General Machado, Port. Vila General Machado. Bié, C Angola
54 L7 **Camaguán** Guárico, C Venezuela
44 G6 **Camagüey** prev. Puerto Príncipe. Camagüey, C Cuba
44 G5 **Camagüey, Archipiélago de** island group C Cuba
40 D5 **Camallí, Sierra de** ▲ NW Mexico
57 G18 **Camana** var. Camaná. Arequipa, SW Peru
29 Z14 **Camanche** Iowa, C USA
35 P8 **Camanche Reservoir** ▣ California, W USA
61 I16 **Camaquã** Rio Grande do Sul, S Brazil
61 H16 **Camaquã, Rio** ≈ S Brazil
64 P6 **Câmara de Lobos** Madeira, Portugal, NE Atlantic Ocean
103 U16 **Camarat, Cap** headland SE France
41 O8 **Camargo** Tamaulipas, C Mexico
103 R15 **Camargue** physical region SE France
104 F2 **Camariñas** Galicia, NW Spain
Camaronero, Laguna del see Caimanero, Laguna del
63 J18 **Camarones** Chaco, S Argentina
63 J18 **Camarones, Bahía** bay S Argentina
104 J14 **Camas** Andalucía, S Spain
167 S15 **Ca Mau** prev. Quan Long. Minh Hai, S Vietnam
82 E11 **Camaxilo** Lunda Norte, NE Angola
104 G3 **Cambados** Galicia, NW Spain
Cambay, Gulf of see Khambhāt, Gulf of
Camberia see Chambéry
97 N22 **Camberley** SE England, UK
167 R12 **Cambodia** off. Kingdom of Cambodia, var. Democratic Kampuchea, Roat Kampuchea, Cam. Kampuchea; prev. People's Democratic Republic of Kampuchea. ◆ republic SE Asia
102 I16 **Cambo-les-Bains** Pyrénées-Atlantiques, SW France
103 P2 **Cambrai** Flem. Kambryk; prev. Cambray, anc. Cameracum. Nord, N France
Cambray see Cambrai
104 H2 **Cambre** Galicia, NW Spain
35 O12 **Cambria** California, W USA
97 J20 **Cambrian Mountains** ▲ C Wales, UK
14 G16 **Cambridge** Ontario, S Canada
44 I12 **Cambridge** W Jamaica
184 M8 **Cambridge** Waikato, North Island, NZ
97 O20 **Cambridge** Lat. Cantabrigia. E England, UK
32 M12 **Cambridge** Idaho, NW USA
30 K11 **Cambridge** Illinois, N USA
21 Y4 **Cambridge** Maryland, NE USA
19 O11 **Cambridge** Massachusetts, NE USA
29 V7 **Cambridge** Minnesota, N USA
29 N16 **Cambridge** Nebraska, C USA
31 U13 **Cambridge** Ohio, NE USA
8 L7 **Cambridge Bay** Victoria Island, Nunavut, NW Canada
97 O20 **Cambridgeshire** cultural region E England, UK
105 U6 **Cambrils de Mar** Cataluña, NE Spain
Cambundi-Catembo see Nova Gaia
137 N11 **Çam Burnu** headland N Turkey
183 S9 **Camden** New South Wales, SE Australia
23 O6 **Camden** Alabama, S USA
27 U14 **Camden** Arkansas, C USA
21 Y3 **Camden** Delaware, NE USA
19 R7 **Camden** Maine, NE USA
18 I16 **Camden** New Jersey, NE USA
18 I9 **Camden** New York, NE USA
21 R12 **Camden** South Carolina, SE USA
20 H8 **Camden** Tennessee, S USA
25 X9 **Camden** Texas, SW USA
39 S5 **Camden Bay** bay S Beaufort Sea
27 U6 **Camdenton** Missouri, C USA
Camellia State see Alabama
18 M7 **Camels Hump** ▲ Vermont, NE USA
117 N8 **Camenca** Rus. Kamenka. N Moldova
Cameracum see Cambrai
22 G9 **Cameron** Louisiana, S USA
25 T9 **Cameron** Texas, SW USA
30 J5 **Cameron** Wisconsin, N USA
10 M12 **Cameron** ≈ British Columbia, W Canada
185 A24 **Cameron Mountains** ▲ South Island, NZ
79 D15 **Cameroon** off. Republic of Cameroon, Fr. Cameroun. ◆ republic W Africa
79 D15 **Cameroon Mountain** ▲ SW Cameroon
Cameroon Ridge see Camerounaise, Dorsale
Cameroun see Cameroon
79 E14 **Camerounaise, Dorsale** Eng. Cameroon Ridge. ridge NW Cameroon
171 N3 **Camiling** Luzon, N Philippines
23 T7 **Camilla** Georgia, SE USA
104 G5 **Caminha** Viana do Castelo, N Portugal
35 P7 **Camino** California, W USA
136 B15 **Çamiçi Gölü** ◎ SW Turkey
107 J24 **Cammarata** Sicilia, Italy, C Mediterranean Sea
42 K10 **Camoapa** Boaco, S Nicaragua
58 O13 **Camocim** Ceará, E Brazil
106 D10 **Camogli** Liguria, NW Italy
181 S5 **Camooweal** Queensland, C Australia
55 Y11 **Camopi** E French Guiana
151 Q22 **Camorta** island Nicobar Islands, India, NE Indian Ocean
42 I6 **Campamento** Olancho, C Honduras
61 D19 **Campana** Buenos Aires, E Argentina
63 F21 **Campana, Isla** island S Chile
104 K11 **Campanario** Extremadura, W Spain
107 L17 **Campania** Eng. Champagne. ◈ region S Italy
27 Y8 **Campbell** Missouri, C USA
185 K15 **Campbell, Cape** headland South Island, NZ
14 J14 **Campbellford** Ontario, SE Canada
31 R13 **Campbell Hill** hill Ohio, N USA
192 K13 **Campbell Island** island S NZ
175 P13 **Campbell Plateau** undersea feature SW Pacific Ocean
10 K17 **Campbell River** Vancouver Island, British Columbia, SW Canada
20 L6 **Campbellsville** Kentucky, S USA
13 O13 **Campbellton** New Brunswick, SE Canada
183 P16 **Campbell Town** Tasmania, SE Australia
183 S9 **Campbelltown** New South Wales, SE Australia
96 G13 **Campbeltown** W Scotland, UK
41 W13 **Campeche** Campeche, SE Mexico
41 W14 **Campeche** ◈ state SE Mexico
41 T14 **Campeche, Bahía de** Eng. Bay of Campeche. bay E Mexico
Campeche, Banco de see Campeche Bank
64 C11 **Campeche Bank** Sp. Banco de Campeche, Sonda de Campeche. undersea feature S Gulf of Mexico
Campeche, Bay of see Campeche, Bahía de
Campeche, Sonda de see Campeche Bank
44 H7 **Campechuela** Granma, E Cuba
182 M13 **Camperdown** Victoria, SE Australia
167 U6 **Cẩm Phả** Quang Ninh, N Vietnam
116 H10 **Câmpia Turzii** Ger. Jerischmarkt, Hung. Aranyosgyéres; prev. Cîmpia Turzii, Ghiriș, Gyéres. Cluj, NW Romania
104 K12 **Campillo de Llerena** Extremadura, W Spain
104 L15 **Campillos** Andalucía, S Spain
116 J13 **Câmpina** prev. Cîmpina. Prahova, SE Romania
59 Q15 **Campina Grande** Paraíba, E Brazil
60 L9 **Campinas** São Paulo, S Brazil
38 L10 **Camp Kulowiye** Saint Lawrence Island, Alaska, USA
79 D17 **Campo** var. Kampo. Sud, SW Cameroon
Campo see Ntem
59 N15 **Campo Alegre de Lourdes** Bahia, E Brazil
107 L16 **Campobasso** Molise, C Italy
107 H24 **Campobello di Mazara** Sicilia, Italy, C Mediterranean Sea
Campo Criptana see Campo de Criptana
105 O10 **Campo de Criptana** var. Campo Criptana. Castilla-La Mancha, C Spain
59 I16 **Campo de Diauarum** var. Pôsto Diuarum. Mato Grosso, W Brazil
54 E5 **Campo de la Cruz** Atlántico, N Colombia
105 P11 **Campo de Montiel** physical region C Spain
Campo dos Goitacazes see Campos
60 H12 **Campo Erê** Santa Catarina, S Brazil
62 L7 **Campo Gallo** Santiago del Estero, N Argentina
59 I20 **Campo Grande** state capital Mato Grosso do Sul, SW Brazil
60 K12 **Campo Largo** Paraná, S Brazil
58 N13 **Campo Maior** Piauí, E Brazil
104 I10 **Campo Maior** Portalegre, C Portugal
60 H10 **Campo Mourão** Paraná, S Brazil
60 Q9 **Campos** var. Campo dos Goitacazes. Rio de Janeiro, SE Brazil
59 L17 **Campos Belos** Goiás, S Brazil
60 N9 **Campos do Jordão** São Paulo, S Brazil
60 I13 **Campos Novos** Santa Catarina, S Brazil
59 O14 **Campos Sales** Ceará, E Brazil
25 Q9 **Camp San Saba** Texas, SW USA
21 N6 **Campton** Kentucky, S USA
116 I13 **Câmpulung** prev. Câmpulung-Mușcel, Cîmpulung. Argeș, S Romania
116 J9 **Câmpulung Moldovenesc** var. Cîmpulung Moldovenesc, Ger. Kimpolung, Hung. Hosszúmezjő. Suceava, NE Romania
Câmpulung-Mușcel see Câmpulung
Campus Stellae see Santiago
36 L12 **Camp Verde** Arizona, SW USA
25 P11 **Camp Wood** Texas, SW USA
167 V13 **Cam Ranh** Khanh Hoa, S Vietnam
11 Q15 **Camrose** Alberta, SW Canada
Camulodunum see Colchester
136 B12 **Çan** Çanakkale, NW Turkey
18 L12 **Canaan** Connecticut, NE USA
9 O13 **Canada** ◆ commonwealth republic N North America
197 P6 **Canada Basin** undersea feature Arctic Ocean
61 B18 **Cañada de Gómez** Santa Fe, C Argentina
197 P6 **Canada Plain** undersea feature Arctic Ocean
61 A18 **Cañada Rosquín** Santa Fe, C Argentina
25 P1 **Canadian** Texas, SW USA
16 K12 **Canadian River** ≈ SW USA
8 L12 **Canadian Shield** physical region Canada
63 I18 **Cañadón Grande, Sierra** ▲ S Argentina
55 P9 **Canaima** Bolívar, SE Venezuela
136 B11 **Çanakkale** var. Dardanelli; prev. Chanak, Kale Sultanie. Çanakkale, W Turkey
136 B12 **Çanakkale** ◈ province NW Turkey
136 B11 **Çanakkale Boğazı** Eng. Dardanelles. strait NW Turkey
187 Q17 **Canala** Province Nord, C New Caledonia
59 A15 **Canamari** Amazonas, W Brazil
18 G10 **Canandaigua** New York, NE USA
18 F10 **Canandaigua Lake** ◎ New York, NE USA
40 G3 **Cananea** Sonora, NW Mexico
56 B8 **Cañar** ◈ province C Ecuador
64 N10 **Canarias, Islas** Eng. Canary Islands. ◈ autonomous community Spain, NE Atlantic Ocean
Canaries Basin see Canary Basin
44 C6 **Canarreos, Archipiélago de los** island group W Cuba
66 K3 **Canary Basin** var. Canaries Basin, Monaco Basin. undersea feature E Atlantic Ocean
Canary Islands see Canarias, Islas
42 L13 **Cañas** Guanacaste, NW Costa Rica
18 I10 **Canastota** New York, NE USA
40 K9 **Canatlán** Durango, C Mexico
104 J9 **Cañaveral** Extremadura, W Spain

◆ Country ◇ Dependent Territory ◈ Administrative Region ▲ Mountain ⛰ Volcano ◎ Lake
● Country Capital ○ Dependent Territory Capital ✕ International Airport ▲ Mountain Range ≈ River ▣ Reservoir

23 Y11 **Canaveral, Cape** *headland* Florida, SE USA
59 O18 **Canavieiras** Bahia, E Brazil
43 R16 **Cañazas** Veraguas, W Panama
106 H6 **Canazei** Trentino-Alto Adige, N Italy
183 P6 **Canbelego** New South Wales, SE Australia
183 R10 **Canberra** ● (Australia) Australian Capital Territory, SE Australia
183 R10 **Canberra** ✕ Australian Capital Territory, SE Australia
35 P2 **Canby** California, W USA
29 S9 **Canby** Minnesota, N USA
103 N2 **Canche** ≈ N France
102 L13 **Cancon** Lot-et-Garonne, SW France
41 Z11 **Cancún** Quintana Roo, SE Mexico
104 K2 **Candás** Asturias, N Spain
102 J7 **Cande** Maine-et-Loire, NW France
41 W14 **Candelaria** Campeche, SE Mexico
24 J11 **Candelaria** Texas, SW USA
41 W15 **Candelaria, Río** ≈ Guatemala/Mexico
104 L8 **Candeleda** Castilla-León, N Spain
Candia *see* Irákleio
41 P8 **Cándido Aguilar** Tamaulipas, C Mexico
39 N8 **Candle** Alaska, USA
11 T14 **Candle Lake** Saskatchewan, C Canada
18 L13 **Candlewood, Lake** ⊞ Connecticut, NE USA
29 O3 **Cando** North Dakota, N USA
Canea *see* Chaniá
45 O12 **Canefield** ✕ (Roseau) SW Dominica
61 F20 **Canelones** *prev.* Guadalupe. Canelones, S Uruguay
61 E20 **Canelones** ◐ *department* S Uruguay
Canendiyú *see* Canindeyú
63 F14 **Cañete** Bío Bío, C Chile
105 Q9 **Cañete** Castilla-La Mancha, C Spain
Cañete *see* San Vicente de Cañete
27 P8 **Caney** Kansas, C USA
27 P8 **Caney River** ≈ Kansas/Oklahoma, C USA
105 S3 **Canfranc-Estación** Aragón, NE Spain
83 E14 **Cangamba** *Port.* Vila de Aljustrel. Moxico, E Angola
82 C12 **Cangandala** Malanje, NW Angola
104 G4 **Cangas** Galicia, NW Spain
104 J2 **Cangas del Narcea** Asturias, N Spain
104 L2 **Cangas de Onís** Asturias, N Spain
161 S11 **Cangnan** *var.* Lingxi. Zhejiang, SE China
82 C10 **Cangola** Uíge, NW Angola
83 E14 **Cangombe** Moxico, E Angola
63 H21 **Cangrejo, Cerro** ▲ S Argentina
61 H17 **Canguçu** Rio Grande do Sul, S Brazil
161 P3 **Cangzhou** Hebei, E China
12 M7 **Caniapiscau** ≈ Québec, E Canada
12 M8 **Caniapiscau, Réservoir de** ⊞ Québec, C Canada
107 J24 **Canicattì** Sicilia, Italy, C Mediterranean Sea
136 L11 **Canik Dağları** ▲ N Turkey
105 P14 **Caniles** Andalucía, S Spain
59 B16 **Canindé** Acre, W Brazil
62 P6 **Canindeyú** *var.* Canendiyú, Canindiyú. ◐ *department* E Paraguay
Canindiyú *see* Canindeyú
194 J10 **Canisteo Peninsula** *peninsula* Antarctica
18 F11 **Canisteo River** ≈ New York, NE USA
40 M10 **Cañitas** *var.* Cañitas de Felipe Pescador. Zacatecas, C Mexico
Cañitas de Felipe Pescador *see* Cañitas
105 P15 **Canjáyar** Andalucía, S Spain
136 I12 **Çankırı** *var.* Chankiri; *anc.* Gangra, Germanicopolis. Çankın, N Turkey
136 I11 **Çankırı** *var.* Chankiri. ◐ *province* N Turkey
171 P6 **Canlaon Volcano** ▲ Negros, C Philippines
11 P16 **Canmore** Alberta, SW Canada
96 F9 **Canna** *island* NW Scotland, UK
155 F20 **Cannanore** *var.* Kananur, Kannur. Kerala, SW India
31 O17 **Cannelton** Indiana, N USA
103 U15 **Cannes** Alpes-Maritimes, SE France
39 R5 **Canning River** ≈ Alaska, USA
106 C6 **Cannobio** Piemonte, NE Italy
97 L19 **Cannock** C England, UK
28 M6 **Cannonball River** ≈ North Dakota, N USA
29 W9 **Cannon Falls** Minnesota, N USA
18 I11 **Cannonsville Reservoir** ⊞ New York, NE USA
183 R12 **Cann River** Victoria, SE Australia
61 I16 **Canoas** Rio Grande do Sul, S Brazil
61 I14 **Canoas, Rio** ≈ S Brazil
14 I12 **Canoe Lake** ◎ Ontario, SE Canada
60 J12 **Canoinhas** Santa Catarina, S Brazil
37 T6 **Canon City** Colorado, C USA
55 P8 **Caño Negro** Bolívar, SE Venezuela
173 X15 **Canonniers Point** *headland* N Mauritius
23 W6 **Canoochee River** ≈ Georgia, SE USA
11 V15 **Canora** Saskatchewan, S Canada
45 Y14 **Canouan** *island* S Saint Vincent and the Grenadines
13 R15 **Canso** Nova Scotia, SE Canada
104 M3 **Cantabria** ◐ *autonomous community* N Spain
104 K3 **Cantábrica, Cordillera** ▲ N Spain
Cantabrigia *see* Cambridge
103 O12 **Cantal** ◐ *department* C France
105 N6 **Cantalejo** Castilla-León, N Spain
103 O12 **Cantal, Monts du** ▲ C France
104 G8 **Cantanhede** Coimbra, C Portugal
Cantaño *see* Cataño
55 O6 **Cantaura** Anzoátegui, NE Venezuela
116 M11 **Cantemir** *Rus.* Kantemir. S Moldova
97 Q22 **Canterbury** *hist.* Cantwaraburh, *anc.* Durovernum, *Lat.* Cantuaria. SE England, UK
185 F19 **Canterbury** *off.* Canterbury Region. ◐ *region* South Island, NZ
185 H20 **Canterbury Bight** *bight* South Island, NZ
185 H19 **Canterbury Plains** *plain* South Island, NZ
167 S14 **Cần Thơ** Cần Thơ, S Vietnam
104 K13 **Cantillana** Andalucía, S Spain
59 N15 **Canto do Buriti** Piauí, NE Brazil
23 S2 **Canton** Georgia, SE USA
30 K12 **Canton** Illinois, N USA
22 L5 **Canton** Mississippi, S USA
27 V2 **Canton** Missouri, C USA
18 J7 **Canton** New York, NE USA
21 O10 **Canton** North Carolina, SE USA
31 U12 **Canton** Ohio, N USA
26 L9 **Canton** Oklahoma, C USA
18 G12 **Canton** Pennsylvania, NE USA
29 R11 **Canton** South Dakota, N USA
25 V7 **Canton** Texas, SW USA
Canton *see* Guangzhou
Canton Island *see* Kanton
26 L9 **Canton Lake** ⊞ Oklahoma, C USA
106 D7 **Cantù** Lombardia, N Italy
Cantuaria/Cantwaraburh *see* Canterbury
39 R10 **Cantwell** Alaska, USA
59 O16 **Canudos** Bahia, E Brazil
47 T7 **Canumã, Rio** ≈ N Brazil
Canusium *see* Puglia, Canosa di
24 G7 **Canutillo** Texas, SW USA
25 N3 **Canyon** Texas, SW USA
33 S12 **Canyon** Wyoming, C USA
32 K13 **Canyon City** Oregon, NW USA
33 R10 **Canyon Ferry Lake** ◎ Montana, NW USA
25 S11 **Canyon Lake** ⊞ Texas, SW USA
167 T5 **Cao Bang** *var.* Caobang. Cao Bằng, N Vietnam
160 J12 **Caodu He** ≈ S China
167 S14 **Cao Lanh** Đồng Thap, S Vietnam
82 C11 **Caombo** Malanje, NW Angola
Caorach, Cuan na g *see* Sheep Haven
Caozhou *see* Heze
171 Q12 **Capalulu** Pulau Mangole, E Indonesia
54 K8 **Capanaparo, Río** ≈ Colombia/Venezuela
58 L12 **Capanema** Pará, NE Brazil
60 L10 **Capão Bonito** São Paulo, S Brazil
60 I13 **Capão Doce, Morro do** ▲ S Brazil
54 I4 **Capatárida** Falcón, N Venezuela
102 I15 **Capbreton** Landes, SW France
Cap-Breton, Île du *see* Cape Breton Island
15 W6 **Cap-Chat** Québec, SE Canada
15 P11 **Cap-de-la-Madeleine** Québec, SE Canada
103 N13 **Capdenac** Aveyron, S France
183 Q15 **Cape Barren Island** *island* Furneaux Group, Tasmania, SE Australia
65 O18 **Cape Basin** *undersea feature* S Atlantic Ocean
13 R14 **Cape Breton Island** *Fr.* Île du Cap-Breton. *island* Nova Scotia, SE Canada
23 Y11 **Cape Canaveral** Florida, SE USA
21 Y6 **Cape Charles** Virginia, NE USA
77 P17 **Cape Coast** *prev.* Cape Coast Castle. S Ghana
Cape Coast Castle *see* Cape Coast
19 Q12 **Cape Cod Bay** *bay* Massachusetts, NE USA
23 W15 **Cape Coral** Florida, SE USA
181 R4 **Cape Crawford Roadhouse** Northern Territory, N Australia
9 Q7 **Cape Dorset** Baffin Island, Nunavut, NE Canada
21 N8 **Cape Fear River** ≈ North Carolina, SE USA
27 Y7 **Cape Girardeau** Missouri, C USA
21 T14 **Cape Island** *island* South Carolina, SE USA
186 A6 **Capella** ▲ NW PNG
98 H12 **Capelle aan den IJssel** Zuid-Holland, SW Netherlands
83 C15 **Capelongo** Huíla, C Angola
18 J17 **Cape May** New Jersey, NE USA
18 J17 **Cape May Court House** New Jersey, NE USA
Cape Palmas *see* Harper
8 I6 **Cape Parry** Northwest Territories, N Canada
65 P19 **Cape Rise** *undersea feature* SW Indian Ocean
Cape Saint Jacques *see* Vung Tau
Capesterre *see* Capesterre-Belle-Eau
45 Y6 **Capesterre-Belle-Eau** *var.* Capesterre. Basse Terre, S Guadeloupe
83 D26 **Cape Town** *var.* Ekapa, *Afr.* Kaapstad, Kapstad. ● (South Africa-legislative capital) Western Cape, SW South Africa
83 E26 **Cape Town** ✕ Western Cape, SW South Africa
76 D9 **Cape Verde** *off.* Republic of Cape Verde, *Port.* Cabo Verde, Ilhas do Cabo Verde. ◆ *republic* E Atlantic Ocean
64 L11 **Cape Verde Basin** *undersea feature* E Atlantic Ocean
66 K5 **Cape Verde Islands** *island group* E Atlantic Ocean
64 L10 **Cape Verde Plain** *undersea feature* E Atlantic Ocean
Cape Verde Plateau/Cape Verde Rise *see* Cape Verde Terrace
64 L11 **Cape Verde Terrace** *var.* Cape Verde Plateau, Cape Verde Rise. *undersea feature* E Atlantic Ocean
181 V2 **Cape York Peninsula** *peninsula* Queensland, N Australia
44 M8 **Cap-Haïtien** *var.* Le Cap. N Haiti
43 T15 **Capira** Panamá, C Panama
14 K8 **Capitachouane** ≈ Québec, SE Canada
14 L8 **Capitachouane, Lac** ◎ Québec, SE Canada
37 T13 **Capitan** New Mexico, SW USA
194 G3 **Capitán Arturo Prat** *Chilean research station* South Shetland Islands, Antarctica
37 S13 **Capitan Mountains** ▲ New Mexico, SW USA
62 M3 **Capitán Pablo Lagerenza** *var.* Mayor Pablo Lagerenza. Chaco, N Paraguay
37 T13 **Capitan Peak** ▲ New Mexico, SW USA
188 H5 **Capitol Hill** Saipan, S Northern Mariana Islands
60 I9 **Capivara, Represa** ⊞ S Brazil
61 J16 **Capivari** Rio Grande do Sul, S Brazil
113 H15 **Čapljina** Federacija Bosna I Hercegovina, S Bosnia and Herzegovina
83 M15 **Capoche** *var.* Kapoche. ≈ Mozambique/Zambia
Capo Delgado, Província de *see* Cabo Delgado
107 K17 **Capodichino** ✕ (Napoli) Campania, S Italy
Capodistria *see* Koper
106 E12 **Capraia, Isola** *island* Archipelago Toscano, C Italy
107 B16 **Caprara, Punta** *var.* Punta dello Scorno. *headland* Isola Asinara, W Italy
Capraria, Isola di to Capraia, Isola *see* Cabrera
14 F10 **Capreol** Ontario, S Canada
107 K18 **Capri** Campania, S Italy
175 S9 **Capricorn Tablemount** *undersea feature* W Pacific Ocean
107 J18 **Capri, Isola di** *island* S Italy
83 G16 **Caprivi** ◐ *district* NE Namibia
Caprivi Concession *see* Caprivi Strip
83 F16 **Caprivi Strip** *Ger.* Caprivizipfel; *prev.* Caprivi Concession. *cultural region* NE Namibia
Caprivizipfel *see* Caprivi Strip
25 O5 **Cap Rock Escarpment** *cliffs* Texas, SW USA
15 R10 **Cap-Rouge** Québec, SE Canada
Cap Saint-Jacques *see* Vung Tau
38 F12 **Captain Cook** Hawai'i, USA, C Pacific Ocean
183 R10 **Captains Flat** New South Wales, SE Australia
102 K14 **Captieux** Gironde, SW France
107 K17 **Capua** Campania, S Italy
54 F14 **Caquetá** *off.* Departamento del Caquetá. ◐ *province* S Colombia
54 E13 **Caquetá, Río** *var.* Rio Japurá, Yapurá. ≈ Brazil/Colombia *see also* Japurá, Rio
CAR *see* Central African Republic
Cara *see* Kara
57 I16 **Carabaya, Cordillera** ▲ E Peru
54 K5 **Carabobo** *off.* Estado Carabobo. ◐ *state* N Venezuela
116 I14 **Caracal** Olt, S Romania
58 F10 **Caracaraí** Rondônia, W Brazil
54 L5 **Caracas** ● (Venezuela) Distrito Federal, N Venezuela
54 I5 **Carache** Trujillo, N Venezuela
60 N10 **Caraguatatuba** São Paulo, S Brazil
48 I7 **Carajás, Serra dos** ▲ N Brazil
Caralis *see* Cagliari
54 E9 **Caramanta** Antioquia, W Colombia
171 P4 **Caramoan** Catanduanes Island, N Philippines
Caramurat *see* Mihail Kogălniceanu
116 F12 **Caransebeş** *Ger.* Karansebesch, *Hung.* Karánsebes. Caraş-Severin, SW Romania
Carapella *see* Carapelle
107 M16 **Carapelle** *var.* Carapella. ≈ SE Italy
55 O9 **Carapo** Bolívar, SE Venezuela
13 P13 **Caraquet** New Brunswick, SE Canada
Caras *see* Caraz
116 F12 **Caraşova** *Hung.* Krassóvár. Caraş-Severin, SW Romania
116 F12 **Caraş-Severin** ◐ *county* SW Romania
42 M5 **Caratasca, Laguna de** *lagoon* NE Honduras
58 C13 **Carauari** Amazonas, NW Brazil
Caravaca *see* Caravaca de la Cruz
105 Q12 **Caravaca de la Cruz** *var.* Caravaca. Murcia, SE Spain
106 E7 **Caravaggio** Lombardia, N Italy
107 C18 **Caravai, Passo di** *pass* Sardegna, Italy, C Mediterranean Sea
59 O19 **Caravelas** Bahia, E Brazil
56 C12 **Caraz** *var.* Caras. Ancash, W Peru
61 H14 **Carazinho** Rio Grande do Sul, S Brazil
42 J11 **Carazo** ◐ *department* SW Nicaragua
Carballiño *see* O Carballiño
104 G2 **Carballo** Galicia, NW Spain
11 W16 **Carberry** Manitoba, S Canada
40 F4 **Carbó** Sonora, NW Mexico
107 C20 **Carbonara, Capo** *headland* Sardegna, Italy, C Mediterranean Sea
37 Q5 **Carbondale** Colorado, C USA
30 L17 **Carbondale** Illinois, N USA
27 Q4 **Carbondale** Kansas, C USA
18 I13 **Carbondale** Pennsylvania, NE USA
13 V12 **Carbonear** Newfoundland and Labrador, SE Canada
105 Q9 **Carboneras de Guadazaón** *var.* Carboneras de Guadazón. Castilla-La Mancha, C Spain
Carboneras de Guadazón *see* Carboneras de Guadazaón
23 O3 **Carbon Hill** Alabama, S USA
107 B20 **Carbonia** *var.* Carbonia Centro. Sardegna, Italy, C Mediterranean Sea
Carbonia Centro *see* Carbonia
105 S10 **Carcaixent** País Valenciano, E Spain
Carcaso *see* Carcassonne
65 B24 **Carcass Island** *island* NW Falkland Islands
103 O16 **Carcassonne** *anc.* Carcaso. Aude, S France
105 R12 **Carche** ▲ S Spain
56 A13 **Carchi** ◐ *province* N Ecuador
10 I8 **Carcross** Yukon Territory, W Canada
Cardamomes, Chaîne des *see* Krâvanh, Chuŏr Phnum
155 G22 **Cardamom Hills** ▲ SW India
Cardamom Mountains *see* Krâvanh, Chuŏr Phnum
104 M12 **Cardeña** Andalucía, S Spain
44 D4 **Cárdenas** Matanzas, W Cuba
41 O11 **Cárdenas** San Luis Potosí C Mexico
41 U15 **Cárdenas** Tabasco, SE Mexico
63 H21 **Cardiel, Lago** ◎ S Argentina
97 K22 **Cardiff** *Wel.* Caerdydd. ◐ S Wales, UK
97 J22 **Cardiff-Wales** ✕ S Wales, UK
97 I21 **Cardigan** *Wel.* Aberteifi. SW Wales, UK
97 I20 **Cardigan** *cultural region* W Wales, UK
97 I20 **Cardigan Bay** *bay* W Wales, UK
19 N8 **Cardigan, Mount** ▲ New Hampshire, NE USA
14 M13 **Cardinal** Ontario, SE Canada
105 V5 **Cardona** Cataluña, NE Spain
61 E19 **Cardona** Soriano, SW Uruguay
105 V4 **Cardoner** ≈ NE Spain
11 Q17 **Cardston** Alberta, SW Canada
181 W5 **Cardwell** Queensland, NE Australia
116 G8 **Carei** *Ger.* Gross-Karol, Karol, *Hung.* Nagykároly; *prev.* Careii-Mari. Satu Mare, NW Romania
Careii-Mari *see* Carei
58 F13 **Careiro** Amazonas, NW Brazil
102 J4 **Carentan** Manche, N France
104 M2 **Cares** ≈ N Spain
33 P14 **Carey** Idaho, NW USA
31 S12 **Carey** Ohio, N USA
25 P4 **Carey** Texas, SW USA
180 L11 **Carey, Lake** ◎ Western Australia
173 O8 **Cargados Carajos Bank** *undersea feature* C Indian Ocean
102 G6 **Carhaix-Plouguer** Finistère, NW France
61 A22 **Carhué** Buenos Aires, E Argentina
55 O5 **Cariaco** Sucre, NE Venezuela
107 O20 **Cariati** Calabria, SW Italy
2 H17 **Caribbean Plate** *tectonic feature*
44 I11 **Caribbean Sea** *sea* W Atlantic Ocean
11 N15 **Cariboo Mountains** ▲ British Columbia, SW Canada
11 W9 **Caribou** Manitoba, C Canada
19 S2 **Caribou** Maine, NE USA
11 P10 **Caribou Mountains** ▲ Alberta, SW Canada
Caribrod *see* Dimitrovgrad
40 I5 **Carichic** Chihuahua, N Mexico
103 R3 **Carignan** Ardennes, N France
183 Q5 **Carinda** New South Wales, SE Australia
105 R6 **Cariñena** Aragón, NE Spain
107 I23 **Carini** Sicilia, Italy, C Mediterranean Sea
107 K17 **Carinola** Campania, S Italy
Carinthi *see* Kärnten
55 O5 **Caripe** Monagas, NE Venezuela
55 P5 **Caripito** Monagas, NE Venezuela
15 W7 **Carleton** Québec, SE Canada
31 S10 **Carleton** Michigan, N USA
13 O14 **Carleton, Mount** ▲ New Brunswick, SE Canada
14 L13 **Carleton Place** Ontario, SE Canada
35 V3 **Carlin** Nevada, W USA
30 K14 **Carlinville** Illinois, N USA
97 K14 **Carlisle** *anc.* Caer Luel, Luguvallium, Luguvallum. NW England, UK
27 V11 **Carlisle** Arkansas, C USA
31 N15 **Carlisle** Indiana, N USA
29 V14 **Carlisle** Iowa, C USA
21 N5 **Carlisle** Kentucky, S USA
18 F15 **Carlisle** Pennsylvania, NE USA
21 Q11 **Carlisle** South Carolina, SE USA
38 J17 **Carlisle Island** *island* Aleutian Islands, Alaska, USA
27 R7 **Carl Junction** Missouri, C USA
107 A20 **Carloforte** Sardegna, Italy, C Mediterranean Sea
Carlopago *see* Karlobag
61 B21 **Carlos Casares** Buenos Aires, E Argentina
61 E18 **Carlos Reyles** Durazno, C Uruguay
61 A21 **Carlos Tejedor** Buenos Aires, E Argentina
97 F19 **Carlow** *Ir.* Ceatharlach. SE Ireland
97 F19 **Carlow** *Ir.* Cheatharlach. *cultural region* SE Ireland
96 F7 **Carloway** NW Scotland, UK
Carlsbad *see* Karlovy Vary
35 U17 **Carlsbad** California, W USA
37 U15 **Carlsbad** New Mexico, SW USA
131 N13 **Carlsberg Ridge** *undersea feature* S Arabian Sea
Carlsruhe *see* Karlsruhe
29 W6 **Carlton** Minnesota, N USA
11 V17 **Carlyle** Saskatchewan, S Canada
30 L15 **Carlyle** Illinois, N USA
30 L15 **Carlyle Lake** ⊞ Illinois, N USA
10 H7 **Carmacks** Yukon Territory, W Canada
106 B9 **Carmagnola** Piemonte, NW Italy
11 X16 **Carman** Manitoba, S Canada
Carmana/Carmania *see* Kermān
97 I21 **Carmarthen** SW Wales, UK
97 I21 **Carmarthen** *cultural region* SW Wales, UK
97 I22 **Carmarthen Bay** *inlet* SW Wales, UK
103 N14 **Carmaux** Tarn, S France
35 N11 **Carmel** California, W USA
31 O13 **Carmel** Indiana, N USA
18 L13 **Carmel** New York, NE USA
97 H18 **Carmel Head** *headland* NW Wales, UK
42 E2 **Carmelita** Petén, N Guatemala
61 D19 **Carmelo** Colonia, SW Uruguay
41 V14 **Carmen** *var.* Ciudad del Carmen. Campeche, SE Mexico
61 A25 **Carmen de Patagones** Buenos Aires, E Argentina
40 F8 **Carmen, Isla** *island* W Mexico
40 M5 **Carmen, Sierra del** ▲ NW Mexico
30 M16 **Carmi** Illinois, N USA
35 O7 **Carmichael** California, W USA
Carmiel *see* Karmi'él
25 U11 **Carmine** Texas, SW USA
104 K14 **Carmona** Andalucía, S Spain
Carmona *see* Uíge
Carnaro *see* Kvarner
14 I13 **Carnarvon** Ontario, SE Canada
83 G24 **Carnarvon** Northern Cape, W South Africa
Carnarvon *see* Caernarfon
180 K9 **Carnarvon Range** ▲ Western Australia
180 G9 **Carnarvon** Western Australia
Carn Domhnach *see* Carndonagh
96 E13 **Carndonagh** *Ir.* Carn Domhnach. NW Ireland
11 V17 **Carnduff** Saskatchewan, S Canada
26 L11 **Carnegie** Oklahoma, C USA
180 L9 **Carnegie, Lake** *salt lake* Western Australia
193 U8 **Carnegie Ridge** *undersea feature* E Pacific Ocean
96 H9 **Carn Eige** ▲ N Scotland, UK
182 F5 **Carnes** South Australia
194 J12 **Carney Island** *island* Antarctica
18 H16 **Carneys Point** New Jersey, NE USA
Carniche, Alpi *see* Karnische Alpen
151 Q21 **Car Nicobar** *island* Nicobar Islands, India, NE Indian Ocean
79 H15 **Carnot** Mambéré-Kadéï, W Central African Republic
182 F10 **Carnot, Cape** *headland* South Australia
96 K11 **Carnoustie** E Scotland, UK
97 F20 **Carnsore Point** *Ir.* Ceann an Chairn. *headland* SE Ireland
8 H7 **Carnwath** ≈ Northwest Territories, NW Canada
31 R8 **Caro** Michigan, N USA
23 Z15 **Carol City** Florida, SE USA
59 L14 **Carolina** Maranhão, E Brazil
45 U5 **Carolina** E Puerto Rico
21 V12 **Carolina Beach** North Carolina, SE USA
Caroline Island *see* Millennium Island
189 N15 **Caroline Islands** *island group* C Micronesia
131 Z14 **Caroline Plate** *tectonic feature*
192 H7 **Caroline Ridge** *undersea feature* E Philippine Sea
Carolopois *see* Châlons-en-Champagne
45 V14 **Caroni Arena Dam** ⊞ Trinidad, Trinidad and Tobago
Caronie, Monti *see* Nebrodi, Monti
55 P7 **Caroní, Río** ≈ E Venezuela
45 U14 **Caroni River** ≈ Trinidad, Trinidad and Tobago
Caronium *see* A Coruña
54 J5 **Carora** Lara, N Venezuela
86 F12 **Carpathian Mountains** *var.* Carpathians, *Cz./Pol.* Karpaty, *Ger.* Karpaten. ▲ E Europe
Carpathians *see* Carpathian Mountains
Carpathos/Carpathus *see* Kárpathos
116 H12 **Carpaţii Meridionali** *var.* Alpi Transilvanici, Carpaţii Sudici, *Eng.* South Carpathians, Transylvanian Alps, *Ger.* Südkarpaten, Transsylvanische Alpen, *Hung.* Déli-Kárpátok, Erdélyi-Havasok. ▲ C Romania
Carpaţii Sudici *see* Carpaţii Meridionali
174 L7 **Carpentaria, Gulf of** *gulf* N Australia
Carpentoracte *see* Carpentras
103 R14 **Carpentras** *anc.* Carpentoracte. Vaucluse, SE France
106 F9 **Carpi** Emilia-Romagna, N Italy
116 E11 **Carpiniş** *Hung.* Gyertyámos. Timiş, W Romania
35 R14 **Carpinteria** California, W USA
23 S9 **Carrabelle** Florida, SE USA
Carraig Aonair *see* Fastnet Rock
Carraig Fhearghais *see* Carrickfergus
Carraig Mhachaire Rois *see* Carrickmacross
Carraig na Siúire *see* Carrick-on-Suir
Carrantual *see* Carrauntoohil
106 E10 **Carrara** Toscana, C Italy
61 F20 **Carrasco** ✕ (Montevideo) Canelones, S Uruguay
105 P9 **Carrascosa del Campo** Castilla-La Mancha, C Spain
54 H4 **Carrasquero** Zulia, NW Venezuela
183 O9 **Carrathool** New South Wales, SE Australia
Carrauntohil *see* Carrauntoohil
97 B21 **Carrauntoohil** *Ir.* Carrantual, Carrauntohil, Corrán Tuathail. ▲ SW Ireland
45 Y15 **Carriacou** *island* N Grenada
97 G15 **Carrickfergus** *Ir.* Carraig Fhearghais. NE Northern Ireland, UK
97 F16 **Carrickmacross** *Ir.* Carraig Mhachaire Rois. N Ireland
97 D16 **Carrick-on-Shannon** *Ir.* Cora Droma Rúisc. NW Ireland
97 E20 **Carrick-on-Suir** *Ir.* Carraig na Siúire. S Ireland
182 I7 **Carrieton** South Australia
40 L7 **Carrillo** Chihuahua, N Mexico
29 O4 **Carrington** North Dakota, N USA
104 M4 **Carrión** ≈ N Spain
104 M4 **Carrión de los Condes** Castilla-León, N Spain
25 P13 **Carrizo Springs** Texas, SW USA
37 S13 **Carrizozo** New Mexico, SW USA
29 T13 **Carroll** Iowa, C USA
23 N4 **Carrollton** Alabama, S USA
23 R3 **Carrollton** Georgia, SE USA
30 K14 **Carrollton** Illinois, N USA
20 L4 **Carrollton** Kentucky, S USA
31 R8 **Carrollton** Michigan, N USA
27 T3 **Carrollton** Missouri, C USA
31 U12 **Carrollton** Ohio, N USA
25 T6 **Carrollton** Texas, SW USA
11 U14 **Carrot** ≈ Saskatchewan, S Canada
11 U14 **Carrot River** Saskatchewan, C Canada
18 J7 **Carry Falls Reservoir** ⊞ New York, NE USA
136 L11 **Çarşamba** Samsun, N Turkey
28 L6 **Carson** North Dakota, N USA
35 Q6 **Carson City** *state capital* Nevada, W USA
35 R6 **Carson River** ≈ Nevada, W USA
35 S5 **Carson Sink** *salt flat* Nevada, W USA
11 Q16 **Carstairs** Alberta, SW Canada
Carstensz, Puntjak *see* Jaya, Puncak
54 E5 **Cartagena** *var.* Cartagena de los Indes. Bolívar, NW Colombia
105 R13 **Cartagena** *anc.* Carthago Nova. Murcia, SE Spain
54 E13 **Cartagena de Chaira** Caquetá, S Colombia
Cartagena de los Indes *see* Cartagena
54 D10 **Cartago** Valle del Cauca, W Colombia
43 N14 **Cartago** Cartago, C Costa Rica
42 M14 **Cartago** *off.* Provincia de Cartago. ◐ *province* C Costa Rica
25 O11 **Carta Valley** Texas, SW USA
104 F10 **Cartaxo** Santarém, C Portugal
104 I14 **Cartaya** Andalucía, S Spain
Carteret Islands *see* Tulun Islands
29 S15 **Carter Lake** Iowa, C USA
23 S3 **Cartersville** Georgia, SE USA
185 M14 **Carterton** Wellington, North Island, NZ
30 J13 **Carthage** Illinois, N USA
22 L5 **Carthage** Mississippi, S USA
27 R7 **Carthage** Missouri, C USA
18 I8 **Carthage** New York, NE USA
21 T10 **Carthage** North Carolina, SE USA
20 K8 **Carthage** Tennessee, S USA
25 X7 **Carthage** Texas, SW USA
74 M5 **Carthage** ✕ (Tunis) N Tunisia
Carthago Nova *see* Cartagena
14 E10 **Cartier** Ontario, S Canada

◆ Country ● Country Capital ◇ Dependent Territory ○ Dependent Territory Capital ◐ Administrative Region ✕ International Airport ▲ Mountain ▲ Mountain Range Volcano ≈ River ◎ Lake ⊞ Reservoir

13 S8 Cartwright Newfoundland and Labrador, E Canada
55 P9 Caruana de Montaña Bolívar, SE Venezuela
59 Q15 Caruaru Pernambuco, E Brazil
55 P5 Carúpano Sucre, NE Venezuela
Carusbur see Cherbourg
58 M12 Carutapera Maranhão, E Brazil
27 Y9 Caruthersville Missouri, C USA
103 O1 Carvin Pas-de-Calais, N France
58 E12 Carvoeiro Amazonas, NW Brazil
104 E10 Carvoeiro, Cabo headland C Portugal
21 U9 Cary North Carolina, SE USA
182 M3 Caryapundy Swamp wetland New South Wales/Queensland, SE Australia
65 E24 Carysfort, Cape headland East Falkland, Falkland Islands
74 F6 Casablanca Ar. Dar-el-Beida. NW Morocco
60 M8 Casa Branca São Paulo, S Brazil
36 L14 Casa Grande Arizona, SW USA
106 C8 Casale Monferrato Piemonte, NW Italy
106 E8 Casalpusterlengo Lombardia, N Italy
54 H10 Casanare off. Intendencia de Casanare. ◈ province C Colombia
55 P5 Casanay Sucre, NE Venezuela
24 K11 Casa Piedra Texas, SW USA
107 Q19 Casarano Puglia, SE Italy
42 J11 Casares Carazo, W Nicaragua
105 R10 Casas Ibáñez Castilla-La Mancha, C Spain
61 I14 Casca Rio Grande do Sul, S Brazil
172 I17 Cascade Mahé, NE Seychelles
33 N13 Cascade Idaho, NW USA
29 Y13 Cascade Iowa, C USA
33 R9 Cascade Montana, NW USA
185 B20 Cascade Point headland South Island, NZ
32 G13 Cascade Range ▲ Oregon/Washington, NW USA
33 N12 Cascade Reservoir ⊟ Idaho, NW USA
0 E8 Cascadia Basin undersea feature NE Pacific Ocean
104 E11 Cascais Lisboa, C Portugal
15 W7 Cascapédia ≈ Québec, SE Canada
59 I22 Cascavel Ceará, E Brazil
60 G11 Cascavel Paraná, S Brazil
106 I13 Cascia Umbria, C Italy
106 F11 Cascina Toscana, C Italy
19 Q8 Casco Bay bay Maine, NE USA
194 J7 Case Island island Antarctica
106 B8 Caselle × (Torino) Piemonte, NW Italy
107 K17 Caserta Campania, S Italy
15 N8 Casey Québec, SE Canada
30 M14 Casey Illinois, N USA
195 Y12 Casey Australian research station Antarctica
195 W3 Casey Bay bay Antarctica
80 Q11 Caseyr, Raas headland NE Somalia
97 D20 Cashel Ir. Caiseal. S Ireland
54 G6 Casigua Zulia, W Venezuela
61 B19 Casilda Santa Fe, C Argentina
Casim see General Toshevo
183 V4 Casino New South Wales, SE Australia
Casinum see Cassino
111 E17 Čáslav Ger. Tschaslau. Střední Čechy, C Czech Republic
56 C13 Casma Ancash, C Peru
167 S7 Ca, Sông ≈ N Vietnam
107 K17 Casoria Campania, S Italy
105 T6 Caspe Aragón, NE Spain
33 X15 Casper Wyoming, C USA
84 M10 Caspian Depression Kaz. Kaspiy Mangy Oypaty, Rus. Prikaspiyskaya Nizmennost'. depression Kazakhstan/Russian Federation
138 Kk9 Caspian Sea Az. Xäzär Dänizi, Kaz. Kaspiy Tengizi, Per. Baḩr-e Khazar, Daryā-ye Khazar, Rus. Kaspiyskoye More. inland sea Asia/Europe
83 L14 Cassacatiza Tete, NW Mozambique
Cassai see Kasai
82 F13 Cassamba Moxico, E Angola
107 N20 Cassano allo Ionio Calabria, SE Italy
31 S8 Cass City Michigan, N USA
Cassel see Kassel
14 M13 Casselman Ontario, SE Canada
29 R5 Casselton North Dakota, N USA
59 M16 Cássia var. Santa Rita de Cassia. Bahia, E Brazil
10 J9 Cassiar British Columbia, W Canada
10 K10 Cassiar Mountains ▲ British Columbia, W Canada
83 C15 Cassinga Huíla, SW Angola
107 J16 Cassino prev. San Germano; anc. Casinum. Lazio, C Italy
29 T4 Cass Lake Minnesota, N USA
29 T4 Cass Lake ◎ Minnesota, N USA
31 P10 Cassopolis Michigan, N USA
31 S8 Cass River ≈ Michigan, N USA
27 S8 Cassville Missouri, C USA
Castamoni see Kastamonu
58 L12 Castanhal Pará, NE Brazil
104 G8 Castanheira de Pêra Leiria, C Portugal
41 N7 Castaños Coahuila de Zaragoza, NE Mexico
108 I10 Castasegna Graubünden, SE Switzerland
106 D8 Casteggio Lombardia, N Italy
107 K23 Castelbuono Sicilia, Italy, C Mediterranean Sea
107 K15 Castel di Sangro Abruzzo, C Italy
106 H7 Castelfranco Veneto Veneto, NE Italy
102 K14 Casteljaloux Lot-et-Garonne, SW France
107 L18 Castellabate var. Santa Maria di Castellabate. Campania, S Italy
107 I23 Castellammare del Golfo Sicilia, Italy, C Mediterranean Sea
107 H22 Castellammare, Golfo di gulf Sicilia, Italy, C Mediterranean Sea
103 U15 Castellane Alpes-de-Haute-Provence, SE France
107 O18 Castellaneta Puglia, SE Italy
106 E9 Castel l'Arquato Emilia-Romagna, C Italy
61 E21 Castelli Buenos Aires, E Argentina
105 T9 Castelló de la Plana var. Castellón. País Valenciano, E Spain
105 S8 Castellón ◈ province País Valenciano, E Spain
Castellón see Castelló de la Plana
105 S7 Castellote Aragón, NE Spain
103 N16 Castelnaudary Aude, S France
102 L16 Castelnau-Magnoac Hautes-Pyrénées, S France
106 F10 Castelnovo ne' Monti Emilia-Romagna, C Italy
Castelnuovo see Herceg-Novi
104 H9 Castelo Branco Castelo Branco, C Portugal
104 H8 Castelo Branco ◈ district C Portugal
104 I10 Castelo de Vide Portalegre, C Portugal
104 G9 Castelo do Bode, Barragem do ⊟ C Portugal
106 G10 Castel San Pietro Terme Emilia-Romagna, C Italy
107 B17 Castelsardo Sardegna, Italy, C Mediterranean Sea
102 M14 Castelsarrasin Tarn-et-Garonne, S France
107 I24 Casteltermini Sicilia, Italy, C Mediterranean Sea
107 H24 Castelvetrano Sicilia, Italy, C Mediterranean Sea
182 L12 Casterton Victoria, SE Australia
102 J15 Castets Landes, SW France
106 H12 Castiglione del Lago Umbria, C Italy
106 F13 Castiglione della Pescaia Toscana, C Italy
106 F8 Castiglione delle Stiviere Lombardia, N Italy
104 M9 Castilla-La Mancha ◈ autonomous community NE Spain
104 L5 Castilla-León var. Castillia y Leon. ◈ autonomous community NW Spain
105 N10 Castilla Nueva cultural region C Spain
105 N6 Castilla Vieja cultural region N Spain
Castillia y Leon see Castilla-León
Castillo de Locubim see Castillo de Locubín
105 N14 Castillo de Locubín var. Castillo de Locubim. Andalucía, S Spain
102 K13 Castillon-la-Bataille Gironde, SW France
63 I19 Castillo, Pampa del plain S Argentina
61 G19 Castillos Rocha, SE Uruguay
97 B16 Castlebar Ir. Caisleán an Bharraigh. W Ireland
97 F16 Castleblayney Ir. Baile na Lorgan. N Ireland
45 O11 Castle Bruce E Dominica
36 M5 Castle Dale Utah, W USA
36 I14 Castle Dome Peak ▲ Arizona, SW USA
97 J14 Castle Douglas S Scotland, UK
97 E14 Castlefinn Ir. Caisleán na Finne. NW Ireland
97 M17 Castleford N England, UK
11 O17 Castlegar British Columbia, SW Canada
64 B12 Castle Harbour inlet Bermuda, NW Atlantic Ocean
21 V12 Castle Hayne North Carolina, SE USA
97 B20 Castleisland Ir. Oileán Ciarral. SW Ireland
183 N12 Castlemaine Victoria, SE Australia
37 R5 Castle Peak ▲ Colorado, C USA
33 O13 Castle Peak ▲ Idaho, NW USA
184 N13 Castlepoint Wellington, North Island, NZ
97 D17 Castlerea Ir. An Caisleán Riabhach. W Ireland
97 G15 Castlereagh Ir. An Caisleán Riabhach. N Northern Ireland, UK
183 R6 Castlereagh River ≈ New South Wales, SE Australia
37 T5 Castle Rock Colorado, C USA
30 K7 Castle Rock Lake ⊟ Wisconsin, N USA
65 G25 Castle Rock Point headland S Saint Helena
97 I16 Castletown SE Isle of Man
29 R9 Castlewood South Dakota, N USA
11 R15 Castor Alberta, SW Canada
14 M13 Castor ≈ Ontario, SE Canada
27 X7 Castor River ≈ Missouri, C USA
Castra Albiensium see Castres
Castra Regina see Regensburg
103 N15 Castres anc. Castra Albiensium. Tarn, S France
98 H9 Castricum Noord-Holland, W Netherlands
45 S11 Castries ● (Saint Lucia) N Saint Lucia
60 J11 Castro Paraná, S Brazil
63 F17 Castro Los Lagos, W Chile
104 H7 Castro Daire Viseu, N Portugal
104 M13 Castro del Río Andalucía, S Spain
Castrogiovanni see Enna
104 H14 Castro Marim Faro, S Portugal
104 J2 Castropol Asturias, N Spain
105 O2 Castro-Urdiales var. Castro Urdiales. Cantabria, N Spain
104 G13 Castro Verde Beja, S Portugal
107 N19 Castrovillari Calabria, SW Italy
35 N10 Castroville California, W USA
25 R12 Castroville Texas, SW USA
104 K11 Castuera Extremadura, W Spain
61 F19 Casupá Florida, S Uruguay
185 A22 Caswell Sound sound South Island, NZ
137 Q13 Çat Erzurum, NE Turkey
42 K6 Catacamas Olancho, C Honduras
56 A10 Catacaos Piura, NW Peru
22 I7 Catahoula Lake ◎ Louisiana, S USA
137 S15 Çatak Van, SE Turkey
137 S15 Çatak Çayi ≈ SE Turkey
114 O12 Çatalca İstanbul, NW Turkey
114 O12 Çatalca Yarımadası physical region NW Turkey
62 H6 Catalina Antofagasta, N Chile
Catalonia see Cataluña
105 U5 Cataluña Cat. Catalunya; Eng. Catalonia. ◈ autonomous community N Spain
Catalunya see Cataluña
62 J7 Catamarca off. Provincia de Catamarca. ◈ province NW Argentina
Catamarca see San Fernando del Valle de Catamarca
83 M16 Catandica Manica, C Mozambique
171 P4 Catanduanes Island island N Philippines
60 K8 Catanduva São Paulo, S Brazil
107 L24 Catania Sicilia, Italy, C Mediterranean Sea
107 M24 Catania, Golfo di gulf Sicilia, Italy, C Mediterranean Sea
45 U5 Cataño var. Cantaño. E Puerto Rico
107 O21 Catanzaro Calabria, SW Italy
107 O22 Catanzaro Marina var. Marina di Catanzaro. Calabria, S Italy
25 Q14 Catarina Texas, SW USA
171 Q5 Catarman Samar, C Philippines
105 S10 Catarroja País Valenciano, E Spain
21 R11 Catawba River ≈ North Carolina/South Carolina, SE USA
171 Q5 Catbalogan Samar, C Philippines
14 I14 Catchacoma Ontario, SE Canada
41 S15 Catemaco Veracruz-Llave, SE Mexico
Cathair na Mart see Westport
Cathair Saidhbhín see Cahersiveen
31 P5 Cat Head Point headland Michigan, N USA
23 Q2 Cathedral Caverns cave Alabama, S USA
35 V16 Cathedral City California, W USA
24 K10 Cathedral Mountain ▲ Texas, SW USA
32 G10 Cathlamet Washington, NW USA
76 G13 Catió S Guinea-Bissau
55 O10 Catisimiña Bolívar, SE Venezuela
44 J3 Cat Island island C Bahamas
12 B9 Cat Lake Ontario, S Canada
21 P5 Catlettsburg Kentucky, S USA
185 D24 Catlins ≈ South Island, NZ
35 R1 Catnip Mountain ▲ Nevada, W USA
41 Z11 Catoche, Cabo headland SE Mexico
27 P9 Catoosa Oklahoma, C USA
41 N10 Catorce San Luis Potosí, C Mexico
63 I14 Catriel Río Negro, C Argentina
62 K13 Catriló La Pampa, C Argentina
58 F11 Catrimani Roraima, N Brazil
58 E10 Catrimani, Rio ≈ N Brazil
18 K11 Catskill New York, NE USA
18 K11 Catskill Creek ≈ New York, NE USA
18 J11 Catskill Mountains ▲ New York, NE USA
18 D11 Cattaraugus Creek ≈ New York, NE USA
Cattaro see Kotor
Cattaro, Bocche di see Kotorska, Boka
107 I24 Cattolica Eraclea Sicilia, Italy, C Mediterranean Sea
83 B14 Catumbela ≈ W Angola
83 N14 Catur Niassa, N Mozambique
82 C10 Cauale ≈ NE Angola
171 O2 Cauayan Luzon, N Philippines
54 C12 Cauca off. Departamento del Cauca. ◈ province SW Colombia
47 P5 Cauca ≈ SE Venezuela
58 P13 Caucaia Ceará, E Brazil
54 E7 Cauca, Río ≈ N Colombia
54 E7 Caucasia Antioquia, NW Colombia
137 Q8 Caucasus Rus. Kavkaz. ▲ Georgia/Russian Federation
62 I10 Caucete San Juan, W Argentina
105 R11 Caudete Castilla-La Mancha, C Spain
103 P2 Caudry Nord, N France
82 D11 Caungula Lunda Norte, NE Angola
62 G13 Cauquenes Maule, C Chile
55 N8 Caura, Río ≈ C Venezuela
15 V7 Causapscal Québec, SE Canada
117 N10 Căuşeni Rus. Kaushany. E Moldova
102 M14 Caussade Tarn-et-Garonne, S France
102 K17 Cauterets Hautes-Pyrénées, S France
10 J15 Caution, Cape headland British Columbia, SW Canada
44 H7 Cauto ≈ E Cuba
Cauvery see Kāveri
102 L3 Caux, Pays de physical region N France
107 L18 Cava dei Tirreni Campania, S Italy
104 G6 Cávado ≈ N Portugal
Cavaia see Kavajë
103 R15 Cavaillon Vaucluse, SE France
103 U16 Cavalaire-sur-Mer Var, SE France
106 G6 Cavalese Ger. Gablös. Trentino-Alto Adige, N Italy
29 Q2 Cavalier North Dakota, N USA
76 L17 Cavalla var. Cavally, Cavally Fleuve. ≈ Ivory Coast/Liberia
105 Y8 Cavalleria, Cap de var. Cabo Caballeria. headland Menorca, Spain, W Mediterranean Sea
184 K2 Cavalli Islands island group N NZ
Cavally/Cavally Fleuve see Cavalla
97 E16 Cavan Ir. Cabhán. N Ireland
97 E16 Cavan Ir. An Cabhán. cultural region N Ireland
106 H8 Cavarzere Veneto, NE Italy
27 W9 Cave City Arkansas, C USA
20 K7 Cave City Kentucky, S USA
65 M25 Cave Point headland S Tristan da Cunha
21 N5 Cave Run Lake ⊟ Kentucky, S USA
58 K11 Caviana de Fora, Ilha var. Ilha Caviana. island N Brazil
Caviana, Ilha see Caviana de Fora, Ilha
113 I16 Cavtat It. Ragusavecchia. Dubrovnik-Neretva, SE Croatia
Cawnpore see Kānpur
Caxamarca see Cajamarca
58 A13 Caxias Amazonas, W Brazil
58 N13 Caxias Maranhão, E Brazil
61 I15 Caxias do Sul Rio Grande do Sul, S Brazil
42 J4 Caxinas, Punta headland N Honduras
82 B11 Caxito Bengo, NW Angola
136 F14 Çay Afyon, W Turkey
40 L15 Cayacal, Punta var. Punta Mongrove. headland S Mexico
56 C6 Cayambe Pichincha, N Ecuador
56 C6 Cayambe ▲ N Ecuador
21 R12 Cayce South Carolina, SE USA
55 Y10 Cayenne ○ (French Guiana) NE French Guiana
55 Y10 Cayenne × NE French Guiana
44 K10 Cayes var. Les Cayes. SW Haiti
45 U6 Cayey C Puerto Rico
45 U6 Cayey, Sierra de ▲ E Puerto Rico
103 N14 Caylus Tarn-et-Garonne, S France
44 E8 Cayman Brac island E Cayman Islands
44 D8 Cayman Islands ◇ UK dependent territory W West Indies
64 D11 Cayman Trench undersea feature NW Caribbean Sea
47 O3 Cayman Trough undersea feature NW Caribbean Sea
80 O13 Caynabo Togdheer, N Somalia
42 F3 Cayo ◈ district SW Belize
Cayo see San Ignacio
43 N9 Cayos Guerrero reef E Nicaragua
43 O9 Cayos King reef E Nicaragua
44 E4 Cay Sal islet SW Bahamas
14 G16 Cayuga Ontario, S Canada
25 V8 Cayuga Texas, SW USA
18 G10 Cayuga Lake ◎ New York, NE USA
104 K13 Cazalla de la Sierra Andalucía, S Spain
116 L14 Căzănești Ialomița, SE Romania
102 M16 Cazères Haute-Garonne, S France
112 E10 Cazin Federacija Bosna I Hercegovina, NW Bosnia and Herzegovina
82 G13 Cazombo Moxico, E Angola
105 O13 Cazorla Andalucía, S Spain
Cazza see Sušac
104 L4 Cea ≈ NW Spain
Ceadâr-Lunga see Ciadîr-Lunga
Ceanannas see Kells
Ceann Toirc see Kanturk
58 O13 Ceará off. Estado do Ceará. ◈ state C Brazil
Ceará see Fortaleza
Ceara Abyssal Plain see Ceará Plain
59 Q14 Ceará Mirim Rio Grande do Norte, E Brazil
64 J13 Ceará Plain var. Ceara Abyssal Plain. undersea feature W Atlantic Ocean
64 I13 Ceará Ridge undersea feature C Atlantic Ocean
Ceatharlach see Carlow
43 Q17 Cébaco, Isla island SW Panama
40 K7 Ceballos Durango, C Mexico
61 G19 Cebollatí Rocha, E Uruguay
61 G19 Cebollatí, Río ≈ E Uruguay
105 P5 Cebollera ▲ N Spain
104 M8 Cebreros Castilla-León, N Spain
171 P6 Cebu off. Cebu City. Cebu, C Philippines
171 P6 Cebu island C Philippines
107 J16 Ceccano Lazio, C Italy
Čechy see Bohemia
106 F12 Cecina Toscana, C Italy
26 K4 Cedar Bluff Reservoir ⊟ Kansas, C USA
30 M8 Cedarburg Wisconsin, N USA
36 J7 Cedar City Utah, W USA
25 T11 Cedar Creek Texas, SW USA
28 L7 Cedar Creek ≈ North Dakota, N USA
25 U7 Cedar Creek Reservoir ⊟ Texas, SW USA
29 W13 Cedar Falls Iowa, C USA
31 N8 Cedar Grove Wisconsin, N USA
21 Y6 Cedar Island island Virginia, NE USA
23 U11 Cedar Key Cedar Keys, Florida, SE USA
23 U11 Cedar Keys island group Florida, SE USA
11 V14 Cedar Lake ◎ Manitoba, C Canada
14 I11 Cedar Lake ◎ Ontario, SE Canada
24 M6 Cedar Lake ◎ Texas, SW USA
29 X13 Cedar Rapids Iowa, C USA
29 X14 Cedar River ≈ Iowa/Minnesota, C USA
29 O14 Cedar River ≈ Nebraska, C USA
31 P8 Cedar Springs Michigan, N USA
23 R3 Cedartown Georgia, SE USA
27 O7 Cedar Vale Kansas, C USA
35 Q2 Cedarville California, W USA
104 H1 Cedeira Galicia, NW Spain
42 H8 Cedeño Choluteca, S Honduras
41 N10 Cedral San Luis Potosí, C Mexico
42 I6 Cedros Francisco Morazán, C Honduras
40 M9 Cedros Zacatecas, C Mexico
40 B5 Cedros, Isla island W Mexico
193 R5 Cedros Trench undersea feature E Pacific Ocean
182 E7 Ceduna South Australia
110 D10 Cedynia Ger. Zehden. Zachodnio-pomorskie, W Poland
80 P12 Ceelaayo Sanaag, N Somalia
81 O16 Ceel Buur It. El Bur; Galguduud, C Somalia
81 N15 Ceel Dheere var. Ceel Dher, It. El Dere. Galguduud, C Somalia
Ceel Dher see Ceel Dheere
81 P14 Ceel Xamure Mudug, E Somalia
80 O12 Ceerigaabo var. Erigabo, Erigavo. Sanaag, N Somalia
107 J23 Cefalù anc. Cephaloedium. Sicilia, Italy, C Mediterranean Sea
105 N6 Cega ≈ N Spain
111 K23 Cegléd prev. Czegléd. Pest, C Hungary
113 N18 Čegrane W FYR Macedonia
105 Q13 Cehegín Murcia, SE Spain
136 K12 Çekerek Yozgat, N Turkey
146 B13 Çekiçler Rus. Chekishlyar, Turkm. Chekichler. Balkan Welaýaty, W Turkmenistan
107 J15 Celano Abruzzo, C Italy
104 H4 Celanova Galicia, NW Spain
42 F6 Celaque, Cordillera de ▲ W Honduras
41 N13 Celaya Guanajuato, C Mexico
Celebes see Sulawesi
192 F7 Celebes Basin undersea feature SE South China Sea
192 F7 Celebes Sea Ind. Laut Sulawesi. sea Indonesia/Philippines
41 W12 Celestún Yucatán, E Mexico
31 Q12 Celina Ohio, N USA
20 L8 Celina Tennessee, S USA
25 U5 Celina Texas, SW USA
112 G11 Čelinac Donji Republika Srpska, N Bosnia and Herzegovina
109 V10 Celje Ger. Cilli. C Slovenia
111 G23 Celldömölk Vas, W Hungary
100 J12 Celle var. Zelle. Niedersachsen, N Germany
99 D19 Celles Hainaut, SW Belgium
104 I7 Celorico da Beira Guarda, N Portugal
Celovec see Klagenfurt
64 M7 Celtic Sea Ir. An Mhuir Cheilteach. sea SW British Isles
64 N7 Celtic Shelf undersea feature E Atlantic Ocean
114 L13 Çeltik Gölu ◎ NW Turkey
146 J17 Çemenibit prev. Rus. Chemenibit. Mary Welaýaty, S Turkmenistan
113 M14 Čemerno ▲ C Serbia and Montenegro (Yugo.)
105 Q12 Cenajo, Embalse del ⊟ S Spain
171 V13 Cenderawasih, Teluk var. Teluk Irian, Teluk Sarera. bay W Pacific Ocean
105 P4 Cenicero La Rioja, N Spain
106 E9 Ceno ≈ NW Italy
102 K13 Cenon Gironde, SW France
14 K13 Centennial Lake ◎ Ontario, SE Canada
Centennial State see Colorado
37 S7 Center Colorado, C USA
29 Q13 Center Nebraska, C USA
28 M5 Center North Dakota, N USA
25 X8 Center Texas, SW USA
29 W8 Center City Minnesota, N USA
36 L5 Centerfield Utah, W USA
20 K9 Center Hill Lake ⊟ Tennessee, S USA
29 X13 Center Point Iowa, C USA
25 R11 Center Point Texas, SW USA
29 W16 Centerville Iowa, C USA
27 W7 Centerville Missouri, C USA
29 R12 Centerville South Dakota, N USA
20 I9 Centerville Tennessee, S USA
25 V9 Centerville Texas, SW USA
40 M5 Centinela, Picacho del ▲ NE Mexico
106 G9 Cento Emilia-Romagna, N Italy
Centrafricaine, République see Central African Republic
39 S8 Central Alaska, USA
37 P15 Central New Mexico, SW USA
83 H18 Central ◈ district E Botswana
138 E10 Central ◈ district C Israel
81 I19 Central ◈ province C Kenya
82 M13 Central ◈ region C Malawi
153 P12 Central ◈ zone C Nepal
186 E9 Central ◈ province S PNG
63 I21 Central ◈ department C Paraguay
186 M9 Central off. Central Province. ◈ province S Solomon Islands
83 J14 Central ◈ province C Zambia
117 P11 Central × (Odesa) Odes'ka Oblast', SW Ukraine
Central see Centre
79 H14 Central African Republic var. République Centrafricaine, abbrev. CAR; prev. Ubangi-Shari, Oubangui-Chari, Territoire de l'Oubangui-Chari. ◆ republic C Africa
192 G6 Central Basin Trough undersea feature W Pacific Ocean
Central Borneo see Kalimantan Tengah
149 P12 Central Brāhui Range ▲ W Pakistan
Central Celebes see Sulawesi Tengah
29 Y13 Central City Iowa, C USA
20 I6 Central City Kentucky, S USA
29 P15 Central City Nebraska, C USA
48 D6 Central, Cordillera ▲ W Bolivia
54 D11 Central, Cordillera ▲ W Colombia
42 M13 Central, Cordillera ▲ C Costa Rica
45 N9 Central, Cordillera ▲ C Dominican Republic
43 R16 Central, Cordillera ▲ C Panama
45 S6 Central, Cordillera ▲ Puerto Rico
42 H7 Central District var. Tegucigalpa. ◈ district C Honduras
30 L15 Centralia Illinois, N USA
27 U4 Centralia Missouri, C USA
32 G9 Centralia Washington, NW USA
Central Indian Ridge see Mid-Indian Ridge
Central Java see Jawa Tengah
Central Kalimantan see Kalimantan Tengah
148 L14 Central Makrān Range ▲ W Pakistan
192 K7 Central Pacific Basin undersea feature C Pacific Ocean
59 M19 Central, Planalto var. Brazilian Highlands. ▲ E Brazil
32 F15 Central Point Oregon, NW USA
155 K25 Central Province ◈ province C Sri Lanka
Central Provinces and Berar see Madhya Pradesh
186 B6 Central Range ▲ NW PNG
Central Russian Upland see Srednerusskaya Vozvyshennost'
Central Siberian Plateau/Central Siberian Uplands see Srednesibirskoye Ploskogor'ye
104 K8 Central, Sistema ▲ C Spain
Central Sulawesi see Sulawesi Tengah
35 N3 Central Valley California, W USA
35 P8 Central Valley valley California, W USA
23 Q3 Centre Alabama, S USA
79 E15 Centre Eng. Central. ◈ province C Cameroon
102 M8 Centre ◈ region N France
173 Y16 Centre de Flacq E Mauritius
55 Y9 Centre Spatial Guyanais space station N French Guiana
23 O5 Centreville Alabama, S USA
21 X3 Centreville Maryland, NE USA
22 J7 Centreville Mississippi, S USA
Centum Cellae see Civitavecchia
160 M14 Cenxi Guangxi Zhuangzu Zizhiqu, S China
Ceos see Kéa
Cephaloedium see Cefalu
112 I9 Čepin Hung. Csepén. Osijek-Baranja, E Croatia
Ceram see Seram, Pulau
171 R13 Ceram Sea Ind. Laut Seram. sea E Indonesia
192 G8 Ceram Trough undersea feature W Pacific Ocean
Cerasus see Giresun
36 I10 Cerbat Mountains ▲ Arizona, SW USA
103 P17 Cerbère, Cap headland S France
104 F13 Cercal do Alentejo Setúbal, S Portugal
111 A18 Čerchov Ger. Czerkow. ▲ W Czech Republic
103 O13 Cère ≈ C France
61 A16 Ceres Santa Fe, C Argentina
59 K18 Ceres Goiás, C Brazil
Ceresio see Lugano, Lago di
103 O17 Céret Pyrénées-Orientales, S France
54 E6 Cereté Córdoba, NW Colombia
172 I17 Cerf, Île au island Inner Islands, NE Seychelles
99 G22 Cerfontaine Namur, S Belgium
Cergy-Pontoise see Pontoise
107 N16 Cerignola Puglia, SE Italy
Cerigo see Kýthira
103 O9 Cérilly Allier, C France

◆ Country ● Country Capital ◇ Dependent Territory ○ Dependent Territory Capital ◈ Administrative Region × International Airport ▲ Mountain ▲ Mountain Range Volcano ≈ River ◎ Lake ⊟ Reservoir

136 I11 **Çerkeş** Çankın, N Turkey
136 D10 **Çerkezköy** Tekirdağ, NW Turkey
109 T12 **Cerknica** *Ger.* Zirknitz. SW Slovenia
109 S11 **Cerkno** W Slovenia
116 F10 **Cermei** *Hung.* Csermő. Arad, W Romania
137 O15 **Çermik** Diyarbakır, SE Turkey
112 I10 **Cerna** Vukovar-Srijem, E Croatia
Cernăuţi *see* Chernivtsi
116 M14 **Cernavodă** Constanţa, SW Romania
103 U7 **Cernay** Haut-Rhin, NE France
Černice *see* Schwarzach
41 O8 **Cerralvo** Nuevo León, NE Mexico
40 G9 **Cerralvo, Isla** *island* W Mexico
107 L16 **Cerreto Sannita** Campania, S Italy
113 L20 **Cërrik** *var.* Cerriku. Elbasan, C Albania
Cerriku *see* Cërrik
41 O11 **Cerritos** San Luis Potosí, C Mexico
60 K11 **Cerro Azul** Paraná, S Brazil
61 F18 **Cerro Chato** Treinta y Tres, E Uruguay
61 F19 **Cerro Colorado** Florida, S Uruguay
56 E13 **Cerro de Pasco** Pasco, C Peru
61 G18 **Cerro Largo** ◈ *department* NE Uruguay
61 G14 **Cêrro Largo** Rio Grande do Sul, S Brazil
42 E7 **Cerrón Grande, Embalse** ⊟ N El Salvador
63 I14 **Cerros Colorados, Embalse** ◎ W Argentina
105 V5 **Cervera** Cataluña, NE Spain
104 M3 **Cervera del Pisuerga** Castilla-León, N Spain
105 Q5 **Cervera del Río Alhama** La Rioja, N Spain
107 H15 **Cerveteri** Lazio, C Italy
106 H10 **Cervia** Emilia-Romagna, N Italy
106 J7 **Cervignano del Friuli** Friuli-Venezia Giulia, NE Italy
107 L17 **Cervinara** Campania, S Italy
Cervinia *see* Breuil-Cervinia
106 B6 **Cervino, Monte** *var.* Matterhorn. ▲ Italy/Switzerland **see also** Matterhorn
103 Y14 **Cervione** Corse, France, C Mediterranean Sea
104 I1 **Cervo** Galicia, NW Spain
54 F5 **Cesar** *off.* Departamento del Cesar. ◈ *province* N Colombia
106 H10 **Cesena** *anc.* Caesena. Emilia-Romagna, N Italy
106 I10 **Cesenatico** Emilia-Romagna, N Italy
118 H8 **Cēsis** *Ger.* Wenden. Cēsis, C Latvia
111 D15 **Česká Lípa** *Ger.* Böhmisch-Leipa. Liberecký Kraj, N Czech Republic
Česká Republika *see* Czech Republic
111 F17 **Česká Třebová** *Ger.* Böhmisch-Trübau. Pardubický Kraj, C Czech Republic
111 D19 **České Budějovice** *Ger.* Budweis. Jihočeský Kraj, S Czech Republic
111 D19 **České Velenice** Jihočeský Kraj, S Czech Republic
111 E18 **Českomoravská Vrchovina** *var.* Českomoravská Vysočina, *Eng.* Bohemian-Moravian Highlands, *Ger.* Böhmisch-Mährische Höhe. ▲ S Czech Republic
Českomoravská Vysočina *see* Českomoravská Vrchovina
111 C19 **Český Krumlov** *var.* Böhmisch-Krumau, *Ger.* Krummau. Jihočeský Kraj, S Czech Republic
Ceský Les *see* Bohemian Forest
112 F8 **Česma** ∽ N Croatia
136 A14 **Çeşme** İzmir, W Turkey
Cess *see* Cestos
183 T8 **Cessnock** New South Wales, SE Australia
76 K17 **Cestos** *var.* Cess. ∽ S Liberia
118 I9 **Cesvaine** Madona, E Latvia
116 G14 **Cetate** Dolj, SW Romania
Cetatea Albă *see* Bilhorod-Dnistrovs'kyy
113 J17 **Cetinje** *It.* Cettigne. Montenegro, SW Serbia and Montenegro (Yugo.)
107 N20 **Cetraro** Calabria, S Italy
Cette *see* Sète
188 A17 **Cetti Bay** *bay* SW Guam
Cettigne *see* Cetinje
104 L17 **Ceuta** *var.* Sebta. Ceuta, Spain, N Africa
88 C15 **Ceuta** *enclave* Spain, N Africa
106 B9 **Ceva** Piemonte, NE Italy
103 P14 **Cévennes** ▲ S France
108 G10 **Cevio** Ticino, S Switzerland
136 K16 **Ceyhan** Adana, S Turkey
136 K17 **Ceyhan Nehri** ∽ S Turkey
137 P17 **Ceylanpınar** Şanlıurfa, SE Turkey
Ceylon *see* Sri Lanka
173 R6 **Ceylon Plain** *undersea feature* N Indian Ocean
Ceyre to the Caribs *see* Marie-Galante
103 Q14 **Cèze** ∽ S France
Chaacha *see* Çäçe
127 P6 **Chaadayevka** Penzenskaya Oblast', W Russian Federation
167 O12 **Cha-Am** Phetchaburi, SW Thailand
143 W15 **Chābahār** *var.* Chāh Bahār, Chahbar. Sīstān va Balūchestān, SE Iran
61 B19 **Chabas** Santa Fe, C Argentina
103 T10 **Chablais** *physical region* E France
61 B20 **Chacabuco** Buenos Aires, E Argentina
42 K8 **Chachagón, Cerro** ▲ N Nicaragua
56 C10 **Chachapoyas** Amazonas, NW Peru
Chäche *see* Çäçe
119 O18 **Chachersk** *Rus.* Chechersk. Homyel'skaya Voblasts', SE Belarus
119 N16 **Chachevichy** *Rus.* Chechevichi. Mahilyowskaya Voblasts', E Belarus
61 B14 **Chaco** *off.* Provincia de Chaco. ◈ *province* NE Argentina
Chaco *see* Gran Chaco
62 M6 **Chaco Austral** *physical region* N Argentina
62 M3 **Chaco Boreal** *physical region* N Paraguay
62 M6 **Chaco Central** *physical region* N Argentina
39 Y15 **Chacon, Cape** *headland* Prince of Wales Island, Alaska, USA
78 H9 **Chad** *off.* Republic of Chad, *Fr.* Tchad. ◆ *republic* C Africa
122 K14 **Chadan** Respublika Tyva, S Russian Federation
21 U12 **Chadbourn** North Carolina, SE USA
83 L14 **Chadiza** Eastern, E Zambia
67 Q7 **Chad, Lake** *Fr.* Lac Tchad. ◎ C Africa
28 J12 **Chadron** Nebraska, C USA
Chadyr-Lunga *see* Ciadîr-Lunga
163 W14 **Chaeryŏng** SW North Korea
105 P17 **Chafarinas, Islas** *island group* S Spain
27 Y7 **Chaffee** Missouri, C USA
148 L12 **Chāgai Hills** *var.* Chāh Gay. ▲ Afghanistan/Pakistan
123 Q11 **Chagda** Respublika Sakha (Yakutiya), NE Russian Federation
Chaghasarāy *see* Asadābād
149 N5 **Chaghcharān** *var.* Chakhcharan, Cheghcheran, Qala Āhangarān. Ghowr, C Afghanistan
103 R9 **Chagny** Saône-et-Loire, C France
173 Q7 **Chagos Archipelago** *var.* Oil Islands. *island group* British Indian Ocean Territory
131 O15 **Chagos Bank** *undersea feature* C Indian Ocean
131 O14 **Chagos-Laccadive Plateau** *undersea feature* N Indian Ocean
173 Q7 **Chagos Trench** *undersea feature* N Indian Ocean
43 T14 **Chagres, Río** ∽ C Panama
45 U14 **Chaguanas** Trinidad, Trinidad and Tobago
54 M6 **Chaguaramas** Guárico, N Venezuela
Chagyl *see* Çagyl
Chahārmahāl and Bakhtiyārī *see* Chahār Maḩall va Bakhtīārī
142 M9 **Chahār Maḩall va Bakhtīārī** *off.* Ostān-e Chahār Maḩall va Bakhtīārī, *var.* Chahārmahāl and Bakhtiyārī. ◈ *province* SW Iran
Chāh Bahār/Chahbar *see* Chābahār
143 V13 **Chāh Derāz** Sīstān va Balūchestān, SE Iran
Chāh Gay *see* Chāgai Hills
167 P10 **Chai Badan** Lop Buri, C Thailand
153 Q16 **Chāībāsa** Jhārkhand, N India
79 E19 **Chaillu, Massif du** ▲ C Gabon
167 O10 **Chai Nat** *var.* Chainat, Jainat, Jayanath. Chai Nat, C Thailand
65 M14 **Chain Fracture Zone** *tectonic feature* E Atlantic Ocean
173 N5 **Chain Ridge** *undersea feature* W Indian Ocean
Chairn, Ceann an *see* Carnsore Point
158 L5 **Chaiwopu** Xinjiang Uygur Zizhiqu, W China
167 Q10 **Chaiyaphum** *var.* Jayabum. Chaiyaphum, C Thailand
62 N10 **Chajarí** Entre Ríos, E Argentina
42 C5 **Chajul** Quiché, W Guatemala
83 K16 **Chakari** Mashonaland West, N Zimbabwe
148 J9 **Chakhānsūr** Nīmrūz, SW Afghanistan
Chakhānsūr *see* Nīmrūz
Chakhcharan *see* Chaghcharān
149 V8 **Chak Jhumra** *var.* Jhumra. Punjab, E Pakistan
146 I16 **Chaknakdysonga** Ahal Welaýaty, S Turkmenistan
153 P16 **Chakradharpur** Jhārkhand, N India
152 J8 **Chakrāta** Uttaranchal, N India
149 U7 **Chakwāl** Punjab, NE Pakistan
57 F17 **Chala** Arequipa, SW Peru
102 K12 **Chalais** Charente, W France
108 D10 **Chalais** Valais, SW Switzerland
115 J20 **Chalándri** *var.* Halandri; *prev.* Khalándrion. *prehistoric site* Sýros, Kykládes, Greece, Aegean Sea
188 H6 **Chalan Kanoa** Saipan, S Northern Mariana Islands
188 C16 **Chalan Pago** C Guam
Chalap Dalam/Chalap Dalan *see* Chehel Abdālān, Kūh-e
42 F7 **Chalatenango** Chalatenango, N El Salvador
42 A9 **Chalatenango** ◈ *department* NW El Salvador
83 P15 **Chalaua** Nampula, NE Mozambique
81 I16 **Chalbi Desert** *desert* N Kenya
42 D7 **Chalchuapa** Santa Ana, W El Salvador
Chalcidice *see* Chalkidikí
Chalcis *see* Chalkída
103 N6 **Châlette-sur-Loing** Loiret, C France
15 X8 **Chaleur Bay** *Fr.* Baie des Chaleurs. *bay* New Brunswick/Québec, E Canada
Chaleurs, Baie des *see* Chaleur Bay
57 G16 **Chalhuanca** Apurímac, S Peru
154 F12 **Chālisgaon** Mahārāshtra, C India
115 N23 **Chálki** *island* Dodekánisos, Greece, Aegean Sea
115 F16 **Chalkiádes** Thessalía, C Greece
115 H18 **Chalkída** *var.* Halkida; *prev.* Khalkís, *anc.* Chalcis. Evvoia, E Greece
115 G14 **Chalkidikí** *var.* Khalkidhikí; *anc.* Chalcidice. *peninsula* NE Greece
185 A24 **Chalky Inlet** *inlet* South Island, NZ
39 S7 **Chalkyitsik** Alaska, USA
102 I9 **Challans** Vendée, NW France
57 K19 **Challapata** Oruro, SW Bolivia
192 H6 **Challenger Deep** *undersea feature* W Pacific Ocean
193 S11 **Challenger Fracture Zone** *tectonic feature* SE Pacific Ocean
192 K11 **Challenger Plateau** *undersea feature* E Tasman Sea
33 P13 **Challis** Idaho, NW USA
22 L9 **Chalmette** Louisiana, S USA
124 J11 **Chalna** Respublika Kareliya, NW Russian Federation
103 Q5 **Châlons-en-Champagne** *prev.* Châlons-sur-Marne, *hist.* Arcae Remorum, *anc.* Carolopois. Marne, NE France
Châlons-sur-Marne *see* Châlons-en-Champagne
103 R9 **Chalon-sur-Saône** *anc.* Cabillonum. Saône-et-Loire, C France
Chaltel, Cerro *see* Fitzroy, Monte
143 N4 **Chālūs** Māzandarān, N Iran
102 M11 **Châlus** Haute-Vienne, C France
101 N20 **Cham** Bayern, SE Germany
108 F7 **Cham** Zug, N Switzerland
37 R8 **Chama** New Mexico, SW USA
Cha Mai *see* Thung Song
83 E22 **Chamaites** Karas, S Namibia
149 O9 **Chaman** Baluchistān, SW Pakistan
37 R9 **Chama, Río** ∽ New Mexico, SW USA
152 I6 **Chamba** Himāchal Pradesh, N India
81 I25 **Chamba** Ruvuma, S Tanzania
150 H12 **Chambal** ∽ C India
11 U16 **Chamberlain** Saskatchewan, S Canada
29 O11 **Chamberlain** South Dakota, N USA
19 R3 **Chamberlain Lake** ◎ Maine, NE USA
39 S5 **Chamberlin, Mount** ▲ Alaska, USA
37 O11 **Chambers** Arizona, SW USA
18 F16 **Chambersburg** Pennsylvania, NE USA
31 N5 **Chambers Island** *island* Wisconsin, N USA
103 T11 **Chambéry** *anc.* Camberia. Savoie, E France
82 L12 **Chambeshi** Northern, NE Zambia
82 L12 **Chambeshi** ∽ NE Zambia
74 M6 **Chambi, Jebel** *var.* Jabal ash Sha'nabī. ▲ W Tunisia
15 Q7 **Chambord** Québec, SE Canada
139 U11 **Chamcham** S Iraq
139 T4 **Chamchamāl** N Iraq
40 J14 **Chamela** Jalisco, SW Mexico
42 G5 **Chamelecón, Río** ∽ NW Honduras
62 J9 **Chamical** La Rioja, C Argentina
115 L23 **Chamilí** *island* Kykládes, Greece, Aegean Sea
167 Q13 **Châmnar** Kaôh Kông, SW Cambodia
152 K9 **Chamoli** Uttaranchal, N India
103 U11 **Chamonix-Mont-Blanc** Haute-Savoie, E France
154 L11 **Chāmpa** Chhattīsgarh, C India
10 H8 **Champagne** Yukon Territory, W Canada
103 Q5 **Champagne** *cultural region* N France
Champagne *see* Campania
103 Q5 **Champagne-Ardenne** ◈ *region* N France
103 S9 **Champagnole** Jura, E France
30 M13 **Champaign** Illinois, N USA
167 S10 **Champasak** Champasak, S Laos
103 U6 **Champ de Feu** ▲ NE France
13 O7 **Champdoré, Lac** ◎ Québec, NE Canada
42 B6 **Champerico** Retalhuleu, SW Guatemala
108 C11 **Champéry** Valais, SW Switzerland
18 L6 **Champlain** New York, NE USA
18 L9 **Champlain Canal** *canal* New York, NE USA
15 P13 **Champlain, Lac** ◎ Canada/USA **see also** Champlain, Lake
18 L7 **Champlain, Lake** ◎ Canada/USA **see also** Champlain, Lac
103 S7 **Champlitte** Haute-Saône, E France
41 W13 **Champotón** Campeche, SE Mexico
104 G10 **Chamusca** Santarém, C Portugal
119 O20 **Chamyarysy** *Rus.* Chemerisy. Homyel'skaya Voblasts', SE Belarus
127 P5 **Chamzinka** Respublika Mordoviya, W Russian Federation
Chanáil Mhór, An *see* Grand Canal
Chanak *see* Çanakkale
64 G7 **Chañaral** Atacama, N Chile
104 H13 **Chança, Rio** *var.* Chanza. ∽ Portugal/Spain
57 D14 **Chancay** Lima, W Peru
Chan-chiang/Chanchiang *see* Zhanjiang
64 G13 **Chanco** Maule, Chile
39 R7 **Chandalar** Alaska, USA
39 R6 **Chandalar River** ∽ Alaska, USA
152 L10 **Chandan Chauki** Uttar Pradesh, N India
153 S16 **Chandannagar** *prev.* Chandernagore. West Bengal, E India
152 K10 **Chandausi** Uttar Pradesh, N India
22 M10 **Chandeleur Islands** *island group* Louisiana, S USA
22 M9 **Chandeleur Sound** *sound* N Gulf of Mexico
152 I8 **Chandīgarh** Punjab, N India
153 Q16 **Chāndil** Jhārkhand, NE India
182 D2 **Chandler** South Australia
15 Y7 **Chandler** Québec, SE Canada
36 L14 **Chandler** Arizona, SW USA
27 O10 **Chandler** Oklahoma, C USA
25 V7 **Chandler** Texas, SW USA
39 Q6 **Chandler River** ∽ Alaska, USA
56 H13 **Chandles, Río** ∽ E Peru
163 N9 **Chandmanĭ** Dornogovĭ, SE Mongolia
14 J13 **Chandos Lake** ◎ Ontario, SE Canada
153 U15 **Chandpur** Chittagong, C Bangladesh
154 I13 **Chandrapur** Mahārāshtra, C India
83 J15 **Changa** Southern, S Zambia
Changan *see* Xi'an, Shaanxi, China
Chang'an *see* Rong'an, Guangxi Zhuangzu Zizhiqu, China
155 G23 **Changanācheri** Kerala, SW India
83 M19 **Changane** ∽ S Mozambique
83 M16 **Changara** Tete, NW Mozambique
163 X11 **Changbai** *var.* Changbai Chosenzu Zizhixian. Jilin, NE China
Changbai Chosenzu Zizhixian *see* Changbai
163 X11 **Changbai Shan** ▲ NE China
163 V10 **Changchun** *var.* Ch'angch'un, Ch'ang-ch'un; *prev.* Hsinking. Jilin, NE China
160 M10 **Changde** Hunan, S China
161 S13 **Changhua** *Jap.* Shōka. C Taiwan
168 L10 **Changi** ✕ (Singapore) E Singapore
158 L5 **Changji** Xinjiang Uygur Zizhiqu, NW China
160 L17 **Changjiang** *var.* Changjiang Lizu Zizhixian, Shiliu. Hainan, S China
157 O13 **Chang Jiang** *var.* Yangtze Kiang, *Eng.* Yangtze. ∽ C China
161 S8 **Changjiang Kou** *delta* E China
Changjiang Lizu Zizhixian *see* Changjiang
167 F12 **Chang, Ko** *island* S Thailand
161 Q2 **Changli** Hebei, E China
163 V10 **Changling** Jilin, NE China
Changning *see* Xunwu
161 N11 **Changsha** *var.* Ch'angsha, Ch'ang-sha. Hunan, S China
161 Q10 **Changshan** Zhejiang, SE China
163 V14 **Changshan Qundao** *island group* NE China
161 S8 **Changshu** *var.* Ch'ang-shu. Jiangsu, E China
163 V11 **Changtu** Liaoning, NE China
43 P14 **Changuinola** Bocas del Toro, NW Panama
159 N9 **Changweiliang** Qinghai, W China
160 K6 **Changwu** *var.* Zhaoren. Shaanxi, C China
163 U13 **Changxing Dao** *island* N China
160 M9 **Changyang** *var.* Longzhouping. Hubei, C China
163 W14 **Changyŏn** SW North Korea
161 N5 **Changzhi** Shanxi, C China
161 R8 **Changzhou** Jiangsu, E China
115 H24 **Chaniá** *var.* Hania, Khaniá, *Eng.* Canea; *anc.* Cydonia. Kríti, Greece, E Mediterranean Sea
62 J5 **Chañi, Nevado de** ▲ NW Argentina
115 H24 **Chanión, Kólpos** *gulf* Kríti, Greece, E Mediterranean Sea
Chankiri *see* Çankırı
30 M11 **Channahon** Illinois, N USA
155 H20 **Channapatna** Karnātaka, E India
97 K26 **Channel Islands** *Fr.* Îles Normandes. *island group* S English Channel
35 R16 **Channel Islands** *island group* California, W USA
13 S13 **Channel-Port aux Basques** Newfoundland and Labrador, SE Canada
Channel, The *see* English Channel
97 Q23 **Channel Tunnel** *tunnel* France/UK
24 M2 **Channing** Texas, SW USA
Chantabun/Chantaburi *see* Chanthaburi
104 H3 **Chantada** Galicia, NW Spain
167 P12 **Chanthaburi** *var.* Chantabun, Chantaburi. Chantaburi, S Thailand
103 O4 **Chantilly** Oise, N France
139 V12 **Chanūn as Sa'ūdī** S Iraq
27 Q6 **Chanute** Kansas, C USA
Chanza *see* Chança, Rio
Ch'ao-an/Chaochow *see* Chaozhou
161 P8 **Chao Hu** ◎ E China
167 P11 **Chao Phraya, Mae Nam** ∽ C Thailand
Chaor He *see* Qulin Gol
Chaouèn *see* Chefchaouen
161 P14 **Chaoyang** Guangdong, S China
163 T12 **Chaoyang** Liaoning, NE China
Chaoyang *see* Jiayin, Heilongjiang, China
Chaoyang *see* Huinan, Jilin, China
161 Q14 **Chaozhou** *var.* Chaoan, Chao'an, Ch'ao-an; *prev.* Chaochow. Guangdong, SE China
58 N13 **Chapadinha** Maranhão, E Brazil
12 K12 **Chapais** Québec, SE Canada
40 L13 **Chapala** Jalisco, SW Mexico
40 L13 **Chapala, Lago de** ◎ C Mexico
146 F13 **Chapan, Gora** ▲ C Turkmenistan
57 M18 **Chapare, Río** ∽ C Bolivia
54 E11 **Chaparral** Tolima, C Colombia
144 F9 **Chapayev** Zapadnyy Kazakhstan, NW Kazakhstan
123 O11 **Chapayevo** Respublika Sakha (Yakutiya), NE Russian Federation
127 R6 **Chapayevsk** Samarskaya Oblast', W Russian Federation
60 H13 **Chapecó** Santa Catarina, S Brazil
60 I13 **Chapecó, Rio** ∽ S Brazil
20 J9 **Chapel Hill** Tennessee, S USA
44 J12 **Chapelton** C Jamaica
14 C8 **Chapleau** Ontario, SE Canada
14 D7 **Chapleau** ∽ Ontario, S Canada
11 T16 **Chaplin** Saskatchewan, S Canada
126 M5 **Chaplygin** Lipetskaya Oblast', W Russian Federation
117 S11 **Chaplynka** Khersons'ka Oblast', S Ukraine
9 O6 **Chapman, Cape** *headland* Nunavut, NE Canada
25 T15 **Chapman Ranch** Texas, SW USA
Chapman's *see* Okwa
21 P5 **Chapmanville** West Virginia, NE USA
28 K15 **Chappell** Nebraska, C USA
Chapra *see* Chhapra
56 D9 **Chapuli, Río** ∽ N Peru
76 I6 **Châr** *well* N Mauritania
123 P12 **Chara** Chitinskaya Oblast', S Russian Federation
123 O11 **Chara** ∽ C Russian Federation
54 G8 **Charala** Santander, C Colombia
41 N10 **Charcas** San Luis Potosí, C Mexico
25 T13 **Charco** Texas, SW USA
194 H7 **Charcot Island** *island* Antarctica
64 M8 **Charcot Seamounts** *undersea feature* E Atlantic Ocean
Chardara *see* Shardara
145 P17 **Chardarinskoye Vodokhranilishche** ⊟ S Kazakhstan
31 U11 **Chardon** Ohio, N USA
44 K9 **Chardonnières** SW Haiti
Chardzhev *see* Türkmenabat
Chardzhevskaya Oblast' *see* Lebap Welaýaty
Chardzhou/Chardzhui *see* Türkmenabat
102 L11 **Charente** ◈ *department* W France
102 J11 **Charente** ∽ W France
102 J10 **Charente-Maritime** ◈ *department* W France
137 U12 **Ch'arents'avan** C Armenia
78 I12 **Chari** *var.* Shari. ∽ Central African Republic/Chad
78 G11 **Chari-Baguirmi** *off.* Préfecture du Chari-Baguirmi. ◈ *prefecture* SW Chad
149 Q4 **Chārīkār** Parwān, NE Afghanistan
29 V15 **Chariton** Iowa, C USA
27 U3 **Chariton River** ∽ Missouri, C USA
55 T7 **Charity** NW Guyana
31 R7 **Charity Island** *island* Michigan, N USA
Chärjew *see* Türkmenabat
Chärjew Oblasty *see* Lebap Welaýaty
Charkhlik/Charkhliq *see* Ruoqiang
99 G20 **Charleroi** Hainaut, S Belgium
11 V12 **Charles** Manitoba, C Canada
15 R10 **Charlesbourg** Québec, SE Canada
21 Y7 **Charles, Cape** *headland* Virginia, NE USA
29 W12 **Charles City** Iowa, C USA
21 W6 **Charles City** Virginia, NE USA
103 O5 **Charles de Gaulle** ✕ (Paris) Seine-et-Marne, N France
12 K1 **Charles Island** *island* Nunavut, NE Canada
Charles Island *see* Santa María, Isla
30 K9 **Charles Mound** *hill* Illinois, N USA
185 A22 **Charles Sound** *sound* South Island, NZ
185 G15 **Charleston** West Coast, South Island, NZ
27 S11 **Charleston** Arkansas, C USA
30 M14 **Charleston** Illinois, N USA
22 L3 **Charleston** Mississippi, S USA
27 Z7 **Charleston** Missouri, C USA
21 T15 **Charleston** South Carolina, SE USA
21 Q5 **Charleston** *state capital* West Virginia, NE USA
14 L14 **Charleston Lake** ◎ Ontario, SE Canada
35 W11 **Charleston Peak** ▲ Nevada, W USA
45 W10 **Charlestown** Nevis, Saint Kitts and Nevis
31 P16 **Charlestown** Indiana, N USA
18 M9 **Charlestown** New Hampshire, NE USA
21 V3 **Charles Town** West Virginia, NE USA
181 W9 **Charleville** Queensland, E Australia
103 R3 **Charleville-Mézières** Ardennes, N France
31 P5 **Charlevoix** Michigan, N USA
31 Q6 **Charlevoix, Lake** ◎ Michigan, N USA
39 T9 **Charley River** ∽ Alaska, USA
64 J6 **Charlie-Gibbs Fracture Zone** *tectonic feature* N Atlantic Ocean
103 Q10 **Charlieu** Loire, E France
31 Q9 **Charlotte** Michigan, N USA
21 R10 **Charlotte** North Carolina, SE USA
20 I8 **Charlotte** Tennessee, S USA
25 R13 **Charlotte** Texas, SW USA
21 R10 **Charlotte** ✕ North Carolina, SE USA
45 T9 **Charlotte Amalie** *prev.* Saint Thomas. ○ (Virgin Islands (US)) Saint Thomas, N Virgin Islands (US)
21 U7 **Charlotte Court House** Virginia, NE USA
23 W14 **Charlotte Harbor** *inlet* Florida, SE USA
Charlotte Island *see* Abaiang
95 J15 **Charlottenberg** Värmland, C Sweden
Charlottenhof *see* Aegviidu
21 U5 **Charlottesville** Virginia, NE USA
Charlotte Town *see* Roseau, Dominica
Charlotte Town *see* Gouyave, Grenada
13 Q14 **Charlottetown** Prince Edward Island, Prince Edward Island, SE Canada
45 Z16 **Charlotteville** Tobago, Trinidad and Tobago
182 M11 **Charlton** Victoria, SE Australia
12 H10 **Charlton Island** *island* Nunavut, C Canada
103 T6 **Charmes** Vosges, NE France
119 F19 **Charnawchytsy** *Rus.* Chernavchitsy. Brestskaya Voblasts', SW Belarus
15 R10 **Charny** Québec, SE Canada
149 T5 **Chārsadda** North-West Frontier Province, NW Pakistan
Charshanga/Charshangngy/Charshangy *see* Köýtendag
Charsk *see* Shar
181 W6 **Charters Towers** Queensland, NE Australia
15 R12 **Chartierville** Québec, SE Canada
102 M6 **Chartres** *anc.* Autricum, Civitas Carnutum. Eure-et-Loir, C France
127 P4 **Charvash Respubliki** *prev.* Chuvashskaya Respublika, *var.* Chavash Respubliki, *Eng.* Chuvashia. ◈ *autonomous republic* W Russian Federation
145 W15 **Charyn** *Kaz.* Sharyn. Almaty, SE Kazakhstan
61 D21 **Chascomús** Buenos Aires, E Argentina
11 N16 **Chase** British Columbia, SW Canada
21 U7 **Chase City** Virginia, NE USA
19 S4 **Chase, Mount** ▲ Maine, NE USA
118 M13 **Chashniki** *Rus.* Chashniki. Vitsyebskaya Voblasts', N Belarus
115 D15 **Chásia** ▲ C Greece
29 V9 **Chaska** Minnesota, N USA
185 D25 **Chaslands Mistake** *headland* South Island, NZ
125 R11 **Chasovo** Respublika Komi, NW Russian Federation
Chasovo *see* Vazhgort
124 H14 **Chastova** Novgorodskaya Oblast', NW Russian Federation
143 R3 **Chāt** Golestān, N Iran
Chatak *see* Chhatak
Chatang *see* Zhanang
39 R9 **Chatanika** Alaska, USA
39 R9 **Chatanika River** ∽ Alaska, USA
147 T8 **Chat-Bazar** Talasskaya Oblast', NW Kyrgyzstan
45 Y14 **Chateaubelair** Saint Vincent, W Saint Vincent and the Grenadines
102 J7 **Châteaubriant** Loire-Atlantique, NW France
103 Q8 **Château-Chinon** Nièvre, C France
108 C10 **Château d'Oex** Vaud, W Switzerland
102 L7 **Château-du-Loir** Sarthe, NW France
102 M6 **Châteaudun** Eure-et-Loir, C France
102 K7 **Château-Gontier** Mayenne, NW France
15 O13 **Châteauguay** Québec, SE Canada
102 F6 **Châteaulin** Finistère, NW France
103 N9 **Châteaumeillant** Cher, C France
102 K11 **Châteauneuf-sur-Charente** Charente, W France
102 M7 **Château-Renault** Indre-et-Loire, C France
103 N9 **Châteauroux** *prev.* Indreville. Indre, C France
103 T5 **Château-Salins** Moselle, NE France
103 P4 **Château-Thierry** Aisne, N France
99 H21 **Châtelet** Hainaut, S Belgium
Châtelherault *see* Châtellerault
102 L9 **Châtellerault** *var.* Châtelherault. Vienne, W France
29 X10 **Chatfield** Minnesota, N USA
13 O14 **Chatham** New Brunswick, SE Canada
14 D17 **Chatham** Ontario, S Canada
97 P22 **Chatham** SE England, UK
30 K14 **Chatham** Illinois, N USA
21 T7 **Chatham** Virginia, NE USA
63 F22 **Chatham, Isla** *island* S Chile
175 R12 **Chatham Island** *island* Chatham Islands, NZ

◆ Country ● Country Capital ◇ Dependent Territory ○ Dependent Territory Capital ◈ Administrative Region ✕ International Airport ▲ Mountain ▲ Mountain Range ⛰ Volcano ∽ River ◎ Lake ⊟ Reservoir

Chatham Island *see* San Cristóbal, Isla
Chatham Island Rise *see* Chatham Rise
192 *L12* **Chatham Islands** *island group* NZ, SW Pacific Ocean
175 *Q12* **Chatham Rise** *var.* Chatham Island Rise. *undersea feature* S Pacific Ocean
39 *X13* **Chatham Strait** *strait* Alaska, USA
Chathóir, Rinn *see* Cahore Point
102 *M9* **Châtillon-sur-Indre** Indre, C France
103 *Q7* **Châtillon-sur-Seine** Côte d'Or, C France
147 *S8* **Chatkal** *Uzb.* Chotqol. ≈ Kyrgyzstan/Uzbekistan
147 *R9* **Chatkal Range** *Rus.* Chatkal'skiy Khrebet. ⛰ Kyrgyzstan/Uzbekistan
Chatkal'skiy Khrebet *see* Chatkal Range
23 *N7* **Chatom** Alabama, S USA
Chatrapur *see* Chhatrapur
143 *S10* **Chatrūd** Kermān, C Iran
23 *S2* **Chatsworth** Georgia, SE USA
Chāttagām *see* Chittagong
23 *S8* **Chattahoochee** Florida, SE USA
23 *R8* **Chattahoochee River** ≈ SE USA
20 *L10* **Chattanooga** Tennessee, S USA
147 *V10* **Chatyr-Këľ, Ozero** ◎ C Kyrgyzstan
147 *W9* **Chatyr-Tash** Narynskaya Oblast', C Kyrgyzstan
15 *R12* **Chaudière** ≈ Québec, SE Canada
167 *S14* **Châu Đôc** *var.* Chauphu, Chau Phu. An Giang, S Vietnam
152 *D13* **Chauhtan** *prev.* Chohtan. Rājasthān, NW India
115 *Ff5* **Chauk** Magwe, W Myanmar
103 *R6* **Chaumont** *prev.* Chaumont-en-Bassigny. Haute-Marne, N France
Chaumont-en-Bassigny *see* Chaumont
123 *T5* **Chaunskaya Guba** *bay* NE Russian Federation
103 *P3* **Chauny** Aisne, N France
Châu Ô *see* Binh Sơn
Chau Phu *see* Châu Đôc
102 *I5* **Chausey, Îles** *island group* N France
Chausy *see* Chavusy
18 *C11* **Chautauqua Lake** ◎ New York, NE USA
102 *L9* **Chauvigny** Vienne, W France
124 *L6* **Chavan'ga** Murmanskaya Oblast', NW Russian Federation
14 *K10* **Chavannes, Lac** ◎ Québec, SE Canada
Chavantes, Represa de *see* Xavantes, Represa de
61 *D15* **Chavarría** Corrientes, NE Argentina
Chavash Respubliki *see* Charvash Respubliki
104 *I5* **Chaves** *anc.* Aquae Flaviae. Vila Real, N Portugal
Chávez, Isla *see* Santa Cruz, Isla
82 *G13* **Chavuma** North Western, NW Zambia
119 *O16* **Chavusy** *Rus.* Chausy. Mahilyowskaya Voblasts', E Belarus
Chayan *see* Shayan
147 *U8* **Chayek** Narynskaya Oblast', C Kyrgyzstan
139 *T6* **Chāy Khānah** E Iraq
125 *T16* **Chaykovskiy** Permskaya Oblast', NW Russian Federation
167 *T12* **Chbar** Môndól Kiri, E Cambodia
23 *Q4* **Cheaha Mountain** ▲ Alabama, S USA
Cheatharlach *see* Carlow
21 *S2* **Cheat River** ≈ NE USA
111 *A16* **Cheb** *Ger.* Eger. Karlovarský Kraj, W Czech Republic
127 *Q3* **Cheboksary** Chuvashskaya Respublika, W Russian Federation
31 *Q5* **Cheboygan** Michigan, N USA
Chechaouèn *see* Chefchaouen
Chechenia *see* Chechenskaya Respublika
127 *O15* **Chechenskaya Respublika** *Eng.* Chechenia, Chechnia, *Rus.* Chechnya. ◈ *autonomous republic* SW Russian Federation
67 *N4* **Chech, Erg** *desert* Algeria/Mali
Chechersk *see* Chachersk
Chechevichi *see* Chachevichy
Che-chiang *see* Zhejiang
Chechnia/Chechnya *see* Chechenskaya Respublika
163 *Y15* **Chech'ŏn** *Jap.* Teisen. N South Korea
111 *L15* **Chęciny** Świętokrzyskie, S Poland
27 *Q10* **Checotah** Oklahoma, C USA
13 *R15* **Chedabucto Bay** *inlet* Nova Scotia, E Canada
166 *J7* **Cheduba Island** *island* W Myanmar
37 *T5* **Cheesman Lake** ▣ Colorado, C USA
195 *S16* **Cheetham, Cape** *headland* Antarctica
74 *G5* **Chefchaouen** *var.* Chaouèn, Chechaouèn, *Sp.* Xauen. N Morocco
Chefoo *see* Yantai
38 *M12* **Chefornak** Alaska, USA
123 *R13* **Chegdomyn** Khabarovskiy Kray, SE Russian Federation
76 *M4* **Chegga** Tiris Zemmour, NE Mauritania
Cheghcheran *see* Chaghcharān
32 *G9* **Chehalis** Washington, NW USA
32 *G9* **Chehalis River** ≈ Washington, NW USA
148 *M6* **Chehel Abdālān, Kūh-e** *var.* Chalap Dalam, *Pash.* Chalap Dalan. ⛰ C Afghanistan
115 *D14* **Cheimadítis, Límni** ◎ N Greece
103 *U15* **Cheiron, Mont** ▲ SE France
163 *X17* **Cheju** *Jap.* Saishū. S South Korea
163 *Y17* **Cheju** ✕ S South Korea
163 *Y17* **Cheju-do** *Jap.* Saishū; *prev.* Quelpart. *island* S South Korea
163 *X17* **Cheju-haehyŏp** *strait* S South Korea
Chekiang *see* Zhejiang
Chekichler/Chekishlyar *see* Çekiçler
188 *F8* **Chelab** Babeldaob, N Palau
147 *N11* **Chelak** *Rus.* Chelek. Samarqand Viloyati, C Uzbekistan
32 *J7* **Chelan, Lake** ▣ Washington, NW USA
Chelek *see* Chelak
Cheleken *see* Hazar
Chélif/Chéliff *see* Chelif, Oued
74 *J5* **Chelif, Oued** *var.* Chélif, Chéliff, Chellif, Shellif. ≈ N Algeria
Chelkar *see* Shalkar
Chelkar, Ozero *see* Shalkar, Ozero
Chellif *see* Chelif, Oued
111 *P14* **Chełm** *Rus.* Kholm. Lubelskie, SE Poland
110 *I9* **Chełmno** *Ger.* Culm, Kulm. Kujawski-pomorskie, C Poland
14 *F10* **Chelmsford** Ontario, S Canada
97 *P21* **Chelmsford** E England, UK
110 *J9* **Chełmża** *Ger.* Culmsee, Kulmsee. Kujawski-pomorskie, C Poland
27 *Q8* **Chelsea** Oklahoma, C USA
18 *M8* **Chelsea** Vermont, NE USA
97 *L21* **Cheltenham** C England, UK
105 *R9* **Chelva** País Valenciano, E Spain
122 *G11* **Chelyabinsk** Chelyabinskaya Oblast', C Russian Federation
122 *F11* **Chelyabinskaya Oblast'** ◈ *province* C Russian Federation
123 *N5* **Chelyuskin, Mys** *headland* N Russian Federation
41 *Y12* **Chemax** Yucatán, SE Mexico
83 *N16* **Chemba** Sofala, C Mozambique
82 *J13* **Chembe** Luapula, NE Zambia
Chemenibit *see* Çemenibit
Chemerisy *see* Chamyarysy
116 *K7* **Chemerivtsi** Khmel'nyts'ka Oblast', W Ukraine
102 *J8* **Chemillé** Maine-et-Loire, NW France
173 *X17* **Chemin Grenier** S Mauritius
101 *N16* **Chemnitz** *prev.* Karl-Marx-Stadt. Sachsen, E Germany
Chemulpo *see* Inch'ŏn
32 *H14* **Chemult** Oregon, NW USA
18 *G12* **Chemung River** ≈ New York/Pennsylvania, NE USA
149 *U8* **Chenāb** ≈ India/Pakistan
39 *S9* **Chena Hot Springs** Alaska, USA
18 *I11* **Chenango River** ≈ New York, NE USA
168 *J7* **Chenderoh, Tasik** ◎ Peninsular Malaysia
15 *Q11* **Chêne, Rivière du** ≈ Québec, SE Canada
32 *L8* **Cheney** Washington, NW USA
26 *M6* **Cheney Reservoir** ▣ Kansas, C USA
Chengchiatun *see* Liaoyuan
Ch'eng-chou/Chengchow *see* Zhengzhou
161 *P1* **Chengde** *var.* Jehol. Hebei, E China
160 *I9* **Chengdu** *var.* Chengtu, Ch'eng-tu. Sichuan, C China
161 *Q14* **Chenghai** Guangdong, S China
Chenghsien *see* Zhengzhou
160 *H13* **Chengjiang** Yunnan, SW China
Chengjiang *see* Taihe
160 *L17* **Chengmai** *var.* Jinjiang. Hainan, S China
Chengtu/Ch'eng-tu *see* Chengdu
159 *W12* **Chengxian** *var.* Cheng Xian. Gansu, C China
Chengyang *see* Juxian
Chengzhong *see* Ningming
Chenkiang *see* Zhenjiang
155 *J19* **Chennai** *prev.* Madras. Tamil Nādu, S India
155 *J19* **Chennai** ✕ Tamil Nādu, S India
103 *R8* **Chenôve** Côte d'Or, C France
Chenstokhov *see* Częstochowa
160 *L11* **Chenxi** *var.* Chenyang. Hunan, S China
Chen Xian/Chenxian/Chen Xiang *see* Chenzhou
Chenyang *see* Chenxi
161 *N12* **Chenzhou** *var.* Chenxian, Chen Xian, Chen Xiang. Hunan, S China
167 *U12* **Cheo Reo** *var.* A Yun Pa. Gia Lai, S Vietnam
114 *I11* **Chepelare** Smolyan, S Bulgaria
114 *I11* **Chepelarska Reka** ≈ S Bulgaria
56 *B11* **Chepén** La Libertad, C Peru
62 *J10* **Chepes** La Rioja, C Argentina
161 *O15* **Chep Lap Kok** ✕ (Hong Kong) S China
43 *U14* **Chepo** Panamá, C Panama
Chepping Wycombe *see* High Wycombe
127 *R14* **Cheptsa** ≈ NW Russian Federation
30 *K3* **Chequamegon Point** *headland* Wisconsin, N USA
103 *O8* **Cher** ◈ *department* C France
102 *M8* **Cher** ≈ C France
Cherangani Hills *see* Cherangany Hills
81 *H17* **Cherangany Hills** *var.* Cherangani Hills. ⛰ W Kenya
21 *S11* **Cheraw** South Carolina, SE USA
102 *I3* **Cherbourg** *anc.* Carusbur. Manche, N France
127 *R5* **Cherdakly** Ul'yanovskaya Oblast', W Russian Federation
125 *U12* **Cherdyn'** Permskaya Oblast', NW Russian Federation
126 *J14* **Cherekha** ≈ W Russian Federation
122 *M13* **Cheremkhovo** Irkutskaya Oblast', S Russian Federation
Cheren *see* Keren
124 *K14* **Cherepovets** Vologodskaya Oblast', NW Russian Federation
125 *O11* **Cherevkovo** Arkhangel'skaya Oblast', NW Russian Federation
74 *I6* **Chergui, Chott ech** *salt lake* NW Algeria
Cherikov *see* Cherykaw
117 *P6* **Cherkas'ka Oblast'** *var.* Cherkasy, *Rus.* Cherkasskaya Oblast'. ◈ *province* C Ukraine
Cherkasskaya Oblast' *see* Cherkas'ka Oblast'
Cherkassy *see* Cherkasy
117 *Q6* **Cherkasy** *Rus.* Cherkassy. Cherkas'ka Oblast', C Ukraine
Cherkasy *see* Cherkas'ka Oblast'
126 *M15* **Cherkessk** Karachayevo-Cherkesskaya Respublika, SW Russian Federation
122 *H12* **Cherlak** Omskaya Oblast', C Russian Federation
122 *H12* **Cherlakskiy** Omskaya Oblast', C Russian Federation
125 *U13* **Chermoz** Permskaya Oblast', NW Russian Federation
Chernavchitsy *see* Charnawchytsy
125 *T3* **Chernaya** Nenetskiy Avtonomnyy Okrug, NW Russian Federation
127 *T4* **Chernaya** ≈ NW Russian Federation
Chernigov *see* Chernihiv
Chernigovskaya Oblast' *see* Chernihivs'ka Oblast'
117 *Q2* **Chernihiv** *Rus.* Chernigov. Chernihivs'ka Oblast', NE Ukraine
Chernihiv *see* Chernihivs'ka Oblast'
117 *V9* **Chernihivka** Zaporiz'ka Oblast', SE Ukraine
117 *P2* **Chernihivs'ka Oblast'** *var.* Chernihiv, *Rus.* Chernigovskaya Oblast'. ◈ *province* NE Ukraine
114 *I9* **Cherni Osŭm** ≈ N Bulgaria
116 *J8* **Chernivets'ka Oblast'** *var.* Chernivtsi, *Rus.* Chernovitskaya Oblast'. ◈ *province* W Ukraine
114 *I9* **Cherni Vit** ≈ NW Bulgaria
114 *G10* **Cherni Vrŭkh** ▲ W Bulgaria
116 *K8* **Chernivtsi** *Ger.* Czernowitz, *Rom.* Cernăuţi, *Rus.* Chernovtsy. Chernivets'ka Oblast', W Ukraine
116 *M7* **Chernivtsi** Vinnyts'ka Oblast', C Ukraine
Chernivtsi *see* Chernivets'ka Oblast'
Chernobyl' *see* Chornobyl'
Cherno More *see* Black Sea
Chernomorskoye *see* Chornomors'ke
145 *T7* **Chernoretskoye** Pavlodar, NE Kazakhstan
Chernovitskaya Oblast' *see* Chernivets'ka Oblast'
Chernovtsy *see* Chernivtsi
145 *U8* **Chernoye** Pavlodar, NE Kazakhstan
Chernoye More *see* Black Sea
125 *U16* **Chernushka** Permskaya Oblast', NW Russian Federation
117 *N4* **Chernyakhiv** *Rus.* Chernyakhov. Zhytomyrs'ka Oblast', N Ukraine
Chernyakhov *see* Chernyakhiv
119 *C14* **Chernyakhovsk** *Ger.* Insterburg. Kaliningradskaya Oblast', W Russian Federation
126 *K8* **Chernyanka** Belgorodskaya Oblast', W Russian Federation
127 *V5* **Chernyshëva, Gryada** ⛰ NW Russian Federation
144 *J14* **Chernyshëva, Zaliv** *gulf* SW Kazakhstan
123 *O10* **Chernyshevskiy** Respublika Sakha (Yakutiya), NE Russian Federation
127 *P13* **Chërnyye Zemli** *plain* SW Russian Federation
Chërnyy Irtysh *see* Ertix He
127 *V7* **Chernyy Otrog** Orenburgskaya Oblast', W Russian Federation
29 *T12* **Cherokee** Iowa, C USA
26 *M8* **Cherokee** Oklahoma, C USA
25 *R9* **Cherokee** Texas, SW USA
21 *O8* **Cherokee Lake** ▣ Tennessee, S USA
Cherokees, Lake O' The *see* Grand Lake O' The Cherokees
44 *H1* **Cherokee Sound** Great Abaco, N Bahamas
153 *V13* **Cherrapunji** Meghālaya, NE India
28 *L9* **Cherry Creek** ≈ South Dakota, N USA
18 *J16* **Cherry Hill** New Jersey, NE USA
27 *Q7* **Cherryvale** Kansas, C USA
21 *Q10* **Cherryville** North Carolina, SE USA
Cherski Range *see* Cherskogo, Khrebet
123 *T6* **Cherskiy** Respublika Sakha (Yakutiya), NE Russian Federation
123 *R8* **Cherskogo, Khrebet** *var.* Cherski Range. ⛰ NE Russian Federation
Cherso *see* Cres
126 *L10* **Chertkovo** Rostovskaya Oblast', SW Russian Federation
Cherven' *see* Chervyen'
114 *H8* **Cherven Bryag** Pleven, N Bulgaria
116 *M4* **Chervonoarmiys'k** Zhytomyrs'ka Oblast', N Ukraine
Chervonograd *see* Chervonohrad
116 *I4* **Chervonohrad** *Rus.* Chervonograd. L'vivs'ka Oblast', NW Ukraine
117 *W6* **Chervonooskil's'ke Vodoskhovyshche** *Rus.* Krasnoosol'skoye Vodokhranilishche. ▣ NE Ukraine
Chervonoye, Ozero *see* Chyrvonaye, Vozyera
117 *S4* **Chervonozavods'ke** Poltavs'ka Oblast', C Ukraine
119 *L16* **Chervyen'** *Rus.* Cherven'. Minskaya Voblasts', C Belarus
119 *P16* **Cherykaw** *Rus.* Cherikov. Mahilyowskaya Voblasts', E Belarus
31 *R9* **Chesaning** Michigan, N USA
21 *X5* **Chesapeake Bay** *inlet* NE USA
Cheshevlya *see* Tsyeshawlya
97 *K18* **Cheshire** *cultural region* C England, UK
127 *P5* **Chëshskaya Guba** *var.* Archangel Bay, Chesha Bay, Dvina Bay. *bay* NW Russian Federation
14 *F14* **Chesley** Ontario, S Canada
21 *Q10* **Chesnee** South Carolina, SE USA
97 *K18* **Chester** *Wel.* Caerleon; *hist.* Legaceaster, *Lat.* Deva, Devana Castra. C England, UK
35 *O4* **Chester** California, W USA
30 *K16* **Chester** Illinois, N USA
33 *S7* **Chester** Montana, NW USA
18 *I16* **Chester** Pennsylvania, NE USA
21 *R1* **Chester** South Carolina, SE USA
25 *X9* **Chester** Texas, SW USA
21 *W6* **Chester** Virginia, NE USA
21 *R11* **Chester** West Virginia, NE USA
97 *M18* **Chesterfield** C England, UK
21 *S11* **Chesterfield** South Carolina, SE USA
21 *W6* **Chesterfield** Virginia, NE USA
192 *J9* **Chesterfield, Îles** *island group* NW New Caledonia
9 *O9* **Chesterfield Inlet** Nunavut, NW Canada
9 *O9* **Chesterfield Inlet** *inlet* Nunavut, N Canada
21 *Y3* **Chester River** ≈ Delaware/Maryland, NE USA
21 *X3* **Chestertown** Maryland, NE USA
19 *R4* **Chesuncook Lake** ◎ Maine, NE USA
30 *J5* **Chetek** Wisconsin, N USA
13 *R14* **Chéticamp** Nova Scotia, SE Canada
27 *Q8* **Chetopa** Kansas, C USA
41 *Y14* **Chetumal** *var.* Payo Obispo. Quintana Roo, SE Mexico
Chetumal, Bahia/Chetumal, Bahía de *see* Chetumal Bay
42 *G1* **Chetumal Bay** *var.* Bahia Chetumal, Bahía de Chetumal. *bay* Belize/Mexico
10 *M13* **Chetwynd** British Columbia, W Canada
38 *M11* **Chevak** Alaska, USA
36 *M12* **Chevelon Creek** ≈ Arizona, SW USA
185 *J17* **Cheviot** Canterbury, South Island, NZ
96 *L13* **Cheviot Hills** *hill range* England/Scotland, UK
96 *L13* **Cheviot, The** ▲ NE England, UK
14 *M11* **Chevreuil, Lac du** ◎ Québec, SE Canada
81 *I16* **Ch'ew Bahir** *var.* Lake Stefanie. ◎ Ethiopia/Kenya
32 *L7* **Chewelah** Washington, NW USA
26 *K10* **Cheyenne** Oklahoma, C USA
33 *Z17* **Cheyenne** *state capital* Wyoming, C USA
26 *L5* **Cheyenne Bottoms** ◎ Kansas, C USA
16 *J8* **Cheyenne River** ≈ South Dakota/Wyoming, N USA
37 *W5* **Cheyenne Wells** Colorado, C USA
108 *C9* **Cheyres** Vaud, W Switzerland
Chezdi-Oşorheiu *see* Târgu Secuiesc
153 *P13* **Chhapra** *prev.* Chapra. Bihār, N India
153 *V13* **Chhatak** *var.* Chatak. Chittagong, NE Bangladesh
154 *J9* **Chhatarpur** Madhya Pradesh, C India
154 *N13* **Chhatrapur** *prev.* Chatrapur; Orissa, E India
154 *L12* **Chhattīsgarh** *plain* C India
154 *K12* **Chhattīsgarh** ◈ *state* E India
154 *I11* **Chhindwāra** Madhya Pradesh, C India
153 *T12* **Chhukha** SW Bhutan
161 *S14* **Chiai** *var.* Chia-i, Chiayi, Kiayi, Jiayi, *Jap.* Kagi. C Taiwan
Chia-mu-ssu *see* Jiamusi
83 *B15* **Chiange** *Port.* Vila de Almoster. Huíla, SW Angola
Chiang-hsi *see* Jiangxi
161 *S12* **Chiang Kai-shek** ✕ (T'aipei) N Taiwan
167 *P8* **Chiang Khan** Loei, E Thailand
167 *O7* **Chiang Mai** *var.* Chiangmai, Chiengmai, Kiangmai. Chiang Mai, NW Thailand
167 *O7* **Chiang Mai** ✕ Chiang Mai, NW Thailand
167 *O6* **Chiang Rai** *var.* Chianpai, Chienrai, Muang Chiang Rai. Chiang Rai, NW Thailand
Chiang-su *see* Jiangsu
Chianning/Chian-ning *see* Nanjing
Chianpai *see* Chiang Rai
106 *G12* **Chianti** *cultural region* C Italy
Chiapa *see* Chiapa de Corzo
41 *U16* **Chiapa de Corzo** *var.* Chiapa. Chiapas, SE Mexico
41 *V16* **Chiapas** ◈ *state* SE Mexico
106 *J12* **Chiaravalle** Marche, C Italy
107 *N22* **Chiaravalle Centrale** Calabria, SW Italy
106 *E7* **Chiari** Lombardia, N Italy
108 *H12* **Chiasso** Ticino, S Switzerland
137 *S9* **Chiat'ura** C Georgia
41 *P15* **Chiautla** *var.* Chiautla de Tapia. Puebla, S Mexico
Chiautla de Tapia *see* Chiautla
106 *D10* **Chiavari** Liguria, NW Italy
106 *E6* **Chiavenna** Lombardia, N Italy
Chiayi *see* Chiai
Chiazza *see* Piazza Armerina
165 *O13* **Chiba** *var.* Tiba. Chiba, Honshū, S Japan
165 *O14* **Chiba** *off.* Chiba-ken, *var.* Tiba. ◈ *prefecture* Honshū, S Japan
83 *M18* **Chibabava** Sofala, C Mozambique
161 *O10* **Chibi** *prev.* Puqi. Hubei, C China
83 *B15* **Chibia** *Port.* João de Almeida, Vila João de Almeida. Huíla, SW Angola
83 *M18* **Chiboma** Sofala, C Mozambique
82 *J12* **Chibondo** Luapula, N Zambia
82 *K11* **Chibote** Luapula, NE Zambia
12 *K12* **Chibougamau** Québec, SE Canada
164 *H11* **Chiburi-jima** *island* Oki-shotō, SW Japan
83 *M20* **Chibuto** Gaza, S Mozambique
31 *N11* **Chicago** Illinois, N USA
31 *N11* **Chicago Heights** Illinois, N USA
15 *W6* **Chic-Chocs, Monts** *Eng.* Shickshock Mountains. ⛰ Québec, SE Canada
39 *W13* **Chichagof Island** *island* Alexander Archipelago, Alaska, USA
57 *K20* **Chichas, Cordillera de** ⛰ SW Bolivia
41 *X12* **Chichén-Itzá, Ruinas** *ruins* Yucatán, SE Mexico
97 *N23* **Chichester** SE England, UK
42 *C5* **Chichicastenango** Quiché, W Guatemala
42 *I9* **Chichigalpa** Chinandega, NW Nicaragua
Ch'i-ch'i-ha-erh *see* Qiqihar
165 *X16* **Chichijima-rettō** *Eng.* Beechy Group. *island group* SE Japan
54 *K4* **Chichiriviche** Falcón, N Venezuela
39 *R11* **Chickaloon** Alaska, USA
20 *L10* **Chickamauga Lake** ▣ Tennessee, S USA
23 *N7* **Chickasawhay River** ≈ Mississippi, S USA
26 *M11* **Chickasha** Oklahoma, C USA
39 *T9* **Chicken** Alaska, USA
104 *J16* **Chiclana de la Frontera** Andalucía, S Spain
56 *B11* **Chiclayo** Lambayeque, NW Peru
35 *N5* **Chico** California, W USA
83 *L15* **Chicoa** Tete, NW Mozambique
83 *M20* **Chicomo** Gaza, S Mozambique
18 *M11* **Chicopee** Massachusetts, NE USA
63 *I19* **Chico, Río** ≈ SE Argentina
63 *I21* **Chico, Río** ≈ S Argentina
27 *W14* **Chicot, Lake** ◎ Arkansas, C USA
15 *R7* **Chicoutimi** Québec, SE Canada
15 *Q8* **Chicoutimi** ≈ Québec, SE Canada
83 *L19* **Chicualacuala** Gaza, SW Mozambique
83 *B14* **Chicuma** Benguela, C Angola
155 *J21* **Chidambaram** Tamil Nādu, SE India
196 *K13* **Chidley, Cape** *headland* Newfoundland and Labrador, E Canada
101 *N24* **Chiemsee** ◎ SE Germany
Chiengmai *see* Chiang Mai
Chienrai *see* Chiang Rai
106 *B8* **Chieri** Piemonte, NW Italy
106 *F8* **Chiese** ≈ N Italy
107 *K14* **Chieti** *var.* Teate. Abruzzo, C Italy
99 *E19* **Chièvres** Hainaut, SW Belgium
163 *S12* **Chifeng** *var.* Ulanhad. Nei Mongol Zizhiqu, N China
82 *F13* **Chifumage** ≈ E Angola
82 *M13* **Chifunda** Eastern, NE Zambia
145 *S14* **Chiganak** *var.* Čiganak. Zhambyl, SE Kazakhstan
39 *P15* **Chiginagak, Mount** ▲ Alaska, USA
Chigirin *see* Chyhyryn
41 *P13* **Chignahuapan** Puebla, S Mexico
39 *O15* **Chignik** Alaska, USA
83 *M19* **Chigombe** ≈ S Mozambique
54 *D7* **Chigorodó** Antioquia, NW Colombia
83 *M19* **Chigubo** Gaza, S Mozambique
162 *D6* **Chihertey** Bayan-Ölgiy, W Mongolia
Chih-fu *see* Yantai
Chihli *see* Hebei
Chihli, Gulf of *see* Bo Hai
40 *J6* **Chihuahua** Chihuahua, NW Mexico
40 *I6* **Chihuahua** ◈ *state* N Mexico
145 *O15* **Chiili** Kzylorda, S Kazakhstan
26 *M7* **Chikaskia River** ≈ Kansas/Oklahoma, C USA
155 *H19* **Chik Ballāpur** Karnātaka, W India
124 *G15* **Chikhachevo** Pskovskaya Oblast', W Russian Federation
155 *F19* **Chikmagalūr** Karnātaka, W India
131 *V7* **Chikoy** ≈ C Russian Federation
83 *J15* **Chikumbi** Lusaka, C Zambia
82 *M13* **Chikwa** Eastern, NE Zambia
Chikwana *see* Chikwawa
83 *N15* **Chikwawa** *var.* Chikwana. Southern, S Malawi
155 *J16* **Chilakalūrupet** Andhra Pradesh, E India
146 *L14* **Chilan** Lebap Welaýaty, E Turkmenistan
Chilapa *see* Chilapa de Alvarez
41 *P16* **Chilapa de Alvarez** *var.* Chilapa. Guerrero, S Mexico
155 *J25* **Chilaw** North Western Province, W Sri Lanka
57 *D15* **Chilca** Lima, W Peru
23 *Q4* **Childersburg** Alabama, S USA
25 *P4* **Childress** Texas, SW USA
63 *G14* **Chile** *off.* Republic of Chile. ◆ *republic* SW South America
47 *R10* **Chile Basin** *undersea feature* E Pacific Ocean
63 *H20* **Chile Chico** Aisén, W Chile
62 *I9* **Chilecito** La Rioja, NW Argentina
62 *H12* **Chilecito** Mendoza, W Argentina
83 *L14* **Chilembwe** Eastern, E Zambia
193 *S11* **Chile Rise** *undersea feature* SE Pacific Ocean
117 *N13* **Chilia Braţul** ≈ SE Romania
Chilia-Nouă *see* Kiliya
145 *V15* **Chilik** Almaty, SE Kazakhstan
145 *V15* **Chilik** ≈ SE Kazakhstan
154 *O13* **Chilika Lake** *var.* Chilka Lake. ◎ E India
82 *J13* **Chililabombwe** Copperbelt, C Zambia
Chi-lin *see* Jilin
Chilka Lake *see* Chilika Lake
10 *H9* **Chilkoot Pass** *pass* British Columbia, W Canada
Chill Ala, Cuan *see* Killala Bay
62 *G13* **Chillán** Bío Bío, C Chile
61 *C22* **Chillar** Buenos Aires, E Argentina
Chill Chiaráin, Cuan *see* Kilkieran Bay
30 *K12* **Chillicothe** Illinois, N USA
27 *S3* **Chillicothe** Missouri, C USA
31 *S14* **Chillicothe** Ohio, N USA
25 *Q4* **Chillicothe** Texas, SW USA
10 *M17* **Chilliwack** British Columbia, SW Canada
Chill Mhantáin, Ceann *see* Wicklow Head
Chill Mhantáin, Sléibhte *see* Wicklow Mountains
108 *C10* **Chillon** Vaud, W Switzerland
Chil'mamedkum, Peski/Chilmämetgum *see* Çilmämmetgum
63 *F17* **Chiloé, Isla de** *var.* Isla Grande de Chiloé. *island* W Chile
32 *H15* **Chiloquin** Oregon, NW USA
41 *O16* **Chilpancingo** *var.* Chilpancingo de los Bravos. Guerrero, S Mexico
Chilpancingo de los Bravos *see* Chilpancingo
97 *N21* **Chiltern Hills** *hill range* S England, UK
30 *M7* **Chilton** Wisconsin, N USA
82 *F11* **Chiluage** Lunda Sul, NE Angola
82 *N12* **Chilumba** *prev.* Deep Bay. Northern, N Malawi
161 *T12* **Chilung** *var.* Keelung, *Jap.* Kirun, Kirun'; *prev. Sp.* Santissima Trinidad. N Taiwan
83 *N15* **Chilwa, Lake** *var.* Lago Chirua, Lake Shirwa. ◎ SE Malawi
167 *R10* **Chi, Mae Nam** ≈ E Thailand
42 *C6* **Chimaltenango** Chimaltenango, C Guatemala
42 *A2* **Chimaltenango** *off.* Departamento de Chimaltenango. ◈ *department* S Guatemala
43 *V15* **Chimán** Panamá, E Panama
83 *M17* **Chimanimani** *prev.* Mandidzudzure, Melsetter. Manicaland, E Zimbabwe
99 *G22* **Chimay** Hainaut, S Belgium
37 *S10* **Chimayo** New Mexico, SW USA
Chimbay *see* Chimboy
56 *A13* **Chimborazo** ◈ *province* C Ecuador
56 *C7* **Chimborazo** ⊼ C Ecuador
56 *C12* **Chimbote** Ancash, W Peru
146 *H7* **Chimboy** *Rus.* Chimbay. Qoraqalpog'iston Respublikasi, NW Uzbekistan
186 *D7* **Chimbu** ◈ *province* C PNG
54 *F6* **Chimichagua** Cesar, N Colombia
Chimishliya *see* Cimişlia
Chimkent *see* Shymkent
Chimkentskaya Oblast' *see* Yuzhnyy Kazakhstan
28 *I14* **Chimney Rock** *rock* Nebraska, C USA
83 *M17* **Chimoio** Manica, C Mozambique
82 *K11* **Chimpembe** Northern, NE Zambia
41 *O8* **China** Nuevo León, NE Mexico
156 *M9* **China** *off.* People's Republic of China, *Chin.* Chung-hua Jen-min Kung-ho-kuo, Zhonghua Renmin Gongheguo; *prev.* Chinese Empire. ◆ *republic* E Asia
19 *Q7* **China Lake** ◎ Maine, NE USA
42 *F8* **Chinameca** San Miguel, E El Salvador
Chi-nan/Chinan *see* Jinan
42 *H9* **Chinandega** Chinandega, NW Nicaragua
42 *H9* **Chinandega** ◈ *department* NW Nicaragua
China, People's Republic of *see* China
China, Republic of *see* Taiwan

◆ Country
● Country Capital
◇ Dependent Territory
○ Dependent Territory Capital
◈ Administrative Region
✕ International Airport
▲ Mountain
⛰ Mountain Range
⊼ Volcano
≈ River
◎ Lake
▣ Reservoir

24 J11 Chinati Mountains ▲ Texas, SW USA
Chinaz see Chinoz
57 E15 Chincha Alta Ica, SW Peru
11 N11 Chinchaga ≈ Alberta, SW Canada
Chin-chiang see Quanzhou
Chinchilla see Chinchilla de Monte Aragón
105 Q11 Chinchilla de Monte Aragón var. Chinchilla. Castilla-La Mancha, C Spain
54 D10 Chinchiná Caldas, W Colombia
105 O8 Chinchón Madrid, C Spain
41 Z14 Chinchorro, Banco island SE Mexico
Chin-chou/Chinchow see Jinzhou
21 Z5 Chincoteague Assateague Island, Virginia, NE USA
83 O17 Chinde Zambézia, NE Mozambique
163 X17 Chin-do Jap. Chin-tō. island SW South Korea
159 R13 Chindu var. Chuqung. Qinghai, C China
166 M2 Chindwin ≈ N Myanmar
Chinese Empire see China
Ch'ing Hai see Qinghai Hu
Chinghai see Qinghai
Chingildi see Shengeldi
144 H9 Chingirlau Kaz. Shyngghyrlaū. Zapadnyy Kazakhstan, W Kazakhstan
82 J13 Chingola Copperbelt, C Zambia
Ching-Tao/Ch'ing-tao see Qingdao
82 C13 Chinguar Huambo, C Angola
76 I7 Chinguețți var. Chinguetti. Adrar, C Mauritania
163 Z16 Chinhae Jap. Chinkai. S South Korea
166 K4 Chin Hills ▲ W Myanmar
83 K16 Chinhoyi prev. Sinoia. Mashonaland West, N Zimbabwe
Chinhsien see Jinzhou
39 Q14 Chiniak, Cape headland Kodiak Island, Alaska, USA
14 G10 Chiniguchi Lake ◎ Ontario, S Canada
149 U8 Chiniot Punjab, NE Pakistan
163 Y16 Chinju Jap. Shinshū. S South Korea
Chinkai see Chinhae
78 M13 Chinko ≈ E Central African Republic
37 O9 Chinle Arizona, SW USA
161 R13 Chinmen Tao var. Jinmen Dao, Quemoy. island W Taiwan
Chinnchâr see Shinshār
Chinnereth see Tiberias, Lake
164 C12 Chino var. Tino. Nagano, Honshū, S Japan
102 L8 Chinon Indre-et-Loire, C France
33 T7 Chinook Montana, NW USA
Chinook State see Washington
192 L4 Chinook Trough undersea feature N Pacific Ocean
36 K11 Chino Valley Arizona, SW USA
147 P10 Chinoz Rus. Chinaz. Toshkent Viloyati, E Uzbekistan
82 L12 Chinsali Northern, NE Zambia
166 K5 Chin State ◆ state W Myanmar
Chinsura see Chunchura
Chin-tō see Chin-do
54 E6 Chinú Córdoba, NW Colombia
99 K24 Chiny, Forêt de forest SE Belgium
83 M15 Chioco Tete, NW Mozambique
106 H8 Chioggia anc. Fossa Claudia. Veneto, NE Italy
114 H12 Chionótrypa ▲ NE Greece
115 L18 Chíos var. Hios, Khíos, It. Scio, Turk. Sakiz-Adasi. Chíos, E Greece
115 K18 Chíos var. Khíos. island E Greece
83 M14 Chipata prev. Fort Jameson. Eastern, E Zambia
83 C14 Chipindo Huíla, C Angola
23 R8 Chipley Florida, SE USA
155 D15 Chiplūn Mahārāshtra, W India
81 H22 Chipogolo Dodoma, C Tanzania
23 R8 Chipola River ≈ Florida, SE USA
97 L22 Chippenham S England, UK
30 J6 Chippewa Falls Wisconsin, N USA
30 J4 Chippewa, Lake ▣ Wisconsin, N USA
31 Q8 Chippewa River ≈ Michigan, N USA
30 I6 Chippewa River ≈ Wisconsin, N USA
Chipping Wycombe see High Wycombe
114 G8 Chiprovtsi Montana, NW Bulgaria
19 T4 Chiputneticook Lakes lakes Canada/USA
56 D13 Chiquián Ancash, W Peru
41 Y11 Chiquilá Quintana Roo, SE Mexico
42 E6 Chiquimula Chiquimula, SE Guatemala
42 A3 Chiquimula off. Departamento de Chiquimula. ◆ department SE Guatemala
42 D7 Chiquimulilla Santa Rosa, S Guatemala
54 F9 Chiquinquirá Boyacá, C Colombia
155 J17 Chīrāla Andhra Pradesh, E India
149 N4 Chīras Ghowr, N Afghanistan
152 H11 Chirāwa Rājasthān, N India
Chirchik see Chirchiq
147 Q9 Chirchiq Rus. Chirchik. Toshkent Viloyati, E Uzbekistan
147 P10 Chirchiq ≈ E Uzbekistan
Chire see Shire
83 L18 Chiredzi Masvingo, SE Zimbabwe
25 X8 Chireno Texas, SW USA
77 X7 Chirfa Agadez, NE Niger
37 O16 Chiricahua Mountains ▲ Arizona, SW USA
37 O16 Chiricahua Peak ▲ Arizona, SW USA
54 F6 Chiriguaná Cesar, N Colombia
39 P15 Chirikof Island island Alaska, USA
43 P16 Chiriquí off. Provincia de Chiriquí. ◆ province SW Panama
43 P17 Chiriquí, Golfo de Eng. Chiriqui Gulf. gulf SW Panama
43 P15 Chiriquí Grande Bocas del Toro, W Panama
Chiriqui Gulf see Chiriquí, Golfo de
43 P15 Chiriquí, Laguna de lagoon NW Panama
43 O16 Chiriquí Viejo, Río ≈ W Panama
Chiriquí, Volcán de see Barú, Volcán
83 N15 Chiromo Southern, S Malawi
114 J10 Chirpan Stara Zagora, C Bulgaria
43 N14 Chirripó Atlántico, Río ≈ E Costa Rica
Chirripó, Cerro see Chirripó Grande, Cerro
43 N14 Chirripó Grande, Cerro var. Cerro Chirripó. ▲ SE Costa Rica
43 N13 Chirripó, Río var. Río Chirripó del Pacífico. ≈ NE Costa Rica
Chirua, Lago see Chilwa, Lake
83 J15 Chirundu Southern, S Zambia
29 W8 Chisago City Minnesota, N USA
83 J14 Chisamba Central, C Zambia
39 T10 Chisana Alaska, USA
82 I13 Chisasa North Western, NW Zambia
12 I9 Chisasibi Québec, C Canada
42 D4 Chisec Alta Verapaz, C Guatemala
127 U5 Chishmy Respublika Bashkortostan, W Russian Federation
29 V4 Chisholm Minnesota, N USA
160 I11 Chishui He ≈ C China
Chisimaio/Chisimayu see Kismaayo
117 N10 Chişinău Rus. Kishinev. ● (Moldova) C Moldova
117 N10 Chişinău ✕ S Moldova
Chişinău-Criş see Chişineu-Criş
116 F10 Chişineu-Criş Hung. Kisjenő; prev. Chişinău-Criş. Arad, W Romania
83 K14 Chisomo Central, C Zambia
106 A8 Chisone ≈ NW Italy
24 K12 Chisos Mountains ▲ Texas, SW USA
149 U10 Chistiān Mandi Punjab, E Pakistan
39 T10 Chistochina Alaska, USA
127 R4 Chistopol' Respublika Tatarstan, W Russian Federation
145 O8 Chistopol'ye Severnyy Kazakhstan, N Kazakhstan
123 O13 Chita Chitinskaya Oblast', S Russian Federation
83 B16 Chitado Cunene, SW Angola
Chitaldroog/Chitaldrug see Chitradurga
83 C15 Chitanda ≈ S Angola
Chitangwiza see Chitungwiza
82 F10 Chitato Lunda Norte, NE Angola
83 C14 Chitembo Bié, C Angola
39 T11 Chitina Alaska, USA
39 T11 Chitina River ≈ Alaska, USA
123 O12 Chitinskaya Oblast' ◆ province S Russian Federation
82 M11 Chitipa Northern, NW Malawi
165 S4 Chitose var. Titose. Hokkaidō, NE Japan
155 G18 Chitradurga prev. Chitaldroog, Chitaldrug. Karnātaka, W India
149 T3 Chitrāl North-West Frontier Province, NW Pakistan
43 S16 Chitré Herrera, S Panama
153 V16 Chittagong Ben. Chāttagām. Chittagong, SE Bangladesh
153 U16 Chittagong ◆ division E Bangladesh
153 Q15 Chittaranjan West Bengal, NE India
152 G14 Chittaurgarh Rājasthān, N India
155 I19 Chittoor Andhra Pradesh, E India
155 G21 Chittūr Kerala, SW India
83 K16 Chitungwiza prev. Chitangwiza. Mashonaland East, NE Zimbabwe
62 H4 Chiuchíu Antofagasta, N Chile
82 F12 Chiumbe var. Tshiumbe. ≈ Angola/Dem. Rep. Congo
83 F15 Chiume Moxico, E Angola
82 K13 Chiundaponde Northern, NE Zambia
106 H13 Chiusi Toscana, C Italy
54 J5 Chivacoa Yaracuy, N Venezuela
106 B8 Chivasso Piemonte, NW Italy
83 L17 Chivhu prev. Enkeldoorn. Midlands, C Zimbabwe
61 C20 Chivilcoy Buenos Aires, E Argentina
82 N12 Chiweta Northern, N Malawi
42 D4 Chixoy, Río var. Río Negro, Río Salinas. ≈ Guatemala/Mexico
82 H13 Chizela North Western, NW Zambia
125 O5 Chizha Nenetskiy Avtonomnyy Okrug, NW Russian Federation
161 Q9 Chizhou var. Guichi. Anhui, E China
164 I12 Chizu Tottori, Honshū, SW Japan
Chkalov see Orenburg
74 J5 Chlef var. Ech Cheliff, Ech Chleff; prev. Al-Asnam, El Asnam, Orléansville. NW Algeria
115 G18 Chlómo ▲ C Greece
111 M15 Chmielnik Świętokrzyskie, C Poland
167 S11 Chŏâm Khsant Preăh Vihéar, N Cambodia
62 G10 Choapa, Río var. Choapo. ≈ C Chile
Choapas see Las Choapas
Choarta see Chwārtā
83 H17 Chobe ◆ district NE Botswana
67 T13 Chobe ≈ N Botswana
14 K8 Chochocouane ≈ Québec, SE Canada
110 E13 Chocianów Ger. Kotzenan. Dolnośląskie, SW Poland
54 C9 Chocó off. Departamento del Chocó. ◆ province W Colombia
35 X16 Chocolate Mountains ▲ California, W USA
21 W9 Chocowinity North Carolina, SE USA
27 N10 Choctaw Oklahoma, C USA
23 Q8 Choctawhatchee Bay bay Florida, SE USA
23 Q8 Choctawhatchee River ≈ Florida, SE USA
Chodau see Chodov
163 V14 Chŏ-do island SW North Korea
Chodorów see Khodoriv
111 A16 Chodov Ger. Chodau. Karlovarský Kraj, W Czech Republic
110 G10 Chodzież Wielkopolskie, C Poland
63 J15 Choele Choel Río Negro, C Argentina
83 L14 Chofombo Tete, NW Mozambique
Chohtan see Chauhtan
11 U14 Choiceland Saskatchewan, C Canada
186 K8 Choiseul var. Lauru. island NW Solomon Islands
63 M23 Choiseul Sound sound East Falkland, Falkland Islands
40 H7 Choix Sinaloa, C Mexico
110 D10 Chojna Zachodnio-pomorskie, W Poland
110 H8 Chojnice Ger. Konitz. Pomorskie, N Poland
111 F14 Chojnów Ger. Hainau, Haynau. Dolnośląskie, SW Poland
167 Q10 Chok Chai Nakhon Ratchasima, C Thailand
80 I12 Ch'ok'ē var. Choke Mountains. ▲ NW Ethiopia
25 R13 Choke Canyon Lake ▣ Texas, SW USA
Choke Mountains see Ch'ok'ē
145 T15 Chokpar Kaz. Shoqpar. Zhambyl, S Kazakhstan
147 W7 Chok-Tal var. Choktal. Issyk-Kul'skaya Oblast', E Kyrgyzstan
Chókué see Chokwé
123 R7 Chokurdakh Respublika Sakha (Yakutiya), NE Russian Federation
83 L20 Chokwé var. Chókuè. Gaza, S Mozambique
188 F8 Chol Babeldaob, N Palau
160 E8 Chola Shan ▲ C China
102 J8 Cholet Maine-et-Loire, NW France
63 H17 Cholila Chubut, W Argentina
Cholo see Thyolo
147 V8 Cholpon Narynskaya Oblast', C Kyrgyzstan
147 X7 Cholpon-Ata Issyk-Kul'skaya Oblast', E Kyrgyzstan
41 P14 Cholula Puebla, S Mexico
42 I8 Choluteca Choluteca, S Honduras
42 H8 Choluteca ◆ department S Honduras
42 G6 Choluteca, Río ≈ SW Honduras
83 I15 Choma Southern, S Zambia
153 T11 Chomo Lhari ▲ NW Bhutan
167 N7 Chom Thong Chiang Mai, NW Thailand
111 B15 Chomutov Ger. Komotau. Ústecký Kraj, NW Czech Republic
123 N11 Chona ≈ C Russian Federation
163 X15 Ch'ŏnan Jap. Tenan. W South Korea
167 P11 Chon Buri prev. Bang Pla Soi. Chon Buri, S Thailand
56 B6 Chone Manabí, W Ecuador
163 W13 Ch'ŏngch'ŏn-gang ≈ W North Korea
163 Y11 Ch'ŏngjin NE North Korea
163 W13 Chŏngju W North Korea
161 S8 Chongming Dao island E China
160 J10 Chongqing var. Ch'ung-ching, Ch'ung-ch'ing, Chungking, Pahsien, Tchongking, Yuzhou. Chongqing Shi, C China
Chŏngup see Chŏnju
161 O10 Chongyang var. Tiancheng. Hubei, C China
160 J15 Chongzuo Guangxi Zhuangzu Zizhiqu, S China
163 Y16 Chŏnju prev. Chŏngup, Jap. Seiyu. SW South Korea
163 Y15 Chŏnju Jap. Zenshū. SW South Korea
Chonnacht see Connaught
163 Q9 Chonogol Sühbaatar, E Mongolia
63 F19 Chonos, Archipiélago de los island group S Chile
42 K10 Chontales ◆ department S Nicaragua
167 T13 Chơn Thanh Sông Be, S Vietnam
158 K17 Cho Oyu var. Qowowuyag. ▲ China/Nepal
116 G7 Chop Cz. Čop, Hung. Csap. Zakarpats'ka Oblast', W Ukraine
21 Y3 Choptank River ≈ Maryland, NE USA
Chorcaí, Cuan see Cork Harbour
43 P15 Chorcha, Cerro ▲ W Panama
Chorku see Chorkŭh
147 R11 Chorkŭh Rus. Chorku. N Tajikistan
97 K17 Chorley NW England, UK
Chorne More see Black Sea
117 R5 Chornobay Cherkas'ka Oblast', C Ukraine
117 O3 Chornobyl' Rus. Chernobyl'. Kyyivs'ka Oblast', N Ukraine
117 R12 Chornomors'ke Rus. Chernomorskoye. Respublika Krym, S Ukraine
117 R4 Chornukhy Poltavs'ka Oblast', C Ukraine
Chorokh/Chorokhi see Çoruh Nehri
110 O9 Choroszcz Podlaskie, NE Poland
116 K6 Chortkiv Rus. Chortkov. Ternopil's'ka Oblast', W Ukraine
Chortkov see Chortkiv
Chorum see Çorum
110 M9 Chorzele Mazowieckie, C Poland
111 J16 Chorzów Ger. Königshütte; prev. Królewska Huta. Śląskie, S Poland
163 W12 Ch'osan N North Korea
Chośebuz see Cottbus
Chōsen-kaikyō see Korea Strait
164 P14 Chōshi var. Tyôsi. Chiba, Honshū, S Japan
63 H14 Chos Malal Neuquén, W Argentina
Chosŏn-minjujuŭi-inmin-kanghwaguk see North Korea
110 E9 Choszczno Ger. Arnswalde. Zachodnio-pomorskie, NW Poland
153 O15 Chota Nāgpur plateau N India
33 R8 Choteau Montana, NW USA
Chotqol see Chatkal
14 M8 Chouart ≈ Québec, SE Canada
76 I7 Choûm Adrar, C Mauritania
27 Q9 Chouteau Oklahoma, C USA
21 X8 Chowan River ≈ North Carolina, SE USA
35 Q10 Chowchilla California, W USA
163 P7 Choybalsan prev. Bayan Tumen. Dornod, E Mongolia
162 M9 Choyr Govĭ Sumber, C Mongolia
185 I19 Christchurch Canterbury, South Island, NZ
97 M24 Christchurch S England, UK
185 I18 Christchurch ✕ Canterbury, South Island, NZ
44 J12 Christiana C Jamaica
83 H22 Christiana Free State, C South Africa
115 J23 Christiáni island Kykládes, Greece, Aegean Sea
Christiania see Oslo
14 G13 Christian Island island Ontario, S Canada
191 P16 Christian, Point headland Pitcairn Island, Pitcairn Islands
38 M11 Christian River ≈ Alaska, USA
Christiansand see Kristiansand
21 S7 Christiansburg Virginia, NE USA
95 G23 Christiansfeld Sønderjylland, SW Denmark
Christianshåb see Qasigiannguit
39 X14 Christian Sound inlet Alaska, USA
45 T9 Christiansted Saint Croix, S Virgin Islands (US)
Christiansund see Kristiansund
25 R13 Christine Texas, SW USA
173 U7 Christmas Island ◇ Australian external territory E Indian Ocean
131 T17 Christmas Island island E Indian Ocean
Christmas Island see Kiritimati
192 M7 Christmas Ridge undersea feature C Pacific Ocean
30 L16 Christopher Illinois, N USA
25 P9 Christoval Texas, SW USA
111 F17 Chrudim Pardubický Kraj, C Czech Republic
115 K25 Chrýsi island SE Greece
121 N2 Chrysochoú, Kólpos var. Khrysokhou Bay. bay E Mediterranean Sea
114 I13 Chrysoúpoli var. Hrisoupoli; prev. Khrisoúpolis. Anatolikí Makedonía kai Thráki, NE Greece
111 K16 Chrzanów var. Chrzanow, Ger. Zaumgarten. Śląskie, S Poland
131 Q7 Chu Kaz. Shū. ≈ Kazakhstan/Kyrgyzstan
42 C5 Chuacús, Sierra de ▲ W Guatemala
153 S15 Chuadanga Khulna, W Bangladesh
Chuan see Sichuan
Ch'uan-chou see Quanzhou
39 O11 Chuathbaluk Alaska, USA
Chubek see Moskva
63 I17 Chubut off. Provincia de Chubut. ◆ province S Argentina
63 I17 Chubut, Río ≈ SE Argentina
43 V15 Chucanti, Cerro ▲ E Panama
Ch'u-chiang see Shaoguan
43 W15 Chucunaque, Río ≈ E Panama
Chudin see Chudzin
116 M5 Chudniv Zhytomyrs'ka Oblast', N Ukraine
124 H13 Chudovo Novgorodskaya Oblast', W Russian Federation
Chudskoye Ozero see Peipus, Lake
119 J18 Chudzin Rus. Chudin. Brestskaya Voblasts', SW Belarus
39 Q13 Chugach Islands island group Alaska, USA
39 S11 Chugach Mountains ▲ Alaska, USA
164 G12 Chūgoku-sanchi ▲ Honshū, SW Japan
Chugqênsumdo see Jigzhi
Chuguyev see Chuhuyiv
117 V5 Chuhuyiv var. Chuguyev. Kharkivs'ka Oblast', E Ukraine
61 H19 Chuí Rio Grande do Sul, S Brazil
Chuí see Chuy
145 S15 Chu-Iliyskiye Gory Kaz. Shū-Ile Taūlary. ▲ S Kazakhstan
Chukai see Cukai
Chukchi Avtonomnyy Okrug see Chukotskiy Avtonomnyy Okrug
Chukchi Peninsula see Chukotskiy Poluostrov
197 R6 Chukchi Plain undersea feature Arctic Ocean
197 R6 Chukchi Plateau undersea feature Arctic Ocean
197 R4 Chukchi Sea Rus. Chukotskoye More. sea Arctic Ocean
125 N14 Chukhloma Kostromskaya Oblast', NW Russian Federation
Chukotka see Chukotskiy Avtonomnyy Okrug
Chukot Range see Anadyrskiy Khrebet
123 V6 Chukotskiy Avtonomnyy Okrug var. Chukchi Avtonomnyy Okrug, Chukotka. ◆ autonomous district NE Russian Federation
123 W5 Chukotskiy, Mys headland NE Russian Federation
123 V5 Chukotskiy Poluostrov Eng. Chukchi Peninsula. peninsula NE Russian Federation
Chukotskoye More see Chukchi Sea
Chukurkak see Chuqurqoq
Chulakkurgan see Sholakkorgan
35 U17 Chula Vista California, W USA
123 Q12 Chul'man Respublika Sakha (Yakutiya), NE Russian Federation
56 B9 Chulucanas Piura, NW Peru
122 J12 Chulym ≈ C Russian Federation
152 K6 Chumar Jammu and Kashmir, N India
114 K9 Chumerna ▲ C Bulgaria
123 R12 Chumikan Khabarovskiy Kray, E Russian Federation
167 Q9 Chum Phae Khon Kaen, C Thailand
167 N13 Chumphon var. Jumporn. Chumphon, SW Thailand
167 O9 Chumsaeng var. Chum Saeng. Nakhon Sawan, C Thailand
122 L12 Chuna ≈ C Russian Federation
161 R9 Chun'an var. Pailing. Zhejiang, SE China
161 S13 Chunan N Taiwan
163 Y14 Ch'unch'ŏn Jap. Shunsen. N South Korea
153 S16 Chunchura prev. Chinsura. West Bengal, NE India
145 W15 Chundzha Almaty, SE Kazakhstan
Ch'ung-ch'ing/Ch'ung-ching see Chongqing
Chung-hua Jen-min Kung-ho-kuo see China
163 Y15 Ch'ungju Jap. Chūshū. C South Korea
Chungking see Chongqing
161 T14 Chungyang Shanmo Chin. Taiwan Shan. ▲ C Taiwan
149 V9 Chūniān Punjab, E Pakistan
122 L12 Chunskiy Irkutskaya Oblast', S Russian Federation
122 M11 Chunya ≈ C Russian Federation
124 J6 Chupa Respublika Kareliya, NW Russian Federation
125 P8 Chuprovo Respublika Komi, NW Russian Federation
57 G17 Chuquibamba Arequipa, SW Peru
62 H4 Chuquicamata Antofagasta, N Chile
57 L21 Chuquisaca ◆ department S Bolivia
Chuquisaca see Sucre
Chuqung see Chindu
146 I8 Chuqurqoq Rus. Chukurkak. Qoraqalpog'iston Respublikasi, NW Uzbekistan
127 T2 Chur Udmurtskaya Respublika, NW Russian Federation
108 I9 Chur Fr. Coire, It. Coira, Rmsch. Cuera, Quera; anc. Curia Rhaetorum. Graubünden, E Switzerland
123 Q10 Churapcha Respublika Sakha (Yakutiya), NE Russian Federation
11 V16 Churchbridge Saskatchewan, S Canada
21 O8 Church Hill Tennessee, S USA
11 X9 Churchill Manitoba, C Canada
11 X10 Churchill ≈ Manitoba /Saskatchewan, C Canada
13 P9 Churchill ≈ Newfoundland and Labrador, E Canada
11 Y9 Churchill, Cape headland Manitoba, C Canada
13 P9 Churchill Falls Newfoundland and Labrador, E Canada
11 S12 Churchill Lake ◎ Saskatchewan, C Canada
19 Q3 Churchill Lake ◎ Maine, NE USA
194 I5 Churchill Peninsula peninsula Antarctica
22 H8 Church Point Louisiana, S USA
29 O3 Churchs Ferry North Dakota, N USA
146 G12 Churchuri Ahal Welaýaty, C Turkmenistan
21 T5 Churchville Virginia, NE USA
152 G10 Chūru Rājasthān, NW India
54 J4 Churuguara Falcón, N Venezuela
167 U11 Chư Sê Gia Lai, C Vietnam
144 J12 Chushkakul, Gory ▲ SW Kazakhstan
Chūshū see Ch'ungju
37 O9 Chuska Mountains ▲ Arizona/New Mexico, SW USA
Chu, Sông see Sam, Nam
125 V14 Chusovoy Permskaya Oblast', NW Russian Federation
147 R10 Chust Namangan Viloyati, E Uzbekistan
Chust see Khust
15 U6 Chute-aux-Outardes Québec, SE Canada
117 U5 Chutove Poltavs'ka Oblast', C Ukraine
189 O15 Chuuk var. Truk. ◆ state C Micronesia
189 P15 Chuuk Islands var. Hogoley Islands; prev. Truk Islands. island group Caroline Islands, C Micronesia
Chuvashia see charvash Respubliki
Chuvashskaya Respublika see charvash Respubliki
Chuwārtah see Chwārtā
Chu Xian/Chuxian see Chuzhou
160 G13 Chuxiong Yunnan, SW China
147 V7 Chuy Chuyskaya Oblast', N Kyrgyzstan
61 H19 Chuy var. Chuí. Rocha, E Uruguay
123 O11 Chuya Respublika Sakha (Yakutiya), NE Russian Federation
Chüy Oblasty see Chuyskaya Oblast'
147 U8 Chuyskaya Oblast' Kir. Chüy Oblasty. ◆ province N Kyrgyzstan
161 Q7 Chuzhou var. Chuxian, Chu Xian. Anhui, E China
139 U3 Chwārtā var. Choarta, Chuwārtah. NE Iraq
119 N16 Chyhirynskaye Vodaskhovishcha ▣ E Belarus
117 R6 Chyhyryn Rus. Chigirin. Cherkas'ka Oblast', N Ukraine
Chyrvonaya Slabada see Krasnaya Slabada
119 L19 Chyrvonaye, Vozyera Rus. Ozero Chervonoye. ◎ SE Belarus
117 N11 Ciadîr-Lunga var. Ceadâr-Lunga, Rus. Chadyr-Lunga. S Moldova
169 P16 Ciamis prev. Tjiamis. Jawa, C Indonesia
107 I16 Ciampino ✕ Lazio, C Italy
169 N16 Cianjur prev. Tjiandjoer. Jawa, C Indonesia
60 H10 Cianorte Paraná, S Brazil
Ciarraí see Kerry
112 N13 Ćićevac Serbia, E Serbia and Montenegro (Yugo.)
187 Z14 Cicia prev. Thithia. island Lau Group, E Fiji
105 P4 Cidacos ≈ N Spain
136 I10 Cide Kastamonu, N Turkey
110 L10 Ciechanów prev. Zichenau. Mazowieckie, C Poland
110 O10 Ciechanowiec Ger. Rudelstadt. Podlaskie, E Poland
110 J10 Ciechocinek Kujawsko-pomorskie, C Poland
44 F6 Ciego de Ávila Ciego de Ávila, C Cuba
54 F4 Ciénaga Magdalena, N Colombia
54 E6 Ciénaga de Oro Córdoba, NW Colombia
44 E5 Cienfuegos Cienfuegos, C Cuba
104 F4 Cíes, Illas island group NW Spain
111 P16 Cieszanów Podkarpackie, SE Poland
111 J17 Cieszyn Cz. Těšín, Ger. Teschen. Śląskie, S Poland
105 R12 Cieza Murcia, SE Spain
136 F13 Çifteler Eskişehir, W Turkey
105 P7 Cifuentes Castilla-La Mancha, C Spain
Čiganak see Chiganak
105 P9 Cigüela ≈ C Spain
136 H14 Cihanbeyli Konya, C Turkey
136 H14 Cihanbeyli Yaylası plateau C Turkey
104 L10 Cijara, Embalse de ▣ C Spain
169 P16 Cikalong Jawa, S Indonesia
169 N16 Cikawung Jawa, S Indonesia
187 Y13 Cikobia prev. Thikombia. island N Fiji
169 P17 Cilacap prev. Tjilatjap. Jawa, C Indonesia
173 O16 Cilaos C Réunion
137 S11 Çıldır Ardahan, NE Turkey
137 S11 Çıldır Gölü ◎ NE Turkey
160 M10 Cili Hunan, S China
121 V10 Cilicia Trough undersea feature E Mediterranean Sea
Cill Airne see Killarney
Cill Chainnigh see Kilkenny
Cill Chaoi see Kilkee
Cill Choca see Kilcock
Cill Dara see Kildare
105 N3 Cilleruelo de Bezana Castilla-León, N Spain
Cilli see Celje
Cill Mhantáin see Wicklow
Cill Rois see Kilrush
146 C11 Çilmämmetgum Rus. Peski Chil'mamedkum, Turkm. Chilmämetgum. desert W Turkmenistan
137 Z11 Çiloy Adası Rus. Ostrov Zhiloy. island E Azerbaijan
26 J6 Cimarron Kansas, C USA
37 T9 Cimarron New Mexico, SW USA
26 M9 Cimarron River ≈ Kansas/Oklahoma, C USA
117 N11 Cimişlia Rus. Chimishliya. S Moldova
Cimpia Turzii see Câmpia Turzii
Cimpina see Câmpina
Cimpulung see Câmpulung

◆ Country ● Country Capital ◇ Dependent Territory ○ Dependent Territory Capital ◆ Administrative Region ✕ International Airport ▲ Mountain ▲ Mountain Range Volcano ≈ River ◎ Lake ▣ Reservoir

Cîmpulung Moldovenesc see Câmpulung Moldovenesc
137 P15 **Çınar** Dıyarbakır, SE Turkey
54 J8 **Cinaruco, Río** ≈ Colombia/Venezuela
Cina Selatan, Laut see South China Sea
105 T5 **Cinca** ≈ NE Spain
112 G13 **Cincar** ▲ SW Bosnia and Herzegovina
31 Q15 **Cincinnati** Ohio, N USA
21 M4 **Cincinnati** ✕ Kentucky, S USA
Cinco de Outubro see Xá-Muteba
136 C15 **Çine** Aydın, SW Turkey
99 J21 **Ciney** Namur, SE Belgium
104 H6 **Cinfães** Viseu, N Portugal
106 J12 **Cingoli** Marche, C Italy
41 U16 **Cintalapa** *var.* Cintalapa de Figueroa. Chiapas, SE Mexico
Cintalapa de Figueroa see Cintalapa
103 X14 **Cinto, Monte** ▲ Corse, France, C Mediterranean Sea
Cintra see Sintra
105 Q5 **Cintruénigo** Navarra, N Spain
Cionn tSáile see Kinsale
116 K13 **Ciorani** Prahova, SE Romania
113 E14 **Čiovo** *It.* Bua. *island* S Croatia
Cipiúr see Kippure
63 I15 **Cipolletti** Río Negro, C Argentina
120 L7 **Circeo, Capo** *headland* C Italy
39 S8 **Circle** *var.* Circle City. Alaska, USA
33 X8 **Circle** Montana, NW USA
Circle City see Circle
31 S14 **Circleville** Ohio, N USA
36 K6 **Circleville** Utah, W USA
169 P16 **Cirebon** *prev.* Tjirebon. Jawa, S Indonesia
97 L21 **Cirencester** *anc.* Corinium, Corinium Dobunorum. C England, UK
Cirkvenica see Crikvenica
107 O20 **Ciro** Calabria, SW Italy
107 O20 **Ciro Marina** Calabria, S Italy
102 K14 **Ciron** ≈ SW France
Cirquenizza see Crikvenica
25 R7 **Cisco** Texas, SW USA
116 I12 **Cisnădie** *Ger.* Heltau, *Hung.* Nagydisznód. Sibiu, SW Romania
63 G18 **Cisnes, Río** ≈ S Chile
25 T11 **Cistern** Texas, SW USA
104 L3 **Cistierna** Castilla-León, N Spain
Citharista see la Ciotat
Citlaltépetl see Orizaba, Volcán Pico de
55 X10 **Citron** NW French Guiana
23 N7 **Citronelle** Alabama, S USA
35 O7 **Citrus Heights** California, W USA
106 H7 **Cittadella** Veneto, NE Italy
106 H13 **Città della Pieve** Umbria, C Italy
106 H12 **Città di Castello** Umbria, C Italy
107 I14 **Cittaducale** Lazio, C Italy
107 N22 **Cittanova** Calabria, SW Italy
Cittavecchia see Starigrad
116 G10 **Ciucea** *Hung.* Csucsa. Cluj, NW Romania
116 M13 **Ciucurova** Tulcea, SE Romania
Ciudad Acuña see Villa Acuña
41 N15 **Ciudad Altamirano** Guerrero, S Mexico
42 G7 **Ciudad Barrios** San Miguel, NE El Salvador
54 I7 **Ciudad Bolívar** Barinas, NW Venezuela
55 N7 **Ciudad Bolívar** *prev.* Angostura. Bolívar, E Venezuela
40 K6 **Ciudad Camargo** Chihuahua, N Mexico
40 E8 **Ciudad Constitución** Baja California Sur, W Mexico
Ciudad Cortés see Cortés
41 V17 **Ciudad Cuauhtémoc** Chiapas, SE Mexico
42 J9 **Ciudad Darío** *var.* Dario. Matagalpa, W Nicaragua
Ciudad de Dolores Hidalgo see Dolores Hidalgo
42 C6 **Ciudad de Guatemala** *Eng.* Guatemala City; *prev.* Santiago de los Caballeros. ● (Guatemala) Guatemala, C Guatemala
Ciudad del Carmen see Carmen
62 Q6 **Ciudad del Este** *prev.* Cuidad Presidente Stroessner, Presidente Stroessner, Puerto Presidente Stroessner. Alto Paraná, SE Paraguay
62 K5 **Ciudad de Libertador General San Martín** *var.* Libertador General San Martín. Jujuy, C Argentina
Ciudad Delicias see Delicias
41 O11 **Ciudad del Maíz** San Luis Potosí, C Mexico
Ciudad de México see México
54 J7 **Ciudad de Nutrias** Barinas, NW Venezuela
Ciudad de Panamá see Panamá
55 P7 **Ciudad Guayana** *prev.* San Tomé de Guayana, Santo Tomé de Guayana. Bolívar, NE Venezuela
40 K14 **Ciudad Guzmán** Jalisco, SW Mexico
41 V17 **Ciudad Hidalgo** Chiapas, SE Mexico
41 N14 **Ciudad Hidalgo** Michoacán de Ocampo, SW Mexico
40 J3 **Ciudad Juárez** Chihuahua, N Mexico
40 L8 **Ciudad Lerdo** Durango, C Mexico
41 Q11 **Ciudad Madero** *var.* Villa Cecilia. Tamaulipas, C Mexico
41 P11 **Ciudad Mante** Tamaulipas, C Mexico
42 F2 **Ciudad Melchor de Mencos** *var.* Melchor de Mencos. Petén, NE Guatemala
41 P8 **Ciudad Miguel Alemán** Tamaulipas, C Mexico
Ciudad Mutis see Bahía Solano
40 G6 **Ciudad Obregón** Sonora, NW Mexico
54 I5 **Ciudad Ojeda** Zulia, NW Venezuela
55 P7 **Ciudad Piar** Bolívar, E Venezuela
Ciudad Porfirio Díaz see Piedras Negras
Ciudad Quesada see Quesada
105 N11 **Ciudad Real** Castilla-La Mancha, C Spain
105 N11 **Ciudad Real** ◐ *province* Castilla-La Mancha, C Spain
104 J7 **Ciudad-Rodrigo** Castilla-León, N Spain
42 A6 **Ciudad Tecún Umán** San Marcos, SW Guatemala
Ciudad Trujillo see Santo Domingo
41 P12 **Ciudad Valles** San Luis Potosí, C Mexico
41 O10 **Ciudad Victoria** Tamaulipas, C Mexico
42 C6 **Ciudad Vieja** Suchitepéquez, S Guatemala
116 L8 **Ciuhuru** *var.* Reuţel. ≈ N Moldova
Ciutadella see Ciutadella de Menorca
105 Z8 **Ciutadella de Menorca** *var.* Ciutadella. Menorca, Spain, W Mediterranean Sea
136 L11 **Civa Burnu** *headland* N Turkey
106 J7 **Cividale del Friuli** Friuli-Venezia Giulia, NE Italy
107 H14 **Civita Castellana** Lazio, C Italy
106 J12 **Civitanova Marche** Marche, C Italy
Civitas Altae Ripae see Brzeg
Civitas Carnutum see Chartres
Civitas Eburovicum see Évreux
Civitas Nemetum see Speyer
107 G15 **Civitavecchia** *anc.* Centum Cellae, Trajani Portus. Lazio, C Italy
102 L10 **Civray** Vienne, W France
136 E14 **Çivril** Denizli, W Turkey
161 O5 **Cixian** Hebei, E China
137 R16 **Cizre** Şırnak, SE Turkey
Clacton see Clacton-on-Sea
97 Q21 **Clacton-on-Sea** *var.* Clacton. E England, UK
22 H5 **Claiborne, Lake** ⊞ Louisiana, S USA
102 L10 **Clain** ≈ W France
11 Q11 **Claire, Lake** ◎ Alberta, C Canada
25 O6 **Clairemont** Texas, SW USA
34 M3 **Clair Engle Lake** ⊞ California, W USA
18 B15 **Clairton** Pennsylvania, NE USA
32 F7 **Clallam Bay** Washington, NW USA
103 P8 **Clamecy** Nièvre, C France
23 P5 **Clanton** Alabama, S USA
61 D17 **Clara** Entre Ríos, E Argentina
97 E18 **Clara** *Ir.* Clóirtheach. C Ireland
29 T9 **Clara City** Minnesota, N USA
61 D23 **Claraz** Buenos Aires, E Argentina
Clár Chlainne Mhuiris see Claremorris
182 I8 **Clare** South Australia
97 C19 **Clare** *Ir.* An Clár. *cultural region* W Ireland
97 C18 **Clare** ≈ W Ireland
97 A16 **Clare Island** *Ir.* Cliara. *island* W Ireland
44 J12 **Claremont** C Jamaica
29 W10 **Claremont** Minnesota, N USA
19 N9 **Claremont** New Hampshire, NE USA
27 Q9 **Claremore** Oklahoma, C USA
97 C17 **Claremorris** *Ir.* Clár Chlainne Mhuiris. W Ireland
185 J16 **Clarence** Canterbury, South Island, NZ
185 J16 **Clarence** ≈ South Island, NZ
65 F15 **Clarence Bay** *bay* Ascension Island, C Atlantic Ocean
63 H25 **Clarence, Isla** *island* S Chile
194 H2 **Clarence Island** *island* South Shetland Islands, Antarctica
183 V5 **Clarence River** ≈ New South Wales, SE Australia
44 J5 **Clarence Town** Long Island, C Bahamas
27 W12 **Clarendon** Arkansas, C USA
25 O3 **Clarendon** Texas, SW USA
13 U12 **Clarenville** Newfoundland and Labrador, SE Canada
11 Q17 **Claresholm** Alberta, SW Canada
29 T16 **Clarinda** Iowa, C USA
55 N5 **Clarines** Anzoátegui, NE Venezuela
29 V12 **Clarion** Iowa, C USA
18 C13 **Clarion** Pennsylvania, NE USA
193 O6 **Clarion Fracture Zone** *tectonic feature* NE Pacific Ocean
18 D13 **Clarion River** ≈ Pennsylvania, NE USA
29 Q9 **Clark** South Dakota, N USA
36 K11 **Clarkdale** Arizona, SW USA
15 W4 **Clarke City** Québec, SE Canada
183 Q15 **Clarke Island** *island* Furneaux Group, Tasmania, SE Australia
181 X6 **Clarke Range** ⛰ Queensland, E Australia
23 T2 **Clarkesville** Georgia, SE USA
29 S9 **Clarkfield** Minnesota, N USA
33 N7 **Clark Fork** Idaho, NW USA
33 N8 **Clark Fork** ≈ Idaho/Montana, NW USA
39 Q12 **Clark, Lake** ◎ Alaska, USA
35 W12 **Clark Mountain** ▲ California, W USA
37 S3 **Clark Peak** ▲ Colorado, C USA
14 D14 **Clark, Point** *headland* Ontario, S Canada
21 S3 **Clarksburg** West Virginia, NE USA
22 K2 **Clarksdale** Mississippi, S USA
33 U12 **Clarks Fork Yellowstone River** ≈ Montana/Wyoming, NW USA
21 P13 **Clark Hill Lake** *var.* J.Storm Thurmond Reservoir. ⊞ Georgia/South Carolina, SE USA
29 R14 **Clarkson** Nebraska, C USA
39 O13 **Clarks Point** Alaska, USA
18 I13 **Clarks Summit** Pennsylvania, NE USA
32 M10 **Clarkston** Washington, NW USA
44 J12 **Clark's Town** C Jamaica
27 T10 **Clarksville** Arkansas, C USA
31 P13 **Clarksville** Indiana, N USA
20 I8 **Clarksville** Tennessee, S USA
25 W5 **Clarksville** Texas, SW USA
21 U8 **Clarksville** Virginia, NE USA
21 U11 **Clarkton** North Carolina, SE USA
61 C24 **Claromecó** *var.* Balneario Claromecó. Buenos Aires, E Argentina
25 N3 **Claude** Texas, SW USA
Clausentum see Southampton
171 O1 **Claveria** Luzon, N Philippines
99 J20 **Clavier** Liège, E Belgium
23 W6 **Claxton** Georgia, SE USA
21 R4 **Clay** West Virginia, NE USA
27 N3 **Clay Center** Kansas, C USA
29 P16 **Clay Center** Nebraska, C USA
21 Y2 **Claymont** Delaware, NE USA
36 M14 **Claypool** Arizona, SW USA
23 R6 **Clayton** Alabama, S USA
23 T1 **Clayton** Georgia, SE USA
22 J5 **Clayton** Louisiana, S USA
27 X5 **Clayton** Missouri, C USA
37 V9 **Clayton** New Mexico, SW USA
21 V9 **Clayton** North Carolina, SE USA
27 Q12 **Clayton** Oklahoma, C USA
182 I4 **Clayton River** *seasonal river* South Australia
21 R7 **Claytor Lake** ⊞ Virginia, NE USA
27 P13 **Clear Boggy Creek** ≈ Oklahoma, C USA
97 B22 **Clear, Cape** *var.* The Bill of Cape Clear, *Ir.* Ceann Cléire. *headland* SW Ireland
36 M12 **Clear Creek** ≈ Arizona, SW USA
39 S12 **Cleare, Cape** *headland* Montague Island, Alaska, USA
18 E13 **Clearfield** Pennsylvania, NE USA
36 L2 **Clearfield** Utah, W USA
25 Q6 **Clear Fork Brazos River** ≈ Texas, SW USA
31 T12 **Clear Fork Reservoir** ⊞ Ohio, N USA
11 N12 **Clear Hills** ⛰ Alberta, SW Canada
29 V12 **Clear Lake** Iowa, C USA
29 R9 **Clear Lake** South Dakota, N USA
34 M6 **Clear Lake** ◎ California, W USA
22 G6 **Clear Lake** ⊞ Louisiana, S USA
34 M6 **Clearlake** California, W USA
35 P1 **Clear Lake Reservoir** ⊞ California, W USA
11 N16 **Clearwater** British Columbia, SW Canada
23 U12 **Clearwater** Florida, SE USA
11 R12 **Clearwater** ≈ Alberta/Saskatchewan, C Canada
27 W7 **Clearwater Lake** ⊞ Missouri, C USA
33 N10 **Clearwater Mountains** ⛰ Idaho, NW USA
33 N10 **Clearwater River** ≈ Idaho, NW USA
29 S4 **Clearwater River** ≈ Minnesota, N USA
25 T7 **Cleburne** Texas, SW USA
32 I9 **Cle Elum** Washington, NW USA
97 O17 **Cleethorpes** E England, UK
Cléire, Ceann see Clear, Cape
21 O11 **Clemson** South Carolina, SE USA
21 Q4 **Clendenin** West Virginia, NE USA
26 M9 **Cleo Springs** Oklahoma, C USA
Clerk Island see Onotoa
181 X8 **Clermont** Queensland, E Australia
15 S8 **Clermont** Québec, SE Canada
103 O4 **Clermont** Oise, N France
29 X12 **Clermont** Iowa, C USA
103 P11 **Clermont-Ferrand** Puy-de-Dôme, C France
103 Q15 **Clermont-l'Hérault** Hérault, S France
99 M22 **Clervaux** Diekirch, N Luxembourg
106 G6 **Cles** Trentino-Alto Adige, N Italy
182 H8 **Cleve** South Australia
Cleve see Kleve
23 T2 **Cleveland** Georgia, SE USA
22 K3 **Cleveland** Mississippi, S USA
31 T11 **Cleveland** Ohio, N USA
27 O9 **Cleveland** Oklahoma, C USA
20 L10 **Cleveland** Tennessee, S USA
25 W10 **Cleveland** Texas, SW USA
31 N7 **Cleveland** Wisconsin, N USA
31 O4 **Cleveland Cliffs Basin** ◎ Michigan, N USA
31 U11 **Cleveland Heights** Ohio, N USA
33 P6 **Cleveland, Mount** ▲ Montana, NW USA
Cleves see Kleve
97 B16 **Clew Bay** *Ir.* Cuan Mó. *inlet* W Ireland
23 Y14 **Clewiston** Florida, SE USA
Cliara see Clare Island
97 A17 **Clifden** *Ir.* An Clochán. W Ireland
37 O14 **Clifton** Arizona, SW USA
18 K14 **Clifton** New Jersey, NE USA
25 S8 **Clifton** Texas, SW USA
21 S6 **Clifton Forge** Virginia, NE USA
182 I1 **Clifton Hills** South Australia
11 S17 **Climax** Saskatchewan, S Canada
21 O8 **Clinch River** ≈ Tennessee /Virginia, S USA
25 P12 **Cline** Texas, SW USA
21 N10 **Clingmans Dome** ▲ North Carolina/Tennessee, SE USA
24 H8 **Clint** Texas, SW USA
10 M16 **Clinton** British Columbia, SW Canada
14 E15 **Clinton** Ontario, S Canada
27 U10 **Clinton** Arkansas, C USA
30 L10 **Clinton** Illinois, N USA
29 Z14 **Clinton** Iowa, C USA
20 G7 **Clinton** Kentucky, S USA
22 J8 **Clinton** Louisiana, S USA
19 N11 **Clinton** Massachusetts, NE USA
31 R10 **Clinton** Michigan, N USA
22 K5 **Clinton** Mississippi, S USA
27 S5 **Clinton** Missouri, C USA
21 V10 **Clinton** North Carolina, SE USA
26 L10 **Clinton** Oklahoma, C USA
21 Q12 **Clinton** South Carolina, SE USA
21 M9 **Clinton** Tennessee, S USA
8 L9 **Clinton-Colden Lake** ◎ Northwest Territories, NW Canada
10 H5 **Clinton Creek** Yukon Territory, NW Canada
30 L13 **Clinton Lake** ⊞ Illinois, N USA
27 Q4 **Clinton Lake** ⊞ Kansas, C USA
21 T11 **Clio** South Carolina, SE USA
193 O7 **Clipperton Fracture Zone** *tectonic feature* E Pacific Ocean
193 Q7 **Clipperton Island** ◇ *French dependency of French Polynesia* E Pacific Ocean
46 K6 **Clipperton Island** *island* E Pacific Ocean
(0) F16 **Clipperton Seamounts** *undersea feature* E Pacific Ocean
102 J8 **Clisson** Loire-Atlantique, NW France
62 K7 **Clodomira** Santiago del Estero, N Argentina
Cloich na Coillte see Clonakilty
Clóirtheach see Clara
97 C21 **Clonakilty** *Ir.* Cloich na Coillte. SW Ireland
181 T6 **Cloncurry** Queensland, C Australia
97 F18 **Clondalkin** *Ir.* Cluain Dolcáin. E Ireland
97 E16 **Clones** *Ir.* Cluain Eois. N Ireland
97 D20 **Clonmel** *Ir.* Cluain Meala. S Ireland
100 G11 **Cloppenburg** Niedersachsen, NW Germany
29 W6 **Cloquet** Minnesota, N USA
37 S14 **Cloudcroft** New Mexico, SW USA
33 W12 **Cloud Peak** ▲ Wyoming, C USA
185 K14 **Cloudy Bay** *inlet* South Island, NZ
21 R10 **Clover** South Carolina, SE USA
34 M6 **Cloverdale** California, W USA
20 J5 **Cloverport** Kentucky, S USA
35 Q10 **Clovis** California, W USA
37 W12 **Clovis** New Mexico, SW USA
14 K13 **Cloyne** Ontario, SE Canada
Cluain Dolcáin see Clondalkin
Cluain Eois see Clones
Cluainín see Manorhamilton
Cluain Meala see Clonmel
116 H10 **Cluj** ◐ *county* NW Romania
Cluj see Cluj-Napoca
116 H10 **Cluj-Napoca** *Ger.* Klausenburg, *Hung.* Kolozsvár; *prev.* Cluj. Cluj, NW Romania
Clunia see Feldkirch
103 R10 **Cluny** Saône-et-Loire, C France
103 T10 **Cluses** Haute-Savoie, E France
106 E7 **Clusone** Lombardia, N Italy
25 W12 **Clute** Texas, SW USA
185 D23 **Clutha** ≈ South Island, NZ
97 J18 **Clwyd** *cultural region* NE Wales, UK
185 D22 **Clyde** Otago, South Island, NZ
27 N3 **Clyde** Kansas, C USA
29 P2 **Clyde** North Dakota, N USA
31 S11 **Clyde** Ohio, N USA
25 Q7 **Clyde** Texas, SW USA
14 K13 **Clyde** ≈ Ontario, SE Canada
96 J13 **Clyde** ≈ W Scotland, UK
96 H12 **Clydebank** S Scotland, UK
96 H13 **Clyde, Firth of** *inlet* S Scotland, UK
33 S11 **Clyde Park** Montana, NW USA
104 I7 **Côa, Rio** ≈ N Portugal
35 W16 **Coachella** California, W USA
35 W16 **Coachella Canal** *canal* California, W USA
40 I9 **Coacoyole** Durango, C Mexico
25 N7 **Coahoma** Texas, SW USA
10 K8 **Coal** ≈ Yukon Territory, NW Canada
40 L14 **Coalcomán** *var.* Coalcomán de Matamoros. Michoacán de Ocampo, S Mexico
Coalcomán de Matamoros see Coalcomán
39 T8 **Coal Creek** Alaska, USA
11 Q17 **Coaldale** Alberta, SW Canada
27 P12 **Coalgate** Oklahoma, C USA
35 P11 **Coalinga** California, W USA
10 L9 **Coal River** British Columbia, W Canada
21 Q6 **Coal River** ≈ West Virginia, NE USA
36 M2 **Coalville** Utah, W USA
58 E13 **Coari** Amazonas, N Brazil
59 D14 **Coari, Rio** ≈ NW Brazil
81 J20 **Coast** ◐ *province* SE Kenya
Coast see Pwani
10 G12 **Coast Mountains** *Fr.* Chaîne Côtière. ⛰ Canada/USA
16 C7 **Coast Ranges** ⛰ W USA
96 I12 **Coatbridge** S Scotland, UK
42 B6 **Coatepeque** Quezaltenango, SW Guatemala
18 H16 **Coatesville** Pennsylvania, NE USA
15 Q13 **Coaticook** Québec, SE Canada
9 P9 **Coats Island** *island* Nunavut, NE Canada
195 O4 **Coats Land** *physical region* Antarctica
41 T14 **Coatzacoalcos** *var.* Quetzalcoalco; *prev.* Puerto México. Veracruz-Llave, E Mexico
41 S14 **Coatzacoalcos, Río** ≈ SE Mexico
116 M15 **Cobadin** Constanța, SW Romania
14 H9 **Cobalt** Ontario, S Canada
42 D5 **Cobán** Alta Verapaz, C Guatemala
183 O6 **Cobar** New South Wales, SE Australia
18 F12 **Cobb Hill** ▲ Pennsylvania, NE USA
(0) D8 **Cobb Seamount** *undersea feature* E Pacific Ocean
14 K12 **Cobden** Ontario, SE Canada
97 D21 **Cobh** *Ir.* An Cóbh; *prev.* Cove of Cork, Queenstown. SW Ireland
57 J14 **Cobija** Pando, NW Bolivia
Coblence/Coblenz see Koblenz
18 J10 **Cobleskill** New York, NE USA
14 I15 **Cobourg** Ontario, SE Canada
181 P1 **Cobourg Peninsula** *headland* Northern Territory, N Australia
183 O10 **Cobram** Victoria, SE Australia
82 N13 **Cóbuè** Niassa, N Mozambique
101 K18 **Coburg** Bayern, SE Germany
19 Q5 **Coburn Mountain** ▲ Maine, NE USA
Coca see Puerto Francisco de Orellana
57 H18 **Cocachacra** Arequipa, SW Peru
59 J17 **Cocalinho** Mato Grosso, W Brazil
Cocanada see Kākināda
105 S11 **Cocentaina** País Valenciano, E Spain
57 L18 **Cochabamba** *hist.* Oropeza. Cochabamba, C Bolivia
57 K18 **Cochabamba** ◐ *department* C Bolivia
57 L18 **Cochabamba, Cordillera de** ⛰ C Bolivia
101 E18 **Cochem** Rheinland-Pfalz, W Germany
37 R6 **Cochetopa Hills** ⛰ Colorado, C USA
155 G22 **Cochin** *var.* Kochi. Kerala, SW India
44 D5 **Cochinos, Bahía de** *Eng.* Bay of Pigs. *bay* SE Cuba
37 O16 **Cochise Head** ▲ Arizona, SW USA
23 U5 **Cochran** Georgia, SE USA
11 P16 **Cochrane** Alberta, SW Canada
12 G12 **Cochrane** Ontario, S Canada
63 G20 **Cochrane** Aisén, S Chile
11 U10 **Cochrane** ≈ Manitoba/Saskatchewan, C Canada
Cochrane, Lago see Pueyrredón, Lago
Cocibolca see Nicaragua, Lago de
Cockade State see Maryland
44 M6 **Cockburn Harbour** South Caicos, S Turks and Caicos Islands
14 C11 **Cockburn Island** *island* Ontario, S Canada
44 J3 **Cockburn Town** San Salvador, E Bahamas
21 X2 **Cockeysville** Maryland, NE USA
181 N12 **Cocklebiddy** Western Australia
44 I12 **Cockpit Country, The** *physical region* W Jamaica
43 S16 **Coclé** *off.* Provincia de Coclé. ◐ *province* C Panama
43 S15 **Coclé del Norte** Colón, C Panama
23 Y12 **Cocoa** Florida, SE USA
23 Y12 **Cocoa Beach** Florida, SE USA
79 D17 **Cocobeach** Estuaire, NW Gabon
44 G5 **Coco, Cayo** *island* C Cuba
151 Q19 **Coco Channel** *strait* Andaman Sea/Bay of Bengal
173 N6 **Coco-de-Mer Seamounts** *undersea feature* W Indian Ocean
36 K10 **Coconino Plateau** *plain* Arizona, SW USA
43 N6 **Coco, Río** *var.* Río Wanki, Segoviao Wangkí. ≈ Honduras/Nicaragua
173 T8 **Cocos (Keeling) Islands** ◇ *Australian external territory* E Indian Ocean
173 T7 **Cocos Basin** *undersea feature* E Indian Ocean
188 B17 **Cocos Island** *island* S Guam
Cocos Island Ridge see Cocos Ridge
131 S17 **Cocos Islands** *island group* E Indian Ocean
(0) G15 **Cocos Plate** *tectonic feature*
193 T7 **Cocos Ridge** *var.* Cocos Island Ridge. *undersea feature* E Pacific Ocean
40 K13 **Cocula** Jalisco, SW Mexico
107 D17 **Coda Cavallo, Capo** *headland* Sardegna, Italy, C Mediterranean Sea
58 E13 **Codajás** Amazonas, N Brazil
Codazzi see Agustín Codazzi
19 Q12 **Cod, Cape** *headland* Massachusetts, NE USA
185 B25 **Codfish Island** *island* SW NZ
106 H9 **Codigoro** Emilia-Romagna, N Italy
13 P5 **Cod Island** *island* Newfoundland and Labrador, E Canada
116 J12 **Codlea** *Ger.* Zeiden, *Hung.* Feketehalom. Brașov, C Romania
58 M13 **Codó** Maranhão, E Brazil
106 E8 **Codogno** Lombardia, N Italy
116 M10 **Codrii** *hill range* C Moldova
45 W9 **Codrington** Barbuda, Antigua and Barbuda
106 J7 **Codroipo** Friuli-Venezia Giulia, NE Italy
28 M12 **Cody** Nebraska, C USA
33 U12 **Cody** Wyoming, C USA
21 P7 **Coeburn** Virginia, NE USA
54 E10 **Coello** Tolima, W Colombia
Coemba see Cuemba
181 V2 **Coen** Queensland, NE Australia
101 E14 **Coesfeld** Nordrhein-Westfalen, W Germany
32 M8 **Coeur d'Alene** Idaho, NW USA
32 M8 **Coeur d'Alene Lake** ⊞ Idaho, NW USA
98 O8 **Coevorden** Drenthe, NE Netherlands
10 H6 **Coffee Creek** Yukon Territory, W Canada
30 L15 **Coffeen Lake** ⊞ Illinois, N USA
22 L3 **Coffeeville** Mississippi, S USA
27 Q8 **Coffeyville** Kansas, C USA
182 G9 **Coffin Bay** South Australia
182 F9 **Coffin Bay Peninsula** *peninsula* South Australia
183 V5 **Coffs Harbour** New South Wales, SE Australia
105 R10 **Cofrentes** País Valenciano, E Spain
Cogîlnic see Kohyl'nyk
102 K11 **Cognac** *anc.* Compniacum. Charente, W France
106 B7 **Cogne** Valle d'Aosta, NW Italy
103 U16 **Cogolin** Var, SE France
105 O7 **Cogolludo** Castilla-La Mancha, C Spain
Cohalm see Rupea
92 L8 **Čohkarášša** *var.* Cuokkarašša. ▲ N Norway
Čohkkiras see Jukkasjärvi
F11 **Cohocton River** ≈ New York, NE USA
18 L10 **Cohoes** New York, NE USA
183 N10 **Cohuna** Victoria, SE Australia
43 P17 **Coiba, Isla de** *island* SW Panama
63 H23 **Coig, Río** ≈ S Argentina
63 G19 **Coihaique** *var.* Coyhaique. Aisén, S Chile
155 G21 **Coimbatore** Tamil Nādu, S India
104 G8 **Coimbra** *anc.* Conimbria, Conimbriga. Coimbra, W Portugal
104 G8 **Coimbra** ◐ *district* N Portugal
104 L15 **Coín** Andalucía, S Spain
57 J20 **Coipasa, Laguna** ◎ W Bolivia
57 J20 **Coipasa, Salar de** *salt lake* W Bolivia
Coira/Coire see Chur
Coirib, Loch see Corrib, Lough
54 K6 **Cojedes** *off.* Estado Cojedes. ◐ *state* N Venezuela
42 F7 **Cojutepeque** Cuscatlán, C El Salvador
Coka see Banbar
33 S16 **Cokeville** Wyoming, C USA
182 M13 **Colac** Victoria, SE Australia
59 O20 **Colatina** Espírito Santo, SE Brazil
27 O13 **Colbert** Oklahoma, C USA
100 L12 **Colbitz-Letzinger Heide** *heathland* N Germany
26 I3 **Colby** Kansas, C USA
57 H17 **Colca, Río** ≈ SW Peru
97 P21 **Colchester** *hist.* Colneceaste, *anc.* Camulodunum. E England, UK
19 N13 **Colchester** Connecticut, NE USA
38 M16 **Cold Bay** Alaska, USA
11 R14 **Cold Lake** Alberta, SW Canada
11 R13 **Cold Lake** ◎ Alberta/Saskatchewan, S Canada
29 U8 **Cold Spring** Minnesota, N USA
25 W10 **Coldspring** Texas, SW USA
11 N17 **Coldstream** British Columbia, SW Canada
96 L13 **Coldstream** SE Scotland, UK
14 H13 **Coldwater** Ontario, S Canada
26 K7 **Coldwater** Kansas, C USA
31 Q10 **Coldwater** Michigan, N USA
25 N1 **Coldwater Creek** ≈ Oklahoma/Texas, SW USA
22 K2 **Coldwater River** ≈ Mississippi, S USA
183 O9 **Coleambally** New South Wales, SE Australia
19 O6 **Colebrook** New Hampshire, NE USA
27 T5 **Cole Camp** Missouri, C USA
39 T6 **Coleen River** ≈ Alaska, USA
11 P17 **Coleman** Alberta, SW Canada
25 Q8 **Coleman** Texas, SW USA
Çölemerik see Hakkâri
83 K22 **Colenso** KwaZulu/Natal, E South Africa
182 L12 **Coleraine** Victoria, SE Australia

◆ Country ● Country Capital ◇ Dependent Territory ○ Dependent Territory Capital ◐ Administrative Region ✕ International Airport ▲ Mountain ⛰ Mountain Range Volcano ≈ River ◎ Lake ⊞ Reservoir

97 F14 Coleraine Ir. Cúil Raithin. N Northern Ireland, UK
185 G18 Coleridge, Lake ◎ South Island, NZ
83 H24 Colesberg Northern Cape, C South Africa
22 H7 Colfax Louisiana, S USA
32 L9 Colfax Washington, NW USA
30 J6 Colfax Wisconsin, N USA
63 I19 Colhué Huapí, Lago ◎ S Argentina
45 Z6 Colibris, Pointe des headland Grande Terre, E Guadeloupe
106 D6 Colico Lombardia, N Italy
99 E14 Colijnsplaat Zeeland, SW Netherlands
40 L14 Colima Colima, S Mexico
40 K14 Colima ◆ state SW Mexico
40 L14 Colima, Nevado de ✻ C Mexico
59 M14 Colinas Maranhão, E Brazil
96 F10 Coll island W Scotland, UK
105 N7 Collado Villalba var. Villalba. Madrid, C Spain
183 R4 Collarenebri New South Wales, SE Australia
37 P5 Collbran Colorado, C USA
106 G12 Colle di Val d'Elsa Toscana, C Italy
39 R9 College Alaska, USA
32 K10 College Place Washington, NW USA
25 U10 College Station Texas, SW USA
183 P4 Collerina New South Wales, SE Australia
180 I13 Collie Western Australia
180 L4 Collier Bay bay Western Australia
21 F10 Collierville Tennessee, S USA
106 F11 Collina, Passo della pass C Italy
14 G14 Collingwood Ontario, S Canada
184 I13 Collingwood Tasman, South Island, NZ
22 L7 Collins Mississippi, S USA
30 K15 Collinsville Illinois, N USA
27 P9 Collinsville Oklahoma, C USA
20 H10 Collinwood Tennessee, S USA
Collipo see Leiria
63 G14 Collipulli Araucanía, C Chile
97 D16 Collooney Ir. Cúil Mhuine. NW Ireland
29 R10 Colman South Dakota, N USA
103 U6 Colmar Ger. Kolmar. Haut-Rhin, NE France
104 M15 Colmenar Andalucía, S Spain
Colmenar see Colmenar de Oreja
105 O9 Colmenar de Oreja var. Colmenar. Madrid, C Spain
105 N7 Colmenar Viejo Madrid, C Spain
25 X9 Colmesneil Texas, SW USA
Cöln see Köln
Colneceaste see Colchester
40 C3 Colnet Baja California, NW Mexico
59 G15 Colniza Mato Grosso, W Brazil
Cologne see Köln
42 B6 Colomba Quezaltenango, SW Guatemala
Colomb-Béchar see Béchar
54 E11 Colombia Huila, C Colombia
54 G10 Colombia off. Republic of Colombia. ◆ republic N South America
64 E12 Colombian Basin undersea feature SW Caribbean Sea
Colombie-Britannique see British Columbia
15 T6 Colombier Québec, SE Canada
155 J25 Colombo ● (Sri Lanka) Western Province, W Sri Lanka
155 J25 Colombo ✕ Western Province, SW Sri Lanka
29 N11 Colome South Dakota, N USA
61 D18 Colon Entre Ríos, E Argentina
61 B19 Colón Buenos Aires, E Argentina
44 D5 Colón Matanzas, C Cuba
43 T14 Colón prev. Aspinwall. Colón, C Panama
42 K5 Colón ◆ department NE Honduras
43 S15 Colón off. Provincia de Colón. ◆ province N Panama
57 A16 Colón, Archipiélago de var. Islas de los Galápagos, Eng. Galapagos Islands, Tortoise Islands. island group Ecuador, E Pacific Ocean
44 K5 Colonel Hill Crooked Island, SE Bahamas
40 B3 Colonet, Cabo headland NW Mexico
188 G14 Colonia Yap, W Micronesia
61 D19 Colonia ◆ department SW Uruguay
Colonia see Kolonia, Micronesia
Colonia see Colonia del Sacramento, Uruguay
Colonia Agrippina see Köln
61 D20 Colonia del Sacramento var. Colonia. Colonia, SW Uruguay
62 L8 Colonia Dora Santiago del Estero, N Argentina
Colonia Julia Fanestris see Fano
21 W5 Colonial Beach Virginia, NE USA
21 V6 Colonial Heights Virginia, NE USA
193 S7 Colón Ridge undersea feature E Pacific Ocean
96 F12 Colonsay island W Scotland, UK
57 K22 Colorada, Laguna ◎ SW Bolivia
37 R6 Colorado off. State of Colorado; also known as Centennial State, Silver State. ◆ state C USA
63 H22 Colorado, Cerro ▲ S Argentina
25 O7 Colorado City Texas, SW USA
36 M7 Colorado Plateau plateau W USA
61 A24 Colorado, Río ≈ E Argentina
43 N12 Colorado, Río ≈ NE Costa Rica
Colorado, Río see Colorado River
16 F12 Colorado River var. Río Colorado. ≈ Mexico/USA
16 K14 Colorado River ≈ Texas, SW USA
35 W15 Colorado River Aqueduct aqueduct California, W USA
44 A4 Colorados, Archipiélago de los island group NW Cuba
62 J9 Colorados, Desagües de los ◎ W Argentina
37 T5 Colorado Springs Colorado, C USA
40 L11 Colotlán Jalisco, SW Mexico
57 L19 Colquechaca Potosí, C Bolivia
23 S7 Colquitt Georgia, SE USA
29 R11 Colton South Dakota, N USA
32 M10 Colton Washington, NW USA
35 P8 Columbia California, W USA
30 K16 Columbia Illinois, N USA
20 L7 Columbia Kentucky, S USA
22 I6 Columbia Louisiana, S USA
21 W3 Columbia Maryland, NE USA
22 L7 Columbia Mississippi, S USA
27 U4 Columbia Missouri, C USA
21 Y9 Columbia North Carolina, SE USA
18 G16 Columbia Pennsylvania, NE USA
21 Q12 Columbia state capital South Carolina, SE USA
20 I9 Columbia Tennessee, S USA
(0) F9 Columbia ≈ Canada/USA
32 K9 Columbia Basin basin Washington, NW USA
197 Q10 Columbia, Cape headland Ellesmere Island, Nunavut, NE Canada
31 Q12 Columbia City Indiana, N USA
21 W3 Columbia, District of ◆ federal district NE USA
33 P7 Columbia Falls Montana, NW USA
11 O15 Columbia Icefield icefield Alberta/British Columbia, S Canada
11 O15 Columbia, Mount ▲ Alberta/British Columbia, SW Canada
11 N15 Columbia Mountains ▲ British Columbia, SW Canada
23 P4 Columbiana Alabama, S USA
31 V12 Columbiana Ohio, N USA
32 M14 Columbia Plateau plateau Idaho/Oregon, NW USA
29 P7 Columbia Road Reservoir ⊡ South Dakota, N USA
65 K16 Columbia Seamount undersea feature C Atlantic Ocean
83 D25 Columbine, Cape headland SW South Africa
105 U9 Columbretes, Islas island group E Spain
23 R5 Columbus Georgia, SE USA
31 P14 Columbus Indiana, N USA
27 R7 Columbus Kansas, C USA
23 N4 Columbus Mississippi, S USA
33 U11 Columbus Montana, NW USA
29 Q15 Columbus Nebraska, C USA
37 Q16 Columbus New Mexico, SW USA
21 P10 Columbus North Carolina, SE USA
28 K2 Columbus North Dakota, N USA
31 S13 Columbus state capital Ohio, N USA
25 U11 Columbus Texas, SW USA
30 L8 Columbus Wisconsin, N USA
31 R12 Columbus Grove Ohio, N USA
29 Y15 Columbus Junction Iowa, C USA
44 J3 Columbus Point headland Cat Island, C Bahamas
35 T8 Columbus Salt Marsh salt marsh Nevada, W USA
35 N6 Colusa California, W USA
32 L7 Colville Washington, NW USA
184 M5 Colville, Cape headland North Island, NZ
184 M5 Colville Channel channel North Island, NZ
39 P6 Colville River ≈ Alaska, USA
97 J18 Colwyn Bay N Wales, UK
106 H9 Comacchio var. Commachio; anc. Comactium. Emilia-Romagna, N Italy
106 H9 Comacchio, Valli di lagoon Adriatic Sea, N Mediterranean Sea
Comactium see Comacchio
41 V17 Comalapa Chiapas, SE Mexico
41 U15 Comalcalco Tabasco, SE Mexico
63 H16 Comallo Río Negro, SW Argentina
26 M12 Comanche Oklahoma, C USA
25 R8 Comanche Texas, SW USA
194 H2 Comandante Ferraz Brazilian research station Antarctica
62 N6 Comandante Fontana Formosa, N Argentina
63 I22 Comandante Luis Peidra Buena Santa Cruz, S Argentina
59 O18 Comandatuba Bahia, SE Brazil
116 K11 Comănești Hung. Kománfalva. Bacău, SW Romania
57 M19 Comarapa Santa Cruz, C Bolivia
116 J13 Comarnic Prahova, SE Romania
42 H6 Comayagua Comayagua, W Honduras
42 H6 Comayagua ◆ department W Honduras
42 I6 Comayagua, Montañas de ▲ C Honduras
21 R15 Combahee River ≈ South Carolina, SE USA
62 G10 Combarbalá Coquimbo, C Chile
103 S7 Combeaufontaine Haute-Saône, E France
97 G15 Comber Ir. An Comar. E Northern Ireland, UK
99 K20 Comblain-au-Pont Liège, E Belgium
102 I6 Combourg Ille-et-Vilaine, NW France
44 M9 Comendador prev. Elías Piña. W Dominican Republic
Comer See see Como, Lago di
25 R11 Comfort Texas, SW USA
153 V15 Comilla Ben. Kumillā. Chittagong, E Bangladesh
99 B18 Comines Hainaut, W Belgium
121 O15 Comino Malt. Kemmuna. island C Malta
107 D18 Comino, Capo headland Sardegna, Italy, C Mediterranean Sea
107 K25 Comiso Sicilia, Italy, C Mediterranean Sea
41 V16 Comitán var. Comitán de Domínguez. Chiapas, SE Mexico
Comitán de Domínguez see Comitán
Commachio see Comacchio
Commander Islands see Komandorskiye Ostrova
103 O10 Commentry Allier, C France
23 T2 Commerce Georgia, SE USA
27 R8 Commerce Oklahoma, C USA
25 V5 Commerce Texas, SW USA
37 T4 Commerce City Colorado, C USA
103 S5 Commercy Meuse, NE France
55 W9 Commewijne var. Commewyne. ◆ district NE Suriname
Commewyne see Commewijne
15 P8 Commissaires, Lac des ◎ Québec, SE Canada
64 A12 Commissioner's Point headland W Bermuda
9 O7 Committee Bay bay Nunavut, N Canada
106 D7 Como anc. Comum. Lombardia, N Italy
63 J19 Comodoro Rivadavia Chubut, SE Argentina
106 D6 Como, Lago di var. Lario, Eng. Lake Como, Ger. Comer See. ◎ N Italy
Como, Lake see Como, Lago di
40 E7 Comondú Baja California Sur, W Mexico
116 F12 Comorâște Hung. Komornok. Caraș-Severin, SW Romania
Comores, République Fédérale Islamique des see Comoros
155 G24 Comorin, Cape headland SE India
172 M8 Comoro Basin undersea feature SW Indian Ocean
172 I14 Comoro Islands island group W Indian Ocean
172 H13 Comoros off. Federal Islamic Republic of the Comoros, Fr. République Fédérale Islamique des Comores. ◆ republic W Indian Ocean
10 L17 Comox Vancouver Island, British Columbia, SW Canada
103 O4 Compiègne Oise, N France
Complutum see Alcalá de Henares
Compniacum see Cognac
40 K12 Compostela Nayarit, C Mexico
Compostella see Santiago
60 L11 Comprida, Ilha island S Brazil
117 N11 Comrat Rus. Komrat. S Moldova
25 O11 Comstock Texas, SW USA
31 P9 Comstock Park Michigan, N USA
193 N3 Comstock Seamount undersea feature N Pacific Ocean
Comum see Como
159 N17 Cona Xizang Zizhiqu, W China
76 H14 Conakry ● (Guinea) Conakry, SW Guinea
76 H14 Conakry ✕ Conakry, SW Guinea
Conamara see Connemara
Conca see Cuenca
25 Q12 Concan Texas, SW USA
102 F6 Concarneau Finistère, NW France
83 O17 Conceição Sofala, C Mozambique
59 K15 Conceição do Araguaia Pará, NE Brazil
58 F10 Conceição do Maú Roraima, W Brazil
61 D14 Concepción var. Concepcion. Corrientes, NE Argentina
62 J8 Concepción Tucumán, N Argentina
57 O17 Concepción Santa Cruz, E Bolivia
62 G13 Concepción Bío Bío, C Chile
54 E14 Concepción Putumayo, S Colombia
62 O5 Concepción var. Villa Concepción. Concepción, C Paraguay
62 O5 Concepción off. Departamento de Concepción. ◆ department E Paraguay
Concepción see La Concepción
Concepción de la Vega see La Vega
41 N9 Concepción del Oro Zacatecas, C Mexico
61 D18 Concepción del Uruguay Entre Ríos, E Argentina
42 K11 Concepción, Volcán ✻ SW Nicaragua
44 J4 Conception Island island C Bahamas
35 P14 Conception, Point headland California, W USA
54 H6 Concha Zulia, W Venezuela
60 L9 Conchas São Paulo, S Brazil
37 U11 Conchas Dam New Mexico, SW USA
37 U10 Conchas Lake ⊡ New Mexico, SW USA
102 M5 Conches-en-Ouche Eure, N France
37 N12 Concho Arizona, SW USA
40 J5 Conchos, Río ≈ NW Mexico
41 O8 Conchos, Río ≈ C Mexico
108 C8 Concise Vaud, W Switzerland
35 N8 Concord California, W USA
19 O9 Concord state capital New Hampshire, NE USA
21 R10 Concord North Carolina, SE USA
61 D17 Concordia Entre Ríos, E Argentina
54 D9 Concordia Antioquia, W Colombia
40 J10 Concordia Sinaloa, C Mexico
57 I19 Concordia Tacna, SW Peru
27 N3 Concordia Kansas, C USA
27 S4 Concordia Missouri, C USA
60 I13 Concórdia Santa Catarina, S Brazil
167 S7 Con Cuông Nghê An, N Vietnam
167 T15 Côn Đao var. Con Son. island S Vietnam
Condate see St-Claude, Jura, France
Condate see Rennes, Ille-et-Vilaine, France
Condate see Montereau-Faut-Yonne, Seine-St-Denis, France
29 P8 Conde South Dakota, N USA
42 J8 Condega Estelí, NW Nicaragua
103 P2 Condé-sur-l'Escaut Nord, N France
102 K5 Condé-sur-Noireau Calvados, N France
Condivincum see Nantes
183 P8 Condobolin New South Wales, SE Australia
102 L15 Condom Gers, S France
32 J11 Condon Oregon, NW USA
54 D9 Condoto Chocó, W Colombia
23 F7 Conecuh River ≈ Alabama/Florida, SE USA
106 H7 Conegliano Veneto, NE Italy
61 C19 Conesa Buenos Aires, E Argentina
14 F15 Conestogo ≈ Ontario, S Canada
Confluentes see Koblenz
102 L10 Confolens Charente, W France
36 J4 Confusion Range ▲ Utah, W USA
62 N6 Confuso, Río ≈ C Paraguay
21 R12 Congaree River ≈ South Carolina, SE USA
Công Hoa Xa Hôi Chu Nghia Viêt Nam see Vietnam
160 K12 Congjiang var. Bingmei. Guizhou, S China
79 K19 Congo off. Democratic Republic of Congo; prev. Zaire, Belgian Congo, Congo (Kinshasa). ◆ republic C Africa
79 G18 Congo off. Republic of the Congo, Fr. Moyen-Congo; prev. Middle Congo. ◆ republic C Africa
67 T11 Congo var. Kongo, Fr. Zaire. ≈ C Africa
Congo see Zaire (province, Angola)
Congo/Congo (Kinshasa) see Congo (Democratic Republic of)
79 K18 Congo Basin drainage basin W Dem. Rep. Congo
67 Q11 Congo Canyon var. Congo Seavalley, Congo Submarine Canyon. undersea feature E Atlantic Ocean
Congo Cone see Congo Fan
65 P15 Congo Fan var. Congo Cone. undersea feature E Atlantic Ocean
Coni see Cuneo
63 H18 Cónico, Cerro ▲ SW Argentina
Conimbria/Conimbriga see Coimbra
Conjeeveram see Kānchīpuram
11 R13 Conklin Alberta, C Canada
24 M1 Conlen Texas, SW USA
Con, Loch see Conn, Lough
Connacht see Connaught
97 B17 Connaught var. Connacht, Ir. Chonnacht, Cúige. cultural region W Ireland
31 V10 Conneaut Ohio, N USA
18 L13 Connecticut off. State of Connecticut; also known as Blue Law State, Constitution State, Land of Steady Habits, Nutmeg State. ◆ state NE USA
19 N8 Connecticut ≈ Canada/USA
19 O6 Connecticut Lakes lakes New Hampshire, NE USA
32 K9 Connell Washington, NW USA
97 B17 Connemara Ir. Conamara. region W Ireland
31 Q14 Connersville Indiana, N USA
97 B16 Conn, Lough Ir. Loch Con. ◎ W Ireland
35 X6 Connors Pass pass Nevada, W USA
181 X7 Connors Range ▲ Queensland, E Australia
56 E7 Cononaco, Río ≈ E Ecuador
29 W13 Conrad Iowa, C USA
33 R7 Conrad Montana, NW USA
25 W10 Conroe Texas, SW USA
25 V10 Conroe, Lake ⊡ Texas, SW USA
61 C17 Conscripto Bernardi Entre Ríos, E Argentina
59 M20 Conselheiro Lafaiete Minas Gerais, SE Brazil
Consentia see Cosenza
97 L14 Consett N England, UK
44 B5 Consolación del Sur Pinar del Río, W Cuba
Con Son see Côn Đao
11 R15 Consort Alberta, SW Canada
Constance see Konstanz
108 I6 Constance, Lake Ger. Bodensee. ◎ C Europe
104 G9 Constância Santarém, C Portugal
117 N14 Constanța var. Küstendje, Eng. Constanza, Ger. Konstanza, Turk. Küstence. Constanța, SE Romania
116 L14 Constanța ◆ county SE Romania
Constantia see Coutances, France
Constantia see Konstanz, Germany
104 K13 Constantina Andalucía, S Spain
74 L5 Constantine var. Qacentina, Ar. Qoussantina. NE Algeria
39 O14 Constantine, Cape headland Alaska, USA
Constantinople see İstanbul
Constantiola see Oltenișa
Constanz see Konstanz
Constanza see Constanța
62 G13 Constitución Maule, C Chile
61 D17 Constitución Salto, N Uruguay
Constitution State see Connecticut
105 N10 Consuegra Castilla-La Mancha, C Spain
181 X9 Consuelo Peak ▲ Queensland, E Australia
56 E11 Contamana Loreto, N Peru
Contrasto, Colle del see Contrasto, Portella del
107 K23 Contrasto, Portella del var. Colle del Contrasto. pass Sicilia, Italy, C Mediterranean Sea
54 G8 Contratación Santander, C Colombia
102 M8 Contres Loir-et-Cher, C France
107 O17 Conversano Puglia, SE Italy
27 U11 Conway Arkansas, C USA
19 O8 Conway New Hampshire, NE USA
21 U13 Conway South Carolina, SE USA
25 N2 Conway Texas, SW USA
27 U11 Conway, Lake ⊡ Arkansas, C USA
27 N7 Conway Springs Kansas, C USA
97 J18 Conwy N Wales, UK
23 T3 Conyers Georgia, SE USA
Coo see Kos
182 F4 Coober Pedy South Australia
181 P2 Cooinda Northern Territory, N Australia
182 B6 Cook South Australia
29 W4 Cook Minnesota, N USA
191 N6 Cook, Baie de bay Moorea, W French Polynesia
10 J16 Cook, Cape headland Vancouver Island, British Columbia, SW Canada
37 Q15 Cookes Peak ▲ New Mexico, SW USA
20 L8 Cookeville Tennessee, S USA
175 P9 Cook Fracture Zone tectonic feature S Pacific Ocean
Cook, Grand Récif de see Cook, Récif de
39 Q12 Cook Inlet inlet Alaska, USA
191 X2 Cook Island island Line Islands, E Kiribati
190 J14 Cook Islands ◇ territory in free association with NZ S Pacific Ocean
Cook, Mount see Aoraki
187 O15 Cook, Récif de var. Grand Récif de Cook. reef S New Caledonia
14 G14 Cookstown Ontario, S Canada
97 F15 Cookstown Ir. An Chorr Chríochach. C Northern Ireland, UK
185 K14 Cook Strait var. Raukawa. strait NZ
181 W3 Cooktown Queensland, NE Australia
183 P6 Coolabah New South Wales, SE Australia
182 J11 Coola Coola Swamp wetland South Australia
183 S7 Coolah New South Wales, SE Australia
183 P9 Coolamon New South Wales, SE Australia
183 T4 Coolatai New South Wales, SE Australia
180 K12 Coolgardie Western Australia
36 L14 Coolidge Arizona, SW USA
25 U8 Coolidge Texas, SW USA
183 Q11 Cooma New South Wales, SE Australia
Coomassie see Kumasi
183 R6 Coonabarabran New South Wales, SE Australia
182 J10 Coonalpyn South Australia
183 R6 Coonamble New South Wales, SE Australia
Coondapoor see Kundāpura
155 G21 Coonoor Tamil Nādu, SE India
29 U14 Coon Rapids Iowa, C USA
29 V8 Coon Rapids Minnesota, N USA
25 V5 Cooper Texas, SW USA
181 U9 Cooper Creek var. Barcoo, Cooper's Creek. seasonal river Queensland/South Australia
39 R12 Cooper Landing Alaska, USA
21 T14 Cooper River ≈ South Carolina, SE USA
Cooper's Creek see Cooper Creek
44 H1 Coopers Town Great Abaco, N Bahamas
18 J10 Cooperstown New York, NE USA
29 P4 Cooperstown North Dakota, N USA
31 P9 Coopersville Michigan, N USA
182 D7 Coorabie South Australia
23 Q3 Coosa River ≈ Alabama/Georgia, S USA
32 E14 Coos Bay Oregon, NW USA
183 Q9 Cootamundra New South Wales, SE Australia
97 E16 Cootehill Ir. Muinchille. N Ireland
Cop see Chop
57 J17 Copacabana La Paz, W Bolivia
63 H14 Copahué, Volcán ▲ C Chile
41 U16 Copainalá Chiapas, SE Mexico
32 F8 Copalis Beach Washington, NW USA
42 F6 Copán ◆ department W Honduras
Copán see Copán Ruinas
25 T14 Copano Bay bay NW Gulf of Mexico
42 F6 Copán Ruinas var. Copán. Copán, W Honduras
Copenhagen see København
107 Q19 Copertino Puglia, SE Italy
62 H7 Copiapó Atacama, N Chile
62 G8 Copiapó, Bahía bay N Chile
62 G7 Copiapó, Río ≈ N Chile
114 M12 Çöpköy Edirne, NW Turkey
182 I5 Copley South Australia
106 H9 Copparo Emilia-Romagna, C Italy
55 V10 Coppename Rivier var. Koppename. ≈ C Suriname
25 S9 Copperas Cove Texas, SW USA
82 J13 Copperbelt ◆ province C Zambia
39 S11 Copper Center Alaska, USA
Coppermine see Kugluktuk
8 K8 Coppermine ≈ Northwest Territories/Nunavut, N Canada
39 T11 Copper River ≈ Alaska, USA
Copper State see Arizona
116 I11 Copșa Mică Ger. Kleinkopisch, Hung. Kiskapus. Sibiu, C Romania
158 J14 Coqên Xizang Zizhiqu, W China
Coquilhatville see Mbandaka
32 E14 Coquille Oregon, NW USA
62 G9 Coquimbo Coquimbo, N Chile
62 G9 Coquimbo off. Región de Coquimbo. ◆ region C Chile
116 I15 Corabia Olt, S Romania
57 F17 Coracora Ayacucho, SW Peru
Cora Droma Rúisc see Carrick-on-Shannon
44 K9 Corail SW Haiti
183 V4 Coraki New South Wales, SE Australia
180 G8 Coral Bay Western Australia
23 Y16 Coral Gables Florida, SE USA
9 P8 Coral Harbour Southampton Island, Northwest Territories, NE Canada
192 I9 Coral Sea sea SW Pacific Ocean
174 M7 Coral Sea Basin undersea feature N Coral Sea
192 H9 Coral Sea Islands ◇ Australian external territory SW Pacific Ocean
182 M12 Corangamite, Lake ◎ Victoria, SE Australia
Corantijn Rivier see Courantyne River
18 B14 Coraopolis Pennsylvania, NE USA
107 N17 Corato Puglia, SE Italy
103 O17 Corbières ▲ S France
103 P8 Corbigny Nièvre, C France
21 N7 Corbin Kentucky, S USA
104 L14 Corbones ≈ SW Spain
Corcaigh see Cork
35 R11 Corcoran California, W USA
47 T14 Corcovado, Golfo gulf S Chile
63 G18 Corcovado, Volcán ✻ S Chile
104 F3 Corcubión Galicia, NW Spain
Corcyra Nigra see Korčula
60 Q9 Cordeiro Rio de Janeiro, SE Brazil
23 T6 Cordele Georgia, SE USA
26 L11 Cordell Oklahoma, C USA
103 N14 Cordes Tarn, S France
62 O6 Cordillera off. Departamento de la Cordillera. ◆ department C Paraguay
182 K1 Cordillo Downs South Australia
62 K10 Córdoba Córdoba, C Argentina
41 R14 Córdoba Veracruz-Llave, E Mexico
104 M13 Córdoba var. Cordoba, Eng. Cordova; anc. Corduba. Andalucía, SW Spain
62 K11 Córdoba off. Provincia de Córdoba. ◆ province C Argentina
54 D7 Córdoba off. Departamento de Córdoba. ◆ province NW Colombia
104 L13 Córdoba ◆ province Andalucía, S Spain
62 K10 Córdoba, Sierras de ▲ C Argentina
23 O3 Cordova Alabama, S USA
39 S12 Cordova Alaska, USA
Cordova/Corduba see Córdoba
Corentyne River see Courantyne River
Corfu see Kérkyra
104 J9 Coria Extremadura, W Spain

104 J14 Coria del Río Andalucía, S Spain
183 S8 Coricudgy, Mount ▲ New South Wales, SE Australia
107 N20 Corigliano Calabro Calabria, SW Italy
Corinium/Corinium Dobunorum see Cirencester
23 N1 Corinth Mississippi, S USA
Corinth see Kórinthos
Corinth Canal see Dióryga Korinthou
Corinth, Gulf of/Corinthiacus Sinus see Korinthiakós Kólpos
Corinthus see Kórinthos
42 I9 Corinto Chinandega, NW Nicaragua
97 C21 Cork Ir. Corcaigh. S Ireland
97 C21 Cork Ir. Corcaigh. cultural region SW Ireland
97 C21 Cork × SW Ireland
97 D21 Cork Harbour Ir. Cuan Chorcaí. inlet SW Ireland
107 I23 Corleone Sicilia, Italy, C Mediterranean Sea
114 N13 Çorlu Tekirdağ, NW Turkey
114 N12 Çorlu Çayı ≈ NW Turkey
Cormaiore see Courmayeur
11 V13 Cormorant Manitoba, C Canada
23 T2 Cornelia Georgia, SE USA
60 J10 Cornélio Procópio Paraná, S Brazil
55 V9 Corneliskondre Sipaliwini, N Suriname
30 J5 Cornell Wisconsin, N USA
13 S12 Corner Brook Newfoundland and Labrador, E Canada
Corner Rise Seamounts see Corner Seamounts
64 I9 Corner Seamounts var. Corner Rise Seamounts. undersea feature NW Atlantic Ocean
116 M9 Corneşti Rus. Korneshty. C Moldova
Corneto see Tarquinia
Cornhusker State see Nebraska
27 X8 Corning Arkansas, C USA
35 N5 Corning California, W USA
29 U15 Corning Iowa, C USA
18 G11 Corning New York, NE USA
Corn Islands see Maíz, Islas del
107 J14 Corno Grande ▲ C Italy
15 N13 Cornwall Ontario, SE Canada
97 H25 Cornwall cultural region SW England, UK
97 G25 Cornwall, Cape headland SW England, UK
54 J4 Coro prev. Santa Ana de Coro. Falcón, NW Venezuela
57 J18 Corocoro La Paz, W Bolivia
57 K17 Coroico La Paz, W Bolivia
184 M5 Coromandel Waikato, North Island, NZ
155 K20 Coromandel Coast coast E India
184 M5 Coromandel Peninsula peninsula North Island, NZ
184 M6 Coromandel Range ⛰ North Island, NZ
171 N5 Coron Busuanga Island, W Philippines
35 T15 Corona California, W USA
37 T12 Corona New Mexico, SW USA
11 U17 Coronach Saskatchewan, S Canada
35 U17 Coronado California, W USA
43 N15 Coronado, Bahía de bay S Costa Rica
11 R15 Coronation Alberta, SW Canada
8 K7 Coronation Gulf gulf Nunavut, N Canada
194 I1 Coronation Island island Antarctica
39 X14 Coronation Island island Alexander Archipelago, Alaska, USA
61 B18 Coronda Santa Fe, C Argentina
63 F14 Coronel Bío Bío, C Chile
61 D20 Coronel Brandsen var. Brandsen. Buenos Aires, E Argentina
62 K4 Coronel Cornejo Salta, N Argentina
61 B24 Coronel Dorrego Buenos Aires, E Argentina
62 P6 Coronel Oviedo Caaguazú, SE Paraguay
61 B23 Coronel Pringles Buenos Aires, E Argentina
61 B23 Coronel Suárez Buenos Aires, E Argentina
61 E22 Coronel Vidal Buenos Aires, E Argentina
55 V9 Coronie ◈ district NW Suriname
57 G17 Coropuna, Nevado ▲ S Peru
Çorovoda see Çorovodë
113 L22 Çorovodë var. Çorovoda. Berat, S Albania
183 P11 Corowa New South Wales, SE Australia
42 G1 Corozal Corozal, N Belize
54 E6 Corozal Sucre, NW Colombia
42 G1 Corozal ◈ district N Belize
25 T14 Corpus Christi Texas, SW USA
25 T14 Corpus Christi Bay inlet Texas, SW USA
25 R14 Corpus Christi, Lake ⊡ Texas, SW USA
63 F16 Corral Los Lagos, C Chile
105 O9 Corral de Almaguer Castilla-La Mancha, C Spain
104 K6 Corrales Castilla-León, N Spain
37 R11 Corrales New Mexico, SW USA
Corrán Tuathail see Carrauntoohil
106 F9 Correggio Emilia-Romagna, C Italy
59 M16 Corrente Piauí, E Brazil
59 I19 Correntes, Rio ≈ SW Brazil
103 N12 Corrèze ◈ department C France
97 C17 Corrib, Lough Ir. Loch Coirib. ◎ W Ireland
61 C14 Corrientes Corrientes, NE Argentina
61 D15 Corrientes off. Provincia de Corrientes. ◈ province NE Argentina
44 A5 Corrientes, Cabo headland W Cuba
40 I13 Corrientes, Cabo headland SW Mexico
Corrientes, Provincia de see Corrientes
61 C16 Corrientes, Río ≈ NE Argentina
56 E8 Corrientes, Río ≈ Ecuador/Peru
25 W9 Corrigan Texas, SW USA
55 U9 Corriverton E Guyana
Corriza see Korçë
183 Q11 Corryong Victoria, SE Australia
103 Y12 Corse Eng. Corsica. ◈ region France, C Mediterranean Sea
103 X13 Corse Eng. Corsica. island France, C Mediterranean Sea
103 Y13 Corse, Cap headland Corse, France, C Mediterranean Sea
103 X15 Corse-du-Sud ◈ department Corse, France, C Mediterranean Sea
29 P11 Corsica South Dakota, N USA
Corsica see Corse
25 U7 Corsicana Texas, SW USA
103 Y15 Corte Corse, France, C Mediterranean Sea
63 G16 Corte Alto Los Lagos, S Chile
104 I13 Cortegana Andalucía, S Spain
43 N15 Cortés var. Ciudad Cortés. Puntarenas, SE Costa Rica
42 G5 Cortés ◈ department NW Honduras
37 P8 Cortez Colorado, C USA
Cortez, Sea of see California, Golfo de
106 H6 Cortina d'Ampezzo Veneto, NE Italy
18 H11 Cortland New York, NE USA
31 V11 Cortland Ohio, N USA
106 H12 Cortona Toscana, C Italy
76 H13 Corubal, Rio ≈ E Guinea-Bissau
104 G10 Coruche Santarém, C Portugal
Çoruh see Rize
137 R11 Çoruh Nehri Geor. Chorokhi, Rus. Chorokh. ≈ Georgia/Turkey
136 K12 Çorum var. Chorum. Çorum, N Turkey
136 J12 Çorum var. Chorum. ◈ province N Turkey
59 H19 Corumbá Mato Grosso do Sul, S Brazil
14 D16 Corunna Ontario, S Canada
Corunna see A Coruña
32 F12 Corvallis Oregon, NW USA
64 M1 Corvo var. Ilha do Corvo. island Azores, Portugal, NE Atlantic Ocean
Corvo, Ilha do see Corvo
31 O16 Corydon Indiana, N USA
29 V16 Corydon Iowa, C USA
Cos see Kos
40 I9 Cosalá Sinaloa, C Mexico
41 R15 Cosamaloapan var. Cosamaloapan de Carpio. Veracruz-Llave, E Mexico
Cosamaloapan de Carpio see Cosamaloapan
107 N21 Cosenza anc. Consentia. Calabria, SW Italy
31 T13 Coshocton Ohio, N USA
42 H9 Cosigüina, Punta headland NW Nicaragua
29 T9 Cosmos Minnesota, N USA
103 O8 Cosne-sur-Loire Nièvre, C France
108 B9 Cossonay Vaud, W Switzerland
Cossyra see Pantelleria
47 R4 Costa, Cordillera de la var. Cordillera de Venezuela. ⛰ N Venezuela
42 K13 Costa Rica off. Republic of Costa Rica. ◆ republic Central America
43 N15 Costeña, Fila ⛰ S Costa Rica
Costermansville see Bukavu
116 I14 Costeşti Argeş, SW Romania
37 S8 Costilla New Mexico, SW USA
35 O7 Cosumnes River ≈ California, W USA
101 O16 Coswig Sachsen, E Germany
101 M14 Coswig Sachsen-Anhalt, E Germany
Cosyra see Pantelleria
171 Q7 Cotabato Mindanao, S Philippines
56 C5 Cotacachi ▲ N Ecuador
57 L21 Cotagaita Potosí, S Bolivia
103 V15 Côte d'Azur prev. Nice. × (Nice) Alpes-Maritimes, SE France
Côte d'Ivoire see Ivory Coast
103 R8 Côte d'Or cultural region C France
103 R7 Côte d'Or ◈ department E France
Côte Française des Somalis see Djibouti
102 J4 Cotentin peninsula N France
102 G6 Côtes d'Armor prev. Côtes-du-Nord. ◈ department NW France
Côtes-du Nord see Côtes d'Armor
Cöthen see Köthen
Côtière, Chaîne see Coast Mountains
40 M13 Cotija var. Cotija de la Paz. Michoacán de Ocampo, SW Mexico
Cotija de la Paz see Cotija
77 R16 Cotonou var. Kotonu. S Benin
77 R16 Cotonou × S Benin
56 B6 Cotopaxi prev. León. ◈ province C Ecuador
56 C6 Cotopaxi 🌋 N Ecuador
Cotrone see Crotone
97 L21 Cotswold Hills var. Cotswolds. hill range S England, UK
Cotswolds see Cotswold Hills
32 F13 Cottage Grove Oregon, NW USA
21 S14 Cottageville South Carolina, SE USA
101 P14 Cottbus Lus. Chośebuz; prev. Kottbus. Brandenburg, E Germany
27 U9 Cotter Arkansas, C USA
106 A9 Cottian Alps Fr. Alpes Cottiennes, It. Alpi Cozie. ⛰ France/Italy
Cottiennes, Alpes see Cottian Alps
Cotton State, The see Alabama
22 G4 Cotton Valley Louisiana, S USA
36 L12 Cottonwood Arizona, SW USA
32 M10 Cottonwood Idaho, NW USA
29 S9 Cottonwood Minnesota, N USA
25 Q7 Cottonwood Texas, SW USA
27 O5 Cottonwood Falls Kansas, C USA
36 L3 Cottonwood Heights Utah, W USA
29 S10 Cottonwood River ≈ Minnesota, N USA
45 O9 Cotuí C Dominican Republic
25 Q13 Cotulla Texas, SW USA
Cotyora see Ordu
102 I11 Coubre, Pointe de la headland W France
18 E12 Coudersport Pennsylvania, NE USA
15 S9 Coudres, Île aux island Québec, SE Canada
182 G11 Couedic, Cape de headland South Australia
Couentrey see Coventry
102 I6 Couesnon ≈ NW France
32 H10 Cougar Washington, NW USA
102 L10 Couhé Vienne, W France
32 K8 Coulee City Washington, NW USA
195 Q15 Coulman Island island Antarctica
103 P5 Coulommiers Seine-et-Marne, N France
14 K11 Coulonge ≈ Québec, SE Canada
14 K11 Coulonge Est ≈ Québec, SE Canada
35 Q9 Coulterville California, W USA
38 M9 Council Alaska, USA
32 M12 Council Idaho, NW USA
29 S15 Council Bluffs Iowa, C USA
27 O5 Council Grove Kansas, C USA
27 O5 Council Grove Lake ⊡ Kansas, C USA
32 G7 Coupeville Washington, NW USA
55 U12 Courantyne River var. Corantijn Rivier, Corentyne River. ≈ Guyana/Suriname
99 G21 Courcelles Hainaut, S Belgium
108 C7 Courgenay Jura, NW Switzerland
126 B2 Courland Lagoon Ger. Kurisches Haff, Rus. Kurskiy Zaliv. lagoon Lithuania/Russian Federation
118 B12 Courland Spit Lith. Kuršių Nerija, Rus. Kurshskaya Kosa. spit Lithuania/Russian Federation
106 A6 Courmayeur prev. Cormaiore. Valle d'Aosta, NW Italy
108 D7 Courroux Jura, NW Switzerland
10 K17 Courtenay Vancouver Island, British Columbia, SW Canada
21 W7 Courtland Virginia, NE USA
25 V10 Courtney Texas, SW USA
30 J4 Court Oreilles, Lac ◎ Wisconsin, N USA
Courtrai see Kortrijk
99 H19 Court-Saint-Étienne Wallon Brabant, C Belgium
22 G6 Coushatta Louisiana, S USA
172 I16 Cousin island Inner Islands, NE Seychelles
172 I16 Cousine island Inner Islands, NE Seychelles
102 J4 Coutances anc. Constantia. Manche, N France
102 K12 Coutras Gironde, SW France
45 U14 Couva Trinidad, Trinidad and Tobago
108 B8 Couvet Neuchâtel, W Switzerland
99 H22 Couvin Namur, S Belgium
116 K12 Covasna Ger. Kowasna, Hung. Kovászna. Covasna, E Romania
116 J11 Covasna ◈ county E Romania
14 E12 Cove Island island Ontario, S Canada
34 M5 Covelo California, W USA
97 M20 Coventry anc. Couentrey. C England, UK
Cove of Cork see Cobh
21 U5 Covesville Virginia, NE USA
104 I8 Covilhã Castelo Branco, E Portugal
23 T3 Covington Georgia, SE USA
31 N13 Covington Indiana, N USA
20 M3 Covington Kentucky, S USA
22 K8 Covington Louisiana, S USA
31 Q13 Covington Ohio, N USA
20 F9 Covington Tennessee, S USA
21 S6 Covington Virginia, NE USA
183 Q8 Cowal, Lake seasonal lake New South Wales, SE Australia
11 W15 Cowan Manitoba, S Canada
18 F12 Cowanesque River ≈ New York/Pennsylvania, NE USA
180 L12 Cowan, Lake ◎ Western Australia
15 P13 Cowansville Québec, SE Canada
182 H8 Cowell South Australia
97 M23 Cowes S England, UK
27 Q10 Coweta Oklahoma, C USA
(0) D6 Cowie Seamount undersea feature NE Pacific Ocean
32 G10 Cowlitz River ≈ Washington, NW USA
21 Q11 Cowpens South Carolina, SE USA
183 R8 Cowra New South Wales, SE Australia
Coxen Hole see Roatán
59 I19 Coxim Mato Grosso do Sul, S Brazil
59 I19 Coxim, Rio ≈ SW Brazil
Coxin Hole see Roatán
153 V17 Cox's Bazar Chittagong, S Bangladesh
76 H14 Coyah Conakry, W Guinea
40 K5 Coyame Chihuahua, N Mexico
24 L9 Coyanosa Draw ≈ Texas, SW USA
Coyhaique see Coihaique
42 C7 Coyolate, Río ≈ S Guatemala
Coyote State see South Dakota
40 I10 Coyotitán Sinaloa, C Mexico
41 N15 Coyuca var. Coyuca de Catalán. Guerrero, S Mexico
41 O16 Coyuca var. Coyuca de Benítez. Guerrero, S Mexico
Coyuca de Benítez/Coyuca de Catalán see Coyuca
29 N15 Cozad Nebraska, C USA
Cozie, Alpi see Cottian Alps
Cozmeni see Kitsman'
40 E3 Cozón, Cerro ▲ NW Mexico
41 Z12 Cozumel Quintana Roo, E Mexico
41 Z12 Cozumel, Isla island SE Mexico
32 K8 Crab Creek ≈ Washington, NW USA
44 H12 Crab Pond Point headland W Jamaica
Cracovia/Cracow see Małopolskie
83 I25 Cradock Eastern Cape, S South Africa
39 Y14 Craig Prince of Wales Island, Alaska, USA
37 Q3 Craig Colorado, C USA
97 F15 Craigavon C Northern Ireland, UK
21 T5 Craigsville Virginia, NE USA
101 J21 Crailsheim Baden-Württemberg, S Germany
116 H14 Craiova Dolj, SW Romania
10 K12 Cranberry Junction British Columbia, SW Canada
18 J8 Cranberry Lake ◎ New York, NE USA
11 V13 Cranberry Portage Manitoba, C Canada
11 P17 Cranbrook British Columbia, SW Canada
30 M5 Crandon Wisconsin, N USA
32 K14 Crane Oregon, NW USA
24 M9 Crane Texas, SW USA
Crane see The Crane
25 S8 Cranfills Gap Texas, SW USA
19 O12 Cranston Rhode Island, NE USA
Cranz see Zelenogradsk
59 L15 Craolândia Tocantins, E Brazil
102 J7 Craon Mayenne, NW France
195 V16 Crary, Cape headland Antarctica
Crasna see Kraszna
32 G14 Crater Lake ◎ Oregon, NW USA
33 P14 Craters of the Moon National Monument national park Idaho, NW USA
59 O14 Crateús Ceará, E Brazil
Crathis see Crati
107 N20 Crati anc. Crathis. ≈ S Italy
11 U16 Craven Saskatchewan, S Canada
54 I8 Cravo Norte Arauca, E Colombia
28 J12 Crawford Nebraska, C USA
25 T8 Crawford Texas, SW USA
11 O17 Crawford Bay British Columbia, SW Canada
65 M19 Crawford Seamount undersea feature S Atlantic Ocean
31 O13 Crawfordsville Indiana, N USA
23 S9 Crawfordville Florida, SE USA
97 O23 Crawley SE England, UK
33 S10 Crazy Mountains ⛰ Montana, NW USA
11 T11 Cree ≈ Saskatchewan, C Canada
37 R7 Creede Colorado, C USA
40 I6 Creel Chihuahua, N Mexico
11 S11 Cree Lake ◎ Saskatchewan, C Canada
11 V13 Creighton Saskatchewan, C Canada
29 Q13 Creighton Nebraska, C USA
103 O4 Creil Oise, N France
106 E8 Crema Lombardia, N Italy
106 E8 Cremona Lombardia, N Italy
Creole State see Louisiana
112 M10 Crepaja Hung. Cserépalja. Serbia, N Serbia and Montenegro (Yugo.)
103 O4 Crépy-en-Valois Oise, N France
112 B10 Cres It. Cherso. Primorje-Gorski Kotar, NW Croatia
112 A11 Cres It. Cherso; anc. Crexa. island W Croatia
32 H14 Crescent Oregon, NW USA
34 K1 Crescent City California, W USA
23 W10 Crescent City Florida, SE USA
167 X10 Crescent Group island group C Paracel Islands
23 W10 Crescent Lake ◎ Florida, SE USA
29 X11 Cresco Iowa, C USA
61 B18 Crespo Entre Ríos, E Argentina
54 E5 Crespo × (Cartagena) Bolívar, NW Colombia
103 R13 Crest Drôme, E France
37 R5 Crested Butte Colorado, C USA
31 S12 Crestline Ohio, N USA
11 O17 Creston British Columbia, SW Canada
29 U15 Creston Iowa, C USA
33 V16 Creston Wyoming, C USA
37 S7 Crestone Peak ▲ Colorado, C USA
23 P8 Crestview Florida, SE USA
121 R10 Cretan Trough undersea feature Aegean Sea, C Mediterranean Sea
29 R16 Crete Nebraska, C USA
Crete see Kríti
103 O5 Créteil Val-de-Marne, N France
Crete, Sea of/Creticum, Mare see Kritikó Pélagos
105 X4 Creus, Cap de headland NE Spain
103 N10 Creuse ◈ department C France
102 L9 Creuse ≈ C France
103 T4 Creutzwald Moselle, NE France
105 S12 Crevillente País Valenciano, E Spain
97 L18 Crewe C England, UK
21 V7 Crewe Virginia, NE USA
Crexa see Cres
43 Q15 Cricamola, Río ≈ NW Panama
61 K14 Criciúma Santa Catarina, S Brazil
96 J11 Crieff C Scotland, UK
112 B10 Crikvenica It. Cirquenizza; prev. Cirkvenica, Crjkvenica. Primorje-Gorski Kotar, NW Croatia
Crimea/Crimean Oblast see Krym, Respublika
101 M16 Crimmitschau var. Krimmitschau. Sachsen, E Germany
116 G11 Crişcior Hung. Kristyor. Hunedoara, W Romania
21 Y5 Crisfield Maryland, NE USA
31 P3 Crisp Point headland Michigan, N USA
59 L19 Cristalina Goiás, C Brazil
44 J7 Cristal, Sierra del ⛰ E Cuba
43 T14 Cristóbal Colón, C Panama
54 F4 Cristóbal Colón, Pico ▲ N Colombia
Cristur/Cristuru Săcuiesc see Cristuru Secuiesc
116 I11 Cristuru Secuiesc prev. Cristur, Cristuru Săcuiesc, Sitaş Cristuru, Ger. Kreutz, Hung. Székelykeresztúr, Szitás-Keresztúr. Harghita, C Romania
116 F10 Crişul Alb var. Weisse Kreisch, Ger. Weisse Körös, Hung. Fehér-Körös. ≈ Hungary/Romania
116 F10 Crişul Negru Ger. Schwarze Körös, Hung. Fekete-Körös. ≈ Hungary/Romania
116 G10 Crişul Repede var. Schnelle Kreisch, Ger. Schnelle Körös, Hung. Sebes-Körös. ≈ Hungary/Romania
117 N10 Criuleni Rus. Kriulyany. C Moldova
Crivadia Vulcanului see Vulcan
Crjkvenica see Crikvenica
113 O17 Crna Gora ⛰ FYR Macedonia/Serbia and Montenegro (Yugo.)
Crna Gora see Montenegro
113 O20 Crna Reka ≈ S FYR Macedonia
Crni Drim see Black Drin
109 V10 Črni vrh ▲ NE Slovenia
109 V13 Črnomelj Ger. Tschernembl. SE Slovenia
97 A17 Croagh Patrick Ir. Cruach Phádraig. ▲ W Ireland
112 D9 Croatia off. Republic of Croatia, Ger. Kroatien, SCr. Hrvatska. ◆ republic SE Europe
Croce, Picco di see Wilde Kreuzspitze
15 P8 Croche ≈ Québec, SE Canada
169 V7 Crocker, Banjaran var. Crocker Range. ⛰ East Malaysia
Crocker Range see Crocker, Banjaran
25 V9 Crockett Texas, SW USA
67 V14 Crocodile var. Krokodil. ≈ N South Africa
Crocodile see Limpopo
20 I7 Crofton Kentucky, S USA
29 Q12 Crofton Nebraska, C USA
Croia see Krujë
103 R16 Croisette, Cap headland SE France
102 G8 Croisic, Pointe du headland NW France
103 S13 Croix Haute, Col de la pass E France
15 U5 Croix, Pointe à la headland Québec, SE Canada
14 F13 Croker, Cape headland Ontario, S Canada
181 P1 Croker Island island Northern Territory, N Australia
96 I8 Cromarty N Scotland, UK
99 M21 Crombach Liège, E Belgium
97 Q18 Cromer E England, UK
185 D22 Cromwell Otago, South Island, NZ
185 H16 Cronadun West Coast, South Island, NZ
39 O11 Crooked Creek Alaska, USA
44 K5 Crooked Island island SE Bahamas
44 J5 Crooked Island Passage channel SE Bahamas
32 I13 Crooked River ≈ Oregon, NW USA
29 R4 Crookston Minnesota, N USA
28 I10 Crooks Tower ▲ South Dakota, N USA
31 T14 Crooksville Ohio, N USA
183 R9 Crookwell New South Wales, SE Australia
14 L14 Crosby Ontario, SE Canada
97 K17 Crosby var. Great Crosby. NW England, UK
29 U6 Crosby Minnesota, N USA
28 K2 Crosby North Dakota, N USA
25 O5 Crosbyton Texas, SW USA
77 V16 Cross ≈ Cameroon/Nigeria
23 U10 Cross City Florida, SE USA
Crossen see Krosno Odrzańskie
27 V14 Crossett Arkansas, C USA
97 K15 Cross Fell ▲ N England, UK
11 P16 Crossfield Alberta, SW Canada
21 Q12 Cross Hill South Carolina, SE USA
19 U6 Cross Island island Maine, NE USA
11 X13 Cross Lake Manitoba, C Canada
22 F5 Cross Lake ⊡ Louisiana, S USA
36 I12 Crossman Peak ▲ Arizona, SW USA
25 Q7 Cross Plains Texas, SW USA
77 V17 Cross River ◈ state SE Nigeria
20 L9 Crossville Tennessee, S USA
31 S8 Croswell Michigan, N USA
14 K13 Crotch Lake ◎ Ontario, SE Canada
Croton/Crotona see Crotone
107 O21 Crotone var. Cotrone; anc. Croton, Crotona. Calabria, SW Italy
33 V11 Crow Agency Montana, NW USA
183 U7 Crowdy Head headland New South Wales, SE Australia
25 Q4 Crowell Texas, SW USA
183 O6 Crowl Creek seasonal river New South Wales, SE Australia
22 H9 Crowley Louisiana, S USA
35 S9 Crowley, Lake ⊡ California, W USA
27 X10 Crowleys Ridge hill range Arkansas, C USA
31 N11 Crown Point Indiana, N USA
37 P10 Crownpoint New Mexico, SW USA
33 R10 Crow Peak ▲ Montana, NW USA
11 P17 Crowsnest Pass pass Alberta/British Columbia, SW Canada
29 T6 Crow Wing River ≈ Minnesota, N USA
97 O22 Croydon SE England, UK
173 P11 Crozet Basin undersea feature S Indian Ocean
173 O12 Crozet Islands island group French Southern and Antarctic Territories
173 N12 Crozet Plateau var. Crozet Plateaus. undersea feature SW Indian Ocean
Crozet Plateaus see Crozet Plateau
102 E6 Crozon Finistère, NW France
Cruacha Dubha, Na see Macgillycuddy's Reeks
Cruach Phádraig see Croagh Patrick
116 M14 Crucea Constanţa, SE Romania
44 E5 Cruces Cienfuegos, C Cuba
107 O20 Crucoli Torretta Calabria, SW Italy
41 P9 Cruillas Tamaulipas, C Mexico
64 K9 Cruiser Tablemount undersea feature E Atlantic Ocean
61 G14 Cruz Alta Rio Grande do Sul, S Brazil
44 G8 Cruz, Cabo headland S Cuba
60 N9 Cruzeiro São Paulo, S Brazil
60 H10 Cruzeiro do Oeste Paraná, S Brazil
59 A15 Cruzeiro do Sul Acre, W Brazil
23 U11 Crystal Bay bay Florida, SE USA
182 I8 Crystal Brook South Australia
11 X17 Crystal City Manitoba, S Canada
27 X5 Crystal City Missouri, C USA
25 P13 Crystal City Texas, SW USA
30 M4 Crystal Falls Michigan, N USA
23 Q8 Crystal Lake Florida, SE USA
31 O6 Crystal Lake ◎ Michigan, N USA
23 V11 Crystal River Florida, SE USA
37 Q5 Crystal River ≈ Colorado, C USA
22 K6 Crystal Springs Mississippi, S USA
Csaca see Čadca
Csakathurn/Csáktornya see Čakovec
Csap see Chop
Csepén see Čepin
Cserépalja see Crepaja
Csermő see Cermei
Csíkszereda see Miercurea-Ciuc
111 L24 Csongrád Csongrád, SE Hungary
111 L24 Csongrád off. Csongrád Megye. ◈ county SE Hungary
111 H22 Csorna Győr-Moson-Sopron, NW Hungary
Csucsa see Ciucea
111 G25 Csurgó Somogy, SW Hungary
Csurog see Čurug
54 L5 Cúa Miranda, N Venezuela
82 C11 Cuale Malanje, NW Angola
67 T12 Cuando var. Kwando. ≈ S Africa
83 E15 Cuando Cubango var. Kuando-Kubango. ◈ province SE Angola
83 E16 Cuangar Cuando Cubango, S Angola
82 D11 Cuango Lunda Norte, NE Angola
82 C10 Cuango Uíge, NW Angola
82 C10 Cuango var. Kwango. ≈ Angola/Dem. Rep. Congo see also Kwango
Cuan, Loch see Strangford Lough
82 C12 Cuanza var. Kwanza. ≈ C Angola
82 B11 Cuanza Norte var. Kuanza Norte. ◈ province NE Angola
82 B12 Cuanza Sul var. Kuanza Sul. ◈ province NE Angola

◆ Country ● Country Capital ◇ Dependent Territory ○ Dependent Territory Capital ◈ Administrative Region × International Airport ▲ Mountain ⛰ Mountain Range 🌋 Volcano ≈ River ◎ Lake ⊡ Reservoir

61 E16 Cuareim, Río var. Rio Quaraí. ≈ Brazil/Uruguay see also Quaraí, Rio
83 D15 Cuatir ≈ S Angola
40 M7 Cuatro Ciénegas var. Cuatro Ciénegas de Carranza. Coahuila de Zaragoza, NE Mexico
Cuatro Ciénegas de Carranza see Cuatro Ciénegas
40 I6 Cuauhtémoc Chihuahua, N Mexico
41 P14 Cuautla Morelos, S Mexico
104 H12 Cuba Beja, S Portugal
27 W6 Cuba Missouri, C USA
37 R10 Cuba New Mexico, SW USA
44 E6 Cuba off. Republic of Cuba. ◆ republic W West Indies
47 O2 Cuba island W West Indies
82 B13 Cubal Benguela, W Angola
83 C15 Cubango var. Kuvango, Port. Vila Artur de Paiva, Vila da Ponte. Huíla, SW Angola
83 D16 Cubango var. Kavango, Kavengo, Kubango, Okavango, Okavanggo. ≈ S Africa see also Okavango
54 H8 Cubará Boyacá, N Colombia
136 I12 Çubuk Ankara, N Turkey
83 D14 Cuchi Cuando Cubango, C Angola
42 C5 Cuchumatanes, Sierra de los ▲ W Guatemala
Cuculaya, Rio see Kukalaya, Rio
82 E12 Cucumbi prev. Trás-os-Montes. Lunda Sul, NE Angola
54 G7 Cúcuta var. San José de Cúcuta. Norte de Santander, N Colombia
31 N9 Cudahy Wisconsin, N USA
155 J21 Cuddalore Tamil Nādu, SE India
155 I18 Cuddapah Andhra Pradesh, S India
104 M6 Cuéllar Castilla-León, N Spain
82 D13 Cuemba var. Coemba. Bié, C Angola
56 B8 Cuenca Azuay, S Ecuador
105 Q9 Cuenca anc. Conca. Castilla-La Mancha, C Spain
105 P9 Cuenca ❖ province Castilla-La Mancha, C Spain
40 L9 Cuencamé var. Cuencamé de Ceniceros. Durango, C Mexico
Cuencamé de Ceniceros see Cuencamé
105 Q8 Cuenca, Serranía de ▲ C Spain
Cuera see Chur
105 P5 Cuerda del Pozo, Embalse de la ⊡ N Spain
41 O14 Cuernavaca Morelos, S Mexico
25 T12 Cuero Texas, SW USA
44 I7 Cueto Holguín, E Cuba
41 Q13 Cuetzalán var. Cuetzalán del Progreso. Puebla, S Mexico
Cuetzalán del Progreso see Cuetzalán
105 Q14 Cuevas de Almanzora Andalucía, S Spain
105 T8 Cuevas de Vinromá País Valenciano, E Spain
116 H12 Cugir Hung. Kudzsir. Alba, SW Romania
59 H18 Cuiabá prev. Cuyabá. state capital Mato Grosso, SW Brazil
59 H19 Cuiabá, Rio ≈ SW Brazil
41 R15 Cuicatlán var. San Juan Bautista Cuicatlán. Oaxaca, SE Mexico
191 W16 Cuidado, Punta headland Easter Island, Chile, E Pacific Ocean
Cuidad Presidente Stroessner see Ciudad del Este
Cúige see Connaught
Cúige Laighean see Leinster
Cúige Mumhan see Munster
Cuihua see Daguan
98 L13 Cuijck Noord-Brabant, SE Netherlands
Cúil an tSúdaire see Portarlington
42 D7 Cuilapa Santa Rosa, S Guatemala
42 B5 Cuilco, Río ≈ W Guatemala
Cúil Mhuine see Collooney
Cúil Raithin see Coleraine
83 C14 Cuima Huambo, C Angola
83 E16 Cuito var. Kwito. ≈ SE Angola
83 E15 Cuito Cuanavale Cuando Cubango, E Angola
41 N14 Cuitzeo, Lago de ◎ C Mexico
27 W4 Cuivre River ≈ Missouri, C USA
Çuka see Çukë
168 L8 Cukai var. Chukai, Kemaman. Terengganu, Peninsular Malaysia
113 L23 Çukë var. Çuka. Vlorë, S Albania
Cularo see Grenoble
33 Y7 Culbertson Montana, NW USA
28 M16 Culbertson Nebraska, C USA
183 P10 Culcairn New South Wales, SE Australia
45 W5 Culebra var. Dewey. E Puerto Rico
45 W6 Culebra, Isla de island E Puerto Rico
37 T8 Culebra Peak ▲ Colorado, C USA
104 J5 Culebra, Sierra de la ▲ NW Spain
98 J12 Culemborg Gelderland, C Netherlands
137 V14 Culfa Rus. Dzhul'fa. SW Azerbaijan
183 P4 Culgoa River ≈ New South Wales/Queensland, SE Australia
40 I9 Culiacán var. Culiacán Rosales, Culiacán-Rosales. Sinaloa, C Mexico
Culiacán-Rosales/Culiacán Rosales see Culiacán
105 P14 Cúllar-Baza Andalucía, S Spain
105 S10 Cullera País Valenciano, E Spain
23 P3 Cullman Alabama, S USA
108 B10 Cully Vaud, W Switzerland
Culm see Chełmno
Culmsee see Chełmża
21 V4 Culpeper Virginia, NE USA
185 I17 Culverden Canterbury, South Island, NZ
55 N5 Cumaná Sucre, NE Venezuela
55 O5 Cumanacoa Sucre, NE Venezuela
54 C13 Cumbal, Nevado de elevation S Colombia
21 O7 Cumberland Kentucky, S USA
21 U2 Cumberland Maryland, NE USA
21 V6 Cumberland Virginia, NE USA
187 P12 Cumberland, Cape var. Cape Nahoi. headland Espiritu Santo, N Vanuatu
11 V14 Cumberland House Saskatchewan, C Canada
23 W8 Cumberland Island island Georgia, SE USA
20 L7 Cumberland, Lake ⊡ Kentucky, S USA
9 R5 Cumberland Peninsula peninsula Baffin Island, Nunavut, NE Canada
2 N9 Cumberland Plateau plateau E USA
30 L1 Cumberland Point headland Michigan, N USA
21 O7 Cumberland River ≈ Kentucky/Tennessee, S USA
9 S6 Cumberland Sound inlet Baffin Island, Nunavut, NE Canada
96 I12 Cumbernauld S Scotland, UK
97 K15 Cumbria cultural region NW England, UK
97 K15 Cumbrian Mountains ▲ NW England, UK
23 S2 Cumming Georgia, SE USA
Cummin in Pommern see Kamień Pomorski
182 G9 Cummins South Australia
96 I13 Cumnock W Scotland, UK
40 G4 Cumpas Sonora, NW Mexico
136 H16 Çumra Konya, C Turkey
63 G15 Cunco Araucanía, C Chile
54 E9 Cundinamarca off. Departamento de Cundinamarca. ❖ province C Colombia
41 U15 Cunduacán Tabasco, SE Mexico
83 C16 Cunene ❖ province S Angola
83 A16 Cunene var. Kunene. ≈ Angola/Namibia see also Kunene
106 A9 Cuneo Fr. Coni. Piemonte, NW Italy
83 E15 Cunjamba Cuando Cubango, E Angola
181 V10 Cunnamulla Queensland, E Australia
Čunusavvon see Junosuando
Cuokkarašša see Čohkarášša
106 B7 Cuorgne Piemonte, NE Italy
96 K11 Cupar E Scotland, UK
116 L8 Cupcina Rus. Kupchino; prev. Calinisc, Kalinisk. N Moldova
54 C8 Cupica Chocó, W Colombia
54 C8 Cupica, Golfo de gulf W Colombia
112 N13 Ćuprija Serbia, E Serbia and Montenegro (Yugo.)
Cura see Villa de Cura
45 P16 Curaçao island Netherlands Antilles
56 H13 Curanja, Río ≈ E Peru
56 F7 Curaray, Río ≈ Ecuador/Peru
116 K14 Curcani Călărași, SE Romania
182 H4 Curdimurka South Australia
103 P7 Cure ≈ C France
173 Y16 Curepipe C Mauritius
55 R6 Curiapo Delta Amacuro, NE Venezuela
Curia Rhaetorum see Chur
62 G12 Curicó Maule, C Chile
Curieta see Krk
172 I15 Curieuse island Inner Islands, NE Seychelles
59 C16 Curitiba Acre, W Brazil
60 K12 Curitiba prev. Curytiba. state capital Paraná, S Brazil
60 J13 Curitibanos Santa Catarina, S Brazil
183 S6 Curlewis New South Wales, SE Australia
182 J6 Curnamona South Australia
83 A15 Curoca ≈ SW Angola
183 T6 Currabubula New South Wales, SE Australia
59 Q14 Currais Novos Rio Grande do Norte, E Brazil
35 W7 Currant Nevada, W USA
35 W6 Currant Mountain ▲ Nevada, W USA
44 H2 Current Eleuthera Island, C Bahamas
27 W8 Current River ≈ Arkansas/Missouri, C USA
182 M14 Currie Tasmania, SE Australia
21 Y8 Currituck North Carolina, SE USA
21 Y8 Currituck Sound sound North Carolina, SE USA
39 R11 Curry Alaska, USA
Curtbunar see Tervel
116 I13 Curtea de Argeș var. Curtea-de-Arges. Argeș, S Romania
116 E10 Curtici Ger. Kurtitsch, Hung. Kürtös. Arad, W Romania
28 M16 Curtis Nebraska, C USA
104 H2 Curtis-Estación Galicia, NW Spain
183 O14 Curtis Group island group Tasmania, SE Australia
181 Y8 Curtis Island island Queensland, SE Australia
58 K11 Curuá, Ilha do island NE Brazil
47 U7 Curuá, Rio ≈ N Brazil
59 A14 Curuçá, Rio ≈ NW Brazil
112 L9 Čurug Hung. Csurog. Serbia, N Serbia and Montenegro (Yugo.)
61 D16 Curuzú Cuatiá Corrientes, NE Argentina
59 M19 Curvelo Minas Gerais, SE Brazil
18 E14 Curwensville Pennsylvania, NE USA
30 M3 Curwood, Mount ▲ Michigan, N USA
Curytiba see Curitiba
Curzola see Korčula
42 A10 Cuscatlán ❖ department C El Salvador
57 H15 Cusco var. Cuzco. Cusco, C Peru
57 H15 Cusco off. Departamento de Cusco; var. Cuzco. ❖ department C Peru
27 O9 Cushing Oklahoma, C USA
25 W8 Cushing Texas, SW USA
40 I6 Cusihuiriachic Chihuahua, N Mexico
103 P10 Cusset Allier, C France
23 S6 Cusseta Georgia, SE USA
28 J10 Custer South Dakota, N USA
Cüstrin see Kostrzyn
33 Q7 Cut Bank Montana, NW USA
Cutch, Gulf of see Kachchh, Gulf of
23 S6 Cuthbert Georgia, SE USA
11 S15 Cut Knife Saskatchewan, S Canada
23 Y16 Cutler Ridge Florida, SE USA
22 K10 Cut Off Louisiana, S USA
63 I15 Cutral-Có Neuquén, C Argentina
107 O21 Cutro Calabria, SW Italy
183 O4 Cuttaburra Channels seasonal river New South Wales, SE Australia
154 O12 Cuttack Orissa, E India
83 C15 Cuvelai Cunene, SW Angola
79 G18 Cuvette var. Région de la Cuvette. ❖ province C Congo
173 V9 Cuvier Basin undersea feature E Indian Ocean
173 U9 Cuvier Plateau undersea feature E Indian Ocean
82 B12 Cuvo ≈ W Angola
100 H9 Cuxhaven Niedersachsen, NW Germany
Cuyabá see Cuiabá
Cuyuni, Río see Cuyuni River
55 S8 Cuyuni River var. Río Cuyuni. ≈ Guyana/Venezuela
Cuzco see Cusco
97 K22 Cwmbran Wel. Cwmbrân. SW Wales, UK
28 K15 C.W.McConaughy, Lake ⊡ Nebraska, C USA
81 D20 Cyangugu SW Rwanda
110 D11 Cybinka Ger. Ziebingen. Lubuskie, W Poland
Cyclades see Kykládes
Cydonia see Chaniá
Cymru see Wales
20 M5 Cynthiana Kentucky, S USA
11 S17 Cypress Hills ▲ Alberta/Saskatchewan, SW Canada
Cypro-Syrian Basin see Cyprus Basin
121 U11 Cyprus off. Republic of Cyprus, Gk. Kypros, Turk. Kıbrıs, Kıbrıs Cumhuriyeti. ◆ republic E Mediterranean Sea
84 L14 Cyprus Gk. Kypros, Turk. Kıbrıs. island E Mediterranean Sea
121 W11 Cyprus Basin var. Cypro-Syrian Basin. undersea feature E Mediterranean Sea
Cythera see Kýthira
Cythnos see Kýthnos
110 F9 Czaplinek Ger. Tempelburg. Zachodnio-pomorskie, NW Poland
Czarna Woda see Wda
110 G8 Czarne Pomorskie, N Poland
110 G10 Czarnków Wielkopolskie, C Poland
111 E17 Czech Republic Cz. Česká Republika. ◆ republic C Europe
Czegléd see Cegléd
110 G12 Czempiń Wielkolpolskie, C Poland
Czenstochau see Częstochowa
Czerkow see Čerchov
Czernowitz see Chernivtsi
110 I8 Czersk Pomorskie, N Poland
111 J15 Częstochowa Ger. Czenstochau, Tschenstochau, Rus. Chenstokhov. Śląskie, S Poland
110 F10 Człopa Ger. Schloppe. Zachodnio-pomorskie, NW Poland
110 H8 Człuchów Ger. Schlochau. Pomorskie, NW Poland

D

163 V9 Da'an var. Dalai. Jilin, NE China
15 S10 Daaquam Québec, SE Canada
Daawo, Webi see Dawa Wenz
54 I4 Dabajuro Falcón, NW Venezuela
77 N15 Dabakala NE Ivory Coast
163 S11 Daban var. Bairin Youqi. Nei Mongol Zizhiqu, N China
111 K23 Dabas Pest, C Hungary
160 L8 Daba Shan ▲ C China
Dabba see Daocheng
140 J5 Dabbāgh, Jabal ▲ NW Saudi Arabia
54 D8 Dabeiba Antioquia, NW Colombia
154 E11 Dabhoi Gujarāt, W India
161 P8 Dabie Shan ▲ C China
76 J13 Dabola Haute-Guinée, C Guinea
77 N17 Dabou S Ivory Coast
162 M15 Dabqig var. Uxin Qi. Nei Mongol Zizhiqu, N China
110 P8 Dąbrowa Białostocka Podlaskie, NE Poland
111 M16 Dąbrowa Tarnowska Małopolskie, S Poland
119 M20 Dabryn' Rus. Dobryn'. Homyel'skaya Voblasts', SE Belarus
159 P10 Dabsan Hu ◎ C China
161 Q13 Dabu var. Huliao. Guangdong, S China
116 H15 Dăbuleni Dolj, SW Romania
Dacca see Dhaka
101 L23 Dachau Bayern, SE Germany
160 K8 Dachuan prev. Daxian, Da Xian. Sichuan, C China
Dacia Bank see Dacia Seamount
64 M10 Dacia Seamount var. Dacia Bank. undersea feature E Atlantic Ocean
37 T3 Dacono Colorado, C USA
Đắc Tô see Đak Tô
Dacura see Dákura
23 W12 Dade City Florida, SE USA
152 L10 Dadeldhura var. Dandeldhura. Far Western, W Nepal
23 Q5 Dadeville Alabama, S USA
Dadong see Donggang
103 N15 Dadou ≈ S France
154 D12 Dādra and Nagar Haveli ❖ union territory W India
149 P14 Dādu Sind, SE Pakistan
167 U11 Da Du Boloc Kon Tum, C Vietnam
160 G9 Dadu He ≈ C China
Daegu see Taegu
Daerah Istimewa Aceh see Aceh
171 P4 Daet Luzon, N Philippines
160 I11 Dafang Guizhou, S China
Dafeng see Shanglin
153 W11 Dafla Hills ▲ NE India
11 U15 Dafoe Saskatchewan, S Canada
76 G10 Dagana N Senegal
Dagana see Dahana, Tajikistan
Dagana see Massakory, Chad
Dagcagoin see Zoigê
118 K11 Dagda Krāslava, SE Latvia
Dagden see Hiiumaa
Dagden-Sund see Soela Väin
127 P16 Dagestan, Respublika prev. Dagestanskaya ASSR, Eng. Daghestan. ❖ autonomous republic SW Russian Federation
Dagestanskaya ASSR see Dagestan, Respublika
127 R17 Dagestanskiye Ogni Respublika Dagestan, SW Russian Federation
185 A23 Dagg Sound sound South Island, NZ
Daghestan see Dagestan, Respublika
141 Y8 Daghmar NE Oman
Dağliq Qarabağ see Nagorno-Karabakh
Dagö see Hiiumaa
54 D11 Dagua Valle del Cauca, W Colombia
160 H11 Daguan var. Cuihua. Yunnan, SW China
171 N3 Dagupan off. Dagupan City. Luzon, N Philippines
159 N16 Dagzê var. Dêqên. Xizang Zizhiqu, W China
147 Q13 Dahana Rus. Dagana, Dakhana. SW Tajikistan
163 V10 Dahei Shan ▲ N China
163 T7 Da Hinggan Ling Eng. Great Khingan Range. ▲ NE China
Dahlac Archipelago see Dahlak Archipelago
80 K9 Dahlak Archipelago var. Dahlac Archipelago. island group E Eritrea
23 T2 Dahlonega Georgia, SE USA
101 O14 Dahme Brandenburg, E Germany
100 O13 Dahme ≈ E Germany
141 O14 Dahm, Ramlat desert NW Yemen
154 E10 Dāhod prev. Dohad. Gujarāt, W India
Dahomey see Benin
158 G10 Dahongliutan Xinjiang Uygur Zizhiqu, NW China
Dahra see Dara
139 R2 Dahūk var. Dohuk, Kurd. Dihōk. N Iraq
116 J15 Daia Giurgiu, S Romania
165 P12 Daigo Ibaraki, Honshū, S Japan
163 O13 Dai Hai ◎ N China
Daihoku see T'aipei
186 M8 Dai Island island N Solomon Islands
166 M8 Daik-u Pegu, SW Myanmar
138 H9 Dā'īl Dar'ā, S Syria
167 U12 Dai Lanh Khanh Hoa, S Vietnam
161 Q13 Daimao Shan ▲ SE China
105 N11 Daimiel Castilla-La Mancha, C Spain
115 F22 Daimoniá Pelopónnisos, S Greece
Dainan see T'ainan
25 W6 Daingerfield Texas, SW USA
Daingin, Bá an see Dingle Bay
159 R13 Dainkognubma Xizang Zizhiqu, W China
164 K14 Daiō-zaki headland Honshū, SW Japan
Dairbhre see Valencia Island
61 B22 Daireaux Buenos Aires, E Argentina
Dairen see Dalian
75 W9 Dairûţ var. Dayrūţ. C Egypt
25 X10 Daisetta Texas, SW USA
192 G5 Daitō-jima island group SW Japan
192 G5 Daitō Ridge undersea feature N Philippine Sea
161 N3 Daixian var. Dai Xian. Shanxi, C China
Daiyue see Shanyin
161 Q12 Daiyun Shan ▲ SE China
44 M8 Dajabón NW Dominican Republic
159 T10 Dajin Chuan ≈ C China
148 J6 Dak ◎ W Afghanistan
76 F11 Dakar ● (Senegal) W Senegal
76 F11 Dakar ✕ W Senegal
167 U10 Đak Glây Kon Tum, C Vietnam
Dakhana see Dahana
153 U16 Dakhin Shahbazpur Island island S Bangladesh
Dakhla see Ad Dakhla
76 F7 Dakhlet Nouâdhibou ❖ region NW Mauritania
Đak Lap see Kiên Đưc
167 U13 Đak Nông Đăc Lăc, S Vietnam
77 U11 Dakoro Maradi, S Niger
29 R12 Dakota City Iowa, C USA
29 R13 Dakota City Nebraska, C USA
113 M17 Đakovica var. Djakovica, Alb. Gjakovë. Serbia, S Serbia and Montenegro (Yugo.)
112 I10 Đakovo var. Djakovo, Hung. Diakovár. Osijek-Baranja, E Croatia
Dakshin see Deccan
167 U11 Đak Tô var. Đăc Tô. Kon Tum, C Vietnam
43 N7 Dákura var. Dacura. Región Autónoma Atlántico Norte, NE Nicaragua
95 I14 Dal Akershus, S Norway
82 E12 Dala Lunda Sul, E Angola
108 J8 Dalaas Vorarlberg, W Austria
76 I13 Dalaba Moyenne-Guinée, W Guinea
Dalai see Da'an
162 I12 Dalain Hob var. Ejin Qi. Nei Mongol Zizhiqu, N China
Dalai Nor see Hulun Nur
163 Q11 Dalai Nur salt lake N China
Dala-Jarna see Järna
95 M14 Dalälven ≈ C Sweden
136 C16 Dalaman Muğla, SW Turkey
136 C16 Dalaman ✕ Muğla, SW Turkey
136 D16 Dalaman Çayı ≈ SW Turkey
162 K11 Dalandzadgad Ömnögovĭ, S Mongolia
95 D17 Dalane physical region S Norway
189 Z2 Dalap-Uliga-Djarrit var. Delap-Uliga-Darrit, D-U-D. island group Ratak Chain, SE Marshall Islands
94 J12 Dalarna prev. Kopparberg. ❖ county C Sweden
94 L13 Dalarna prev. Eng. Dalecarlia. cultural region C Sweden
95 P16 Dalarö Stockholm, C Sweden
167 U13 Đa Lat Lâm Đông, S Vietnam
162 J11 Dalay Ömnögovĭ, S Mongolia
148 L12 Dālbandīn var. Dāl Bandin. Baluchistān, SW Pakistan
95 J17 Dalbosjön lake bay S Sweden
181 Y10 Dalby Queensland, E Australia
94 D13 Dale Hordaland, S Norway
94 C12 Dale Sogn og Fjordane, S Norway
32 K12 Dale Oregon, NW USA
25 T11 Dale Texas, SW USA
Dalecarlia see Dalarna
21 W4 Dale City Virginia, NE USA
20 L8 Dale Hollow Lake ⊡ Kentucky/Tennessee, S USA
98 O8 Dalen Drenthe, NE Netherlands
95 E15 Dalen Telemark, S Norway
166 K14 Daletme Chin State, W Myanmar
23 Q7 Daleville Alabama, S USA
98 M9 Dalfsen Overijssel, E Netherlands
24 M1 Dalhart Texas, SW USA
13 O13 Dalhousie New Brunswick, SE Canada
152 I6 Dalhousie Himāchal Pradesh, N India
160 F12 Dali var. Xiaguan. Yunnan, SW China
Dali see Idálion
163 U14 Dalian var. Dairen, Dalien, Lüda, Ta-lien, Rus. Dalny. Liaoning, NE China
105 O15 Dalías Andalucía, S Spain
Dalien see Dalian
Dalijan see Delījān
112 J9 Dalj Hung. Dalja. Osijek-Baranja, E Croatia
Dalja see Dalj
32 F12 Dallas Oregon, NW USA
25 U6 Dallas Texas, SW USA
25 T7 Dallas-Fort Worth ✕ Texas, SW USA
154 K12 Dalli Rājhara Chhattīsgarh, C India
39 X15 Dall Island island Alexander Archipelago, Alaska, USA
38 M12 Dall Lake ◎ Alaska, USA
Dállogilli see Korpilombolo
77 S12 Dallol Bosso seasonal river W Niger
141 U7 Dalmā island W UAE
113 E14 Dalmacija Eng. Dalmatia, Ger. Dalmatien, It. Dalmazia. cultural region S Croatia
Dalmatia/Dalmatien/Dalmazia see Dalmacija
123 S15 Dal'negorsk Primorskiy Kray, SE Russian Federation
Dalny see Dalian
76 M16 Daloa C Ivory Coast
160 J11 Dalou Shan ▲ S China
181 X7 Dalrymple Lake ◎ Queensland, E Australia
14 H14 Dalrymple Lake ◎ Ontario, S Canada
181 X7 Dalrymple, Mount ▲ Queensland, E Australia
93 K20 Dalsbruk Fin. Taalintehdas. Länsi-Suomi, W Finland
95 K19 Dalsjöfors Västra Götaland, S Sweden
95 J17 Dals Långed var. Långed. Västra Götaland, S Sweden
153 O15 Dāltenganj prev. Daltonganj. Jhārkhand, N India
23 R2 Dalton Georgia, SE USA
Daltonganj see Dāltenganj
195 X14 Dalton Iceberg Tongue ice feature Antarctica
Dálvvadis see Jokkmokk
92 J1 Dalvík Norðurland Eystra, N Iceland
35 N8 Daly City California, W USA
181 P2 Daly River ≈ Northern Territory, N Australia
181 Q3 Daly Waters Northern Territory, N Australia
119 F20 Damachava var. Damachova, Pol. Domaczewo, Rus. Domachëvo. Brestskaya Voblasts', SW Belarus
Damachova see Damachava
77 W11 Damagaram Takaya Zinder, S Niger
154 D12 Damān Damān and Diu, W India
154 B12 Damān and Diu ❖ union territory W India
75 V7 Damanhûr anc. Hermopolis Parva. N Egypt
Damão see Damān
161 O1 Damaqun Shan ▲ E China
79 I15 Damara Ombella-Mpoko, S Central African Republic
83 D18 Damaraland physical region C Namibia
171 S15 Damar, Kepulauan var. Baraf Daja Islands, Kepulauan Barat Daya. island group C Indonesia
168 J8 Damar Laut Perak, Peninsular Malaysia
171 S15 Damar, Pulau island Maluku, E Indonesia
Damas see Dimashq
77 Y12 Damasak Borno, NE Nigeria
Damasco see Dimashq
21 Q8 Damascus Virginia, NE USA
Damascus see Dimashq
77 X13 Damaturu Yobe, NE Nigeria
171 R9 Damau Pulau Kaburuang, N Indonesia
143 O5 Damāvand, Qolleh-ye ▲ N Iran
82 B10 Damba Uíge, NW Angola
114 M12 Dambaslar Tekirdağ, NW Turkey
116 J13 Dâmbovița prev. Dîmbovița. ❖ county SE Romania
116 J13 Dâmbovița prev. Dîmbovița. ≈ S Romania
173 Y15 D'Ambre, Île island NE Mauritius
155 K24 Dambulla Central Province, C Sri Lanka
44 K9 Dame-Marie SW Haiti
44 J9 Dame Marie, Cap headland SW Haiti
143 Q4 Dāmghān Semnān, N Iran
Damietta see Dumyāt
138 G10 Dāmiyā Al Balqā', NW Jordan
146 G11 Damla Daşoguz Welaýaty, N Turkmenistan
Dammām see Ad Dammān
100 G12 Damme Niedersachsen, NW Germany
153 R15 Dāmodar ≈ NE India
154 J9 Damoh Madhya Pradesh, C India
77 P15 Damongo NW Ghana
138 G7 Damour var. Ad Dāmūr. W Lebanon
171 N11 Dampal, Teluk bay Sulawesi, C Indonesia
180 H7 Dampier Western Australia
180 H6 Dampier Archipelago island group Western Australia
141 U14 Damqawt var. Damqut. E Yemen
159 O13 Dam Qu ≈ C China
Damqut see Damqawt
167 R13 Dâmrei, Chuŏr Phnum Fr. Chaîne de l'Éléphant. ▲ SW Cambodia
108 C7 Damvant Jura, NW Switzerland
Damwâld see Damwoude
98 L5 Damwoude Fris. Damwâld. Friesland, N Netherlands
159 N15 Damxung var. Gongtang. Xizang Zizhiqu, W China
80 K11 Danakil Desert var. Afar Depression, Danakil Plain. desert E Africa
Danakil Plain see Danakil Desert
35 R8 Dana, Mount ▲ California, W USA
76 L16 Danané W Ivory Coast
167 U10 Đa Nẵng prev. Tourane. Quang Nam-Đa Nẵng, C Vietnam
160 G9 Danba var. Zhanggu, Tib. Rongzhag. Sichuan, C China
Danborg see Daneborg
18 L13 Danbury Connecticut, NE USA
25 W12 Danbury Texas, SW USA
35 X15 Danby Lake ◎ California, W USA
194 H4 Danco Coast physical region Antarctica
82 B11 Dande ≈ NW Angola
Dandeldhura see Dadeldhura
155 E17 Dandeli Karnātaka, W India
183 O12 Dandenong Victoria, SE Australia
163 V13 Dandong var. Tan-tung; prev. An-tung. Liaoning, NE China
197 Q14 Daneborg var. Danborg. Tunu, N Greenland
25 V12 Danevang Texas, SW USA
Dänew see Galkynyş
Danfeng see Shizong
14 L12 Danford Lake Québec, SE Canada
19 T4 Danforth Maine, NE USA
37 P3 Danforth Hills ▲ Colorado, C USA
Dangara see Danghara
159 V12 Dangchang Gansu, C China
159 P8 Dangchengwan var. Subei, Subei Mongolzu Zizhixian. Gansu, N China
82 B10 Dange Uíge, NW Angola
Dangerous Archipelago see Tuamotu, Îles
83 E26 Danger Point headland SW South Africa
147 Q13 Danghara Rus. Dangara. SW Tajikistan
159 P8 Danghe Nanshan ▲ W China
80 I12 Dangila var. Dänglä. Amhara, NW Ethiopia

◆ Country ● Country Capital ◇ Dependent Territory ○ Dependent Territory Capital ❖ Administrative Region ✕ International Airport ▲ Mountain ▲ Mountain Range Volcano ≈ River ◎ Lake ⊡ Reservoir

159 P8 **Dangjin Shankou** *pass* N China
Dangla *see* Tanggula Shan, China
Dang La *see* Tanggula Shankou, China
Dānglā *see* Dangila, Ethiopia
Dangme Chu *see* Manās
153 Y11 **Dāngori** Assam, NE India
Dang Raek, Phanom/Dangrek, Chaîne des *see* Dângrêk, Chuŏr Phnum
167 S11 **Dângrêk, Chuŏr Phnum** *var.* Phanom Dang Raek, Phanom Dong Rak, *Fr.* Chaîne des Dangrek. ▲ Cambodia/Thailand
42 G3 **Dangriga** *prev.* Stann Creek. Stann Creek, E Belize
161 P6 **Dangshan** Anhui, E China
33 T15 **Daniel** Wyoming, C USA
83 H22 **Daniëlskuil** Northern Cape, N South Africa
19 N12 **Danielson** Connecticut, NE USA
124 M15 **Danilov** Yaroslavskaya Oblast', W Russian Federation
127 O9 **Danilovka** Volgogradskaya Oblast', SW Russian Federation
Danish West Indies *see* Virgin Islands (US)
160 L7 **Dan Jiang** ∽ C China
160 M7 **Danjiangkou Shuiku** ⊠ C China
141 W8 **Ḍank** *var.* Dhank. NW Oman
152 J7 **Dankhar** Himāchal Pradesh, N India
126 L6 **Dankov** Lipetskaya Oblast', W Russian Federation
42 J7 **Danlí** El Paraíso, S Honduras
Danmark *see* Denmark
Danmarksstraedet *see* Denmark Strait
95 O14 **Dannemora** Uppsala, C Sweden
18 L6 **Dannemora** New York, NE USA
100 K11 **Dannenberg** Niedersachsen, N Germany
184 N12 **Dannevirke** Manawatu-Wanganui, North Island, NZ
21 U8 **Dan River** ∽ Virginia, NE USA
167 P8 **Dan Sai** Loei, C Thailand
18 F10 **Dansville** New York, NE USA
Dantzig *see* Gdańsk
86 E12 **Danube** *Bul.* Dunav, *Cz.* Dunaj, *Ger.* Donau, *Hung.* Duna, *Rom.* Dunărea. ∽ C Europe
Danubian Plain *see* Dunavska Ravnina
166 L8 **Danubyu** Irrawaddy, SW Myanmar
Danum *see* Doncaster
19 P11 **Danvers** Massachusetts, NE USA
27 T11 **Danville** Arkansas, C USA
31 N13 **Danville** Illinois, N USA
31 O14 **Danville** Indiana, N USA
29 Y15 **Danville** Iowa, C USA
20 M6 **Danville** Kentucky, S USA
18 G14 **Danville** Pennsylvania, NE USA
21 T6 **Danville** Virginia, NE USA
Danxian/Dan Xian *see* Danzhou
160 L17 **Danzhou** *prev.* Danxian, Dan Xian, Nada. Hainan, S China
Danzig *see* Gdańsk
Danziger Bucht *see* Danzig, Gulf of
110 J6 **Danzig, Gulf of** *var.* Gulf of Gdańsk, *Ger.* Danziger Bucht, *Pol.* Zakota Gdańska, *Rus.* Gdan'skaya Bukhta. *gulf* N Poland
160 F10 **Daocheng** *var.* Jinzhu, *Tib.* Dabba. Sichuan, C China
Daojiang *see* Daoxian
Daokou *see* Huaxian
104 H7 **Dão, Rio** ∽ N Portugal
Daosa *see* Dausa
77 Y7 **Dao Timmi** Agadez, NE Niger
160 M13 **Daoxian** *var.* Daojiang, Dao Xian. Hunan, S China
77 Q14 **Dapaong** N Togo
23 N8 **Daphne** Alabama, S USA
171 P7 **Dapitan** Mindanao, S Philippines
159 P9 **Da Qaidam** Qinghai, C China
163 V8 **Daqing** *var.* Sartu. Heilongjiang, NE China
163 O13 **Daqing Shan** ▲ N China
163 T11 **Daqin Tal** *var.* Naiman Qi. Nei Mongol Zizhiqu, N China
Daqm *see* Duqm
160 G8 **Da Qu** *var.* Do Qu. ∽ C China
139 T5 **Dāqūq** *var.* Tāwūq. N Iraq
76 G10 **Dara** *var.* Dahra. NW Senegal
138 H9 **Dar'ā** *var.* Der'a, *Fr.* Déraa. Dar'ā, SW Syria
138 H8 **Dar'ā** *off.* Muḥāfaẓat Dar'ā, *var.* Dará, Derá, Derrá. ◆ *governorate* S Syria
143 Q12 **Dārāb** Fārs, S Iran
116 K8 **Darabani** Botoşani, NW Romania
Daraj *see* Dirj
142 M8 **Darān** Eşfahān, W Iran
167 U12 **Đa Răng, Sông** *var.* Ba. ∽ S Vietnam
Daraut-Kurgan *see* Daroot-Korgon
77 W13 **Darazo** Bauchi, E Nigeria
139 S3 **Darband** N Iraq
139 V4 **Darband-i Khān, Sadd** *dam* NE Iraq
139 N1 **Darbāsīyah** *var.* Derbisīye. Al Ḥasakah, N Syria
118 C11 **Darbėnai** Klaipėda, NW Lithuania
153 Q13 **Darbhanga** Bihār, N India
38 M9 **Darby, Cape** *headland* Alaska, USA
112 I9 **Darda** *Hung.* Dárda. Osijek-Baranja, E Croatia
27 T11 **Dardanelle** Arkansas, C USA
27 S11 **Dardanelle, Lake** ⊠ Arkansas, C USA
Dardanelles *see* Çanakkale Boğazı
Dardanelli *see* Çanakkale
Dardo *see* Kangding
Dar-el-Beida *see* Casablanca
136 M14 **Darende** Malatya, C Turkey
81 J22 **Dar es Salaam** Dar es Salaam, E Tanzania
81 J22 **Dar es Salaam** ✕ Pwani, E Tanzania
185 H18 **Darfield** Canterbury, South Island, NZ
106 F7 **Darfo** Lombardia, N Italy
80 B10 **Darfur** *var.* Darfur Massif. *cultural region* W Sudan
Darfur Massif *see* Darfur
Darganata/Dargan-Ata *see* Birata
143 T3 **Dargaz** *var.* Darreh Gaz; *prev.* Moḥammadābād. Khorāsān, NE Iran
139 U4 **Dargazayn** NE Iraq
183 P12 **Dargo** Victoria, SE Australia
162 K7 **Darhan** Bulgan, C Mongolia
162 L6 **Darhan** Darhan Uul, N Mongolia
163 N8 **Darhan** Hentiy, C Mongolia
Darhan Muminggan Lianheqi *see* Bailingmiao
162 L6 **Darhan Uul** ◆ *province* N Mongolia
23 W7 **Darien** Georgia, SE USA
43 W16 **Darién** *off.* Provincia del Darién. ◆ *province* SE Panama
Darién, Golfo del *see* Darien, Gulf of
43 X14 **Darien, Gulf of** *Sp.* Golfo del Darién. *gulf* S Caribbean Sea
Darien, Isthmus of *see* Panamá, Istmo de
42 K9 **Dariense, Cordillera** ▲ C Nicaragua
43 W15 **Darién, Serranía del** ▲ Colombia/Panama
Dario *see* Ciudad Darío
Dariorigum *see* Vannes
Dariv *see* Darvi
Darj *see* Dirj
Darjeeling *see* Darjiling
153 S12 **Darjiling** *prev.* Darjeeling. West Bengal, NE India
Darkehnen *see* Ozersk
159 S12 **Darlag** *var.* Gümai. Qinghai, C China
183 T3 **Darling Downs** *hill range* Queensland, E Australia
28 M2 **Darling, Lake** ⊠ North Dakota, N USA
180 I12 **Darling Range** ▲ Western Australia
182 L8 **Darling River** ∽ New South Wales, SE Australia
97 M15 **Darlington** N England, UK
21 T12 **Darlington** South Carolina, SE USA
30 K9 **Darlington** Wisconsin, N USA
110 G7 **Darłowo** Zachodnio-pomorskie, NW Poland
101 G19 **Darmstadt** Hessen, SW Germany
75 S7 **Darnah** *var.* Dérna. NE Libya
103 S6 **Darney** Vosges, NE France
182 M7 **Darnick** New South Wales, SE Australia
195 Y6 **Darnley, Cape** *headland* Antarctica
105 R7 **Daroca** Aragón, NE Spain
147 S11 **Daroot-Korgon** *var.* Daraut-Kurgan. Oshskaya Oblast', SW Kyrgyzstan
61 A23 **Darragueira** *var.* Darregueira. Buenos Aires, E Argentina
Darregueira *see* Darragueira
Darreh Gaz *see* Dargaz
142 K7 **Darreh Shahr** *var.* Darreh-ye Shahr. Īlām, W Iran
Darreh-ye Shahr *see* Darreh Shahr
32 I7 **Darrington** Washington, NW USA
25 P1 **Darrouzett** Texas, SW USA
153 S15 **Darsana** *var.* Darshana. Khulna, N Bangladesh
Darshana *see* Darsana
100 M7 **Darss** *peninsula* NE Germany
100 M7 **Darsser Ort** *headland* NE Germany
97 J24 **Dart** ∽ SW England, UK
Dartang *see* Baqên
97 P22 **Dartford** SE England, UK
182 L12 **Dartmoor** Victoria, SE Australia
97 I24 **Dartmoor** *moorland* SW England, UK
13 Q15 **Dartmouth** Nova Scotia, SE Canada
97 J24 **Dartmouth** SW England, UK
15 Y6 **Dartmouth** ∽ Québec, SE Canada
183 Q11 **Dartmouth Reservoir** ⊚ Victoria, SE Australia
Dartuch, Cabo *see* Artrutx, Cap d'
186 C9 **Daru** Western, SW PNG
112 G9 **Daruvar** *Hung.* Daruvár. Bjelovar-Bilogora, NE Croatia
Darvaza, Turkmenistan *see* Derweze
Darvaza, Uzbekistan *see* Darvoza
Darvazskiy Khrebet *see* Darvoz, Qatorkŭhi
162 F8 **Darvi** *var.* Dariv. Govĭ-Altay, W Mongolia
148 L9 **Darvīshān** *var.* Darweshan, Garmser. Helmand, S Afghanistan
147 R13 **Darvoz, Qatorkŭhi** *Rus.* Darvazskiy Khrebet. ▲ C Tajikistan
Darweshan *see* Darvīshān
63 J15 **Darwin** Río Negro, S Argentina
181 O1 **Darwin** *prev.* Palmerston, Port Darwin. *territory capital* Northern Territory, N Australia
65 D24 **Darwin** *var.* Darwin Settlement. East Falkland, Falkland Islands
62 H8 **Darwin, Cordillera** ▲ N Chile
57 B17 **Darwin, Volcán** ⚠ Galapagos Islands, Ecuador, E Pacific Ocean
147 O10 **Darvoza** *Rus.* Darvaza. Jizzax Viloyati, C Uzbekistan
149 S8 **Darya Khān** Punjab, E Pakistan
145 O15 **Dar'yalyktakyr, Ravnina** *plain* S Kazakhstan
143 T11 **Dārzīn** Kermān, S Iran
Dashennongjia *see* Shennong Ding
Dashhowuz *see* Daşoguz
Dashhowuz Welayaty *see* Daşoguz Welaýaty
119 O16 **Dashkawka** *Rus.* Dashkovka. Mahilyowskaya Voblasts', E Belarus
Dashkhovuz *see* Daşoguz/Daşoguz Welaýaty
Dashkhovuzskiy Velayat *see* Daşoguz Welaýaty
Dashköpri *see* Daşköpri
Dashkovka *see* Dashkawka
148 J15 **Dasht** ∽ SW Pakistan
Dashtidzhum *see* Dashtijum
147 R13 **Dashtijum** *Rus.* Dashtidzhum. SW Tajikistan
149 W7 **Daska** Punjab, NE Pakistan
146 J16 **Daşköpri** *var.* Dashköpri, *Rus.* Tashkepri. Mary Welaýaty, S Turkmenistan
146 H8 **Daşoguz** *Rus.* Dashkhovuz, *Turkm.* Dashhowuz; *prev.* Tashauz. Daşoguz Welaýaty, N Turkmenistan
146 E9 **Daşoguz Welaýaty** *var.* Dashhowuz Welayaty, *Rus.* Dashkhovuz, Dashkhovuzskiy Velayat. ◆ *province* N Turkmenistan
Đa, Sông *see* Black River
77 R15 **Dassa** *var.* Dassa-Zoumé. S Benin
Dassa-Zoumé *see* Dassa
29 U8 **Dassel** Minnesota, N USA
152 H3 **Dastegil Sar** *var.* Disteghil Sār. ▲ N India
136 C16 **Datça** Muğla, SW Turkey
165 R4 **Date** Hokkaidō, NE Japan
154 I8 **Datia** *prev.* Duttia. Madhya Pradesh, C India
Dåtnejaevrie *see* Tunnsjøen
159 T10 **Datong** *var.* Qiaotou. Qinghai, C China
161 N2 **Datong** *var.* Tatung, Ta-t'ung. Shanxi, C China
Datong *see* Tong'an
159 S9 **Datong He** ∽ C China
159 S9 **Datong Shan** ▲ C China
169 O10 **Datu, Tanjung** *headland* Indonesia/Malaysia
Daua *see* Dawa Wenz
172 H16 **Dauban, Mount** ▲ Silhouette, NE Seychelles
149 T7 **Dāūd Khel** Punjab, E Pakistan
119 G15 **Daugai** Alytus, S Lithuania
Daugava *see* Western Dvina
118 J11 **Daugavpils** *Ger.* Dünaburg; *prev. Rus.* Dvinsk. *municipality* Daugvapils, SE Latvia
Dauka *see* Dawkah
Daulatabad *see* Malāyer
101 D18 **Daun** Rheinland-Pfalz, W Germany
155 E14 **Daund** *prev.* Dhond. Mahārāshtra, W India
166 M12 **Daung Kyun** *island* S Myanmar
11 W15 **Dauphin** Manitoba, S Canada
103 S13 **Dauphiné** *cultural region* E France
23 N9 **Dauphin Island** *island* Alabama, S USA
11 X15 **Dauphin River** Manitoba, S Canada
77 V12 **Daura** Katsina, N Nigeria
152 H12 **Dausa** *prev.* Daosa. Rājasthān, N India
Dauwa *see* Dawwah
137 Y10 **Däväçi** *Rus.* Divichi. NE Azerbaijan
155 F18 **Dāvangere** Karnātaka, W India
171 Q8 **Davao** *off.* Davao City. Mindanao, S Philippines
171 Q8 **Davao Gulf** *gulf* Mindanao, S Philippines
15 Q11 **Daveluyville** Québec, SE Canada
29 Z14 **Davenport** Iowa, C USA
32 L8 **Davenport** Washington, NW USA
43 P16 **David** Chiriquí, W Panama
15 O11 **David** ∽ Québec, SE Canada
29 R15 **David City** Nebraska, C USA
David-Gorodok *see* Davyd-Haradok
11 T16 **Davidson** Saskatchewan, S Canada
21 R10 **Davidson** North Carolina, SE USA
26 K12 **Davidson** Oklahoma, C USA
39 S6 **Davidson Mountains** ▲ Alaska, USA
172 M8 **Davie Ridge** *undersea feature* W Indian Ocean
182 A1 **Davies, Mount** ▲ South Australia
35 O7 **Davis** California, W USA
27 N12 **Davis** Oklahoma, C USA
195 Y7 **Davis** *Australian research station* Antarctica
194 H3 **Davis Coast** *physical region* Antarctica
18 C16 **Davis, Mount** ▲ Pennsylvania, NE USA
24 K9 **Davis Mountains** ▲ Texas, SW USA
195 Z9 **Davis Sea** *sea* Antarctica
65 O20 **Davis Seamounts** *undersea feature* S Atlantic Ocean
196 M13 **Davis Strait** *strait* Baffin Bay/Labrador Sea
127 U5 **Davlekanovo** Respublika Bashkortostan, W Russian Federation
108 J9 **Davos** *Rmsch.* Tavau. Graubünden, E Switzerland
119 J20 **Davyd-Haradok** *Pol.* Dawidgródek, *Rus.* David-Gorodok. Brestskaya Voblasts', SW Belarus
163 U12 **Dawa** Liaoning, NE China
141 O11 **Dawāsir, Wādī ad** *dry watercourse* S Saudi Arabia
81 K15 **Dawa Wenz** *var.* Daua, Webi Daawo. ∽ E Africa
Dawaymah, Birkat ad *see* Umm al Baqar, Hawr
Dawei *see* Tavoy
119 K14 **Dawhinava** *Rus.* Dolginovo. Minskaya Voblasts', N Belarus
Dawidgródek *see* Davyd-Haradok
141 V12 **Dawkah** *var.* Dauka. SW Oman
Dawlat Qaṭar *see* Qatar
24 M3 **Dawn** Texas, SW USA
Dawo *see* Maqên
140 M11 **Daws** Al Bāḥah, SW Saudi Arabia
10 H5 **Dawson** *var.* Dawson City. Yukon Territory, NW Canada
23 S6 **Dawson** Georgia, SE USA
29 S9 **Dawson** Minnesota, N USA
Dawson City *see* Dawson
11 N13 **Dawson Creek** British Columbia, W Canada
8 H7 **Dawson Range** ▲ Yukon Territory, W Canada
181 Y9 **Dawson River** ∽ Queensland, E Australia
10 J15 **Dawsons Landing** British Columbia, SW Canada
20 I7 **Dawson Springs** Kentucky, S USA
23 S2 **Dawsonville** Georgia, SE USA
160 G8 **Dawu** *var.* Xianshui. Sichuan, C China
Dawu *see* Maqên
Dawukou *see* Shizuishan
141 Y10 **Dawwah** *var.* Dauwa. W Oman
102 J15 **Dax** *var.* Ax; *anc.* Aquae Augustae, Aquae Tarbelicae. Landes, SW France
Da Xian/Daxian *see* Dachuan
Daxue *see* Wencheng
160 G9 **Daxue Shan** ▲ C China
Dayan *see* Lijiang
160 G12 **Dayao** *var.* Jinbi. Yunnan, SW China
Dayishan *see* Gaoyou
183 N12 **Daylesford** Victoria, SE Australia
35 U10 **Daylight Pass** *pass* California, W USA
61 D17 **Daymán, Río** ∽ N Uruguay
Dayr *see* Ad Dayr
138 G10 **Dayr 'Allā** *var.* Deir 'Alla. Al Balqā', N Jordan
139 N4 **Dayr az Zawr** *var.* Deir ez Zor. Dayr az Zawr, E Syria
138 M5 **Dayr az Zawr** *off.* Muḥāfaẓat Dayr az Zawr, *var.* Dayr Az-Zor. ◆ *governorate* E Syria
Dayr Az-Zor *see* Dayr az Zawr
Dayrūṭ *see* Dairûṭ
11 Q15 **Daysland** Alberta, SW Canada
31 R14 **Dayton** Ohio, N USA
20 L10 **Dayton** Tennessee, S USA
25 W11 **Dayton** Texas, SW USA
32 L10 **Dayton** Washington, NW USA
23 X10 **Daytona Beach** Florida, SE USA
169 U12 **Dayu** Borneo, C Indonesia
161 O13 **Dayu Ling** ▲ S China
161 R7 **Da Yunhe** *Eng.* Grand Canal. *canal* E China
161 S11 **Dayu Shan** *island* SE China
160 J9 **Dazhu** *var.* Zhuyang. Sichuan, C China
160 J9 **Dazu** *var.* Longgang. Chongqing Shi, C China
83 H24 **De Aar** Northern Cape, C South Africa
194 K5 **Deacon, Cape** *headland* Antarctica
39 R5 **Deadhorse** Alaska, USA
33 T12 **Dead Indian Peak** ▲ Wyoming, C USA
23 R9 **Dead Lake** ⊚ Florida, SE USA
44 J4 **Deadman's Cay** Long Island, C Bahamas
138 G11 **Dead Sea** *var.* Bahret Lut, Lacus Asphaltites, *Ar.* Al Baḥr al Mayyit, Baḥrat Lūt, *Heb.* Yam HaMelaḥ. *salt lake* Israel/Jordan
28 J9 **Deadwood** South Dakota, N USA
97 Q22 **Deal** SE England, UK
83 I22 **Dealesville** Free State, C South Africa
161 P10 **De'an** *var.* Puting. Jiangxi, S China
62 K9 **Deán Funes** Córdoba, C Argentina
194 L12 **Dean Island** *island* Antarctica
Deanuvuotna *see* Tanafjorden
31 S10 **Dearborn** Michigan, N USA
27 R3 **Dearborn** Missouri, C USA
Deargget *see* Tärendö
32 K9 **Deary** Idaho, NW USA
32 M9 **Deary** Washington, NW USA
10 J10 **Dease** ∽ British Columbia, W Canada
10 J10 **Dease Lake** British Columbia, W Canada
35 U11 **Death Valley** California, W USA
35 U11 **Death Valley** *valley* California, W USA
92 M8 **Deatnu** *Fin.* Tenojoki, *Nor.* Tana. ∽ Finland/Norway *see also* Tenojoki
102 L4 **Deauville** Calvados, N France
117 X7 **Debal'tseve** *Rus.* Debal'tsevo. Donets'ka Oblast', SE Ukraine
Debal'tsevo *see* Debal'tseve
113 M19 **Debar** *Ger.* Dibra, *Turk.* Debre. W FYR Macedonia
39 O9 **Debauch Mountain** ▲ Alaska, USA
De Behagle *see* Laï
25 X7 **De Berry** Texas, SW USA
127 T2 **Debessy** Udmurtskaya Respublika, NW Russian Federation
111 N16 **Dębica** Podkarpackie, SE Poland
De Bildt *see* De Bilt
98 J11 **De Bilt** *var.* De Bildt. Utrecht, C Netherlands
123 T9 **Debin** Magadanskaya Oblast', E Russian Federation
110 N13 **Dęblin** *Rus.* Ivangorod. Lubelskie, E Poland
110 D10 **Dębno** Zachodnio-pomorskie, NW Poland
39 S10 **Deborah, Mount** ▲ Alaska, USA
33 N8 **De Borgia** Montana, NW USA
Debra Birhan *see* Debre Birhan
Debra Marcos *see* Debre Mark'os
Debra Tabor *see* Debre Tabor
Debre *see* Debar
80 J13 **Debre Birhan** *var.* Debra Birhan. Amhara, N Ethiopia
111 N22 **Debrecen** *Ger.* Debreczin, *Rom.* Debreţin; *prev.* Debreczen. Hajdú-Bihar, E Hungary
Debreczen/Debreczin *see* Debrecen
80 I12 **Debre Mark'os** *var.* Debra Marcos. Amhara, N Ethiopia
113 N19 **Debrešte** SW FYR Macedonia
80 J11 **Debre Tabor** *var.* Debra Tabor. Amhara, N Ethiopia
Debreţin *see* Debrecen
80 J13 **Debre Zeyt** Oromo, C Ethiopia
113 L16 **Dečani** Serbia, S Serbia and Montenegro (Yugo.)
23 P2 **Decatur** Alabama, S USA
23 S3 **Decatur** Georgia, SE USA
30 L13 **Decatur** Illinois, N USA
31 Q12 **Decatur** Indiana, N USA
22 M5 **Decatur** Mississippi, S USA
29 S14 **Decatur** Nebraska, C USA
25 S6 **Decatur** Texas, SW USA
20 H9 **Decaturville** Tennessee, S USA
103 O13 **Decazeville** Aveyron, S France
155 H17 **Deccan** *Hind.* Dakshin. *plateau* C India
14 J8 **Decelles, Réservoir** ⊠ Québec, SE Canada
12 K2 **Déception** Québec, NE Canada
160 G11 **Dechang** *var.* Dezhou. Sichuan, C China
111 C15 **Děčín** *Ger.* Tetschen. Ústecký Kraj, NW Czech Republic
103 P9 **Decize** Nièvre, C France
98 I6 **De Cocksdorp** Noord-Holland, NW Netherlands
29 X11 **Decorah** Iowa, C USA
Dedeagaç/Dedeagach *see* Alexandroúpoli
188 C15 **Dededo** N Guam
98 N9 **Dedemsvaart** Overijssel, E Netherlands
19 O11 **Dedham** Massachusetts, NE USA
63 H19 **Dedo, Cerro** ▲ SW Argentina
77 O13 **Dédougou** W Burkina
124 G15 **Dedovichi** Pskovskaya Oblast', W Russian Federation
Dedu *see* Wudalianchi
155 J24 **Deduru Oya** ∽ W Sri Lanka
83 N14 **Dedza** Central, S Malawi
83 N14 **Dedza Mountain** ▲ C Malawi
97 J19 **Dee** *Wel.* Afon Dyfrdwy. ∽ England/Wales, UK
96 K9 **Dee** ∽ NE Scotland, UK
Deep Bay *see* Chilumba
21 T3 **Deep Creek Lake** ⊠ Maryland, NE USA
36 J4 **Deep Creek Range** ▲ Utah, W USA
27 P10 **Deep Fork** ∽ Oklahoma, C USA
14 J11 **Deep River** Ontario, SE Canada
21 T10 **Deep River** ∽ North Carolina, SE USA
183 U4 **Deepwater** New South Wales, SE Australia
31 S14 **Deer Creek Lake** ⊚ Ohio, N USA
23 Z15 **Deerfield Beach** Florida, SE USA
39 N8 **Deering** Alaska, USA
38 M16 **Deer Island** *island* Alaska, USA
19 S7 **Deer Isle** *island* Maine, NE USA
13 S11 **Deer Lake** Newfoundland and Labrador, SE Canada
99 D18 **Deerlijk** West-Vlaanderen, W Belgium
33 Q10 **Deer Lodge** Montana, NW USA
32 L8 **Deer Park** Washington, NW USA
29 U5 **Deer River** Minnesota, N USA
Deés *see* Dej
Defeng *see* Liping
31 R11 **Defiance** Ohio, N USA
23 Q8 **De Funiak Springs** Florida, SE USA
95 L23 **Degeberga** Skåne, S Sweden
104 H12 **Degebe, Ribeira** ∽ S Portugal
80 M13 **Degeh Bur** Somali, E Ethiopia
15 U9 **Dégelis** Québec, SE Canada
77 U17 **Degema** Rivers, S Nigeria
95 L16 **Degerfors** Örebro, C Sweden
193 R14 **De Gerlache Seamounts** *undersea feature* SE Pacific Ocean
101 N21 **Deggendorf** Bayern, SE Germany
80 I11 **Degoma** Amhara, N Ethiopia
De Gordyk *see* Gorredijk
27 T12 **De Gray Lake** ⊠ Arkansas, C USA
180 J6 **De Grey River** ∽ Western Australia
126 M10 **Degtevo** Rostovskaya Oblast', SW Russian Federation
143 X13 **Dehak** Sīstān va Balūchestān, SE Iran
143 R9 **Deh 'Alī** Kermān, C Iran
143 S13 **Dehbārez** *var.* Rūdān. Hormozgān, S Iran
143 P10 **Deh Bīd** Fārs, C Iran
142 M10 **Deh Dasht** Kohgīlūyeh va Būyer Aḥmad, SW Iran
75 N8 **Dehibat** SE Tunisia
Dehli *see* Delhi
142 K8 **Dehlorān** Īlām, W Iran
147 N13 **Dehqonobod** *Rus.* Dekhkanabad. Qashqadaryo Viloyati, S Uzbekistan
152 J9 **Dehra Dūn** Uttaranchal, N India
153 O14 **Dehri** Bihār, N India
148 K10 **Deh Shū** *var.* Deshu. Helmand, S Afghanistan
99 D17 **Deinze** Oost-Vlaanderen, NW Belgium
Deir 'Alla *see* Dayr 'Allā
Deir ez Zor *see* Dayr az Zawr
Deirgeirt, Loch *see* Derg, Lough
116 H9 **Dej** *Hung.* Dés; *prev.* Deés. Cluj, NW Romania
95 K15 **Deje** Värmland, C Sweden
171 Y15 **De Jongs, Tanjung** *headland* Papua, SE Indonesia
De Jouwer *see* Joure
30 M10 **De Kalb** Illinois, N USA
22 M5 **De Kalb** Mississippi, S USA
25 W5 **De Kalb** Texas, SW USA
Dekéleia *see* Dhekéleia
79 K20 **Dekese** Kasai Occidental, C Dem. Rep. Congo
Dekhkanabad *see* Dehqonobod
79 I14 **Dékoa** Kémo, C Central African Republic
98 H6 **De Koog** Noord-Holland, NW Netherlands
30 M9 **Delafield** Wisconsin, N USA
61 C23 **De La Garma** Buenos Aires, E Argentina
14 K10 **Delahey, Lac** ⊚ Québec, SE Canada
80 E11 **Delami** Southern Kordofan, C Sudan
23 X11 **De Land** Florida, SE USA
35 R12 **Delano** California, W USA
29 V8 **Delano** Minnesota, N USA
36 K6 **Delano Peak** ▲ Utah, W USA
Delap-Uliga-Darrit *see* Dalap-Uliga-Djarrit
148 L7 **Delārām** Farāh, SW Afghanistan
38 F17 **Delarof Islands** *island group* Aleutian Islands, Alaska, USA
30 M9 **Delavan** Wisconsin, N USA
31 S13 **Delaware** Ohio, N USA
18 I17 **Delaware** *off.* State of Delaware; also known as Blue Hen State, Diamond State, First State. ◆ *state* NE USA
18 I17 **Delaware Bay** *bay* NE USA
24 J8 **Delaware Mountains** ▲ Texas, SW USA
18 I12 **Delaware River** ∽ NE USA
27 Q3 **Delaware River** ∽ Kansas, C USA
18 J14 **Delaware Water Gap** *valley* New Jersey/Pennsylvania, NE USA
101 G14 **Delbrück** Nordrhein-Westfalen, W Germany
11 Q15 **Delburne** Alberta, SW Canada
172 M12 **Del Cano Rise** *undersea feature* SW Indian Ocean
113 Q18 **Delčevo** NE FYR Macedonia
Delcommune, Lac *see* Nzilo, Lac
98 O10 **Delden** Overijssel, E Netherlands
183 R12 **Delegate** New South Wales, SE Australia
De Lemmer *see* Lemmer
108 D7 **Delémont** *Ger.* Delsberg. Jura, NW Switzerland
25 R7 **De Leon** Texas, SW USA
115 F18 **Delfoí** Stereá Ellás, C Greece
98 G12 **Delft** Zuid-Holland, W Netherlands
155 J23 **Delft** *island* NW Sri Lanka
98 O5 **Delfzijl** Groningen, NE Netherlands
(0) E9 **Delgada Fan** *undersea feature* NE Pacific Ocean
42 F7 **Delgado** San Salvador, SW El Salvador
82 Q12 **Delgado, Cabo** *headland* N Mozambique
80 E6 **Delgo** Northern, N Sudan
159 R10 **Delhi** *var.* Delingha. Qinghai, C China
152 I10 **Delhi** *var.* Dehli, *Hind.* Dilli; *hist.* Shahjahanabad. Delhi, N India
22 J5 **Delhi** Louisiana, S USA
18 J11 **Delhi** New York, NE USA
152 I10 **Delhi** ◆ *union territory* NW India
136 J17 **Deli Burnu** *headland* S Turkey
55 X10 **Délices** C French Guiana
136 J12 **Delice Çayı** ∽ C Turkey
40 J6 **Delicias** *var.* Ciudad Delicias. Chihuahua, N Mexico
143 N7 **Delījān** *var.* Dalijan, Dilijan. Markazī, W Iran
112 P12 **Deli Jovan** ▲ E Serbia and Montenegro (Yugo.)
Déli-Kárpátok *see* Carpaţii Meridionali
8 I8 **Déline** *prev.* Fort Franklin. Northwest Territories, NW Canada
Delingha *see* Delhi
15 Q7 **Delisle** Québec, SE Canada
11 T15 **Delisle** Saskatchewan, S Canada
101 M15 **Delitzsch** Sachsen, E Germany
33 Q12 **Dell** Montana, NW USA
24 I7 **Dell City** Texas, SW USA
103 U7 **Delle** Territoire-de-Belfort, E France
36 J9 **Dellenbaugh, Mount** ▲ Arizona, SW USA
29 R11 **Dell Rapids** South Dakota, N USA
21 Y4 **Delmar** Maryland, NE USA
18 K11 **Delmar** New York, NE USA
100 G11 **Delmenhorst** Niedersachsen, NW Germany
112 C9 **Delnice** Primorje-Gorski Kotar, NW Croatia
37 R7 **Del Norte** Colorado, C USA
39 N6 **De Long Mountains** ▲ Alaska, USA
183 P16 **Deloraine** Tasmania, SE Australia
11 W17 **Deloraine** Manitoba, S Canada
31 O12 **Delphi** Indiana, N USA
31 Q12 **Delphos** Ohio, N USA
23 Z15 **Delray Beach** Florida, SE USA
25 O12 **Del Rio** Texas, SW USA
Delsberg *see* Delémont
94 N11 **Delsbo** Gävleborg, C Sweden

◆ COUNTRY ● COUNTRY CAPITAL ◇ DEPENDENT TERRITORY ○ DEPENDENT TERRITORY CAPITAL ◆ ADMINISTRATIVE REGION ✕ INTERNATIONAL AIRPORT ▲ MOUNTAIN ▲ MOUNTAIN RANGE ⚠ VOLCANO ∽ RIVER ⊚ LAKE ⊠ RESERVOIR

37 P6 **Delta** Colorado, C USA
36 K5 **Delta** Utah, W USA
77 T17 **Delta** ◈ *state* S Nigeria
55 Q6 **Delta Amacuro** *off.* Territorio Delta Amacuro. ◈ *federal district* NE Venezuela
39 S9 **Delta Junction** Alaska, USA
23 X11 **Deltona** Florida, SE USA
183 T5 **Delungra** New South Wales, SE Australia
154 C12 **Delvāda** Gujarāt, W India
61 B21 **Del Valle** Buenos Aires, E Argentina
Delvina *see* Delvinë
115 C15 **Delvináki** *var.* Dhelvinákion; *prev.* Pogónion. Ípeiros, W Greece
113 L23 **Delvinë** *var.* Delvina, *It.* Delvino. Vlorë, S Albania
Delvino *see* Delvinë
116 I7 **Delyatyn** Ivano-Frankivs'ka Oblast', W Ukraine
127 U5 **Dëma** ∽ W Russian Federation
105 O5 **Demanda, Sierra de la** ▲ W Spain
39 T5 **Demarcation Point** *headland* Alaska, USA
79 K21 **Demba** Kasai Occidental, C Dem. Rep. Congo
172 H13 **Dembéni** Grande Comore, NW Comoros
79 M15 **Dembia** Mbomou, SE Central African Republic
Dembidollo *see* Dembī Dolo
80 H13 **Dembī Dolo** *var.* Dembidollo. Oromo, C Ethiopia
152 K6 **Demchok** *var.* Dêmqog. China/India *see also* Dêmqog
152 L6 **Demchok** *var.* Dêmqog. *disputed region* China/India *see also* Dêmqog
98 I12 **De Meern** Utrecht, C Netherlands
99 I17 **Demer** ∽ C Belgium
64 H12 **Demerara Plain** *undersea feature* W Atlantic Ocean
64 H12 **Demerara Plateau** *undersea feature* W Atlantic Ocean
55 T9 **Demerara River** ∽ NE Guyana
126 H3 **Demidov** Smolenskaya Oblast', W Russian Federation
37 Q15 **Deming** New Mexico, SW USA
32 H6 **Deming** Washington, NW USA
58 E10 **Demini, Rio** ∽ NW Brazil
136 D13 **Demirci** Manisa, W Turkey
113 P19 **Demir Kapija** *prev.* Železna Vrata. SE FYR Macedonia
114 N11 **Demirköy** Kırklareli, NW Turkey
100 N9 **Demmin** Mecklenburg-Vorpommern, NE Germany
23 O5 **Demopolis** Alabama, S USA
31 N11 **Demotte** Indiana, N USA
158 F13 **Dêmqog** *var.* Demchok. China/India *see also* Demchok
152 L6 **Dêmqog** *var.* Demchok. *disputed region* China/India *see also* Demchok
171 Y13 **Demta** Papua, E Indonesia
122 H11 **Dem'yanka** ∽ C Russian Federation
124 H15 **Demyansk** Novgorodskaya Oblast', W Russian Federation
122 H10 **Dem'yanskoye** Tyumenskaya Oblast', C Russian Federation
103 P2 **Denain** Nord, N France
39 S10 **Denali** Alaska, USA
Denali *see* McKinley, Mount
81 M14 **Denan** Somali, E Ethiopia
Denau *see* Denov
97 J18 **Denbigh** *Wel.* Dinbych. NE Wales, UK
97 J18 **Denbigh** *cultural region* N Wales, UK
98 I6 **Den Burg** Noord-Holland, NW Netherlands
99 F18 **Dender** *Fr.* Dendre. ∽ W Belgium
99 F18 **Denderleeuw** Oost-Vlaanderen, NW Belgium
99 F17 **Dendermonde** *Fr.* Termonde. Oost-Vlaanderen, NW Belgium
Dendre *see* Dender
194 I9 **Dendtler Island** *island* Antarctica
98 P10 **Denekamp** Overijssel, E Netherlands
77 W12 **Dengas** Zinder, S Niger
Dêngkagoin *see* T'ewo
162 L13 **Dengkou** *var.* Bayan Gol. Nei Mongol Zizhiqu, N China
159 Q14 **Dêngqên** *var.* Gyamotang. Xizang Zizhiqu, W China
Deng Xian *see* Dengzhou
160 M7 **Dengzhou** *prev.* Deng Xian. Henan, C China
Dengzhou *see* Penglai
Den Haag *see* 's-Gravenhage
98 N9 **Den Ham** Overijssel, E Netherlands
180 H10 **Denham** Western Australia
44 J12 **Denham, Mount** ▲ C Jamaica
22 J8 **Denham Springs** Louisiana, S USA
98 I7 **Den Helder** Noord-Holland, NW Netherlands
105 T11 **Dénia** País Valenciano, E Spain
189 Q8 **Denig** W Nauru
183 N10 **Deniliquin** New South Wales, SE Australia
29 T14 **Denison** Iowa, C USA
25 U5 **Denison** Texas, SW USA
144 L8 **Denisovka** *prev.* Ordzhonikidze. Kostanay, N Kazakhstan
136 D15 **Denizli** Denizli, SW Turkey
136 D15 **Denizli** ◈ *province* SW Turkey
Denjong *see* Sikkim
183 S7 **Denman** New South Wales, SE Australia
195 Y10 **Denman Glacier** *glacier* Antarctica
21 R14 **Denmark** South Carolina, SE USA
95 G23 **Denmark** *off.* Kingdom of Denmark, *Dan.* Danmark; *anc.* Hafnia. ◆ *monarchy* N Europe
92 H1 **Denmark Strait** *var.* Danmarksstraedet. *strait* Greenland/Iceland
45 T11 **Dennery** E Saint Lucia
98 I7 **Den Oever** Noord-Holland, NW Netherlands
147 O13 **Denov** *Rus.* Denau. Surxondaryo Viloyati, S Uzbekistan
169 U17 **Denpasar** *prev.* Paloe. Bali, C Indonesia
116 E12 **Denta** Timiş, W Romania
21 Y3 **Denton** Maryland, NE USA
25 T6 **Denton** Texas, SW USA
186 G9 **D'Entrecasteaux Islands** *island group* SE PNG
37 T4 **Denver** *state capital* Colorado, C USA
37 T4 **Denver** ✕ Colorado, C USA
24 L6 **Denver City** Texas, SW USA
152 J9 **Deoband** Uttar Pradesh, N India
Deoghar *see* Devghar
154 E13 **Deolāli** Mahārāshtra, W India
154 I10 **Deori** Madhya Pradesh, C India
153 O12 **Deoria** Uttar Pradesh, N India
99 A17 **De Panne** West-Vlaanderen, W Belgium
54 M5 **Dependencia Federal** *off.* Territorio Dependencia Federal. ◈ *federal dependency* N Venezuela
Dependencia Federal, Territorio *see* Dependencia Federal
30 M7 **De Pere** Wisconsin, N USA
18 D10 **Depew** New York, NE USA
99 E17 **De Pinte** Oost-Vlaanderen, NW Belgium
25 V5 **Deport** Texas, SW USA
123 Q8 **Deputatskiy** Respublika Sakha (Yakutiya), NE Russian Federation
Dêqên *see* Dagzê
27 S13 **De Queen** Arkansas, C USA
22 G8 **De Quincy** Louisiana, S USA
81 J20 **Dera** *spring/well* S Kenya
Der'a/Derá/Déraa *see* Dar'ā
149 S10 **Dera Ghāzi Khān** *var.* Dera Ghāzikhān. Punjab, C Pakistan
149 S8 **Dera Ismāīl Khān** North-West Frontier Province, C Pakistan
113 L16 **Đeravica** ▲ S Serbia and Montenegro (Yugo.)
116 L6 **Derazhnya** Khmel'nyts'ka Oblast', W Ukraine
127 R17 **Derbent** Respublika Dagestan, SW Russian Federation
147 N13 **Derbent** Surxondaryo Viloyati, S Uzbekistan
Derbisīye *see* Darbāsīyah
79 M15 **Derbissaka** Mbomou, SE Central African Republic
180 L4 **Derby** Western Australia
97 M19 **Derby** C England, UK
27 N7 **Derby** Kansas, C USA
97 L18 **Derbyshire** *cultural region* C England, UK
112 O11 **Derdap** *physical region* E Serbia and Montenegro (Yugo.)
Derelí *see* Gónnoi
171 W13 **Derew** ∽ Papua, E Indonesia
127 R8 **Dergachi** Saratovskaya Oblast', W Russian Federation
Dergachi *see* Derhachi
97 C19 **Derg, Lough** *Ir.* Loch Deirgeirt. ◎ W Ireland
117 V5 **Derhachi** *Rus.* Dergachi. Kharkivs'ka Oblast', E Ukraine
22 G8 **De Ridder** Louisiana, S USA
137 P16 **Derik** Mardin, SE Turkey
83 E20 **Derm** Hardap, C Namibia
144 M14 **Dermentobe** *prev.* Dyurmen'tyube. Kzylorda, S Kazakhstan
27 W14 **Dermott** Arkansas, C USA
Dérna *see* Darnah
Dernberg, Cape *see* Dolphin Head
22 J11 **Dernieres, Isles** *island group* Louisiana, S USA
Dernis *see* Drniš
102 I4 **Déroute, Passage de la** *strait* Channel Islands/France
Derrá *see* Dar'ā
Derry *see* Londonderry
Dertona *see* Tortona
Dertosa *see* Tortosa
80 H8 **Derudeb** Red Sea, NE Sudan
112 H10 **Derventa** Republika Srpska, N Bosnia and Herzegovina
183 O16 **Derwent Bridge** Tasmania, SE Australia
183 O17 **Derwent, River** ∽ Tasmania, SE Australia
146 F10 **Derweze** *Rus.* Darvaza. Ahal Welaýaty, C Turkmenistan
Deržavinsk *see* Derzhavinsk
145 O9 **Derzhavinsk** *var.* Deržavinsk. Akmola, C Kazakhstan
Dés *see* Dej
57 J18 **Desaguadero** Puno, S Peru
57 J18 **Desaguadero, Río** ∽ Bolivia/Peru
191 W9 **Désappointement, Îles du** *island group* Îles Tuamotu, C French Polynesia
27 W11 **Des Arc** Arkansas, C USA
14 C10 **Desbarats** Ontario, S Canada
62 H13 **Descabezado Grande, Volcán** ⛰ C Chile
40 B2 **Descanso** Baja California, NW Mexico
102 L9 **Descartes** Indre-et-Loire, C France
11 T13 **Deschambault Lake** ◎ Saskatchewan, C Canada
Deschnaer Koppe *see* Velká Deštná
32 I11 **Deschutes River** ∽ Oregon, NW USA
80 J12 **Desē** *var.* Desse, *It.* Dessie. Amhara, N Ethiopia
63 I20 **Deseado, Río** ∽ S Argentina
106 F8 **Desenzano del Garda** Lombardia, N Italy
36 K3 **Deseret Peak** ▲ Utah, W USA
64 P6 **Deserta Grande** *island* Madeira, Portugal, NE Atlantic Ocean
64 P6 **Desertas, Ilhas** *island group* Madeira, Portugal, NE Atlantic Ocean
35 X16 **Desert Center** California, W USA
35 V15 **Desert Hot Springs** California, W USA
14 K10 **Désert, Lac** ◎ Québec, SE Canada
36 J2 **Desert Peak** ▲ Utah, W USA
31 R11 **Deshler** Ohio, N USA
Deshu *see* Deh Shū
Desiderii Fanum *see* St-Dizier
106 D7 **Desio** Lombardia, N Italy
115 E15 **Deskáti** *var.* Dheskáti. Dytikí Makedonía, N Greece
28 L2 **Des Lacs River** ∽ North Dakota, N USA
27 X6 **Desloge** Missouri, C USA
11 Q12 **Desmarais** Alberta, W Canada
29 Q10 **De Smet** South Dakota, N USA
29 V14 **Des Moines** *state capital* Iowa, C USA
17 N9 **Des Moines River** ∽ C USA
117 P4 **Desna** ∽ Russian Federation/Ukraine
116 G14 **Desnăţui** ∽ S Romania
63 F24 **Desolación, Isla** *island* S Chile
29 V14 **De Soto** Iowa, C USA
23 Q4 **De Soto Falls** *waterfall* Alabama, S USA
83 I25 **Despatch** Eastern Cape, S South Africa
105 N12 **Despeñaperros, Desfiladero de** *pass* S Spain
31 N10 **Des Plaines** Illinois, N USA
115 J21 **Despotikó** *island* Kykládes, Greece, Aegean Sea
112 N12 **Despotovac** Serbia, E Serbia and Montenegro (Yugo.)
101 M14 **Dessau** Sachsen-Anhalt, E Germany
Desse *see* Desē
99 J16 **Dessel** Antwerpen, N Belgium
Dessie *see* Desē
Destêrro *see* Florianópolis
23 P9 **Destin** Florida, SE USA
Deštná *see* Velká Deštná
193 T10 **Desventurados, Islas de los** *island group* W Chile
103 N1 **Desvres** Pas-de-Calais, N France
116 E12 **Deta** *Ger.* Detta. Timiş, W Romania
101 H14 **Detmold** Nordrhein-Westfalen, W Germany
31 S10 **Detroit** Michigan, N USA
25 W5 **Detroit** Texas, SW USA
31 S10 **Detroit** ∽ Canada/USA
29 S6 **Detroit Lakes** Minnesota, N USA
31 S10 **Detroit Metropolitan** ✕ Michigan, N USA
Detta *see* Deta
167 S10 **Det Udom** Ubon Ratchathani, E Thailand
111 K20 **Detva** *Hung.* Gyeva. Banskobystrický Kraj, C Slovakia
154 G13 **Deūlgaon Rāja** Mahārāshtra, C India
99 L15 **Deurne** Noord-Brabant, SE Netherlands
99 H16 **Deurne** ✕ (Antwerpen) Antwerpen, N Belgium
Deutsch-Brod *see* Havlíčkův Brod
Deutschendorf *see* Poprad
Deutsch-Eylau *see* Iława
109 Y6 **Deutschkreutz** Burgenland, E Austria
Deutsch Krone *see* Wałcz
Deutschland/Deutschland, Bundesrepublik *see* Germany
109 V9 **Deutschlandsberg** Steiermark, SE Austria
Deutsch-Südwestafrika *see* Namibia
109 Y3 **Deutsch-Wagram** Niederösterreich, E Austria
Deux-Ponts *see* Zweibrücken
14 I11 **Deux Rivieres** Ontario, SE Canada
102 K9 **Deux-Sèvres** ◈ *department* W France
116 G11 **Deva** *Ger.* Diemrich, *Hung.* Déva. Hunedoara, W Romania
Deva *see* Chester
Devana *see* Aberdeen
Devana Castra *see* Chester
Đevđelija *see* Gevgelija
136 L12 **Deveci Dağları** ▲ N Turkey
137 P15 **Devegeçidi Barajı** ⊠ SE Turkey
136 K15 **Develi** Kayseri, C Turkey
98 M11 **Deventer** Overijssel, E Netherlands
15 O10 **Devenyns, Lac** ◎ Québec, SE Canada
96 K8 **Deveron** ∽ NE Scotland, UK
153 R14 **Devghar** *prev.* Deoghar. Jhārkhand, NE India
27 R10 **Devil's Den** *plateau* Arkansas, C USA
35 R7 **Devils Gate** *pass* California, W USA
30 J2 **Devils Island** *island* Apostle Islands, Wisconsin, N USA
Devil's Island *see* Diable, Île du
29 P3 **Devils Lake** North Dakota, N USA
31 R10 **Devils Lake** ◎ Michigan, N USA
29 O3 **Devils Lake** ◎ North Dakota, N USA
35 W13 **Devils Playground** *desert* California, W USA
25 O11 **Devils River** ∽ Texas, SW USA
33 Y12 **Devils Tower** ▲ Wyoming, C USA
114 I11 **Devin** *prev.* Dovlen. Smolyan, SW Bulgaria
25 R12 **Devine** Texas, SW USA
152 H13 **Devli** Rājasthān, N India
Devne *see* Devnya
114 N8 **Devnya** *prev.* Devne. Varna, E Bulgaria
31 U14 **Devola** Ohio, N USA
Devoll *see* Devollit, Lumi i
113 M21 **Devollit, Lumi i** *var.* Devoll. ∽ SE Albania
11 Q14 **Devon** Alberta, SW Canada
97 I23 **Devon** *cultural region* SW England, UK
9 O4 **Devon Ice Cap** *ice feature* Nunavut, N Canada
8 N4 **Devon Island** *prev.* North Devon Island. *island* Parry Islands, Nunavut, NE Canada
183 O16 **Devonport** Tasmania, SE Australia
136 H11 **Devrek** Zonguldak, N Turkey
154 G10 **Dewās** Madhya Pradesh, C India
De Westerein *see* Zwaagwesteinde
27 P8 **Dewey** Oklahoma, C USA
Dewey *see* Culebra
98 M8 **De Wijk** Drenthe, NE Netherlands
27 W12 **De Witt** Arkansas, C USA
29 Z14 **De Witt** Iowa, C USA
29 R16 **De Witt** Nebraska, C USA
97 M17 **Dewsbury** N England, UK
161 Q10 **Dexing** Jiangxi, S China
27 Y8 **Dexter** Missouri, C USA
37 U14 **Dexter** New Mexico, SW USA
160 I8 **Deyang** Sichuan, C China
182 C4 **Dey-Dey, Lake** *salt lake* South Australia
143 S7 **Deyhūk** Yazd, E Iran
Deynau *see* Galkynyş
142 L8 **Dezfūl** *var.* Dizful. Khūzestān, SW Iran
131 X4 **Dezhneva, Mys** *headland* NE Russian Federation
161 P4 **Dezhou** Shandong, E China
Dezhou *see* Dechang
Dezh Shāhpūr *see* Marīvān
Dhahran *see* Az Zahrān
Dhahran Al Khobar *see* Az Zahrān al Khubar
153 U14 **Dhaka** *prev.* Dacca. ● (Bangladesh) Dhaka, C Bangladesh
153 T15 **Dhaka** ◈ *division* C Bangladesh
Dhali *see* Idálion
141 O15 **Dhamār** W Yemen
Dhambul *see* Taraz
154 K12 **Dhamtari** Chhattīsgarh, C India
153 Q15 **Dhanbād** Jhārkhand, NE India
152 L10 **Dhangadhi** *var.* Dhangarhi. Far Western, W Nepal
Dhangarhi *see* Dhangadhi
Dhank *see* Đank
153 R12 **Dhankuta** Eastern, E Nepal
152 I6 **Dhaola Dhār** ▲ NE India
154 F10 **Dhār** Madhya Pradesh, C India
153 R12 **Dharan** *var.* Dharan Bazar. Eastern, E Nepal
155 H21 **Dhārāpuram** Tamil Nādu, SE India
155 H20 **Dharmapuri** Tamil Nādu, SE India
155 H18 **Dharmavaram** Andhra Pradesh, E India
154 M11 **Dharmjaygarh** Chhattīsgarh, C India
Dharmsāla *see* Dharmshāla
152 I7 **Dharmshāla** *prev.* Dharmsāla. Himāchal Pradesh, N India
155 F17 **Dhārwād** *prev.* Dharwar. Karnātaka, SW India
Dharwar *see* Dhārwād
153 O10 **Dhaulāgiri** ▲ C Nepal
81 L18 **Dheere Laaq** *var.* Lak Dera, *It.* Lach Dera. *seasonal river* Kenya/Somalia
121 Q3 **Dhekéleia Sovereign Base Area** *UK military installation* E Cyprus
121 Q3 **Dhekélia** *Eng.* Dhekelia, *Gk.* Dekéleia. *UK air base* SE Cyprus
Dhelvinákion *see* Delvináki
113 M22 **Dhëmbelit, Majae** ▲ S Albania
154 O12 **Dhenkānāl** Orissa, E India
Dheskáti *see* Deskáti
138 G11 **Dhībān** 'Al Āşimah, NW Jordan
Dhidhimótikhon *see* Didymóteicho
Dhíkti Ori *see* Díkti
138 I12 **Dhirwah, Wādī adh** *dry watercourse* C Jordan
Dhístomon *see* Dístomo
Dhodhekánisos *see* Dodekánisos
Dhodhóni *see* Dodóni
Dhofar *see* Zufār
Dhomokós *see* Domokós
Dhond *see* Daund
155 H17 **Dhone** Andhra Pradesh, C India
154 B11 **Dhorāji** Gujarāt, W India
Dhráma *see* Dráma
154 C10 **Dhrāngadhra** Gujarāt, W India
Dhrepanon, Akrotírio *see* Drépano, Akrotírio
153 T13 **Dhuburi** Assam, NE India
154 F12 **Dhule** *prev.* Dhulia. Mahārāshtra, C India
Dhulia *see* Dhule
Dhún Dealgan, Cuan *see* Dundalk Bay
Dhún Droma, Cuan *see* Dundrum Bay
Dhún na nGall, Bá *see* Donegal Bay
Dhū Shaykh *see* Qazānīyah
80 Q13 **Dhuudo** Bari, NE Somalia
81 N15 **Dhuusa Marreeb** *var.* Dusa Marreb, *It.* Dusa Mareb. Galguduud, C Somalia
115 I24 **Día** *island* SE Greece
55 Y9 **Diable, Île du** *var.* Devil's Island. *island* N French Guiana
15 N12 **Diable, Rivière du** ∽ Québec, SE Canada
35 N8 **Diablo, Mount** ▲ California, W USA
35 O9 **Diablo Range** ▲ California, W USA
24 I8 **Diablo, Sierra** ▲ Texas, SW USA
45 O11 **Diablotins, Morne** ▲ N Dominica
77 N11 **Diafarabé** Mopti, C Mali
77 N11 **Diaka** ∽ SW Mali
Diakovár *see* Đakovo
76 I12 **Dialakoto** S Senegal
61 B18 **Diamante** Entre Ríos, E Argentina
62 I12 **Diamante, Río** ∽ C Argentina
59 M19 **Diamantina** Minas Gerais, SE Brazil
59 N17 **Diamantina, Chapada** ▲ E Brazil
173 U11 **Diamantina Fracture Zone** *tectonic feature* E Indian Ocean
181 T8 **Diamantina River** ∽ Queensland/South Australia
38 D9 **Diamond Head** *headland* O'ahu, Hawai'i, USA, C Pacific Ocean
37 P2 **Diamond Peak** ▲ Colorado, C USA
35 W5 **Diamond Peak** ▲ Nevada, W USA
Diamond State *see* Delaware
76 J11 **Diamou** Kayes, SW Mali
95 I23 **Dianalund** Vestsjælland, C Denmark
65 G25 **Diana's Peak** ▲ C Saint Helena
160 M16 **Dianbai** *var.* Shuidong. Guangdong, S China
160 G13 **Dian Chi** ◎ SW China
106 B10 **Diano Marina** Liguria, NW Italy
163 V11 **Diaobingshan** *var.* Tiefa. Liaoning, NE China
77 R13 **Diapaga** E Burkina
Diarbekr *see* Diyarbakır
107 J15 **Diavolo, Passo del** *pass* C Italy
61 B18 **Díaz** Santa Fe, C Argentina
141 W6 **Dibā al Ḩiṣn** *var.* Dibāh, Dibba. Ash Shāriqah, NE UAE
139 S3 **Dībaga** N Iraq
Dibāh *see* Dibā al Ḩiṣn
79 L22 **Dibaya** Kasai Occidental, S Dem. Rep. Congo
Dibba *see* Dibā al Ḩiṣn
195 W15 **Dibble Iceberg Tongue** *ice feature* Antarctica
113 L19 **Dibër** ◈ *district* E Albania
83 I20 **Dibete** Central, SE Botswana
25 W9 **Diboll** Texas, SW USA
Dibra *see* Debar
153 X11 **Dibrugarh** Assam, NE India
54 G4 **Dibulla** La Guajira, N Colombia
25 O5 **Dickens** Texas, SW USA
19 R2 **Dickey** Maine, NE USA
30 K9 **Dickeyville** Wisconsin, N USA
28 K5 **Dickinson** North Dakota, N USA
(0) E6 **Dickins Seamount** *undersea feature* NE Pacific Ocean
27 O13 **Dickson** Oklahoma, C USA
20 I9 **Dickson** Tennessee, S USA
Dicle *see* Tigris
Dicsőszentmárton *see* Târnăveni
98 M12 **Didam** Gelderland, E Netherlands
163 Y8 **Didao** Heilongjiang, NE China
76 L12 **Didiéni** Koulikoro, W Mali
Didimo *see* Dídymo
Didimotiho *see* Didymóteicho
81 K17 **Didimtu** *spring/well* NE Kenya
67 U9 **Didinga Hills** ▲ S Sudan
11 Q16 **Didsbury** Alberta, SW Canada
152 G11 **Dīdwāna** Rājasthān, N India
115 G20 **Dídymo** *var.* Didimo. ▲ S Greece
114 L12 **Didymóteicho** *var.* Dhidhimótikhon, Didimotiho. Anatolikí Makedonía kai Thráki, NE Greece
103 S13 **Die** Drôme, E France
77 O13 **Diébougou** SW Burkina
Diedenhofen *see* Thionville
11 S16 **Diefenbaker, Lake** ⊠ Saskatchewan, S Canada
62 H7 **Diego de Almagro** Atacama, N Chile
63 F23 **Diego de Almagro, Isla** *island* S Chile
61 A20 **Diego de Alvear** Santa Fe, C Argentina
173 Q7 **Diego Garcia** *island* S British Indian Ocean Territory
Diégo-Suarez *see* Antsirañana
99 M23 **Diekirch** Diekirch, C Luxembourg
99 L23 **Diekirch** ◈ *district* N Luxembourg
76 K11 **Diéma** Kayes, W Mali
101 H15 **Diemel** ∽ W Germany
98 I10 **Diemen** Noord-Holland, C Netherlands
Diemrich *see* Deva
167 R6 **Điện Biên** *var.* Bien Bien, Dien Bien Phu. Lai Châu, N Vietnam
Dien Bien Phu *see* Điện Biên
167 S7 **Diễn Châu** Nghệ An, N Vietnam
99 K18 **Diepenbeek** Limburg, NE Belgium
98 N11 **Diepenheim** Overijssel, E Netherlands
98 M10 **Diepenveen** Overijssel, E Netherlands
100 G12 **Diepholz** Niedersachsen, NW Germany
102 M3 **Dieppe** Seine-Maritime, N France
98 M12 **Dieren** Gelderland, E Netherlands
27 S13 **Dierks** Arkansas, C USA
99 J17 **Diest** Vlaams Brabant, C Belgium
108 F7 **Dietikon** Zürich, NW Switzerland
103 R13 **Dieulefit** Drôme, E France
103 T5 **Dieuze** Moselle, NE France
119 H15 **Dieveniškės** Vilnius, SE Lithuania
98 N7 **Diever** Drenthe, NE Netherlands
101 F17 **Diez** Rheinland-Pfalz, W Germany
77 Y12 **Diffa** Diffa, SE Niger
77 Y10 **Diffa** ◈ *department* SE Niger
99 L25 **Differdange** Luxembourg, SW Luxembourg
13 O16 **Digby** Nova Scotia, SE Canada
26 J5 **Dighton** Kansas, C USA
Dignano d'Istria *see* Vodnjan
103 T14 **Digne** *var.* Digne-les-Bains. Alpes-de-Haute-Provence, SE France
Digne-les-Bains *see* Digne
Digoel *see* Digul, Sungai
103 Q10 **Digoin** Saône-et-Loire, C France
171 Q8 **Digos** Mindanao, S Philippines
149 Q16 **Digri** Sind, SE Pakistan
171 Y14 **Digul Barat, Sungai** ∽ Papua, E Indonesia
171 Y15 **Digul, Sungai** *prev.* Digoel. ∽ Papua, E Indonesia
171 Z14 **Digul Timur, Sungai** ∽ Papua, E Indonesia
Dihang *see* Brahmaputra
153 X10 **Dihāng** ∽ NE India
Dihōk *see* Dahūk
81 L17 **Diinsoor** Bay, S Somalia
Dijlah *see* Tigris
99 H17 **Dijle** ∽ C Belgium
103 R8 **Dijon** *anc.* Dibio. Côte d'Or, C France
93 H14 **Dikanäs** Västerbotten, N Sweden
80 L12 **Dikhil** SW Djibouti
136 B13 **Dikili** İzmir, W Turkey
99 B17 **Diksmuide** *var.* Dixmuide, *Fr.* Dixmude. West-Vlaanderen, W Belgium
122 K7 **Dikson** Taymyrskiy (Dolgano-Nenetskiy) Avtonomnyy Okrug, N Russian Federation
115 K25 **Díkti** *var.* Dhíkti Ori. ▲ Kríti, Greece, E Mediterranean Sea
77 Z13 **Dikwa** Borno, NE Nigeria
81 J15 **Dīla** Southern, S Ethiopia
99 G18 **Dilbeek** Vlaams Brabant, C Belgium
171 Q16 **Dili** *var.* Dilli, Dilly. ○ (East Timor) N East Timor
77 Y11 **Dilia** *var.* Dillia. ∽ SE Niger
Dilijan *see* Delijan
167 U13 **Di Linh** Lâm Đông, S Vietnam
101 G16 **Dillenburg** Hessen, W Germany
25 Q13 **Dilley** Texas, SW USA
Dilli *see* Delhi, India
Dilli *see* Dili, East Timor
Dillia *see* Dilia
80 E11 **Dilling** *var.* Ad Dalanj. Southern Kordofan, C Sudan
101 D20 **Dillingen** Saarland, SW Germany
Dillingen *see* Dillingen an der Donau
101 J22 **Dillingen an der Donau** *var.* Dillingen. Bayern, S Germany
39 O13 **Dillingham** Alaska, USA
33 Q12 **Dillon** Montana, NW USA
21 T12 **Dillon** South Carolina, SE USA
31 T13 **Dillon Lake** ◎ Ohio, N USA
Dilly *see* Dili
Dilman *see* Salmās
79 K24 **Dilolo** Katanga, S Dem. Rep. Congo
115 J20 **Dílos** *island* Kykládes, Greece, Aegean Sea
141 Y11 **Dil', Ra's ad** *headland* E Oman
29 R5 **Dilworth** Minnesota, N USA
138 H7 **Dimashq** *var.* Ash Shām, Esh Sham, *Eng.* Damascus, *Fr.* Damas, *It.* Damasco. ● (Syria) Dimashq, SW Syria
138 I8 **Dimashq** *off.* Muḩāfaẓat Dimashq, *var.* Damascus, *Ar.* Ash Sham, Ash Shām, Damasco, Esh Sham, *Fr.* Damas. ◈ *governorate* S Syria
138 I7 **Dimashq** ✕ Dimashq, S Syria
79 L21 **Dimbelenge** Kasai Occidental, C Dem. Rep. Congo
77 N16 **Dimbokro** E Ivory Coast
182 L11 **Dimboola** Victoria, SE Australia
Dîmboviţa *see* Dâmboviţa
Dimitrov *see* Dymytrov
114 K11 **Dimitrovgrad** Khaskovo, S Bulgaria
127 R5 **Dimitrovgrad** Ul'yanovskaya Oblast', W Russian Federation
113 Q15 **Dimitrovgrad** *prev.* Caribrod. Serbia, SE Serbia and Montenegro (Yugo.)
Dimitrovo *see* Pernik
Dimlang *see* Vogel Peak
24 M3 **Dimmitt** Texas, SW USA
114 F7 **Dimovo** Vidin, NW Bulgaria
59 A16 **Dimpolis** Acre, W Brazil
115 O23 **Dimyliá** Ródos, Dodekánisos, Greece, Aegean Sea
171 Q6 **Dinagat Island** *island* S Philippines
153 S13 **Dinajpur** Rajshahi, NW Bangladesh
102 I6 **Dinan** Côtes d'Armor, NW France
99 I21 **Dinant** Namur, S Belgium
136 E15 **Dinar** Afyon, SW Turkey
112 F13 **Dinara** ▲ W Croatia
Dinara *see* Dinaric Alps
102 I5 **Dinard** Ille-et-Vilaine, NW France
112 F13 **Dinaric Alps** *var.* Dinara. ▲ Bosnia and Herzegovina/Croatia
143 N10 **Dīnār, Kūh-e** ▲ C Iran
Dinbych *see* Denbigh
155 H22 **Dindigul** Tamil Nādu, SE India
83 M19 **Dindiza** Gaza, S Mozambique
149 V7 **Dinga** Punjab, E Pakistan
79 H21 **Dinga** Bandundu, SW Dem. Rep. Congo
158 L16 **Dinggyê** *var.* Gyangkar. Xizang Zizhiqu, W China
97 A20 **Dingle** *Ir.* An Daingean. SW Ireland
97 A20 **Dingle Bay** *Ir.* Bá an Daingin. *bay* SW Ireland
18 I13 **Dingmans Ferry** Pennsylvania, NE USA

◆ Country ● Country Capital ◇ Dependent Territory ○ Dependent Territory Capital ◈ Administrative Region ✕ International Airport ▲ Mountain ▲ Mountain Range ⛰ Volcano ∽ River ◎ Lake ⊠ Reservoir

101 N22 **Dingolfing** Bayern, SE Germany
171 O1 **Dingras** Luzon, N Philippines
76 J13 **Dinguiraye** Haute-Guinée, N Guinea
96 I8 **Dingwall** N Scotland, UK
159 V10 **Dingxi** Gansu, C China
161 Q7 **Dingyuan** Anhui, E China
161 O3 **Dingzhou** *prev.* Ding Xian. Hebei, E China
167 U6 **Đinh Lâp** Lang Sơn, N Vietnam
167 T13 **Đinh Quan** Đông Nai, S Vietnam
100 E13 **Dinkel** ≈ Germany/Netherlands
101 J21 **Dinkelsbühl** Bayern, S Germany
101 D14 **Dinslaken** Nordrhein-Westfalen, W Germany
35 R11 **Dinuba** California, W USA
21 W7 **Dinwiddie** Virginia, NE USA
98 N13 **Dinxperlo** Gelderland, E Netherlands
115 F14 **Dió** *anc.* Dium. *site of ancient city* Kentrikí Makedonía, N Greece
Diófás *see* Nucet
76 M12 **Dioïla** Koulikoro, W Mali
115 G19 **Dióryga Korinthou** *Eng.* Corinth Canal. *canal* S Greece
76 G12 **Diouloulou** SW Senegal
77 N11 **Dioura** Mopti, W Mali
76 G11 **Diourbel** W Senegal
152 L10 **Dipayal** Far Western, W Nepal
121 R1 **Dipkarpaz** *Gk.* Rizokarpaso, Rizokárpason. NE Cyprus
149 R17 **Diplo** Sind, SE Pakistan
171 P7 **Dipolog** *var.* Dipolog City. Mindanao, S Philippines
185 C23 **Dipton** Southland, South Island, NZ
77 O10 **Diré** Tombouctou, C Mali
80 L13 **Dirē Dawa** Dirē Dawa, E Ethiopia
Dirfis *see* Dírfys
115 H18 **Dírfys** *var.* Dirfis. ⛰ Évvioa, C Greece
75 N9 **Dirj** *var.* Daraj, Darj. W Libya
180 G10 **Dirk Hartog Island** *island* Western Australia
77 Y8 **Dirkou** Agadez, NE Niger
181 X11 **Dirranbandi** Queensland, E Australia
81 O16 **Dirri** Galguduud, C Somalia
Dirschau *see* Tczew
37 N6 **Dirty Devil River** ≈ Utah, W USA
32 E10 **Disappointment, Cape** *headland* Washington, NW USA
180 L8 **Disappointment, Lake** *salt lake* Western Australia
183 R12 **Disaster Bay** *bay* New South Wales, SE Australia
44 J11 **Discovery Bay** C Jamaica
182 K13 **Discovery Bay** *inlet* SE Australia
67 Y15 **Discovery II Fracture Zone** *tectonic feature* SW Indian Ocean
Discovery Seamount/Discovery Seamounts *see* Discovery Tablemount
65 O19 **Discovery Tablemount** *var.* Discovery Seamount, Discovery Seamounts. *undersea feature* SW Indian Ocean
108 G9 **Disentis** *Rmsch.* Mustér. Graubünden, S Switzerland
39 O10 **Dishna River** ≈ Alaska, USA
195 X4 **Dismal Mountains** ⛰ Antarctica
28 M14 **Dismal River** ≈ Nebraska, C USA
Disna *see* Dzisna
99 L19 **Dison** Liège, E Belgium
153 V12 **Dispur** Assam, NE India
15 R11 **Disraeli** Québec, SE Canada
115 F18 **Dístomo** *prev.* Dhístomon. Stereá Ellás, C Greece
115 H18 **Dístos, Límni** ◎ Évvoia, C Greece
59 L18 **Distrito Federal** *Eng.* Federal District. ◈ *federal district* C Brazil
41 P14 **Distrito Federal** ◈ *federal district* S Mexico
54 L4 **Distrito Federal** *off.* Territorio Distrito Federal. ◈ *federal district* N Venezuela
Distrito Federal, Territorio *see* Distrito Federal
116 J10 **Ditrău** *Hung.* Ditró. Harghita, C Romania
Ditró *see* Ditrău
154 B12 **Diu** Damān and Diu, W India
Dium *see* Dió
109 S13 **Divača** SW Slovenia
102 K5 **Dives** ≈ N France
Divichi *see* Däväçi
33 Q11 **Divide** Montana, NW USA
Divin *see* Dzivin
83 N18 **Divinhe** Sofala, E Mozambique
59 L20 **Divinópolis** Minas Gerais, SE Brazil
127 N13 **Divnoye** Stavropol'skiy Kray, SW Russian Federation
76 M17 **Divo** S Ivory Coast
Divodurum Mediomatricum *see* Metz
137 N13 **Divriği** Sivas, C Turkey
Diwaniyah *see* Ad Dīwānīyah
14 J10 **Dix Milles, Lac** ◎ Québec, SE Canada
14 M8 **Dix Milles, Lac des** ◎ Québec, SE Canada
Dixmude/Dixmuide *see* Diksmuide
35 N7 **Dixon** California, W USA
30 L10 **Dixon** Illinois, N USA
20 I6 **Dixon** Kentucky, S USA
27 V6 **Dixon** Missouri, C USA
37 S9 **Dixon** New Mexico, SW USA
39 Y15 **Dixon Entrance** *strait* Canada/USA
18 D14 **Dixonville** Pennsylvania, NE USA
137 T13 **Diyadin** Ağrı, E Turkey
139 V5 **Diyālá, Nahr** *var.* Rudkhaneh-ye Sīrvān, Sīrwan. ≈ Iran/Iraq *see also* Sīrvān, Rudkhaneh-ye
137 P15 **Diyarbakır** *var.* Diarbekr; *anc.* Amida. Diyarbakır, SE Turkey
137 P15 **Diyarbakır** *var.* Diarbekr. ◈ *province* SE Turkey
Dizful *see* Dezfūl
79 F16 **Dja** ≈ SE Cameroon
Djadié *see* Zadié
77 X7 **Djado** Agadez, NE Niger
77 X6 **Djado, Plateau du** ⛰ NE Niger
Djailolo *see* Halmahera, Pulau
Djajapura *see* Jayapura
Djakarta *see* Jakarta
Djakovica *see* Đakovica
Djakovo *see* Đakovo
79 G20 **Djambala** Plateaux, C Congo
Djambi *see* Jambi
Djambi *see* Hari, Batang, Sumatera, W Indonesia
74 M9 **Djanet** E Algeria
74 M11 **Djanet** *prev.* Fort Charlet. SE Algeria
Djatiwangi *see* Jatiwangi
Djaul *see* Dyaul Island
Djawa *see* Jawa
Djéblé *see* Jablah
78 I10 **Djédaa** Batha, C Chad
74 J6 **Djelfa** *var.* El Djelfa. N Algeria
79 M14 **Djéma** Haut-Mbomou, E Central African Republic
Djeneponto *see* Jeneponto
77 N12 **Djenné** *var.* Jenné. Mopti, C Mali
Djérablous *see* Jarābulus
Djerba *see* Jerba, Île de
79 F15 **Djérem** ≈ C Cameroon
Djevdjelija *see* Gevgelija
77 P11 **Djibo** N Burkina
80 L12 **Djibouti** *var.* Jibuti. ● (Djibouti) E Djibouti
80 L12 **Djibouti** *off.* Republic of Djibouti, *var.* Jibuti; *prev.* French Somaliland, French Territory of the Afars and Issas, *Fr.* Côte Française des Somalis, Territoire Français des Afars et des Issas. ◆ *republic* E Africa
80 L12 **Djibouti** ✕ C Djibouti
Djidjel/Djidjelli *see* Jijel
55 W10 **Djoemoe** Sipaliwini, C Suriname
Djokjakarta *see* Yogyakarta
79 K21 **Djoku-Punda** Kasai Occidental, S Dem. Rep. Congo
79 K18 **Djolu** Equateur, N Dem. Rep. Congo
Djorče Petrov *see* Đorče Petrov
79 F17 **Djoua** ≈ Congo/Gabon
77 R14 **Djougou** W Benin
79 F16 **Djoum** Sud, S Cameroon
78 I8 **Djourab, Erg du** *dunes* N Chad
79 P17 **Djugu** Orientale, NE Dem. Rep. Congo
Djumbir *see* Ďumbier
92 L3 **Djúpivogur** Austurland, SE Iceland
94 L13 **Djura** Dalarna, C Sweden
Djurdjevac *see* Đurđevac
83 G18 **D'Kar** Ghanzi, NW Botswana
197 U6 **Dmitriya Lapteva, Proliv** *strait* N Russian Federation
126 J7 **Dmitriyev-L'govskiy** Kurskaya Oblast', W Russian Federation
Dmitriyevsk *see* Makiyivka
126 K3 **Dmitrov** Moskovskaya Oblast', W Russian Federation
Dmitrovichi *see* Dzmitravichy
126 J6 **Dmitrovsk-Orlovskiy** Orlovskaya Oblast', W Russian Federation
117 R3 **Dmytrivka** Chernihivs'ka Oblast', N Ukraine
Dnepr *see* Dnieper
Dneprodzerzhinsk *see* Dniprodzerzhyns'k
Dneprodzerzhinskoye Vodokhranilishche *see* Dniprodzerzhyns'ke Vodoskhovyshche
Dnepropetrovsk *see* Dnipropetrovs'k
Dnepropetrovskaya Oblast' *see* Dnipropetrovs'ka Oblast'
Dneprorudnoye *see* Dniprorudne
Dneprovskiy Liman *see* Dniprovs'kyy Lyman
Dneprovsko-Bugskiy Kanal *see* Dnyaprowska-Buhski, Kanal
Dnestr *see* Dniester
Dnestrovskiy Liman *see* Dnistrovs'kyy Lyman
86 H11 **Dnieper** *Bel.* Dnyapro, *Rus.* Dnepr, *Ukr.* Dnipro. ≈ E Europe
117 P3 **Dnieper Lowland** *Bel.* Prydnyaprowskaya Nizina, *Ukr.* Prydniprovs'ka Nyzovyna. *lowlands* Belarus/Ukraine
116 M8 **Dniester** *Rom.* Nistru, *Rus.* Dnestr, *Ukr.* Dnister; *anc.* Tyras. ≈ Moldova/Ukraine
Dnipro *see* Dnieper
117 T7 **Dniprodzerzhyns'k** *Rus.* Dneprodzerzhinsk; *prev.* Kamenskoye. Dnipropetrovs'ka Oblast', E Ukraine
117 T7 **Dniprodzerzhyns'ke Vodoskhovyshche** *Rus.* Dneprodzerzhinskoye Vodokhranilishche. ⊞ C Ukraine
117 U7 **Dnipropetrovs'k** *Rus.* Dnepropetrovsk; *prev.* Yekaterinoslav. Dnipropetrovs'ka Oblast', E Ukraine
117 U8 **Dnipropetrovs'k** ✕ Dnipropetrovs'ka Oblast', S Ukraine
Dnipropetrovs'k *see* Dnipropetrovs'ka Oblast'
117 T7 **Dnipropetrovs'ka Oblast'** *var.* Dnipropetrovs'k, *Rus.* Dnepropetrovskaya Oblast'. ◈ *province* E Ukraine
117 U9 **Dniprorudne** *Rus.* Dneprorudnoye. Zaporiz'ka Oblast', SE Ukraine
117 Q11 **Dniprovs'kyy Lyman** *Rus.* Dneprovskiy Liman. *bay* S Ukraine
Dnister *see* Dniester
117 O11 **Dnistrovs'kyy Lyman** *Rus.* Dnestrovskiy Liman. *inlet* S Ukraine
124 G14 **Dno** Pskovskaya Oblast', W Russian Federation
Dnyapro *see* Dnieper
119 H20 **Dnyaprowska-Buhski, Kanal** *Rus.* Dneprovsko-Bugskiy Kanal. *canal* SW Belarus
13 O14 **Doaktown** New Brunswick, SE Canada
78 H13 **Doba** Logone-Oriental, S Chad
118 E9 **Dobele** *Ger.* Doblen. Dobele, W Latvia
101 N16 **Döbeln** Sachsen, E Germany
171 U12 **Doberai, Jazirah** *Dut.* Vogelkop. *peninsula* Papua, E Indonesia
110 F10 **Dobiegniew** *Ger.* Lubuskie, W Poland
Doblen *see* Dobele
81 K18 **Dobli** *spring/well* SW Somalia
112 H11 **Doboj** Republika Srpska, N Bosnia and Herzegovina
110 L8 **Dobre Miasto** *Ger.* Guttstadt. Warmińsko-Mazurskie, NE Poland
114 N7 **Dobrich** *Rom.* Bazargic; *prev.* Tolbukhin. Dobrich, NE Bulgaria
114 N7 **Dobrich** ◈ *province* NE Bulgaria
126 M8 **Dobrinka** Lipetskaya Oblast', W Russian Federation
126 M7 **Dobrinka** Volgogradskaya Oblast', SW Russian Federation
Dobrla Vas *see* Eberndorf
111 I15 **Dobrodzień** *Ger.* Guttentag. Opolskie, S Poland
Dobrogea *see* Dobruja
117 W7 **Dobropillya** *Rus.* Dobropol'ye. Donets'ka Oblast', SE Ukraine
Dobropol'ye *see* Dobropillya
117 P8 **Dobrovelychkivka** Kirovohrads'ka Oblast', C Ukraine
Dobrudja/Dobrudzha *see* Dobruja
114 O7 **Dobruja** *var.* Dobrudja, *Bul.* Dobrudzha, *Rom.* Dobrogea. *physical region* Bulgaria/Romania
119 P19 **Dobrush** Homyel'skaya Voblasts', SE Belarus
125 U14 **Dobryanka** Permskaya Oblast', NW Russian Federation
117 P2 **Dobryanka** Chernihivs'ka Oblast', N Ukraine
Dobryn' *see* Dabryn'
21 R8 **Dobson** North Carolina, SE USA
59 N20 **Doce, Rio** ≈ SE Brazil
93 I16 **Docksta** Västernorrland, C Sweden
41 N10 **Doctor Arroyo** Nuevo León, NE Mexico
62 L4 **Doctor Pedro P. Peña** Boquerón, W Paraguay
171 S11 **Dodaga** Pulau Halmahera, E Indonesia
155 G21 **Dodda Betta** ▲ S India
Dodecanese *see* Dodekánisos
115 M22 **Dodekánisos** *var.* Nóties Sporádes, *Eng.* Dodecanese; *prev.* Dhodhekánisos. *island group* SE Greece
26 J6 **Dodge City** Kansas, C USA
30 K9 **Dodgeville** Wisconsin, N USA
97 H25 **Dodman Point** *headland* SW England, UK
81 J14 **Dodola** Oromo, C Ethiopia
81 H22 **Dodoma** ● (Tanzania) Dodoma, C Tanzania
81 H22 **Dodoma** ◈ *region* C Tanzania
115 C16 **Dodóni** *var.* Dhodhóni. *site of ancient city* Ípeiros, W Greece
33 U7 **Dodson** Montana, NW USA
25 P3 **Dodson** Texas, SW USA
98 M12 **Doesburg** Gelderland, E Netherlands
98 N12 **Doetinchem** Gelderland, E Netherlands
158 L12 **Dogai Coring** *var.* Lake Montcalm. ◎ W China
137 N15 **Doğanşehir** Malatya, C Turkey
84 E9 **Dogger Bank** *undersea feature* C North Sea
23 S10 **Dog Island** *island* Florida, SE USA
14 C7 **Dog Lake** ◎ Ontario, S Canada
106 B9 **Dogliani** Piemonte, NE Italy
164 H11 **Dōgo** *island* Oki-shotō, SW Japan
Do Gonbadān *see* Dow Gonbadān
77 S12 **Dogondoutchi** Dosso, SW Niger
Dogrular *see* Pravda
137 T13 **Doğubayazıt** Ağrı, E Turkey
137 P12 **Doğu Karadeniz Dağları** *var.* Anadolu Dağları. ⛰ NE Turkey
158 K16 **Dogxung Zangbo** ≈ W China
Doha *see* Ad Dawḩah
Dohad *see* Dāhod
Dohuk *see* Dahūk
159 N16 **Doilungdêqên** *var.* Namka. Xizang Zizhiqu, W China
114 F12 **Doïranis, Límnis** *Bul.* Ezero Doyransko. ◎ N Greece
Doire *see* Londonderry
99 H22 **Doische** Namur, S Belgium
59 P17 **Dois de Julho** ✕ (Salvador) Bahia, NE Brazil
60 H12 **Dois Vizinhos** Paraná, S Brazil
80 H10 **Doka** Gedaref, E Sudan
Doka *see* Kéita, Bahr
139 T3 **Dokan** *var.* Dūkān. E Iraq
94 H13 **Dokka** Oppland, S Norway
98 L5 **Dokkum** Friesland, N Netherlands
98 L5 **Dokkumer Ee** ≈ N Netherlands
76 K13 **Doko** Haute-Guinée, NE Guinea
Dokshitsy *see* Dokshytsy
118 K13 **Dokshytsy** *Rus.* Dokshitsy. Vitsyebskaya Voblasts', N Belarus
117 X8 **Dokuchayevs'k** *var.* Dokuchayevsk. Donets'ka Oblast', SE Ukraine
Dolak, Pulau *see* Yos Sudarso, Pulau
29 P9 **Doland** South Dakota, N USA
63 J18 **Dolavón** Chaco, S Argentina
15 P6 **Dolbeau** Québec, SE Canada
102 I5 **Dol-de-Bretagne** Ille-et-Vilaine, NW France
64 J13 **Doldrums Fracture Zone** *tectonic feature* W Atlantic Ocean
103 S8 **Dôle** Jura, E France
97 J19 **Dolgellau** NW Wales, UK
Dolginovo *see* Dawhinava
Dolgi, Ostrov *see* Dolgiy, Ostrov
127 U2 **Dolgiy, Ostrov** *var.* Ostrov Dolgi. *island* NW Russian Federation
162 J9 **Dölgöön** Övörhangay, C Mongolia
107 C20 **Dolianova** Sardegna, Italy, C Mediterranean Sea
Dolina *see* Dolyna
123 T13 **Dolinsk** Ostrov Sakhalin, Sakhalinskaya Oblast', SE Russian Federation
Dolinskaya *see* Dolyns'ka
79 F21 **Dolisie** *prev.* Loubomo. Le Niari, S Congo
116 G14 **Dolj** ◈ *county* SW Romania
98 P5 **Dollard** *bay* NW Germany
194 J5 **Dolleman Island** *island* Antarctica
114 I8 **Dolni Dŭbnik** Pleven, N Bulgaria
114 F8 **Dolni Lom** Vidin, NW Bulgaria
Dolnja Lendava *see* Lendava
114 K9 **Dolno Panicherevo** *var.* Panicherevo. Sliven, C Bulgaria
111 F14 **Dolnośląskie** ◈ *province* SW Poland
111 K18 **Dolný Kubín** *Hung.* Alsókubin. Žilinský Kraj, N Slovakia
106 H8 **Dolo** Veneto, NE Italy
Dolomites/Dolomiti *see* Dolomitiche, Alpi
106 H6 **Dolomitiche, Alpi** *var.* Dolomiti, *Eng.* Dolomites. ⛰ NE Italy
Dolonnur *see* Duolun
162 K10 **Doloon** Ömnögovĭ, S Mongolia
61 E21 **Dolores** Buenos Aires, E Argentina
42 E3 **Dolores** Petén, N Guatemala
171 Q5 **Dolores** Samar, C Philippines
105 S12 **Dolores** País Valenciano, E Spain
61 D19 **Dolores** Soriano, SW Uruguay
41 N12 **Dolores Hidalgo** *var.* Ciudad de Dolores Hidalgo. Guanajuato, C Mexico
8 J7 **Dolphin and Union Strait** *strait* Northwest Territories / Nunavut, N Canada
65 D23 **Dolphin, Cape** *headland* East Falkland, Falkland Islands
44 H12 **Dolphin Head** *hill* W Jamaica
83 B21 **Dolphin Head** *var.* Cape Dernberg. *headland* SW Namibia
110 G12 **Dolsk** *Ger.* Dolzig. Wielkolpolskie, C Poland
167 S8 **Đô Lương** Nghê An, N Vietnam
116 I6 **Dolyna** *Rus.* Dolina. Ivano-Frankivs'ka Oblast', W Ukraine
117 R8 **Dolyns'ka** *Rus.* Dolinskaya. Kirovohrads'ka Oblast', S Ukraine
Dolzig *see* Dolsk
Domachëvo/Domaczewo *see* Damachava
117 P9 **Domanivka** Mykolayivs'ka Oblast', S Ukraine
153 S13 **Domar** Rajshahi, N Bangladesh
108 I9 **Domat/Ems** Graubünden, SE Switzerland
111 A18 **Domažlice** *Ger.* Taus. Plzeňský Kraj, W Czech Republic
127 X8 **Dombarovskiy** Orenburgskaya Oblast', W Russian Federation
94 G10 **Dombås** Oppland, S Norway
83 M17 **Dombe** Manica, C Mozambique
82 A13 **Dombe Grande** Benguela, C Angola
103 R10 **Dombes** *physical region* E France
111 I25 **Dombóvár** Tolna, S Hungary
99 D14 **Domburg** Zeeland, SW Netherlands
58 L13 **Dom Eliseu** Pará, NE Brazil
Domel Island *see* Letsôk-aw Kyun
103 O11 **Dôme, Puy de** ▲ C France
36 H13 **Dome Rock Mountains** ⛰ Arizona, SW USA
Domesnes, Cape *see* Kolkasrags
62 G8 **Domeyko** Atacama, N Chile
62 H5 **Domeyko, Cordillera** ⛰ N Chile
102 K5 **Domfront** Orne, N France
171 X13 **Dom, Gunung** ▲ Papua, E Indonesia
45 X11 **Dominica** *off.* Commonwealth of Dominica. ◆ *republic* E West Indies
47 S3 **Dominica** *island* Dominica
Dominica Channel *see* Martinique Passage
43 N15 **Dominical** Puntarenas, SE Costa Rica
45 Q8 **Dominican Republic** ◆ *republic* C West Indies
45 X11 **Dominica Passage** *passage* E Caribbean Sea
99 K14 **Dommel** ≈ S Netherlands
81 O14 **Domo** Somali, E Ethiopia
126 L4 **Domodedovo** ✕ (Moskva) Moskovskaya Oblast', W Russian Federation
106 C6 **Domodossola** Piemonte, NE Italy
115 F17 **Domokós** *var.* Dhomokós. Stereá Ellás, C Greece
172 I14 **Domoni** Anjouan, SE Comoros
61 G16 **Dom Pedrito** Rio Grande do Sul, S Brazil
Dompoe *see* Dompu
170 M16 **Dompu** *prev.* Dompoe. Sumbawa, C Indonesia
Domschale *see* Domžale
62 H13 **Domuyo, Volcán** ⩚ W Argentina
109 U11 **Domžale** *Ger.* Domschale. C Slovenia
127 O10 **Don** *var.* Duna, Tanais. ≈ SW Russian Federation
96 K9 **Don** ≈ NE Scotland, UK
182 M11 **Donald** Victoria, SE Australia
22 J9 **Donaldsonville** Louisiana, S USA
23 S8 **Donalsonville** Georgia, SE USA
Donau *see* Danube
101 G23 **Donaueschingen** Baden-Württemberg, SW Germany
101 K22 **Donaumoos** *wetland* S Germany
101 K22 **Donauwörth** Bayern, S Germany
109 U7 **Donawitz** Steiermark, SE Austria
117 X7 **Donbass** *industrial region* Russian Federation/Ukraine
104 K11 **Don Benito** Extremadura, W Spain
97 M17 **Doncaster** *anc.* Danum. N England, UK
44 K12 **Don Christophers Point** *headland* C Jamaica
55 V9 **Donderkamp** Sipaliwini, NW Suriname
82 B12 **Dondo** Cuanza Norte, NW Angola
171 O12 **Dondo** Sulawesi, N Indonesia
83 N17 **Dondo** Sofala, C Mozambique
155 K26 **Dondra Head** *headland* S Sri Lanka
Dondușani *see* Dondușeni
116 M8 **Dondușeni** *var.* Dondușani, *Rus.* Dondyushany. N Moldova
Dondyushany *see* Dondușeni
97 D15 **Donegal** *Ir.* Dún na nGall. NW Ireland
97 D14 **Donegal** *Ir.* Dún na nGall. *cultural region* NW Ireland
97 C15 **Donegal Bay** *Ir.* Bá Dhún na nGall. *bay* NW Ireland
84 K10 **Donets** ≈ Russian Federation/Ukraine
117 X8 **Donets'k** *Rus.* Donetsk; *prev.* Stalino. Donets'ka Oblast', E Ukraine
117 W8 **Donets'k** ✕ Donets'ka Oblast', E Ukraine
Donets'k *see* Donets'ka Oblast'
117 W8 **Donets'ka Oblast'** *var.* Donets'k, *Rus.* Donetskaya Oblast'; *prev. Rus.* Stalinskaya Oblast'. ◈ *province* SE Ukraine
Donetskaya Oblast' *see* Donets'ka Oblast'
67 P8 **Donga** ≈ Cameroon/Nigeria
157 O13 **Dongchuan** Yunnan, SW China
99 I14 **Dongen** Noord-Brabant, S Netherlands
160 K17 **Dongfang** *var.* Basuo. Hainan, S China
163 Z7 **Dongfanghong** Heilongjiang, NE China
163 W11 **Dongfeng** Jilin, NE China
171 N12 **Donggala** Sulawesi, C Indonesia
163 V13 **Donggang** *var.* Dadong, *prev.* Donggou. Liaoning, NE China
Donggou *see* Donggang
161 O14 **Dongguan** Guangdong, S China
167 T9 **Đông Ha** Quang Tri, C Vietnam
Dong Hai *see* East China Sea
160 M16 **Donghai Dao** *island* S China
162 I12 **Dong He** *Mong.* Narin Gol. ≈ N China
167 T9 **Đông Hơi** Quang Binh, C Vietnam
108 H10 **Dongio** Ticino, S Switzerland
Dongkan *see* Binhai
160 L11 **Dongkou** Hunan, S China
Dongliao *see* Liaoyuan
Dong-nai *see* Đông Nai, Sông
167 U13 **Đông Nai, Sông** *var.* Dong-nai, Dong Noi, Donnai. ≈ S Vietnam
161 N14 **Dongnan Qiuling** *plateau* SE China
163 Y9 **Dongning** Heilongjiang, NE China
Dong Noi *see* Đông Nai, Sông
83 C14 **Dongo** Huíla, C Angola
80 E7 **Dongola** *var.* Donqola, Dunqulah. Northern, N Sudan
79 I17 **Dongou** La Likouala, NE Congo
Đông Phu *see* Đông Xoai
Dongping *see* Anhua
Dong Rak, Phanom *see* Dângrêk, Chuŏr Phnum
161 Q14 **Dongshan Dao** *island* SE China
Dongsheng *see* Ordos
161 R7 **Dongtai** Jiangsu, E China
161 N10 **Dongting Hu** *var.* Tung-t'ing Hu. ◎ S China
161 P10 **Dongxiang** *var.* Xiaogang. Jiangxi, S China
167 T13 **Đông Xoai** *var.* Đông Phu. Sông Be, S Vietnam
161 Q4 **Dongying** Shandong, E China
27 X8 **Doniphan** Missouri, C USA
Donja Łużyca *see* Niederlausitz
10 G7 **Donjek** ≈ Yukon Territory, W Canada
112 E11 **Donji Lapac** Lika-Senj, W Croatia
112 H8 **Donji Miholjac** Osijek-Baranja, NE Croatia
112 P12 **Donji Milanovac** Serbia, E Serbia and Montenegro (Yugo.)
112 G12 **Donji Vakuf** *var.* Srbobran, Federacija Bosna I Hercegovina, C Bosnia & Herzegovina
98 M6 **Donkerbroek** Friesland, N Netherlands
167 P11 **Don Muang** ✕ (Krung Thep) Nonthaburi, C Thailand
25 S17 **Donna** Texas, SW USA
15 Q10 **Donnacona** Québec, SE Canada
Donnai *see* Đông Nai, Sông
29 Y16 **Donnellson** Iowa, C USA
11 O13 **Donnelly** Alberta, W Canada
35 H6 **Donner Pass** *pass* California, W USA
101 F19 **Donnersberg** ▲ W Germany
Donoso *see* Miguel de la Borda
105 P2 **Donostia-San Sebastián** País Vasco, N Spain
115 K21 **Donoússa** *island* Kykládes, Greece, Aegean Sea
35 P8 **Don Pedro Reservoir** ⊞ California, W USA
Donqola *see* Dongola
126 L5 **Donskoy** Tul'skaya Oblast', W Russian Federation
81 L16 **Doolow** Somali, E Ethiopia
39 Q7 **Doonerak, Mount** ▲ Alaska, USA
98 J12 **Doorn** Utrecht, C Netherlands
Doornik *see* Tournai
31 N6 **Door Peninsula** *peninsula* Wisconsin, N USA
80 P13 **Dooxo Nugaaleed** *var.* Nogal Valley. *valley* E Somalia
Do Qu *see* Da Qu
106 B7 **Dora Baltea** *anc.* Duria Major. ≈ NW Italy
180 K7 **Dora, Lake** *salt lake* Western Australia
106 A8 **Dora Riparia** *anc.* Duria Minor. ≈ NW Italy
Dorbiljin *see* Emin
Dorbod/Dorbod Mongolzu Zizhixian *see* Taikang
113 N18 **Đorče Petrov** *var.* Djorče Petrov, Gorče Petrov. N FYR Macedonia
14 F16 **Dorchester** Ontario, S Canada
97 L24 **Dorchester** *anc.* Durnovaria. S England, UK
9 P7 **Dorchester, Cape** *headland* Baffin Island, Nunavut, NE Canada
83 D19 **Dordabis** Khomas, C Namibia
102 L12 **Dordogne** ◈ *department* SW France
103 N12 **Dordogne** ≈ W France
98 H13 **Dordrecht** *var.* Dordt, Dort. Zuid-Holland, SW Netherlands
Dordt *see* Dordrecht
103 P11 **Dore** ≈ C France
11 S13 **Doré Lake** Saskatchewan, C Canada
103 O12 **Dore, Monts** ⛰ C France
101 M23 **Dorfen** Bayern, SE Germany
107 D18 **Dorgali** Sardegna, Italy, C Mediterranean Sea
159 N11 **Dorgê Co** *var.* Elsen Nur. ◎ C China
162 F7 **Dörgön Nuur** ◎ NW Mongolia
77 Q12 **Dori** N Burkina
83 E24 **Doring** ≈ S South Africa
101 E16 **Dormagen** Nordrhein-Westfalen, W Germany
103 P4 **Dormans** Marne, N France
108 E6 **Dornach** Solothurn, NW Switzerland
Dorna Watra *see* Vatra Dornei
108 J7 **Dornbirn** Vorarlberg, W Austria
96 I7 **Dornoch** N Scotland, UK
96 J7 **Dornoch Firth** *inlet* N Scotland, UK
163 P7 **Dornod** ◈ *province* E Mongolia
163 N10 **Dornogovĭ** ◈ *province* SE Mongolia
77 P10 **Doro** Tombouctou, S Mali
116 L14 **Dorobanțu** Călărași, S Romania
111 J22 **Dorog** Komárom-Esztergom, N Hungary
126 I4 **Dorogobuzh** Smolenskaya Oblast', W Russian Federation
116 K8 **Dorohoi** Botoșani, NE Romania
93 H15 **Dorotea** Västerbotten, N Sweden
Dorpat *see* Tartu
180 G10 **Dorre Island** *island* Western Australia
183 U5 **Dorrigo** New South Wales, SE Australia
35 N1 **Dorris** California, W USA
14 H13 **Dorset** Ontario, SE Canada
97 K23 **Dorset** *cultural region* S England, UK
101 E14 **Dorsten** Nordrhein-Westfalen, W Germany
Dort *see* Dordrecht
101 F15 **Dortmund** Nordrhein-Westfalen, W Germany
100 F12 **Dortmund-Ems-Kanal** *canal* W Germany
136 L17 **Dörtyol** Hatay, S Turkey
142 L7 **Do Rūd** *var.* Dow Rūd, Durud. Lorestān, W Iran
79 O15 **Doruma** Orientale, N Dem. Rep. Congo
15 O12 **Dorval** ✕ (Montréal) Québec, SE Canada
45 T5 **Dos Bocas, Lago** ◎ C Puerto Rico
104 K14 **Dos Hermanas** Andalucía, S Spain

◆ Country ● Country Capital ◇ Dependent Territory ○ Dependent Territory Capital ◈ Administrative Region ✕ International Airport ▲ Mountain ⛰ Mountain Range ⩚ Volcano ≈ River ◎ Lake ⊞ Reservoir

Dospad Dagh see Rhodope Mountains
35 P10 **Dos Palos** California, W USA
114 I11 **Dospat** Smolyan, S Bulgaria
114 H11 **Dospat, Yazovir** ⊞ SW Bulgaria
100 M11 **Dosse** ≈ NE Germany
77 S12 **Dosso** Dosso, SW Niger
77 S12 **Dosso** ◈ department SW Niger
144 G12 **Dossor** Atyrau, SW Kazakhstan
147 O10 **Do'stlik** Jizzax Viloyati, C Uzbekistan
147 V9 **Dostuk** Narynskaya Oblast', C Kyrgyzstan
145 X13 **Dostyk** prev. Druzhba. Almaty, SE Kazakhstan
23 R7 **Dothan** Alabama, S USA
39 T9 **Dot Lake** Alaska, USA
118 F12 **Dotnuva** Kaunas, C Lithuania
99 D19 **Dottignies** Hainaut, W Belgium
103 P2 **Douai** prev. Douay, anc. Duacum. Nord, N France
14 L9 **Douaire, Lac** ◎ Québec, SE Canada
79 D16 **Douala** var. Duala. Littoral, W Cameroon
79 D16 **Douala** ✕ Littoral, W Cameroon
102 F6 **Douarnenez** Finistère, NW France
102 E6 **Douarnenez, Baie de** bay NW France
Douay see Douai
25 O6 **Double Mountain Fork Brazos River** ≈ Texas, SW USA
23 O3 **Double Springs** Alabama, S USA
103 T8 **Doubs** ◈ department E France
108 C8 **Doubs** ≈ France/Switzerland
185 A22 **Doubtful Sound** sound South Island, NZ
184 J2 **Doubtless Bay** bay North Island, NZ
25 X9 **Doucette** Texas, SW USA
102 K8 **Doué-la-Fontaine** Maine-et-Loire, NW France
77 O11 **Douentza** Mopti, S Mali
65 D24 **Douglas** East Falkland, Falkland Islands
97 I16 **Douglas** ○ (Isle of Man) E Isle of Man
83 H23 **Douglas** Northern Cape, C South Africa
39 X13 **Douglas** Alexander Archipelago, Alaska, USA
37 O17 **Douglas** Arizona, SW USA
23 U7 **Douglas** Georgia, SE USA
33 Y15 **Douglas** Wyoming, C USA
38 L9 **Douglas, Cape** headland Alaska USA
10 J14 **Douglas Channel** channel British Columbia, W Canada
182 G3 **Douglas Creek** seasonal river South Australia
31 P5 **Douglas Lake** ◎ Michigan, N USA
21 O9 **Douglas Lake** ⊞ Tennessee, S USA
39 Q13 **Douglas, Mount** ▲ Alaska, USA
194 I6 **Douglas Range** ⛰ Alexander Island, Antarctica
121 P9 **Doukáto, Akrotírio** headland Lefkáda, W Greece
103 O2 **Doullens** Somme, N France
Douma see Dūmā
79 F15 **Doumé** Est, E Cameroon
99 E21 **Dour** Hainaut, S Belgium
59 K18 **Dourada, Serra** ⛰ S Brazil
59 I21 **Dourados** Mato Grosso do Sul, S Brazil
103 N5 **Dourdan** Essonne, N France
104 I6 **Douro** Sp. Duero. ≈ Portugal/Spain see also Duero
104 G6 **Douro Litoral** former province N Portugal
Douvres see Dover
102 K15 **Douze** ≈ SW France
183 P17 **Dover** Tasmania, SE Australia
97 Q22 **Dover** Fr. Douvres; Lat. Dubris Portus. SE England, UK
21 Y3 **Dover** state capital Delaware, NE USA
19 P9 **Dover** New Hampshire, NE USA
18 J14 **Dover** New Jersey, NE USA
31 U12 **Dover** Ohio, N USA
20 H8 **Dover** Tennessee, S USA
97 Q23 **Dover, Strait of** var. Straits of Dover, Fr. Pas de Calais. strait England, UK/France
Dover, Straits of see Dover, Strait of
Dovlen see Devin
94 G11 **Dovre** Oppland, S Norway
94 G10 **Dovrefjell** plateau S Norway
Dovsk see Dowsk
83 M14 **Dowa** Central, C Malawi
31 O10 **Dowagiac** Michigan, N USA
143 N10 **Dow Gonbadān** var. Do Gonbadān, Gonbadān. Kohgīlūyeh va Būyer Aḩmad, SW Iran
148 M2 **Dowlatābād** Fāryāb, N Afghanistan
97 G16 **Down** cultural region SE Northern Ireland, UK
33 R16 **Downey** Idaho, NW USA
35 P5 **Downieville** California, W USA
97 G16 **Downpatrick** Ir. Dún Pádraig. SE Northern Ireland, UK
26 M3 **Downs** Kansas, C USA
18 J12 **Downsville** New York, NE USA
Dow Rūd see Do Rūd
29 V12 **Dows** Iowa, C USA
119 O17 **Dowsk** Rus. Dovsk. Homyel'skaya Voblasts', SE Belarus
35 Q4 **Doyle** California, W USA
18 I15 **Doylestown** Pennsylvania, NE USA
Doyransko, Ezero see Doïranis, Límnis
114 I8 **Doyrentsi** Lovech, N Bulgaria
164 G11 **Dōzen** island Oki-shotō, SW Japan
14 K9 **Dozois, Réservoir** ⊞ Québec, SE Canada
74 D9 **Drâa** seasonal river S Morocco
Drâa, Hammada du see Dra, Hamada du
Drabble see José Enrique Rodó
117 Q5 **Drabiv** Cherkas'ka Oblast', C Ukraine
Drable see José Enrique Rodó
103 S13 **Drac** ≈ E France
Drač/Draç see Durrës
60 I8 **Dracena** São Paulo, S Brazil
98 M6 **Drachten** Friesland, N Netherlands
92 H11 **Drag** Lapp. Ájluokta. Nordland, C Norway
116 L14 **Dragalina** Călăraşi, SE Romania
116 I14 **Drăgăneşti-Olt** Olt, S Romania
116 J14 **Drăgăneşti-Vlaşca** Teleorman, S Romania
116 I13 **Drăgăşani** Vâlcea, SW Romania
114 G9 **Dragoman** Sofiya, W Bulgaria
115 L25 **Dragonáda** island SE Greece
Dragonera, Isla see Sa Dragonera
45 T14 **Dragon's Mouths, The** strait Trinidad and Tobago/Venezuela
95 J23 **Dragør** København, E Denmark
114 F10 **Dragovishitsa** Kyustendil, W Bulgaria
103 U15 **Draguignan** Var, SE France
74 E9 **Dra, Hamada du** var. Hammada du Drâa, Haut Plateau du Dra. plateau W Algeria
Dra, Haut Plateau du see Dra, Hamada du
119 H19 **Drahichyn** Pol. Drohiczyn Poleski, Rus. Drogichin. Brestskaya Voblasts', SW Belarus
29 N4 **Drake** North Dakota, N USA
83 K23 **Drakensberg** ⛰ Lesotho/South Africa
194 F3 **Drake Passage** passage Atlantic Ocean/Pacific Ocean
114 L8 **Dralfa** Tŭrgovishte, N Bulgaria
114 I12 **Dráma** var. Dhráma. Anatolikí Makedonía kai Thráki, NE Greece
Dramburg see Drawsko Pomorskie
95 H15 **Drammen** Buskerud, S Norway
95 H15 **Drammensfjorden** fjord S Norway
92 H1 **Drangajökull** ▲ NW Iceland
95 F16 **Drangedal** Telemark, S Norway
92 I2 **Drangsnes** Vestfirdhir, NW Iceland
Drann see Dravinja
109 T10 **Drau** var. Drava, Eng. Drave, Hung. Dráva. ≈ C Europe see also Drava
84 I11 **Drava** var. Drau, Eng. Drave, Hung. Dráva. ≈ C Europe see also Drau
Dráva see Drau/Drava
Drave see Drau/Drava
109 W10 **Dravinja** Ger. Drann. ≈ NE Slovenia
109 V9 **Dravograd** Ger. Unterdrauburg; prev. Spodnji Dravograd. N Slovenia
110 F10 **Drawa** ≈ NW Poland
110 F9 **Drawno** Zachodnio-pomorskie, NW Poland
110 F9 **Drawsko Pomorskie** Ger. Dramburg. Zachodnio-pomorskie, NW Poland
29 R3 **Drayton** North Dakota, N USA
11 P14 **Drayton Valley** Alberta, SW Canada
186 B6 **Dreikikir** East Sepik, NW PNG
Dreikirchen see Teiuş
98 N7 **Drenthe** ◈ province NE Netherlands
115 H15 **Drépano, Akrotírio** var. Akra Dhrepanon. headland N Greece
Drepanum see Trapani
14 D17 **Dresden** Ontario, S Canada
101 O16 **Dresden** Sachsen, E Germany
20 G8 **Dresden** Tennessee, S USA
118 M11 **Dretun'** Rus. Dretun'. Vitsyebskaya Voblasts', N Belarus
102 M5 **Dreux** anc. Drocae, Durocasses. Eure-et-Loir, C France
94 I11 **Drevsjø** Hedmark, S Norway
22 K3 **Drew** Mississippi, S USA
110 F10 **Drezdenko** Ger. Driesen. Lubuskie, W Poland
98 J12 **Driebergen** var. Driebergen-Rijsenburg. Utrecht, C Netherlands
Driebergen-Rijsenburg see Driebergen
Driesen see Drezdenko
97 N16 **Driffield** E England, UK
65 D25 **Driftwood Point** headland East Falkland, Falkland Islands
33 S14 **Driggs** Idaho, NW USA
Drin see Drinit, Lumi i
112 K12 **Drina** ≈ Bosnia and Herzegovina/Serbia and Montenegro (Yugo.)
Drin, Gulf of see Drinit, Gjiri i
113 K18 **Drinit, Gjiri i** var. Pellg i Drinit, Eng. Gulf of Drin. gulf NW Albania
113 L17 **Drinit, Lumi i** var. Drin. ≈ NW Albania
Drinit, Pellg i see Drinit, Gjiri i
Drinit të Zi, Lumi i see Black Drin
113 L22 **Drino** var. Drinos, Drínos Pótamos, Alb. Lumi i Drinos. ≈ Albania/Greece
Drinos, Lumi i/Drínos Pótamos see Drino
25 S11 **Dripping Springs** Texas, SW USA
25 S15 **Driscoll** Texas, SW USA
22 H5 **Driskill Mountain** ▲ Louisiana, S USA
Drissa see Drysa
94 G10 **Driva** ≈ S Norway
112 E13 **Drniš** It. Šibenik-Knin, S Croatia
95 H15 **Drøbak** Akershus, S Norway
116 G13 **Drobeta-Turnu Severin** prev. Turnu Severin. Mehedinți, SW Romania
Drocae see Dreux
116 M8 **Drochia** Rus. Drokiya. N Moldova
97 F17 **Drogheda** Ir. Droichead Átha. NE Ireland
Drogichin see Drahichyn
Drogobych see Drohobych
Drohiczyn Poleski see Drahichyn
116 H6 **Drohobych** Pol. Drohobycz, Rus. Drogobych. L'vivs'ka Oblast', NW Ukraine
Drohobycz see Drohobych
Droichead Átha see Drogheda
Droicheadna Bandan see Bandon
Droichead na Banna see Banbridge
Droim Mór see Dromore
Drokiya see Drochia
103 R13 **Drôme** ◈ department E France
103 S13 **Drôme** ≈ E France
97 G15 **Dromore** Ir. Droim Mór. SE Northern Ireland, UK
106 A9 **Dronero** Piemonte, NE Italy
102 L12 **Dronne** ≈ SW France
195 Q3 **Dronning Maud Land** physical region Antarctica
98 K6 **Dronrijp** Fris. Dronryp. Friesland, N Netherlands
Dronryp see Dronrijp
98 L9 **Dronten** Flevoland, C Netherlands
Drontheim see Trondheim
102 L13 **Dropt** ≈ SW France
149 T4 **Drosh** North-West Frontier Province, NW Pakistan
Drossen see Ośno Lubuskie
Drug see Durg
118 I12 **Drūkšiai** ◎ NE Lithuania
Druk-yul see Bhutan
11 Q16 **Drumheller** Alberta, SW Canada
33 Q10 **Drummond** Montana, NW USA
31 R4 **Drummond Island** island Michigan, N USA
Drummond Island see Tabiteuea
21 X7 **Drummond, Lake** ◎ Virginia, NE USA
15 P12 **Drummondville** Québec, SE Canada
39 T11 **Drum, Mount** ▲ Alaska, USA
27 O9 **Drumright** Oklahoma, C USA
99 J14 **Drunen** Noord-Brabant, S Netherlands
Druskienniki see Druskininkai
119 F15 **Druskininkai** Pol. Druskienniki. Alytus, S Lithuania
98 K13 **Druten** Gelderland, SE Netherlands
118 K11 **Druya** Vitsyebskaya Voblasts', NW Belarus
117 S2 **Druzhba** Sums'ka Oblast', NE Ukraine
Druzhba see Dostyk, Kazakhstan
Druzhba see Pitnak, Uzbekistan
123 R7 **Druzhina** Respublika Sakha (Yakutiya), NE Russian Federation
117 X7 **Druzhkivka** Donets'ka Oblast', E Ukraine
112 E12 **Drvar** Federacija Bosna I Hercegovina, Bosnia and Herzegovina
113 G15 **Drvenik** Split-Dalmacija, SE Croatia
114 K9 **Dryanovo** Gabrovo, N Bulgaria
26 G7 **Dry Cimarron River** ≈ Kansas/Oklahoma, C USA
12 B11 **Dryden** Ontario, C Canada
24 M11 **Dryden** Texas, SW USA
195 Q14 **Drygalski Ice Tongue** ice feature Antarctica
118 L11 **Drysa** Rus. Drissa. ≈ N Belarus
23 V17 **Dry Tortugas** island Florida, SE USA
79 D15 **Dschang** Ouest, W Cameroon
54 J5 **Duaca** Lara, N Venezuela
Duacum see Douai
Duala see Douala
45 N9 **Duarte, Pico** ▲ C Dominican Republic
140 J5 **Ḑubā** Tabūk, NW Saudi Arabia
Dubai see Dubayy
117 N9 **Dubăsari** Rus. Dubossary. NE Moldova
117 N9 **Dubăsari Reservoir** ⊞ NE Moldova
8 M10 **Dubawnt** ≈ Nunavut, NW Canada
8 L9 **Dubawnt Lake** ◎ Northwest Territories/Nunavut, N Canada
30 L6 **Du Bay, Lake** ⊞ Wisconsin, N USA
141 U7 **Dubayy** Eng. Dubai. Dubayy, NE UAE
141 W7 **Dubayy** Eng. Dubai. ✕ Dubayy, NE UAE
183 R7 **Dubbo** New South Wales, SE Australia
108 G7 **Dübendorf** Zürich, NW Switzerland
97 F18 **Dublin** Ir. Baile Átha Cliath; anc. Eblana. ● (Ireland), E Ireland
23 U5 **Dublin** Georgia, SE USA
25 R7 **Dublin** Texas, SW USA
97 G18 **Dublin** Ir. Baile Átha Cliath; anc. Eblana. cultural region E Ireland
97 G18 **Dublin Airport** ✕ E Ireland
189 V12 **Dublon** var. Tonoas. island Chuuk Islands, C Micronesia
126 K2 **Dubna** Moskovskaya Oblast', W Russian Federation
111 G19 **Dubňany** Ger. Dubnian. Jihomoravský Kraj, SE Czech Republic
Dubnian see Dubňany
111 I19 **Dubnica nad Váhom** Hung. Máriatölgyes; prev. Dubnicz. Trenčiansky Kraj, W Slovakia
Dubnicz see Dubnica nad Váhom
116 K4 **Dubno** Rivnens'ka Oblast', NW Ukraine
18 D13 **Du Bois** Pennsylvania, NE USA
33 R13 **Dubois** Idaho, NW USA
33 T14 **Dubois** Wyoming, C USA
Dubossary see Dubăsari
127 O10 **Dubovka** Volgogradskaya Oblast', SW Russian Federation
76 H14 **Dubréka** Guinée-Maritime, SW Guinea
14 B7 **Dubreuilville** Ontario, S Canada
Dubris Portus see Dover
119 L20 **Dubrova** Rus. Dubrova. Homyel'skaya Voblasts', SE Belarus
126 I5 **Dubrovka** Bryanskaya Oblast', W Russian Federation
113 H16 **Dubrovnik** It. Ragusa. Dubrovnik-Neretva, SE Croatia
113 I16 **Dubrovnik** ✕ Dubrovnik-Neretva, SE Croatia
113 F16 **Dubrovnik-Neretva** off. Dubrovačko-Neretvanska Županija. ◈ province SE Croatia
Dubrovno see Dubrowna
116 L2 **Dubrovytsya** Rivnens'ka Oblast', NW Ukraine
119 O14 **Dubrowna** Rus. Dubrovno. Vitsyebskaya Voblasts', N Belarus
29 Z13 **Dubuque** Iowa, C USA
118 E12 **Dubysa** ≈ C Lithuania
167 U11 **Đưc Cơ** Gia Lai, C Vietnam
191 V12 **Duc de Gloucester, Îles du** Eng. Duke of Gloucester Islands. island group C French Polynesia
111 C15 **Duchcov** Ger. Dux. Ústecký Kraj, NW Czech Republic
37 N3 **Duchesne** Utah, W USA
191 P17 **Ducie Island** atoll E Pitcairn Islands
11 W15 **Duck Bay** Manitoba, S Canada
23 X17 **Duck Key** island Florida Keys, Florida, SE USA
11 T14 **Duck Lake** Saskatchewan, S Canada
11 V15 **Duck Mountain** ⛰ Manitoba, S Canada
20 I9 **Duck River** ≈ Tennessee, S USA
20 M10 **Ducktown** Tennessee, S USA
167 U10 **Đức Phô** Quang Ngai, C Vietnam
Đức Tho see Lin Camh
167 U13 **Đức Trọng** var. Liên Nghia. Lâm Đồng, S Vietnam
D-U-D see Dalap-Uliga-Djarrit
99 M25 **Dudelange** var. Forge du Sud, Ger. Dudelingen. Luxembourg, S Luxembourg
Dudelingen see Dudelange
101 J15 **Duderstadt** Niedersachsen, C Germany
153 N15 **Dūdhi** Uttar Pradesh, N India
122 K8 **Dudinka** Taymyrskiy (Dolgano-Nenetskiy) Avtonomnyy Okrug, N Russian Federation
97 L20 **Dudley** C England, UK
154 G13 **Dudna** ≈ C India
76 L16 **Duékoué** W Ivory Coast
104 M5 **Dueñas** Castilla-León, N Spain
104 K4 **Duerna** ≈ NW Spain
105 O6 **Duero** Port. Douro. ≈ Portugal/Spain see also Douro
Duesseldorf see Düsseldorf
21 P12 **Due West** South Carolina, SE USA
195 P11 **Dufek Coast** physical region Antarctica
99 H17 **Duffel** Antwerpen, C Belgium
35 S2 **Duffer Peak** ▲ Nevada, W USA
187 Q9 **Duff Islands** island group E Solomon Islands
Dufour, Pizzo/Dufour, Punta see Dufour Spitze
108 E12 **Dufour Spitze** It. Pizzo Dufour, Punta Dufour. ▲ Italy/Switzerland
112 D9 **Duga Resa** Karlovac, C Croatia
22 H5 **Dugdemona River** ≈ Louisiana, S USA
154 J12 **Duggīpar** Mahārāshtra, C India
112 B13 **Dugi Otok** var. Isola Grossa, It. Isola Lunga. island W Croatia
113 F14 **Dugopolje** Split-Dalmacija, S Croatia
160 L8 **Du He** ≈ C China
54 M11 **Duida, Cerro** ▲ S Venezuela
Duinekerke see Dunkerque
101 E15 **Duisburg** prev. Duisburg-Hamborn. Nordrhein-Westfalen, W Germany
Duisburg-Hamborn see Duisburg
99 F14 **Duiveland** island SW Netherlands
98 M12 **Duiven** Gelderland, E Netherlands
139 W10 **Dujaylah, Hawr ad** ◎ S Iraq
160 H9 **Dujiangyan** var. Guanxian, Guan Xian. Sichuan, C China
81 L18 **Dujuuma** Shabeellaha Hoose, S Somalia
Dūkān see Dokan
39 Z14 **Duke Island** island Alexander Archipelago, Alaska, USA
Dukelský Priesmy/Dukelský Průsmyk see Dukla Pass
Duke of Gloucester Islands see Duc de Gloucester, Îles du
81 F14 **Duk Faiwil** Jonglei, SE Sudan
141 T7 **Dukhān** C Qatar
Dukhan Heights see Dukhān, Jabal
143 N16 **Dukhān, Jabal** var. Dukhan Heights. hill range S Qatar
127 Q7 **Dukhovnitskoye** Saratovskaya Oblast', W Russian Federation
126 H4 **Dukhovshchina** Smolenskaya Oblast', W Russian Federation
Dukielska, Przełęcz see Dukla Pass
111 N17 **Dukla** Podkarpackie, SE Poland
Duklai Hág see Dukla Pass
111 N18 **Dukla Pass** Cz. Dukelský Průsmyk, Ger. Dukla-Pass, Hung. Duklai Hág, Pol. Przełęcz Dukielska, Slvk. Dukelský Priesmy. pass Poland/Slovakia
Dukou see Panzhihua
118 I12 **Dūkštas** Utena, E Lithuania
162 M8 **Dulaan** Hentiy, C Mongolia
159 R10 **Dulan** var. Qagan Us. Qinghai, C China
37 R8 **Dulce** New Mexico, SW USA
43 N16 **Dulce, Golfo** gulf S Costa Rica
Dulce, Golfo see Izabal, Lago de
42 K6 **Dulce Nombre de Culmí** Olancho, C Honduras
62 L9 **Dulce, Río** ≈ C Argentina
123 Q9 **Dulgalakh** ≈ NE Russian Federation
114 M8 **Dŭlgopol** Varna, E Bulgaria
153 V14 **Dullabchara** Assam, NE India
20 D3 **Dulles** ✕ (Washington DC) Virginia, NE USA
101 E14 **Dülmen** Nordrhein-Westfalen, W Germany
114 M7 **Dulovo** Silistra, NE Bulgaria
29 W5 **Duluth** Minnesota, N USA
138 H7 **Dūmā** Fr. Douma. Dimashq, SW Syria
171 O8 **Dumagasa Point** headland Mindanao, S Philippines
171 P6 **Dumaguete** var. Dumaguete City. Negros, C Philippines
168 J10 **Dumai** Sumatera, W Indonesia
183 T4 **Dumaresq River** ≈ New South Wales/Queensland, SE Australia
27 W13 **Dumas** Arkansas, C USA
25 N1 **Dumas** Texas, SW USA
138 I7 **Ḑumayr** Dimashq, W Syria
96 I12 **Dumbarton** W Scotland, UK
96 I12 **Dumbarton** cultural region C Scotland, UK
187 Q17 **Dumbéa** Province Sud, S New Caledonia
111 K19 **Ďumbier** Ger. Djumbir, Hung. Gyömbér. ▲ C Slovakia
116 I11 **Dumbrăveni** Ger. Elisabethstedt, Hung. Erzsébetváros; prev. Ebesfalva, Eppeschdorf, Ibaşfalău. Sibiu, C Romania
116 L12 **Dumbrăveni** Vrancea, E Romania
97 J14 **Dumfries** S Scotland, UK
97 J14 **Dumfries** cultural region SW Scotland, UK
153 R15 **Dumka** Jhārkhand, NE India
Dümmer see Dümmersee
100 G12 **Dümmersee** var. Dümmer. ◎ NW Germany
14 J11 **Dumoine** ≈ Québec, SE Canada
14 J10 **Dumoine, Lac** ◎ Québec, SE Canada
195 V16 **Dumont d'Urville** French research station Antarctica
195 W15 **Dumont d'Urville Sea** S Pacific Ocean
14 K11 **Dumont, Lac** ◎ Québec, SE Canada
75 W7 **Dumyâṭ** Eng. Damietta. N Egypt
Duna see Don, Russian Federation
Duna see Danube, C Europe
Düna see Western Dvina
Dünaburg see Daugavpils
111 J24 **Dunaföldvár** Tolna, C Hungary
Dunaj see Wien, Austria
Dunaj see Danube, C Europe
111 L18 **Dunajec** ≈ S Poland
111 H21 **Dunajská Streda** Hung. Dunaszerdahely. Trnavský Kraj, W Slovakia
Dunapentele see Dunaújváros
Dunărea see Danube
116 M13 **Dunărea Veche, Braţul** ≈ SE Romania
117 N13 **Dunării, Delta** delta SE Romania
Dunaszerdahely see Dunajská Streda
111 J23 **Dunaújváros** prev. Dunapentele, Sztálinváros. Fejér, C Hungary
Dunav see Danube
114 J8 **Dunavska Ravnina** Eng. Danubian Plain. plain N Bulgaria
114 G7 **Dunavtsi** Vidin, NW Bulgaria
123 S15 **Dunay** Primorskiy Kray, SE Russian Federation
Dunayevtsy see Dunayivtsi
116 L7 **Dunayivtsi** Rus. Dunayevtsy. Khmel'nyts'ka Oblast', NW Ukraine
185 F22 **Dunback** Otago, South Island, NZ
10 L17 **Duncan** Vancouver Island, British Columbia, SW Canada
37 O15 **Duncan** Arizona, SW USA
26 M12 **Duncan** Oklahoma, C USA
Duncan Island see Pinzón, Isla
151 Q20 **Duncan Passage** strait Andaman Sea/Bay of Bengal
96 K6 **Duncansby Head** headland N Scotland, UK
14 G12 **Dunchurch** Ontario, S Canada
118 D7 **Dundaga** Talsi, NW Latvia
14 G14 **Dundalk** Ontario, S Canada
97 F16 **Dundalk** Ir. Dún Dealgan. NE Ireland
21 X3 **Dundalk** Maryland, NE USA
97 F16 **Dundalk Bay** Ir. Cuan Dhún Dealgan. bay NE Ireland
14 G16 **Dundas** Ontario, S Canada
180 L12 **Dundas, Lake** salt lake Western Australia
163 O7 **Dundbürd** Hentiy, E Mongolia
Dún Dealgan see Dundalk
15 N13 **Dundee** Québec, SE Canada
83 K22 **Dundee** KwaZulu/Natal, E South Africa
96 K11 **Dundee** E Scotland, UK
31 R10 **Dundee** Michigan, N USA
25 R5 **Dundee** Texas, SW USA
194 H3 **Dundee Island** island Antarctica
162 L9 **Dundgovĭ** ◈ province C Mongolia
97 G16 **Dundrum Bay** Ir. Cuan Dhún Droma. inlet NW Irish Sea
11 T15 **Dundurn** Saskatchewan, S Canada
162 E6 **Dund-Us** Hovd, W Mongolia
185 F23 **Dunedin** Otago, South Island, NZ
183 R7 **Dunedoo** New South Wales, SE Australia
97 D14 **Dunfanaghy** Ir. Dún Fionnachaidh. NW Ireland
96 J12 **Dunfermline** C Scotland, UK
Dún Fionnachaidh see Dunfanaghy
149 V10 **Dunga Bunga** Punjab, E Pakistan
97 F15 **Dungannon** Ir. Dún Geanainn. C Northern Ireland, UK
Dun Garbháin see Dungarvan
152 F15 **Dūngarpur** Rājasthān, N India
97 E21 **Dungarvan** Ir. Dun Garbháin. S Ireland
101 N21 **Dungau** cultural region SE Germany
Dún Geanainn see Dungannon
97 P23 **Dungeness** headland SE England, UK
63 I23 **Dungeness, Punta** headland S Argentina
Dungloe see Dunglow
97 D14 **Dunglow** var. Dungloe, Ir. An Clochán Liath. NW Ireland
183 T7 **Dungog** New South Wales, SE Australia
79 O16 **Dungu** Orientale, NE Dem. Rep. Congo
168 L8 **Dungun** var. Kuala Dungun. Terengganu, Peninsular Malaysia
80 I6 **Dungûnab** Red Sea, NE Sudan
15 P13 **Dunham** Québec, SE Canada
Dunheved see Launceston
Dunholme see Durham
163 X10 **Dunhua** Jilin, NE China
159 P8 **Dunhuang** Gansu, N China
182 L12 **Dunkeld** Victoria, SE Australia
103 O1 **Dunkerque** Eng. Dunkirk, Flem. Duinekerke; prev. Dunquerque. Nord, N France
97 K23 **Dunkery Beacon** ▲ SW England, UK
18 C11 **Dunkirk** New York, NE USA
Dunkirk see Dunkerque
77 P17 **Dunkwa** SW Ghana
97 G18 **Dún Laoghaire** Eng. Dunleary; prev. Kingstown. E Ireland
29 S14 **Dunlap** Iowa, C USA
20 L10 **Dunlap** Tennessee, S USA
Dunleary see Dún Laoghaire
Dún Mánmhaí see Dunmanway
97 B21 **Dunmanway** Ir. Dún Mánmhaí. SW Ireland
18 I13 **Dunmore** Pennsylvania, NE USA
21 U10 **Dunn** North Carolina, SE USA
Dún na nGall see Donegal
23 V11 **Dunnellon** Florida, SE USA
96 J6 **Dunnet Head** headland N Scotland, UK
29 N14 **Dunning** Nebraska, C USA
65 B24 **Dunnose Head Settlement** West Falkland, Falkland Islands
14 G17 **Dunnville** Ontario, S Canada
Dún Pádraig see Downpatrick
Dunquerque see Dunkerque
Dunqulah see Dongola
96 L12 **Duns** SE Scotland, UK
29 N2 **Dunseith** North Dakota, N USA
35 N2 **Dunsmuir** California, W USA
97 N21 **Dunstable** Lat. Durocobrivae. E England, UK
185 D21 **Dunstan Mountains** ⛰ South Island, NZ
103 O9 **Dun-sur-Auron** Cher, C France
185 F21 **Duntroon** Canterbury, South Island, NZ
149 T10 **Dunyāpur** Punjab, E Pakistan
163 U5 **Duobukur He** ≈ NE China
163 R12 **Duolun** var. Dolonnur. Nei Mongol Zizhiqu, N China
167 Q14 **Dương Đông** Kiên Giang, S Vietnam
114 G10 **Dupnitsa** prev. Marek, Stanke Dimitrov. Kyustendil, W Bulgaria
28 L8 **Dupree** South Dakota, N USA
33 Q7 **Dupuyer** Montana, NW USA
141 Y11 **Duqm** var. Daqm. E Oman
63 F23 **Duque de York, Isla** island S Chile

◆ Country ● Country Capital ◇ Dependent Territory ○ Dependent Territory Capital ◈ Administrative Region ✕ International Airport ▲ Mountain ⛰ Mountain Range Volcano ≈ River ◎ Lake ⊞ Reservoir

181 *N4* **Durack Range** ⛰ Western Australia
136 *K10* **Durağan** Sinop, N Turkey
103 *S15* **Durance** ≈ SE France
31 *R9* **Durand** Michigan, N USA
30 *I6* **Durand** Wisconsin, N USA
40 *K10* **Durango** *var.* Victoria de Durango. Durango, W Mexico
105 *P3* **Durango** País Vasco, N Spain
37 *Q8* **Durango** Colorado, C USA
40 *J9* **Durango** ◈ *state* C Mexico
114 *O7* **Durankulak** ***Rom.*** Răcari; ***prev.*** Blatnitsa, Duranulac. Dobrich, NE Bulgaria
22 *L4* **Durant** Mississippi, S USA
27 *P13* **Durant** Oklahoma, C USA
Duranulac *see* Durankulak
105 *N6* **Duratón** ≈ N Spain
61 *E19* **Durazno** *var.* San Pedro de Durazno. Durazno, C Uruguay
61 *E19* **Durazno** ◈ *department* C Uruguay
Durazzo *see* Durrës
83 *K23* **Durban** *var.* Port Natal. KwaZulu/Natal, E South Africa
83 *K23* **Durban** × KwaZulu/Natal, E South Africa
118 *C9* **Durbe** ***Ger.*** Durben. Liepāja, W Latvia
Durben *see* Durbe
99 *K21* **Durbuy** Luxembourg, SE Belgium
105 *N15* **Dúrcal** Andalucía, S Spain
112 *F8* **Đurđevac** ***Ger.*** Sankt Georgen, ***Hung.*** Szentgyörgy; ***prev.*** Djurdjevac, Gjurgjevac. Koprivnica-Križevci, N Croatia
113 *K15* **Đurđevica Tara** Montenegro, SW Serbia and Montenegro (Yugo.)
97 *L24* **Durdle Door** *natural arch* S England, UK
158 *L3* **Düre** Xinjiang Uygur Zizhiqu, W China
101 *D16* **Düren** ***anc.*** Marcodurum. Nordrhein-Westfalen, W Germany
154 *K12* **Durg** ***prev.*** Drug. Chhattīsgarh, C India
153 *U13* **Durgapur** Dhaka, N Bangladesh
153 *R15* **Durgāpur** West Bengal, NE India
14 *F14* **Durham** Ontario, S Canada
97 *M14* **Durham** ***hist.*** Dunholme. N England, UK
21 *U9* **Durham** North Carolina, SE USA
97 *L15* **Durham** *cultural region* N England, UK
168 *J10* **Duri** Sumatera, W Indonesia
Duria Major *see* Dora Baltea
Duria Minor *see* Dora Riparia
Durlas *see* Thurles
141 *P8* **Ḑurmā** Ar Riyāḑ, C Saudi Arabia
113 *J15* **Durmitor** ▲ N Serbia and Montenegro (Yugo.)
96 *H6* **Durness** N Scotland, UK
109 *Y3* **Dürnkrut** Niederösterreich, E Austria
Durnovaria *see* Dorchester
Durobrivae *see* Rochester
Durocasses *see* Dreux
Durocobrivae *see* Dunstable
Durocortorum *see* Reims
Durostorum *see* Silistra
Durovernum *see* Canterbury
113 *K20* **Durrës** *var.* Durrësi, Dursi, ***It.*** Durazzo, ***SCr.*** Drač, ***Turk.*** Draç. Durrës, W Albania
113 *K19* **Durrës** ◈ *district* W Albania
Durrësi *see* Durrës
97 *A21* **Dursey Island** ***Ir.*** Oileán Baoi. *island* SW Ireland
Dursi *see* Durrës
Duru *see* Wuchuan
Durud *see* Do Rūd
114 *P12* **Durusu** İstanbul, NW Turkey
114 *O12* **Durusu Gölü** ◎ NW Turkey
138 *I9* **Durūz, Jabal ad** ▲ SW Syria
184 *K13* **D'Urville Island** *island* C NZ
171 *X12* **D'Urville, Tanjung** *headland* Papua, E Indonesia
146 *H14* **Duşak** ***Rus.*** Dushak. Ahal Welaýaty, S Turkmenistan
Dusa Mareb/Dusa Marreb *see* Dhuusa Marreeb
118 *I11* **Dusetos** Utena, NE Lithuania
Dushak *see* Duşak
160 *K12* **Dushan** Guizhou, S China
147 *P13* **Dushanbe** ***var.*** Dyushambe; ***prev.*** Stalinabad, ***Taj.*** Stalinobod. ● (Tajikistan) W Tajikistan
147 *P13* **Dushanbe** × W Tajikistan
137 *T9* **Dushet'i** E Georgia
18 *H13* **Dushore** Pennsylvania, NE USA
185 *A23* **Dusky Sound** *sound* South Island, NZ
101 *E15* **Düsseldorf** ***var.*** Duesseldorf. Nordrhein-Westfalen, W Germany
147 *P14* **Dŭstí** ***Rus.*** Dusti. SW Tajikistan
194 *I9* **Dustin Island** *island* Antarctica
Dutch East Indies *see* Indonesia
Dutch Guiana *see* Suriname
38 *L17* **Dutch Harbor** Unalaska Island, Alaska, USA
36 *J3* **Dutch Mount** ▲ Utah, W USA
Dutch New Guinea *see* Papua
Dutch West Indies *see* Netherlands Antilles
83 *H20* **Dutlwe** Kweneng, S Botswana
67 *V16* **Du Toit Fracture Zone** *tectonic feature* SW Indian Ocean
125 *U8* **Dutovo** Respublika Komi, NW Russian Federation
77 *V13* **Dutsan Wai** *var.* Dutsen Wai. Kaduna, C Nigeria
77 *W13* **Dutse** Jigawa, N Nigeria
Dutsen Wai *see* Dutsan Wai
Duttia *see* Datia
14 *E17* **Dutton** Ontario, S Canada
36 *L7* **Dutton, Mount** ▲ Utah, W USA
162 *E7* **Duut** Hovd, W Mongolia
14 *K11* **Duval, Lac** ◎ Québec, SE Canada
127 *W3* **Duvan** Respublika Bashkortostan, W Russian Federation
138 *L9* **Duwaykhilat Satīḩ ar Ruwayshid** *seasonal river* SE Jordan
Dux *see* Duchcov
160 *J13* **Duyang Shan** ⛰ S China
167 *T14* **Duyên Hai** Tra Vinh, S Vietnam
160 *K12* **Duyun** Guizhou, S China
136 *G11* **Düzce** Bolu, NW Turkey
Duzdab *see* Zāhedān
Duzenkyr, Khrebet *see* Duzkyr, Khrebet
146 *I16* **Duzkyr, Khrebet** ***prev.*** Khrebet Duzenkyr. ⛰ S Turkmenistan
Dvina Bay *see* Chëshskaya Guba
Dvinsk *see* Daugavpils
126 *L7* **Dvinskaya Guba** *bay* NW Russian Federation
112 *E10* **Dvor** Sisak-Moslavina, C Croatia
117 *W5* **Dvorichna** Kharkivs'ka Oblast', E Ukraine
111 *F16* **Dvůr Králové nad Labem** ***Ger.*** Königinhof an der Elbe. Královéhradecký Kraj, NE Czech Republic
154 *A10* **Dwārka** Gujarāt, W India
30 *M12* **Dwight** Illinois, N USA
98 *N8* **Dwingeloo** Drenthe, NE Netherlands
33 *N10* **Dworshak Reservoir** ▣ Idaho, NW USA
Dyal *see* Dyaul Island
Dyanev *see* Galkynyş
Dyatlovo *see* Dzyatlava
186 *G5* **Dyaul Island** *var.* Djaul, Dyal. *island* NE PNG
20 *G8* **Dyer** Tennessee, S USA
9 *S5* **Dyer, Cape** *headland* Baffin Island, Nunavut, NE Canada
20 *F8* **Dyersburg** Tennessee, S USA
29 *Y13* **Dyersville** Iowa, C USA
97 *I21* **Dyfed** *cultural region* SW Wales, UK
Dyfrdwy, Afon *see* Dee
Dyhernfurth *see* Brzeg Dolny
111 *E19* **Dyje** *var.* Thaya. ≈ Austria/Czech Rep. ***see also*** Thaya
117 *T5* **Dykanska** Poltavs'ka Oblast', C Ukraine
127 *N16* **Dykhtau** ▲ SW Russian Federation
111 *A16* **Dyleń** ***Ger.*** Tillenberg. ▲ NW Czech Republic
110 *K9* **Dylewska Góra** ▲ N Poland
117 *O4* **Dymer** Kyyivs'ka Oblast', N Ukraine
117 *W7* **Dymytrov** ***Rus.*** Dimitrov. Donets'ka Oblast', SE Ukraine
111 *O17* **Dynów** Podkarpackie, SE Poland
29 *X13* **Dysart** Iowa, C USA
Dysna *see* Dzisna
115 *D18* **Dytikí Ellás** ***Eng.*** Greece West. ◈ *region* C Greece
115 *C14* **Dytikí Makedonía** ***Eng.*** Macedonia West. ◈ *region* N Greece
Dyurmen'tyube *see* Dermentobe
127 *U4* **Dyurtyuli** Respublika Bashkortostan, W Russian Federation
Dyushambe *see* Dushanbe
162 *I7* **Dzaanhushuu** Arhangay, C Mongolia
Dza Chu *see* Mekong
162 *I8* **Dzadgay** Bayanhongor, C Mongolia
162 *H8* **Dzag** Bayanhongor, C Mongolia
162 *H10* **Dzalaa** Bayanhongor, C Mongolia
172 *J14* **Dzaoudzi** E Mayotte
Dzaudzhikau *see* Vladikavkaz
162 *G7* **Dzavhan** ◈ *province* NW Mongolia
162 *G7* **Dzavhan Gol** ≈ NW Mongolia
162 *J7* **Dzegstey** Arhangay, C Mongolia
127 *O3* **Dzerzhinsk** Nizhegorodskaya Oblast', W Russian Federation
Dzerzhinsk *see* Dzyarzhynsk, Belarus
Dzerzhinsk *see* Dzerzhyns'k, Ukraine
Dzerzhinskiy *see* Nar'yan-Mar
Dzerzhinskoye *see* Tokzhaylau
117 *X7* **Dzerzhyns'k** ***Rus.*** Dzerzhinsk. Donets'ka Oblast', SE Ukraine
116 *M5* **Dzerzhyns'k** Zhytomyrs'ka Oblast', N Ukraine
Dzhailgan *see* Jayilgan
145 *N14* **Dzhalagash** ***Kaz.*** Zhalashash. Kzylorda, S Kazakhstan
147 *T10* **Dzhalal-Abad** ***Kir.*** Jalal-Abad. Dzhalal-Abadskaya Oblast', W Kyrgyzstan
147 *S9* **Dzhalal-Abadskaya Oblast'** ***Kir.*** Jalal-Abad Oblasty. ◈ *province* W Kyrgyzstan
Dzhalilabad *see* Cälilabad
Dzhambeyty *see* Zhympīty
Dzhambulskaya Oblast' *see* Zhambyl
144 *D9* **Dzhanibek** ***var.*** Dzhanybek, ***Kaz.*** Zhanibek, Zhänibek. Zapadnyy Kazakhstan, W Kazakhstan
Dzhankel'dy *see* Jongeldi
117 *T12* **Dzhankoy** Respublika Krym, S Ukraine
145 *V14* **Dzhansugurov** ***Kaz.*** Zhansügirov. Almaty, SE Kazakhstan
147 *R9* **Dzhany-Bazar** ***var.*** Yangibazar. Dzhalal-Abadskaya Oblast', W Kyrgyzstan
Dzhanybek *see* Dzhanibek
123 *P8* **Dzhardzhan** Respublika Sakha (Yakutiya), NE Russian Federation
Dzharkurgan *see* Jarqo'rg'on
117 *S11* **Dzharylhats'ka Zatoka** *gulf* S Ukraine
Dzhavilgan *see* Jayilgan
Dzhebel *see* Jebel
147 *T14* **Dzhelandy** SE Tajikistan
147 *Y7* **Dzhergalan** ***Kir.*** Jyrgalan. Issyk-Kul'skaya Oblast', NE Kyrgyzstan
Dzherzinskoye *see* Tokzhaylau
Dzhetygara *see* Zhitikara
Dzhetysay ***see*** Zhetysay.
Dzhezkazgan *see* Zhezkazgan
Dzhigirbent *see* Jigerbent
Dzhirgatal' *see* Jirgatol
Dzhizak *see* Jizzakh
Dzhizakskaya Oblast' *see* Jizzax Viloyati
123 *P8* **Dzhugdzhur, Khrebet** ⛰ E Russian Federation
Dzhul'fa *see* Culfa
Dzhuma *see* Juma
145 *W14* **Dzhungarskiy Alatau** ⛰ China/Kazakhstan
144 *M14* **Dzhusaly** ***Kaz.*** Zholsaly. Kzylorda, SW Kazakhstan
146 *J12* **Dzhynlykum, Peski** *desert* E Turkmenistan
110 *L9* **Działdowo** Warmińsko-Mazurskie, C Poland
111 *L16* **Działoszyce** Świętokrzyskie, C Poland
41 *X11* **Dzidzantún** Yucatán, E Mexico
111 *G15* **Dzierżoniów** ***Ger.*** Reichenbach. Dolnośląskie, SW Poland
41 *X11* **Dzilam de Bravo** Yucatán, E Mexico
118 *L12* **Dzisna** ***Rus.*** Disna. Vitsyebskaya Voblasts', N Belarus
118 *K12* **Dzisna** ***Lith.*** Dysna, ***Rus.*** Disna. ≈ Belarus/Lithuania
119 *G20* **Dzivin** ***Rus.*** Divin. Brestskaya Voblasts', SW Belarus
119 *M15* **Dzmitravichy** ***Rus.*** Dmitrovichi. Minskaya Voblasts', C Belarus
162 *M8* **Dzogsool** Töv, C Mongolia
131 *S8* **Dzungaria** *var.* Sungaria, Zungaria. *physical region* W China
Dzungarian Basin *see* Junggar Pendi
162 *G5* **Dzür** Dzavhan, W Mongolia
163 *Q8* **Dzüünbulag** Dornod, E Mongolia
163 *O8* **Dzüünbulag** Sühbaatar, E Mongolia
162 *H7* **Dzuunmod** Dzavhan, C Mongolia
162 *L8* **Dzuunmod** Töv, C Mongolia
Dzüün Soyonī Nuruu *see* Eastern Sayans
162 *F8* **Dzüyl** Govĭ-Altay, SW Mongolia
Dzvina *see* Western Dvina
119 *J16* **Dzyarzhynsk** ***Rus.*** Dzerzhinsk; ***prev.*** Kaydanovo. Minskaya Voblasts', C Belarus
119 *H17* **Dzyatlava** ***Pol.*** Zdzięcioł, ***Rus.*** Dyatlovo. Hrodzyenskaya Voblasts', W Belarus

E

E *see* Hubei
Éadan Doire *see* Edenderry
37 *W6* **Eads** Colorado, C USA
37 *O13* **Eagar** Arizona, SW USA
39 *T8* **Eagle** Alaska, USA
13 *S8* **Eagle** ≈ Newfoundland and Labrador, E Canada
10 *I3* **Eagle** ≈ Yukon Territory, NW Canada
29 *T7* **Eagle Bend** Minnesota, N USA
28 *M8* **Eagle Butte** South Dakota, N USA
29 *V12* **Eagle Grove** Iowa, C USA
19 *R2* **Eagle Lake** Maine, NE USA
25 *U11* **Eagle Lake** Texas, SW USA
12 *A11* **Eagle Lake** ◎ Ontario, S Canada
35 *P3* **Eagle Lake** ◎ California, W USA
19 *R3* **Eagle Lake** ◎ Maine, NE USA
29 *Y3* **Eagle Mountain** ▲ Minnesota, N USA
25 *T6* **Eagle Mountain Lake** ▣ Texas, SW USA
37 *S9* **Eagle Nest Lake** ▣ New Mexico, SW USA
25 *P13* **Eagle Pass** Texas, SW USA
65 *C25* **Eagle Passage** *passage* SW Atlantic Ocean
35 *R8* **Eagle Peak** ▲ California, W USA
35 *Q2* **Eagle Peak** ▲ California, W USA
37 *P13* **Eagle Peak** ▲ New Mexico, SW USA
10 *I4* **Eagle Plain** Yukon Territory, NW Canada
32 *G15* **Eagle Point** Oregon, NW USA
186 *P10* **Eagle Point** *headland* SE PNG
39 *R11* **Eagle River** Alaska, USA
30 *M2* **Eagle River** Michigan, N USA
30 *L4* **Eagle River** Wisconsin, N USA
21 *S6* **Eagle Rock** Virginia, NE USA
36 *J13* **Eagletail Mountains** ⛰ Arizona, SW USA
167 *U12* **Ea Hleo** Đăc Lăc, S Vietnam
167 *U12* **Ea Kar** Đăc Lăc, S Vietnam
Eanjum *see* Anjum
Eanodat *see* Enontekiö
12 *B10* **Ear Falls** Ontario, C Canada
27 *X10* **Earle** Arkansas, C USA
35 *R12* **Earlimart** California, W USA
20 *I6* **Earlington** Kentucky, S USA
14 *H8* **Earlton** Ontario, S Canada
29 *T13* **Early** Iowa, C USA
96 *J11* **Earn** ≈ N Scotland, UK
185 *C21* **Earnslaw, Mount** ▲ South Island, NZ
24 *M4* **Earth** Texas, SW USA
21 *P11* **Easley** South Carolina, SE USA
East *see* Est
East Açores Fracture Zone *see* East Azores Fracture Zone
97 *P19* **East Anglia** *physical region* E England, UK
15 *Q12* **East Angus** Québec, SE Canada
East Antarctica *see* Greater Antarctica
18 *E10* **East Aurora** New York, NE USA
East Australian Basin *see* Tasman Basin
East Azerbaijan *see* Āzarbāyān-e Sharqī
64 *L9* **East Azores Fracture Zone** *var.* East Açores Fracture Zone. *tectonic feature* E Atlantic Ocean
22 *M11* **East Bay** *bay* Louisiana, S USA
25 *V11* **East Bernard** Texas, SW USA
29 *V8* **East Bethel** Minnesota, N USA
East Borneo *see* Kalimantan Timur
97 *P23* **Eastbourne** SE England, UK
15 *R11* **East-Broughton** Québec, SE Canada
44 *M6* **East Caicos** *island* E Turks and Caicos Islands
184 *R7* **East Cape** *headland* North Island, NZ
174 *M4* **East Caroline Basin** *undersea feature* SW Pacific Ocean
192 *P4* **East China Sea** ***Chin.*** Dong Hai. *sea* W Pacific Ocean
97 *P19* **East Dereham** E England, UK
30 *J9* **East Dubuque** Illinois, N USA
11 *S17* **Eastend** Saskatchewan, S Canada
193 *S10* **Easter Fracture Zone** *tectonic feature* E Pacific Ocean
Easter Island *see* Pascua, Isla de
81 *J18* **Eastern** ◈ *province* Kenya
153 *Q12* **Eastern** ◈ *zone* E Nepal
82 *L13* **Eastern** ◈ *province* E Zambia
83 *H24* **Eastern Cape** ***off.*** Eastern Cape Province, ***Afr.*** Oos-Kaap. ◈ *province* SE South Africa
Eastern Desert *see* Sahara el Sharqîya
81 *F15* **Eastern Equatoria** ◈ *state* SE Sudan
Eastern Euphrates *see* Murat Nehri
155 *J17* **Eastern Ghats** ⛰ SE India
186 *E7* **Eastern Highlands** ◈ *province* C PNG
155 *K25* **Eastern Province** ◈ *province* E Sri Lanka
Eastern Region *see* Ash Sharqīyah
122 *L13* **Eastern Sayans** ***Mong.*** Dzüün Soyonī Nuruu, ***Rus.*** Vostochnyy Sayan. ⛰ Mongolia/Russian Federation
Eastern Scheldt *see* Oosterschelde
Eastern Sierra Madre *see* Madre Oriental, Sierra
Eastern Transvaal *see* Mpumalanga
11 *W14* **Easterville** Manitoba, C Canada
Easterwâlde *see* Oosterwolde
63 *M23* **East Falkland** *var.* Isla Soledad. *island* E Falkland Islands
19 *P12* **East Falmouth** Massachusetts, NE USA
East Fayu *see* Fayu
East Flanders *see* Oost Vlaanderen
39 *S6* **East Fork Chandalar River** ≈ Alaska, USA
29 *U12* **East Fork Des Moines River** ≈ Iowa/Minnesota, C USA
East Frisian Islands *see* Ostfriesische Inseln
18 *K10* **East Glenville** New York, NE USA
29 *R4* **East Grand Forks** Minnesota, N USA
97 *O23* **East Grinstead** SE England, UK
18 *M12* **East Hartford** Connecticut, NE USA
18 *M13* **East Haven** Connecticut, NE USA
173 *T9* **East Indiaman Ridge** *undersea feature* E Indian Ocean
131 *V16* **East Indies** *island group* SE Asia
East Java *see* Jawa Timur
31 *Q6* **East Jordan** Michigan, N USA
East Kalimantan *see* Kalimantan Timur
East Kazakhstan *see* Vostochnyy Kazakhstan
96 *I12* **East Kilbride** S Scotland, UK
25 *R7* **Eastland** Texas, SW USA
31 *Q9* **East Lansing** Michigan, N USA
35 *X11* **East Las Vegas** Nevada, W USA
97 *M23* **Eastleigh** S England, UK
31 *V12* **East Liverpool** Ohio, N USA
83 *J25* **East London** ***Afr.*** Oos-Londen; ***prev.*** Emonti, Port Rex. Eastern Cape, S South Africa
96 *K12* **East Lothian** *cultural region* SE Scotland, UK
12 *I10* **Eastmain** Québec, E Canada
12 *J10* **Eastmain** ≈ Québec, C Canada
15 *P13* **Eastman** Québec, SE Canada
23 *U6* **Eastman** Georgia, SE USA
175 *O3* **East Mariana Basin** *undersea feature* W Pacific Ocean
30 *K11* **East Moline** Illinois, N USA
186 *H7* **East New Britain** ◈ *province* E PNG
29 *T15* **East Nishnabotna River** ≈ Iowa, C USA
197 *V12* **East Novaya Zemlya Trough** *var.* Novaya Zemlya Trough. *undersea feature* W Kara Sea
East Nusa Tenggara *see* Nusa Tenggara Timur
21 *X4* **Easton** Maryland, NE USA
18 *I14* **Easton** Pennsylvania, NE USA
193 *R16* **East Pacific Rise** *undersea feature* E Pacific Ocean
East Pakistan *see* Bangladesh
31 *V12* **East Palestine** Ohio, N USA
30 *L12* **East Peoria** Illinois, N USA
23 *S3* **East Point** Georgia, SE USA
19 *U6* **Eastport** Maine, NE USA
27 *Z8* **East Prairie** Missouri, C USA
19 *O12* **East Providence** Rhode Island, NE USA
20 *L11* **East Ridge** Tennessee, S USA
97 *N16* **East Riding** *cultural region* N England, UK
18 *F9* **East Rochester** New York, NE USA
30 *K15* **East Saint Louis** Illinois, N USA
65 *K21* **East Scotia Basin** *undersea feature* SE Scotia Sea
129 *Y8* **East Sea** *var.* Sea of Japan, ***Rus.*** Yapanskoye More. *sea* NW Pacific Ocean ***see also*** Japan, Sea of
186 *B6* **East Sepik** ◈ *province* NW PNG
173 *N4* **East Sheba Ridge** *undersea feature* W Arabian Sea
East Siberian Sea *see* Vostochno-Sibirskoye More
18 *I14* **East Stroudsburg** Pennsylvania, NE USA
East Tasmanian Rise/East Tasmania Plateau/East Tasmania Rise *see* East Tasman Plateau
192 *I12* **East Tasman Plateau** ***var.*** East Tasmanian Rise, East Tasmania Plateau, East Tasmania Rise. *undersea feature* SW Tasman Sea
64 *L7* **East Thulean Rise** *undersea feature* N Atlantic Ocean
171 *R16* **East Timor** *var* Loro Sae *prev.* Portuguese Timor, Timor Timur ◆ *country* SE Asia
21 *Y6* **Eastville** Virginia, NE USA
35 *R7* **East Walker River** ≈ California/Nevada, W USA
182 *D1* **Eateringinna Creek** ≈ South Australia
37 *T3* **Eaton** Colorado, C USA
15 *Q12* **Eaton** ≈ Québec, SE Canada
11 *S16* **Eatonia** Saskatchewan, S Canada
31 *Q10* **Eaton Rapids** Michigan, N USA
23 *U4* **Eatonton** Georgia, SE USA
32 *H9* **Eatonville** Washington, NW USA
30 *J6* **Eau Claire** Wisconsin, N USA
Eau Claire, Lac à L' *see* St.Clair, Lake
12 *J7* **Eau Claire, Lac à l'** ◎ Québec, SE Canada
30 *L6* **Eau Claire River** ≈ Wisconsin, N USA
188 *J16* **Eauripik Atoll** *atoll* Caroline Islands, C Micronesia
192 *H7* **Eauripik Rise** *undersea feature* W Pacific Ocean
102 *K15* **Eauze** Gers, S France
41 *P11* **Ébano** San Luis Potosí, C Mexico
97 *K21* **Ebbw Vale** SE Wales, UK
79 *E17* **Ebebiyin** NE Equatorial Guinea
95 *H22* **Ebeltoft** Århus, C Denmark
109 *X5* **Ebenfurth** Niederösterreich, E Austria
18 *D14* **Ebensburg** Pennsylvania, NE USA
109 *S5* **Ebensee** Oberösterreich, N Austria
101 *H20* **Eberbach** Baden-Württemberg, SW Germany
121 *U8* **Eber Gölü** *salt lake* C Turkey
109 *U9* **Eberndorf** ***Slvn.*** Dobrla Vas. Kärnten, S Austria
109 *R4* **Eberschwang** Oberösterreich, N Austria
100 *O11* **Eberswalde-Finow** Brandenburg, E Germany
Ebesfalva *see* Dumbrăveni
165 *T4* **Ebetsu** *var.* Ebetu. Hokkaidō, NE Japan
Ebetu *see* Ebetsu
Ebinayon *see* Evinayong
158 *I4* **Ebinur Hu** ◎ NW China
138 *I3* **Ebla** ***Ar.*** Tell Mardīkh. *site of ancient city* Idlib, NW Syria
Eblana *see* Dublin
108 *H7* **Ebnat** Sankt Gallen, NE Switzerland
107 *L18* **Eboli** Campania, S Italy
79 *E16* **Ebolowa** Sud, S Cameroon
79 *N21* **Ebombo** Kasai Oriental, C Dem. Rep. Congo
189 *T9* **Ebon Atoll** *var.* Epoon. *atoll* Ralik Chain, S Marshall Islands
Ebora *see* Évora
Eboracum *see* York
Eborodunum *see* Yverdon
101 *J19* **Ebrach** Bayern, C Germany
109 *X5* **Ebreichsdorf** Niederösterreich, E Austria
105 *S6* **Ebro** ≈ NE Spain
105 *N3* **Ebro, Embalse del** ▣ N Spain
120 *G7* **Ebro Fan** *undersea feature* W Mediterranean Sea
Eburacum *see* York
Ebusus *see* Eivissa
99 *F20* **Écaussinnes-d'Enghien** Hainaut, SW Belgium
Ecbatana *see* Hamadān
21 *Q6* **Eccles** West Virginia, NE USA
115 *L14* **Eceabat** Çanakkale, NW Turkey
171 *O2* **Echague** Luzon, N Philippines
Ech Cheliff/Ech Chleff *see* Chlef
Echeng *see* Ezhou
115 *C18* **Echinádes** *island group* W Greece
114 *J12* **Echínos** *var.* Ehinos, Ekhínos. Anatolikí Makedonía kai Thráki, NE Greece
164 *J12* **Echizen-misaki** *headland* Honshū, SW Japan
Echmiadzin *see* Ejmiatsin
8 *J8* **Echo Bay** Northwest Territories, NW Canada
35 *Y11* **Echo Bay** Nevada, W USA
36 *L9* **Echo Cliffs** *cliff* Arizona, SW USA
14 *C10* **Echo Lake** ◎ Ontario, S Canada
35 *Q7* **Echo Summit** ▲ California, W USA
14 *L8* **Échouani, Lac** ◎ Québec, SE Canada
99 *L17* **Echt** Limburg, SE Netherlands
101 *H22* **Echterdingen** × (Stuttgart) Baden-Württemberg, SW Germany
99 *N24* **Echternach** Grevenmacher, E Luxembourg
183 *N11* **Echuca** Victoria, SE Australia
104 *L14* **Ecija** ***anc.*** Astigi. Andalucía, SW Spain
Eckengraf *see* Viesīte
100 *I7* **Eckernförde** Schleswig-Holstein, N Germany
100 *J7* **Eckernförder Bucht** *inlet* N Germany
102 *L7* **Écommoy** Sarthe, NW France
14 *L10* **Écorce, Lac de l'** ◎ Québec, SE Canada
15 *Q8* **Écorces, Rivière aux** ≈ Québec, SE Canada
56 *C7* **Ecuador** ***off.*** Republic of Ecuador. ◆ *republic* NW South America
80 *L10* **Ed** ***var.*** Edd. SE Eritrea
95 *I17* **Ed** Västra Götaland, S Sweden
98 *I9* **Edam** Noord-Holland, C Netherlands
96 *K4* **Eday** *island* NE Scotland, UK
25 *S17* **Edcouch** Texas, SW USA
Edd *see* Ed
80 *C11* **Ed Da'ein** Southern Darfur, W Sudan
80 *G11* **Ed Damazin** *var.* Ad Damazīn. Blue Nile, E Sudan
80 *G8* **Ed Damer** *var.* Ad Damar, Ad Dāmir. River Nile, NE Sudan
80 *E8* **Ed Debba** Northern, N Sudan
80 *F10* **Ed Dueim** *var.* Ad Duwaym, Ad Duwēm. White Nile, C Sudan
183 *Q16* **Eddystone Point** *headland* Tasmania, SE Australia
97 *I25* **Eddystone Rocks** *rocks* SW England, UK
29 *W15* **Eddyville** Iowa, C USA
20 *H7* **Eddyville** Kentucky, S USA
98 *L12* **Ede** Gelderland, C Netherlands
77 *T16* **Ede** Osun, SW Nigeria
79 *D16* **Edéa** Littoral, SW Cameroon
111 *M20* **Edelény** Borsod-Abaúj-Zemplén, NE Hungary
183 *R12* **Eden** New South Wales, SE Australia
21 *T8* **Eden** North Carolina, SE USA
25 *P9* **Eden** Texas, SW USA
97 *K14* **Eden** ≈ NW England, UK
83 *I23* **Edenburg** Free State, C South Africa
185 *D24* **Edendale** Southland, South Island, NZ
97 *E18* **Edenderry** ***Ir.*** Éadan Doire. C Ireland
182 *L11* **Edenhope** Victoria, SE Australia
21 *X8* **Edenton** North Carolina, SE USA
101 *G16* **Eder** ≈ NW Germany
101 *H15* **Edersee** ◎ W Germany
Edessa *see* Şanlıurfa
114 *E13* **Édessa** *var.* Édhessa. Kentrikí Makedonía, N Greece
Edfu *see* Idfu
29 *P16* **Edgar** Nebraska, C USA
19 *P13* **Edgartown** Martha's Vineyard, Massachusetts, NE USA
39 *X13* **Edgecumbe, Mount** ▲ Baranof Island, Alaska, USA
21 *Q13* **Edgefield** South Carolina, SE USA
29 *P6* **Edgeley** North Dakota, N USA
28 *I11* **Edgemont** South Dakota, N USA
92 *O3* **Edgeøya** *island* S Svalbard
27 *Q4* **Edgerton** Kansas, C USA
29 *S10* **Edgerton** Minnesota, N USA
21 *X3* **Edgewood** Maryland, NE USA
25 *V6* **Edgewood** Texas, SW USA
Édhessa *see* Édessa
29 *V9* **Edina** Minnesota, N USA
27 *U2* **Edina** Missouri, C USA
25 *S17* **Edinburg** Texas, SW USA
65 *M24* **Edinburgh** *var.* Settlement of Edinburgh. ○ (Tristan da Cunha) NW Tristan da Cunha
96 *J12* **Edinburgh** ◐ S Scotland, UK
31 *P14* **Edinburgh** Indiana, N USA
96 *J12* **Edinburgh** × S Scotland, UK
116 *L8* **Edineț** *var.* Edineți, ***Rus.*** Yedintsy. NW Moldova
Edineți *see* Edineț
Edingen *see* Enghien
136 *B9* **Edirne** ***Eng.*** Adrianople; ***anc.*** Adrianopolis, Hadrianopolis. Edirne, NW Turkey
136 *B11* **Edirne** ◈ *province* NW Turkey
18 *K15* **Edison** New Jersey, NE USA
21 *S15* **Edisto Island** South Carolina, SE USA
21 *R14* **Edisto River** ≈ South Carolina, SE USA
33 *S10* **Edith, Mount** ▲ Montana, NW USA
27 *N10* **Edmond** Oklahoma, C USA
32 *H8* **Edmonds** Washington, NW USA
11 *Q14* **Edmonton** Alberta, SW Canada

◆ COUNTRY ● COUNTRY CAPITAL ◇ DEPENDENT TERRITORY ○ DEPENDENT TERRITORY CAPITAL ◈ ADMINISTRATIVE REGION × INTERNATIONAL AIRPORT ▲ MOUNTAIN ⛰ MOUNTAIN RANGE ⚶ VOLCANO ≈ RIVER ◎ LAKE ▣ RESERVOIR

20 K7 **Edmonton** Kentucky, S USA
11 Q14 **Edmonton** ✕ Alberta, SW Canada
29 P3 **Edmore** North Dakota, N USA
13 N13 **Edmundston** New Brunswick, SE Canada
25 U12 **Edna** Texas, SW USA
39 X14 **Edna Bay** Kosciusko Island, Alaska, USA
77 U16 **Edo** ◆ *state* S Nigeria
106 F6 **Edolo** Lombardia, N Italy
64 L6 **Edoras Bank** *undersea feature* C Atlantic Ocean
96 G7 **Edrachillis Bay** *bay* NW Scotland, UK
136 B12 **Edremit** Balıkesir, NW Turkey
136 B12 **Edremit Körfezi** *gulf* NW Turkey
95 P14 **Edsbro** Stockholm, C Sweden
95 N18 **Edsbruk** Kalmar, S Sweden
94 M12 **Edsbyn** Gävleborg, C Sweden
11 O14 **Edson** Alberta, SW Canada
62 K13 **Eduardo Castex** La Pampa, C Argentina
58 F12 **Eduardo Gomes** ✕ (Manaus) Amazonas, NW Brazil
Edwardesabad *see* Bannu
67 U9 **Edward, Lake** *var.* Albert Edward Nyanza, Edward Nyanza, Lac Idi Amin, Lake Rutanzige. ◎ Uganda/Dem. Rep. Congo
Edward Nyanza *see* Edward, Lake
22 K5 **Edwards** Mississippi, S USA
25 O10 **Edwards Plateau** *plain* Texas, SW USA
30 J11 **Edwards River** ⁓ Illinois, N USA
30 K15 **Edwardsville** Illinois, N USA
195 O13 **Edward VII Peninsula** *peninsula* Antarctica
195 X4 **Edward VIII Gulf** *bay* Antarctica
10 J11 **Edziza, Mount** ▲ British Columbia, W Canada
8 K10 **Edzo** *prev.* Rae-Edzo. Northwest Territories, NW Canada
39 N12 **Eek** Alaska, USA
99 D16 **Eeklo** *var.* Eekloo. Oost-Vlaanderen, NW Belgium
Eekloo *see* Eeklo
39 N12 **Eek River** ⁓ Alaska, USA
98 N6 **Eelde** Drenthe, NE Netherlands
34 L5 **Eel River** ⁓ California, W USA
31 P12 **Eel River** ⁓ Indiana, N USA
Eems *see* Ems
98 O4 **Eemshaven** Groningen, NE Netherlands
98 O5 **Eems Kanaal** *canal* NE Netherlands
98 M11 **Eerbeek** Gelderland, E Netherlands
99 C17 **Eernegem** West-Vlaanderen, W Belgium
99 J15 **Eersel** Noord-Brabant, S Netherlands
Eesti Vabariik *see* Estonia
187 R14 **Efate** *var.* Éfaté, Fr. Vaté *prev.* Sandwich Island. *island* C Vanuatu
109 S4 **Eferding** Oberösterreich, N Austria
30 M15 **Effingham** Illinois, N USA
117 N15 **Eforie-Nord** Constanța, SE Romania
117 N15 **Eforie Sud** Constanța, E Romania
Efyrnwy, Afon *see* Vyrnwy
163 N7 **Eg** Hentiy, N Mongolia
107 G23 **Egadi, Isole** *island group* S Italy
35 X6 **Egan Range** ▲▲ Nevada, W USA
14 K12 **Eganville** Ontario, SE Canada
Ege Denizi *see* Aegean Sea
39 O14 **Egegik** Alaska, USA
111 L21 **Eger** *Ger.* Erlau. Heves, NE Hungary
Eger *see* Cheb, Czech Republic
Eger *see* Ohre, Czech Republic/Germany
173 P8 **Egeria Fracture Zone** *tectonic feature* W Indian Ocean
95 C17 **Egersund** Rogaland, S Norway
108 J7 **Egg** Vorarlberg, NW Austria
101 H14 **Egge-gebirge** ▲▲ C Germany
109 Q4 **Eggelsberg** Oberösterreich, N Austria
109 W2 **Eggenburg** Niederösterreich, NE Austria
101 N22 **Eggenfelden** Bayern, SE Germany
18 J17 **Egg Harbor City** New Jersey, NE USA
65 G25 **Egg Island** *island* W Saint Helena
183 N14 **Egg Lagoon** Tasmania, SE Australia
99 I20 **Éghezèe** Namur, C Belgium
92 L2 **Egilsstadhir** Austurland, E Iceland
Egina *see* Aígina
Egindibulaq *see* Yegindybulak
Egio *see* Aígio
103 N12 **Égletons** Corrèze, C France
98 H9 **Egmond aan Zee** Noord-Holland, NW Netherlands
Egmont *see* Taranaki, Mount
184 J10 **Egmont, Cape** *headland* North Island, NZ
Egoli *see* Johannesburg
Eğri Palanka *see* Kriva Palanka
95 G23 **Egtved** Vejle, C Denmark
123 U5 **Egvekinot** Chukotskiy Avtonomnyy Okrug, NE Russian Federation
75 V9 **Egypt** *off.* Arab Republic of Egypt, *Ar.* Jumhūrīyah Mişr al 'Arabīyah; *prev.* United Arab Republic, *anc.* Aegyptus. ◆ *republic* NE Africa
30 L17 **Egypt, Lake Of** ▣ Illinois, N USA
162 I14 **Ehen Hudag** *var.* Alx Youqi. Nei Mongol Zizhiqu, N China
164 F14 **Ehime** *off.* Ehime-ken. ◆ *prefecture* Shikoku, SW Japan
101 I23 **Ehingen** Baden-Württemberg, S Germany
21 R14 **Ehrhardt** South Carolina, SE USA
108 L7 **Ehrwald** Tirol, W Austria
191 W6 **Eiao** *island* Îles Marquises, NE French Polynesia
105 P2 **Eibar** País Vasco, N Spain
98 O11 **Eibergen** Gelderland, E Netherlands
109 V9 **Eibiswald** Steiermark, SE Austria
109 P8 **Eichham** ▲ SW Austria
101 J15 **Eichsfeld** *hill range* C Germany
101 K21 **Eichstätt** Bayern, SE Germany
100 H8 **Eider** ⁓ N Germany
94 E13 **Eidfjord** Hordaland, S Norway
94 D13 **Eidfjorden** *fjord* S Norway
94 F9 **Eidsvåg** Møre og Romsdal, S Norway
95 I14 **Eidsvoll** Akershus, S Norway
92 N2 **Eidsvollfjellet** ▲ NW Svalbard
Eier-Berg *see* Suur Munamägi
101 D18 **Eifel** *plateau* W Germany
108 E9 **Eiger** ▲ C Switzerland
96 G10 **Eigg** *island* W Scotland, UK
155 D24 **Eight Degree Channel** *channel* India/Maldives
44 G1 **Eight Mile Rock** Grand Bahama Island, N Bahamas
194 J9 **Eights Coast** *physical region* Antarctica
180 K6 **Eighty Mile Beach** *beach* Western Australia
99 L18 **Eijsden** Limburg, SE Netherlands
95 G15 **Eikeren** ◎ S Norway
Eil *see* Eyl
Eilat *see* Elat
183 O12 **Eildon** Victoria, SE Australia
183 O12 **Eildon, Lake** ◎ Victoria, SE Australia
80 E8 **Eilei** Northern Kordofan, C Sudan
101 N15 **Eilenburg** Sachsen, E Germany
94 H13 **Eina** Oppland, S Norway
Ein 'Avedat *see* En 'Avedat
101 I14 **Einbeck** Niedersachsen, C Germany
99 K15 **Eindhoven** Noord-Brabant, S Netherlands
108 G8 **Einsiedeln** Schwyz, NE Switzerland
Eipel *see* Ipel'
Éire *see* Ireland, Republic of
Éireann, Muir *see* Irish Sea
Eirik Outer Ridge *see* Eirik Ridge
64 I6 **Eirik Ridge** *var.* Eirik Outer Ridge. *undersea feature* E Labrador Sea
92 I3 **Eiríksjökull** ▲ C Iceland
59 B14 **Eirunepé** Amazonas, N Brazil
99 L17 **Eisden** Limburg, NE Belgium
83 F18 **Eiseb** ⁓ Botswana/Namibia
Eisen *see* Yŏngch'ŏn
101 J16 **Eisenach** Thüringen, C Germany
Eisenburg *see* Vasvár
109 U6 **Eisenerz** Steiermark, SE Austria
100 Q13 **Eisenhüttenstadt** Brandenburg, E Germany
109 U10 **Eisenkappel** *Slvn.* Železna Kapela. Kärnten, S Austria
Eisenmarkt *see* Hunedoara
109 Y5 **Eisenstadt** Burgenland, E Austria
Eishū *see* Yŏngju
119 H15 **Eišiškės** Vilnius, SE Lithuania
101 L15 **Eisleben** Sachsen-Anhalt, C Germany
190 I3 **Eita** Tarawa, W Kiribati
Eitape *see* Aitape
105 V11 **Eivissa** *var.* Iviza, *Cast.* Ibiza; *anc.* Ebusus. Eivissa, Spain, W Mediterranean Sea
105 V10 **Eivissa** *var.* Iviza, *Cast.* Ibiza; *anc.* Ebusus. *island* Islas Baleares, Spain, W Mediterranean Sea
105 R4 **Ejea de los Caballeros** Aragón, NE Spain
40 E8 **Ejido Insurgentes** Baja California Sur, W Mexico
Ejin Qi *see* Dalain Hob
Ejmiadzın *see* Ejmiatsin
137 T12 **Ejmiatsin** *var.* Ejmiadzın, Etchmiadzin, *Rus.* Echmiadzin. W Armenia
77 P16 **Ejura** C Ghana
41 R16 **Ejutla** *var.* Ejutla de Crespo. Oaxaca, SE Mexico
Ejutla de Crespo *see* Ejutla
33 Y10 **Ekalaka** Montana, NW USA
Ekapa *see* Cape Town
Ekaterinodar *see* Krasnodar
93 L20 **Ekenäs** *Fin.* Tammisaari. Etelä-Suomi, SW Finland
146 B13 **Ekerem** *Rus.* Okarem. Balkan Welaýaty, W Turkmenistan
184 M13 **Eketahuna** Manawatu-Wanganui, North Island, NZ
Ekhínos *see* Echínos
123 U5 **Ekiatapskiy Khrebet** ▲▲ NE Russian Federation
145 T8 **Ekibastuz** Pavlodar, NE Kazakhstan
123 R13 **Ekimchan** Amurskaya Oblast', SE Russian Federation
95 O15 **Ekoln** ◎ C Sweden
80 I7 **Ekowit** Red Sea, NE Sudan
95 L19 **Eksjö** Jönköping, S Sweden
93 I15 **Ekträsk** Västerbotten, N Sweden
39 O13 **Ekuk** Alaska, USA
12 F9 **Ekwan** ⁓ Ontario, C Canada
39 O13 **Ekwok** Alaska, USA
166 M6 **Ela** Mandalay, C Myanmar
El Aaiun *see* El Ayoun
81 N15 **El Ābrēd** Somali, E Ethiopia
115 F22 **Elafónisos** *island* S Greece
115 F22 **Elafonísou, Porthmós** *strait* S Greece
El-Aïoun *see* El Ayoun
75 U8 **El 'Alamein** *var.* Al 'Alamayn. N Egypt
41 Q12 **El Alazán** Veracruz-Llave, C Mexico
57 J18 **El Alto** *var.* La Paz. ✕ (La Paz) La Paz, W Bolivia
Elam *see* Īlām
El Amparo *see* El Amparo de Apure
54 I8 **El Amparo de Apure** *var.* El Amparo. Apure, C Venezuela
171 R13 **Elara** Pulau Ambelau, E Indonesia
El Araïch/El Araïche *see* Larache
40 D6 **El Arco** Baja California, NW Mexico
75 X7 **El 'Arîsh** *var.* Al 'Arīsh. NE Egypt
115 L25 **Elása** *island* SE Greece
El Asnam *see* Chlef
Elassón *see* Elassóna
115 E15 **Elassóna** *prev.* Elassón. Thessalía, C Greece
105 N2 **El Astillero** Cantabria, N Spain
138 F14 **Elat** *var.* Eilat, Elath. Southern, S Israel
Elat, Gulf of *see* Aqaba, Gulf of
Elath *see* Elat, Israel
Elath *see* Al 'Aqabah, Jordan
115 C17 **Eláti** ▲ Lefkáda, Iónioi Nísoi, Greece, C Mediterranean Sea
188 L16 **Elato Atoll** *atoll* Caroline Islands, C Micronesia
80 C7 **El'Atrun** Northern Darfur, NW Sudan
74 H6 **El Ayoun** *var.* El Aaiun, El-Aïoun, La Youne. NE Morocco
137 N14 **Elazığ** *var.* Elâziğ, Elâziz. Elazığ, E Turkey
137 O14 **Elazığ** *var.* Elâziğ, Elâziz. ◆ *province* C Turkey
Elâziz *see* Elazığ
Azraq, Bahr el *see* Blue Nile
23 Q7 **Elba** Alabama, S USA
106 E13 **Elba, Isola d'** *island* Archipelago Toscano, C Italy
123 S13 **El'ban** Khabarovskiy Kray, E Russian Federation
54 F6 **El Banco** Magdalena, N Colombia
El Barco *see* O Barco
104 L8 **El Barco de Ávila** Castilla-León, N Spain
El Barco de Valdeorras *see* O Barco
138 H7 **El Barouk, Jabal** ▲▲ C Lebanon
113 L20 **Elbasan** *var.* Elbasani. Elbasan, C Albania
113 L20 **Elbasan** ◆ *district* C Albania
Elbasani *see* Elbasan
54 K6 **El Baúl** Cojedes, C Venezuela
86 D11 **Elbe** *Cz.* Labe. ⁓ Czech Republic/Germany
100 L13 **Elbe-Havel-Kanal** *canal* E Germany
100 K9 **Elbe-Lübeck-Kanal** *canal* N Germany
El Beni *see* Beni
138 H7 **El Beqaa** *var.* Al Biqā', Bekaa Valley. *valley* E Lebanon
25 R6 **Elbert** Texas, SW USA
37 R5 **Elbert, Mount** ▲ Colorado, C USA
23 U3 **Elberton** Georgia, SE USA
100 K11 **Elbe-Seiten-Kanal** *canal* N Germany
102 M4 **Elbeuf** Seine-Maritime, N France
Elbing *see* Elbląg
136 M15 **Elbistan** Kahramanmaraş, S Turkey
110 K7 **Elbląg** *var.* Elblag, *Ger.* Elbing. Warmińsko-Mazurskie, NE Poland
43 N10 **El Bluff** Región Autónoma Atlántico Sur, SE Nicaragua
63 H17 **El Bolsón** Río Negro, W Argentina
105 P11 **El Bonillo** Castilla-La Mancha, C Spain
El Bordo *see* Patía
El Boulaida/El Boulaïda *see* Blida
11 T16 **Elbow** Saskatchewan, S Canada
29 S7 **Elbow Lake** Minnesota, N USA
127 N16 **El'brus** *var.* Gora El'brus. ▲ SW Russian Federation
El'brus, Gora *see* El'brus
126 M15 **El'brusskiy** Karachayevo-Cherkesskaya Respublika, SW Russian Federation
81 D14 **El Buhayrat** *var.* Lakes State. ◆ *state* S Sudan
El Bur *see* Ceel Buur
98 L10 **Elburg** Gelderland, E Netherlands
105 O6 **El Burgo de Osma** Castilla-León, C Spain
Elburz Mountains *see* Alborz, Reshteh-ye Kūhhā-ye
35 V17 **El Cajon** California, W USA
63 H22 **El Calafate** *var.* Calafate. Santa Cruz, S Argentina
55 Q8 **El Callao** Bolívar, E Venezuela
25 U12 **El Campo** Texas, SW USA
54 I7 **El Cantón** Barinas, W Venezuela
35 Q8 **El Capitan** ▲ California, W USA
54 H5 **El Carmelo** Zulia, NW Venezuela
62 J5 **El Carmen** Jujuy, NW Argentina
54 E5 **El Carmen de Bolívar** Bolívar, NW Colombia
55 O8 **El Casabe** Bolívar, SE Venezuela
42 M12 **El Castillo de La Concepción** Río San Juan, SE Nicaragua
El Cayo *see* San Ignacio
35 X17 **El Centro** California, W USA
55 N6 **El Chaparro** Anzoátegui, NE Venezuela
105 S12 **Elche** *Cat.* Elx; *anc.* Ilici, *Lat.* Illicis. País Valenciano, E Spain
105 Q12 **Elche de la Sierra** Castilla-La Mancha, C Spain
41 U15 **El Chichonal, Volcán** ☒ SE Mexico
40 C2 **El Chinero** Baja California, NW Mexico
181 R1 **Elcho Island** *island* Wessel Islands, Northern Territory, N Australia
63 H18 **El Corcovado** Chubut, SW Argentina
105 R12 **Elda** País Valenciano, E Spain
100 M10 **Elde** ⁓ NE Germany
98 L12 **Elden** Gelderland, E Netherlands
81 J16 **El Der** *spring/well* S Ethiopia
El Dere *see* Ceel Dheere
40 E3 **El Desemboque** Sonora, NW Mexico
54 F5 **El Difícil** *var.* Ariguaní. Magdalena, N Colombia
123 R10 **El'dikan** Respublika Sakha (Yakutiya), NE Russian Federation
El Djazaïr *see* Alger
El Djelfa *see* Djelfa
29 X15 **Eldon** Iowa, C USA
27 U5 **Eldon** Missouri, C USA
54 E13 **El Doncello** Caquetá, S Colombia
29 W13 **Eldora** Iowa, C USA
60 G12 **Eldorado** Misiones, NE Argentina
40 I9 **El Dorado** Sinaloa, C Mexico
27 U14 **El Dorado** Arkansas, C USA
30 M17 **Eldorado** Illinois, N USA
27 O6 **El Dorado** Kansas, C USA
26 K12 **Eldorado** Oklahoma, C USA
25 O9 **Eldorado** Texas, SW USA
55 Q8 **El Dorado** Bolívar, E Venezuela
54 F10 **El Dorado** ✕ (Bogotá) Cundinamarca, C Colombia
El Dorado *see* California
27 O6 **El Dorado Lake** ▣ Kansas, C USA
27 S6 **El Dorado Springs** Missouri, C USA
81 H18 **Eldoret** Rift Valley, W Kenya
29 Z14 **Eldridge** Iowa, C USA
95 J21 **Eldsberga** Halland, S Sweden
25 R4 **Electra** Texas, SW USA
37 Q7 **Electra Lake** ▣ Colorado, C USA
38 B8 **'Ele'ele** *var.* Eleele. Kaua'i, Hawai'i, USA, C Pacific Ocean
Elefantes *see* Olifants
115 H19 **Elefsína** *prev.* Elevsís. Attikí, C Greece
115 G19 **Eléftheres** *anc.* Eleutherae. *site of ancient city* Attikí/Stereá Ellás, C Greece
114 I13 **Eleftheroúpoli** *prev.* Elevtheroúpolis. Anatolikí Makedonía kai Thráki, NE Greece
74 F10 **El Eglab** ▲▲ SW Algeria
118 F10 **Eleja** Jelgava, C Latvia
Elek *see* Ilek
119 G14 **Elektrėnai** Vilnius, SE Lithuania
126 L3 **Elektrostal'** Moskovskaya Oblast', W Russian Federation
81 H15 **Elemi Triangle** *disputed region* Kenya/Sudan
54 G16 **El Encanto** Amazonas, S Colombia
37 R14 **Elephant Butte Reservoir** ▣ New Mexico, SW USA
Éléphant, Chaîne de l' *see* Dâmrei, Chuŏr Phmun
194 G2 **Elephant Island** *island* South Shetland Islands, Antarctica
Elephant River *see* Olifants
El Escorial *see* San Lorenzo de El Escorial
Élesd *see* Aleşd
114 F11 **Eleshnitsa** ⁓ W Bulgaria
137 S13 **Eleşkirt** Ağrı, E Turkey
42 F5 **El Estor** Izabal, E Guatemala
Eleutherae *see* Eléftheres
44 I2 **Eleuthera Island** *island* N Bahamas
37 S5 **Elevenmile Canyon Reservoir** ▣ Colorado, C USA
27 W8 **Eleven Point River** ⁓ Arkansas/Missouri, C USA
Elevsís *see* Elefsína
Elevtheroúpolis *see* Eleftheroúpoli
75 W8 **El Faiyûm** *var.* Al Fayyūm. N Egypt
80 B10 **El Fasher** *var.* Al Fāshir. Northern Darfur, W Sudan
75 W8 **El Fashn** *var.* Al Fashn. C Egypt
El Ferrol/El Ferrol del Caudillo *see* Ferrol
39 W13 **Elfin Cove** Chichagof Island, Alaska, USA
105 W4 **El Fluvià** ⁓ NE Spain
40 H7 **El Fuerte** Sinaloa, W Mexico
80 D11 **El Fula** Western Kordofan, C Sudan
El Gedaref *see* Gedaref
80 A10 **El Geneina** *var.* Ajjinena, Al-Genain, Al Junaynah. Western Darfur, W Sudan
96 J8 **Elgin** NE Scotland, UK
30 M10 **Elgin** Illinois, N USA
29 P14 **Elgin** Nebraska, C USA
35 Y9 **Elgin** Nevada, W USA
28 L6 **Elgin** North Dakota, N USA
26 M12 **Elgin** Oklahoma, C USA
25 T10 **Elgin** Texas, SW USA
123 R9 **El'ginskiy** Respublika Sakha (Yakutiya), NE Russian Federation
75 W8 **El Gîza** *var.* Al Jīzah, Gîza, Gizeh. N Egypt
74 J8 **El Goléa** *var.* Al Golea. C Algeria
40 D2 **El Golfo de Santa Clara** Sonora, NW Mexico
81 G18 **Elgon, Mount** ▲ E Uganda
105 T4 **El Grado** Aragón, NE Spain
94 I10 **Elgspiggen** ▲ S Norway
40 L6 **El Guaje, Laguna** ▣ NE Mexico
54 H6 **El Guayabo** Zulia, W Venezuela
77 O6 **El Guettâra** *oasis* N Mali
76 J6 **El Hammâmi** *desert* N Mauritania
76 M5 **El Hank** *cliff* N Mauritania
El Haseke *see* Al Ḩasakah
80 H10 **El Hawata** Gedaref, E Sudan
El Higo *see* Higos
171 T16 **Eliase** Pulau Selaru, E Indonesia
Elías Piña *see* Comendador
25 R6 **Eliasville** Texas, SW USA
Elichpur *see* Achalpur
37 V13 **Elida** New Mexico, SW USA
115 F18 **Elikónas** ▲ C Greece
67 T10 **Elila** ⁓ W Dem. Rep. Congo
39 N9 **Elim** Alaska, USA
Elimberrum *see* Auch
Eliocroca *see* Lorca
61 B16 **Elisa** Santa Fe, C Argentina
Elisabethstedt *see* Dumbrăveni
Élisabethville *see* Lubumbashi
127 O13 **Elista** Respublika Kalmykiya, SW Russian Federation
182 I9 **Elizabeth** South Australia
21 Q3 **Elizabeth** West Virginia, NE USA
19 Q9 **Elizabeth, Cape** *headland* Maine, NE USA
21 Y8 **Elizabeth City** North Carolina, SE USA
21 P8 **Elizabethton** Tennessee, S USA
30 M17 **Elizabethtown** Illinois, N USA
20 K6 **Elizabethtown** Kentucky, S USA
18 L7 **Elizabethtown** New York, NE USA
21 U11 **Elizabethtown** North Carolina, SE USA
18 G15 **Elizabethtown** Pennsylvania, NE USA
74 E6 **El-Jadida** *prev.* Mazagan. W Morocco
El Jafr *see* Jafr, Qā' al
80 F11 **El Jebelein** White Nile, E Sudan
110 N8 **Ełk** *Ger.* Lyck. Warmińsko-Mazurskie, NE Poland
110 O8 **Ełk** ⁓ NE Poland
29 Y12 **Elkader** Iowa, C USA
80 G9 **El Kamlin** Gezira, C Sudan
33 N11 **Elk City** Idaho, NW USA
26 K10 **Elk City** Oklahoma, C USA
27 P7 **Elk City Lake** ▣ Kansas, C USA
34 M5 **Elk Creek** California, W USA
28 J10 **Elk Creek** ⁓ South Dakota, N USA
74 M5 **El Kef** *var.* Al Kāf, Le Kef. NW Tunisia
74 F7 **El Kelâa Srarhna** *var.* Kal al Sraghna. C Morocco
El Kerak *see* Al Karak
11 P17 **Elkford** British Columbia, SW Canada
El Khalil *see* Hebron
80 E7 **El Khandaq** Northern, N Sudan
75 W10 **El Khârga** *var.* Al Khārijah. C Egypt
31 P11 **Elkhart** Indiana, N USA
26 H7 **Elkhart** Kansas, C USA
25 V8 **Elkhart** Texas, SW USA
30 M7 **Elkhart Lake** ◎ Wisconsin, N USA
El Khartûm *see* Khartoum
37 Q3 **Elkhead Mountains** ▲▲ Colorado, C USA
18 I12 **Elk Hill** ▲ Pennsylvania, NE USA
138 G8 **El Khiyam** *var.* Al Khiyām, Khiam. S Lebanon
29 S15 **Elkhorn** Nebraska, C USA
30 M9 **Elkhorn** Wisconsin, N USA
29 R14 **Elkhorn River** ⁓ Nebraska, C USA
127 O16 **El'khotovo** Respublika Severnaya Osetiya, SW Russian Federation
114 L10 **Elkhovo** *prev.* Kizilagach. Yambol, E Bulgaria
21 R8 **Elkin** North Carolina, SE USA
21 S4 **Elkins** West Virginia, NE USA
195 X3 **Elkins, Mount** ▲ Antarctica
14 G8 **Elk Lake** Ontario, S Canada
31 P6 **Elk Lake** ◎ Michigan, N USA
18 F12 **Elkland** Pennsylvania, NE USA
35 W3 **Elko** Nevada, W USA
11 R14 **Elk Point** Alberta, SW Canada
29 R12 **Elk Point** South Dakota, N USA
29 V8 **Elk River** Minnesota, N USA
20 J10 **Elk River** ⁓ Alabama/Tennessee, S USA
21 R4 **Elk River** ⁓ West Virginia, NE USA
20 I7 **Elkton** Kentucky, S USA
21 Y2 **Elkton** Maryland, NE USA
29 R10 **Elkton** South Dakota, N USA
20 I10 **Elkton** Tennessee, S USA
21 U5 **Elkton** Virginia, NE USA
El Kuneitra *see* Al Qunayţirah
81 L15 **El Kure** Somali, E Ethiopia
80 D12 **El Lagowa** Western Kordofan, C Sudan
39 S12 **Ellamar** Alaska, USA
Ellás *see* Greece
23 S6 **Ellaville** Georgia, SE USA
8 I3 **Ellef Ringnes Island** *island* Nunavut, N Canada
29 V10 **Ellendale** Minnesota, N USA
29 P7 **Ellendale** North Dakota, N USA
36 M6 **Ellen, Mount** ▲ Utah, W USA
32 I9 **Ellensburg** Washington, NW USA
18 K12 **Ellenville** New York, NE USA
Ellep *see* Lib
21 T10 **Ellerbe** North Carolina, SE USA
9 N2 **Ellesmere Island** *island* Queen Elizabeth Islands, Nunavut, N Canada
185 H19 **Ellesmere, Lake** ◎ South Island, NZ
97 K18 **Ellesmere Port** C England, UK
31 O14 **Ellettsville** Indiana, N USA
99 E19 **Ellezelles** Hainaut, SW Belgium
8 L7 **Ellice** ⁓ Nunavut, NE Canada
Ellice Islands *see* Tuvalu
Ellichpur *see* Achalpur
21 W3 **Ellicott City** Maryland, NE USA
23 S2 **Ellijay** Georgia, SE USA
27 W7 **Ellington** Missouri, C USA
26 L5 **Ellinwood** Kansas, C USA
83 J24 **Elliot** Eastern Cape, SE South Africa
14 D10 **Elliot Lake** Ontario, S Canada
181 X6 **Elliot, Mount** ▲ Queensland, E Australia
21 T5 **Elliott Knob** ▲ Virginia, NE USA
26 K4 **Ellis** Kansas, C USA
182 F8 **Elliston** South Australia
22 M7 **Ellisville** Mississippi, S USA
105 V5 **El Llobregat** ⁓ NE Spain
96 L9 **Ellon** NE Scotland, UK
Ellore *see* Elūru
21 S13 **Elloree** South Carolina, SE USA
26 M4 **Ellsworth** Kansas, C USA
19 S7 **Ellsworth** Maine, NE USA
30 I6 **Ellsworth** Wisconsin, N USA
26 M11 **Ellsworth, Lake** ▣ Oklahoma, C USA
194 K9 **Ellsworth Land** *physical region* Antarctica
194 L9 **Ellsworth Mountains** ▲▲ Antarctica
101 J21 **Ellwangen** Baden-Württemberg, S Germany
18 B14 **Ellwood City** Pennsylvania, NE USA
108 H8 **Elm** Glarus, NE Switzerland
32 G9 **Elma** Washington, NW USA
121 V13 **El Maḩalla el Kubra** *var.* Al Maḩallah al Kubrá, Mahalla el Kubra. N Egypt
74 E9 **El Mahbas** *var.* Mahbés. SW Western Sahara
63 H17 **El Maitén** Chubut, W Argentina
136 E16 **Elmalı** Antalya, SW Turkey
80 G10 **El Managil** Gezira, C Sudan
54 M12 **El Mango** Amazonas, S Venezuela
75 W7 **El Manṣûra** *var.* Al Manşūrah, Manşūra. N Egypt
55 P8 **El Manteco** Bolívar, E Venezuela
29 O16 **Elm Creek** Nebraska, C USA
El Mediyya *see* Médéa
77 V9 **Elméki** Agadez, C Niger
108 K7 **Elmen** Tirol, W Austria
18 I16 **Elmer** New Jersey, NE USA
138 G6 **El Mina** *var.* Al Mīnā'. N Lebanon
75 W9 **El Minya** *var.* Al Minyā, Minya. C Egypt
14 F15 **Elmira** Ontario, S Canada
18 G11 **Elmira** New York, NE USA
36 K13 **El Mirage** Arizona, SW USA
29 O7 **Elm Lake** ▣ South Dakota, N USA
El Moján *see* San Rafael
105 N7 **El Molar** Madrid, C Spain
76 L7 **El Mrâyer** *well* C Mauritania
76 L5 **El Mreiti** *well* N Mauritania
76 L8 **El Mreyyé** *desert* E Mauritania
29 P8 **Elm River** ⁓ North Dakota/South Dakota, N USA
100 I9 **Elmshorn** Schleswig-Holstein, N Germany
80 D12 **El Muglad** Western Kordofan, C Sudan
El Muwaqqar *see* Al Muwaqqar
14 G14 **Elmvale** Ontario, S Canada
30 K12 **Elmwood** Illinois, N USA
26 J8 **Elmwood** Oklahoma, C USA
103 P17 **Elne** *anc.* Illiberis. Pyrénées-Orientales, S France
54 F11 **El Nevado, Cerro** *elevation* C Colombia
171 N5 **El Nido** Palawan, W Philippines
62 I12 **El Nihuil** Mendoza, W Argentina
75 W7 **El Nouzha** ✕ (Alexandria) N Egypt
80 E10 **El Obeid** *var.* Al Obayyid, Al Ubayyiḑ. Northern Kordofan, C Sudan
41 O13 **El Oro** México, S Mexico
56 B8 **El Oro** ◆ *province* SW Ecuador
61 B19 **Elortondo** Santa Fe, C Argentina
54 J8 **Elorza** Apure, C Venezuela
El Ouâdi *see* El Oued
74 L7 **El Oued** *var.* Al Oued, El Ouâdi, El Wad. NE Algeria
36 L15 **Eloy** Arizona, SW USA
55 Q7 **El Palmar** Bolívar, E Venezuela
40 K8 **El Palmito** Durango, W Mexico
55 P7 **El Pao** Bolívar, E Venezuela
54 K5 **El Pao** Cojedes, N Venezuela
42 J7 **El Paraíso** El Paraíso, S Honduras
42 I7 **El Paraíso** ◆ *department* SE Honduras
30 L12 **El Paso** Illinois, N USA
24 G8 **El Paso** Texas, SW USA
24 G8 **El Paso** ✕ Texas, SW USA
105 U7 **El Perello** Cataluña, NE Spain
55 P5 **El Pilar** Sucre, NE Venezuela
42 F7 **El Pital, Cerro** ▲ El Salvador/Honduras
35 Q9 **El Portal** California, W USA
40 J3 **El Porvenir** Chihuahua, N Mexico
43 U14 **El Porvenir** San Blas, N Panama
105 W6 **El Prat de Llobregat** Cataluña, NE Spain
42 H5 **El Progreso** Yoro, NW Honduras
42 A2 **El Progreso** *off.* Departamento de El Progreso. ◆ *department* C Guatemala
El Progreso *see* Guastatoya
104 L9 **El Puente del Arzobispo** Castilla-La Mancha, C Spain

◆ COUNTRY ◇ DEPENDENT TERRITORY ◆ ADMINISTRATIVE REGION ▲ MOUNTAIN ☒ VOLCANO ◎ LAKE
● COUNTRY CAPITAL ○ DEPENDENT TERRITORY CAPITAL ✕ INTERNATIONAL AIRPORT ▲▲ MOUNTAIN RANGE ⁓ RIVER ▣ RESERVOIR

104 *J15* **El Puerto de Santa María** Andalucía, S Spain
62 *I8* **El Puesto** Catamarca, NW Argentina
El Qâhira *see* Cairo
75 *V10* **El Qaşr** ***var.*** Al Qaşr. C Egypt
El Qatrani *see* Al Qaţrānah
40 *I10* **El Quelite** Sinaloa, C Mexico
62 *G9* **Elqui, Río** ≈ N Chile
El Quneitra *see* Al Qunayţirah
El Quseir *see* Al Quşayr
El Quweira *see* Al Quwayrah
141 *O15* **El-Rahaba** × (Şan'ā') W Yemen
42 *M10* **El Rama** Región Autónoma Atlántico Sur, SE Nicaragua
43 *W16* **El Real** ***var.*** El Real de Santa María. Darién, SE Panama
El Real de Santa María *see* El Real
26 *M10* **El Reno** Oklahoma, C USA
40 *K9* **El Rodeo** Durango, C Mexico
104 *J13* **El Ronquillo** Andalucía, S Spain
11 *S16* **Elrose** Saskatchewan, S Canada
30 *K8* **Elroy** Wisconsin, N USA
25 *S17* **Elsa** Texas, SW USA
75 *W8* **El Şaff** ***var.*** Aş Şaff. N Egypt
40 *J10* **El Salto** Durango, C Mexico
42 *D8* **El Salvador** ***off.*** Republica de El Salvador. ◆ *republic* Central America
54 *K7* **El Samán de Apure** Apure, C Venezuela
14 *D7* **Elsas** Ontario, S Canada
40 *F3* **El Sásabe** ***var.*** Aduana del Sásabe. Sonora, NW Mexico
Elsass *see* Alsace
40 *J5* **El Sáuz** Chihuahua, N Mexico
27 *W4* **Elsberry** Missouri, C USA
45 *P9* **El Seibo** ***var.*** Santa Cruz de El Seibo, Santa Cruz del Seibo. E Dominican Republic
42 *B7* **El Semillero Barra Nahualate** Escuintla, SW Guatemala
Elsene *see* Ixelles
Elsen Nur *see* Dorgê Co
36 *L6* **Elsinore** Utah, W USA
Elsinore *see* Helsingør
99 *L18* **Elsloo** Limburg, SE Netherlands
60 *G13* **El Soberbio** Misiones, NE Argentina
55 *N6* **El Socorro** Guárico, C Venezuela
54 *L6* **El Sombrero** Guárico, N Venezuela
98 *L10* **Elspeet** Gelderland, E Netherlands
98 *L12* **Elst** Gelderland, E Netherlands
101 *O15* **Elsterwerda** Brandenburg, E Germany
40 *J4* **El Sueco** Chihuahua, N Mexico
El Suweida *see* As Suwaydā'
El Suweis *see* Suez
54 *D12* **El Tambo** Cauca, SW Colombia
175 *T13* **Eltanin Fracture Zone** *tectonic feature* SE Pacific Ocean
105 *X5* **El Ter** ≈ NE Spain
184 *K11* **Eltham** Taranaki, North Island, NZ
55 *O6* **El Tigre** Anzoátegui, NE Venezuela
El Tigrito *see* San José de Guanipa
54 *J5* **El Tocuyo** Lara, N Venezuela
127 *Q10* **El'ton** Volgogradskaya Oblast', SW Russian Federation
32 *K10* **Eltopia** Washington, NW USA
105 *Z8* **El Toro** ***var.*** Mare de Déu del Toro. ▲ Menorca, Spain, W Mediterranean Sea
61 *A18* **El Trébol** Santa Fe, C Argentina
40 *J13* **El Tuito** Jalisco, SW Mexico
75 *X8* **El Ţûr** ***var.*** Aţ Ţūr. NE Egypt
155 *K16* **Elūru** ***prev.*** Ellore. Andhra Pradesh, E India
118 *H13* **Elva** ***Ger.*** Elwa. Tartumaa, SE Estonia
37 *R9* **El Vado Reservoir** ▣ New Mexico, SW USA
43 *S15* **El Valle** Coclé, C Panama
104 *I11* **Elvas** Portalegre, C Portugal
54 *K7* **El Venado** Apure, C Venezuela
105 *V6* **El Vendrell** Cataluña, NE Spain
94 *I13* **Elverum** Hedmark, S Norway
42 *I9* **El Viejo** Chinandega, NW Nicaragua
54 *G7* **El Viejo, Cerro** ▲ C Colombia
54 *H6* **El Vigía** Mérida, NW Venezuela
105 *Q4* **El Villar de Arnedo** La Rioja, N Spain
59 *A14* **Elvira** Amazonas, W Brazil
Elwa *see* Elva
El Wad *see* El Oued
81 *K17* **El Wak** North Eastern, NE Kenya
33 *R7* **Elwell, Lake** ▣ Montana, NW USA
31 *P13* **Elwood** Indiana, N USA
27 *R3* **Elwood** Kansas, C USA
29 *N16* **Elwood** Nebraska, C USA
Elx *see* Elche
97 *O20* **Ely** E England, UK
29 *X4* **Ely** Minnesota, N USA
35 *X6* **Ely** Nevada, W USA
El Yopal *see* Yopal
31 *T11* **Elyria** Ohio, N USA
45 *S9* **El Yunque** ▲ E Puerto Rico
101 *F23* **Elz** ≈ SW Germany
187 *R14* **Emae** *island* Shepherd Islands, C Vanuatu
118 *I5* **Emajõgi** ***Ger.*** Embach. ≈ SE Estonia
Emāmrūd *see* Shāhrūd
149 *Q2* **Emām Şāḩeb** ***var.*** Emam Saheb, Hazarat Imam. Kunduz, NE Afghanistan
Emāmshahr *see* Shāhrūd
95 *M20* **Emån** ≈ S Sweden
144 *J11* **Emba** ***Kaz.*** Embi. Aktyubinsk, W Kazakhstan
144 *H12* **Emba** ***Kaz.*** Zhem. ≈ W Kazakhstan
Embach *see* Emajõgi
62 *K5* **Embarcación** Salta, N Argentina
30 *M15* **Embarras River** ≈ Illinois, N USA
Embi *see* Emba
81 *I19* **Embu** Eastern, C Kenya
100 *E10* **Emden** Niedersachsen, NW Germany
160 *H9* **Emei Shan** ▲ Sichuan, C China
29 *Q4* **Emerado** North Dakota, N USA
181 *X8* **Emerald** Queensland, E Australia
Emerald Isle *see* Montserrat
57 *J15* **Emero, Río** ≈ W Bolivia
11 *Y17* **Emerson** Manitoba, S Canada
29 *T15* **Emerson** Iowa, C USA
29 *R13* **Emerson** Nebraska, C USA
36 *M5* **Emery** Utah, W USA
Emesa *see* Ḩimş
136 *E13* **Emet** Kütahya, W Turkey
186 *B8* **Emeti** Western, SW PNG
35 *V3* **Emigrant Pass** *pass* Nevada, W USA
78 *I6* **Emi Koussi** ▲ N Chad
Emilia *see* Emilia-Romagna
41 *V15* **Emiliano Zapata** Chiapas, SE Mexico
106 *E9* **Emilia-Romagna** ***prev.*** Emilia, ***anc.*** Æmilia. ◈ *region* N Italy
158 *J3* **Emin** ***var.*** Dorbiljin. Xinjiang Uygur Zizhiqu, NW China
149 *W8* **Eminābād** Punjab, E Pakistan
21 *L5* **Eminence** Kentucky, S USA
27 *W7* **Eminence** Missouri, C USA
114 *N9* **Emine, Nos** *headland* E Bulgaria
158 *I3* **Emin He** ≈ NW China
186 *G4* **Emirau Island** *island* N PNG
136 *F13* **Emirdağ** Afyon, W Turkey
95 *M21* **Emmaboda** Kalmar, S Sweden
118 *E5* **Emmaste** Hiiumaa, W Estonia
18 *I15* **Emmaus** Pennsylvania, NE USA
183 *U4* **Emmaville** New South Wales, SE Australia
108 *E9* **Emme** ≈ W Switzerland
98 *L8* **Emmeloord** Flevoland, N Netherlands
98 *O8* **Emmen** Drenthe, NE Netherlands
108 *F8* **Emmen** Luzern, C Switzerland
101 *F23* **Emmendingen** Baden-Württemberg, SW Germany
98 *P8* **Emmer-Compascuum** Drenthe, NE Netherlands
101 *D14* **Emmerich** Nordrhein-Westfalen, W Germany
29 *U12* **Emmetsburg** Iowa, C USA
32 *M14* **Emmett** Idaho, NW USA
38 *M10* **Emmonak** Alaska, USA
Emona *see* Ljubljana
Emonti *see* East London
24 *L12* **Emory Peak** ▲ Texas, SW USA
40 *F6* **Empalme** Sonora, NW Mexico
83 *L23* **Empangeni** KwaZulu/Natal, E South Africa
61 *C14* **Empedrado** Corrientes, NE Argentina
192 *K3* **Emperor Seamounts** *undersea feature* NW Pacific Ocean
192 *L3* **Emperor Trough** *undersea feature* N Pacific Ocean
35 *R4* **Empire** Nevada, W USA
Empire State of the South *see* Georgia
Emplawas *see* Amplawas
106 *F11* **Empoli** Toscana, C Italy
27 *P5* **Emporia** Kansas, C USA
21 *W7* **Emporia** Virginia, NE USA
18 *E13* **Emporium** Pennsylvania, NE USA
Empty Quarter *see* Ar Rub' al Khālī
100 *E10* **Ems** ***Dut.*** Eems. ≈ NW Germany
100 *F13* **Emsdetten** Nordrhein-Westfalen, NW Germany
Ems-Hunte Canal *see* Küstenkanal
100 *F10* **Ems-Jade-Kanal** *canal* NW Germany
100 *F11* **Emsland** *cultural region* NW Germany
182 *D3* **Emu Junction** South Australia
163 *T3* **Emur He** ≈ NE China
55 *R8* **Enachu Landing** NW Guyana
93 *F16* **Enafors** Jämtland, C Sweden
94 *N11* **Enånger** Gävleborg, C Sweden
96 *G7* **Enard Bay** *bay* NW Scotland, UK
Enareträsk *see* Inarijärvi
171 *X14* **Enarotali** Papua, E Indonesia
138 *E12* **En 'Avedat** *var.* Ein 'Avedat, *well* S Israel
165 *T2* **Enbetsu** Hokkaidō, NE Japan
61 *H16* **Encantadas, Serra das** ▲ S Brazil
40 *E7* **Encantado, Cerro** ▲ NW Mexico
62 *P7* **Encarnación** Itapúa, S Paraguay
40 *M12* **Encarnación de Díaz** Jalisco, SW Mexico
77 *O17* **Enchi** SW Ghana
25 *Q14* **Encinal** Texas, SW USA
35 *U17* **Encinitas** California, W USA
25 *S16* **Encino** Texas, SW USA
54 *H6* **Encontrados** Zulia, NW Venezuela
182 *I10* **Encounter Bay** *inlet* South Australia
61 *F15* **Encruzilhada** Rio Grande do Sul, S Brazil
61 *H16* **Encruzilhada do Sul** Rio Grande do Sul, S Brazil
111 *M20* **Encs** Borsod-Abaúj-Zemplén, NE Hungary
193 *P3* **Endeavour Seamount** *undersea feature* N Pacific Ocean
181 *V1* **Endeavour Strait** *strait* Queensland, NE Australia
171 *O16* **Endeh** Flores, S Indonesia
95 *G23* **Endelave** *island* C Denmark
191 *T4* **Enderbury Island** *atoll* Phoenix Islands, C Kiribati
11 *N16* **Enderby** British Columbia, SW Canada
195 *W4* **Enderby Land** *physical region* Antarctica
173 *N14* **Enderby Plain** *undersea feature* S Indian Ocean
29 *Q6* **Enderlin** North Dakota, N USA
Endersdorf *see* Jędrzejów
28 *K16* **Enders Reservoir** ▣ Nebraska, C USA
18 *H11* **Endicott** New York, NE USA
39 *P7* **Endicott Mountains** ▲ Alaska, USA
118 *I5* **Endla Raba** *wetland* C Estonia
117 *T9* **Enerhodar** Zaporiz'ka Oblast', SE Ukraine
57 *F14* **Ene, Río** ≈ C Peru
189 *N4* **Enewetak Atoll** ***var.*** Ānewetak, Eniwetok. *atoll* Ralik Chain, W Marshall Islands
114 *L13* **Enez** Edirne, NW Turkey
21 *W8* **Enfield** North Carolina, SE USA
186 *B7* **Enga** ◈ *province* W PNG
45 *Q9* **Engaño, Cabo** *headland* E Dominican Republic
164 *U3* **Engaru** Hokkaidō, NE Japan
138 *F11* **'En Gedi** Southern, E Israel
108 *F9* **Engelberg** Unterwalden, C Switzerland
21 *Y9* **Engelhard** North Carolina, SE USA
127 *P8* **Engel's** Saratovskaya Oblast', W Russian Federation
101 *G24* **Engen** Baden-Württemberg, SW Germany
Engeten *see* Aiud
168 *K15* **Enggano, Pulau** *island* W Indonesia
80 *J8* **Enghershatu** ▲ N Eritrea
99 *F19* **Enghien** ***Dut.*** Edingen. Hainaut, SW Belgium
27 *V12* **England** Arkansas, C USA
97 *M20* **England** ***Lat.*** Anglia. *national region* UK
14 *H8* **Englehart** Ontario, S Canada
37 *T4* **Englewood** Colorado, C USA
31 *O16* **English** Indiana, N USA
39 *Q13* **English Bay** Alaska, USA
English Bazar *see* Ingrāj Bāzār
97 *N25* **English Channel** ***var.*** The Channel, ***Fr.*** la Manche. *channel* NW Europe
194 *J7* **English Coast** *physical region* Antarctica
105 *S11* **Enguera** País Valenciano, E Spain
118 *E8* **Engure** Tukums, W Latvia
118 *E8* **Engures Ezers** ◎ NW Latvia
137 *R9* **Enguri** ***Rus.*** Inguri. ≈ NW Georgia
Engyum *see* Gangi
26 *M9* **Enid** Oklahoma, C USA
22 *L3* **Enid Lake** ▣ Mississippi, S USA
189 *Y2* **Enigu** *island* Ratak Chain, SE Marshall Islands
Enikale Strait *see* Kerch Strait
147 *Z8* **Enil'chek** Issyk-Kul'skaya Oblast', E Kyrgyzstan
115 *F17* **Enipéfs** ≈ C Greece
165 *S4* **Eniwa** Hokkaidō, NE Japan
Eniwetok *see* Enewetak Atoll
Enjiang *see* Yongfeng
123 *S11* **Enkan, Mys** *headland* NE Russian Federation
Enkeldoorn *see* Chivhu
98 *J8* **Enkhuizen** Noord-Holland, NW Netherlands
109 *Q4* **Enknach** ≈ N Austria
95 *N15* **Enköping** Uppsala, C Sweden
107 *K24* **Enna** ***var.*** Castrogiovanni, Henna. Sicilia, Italy, C Mediterranean Sea
80 *D11* **En Nahud** Western Kordofan, C Sudan
138 *F8* **En Nâqoûra** ***var.*** An Nāqūrah. SW Lebanon
En Nazira *see* Nazerat
78 *K8* **Ennedi** *plateau* E Chad
101 *E15* **Ennepetal** Nordrhein-Westfalen, W Germany
183 *P4* **Enngonia** New South Wales, SE Australia
97 *C19* **Ennis** ***Ir.*** Inis. W Ireland
33 *R11* **Ennis** Montana, NW USA
25 *U7* **Ennis** Texas, SW USA
97 *F20* **Enniscorthy** ***Ir.*** Inis Córthaidh. SE Ireland
97 *E15* **Enniskillen** ***var.*** Inniskilling, ***Ir.*** Inis Ceithleann. SW Northern Ireland, UK
97 *B19* **Ennistimon** ***Ir.*** Inis Díomáin. W Ireland
109 *T4* **Enns** Oberösterreich, N Austria
109 *T4* **Enns** ≈ C Austria
93 *O16* **Eno** Itä-Suomi, E Finland
24 *M5* **Enochs** Texas, SW USA
93 *N17* **Enonkoski** Isä-Suomi, E Finland
92 *K10* **Enontekiö** ***Lapp.*** Eanodat. Lappi, N Finland
21 *Q11* **Enoree** South Carolina, SE USA
21 *P11* **Enoree River** ≈ South Carolina, SE USA
18 *M6* **Enosburg Falls** Vermont, NE USA
171 *N13* **Enrekang** Sulawesi, C Indonesia
45 *N10* **Enriquillo** SW Dominican Republic
45 *N9* **Enriquillo, Lago** ◎ SW Dominican Republic
98 *L9* **Ens** Flevoland, N Netherlands
98 *P11* **Enschede** Overijssel, E Netherlands
40 *B2* **Ensenada** Baja California, NW Mexico
101 *E20* **Ensheim** × (Saarbrücken) Saarland, W Germany
160 *L9* **Enshi** Hubei, C China
164 *L14* **Enshū-nada** *gulf* SW Japan
23 *O8* **Ensley** Florida, SE USA
Enso *see* Svetogorsk
81 *F18* **Entebbe** S Uganda
81 *F18* **Entebbe** × C Uganda
101 *M18* **Entenbühl** ▲ Czech Republic/Germany
98 *N10* **Enter** Overijssel, E Netherlands
23 *Q7* **Enterprise** Alabama, S USA
32 *L11* **Enterprise** Oregon, NW USA
36 *J7* **Enterprise** Utah, W USA
32 *J8* **Entiat** Washington, NW USA
105 *P15* **Entinas, Punta de las** *headland* S Spain
108 *F8* **Entlebuch** Luzern, W Switzerland
108 *F8* **Entlebuch** *valley* C Switzerland
63 *I22* **Entrada, Punta** *headland* S Argentina
103 *O13* **Entraygues-sur-Truyère** Aveyron, S France
187 *O14* **Entrecasteaux, Récifs d'** *reef* N New Caledonia
61 *C17* **Entre Ríos** ***off.*** Provincia de Entre Ríos. ◈ *province* NE Argentina
42 *K7* **Entre Ríos, Cordillera** ▲ Honduras/Nicaragua
104 *G9* **Entroncamento** Santarém, C Portugal
77 *V16* **Enugu** Enugu, S Nigeria
77 *U16* **Enugu** ◈ *state* SE Nigeria
123 *V5* **Enurmino** Chukotskiy Avtonomnyy Okrug, NE Russian Federation
54 *E9* **Envigado** Antioquia, W Colombia
59 *B15* **Envira** Amazonas, W Brazil
Enyélé *see* Enyellé
79 *I16* **Enyellé** ***var.*** Enyélé. La Likouala, NE Congo
101 *H21* **Enz** ≈ SW Germany
165 *N13* **Enzan** Yamanashi, Honshū, S Japan
104 *I2* **Eo** ≈ NW Spain
Eochaill *see* Youghal
Eochaille, Cuan *see* Youghal Bay
107 *K22* **Eolie, Isole** ***var.*** Isole Lipari, ***Eng.*** Aeolian Islands, Lipari Islands. *island group* S Italy
189 *U12* **Eot** *island* Chuuk, C Micronesia
115 *J25* **Epáno Archánes** ***var.*** Áno Arkhánai; ***prev.*** Epáno Arkhánai. Kríti, Greece, E Mediterranean Sea
Epáno Arkhánai *see* Epáno Archánes
115 *G14* **Epanomí** Kentrikí Makedonía, N Greece
98 *M10* **Epe** Gelderland, E Netherlands
77 *S16* **Epe** Lagos, S Nigeria
79 *I17* **Epéna** La Likouala, NE Congo
Eperies/Eperjes *see* Prešov
103 *Q4* **Épernay** ***anc.*** Sparnacum. Marne, N France
36 *L5* **Ephraim** Utah, W USA
18 *H15* **Ephrata** Pennsylvania, NE USA
32 *J8* **Ephrata** Washington, NW USA
187 *R14* **Epi** *var.* Épi *island* C Vanuatu
105 *R6* **Épila** Aragón, NE Spain
103 *T6* **Épinal** Vosges, NE France
Epiphania *see* Ḩamāh
Epirus *see* Ípeiros
121 *P3* **Episkopí** SW Cyprus
Episkopi Bay *see* Episkopí, Kólpos
121 *P3* **Episkopí, Kólpos** ***var.*** Episkopi Bay. *bay* SE Cyprus
Epitoli *see* Pretoria
Epoon *see* Ebon Atoll
Eporedia *see* Ivrea
Eppeschdorf *see* Dumbrăveni
101 *H21* **Eppingen** Baden-Württemberg, SW Germany
83 *E18* **Epukiro** Omaheke, E Namibia
29 *Y13* **Epworth** Iowa, C USA
143 *O10* **Eqlīd** ***var.*** Iqlid. Fārs, C Iran
Equality State *see* Wyoming
79 *J18* **Equateur** ***off.*** Région de l' Equateur. ◈ *region* N Dem. Rep. Congo
151 *K22* **Equatorial Channel** *channel* S Maldives
79 *B17* **Equatorial Guinea** ***off.*** Republic of Equatorial Guinea. ◆ *republic* C Africa
121 *V11* **Eratosthenes Tablemount** *undersea feature* E Mediterranean Sea
Erautini *see* Johannesburg
136 *L12* **Erbaa** Tokat, N Turkey
101 *E19* **Erbeskopf** ▲ W Germany
Erbil *see* Arbīl
121 *P2* **Ercan** × (Nicosia) N Cyprus
Ercegnovi *see* Herceg-Novi
137 *T14* **Erçek Gölü** ◎ E Turkey
137 *S14* **Erciş** Van, E Turkey
136 *K14* **Erciyes Dağı** ***anc.*** Argaeus. ▲ C Turkey
111 *J22* **Érd** ***Ger.*** Hanselbeck. Pest, C Hungary
Erdaobaihe *see* Baihe
159 *O12* **Erdaogou** Qinghai, W China
163 *X11* **Erdao Jiang** ▲ NE China
Erdăt-Sângeorz *see* Sângeorgiu de Pădure
136 *C11* **Erdek** Balıkesir, NW Turkey
Erdély *see* Transylvania
Erdélyi-Havasok *see* Carpaţii Meridionali
136 *J17* **Erdemli** İçel, S Turkey
162 *K6* **Erdenet** Orhon, N Mongolia
162 *I8* **Erdenetsogt** Bayanhongor, C Mongolia
78 *K7* **Erdi** *plateau* NE Chad
78 *L7* **Erdi Ma** *desert* NE Chad
101 *M23* **Erding** Bayern, SE Germany
Erdőszáda *see* Ardusat
Erdőszentgyörgy *see* Sângeorgiu de Pădure
102 *I7* **Erdre** ≈ NW France
195 *R13* **Erebus, Mount** ▲ Ross Island, Antarctica
61 *H14* **Erechim** Rio Grande do Sul, S Brazil
163 *O7* **Ereen Davaanï Nuruu** ▲ NE Mongolia
163 *Q6* **Ereentsav** Dornod, NE Mongolia
136 *I16* **Ereğli** Konya, S Turkey
136 *I15* **Ereğli Gölü** ◎ W Turkey
115 *A15* **Ereíkoussa** *island* Iónioi Nísoi, Greece, C Mediterranean Sea
163 *O11* **Erenhot** ***var.*** Erlian. Nei Mongol Zizhiqu, NE China
104 *M6* **Eresma** ≈ N Spain
115 *K17* **Eresós** ***var.*** Eressós. Lésvos, E Greece
Eressós *see* Eresós
Erevan *see* Yerevan
Ereymentaū *see* Yereymentau
99 *K21* **Érezée** Luxembourg, SE Belgium
74 *G7* **Erfoud** SE Morocco
101 *D16* **Erft** ≈ W Germany
101 *K16* **Erfurt** Thüringen, C Germany
137 *P15* **Ergani** Dıyarbakır, SE Turkey
163 *N11* **Ergel** Dornogovĭ, SE Mongolia
Ergene Irmağı *see* Ergene Çayı
162 *L11* **Ergenetsogt** Ömnögovĭ, S Mongolia
136 *C10* **Ergene Çayı** ***var.*** Ergene Irmağı. ≈ NW Turkey
118 *I9* **Ērgļi** Madona, C Latvia
78 *H11* **Erguig, Bahr** ≈ SW Chad
163 *S5* **Ergun** ***var.*** Labudalin, ***prev.*** Ergun Youqi. Nei Mongol Zizhiqu, N China
Ergun He *see* Argun
Ergun Youqi *see* Ergun
Ergun Zuoqi *see* Genhe
160 *F12* **Er Hai** ▣ SW China
102 *G4* **Er, Îles d'** *island group* NW France
106 *K4* **Ería** ≈ NW Spain
80 *H8* **Eriba** Kassala, NE Sudan
96 *I6* **Eriboll, Loch** *inlet* NW Scotland, UK
65 *Q18* **Erica Seamount** *undersea feature* SW Indian Ocean
107 *H23* **Erice** Sicilia, Italy, C Mediterranean Sea
104 *E10* **Ericeira** Lisboa, C Portugal
96 *H10* **Ericht, Loch** ◎ C Scotland, UK
26 *J11* **Erick** Oklahoma, C USA
18 *B11* **Erie** Pennsylvania, NE USA
18 *E9* **Erie Canal** *canal* New York, NE USA
Érié, Lac *see* Erie, Lake
31 *T10* **Erie, Lake** ***Fr.*** Lac Érié. ◎ Canada/USA
Erigabo *see* Ceerigaabo
77 *N8* **'Erîgât** *desert* N Mali
Erigavo *see* Ceerigaabo
92 *P2* **Erik Eriksenstretet** *strait* E Svalbard
11 *X15* **Eriksdale** Manitoba, S Canada
189 *V6* **Erikub Atoll** ***var.*** Ādkup. *atoll* Ratak Chain, C Marshall Islands
Erimanthos *see* Erýmanthos
165 *T6* **Erimo** Hokkaidō, NE Japan
165 *T6* **Erimo-misaki** *headland* Hokkaidō, NE Japan
20 *H8* **Erin** Tennessee, S USA
96 *E9* **Eriskay** *island* NW Scotland, UK
Erithraí *see* Erythrés
80 *I9* **Eritrea** ***off.*** State of Eritrea, ***Tig.*** Ērtra. ◆ *transitional government* E Africa
Erivan *see* Yerevan
101 *D16* **Erkelenz** Nordrhein-Westfalen, W Germany
95 *P15* **Erken** ◎ C Sweden
101 *K19* **Erlangen** Bayern, S Germany
160 *G9* **Erlang Shan** ▲ C China
Erlau *see* Eger
109 *V5* **Erlauf** ≈ NE Austria
181 *Q8* **Erldunda Roadhouse** Northern Territory, N Australia
Erlian *see* Erenhot
27 *T15* **Erling, Lake** ▣ Arkansas, USA
109 *O8* **Erlsbach** Tirol, W Austria
Ermak *see* Aksu
98 *K10* **Ermelo** Gelderland, C Netherlands
83 *K21* **Ermelo** Mpumalanga, NE South Africa
136 *H17* **Ermenek** Karaman, S Turkey
Érmihályfalva *see* Valea lui Mihai
115 *G20* **Ermióni** Pelopónnisos, S Greece
115 *J20* **Ermoúpoli** ***var.*** Hermoupolis; ***prev.*** Ermoúpolis. Sýros, Kykládes, Greece, Aegean Sea
Ermoúpolis *see* Ermoúpoli
Ernabella *see* Pukatja
155 *G22* **Ernākulam** Kerala, SW India
102 *J6* **Ernée** Mayenne, NW France
61 *H14* **Ernestina, Barragem** ▣ S Brazil
54 *E4* **Ernesto Cortissoz** × (Barranquilla) Atlántico, N Colombia
155 *H21* **Erode** Tamil Nādu, SE India
Eroj *see* Iroj
83 *C19* **Erongo** ◈ *district* W Namibia
99 *F21* **Erquelinnes** Hainaut, S Belgium
74 *G7* **Er-Rachidia** ***var.*** Ksar al Soule. E Morocco
80 *E11* **Er Rahad** ***var.*** Ar Rahad. Northern Kordofan, C Sudan
Er Ramle *see* Ramla
83 *O15* **Errego** Zambézia, NE Mozambique
Errenteria *see* Rentería
Er Rif/Er Riff *see* Rif
97 *D14* **Errigal Mountain** ***Ir.*** An Earagail. ▲ N Ireland
97 *A15* **Erris Head** ***Ir.*** Ceann Iorrais. *headland* W Ireland
187 *S15* **Erromango** *island* S Vanuatu
Error Guyot *see* Error Tablemount
173 *O4* **Error Tablemount** ***var.*** Error Guyot. *undersea feature* W Indian Ocean
80 *G11* **Er Roseires** Blue Nile, E Sudan
Erseka *see* Ersekë
113 *M22* **Ersekë** ***var.*** Erseka, Kolonjë. Korçë, SE Albania
Érsekújvár *see* Nové Zámky
29 *S4* **Erskine** Minnesota, N USA
103 *V6* **Erstein** Bas-Rhin, NE France
108 *G9* **Erstfeld** Uri, C Switzerland
158 *M3* **Ertai** Xinjiang Uygur Zizhiqu, NW China
126 *M7* **Ertil'** Voronezhskaya Oblast', W Russian Federation
Ertis *see* Irtysh, C Asia
Ertis *see* Irtyshsk, Kazakhstan
158 *K2* **Ertix He** ***Rus.*** Chërnyy Irtysh. ≈ China/Kazakhstan
Ērtra *see* Eritrea
21 *P9* **Erwin** North Carolina, SE USA
114 *L12* **Erydropótamos** ***Bul.*** Byala Reka. ≈ Bulgaria/Greece
115 *E19* **Erýmanthos** ***var.*** Erimanthos. ▲ S Greece
115 *G19* **Erythrés** ***prev.*** Erithraí. Stereá Ellás, C Greece
160 *F12* **Eryuan** ***var.*** Yuhu. Yunnan, SW China
109 *U6* **Erzbach** ≈ W Austria
Erzerum *see* Erzurum
101 *N17* **Erzgebirge** ***Cz.*** Krušné Hory, ***Eng.*** Ore Mountains. ▲ Czech Republic/Germany ***see also*** Krušné Hory
122 *L14* **Erzin** Respublika Tyva, S Russian Federation
137 *O13* **Erzincan** ***var.*** Erzinjan. Erzincan, E Turkey
137 *N13* **Erzincan** ***var.*** Erzinjan. ◈ *province* NE Turkey
Erzinjan *see* Erzincan
Erzsébetváros *see* Dumbrăveni
137 *Q13* **Erzurum** ***prev.*** Erzerum. Erzurum, NE Turkey
137 *Q12* **Erzurum** ***prev.*** Erzerum. ◈ *province* NE Turkey
186 *G9* **Esa'ala** Normanby Island, SE PNG
165 *T2* **Esashi** Hokkaidō, NE Japan
165 *Q9* **Esashi** ***var.*** Esasi. Iwate, Honshū, C Japan
165 *Q5* **Esasho** Hokkaidō, N Japan
Esasi *see* Esashi
95 *F23* **Esbjerg** Ribe, W Denmark
Esbo *see* Espoo
36 *L7* **Escalante** Utah, W USA
36 *M7* **Escalante River** ≈ Utah, W USA
14 *L12* **Escalier, Réservoir l'** ▣ Québec, SE Canada
40 *K7* **Escalón** Chihuahua, N Mexico
104 *M8* **Escalona** Castilla-La Mancha, C Spain
23 *O8* **Escambia River** ≈ Florida, SE USA
31 *N5* **Escanaba** Michigan, N USA
31 *N4* **Escanaba River** ≈ Michigan, N USA
105 *R8* **Escandón, Puerto de** *pass* E Spain
41 *W14* **Escárcega** Campeche, SE Mexico
171 *O1* **Escarpada Point** *headland* Luzon, N Philippines
23 *N8* **Escatawpa River** ≈ Alabama/Mississippi, S USA
103 *P2* **Escaut** ≈ N France
Escaut *see* Scheldt
99 *M25* **Esch-sur-Alzette** Luxembourg, S Luxembourg
101 *J15* **Eschwege** Hessen, C Germany
101 *D16* **Eschweiler** Nordrhein-Westfalen, W Germany
Esclaves, Grand Lac des *see* Great Slave Lake
45 *O8* **Escocesa, Bahía** *bay* N Dominican Republic
43 *W15* **Escocés, Punta** *headland* NE Panama
35 *U17* **Escondido** California, W USA
42 *M10* **Escondido, Río** ≈ SE Nicaragua
15 *S7* **Escoumins, Rivière des** ≈ Québec, SE Canada
37 *O13* **Escudilla Mountain** ▲ Arizona, SW USA
40 *J11* **Escuinapa** ***var.*** Escuinapa de Hidalgo. Sinaloa, C Mexico
Escuinapa de Hidalgo *see* Escuinapa
42 *C6* **Escuintla** Escuintla, S Guatemala
41 *V17* **Escuintla** Chiapas, SE Mexico
42 *A2* **Escuintla** ***off.*** Departamento de Escuintla. ◈ *department* S Guatemala
15 *W7* **Escuminac** ≈ Québec, SE Canada
79 *D16* **Eséka** Centre, SW Cameroon
136 *I12* **Esenboğa** × (Ankara) Ankara, C Turkey
146 *B13* **Esenguly** ***Rus.*** Gasan-Kuli. Balkan Welaýaty, W Turkmenistan
136 *D17* **Eşen Çayı** ≈ SW Turkey
105 *T4* **Ésera** ≈ NE Spain
143 *N8* **Eşfahān** ***Eng.*** Isfahan; ***anc.*** Aspadana. Eşfahān, C Iran
143 *O7* **Eşfahān** ***off.*** Ostān-e Eşfahān. ◈ *province* C Iran
105 *N5* **Esgueva** ≈ N Spain
149 *Q3* **Eshkamesh** Takhār, NE Afghanistan
149 *T2* **Eshkāshem** Badakhshān, NE Afghanistan
83 *L23* **Eshowe** KwaZulu/Natal, E South Africa
143 *T5* **'Eshqābād** Khorāsān, NE Iran
Esh Sham *see* Dimashq
Esh Sharā *see* Ash Sharāh
Esik *see* Yesik
Esil *see* Ishim, Kazakhstan/Russian Federation
Esil *see* Yesil', Kazakhstan
183 *V2* **Esk** Queensland, E Australia
184 *O11* **Eskdale** Hawke's Bay, North Island, NZ
Eski Dzhumaya *see* Tŭrgovishte
92 *L2* **Eskifjördhur** Austurland, E Iceland
139 *S3* **Eski Kaļak** ***var.*** Askī Kalak, Kalak. N Iraq
95 *N16* **Eskilstuna** Södermanland, C Sweden
8 *H6* **Eskimo Lakes** *lakes* Northwest Territories, NW Canada
0 *O10* **Eskimo Point** *headland* Nunavut, E Canada
Eskimo Point *see* Arviat
139 *Q2* **Eski Mosul** N Iraq
147 *T10* **Eski-Nookat** ***var.*** Iski-Nauket. Oshskaya Oblast', SW Kyrgyzstan
136 *F12* **Eskişehir** ***var.*** Eskishehr. Eskişehir, W Turkey

◆ Country ● Country Capital ◇ Dependent Territory ○ Dependent Territory Capital ◈ Administrative Region × International Airport ▲ Mountain ▲ Mountain Range ⩘ Volcano ≈ River ◎ Lake ▣ Reservoir

136 F13 **Eskişehir** *var.* Eski shehr. ◈ *province* NW Turkey
Eskishehr *see* Eskişehir
104 K5 **Esla** ≈ NW Spain
142 J6 **Eslāmābād** *var.* Eslāmābād-e Gharb; *prev.* Harunabad, Shāhābād. Kermānshāhān, W Iran
Eslāmābād-e Gharb *see* Eslāmābād
148 J4 **Eslām Qal'eh** *Pash.* Islam Qala. Herāt, W Afghanistan
95 K23 **Eslöv** Skåne, S Sweden
143 S12 **Esmā'īlābād** Kermān, S Iran
143 U8 **Esmā'īlābād** Khorāsān, E Iran
136 D14 **Eşme** Uşak, W Turkey
44 G6 **Esmeralda** Camagüey, E Cuba
63 F21 **Esmeralda, Isla** *island* S Chile
56 B5 **Esmeraldas** Esmeraldas, N Ecuador
56 B5 **Esmeraldas** ◈ *province* NW Ecuador
Esna *see* Isna
14 B6 **Esnagi Lake** ◎ Ontario, S Canada
143 V14 **Espakeh** Sīstān va Balūchestān, SE Iran
103 O13 **Espalion** Aveyron, S France
España *see* Spain
14 E11 **Espanola** Ontario, S Canada
37 S10 **Espanola** New Mexico, SW USA
57 C18 **Española, Isla** *var.* Hood Island. *island* Galapagos Islands, Ecuador, E Pacific Ocean
104 M13 **Espejo** Andalucía, S Spain
94 C13 **Espeland** Hordaland, S Norway
100 G12 **Espelkamp** Nordrhein-Westfalen, NW Germany
38 M8 **Espenberg, Cape** *headland* Alaska, USA
180 L13 **Esperance** Western Australia
186 L9 **Esperance, Cape** *headland* Guadacanal, C Solomon Islands
57 P18 **Esperancita** Santa Cruz, E Bolivia
61 B17 **Esperanza** Santa Fe, C Argentina
40 G6 **Esperanza** Sonora, NW Mexico
24 H9 **Esperanza** Texas, SW USA
194 H3 **Esperanza** *Argentinian research station* Antarctica
104 E12 **Espichel, Cabo** *headland* S Portugal
54 E10 **Espinal** Tolima, C Colombia
48 K10 **Espinhaço, Serra do** ▲▲ SE Brazil
104 G6 **Espinho** Aveiro, N Portugal
59 N18 **Espinosa** Minas Gerais, SE Brazil
103 O15 **Espinouse** ▲▲ S France
60 Q8 **Espírito Santo** *off.* Estado do Espírito Santo. ◈ *state* E Brazil
187 P13 **Espiritu Santo** *var.* Santo. *island* W Vanuatu
41 Z13 **Espíritu Santo, Bahía del** *bay* SE Mexico
40 F9 **Espíritu Santo, Isla del** *island* W Mexico
41 Y12 **Espita** Yucatán, SE Mexico
15 Y7 **Espoir, Cap d'** *headland* Québec, SE Canada
Esponsede/Esponsende *see* Esposende
93 L20 **Espoo** *Swe.* Esbo. Etelä-Suomi, S Finland
104 G5 **Esposende** *var.* Esponsede, Esponsende. Braga, N Portugal
83 M18 **Espungabera** Manica, SW Mozambique
63 H17 **Esquel** Chubut, SW Argentina
10 L17 **Esquimalt** Vancouver Island, British Columbia, SW Canada
61 C16 **Esquina** Corrientes, NE Argentina
42 E6 **Esquipulas** Chiquimula, SE Guatemala
42 K9 **Esquipulas** Matagalpa, C Nicaragua
94 I8 **Essandjøen** ◎ S Norway
74 E7 **Essaouira** *prev.* Mogador. W Morocco
Esseg *see* Osijek
Es Semara *see* Smara
99 G15 **Essen** Antwerpen, N Belgium
101 E15 **Essen** *var.* Essen an der Ruhr. Nordrhein-Westfalen, W Germany
Essen an der Ruhr *see* Essen
74 I5 **Es Senia** ✕ (Oran) NW Algeria
55 T8 **Essequibo Islands** *island group* N Guyana
55 T11 **Essequibo River** ≈ C Guyana
14 C18 **Essex** Ontario, S Canada
29 T16 **Essex** Iowa, C USA
97 P21 **Essex** *cultural region* E England, UK
31 R8 **Essexville** Michigan, N USA
101 H22 **Esslingen** *var.* Esslingen am Neckar. Baden-Württemberg, SW Germany
Esslingen am Neckar *see* Esslingen
103 N6 **Essonne** ◈ *department* N France
Es Suweida *see* As Suwaydā'
79 F16 **Est** *Eng.* East. ◈ *province* SE Cameroon
104 I1 **Estaca de Bares, Punta da** *point* NW Spain
24 M5 **Estacado, Llano** *plain* New Mexico/Texas, SW USA
63 K25 **Estados, Isla de los** *prev. Eng.* Staten Island. *island* S Argentina
143 P12 **Eşţahbān** Fārs, S Iran
14 F11 **Estaire** Ontario, S Canada
37 S12 **Estancia** New Mexico, SW USA
59 P16 **Estância** Sergipe, E Brazil
104 G7 **Estarreja** Aveiro, N Portugal
102 M17 **Estats, Pic d'** *Sp.* Pico d'Estats. ▲ France/Spain
Estats, Pico d' *see* Estats, Pic d'
83 K23 **Estcourt** KwaZulu/Natal, E South Africa
106 H8 **Este** *anc.* Ateste. Veneto, NE Italy
42 J9 **Estelí** Estelí, NW Nicaragua
42 J9 **Estelí** ◈ *department* NW Nicaragua
105 Q4 **Estella** *Bas.* Lizarra. Navarra, N Spain
29 R9 **Estelline** South Dakota, N USA
25 P4 **Estelline** Texas, SW USA
104 L14 **Estepa** Andalucía, S Spain
104 L16 **Estepona** Andalucía, S Spain
39 R9 **Ester** Alaska, USA
11 V16 **Esterhazy** Saskatchewan, S Canada
37 S3 **Estes Park** Colorado, C USA
11 V17 **Estevan** Saskatchewan, S Canada
29 T11 **Estherville** Iowa, C USA
21 R15 **Estill** South Carolina, SE USA
103 Q6 **Estissac** Aube, N France
15 T9 **Est, Lac de l'** ◎ Québec, SE Canada
Estland *see* Estonia
11 S16 **Eston** Saskatchewan, S Canada
118 G5 **Estonia** *off.* Republic of Estonia, *Est.* Eesti Vabariik, *Ger.* Estland, *Latv.* Igaunija; *prev.* Estonian SSR, *Rus.* Estonskaya SSR. ◆ *republic* NE Europe
Estonskaya SSR *see* Estonia
104 E11 **Estoril** Lisboa, W Portugal
59 L14 **Estreito** Maranhão, E Brazil
104 I8 **Estrela, Serra da** ▲▲ C Portugal
40 D3 **Estrella, Punta** *headland* NW Mexico
Estremadura *see* Extremadura
104 F10 **Estremadura** *cultural and historical region* W Portugal
104 H11 **Estremoz** Évora, S Portugal
79 D18 **Estuaire** *off.* Province de l'Estuaire, *var.* L'Estuaire. ◈ *province* NW Gabon
Eszék *see* Osijek
111 I22 **Esztergom** *Ger.* Gran; *anc.* Strigonium. Komárom-Esztergom, N Hungary
152 K11 **Etah** Uttar Pradesh, N India
189 R17 **Etal Atoll** *atoll* Mortlock Islands, C Micronesia
99 K24 **Étalle** Luxembourg, SE Belgium
103 N6 **Étampes** Essonne, N France
182 J1 **Etamunbanie, Lake** *salt lake* South Australia
103 N1 **Étaples** Pas-de-Calais, N France
152 K12 **Etāwah** Uttar Pradesh, N India
15 R10 **Etchemin** ≈ Québec, SE Canada
Etchmiadzin *see* Ejmiatsin
40 G7 **Etchojoa** Sonora, NW Mexico
93 L19 **Etelä-Suomi** ◈ *province* S Finland
83 B16 **Etengua** Kunene, NW Namibia
99 K25 **Éthe** Luxembourg, SE Belgium
11 W15 **Ethelbert** Manitoba, S Canada
80 H12 **Ethiopia** *off.* Federal Democratic Republic of Ethiopia; *prev.* Abyssinia, People's Democratic Republic of Ethiopia. ◆ *republic* E Africa
80 I13 **Ethiopian Highlands** *var.* Ethiopian Plateau. *plateau* N Ethiopia
Ethiopian Plateau *see* Ethiopian Highlands
34 M2 **Etna** California, W USA
18 B14 **Etna** Pennsylvania, NE USA
94 G12 **Etna** ≈ S Norway
107 L24 **Etna, Monte** *Eng.* Mount Etna. ☒ Sicilia, Italy, C Mediterranean Sea
Etna, Mount *see* Etna, Monte
95 C15 **Etne** Hordaland, S Norway
Etoliko *see* Aitolikó
39 Y14 **Etolin Island** *island* Alexander Archipelago, Alaska, USA
38 L12 **Etolin Strait** *strait* Alaska, USA
83 C17 **Etosha Pan** *salt lake* N Namibia
79 G18 **Etoumbi** Cuvette, NW Congo
20 M10 **Etowah** Tennessee, S USA
23 S2 **Etowah River** ≈ Georgia, SE USA
146 B13 **Etrek** *var.* Gyzyletrek, *Rus.* Kizyl-Atrek. Balkan Welaýaty, W Turkmenistan
146 C13 **Etrek** *Per.* Rūd-e Atrak, *Rus.* Atrak, Atrek. ≈ Iran/Turkmenistan
102 L3 **Étretat** Seine-Maritime, N France
114 H9 **Etropole** Sofiya, W Bulgaria
Etsch *see* Adige
Et Tafila *see* Aţ Ţafīlah
99 M23 **Ettelbrück** Diekirch, C Luxembourg
189 V12 **Etten** *atoll* Chuuk Islands, C Micronesia
99 H14 **Etten-Leur** Noord-Brabant, S Netherlands
76 G7 **Et Tidra** *var.* Ile Tidra. *island* Dakhlet Nouâdhibou, NW Mauritania
101 G21 **Ettlingen** Baden-Württemberg, SW Germany
102 M2 **Eu** Seine-Maritime, N France
193 W16 **'Eua** *prev.* Middleburg Island. *island* Tongatapu Group, SE Tonga
193 W15 **Eua Iki** *island* Tongatapu Group, S Tonga
Euboea *see* Évvoia
181 O12 **Eucla** Western Australia
31 U11 **Euclid** Ohio, N USA
27 W14 **Eudora** Arkansas, C USA
27 Q4 **Eudora** Kansas, C USA
182 J9 **Eudunda** South Australia
23 R6 **Eufaula** Alabama, S USA
27 Q11 **Eufaula** Oklahoma, C USA
27 Q11 **Eufaula Lake** *var.* Eufaula Reservoir. ▣ Oklahoma, C USA
Eufaula Reservoir *see* Eufaula Lake
32 F13 **Eugene** Oregon, NW USA
40 B6 **Eugenia, Punta** *headland* W Mexico
183 Q8 **Eugowra** New South Wales, SE Australia
104 I2 **Eume** ≈ NW Spain
104 H2 **Eume, Embalse do** ▣ NW Spain
Eumolpias *see* Plovdiv
59 O18 **Eunápolis** Bahia, SE Brazil
22 H8 **Eunice** Louisiana, S USA
37 W15 **Eunice** New Mexico, SW USA
99 M19 **Eupen** Liège, E Belgium
138 Jj9 **Euphrates** *Ar.* Al Furāt, *Turk.* Firat Nehri. ≈ SW Asia
138 L3 **Euphrates Dam** *dam* N Syria
22 M4 **Eupora** Mississippi, S USA
93 K19 **Eura** Länsi-Suomi, W Finland
93 K19 **Eurajoki** Länsi-Suomi, W Finland
84 **Eurasian Plate** *tectonic feature*
102 L4 **Eure** ◈ *department* N France
102 M4 **Eure** ≈ N France
102 M6 **Eure-et-Loir** ◈ *department* C France
34 K3 **Eureka** California, W USA
27 P6 **Eureka** Kansas, C USA
33 O6 **Eureka** Montana, NW USA
35 V5 **Eureka** Nevada, W USA
29 O7 **Eureka** South Dakota, N USA
36 L4 **Eureka** Utah, W USA
32 K10 **Eureka** Washington, NW USA
27 S9 **Eureka Springs** Arkansas, C USA
182 K6 **Eurinilla Creek** *seasonal river* South Australia
183 O11 **Euroa** Victoria, SE Australia
172 M9 **Europa** *island* W Madagascar
104 L3 **Europa, Picos de** ▲▲ N Spain
104 L16 **Europa Point** *headland* S Gibraltar
86-87 **Europe** *continent*
98 F12 **Europoort** Zuid-Holland, W Netherlands
Euskadi *see* País Vasco
101 D17 **Euskirchen** Nordrhein-Westfalen, W Germany
23 W11 **Eustis** Florida, SE USA
182 M9 **Euston** New South Wales, SE Australia
23 N5 **Eutaw** Alabama, S USA
100 K8 **Eutin** Schleswig-Holstein, N Germany
10 K14 **Eutsuk Lake** ▣ British Columbia, SW Canada
Euxine Sea *see* Black Sea
83 C16 **Evale** Cunene, SW Angola
37 T3 **Evans** Colorado, C USA
11 P14 **Evansburg** Alberta, SW Canada
29 X13 **Evansdale** Iowa, C USA
183 V4 **Evans Head** New South Wales, SE Australia
12 J11 **Evans, Lac** ◎ Québec, SE Canada
37 S5 **Evans, Mount** ▲ Colorado, C USA
9 Q8 Nunavut, N Canada
31 N10 **Evanston** Illinois, N USA
33 S17 **Evanston** Wyoming, C USA
14 D11 **Evansville** Manitoulin Island, Ontario, S Canada
31 N16 **Evansville** Indiana, N USA
30 L9 **Evansville** Wisconsin, N USA
25 S8 **Evant** Texas, SW USA
143 P13 **Evaz** Fārs, S Iran
29 W4 **Eveleth** Minnesota, N USA
182 E3 **Evelyn Creek** *seasonal river* South Australia
181 Q2 **Evelyn, Mount** ▲ Northern Territory, N Australia
122 K10 **Evenkiyskiy Avtonomnyy Okrug** ◈ *autonomous district* N Russian Federation
183 R13 **Everard, Cape** *headland* Victoria, SE Australia
182 F6 **Everard, Lake** *salt lake* South Australia
182 C2 **Everard Ranges** ▲▲ South Australia
153 R11 **Everest, Mount** *Chin.* Qomolangma Feng, *Nep.* Sagarmatha. ▲ China/Nepal
18 E15 **Everett** Pennsylvania, NE USA
32 H7 **Everett** Washington, NW USA
99 E17 **Evergem** Oost-Vlaanderen, NW Belgium
23 X16 **Everglades City** Florida, SE USA
23 Y16 **Everglades, The** *wetland* Florida, SE USA
23 P7 **Evergreen** Alabama, S USA
37 T4 **Evergreen** Colorado, C USA
Evergreen State *see* Washington
97 L21 **Evesham** C England, UK
103 T10 **Évian-les-Bains** Haute-Savoie, E France
93 K16 **Evijärvi** Länsi-Suomi, W Finland
79 D17 **Evinayong** *var.* Ebinayon, Evinayoung. C Equatorial Guinea
Evinayoung *see* Evinayong
115 E18 **Évinos** ≈ C Greece
95 E17 **Evje** Aust-Agder, S Norway
Evmolpia *see* Plovdiv
104 H11 **Évora** *anc.* Ebora, *Lat.* Liberalitas Julia. Évora, C Portugal
104 G11 **Évora** ◈ *district* S Portugal
102 M4 **Évreux** *anc.* Civitas Eburovicum. Eure, N France
102 K6 **Évron** Mayenne, NW France
114 L13 **Évros** *Bul.* Maritsa, *Turk.* Meriç; *anc.* Hebrus. ≈ SE Europe *see also* Maritsa/Meriç
115 F21 **Evrótas** ≈ S Greece
103 O5 **Évry** Essonne, N France
25 O8 **E.V.Spence Reservoir** ▣ Texas, SW USA
115 I18 **Évvoia** *Lat.* Euboea. *island* C Greece
38 D9 **'Ewa Beach** *var.* Ewa Beach. O'ahu, Hawai'i, USA, C Pacific Ocean
32 L9 **Ewan** Washington, NW USA
44 K12 **Ewarton** C Jamaica
81 J18 **Ewaso Ng'iro** *var.* Nyiro. ≈ C Kenya
29 P13 **Ewing** Nebraska, C USA
194 J5 **Ewing Island** *island* Antarctica
65 P17 **Ewing Seamount** *undersea feature* E Atlantic Ocean
158 L6 **Ewirgol** Xinjiang Uygur Zizhiqu, W China
79 G19 **Ewo** Cuvette, W Congo
27 S3 **Excelsior Springs** Missouri, C USA
97 J23 **Exe** ≈ SW England, UK
194 L12 **Executive Committee Range** ▲▲ Antarctica
14 E16 **Exeter** Ontario, S Canada
97 J24 **Exeter** *anc.* Isca Damnoniorum. SW England, UK
35 R11 **Exeter** California, W USA
19 P10 **Exeter** New Hampshire, NE USA
Exin *see* Kcynia
29 T14 **Exira** Iowa, C USA
97 J23 **Exmoor** *moorland* SW England, UK
21 Y6 **Exmore** Virginia, NE USA
180 G8 **Exmouth** Western Australia
97 J24 **Exmouth** SW England, UK
180 G8 **Exmouth Gulf** *gulf* Western Australia
173 V8 **Exmouth Plateau** *undersea feature* E Indian Ocean
115 J20 **Exompourgo** *ancient monument* Tínos, Kykládes, Greece, Aegean Sea
104 I10 **Extremadura** *var.* Estremadura. ◈ *autonomous community* W Spain
78 F12 **Extrême-Nord** *Eng.* Extreme North. ◈ *province* N Cameroon
Extreme North *see* Extrême-Nord
44 I3 **Exuma Cays** *islets* C Bahamas
44 I3 **Exuma Sound** *sound* C Bahamas
81 H20 **Eyasi, Lake** ◎ N Tanzania
95 F17 **Eydehavn** Aust-Agder, S Norway
96 L12 **Eyemouth** SE Scotland, UK
96 G7 **Eye Peninsula** *peninsula* NW Scotland, UK
80 Q13 **Eyl** *It.* Eil. Nugaal, E Somalia
103 N11 **Eymoutiers** Haute-Vienne, C France
Eyo (lower course) *see* Uolo, Río
29 X10 **Eyota** Minnesota, N USA
182 H2 **Eyre Basin, Lake** *salt lake* South Australia
182 I1 **Eyre Creek** *seasonal river* Northern Territory/South Australia
174 L9 **Eyre, Lake** *salt lake* South Australia
185 C22 **Eyre Mountains** ▲▲ South Island, NZ
182 H3 **Eyre North, Lake** *salt lake* South Australia
182 G7 **Eyre Peninsula** *peninsula* South Australia
182 H4 **Eyre South, Lake** *salt lake* South Australia
95 B18 **Eysturoy** *Dan.* Østerø *Island* Faeroe Islands
61 D20 **Ezeiza** ✕ (Buenos Aires) Buenos Aires, E Argentina
Ezeres *see* Ezeriş
116 F12 **Ezeriş** *Hung.* Ezeres. Caraş-Severin, W Romania
161 O9 **Ezhou** *prev.* Echeng. Hubei, C China
125 R11 **Ezhva** Respublika Komi, NW Russian Federation
136 B12 **Ezine** Çanakkale, NW Turkey
Ezo *see* Hokkaidō
Ezra/Ezraa *see* Izra'

F

191 P7 **Faaa** Tahiti, W French Polynesia
191 P7 **Faaa** ✕ (Papeete) Tahiti, W French Polynesia
95 H24 **Faaborg** *var.* Fåborg. Fyn, C Denmark
151 K19 **Faadhippolhu Atoll** *var.* Fadiffolu, Lhaviyani Atoll. *atoll* N Maldives
191 U10 **Faaite** *atoll* Îles Tuamotu, C French Polynesia
191 Q8 **Faaone** Tahiti, W French Polynesia
24 H8 **Fabens** Texas, SW USA
94 H12 **Fåberg** Oppland, S Norway
Fåborg *see* Faaborg
106 I12 **Fabriano** Marche, C Italy
145 U16 **Fabrichnyy** Almaty, SE Kazakhstan
54 F10 **Facatativá** Cundinamarca, C Colombia
77 X9 **Fachi** Agadez, C Niger
188 B16 **Facpi Point** *headland* W Guam
18 I13 **Factoryville** Pennsylvania, NE USA
78 K8 **Fada** Borkou-Ennedi-Tibesti, E Chad
77 Q13 **Fada-Ngourma** E Burkina
123 N6 **Faddeya, Zaliv** *bay* N Russian Federation
123 Q5 **Faddeyevskiy, Ostrov** *island* Novosibirskiye Ostrova, NE Russian Federation
141 W12 **Fadhī** S Oman
106 H10 **Faenza** *anc.* Faventia. Emilia-Romagna, N Italy
64 M5 **Faeroe-Iceland Ridge** *undersea feature* NW Norwegian Sea
64 M5 **Faeroe Islands** *Dan.* Færøerne, *Faer.* Føroyar. ◇ *Danish external territory* N Atlantic Ocean
86 C8 **Faeroe Islands** *island group* N Atlantic Ocean
Færøerne *see* Faeroe Islands
64 N6 **Faeroe-Shetland Trough** *undersea feature* NE Atlantic Ocean
104 H6 **Fafe** Braga, N Portugal
80 K13 **Fafen Shet'** ≈ E Ethiopia
193 V15 **Fafo** *island* Tongatapu Group, S Tonga
192 I16 **Fagaloa Bay** *bay* Upolu, E Samoa
192 H15 **Fagamālo** Savai'i, N Samoa
116 I12 **Făgăraş** *Ger.* Fogarasch, *Hung.* Fogaras. Braşov, C Romania
95 M20 **Fagerhult** Kalmar, S Sweden
94 G13 **Fagernes** Oppland, S Norway
92 I9 **Fagernes** Troms, N Norway
95 M14 **Fagersta** Västmanland, C Sweden
77 W13 **Faggo** *var.* Foggo. Bauchi, N Nigeria
Faghman *see* Fughmah
Fagibina, Lake *see* Faguibine, Lac
63 J25 **Fagnano, Lago** ◎ S Argentina
99 G22 **Fagne** *hill range* S Belgium
77 N10 **Faguibine, Lac** *var.* Lake Fagibina. ◎ NW Mali
Fahaheel *see* Al Fuḩayḩīl
Fahlun *see* Falun
143 U12 **Fahraj** Kermān, SE Iran
64 P5 **Faial** Madeira, Portugal, NE Atlantic Ocean
64 N2 **Faial** *var.* Ilha do Faial. *island* Azores, Portugal, NE Atlantic Ocean
Faial, Ilha do *see* Faial
108 G10 **Faido** Ticino, S Switzerland
Faifo *see* Hội An
Failaka Island *see* Faylakah
190 G12 **Faioa, Île** *island* N Wallis and Futuna
181 W8 **Fairbairn Reservoir** ▣ Queensland, E Australia
39 R9 **Fairbanks** Alaska, USA
21 U12 **Fair Bluff** North Carolina, SE USA
31 R14 **Fairborn** Ohio, N USA
23 S3 **Fairburn** Georgia, SE USA
30 M12 **Fairbury** Illinois, N USA
29 Q17 **Fairbury** Nebraska, C USA
29 T9 **Fairfax** Minnesota, N USA
27 O8 **Fairfax** Oklahoma, C USA
21 R14 **Fairfax** South Carolina, SE USA
35 N8 **Fairfield** California, W USA
33 O14 **Fairfield** Idaho, NW USA
30 M16 **Fairfield** Illinois, N USA
29 X15 **Fairfield** Iowa, C USA
33 R8 **Fairfield** Montana, NW USA
31 Q14 **Fairfield** Ohio, N USA
25 U8 **Fairfield** Texas, SW USA
27 T7 **Fair Grove** Missouri, C USA
19 P12 **Fairhaven** Massachusetts, NE USA
23 N8 **Fairhope** Alabama, S USA
96 L4 **Fair Isle** *island* NE Scotland, UK
185 F20 **Fairlie** Canterbury, South Island, NZ
29 U11 **Fairmont** Minnesota, N USA
29 Q16 **Fairmont** Nebraska, C USA
21 S3 **Fairmont** West Virginia, NE USA
31 P13 **Fairmount** Indiana, N USA
18 H10 **Fairmount** New York, NE USA
29 R7 **Fairmount** North Dakota, N USA
37 S5 **Fairplay** Colorado, C USA
18 F9 **Fairport** New York, NE USA
11 O12 **Fairview** Alberta, W Canada
26 L9 **Fairview** Oklahoma, C USA
36 L4 **Fairview** Utah, W USA
35 T6 **Fairview Peak** ▲ Nevada, W USA
188 H14 **Fais** *atoll* Caroline Islands, W Micronesia
149 U8 **Faisalābād** *prev.* Lyallpur. Punjab, NE Pakistan
Faisaliya *see* Fayşalīyah
28 L8 **Faith** South Dakota, N USA
153 N12 **Faizābād** Uttar Pradesh, N India
Faizabad/Faizābād *see* Feyẕābād
45 S9 **Fajardo** E Puerto Rico
139 R9 **Fajj, Wādī al** *dry watercourse* S Iraq
140 K4 **Fajr, Bi'r** *well* NW Saudi Arabia
191 W10 **Fakahina** *atoll* Îles Tuamotu, C French Polynesia
190 L10 **Fakaofo Atoll** *island* SE Tokelau
191 U10 **Fakarava** *atoll* Îles Tuamotu, C French Polynesia
127 T2 **Fakel** Udmurtskaya Respublika, NW Russian Federation
97 P19 **Fakenham** E England, UK
171 U13 **Fakfak** Papua, E Indonesia
153 T12 **Fakīragrām** Assam, NE India
114 M10 **Fakiyska Reka** ≈ SE Bulgaria
95 J24 **Fakse** Storstrøm, SE Denmark
95 J24 **Fakse Bugt** *bay* SE Denmark
95 J24 **Fakse Ladeplads** Storstrøm, SE Denmark
163 V11 **Faku** Liaoning, NE China
76 J14 **Falaba** N Sierra Leone
102 K5 **Falaise** Calvados, N France
114 H12 **Falakró** ▲ NE Greece
189 T12 **Falalu** *island* Chuuk, C Micronesia
166 L4 **Falam** Chin State, W Myanmar
143 N8 **Falāvarjān** Eşfahān, C Iran
116 M11 **Fălciu** Vaslui, E Romania
54 I4 **Falcón** *off.* Estado Falcón. ◈ *state* NW Venezuela
106 J12 **Falconara Marittima** Marche, C Italy
Falcone, Capo del *see* Falcone, Punta del
107 A16 **Falcone, Punta del** *var.* Capo del Falcone. *headland* Sardegna, Italy, C Mediterranean Sea
11 Y16 **Falcon Lake** Manitoba, S Canada
Falcon Lake *see* Falcón, Presa/Falcon Reservoir
41 O7 **Falcón, Presa** *var.* Falcon Lake, Falcon Reservoir. ▣ Mexico/USA *see also* Falcon Reservoir
25 Q16 **Falcon Reservoir** *var.* Falcon Lake, Presa Falcón. ▣ Mexico/USA *see also* Falcón, Presa
190 L10 **Fale** *island* Fakaofo Atoll, SE Tokelau
192 F15 **Faleālupo** Savai'i, NW Samoa
190 B10 **Falefatu** *island* Funafuti Atoll, C Tuvalu
192 G15 **Fālelima** Savai'i, NW Samoa
95 N18 **Falerum** Östergötland, S Sweden
Faleshty *see* Făleşti
116 M9 **Făleşti** *Rus.* Faleshty. NW Moldova
25 S15 **Falfurrias** Texas, SW USA
11 O13 **Falher** Alberta, W Canada
Falkenau an der Eger *see* Sokolov
95 J21 **Falkenberg** Halland, S Sweden
Falkenberg *see* Niemodlin
Falkenburg in Pommern *see* Złocieniec
100 N12 **Falkensee** Brandenburg, NE Germany
96 J12 **Falkirk** C Scotland, UK
65 I20 **Falkland Escarpment** *undersea feature* SW Atlantic Ocean
63 K24 **Falkland Islands** *var.* Falklands, Islas Malvinas. ◇ *UK dependent territory* SW Atlantic Ocean
47 W14 **Falkland Islands** *island group* SW Atlantic Ocean
65 I20 **Falkland Plateau** *var.* Argentine Rise. *undersea feature* SW Atlantic Ocean
Falklands *see* Falkland Islands
63 M23 **Falkland Sound** *var.* Estrecho de San Carlos. *strait* C Falkland Islands
Falknov nad Ohří *see* Sokolov
115 H21 **Falkonéra** *island* S Greece
95 K18 **Falköping** Västra Götaland, S Sweden
139 U8 **Fallāḩ** E Iraq
35 U16 **Fallbrook** California, W USA
189 U12 **Falleallej Pass** *passage* Chuuk Islands, C Micronesia
93 J14 **Fällfors** Västerbotten, N Sweden
194 I6 **Fallières Coast** *physical region* Antarctica
100 I11 **Fallingbostel** Niedersachsen, NW Germany
33 X9 **Fallon** Montana, NW USA
35 S5 **Fallon** Nevada, W USA
19 O12 **Fall River** Massachusetts, NE USA
27 P6 **Fall River Lake** ▣ Kansas, C USA
35 O3 **Fall River Mills** California, W USA
21 W4 **Falls Church** Virginia, NE USA
29 S17 **Falls City** Nebraska, C USA
25 S12 **Falls City** Texas, SW USA
Falluja *see* Al Fallūjah
77 S12 **Falmey** Dosso, SW Niger
45 W10 **Falmouth** Antigua, Antigua and Barbuda
44 J11 **Falmouth** W Jamaica
97 H25 **Falmouth** SW England, UK
20 M4 **Falmouth** Kentucky, S USA
19 P13 **Falmouth** Massachusetts, NE USA
21 W5 **Falmouth** Virginia, NE USA
189 U12 **Falos** *island* Chuuk, C Micronesia
83 E26 **False Bay** *Afr.* Valsbaai. *bay* SW South Africa
155 K17 **False Divi Point** *headland* E India
38 M16 **False Pass** Unimak Island, Alaska, USA
154 P12 **False Point** *headland* E India
105 U6 **Falset** Cataluña, NE Spain
95 I25 **Falster** *island* SE Denmark
116 K9 **Fălticeni** *Hung.* Falticsén. Suceava, NE Romania
Falticsén *see* Fălticeni
94 M13 **Falun** *var.* Fahlun. Dalarna, C Sweden
Famagusta *see* Gazimağusa
Famagusta Bay *see* Gazimağusa Körfezi
62 I8 **Famatina** La Rioja, NW Argentina
99 J21 **Famenne** *physical region* SE Belgium
113 D22 **Fan** *var.* Fani. ≈ N Albania
77 X15 **Fan** ≈ E Nigeria
76 M12 **Fana** Koulikoro, SW Mali
115 K19 **Fána** *ancient harbour* Chíos, SE Greece
189 V13 **Fanan** *island* Chuuk, C Micronesia
189 U12 **Fanapanges** *island* Chuuk, C Micronesia
115 L20 **Fanári, Akrotírio** *headland* Ikaría, Dodekánisos, Greece, Aegean Sea
45 Q13 **Fancy** Saint Vincent, Saint Vincent and the Grenadines
172 I5 **Fandriana** Fianarantsoa, SE Madagascar
167 O6 **Fang** Chiang Mai, NW Thailand
80 E13 **Fangak** Jonglei, SE Sudan
191 W10 **Fangatau** *atoll* Îles Tuamotu, C French Polynesia
191 X12 **Fangataufa** *island* Îles Tuamotu, SE French Polynesia
193 V15 **Fanga Uta** *bay* S Tonga
161 N7 **Fangcheng** Henan, C China
160 K15 **Fangchenggang** *var.* Fangcheng Gezu Zizhixian; *prev.* Fangcheng. Guangxi Zhuangzu Zizhiqu, S China
161 S15 **Fangshan** S Taiwan
163 X8 **Fangzheng** Heilongjiang, NE China
Fani *see* Fan
119 K16 **Fanipal'** *Rus.* Fanipol'. Minskaya Voblasts', C Belarus
Fanipol' *see* Fanipal'
25 T13 **Fannin** Texas, SW USA
Fanning Island *see* Tabuaeran
94 G8 **Fannrem** Sør-Trøndelag, S Norway
106 I11 **Fano** *anc.* Colonia Julia Fanestris, Fanum Fortunae. Marche, C Italy
95 E23 **Fanø** *island* W Denmark
167 R5 **Fan Si Pan** ▲ N Vietnam
Fanum Fortunae *see* Fano
Fao *see* Al Fāw
141 W7 **Faq'** *var.* Al Faqa. Dubayy, E UAE
Farab *see* Farap
194 H5 **Faraday** *UK research station* Antarctica

◆ Country ● Country Capital ◇ Dependent Territory ○ Dependent Territory Capital ◈ Administrative Region ▲ Mountain ▲▲ Mountain Range ☒ Volcano ≈ River ◎ Lake ▣ Reservoir ✕ International Airport

185 G16 **Faraday, Mount** ▲ South Island, NZ
79 P16 **Faradje** Orientale, NE Dem. Rep. Congo
Faradofay *see* Tôlañaro
172 I7 **Farafangana** Fianarantsoa, SE Madagascar
148 J7 **Farāh** *var.* Farah, Fararud. Farāh, W Afghanistan
148 K7 **Farāh** ◈ *province* W Afghanistan
148 J7 **Farāh Rūd** ≈ W Afghanistan
188 K7 **Farallon de Medinilla** *island* C Northern Mariana Islands
188 J2 **Farallon de Pajaros** *var.* Uracas. *island* N Northern Mariana Islands
76 J14 **Faranah** Haute-Guinée, S Guinea
146 K12 **Farap** *Rus.* Farab. Lebap Welaýaty, NE Turkmenistan
Fararud *see* Farāh
140 M13 **Farasān, Jazā'ir** *island group* SW Saudi Arabia
172 I5 **Faratsiho** Antananarivo, C Madagascar
188 K15 **Faraulep Atoll** *atoll* Caroline Islands, C Micronesia
99 H20 **Farciennes** Hainaut, S Belgium
105 O14 **Fardes** ≈ S Spain
191 S10 **Fare** Huahine, W French Polynesia
97 M23 **Fareham** S England, UK
39 P11 **Farewell** Alaska, USA
184 H13 **Farewell, Cape** *headland* South Island, NZ
Farewell, Cape *see* Nunap Isua
184 I13 **Farewell Spit** *spit* South Island, NZ
95 I17 **Färgelanda** Västra Götaland, S Sweden
Farghona Valley *see* Fergana Valley
147 R10 **Farg'ona Viloyati** *Rus.* Ferganskaya Oblast'. ◈ *province* E Uzbekistan
Farghona, Wodii/Farghona Wodiysi *see* Fergana Valley
23 V8 **Fargo** Georgia, SE USA
29 R5 **Fargo** North Dakota, N USA
147 S10 **Farg'ona** *Rus.* Fergana; *prev.* Novyy Margilan. Farg'ona Viloyati, E Uzbekistan
29 V10 **Faribault** Minnesota, N USA
152 J11 **Farīdābād** Haryāna, N India
152 H8 **Farīdkot** Punjab, NW India
153 T15 **Faridpur** Dhaka, C Bangladesh
121 P14 **Fārigh, Wādī al** ≈ N Libya
172 I4 **Farihy Alaotra** ◎ C Madagascar
94 M11 **Färila** Gävleborg, C Sweden
104 E9 **Farilhões** *island* C Portugal
76 G12 **Farim** NW Guinea-Bissau
Farish *see* Forish
141 T11 **Fāris, Qalamat** *well* SE Saudi Arabia
95 N21 **Färjestaden** Kalmar, S Sweden
149 R2 **Farkhār** Takhār, NE Afghanistan
147 Q14 **Farkhor** *Rus.* Parkhar. SW Tajikistan
116 F12 **Fârliug** *prev.* Fîrliug, *Hung.* Furluk. Caraş-Severin, SW Romania
115 M21 **Farmakonísi** *island* Dodekánisos, Greece, Aegean Sea
30 M13 **Farmer City** Illinois, N USA
31 N14 **Farmersburg** Indiana, N USA
25 U6 **Farmersville** Texas, SW USA
22 H5 **Farmerville** Louisiana, S USA
29 X16 **Farmington** Iowa, C USA
19 Q6 **Farmington** Maine, NE USA
29 V9 **Farmington** Minnesota, N USA
27 X6 **Farmington** Missouri, C USA
19 O9 **Farmington** New Hampshire, NE USA
37 P9 **Farmington** New Mexico, SW USA
36 L2 **Farmington** Utah, W USA
21 W9 **Farmville** North Carolina, SE USA
21 U6 **Farmville** Virginia, NE USA
97 N22 **Farnborough** S England, UK
97 N22 **Farnham** S England, UK
10 J7 **Faro** Yukon Territory, W Canada
104 G14 **Faro** Faro, S Portugal
104 G14 **Faro** ◈ *district* S Portugal
104 G14 **Faro** ✕ Faro, S Portugal
78 F13 **Faro** ≈ Cameroon/Nigeria
95 Q18 **Fårö** Gotland, SE Sweden
Faro, Punta del *see* Peloro, Capo
95 Q18 **Fårösund** Gotland, SE Sweden
173 N7 **Farquhar Group** *island group* S Seychelles
18 B13 **Farrell** Pennsylvania, NE USA
152 K11 **Farrukhābād** Uttar Pradesh, N India
143 P11 **Fārs** *off.* Ostān-e Fārs; *anc.* Persis. ◈ *province* S Iran
115 F16 **Fársala** Thessalía, C Greece
143 R4 **Fārsīān** Golestān, N Iran
Fārs, Khalīj-e *see* The Gulf
95 G21 **Farsø** Nordjylland, N Denmark
95 D18 **Farsund** Vest-Agder, S Norway
141 U14 **Fartak, Ra's** *headland* E Yemen
60 H13 **Fartura, Serra da** ▲ S Brazil
Farvel, Kap *see* Nunap Isua
24 L4 **Farwell** Texas, SW USA
194 I9 **Farwell Island** *island* Antarctica
152 L9 **Far Western** ◈ *zone* W Nepal
148 M3 **Fāryāb** ◈ *province* N Afghanistan
143 P12 **Fasā** Fārs, S Iran
141 U12 **Fasad, Ramlat** *desert* SW Oman
107 P17 **Fasano** Puglia, SE Italy
92 L3 **Fáskrúdhsfjördhur** Austurland, E Iceland
117 O5 **Fastiv** *Rus.* Fastov. Kyyivs'ka Oblast', NW Ukraine
97 B22 **Fastnet Rock** *Ir.* Carraig Aonair. *island* SW Ireland
Fastov *see* Fastiv
190 C9 **Fatato** *island* Funafuti Atoll, C Tuvalu
152 K12 **Fatehgarh** Uttar Pradesh, N India
149 U6 **Fatehjang** Punjab, E Pakistan
152 G11 **Fatehpur** Rājasthān, N India
152 L13 **Fatehpur** Uttar Pradesh, N India
126 J7 **Fatezh** Kurskaya Oblast', W Russian Federation
76 G11 **Fatick** W Senegal
104 G9 **Fátima** Santarém, W Portugal
136 M11 **Fatsa** Ordu, N Turkey
Fatshan *see* Foshan
190 D12 **Fatua, Pointe** *var.* Pointe Nord. *headland* Île Futuna, S Wallis and Futuna
191 X7 **Fatu Hiva** *island* Îles Marquises, NE French Polynesia
Fatunda *see* Fatundu
79 H21 **Fatundu** *var.* Fatunda. Bandundu, W Dem. Rep. Congo
187 S11 **Fatutaka** *island*, E Soloman Islands
29 O8 **Faulkton** South Dakota, N USA
116 L13 **Făurei** *prev.* Filimon Sîrbu. Brăila, SE Romania
92 G12 **Fauske** Nordland, C Norway
11 P13 **Faust** Alberta, W Canada
99 L23 **Fauvillers** Luxembourg, SE Belgium
107 J24 **Favara** Sicilia, Italy, C Mediterranean Sea
Faventia *see* Faenza
107 G23 **Favignana, Isola** *island* Isole Egadi, S Italy
12 D8 **Fawn** ≈ Ontario, SE Canada
Faxa Bay *see* Faxaflói
92 H3 **Faxaflói** *Eng.* Faxa Bay. *bay* W Iceland
78 I7 **Faya** *prev.* Faya-Largeau, Largeau. Borkou-Ennedi-Tibesti, N Chad
Faya-Largeau *see* Faya
187 Q16 **Fayaoué** Province des Îles Loyauté, C New Caledonia
138 M5 **Fayḑāt** *hill range* E Syria
23 O3 **Fayette** Alabama, S USA
29 X12 **Fayette** Iowa, C USA
22 J6 **Fayette** Mississippi, S USA
27 U4 **Fayette** Missouri, C USA
27 S9 **Fayetteville** Arkansas, C USA
21 U10 **Fayetteville** North Carolina, SE USA
20 J10 **Fayetteville** Tennessee, S USA
25 U11 **Fayetteville** Texas, SW USA
21 R5 **Fayetteville** West Virginia, NE USA
141 R4 **Faylakah** *var.* Failaka Island. *island* E Kuwait
139 T10 **Fayṣalīyah** *var.* Faisaliya. S Iraq
189 P15 **Fayu** *var.* East Fayu. *island* Hall Islands, C Micronesia
152 G8 **Fāzilka** Punjab, NW India
Fdérick *see* Fdérik
76 I6 **Fdérik** *var.* Fdérick, *Fr.* Fort Gouraud. Tiris Zemmour, NW Mauritania
Feabhail, Loch *see* Foyle, Lough
97 B20 **Feale** ≈ SW Ireland
21 V12 **Fear, Cape** *headland* Bald Head Island, North Carolina, SE USA
35 O6 **Feather River** ≈ California, W USA
185 M14 **Featherston** Wellington, North Island, NZ
102 L3 **Fécamp** Seine-Maritime, N France
Fédala *see* Mohammedia
61 D17 **Federación** Entre Ríos, E Argentina
61 D17 **Federal** Entre Ríos, E Argentina
77 T15 **Federal Capital District** ◈ *capital territory* C Nigeria
Federal Capital Territory *see* Australian Capital Territory
Federal District *see* Distrito Federal
21 Y4 **Federalsburg** Maryland, NE USA
74 M6 **Fedjaj, Chott el** *var.* Chott el Fejaj, Shaṭṭ al Fijāj. *salt lake* C Tunisia
94 B13 **Fedje** *island* S Norway
144 M7 **Fedorovka** Kostanay, N Kazakhstan
127 U6 **Fedorovka** Respublika Bashkortostan, W Russian Federation
Fëdory *see* Fyadory
117 U11 **Fedotova Kosa** *spit* SE Ukraine
189 V13 **Fefan** *atoll* Chuuk Islands, C Micronesia
111 O21 **Fehérgyarmat** Szabolcs-Szatmár-Bereg, E Hungary
Fehér-Körös *see* Crişul Alb
Fehértemplom *see* Bela Crkva
Fehérvölgy *see* Albac
100 L7 **Fehmarn** *island* N Germany
95 H25 **Fehmarn Belt** *Dan.* Femern Bælt, *Ger.* Fehmarnbelt. *strait* Denmark/Germany *see also* Femern Bælt
Fehmarnbelt *see* Fehmarn Belt/Femern Bælt
109 X8 **Fehring** Steiermark, SE Austria
59 B15 **Feijó** Acre, W Brazil
184 M12 **Feilding** Manawatu-Wanganui, North Island, NZ
Feira *see* Feira de Santana
59 O17 **Feira de Santana** *var.* Feira. Bahia, E Brazil
109 X7 **Feistritz** ≈ SE Austria
Feistritz *see* Ilirska Bistrica
161 P8 **Feixi** *var.* Shangpai. Anhui, E China
Fejaj, Chott el *see* Fedjaj, Chott el
111 I23 **Fejér** *off.* Fejér Megye. ◈ *county* W Hungary
95 I24 **Fejø** *island* SE Denmark
136 K15 **Feke** Adana, S Turkey
Feketehalom *see* Codlea
Fekete-Körös *see* Crişul Negru
109 T3 **Feldaist** ≈ N Austria
109 W8 **Feldbach** Steiermark, SE Austria
101 F24 **Feldberg** ▲ SW Germany
116 J12 **Feldioara** *Ger.* Marienburg, *Hung.* Földvár. Braşov, C Romania
108 I7 **Feldkirch** *anc.* Clunia. Vorarlberg, W Austria
109 S9 **Feldkirchen in Kärnten** *Slvn.* Trg. Kärnten, S Austria
Félegyháza *see* Kiskunfélegyháza
192 H16 **Feleolo** ✕ (Āpia) Upolu, C Samoa
104 H6 **Felgueiras** Porto, N Portugal
Felicitas Julia *see* Lisboa
172 J16 **Félicité** *island* Inner Islands, NE Seychelles
151 K20 **Felidhu Atoll** *atoll* C Maldives
41 Y13 **Felipe Carrillo Puerto** Quintana Roo, SE Mexico
97 Q21 **Felixstowe** E England, UK
103 N11 **Felletin** Creuse, C France
Fellin *see* Viljandi
Felsőbánya *see* Baia Sprie
Felsőmuzslya *see* Mužlja
Felsővisó *see* Vişeu de Sus
35 N10 **Felton** California, W USA
106 H7 **Feltre** Veneto, NE Italy
95 H25 **Femern Bælt** *Ger.* Fehmarnbelt, Fehmarn Belt. *strait* Denmark/Germany *see also* Fehmarn Belt
95 I24 **Femø** *island* SE Denmark
94 I10 **Femunden** ◎ S Norway
104 H2 **Fene** Galicia, NW Spain
14 I14 **Fenelon Falls** Ontario, SE Canada
189 U13 **Feneppi** *atoll* Chuuk Islands, C Micronesia
137 O11 **Fener Burnu** *headland* N Turkey
115 J14 **Fengári** ▲ Samothráki, E Greece
163 V13 **Fengcheng** *var.* Feng-cheng, Fenghwangcheng. Liaoning, NE China
160 K11 **Fenggang** *var.* Longquan. Guizhou, S China
161 S9 **Fenghua** Zhejiang, SE China
Fenghwangcheng *see* Fengcheng
Fengjiaba *see* Wangcang
160 L9 **Fengjie** *var.* Yong'an. Chongqing Shi, C China
160 M14 **Fengkai** *var.* Jiangkou. Guangdong, S China
161 T13 **Fenglin** *Jap.* Hōrin. C Taiwan
161 P1 **Fengning** *prev.* Dagezhen. Hebei, E China
160 E13 **Fengqing** *var.* Fengshan. Yunnan, SW China
161 O6 **Fengqiu** Henan, C China
161 Q2 **Fengrun** Hebei, E China
Fengshan *see* Fengqing
Fengshan *see* Luoyuan, Fujian, China
163 T4 **Fengshui Shan** ▲ NE China
161 P14 **Fengshun** Guangdong, S China
Fengtien *see* Liaoning, China
Fengtien *see* Shenyang, China
160 J7 **Fengxian** *var.* Feng Xian; *prev.* Shuangshipu. Shaanxi, C China
Fengxiang *see* Luobei
163 P13 **Fengzhen** Nei Mongol Zizhiqu, N China
160 M6 **Fen He** ≈ C China
153 V15 **Feni** Chittagong, E Bangladesh
186 I6 **Feni Islands** *island group* NE PNG
38 H17 **Fenimore Pass** *strait* Aleutian Islands, Alaska, USA
84 B9 **Feni Ridge** *undersea feature* N Atlantic Ocean
Fennern *see* Vändra
30 J9 **Fennimore** Wisconsin, N USA
172 J4 **Fenoarivo** Toamasina, E Madagascar
95 I25 **Fensmark** Storstrøm, SE Denmark
97 O19 **Fens, The** *wetland* E England, UK
31 R9 **Fenton** Michigan, N USA
190 K10 **Fenua Fala** *island* SE Tokelau
190 F12 **Fenuafo'ou, Île** *island* E Wallis and Futuna
190 L10 **Fenua Loa** *island* Fakaofo Atoll, E Tokelau
160 M4 **Fenyang** Shanxi, C China
117 U13 **Feodosiya** *var.* Kefe, *It.* Kaffa; *anc.* Theodosia. Respublika Krym, S Ukraine
94 I10 **Feragen** ◎ S Norway
74 L5 **Fer, Cap de** *headland* NE Algeria
31 O16 **Ferdinand** Indiana, N USA
Ferdinand *see* Montana, Bulgaria
Ferdinand *see* Mihail Kogălniceanu, Romania
Ferdinandsberg *see* Oţelu Roşu
143 T7 **Ferdows** *var.* Firdaus; *prev.* Tūn. Khorāsān, E Iran
103 Q5 **Fère-Champenoise** Marne, N France
Ferencz-József Csúcs *see* Gerlachovský štít
107 J16 **Ferentino** Lazio, C Italy
114 L13 **Féres** Anatolikí Makedonía kai Thráki, NE Greece
Fergana *see* Farg'ona
147 S10 **Fergana Valley** *var.* Farghona Valley, *Rus.* Ferganskaya Dolina, *Taj.* Wodii Farghona, *Uzb.* Farghona Wodiysi. *basin* Tajikistan/Uzbekistan
Ferganskaya Dolina *see* Fergana Valley
Ferganskaya Oblast' *see* Farg'ona Viloyati
147 U9 **Ferganskiy Khrebet** ▲ C Kyrgyzstan
14 F15 **Fergus** Ontario, S Canada
29 S6 **Fergus Falls** Minnesota, N USA
186 G9 **Fergusson Island** *var.* Kaluwawa. *island* SE PNG
111 K22 **Ferihegy** ✕ (Budapest) Budapest, C Hungary
Ferizaj *see* Uroševac
77 N14 **Ferkessédougou** N Ivory Coast
109 T10 **Ferlach** *Slvn.* Borovlje. Kärnten, S Austria
97 E16 **Fermanagh** *cultural region* SW Northern Ireland, UK
106 J13 **Fermo** *anc.* Firmum Picenum. Marche, C Italy
104 J6 **Fermoselle** Castilla-León, N Spain
97 D20 **Fermoy** *Ir.* Mainistir Fhear Maí. SW Ireland
23 W8 **Fernandina Beach** Amelia Island, Florida, SE USA
57 A17 **Fernandina, Isla** *var.* Narborough Island. *island* Galapagos Islands, Ecuador, E Pacific Ocean
47 Y5 **Fernando de Noronha** *island* E Brazil
Fernando Po/Fernando Póo *see* Bioco, Isla de
60 J7 **Fernandópolis** São Paulo, S Brazil
104 M13 **Fernán Núñez** Andalucía, S Spain
83 Q14 **Fernão Veloso, Baia de** *bay* NE Mozambique
34 K3 **Ferndale** California, W USA
32 H6 **Ferndale** Washington, NW USA
11 P17 **Fernie** British Columbia, SW Canada
35 R5 **Fernley** Nevada, W USA
Ferozepore *see* Fīrozpur
107 N18 **Ferrandina** Basilicata, S Italy
106 G9 **Ferrara** *anc.* Forum Alieni. Emilia-Romagna, N Italy
120 F9 **Ferrat, Cap** *headland* NW Algeria
107 D20 **Ferrato, Capo** *headland* Sardegna, Italy, C Mediterranean Sea
104 G12 **Ferreira do Alentejo** Beja, S Portugal
56 B11 **Ferreñafe** Lambayeque, W Peru
108 C12 **Ferret** Valais, SW Switzerland
102 I13 **Ferret, Cap** *headland* W France
22 I6 **Ferriday** Louisiana, S USA
Ferro *see* Hierro
107 D16 **Ferro, Capo** *headland* Sardegna, Italy, C Mediterranean Sea
104 H2 **Ferrol** *var.* El Ferrol; *prev.* El Ferrol del Caudillo. Galicia, NW Spain
56 B12 **Ferrol, Península de** *peninsula* W Peru
36 M5 **Ferron** Utah, W USA
21 S7 **Ferrum** Virginia, NE USA
23 O8 **Ferry Pass** Florida, SE USA
Ferryville *see* Menzel Bourguiba
29 S4 **Fertile** Minnesota, N USA
Fertő *see* Neusiedler See
98 L5 **Ferwerd** *Fris.* Ferwert. Friesland, N Netherlands
Ferwert *see* Ferwerd
74 G6 **Fès** *Eng.* Fez. N Morocco
79 I22 **Feshi** Bandundu, SW Dem. Rep. Congo
29 O4 **Fessenden** North Dakota, N USA
Festenberg *see* Twardogóra
27 X5 **Festus** Missouri, C USA
116 M14 **Feteşti** Ialomiţa, SE Romania
136 D17 **Fethiye** Muğla, SW Turkey
96 M1 **Fetlar** *island* NE Scotland, UK
95 I15 **Fetsund** Akershus, S Norway
12 L5 **Feuilles, Lac aux** ◎ Québec, E Canada
12 L5 **Feuilles, Rivière aux** ≈ Québec, E Canada
99 M23 **Feulen** Diekirch, C Luxembourg
103 Q11 **Feurs** Loire, E France
95 F18 **Fevik** Aust-Agder, S Norway
123 R13 **Fevral'sk** Amurskaya Oblast', SE Russian Federation
149 S2 **Feyzābād** *var.* Faizabad, Faizābād, Feyzābād, Fyzabad. Badakhshān, NE Afghanistan
Fez *see* Fès
97 J19 **Ffestiniog** NW Wales, UK
Fhóid Duibh, Cuan an *see* Blacksod Bay
62 I8 **Fiambalá** Catamarca, NW Argentina
172 I6 **Fianarantsoa** Fianarantsoa, C Madagascar
172 H6 **Fianarantsoa** ◈ *province* SE Madagascar
78 G12 **Fianga** Mayo-Kébbi, SW Chad
Ficce *see* Fichē
80 J12 **Fichē** *It.* Ficce. Oromo, C Ethiopia
101 N17 **Fichtelberg** ▲ Czech Republic/Germany
101 M18 **Fichtelgebirge** ▲ SE Germany
101 M19 **Fichtelnaab** ≈ SE Germany
106 E9 **Fidenza** Emilia-Romagna, N Italy
113 K21 **Fier** *var.* Fieri. Fier, SW Albania
113 K21 **Fier** ◈ *district* W Albania
Fieri *see* Fier
Fierza *see* Fierzë
113 L17 **Fierzë** *var.* Fierza. Shkodër, N Albania
113 L17 **Fierzës, Liqeni i** ◎ N Albania
108 F10 **Fiesch** Valais, SW Switzerland
106 G11 **Fiesole** Toscana, C Italy
138 G12 **Fifah** Aṭ Ṭafīlah, W Jordan
96 K11 **Fife** *var.* Kingdom of Fife. *cultural region* E Scotland, UK
96 K11 **Fife Ness** *headland* E Scotland, UK
Fifteen Twenty Fracture Zone *see* Barracuda Fracture Zone
103 N13 **Figeac** Lot, S France
95 N19 **Figeholm** Kalmar, SE Sweden
Figig *see* Figuig
83 J18 **Figtree** Matabeleland South, SW Zimbabwe
104 F8 **Figueira da Foz** Coimbra, W Portugal
105 X4 **Figueres** Cataluña, E Spain
74 H7 **Figuig** *var.* Figig. E Morocco
Fijāj, Shaṭṭ al *see* Fedjaj, Chott el
187 Y15 **Fiji** *off.* Sovereign Democratic Republic of Fiji, *Fij.* Viti. ◆ *republic* SW Pacific Ocean
192 K9 **Fiji** *island group* SW Pacific Ocean
175 Q8 **Fiji Plate** *tectonic feature*
105 P14 **Filabres, Sierra de los** ▲ SE Spain
83 K18 **Filabusi** Matabeleland South, S Zimbabwe
42 K13 **Filadelfia** Guanacaste, W Costa Rica
111 K20 **Fil'akovo** *Hung.* Fülek. Banskobystrický Kraj, C Slovakia
195 N5 **Filchner Ice Shelf** *ice shelf* Antarctica
14 J11 **Fildegrand** ≈ Québec, SE Canada
33 O15 **Filer** Idaho, NW USA
Filevo *see* Vŭrbitsa
116 H14 **Filiaşi** Dolj, SW Romania
115 B16 **Filiátes** Ípeiros, W Greece
115 D21 **Filiatrá** Pelopónnisos, S Greece
107 K22 **Filicudi, Isola** *island* Isole Eolie, S Italy
141 Y10 **Filim** E Oman
Filimon Sîrbu *see* Făurei
77 S11 **Filingué** Tillabéri, W Niger
114 K13 **Filiourí** ≈ NE Greece
114 I13 **Fílippoi** *anc.* Philippi. *site of ancient city* Anatolikí Makedonía kai Thráki, NE Greece
95 L15 **Filipstad** Värmland, C Sweden
108 I9 **Filisur** Graubünden, S Switzerland
94 E12 **Filefjell** ▲ S Norway
35 R14 **Fillmore** California, W USA
36 K5 **Fillmore** Utah, W USA
14 J10 **Fils, Lac du** ◎ Québec, SE Canada
136 H11 **Filyos Çayı** ≈ N Turkey
195 Q2 **Fimbulheimen** *physical region* Antarctica
195 Q1 **Fimbul Ice Shelf** *ice shelf* Antarctica
106 G9 **Finale Emilia** Emilia-Romagna, C Italy
106 C10 **Finale Ligure** Liguria, NW Italy
105 P14 **Fiñana** Andalucía, S Spain
172 I6 **Finandrahana** Fianarantsoa, SE Madagascar
21 S6 **Fincastle** Virginia, NE USA
99 M25 **Findel** ✕ (Luxembourg) Luxembourg, C Luxembourg
96 J9 **Findhorn** ≈ N Scotland, UK
31 R12 **Findlay** Ohio, N USA
18 G11 **Finger Lakes** *lakes* New York, NE USA
83 L14 **Fingoè** Tete, NW Mozambique
136 E17 **Finike** Antalya, SW Turkey
102 F6 **Finistère** ◈ *department* NW France
186 D7 **Finisterre Range** ▲ N PNG
181 Q8 **Finke** Northern Territory, N Australia
109 S10 **Finkenstein** Kärnten, S Austria
189 Y15 **Finkol, Mount** *var.* Mount Crozer. ▲ Kosrae, E Micronesia
93 L17 **Finland** *off.* Republic of Finland, *Fin.* Suomen Tasavalta, Suomi. ◆ *republic* N Europe
126 F12 **Finland, Gulf of** *Est.* Soome Laht, *Fin.* Suomenlahti, *Ger.* Finnischer Meerbusen, *Rus.* Finskiy Zaliv, *Swe.* Finska Viken. *gulf* E Baltic Sea
10 L11 **Finlay** ≈ British Columbia, W Canada
183 O10 **Finley** New South Wales, SE Australia
29 Q4 **Finley** North Dakota, N USA
Finnischer Meerbusen *see* Finland, Gulf of
92 K9 **Finnmark** ◈ *county* N Norway
92 K9 **Finnmarksvidda** *physical region* N Norway
92 I9 **Finnsnes** Troms, N Norway
186 E7 **Finschhafen** Morobe, C PNG
94 E13 **Finse** Hordaland, S Norway
Finska Viken/Finskiy Zaliv *see* Finland, Gulf of
95 M17 **Finspång** Östergötland, S Sweden
108 F10 **Finsteraarhorn** ▲ Switzerland
101 O14 **Finsterwalde** Brandenburg, E Germany
185 A23 **Fiordland** *physical region* South Island, NZ
106 E9 **Fiorenzuola d'Arda** Emilia-Romagna, C Italy
Firat Nehri *see* Euphrates
Firdaus *see* Ferdows
18 M14 **Fire Island** *island* New York, NE USA
106 G11 **Firenze** *Eng.* Florence; *anc.* Florentia. Toscana, C Italy
106 G10 **Firenzuola** Toscana, C Italy
14 C6 **Fire River** Ontario, S Canada
Fîrliug *see* Fârliug
61 B19 **Firmat** Santa Fe, C Argentina
103 Q12 **Firminy** Loire, E France
Firmum Picenum *see* Fermo
152 J12 **Fīrozābād** Uttar Pradesh, N India
152 G8 **Fīrozpur** *var.* Ferozepore. Punjab, NW India
First State *see* Delaware
143 O12 **Fīrūzābād** Fārs, S Iran
Fischamend *see* Fischamend Markt
109 Y4 **Fischamend Markt** *var.* Fischamend. Niederösterreich, NE Austria
109 W6 **Fischbacher Alpen** ▲ E Austria
Fischhausen *see* Primorsk
83 D21 **Fish** *var.* Vis. ≈ S Namibia
83 F24 **Fish** *Afr.* Vis. ≈ SW South Africa
11 X15 **Fisher Branch** Manitoba, S Canada
11 X15 **Fisher River** Manitoba, S Canada
19 N13 **Fishers Island** *island* New York, NE USA
37 U8 **Fishers Peak** ▲ Colorado, C USA
9 P9 **Fisher Strait** *strait* Nunavut, N Canada
97 H21 **Fishguard** *Wel.* Abergwaun. SW Wales, UK
19 R2 **Fish River Lake** ◎ Maine, NE USA
194 K6 **Fiske, Cape** *headland* Antarctica
103 P4 **Fismes** Marne, N France
104 F3 **Fisterra, Cabo** *headland* NW Spain
19 N11 **Fitchburg** Massachusetts, NE USA
96 L3 **Fitful Head** *headland* NE Scotland, UK
95 C14 **Fitjar** Hordaland, S Norway
192 H16 **Fito** ▲ Upolu, C Samoa
23 U6 **Fitzgerald** Georgia, SE USA
180 M5 **Fitzroy Crossing** Western Australia
63 G21 **Fitzroy, Monte** *var.* Cerro Chaltel. ▲ S Argentina
181 Y8 **Fitzroy River** ≈ Queensland, E Australia
180 L5 **Fitzroy River** ≈ Western Australia
14 E12 **Fitzwilliam Island** *island* Ontario, S Canada
107 J15 **Fiuggi** Lazio, C Italy
Fiume *see* Rijeka
107 H15 **Fiumicino** Lazio, C Italy
Fiumicino *see* Leonardo da Vinci
106 E10 **Fivizzano** Toscana, C Italy
79 O21 **Fizi** Sud Kivu, E Dem. Rep. Congo
Fizuli *see* Füzuli
92 I11 **Fjällåsen** Norrbotten, N Sweden
95 G20 **Fjerritslev** Nordjylland, N Denmark
F.J.S. *see* Franz Josef Strauss
95 L16 **Fjugesta** Örebro, C Sweden
Fladstrand *see* Frederikshavn
37 V5 **Flagler** Colorado, C USA
23 X10 **Flagler Beach** Florida, SE USA
36 L11 **Flagstaff** Arizona, SW USA
65 H24 **Flagstaff Bay** *bay* Saint Helena, C Atlantic Ocean
19 P5 **Flagstaff Lake** ◎ Maine, NE USA
94 E13 **Flåm** Sogn og Fjordane, S Norway
15 O8 **Flamand** ≈ Québec, SE Canada
30 J5 **Flambeau River** ≈ Wisconsin, N USA
97 O16 **Flamborough Head** *headland* E England, UK
100 N13 **Fläming** *hill range* NE Germany
16 H8 **Flaming Gorge Reservoir** ⊞ Utah/Wyoming, NW USA
99 B18 **Flanders** *Dut.* Vlaanderen, *Fr.* Flandre. *cultural region* Belgium/France
Flandre *see* Flanders
29 R10 **Flandreau** South Dakota, N USA
96 D6 **Flannan Isles** *island group* NW Scotland, UK
28 M6 **Flasher** North Dakota, N USA
93 G15 **Flåsjön** ◎ N Sweden
39 O11 **Flat** Alaska, USA
92 H1 **Flateyri** Vestfirdhir, Nw Iceland
33 P8 **Flathead Lake** ◎ Montana, NW USA
173 Y15 **Flat Island** *Fr.* Île Plate. *island* N Mauritius
25 T11 **Flatonia** Texas, SW USA
185 M14 **Flat Point** *headland* North Island, NZ
27 X6 **Flat River** Missouri, C USA
31 P8 **Flat River** ≈ Michigan, N USA
31 P14 **Flatrock River** ≈ Indiana, N USA
32 E6 **Flattery, Cape** *headland* Washington, NW USA
64 B12 **Flatts Village** *var.* The Flatts Village. C Bermuda
108 H7 **Flawil** Sankt Gallen, NE Switzerland
97 N22 **Fleet** S England, UK
97 K16 **Fleetwood** NW England, UK
18 H15 **Fleetwood** Pennsylvania, NE USA
95 D18 **Flekkefjord** Vest-Agder, S Norway
21 N5 **Flemingsburg** Kentucky, S USA
18 J15 **Flemington** New Jersey, NE USA
64 I7 **Flemish Cap** *undersea feature* NW Atlantic Ocean
95 N16 **Flen** Södermanland, C Sweden
100 I6 **Flensburg** Schleswig-Holstein, N Germany
100 J6 **Flensburger Förde** *inlet* Denmark/Germany
102 K5 **Flers** Orne, N France
95 C14 **Flesland** ✕ (Bergen) Hordaland, S Norway
Flessingue *see* Vlissingen
21 P10 **Fletcher** North Carolina, SE USA
31 R6 **Fletcher Pond** ◎ Michigan, N USA
102 L15 **Fleurance** Gers, S France
108 B8 **Fleurier** Neuchâtel, W Switzerland
99 H20 **Fleurus** Hainaut, S Belgium
103 N7 **Fleury-les-Aubrais** Loiret, C France
98 K10 **Flevoland** ◈ *province* C Netherlands
Flickertail State *see* North Dakota
108 H9 **Flims** Glarus, NE Switzerland
182 F8 **Flinders Island** *island* Investigator Group, South Australia
183 P14 **Flinders Island** *island* Furneaux Group, Tasmania, SE Australia

◆ COUNTRY ● COUNTRY CAPITAL ◇ DEPENDENT TERRITORY ○ DEPENDENT TERRITORY CAPITAL ◈ ADMINISTRATIVE REGION ✕ INTERNATIONAL AIRPORT ▲ MOUNTAIN ▲ MOUNTAIN RANGE ⚲ VOLCANO ≈ RIVER ◎ LAKE ⊞ RESERVOIR

182 I6 **Flinders Ranges** ▲ South Australia
181 U5 **Flinders River** ≈ Queensland, NE Australia
11 V13 **Flin Flon** Manitoba, C Canada
97 K18 **Flint** NE Wales, UK
31 R9 **Flint** Michigan, N USA
97 J18 **Flint** cultural region NE Wales, UK
27 O7 **Flint Hills** hill range Kansas, C USA
191 Y6 **Flint Island** island Line Islands, E Kiribati
23 S4 **Flint River** ≈ Georgia, SE USA
31 R9 **Flint River** ≈ Michigan, N USA
189 X12 **Flipper Point** headland C Wake Island
94 I13 **Flisa** Hedmark, S Norway
94 J13 **Flisa** ≈ S Norway
122 J5 **Flissingskiy, Mys** headland Novaya Zemlya, NW Russian Federation
Flitsch see Bovec
105 U6 **Flix** Cataluña, NE Spain
95 J19 **Floda** Västra Götaland, S Sweden
101 O16 **Flöha** ≈ E Germany
25 O4 **Flomot** Texas, SW USA
29 V5 **Floodwood** Minnesota, N USA
30 M15 **Flora** Illinois, N USA
103 P14 **Florac** Lozère, S France
23 Q8 **Florala** Alabama, S USA
103 S4 **Florange** Moselle, NE France
Floreana, Isla see Santa María, Isla
23 O2 **Florence** Alabama, S USA
36 L14 **Florence** Arizona, SW USA
37 T6 **Florence** Colorado, C USA
27 O5 **Florence** Kansas, C USA
20 M4 **Florence** Kentucky, S USA
32 E13 **Florence** Oregon, NW USA
21 T12 **Florence** South Carolina, SE USA
25 S9 **Florence** Texas, SW USA
Florence see Firenze
54 E13 **Florencia** Caquetá, S Colombia
99 H21 **Florennes** Namur, S Belgium
Florentia see Firenze
63 J18 **Florentino Ameghino, Embalse** ◎ S Argentina
99 J24 **Florenville** Luxembourg, SE Belgium
42 E3 **Flores** Petén, N Guatemala
61 E19 **Flores** ◈ department S Uruguay
171 O16 **Flores** island Nusa Tenggara, C Indonesia
64 M1 **Flores** island Azores, Portugal, NE Atlantic Ocean
Floreshty see Florești
Flores, Lago de see Petén Itzá, Lago
Flores, Laut see Flores Sea
171 N15 **Flores Sea** Ind. Laut Flores. sea C Indonesia
116 M8 **Florești** Rus. Floreshty. N Moldova
25 S12 **Floresville** Texas, SW USA
59 N14 **Floriano** Piauí, E Brazil
61 K14 **Florianópolis** prev. Destêrro. state capital Santa Catarina, S Brazil
44 G6 **Florida** Camagüey, C Cuba
61 F19 **Florida** Florida, S Uruguay
61 F19 **Florida** ◈ department S Uruguay
23 U9 **Florida** off. State of Florida; also known as Peninsular State, Sunshine State. ◈ state SE USA
23 Y17 **Florida Bay** bay Florida, SE USA
54 G8 **Floridablanca** Santander, N Colombia
23 Y17 **Florida Keys** island group Florida, SE USA
37 Q16 **Florida Mountains** ▲ New Mexico, SW USA
64 D10 **Florida, Straits of** strait Atlantic Ocean/Gulf of Mexico
114 D13 **Flórina** var. Phlórina. Dytikí Makedonía, N Greece
27 X4 **Florissant** Missouri, C USA
94 C11 **Florø** Sogn og Fjordane, S Norway
115 L22 **Floúda, Akrotírio** headland Astypálaia, Kykládes, Greece, Aegean Sea
21 S7 **Floyd** Virginia, NE USA
25 N4 **Floydada** Texas, SW USA
Flüela Wisshorn see Weisshorn
98 K7 **Fluessen** ◎ N Netherlands
105 S5 **Flúmen** ≈ NE Spain
107 C20 **Flumendosa** ≈ Sardegna, Italy, C Mediterranean Sea
31 R9 **Flushing** Michigan, N USA
Flushing see Vlissingen
25 O6 **Fluvanna** Texas, SW USA
186 B8 **Fly** ≈ Indonesia/PNG
194 I10 **Flying Fish, Cape** headland Thurston Island, Antarctica
Flylân see Vlieland
193 Y15 **Foa** island Ha'apai Group, C Tonga
11 U15 **Foam Lake** Saskatchewan, S Canada
113 J14 **Foča** var Srbinje, Republika Srpska, Bosnia and Herzegovina
116 L12 **Focșani** Vrancea, E Romania
Fogaras/Fogarasch see Făgăraș
107 M16 **Foggia** Puglia, SE Italy
Foggo see Faggo
76 D10 **Fogo** island Ilhas de Sotavento, SW Cape Verde
13 U11 **Fogo Island** island Newfoundland and Labrador, E Canada
109 U7 **Fohnsdorf** Steiermark, SE Austria
100 G7 **Föhr** island NW Germany
104 F14 **Fóia** ▲ S Portugal
14 I10 **Foins, Lac aux** ◎ Québec, SE Canada
103 N17 **Foix** Ariège, S France
126 I5 **Fokino** Bryanskaya Oblast', W Russian Federation
123 S15 **Fokino** Primorskiy Oblast', SE Russian Federation
Fola, Cnoc see Bloody Foreland
94 E13 **Folarskardnuten** ▲ S Norway
92 G11 **Folda** fjord C Norway
93 E14 **Folda** fjord C Norway
Földvár see Feldioara
93 F14 **Foldereid** Nord-Trøndelag, C Norway
115 J22 **Folégandros** island Kykládes, Greece, Aegean Sea
23 O9 **Foley** Alabama, S USA
29 U7 **Foley** Minnesota, N USA
14 E7 **Foleyet** Ontario, S Canada
95 D14 **Folgefonni** glacier S Norway
106 I13 **Foligno** Umbria, C Italy
97 Q23 **Folkestone** SE England, UK
23 W8 **Folkston** Georgia, SE USA
94 H10 **Folldal** Hedmark, S Norway
25 P1 **Follett** Texas, SW USA
106 F13 **Follonica** Toscana, C Italy
21 T15 **Folly Beach** South Carolina, SE USA
35 O7 **Folsom** California, W USA
116 M12 **Foltești** Galați, E Romania
172 H14 **Fomboni** Mohéli, S Comoros
18 K10 **Fonda** New York, NE USA
11 S10 **Fond-du-Lac** Saskatchewan, C Canada
30 M8 **Fond du Lac** Wisconsin, N USA
11 T10 **Fond-du-Lac** ≈ Saskatchewan, C Canada
190 C9 **Fongafale** var. Funafuti. • (Tuvalu) Funafuti Atoll, SE Tuvalu
190 G8 **Fongafale** atoll C Tuvalu
107 C18 **Fonni** Sardegna, Italy, C Mediterranean Sea
189 V12 **Fono** island Chuuk, C Micronesia
54 G4 **Fonseca** La Guajira, N Colombia
Fonseca, Golfo de see Fonseca, Gulf of
42 H8 **Fonseca, Gulf of** Sp. Golfo de Fonseca. gulf Central America
103 O6 **Fontainebleau** Seine-et-Marne, N France
63 G19 **Fontana, Lago** ◎ W Argentina
21 N10 **Fontana Lake** ⊟ North Carolina, SE USA
107 L24 **Fontanarossa** ✕ (Catania) Sicilia, Italy, C Mediterranean Sea
11 N11 **Fontas** ≈ British Columbia, W Canada
58 D12 **Fonte Boa** Amazonas, N Brazil
102 J10 **Fontenay-le-Comte** Vendée, NW France
33 T16 **Fontenelle Reservoir** ⊟ Wyoming, C USA
193 Y14 **Fonualei** island Vava'u Group, N Tonga
111 H24 **Fonyód** Somogy, W Hungary
Foochow see Fuzhou
39 Q10 **Foraker, Mount** ▲ Alaska, USA
187 R14 **Forari** Éfaté, C Vanuatu
103 U4 **Forbach** Moselle, NE France
183 Q8 **Forbes** New South Wales, SE Australia
77 T17 **Forcados** Delta, S Nigeria
103 S14 **Forcalquier** Alpes-de-Haute-Provence, SE France
101 K19 **Forchheim** Bayern, SE Germany
35 R13 **Ford City** California, W USA
94 D11 **Førde** Sogn og Fjordane, S Norway
31 N4 **Ford River** ≈ Michigan, N USA
183 O4 **Fords Bridge** New South Wales, SE Australia
20 J6 **Fordsville** Kentucky, S USA
27 U13 **Fordyce** Arkansas, C USA
76 I14 **Forécariah** Guinée-Maritime, SW Guinea
197 O14 **Forel, Mont** ▲ SE Greenland
11 R17 **Foremost** Alberta, SW Canada
14 D16 **Forest** Ontario, S Canada
22 L5 **Forest** Mississippi, S USA
31 S12 **Forest** Ohio, N USA
29 V11 **Forest City** Iowa, C USA
21 Q10 **Forest City** North Carolina, SE USA
32 G11 **Forest Grove** Oregon, NW USA
183 P17 **Forestier Peninsula** peninsula Tasmania, SE Australia
29 V8 **Forest Lake** Minnesota, N USA
23 S3 **Forest Park** Georgia, SE USA
29 Q3 **Forest River** ≈ North Dakota, N USA
15 T6 **Forestville** Québec, SE Canada
103 Q11 **Forez, Monts du** ▲ C France
96 K10 **Forfar** E Scotland, UK
26 J8 **Forgan** Oklahoma, C USA
Forge du Sud see Dudelange
101 J24 **Forggensee** ◎ S Germany
147 N10 **Forish** Rus. Farish. Jizzax Viloyati, C Uzbekistan
20 F9 **Forked Deer River** ≈ Tennessee, S USA
32 F7 **Forks** Washington, NW USA
92 N2 **Forlandsundet** sound W Svalbard
106 H10 **Forlì** anc. Forum Livii. Emilia-Romagna, N Italy
29 Q7 **Forman** North Dakota, N USA
97 K17 **Formby** NW England, UK
105 V11 **Formentera** anc. Ophiusa, Lat. Frumentum. island Islas Baleares, Spain, W Mediterranean Sea
Formentor, Cabo de see Formentor, Cap de
105 Y9 **Formentor, Cap de** var. Cabo de Formentor, Cape Formentor. headland Mallorca, Spain, W Mediterranean Sea
Formentor, Cape see Formentor, Cap de
107 J16 **Formia** Lazio, C Italy
62 O7 **Formosa** Formosa, NE Argentina
62 M6 **Formosa** off. Provincia de Formosa. ◈ province NE Argentina
Formosa/Formo'sa see Taiwan
59 I17 **Formosa, Serra** ▲ C Brazil
Formosa Strait see Taiwan Strait
95 H15 **Fornebu** ✕ (Oslo) Akershus, S Norway
25 U6 **Forney** Texas, SW USA
95 H21 **Fornæs** headland C Denmark
106 E9 **Fornovo di Taro** Emilia-Romagna, C Italy
117 T14 **Foros** Respublika Krym, S Ukraine
Føroyar see Faeroe Islands
96 J8 **Forres** NE Scotland, UK
27 X11 **Forrest City** Arkansas, C USA
39 Y15 **Forrester Island** island Alexander Archipelago, Alaska, USA
25 N7 **Forsan** Texas, SW USA
181 V5 **Forsayth** Queensland, NE Australia
95 L19 **Forserum** Jönköping, S Sweden
95 K15 **Forshaga** Värmland, C Sweden
93 L19 **Forssa** Etelä-Suomi, S Finland
101 Q14 **Forst** Lus. Baršć Łužyca. Brandenburg, E Germany
183 U7 **Forster-Tuncurry** New South Wales, SE Australia
23 T4 **Forsyth** Georgia, SE USA
27 T8 **Forsyth** Missouri, C USA
33 W10 **Forsyth** Montana, NW USA
149 U11 **Fort Abbās** Punjab, E Pakistan
12 G10 **Fort Albany** Ontario, C Canada
56 L13 **Fortaleza** Pando, N Bolivia
58 P13 **Fortaleza** prev. Ceará. state capital Ceará, NE Brazil
59 D16 **Fortaleza** Rondônia, W Brazil
56 C13 **Fortaleza, Río** ≈ W Peru
Fort-Archambault see Sarh
21 U3 **Fort Ashby** West Virginia, NE USA
96 I9 **Fort Augustus** N Scotland, UK
Fort-Bayard see Zhanjiang
33 S8 **Fort Benton** Montana, NW USA
35 Q1 **Fort Bidwell** California, W USA
34 L5 **Fort Bragg** California, W USA
31 N16 **Fort Branch** Indiana, N USA
Fort-Bretonnet see Bousso
33 T17 **Fort Bridger** Wyoming, C USA
Fort-Cappolani see Tidjikja
Fort Charlet see Djanet
Fort-Chimo see Kuujjuaq
11 R10 **Fort Chipewyan** Alberta, C Canada
Fort Cobb Lake see Fort Cobb Reservoir
26 L11 **Fort Cobb Reservoir** var. Fort Cobb Lake. ⊟ Oklahoma, C USA
37 T3 **Fort Collins** Colorado, C USA
14 K12 **Fort-Coulonge** Québec, SE Canada
Fort-Crampel see Kaga Bandoro
Fort-Dauphin see Tôlañaro
24 K10 **Fort Davis** Texas, SW USA
37 O10 **Fort Defiance** Arizona, SW USA
45 Q12 **Fort-de-France** prev. Fort-Royal. ○ (Martinique) W Martinique
45 P12 **Fort-de-France, Baie de** bay W Martinique
Fort de Kock see Bukittinggi
23 P6 **Fort Deposit** Alabama, S USA
29 U13 **Fort Dodge** Iowa, C USA
13 S10 **Forteau** Québec, E Canada
106 E11 **Forte dei Marmi** Toscana, C Italy
14 H17 **Fort Erie** Ontario, S Canada
180 H7 **Fortescue River** ≈ Western Australia
19 S2 **Fort Fairfield** Maine, NE USA
Fort-Foureau see Kousséri
12 A11 **Fort Frances** Ontario, S Canada
Fort Franklin see Déljne
23 R7 **Fort Gaines** Georgia, SE USA
37 T8 **Fort Garland** Colorado, C USA
21 P5 **Fort Gay** West Virginia, NE USA
Fort George see La Grande Rivière
27 Q10 **Fort Gibson** Oklahoma, C USA
27 Q9 **Fort Gibson Lake** ⊟ Oklahoma, C USA
8 H7 **Fort Good Hope** var. Good Hope. Northwest Territories, NW Canada
23 V4 **Fort Gordon** Georgia, SE USA
Fort Gouraud see Fdérik
96 I11 **Forth** ≈ C Scotland, UK
Fort Hall see Murang'a
24 H8 **Fort Hancock** Texas, SW USA
Fort Hertz see Putao
96 K12 **Forth, Firth of** estuary E Scotland, UK
14 L14 **Forthton** Ontario, SE Canada
14 M8 **Fortier** ≈ Québec, SE Canada
Fortín General Eugenio Garay see General Eugenio A. Garay
Fort Jameson see Chipata
Fort Johnston see Mangochi
19 R1 **Fort Kent** Maine, NE USA
Fort-Lamy see Ndjamena
23 Z15 **Fort Lauderdale** Florida, SE USA
21 R11 **Fort Lawn** South Carolina, SE USA
8 H10 **Fort Liard** var. Liard. Northwest Territories, W Canada
44 M8 **Fort-Liberté** NE Haiti
21 N9 **Fort Loudoun Lake** ⊟ Tennessee, S USA
37 T3 **Fort Lupton** Colorado, C USA
11 R12 **Fort MacKay** Alberta, C Canada
11 Q17 **Fort Macleod** var. MacLeod. Alberta, SW Canada
29 Y16 **Fort Madison** Iowa, C USA
Fort Manning see Mchinji
25 P9 **Fort McKavett** Texas, SW USA
11 R12 **Fort McMurray** Alberta, C Canada
8 G7 **Fort McPherson** var. McPherson. Northwest Territories, NW Canada
21 R11 **Fort Mill** South Carolina, SE USA
Fort-Millot see Ngouri
37 U3 **Fort Morgan** Colorado, C USA
23 W14 **Fort Myers** Florida, SE USA
23 W15 **Fort Myers Beach** Florida, SE USA
10 M10 **Fort Nelson** British Columbia, W Canada
10 M10 **Fort Nelson** ≈ British Columbia, W Canada
Fort Norman see Tulita
23 Q2 **Fort Payne** Alabama, S USA
33 W7 **Fort Peck** Montana, NW USA
33 V8 **Fort Peck Lake** ⊟ Montana, NW USA
23 Y13 **Fort Pierce** Florida, SE USA
29 N10 **Fort Pierre** South Dakota, N USA
81 E18 **Fort Portal** SW Uganda
8 J10 **Fort Providence** var. Providence. Northwest Territories, W Canada
11 U16 **Fort Qu'Appelle** Saskatchewan, S Canada
Fort-Repoux see Akjoujt
8 K10 **Fort Resolution** var. Resolution. Northwest Territories, W Canada
33 T13 **Fortress Mountain** ▲ Wyoming, C USA
Fort Rosebery see Mansa
Fort-Rousset see Owando
Fort-Royal see Fort-de-France
12 I10 **Fort Rupert** prev. Rupert House. Québec, SE Canada
8 H13 **Fort St.James** British Columbia, SW Canada
11 N12 **Fort St.John** British Columbia, W Canada
Fort Sandeman see Zhob
11 Q14 **Fort Saskatchewan** Alberta, SW Canada
27 R6 **Fort Scott** Kansas, C USA
12 E6 **Fort Severn** Ontario, C Canada
31 R12 **Fort Shawnee** Ohio, N USA
144 E14 **Fort-Shevchenko** Mangistau, W Kazakhstan
Fort-Sibut see Sibut
8 I10 **Fort Simpson** var. Simpson. Northwest Territories, W Canada
8 K11 **Fort Smith** district capital Northwest Territories, W Canada
27 R10 **Fort Smith** Arkansas, C USA
37 T13 **Fort Stanton** New Mexico, SW USA
24 L9 **Fort Stockton** Texas, SW USA
37 U12 **Fort Sumner** New Mexico, SW USA
26 K8 **Fort Supply** Oklahoma, C USA
26 K8 **Fort Supply Lake** ⊟ Oklahoma, C USA
29 O10 **Fort Thompson** South Dakota, N USA
Fort-Trinquet see Bîr Mogreïn
105 R12 **Fortuna** Murcia, SE Spain
34 K3 **Fortuna** California, W USA
28 J2 **Fortuna** North Dakota, N USA
23 T5 **Fort Valley** Georgia, SE USA
11 P11 **Fort Vermilion** Alberta, W Canada
Fort Victoria see Masvingo
31 P13 **Fortville** Indiana, N USA
23 P9 **Fort Walton Beach** Florida, SE USA
31 P12 **Fort Wayne** Indiana, N USA
96 H10 **Fort William** N Scotland, UK
25 T6 **Fort Worth** Texas, SW USA
28 M7 **Fort Yates** North Dakota, N USA
39 S7 **Fort Yukon** Alaska, USA
Forum Alieni see Ferrara
Forum Julii see Fréjus
Forum Livii see Forlì
143 Q15 **Forūr, Jazīreh-ye** island S Iran
94 H7 **Fosen** physical region S Norway
161 N14 **Foshan** var. Fatshan, Fo-shan, Namhoi. Guangdong, S China
Fossa Claudia see Chioggia
106 B9 **Fossano** Piemonte, NW Italy
99 H21 **Fosses-la-Ville** Namur, S Belgium
32 J12 **Fossil** Oregon, NW USA
Foss Lake see Foss Reservoir
106 I11 **Fossombrone** Marche, C Italy
26 K10 **Foss Reservoir** var. Foss Lake. ⊟ Oklahoma, C USA
29 S4 **Fosston** Minnesota, N USA
183 O13 **Foster** Victoria, SE Australia
11 T12 **Foster Lakes** ◎ Saskatchewan, C Canada
31 S12 **Fostoria** Ohio, N USA
79 D19 **Fougamou** Ngounié, C Gabon
102 J6 **Fougères** Ille-et-Vilaine, NW France
Fou-hsin see Fuxin
27 S14 **Fouke** Arkansas, C USA
96 K2 **Foula** island NE Scotland, UK
65 D24 **Foul Bay** bay East Falkland, Falkland Islands
97 P21 **Foulness Island** island SE England, UK
185 F15 **Foulwind, Cape** headland South Island, NZ
79 E15 **Foumban** Ouest, NW Cameroon
172 H13 **Foumbouni** Grande Comore, NW Comoros
195 N8 **Foundation Ice Stream** glacier Antarctica
37 T6 **Fountain** Colorado, C USA
36 L4 **Fountain Green** Utah, W USA
21 P11 **Fountain Inn** South Carolina, SE USA
27 S11 **Fourche LaFave River** ≈ Arkansas, C USA
33 Z13 **Four Corners** Wyoming, C USA
103 Q2 **Fourmies** Nord, N France
38 J17 **Four Mountains, Islands of** island group Aleutian Islands, Alaska, USA
173 P17 **Fournaise, Piton de la** ▲ SE Réunion
14 J8 **Fournière, Lac** ◎ Québec, SE Canada
115 L20 **Foúrnoi** island Dodekánisos, Greece, Aegean Sea
64 K13 **Four North Fracture Zone** tectonic feature W Atlantic Ocean
Fouron-Saint-Martin see Sint-Martens-Voeren
30 L3 **Fourteen Mile Point** headland Michigan, N USA
76 I13 **Fouta Djallon** var. Futa Jallon. ▲ W Guinea
185 C25 **Foveaux Strait** strait S NZ
35 Q11 **Fowler** California, W USA
37 U6 **Fowler** Colorado, C USA
31 N12 **Fowler** Indiana, N USA
182 D7 **Fowlers Bay** bay South Australia
25 R13 **Fowlerton** Texas, SW USA
142 M3 **Fowman** var. Fuman, Fumen. Gīlān, NW Iran
65 C25 **Fox Bay East** West Falkland, Falkland Islands
65 C25 **Fox Bay West** West Falkland, Falkland Islands
14 J14 **Foxboro** Ontario, SE Canada
11 O14 **Fox Creek** Alberta, W Canada
64 G5 **Foxe Basin** sea Nunavut, N Canada
64 G5 **Foxe Channel** channel Nunavut, N Canada
95 I16 **Foxen** ◎ C Sweden
9 Q7 **Foxe Peninsula** peninsula Baffin Island, Nunavut, NE Canada
185 E19 **Fox Glacier** West Coast, South Island, NZ
38 L17 **Fox Islands** island Aleutian Islands, Alaska, USA
30 M10 **Fox Lake** Illinois, N USA
11 V12 **Fox Mine** Manitoba, C Canada
35 R3 **Fox Mountain** ▲ Nevada, W USA
65 E25 **Fox Point** headland East Falkland, Falkland Islands
30 M11 **Fox River** ≈ Illinois/Wisconsin, N USA
30 L7 **Fox River** ≈ Wisconsin, N USA
184 L13 **Foxton** Manawatu-Wanganui, North Island, NZ
11 S16 **Fox Valley** Saskatchewan, S Canada
11 W16 **Foxwarren** Manitoba, S Canada
97 E14 **Foyle, Lough** Ir. Loch Feabhail. inlet N Ireland
194 H5 **Foyn Coast** physical region Antarctica
104 I2 **Foz** Galicia, NW Spain
60 I12 **Foz do Areia, Represa de** ⊟ S Brazil
59 A16 **Foz do Breu** Acre, W Brazil
83 A16 **Foz do Cunene** Namibe, SW Angola
60 G12 **Foz do Iguaçu** Paraná, S Brazil
58 C12 **Foz do Mamoriá** Amazonas, NW Brazil
105 T6 **Fraga** Aragón, NE Spain
44 F5 **Fragoso, Cayo** island C Cuba
61 G18 **Fraile Muerto** Cerro Largo, NE Uruguay
99 H21 **Fraire** Namur, S Belgium
99 L21 **Fraiture, Baraque de** hill SE Belgium
Frakštát see Hlohovec
197 S10 **Fram Basin** var. Amundsen Basin. undersea feature Arctic Ocean
99 F20 **Frameries** Hainaut, S Belgium
19 O11 **Framingham** Massachusetts, NE USA
60 L7 **Franca** São Paulo, S Brazil
187 O15 **Français, Récif des** reef W New Caledonia
107 K14 **Francavilla al Mare** Abruzzo, C Italy
107 P18 **Francavilla Fontana** Puglia, SE Italy
102 M8 **France** off. French Republic, It./Sp. Francia; prev. Gaul, Gaule, Lat. Gallia. ◆ republic W Europe
45 O8 **Francés Viejo, Cabo** headland NE Dominican Republic
79 F19 **Franceville** var. Massoukou, Masuku. Haut-Ogooué, E Gabon
79 F19 **Franceville** ✕ Haut-Ogooué, E Gabon
Francfort see Frankfurt am Main
103 T8 **Franche-Comté** ◈ region E France
Francia see France
29 O11 **Francis Case, Lake** ⊟ South Dakota, N USA
60 H12 **Francisco Beltrão** Paraná, S Brazil
Francisco I. Madero see Villa Madero
61 A21 **Francisco Madero** Buenos Aires, E Argentina
42 H6 **Francisco Morazán** prev. Tegucigalpa. ◈ department C Honduras
83 J18 **Francistown** North East, NE Botswana
Franconian Forest see Frankenwald
Franconian Jura see Fränkische Alb
98 K6 **Franeker** Fris. Frjentsjer. Friesland, N Netherlands
Frankenalb see Fränkische Alb
101 H16 **Frankenberg** Hessen, C Germany
101 J20 **Frankenhöhe** hill range C Germany
31 R8 **Frankenmuth** Michigan, N USA
101 F20 **Frankenstein** hill W Germany
Frankenstein/Frankenstein in Schlesien see Ząbkowice Śląskie
101 G20 **Frankenthal** Rheinland-Pfalz, W Germany
101 L18 **Frankenwald** Eng. Franconian Forest. ▲ C Germany
44 J12 **Frankfield** C Jamaica
14 J14 **Frankford** Ontario, SE Canada
31 O13 **Frankfort** Indiana, N USA
27 O3 **Frankfort** Kansas, C USA
20 L5 **Frankfort** state capital Kentucky, S USA
Frankfort on the Main see Frankfurt am Main
Frankfurt see Słubice, Poland
Frankfurt see Frankfurt am Main, Germany
101 G18 **Frankfurt am Main** var. Frankfurt, Fr. Francfort; prev. Eng. Frankfort on the Main. Hessen, SW Germany
100 Q12 **Frankfurt an der Oder** Brandenburg, E Germany
101 L21 **Fränkische Alb** var. Frankenalb, Eng. Franconian Jura. ▲ S Germany
101 I18 **Fränkische Saale** ≈ C Germany
101 L19 **Fränkische Schweiz** hill range C Germany
23 R4 **Franklin** Georgia, SE USA
31 P14 **Franklin** Indiana, N USA
20 J7 **Franklin** Kentucky, S USA
22 I9 **Franklin** Louisiana, S USA
29 O17 **Franklin** Nebraska, C USA
21 N10 **Franklin** North Carolina, SE USA
18 C13 **Franklin** Pennsylvania, NE USA
20 J9 **Franklin** Tennessee, S USA
25 U9 **Franklin** Texas, SW USA
21 X7 **Franklin** Virginia, NE USA
21 T4 **Franklin** West Virginia, NE USA
30 M9 **Franklin** Wisconsin, N USA
8 I6 **Franklin Bay** inlet Northwest Territories, N Canada
32 K7 **Franklin D.Roosevelt Lake** ⊟ Washington, NW USA
35 W4 **Franklin Lake** ◎ Nevada, W USA
185 B22 **Franklin Mountains** ▲ South Island, NZ
39 R5 **Franklin Mountains** ▲ Alaska, USA
39 N4 **Franklin, Point** headland Alaska, USA
183 O17 **Franklin River** ≈ Tasmania, SE Australia
22 K8 **Franklinton** Louisiana, S USA
21 U9 **Franklinton** North Carolina, SE USA
Frankstadt see Frenštát pod Radhoštěm
25 V7 **Frankston** Texas, SW USA
33 U12 **Frannie** Wyoming, C USA
15 U5 **Franquelin** Québec, SE Canada
15 U5 **Franquelin** ≈ Québec, SE Canada
83 C18 **Fransfontein** Kunene, NW Namibia
93 H17 **Fränsta** Västernorrland, C Sweden
122 J3 **Frantsa-Iosifa, Zemlya** Eng. Franz Josef Land. island group N Russian Federation
185 E18 **Franz Josef Glacier** West Coast, South Island, NZ
Franz Josef Land see Frantsa-Iosifa, Zemlya
Franz-Josef Spitze see Gerlachovský štít
101 L23 **Franz Josef Strauss** abbrev. F.J.S. ✕ (München) Bayern, SE Germany
107 A19 **Frasca, Capo della** headland Sardegna, Italy, C Mediterranean Sea
107 I15 **Frascati** Lazio, C Italy
11 N14 **Fraser** ≈ British Columbia, SW Canada
83 G24 **Fraserburg** Western Cape, SW South Africa
96 L8 **Fraserburgh** NE Scotland, UK
181 Z9 **Fraser Island** var. Great Sandy Island. island Queensland, E Australia
10 L14 **Fraser Lake** British Columbia, SW Canada
10 L15 **Fraser Plateau** plateau British Columbia, SW Canada
184 P10 **Frasertown** Hawke's Bay, North Island, NZ
99 E19 **Frasnes-lez-Buissenal** Hainaut, SW Belgium
108 I7 **Frastanz** Vorarlberg, NW Austria
14 B8 **Frater** Ontario, S Canada
Frauenbach see Baia Mare
Frauenburg see Saldus, Latvia
Frauenburg see Frombork, Poland
108 H6 **Frauenfeld** Thurgau, NE Switzerland
109 Z5 **Frauenkirchen** Burgenland, E Austria
61 D19 **Fray Bentos** Río Negro, W Uruguay
61 F19 **Fray Marcos** Florida, S Uruguay
29 S6 **Frazee** Minnesota, N USA
104 M5 **Frechilla** Castilla-León, N Spain
30 J4 **Frederic** Wisconsin, N USA
95 G23 **Fredericia** Vejle, C Denmark
21 W3 **Frederick** Maryland, NE USA
26 L12 **Frederick** Oklahoma, C USA
29 P7 **Frederick** South Dakota, N USA
29 X12 **Fredericksburg** Iowa, C USA
25 R10 **Fredericksburg** Texas, SW USA
21 W5 **Fredericksburg** Virginia, NE USA
39 X13 **Frederick Sound** sound Alaska, USA

◆ Country • Country Capital ◇ Dependent Territory ○ Dependent Territory Capital ◈ Administrative Region ✕ International Airport ▲ Mountain ▲ Mountain Range ✱ Volcano ≈ River ◎ Lake ⊟ Reservoir

27 X6 **Fredericktown** Missouri, C USA
60 H13 **Frederico Westphalen** Rio Grande do Sul, S Brazil
13 O15 **Fredericton** New Brunswick, SE Canada
95 I22 **Frederiksborg** *off.* Frederiksborgs Amt. ◈ *county* E Denmark
Frederikshåb *see* Paamiut
95 H19 **Frederikshavn** *prev.* Fladstrand. Nordjylland, N Denmark
95 J22 **Frederikssund** Frederiksborg, E Denmark
45 T9 **Frederiksted** Saint Croix, S Virgin Islands (US)
95 I22 **Frederiksværk** *var.* Frederiksværk og Hanehoved. Frederiksborg, E Denmark
Frederiksværk og Hanehoved *see* Frederiksværk
54 E9 **Fredonia** Antioquia, W Colombia
36 K8 **Fredonia** Arizona, SW USA
27 P7 **Fredonia** Kansas, C USA
18 C11 **Fredonia** New York, NE USA
35 P4 **Fredonyer Pass** *pass* California, W USA
93 I15 **Fredrika** Västerbotten, N Sweden
95 L14 **Fredriksberg** Dalarna, C Sweden
Fredrikshald *see* Halden
Fredrikshamn *see* Hamina
95 H16 **Fredrikstad** Østfold, S Norway
30 K16 **Freeburg** Illinois, N USA
18 K15 **Freehold** New Jersey, NE USA
18 H14 **Freeland** Pennsylvania, NE USA
182 J5 **Freeling Heights** ▲ South Australia
35 Q7 **Freel Peak** ▲ California, W USA
9 Z9 **Freels, Cape** *headland* Newfoundland and Labrador, E Canada
29 Q11 **Freeman** South Dakota, N USA
44 G1 **Freeport** Grand Bahama Island, N Bahamas
30 L10 **Freeport** Illinois, N USA
25 W12 **Freeport** Texas, SW USA
44 G1 **Freeport** ✕ Grand Bahama Island, N Bahamas
25 R14 **Freer** Texas, SW USA
83 I22 **Free State** *off.* Free State Province; *prev.* Orange Free State, *Afr.* Oranje Vrystaat. ◈ *province* C South Africa
Free State *see* Maryland
76 G15 **Freetown** ● (Sierra Leone) W Sierra Leone
172 J16 **Frégate** *island* Inner Islands, NE Seychelles
104 J12 **Fregenal de la Sierra** Extremadura, W Spain
182 C2 **Fregon** South Australia
102 H5 **Fréhel, Cap** *headland* NW France
94 F8 **Frei** Møre og Romsdal, S Norway
101 O16 **Freiberg** Sachsen, E Germany
101 O16 **Freiberger Mulde** ≈ E Germany
Freiburg *see* Fribourg, Switzerland
Freiburg *see* Freiburg im Breisgau, Germany
101 F23 **Freiburg im Breisgau** *var.* Freiburg, *Fr.* Fribourg-en-Brisgau. Baden-Württemberg, SW Germany
Freiburg in Schlesien *see* Świebodzice
Freie Hansestadt Bremen *see* Bremen
Freie und Hansestadt Hamburg *see* Brandenburg
101 L22 **Freising** Bayern, SE Germany
109 T3 **Freistadt** Oberösterreich, N Austria
Freistadtl *see* Hlohovec
101 O16 **Freital** Sachsen, E Germany
Freiwaldau *see* Jeseník
104 J6 **Freixo de Espada à Cinta** Bragança, N Portugal
103 U15 **Fréjus** *anc.* Forum Julii. Var, SE France
180 I13 **Fremantle** Western Australia
35 N9 **Fremont** California, W USA
31 Q11 **Fremont** Indiana, N USA
29 W15 **Fremont** Iowa, C USA
31 P8 **Fremont** Michigan, N USA
29 R15 **Fremont** Nebraska, C USA
31 S11 **Fremont** Ohio, N USA
33 T14 **Fremont Peak** ▲ Wyoming, C USA
36 M6 **Fremont River** ≈ Utah, W USA
21 O9 **French Broad River** ≈ Tennessee, S USA
21 N5 **Frenchburg** Kentucky, S USA
18 C12 **French Creek** ≈ Pennsylvania, NE USA
32 K15 **Frenchglen** Oregon, NW USA
55 Y10 **French Guiana** *var.* Guiana, Guyane. ◇ *French overseas department* N South America
French Guinea *see* Guinea
31 O15 **French Lick** Indiana, N USA
185 J14 **French Pass** Marlborough, South Island, NZ
191 T11 **French Polynesia** ◇ *French overseas territory* C Polynesia
French Republic *see* France
14 F11 **French River** ≈ Ontario, S Canada
French Somaliland *see* Djibouti
173 P12 **French Southern and Antarctic Territories** *Fr.* Terres Australes et Antarctiques Françaises. ◇ *French overseas territory* S Indian Ocean
French Sudan *see* Mali
French Territory of the Afars and Issas *see* Djibouti
French Togoland *see* Togo
74 J6 **Frenda** NW Algeria
111 I18 **Frenštát pod Radhoštěm** *Ger.* Frankstadt. Moravskoslezský Kraj, E Czech Republic
76 M17 **Fresco** S Ivory Coast
195 U16 **Freshfield, Cape** *headland* Antarctica
40 L10 **Fresnillo** *var.* Fresnillo de González Echeverría. Zacatecas, C Mexico
Fresnillo de González Echeverría *see* Fresnillo
35 Q10 **Fresno** California, W USA
Freu, Cabo del *see* Freu, Cap des
105 Y9 **Freu, Cap des** *var.* Cabo del Freu. *headland* Mallorca, Spain, W Mediterranean Sea
101 G22 **Freudenstadt** Baden-Württemberg, SW Germany
Freudenthal *see* Bruntál
183 Q17 **Freycinet Peninsula** *peninsula* Tasmania, SE Australia
76 H14 **Fria** Guinée-Maritime, W Guinea
83 A17 **Fria, Cape** *headland* NW Namibia
35 Q10 **Friant** California, W USA
62 K8 **Frías** Catamarca, N Argentina
108 D9 **Fribourg** *Ger.* Freiburg. Fribourg, W Switzerland
108 C9 **Fribourg** *Ger.* Freiburg. ◈ *canton* W Switzerland
Fribourg-en-Brisgau *see* Freiburg im Breisgau
32 G7 **Friday Harbor** San Juan Islands, Washington, NW USA
Friedau *see* Ormož
101 K23 **Friedberg** Bayern, S Germany
101 H18 **Friedberg** Hessen, W Germany
Friedeberg Neumark *see* Strzelce Krajeńskie
Friedek-Mistek *see* Frýdek-Místek
Friedland *see* Pravdinsk
101 I24 **Friedrichshafen** Baden-Württemberg, S Germany
Friedrichstadt *see* Jaunjelgava
29 Q16 **Friend** Nebraska, C USA
Friendly Islands *see* Tonga
55 V9 **Friendship** Coronie, N Suriname
30 L7 **Friendship** Wisconsin, N USA
109 T8 **Friesach** Kärnten, S Austria
Friesche Eilanden *see* Frisian Islands
101 F22 **Friesenheim** Baden-Württemberg, SW Germany
Friesische Inseln *see* Frisian Islands
98 K6 **Friesland** ◈ *province* N Netherlands
60 Q10 **Frio, Cabo** *headland* SE Brazil
24 M3 **Friona** Texas, SW USA
42 L12 **Frío, Río** ≈ N Costa Rica
25 R13 **Frio River** ≈ Texas, SW USA
99 M25 **Frisange** Luxembourg, S Luxembourg
Frisches Haff *see* Vistula Lagoon
36 J6 **Frisco Peak** ▲ Utah, W USA
84 F9 **Frisian Islands** *Dut.* Friesche Eilanden, *Ger.* Friesische Inseln. *island group* N Europe
18 L12 **Frissell, Mount** ▲ Connecticut, NE USA
95 J19 **Fristad** Västra Götaland, S Sweden
25 N2 **Fritch** Texas, SW USA
95 J19 **Fritsla** Västra Götaland, S Sweden
101 H16 **Fritzlar** Hessen, C Germany
106 H6 **Friuli-Venezia Giulia** ◈ *region* NE Italy
Frjentsjer *see* Franeker
196 L13 **Frobisher Bay** *inlet* Baffin Island, Nunavut, NE Canada
Frobisher Bay *see* Iqaluit
11 S12 **Frobisher Lake** ◎ Saskatchewan, C Canada
94 G7 **Frohavet** *sound* C Norway
Frohenbruck *see* Veselí nad Lužnicí
109 V7 **Frohnleiten** Steiermark, SE Austria
99 G22 **Froidchapelle** Hainaut, S Belgium
127 O9 **Frolovo** Volgogradskaya Oblast', SW Russian Federation
110 K7 **Frombork** *Ger.* Frauenburg. Warmińsko-Mazurskie, NE Poland
97 L22 **Frome** SW England, UK
182 I4 **Frome Creek** *seasonal river* South Australia
182 J6 **Frome Downs** South Australia
182 J5 **Frome, Lake** *salt lake* South Australia
Fronicken *see* Wronki
104 H10 **Fronteira** Portalegre, C Portugal
40 M7 **Frontera** Coahuila de Zaragoza, NE Mexico
41 U14 **Frontera** Tabasco, SE Mexico
40 G3 **Fronteras** Sonora, NW Mexico
103 Q16 **Frontignan** Hérault, S France
54 D8 **Frontino** Antioquia, NW Colombia
21 V4 **Front Royal** Virginia, NE USA
107 J16 **Frosinone** *anc.* Frusino. Lazio, C Italy
107 K16 **Frosolone** Molise, C Italy
25 U7 **Frost** Texas, SW USA
21 U2 **Frostburg** Maryland, NE USA
23 X13 **Frostproof** Florida, SE USA
Frostviken *see* Kvarnbergsvattnet
95 M15 **Frövi** Örebro, C Sweden
94 F7 **Frøya** *island* W Norway
37 P5 **Fruita** Colorado, C USA
28 J9 **Fruitdale** South Dakota, N USA
23 W11 **Fruitland Park** Florida, SE USA
Frumentum *see* Formentera
147 S11 **Frunze** Batkenskaya Oblast', SW Kyrgyzstan
Frunze *see* Bishkek
117 O9 **Frunzivka** Odes'ka Oblast', SW Ukraine
Frusino *see* Frosinone
108 E9 **Frutigen** Bern, W Switzerland
111 I17 **Frýdek-Místek** *Ger.* Friedek-Mistek. Moravskoslezský Kraj, E Czech Republic
193 V16 **Fua'amotu** Tongatapu, S Tonga
190 A9 **Fuafatu** *island* Funafuti Atoll, C Tuvalu
190 A9 **Fuagea** *island* Funafuti Atoll, C Tuvalu
190 B8 **Fualifeke** *atoll* C Tuvalu
190 A8 **Fualopa** *island* Funafuti Atoll, C Tuvalu
151 K22 **Fuammulah** *var.* Gnaviyani Atoll. *atoll* S Maldives
161 R11 **Fu'an** Fujian, SE China
Fu-chien *see* Fujian
Fu-chou *see* Fuzhou
164 G13 **Fuchū** *var.* Hutyû. Hiroshima, Honshū, SW Japan
160 M13 **Fuchuan** Guangxi Zhuangzu Zizhiqu, S China
165 R8 **Fudai** Iwate, Honshū, C Japan
161 S11 **Fuding** Fujian, SE China
81 J20 **Fudua** *spring/well* S Kenya
104 M16 **Fuengirola** Andalucía, S Spain
104 J12 **Fuente de Cantos** Extremadura, W Spain
104 J11 **Fuente del Maestre** Extremadura, W Spain
104 L12 **Fuente Obejuna** Andalucía, S Spain
104 L6 **Fuentesaúco** Castilla-León, N Spain
62 O3 **Fuerte Olimpo** *var.* Olimpo. Alto Paraguay, NE Paraguay
40 H8 **Fuerte, Río** ≈ C Mexico
64 Q11 **Fuerteventura** *island* Islas Canarias, Spain, NE Atlantic Ocean
141 S14 **Fughmah** *var.* Faghman, Fugma. C Yemen
92 M2 **Fuglehuken** *headland* W Svalbard
95 B18 **Fugloy** *Dan.* Fuglø *Island* Faeroe Islands
197 T15 **Fugløya Bank** *undersea feature* E Norwegian Sea
166 E11 **Fugong** Yunnan, SW China
Fugma *see* Fughmah
81 K16 **Fugugo** *spring/well* NE Kenya
158 L2 **Fuhai** *var.* Burultokay. Xinjiang Uygur Zizhiqu, NW China
161 P10 **Fu He** ≈ S China
Fuhkien *see* Fujian
100 J9 **Fuhlsbüttel** ✕ (Hamburg) Hamburg, N Germany
101 L14 **Fuhne** ≈ C Germany
Fu-hsin *see* Fuxin
Fujairah *see* Al Fujayrah
164 M14 **Fuji** *var.* Huzi. Shizuoka, Honshū, S Japan
161 Q12 **Fujian** *var.* Fu-chien, Fuhkien, Fujian Sheng, Fukien, Min. ◈ *province* SE China
160 I9 **Fu Jiang** ≈ C China
Fujian Sheng *see* Fujian
164 M14 **Fujieda** *var.* Huzieda. Shizuoka, Honshū, S Japan
Fuji, Mount/Fujiyama *see* Fuji-san
163 Y7 **Fujin** Heilongjiang, NE China
164 M13 **Fujinomiya** *var.* Huzinomiya. Shizuoka, Honshū, S Japan
164 N13 **Fuji-san** *var.* Fujiyama, *Eng.* Mount Fuji. ▲ Honshū, SE Japan
165 N14 **Fujisawa** *var.* Huzisawa. Kanagawa, Honshū, S Japan
165 T3 **Fukagawa** *var.* Hukagawa. Hokkaidō, NE Japan
158 L5 **Fukang** Xinjiang Uygur Zizhiqu, W China
165 P7 **Fukaura** Aomori, Honshū, C Japan
193 W15 **Fukave** *island* Tongatapu Group, S Tonga
Fukien *see* Fujian
164 J13 **Fukuchiyama** *var.* Hukutiyama. Kyōto, Honshū, SW Japan
164 A14 **Fukue** *var.* Hukue. Nagasaki, Fukue-jima, SW Japan
164 A13 **Fukue-jima** *island* Gotō-rettō, SW Japan
164 K12 **Fukui** *var.* Hukui. Fukui, Honshū, SW Japan
164 K12 **Fukui** *off.* Fukui-ken, *var.* Hukui. ◈ *prefecture* Honshū, SW Japan
164 D13 **Fukuoka** *var.* Hukuoka; *hist.* Najima. Fukuoka, Kyūshū, SW Japan
164 D13 **Fukuoka** *off.* Fukuoka-ken, *var.* Hukuoka. ◈ *prefecture* Kyūshū, SW Japan
165 P11 **Fukushima** *var.* Hukusima. Fukushima, Honshū, C Japan
165 Q6 **Fukushima** Hokkaidō, NE Japan
165 Q12 **Fukushima** *off.* Fukushima-ken, *var.* Hukusima. ◈ *prefecture* Honshū, C Japan
164 G13 **Fukuyama** *var.* Hukuyama. Hiroshima, Honshū, SW Japan
76 G13 **Fulacunda** C Guinea-Bissau
131 P8 **Fūlādī, Kūh-e** ▲ E Afghanistan
187 Z15 **Fulaga** *island* Lau Group, E Fiji
101 I17 **Fulda** Hessen, C Germany
29 S10 **Fulda** Minnesota, N USA
101 I16 **Fulda** ≈ C Germany
Fülek *see* Fil'akovo
Fulin *see* Hanyuan
160 K10 **Fuling** Chongqing Shi, C China
35 T15 **Fullerton** California, SE USA
29 P15 **Fullerton** Nebraska, C USA
108 M8 **Fulpmes** Tirol, W Austria
20 G8 **Fulton** Kentucky, S USA
22 N2 **Fulton** Mississippi, S USA
27 V4 **Fulton** Missouri, C USA
18 H9 **Fulton** New York, NE USA
Fuman/Fumen *see* Fowman
103 R3 **Fumay** Ardennes, N France
102 M13 **Fumel** Lot-et-Garonne, SW France
190 B10 **Funafara** *atoll* C Tuvalu
190 C9 **Funafuti** ✕ Funafuti Atoll, C Tuvalu
Funafuti *see* Fongafale
190 F8 **Funafuti Atoll** *atoll* C Tuvalu
190 B9 **Funangongo** *atoll* C Tuvalu
93 F17 **Funäsdalen** Jämtland, C Sweden
64 O6 **Funchal** Madeira, Portugal, NE Atlantic Ocean
64 P5 **Funchal** ✕ Madeira, Portugal, NE Atlantic Ocean
54 F5 **Fundación** Magdalena, N Colombia
104 I8 **Fundão** *var.* Fundáo. Castelo Branco, C Portugal
13 O16 **Fundy, Bay of** *bay* Canada/USA
Fünen *see* Fyn
54 C13 **Fúnes** Nariño, SW Colombia
Fünfkirchen *see* Pécs
83 M19 **Funhalouro** Inhambane, S Mozambique
161 R6 **Funing** Jiangsu, E China
160 I14 **Funing** *var.* Xinhua. Yunnan, SW China
160 M7 **Funiu Shan** ▲▲ C China
77 U13 **Funtua** Katsina, N Nigeria
161 R12 **Fuqing** Fujian, SE China
83 M14 **Furancungo** Tete, NW Mozambique
116 I15 **Furculeşti** Teleorman, S Romania
Füred *see* Balatonfüred
165 W4 **Füren-ko** ◎ Hokkaidō, NE Japan
143 R12 **Fürg** Färs, S Iran
Furluk *see* Fârliug
Fürmanov/Furmanovka *see* Moyynkum
Furmanovo *see* Zhalpaktal
59 L20 **Furnas, Represa de** ⊡ SE Brazil
183 Q14 **Furneaux Group** *island group* Tasmania, SE Australia
Furnes *see* Veurne
160 J10 **Furong Jiang** ≈ S China
138 I5 **Furqlus** Ḥimṣ, W Syria
100 F12 **Fürstenau** Niedersachsen, NW Germany
109 X8 **Fürstenfeld** Steiermark, SE Austria
101 L23 **Fürstenfeldbruck** Bayern, S Germany
100 P12 **Fürstenwalde** Brandenburg, NE Germany
101 K20 **Fürth** Bayern, S Germany
109 W3 **Furth bei Göttweig** Niederösterreich, NW Austria
165 R3 **Furubira** Hokkaidō, NE Japan
94 L12 **Furudal** Dalarna, C Sweden
164 L12 **Furukawa** Gifu, Honshū, SW Japan
165 Q10 **Furukawa** *var.* Hurukawa. Miyagi, Honshū, C Japan
54 F10 **Fusagasugá** Cundinamarca, C Colombia
Fusan *see* Pusan
Fushë-Arëzi/Fushë-Arrësi *see* Fushë-Arrëz
113 L18 **Fushë-Arrëz** *var.* Fushë-Arëzi, Fushë-Arrësi. Shkodër, N Albania
Fushë-Kruja *see* Fushë-Krujë
113 K19 **Fushë-Krujë** *var.* Fushë-Kruja. Durrës, C Albania
163 V12 **Fushun** *var.* Fou-shan, Fu-shun. Liaoning, NE China
Fusin *see* Fuxin
108 G10 **Fusio** Ticino, S Switzerland
163 X11 **Fusong** Jilin, NE China
101 K24 **Füssen** Bayern, S Germany
160 K15 **Fusui** *prev.* Funan. Guangxi Zhuangzu Zizhiqu, S China
Futa Jallon *see* Fouta Djallon
63 G18 **Futaleufú** Los Lagos, S Chile
112 K10 **Futog** Serbia, NW Serbia and Montenegro (Yugo.)
165 O14 **Futtsu** *var.* Huttu. Chiba, Honshū, S Japan
187 S15 **Futuna** *island* S Vanuatu
190 D12 **Futuna, Île** *island* S Wallis and Futuna
161 Q11 **Futun Xi** ≈ SE China
160 L5 **Fuxian** *var.* Fu Xian. Shaanxi, C China
Fuxian *see* Wafangdian
160 G13 **Fuxian Hu** ◎ SW China
163 U12 **Fuxin** *var.* Fou-hsin, Fu-hsin, Fusin. Liaoning, NE China
Fuxing *see* Wangmo
161 P7 **Fuyang** Anhui, E China
161 O4 **Fuyang He** ≈ E China
163 U7 **Fuyu** Heilongjiang, NE China
Fuyu/Fu-yü *see* Songyuan
163 Z6 **Fuyuan** Heilongjiang, NE China
158 M3 **Fuyun** *var.* Koktokay. Xinjiang Uygur Zizhiqu, NW China
111 L22 **Füzesabony** Heves, E Hungary
161 R12 **Fuzhou** *var.* Foochow, Fu-chou. Fujian, SE China
161 P11 **Fuzhou** *prev.* Linchuan. Jiangxi, S China
137 W13 **Füzuli** *Rus.* Fizuli. SW Azerbaijan
119 I20 **Fyadory** *Rus.* Fëdory. Brestskaya Voblasts', SW Belarus
95 G24 **Fyn** *off.* Fyns Amt, *var.* Fünen. ◈ *county* C Denmark
95 G23 **Fyn** *Ger.* Fünen. *island* C Denmark
96 H12 **Fyne, Loch** *inlet* W Scotland, UK
95 E16 **Fyresvatn** ◎ S Norway
FYR Macedonia/FYROM *see* Macedonia, FYR
Fyzabad *see* Feyzābād

G

81 O14 **Gaalkacyo** *var.* Galka'yo, *It.* Galcaio. Mudug, C Somalia
146 J11 **Gabakly** *Rus.* Kabakly. Lebap Welaýaty, NE Turkmenistan
114 H8 **Gabare** Vratsa, NW Bulgaria
102 K15 **Gabas** ≈ SW France
Gabasumdo *see* Tongde
35 T7 **Gabbs** Nevada, W USA
82 B12 **Gabela** Cuanza Sul, W Angola
Gaberones *see* Gaborone
189 X14 **Gabert** *island* Caroline Islands, E Micronesia
74 M7 **Gabès** *var.* Qābis. E Tunisia
74 M6 **Gabès, Golfe de** *Ar.* Khalīj Qābis. *gulf* E Tunisia
Gablonz an der Neisse *see* Jablonec nad Nisou
Gablös *see* Cavalese
79 E18 **Gabon** *off.* Gabonese Republic. ◆ *republic* C Africa
83 I20 **Gaborone** *prev.* Gaberones. ● (Botswana) South East, SE Botswana
83 I20 **Gaborone** ✕ South East, SE Botswana
104 K8 **Gabriel y Galán, Embalse de** ⊡ W Spain
143 U15 **Gābrīk, Rūd-e** ≈ SE Iran
114 J9 **Gabrovo** Gabrovo, N Bulgaria
114 J9 **Gabrovo** ◈ *province* N Bulgaria
76 H12 **Gabú** *prev.* Nova Lamego. E Guinea-Bissau
29 O6 **Gackle** North Dakota, N USA
113 I15 **Gacko** Republika Srpska, Bosnia and Herzegovina
155 F17 **Gadag** Karnātaka, W India
93 G15 **Gäddede** Jämtland, C Sweden
159 S12 **Gadê** Qinghai, C China
Gades/Gadier/Gadir/Gadire *see* Cádiz
105 P15 **Gádor, Sierra de** ▲▲ S Spain
149 S15 **Gadra** Sind, SE Pakistan
23 Q3 **Gadsden** Alabama, S USA
36 H15 **Gadsden** Arizona, SW USA
Gadyach *see* Hadyach
79 H15 **Gadzi** Mambéré-Kadéï, SW Central African Republic
116 J13 **Găeşti** Dâmboviţa, S Romania
107 J17 **Gaeta** Lazio, C Italy
107 J17 **Gaeta, Golfo di** *var.* Gulf of Gaeta. *gulf* C Italy
188 L14 **Gaferut** *atoll* Caroline Islands, W Micronesia
21 Q10 **Gaffney** South Carolina, SE USA
Gäfle *see* Gävle
Gäfleborg *see* Gävleborg
74 M6 **Gafsa** *var.* Qafṣah. W Tunisia
Gafurov *see* Ghafurov
147 O10 **Gagarin** Jizzax Viloyati, C Uzbekistan
101 G21 **Gaggenau** Baden-Württemberg, SW Germany
188 F16 **Gagil Tamil** *var.* Gagil-Tomil. *island* Caroline Islands, W Micronesia
Gagil-Tomil *see* Gagil Tamil
127 O4 **Gagino** Nizhegorodskaya Oblast', W Russian Federation
107 Q19 **Gagliano del Capo** Puglia, SE Italy
94 L13 **Gagnef** Dalarna, C Sweden
76 M17 **Gagnoa** C Ivory Coast
13 N10 **Gagnon** Québec, E Canada
Gago Coutinho *see* Lumbala N'Guimbo
137 P8 **Gagra** NW Georgia
31 S13 **Gahanna** Ohio, N USA
143 R13 **Gahkom** Hormozgān, S Iran
Gahnpa *see* Ganta
57 Q19 **Gaíba, Laguna** ◎ E Bolivia
153 T13 **Gaibanda** *var.* Gaibandah. Rajshahi, NW Bangladesh
Gaibandah *see* Gaibanda
Gaibhlte, Cnoc Mór na n *see* Galtymore Mountain
109 R9 **Gail** ≈ S Austria
101 I21 **Gaildorf** Baden-Württemberg, S Germany
103 N15 **Gaillac** *var.* Gaillac-sur-Tarn. Tarn, S France
Gaillac-sur-Tarn *see* Gaillac
Gaillimh *see* Galway
Gaillimhe, Cuan na *see* Galway Bay
109 Q9 **Gailtaler Alpen** ▲▲ S Austria
63 J17 **Gaimán** Chaco, S Argentina
20 K8 **Gainesboro** Tennessee, S USA
23 V10 **Gainesville** Florida, SE USA
23 T2 **Gainesville** Georgia, SE USA
27 U8 **Gainesville** Missouri, C USA
25 T5 **Gainesville** Texas, SW USA
109 X5 **Gainfarn** Niederösterreich, NE Austria
97 N18 **Gainsborough** E England, UK
182 G6 **Gairdner, Lake** *salt lake* South Australia
Gaissane *see* Gáissát
92 L8 **Gáissát** *var.* Gaissane. ▲▲ N Norway
43 T15 **Gaital, Cerro** ▲ C Panama
21 W3 **Gaithersburg** Maryland, NE USA
163 U13 **Gaizhou** Liaoning, NE China
Gaizina Kalns *see* Gaiziņkalns
118 H7 **Gaiziņkalns** *var.* Gaizina Kalns. ▲ E Latvia
Gajac *see* Villeneuve-sur-Lot
39 S10 **Gakona** Alaska, USA
Galaassiya *see* Galaosiyo
Galāğil *see* Jalājil
Galam, Pulau *see* Gelam, Pulau
62 J6 **Galán, Cerro** ▲ NW Argentina
111 H21 **Galanta** *Hung.* Galánta. Trnavský Kraj, W Slovakia
146 L11 **Galaosiyo** *Rus.* Galaassiya. Buxoro Viloyati, C Uzbekistan
57 B17 **Galápagos** *off.* Provincia de Galápagos. ◈ *province* Ecuador, E Pacific Ocean
193 P8 **Galapagos Fracture Zone** *tectonic feature* E Pacific Ocean
193 S9 **Galapagos Rise** *undersea feature* E Pacific Ocean
96 K13 **Galashiels** SE Scotland, UK
116 M12 **Galaţi** *Ger.* Galatz. Galaţi, E Romania
116 L12 **Galaţi** ◈ *county* E Romania
107 Q19 **Galatina** Puglia, SE Italy
107 Q19 **Galatone** Puglia, SE Italy
Galatz *see* Galaţi
21 R8 **Galax** Virginia, NE USA
146 J16 **Galaýmor** *Rus.* Kala-i-Mor. Mary Welaýaty, S Turkmenistan
Galcaio *see* Gaalkacyo
64 P11 **Gáldar** Gran Canaria, Islas Canarias, NE Atlantic Ocean
94 F11 **Galdhøpiggen** ▲ S Norway
40 I4 **Galeana** Chihuahua, N Mexico
41 O9 **Galeana** Nuevo León, NE Mexico
60 P9 **Galeão** ✕ (Rio de Janeiro) Rio de Janeiro, SE Brazil
171 R10 **Galela** Pulau Halmahera, E Indonesia
39 O9 **Galena** Alaska, USA
30 K10 **Galena** Illinois, N USA
27 R7 **Galena** Kansas, C USA
27 T8 **Galena** Missouri, C USA
45 V15 **Galeota Point** *headland* Trinidad, Trinidad and Tobago
105 P13 **Galera** Andalucía, S Spain
45 Y16 **Galera Point** *headland* Trinidad, Trinidad and Tobago
56 A5 **Galera, Punta** *headland* NW Ecuador
30 K12 **Galesburg** Illinois, N USA
30 J7 **Galesville** Wisconsin, N USA
18 F12 **Galeton** Pennsylvania, NE USA
116 H9 **Gâlgău** *Hung.* Galgó; *prev.* Gîlgău. Sălaj, NW Romania
Galgó *see* Gâlgău
Galgóc *see* Hlohovec
81 N15 **Galguduud** *off.* Gobolka Galguduud. ◈ *region* E Somalia
137 Q9 **Gali** W Georgia
125 N14 **Galich** Kostromskaya Oblast', NW Russian Federation
114 H7 **Galiche** Vratsa, NW Bulgaria
104 H3 **Galicia** *anc.* Gallaecia. ◈ *autonomous community* NW Spain
64 M8 **Galicia Bank** *undersea feature* E Atlantic Ocean
Galilee *see* HaGalil
181 W7 **Galilee, Lake** ◎ Queensland, NE Australia
Galilee, Sea of *see* Tiberias, Lake
106 E11 **Galileo Galilei** ✕ (Pisa) Toscana, C Italy
31 S12 **Galion** Ohio, N USA
Galka'yo *see* Gaalkacyo
146 K12 **Galkynyş** *prev. Rus.* Deynau, Dyanev, *Turkm.* Dänew. Lebap Welaýaty, NE Turkmenistan
80 H11 **Gallabat** Gedaref, E Sudan
Gallaecia *see* Galicia
106 C7 **Gallarate** Lombardia, NW Italy
27 S2 **Gallatin** Missouri, C USA
20 J8 **Gallatin** Tennessee, S USA
33 R11 **Gallatin Peak** ▲ Montana, NW USA
33 R12 **Gallatin River** ≈ Montana/Wyoming, NW USA
155 J26 **Galle** *prev.* Point de Galle. Southern Province, SW Sri Lanka
105 S5 **Gállego** ≈ NE Spain
193 Q8 **Gallego Rise** *undersea feature* E Pacific Ocean
Gallegos *see* Río Gallegos
63 H23 **Gallegos, Río** ≈ Argentina/Chile
Gallia *see* France
22 K10 **Galliano** Louisiana, S USA
114 G13 **Gallikós** ≈ N Greece
37 S12 **Gallinas Peak** ▲ New Mexico, SW USA
54 H3 **Gallinas, Punta** *headland* NE Colombia
37 T11 **Gallinas River** ≈ New Mexico, SW USA
107 Q19 **Gallipoli** Puglia, SE Italy
Gallipoli *see* Gelibolu
Gallipoli Peninsula *see* Gelibolu Yarımadası
31 T15 **Gallipolis** Ohio, N USA
92 J12 **Gällivare** *Lapp.* Váhtjer. Norrbotten, N Sweden
109 T4 **Gallneukirchen** Oberösterreich, N Austria
105 Q7 **Gallo** ≈ C Spain
93 G17 **Gällö** Jämtland, C Sweden
107 I23 **Gallo, Capo** *headland* Sicilia, Italy, C Mediterranean Sea
37 P13 **Gallo Mountains** ▲▲ New Mexico, SW USA
18 G8 **Galloo Island** *island* New York, NE USA
97 H15 **Galloway, Mull of** *headland* S Scotland, UK
37 P10 **Gallup** New Mexico, SW USA
105 R5 **Gallur** Aragón, NE Spain
Gâlma *see* Guelma
35 O8 **Galt** California, W USA
74 C10 **Galtat-Zemmour** C Western Sahara
95 G22 **Galten** Århus, C Denmark
97 D20 **Galtymore Mountain** *Ir.* Cnoc Mór na nGaibhlte. ▲ S Ireland
97 D20 **Galty Mountains** *Ir.* Na Gaibhlte. ▲▲ S Ireland
30 K11 **Galva** Illinois, N USA
25 X12 **Galveston** Texas, SW USA
25 W11 **Galveston Bay** *inlet* Texas, SW USA
25 W12 **Galveston Island** *island* Texas, SW USA
61 B18 **Gálvez** Santa Fe, C Argentina
97 C18 **Galway** *Ir.* Gaillimh. W Ireland
97 B18 **Galway** *Ir.* Gaillimh. *cultural region* W Ireland
97 B18 **Galway Bay** *Ir.* Cuan na Gaillimhe. *bay* W Ireland
83 F18 **Gam** Otjozondjupa, NE Namibia
164 L14 **Gamagōri** Aichi, Honshū, SW Japan
54 F7 **Gamarra** Cesar, N Colombia
Gámas *see* Kaamanen
158 L17 **Gamba** Xizang Zizhiqu, W China
Gamba *see* Zamtang

◆ Country ● Country Capital ◇ Dependent Territory ○ Dependent Territory Capital ◈ Administrative Region ✕ International Airport ▲ Mountain ▲▲ Mountain Range △ Volcano ≈ River ◎ Lake ⊡ Reservoir

77 P14 Gambaga NE Ghana
80 G13 Gambēla Gambēla, W Ethiopia
83 H14 Gambēla ◈ region, W Ethiopia
38 K10 Gambell Saint Lawrence Island, Alaska, USA
76 E12 Gambia off. Republic of The Gambia, The Gambia. ◆ republic W Africa
76 I12 Gambia Fr. Gambie. ≈ W Africa
64 K12 Gambia Plain undersea feature E Atlantic Ocean
Gambie see Gambia
31 T13 Gambier Ohio, N USA
191 Y13 Gambier, Îles island group E French Polynesia
182 G10 Gambier Islands island group South Australia
79 H19 Gamboma Plateaux, E Congo
79 G16 Gamboula Mambéré-Kadéï, SW Central African Republic
37 P10 Gamerco New Mexico, SW USA
137 V12 Gamış Dağı ▲ W Azerbaijan
Gamlakarleby see Kokkola
95 N18 Gamleby Kalmar, S Sweden
Gammelstad see Gammelstaden
93 J14 Gammelstaden var. Gammelstad. Norrbotten, N Sweden
Gammouda see Sidi Bouzid
155 J25 Gampaha Western Province, W Sri Lanka
155 K25 Gampola Central Province, C Sri Lanka
167 S5 Gâm, Sông ≈ N Vietnam
92 L7 Gamvik Finnmark, N Norway
150 H13 Gan Addu Atoll, C Maldives
Gan see Gansu, China
Gan see Jiangxi, China
Ganaane see Juba
37 O10 Ganado Arizona, SW USA
25 U12 Ganado Texas, SW USA
14 L14 Gananoque Ontario, SE Canada
Ganāveh see Bandar-e Gonāveh
137 V11 Gäncä Rus. Gyandzha; prev. Kirovabad, Yelisavetpol. W Azerbaijan
Ganchi see Ghonchí
Gand see Gent
82 B13 Ganda var. Mariano Machado, Port. Vila Mariano Machado. Benguela, W Angola
79 L22 Gandajika Kasai Oriental, S Dem. Rep. Congo
153 O12 Gandak Nep. Nārāyāni. ≈ India/Nepal
13 U11 Gander Newfoundland and Labrador, SE Canada
13 U11 Gander × Newfoundland and Labrador, E Canada
100 G11 Ganderkesee Niedersachsen, NW Germany
105 T7 Gandesa Cataluña, NE Spain
154 B10 Gāndhīdhām Gujarāt, W India
154 D10 Gāndhīnagar Gujarāt, W India
154 F9 Gāndhi Sāgar ◎ C India
105 T11 Gandía País Valenciano, E Spain
159 O10 Gang Qinghai, W China
152 G9 Gangānagar Rājasthān, NW India
152 I12 Gangāpur Rājasthān, N India
153 S17 Ganga Sāgar West Bengal, NE India
Gangavathi see Gangāwati
155 G17 Gangāwati var. Gangavathi. Karnātaka, C India
159 S9 Gangca var. Shaliuhe. Qinghai, C China
158 H14 Gangdisê Shan Eng. Kailas Range. ▲ W China
103 Q15 Ganges Hérault, S France
153 P13 Ganges Ben. Padma. ≈ Bangladesh/India see also Padma
Ganges Cone see Ganges Fan
173 S3 Ganges Fan var. Ganges Cone. undersea feature N Bay of Bengal
153 U17 Ganges, Mouths of the delta Bangladesh/India
107 K23 Gangi anc. Engyum. Sicilia, Italy, C Mediterranean Sea
152 K8 Gangotri Uttaranchal, N India
Gangra see Çankırı
153 S11 Gangtok Sikkim, N India
159 W11 Gangu Gansu, C China
163 U5 Gan He ≈ NE China
171 S12 Gani Pulau Halmahera, E Indonesia
161 O12 Gan Jiang ≈ S China
163 U11 Ganjig var. Horqin Zuoyi Houqi. Nei Mongol Zizhiqu, N China
146 H15 Gannaly Ahal Welaýaty, S Turkmenistan
163 U7 Gannan Heilongjiang, NE China
103 P10 Gannat Allier, C France
33 T14 Gannett Peak ▲ Wyoming, C USA
29 O10 Gannvalley South Dakota, N USA
Ganqu see Lhünzhub
109 Y3 Gänserndorf Niederösterreich, NE Austria
Gansos, Lago dos see Goose Lake
159 T9 Gansu var. Gan, Gansu Sheng, Kansu. ◈ province N China
Gansu Sheng see Gansu
76 K16 Ganta var. Gahnpa. NE Liberia
182 H11 Gantheaume, Cape headland South Australia
Gantsevichi see Hantsavichy
161 Q6 Ganyu var. Qingkou. Jiangsu, E China
144 D12 Ganyushkino Atyrau, SW Kazakhstan
161 O12 Ganzhou Jiangxi, S China
Ganzhou see Zhangye
77 Q10 Gao Gao, E Mali
77 R10 Gao ◈ region SE Mali
161 O10 Gao'an Jiangxi, S China
Gaocheng see Litang
Gaoleshan see Xianfeng
161 R5 Gaomi Shandong, E China
161 N5 Gaoping Shanxi, C China
159 S8 Gaotai Gansu, N China
Gaoth Dobhair see Gweedore
77 O14 Gaoua SW Burkina
76 I13 Gaoual Moyenne-Guinée, N Guinea
Gaoxiong see Kaohsiung
161 R7 Gaoyou var. Dayishan. Jiangsu, E China
161 R7 Gaoyou Hu ◎ E China
160 M15 Gaozhou Guangdong, S China
103 T13 Gap anc. Vapincum. Hautes-Alpes, SE France
146 E9 Gaplaňgyr Platosy Rus. Plato Kaplangky. ridge Turkmenistan/Uzbekistan
158 G13 Gar var. Gar Xincun. Xizang Zizhiqu, W China
Garabekevyul see Garabekewül
146 L13 Garabekewül Rus. Garabekevyul, Karabekaul. Lebap Welaýaty, E Turkmenistan
146 K15 Garabil Belentligi Rus. Vozvyshennost' Karabil'. ▲ S Turkmenistan
146 B9 Garabogaz Aylagy Rus. Zaliv Kara-Bogaz-Gol. bay NW Turkmenistan
146 A9 Garabogazköl Rus. Kara-Bogaz-Kol. Balkan Welaýaty, NW Turkmenistan
43 V16 Garachiné Darién, SE Panama
43 V16 Garachiné, Punta headland SE Panama
146 K12 Garagan Rus. Karagan. Ahal Welaýaty, C Turkmenistan
54 G10 Garagoa Boyacá, C Colombia
146 A11 Garagöl Rus. Karagel'. Balkan Welaýaty, W Turkmenistan
146 F12 Garagum var. Garagumy, Qara Qum, Eng. Black Sand Desert, Kara Kum; prev. Peski Karakumy. desert C Turkmenistan
146 E12 Garagum Kanaly var. Kara Kum Canal, Rus. Garagumskiy Kanal, Karakumskiy Kanal. canal C Turkmenistan
Garagumskiy Kanal see Garagum Kanaly
Garagumy see Garagum
183 S4 Garah New South Wales, SE Australia
64 O11 Garajonay ▲ Gomera, Islas Canarias, NE Atlantic Ocean
114 M8 Gara Khitrino Shumen, NE Bulgaria
76 L13 Garalo Sikasso, SW Mali
Garam see Hron
146 L14 Garamätnyýaz Rus. Karamet-Niyaz. Lebap Welaýaty, E Turkmenistan
Garamszentkereszt see Žiar nad Hronom
77 Q13 Garango S Burkina
59 Q15 Garanhuns Pernambuco, E Brazil
188 H5 Garapan Saipan, S Northern Mariana Islands
Gárasavvon see Karesuando
Gárassavon see Kaaresuvanto
78 J13 Garba Bamingui-Bangoran, N Central African Republic
Garba see Jiulong
81 L16 Garbahaarrey It. Garba Harre. Gedo, SW Somalia
Garba Harre see Garbahaarrey
81 J18 Garba Tula Eastern, C Kenya
27 N9 Garber Oklahoma, C USA
34 L4 Garberville California, W USA
100 I12 Garbsen Niedersachsen, N Germany
Garbo see Lhozhag
60 K9 Garça São Paulo, S Brazil
104 L10 García de Solá, Embalse de ⊡ C Spain
103 Q14 Gard ◈ department S France
103 Q14 Gard ≈ S France
106 F7 Garda, Lago di var. Benaco, Eng. Lake Garda, Ger. Gardasee. ◎ NE Italy
Garda, Lake see Garda, Lago di
Gardan Divāl see Gardan Dīwāl
149 Q5 Gardan Dīwāl var. Gardan Divāl. Wardag, C Afghanistan
103 S15 Gardanne Bouches-du-Rhône, SE France
Gardasee see Garda, Lago di
100 L12 Gardelegen Sachsen-Anhalt, C Germany
14 B10 Garden ≈ Ontario, S Canada
23 X6 Garden City Georgia, SE USA
26 I6 Garden City Kansas, C USA
27 S5 Garden City Missouri, C USA
25 N8 Garden City Texas, SW USA
23 P3 Gardendale Alabama, S USA
31 P5 Garden Island island Michigan, N USA
22 M11 Garden Island Bay bay Louisiana, S USA
31 O5 Garden Peninsula peninsula Michigan, N USA
Garden State see New Jersey
95 I14 Gardermoen Akershus, S Norway
Gardeyz see Gardēz
149 Q6 Gardēz var. Gardeyz, Gordiaz. Paktīā, E Afghanistan
93 G14 Gardiken ◎ N Sweden
19 Q7 Gardiner Maine, NE USA
33 S12 Gardiner Montana, NW USA
19 N13 Gardiners Island island New York, NE USA
Gardner Island see Nikumaroro
19 T6 Gardner Lake ◎ Maine, NE USA
35 Q6 Gardnerville Nevada, W USA
Gardo see Qardho
106 F7 Gardone Val Trompia Lombardia, N Italy
Garegegasnjárga see Karigasniemi
38 F17 Gareloi Island island Aleutian Islands, Alaska, USA
Gares see Puente la Reina
106 B10 Garessio Piemonte, NE Italy
32 M9 Garfield Washington, NW USA
31 U11 Garfield Heights Ohio, N USA
Gargaliani see Gargaliánoi
115 D21 Gargaliánoi var. Gargaliani. Pelopónnisos, S Greece
107 N15 Gargano, Promontorio del headland SE Italy
108 J8 Gargellen Graubünden, W Switzerland
93 I14 Gargnäs Västerbotten, N Sweden
118 C11 Gargždai Klaipėda, W Lithuania
154 J13 Garhchiroli Mahārāshtra, C India
153 O15 Garhwa Jhārkhand, N India
171 V13 Gariau Papua, E Indonesia
83 E24 Garies Northern Cape, W South Africa
109 K17 Garigliano ≈ C Italy
81 K19 Garissa Coast, E Kenya
21 V11 Garland North Carolina, SE USA
25 T6 Garland Texas, SW USA
36 L1 Garland Utah, W USA
106 D8 Garlasco Lombardia, N Italy
119 F14 Garliava Kaunas, S Lithuania
Garm see Gharm
142 M9 Garm, Āb-e var. Rūd-e Khersān. ≈ SW Iran
101 K25 Garmisch-Partenkirchen Bayern, S Germany
143 O5 Garmsār prev. Qishlaq. Semnān, N Iran
Garmser see Darvīshān
29 V12 Garner Iowa, C USA
21 U9 Garner North Carolina, SE USA
27 Q5 Garnett Kansas, C USA
99 M25 Garnich Luxembourg, SW Luxembourg
182 M8 Garnpung, Lake salt lake New South Wales, SE Australia
Garoe see Garoowe
Garoet see Garut
153 U13 Gāro Hills hill range NE India
102 K13 Garonne anc. Garumna. ≈ S France
80 P13 Garoowe var. Garoe. Nugaal, N Somalia
78 F12 Garoua var. Garua. Nord, N Cameroon
79 G14 Garoua Boulaï Est, E Cameroon
77 O10 Garou, Lac ◎ C Mali
95 L16 Garphyttan Örebro, C Sweden
29 R11 Garretson South Dakota, N USA
31 Q11 Garrett Indiana, N USA
33 Q10 Garrison Montana, NW USA
28 M4 Garrison North Dakota, N USA
25 X8 Garrison Texas, SW USA
28 L4 Garrison Dam dam North Dakota, N USA
104 J9 Garrovillas Extremadura, W Spain
146 D12 Garrygala Rus. Kara-Kala. Balkan Welaýaty, W Turkmenistan
8 L8 Garry Lake ◎ Nunavut, N Canada
Gars see Gars am Kamp
109 W3 Gars am Kamp var. Gars. Niederösterreich, NE Austria
81 K20 Garsen Coast, S Kenya
Garshy see Garşy
14 F10 Garson Ontario, S Canada
109 T5 Garsten Oberösterreich, N Austria
146 A9 Garşy var. Garshy, Rus. Karshi. Balkan Welaýaty, NW Turkmenistan
Gartar see Qianning
102 M10 Gartempe ≈ C France
Gartog see Markam
Garua see Garoua
83 D21 Garub Karas, SW Namibia
Garumna see Garonne
169 P16 Garut prev. Garoet. Jawa, C Indonesia
185 C20 Garvie Mountains ▲ South Island, NZ
110 N12 Garwolin Mazowieckie, E Poland
25 U12 Garwood Texas, SW USA
Gar Xincun see Gar
31 N11 Gary Indiana, N USA
25 X7 Gary Texas, SW USA
158 G13 Gar Zangbo ≈ W China
160 F8 Garzê Sichuan, C China
54 E12 Garzón Huila, S Colombia
Gasan-Kuli see Esenguly
31 P13 Gas City Indiana, N USA
102 K15 Gascogne Eng. Gascony. cultural region S France
Gascogne, Golfe de see Gascony, Gulf of
26 V5 Gasconade River ≈ Missouri, C USA
Gascony see Gascogne
180 H9 Gascoyne Junction Western Australia
173 V8 Gascoyne Plain undersea feature E Indian Ocean
180 H9 Gascoyne River ≈ Western Australia
192 J11 Gascoyne Tablemount undersea feature N Tasman Sea
67 U6 Gash var. Nahr al Qāsh. ≈ W Sudan
149 X3 Gasherbrum ▲ NE Pakistan
Gas Hu see Gas Hure Hu
77 X12 Gashua Yobe, NE Nigeria
159 N9 Gas Hure Hu var. Gas Hu. ◎ C China
186 G7 Gasmata New Britain, E PNG
23 V14 Gasparilla Island island Florida, SE USA
169 O13 Gaspar, Selat strait W Indonesia
15 Y6 Gaspé Québec, SE Canada
15 Z6 Gaspé, Cap de headland Québec, SE Canada
15 X6 Gaspé, Péninsule de var. Péninsule de la Gaspésie. peninsula Québec, SE Canada
Gaspésie, Péninsule de la see Gaspé, Péninsule de
77 W15 Gassol Taraba, E Nigeria
Gastein see Badgastein
21 R10 Gastonia North Carolina, SE USA
21 V8 Gaston, Lake ⊡ North Carolina/Virginia, SE USA
115 D19 Gastoúni Dytikí Ellás, S Greece
63 I17 Gastre Chubut, S Argentina
Gat see Ghāt
105 P15 Gata, Cabo de headland S Spain
Gata, Cape see Gátas, Akrotíri
105 T11 Gata de Gorgos País Valenciano, E Spain
116 E12 Gătaia Ger. Gataja, Hung. Gátalja; prev. Gáttája. Timiş, W Romania
Gataja/Gátalja see Gătaia
121 P3 Gátas, Akrotíri var. Cape Gata. headland S Cyprus
104 J8 Gata, Sierra de ▲ W Spain
124 G13 Gatchina Leningradskaya Oblast', NW Russian Federation
21 P8 Gate City Virginia, NE USA
97 M14 Gateshead NE England, UK
21 X8 Gatesville North Carolina, SE USA
25 S8 Gatesville Texas, SW USA
14 L12 Gatineau Québec, SE Canada
14 L11 Gatineau ≈ Ontario/Québec, SE Canada
21 N9 Gatlinburg Tennessee, S USA
Gatooma see Kadoma
Gáttája see Gătaia
43 T14 Gatún, Lago ⊡ C Panama
59 N14 Gaturiano Piauí, NE Brazil
97 O22 Gatwick × (London) SE England, UK
187 Y14 Gau prev. Ngau. island C Fiji
187 R12 Gaua var Santa Maria, island Banks Islands, N Vanuatu
104 L16 Gaucín Andalucía, S Spain
Gauhāti see Guwāhāti
118 I8 Gauja Ger. Aa. ≈ Estonia/Latvia
118 I7 Gaujiena Alūksne, NE Latvia
Gaul/Gaule see France
94 H9 Gauldalen valley S Norway
21 R5 Gauley River ≈ West Virginia, NE USA
99 D19 Gaurain-Ramecroix Hainaut, SW Belgium
95 F15 Gaustatoppen ▲ S Norway
83 J21 Gauteng off. Gauteng Province; prev. Pretoria-Witwatersrand-Vereeniging. ◈ province NE South Africa
Gauteng see Germiston, South Africa
Gauteng see Johannesburg, South Africa
143 P14 Gāvbandī Hormozgān, S Iran
115 H25 Gavdopoúla island SE Greece
115 H26 Gávdos island SE Greece
102 K16 Gave de Pau var. Gave-de-Pay. ≈ SW France
Gave-de-Pay see Gave de Pau
102 J16 Gave d'Oloron ≈ SW France
99 E18 Gavere Oost-Vlaanderen, NW Belgium
94 N13 Gävle var. Gäfle; prev. Gefle. Gävleborg, C Sweden
94 M11 Gävleborg var. Gäfleborg, Gefleborg. ◈ county C Sweden
94 O13 Gävlebukten bay C Sweden
124 L16 Gavrilov-Yam Yaroslavskaya Oblast', W Russian Federation
182 I9 Gawler South Australia
182 G7 Gawler Ranges hill range South Australia
Gawso see Goaso
162 H11 Gaxun Nur ◎ N China
153 P14 Gaya Bihār, N India
77 S13 Gaya Dosso, SW Niger
Gaya see Kyjov
31 Q6 Gaylord Michigan, N USA
29 U9 Gaylord Minnesota, N USA
181 Y9 Gayndah Queensland, E Australia
125 T12 Gayny Komi-Permyatskiy Avtonomnyy Okrug, NW Russian Federation
Gaysin see Haysyn
Gayvorno see Hayvoron
138 E11 Gaza Ar. Ghazzah, Heb. 'Azza. NE Gaza Strip
83 L20 Gaza off. Província de Gaza. ◈ province SW Mozambique
Gaz-Achak see Gazojak
Gazalkent see G'azalkent
147 Q9 G'azalkent Rus. Gazalkent. Toshkent Viloyati, E Uzbekistan
Gazandzhyk/Gazanjyk see Bereket
77 V12 Gazaoua Maradi, S Niger
138 E11 Gaza Strip Ar. Qiţā' Ghazzah. disputed region SW Asia
Gazgan see G'ozg'on
Gazi Antep see Gaziantep
136 M16 Gaziantep var. Gazi Antep; prev. Aintab, Antep. Gaziantep, S Turkey
136 M17 Gaziantep var. Gazi Antep. ◈ province S Turkey
114 M13 Gaziköy Tekirdağ, NW Turkey
121 Q2 Gazimağusa var. Famagusta, Gk. Ammóchostos. E Cyprus
121 Q2 Gazimağusa Körfezi var. Famagusta Bay, Gk. Kólpos Ammóchostos. bay E Cyprus
146 K11 Gazli Buxoro Viloyati, C Uzbekistan
146 I9 Gazojak Rus. Gaz-Achak. Lebap Welaýaty, NE Turkmenistan
79 K15 Gbadolite Equateur, NW Dem. Rep. Congo
76 K16 Gbanga var. Gbarnga. N Liberia
Gbarnga see Gbanga
77 S14 Gbéroubouè var. Béroubouay. N Benin
77 W16 Gboko Benue, S Nigeria
Gcuwa see Butterworth
110 J7 Gdańsk Fr. Dantzig, Ger. Danzig. Pomorskie, N Poland
Gdan'skaya Bukhta/Gdańsk, Gulf of see Danzig, Gulf of
Gdańska, Zakota see Danzig, Gulf of
Gdingen see Gdynia
124 F13 Gdov Pskovskaya Oblast', W Russian Federation
110 I6 Gdynia Ger. Gdingen. Pomorskie, N Poland
26 M10 Geary Oklahoma, C USA
Geavvú see Kevo
76 H12 Géba, Rio ≈ C Guinea-Bissau
136 E11 Gebze Kocaeli, NW Turkey
80 H10 Gedaref var. Al Qaḍārif, El Gedaref. Gedaref, E Sudan
80 H10 Gedaref ◈ state E Sudan
80 B11 Gedid Ras el Fil Southern Darfur, W Sudan
101 I23 Gedinne Namur, SE Belgium
136 E13 Gediz Kütahya, W Turkey
136 C14 Gediz Nehri ≈ W Turkey
81 N14 Gedlegubē Somali, E Ethiopia
81 L17 Gedo off. Gobolka Gedo. ◈ region SW Somalia
95 I25 Gedser Storstrøm, SE Denmark
99 I16 Geel var. Gheel. Antwerpen, N Belgium
183 N13 Geelong Victoria, SE Australia
Ge'e'mu see Golmud
99 I14 Geertruidenberg Noord-Brabant, S Netherlands
100 H10 Geeste ≈ NW Germany
100 J10 Geesthacht Schleswig-Holstein, N Germany
183 P17 Geeveston Tasmania, SE Australia
Gefle see Gävle
Gefleborg see Gävleborg
158 G13 Gê'gyai Xizang Zizhiqu, W China
77 X12 Geidam Yobe, NE Nigeria
11 T11 Geikie ≈ Saskatchewan, C Canada
94 F13 Geilo Buskerud, S Norway
94 E10 Geiranger Møre og Romsdal, S Norway
101 I22 Geislingen var. Geislingen an der Steige. Baden-Württemberg, SW Germany
Geislingen an der Steige see Geislingen
81 F20 Geita Mwanza, NW Tanzania
95 G15 Geithus Buskerud, S Norway
160 H14 Gejiu var. Kochiu. Yunnan, S China
Gëkdepe see Gökdepe
146 E9 Geklengkui, Solonchak var. Solonchak Goklenkuy. salt marsh NW Turkmenistan
81 D14 Gel ≈ W Sudan
107 K25 Gela prev. Terranova di Sicilia. Sicilia, Italy, C Mediterranean Sea
159 N13 Gêladaindong ▲ C China
81 N14 Geladī Somali, E Ethiopia
169 P13 Gelam, Pulau var. Pulau Galam. island N Indonesia
Gelaozu Miaozu Zizhixian see Wuchuan
98 L11 Gelderland prev. Eng. Guelders. ◈ province E Netherlands
98 J13 Geldermalsen Gelderland, C Netherlands
101 D14 Geldern Nordrhein-Westfalen, W Germany
99 K15 Geldrop Noord-Brabant, SE Netherlands
99 L17 Geleen Limburg, SE Netherlands
126 K14 Gelendzhik Krasnodarskiy Kray, SW Russian Federation
Gelib see Jilib
136 B11 Gelibolu Eng. Gallipoli. Çanakkale, NW Turkey
115 L14 Gelibolu Yarımadası Eng. Gallipoli Peninsula. peninsula NW Turkey
81 O14 Gellinsor Mudug, C Somalia
101 H18 Gelnhausen Hessen, C Germany
101 E14 Gelsenkirchen Nordrhein-Westfalen, W Germany
83 C20 Geluk Hardap, SW Namibia
99 H20 Gembloux Namur, Belgium
79 J16 Gemena Equateur, NW Dem. Rep. Congo
99 L14 Gemert Noord-Brabant, SE Netherlands
136 E11 Gemlik Bursa, NW Turkey
Gem of the Mountains see Idaho
106 J6 Gemona del Friuli Friuli-Venezia Giulia, NE Italy
Gem State see Idaho
Genalē Wenz see Juba
169 R10 Genali, Danau ◎ Borneo, N Indonesia
99 G19 Genappe Wallon Brabant, C Belgium
137 P14 Genç Bingöl, E Turkey
Genck see Genk
98 M9 Genemuiden Overijssel, E Netherlands
63 K14 General Acha La Pampa, C Argentina
61 C21 General Alvear Buenos Aires, E Argentina
62 I12 General Alvear Mendoza, W Argentina
61 B20 General Arenales Buenos Aires, E Argentina
61 D21 General Belgrano Buenos Aires, E Argentina
194 H3 General Bernardo O'Higgins Chilean research station Antarctica
41 O8 General Bravo Nuevo León, NE Mexico
62 M7 General Capdevila Chaco, N Argentina
General Carrera, Lago see Buenos Aires, Lago
41 N9 General Cepeda Coahuila de Zaragoza, NE Mexico
63 K15 General Conesa Río Negro, E Argentina
61 G18 General Enrique Martínez Treinta y Tres, E Uruguay
62 L3 General Eugenio A. Garay var. Fortín General Eugenio Garay; prev. Yrendagüé. Nueva Asunción, NW Paraguay
61 C18 General Galarza Entre Ríos, E Argentina
61 E22 General Guido Buenos Aires, E Argentina
General José F.Uriburu see Zárate
61 E22 General Juan Madariaga Buenos Aires, E Argentina
41 O16 General Juan N Alvarez × (Acapulco) Guerrero, S Mexico
61 B22 General La Madrid Buenos Aires, E Argentina
61 E21 General Lavalle Buenos Aires, E Argentina
General Machado see Camacupa
62 I8 General Manuel Belgrano, Cerro ▲ W Argentina
41 O8 General Mariano Escobero × (Monterrey) Nuevo León, NE Mexico
61 B20 General O'Brien Buenos Aires, E Argentina
62 K13 General Pico La Pampa, C Argentina
62 M7 General Pinedo Chaco, N Argentina
61 B20 General Pinto Buenos Aires, E Argentina
61 E22 General Pirán Buenos Aires, E Argentina
43 N15 General, Río ≈ S Costa Rica
63 I15 General Roca Río Negro, C Argentina
171 Q8 General Santos off. General Santos City. Mindanao, S Philippines
41 O9 General Terán Nuevo León, NE Mexico
114 N7 General Toshevo Rom. I.G.Duca, prev. Casim, Kasimköj. Dobrich, NE Bulgaria
61 B20 General Viamonte Buenos Aires, E Argentina
61 A20 General Villegas Buenos Aires, E Argentina
Gênes see Genova
18 E11 Genesee River ≈ New York/Pennsylvania, NE USA
30 K11 Geneseo Illinois, N USA
18 F10 Geneseo New York, NE USA
57 L14 Geneshuaya, Río ≈ N Bolivia
23 Q8 Geneva Alabama, S USA
30 M10 Geneva Illinois, N USA
29 Q16 Geneva Nebraska, C USA
18 G10 Geneva New York, NE USA
31 U10 Geneva Ohio, NE USA
Geneva see Genève
108 B10 Geneva, Lake Fr. Lac de Genève, Lac Léman, le Léman, Ger. Genfer See. ◎ France/Switzerland
108 A10 Genève Eng. Geneva, Ger. Genf, It. Ginevra. Genève, SW Switzerland
108 A11 Genève Eng. Geneva, Ger. Genf, It. Ginevra. ◈ canton SW Switzerland
108 A10 Genève var. Geneva. × Vaud, SW Switzerland
Genève, Lac de see Geneva, Lake
Genf see Genève
Genfer See see Geneva, Lake
163 T5 Genhe prev. Ergun Zuoqi. Nei Mongol Zizhiqu, N China
163 S5 Gen He ≈ NE China
Genichesk see Heniches'k
104 L14 Genil ≈ S Spain
99 K18 Genk var. Genck. Limburg, NE Belgium
164 C13 Genkai-nada gulf Kyūshū, SW Japan
107 C19 Gennargentu, Monti del ▲ Sardegna, Italy, C Mediterranean Sea
99 M14 Gennep Limburg, SE Netherlands
30 M10 Genoa Illinois, N USA
29 Q15 Genoa Nebraska, C USA
Genoa see Genova
Genoa, Gulf of see Genova, Golfo di
106 D10 Genova Eng. Genoa, Fr. Gênes; anc. Genua. Liguria, NW Italy
106 D10 Genova, Golfo di Eng. Gulf of Genoa. gulf NW Italy
57 C17 Genovesa, Isla var. Tower Island. island Galapagos Islands, Ecuador, E Pacific Ocean
Genshū see Wŏnju
99 E17 Gent Eng. Ghent, Fr. Gand. Oost-Vlaanderen, NW Belgium
169 N16 Genteng Jawa, C Indonesia
100 M12 Genthin Sachsen-Anhalt, E Germany
27 R9 Gentry Arkansas, C USA
Genua see Genova
107 I15 Genzano di Roma Lazio, C Italy
Geokchay see Göyçay
Geok-Tepe see Gökdepe
122 I3 Georga, Zemlya Eng. George Land. island Zemlya Frantsa-Iosifa, N Russian Federation
83 G26 George Western Cape, S South Africa
29 S11 George Iowa, C USA
13 O5 George ≈ Newfoundland and Labrador/Québec, E Canada
45 T11 George FL Charles × (Castries) prev. Vigie NE Saint Lucia
65 C25 George Island island S Falkland Islands
183 R10 George, Lake ◎ New South Wales, SE Australia
81 E18 George, Lake ◎ SW Uganda
23 W10 George, Lake ◎ Florida, SE USA
18 L8 George, Lake ⊡ New York, NE USA
George Land see Georga, Zemlya
Georgenburg see Jurbarkas
George River see Kangiqsualujjuaq
64 G8 Georges Bank undersea feature W Atlantic Ocean

◆ Country ● Country Capital ◇ Dependent Territory ○ Dependent Territory Capital ◈ Administrative Region × International Airport ▲ Mountain ▲ Mountain Range Volcano ≈ River ◎ Lake ⊡ Reservoir

185 A21 **George Sound** *sound* South Island, NZ
65 F15 **Georgetown** ○ (Ascension Island) NW Ascension Island
181 V5 **Georgetown** Queensland, NE Australia
183 P15 **George Town** Tasmania, SE Australia
44 I4 **George Town** Great Exuma Island, C Bahamas
44 D8 **George Town** *var.* Georgetown. ○ (Cayman Islands) Grand Cayman, SW Cayman Islands
76 H12 **Georgetown** E Gambia
55 T8 **Georgetown** ● (Guyana) N Guyana
168 I7 **George Town** *var.* Penang, Pinang. Pinang, Peninsular Malaysia
45 Y14 **Georgetown** Saint Vincent, Saint Vincent and the Grenadines
21 Y4 **Georgetown** Delaware, NE USA
23 R6 **Georgetown** Georgia, SE USA
20 M5 **Georgetown** Kentucky, S USA
21 T13 **Georgetown** South Carolina, SE USA
25 S10 **Georgetown** Texas, SW USA
55 T8 **Georgetown** × N Guyana
195 U16 **George V Coast** *physical region* Antarctica
195 T15 **George V Land** *physical region* Antarctica
194 J7 **George VI Ice Shelf** *ice shelf* Antarctica
194 J6 **George VI Sound** *sound* Antarctica
25 S14 **George West** Texas, SW USA
137 R9 **Georgia** *off.* Republic of Georgia, *Geor.* Sak'art'velo, *Rus.* Gruzinskaya SSR, Gruziya; *prev.* Georgian SSR. ◆ *republic* SW Asia
23 S5 **Georgia** *off.* State of Georgia; also known as Empire State of the South, Peach State. ◈ *state* SE USA
14 F12 **Georgian Bay** *lake bay* Ontario, S Canada
10 L17 **Georgia, Strait of** *strait* British Columbia, W Canada
Georgi Dimitrov *see* Kostenets
Georgi Dimitrov, Yazovir *see* Koprinka, Yazovir
114 M9 **Georgi Traykov, Yazovir** ▣ NE Bulgaria
Georgiu-Dezh *see* Liski
145 W10 **Georgiyevka** Vostochnyy Kazakhstan, E Kazakhstan
Georgiyevka *see* Korday
127 N15 **Georgiyevsk** Stavropol'skiy Kray, SW Russian Federation
100 G13 **Georgsmarienhütte** Niedersachsen, NW Germany
195 O1 **Georg von Neumayer** *German research station* Antarctica
101 M16 **Gera** Thüringen, E Germany
101 K16 **Gera** ≈ C Germany
99 E19 **Geraardsbergen** Oost-Vlaanderen, SW Belgium
115 F21 **Geráki** Pelopónnisos, S Greece
27 W5 **Gerald** Missouri, C USA
47 V8 **Geral de Goiás, Serra** ▲ E Brazil
185 G20 **Geraldine** Canterbury, South Island, NZ
180 H11 **Geraldton** Western Australia
12 E11 **Geraldton** Ontario, S Canada
60 J12 **Geral, Serra** ▲ S Brazil
103 U6 **Gérardmer** Vosges, NE France
Gerasa *see* Jarash
Gerdauen *see* Zheleznodorozhnyy
39 Q11 **Gerdine, Mount** ▲ Alaska, USA
136 H11 **Gerede** Bolu, N Turkey
136 H11 **Gerede Çayı** ≈ N Turkey
148 M8 **Gereshk** Helmand, SW Afghanistan
101 L24 **Geretsried** Bayern, S Germany
105 P14 **Gérgal** Andalucía, S Spain
28 I14 **Gering** Nebraska, C USA
35 R3 **Gerlach** Nevada, W USA
Gerlachfalvi Csúcs/Gerlachovka *see* Gerlachovský štít
111 L18 **Gerlachovský štít** *var.* Gerlachovka, *Ger.* Gerlsdorfer Spitze, *Hung.* Gerlachfalvi Csúcs; *prev.* Stalinov Štít, *Ger.* Franz-Josef Spitze, *Hung.* Ferencz-József Csúcs. ▲ N Slovakia
108 E8 **Gerlafingen** Solothurn, NW Switzerland
Gerlsdorfer Spitze *see* Gerlachovský štít
139 V3 **Germak** E Iraq
German East Africa *see* Tanzania
Germanicopolis *see* Çankırı
Germanicum, Mare/German Ocean *see* North Sea
Germanovichi *see* Hyermanavichy
German Southwest Africa *see* Namibia
20 E10 **Germantown** Tennessee, S USA
101 I15 **Germany** *off.* Federal Republic of Germany, *Ger.* Bundesrepublik Deutschland, Deutschland. ◆ *federal republic* N Europe
101 L23 **Germering** Bayern, SE Germany
83 J21 **Germiston** *var.* Gauteng. Gauteng, NE South Africa
Gernika *see* Gernika-Lumo
105 P2 **Gernika-Lumo** *var.* Gernika, Guernica, Guernica y Lumo. País Vasco, N Spain
164 L12 **Gero** Gifu, Honshū, SW Japan
115 F22 **Geroliménas** Pelopónnisos, S Greece
Gerona *see* Girona
99 H21 **Gerpinnes** Hainaut, S Belgium
102 L15 **Gers** ◈ *department* S France
102 L14 **Gers** ≈ S France
Gerunda *see* Girona
136 K10 **Gerze** Sinop, N Turkey
158 I13 **Gêrzê** *var.* Luring. Xizang Zizhiqu, W China
Gesoriacum/Gessoriacum *see* Boulogne-sur-Mer
99 J21 **Gesves** Namur, SE Belgium
93 J20 **Geta** Åland, SW Finland
105 N8 **Getafe** Madrid, C Spain
95 J21 **Getinge** Halland, S Sweden
18 F16 **Gettysburg** Pennsylvania, NE USA
29 N8 **Gettysburg** South Dakota, N USA
194 K12 **Getz Ice Shelf** *ice shelf* Antarctica
137 S15 **Gevaş** Van, SE Turkey
Gevgeli *see* Gevgelija
113 Q20 **Gevgelija** *var.* Đevđelija, Djevdjelija, *Turk.* Gevgeli. SE FYR Macedonia
103 T10 **Gex** Ain, E France
92 I3 **Geysir** *physical region* SW Iceland
136 F11 **Geyve** Sakarya, NW Turkey
80 G10 **Gezira** ◈ *state* E Sudan
109 V3 **Gföhl** Niederösterreich, N Austria
83 H22 **Ghaap Plateau** *Afr.* Ghaapplato. *plateau* C South Africa
Ghaapplato *see* Ghaap Plateau
Ghaba *see* Al Ghābah
138 J8 **Ghāb, Tall** ▲ SE Syria
139 Q9 **Ghadaf, Wādī al** *dry watercourse* C Iraq
Ghadamès *see* Ghadāmis
74 M9 **Ghadāmis** *var.* Ghadamès, Rhadames. W Libya
141 Y10 **Ghadan** E Oman
75 O10 **Ghaddūwah** C Libya
147 Q11 **Ghafurov** *Rus.* Gafurov; *prev.* Sovetabad. NW Tajikistan
153 N12 **Ghāghara** ≈ S Asia
149 P13 **Ghaibi Dero** Sind, SE Pakistan
141 Y10 **Ghalat** E Oman
147 O11 **G'allaorol** Jizzax Viloyati, C Uzbekistan
139 W11 **Ghamūkah, Hawr** ◎ S Iraq
77 P15 **Ghana** *off.* Republic of Ghana. ◆ *republic* W Africa
141 X12 **Ghānah** *spring/well* S Oman
Ghanongga *see* Ranongga
Ghansi/Ghansiland *see* Ghanzi
83 F18 **Ghanzi** *var.* Khanzi. Ghanzi, W Botswana
83 G19 **Ghanzi** *var.* Ghansi, Ghansiland, Khanzi. ◈ *district* C Botswana
67 T14 **Ghanzi** *var.* Knanzi. ≈ Botswana/South Africa
Ghap'an *see* Kapan
138 F13 **Gharandal** Ma'ān, SW Jordan
Gharbt, Jabal al *see* Liban, Jebel
74 K7 **Ghardaïa** N Algeria
139 U14 **Gharibīyah, Sha'īb al** ≈ S Iraq
147 R12 **Gharm** *Rus.* Garm. C Tajikistan
149 P17 **Gharo** Sind, SE Pakistan
139 W10 **Gharrāf, Shaṭṭ al** ≈ S Iraq
Gharvān *see* Gharyān
75 O7 **Gharyān** *var.* Gharvān. NW Libya
74 M11 **Ghāt** *var.* Gat. SW Libya
Ghawdex *see* Gozo
141 U8 **Ghayathi** Abū Ẓaby, W UAE
Ghazāl, Baḥr al *see* Ghazal, Bahr el
78 H9 **Ghazal, Bahr el** *var.* Soro. *seasonal river* C Chad
80 E13 **Ghazal, Bahr el** *var.* Baḥr al Ghazāl. ≈ S Sudan
74 H6 **Ghazaouet** NW Algeria
152 J10 **Ghāziābād** Uttar Pradesh, N India
153 O13 **Ghāzīpur** Uttar Pradesh, N India
149 Q6 **Ghaznī** *var.* Ghazni. Ghaznī, E Afghanistan
149 P7 **Ghaznī** ◈ *province* SE Afghanistan
Ghazzah *see* Gaza
Gheel *see* Geel
Ghelizâne *see* Relizane
Ghent *see* Gent
Gheorghe Brațul *see* Sfântu Gheorghe, Brațul
Gheorghe Gheorghiu-Dej *see* Onești
116 J10 **Gheorgheni** *prev.* Gheorghieni, Sînt-Miclăuș, *Ger.* Niklasmarkt, *Hung.* Gyergyószentmiklós. Harghita, C Romania
Gheorghieni *see* Gheorgheni
116 H10 **Gherla** *Ger.* Neuschliss, *Hung.* Szamosújvár; *prev.* Armenierstadt. Cluj, NW Romania
Gheweifat *see* Ghuwayfāt
Ghilan *see* Gīlān
107 C18 **Ghilarza** Sardegna, Italy, C Mediterranean Sea
Ghilizane *see* Relizane
Ghimbi *see* Gīmbī
Ghiriş *see* Câmpia Turzii
103 Y15 **Ghisonaccia** Corse, France, C Mediterranean Sea
147 Q11 **Ghonchí** *Rus.* Ganchi. NW Tajikistan
Ghor *see* Ghowr
153 T13 **Ghoraghat** Rajshahi, NW Bangladesh
149 R13 **Ghotki** Sind, SE Pakistan
148 M5 **Ghowr** *var.* Ghor. ◈ *province* C Afghanistan
147 T13 **Ghŭdara** *var.* Gudara, *Rus.* Kudara. SE Tajikistan
153 R13 **Ghugri** ≈ N India
147 S14 **Ghund** *Rus.* Gunt. ≈ SE Tajikistan
Ghurdaqah *see* Hurghada
148 J5 **Ghūrīān** Herāt, W Afghanistan
141 T8 **Ghuwayfāt** *var.* Gheweifat. Abū Ẓaby, W UAE
121 O14 **Ghuzayyil, Sabkhat** *salt lake* N Libya
115 G17 **Giáltra** Évvoia, C Greece
Giamame *see* Jamaame
167 U13 **Gia Nghia** *var.* Äak Nông. Đăc Lăc, S Vietnam
114 F13 **Giannitsá** *var.* Yiannitsá. Kentrikí Makedonía, N Greece
107 F14 **Giannutri, Isola di** *island* Archipelago Toscano, C Italy
96 F13 **Giant's Causeway** *Ir.* Clochán an Aifir. *lava flow* N Northern Ireland, UK
167 S15 **Gia Rai** Minh Hai, S Vietnam
107 L24 **Giarre** Sicilia, Italy, C Mediterranean Sea
44 I7 **Gibara** Holguín, E Cuba
29 O16 **Gibbon** Nebraska, C USA
32 K11 **Gibbon** Oregon, NW USA
33 P11 **Gibbonsville** Idaho, NW USA
64 A13 **Gibb's Hill** *hill* S Bermuda
92 I9 **Gibostad** Troms, N Norway
104 I14 **Gibraleón** Andalucía, S Spain
104 L16 **Gibraltar** ○ (Gibraltar) S Gibraltar
104 L16 **Gibraltar** ◇ *UK dependent territory* SW Europe
Gibraltar, Détroit de/Gibraltar, Estrecho de *see* Gibraltar, Strait of
104 J17 **Gibraltar, Strait of** *Fr.* Détroit de Gibraltar, *Sp.* Estrecho de Gibraltar. *strait* Atlantic Ocean/ Mediterranean Sea
31 S11 **Gibsonburg** Ohio, N USA
30 M13 **Gibson City** Illinois, N USA
180 L8 **Gibson Desert** *desert* Western Australia
10 L17 **Gibsons** British Columbia, SW Canada
149 N12 **Gīdār** Baluchistān, SW Pakistan
155 I17 **Giddalūr** Andhra Pradesh, E India
24 U10 **Giddings** Texas, SW USA
27 Y8 **Gideon** Missouri, C USA
81 I15 **Gīdolē** Southern, S Ethiopia
118 H13 **Giedraičiai** Utena, E Lithuania
103 O7 **Gien** Loiret, C France
101 G17 **Giessen** Hessen, W Germany
98 O6 **Gieten** Drenthe, NE Netherlands
23 Y13 **Gifford** Florida, SE USA
9 O5 **Gifford** ≈ Baffin Island, Nunavut, NE Canada
100 J12 **Gifhorn** Niedersachsen, N Germany
11 P13 **Gift Lake** Alberta, W Canada
164 K13 **Gifu** *var.* Gihu. Gifu, Honshū, SW Japan
164 L13 **Gifu** *off.* Gifu-ken, *var.* Gihu. ◈ *prefecture* Honshū, SW Japan
126 M13 **Gigant** Rostovskaya Oblast', SW Russian Federation
40 E8 **Giganta, Sierra de la** ▲ W Mexico
54 E12 **Gigante** Huila, S Colombia
114 I7 **Gigen** Pleven, N Bulgaria
Gigiga *see* Jijiga
96 G12 **Gigha Island** *island* SW Scotland, UK
107 E14 **Giglio, Isola del** *island* Archipelago Toscano, C Italy
Gihu *see* Gifu
146 L11 **G'ijduwon** *Rus.* Gizhduvan. Buxoro Viloyati, C Uzbekistan
104 L2 **Gijón** *var.* Xixón. Asturias, NW Spain
81 D20 **Gikongoro** SW Rwanda
36 K14 **Gila Bend** Arizona, SW USA
36 J14 **Gila Bend Mountains** ▲ Arizona, SW USA
37 N14 **Gila Mountains** ▲ Arizona, SW USA
36 I15 **Gila Mountains** ▲ Arizona, SW USA
142 M4 **Gīlān** *off.* Ostān-e Gīlān; *var.* Ghilan, Guilan. ◈ *province* NW Iran
Gilani *see* Gnjilane
36 L14 **Gila River** ≈ Arizona, SW USA
29 W4 **Gilbert** Minnesota, N USA
Gilbert Islands *see* Tungaru
10 L16 **Gilbert, Mount** ▲ British Columbia, SW Canada
181 U4 **Gilbert River** ≈ Queensland, NE Australia
(0) C6 **Gilbert Seamounts** *undersea feature* NE Pacific Ocean
33 S7 **Gildford** Montana, NW USA
83 P15 **Gilé** Zambézia, NE Mozambique
30 K4 **Gile Flowage** ◎ Wisconsin, N USA
182 G7 **Giles, Lake** *salt lake* South Australia
75 U12 **Gilf Kebir Plateau** *Ar.* Haḍabat al Jilf al Kabīr. *plateau* SW Egypt
183 R6 **Gilgandra** New South Wales, SE Australia
Gilgău *see* Gâlgău
81 I19 **Gilgil** Rift Valley, SW Kenya
183 S4 **Gil Gil Creek** ≈ New South Wales, SE Australia
149 V3 **Gilgit** Jammu and Kashmir, NE Pakistan
149 V3 **Gilgit** ≈ N Pakistan
11 X11 **Gillam** Manitoba, C Canada
95 J22 **Gilleleje** Frederiksborg, E Denmark
30 K14 **Gillespie** Illinois, N USA
27 W13 **Gillett** Arkansas, C USA
33 X12 **Gillette** Wyoming, C USA
97 P22 **Gillingham** SE England, UK
195 X6 **Gillock Island** *island* Antarctica
173 O16 **Gillot** × (St-Denis) N Réunion
65 H25 **Gill Point** *headland* E Saint Helena
30 M12 **Gilman** Illinois, N USA
25 W6 **Gilmer** Texas, SW USA
Gilolo *see* Halmahera, Pulau
81 G14 **Gīlo Wenz** ≈ SW Ethiopia
35 O10 **Gilroy** California, W USA
123 Q12 **Gilyuy** ≈ SE Russian Federation
99 I14 **Gilze** Noord-Brabant, S Netherlands
165 R16 **Gima** Okinawa, Kume-jima, SW Japan
80 H13 **Gīmbī** *It.* Ghimbi. Oromo, C Ethiopia
45 T12 **Gimie, Mount** ▲ C Saint Lucia
11 X16 **Gimli** Manitoba, S Canada
Gimma *see* Jīma
95 O14 **Gimo** Uppsala, C Sweden
102 L15 **Gimone** ≈ S France
Gimpoe *see* Gimpu
171 N12 **Gimpu** *prev.* Gimpoe. Sulawesi, C Indonesia
182 F5 **Gina** South Australia
Ginevra *see* Genève
99 J19 **Gingelom** Limburg, NE Belgium
180 I12 **Gingin** Western Australia
171 Q7 **Gingoog** Mindanao, S Philippines
81 K14 **Gīnīr** Oromo, C Ethiopia
Giohar *see* Jawhar
107 O17 **Gioia del Colle** Puglia, SE Italy
107 M22 **Gioia, Golfo di** *gulf* S Italy
Giona *see* Gkióna
115 I16 **Gioúra** *island* Vóreioi Sporádes, Greece, Aegean Sea
107 O17 **Giovinazzo** Puglia, SE Italy
Gipeswic *see* Ipswich
Gipuzkoa *see* Guipúzcoa
Giran *see* Ilan
30 K14 **Girard** Illinois, N USA
27 R7 **Girard** Kansas, C USA
25 O6 **Girard** Texas, SW USA
54 E10 **Girardot** Cundinamarca, C Colombia
172 M7 **Giraud Seamount** *undersea feature* SW Indian Ocean
83 A15 **Giraul** ≈ SW Angola
96 L9 **Girdle Ness** *headland* NE Scotland, UK
137 N11 **Giresun** *var.* Kerasunt; *anc.* Cerasus, Pharnacia. Giresun, NE Turkey
137 N12 **Giresun** *var.* Kerasunt. ◈ *province* NE Turkey
137 N12 **Giresun Dağları** ▲ N Turkey
75 X10 **Girga** *var.* Girgeh, Jirjā. C Egypt
Girgeh *see* Girga
Girgenti *see* Agrigento
153 Q15 **Girīdīh** Jhārkhand, NE India
183 P6 **Girilambone** New South Wales, SE Australia
Girin *see* Jilin
121 W10 **Girne** *Gk.* Kerýneia, Kyrenia. N Cyprus
Giron *see* Kiruna
105 X5 **Girona** *var.* Gerona; *anc.* Gerunda. Cataluña, NE Spain
105 W5 **Girona** *var.* Gerona ◈ *province* Cataluña, NE Spain
102 J12 **Gironde** ◈ *department* SW France
102 J11 **Gironde** *estuary* SW France
105 V5 **Gironella** Cataluña, NE Spain
103 N15 **Girou** ≈ S France
97 H14 **Girvan** W Scotland, UK
24 M9 **Girvin** Texas, SW USA
184 Q9 **Gisborne** Gisborne, North Island, NZ
184 P9 **Gisborne** *off.* Gisborne District. ◈ *unitary authority* North Island, NZ
Giseifu *see* Ŭijŏngbu
Gisenye *see* Gisenyi
81 D19 **Gisenyi** *var.* Gisenye. NW Rwanda
95 K20 **Gislaved** Jönköping, S Sweden
103 N4 **Gisors** Eure, N France
Gissar *see* Hisor
147 P12 **Gissar Range** *Rus.* Gissarskiy Khrebet. ▲ Tajikistan/Uzbekistan
Gissarskiy Khrebet *see* Gissar Range
99 B16 **Gistel** West-Vlaanderen, W Belgium
108 F9 **Giswil** Unterwalden, C Switzerland
115 B16 **Gitánes** *ancient monument* Ípeiros, W Greece
81 E20 **Gitarama** C Rwanda
81 E20 **Gitega** C Burundi
Githio *see* Gýtheio
108 H11 **Giubiasco** Ticino, S Switzerland
106 K13 **Giulianova** Abruzzo, C Italy
Giulie, Alpi *see* Julian Alps
Giumri *see* Gyumri
116 M13 **Giurgeni** Ialomiţa, SE Romania
116 J15 **Giurgiu** Giurgiu, S Romania
116 J14 **Giurgiu** ◈ *county* SE Romania
95 F22 **Give** Vejle, C Denmark
103 R2 **Givet** Ardennes, N France
103 R11 **Givors** Rhône, E France
83 K19 **Giyani** Limpopo, NE South Africa
80 I13 **Giyon** Oromo, C Ethiopia
Giza/Gizeh *see* El Gîza
75 V8 **Giza, Pyramids of** *ancient monument* N Egypt
Gizhduvan *see* G'ijduwon
123 U8 **Gizhiga** Magadanskaya Oblast', E Russian Federation
123 T9 **Gizhiginskaya Guba** *bay* E Russian Federation
186 K8 **Gizo** Gizo, NW Solomon Islands
110 N7 **Giżycko** *Ger.* Warmińsko-Mazurskie, NE Poland
Gízymałów *see* Hrymayliv
Gjakovë *see* Đakovica
94 F12 **Gjende** ◎ S Norway
95 F17 **Gjerstad** Aust-Agder, S Norway
Gjilan *see* Gnjilane
Gjinokastër *see* Gjirokastër
113 L23 **Gjirokastër** *var.* Gjirokastra; *prev.* Gjinokastër, *Gk.* Argyrokastron, *It.* Argirocastro. Gjirokastër, S Albania
113 L22 **Gjirokastër** ◈ *district* S Albania
8 M7 **Gjoa Haven** King William Island, Nunavut, NW Canada
94 H13 **Gjøvik** Oppland, S Norway
113 J22 **Gjuhëzës, Kepi i** *headland* SW Albania
Gjurgjevac *see* Đurđevac
115 E18 **Gkióna** *var.* Giona. ▲ C Greece
121 R3 **Gkréko, Akrotíri** *var.* Cape Greco, Pidálion. *headland* E Cyprus
99 I18 **Glabbeek-Zuurbemde** Vlaams Brabant, C Belgium
13 R14 **Glace Bay** Cape Breton Island, Nova Scotia, SE Canada
11 O16 **Glacier** British Columbia, SW Canada
39 W12 **Glacier Bay** *inlet* Alaska, USA
32 I7 **Glacier Peak** ▲ Washington, NW USA
21 Q7 **Glade Spring** Virginia, NE USA
25 W7 **Gladewater** Texas, SW USA
181 Y8 **Gladstone** Queensland, E Australia
182 I8 **Gladstone** South Australia
11 X16 **Gladstone** Manitoba, S Canada
31 O5 **Gladstone** Michigan, N USA
27 R4 **Gladstone** Missouri, C USA
31 Q7 **Gladwin** Michigan, N USA
95 J15 **Glafsfjorden** ◎ C Sweden
92 H2 **Gláma** *physical region* NW Iceland
94 I12 **Gláma** *var.* Glommen, Glomma. ≈ S Norway
112 F13 **Glamoč** Federacija Bosna I Hercegovina, NE Bosnia and Herzegovina
97 J22 **Glamorgan** *cultural region* S Wales, UK
95 G24 **Glamsbjerg** Fyn, C Denmark
171 Q8 **Glan** Mindanao, S Philippines
95 M17 **Glan** ◎ S Sweden
109 T9 **Glan** ≈ SE Austria
101 F19 **Glan** ≈ W Germany
Glaris *see* Glarus
108 H9 **Glarner Alpen** *Eng.* Glarus Alps. ▲ E Switzerland
108 H8 **Glarus** Glarus, E Switzerland
108 H9 **Glarus** *Fr.* Glaris. ◈ *canton* C Switzerland
Glarus Alps *see* Glarner Alpen
27 N3 **Glasco** Kansas, C USA
96 I12 **Glasgow** S Scotland, UK
20 K7 **Glasgow** Kentucky, S USA
27 T4 **Glasgow** Missouri, C USA
33 W7 **Glasgow** Montana, NW USA
21 T6 **Glasgow** Virginia, NE USA
96 I12 **Glasgow** × W Scotland, UK
11 S14 **Glaslyn** Saskatchewan, S Canada
18 I16 **Glassboro** New Jersey, NE USA
24 L10 **Glass Mountains** ▲ Texas, SW USA
97 K23 **Glastonbury** SW England, UK
Glatz *see* Kłodzko
101 N16 **Glauchau** Sachsen, E Germany
Glavn'a Morava *see* Velika Morava
113 N16 **Glavnik** Serbia, S Serbia and Montenegro (Yugo.)
127 T1 **Glazov** Udmurtskaya Respublika, NW Russian Federation
Głda *see* Gwda
109 U8 **Gleinalpe** ▲ SE Austria
109 W8 **Gleisdorf** Steiermark, SE Austria
Gleiwitz *see* Gliwice
39 S11 **Glenallen** Alaska, USA
102 F7 **Glénan, Îles** *island group* NW France
185 G21 **Glenavy** Canterbury, South Island, NZ
10 H5 **Glenboyle** Yukon Territory, NW Canada
21 X3 **Glen Burnie** Maryland, NE USA
36 L8 **Glen Canyon** *canyon* Utah, W USA
36 L8 **Glen Canyon Dam** *dam* Arizona, SW USA
30 K15 **Glen Carbon** Illinois, N USA
14 E17 **Glencoe** Ontario, S Canada
83 K22 **Glencoe** KwaZulu/Natal, E South Africa
29 U9 **Glencoe** Minnesota, N USA
96 H10 **Glen Coe** *valley* N Scotland, UK
36 K13 **Glendale** Arizona, SW USA
35 S15 **Glendale** California, W USA
182 G5 **Glendambo** South Australia
33 Y8 **Glendive** Montana, NW USA
33 Y15 **Glendo** Wyoming, C USA
55 S10 **Glendor Mountians** ▲ C Guyana
182 K12 **Glenelg River** ≈ South Australia/Victoria, SE Australia
29 P4 **Glenfield** North Dakota, N USA
25 V12 **Glen Flora** Texas, SW USA
181 P7 **Glen Helen** Northern Territory, N Australia
183 U5 **Glen Innes** New South Wales, SE Australia
31 P6 **Glen Lake** ◎ Michigan, N USA
10 I7 **Glenlyon Peak** ▲ Yukon Territory, W Canada
37 N16 **Glenn, Mount** ▲ Arizona, SW USA
33 N15 **Glenns Ferry** Idaho, NW USA
23 W6 **Glennville** Georgia, SE USA
10 J10 **Glenora** British Columbia, W Canada
182 M11 **Glenorchy** Victoria, SE Australia
183 V5 **Glenreagh** New South Wales, SE Australia
33 X15 **Glenrock** Wyoming, C USA
96 K11 **Glenrothes** E Scotland, UK
18 L9 **Glens Falls** New York, NE USA
97 D14 **Glenties** *Ir.* Na Gleannta. NW Ireland
28 L5 **Glen Ullin** North Dakota, N USA
21 R4 **Glenville** West Virginia, NE USA
27 T12 **Glenwood** Arkansas, C USA
29 S15 **Glenwood** Iowa, C USA
29 T7 **Glenwood** Minnesota, N USA
36 L5 **Glenwood** Utah, W USA
30 I5 **Glenwood City** Wisconsin, N USA
37 Q4 **Glenwood Springs** Colorado, C USA
108 F10 **Gletsch** Valais, S Switzerland
Glevum *see* Gloucester
29 U14 **Glidden** Iowa, C USA
112 E9 **Glina** Sisak-Moslavina, NE Croatia
94 F11 **Glittertind** ▲ S Norway
111 J16 **Gliwice** *Ger.* Gleiwitz. Śląskie, S Poland
36 M14 **Globe** Arizona, SW USA
Globino *see* Hlobyne
108 L9 **Glockturm** ▲ SW Austria
116 L9 **Glodeni** *Rus.* Glodyany. N Moldova
109 S9 **Glödnitz** Kärnten, S Austria
Glodyany *see* Glodeni
Glogau *see* Głogów
109 W6 **Gloggnitz** Niederösterreich, E Austria
110 F13 **Głogów** *Ger.* Glogau, Glogow. Dolnośląskie, SW Poland
111 I16 **Głogówek** *Ger.* Oberglogau. Opolskie, S Poland
92 G12 **Glomfjord** Nordland, C Norway
Glommen *see* Gláma
93 I14 **Glommersträsk** Norrbotten, N Sweden
172 I1 **Glorieuses, Nosy** *island group* N Madagascar
65 C25 **Glorious Hill** *hill* East Falkland, Falkland Islands
38 J12 **Glory of Russia Cape** *headland* Saint Matthew Island, Alaska, USA
22 J7 **Gloster** Mississippi, S USA
183 U7 **Gloucester** New South Wales, SE Australia
186 F7 **Gloucester** New Britain, E PNG
97 L21 **Gloucester** *hist.* Caer Glou, *Lat.* Glevum. C England, UK
19 P10 **Gloucester** Massachusetts, NE USA
21 X6 **Gloucester** Virginia, NE USA
97 K21 **Gloucestershire** *cultural region* C England, UK
31 T14 **Glouster** Ohio, N USA
42 H3 **Glovers Reef** *reef* E Belize
18 K10 **Gloversville** New York, NE USA
110 K12 **Głowno** Łódź, C Poland
111 H16 **Głubczyce** *Ger.* Leobschütz. Opolskie, S Poland
126 L11 **Glubokiy** Rostovskaya Oblast', SW Russian Federation
145 W9 **Glubokoye** Vostochnyy Kazakhstan, E Kazakhstan
Glubokoye *see* Hlybokaye
111 H16 **Głuchołazy** *Ger.* Ziegenhais. Opolskie, S Poland
100 I9 **Glückstadt** Schleswig-Holstein, N Germany
Glukhov *see* Hlukhiv
Glushkevichi *see* Hlushkavichy
Glusk/Glussk *see* Hlusk
Glybokaya *see* Hlyboka
95 F21 **Glyngøre** Viborg, NW Denmark
127 Q9 **Gmelinka** Volgogradskaya Oblast', SW Russian Federation
109 R8 **Gmünd** Kärnten, S Austria
109 U2 **Gmünd** Niederösterreich, N Austria
Gmünd *see* Schwäbisch Gmünd
109 S5 **Gmunden** Oberösterreich, N Austria
Gmundner See *see* Traunsee
94 N10 **Gnarp** Gävleborg, C Sweden
109 W8 **Gnas** Steiermark, SE Austria
Gnesen *see* Gniezno
95 O16 **Gnesta** Södermanland, C Sweden
110 H11 **Gniezno** *Ger.* Gnesen. Wielkolpolskie, C Poland
113 O17 **Gnjilane** *var.* Gilani, *Alb.* Gjilan. Serbia, S Serbia and Montenegro (Yugo.)
95 K20 **Gnosjö** Jönköping, S Sweden
155 E17 **Goa** *prev.* Old Goa, Vela Goa, Velha Goa. Goa, W India
155 E17 **Goa** *var.* Old Goa. ◈ *state* W India
Goabddális *see* Kåbdalis
42 H7 **Goascorán, Río** ≈ El Salvador/Honduras
77 O16 **Goaso** *var.* Gawso. W Ghana
81 K14 **Goba** *It.* Oromo, S Ethiopia
83 C20 **Gobabed** Erongo, W Namibia
83 E19 **Gobabis** Omaheke, E Namibia
Gobannium *see* Abergavenny
64 M7 **Goban Spur** *undersea feature* NW Atlantic Ocean
Gobbà *see* Goba
63 H21 **Gobernador Gregores** Santa Cruz, S Argentina
61 F14 **Gobernador Ingeniero Virasoro** Corrientes, NE Argentina
162 L12 **Gobi** *desert* China/Mongolia
164 I14 **Gobō** Wakayama, Honshū, SW Japan
101 D14 **Goch** Nordrhein-Westfalen, W Germany
83 E20 **Gochas** Hardap, S Namibia
155 I14 **Godāvari** *var.* Godavari. ≈ C India
155 L16 **Godāvari, Mouths of the** *delta* E India
15 V5 **Godbout** Québec, SE Canada
15 U5 **Godbout** ≈ Québec, SE Canada
15 U5 **Godbout Est** ≈ Québec, SE Canada
27 N6 **Goddard** Kansas, C USA
14 E15 **Goderich** Ontario, S Canada
Godhavn *see* Qeqertarsuaq
154 E10 **Godhra** Gujarāt, W India
Göding *see* Hodonín
111 K22 **Gödöllő** Pest, N Hungary
62 H11 **Godoy Cruz** Mendoza, W Argentina
11 Y11 **Gods** ≈ Manitoba, C Canada
11 Y13 **Gods Lake** Manitoba, C Canada
11 X13 **Gods Lake** ◎ Manitoba, C Canada

Godthaab/Godthåb see Nuuk
Godwin Austen, Mount see K2
Goede Hoop, Kaap de see Good Hope, Cape of
Goedgegun see Nhlangano
Goeie Hoop, Kaap die see Good Hope, Cape of
13 O7 Goéland, Lac au ◎ Québec, SE Canada
98 E13 Goeree island SW Netherlands
99 F15 Goes Zeeland, SW Netherlands
Goettingen see Göttingen
19 O10 Goffstown New Hampshire, NE USA
14 E8 Gogama Ontario, S Canada
30 L3 Gogebic, Lake ◎ Michigan, N USA
30 K3 Gogebic Range hill range Michigan/Wisconsin, N USA
137 V13 Gogi, Mount Arm. Gogi Lerr, Az. Küküdağ. ▲ Armenia/Azerbaijan
126 F12 Gogland, Ostrov island NW Russian Federation
111 I15 Gogolin Opolskie, S Poland
Gogonou see Gogounou
77 S14 Gogounou var. Gogonou. N Benin
152 I10 Gohāna Haryāna, N India
59 K18 Goianésia Goiás, C Brazil
59 K18 Goiânia prev. Goyania. state capital Goiás, C Brazil
59 K18 Goiás Goiás, C Brazil
59 J18 Goiás off. Estado de Goiás; prev. Goiaz, Goyaz. ◆ state C Brazil
Goiaz see Goiás
159 R14 Goinsargoin Xizang Zizhiqu, W China
60 H10 Goio-Erê Paraná, SW Brazil
99 I15 Goirle Noord-Brabant, S Netherlands
104 H8 Góis Coimbra, N Portugal
165 Q8 Gojōme Akita, Honshū, NW Japan
149 U9 Gojra Punjab, E Pakistan
136 A11 Gökçeada var. Imroz Adasi, Gk. Imbros. island NW Turkey
Gökçeada see İmroz
146 F13 Gökdepe Rus. Gëkdepe, Geok-Tepe. Ahal Welaýaty, C Turkmenistan
136 I10 Gökırmak ~ N Turkey
Goklenkuy, Solonchak see Geklengkui, Solonchak
136 C16 Gökova Körfezi gulf SW Turkey
136 K15 Göksu ~ S Turkey
136 L15 Göksun Kahramanmaraş, C Turkey
136 I17 Göksu Nehri ~ S Turkey
83 J16 Gokwe Midlands, NW Zimbabwe
94 F13 Gol Buskerud, S Norway
153 X12 Golāghāt Assam, NE India
110 H10 Gołańcz Wielkopolskie, C Poland
138 G8 Golan Heights Ar. Al Jawlān, Heb. HaGolan. ⛰ SW Syria
Golārā see Ārān
Golaya Pristan see Hola Prystan'
143 T11 Golbāf Kermān, C Iran
136 M15 Gölbaşı Adıyaman, S Turkey
109 P9 Gölbner ▲ SW Austria
30 M17 Golconda Illinois, N USA
35 T3 Golconda Nevada, W USA
136 E11 Gölcük Kocaeli, NW Turkey
108 I7 Goldach Sankt Gallen, NE Switzerland
110 N7 Gołdap Ger. Goldap. Warmińsko-Mazurskie, NE Poland
32 E15 Gold Beach Oregon, NW USA
Goldberg see Złotoryja
68 D11 Gold Coast coastal region S Ghana
183 V3 Gold Coast cultural region Queensland, E Australia
39 R10 Gold Creek Alaska, USA
11 O16 Golden British Columbia, SW Canada
37 T4 Golden Colorado, C USA
184 I13 Golden Bay bay South Island, NZ
27 R7 Golden City Missouri, C USA
32 I11 Goldendale Washington, NW USA
Goldener Tisch see Zlatý Stôl
44 L13 Golden Grove E Jamaica
14 J12 Golden Lake ◎ Ontario, SE Canada
22 K10 Golden Meadow Louisiana, S USA
45 V10 Golden Rock ✕ (Basseterre) Saint Kitts, Saint Kitts and Nevis
Golden State, The see California
83 K16 Golden Valley Mashonaland West, N Zimbabwe
35 U9 Goldfield Nevada, W USA
Goldingen see Kuldīga
Goldmarkt see Zlatna
10 K17 Gold River Vancouver Island, British Columbia, SW Canada
21 V10 Goldsboro North Carolina, SE USA
24 M8 Goldsmith Texas, SW USA
25 R8 Goldthwaite Texas, SW USA
137 R11 Göle Ardahan, NE Turkey
Golema Ada see Ostrovo
114 H9 Golema Planina ⛰ W Bulgaria
114 F9 Golemi Vrŭkh ▲ W Bulgaria
110 D8 Goleniów Ger. Gollnow. Zachodnio-pomorskie, NW Poland
149 R3 Golestān ◆ province N Iran
35 Q14 Goleta California, W USA
43 O16 Golfito Puntarenas, SE Costa Rica
25 T13 Goliad Texas, SW USA
113 L14 Golija ⛰ SW Serbia and Montenegro (Yugo.)
Golinka see Gongbo'gyamda
113 O16 Goljak ⛰ SE Serbia and Montenegro (Yugo.)
136 M12 Gölköy Ordu, N Turkey
Gollel see Lavumisa
109 X3 Göllersbach ~ NE Austria
Gollnow see Goleniów
Golmo see Golmud
159 P10 Golmud var. Ge'e'mu, Golmo, Chin. Ko-erh-mu. Qinghai, C China
103 Y14 Golo ~ Corse, France, C Mediterranean Sea
Golovanevsk see Holovanivs'k
Golovchin see Halowchyn
39 N9 Golovin Alaska, USA
142 M7 Golpāyegān var. Gulpaigan. Eşfahān, W Iran
Golshan see Ţabas
Gol'shany see Hal'shany
96 J7 Golspie N Scotland, UK
112 O11 Golubac Serbia, NE Serbia and Montenegro (Yugo.)
110 J9 Golub-Dobrzyń Kujawski-pomorskie, C Poland
145 S7 Golubovka Pavlodar, N Kazakhstan
82 B11 Golungo Alto Cuanza Norte, NW Angola
114 M8 Golyama Kamchiya ~ E Bulgaria
114 L8 Golyama Reka ~ N Bulgaria
114 H11 Golyama Syutkya ▲ SW Bulgaria
114 I12 Golyam Perelik ▲ S Bulgaria
114 I11 Golyam Persenk ▲ S Bulgaria
79 P19 Goma Nord Kivu, NE Dem. Rep. Congo
Gomati see Gumti
77 X14 Gombe Gombe, E Nigeria
67 U10 Gombe var. Igombe. ~ E Tanzania
77 Y14 Gombi Adamawa, E Nigeria
Gombroon see Bandar-e 'Abbās
Gomel' see Homyel'
Gomel'skaya Oblast' see Homyel'skaya Voblasts'
64 N11 Gomera island Islas Canarias, Spain, NE Atlantic Ocean
40 I5 Gómez Farias Chihuahua, N Mexico
40 L8 Gómez Palacio Durango, C Mexico
158 J13 Gomo Xizang Zizhiqu, W China
143 T6 Gonābād var. Gunabad. Khorāsān, NE Iran
44 L8 Gonaïves var. Les Gonaïves. N Haiti
123 Q12 Gonam ~ NE Russian Federation
44 L9 Gonâve, Canal de la var. Canal de Sud. channel N Caribbean Sea
44 K9 Gonâve, Golfe de la gulf N Caribbean Sea
Gonāveh see Bandar-e Gonāveh
44 K9 Gonâve, Île de la island C Haiti
Gonbadān see Dow Gonbadān
143 Q3 Gonbad-e Kāvūs var. Gunbad-i-Qawus. Golestān, N Iran
152 M12 Gonda Uttar Pradesh, N India
Gondar see Gonder
80 I11 Gonder var. Gondar. Amhara, N Ethiopia
78 J13 Gondey Moyen-Chari, S Chad
154 J12 Gondia Mahārāshtra, C India
104 G6 Gondomar Porto, NW Portugal
136 C12 Gönen Balıkesir, W Turkey
136 C12 Gönen Çayı ~ NW Turkey
159 O15 Gongbo'gyamda var. Golinka. Xizang Zizhiqu, W China
159 N16 Gonggar var. Gyixong. Xizang Zizhiqu, W China
160 G9 Gongga Shan ▲ C China
159 T10 Gonghe var. Qabqa. Qinghai, C China
Gongjiang see Yudu
158 I5 Gongliu var. Tokkuztara. Xinjiang Uygur Zizhiqu, NW China
77 W14 Gongola ~ E Nigeria
Gongoleh State see Jonglei
183 P5 Gongolgon New South Wales, SE Australia
159 Q6 Gongpoquan Gansu, N China
Gongquan see Gongxian
Gongtang see Damxung
160 I10 Gongxian var. Gongquan, Gong Xian. Sichuan, C China
157 V10 Gongzhuling prev. Huaide. Jilin, NE China
159 S14 Gonjo Xizang Zizhiqu, W China
107 B20 Gonnesa Sardegna, Italy, C Mediterranean Sea
Gonni/Gónnos see Gónnoi
115 F15 Gónnoi var. Gonni, Gónnos; prev. Derelí. Thessalía, C Greece
164 C13 Gōnoura Nagasaki, Iki, SW Japan
35 O11 Gonzales California, W USA
22 J9 Gonzales Louisiana, S USA
25 T12 Gonzales Texas, SW USA
41 P11 González Tamaulipas, C Mexico
21 V6 Goochland Virginia, NE USA
195 X14 Goodenough, Cape headland Antarctica
186 F9 Goodenough Island var. Morata. island SE PNG
Good Hope see Fort Good Hope
39 N8 Goodhope Bay bay Alaska, USA
83 D26 Good Hope, Cape of Afr. Kaap de Goede Hoop, Kaap die Goeie Hoop. headland SW South Africa
10 K10 Good Hope Lake British Columbia, W Canada
83 E23 Goodhouse Northern Cape, W South Africa
33 O15 Gooding Idaho, NW USA
26 H3 Goodland Kansas, C USA
173 Y15 Goodlands NW Mauritius
20 J8 Goodlettsville Tennessee, S USA
39 N13 Goodnews Alaska, USA
25 O3 Goodnight Texas, SW USA
183 Q4 Goodooga New South Wales, SE Australia
29 N4 Goodrich North Dakota, N USA
25 W10 Goodrich Texas, SW USA
29 X10 Goodview Minnesota, N USA
26 H8 Goodwell Oklahoma, C USA
97 N17 Goole E England, UK
183 O8 Goolgowi New South Wales, SE Australia
182 I10 Goolwa South Australia
181 Y11 Goondiwindi Queensland, E Australia
98 O11 Goor Overijssel, E Netherlands
Goose Bay see Happy Valley-Goose Bay
33 V13 Gooseberry Creek ~ Wyoming, C USA
21 S14 Goose Creek South Carolina, SE USA
63 M23 Goose Green var. Prado del Ganso. East Falkland, Falkland Islands
16 D8 Goose Lake var. Lago dos Gansos. ◎ California/Oregon, W USA
29 Q4 Goose River ~ North Dakota, N USA
153 T16 Gopalganj Dhaka, S Bangladesh
153 O12 Gopālganj Bihār, N India
Gopher State see Minnesota
101 I22 Göppingen Baden-Württemberg, SW Germany
110 G13 Góra Ger. Guhrau. Dolnośląskie, SW Poland
110 M12 Góra Kalwaria Mazowieckie, C Poland
153 O12 Gorakhpur Uttar Pradesh, N India
Gorany see Harany
113 J14 Goražde Federacija Bosna I Hercegovina, Bosnia and Herzegovina
Gorbovichi see Harbavichy
Gorče Petrov see Đorče Petrov
(0) E9 Gorda Ridges undersea feature NE Pacific Ocean
Gordiaz see Gardēz
78 K12 Gordil Vakaga, N Central African Republic
23 U5 Gordon Georgia, SE USA
28 K12 Gordon Nebraska, C USA
25 R7 Gordon Texas, SW USA
28 L13 Gordon Creek ~ Nebraska, C USA
63 I25 Gordon, Isla island S Chile
183 O17 Gordon, Lake ◎ Tasmania, SE Australia
183 O17 Gordon River ~ Tasmania, SE Australia
21 V5 Gordonsville Virginia, NE USA
80 H13 Gorē Oromo, C Ethiopia
185 D24 Gore Southland, South Island, NZ
78 H13 Goré Logone-Oriental, S Chad
14 D11 Gore Bay Manitoulin Island, Ontario, S Canada
25 Q5 Goree Texas, SW USA
137 O11 Görele Giresun, NE Turkey
19 N6 Gore Mountain ▲ Vermont, NE USA
39 R13 Gore Point headland Alaska, USA
37 R4 Gore Range ⛰ Colorado, C USA
97 F19 Gorey Ir. Guaire. SE Ireland
143 R12 Gorgāb Kermān, S Iran
143 Q4 Gorgān var. Astarabad, Astrabad, Gurgan; prev. Asterābād, anc. Hyrcania. Golestān, N Iran
143 Q4 Gorgān, Rūd-e ~ N Iran
76 I10 Gorgol ◆ region S Mauritania
106 D12 Gorgona, Isola di island Archipelago Toscano, C Italy
19 P8 Gorham Maine, NE USA
137 T10 Gori C Georgia
98 I13 Gorinchem var. Gorkum. Zuid-Holland, C Netherlands
137 V13 Goris SE Armenia
124 K16 Goritsy Tverskaya Oblast', W Russian Federation
106 J7 Gorizia Ger. Görz. Friuli-Venezia Giulia, NE Italy
116 G13 Gorj ◆ county SW Romania
109 W12 Gorjanci var. Uskočke Planine, Žumberak, Žumberačko Gorje, Ger. Uskokengebirge; prev. Sichelburger Gerbirge. ⛰ Croatia/Slovenia see also Žumberačko Gorje
Görkau see Jirkov
Gorki see Horki
Gor'kiy see Nizhniy Novgorod
Gor'kiy Reservoir see Gor'kovskoye Vodokhranilishche
Gorkum see Gorinchem
95 I23 Gørlev Vestsjælland, E Denmark
111 M17 Gorlice Małopolskie, S Poland
101 Q15 Görlitz Sachsen, E Germany
Görlitz see Zgorzelec
Gorlovka see Horlivka
25 R7 Gorman Texas, SW USA
21 T3 Gormania West Virginia, NE USA
Gorna Dzhumaya see Blagoevgrad
114 K8 Gorna Oryakhovitsa Veliko Tŭrnovo, N Bulgaria
114 J8 Gorna Studena Veliko Tŭrnovo, N Bulgaria
Gornja Mužlja see Mužlja
109 X9 Gornja Radgona Ger. Oberradkersburg. NE Slovenia
112 M13 Gornji Milanovac Serbia, C Serbia and Montenegro (Yugo.)
112 G13 Gornji Vakuf var. Uskoplje. Federacija Bosna I Hercegovina, W Bosnia and Herzegovina
122 J13 Gorno-Altaysk Respublika Altay, S Russian Federation
Gorno-Altayskaya Respublika see Altay, Respublika
123 N12 Gorno-Chuyskiy Irkutskaya Oblast', C Russian Federation
125 V14 Gornozavodsk Permskaya Oblast', NW Russian Federation
122 I13 Gornyak Altayskiy Kray S Russian Federation
123 O14 Gornyy Chitinskaya Oblast', S Russian Federation
127 R8 Gornyy Saratovskaya Oblast', W Russian Federation
Gornyy Altay see Altay, Respublika
127 O10 Gornyy Balykley Volgogradskaya Oblast', SW Russian Federation
80 I13 Goroch'an ▲ W Ethiopia
Gorodenka see Horodenka
127 O3 Gorodets Nizhegorodskaya Oblast', W Russian Federation
Gorodets see Haradzyets
Gorodeya see Haradzyeya
127 P6 Gorodishche Penzenskaya Oblast', W Russian Federation
Gorodishche see Horodyshche
Gorodnya see Horodnya
Gorodok see Haradok
Gorodok/Gorodok Yagellonski see Horodok
126 M13 Gorodovikovsk Respublika Kalmykiya, SW Russian Federation
186 D7 Goroka Eastern Highlands, C PNG
Gorokhov see Horokhiv
127 N3 Gorokhovets Vladimirskaya Oblast', W Russian Federation
77 Q11 Gorom-Gorom NE Burkina
171 U13 Gorong, Kepulauan island group E Indonesia
83 M17 Gorongosa Sofala, C Mozambique
171 P11 Gorontalo Sulawesi, C Indonesia
171 P11 Gorontalo off. Propinsi Gorontalo. ◆ province N Indonesia
Gorontalo, Teluk see Tomini, Gulf of
110 L7 Górowo Iławeckie Ger. Landsberg. Warmińsko-Mazurskie, NE Poland,
98 M7 Gorredijk Fris. De Gordyk. Friesland, N Netherlands
84 C14 Gorringe Ridge undersea feature E Atlantic Ocean
98 M11 Gorssel Gelderland, E Netherlands
109 T8 Görtschitz ~ S Austria
Goryn see Horyn'
Görz see Gorizia
110 E10 Gorzów Wielkopolski Ger. Landsberg, Landsberg an der Warthe. Lubuskie, W Poland
108 G9 Göschenen Uri, C Switzerland
165 O11 Gosen Niigata, Honshū, C Japan
183 T8 Gosford New South Wales, SE Australia
31 P11 Goshen Indiana, N USA
18 K13 Goshen New York, NE USA
Goshoba see Goşoba
165 Q7 Goshogawara var. Gosyogawara. Aomori, Honshū, C Japan
101 J14 Goslar Niedersachsen, C Germany
27 Y9 Gosnell Arkansas, C USA
146 B10 Goşoba var. Goshoba, Rus. Koshoba. Balkanskiy Velayat, NW Turkmenistan
112 C11 Gospić Lika-Senj, C Croatia
97 N23 Gosport S England, UK
94 D9 Gossa island S Norway
108 H7 Gossau Sankt Gallen, NE Switzerland
99 G20 Gosselies var. Goss'lies. Hainaut, S Belgium
77 P10 Gossi Tombouctou, C Mali
Goss'lies see Gosselies
113 N18 Gostivar W FYR Macedonia
Gostomel' see Hostomel'
110 G12 Gostyń var. Gostyn. Wielkopolskie, C Poland
110 K11 Gostynin Mazowieckie, C Poland
Gosyogawara see Goshogawara
95 J18 Göta Älv ~ S Sweden
95 N17 Göta kanal canal S Sweden
95 K18 Götaland cultural region S Sweden
95 H17 Göteborg Eng. Gothenburg. Västra Götaland, S Sweden
77 X16 Gotel Mountains ⛰ E Nigeria
95 K17 Götene Västra Götaland, S Sweden
Gotera see San Francisco
101 K16 Gotha Thüringen, C Germany
29 N15 Gothenburg Nebraska, C USA
Gothenburg see Göteborg
77 R12 Gothèye Tillabéri, SW Niger
Gothland see Gotland
95 P19 Gotland var. Gothland, Gottland. ◆ county SE Sweden
95 O18 Gotland island SE Sweden
164 B13 Gotō-rettō island group SW Japan
114 H12 Gotse Delchev prev. Nevrokop. Blagoevgrad, SW Bulgaria
95 P17 Gotska Sandön island SE Sweden
101 I15 Göttingen var. Goettingen. Niedersachsen, C Germany
Gottland see Gotland
93 I16 Gottne Västernorrland, C Sweden
Gottschee see Kočevje
Gottwaldov see Zlín
Gôtu see Gōtsu
146 B11 Goturdepe Rus. Koturdepe. Balkan Welaýaty, W Turkmenistan
108 I7 Götzis Vorarlberg, NW Austria
98 H12 Gouda Zuid-Holland, C Netherlands
76 I11 Goudiri var. Goudiry. E Senegal
Goudiry see Goudiri
77 X12 Goudoumaria Diffa, S Niger
15 R9 Gouffre, Rivière du ~ Québec, SE Canada
65 M19 Gough Fracture Zone tectonic feature S Atlantic Ocean
65 M19 Gough Island island Tristan da Cunha, S Atlantic Ocean
15 N8 Gouin, Réservoir ▣ Québec, SE Canada
14 B10 Goulais River Ontario, S Canada
183 R9 Goulburn New South Wales, SE Australia
183 O11 Goulburn River ~ Victoria, SE Australia
195 O10 Gould Coast physical region Antarctica
Goulimime see Guelmime
114 F13 Gouménissa Kentrikí Makedonía, N Greece
77 O10 Goundam Tombouctou, NW Mali
78 H12 Goundi Moyen-Chari, S Chad
78 G12 Gounou-Gaya Mayo-Kébbi, SW Chad
77 O12 Gourci var. Gourcy. NW Burkina
Gourcy see Gourci
102 M13 Gourdon Lot, S France
77 W11 Gouré Zinder, SE Niger
102 G6 Gourin Morbihan, NW France
77 P10 Gourma-Rharous Tombouctou, C Mali
103 N4 Gournay-en-Bray Seine-Maritime, N France
78 J6 Gouro Borkou-Ennedi-Tibesti, N Chad
104 H8 Gouveia Guarda, N Portugal
18 I7 Gouverneur New York, NE USA
99 L21 Gouvy Luxembourg, E Belgium
45 R14 Gouyave var. Charlotte Town. NW Grenada
Goverla, Gora see Hoverla, Hora
59 N20 Governador Valadares Minas Gerais, SE Brazil
171 R8 Governor Generoso Mindanao, S Philippines
44 I2 Governor's Harbour Eleuthera Island, C Bahamas
162 F9 Govĭ-Altay ◆ province SW Mongolia
162 I10 Govĭ Altayn Nuruu ⛰ S Mongolia
154 L9 Govind Ballabh Pant Sāgar ▣ C India
152 J7 Govind Sāgar ▣ NE India
162 M8 Govĭ-Sumber ◆ province C Mongolia
Govurdak see Gowurdak
18 D11 Gowanda New York, NE USA
148 J10 Gowd-e Zereh, Dasht-e var. Guad-i-Zirreh. marsh SW Afghanistan
14 F8 Gowganda Ontario, S Canada
14 G8 Gowganda Lake ◎ Ontario, S Canada
29 U13 Gowrie Iowa, C USA
147 N14 Gowurdak Rus. Govurdak; prev. Guardak. Lebap Welaýaty, E Turkmenistan
61 C15 Goya Corrientes, NE Argentina
Goyania see Goiânia
137 X11 Göyçay Rus. Geokchay. C Azerbaijan
146 D10 Goymat Rus. Koymat. Balkan Welaýaty, NW Turkmenistan
146 D10 Goymatdag Rus. Gory Koymatdag. hill range NW Turkmenistan
136 F12 Göynük Bolu, NW Turkey
165 R9 Goyō-san ▲ Honshū, C Japan
78 K11 Goz Beïda Ouaddaï, SE Chad
146 M10 G'ozg'on Rus. Gazgan. Navoiy Viloyati, C Uzbekistan
158 H11 Gozha Co ◎ W China
121 O15 Gozo Malt. Ghawdex. island N Malta
80 H9 Göz Regeb Kassala, NE Sudan
Gozyô see Gojō
83 H25 Graaff-Reinet Eastern Cape, S South Africa
Graasten see Gråsten
76 L17 Grabo SW Ivory Coast
112 P11 Grabovica Serbia, E Serbia and Montenegro (Yugo.)
110 I13 Grabów nad Prosną Wielkopolskie, C Poland
108 I8 Grabs Sankt Gallen, NE Switzerland
112 D12 Gračac Zadar, C Croatia
112 I11 Gračanica Federacija Bosna I Hercegovina, NE Bosnia and Herzegovina
14 L11 Gracefield Québec, SE Canada
99 K19 Grâce-Hollogne Liège, E Belgium
23 R8 Graceville Florida, SE USA
29 R8 Graceville Minnesota, N USA
42 G6 Gracias Lempira, W Honduras
Gracias see Lempira
42 L5 Gracias a Dios ◆ department E Honduras
43 O6 Gracias a Dios, Cabo de headland Honduras/Nicaragua
64 O2 Graciosa var. Ilha Graciosa. island Azores, Portugal, NE Atlantic Ocean
64 Q11 Graciosa island Islas Canarias, Spain, NE Atlantic Ocean
Graciosa, Ilha see Graciosa
112 I11 Gradačac Federacija Bosna I Hercegovina, N Bosnia and Herzegovina
59 J15 Gradaús, Serra dos ⛰ C Brazil
104 L3 Gradefes Castilla-León, N Spain
Gradiška see Bosanska Gradiška
Gradizhsk see Hradyz'k
106 J7 Grado Friuli-Venezia Giulia, NE Italy
104 K2 Grado Asturias, N Spain
113 P19 Gradsko C FYR Macedonia
37 V11 Grady New Mexico, SW USA
29 T12 Graettinger Iowa, C USA
101 M23 Grafing Bayern, SE Germany
25 S6 Graford Texas, SW USA
183 V5 Grafton New South Wales, SE Australia
29 Q3 Grafton North Dakota, N USA
21 S3 Grafton West Virginia, NE USA
21 T9 Graham North Carolina, SE USA
25 R6 Graham Texas, SW USA
Graham Bell Island see Greem-Bell, Ostrov
10 I13 Graham Island island Queen Charlotte Islands, British Columbia, SW Canada
19 S6 Graham Lake ◎ Maine, NE USA
194 H4 Graham Land physical region Antarctica
37 N15 Graham, Mount ▲ Arizona, SW USA
Grahamstad see Grahamstown
83 I25 Grahamstown Afr. Grahamstad. Eastern Cape, S South Africa
Grahovo see Bosansko Grahovo
68 C11 Grain Coast coastal region S Liberia
169 S17 Grajagan, Teluk bay Jawa, S Indonesia
59 L14 Grajaú Maranhão, E Brazil
58 M13 Grajaú, Rio ~ NE Brazil
110 O8 Grajewo Podlaskie, NE Poland
95 F24 Gram Sønderjylland, SW Denmark
103 N13 Gramat Lot, S France
22 H5 Grambling Louisiana, S USA
115 C14 Grámmos ⛰ Albania/Greece
96 I9 Grampian Mountains ⛰ C Scotland, UK
182 L12 Grampians, The ⛰ Victoria, SE Australia
98 O9 Gramsbergen Overijssel, E Netherlands
113 L21 Gramsh var. Gramshi. Elbasan, C Albania
Gramshi see Gramsh
Gran see Hron, Slovakia
Gran see Esztergom, N Hungary
54 F11 Granada Meta, C Colombia
42 J10 Granada Granada, SW Nicaragua
105 N14 Granada Andalucía, S Spain
37 W6 Granada Colorado, C USA
42 J11 Granada ◆ department SW Nicaragua
105 N14 Granada ◆ province Andalucía, S Spain
63 I21 Gran Altiplanicie Central plain S Argentina
97 E17 Granard Ir. Gránard. C Ireland
63 J20 Gran Bajo basin S Argentina
63 J15 Gran Bajo del Gualicho basin E Argentina
63 I21 Gran Bajo de San Julián basin SE Argentina
25 S7 Granbury Texas, SW USA
15 P12 Granby Québec, SE Canada
27 S8 Granby Missouri, C USA
37 S3 Granby, Lake ▣ Colorado, C USA
64 O12 Gran Canaria var. Grand Canary. island Islas Canarias, Spain, NE Atlantic Ocean
47 T11 Gran Chaco var. Chaco. lowland plain South America
45 R14 Grand Anse SW Grenada
Grand-Anse see Portsmouth
44 G1 Grand Bahama Island island N Bahamas
Grand Balé see Tui
103 U7 Grand Ballon Ger. Ballon de Guebwiller. ▲ NE France
13 T13 Grand Bank Newfoundland and Labrador, SE Canada
64 I7 Grand Banks of Newfoundland and Labrador undersea feature NW Atlantic Ocean
Grand Bassa see Buchanan
77 N17 Grand-Bassam var. Bassam. SE Ivory Coast
14 E16 Grand Bend Ontario, S Canada
76 L17 Grand-Bérébi var. Grand-Béréby. SW Ivory Coast
Grand-Béréby see Grand-Bérébi
45 X11 Grand-Bourg Marie-Galante, SE Guadeloupe
44 M6 Grand Caicos var. Middle Caicos. island C Turks and Caicos Islands
14 K12 Grand Calumet, Île du island Québec, SE Canada
97 E18 Grand Canal Ir. An Chanáil Mhór. canal C Ireland
Grand Canary see Gran Canaria
36 K10 Grand Canyon Arizona, SW USA
36 J9 Grand Canyon canyon Arizona, SW USA
Grand Canyon State see Arizona
44 D8 Grand Cayman island SW Cayman Islands
11 R14 Grand Centre Alberta, SW Canada
76 L17 Grand Cess SE Liberia
108 D12 Grand Combin ▲ S Switzerland
32 K8 Grand Coulee Washington, NW USA
32 J8 Grand Coulee valley Washington, NW USA
45 X5 Grand Cul-de-Sac Marin bay N Guadeloupe
Grand Duchy of Luxembourg see Luxembourg
63 I22 Grande, Bahía bay S Argentina
11 N14 Grande Cache Alberta, W Canada
103 U12 Grande Casse ▲ E France
172 G12 Grande Comore var. Njazidja, Great Comoro. island NW Comoros
61 G18 Grande, Cuchilla hill range E Uruguay
45 S5 Grande de Añasco, Río ~ W Puerto Rico
Grande de Chiloé, Isla see Chiloé, Isla de

◆ Country ● Country Capital ◇ Dependent Territory ○ Dependent Territory Capital ◆ Administrative Region ✕ International Airport ▲ Mountain ⛰ Mountain Range ▲ Volcano ~ River ◎ Lake ▣ Reservoir

58 J12 **Grande de Gurupá, Ilha** *river island* NE Brazil
57 K21 **Grande de Lipez, Río** ≈ SW Bolivia
45 U6 **Grande de Loíza, Río** ≈ E Puerto Rico
45 T5 **Grande de Manatí, Río** ≈ C Puerto Rico
42 L9 **Grande de Matagalpa, Río** ≈ C Nicaragua
40 K12 **Grande de Santiago, Río** *var.* Santiago. ≈ C Mexico
43 O15 **Grande de Térraba, Río** *var.* Río Térraba. ≈ SE Costa Rica
12 J9 **Grande Deux, Réservoir la** ⊡ Québec, E Canada
60 O10 **Grande, Ilha** *island* SE Brazil
11 O13 **Grande Prairie** Alberta, W Canada
74 I8 **Grand Erg Occidental** *desert* W Algeria
74 L9 **Grand Erg Oriental** *desert* Algeria/Tunisia
59 J20 **Grande, Rio** ≈ S Brazil
2 F15 **Grande, Rio** *var.* Río Bravo, *Sp.* Río Bravo del Norte, Bravo del Norte. ≈ Mexico/USA
57 M18 **Grande, Río** ≈ C Bolivia
15 Y7 **Grande-Rivière** Québec, SE Canada
15 Y6 **Grande Rivière** ≈ Québec, SE Canada
44 M8 **Grande-Rivière-du-Nord** N Haiti
62 K9 **Grande, Salina** *var.* Gran Salitral. *salt lake* C Argentina
15 S7 **Grandes-Bergeronnes** Québec, SE Canada
47 W6 **Grande, Serra** ▲ W Brazil
40 K4 **Grande, Sierra** ▲ N Mexico
103 S12 **Grandes Rousses** ▲ E France
63 K17 **Grandes, Salinas** *salt lake* E Argentina
45 Y5 **Grande Terre** *island* E West Indies
15 X5 **Grande-Vallée** Québec, SE Canada
45 Y5 **Grande Vigie, Pointe de la** *headland* Grande Terre, N Guadeloupe
13 N14 **Grand Falls** New Brunswick, SE Canada
13 T11 **Grand Falls** Newfoundland and Labrador, SE Canada
24 L9 **Grandfalls** Texas, SW USA
21 P9 **Grandfather Mountain** ▲ North Carolina, SE USA
26 L13 **Grandfield** Oklahoma, C USA
11 N17 **Grand Forks** British Columbia, SW Canada
29 R4 **Grand Forks** North Dakota, N USA
31 O9 **Grand Haven** Michigan, N USA
Grandichi *see* Hrandzichy
29 P15 **Grand Island** Nebraska, C USA
31 O3 **Grand Island** *island* Michigan, N USA
22 K10 **Grand Isle** Louisiana, S USA
65 A23 **Grand Jason** *island* Jason Islands, NW Falkland Islands
37 P5 **Grand Junction** Colorado, C USA
20 F10 **Grand Junction** Tennessee, S USA
14 J9 **Grand-Lac-Victoria** Québec, SE Canada
14 J9 **Grand lac Victoria** ◎ Québec, SE Canada
77 N17 **Grand-Lahou** *var.* Grand Lahu. S Ivory Coast
Grand Lahu *see* Grand-Lahou
37 S3 **Grand Lake** Colorado, C USA
13 S11 **Grand Lake** ◎ Newfoundland and Labrador, E Canada
22 G9 **Grand Lake** ◎ Louisiana, S USA
31 R5 **Grand Lake** ◎ Michigan, N USA
31 Q13 **Grand Lake** ⊡ Ohio, N USA
27 R9 **Grand Lake O' The Cherokees** *var.* Lake O' The Cherokees. ⊡ Oklahoma, C USA
31 Q9 **Grand Ledge** Michigan, N USA
102 I8 **Grand-Lieu, Lac de** ◎ NW France
19 U6 **Grand Manan Channel** *channel* Canada/USA
13 O15 **Grand Manan Island** *island* New Brunswick, SE Canada
29 Y4 **Grand Marais** Minnesota, N USA
15 P10 **Grand-Mère** Quebec, SE Canada
37 P5 **Grand Mesa** ▲ Colorado, C USA
108 C10 **Grand Muveran** ▲ W Switzerland
104 G12 **Grândola** Setúbal, S Portugal
Grand Paradis *see* Gran Paradiso
187 O15 **Grand Passage** *passage* N New Caledonia
77 R16 **Grand-Popo** S Benin
29 Z3 **Grand Portage** Minnesota, N USA
25 T6 **Grand Prairie** Texas, SW USA
11 W14 **Grand Rapids** Manitoba, C Canada
31 P9 **Grand Rapids** Michigan, N USA
29 V5 **Grand Rapids** Minnesota, N USA
14 L10 **Grand-Remous** Québec, SE Canada
14 F15 **Grand River** ≈ Ontario, S Canada
31 P9 **Grand River** ≈ Michigan, N USA
27 T3 **Grand River** ≈ Missouri, C USA
28 M7 **Grand River** ≈ South Dakota, N USA
45 Q11 **Grand' Rivière** N Martinique
32 F11 **Grand Ronde** Oregon, NW USA
32 L11 **Grand Ronde River** ≈ Oregon/Washington, NW USA
Grand-Saint-Bernard, Col du *see* Great Saint Bernard Pass
25 V6 **Grand Saline** Texas, SW USA
55 X10 **Grand-Santi** W French Guiana
Grandsee *see* Grandson
108 B9 **Grandson** *prev.* Grandsee. Vaud, W Switzerland
172 J16 **Grand Sœur** *island* Les Sœurs, NE Seychelles
33 S14 **Grand Teton** ▲ Wyoming, C USA
31 P5 **Grand Traverse Bay** *lake bay* Michigan, N USA
45 N6 **Grand Turk** ○ (Turks and Caicos Islands) Grand Turk Island, S Turks and Caicos Islands
45 N6 **Grand Turk Island** *island* SE Turks and Caicos Islands
103 S13 **Grand Veymont** ▲ E France
11 W15 **Grandview** Manitoba, S Canada
27 R4 **Grandview** Missouri, C USA
36 I10 **Grand Wash Cliffs** *cliff* Arizona, SW USA
14 J8 **Granet, Lac** ◎ Québec, SE Canada
95 L14 **Grangärde** Dalarna, C Sweden
44 H12 **Grange Hill** W Jamaica
96 J12 **Grangemouth** C Scotland, UK
25 T10 **Granger** Texas, SW USA
32 J10 **Granger** Washington, NW USA
33 T17 **Granger** Wyoming, C USA
Granges *see* Grenchen
95 L14 **Grängesberg** Dalarna, C Sweden
33 N11 **Grangeville** Idaho, NW USA
10 K13 **Granisle** British Columbia, SW Canada
30 K15 **Granite City** Illinois, N USA
29 S9 **Granite Falls** Minnesota, N USA
21 Q9 **Granite Falls** North Carolina, SE USA
36 K12 **Granite Mountain** ▲ Arizona, SW USA
33 T12 **Granite Peak** ▲ Montana, NW USA
35 T2 **Granite Peak** ▲ Nevada, W USA
36 J3 **Granite Peak** ▲ Utah, W USA
Granite State *see* New Hampshire
107 H24 **Granitola, Capo** *headland* Sicilia, Italy, C Mediterranean Sea
185 H15 **Granity** West Coast, South Island, NZ
Gran Lago *see* Nicaragua, Lago de
63 J18 **Gran Laguna Salada** ◎ S Argentina
Gran Malvina, Isla *see* West Falkland
95 L18 **Gränna** Jönköping, S Sweden
105 W5 **Granollers** *var.* Granollérs. Cataluña, NE Spain
106 A7 **Gran Paradiso** *Fr.* Grand Paradis. ▲ NW Italy
Gran Pilastro *see* Hochfeiler
Gran Salitral *see* Grande, Salina
Gran San Bernardo, Passo di *see* Great Saint Bernard Pass
Gran Santiago *see* Santiago
107 J14 **Gran Sasso d'Italia** ▲ C Italy
100 N11 **Gransee** Brandenburg, NE Germany
28 L15 **Grant** Nebraska, C USA
27 R1 **Grant City** Missouri, C USA
97 N19 **Grantham** E England, UK
65 D24 **Grantham Sound** *sound* East Falkland, Falkland Islands
194 K13 **Grant Island** *island* Antarctica
45 Z14 **Grantley Adams** ✕ (Bridgetown) SE Barbados
35 S7 **Grant, Mount** ▲ Nevada, W USA
96 J9 **Grantown-on-Spey** N Scotland, UK
35 W8 **Grant Range** ▲ Nevada, W USA
37 Q11 **Grants** New Mexico, SW USA
30 I4 **Grantsburg** Wisconsin, N USA
32 F15 **Grants Pass** Oregon, NW USA
36 K3 **Grantsville** Utah, W USA
21 R4 **Grantsville** West Virginia, NE USA
102 I5 **Granville** Manche, N France
11 V12 **Granville Lake** ◎ Manitoba, C Canada
25 V8 **Grapeland** Texas, SW USA
25 T6 **Grapevine** Texas, SW USA
83 K20 **Graskop** Mpumalanga, NE South Africa
95 P14 **Gräsö** Uppsala, C Sweden
93 I19 **Gräsö** *island* C Sweden
103 U15 **Grasse** Alpes-Maritimes, SE France
18 E14 **Grassflat** Pennsylvania, NE USA
33 U9 **Grassrange** Montana, NW USA
18 J6 **Grass River** ≈ New York, NE USA
35 P6 **Grass Valley** California, W USA
183 N14 **Grassy** Tasmania, SE Australia
28 K4 **Grassy Butte** North Dakota, N USA
21 R5 **Grassy Knob** ▲ West Virginia, NE USA
95 G24 **Gråsten** *var.* Graasten. Sønderjylland, SW Denmark
95 J18 **Grästorp** Västra Götaland, S Sweden
Gratianopolis *see* Grenoble
109 V8 **Gratwein** Steiermark, SE Austria
Gratz *see* Graz
108 I9 **Graubünden** *Fr.* Grisons, *It.* Grigioni. ◆ *canton* SE Switzerland
Graudenz *see* Grudziądz
103 N15 **Graulhet** Tarn, S France
105 T4 **Graus** Aragón, NE Spain
61 I16 **Gravataí** Rio Grande do Sul, S Brazil
98 L13 **Grave** Noord-Brabant, SE Netherlands
11 T17 **Gravelbourg** Saskatchewan, S Canada
103 N1 **Gravelines** Nord, N France
Graven *see* Grez-Doiceau
14 H13 **Gravenhurst** Ontario, S Canada
33 O10 **Grave Peak** ▲ Idaho, NW USA
102 I11 **Grave, Pointe de** *headland* W France
183 S4 **Gravesend** New South Wales, SE Australia
97 P22 **Gravesend** SE England, UK
107 N17 **Gravina in Puglia** Puglia, SE Italy
103 S8 **Gray** Haute-Saône, E France
23 T4 **Gray** Georgia, SE USA
195 V16 **Gray, Cape** *headland* Antarctica
32 F9 **Grayland** Washington, NW USA
39 N10 **Grayling** Alaska, USA
31 Q6 **Grayling** Michigan, N USA
32 F9 **Grays Harbor** *inlet* Washington, NW USA
21 O5 **Grayson** Kentucky, S USA
37 S4 **Grays Peak** ▲ Colorado, C USA
30 M16 **Grayville** Illinois, N USA
109 V8 **Graz** *prev.* Gratz. Steiermark, SE Austria
104 L15 **Grazalema** Andalucía, S Spain
113 P15 **Grdelica** Serbia, SE Serbia and Montenegro (Yugo.)
44 H1 **Great Abaco** *var.* Abaco Island. *island* N Bahamas
Great Admiralty Island *see* Manus Island
Great Alfold *see* Great Hungarian Plain
Great Ararat *see* Büyükağrı Dağı
181 U8 **Great Artesian Basin** *lowlands* Queensland, C Australia
181 O12 **Great Australian Bight** *bight* S Australia
64 E11 **Great Bahama Bank** *undersea feature* E Gulf of Mexico
184 M4 **Great Barrier Island** *island* N NZ
181 X4 **Great Barrier Reef** *reef* Queensland, NE Australia
18 L11 **Great Barrington** Massachusetts, NE USA
(0) F10 **Great Basin** *basin* W USA
8 I8 **Great Bear Lake** *Fr.* Grand Lac de l'Ours. ◎ Northwest Territories, NW Canada
Great Belt *see* Storebælt
26 L5 **Great Bend** Kansas, C USA
Great Bermuda *see* Bermuda
97 A20 **Great Blasket Island** *Ir.* An Blascaod Mór. *island* SW Ireland
Great Britain *see* Britain
151 Q23 **Great Channel** *channel* Andaman Sea/Indian Ocean
166 J10 **Great Coco Island** *island* SW Myanmar
Great Crosby *see* Crosby
21 X7 **Great Dismal Swamp** *wetland* North Carolina/Virginia, SE USA
33 V16 **Great Divide Basin** *basin* Wyoming, C USA
181 W7 **Great Dividing Range** ▲ NE Australia
14 D12 **Great Duck Island** *island* Ontario, S Canada
Great Elder Reservoir *see* Waconda Lake
195 V8 **Greater Antarctica** *var.* East Antarctica. *physical region* Antarctica
44 G8 **Greater Antilles** *island group* West Indies
131 V16 **Greater Sunda Islands** *var.* Sunda Islands. *island group* Indonesia
184 I1 **Great Exhibition Bay** *inlet* North Island, NZ
44 H4 **Great Exuma Island** *island* C Bahamas
33 R8 **Great Falls** Montana, NW USA
21 R11 **Great Falls** South Carolina, SE USA
84 F9 **Great Fisher Bank** *undersea feature* C North Sea
Great Glen *see* Mor, Glen
Great Grimsby *see* Grimsby
44 I4 **Great Guana Cay** *island* C Bahamas
64 I5 **Great Hellefiske Bank** *undersea feature* N Atlantic Ocean
111 L24 **Great Hungarian Plain** *var.* Great Alfold, Plain of Hungary, *Hung.* Alföld. *plain* SE Europe
44 L7 **Great Inagua** *var.* Inagua Islands. *island* S Bahamas
Great Indian Desert *see* Thar Desert
83 G25 **Great Karoo** *var.* Great Karroo, High Veld, *Afr.* Groot Karoo, Hoë Karoo. *plateau region* S South Africa
Great Karroo *see* Great Karoo
Great Kei *see* Groot-Kei
Great Khingan Range *see* Da Hinggan Ling
14 E11 **Great La Cloche Island** *island* Ontario, S Canada
183 P16 **Great Lake** ◎ Tasmania, SE Australia
Great Lake *see* Tônlé Sap
9 R15 **Great Lakes** *lakes* Ontario, Canada/USA
Great Lakes State *see* Michigan
97 L20 **Great Malvern** W England, UK
184 M5 **Great Mercury Island** *island* N NZ
Great Meteor Seamount *see* Great Meteor Tablemount
64 K10 **Great Meteor Tablemount** *var.* Great Meteor Seamount. *undersea feature* E Atlantic Ocean
31 Q14 **Great Miami River** ≈ Ohio, N USA
151 Q24 **Great Nicobar** *island* Nicobar Islands, India, NE Indian Ocean
97 O19 **Great Ouse** *var.* Ouse. ≈ E England, UK
183 Q17 **Great Oyster Bay** *bay* Tasmania, SE Australia
44 I13 **Great Pedro Bluff** *headland* W Jamaica
21 T12 **Great Pee Dee River** ≈ North Carolina/South Carolina, SE USA
131 W9 **Great Plain of China** *plain* E China
(0) F12 **Great Plains** *var.* High Plains. *plains* Canada/USA
37 W6 **Great Plains Reservoirs** ⊡ Colorado, C USA
19 Q13 **Great Point** *headland* Nantucket Island, Massachusetts, NE USA
68 I13 **Great Rift Valley** *var.* Rift Valley. *depression* Asia/Africa
81 I23 **Great Ruaha** ≈ S Tanzania
18 K10 **Great Sacandaga Lake** ⊡ New York, NE USA
108 C12 **Great Saint Bernard Pass** *Fr.* Col du Grand-Saint-Bernard, *It.* Passo di Gran San Bernardo. *pass* Italy/Switzerland
44 F1 **Great Sale Cay** *island* N Bahamas
Great Salt Desert *see* Kavīr, Dasht-e
36 K1 **Great Salt Lake** *salt lake* Utah, W USA
36 J3 **Great Salt Lake Desert** *plain* Utah, W USA
26 M8 **Great Salt Plains Lake** ⊡ Oklahoma, C USA
75 T9 **Great Sand Sea** *desert* Egypt/Libya
180 L6 **Great Sandy Desert** *desert* Western Australia
Great Sandy Desert *see* Ar Rub' al Khālī
Great Sandy Island *see* Fraser Island
187 Y13 **Great Sea Reef** *reef* Vanua Levu, N Fiji
38 H17 **Great Sitkin Island** *island* Aleutian Islands, Alaska, USA
8 J10 **Great Slave Lake** *Fr.* Grand Lac des Esclaves. ◎ Northwest Territories, NW Canada
21 O10 **Great Smoky Mountains** ▲ North Carolina/Tennessee, SE USA
10 L11 **Great Snow Mountain** ▲ British Columbia, W Canada
64 A12 **Great Sound** *bay* Bermuda, NW Atlantic Ocean
180 M10 **Great Victoria Desert** *desert* South Australia/Western Australia
194 H2 **Great Wall** *Chinese research station* South Shetland Islands, Antarctica
19 T7 **Great Wass Island** *island* Maine, NE USA
97 Q19 **Great Yarmouth** *var.* Yarmouth. E England, UK
139 S1 **Great Zab** *Ar.* Az Zāb al Kabīr, *Kurd.* Zē-i Bādīnān, *Turk.* Büyükzap Suyu. ≈ Iraq/Turkey
95 I17 **Grebbestad** Västra Götaland, S Sweden
Grebenka *see* Hrebinka
42 M13 **Grecia** Alajuela, C Costa Rica
61 E18 **Greco** Río Negro, W Uruguay
Greco, Cape *see* Gkréko, Akrotíri
104 L8 **Gredos, Sierra de** ▲ W Spain
18 F9 **Greece** New York, NE USA
115 E17 **Greece** *off.* Hellenic Republic, *Gk.* Ellás; *anc.* Hellas. ◆ *republic* SE Europe
Greece Central *see* Stereá Ellás
Greece West *see* Dytikí Ellás
37 T3 **Greeley** Colorado, C USA
29 P14 **Greeley** Nebraska, C USA
122 K3 **Greem-Bell, Ostrov** *Eng.* Graham Bell Island. *island* Zemlya Frantsa-Iosifa, N Russian Federation
30 M6 **Green Bay** Wisconsin, N USA
31 N6 **Green Bay** *lake bay* Michigan/Wisconsin, N USA
21 S5 **Greenbrier River** ≈ West Virginia, NE USA
29 S2 **Greenbush** Minnesota, N USA
183 R12 **Green Cape** *headland* New South Wales, SE Australia
31 O14 **Greencastle** Indiana, N USA
18 F16 **Greencastle** Pennsylvania, NE USA
27 T2 **Green City** Missouri, C USA
21 O9 **Greeneville** Tennessee, S USA
35 O11 **Greenfield** California, W USA
31 P14 **Greenfield** Indiana, N USA
29 U15 **Greenfield** Iowa, C USA
18 M11 **Greenfield** Massachusetts, NE USA
27 S7 **Greenfield** Missouri, C USA
31 S14 **Greenfield** Ohio, N USA
20 G8 **Greenfield** Tennessee, S USA
30 M9 **Greenfield** Wisconsin, N USA
27 T9 **Green Forest** Arkansas, C USA
37 T7 **Greenhorn Mountain** ▲ Colorado, C USA
Green Island *see* Lü Tao
186 I6 **Green Islands** *var.* Nissan Islands. *island group* NE PNG
11 S14 **Green Lake** Saskatchewan, C Canada
30 L8 **Green Lake** ◎ Wisconsin, N USA
197 O14 **Greenland** *Dan.* Grønland, *Inuit* Kalaallit Nunaat. ◇ *Danish external territory* NE North America
84 D4 **Greenland** *island* NE North America
197 R13 **Greenland Plain** *undersea feature* N Greenland Sea
197 R14 **Greenland Sea** *sea* Arctic Ocean
37 R4 **Green Mountain Reservoir** ⊡ Colorado, C USA
18 M8 **Green Mountains** ▲ Vermont, NE USA
Green Mountain State *see* Vermont
96 H12 **Greenock** W Scotland, UK
39 T5 **Greenough, Mount** ▲ Alaska, USA
186 A6 **Green River** Sandaun, NW PNG
37 N5 **Green River** Utah, W USA
33 U17 **Green River** Wyoming, C USA
16 H9 **Green River** ≈ W USA
30 K11 **Green River** ≈ Illinois, N USA
20 J7 **Green River** ≈ Kentucky, S USA
28 K5 **Green River** ≈ North Dakota, N USA
37 N6 **Green River** ≈ Utah, W USA
33 T16 **Green River** ≈ Wyoming, C USA
20 L7 **Green River Lake** ⊡ Kentucky, S USA
23 O5 **Greensboro** Alabama, S USA
23 U3 **Greensboro** Georgia, SE USA
21 T9 **Greensboro** North Carolina, SE USA
31 P14 **Greensburg** Indiana, N USA
26 K6 **Greensburg** Kansas, C USA
20 L7 **Greensburg** Kentucky, S USA
18 C15 **Greensburg** Pennsylvania, NE USA
37 O13 **Greens Peak** ▲ Arizona, SW USA
21 V12 **Green Swamp** *wetland* North Carolina, SE USA
21 O4 **Greenup** Kentucky, S USA
36 M16 **Green Valley** Arizona, SW USA
76 K17 **Greenville** *var.* Sino, Sinoe. SE Liberia
23 P6 **Greenville** Alabama, S USA
23 T8 **Greenville** Florida, SE USA
23 S4 **Greenville** Georgia, SE USA
30 L15 **Greenville** Illinois, N USA
20 I7 **Greenville** Kentucky, S USA
19 Q5 **Greenville** Maine, NE USA
31 P9 **Greenville** Michigan, N USA
22 J4 **Greenville** Mississippi, S USA
21 W9 **Greenville** North Carolina, SE USA
31 Q13 **Greenville** Ohio, N USA
19 O12 **Greenville** Rhode Island, NE USA
21 P11 **Greenville** South Carolina, SE USA
25 U6 **Greenville** Texas, SW USA
31 T12 **Greenwich** Ohio, N USA
27 S11 **Greenwood** Arkansas, C USA
31 O14 **Greenwood** Indiana, N USA
22 K4 **Greenwood** Mississippi, S USA
21 P12 **Greenwood** South Carolina, SE USA
21 Q12 **Greenwood, Lake** ⊡ South Carolina, SE USA
21 P11 **Greer** South Carolina, SE USA
27 V10 **Greers Ferry Lake** ⊡ Arkansas, C USA
27 S13 **Greeson, Lake** ⊡ Arkansas, C USA
29 O12 **Gregory** South Dakota, N USA
182 J3 **Gregory, Lake** *salt lake* South Australia
180 J9 **Gregory Lake** ◎ Western Australia
181 V5 **Gregory Range** ▲ Queensland, E Australia
Greifenberg/Greifenberg in Pommern *see* Gryfice
Greifenhagen *see* Gryfino
100 O8 **Greifswald** Mecklenburg-Vorpommern, NE Germany
100 O8 **Greifswalder Bodden** *bay* NE Germany
109 U4 **Grein** Oberösterreich, N Austria
101 M17 **Greiz** Thüringen, C Germany
Gremicha/Gremiha *see* Gremikha
124 M4 **Gremikha** *var.* Gremicha, Gremiha. Murmanskaya Oblast', NW Russian Federation
125 V14 **Gremyachinsk** Permskaya Oblast', NW Russian Federation
Grenå *see* Grenaa
95 H21 **Grenaa** *var.* Grenå. Århus, C Denmark
22 L3 **Grenada** Mississippi, S USA
45 W15 **Grenada** ◆ *commonwealth republic* SE West Indies
47 S4 **Grenada** *island* Grenada
47 R4 **Grenada Basin** *undersea feature* W Atlantic Ocean
22 L3 **Grenada Lake** ⊡ Mississippi, S USA
45 Y14 **Grenadines, The** *island group* Grenada/St Vincent and the Grenadines
108 D7 **Grenchen** *Fr.* Granges. Solothurn, NW Switzerland
183 Q9 **Grenfell** New South Wales, SE Australia
11 V16 **Grenfell** Saskatchewan, S Canada
92 J1 **Grenivík** Nordhurland Eystra, N Iceland
103 S12 **Grenoble** *anc.* Cularo, Gratianopolis. Isère, E France
28 J2 **Grenora** North Dakota, N USA
92 N8 **Grense-Jakobselv** Finnmark, N Norway
45 S14 **Grenville** E Grenada
32 G11 **Gresham** Oregon, NW USA
Gresk *see* Hresk
106 B7 **Gressoney-St-Jean** Valle d'Aosta, NW Italy
22 K9 **Gretna** Louisiana, S USA
21 T7 **Gretna** Virginia, NE USA
98 F13 **Grevelingen** *inlet* S North Sea
100 F13 **Greven** Nordrhein-Westfalen, NW Germany
115 D15 **Grevená** Dytikí Makedonía, N Greece
101 D16 **Grevenbroich** Nordrhein-Westfalen, W Germany
99 N24 **Grevenmacher** Grevenmacher, E Luxembourg
99 M24 **Grevenmacher** ◆ *district* E Luxembourg
100 K9 **Grevesmühlen** Mecklenburg-Vorpommern, N Germany
185 H16 **Grey** ≈ South Island, NZ
33 V12 **Greybull** Wyoming, C USA
33 U13 **Greybull River** ≈ Wyoming, C USA
65 A24 **Grey Channel** *sound* Falkland Islands
Greyerzer See *see* Gruyère, Lac de la
13 T10 **Grey Islands** *island group* Newfoundland and Labrador, E Canada
18 L10 **Greylock, Mount** ▲ Massachusetts, NE USA
185 G17 **Greymouth** West Coast, South Island, NZ
181 U10 **Grey Range** ▲ New South Wales/Queensland, E Australia
97 G18 **Greystones** *Ir.* Na Clocha Liatha. E Ireland
185 M14 **Greytown** Wellington, North Island, NZ
83 K23 **Greytown** KwaZulu/Natal, E South Africa
Greytown *see* San Juan del Norte
99 H19 **Grez-Doiceau** *Dut.* Graven. Wallon Brabant, C Belgium
115 J19 **Griá, Akrotírio** *headland* Ándros, Kykládes, Greece, Aegean Sea
127 N8 **Gribanovskiy** Voronezhskaya Oblast', W Russian Federation
78 I13 **Gribingui** ≈ N Central African Republic
35 O6 **Gridley** California, W USA
83 G23 **Griekwastad** Northern Cape, C South Africa
23 S4 **Griffin** Georgia, SE USA
183 O9 **Griffith** New South Wales, SE Australia
14 F13 **Griffith Island** *island* Ontario, S Canada
21 W10 **Grifton** North Carolina, SE USA
Grigioni *see* Graubünden
119 H14 **Grigiškes** Vilnius, SE Lithuania
117 N10 **Grigoriopol** C Moldova
147 X7 **Grigor'yevka** Issyk-Kul'skaya Oblast', E Kyrgyzstan
193 U8 **Grijalva Ridge** *undersea feature* E Pacific Ocean
41 U15 **Grijalva, Río** *var.* Tabasco. ≈ Guatemala/Mexico
98 N5 **Grijpskerk** Groningen, NE Netherlands
83 C22 **Grillenthal** Karas, SW Namibia
79 J15 **Grimari** Ouaka, C Central African Republic
Grimaylov *see* Hrymayliv
99 G18 **Grimbergen** Vlaams Brabant, C Belgium
183 N15 **Grim, Cape** *headland* Tasmania, SE Australia
100 N8 **Grimmen** Mecklenburg-Vorpommern, NE Germany
14 G16 **Grimsby** Ontario, S Canada
97 O17 **Grimsby** *prev.* Great Grimsby. E England, UK
92 J1 **Grímsey** *var.* Grimsey. *island* N Iceland
11 O12 **Grimshaw** Alberta, W Canada
95 F18 **Grimstad** Aust-Agder, S Norway
92 H4 **Grindavík** Reykjanes, W Iceland
108 F9 **Grindelwald** Bern, S Switzerland
95 F23 **Grindsted** Ribe, W Denmark
29 W14 **Grinnell** Iowa, C USA
8 K4 **Grinnell Peninsula** *peninsula* Nunavut, N Canada
109 U10 **Grintovec** ▲ N Slovenia
9 N3 **Grise Fiord** *var.* Aujuittuq. Nunavut, N Canada
182 H1 **Griselda, Lake** *salt lake* South Australia
Grisons *see* Graubünden
95 P14 **Grisslehamn** Stockholm, C Sweden
29 T15 **Griswold** Iowa, C USA
102 M1 **Griz Nez, Cap** *headland* N France
112 P13 **Grljan** Serbia, E Serbia and Montenegro (Yugo.)
112 E11 **Grmeč** ▲ NW Bosnia and Herzegovina
99 H16 **Grobbendonk** Antwerpen, N Belgium
Grobin *see* Grobiņa
118 C10 **Grobiņa** *Ger.* Grobin. Liepāja, W Latvia
83 K20 **Groblersdal** Mpumalanga, NE South Africa
83 G23 **Groblershoop** Northern Cape, W South Africa
Gródek Jagielloński *see* Horodok
109 Q6 **Grödig** Salzburg, W Austria
111 H15 **Grodków** Opolskie, S Poland
Grodnenskaya Oblast' *see* Hrodzyenskaya Voblasts'
Grodno *see* Hrodna
110 L12 **Grodzisk Mazowiecki** Mazowieckie, C Poland
110 F12 **Grodzisk Wielkopolski** Wielkolpolskie, C Poland
Grodzyanka *see* Hradzyanka
98 O12 **Groenlo** Gelderland, E Netherlands
83 E22 **Groenrivier** Karas, SE Namibia
25 U8 **Groesbeck** Texas, SW USA
98 L13 **Groesbeek** Gelderland, SE Netherlands
102 G7 **Groix, Îles de** *island group* NW France
110 M12 **Grójec** Mazowieckie, C Poland
65 K15 **Gröll Seamount** *undersea feature* C Atlantic Ocean
100 E13 **Gronau** *var.* Gronau in Westfalen. Nordrhein-Westfalen, NW Germany
Gronau in Westfalen *see* Gronau
93 F15 **Grong** Nord-Trøndelag, C Norway

◆ COUNTRY ● COUNTRY CAPITAL ◇ DEPENDENT TERRITORY ○ DEPENDENT TERRITORY CAPITAL ◆ ADMINISTRATIVE REGION ✕ INTERNATIONAL AIRPORT ▲ MOUNTAIN ▲ MOUNTAIN RANGE ⚠ VOLCANO ≈ RIVER ◎ LAKE ⊡ RESERVOIR

95 N22 **Grönhögen** Kalmar, S Sweden
98 N5 **Groningen** Groningen, NE Netherlands
55 W9 **Groningen** Saramacca, N Suriname
98 N5 **Groningen** ◆ *province* NE Netherlands
Grønland *see* Greenland
108 H11 **Grono** Graubünden, S Switzerland
95 M20 **Grönskåra** Kalmar, S Sweden
25 O2 **Groom** Texas, SW USA
35 W9 **Groom Lake** ◎ Nevada, W USA
83 H25 **Groot** ≈ South Africa
181 S2 **Groote Eylandt** *island* Northern Territory, N Australia
98 M6 **Grootegast** Groningen, NE Netherlands
83 D17 **Grootfontein** Otjozondjupa, N Namibia
83 E22 **Groot Karasberge** ⛰ S Namibia
Groot Karoo *see* Great Karoo
83 J25 **Groot-Kei** *Eng.* Great Kei. ≈ S South Africa
45 T10 **Gros Islet** N Saint Lucia
44 L8 **Gros-Morne** NW Haiti
13 S11 **Gros Morne** ▲ Newfoundland and Labrador, E Canada
103 R9 **Grosne** ≈ C France
45 S12 **Gros Piton** ▲ SW Saint Lucia
Grossa, Isola *see* Dugi Otok
Grossbetschkerek *see* Zrenjanin
Grosse Isper *see* Grosse Ysper
Grosse Kokel *see* Târnava Mare
101 M21 **Grosse Laaber** *var.* Grosse Laber. ≈ SE Germany
Grosse Laber *see* Grosse Laaber
Grosse Morava *see* Velika Morava
101 O15 **Grossenhain** Sachsen, E Germany
109 Y4 **Grossenzersdorf** Niederösterreich, NE Austria
101 O21 **Grosser Arber** ▲ SE Germany
101 K17 **Grosser Beerberg** ▲ C Germany
101 G18 **Grosser Feldberg** ▲ W Germany
109 O8 **Grosser Löffler** *It.* Monte Lovello. ▲ Austria/Italy
109 N8 **Grosser Möseler** *var.* Mesule. ▲ Austria/Italy
100 J8 **Grosser Plöner See** ◎ N Germany
101 O21 **Grosser Rachel** ▲ SE Germany
Grosser Sund *see* Suur Väin
15 V6 **Grosses-Roches** Québec, SE Canada
109 P8 **Grosses Weiesbachhorn** *var.* Wiesbachhorn. ▲ W Austria
106 F13 **Grosseto** Toscana, C Italy
101 M22 **Grosse Vils** ≈ SE Germany
109 U4 **Grosse Ysper** *var.* Grosse Isper. ≈ N Austria
101 G19 **Gross-Gerau** Hessen, W Germany
109 U3 **Gross Gerungs** Niederösterreich, N Austria
109 P8 **Grossglockner** ▲ W Austria
Grosskanizsa *see* Nagykanizsa
Gross-Karol *see* Carei
Grosskikinda *see* Kikinda
109 W9 **Grossklein** Steiermark, SE Austria
Grosskoppe *see* Velká Deštná
Grossmeseritsch *see* Velké Meziříčí
Grossmichel *see* Michalovce
101 H19 **Grossostheim** Bayern, C Germany
109 X7 **Grosspetersdorf** Burgenland, SE Austria
109 T5 **Grossraming** Oberösterreich, C Austria
101 P14 **Grossräschen** Brandenburg, E Germany
Grossrauschenbach *see* Revúca
Gross-Sankt-Johannis *see* Suure-Jaani
Gross-Schlatten *see* Abrud
109 V2 **Gross-Siegharts** Niederösterreich, N Austria
Gross-Skaisgirren *see* Bol'shakovo
Gross-Steffelsdorf *see* Rimavská Sobota
Gross Strehlitz *see* Strzelce Opolskie
109 O8 **Grossvenediger** ▲ W Austria
Grosswardein *see* Oradea
Gross Wartenberg *see* Syców
109 U11 **Grosuplje** C Slovenia
99 H17 **Grote Nete** ≈ N Belgium
94 E10 **Grotli** Oppland, S Norway
19 N13 **Groton** Connecticut, NE USA
29 P8 **Groton** South Dakota, N USA
107 P18 **Grottaglie** Puglia, SE Italy
107 L17 **Grottaminarda** Campania, S Italy
106 K13 **Grottammare** Marche, C Italy
21 U5 **Grottoes** Virginia, NE USA
Grou *see* Grouw
13 N10 **Groulx, Monts** ⛰ Québec, E Canada
14 E7 **Groundhog** ≈ Ontario, S Canada
36 J1 **Grouse Creek** Utah, W USA
36 J1 **Grouse Creek Mountains** ⛰ Utah, W USA
98 L6 **Grouw** *Fris.* Grou. Friesland, N Netherlands
27 R8 **Grove** Oklahoma, C USA
31 S13 **Grove City** Ohio, N USA
18 B13 **Grove City** Pennsylvania, NE USA
23 O6 **Grove Hill** Alabama, S USA
33 S15 **Grover** Wyoming, C USA
35 P13 **Grover City** California, W USA
25 Y11 **Groves** Texas, SW USA
19 O7 **Groveton** New Hampshire, NE USA
25 W9 **Groveton** Texas, SW USA
36 J15 **Growler Mountains** ⛰ Arizona, SW USA
Grozdovo *see* Bratya Daskalovi
127 P16 **Groznyy** Chechenskaya Respublika, SW Russian Federation
Grubeshov *see* Hrubieszów
112 G9 **Grubišno Polje** Bjelovar-Bilogora, NE Croatia
Grudovo *see* Sredets
110 J9 **Grudziądz** *Ger.* Graudenz. Kujawsko-pomorskie, C Poland
25 R17 **Grulla** *var.* La Grulla. Texas, SW USA
40 K14 **Grullo** Jalisco, SW Mexico
67 V10 **Grumeti** ≈ N Tanzania
95 K16 **Grums** Värmland, C Sweden
109 S5 **Grünau im Almtal** Oberösterreich, N Austria
101 H17 **Grünberg** Hessen, W Germany
Grünberg/Grünberg in Schlesien *see* Zielona Góra
Grünberg in Schlesien *see* Zielona Góra
92 H3 **Grundarfjördhur** Vestfirdhir, W Iceland
21 P7 **Grundy** Virginia, NE USA
29 W13 **Grundy Center** Iowa, C USA
Grüneberg *see* Zielona Góra
25 N1 **Gruver** Texas, SW USA
108 C9 **Gruyère, Lac de la** *Ger.* Greyerzer See. ◎ SW Switzerland
108 C9 **Gruyères** Fribourg, W Switzerland
118 E11 **Gruzdžiai** Šiauliai, N Lithuania
Gruzinskaya SSR/Gruziya *see* Georgia
Gryada Akkyr *see* Akgyr Erezi
126 L7 **Gryazi** Lipetskaya Oblast', W Russian Federation
124 M14 **Gryazovets** Vologodskaya Oblast', NW Russian Federation
111 M17 **Grybów** Małopolskie, SE Poland
94 M13 **Grycksbo** Dalarna, C Sweden
110 E8 **Gryfice** *Ger.* Greifenberg, Greifenberg in Pommern. Zachodnio-pomorskie, NW Poland
110 D9 **Gryfino** *Ger.* Greifenhagen. Zachodnio-pomorskie, NW Poland
92 H9 **Gryllefjord** Troms, N Norway
95 L15 **Grythyttan** Örebro, C Sweden
108 D10 **Gstaad** Bern, W Switzerland
43 P14 **Guabito** Bocas del Toro, NW Panama
44 G7 **Guacanayabo, Golfo de** *gulf* S Cuba
40 I7 **Guachochi** Chihuahua, N Mexico
104 J11 **Guadajira** ≈ SW Spain
104 M13 **Guadajoz** ≈ S Spain
40 L13 **Guadalajara** Jalisco, C Mexico
105 O8 **Guadalajara** *Ar.* Wad Al-Hajarah; *anc.* Arriaca. Castilla-La Mancha, C Spain
105 O7 **Guadalajara** ◆ *province* Castilla-La Mancha, C Spain
104 K12 **Guadalcanal** Andalucía, S Spain
186 L10 **Guadalcanal** *off.* Guadalcanal Province. ◆ *province* C Solomon Islands
186 M9 **Guadalcanal** *island* C Solomon Islands
105 O12 **Guadalén** ≈ S Spain
105 R13 **Guadalentín** ≈ SE Spain
104 K15 **Guadalete** ≈ SW Spain
105 O13 **Guadalimar** ≈ S Spain
105 P12 **Guadalmena** ≈ S Spain
104 L11 **Guadalmez** ≈ W Spain
105 S7 **Guadalope** ≈ E Spain
104 K13 **Guadalquivir** ≈ W Spain
104 J14 **Guadalquivir, Marismas del** *var.* Las Marismas. *wetland* SW Spain
40 M11 **Guadalupe** Zacatecas, C Mexico
57 E16 **Guadalupe** Ica, W Peru
104 L10 **Guadalupe** Extremadura, W Spain
36 L14 **Guadalupe** Arizona, SW USA
35 P13 **Guadalupe** California, W USA
Guadalupe *see* Canelones
40 J3 **Guadalupe Bravos** Chihuahua, N Mexico
40 A4 **Guadalupe, Isla** *island* NW Mexico
37 U15 **Guadalupe Mountains** ⛰ New Mexico/Texas, SW USA
24 J8 **Guadalupe Peak** ▲ Texas, SW USA
25 R11 **Guadalupe River** ≈ SW USA
104 K10 **Guadalupe, Sierra de** ⛰ W Spain
40 K9 **Guadalupe Victoria** Durango, C Mexico
40 I8 **Guadalupe y Calvo** Chihuahua, N Mexico
105 N7 **Guadarrama** Madrid, C Spain
105 N7 **Guadarrama** ≈ C Spain
104 M7 **Guadarrama, Puerto de** *pass* C Spain
105 N9 **Guadarrama, Sierra de** ⛰ C Spain
105 Q9 **Guadazaón** ≈ C Spain
45 X10 **Guadeloupe** ◇ *French overseas department* E West Indies
47 S3 **Guadeloupe** *island group* E West Indies
45 W10 **Guadeloupe Passage** *passage* E Caribbean Sea
104 H13 **Guadiana** ≈ Portugal/Spain
105 O13 **Guadiana Menor** ≈ S Spain
105 Q8 **Guadiela** ≈ C Spain
105 O14 **Guadix** Andalucía, S Spain
Guad-i-Zirreh *see* Gowd-e Zereh, Dasht-e
193 T12 **Guafo Fracture Zone** *tectonic feature* SE Pacific Ocean
63 F18 **Guafo, Isla** *island* S Chile
42 I6 **Guaimaca** Francisco Morazán, C Honduras
54 J12 **Guainía** *off.* Comisaría del Guainía. ◆ *province* E Colombia
54 K12 **Guainía, Río** ≈ Colombia/Venezuela
55 O9 **Guaiquinima, Cerro** *elevation* SE Venezuela
62 O7 **Guairá** *off.* Departamento del Guairá. ◆ *department* S Paraguay
60 G10 **Guaíra** Paraná, S Brazil
60 L7 **Guaíra** São Paulo, S Brazil
Guaire *see* Gorey
63 F18 **Guaiteca, Isla** *island* S Chile
63 G6 **Guajaba, Cayo** *headland* C Cuba
59 D16 **Guajará-Mirim** Rondônia, W Brazil
Guajira *see* La Guajira
54 H3 **Guajira, Península de la** *peninsula* N Colombia
42 J6 **Gualaco** Olancho, C Honduras
34 L7 **Gualala** California, W USA
42 E5 **Gualán** Zacapa, C Guatemala
61 C19 **Gualeguay** Entre Ríos, E Argentina
61 D18 **Gualeguaychú** Entre Ríos, E Argentina
61 C18 **Gualeguay, Río** ≈ E Argentina
63 K16 **Gualicho, Salina del** *salt lake* E Argentina
188 B15 **Guam** ◇ *US unincorporated territory* W Pacific Ocean
63 F19 **Guamblin, Isla** *island* Archipiélago de los Chonos, S Chile
61 A22 **Guaminí** Buenos Aires, E Argentina
40 H8 **Guamúchil** Sinaloa, C Mexico
54 H4 **Guana** *var.* Misión de Guana. Zulia, NW Venezuela
44 C4 **Guanabacoa** La Habana, W Cuba
42 K13 **Guanacaste** *off.* Provincia de Guanacaste. ◆ *province* NW Costa Rica
42 K12 **Guanacaste, Cordillera de** ⛰ NW Costa Rica
40 J8 **Guanaceví** Durango, C Mexico
44 A5 **Guanahacabibes, Golfo de** *gulf* W Cuba
42 K4 **Guanaja, Isla de** *island* Islas de la Bahía, N Honduras
44 C4 **Guanajay** La Habana, W Cuba
41 N12 **Guanajuato** Guanajuato, C Mexico
40 M12 **Guanajuato** ◆ *state* C Mexico
54 J6 **Guanare** Portuguesa, N Venezuela
54 K7 **Guanare, Río** ≈ W Venezuela
54 J6 **Guanarito** Portuguesa, NW Venezuela
160 M3 **Guancen Shan** ⛰ C China
62 I9 **Guandacol** La Rioja, W Argentina
44 A5 **Guane** Pinar del Río, W Cuba
161 N14 **Guangdong** *var.* Guangdong Sheng, Kuang-tung, Kwangtung, Yue. ◆ *province* S China
Guangdong Sheng *see* Guangdong
Guanghua *see* Laohekou
Guangju *see* Kwangju
160 I13 **Guangnan** *var.* Liancheng. Yunnan, SW China
161 N8 **Guangshui** *prev.* Yingshan. Hubei, C China
Guangxi *see* Guangxi Zhuangzu Zizhiqu
160 K14 **Guangxi Zhuangzu Zizhiqu** *var.* Guangxi, Gui, Kuang-hsi, Kwangsi, *Eng.* Kwangsi Chuang Autonomous Region. ◆ *autonomous region* S China
160 J8 **Guangyuan** *var.* Kuang-yuan, Kwangyuan. Sichuan, C China
161 N14 **Guangzhou** *var.* Kuang-chou, Kwangchow, *Eng.* Canton. Guangdong, S China
59 N19 **Guanhães** Minas Gerais, SE Brazil
160 I12 **Guanling** *var.* Guanling Buyeizu Miaozu Zizhixian. Guizhou, S China
Guanling Buyeizu Miaozu Zizhixian *see* Guanling
55 N5 **Guanta** Anzoátegui, NE Venezuela
44 J8 **Guantánamo** Guantánamo, SE Cuba
44 J8 **Guantánamo, Bahía de** *Eng.* Guantanamo Bay. *US military installation* SE Cuba
Guantánamo Bay *see* Guantánamo, Bahía de
Guanxian *see* Dujiangyan
161 Q6 **Guanyun** Jiangsu, E China
54 C12 **Guapí** Cauca, SW Colombia
43 N13 **Guápiles** Limón, NE Costa Rica
61 I15 **Guaporé** Rio Grande do Sul, S Brazil
47 S8 **Guaporé, Rio** *var.* Río Iténez. ≈ Bolivia/Brazil *see also* Iténez, Río
56 B7 **Guaranda** Bolívar, C Ecuador
60 H11 **Guaraniaçu** Paraná, S Brazil
59 O20 **Guarapari** Espírito Santo, SE Brazil
60 I12 **Guarapuava** Paraná, S Brazil
60 J8 **Guararapes** São Paulo, S Brazil
105 S4 **Guara, Sierra de** ⛰ NE Spain
60 N10 **Guaratinguetá** São Paulo, S Brazil
104 I7 **Guarda** Guarda, N Portugal
104 I7 **Guarda** ◆ *district* N Portugal
Guardak *see* Gowurdak
104 M3 **Guardo** Castilla-León, N Spain
104 K11 **Guareña** Extremadura, W Spain
60 J11 **Guaricana, Pico** ▲ S Brazil
54 L6 **Guárico** *off.* Estado Guárico. ◆ *state* N Venezuela
44 J7 **Guarico, Punta** *headland* E Cuba
54 L7 **Guárico, Río** ≈ C Venezuela
60 M10 **Guarujá** São Paulo, SE Brazil
61 L22 **Guarulhos** × (São Paulo) São Paulo, S Brazil
43 R17 **Guarumal** Veraguas, S Panama
Guasapa *see* Guasopa
40 H8 **Guasave** Sinaloa, C Mexico
54 I8 **Guasdualito** Apure, C Venezuela
55 Q7 **Guasipati** Bolívar, E Venezuela
186 I9 **Guasopa** *var.* Guasapa. Woodlark Island, SE PNG
106 F9 **Guastalla** Emilia-Romagna, C Italy
42 D6 **Guastatoya** *var.* El Progreso. El Progreso, C Guatemala
42 D5 **Guatemala** *off.* Republic of Guatemala. ◆ *republic* Central America
42 A2 **Guatemala** *off.* Departamento de Guatemala. ◆ *department* S Guatemala
193 S7 **Guatemala Basin** *undersea feature* E Pacific Ocean
Guatemala City *see* Ciudad de Guatemala
45 V14 **Guatuaro Point** *headland* Trinidad, Trinidad and Tobago
186 B8 **Guavi** ≈ SW PNG
54 G13 **Guaviare** *off.* Comisaría Guaviare. ◆ *province* S Colombia
54 J11 **Guaviare, Río** ≈ E Colombia
61 E15 **Guaviravi** Corrientes, NE Argentina
54 G12 **Guayabero, Río** ≈ SW Colombia
45 U6 **Guayama** E Puerto Rico
42 J7 **Guayambre, Río** ≈ S Honduras
Guayanas, Macizo de las *see* Guiana Highlands
45 V6 **Guayanés, Punta** *headland* E Puerto Rico
42 J6 **Guayape, Río** ≈ C Honduras
56 B7 **Guayaquil** *var.* Santiago de Guayaquil. Guayas, SW Ecuador
Guayaquil *see* Simon Bolivar
56 A8 **Guayaquil, Golfo de** *var.* Gulf of Guayaquil. *gulf* SW Ecuador
Guayaquil, Gulf of *see* Guayaquil, Golfo de
56 A7 **Guayas** ◆ *province* W Ecuador
62 N7 **Guaycurú, Río** ≈ NE Argentina
40 F6 **Guaymas** Sonora, NW Mexico
45 U5 **Guaynabo** E Puerto Rico
80 H12 **Guba** Benishangul, W Ethiopia
146 H8 **Gubadag** *Turkm.* Tel'man; *prev.* Tel'mansk. Daşoguz Welaýaty, N Turkmenistan
125 T1 **Guba Dolgaya** Nenetskiy Avtonomnyy Okrug, NW Russian Federation
125 V13 **Gubakha** Permskaya Oblast', NW Russian Federation
106 I12 **Gubbio** Umbria, C Italy
100 Q13 **Guben** *var.* Wilhelm-Pieck-Stadt. Brandenburg, E Germany
Guben *see* Gubin
110 D12 **Gubin** *Ger.* Guben. Lubuskie, W Poland
126 K8 **Gubkin** Belgorodskaya Oblast', W Russian Federation
Gudara *see* Ghŭdara
105 S8 **Gúdar, Sierra de** ⛰ E Spain
137 P8 **Gudaut'a** NW Georgia
94 G12 **Gudbrandsdalen** *valley* S Norway
95 G21 **Gudenå** *var.* Gudenaa. ≈ C Denmark
Gudenaa *see* Gudenå
127 P16 **Gudermes** Chechenskaya Respublika, SW Russian Federation
155 J18 **Gūdūr** Andhra Pradesh, E India
146 B13 **Gudurolum** Balkan Welaýaty, W Turkmenistan
94 D13 **Gudvangen** Sogn og Fjordane, S Norway
103 U7 **Guebwiller** Haut-Rhin, NE France
Guéckédou *see* Guékédou
14 K8 **Guéguen, Lac** ◎ Québec, SE Canada
76 J15 **Guékédou** *var.* Guéckédou. Guinée-Forestière, S Guinea
41 R16 **Guelatao** Oaxaca, SE Mexico
Guelders *see* Gelderland
78 G11 **Guélengdeng** Mayo-Kébbi, W Chad
74 L5 **Guelma** *var.* Gâlma. NE Algeria
74 D8 **Guelmime** *var.* Goulimime. SW Morocco
14 G15 **Guelph** Ontario, S Canada
102 I7 **Guémené-Penfao** Loire-Atlantique, NW France
102 I7 **Guer** Morbihan, NW France
78 I11 **Guéra** *off.* Préfecture du Guéra. ◆ *prefecture* S Chad
102 H8 **Guérande** Loire-Atlantique, NW France
78 K9 **Guéréda** Biltine, E Chad
103 N10 **Guéret** Creuse, C France
Guernica/Guernica y Lumo *see* Gernika-Lumo
33 Z15 **Guernsey** Wyoming, C USA
97 K25 **Guernsey** *island* Channel Islands, NW Europe
76 J10 **Guérou** Assaba, S Mauritania
25 R16 **Guerra** Texas, SW USA
41 O15 **Guerrero** ◆ *state* S Mexico
40 D6 **Guerrero Negro** Baja California Sur, NW Mexico
103 P9 **Gueugnon** Saône-et-Loire, C France
76 M17 **Guéyo** S Ivory Coast
107 L15 **Guglionesi** Molise, C Italy
188 K5 **Guguan** *island* C Northern Mariana Islands
Guhrau *see* Góra
Gui *see* Guangxi Zhuangzu Zizhiqu
Guiana *see* French Guiana
47 V4 **Guiana Basin** *undersea feature* W Atlantic Ocean
48 G6 **Guiana Highlands** *var.* Macizo de las Guayanas. ⛰ N South America
Guiba *see* Juba
102 I7 **Guichen** Ille-et-Vilaine, NW France
Guichi *see* Chizhou
61 E18 **Guichón** Paysandú, W Uruguay
77 U12 **Guidan-Roumji** Maradi, S Niger
Guidder *see* Guider
159 T10 **Guide** *var.* Heyin. Qinghai, C China
78 F12 **Guider** *var.* Guidder. Nord, N Cameroon
76 I11 **Guidimaka** ◆ *region* S Mauritania
77 W12 **Guidimouni** Zinder, S Niger
76 G10 **Guier, Lac de** *var.* Lac de Guiers. ◎ N Senegal
160 L14 **Guigang** *prev.* Guixian, Gui Xian. Guangxi Zhuangzu Zizhiqu, S China
76 L16 **Guiglo** W Ivory Coast
54 L5 **Güigüe** Carabobo, N Venezuela
83 M20 **Guijá** Gaza, S Mozambique
42 E7 **Güija, Lago de** ◎ El Salvador/Guatemala
160 L14 **Gui Jiang** *var.* Gui Shui. ≈ S China
104 K8 **Guijuelo** Castilla-León, N Spain
Guilan *see* Gīlān
97 N22 **Guildford** SE England, UK
19 R5 **Guildford** Maine, NE USA
19 O7 **Guildhall** Vermont, NE USA
103 R13 **Guilherand** Ardèche, E France
160 L13 **Guilin** *var.* Kuei-lin, Kweilin. Guangxi Zhuangzu Zizhiqu, S China
12 J6 **Guillaume-Delisle, Lac** ◎ Québec, NE Canada
103 U13 **Guillestre** Hautes-Alpes, SE France
104 H6 **Guimarães** *var.* Guimaráes. Braga, N Portugal
58 D11 **Guimarães Rosas, Pico** ▲ NW Brazil
23 N3 **Guin** Alabama, S USA
Güina *see* Wina
76 I14 **Guinea** *off.* Republic of Guinea, *var.* Guinée; *prev.* French Guinea, People's Revolutionary Republic of Guinea. ◆ *republic* W Africa
64 N13 **Guinea Basin** *undersea feature* E Atlantic Ocean
76 E12 **Guinea-Bissau** *off.* Republic of Guinea-Bissau, *Fr.* Guinée-Bissau, *Port.* Guiné-Bissau; *prev.* Portuguese Guinea. ◆ *republic* W Africa
66 K7 **Guinea Fracture Zone** *tectonic feature* E Atlantic Ocean
64 O13 **Guinea, Gulf of** *Fr.* Golfe de Guinée. *gulf* E Atlantic Ocean
Guiné-Bissau *see* Guinea-Bissau
Guinée *see* Guinea
Guinée-Bissau *see* Guinea-Bissau
76 K15 **Guinée-Forestière** ◆ *state* SE Guinea
Guinée, Golfe de *see* Guinea, Gulf of
76 H13 **Guinée-Maritime** ◆ *state* W Guinea
44 C4 **Güines** La Habana, W Cuba
102 G5 **Guingamp** Côtes d'Armor, NW France
105 P3 **Guipúzcoa** *Basq.* Gipuzkoa. ◆ *province* País Vasco, N Spain
44 C5 **Güira de Melena** La Habana, W Cuba
74 G8 **Guir, Hamada du** *desert* Algeria/Morocco
55 P5 **Güiria** Sucre, NE Venezuela
Gui Shui *see* Gui Jiang
104 H2 **Guitiriz** Galicia, NW Spain
77 N17 **Guitri** S Ivory Coast
171 Q5 **Guiuan** Samar, C Philippines
Gui Xian/Guixian *see* Guigang
160 J12 **Guiyang** *var.* Kuei-Yang, Kuei-yang, Kueyang, Kweiyang; *prev.* Kweichu. Guizhou, S China
160 J12 **Guizhou** *var.* Guizhou Sheng, Kuei-chou, Kweichow, Qian. ◆ *province* S China
Guizhou Sheng *see* Guizhou
102 J13 **Gujan-Mestras** Gironde, SW France
154 B10 **Gujarāt** *var.* Gujerat. ◆ *state* W India
149 V6 **Gujar Khān** Punjab, E Pakistan
Gujerat *see* Gujarāt
149 V7 **Gujrānwāla** Punjab, NE Pakistan
149 V7 **Gujrāt** Punjab, E Pakistan
146 B8 **Gulandag** *Rus.* Gory Kulandag. ⛰ W Turkmenistan
159 U9 **Gulang** Gansu, C China
183 R6 **Gulargambone** New South Wales, SE Australia
155 G15 **Gulbarga** Karnātaka, C India
118 J8 **Gulbene** *Ger.* Alt-Schwanenburg. Gulbene, NE Latvia
147 U10 **Gul'cha** *Kir.* Gülchö. Oshskaya Oblast', SW Kyrgyzstan
Gülchö *see* Gul'cha
173 T10 **Gulden Draak Seamount** *undersea feature* E Indian Ocean
136 J16 **Gülek Boğazı** *var.* Cilician Gates. *pass* S Turkey
186 D8 **Gulf** ◆ *province* S PNG
23 O9 **Gulf Breeze** Florida, SE USA
23 V13 **Gulfport** Florida, SE USA
22 M9 **Gulfport** Mississippi, S USA
23 O9 **Gulf Shores** Alabama, S USA
Gulf, The *see* Persian Gulf
183 R7 **Gulgong** New South Wales, SE Australia
160 I11 **Gulin** Sichuan, C China
171 U14 **Gulir** Pulau Kasiui, E Indonesia
Gulistan *see* Guliston
147 P10 **Guliston** *Rus.* Gulistan. Sirdaryo Viloyati, E Uzbekistan
163 T6 **Guliya Shan** ▲ NE China
Gulja *see* Yining
39 S11 **Gulkana** Alaska, USA
11 S17 **Gull Lake** Saskatchewan, S Canada
31 P10 **Gull Lake** ◎ Michigan, N USA
29 T6 **Gull Lake** ◎ Minnesota, N USA
95 L16 **Gullspång** Västra Götaland, S Sweden
136 B15 **Güllük Körfezi** *prev.* Akbük Limanı. *bay* W Turkey
152 H5 **Gulmarg** Jammu and Kashmir, NW India
Gulpaigan *see* Golpāyegān
99 L18 **Gulpen** Limburg, SE Netherlands
Gul'shad *see* Gul'shat
145 S13 **Gul'shat** *var.* Gul'shad. Karaganda, E Kazakhstan
81 F17 **Gulu** N Uganda
114 K10 **Gŭlŭbovo** Stara Zagora, C Bulgaria
114 I7 **Gulyantsi** Pleven, N Bulgaria
Gulyaypole *see* Hulyaypole
Guma *see* Pishan
Gümai *see* Darlag
79 K16 **Gumba** Equateur, NW Dem. Rep. Congo
Gumbinnen *see* Gusev
81 H24 **Gumbiro** Ruvuma, S Tanzania
146 B11 **Gumdag** *prev.* Kum-Dag. Balkan Welaýaty, W Turkmenistan
77 W12 **Gumel** Jigawa, N Nigeria
105 N5 **Gumiel de Hizán** Castilla-León, N Spain
Gumire *see* Gumine
153 P16 **Gumla** Jhārkhand, N India
Gumma *see* Gunma
101 F16 **Gummersbach** Nordrhein-Westfalen, W Germany
77 T13 **Gummi** Zamfara, NW Nigeria
Gumpolds *see* Humpolec
153 N13 **Gumti** *var.* Gomati. ≈ N India
Gümülcine/Gümüljina *see* Komotiní
Gümüşane *see* Gümüşhane
137 O12 **Gümüşhane** *var.* Gümüşane, Gumushkhane. Gümüşhane, NE Turkey
137 O12 **Gümüşhane** *var.* Gümüşane, Gumushkhane. ◆ *province* NE Turkey
Gumushkhane *see* Gümüşhane
171 V14 **Gumzai** Pulau Kola, E Indonesia
154 H9 **Guna** Madhya Pradesh, C India
Gunabad *see* Gonābād
Gunan *see* Qijiang
Gunbad-i-Qawus *see* Gonbad-e Kāvūs
183 O9 **Gunbar** New South Wales, SE Australia
183 O9 **Gun Creek** *seasonal river* New South Wales, SE Australia
183 Q10 **Gundagai** New South Wales, SE Australia
79 K17 **Gundji** Equateur, N Dem. Rep. Congo
155 G20 **Gundlupet** Karnātaka, W India
136 G16 **Gündoğmuş** Antalya, S Turkey
137 O14 **Güney Doğu Toroslar** ⛰ SE Turkey
79 J21 **Gungu** Bandundu, SW Dem. Rep. Congo
127 P17 **Gunib** Respublika Dagestan, SW Russian Federation
112 J11 **Gunja** Vukovar-Srijem, E Croatia
31 P9 **Gun Lake** ◎ Michigan, N USA
165 N12 **Gunma** *off.* Gunma-ken, *var.* Gumma. ◆ *prefecture* Honshū, S Japan
197 P15 **Gunnbjørn Fjeld** *var.* Gunnbjörns Bjerge. ▲ C Greenland
183 S6 **Gunnedah** New South Wales, SE Australia
173 Y15 **Gunner's Quoin** *var.* Coin de Mire. *island* N Mauritius
37 R6 **Gunnison** Colorado, C USA
36 L5 **Gunnison** Utah, W USA
37 P5 **Gunnison River** ≈ Colorado, C USA
21 X2 **Gunpowder River** ≈ Maryland, NE USA
Güns *see* Kőszeg
Gunsan *see* Kunsan
109 S4 **Gunskirchen** Oberösterreich, N Austria
Gunt *see* Ghund
155 H17 **Guntakal** Andhra Pradesh, C India
23 Q2 **Guntersville** Alabama, S USA
23 Q2 **Guntersville Lake** ▣ Alabama, S USA
109 X4 **Guntramsdorf** Niederösterreich, E Austria
155 J16 **Guntūr** *var.* Guntur. Andhra Pradesh, SE India
168 H10 **Gunungsitoli** Pulau Nias, W Indonesia
155 M14 **Gunupur** Orissa, E India
101 J23 **Günz** ≈ S Germany
Gunzan *see* Kunsan
101 J22 **Günzburg** Bayern, S Germany
101 K21 **Gunzenhausen** Bayern, S Germany
Guovdageaidu *see* Kautokeino
161 P7 **Guoyang** Anhui, E China
116 G11 **Gurahonț** *Hung.* Honctő. Arad, W Romania
Gurahumora *see* Gura Humorului

◆ Country ◇ Dependent Territory ◆ Administrative Region ▲ Mountain ▲ Volcano ◎ Lake
● Country Capital ○ Dependent Territory Capital × International Airport ⛰ Mountain Range ≈ River ▣ Reservoir

116 K9 **Gura Humorului** Ger. Gurahumora. Suceava, NE Romania
158 K4 **Gurbantünggüt Shamo** desert W China
152 H7 **Gurdāspur** Punjab, N India
27 T13 **Gurdon** Arkansas, C USA
Gurdzhaani see Gurjaani
Gurgan see Gorgān
152 I10 **Gurgaon** Haryāna, N India
59 M15 **Gurguéia, Rio** ~ NE Brazil
55 Q7 **Guri, Embalse de** ▣ E Venezuela
137 V10 **Gurjaani** Rus. Gurdzhaani. E Georgia
109 T8 **Gurk** Kärnten, S Austria
109 T9 **Gurk** Slvn. Krka. ~ S Austria
Gurkfeld see Krško
114 K9 **Gurkovo** prev. Kolupchii. Stara Zagora, C Bulgaria
109 S9 **Gurktaler Alpen** ▲▲ S Austria
146 H8 **Gurlan** Rus. Gurlen. Xorazm Viloyati, W Uzbekistan
Gurlen see Gurlan
83 M16 **Guro** Manica, C Mozambique
136 M14 **Gürün** Sivas, C Turkey
59 K16 **Gurupi** Tocantins, C Brazil
58 L12 **Gurupi, Rio** ~ NE Brazil
152 E14 **Guru Sikhar** ▲ NW India
Gur'yev/Gur'yevskaya Oblast' see Atyrau
77 U13 **Gusau** Zamfara, NW Nigeria
126 C3 **Gusev** Ger. Gumbinnen. Kaliningradskaya Oblast', W Russian Federation
146 J17 **Gushgy** Rus. Kushka. ~ S Turkmenistan
Gushgy see Serhetabat
Gushiago see Gushiegu
77 Q14 **Gushiegu** var. Gushiago. NE Ghana
165 S17 **Gushikawa** Okinawa, Okinawa, SW Japan
113 L16 **Gusinje** Montenegro, SW Serbia and Montenegro (Yugo.)
126 M4 **Gus'-Khrustal'nyy** Vladimirskaya Oblast', W Russian Federation
107 B19 **Guspini** Sardegna, Italy, C Mediterranean Sea
109 X8 **Güssing** Burgenland, SE Austria
109 V6 **Gusswerk** Steiermark, E Austria
92 O2 **Gustav Adolf Land** physical region NE Svalbard
195 X5 **Gustav Bull Mountains** ▲▲ Antarctica
39 W13 **Gustavus** Alaska, USA
92 O1 **Gustav V Land** physical region NE Svalbard
35 P9 **Gustine** California, W USA
25 R8 **Gustine** Texas, SW USA
100 M9 **Güstrow** Mecklenburg-Vorpommern, NE Germany
95 N18 **Gusum** Östergötland, S Sweden
Guta/Gúta see Kolárovo
Gutenstein see Ravne na Koroškem
101 G14 **Gütersloh** Nordrhein-Westfalen, W Germany
27 N10 **Guthrie** Oklahoma, C USA
25 P5 **Guthrie** Texas, SW USA
29 U14 **Guthrie Center** Iowa, C USA
41 Q13 **Gutiérrez Zamora** Veracruz-Llave, E Mexico
Gutta see Kolárovo
29 Y12 **Guttenberg** Iowa, C USA
Guttentag see Dobrodzień
Guttstadt see Dobre Miasto
162 G8 **Guulin** Govĭ-Altay, C Mongolia
153 V12 **Guwāhāti** prev. Gauhāti. Assam, NE India
139 R3 **Guwēr** var. Al Kuwayr, Al Quwayr, Quwair. N Iraq
146 A10 **Guwlumaýak** Rus. Kuuli-Mayak. Balkan Welaýaty, NW Turkmenistan
55 R9 **Guyana** off. Cooperative Republic of Guyana; prev. British Guiana. ◆ republic N South America
21 P5 **Guyandotte River** ~ West Virginia, NE USA
Guyane see French Guiana
Guyi see Sanjiang
26 H8 **Guymon** Oklahoma, C USA
146 K12 **Guynuk** Lebap Welaýaty, NE Turkmenistan
Guyong see Jiangle
21 O9 **Guyot, Mount** ▲ North Carolina/Tennessee, SE USA
183 U5 **Guyra** New South Wales, SE Australia
159 W10 **Guyuan** Ningxia, N China
Guzar see G'uzor
147 N13 **G'uzor** Rus. Guzar. Qashqadaryo Viloyati, S Uzbekistan
121 P2 **Güzelyurt** Gk. Mórfou, Morphou. W Cyprus
121 N2 **Güzelyurt Körfezi** var. Morfou Bay, Morphou Bay, Gk. Kólpos Mórfou. bay W Cyprus
Guzhou see Rongjiang
40 I3 **Guzmán** Chihuahua, N Mexico
119 B14 **Gvardeysk** Ger. Tapaiu. Kaliningradskaya Oblast', W Russian Federation
Gvardeyskoye see Hvardiys'ke
183 R5 **Gwabegar** New South Wales, SE Australia
148 J16 **Gwādar** var. Gwadur. Baluchistān, SW Pakistan
148 J16 **Gwādar East Bay** bay SW Pakistan
148 J16 **Gwādar West Bay** bay SW Pakistan
Gwadur see Gwādar
83 J17 **Gwai** Matabeleland North, W Zimbabwe
154 I7 **Gwalior** Madhya Pradesh, C India
83 J18 **Gwanda** Matabeleland South, SW Zimbabwe
79 N15 **Gwane** Orientale, N Dem. Rep. Congo
83 I17 **Gwayi** ~ W Zimbabwe
110 G8 **Gwda** var. Glda, Ger. Küddow. ~ NW Poland
97 C14 **Gweebarra Bay** Ir. Béal an Bheara. inlet W Ireland
97 D14 **Gweedore** Ir. Gaoth Dobhair. NW Ireland
Gwelo see Gweru
97 K21 **Gwent** cultural region S Wales, UK
83 K17 **Gweru** prev. Gwelo. Midlands, C Zimbabwe
29 Q7 **Gwinner** North Dakota, N USA
77 Y13 **Gwoza** Borno, NE Nigeria
Gwy see Wye
183 R4 **Gwydir River** ~ New South Wales, SE Australia
97 I19 **Gwynedd** var. Gwyneth. cultural region NW Wales, UK
Gwyneth see Gwynedd
159 O16 **Gyaca** var. Ngarrab. Xizang Zizhiqu, W China
Gya'gya see Saga
Gyaijêpozhanggê see Zhidoi
Gyaisi see Jiulong
115 M22 **Gyalí** var. Yialí. island Dodekánisos, Greece, Aegean Sea
Gyamotang see Dêngqên
Gyandzha see Gäncä
Gyangkar see Dinggyê
158 M16 **Gyangzê** Xizang Zizhiqu, W China
158 L14 **Gyaring Co** ◎ W China
159 Q12 **Gyaring Hu** ◎ C China
115 I20 **Gyáros** var. Yioúra. island Kykládes, Greece, Aegean Sea
122 J7 **Gyda** Yamalo-Nenetskiy Avtonomnyy Okrug, N Russian Federation
122 J7 **Gydanskiy Poluostrov** Eng. Gyda Peninsula. peninsula N Russian Federation
Gyda Peninsula see Gydanskiy Poluostrov
Gyêgu see Yushu
Gyéres see Câmpia Turzii
Gyergyószentmiklós see Gheorgheni
Gyergyótölgyes see Tulgheş
Gyertyámos see Cărpiniş
Gyeva see Detva
Gyigang see Zayü
Gyixong see Gonggar
95 I23 **Gyldenløveshøj** hill range C Denmark
181 Z10 **Gympie** Queensland, E Australia
166 L7 **Gyobingauk** Pegu, SW Myanmar
111 M23 **Gyomaendrőd** Békés, SE Hungary
Gyömbér see Ďumbier
111 L22 **Gyöngyös** Heves, NE Hungary
111 H22 **Győr** Ger. Raab; Lat. Arrabona. Győr-Moson-Sopron, NW Hungary
111 G22 **Győr-Moson-Sopron** off. Győr-Moson-Sopron Megye. ◈ county NW Hungary
11 X15 **Gypsumville** Manitoba, S Canada
12 M4 **Gyrfalcon Islands** island group Nunavut, NE Canada
95 N14 **Gysinge** Gävleborg, C Sweden
115 F22 **Gýtheio** var. Githio; prev. Yíthion. Pelepónnisos, S Greece
146 L13 **Gyuichbirleshik** Lebap Welaýaty, E Turkmenistan
111 N24 **Gyula** Rom. Jula. Békés, SE Hungary
Gyulafehérvár see Alba Iulia
Gyulovo see Roza
137 T11 **Gyumri** var. Giumri, Rus. Kumayri; prev. Aleksandropol', Leninakan. W Armenia
146 D13 **Gyunuzyndag, Gora** ▲ W Turkmenistan
Gyzylarbat see Serdar
146 J15 **Gyzylbaýdak** Rus. Krasnoye Znamya. Mary Welaýaty, S Turkmenistan
Gyzyletrek see Etrek
146 D10 **Gyzylgaýa** Rus. Kizyl-Kaya. Balkan Welaýaty, NW Turkmenistan
146 K12 **Gyzylsuw** Rus. Kizyl-Su. Balkan Welaýaty, W Turkmenistan
126 J3 **Gzhatsk** Smolenskaya Oblast', W Russian Federation

H

159 T12 **Ha** W Bhutan
Haabai see Ha'apai Group
99 H17 **Haacht** Vlaams Brabant, C Belgium
109 T4 **Haag** Niederösterreich, NE Austria
194 L8 **Haag Nunataks** ▲ Antarctica
92 N2 **Haakon VII Land** physical region NW Svalbard
98 O11 **Haaksbergen** Overijssel, E Netherlands
99 E14 **Haamstede** Zeeland, SW Netherlands
193 Y15 **Ha'ano** island Ha'apai Group, C Tonga
193 Y15 **Ha'apai Group** var. Haabai. island group C Tonga
93 L15 **Haapajärvi** Oulu, C Finland
93 L17 **Haapamäki** Länsi-Suomi, W Finland
93 L15 **Haapavesi** Oulu, C Finland
191 N7 **Haapiti** Moorea, W French Polynesia
118 F4 **Haapsalu** Ger. Hapsal. Läänemaa, W Estonia
Ha'Arava see 'Arabah, Wādī al
95 G24 **Haarby** var. Hårby. Fyn, C Denmark
98 H10 **Haarlem** prev. Harlem. Noord-Holland, W Netherlands
185 D19 **Haast** West Coast, South Island, NZ
185 C20 **Haast** ~ South Island, NZ
185 D20 **Haast Pass** pass South Island, NZ
193 W16 **Ha'atua** 'Eau, E Tonga
149 P15 **Hab** ~ SW Pakistan
141 W7 **Haba** var. Al Haba. Dubayy, NE UAE
158 K2 **Habahe** var. Kaba. Xinjiang Uygur Zizhiqu, NW China
141 U13 **Ḩabarūt** var. Habrut. SW Oman
81 J18 **Habaswein** North Eastern, NE Kenya
99 L24 **Habay-la-Neuve** Luxembourg, SE Belgium
139 S8 **Ḩabbānīyah, Buḩayrat** ◎ C Iraq
Habelschwerdt see Bystrzyca Kłodzka
153 V14 **Habiganj** Chittagong, NE Bangladesh
163 Q12 **Habirag** Nei Mongol Zizhiqu, N China
95 L19 **Habo** Västra Götaland, S Sweden
123 V14 **Habomai Islands** island group Kuril'skiye Ostrova, SE Russian Federation
165 S2 **Haboro** Hokkaidō, NE Japan
153 S16 **Habra** West Bengal, NE India
Habrut see Ḩabarūt
143 P17 **Ḩabshān** Abū Ẓaby, C UAE
54 E14 **Hacha** Putumayo, S Colombia
165 X13 **Hachijō** Tōkyō, Hachijō-jima, SE Japan
165 X13 **Hachijō-jima** var. Hatizyô Zima. island Izu-shotō, SE Japan
164 L12 **Hachiman** Gifu, Honshū, SW Japan
165 P7 **Hachimori** Akita, Honshū, C Japan
165 R7 **Hachinohe** Aomori, Honshū, C Japan
93 G17 **Hackås** Jämtland, C Sweden
18 K14 **Hackensack** New Jersey, NE USA
Hadama see Nazrēt
141 W13 **Ḩadbaram** S Oman
139 U13 **Ḩaddānīyah** well S Iraq
96 K12 **Haddington** SE Scotland, UK
141 Z8 **Ḩadd, Ra's al** headland NE Oman
Haded see Xadeed
77 W12 **Hadejia** Jigawa, N Nigeria
77 W12 **Hadejia** ~ N Nigeria
138 F9 **Ḩadera** var. Khadera. Haifa, C Israel
Hadersleben see Haderslev
95 G24 **Haderslev** Ger. Hadersleben. Sønderjylland, SW Denmark
151 J21 **Hadhdhunmathi Atoll** var. Haddummati Atoll, Laamu Atoll. atoll S Maldives
Hadhramaut see Ḩaḑramawt
141 W17 **Hadīboh** Suquṭrā, SE Yemen
158 K9 **Hadilik** Xinjiang Uygur Zizhiqu, W China
136 H16 **Hadım** Konya, S Turkey
140 K7 **Hadīyah** Al Madīnah, W Saudi Arabia
8 L5 **Hadley Bay** bay Victoria Island, Nunavut, N Canada
167 S6 **Ha Đông** var. Hadong. Ha Tây, N Vietnam
141 R15 **Ḩaḑramawt** Eng. Hadhramaut. ▲▲ S Yemen
Hadria see Adria
Hadrianopolis see Edirne
Hadria Picena see Apricena
95 G22 **Hadsten** Århus, C Denmark
95 G21 **Hadsund** Nordjylland, N Denmark
117 S4 **Hadyach** Rus. Gadyach. Poltavs'ka Oblast', NE Ukraine
112 I13 **Hadžići** Federacija Bosna I Hercegovina, SE Bosnia and Herzegovina
163 W14 **Haeju** S North Korea
Haerbin/Haerhpin/Ha-erh-pin see Harbin
141 P5 **Ḩafar al Bāţin** Ash Sharqīyah, N Saudi Arabia
11 T15 **Hafford** Saskatchewan, S Canada
136 M13 **Hafik** Sivas, N Turkey
149 V8 **Hāfizābād** Punjab, E Pakistan
92 H4 **Hafnarfjördhur** Reykjanes, W Iceland
Hafnia see København, Denmark
Hafnia see Denmark
Hafren see Severn
Hafun see Xaafuun
Hafun, Ras see Xaafuun, Raas
80 G10 **Hag 'Abdullah** Sinnar, E Sudan
81 K18 **Hagadera** North Eastern, E Kenya
138 G8 **HaGalil** Eng. Galilee. ▲ N Israel
14 G10 **Hagar** Ontario, S Canada
155 G18 **Hagari** var. Vedāvati. ~ W India
188 B16 **Hagåtña** var. Agana, Agaña. ○ (Guam) NW Guam
100 M13 **Hagelberg** hill NE Germany
39 N14 **Hagemeister Island** island Alaska, USA
101 F15 **Hagen** Nordrhein-Westfalen, W Germany
100 K10 **Hagenow** Mecklenburg-Vorpommern, N Germany
10 K15 **Hagensborg** British Columbia, SW Canada
80 I13 **Hägere Hiywet** var. Agere Hiywet, Ambo. Oromo, C Ethiopia
33 O15 **Hagerman** Idaho, NW USA
37 U14 **Hagerman** New Mexico, SW USA
21 V2 **Hagerstown** Maryland, NE USA
14 G16 **Hagersville** Ontario, S Canada
102 J15 **Hagetmau** Landes, SW France
95 K14 **Hagfors** Värmland, C Sweden
93 G16 **Häggenås** Jämtland, C Sweden
164 E12 **Hagi** Yamaguchi, Honshū, SW Japan
167 S5 **Ha Giang** Ha Giang, N Vietnam
Hagios Evstrátios see Ágios Efstrátios
HaGolan see Golan Heights
103 T4 **Hagondange** Moselle, NE France
97 B18 **Hag's Head** Ir. Ceann Caillí. headland W Ireland
102 I3 **Hague, Cap de la** headland N France
103 V5 **Haguenau** Bas-Rhin, NE France
165 X16 **Hahajima-rettō** island group SE Japan
15 R8 **Ha! Ha!, Lac** ◎ Québec, SE Canada
172 H13 **Hahaya** × (Moroni) Grande Comore, NW Comoros
22 K9 **Hahnville** Louisiana, S USA
83 E22 **Haib** Karas, S Namibia
Haibak see Āybak
149 N15 **Haibo** ~ SW Pakistan
Haibowan see Wuhai
163 U12 **Haicheng** Liaoning, NE China
Haida see Nový Bor
Haidarabad see Hyderābād
Haidenschaft see Ajdovščina
167 T6 **Hai Dương** Hai Hưng, N Vietnam
138 F9 **Haifa** ◈ district NW Israel
Haifa see Ḩefa
Haifa, Bay of see Ḩefa, Mifraẓ
161 P14 **Haifeng** Guangdong, S China
Haifong see Hai Phong
161 P3 **Hai He** ~ E China
Haikang see Leizhou
160 L17 **Haikou** var. Hai-k'ou, Hoihow, Fr. Hoï-Hao. Hainan, S China
140 M6 **Ḩā'il** Ḩā'il, NW Saudi Arabia
141 N5 **Ḩā'il** off. Minṭaqah Ḩā'il. ◈ province N Saudi Arabia
Hai-la-erh see Hailar
163 S6 **Hailar** var. Hai-la-erh; prev. Hulun. Nei Mongol Zizhiqu, N China
163 S6 **Hailar He** ~ NE China
33 P14 **Hailey** Idaho, NW USA
14 H9 **Haileybury** Ontario, S Canada
163 X9 **Hailin** Heilongjiang, NE China
Ḩā'il, Minṭaqah see Ḩā'il
Hailong see Meihekou
93 K14 **Hailuoto** Swe. Karlö. island W Finland
Haima see Haymā'
Haimen see Taizhou
160 M17 **Hainan** var. Hainan Sheng, Qiong. ◈ province S China
160 K17 **Hainan Dao** island S China
Hainan Sheng see Hainan
Hainan Strait see Qiongzhou Haixia
Hainasch see Ainaži
Hainau see Chojnów
99 E20 **Hainaut** ◈ province SW Belgium
Hainburg see Hainburg an der Donau
109 Z4 **Hainburg an der Donau** var. Hainburg. Niederösterreich, NE Austria
39 W12 **Haines** Alaska, USA
32 L12 **Haines** Oregon, NW USA
23 W12 **Haines City** Florida, SE USA
10 H8 **Haines Junction** Yukon Territory, W Canada
109 W4 **Hainfeld** Niederösterreich, NE Austria
101 N16 **Hainichen** Sachsen, E Germany
167 T6 **Hai Phong** var. Haifong, Haiphong. N Vietnam
161 S12 **Haitan Dao** island SE China
44 K8 **Haiti** off. Republic of Haiti. ◆ republic C West Indies
35 T11 **Haiwee Reservoir** ▣ California, W USA
80 I7 **Haiya** Red Sea, NE Sudan
159 T10 **Haiyan** var. Sanjiaocheng. Qinghai, W China
160 M13 **Haiyang Shan** ▲▲ S China
159 V10 **Haiyuan** Ningxia, N China
Hajda see Nový Bor
111 M22 **Hajdú-Bihar** off. Hajdú-Bihar Megye. ◈ county E Hungary
111 N22 **Hajdúböszörmény** Hajdú-Bihar, E Hungary
111 N22 **Hajdúhadház** Hajdú-Bihar, E Hungary
111 N21 **Hajdúnánás** Hajdú-Bihar, E Hungary
111 N22 **Hajdúszoboszló** Hajdú-Bihar, E Hungary
142 I3 **Ḩājī Ebrāhīm, Kūh-e** ▲ Iran/Iraq
165 O9 **Hajiki-zaki** headland Sado, C Japan
Hajine see Abū Ḩardān
153 P13 **Hājīpur** Bihār, N India
141 N14 **Ḩajjah** W Yemen
139 U11 **Ḩajjama** S Iraq
143 R12 **Ḩājjīābād** Hormozgān, C Iran
139 U14 **Ḩājj, Thaqb al** well S Iraq
113 L16 **Hajla** ▲ SW Serbia and Montenegro (Yugo.)
110 P10 **Hajnówka** Ger. Hermhausen. Podlaskie, NE Poland
166 K4 **Haka** Chin State, W Myanmar
Hakapehi see Punaauia
Hakâri see Hakkâri
137 T16 **Hakkâri** var. Çölemerik, Hakâri. Hakkâri, SE Turkey
137 T16 **Hakkâri** var. Hakkari. ◈ province SE Turkey
92 J12 **Hakkas** Norrbotten, N Sweden
164 J14 **Hakken-zan** ▲ Honshū, SW Japan
165 R7 **Hakkōda-san** ▲ Honshū, C Japan
165 T2 **Hako-dake** ▲ Hokkaidō, NE Japan
165 R5 **Hakodate** Hokkaidō, NE Japan
164 L11 **Hakui** Ishikawa, Honshū, SW Japan
190 B16 **Hakupu** SE Niue
164 L12 **Haku-san** ▲ Honshū, SW Japan
Hal see Halle
149 Q15 **Hāla** Sind, SE Pakistan
138 J3 **Ḩalab** Eng. Aleppo, Fr. Alep; anc. Beroea. Ḩalab, NW Syria
138 J3 **Ḩalab** off. Muḩāfaẓat Ḩalab, var. Aleppo, Halab. ◈ governorate NW Syria
138 J3 **Ḩalab** × Ḩalab, NW Syria
141 O8 **Ḩalabān** var. Halībān. Ar Riyāḑ, C Saudi Arabia
139 V4 **Ḩalabja** NE Iraq
146 L13 **Halaç** Rus. Khalach. Lebap Welaýaty, E Turkmenistan
190 A16 **Halagigie Point** headland W Niue
75 Z11 **Halaib** SE Egypt
190 G12 **Halalo** Île Uvea, N Wallis and Futuna
Halandri see Chalándri
141 X13 **Ḩalāniyāt, Juzur al** var. Jazā'ir Bin Ghalfān, Eng. Kuria Muria Islands. island group S Oman
141 W13 **Ḩalāniyāt, Khalīj al** Eng. Kuria Muria Bay. bay S Oman
Halas see Kiskunhalas
38 G11 **Hālawa** var. Halawa. Hawai'i, USA, C Pacific Ocean
38 F9 **Hālawa, Cape** var. Cape Halawa headland Moloka'i, Hawai'i, USA, C Pacific Ocean
162 H6 **Halban** Hövsgöl, N Mongolia
101 K14 **Halberstadt** Sachsen-Anhalt, C Germany
184 M12 **Halcombe** Manawatu-Wanganui, North Island, NZ
95 I16 **Halden** prev. Fredrikshald. Østfold, S Norway
100 L13 **Haldensleben** Sachsen-Anhalt, C Germany
Háldi see Halti
153 S17 **Haldia** West Bengal, NE India
152 K10 **Haldwāni** Uttaranchal, N India
38 F10 **Haleakalā** var. Haleakala crater Maui, Hawai'i, USA, C Pacific Ocean
25 N4 **Hale Center** Texas, SW USA
99 J18 **Halen** Limburg, NE Belgium
23 O2 **Haleyville** Alabama, S USA
77 O17 **Half Assini** SW Ghana
35 R8 **Half Dome** ▲ California, W USA
185 C25 **Halfmoon Bay** var. Oban. Stewart Island, Southland, NZ
182 E5 **Half Moon Lake** salt lake South Australia
163 R7 **Halhgol** Dornod, E Mongolia
Haliacmon see Aliákmonas
Halibān see Ḩalabān
14 I13 **Haliburton** Ontario, SE Canada
14 I12 **Haliburton Highlands** var. Madawaska Highlands. hill range Ontario, SE Canada
13 Q15 **Halifax** Nova Scotia, SE Canada
97 L17 **Halifax** N England, UK
21 W8 **Halifax** North Carolina, SE USA
21 U7 **Halifax** Virginia, NE USA
13 Q15 **Halifax** × Nova Scotia, SE Canada
143 T13 **Halīl Rūd** seasonal river SE Iran
138 I6 **Ḩalīmah** ▲ Lebanon/Syria
162 G8 **Haliun** Govĭ-Altay, W Mongolia
118 I3 **Haljala** Ger. Halljal. Lääne-Virumaa, N Estonia
39 Q4 **Halkett, Cape** headland Alaska, USA
Halkida see Chalkída
96 J6 **Halkirk** N Scotland, UK
15 X7 **Hall** ~ Québec, SE Canada
Hall see Schwäbisch Hall
93 H15 **Hälla** Västerbotten, N Sweden
96 J6 **Halladale** ~ N Scotland, UK
95 J21 **Halland** ◈ county S Sweden
23 Z15 **Hallandale** Florida, SE USA
95 K22 **Hallandsås** physical region S Sweden
9 P6 **Hall Beach** Nunavut, N Canada
99 G19 **Halle** Fr. Hal. Vlaams Brabant, C Belgium
101 M15 **Halle** var. Halle an der Saale. Sachsen-Anhalt, C Germany
Halle an der Saale see Halle
35 W3 **Halleck** Nevada, W USA
95 L15 **Hällefors** Örebro, C Sweden
95 N16 **Hälleforsnäs** Södermanland, C Sweden
109 Q6 **Hallein** Salzburg, N Austria
101 L15 **Halle-Neustadt** Sachsen-Anhalt, C Germany
25 U12 **Hallettsville** Texas, SW USA
195 N4 **Halley** UK research station Antarctica
28 L4 **Halliday** North Dakota, N USA
37 S2 **Halligan Reservoir** ▣ Colorado, C USA
100 G7 **Halligen** island group N Germany
94 G13 **Hallingdal** valley S Norway
38 J12 **Hall Island** island Alaska, USA
Hall Island see Maiana
189 P15 **Hall Islands** island group C Micronesia
118 H6 **Halliste** ~ S Estonia
Halljal see Haljala
93 I15 **Hällnäs** Västerbotten, N Sweden
29 R2 **Hallock** Minnesota, N USA
9 S6 **Hall Peninsula** peninsula Baffin Island, Nunavut, NE Canada
20 F9 **Halls** Tennessee, S USA
95 M16 **Hallsberg** Örebro, C Sweden
181 N5 **Halls Creek** Western Australia
182 L12 **Halls Gap** Victoria, SE Australia
95 N15 **Hallstahammar** Västmanland, C Sweden
109 R6 **Hallstatt** Salzburg, W Austria
109 R6 **Hallstatter See** ◎ C Austria
95 P14 **Hallstavik** Stockholm, C Sweden
24 X7 **Hallsville** Texas, SW USA
103 P1 **Halluin** Nord, N France
Halmahera, Laut see Halmahera Sea
171 R11 **Halmahera, Pulau** prev. Djailolo, Gilolo, Jailolo. island E Indonesia
171 S12 **Halmahera Sea** Ind. Laut Halmahera. sea E Indonesia
95 J21 **Halmstad** Halland, S Sweden
119 N15 **Halowchyn** Rus. Golovchin. Mahilyowskaya Voblasts', E Belarus
95 H20 **Hals** Nordjylland, N Denmark
94 F8 **Halsa** Møre og Romsdal, S Norway
119 I15 **Hal'shany** Rus. Gol'shany. Hrodzyenskaya Voblasts', W Belarus
Hälsingborg see Helsingborg
29 R5 **Halstad** Minnesota, N USA
27 N6 **Halstead** Kansas, C USA
99 G15 **Halsteren** Noord-Brabant, S Netherlands
93 L16 **Halsua** Länsi-Suomi, W Finland
101 E14 **Haltern** Nordrhein-Westfalen, W Germany
92 J9 **Halti** var. Haltiatunturi, Lapp. Háldi. ▲ Finland/Norway
Haltiatunturi see Halti
116 J6 **Halych** Ivano-Frankivs'ka Oblast', W Ukraine
Halycus see Platani
103 P3 **Ham** Somme, N France
Hama see Ḩamāh
164 F12 **Hamada** Shimane, Honshū, SW Japan
142 L6 **Hamadān** anc. Ecbatana. Hamadān, W Iran
142 L6 **Hamadān** off. Ostān-e Hamadān. ◈ province W Iran
138 I5 **Ḩamāh** var. Hama; anc. Epiphania, Bibl. Hamath. Ḩamāh, W Syria
138 I5 **Ḩamāh** off. Muḩāfaẓat Ḩamāh, var. Hama. ◈ governorate C Syria
165 S3 **Hamamasu** Hokkaidō, NE Japan
164 L14 **Hamamatsu** var. Hamamatu. Shizuoka, Honshū, S Japan
Hamamatu see Hamamatsu
165 W14 **Hamanaka** Hokkaidō, NE Japan
164 L14 **Hamana-ko** ◎ Honshū, S Japan
94 I13 **Hamar** prev. Storhammer. Hedmark, S Norway
141 U10 **Ḩamārīr al Kidan, Qalamat** well E Saudi Arabia
164 I12 **Hamasaka** Hyōgo, Honshū, SW Japan
Hamath see Ḩamāh
165 T1 **Hamatonbetsu** Hokkaidō, NE Japan
155 K26 **Hambantota** Southern Province, SE Sri Lanka
Hambourg see Hamburg
100 J9 **Hamburg** Hamburg, N Germany
27 V14 **Hamburg** Arkansas, C USA
29 S16 **Hamburg** Iowa, C USA
18 D10 **Hamburg** New York, NE USA
100 I10 **Hamburg** Fr. Hambourg. ◈ state N Germany
148 K5 **Hamdam Āb, Dasht-e** Pash. Dasht-i Hamdamab. ▲ W Afghanistan
Hamdamab, Dasht-i see Hamdam Āb, Dasht-e
18 M13 **Hamden** Connecticut, NE USA
140 K6 **Ḩamḑ, Wādī al** dry watercourse W Saudi Arabia
93 K18 **Hämeenkyrö** Länsi-Suomi, W Finland
93 L19 **Hämeenlinna** Swe. Tavastehus. Etelä-Suomi, S Finland
HaMelah, Yam see Dead Sea
Hamelin see Hameln
100 I13 **Hameln** Eng. Hamelin. Niedersachsen, N Germany
180 I8 **Hamersley Range** ▲▲ Western Australia
163 Y12 **Hamgyŏng-sanmaek** ▲▲ N North Korea
163 X13 **Hamhŭng** C North Korea
159 O6 **Hami** var. Ha-mi, Uigh. Kumul, Qomul. Xinjiang Uygur Zizhiqu, NW China
139 X10 **Ḩāmid Amīn** E Iraq
141 W11 **Ḩāmidān, Khawr** oasis SE Saudi Arabia
138 H5 **Ḩamīdīyah** var. Hamīdīyé. Ṭarṭūs, W Syria
114 L12 **Hamidiye** Edirne, NW Turkey
Hamīdīyé see Ḩamīdīyah
182 L12 **Hamilton** Victoria, SE Australia
64 B12 **Hamilton** ○ (Bermuda) C Bermuda
14 G16 **Hamilton** Ontario, S Canada
184 M7 **Hamilton** Waikato, North Island, NZ
96 I12 **Hamilton** S Scotland, UK
23 N3 **Hamilton** Alabama, S USA
38 M10 **Hamilton** Alaska, USA
30 J13 **Hamilton** Illinois, N USA
27 S3 **Hamilton** Missouri, C USA
33 P10 **Hamilton** Montana, NW USA
25 S8 **Hamilton** Texas, SW USA
14 G16 **Hamilton** × Ontario, SE Canada
64 I6 **Hamilton Bank** undersea feature SE Labrador Sea
182 E1 **Hamilton Creek** seasonal river South Australia
13 R8 **Hamilton Inlet** inlet Newfoundland and Labrador, E Canada
27 T12 **Hamilton, Lake** ▣ Arkansas, C USA
35 W6 **Hamilton, Mount** ▲ Nevada, W USA
75 S8 **Ḩamīm, Wādī al** ~ NE Libya
93 N19 **Hamina** Swe. Fredrikshamn. Etelä-Suomi, S Finland
11 W16 **Hamiota** Manitoba, S Canada
152 L13 **Hamīrpur** Uttar Pradesh, N India
Hamïs Musait see Khamīs Mushayt
21 T11 **Hamlet** North Carolina, SE USA
25 P6 **Hamlin** Texas, SW USA
21 P5 **Hamlin** West Virginia, NE USA
31 O7 **Hamlin Lake** ◎ Michigan, N USA

◆ Country ● Country Capital ◇ Dependent Territory ○ Dependent Territory Capital ◈ Administrative Region × International Airport ▲ Mountain ▲▲ Mountain Range ☒ Volcano ~ River ◎ Lake ▣ Reservoir

101 F14 **Hamm** var. Hamm in Westfalen. Nordrhein-Westfalen, W Germany
Ḩammāmāt, Khalīj al see Hammamet, Golfe de
75 N5 **Hammamet, Golfe de** Ar. Khalīj al Ḩammāmāt. gulf NE Tunisia
139 R3 **Ḩammān al 'Alīl** N Iraq
139 X12 **Ḩammār, Hawr al** ◎ SE Iraq
93 J20 **Hammarland** Åland, SW Finland
93 H16 **Hammarstrand** Jämtland, C Sweden
93 O17 **Hammaslahti** Itä-Suomi, E Finland
99 F17 **Hamme** Oost-Vlaanderen, NW Belgium
100 H10 **Hamme** ≈ NW Germany
95 G22 **Hammel** Århus, C Denmark
101 I18 **Hammelburg** Bayern, C Germany
99 H18 **Hamme-Mille** Wallon Brabant, C Belgium
100 H10 **Hamme-Oste-Kanal** canal NW Germany
93 G16 **Hammerdal** Jämtland, C Sweden
92 K8 **Hammerfest** Finnmark, N Norway
101 D14 **Hamminkeln** Nordrhein-Westfalen, W Germany
Hamm in Westfalen see Hamm
26 K10 **Hammon** Oklahoma, C USA
31 N11 **Hammond** Indiana, N USA
22 K8 **Hammond** Louisiana, S USA
99 K20 **Hamoir** Liège, E Belgium
99 J21 **Hamois** Namur, SE Belgium
99 K16 **Hamont** Limburg, NE Belgium
185 F22 **Hampden** Otago, South Island, NZ
19 R6 **Hampden** Maine, NE USA
97 M23 **Hampshire** cultural region S England, UK
13 O15 **Hampton** New Brunswick, SE Canada
27 U14 **Hampton** Arkansas, C USA
29 V12 **Hampton** Iowa, C USA
19 P10 **Hampton** New Hampshire, NE USA
21 R14 **Hampton** South Carolina, SE USA
21 P8 **Hampton** Tennessee, S USA
21 X7 **Hampton** Virginia, NE USA
94 L11 **Hamra** Gävleborg, C Sweden
80 D10 **Hamrat esh Sheikh** Northern Kordofan, C Sudan
139 S5 **Ḩamrīn, Jabal** ▲ N Iraq
121 P16 **Hamrun** C Malta
167 U14 **Ham Thuân Nam** Binh Thuân, S Vietnam
Hāmūn, Daryācheh-ye see Şāberī, Hāmūn-e/Sīstān, Daryācheh-ye
Hamwih see Southampton
38 G10 **Hāna** var. Hana. Maui, Hawai'i, USA, C Pacific Ocean
21 S14 **Hanahan** South Carolina, SE USA
38 B8 **Hanalei** Kaua'i, Hawai'i, USA, C Pacific Ocean
167 U10 **Ha Nam** Quang Nam-Đa Nãng, C Vietnam
165 Q9 **Hanamaki** Iwate, Honshū, C Japan
38 F10 **Hanamanioa, Cape** headland Maui, Hawai'i, USA, C Pacific Ocean
190 B16 **Hanan** × (Alofi) SW Niue
101 H18 **Hanau** Hessen, W Germany
8 L9 **Hanbury** ≈ Northwest Territories, NW Canada
Hâncești see Hîncești
10 M15 **Hanceville** British Columbia, SW Canada
23 P3 **Hanceville** Alabama, S USA
Hancewicze see Hantsavichy
160 L6 **Hancheng** Shaanxi, C China
21 V2 **Hancock** Maryland, NE USA
30 M3 **Hancock** Michigan, N USA
29 S8 **Hancock** Minnesota, N USA
18 I12 **Hancock** New York, NE USA
80 Q12 **Handa** Bari, NE Somalia
161 O5 **Handan** var. Han-tan. Hebei, E China
95 P16 **Handen** Stockholm, C Sweden
81 J22 **Handeni** Tanga, E Tanzania
37 Q7 **Handies Peak** ▲ Colorado, C USA
111 J19 **Handlová** Ger. Krickerhäu, Hung. Nyitrabánya; prev. Ger. Kriegerhaj. Trenčiansky Kraj, W Slovakia
165 O13 **Haneda** × (Tōkyō) Tōkyō, Honshū, S Japan
138 F13 **HaNegev** Eng. Negev. desert S Israel
35 Q11 **Hanford** California, W USA
191 V16 **Hanga Roa** Easter Island, Chile, E Pacific Ocean
162 H7 **Hangayn Nuruu** ▲▲ C Mongolia
Hang-chou/Hangchow see Hangzhou
95 K20 **Hånger** Jönköping, S Sweden
Hangö see Hanko
161 R9 **Hangzhou** var. Hang-chou, Hangchow. Zhejiang, SE China
162 F5 **Hanhöhiy Uul** ▲▲ NW Mongolia
146 I14 **Hanhowuz** Rus. Khauz-Khan. Ahal Welaýaty, S Turkmenistan
146 I14 **Hanhowuz Suw Howdany** Rus. Khauzkhanskoye Vodokhranilishche. ⊠ S Turkmenistan
137 P15 **Hani** Diyarbakır, SE Turkey
Hania see Chaniá
141 R11 **Ḩanīsh al Kabīr, Jazīrat al** island SW Yemen
Hanka, Lake see Khanka, Lake
93 M17 **Hankasalmi** Länsi-Suomi, W Finland
29 R7 **Hankinson** North Dakota, N USA
93 K20 **Hanko** Swe. Hangö. Etelä-Suomi, SW Finland
Han-kou/Han-k'ou/Hankow see Wuhan
36 M6 **Hanksville** Utah, W USA
152 K6 **Hanle** Jammu and Kashmir, NW India
185 I17 **Hanmer Springs** Canterbury, South Island, NZ
11 R16 **Hanna** Alberta, SW Canada
27 V3 **Hannibal** Missouri, C USA
180 M3 **Hann, Mount** ▲ Western Australia
100 I12 **Hannover** Eng. Hanover. Niedersachsen, NW Germany
99 J19 **Hannut** Liège, C Belgium
95 L22 **Hanöbukten** bay S Sweden
167 T6 **Ha Nôi** Eng. Hanoi, Fr. Hanoï. ● (Vietnam) N Vietnam
14 F14 **Hanover** Ontario, S Canada
31 P15 **Hanover** Indiana, N USA
18 G16 **Hanover** Pennsylvania, NE USA
21 W6 **Hanover** Virginia, NE USA
Hanover see Hannover
63 G23 **Hanover, Isla** island S Chile
Hanselbeck see Érd
195 X5 **Hansen Mountains** ▲▲ Antarctica
160 M8 **Han Shui** ≈ C China
152 H10 **Hānsi** Haryāna, NW India
95 F20 **Hanstholm** Viborg, NW Denmark
Han-tan see Handan
158 H6 **Hantengri Feng** var. Pik Khan-Tengri. ▲ China/Kazakhstan see also Khan-Tengri, Pik
119 I18 **Hantsavichy** Pol. Hancewicze, Rus. Gantsevichi. Brestskaya Voblasts', SW Belarus
9 Q6 **Hantzsch** ≈ Baffin Island, Nunavut, NE Canada
152 G9 **Hanumāngarh** Rājasthān, NW India
183 O9 **Hanwood** New South Wales, SE Australia
Hanyang see Caidian
Hanyang see Wuhan
160 H10 **Hanyuan** var. Fulin. Sichuan, C China
Hanyuan see Xihe
160 J7 **Hanzhong** Shaanxi, C China
191 W11 **Hao** atoll Îles Tuamotu, C French Polynesia
153 S16 **Hāora** prev. Howrah. West Bengal, NE India
78 K8 **Haouach, Ouadi** dry watercourse E Chad
92 K13 **Haparanda** Norrbotten, N Sweden
25 N3 **Happy** Texas, SW USA
34 M1 **Happy Camp** California, W USA
13 Q9 **Happy Valley-Goose Bay** prev. Goose Bay. Newfoundland and Labrador, E Canada
Hapsal see Haapsalu
152 J10 **Hāpur** Uttar Pradesh, N India
138 F12 **HaQatan, HaMakhtesh** ▲ S Israel
140 I4 **Ḩaql** Tabūk, NW Saudi Arabia
171 U14 **Har** Pulau Kai Besar, E Indonesia
162 M8 **Haraat** Dundgovĭ, C Mongolia
141 R8 **Ḩaraḑ** var. Haradh. Ash Sharqīyah, E Saudi Arabia
Haradh see Ḩaraḑ
118 N12 **Haradok** Rus. Gorodok. Vitsyebskaya Voblasts', N Belarus
92 J13 **Harads** Norrbotten, N Sweden
119 G19 **Haradzyets** Rus. Gorodets. Brestskaya Voblasts', SW Belarus
119 J17 **Haradzyeya** Rus. Gorodeya. Minskaya Voblasts', C Belarus
191 V10 **Haraiki** atoll Îles Tuamotu, C French Polynesia
165 Q11 **Haramachi** Fukushima, Honshū, E Japan
118 M12 **Harany** Rus. Gorany. Vitsyebskaya Voblasts', N Belarus
83 L16 **Harare** prev. Salisbury. ● (Zimbabwe) Mashonaland East, NE Zimbabwe
83 L16 **Harare** × Mashonaland East, NE Zimbabwe
78 J10 **Haraz-Djombo** Batha, C Chad
119 O16 **Harbavichy** Rus. Gorbovichi. Mahilyowskaya Voblasts', E Belarus
76 J16 **Harbel** W Liberia
163 W8 **Harbin** var. Haerbin, Ha-erh-pin, Kharbin; prev. Haerhpin, Pingkiang, Pinkiang. Heilongjiang, NE China
31 S7 **Harbor Beach** Michigan, N USA
13 T13 **Harbour Breton** Newfoundland and Labrador, E Canada
65 D25 **Harbours, Bay of** bay East Falkland, Falkland Islands
Hårby see Haarby
36 I13 **Harcuvar Mountains** ▲▲ Arizona, SW USA
108 I7 **Hard** Vorarlberg, NW Austria
154 H11 **Harda Khās** Madhya Pradesh, C India
95 D14 **Hardanger** physical region S Norway
95 D14 **Hardangerfjorden** fjord S Norway
94 E13 **Hardangerjøkulen** glacier S Norway
95 E14 **Hardangervidda** plateau S Norway
83 D20 **Hardap** ◈ district S Namibia
21 R15 **Hardeeville** South Carolina, SE USA
98 L5 **Hardegarijp** Fris. Hurdegaryp. Friesland, N Netherlands
98 O9 **Hardenberg** Overijssel, E Netherlands
183 Q9 **Harden-Murrumburrah** New South Wales, SE Australia
98 K10 **Harderwijk** Gelderland, C Netherlands
30 J14 **Hardin** Illinois, N USA
33 V11 **Hardin** Montana, NW USA
23 R5 **Harding, Lake** ⊠ Alabama/Georgia, SE USA
20 J6 **Hardinsburg** Kentucky, S USA
98 I13 **Hardinxveld-Giessendam** Zuid-Holland, C Netherlands
11 R15 **Hardisty** Alberta, SW Canada
152 L12 **Hardoi** Uttar Pradesh, N India
23 U4 **Hardwick** Georgia, SE USA
27 W9 **Hardy** Arkansas, C USA
94 D10 **Hareid** Møre og Romsdal, S Norway
8 H7 **Hare Indian** ≈ Northwest Territories, NW Canada
99 D18 **Harelbeke** var. Harlebeke. West-Vlaanderen, W Belgium
Harem see Ḩārim
100 E11 **Haren** Niedersachsen, NW Germany
98 N6 **Haren** Groningen, NE Netherlands
80 L13 **Hārer** Hārer, E Ethiopia
95 P14 **Harg** Uppsala, C Sweden
Hargeisa see Hargeysa
80 M13 **Hargeysa** var. Hargeisa. Woqooyi Galbeed, NW Somalia
116 J10 **Harghita** ◈ county NE Romania
25 S17 **Hargill** Texas, SW USA
162 J8 **Harhorin** Övörhangay, C Mongolia
159 Q9 **Har Hu** ◎ C China
Hariana see Haryāna
141 P15 **Ḩarīb** W Yemen
168 M12 **Hari, Batang** prev. Djambi. ≈ Sumatera, W Indonesia
152 J9 **Haridwār** prev. Hardwar. Uttaranchal, N India
155 F18 **Harihar** Karnātaka, W India
185 F18 **Harihari** West Coast, South Island, NZ
138 I3 **Ḩārim** var. Harem. Idlib, W Syria
98 F13 **Haringvliet** channel SW Netherlands
98 F13 **Haringvlietdam** dam SW Netherlands
149 U5 **Harīpur** North-West Frontier Province, NW Pakistan
148 J4 **Harīrūd** var. Tedzhen, Turkm. Tejen. ≈ Afghanistan/Iran see also Tejen
93 K18 **Harjavalta** Länsi-Suomi, W Finland
Härjehågna see Østrehogna
118 G4 **Harjumaa** off. Harju Maakond. ◈ province NW Estonia
21 X11 **Harkers Island** North Carolina, SE USA
139 S1 **Harki** N Iraq
29 T14 **Harlan** Iowa, C USA
21 O7 **Harlan** Kentucky, S USA
29 N17 **Harlan County Lake** ⊠ Nebraska, C USA
116 L9 **Hârlău** var. Hîrlău. Iași, NE Romania
Harlebeke see Harelbeke
33 U7 **Harlem** Montana, NW USA
Harlem see Haarlem
95 G22 **Harlev** Århus, C Denmark
98 K6 **Harlingen** Fris. Harns. Friesland, N Netherlands
25 T17 **Harlingen** Texas, SW USA
97 O21 **Harlow** E England, UK
33 T10 **Harlowton** Montana, NW USA
94 N11 **Harmånger** Gävleborg, C Sweden
98 I11 **Harmelen** Utrecht, C Netherlands
29 X11 **Harmony** Minnesota, N USA
32 J14 **Harney Basin** basin Oregon, NW USA
(0) F9 **Harney Basin** ▲▲ Oregon, NW USA
32 J14 **Harney Lake** ◎ Oregon, NW USA
28 J10 **Harney Peak** ▲ South Dakota, N USA
93 H17 **Härnösand** var. Hernösand. Västernorrland, C Sweden
Harns see Harlingen
162 F6 **Har Nuur** ◎ NW Mongolia
105 P4 **Haro** La Rioja, N Spain
40 F6 **Haro, Cabo** headland NW Mexico
94 D9 **Harøy** island S Norway
97 N21 **Harpenden** E England, UK
76 L18 **Harper** var. Cape Palmas. NE Liberia
26 M7 **Harper** Kansas, C USA
32 L13 **Harper** Oregon, NW USA
25 Q10 **Harper** Texas, SW USA
35 U13 **Harper Lake** salt flat California, W USA
39 T9 **Harper, Mount** ▲ Alaska, USA
95 J21 **Harplinge** Halland, S Sweden
36 J13 **Harquahala Mountains** ▲▲ Arizona, SW USA
141 T15 **Ḩarrah** SE Yemen
12 H11 **Harricana** ≈ Québec, SE Canada
20 M9 **Harriman** Tennessee, S USA
13 R11 **Harrington Harbour** Québec, E Canada
64 B12 **Harrington Sound** bay Bermuda, NW Atlantic Ocean
96 F8 **Harris** physical region NW Scotland, UK
27 X10 **Harrisburg** Arkansas, C USA
30 M17 **Harrisburg** Illinois, N USA
28 I14 **Harrisburg** Nebraska, C USA
32 F12 **Harrisburg** Oregon, NW USA
18 G15 **Harrisburg** state capital Pennsylvania, NE USA
182 F6 **Harris, Lake** ◎ South Australia
23 W11 **Harris, Lake** ◎ Florida, SE USA
83 J22 **Harrismith** Free State, E South Africa
27 T9 **Harrison** Arkansas, C USA
31 Q7 **Harrison** Michigan, N USA
28 I12 **Harrison** Nebraska, C USA
39 Q5 **Harrison Bay** inlet Alaska, USA
22 I6 **Harrisonburg** Louisiana, S USA
21 U4 **Harrisonburg** Virginia, NE USA
13 R7 **Harrison, Cape** headland Newfoundland and Labrador, E Canada
27 R5 **Harrisonville** Missouri, C USA
Harris Ridge see Lomonosov Ridge
192 M3 **Harris Seamount** undersea feature N Pacific Ocean
96 F8 **Harris, Sound of** strait NW Scotland, UK
31 R6 **Harrisville** Michigan, N USA
21 R3 **Harrisville** West Virginia, NE USA
20 M6 **Harrodsburg** Kentucky, S USA
97 M16 **Harrogate** N England, UK
25 Q4 **Harrold** Texas, SW USA
27 S5 **Harry S.Truman Reservoir** ⊠ Missouri, C USA
100 G13 **Harsewinkel** Nordrhein-Westfalen, W Germany
116 M14 **Hârşova** prev. Hîrşova. Constanţa, SE Romania
92 H10 **Harstad** Troms, N Norway
31 O8 **Hart** Michigan, N USA
24 M4 **Hart** Texas, SW USA
10 I5 **Hart** ≈ Yukon Territory, NW Canada
83 F23 **Hartbees** ≈ C South Africa
109 X7 **Hartberg** Steiermark, SE Austria
182 I10 **Hart, Cape** headland South Australia
95 E14 **Hårteigen** ▲ S Norway
23 Q7 **Hartford** Alabama, S USA
27 R11 **Hartford** Arkansas, C USA
18 M12 **Hartford** state capital Connecticut, NE USA
20 J6 **Hartford** Kentucky, S USA
31 P10 **Hartford** Michigan, N USA
29 R11 **Hartford** South Dakota, N USA
30 M8 **Hartford** Wisconsin, N USA
31 P13 **Hartford City** Indiana, N USA
29 Q13 **Hartington** Nebraska, C USA
13 N14 **Hartland** New Brunswick, SE Canada
97 H23 **Hartland Point** headland SW England, UK
97 M15 **Hartlepool** N England, UK
29 T12 **Hartley** Iowa, C USA
24 M1 **Hartley** Texas, SW USA
32 J15 **Hart Mountain** ▲ Oregon, W USA
173 U10 **Hartog Ridge** undersea feature W Indian Ocean
93 M18 **Hartola** Etelä-Suomi, S Finland
67 U14 **Harts** var. Hartz. ≈ N South Africa
23 P2 **Hartselle** Alabama, S USA
23 S3 **Hartsfield Atlanta** × Georgia, SE USA
27 Q11 **Hartshorne** Oklahoma, C USA
21 S12 **Hartsville** South Carolina, SE USA
20 K8 **Hartsville** Tennessee, S USA
27 U7 **Hartville** Missouri, C USA
23 U2 **Hartwell** Georgia, SE USA
21 O11 **Hartwell Lake** ⊠ Georgia/South Carolina, SE USA
Hartz see Harts
Harunabad see Eslāmābād
162 E6 **Har-Us** Hovd, W Mongolia
162 E6 **Har Us Nuur** ◎ NW Mongolia
30 M10 **Harvard** Illinois, N USA
29 P16 **Harvard** Nebraska, C USA
37 R5 **Harvard, Mount** ▲ Colorado, C USA
31 N11 **Harvey** Illinois, N USA
29 N4 **Harvey** North Dakota, N USA
97 Q21 **Harwich** E England, UK
152 H10 **Haryāna** var. Hariana. ◈ state N India
141 Y9 **Ḩaryān, Ţawī al** spring/well NE Oman
101 J14 **Harz** ▲▲ C Germany
Hasakah see Al Ḩasakah
165 Q9 **Hasama** Miyagi, Honshū, C Japan
136 J15 **Hasan Dağı** ▲ C Turkey
139 T9 **Ḩasan Ibn Ḩassūn** C Iraq
149 R6 **Ḩasan Khēl** var. Ahmad Khel. Paktīā, SE Afghanistan
100 F12 **Hase** ≈ NW Germany
Haselberg see Krasnoznamensk
100 F12 **Haselünne** Niedersachsen, NW Germany
162 K9 **Hashaat** Dundgovĭ, C Mongolia
Hashemite Kingdom of Jordan see Jordan
139 V8 **Hāshimah** E Iraq
141 W13 **Ḩāsik** S Oman
149 U9 **Hāsilpur** Punjab, E Pakistan
Hasimoto see Hashimoto
27 Q10 **Haskell** Oklahoma, C USA
25 Q6 **Haskell** Texas, SW USA
114 M11 **Hasköy** Edirne, NW Turkey
95 L24 **Hasle** Bornholm, E Denmark
97 N23 **Haslemere** SE England, UK
102 I16 **Hasparren** Pyrénées-Atlantiques, SW France
Hassakeh see Al Ḩasakah
155 G19 **Hassan** Karnātaka, W India
36 J13 **Hassayampa River** ≈ Arizona, SW USA
101 J18 **Hassberge** hill range C Germany
94 N10 **Hassela** Gävleborg, C Sweden
99 J18 **Hasselt** Limburg, NE Belgium
98 M9 **Hasselt** Overijssel, E Netherlands
Hassetché see Al Ḩasakah
101 J18 **Hassfurt** Bayern, C Germany
74 L9 **Hassi Bel Guebbour** E Algeria
74 L8 **Hassi Messaoud** E Algeria
95 K22 **Hässleholm** Skåne, S Sweden
Hasta Colonia/Hasta Pompeia see Asti
183 O13 **Hastings** Victoria, SE Australia
184 O11 **Hastings** Hawke's Bay, North Island, NZ
97 P23 **Hastings** SE England, UK
31 P9 **Hastings** Michigan, N USA
29 W9 **Hastings** Minnesota, N USA
29 P16 **Hastings** Nebraska, C USA
95 K22 **Hästveda** Skåne, S Sweden
92 J8 **Hasvik** Finnmark, N Norway
37 V6 **Haswell** Colorado, C USA
162 I10 **Hatansuudal** Bayanhongor, C Mongolia
163 P9 **Hatavch** Sühbaatar, E Mongolia
136 K17 **Hatay** ◈ province S Turkey
37 R15 **Hatch** New Mexico, SW USA
36 K7 **Hatch** Utah, W USA
20 F9 **Hatchie River** ≈ Tennessee, S USA
116 G12 **Haţeg** Ger. Wallenthal, Hung. Hátszeg; prev. Hatzeg, Hötzing. Hunedoara, SW Romania
165 O17 **Hateruma-jima** island Yaeyama-shotō, SW Japan
183 N8 **Hatfield** New South Wales, SE Australia
162 I5 **Hatgal** Hövsgöl, N Mongolia
153 V16 **Hathazari** Chittagong, SE Bangladesh
141 T13 **Hathūt, Hişā'** oasis NE Yemen
167 R14 **Ha Tiên** Kiên Giang, S Vietnam
167 T8 **Ha Tinh** Ha Tinh, N Vietnam
Hatiözi see Hachiōji
138 F12 **Ḩatira, Haré** hill range S Israel
167 R6 **Hat Lot** Sơn La, N Vietnam
45 P16 **Hato Airport** × (Willemstad) Curaçao, SW Netherlands Antilles
54 H9 **Hato Corozal** Casanare, C Colombia
Hato del Volcán see Volcán
45 P9 **Hato Mayor** E Dominican Republic
Hatra see Al Ḩaḑr
Hatria see Adria
Hátszeg see Haţeg
143 R16 **Ḩattā** Dubayy, NE UAE
182 L9 **Hattah** Victoria, SE Australia
98 M9 **Hattem** Gelderland, E Netherlands
21 Z10 **Hatteras** Hatteras Island, North Carolina, SE USA
21 Z10 **Hatteras, Cape** headland North Carolina, SE USA
21 Z9 **Hatteras Island** island North Carolina, SE USA
64 F10 **Hatteras Plain** undersea feature W Atlantic Ocean
93 G14 **Hattfjelldal** Troms, N Norway
22 M7 **Hattiesburg** Mississippi, S USA
29 Q4 **Hatton** North Dakota, N USA
Hatton Bank see Hatton Ridge
64 L6 **Hatton Ridge** var. Hatton Bank. undersea feature N Atlantic Ocean
191 W6 **Hatutu** island Îles Marquises, NE French Polynesia
111 K22 **Hatvan** Heves, NE Hungary
167 O16 **Hat Yai** var. Ban Hat Yai. Songkhla, SW Thailand
Hatzeg see Haţeg
Hatzfeld see Jimbolia
80 N13 **Haud** plateau Ethiopia/Somalia
95 D18 **Hauge** Rogaland, S Norway
95 C15 **Haugesund** Rogaland, S Norway
109 X2 **Haugsdorf** Niederösterreich, NE Austria
184 M9 **Hauhungaroa Range** ▲▲ North Island, NZ
95 E15 **Haukeligrend** Telemark, S Norway
93 L14 **Haukipudas** Oulu, C Finland
93 M17 **Haukivesi** ◎ SE Finland
93 M17 **Haukivuori** Isä-Suomi, E Finland
Hauptkanal see Havelländ Grosse
187 N10 **Hauraha** San Cristobal, SE Solomon Islands
184 L5 **Hauraki Gulf** gulf North Island, NZ
185 B24 **Hauroko, Lake** ◎ South Island, NZ
167 S14 **Hâu, Sông** ≈ S Vietnam
92 N12 **Hautajärvi** Lappi, NE Finland
74 F7 **Haut Atlas** Eng. High Atlas. ▲▲ C Morocco
79 M17 **Haut-Congo** off. Région du Haut-Congo; prev. Haut-Zaïre. ◈ region NE Dem. Rep. Congo
103 Y14 **Haute-Corse** ◈ department Corse, France, C Mediterranean Sea
102 L16 **Haute-Garonne** ◈ department S France
76 J13 **Haute-Guinée** ◈ state NE Guinea
79 K14 **Haute-Kotto** ◈ prefecture E Central African Republic
103 P12 **Haute-Loire** ◈ department C France
103 R6 **Haute-Marne** ◈ department N France
102 M3 **Haute-Normandie** ◈ region N France
15 U6 **Hauterive** Québec, SE Canada
103 T13 **Hautes-Alpes** ◈ department SE France
103 S7 **Haute-Saône** ◈ department E France
103 T10 **Haute-Savoie** ◈ department E France
99 M20 **Hautes Fagnes** Ger. Hohes Venn. ▲ E Belgium
102 K16 **Hautes-Pyrénées** ◈ department S France
99 L23 **Haute Sûre, Lac de la** ⊠ NW Luxembourg
102 M11 **Haute-Vienne** ◈ department C France
19 S8 **Haut, Isle au** island Maine, NE USA
79 M14 **Haut-Mbomou** ◈ préfecture SE Central African Republic
103 Q2 **Hautmont** Nord, N France
79 F19 **Haut-Ogooué** off. Province du Haut-Ogooué, var. Le Haut-Ogooué. ◈ province SE Gabon
Haut-Ogooué, Le see Haut-Ogooué
103 U7 **Haut-Rhin** ◈ department NE France
74 I6 **Hauts Plateaux** plateau Algeria/Morocco
38 D9 **Hau'ula** var. Hauula. O'ahu, Hawai'i, USA, C Pacific Ocean
101 O22 **Hauzenberg** Bayern, SE Germany
30 K13 **Havana** Illinois, N USA
Havana see La Habana
97 N23 **Havant** S England, UK
35 Y14 **Havasu, Lake** ⊠ Arizona/California, W USA
95 J23 **Havdrup** Roskilde, E Denmark
100 N10 **Havel** ≈ NE Germany
99 J21 **Havelange** Namur, SE Belgium
100 M11 **Havelberg** Sachsen-Anhalt, NE Germany
149 U5 **Haveliān** North-West Frontier Province, NW Pakistan
100 N12 **Havelländ Grosse** var. Hauptkanal. canal NE Germany
14 J14 **Havelock** Ontario, SE Canada
185 J14 **Havelock** Marlborough, South Island, NZ
21 X11 **Havelock** North Carolina, SE USA
184 O11 **Havelock North** Hawke's Bay, North Island, NZ
98 M8 **Havelte** Drenthe, NE Netherlands
27 N6 **Haven** Kansas, C USA
97 H21 **Haverfordwest** SW Wales, UK
97 P20 **Haverhill** E England, UK
19 O10 **Haverhill** Massachusetts, NE USA
93 G17 **Haverö** Västernorrland, C Sweden
111 I17 **Havířov** Moravskoslezský Kraj, E Czech Republic
111 E17 **Havlíčkův Brod** Ger. Deutsch-Brod; prev. Německý Brod. Vysočina, C Czech Republic
92 K7 **Havøysund** Finnmark, N Norway
33 T7 **Havre** Montana, NW USA
Havre see le Havre
99 F20 **Havré** Hainaut, S Belgium
13 P11 **Havre-St-Pierre** Québec, E Canada
136 B10 **Havsa** Edirne, NW Turkey
38 D8 **Hawai'i** off. State of Hawai'i; also known as Aloha State, Paradise of the Pacific var. Hawaii. ◈ state USA, C Pacific Ocean
38 G12 **Hawai'i** var. Hawaii. island Hawaiian Islands, USA, C Pacific Ocean
192 M5 **Hawaiian Islands** prev. Sandwich Islands. island group Hawaii, USA, C Pacific Ocean
192 L5 **Hawaiian Ridge** undersea feature N Pacific Ocean
193 N6 **Hawaiian Trough** undersea feature N Pacific Ocean
29 R12 **Hawarden** Iowa, C USA
Hawash see Āwash
139 P6 **Ḩawbayn al Gharbīyah** C Iraq
185 D21 **Hawea, Lake** ◎ South Island, NZ
184 K11 **Hawera** Taranaki, North Island, NZ
20 J5 **Hawesville** Kentucky, S USA
38 G11 **Hāwī** var. Hawi. Hawai'i, USA, C Pacific Ocean
96 K13 **Hawick** SE Scotland, UK
139 S4 **Ḩawījah** C Iraq
139 Y10 **Ḩawīzah, Hawr al** ◎ S Iraq
185 E21 **Hawkdun Range** ▲▲ South Island, NZ
184 P10 **Hawke Bay** bay North Island, NZ
182 I6 **Hawker** South Australia
184 N11 **Hawke's Bay** off. Hawkes Bay Region. ◈ region North Island, NZ
149 O16 **Hawkes Bay** bay SE Pakistan
15 N12 **Hawkesbury** Ontario, SE Canada
Hawkeye State see Iowa
23 T5 **Hawkinsville** Georgia, SE USA
14 B7 **Hawk Junction** Ontario, S Canada
21 N10 **Haw Knob** ▲ North Carolina/Tennessee, SE USA
21 Q9 **Hawksbill Mountain** ▲ North Carolina, SE USA
33 Z16 **Hawk Springs** Wyoming, C USA
Hawlēr see Arbīl
29 S5 **Hawley** Minnesota, N USA
25 P7 **Hawley** Texas, SW USA
141 R14 **Ḩawrā'** C Yemen
139 P7 **Ḩawrān, Wadi** dry watercourse W Iraq
21 T9 **Haw River** ≈ North Carolina, SE USA
139 U5 **Hawshqūrah** E Iraq
35 S7 **Hawthorne** Nevada, W USA
37 W3 **Haxtun** Colorado, C USA
183 N9 **Hay** New South Wales, SE Australia
11 O10 **Hay** ≈ W Canada
171 S13 **Haya** Pulau Seram, E Indonesia
165 R9 **Hayachine-san** ▲ Honshū, C Japan
103 S4 **Hayange** Moselle, NE France
HaYarden see Jordan
Hayastani Hanrapetut'yun see Armenia
Hayasui-seto see Hōyo-kaikyō
39 N9 **Haycock** Alaska, USA
36 M14 **Hayden** Arizona, SW USA
37 Q3 **Hayden** Colorado, C USA
28 M10 **Hayes** South Dakota, N USA
11 X13 **Hayes** ≈ Manitoba, C Canada
9 P12 **Hayes** ≈ Nunavut, NE Canada

◆ Country ● Country Capital ◇ Dependent Territory ○ Dependent Territory Capital ◈ Administrative Region × International Airport ▲ Mountain ▲▲ Mountain Range Ж Volcano ≈ River ◎ Lake ⊠ Reservoir

28 M16 **Hayes Center** Nebraska, C USA
39 S10 **Hayes, Mount** ▲ Alaska, USA
21 N11 **Hayesville** North Carolina, SE USA
35 X10 **Hayford Peak** ▲ Nevada, W USA
34 M3 **Hayfork** California, W USA
Hayir, Qasr al see Ḩayr al Gharbī, Qaşr al
163 P8 **Haylaastay** Sühbaatar, E Mongolia
14 I12 **Hay Lake** ◎ Ontario, SE Canada
141 X11 **Haymā'** var. Haima. C Oman
136 H13 **Haymana** Ankara, C Turkey
138 J7 **Ḩaymūr, Jabal** ▲▲ W Syria
Haynau see Chojnów
22 G4 **Haynesville** Louisiana, S USA
23 P6 **Hayneville** Alabama, S USA
114 M12 **Hayrabolu** Tekirdağ, NW Turkey
136 C10 **Hayrabolu Deresi** ≈ NW Turkey
138 J6 **Ḩayr al Gharbī, Qaşr al** var. Qasr al Hayir, Qasr al Hir al Gharbi. ruins Ḩimş, C Syria
138 L5 **Ḩayr ash Sharqī, Qaşr al** var. Qasr al Hir Ash Sharqī. ruins Ḩimş, C Syria
8 J10 **Hay River** Northwest Territories, W Canada
26 K4 **Hays** Kansas, C USA
28 K12 **Hay Springs** Nebraska, C USA
65 H25 **Haystack, The** ▲ NE Saint Helena
27 N7 **Haysville** Kansas, C USA
117 O7 **Haysyn** Rus. Gaysin. Vinnyts'ka Oblast', C Ukraine
27 Y9 **Hayti** Missouri, C USA
29 Q9 **Hayti** South Dakota, N USA
117 O8 **Hayvoron** Rus. Gayvorno. Kirovohrads'ka Oblast', C Ukraine
35 N9 **Hayward** California, W USA
30 J4 **Hayward** Wisconsin, N USA
97 O23 **Haywards Heath** SE England, UK
146 A11 **Hazar** prev. Rus. Cheleken. Balkan Welaýaty, W Turkmenistan
143 S11 **Hazārān, Kūh-e** var. Kūh-e ā Hazr. ▲ SE Iran
Hazarat Imam see Emām Şāḩeb
21 O7 **Hazard** Kentucky, S USA
137 O15 **Hazar Gölü** ◎ C Turkey
153 P15 **Hazārībāg** var. Hazārībāgh. Jhārkhand, N India
Hazārībāgh see Hazārībāg
103 O1 **Hazebrouck** Nord, N France
30 K9 **Hazel Green** Wisconsin, N USA
192 K9 **Hazel Holme Bank** undersea feature S Pacific Ocean
10 K13 **Hazelton** British Columbia, SW Canada
29 N6 **Hazelton** North Dakota, N USA
35 R5 **Hazen** Nevada, W USA
28 L5 **Hazen** North Dakota, N USA
38 L12 **Hazen Bay** bay E Bering Sea
9 N1 **Hazen, Lake** ◎ Nunavut, N Canada
139 S5 **Hazim, Bi'r** well C Iraq
23 V6 **Hazlehurst** Georgia, SE USA
22 K6 **Hazlehurst** Mississippi, S USA
18 K15 **Hazlet** New Jersey, NE USA
146 I9 **Hazorasp** Rus. Khazarosp. Xorazm Viloyati, W Uzbekistan
147 R13 **Hazratishoh, Qatorkŭhi** var. Khrebet Khazretishi, Rus. Khrebet Khozretishi. ▲▲ S Tajikistan
Hazr, Kūh-e ā see Hazārān, Kūh-e
149 U6 **Hazro** Punjab, E Pakistan
23 R7 **Headland** Alabama, S USA
182 C6 **Head of Bight** headland South Australia
33 N10 **Headquarters** Idaho, NW USA
34 M7 **Healdsburg** California, W USA
27 N13 **Healdton** Oklahoma, C USA
183 O12 **Healesville** Victoria, SE Australia
39 R10 **Healy** Alaska, USA
173 R13 **Heard and McDonald Islands** ◇ Australian external territory S Indian Ocean
173 R13 **Heard Island** island Heard and McDonald Islands, S Indian Ocean
25 U9 **Hearne** Texas, SW USA
12 F12 **Hearst** Ontario, S Canada
194 J5 **Hearst Island** island Antarctica
Heart of Dixie see Alabama
28 L5 **Heart River** ≈ North Dakota, N USA
31 T13 **Heath** Ohio, N USA
183 N11 **Heathcote** Victoria, SE Australia
97 N22 **Heathrow** ✕ (London)SE England, UK
21 X5 **Heathsville** Virginia, NE USA
27 R11 **Heavener** Oklahoma, C USA
25 R15 **Hebbronville** Texas, SW USA
163 Q13 **Hebei** var. Hebei Sheng, Hopeh, Hopei, Ji; prev. Chihli. ◈ province E China
Hebei Sheng see Hebei
36 M3 **Heber City** Utah, W USA
27 V10 **Heber Springs** Arkansas, C USA
161 N5 **Hebi** Henan, C China
32 F11 **Hebo** Oregon, NW USA
96 F9 **Hebrides, Sea of the** sea NW Scotland, UK
13 P5 **Hebron** Newfoundland and Labrador, E Canada
31 N11 **Hebron** Indiana, N USA
29 Q17 **Hebron** Nebraska, C USA
28 L5 **Hebron** North Dakota, N USA
138 F11 **Hebron** var. Al Khalīl, El Khalil, Heb. Hevron; anc. Kiriath-Arba. S West Bank
Hebrus see Évros/Maritsa/Meriç
95 N14 **Heby** Västmanland, C Sweden
10 I14 **Hecate Strait** strait British Columbia, W Canada
41 W12 **Hecelchakán** Campeche, SE Mexico
160 K13 **Hechi** var. Jinchengjiang. Guangxi Zhuangzu Zizhiqu, S China
101 H23 **Hechingen** Baden-Württemberg, S Germany
99 K17 **Hechtel** Limburg, NE Belgium
160 J9 **Hechuan** Chongqing Shi, C China
29 P7 **Hecla** South Dakota, N USA
9 N1 **Hecla, Cape** headland Nunavut, N Canada
29 T9 **Hector** Minnesota, N USA
93 F17 **Hede** Jämtland, C Sweden
95 M14 **Hedemora** Dalarna, C Sweden
92 K13 **Hedenäset** Norrbotten, N Sweden
95 G23 **Hedensted** Vejle, C Denmark
95 N14 **Hedesunda** Gävleborg, C Sweden
95 N14 **Hedesundafjord** ◎ C Sweden
25 O3 **Hedley** Texas, SW USA
94 I12 **Hedmark** ◈ county S Norway
165 T16 **Hedo-misaki** headland Okinawa, SW Japan
29 X15 **Hedrick** Iowa, C USA
99 L16 **Heel** Limburg, SE Netherlands
189 Y12 **Heel Point** point Wake Island
98 H9 **Heemskerk** Noord-Holland, W Netherlands
98 M10 **Heerde** Gelderland, E Netherlands
98 L7 **Heerenveen** Fris. It Hearrenfean. Friesland, N Netherlands
98 I8 **Heerhugowaard** Noord-Holland, NW Netherlands
92 O3 **Heer Land** physical region C Svalbard
99 M18 **Heerlen** Limburg, SE Netherlands
99 J19 **Heers** Limburg, NE Belgium
Heerwegen see Polkowice
98 K13 **Heesch** Noord-Brabant, S Netherlands
99 K15 **Heeze** Noord-Brabant, SE Netherlands
138 F8 **Ḩefa** var. Haifa; hist. Caiffa, Caiphas, anc. Sycaminum. Haifa, N Israel
138 F8 **Ḩefa, Mifraz** Eng. Bay of Haifa. bay N Israel
161 Q8 **Hefei** var. Hofei; hist. Luchow. Anhui, E China
23 R3 **Heflin** Alabama, S USA
163 X7 **Hegang** Heilongjiang, NE China
164 L10 **Hegura-jima** island SW Japan
Heguri-jima see Heigun-tō
Hei see Heilongjiang
100 H8 **Heide** Schleswig-Holstein, N Germany
101 G20 **Heidelberg** Baden-Württemberg, SW Germany
83 J21 **Heidelberg** Gauteng, NE South Africa
22 M6 **Heidelberg** Mississippi, S USA
Heidenheim see Heidenheim an der Brenz
101 J22 **Heidenheim an der Brenz** var. Heidenheim. Baden-Württemberg, S Germany
109 U2 **Heidenreichstein** Niederösterreich, N Austria
164 F14 **Heigun-tō** var. Heguri-jima. island SW Japan
163 W5 **Heihe** prev. Ai-hun. Heilongjiang, NE China
159 S8 **Hei He** ≈ C China
Hei-ho see Nagqu
83 J22 **Heilbron** Free State, N South Africa
101 H21 **Heilbronn** Baden-Württemberg, SW Germany
Heiligenbeil see Mamonovo
109 Q8 **Heiligenblut** Tirol, W Austria
100 K7 **Heiligenhafen** Schleswig-Holstein, N Germany
Heiligenkreuz see Žiar nad Hronom
101 J15 **Heiligenstadt** Thüringen, C Germany
Heilong Jiang see Amur
163 W8 **Heilongjiang** var. Hei, Heilongjiang Sheng, Hei-lung-chiang, Heilungkiang. ◈ province NE China
Heilongjiang Sheng see Heilongjiang
98 H9 **Heiloo** Noord-Holland, NW Netherlands
Heilsberg see Lidzbark Warmiński
Hei-lung-chiang/Heilungkiang see Heilongjiang
92 I4 **Heimaey** var. Heimaæy. island S Iceland
94 H8 **Heimdal** Sør-Trøndelag, S Norway
Heinaste see Ainaži
93 N17 **Heinävesi** Itä-Suomi, E Finland
99 M22 **Heinerscheid** Diekirch, N Luxembourg
98 M10 **Heino** Overijssel, E Netherlands
93 M18 **Heinola** Etelä-Suomi, S Finland
101 C16 **Heinsberg** Nordrhein-Westfalen, W Germany
163 U12 **Heishan** Liaoning, NE China
160 H8 **Heishui** var. Luhua. Sichuan, C China
99 H17 **Heist-op-den-Berg** Antwerpen, C Belgium
Heitō see P'ingtung
171 X15 **Heitske** Papua, E Indonesia
Hejanah see Al Hījānah
Hejaz see Al Ḩijāz
160 M14 **He Jiang** ≈ S China
Hejiayan see Lüeyang
158 K6 **Hejing** Xinjiang Uygur Zizhiqu, NW China
Héjjasfalva see Vânători
Heka see Hoika
137 N14 **Hekimhan** Malatya, C Turkey
92 J4 **Hekla** ▲ S Iceland
Hekou see Yajiang, Sichuan, China
Hekou see Yanshan, Jiangxi, China
110 J6 **Hel** Ger. Hela. Pomorskie, N Poland
Hela see Hel
93 F17 **Helagsfjället** ▲ C Sweden
159 W8 **Helan** var. Xigang. Ningxia, N China
162 K14 **Helan Shan** ▲▲ N China
99 M16 **Helden** Limburg, SE Netherlands
27 X12 **Helena** Arkansas, C USA
33 R10 **Helena** state capital Montana, NW USA
96 H12 **Helensburgh** W Scotland, UK
184 K5 **Helensville** Auckland, North Island, NZ
95 L20 **Helgasjön** ◎ S Sweden
100 G8 **Helgoland** Eng. Heligoland. island NW Germany
Helgoland Bay see Helgoländer Bucht
100 G8 **Helgoländer Bucht** var. Helgoland Bay, Heligoland Bight. bay NW Germany
Heligoland see Helgoland
Heligoland Bight see Helgoländer Bucht
Heliopolis see Baalbek
92 I4 **Hella** Sudhurland, SW Iceland
Hellas see Greece
143 N11 **Ḩelleh, Rūd-e** ≈ S Iran
98 N10 **Hellendoorn** Overijssel, E Netherlands
Hellenic Republic see Greece
121 Q10 **Hellenic Trough** undersea feature Aegean Sea, C Mediterranean Sea
94 E10 **Hellesylt** Møre og Romsdal, S Norway
98 F13 **Hellevoetsluis** Zuid-Holland, SW Netherlands
105 Q12 **Hellín** Castilla-La Mancha, C Spain
115 H19 **Hellinikon** ✕ (Athína) Attikí, C Greece
32 M12 **Hells Canyon** valley Idaho/Oregon, NW USA
148 L9 **Helmand** ◈ province S Afghanistan
148 K10 **Helmand, Daryā-ye** var. Rūd-e Hīrmand. ≈ Afghanistan/Iran see also Hīrmand, Rūd-e
Helmantica see Salamanca
101 K15 **Helme** ≈ C Germany
99 L15 **Helmond** Noord-Brabant, S Netherlands
96 J7 **Helmsdale** N Scotland, UK
100 K13 **Helmstedt** Niedersachsen, N Germany
163 Y10 **Helong** Jilin, NE China
36 M4 **Helper** Utah, W USA
100 O10 **Helpter Berge** hill NE Germany
95 J22 **Helsingborg** prev. Hälsingborg. Skåne, S Sweden
Helsingfors see Helsinki
95 J22 **Helsingør** Eng. Elsinore. Frederiksborg, E Denmark
93 M20 **Helsinki** Swe. Helsingfors. ● (Finland) Etelä-Suomi, S Finland
97 H25 **Helston** SW England, UK
Heltau see Cisnădie
61 C17 **Helvecia** Santa Fe, C Argentina
97 K15 **Helvellyn** ▲ NW England, UK
Helvetia see Switzerland
75 W8 **Helwân** var. Hilwân, Hulwan, Hulwân. N Egypt
97 N21 **Hemel Hempstead** E England, UK
35 U16 **Hemet** California, W USA
28 J13 **Hemingford** Nebraska, C USA
21 T13 **Hemingway** South Carolina, SE USA
92 G13 **Hemnesberget** Nordland, C Norway
25 Y8 **Hemphill** Texas, SW USA
25 V11 **Hempstead** Texas, SW USA
95 P20 **Hemse** Gotland, SE Sweden
94 F13 **Hemsedal** valley S Norway
159 T11 **Henan** var. Henan Mongolzu Zizhixian, Yêgainnyin. Qinghai, C China
161 N6 **Henan** var. Henan Sheng, Honan, Yu. ◈ province C China
184 L4 **Hen and Chickens** island group N NZ
Henan Mongolzu Zizhixian/Henan Sheng see Henan
105 O7 **Henares** ≈ C Spain
165 P7 **Henashi-zaki** headland Honshū, C Japan
102 I16 **Hendaye** Pyrénées-Atlantiques, SW France
136 F11 **Hendek** Sakarya, NW Turkey
61 B21 **Henderson** Buenos Aires, E Argentina
20 I5 **Henderson** Kentucky, S USA
35 X11 **Henderson** Nevada, W USA
21 V8 **Henderson** North Carolina, SE USA
20 G10 **Henderson** Tennessee, S USA
25 W7 **Henderson** Texas, SW USA
30 J12 **Henderson Creek** ≈ Illinois, N USA
186 M9 **Henderson Field** ✕ (Honiara) Guadalcanal, C Solomon Islands
191 O17 **Henderson Island** atoll N Pitcairn Islands
21 O10 **Hendersonville** North Carolina, SE USA
20 J8 **Hendersonville** Tennessee, S USA
143 O14 **Hendorābī, Jazīreh-ye** island S Iran
55 V10 **Hendrik Top** var. Hendriktop. elevation C Suriname
Hendū Kosh see Hindu Kush
14 L12 **Heney, Lac** ◎ Québec, SE Canada
Hengchow see Hengyang
161 S15 **Hengchun** S Taiwan
159 R16 **Hengduan Shan** ▲▲ SW China
98 N12 **Hengelo** Gelderland, E Netherlands
98 O10 **Hengelo** Overijssel, E Netherlands
Hengnan see Hengyang
161 N11 **Hengshan** Hunan, S China
160 L4 **Hengshan** Shaanxi, C China
161 O4 **Hengshui** Hebei, E China
161 N12 **Hengyang** var. Hengnan, Heng-yang; prev. Hengchow. Hunan, S China
117 U11 **Heniches'k** Rus. Genichesk. Khersons'ka Oblast', S Ukraine
21 Z4 **Henlopen, Cape** headland Delaware, NE USA
Henna see Enna
94 M10 **Hennan** Gävleborg, C Sweden
102 G7 **Hennebont** Morbihan, NW France
30 L11 **Hennepin** Illinois, N USA
26 M9 **Hennessey** Oklahoma, C USA
100 N12 **Hennigsdorf** var. Hennigsdorf bei Berlin. Brandenburg, NE Germany
Hennigsdorf bei Berlin see Hennigsdorf
19 N9 **Henniker** New Hampshire, NE USA
25 S5 **Henrietta** Texas, SW USA
Henrique de Carvalho see Saurimo
30 L12 **Henry** Illinois, N USA
21 Y7 **Henry, Cape** headland Virginia, NE USA
27 P10 **Henryetta** Oklahoma, C USA
194 M7 **Henry Ice Rise** ice cap Antarctica
9 Q5 **Henry Kater, Cape** headland Baffin Island, Nunavut, NE Canada
33 R13 **Henrys Fork** ≈ Idaho, NW USA
14 E15 **Hensall** Ontario, S Canada
100 J9 **Henstedt-Ulzburg** Schleswig-Holstein, N Germany
163 N7 **Hentiy** ◈ province N Mongolia
162 M7 **Hentiyn Nuruu** ▲▲ N Mongolia
183 P10 **Henty** New South Wales, SE Australia
166 L8 **Henzada** Irrawaddy, SW Myanmar
Heping see Huishui
101 G19 **Heppenheim** Hessen, W Germany
32 J11 **Heppner** Oregon, NW USA
160 L15 **Hepu** var. Lianzhou. Guangxi Zhuangzu Zizhiqu, S China
92 J2 **Heradhsvötn** ≈ C Iceland
Herakleion see Irákleio
148 K5 **Herāt** var. Herat; anc. Aria. Herāt, W Afghanistan
148 J5 **Herāt** ◈ province W Afghanistan
103 P14 **Hérault** ◈ department S France
103 P15 **Hérault** ≈ S France
11 T16 **Herbert** Saskatchewan, S Canada
185 F22 **Herbert** Otago, South Island, NZ
38 J17 **Herbert Island** island Aleutian Islands, Alaska, USA
Herbertshöhe see Kokopo
15 Q7 **Hérbertville** Québec, SE Canada
101 G17 **Herborn** Hessen, W Germany
113 I17 **Herceg-Novi** It. Castelnuovo; prev. Ercegnovi. Montenegro, SW Serbia and Montenegro (Yugo.)
11 X10 **Herchmer** Manitoba, C Canada
186 E8 **Hercules Bay** bay E PNG
92 K2 **Herdhubreidh** ▲ C Iceland
42 M13 **Heredia** Heredia, C Costa Rica
42 M12 **Heredia** off. Provincia de Heredia. ◈ province N Costa Rica
97 K21 **Hereford** W England, UK
24 M3 **Hereford** Texas, SW USA
15 Q13 **Hereford, Mont** ▲ Québec, SE Canada
97 K21 **Herefordshire** cultural region W England, UK
191 U11 **Hereheretue** atoll Îles Tuamotu, C French Polynesia
105 N10 **Herencia** Castilla-La Mancha, C Spain
99 H18 **Herent** Vlaams Brabant, C Belgium
99 I16 **Herentals** var. Herenthals. Antwerpen, N Belgium
Herenthals see Herentals
99 H17 **Herenthout** Antwerpen, N Belgium
95 J23 **Herfølge** Roskilde, E Denmark
100 G13 **Herford** Nordrhein-Westfalen, NW Germany
27 O5 **Herington** Kansas, C USA
108 H7 **Herisau** Fr. Hérisau. Appenzell Ausser Rhoden, NE Switzerland
Héristal see Herstal
99 J18 **Herk-de-Stad** Limburg, NE Belgium
Herkulesbad/Herkulesfürdő see Băile Herculane
Herlen Gol/Herlen He see Kerulen
35 Q4 **Herlong** California, W USA
97 L26 **Herm** island Channel Islands
109 R9 **Hermagor** Slvn. Šmohor. Kärnten, S Austria
29 S7 **Herman** Minnesota, N USA
96 L1 **Herma Ness** headland NE Scotland, UK
27 V4 **Hermann** Missouri, C USA
181 Q8 **Hermannsburg** Northern Territory, N Australia
Hermannstadt see Sibiu
94 E12 **Hermansverk** Sogn og Fjordane, S Norway
138 H6 **Hermel** var. Hirmil. NE Lebanon
Hermhausen see Hajnówka
183 P6 **Hermidale** New South Wales, SE Australia
55 X9 **Herminadorp** Sipaliwini, NE Suriname
32 K11 **Hermiston** Oregon, NW USA
27 T6 **Hermitage** Missouri, C USA
186 D4 **Hermit Islands** island group N PNG
25 O7 **Hermleigh** Texas, SW USA
138 G7 **Hermon, Mount** Ar. Jabal ash Shaykh. ▲ S Syria
Hermopolis Parva see Damanhûr
28 J10 **Hermosa** South Dakota, N USA
40 F5 **Hermosillo** Sonora, NW Mexico
Hermoupolis see Ermoúpoli
111 N20 **Hernád** var. Hornád, Ger. Kundert. ≈ Hungary /Slovakia
61 C18 **Hernández** Entre Ríos, E Argentina
23 V11 **Hernando** Florida, SE USA
22 L1 **Hernando** Mississippi, S USA
105 Q2 **Hernani** País Vasco, N Spain
99 F19 **Herne** Vlaams Brabant, C Belgium
101 E14 **Herne** Nordrhein-Westfalen, W Germany
95 F22 **Herning** Ringkøbing, W Denmark
Hernösand see Härnösand
121 U11 **Herodotus Basin** undersea feature E Mediterranean Sea
121 Q12 **Herodotus Trough** undersea feature C Mediterranean Sea
29 T11 **Heron Lake** Minnesota, N USA
Herowābād see Khalkhāl
95 G16 **Herre** Telemark, S Norway
29 N7 **Herreid** South Dakota, N USA
101 H22 **Herrenberg** Baden-Württemberg, S Germany
104 L14 **Herrera** Andalucía, S Spain
43 R17 **Herrera** off. Provincia de Herrera. ◈ province S Panama
104 L10 **Herrera del Duque** Extremadura, W Spain
104 M4 **Herrera de Pisuerga** Castilla-León, N Spain
41 Z13 **Herrero, Punta** headland SE Mexico
183 P16 **Herrick** Tasmania, SE Australia
30 L17 **Herrin** Illinois, N USA
20 M6 **Herrington Lake** ⊞ Kentucky, S USA
95 K18 **Herrljunga** Västra Götaland, S Sweden
103 N16 **Hers** ≈ S France
10 I1 **Herschel Island** island Yukon Territory, NW Canada
99 I17 **Herselt** Antwerpen, C Belgium
18 G15 **Hershey** Pennsylvania, NE USA
99 K19 **Herstal** Fr. Héristal. Liège, E Belgium
97 O21 **Hertford** E England, UK
21 X8 **Hertford** North Carolina, SE USA
97 O21 **Hertfordshire** cultural region E England, UK
181 Z9 **Hervey Bay** Queensland, E Australia
101 O14 **Herzberg** Brandenburg, E Germany
99 E18 **Herzele** Oost-Vlaanderen, NW Belgium
101 K20 **Herzogenaurach** Bayern, SE Germany
109 W4 **Herzogenburg** Niederösterreich, NE Austria
Herzogenbusch see 's-Hertogenbosch
103 N2 **Hesdin** Pas-de-Calais, N France
160 K14 **Heshan** Guangxi Zhuangzu Zizhiqu, S China
159 X10 **Heshui** var. Xihuachi. Gansu, C China
99 M25 **Hespérange** Luxembourg, SE Luxembourg
35 U14 **Hesperia** California, W USA
37 P7 **Hesperus Mountain** ▲ Colorado, C USA
10 J6 **Hess** ≈ Yukon Territory, NW Canada
Hesse see Hessen
101 J21 **Hesselberg** ▲ S Germany
95 I22 **Hesselo** island E Denmark
101 H17 **Hessen** Eng./Fr. Hesse. ◈ state C Germany
192 L6 **Hess Tablemount** undersea feature C Pacific Ocean
27 N6 **Hesston** Kansas, C USA
93 G15 **Hestskjøltoppen** ▲ C Norway
97 K18 **Heswall** NW England, UK
153 P12 **Hetauda** Central, C Nepal
Hétfalu see Săcele
28 K7 **Hettinger** North Dakota, N USA
101 L14 **Hettstedt** Sachsen-Anhalt, C Germany
92 P3 **Heuglin, Kapp** headland SE Svalbard
187 N10 **Heuru** San Cristobal, SE Solomon Islands
99 J17 **Heusden** Limburg, NE Belgium
98 J13 **Heusden** Noord-Brabant, S Netherlands
102 K3 **Hève, Cap de la** headland N France
99 H18 **Heverlee** Vlaams Brabant, C Belgium
111 L22 **Heves** Heves, NE Hungary
111 L22 **Heves** off. Heves Megye. ◈ county NE Hungary
Hevron see Hebron
45 Y13 **Hewanorra** ✕ (Saint Lucia) S Saint Lucia
Hexian see Hezhou
160 L6 **Heyang** Shaanxi, C China
Heydebrech see Kędzierzyn-Koźle
Heydekrug see Šilutė
Heyin see Guide
97 K16 **Heysham** NW England, UK
161 O14 **Heyuan** Guangdong, S China
182 L12 **Heywood** Victoria, SE Australia
180 K3 **Heywood Islands** island group Western Australia
161 O6 **Heze** var. Caozhou. Shandong, E China
159 U11 **Hezheng** Gansu, C China
160 M13 **Hezhou** var. Babu; prev. Hexian. Guangxi Zhuangzu Zizhiqu, S China
159 U11 **Hezuo** Gansu, C China
23 Z16 **Hialeah** Florida, SE USA
27 Q3 **Hiawatha** Kansas, C USA
36 M4 **Hiawatha** Utah, W USA
29 V4 **Hibbing** Minnesota, N USA
183 N17 **Hibbs, Point** headland Tasmania, SE Australia
Hibernia see Ireland
20 F8 **Hickman** Kentucky, S USA
21 Q9 **Hickory** North Carolina, SE USA
21 Q9 **Hickory, Lake** ◎ North Carolina, SE USA
184 Q7 **Hicks Bay** Gisborne, North Island, NZ
25 S8 **Hico** Texas, SW USA
165 T4 **Hidaka** Hokkaidō, NE Japan
164 I12 **Hidaka** Hyōgo, Honshū, SW Japan
165 T5 **Hidaka-sanmyaku** ▲▲ Hokkaidō, NE Japan
41 O6 **Hidalgo** var. Villa Hidalgo. Coahuila de Zaragoza, NE Mexico
41 N8 **Hidalgo** Nuevo León, NE Mexico
41 O10 **Hidalgo** Tamaulipas, C Mexico
41 O13 **Hidalgo** ◈ state C Mexico
40 J7 **Hidalgo del Parral** var. Parral. Chihuahua, N Mexico
100 N7 **Hiddensee** island NE Germany
80 G6 **Hidiglib, Wadi** ≈ NE Sudan
109 U6 **Hieflau** Salzburg, E Austria
187 P16 **Hienghène** Province Nord, C New Caledonia
Hierosolyma see Jerusalem
64 N12 **Hierro** var. Ferro. island Islas Canarias, Spain, NE Atlantic Ocean
164 G13 **Higashi-Hiroshima** var. Higasihirosima. Hiroshima, Honshū, SW Japan
164 C12 **Higashi-suidō** strait SW Japan
Higasihirosima see Higashi-Hiroshima
Higasine see Higashine
25 P1 **Higgins** Texas, SW USA
31 P7 **Higgins Lake** ◎ Michigan, N USA
27 S4 **Higginsville** Missouri, C USA
High Atlas see Haut Atlas
30 M5 **High Falls Reservoir** ⊞ Wisconsin, N USA
44 K12 **Highgate** C Jamaica
25 X11 **High Island** Texas, SW USA
31 O5 **High Island** island Michigan, N USA
30 K15 **Highland** Illinois, N USA
31 N10 **Highland Park** Illinois, N USA
21 O10 **Highlands** North Carolina, SE USA
11 O11 **High Level** Alberta, W Canada
29 O9 **Highmore** South Dakota, N USA
171 N3 **High Peak** ▲ Luzon, N Philippines
High Plains see Great Plains
21 S9 **High Point** North Carolina, SE USA
18 J13 **High Point** hill New Jersey, NE USA
11 P13 **High Prairie** Alberta, W Canada
11 Q16 **High River** Alberta, SW Canada
21 S9 **High Rock Lake** ⊞ North Carolina, SE USA
23 V9 **High Springs** Florida, SE USA
High Veld see Great Karoo
97 J24 **High Willhays** ▲ SW England, UK
97 N22 **High Wycombe** prev. Chepping Wycombe, Chipping Wycombe. SE England, UK
41 P12 **Higos** var. El Higo. Veracruz-Llave, E Mexico
102 I16 **Higuer, Cap** headland NE Spain
45 R5 **Higüero, Punta** headland W Puerto Rico
45 P9 **Higüey** var. Salvaleón de Higüey. E Dominican Republic
190 G11 **Hihifo** ✕ (Matā'utu) Île Uvea, N Wallis and Futuna
81 N16 **Hiiraan** off. Gobolka Hiiraan. ◈ region C Somalia
118 E4 **Hiiumaa** off. Hiiumaa Maakond. ◈ province W Estonia
118 D4 **Hiiumaa** Ger. Dagden, Swe. Dagö. island W Estonia
Hijanah see Al Hījānah
105 S6 **Híjar** Aragón, NE Spain
191 V10 **Hikueru** atoll Îles Tuamotu, C French Polynesia
184 K3 **Hikurangi** Northland, North Island, NZ
184 Q8 **Hikurangi** ▲ North Island, NZ
192 L11 **Hikurangi Trench** var. Hikurangi Trough. undersea feature SW Pacific Ocean
Hikurangi Trough see Hikurangi Trench
190 B15 **Hikutavake** NW Niue
121 Q12 **Hilāl, Ra's al** headland N Libya
61 A24 **Hilario Ascasubi** Buenos Aires, E Argentina
101 K17 **Hildburghausen** Thüringen, C Germany
101 E15 **Hilden** Nordrhein-Westfalen, W Germany
100 I13 **Hildesheim** Niedersachsen, N Germany
33 T9 **Hilger** Montana, NW USA
Hili see Hilli
Hilla see Al Ḩillah
45 O14 **Hillaby, Mount** ▲ N Barbados
95 K19 **Hillared** Västra Götaland, S Sweden
195 R12 **Hillary Coast** physical region Antarctica
42 G2 **Hill Bank** Orange Walk, N Belize
33 O14 **Hill City** Idaho, NW USA
26 K3 **Hill City** Kansas, C USA
29 V5 **Hill City** Minnesota, N USA

◆ Country ● Country Capital ◇ Dependent Territory ○ Dependent Territory Capital ◈ Administrative Region ✕ International Airport ▲ Mountain ▲▲ Mountain Range ⌘ Volcano ≈ River ◎ Lake ⊞ Reservoir

28 J10 **Hill City** South Dakota, N USA
65 C24 **Hill Cove Settlement** West Falkland, Falkland Islands
98 H10 **Hillegom** Zuid-Holland, W Netherlands
95 J22 **Hillerød** Frederiksborg, E Denmark
36 M7 **Hillers, Mount** ▲ Utah, W USA
153 S13 **Hilli** *var.* Hili. Rajshahi, NW Bangladesh
29 R11 **Hills** Minnesota, N USA
30 L14 **Hillsboro** Illinois, N USA
27 N5 **Hillsboro** Kansas, C USA
27 X5 **Hillsboro** Missouri, C USA
19 N10 **Hillsboro** New Hampshire, NE USA
37 Q14 **Hillsboro** New Mexico, SW USA
29 R4 **Hillsboro** North Dakota, N USA
31 R14 **Hillsboro** Ohio, N USA
32 G11 **Hillsboro** Oregon, NW USA
25 T8 **Hillsboro** Texas, SW USA
30 K8 **Hillsboro** Wisconsin, N USA
23 Y14 **Hillsboro Canal** *canal* Florida, SE USA
45 Y15 **Hillsborough** Carriacou, N Grenada
97 G15 **Hillsborough** E Northern Ireland, UK
21 U9 **Hillsborough** North Carolina, SE USA
31 Q10 **Hillsdale** Michigan, N USA
183 O8 **Hillston** New South Wales, SE Australia
21 R7 **Hillsville** Virginia, NE USA
96 L2 **Hillswick** NE Scotland, UK
Hill Tippera *see* Tripura
38 H11 **Hilo** Hawai'i, USA, C Pacific Ocean
18 F9 **Hilton** New York, NE USA
14 C10 **Hilton Beach** Ontario, S Canada
21 R16 **Hilton Head Island** South Carolina, SE USA
21 R16 **Hilton Head Island** *island* South Carolina, SE USA
99 J15 **Hilvarenbeek** Noord-Brabant, S Netherlands
98 J11 **Hilversum** Noord-Holland, C Netherlands
Hilwân *see* Helwân
152 J7 **Himāchal Pradesh** ❖ *state* NW India
Himalaya/Himalaya Shan *see* Himalayas
152 M9 **Himalayas** *var.* Himalaya, *Chin.* Himalaya Shan. ▲ S Asia
171 P6 **Himamaylan** Negros, C Philippines
93 K15 **Himanka** Länsi-Suomi, W Finland
Himara *see* Himarë
113 L23 **Himarë** *var.* Himara. Vlorë, S Albania
138 M2 **Ḩimār, Wādī al** *dry watercourse* N Syria
154 D9 **Himatnagar** Gujarāt, W India
109 Y4 **Himberg** Niederösterreich, E Austria
164 I13 **Himeji** *var.* Himezi. Hyōgo, Honshū, SW Japan
164 E14 **Hime-jima** *island* SW Japan
Himezi *see* Himeji
164 L13 **Himi** Toyama, Honshū, SW Japan
109 S9 **Himmelberg** Kärnten, S Austria
138 I5 **Ḩimş** *var.* Homs; *anc.* Emesa. Ḩimş, C Syria
138 K6 **Ḩimş** *off.* Muḩāfaẓat Ḩimş, *var.* Homs. ❖ *governorate* C Syria
138 I5 **Ḩimş, Buḩayrat** *var.* Buḩayrat Qaţţīnah. ◎ W Syria
171 R7 **Hinatuan** Mindanao, S Philippines
117 N10 **Hînceşti** *var.* Hânceşti; *prev.* Kotovsk. C Moldova
44 M9 **Hinche** C Haiti
181 X5 **Hinchinbrook Island** *island* Queensland, NE Australia
39 S12 **Hinchinbrook Island** *island* Alaska, USA
97 M19 **Hinckley** C England, UK
29 V7 **Hinckley** Minnesota, N USA
36 K5 **Hinckley** Utah, W USA
18 J9 **Hinckley Reservoir** ⊡ New York, NE USA
152 I12 **Hindaun** Rājasthān, N India
Hindenburg/Hindenburg in Oberschlesien *see* Zabrze
Hindiya *see* Al Hindīyah
21 O6 **Hindman** Kentucky, S USA
182 L10 **Hindmarsh, Lake** ◎ Victoria, SE Australia
185 G19 **Hinds** Canterbury, South Island, NZ
185 G19 **Hinds** ≈ South Island, NZ
95 H23 **Hindsholm** *island* C Denmark
149 S4 **Hindu Kush** *Per.* Hendū Kosh. ▲ Afghanistan/Pakistan
155 H19 **Hindupur** Andhra Pradesh, E India
11 O12 **Hines Creek** Alberta, W Canada
23 W6 **Hinesville** Georgia, SE USA
154 I12 **Hinganghāt** Mahārāshtra, C India
149 N15 **Hingol** ≈ SW Pakistan
154 H13 **Hingoli** Mahārāshtra, C India
137 R13 **Hınıs** Erzurum, E Turkey
92 O2 **Hinlopenstretet** *strait* N Svalbard
92 G10 **Hinnøya** *Lapp.* Iinnasuolu. *island* C Norway
108 H10 **Hinterrhein** ≈ SW Switzerland
11 O14 **Hinton** Alberta, SW Canada
26 M10 **Hinton** Oklahoma, C USA
21 R6 **Hinton** West Virginia, NE USA
Hios *see* Chíos
41 N8 **Hipolito** Coahuila de Zaragoza, NE Mexico
Hipponium *see* Vibo Valentia
164 B13 **Hirado** Nagasaki, Hirado-shima, SW Japan
164 B13 **Hirado-shima** *island* SW Japan
165 P16 **Hirakubo-saki** *headland* Ishigaki-jima, SW Japan
154 M11 **Hīrākud Reservoir** ⊡ E India
Hir al Gharbi, Qasr al *see* Ḩayr al Gharbī, Qaşr al
165 Q16 **Hirara** Okinawa, Miyako-jima, SW Japan
Qasr al Hir Ash Sharqī *see* Ḩayr ash Sharqī, Qaşr al
164 G12 **Hirata** Shimane, Honshū, SW Japan
Hiratuka *see* Hiratsuka
136 I13 **Hirfanlı Barajı** ⊡ C Turkey
155 G18 **Hiriyūr** Karnātaka, W India
Hîrlău *see* Hârlău
148 K10 **Hirmand, Rūd-e** *var.* Daryā-ye Helmand. ≈ Afghanistan/Iran *see also* Helmand, Daryā-ye
Hirmil *see* Hermel
165 T5 **Hiroo** Hokkaidō, NE Japan
165 Q7 **Hirosaki** Aomori, Honshū, C Japan
164 F13 **Hiroshima** *var.* Hirosima. Hiroshima, Honshū, SW Japan
164 G13 **Hiroshima** *off.* Hiroshima-ken, *var.* Hirosima. ❖ *prefecture* Honshū, SW Japan
Hirosima *see* Hiroshima
Hirschberg/Hirschberg im Riesengebirge/Hirschberg in Schlesien *see* Jelenia Góra
103 Q3 **Hirson** Aisne, N France
Hîrşova *see* Hârşova
95 G19 **Hirtshals** Nordjylland, N Denmark
152 H10 **Hisār** Haryāna, NW India
186 E9 **Hisiu** Central, SW PNG
147 P13 **Hisor** *Rus.* Gissar. W Tajikistan
Hispalis *see* Sevilla
Hispana/Hispania *see* Spain
44 M7 **Hispaniola** *island* Dominion Republic/Haiti
64 F11 **Hispaniola Basin** *var.* Hispaniola Trough. *undersea feature* SW Atlantic Ocean
Hispaniola Trough *see* Hispaniola Basin
Histonium *see* Vasto
139 R7 **Hīt** SW Iraq
165 P14 **Hita** Ōita, Kyūshū, SW Japan
165 P12 **Hitachi** *var.* Hitati. Ibaraki, Honshū, S Japan
165 P12 **Hitachi-Ōta** *var.* Hitatiôta. Ibaraki, Honshū, S Japan
Hitati *see* Hitachi
Hitatiôta *see* Hitachi-Ōta
97 O21 **Hitchin** E England, UK
191 Q7 **Hitiaa** Tahiti, W French Polynesia
164 D15 **Hitoyoshi** *var.* Hitoyosi. Kumamoto, Kyūshū, SW Japan
Hitoyosi *see* Hitoyoshi
94 F7 **Hitra** *prev.* Hitteren. *island* S Norway
Hitteren *see* Hitra
187 Q11 **Hiu** *island* Torres Islands, N Vanuatu
165 O11 **Hiuchiga-take** ▲ Honshū, C Japan
191 X7 **Hiva Oa** *island* Îles Marquises, N French Polynesia
20 M10 **Hiwassee Lake** ⊡ North Carolina, SE USA
20 M10 **Hiwassee River** ≈ SE USA
95 H20 **Hjallerup** Nordjylland, N Denmark
95 M16 **Hjälmaren** *Eng.* Lake Hjalmar. ◎ C Sweden
Hjalmar, Lake *see* Hjälmaren
95 C14 **Hjellestad** Hordaland, S Norway
95 D16 **Hjelmeland** Rogaland, S Norway
94 G10 **Hjerkinn** Oppland, S Norway
95 L18 **Hjo** Västra Götaland, S Sweden
95 G19 **Hjørring** Nordjylland, N Denmark
167 O1 **Hkakabo Razi** ▲ Myanmar/China
167 N1 **Hkring Bum** ▲ N Myanmar
83 L21 **Hlathikulu** *var.* Hlatikulu. S Swaziland
Hlatikulu *see* Hlathikulu
Hliboka *see* Hlyboka
111 F17 **Hlinsko** *var.* Hlinsko v Čechách. Pardubický Kraj, C Czech Republic
Hlinsko v Čechách *see* Hlinsko
117 S6 **Hlobyne** *Rus.* Globino. Poltavs'ka Oblast', NE Ukraine
111 H20 **Hlohovec** *Ger.* Freistadtl, *Hung.* Galgóc; *prev.* Frakštát. Trnavský Kraj, W Slovakia
83 J23 **Hlotse** *var.* Leribe. NW Lesotho
111 I17 **Hlučín** *Ger.* Hultschin, *Pol.* Hulczyn. Moravskoslezský Kraj, E Czech Republic
117 S2 **Hlukhiv** *Rus.* Glukhov. Sums'ka Oblast', NE Ukraine
119 K21 **Hlushkavichy** *Rus.* Glushkevichi. Homyel'skaya Voblasts', SE Belarus
119 L18 **Hlusk** *Rus.* Glusk, Glussk. Mahilyowskaya Voblasts', E Belarus
116 K8 **Hlyboka** *Ger.* Hliboka, *Rus.* Glybokaya. Chernivets'ka Oblast', W Ukraine
118 K13 **Hlybokaye** *Rus.* Glubokoye. Vitsyebskaya Voblasts', N Belarus
77 Q16 **Ho** SE Ghana
167 S6 **Hoa Binh** Hoa Binh, N Vietnam
83 E20 **Hoachanas** Hardap, C Namibia
Hoai Nhơn *see* Bông Sơn
167 T8 **Hoa Lac** Quang Binh, C Vietnam
167 S5 **Hoang Liên Sơn** ▲ N Vietnam
83 B17 **Hoanib** ≈ NW Namibia
33 S15 **Hoback Peak** ▲ Wyoming, C USA
183 P17 **Hobart** *prev.* Hobarton, Hobart Town. *state capital* Tasmania, SE Australia
26 L11 **Hobart** Oklahoma, C USA
183 P17 **Hobart** ✕ Tasmania, SE Australia
Hobarton/Hobart Town *see* Hobart
37 W14 **Hobbs** New Mexico, SW USA
194 L12 **Hobbs Coast** *physical region* Antarctica
23 Z14 **Hobe Sound** Florida, SE USA
Hobicaurikány *see* Uricani
54 E12 **Hobo** Huila, S Colombia
99 G16 **Hoboken** Antwerpen, N Belgium
158 K3 **Hoboksar** *var.* Hoboksar Mongol Zizhixian. Xinjiang Uygur Zizhiqu, NW China
Hoboksar Mongol Zizhixian *see* Hoboksar
95 G21 **Hobro** Nordjylland, N Denmark
21 X10 **Hobucken** North Carolina, SE USA
95 O20 **Hoburgen** *headland* SE Sweden
81 P15 **Hobyo** *It.* Obbia. Mudug, E Somalia
109 R8 **Hochalmspitze** ▲ SW Austria
109 Q4 **Hochburg** Oberösterreich, N Austria
108 F8 **Hochdorf** Luzern, N Switzerland
109 N8 **Hochfeiler** *It.* Gran Pilastro. ▲ Austria/Italy
167 T14 **Hô Chi Minh** *var.* Ho Chi Minh City; *prev.* Saigon. S Vietnam
Ho Chi Minh City *see* Hô Chi Minh
108 I7 **Höchst** Vorarlberg, NW Austria
Höchstadt *see* Höchstadt an der Aisch
101 K19 **Höchstadt an der Aisch** *var.* Höchstadt. Bayern, C Germany
108 L9 **Hochwilde** *It.* L'Altissima. ▲ Austria/Italy
109 S7 **Hochwildstelle** ▲ C Austria
31 T14 **Hocking River** ≈ Ohio, N USA
Hoctúm *see* Hoctún
41 X12 **Hoctún** *var.* Hoctúm. Yucatán, E Mexico
Hodeida *see* Al Ḩudaydah
20 K6 **Hodgenville** Kentucky, S USA
11 T17 **Hodgeville** Saskatchewan, S Canada
76 L9 **Hodh ech Chargui** ❖ *region* E Mauritania
Hodh el Garbi *see* Hodh el Gharbi
76 J10 **Hodh el Gharbi** *var.* Hodh el Garbi. ❖ *region* S Mauritania
111 L25 **Hódmezővásárhely** Csongrád, SE Hungary
74 J6 **Hodna, Chott El** *var.* Chott el-Hodna, *Ar.* Shatt al-Hodna. *salt lake* N Algeria
Hodna, Shatt al- *see* Hodna, Chott El
111 G19 **Hodonín** *Ger.* Göding. Jihomoravský Kraj, SE Czech Republic
162 G6 **Hödrögö** Dzavhan, N Mongolia
Hodság/Hodschag *see* Odžaci
39 R7 **Hodzana River** ≈ Alaska, USA
Hoei *see* Huy
99 H19 **Hoeilaart** Vlaams Brabant, C Belgium
Hoë Karoo *see* Great Karoo
98 F12 **Hoek van Holland** *Eng.* Hook of Holland. Zuid-Holland, W Netherlands
98 L11 **Hoenderloo** Gelderland, E Netherlands
99 L18 **Hoensbroek** Limburg, SE Netherlands
163 Y11 **Hoeryŏng** NE North Korea
99 K18 **Hoeselt** Limburg, NE Belgium
98 K11 **Hoevelaken** Gelderland, C Netherlands
Hoey *see* Huy
101 M18 **Hof** Bayern, SE Germany
Höfdhakaupstadhur *see* Skagaströnd
Hofei *see* Hefei
101 G18 **Hofheim am Taunus** Hessen, W Germany
Hofmarkt *see* Odorheiu Secuiesc
92 L3 **Höfn** Austurland, SE Iceland
94 N13 **Hofors** Gävleborg, C Sweden
92 J6 **Hofsjökull** *glacier* C Iceland
92 J1 **Hofsós** Nordhurland Vestra, N Iceland
164 E13 **Hōfu** Yamaguchi, Honshū, SW Japan
Hofuf *see* Al Hufūf
95 J22 **Höganäs** Skåne, S Sweden
183 P14 **Hogan Group** *island group* Tasmania, SE Australia
23 R4 **Hogansville** Georgia, SE USA
39 P8 **Hogatza River** ≈ Alaska, USA
28 I14 **Hogback Mountain** ▲ Nebraska, C USA
95 G14 **Høgevarde** ▲ S Norway
Högfors *see* Karkkila
31 P5 **Hog Island** *island* Michigan, N USA
21 Y6 **Hog Island** *island* Virginia, NE USA
Hogoley Islands *see* Chuuk Islands
95 N20 **Högsby** Kalmar, S Sweden
36 K1 **Hogup Mountains** ▲ Utah, W USA
101 E17 **Hohe Acht** ▲ W Germany
Hohenelbe *see* Vrchlabí
108 I7 **Hohenems** Vorarlberg, W Austria
Hohenmauth *see* Vysoké Mýto
Hohensalza *see* Inowrocław
Hohenstadt *see* Zábřeh
Hohenstein in Ostpreussen *see* Olsztynek
20 I9 **Hohenwald** Tennessee, S USA
101 L17 **Hohenwarte-Stausee** ⊡ C Germany
Hohes Venn *see* Hautes Fagnes
109 Q8 **Hohe Tauern** ▲ W Austria
163 O13 **Hohhot** *var.* Huhehot, Huhuohaote, *Mong.* Kukukhoto; *prev.* Kweisui, Kwesui. Nei Mongol Zizhiqu, N China
103 U6 **Hohneck** ▲ NE France
77 Q16 **Hohoe** E Ghana
164 E12 **Hōhoku** Yamaguchi, Honshū, SW Japan
159 O11 **Hoh Sai Hu** ◎ C China
159 N11 **Hoh Xil Hu** ◎ C China
158 L11 **Hoh Xil Shan** ▲ W China
167 U10 **Hôi An** *prev.* Faifo. Quang Nam-Đa Nẵng, C Vietnam
Hoï-Hao/Hoihow *see* Haikou
159 S11 **Hoika** *prev.* Heka. Qinghai, W China
81 F17 **Hoima** W Uganda
26 L5 **Hoisington** Kansas, C USA
146 D12 **Hojagala** *Rus.* Khodzhakala. Balkan Welaýaty, W Turkmenistan
146 M13 **Hojambaz** *Rus.* Khodzhambas. Lebap Welaýaty, E Turkmenistan
95 H23 **Højby** Fyn, C Denmark
95 F24 **Højer** Sønderjylland, SW Denmark
164 E14 **Hōjō** *var.* Hôzyô. Ehime, Shikoku, SW Japan
184 J3 **Hokianga Harbour** *inlet* SE Tasman Sea
185 F17 **Hokitika** West Coast, South Island, NZ
165 U4 **Hokkai-dō** ❖ *territory* Hokkaidō, NE Japan
165 T3 **Hokkaidō** *prev.* Ezo, Yeso, Yezo. *island* NE Japan
95 G15 **Hokksund** Buskerud, S Norway
143 S4 **Hokmābād** Khorāsān, N Iran
Hokō *see* P'ohang
Hoko-guntō/Hoko-shotō *see* P'enghu Liehtao
Hoktemberyan *see* Armavir
94 F13 **Hol** Buskerud, S Norway
117 R11 **Hola Prystan'** *Rus.* Golaya Pristan. Khersons'ka Oblast', S Ukraine
95 I23 **Holbæk** Vestsjælland, E Denmark
162 G6 **Holboo** Dzavhan, W Mongolia
183 P10 **Holbrook** New South Wales, SE Australia
37 N11 **Holbrook** Arizona, SW USA
27 S5 **Holden** Missouri, C USA
36 K5 **Holden** Utah, W USA
27 O11 **Holdenville** Oklahoma, C USA
29 O16 **Holdrege** Nebraska, C USA
35 X3 **Hole in the Mountain Peak** ▲ Nevada, W USA
155 G20 **Hole Narsipur** Karnātaka, W India
111 H18 **Holešov** *Ger.* Holleschau. Zlínský Kraj, E Czech Republic
45 N14 **Holetown** *prev.* Jamestown. W Barbados
31 Q12 **Holgate** Ohio, N USA
44 I7 **Holguín** Holguín, SE Cuba
23 V12 **Holiday** Florida, SE USA
39 O12 **Holitna River** ≈ Alaska, USA
94 J13 **Höljes** Värmland, C Sweden
109 X3 **Hollabrunn** Niederösterreich, NE Austria
36 L3 **Holladay** Utah, W USA
11 X16 **Holland** Manitoba, S Canada
31 O9 **Holland** Michigan, N USA
25 T9 **Holland** Texas, SW USA
Holland *see* Netherlands
22 K4 **Hollandale** Mississippi, S USA
Hollandia *see* Jayapura
Hollandsch Diep *see* Hollands Diep
99 H14 **Hollands Diep** *var.* Hollandsch Diep. *channel* SW Netherlands
Holleschau *see* Holešov
25 R5 **Holliday** Texas, SW USA
18 E15 **Hollidaysburg** Pennsylvania, NE USA
21 S6 **Hollins** Virginia, NE USA
26 J12 **Hollis** Oklahoma, C USA
35 O10 **Hollister** California, W USA
27 T8 **Hollister** Missouri, C USA
93 M19 **Hollola** Etelä-Suomi, S Finland
98 K4 **Hollum** Friesland, N Netherlands
95 J23 **Höllviksnäs** Skåne, S Sweden
37 W6 **Holly** Colorado, C USA
31 R9 **Holly** Michigan, N USA
21 S14 **Holly Hill** South Carolina, SE USA
21 W11 **Holly Ridge** North Carolina, SE USA
22 L1 **Holly Springs** Mississippi, S USA
23 Z15 **Hollywood** Florida, SE USA
8 J6 **Holman** Victoria Island, Northwest Territories, N Canada
92 I2 **Hólmavík** Vestfirdhir, NW Iceland
30 J7 **Holmen** Wisconsin, N USA
23 R8 **Holmes Creek** ≈ Alabama/Florida, SE USA
95 H16 **Holmestrand** Vestfold, S Norway
93 J16 **Holmön** *island* N Sweden
95 E22 **Holmsland Klit** *beach* W Denmark
93 J16 **Holmsund** Västerbotten, N Sweden
95 Q18 **Holmudden** *headland* SE Sweden
138 F10 **Ḩolon** *var.* Kholon. Tel Aviv, C Israel
117 P8 **Holovanivs'k** *Rus.* Golovanevsk. Kirovohrads'ka Oblast', C Ukraine
95 F21 **Holstebro** Ringkøbing, W Denmark
95 F23 **Holsted** Ribe, W Denmark
29 T13 **Holstein** Iowa, C USA
Holsteinborg/Holsteinsborg/Holstenborg/Holstensborg *see* Sisimiut
21 O8 **Holston River** ≈ Tennessee, S USA
31 Q9 **Holt** Michigan, N USA
98 N10 **Holten** Overijssel, E Netherlands
27 P3 **Holton** Kansas, C USA
27 U5 **Holts Summit** Missouri, C USA
35 X17 **Holtville** California, W USA
98 L5 **Holwerd** *Fris.* Holwert. Friesland, N Netherlands
Holwert *see* Holwerd
39 O11 **Holy Cross** Alaska, USA
37 R4 **Holy Cross, Mount Of The** ▲ Colorado, C USA
97 I18 **Holyhead** *Wel.* Caer Gybi. NW Wales, UK
97 H18 **Holy Island** *island* NW Wales, UK
96 L12 **Holy Island** *island* NE England, UK
37 W3 **Holyoke** Colorado, C USA
18 M11 **Holyoke** Massachusetts, NE USA
101 I14 **Holzminden** Niedersachsen, C Germany
81 G19 **Homa Bay** Nyanza, W Kenya
Homāyūnshahr *see* Khomeynīshahr
77 P11 **Hombori** Mopti, S Mali
101 E20 **Homburg** Saarland, SW GermanyQ5
9 R5 **Home Bay** *bay* Baffin Bay, Nunavut, NE Canada
Homenau *see* Humenné
39 Q13 **Homer** Alaska, USA
22 H4 **Homer** Louisiana, S USA
18 H10 **Homer** New York, NE USA
23 V7 **Homerville** Georgia, SE USA
23 Y16 **Homestead** Florida, SE USA
27 O9 **Hominy** Oklahoma, C USA
94 H8 **Hommelvik** Sør-Trøndelag, S Norway
95 C16 **Hommersåk** Rogaland, S Norway
155 H15 **Homnābād** Karnātaka, C India
22 J7 **Homochitto River** ≈ Mississippi, S USA
83 N20 **Homoine** Inhambane, SE Mozambique
112 O12 **Homoljske Planine** ▲ E Serbia and Montenegro (Yugo.)
Homonna *see* Humenné
Homs *see* Al Khums, Libya
Homs *see* Ḩimş, Syria
119 P19 **Homyel'** *Rus.* Gomel'. Homyel'skaya Voblasts', SE Belarus
118 L12 **Homyel'** Vitsyebskaya Voblasts', N Belarus
119 L19 **Homyel'skaya Voblasts'** *prev. Rus.* Gomel'skaya Oblast'. ❖ *province* SE Belarus
Honan *see* Henan, China
Honan *see* Luoyang, China
165 U4 **Honbetsu** Hokkaidō, NE Japan
Honctő *see* Gurahonţ
54 E9 **Honda** Tolima, C Colombia
83 D24 **Hondeklip** *Afr.* Hondeklipbaai. Northern Cape, W South Africa
Hondeklipbaai *see* Hondeklip
11 Q13 **Hondo** Alberta, W Canada
164 C15 **Hondo** Kumamoto, Shimo-jima, SW Japan
25 Q12 **Hondo** Texas, SW USA
42 G1 **Hondo** ≈ Central America
Hondo *see* Honshū
42 G6 **Honduras** *off.* Republic of Honduras. ◆ *republic* Central America
Honduras, Golfo de *see* Honduras, Gulf of
42 H4 **Honduras, Gulf of** *Sp.* Golfo de Honduras. *gulf* W Caribbean Sea
11 V12 **Hone** Manitoba, C Canada
21 P12 **Honea Path** South Carolina, SE USA
95 H14 **Hønefoss** Buskerud, S Norway
31 S12 **Honey Creek** ≈ Ohio, N USA
25 V5 **Honey Grove** Texas, SW USA
35 Q4 **Honey Lake** ◎ California, W USA
102 L4 **Honfleur** Calvados, N France
Hon Gai *see* Hông Gai
161 O8 **Hong'an** *prev.* Huang'an. Hubei, C China
Hongay *see* Hông Gai
167 T6 **Hông Gai** *var.* Hon Gai, Hongay. Quang Ninh, N Vietnam
161 O15 **Honghai Wan** *bay* N South China Sea
Hông Hà, Sông *see* Red River
161 O7 **Hong He** ≈ C China
161 N9 **Hong Hu** ◎ C China
160 L11 **Hongjiang** Hunan, S China
Hongjiang *see* Wangcang
161 O15 **Hong Kong** *Chin.* Xianggang. S China
160 L4 **Hongliu He** ≈ C China
159 P8 **Hongliuwan** *var.* Aksay, Aksay Kazakzu Zizhixian. Gansu, N China
159 P7 **Hongliuyuan** Gansu, N China
163 O9 **Hongor** Dornogovĭ, SE Mongolia
161 S8 **Hongqiao** ✕ (Shanghai) Shanghai Shi, E China
160 K14 **Hongshui He** ≈ S China
160 M5 **Hongtong** Shanxi, C China
164 J15 **Hongū** Wakayama, Honshū, SW Japan
Honguedo, Détroit d' *see* Honguedo Passage
15 Y5 **Honguedo Passage** *var.* Honguedo Strait, *Fr.* Détroit d'Honguedo. *strait* Québec, E Canada
Honguedo Strait *see* Honguedo Passage
Hongwan *see* Hongwansi
159 S8 **Hongwansi** *var.* Sunan, Sunan Yugurzu Zizhixian *prev.* Hongwan. Gansu, N China
163 X13 **Hongwŏn** E North Korea
160 H7 **Hongyuan** *var.* Qiongxi, *prev.* Hurama. Sichuan, C China
161 Q7 **Hongze Hu** *var.* Hung-tse Hu. ◎ E China
186 L9 **Honiara** ● (Solomon Islands) Guadalcanal, C Solomon Islands
165 P8 **Honjō** *var.* Honzyô. Akita, Honshū, C Japan
93 K18 **Honkajoki** Länsi-Suomi, W Finland
92 K7 **Honningsvåg** Finnmark, N Norway
95 I19 **Hönö** Västra Götaland, S Sweden
38 G11 **Honoka'a** *var.* Honokaa. Hawai'i, USA, C Pacific Ocean
38 D9 **Honolulu** ◉ O'ahu, Hawai'i, USA, C Pacific Ocean
38 H11 **Honomū** *var.* Honomu. Hawai'i, USA, C Pacific Ocean
105 P10 **Honrubia** Castilla-La Mancha, C Spain
164 M12 **Honshū** *var.* Hondo, Honsyû. *island* SW Japan
Honsyû *see* Honshū
Honte *see* Westerschelde
Honzyô *see* Honjō
8 K8 **Hood** ≈ Nunavut, NW Canada
Hood Island *see* Española, Isla
32 H11 **Hood, Mount** ▲ Oregon, NW USA
32 H11 **Hood River** Oregon, NW USA
98 H10 **Hoofddorp** Noord-Holland, W Netherlands
99 G15 **Hoogerheide** Noord-Brabant, S Netherlands
98 N8 **Hoogeveen** Drenthe, NE Netherlands
98 O6 **Hoogezand-Sappemeer** Groningen, NE Netherlands
98 J8 **Hoogkarspel** Noord-Holland, NW Netherlands
98 N5 **Hoogkerk** Groningen, NE Netherlands
98 G13 **Hoogvliet** Zuid-Holland, SW Netherlands
26 I8 **Hooker** Oklahoma, C USA
97 E21 **Hook Head** *Ir.* Rinn Duáin. *headland* SE Ireland
Hook of Holland *see* Hoek van Holland
162 J9 **Hoolt** Övörhangay, C Mongolia
39 W13 **Hoonah** Chichagof Island, Alaska, USA
38 L11 **Hooper Bay** Alaska, USA
31 N13 **Hoopeston** Illinois, N USA
95 K22 **Höör** Skåne, S Sweden
98 I9 **Hoorn** Noord-Holland, NW Netherlands
18 L10 **Hoosic River** ≈ New York, NE USA
Hoosier State *see* Indiana
35 Y11 **Hoover Dam** *dam* Arizona/Nevada, W USA
162 I9 **Höövör** Övörhangay, C Mongolia
137 Q11 **Hopa** Artvin, NE Turkey
18 J14 **Hopatcong** New Jersey, NE USA
10 M17 **Hope** British Columbia, SW Canada
39 R12 **Hope** Alaska, USA
27 T14 **Hope** Arkansas, C USA
31 P14 **Hope** Indiana, N USA
29 Q5 **Hope** North Dakota, N USA
13 Q7 **Hopedale** Newfoundland and Labrador, NE Canada
Hopeh/Hopei *see* Hebei
180 K13 **Hope, Lake** *salt lake* Western Australia
41 X13 **Hopelchén** Campeche, SE Mexico
21 U11 **Hope Mills** North Carolina, SE USA
183 O7 **Hope, Mount** New South Wales, SE Australia
92 P4 **Hopen** *island* SE Svalbard
197 Q4 **Hope, Point** *headland* Alaska, USA
12 M3 **Hopes Advance, Cap** *headland* Québec, NE Canada
182 L10 **Hopetoun** Victoria, SE Australia
83 H23 **Hopetown** Northern Cape, W South Africa
21 W6 **Hopewell** Virginia, NE USA
109 O7 **Hopfgarten-im-Brixental** Tirol, W Austria
181 N8 **Hopkins Lake** *salt lake* Western Australia
182 M12 **Hopkins River** ≈ Victoria, SE Australia
20 I7 **Hopkinsville** Kentucky, S USA
34 M6 **Hopland** California, W USA
95 G24 **Hoptrup** Sønderjylland, SW Denmark
Hoqin Zuoyi Zhongji *see* Baokang
32 F9 **Hoquiam** Washington, NW USA
29 R6 **Horace** North Dakota, N USA
137 R12 **Horasan** Erzurum, NE Turkey
101 G22 **Horb am Neckar** Baden-Württemberg, S Germany
95 K23 **Hörby** Skåne, S Sweden
43 P16 **Horconcitos** Chiriquí, W Panama
95 C14 **Hordaland** ❖ *county* S Norway
116 H13 **Horezu** Vâlcea, SW Romania
108 G7 **Horgen** Zürich, N Switzerland
162 I7 **Horgo** Arhangay, C Mongolia
Hörin *see* Fenglin
163 O13 **Horinger** Nei Mongol Zizhiqu, N China
162 I9 **Horiult** Bayanhongor, C Mongolia
11 U17 **Horizon** Saskatchewan, S Canada
192 K9 **Horizon Bank** *undersea feature* S Pacific Ocean
192 L10 **Horizon Deep** *undersea feature* W Pacific Ocean
95 L14 **Hörken** Örebro, S Sweden
119 O15 **Horki** *Rus.* Gorki. Mahilyowskaya Voblasts', E Belarus
195 O10 **Horlick Mountains** ▲ Antarctica
117 X7 **Horlivka** *Rom.* Adâncata, *Rus.* Gorlovka. Donets'ka Oblast', E Ukraine
143 V11 **Hormak** Sīstān va Balūchestān, SE Iran
143 R13 **Hormozgān** *off.* Ostān-e Hormozgān. ❖ *province* S Iran
Hormoz, Tangeh-ye *see* Hormuz, Strait of

◆ COUNTRY ● COUNTRY CAPITAL ◇ DEPENDENT TERRITORY ○ DEPENDENT TERRITORY CAPITAL ❖ ADMINISTRATIVE REGION ✕ INTERNATIONAL AIRPORT ▲ MOUNTAIN ▲ MOUNTAIN RANGE ⁂ VOLCANO ≈ RIVER ◎ LAKE ⊡ RESERVOIR

141 W6 **Hormuz, Strait of** *var.* Strait of Ormuz, *Per.* Tangeh-ye Hormoz. *strait* Iran/Oman
109 W2 **Horn** Niederösterreich, NE Austria
95 M18 **Horn** Östergötland, S Sweden
8 J9 **Horn** ≈ Northwest Territories, NW Canada
Hornád *see* Hernád
8 I6 **Hornaday** ≈ Northwest Territories, NW Canada
92 H13 **Hornavan** ◎ N Sweden
65 C24 **Hornby Mountains** *hill range* West Falkland, Falkland Islands
Horn, Cape *see* Hornos, Cabo de
97 O18 **Horncastle** E England, UK
95 N14 **Horndal** Dalarna, C Sweden
93 I16 **Hörnefors** Västerbotten, N Sweden
18 F11 **Hornell** New York, NE USA
Horné Nové Mesto *see* Kysucké Nové Mesto
12 F12 **Hornepayne** Ontario, S Canada
94 D10 **Hornindalsvatnet** ◎ S Norway
101 G22 **Hornisgrinde** ▲ SW Germany
22 M9 **Horn Island** *island* Mississippi, S USA
Hornja Łužica *see* Oberlausitz
63 J26 **Hornos, Cabo de** *Eng.* Cape Horn. *headland* S Chile
117 S10 **Hornostayivka** Khersons'ka Oblast', S Ukraine
183 T9 **Hornsby** New South Wales, SE Australia
97 O16 **Hornsea** E England, UK
94 O11 **Hornslandet** *peninsula* C Sweden
95 H22 **Hornslet** Århus, C Denmark
92 O4 **Hornsundtind** ▲ S Svalbard
Horochów *see* Horokhiv
116 J7 **Horodenka** *Rus.* Gorodenka. Ivano-Frankivs'ka Oblast', W Ukraine
117 Q2 **Horodnya** *Rus.* Gorodnya. Chernihivs'ka Oblast', NE Ukraine
116 K6 **Horodok** Khmel'nyts'ka Oblast', W Ukraine
116 H5 **Horodok** *Pol.* Gródek Jagielloński, *Rus.* Gorodok, Gorodok Yagellonski. L'vivs'ka Oblast', NW Ukraine
117 Q6 **Horodyshche** *Rus.* Gorodishche. Cherkas'ka Oblast', C Ukraine
165 T3 **Horokanai** Hokkaidō, NE Japan
116 J4 **Horokhiv** *Pol.* Horochów, *Rus.* Gorokhov. Volyns'ka Oblast', NW Ukraine
165 T4 **Horoshiri-dake** *var.* Horosiri Dake. ▲ Hokkaidō, N Japan
Horosiri Dake *see* Horoshiri-dake
111 C17 **Hořovice** *Ger.* Horowitz. Středočeský Kraj, W Czech Republic
Horowitz *see* Hořovice
Horqin Zuoyi Houqi *see* Ganjig
Horqin Zuoyi Zhongji *see* Bayan Huxu
62 O5 **Horqueta** Concepción, C Paraguay
55 O12 **Horqueta Minas** Amazonas, S Venezuela
95 J20 **Horred** Västra Götaland, S Sweden
151 J19 **Horsburgh Atoll** *atoll* N Maldives
20 K7 **Horse Cave** Kentucky, S USA
37 V6 **Horse Creek** ≈ Colorado, C USA
27 S6 **Horse Creek** ≈ Missouri, C USA
18 G11 **Horseheads** New York, NE USA
37 P13 **Horse Mount** ▲ New Mexico, SW USA
95 G22 **Horsens** Vejle, C Denmark
65 F25 **Horse Pasture Point** *headland* W Saint Helena
33 N13 **Horseshoe Bend** Idaho, NW USA
36 L13 **Horseshoe Reservoir** ⊠ Arizona, SW USA
64 M9 **Horseshoe Seamounts** *undersea feature* E Atlantic Ocean
182 L11 **Horsham** Victoria, SE Australia
97 O23 **Horsham** SE England, UK
99 M15 **Horst** Limburg, SE Netherlands
64 N2 **Horta** Faial, Azores, Portugal, NE Atlantic Ocean
95 H16 **Horten** Vestfold, S Norway
111 M23 **Hortobágy-Berettyó** ≈ E Hungary
27 Q3 **Horton** Kansas, C USA
8 I7 **Horton** ≈ Northwest Territories, NW Canada
95 I23 **Hørve** Vestsjælland, E Denmark
95 L22 **Hörvik** Blekinge, S Sweden
138 E11 **Horvot Haluza** *var.* Khorvot Khalutsa. *ruins* Southern, S Israel
14 E7 **Horwood Lake** ◎ Ontario, S Canada
116 K4 **Horyn'** *Rus.* Goryn. ≈ NW Ukraine
81 I14 **Hosa'ina** *var.* Hosseina, *It.* Hosanna. Southern, S Ethiopia
Hosanna *see* Hosa'ina
101 H18 **Hösbach** Bayern, C Germany
Hose Mountains *see* Hose, Pegunungan
169 T9 **Hose, Pegunungan** *var.* Hose Mountains. ⛰ East Malaysia
148 L15 **Hoshāb** Baluchistān, SW Pakistan
154 H10 **Hoshangābād** Madhya Pradesh, C India
116 L4 **Hoshcha** Rivnens'ka Oblast', NW Ukraine
152 I7 **Hoshiārpur** Punjab, NW India
162 J7 **Höshööt** Arhangay, C Mongolia
99 M23 **Hosingen** Diekirch, NE Luxembourg
186 G7 **Hoskins** New Britain, E PNG
155 G17 **Hospet** Karnātaka, C India
104 K4 **Hospital de Orbigo** Castilla-León, N Spain
Hospitalet *see* L'Hospitalet de Llobregat
92 N13 **Hossa** Oulu, E Finland
Hosseina *see* Hosa'ina
Hosszúmezjő *see* Câmpulung Moldovenesc
63 I25 **Hoste, Isla** *island* S Chile
117 O4 **Hostomel'** *Rus.* Gostomel'. Kyyivs'ka Oblast', N Ukraine
155 H20 **Hosūr** Tamil Nādu, SE India
167 N8 **Hot** Chiang Mai, NW Thailand
158 G10 **Hotan** *var.* Khotan, *Chin.* Ho-t'ien. Xinjiang Uygur Zizhiqu, NW China
158 H9 **Hotan He** ≈ NW China
83 G22 **Hotazel** Northern Cape, N South Africa
37 Q5 **Hotchkiss** Colorado, C USA
35 V7 **Hot Creek Range** ⛰ Nevada, W USA
Hote *see* Hoti
171 T13 **Hoti** *var.* Hote. Pulau Seram, E Indonesia
Ho-t'ien *see* Hotan
Hotin *see* Khotyn
93 H15 **Hoting** Jämtland, C Sweden
162 L14 **Hotong Qagan Nur** ◎ N China
162 J8 **Hotont** Arhangay, C Mongolia
27 T12 **Hot Springs** Arkansas, C USA
28 J11 **Hot Springs** South Dakota, N USA
21 S5 **Hot Springs** Virginia, NE USA
35 Q4 **Hot Springs Peak** ▲ California, W USA
27 T12 **Hot Springs Village** Arkansas, C USA
Hotspur Bank *see* Hotspur Seamount
65 J16 **Hotspur Seamount** *var.* Hotspur Bank. *undersea feature* C Atlantic Ocean
8 J8 **Hottah Lake** ◎ Northwest Territories, NW Canada
44 K9 **Hotte, Massif de la** ⛰ SW Haiti
99 K21 **Hotton** Luxembourg, SE Belgium
Hötzing *see* Haţeg
187 P17 **Houaïlou** Province Nord, C New Caledonia
74 K5 **Houari Boumediène** ✕ (Alger) N Algeria
167 P6 **Houayxay** *var.* Ban Houayxay, Ban Houei Sai. Bokèo, N Laos
103 N5 **Houdan** Yvelines, N France
99 F20 **Houdeng-Goegnies** *var.* Houdeng-Gœgnies. Hainaut, S Belgium
102 K14 **Houeillès** Lot-et-Garonne, SW France
99 L22 **Houffalize** Luxembourg, SE Belgium
30 M3 **Houghton** Michigan, N USA
31 Q7 **Houghton Lake** Michigan, N USA
31 Q7 **Houghton Lake** ◎ Michigan, N USA
19 T3 **Houlton** Maine, NE USA
160 M5 **Houma** Shanxi, C China
193 U15 **Houma** 'Eua, C Tonga
193 U16 **Houma** Tongatapu, S Tonga
22 J10 **Houma** Louisiana, S USA
196 V16 **Houma Taloa** *headland* Tongatapu, S Tonga
77 O13 **Houndé** SW Burkina
102 J12 **Hourtin-Carcans, Lac d'** ◎ SW France
36 J5 **House Range** ⛰ Utah, W USA
10 K13 **Houston** British Columbia, SW Canada
39 R11 **Houston** Alaska, USA
29 X10 **Houston** Minnesota, N USA
22 M3 **Houston** Mississippi, S USA
27 V7 **Houston** Missouri, C USA
25 W11 **Houston** Texas, SW USA
25 W11 **Houston** ✕ Texas, SW USA
98 J12 **Houten** Utrecht, C Netherlands
99 K17 **Houthalen** Limburg, NE Belgium
99 I22 **Houyet** Namur, SE Belgium
95 H22 **Hov** Århus, C Denmark
95 L17 **Hova** Västra Götaland, S Sweden
162 E6 **Hovd** *var.* Khovd, Kobdo; *prev.* Jirgalanta. Hovd, W Mongolia
162 J10 **Hovd** Övörhangay, C Mongolia
162 E7 **Hovd** ◈ *province* W Mongolia
162 C5 **Hovd Gol** ≈ NW Mongolia
97 O23 **Hove** SE England, UK
29 N8 **Hoven** South Dakota, N USA
116 I8 **Hoverla, Hora** *Rus.* Gora Goverla. ▲ W Ukraine
162 H8 **Höviyn Am** Bayanhongor, C Mongolia
95 M21 **Hovmantorp** Kronoberg, S Sweden
163 N11 **Hövsgöl** Dornogovĭ, SE Mongolia
162 I5 **Hṇvsgṇl** Hṇvsgṇl ◈ *province* N Mongolia
Hovsgol, Lake *see* Hövsgöl Nuur
162 J5 **Hövsgöl Nuur** *var.* Lake Hovsgol. ◎ N Mongolia
78 L9 **Howa, Ouadi** *var.* Wādi Howar. ≈ Chad/Sudan *see also* Howar, Wādi
27 P7 **Howard** Kansas, C USA
29 Q10 **Howard** South Dakota, N USA
25 N10 **Howard Draw** *valley* Texas, SW USA
29 U8 **Howard Lake** Minnesota, N USA
80 B8 **Howar, Wādi** *var.* Ouadi Howa. ≈ Chad/Sudan *see also* Howa, Ouadi
25 U5 **Howe** Texas, SW USA
183 R12 **Howe, Cape** *headland* New South Wales/Victoria, SE Australia
31 R9 **Howell** Michigan, N USA
28 L9 **Howes** South Dakota, N USA
83 K23 **Howick** KwaZulu/Natal, E South Africa
Howrah *see* Hāora
27 W9 **Hoxie** Arkansas, C USA
26 J3 **Hoxie** Kansas, C USA
101 I14 **Höxter** Nordrhein-Westfalen, W Germany
158 K6 **Hoxud** Xinjiang Uygur Zizhiqu, NW China
96 J5 **Hoy** *island* N Scotland, UK
43 S17 **Hoya, Cerro** ▲ S Panama
94 D12 **Høyanger** Sogn og Fjordane, S Norway
101 P15 **Hoyerswerda** *Lus.* Wojerecy. Sachsen, E Germany
164 E14 **Hōyo-kaikyō** *var.* Hayasui-seto. *strait* SW Japan
104 J8 **Hoyos** Extremadura, W Spain
29 W4 **Hoyt Lakes** Minnesota, N USA
87 V2 **Hoyvík** Streymoy, N Faeroe Islands
137 O14 **Hozat** Tunceli, E Turkey
Hôzyô *see* Hōjō
111 F16 **Hradec Králové** *Ger.* Königgrätz. Královéhradecký Kraj, N Czech Republic
Hradecký Kraj *see* Královéhradecký Kraj
111 B16 **Hradiště** *Ger.* Burgstadlberg. ▲ NW Czech Republic
117 R6 **Hradyz'k** *Rus.* Gradizhsk. Poltavs'ka Oblast', NE Ukraine
119 M16 **Hradzyanka** *Rus.* Grodzyanka. Mahilyowskaya Voblasts', E Belarus
119 F16 **Hrandzichy** *Rus.* Grandichi. Hrodzyenskaya Voblasts', W Belarus
111 H18 **Hranice** *Ger.* Mährisch-Weisskirchen. Olomoucký Kraj, E Czech Republic
112 I13 **Hrasnica** Federacija Bosna I Hercegovina, SE Bosnia and Herzegovina
109 V11 **Hrastnik** C Slovenia
137 U12 **Hrazdan** *Rus.* Razdan. C Armenia
137 T12 **Hrazdan** *var.* Zanga, *Rus.* Razdan. ≈ C Armenia
117 R5 **Hrebinka** *Rus.* Grebenka. Poltavs'ka Oblast', NE Ukraine
119 K17 **Hresk** *Rus.* Gresk. Minskaya Voblasts', C Belarus
Hrisoupoli *see* Chrysoúpoli
119 F16 **Hrodna** *Pol.* Grodno. Hrodzyenskaya Voblasts', W Belarus
119 F16 **Hrodzyenskaya Voblasts'** *prev. Rus.* Grodnenskaya Oblast'. ◈ *province* W Belarus
111 J21 **Hron** *Ger.* Gran, *Hung.* Garam. ≈ C Slovakia
111 Q14 **Hrubieszów** *Rus.* Grubeshov. Lubelskie, E Poland
112 F13 **Hrvace** Split-Dalmacija, SE Croatia
Hrvatska *see* Croatia
112 F10 **Hrvatska Kostajnica** *var.* Kostajnica. Sisak-Moslavina, C Croatia
Hrvatsko Grahovo *see* Bosansko Grahovo
116 K6 **Hrymayliv** *Pol.* Gízymałów, *Rus.* Grimaylov. Ternopil's'ka Oblast', W Ukraine
167 N4 **Hsenwi** Shan State, E Myanmar
Hsia-men *see* Xiamen
Hsiang-t'an *see* Xiangtan
Hsi Chiang *see* Xi Jiang
167 N6 **Hsihseng** Shan State, C Myanmar
161 S13 **Hsinchu** *municipality* N Taiwan
Hsing-k'ai Hu *see* Khanka, Lake
Hsi-ning/Hsining *see* Xining
Hsinking *see* Changchun
Hsin-yang *see* Xinyang
161 S14 **Hsinying** *var.* Sinying, *Jap.* Shinei. C Taiwan
167 N4 **Hsipaw** Shan State, C Myanmar
Hsu-chou *see* Xuzhou
161 S13 **Hsüeh Shan** ▲ N Taiwan
Hu *see* Shanghai Shi
83 B18 **Huab** ≈ W Namibia
57 M21 **Huacaya** Chuquisaca, S Bolivia
57 J19 **Huachacalla** Oruro, SW Bolivia
159 X9 **Huachi** *var.* Rouyuanchengzi. Gansu, C China
57 N16 **Huachi, Laguna** ◎ N Bolivia
57 D14 **Huacho** Lima, W Peru
163 Y8 **Huachuan** Heilongjiang, NE China
163 P12 **Huade** Nei Mongol Zizhiqu, N China
163 W10 **Huadian** Jilin, NE China
56 E13 **Huagaruncho, Cordillera** ⛰ C Peru
Hua Hin *see* Ban Hua Hin
191 S10 **Huahine** *island* Îles Sous le Vent, W French Polynesia
Huahua, Rio *see* Wawa, Río
167 R8 **Huai** ≈ E Thailand
161 Q7 **Huai'an** *var.* Qingjiang; *prev.* Huaiyin. Jiangsu, E China
161 P6 **Huaibei** Anhui, E China
Huaide *see* Gongzhuling
157 T10 **Huai He** ≈ C China
160 L11 **Huaihua** Hunan, S China
161 N14 **Huaiji** Guangdong, S China
161 O2 **Huailai** *var.* Shacheng. Hebei, E China
161 P7 **Huainan** *var.* Huai-nan, Hwainan. Anhui, E China
161 N2 **Huairen** Shanxi, C China
161 O7 **Huaiyang** Henan, C China
Huaiyin *see* Huai'an
167 N16 **Huai Yot** Trang, SW Thailand
41 Q15 **Huajuapan** *var.* Huajuapan de León. Oaxaca, SE Mexico
Huajuapan de León *see* Huajuapan
41 O9 **Hualahuises** Nuevo León, NE Mexico
36 I11 **Hualapai Mountains** ⛰ Arizona, SW USA
36 I11 **Hualapai Peak** ▲ Arizona, SW USA
62 J7 **Hualfín** Catamarca, N Argentina
161 T13 **Hualien** *var.* Hwalien, *Jap.* Karen. C Taiwan
56 E10 **Huallaga, Río** ≈ N Peru
56 C11 **Huamachuco** La Libertad, C Peru
41 Q14 **Huamantla** Tlaxcala, S Mexico
82 C13 **Huambo** *Port.* Nova Lisboa. Huambo, C Angola
82 B13 **Huambo** ◈ *province* C Angola
41 P15 **Huamuxtitlán** Guerrero, S Mexico
163 Y8 **Huanan** Heilongjiang, NE China
63 H17 **Huancache, Sierra** ⛰ SW Argentina
57 I17 **Huancané** Puno, SE Peru
57 F16 **Huancapi** Ayacucho, C Peru
57 E15 **Huancavelica** Huancavelica, SW Peru
57 E15 **Huancavelica** *off.* Departamento de Huancavelica. ◈ *department* W Peru
57 E14 **Huancayo** Junín, C Peru
57 K20 **Huanchaca, Cerro** ▲ S Bolivia
56 C12 **Huandoy, Nevado** ▲ W Peru
161 O8 **Huangchuan** Henan, C China
161 O9 **Huanggang** Hubei, C China
Huang Hai *see* Yellow Sea
157 Q8 **Huang He** *var.* Yellow River. ≈ C China
161 Q4 **Huanghe Kou** *delta* E China
160 L5 **Huangling** Shaanxi, C China
163 P13 **Huangqi Hai** ◎ N China
161 Q9 **Huang Shan** ▲ Anhui, E China
161 Q9 **Huangshan** *var.* Tunxi. Anhui, E China
161 O9 **Huangshi** *var.* Huang-shih, Hwangshih. Hubei, C China
Huang-shih *see* Huangshi
160 L5 **Huangtu Gaoyuan** *plateau* C China
61 B22 **Huanguelén** Buenos Aires, E Argentina
161 S10 **Huangyan** Zhejiang, SE China
159 T10 **Huangyuan** Qinghai, C China
159 T10 **Huangzhong** *var.* Lushar. Qinghai, C China
163 W12 **Huanren** *var.* Huanren Manzu Zizhixian. Liaoning, NE China
Huanren Manzu Zizhixian *see* Huanren
57 F15 **Huanta** Ayacucho, C Peru
56 E13 **Huánuco** Huánuco, C Peru
56 D13 **Huánuco** *off.* Departamento de Huánuco. ◈ *department* C Peru
57 K19 **Huanuni** Oruro, W Bolivia
159 X9 **Huanxian** Gansu, C China
161 S12 **Huap'ing Yu** *island* N Taiwan
62 H3 **Huara** Tarapacá, N Chile
57 D14 **Huaral** Lima, W Peru
Huarás *see* Huaraz
56 D13 **Huaraz** *var.* Huarás. Ancash, W Peru
57 I16 **Huari Huari, Río** ≈ S Peru
56 C13 **Huarmey** Ancash, W Peru
40 H4 **Huásabas** Sonora, NW Mexico
56 D8 **Huasaga, Río** ≈ Ecuador/Peru
167 O15 **Hua Sai** Nakhon Si Thammarat, SW Thailand
56 D12 **Huascarán, Nevado** ▲ W Peru
62 G8 **Huasco** Atacama, N Chile
62 G8 **Huasco, Río** ≈ C Chile
159 S11 **Huashikia** Qinghai, W China
40 G7 **Huatabampo** Sonora, NW Mexico
159 W10 **Huating** Gansu, C China
167 S7 **Huatt, Phou** ▲ N Vietnam
41 Q14 **Huatusco** *var.* Huatusco de Chicuellar. Veracruz-Llave, C Mexico
Huatusco de Chicuellar *see* Huatusco
41 P13 **Huauchinango** Puebla, S Mexico
Huaunta *see* Wounta
41 R15 **Huautla** *var.* Huautla de Jiménez. Oaxaca, SE Mexico
Huautla de Jiménez *see* Huautla
161 O5 **Huaxian** *var.* Daokou, Hua Xian. Henan, C China
Huazangsi *see* Tianzhu
29 V13 **Hubbard** Iowa, C USA
25 U8 **Hubbard** Texas, SW USA
25 Q6 **Hubbard Creek Lake** ◎ Texas, SW USA
31 R6 **Hubbard Lake** ◎ Michigan, N USA
160 M9 **Hubei** *var.* E, Hubei Sheng, Hupeh, Hupei. ◈ *province* C China
Hubei Sheng *see* Hubei
109 P8 **Huben** Tirol, W Austria
31 R13 **Huber Heights** Ohio, N USA
155 F17 **Hubli** Karnātaka, SW India
163 X12 **Huch'ang** N North Korea
97 M18 **Hucknall** C England, UK
97 L17 **Huddersfield** N England, UK
95 O16 **Huddinge** Stockholm, C Sweden
94 N11 **Hudiksvall** Gävleborg, C Sweden
29 W13 **Hudson** Iowa, C USA
19 O11 **Hudson** Massachusetts, NE USA
31 Q11 **Hudson** Michigan, N USA
30 H6 **Hudson** Wisconsin, N USA
11 V14 **Hudson Bay** Saskatchewan, S Canada
12 G6 **Hudson Bay** *bay* NE Canada
195 T16 **Hudson, Cape** *headland* Antarctica
Hudson, Détroit d' *see* Hudson Strait
27 Q9 **Hudson, Lake** ⊠ Oklahoma, C USA
18 K9 **Hudson River** ≈ New Jersey/New York, NE USA
10 M12 **Hudson's Hope** British Columbia, W Canada
12 L2 **Hudson Strait** *Fr.* Détroit d'Hudson. *strait* Nunavut/Québec, NE Canada
Hudūd ash Shamālīyah, Minṭaqat al *see* Al Ḥudūd ash Shamālīyah
Hudur *see* Xuddur
167 U9 **Huê** Thưa Thiên-Huê, C Vietnam
104 J7 **Huebra** ≈ W Spain
24 H8 **Hueco Mountains** ⛰ Texas, SW USA
116 G10 **Huedin** *Hung.* Bánffyhunyad. Cluj, NW Romania
40 J10 **Huehueto, Cerro** ▲ C Mexico
42 B5 **Huehuetenango** Huehuetenango, W Guatemala
42 B4 **Huehuetenango** *off.* Departamento de Huehuetenango. ◈ *department* W Guatemala
40 L11 **Huejuquilla** Jalisco, SW Mexico
41 P12 **Huejutla** *var.* Huejutla de Reyes. Hidalgo, C Mexico
Huejutla de Reyes *see* Huejutla
102 G6 **Huelgoat** Finistère, NW France
105 O13 **Huelma** Andalucía, S Spain
104 I14 **Huelva** *anc.* Onuba. Andalucía, SW Spain
104 I13 **Huelva** ◈ *province* Andalucía, SW Spain
104 J13 **Huelva** ≈ SW Spain
105 Q14 **Huercal-Overa** Andalucía, S Spain
37 Q9 **Huerfano Mountain** ▲ New Mexico, SW USA
37 T7 **Huerfano River** ≈ Colorado, C USA
105 S12 **Huertas, Cabo** *headland* SE Spain
105 R6 **Huerva** ≈ N Spain
105 S4 **Huesca** *anc.* Osca. Aragón, NE Spain
105 T4 **Huesca** ◈ *province* Aragón, NE Spain
105 P13 **Huéscar** Andalucía, S Spain
41 N15 **Huetamo** *var.* Huetamo de Núñez. Michoacán de Ocampo, SW Mexico
Huetamo de Núñez *see* Huetamo
105 P8 **Huete** Castilla-La Mancha, C Spain
23 P4 **Hueytown** Alabama, S USA
28 L16 **Hugh Butler Lake** ⊠ Nebraska, C USA
181 V6 **Hughenden** Queensland, NE Australia
182 A6 **Hughes** South Australia
39 P8 **Hughes** Alaska, USA
27 X11 **Hughes** Arkansas, C USA
25 W6 **Hughes Springs** Texas, SW USA
37 V5 **Hugo** Colorado, C USA
27 Q13 **Hugo** Oklahoma, C USA
27 Q13 **Hugo Lake** ⊠ Oklahoma, C USA
26 H7 **Hugoton** Kansas, C USA
Huhehot/Huhuohaote *see* Hohhot
Huhttán *see* Kvikkjokk
161 R13 **Hui'an** *var.* Luocheng. Fujian, SE China
184 O9 **Huiarau Range** ⛰ North Island, NZ
83 D22 **Huib-Hoch Plateau** *plateau* S Namibia
41 O13 **Huichapán** Hidalgo, C Mexico
Huicheng *see* Shexian
163 W13 **Hŭich'ŏn** C North Korea
54 E12 **Huila** *off.* Departamento del Huila. ◈ *province* S Colombia
83 B15 **Huíla** ◈ *province* SW Angola
54 D11 **Huila, Nevado del** *elevation* C Colombia
83 B15 **Huíla Plateau** *plateau* S Angola
160 G12 **Huili** Sichuan, C China
161 P4 **Huimin** Shandong, E China
163 W11 **Huinan** *var.* Chaoyang. Jilin, NE China
62 K12 **Huinca Renancó** Córdoba, C Argentina
159 V10 **Huining** *var.* Huishi. Gansu, C China
Huishi *see* Huining
160 J12 **Huishui** *var.* Heping. Guizhou, S China
102 L6 **Huisne** ≈ NW France
98 L12 **Huissen** Gelderland, SE Netherlands
159 N11 **Huiten Nur** ◎ C China
93 K19 **Huittinen** Länsi-Suomi, W Finland
41 O15 **Huitzuco** *var.* Huitzuco de los Figueroa. Guerrero, S Mexico
Huitzuco de los Figueroa *see* Huitzuco
159 W11 **Huixian** *var.* Hui Xian. Gansu, C China
41 V17 **Huixtla** Chiapas, SE Mexico
160 H12 **Huize** *var.* Zhongping. Yunnan, SW China
98 J10 **Huizen** Noord-Holland, C Netherlands
161 O14 **Huizhou** Guangdong, S China
162 J6 **Hujirt** Arhangay, C Mongolia
162 J8 **Hujirt** Övörhangay, C Mongolia
162 K8 **Hujrt** Töv, C Mongolia
Hukagawa *see* Fukagawa
Hŭksan-chedo *see* Hŭksan-gundo
163 W17 **Hŭksan-gundo** *var.* Hŭksan-chedo. *island group* SW South Korea
Hukue *see* Fukue
Hukui *see* Fukui
83 G20 **Hukuntsi** Kgalagadi, SW Botswana
Hukuoka *see* Fukuoka
Hukusima *see* Fukushima
Hukutiyama *see* Fukuchiyama
Hukuyama *see* Fukuyama
163 W8 **Hulan** Heilongjiang, NE China
163 W8 **Hulan He** ≈ NE China
31 Q4 **Hulbert Lake** ◎ Michigan, N USA
Hulczyn *see* Hlučín
Huliao *see* Dabu
163 Z8 **Hulin** Heilongjiang, NE China
163 S9 **Hulingol** *prev.* Huolin Gol. Nei Mongol Zizhiqu, N China
14 L12 **Hull** Québec, SE Canada
29 S12 **Hull** Iowa, C USA
Hull *see* Kingston upon Hull
Hull Island *see* Orona
99 F16 **Hulst** Zeeland, SW Netherlands
163 Q7 **Hulstay** Dornod, NE Mongolia
Hultschin *see* Hlučín
95 M19 **Hultsfred** Kalmar, S Sweden
163 T13 **Huludao** *prev.* Jinxi, Lianshan. Liaoning, NE China
Hulun *see* Hailar
Hu-lun Ch'ih *see* Hulun Nur
163 Q6 **Hulun Nur** *var.* Hu-lun Ch'ih; *prev.* Dalai Nor. ◎ NE China
Hulwan/Hulwân *see* Helwân
117 V8 **Hulyaypole** *Rus.* Gulyaypole. Zaporiz'ka Oblast', SE Ukraine
163 V4 **Huma** Heilongjiang, NE China
45 V6 **Humacao** E Puerto Rico
163 U4 **Huma He** ≈ NE China
62 J5 **Humahuaca** Jujuy, N Argentina
59 E14 **Humaitá** Amazonas, N Brazil
62 N7 **Humaitá** Ñeembucú, S Paraguay
83 H26 **Humansdorp** Eastern Cape, S South Africa
27 S6 **Humansville** Missouri, C USA
40 I8 **Humaya, Río** ≈ C Mexico
83 C16 **Humbe** Cunene, SW Angola
97 N17 **Humber** *estuary* E England, UK
97 N17 **Humberside** *cultural region* E England, UK
Humberto *see* Umberto
25 W11 **Humble** Texas, SW USA
11 U15 **Humboldt** Saskatchewan, S Canada
29 U12 **Humboldt** Iowa, C USA
27 Q6 **Humboldt** Kansas, C USA
29 S17 **Humboldt** Nebraska, C USA
35 S3 **Humboldt** Nevada, W USA
20 G9 **Humboldt** Tennessee, S USA
34 K3 **Humboldt Bay** *bay* California, W USA
35 S4 **Humboldt Lake** ◎ Nevada, W USA
35 S4 **Humboldt River** ≈ Nevada, W USA
35 T5 **Humboldt Salt Marsh** *wetland* Nevada, W USA
183 P11 **Hume, Lake** ◎ New South Wales/Victoria, SE Australia
111 N19 **Humenné** *Ger.* Homenau, *Hung.* Homonna. Prešovský Kraj, E Slovakia
29 V15 **Humeston** Iowa, C USA
54 J5 **Humocaro Bajo** Lara, N Venezuela
29 Q14 **Humphrey** Nebraska, C USA
35 S9 **Humphreys, Mount** ▲ California, W USA
36 L11 **Humphreys Peak** ▲ Arizona, SW USA
111 E17 **Humpolec** *Ger.* Gumpolds, Humpoletz. Vysočina, C Czech Republic
Humpoletz *see* Humpolec
93 K19 **Humppila** Etelä-Suomi, S Finland
32 F8 **Humptulips** Washington, NW USA
42 H7 **Humuya, Río** ≈ W Honduras
75 P9 **Hūn** N Libya
Hunabasi *see* Funabashi
92 I1 **Húnaflói** *bay* NW Iceland
160 M11 **Hunan** *var.* Hunan Sheng, Xiang. ◈ *province* S China
Hunan Sheng *see* Hunan
163 Y10 **Hunchun** Jilin, NE China
95 I22 **Hundested** Frederiksborg, E Denmark
Hundred Mile House *see* 100 Mile House
116 G12 **Hunedoara** *Ger.* Eisenmarkt, *Hung.* Vajdahunyad. Hunedoara, SW Romania
116 G12 **Hunedoara** ◈ *county* W Romania
101 I17 **Hünfeld** Hessen, C Germany
111 H23 **Hungary** *off.* Republic of Hungary, *Ger.* Ungarn, *Hung.* Magyarország, *Rom.* Ungaria, *SCr.* Mađarska, *Ukr.* Uhorshchyna; *prev.* Hungarian People's Republic. ◆ *republic* C Europe
Hungary, Plain of *see* Great Hungarian Plain
162 F6 **Hungiy** Dzavhan, W Mongolia
163 X13 **Hŭngnam** E North Korea
33 P8 **Hungry Horse Reservoir** ⊠ Montana, NW USA
Hungt'ou *see* Lan Yü
Hung-tse Hu *see* Hongze Hu
167 T6 **Hưng Yên** Hai Hưng, N Vietnam
Hunjiang *see* Baishan
95 I18 **Hunnebostrand** Västra Götaland, S Sweden
101 E19 **Hunsrück** ⛰ W Germany
97 P18 **Hunstanton** E England, UK
155 G20 **Hunsūr** Karnātaka, E India
162 I7 **Hunt** Arhangay, C Mongolia
100 G12 **Hunte** ≈ NW Germany
29 Q5 **Hunter** North Dakota, N USA
25 S11 **Hunter** Texas, SW USA
185 D20 **Hunter** ≈ South Island, NZ
183 N15 **Hunter Island** *island* Tasmania, SE Australia
18 K11 **Hunter Mountain** ▲ New York, NE USA
185 B23 **Hunter Mountains** ⛰ South Island, NZ
183 S7 **Hunter River** ≈ New South Wales, SE Australia
32 L7 **Hunters** Washington, NW USA

◆ Country ● Country Capital ◇ Dependent Territory ○ Dependent Territory Capital ◈ Administrative Region ✕ International Airport ▲ Mountain ⛰ Mountain Range Volcano ≈ River ◎ Lake ⊠ Reservoir

185 F20 **Hunters Hills, The** hill range South Island, NZ
184 M12 **Hunterville** Manawatu-Wanganui, North Island, NZ
31 N16 **Huntingburg** Indiana, N USA
97 O20 **Huntingdon** E England, UK
18 E15 **Huntingdon** Pennsylvania, NE USA
20 G9 **Huntingdon** Tennessee, S USA
97 O20 **Huntingdonshire** cultural region C England, UK
31 P12 **Huntington** Indiana, N USA
32 L13 **Huntington** Oregon, NW USA
25 X9 **Huntington** Texas, SW USA
36 M5 **Huntington** Utah, W USA
21 P5 **Huntington** West Virginia, NE USA
35 T16 **Huntington Beach** California, W USA
35 W4 **Huntington Creek** ≈ Nevada, W USA
184 L7 **Huntly** Waikato, North Island, NZ
96 K8 **Huntly** NE Scotland, UK
10 K8 **Hunt, Mount** ▲ Yukon Territory, NW Canada
14 H12 **Huntsville** Ontario, S Canada
23 P2 **Huntsville** Alabama, S USA
27 S9 **Huntsville** Arkansas, C USA
27 U3 **Huntsville** Missouri, C USA
20 M8 **Huntsville** Tennessee, S USA
25 V10 **Huntsville** Texas, SW USA
36 L2 **Huntsville** Utah, W USA
41 W12 **Hunucmá** Yucatán, SE Mexico
149 W3 **Hunza** var. Karīmābād. Jammu and Kashmir, NE Pakistan
149 W3 **Hunza** ≈ NE Pakistan
Hunze see Oostermoers Vaart
158 H4 **Huocheng** var. Shuiding. Xinjiang Uygur Zizhiqu, NW China
161 N6 **Huojia** Henan, C China
Huolin Gol see Hulingol
186 N14 **Huon** reef N New Caledonia
186 E7 **Huon Peninsula** headland C PNG
Huoshao Dao see Lü Tao
Huoshao Tao see Lan Yü
Hupeh/Hupei see Hubei
Hurama see Hongyuan
Hurano see Furano
95 H14 **Hurdalssjøen** ◎ S Norway
14 E13 **Hurd, Cape** headland Ontario, S Canada
Hurdegaryp see Hardegarijp
29 N4 **Hurdsfield** North Dakota, N USA
162 J7 **Hüremt** Bulgan, C Mongolia
162 J8 **Hüremt** Övörhangay, C Mongolia
75 X9 **Hurghada** var. Al Ghurdaqah, Ghurdaqah. E Egypt
67 V9 **Huri Hills** ⛰ NW Kenya
37 P15 **Hurley** New Mexico, SW USA
30 K4 **Hurley** Wisconsin, N USA
21 Y4 **Hurlock** Maryland, NE USA
29 P10 **Huron** South Dakota, N USA
31 S6 **Huron, Lake** ◎ Canada/USA
31 N3 **Huron Mountains** hill range Michigan, N USA
36 J8 **Hurricane** Utah, W USA
21 P5 **Hurricane** West Virginia, NE USA
36 J8 **Hurricane Cliffs** cliff Arizona, SW USA
23 V6 **Hurricane Creek** ≈ Georgia, SE USA
94 E12 **Hurrungane** ▲ S Norway
101 E16 **Hürth** Nordrhein-Westfalen, W Germany
Hurukawa see Furukawa
185 I17 **Hurunui** ≈ South Island, NZ
95 F21 **Hurup** Viborg, NW Denmark
117 T14 **Hurzuf** Respublika Krym, S Ukraine
Huş see Huşi
95 B19 **Húsavík** Dan. Husevig Faeroe Islands
92 K1 **Húsavík** Nordhurland Eystra, NE Iceland
116 M10 **Huşi** var. Huş. Vaslui, E Romania
95 L19 **Huskvarna** Jönköping, S Sweden
39 P8 **Huslia** Alaska, USA
Husn see Al Ḩuşn
95 C15 **Husnes** Hordaland, S Norway
94 D8 **Hustadvika** sea area S Norway
Husté see Khust
100 H7 **Husum** Schleswig-Holstein, N Germany
93 I16 **Husum** Västernorrland, C Sweden
116 K6 **Husyatyn** Ternopil's'ka Oblast', W Ukraine
Huszt see Khust
162 K6 **Hutag** Bulgan, N Mongolia
26 M6 **Hutchinson** Kansas, C USA
29 U9 **Hutchinson** Minnesota, N USA
23 Y13 **Hutchinson Island** island Florida, SE USA
36 L11 **Hutch Mountain** ▲ Arizona, SW USA
141 O14 **Ḩūth** NW Yemen
186 I7 **Hutjena** Buka Island, NE PNG
109 T8 **Hüttenberg** Kärnten, S Austria
25 T10 **Hutto** Texas, SW USA
Huttu see Futtsu
108 E8 **Huttwil** Bern, W Switzerland
158 K5 **Hutubi** Xinjiang Uygur Zizhiqu, NW China
161 N4 **Hutuo He** ≈ C China
Hutyû see Fuchū
185 E20 **Huxley, Mount** ▲ South Island, NZ
99 J20 **Huy** Dut. Hoei, Hoey. Liège, E Belgium
161 R8 **Huzhou** var. Wuxing. Zhejiang, SE China
Huzi see Fuji
Huzieda see Fujieda
Huzinomiya see Fujinomiya
Huzisawa see Fujisawa
Huziyosida see Fuji-Yoshida
92 I2 **Hvammstangi** Nordhurland Vestra, N Iceland
92 K4 **Hvannadalshnúkur** ▲ S Iceland
113 E15 **Hvar** It. Lesina. Split-Dalmacija, S Croatia
113 F15 **Hvar** It. Lesina; anc. Pharus. island S Croatia
117 T13 **Hvardiys'ke** Rus. Gvardeyskoye. Respublika Krym, S Ukraine
92 I4 **Hveragerdhi** Sudhurland, SW Iceland
95 E22 **Hvide Sande** Ringkøbing, W Denmark
92 I3 **Hvitá** ≈ C Iceland
95 G15 **Hvittingfoss** Buskerud, S Norway
92 I4 **Hvolsvöllur** Sudhurland, SW Iceland
Hwach'ŏn-chŏsuji see P'aro-ho
Hwainan see Huainan
Hwalien see Hualien
83 I16 **Hwange** prev. Wankie. Matabeleland North, W Zimbabwe
Hwang-Hae see Yellow Sea
Hwangshih see Huangshi
83 L17 **Hwedza** Mashonaland East, E Zimbabwe
63 G20 **Hyades, Cerro** ▲ S Chile
19 Q12 **Hyannis** Massachusetts, NE USA
28 L13 **Hyannis** Nebraska, C USA
162 F6 **Hyargas Nuur** ◎ NW Mongolia
Hybla/Hybla Major see Paternò
39 Y14 **Hydaburg** Prince of Wales Island, Alaska, USA
185 F22 **Hyde** Otago, South Island, NZ
21 O7 **Hyden** Kentucky, S USA
18 K12 **Hyde Park** New York, NE USA
39 Z14 **Hyder** Alaska, USA
155 I15 **Hyderābād** var. Haidarabad. Andhra Pradesh, C India
149 Q16 **Hyderābād** var. Haidarabad. Sind, SE Pakistan
103 T16 **Hyères** Var, SE France
103 T16 **Hyères, Îles d'** island group S France
118 K12 **Hyermanavichy** Rus. Germanovichi. Vitsyebskaya Voblasts', N Belarus
163 X12 **Hyesan** NE North Korea
10 K8 **Hyland** ≈ Yukon Territory, NW Canada
95 K20 **Hyltebruk** Halland, S Sweden
18 D16 **Hyndman** Pennsylvania, NE USA
33 P14 **Hyndman Peak** ▲ Idaho, NW USA
164 I13 **Hyōgo** off. Hyōgo-ken. ◈ prefecture Honshū, SW Japan
Hypanis see Kuban'
Hypsas see Belice
Hyrcania see Gorgān
36 L1 **Hyrum** Utah, W USA
93 N14 **Hyrynsalmi** Oulu, C Finland
33 V10 **Hysham** Montana, NW USA
11 N13 **Hythe** Alberta, W Canada
97 Q23 **Hythe** SE England, UK
164 D15 **Hyūga** Miyazaki, Kyūshū, SW Japan
Hyvinge see Hyvinkää
93 L19 **Hyvinkää** Swe. Hyvinge. Etelä-Suomi, S Finland

I

118 J9 **Iacobeni** Ger. Jakobeny. Suceava, NE Romania
Iader see Zadar
172 I7 **Iakora** Fianarantsoa, SE Madagascar
116 K14 **Ialomiţa** var. Jalomitsa. ◈ county SE Romania
116 K14 **Ialomiţa** ≈ SE Romania
117 N10 **Ialoveni** Rus. Yaloveny. C Moldova
117 N11 **Ialpug** var. Ialpugul Mare, Rus. Yalpug. ≈ Moldova/Ukraine
Ialpugul Mare see Ialpug
23 T8 **Iamonia, Lake** ◎ Florida, SE USA
116 L13 **Ianca** Brăila, SE Romania
116 M10 **Iaşi** Ger. Jassy. Iaşi, NE Romania
116 L9 **Iaşi** Ger. Jassy, Yassy. ◈ county NE Romania
114 J13 **Íasmos** Anatolikí Makedonía kai Thráki, NE Greece
22 H6 **Iatt, Lake** ▣ Louisiana, S USA
58 B11 **Iauaretê** Amazonas, NW Brazil
171 N3 **Iba** Luzon, N Philippines
77 S16 **Ibadan** Oyo, SW Nigeria
54 E10 **Ibagué** Tolima, C Colombia
60 J10 **Ibaiti** Paraná, S Brazil
36 J4 **Ibapah Peak** ▲ Utah, W USA
113 M15 **Ibar** Alb. Ibër. ≈ C Serbia and Montenegro (Yugo.)
165 P13 **Ibaraki** off. Ibaraki-ken. ◈ prefecture Honshū, S Japan
56 C5 **Ibarra** var. San Miguel de Ibarra. Imbabura, N Ecuador
Ibaşfalău see Dumbrăveni
141 O16 **Ibb** W Yemen
100 F13 **Ibbenbüren** Nordrhein-Westfalen, NW Germany
79 H16 **Ibenga** ≈ N Congo
Ibër see Ibar
57 I14 **Iberia** Madre de Dios, E Peru
Iberia see Spain
66 M1 **Iberian Basin** undersea feature E Atlantic Ocean
Iberian Mountains see Ibérico, Sistema
84 D12 **Iberian Peninsula** physical region Portugal/Spain
64 M8 **Iberian Plain** undersea feature E Atlantic Ocean
Ibérica, Cordillera see Ibérico, Sistema
105 P6 **Ibérico, Sistema** var. Cordillera Ibérica, Eng. Iberian Mountains. ⛰ NE Spain
12 K7 **Iberville, Lac d'** ◎ Québec, NE Canada
77 T14 **Ibeto** Niger, W Nigeria
77 W15 **Ibi** Taraba, C Nigeria
105 S11 **Ibi** País Valenciano, E Spain
59 L20 **Ibiá** Minas Gerais, SE Brazil
61 F15 **Ibicuí, Rio** ≈ S Brazil
61 C19 **Ibicuy** Entre Ríos, E Argentina
61 F16 **Ibirapuitã** ≈ S Brazil
Ibiza see Eivissa
138 J4 **Ibn Wardān, Qaşr** ruins Ḩamāh, C Syria
Ibo see Sassandra
188 E9 **Ibobang** Babeldaob, N Palau
171 V13 **Ibonma** Papua, E Indonesia
59 N17 **Ibotirama** Bahia, E Brazil
141 Y8 **Ibrā** NE Oman
127 Q4 **Ibresi** Chuvashskaya Respublika, W Russian Federation
141 X8 **ʻIbrī** NW Oman
164 C16 **Ibusuki** Kagoshima, Kyūshū, SW Japan
57 E16 **Ica** Ica, SW Peru
57 E16 **Ica** off. Departamento de Ica. ◈ department SW Peru
58 C11 **Içana** Amazonas, NW Brazil
Icaria see Ikaría
58 B13 **Içá, Rio** var. Río Putumayo. ≈ NW South America see also Putumayo, Río
136 I17 **İçel** var. Ichili. ◈ province S Turkey
92 I3 **Iceland** off. Republic of Iceland, Dan. Island, Icel. Ísland. ◆ republic N Atlantic Ocean
86 B7 **Iceland** island N Atlantic Ocean
64 L5 **Iceland Basin** undersea feature N Atlantic Ocean
Icelandic Plateau see Iceland Plateau
197 Q15 **Iceland Plateau** var. Icelandic Plateau. undersea feature S Greenland Sea
155 E16 **Ichalkaranji** Mahārāshtra, W India
164 D15 **Ichifusa-yama** ▲ Kyūshū, SW Japan
Ichili see İçel
164 K13 **Ichinomiya** var. Itinomiya. Aichi, Honshū, SW Japan
165 Q9 **Ichinoseki** var. Itinoseki. Iwate, Honshū, C Japan
117 R3 **Ichnya** Chernihivs'ka Oblast', NE Ukraine
57 L17 **Ichoa, Río** ≈ C Bolivia
I-ch'un see Yichun
Iconium see Konya
Iculisma see Angoulême
39 U12 **Icy Bay** inlet Alaska, USA
39 N5 **Icy Cape** headland Alaska, USA
39 W13 **Icy Strait** strait Alaska, USA
27 R13 **Idabel** Oklahoma, C USA
29 T13 **Ida Grove** Iowa, C USA
77 U16 **Idah** Kogi, S Nigeria
33 N13 **Idaho** off. State of Idaho; also known as Gem of the Mountains, Gem State. ◈ state NW USA
33 N14 **Idaho City** Idaho, NW USA
33 R14 **Idaho Falls** Idaho, NW USA
121 P2 **Idálion** var. Dali, Dhali. C Cyprus
25 N5 **Idalou** Texas, SW USA
104 I9 **Idanha-a-Nova** Castelo Branco, C Portugal
101 E19 **Idar-Oberstein** Rheinland-Pfalz, SW Germany
118 J3 **Ida-Virumaa** off. Ida-Viru Maakond. ◈ province NE Estonia
124 J8 **Idel'** Respublika Kareliya, NW Russian Federation
79 C15 **Idenao** Sud-Ouest, SW Cameroon
Idenburg-rivier see Taritatu, Sungai
Idensalmi see Iisalmi
162 I6 **Ider** Hövsgöl, C Mongolia
75 X10 **Idfu** var. Edfu. SE Egypt
Ídhi Óros see Ídi
Ídhra see Ýdra
168 H7 **Idi** Sumatera, W Indonesia
115 I25 **Ídi** var. Ídhi Óros. ⛰ Kríti, Greece, E Mediterranean Sea
Idi Amin, Lac see Edward, Lake
106 G10 **Idice** ≈ N Italy
76 G9 **Idini** Trarza, W Mauritania
79 J21 **Idiofa** Bandundu, SW Dem. Rep. Congo
39 O10 **Iditarod River** ≈ Alaska, USA
95 M14 **Idkerberget** Dalarna, C Sweden
138 I3 **Idlib** Idlib, NW Syria
138 I4 **Idlib** off. Muḩāfaẓat Idlib. ◈ governorate NW Syria
Idra see Ýdra
94 J11 **Idre** Dalarna, C Sweden
Idria see Idrija
109 S11 **Idrija** It. Idria. W Slovenia
101 G18 **Idstein** Hessen, W Germany
83 J25 **Idutywa** Eastern Cape, SE South Africa
Idzhevan see Ijevan
118 G9 **Iecava** Bauska, S Latvia
165 T16 **Ie-jima** var. Ii-shima. island Nansei-shotō, SW Japan
99 B18 **Ieper** Fr. Ypres. West-Vlaanderen, W Belgium
115 K25 **Ierápetra** Kríti, Greece, E Mediterranean Sea
115 G22 **Iérax, Akrotírio** headland S Greece
Ierisós see Ierissós
115 H14 **Ierissós** var. Ierisós. Kentrikí Makedonía, N Greece
116 I11 **Iernut** Hung. Radnót. Mureş, C Romania
106 J12 **Iesi** var. Jesi. Marche, C Italy
92 K9 **Iešjávri** var. Jiesjavrre. ◎ N Norway
Iesolo see Jesolo
188 K16 **Ifalik Atoll** atoll Caroline Islands, C Micronesia
172 I6 **Ifanadiana** Fianarantsoa, SE Madagascar
77 T16 **Ife** Osun, SW Nigeria
77 V8 **Iferouâne** Agadez, N Niger
Iferten see Yverdon
92 L8 **Ifjord** Finnmark, N Norway
77 R8 **Ifôghas, Adrar des** var. Adrar des Iforas. ⛰ NE Mali
Iforas, Adrar des see Ifôghas, Adrar des
182 D6 **Ifould lake** salt lake South Australia
74 G6 **Ifrane** C Morocco
171 S11 **Iga** Pulau Halmahera, E Indonesia
81 G18 **Iganga** SE Uganda
60 L7 **Igarapava** São Paulo, S Brazil
122 K9 **Igarka** Krasnoyarskiy Kray, N Russian Federation
Igaunija see Estonia
I.G.Duca see General Toshevo
Igel see Jihlava
137 T12 **Iğdır** ◈ province E Turkey
94 N11 **Iggesund** Gävleborg, C Sweden
39 P7 **Igikpak, Mount** ▲ Alaska, USA
39 P13 **Igiugig** Alaska, USA
Iglau/Iglawa/Igława see Jihlava
107 B20 **Iglesias** Sardegna, Italy, C Mediterranean Sea
127 V4 **Iglino** Respublika Bashkortostan, W Russian Federation
Igló see Spišská Nová Ves
9 O6 **Igloolik** Nunavut, N Canada
12 B11 **Ignace** Ontario, S Canada
118 I12 **Ignalina** Utena, E Lithuania
127 Q5 **Ignatovka** Ul'yanovskaya Oblast', W Russian Federation
124 K12 **Ignatovo** Vologodskaya Oblast', NW Russian Federation
114 N11 **İğneada** Kırklareli, NW Turkey
121 S7 **İğneada Burnu** headland NW Turkey
Igombe see Gombe
115 B16 **Igoumenítsa** Ípeiros, W Greece
127 T2 **Igra** Udmurtskaya Respublika, NW Russian Federation
122 H9 **Igrim** Khanty-Mansiyskiy Avtonomnyy Okrug, N Russian Federation
60 G12 **Iguaçu, Rio** Sp. Río Iguazú. ≈ Argentina/Brazil see also Iguazú, Río
59 I22 **Iguaçu, Salto do** Sp. Cataratas del Iguazú; prev. Victoria Falls. waterfall Argentina/Brazil see also Iguazú, Cataratas del
41 O15 **Iguala** var. Iguala de la Independencia. Guerrero, S Mexico
105 V5 **Igualada** Cataluña, NE Spain
Iguala de la Independencia see Iguala
60 G12 **Iguazú, Cataratas del** Port. Salto do Iguaçu, prev. Victoria Falls. waterfall Argentina/Brazil see also Iguaçu, Salto do
62 Q6 **Iguazú, Río** Port. Rio Iguaçu. ≈ Argentina/Brazil see also Iguaçu, Rio
79 D19 **Iguéla** Ogooué-Maritime, SW Gabon
Iguid, Erg see Iguîdi, 'Erg
67 M5 **Iguîdi, 'Erg** var. Erg Iguid. desert Algeria/Mauritania
172 K2 **Iharaña** prev. Vohémar. Antsiraňana, NE Madagascar
151 K18 **Ihavandippolhu Atoll** var. Ihavandiffulu Atoll. atoll N Maldives
162 M11 **Ih Bulag** Ömnögovĭ, S Mongolia
165 T16 **Iheya-jima** island Nansei-shotō, SW Japan
162 L8 **Ihhayrhan** Töv, C Mongolia
172 I6 **Ihosy** Fianarantsoa, S Madagascar
162 L7 **Ihsüüj** Töv, C Mongolia
93 L14 **Ii** Oulu, C Finland
164 M13 **Iida** Nagano, Honshū, S Japan
93 M14 **Iijoki** ≈ C Finland
Iinnasuolu see Hinnøya
118 J4 **Iisaku** Ger. Isaak. Ida-Virumaa, NE Estonia
93 M16 **Iisalmi** var. Idensalmi. Itä-Suomi, C Finland
165 N11 **Iiyama** Nagano, Honshū, S Japan
77 S16 **Ijebu-Ode** Ogun, SW Nigeria
137 U11 **Ijevan** Rus. Idzhevan. N Armenia
98 H9 **IJmuiden** Noord-Holland, W Netherlands
98 M12 **IJssel** var. Yssel. ≈ Netherlands/Germany
98 J8 **IJsselmeer** prev. Zuider Zee. ◎ N Netherlands
98 L9 **IJsselmuiden** Overijssel, E Netherlands
98 I12 **IJsselstein** Utrecht, C Netherlands
61 G14 **Ijuí** Rio Grande do Sul, S Brazil
61 G14 **Ijuí, Rio** ≈ S Brazil
189 R8 **Ijuw** NE Nauru
99 E16 **IJzendijke** Zeeland, SW Netherlands
99 A18 **Ijzer** ≈ W Belgium
93 K18 **Ikaalinen** Länsi-Suomi, W Finland
172 I6 **Ikalamavony** Fianarantsoa, SE Madagascar
185 G16 **Ikamatua** West Coast, South Island, NZ
77 U16 **Ikare** Ondo, SW Nigeria
115 L20 **Ikaría** var. Kariot, Nicaria, Nikaria; anc. Icaria. island Dodekánisos, Greece, Aegean Sea
95 F22 **Ikast** Ringkøbing, W Denmark
184 O9 **Ikawhenua Range** ⛰ North Island, NZ
165 U4 **Ikeda** Hokkaidō, NE Japan
164 H14 **Ikeda** Tokushima, Shikoku, SW Japan
77 S16 **Ikeja** Lagos, SW Nigeria
79 L19 **Ikela** Equateur, C Dem. Rep. Congo
114 H10 **Ikhtiman** Sofiya, W Bulgaria
164 C13 **Iki** island SW Japan
127 O13 **Iki Burul** Respublika Kalmykiya, SW Russian Federation
137 P11 **İkizdere** Rize, NE Turkey
39 P14 **Ikolik, Cape** headland Kodiak Island, Alaska, USA
77 V17 **Ikom** Cross River, SE Nigeria
172 I6 **Ikongo** prev. Fort-Carnot. Fianarantsoa, SE Madagascar
39 P5 **Ikpikpuk River** ≈ Alaska, USA
190 H1 **Iku** prev. Lone Tree Islet. atoll Tungaru, W Kiribati
164 I12 **Ikuno** Hyōgo, Honshū, SW Japan
190 H16 **Ikurangi** ▲ Rarotonga, S Cook Islands
171 X14 **Ilaga** Papua, E Indonesia
171 O2 **Ilagan** Luzon, N Philippines
153 R12 **Ilam** Eastern, E Nepal
142 J7 **Īlām** var. Elam. Īlām, W Iran
142 J8 **Īlām** off. Ostān-e Īlām. ◈ province W Iran
161 T13 **Ilan** Jap. Giran. N Taiwan
146 G9 **Ilanly Obvodnitel'nyy Kanal** canal N Turkmenistan
122 L12 **Ilanskiy** Krasnoyarskiy Kray, S Russian Federation
108 H9 **Ilanz** Graubünden, S Switzerland
77 S16 **Ilaro** Ogun, SW Nigeria
57 I17 **Ilave** Puno, S Peru
110 K8 **Iława** Ger. Deutsch-Eylau. Warmińsko-Mazurskie, NE Poland
123 P10 **Il'benge** Respublika Sakha (Yakutiya), NE Russian Federation
29 R7 **Ile** var. Ili, Chin. Ili He, Rus. Reka Ili. ≈ China/Kazakhstan see also Ili He
11 S13 **Île-à-la-Crosse** Saskatchewan, C Canada
79 J21 **Ilebo** prev. Port-Francqui. Kasai Occidental, W Dem. Rep. Congo
103 N5 **Île-de-France** ◈ region N France
144 I9 **Ilek** Kaz. Elek. ≈ Kazakhstan/Russian Federation
Ilerda see Lleida
77 T16 **Ilesha** Osun, SW Nigeria
187 Q16 **Îles Loyauté, Province des** ◈ province E New Caledonia
11 X12 **Ilford** Manitoba, C Canada
97 I23 **Ilfracombe** SW England, UK
136 I11 **Ilgaz Dağları** ⛰ N Turkey
136 G15 **Ilgın** Konya, W Turkey
60 I7 **Ilha Solteira** São Paulo, S Brazil
104 G7 **Ílhavo** Aveiro, N Portugal
59 O18 **Ilhéus** Bahia, E Brazil
Ili see Ile/Ili He
116 G11 **Ilia** Hung. Marosillye. Hunedoara, SW Romania
39 P13 **Iliamna** Alaska, USA
39 P13 **Iliamna Lake** ◎ Alaska, USA
137 N13 **Iliç** Erzincan, C Turkey
Il'ichevsk see Şärur, Azerbaijan
Il'ichevsk see Illichivs'k, Ukraine
Ilici see Elche
37 V2 **Iliff** Colorado, C USA
171 Q7 **Iligan** off. Iligan City. Mindanao, S Philippines
171 Q7 **Iligan Bay** bay S Philippines
158 I5 **Ili He** var. Ili, Kaz. Ile, Rus. Reka Ili. ≈ China/Kazakhstan see also Ile
56 C6 **Iliniza** ▲ N Ecuador
Ilinski see Il'inskiy
125 U14 **Il'inskiy** var. Ilinski. Permskaya Oblast', NW Russian Federation
123 T13 **Il'inskiy** Ostrov Sakhalin, Sakhalinskaya Oblast', SE Russian Federation
18 I10 **Ilion** New York, NE USA
38 E9 **ʻĪlio Point** var. Ilio Point. headland Molokaʻi, Hawaiʻi, USA, C Pacific Ocean
109 T13 **Ilirska Bistrica** prev. Bistrica, Ger. Feistritz, Illyrisch-Feistritz, It. Villa del Nevoso. SW Slovenia
137 Q16 **Ilısu Barajı** ▣ SE Turkey
155 G17 **Ilkal** Karnātaka, C India
97 M19 **Ilkeston** C England, UK
121 O16 **Il-Kullana** headland SW Malta
108 J8 **Ill** ≈ W Austria
103 U6 **Ill** ≈ NE France
62 G10 **Illapel** Coquimbo, C Chile
Illaue Fartak Trench see Alula-Fartak Trench
182 C2 **Illbillee, Mount** ▲ South Australia
102 I6 **Ille-et-Vilaine** ◈ department NW France
77 T11 **Illéla** Tahoua, SW Niger
101 J24 **Iller** ≈ S Germany
101 J23 **Illertissen** Bayern, S Germany
105 N8 **Illescas** Castilla-La Mancha, C Spain
Ille-sur-la-Têt see Ille-sur-Têt
103 O17 **Ille-sur-Têt** var. Ille-sur-la-Têt. Pyrénées-Orientales, S France
Illiberis see Elne
117 P11 **Illichivs'k** Rus. Il'ichevsk. Odes'ka Oblast', SW Ukraine
Illicis see Elche
102 M6 **Illiers-Combray** Eure-et-Loir, C France
30 K12 **Illinois** off. State of Illinois; also known as Prairie State, Sucker State. ◈ state C USA
30 J13 **Illinois River** ≈ Illinois, N USA
117 N6 **Illintsi** Vinnyts'ka Oblast', C Ukraine
Illiturgis see Andújar
74 M10 **Illizi** SE Algeria
27 Y7 **Illmo** Missouri, C USA
Illur co see Lorca
Illuro see Mataró
Illyrisch-Feistritz see Ilirska Bistrica
101 K16 **Ilm** ≈ C Germany
101 K17 **Ilmenau** Thüringen, C Germany
126 H14 **Il'men', Ozero** ◎ NW Russian Federation
57 H18 **Ilo** Moquegua, SW Peru
171 O6 **Iloilo** off. Iloilo City. Panay Island, C Philippines
112 K10 **Ilok** Hung. Újlak. Serbia, NW Serbia and Montenegro (Yugo.)
93 O16 **Ilomantsi** Itä-Suomi, E Finland
42 F8 **Ilopango, Lago de** volcanic lake C El Salvador
77 T15 **Ilorin** Kwara, W Nigeria
117 X8 **Ilovays'k** Rus. Ilovaysk. Donets'ka Oblast', SE Ukraine
127 O10 **Ilovlya** Volgogradskaya Oblast', SW Russian Federation
127 O10 **Ilovlya** ≈ SW Russian Federation
123 V8 **Il'pyrskoy** Koryakskiy Avtonomnyy Okrug, E Russian Federation
126 K14 **Il'skiy** Krasnodarskiy Kray, SW Russian Federation
182 B2 **Iltur** South Australia
171 Y13 **Ilugwa** Papua, E Indonesia
Iluh see Batman
118 I11 **Ilūkste** Daugvapils, SE Latvia
171 U14 **Ilur** Pulau Gorong, E Indonesia
32 F10 **Ilwaco** Washington, NW USA
Il'yaly see Ÿylanly
Ilyasbaba Burnu see Tekke Burnu
127 U9 **Ilych** ≈ NW Russian Federation
101 O21 **Ilz** ≈ SE Germany
111 M14 **Iłża** Radom, SE Poland
164 G13 **Imabari** var. Imaharu. Ehime, Shikoku, SW Japan
Imaharu see Imabari
165 O12 **Imaichi** var. Imaiti. Tochigi, Honshū, S Japan
Imaiti see Imaichi
164 K12 **Imajō** Fukui, Honshū, SW Japan
139 R9 **Imām Ibn Hāshim** C Iraq
139 T11 **Imān ʻAbd Allāh** S Iraq
126 J4 **Imandra, Ozero** ◎ NW Russian Federation
164 F15 **Imano-yama** ▲ Shikoku, SW Japan
164 C13 **Imari** Saga, Kyūshū, SW Japan
Imarssuak Mid-Ocean Seachannel see Imarssuak Seachannel
64 J6 **Imarssuak Seachannel** var. Imarssuak Mid-Ocean Seachannel. channel N Atlantic Ocean
93 N18 **Imatra** Etelä-Suomi, S Finland
164 K13 **Imazu** Shiga, Honshū, SW Japan
56 C6 **Imbabura** ◈ province N Ecuador
55 R9 **Imbaimadai** W Guyana
61 K14 **Imbituba** Santa Catarina, S Brazil
27 W9 **Imboden** Arkansas, C USA
Imbros see Gökçeada
Imeni 26 Bakinskikh Komissarov see 26 Bakı Komissarı/Uzboý
125 N13 **Imeni Babushkina** Vologodskaya Oblast', NW Russian Federation
126 J7 **Imeni Karla Libknekhta** Kurskaya Oblast', W Russian Federation
Imeni Mollanepesa see Mollanepes Adyndaky
Imeni S.A.Niyazova see S.A.Nyýazow Adyndaky
Imeni Sverdlova Rudnik see Sverdlovs'k
188 E9 **Imeong** Babeldaob, N Palau
81 L14 **Īmī** Somali, E Ethiopia
115 M21 **Imia** Turk. Kardak. island Dodekánisos, Greece, Aegean Sea
Imishli see İmişli
137 X12 **İmişli** Rus. Imishli. C Azerbaijan
163 X14 **Imjin-gang** ≈ North Korea/South Korea
35 S3 **Imlay** Nevada, W USA
31 S9 **Imlay City** Michigan, N USA
23 X15 **Immokalee** Florida, SE USA
77 U17 **Imo** ◈ state SE Nigeria
106 G10 **Imola** Emilia-Romagna, N Italy
186 A5 **Imonda** Sandaun, NW PNG
Imoschi see Imotski
113 G14 **Imotski** It. Imoschi. Split-Dalmacija, SE Croatia
59 L14 **Imperatriz** Maranhão, NE Brazil
106 B10 **Imperia** Liguria, NW Italy
57 E15 **Imperial** Lima, W Peru
35 X17 **Imperial** California, W USA
28 L16 **Imperial** Nebraska, C USA
24 M9 **Imperial** Texas, SW USA
35 Y17 **Imperial Dam** dam California, W USA
79 I17 **Impfondo** La Likouala, NE Congo
153 X14 **Imphāl** Manipur, NE India
103 P9 **Imphy** Nièvre, C France
106 G11 **Impruneta** Toscana, C Italy
115 K15 **İmroz** var. Gökçeada. Çanakkale, NW Turkey
Imroz Adası see Gökçeada
108 L7 **Imst** Tirol, W Austria
40 F3 **Imuris** Sonora, NW Mexico
164 M13 **Ina** Nagano, Honshū, S Japan
65 M18 **Inaccessible Island** island W Tristan da Cunha
115 F20 **Ínachos** ≈ S Greece
188 H6 **I Naftan, Puntan** headland Saipan, S Northern Mariana Islands
Inagua Islands see Great Inagua/Little Inagua
185 H15 **Inangahua** West Coast, South Island, NZ
57 I14 **Iñapari** Madre de Dios, E Peru
188 B17 **Inarajan** SE Guam
92 L10 **Inari** Lapp. Anár, Aanaar. Lappi, N Finland
92 L10 **Inarijärvi** Lapp. Aanaarjävri, Swe. Enareträsk. ◎ N Finland
92 L9 **Inarijoki** Lapp. Anárjohka. ≈ Finland/Norway
Inău see Ineu
165 P11 **Inawashiro-ko** var. Inawasiro Ko. ◎ Honshū, C Japan
Inawasiro Ko see Inawashiro-ko
62 H7 **Inca de Oro** Atacama, N Chile

◆ Country ● Country Capital ◇ Dependent Territory ○ Dependent Territory Capital ◈ Administrative Region ✈ International Airport ▲ Mountain ⛰ Mountain Range ✱ Volcano ≈ River ◎ Lake ▣ Reservoir

115 J15 **İnce Burnu** *headland* NW Turkey
136 K9 **İnce Burnu** *headland* N Turkey
136 I17 **İncekum Burnu** *headland* S Turkey
76 G7 **Inchiri** ◈ *region* NW Mauritania
163 X15 **Inch'ŏn** *off.* Inch'ŏn-gwangyŏksi, *Jap.* Jinsen; *prev.* Chemulpo. NW South Korea
163 X15 **Inch'on** × (Sŏul) NW South Korea
83 M17 **Inchope** Manica, C Mozambique
Incoronata *see* Kornat
103 Y15 **Incudine, Monte** ▲ Corse, France, C Mediterranean Sea
60 M10 **Indaiatuba** São Paulo, S Brazil
93 H17 **Indal** Västernorrland, C Sweden
93 H17 **Indalsälven** ≈ C Sweden
40 K8 **Inde** Durango, C Mexico
Indefatigable Island *see* Santa Cruz, Isla
35 S10 **Independence** California, W USA
29 X13 **Independence** Iowa, C USA
27 P7 **Independence** Kansas, C USA
20 M4 **Independence** Kentucky, S USA
27 R4 **Independence** Missouri, C USA
21 R8 **Independence** Virginia, NE USA
30 J7 **Independence** Wisconsin, N USA
197 R12 **Independence Fjord** *fjord* N Greenland
Independence Island *see* Malden Island
35 W2 **Independence Mountains** ▲▲ Nevada, W USA
57 K18 **Independencia** Cochabamba, C Bolivia
57 E16 **Independencia, Bahía de la** *bay* W Peru
Independencia, Monte *see* Adam, Mount
116 M12 **Independenţa** Galaţi, SE Romania
Inderagiri *see* Indragiri, Sungai
Inderbor *see* Inderborskiy
144 F11 **Inderborskiy** *Kaz.* Inderbor. Atyrau, W Kazakhstan
151 I14 **India** *off.* Republic of India, *var.* Indian Union, Union of India, *Hind.* Bhārat. ◆ *republic* S Asia
India *see* Inđija
18 D14 **Indiana** Pennsylvania, NE USA
31 N13 **Indiana** *off.* State of Indiana; also known as The Hoosier State. ◈ *state* N USA
31 O14 **Indianapolis** *state capital* Indiana, N USA
11 O10 **Indian Cabins** Alberta, W Canada
42 G1 **Indian Church** Orange Walk, N Belize
Indian Desert *see* Thar Desert
11 U16 **Indian Head** Saskatchewan, S Canada
31 O4 **Indian Lake** ◎ Michigan, N USA
18 K9 **Indian Lake** ◎ New York, NE USA
31 R13 **Indian Lake** ▣ Ohio, N USA
180-181 **Indian Ocean** *ocean*
29 V15 **Indianola** Iowa, C USA
22 K4 **Indianola** Mississippi, S USA
36 J6 **Indian Peak** ▲ Utah, W USA
23 Y13 **Indian River** *lagoon* Florida, SE USA
35 W10 **Indian Springs** Nevada, W USA
23 Y14 **Indiantown** Florida, SE USA
59 K19 **Indiara** Goiás, S Brazil
125 Q4 **Indiga** Nenetskiy Avtonomnyy Okrug, NW Russian Federation
123 R9 **Indigirka** ≈ NE Russian Federation
112 L10 **Inđija** *Hung.* India; *prev.* Indjija. Serbia, N Serbia and Montenegro (Yugo.)
35 V16 **Indio** California, W USA
42 M12 **Indio, Río** ≈ SE Nicaragua
152 I10 **Indira Gandhi International** × (Delhi) Delhi, N India
151 Q23 **Indira Point** *headland* Andaman and Nicobar Islands, India, NE Indian Ocean
Indjija *see* Inđija
131 Q13 **Indo-Australian Plate** *tectonic feature*
173 N11 **Indomed Fracture Zone** *tectonic feature* SW Indian Ocean
170 L12 **Indonesia** *off.* Republic of Indonesia, *Ind.* Republik Indonesia; *prev.* Dutch East Indies, Netherlands East Indies, United States of Indonesia. ◆ *republic* SE Asia
Indonesian Borneo *see* Kalimantan
154 G10 **Indore** Madhya Pradesh, C India
168 L11 **Indragiri, Sungai** *var.* Batang Kuantan, Inderagiri. ≈ Sumatera, W Indonesia
Indramajoe/Indramaju *see* Indramayu
169 P15 **Indramayu** *prev.* Indramajoe, Indramaju. Jawa, C Indonesia
155 K14 **Indrāvati** ≈ S India
103 N9 **Indre** ◈ *department* C France
102 M8 **Indre** ≈ C France
94 D13 **Indre Ålvik** Hordaland, S Norway
102 L8 **Indre-et-Loire** ◈ *department* C France
Indreville *see* Châteauroux
152 G3 **Indus** *Chin.* Yindu He; *prev.* Yin-tu Ho. ≈ S Asia
Indus Cone *see* Indus Fan
173 P3 **Indus Fan** *var.* Indus Cone. *undersea feature* N Arabian Sea
149 P17 **Indus, Mouths of the** *delta* S Pakistan
83 I24 **Indwe** Eastern Cape, SE South Africa
136 I10 **İnebolu** Kastamonu, N Turkey
77 P8 **I-n-Échaï** *oasis* C Mali
114 M13 **İnecik** Tekirdağ, NW Turkey
136 E12 **İnegöl** Bursa, NW Turkey
Inessa *see* Biancavilla
116 F10 **Ineu** *Hung.* Borosjenő; *prev.* Inău. Arad, W Romania
Ineul/Ineu, Vîrful *see* Ineu, Vârful
116 J9 **Ineu, Vârful** *var.* Ineul; *prev.* Vîrful Ineu. ▲ N Romania
21 P6 **Inez** Kentucky, S USA
74 E8 **Inezgane** × (Agadir) W Morocco
41 T17 **Inferior, Laguna** *lagoon* S Mexico
40 M15 **Infiernillo, Presa del** ▣ S Mexico
104 L2 **Infiesto** Asturias, N Spain
93 L20 **Ingå** *Fin.* Inkoo. Etelä-Suomi, S Finland
77 U10 **Ingal** *var.* I-n-Gall. Agadez, C Niger
I-n-Gall *see* Ingal
99 C18 **Ingelmunster** West-Vlaanderen, W Belgium
79 I18 **Ingende** Equateur, W Dem. Rep. Congo
62 L5 **Ingeniero Guillermo Nueva Juárez** Formosa, N Argentina
63 H16 **Ingeniero Jacobacci** Río Negro, C Argentina
14 F16 **Ingersoll** Ontario, S Canada
162 K6 **Ingettolgoy** Bulgan, N Mongolia
181 W5 **Ingham** Queensland, NE Australia
146 M11 **Ingichka** Samarqand Viloyati, C Uzbekistan
97 L16 **Ingleborough** ▲ N England, UK
25 T14 **Ingleside** Texas, SW USA
184 K10 **Inglewood** Taranaki, North Island, NZ
35 S15 **Inglewood** California, W USA
101 L21 **Ingolstadt** Bayern, S Germany
33 V9 **Ingomar** Montana, NW USA
13 R14 **Ingonish Beach** Cape Breton Island, Nova Scotia, SE Canada
153 S14 **Ingrāj Bāzār** *prev.* English Bazar. West Bengal, NE India
25 Q11 **Ingram** Texas, SW USA
195 X7 **Ingrid Christensen Coast** *physical region* Antarctica
74 K14 **I-n-Guezzam** S Algeria
Ingulets *see* Inhulets'
Inguri *see* Enguri
Ingushetia/Ingushetiya, Respublika *see* Ingushskaya Respublika
127 O15 **Ingushskaya Respublika** *var.* Respublika Ingushetiya, *Eng.* Ingushetia. ◈ *autonomous republic* SW Russian Federation
83 N20 **Inhambane** Inhambane, SE Mozambique
83 M20 **Inhambane** *off.* Província de Inhambane. ◈ *province* S Mozambique
83 N17 **Inhaminga** Sofala, C Mozambique
83 N20 **Inharrime** Inhambane, SE Mozambique
83 M18 **Inhassoro** Inhambane, E Mozambique
117 S9 **Inhulets'** *Rus.* Ingulets. Dnipropetrovs'ka Oblast', E Ukraine
117 R10 **Inhulets'** *Rus.* Ingulets. ≈ S Ukraine
105 Q10 **Iniesta** Castilla-La Mancha, C Spain
I-ning *see* Yining
54 K11 **Inírida, Río** ≈ E Colombia
Inis *see* Ennis
Inis Ceithleann *see* Enniskillen
Inis Córthaidh *see* Enniscorthy
Inis Díomáin *see* Ennistimon
97 A17 **Inishbofin** *Ir.* Inis Bó Finne. *island* W Ireland
97 B18 **Inisheer** *var.* Inishere, *Ir.* Inis Oírr. *island* W Ireland
Inishere *see* Inisheer
97 B18 **Inishmaan** *Ir.* Inis Meáin. *island* W Ireland
97 A18 **Inishmore** *Ir.* Árainn. *island* W Ireland
96 E13 **Inishtrahull** *Ir.* Inis Trá Tholl. *island* NW Ireland
97 A17 **Inishturk** *Ir.* Inis Toirc. *island* W Ireland
Inkoo *see* Ingå
185 J16 **Inland Kaikoura Range** ▲▲ South Island, NZ
Inland Sea *see* Seto-naikai
21 P11 **Inman** South Carolina, SE USA
108 L7 **Inn** ≈ C Europe
197 O11 **Innaanganeq** *var.* Kap York. *headland* NW Greenland
182 K2 **Innamincka** South Australia
92 G12 **Inndyr** Nordland, C Norway
42 G3 **Inner Channel** *inlet* SE Belize
96 F11 **Inner Hebrides** *island group* W Scotland, UK
172 H15 **Inner Islands** *var.* Central Group. *island group* NE Seychelles
Inner Mongolia/Inner Mongolian Autonomous Region *see* Nei Mongol Zizhiqu
96 G8 **Inner Sound** *strait* NW Scotland, UK
100 J13 **Innerste** ≈ C Germany
181 W5 **Innisfail** Queensland, NE Australia
11 Q15 **Innisfail** Alberta, SW Canada
Inniskilling *see* Enniskillen
39 O11 **Innoko River** ≈ Alaska, USA
Innosima *see* Innoshima
Innsbruch *see* Innsbruck
108 M7 **Innsbruck** *var.* Innsbruch. Tirol, W Austria
79 I19 **Inongo** Bandundu, W Dem. Rep. Congo
Inoucdjouac *see* Inukjuak
Inowrazlaw *see* Inowrocław
110 I10 **Inowrocław** *Ger.* Hohensalza; *prev.* Inowrazlaw. Kujawski-pomorskie, C Poland
57 K18 **Inquisivi** La Paz, W Bolivia
Inrin *see* Yüanlin
77 O8 **I-n-Sâkâne, 'Erg** *desert* N Mali
74 J10 **I-n-Salah** *var.* In Salah. C Algeria
127 O5 **Insar** Respublika Mordoviya, W Russian Federation
189 X15 **Insiaf** Kosrae, E Micronesia
94 L13 **Insjön** Dalarna, C Sweden
Insterburg *see* Chernyakhovsk
Insula *see* Lille
116 L13 **Însurăţei** Brăila, SE Romania
125 V6 **Inta** Respublika Komi, NW Russian Federation
77 R9 **I-n-Tebezas** Kidal, E Mali
Interamna *see* Teramo
Interamna Nahars *see* Terni
28 L11 **Interior** South Dakota, N USA
108 E9 **Interlaken** Bern, SW Switzerland
29 V2 **International Falls** Minnesota, N USA
167 O7 **Inthanon, Doi** ▲ NW Thailand
42 G7 **Intibucá** ◈ *department* SW Honduras
42 G8 **Intipucá** La Unión, SE El Salvador
61 B15 **Intiyaco** Santa Fe, C Argentina
116 K12 **Întorsura Buzăului** *Ger.* Bozau, *Hung.* Bodzafordulő. Covasna, E Romania
22 H9 **Intracoastal Waterway** *inland waterway system* Louisiana, S USA
25 V13 **Intracoastal Waterway** *inland waterway system* Texas, SW USA
108 G11 **Intragna** Ticino, S Switzerland
165 P14 **Inubō-zaki** *headland* Honshū, S Japan
164 E14 **Inukai** Ōita, Kyūshū, SW Japan
12 I5 **Inukjuak** *var.* Inoucdjouac; *prev.* Port Harrison. Québec, NE Canada
63 I24 **Inútil, Bahía** *bay* S Chile
Inuuvik *see* Inuvik
9 R8 **Inuvik** *var.* Inuuvik. Northwest Territories, NW Canada
164 L13 **Inuyama** Aichi, Honshū, SW Japan
56 G13 **Inuya, Río** ≈ E Peru
127 U13 **In'va** ≈ NW Russian Federation
96 H11 **Inveraray** W Scotland, UK
185 C24 **Invercargill** Southland, South Island, NZ
183 T5 **Inverell** New South Wales, SE Australia
96 I8 **Invergordon** N Scotland, UK
11 P16 **Invermere** British Columbia, SW Canada
13 R14 **Inverness** Cape Breton Island, Nova Scotia, SE Canada
96 I8 **Inverness** N Scotland, UK
23 V11 **Inverness** Florida, SE USA
96 I9 **Inverness** *cultural region* NW Scotland, UK
96 K9 **Inverurie** NE Scotland, UK
182 F8 **Investigator Group** *island group* South Australia
173 T7 **Investigator Ridge** *undersea feature* E Indian Ocean
182 H10 **Investigator Strait** *strait* South Australia
29 R11 **Inwood** Iowa, C USA
123 S10 **Inya** ≈ E Russian Federation
Inyanga *see* Nyanga
83 M16 **Inyangani** ▲ NE Zimbabwe
83 J17 **Inyathi** Matabeleland North, SW Zimbabwe
35 T12 **Inyokern** California, W USA
35 T10 **Inyo Mountains** ▲▲ California, W USA
127 P6 **Inza** Ul'yanovskaya Oblast', W Russian Federation
127 W5 **Inzer** Respublika Bashkortostan, W Russian Federation
127 N7 **Inzhavino** Tambovskaya Oblast', W Russian Federation
115 C16 **Ioánnina** *var.* Janina, Yannina. Ípeiros, W Greece
164 B17 **Iō-jima** *var.* Iwojima. *island* Nansei-shotō, SW Japan
126 L4 **Iokan'ga** ≈ NW Russian Federation
27 Q6 **Iola** Kansas, C USA
Iolcus *see* Iolkós
115 G16 **Iolkós** *anc.* Iolcus. *site of ancient city* Thessalía, C Greece
Iolotan' *see* Ýolöten
83 A16 **Iona** Namibe, SW Angola
96 F11 **Iona** *island* W Scotland, UK
116 M15 **Ion Corvin** Constanţa, SE Romania
35 P7 **Ione** California, W USA
116 I13 **Ioneşti** Vâlcea, SW Romania
31 Q9 **Ionia** Michigan, N USA
Ionia Basin *see* Ionian Basin
121 O10 **Ionian Basin** *var.* Ionia Basin. *undersea feature* Ionian Sea, C Mediterranean Sea
Ionian Islands *see* Iónioi Nísoi
121 O10 **Ionian Sea** *Gk.* Iónio Pélagos, *It.* Mar Ionio. *sea* C Mediterranean Sea
115 B17 **Iónioi Nísoi** *Eng.* Ionian Islands. ◈ *region* W Greece
115 B17 **Iónioi Nísoi** *Eng.* Ionian Islands. *island group* W Greece
Ionio, Mar/Iónio Pélagos *see* Ionian Sea
Iordan *see* Yordon
137 U10 **Iori** *var.* Qabırrı. ≈ Azerbaijan/Georgia
Iorrais, Ceann *see* Erris Head
115 J22 **Íos** Íos, Kykládes, Greece, Aegean Sea
115 J22 **Íos** *var.* Nio. *island* Kykládes, Greece, Aegean Sea
22 G9 **Iowa** Louisiana, S USA
29 V13 **Iowa** *off.* State of Iowa; also known as The Hawkeye State. ◈ *state* C USA
29 Y14 **Iowa City** Iowa, C USA
29 V13 **Iowa Falls** Iowa, C USA
25 R4 **Iowa Park** Texas, SW USA
29 Y14 **Iowa River** ≈ Iowa, C USA
119 M19 **Ipa** *Rus.* Ipa. ≈ SE Belarus
59 N20 **Ipatinga** Minas Gerais, SE Brazil
127 N13 **Ipatovo** Stavropol'skiy Kray, SW Russian Federation
115 C16 **Ípeiros** *Eng.* Epirus. ◈ *region* W Greece
Ipek *see* Peć
111 J21 **Ipel'** *var.* Ipoly, *Ger.* Eipel. ≈ Hungary/Slovakia
54 C13 **Ipiales** Nariño, SW Colombia
189 V14 **Ipis** *atoll* Chuuk Islands, C Micronesia
59 A14 **Ipixuna** Amazonas, W Brazil
168 J8 **Ipoh** Perak, Peninsular Malaysia
Ipoly *see* Ipel'
187 S15 **Ipota** Erromango, S Vanuatu
79 K14 **Ippy** Ouaka, C Central African Republic
114 L13 **İpsala** Edirne, NW Turkey
Ipsario *see* Ypsário
183 V3 **Ipswich** Queensland, E Australia
97 Q20 **Ipswich** *hist.* Gipeswic. E England, UK
29 O8 **Ipswich** South Dakota, N USA
Iput' *see* Iputs'
119 P18 **Iputs'** *Rus.* Iput'. ≈ Belarus /Russian Federation
9 R7 **Iqaluit** *prev.* Frobisher Bay. Baffin Island, Nunavut, NE Canada
159 P9 **Iqe** Qinghai, W China
159 P9 **Iqe He** ≈ C China
Iqlid *see* Eqlīd
62 G3 **Iquique** Tarapacá, N Chile
56 G8 **Iquitos** Loreto, N Peru
25 N9 **Iraan** Texas, SW USA
79 K14 **Ira Banda** Haute-Kotto, E Central African Republic
165 P16 **Irabu-jima** *island* Miyako-shotō, SW Japan
55 Y9 **Iracoubo** N French Guiana
60 H13 **Iraí** Rio Grande do Sul, S Brazil
114 G12 **Irákleia** Kentrikí Makedonía, N Greece
115 J21 **Irákleia** *island* Kykládes, Greece, Aegean Sea
115 J25 **Irákleio** *var.* Herakleion, *Eng.* Candia; *prev.* Iráklion. Kríti, Greece, E Mediterranean Sea
115 J25 **Irákleio** × Kríti, Greece, E Mediterranean Sea
115 F15 **Irákleio** *anc.* Heracleum. *castle* Kentrikí Makedonía, N Greece
Iráklion *see* Irákleio
143 O7 **Iran** *off.* Islamic Republic of Iran; *prev.* Persia. ◆ *republic* SW Asia
58 F13 **Iranduba** Amazonas, NW Brazil
85 P13 **Iranian Plate** *tectonic feature*
143 Q9 **Iranian Plateau** *var.* Plateau of *Iran. plateau* N Iran
169 U9 **Iran, Pegunungan** *var.* Iran Mountains. ▲▲ Indonesia/Malaysia
Iran, Plateau of *see* Iranian Plateau
143 W13 **Īrānshahr** Sīstān va Balūchestān, SE Iran
55 P5 **Irapa** Sucre, NE Venezuela
41 N13 **Irapuato** Guanajuato, C Mexico
139 R7 **Iraq** *off.* Republic of Iraq, *Ar.* 'Irāq. ◆ *republic* SW Asia
60 J12 **Irati** Paraná, S Brazil
105 R3 **Irati** ≈ N Spain
125 T8 **Irayël'** Respublika Komi, NW Russian Federation
43 N13 **Irazú, Volcán** 🌋 C Costa Rica
Irbenskiy Zaliv/Irbes Šaurums *see* Irbe Strait
118 D7 **Irbe Strait** *Est.* Kura Kurk, *Latv.* Irbes Šaurums, *Rus.* Irbenskiy Zaliv; *prev. Est.* Irbe Väin. *strait* Estonia/Latvia
Irbe Väin *see* Irbe Strait
138 G9 **Irbid** Irbid, N Jordan
138 G9 **Irbid** *off.* Muḥāfaẓat Irbid. ◈ *governorate* N Jordan
Irbīl *see* Arbīl
109 S6 **Irdning** Steiermark, SE Austria
79 I18 **Irebu** Equateur, W Dem. Rep. Congo
84 C9 **Ireland** *Lat.* Hibernia. *island* Ireland/UK
97 D17 **Ireland** *var.* Republic of Ireland, *Ir.* Éire. ◆ *republic* NW Europe
64 A12 **Ireland Island North** *island* W Bermuda
64 A12 **Ireland Island South** *island* W Bermuda
Ireland, Republic of *see* Ireland
127 V15 **Iren'** ≈ NW Russian Federation
185 A22 **Irene, Mount** ▲ South Island, NZ
Irgalem *see* Yirga 'Alem
144 L11 **Irgiz** Aktyubinsk, C Kazakhstan
Irian *see* New Guinea
Irian Barat *see* Papua
Irian Jaya *see* Papua
Irian, Teluk *see* Cenderawasih, Teluk
78 K9 **Iriba** Biltine, NE Chad
127 X7 **Iriklinskoye Vodokhranilishche** ▣ W Russian Federation
81 H23 **Iringa** Iringa, C Tanzania
81 H23 **Iringa** ◈ *region* S Tanzania
165 O16 **Iriomote-jima** *island* Sakishima-shotō, SW Japan
42 L4 **Iriona** Colón, NE Honduras
47 U7 **Iriri** ≈ N Brazil
58 I13 **Iriri, Rio** ≈ C Brazil
Iris *see* Yeşilırmak
35 W9 **Irish, Mount** ▲ Nevada, W USA
97 H17 **Irish Sea** *Ir.* Muir Éireann. *sea* C British Isles
139 U12 **Irjal ash Shaykhīyah** S Iraq
147 U11 **Irkeshtam** Oshskaya Oblast', SW Kyrgyzstan
122 M13 **Irkutsk** Irkutskaya Oblast', S Russian Federation
122 M12 **Irkutskaya Oblast'** ◈ *province* S Russian Federation
Irlir, Gora *see* Irlir Tog'l
146 K8 **Irlir Tog'l** *var.* Gora Irlir. ▲ N Uzbekistan
Irminger Basin *see* Reykjanes Basin
21 R12 **Irmo** South Carolina, SE USA
102 E6 **Iroise** *sea* NW France
189 X2 **Iroj** *var.* Eroj. *island* Ratak Chain, SE Marshall Islands
182 H7 **Iron Baron** South Australia
14 C10 **Iron Bridge** Ontario, S Canada
20 H10 **Iron City** Tennessee, S USA
14 I13 **Irondale** ≈ Ontario, SE Canada
182 H7 **Iron Knob** South Australia
30 M5 **Iron Mountain** Michigan, N USA
30 M4 **Iron River** Michigan, N USA
30 J3 **Iron River** Wisconsin, N USA
27 X6 **Ironton** Missouri, C USA
31 S15 **Ironton** Ohio, N USA
30 K4 **Ironwood** Michigan, N USA
12 H12 **Iroquois Falls** Ontario, S Canada
31 N12 **Iroquois River** ≈ Illinois/Indiana, N USA
164 M15 **Irō-zaki** *headland* Honshū, S Japan
Irpen' *see* Irpin'
117 O4 **Irpin'** *Rus.* Irpen'. Kyyivs'ka Oblast', N Ukraine
117 O4 **Irpin'** *Rus.* Irpen'. ≈ N Ukraine
141 Q16 **'Irqah** SW Yemen
166 K8 **Irrawaddy** *var.* Ayeyarwady. ◈ *division* SW Myanmar
166 L6 **Irrawaddy** *var.* Ayeyarwady. ≈ W Myanmar
166 K8 **Irrawaddy, Mouths of the** *delta* SW Myanmar
117 N4 **Irsha** ≈ N Ukraine
116 H7 **Irshava** Zakarpats'ka Oblast', W Ukraine
107 N18 **Irsina** Basilicata, S Italy
Irtish *see* Irtysh
131 R5 **Irtysh** *var.* Irtish, *Kaz.* Ertis. ≈ C Asia
145 S7 **Irtyshsk** *Kaz.* Ertis. Pavlodar, NE Kazakhstan
79 P17 **Irumu** Orientale, E Dem. Rep. Congo
105 Q2 **Irún** País Vasco, N Spain
Iruña *see* Pamplona
105 Q3 **Irurtzun** Navarra, N Spain
96 I13 **Irvine** W Scotland, UK
21 N6 **Irvine** Kentucky, S USA
25 T6 **Irving** Texas, SW USA
20 K5 **Irvington** Kentucky, S USA
Isaak *see* Iisaku
28 L8 **Isabel** South Dakota, N USA
186 L8 **Isabel** *off.* Isabel Province. ◈ *province* N Solomon Islands
171 O8 **Isabela** Basilan Island, SW Philippines
45 S5 **Isabela** W Puerto Rico
45 N8 **Isabela, Cabo** *headland* NW Dominican Republic
57 A18 **Isabela, Isla** *var.* Albemarle Island. *island* Galapagos Islands, Ecuador, E Pacific Ocean
40 I12 **Isabela, Isla** *island* C Mexico
42 K9 **Isabella, Cordillera** ▲▲ NW Nicaragua
35 S12 **Isabella Lake** ▣ California, W USA
31 N2 **Isabelle, Point** *headland* Michigan, N USA
Isabel Segunda *see* Vieques
116 M13 **Isaccea** Tulcea, E Romania
92 H1 **Ísafjarðardjúp** *inlet* NW Iceland
92 H1 **Ísafjördhur** Vestfirdhir, NW Iceland
164 C14 **Isahaya** Nagasaki, Kyūshū, SW Japan
149 S7 **Īsa Khel** Punjab, E Pakistan
172 H7 **Isalo** *var.* Massif de L'Isalo. ▲▲ SW Madagascar
Isalo, Massif de L' *see* Isalo
79 K20 **Isandja** Kasai Occidental, C Dem. Rep. Congo
187 R15 **Isangel** Tanna, S Vanuatu
79 M18 **Isangi** Orientale, C Dem. Rep. Congo
101 L24 **Isar** ≈ Austria/Germany
101 M23 **Isar-Kanal** *canal* SE Germany
Isbarta *see* İsparta
Isca Damnoniorum *see* Exeter
107 K18 **Ischia** *var.* Isola d'Ischia; *anc.* Aenaria. Campania, S Italy
107 J18 **Ischia, Isola d'** *island* S Italy
54 B12 **Iscuandé** *var.* Santa Bárbara. Nariño, SW Colombia
164 K14 **Ise** Mie, Honshū, SW Japan
100 J12 **Ise** ≈ N Germany
95 I23 **Isefjord** *fjord* E Denmark
Iseghem *see* Izegem
192 M14 **Iselin Seamount** *undersea feature* S Pacific Ocean
Isenhof *see* Püssi
106 E7 **Iseo** Lombardia, N Italy
103 U12 **Iseran, Col de l'** *pass* E France
103 S11 **Isère** ◈ *department* E France
103 S12 **Isère** ≈ E France
101 F15 **Iserlohn** Nordrhein-Westfalen, W Germany
107 K16 **Isernia** *var.* Æsernia. Molise, C Italy
165 N12 **Isesaki** Gunma, Honshū, S Japan
131 Q5 **Iset'** ≈ C Russian Federation
77 S15 **Iseyin** Oyo, W Nigeria
Isfahan *see* Eşfahān
147 Q11 **Isfana** Batkenskaya Oblast', SW Kyrgyzstan
147 R11 **Isfara** N Tajikistan
149 O4 **Isfi Maidān** Ghowr, N Afghanistan
92 O3 **Isfjorden** *fjord* W Svalbard
Isha Baydhabo *see* Baydhabo
127 V11 **Isherim, Gora** ▲ NW Russian Federation
127 Q5 **Isheyevka** Ul'yanovskaya Oblast', W Russian Federation
165 P16 **Ishigaki** Okinawa, Ishigaki-jima, SW Japan
165 P16 **Ishigaki-jima** *var.* Isigaki Zima. *island* Sakishima-shotō, SW Japan
165 R3 **Ishikari-wan** *bay* Hokkaidō, NE Japan
165 S16 **Ishikawa** *var.* Isikawa. Okinawa, Okinawa, SW Japan
164 K11 **Ishikawa** *off.* Ishikawa-ken, *var.* Isikawa. ◈ *prefecture* Honshū, SW Japan
122 H11 **Ishim** Tyumenskaya Oblast', C Russian Federation
131 R6 **Ishim** *Kaz.* Esil. ≈ Kazakhstan/Russian Federation
127 V6 **Ishimbay** Respublika Bashkortostan, W Russian Federation
145 O9 **Ishimskoye** Akmola, C Kazakhstan
165 Q10 **Ishinomaki** *var.* Isinomaki. Miyagi, Honshū, C Japan
165 P13 **Ishioka** *var.* Isioka. Ibaraki, Honshū, S Japan
Ishkashim *see* Ishkoshim
Ishkashimskiy Khrebet *see* Ishkoshim, Qatorkŭhi
147 S15 **Ishkoshim** *Rus.* Ishkashim. S Tajikistan
147 S15 **Ishkoshim, Qatorkŭhi** *Rus.* Ishkashimskiy Khrebet. ▲▲ SE Tajikistan
31 N4 **Ishpeming** Michigan, N USA
147 N11 **Ishtixon** *Rus.* Ishtykhan. Samarqand Viloyati, C Uzbekistan
Ishtykhan *see* Ishtixon
153 T15 **Ishurdi** *var.* Iswardi. Rajshahi, W Bangladesh
61 G17 **Isidoro Noblia** Cerro Largo, NE Uruguay
102 J4 **Isigny-sur-Mer** Calvados, N France
Isikari Gawa *see* Ishikari-gawa
Isikawa *see* Ishikawa
136 C11 **Işıklar Dağı** ▲▲ NW Turkey
107 C19 **Isili** Sardegna, Italy, C Mediterranean Sea
122 H12 **Isil'kul'** Omskaya Oblast', C Russian Federation
Isinomaki *see* Ishinomaki
Isioka *see* Ishioka
81 I18 **Isiolo** Eastern, C Kenya
79 O16 **Isiro** Orientale, NE Dem. Rep. Congo
92 P2 **Isispynten** *headland* NE Svalbard
123 P11 **Isit** Respublika Sakha (Yakutiya), NE Russian Federation
149 O2 **Iskabad Canal** *canal* N Afghanistan
147 Q9 **Iskandar** *Rus.* Iskander. Toshkent Viloyati, E Uzbekistan
Iskander *see* Iskandar
Iskăr *see* Iskŭr
121 Q2 **İskele** *var.* Trikomo, *Gk.* Tríkomon. E Cyprus
136 K17 **İskenderun** *Eng.* Alexandretta. Hatay, S Turkey
138 H2 **İskenderun Körfezi** *Eng.* Gulf of Alexandretta. *gulf* S Turkey
136 J11 **İskilip** Çorum, N Turkey
Iski-Nauket *see* Eski-Nookat
114 J11 **Iskra** *prev.* Popovo. Kŭrdzhali, S Bulgaria
114 G10 **Iskŭr** *var.* Iskăr. ≈ NW Bulgaria
114 H10 **Iskŭr, Yazovir** *prev.* Yazovir Stalin. ▣ W Bulgaria
41 S15 **Isla** Veracruz-Llave, SE Mexico
119 J15 **Islach** *Rus.* Isloch'. ≈ C Belarus
104 H14 **Isla Cristina** Andalucía, S Spain
Isla de León *see* San Fernando
149 U6 **Islāmābād** ● (Pakistan) Federal Capital Territory Islāmābād, NE Pakistan
149 V6 **Islāmābād** × Federal Capital Territory Islāmābād, NE Pakistan
Islamabad *see* Anantnāg
149 R17 **Islāmkot** Sind, SE Pakistan
23 Y17 **Islamorada** Florida Keys, Florida, SE USA
153 P14 **Islāmpur** Bihār, N India
Islam Qala *see* Eslām Qal'eh
Island/Ísland *see* Iceland
18 K16 **Island Beach** *spit* New Jersey, NE USA
19 S4 **Island Falls** Maine, NE USA
182 H6 **Island Lagoon** ◎ South Australia
11 Y13 **Island Lake** ◎ Manitoba, C Canada
29 W5 **Island Lake Reservoir** ▣ Minnesota, N USA
33 R13 **Island Park** Idaho, NW USA
19 N6 **Island Pond** Vermont, NE USA
184 K2 **Islands, Bay of** *inlet* North Island, NZ
103 R7 **Is-sur-Tille** Côte d'Or, C France
42 J3 **Islas de la Bahía** ◈ *department* N Honduras
65 L20 **Islas Orcadas Rise** *undersea feature* S Atlantic Ocean
96 F12 **Islay** *island* SW Scotland, UK
116 I15 **Islaz** Teleorman, S Romania
29 V7 **Isle** Minnesota, N USA
102 M12 **Isle** ≈ W France
97 I16 **Isle of Man** ◇ *UK crown dependency* NW Europe
21 X7 **Isle of Wight** Virginia, NE USA
97 M24 **Isle of Wight** *cultural region* S England, UK
191 Y3 **Isles Lagoon** ◎ Kiritimati, E Kiribati
37 R11 **Isleta Pueblo** New Mexico, SW USA
Isloch' *see* Islach

◆ Country ● Country Capital ◇ Dependent Territory ○ Dependent Territory Capital ◈ Administrative Region × International Airport ▲ Mountain ▲▲ Mountain Range 🌋 Volcano ≈ River ◎ Lake ▣ Reservoir

61 *E19* **Ismael Cortinas** Flores, S Uruguay
Ismailia *see* Ismâ'ilîya
75 *W7* **Ismâ'ilîya** ***var.*** Ismailia. N Egypt
Ismailly *see* İsmayıllı
137 *X11* **İsmayıllı** ***Rus.*** Ismailly. C Azerbaijan
Ismid *see* İzmit
75 *X10* **Isna** ***var.*** Esna. SE Egypt
93 *K18* **Isojoki** Länsi-Suomi, W Finland
82 *M12* **Isoka** Northern, NE Zambia
Isola d'Ischia *see* Ischia
Isola d'Istria *see* Izola
Isonzo *see* Soča
15 *U4* **Isoukustouc** ≈ Québec, SE Canada
136 *F15* **İsparta** ***var.*** Isbarta. İsparta, SW Turkey
136 *F15* **İsparta** ***var.*** Isbarta. ◈ *province* SW Turkey
114 *M7* **Isperikh** ***prev.*** Kemanlar. Razgrad, N Bulgaria
107 *L26* **Ispica** Sicilia, Italy, C Mediterranean Sea
148 *J14* **Ispikān** Baluchistān, SW Pakistan
137 *Q12* **İspir** Erzurum, NE Turkey
138 *E12* **Israel** ***off.*** State of Israel, ***var.*** Medinat Israel, ***Heb.*** Yisrael, Yisra'el. ◆ *republic* SW Asia
Issa *see* Vis
55 *S9* **Issano** C Guyana
76 *M16* **Issia** SW Ivory Coast
Issiq Köl *see* Issyk-Kul', Ozero
103 *P11* **Issoire** Puy-de-Dôme, C France
103 *N9* **Issoudun** ***anc.*** Uxellodunum. Indre, C France
81 *H22* **Issuna** Singida, C Tanzania
Issyk *see* Yesik
Issyk-Kul' *see* Balykchy
147 *X7* **Issyk-Kul', Ozero** ***var.*** Issiq Köl, ***Kir.*** Ysyk-Köl. ◎ E Kyrgyzstan
147 *X7* **Issyk-Kul'skaya Oblast'** ***Kir.*** Ysyk-Köl Oblasty. ◈ *province* E Kyrgyzstan
149 *Q7* **Istādeh-ye Moqor, Āb-e-** ***var.*** Āb-i-Istāda. ◎ SE Afghanistan
136 *D11* **İstanbul** ***Bul.*** Tsarigrad, ***Eng.*** Istanbul; ***prev.*** Constantinople, ***anc.*** Byzantium. İstanbul, NW Turkey
114 *P12* **İstanbul** ◈ *province* NW Turkey
114 *P12* **İstanbul Boğazı** ***var.*** Bosporus Thracius, ***Eng.*** Bosphorus, Bosporus, ***Turk.*** Karadeniz Boğazı. *strait* NW Turkey
Istarska Županija *see* Istra
115 *G19* **Isthmía** Pelopónnisos, S Greece
115 *G17* **Istiaía** Évvoia, C Greece
54 *D9* **Istmina** Chocó, W Colombia
23 *W13* **Istokpoga, Lake** ◎ Florida, SE USA
112 *A9* **Istra** ***off.*** Istarska županija. ◈ *province* NW Croatia
112 *I10* **Istra** ***Eng.*** Istria, ***Ger.*** Istrien. *cultural region* NW Croatia
103 *R15* **Istres** Bouches-du-Rhône, SE France
Istria/Istrien *see* Istra
Iswardi *see* Ishurdi
127 *V7* **Isyangulovo** Respublika Bashkortostan, W Russian Federation
62 *O6* **Itá** Central, S Paraguay
59 *O17* **Itaberaba** Bahia, E Brazil
59 *M20* **Itabira** ***prev.*** Presidente Vargas. Minas Gerais, SE Brazil
59 *O18* **Itabuna** Bahia, E Brazil
59 *J18* **Itacaiu** Mato Grosso, S Brazil
58 *G12* **Itacoatiara** Amazonas, N Brazil
54 *D9* **Itagüí** Antioquia, W Colombia
60 *D13* **Itá Ibaté** Corrientes, NE Argentina
60 *G11* **Itaipú, Represa de** ▣ Brazil/Paraguay
58 *H13* **Itaituba** Pará, NE Brazil
60 *K13* **Itajaí** Santa Catarina, S Brazil
Italia/Italiana, Republica/Italian Republic, The *see* Italy
Italian Somaliland *see* Somalia
25 *T7* **Italy** Texas, SW USA
106 *G12* **Italy** ***off.*** The Italian Republic, ***It.*** Italia, Republica Italiana. ◆ *republic* S Europe
59 *O19* **Itamaraju** Bahia, E Brazil
59 *C14* **Itamarati** Amazonas, W Brazil
59 *M19* **Itambé, Pico de** ▲ SE Brazil
164 *J13* **Itami** × (Ōsaka) Ōsaka, Honshū, SW Japan
115 *H15* **Ítamos** ▲ N Greece
153 *W11* **Itānagar** Arunāchal Pradesh, NE India
Itany *see* Litani
59 *N19* **Itaobim** Minas Gerais, SE Brazil
59 *P15* **Itaparica, Represa de** ▣ E Brazil
58 *M13* **Itapecuru-Mirim** Maranhão, E Brazil
60 *Q8* **Itaperuna** Rio de Janeiro, SE Brazil
59 *O18* **Itapetinga** Bahia, E Brazil
60 *L10* **Itapetininga** São Paulo, S Brazil
60 *K10* **Itapeva** São Paulo, S Brazil
47 *W6* **Itapicuru, Rio** ≈ NE Brazil
58 *O13* **Itapipoca** Ceará, E Brazil
60 *M9* **Itapira** São Paulo, S Brazil
60 *K8* **Itápolis** São Paulo, S Brazil
60 *K10* **Itaporanga** São Paulo, S Brazil
62 *P7* **Itapúa** ***off.*** Departamento de Itapúa. ◈ *department* SE Paraguay
59 *E15* **Itapuã do Oeste** Rondônia, W Brazil
61 *E15* **Itaqui** Rio Grande do Sul, S Brazil
60 *K10* **Itararé** São Paulo, S Brazil
60 *K10* **Itararé, Rio** ≈ S Brazil
154 *H11* **Itārsi** Madhya Pradesh, C India
25 *T7* **Itasca** Texas, SW USA
Itassi *see* Vieille Case
93 *N17* **Itä-Suomi** ◈ *province* E Finland
60 *D13* **Itatí** Corrientes, NE Argentina
60 *K10* **Itatinga** São Paulo, S Brazil
115 *F18* **Itéas, Kólpos** *gulf* C Greece
57 *N15* **Iténez, Río** ***var.*** Rio Guaporé. ≈ Bolivia/Brazil ***see also*** Guaporé, Rio
54 *H11* **Iteviate, Río** ≈ C Colombia
100 *I13* **Ith** *hill range* C Germany
31 *Q8* **Ithaca** Michigan, N USA
18 *H11* **Ithaca** New York, NE USA
115 *C18* **Itháki** Itháki, Iónioi Nísoi, Greece, C Mediterranean Sea
115 *C18* **Itháki** *island* Iónioi Nísoi, Greece, C Mediterranean Sea
It Hearrenfean *see* Heerenveen
79 *L17* **Itimbiri** ≈ N Dem. Rep. Congo
Itinomiya *see* Ichinomiya
Itinoseki *see* Ichinoseki
39 *Q5* **Itkilik River** ≈ Alaska, USA
164 *M11* **Itoigawa** Niigata, Honshū, C Japan
15 *R6* **Itomamo, Lac** ◎ Québec, SE Canada
165 *S17* **Itoman** Okinawa, SW Japan
102 *M5* **Iton** ≈ N France
57 *M16* **Itonamas Río** ≈ NE Bolivia
Itoupé, Mont *see* Sommet Tabulaire
Itseqqortoormiit *see* Ittoqqortoormiit
22 *K4* **Itta Bena** Mississippi, S USA
107 *B17* **Ittiri** Sardegna, Italy, C Mediterranean Sea
197 *Q14* **Ittoqqortoormiit** *var.* Itseqqortoormiit, ***Dan.*** Scoresbysund, ***Eng.*** Scoresby Sound. Tunu, C Greenland
60 *M10* **Itu** São Paulo, S Brazil
54 *D8* **Ituango** Antioquia, NW Colombia
59 *A14* **Ituí, Rio** ≈ NW Brazil
79 *O20* **Itula** Sud Kivu, E Dem. Rep. Congo
59 *K19* **Itumbiara** Goiás, C Brazil
55 *T9* **Ituni** E Guyana
41 *X13* **Iturbide** Campeche, SE Mexico
Ituri *see* Aruwimi
123 *V13* **Iturup, Ostrov** *island* Kuril'skiye Ostrova, SE Russian Federation
60 *L7* **Ituverava** São Paulo, S Brazil
59 *C15* **Ituxi, Rio** ≈ W Brazil
61 *E14* **Ituzaingó** Corrientes, NE Argentina
101 *K18* **Itz** ≈ C Germany
100 *I9* **Itzehoe** Schleswig-Holstein, N Germany
23 *N2* **Iuka** Mississippi, S USA
60 *I11* **Ivaiporã** Paraná, S Brazil
60 *I11* **Ivaí, Rio** ≈ S Brazil
92 *L10* **Ivalo** ***Lapp.*** Avveel, Avvil. Lappi, N Finland
92 *L10* **Ivalojoki** ***Lapp.*** Avreel. ≈ N Finland
119 *H20* **Ivanava** ***Pol.*** Janów, Janów Poleski, ***Rus.*** Ivanovo. Brestskaya Voblasts', SW Belarus
Ivangorod *see* Dęblin
Ivangrad *see* Berane
183 *N7* **Ivanhoe** New South Wales, SE Australia
29 *S9* **Ivanhoe** Minnesota, N USA
14 *D8* **Ivanhoe** ≈ Ontario, S Canada
112 *E8* **Ivanić-Grad** Sisak-Moslavina, N Croatia
117 *T10* **Ivanivka** Khersons'ka Oblast', S Ukraine
117 *P10* **Ivanivka** Odes'ka Oblast', SW Ukraine
113 *L14* **Ivanjica** Serbia, C Serbia and Montenegro (Yugo.)
112 *G11* **Ivanjska** ***var.*** Potkozarje. Republika Srpska, NW Bosnia & Herzegovina
111 *H21* **Ivanka** × (Bratislava) Bratislavský Kraj, W Slovakia
117 *O3* **Ivankiv** ***Rus.*** Ivankov. Kyyivs'ka Oblast', N Ukraine
Ivankov *see* Ivankiv
39 *O15* **Ivanof Bay** Alaska, USA
116 *J7* **Ivano-Frankivs'k** ***Ger.*** Stanislau, ***Pol.*** Stanisławów, ***Rus.*** Ivano-Frankovsk; ***prev.*** Stanislav. Ivano-Frankivs'ka Oblast', W Ukraine
Ivano-Frankivs'k *see* Ivano-Frankivs'ka Oblast'
116 *I7* **Ivano-Frankivs'ka Oblast'** ***var.*** Ivano-Frankivs'k, ***Rus.*** Ivano-Frankovskaya Oblast'; ***prev.*** Stanislavskaya Oblast'. ◈ *province* W Ukraine
Ivano-Frankovsk *see* Ivano-Frankivs'k
Ivano-Frankovskaya Oblast' *see* Ivano-Frankivs'ka Oblast'
124 *M16* **Ivanovo** Ivanovskaya Oblast', W Russian Federation
Ivanovo *see* Ivanava
124 *M16* **Ivanovskaya Oblast'** ◈ *province* W Russian Federation
35 *X12* **Ivanpah Lake** ◎ California, W USA
112 *E7* **Ivanščica** ▲▲ NE Croatia
114 *M8* **Ivanski** Shumen, NE Bulgaria
127 *R7* **Ivanteyevka** Saratovskaya Oblast', W Russian Federation
Ivantsevichi/Ivatsevichi *see* Ivatsevichy
116 *I4* **Ivanychi** Volyns'ka Oblast', NW Ukraine
119 *H18* **Ivatsevichy** ***Pol.*** Iwacewicze, ***Rus.*** Ivantsevichi, Ivatsevichi. Brestskaya Voblasts', SW Belarus
114 *L12* **Ivaylovgrad** Khaskovo, S Bulgaria
114 *K11* **Ivaylovgrad, Yazovir** ▣ S Bulgaria
122 *G9* **Ivdel'** Sverdlovskaya Oblast', C Russian Federation
Ivenets *see* Ivyanyets
116 *L12* **Ivești** Galați, E Romania
Ivgovuotna *see* Lyngen
Ivigtut *see* Ivittuut
79 *F18* **Ivindo** ≈ Congo/Gabon
59 *I21* **Ivinheima** Mato Grosso do Sul, SW Brazil
196 *M15* **Ivittuut** ***var.*** Ivigtut. Kitaa, S Greenland
Iviza *see* Eivissa
172 *I6* **Ivohibe** Fianarantsoa, SE Madagascar
Ivoire, Côte d' *see* Ivory Coast
76 *L15* **Ivory Coast** ***off.*** Republic of the Ivory Coast, ***Fr.*** Côte d'Ivoire, République de la Côte d'Ivoire. ◆ *republic* W Africa
68 *C11* **Ivory Coast** ***Fr.*** Côte d'Ivoire. *coastal region* S Ivory Coast
95 *L22* **Ivösjön** ◎ S Sweden
106 *B7* **Ivrea** ***anc.*** Eporedia. Piemonte, NW Italy
12 *J2* **Ivujivik** Québec, NE Canada
119 *J16* **Ivyanyets** ***Rus.*** Ivenets. Minskaya Voblasts', C Belarus
Iv'ye *see* Iwye
Iwacewicze *see* Ivatsevichy
165 *R8* **Iwaizumi** Iwate, Honshū, NE Japan
165 *P12* **Iwaki** Fukushima, Honshū, N Japan
164 *F13* **Iwakuni** Yamaguchi, Honshū, SW Japan
165 *S4* **Iwamizawa** Hokkaidō, NE Japan
165 *R4* **Iwanai** Hokkaidō, NE Japan
165 *Q10* **Iwanuma** Miyagi, Honshū, C Japan
164 *L14* **Iwata** Shizuoka, Honshū, S Japan
165 *R8* **Iwate** Iwate, Honshū, N Japan
165 *R8* **Iwate** ***off.*** Iwate-ken. ◈ *prefecture* Honshū, C Japan
Iwje *see* Iwye
77 *S16* **Iwo** Oyo, SW Nigeria
Iwojima *see* Iō-jima
119 *I16* **Iwye** ***Pol.*** Iwje, ***Rus.*** Iv'ye. Hrodzyenskaya Voblasts', W Belarus
42 *C4* **Ixcán, Río** ≈ Guatemala/Mexico
99 *G18* **Ixelles** ***Dut.*** Elsene. Brussels, C Belgium
57 *J16* **Ixiamas** La Paz, NW Bolivia
41 *O13* **Ixmiquilpan** ***var.*** Ixmiquilpán. Hidalgo, C Mexico
83 *K23* **Ixopo** KwaZulu/Natal, E South Africa
Ixtaccíhuatal, Volcán *see* Iztaccíhuati, Volcán
40 *M16* **Ixtapa** Guerrero, S Mexico
41 *S16* **Ixtepec** Oaxaca, SE Mexico
40 *K12* **Ixtlán** ***var.*** Ixtlán del Río. Nayarit, C Mexico
Ixtlán del Río *see* Ixtlán
122 *H11* **Iyevlevo** Tyumenskaya Oblast', C Russian Federation
164 *F14* **Iyo** Ehime, Shikoku, SW Japan
Iyomisima *see* Iyomishima
164 *E14* **Iyo-nada** *sea* S Japan
42 *E4* **Izabal** ***off.*** Departamento de Izabal. ◈ *department* E Guatemala
42 *F5* **Izabal, Lago de** ***prev.*** Golfo Dulce. ◎ E Guatemala
143 *O9* **Īzad Khvāst** Fārs, C Iran
41 *X12* **Izamal** Yucatán, SE Mexico
127 *Q16* **Izberbash** Respublika Dagestan, SW Russian Federation
99 *C18* **Izegem** ***prev.*** Iseghem. West-Vlaanderen, W Belgium
142 *M9* **Īzeh** Khūzestān, SW Iran
165 *T16* **Izena-jima** *island* Nansei-shotō, SW Japan
114 *N10* **Izgrev** Burgas, E Bulgaria
127 *T2* **Izhevsk** ***prev.*** Ustinov. Udmurtskaya Respublika, NW Russian Federation
125 *S7* **Izhma** Respublika Komi, NW Russian Federation
127 *S7* **Izhma** ≈ NW Russian Federation
141 *X8* **Izkī** NE Oman
Izmail *see* Izmayil
117 *N13* **Izmayil** ***Rus.*** Izmail. Odes'ka Oblast', SW Ukraine
136 *B14* **İzmir** ***prev.*** Smyrna. İzmir, W Turkey
136 *C14* **İzmir** ***prev.*** Smyrna. ◈ *province* W Turkey
136 *E11* **İzmit** ***var.*** Ismid; ***anc.*** Astacus. Kocaeli, NW Turkey
104 *M14* **Iznájar** Andalucía, S Spain
104 *M14* **Iznajar, Embalse de** ▣ S Spain
105 *N14* **Iznalloz** Andalucía, S Spain
136 *E11* **İznik** Bursa, NW Turkey
136 *E12* **İznik Gölü** ◎ NW Turkey
126 *M14* **Izobil'nyy** Stavropol'skiy Kray, SW Russian Federation
109 *S13* **Izola** ***It.*** Isola d'Istria. SW Slovenia
138 *H9* **Izra'** ***var.*** Ezra, Ezraa. Dar'ā, S Syria
41 *P14* **Iztaccíhuati, Volcán** ***var.*** Volcán Ixtaccíhuatal. ※ S Mexico
42 *C7* **Iztapa** Escuintla, SE Guatemala
Izúcar de Matamoros *see* Matamoros
165 *N14* **Izu-hantō** *peninsula* Honshū, S Japan
164 *C12* **Izuhara** Nagasaki, Tsushima, SW Japan
164 *J14* **Izumiōtsu** Ōsaka, Honshū, SW Japan
164 *I14* **Izumi-Sano** Ōsaka, Honshū, SW Japan
164 *G12* **Izumo** Shimane, Honshū, SW Japan
Izu Shichito *see* Izu-shotō
192 *H5* **Izu Trench** *undersea feature* NW Pacific Ocean
122 *K6* **Izvestiy TsIK, Ostrova** *island* N Russian Federation
114 *G10* **Izvor** Pernik, W Bulgaria
116 *L5* **Izyaslav** Khmel'nyts'ka Oblast', W Ukraine
117 *W6* **Izyum** Kharkivs'ka Oblast', E Ukraine

J

95 *M18* **Jaala** Etelä-Suomi, S Finland
140 *J5* **Jabal ash Shifā** *desert* NW Saudi Arabia
141 *U8* **Jabal aẓ Ẓannah** ***var.*** Jebel Dhanna. Abū Ẓaby, W UAE
138 *E11* **Jabalīya** ***var.*** Jabāliyah. NE Gaza Strip
Jabāliyah *see* Jabalīya
105 *N11* **Jabalón** ≈ C Spain
154 *J10* **Jabalpur** ***prev.*** Jubbulpore. Madhya Pradesh, C India
141 *N15* **Jabal Zuqar, Jazīrat** ***var.*** Az Zuqur. *island* SW Yemen
Jabat *see* Jabwot
138 *J3* **Jabbūl, Sabkhat al** *salt flat* NW Syria
181 *P1* **Jabiru** Northern Territory, N Australia
138 *H4* **Jablah** ***var.*** Jeble, ***Fr.*** Djéblé. Al Lādhiqīyah, W Syria
112 *C11* **Jablanac** Lika-Senj, W Croatia
113 *H14* **Jablanica** Federacija Bosna I Hercegovina, SW Bosnia and Herzegovina
113 *M20* **Jablanica** ***Alb.*** Mali i Jabllanicës, ***var.*** Malet e Jabllanicës. ▲▲ Albania/FYR Macedonia ***see also*** Jabllanicës, Mali i
Jabllanicës, Malet e *see* Jablanica/Jabllanicës, Mali i
113 *M20* **Jabllanicës, Mali i** ***var.*** Malet e Jabllanicës, ***Mac.*** Jablanica. ▲▲ Albania/FYR Macedonia ***see also*** Jablanica
111 *E15* **Jablonec nad Nisou** ***Ger.*** Gablonz an der Neisse. Liberecký Kraj, N Czech Republic
Jabłonków/Jablunkau *see* Jablunkov
110 *J9* **Jabłonowo Pomorskie** Kujawski-pomorskie, C Poland
111 *J17* **Jablunkov** ***Ger.*** Jablunkau, ***Pol.*** Jabłonków. Moravskoslezský Kraj, E Czech Republic
59 *Q15* **Jaboatão** Pernambuco, E Brazil
60 *L8* **Jaboticabal** São Paulo, S Brazil
189 *U7* **Jabwot** ***var.*** Jabat, Jebat, Jōwat. *island* Ralik Chain, S Marshall Islands
105 *S4* **Jaca** Aragón, NE Spain
42 *B4* **Jacaltenango** Huehuetenango, W Guatemala
59 *G14* **Jacaré-a-Canga** Pará, NE Brazil
60 *N10* **Jacareí** São Paulo, S Brazil
59 *I18* **Jaciara** Mato Grosso, W Brazil
59 *E15* **Jaciparaná** Rondônia, W Brazil
19 *P5* **Jackman** Maine, NE USA
35 *X1* **Jackpot** Nevada, W USA
20 *M8* **Jacksboro** Tennessee, S USA
25 *S6* **Jacksboro** Texas, SW USA
23 *N7* **Jackson** Alabama, S USA
35 *P7* **Jackson** California, W USA
23 *T4* **Jackson** Georgia, SE USA
21 *O6* **Jackson** Kentucky, S USA
22 *J8* **Jackson** Louisiana, S USA
31 *Q10* **Jackson** Michigan, N USA
29 *T11* **Jackson** Minnesota, N USA
22 *K5* **Jackson** *state capital* Mississippi, S USA
27 *Y7* **Jackson** Missouri, C USA
21 *W8* **Jackson** North Carolina, SE USA
31 *T15* **Jackson** Ohio, NE USA
20 *G9* **Jackson** Tennessee, S USA
33 *S14* **Jackson** Wyoming, C USA
185 *C19* **Jackson Bay** *bay* South Island, NZ
186 *E9* **Jackson Field** × (Port Moresby) Central/National Capital District, S PNG
185 *C20* **Jackson Head** *headland* South Island, NZ
23 *S8* **Jackson, Lake** ◎ Florida, SE USA
33 *S13* **Jackson Lake** ◎ Wyoming, C USA
194 *J6* **Jackson, Mount** ▲ Antarctica
37 *U3* **Jackson Reservoir** ◎ Colorado, C USA
23 *Q3* **Jacksonville** Alabama, S USA
27 *V11* **Jacksonville** Arkansas, C USA
23 *W8* **Jacksonville** Florida, SE USA
30 *K14* **Jacksonville** Illinois, N USA
21 *W11* **Jacksonville** North Carolina, SE USA
25 *W7* **Jacksonville** Texas, SW USA
23 *X9* **Jacksonville Beach** Florida, SE USA
44 *L9* **Jacmel** ***var.*** Jaquemel. S Haiti
Jacob *see* Nkayi
149 *Q12* **Jacobābād** Sind, SE Pakistan
55 *T11* **Jacobs Ladder Falls** *waterfall* S Guyana
45 *O11* **Jaco, Pointe** *headland* N Dominica
15 *Q9* **Jacques-Cartier** ≈ Québec, SE Canada
13 *P11* **Jacques-Cartier, Détroit de** ***var.*** Jacques-Cartier Passage. *strait* Gulf of St. Lawrence/St. Lawrence River
15 *W6* **Jacques-Cartier, Mont** ▲ Québec, SE Canada
Jacques-Cartier Passage *see* Jacques-Cartier, Détroit de
61 *H16* **Jacuí, Rio** ≈ S Brazil
60 *L11* **Jacupiranga** São Paulo, S Brazil
100 *G10* **Jade** ≈ NW Germany
100 *G10* **Jadebusen** *bay* NW Germany
Jadotville *see* Likasi
Jadransko More/Jadransko Morje *see* Adriatic Sea
105 *O7* **Jadraque** Castilla-La Mancha, C Spain
56 *C10* **Jaén** Cajamarca, N Peru
105 *N13* **Jaén** Andalucía, SW Spain
105 *N13* **Jaén** ◈ *province* Andalucía, S Spain
155 *J23* **Jaffna** Northern Province, N Sri Lanka
155 *K23* **Jaffna Lagoon** *lagoon* N Sri Lanka
19 *N10* **Jaffrey** New Hampshire, NE USA
138 *H13* **Jafr, Qā' al** ***var.*** El Jafr. *salt pan* S Jordan
152 *J9* **Jagādhri** Haryāna, N India
118 *H4* **Jägala** ***var.*** Jägala Jõgi, ***Ger.*** Jaggowal. ≈ NW Estonia
Jägala Jõgi *see* Jägala
Jagannath *see* Puri
155 *L14* **Jagdalpur** Chhattīsgarh, C India
163 *U5* **Jagdaqi** Nei Mongol Zizhiqu, N China
Jägerndorf *see* Krnov
Jaggowal *see* Jägala
139 *O2* **Jaghjaghah, Nahr** ≈ N Syria
112 *N13* **Jagodina** ***prev.*** Svetozarevo. Serbia, C Serbia and Montenegro (Yugo.)
112 *K12* **Jagodnja** ▲▲ W Serbia and Montenegro (Yugo.)
101 *I20* **Jagst** ≈ SW Germany
155 *I14* **Jagtiāl** Andhra Pradesh, C India
61 *H18* **Jaguarão** Rio Grande do Sul, S Brazil
61 *H18* **Jaguarão, Rio** ***var.*** Río Yaguarón. ≈ Brazil/Uruguay
60 *K11* **Jaguariaíva** Paraná, S Brazil
44 *D5* **Jagüey Grande** Matanzas, W Cuba
153 *P14* **Jahānābād** Bihār, N India
Jahra *see* Al Jahrā'
143 *P12* **Jahrom** ***var.*** Jahrum. Fārs, S Iran
Jahrum *see* Jahrom
Jailolo *see* Halmahera, Pulau
Jainat *see* Chai Nat
Jainti *see* Jayanti
152 *H12* **Jaipur** ***prev.*** Jeypore. Rājasthān, N India
153 *T14* **Jaipur Hat** Rajshahi, NW Bangladesh
152 *D11* **Jaisalmer** Rājasthān, NW India
154 *O12* **Jājapur** Orissa, E India
143 *R4* **Jājarm** Khorāsān, NE Iran
112 *G12* **Jajce** Federacija Bosna I Hercegovina, W Bosnia and Herzegovina
Jajı *see* 'Alī Kheyl
83 *D17* **Jakalsberg** Otjozondjupa, N Namibia
169 *O15* **Jakarta** ***prev.*** Djakarta, ***Dut.*** Batavia. ● (Indonesia) Jawa, C Indonesia
10 *I8* **Jakes Corner** Yukon Territory, W Canada
152 *H9* **Jākhal** Haryāna, NW India
Jakobeny *see* Iacobeni
93 *K16* **Jakobstad** ***Fin.*** Pietarsaari. Länsi-Suomi, W Finland
Jakobstadt *see* Jēkabpils
113 *O18* **Jakupica** ▲▲ C FYR Macedonia
37 *W15* **Jal** New Mexico, SW USA
141 *P7* **Jalājil** ***var.*** Ğalāğıl. Ar Riyāḍ, C Saudi Arabia
Jalal-Abad *see* Dzhalal-Abad, Dzhalal-Abadskaya Oblast', W Kyrgyzstan
149 *S5* **Jalālābād** ***var.*** Jalalabad, Jelalabad. Nangarhār, E Afghanistan
Jalal-Abad Oblasty *see* Dzhalal-Abadskaya Oblast'
149 *V7* **Jalālpur** Punjab, E Pakistan
149 *T11* **Jalālpur Pīrwāla** Punjab, E Pakistan
152 *H8* **Jalandhar** ***prev.*** Jullundur. Punjab, N India
42 *J7* **Jalán, Río** ≈ S Honduras
42 *E6* **Jalapa** Jalapa, C Guatemala
42 *J7* **Jalapa** Nueva Segovia, NW Nicaragua
42 *A3* **Jalapa** ***off.*** Departamento de Jalapa. ◈ *department* SE Guatemala
42 *E6* **Jalapa, Río** ≈ SE Guatemala
143 *X13* **Jālaq** Sīstān va Balūchestān, SE Iran
93 *K17* **Jalasjärvi** Länsi-Suomi, W Finland
149 *O8* **Jaldak** Zābul, SE Afghanistan
60 *J7* **Jales** São Paulo, S Brazil
154 *P11* **Jaleshwar** ***var.*** Jaleswar. Orissa, NE India
Jaleswar *see* Jaleshwar
154 *F12* **Jalgaon** Mahārāshtra, C India
139 *W12* **Jalībah** S Iraq
139 *W13* **Jalīb Shahāb** S Iraq
77 *X15* **Jalingo** Taraba, E Nigeria
40 *K13* **Jalisco** ◈ *state* SW Mexico
154 *G13* **Jālna** Mahārāshtra, W India
Jalomitsa *see* Ialomiţa
105 *R5* **Jalón** ≈ N Spain
152 *E13* **Jālor** Rājasthān, N India
112 *K11* **Jalovik** Serbia, W Serbia and Montenegro (Yugo.)
40 *L12* **Jalpa** Zacatecas, C Mexico
153 *S12* **Jalpāiguri** West Bengal, NE India
41 *O12* **Jalpán** ***var.*** Jalpan. Querétaro de Arteaga, C Mexico
67 *P2* **Jalta** *island* N Tunisia
75 *S9* **Jālū** ***var.*** Jūlā. NE Libya
189 *U8* **Jaluit Atoll** ***var.*** Jālwōj. *atoll* Ralik Chain, S Marshall Islands
Jālwōj *see* Jaluit Atoll
81 *L18* **Jamaame** ***It.*** Giamame; ***prev.*** Margherita. Jubbada Hoose, S Somalia
77 *W13* **Jamaare** ≈ NE Nigeria
44 *G9* **Jamaica** ◆ *commonwealth republic* W West Indies
47 *P3* **Jamaica** *island* W West Indies
44 *I9* **Jamaica Channel** *channel* Haiti/Jamaica
153 *T14* **Jamalpur** Dhaka, N Bangladesh
153 *Q14* **Jamālpur** Bihār, NE India
168 *L9* **Jamaluang** ***var.*** Jemaluang. Johor, Peninsular Malaysia
59 *I14* **Jamanxim, Rio** ≈ C Brazil
56 *B8* **Jambeli, Canal de** *channel* S Ecuador
99 *I20* **Jambes** Namur, SE Belgium
168 *L12* **Jambi** ***var.*** Telanaipura; ***prev.*** Djambi. Sumatera, W Indonesia
168 *K12* **Jambi** ***off.*** Propinsi Jambi, ***var.*** Djambi. ◈ *province* W Indonesia
Jamdena *see* Yamdena, Pulau
12 *H8* **James Bay** *bay* Ontario/Québec, E Canada
63 *F19* **James, Isla** *island* Archipiélago de los Chonos, S Chile
181 *Q8* **James Ranges** ▲▲ Northern Territory, C Australia
29 *P8* **James River** ≈ North Dakota/South Dakota, N USA
21 *X7* **James River** ≈ Virginia, NE USA
194 *H4* **James Ross Island** *island* Antarctica
182 *I8* **Jamestown** South Australia
65 *G25* **Jamestown** ○ (Saint Helena) NW Saint Helena
35 *P8* **Jamestown** California, W USA
20 *L7* **Jamestown** Kentucky, S USA
18 *D11* **Jamestown** New York, NE USA
29 *P5* **Jamestown** North Dakota, N USA
20 *L8* **Jamestown** Tennessee, S USA
Jamestown *see* Holetown
15 *N10* **Jamet** ≈ Québec, SE Canada
41 *Q17* **Jamiltepec** ***var.*** Santiago Jamiltepec. Oaxaca, SE Mexico
95 *F20* **Jammerbugten** *bay* Skagerrak, E North Sea
152 *H6* **Jammu** ***prev.*** Jummoo. Jammu and Kashmir, NW India
152 *I5* **Jammu and Kashmir** ***var.*** Jammu-Kashmir, Kashmir. ◈ *state* NW India
149 *V4* **Jammu and Kashmir** *disputed region* India/Pakistan
154 *B10* **Jāmnagar** ***prev.*** Navanagar. Gujarāt, W India
149 *S11* **Jāmpur** Punjab, E Pakistan
93 *L18* **Jämsä** Länsi-Suomi, W Finland
93 *L18* **Jämsänkoski** Länsi-Suomi, W Finland
153 *Q16* **Jamshedpur** Jhārkhand, NE India
94 *K9* **Jämtland** ◈ *county* C Sweden
153 *Q14* **Jamūi** Bihār, NE India
153 *T14* **Jamuna** ≈ N Bangladesh
Jamuna *see* Brahmaputra
Jamundá *see* Nhamundá, Rio
54 *D11* **Jamundí** Valle del Cauca, SW Colombia
153 *Q12* **Janakpur** Central, C Nepal
59 *N18* **Janaúba** Minas Gerais, SE Brazil
58 *K11* **Janaucu, Ilha** *island* NE Brazil
143 *Q7* **Jandaq** Eşfahān, C Iran
64 *Q11* **Jandia, Punta de** *headland* Fuerteventura, Islas Canarias, Spain, NE Atlantic Ocean
59 *B14* **Jandiatuba, Rio** ≈ NW Brazil
105 *N12* **Jándula** ≈ S Spain
29 *V10* **Janesville** Minnesota, N USA
30 *L9* **Janesville** Wisconsin, N USA
149 *N13* **Jangal** Baluchistān, SW Pakistan
83 *N20* **Jangamo** Inhambane, SE Mozambique
155 *J14* **Jangaon** Andhra Pradesh, C India
153 *S14* **Jangīpur** West Bengal, NE India
Janina *see* Ioánnina
Janischken *see* Joniškis
112 *J11* **Janja** Republika Srpska, NE Bosnia and Herzegovina
Jankovac *see* Jánoshalma
197 *Q15* **Jan Mayen** ◇ *Norwegian dependency* N Atlantic Ocean
84 *D5* **Jan Mayen** *island* N Atlantic Ocean
197 *R15* **Jan Mayen Fracture Zone** *tectonic feature* Greenland Sea/Norwegian Sea
197 *R15* **Jan Mayen Ridge** *undersea feature* Greenland Sea/Norwegian Sea
40 *H3* **Janos** Chihuahua, N Mexico
111 *K25* **Jánoshalma** ***SCr.*** Jankovac. Bács-Kiskun, S Hungary
Janow/Janów *see* Jonava, Lithuania
Janów *see* Ivanava, Belarus
110 *H10* **Janowiec Wielkopolski** ***Ger.*** Janowitz. Kujawski-pomorskie, C Poland
Janowitz *see* Janowiec Wielkopolski
111 *O15* **Janów Lubelski** Lubelskie, E Poland
Janów Poleski *see* Ivanava
83 *H25* **Jansenville** Eastern Cape, S South Africa
59 *M18* **Januária** Minas Gerais, SE Brazil
Janūbīyah, Al Bādiyah al *see* Ash Shāmīyah
102 *I7* **Janzé** Ille-et-Vilaine, NW France
154 *F10* **Jaora** Madhya Pradesh, C India
164 *K11* **Japan** ***var.*** Nippon, ***Jap.*** Nihon. ◆ *monarchy* E Asia
131 *Y9* **Japan** *island group* E Asia
192 *H4* **Japan Basin** *undersea feature* N Sea of Japan
131 *Y8* **Japan, Sea of** ***var.*** East Sea, ***Rus.*** Yapanskoye More. *sea* NW Pacific Ocean ***see also*** East Sea
192 *H4* **Japan Trench** *undersea feature* NW Pacific Ocean
Japen *see* Yapen, Pulau
59 *A15* **Japiim** ***var.*** Máncio Lima. Acre, W Brazil
58 *D12* **Japurá** Amazonas, N Brazil
58 *C12* **Japurá, Rio** ***var.*** Río Caquetá, Yapurá. ≈ Brazil/Colombia ***see also*** Caquetá, Río
43 *W17* **Jaqué** Darién, SE Panama
Jaquemel *see* Jacmel
Jarablos *see* Jarābulus
138 *K2* **Jarābulus** ***var.*** Jarablos, Jerablus, ***Fr.*** Djérablous. Ḥalab, N Syria
60 *K13* **Jaraguá do Sul** Santa Catarina, S Brazil
104 *K9* **Jaraicejo** Extremadura, W Spain
104 *K9* **Jaráiz de la Vera** Extremadura, W Spain
105 *O7* **Jarama** ≈ C Spain
63 *J20* **Jaramillo** Santa Cruz, SE Argentina

◆ Country ● Country Capital ◇ Dependent Territory ○ Dependent Territory Capital ◈ Administrative Region × International Airport ▲ Mountain ▲▲ Mountain Range ※ Volcano ≈ River ◎ Lake ▣ Reservoir

Jarandilla de la Vega see Jarandilla de la Vera
104 K8 **Jarandilla de la Vera** var. Jarandilla de la Vega. Extremadura, W Spain
149 V9 **Jaranwāla** Punjab, E Pakistan
138 G9 **Jarash** var. Jerash; anc. Gerasa. Irbid, NW Jordan
Jarbah, Jazīrat see Jerba, Île de
94 N13 **Järbo** Gävleborg, C Sweden
Jardan see Yordon
44 F7 **Jardines de la Reina, Archipiélago de los** island group C Cuba
162 J7 **Jargalant** Arhangay, C Mongolia
162 I8 **Jargalant** Bayanhongor, C Mongolia
162 D7 **Jargalant** Bayan-Ölgiy, W Mongolia
162 K6 **Jargalant** Bulgan, N Mongolia
162 G9 **Jargalant** Govĭ-Altay, W Mongolia
Jarīd, Shaṭṭ al see Jerid, Chott el
58 I11 **Jari, Rio** var. Jary. ↝ N Brazil
141 N7 **Jarīr, Wādī al** dry watercourse C Saudi Arabia
Jarja see Yur'ya
94 L13 **Järna** var. Dala-Jarna. Dalarna, C Sweden
95 O16 **Järna** Stockholm, C Sweden
102 K11 **Jarnac** Charente, W France
110 H12 **Jarocin** Wielkopolskie, C Poland
111 F16 **Jaroměř** Ger. Jermer. Královéhradecký Kraj, N Czech Republic
Jaroslau see Jarosław
111 O16 **Jarosław** Ger. Jaroslau, Rus. Yaroslav. Podkarpackie, SE Poland
93 F16 **Järpen** Jämtland, C Sweden
147 O14 **Jarqo'rg'on** Rus. Dzharkurgan. Surxondaryo Viloyati, S Uzbekistan
139 P2 **Jarrāh, Wadi** dry watercourse NE Syria
Jars, Plain of see Xiangkhoang, Plateau de
162 K14 **Jartai Yanchi** ◎ N China
59 E16 **Jaru** Rondônia, W Brazil
Jarud Qi see Lubei
118 I4 **Järva-Jaani** Ger. Sankt-Johannis. Järvamaa, N Estonia
118 G5 **Järvakandi** Ger. Jerwakant. Raplamaa, NW Estonia
118 H4 **Järvamaa** off. Järva Maakond. ◈ province N Estonia
93 L19 **Järvenpää** Etelä-Suomi, S Finland
14 G17 **Jarvis** Ontario, S Canada
177 R8 **Jarvis Island** ◇ US unincorporated territory C Pacific Ocean
94 M11 **Järvsö** Gävleborg, C Sweden
Jary see Jari, Rio
112 M9 **Jaša Tomić** Serbia, NE Serbia and Montenegro (Yugo.)
112 D12 **Jasenice** Zadar, SW Croatia
138 I11 **Jashshat al 'Adlah, Wādī al** dry watercourse C Jordan
77 Q16 **Jasikan** E Ghana
143 T15 **Jāsk** Hormozgān, SE Iran
146 F6 **Jasliq** Rus. Zhaslyk. Qoraqalpog'iston Respublikasi, NW Uzbekistan
111 N17 **Jasło** Podkarpackie, SE Poland
11 U16 **Jasmin** Saskatchewan, S Canada
65 A23 **Jason Islands** island group NW Falkland Islands
194 I4 **Jason Peninsula** peninsula Antarctica
31 N15 **Jasonville** Indiana, N USA
11 O15 **Jasper** Alberta, SW Canada
14 L13 **Jasper** Ontario, SE Canada
23 O3 **Jasper** Alabama, S USA
27 T9 **Jasper** Arkansas, C USA
23 U8 **Jasper** Florida, SE USA
31 N16 **Jasper** Indiana, N USA
29 R11 **Jasper** Minnesota, N USA
27 S7 **Jasper** Missouri, C USA
20 K10 **Jasper** Tennessee, S USA
25 Y9 **Jasper** Texas, SW USA
11 O15 **Jasper National Park** national park Alberta/British Columbia, SW Canada
Jassy see Iaşi
113 N14 **Jastrebac** ▲ SE Serbia and Montenegro (Yugo.)
112 D9 **Jastrebarsko** Zagreb, N Croatia
Jastrow see Jastrowie
110 G9 **Jastrowie** Ger. Jastrow. Wielkopolskie, C Poland
111 J17 **Jastrzębie-Zdrój** Śląskie, S Poland
111 L22 **Jászapáti** Jász-Nagykun-Szolnok, E Hungary
111 L22 **Jászberény** Jász-Nagykun-Szolnok, E Hungary
111 L23 **Jász-Nagykun-Szolnok** off. Jász-Nagykun-Szolnok Megye. ◈ county E Hungary
59 J19 **Jataí** Goiás, C Brazil
58 G12 **Jatapu, Serra do** ▲ N Brazil
41 W16 **Jatate, Río** ↝ SE Mexico
149 P17 **Jāti** Sind, SE Pakistan
44 F6 **Jatibonico** Sancti Spíritus, C Cuba
169 O16 **Jatiluhur, Danau** ◎ Jawa, S Indonesia
Jativa see Xátiva
149 S11 **Jattoi** Punjab, E Pakistan
60 L9 **Jaú** São Paulo, S Brazil
58 F11 **Jauaperi, Rio** ↝ N Brazil
99 I19 **Jauche** Wallon Brabant, C Belgium
Jauer see Jawor
Jauf see Al Jawf
149 U7 **Jauharābād** Punjab, E Pakistan
57 E14 **Jauja** Junín, C Peru
41 O10 **Jaumave** Tamaulipas, C Mexico
118 H10 **Jaunjelgava** Ger. Friedrichstadt. Aizkraukle, S Latvia
Jaunlatgale see Pytalovo
118 I8 **Jaunpiebalga** Gulbene, NE Latvia
118 E9 **Jaunpils** Tukums, C Latvia
153 N13 **Jaunpur** Uttar Pradesh, N India
29 N8 **Java** South Dakota, N USA
Java see Jawa
105 R9 **Javalambre** ▲ E Spain
173 V7 **Java Ridge** undersea feature E Indian Ocean
59 A14 **Javari, Rio** var. Yavarí. ↝ Brazil/Peru
163 O7 **Javarthushuu** Dornod, NE Mongolia
169 Q15 **Java Sea** Ind. Laut Jawa. sea W Indonesia
173 U7 **Java Trench** var. Sunda Trench. undersea feature E Indian Ocean
105 T11 **Jávea** Cat. Xàbia. País Valenciano, E Spain
163 O7 **Javhlant** Hentiy, E Mongolia
63 G20 **Javier, Isla** island S Chile
113 L14 **Javor** ▲ Bosnia and Herzegovina/Serbia and Montenegro (Yugo.)
111 K20 **Javorie** Hung. Jávoros. ▲ S Slovakia
Jávoros see Javorie
93 J14 **Jävre** Norrbotten, N Sweden
192 E8 **Jawa** Eng. Java; prev. Djawa. island C Indonesia
169 O16 **Jawa Barat** off. Propinsi Jawa Barat, Eng. West Java. ◈ province S Indonesia
Jawa, Laut see Java Sea
139 R3 **Jawān** NW Iraq
169 P16 **Jawa Tengah** off. Propinsi Jawa Tengah, Eng. Central Java. ◈ province S Indonesia
169 R16 **Jawa Timur** off. Propinsi Jawa Timur, Eng. East Java. ◈ province S Indonesia
81 N17 **Jawhar** var. Jowhar, It. Giohar. Shabeellaha Dhexe, S Somalia
111 F14 **Jawor** Ger. Jauer. Dolnośląskie, SW Poland
Jaworów see Yavoriv
111 J16 **Jaworzno** Śląskie, S Poland
Jaxartes see Syr Darya
27 R9 **Jay** Oklahoma, C USA
Jayabum see Chaiyaphum
Jayanath see Chai Nat
153 T12 **Jayanti** prev. Jainti. West Bengal, NE India
171 X14 **Jaya, Puncak** prev. Puntjak Carstensz, Puntjak Sukarno. ▲ Papua, E Indonesia
171 Z13 **Jayapura** var. Djajapura, Dut. Hollandia; prev. Kotabaru, Sukarnapura. Papua, E Indonesia
Jay Dairen see Dalian
Jayhawker State see Kansas
147 S12 **Jayilgan** Rus. Dzhailgan, Dzhayilgan. C Tajikistan
155 L14 **Jaypur** var. Jeypore, Jeypur. Orissa, E India
25 O6 **Jayton** Texas, SW USA
143 U13 **Jaz Murian, Hāmūn-e** ◎ SE Iran
138 M4 **Jazrah** Ar Raqqah, C Syria
138 G6 **Jbaïl** var. Jebeil, Jubayl, Jubeil; anc. Biblical Gebal, Bybles. W Lebanon
25 O7 **J.B.Thomas, Lake** ⊠ Texas, SW USA
Jdaïdé see Judaydah
35 X12 **Jean** Nevada, W USA
22 I9 **Jeanerette** Louisiana, S USA
44 L8 **Jean-Rabel** NW Haiti
143 T12 **Jebāl Bārez, Kūh-e** ▲ SE Iran
Jebat see Jabwot
77 T15 **Jebba** Kwara, W Nigeria
Jebeil see Jbaïl
116 E12 **Jebel** Hung. Széphely; prev. Hung. Zsebely. Timiş, W Romania
146 B11 **Jebel** Rus. Dzhebel. Balkan Welaýaty, W Turkmenistan
Jebel, Bahr el see White Nile
Jebel Dhanna see Jabal az Zannah
Jeble see Jablah
96 K13 **Jedburgh** SE Scotland, UK
Jedda see Jiddah
111 L15 **Jędrzejów** Ger. Endersdorf. Świętokrzyskie, C Poland
100 K12 **Jeetze** var. Jeetzel. ↝ C Germany
Jeetzel see Jeetze
29 U14 **Jefferson** Iowa, C USA
21 Q8 **Jefferson** North Carolina, SE USA
25 X6 **Jefferson** Texas, SW USA
30 M9 **Jefferson** Wisconsin, N USA
27 U5 **Jefferson City** state capital Missouri, C USA
33 R10 **Jefferson City** Montana, NW USA
21 N9 **Jefferson City** Tennessee, S USA
35 U7 **Jefferson, Mount** ▲ Nevada, W USA
32 H12 **Jefferson, Mount** ▲ Oregon, NW USA
20 L5 **Jeffersontown** Kentucky, S USA
31 P16 **Jeffersonville** Indiana, N USA
33 V15 **Jeffrey City** Wyoming, C USA
77 T13 **Jega** Kebbi, NW Nigeria
Jehol see Chengde
62 P5 **Jejui-Guazú, Río** ↝ E Paraguay
118 I10 **Jēkabpils** Ger. Jakobstadt. Jēkabpils, S Latvia
23 W7 **Jekyll Island** island Georgia, SE USA
169 R13 **Jelai, Sungai** ↝ Borneo, N Indonesia
Jelalabad see Jalālābād
111 H14 **Jelcz-Laskowice** Dolnośląskie, SW Poland
111 E14 **Jelenia Góra** Ger. Hirschberg, Hirschberg im Riesengebirge, Hirschberg in Riesengebirge, Hirschberg in Schlesien. Dolnośląskie, SW Poland
153 S11 **Jelep La** pass N India
118 F9 **Jelgava** Ger. Mitau. Jelgava, C Latvia
112 L13 **Jelica** ▲ C Serbia and Montenegro (Yugo.)
20 M8 **Jellico** Tennessee, S USA
95 G23 **Jelling** Vejle, C Denmark
169 N9 **Jemaja, Pulau** island W Indonesia
Jemaluang see Jamaluang
99 E20 **Jemappes** Hainaut, S Belgium
169 S17 **Jember** prev. Djember. Jawa, C Indonesia
99 I20 **Jemeppe-sur-Sambre** Namur, S Belgium
37 R10 **Jemez Pueblo** New Mexico, SW USA
158 K2 **Jeminay** Xinjiang Uygur Zizhiqu, NW China
189 U5 **Jemo Island** atoll Ratak Chain, C Marshall Islands
169 U11 **Jempang, Danau** ◎ Borneo, N Indonesia
101 L16 **Jena** Thüringen, C Germany
22 I6 **Jena** Louisiana, S USA
108 I8 **Jenaz** Graubünden, SE Switzerland
109 N7 **Jenbach** Tirol, W Austria
171 N15 **Jeneponto** prev. Djeneponto. Sulawesi, C Indonesia
138 F9 **Jenīn** N West Bank
21 P7 **Jenkins** Kentucky, S USA
27 P9 **Jenks** Oklahoma, C USA
Jenné see Djenné
109 X8 **Jennersdorf** Burgenland, SE Austria
22 H9 **Jennings** Louisiana, S USA
9 N7 **Jenny Lind Island** island Nunavut, N Canada
23 Y13 **Jensen Beach** Florida, SE USA
9 P6 **Jens Munk Island** island Nunavut, NE Canada
59 O17 **Jequié** Bahia, E Brazil
59 O18 **Jequitinhonha, Rio** ↝ E Brazil
Jerablus see Jarābulus
74 H6 **Jerada** NE Morocco
Jerash see Jarash
75 N7 **Jerba, Île de** var. Djerba, Jazīrat Jarbah. island E Tunisia
44 K9 **Jérémie** SW Haiti
Jerez see Jeréz de la Frontera, Spain
Jeréz see Jerez de García Salinas, Mexico
40 L11 **Jerez de García Salinas** var. Jeréz. Zacatecas, C Mexico
104 J15 **Jeréz de la Frontera** var. Jerez; prev. Xeres. Andalucía, SW Spain
104 I12 **Jeréz de los Caballeros** Extremadura, W Spain
Jergucati see Jorgucat
138 G10 **Jericho** Ar. Arīḥā, Heb. Yeriḥo. E West Bank
74 M7 **Jerid, Chott el** var. Shaṭṭ al Jarīd. salt lake SW Tunisia
183 O10 **Jerilderie** New South Wales, SE Australia
Jerischmarkt see Câmpia Turzii
92 K11 **Jerisjärvi** ◎ NW Finland
Jermentau see Yereymentau
Jermer see Jaroměř
36 K11 **Jerome** Arizona, SW USA
33 O15 **Jerome** Idaho, NW USA
97 L26 **Jersey** island Channel Islands, NW Europe
18 K14 **Jersey City** New Jersey, NE USA
18 F13 **Jersey Shore** Pennsylvania, NE USA
30 K14 **Jerseyville** Illinois, N USA
104 K8 **Jerte** ↝ W Spain
138 F10 **Jerusalem** Ar. Al Quds, Al Quds ash Sharīf, Heb. Yerushalayim; anc. Hierosolyma. ● (Israel) Jerusalem, NE Israel
138 G10 **Jerusalem** ◈ district E Israel
183 S10 **Jervis Bay** New South Wales, SE Australia
183 S10 **Jervis Bay Territory** ◈ territory SE Australia
Jerwakant see Järvakandi
109 S10 **Jesenice** Ger. Assling. NW Slovenia
111 H16 **Jeseník** Ger. Freiwaldau. Olomoucký Kraj, E Czech Republic
Jesi see Iesi
106 I8 **Jesolo** var. Iesolo. Veneto, NE Italy
Jesselton see Kota Kinabalu
95 I14 **Jessheim** Akershus, S Norway
153 T15 **Jessore** Khulna, W Bangladesh
23 W6 **Jesup** Georgia, SE USA
41 S15 **Jesús Carranza** Veracruz-Llave, SE Mexico
62 K10 **Jesús María** Córdoba, C Argentina
26 K6 **Jetmore** Kansas, C USA
103 Q2 **Jeumont** Nord, N France
95 H14 **Jevnaker** Oppland, S Norway
Jewe see Jõhvi
25 V9 **Jewett** Texas, SW USA
19 N12 **Jewett City** Connecticut, NE USA
Jewish Autonomous Oblast see Yevreyskaya Avtonomnaya Oblast'
Jeypore/Jeypur see Jaypur, Orissa, India
Jeypore see Jaipur, Rājasthān, India
113 L17 **Jezercës, Maja e** ▲ N Albania
111 B18 **Jezerní Hora** ▲ SW Czech Republic
154 F10 **Jhābua** Madhya Pradesh, C India
152 H14 **Jhālāwār** Rājasthān, N India
Jhang/Jhang Sadar see Jhang Sadr
149 U9 **Jhang Sadr** var. Jhang, Jhang Sadar. Punjab, NE Pakistan
152 J13 **Jhānsi** Uttar Pradesh, N India
153 O16 **Jhārkhand** ◈ state NE India
154 M11 **Jhārsuguda** Orissa, E India
149 V7 **Jhelum** Punjab, NE Pakistan
131 P9 **Jhelum** ↝ E Pakistan
Jhenaidaha see Jhenida
153 T15 **Jhenida** var. Jhenaidaha. Dhaka, W Bangladesh
149 P16 **Jhimpīr** Sind, SE Pakistan
Jhind see Jīnd
149 R16 **Jhudo** Sind, SE Pakistan
Jhumra see Chak Jhumra
152 H11 **Jhunjhunūn** Rājasthān, N India
Ji see Hebei, China
Ji see Jilin, China
Jiading see Xinfeng
153 S14 **Jiāganj** West Bengal, NE India
160 J7 **Jialing Jiang** ↝ C China
163 Y7 **Jiamusi** var. Chia-mu-ssu, Kiamusze. Heilongjiang, NE China
161 O11 **Ji'an** Jiangxi, S China
163 W12 **Ji'an** Jilin, NE China
163 T13 **Jianchang** Liaoning, NE China
Jianchang see Nancheng
160 F11 **Jianchuan** var. Jinhuan. Yunnan, SW China
158 M4 **Jiangjunmiao** Xinjiang Uygur Zizhiqu, W China
160 K11 **Jiangkou** var. Shuangjiang. Guizhou, S China
Jiangkou see Fengkai
161 Q12 **Jiangle** var. Guyong. Fujian, SE China
161 N15 **Jiangmen** Guangdong, S China
Jiangna see Yanshan
161 Q10 **Jiangshan** Zhejiang, SE China
161 Q7 **Jiangsu** var. Chiang-su, Jiangsu Sheng, Kiangsu, Su. ◈ province E China
Jiangsu Sheng see Jiangsu
161 O11 **Jiangxi** var. Chiang-hsi, Gan, Jiangxi Sheng, Kiangsi. ◈ province S China
Jiangxi Sheng see Jiangxi
160 I8 **Jiangyou** prev. Zhongba. Sichuan, C China
161 N9 **Jianli** var. Rongcheng. Hubei, C China
161 Q11 **Jian'ou** Fujian, SE China
163 S12 **Jianping** var. Yebaishou. Liaoning, NE China
Jianshe see Baiyü
160 L9 **Jianshi** var. Yezhou. Hubei, C China
131 V11 **Jian Xi** ↝ SE China
161 Q11 **Jianyang** Fujian, SE China
160 I9 **Jianyang** Sichuan, C China
163 X10 **Jiaohe** Jilin, NE China
Jiaojiang see Taizhou
Jiaoxian see Jiaozhou
161 R5 **Jiaozhou** prev. Jiaoxian. Shandong, E China
161 N6 **Jiaozuo** Henan, C China
Jiashan see Mingguang
158 F8 **Jiashi** var. Payzawat. Xinjiang Uygur Zizhiqu, NW China
154 L9 **Jiāwān** Madhya Pradesh, C India
161 S9 **Jiaxing** Zhejiang, SE China
Jiayi see Chiai
163 X6 **Jiayin** var. Chaoyang. Heilongjiang, NE China
159 R8 **Jiayuguan** Gansu, N China
Jibhalanta see Uliastay
138 M4 **Jibli** Ar Raqqah, C Syria
116 H9 **Jibou** Hung. Zsibó. Sălaj, NW Romania
141 Z9 **Jibsh, Ra's al** headland E Oman
Jibuti see Djibouti
111 E15 **Jičín** Ger. Jitschin. Královéhradecký Kraj, N Czech Republic
140 K10 **Jiddah** Eng. Jedda. ● (Saudi Arabia) Makkah, W Saudi Arabia
141 W11 **Jiddat al Ḥarāsīs** desert C Oman
Jiesjavrre see Iešjávri
160 M4 **Jiexiu** Shanxi, C China
161 P14 **Jieyang** Guangdong, S China
119 F14 **Jieznas** Kaunas, S Lithuania
Jīfa', Bi'r see Jif'īyah, Bi'r
141 P15 **Jif'īyah, Bi'r** var. Bi'r Jīfa'. well C Yemen
77 W13 **Jigawa** ◈ state N Nigeria
146 J10 **Jigerbent** Rus. Dzhigirbent. Lebap Welaýaty, NE Turkmenistan
44 I7 **Jiguaní** Granma, E Cuba
159 T12 **Jigzhi** var. Chugqênsumdo. Qinghai, C China
Jih-k'a-tse see Xigazê
111 E18 **Jihlava** Ger. Iglau, Pol. Igława. Vysočina, C Czech Republic
111 E18 **Jihlava** var. Igel, Ger. Iglawa. ↝ S Czech Republic
Jihlavský Kraj see Vysočina
111 C18 **Jihočeský Kraj** prev. Budějovický Kraj. ◈ region S Czech Republic
111 G19 **Jihomoravský Kraj** prev. Brněnský Kraj. ◈ region SE Czech Republic
74 L5 **Jijel** var. Djidjel; prev. Djidjelli. NE Algeria
116 L9 **Jijia** ↝ N Romania
80 L13 **Jijiga** It. Giggiga. Somali, E Ethiopia
105 S12 **Jijona** var. Xixona. País Valenciano, E Spain
Jilf al Kabīr, Haḍabat al see Gilf Kebir Plateau
81 L18 **Jilib** It. Gelib. Jubbada Dhexe, S Somalia
163 W10 **Jilin** var. Chi-lin, Girin, Kirin; prev. Yungki, Yunki. Jilin, NE China
163 W10 **Jilin** var. Chi-lin, Girin, Ji, Jilin Sheng, Kirin. ◈ province NE China
163 W11 **Jilin Hada Ling** ▲ NE China
Jilin Sheng see Jilin
163 S4 **Jiliu He** ↝ NE China
105 Q6 **Jiloca** ↝ N Spain
81 I14 **Jīma** var. Jimma, It. Gimma. Oromo, C Ethiopia
44 M9 **Jimaní** W Dominican Republic
116 E11 **Jimbolia** Ger. Hatzfeld, Hung. Zsombolya. Timiş, W Romania
104 K16 **Jimena de la Frontera** Andalucía, S Spain
40 K7 **Jiménez** Chihuahua, N Mexico
41 N5 **Jiménez** Coahuila de Zaragoza, NE Mexico
41 P9 **Jiménez** var. Santander Jiménez. Tamaulipas, C Mexico
40 L10 **Jiménez del Teul** Zacatecas, C Mexico
77 Y14 **Jimeta** Adamawa, E Nigeria
Jimma see Jīma
158 M5 **Jimsar** Xinjiang Uygur Zizhiqu, NW China
18 I14 **Jim Thorpe** Pennsylvania, NE USA
Jin see Shanxi, China
Jin see Tianjin Shi, China
161 P5 **Jinan** var. Chinan, Chi-nan, Tsinan. Shandong, E China
Jin'an see Songpan
Jinbi see Dayao
159 T8 **Jinchang** Gansu, N China
161 N5 **Jincheng** Shanxi, C China
Jincheng see Wuding
Jinchengjiang see Hechi
152 I9 **Jīnd** prev. Jhind. Haryāna, NW India
183 Q11 **Jindabyne** New South Wales, SE Australia
111 O18 **Jindřichův Hradec** Ger. Neuhaus. Jihočeský Kraj, S Czech Republic
Jing see Beijing Shi, China
Jing see Jinghe, China
159 X10 **Jingchuan** Gansu, C China
161 Q10 **Jingdezhen** Jiangxi, S China
161 O12 **Jinggangshan** Jiangxi, S China
161 P3 **Jinghai** Tianjin Shi, E China
158 K6 **Jing He** ↝ C China
158 I4 **Jinghe** var. Jing. Xinjiang Uygur Zizhiqu, NW China
160 F15 **Jinghong** var. Yunjinghong. Yunnan, SW China
160 M9 **Jingmen** Hubei, C China
163 X10 **Jingpo Hu** ◎ NE China
160 M8 **Jing Shan** ▲ C China
159 V9 **Jingtai** var. Yitiaoshan. Gansu, C China
160 J14 **Jingxi** var. Xinjing. Guangxi Zhuangzu Zizhiqu, S China
Jing Xian see Jingzhou, Hunan
163 W11 **Jingyu** Jilin, NE China
159 V10 **Jingyuan** Gansu, C China
160 M9 **Jingzhou** prev. Shashi, Sha-shih, Shasi. Hubei, C China
160 L12 **Jingzhou** var. Jing Xian. Jingzhou Miaozu Dongzu Zizhixian, Quyang. Hunan, S China
Jingzhou Miaozu Dongzu Zizhixian see Jingzhou, Hunan
161 R10 **Jinhua** Zhejiang, SE China
Jinhuan see Jianchuan
163 P13 **Jining** Nei Mongol Zizhiqu, N China
161 P5 **Jining** Shandong, E China
81 G18 **Jinja** S Uganda
161 R13 **Jinjiang** var. Qingyang. Fujian, SE China
161 O11 **Jin Jiang** ↝ S China
Jinjiang see Chengmai
171 V15 **Jin, Kepulauan** island group E Indonesia
Jinmen Dao see Chinmen Tao
42 J9 **Jinotega** Jinotega, NW Nicaragua
42 K7 **Jinotega** ◈ department N Nicaragua
42 J11 **Jinotepe** Carazo, SW Nicaragua
160 L13 **Jinping** var. Sanjiang. Guizhou, S China
160 H14 **Jinping** Yunnan, SW China
Jinsen see Inch'ŏn
160 J11 **Jinsha** Guizhou, S China
157 N12 **Jinsha Jiang** Eng. Yangtze. ↝ SW China
160 M10 **Jinshi** Hunan, S China
Jinshi see Xinning
159 R7 **Jinta** Gansu, N China
161 Q12 **Jin Xi** ↝ SE China
Jinxian see Huludao
161 P6 **Jinxiang** Shandong, E China
161 P8 **Jinzhai** var. Meishan. Anhui, E China
161 N4 **Jinzhong** var. Yuci. Shanxi, C China
163 U14 **Jinzhou** prev. Jinxian. Liaoning, NE China
163 T12 **Jinzhou** var. Chin-chou, Chinchow; prev. Chinhsien. Liaoning, NE China
Jinzhu see Daocheng
138 H12 **Jinz, Qā' al** ◎ C Jordan
47 S8 **Jiparaná, Rio** ↝ W Brazil
56 A7 **Jipijapa** Manabí, W Ecuador
42 F8 **Jiquilisco** Usulután, S El Salvador
Jirgalanta see Hovd
147 S12 **Jirgatol** Rus. Dzhirgatal'. C Tajikistan
Jirjā see Girga
111 B15 **Jirkov** Ger. Görkau. Ústecký Kraj, NW Czech Republic
Jiroft see Sabzvārān
160 L11 **Jishou** Hunan, S China
Jisr ash Shadadi see Ash Shadādah
116 I14 **Jitaru** Olt, S Romania
Jitschin see Jičín
116 H14 **Jiu** Ger. Schil, Schyl, Hung. Zsil, Zsily. ↝ S Romania
161 R11 **Jiufeng Shan** ▲ SE China
161 P9 **Jiujiang** Jiangxi, S China
161 O10 **Jiuling Shan** ▲ S China
160 G10 **Jiulong** var. Garba, Tib. Gyaisi. Sichuan, C China
161 Q13 **Jiulong Jiang** ↝ SE China
161 Q12 **Jiulong Xi** ↝ SE China
159 R8 **Jiuquan** var. Suzhou. Gansu, N China
160 K17 **Jiusuo** Hainan, S China
163 W10 **Jiutai** Jilin, NE China
160 K13 **Jiuwan Dashan** ▲ S China
160 I7 **Jiuzhaigou** prev. Nanping. Sichuan, C China
148 J16 **Jīwani** Baluchistān, SW Pakistan
163 Y8 **Jixi** Heilongjiang, NE China
163 Y7 **Jixian** Heilongjiang, NE China
160 M5 **Jixian** var. Ji Xian. Shanxi, C China
Jiza see Al Jīzah
141 N13 **Jīzān** var. Qīzān. Jīzān, SW Saudi Arabia
141 N13 **Jīzān** var. Minṭaqat Jīzān. ◈ province SW Saudi Arabia
140 K6 **Jīzl, Wādī al** dry watercourse W Saudi Arabia
164 H12 **Jizō-zaki** headland Honshū, SW Japan
141 U14 **Jiz', Wādī al** dry watercourse E Yemen
147 O11 **Jizzakh** Rus. Dzhizak. Jizzax Viloyati, C Uzbekistan
147 N10 **Jizzax Viloyati** Rus. Dzhizakskaya Oblast'. ◈ province C Uzbekistan
60 I13 **Joaçaba** Santa Catarina, S Brazil
Joal see Joal-Fadiout
76 F11 **Joal-Fadiout** prev. Joal. W Senegal
76 E10 **João Barrosa** Boa Vista, E Cape Verde
João Belo see Xai-Xai
João de Almeida see Chibia
59 Q15 **João Pessoa** prev. Paraíba. state capital Paraíba, E Brazil
25 X7 **Joaquin** Texas, SW USA
62 K6 **Joaquín V.González** Salta, N Argentina
Joazeiro see Juazeiro
Jo'burg see Johannesburg
109 O7 **Jochberger Ache** ↝ W Austria
Jo-ch'iang see Ruoqiang
92 K12 **Jock** Norrbotten, N Sweden
42 I5 **Jocón** Yoro, N Honduras
105 O13 **Jódar** Andalucía, S Spain
152 F12 **Jodhpur** Rājasthān, NW India
99 I19 **Jodoigne** Wallon Brabant, C Belgium
95 I22 **Jægerspris** Frederiksborg, E Denmark
93 O16 **Joensuu** Itä-Suomi, E Finland
95 C17 **Jæren** physical region S Norway
37 W4 **Joes** Colorado, C USA
191 Z3 **Joe's Hill** hill Kiritimati, NE Kiribati
165 N11 **Jōetsu** var. Zyôetu. Niigata, Honshū, C Japan
83 M18 **Jofane** Inhambane, S Mozambique
153 R12 **Jogbani** Bihār, NE India
118 I5 **Jõgeva** Ger. Laisholm. Jõgevamaa, E Estonia
118 I4 **Jõgevamaa** off. Jõgeva Maakond. ◈ province E Estonia
155 E18 **Jog Falls** waterfall Karnātaka, W India
143 S4 **Joghatāy** Khorāsān, NE Iran
153 U12 **Jogīghopa** Assam, NE India
152 I7 **Jogindarnagar** Himāchal Pradesh, N India
Jogjakarta see Yogyakarta
164 L11 **Jōhana** Toyama, Honshū, SW Japan
83 J21 **Johannesburg** var. Egoli, Erautini, Gauteng, abbrev. Jo'burg. Gauteng, NE South Africa
35 T13 **Johannesburg** California, W USA
83 I21 **Johannesburg** ✕ Gauteng, NE South Africa
Johannisburg see Pisz
149 P14 **Johi** Sind, SE Pakistan
55 T13 **Johi Village** S Guyana
32 K13 **John Day** Oregon, NW USA
32 I11 **John Day River** ↝ Oregon, NW USA
18 L14 **John F Kennedy** ✕ (New York) Long Island, New York, NE USA
21 V8 **John H.Kerr Reservoir** var. Buggs Island Lake, Kerr Lake. ⊠ North Carolina/Virginia, SE USA
37 V6 **John Martin Reservoir** ⊠ Colorado, C USA
96 K6 **John o'Groats** N Scotland, UK
27 P5 **John Redmond Reservoir** ⊠ Kansas, C USA
39 Q7 **John River** ↝ Alaska, USA
26 H6 **Johnson** Kansas, C USA
18 M7 **Johnson** Vermont, NE USA
18 D13 **Johnsonburg** Pennsylvania, NE USA
18 H11 **Johnson City** New York, NE USA
21 P8 **Johnson City** Tennessee, S USA
25 R10 **Johnson City** Texas, SW USA
35 S12 **Johnsondale** California, W USA
10 I8 **Johnsons Crossing** Yukon Territory, W Canada
21 T13 **Johnsonville** South Carolina, SE USA
21 Q13 **Johnston** South Carolina, SE USA
192 M6 **Johnston Atoll** ◇ US unincorporated territory C Pacific Ocean
175 Q3 **Johnston Atoll** atoll C Pacific Ocean
30 L17 **Johnston City** Illinois, N USA
180 K12 **Johnston, Lake** salt lake Western Australia
31 S13 **Johnstown** Ohio, N USA
18 D15 **Johnstown** Pennsylvania, NE USA
168 L10 **Johor** var. Johore. ◈ state Peninsular Malaysia
Johor Baharu see Johor Bahru
168 K10 **Johor Bahru** var. Johor Baharu, Johore Bahru. Johor, Peninsular Malaysia
Johore see Johor
Johore Bahru see Johor Bahru
118 K3 **Jõhvi** Ger. Jewe. Ida-Virumaa, NE Estonia
103 P7 **Joigny** Yonne, C France
Joinvile see Joinville
60 K12 **Joinville** var. Joinvile. Santa Catarina, S Brazil
103 R6 **Joinville** Haute-Marne, N France
194 H3 **Joinville Island** island Antarctica
41 O15 **Jojutla** var. Jojutla de Juárez. Morelos, S Mexico
Jojutla de Juárez see Jojutla
92 I12 **Jokkmokk** Lapp. Dálvvadis. Norrbotten, N Sweden
92 L2 **Jökulsá á Dal** ↝ E Iceland
92 K2 **Jökulsá á Fjöllum** ↝ NE Iceland
Jokyakarta see Yogyakarta
30 M11 **Joliet** Illinois, N USA
15 O11 **Joliette** Québec, SE Canada
171 O8 **Jolo** Jolo Island, SW Philippines
94 D11 **Jølstravatnet** ◎ S Norway
169 S16 **Jombang** prev. Djombang. Jawa, S Indonesia
159 R14 **Jomda** Xizang Zizhiqu, W China
118 G13 **Jonava** Ger. Janow, Pol. Janów. Kaunas, C Lithuania
146 L11 **Jondor** Rus. Zhondor. Buxoro Viloyati, C Uzbekistan
159 V11 **Jonê** Gansu, C China
27 X9 **Jonesboro** Arkansas, C USA
23 S4 **Jonesboro** Georgia, SE USA
30 L17 **Jonesboro** Illinois, N USA
22 H5 **Jonesboro** Louisiana, S USA

◆ Country ● Country Capital ◇ Dependent Territory ○ Dependent Territory Capital ◈ Administrative Region ✕ International Airport ▲ Mountain ▲ Mountain Range ⚲ Volcano ↝ River ◎ Lake ⊠ Reservoir

21 P8 **Jonesboro** Tennessee, S USA
19 T6 **Jonesport** Maine, NE USA
9 N4 **Jones Sound** *channel* Nunavut, N Canada
22 I6 **Jonesville** Louisiana, S USA
31 Q10 **Jonesville** Michigan, N USA
21 Q11 **Jonesville** South Carolina, SE USA
146 K10 **Jongeldi** *Rus.* Dzhankel'dy. Buxoro Viloyati, C Uzbekistan
81 F14 **Jonglei** Jonglei, SE Sudan
81 F14 **Jonglei** *var.* Gongoleh State. ◈ *state* SE Sudan
81 F14 **Jonglei Canal** *canal* S Sudan
118 F11 **Joniškėlis** Panevėžys, N Lithuania
118 F10 **Joniškis** *Ger.* Janischken. Šiauliai, N Lithuania
95 L19 **Jönköping** Jönköping, S Sweden
95 K20 **Jönköping** ◈ *county* S Sweden
15 Q7 **Jonquière** Québec, SE Canada
41 V15 **Jonuta** Tabasco, SE Mexico
102 K12 **Jonzac** Charente-Maritime, W France
27 R7 **Joplin** Missouri, C USA
33 W8 **Jordan** Montana, NW USA
138 H12 **Jordan** *off.* Hashemite Kingdom of Jordan, *Ar.* Al Mamlakah al Urdunīyah al Hāshimīyah, Al Urdunn; *prev.* Transjordan. ◆ *monarchy* SW Asia
138 G9 **Jordan** *Ar.* Urdunn, *Heb.* HaYarden. ≈ SW Asia
Jordan Lake *see* B.Everett Jordan Reservoir
111 K17 **Jordanów** Małopolskie, S Poland
32 M15 **Jordan Valley** Oregon, NW USA
138 G9 **Jordan Valley** *valley* N Israel
57 D15 **Jorge Chávez International** *var.* Lima. ✕ (Lima) Lima, W Peru
113 L23 **Jorgucat** *var.* Jergucati, Jorgucati. Gjirokastër, S Albania
Jorgucati *see* Jorgucat
153 X12 **Jorhāt** Assam, NE India
93 J14 **Jörn** Västerbotten, N Sweden
37 R14 **Jornada Del Muerto** *valley* New Mexico, SW USA
93 N17 **Joroinen** Isä-Suomi, E Finland
95 C16 **Jørpeland** Rogaland, S Norway
77 W14 **Jos** Plateau, C Nigeria
171 Q8 **Jose Abad Santos** *var.* Trinidad. Mindanao, S Philippines
61 F19 **José Batlle y Ordóñez** *var.* Batlle y Ordóñez. Florida, C Uruguay
63 H18 **José de San Martín** Chubut, S Argentina
61 E19 **José Enrique Rodó** *var.* Rodó, José E.Rodo; *prev.* Drabble, Drable. Soriano, SW Uruguay
José E.Rodo *see* José Enrique Rodó
Josefsdorf *see* Žabalj
44 C4 **José Martí** ✕ (La Habana) Cuidad de La Habana, N Cuba
61 F19 **José Pedro Varela** *var.* José P.Varela. Lavalleja, S Uruguay
181 N2 **Joseph Bonaparte Gulf** *gulf* N Australia
37 N11 **Joseph City** Arizona, SW USA
13 O9 **Joseph, Lake** ◎ Newfoundland and Labrador, E Canada
14 G13 **Joseph, Lake** ◎ Ontario, S Canada
186 C6 **Josephstaal** Madang, N PNG
José P.Varela *see* José Pedro Varela
59 J14 **José Rodrigues** Pará, N Brazil
152 K9 **Joshīmath** Uttaranchal, N India
25 T7 **Joshua** Texas, SW USA
35 V15 **Joshua Tree** California, W USA
77 V14 **Jos Plateau** *plateau* C Nigeria
102 H6 **Josselin** Morbihan, NW France
Jos Sudarso *see* Yos Sudarso, Pulau
94 E11 **Jostedalsbreen** *glacier* S Norway
94 F12 **Jotunheimen** ▲▲ S Norway
138 G7 **Joûnié** *var.* Junīyah. W Lebanon
25 R13 **Jourdanton** Texas, SW USA
98 L7 **Joure** *Fris.* De Jouwer. Friesland, N Netherlands
93 M18 **Joutsa** Länsi-Suomi, W Finland
93 N18 **Joutseno** Etelä-Suomi, S Finland
92 M12 **Joutsijärvi** Lappi, NE Finland
108 A9 **Joux, Lac de** ◎ W Switzerland
44 D5 **Jovellanos** Matanzas, W Cuba
153 V13 **Jowai** Meghālaya, NE India
Jōwat *see* Jabwot
Jowhar *see* Jawhar
143 O12 **Jowkān** Fārs, S Iran
143 Q10 **Jowzam** Kermān, C Iran
149 N2 **Jowzjān** ◈ *province* N Afghanistan
Józseffalva *see* Žabalj
J.Storm Thurmond Reservoir *see* Clark Hill Lake
45 T6 **Juana Díaz** C Puerto Rico
40 L9 **Juan Aldama** Zacatecas, C Mexico
(0) E9 **Juan de Fuca Plate** *tectonic feature*
32 F7 **Juan de Fuca, Strait of** *strait* Canada/USA
Juan Fernandez Islands *see* Juan Fernández, Islas
193 S11 **Juan Fernández, Islas** *Eng.* Juan Fernandez Islands. *island group* W Chile
55 O4 **Juangriego** Nueva Esparta, NE Venezuela
56 D11 **Juanjuí** *var.* Juanjuy. San Martín, N Peru
Juanjuy *see* Juanjuí
93 N16 **Juankoski** Itä-Suomi, C Finland
Juan Lacaze *see* Juan L.Lacaze
61 E20 **Juan L.Lacaze** *var.* Juan Lacaze, Puerto Sauce; *prev.* Sauce. Colonia, SW Uruguay
62 L5 **Juan Solá** Salta, N Argentina
63 F21 **Juan Stuven, Isla** *island* S Chile
59 H16 **Juará** Mato Grosso, W Brazil
41 N7 **Juárez** *var.* Villa Juárez. Coahuila de Zaragoza, NE Mexico
40 C2 **Juárez, Sierra de** ▲▲ NW Mexico
59 O15 **Juazeiro** *prev.* Joazeiro. Bahia, E Brazil
59 P14 **Juazeiro do Norte** Ceará, E Brazil
81 F15 **Juba** *var.* Jūbā. Bahr el Gabel, S Sudan
81 L17 **Juba** *Amh.* Genalē Wenz, *It.* Guiba, *Som.* Ganaane, Webi Jubba. ≈ Ethiopia/Somalia
194 H2 **Jubany** *Argentinian research station* Antarctica
Jubayl *see* Jbaïl
81 L18 **Jubbada Dhexe** *off.* Gobolka Jubbada Dhexe. ◈ *region* SW Somalia
81 K18 **Jubbada Hoose** ◈ *region* SW Somalia
Jubba, Webi *see* Juba
Jubbulpore *see* Jabalpur
Jubeil *see* Jbaïl
74 B9 **Juby, Cap** *headland* SW Morocco
105 R10 **Júcar** *var.* Jucar. ≈ C Spain
40 L12 **Juchipila** Zacatecas, C Mexico
41 S16 **Juchitán** *var.* Juchitán de Zaragosa. Oaxaca, SE Mexico
Juchitán de Zaragosa *see* Juchitán
138 G11 **Judaea** *cultural region* Israel/West Bank
138 F11 **Judaean Hills** *Heb.* Haré Yehuda. *hill range* E Israel
138 H8 **Judaydah** *Fr.* Jdaïdé. Dimashq, W Syria
139 P11 **Judayyidat Hāmir** S Iraq
109 U8 **Judenburg** Steiermark, C Austria
33 T8 **Judith River** ≈ Montana, NW USA
27 V11 **Judsonia** Arkansas, C USA
141 P14 **Jufrah, Wādī al** *dry watercourse* NW Yemen
Jugar *see* Sêrxü
Jugoslavija/Jugoslavija, Savezna Republika *see* Serbia and Montenegro (Yugo.)
42 K10 **Juigalpa** Chontales, S Nicaragua
161 T13 **Juishui** C Taiwan
100 E9 **Juist** *island* NW Germany
59 M21 **Juiz de Fora** Minas Gerais, SE Brazil
62 J5 **Jujuy** *off.* Provincia de Jujuy. ◈ *province* N Argentina
Jujuy *see* San Salvador de Jujuy
92 J11 **Jukkasjärvi** *Lapp.* Čohkkiras. Norrbotten, N Sweden
Jula *see* Gyula, Hungary
Jūlā *see* Jālū, Libya
37 W2 **Julesburg** Colorado, C USA
Julia Beterrae *see* Béziers
57 I17 **Juliaca** Puno, SE Peru
181 U6 **Julia Creek** Queensland, C Australia
35 V17 **Julian** California, W USA
98 H7 **Julianadorp** Noord-Holland, NW Netherlands
109 S11 **Julian Alps** *Ger.* Julische Alpen, *It.* Alpi Giulie, *Slvn.* Julijske Alpe ▲▲ Italy/Slovenia
55 V11 **Juliana Top** ▲ C Suriname
Julianehåb *see* Qaqortoq
Julijske Alpe *see* Julian Alps
40 J6 **Julimes** Chihuahua, N Mexico
Julio Briga *see* Bragança, Portugal
Juliobriga *see* Logroño, Spain
61 G15 **Júlio de Castilhos** Rio Grande do Sul, S Brazil
Juliomagus *see* Angers
Julische Alpen *see* Julian Alps
Jullundur *see* Jalandhar
147 N11 **Juma** *Rus.* Dzhuma. Samarqand Viloyati, C Uzbekistan
161 O3 **Juma He** ≈ E China
81 L18 **Jumboo** Jubbada Hoose, S Somalia
35 Y11 **Jumbo Peak** ▲ Nevada, W USA
105 R12 **Jumilla** Murcia, SE Spain
153 N10 **Jumla** Mid Western, NW Nepal
Jummoo *see* Jammu
Jumna *see* Yamuna
Jumporn *see* Chumphon
30 K5 **Jump River** ≈ Wisconsin, N USA
154 B11 **Jūnāgadh** *var.* Junagarh. Gujarāt, W India
Junagarh *see* Jūnāgadh
161 Q6 **Junan** *var.* Shizilu. Shandong, E China
62 G11 **Juncal, Cerro** ▲ C Chile
25 Q10 **Junction** Texas, SW USA
36 K6 **Junction** Utah, W USA
27 O4 **Junction City** Kansas, C USA
32 F13 **Junction City** Oregon, NW USA
60 M10 **Jundiaí** São Paulo, S Brazil
39 X12 **Juneau** *state capital* Alaska, USA
30 M8 **Juneau** Wisconsin, N USA
105 U6 **Juneda** Cataluña, NE Spain
183 Q9 **Junee** New South Wales, SE Australia
35 R8 **June Lake** California, W USA
Jungbunzlau *see* Mladá Boleslav
158 L4 **Junggar Pendi** *Eng.* Dzungarian Basin. *basin* NW China
99 N24 **Junglinster** Grevenmacher, C Luxembourg
18 F14 **Juniata River** ≈ Pennsylvania, NE USA
61 B20 **Junín** Buenos Aires, E Argentina
57 E14 **Junín** Junín, C Peru
57 F14 **Junín** *off.* Departamento de Junín. ◈ *department* C Peru
63 H15 **Junín de los Andes** Neuquén, W Argentina
57 D14 **Junín, Lago de** ◎ C Peru
Junīyah *see* Joûnié
Junkseylon *see* Phuket
160 I11 **Junlian** Sichuan, C China
25 O11 **Juno** Texas, SW USA
92 J11 **Junosuando** *Lapp.* Čunusavvon. Norrbotten, N Sweden
93 H16 **Junsele** Västernorrland, C Sweden
Junten *see* Sunch'ŏn
32 L14 **Juntura** Oregon, NW USA
93 N14 **Juntusranta** Oulu, E Finland
118 H11 **Juodupė** Panevėžys, NE Lithuania
119 H14 **Juozapinės Kalnas** ▲ SE Lithuania
99 K19 **Juprelle** Liège, E Belgium
80 D13 **Jur** ≈ C Sudan
103 S9 **Jura** ◈ *department* E France
108 C7 **Jura** ◈ *canton* NW Switzerland
108 B8 **Jura** *var.* Jura Mountains. ▲▲ France/Switzerland
96 G12 **Jura** *island* SW Scotland, UK
Juraciszki *see* Yuratsishki
54 C8 **Juradó** Chocó, NW Colombia
Jura Mountains *see* Jura
96 G12 **Jura, Sound of** *strait* W Scotland, UK
139 V15 **Juraybīyāt, Bi'r** *well* S Iraq
118 E13 **Jurbarkas** *Ger.* Georgenburg, Jurburg. Tauragė, W Lithuania
99 F20 **Jurbise** Hainaut, SW Belgium
Jurburg *see* Jurbarkas
118 F9 **Jūrmala** Rīga, C Latvia
58 D13 **Juruá** Amazonas, NW Brazil
48 F7 **Juruá, Rio** *var.* Río Yuruá. ≈ Brazil/Peru
59 G16 **Juruena** Mato Grosso, W Brazil
59 G16 **Juruena** ≈ W Brazil
165 Q6 **Jūsan-ko** ◎ Honshū, C Japan
25 O6 **Justiceburg** Texas, SW USA
Justinianopolis *see* Kirşehir
62 K11 **Justo Daract** San Luis, C Argentina
59 C14 **Jutaí** Amazonas, W Brazil
58 C13 **Jutaí, Rio** ≈ NW Brazil
100 N13 **Jüterbog** Brandenburg, E Germany
42 E6 **Jutiapa** Jutiapa, S Guatemala
42 A3 **Jutiapa** *off.* Departamento de Jutiapa. ◈ *department* SE Guatemala
42 J6 **Juticalpa** Olancho, C Honduras
82 I13 **Jutila** North Western, NW Zambia
Jutland *see* Jylland
84 F8 **Jutland Bank** *undersea feature* SE North Sea
93 N16 **Juuka** Itä-Suomi, E Finland
93 N17 **Juva** Isä-Suomi, SE Finland
Juvavum *see* Salzburg
44 A6 **Juventud, Isla de la** *var.* Isla de Pinos, *Eng.* Isle of Youth; *prev.* The Isle of the Pines. *island* W Cuba
161 Q5 **Juxian** *var.* Chengyang, Ju Xian. Shandong, E China
161 P6 **Juye** Shandong, E China
113 O15 **Južna Morava** *Ger.* Südliche Morava. ≈ SE Serbia and Montenegro (Yugo.)
83 H20 **Jwaneng** Southern, S Botswana
95 I23 **Jyderup** Vestsjælland, E Denmark
95 F22 **Jylland** *Eng.* Jutland. *peninsula* W Denmark
Jyrgalan *see* Dzhergalan
93 M17 **Jyväskylä** Länsi-Suomi, W Finland

K

155 X3 **K2** *Chin.* Qogir Feng, *Eng.* Mount Godwin Austen. ▲ China/Pakistan
38 D9 **Ka'a'awa** *var.* Kaaawa. O'ahu, Hawai'i, USA, C Pacific Ocean
81 G16 **Kaabong** NE Uganda
Kaaden *see* Kadaň
55 V9 **Kaaimanston** Sipaliwini, N Suriname
Kaakhka *see* Kaka
Kaala *see* Caála
187 O16 **Kaala-Gomen** Province Nord, W New Caledonia
92 L9 **Kaamanen** *Lapp.* Gámas. Lappi, N Finland
Kaapstad *see* Cape Town
Kaarasjoki *see* Karasjok
Kaaresuanto *see* Karesuando
92 J10 **Kaaresuvanto** *Lapp.* Gárassavon. Lappi, N Finland
93 K19 **Kaarina** Länsi-Suomi, W Finland
99 I14 **Kaatsheuvel** Noord-Brabant, S Netherlands
93 N16 **Kaavi** Itä-Suomi, C Finland
Ka'a'wa *see* Kaaawa
Kaba *see* Habahe
171 O14 **Kabaena, Pulau** *island* C Indonesia
Kabakly *see* Gabakly
76 J14 **Kabala** N Sierra Leone
81 E19 **Kabale** SW Uganda
55 U10 **Kabalebo Rivier** ≈ W Suriname
79 N22 **Kabalo** Katanga, SE Dem. Rep. Congo
145 W13 **Kabanbay** *Kaz.* Qabanbay *prev.* Andreyevka, *Kaz.* Andreevka. Almaty, SE Kazakhstan
79 O21 **Kabambare** Maniema, E Dem. Rep. Congo
187 Y15 **Kabara** *prev.* Kambara. *island* Lau Group, E Fiji
Kabardino-Balkaria *see* Kabardino-Balkarskaya Respublika
126 M15 **Kabardino-Balkarskaya Respublika** *Eng.* Kabardino-Balkaria. ◈ *autonomous republic* SW Russian Federation
79 O19 **Kabare** Sud Kivu, E Dem. Rep. Congo
171 T11 **Kabarei** Papua, E Indonesia
171 P7 **Kabasalan** Mindanao, S Philippines
77 U15 **Kabba** Kogi, S Nigeria
92 I13 **Kåbdalis** *Lapp.* Goabddális. Norrbotten, N Sweden
138 M6 **Kabd aş Şārim** *hill range* E Syria
14 B7 **Kabenung Lake** ◎ Ontario, S Canada
29 W3 **Kabetogama Lake** ◎ Minnesota, N USA
Kabia, Pulau *see* Kabin, Pulau
79 M22 **Kabinda** Kasai Oriental, SE Dem. Rep. Congo
Kabinda *see* Cabinda
171 O15 **Kabin, Pulau** *var.* Pulau Kabia. *island* W Indonesia
171 P16 **Kabir** Pulau Pantar, S Indonesia
149 T10 **Kabīrwāla** Punjab, E Pakistan
78 I13 **Kabo** Ouham, NW Central African Republic
Kābol *see* Kābul
83 H14 **Kabompo** North Western, W Zambia
83 H14 **Kabompo** ≈ W Zambia
79 M22 **Kabongo** Katanga, SE Dem. Rep. Congo
120 K11 **Kaboudia, Rass** *headland* E Tunisia
143 U4 **Kabūd Gonbad** Khorāsān, NE Iran
142 L5 **Kabūd Rāhang** Hamadān, W Iran
82 L12 **Kabuko** Northern, NE Zambia
149 Q5 **Kābul** *var.* Kabul, *Per.* Kābol. ● (Afghanistan) Kābul, E Afghanistan
149 Q5 **Kābul** *Eng.* Kabul, *Per.* Kābol. ◈ *province* E Afghanistan
149 Q5 **Kābul** ✕ Kābul, E Afghanistan
149 R5 **Kabul** *var.* Daryā-ye Kābul. ≈ Afghanistan/Pakistan *see also* Kābul, Daryā-ye
149 S5 **Kābul, Daryā-ye** *var.* Kabul. ≈ Afghanistan/Pakistan *see also* Kabul
79 O25 **Kabunda** Katanga, SE Dem. Rep. Congo
171 R9 **Kaburuang, Pulau** *island* Kepulauan Talaud, N Indonesia
80 G8 **Kabushiya** River Nile, NE Sudan
83 J14 **Kabwe** Central, C Zambia
186 E7 **Kabwum** Morobe, C PNG
113 N17 **Kačanik** Serbia, S Serbia and Montenegro (Yugo.)
118 F13 **Kačerginė** Kaunas, C Lithuania
117 S13 **Kacha** Respublika Krym, S Ukraine
154 A10 **Kachchh, Gulf of** *var.* Gulf of Cutch, Gulf of Kutch. *gulf* W India
154 I11 **Kachchhidhāna** Madhya Pradesh, C India
149 Q11 **Kachchh, Rann of** *var.* Rann of Kachh, Rann of Kutch. *salt marsh* India/Pakistan
39 Q13 **Kachemak Bay** *bay* Alaska, USA
Kachh, Rann of *see* Kachchh, Rann of
77 V14 **Kachia** Kaduna, C Nigeria
167 N2 **Kachin State** ◈ *state* N Myanmar
145 T7 **Kachiry** Pavlodar, NE Kazakhstan
137 Q11 **Kaçkar Dağları** ▲▲ NE Turkey
155 C21 **Kadamatt Island** *island* Lakshadweep, India, N Indian Ocean
111 B15 **Kadaň** *Ger.* Kaaden. Ústecký Kraj, NW Czech Republic
167 N11 **Kadan Kyun** *prev.* King Island. *island* Mergui Archipelago, S Myanmar
187 X15 **Kadavu** *prev.* Kandavu. *island* S Fiji
187 X15 **Kadavu Passage** *channel* S Fiji
79 G16 **Kadéï** ≈ Cameroon/Central African Republic
Kadhimain *see* Al Kāẓimīyah
Kadijica *see* Kadiytsa
114 M13 **Kadıköy Barajı** ⊡ NW Turkey
182 I8 **Kadina** South Australia
136 H15 **Kadınhanı** Konya, C Turkey
76 M14 **Kadiolo** Sikasso, S Mali
136 L16 **Kadirli** Osmaniye, S Turkey
114 G11 **Kadiytsa** *Mac.* Kadijica. ▲ Bulgaria/FYR Macedonia
28 L10 **Kadoka** South Dakota, N USA
127 N5 **Kadom** Ryazanskaya Oblast', W Russian Federation
83 K16 **Kadoma** *prev.* Gatooma. Mashonaland West, C Zimbabwe
80 E12 **Kadugli** Southern Kordofan, S Sudan
77 V14 **Kaduna** Kaduna, C Nigeria
77 V14 **Kaduna** ◈ *state* C Nigeria
77 V15 **Kaduna** ≈ N Nigeria
124 K14 **Kaduy** Vologodskaya Oblast', NW Russian Federation
154 E13 **Kadwa** ≈ W India
123 S9 **Kadykchan** Magadanskaya Oblast', E Russian Federation
Kadzharan *see* K'ajaran
125 T7 **Kadzherom** Respublika Komi, NW Russian Federation
147 X8 **Kadzhi-Say** *Kir.* Kajisay. Issyk-Kul'skaya Oblast', NE Kyrgyzstan
76 I10 **Kaédi** Gorgol, S Mauritania
78 G12 **Kaélé** Extrême-Nord, N Cameroon
38 C9 **Ka'ena Point** *var.* Kaena Point *headland* O'ahu, Hawai'i, USA, C Pacific Ocean
184 J2 **Kaeo** Northland, North Island, NZ
163 X14 **Kaesŏng** *var.* Kaesŏng-si. S North Korea
Kaesŏng-si *see* Kaesŏng
Kaewieng *see* Kavieng
79 L24 **Kafakumba** Katanga, S Dem. Rep. Congo
Kafan *see* Kapan
77 V14 **Kafanchan** Kaduna, C Nigeria
Kaffa *see* Feodosiya
76 G11 **Kaffrine** C Senegal
Kafiau *see* Kofiau, Pulau
115 I19 **Kafiréas, Akrotírio** *headland* Évvoia, C Greece
115 I19 **Kafiréas, Stenó** *strait* Évvoia/Kykládes, Greece, Aegean Sea
Kafirnigan *see* Kofarnihon
Kafo *see* Kafu
Kafr ash Shaykh/Kafrel Sheik *see* Kafr el Sheikh
75 W7 **Kafr el Sheikh** *var.* Kafr ash Shaykh, Kafrel Sheik. N Egypt
81 F17 **Kafu** *var.* Kafo. ≈ W Uganda
83 J15 **Kafue** Lusaka, SE Zambia
83 I14 **Kafue** ≈ C Zambia
67 T13 **Kafue Flats** *plain* C Zambia
164 K12 **Kaga** Ishikawa, Honshū, SW Japan
79 J14 **Kaga Bandoro** *prev.* Fort-Crampel. Nana-Grébizi, C Central African Republic
81 E18 **Kagadi** W Uganda
38 H17 **Kagalaska Island** *island* Aleutian Islands, Alaska, USA
Kagan *see* Kogon
Kaganovichabad *see* Kolkhozobod
Kagarlyk *see* Kaharlyk
164 H14 **Kagawa** *off.* Kagawa-ken. ◈ *prefecture* Shikoku, SW Japan
154 J13 **Kagaznagar** Andhra Pradesh, C India
93 J14 **Kåge** Västerbotten, N Sweden
81 E19 **Kagera** *var.* Ziwa Magharibi, *Eng.* West Lake. ◈ *region* NW Tanzania
81 E19 **Kagera** *var.* Akagera. ≈ Rwanda/Tanzania *see also* Akagera
76 L5 **Kâghet** *var.* Karet. *physical region* N Mauritania
Kagi *see* Chiai
137 S12 **Kağızman** Kars, NE Turkey
188 I6 **Kagman Point** *headland* Saipan, S Northern Mariana Islands
164 C16 **Kagoshima** *var.* Kagosima. Kagoshima, Kyūshū, SW Japan
164 C16 **Kagoshima** *off.* Kagoshima-ken, *var.* Kagosima. ◈ *prefecture* Kyūshū, SW Japan
Kagosima *see* Kagoshima
Kagul *see* Cahul
Kagul, Ozero *see* Kahul, Ozero
38 B8 **Kahala Point** *headland* Kaua'i, Hawai'i, USA, C Pacific Ocean
81 F21 **Kahama** Shinyanga, NW Tanzania
117 P5 **Kaharlyk** *Rus.* Kagarlyk. Kyyivs'ka Oblast', N Ukraine
169 T13 **Kahayan, Sungai** ≈ Borneo, C Indonesia
79 I22 **Kahemba** Bandundu, SW Dem. Rep. Congo
185 A23 **Kaherekoau Mountains** ▲▲ South Island, NZ
143 W14 **Kahīrī** *var.* Kūhīrī. Sīstān va Balūchestān, SE Iran
101 L16 **Kahla** Thüringen, C Germany
101 G15 **Kahler Asten** ▲ W Germany
149 Q4 **Kahmard, Daryā-ye** *prev.* Darya-i-Surkhab. ≈ NE Afghanistan
143 T13 **Kahnūj** Kermān, SE Iran
27 V1 **Kahoka** Missouri, C USA
38 E10 **Kaho'olawe** *var.* Kahoolawe *island* Hawai'i, USA, C Pacific Ocean
136 M16 **Kahramanmaraş** *var.* Kahraman Maraş, Maraş, Marash. Kahramanmaraş, S Turkey
136 L15 **Kahramanmaraş** *var.* Kahraman Maraş, Maraş, Marash. ◈ *province* C Turkey
Kahror/Kahror Pakka *see* Karor Pacca
137 N15 **Kâhta** Adıyaman, S Turkey
38 D8 **Kahuku** O'ahu, Hawai'i, USA, C Pacific Ocean
38 D8 **Kahuku Point** *headland* O'ahu, Hawai'i, USA, C Pacific Ocean
116 M12 **Kahul, Ozero** *var.* Lacul Cahul, *Rus.* Ozero Kagul. ◎ Moldova/Ukraine
143 V11 **Kahūrak** Sīstān va Balūchestān, SE Iran
184 G13 **Kahurangi Point** *headland* South Island, NZ
149 V6 **Kahūta** Punjab, E Pakistan
77 S14 **Kaiama** Kwara, W Nigeria
186 D7 **Kaiapit** Morobe, C PNG
185 I18 **Kaiapoi** Canterbury, South Island, NZ
36 K9 **Kaibab Plateau** *plain* Arizona, SW USA
171 U14 **Kai Besar, Pulau** *island* Kepulauan Kai, E Indonesia
36 L9 **Kaibito Plateau** *plain* Arizona, SW USA
158 K6 **Kaidu He** *var.* Karaxahar. ≈ NW China
55 S10 **Kaieteur Falls** *waterfall* C Guyana
161 O6 **Kaifeng** Henan, C China
184 J3 **Kaihu** Northland, North Island, NZ
Kaihua *see* Wenshan
171 U14 **Kai Kecil, Pulau** *island* Kepulauan Kai, E Indonesia
169 U16 **Kai, Kepulauan** *prev.* Kei Islands. *island group* Maluku, SE Indonesia
184 J3 **Kaikohe** Northland, North Island, NZ
185 J16 **Kaikoura** Canterbury, South Island, NZ
185 J16 **Kaikoura Peninsula** *peninsula* South Island, NZ
Kailas Range *see* Gangdisê Shan
160 K12 **Kaili** Guizhou, S China
38 F10 **Kailua** Maui, Hawai'i, USA, C Pacific Ocean
Kailua *see* Kalaoa
38 G11 **Kalaoa** *var.* Kailua. Hawai'i, USA, C Pacific Ocean
38 G11 **Kailua-Kona** *var.* Kona. Hawai'i, USA, C Pacific Ocean
186 B7 **Kaim** ≈ W PNG
171 X14 **Kaima** Papua, E Indonesia
184 M7 **Kaimai Range** ▲▲ North Island, NZ
114 E13 **Kaïmaktsalán** ▲ Greece/FYR Macedonia
185 C20 **Kaimanawa Mountains** ▲▲ North Island, NZ
118 E4 **Käina** *Ger.* Keinis; *prev.* Keina. Hiiumaa, W Estonia
109 V7 **Kainach** ≈ SE Austria
164 I14 **Kainan** Tokushima, Shikoku, SW Japan
164 H15 **Kainan** Wakayama, Honshū, SW Japan
147 U7 **Kaindy** *Kir.* Kayyngdy. Chuyskaya Oblast', N Kyrgyzstan
77 T14 **Kainji Dam** *dam* W Nigeria
Kainji Lake *see* Kainji Reservoir
77 T14 **Kainji Reservoir** *var.* Kainji Lake. ⊡ W Nigeria
186 D8 **Kaintiba** *var.* Kamina. Gulf, S PNG
92 K12 **Kainulaisjärvi** Norrbotten, N Sweden
184 K5 **Kaipara Harbour** *harbour* North Island, NZ
152 I10 **Kairāna** Uttar Pradesh, N India
74 M6 **Kairouan** *var.* Al Qayrawān. E Tunisia
Kaisaria *see* Kayseri
101 F20 **Kaiserslautern** Rheinland-Pfalz, SW Germany
118 G13 **Kaišiadorys** Kaunas, S Lithuania
184 I2 **Kaitaia** Northland, North Island, NZ
185 E24 **Kaitangata** Otago, South Island, NZ
152 I9 **Kaithal** Haryāna, NW India
Kaitong *see* Tongyu
169 N13 **Kait, Tanjung** *headland* Sumatera, W Indonesia
38 E9 **Kaiwi Channel** *channel* Hawai'i, USA, C Pacific Ocean
160 K9 **Kaixian** *var.* Kai Xian. Sichuan, C China
163 V11 **Kaiyuan** *var.* K'ai-yüan. Liaoning, NE China
160 H14 **Kaiyuan** Yunnan, SW China
39 O9 **Kaiyuh Mountains** ▲▲ Alaska, USA
93 M15 **Kajaani** *Swe.* Kajana. Oulu, C Finland
149 N7 **Kajakī, Band-e** ◎ C Afghanistan
Kajan *see* Kayan, Sungai
Kajana *see* Kajaani
137 V13 **K'ajaran** *Rus.* Kadzharan. SE Armenia
Kajisay *see* Kadzhi-Say
113 O20 **Kajmakčalan** ▲ S FYR Macedonia
Kajnar *see* Kaynar
149 N6 **Kajrān** Urūzgān, C Afghanistan
149 N5 **Kaj Rūd** ≈ C Afghanistan
146 G14 **Kaka** *Rus.* Kaakhka. Ahal Welaýaty, S Turkmenistan
12 C12 **Kakabeka Falls** Ontario, S Canada
83 F23 **Kakamas** Northern Cape, W South Africa
81 H18 **Kakamega** Western, W Kenya
112 H13 **Kakanj** Federacija Bosna I Hercegovina, Bosnia and Herzegovina
185 F22 **Kakanui Mountains** ▲▲ South Island, NZ
184 K11 **Kakaramea** Taranaki, North Island, NZ
76 J16 **Kakata** C Liberia
184 M11 **Kakatahi** Manawatu-Wanganui, North Island, NZ
113 M23 **Kakavi** Gjirokastër, S Albania
147 O14 **Kakaydi** Surxondaryo Viloyati, S Uzbekistan
164 F13 **Kake** Hiroshima, Honshū, SW Japan
39 X13 **Kake** Kupreanof Island, Alaska, USA
171 P14 **Kakea** Pulau Wowoni, C Indonesia
164 M14 **Kakegawa** Shizuoka, Honshū, S Japan
165 V16 **Kakeromajima** Kagoshima, SW Japan
143 T6 **Kākhak** *var.* Kākhk. Khorāsān, E Iran
118 L11 **Kakhanavichy** *Rus.* Kokhanovichi. Vitsyebskaya Voblasts', N Belarus
39 P13 **Kakhonak** Alaska, USA
117 S10 **Kakhovka** Khersons'ka Oblast', S Ukraine
117 U9 **Kakhovs'ka Vodoskhovyshche** *Rus.* Kakhovskoye Vodokhranilishche. ⊡ SE Ukraine
Kakhovskoye Vodokhranilishche *see* Kakhovs'ka Vodoskhovyshche
117 T11 **Kakhovs'kyy Kanal** *canal* S Ukraine
Kakia *see* Khakhea
155 L16 **Kākināda** *prev.* Cocanada. Andhra Pradesh, E India
Kākisalmi *see* Priozersk
164 I13 **Kakogawa** Hyōgo, Honshū, SW Japan
81 F18 **Kakoge** C Uganda
145 O7 **Kak, Ozero** ◎ N Kazakhstan
Ka-Krem *see* Malyy Yenisey
Kakshaal-Too, Khrebet *see* Kokshaal-Tau
39 S5 **Kaktovik** Alaska, USA
165 Q11 **Kakuda** Miyagi, Honshū, C Japan
165 Q8 **Kakunodate** Akita, Honshū, C Japan
Kalaallit Nunaat *see* Greenland
149 T7 **Kālābāgh** Punjab, E Pakistan
171 Q16 **Kalabahi** Pulau Alor, S Indonesia
188 I5 **Kalabera** Saipan, S Northern Mariana Islands
83 G14 **Kalabo** Western, W Zambia
126 M9 **Kalach** Voronezhskaya Oblast', W Russian Federation

◆ Country ● Country Capital ◇ Dependent Territory ○ Dependent Territory Capital ◈ Administrative Region ✕ International Airport ▲ Mountain ▲▲ Mountain Range ⩟ Volcano ≈ River ◎ Lake ⊡ Reservoir

127 *N10* **Kalach-na-Donu** Volgogradskaya Oblast', SW Russian Federation
166 *K5* **Kaladan** ≈ W Myanmar
14 *K14* **Kaladar** Ontario, SE Canada
38 *G13* **Ka Lae** *var.* South Cape, South Point. *headland* Hawai'i, USA, C Pacific Ocean
83 *G19* **Kalahari Desert** *desert* Southern Africa
38 *B8* **Kalāheo** *var.* Kalaheo. Kaua'i, Hawai'i, USA, C Pacific Ocean
Kalaikhum *see* Qal'aikhum
Kala-i-Mor *see* Galaýmor
93 *K15* **Kalajoki** Oulu, W Finland
Kalak *see* Eski Kaļak
Kal al Sraghna *see* El Kelâa Srarhna
32 *G10* **Kalama** Washington, NW USA
Kalámai *see* Kalámata
115 *G14* **Kalamariá** Kentrikí Makedonía, N Greece
115 *E21* **Kalámata** *prev.* Kalámai. Pelopónnisos, S Greece
31 *P10* **Kalamazoo** Michigan, N USA
31 *P9* **Kalamazoo River** ≈ Michigan, N USA
Kalambaka *see* Kalampáka
117 *S13* **Kalamits'ka Zatoka** *Rus.* Kalamitskiy Zaliv. *gulf* S Ukraine
Kalamitskiy Zaliv *see* Kalamits'ka Zatoka
115 *H18* **Kálamos** Attikí, C Greece
115 *C18* **Kálamos** *island* Iónioi Nísoi, Greece, C Mediterranean Sea
115 *D15* **Kalampáka** *var.* Kalambaka. Thessalía, C Greece
Kalan *see* Călan, Romania
Kalan *see* Tunceli, Turkey
117 *S11* **Kalanchak** Khersons'ka Oblast', S Ukraine
38 *G11* **Kalaoa** *var.* Kailua. Hawai'i, USA, C Pacific Ocean
171 *O15* **Kalaotoa, Pulau** *island* W Indonesia
155 *J24* **Kala Oya** ≈ NW Sri Lanka
Kalarash *see* Călăraşi
93 *H17* **Kälarne** Jämtland, C Sweden
143 *V15* **Kalar Rūd** ≈ SE Iran
167 *R9* **Kalasin** *var.* Muang Kalasin. Kalasin, E Thailand
149 *O8* **Kalāt** *Per.* Qalāt. Zābul, S Afghanistan
149 *O11* **Kālat** *var.* Kelat, Khelat. Baluchistān, SW Pakistan
115 *J14* **Kalathriá, Akrotírio** *headland* Samothráki, NE Greece
193 *W17* **Kalau** *island* Tongatapu Group, SE Tonga
38 *E9* **Kalaupapa** Moloka'i, Hawai'i, USA, C Pacific Ocean
127 *N13* **Kalaus** ≈ SW Russian Federation
Kalávrita *see* Kalávryta
115 *E19* **Kalávryta** *var.* Kalávrita. Dytikí Ellás, S Greece
141 *Y10* **Kalbān** W Oman
180 *H11* **Kalbarri** Western Australia
145 *X10* **Kalbinskiy Khrebet** *Kaz.* Qalba Zhotasy. ⛰ E Kazakhstan
144 *G10* **Kaldygayty** ≈ W Kazakhstan
136 *I12* **Kalecik** Ankara, N Turkey
79 *O19* **Kalehe** Sud Kivu, E Dem. Rep. Congo
79 *P22* **Kalemie** *prev.* Albertville. Katanga, SE Dem. Rep. Congo
166 *L4* **Kalemyo** Sagaing, W Myanmar
82 *H12* **Kalene Hill** North Western, NW Zambia
Kale Sultanie *see* Çanakkale
124 *I7* **Kalevala** Respublika Kareliya, NW Russian Federation
166 *L4* **Kalewa** Sagaing, C Myanmar
Kalgan *see* Zhangjiakou
39 *Q12* **Kalgin Island** *island* Alaska, USA
180 *L12* **Kalgoorlie** Western Australia
Kali *see* Sārda
115 *E17* **Kaliakoúda** ▲ C Greece
114 *O8* **Kaliakra, Nos** *headland* NE Bulgaria
115 *F19* **Kaliánoi** Pelopónnisos, S Greece
115 *N24* **Kalí Límni** ▲ Kárpathos, SE Greece
79 *N20* **Kalima** Maniema, E Dem. Rep. Congo
169 *S11* **Kalimantan** *Eng.* Indonesian Borneo. *geopolitical region* Borneo, C Indonesia
169 *Q11* **Kalimantan Barat** *off.* Propinsi Kalimantan Barat, *Eng.* West Borneo, West Kalimantan. ⬖ *province* N Indonesia
169 *T13* **Kalimantan Selatan** *off.* Propinsi Kalimantan Selatan, *Eng.* South Borneo, South Kalimantan. ⬖ *province* N Indonesia
169 *R12* **Kalimantan Tengah** *off.* Propinsi Kalimantan Tengah, *Eng.* Central Borneo, Central Kalimantan. ⬖ *province* N Indonesia
169 *U10* **Kalimantan Timur** *off.* Propinsi Kalimantan Timur, *Eng.* East Borneo, East Kalimantan. ⬖ *province* N Indonesia
Kálimnos *see* Kálymnos
153 *S12* **Kālimpang** West Bengal, NE India
Kalinin *see* Tver', Russian Federation
Kalinin *see* Boldumsaz, Turkmenistan
Kalininabad *see* Kaliniobod
126 *B3* **Kaliningrad** Kaliningradskaya Oblast', W Russian Federation
Kaliningrad *see* Kaliningradskaya Oblast'
126 *A3* **Kaliningradskaya Oblast'** *var.* Kaliningrad. ⬖ *province and enclave* W Russian Federation
Kalinino *see* Tashir
147 *P14* **Kalininobod** *Rus.* Kalininabad. SW Tajikistan
127 *O8* **Kalininsk** Saratovskaya Oblast', W Russian Federation
Kalininsk *see* Boldumsaz
Kalinisk *see* Cupcina
119 *M19* **Kalinkavichy** *Rus.* Kalinkovichi. Homyel'skaya Voblasts', SE Belarus
Kalinkovichi *see* Kalinkavichy
81 *G18* **Kaliro** SE Uganda
Kalisch/Kalish *see* Kalisz
33 *O7* **Kalispell** Montana, NW USA
110 *I13* **Kalisz** *Ger.* Kalisch, *Rus.* Kalish; *anc.* Calisia. Wielkopolskie, C Poland
110 *F9* **Kalisz Pomorski** *Ger.* Kallies. Zachodnio-pomorskie, NW Poland
126 *M10* **Kalitva** ≈ SW Russian Federation
81 *F21* **Kaliua** Tabora, C Tanzania
92 *K13* **Kalix** Norrbotten, N Sweden
92 *J11* **Kalixfors** Norrbotten, N Sweden
145 *T8* **Kalkaman** Pavlodar, NE Kazakhstan
Kalkandelen *see* Tetovo
181 *O4* **Kalkarindji** Northern Territory, N Australia
31 *P6* **Kalkaska** Michigan, N USA
93 *F16* **Kall** Jämtland, C Sweden
189 *X2* **Kallalen** *var.* Calalen. *island* Ratak Chain, SE Marshall Islands
118 *J5* **Kallaste** *Ger.* Krasnogor. Tartumaa, SE Estonia
93 *N16* **Kallavesi** ◎ SE Finland
115 *F17* **Kallídromo** ⛰ C Greece
Kallies *see* Kalisz Pomorski
95 *M22* **Kallinge** Blekinge, S Sweden
115 *L16* **Kalloní** Lésvos, E Greece
93 *F16* **Kallsjön** ◎ C Sweden
95 *N21* **Kalmar** *var.* Calmar. Kalmar, S Sweden
95 *M19* **Kalmar** *var.* Calmar. ⬖ *county* S Sweden
95 *N20* **Kalmarsund** *strait* S Sweden
148 *L16* **Kalmat, Khor** *Eng.* Kalmat Lagoon. *lagoon* SW Pakistan
Kalmat Lagoon *see* Kalmat, Khor
117 *X9* **Kal'mius** ≈ E Ukraine
99 *H15* **Kalmthout** Antwerpen, N Belgium
Kalmykia/Kalmykiya-Khal'mg Tangch, Respublika *see* Kalmykiya, Respublika
127 *O12* **Kalmykiya, Respublika** *var.* Respublika Kalmykiya-Khal'mg Tangch, *Eng.* Kalmykia; *prev.* Kalmytskaya ASSR. ⬖ *autonomous republic* SW Russian Federation
Kalmytskaya ASSR *see* Kalmykiya, Respublika
118 *F9* **Kalnciems** Jelgava, C Latvia
114 *L10* **Kalnitsa** ≈ SE Bulgaria
111 *J24* **Kalocsa** Bács-Kiskun, S Hungary
114 *J9* **Kalofer** Plovdiv, C Bulgaria
38 *E10* **Kalohi Channel** *channel* Hawai'i, USA, C Pacific Ocean
83 *I16* **Kalomo** Southern, S Zambia
29 *X14* **Kalona** Iowa, C USA
115 *K22* **Kalotási, Akrotírio** *headland* Amorgós, Kykládes, Greece, Aegean Sea
152 *J8* **Kalpa** Himāchal Pradesh, N India
115 *C15* **Kalpáki** Ípeiros, W Greece
155 *C22* **Kalpeni Island** *island* Lakshadweep, India, N Indian Ocean
152 *K13* **Kālpi** Uttar Pradesh, N India
158 *G7* **Kalpin** Xinjiang Uygur Zizhiqu, NW China
149 *P16* **Kalri Lake** ◎ SE Pakistan
143 *R5* **Kāl Shūr** N Iran
39 *N11* **Kalskag** Alaska, USA
95 *B18* **Kalsoy** *Dan.* Kalsø *Island* Faeroe Islands
39 *O9* **Kaltag** Alaska, USA
108 *H7* **Kaltbrunn** Sankt Gallen, NE Switzerland
Kaltdorf *see* Pruszków
77 *X14* **Kaltungo** Gombe, E Nigeria
126 *K4* **Kaluga** Kaluzhskaya Oblast', W Russian Federation
155 *J26* **Kalu Ganga** ≈ S Sri Lanka
82 *J13* **Kalulushi** Copperbelt, C Zambia
180 *M2* **Kalumburu** Western Australia
95 *H23* **Kalundborg** Vestsjælland, E Denmark
82 *K11* **Kalungwishi** ≈ N Zambia
149 *T8* **Kalūr Kot** Punjab, E Pakistan
116 *I6* **Kalush** *Pol.* Kałusz. Ivano-Frankivs'ka Oblast', W Ukraine
Kałusz *see* Kalush
110 *N11* **Kałuszyn** Mazowieckie, C Poland
155 *J26* **Kalutara** Western Province, SW Sri Lanka
Kaluwawa *see* Fergusson Island
126 *I5* **Kaluzhskaya Oblast'** ⬖ *province* W Russian Federation
119 *E14* **Kalvarija** *Pol.* Kalwaria. Marijampolė, S Lithuania
93 *K15* **Kälviä** Länsi-Suomi, W Finland
109 *U6* **Kalwang** Steiermark, E Austria
Kalwaria *see* Kalvarija
154 *D13* **Kalyān** Mahārāshtra, W India
124 *K16* **Kalyazin** Tverskaya Oblast', W Russian Federation
115 *D18* **Kalydón** *anc.* Calydon. *site of ancient city* Dytikí Ellás, C Greece
115 *M21* **Kálymnos** *var.* Kálimnos. Kálymnos, Dodekánisos, Greece, Aegean Sea
115 *M21* **Kálymnos** *var.* Kálimnos. *island* Dodekánisos, Greece, Aegean Sea
117 *O5* **Kalynivka** Kyyivs'ka Oblast', N Ukraine
117 *N6* **Kalynivka** Vinnyts'ka Oblast', C Ukraine
42 *M10* **Kama** *var.* Cama. Región Autónoma Atlántico Sur, SE Nicaragua
165 *R9* **Kamaishi** *var.* Kamaisi. Iwate, Honshū, C Japan
Kamaisi *see* Kamaishi
118 *H11* **Kamajai** Panevėžys, NE Lithuania
118 *H13* **Kamajai** Utena, E Lithuania
149 *U9* **Kamālia** Punjab, NE Pakistan
83 *I14* **Kamalondo** North Western, NW Zambia
136 *I13* **Kaman** Kirşehir, C Turkey
79 *O20* **Kamanyola** Sud Kivu, E Dem. Rep. Congo
141 *N14* **Kamarān** *island* W Yemen
55 *R9* **Kamarang** W Guyana
Kāmāreddi/Kamareddy *see* Rāmāreddi
Kama Reservoir *see* Kamskoye Vodokhranilishche
148 *K13* **Kamarod** Baluchistān, SW Pakistan
171 *P14* **Kamaru** Pulau Buton, C Indonesia
77 *S13* **Kamba** Kebbi, NW Nigeria
Kambaeng Petch *see* Kamphaeng Phet
180 *L12* **Kambalda** Western Australia
149 *P13* **Kambar** *var.* Qambar. Sind, SE Pakistan
Kambara *see* Kabara
76 *I14* **Kambia** W Sierra Leone
Kambos *see* Kámpos
79 *N25* **Kambove** Katanga, SE Dem. Rep. Congo
Kambryk *see* Cambrai
123 *V10* **Kamchatka** ≈ E Russian Federation
Kamchatka *see* Kamchatka, Poluostrov
Kamchatka Basin *see* Komandorskaya Basin
123 *U10* **Kamchatka, Poluostrov** *Eng.* Kamchatka. *peninsula* E Russian Federation
123 *V10* **Kamchatskaya Oblast'** ⬖ *province* E Russian Federation
123 *V10* **Kamchatskiy Zaliv** *gulf* E Russian Federation
114 *N9* **Kamchiya** ≈ E Bulgaria
114 *L9* **Kamchiya, Yazovir** ▣ E Bulgaria
Kamdesh *see* Kāmdeysh
149 *T4* **Kāmdeysh** *var.* Kamdesh. Kunar, E Afghanistan
118 *M13* **Kamen'** *Rus.* Kamen'. Vitsyebskaya Voblasts', N Belarus
Kamenets *see* Kamyanyets
Kamenets-Podol'skaya Oblast' *see* Khmel'nyts'ka Oblast'
Kamenets-Podol'skiy *see* Kam"yanets'-Podil's'kyy
113 *Q18* **Kamenica** NE FYR Macedonia
112 *A11* **Kamenjak, Rt** *headland* NW Croatia
144 *F8* **Kamenka** Zapadnyy Kazakhstan, NW Kazakhstan
125 *O6* **Kamenka** Arkhangel'skaya Oblast', NW Russian Federation
126 *O6* **Kamenka** Penzenskaya Oblast', W Russian Federation
127 *L8* **Kamenka** Voronezhskaya Oblast', W Russian Federation
Kamenka *see* Camenca, Moldova
Kamenka *see* Kam"yanka, Ukraine
Kamenka-Bugskaya *see* Kam"yanka-Buz'ka
Kamenka Dneprovskaya *see* Kam"yanka-Dniprovs'ka
Kamen Kashirskiy *see* Kamin'-Kashyrs'kyy
1028*L15* **Kamennomostskiy** Respublika Adygeya, SW Russian Federation
126 *L11* **Kamenolomni** Rostovskaya Oblast', SW Russian Federation
127 *P8* **Kamenskiy** Saratovskaya Oblast', W Russian Federation
Kamenskoye *see* Dniprodzerzhyns'k
126 *L11* **Kamensk-Shakhtinskiy** Rostovskaya Oblast', SW Russian Federation
101 *P15* **Kamenz** Sachsen, E Germany
164 *J13* **Kameoka** Kyōto, Honshū, SW Japan
126 *M3* **Kameshkovo** Vladimirskaya Oblast', W Russian Federation
164 *C11* **Kami-Agata** Nagasaki, Tsushima, SW Japan
33 *N10* **Kamiah** Idaho, NW USA
Kamień Koszyrski *see* Kamin'-Kashyrs'kyy
110 *H9* **Kamień Krajeński** *Ger.* Kamin in Westpreussen. Kujawsko-pomorskie, C Poland
111 *F15* **Kamienna Góra** *Ger.* Landeshut, Landeshut in Schlesien. Dolnośląskie, SW Poland
110 *D8* **Kamień Pomorski** *Ger.* Cammin in Pommern. Zachodnio-pomorskie, NW Poland
165 *R5* **Kamiiso** Hokkaidō, NE Japan
79 *L22* **Kamiji** Kasai Oriental, S Dem. Rep. Congo
165 *T3* **Kamikawa** Hokkaidō, NE Japan
164 *B15* **Kami-Koshiki-jima** *island* SW Japan
79 *M23* **Kamina** Katanga, S Dem. Rep. Congo
Kamina *see* Kaintiba
42 *C6* **Kaminaljuyú** *ruins* Guatemala, C Guatemala
Kamin in Westpreussen *see* Kamień Krajeński
116 *J2* **Kamin'-Kashyrs'kyy** *Pol.* Kamień Koszyrski, *Rus.* Kamen Kashirskiy. Volyns'ka Oblast', NW Ukraine
165 *Q5* **Kaminokuni** Hokkaidō, NE Japan
165 *P10* **Kaminoyama** Yamagata, Honshū, C Japan
39 *Q13* **Kamishak Bay** *bay* Alaska, USA
165 *U4* **Kami-Shihoro** Hokkaidō, NE Japan
Kamishli *see* Al Qāmishlī
Kamissar *see* Kamsar
164 *C11* **Kami-Tsushima** Nagasaki, Tsushima, SW Japan
79 *O20* **Kamituga** Sud Kivu, E Dem. Rep. Congo
164 *B17* **Kamiyaku** Kagoshima, Yaku-shima, SW Japan
11 *N16* **Kamloops** British Columbia, SW Canada
107 *G25* **Kamma** Sicilia, Italy, C Mediterranean Sea
192 *K4* **Kammu Seamount** *undersea feature* N Pacific Ocean
109 *U11* **Kamnik** *Ger.* Stein. C Slovenia
Kamniške Alpe *see* Kamniško-Savinjske Alpe
109 *T10* **Kamniško-Savinjske Alpe** *var.* Kamniške Alpe, Sanntaler Alpen, *Ger.* Steiner Alpen. ⛰ N Slovenia
165 *O14* **Kamogawa** Chiba, Honshū, S Japan
149 *W8* **Kāmoke** Punjab, E Pakistan
82 *L13* **Kamoto** Eastern, E Zambia
109 *V3* **Kamp** ≈ N Austria
81 *F18* **Kampala** ● (Uganda) S Uganda
168 *K11* **Kampar, Sungai** ≈ Sumatera, W Indonesia
98 *L9* **Kampen** Overijssel, E Netherlands
79 *N20* **Kampene** Maniema, E Dem. Rep. Congo
29 *Q9* **Kampeska, Lake** ◎ South Dakota, N USA
167 *O9* **Kamphaeng Phet** *var.* Kambaeng Petch. Kamphaeng Phet, W Thailand
Kampo *see* Campo, Cameroon
Kampo *see* Ntem, Cameroon/Equatorial Guinea
167 *S12* **Kâmpóng Cham** *prev.* Kompong Cham. Kâmpóng Cham, C Cambodia
167 *R12* **Kâmpóng Chhnăng** *prev.* Kompong. Kâmpóng Chhnăng, C Cambodia
167 *R12* **Kâmpóng Khleăng** *prev.* Kompong Kleang. Siĕmréab, NW Cambodia
167 *Q14* **Kâmpóng Saôm** *prev.* Kompong Som, Sihanoukville. Kâmpóng Saôm, SW Cambodia
167 *R13* **Kâmpóng Spoe** *prev.* Kompong Speu. Kâmpóng Spœ, S Cambodia
121 *O2* **Kámpos** *var.* Kambos. NW Cyprus
167 *R14* **Kâmpôt** Kâmpôt, SW Cambodia
Kamptee *see* Kāmthi
77 *O14* **Kampti** SW Burkina
Kampuchea *see* Cambodia
169 *Q9* **Kampung Sirik** Sarawak, East Malaysia
11 *V15* **Kamsack** Saskatchewan, S Canada
76 *H13* **Kamsar** *var.* Kamissar. Guinée-Maritime, W Guinea
127 *R4* **Kamskoye Ust'ye** Respublika Tatarstan, W Russian Federation
127 *U14* **Kamskoye Vodokhranilishche** *var.* Kama Reservoir. ▣ NW Russian Federation
154 *I12* **Kāmthi** *prev.* Kamptee. Mahārāshtra, C India
Kamuela *see* Waimea
165 *R3* **Kamuenai** Hokkaidō, NE Japan
165 *T5* **Kamui-dake** ✻ Hokkaidō, NE Japan
165 *R3* **Kamui-misaki** *headland* Hokkaidō, NE Japan
43 *O15* **Kámuk, Cerro** ▲ SE Costa Rica
116 *K7* **Kam"yanets'-Podil's'kyy** *Rus.* Kamenets-Podol'skiy. Khmel'nyts'ka Oblast', W Ukraine
117 *Q6* **Kam"yanka** *Rus.* Kamenka. Cherkas'ka Oblast', C Ukraine
116 *I5* **Kam"yanka-Buz'ka** *Rus.* Kamenka-Bugskaya. L'vivs'ka Oblast', NW Ukraine
117 *T9* **Kam"yanka-Dniprovs'ka** *Rus.* Kamenka Dneprovskaya. Zaporiz'ka Oblast', SE Ukraine
119 *F19* **Kamyanyets** *Rus.* Kamenets. Brestskaya Voblasts', SW Belarus
127 *P9* **Kamyshin** Volgogradskaya Oblast', SW Russian Federation
127 *Q13* **Kamyzyak** Astrakhanskaya Oblast', SW Russian Federation
12 *K8* **Kanaaupscow** ≈ Québec, C Canada
36 *K8* **Kanab** Utah, W USA
36 *K9* **Kanab Creek** ≈ Arizona/Utah, SW USA
187 *Y14* **Kanacea** *prev.* Kanathea. Taveuni, N Fiji
38 *G17* **Kanaga Island** *island* Aleutian Islands, Alaska, USA
38 *G17* **Kanaga Volcano** ▲ Kanaga Island, Alaska, USA
165 *N14* **Kanagawa** *off.* Kanagawa-ken. ⬖ *prefecture* Honshū, S Japan
13 *Q8* **Kanairiktok** ≈ Newfoundland and Labrador, E Canada
Kanaky *see* New Caledonia
79 *K22* **Kananga** *prev.* Luluabourg. Kasai Occidental, S Dem. Rep. Congo
Kananur *see* Cannanore
Kanara *see* Karnātaka
36 *J7* **Kanarraville** Utah, W USA
127 *Q4* **Kanash** Chuvashskaya Respublika, W Russian Federation
Kanathea *see* Kanacea
21 *Q4* **Kanawha River** ≈ West Virginia, NE USA
164 *L13* **Kanayama** Gifu, Honshū, SW Japan
164 *L11* **Kanazawa** Ishikawa, Honshū, SW Japan
166 *M4* **Kanbalu** Sagaing, C Myanmar
166 *L8* **Kanbe** Yangon, SW Myanmar
167 *O11* **Kanchanaburi** Kanchanaburi, W Thailand
Kānchenjunga *see* Kangchenjunga
145 *V11* **Kanchingiz, Khrebet** ⛰ E Kazakhstan
155 *J19* **Kānchīpuram** *prev.* Conjeeveram. Tamil Nādu, SE India
149 *N8* **Kandahār** *Per.* Qandahār. Kandahār, S Afghanistan
149 *N9* **Kandahār** *Per.* Qandahār. ⬖ *province* SE Afghanistan
Kandalakša *see* Kandalaksha
124 *I5* **Kandalaksha** *var.* Kandalakša, *Fin.* Kantalahti. Murmanskaya Oblast', NW Russian Federation
Kandalaksha Gulf/Kandalakshskaya Guba *see* Kandalakshskiy Zaliv
126 *K6* **Kandalakshskiy Zaliv** *var.* Kandalakshskaya Guba, *Eng.* Kandalaksha Gulf. *bay* NW Russian Federation
Kandalangodi *see* Kandalangoti
83 *G17* **Kandalangoti** *var.* Kandalangodi. Ngamiland, NW Botswana
169 *U13* **Kandangan** Borneo, C Indonesia
Kandau *see* Kandava
118 *E8* **Kandava** *Ger.* Kandau. Tukums, W Latvia
Kandavu *see* Kadavu
77 *R14* **Kandé** *var.* Kanté. NE Togo
101 *F23* **Kandel** ▲ SW Germany
186 *C7* **Kandep** Enga, W PNG
149 *R12* **Kandh Kot** Sind, SE Pakistan
77 *S13* **Kandi** N Benin
149 *P14* **Kandiāro** Sind, SE Pakistan
136 *F11* **Kandıra** Kocaeli, NW Turkey
183 *S8* **Kandos** New South Wales, SE Australia
148 *M16* **Kandrāch** *var.* Kanrach. Baluchistān, SW Pakistan
172 *I4* **Kandreho** Mahajanga, C Madagascar
186 *F7* **Kandrian** New Britain, E PNG
Kandukur *see* Kondukūr
155 *K25* **Kandy** Central Province, C Sri Lanka
144 *I10* **Kandyagash** *Kaz.* Qandyaghash; *prev.* Oktyabr'sk. Aktyubinsk, W Kazakhstan
18 *D12* **Kane** Pennsylvania, NE USA
64 *I11* **Kane Fracture Zone** *tectonic feature* NW Atlantic Ocean
Kanëka *see* Kanëvka
78 *G9* **Kanem** *off.* Préfecture du Kanem. ⬖ *prefecture* W Chad
38 *D9* **Kāne'ohe** *var.* Kaneohe. O'ahu, Hawai'i, USA, C Pacific Ocean
Kanestron, Akrotírio *see* Palioúri, Akrotírio
Kanëv *see* Kaniv
124 *M5* **Kanëvka** *var.* Kanëka. Murmanskaya Oblast', NW Russian Federation
126 *K13* **Kanevskaya** Krasnodarskiy Kray, SW Russian Federation
Kanevskoye Vodokhranilishche *see* Kanivs'ke Vodoskhovyshche
165 *P9* **Kaneyama** Yamagata, Honshū, C Japan
83 *G20* **Kang** Kgalagadi, C Botswana
76 *L13* **Kangaba** Koulikoro, SW Mali
136 *M13* **Kangal** Sivas, C Turkey
143 *O13* **Kangān** Būshehr, S Iran
143 *S15* **Kangān** Hormozgān, SE Iran
168 *J6* **Kangar** Perlis, Peninsular Malaysia
76 *L13* **Kangaré** Sikasso, S Mali
182 *F10* **Kangaroo Island** *island* South Australia
93 *M17* **Kangasniemi** Itä-Suomi, E Finland
142 *K6* **Kangāvar** *var.* Kangāwar. Kermānshāh, W Iran
Kangāwar *see* Kangāvar
153 *S11* **Kangchenjunga** *var.* Kānchenjunga. ▲ NE India
160 *G9* **Kangding** *var.* Lucheng, *Tib.* Dardo. Sichuan, C China
169 *U16* **Kangean, Kepulauan** *island group* S Indonesia
169 *T16* **Kangean, Pulau** *island* Kepulauan Kangean, S Indonesia
67 *U8* **Kangen** *var.* Kengen. ≈ SE Sudan
197 *N14* **Kangerlussuaq** *Dan.* Sondre Strømfjord. ✕ Kitaa, W Greenland
197 *Q15* **Kangertittivaq** *Dan.* Scoresby Sund. *fjord* E Greenland
167 *O2* **Kangfang** Kachin State, N Myanmar
163 *X12* **Kanggye** N North Korea
197 *P15* **Kangikajik** *var.* Kap Brewster. *headland* E Greenland
13 *N5* **Kangiqsualujjuaq** *prev.* George River, Port-Nouveau-Québec. Québec, E Canada
12 *L2* **Kangiqsujuaq** *prev.* Maricourt, Wakeham Bay. Québec, NE Canada
12 *M4* **Kangirsuk** *prev.* Bellin, Payne. Québec, E Canada
Kangle *see* Wanzai
158 *J15* **Kangmar** Xizang Zizhiqu, W China
158 *M16* **Kangmar** Xizang Zizhiqu, W China
163 *Y14* **Kangnŭng** *Jap.* Kōryō. NE South Korea
79 *D18* **Kango** Estuaire, NW Gabon
152 *I7* **Kāngra** Himāchal Pradesh, NW India
153 *Q16* **Kangsabati Reservoir** ▣ N India
159 *O17* **Kangto** ▲ China/India
159 *W12* **Kangxian** *var.* Kang Xian, Zuitai, Zuitaizi. Gansu, C China
166 *L4* **Kani** Sagaing, C Myanmar
76 *M15* **Kani** NW Ivory Coast
79 *M23* **Kaniama** Katanga, S Dem. Rep. Congo
Kanibadam *see* Konibodom
169 *V6* **Kanibongan** Sabah, East Malaysia
185 *F17* **Kaniere** West Coast, South Island, NZ
185 *G17* **Kaniere, Lake** ◎ South Island, NZ
188 *E17* **Kanifaay** Yap, W Micronesia
127 *O4* **Kanin Kamen'** ⛰ NW Russian Federation
125 *N3* **Kanin Nos** Nenetskiy Avtonomnyy Okrug, NW Russian Federation
127 *N3* **Kanin Nos, Mys** *headland* NW Russian Federation
127 *O5* **Kanin, Poluostrov** *peninsula* NW Russian Federation
139 *V8* **Kānī Sakht** E Iraq
139 *T3* **Kānī Sulaymān** N Iraq
165 *Q6* **Kanita** Aomori, Honshū, C Japan
117 *Q5* **Kaniv** *Rus.* Kanëv. Cherkas'ka Oblast', C Ukraine
182 *K11* **Kaniva** Victoria, SE Australia
117 *Q5* **Kanivs'ke Vodoskhovyshche** *Rus.* Kanevskoye Vodokhranilishche. ▣ C Ukraine
112 *L8* **Kanjiža** *Ger.* Altkanischa, *Hung.* Magyarkanizsa, Ókanizsa; *prev.* Stara Kanjiža. Serbia, N Serbia and Montenegro (Yugo.)
93 *K18* **Kankaanpää** Länsi-Suomi, W Finland
30 *M12* **Kankakee** Illinois, N USA
31 *O11* **Kankakee River** ≈ Illinois/Indiana, N USA
76 *K14* **Kankan** Haute-Guinée, E Guinea
154 *K13* **Kānker** Chhattīsgarh, C India
76 *J10* **Kankossa** Assaba, S Mauritania
167 *N12* **Kanmaw Kyun** *var.* Kisseraing, Kithareng. *island* Mergui Archipelago, S Myanmar
164 *F12* **Kanmuri-yama** ▲ Kyūshū, SW Japan
21 *R10* **Kannapolis** North Carolina, SE USA
93 *L16* **Kannonkoski** Länsi-Suomi, W Finland
Kannur *see* Cannanore
93 *K15* **Kannus** Länsi-Suomi, W Finland
77 *V13* **Kano** Kano, N Nigeria
77 *V13* **Kano** ⬖ *state* N Nigeria
77 *V13* **Kano** ✕ Kano, N Nigeria
164 *G14* **Kan'onji** *var.* Kanonzi. Kagawa, Shikoku, SW Japan
Kanonzi *see* Kan'onji
26 *M5* **Kanopolis Lake** ▣ Kansas, C USA
36 *K5* **Kanosh** Utah, W USA
169 *R9* **Kanowit** Sarawak, East Malaysia
164 *C16* **Kanoya** Kagoshima, Kyūshū, SW Japan
152 *L13* **Kānpur** *Eng.* Cawnpore. Uttar Pradesh, N India
Kanrach *see* Kandrāch
164 *I14* **Kansai** ✕ (Ōsaka) Ōsaka, Honshū, SW Japan
27 *R9* **Kansas** Oklahoma, C USA
26 *L5* **Kansas** *off.* State of Kansas; also known as Jayhawker State, Sunflower State. ⬖ *state* C USA
27 *R4* **Kansas City** Kansas, C USA
27 *R4* **Kansas City** Missouri, C USA
27 *R3* **Kansas City** ✕ Missouri, C USA
27 *P4* **Kansas River** ≈ Kansas, C USA
122 *L14* **Kansk** Krasnoyarskiy Kray, S Russian Federation
Kansu *see* Gansu
147 *V7* **Kant** Chuyskaya Oblast', N Kyrgyzstan
Kantalahti *see* Kandalaksha
167 *N16* **Kantang** *var.* Ban Kantang. Trang, SW Thailand
115 *H25* **Kántanos** Kríti, Greece, E Mediterranean Sea
77 *R12* **Kantchari** E Burkina
Kanté *see* Kandé
Kantemir *see* Cantemir
126 *L9* **Kantemirovka** Voronezhskaya Oblast', W Russian Federation
167 *R11* **Kantharalak** Si Sa Ket, E Thailand
Kantipur *see* Kathmandu
39 *Q9* **Kantishna** ≈ Alaska, USA
191 *S3* **Kanton** *var.* Abariringa, Canton Island; *prev.* Mary Island. *atoll* Phoenix Islands, C Kiribati
97 *C20* **Kanturk** *Ir.* Ceann Toirc. SW Ireland
55 *T11* **Kanuku Mountains** ⛰ S Guyana
165 *O12* **Kanuma** Tochigi, Honshū, S Japan
83 *H20* **Kanye** Southern, SE Botswana
83 *H17* **Kanyu** Ngamiland, C Botswana
166 *M7* **Kanyutkwin** Pegu, C Myanmar
79 *M24* **Kanzenze** Katanga, SE Dem. Rep. Congo
193 *Y15* **Kao** *island* Kotu Group, W Tonga
161 *S14* **Kaohsiung** *var.* Gaoxiong, *Jap.* Takao, Takow. S Taiwan
161 *S14* **Kaohsiung** ✕ S Taiwan
Kaokaona *see* Kirakira
83 *B17* **Kaoko Veld** ⛰ N Namibia
76 *G11* **Kaolack** *var.* Kaolak. W Senegal
Kaolak *see* Kaolack
Kaolan *see* Lanzhou
186 *M8* **Kaolo** San Jorge, N Solomon Islands
83 *H14* **Kaoma** Western, W Zambia
38 *B8* **Kapa'a** *var.* Kapaa. Kaua'i, Hawai'i, USA, C Pacific Ocean
113 *J16* **Kapa Moračka** ▲ SW Serbia and Montenegro (Yugo.)
137 *V13* **Kapan** *Rus.* Kafan; *prev.* Ghap'an. SE Armenia

◆ Country ● Country Capital ◇ Dependent Territory ○ Dependent Territory Capital ⬖ Administrative Region ✕ International Airport ▲ Mountain ⛰ Mountain Range ✻ Volcano ≈ River ◎ Lake ▣ Reservoir

82 L13 **Kapandashila** Northern, NE Zambia
79 L23 **Kapanga** Katanga, S Dem. Rep. Congo
145 U15 **Kapchagay** *Kaz.* Kapshaghay. Almaty, SE Kazakhstan
145 V15 **Kapchagayskoye Vodokhranilishche** *Kaz.* Qapshagay Böyeni. ▣ SE Kazakhstan
99 F15 **Kapelle** Zeeland, SW Netherlands
99 G16 **Kapellen** Antwerpen, N Belgium
95 P15 **Kapellskär** Stockholm, C Sweden
81 H18 **Kapenguria** Rift Valley, W Kenya
109 V6 **Kapfenberg** Steiermark, C Austria
83 J14 **Kapiri Mposhi** Central, C Zambia
149 R4 **Kāpīsā** ◆ *province* E Afghanistan
12 G10 **Kapiskau** ~ Ontario, C Canada
184 K13 **Kapiti Island** *island* C NZ
78 K9 **Kapka, Massif du** ▲ E Chad
Kaplamada *see* Kaubalatmada, Gunung
22 H9 **Kaplan** Louisiana, S USA
Kaplangky, Plato *see* Gaplaňgyr Platosy
111 D19 **Kaplice** *Ger.* Kaplitz. Jihočeský Kraj, S Czech Republic
Kaplitz *see* Kaplice
Kapoche *see* Capoche
171 T12 **Kapocol** Papua, E Indonesia
167 N14 **Kapoe** Ranong, SW Thailand
Kapoeas *see* Kapuas, Sungai
81 G15 **Kapoeta** Eastern Equatoria, SE Sudan
111 I25 **Kapos** ~ S Hungary
111 H25 **Kaposvár** Somogy, SW Hungary
94 H13 **Kapp** Oppland, S Norway
100 I7 **Kappeln** Schleswig-Holstein, N Germany
Kaproncza *see* Koprivnica
109 P7 **Kaprun** Salzburg, C Austria
Kapshaghay *see* Kapchagay
Kapstad *see* Cape Town
Kapsukas *see* Marijampolė
171 Y13 **Kaptiau** Papua, E Indonesia
119 L19 **Kaptsevichy** *Rus.* Koptsevichi. Homyel'skaya Voblasts', SE Belarus
Kapuas Hulu, Banjaran/Kapuas Hulu, Pegunungan *see* Kapuas Mountains
169 S10 **Kapuas Mountains** *Ind.* Banjaran Kapuas Hulu, Pegunungan Kapuas Hulu. ▲ Indonesia/Malaysia
169 P11 **Kapuas, Sungai** ~ Borneo, N Indonesia
169 T13 **Kapuas, Sungai** *prev.* Kapoeas. ~ Borneo, C Indonesia
182 J9 **Kapunda** South Australia
152 H8 **Kapūrthala** Punjab, N India
12 G12 **Kapuskasing** Ontario, S Canada
14 D6 **Kapuskasing** ~ Ontario, S Canada
127 P11 **Kapustin Yar** Astrakhanskaya Oblast', SW Russian Federation
82 K11 **Kaputa** Northern, NE Zambia
111 G22 **Kapuvár** Győr-Moson-Sopron, NW Hungary
Kapydzhik, Gora *see* Qazangödağ
119 J17 **Kapyl'** *Rus.* Kopyl'. Minskaya Voblasts', C Belarus
43 N9 **Kara** *var.* Cara. Región Autónoma Atlántico Sur, E Nicaragua
77 R14 **Kara** *var.* Lama-Kara. NE Togo
77 Q14 **Kara** ~ N Togo
144 L7 **Karabalyk** *Kaz.* Komsomol, Komsomolets. Kostanay, N Kazakhstan
147 U7 **Kara-Balta** Chuyskaya Oblast', N Kyrgyzstan
144 G11 **Karabau** Atyrau, W Kazakhstan
146 E7 **Karabaur', Uval** *Kaz.* Korabavur Pastligi, *Uzb.* Qorabowur Kirlari. *physical region* Kazakhstan/Uzbekistan
Karabekaul *see* Garabekewül
Karabil', Vozvyshennost' *see* Garabil Belentligi
Kara-Bogaz-Gol *see* Garabogazköl
Kara-Bogaz-Gol, Zaliv *see* Garabogaz Aylagy
145 R15 **Karaboget** *Kaz.* Qaraböget. Zhambyl, S Kazakhstan
136 H11 **Karabük** Karabük, NW Turkey
136 H11 **Karabük** ◆ *province* NW Turkey
122 L12 **Karabula** Krasnoyarskiy Kray, C Russian Federation
145 V14 **Karabulak** *Kaz.* Qarabulaq. Almaty, SE Kazakhstan
145 Y11 **Karabulak** *Kaz.* Qarabulaq. Vostochnyy Kazakhstan, E Kazakhstan
145 Q17 **Karabulak** *Kaz.* Qarabulaq. Yuzhnyy Kazakhstan, S Kazakhstan
136 C17 **Kara Burnu** *headland* SW Turkey
144 K10 **Karabutak** *Kaz.* Qarabutaq. Aktyubinsk, W Kazakhstan
136 D12 **Karacabey** Bursa, NW Turkey
114 O12 **Karacaköy** İstanbul, NW Turkey
114 M12 **Karacaoğlan** Kırklareli, NW Turkey
Karachay-Cherkessia *see* Karachayevo-Cherkesskaya Respublika
126 L15 **Karachayevo-Cherkesskaya Respublika** *Eng.* Karachay-Cherkessia. ◆ *autonomous republic* SW Russian Federation
126 M15 **Karachayevsk** Karachayevo-Cherkesskaya Respublika, SW Russian Federation
126 J6 **Karachev** Bryanskaya Oblast', W Russian Federation
149 O16 **Karāchi** Sind, SE Pakistan
149 O16 **Karāchi** ✕ Sind, S Pakistan
Karácsonkő *see* Piatra-Neamț
155 E15 **Karād** Mahārāshtra, W India
136 H16 **Karadağ** ▲ S Turkey
147 T10 **Karadar'ya** *Uzb.* Qoradaryo. ~ Kyrgyzstan/Uzbekistan
Karadeniz *see* Black Sea
Karadeniz Boğazı *see* İstanbul Boğazı
146 B13 **Karadepe** Balkan Welaýaty, W Turkmenistan
Karadzhar *see* Qorajar
Karaferiye *see* Véroia
Karagan *see* Garagan
145 R10 **Karaganda** *Kaz.* Qaraghandy. Karaganda, C Kazakhstan
145 R10 **Karaganda** *off.* Karagandinskaya Oblast', *Kaz.* Qaraghandy Oblysy. ◆ *province* C Kazakhstan
Karagandinskaya Oblast' *see* Karaganda
145 T10 **Karagayly** *Kaz.* Qaraghayly. Karaganda, C Kazakhstan
Karagel' *see* Garagöl
123 U9 **Karaginskiy, Ostrov** *island* E Russian Federation
197 T1 **Karaginskiy Zaliv** *bay* E Russian Federation
137 P13 **Karagöl Dağları** ▲ NE Turkey
114 L13 **Karahisar** Edirne, NW Turkey
127 V3 **Karaidel'** Respublika Bashkortostan, W Russian Federation
127 V3 **Karaidel'skiy** Respublika Bashkortostan, W Russian Federation
114 L13 **Karaidemir Barajı** ▣ NW Turkey
155 J21 **Kāraikāl** Pondicherry, SE India
155 I22 **Kāraikkudi** Tamil Nādu, SE India
145 Y11 **Kara Irtysh** *Rus.* Chërnyy Irtysh. ~ NE Kazakhstan
143 N5 **Karaj** Tehrān, N Iran
168 K8 **Karak** Pahang, Peninsular Malaysia
Karak *see* Al Karak
147 T11 **Kara-Kabak** Oshskaya Oblast', SW Kyrgyzstan
Kara-Kala *see* Garrygala
Karakala *see* Oqqal'a
Karakalpakstan, Respublika *see* Qoraqalpog'iston Respublikasi
Karakalpakya *see* Qoraqalpog'iston
Karakax *see* Moyu
158 G10 **Karakax He** ~ NW China
121 X8 **Karakaya Barajı** ▣ C Turkey
171 Q9 **Karakelang, Pulau** *island* N Indonesia
Karakılısse *see* Ağrı
Karak, Muḩāfaẓat al *see* Al Karak
Kara-Köl *see* Kara-Kul'
147 Y7 **Karakol** *prev.* Przheval'sk. Issyk-Kul'skaya Oblast', NE Kyrgyzstan
147 X8 **Karakol** *var.* Karakolka. Issyk-Kul'skaya Oblast', NE Kyrgyzstan
Karakolka *see* Karakol
149 W2 **Karakoram Highway** *road* China/Pakistan
149 Z3 **Karakoram Pass** *Chin.* Karakoram Shankou. *pass* C Asia
152 I3 **Karakoram Range** ▲ C Asia
Karakoram Shankou *see* Karakoram Pass
Karaköse *see* Ağrı
145 P14 **Karakoyyn, Ozero** *Kaz.* Qaraqoyyn. ◎ C Kazakhstan
83 F19 **Karakubis** Ghanzi, W Botswana
147 T9 **Kara-Kul'** *Kir.* Kara-Köl. Dzhalal-Abadskaya Oblast', W Kyrgyzstan
Karakul' *see* Qarokŭl, Tajikistan
Karakul' *see* Qorako'l, Uzbekistan
147 U10 **Kara-Kul'dzha** Oshskaya Oblast', SW Kyrgyzstan
127 T3 **Karakulino** Udmurtskaya Respublika, NW Russian Federation
Karakul', Ozero *see* Qarokŭl
Kara Kum *see* Garagum
Kara Kum Canal/Karakumskiy Kanal *see* Garagum Kanaly
Karakumy, Peski *see* Garagum
83 E17 **Karakuwisa** Okavango, NE Namibia
122 M13 **Karam** Irkutskaya Oblast', S Russian Federation
Karamai *see* Karamay
169 T14 **Karamain, Pulau** *island* N Indonesia
136 I16 **Karaman** Karaman, S Turkey
136 H16 **Karaman** ◆ *province* S Turkey
114 M8 **Karamandere** ~ NE Bulgaria
158 J4 **Karamay** *var.* Karamai, Kelamayi, *prev. Chin.* K'o-la-ma-i. Xinjiang Uygur Zizhiqu, NW China
169 U14 **Karambu** Borneo, N Indonesia
185 H14 **Karamea** West Coast, South Island, NZ
185 H14 **Karamea** ~ South Island, NZ
185 G15 **Karamea Bight** *gulf* South Island, NZ
Karamet-Niyaz *see* Garamätnyýaz
158 K10 **Karamiran He** ~ NW China
147 S11 **Karamyk** Oshskaya Oblast', SW Kyrgyzstan
169 U17 **Karangasem** Bali, S Indonesia
154 H12 **Kāranja** Mahārāshtra, C India
Karanpur *see* Karanpura
152 F9 **Karanpura** *var.* Karanpur. Rājasthān, NW India
Karánsebes/Karansebesch *see* Caransebeş
145 T14 **Karaoy** *Kaz.* Qaraoy. Almaty, SE Kazakhstan
114 N7 **Karapelit** *Rom.* Stejarul. Dobrich, NE Bulgaria
136 I15 **Karapınar** Konya, C Turkey
83 D22 **Karas** ◆ *district* S Namibia
147 Y8 **Kara-Say** Issyk-Kul'skaya Oblast', NE Kyrgyzstan
83 E22 **Karasburg** Karas, S Namibia
Kara Sea *see* Karskoye More
92 K9 **Kárášjohka** *var.* Karašjokka. ~ N Norway
92 L9 **Karasjok** *Fin.* Kaarasjoki, *Lap.* Kárášjohka. Finnmark, N Norway
Karašjokka *see* Kárášjohka
Kara Strait *see* Karskiye Vorota, Proliv
Kara Su *see* Mesta/Néstos
145 N8 **Karasu** *Kaz.* Qarasū. Kostanay, N Kazakhstan
136 F11 **Karasu** Sakarya, NW Turkey
Karasubazar *see* Bilohirs'k
122 I12 **Karasuk** Novosibirskaya Oblast', C Russian Federation
145 U13 **Karatal** *Kaz.* Qaratal. ~ SE Kazakhstan
136 K17 **Karataş** Adana, S Turkey
145 Q16 **Karatau** *Kaz.* Qaratau. Zhambyl, S Kazakhstan
Karatau *see* Karatau, Khrebet
145 P16 **Karatau, Khrebet** *var.* Karatau, *Kaz.* Qaratau. ▲ S Kazakhstan
144 G13 **Karaton** *Kaz.* Qaraton. Atyrau, W Kazakhstan
164 C13 **Karatsu** *var.* Karatu. Saga, Kyūshū, SW Japan
Karatu *see* Karatsu
122 K8 **Karaul** Taymyrskiy (Dolgano-Nenetskiy) Avtonomnyy Okrug, N Russian Federation
Karaulbazar *see* Qorovulbozor
Karauzyak *see* Qorao'zak
115 D16 **Karáva** ▲ C Greece
Karavanke *see* Karawanken
115 F22 **Karavás** Kýthira, S Greece
113 J20 **Karavastasë, Laguna e** *var.* Kënet' e Karavastas, Kravasta Lagoon. *lagoon* W Albania
Karavastas, Kënet' e *see* Karavastasë, Laguna e
118 I5 **Karavere** Tartumaa, E Estonia
115 L23 **Karavonísia** *island* Kykládes, Greece, Aegean Sea
169 O15 **Karawang** *prev.* Krawang. Jawa, C Indonesia
109 T10 **Karawanken** *Slvn.* Karavanke. ▲ Austria/Serbia and Montenegro (Yugo.)
Karaxahar *see* Kaidu He
137 R13 **Karayazı** Erzurum, NE Turkey
145 Q12 **Karazhal** Karaganda, C Kazakhstan
139 S9 **Karbalā'** *var.* Kerbala, Kerbela. S Iraq
94 L11 **Kårböle** Gävleborg, C Sweden
111 M23 **Karcag** Jász-Nagykun-Szolnok, E Hungary
Kardak *see* Imia
114 N7 **Kardam** Dobrich, NE Bulgaria
115 M22 **Kardámaina** Kos, Dodekánisos, Greece, Aegean Sea
Kardamila *see* Kardámyla
115 L18 **Kardámyla** *var.* Kardamila, Kardhámila. Chíos, E Greece
Kardeljevo *see* Ploče
Kardh *see* Qardho
Kardhámila *see* Kardámyla
Kardhítsa *see* Kardítsa
115 E16 **Kardítsa** *var.* Kardhítsa. Thessalía, C Greece
118 E4 **Kärdla** *Ger.* Kertel. Hiiumaa, W Estonia
Karelia *see* Kareliya, Respublika
119 I16 **Karelichy** *Pol.* Korelicze, *Rus.* Korelichi. Hrodzyenskaya Voblasts', W Belarus
126 I10 **Kareliya, Respublika** *prev.* Karel'skaya ASSR, *Eng.* Karelia. ◆ *autonomous republic* NW Russian Federation
Karel'skaya ASSR *see* Kareliya, Respublika
81 E22 **Karema** Rukwa, W Tanzania
Karen *see* Hualien
83 I14 **Karenda** Central, C Zambia
167 N8 **Karen State** *var.* Kawthule State, Kayin State. ◆ *state* S Myanmar
92 J10 **Karesuando** *Fin.* Kaaresuanto, *Lapp.* Gárasavvon. Norrbotten, N Sweden
Karet *see* Kâghet
Kareyz-e-Elyās/Kārez Iliās *see* Kārīz-e Elyās
122 J11 **Kargasok** Tomskaya Oblast', C Russian Federation
122 I12 **Kargat** Novosibirskaya Oblast', C Russian Federation
136 J11 **Kargı** Çorum, N Turkey
152 I5 **Kargil** Jammu and Kashmir, NW India
Kargilik *see* Yecheng
124 L11 **Kargopol'** Arkhangel'skaya Oblast', NW Russian Federation
110 F12 **Kargowa** *Ger.* Unruhstadt. Lubuskie, W Poland
77 X13 **Kari** Bauchi, E Nigeria
83 J15 **Kariba** Mashonaland West, N Zimbabwe
83 J16 **Kariba, Lake** ▣ Zambia/Zimbabwe
165 Q4 **Kariba-yama** ▲ Hokkaidō, NE Japan
83 C19 **Karibib** Erongo, C Namibia
Karies *see* Karyés
92 L9 **Karigasniemi** *Lapp.* Garegegasnjárga. Lappi, N Finland
184 J2 **Karikari, Cape** *headland* North Island, NZ
Karimābād *see* Hunza
169 P12 **Karimata, Kepulauan** *island group* N Indonesia
169 P12 **Karimata, Pulau** *island* Kepulauan Karimata, N Indonesia
169 O11 **Karimata, Selat** *strait* W Indonesia
155 I14 **Karīmnagar** Andhra Pradesh, C India
186 C7 **Karimui** Chimbu, C PNG
169 Q15 **Karimunjawa, Pulau** *island* S Indonesia
80 N12 **Karin** Woqooyi Galbeed, N Somalia
Kariot *see* Ikaría
93 L20 **Karis** *Fin.* Karjaa. Etelä-Suomi, SW Finland
Káristos *see* Kárystos
148 J4 **Kārīz-e Elyās** *var.* Kareyz-e-Elyās, Kārez Iliās. Herāt, NW Afghanistan
Karjaa *see* Karis
145 T10 **Karkaralinsk** *Kaz.* Qarqaraly. Karaganda, E Kazakhstan
186 D6 **Karkar Island** *island* N PNG
143 N7 **Karkas, Kūh-e** ▲ C Iran
142 K8 **Karkheh, Rūd-e** ~ SW Iran
115 L20 **Karkinágrio** Ikaría, Dodekánisos, Greece, Aegean Sea
117 R12 **Karkinits'ka Zatoka** *Rus.* Karkinitskiy Zaliv. *gulf* S Ukraine
Karkinitskiy Zaliv *see* Karkinits'ka Zatoka
93 L19 **Karkkila** *Swe.* Högfors. Etelä-Suomi, S Finland
93 M19 **Kärkölä** Etelä-Suomi, S Finland
182 G9 **Karkoo** South Australia
Karkūk *see* Kirkūk
118 D5 **Kärla** *Ger.* Kergel. Saaremaa, W Estonia
Karleby *see* Kokkola
110 F7 **Karlino** *Ger.* Körlin an der Persante. Zachodnio-pomorskie, NW Poland
137 Q13 **Karlıova** Bingöl, E Turkey
117 U6 **Karlivka** Poltavs'ka Oblast', C Ukraine
Karl-Marx-Stadt *see* Chemnitz
Karlö *see* Hailuoto
112 C11 **Karlobag** *It.* Carlopago. Lika-Senj, W Croatia
112 D9 **Karlovac** *Ger.* Karlstadt, *Hung.* Károlyváros. Karlovac, C Croatia
112 C10 **Karlovac** *off.* Karlovačka Županija. ◆ *province* C Croatia
Karlovačka Županija *see* Karlovac
111 A16 **Karlovarský Kraj** ◆ W Czech Republic
114 J9 **Karlovo** *prev.* Levskigrad. Plovdiv, C Bulgaria
111 A16 **Karlovy Vary** *Ger.* Karlsbad; *prev. Eng.* Carlsbad. Karlovarský Kraj, W Czech Republic
Karlsbad *see* Karlovy Vary
95 L17 **Karlsborg** Västra Götaland, S Sweden
Karlsburg *see* Alba Iulia
95 L22 **Karlshamn** Blekinge, S Sweden
95 L16 **Karlskoga** Örebro, C Sweden
95 M22 **Karlskrona** Blekinge, S Sweden
101 G21 **Karlsruhe** *var.* Carlsruhe. Baden-Württemberg, SW Germany
95 K16 **Karlstad** Värmland, C Sweden
29 R3 **Karlstad** Minnesota, N USA
101 I18 **Karlstadt** Bayern, C Germany
Karlstadt *see* Karlovac
39 Q14 **Karluk** Kodiak Island, Alaska, USA
Karluk *see* Qarluq
119 O17 **Karma** *Rus.* Korma. Homyel'skaya Voblasts', SE Belarus
155 F14 **Karmāla** Mahārāshtra, W India
146 M11 **Karmana** Navoiy Viloyati, C Uzbekistan
138 G8 **Karmi'él** *var.* Carmiel. Northern, N Israel
95 B16 **Karmøy** *island* S Norway
152 I9 **Karnāl** Haryāna, N India
153 W15 **Karnaphuli Reservoir** ▣ NE India
155 F17 **Karnātaka** *var.* Kanara; *prev.* Maisur, Mysore. ◆ *state* W India
25 S13 **Karnes City** Texas, SW USA
109 P9 **Karnische Alpen** *It.* Alpi Carniche. ▲ Austria/Italy
114 M9 **Karnobat** Burgas, E Bulgaria
109 Q9 **Kärnten** *off.* Land Kärnten, *Eng.* Carinthia, *Slvn.* Koroška. ◆ *state* S Austria
Karnul *see* Kurnool
83 K16 **Karoi** Mashonaland West, N Zimbabwe
Karol *see* Carei
Károly-Fehérvár *see* Alba Iulia
Károlyváros *see* Karlovac
82 M12 **Karonga** Northern, N Malawi
147 W10 **Karool-Tëbë** Narynskaya Oblast', C Kyrgyzstan
182 J9 **Karoonda** South Australia
149 S9 **Karor Lāl Esan** Punjab, E Pakistan
149 T11 **Karor Pacca** *var.* Kahror, Kahror Pakka. Punjab, E Pakistan
171 N12 **Karosa** Sulawesi, C Indonesia
Karpaten *see* Carpathian Mountains
115 L22 **Karpáthio Pélagos** *sea* Dodekánisos, Greece, Aegean Sea
115 N24 **Kárpathos** Kárpathos, SE Greece
115 N24 **Kárpathos** *It.* Scarpanto; *anc.* Carpathos, Carpathus. *island* SE Greece
Karpathos Strait *see* Karpathou, Stenó
115 N24 **Karpathou, Stenó** *var.* Karpathos Strait, Scarpanto Strait. *strait* Dodekánisos, Greece, Aegean Sea
Karpaty *see* Carpathian Mountains
115 E17 **Karpenísi** *prev.* Karpenísion. Stereá Ellás, C Greece
Karpenísion *see* Karpenísi
Karpilovka *see* Aktsyabrski
125 O8 **Karpogory** Arkhangel'skaya Oblast', NW Russian Federation
180 I7 **Karratha** Western Australia
137 S12 **Kars** *var.* Qars. Kars, NE Turkey
137 S12 **Kars** *var.* Qars. ◆ *province* NE Turkey
145 O12 **Karsakpay** *Kaz.* Qarsaqbay. Karaganda, C Kazakhstan
93 L15 **Kärsämäki** Oulu, C Finland
Karsau *see* Kārsava
118 K9 **Kārsava** *Ger.* Karsau; *prev. Rus.* Korsovka. Ludza, E Latvia
Karshi Turkmenistan *see* Garşy
Karshi Uzbekistan *see* Qarshi
Karshinskaya Step *see* Qarshi Cho'li
Karshinskiy Kanal *see* Qarshi Kanali
84 I5 **Karskiye Vorota, Proliv** *Eng.* Kara Strait. *strait* N Russian Federation
122 J6 **Karskoye More** *Eng.* Kara Sea. *sea* Arctic Ocean
93 L17 **Karstula** Länsi-Suomi, W Finland
127 Q5 **Karsun** Ul'yanovskaya Oblast', W Russian Federation
122 F11 **Kartaly** Chelyabinskaya Oblast', C Russian Federation
18 E13 **Karthaus** Pennsylvania, NE USA
110 I7 **Kartuzy** Pomorskie, NW Poland
165 R8 **Karumai** Iwate, Honshū, C Japan
181 U4 **Karumba** Queensland, NE Australia
142 L10 **Kārūn** *var.* Rūd-e Kārūn. ~ SW Iran
92 K13 **Karungi** Norrbotten, N Sweden
92 K13 **Karunki** Lappi, N Finland
Kārūn, Rūd-e *see* Kārūn
155 H21 **Karūr** Tamil Nādu, SE India
93 K17 **Karvia** Länsi-Suomi, W Finland
111 J17 **Karviná** *Ger.* Karwin, *Pol.* Karwina; *prev.* Nová Karvinná. Moravskoslezský Kraj, E Czech Republic
155 E17 **Kārwār** Karnātaka, W India
108 M7 **Karwendelgebirge** ▲ Austria/Germany
Karwin/Karwina *see* Karviná
115 I14 **Karyés** *var.* Karies. Ágion Óros, N Greece
115 I19 **Kárystos** *var.* Káristos. Évvoia, C Greece
136 E17 **Kaş** Antalya, SW Turkey
39 Y14 **Kasaan** Prince of Wales Island, Alaska, USA
164 I13 **Kasai** Hyōgo, Honshū, SW Japan
79 K21 **Kasai** *var.* Cassai, Kassai. ~ Angola/Dem. Rep. Congo
79 K22 **Kasai Occidental** *off.* Région Kasai Occidental. ◆ *region* S Dem. Rep. Congo
79 L21 **Kasai Oriental** *off.* Région Kasai Oriental. ◆ *region* C Dem. Rep. Congo
79 L24 **Kasaji** Katanga, S Dem. Rep. Congo
82 L12 **Kasama** Northern, N Zambia
Kasan *see* Koson
83 H16 **Kasane** Chobe, NE Botswana
81 E23 **Kasanga** Rukwa, W Tanzania
79 G21 **Kasangulu** Bas-Congo, W Dem. Rep. Congo
Kasansay *see* Kosonsoy
Kasargen *see* Kasari
155 E20 **Kāsaragod** Kerala, SW India
118 P13 **Kasari** *var.* Kasari Jõgi, *Ger.* Kasargen. ~ W Estonia
Kasari Jõgi *see* Kasari
8 L11 **Kasba Lake** ◎ Northwest Territories/Nunavut, N Canada
Kaschau *see* Košice
164 B16 **Kaseda** Kagoshima, Kyūshū, SW Japan
83 I14 **Kasempa** North Western, NW Zambia
79 O24 **Kasenga** Katanga, SE Dem. Rep. Congo
79 P17 **Kasenye** *var.* Kasenyi. Orientale, NE Dem. Rep. Congo
Kasenyi *see* Kasenye
81 E18 **Kasese** SW Uganda
79 O19 **Kasese** Maniema, E Dem. Rep. Congo
152 J11 **Kāsganj** Uttar Pradesh, N India
143 U4 **Kashaf Rūd** ~ NE Iran
143 N7 **Kāshān** Eşfahān, C Iran
126 M10 **Kashary** Rostovskaya Oblast', SW Russian Federation
39 O12 **Kashegelok** Alaska, USA
Kashgar *see* Kashi
158 E7 **Kashi** *Chin.* Kaxgar, K'o-shih, *Uigh.* Kashgar. Xinjiang Uygur Zizhiqu, NW China
164 J14 **Kashihara** *var.* Kasihara. Nara, Honshū, SW Japan
165 P13 **Kashima-nada** *gulf* S Japan
124 K15 **Kashin** Tverskaya Oblast', W Russian Federation
152 K10 **Kāshīpur** Uttaranchal, N India
126 L4 **Kashira** Moskovskaya Oblast', W Russian Federation
165 N11 **Kashiwazaki** *var.* Kasiwazaki. Niigata, Honshū, C Japan
Kashkadar'inskaya Oblast' *see* Qashqadaryo Viloyati
143 T5 **Kāshmar** *var.* Turshiz; *prev.* Solṭānābād, Torshiz. Khorāsān, NE Iran
Kashmir *see* Jammu and Kashmir
149 R12 **Kashmor** Sind, SE Pakistan
149 S5 **Kashmūnd Ghar** *Eng.* Kashmund Range. ▲ E Afghanistan
Kashmund Range *see* Kashmūnd Ghar
Kasi *see* Vārānasi
153 O12 **Kasia** Uttar Pradesh, N India
39 N12 **Kasigluk** Alaska, USA
Kasihara *see* Kashihara
39 R12 **Kasilof** Alaska, USA
Kasima *see* Kashima
Kasimköj *see* General Toshevo
126 M4 **Kasimov** Ryazanskaya Oblast', W Russian Federation
79 P18 **Kasindi** Nord Kivu, E Dem. Rep. Congo
82 M12 **Kasitu** ~ N Malawi
Kasiwa *see* Kashiwa
Kasiwazaki *see* Kashiwazaki
30 L14 **Kaskaskia River** ~ Illinois, N USA
93 J17 **Kaskinen** *Swe.* Kaskö. Länsi-Suomi, W Finland
Kaskö *see* Kaskinen
Kas Kong *see* Kŏng, Kaôh
11 O17 **Kaslo** British Columbia, SW Canada
Käsmark *see* Kežmarok
169 T12 **Kasongan** Borneo, C Indonesia
79 N21 **Kasongo** Maniema, E Dem. Rep. Congo
79 H22 **Kasongo-Lunda** Bandundu, SW Dem. Rep. Congo
115 M24 **Kásos** *island* S Greece
Kasos Strait *see* Kasou, Stenó
115 M25 **Kasou, Stenó** *var.* Kasos Strait. *strait* Dodekánisos /Kríti, Greece, Aegean Sea
137 T10 **Kaspi** C Georgia
114 M8 **Kaspichan** Shumen, NE Bulgaria
Kaspīy Mangy Oypaty *see* Caspian Depression
127 Q16 **Kaspiysk** Respublika Dagestan, SW Russian Federation
Kaspiyskiy *see* Lagan'
Kaspiyskoye More/Kaspiy Tengizi *see* Caspian Sea
Kassa *see* Košice
Kassai *see* Kasai
80 I9 **Kassala** Kassala, E Sudan
80 H9 **Kassala** ◆ *state* NE Sudan
115 G15 **Kassándra** *prev.* Pallíni; *anc.* Pallene. *peninsula* NE Greece
115 G15 **Kassándras, Akrotírio** *headland* N Greece
115 H15 **Kassándras, Kólpos** *var.* Kólpos Toronaíos. *gulf* N Greece
139 Y11 **Kassārah** E Iraq
101 I15 **Kassel** *prev.* Cassel. Hessen, C Germany
74 M6 **Kasserine** *var.* Al Qaşrayn. W Tunisia
14 J14 **Kasshabog Lake** ◎ Ontario, SE Canada
139 O5 **Kassīr, Sabkhat al** ◎ E Syria
29 W10 **Kasson** Minnesota, N USA
115 C17 **Kassópi** *site of ancient city* Ípeiros, W Greece
115 N24 **Kastállou, Akrotírio** *headland* Kárpathos, SE Greece
136 I11 **Kastamonu** *var.* Castamoni, Kastamuni. Kastamonu, N Turkey
136 I10 **Kastamonu** *var.* Kastamuni. ◆ *province* N Turkey
Kastamuni *see* Kastamonu
115 E14 **Kastaneá** Kentrikí Makedonía, N Greece
115 H24 **Kastélli** Kríti, Greece, E Mediterranean Sea
Kastellórizon *see* Megísti
95 N21 **Kastlösa** Kalmar, S Sweden
115 D14 **Kastoría** Dytikí Makedonía, N Greece
126 K7 **Kastornoye** Kurskaya Oblast', W Russian Federation
115 I21 **Kástro** Sífnos, Kykládes, Greece, Aegean Sea
95 J23 **Kastrup** ✕ (København) København, E Denmark
119 Q17 **Kastsyukovichy** *Rus.* Kostyukovichi. Mahilyowskaya Voblasts', E Belarus
119 O18 **Kastsyukowka** *Rus.* Kostyukovka. Homyel'skaya Voblasts', SE Belarus
164 D13 **Kasuga** Fukuoka, Kyūshū, SW Japan
164 L13 **Kasugai** Aichi, Honshū, SW Japan
81 E21 **Kasulu** Kigoma, W Tanzania
164 I12 **Kasumi** Hyōgo, Honshū, SW Japan
127 R17 **Kasumkent** Respublika Dagestan, SW Russian Federation
82 M13 **Kasungu** Central, C Malawi
149 W9 **Kasūr** Punjab, E Pakistan
83 G15 **Kataba** Western, W Zambia
19 R4 **Katahdin, Mount** ▲ Maine, NE USA
79 M20 **Katako-Kombe** Kasai Oriental, C Dem. Rep. Congo
39 T12 **Katalla** Alaska, USA
Katana *see* Qaṭanā
79 L24 **Katanga** *off.* Région du Katanga; *prev.* Shaba. ◆ *region* SE Dem. Rep. Congo
122 M11 **Katanga** ~ C Russian Federation
154 J11 **Katangi** Madhya Pradesh, C India
180 J13 **Katanning** Western Australia
189 P8 **Kata Tjuta** *var.* Mount Olga ▲ Northern Territory, C Australia
Katawaz *see* Zarghūn Shahr
151 Q22 **Katchall Island** *island* Nicobar Islands, India, NE Indian Ocean
115 F14 **Kateríni** Kentrikí Makedonía, N Greece
117 P7 **Katerynopil'** Cherkas'ka Oblast', C Ukraine

166 M3 **Katha** Sagaing, N Myanmar
181 P2 **Katherine** Northern Territory, N Australia
154 B11 **Kāthiāwār Peninsula** peninsula W India
153 P11 **Kathmandu** prev. Kantipur. ● (Nepal) Central, C Nepal
152 H7 **Kathua** Jammu and Kashmir, NW India
76 L12 **Kati** Koulikoro, SW Mali
153 R13 **Katihār** Bihār, NE India
184 N7 **Katikati** Bay of Plenty, North Island, NZ
83 H16 **Katima Mulilo** Caprivi, NE Namibia
77 N15 **Katiola** C Ivory Coast
191 V10 **Katiu** atoll Îles Tuamotu, C French Polynesia
117 N12 **Katlabukh, Ozero** ◎ SW Ukraine
39 P14 **Katmai, Mount** ▲ Alaska, USA
154 J9 **Katni** Madhya Pradesh, C India
115 D19 **Káto Achaïa** var. Kato Ahaia, Káto Akhaía. Dytikí Ellás, S Greece
Kato Ahaia/Káto Akhaía see Káto Achaïa
121 P2 **Kato Lakatámeia** var. Kato Lakatamia. C Cyprus
Kato Lakatamia see Kato Lakatámeia
79 N22 **Katompi** Katanga, SE Dem. Rep. Congo
83 K14 **Katondwe** Lusaka, C Zambia
114 H12 **Káto Nevrokópi** prev. Káto Nevrokópion. Anatolikí Makedonía kai Thráki, NE Greece
Káto Nevrokópion see Káto Nevrokópi
81 E18 **Katonga** ≈ S Uganda
115 F15 **Káto Ólympos** ▲▲ C Greece
115 D17 **Katoúna** Dytikí Ellás, C Greece
115 E19 **Káto Vlasiá** Dytikí Makedonía, S Greece
111 J16 **Katowice** Ger. Kattowitz. Śląskie, S Poland
153 S15 **Kātoya** West Bengal, NE India
136 E16 **Katrançik Dağı** ▲▲ SW Turkey
95 N16 **Katrineholm** Södermanland, C Sweden
96 I11 **Katrine, Loch** ◎ C Scotland, UK
77 V12 **Katsina** Katsina, N Nigeria
77 U12 **Katsina** ◈ state N Nigeria
67 P8 **Katsina Ala** ≈ S Nigeria
164 C13 **Katsumoto** Nagasaki, Iki, SW Japan
165 P13 **Katsuta** var. Katuta. Ibaraki, Honshū, S Japan
165 O14 **Katsuura** var. Katuura. Chiba, Honshū, S Japan
164 K12 **Katsuyama** var. Katuyama. Fukui, Honshū, SW Japan
164 H12 **Katsuyama** Okayama, Honshū, SW Japan
Kattakurgan see Kattaqo'rg'on
147 N11 **Kattaqo'rg'on** Rus. Kattakurgan. Samarqand Viloyati, C Uzbekistan
115 O23 **Kattavía** Ródos, Dodekánisos, Greece, Aegean Sea
95 I21 **Kattegat** Dan. Kattegatt. strait N Europe
Kattegatt see Kattegat
95 P19 **Katthammarsvik** Gotland, SE Sweden
Kattowitz see Katowice
122 J13 **Katun'** ≈ S Russian Federation
Katuta see Katsuta
Katuura see Katsuura
Katuyama see Katsuyama
Katwijk see Katwijk aan Zee
98 G11 **Katwijk aan Zee** var. Katwijk. Zuid-Holland, W Netherlands
38 B8 **Kaua'i** var. Kauai. island Hawaiian Islands, Hawai'i, USA, C Pacific Ocean
38 C8 **Kaua'i Channel** var. Kauai Channel channel Hawai'i, USA, C Pacific Ocean
171 R13 **Kaubalatmada, Gunung** var. Kaplamada. ▲ Pulau Buru, E Indonesia
191 U10 **Kauehi** atoll Îles Tuamotu, C French Polynesia
Kauen see Kaunas
101 K24 **Kaufbeuren** Bayern, S Germany
25 U7 **Kaufman** Texas, SW USA
101 I15 **Kaufungen** Hessen, C Germany
93 K17 **Kauhajoki** Länsi-Suomi, W Finland
93 K16 **Kauhava** Länsi-Suomi, W Finland
30 M7 **Kaukauna** Wisconsin, N USA
92 L11 **Kaukonen** Lappi, N Finland
38 A8 **Kaulakahi Channel** channel Hawai'i, USA, C Pacific Ocean
38 E9 **Kaunakakai** Moloka'i, Hawai'i, USA, C Pacific Ocean
38 F12 **Kaunā Point** var. Kauna Point headland Hawai'i, USA, C Pacific Ocean
118 F13 **Kaunas** Ger. Kauen, Pol. Kowno; prev. Rus. Kovno. Kaunas, C Lithuania
118 F13 **Kaunas** ◈ province C Lithuania
186 C6 **Kaup** East Sepik, NW PNG
77 U12 **Kaura Namoda** Zamfara, NW Nigeria
Kaushany see Căuşeni
93 K16 **Kaustinen** Länsi-Suomi, W Finland
99 M23 **Kautenbach** Diekirch, NE Luxembourg
92 K10 **Kautokeino** Lap. Guovdageaidnu. Finnmark, N Norway
Kavadar see Kavadarci
113 P19 **Kavadarci** Turk. Kavadar. C FYR Macedonia
Kavaja see Kavajë
113 K20 **Kavajë** It. Cavaia, Kavaja. Tiranë, W Albania
114 M13 **Kavak Çayı** ≈ NW Turkey
Kavakli see Topolovgrad
114 I13 **Kavála** prev. Kaválla. Anatolikí Makedonía kai Thráki, NE Greece
114 I13 **Kaválas, Kólpos** gulf Aegean Sea, NE Mediterranean Sea
155 J17 **Kāvali** Andhra Pradesh, E India
Kaválla see Kavála
Kavango see Cubango/Okavango
155 C21 **Kavaratti** Lakshadweep, SW India
114 O8 **Kavarna** Dobrich, NE Bulgaria
118 G12 **Kavarskas** Utena, E Lithuania
76 I13 **Kavendou** ▲ C Guinea
Kavengo see Cubango/Okavango
155 F20 **Kāveri** var. Cauvery. ≈ S India
186 G5 **Kavieng** var. Kaewieng. NE PNG
83 H16 **Kavimba** Chobe, NE Botswana
83 I15 **Kavingu** Southern, S Zambia
143 Q6 **Kavīr, Dasht-e** var. Great Salt Desert. salt pan N Iran
Kavirondo Gulf see Winam Gulf
Kavkaz see Caucasus
95 K23 **Kävlinge** Skåne, S Sweden
82 G12 **Kavungo** Moxico, E Angola
165 Q8 **Kawabe** Akita, Honshū, C Japan
165 R9 **Kawai** Iwate, Honshū, C Japan
38 A8 **Kawaihoa Point** headland Ni'ihau, Hawai'i, USA, C Pacific Ocean
184 K3 **Kawakawa** Northland, North Island, NZ
82 I13 **Kawama** North Western, NW Zambia
82 K11 **Kawambwa** Luapula, N Zambia
154 K11 **Kawardha** Chhattīsgarh, C India
14 I14 **Kawartha Lakes** ◎ Ontario, SE Canada
165 O13 **Kawasaki** Kanagawa, Honshū, S Japan
171 R12 **Kawassi** Pulau Obi, E Indonesia
165 R6 **Kawauchi** Aomori, Honshū, C Japan
184 L5 **Kawau Island** island N NZ
184 N10 **Kaweka Range** ▲▲ North Island, NZ
Kawelecht see Puhja
184 O8 **Kawerau** Bay of Plenty, North Island, NZ
184 L8 **Kawhia** Waikato, North Island, NZ
184 K8 **Kawhia Harbour** inlet North Island, NZ
35 V8 **Kawich Peak** ▲ Nevada, W USA
35 V9 **Kawich Range** ▲▲ Nevada, W USA
14 G12 **Kawigamog Lake** ◎ Ontario, S Canada
171 P9 **Kawio, Kepulauan** island group N Indonesia
167 N9 **Kawkareik** Karen State, S Myanmar
27 O8 **Kaw Lake** ⊞ Oklahoma, C USA
166 M3 **Kawlin** Sagaing, N Myanmar
Kawm Umbū see Kôm Ombo
Kawthule State see Karen State
Kaxgar see Kashi
158 D7 **Kaxgar He** ≈ NW China
158 J5 **Kax He** ≈ NW China
77 P12 **Kaya** C Burkina
167 N6 **Kayah State** ◈ state C Myanmar
39 T12 **Kayak Island** island Alaska, USA
114 M11 **Kayalıköy Barajı** ⊞ NW Turkey
155 G23 **Kāyamkulam** Kerala, SW India
166 M8 **Kayan** Yangon, SW Myanmar
169 V9 **Kayan, Sungai** prev. Kajan. ≈ Borneo, C Indonesia
144 F14 **Kaydak, Sor** salt flat SW Kazakhstan
Kaydanovo see Dzyarzhynsk
37 N9 **Kayenta** Arizona, SW USA
76 J11 **Kayes** Kayes, W Mali
76 J11 **Kayes** ◈ region SW Mali
Kayin State see Karen State
145 U10 **Kaynar** var. Kajnar. Vostochnyy Kazakhstan, E Kazakhstan
Kaynary see Căinari
83 H15 **Kayoya** Western, W Zambia
Kayrakkum see Qayroqqum
Kayrakkumskoye Vodokhranilishche see Qayroqqum, Obanbori
136 K14 **Kayseri** var. Kaisaria; anc. Caesarea Mazaca, Mazaca. Kayseri, C Turkey
136 K14 **Kayseri** var. Kaisaria. ◈ province C Turkey
36 L2 **Kaysville** Utah, W USA
Kayyngdy see Kaindy
14 L11 **Kazabazua** Québec, SE Canada
14 L12 **Kazabazua** ≈ Québec, SE Canada
123 Q7 **Kazach'ye** Respublika Sakha (Yakutiya), NE Russian Federation
Kazakdar'ya see Qozoqdaryo
146 E9 **Kazakhlyshor, Solonchak** var. Solonchak Shorkazakhly. salt marsh NW Turkmenistan
Kazakhskaya SSR/ Kazakh Soviet Socialist Republic see Kazakhstan
145 R9 **Kazakhskiy Melkosopochnik** Eng. Kazakh Uplands, Kirghiz Steppe, Kaz. Saryarqa. uplands C Kazakhstan
144 L12 **Kazakhstan** off. Republic of Kazakhstan, var. Kazakstan, Kaz. Qazaqstan, Qazaqstan Respublikasy; prev. Kazakh Soviet Socialist Republic, Rus. Kazakhskaya SSR. ◆ republic C Asia
Kazakh Uplands see Kazakhskiy Melkosopochnik
Kazakstan see Kazakhstan
144 L14 **Kazalinsk** Kzylorda, S Kazakhstan
127 R4 **Kazan'** Respublika Tatarstan, W Russian Federation
127 R4 **Kazan'** ✕ Respublika Tatarstan, W Russian Federation
8 M10 **Kazan** ≈ Nunavut, NW Canada
Kazandzhik see Bereket
117 R8 **Kazanka** Mykolayivs'ka Oblast', S Ukraine
Kazanketken see Qozonketkan
Kazanlik see Kazanlŭk
114 J9 **Kazanlŭk** prev. Kazanlik. Stara Zagora, C Bulgaria
165 Y16 **Kazan-rettō** Eng. Volcano Islands. island group SE Japan
117 V12 **Kazantip, Mys** headland S Ukraine
147 U9 **Kazarman** Narynskaya Oblast', C Kyrgyzstan
Kazatin see Kozyatyn
Kazbegi see Kazbek
Kazbegi see Qazbegi
137 T9 **Kazbek** var. Kazbegi, Geor. Mqinvartsveri. ▲ N Georgia
82 M13 **Kazembe** Eastern, NE Zambia
143 N11 **Kāzerūn** Fārs, S Iran
125 R12 **Kazhym** Respublika Komi, NW Russian Federation
Kazi Ahmad see Qāzi Ahmad
Kazi Magomed see Qazimämmäd
136 H16 **Kâzımkarabekir** Karaman, S Turkey
111 M20 **Kazincbarcika** Borsod-Abaúj-Zemplén, NE Hungary
119 H17 **Kazlowshchyna** Pol. Kozlowszczyzna, Rus. Kozlovshchina. Hrodzyenskaya Voblasts', W Belarus
119 E14 **Kazlų Rūda** Marijampolė, S Lithuania
144 E9 **Kaztalovka** Zapadnyy Kazakhstan, W Kazakhstan
79 K22 **Kazumba** Kasai Occidental, S Dem. Rep. Congo
165 Q8 **Kazuno** Akita, Honshū, C Japan
Kazvin see Qazvīn
118 J12 **Kaz'yany** Rus. Koz'yany. Vitsyebskaya Voblasts', NW Belarus
122 H9 **Kazym** ≈ N Russian Federation
110 H10 **Kcynia** Ger. Exin. Kujawsko-pomorskie, C Poland
115 I20 **Kéa** Kéa, Kykládes, Greece, Aegean Sea
115 I20 **Kéa** prev. Kéos, anc. Ceos. island Kykládes, Greece, Aegean Sea
38 H11 **Kea'au** var. Keaau. Hawai'i, USA, C Pacific Ocean
38 F11 **Keāhole Point** var. Keahole Point headland Hawai'i, USA, C Pacific Ocean
38 G12 **Kealakekua** Hawai'i, USA, C Pacific Ocean
38 H11 **Kea, Mauna** ▲ Hawai'i, USA, C Pacific Ocean
37 N10 **Keams** Arizona, SW USA
Kéamu see Aneityum
29 O16 **Kearney** Nebraska, C USA
36 L3 **Kearns** Utah, W USA
115 H20 **Kéas, Stenó** strait SE Greece
137 O14 **Keban Barajı** dam C Turkey
137 O14 **Keban Barajı** ⊞ C Turkey
77 S13 **Kebbi** ◈ state NW Nigeria
76 G10 **Kébémèr** NW Senegal
74 M7 **Kebili** var. Qibilī. C Tunisia
138 H4 **Kebir, Nahr el** ≈ NW Syria
80 A10 **Kebkabiya** Northern Darfur, W Sudan
92 I11 **Kebnekaise** ▲ N Sweden
81 M14 **K'ebrī Dehar** Somali, E Ethiopia
148 K15 **Kech** ≈ SW Pakistan
10 K10 **Kechika** ≈ British Columbia, W Canada
111 K23 **Kecskemét** Bács-Kiskun, C Hungary
168 J6 **Kedah** ◈ state Peninsular Malaysia
118 F12 **Kėdainiai** Kaunas, C Lithuania
Kedder see Kehra
13 N13 **Kedgwick** New Brunswick, SE Canada
169 R16 **Kediri** Jawa, C Indonesia
171 Y13 **Kedir Sarmi** Papua, E Indonesia
163 V7 **Kedong** Heilongjiang, NE China
76 I12 **Kédougou** SE Senegal
122 I11 **Kedrovyy** Tomskaya Oblast', C Russian Federation
111 H16 **Kędzierzyn-Koźle** Ger. Heydebrech. Opolskie, S Poland
8 H8 **Keele** ≈ Northwest Territories, NW Canada
10 K6 **Keele Peak** ▲ Yukon Territory, NW Canada
Keelung see Chilung
19 N10 **Keene** New Hampshire, NE USA
99 H17 **Keerbergen** Vlaams Brabant, C Belgium
83 E21 **Keetmanshoop** Karas, S Namibia
12 A11 **Keewatin** Ontario, S Canada
29 V4 **Keewatin** Minnesota, N USA
115 B18 **Kefallinía** var. Kefallonía. island Iónioi Nísoi, Greece, C Mediterranean Sea
Kefallonía see Kefallinía
115 M22 **Kéfalos** Kos, Dodekánisos, Greece, Aegean Sea
171 Q17 **Kefamenanu** Timor, C Indonesia
138 F10 **Kefar Sava** var. Kfar Saba. Central, C Israel
Kefe see Feodosiya
77 V15 **Keffi** Nassarawa, C Nigeria
92 H4 **Keflavík** ✕ (Reykjavík) Reykjanes, W Iceland
92 H4 **Keflavík** Reykjanes, W Iceland
Kegalee see Kegalla
155 J25 **Kegalla** var. Kegalee, Kegalle. Sabaragamuwa Province, C Sri Lanka
Kegalle see Kegalla
Kegayli see Kegeyli
Kegel see Keila
145 W16 **Kegen** Almaty, SE Kazakhstan
146 H7 **Kegeyli** prev. Kegayli. Qoraqalpogʻiston Respublikasi, W Uzbekistan
101 F22 **Kehl** Baden-Württemberg, SW Germany
118 H3 **Kehra** Ger. Kedder. Harjumaa, NW Estonia
117 U6 **Kehychivka** Kharkivs'ka Oblast', E Ukraine
97 L17 **Keighley** N England, UK
Kei Islands see Kai, Kepulauan
Keijō see Sŏul
118 G3 **Keila** Ger. Kegel. Harjumaa, NW Estonia
Keilberg see Klínovec
83 F23 **Keimoes** Northern Cape, W South Africa
Keina/Keinis see Käina
Keishū see Kyŏngju
77 T11 **Keïta** Tahoua, C Niger
78 J12 **Kéita, Bahr** var. Doka. ≈ S Chad
182 K10 **Keith** South Australia
96 K8 **Keith** NE Scotland, UK
26 K3 **Keith Sebelius Lake** ⊞ Kansas, C USA
32 G11 **Keizer** Oregon, NW USA
38 A8 **Kekaha** Kaua'i, Hawai'i, USA, C Pacific Ocean
147 U10 **Këk-Art** prev. Alaykel', Alay-Kuu. Oshskaya Oblast', SW Kyrgyzstan
147 W10 **Këk-Aygyr** var. Keyaygyr. Narynskaya Oblast', C Kyrgyzstan
147 V9 **Këk-Dzhar** Narynskaya Oblast', C Kyrgyzstan
14 L8 **Kekek** ≈ Québec, SE Canada
185 K15 **Kekerengu** Canterbury, South Island, NZ
111 L21 **Kékes** ▲ N Hungary
171 P17 **Kekneno, Gunung** ▲ Timor, S Indonesia
147 S9 **Këk-Tash** Kir. Kök-Tash. Dzhalal-Abadskaya Oblast', W Kyrgyzstan
81 M15 **K'elafo** Somali, E Ethiopia
169 U10 **Kelai, Sungai** ≈ Borneo, N Indonesia
Kelamayi see Karamay
Kelang see Klang
168 K7 **Kelantan** ◈ state Peninsular Malaysia
Kelantan see Kelantan, Sungai
168 K7 **Kelantan, Sungai** var. Kelantan. ≈ Peninsular Malaysia
Kelat see Kālat
Kelcyra see Këlcyrë
113 L22 **Këlcyrë** var. Këlcyra. Gjirokastër, S Albania
Kelifskiy Uzboy see Kelif Uzboýy
146 L14 **Kelif Uzboýy** Rus. Kelifskiy Uzboy. salt marsh E Turkmenistan
137 O12 **Kelkit** Gümüşhane, NE Turkey
136 M12 **Kelkit Çayı** ≈ N Turkey
77 W11 **Kellé** Zinder, S Niger
79 G18 **Kéllé** Cuvette, W Congo
145 P7 **Kellerovka** Severnyy Kazakhstan, N Kazakhstan
8 I5 **Kellett, Cape** headland Banks Island, Northwest Territories, NW Canada
31 S11 **Kelleys Island** island Ohio, N USA
33 N8 **Kellogg** Idaho, NW USA
92 M12 **Kelloselkä** Lappi, N Finland
97 F17 **Kells** Ir. Ceanannas. E Ireland
118 E12 **Kelmė** Šiauliai, C Lithuania
99 M19 **Kelmis** var. La Calamine. Liège, E Belgium
78 H12 **Kélo** Tandjilé, SW Chad
83 I14 **Kelongwa** North Western, NW Zambia
11 N17 **Kelowna** British Columbia, SW Canada
11 X12 **Kelsey** Manitoba, C Canada
34 M6 **Kelseyville** California, W USA
96 K13 **Kelso** SE Scotland, UK
32 G10 **Kelso** Washington, NW USA
195 W15 **Keltie, Cape** headland Antarctica
Keltsy see Kielce
168 L9 **Keluang** var. Kluang. Johor, Peninsular Malaysia
168 M11 **Kelume** Pulau Lingga, W Indonesia
11 U15 **Kelvington** Saskatchewan, S Canada
124 J7 **Kem'** Respublika Kareliya, NW Russian Federation
126 I7 **Kem'** ≈ NW Russian Federation
137 O13 **Kemah** Erzincan, E Turkey
137 N13 **Kemaliye** Erzincan, C Turkey
Kemaman see Cukai
Kemanlar see Isperikh
10 K14 **Kemano** British Columbia, SW Canada
Kemarat see Khemmarat
171 P12 **Kembani** Pulau Peleng, N Indonesia
136 F17 **Kemer** Antalya, SW Turkey
122 J12 **Kemerovo** prev. Shcheglovsk. Kemerovskaya Oblast', C Russian Federation
122 K12 **Kemerovskaya Oblast'** ◈ province S Russian Federation
92 L13 **Kemi** Lappi, NW Finland
92 M12 **Kemijärvi** Swe. Kemiträsk. Lappi, N Finland
92 M12 **Kemijärvi** ◎ N Finland
92 L13 **Kemijoki** ≈ NW Finland
147 V7 **Kemin** prev. Bystrovka. Chuyskaya Oblast', N Kyrgyzstan
92 L13 **Keminmaa** Lappi, NW Finland
Kemins Island see Nikumaroro
Kemiö see Kimito
Kemiträsk see Kemijärvi
127 P5 **Kemlya** Respublika Mordoviya, W Russian Federation
99 B18 **Kemmel** West-Vlaanderen, W Belgium
33 S16 **Kemmerer** Wyoming, C USA
Kemmuna see Comino
79 I14 **Kémo** ◈ prefecture S Central African Republic
25 U7 **Kemp** Texas, SW USA
93 L14 **Kempele** Oulu, C Finland
101 D15 **Kempen** Nordrhein-Westfalen, W Germany
25 Q5 **Kemp, Lake** ◎ Texas, SW USA
195 W5 **Kemp Land** physical region Antarctica
25 S9 **Kempner** Texas, SW USA
44 H3 **Kemp's Bay** Andros Island, W Bahamas
183 U6 **Kempsey** New South Wales, SE Australia
101 J24 **Kempten** Bayern, S Germany
15 N9 **Kempt, Lac** ◎ Québec, SE Canada
183 P17 **Kempton** Tasmania, SE Australia
154 J9 **Ken** ≈ C India
39 R12 **Kenai** Alaska, USA
(0) D5 **Kenai Mountains** ▲▲ Alaska, USA
39 R12 **Kenai Peninsula** peninsula Alaska, USA
21 V11 **Kenansville** North Carolina, SE USA
146 A10 **Kenar** prev. Rus. Ufra. Balkan Welaýaty, NW Turkmenistan
121 U13 **Kenâyis, Râs el** headland N Egypt
97 K16 **Kendal** NW England, UK
23 Y16 **Kendall** Florida, SE USA
9 O8 **Kendall, Cape** headland Nunavut, E Canada
18 J15 **Kendall Park** New Jersey, NE USA
31 Q11 **Kendallville** Indiana, N USA
171 P14 **Kendari** Sulawesi, C Indonesia
169 Q13 **Kendawangan** Borneo, C Indonesia
154 O12 **Kendrāpāra** var. Kendrāparha. Orissa, E India
Kendrāparha see Kendrāpāra
154 O11 **Kendujhargarh** prev. Keonjihargarh. Orissa, E India
25 S13 **Kenedy** Texas, SW USA
Kënekesir see Könekesir
76 J15 **Kenema** SE Sierra Leone
29 P16 **Kenesaw** Nebraska, C USA
Këneurgench see Köneürgenç
79 H21 **Kenge** Bandundu, SW Dem. Rep. Congo
Kengen see Kangen
167 O5 **Keng Tung** var. Kentung. Shan State, E Myanmar
83 F23 **Kenhardt** Northern Cape, W South Africa
76 J12 **Kéniéba** Kayes, W Mali
Kenimekh see Konimex
169 U7 **Keningau** Sabah, East Malaysia
74 F6 **Kénitra** prev. Port-Lyautey. NW Morocco
21 V9 **Kenly** North Carolina, SE USA
97 B21 **Kenmare** Ir. Neidín. S Ireland
28 L2 **Kenmare** North Dakota, N USA
97 A21 **Kenmare River** Ir. An Ribhéar. inlet NE Atlantic Ocean
18 D10 **Kenmore** New York, NE USA
25 W8 **Kennard** Texas, SW USA
29 N10 **Kennebec** South Dakota, N USA
19 Q7 **Kennebec River** ≈ Maine, NE USA
19 P9 **Kennebunk** Maine, NE USA
39 R13 **Kennedy Entrance** strait Alaska, USA
166 L3 **Kennedy Peak** ▲ W Myanmar
22 K9 **Kenner** Louisiana, S USA
180 I8 **Kenneth Range** ▲▲ Western Australia
27 Y9 **Kennett** Missouri, C USA
18 I16 **Kennett Square** Pennsylvania, NE USA
32 K10 **Kennewick** Washington, NW USA
12 E11 **Kenogami** ≈ Ontario, S Canada
15 Q7 **Kénogami, Lac** ◎ Québec, SE Canada
14 G8 **Kenogami Lake** Ontario, S Canada
14 F7 **Kenogamissi Lake** ◎ Ontario, S Canada
10 I6 **Keno Hill** Yukon Territory, NW Canada
12 A11 **Kenora** Ontario, S Canada
31 N9 **Kenosha** Wisconsin, N USA
13 P14 **Kensington** Prince Edward Island, SE Canada
26 L3 **Kensington** Kansas, C USA
32 I11 **Kent** Oregon, NW USA
24 J9 **Kent** Texas, SW USA
32 H8 **Kent** Washington, NW USA
97 P22 **Kent** cultural region SE England, UK
145 P16 **Kentau** Yuzhnyy Kazakhstan, S Kazakhstan
183 P14 **Kent Group** island group Tasmania, SE Australia
31 N12 **Kentland** Indiana, N USA
31 R12 **Kenton** Ohio, N USA
8 K7 **Kent Peninsula** peninsula Nunavut, N Canada
115 F14 **Kentrikí Makedonía** Eng. Macedonia Central. ◈ region N Greece
20 J6 **Kentucky** off. Commonwealth of Kentucky; also known as The Bluegrass State. ◈ state C USA
20 H8 **Kentucky Lake** ⊞ Kentucky/Tennessee, S USA
Kentung see Keng Tung
13 P15 **Kentville** Nova Scotia, SE Canada
22 K8 **Kentwood** Louisiana, S USA
31 P9 **Kentwood** Michigan, N USA
81 H17 **Kenya** off. Republic of Kenya. ◆ republic E Africa
Kenya, Mount see Kirinyaga
168 L7 **Kenyir, Tasik** var. Tasek Kenyir. ◎ Peninsular Malaysia
29 W10 **Kenyon** Minnesota, N USA
29 Y16 **Keokuk** Iowa, C USA
Keonjihargarh see Kendujhargarh
Kéos see Kéa
29 X16 **Keosauqua** Iowa, C USA
29 X15 **Keota** Iowa, C USA
21 O11 **Keowee, Lake** ⊞ South Carolina, SE USA
124 I7 **Kepa** var. Kepe. Respublika Kareliya, NW Russia
Kepe see Kepa
189 O13 **Kepirohi Falls** waterfall Pohnpei, E Micronesia
185 B22 **Kepler Mountains** ▲▲ South Island, NZ
111 I14 **Kępno** Wielkopolskie, C Poland
65 C24 **Keppel Island** island N Falkland Islands
Keppel Island see Niuatoputapu
65 C23 **Keppel Sound** sound N Falkland Islands
136 D12 **Kepsut** Balıkesir, NW Turkey
168 M11 **Kepulauan Riau** off. Propinsi Kepulauan Riau. ◈ province NW Indonesia
171 V13 **Kerai** Papua, E Indonesia
Kerak see Al Karak
155 F22 **Kerala** ◈ state S India
165 R16 **Kerama-rettō** island group SW Japan
183 N10 **Kerang** Victoria, SE Australia
Kerasunt see Giresun
115 H19 **Keratéa** var. Keratea. Attikí, C Greece
93 M19 **Kerava** Swe. Kervo. Etelä-Suomi, S Finland
Kerbala/Kerbela see Karbalā'
32 F15 **Kerby** Oregon, NW USA
117 W12 **Kerch** Rus. Kerch'. Respublika Krym, SE Ukraine
Kerchens'ka Protska/ Kerchenskiy Proliv see Kerch Strait
117 V13 **Kerchens'kyy Pivostriv** peninsula S Ukraine
121 V4 **Kerch Strait** var. Bosporus Cimmerius, Enikale Strait, Rus. Kerchenskiy Proliv, Ukr. Kerchens'ka Protska. strait Black Sea/Sea of Azov
152 K8 **Kerdārnāth** Uttaranchal, N India
Kerdilio see Kerdýlio
114 H13 **Kerdýlio** var. Kerdilio. ▲ N Greece
186 D8 **Kerema** Gulf, S PNG
Keremitlik see Lyulyakovo
136 I9 **Kerempe Burnu** headland N Turkey
80 J9 **Keren** var. Cheren. C Eritrea
25 U7 **Kerens** Texas, SW USA
184 M6 **Kerepehi** Waikato, North Island, NZ
145 P10 **Kerey, Ozero** ◎ C Kazakhstan
Kergel see Kärla
173 Q12 **Kerguelen** island C French Southern and Antarctic Territories
173 Q13 **Kerguelen Plateau** undersea feature S Indian Ocean
115 C20 **Kerí** Zákynthos, Iónioi Nísoi, Greece
81 H19 **Kericho** Rift Valley, W Kenya
184 K2 **Kerikeri** Northland, North Island, NZ
93 O17 **Kerimäki** Isä-Suomi, E Finland
168 K12 **Kerinci, Gunung** ▲ Sumatera, W Indonesia
Keriya see Yutian
158 H9 **Keriya He** ≈ NW China
98 J9 **Kerkbuurt** Noord-Holland, C Netherlands
98 J13 **Kerkdriel** Gelderland, C Netherlands
75 N6 **Kerkenah, Îles de** var. Kerkenna Islands, Ar. Juzur Qarqannah. island group E Tunisia
Kerkenna Islands see Kerkenah, Îles de
115 M20 **Kerketévs** ▲ Sámos, Dodekánisos, Greece, Aegean Sea
29 T8 **Kerkhoven** Minnesota, N USA
Kerki see Atamyrat
Kerkichi see Kerkiçi
146 M14 **Kerkiçi** Rus. Kerkichi. Lebap Welaýaty, E Turkmenistan
115 F16 **Kerkíneo** prehistoric site Thessalía, C Greece
114 G12 **Kerkinítis, Límni** ◎ N Greece
Kérkira see Kérkyra
99 M18 **Kerkrade** Limburg, SE Netherlands
Kerkuk see Kirkūk
115 B16 **Kerkyra** ✕ Kérkyra, Iónioi Nísoi, Greece
115 B16 **Kérkyra** var. Kérkira, Eng. Corfu. Kérkyra, Iónioi Nísoi, Greece, C Mediterranean Sea
115 A16 **Kérkyra** var. Kérkira, Eng. Corfu. island Iónioi Nísoi, Greece, C Mediterranean Sea
192 K10 **Kermadec Islands** island group NZ, SW Pacific Ocean
175 R10 **Kermadec Ridge** undersea feature SW Pacific Ocean
175 R11 **Kermadec Trench** undersea feature SW Pacific Ocean
143 S10 **Kermān** var. Kirman; anc. Carmana. Kermān, C Iran
143 R11 **Kermān** off. Ostān-e Kermān, var. Kirman; anc. Carmania. ◈ province SE Iran
143 U12 **Kermān, Bīābān-e** var. Kerman Desert. desert SE Iran
142 K6 **Kermānshāh** var. Qahremānshahr; prev. Bākhtarān. Kermānshāh, W Iran
143 Q9 **Kermānshāh** Yazd, C Iran
142 J6 **Kermānshāh** off. Ostān-e Kermānshāh; prev. Bākhtarān, Kermānshāhān. ◈ province W Iran
Kermānshāhān see Kermānshāh
114 L10 **Kermen** Sliven, C Bulgaria
24 L8 **Kermit** Texas, SW USA
21 P6 **Kermit** West Virginia, NE USA
21 S9 **Kernersville** North Carolina, SE USA

◆ Country ● Country Capital ◇ Dependent Territory ○ Dependent Territory Capital ◈ Administrative Region ✕ International Airport ▲ Mountain ▲▲ Mountain Range Volcano ≈ River ◎ Lake ⊞ Reservoir

35 S12 **Kern River** ≈ California, W USA
35 S12 **Kernville** California, W USA
115 K21 **Kéros** *island* Kykládes, Greece, Aegean Sea
76 K14 **Kérouané** Haute-Guinée, SE Guinea
101 D16 **Kerpen** Nordrhein-Westfalen, W Germany
146 I11 **Kerpichli** Lebap Welaýaty, NE Turkmenistan
24 M1 **Kerrick** Texas, SW USA
Kerr Lake *see* John H.Kerr Reservoir
11 S15 **Kerrobert** Saskatchewan, S Canada
25 Q11 **Kerrville** Texas, SW USA
97 B20 **Kerry** *Ir.* Ciarraí. *cultural region* SW Ireland
21 S11 **Kershaw** South Carolina, SE USA
Kertel *see* Kärdla
95 H23 **Kerteminde** Fyn, C Denmark
163 Q7 **Kerulen** *Chin.* Herlen He, *Mong.* Herlen Gol. ≈ China/Mongolia
Kervo *see* Kerava
Kerýneia *see* Girne
12 H11 **Kesagami Lake** ◎ Ontario, SE Canada
93 O17 **Kesälahti** Itä-Suomi, E Finland
136 B11 **Keşan** Edirne, NW Turkey
165 R9 **Kesennuma** Miyagi, Honshū, C Japan
163 V7 **Keshan** Heilongjiang, NE China
30 M6 **Keshena** Wisconsin, N USA
136 I13 **Keskin** Kırıkkale, C Turkey
Késmárk *see* Kežmarok
124 I6 **Kesten'ga** *var.* Kest Enga. Respublika Kareliya, NW Russian Federation
98 K12 **Kesteren** Gelderland, C Netherlands
14 H14 **Keswick** Ontario, S Canada
97 K15 **Keswick** NW England, UK
111 H24 **Keszthely** Zala, SW Hungary
122 K11 **Ket'** ≈ C Russian Federation
77 R17 **Keta** SE Ghana
169 Q12 **Ketapang** Borneo, C Indonesia
127 O12 **Ketchenery** *prev.* Sovetskoye. Respublika Kalmykiya, SW Russian Federation
39 Y14 **Ketchikan** Revillagigedo Island, Alaska, USA
33 O14 **Ketchum** Idaho, NW USA
Kete/Kete Krakye *see* Kete-Krachi
77 Q15 **Kete-Krachi** *var.* Kete, Kete Krakye. E Ghana
98 L9 **Ketelmeer** *channel* E Netherlands
149 P17 **Keti Bandar** Sind, SE Pakistan
145 W16 **Ketmen', Khrebet** ▲▲ SE Kazakhstan
77 S16 **Kétou** SE Benin
110 M7 **Kętrzyn** *Ger.* Rastenburg. Warmińsko-Mazurskie, NE Poland,
97 N20 **Kettering** C England, UK
31 R14 **Kettering** Ohio, N USA
18 F13 **Kettle Creek** ≈ Pennsylvania, NE USA
32 L7 **Kettle Falls** Washington, NW USA
14 D16 **Kettle Point** *headland* Ontario, S Canada
29 V6 **Kettle River** ≈ Minnesota, N USA
186 B7 **Ketu** ≈ W PNG
18 G10 **Keuka Lake** ◎ New York, NE USA
Keupriya *see* Primorsko
93 L17 **Keuruu** Länsi-Suomi, W Finland
Kevevára *see* Kovin
92 L9 **Kevo** *Lapp.* Geavvú. Lappi, N Finland
44 M6 **Kew** North Caicos, N Turks and Caicos Islands
30 K11 **Kewanee** Illinois, N USA
31 N7 **Kewaunee** Wisconsin, N USA
30 M3 **Keweenaw Bay** ◎ Michigan, N USA
31 N2 **Keweenaw Peninsula** *peninsula* Michigan, N USA
31 N2 **Keweenaw Point** *headland* Michigan, N USA
29 N12 **Keya Paha River** ≈ Nebraska/South Dakota, N USA
Keyaygyr *see* Këk-Aygyr
23 Z16 **Key Biscayne** Florida, SE USA
26 G8 **Keyes** Oklahoma, C USA
23 Y17 **Key Largo** Key Largo, Florida, SE USA
21 U3 **Keyser** West Virginia, NE USA
27 O9 **Keystone Lake** ▣ Oklahoma, C USA
36 L16 **Keystone Peak** ▲ Arizona, SW USA
Keystone State *see* Pennsylvania
21 U7 **Keysville** Virginia, NE USA
27 T3 **Keytesville** Missouri, C USA
23 W17 **Key West** Florida Keys, Florida, SE USA
127 T1 **Kez** Udmurtskaya Respublika, NW Russian Federation
Kezdivásárhely *see* Târgu Secuiesc
122 M12 **Kezhma** Krasnoyarskiy Kray, C Russian Federation
111 L18 **Kežmarok** *Ger.* Käsmark, *Hung.* Késmárk. Prešovský Kraj, E Slovakia
Kfar Saba *see* Kefar Sava
83 F20 **Kgalagadi** ◈ *district* SW Botswana
83 I20 **Kgatleng** ◈ *district* SE Botswana
188 F8 **Kgkeklau** Babeldaob, N Palau
125 R6 **Khabarikha** *var.* Chabaricha. Respublika Komi, NW Russian Federation
123 S14 **Khabarovsk** Khabarovskiy Kray, SE Russian Federation
123 R11 **Khabarovskiy Kray** ◈ *territory* E Russian Federation
141 W7 **Khabb** Abū Ẓaby, E UAE
Khabour, Nahr al *see* Khābūr, Nahr al
Khabura *see* Al Khābūrah
139 N2 **Khābūr, Nahr al** *var.* Nahr al Khabour. ≈ Syria/Turkey
Khachmas *see* Xaçmaz
80 B12 **Khadari** ≈ W Sudan
Khadera *see* Hadera
141 X12 **Khādhil** *var.* Khudal. SE Oman
155 E14 **Khadki** *prev.* Kirkee. Mahārāshtra, W India
126 L14 **Khadyzhensk** Krasnodarskiy Kray, SW Russian Federation
114 N9 **Khadzhiyska Reka** ≈ E Bulgaria
117 P10 **Khadzhybeys'kyy Lyman** ◎ SW Ukraine
138 K3 **Khafsah** Ḥalab, N Syria
152 M13 **Khāga** Uttar Pradesh, N India
153 Q13 **Khagaria** Bihār, NE India
149 Q13 **Khairpur** Sind, SE Pakistan
122 K13 **Khakasiya, Respublika** *prev.* Khakasskaya Avtonomnaya Oblast', *Eng.* Khakassia. ◈ *autonomous republic* C Russian Federation
Khakassia/Khakasskaya Avtonomnaya Oblast' *see* Khakasiya, Respublika
167 N9 **Kha Khaeng, Khao** ▲ W Thailand
83 G20 **Khakhea** *var.* Kakia. Southern, S Botswana
Khalach *see* Halaç
Khalándrion *see* Chalándri
127 W7 **Khalilovo** Orenburgskaya Oblast', W Russian Federation
Khalkabad *see* Xalqobod
142 L3 **Khalkhāl** *prev.* Herowābād. Ardabīl, NW Iran
Khalkidhikí *see* Chalkidikí
Khalkís *see* Chalkída
125 W3 **Khal'mer-Yu** Respublika Komi, NW Russian Federation
119 M14 **Khalopyenichy** *Rus.* Kholopenichi. Minskaya Voblasts', NE Belarus
Khalturin *see* Orlov
141 Y10 **Khalūf** *var.* Al Khaluf. E Oman
154 K10 **Khamaria** Madhya Pradesh, C India
154 D11 **Khambhāt** Gujarāt, W India
154 C12 **Khambhāt, Gulf of** *Eng.* Gulf of Cambay. *gulf* W India
167 U10 **Khâm Đưc** Quang Nam-Đa Nāng, C Vietnam
154 G12 **Khāmgaon** Mahārāshtra, C India
141 O14 **Khamir** *var.* Khamr. W Yemen
141 N12 **Khamīs Mushayt** *var.* Hamīs Musait. 'Asīr, SW Saudi Arabia
123 P10 **Khampa** Respublika Sakha (Yakutiya), NE Russian Federation
Khamr *see* Khamir
83 C19 **Khan** ≈ W Namibia
149 Q2 **Khānābād** Kunduz, NE Afghanistan
Khān Abou Châmâte/Khan Abou Ech Cham *see* Khān Abū Shāmāt
138 I7 **Khān Abū Shāmāt** *var.* Khān Abou Châmâte, Khan Abou Ech Cham. Dimashq, W Syria
Khān al Baghdādī *see* Al Baghdādī
Khān al Maḥāwīl *see* Al Maḥāwīl
139 T7 **Khān al Mashāhidah** C Iraq
139 T10 **Khān al Muṣallá** S Iraq
139 U6 **Khānaqīn** E Iraq
139 T11 **Khān ar Ruḥbah** S Iraq
139 P2 **Khān as Sūr** N Iraq
139 T8 **Khān Āzād** C Iraq
154 N13 **Khandaparha** *prev.* Khandpara. Orissa, E India
Khandpara *see* Khandaparha
149 T2 **Khandūd** *var.* Khandud, Wakhan. Badakhshān, NE Afghanistan
154 G11 **Khandwa** Madhya Pradesh, C India
123 R10 **Khandyga** Respublika Sakha (Yakutiya), NE Russian Federation
149 T10 **Khānewāl** Punjab, NE Pakistan
149 S10 **Khāngarh** Punjab, E Pakistan
Khanh Hung *see* Soc Trăng
Khaniá *see* Chaniá
Khanka *see* Xonqa
163 Z8 **Khanka, Lake** *var.* Hsing-k'ai Hu, Lake Hanka, *Chin.* Xingkai Hu, *Rus.* Ozero Khanka. ◎ China/Russian Federation
Khanka, Ozero *see* Khanka, Lake
Khankendi *see* Xankändi
Khanlar *see* Xanlar
123 O9 **Khannya** ≈ NE Russian Federation
149 S12 **Khānpur** Punjab, SE Pakistan
149 S12 **Khānpur** Punjab, E Pakistan
138 I4 **Khān Shaykhūn** *var.* Khan Sheikhun. Idlib, NW Syria
Khan Sheikhun *see* Khān Shaykhūn
145 S15 **Khantau** Zhambyl, S Kazakhstan
145 W16 **Khan Tengri, Pik** ▲ SE Kazakhstan
167 S9 **Khanthabouli** *prev.* Savannakhét. Savannakhét, S Laos
127 V8 **Khanty-Mansiyskiy Avtonomnyy Okrug** ◈ *autonomous district* C Russian Federation
139 R4 **Khānūqah** C Iraq
138 E11 **Khān Yūnis** *var.* Khān Yūnus. S Gaza Strip
Khān Yūnus *see* Khān Yūnis
Khanzi *see* Ghanzi
139 U5 **Khān Zūr** E Iraq
167 N10 **Khao Laem Reservoir** ▣ W Thailand
123 O14 **Khapcheranga** Chitinskaya Oblast', S Russian Federation
127 Q12 **Kharabali** Astrakhanskaya Oblast', SW Russian Federation
153 R16 **Kharagpur** West Bengal, NE India
139 V11 **Kharā'ib 'Abd al Karīm** S Iraq
143 Q8 **Kharānaq** Yazd, C Iran
Kharbin *see* Harbin
146 H13 **Khardzhagaz** Ahal Welaýaty, C Turkmenistan
Khārga Oasis *see* Great Oasis, The
154 F11 **Khargon** Madhya Pradesh, C India
149 V7 **Khāriān** Punjab, NE Pakistan
117 X8 **Kharisyz'k** Donets'ka Oblast', E Ukraine
117 V5 **Kharkiv** *Rus.* Khar'kov. Kharkivs'ka Oblast', NE Ukraine
117 V5 **Kharkiv** ✕ Kharkivs'ka Oblast', E Ukraine
Kharkiv *see* Kharkivs'ka Oblast'
117 U5 **Kharkivs'ka Oblast'** *var.* Kharkiv, *Rus.* Khar'kovskaya Oblast'. ◈ *province* E Ukraine
Khar'kov *see* Kharkiv
Khar'kovskaya Oblast' *see* Kharkivs'ka Oblast'
124 L3 **Kharlovka** Murmanskaya Oblast', NW Russian Federation
114 K11 **Kharmanli** Khaskovo, S Bulgaria
114 K11 **Kharmanliyska Reka** ≈ S Bulgaria
124 M13 **Kharovsk** Vologodskaya Oblast', NW Russian Federation
80 F9 **Khartoum** *var.* El Khartûm, Khartum. ● (Sudan) Khartoum, C Sudan
80 F9 **Khartoum** ◈ *state* NE Sudan
80 F9 **Khartoum** ✕ Khartoum, C Sudan
80 F9 **Khartoum North** Khartoum, C Sudan
117 X8 **Khartsyz'k** *Rus.* Khartsyzsk. Donets'ka Oblast', SE Ukraine
Khartsyzsk *see* Khartsyz'k
Khartum *see* Khartoum
Khasab *see* Al Khaṣab
123 S15 **Khasan** Primorskiy Kray, SE Russian Federation
127 P16 **Khasavyurt** Respublika Dagestan, SW Russian Federation
143 W12 **Khāsh** *prev.* Vāsht. Sīstān va Balūchestān, SE Iran
148 K8 **Khāsh, Dasht-e** *Eng.* Khash Desert. *desert* SW Afghanistan
Khash Desert *see* Khāsh, Dasht-e
Khashim Al Qirba/Khashm al Qirbah *see* Khashm el Girba
80 H9 **Khashm el Girba** *var.* Khashim Al Qirba, Khashm al Qirbah. Kassala, E Sudan
138 G14 **Khashsh, Jabal al** ▲ S Jordan
137 S10 **Khashuri** C Georgia
153 V13 **Khāsi Hills** *hill range* NE India
114 K11 **Khaskovo** Khaskovo, S Bulgaria
114 K11 **Khaskovo** ◈ *province* S Bulgaria
122 M7 **Khatanga** ≈ N Russian Federation
Khatanga, Gulf of *see* Khatangskiy Zaliv
123 N7 **Khatangskiy Zaliv** *var.* Gulf of Khatanga. *bay* N Russian Federation
141 W7 **Khatmat al Malāḥah** N Oman
143 S16 **Khaṭmat al Malāḥah** Ash Shāriqah, E UAE
123 V7 **Khatyrka** Chukotskiy Avtonomnyy Okrug, NE Russian Federation
Khauz-Khan *see* Hanhowuz
Khauzkhanskoye Vodokhranilishche *see* Hanhowuz Suw Howdany
Khavaling *see* Khovaling
Khavast *see* Xovos
139 W10 **Khawrah, Nahr al** ≈ S Iraq
Khawr Barakah *see* Baraka
141 W7 **Khawr Fakkān** *var.* Khor Fakkan. Ash Shāriqah, NE UAE
140 L6 **Khaybar** Al Madīnah, NW Saudi Arabia
Khaybar, Kowtal-e *see* Khyber Pass
147 S11 **Khaydarkan** *var.* Khaydarken. Batkenskaya Oblast', SW Kyrgyzstan
Khaydarken *see* Khaydarkan
127 U2 **Khaypudyrskaya Guba** *bay* NW Russian Federation
139 S1 **Khayrūzuk** E Iraq
Khazar, Baḥr-e/Khazar, Daryā-ye *see* Caspian Sea
Khazarosp *see* Hazorasp
Khazretishi, Khrebet *see* Hazratishoh, Qatorkŭhi
Khelat *see* Kālat
74 F6 **Khemisset** NW Morocco
167 R10 **Khemmarat** *var.* Kemarat. Ubon Ratchathani, E Thailand
74 L6 **Khenchela** *var.* Khenchla. NE Algeria
Khenchla *see* Khenchela
74 G7 **Khénifra** C Morocco
Khersān, Rūd-e *see* Garm, Āb-e
117 R10 **Kherson** Khersons'ka Oblast', S Ukraine
Kherson *see* Khersons'ka Oblast'
117 S14 **Khersones, Mys** *Rus.* Mys Khersonesskiy. *headland* S Ukraine
Khersonesskiy, Mys *see* Khersones, Mys
117 R10 **Khersons'ka Oblast'** *var.* Kherson, *Rus.* Khersonskaya Oblast'. ◈ *province* S Ukraine
Khersonskaya Oblast' *see* Khersons'ka Oblast'
122 L8 **Kheta** ≈ N Russian Federation
167 S8 **Khe Ve** Quang Binh, C Vietnam
149 U7 **Khewra** Punjab, E Pakistan
Khiam *see* El Khiyam
126 J4 **Khibiny** ▲▲ NW Russian Federation
126 K3 **Khimki** Moskovskaya Oblast', W Russian Federation
147 S12 **Khingov** *Rus.* Obi-Khingou. ≈ C Tajikistan
Khíos *see* Chíos
149 R15 **Khipro** Sind, SE Pakistan
139 S10 **Khirr, Wādī al** *dry watercourse* S Iraq
114 I10 **Khisarya** Plovdiv, C Bulgaria
Khiva *see* Xiva
167 N9 **Khlong Khlung** Kamphaeng Phet, W Thailand
167 N15 **Khlong Thom** Krabi, SW Thailand
167 P12 **Khlung** Chantaburi, S Thailand
Khmel'nik *see* Khmil'nyk
Khmel'nitskaya Oblast' *see* Khmel'nyts'ka Oblast'
Khmel'nitskiy *see* Khmel 'nyts'kyy
116 K5 **Khmel'nyts'ka Oblast'** *var.* Khmel'nyts'kyy, *Rus.* Khmel'nitskaya Oblast'; *prev.* Kamenets-Podol'skaya Oblast'. ◈ *province* NW Ukraine
116 L6 **Khmel 'nyts'kyy** *Rus.* Khmel'nitskiy; *prev.* Proskurov. Khmel'nyts'ka Oblast', W Ukraine
Khmel'nyts'kyy *see* Khmel'nyts'ka Oblast'
116 M6 **Khmil'nyk** *Rus.* Khmel'nik. Vinnyts'ka Oblast', C Ukraine
144 I10 **Khobda** *prev.* Novoalekseyevka. Aktyubinsk, W Kazakhstan
137 R9 **Khobi** W Georgia
119 P15 **Khodasy** *Rus.* Khodosy. Mahilyowskaya Voblasts', E Belarus
116 I6 **Khodoriv** *Pol.* Chodorów, *Rus.* Khodorov. L'vivs'ka Oblast', NW Ukraine
Khodorov *see* Khodoriv
Khodosy *see* Khodasy
Khodzhakala *see* Hojagala
Khodzhambas *see* Hojambaz
Khodzhent *see* Khŭjand
Khodzheyli *see* Xo'jayli
Khoi *see* Khvoy
Khojend *see* Khŭjand
Khokand *see* Qo'qon
126 L8 **Khokhol'skiy** Voronezhskaya Oblast', W Russian Federation
167 P10 **Khok Samrong** Lop Buri, C Thailand
149 P2 **Kholm** *var.* Tashqurghan, *Pash.* Khulm. Balkh, N Afghanistan
124 H15 **Kholm** Novgorodskaya Oblast', W Russian Federation
Kholm *see* Chełm
Kholmech' *see* Kholmyech
123 T13 **Kholmsk** Ostrov Sakhalin, Sakhalinskaya Oblast', SE Russian Federation
119 O19 **Kholmyech** *Rus.* Kholmech'. Homyel'skaya Voblasts', SE Belarus
Kholon *see* Holon
Kholopenichi *see* Khalopyenichy
83 D19 **Khomas** ◈ *district* C Namibia
83 D19 **Khomas Hochland** *var.* Khomasplato. *plateau* C Namibia
Khomasplato *see* Khomas Hochland
Khomein *see* Khomeyn
142 M7 **Khomeyn** *var.* Khomein, Khumain. Markazī, W Iran
143 N8 **Khomeynīshahr** *prev.* Homāyūnshahr. Eṣfahān, C Iran
Khoms *see* Al Khums
Khong Sedone *see* Muang Khôngxédôn
167 Q9 **Khon Kaen** *var.* Muang Khon Kaen. Khon Kaen, E Thailand
167 Q9 **Khon San** Khon Kaen, E Thailand
123 R8 **Khonuu** Respublika Sakha (Yakutiya), NE Russian Federation
127 N8 **Khopër** *var.* Khoper. ≈ SW Russian Federation
123 S14 **Khor** Khabarovskiy Kray, SE Russian Federation
143 S6 **Khorāsān** *off.* Ostān-e Khorāsān, *var.* Khorassan, Khurasan. ◈ *province* NE Iran
Khorassan *see* Khorāsān
Khorat *see* Nakhon Ratchasima
154 O13 **Khordha** *prev.* Khurda. Orissa, E India
125 U4 **Khorey-Ver** Nenetskiy Avtonomnyy Okrug, NW Russian Federation
Khorezmskaya Oblast' *see* Xorazm Viloyati
Khor Fakkan *see* Khawr Fakkān
145 W15 **Khorgos** Almaty, SE Kazakhstan
123 N13 **Khorinsk** Respublika Buryatiya, S Russian Federation
83 C18 **Khorixas** Kunene, NW Namibia
141 O17 **Khormaksar** *var.* Aden. ✕ ('Aden) SW Yemen
Khormal *see* Khurmāl
Khormuj *see* Khvormūj
Khorog *see* Khorugh
117 S5 **Khorol** Poltavs'ka Oblast', NE Ukraine
142 L7 **Khorramābād** *var.* Khurramabad. Lorestān, W Iran
142 K10 **Khorramshahr** *var.* Khurramshahr, Muhammerah; *prev.* Mohammerah. Khūzestān, SW Iran
147 S14 **Khorugh** *Rus.* Khorog. S Tajikistan
127 Q12 **Khosheutovo** Astrakhanskaya Oblast', SW Russian Federation
Khotan *see* Hotan
Khorvot Khalutsa *see* Horvot Haluza
Khotimsk *see* Khotsimsk
Khotin *see* Khotyn
119 R16 **Khotsimsk** *Rus.* Khotimsk. Mahilyowskaya Voblasts', E Belarus
116 K7 **Khotyn** *Rom.* Hotin, *Rus.* Khotin. Chernivets'ka Oblast', W Ukraine
74 F7 **Khouribga** C Morocco
147 Q13 **Khovaling** *Rus.* Khavaling. SW Tajikistan
Khovd *see* Hovd
149 R6 **Khowst** Paktiā, E Afghanistan
Khoy *see* Khvoy
119 N20 **Khoyniki** *Rus.* Khoyniki. Homyel'skaya Voblasts', SE Belarus
Khozretishi, Khrebet *see* Hazratishoh, Qatorkŭhi
Khrisoúpolis *see* Chrysoúpoli
144 J10 **Khromtau** *Kaz.* Khromtaū. Aktyubinsk, W Kazakhstan
Khrysokhou Bay *see* Chrysochoú, Kólpos
117 O7 **Khrystynivka** Cherkas'ka Oblast', C Ukraine
167 R10 **Khuang Nai** Ubon Ratchathani, E Thailand
Khudal *see* Khādhil
Khudat *see* Xudat
149 W9 **Khudiān** Punjab, E Pakistan
Khudzhand *see* Khŭjand
147 O13 **Khufar** Surxondaryo Viloyati, S Uzbekistan
83 G21 **Khuis** Kgalagadi, SW Botswana
147 Q11 **Khŭjand** *var.* Khodzhent, Khojend, *Rus.* Khudzhand; *prev.* Leninabad, *Taj.* Leninobod. N Tajikistan
167 R11 **Khukhan** Si Sa Ket, E Thailand
Khulm *see* Kholm
153 T16 **Khulna** Khulna, SW Bangladesh
153 T16 **Khulna** ◈ *division* SW Bangladesh
Khumain *see* Khomeyn
Khums *see* Al Khums
149 W2 **Khunjerāb Pass** *Chin.* Kunjirap Daban. *pass* China/Pakistan *see also* Kunjirap Daban
153 P16 **Khunti** Jhārkhand, N India
167 N7 **Khun Yuam** Mae Hong Son, NW Thailand
Khurais *see* Khurayṣ
Khurasan *see* Khorāsān
141 R7 **Khurayṣ** *var.* Khurais. Ash Sharqīyah, C Saudi Arabia
Khurda *see* Khordha
152 J11 **Khurja** Uttar Pradesh, N India
139 V4 **Khurmāl** *var.* Khormal. NE Iraq
Khurramabad *see* Khorramābād
Khurramshahr *see* Khorramshahr
149 U7 **Khushāb** Punjab, NE Pakistan
116 H8 **Khust** *Cz.* Chust, Husté, *Hung.* Huszt. Zakarpats'ka Oblast', W Ukraine
80 D11 **Khuwei** Western Kordofan, C Sudan
149 O13 **Khuzdār** Baluchistān, SW Pakistan
142 L9 **Khūzestān** *off.* Ostān-e Khūzestān, *var.* Khuzistan; *prev.* Arabistan, *anc.* Susiana. ◈ *province* SW Iran
Khuzistan *see* Khūzestān
149 R2 **Khvājeh Ghār** *var.* Khwajaghar, Khwaja-i-Ghar. Takhār, NE Afghanistan
127 Q7 **Khvalynsk** Saratovskaya Oblast', W Russian Federation
143 N12 **Khvormūj** *var.* Khormuj. Būshehr, S Iran
142 I2 **Khvoy** *var.* Khoi, Khoy. Āžarbāyjān-e Bākhtarī, NW Iran
Khwajaghar/Khwaja-i-Ghar *see* Khvājeh Ghār
149 S5 **Khyber Pass** *var.* Kowtal-e Khaybar. *pass* Afghanistan/Pakistan
186 L8 **Kia** Santa Isabel, N Solomon Islands
183 S10 **Kiama** New South Wales, SE Australia
79 O22 **Kiambi** Katanga, SE Dem. Rep. Congo
27 Q12 **Kiamichi Mountains** ▲▲ Oklahoma, C USA
27 Q12 **Kiamichi River** ≈ Oklahoma, C USA
14 M10 **Kiamika, Réservoir** ▣ Québec, SE Canada
Kiamusze *see* Jiamusi
39 N7 **Kiana** Alaska, USA
Kiangmai *see* Chiang Mai
Kiang-ning *see* Nanjing
Kiangsi *see* Jiangxi
Kiangsu *see* Jiangsu
93 M14 **Kiantajärvi** ◎ E Finland
115 F19 **Kiáto** *prev.* Kiáton. Pelopónnisos, S Greece
Kiáton *see* Kiáto
Kiayi *see* Chiai
67 T9 **Kibali** *var.* Uele (upper course). ≈ NE Dem. Rep. Congo
79 E20 **Kibangou** Le Niari, SW Congo
Kibarty *see* Kybartai
92 M8 **Kiberg** Finnmark, N Norway
95 F22 **Kibæk** Ringkøbing, W Denmark
79 N20 **Kibombo** Maniema, E Dem. Rep. Congo
81 E20 **Kibondo** Kigoma, NW Tanzania
81 J15 **Kibre Mengist** *var.* Adola. Oromo, C Ethiopia
Kıbrıs/Kıbrıs Cumhuriyeti *see* Cyprus
81 E20 **Kibungo** *var.* Kibungu. SE Rwanda
Kibungu *see* Kibungo
113 N19 **Kičevo** SW FYR Macedonia
125 P13 **Kichmengskiy Gorodok** Vologodskaya Oblast', NW Russian Federation
30 J8 **Kickapoo River** ≈ Wisconsin, N USA
11 P16 **Kicking Horse Pass** *pass* Alberta/British Columbia, SW Canada
77 R9 **Kidal** Kidal, C Mali
77 Q8 **Kidal** ◈ *region* NE Mali
171 Q7 **Kidapawan** Mindanao, S Philippines
97 L20 **Kidderminster** C England, UK
76 I11 **Kidira** E Senegal
184 O11 **Kidnappers, Cape** *headland* North Island, NZ
100 J8 **Kiel** Schleswig-Holstein, N Germany
111 L15 **Kielce** *Rus.* Keltsy. Świętokrzyskie, C Poland
100 K7 **Kieler Bucht** *bay* N Germany
100 J7 **Kieler Förde** *inlet* N Germany
167 U13 **Kiên Đưc** *var.* Đak Lap. Đăc Lăc, S Vietnam
79 N24 **Kienge** Katanga, SE Dem. Rep. Congo
100 Q12 **Kietz** Brandenburg, NE Germany
Kiev *see* Kyyiv
Kiev Reservoir *see* Kyyivs'ke Vodoskhovyshche
76 J10 **Kiffa** Assaba, S Mauritania
115 H19 **Kifisiá** Attikí, C Greece
115 F18 **Kifisós** ≈ C Greece
139 U5 **Kifrī** N Iraq
81 D20 **Kigali** ● (Rwanda) C Rwanda
81 E20 **Kigali** ✕ C Rwanda
137 P13 **Kiğı** Bingöl, E Turkey
81 E21 **Kigoma** Kigoma, W Tanzania
81 E21 **Kigoma** ◈ *region* W Tanzania
38 F10 **Kīhei** *var.* Kihei. Maui, Hawai'i, USA, C Pacific Ocean
93 K17 **Kihniö** Länsi-Suomi, W Finland
118 F6 **Kihnu** *var.* Kihnu Saar, *Ger.* Kühnö. *island* SW Estonia
Kihnu Saar *see* Kihnu
38 A8 **Kii Landing** Ni'ihau, Hawai'i, USA, C Pacific Ocean
93 L14 **Kiiminki** Oulu, C Finland
164 J14 **Kii-Nagashima** *var.* Nagashima. Mie, Honshū, SW Japan
164 J14 **Kii-sanchi** ▲▲ Honshū, SW Japan
92 L11 **Kiistala** Lappi, N Finland
164 I15 **Kii-suidō** *strait* S Japan
165 V16 **Kikai-shima** *var.* Kikaiga-shima. *island* Nansei-shotō, SW Japan
112 M8 **Kikinda** *Ger.* Grosskikinda, *Hung.* Nagykikinda; *prev.* Velika Kikinda. Serbia, N Serbia and Montenegro (Yugo.)
Kikládhes *see* Kykládes
165 Q5 **Kikonai** Hokkaidō, NE Japan
186 C8 **Kikori** Gulf, S PNG
186 C8 **Kikori** ≈ W PNG
165 O14 **Kikuchi** *var.* Kikuti. Kumamoto, Kyūshū, SW Japan
Kikuti *see* Kikuchi
127 N8 **Kikvidze** Volgogradskaya Oblast', SW Russian Federation
14 I10 **Kikwissi, Lac** ◎ Québec, SE Canada
79 I21 **Kikwit** Bandundu, W Dem. Rep. Congo
95 K15 **Kil** Värmland, C Sweden
94 N12 **Kilafors** Gävleborg, C Sweden
38 B8 **Kilauea** *var.* Kilauea. Kaua'i, Hawai'i, USA, C Pacific Ocean
38 H12 **Kilauea Caldera** *var.* Kilauea Caldera *crater* Hawai'i, USA, C Pacific Ocean
109 V4 **Kilb** Niederösterreich, C Austria
39 O12 **Kilbuck Mountains** ▲▲ Alaska, USA
163 Y12 **Kilchu** NE North Korea
97 F18 **Kilcock** *Ir.* Cill Choca. E Ireland
183 V2 **Kilcoy** Queensland, E Australia
97 F18 **Kildare** *Ir.* Cill Dara. E Ireland
97 F18 **Kildare** *Ir.* Cill Dara. *cultural region* E Ireland
126 K2 **Kil'din, Ostrov** *island* NW Russian Federation
25 W7 **Kilgore** Texas, SW USA
Kilien Mountains *see* Qilian Shan
114 K9 **Kilifarevo** Veliko Tŭrnovo, N Bulgaria
81 K20 **Kilifi** Coast, SE Kenya
189 U9 **Kili Island** *var.* Kōle. *island* Ralik Chain, S Marshall Islands
149 V2 **Kilik Pass** *pass* Afghanistan/China
Kilimane *see* Quelimane
81 I21 **Kilimanjaro** ◈ *region* E Tanzania
81 I20 **Kilimanjaro** *var.* Uhuru Peak. ▲ NE Tanzania
Kilimbangara *see* Kolombangara
Kilinailau Islands *see* Tulun Islands
81 K23 **Kilindoni** Pwani, E Tanzania
118 H6 **Kilingi-Nõmme** *Ger.* Kurkund. Pärnumaa, SW Estonia
136 M17 **Kilis** Kilis, S Turkey
136 M16 **Kilis** ◈ *province* S Turkey
117 N12 **Kiliya** *Rom.* Chilia-Nouă. Odes'ka Oblast', SW Ukraine
97 B19 **Kilkee** *Ir.* Cill Chaoi. W Ireland
97 E19 **Kilkenny** *Ir.* Cill Chainnigh. S Ireland
97 E19 **Kilkenny** *Ir.* Cill Chainnigh. *cultural region* S Ireland
97 B18 **Kilkieran Bay** *Ir.* Cuan Chill Chiaráin. *bay* W Ireland
114 G13 **Kilkís** Kentrikí Makedonía, N Greece
97 C15 **Killala Bay** *Ir.* Cuan Chill Ala. *inlet* NW Ireland
11 R15 **Killam** Alberta, SW Canada
183 U3 **Killarney** Queensland, E Australia
11 W17 **Killarney** Manitoba, S Canada

◆ Country ● Country Capital ◇ Dependent Territory ○ Dependent Territory Capital ◈ Administrative Region ✕ International Airport ▲ Mountain ▲▲ Mountain Range Volcano ≈ River ◎ Lake ▣ Reservoir

14 E11 **Killarney** Ontario, S Canada
97 B20 **Killarney** *Ir.* Cill Airne. SW Ireland
28 K4 **Killdeer** North Dakota, N USA
28 J4 **Killdeer Mountains** ⛰ North Dakota, N USA
45 V15 **Killdeer River** ∽ Trinidad, Trinidad and Tobago
25 S9 **Killeen** Texas, SW USA
39 P6 **Killik River** ∽ Alaska, USA
9 T7 **Killinek Island** *island* Nunavut, NE Canada
Killini *see* Kyllíni
115 C19 **Killínis, Akrotírio** *headland* S Greece
97 D15 **Killybegs** *Ir.* Na Cealla Beaga. NW Ireland
Kilmain *see* Quelimane
96 I13 **Kilmarnock** W Scotland, UK
21 X6 **Kilmarnock** Virginia, NE USA
125 S16 **Kil'mez'** Kirovskaya Oblast', NW Russian Federation
127 S2 **Kil'mez'** Udmurtskaya Respublika, NW Russian Federation
127 R16 **Kil'mez'** ∽ NW Russian Federation
67 V11 **Kilombero** ∽ S Tanzania
92 J10 **Kilpisjarvi** Lappi, N Finland
97 B19 **Kilrush** *Ir.* Cill Rois. W Ireland
79 O24 **Kilwa** Katanga, SE Dem. Rep. Congo
Kilwa *see* Kilwa Kivinje
81 J24 **Kilwa Kivinje** *var.* Kilwa. Lindi, SE Tanzania
81 J24 **Kilwa Masoko** Lindi, SE Tanzania
171 T13 **Kilwo** Pulau Seram, E Indonesia
114 P12 **Kilyos** İstanbul, NW Turkey
37 V8 **Kim** Colorado, C USA
169 U7 **Kimanis, Teluk** *bay* Sabah, East Malaysia
182 H8 **Kimba** South Australia
28 I15 **Kimball** Nebraska, C USA
29 O11 **Kimball** South Dakota, N USA
79 I21 **Kimbao** Bandundu, SW Dem. Rep. Congo
186 F7 **Kimbe** New Britain, E PNG
186 G7 **Kimbe Bay** *inlet* New Britain, E PNG
11 P17 **Kimberley** British Columbia, SW Canada
83 H23 **Kimberley** Northern Cape, C South Africa
180 M4 **Kimberley Plateau** *plateau* Western Australia
33 P15 **Kimberly** Idaho, NW USA
163 Y12 **Kimch'aek** *prev.* Sŏngjin. E North Korea
163 Y15 **Kimch'ŏn** C South Korea
163 Z16 **Kim Hae** *var.* Pusan. × (Pusan) SE South Korea
Kími *see* Kými
93 K20 **Kimito** *Swe.* Kemiö. Länsi-Suomi, W Finland
165 R4 **Kimobetsu** Hokkaidō, NE Japan
115 I21 **Kímolos** *island* Kykládes, Greece, Aegean Sea
115 I21 **Kímolou Sífnou, Stenó** *strait* Kykládes, Greece, Aegean Sea
126 L5 **Kimovsk** Tul'skaya Oblast', W Russian Federation
Kimpolung *see* Câmpulung Moldovenesc
124 K16 **Kimry** Tverskaya Oblast', W Russian Federation
79 H21 **Kimvula** Bas-Congo, SW Dem. Rep. Congo
169 U6 **Kinabalu, Gunung** ▲ East Malaysia
Kinabatangan *see* Kinabatangan, Sungai
169 V7 **Kinabatangan, Sungai** *var.* Kinabatangan. ∽ East Malaysia
115 L21 **Kínaros** *island* Kykládes, Greece, Aegean Sea
11 O15 **Kinbasket Lake** ⊟ British Columbia, SW Canada
96 I7 **Kinbrace** N Scotland, UK
14 E14 **Kincardine** Ontario, S Canada
96 K10 **Kincardine** *cultural region* E Scotland, UK
79 K21 **Kinda** Kasai Occidental, SE Dem. Rep. Congo
79 M24 **Kinda** Katanga, SE Dem. Rep. Congo
166 L3 **Kindat** Sagaing, N Myanmar
109 V6 **Kindberg** Steiermark, C Austria
22 H8 **Kinder** Louisiana, S USA
98 H13 **Kinderdijk** Zuid-Holland, SW Netherlands
97 M17 **Kinder Scout** ▲ C England, UK
11 S16 **Kindersley** Saskatchewan, S Canada
76 I14 **Kindia** Guinée-Maritime, SW Guinea
64 B11 **Kindley Field** *air base* E Bermuda
29 R6 **Kindred** North Dakota, N USA
79 N20 **Kindu** *prev.* Kindu-Port-Empain. Maniema, C Dem. Rep. Congo
Kindu-Port-Empain *see* Kindu
127 S6 **Kinel'** Samarskaya Oblast', W Russian Federation
125 N15 **Kineshma** Ivanovskaya Oblast', W Russian Federation
King *see* King William's Town
140 K10 **King Abdul Aziz** × (Makkah) Makkah, W Saudi Arabia
21 X6 **King and Queen Court House** Virginia, NE USA
King Charles Islands *see* Kong Karls Land
King Christian IX Land *see* Kong Christian IX Land
King Christian X Land *see* Kong Christian X Land
35 O11 **King City** California, W USA
27 R2 **King City** Missouri, C USA
38 M16 **King Cove** Alaska, USA
26 M10 **Kingfisher** Oklahoma, C USA
King Frederik VI Coast *see* Kong Frederik VI Kyst
King Frederik VIII Land *see* Kong Frederik VIII Land
65 B24 **King George Bay** *bay* West Falkland, Falkland Islands
194 G3 **King George Island** *var.* King George Land. *island* South Shetland Islands, Antarctica
12 I6 **King George Islands** *island group* Nunavut, C Canada
King George Land *see* King George Island
124 G13 **Kingisepp** Leningradskaya Oblast', NW Russian Federation
183 N14 **King Island** *island* Tasmania, SE Australia
10 J15 **King Island** *island* British Columbia, SW Canada
King Island *see* Kadan Kyun
Kingissepp *see* Kuressaare
141 Q7 **King Khalid** × (Ar Riyāḍ) Ar Riyāḍ, C Saudi Arabia
35 S2 **King Lear Peak** ▲ Nevada, W USA
195 Y8 **King Leopold and Queen Astrid Land** *physical region* Antarctica
180 M4 **King Leopold Ranges** ⛰ Western Australia
36 I11 **Kingman** Arizona, SW USA
26 M6 **Kingman** Kansas, C USA
192 L7 **Kingman Reef** ◇ *US territory* C Pacific Ocean
79 N20 **Kingombe** Maniema, E Dem. Rep. Congo
182 F5 **Kingoonya** South Australia
194 J10 **King Peninsula** *peninsula* Antarctica
39 P13 **King Salmon** Alaska, USA
35 Q6 **Kings Beach** California, W USA
35 R11 **Kingsburg** California, W USA
182 I10 **Kingscote** South Australia
King's County *see* Offaly
194 H2 **King Sejong** *South Korean research station* Antarctica
183 T9 **Kingsford Smith** × (Sydney) New South Wales, SE Australia
11 P17 **Kingsgate** British Columbia, SW Canada
23 W8 **Kingsland** Georgia, SE USA
29 S13 **Kingsley** Iowa, C USA
97 O19 **King's Lynn** *var.* Bishop's Lynn, Kings Lynn, Lynn, Lynn Regis. E England, UK
21 Q10 **Kings Mountain** North Carolina, SE USA
180 K4 **King Sound** *sound* Western Australia
37 N2 **Kings Peak** ▲ Utah, W USA
21 O8 **Kingsport** Tennessee, S USA
35 R11 **Kings River** ∽ California, W USA
183 P17 **Kingston** Tasmania, SE Australia
14 K14 **Kingston** Ontario, SE Canada
44 K13 **Kingston** ● (Jamaica) E Jamaica
185 C22 **Kingston** Otago, South Island, NZ
19 P12 **Kingston** Massachusetts, NE USA
27 S3 **Kingston** Missouri, C USA
18 K12 **Kingston** New York, NE USA
31 S14 **Kingston** Ohio, N USA
19 O13 **Kingston** Rhode Island, NE USA
20 M9 **Kingston** Tennessee, S USA
35 W12 **Kingston Peak** ▲ California, W USA
182 J11 **Kingston Southeast** South Australia
97 N17 **Kingston upon Hull** *var.* Hull. E England, UK
97 N22 **Kingston upon Thames** SE England, UK
45 P14 **Kingstown** ● (Saint Vincent and the Grenadines) Saint Vincent, Saint Vincent and the Grenadines
Kingstown *see* Dún Laoghaire
21 T13 **Kingstree** South Carolina, SE USA
64 L8 **Kings Trough** *undersea feature* E Atlantic Ocean
14 C18 **Kingsville** Ontario, S Canada
25 S15 **Kingsville** Texas, SW USA
21 W6 **King William** Virginia, NE USA
8 M7 **King William Island** *island* Nunavut, N Canada Arctic Ocean
83 I25 **King William's Town** *var.* King, Kingwilliamstown. Eastern Cape, S South Africa
21 T3 **Kingwood** West Virginia, NE USA
136 C13 **Kınık** İzmir, W Turkey
79 G21 **Kinkala** Le Pool, S Congo
165 R10 **Kinka-san** *headland* Honshū, C Japan
184 M8 **Kinleith** Waikato, North Island, NZ
95 J19 **Kinna** Västra Götaland, S Sweden
96 L8 **Kinnaird Head** *var.* Kinnairds Head. *headland* NE Scotland, UK
95 K20 **Kinnared** Halland, S Sweden
Kinneret, Yam *see* Tiberias, Lake
155 K24 **Kinniyai** Eastern Province, NE Sri Lanka
93 L16 **Kinnula** Länsi-Suomi, W Finland
14 I8 **Kinojévis** ∽ Québec, SE Canada
164 I14 **Kino-kawa** ∽ Honshū, SW Japan
11 U11 **Kinoosao** Saskatchewan, C Canada
99 L17 **Kinrooi** Limburg, NE Belgium
96 J11 **Kinross** C Scotland, UK
96 J11 **Kinross** *cultural region* C Scotland, UK
97 C21 **Kinsale** *Ir.* Cionn tSáile. SW Ireland
95 D14 **Kinsarvik** Hordaland, S Norway
79 G21 **Kinshasa** *prev.* Léopoldville. ● (Dem. Rep. Congo) Kinshasa, W Dem. Rep. Congo
79 G21 **Kinshasa** *off.* Ville de Kinshasa, *var.* Kinshasa City. ◈ *region* SW Dem. Rep. Congo
79 G21 **Kinshasa** × Kinshasa, SW Dem. Rep. Congo
Kinshasa City *see* Kinshasa
117 U9 **Kins'ka** ∽ SE Ukraine
26 K6 **Kinsley** Kansas, C USA
21 W10 **Kinston** North Carolina, SE USA
77 P15 **Kintampo** W Ghana
182 B1 **Kintore, Mount** ▲ South Australia
96 G13 **Kintyre** *peninsula* W Scotland, UK
96 G13 **Kintyre, Mull of** *headland* W Scotland, UK
166 M4 **Kin-u** Sagaing, C Myanmar
12 G8 **Kinushseo** ∽ Ontario, C Canada
11 P13 **Kinuso** Alberta, W Canada
154 I13 **Kinwat** Mahārāshtra, C India
81 F16 **Kinyeti** ▲ S Sudan
101 I17 **Kinzig** ∽ SW Germany
Kioga, Lake *see* Kyoga, Lake
26 M8 **Kiowa** Kansas, C USA
27 P12 **Kiowa** Oklahoma, C USA
Kiparissía *see* Kyparissía
14 H10 **Kipawa, Lac** ◎ Québec, SE Canada
81 G24 **Kipengere Range** ⛰ SW Tanzania
81 E23 **Kipili** Rukwa, W Tanzania
81 K20 **Kipini** Coast, SE Kenya
11 V16 **Kipling** Saskatchewan, S Canada
38 M13 **Kipnuk** Alaska, USA
97 F18 **Kippure** *Ir.* Cipiúr. ▲ E Ireland
79 N25 **Kipushi** Katanga, SE Dem. Rep. Congo
187 N10 **Kirakira** *var.* Kaokaona. San Cristobal, SE Solomon Islands
155 K14 **Kirandul** *var.* Bailādila. Chhattīsgarh, C India
155 I21 **Kīranūr** Tamil Nādu, SE India
119 N21 **Kiraw** *Rus.* Kirovo. Homyel'skaya Voblasts', SE Belarus
119 M17 **Kirawsk** *Rus.* Kirovsk; *prev.* Startsy. Mahilyowskaya Voblasts', E Belarus
118 F5 **Kirbla** Läänemaa, W Estonia
25 Y9 **Kirbyville** Texas, SW USA
114 M12 **Kırcasalih** Edirne, NW Turkey
109 W8 **Kirchbach** *var.* Kirchbach in Steiermark. Steiermark, SE Austria
Kirchbach in Steiermark *see* Kirchbach
108 H7 **Kirchberg** Sankt Gallen, NE Switzerland
109 S5 **Kirchdorf an der Krems** Oberösterreich, N Austria
Kirchheim *see* Kirchheim unter Teck
101 I22 **Kirchheim unter Teck** *var.* Kirchheim. Baden-Württemberg, SW Germany
Kirdzhali *see* Kŭrdzhali
123 N13 **Kirenga** ∽ S Russian Federation
123 N12 **Kirensk** Irkutskaya Oblast', C Russian Federation
Kirghizia *see* Kyrgyzstan
145 S16 **Kirghiz Range** *Rus.* Kirgizskiy Khrebet; *prev.* Alexander Range. ⛰ Kazakhstan/Kyrgyzstan
Kirghiz SSR *see* Kyrgyzstan
Kirghiz Steppe *see* Kazakhskiy Melkosopochnik
Kirgizskaya SSR *see* Kyrgyzstan
Kirgizskiy Khrebet *see* Kirghiz Range
79 I19 **Kiri** Bandundu, W Dem. Rep. Congo
Kiriath-Arba *see* Hebron
191 R3 **Kiribati** *off.* Republic of Kiribati. ◆ *republic* C Pacific Ocean
136 L17 **Kırıkhan** Hatay, S Turkey
136 I13 **Kırıkkale** Kırıkkale, C Turkey
136 C10 **Kırıkkale** ◈ *province* C Turkey
124 L13 **Kirillov** Vologodskaya Oblast', NW Russian Federation
Kirin *see* Jilin
81 I18 **Kirinyaga** *prev.* Mount Kenya. Ⓥ C Kenya
124 H13 **Kirishi** *var.* Kirisi. Leningradskaya Oblast', NW Russian Federation
164 C16 **Kirishima-yama** ▲ Kyūshū, SW Japan
Kirisi *see* Kirishi
191 Y2 **Kiritimati** × Kiritimati, E Kiribati
191 Y2 **Kiritimati** *prev.* Christmas Island. *atoll* Line Islands, E Kiribati
186 G9 **Kiriwina Island** *Eng.* Trobriand Island. *island* SE PNG
186 G9 **Kiriwina Islands** *var.* Trobriand Islands. *island group* S PNG
96 K12 **Kirkcaldy** E Scotland, UK
97 I14 **Kirkcudbright** S Scotland, UK
97 I14 **Kirkcudbright** *cultural region* S Scotland, UK
Kirkee *see* Khadki
92 M8 **Kirkenes** *Fin.* Kirkkoniemi. Finnmark, N Norway
95 I14 **Kirkenær** Hedmark, S Norway
92 J4 **Kirkjubæjarklaustur** Sudhurland, S Iceland
Kirk-Kilissa *see* Kırklareli
Kirkkoniemi *see* Kirkenes
93 L20 **Kirkkonummi** *Swe.* Kyrkslätt. Etelä-Suomi, S Finland
14 G7 **Kirkland Lake** Ontario, S Canada
136 C9 **Kırklareli** *prev.* Kirk-Kilissa. Kırklareli, NW Turkey
136 I13 **Kırklareli** ◈ *province* NW Turkey
185 F20 **Kirkliston Range** ⛰ South Island, NZ
14 D10 **Kirkpatrick Lake** ◎ Ontario, S Canada
195 Q11 **Kirkpatrick, Mount** ▲ Antarctica
27 U2 **Kirksville** Missouri, C USA
139 T4 **Kirkūk** *var.* Karkūk, Kerkuk. N Iraq
139 U7 **Kir Kush** E Iraq
96 K5 **Kirkwall** NE Scotland, UK
83 H25 **Kirkwood** Eastern Cape, S South Africa
27 X5 **Kirkwood** Missouri, C USA
Kirman *see* Kermān
Kir Moab/Kir of Moab *see* Al Karak
126 I5 **Kirov** Kaluzhskaya Oblast', W Russian Federation
125 R14 **Kirov** *prev.* Vyatka. Kirovskaya Oblast', NW Russian Federation
Kirov *see* Balpyk Bi, Kazakhstan
Kirov/Kirova *see* Kopbirlik, Kazakhstan
Kirovabad *see* Gäncä, Azerbaijan
Kirovabad *see* Panj, Tajikistan
Kirovakan *see* Vanadzor
Kirovo *see* Kiraw, Belarus
Kirovo/Kirovograd *see* Kirovohrad, Ukraine
Kirovo *see* Beshariq, Uzbekistan
125 R14 **Kirovo-Chepetsk** Kirovskaya Oblast', NW Russian Federation
Kirovogradskaya Oblast'/Kirovohrad *see* Kirovohrads'ka Oblast'
117 R7 **Kirovohrad** *Rus.* Kirovograd; *prev.* Kirovo, Yelizavetgrad, Zinov'yevsk. Kirovohrads'ka Oblast', C Ukraine
117 P7 **Kirovohrads'ka Oblast'** *var.* Kirovohrad, *Rus.* Kirovogradskaya Oblast'. ◈ *province* C Ukraine
124 J4 **Kirovsk** Murmanskaya Oblast', NW Russian Federation
Kirovsk *see* Babadaýhan, Turkmenistan
Kirovsk *see* Kirawsk, Belarus
117 X7 **Kirovs'k** Luhans'ka Oblast', E Ukraine
122 E9 **Kirovskaya Oblast'** ◈ *province* NW Russian Federation
117 X8 **Kirovs'ke** Donets'ka Oblast', E Ukraine
117 U13 **Kirovs'ke** *Rus.* Kirovskoye. Respublika Krym, S Ukraine
Kirovskiy *see* Balpyk Bi/Ust'yevoye
Kirovskoye *see* Kyzyl-Adyr
Kirovskoye *see* Kirovs'ke
146 E11 **Kirpili** Ahal Welaýaty, C Turkmenistan
96 K10 **Kirriemuir** E Scotland, UK
125 S13 **Kirs** Kirovskaya Oblast', NW Russian Federation
127 N7 **Kirsanov** Tambovskaya Oblast', W Russian Federation
136 J14 **Kırşehir** *anc.* Justinianopolis. Kırşehir, C Turkey
136 I13 **Kırşehir** ◈ *province* C Turkey
149 P4 **Kīrthar Range** ⛰ S Pakistan
37 P9 **Kirtland** New Mexico, SW USA
Kirun/Kirun' *see* Chilung
92 J11 **Kiruna** *Lapp.* Giron. Norrbotten, N Sweden
79 M18 **Kirundu** Orientale, NE Dem. Rep. Congo
26 L3 **Kirwin Reservoir** ⊟ Kansas, C USA
127 Q4 **Kirya** Chuvashskaya Respublika, W Russian Federation
Kiryat Gat *see* Qiryat Gat
95 M18 **Kisa** Östergötland, S Sweden
165 P9 **Kisakata** Akita, Honshū, C Japan
Kisalföld *see* Little Alföld
79 L18 **Kisangani** *prev.* Stanleyville. Orientale, NE Dem. Rep. Congo
39 N12 **Kisaralik River** ∽ Alaska, USA
165 O14 **Kisarazu** Chiba, Honshū, S Japan
111 I22 **Kisbér** Komárom-Esztergom, NW Hungary
11 V17 **Kisbey** Saskatchewan, S Canada
122 J13 **Kiselevsk** Kemerovskaya Oblast', S Russian Federation
153 R13 **Kishanganj** Bihār, NE India
152 G12 **Kishangarh** Rājasthān, N India
Kishegyes *see* Mali Iđoš
77 S15 **Kishi** Oyo, W Nigeria
Kishinev *see* Chişinău
Kishiözen *see* Malyy Uzen'
164 I14 **Kishiwada** *var.* Kisiwada. Ōsaka, Honshū, SW Japan
143 P14 **Kish, Jazīreh-ye** *var.* Qeys. *island* S Iran
145 R7 **Kishkenekol'** *prev.* Kzyltu, *Kaz.* Qyzyltu; Severnyy Kazakhstan, N Kazakhstan
152 I6 **Kishtwār** Jammu and Kashmir, NW India
81 H19 **Kisii** Nyanza, SW Kenya
81 J23 **Kisiju** Pwani, E Tanzania
Kisiwada *see* Kishiwada
Kisjenő *see* Chişineu-Criş
38 E17 **Kiska Island** *island* Aleutian Islands, Alaska, USA
Kiskapus *see* Copşa Mică
111 M22 **Kiskörei-víztároló** ⊟ E Hungary
Kis-Küküllo *see* Târnava Mică
111 L24 **Kiskunfélegyháza** *var.* Félegyháza. Bács-Kiskun, C Hungary
111 K25 **Kiskunhalas** *var.* Halas. Bács-Kiskun, S Hungary
111 K24 **Kiskunmajsa** Bács-Kiskun, S Hungary
127 N15 **Kislovodsk** Stavropol'skiy Kray, SW Russian Federation
81 L18 **Kismaayo** *var.* Chisimayu, Kismayu, *It.* Chisimaio. Jubbada Hoose, S Somalia
Kismayu *see* Kismaayo
164 M13 **Kiso-sanmyaku** ⛰ Honshū, S Japan
Kisseraing *see* Kanmaw Kyun
76 K14 **Kissidougou** Guinée-Forestière, S Guinea
23 X12 **Kissimmee** Florida, SE USA
23 X12 **Kissimmee, Lake** ◎ Florida, SE USA
23 X13 **Kissimmee River** ∽ Florida, SE USA
11 V13 **Kississing Lake** ◎ Manitoba, C Canada
111 L24 **Kistelek** Csongrád, SE Hungary
Kistna *see* Krishna
111 M23 **Kisújszállás** Jász-Nagykun-Szolnok, E Hungary
164 G12 **Kisuki** Shimane, Honshū, SW Japan
81 H18 **Kisumu** *prev.* Port Florence. Nyanza, W Kenya
Kisutzaneustadtl *see* Kysucké Nové Mesto
111 O20 **Kisvárda** *Ger.* Kleinwardein. Szabolcs-Szatmár-Bereg, E Hungary
81 J24 **Kiswere** Lindi, SE Tanzania
Kiszucaújhely *see* Kysucké Nové Mesto
76 K12 **Kita** Kayes, W Mali
207 N14 **Kitaa** ◈ *province* W Greenland
Kitab *see* Kitob
165 Q4 **Kitahiyama** Hokkaidō, NE Japan
165 P12 **Kita-Ibaraki** Ibaraki, Honshū, S Japan
165 X16 **Kita-Iō-jima** *Eng.* San Alessandro. *island* SE Japan
165 Q9 **Kitakami** Iwate, Honshū, C Japan
165 P11 **Kitakata** Fukushima, Honshū, C Japan
164 D13 **Kitakyūshū** *var.* Kitakyûsyû. Fukuoka, Kyūshū, SW Japan
Kitakyûsyû *see* Kitakyūshū
81 H18 **Kitale** Rift Valley, W Kenya
165 U3 **Kitami** Hokkaidō, NE Japan
165 T2 **Kitami-sanchi** ⛰ Hokkaidō, NE Japan
37 W5 **Kit Carson** Colorado, C USA
180 M12 **Kitchener** Western Australia
14 F16 **Kitchener** Ontario, S Canada
93 O17 **Kitee** Itä-Suomi, E Finland
81 G16 **Kitgum** N Uganda
Kithareng *see* Kanmaw Kyun
Kíthira *see* Kýthira
Kíthnos *see* Kýthnos
10 J13 **Kitimat** British Columbia, SW Canada
92 L11 **Kitinen** ∽ N Finland
147 N12 **Kitob** *Rus.* Kitab. Qashqadaryo Viloyati, S Uzbekistan
116 K7 **Kitsman'** *Ger.* Kotzman, *Rom.* Cozmeni, *Rus.* Kitsman. Chernivets'ka Oblast', W Ukraine
164 E14 **Kitsuki** *var.* Kituki. Ōita, Kyūshū, SW Japan
18 C14 **Kittanning** Pennsylvania, NE USA
19 P10 **Kittery** Maine, NE USA
92 L11 **Kittilä** Lappi, N Finland
109 Z4 **Kittsee** Burgenland, E Austria
81 J19 **Kitui** Eastern, S Kenya
Kituki *see* Kitsuki
81 G22 **Kitunda** Tabora, C Tanzania
10 K13 **Kitwanga** British Columbia, SW Canada
82 J13 **Kitwe** *var.* Kitwe-Nkana. Copperbelt, C Zambia
Kitwe-Nkana *see* Kitwe
109 O7 **Kitzbühel** Tirol, W Austria
109 O7 **Kitzbüheler Alpen** ⛰ W Austria
101 J19 **Kitzingen** Bayern, SE Germany
153 Q14 **Kiul** Bihār, NE India
186 A7 **Kiunga** Western, SW PNG
93 M16 **Kiuruvesi** Itä-Suomi, C Finland
38 M7 **Kivalina** Alaska, USA
92 L13 **Kivalo** *ridge* C Finland
116 J3 **Kivertsi** *Pol.* Kiwerce, *Rus.* Kivertsy. Volyns'ka Oblast', NW Ukraine
Kivertsy *see* Kivertsi
93 L16 **Kivijärvi** Länsi-Suomi, W Finland
95 L23 **Kivik** Skåne, S Sweden
118 J3 **Kiviõli** Ida-Virumaa, NE Estonia
Kivu, Lac *see* Kivu, Lake
67 U10 **Kivu, Lake** *Fr.* Lac Kivu. ◎ Rwanda/Dem. Rep. Congo
186 C9 **Kiwai Island** *island* SW PNG
39 N8 **Kiwalik** Alaska, USA
Kiwerce *see* Kivertsi
Kiyev *see* Kyyiv
145 R10 **Kiyevka** Karaganda, C Kazakhstan
Kiyevskaya Oblast' *see* Kyyivs'ka Oblast'
Kiyevskoye Vodokhranilishche *see* Kyyivs'ke Vodoskhovyshche
136 D10 **Kıyıköy** Kırklareli, NW Turkey
145 O9 **Kiyma** Akmola, C Kazakhstan
125 V13 **Kizel** Permskaya Oblast', NW Russian Federation
125 O12 **Kizema** *var.* Kizëma. Arkhangel'skaya Oblast', NW Russian Federation
Kizilagach *see* Elkhovo
136 H12 **Kızılcahamam** Ankara, N Turkey
136 J10 **Kızıl Irmak** ∽ C Turkey
Kızılkoca *see* Şefaatli
Kizil Kum *see* Kyzyl Kum
137 P16 **Kızıltepe** Mardin, SE Turkey
Ki Zil Uzen *see* Qezel Owzan, Rūd-e
127 Q16 **Kizilyurt** Respublika Dagestan, SW Russian Federation
127 Q15 **Kizlyar** Respublika Dagestan, SW Russian Federation
127 S3 **Kizner** Udmurtskaya Respublika, NW Russian Federation
Kizyl-Arvat *see* Serdar
Kizyl-Atrek *see* Etrek
Kizyl-Kaya *see* Gyzylgaya
Kizyl-Su *see* Gyzylsuw
95 H16 **Kjerkøy** *island* S Norway
Kjølen *see* Kölen
92 L7 **Kjøllefjord** Finnmark, N Norway
92 H11 **Kjøpsvik** Nordland, C Norway
169 N12 **Klabat, Teluk** *bay* Pulau Bangka, W Indonesia
112 I12 **Kladanj** Federacija Bosna I Hercegovina, C Bosnia and Herzegovina
171 X16 **Kladar** Papua, E Indonesia
111 C16 **Kladno** Středočeský Kraj, NW Czech Republic
112 P11 **Kladovo** Serbia, E Serbia and Montenegro (Yugo.)
167 P12 **Klaeng** Rayong, S Thailand
109 T9 **Klagenfurt** *Slvn.* Celovec. Kärnten, S Austria
118 B11 **Klaipėda** *Ger.* Memel. Klaipėda, NW Lithuania
118 C11 **Klaipėda** ◈ *province* W Lithuania
95 B18 **Klaksvík** *Dan.* Klaksvig Faeroe Islands
34 L2 **Klamath** California, W USA
32 H16 **Klamath Falls** Oregon, NW USA
34 M1 **Klamath Mountains** ⛰ California/Oregon, W USA
34 L2 **Klamath River** ∽ California/Oregon, W USA
168 K9 **Klang** *var.* Kelang; *prev.* Port Swettenham. Selangor, Peninsular Malaysia
94 J13 **Klarälven** ∽ Norway/Sweden
111 B15 **Klášterec nad Ohří** *Ger.* Klösterle an der Eger. Ústecký Kraj, NW Czech Republic
111 B18 **Klatovy** *Ger.* Klattau. Plzeňský Kraj, W Czech Republic
Klattau *see* Klatovy
Klausenburg *see* Cluj-Napoca
39 Y14 **Klawock** Prince of Wales Island, Alaska, USA
98 P8 **Klazienaveen** Drenthe, NE Netherlands
Kleck *see* Klyetsk
110 H11 **Kłecko** Wielkolpolskie, C Poland
110 I11 **Kleczew** Wielkopolskie, C Poland
10 L15 **Kleena Kleene** British Columbia, SW Canada
83 D20 **Klein Aub** Hardap, C Namibia
Kleine Donau *see* Mosoni-Duna
101 O14 **Kleine Elster** ∽ E Germany
Kleine Kokel *see* Târnava Mică
99 I16 **Kleine Nete** ∽ N Belgium
Kleines Ungarisches Tiefland *see* Little Alföld
83 E22 **Klein Karas** Karas, S Namibia
Kleinkopisch *see* Copşa Mică
Klein-Marien *see* Väike-Maarja
Kleinschlatten *see* Zlatna
83 D23 **Kleinsee** Northern Cape, W South Africa
Kleinwardein *see* Kisvárda
115 C16 **Kleisoúra** Ípeiros, W Greece
95 C17 **Klepp** Rogaland, S Norway
83 I22 **Klerksdorp** North-West, N South Africa
126 I5 **Kletnya** Bryanskaya Oblast', W Russian Federation
Kletsk *see* Klyetsk
101 D14 **Kleve** *Eng.* Cleves, *Fr.* Clèves; *prev.* Cleve. Nordrhein-Westfalen, W Germany
113 J16 **Kličevo** Montenegro, SW Serbia and Montenegro (Yugo.)
119 M16 **Klichaw** *Rus.* Klichev. Mahilyowskaya Voblasts', E Belarus
Klichev *see* Klichaw
119 Q16 **Klimavichy** *Rus.* Klimovichi. Mahilyowskaya Voblasts', E Belarus
114 M7 **Kliment** Shumen, NE Bulgaria
Klimovichi *see* Klimavichy
93 G14 **Klimpfjäll** Västerbotten, N Sweden
126 K3 **Klin** Moskovskaya Oblast', W Russian Federation
113 M16 **Klina** Serbia, S Serbia and Montenegro (Yugo.)
111 B15 **Klínovec** *Ger.* Keilberg. ▲ NW Czech Republic
95 P19 **Klintehamn** Gotland, SE Sweden
127 R8 **Klintsovka** Saratovskaya Oblast', W Russian Federation
126 H6 **Klintsy** Bryanskaya Oblast', W Russian Federation
95 K22 **Klippan** Skåne, S Sweden
92 G13 **Klippen** Västerbotten, N Sweden
121 P2 **Klírou** W Cyprus
114 I9 **Klisura** Plovdiv, C Bulgaria
95 F20 **Klitmøller** Viborg, NW Denmark
112 F11 **Ključ** Federacija Bosna I Hercegovina, NW Bosnia and Herzegovina
111 J14 **Kłobuck** Śląskie, S Poland
110 J11 **Kłodawa** Wielkopolskie, C Poland
111 G16 **Kłodzko** *Ger.* Glatz. Dolnośląskie, SW Poland
95 I14 **Kløfta** Akershus, S Norway
112 P12 **Kokočevac** Serbia, E Serbia and Montenegro (Yugo.)
118 G3 **Klooga** *Ger.* Lodensee. Harjumaa, NW Estonia
99 F15 **Kloosterzande** Zeeland, SW Netherlands
113 L19 **Klos** *var.* Klosi. Dibër, C Albania
Klosi *see* Klos
Klösterle an der Eger *see* Klášterec nad Ohří

◆ Country ● Country Capital ◇ Dependent Territory ○ Dependent Territory Capital ◈ Administrative Region × International Airport ▲ Mountain ⛰ Mountain Range Ⓥ Volcano ∽ River ◎ Lake ⊟ Reservoir

109 *X3* **Klosterneuburg** Niederösterreich, NE Austria
108 *J9* **Klosters** Graubünden, SE Switzerland
108 *G7* **Kloten** Zürich, N Switzerland
108 *G7* **Kloten** × (Zürich) Zürich, N Switzerland
100 *K12* **Klötze** Sachsen-Anhalt, C Germany
12 *K3* **Klotz, Lac** ◎ Québec, NE Canada
101 *O15* **Klotzsche** × (Dresden) Sachsen, E Germany
10 *H7* **Kluane Lake** ◎ Yukon Territory, W Canada
Kluang *see* Keluang
111 *I14* **Kluczbork** *Ger.* Kreuzburg, Kreuzburg in Oberschlesien. Opolskie, S Poland
39 *W12* **Klukwan** Alaska, USA
Klyastitsy *see* Klyastsitsy
118 *L11* **Klyastsitsy** *Rus.* Klyastitsy. Vitsyebskaya Voblasts', N Belarus
127 *T5* **Klyavlino** Samarskaya Oblast', W Russian Federation
84 *K9* **Klyaz'in** ≈ W Russian Federation
127 *N3* **Klyaz'ma** ≈ W Russian Federation
119 *J17* **Klyetsk** *Pol.* Kleck, *Rus.* Kletsk. Minskaya Voblasts', SW Belarus
147 *S8* **Klyuchevka** Talasskaya Oblast', NW Kyrgyzstan
123 *V10* **Klyuchevskaya Sopka, Vulkan** 🌋 E Russian Federation
95 *D17* **Knaben** Vest-Agder, S Norway
Knanzi *see* Ghanzi
95 *K21* **Knäred** Halland, S Sweden
97 *M16* **Knaresborough** N England, UK
114 *H8* **Knezha** Vratsa , NW Bulgaria
25 *O9* **Knickerbocker** Texas, SW USA
28 *K5* **Knife River** ≈ North Dakota, N USA
10 *K16* **Knight Inlet** *inlet* British Columbia, W Canada
39 *S12* **Knight Island** *island* Alaska, USA
97 *K20* **Knighton** E Wales, UK
35 *O7* **Knights Landing** California, W USA
112 *E13* **Knin** Šibenik-Knin, S Croatia
25 *Q12* **Knippal** Texas, SW USA
109 *U7* **Knittelfeld** Steiermark, C Austria
95 *O15* **Knivsta** Uppsala, C Sweden
113 *P14* **Knjaževac** Serbia, E Serbia and Montenegro (Yugo.)
27 *S4* **Knob Noster** Missouri, C USA
99 *D15* **Knokke-Heist** West-Vlaanderen, NW Belgium
95 *H20* **Knøsen** *hill* N Denmark
Knosós *see* Knossos
115 *J25* **Knossos** *Gk.* Knosós. *prehistoric site* Kríti, Greece, E Mediterranean Sea
25 *N7* **Knott** Texas, SW USA
194 *K5* **Knowles, Cape** *headland* Antarctica
31 *O11* **Knox** Indiana, N USA
29 *O3* **Knox** North Dakota, N USA
18 *C13* **Knox** Pennsylvania, NE USA
189 *X8* **Knox Atoll** *var.* Ṇadikdik, Narikrik. *atoll* Ratak Chain, SE Marshall Islands
10 *H13* **Knox, Cape** *headland* Graham Island, British Columbia, SW Canada
25 *P5* **Knox City** Texas, SW USA
195 *Y11* **Knox Coast** *physical region* Antarctica
31 *T12* **Knox Lake** ⊡ Ohio, N USA
23 *T5* **Knoxville** Georgia, SE USA
30 *K12* **Knoxville** Illinois, N USA
29 *W15* **Knoxville** Iowa, C USA
21 *N9* **Knoxville** Tennessee, S USA
197 *P11* **Knud Rasmussen Land** *physical region* N Greenland
Knüll *see* Knüllgebirge
101 *I16* **Knüllgebirge** *var.* Knüll. ▲▲ C Germany
Knyazhevo *see* Sredishte
Knyazhitsy *see* Knyazhytsy
119 *O15* **Knyazhytsy** *Rus.* Knyazhitsy. Mahilyowskaya Voblasts', E Belarus
83 *G26* **Knysna** Western Cape, SW South Africa
Koartac *see* Quaqtaq
169 *N13* **Koba** Pulau Bangka, W Indonesia
164 *D16* **Kobayashi** *var.* Kobayasi. Miyazaki, Kyūshū, SW Japan
Kobayasi *see* Kobayashi
Kobdo *see* Hovd
164 *I13* **Kōbe** Hyōgo, Honshū, SW Japan
Kobelyaki *see* Kobelyaky
117 *T6* **Kobelyaky** *Rus.* Kobelyaki. Poltavs'ka Oblast', NE Ukraine
95 *J22* **København** *Eng.* Copenhagen; *anc.* Hafnia. ● (Denmark) Sjælland, København, E Denmark
95 *J23* **København** *off.* Københavns Amt. ◈ *county* E Denmark
76 *K10* **Kobenni** Hodh el Gharbi, S Mauritania
171 *T13* **Kobi** Pulau Seram, E Indonesia
101 *F17* **Koblenz** *prev.* Coblenz, *Fr.* Coblence, *anc.* Confluentes. Rheinland-Pfalz, W Germany
108 *F6* **Koblenz** Aargau, N Switzerland
124 *J14* **Kobozha** Novgorodskaya Oblast', W Russian Federation
Kobrin *see* Kobryn
171 *V15* **Kobroor, Pulau** *island* Kepulauan Aru, E Indonesia
119 *G19* **Kobryn** *Pol.* Kobryn, *Rus.* Kobrin. Brestskaya Voblasts', SW Belarus
39 *O7* **Kobuk** Alaska, USA
39 *O7* **Kobuk River** ≈ Alaska, USA
137 *Q10* **K'obulet'i** W Georgia
123 *P10* **Kobyay** Respublika Sakha (Yakutiya). NE Russian Federation
136 *E11* **Kocaeli** ◈ *province* NW Turkey
113 *P18* **Kočani** NE FYR Macedonia
112 *K12* **Koceljevo** Serbia, W Serbia and Montenegro (Yugo.)
109 *U12* **Kočevje** *Ger.* Gottschee. S Slovenia
153 *T12* **Koch Bihār** West Bengal, NE India
122 *M9* **Kochechum** ≈ N Russian Federation
101 *I20* **Kocher** ≈ SW Germany
125 *T13* **Kochevo** Komi-Permyatskiy Avtonomnyy Okrug, NW Russian Federation
164 *G14* **Kōchi** *var.* Kôti. Kōchi, Shikoku, SW Japan
164 *G14* **Kōchi** *off.* Kōchi-ken, *var.* Kôti. ◈ *prefecture* Shikoku, SW Japan
Kochi *see* Cochin
Kochiu *see* Gejiu
Kochkor *see* Kochkorka
147 *V8* **Kochkorka** *Kir.* Kochkor. Narynskaya Oblast', C Kyrgyzstan
125 *V5* **Kochmes** Respublika Komi, NW Russian Federation
127 *P15* **Kochubey** Respublika Dagestan, SW Russian Federation
115 *I17* **Kochýlas** ▲ Skýros, Vóreioi Sporádes, Greece, Aegean Sea
110 *O13* **Kock** Lubelskie, E Poland
81 *J19* **Kodacho** *spring/well* S Kenya
155 *K24* **Koddiyar Bay** *bay* NE Sri Lanka
39 *Q14* **Kodiak** Kodiak Island, Alaska, USA
39 *Q14* **Kodiak Island** *island* Alaska, USA
154 *B12* **Kodīnār** Gujarāt, W India
124 *M9* **Kodino** Arkhangel'skaya Oblast', NW Russian Federation
122 *M12* **Kodinsk** Krasnoyarskiy Kray, C Russian Federation
80 *F12* **Kodok** Upper Nile, SE Sudan
117 *N8* **Kodyma** Odes'ka Oblast', SW Ukraine
99 *B17* **Koekelare** West-Vlaanderen, W Belgium
Koeln *see* Köln
Koepang *see* Kupang
Ko-erh-mu *see* Golmud
99 *J17* **Koersel** Limburg, NE Belgium
83 *E21* **Koës** Karas, SE Namibia
Koetai *see* Mahakam, Sungai
Koetaradja *see* Bandaaceh
36 *I14* **Kofa Mountains** ▲▲ Arizona, SW USA
171 *Y15* **Kofarau** Papua, E Indonesia
147 *P13* **Kofarnihon** *Rus.* Kofarnikhon; *prev.* Ordzhonikidzeabad, *Taj.* Orjonikidzeobod, Yangi-Bazar. W Tajikistan
147 *P14* **Kofarnihon** *Rus.* Kafirnigan. ≈ SW Tajikistan
Kofarnikhon *see* Kofarnihon
114 *M11* **Kofçaz** Kırklareli, NW Turkey
115 *J25* **Kófinas** ▲ Kríti, Greece, E Mediterranean Sea
121 *P3* **Kofínou** *var.* Kophinou. S Cyprus
109 *V8* **Köflach** Steiermark, SE Austria
77 *Q17* **Koforidua** SE Ghana
164 *H12* **Kōfu** Tottori, Honshū, SW Japan
164 *M13* **Kōfu** *var.* Kôhu. Yamanashi, Honshū, S Japan
81 *F22* **Koga** Tabora, C Tanzania
Kogălniceanu *see* Mihail Kogălniceanu
13 *P6* **Kogaluk** ≈ Newfoundland and Labrador, E Canada
12 *J4* **Kogaluk** ≈ Québec, NE Canada
122 *I10* **Kogalym** Khanty-Mansiyskiy Avtonomnyy Okrug, C Russian Federation
95 *J23* **Køge** Roskilde, E Denmark
95 *J23* **Køge Bugt** *bay* E Denmark
77 *U16* **Kogi** ◈ *state* C Nigeria
146 *L11* **Kogon** *Rus.* Kagan. Buxoro Viloyati, C Uzbekistan
163 *Y17* **Kōgŭm-do** *island* S South Korea
Kőhalom *see* Rupea
149 *T6* **Kohāt** North-West Frontier Province, NW Pakistan
118 *G4* **Kohila** *Ger.* Koil. Raplamaa, NW Estonia
153 *X13* **Kohīma** Nāgāland, E India
Koh I Noh *see* Büyükağrı Dağı
142 *L10* **Kohgīlūyeh va Būyer Aḥmad** *off.* Ostān-e Kohgīlūyeh va Būyer Aḥmad, *var.* Boyer Ahmadī va Kohkīlūyeh. ◈ *province* SW Iran
Kohsān *see* Kūhestān
118 *J3* **Kohtla-Järve** Ida-Virumaa, NE Estonia
Kôhu *see* Kōfu
117 *N10* **Kohyl'nyk** *Rom.* Cogîlnic. ≈ Moldova/Ukraine
165 *N11* **Koide** Niigata, Honshū, C Japan
10 *G7* **Koidern** Yukon Territory, W Canada
76 *J15* **Koidu** E Sierra Leone
118 *I4* **Koigi** Järvamaa, C Estonia
Koil *see* Kohila
172 *H13* **Koimbani** Grande Comore, NW Comoros
139 *T3* **Koi Sanjaq** *var.* Koysanjaq, Kūysanjaq. N Iraq
93 *O16* **Koitere** ◎ E Finland
Koivisto *see* Primorsk
163 *Z16* **Kōje-do** *Jap.* Kyōsai-tō. *island* S South Korea
80 *J13* **K'ok'a Hāyk'** ◎ C Ethiopia
Kokand *see* Qo'qon
182 *F6* **Kokatha** South Australia
Kokcha *see* Ko'kcha
Kokchetav *see* Kokshetau
93 *K18* **Kokemäenjoki** ≈ SW Finland
171 *W14* **Kokenau** *var.* Kokonau. Papua, E Indonesia
83 *E22* **Kokerboom** Karas, SE Namibia
119 *N14* **Kokhanava** *Rus.* Kokhanovo. Vitsyebskaya Voblasts', NE Belarus
Kokhanovichi *see* Kakhanavichy
Kokhanovo *see* Kokhanava
Kök-Janggak *see* Kok-Yangak
93 *K16* **Kokkola** *Swe.* Karleby; *prev.* *Swe.* Gamlakarleby. Länsi-Suomi, W Finland
158 *L3* **Kok Kuduk** *well* N China
118 *H9* **Koknese** Aizkraukle, C Latvia
77 *T13* **Koko** Kebbi, W Nigeria
186 *E9* **Kokoda** Northern, S PNG
76 *K12* **Kokofata** Kayes, W Mali
39 *N6* **Kokolik River** ≈ Alaska, USA
31 *O13* **Kokomo** Indiana, N USA
Kokonau *see* Kokenau
Koko Nor *see* Qinghai Hu, China
Koko Nor *see* Qinghai, China
186 *H6* **Kokopo** *var.* Kopopo; *prev.* Herbertshöhe. New Britain, E PNG
145 *X10* **Kokpekti** *Kaz.* Kökpekti. Vostochnyy Kazakhstan, E Kazakhstan
145 *X11* **Kokpekti** ≈ E Kazakhstan
39 *P9* **Kokrines** Alaska, USA
39 *P9* **Kokrines Hills** ▲▲ Alaska, USA
145 *P17* **Koksaray** Yuzhnyy Kazakhstan, S Kazakhstan
147 *X9* **Kokshaal-Tau** *Rus.* Khrebet Kakshaal-Too. ▲▲ China/Kyrgyzstan
145 *P7* **Kokshetau** *Kaz.* Kökshetaū; *prev.* Kokchetav. Akmola, N Kazakhstan
99 *A17* **Koksijde** West-Vlaanderen, W Belgium
12 *M5* **Koksoak** ≈ Québec, E Canada
83 *K24* **Kokstad** KwaZulu/Natal, E South Africa
145 *W15* **Koktal** *Kaz.* Köktal. Almaty, SE Kazakhstan
145 *Q12* **Koktas** ≈ C Kazakhstan
Kök-Tash *see* Kĕk-Tash
Koktokay *see* Fuyun
147 *T9* **Kok-Yangak** *Kir.* Kök-Janggak. Dzhalal-Abadskaya Oblast', W Kyrgyzstan
158 *F9* **Kokyar** Xinjiang Uygur Zizhiqu, W China
149 *O13* **Kolāchi** *var.* Kulachi. ≈ SW Pakistan
76 *J15* **Kolahun** N Liberia
171 *O14* **Kolaka** Sulawesi, C Indonesia
Kolam *see* Quilon
K'o-la-ma-i *see* Karamay
Kola Peninsula *see* Kol'skiy Poluostrov
155 *H19* **Kolār** Karnātaka, E India
155 *H19* **Kolār Gold Fields** Karnātaka, E India
92 *K11* **Kolari** Lappi, NW Finland
111 *I21* **Kolárovo** *Ger.* Gutta; *prev.* Guta, *Hung.* Gúta. Nitriansky Kraj, SW Slovakia
113 *K16* **Kolašin** Montenegro, SW Serbia and Montenegro (Yugo.)
152 *F11* **Kolāyat** Rājasthān, NW India
95 *N15* **Kolbäck** Västmanland, C Sweden
Kolbcha *see* Kowbcha
197 *Q15* **Kolbeinsey Ridge** *undersea feature* Denmark Strait/Norwegian Sea
Kolberg *see* Kołobrzeg
95 *H15* **Kolbotn** Akershus, S Norway
111 *N16* **Kolbuszowa** Podkarpackie, SE Poland
126 *L3* **Kol'chugino** Vladimirskaya Oblast', W Russian Federation
76 *H12* **Kolda** S Senegal
95 *G23* **Kolding** Vejle, C Denmark
79 *M17* **Kole** Orientale, N Dem. Rep. Congo
79 *K20* **Kole** Kasai Oriental, SW Dem. Rep. Congo
Kōle *see* Kili Island
84 *F6* **Kölen** *Nor.* Kjølen. ▲▲ Norway/Sweden
Kolepom, Pulau *see* Yos Sudarso, Pulau
118 *H3* **Kolga Laht** *Ger.* Kolko-Wiek. *bay* N Estonia
127 *Q3* **Kolguyev, Ostrov** *island* NW Russian Federation
155 *E16* **Kolhāpur** Mahārāshtra, SW India
151 *K21* **Kolhumadulu Atoll** *var.* Kolumadulu Atoll, Thaa Atoll. *atoll* S Maldives
93 *O16* **Koli** *var.* Kolinkylä. Itä-Suomi, E Finland
39 *O13* **Koliganek** Alaska, USA
111 *E16* **Kolín** *Ger.* Kolin. Středočeský Kraj, C Czech Republic
Kolinkylä *see* Koli
190 *E12* **Koliu** Île Futuna, W Wallis and Futuna
118 *E7* **Kolka** Talsi, NW Latvia
118 *E7* **Kolkasrags** *prev. Eng.* Cape Domesnes. *headland* NW Latvia
Kolkhozabad *see* Kolkhozobod
147 *P14* **Kolkhozobod** *Rus.* Kolkhozabad; *prev.* Kaganovichabad, Tugalan. SW Tajikistan
Kolki/Kołki *see* Kolky
Kolko-Wiek *see* Kolga Laht
116 *K3* **Kolky** *Pol.* Kołki, *Rus.* Kolki. Volyns'ka Oblast', NW Ukraine
Kollam *see* Quilon
155 *G20* **Kollegāl** Karnātaka, W India
98 *M5* **Kollum** Friesland, N Netherlands
Kolmar *see* Colmar
101 *E16* **Köln** *var.* Koeln, *Eng./Fr.* Cologne; *prev.* Cöln, *anc.* Colonia Agrippina, Oppidum Ubiorum. Nordrhein-Westfalen, W Germany
110 *N9* **Kolno** Podlaskie, NE Poland
110 *J12* **Koło** Wielkopolskie, C Poland
38 *B8* **Kōloa** *var.* Koloa. Kaua'i, Hawai'i, USA, C Pacific Ocean
110 *E7* **Kołobrzeg** *Ger.* Kolberg. Zachodnio-pomorskie, NW Poland
126 *H4* **Kolodnya** Smolenskaya Oblast', W Russian Federation
190 *E13* **Kolofau, Mont** 🌋 Île Alofi, S Wallis and Futuna
125 *O14* **Kologriv** Kostromskaya Oblast', NW Russian Federation
76 *L12* **Kolokani** Koulikoro, W Mali
77 *N13* **Koloko** W Burkina
186 *K8* **Kolombangara** *var.* Kilimbangara, Nduke. *island* New Georgia Islands, NW Solomon Islands
Kolomea *see* Kolomyya
126 *L4* **Kolomna** Moskovskaya Oblast', W Russian Federation
116 *J7* **Kolomyya** *Ger.* Kolomea. Ivano-Frankivs'ka Oblast', W Ukraine
76 *M13* **Kolondiéba** Sikasso, SW Mali
193 *V15* **Kolonga** Tongatapu, S Tonga
189 *U16* **Kolonia** *var.* Colonia. Pohnpei, E Micronesia
Kolonja *see* Kolonjë
113 *K21* **Kolonjë** *var.* Kolonja. Fier, C Albania
Kolonjë *see* Ersekë
Kolotambu *see* Avuavu
193 *U15* **Kolovai** Tongatapu, S Tonga
Kolozsvár *see* Cluj-Napoca
112 *C9* **Kolpa** *Ger.* Kulpa, *SCr.* Kupa. ≈ Croatia/Slovenia
122 *J11* **Kolpashevo** Tomskaya Oblast', C Russian Federation
124 *H13* **Kolpino** Leningradskaya Oblast', NW Russian Federation
100 *M10* **Kölpinsee** ◎ NE Germany
146 *K8* **Ko'lquduq** *Rus.* Kulkuduk. Navoiy Viloyati, N Uzbekistan
126 *K5* **Kol'skiy Poluostrov** *Eng.* Kola Peninsula. *peninsula* NW Russian Federation
127 *T6* **Koltubanovskiy** Orenburgskaya Oblast', W Russian Federation
112 *L11* **Kolubara** ≈ C Serbia and Montenegro (Yugo.)
Kolupchii *see* Gurkovo
110 *K13* **Koluszki** Łodzkie, C Poland
127 *T6* **Kolva** ≈ NW Russian Federation
93 *E14* **Kolvereid** Nord-Trøndelag, W Norway
148 *L15* **Kolwa** Baluchistān, SW Pakistan
79 *M24* **Kolwezi** Katanga, S Dem. Rep. Congo
123 *S7* **Kolyma** ≈ NE Russian Federation
Kolyma Lowland *see* Kolymskaya Nizmennost'
Kolyma Range/Kolymskiy, Khrebet *see* Kolymskoye Nagor'ye
123 *S7* **Kolymskaya Nizmennost'** *Eng.* Kolyma Lowland. *lowlands* NE Russian Federation
123 *S7* **Kolymskoye** Respublika Sakha (Yakutiya), NE Russian Federation
123 *U8* **Kolymskoye Nagor'ye** *var.* Khrebet Kolymskiy, *Eng.* Kolyma Range. ▲▲ E Russian Federation
123 *V5* **Kolyuchinskaya Guba** *bay* NE Russian Federation
145 *W15* **Kol'zhat** Almaty, SE Kazakhstan
114 *G8* **Kom** ▲ NW Bulgaria
80 *I13* **Koma** Oromo, C Ethiopia
77 *X12* **Komadugu Gana** ≈ NE Nigeria
164 *M13* **Komagane** Nagano, Honshū, S Japan
79 *P17* **Komanda** Orientale, NE Dem. Rep. Congo
197 *U1* **Komandorskaya Basin** *var.* Kamchatka Basin. *undersea feature* SW Bering Sea
123 *W9* **Komandorskiye Ostrova** *Eng.* Commander Islands. *island group* E Russian Federation
Kománfalva *see* Comănești
111 *I22* **Komárno** *Ger.* Komorn, *Hung.* Komárom. Nitriansky Kraj, SW Slovakia
111 *I22* **Komárom** Komárom-Esztergom, NW Hungary
Komárom *see* Komárno
111 *I22* **Komárom-Esztergom** *off.* Komárom-Esztergom Megye. ◈ *county* N Hungary
164 *K11* **Komatsu** *var.* Komatu. Ishikawa, Honshū, SW Japan
Komatu *see* Komatsu
83 *D17* **Kombat** Otjozondjupa, N Namibia
Kombissiguiri *see* Kombissiri
77 *P13* **Kombissiri** *var.* Kombissiguiri. C Burkina
188 *E10* **Komebail Lagoon** *lagoon* N Palau
81 *F20* **Kome Island** *island* N Tanzania
Komeyo *see* Wandai
117 *P10* **Kominternivs'ke** Odes'ka Oblast', SW Ukraine
125 *R12* **Komi-Permyatskiy Avtonomnyy Okrug** ◈ *autonomous district* W Russian Federation
127 *R8* **Komi, Respublika** ◈ *autonomous republic* NW Russian Federation
111 *I25* **Komló** Baranya, SW Hungary
Kommunarsk *see* Alchevs'k
147 *S12* **Kommunizm, Qullai** ▲ E Tajikistan
186 *B7* **Komo** Southern Highlands, W PNG
170 *M16* **Komodo, Pulau** *island* Nusa Tenggara, S Indonesia
77 *N15* **Komoé** *var.* Komoé Fleuve. ≈ E Ivory Coast
Komoé Fleuve *see* Komoé
75 *X11* **Kôm Ombo** *var.* Kawm Umbū. SE Egypt
79 *F20* **Komono** La Lékoumou, SW Congo
171 *Y16* **Komoran** Papua, E Indonesia
171 *Y16* **Komoran, Pulau** *island* E Indonesia
Komorn *see* Komárno
Komornok *see* Comorâște
Komosolabad *see* Komsomolobod
Komotau *see* Chomutov
114 *K13* **Komotiní** *var.* Gümüljina, *Turk.* Gümülcine. Anatolikí Makedonía kai Thráki, NE Greece
113 *K16* **Komovi** ▲▲ SW Serbia and Montenegro (Yugo.)
117 *R8* **Kompaniyivka** Kirovohrads'ka Oblast', C Ukraine
Kompong *see* Kâmpóng Chhnăng
Kompong Cham *see* Kâmpóng Cham
Kompong Kleang *see* Kâmpóng Khleăng
Kompong Som *see* Kâmpóng Saôm
Kompong Speu *see* Kâmpóng Spoe
Komrat *see* Comrat
Komsomol *see* Komsomol'skiy, Atyrau, Kazakhstan
Komsomol/Komsomolets *see* Karabalyk, Kostanay, Kazakhstan
122 *K14* **Komsomolets, Ostrov** *island* Severnaya Zemlya, N Russian Federation
144 *F13* **Komsomolets, Zaliv** *lake gulf* SW Kazakhstan
147 *Q12* **Komsomolobod** *Rus.* Komosolabad. C Tajikistan
124 *M16* **Komsomol'sk** Ivanovskaya Oblast', W Russian Federation
117 *S6* **Komsomol's'k** Poltavs'ka Oblast', C Ukraine
146 *M11* **Komsomol'sk** Navoiy Viloyati, N Uzbekistan
144 *G12* **Komsomol'skiy** *Kaz.* Komsomol. Atyrau, W Kazakhstan
125 *W4* **Komsomol'skiy** Respublika Komi, NW Russian Federation
123 *S13* **Komsomol'sk-na-Amure** Khabarovskiy Kray, SE Russian Federation
Komsomol'sk-na-Ustyurte *see* Kubla-Ustyurt
144 *K10* **Komsomol'skoye** Aktyubinsk, NW Kazakhstan
127 *Q8* **Komsomol'skoye** Saratovskaya Oblast', W Russian Federation
145 *P10* **Kon** ≈ C Kazakhstan
Kona *see* Kailua-Kona
124 *K16* **Konakovo** Tverskaya Oblast', W Russian Federation
143 *V15* **Konārak** Sīstān va Balūchestān, SE Iran
Konarhā *see* Kunar
27 *O11* **Konawa** Oklahoma, C USA
122 *H10* **Konda** ≈ C Russian Federation
154 *L13* **Kondagaon** Chhattīsgarh, C India
14 *K10* **Kondiaronk, Lac** ◎ Québec, SE Canada
180 *J13* **Kondinin** Western Australia
81 *H21* **Kondoa** Dodoma, C Tanzania
127 *P6* **Kondol'** Penzenskaya Oblast', W Russian Federation
114 *N10* **Kondolovo** Burgas, E Bulgaria
171 *Z16* **Kondomirat** Papua, E Indonesia
124 *J10* **Kondopoga** Respublika Kareliya, NW Russian Federation
Kondoz *see* Kunduz
155 *J17* **Kondukūr** *var.* Kandukur. Andhra Pradesh, E India
Kondūz *see* Kunduz
187 *P16* **Koné** Province Nord, W New Caledonia
146 *E13* **Könekesir** *Rus.* Kënekesir. Balkan Welaýaty, W Turkmenistan
146 *G8* **Köneürgenç** *var.* Köneürgench, *Rus.* Këneurgench; *prev.* Kunya-Urgench. Daşoguz Welaýaty, N Turkmenistan
Köneürgench *see* Köneürgenç
77 *N15* **Kong** N Ivory Coast
39 *S5* **Kongakut River** ≈ Alaska, USA
197 *O14* **Kong Christian IX Land** *Eng.* King Christian IX Land. *physical region* SE Greenland
197 *P13* **Kong Christian X Land** *Eng.* King Christian X Land. *physical region* E Greenland
197 *N13* **Kong Frederik IX Land** *Eng.* King Frederik IX Land. *physical region* SW Greenland
197 *Q12* **Kong Frederik VIII Land** *Eng.* King Frederik VIII Land. *physical region* NE Greenland
197 *N15* **Kong Frederik VI Kyst** *Eng.* King Frederik VI Coast. *physical region* SE Greenland
167 *P13* **Kŏng, Kaôh** *prev.* Kas Kong. *island* SW Cambodia
92 *P2* **Kong Karls Land** *Eng.* King Charles Islands. *island group* SE Svalbard
81 *G14* **Kong Kong** ≈ SE Sudan
Kongo *see* Congo (river)
83 *G16* **Kongola** Caprivi, NE Namibia
79 *N21* **Kongolo** Katanga, E Dem. Rep. Congo
81 *F14* **Kongor** Jonglei, SE Sudan
197 *Q14* **Kong Oscar Fjord** *fjord* E Greenland
77 *P12* **Kongoussi** N Burkina
95 *G15* **Kongsberg** Buskerud, S Norway
92 *Q2* **Kongsøya** *island* Kong Karls Land, E Svalbard
95 *I14* **Kongsvinger** Hedmark, S Norway
Kongtong *see* Pingliang
167 *T11* **Kông, Tônle** *Lao.* Xê Kong. ≈ Cambodia/Laos
158 *E8* **Kongur Shan** ▲ NW China
81 *I22* **Kongwa** Dodoma, C Tanzania
Kong, Xê *see* Kông, Tônle
Konia *see* Konya
147 *R11* **Konibodom** *Rus.* Kanibadam. N Tajikistan
111 *K15* **Koniecpol** Śląskie, S Poland
Konieh *see* Konya
Königgrätz *see* Hradec Králové
Königinhof an der Elbe *see* Dvůr Králové nad Labem
101 *K23* **Königsbrunn** Bayern, S Germany
Königshütte *see* Chorzów
101 *O24* **Königssee** ◎ SE Germany
109 *S8* **Königstuhl** ▲ S Austria
109 *U3* **Konigswiesen** Oberösterreich, N Austria
101 *E17* **Königswinter** Nordrhein-Westfalen, W Germany
146 *M11* **Konimex** *Rus.* Kenimekh. Navoiy Viloyati, N Uzbekistan
110 *I12* **Konin** *Ger.* Kuhnau. Wielkopolskie, C Poland
Koninkrijk der Nederlanden *see* Netherlands
113 *L24* **Konispol** *var.* Konispoli. Vlorë, S Albania
Konispoli *see* Konispol
115 *C15* **Kónitsa** Ípeiros, W Greece
Konitz *see* Chojnice
108 *D8* **Köniz** Bern, W Switzerland
113 *H14* **Konjic** Federacija Bosna I Hercegovina, C Bosnia and Herzegovina
92 *J10* **Könkämäälven** ≈ Finland/Sweden
155 *D14* **Konkan** W India
83 *D22* **Konkiep** ≈ S Namibia
76 *I14* **Konkouré** ≈ W Guinea
77 *O11* **Konna** Mopti, S Mali
186 *H6* **Konogaiang, Mount** ▲ New Ireland, NE PNG
186 *H5* **Konogogo** New Ireland, NE PNG
108 *E9* **Konolfingen** Bern, W Switzerland
77 *P16* **Konongo** C Ghana
186 *H5* **Konos** New Ireland, NE PNG
124 *M12* **Konosha** Arkhangel'skaya Oblast', NW Russian Federation
117 *R3* **Konotop** Sums'ka Oblast', NE Ukraine
158 *L7* **Konqi He** ≈ NW China
111 *L14* **Końskie** Świętokrzyskie, C Poland
Konstantinovka *see* Kostyantynivka
126 *M11* **Konstantinovsk** Rostovskaya Oblast', SW Russian Federation
101 *H24* **Konstanz** *var.* Constanz, *Eng.* Constance; *hist.* Kostnitz, *anc.* Constantia. Baden-Württemberg, S Germany
Konstanza *see* Constanța
77 *T14* **Kontagora** Niger, W Nigeria
78 *E13* **Kontcha** Nord, N Cameroon
99 *G17* **Kontich** Antwerpen, N Belgium
93 *O16* **Kontiolahti** Itä-Suomi, E Finland
93 *M15* **Kontiomäki** Oulu, C Finland
167 *U11* **Kon Tum** *var.* Kontum. Kon Tum, C Vietnam
Konur *see* Sulakyurt
136 *H15* **Konya** *var.* Konieh; *prev.* Konia, *anc.* Iconium. Konya, C Turkey
136 *H15* **Konya** *var.* Konia, Konieh. ◈ *province* C Turkey
145 *T13* **Konyrat** *var.* Kounradskiy, *Kaz.* Qongyrat. Karaganda, C Kazakhstan
145 *W15* **Konyrolen** Almaty, SE Kazakhstan
81 *I19* **Konza** Eastern, S Kenya
98 *I9* **Koog aan den Zaan** Noord-Holland, C Netherlands
182 *E7* **Koonibba** South Australia
31 *O11* **Koontz Lake** Indiana, N USA
171 *U12* **Koor** Papua, E Indonesia
183 *R9* **Koorawatha** New South Wales, SE Australia
118 *J5* **Koosa** Tartumaa, E Estonia
33 *N7* **Kootenai** *var.* Kootenay. ≈ Canada/USA *see also* Kootenay
11 *P17* **Kootenay** *var.* Kootenai. ≈ Canada/USA *see also* Kootenai
83 *F24* **Kootjieskolk** Northern Cape, W South Africa
113 *M15* **Kopaonik** ▲▲ S Serbia and Montenegro (Yugo.)
Kopar *see* Koper
92 *K1* **Kópasker** Nordhurland Eystra, N Iceland
92 *H4* **Kópavogur** Reykjanes, W Iceland
145 *U13* **Kopbirlik** *prev.* Kīrov, Kirova. Almaty, SE Kazakhstan
109 *S13* **Koper** *It.* Capodistria; *prev.* Kopar. SW Slovenia
95 *C16* **Kopervik** Rogaland, S Norway
Köpetdag Gershi/Kopetdag, Khrebet *see* Koppeh Dāgh
Kophinou *see* Kofínou
182 *G8* **Kopi** South Australia
Kopiago *see* Lake Copiago
153 *W12* **Kopili** ≈ NE India
95 *M15* **Köping** Västmanland, C Sweden
113 *K17* **Koplik** *var.* Kopliku. Shkodër, NW Albania
Kopliku *see* Koplik
Kopopo *see* Kokopo
94 *I11* **Koppang** Hedmark, S Norway
Kopparberg *see* Dalarna
143 *S3* **Koppeh Dāgh** *Rus.* Khrebet Kopetdag, *Turkm.* Köpetdag Gershi. ▲▲ Iran/Turkmenistan
Koppename *see* Coppename Rivier
95 *J15* **Koppom** Värmland, C Sweden
Kopreinitz *see* Koprivnica
114 *K9* **Koprinka, Yazovir** *prev.* Yazovir Georgi Dimitrov. ⊡ C Bulgaria
112 *F7* **Koprivnica** *Ger.* Kopreinitz, *Hung.* Kaproncza. Koprivnica-Križevci, N Croatia

◆ Country ● Country Capital ◇ Dependent Territory ○ Dependent Territory Capital ◈ Administrative Region × International Airport ▲ Mountain ▲▲ Mountain Range 🌋 Volcano ≈ River ◎ Lake ⊡ Reservoir

Koprivnica-Križevci *off.* Koprivničko-Križevačka Županija. ◆ *province* N Croatia
111 I17 **Kopřivnice** *Ger.* Nesselsdorf. Moravskoslezský Kraj, E Czech Republic
Köprülü *see* Veles
Koptsevichi *see* Kaptsevichy
Kopyl' *see* Kapyl'
119 O14 **Kopys'** *Rus.* Kopys'. Vitsyebskaya Voblasts', NE Belarus
113 M18 **Korab** ▲ Albania/FYR Macedonia
Korabavur Pastligi *see* Karabaur', Uval
81 M14 **K'orahē** Somali, E Ethiopia
115 L16 **Kórakas, Akrotírio** *headland* Lésvos, E Greece
112 D9 **Korana** ∾ C Croatia
155 L14 **Korāput** Orissa, E India
Korat *see* Nakhon Ratchasima
167 Q9 **Korat Plateau** *plateau* E Thailand
139 T1 **Kōrāwa, Sar-i** ▲ NE Iraq
154 L11 **Korba** Chhattīsgarh, C India
101 H15 **Korbach** Hessen, C Germany
Korça *see* Korçë
113 M21 **Korçë** *var.* Korça, *Gk.* Korytsa, *It.* Corriza; *prev.* Koritsa. Korçë, SE Albania
113 M21 **Korçë** ◆ *district* SE Albania
113 G15 **Korčula** *It.* Curzola. Dubrovnik-Neretva, S Croatia
113 F15 **Korčula** *It.* Curzola; *anc.* Corcyra Nigra. *island* S Croatia
113 F15 **Korčulanski Kanal** *channel* S Croatia
145 T6 **Korday** *prev.* Georgiyevka. Zhambyl, SE Kazakhstan
142 J5 **Kordestān** *off.* Ostān-e Kordestān, *var.* Kurdestan. ◆ *province* W Iran
143 P4 **Kord Kūy** *var.* Kurd Kui. Golestān, N Iran
163 V13 **Korea Bay** *bay* China/North Korea
Korea, Democratic People's Republic of *see* North Korea
171 T15 **Koreare** Pulau Yamdena, E Indonesia
Korea, Republic of *see* South Korea
163 Z17 **Korea Strait** *Jap.* Chōsen-kaikyō, *Kor.* Taehan-haehyŏp. *channel* Japan/South Korea
Korelichi/Korelicze *see* Karelichy
80 J11 **Korem** Tigray, N Ethiopia
77 U11 **Korén Adoua** ∾ C Niger
126 I7 **Korenevo** Kurskaya Oblast', W Russian Federation
126 L13 **Korenovsk** Krasnodarskiy Kray, SW Russian Federation
116 L4 **Korets'** *Pol.* Korzec, *Rus.* Korets. Rivnens'ka Oblast', NW Ukraine
194 L7 **Korff Ice Rise** *ice cap* Antarctica
145 Q10 **Korgalzhyn** *var.* Kurgal'dzhino, Kurgal'dzhinsky, *Kaz.* Qorgazhyn. Akmola, C Kazakhstan
92 G13 **Korgen** Troms, N Norway
147 R9 **Korgon-Dĕbĕ** Dzhalal-Abadskaya Oblast', W Kyrgyzstan
76 M14 **Korhogo** N Ivory Coast
115 F19 **Korinthiakós Kólpos** *Eng.* Gulf of Corinth; *anc.* Corinthiacus Sinus. *gulf* C Greece
115 F19 **Kórinthos** *Eng.* Corinth; *anc.* Corinthus. Pelopónnisos, S Greece
113 M18 **Koritnik** ▲ S Serbia and Montenegro (Yugo.)
Koritsa *see* Korçë
165 P11 **Kōriyama** Fukushima, Honshū, C Japan
136 E16 **Korkuteli** Antalya, SW Turkey
158 K6 **Korla** *Chin.* K'u-erh-lo. Xinjiang Uygur Zizhiqu, NW China
122 J10 **Korliki** Khanty-Mansiyskiy Avtonomnyy Okrug, C Russian Federation
Körlin an der Persante *see* Karlino
Korma *see* Karma
14 D8 **Kormak** Ontario, S Canada
Kormakíti, Akrotíri/Kormakiti, Cape/Kormakítis *see* Koruçam Burnu
111 G23 **Körmend** Vas, W Hungary
139 T5 **Kōrmōr** E Iraq
112 C13 **Kornat** *It.* Incoronata. *island* W Croatia
Korneshty *see* Cornești
109 X3 **Korneuburg** Niederösterreich, NE Austria
145 P7 **Korneyevka** Severnyy Kazakhstan, N Kazakhstan
95 I17 **Kornsjø** Østfold, S Norway
77 O11 **Koro** Mopti, S Mali
187 Y14 **Koro** *island* C Fiji
186 B7 **Koroba** Southern Highlands, W PNG
126 K8 **Korocha** Belgorodskaya Oblast', W Russian Federation
136 H12 **Köroğlu Dağları** ▲ C Turkey
183 V6 **Korogoro Point** *headland* New South Wales, SE Australia
81 J21 **Korogwe** Tanga, E Tanzania
182 L13 **Koroit** Victoria, SE Australia
187 X15 **Korolevu** Viti Levu, W Fiji
190 I17 **Koromiri** *island* S Cook Islands
171 Q8 **Koronadal** Mindanao, S Philippines
115 E22 **Koróni** Pelopónnisos, S Greece
114 G13 **Korónia, Límni** ◎ N Greece
110 I9 **Koronowo** *Ger.* Krone an der Brahe. Kujawski-pomorskie, C Poland
117 R2 **Korop** Chernihivs'ka Oblast', N Ukraine
115 H19 **Koropí** Attikí, C Greece
188 C8 **Koror** *var.* Oreor. ● (Palau) Oreor, N Palau
Koror *see* Oreor
Kőrös *see* Križevci
111 L23 **Körös** ∾ E Hungary
Körösbánya *see* Baia de Criş
187 Y14 **Koro Sea** *sea* C Fiji
Koroška *see* Kärnten
117 N3 **Korosten'** Zhytomyrs'ka Oblast', NW Ukraine
Korostyshev *see* Korostyshiv
117 N4 **Korostyshiv** *Rus.* Korostyshev. Zhytomyrs'ka Oblast', N Ukraine
127 V3 **Korotaikha** ∾ NW Russian Federation
122 J9 **Korotchayevo** Yamalo-Nenetskiy Avtonomnyy Okrug, N Russian Federation
78 I8 **Koro Toro** Borkou-Ennedi-Tibesti, N Chad
39 N16 **Korovin Island** *island* Shumagin Islands, Alaska, USA
187 X14 **Korovou** Viti Levu, W Fiji
93 M17 **Korpilahti** Länsi-Suomi, W Finland
92 K12 **Korpilombolo** *Lapp.* Dállogilli. Norrbotten, N Sweden
123 T13 **Korsakov** Ostrov Sakhalin, Sakhalinskaya Oblast', SE Russian Federation
93 J16 **Korsholm** *Fin.* Mustasaari. Länsi-Suomi, W Finland
95 I23 **Korsør** Vestsjælland, E Denmark
Korsovka *see* Kārsava
117 P6 **Korsun'-Shevchenkivs'kyy** *Rus.* Korsun'-Shevchenkovskiy. Cherkas'ka Oblast', C Ukraine
Korsun'-Shevchenkovskiy *see* Korsun'-Shevchenkivs'kyy
99 C17 **Kortemark** West-Vlaanderen, W Belgium
99 H18 **Kortenberg** Vlaams Brabant, C Belgium
99 K18 **Kortessem** Limburg, NE Belgium
99 E14 **Kortgene** Zeeland, SW Netherlands
80 F8 **Korti** Northern, N Sudan
99 C18 **Kortrijk** *Fr.* Courtrai. West-Vlaanderen, W Belgium
121 O2 **Koruçam Burnu** *var.* Cape Kormakiti, Kormakítis, *Gk.* Akrotíri Kormakíti. *headland* N Cyprus
183 O13 **Korumburra** Victoria, SE Australia
Koryak Range *see* Koryakskoye Nagor'ye
123 V8 **Koryakskiy Avtonomnyy Okrug** ◆ *autonomous district* E Russian Federation
Koryakskiy Khrebet *see* Koryakskoye Nagor'ye
123 V7 **Koryakskoye Nagor'ye** *var.* Koryakskiy Khrebet, *Eng.* Koryak Range. ▲ NE Russian Federation
125 P11 **Koryazhma** Arkhangel'skaya Oblast', NW Russian Federation
Koryŏ *see* Kangnŭng
Korytsa *see* Korçë
117 Q2 **Koryukivka** Chernihivs'ka Oblast', N Ukraine
Korzec *see* Korets'
115 N21 **Kos** Kos, Dodekánisos, Greece, Aegean Sea
115 M21 **Kos** *It.* Coo; *anc.* Cos. *island* Dodekánisos, Greece, Aegean Sea
125 T12 **Kosa** Komi-Permyatskiy Avtonomnyy Okrug, NW Russian Federation
127 T13 **Kosa** ∾ NW Russian Federation
164 B12 **Kō-saki** *headland* Nagasaki, Tsushima, SW Japan
163 X13 **Kosan** SE North Korea
119 H18 **Kosava** *Rus.* Kosovo. Brestskaya Voblasts', SW Belarus
Kosch *see* Kose
144 G12 **Koschagyl** *Kaz.* Qosshaghyl. Atyrau, W Kazakhstan
110 G12 **Kościan** *Ger.* Kosten. Wielkopolskie, C Poland
110 I7 **Kościerzyna** Pomorskie, NW Poland
22 L4 **Kosciusko** Mississippi, S USA
Kosciusko, Mount *see* Kosciuszko, Mount
183 R11 **Kosciuszko, Mount** *prev.* Mount Kosciusko ▲ New South Wales, SE Australia
118 H4 **Kose** *Ger.* Kosch. Harjumaa, NW Estonia
114 G6 **Koshava** Vidin, NW Bulgaria
147 U9 **Kosh-Dĕbĕ** *var.* Koshtebë. Narynskaya Oblast', C Kyrgyzstan
K'o-shih *see* Kashi
164 B16 **Koshikijima-rettō** *var.* Kosikizima Rettô. *island group* SW Japan
145 W13 **Koshkarkol', Ozero** ◎ SE Kazakhstan
30 L9 **Koshkonong, Lake** ◎ Wisconsin, N USA
Koshoba *see* Goşoba
164 M12 **Kōshoku** *var.* Kôsyoku. Nagano, Honshū, S Japan
Koshtebë *see* Kosh-Dĕbĕ
Kōshū *see* Kwangju
111 N19 **Košice** *Ger.* Kaschau, *Hung.* Kassa. Košický Kraj, E Slovakia
111 M20 **Košický Kraj** ◆ *region* E Slovakia
Kosigaya *see* Koshigaya
Kosikizima Rettô *see* Koshikijima-retto
153 R12 **Kosi Reservoir** ⊠ E Nepal
116 J8 **Kosiv** Ivano-Frankivs'ka Oblast', W Ukraine
145 O11 **Koskol'** Karaganda, C Kazakhstan
125 Q9 **Koslan** Respublika Komi, NW Russian Federation
Köslin *see* Koszalin
146 M12 **Koson** *Rus.* Kasan. Qashqadaryo Viloyati, S Uzbekistan
163 Y13 **Kosŏng** SE North Korea
147 S9 **Kosonsoy** *Rus.* Kasansay. Namangan Viloyati, E Uzbekistan
113 M16 **Kosovo** *prev.* Autonomous Province of Kosovo and Metohija. *region* S Serbia and Montenegro (Yugo.)
Kosovo *see* Kosava
Kosovo and Metohija, Autonomous Province of *see* Kosovo
113 N16 **Kosovo Polje** Serbia, S Serbia and Montenegro (Yugo.)
113 O16 **Kosovska Kamenica** Serbia, SE Serbia and Montenegro (Yugo.)
113 M16 **Kosovska Mitrovica** *Alb.* Mitrovicë; *prev.* Mitrovica, Titova Mitrovica. Serbia, S Serbia and Montenegro (Yugo.)
189 X17 **Kosrae** ◆ *state* E Micronesia
189 Y14 **Kosrae** *prev.* Kusaie. *island* Caroline Islands, E Micronesia
25 U9 **Kosse** Texas, SW USA
109 P6 **Kössen** Tirol, W Austria
76 M16 **Kossou, Lac de** ◎ C Ivory Coast
Kossukavak *see* Krumovgrad
Kostajnica *see* Hrvatska Kostajnica
150 M7 **Kostanay** *var.* Kustanay, *Kaz.* Qostanay. N Kazakhstan
150 L8 **Kostanay** *var.* Kostanayskaya Oblast, *Kaz.* Qostanay Oblysy. ◆ *province* N Kazakhstan
Kostanayskaya Oblast *see* Kostanay
Kostamus *see* Kostomuksha
Kosten *see* Kościan
114 H10 **Kostenets** *prev.* Georgi Dimitrov. Sofiya, W Bulgaria
80 F10 **Kosti** White Nile, C Sudan
Kostnitz *see* Konstanz
124 H7 **Kostomuksha** *Fin.* Kostamus. Respublika Kareliya, NW Russian Federation
116 K3 **Kostopil'** *Rus.* Kostopol'. Rivnens'ka Oblast', NW Ukraine
Kostopol' *see* Kostopil'
124 M15 **Kostroma** Kostromskaya Oblast', NW Russian Federation
127 N14 **Kostroma** ∾ NW Russian Federation
125 N14 **Kostromskaya Oblast'** ◆ *province* NW Russian Federation
110 D11 **Kostrzyn** *Ger.* Cüstrin, Küstrin. Lubuskie, W Poland
110 H11 **Kostrzyn** Wielkopolskie, C Poland
117 X7 **Kostyantynivka** *Rus.* Konstantinovka. Donets'ka Oblast', SE Ukraine
Kostyukovichi *see* Kastsyukovichy
Kostyukovka *see* Kastsyukowka
Kôsyoku *see* Kōshoku
125 U6 **Kos'yu** Respublika Komi, NW Russian Federation
127 U6 **Kos'yu** ∾ NW Russian Federation
110 F7 **Koszalin** *Ger.* Köslin. Zachodnio-pomorskie, NW Poland
111 F22 **Kőszeg** *Ger.* Güns. Vas, W Hungary
152 H13 **Kota** *prev.* Kotah. Rājasthān, N India
168 K12 **Kota Baru** Sumatera, W Indonesia
169 U13 **Kotabaru** Pulau Laut, C Indonesia
Kotabaru *see* Jayapura
168 K6 **Kota Bharu** *var.* Kota Baharu, Kota Bahru. Kelantan, Peninsular Malaysia
Kotaboemi *see* Kotabumi
168 M14 **Kotabumi** *prev.* Kotaboemi. Sumatera, W Indonesia
149 S10 **Kot Addu** Punjab, E Pakistan
Kotah *see* Kota
169 U7 **Kota Kinabalu** *prev.* Jesselton. Sabah, East Malaysia
169 U7 **Kota Kinabalu** ✕ Sabah, East Malaysia
92 M12 **Kotala** Lappi, N Finland
Kotamobagoe *see* Kotamobagu
171 Q11 **Kotamobagu** *prev.* Kotamobagoe. Sulawesi, C Indonesia
155 L14 **Kotapad** *var.* Kotapārh. Orissa, E India
Kotapārh *see* Kotapad
166 N17 **Ko Ta Ru Tao** *island* SW Thailand
169 R13 **Kotawaringin, Teluk** *bay* Borneo, C Indonesia
149 Q13 **Kot Dīji** Sind, SE Pakistan
152 K9 **Kotdwāra** Uttaranchal, N India
125 Q14 **Kotel'nich** Kirovskaya Oblast', NW Russian Federation
127 N12 **Kotel'nikovo** Volgogradskaya Oblast', SW Russian Federation
123 Q6 **Kotel'nyy, Ostrov** *island* Novosibirskiye Ostrova, N Russian Federation
117 T5 **Kotel'va** Poltavs'ka Oblast', C Ukraine
101 M14 **Köthen** *var.* Cöthen. Sachsen-Anhalt, C Germany
Kôti *see* Kōchi
81 G17 **Kotido** NE Uganda
93 N19 **Kotka** Etelä-Suomi, S Finland
125 P11 **Kotlas** Arkhangel'skaya Oblast', NW Russian Federation
38 M10 **Kotlik** Alaska, USA
77 Q17 **Kotoka** ✕ (Accra) S Ghana
Kotonu *see* Cotonou
113 J17 **Kotor** *It.* Cattaro. Montenegro, SW Serbia and Montenegro (Yugo.)
Kotor *see* Kotoriba
112 F7 **Kotoriba** *Hung.* Kotor. Međimurje, N Croatia
113 I17 **Kotorska, Boka** *It.* Bocche di Cattaro. *bay* Montenegro, SW Serbia and Montenegro (Yugo.)
112 H11 **Kotorsko** Republika Srpska, N Bosnia and Herzegovina
112 G11 **Kotor Varoš** Republika Srpska, N Bosnia and Herzegovina
Koto Sho/Kotosho *see* Lan Yü
126 M7 **Kotovsk** Tambovskaya Oblast', W Russian Federation
117 O9 **Kotovs'k** *Rus.* Kotovsk. Odes'ka Oblast', SW Ukraine
Kotovsk *see* Hînceşti
119 G16 **Kotra** *Rus.* Kotra. ∾ W Belarus
149 P16 **Kotri** Sind, SE Pakistan
109 Q9 **Kötschach** Kärnten, S Austria
155 K15 **Kottagūdem** Andhra Pradesh, E India
155 F21 **Kottappadi** Kerala, SW India
155 G23 **Kottayam** Kerala, SW India
Kottbus *see* Cottbus
Kotte *see* Sri Jayawardanapura
79 K15 **Kotto** ∾ Central African Republic/Dem. Rep. Congo
193 X15 **Kotu Group** *island group* W Tonga
Koturdepe *see* Goturdepe
122 M9 **Kotuy** ∾ N Russian Federation
83 M16 **Kotwa** Mashonaland East, NE Zimbabwe
39 N7 **Kotzebue** Alaska, USA
38 M7 **Kotzebue Sound** *inlet* Alaska, USA
Kotzenan *see* Chocianów
Kotzman *see* Kitsman'
77 R14 **Kouandé** NW Benin
79 J15 **Kouango** Ouaka, S Central African Republic
77 O13 **Koudougou** C Burkina
98 K7 **Koudum** Friesland, N Netherlands
115 L25 **Koufonísi** *island* SE Greece
115 K21 **Koufonísi** *island* Kykládes, Greece, Aegean Sea
38 M8 **Kougarok Mountain** ▲ Alaska, USA
79 E20 **Kouilou** ∾ S Congo
121 O3 **Koúklia** SW Cyprus
79 E19 **Koulamoutou** Ogooué-Lolo, C Gabon
76 L12 **Koulikoro** Koulikoro, SW Mali
76 L11 **Koulikoro** ◆ *region* SW Mali
187 P16 **Koumac** Province Nord, W New Caledonia
165 N12 **Koumi** Nagano, Honshū, S Japan
78 I13 **Koumra** Moyen-Chari, S Chad
Kounadougou *see* Koundougou
76 M15 **Kounahiri** C Ivory Coast
76 I12 **Koundâra** Moyenne-Guinée, NW Guinea
77 N13 **Koundougou** *var.* Kounadougou. C Burkina
76 H11 **Koungheul** C Senegal
Kounradskiy *see* Konyrat
25 X10 **Kountze** Texas, SW USA
77 Q13 **Koupéla** C Burkina
77 N13 **Kouri** Sikasso, SW Mali
55 Y9 **Kourou** N French Guiana
114 J12 **Kouroú** ∾ NE Greece
76 K14 **Kouroussa** Haute-Guinée, C Guinea
Kousseir *see* Al Quşayr
78 G11 **Kousséri** *prev.* Fort-Foureau. Extrême-Nord, NE Cameroon
Kouteifé *see* Al Quţayfah
76 M13 **Koutiala** Sikasso, S Mali
76 M14 **Kouto** NW Ivory Coast
93 M19 **Kouvola** Etelä-Suomi, S Finland
79 G18 **Kouyou** ∾ C Congo
112 M10 **Kovačica** *Hung.* Antafalva; *prev.* Kovacsicza. Serbia, N Serbia and Montenegro (Yugo.)
Kovacsicza *see* Kovačica
Kővárhosszúfalu *see* Satulung
Kovászna *see* Covasna
124 I4 **Kovdor** Murmanskaya Oblast', NW Russian Federation
126 I5 **Kovdozero, Ozero** ◎ NW Russian Federation
116 J3 **Kovel'** *Pol.* Kowel. Volyns'ka Oblast', NW Ukraine
112 M11 **Kovin** *Hung.* Kevevára; *prev.* Temes-Kubin. Serbia, NE Serbia and Montenegro (Yugo.)
Kovno *see* Kaunas
127 N3 **Kovrov** Vladimirskaya Oblast', W Russian Federation
127 O5 **Kovylkino** Respublika Mordoviya, W Russian Federation
110 J11 **Kowal** Kujawsko-pomorskie, C Poland
110 J9 **Kowalewo Pomorskie** *Ger.* Schönsee. Kujawsko-pomorskie, C Poland
Kowasna *see* Covasna
119 M16 **Kowbcha** *Rus.* Kolbcha. Mahilyowskaya Voblasts', E Belarus
Koweit *see* Kuwait
Kowel *see* Kovel'
185 F17 **Kowhitirangi** West Coast, South Island, NZ
161 O15 **Kowloon** *Chin.* Jiulong. Hong Kong, S China
Kowno *see* Kaunas
159 N7 **Kox Kuduk** *well* NW China
136 D16 **Köyceğiz** Muğla, SW Turkey
125 N6 **Koyda** Arkhangel'skaya Oblast', NW Russian Federation
Koymat *see* Goymat
Koymatdag, Gory *see* Goymatdag
Koyna Reservoir *see* Shivāji Sāgar
165 P9 **Koyoshi-gawa** ∾ Honshū, C Japan
Koysanjaq *see* Koi Sanjaq
Koytash *see* Qo'ytosh
146 M14 **Köýtendag** *prev. Rus.* Charshanga, Charshangy, *Turkm.* Charshangngy. Lebap Welaýaty, E Turkmenistan
39 N9 **Koyuk** Alaska, USA
39 N9 **Koyuk River** ∾ Alaska, USA
39 O9 **Koyukuk** Alaska, USA
39 O9 **Koyukuk River** ∾ Alaska, USA
136 J13 **Kozaklı** Nevşehir, C Turkey
136 K16 **Kozan** Adana, S Turkey
115 E14 **Kozáni** Dytikí Makedonía, N Greece
112 F10 **Kozara** ▲ NW Bosnia and Herzegovina
Kozarska Dubica *see* Bosanska Dubica
117 P3 **Kozelets'** *Rus.* Kozelets. Chernihivs'ka Oblast', NE Ukraine
117 S6 **Kozel'shchyna** Poltavs'ka Oblast', C Ukraine
126 J5 **Kozel'sk** Kaluzhskaya Oblast', W Russian Federation
Kozhikode *see* Calicut
127 V9 **Kozhimiz, Gora** ▲ NW Russian Federation
126 L9 **Kozhozero, Ozero** ◎ NW Russian Federation
125 T7 **Kozhva** *var.* Kozya. Respublika Komi, NW Russian Federation
127 T7 **Kozhva** ∾ NW Russian Federation
110 N13 **Kozienice** Mazowieckie, C Poland
125 U6 **Kozhim** Respublika Komi, NW Russian Federation
109 S13 **Kozina** SW Slovenia
114 H7 **Kozloduy** Vratsa, NW Bulgaria
127 Q3 **Kozlovka** Chuvashskaya Respublika, W Russian Federation
Kozlovshchina/Kozlowszczyzna *see* Kazlowshchyna
127 P3 **Koz'modem'yansk** Respublika Mariy El, W Russian Federation
116 J6 **Kozova** Ternopil's'ka Oblast', W Ukraine
113 P20 **Kožuf** ▲ S FYR Macedonia
165 N15 **Kōzu-shima** *island* E Japan
Kozya *see* Kozhva
Koz'yany *see* Kaz'yany
117 N5 **Kozyatyn** *Rus.* Kazatin. Vinnyts'ka Oblast', C Ukraine
77 Q16 **Kpalimé** *var.* Palimé. SW Togo
77 Q16 **Kpandu** E Ghana
99 F15 **Krabbendijke** Zeeland, SW Netherlands
167 N15 **Krabi** *var.* Muang Krabi. Krabi, SW Thailand
167 N13 **Kra Buri** Ranong, SW Thailand
167 S12 **Krâchéh** *prev.* Kratie. Krâchéh, E Cambodia
95 G17 **Kragerø** Telemark, S Norway
112 M13 **Kragujevac** Serbia, C Serbia and Montenegro (Yugo.)
Krainburg *see* Kranj
166 N13 **Kra, Isthmus of** *isthmus* Malaysia/Thailand
112 D12 **Krajina** *cultural region* SW Croatia
Krakatau, Pulau *see* Rakata, Pulau
Krakau *see* Małopolskie
111 L16 **Kraków** *Eng.* Cracow, *Ger.* Krakau; *anc.* Cracovia. Małopolskie, S Poland
100 L9 **Krakower See** ◎ NE Germany
167 Q11 **Krâlănh** Siĕmréab, NW Cambodia
45 Q16 **Kralendijk** Bonaire, E Netherlands Antilles
112 B10 **Kraljevica** *It.* Porto Re. Primorje-Gorski Kotar, NW Croatia
112 M13 **Kraljevo** *prev.* Rankovićevo. Serbia, C Serbia and Montenegro (Yugo.)
111 E16 **Královéhradecký Kraj** *prev.* Hradecký Kraj. ◆ *region* N Czech Republic
Kralup an der Moldau *see* Kralupy nad Vltavou
111 C16 **Kralupy nad Vltavou** *Ger.* Kralup an der Moldau. Středočeský Kraj, NW Czech Republic
117 W7 **Kramators'k** *Rus.* Kramatorsk. Donets'ka Oblast', SE Ukraine
93 H17 **Kramfors** Västernorrland, C Sweden
115 D15 **Kranéa** Dytikí Makedonía, N Greece
108 M7 **Kranebitten** ✕ (Innsbruck) Tirol, W Austria
115 G20 **Kranídi** Pelopónnisos, S Greece
109 T11 **Kranj** *Ger.* Krainburg. NW Slovenia
115 F16 **Krannón** *battleground* Thessalía, C Greece
Kranz *see* Zelenogradsk
112 D7 **Krapina** Krapina-Zagorje, N Croatia
112 E8 **Krapina** ∾ N Croatia
112 D8 **Krapina-Zagorje** *off.* Krapinsko-Zagorska Županija. ◆ *province* N Croatia
114 L7 **Krapinets** ∾ NE Bulgaria
111 I15 **Krapkowice** *Ger.* Krappitz. Opolskie, S Poland
Krappitz *see* Krapkowice
125 O12 **Krasavino** Vologodskaya Oblast', NW Russian Federation
122 H6 **Krasino** Novaya Zemlya, Arkhangel'skaya Oblast', N Russian Federation
123 S15 **Kraskino** Primorskiy Kray, SE Russian Federation
118 J11 **Krāslava** Krāslava, SE Latvia
119 M14 **Krasnaluki** *Rus.* Krasnoluki. Vitsyebskaya Voblasts', N Belarus
119 P17 **Krasnapollye** *Rus.* Krasnopol'ye. Mahilyowskaya Voblasts', E Belarus
126 L15 **Krasnaya Polyana** Krasnodarskiy Kray, SW Russian Federation
119 J18 **Krasnaya Slabada** *var.* Chyrvonaya Slabada, *Rus.* Krasnaya Sloboda. Minskaya Voblasts', S Belarus
Krasnaya Sloboda *see* Krasnaya Slabada
119 J15 **Krasnaye** *Rus.* Krasnoye. Minskaya Voblasts', C Belarus
111 O14 **Kraśnik** *Ger.* Kratznick. Lubelskie, E Poland
117 O9 **Krasni Okny** Odes'ka Oblast', SW Ukraine
145 P7 **Krasnoarmeysk** Severnyy Kazakhstan, N Kazakhstan
127 P8 **Krasnoarmeysk** Saratovskaya Oblast', W Russian Federation
Krasnoarmeysk *see* Krasnoarmiys'k/Tayynsha
123 T6 **Krasnoarmeyskiy** Chukotskiy Avtonomnyy Okrug, NE Russian Federation
117 W7 **Krasnoarmiys'k** *Rus.* Krasnoarmeysk. Donets'ka Oblast', SE Ukraine
125 P11 **Krasnoborsk** Arkhangel'skaya Oblast', NW Russian Federation
126 K14 **Krasnodar** *prev.* Ekaterinodar, Yekaterinodar. Krasnodarskiy Kray, SW Russian Federation
126 K13 **Krasnodarskiy Kray** ◆ *territory* SW Russian Federation
117 Z7 **Krasnodon** Luhans'ka Oblast', E Ukraine
Krasnogor *see* Kallaste
127 T2 **Krasnogorskoye** *Latv.* Sarkaņi. Udmurtskaya Respublika, NW Russian Federation
Krasnograd *see* Krasnohrad
Krasnogvardeysk *see* Bulung'ur
126 M13 **Krasnogvardeyskoye** Stavropol'skiy Kray, SW Russian Federation
Krasnogvardeyskoye *see* Krasnohvardiys'ke
117 U6 **Krasnohrad** *Rus.* Krasnograd. Kharkivs'ka Oblast', E Ukraine
117 S12 **Krasnohvardiys'ke** *Rus.* Krasnogvardeyskoye. Respublika Krym, S Ukraine
123 P14 **Krasnokamensk** Chitinskaya Oblast', S Russian Federation
125 U14 **Krasnokamsk** Permskaya Oblast', W Russian Federation
127 U8 **Krasnokholm** Orenburgskaya Oblast', W Russian Federation
117 U5 **Krasnokuts'k** *Rus.* Krasnokutsk. Kharkivs'ka Oblast', E Ukraine
126 L7 **Krasnolesnyy** Voronezhskaya Oblast', W Russian Federation
Krasnoluki *see* Krasnaluki
Krasnoosol'skoye Vodokhranilishche *see* Chervonooskil's'ke Vodoskhovyshche
117 S11 **Krasnoperekops'k** *Rus.* Krasnoperekopsk. Respublika Krym, S Ukraine
117 U4 **Krasnopillya** Sums'ka Oblast', NE Ukraine
Krasnopol'ye *see* Krasnapollye
124 L5 **Krasnoshchel'ye** Murmanskaya Oblast', NW Russian Federation
127 O5 **Krasnoslobodsk** Respublika Mordoviya, W Russian Federation
127 T2 **Krasnoslobodsk** Volgogradskaya Oblast', SW Russian Federation
Krasnostav *see* Krasnystaw
127 V5 **Krasnousol'skiy** Respublika Bashkortostan, W Russian Federation
125 U12 **Krasnovishersk** Permskaya Oblast', NW Russian Federation
Krasnovodsk *see* Türkmenbaşy
Krasnovodskiy Zaliv *see* Türkmenbaşy Aylagy
146 B10 **Krasnovodskoye Plato** *Turkm.* Krasnowodsk Platosy. *plateau* NW Turkmenistan
Krasnowodsk Aylagy *see* Türkmenbaşy Aylagy
Krasnowodsk Platosy *see* Krasnovodskoye Plato
122 K12 **Krasnoyarsk** Krasnoyarskiy Kray, S Russian Federation
127 X7 **Krasnoyarskiy** Orenburgskaya Oblast', W Russian Federation
122 K11 **Krasnoyarskiy Kray** ◆ *territory* C Russian Federation
Krasnoye *see* Krasnaye
Krasnoye Znamya *see* Gyzylbaydak
125 R11 **Krasnozatonskiy** Respublika Komi, NW Russian Federation
118 D13 **Krasnoznamensk** *prev.* Lasdehnen, *Ger.* Haselberg. Kaliningradskaya Oblast', W Russian Federation
126 K4 **Krasnoznamensk** Moskovskaya Oblast', W Russian Federation
117 R11 **Krasnoznam"yans'kyy Kanal** *canal* S Ukraine
111 P14 **Krasnystaw** *Rus.* Krasnostav. Lubelskie, SE Poland
126 H4 **Krasnyy** Smolenskaya Oblast', W Russian Federation
127 P2 **Krasnyye Baki** Nizhegorodskaya Oblast', W Russian Federation
127 Q13 **Krasnyye Barrikady** Astrakhanskaya Oblast', SW Russian Federation
124 K15 **Krasnyy Kholm** Tverskaya Oblast', W Russian Federation
127 Q8 **Krasnyy Kut** Saratovskaya Oblast', W Russian Federation
Krasnyy Liman *see* Krasnyy Lyman
117 Y7 **Krasnyy Luch** *prev.* Krindachevka. Luhans'ka Oblast', E Ukraine
117 X6 **Krasnyy Lyman** *Rus.* Krasnyy Liman. Donets'ka Oblast', SE Ukraine

◆ Country ● Country Capital ◇ Dependent Territory ○ Dependent Territory Capital ◆ Administrative Region ✕ International Airport ▲ Mountain ▲ Mountain Range ⚠ Volcano ∾ River ◎ Lake ⊠ Reservoir

127 R3 **Krasnyy Steklovar** Respublika Mariy El, W Russian Federation
127 P8 **Krasnyy Tekstil'shchik** Saratovskaya Oblast', W Russian Federation
127 R13 **Krasnyy Yar** Astrakhanskaya Oblast', SW Russian Federation
116 L5 **Krasyliv** Khmel'nyts'ka Oblast', W Ukraine
111 O21 **Kraszna** Rom. Crasna. ≈ Hungary/Romania
Kratie see Krâchéh
113 P17 **Kratovo** NE FYR Macedonia
Kratznick see Kraśnik
171 Y13 **Krau** Papua, E Indonesia
167 Q13 **Krâvanh, Chuŏr Phnum** Eng. Cardamom Mountains, Fr. Chaîne des Cardamomes. ▲▲ W Cambodia
Kravasta Lagoon see Karavastasë, Laguna e
Krawang see Karawang
Kraxatau see Rakata, Pulau
127 Q15 **Kraynovka** Respublika Dagestan, SW Russian Federation
118 D12 **Kražiai** Šiauliai, C Lithuania
27 P11 **Krebs** Oklahoma, C USA
101 D15 **Krefeld** Nordrhein-Westfalen, W Germany
Kreisstadt see Krosno Odrzańskie
115 D17 **Kremastón, Technití Límni** ⊠ C Greece
Kremenchug see Kremenchuk
Kremenchugskoye Vodokhranilishche/ Kremenchuk Reservoir see Kremenchuts'ke Vodoskhovyshche
117 S6 **Kremenchuk** Rus. Kremenchug. Poltavs'ka Oblast', NE Ukraine
117 R6 **Kremenchuts'ke Vodoskhovyshche** Eng. Kremenchuk Reservoir, Rus. Kremenchugskoye Vodokhranilishche. ⊠ C Ukraine
116 K5 **Kremenets'** Pol. Krzemieniec, Rus. Kremenets. Ternopil's'ka Oblast', W Ukraine
Kremennaya see Kreminna
117 X6 **Kreminna** Rus. Kremennaya. Luhans'ka Oblast', E Ukraine
37 R4 **Kremmling** Colorado, C USA
109 V3 **Krems** ≈ NE Austria
Krems see Krems an der Donau
109 W3 **Krems an der Donau** var. Krems. Niederösterreich, N Austria
Kremsier see Kroměříž
109 S4 **Kremsmünster** Oberösterreich, N Austria
38 M17 **Krenitzin Islands** island Aleutian Islands, Alaska, USA
Kresena see Kresna
114 G11 **Kresna** var. Kresena. Blagoevgrad, SW Bulgaria
112 O12 **Krespoljin** Serbia, E Serbia and Montenegro (Yugo.)
25 N4 **Kress** Texas, SW USA
123 V6 **Kresta, Zaliv** bay E Russian Federation
115 D20 **Kréstena** prev. Selinoús. Dytikí Ellás, S Greece
124 H14 **Kresttsy** Novgorodskaya Oblast', W Russian Federation
Kretikon Delagos see Kritikó Pélagos
118 C11 **Kretinga** Ger. Krottingen. Klaipėda, NW Lithuania
Kreutz see Cristuru Secuiesc
Kreuz see Križevci, Croatia
Kreuz see Risti, Estonia
Kreuzburg/Kreuzburg in Oberschlesien see Kluczbork
Kreuzingen see Bol'shakovo
108 H6 **Kreuzlingen** Thurgau, NE Switzerland
101 K25 **Kreuzspitze** ▲ S Germany
101 F16 **Kreuztal** Nordrhein-Westfalen, W Germany
119 I15 **Kreva** Rus. Krevo. Hrodzyenskaya Voblasts', W Belarus
Krevo see Kreva
Kría Vrísi see Krýa Vrýsi
79 D16 **Kribi** Sud, SW Cameroon
Krichëv see Krychaw
Krickerhäu/Kriegerhaj see Handlová
109 W6 **Krieglach** Steiermark, E Austria
108 F8 **Kriens** Luzern, W Switzerland
Krimmitschau see Crimmitschau
98 H12 **Krimpen aan den IJssel** Zuid-Holland, SW Netherlands
Krindachevka see Krasnyy Luch
115 G25 **Kríos, Akrotírio** headland Kríti, Greece, E Mediterranean Sea
155 J16 **Krishna** prev. Kistna. ≈ C India
155 H20 **Krishnagiri** Tamil Nādu, SE India
155 K17 **Krishna, Mouths of the** delta SE India
153 S15 **Krishnanagar** West Bengal, N India
155 G20 **Krishnarājāsāgara Reservoir** ⊠ W India
95 N19 **Kristdala** Kalmar, S Sweden
Kristiania see Oslo
95 E18 **Kristiansand** var. Christiansand. Vest-Agder, S Norway
95 L22 **Kristianstad** Skåne, S Sweden
94 F8 **Kristiansund** var. Christiansund. Møre og Romsdal, S Norway
Kristiinankaupunki see Kristinestad
93 I14 **Kristineberg** Västerbotten, N Sweden
95 L16 **Kristinehamn** Värmland, C Sweden
93 J17 **Kristinestad** Fin. Kristiinankaupunki. Länsi-Suomi, W Finland
Kristyor see Crişcior
115 J25 **Kríti** Eng. Crete. ◈ region Greece, Aegean Sea
115 J24 **Kríti** Eng. Crete. island Greece, Aegean Sea
115 J23 **Kritikó Pélagos** var. Kretikon Delagos, Eng. Sea of Crete; anc. Mare Creticum. sea Greece, Aegean Sea
Kriulyany see Criuleni
112 I12 **Krivaja** ≈ NE Bosnia and Herzegovina
Krivaja see Mali Iđoš
113 P17 **Kriva Palanka** Turk. Eğri Palanka. NE FYR Macedonia
Krivichi see Kryvychy
114 H8 **Krivodol** Vratsa, NW Bulgaria
126 M10 **Krivorozh'ye** Rostovskaya Oblast', SW Russian Federation
Krivoshin see Kryvoshyn
Krivoy Rog see Kryvyy Rih
112 F7 **Križevci** Ger. Kreuz, Hung. Kőrös. Varaždin, NE Croatia
112 B10 **Krk** It. Veglia. Primorje-Gorski Kotar, NW Croatia
112 B10 **Krk** It. Veglia; anc. Curieta. island NW Croatia
109 V12 **Krka** ≈ SE Slovenia
Krka see Gurk
109 R11 **Krn** ▲ NW Slovenia
111 H16 **Krnov** Ger. Jägerndorf. Moravskoslezský Kraj, E Czech Republic
Kroatien see Croatia
95 G14 **Krøderen** Buskerud, S Norway
95 G14 **Krøderen** ◎ S Norway
Kroi see Krui
95 N17 **Krokek** Östergötland, S Sweden
Krokodil see Crocodile
93 G16 **Krokom** Jämtland, C Sweden
117 S2 **Krolevets'** Rus. Krolevets. Sums'ka Oblast', NE Ukraine
Królewska Huta see Chorzów
111 H18 **Kroměříž** Ger. Kremsier. Zlínský Kraj, E Czech Republic
98 I9 **Krommenie** Noord-Holland, C Netherlands
126 J6 **Kromy** Orlovskaya Oblast', W Russian Federation
101 L18 **Kronach** Bayern, E Germany
Krone an der Brahe see Koronowo
167 Q13 **Krŏng Kaôh Kŏng** Kaôh Kŏng, SW Cambodia
95 K21 **Kronoberg** ◈ county S Sweden
123 V10 **Kronotskiy Zaliv** bay E Russian Federation
195 O2 **Kronprinsesse Märtha Kyst** physical region Antarctica
195 V3 **Kronprins Olav Kyst** physical region Antarctica
124 G12 **Kronshtadt** Leningradskaya Oblast', NW Russian Federation
Kronstadt see Braşov
83 I22 **Kroonstad** Free State, C South Africa
123 O12 **Kropotkin** Irkutskaya Oblast', C Russian Federation
126 L14 **Kropotkin** Krasnodarskiy Kray, SW Russian Federation
110 J11 **Krośniewice** Łódzkie, C Poland
111 N17 **Krosno** Ger. Krossen. Podkarpackie, SE Poland
110 E12 **Krosno Odrzańskie** Ger. Crossen, Kreisstadt. Lubuskie, W Poland
Krossen see Krosno
Krotoschin see Krotoszyn
110 H13 **Krotoszyn** Ger. Krotoschin. Wielkopolskie, C Poland
Krottingen see Kretinga
Krousón see Krousónas
115 J25 **Krousónas** prev. Krousón, Kroussón. Kríti, Greece, E Mediterranean Sea
Kroussón see Krousónas
Krraba see Krrabë
113 L20 **Krrabë** var. Krraba. Tiranë, C Albania
113 L17 **Krrabit, Mali i** ▲▲ N Albania
109 W12 **Krško** Ger. Gurkfeld; prev. Videm-Krško. E Slovenia
83 K19 **Kruger National Park** national park Limpopo, N South Africa
83 J21 **Krugersdorp** Gauteng, NE South Africa
38 D16 **Krugloi Point** headland Agattu Island, Alaska, USA
Krugloye see Kruhlaye
119 N15 **Kruhlaye** Rus. Krugloye. Mahilyowskaya Voblasts', E Belarus
168 L15 **Krui** var. Kroi. Sumatera, SW Indonesia
99 G16 **Kruibeke** Oost-Vlaanderen, N Belgium
83 G25 **Kruidfontein** Western Cape, SW South Africa
99 F15 **Kruiningen** Zeeland, SW Netherlands
Kruja see Krujë
113 L19 **Krujë** var. Kruja, It. Croia. Durrës, C Albania
Krulevshchina see Krulewshchyna
118 K13 **Krulewshchyna** Rus. Krulevshchina. Vitsyebskaya Voblasts', N Belarus
25 T6 **Krum** Texas, SW USA
101 J23 **Krumbach** Bayern, S Germany
113 M17 **Krumë** Kukës, NE Albania
Krummau see Český Krumlov
114 K12 **Krumovgrad** prev. Kossukavak. Kŭrdzhali, S Bulgaria
114 K12 **Krumovitsa** ≈ S Bulgaria
114 L10 **Krumovo** Yambol, E Bulgaria
167 O11 **Krung Thep** var. Krung Thep Mahanakhon, Eng. Bangkok. ● (Thailand) Bangkok, C Thailand
167 O11 **Krung Thep, Ao** var. Bight of Bangkok. bay S Thailand
Krung Thep Mahanakhon see Krung Thep
Krupa/Krupa na Uni see Bosanska Krupa
119 M15 **Krupki** Rus. Krupki. Minskaya Voblasts', C Belarus
95 G24 **Kruså** var. Krusaa. Sønderjylland, SW Denmark
Krusaa see Kruså
113 N14 **Kruševac** Serbia, C Serbia and Montenegro (Yugo.)
113 N19 **Kruševo** SW FYR Macedonia
111 A15 **Krušné Hory** Eng. Ore Mountains, Ger. Erzgebirge. ▲▲ Czech Republic/Germany see also Erzgebirge
39 W13 **Kruzof Island** island Alexander Archipelago, Alaska, USA
114 F13 **Krýa Vrýsi** var. Kría Vrísi. Kentrikí Makedonía, N Greece
119 P16 **Krychaw** Rus. Krichëv. Mahilyowskaya Voblasts', E Belarus
64 K11 **Krylov Seamount** undersea feature E Atlantic Ocean
Krym see Krym, Respublika
117 S13 **Krym, Respublika** var. Krym, Eng. Crimea, Crimean Oblast; prev. Rus. Krymskaya ASSR, Krymskaya Oblast'. ◈ province SE Ukraine
126 K14 **Krymsk** Krasnodarskiy Kray, SW Russian Federation
Krymskaya ASSR/ Krymskaya Oblast' see Krym, Respublika
117 T13 **Kryms'ki Hory** ▲▲ S Ukraine
117 T13 **Kryms'kyy Pivostriv** peninsula S Ukraine
111 M18 **Krynica** Ger. Tannenhof. Małopolskie, S Poland
117 P8 **Kryve Ozero** Odes'ka Oblast', SW Ukraine
119 I18 **Kryvoshyn** Rus. Krivoshin. Brestskaya Voblasts', SW Belarus
119 K14 **Kryvychy** Rus. Krivichi. Minskaya Voblasts', C Belarus
117 S8 **Kryvyy Rih** Rus. Krivoy Rog. Dnipropetrovs'ka Oblast', SE Ukraine
117 N8 **Kryzhopil'** Vinnyts'ka Oblast', C Ukraine
Krzemieniec see Kremenets'
111 J14 **Krzepice** Śląskie, S Poland
110 F10 **Krzyż Wielkopolski** Wielkopolskie, C Poland
Ksar al Kabir see Ksar-el-Kebir
Ksar al Soule see Er-Rachidia
74 J5 **Ksar El Boukhari** N Algeria
74 G5 **Ksar-el-Kebir** var. Alcázar, Ksar al Kabir, Ksar-el-Kébir, Ar. Al-Kasr al-Kebir, Al-Qsar al-Kbir, Sp. Alcazarquivir. NW Morocco
110 H12 **Książ Wielkopolski** Ger. Xions. Wielkopolskie, C Poland
127 O3 **Kstovo** Nizhegorodskaya Oblast', W Russian Federation
169 T8 **Kuala Belait** W Brunei
Kuala Dungun see Dungun
169 Q10 **Kualakerian** Borneo, C Indonesia
169 S12 **Kualakuayan** Borneo, C Indonesia
168 K8 **Kuala Lipis** Pahang, Peninsular Malaysia
168 K9 **Kuala Lumpur** ● (Malaysia) Kuala Lumpur, Peninsular Malaysia
168 K9 **Kuala Lumpur International** ✈ Selangor, Peninsular Malaysia
Kuala Pelabohan Kelang see Pelabuhan Klang
169 U7 **Kuala Penyu** Sabah, East Malaysia
38 E9 **Kualapu'u** var. Kualapuu. Moloka'i, Hawai'i, USA, C Pacific Ocean
168 L7 **Kuala Terengganu** var. Kuala Trengganu. Terengganu, Peninsular Malaysia
168 L11 **Kualatungkal** Sumatera, W Indonesia
171 P11 **Kuandang** Sulawesi, N Indonesia
163 V12 **Kuandian** var. Kuandian Manzu Zizhixian. Liaoning, NE China
Kuandian Manzu Zizhixian see Kuandian
Kuando-Kubango see Cuando Cubango
Kuang-chou see Guangzhou
Kuang-hsi see Guangxi Zhuangzu Zizhiqu
Kuang-tung see Guangdong
Kuang-yuan see Guangyuan
Kuantan, Batang see Indragiri, Sungai
Kuanza Norte see Cuanza Norte
Kuanza Sul see Cuanza Sul
Kuba see Quba
Kubango see Cubango/Okavango
141 X8 **Kubārah** NW Oman
93 H16 **Kubbe** Västernorrland, C Sweden
80 A11 **Kubbum** Southern Darfur, W Sudan
126 L13 **Kubenskoye, Ozero** ◎ NW Russian Federation
146 G6 **Kubla-Ustyurt** Rus. Komsomol'sk-na-Ustyurte. Qoraqalpog'iston Respublikasi, NW Uzbekistan
164 G15 **Kubokawa** Kōchi, Shikoku, SW Japan
114 L7 **Kubrat** prev. Balbunar. Razgrad, N Bulgaria
112 O13 **Kučajske Planine** ▲▲ E Serbia and Montenegro (Yugo.)
165 T1 **Kuccharo-ko** ◎ Hokkaidō, N Japan
112 O11 **Kučevo** Serbia, NE Serbia and Montenegro (Yugo.)
Kuchan see Qūchān
169 Q10 **Kuching** prev. Sarawak. Sarawak, East Malaysia
169 Q10 **Kuching** ✈ Sarawak, East Malaysia
164 B17 **Kuchinoerabu-jima** island Nansei-shotō, SW Japan
164 C14 **Kuchinotsu** Nagasaki, Kyūshū, SW Japan
109 Q6 **Kuchl** Salzburg, NW Austria
148 L9 **Kūchnay Darweyshān** Helmand, S Afghanistan
Kuchurgan see Kuchurhan
117 O9 **Kuchurhan** Rus. Kuchurgan. ≈ NE Ukraine
Kuçova see Kuçovë
113 L21 **Kuçovë** var. Kuçova; prev. Qyteti Stalin. Berat, C Albania
136 D11 **Küçük Çekmece** İstanbul, NW Turkey
164 F14 **Kudamatsu** var. Kudamatu. Yamaguchi, Honshū, SW Japan
Kudamatu see Kudamatsu
Kudara see Ghŭdara
169 V6 **Kudat** Sabah, East Malaysia
Küddow see Gwda
155 G17 **Kūdligi** Karnātaka, W India
Kudowa see Kudowa-Zdrój
111 F16 **Kudowa-Zdrój** Ger. Kudowa. Wałbrzych, SW Poland
117 P9 **Kudryavtsivka** Mykolayivs'ka Oblast', S Ukraine
169 R16 **Kudus** prev. Koedoes. Jawa, C Indonesia
125 T13 **Kudymkar** Komi-Permyatskiy Avtonomnyy Okrug, NW Russian Federation
Kudzsir see Cugir
Kuei-chou see Guizhou
Kuei-lin see Guilin
Kuei-yang see Guiyang
K'u-erh-lo see Korla
Kueyang see Guiyang
Kufa see Al Kūfah
136 E14 **Kūfiçayı** ≈ C Turkey
109 O6 **Kufstein** Tirol, W Austria
145 V14 **Kugaly** Kaz. Qoghaly. Almaty, SE Kazakhstan
8 K8 **Kugluktuk** var. Qurlurtuuq; prev. Coppermine. Nunavut, NW Canada
143 Y13 **Kūhak** Sīstān va Balūchestān, SE Iran
143 R9 **Kūhbonān** Kermān, C Iran
148 J5 **Kūhestān** var. Kohsān. Herāt, W Afghanistan
93 N15 **Kuhmo** Oulu, E Finland
93 L18 **Kuhmoinen** Länsi-Suomi, W Finland
Kuhnau see Konin
Kūhnō see Kihnu
143 O8 **Kūhpāyeh** Eşfahān, C Iran
167 O12 **Kui Buri** var. Ban Kui Nua. Prachuap Khiri Khan, SW Thailand
Kuibyshev see Kuybyshevskoye Vodokhranilishche
82 D13 **Kuito** Port. Silva Porto. Bié, C Angola
39 X14 **Kuiu Island** island Alexander Archipelago, Alaska, USA
92 L13 **Kuivaniemi** Oulu, C Finland
77 V14 **Kujama** Kaduna, C Nigeria
110 I10 **Kujawsko-pomorskie** ◈ province, C Poland
165 R8 **Kuji** var. Kuzi. Iwate, Honshū, C Japan
Kujto, Ozero see Kuyto, Ozero
Kujū-renzan see Kujū-san
164 D14 **Kujū-san** var. Kujū-renzan. ▲ Kyūshū, SW Japan
43 N7 **Kukalaya, Rio** var. Rio Cuculaya, Rio Kukulaya. ≈ NE Nicaragua
113 O16 **Kukavica** var. Vlajna. ▲ SE Serbia and Montenegro (Yugo.)
146 M10 **Ko'kcha** Rus. Kokcha. Buxoro Viloyati, C Uzbekistan
113 M18 **Kukës** var. Kukësi. Kukës, NE Albania
113 L18 **Kukës** ◈ district NE Albania
Kukësi see Kukës
186 D8 **Kukipi** Gulf, S PNG
127 S3 **Kukmor** Respublika Tatarstan, W Russian Federation
Kukong see Shaoguan
39 N6 **Kukpowruk River** ≈ Alaska, USA
38 M6 **Kukpuk River** ≈ Alaska, USA
Kukukhoto see Hohhot
Kukulaya, Rio see Kukalaya, Rio
189 W12 **Kuku Point** headland NW Wake Island
146 G11 **Kukurtli** Ahal Welaýaty, C Turkmenistan
Kül see Kül, Rūd-e
114 F7 **Kula** Vidin, NW Bulgaria
136 D14 **Kula** Manisa, W Turkey
112 K9 **Kula** Serbia, NW Serbia and Montenegro (Yugo.)
149 S8 **Kulāchi** North-West Frontier Province, NW Pakistan
Kulachi see Kolāchi
144 F11 **Kulagino** Kaz. Kūlagīno. Atyrau, W Kazakhstan
168 L10 **Kulai** Johor, Peninsular Malaysia
114 M7 **Kulak** ≈ NE Bulgaria
153 T11 **Kula Kangri** var. Kulhakangri. ▲ Bhutan/China
144 E13 **Kulaly, Ostrov** island SW Kazakhstan
145 S16 **Kulan** Kaz. Qulan; prev. Lugovoy, Lugovoye. Zhambyl, S Kazakhstan
147 V9 **Kulanak** Narynskaya Oblast', C Kyrgyzstan
Kulandag, Gory see Gulandag
153 V14 **Kulaura** Chittagong, NE Bangladesh
118 D9 **Kuldīga** Ger. Goldingen. Kuldiga, W Latvia
Kuldja see Yining
Kul'dzhuktau, Gory see Quljuqtov-Toghi
127 N4 **Kulebaki** Nizhegorodskaya Oblast', W Russian Federation
112 E11 **Kulen Vakuf** var. Spasovo. Federacija Bosna I Hercegovina, NW Bosnia and Herzegovina
181 Q9 **Kulgera Roadhouse** Northern Territory, N Australia
Kulhakangri see Kula Kangri
127 T1 **Kuliga** Udmurtskaya Respublika, NW Russian Federation
Kulkuduk see Ko'lquduq
118 G4 **Kullamaa** Läänemaa, W Estonia
197 O12 **Kullorsuaq** var. Kuvdlorssuak. Kitaa, C Greenland
29 O6 **Kulm** North Dakota, N USA
Kulm see Chełmno
146 D12 **Kul'mach** prev. Turkm. Isgender. Balkan Welaýaty, W Turkmenistan
101 L18 **Kulmbach** Bayern, SE Germany
Kulmsee see Chełmża
147 Q14 **Kŭlob** Rus. Kulyab. SW Tajikistan
92 M13 **Kuloharju** Lappi, N Finland
125 N7 **Kuloy** Arkhangel'skaya Oblast', NW Russian Federation
127 N7 **Kuloy** ≈ NW Russian Federation
137 Q14 **Kulp** Diyarbakır, SE Turkey
Kulpa see Kolpa
77 P14 **Kulpawn** ≈ N Ghana
143 R13 **Kūl, Rūd-e** var. Kül. ≈ S Iran
144 G12 **Kul'sary** Kaz. Qulsary. Atyrau, W Kazakhstan
153 R15 **Kulti** West Bengal, NE India
93 G14 **Kultsjön** ◎ N Sweden
136 I14 **Kulu** Konya, W Turkey
123 S9 **Kulu** ≈ E Russian Federation
122 I13 **Kulunda** Altayskiy Kray, S Russian Federation
145 T7 **Kulunda Steppe** Kaz. Qulyndy Zhazyghy, Rus. Kulundinskaya Ravnina. grassland Kazakhstan/Russian Federation
Kulundinskaya Ravnina see Kulunda Steppe
182 M9 **Kulwin** Victoria, SE Australia
Kulyab see Kŭlob
117 Q3 **Kulykivka** Chernihivs'ka Oblast', N Ukraine
Kum see Qom
164 F14 **Kuma** Ehime, Shikoku, SW Japan
127 P14 **Kuma** ≈ SW Russian Federation
165 O12 **Kumagaya** Saitama, Honshū, S Japan
165 Q5 **Kumaishi** Hokkaidō, NE Japan
169 R13 **Kumai, Teluk** bay Borneo, C Indonesia
127 Y7 **Kumak** Orenburgskaya Oblast', W Russian Federation
164 C14 **Kumamoto** Kumamoto, Kyūshū, SW Japan
164 D15 **Kumamoto** off. Kumamoto-ken. ◈ prefecture Kyūshū, SW Japan
164 J15 **Kumano** Mie, Honshū, SW Japan
Kumanova see Kumanovo
113 O17 **Kumanovo** Turk. Kumanova. N FYR Macedonia
185 G17 **Kumara** West Coast, South Island, NZ
180 J8 **Kumarina Roadhouse** Western Australia
153 T15 **Kumarkhali** Khulna, W Bangladesh
77 P16 **Kumasi** prev. Coomassie. C Ghana
Kumayri see Gyumri
79 D15 **Kumba** Sud-Ouest, W Cameroon
114 N13 **Kumbağ** Tekirdağ, NW Turkey
155 J21 **Kumbakonam** Tamil Nādu, SE India
Kum-Dag see Gumdag
165 R16 **Kume-jima** island Nansei-shotō, SW Japan
127 V6 **Kumertau** Respublika Bashkortostan, W Russia
35 R4 **Kumiva Peak** ▲ Nevada, W USA
159 N8 **Kum Kuduk** well NW China
159 N7 **Kumkuduk** Xinjiang Uygur Zizhiqu, W China
Kumkurgan see Qumqo'rg'on
95 M16 **Kumla** Örebro, C Sweden
136 E17 **Kumluca** Antalya, SW Turkey
100 N9 **Kummerower See** ◎ NE Germany
77 X14 **Kumo** Gombe, E Nigeria
145 O13 **Kumola** ≈ C Kazakhstan
167 N1 **Kumon Range** ▲▲ N Myanmar
83 F22 **Kums** Karas, SE Namibia
155 E18 **Kumta** Karnātaka, W India
158 L6 **Kümük** Xinjiang Uygur Zizhiqu, W China
38 H12 **Kumukahi, Cape** headland Hawai'i, USA, C Pacific Ocean
127 Q17 **Kumukh** Respublika Dagestan, SW Russian Federation
Kumul see Hami
127 N9 **Kumylzhenskaya** Volgogradskaya Oblast', SW Russian Federation
141 W6 **Kumzār** N Oman
149 S4 **Kunar** Per. Konarhā. ◈ province E Afghanistan
Kunashiri see Kunashir, Ostrov
123 U14 **Kunashir, Ostrov** var. Kunashiri. island Kuril'skiye Ostrova, SE Russian Federation
118 I3 **Kunda** Lääne-Virumaa, NE Estonia
152 M13 **Kunda** Uttar Pradesh, N India
155 E19 **Kundāpura** var. Coondapoor. Karnātaka, W India
79 O24 **Kundelungu, Monts** ▲ S Dem. Rep. Congo
Kundert see Hernád
186 D7 **Kundiawa** Chimbu, W PNG
Kundla see Sāvarkundla
168 L10 **Kundur, Pulau** island W Indonesia
149 Q2 **Kunduz** var. Kondoz, Kundūz, Qondūz, Per. Kondūz. Kunduz, NE Afghanistan
149 Q2 **Kunduz** Per. Kondūz. ◈ province NE Afghanistan
Kuneitra see Al Qunayṭirah
83 B18 **Kunene** ◈ district NE Namibia
83 A16 **Kunene** var. Cunene. ≈ Angola/Namibia see also Cunene
Kūnes see Xinyuan
158 J5 **Künes He** ≈ NW China
95 I19 **Kungälv** Västra Götaland, S Sweden
147 W7 **Kungei Ala-Tau** Rus. Khrebet Kyungëy Ala-Too, Kir. Küngöy Ala-Too. ▲▲ Kazakhstan/Kyrgyzstan
Küngöy Ala-Too see Kungei Ala-Tau
Kungrad see Qo'ng'irot
95 J19 **Kungsbacka** Halland, S Sweden
95 I18 **Kungshamn** Västra Götaland, S Sweden
95 M16 **Kungsör** Västmanland, C Sweden
79 J16 **Kungu** Equateur, NW Dem. Rep. Congo
125 V15 **Kungur** Permskaya Oblast', NW Russian Federation
166 L9 **Kungyangon** Yangon, SW Myanmar
111 M22 **Kunhegyes** Jász-Nagykun-Szolnok, E Hungary
167 O5 **Kunhing** Shan State, E Myanmar
158 D9 **Kunjirap Daban** var. Khūnjerāb Pass. pass China/Pakistan see also Khūnjerāb Pass
Kunlun Mountains see Kunlun Shan
158 H10 **Kunlun Shan** Eng. Kunlun Mountains. ▲▲ NW China
159 P11 **Kunlun Shankou** pass C China
160 G13 **Kunming** var. K'un-ming; prev. Yunnan. Yunnan, SW China
165 R4 **Kunnui** Hokkaidō, NE Japan
95 B18 **Kunoy** Dan. Kunø Island Faeroe Islands
163 X16 **Kunsan** var. Gunsan, Jap. Gunzan. W South Korea
111 L24 **Kunszentmárton** Jász-Nagykun-Szolnok, E Hungary
111 J23 **Kunszentmiklós** Bács-Kiskun, C Hungary
181 N3 **Kununurra** Western Australia
Kunyang see Pingyang
Kunya-Urgench see Köneürgenç
Kunyé see Pins, Île des
169 T11 **Kunyi** Borneo, C Indonesia
101 I20 **Künzelsau** Baden-Württemberg, S Germany
161 S10 **Kuocang Shan** ▲▲ SE China
124 H5 **Kuoloyarvi** var. Luolajarvi. Murmanskaya Oblast', NW Russian Federation
93 N16 **Kuopio** Itä-Suomi, C Finland
93 K17 **Kuortane** Länsi-Suomi, W Finland
93 M18 **Kuortti** Itä-Suomi, E Finland
Kupa see Kolpa
171 P17 **Kupang** prev. Koepang. Timor, C Indonesia
39 Q5 **Kuparuk River** ≈ Alaska, USA
Kupchino see Cupcina
186 E9 **Kupiano** Central, S PNG
180 M4 **Kupingarri** Western Australia
122 I12 **Kupino** Novosibirskaya Oblast', C Russian Federation
118 H11 **Kupiškis** Panevėžys, NE Lithuania
114 L13 **Küplü** Edirne, NW Turkey
39 X13 **Kupreanof Island** island Alexander Archipelago, Alaska, USA
39 O16 **Kupreanof Point** headland Alaska, USA
112 G13 **Kupres** Federacija Bosna I Hercegovina, SW Bosnia and Herzegovina
117 W5 **Kup"yans'k** Rus. Kupyansk. Kharkivs'ka Oblast', E Ukraine
117 W5 **Kup"yans'k-Vuzlovyy** Kharkivs'ka Oblast', E Ukraine
158 I6 **Kuqa** Xinjiang Uygur Zizhiqu, NW China
Kür see Kura
137 W11 **Kura** Az. Kür, Geor. Mtkvari, Turk. Kura Nehri. ≈ SW Asia
55 R8 **Kuracki** NW Guyana
Kura Kurk see Irbe Strait
147 Q10 **Kurama Range** Rus. Kuraminskiy Khrebet. ▲▲ Tajikistan/Uzbekistan
Kuraminskiy Khrebet see Kurama Range
Kura Nehri see Kura
119 J14 **Kuranyets** Rus. Kurenets. Minskaya Voblasts', C Belarus
164 H13 **Kurashiki** var. Kurasiki. Okayama, Honshū, SW Japan
154 L10 **Kurasia** Chhattīsgarh, C India
Kurasiki see Kurashiki
164 H12 **Kurayoshi** var. Kurayosi. Tottori, Honshū, SW Japan
Kurayosi see Kurayoshi
163 X6 **Kurbin He** ≈ NE China
145 X10 **Kurchum** Kaz. Kürshim. Vostochnyy Kazakhstan, E Kazakhstan
145 Y10 **Kurchum** ≈ E Kazakhstan
137 X11 **Kürdämir** Rus. Kyurdamir. C Azerbaijan
Kurdestan see Kordestān
139 S1 **Kurdistan** cultural region SW Asia
Kurd Kui see Kord Kūy
155 F15 **Kurduvādi** Mahārāshtra, W India
114 J11 **Kŭrdzhali** var. Kirdzhali. Kŭrdzhali, S Bulgaria
114 K11 **Kŭrdzhali** ◈ province S Bulgaria
114 J11 **Kŭrdzhali, Yazovir** ⊠ S Bulgaria

◆ COUNTRY ● COUNTRY CAPITAL ◇ DEPENDENT TERRITORY ○ DEPENDENT TERRITORY CAPITAL ◈ ADMINISTRATIVE REGION ✈ INTERNATIONAL AIRPORT ▲ MOUNTAIN ▲▲ MOUNTAIN RANGE VOLCANO ≈ RIVER ◎ LAKE ⊠ RESERVOIR

164 F13 **Kure** Hiroshima, Honshū, SW Japan
192 K5 **Kure Atoll** var. Ocean Island. atoll Hawaiian Islands, Hawaii, USA, C Pacific Ocean
136 J10 **Küre Dağları** ▲▲ N Turkey
Kurenets see Kuranyets
118 E6 **Kuressaare** Ger. Arensburg; prev. Kingissepp. Saaremaa, W Estonia
122 K9 **Kureyka** Krasnoyarskiy Kray, N Russian Federation
122 K9 **Kureyka** ≈ N Russian Federation
Kurgal'dzhino/Kurgal'dzhinskiy see Korgalzhyn
122 G11 **Kurgan** Kurganskaya Oblast', C Russian Federation
126 L14 **Kurganinsk** Krasnodarskiy Kray, SW Russian Federation
122 G11 **Kurganskaya Oblast'** ◈ province C Russian Federation
Kurgan-Tyube see Qŭrghonteppa
191 O2 **Kuria** prev. Woodle Island. island Tungaru, W Kiribati
Kuria Muria Bay see Ḩalānīyāt, Khalīj al
Kuria Muria Islands see Ḩalānīyāt, Juzur al
153 T13 **Kurigram** Rajshahi, N Bangladesh
93 K17 **Kurikka** Länsi-Suomi, W Finland
192 I3 **Kurile Basin** undersea feature NW Pacific Ocean
Kurile Islands see Kuril'skiye Ostrova
Kurile-Kamchatka Depression see Kurile Trench
192 J3 **Kurile Trench** var. Kurile-Kamchatka Depression. undersea feature NW Pacific Ocean
127 Q9 **Kurilovka** Saratovskaya Oblast', W Russian Federation
123 U13 **Kuril'sk** Kuril'skiye Ostrova, Sakhalinskaya Oblats', SE Russian Federation
122 G11 **Kuril'skiye Ostrova** Eng. Kurile Islands. island group SE Russian Federation
42 M9 **Kurinwas, Río** ≈ E Nicaragua
Kurisches Haff see Courland Lagoon
Kurkund see Kilingi-Nõmme
126 M4 **Kurlovskiy** Vladimirskaya Oblast', W Russian Federation
80 G12 **Kurmuk** Blue Nile, SE Sudan
Kurna see Al Qurnah
155 H17 **Kurnool** var. Karnul. Andhra Pradesh, S India
164 M11 **Kurobe** Toyama, Honshū, SW Japan
165 Q7 **Kuroishi** var. Kuroisi. Aomori, Honshū, C Japan
Kuroisi see Kuroishi
165 O12 **Kuroiso** Tochigi, Honshū, S Japan
165 Q4 **Kuromatsunai** Hokkaidō, NE Japan
164 B17 **Kuro-shima** island SW Japan
185 F21 **Kurow** Canterbury, South Island, NZ
127 N15 **Kursavka** Stavropol'skiy Kray, SW Russian Federation
118 E11 **Kuršėnai** Šiauliai, N Lithuania
Kürshim see Kurchum
Kurshskaya Kosa/Kuršių Nerija see Courland Spit
126 J7 **Kursk** Kurskaya Oblast', W Russian Federation
126 I7 **Kurskaya Oblast'** ◈ province W Russian Federation
Kurskiy Zaliv see Courland Lagoon
113 N15 **Kuršumlija** Serbia, S Serbia and Montenegro (Yugo.)
137 R15 **Kurtalan** Siirt, SE Turkey
Kurtbunar see Tervel
Kurt-Dere see Vŭlchidol
Kurtitsch/Kürtös see Curtici
Kurtty see Kurty
145 U15 **Kurty** var. Kurtty. ≈ SE Kazakhstan
93 L18 **Kuru** Länsi-Suomi, W Finland
80 C13 **Kuru** ≈ W Sudan
114 M13 **Kuru Dağı** ▲▲ NW Turkey
158 L7 **Kuruktag** ▲▲ NW China
83 G22 **Kuruman** Northern Cape, N South Africa
67 T14 **Kuruman** ≈ W South Africa
164 D14 **Kurume** Fukuoka, Kyūshū, SW Japan
123 N13 **Kurumkan** Respublika Buryatiya, S Russian Federation
155 J25 **Kurunegala** North Western Province, C Sri Lanka
55 T10 **Kurupukari** C Guyana
125 U10 **Kur"ya** Respublika Komi, NW Russian Federation
144 E15 **Kuryk** prev. Yeraliyev. Mangistau, SW Kazakhstan
136 B15 **Kuşadası** Aydın, SW Turkey
115 M19 **Kuşadası Körfezi** gulf SW Turkey
164 A17 **Kusagaki-guntō** island SW Japan
Kusaie see Kosrae
145 T12 **Kusak** ≈ C Kazakhstan
Kusary see Qusar
167 P7 **Ku Sathan, Doi** ▲ NW Thailand
164 J13 **Kusatsu** var. Kusatu. Shiga, Honshū, SW Japan
Kusatu see Kusatsu
138 F11 **Kuseifa** Southern, C Israel
136 C12 **Kuş Gölü** ◎ NW Turkey
126 L12 **Kushchevskaya** Krasnodarskiy Kray, SW Russian Federation
164 D16 **Kushima** var. Kusima. Miyazaki, Kyūshū, SW Japan
164 I15 **Kushimoto** Wakayama, Honshū, SW Japan
165 V4 **Kushiro** var. Kusiro. Hokkaidō, NE Japan
148 K4 **Kūshk** Herāt, W Afghanistan
Kushka see Gushgy/Serhetabat
145 N8 **Kushmurun** Kaz. Qusmuryn. Kostanay, N Kazakhstan
145 N8 **Kushmurun, Ozero** Kaz. Qusmuryn. ◎ N Kazakhstan
127 U4 **Kushnarenkovo** Respublika Bashkortostan, W Russian Federation
Kushrabat see Qo'shrabot
153 T15 **Kushtia** var. Kustia. Khulna, W Bangladesh
Kusikino see Kushikino
Kusima see Kushima
Kusiro see Kushiro
38 M13 **Kuskokwim Bay** bay Alaska, USA
39 P11 **Kuskokwim Mountains** ▲▲ Alaska, USA
39 N12 **Kuskokwim River** ≈ Alaska, USA
108 G7 **Küsnacht** Zürich, N Switzerland
165 V4 **Kussharo-ko** var. Kussyaro. ◎ Hokkaidō, NE Japan
Küssnacht see Küssnacht am Rigi
108 F8 **Küssnacht am Rigi** var. Küssnacht. Schwyz, C Switzerland
Kussyaro see Kussharo-ko
Kustanay see Kostanay
Küstence/Küstendje see Constanța
100 F11 **Küstenkanal** var. Ems-Hunte Canal. canal NW Germany
Küstrin see Kostrzyn
Kustia see Kushtia
171 R11 **Kusu** Pulau Halmahera, E Indonesia
170 L16 **Kuta** Pulau Lombok, S Indonesia
139 T4 **Kutabān** N Iraq
136 E13 **Kütahya** prev. Kutaia. Kütahya, W Turkey
136 E13 **Kütahya** var. Kutaia. ◈ province W Turkey
Kutai see Mahakam, Sungai
Kutaia see Kütahya
137 R9 **K'ut'aisi** W Georgia
Kūt al 'Amārah see Al Kūt
Kut al Hai/Kūt al Ḩayy see Al Ḩayy
Kut al Imara see Al Kūt
123 Q11 **Kutana** Respublika Sakha (Yakutiya), NE Russian Federation
Kutaradja/Kutaraja see Bandaaceh
165 R4 **Kutchan** Hokkaidō, NE Japan
Kutch, Gulf of see Kachchh, Gulf of
Kutch, Rann of see Kachchh, Rann of
112 F9 **Kutina** Sisak-Moslavina, NE Croatia
112 H9 **Kutjevo** Požega-Slavonija, NE Croatia
111 E17 **Kutná Hora** Ger. Kuttenberg. Středočeský Kraj, C Czech Republic
110 K12 **Kutno** Łódzkie, C Poland
Kuttenberg see Kutná Hora
79 I20 **Kutu** Bandundu, W Dem. Rep. Congo
153 V17 **Kutubdia Island** island SE Bangladesh
80 B10 **Kutum** Northern Darfur, W Sudan
147 Y7 **Kuturgu** Issyk-Kul'skaya Oblast', E Kyrgyzstan
12 M5 **Kuujjuaq** prev. Fort-Chimo. Québec, E Canada
12 I7 **Kuujjuarapik** Québec, C Canada
Kuuli-Mayak see Guwlumaýak
118 I6 **Kuulse magi** ▲ S Estonia
92 N13 **Kuusamo** Oulu, E Finland
93 M19 **Kuusankoski** Etelä-Suomi, S Finland
127 W7 **Kuvandyk** Orenburgskaya Oblast', W Russian Federation
Kuvango see Cubango
Kuvasay see Quvasoy
Kuvdlorssuak see Kullorsuaq
124 I16 **Kuvshinovo** Tverskaya Oblast', W Russian Federation
141 Q4 **Kuwait** off. State of Kuwait, var. Dawlat al Kuwait, Koweit, Kuweit. ◆ monarchy SW Asia
Kuwait see Al Kuwayt
Kuwait Bay see Kuwayt, Jūn al
Kuwait City see Al Kuwayt
Kuwait, Dawlat al see Kuwait
Kuwajleen see Kwajalein Atoll
164 K13 **Kuwana** Mie, Honshū, SW Japan
139 X9 **Kuwayt** E Iraq
142 K11 **Kuwayt, Jūn al** var. Kuwait Bay. bay E Kuwait
Kuweit see Kuwait
117 P10 **Kuyal'nyts'kyy Lyman** ◎ SW Ukraine
122 I12 **Kuybyshev** Novosibirskaya Oblast', C Russian Federation
Kuybyshev see Bolgar, Respublika Tatarstan, Russian Federation
Kuybyshev see Samara
117 W9 **Kuybysheve** Rus. Kuybyshevo. Zaporiz'ka Oblast', SE Ukraine
Kuybyshevo see Kuybysheve
Kuybyshev Reservoir see Kuybyshevskoye Vodokhranilishche
Kuybyshevskaya Oblast' see Samarskaya Oblast'
Kuybyshevskiy see Novoishimskiy
127 R4 **Kuybyshevskoye Vodokhranilishche** var. Kuibyshev, Eng. Kuybyshev Reservoir. ▣ W Russian Federation
123 S9 **Kuydusun** Respublika Sakha (Yakutiya), NE Russian Federation
125 U16 **Kuyeda** Permskaya Oblast', NW Russian Federation
Küysanjaq see Koi Sanjaq
126 I7 **Kuyto, Ozero** var. Ozero Kujto. ◎ NW Russian Federation
158 J4 **Kuytun** Xinjiang Uygur Zizhiqu, NW China
122 M13 **Kuytun** Irkutskaya Oblast', S Russian Federation
55 S12 **Kuyuwini Landing** S Guyana
Kuzi see Kuji
38 M9 **Kuzitrin River** ≈ Alaska, USA
127 P6 **Kuznetsk** Penzenskaya Oblast', W Russian Federation
116 K3 **Kuznetsovs'k** Rivnens'ka Oblast', NW Ukraine
124 K6 **Kuzomen'** Murmanskaya Oblast', NW Russian Federation
165 R8 **Kuzumaki** Iwate, Honshū, C Japan
92 H9 **Kvaløya** island N Norway
92 K8 **Kvalsund** Finnmark, N Norway
94 G11 **Kvam** Oppland, S Norway
127 X7 **Kvarkeno** Orenburgskaya Oblast', W Russian Federation
93 G15 **Kvarnbergsvattnet** var. Frostviken. ◎ N Sweden
112 A11 **Kvarner** var. Carnaro, It. Quarnero. gulf W Croatia
112 B11 **Kvarnerić** channel W Croatia
39 O14 **Kvichak Bay** bay Alaska, USA
92 H12 **Kvikkjokk** Lapp. Huhttán. Norrbotten, N Sweden
95 D17 **Kvina** ≈ S Norway
92 Q1 **Kvitøya** island NE Svalbard
95 F16 **Kviteseid** Telemark, S Norway
95 H24 **Kværndrup** Fyn, C Denmark
79 H20 **Kwa** ≈ W Dem. Rep. Congo
77 Q15 **Kwadwokurom** C Ghana
186 M8 **Kwailibesi** Malaita, N Solomon Islands
189 S6 **Kwajalein Atoll** var. Kuwajleen. atoll Ralik Chain, C Marshall Islands
55 W9 **Kwakoegron** Brokopondo, N Suriname
81 J21 **Kwale** Coast, S Kenya
77 U17 **Kwale** Delta, S Nigeria
79 H20 **Kwamouth** Bandundu, W Dem. Rep. Congo
Kwando see Cuando
Kwangchow see Guangzhou
Kwangchu see Kwangju
163 X16 **Kwangju** off. Kwangju-gwangyŏksi, var. Guangju, Kwangchu, Jap. Kōshū. SW South Korea
79 H20 **Kwango** Port. Cuango. ≈ Angola/Dem. Rep. Congo see also Cuango
Kwangsi/Kwangsi Chuang Autonomous Region see Guangxi Zhuangzu Zizhiqu
Kwangtung see Guangdong
Kwangyuan see Guangyuan
81 F17 **Kwania, Lake** ◎ C Uganda
Kwanza see Cuanza
77 S15 **Kwara** ◈ state SW Nigeria
83 K22 **KwaZulu/Natal** off. KwaZulu/Natal Province; prev. Natal. ◈ province E South Africa
Kweichow see Guizhou
Kweichu see Guiyang
Kweilin see Guilin
Kweisui see Hohhot
Kweiyang see Guiyang
83 K17 **Kwekwe** prev. Que Que. Midlands, C Zimbabwe
83 G20 **Kweneng** ◈ district S Botswana
Kwesui see Hohhot
39 N12 **Kwethluk** Alaska, USA
39 N12 **Kwethluk River** ≈ Alaska, USA
110 J8 **Kwidzyń** Ger. Marienwerder. Pomorskie, N Poland
38 M13 **Kwigillingok** Alaska, USA
186 E9 **Kwikila** Central, S PNG
79 I20 **Kwilu** ≈ W Dem. Rep. Congo
Kwito see Cuito
171 U12 **Kwoka, Gunung** ▲ Papua, E Indonesia
78 I12 **Kyabé** Moyen-Chari, S Chad
183 O11 **Kyabram** Victoria, SE Australia
166 M9 **Kyaikkami** prev. Amherst. Mon State, S Myanmar
166 L9 **Kyaiklat** Irrawaddy, SW Myanmar
166 M8 **Kyaikto** Mon State, S Myanmar
123 N14 **Kyakhta** Respublika Buryatiya, S Russian Federation
182 G8 **Kyancutta** South Australia
167 T8 **Ky Anh** Ha Tinh, N Vietnam
166 L5 **Kyaukpadaung** Mandalay, C Myanmar
166 J6 **Kyaukpyu** Arakan State, W Myanmar
166 M5 **Kyaukse** Mandalay, C Myanmar
166 L8 **Kyaunggon** Irrawaddy, SW Myanmar
119 E14 **Kybartai** Pol. Kibarty. Marijampolė, S Lithuania
152 I7 **Kyelang** Himāchal Pradesh, NW India
111 G19 **Kyjov** Ger. Gaya. Jihomoravský Kraj, SE Czech Republic
115 J21 **Kykládes** var. Kikládhes, Eng. Cyclades. island group SE Greece
25 S11 **Kyle** Texas, SW USA
96 G9 **Kyle of Lochalsh** N Scotland, UK
101 D18 **Kyll** ≈ W Germany
115 F19 **Kyllíni** var. Killini. ▲ S Greece
93 M19 **Kymijoki** ≈ S Finland
115 H18 **Kýmis, Akrotírio** headland Évvoia, C Greece
125 W14 **Kyn** Permskaya Oblast', NW Russian Federation
183 N12 **Kyneton** Victoria, SE Australia
81 G17 **Kyoga, Lake** var. Lake Kioga. ◎ C Uganda
164 J12 **Kyōga-misaki** headland Honshū, SW Japan
183 V4 **Kyogle** New South Wales, SE Australia
163 W15 **Kyŏnggi-man** bay NW South Korea
163 Z16 **Kyŏngju** Jap. Keishū. SE South Korea
Kyŏngsŏng see Sŏul
Kyōsai-tō see Kōje-do
81 F19 **Kyotera** S Uganda
164 J13 **Kyōto** Kyōto, Honshū, SW Japan
164 J13 **Kyōto** off. Kyōto-fu, var. Kyōto Hu. ◈ urban prefecture Honshū, SW Japan
Kyōto-fu/Kyōto Hu see Kyōto
115 D21 **Kyparissía** var. Kiparissía. Pelopónnisos, S Greece
115 D20 **Kyparissiakós Kólpos** gulf S Greece
Kyperounda see Kyperoúnta
121 P3 **Kyperoúnta** var. Kyperounda. C Cyprus
Kypros see Cyprus
115 H16 **Kyrá Panagía** island Vóreioi Sporádes, Greece, Aegean Sea
Kyrenia see Girne
Kyrenia Mountains see Beşparmak Dağları
Kyrgyz Republic see Kyrgyzstan
147 U9 **Kyrgyzstan** off. Kyrgyz Republic, var. Kirghizia; prev. Kirgizskaya SSR, Kirghiz SSR, Republic of Kyrgyzstan. ◆ republic C Asia
100 M11 **Kyritz** Brandenburg, NE Germany
Kyrkslätt see Kirkkonummi
94 G8 **Kyrksæterøra** Sør-Trøndelag, S Norway
125 U8 **Kyrta** Respublika Komi, NW Russian Federation
111 J18 **Kysucké Nové Mesto** prev. Horné Nové Mesto, Ger. Kisutzaneustadtl, Oberneustadtl, Hung. Kiszucaújhely. Žilinský Kraj, N Slovakia
117 N12 **Kytay, Ozero** ◎ SW Ukraine
115 F23 **Kýthira** var. Kíthira, It. Cerigo; Lat. Cythera. Kýthira, S Greece
115 F23 **Kýthira** var. Kíthira, It. Cerigo; Lat. Cythera. island S Greece
115 I20 **Kýthnos** Kýthnos, Kykládes, Greece, Aegean Sea
115 I20 **Kýthnos** var. Kíthnos, Thermiá, It. Termia; anc. Cythnos. island Kykládes, Greece, Aegean Sea
115 I20 **Kýthnou, Stenó** strait Kykládes, Greece, Aegean Sea
Kyungëy Ala-Too, Khrebet see Kungei Ala-Tau
Kyurdamir see Kürdämir
146 C11 **Kürendag** Rus. Gora Kyuren. ▲ W Turkmenistan
Kyuren, Gora see Kürendag
164 D15 **Kyūshū** var. Kyûsyû. island SW Japan
192 H6 **Kyushu-Palau Ridge** var. Kyusyu-Palau Ridge. undersea feature W Pacific Ocean
114 F10 **Kyustendil** anc. Pautalia. Kyustendil, W Bulgaria
114 G11 **Kyustendil** ◈ province W Bulgaria
Kyûsyû see Kyūshū
Kyusyu-Palau Ridge see Kyushu-Palau Ridge
123 P8 **Kyusyur** Respublika Sakha (Yakutiya), NE Russian Federation
183 P10 **Kywong** New South Wales, SE Australia
117 P4 **Kyyiv** Eng. Kiev, Rus. Kiyev. ● (Ukraine) Kyyivs'ka Oblast', N Ukraine
Kyyiv see Kyyivs'ka Oblast'
117 O4 **Kyyivs'ka Oblast'** var. Kyyiv, Rus. Kiyevskaya Oblast'. ◈ province N Ukraine
117 P3 **Kyyivs'ke Vodoskhovyshche** Eng. Kiev Reservoir, Rus. Kiyevskoye Vodokhranilishche. ▣ N Ukraine
93 L16 **Kyyjärvi** Länsi-Suomi, W Finland
122 K14 **Kyzyl** Respublika Tyva, C Russian Federation
147 S8 **Kyzyl-Adyr** prev. Kirovskoye. Talasskaya Oblast', NW Kyrgyzstan
145 V14 **Kyzylagash** Almaty, SE Kazakhstan
146 C13 **Kyzylbair** Balkan Welaýaty, W Turkmenistan
Kyzyl-Dzhiik, Pereval see Uzbel Shankou
145 S7 **Kyzylkak, Ozero** ◎ NE Kazakhstan
145 X11 **Kyzylkesek** Vostochnyy Kazakhstan, E Kazakhstan
147 S10 **Kyzyl-Kiya** Kir. Kyzyl-Kyya. Batkenskaya Oblast', SW Kyrgyzstan
144 L11 **Kyzylkol', Ozero** ◎ C Kazakhstan
151 N15 **Kyzylorda** var. Kzyl-Orda, Qizil Orda Kaz. Qyzylorda; prev. Perovsk. Kyzylorda, S Kazakhstan
150 L14 **Kyzylorda** off. Kyzylordinskaya Oblast' Kaz. Qyzylorda Oblysy. ◈ province S Kazakhstan
122 K14 **Kyzyl Kum** var. Kizil Kum, Qizil Qum, Uzb. Qizilqum. desert Kazakhstan/Uzbekistan
Kyzyl-Kyya see Kyzyl-Kiya
Kyzylrabat see Qizilravot
Kyzylrabot see Qizilrabot
Kyzylsu see Kyzyl-Suu
147 X7 **Kyzyl-Suu** prev. Pokrovka. Issyk-Kul'skaya Oblast', NE Kyrgyzstan
147 S12 **Kyzyl-Suu** var. Kyzylsu. ≈ Kyrgyzstan/Tajikistan
147 X8 **Kyzyl-Tuu** Issyk-Kul'skaya Oblast', E Kyrgyzstan
145 Q12 **Kyzylzhar** Kaz. Qyzylzhar. Karaganda, C Kazakhstan
Kzyl-Orda see Kyzylorda
Kzylordinskaya Oblast' see Kyzylorda
Kzyltu see Kishkenekol'

L

109 X2 **Laa an der Thaya** Niederösterreich, NE Austria
63 K15 **La Adela** La Pampa, SE Argentina
Laagen see Numedalslågen
109 S5 **Laakirchen** Oberösterreich, N Austria
Laaland see Lolland
104 I11 **La Albuera** Extremadura, W Spain
105 O7 **La Alcarria** physical region C Spain
104 K14 **La Algaba** Andalucía, S Spain
105 P9 **La Almarcha** Castilla-La Mancha, C Spain
105 R6 **La Almunia de Doña Godina** Aragón, NE Spain
41 N5 **La Amistad, Presa** ▣ NW Mexico
118 F4 **Läänemaa** off. Lääne Maakond. ◈ province NW Estonia
118 I3 **Lääne-Virumaa** off. Lääne-Viru Maakond. ◈ province NE Estonia
62 J9 **La Antigua, Salina** salt lake W Argentina
99 E17 **Laarne** Oost-Vlaanderen, NW Belgium
80 O13 **Laas Caanood** Nugaal, N Somalia
41 O9 **La Ascensión** Nuevo León, NE Mexico
80 N12 **Laas Dhaareed** Woqooyi Galbeed, N Somalia
55 O4 **La Asunción** Nueva Esparta, NE Venezuela
Laatokka see Ladozhskoye Ozero
100 I13 **Laatzen** Niedersachsen, NW Germany
38 E9 **Lā'au Point** var. Laau Point headland Moloka'i, Hawai'i, USA, C Pacific Ocean
42 D6 **La Aurora** ✕ (Ciudad de Guatemala) Guatemala, C Guatemala
74 C9 **Laâyoune** var. Aaiún. ○ (Western Sahara) NW Western Sahara
126 L14 **Laba** ≈ SW Russian Federation
40 M6 **La Babia** Coahuila de Zaragoza, NE Mexico
15 R7 **La Baie** Québec, SE Canada
171 P16 **Labala** Pulau Lomblen, S Indonesia
62 K8 **La Banda** Santiago del Estero, N Argentina
La Banda Oriental see Uruguay
104 K4 **La Bañeza** Castilla-León, N Spain
40 M13 **La Barca** Jalisco, SW Mexico
40 K14 **La Barra de Navidad** Jalisco, C Mexico
187 Y13 **Labasa** prev. Lambasa. Vanua Levu, N Fiji
102 H8 **la Baule-Escoublac** Loire-Atlantique, NW France
Labe see Elbe
76 I13 **Labé** Moyenne-Guinée, NW Guinea
23 X14 **La Belle** Florida, SE USA
15 N11 **Labelle** Québec, SE Canada
10 H7 **Laberge, Lake** ◎ Yukon Territory, W Canada
Labes see Łobez
Labiau see Polessk
112 A10 **Labin** It. Albona. Istra, NW Croatia
126 L14 **Labinsk** Krasnodarskiy Kray, SW Russian Federation
105 X5 **La Bisbal d'Empordà** Cataluña, NE Spain
119 P16 **Labkovichy** Rus. Lobkovichi. Mahilyowskaya Voblasts', E Belarus
15 S4 **La Blache, Lac de** ◎ Québec, SE Canada
171 P4 **Labo** Luzon, N Philippines
Laboehanbadjo see Labuhanbajo
Laborca see Laborec
111 N18 **Laborec** Hung. Laborca. ≈ E Slovakia
108 D11 **La Borgne** ≈ S Switzerland
45 T12 **Laborie** SW Saint Lucia
79 F21 **La Bouenza** ◈ province S Congo
102 J14 **Labouheyre** Landes, SW France
62 L12 **Laboulaye** Córdoba, C Argentina
13 Q7 **Labrador** cultural region Newfoundland and Labrador, SW Canada
64 I6 **Labrador Basin** var. Labrador Sea Basin. undersea feature Labrador Sea
13 N9 **Labrador City** Newfoundland and Labrador, E Canada
13 Q5 **Labrador Sea** sea NW Atlantic Ocean
Labrador Sea Basin see Labrador Basin
Labrang see Xiahe
54 G9 **Labranzagrande** Boyacá, C Colombia
45 U15 **La Brea** Trinidad, Trinidad and Tobago
59 D14 **Lábrea** Amazonas, N Brazil
15 S6 **Labrieville** Québec, SE Canada
102 K14 **Labrit** Landes, SW France
108 C9 **La Broye** ≈ SW Switzerland
103 N15 **Labruguière** Tarn, S France
168 M11 **Labu** Pulau Singkep, W Indonesia
169 T7 **Labuan** var. Victoria. Labuan, East Malaysia
169 T7 **Labuan** ◈ federal territory East Malaysia
Labuan see Labuan, Pulau
169 T7 **Labuan, Pulau** var. Labuan. island East Malaysia
Labudalin see Ergun
171 N16 **Labuhanbajo** prev. Laboehanbadjo. Flores, S Indonesia
168 J9 **Labuhanbilik** Sumatera, N Indonesia
168 G8 **Labuhanhaji** Sumatera, W Indonesia
Labuk see Labuk, Sungai
Labuk Bay see Labuk, Teluk
169 V7 **Labuk, Sungai** var. Labuk. ≈ East Malaysia
169 W6 **Labuk, Teluk** var. Labuk Bay, Telukan Labuk. bay S Sulu Sea
Labuk, Telukan see Labuk, Teluk
166 K9 **Labutta** Irrawaddy, SW Myanmar
122 I8 **Labytnangi** Yamalo-Nenetskiy Avtonomnyy Okrug, N Russian Federation
78 F10 **Lac** off. Préfecture du Lac. ◈ prefecture W Chad
113 K19 **Laç** var. Laci. Lezhë, C Albania
57 K19 **Lacajahuira, Rio** ≈ W Bolivia
La Calamine see Kelmis
62 G11 **La Calera** Valparaíso, C Chile
13 P11 **Lac-Allard** Québec, E Canada
104 L13 **La Campana** Andalucía, S Spain
102 J12 **Lacanau** Gironde, SW France
42 C2 **Lacandón, Sierra del** ▲▲ Guatemala/Mexico
La Cañiza see A Cañiza
41 W16 **Lacantún, Río** ≈ SE Mexico
103 Q3 **la Capelle** Aisne, N France
112 K10 **Laćarak** Serbia, NW Serbia and Montenegro (Yugo.)
62 L11 **La Carlota** Córdoba, C Argentina
104 L13 **La Carlota** Andalucía, S Spain
105 N12 **La Carolina** Andalucía, S Spain
103 O15 **Lacaune** Tarn, S France
15 P7 **Lac-Bouchette** Québec, SE Canada
Laccadive Islands/Laccadive Minicoy and Amindivi Islands, the see Lakshadweep
11 Y16 **Lac du Bonnet** Manitoba, S Canada
30 L4 **Lac du Flambeau** Wisconsin, N USA
15 P8 **Lac-Édouard** Québec, SE Canada
42 I4 **La Ceiba** Atlántida, N Honduras
54 E9 **La Ceja** Antioquia, W Colombia
182 J11 **Lacepede Bay** bay South Australia
32 G9 **Lacey** Washington, NW USA
103 P12 **la Chaise-Dieu** Haute-Loire, C France
114 G13 **Lachanás** Kentrikí Makedonía, N Greece
126 L11 **Lacha, Ozero** ◎ NW Russian Federation
103 O8 **la Charité-sur-Loire** Nièvre, C France
103 N9 **la Châtre** Indre, C France
108 C8 **La Chaux-de-Fonds** Neuchâtel, W Switzerland
Lach Dera see Dheere Laaq
108 G8 **Lachen** Schwyz, C Switzerland
183 Q8 **Lachlan River** ≈ New South Wales, SE Australia
43 T15 **La Chorrera** Panamá, C Panama
15 V7 **Lac-Humqui** Québec, SE Canada
15 N12 **Lachute** Québec, SE Canada
Lachyn see Laçın
Laci see Laç
137 W13 **Laçın** Rus. Lachyn. SW Azerbaijan
103 S16 **la Ciotat** anc. Citharista. Bouches-du-Rhône, SE France
18 D10 **Lackawanna** New York, NE USA
11 Q13 **Lac La Biche** Alberta, SW Canada
Lac La Martre see Wha Ti
15 R12 **Lac-Mégantic** var. Mégantic. Québec, SE Canada
Lacobriga see Lagos
40 G5 **La Colorada** Sonora, NW Mexico
11 Q15 **Lacombe** Alberta, SW Canada
30 L12 **Lacon** Illinois, N USA
43 P16 **La Concepción** var. Concepción. Chiriquí, W Panama
54 H5 **La Concepción** Zulia, NW Venezuela
54 H5 **La Concepción** Zulia, NW Venezuela
107 C19 **Laconi** Sardegna, Italy, C Mediterranean Sea
19 O9 **Laconia** New Hampshire, NE USA
61 H19 **La Coronilla** Rocha, E Uruguay
La Coruña see A Coruña
103 O11 **la Courtine** Creuse, C France
102 J16 **Lacq** Pyrénées-Atlantiques, SW France
15 P9 **La Croche** Québec, SE Canada
29 X3 **la Croix, Lac** ◎ Canada/USA
26 K5 **La Crosse** Kansas, C USA
21 V7 **La Crosse** Virginia, NE USA
32 L9 **La Crosse** Washington, NW USA
30 J7 **La Crosse** Wisconsin, N USA
54 C13 **La Cruz** Nariño, SW Colombia
42 K12 **La Cruz** Guanacaste, NW Costa Rica
40 I10 **La Cruz** Sinaloa, W Mexico
61 F19 **La Cruz** Florida, S Uruguay
42 M9 **La Cruz de Río Grande** Región Autónoma Atlántico Sur, E Nicaragua
54 J4 **La Cruz de Taratara** Falcón, N Venezuela
15 Q10 **Lac-St-Charles** Québec, SE Canada
40 M6 **La Cuesta** Coahuila de Zaragoza, NE Mexico
57 A17 **La Cumbra, Volcán** ☒ Galapagos Islands, Ecuador, E Pacific Ocean
152 J5 **Ladākh Range** ▲▲ NE India
26 J5 **Ladder Creek** ≈ Kansas, C USA
45 X10 **la Désirade** atoll E Guadeloupe
Lādhiqīyah, Muḥāfaẓat al see Al Lādhiqīyah
83 F25 **Ladismith** Western Cape, SW South Africa
152 G11 **Lādnūn** Rājasthān, NW India

◆ Country ● Country Capital ◇ Dependent Territory ○ Dependent Territory Capital ◈ Administrative Region ✕ International Airport ▲ Mountain ▲▲ Mountain Range ☒ Volcano ≈ River ◎ Lake ▣ Reservoir

Ladoga, Lake see Ladozhskoye Ozero
115 E19 Ládon ≈ S Greece
54 E9 La Dorada Caldas, C Colombia
126 H11 Ladozhskoye Ozero Eng. Lake Ladoga, Fin. Laatokka. ◎ NW Russian Federation
37 R12 Ladron Peak ▲ New Mexico, SW USA
124 J11 Ladva-Vetka Respublika Kareliya, NW Russian Federation
183 Q15 Lady Barron Tasmania, SE Australia
14 G9 Lady Evelyn Lake ◎ Ontario, S Canada
23 W11 Lady Lake Florida, SE USA
10 L17 Ladysmith Vancouver Island, British Columbia, SW Canada
83 J22 Ladysmith KwaZulu/Natal, E South Africa
30 J5 Ladysmith Wisconsin, N USA
145 P9 Ladyzhenka Akmola, C Kazakhstan
186 E7 Lae Morobe, W PNG
189 R6 Lae Atoll atoll Ralik Chain, W Marshall Islands
40 C3 La Encantada, Cerro de ▲ NW Mexico
94 E12 Lærdalsøyri Sogn og Fjordane, S Norway
55 N11 La Esmeralda Amazonas, S Venezuela
42 G7 La Esperanza Intibucá, SW Honduras
30 K8 La Farge Wisconsin, N USA
23 R5 Lafayette Alabama, S USA
37 T4 Lafayette Colorado, C USA
23 R2 La Fayette Georgia, SE USA
31 O13 Lafayette Indiana, N USA
22 I9 Lafayette Louisiana, S USA
20 K8 Lafayette Tennessee, S USA
19 N7 Lafayette, Mount ▲ New Hampshire, NE USA
La Fe see Santa Fé
103 P3 la Fère Aisne, N France
102 L6 la Ferté-Bernard Sarthe, NW France
102 K5 la Ferté-Macé Orne, N France
103 N7 la Ferté-St-Aubin Loiret, C France
103 P5 la Ferté-sous-Jouarre Seine-et-Marne, N France
77 V15 Lafia Nassarawa, C Nigeria
77 T15 Lafiagi Kwara, W Nigeria
11 T17 Lafleche Saskatchewan, S Canada
102 K7 la Flèche Sarthe, NW France
109 X7 Lafnitz Hung. Lapines. ≈ Austria/Hungary
187 P17 La Foa Province Sud, S New Caledonia
20 M8 La Follette Tennessee, S USA
15 N12 Lafontaine Québec, SE Canada
22 K10 Lafourche, Bayou ≈ Louisiana, S USA
62 K6 La Fragua Santiago del Estero, N Argentina
54 H7 La Fría Táchira, NW Venezuela
104 J7 La Fuente de San Esteban Castilla-León, N Spain
186 C7 Lagaip ≈ W PNG
61 B15 La Gallareta Santa Fe, C Argentina
127 Q14 Lagan' prev. Kaspiyskiy. Respublika Kalmykiya, SW Russian Federation
95 L20 Lagan Kronoberg, S Sweden
95 K21 Lågan ≈ S Sweden
92 L2 Lagarfljót var. Lögurinn. ◎ E Iceland
37 R7 La Garita Mountains ▲▲ Colorado, C USA
171 O2 Lagawe Luzon, N Philippines
78 F13 Lagdo Nord, N Cameroon
78 F13 Lagdo, Lac de ◎ N Cameroon
100 H13 Lage Nordrhein-Westfalen, W Germany
94 H12 Lågen ≈ S Norway
61 J14 Lages Santa Catarina, S Brazil
Lágesvuotna see Laksefjorden
149 R4 Laghmān ◈ province E Afghanistan
74 J6 Laghouat N Algeria
105 Q10 La Gineta Castilla-La Mancha, C Spain
115 E21 Lagkáda var. Langada. Pelopónnisos, S Greece
114 G13 Lagkadás var. Langades, Langadhás. Kentrikí Makedonía, N Greece
115 E20 Lagkádia var. Langádhia, Langadia. Pelopónnisos, S Greece
54 F6 La Gloria Cesar, N Colombia
41 O7 La Gloria Nuevo León, NE Mexico
92 N3 Lågneset headland W Svalbard
104 G14 Lagoa Faro, S Portugal
La Goagira see La Guajira
Lago Agrio see Nueva Loja
61 I14 Lagoa Vermelha Rio Grande do Sul, S Brazil
137 V10 Lagodekhi SE Georgia
42 C7 La Gomera Escuintla, S Guatemala
Lagone see Logone
107 M19 Lagonegro Basilicata, S Italy
63 G16 Lago Ranco Los Lagos, S Chile
77 S16 Lagos Lagos, SW Nigeria
104 F14 Lagos anc. Lacobriga. Faro, S Portugal
77 S16 Lagos ◈ state SW Nigeria
40 M12 Lagos de Moreno Jalisco, SW Mexico
Lagosta see Lastovo
74 A12 Lagouira SW Western Sahara
92 O1 Lågøya island N Svalbard
32 L11 La Grande Oregon, NW USA
103 Q14 la Grande-Combe Gard, S France
12 K9 La Grande Rivière var. Fort George. ≈ Québec, SE Canada
23 R4 La Grange Georgia, SE USA
31 P11 Lagrange Indiana, N USA
20 L5 La Grange Kentucky, S USA
27 V2 La Grange Missouri, C USA
21 V10 La Grange North Carolina, SE USA
25 U11 La Grange Texas, SW USA
105 N7 La Granja Castilla-León, N Spain
55 Q9 La Gran Sabana grassland E Venezuela
54 H7 La Grita Táchira, NW Venezuela
La Grulla see Grulla
15 R11 La Guadeloupe Québec, SE Canada
64 F12 La Guaira Distrito Federal, N Venezuela
54 G4 La Guajira off. Departamento de La Guajira, var. Guajira, La Goagira. ◈ province NE Colombia
188 I4 Lagua Lichan, Punta headland Saipan, S Northern Mariana Islands
18 K14 La Guardia ✕ (New York) Long Island, New York, NE USA
La Guardia/Laguardia see A Guarda
105 P4 Laguardia País Vasco, N Spain
La Gudiña see A Gudiña
103 O9 la Guerche-sur-l'Aubois Cher, C France
103 O13 Laguiole Aveyron, S France
83 F26 L'Agulhas var. Agulhas. W Cape, SW South Africa
61 K14 Laguna Santa Catarina, S Brazil
37 Q11 Laguna New Mexico, SW USA
35 T16 Laguna Beach California, W USA
35 Y17 Laguna Dam dam Arizona/California, W USA
40 L7 Laguna El Rey Coahuila de Zaragoza, N Mexico
35 V17 Laguna Mountains ▲▲ California, W USA
61 B17 Laguna Paiva Santa Fe, C Argentina
62 H3 Lagunas Tarapacá, N Chile
56 E9 Lagunas Loreto, N Peru
57 M20 Lagunillas Santa Cruz, SE Bolivia
54 H6 Lagunillas Mérida, NW Venezuela
44 C4 La Habana var. Havana. ● (Cuba) Ciudad de La Habana, W Cuba
169 W7 Lahad Datu Sabah, East Malaysia
169 W7 Lahad Datu, Teluk var. Telukan Lahad Datu, Teluk Darvel, Teluk Datu; prev. Darvel Bay. bay Sabah, East Malaysia
38 F10 Lahaina Maui, Hawai'i, USA, C Pacific Ocean
168 L14 Lahat Sumatera, W Indonesia
La Haye see 's-Gravenhage
Lahej see Laḩij
62 G9 La Higuera Coquimbo, N Chile
141 S13 Lahī, Ḩisā' al spring/well NE Yemen
141 O16 Laḩij var. Laḩj, Eng. Lahej. SW Yemen
142 M3 Lāhījān Gīlān, NW Iran
119 I19 Lahishyn Pol. Lohiszyn, Rus. Logishin. Brestskaya Voblasts', SW Belarus
Laḩj see Laḩij
101 F18 Lahn ≈ W Germany
Lähn see Wleń
95 J21 Laholm Halland, S Sweden
95 J21 Laholmsbukten bay S Sweden
35 R6 Lahontan Reservoir ⊡ Nevada, W USA
149 W8 Lahore Punjab, NE Pakistan
149 W8 Lahore ✕ Punjab, E Pakistan
55 Q6 La Horqueta Delta Amacuro, NE Venezuela
119 K15 Lahoysk Rus. Logoysk. Minskaya Voblasts', C Belarus
101 F22 Lahr Baden-Württemberg, S Germany
93 M19 Lahti Swe. Lahtis. Etelä-Suomi, S Finland
Lahtis see Lahti
40 M14 La Huacana Michoacán de Ocampo, SW Mexico
40 K14 La Huerta Jalisco, SW Mexico
78 H12 Laï prev. Behagle, De Behagle. Tandjilé, S Chad
Laibach see Ljubljana
167 Q5 Lai Châu Lai Châu, N Vietnam
38 D9 Lā'ie var. Laie. O'ahu, Hawai'i, USA, C Pacific Ocean
102 L5 l'Aigle Orne, N France
103 Q7 Laignes Côte d'Or, C France
93 K17 Laihia Länsi-Suomi, W Finland
Laila see Laylā
83 F25 Laingsburg Western Cape, SW South Africa
109 U2 Lainsitz Cz. Lužnice. ≈ Austria/Czech Republic
96 I7 Lairg N Scotland, UK
81 I17 Laisamis Eastern, N Kenya
Laisberg see Leisi
127 R4 Laishevo Respublika Tatarstan, W Russian Federation
Laisholm see Jõgeva
92 H13 Laisvall Norrbotten, N Sweden
93 K19 Laitila Länsi-Suomi, W Finland
161 P5 Laiwu Shandong, E China
161 R4 Laixi var. Shuiji. Shandong, E China
161 R4 Laiyang Shandong, E China
161 O3 Laiyuan Hebei, E China
161 R4 Laizhou var. Ye Xian. Shandong, E China
161 Q4 Laizhou Wan var. Laichow Bay. bay E China
37 S8 La Jara Colorado, C USA
61 I15 Lajeado Rio Grande do Sul, S Brazil
112 L12 Lajkovac Serbia, C Serbia and Montenegro (Yugo.)
111 K23 Lajosmizse Bács-Kiskun, C Hungary
Lajta see Leitha
40 I6 La Junta Chihuahua, N Mexico
37 V7 La Junta Colorado, C USA
92 J13 Lakaträsk Norrbotten, N Sweden
Lak Dera see Dheere Laaq
Lakeamu see Lakekamu
29 P12 Lake Andes South Dakota, N USA
22 H9 Lake Arthur Louisiana, S USA
187 Z15 Lakeba prev. Lakemba. island Lau Group, E Fiji
187 Z14 Lakeba Passage channel E Fiji
29 S10 Lake Benton Minnesota, N USA
23 V9 Lake Butler Florida, SE USA
183 P8 Lake Cargelligo New South Wales, SE Australia
22 G9 Lake Charles Louisiana, S USA
27 X9 Lake City Arkansas, C USA
37 Q7 Lake City Colorado, C USA
23 V9 Lake City Florida, SE USA
29 U13 Lake City Iowa, C USA
31 P7 Lake City Michigan, N USA
29 W9 Lake City Minnesota, N USA
21 T13 Lake City South Carolina, SE USA
29 Q7 Lake City South Dakota, N USA
20 M8 Lake City Tennessee, S USA
10 L17 Lake Cowichan Vancouver Island, British Columbia, SW Canada
29 U10 Lake Crystal Minnesota, N USA
25 T6 Lake Dallas Texas, SW USA
97 K15 Lake District physical region NW England, UK
18 D10 Lake Erie Beach New York, NE USA
29 T11 Lakefield Minnesota, N USA
25 V6 Lake Fork Reservoir ⊡ Texas, SW USA
30 M9 Lake Geneva Wisconsin, N USA
18 L9 Lake George New York, NE USA
9 R7 Lake Harbour Baffin Island, Nunavut, NE Canada
36 I12 Lake Havasu City Arizona, SW USA
25 W12 Lake Jackson Texas, SW USA
186 D8 Lakekamu var. Lakeamu. ≈ S PNG
180 K13 Lake King Western Australia
23 V12 Lakeland Florida, SE USA
23 U7 Lakeland Georgia, SE USA
181 W4 Lakeland Downs Queensland, NE Australia
11 P16 Lake Louise Alberta, SW Canada
Lakemba see Lakeba
29 V11 Lake Mills Iowa, C USA
39 Q10 Lake Minchumina Alaska, USA
Lakemti see Nek'emtē
186 A7 Lake Murray Western, SW PNG
80 F5 Lake Nasser var. Buhayrat Nasir, Buḩayrat Nāşir, Buḩeiret Nâşir. ◎ Egypt/Sudan
31 R9 Lake Orion Michigan, N USA
190 B16 Lakepa NE Niue
29 T11 Lake Park Iowa, C USA
18 K7 Lake Placid New York, NE USA
18 K9 Lake Pleasant New York, NE USA
34 M6 Lakeport California, W USA
29 Q10 Lake Preston South Dakota, N USA
22 J5 Lake Providence Louisiana, S USA
185 E20 Lake Pukaki Canterbury, South Island, NZ
183 Q12 Lakes Entrance Victoria, SE Australia
37 N12 Lakeside Arizona, SW USA
35 V17 Lakeside California, W USA
23 S9 Lakeside Florida, SE USA
28 K13 Lakeside Nebraska, C USA
32 E13 Lakeside Oregon, NW USA
21 W6 Lakeside Virginia, NE USA
Lakes State see El Buhayrat
Lake State see Michigan
185 F20 Lake Tekapo Canterbury, South Island, NZ
21 O10 Lake Toxaway North Carolina, SE USA
29 T13 Lake View Iowa, C USA
32 I16 Lakeview Oregon, NW USA
25 O3 Lakeview Texas, SW USA
27 W14 Lake Village Arkansas, C USA
23 W12 Lake Wales Florida, SE USA
37 T4 Lakewood Colorado, C USA
18 K15 Lakewood New Jersey, NE USA
18 C11 Lakewood New York, NE USA
31 T11 Lakewood Ohio, N USA
23 Y13 Lakewood Park Florida, SE USA
23 Z14 Lake Worth Florida, SE USA
152 H4 Lake Wular ◎ NE India
124 H11 Lakhdenpokh'ya Respublika Kareliya, NW Russian Federation
152 L11 Lakhīmpur Uttar Pradesh, N India
154 J11 Lakhnādon Madhya Pradesh, C India
Lakhnau see Lucknow
154 A9 Lakhpat Gujarāt, W India
119 K19 Lakhva Rus. Lakhva. Brestskaya Voblasts', SW Belarus
26 I6 Lakin Kansas, C USA
149 S7 Lakki Marwat North-West Frontier Province, NW Pakistan
115 F21 Lakonía historical region S Greece
115 F22 Lakonikós Kólpos gulf S Greece
76 M17 Lakota S Ivory Coast
29 U11 Lakota Iowa, C USA
29 P3 Lakota North Dakota, N USA
Lak Sao see Ban Lakxao
92 L8 Laksefjorden Lapp. Lágesvuotna. fjord N Norway
92 K8 Lakselv Lapp. Leavdnja. Finnmark, N Norway
155 B21 Lakshadweep prev. the Laccadive, Minicoy and Amindivi Islands. ◈ union territory India, N Indian Ocean
155 C22 Lakshadweep Eng. Laccadive Islands. island group India, N Indian Ocean
153 S17 Lakshmikāntapur West Bengal, NE India
112 G11 Laktaši Republika Srpska, N Bosnia and Herzegovina
149 V7 Lāla Mūsa Punjab, NE Pakistan
la Laon see Laon
114 M11 Lalapaşa Edirne, NW Turkey
83 P14 Lalaua Nampula, N Mozambique
105 S10 L'Alcúdia var. L'Alcúdia. País Valenciano, E Spain
80 J11 Lalibela Amhara, N Ethiopia,
153 T12 Lalmanirhat Rajshahi, N Bangladesh
79 F20 La Lékoumou ◈ province SW Congo
42 E8 La Libertad La Libertad, SW El Salvador
42 E3 La Libertad Petén, N Guatemala
42 H6 La Libertad Comayagua, SW Honduras
40 E4 La Libertad var. Puerto Libertad. Sonora, NW Mexico
42 K10 La Libertad Chontales, S Nicaragua
42 A9 La Libertad ◈ department SW El Salvador
56 B11 La Libertad off. Departamento de La Libertad. ◈ department W Peru
62 G11 La Ligua Valparaíso, C Chile
139 U5 La'li Khān E Iraq
79 H16 La Likouala ◈ province NE Congo
104 H3 Lalín Galicia, NW Spain
102 L13 Lalinde Dordogne, SW France
104 K16 La Línea var. La Línea de la Concepción. Andalucía, S Spain
La Línea de la Concepción see La Línea
152 J14 Lalitpur Uttar Pradesh, N India
153 P11 Lalitpur Central, C Nepal
152 K10 Lālkua Uttaranchal, N India
11 R12 La Loche Saskatchewan, C Canada
102 M6 la Loupe Eure-et-Loir, C France
99 G20 La Louvière Hainaut, S Belgium
L'Altissima see Hochwilde
104 L14 La Luisiana Andalucía, S Spain
37 S14 La Luz New Mexico, SW USA
107 D16 La Maddalena Sardegna, Italy, C Mediterranean Sea
62 J7 La Madrid Tucumán, N Argentina
Lama-Kara see Kara
15 S8 La Malbaie Québec, SE Canada
167 T10 Lamam Xékong, S Laos
105 P10 La Mancha physical region C Spain
la Manche see English Channel
187 R13 Lamap Malekula, C Vanuatu
37 W6 Lamar Colorado, C USA
27 S7 Lamar Missouri, C USA
21 S12 Lamar South Carolina, SE USA
107 C19 La Marmora, Punta ▲ Sardegna, Italy, C Mediterranean Sea
8 I9 La Martre, Lac ◎ Northwest Territories, NW Canada
56 D10 Lamas San Martín, N Peru
42 I5 La Masica Atlántida, NW Honduras
103 R12 Lamastre Ardèche, E France
La Matepec see Santa Ana, Volcán de
44 I7 La Maya Santiago de Cuba, E Cuba
109 S5 Lambach Oberösterreich, N Austria
168 I11 Lambak Pulau Pini, W Indonesia
102 H5 Lamballe Côtes d'Armor, NW France
79 D18 Lambaréné Moyen-Ogooué, W Gabon
Lambasa see Labasa
56 B11 Lambayeque Lambayeque, W Peru
56 A10 Lambayeque off. Departamento de Lambayeque. ◈ department NW Peru
97 G17 Lambay Island Ir. Reachrainn. island E Ireland
186 G6 Lambert, Cape headland New Britain, E PNG
195 W6 Lambert Glacier glacier Antarctica
29 T10 Lamberton Minnesota, N USA
27 X4 Lambert-Saint Louis ✕ Missouri, C USA
31 R11 Lambertville Michigan, N USA
18 J15 Lambertville New Jersey, NE USA
171 N12 Lambogo Sulawesi, N Indonesia
106 D8 Lambro ≈ N Italy
33 W11 Lame Deer Montana, NW USA
104 H6 Lamego Viseu, N Portugal
187 Q14 Lamen Bay Épi, C Vanuatu
45 X6 Lamentin Basse Terre, N Guadeloupe
Lamentin see le Lamentin
182 K10 Lameroo South Australia
54 F10 La Mesa Cundinamarca, C Colombia
35 U17 La Mesa California, W USA
37 R16 La Mesa New Mexico, SW USA
25 N6 Lamesa Texas, SW USA
107 N21 Lamezia Terme Calabria, SE Italy
115 F17 Lamía Stereá Ellás, C Greece
171 O8 Lamitan Basilan Island, SW Philippines
187 Y14 Lamiti Gau, C Fiji
171 T11 Lamlam Papua, E Indonesia
188 B16 Lamlam, Mount ▲ SW Guam
109 Q6 Lammer ≈ E Austria
185 E23 Lammerlaw Range ▲▲ South Island, NZ
95 L20 Lammhult Kronoberg, S Sweden
93 L18 Lammi Etelä-Suomi, S Finland
189 U11 Lamoil island Chuuk, C Micronesia
35 W3 Lamoille Nevada, W USA
18 M7 Lamoille River ≈ Vermont, NE USA
30 J13 La Moine River ≈ Illinois, N USA
171 P4 Lamon Bay bay Luzon, N Philippines
29 V16 Lamoni Iowa, C USA
35 R13 Lamont California, W USA
27 N8 Lamont Oklahoma, C USA
54 E13 La Montañita var. Montañita. Caquetá, S Colombia
43 N8 La Mosquitia var. Miskito Coast, Eng. Mosquito Coast. coastal region E Nicaragua
102 I9 la Mothe-Achard Vendée, NW France
188 L15 Lamotrek Atoll atoll Caroline Islands, C Micronesia
29 P6 La Moure North Dakota, N USA
167 O8 Lampang var. Muang Lampang. Lampang, NW Thailand
167 R9 Lam Pao Reservoir ⊡ E Thailand
25 S9 Lampasas Texas, SW USA
25 S9 Lampasas River ≈ Texas, SW USA
41 N7 Lampazos var. Lampazos de Naranjo. Nuevo León, NE Mexico
Lampazos de Naranjo see Lampazos
115 E19 Lámpeia Dytikí Ellás, S Greece
101 G19 Lampertheim Hessen, W Germany
97 I20 Lampeter SW Wales, UK
167 O7 Lamphun var. Lampun, Muang Lamphun. Lamphun, NW Thailand
11 X10 Lamprey Manitoba, C Canada
Lampun see Lamphun
168 M15 Lampung off. Propinsi Lampung. ◈ province SW Indonesia
126 K6 Lamskoye Lipetskaya Oblast', W Russian Federation
81 K20 Lamu Coast, SE Kenya
43 N14 La Muerte, Cerro ▲ C Costa Rica
103 S13 la Mure Isère, E France
37 S10 Lamy New Mexico, SW USA
119 J18 Lan' Rus. Lan'. ≈ C Belarus
38 E10 Lāna'i var. Lanai. island Hawai'i, USA, C Pacific Ocean
38 E10 Lāna'i City var. Lanai City. Lāna'i, Hawai'i, USA, C Pacific Ocean
99 L18 Lanaken Limburg, NE Belgium
171 Q7 Lanao, Lake var. Lake Sultan Alonto. ◎ Mindanao, S Philippines
96 J12 Lanark S Scotland, UK
96 I13 Lanark cultural region C Scotland, UK
104 L9 La Nava de Ricomalillo Castilla-La Mancha, C Spain
166 M13 Lanbi Kyun prev. Sullivan Island. island Mergui Archipelago, S Myanmar
Lancang Jiang see Mekong
97 K17 Lancashire cultural region NW England, UK
15 N13 Lancaster Ontario, SE Canada
97 K16 Lancaster NW England, UK
35 T14 Lancaster California, W USA
20 M6 Lancaster Kentucky, S USA
27 U1 Lancaster Missouri, C USA
19 O7 Lancaster New Hampshire, NE USA
18 D10 Lancaster New York, NE USA
31 T14 Lancaster Ohio, N USA
18 H16 Lancaster Pennsylvania, NE USA
21 R11 Lancaster South Carolina, SE USA
25 U7 Lancaster Texas, SW USA
21 X5 Lancaster Virginia, NE USA
30 J9 Lancaster Wisconsin, N USA
9 O4 Lancaster Sound sound Nunavut, N Canada
Lan-chou/Lan-chow/Lanchow see Lanzhou
107 K14 Lanciano Abruzzo, C Italy
111 O16 Łańcut Podkarpackie, SE Poland
169 Q11 Landak, Sungai ≈ Borneo, N Indonesia
Landao see Lantau Island
Landau see Landau an der Isar, Bayern, Germany
Landau see Landau in der Pfalz, Rheinland-Pfalz, Germany
101 N22 Landau an der Isar var. Landau. Bayern, SE Germany
101 F20 Landau in der Pfalz var. Landau. Rheinland-Pfalz, SW Germany
Land Burgenland see Burgenland
108 K8 Landeck Tirol, W Austria
99 J19 Landen Vlaams Brabant, C Belgium
33 U15 Lander Wyoming, C USA
102 F5 Landerneau Finistère, NW France
95 K20 Landeryd Halland, S Sweden
102 J15 Landes ◈ department SW France
Landeshut/Landeshut in Schlesien see Kamienna Góra
105 R9 Landete Castilla-La Mancha, C Spain
99 M18 Landgraaf Limburg, SE Netherlands
102 F5 Landivisiau Finistère, NW France
Land of Enchantment see New Mexico
Land of Opportunity see Arkansas
Land of Steady Habits see Connecticut
Land of the Midnight Sun see Alaska
108 I8 Landquart Graubünden, SE Switzerland
108 J9 Landquart ≈ Austria/Switzerland
21 P10 Landrum South Carolina, SE USA
Landsberg see Górowo Iławeckie, Warmińsko-Mazurskie, NE Poland
Landsberg see Gorzów Wielkopolski, Gorzów, Poland
101 K23 Landsberg am Lech Bayern, S Germany
Landsberg an der Warthe see Gorzów Wielkopolski
8 J4 Lands End headland Northwest Territories, NW Canada
97 G25 Land's End headland SW England, UK
101 M22 Landshut Bayern, SE Germany
Landskron see Lanškroun
95 J22 Landskrona Skåne, S Sweden
98 I10 Landsmeer Noord-Holland, C Netherlands
95 J19 Landvetter ✕ (Göteborg) Västra Götaland, S Sweden
Landwarów see Lentvaris
23 R5 Lanett Alabama, S USA
108 C8 La Neuveville var. Neuveville, Ger. Neuenstadt. Neuchâtel, W Switzerland
95 G21 Langå var. Langaa. Århus, C Denmark
Langaa see Langå
158 G14 La'nga Co ◎ W China
Langada see Lagkáda
Langades/Langadhás see Lagkadás
Langádhia/Langadia see Lagkádia
147 T14 Langar Rus. Lyangar. SE Tajikistan
146 M10 Langar Rus. Lyangar. Navoiy Viloyati, C Uzbekistan
142 M3 Langarūd Gīlān, NW Iran
11 V16 Langbank Saskatchewan, S Canada
29 P2 Langdon North Dakota, N USA
103 P12 Langeac Haute-Loire, C France
102 L8 Langeais Indre-et-Loire, C France
80 I8 Langeb, Wadi ≈ NE Sudan
Långed see Dals Långed
95 G25 Langeland island S Denmark
99 B18 Langemark West-Vlaanderen, W Belgium
101 G18 Langen Hessen, W Germany
101 J22 Langenau Baden-Württemberg, S Germany
11 V16 Langenburg Saskatchewan, S Canada
101 E16 Langenfeld Nordrhein-Westfalen, W Germany
108 L8 Längenfeld Tirol, W Austria
100 I12 Langenhagen Niedersachsen, N Germany
100 I12 Langenhagen ✕ (Hannover) Niedersachsen, NW Germany
109 W3 Langenlois Niederösterreich, NE Austria
108 E7 Langenthal Bern, NW Switzerland
109 W6 Langenwang Steiermark, E Austria
109 X3 Langenzersdorf Niederösterreich, E Austria
100 F9 Langeoog island NW Germany
95 H23 Langeskov Fyn, C Denmark
95 G16 Langesund Telemark, S Norway
95 G17 Langesundsfjorden fjord S Norway
94 D10 Langevåg Møre og Romsdal, S Norway
161 P3 Langfang Hebei, E China
94 E9 Langfjorden fjord S Norway
29 Q8 Langford South Dakota, N USA
168 I10 Langgapayung Sumatera, W Indonesia
106 E9 Langhirano Emilia-Romagna, C Italy
97 K14 Langholm S Scotland, UK
92 I3 Langjökull glacier C Iceland
168 I6 Langkawi, Pulau island Peninsular Malaysia
166 M14 Langkha Tuk, Khao ▲ SW Thailand
14 L8 Langlade Québec, SE Canada
10 M17 Langley British Columbia, SW Canada
167 S7 Lang Mô Thanh Hoa, N Vietnam
Langnau see Langnau im Emmental
108 E8 Langnau im Emmental var. Langnau. Bern, W Switzerland
103 Q13 Langogne Lozère, S France
102 K13 Langon Gironde, SW France
La Ngounié see Ngounié
92 G10 Langøya island C Norway
158 G14 Langqên Zangbo ≈ China/India
104 K2 Langreo var. Sama de Langreo. Asturias, N Spain
103 S7 Langres Haute-Marne, N France
103 R8 Langres, Plateau de plateau C France

◆ Country ● Country Capital ◇ Dependent Territory ○ Dependent Territory Capital ◈ Administrative Region ✕ International Airport ▲ Mountain ▲▲ Mountain Range ☒ Volcano ≈ River ◎ Lake ⊡ Reservoir

168 H8 **Langsa** Sumatera, W Indonesia
93 H16 **Långsele** Västernorrland, C Sweden
162 L12 **Lang Shan** ▲▲ N China
95 M14 **Långshyttan** Dalarna, C Sweden
167 T5 **Lang Sơn** *var.* Langson. Lang Sơn, N Vietnam
167 N14 **Lang Suan** Chumphon, SW Thailand
93 J14 **Långträsk** Norrbotten, N Sweden
25 N11 **Langtry** Texas, SW USA
103 P16 **Languedoc** *cultural region* S France
103 P15 **Languedoc-Roussillon** ◈ *region* S France
27 X10 **L'Anguille River** ≈ Arkansas, C USA
93 I16 **Långviksmon** Västernorrland, N Sweden
101 K22 **Langweid** Bayern, S Germany
160 J8 **Langzhong** Sichuan, C China
Lan Hsü *see* Lan Yü
11 U15 **Lanigan** Saskatchewan, S Canada
116 K5 **Lanivtsi** Ternopil's'ka Oblast', W Ukraine
137 Y13 **Länkäran** *Rus.* Lenkoran'. S Azerbaijan
102 L16 **Lannemezan** Hautes-Pyrénées, S France
102 G5 **Lannion** Côtes d'Armor, NW France
14 M11 **L'Annonciation** Québec, SE Canada
105 V5 **L'Anoia** ≈ NE Spain
18 I15 **Lansdale** Pennsylvania, NE USA
14 L14 **Lansdowne** Ontario, SE Canada
152 K9 **Lansdowne** Uttaranchal, N India
30 M3 **L'Anse** Michigan, N USA
15 S7 **L'Anse-St-Jean** Québec, SE Canada
93 K18 **Länsi-Suomi** ◈ *province* W Finland
29 Y11 **Lansing** Iowa, C USA
27 R4 **Lansing** Kansas, C USA
31 Q9 **Lansing** *state capital* Michigan, N USA
92 J12 **Lansjärv** Norrbotten, N Sweden
111 G17 **Lanškroun** *Ger.* Landskron. Pardubický Kraj, C Czech Republic
167 N16 **Lanta, Ko** *island* S Thailand
161 O15 **Lantau Island** *Cant.* Tai Yue Shan, *Chin.* Landao. *island* Hong Kong, S China
Lan-ts'ang Chiang *see* Mekong
171 O11 **Lanu** Sulawesi, N Indonesia
107 D19 **Lanusei** Sardegna, Italy, C Mediterranean Sea
102 H7 **Lanvaux, Landes de** *physical region* NW France
163 W8 **Lanxi** Heilongjiang, NE China
161 R10 **Lanxi** Zhejiang, SE China
La Nyanga *see* Nyanga
161 T15 **Lan Yü** *var.* Huoshao Tao, *var.* Hungt'ou, Lan Hsü, Lanyü, *Eng.* Orchid Island; *prev.* Kotosho, Koto Sho. *island* SE Taiwan
64 P11 **Lanzarote** *island* Islas Canarias, Spain, NE Atlantic Ocean
159 V10 **Lanzhou** *var.* Lan-chou, Lanchow, Lan-chow; *prev.* Kaolan. Gansu, C China
106 B8 **Lanzo Torinese** Piemonte, NE Italy
171 O1 **Laoag** Luzon, N Philippines
171 Q5 **Laoang** Samar, C Philippines
167 R5 **Lao Cai** Lao Cai, N Vietnam
Laodicea/Laodicea ad Mare *see* Al Lādhiqīyah
Laoet *see* Laut, Pulau
163 T11 **Laoha He** ≈ NE China
160 M8 **Laohekou** *prev.* Guanghua. Hubei, C China
Laoi, An *see* Lee
97 E19 **Laois** *prev.* Leix, Queen's County. *cultural region* C Ireland
Laojunmiao *see* Yumen
163 W12 **Lao Ling** ▲▲ N China
64 Q11 **La Oliva** *var.* Oliva. Fuerteventura, Islas Canarias, Spain, NE Atlantic Ocean
Lao, Loch *see* Belfast Lough
Laolong *see* Longchuan
Lao Mangnai *see* Mangnai
103 P3 **Laon** *var.* la Laon; *anc.* Laudunum. Aisne, N France
Lao People's Democratic Republic *see* Laos
54 M3 **La Orchila, Isla** *island* N Venezuela
64 O11 **La Orotava** Tenerife, Islas Canarias, Spain, NE Atlantic Ocean
57 E14 **La Oroya** Junín, C Peru
167 Q7 **Laos** *off.* Lao People's Democratic Republic. ◆ *republic* SE Asia
161 R5 **Laoshan Wan** *bay* E China
163 Y10 **Laoye Ling** ▲▲ NE China
60 J12 **Lapa** Paraná, S Brazil
103 P10 **Lapalisse** Allier, C France
54 F9 **La Palma** Cundinamarca, C Colombia
42 F7 **La Palma** Chalatenango, N El Salvador
43 W16 **La Palma** Darién, SE Panama
64 N11 **La Palma** *island* Islas Canarias, Spain, NE Atlantic Ocean
104 J14 **La Palma del Condado** Andalucía, S Spain
61 F18 **La Paloma** Durazno, C Uruguay
61 G20 **La Paloma** Rocha, E Uruguay
61 A21 **La Pampa** *off.* Provincia de La Pampa. ◈ *province* C Argentina
55 P8 **La Paragua** Bolívar, E Venezuela
119 O16 **Lapatsichy** *Rus.* Lopatichi. Mahilyowskaya Voblasts', E Belarus
61 C16 **La Paz** Entre Ríos, E Argentina
62 I11 **La Paz** Mendoza, C Argentina
57 J18 **La Paz** *var.* La Paz de Ayacucho. ● (Bolivia-legislative and administrative capital) La Paz, W Bolivia
42 H6 **La Paz** La Paz, SW Honduras
40 F9 **La Paz** Baja California Sur, NW Mexico
61 F20 **La Paz** Canelones, S Uruguay
57 J16 **La Paz** ◈ *department* W Bolivia
42 B9 **La Paz** ◈ *department* S El Salvador
42 G7 **La Paz** ◈ *department* SW Honduras
La Paz *see* El Alto, Bolivia
La Paz *see* Robles, Colombia
La Paz *see* La Paz Centro, Nicaragua
40 F9 **La Paz, Bahía de** *bay* W Mexico
42 I10 **La Paz Centro** *var.* La Paz. León, W Nicaragua
La Paz de Ayacucho *see* La Paz
54 J15 **La Pedrera** Amazonas, SE Colombia
31 S9 **Lapeer** Michigan, N USA
40 K6 **La Perla** Chihuahua, N Mexico
165 T1 **La Perouse Strait** *Jap.* Sōya-kaikyō, *Rus.* Proliv Laperuza. *strait* Japan/Russian Federation
63 I14 **La Perra, Salitral de** *salt lake* C Argentina
Laperuza, Proliv *see* La Perouse Strait
41 Q10 **La Pesca** Tamaulipas, C Mexico
40 M13 **La Piedad Cavadas** Michoacán de Ocampo, C Mexico
Lapines *see* Lafnitz
93 M16 **Lapinlahti** Itä-Suomi, C Finland
Lápithos *see* Lapta
22 K9 **Laplace** Louisiana, S USA
45 X12 **La Plaine** SE Dominica
173 P16 **la Plaine-des-Palmistes** C Réunion
92 K11 **Lapland** *Fin.* Lappi, *Swe.* Lappland. *cultural region* N Europe
28 M8 **La Plant** South Dakota, N USA
61 D20 **La Plata** Buenos Aires, E Argentina
54 D12 **La Plata** Huila, SW Colombia
21 W4 **La Plata** Maryland, NE USA
La Plata *see* Sucre
45 U6 **la Plata, Río de** ≈ C Puerto Rico
105 W4 **La Pobla de Lillet** Cataluña, NE Spain
105 U4 **La Pobla de Segur** Cataluña, NE Spain
15 S9 **La Pocatière** Québec, SE Canada
104 L3 **La Pola de Gordón** Castilla-León, N Spain
31 O11 **La Porte** Indiana, N USA
18 H13 **Laporte** Pennsylvania, NE USA
29 X13 **La Porte City** Iowa, C USA
62 J8 **La Posta** Catamarca, C Argentina
40 E8 **La Poza Grande** Baja California Sur, W Mexico
93 K16 **Lappajärvi** Länsi-Suomi, W Finland
93 L16 **Lappajärvi** ◎ W Finland
93 N18 **Lappeenranta** *Swe.* Villmanstrand. Etelä-Suomi, S Finland
93 J17 **Lappfjärd** *Fin.* Lapväärtti. Länsi-Suomi, W Finland
92 L12 **Lappi** *Swe.* Lappland. ◈ *province* N Finland
Lappi *see* Lapland
Lappland *see* Lappi
Lappland *see* Lapland, N Europe
Lappo *see* Lapua
61 C23 **Laprida** Buenos Aires, E Argentina
25 P13 **La Pryor** Texas, SW USA
136 B11 **Lâpseki** Çanakkale, NW Turkey
121 P2 **Lapta** *Gk.* Lápithos. NW Cyprus
Laptev Sea *see* Laptevykh, More
122 N6 **Laptevykh, More** *Eng.* Laptev Sea. *sea* Arctic Ocean
93 K16 **Lapua** *Swe.* Lappo. Länsi-Suomi, W Finland
105 P3 **La Puebla de Arganzón** País Vasco, N Spain
104 L14 **La Puebla de Cazalla** Andalucía, S Spain
104 M9 **La Puebla de Montalbán** Castilla-La Mancha, C Spain
54 I6 **La Puerta** Trujillo, NW Venezuela
Lapurdum *see* Bayonne
40 E7 **La Purísima** Baja California Sur, W Mexico
Lapväärtti *see* Lappfjärd
110 O10 **Łapy** Podlaskie, NE Poland
80 D6 **Laqiya Arba'in** Northern, NW Sudan
62 J4 **La Quiaca** Jujuy, N Argentina
107 J14 **L'Aquila** *var.* Aquila, Aquila degli Abruzzo. Abruzzo, C Italy
143 Q13 **Lār** Fārs, S Iran
54 J5 **Lara** *off.* Estado Lara. ◈ *state* NW Venezuela
104 G2 **Laracha** Galicia, NW Spain
74 G5 **Larache** *var.* al Araïch, El Araïch, El Araïche, *anc.* Lixus. NW Morocco
103 T14 **Laragne-Montéglin** Hautes-Alpes, SE France
104 M13 **La Rambla** Andalucía, S Spain
33 Y17 **Laramie** Wyoming, C USA
33 X15 **Laramie Mountains** ▲▲ Wyoming, C USA
33 Y16 **Laramie River** ≈ Wyoming, C USA
60 H12 **Laranjeiras do Sul** Paraná, S Brazil
Larantoeka *see* Larantuka
171 P16 **Larantuka** *prev.* Larantoeka. Flores, C Indonesia
171 U15 **Larat** Pulau Larat, E Indonesia
171 U15 **Larat, Pulau** *island* Kepulauan Tanimbar, E Indonesia
95 P19 **Lärbro** Gotland, SE Sweden
106 A9 **Larche, Col de** *pass* France/Italy
14 H8 **Larder Lake** Ontario, S Canada
105 O2 **Laredo** Cantabria, N Spain
25 Q15 **Laredo** Texas, SW USA
40 H9 **La Reforma** Sinaloa, W Mexico
98 N11 **Laren** Gelderland, E Netherlands
98 J11 **Laren** Noord-Holland, C Netherlands
102 K13 **la Réole** Gironde, SW France
La Réunion *see* Réunion
Largeau *see* Faya
103 U13 **l'Argentière-la-Bessée** Hautes-Alpes, SE France
149 O4 **Lar Gerd** *var.* Largird. Balkh, N Afghanistan
Largird *see* Lar Gerd
23 V12 **Largo** Florida, SE USA
37 Q9 **Largo, Canon** *valley* New Mexico, SW USA
44 D6 **Largo, Cayo** *island* W Cuba
23 Z17 **Largo, Key** *island* Florida Keys, Florida, SE USA
96 H12 **Largs** W Scotland, UK
102 I16 **la Rhune** *var.* Larrún. ▲ France/Spain *see also* Larrún
la Riege *see* Ariège
29 Q4 **Larimore** North Dakota, N USA
107 L15 **Larino** Molise, C Italy
Lario *see* Como, Lago di
62 J9 **La Rioja** La Rioja, NW Argentina
62 I9 **La Rioja** *off.* Provincia de La Rioja. ◈ *province* NW Argentina
105 O4 **La Rioja** ◈ *autonomous community* N Spain
115 F16 **Lárisa** *var.* Larissa. Thessalía, C Greece
Larissa *see* Lárisa
149 Q13 **Lārkāna** *var.* Larkhana. Sind, SE Pakistan
Larkhana *see* Lārkāna
Larnaca *see* Lárnaka
121 Q3 **Lárnaka** *var.* Larnaca, Larnax. SE Cyprus
121 Q3 **Lárnaka** ✕ SE Cyprus
Larnax *see* Lárnaka
97 G14 **Larne** *Ir.* Latharna. E Northern Ireland, UK
26 L5 **Larned** Kansas, C USA
104 L3 **La Robla** Castilla-León, N Spain
104 J10 **La Roca de la Sierra** Extremadura, W Spain
99 K22 **La Roche-en-Ardenne** Luxembourg, SE Belgium
102 L11 **la Rochefoucauld** Charente, W France
102 J10 **la Rochelle** *anc.* Rupella. Charente-Maritime, W France
102 I9 **la Roche-sur-Yon** *prev.* Bourbon Vendée, Napoléon-Vendée. Vendée, NW France
105 Q10 **La Roda** Castilla-La Mancha, C Spain
104 L14 **La Roda de Andalucía** Andalucía, S Spain
45 P9 **La Romana** E Dominican Republic
11 T13 **La Ronge** Saskatchewan, C Canada
11 U13 **La Ronge, Lac** ◎ Saskatchewan, C Canada
22 K10 **Larose** Louisiana, S USA
42 M7 **La Rosita** Región Autónoma Atlántico Norte, NE Nicaragua
181 Q3 **Larrimah** Northern Territory, N Australia
62 N11 **Larroque** Entre Ríos, E Argentina
105 Q2 **Larrún** *Fr.* la Rhune. ▲ France/Spain *see also* la Rhune
195 X6 **Lars Christensen Coast** *physical region* Antarctica
39 Q14 **Larsen Bay** Kodiak Island, Alaska, USA
194 I5 **Larsen Ice Shelf** *ice shelf* Antarctica
8 M6 **Larsen Sound** *sound* Nunavut, N Canada
La Rúa *see* A Rúa de Valdeorras
102 K16 **Laruns** Pyrénées-Atlantiques, SW France
95 G16 **Larvik** Vestfold, S Norway
La-sa *see* Lhasa
171 S13 **Lasahata** Pulau Seram, E Indonesia
Lasahau *see* Lasihao
37 O6 **La Sal** Utah, W USA
14 C17 **La Salle** Ontario, S Canada
30 L11 **La Salle** Illinois, N USA
45 O9 **Las Americas** ✕ (Santo Domingo) S Dominican Republic
79 G17 **La Sangha** ◈ *province* N Congo
37 V6 **Las Animas** Colorado, C USA
108 D10 **La Sarine** *var.* Sarine. ≈ SW Switzerland
108 B9 **La Sarraz** Vaud, W Switzerland
12 H12 **La Sarre** Québec, SE Canada
54 L3 **Las Aves, Islas** *var.* Islas de Aves. *island group* N Venezuela
55 N7 **Las Bonitas** Bolívar, C Venezuela
104 K15 **Las Cabezas de San Juan** Andalucía, S Spain
61 G19 **Lascano** Rocha, E Uruguay
62 I5 **Lascar, Volcán** ▲ N Chile
41 T15 **Las Choapas** *var.* Choapas. Veracruz-Llave, SE Mexico
37 R15 **Las Cruces** New Mexico, SW USA
Lasdehnen *see* Krasnoznamensk
105 V4 **La See d'Urgel** *var.* La Seu d'Urgell, Seo de Urgel. Cataluña, NE Spain
La Selle *see* Selle, Pic de la
62 G9 **La Serena** Coquimbo, C Chile
104 K11 **La Serena** *physical region* W Spain
La Seu d'Urgell *see* La See d'Urgel
103 T16 **la Seyne-sur-Mer** Var, SE France
61 D21 **Las Flores** Buenos Aires, E Argentina
62 H9 **Las Flores** San Juan, W Argentina
11 S14 **Lashburn** Saskatchewan, S Canada
62 I11 **Las Heras** Mendoza, W Argentina
167 N4 **Lashio** Shan State, E Myanmar
148 M8 **Lashkar Gāh** *var.* Lash-Kar-Gar'. Helmand, S Afghanistan
Lash-Kar-Gar' *see* Lashkar Gāh
171 P14 **Lasihao** *var.* Lasahau. Pulau Muna, C Indonesia
107 N21 **La Sila** ▲▲ SW Italy
63 H23 **La Silueta, Cerro** ▲ S Chile
42 L9 **La Sirena** Región Autónoma Atlántico Sur, E Nicaragua
110 J13 **Łask** Łódzkie, C Poland
109 V11 **Laško** *Ger.* Tüffer. C Slovenia
63 H14 **Las Lajas** Neuquén, W Argentina
63 H15 **Las Lajas, Cerro** ▲ W Argentina
62 M6 **Las Lomitas** Formosa, N Argentina
41 V16 **Las Margaritas** Chiapas, SE Mexico
Las Marismas *see* Guadalquivir, Marismas del
54 M6 **Las Mercedes** Guárico, N Venezuela
42 F6 **Las Minas, Cerro** ▲ W Honduras
105 O11 **La Solana** Castilla-La Mancha, C Spain
45 Q14 **La Soufrière** ✱ Saint Vincent, Saint Vincent and the Grenadines
102 M10 **la Souterraine** Creuse, C France
62 N7 **Las Palmas** Chaco, N Argentina
43 Q16 **Las Palmas** Veraguas, W Panama
64 P12 **Las Palmas** *var.* Las Palmas de Gran Canaria. Gran Canaria, Islas Canarias, Spain, NE Atlantic Ocean
64 P12 **Las Palmas** ◈ *province* Islas Canarias, Spain, NE Atlantic Ocean
64 Q12 **Las Palmas** ✕ Gran Canaria, Islas Canarias, Spain, NE Atlantic Ocean
Las Palmas de Gran Canaria *see* Las Palmas
40 D6 **Las Palomas** Baja California Sur, W Mexico
105 P10 **Las Pedroñeras** Castilla-La Mancha, C Spain
106 E10 **La Spezia** Liguria, NW Italy
61 F20 **Las Piedras** Canelones, S Uruguay
63 J18 **Las Plumas** Chubut, S Argentina
61 B18 **Las Rosas** Santa Fe, C Argentina
Lassa *see* Lhasa
35 O4 **Lassen Peak** ▲ California, W USA
194 K6 **Lassiter Coast** *physical region* Antarctica
109 V9 **Lassnitz** ≈ SE Austria
15 O12 **L'Assomption** Québec, SE Canada
15 N11 **L'Assomption** ≈ Québec, SE Canada
43 S17 **Las Tablas** Los Santos, S Panama
Lastarria, Volcán *see* Azufre, Volcán
37 V4 **Last Chance** Colorado, C USA
Last Frontier, The *see* Alaska
11 U16 **Last Mountain Lake** ◎ Saskatchewan, S Canada
62 H9 **Las Tórtolas, Cerro** ▲ W Argentina
61 C14 **Las Toscas** Santa Fe, C Argentina
79 F19 **Lastoursville** Ogooué-Lolo, E Gabon
113 F16 **Lastovo** *It.* Lagosta. *island* SW Croatia
113 F16 **Lastovski Kanal** *channel* SW Croatia
40 E6 **Las Tres Vírgenes, Volcán** ✱ W Mexico
40 F4 **Las Trincheras** Sonora, NW Mexico
55 N8 **Las Trincheras** Bolívar, E Venezuela
44 H7 **Las Tunas** *var.* Victoria de las Tunas. Las Tunas, E Cuba
La Suisse *see* Switzerland
40 I5 **Las Varas** Chihuahua, N Mexico
40 J12 **Las Varas** Nayarit, C Mexico
62 L10 **Las Varillas** Córdoba, E Argentina
35 X11 **Las Vegas** Nevada, W USA
37 T10 **Las Vegas** New Mexico, SW USA
187 P10 **Lata** Nendö, Solomon Islands
13 R10 **La Tabatière** Québec, E Canada
56 C6 **Latacunga** Cotopaxi, C Ecuador
194 I7 **Latady Island** *island* Antarctica
54 E14 **La Tagua** Putumayo, S Colombia
Latakia *see* Al Lādhiqīyah
92 J10 **Lätäseno** ≈ NW Finland
14 H9 **Latchford** Ontario, S Canada
14 J13 **Latchford Bridge** Ontario, SE Canada
193 Y14 **Late** *island* Vava'u Group, N Tonga
153 P15 **Lātehār** Jhārkhand, N India
15 R7 **Laterrière** Québec, SE Canada
102 J13 **la Teste** Gironde, SW France
25 V8 **Latexo** Texas, SW USA
18 L10 **Latham** New York, NE USA
Latharna *see* Larne
108 B9 **La Thielle** *var.* Thièle. ≈ W Switzerland
27 R3 **Lathrop** Missouri, C USA
107 I16 **Latina** *prev.* Littoria. Lazio, C Italy
41 R14 **La Tinaja** Veracruz-Llave, S Mexico
106 J7 **Latisana** Friuli-Venezia Giulia, NE Italy
Latium *see* Lazio
115 K25 **Lató** *site of ancient city* Kríti, Greece, E Mediterranean Sea
187 Q17 **La Tontouta** ✕ (Noumea) Province Sud, S New Caledonia
55 N4 **La Tortuga, Isla** *var.* Isla Tortuga. *island* N Venezuela
108 C10 **La Tour-de-Peilz** *var.* La Tour de Peilz. Vaud, SW Switzerland
103 S11 **la Tour-du-Pin** Isère, E France
102 J11 **la Tremblade** Charente-Maritime, W France
102 L10 **la Trimouille** Vienne, W France
42 J9 **La Trinidad** Estelí, NW Nicaragua
41 V16 **La Trinitaria** Chiapas, SE Mexico
45 Q11 **la Trinité** E Martinique
15 U7 **La Trinité-des-Monts** Québec, SE Canada
18 C15 **Latrobe** Pennsylvania, NE USA
183 P13 **La Trobe River** ≈ Victoria, SE Australia
Lattakia/Lattaquié *see* Al Lādhiqīyah
171 S13 **Latu** Pulau Seram, E Indonesia
15 P9 **La Tuque** Québec, SE Canada
155 G14 **Lātūr** Mahārāshtra, C India
118 G8 **Latvia** *off.* Republic of Latvia, *Ger.* Lettland, *Latv.* Latvija, Latvijas Republika; *prev.* Latvian SSR, *Rus.* Latviyskaya SSR. ◆ *republic* NE Europe
Latvian SSR/Latvija/Latvijas Republika/Latviyskaya SSR *see* Latvia
186 H7 **Lau** New Britain, E PNG
175 R9 **Lau Basin** *undersea feature* S Pacific Ocean
101 O15 **Lauchhammer** Brandenburg, E Germany
Laudunum *see* Laon
Laudus *see* St-Lô
Lauenburg/Lauenburg in Pommern *see* Lębork
101 L20 **Lauf an der Pegnitz** Bayern, SE Germany
108 D7 **Laufen** Basel, NW Switzerland
109 P5 **Lauffen** Salzburg, NW Austria
92 I2 **Laugarbakki** Nordhurland Vestra, N Iceland
92 I4 **Laugarvatn** Sudhurland, SW Iceland
31 O3 **Laughing Fish Point** *headland* Michigan, N USA
187 Z14 **Lau Group** *island group* E Fiji
Lauis *see* Lugano
93 M17 **Laukaa** Länsi-Suomi, W Finland
118 D12 **Laukuva** Tauragė, W Lithuania
Laun *see* Louny
183 P16 **Launceston** Tasmania, SE Australia
97 I24 **Launceston** *anc.* Dunheved. SW England, UK
54 C13 **La Unión** Nariño, SW Colombia
42 H8 **La Unión** La Unión, SE El Salvador
42 I6 **La Unión** Olancho, C Honduras
40 M15 **La Unión** Guerrero, S Mexico
41 Y14 **La Unión** Quintana Roo, E Mexico
105 S13 **La Unión** Murcia, SE Spain
54 L7 **La Unión** Barinas, C Venezuela
42 B10 **La Unión** ◈ *department* E El Salvador
38 H11 **Laupāhoehoe** *var.* Laupahoehoe. Hawai'i, USA, C Pacific Ocean
101 I23 **Laupheim** Baden-Württemberg, S Germany
181 W3 **Laura** Queensland, NE Australia
189 X2 **Laura** *atoll* Majuro Atoll, SE Marshall Islands
Laurana *see* Lovran
54 L8 **La Urbana** Bolívar, C Venezuela
21 Y4 **Laurel** Delaware, NE USA
23 V14 **Laurel** Florida, SE USA
21 W3 **Laurel** Maryland, NE USA
22 M6 **Laurel** Mississippi, S USA
33 U11 **Laurel** Montana, NW USA
29 R13 **Laurel** Nebraska, C USA
18 H15 **Laureldale** Pennsylvania, NE USA
18 C16 **Laurel Hill** *ridge* Pennsylvania, NE USA
29 T12 **Laurens** Iowa, C USA
21 P11 **Laurens** South Carolina, SE USA
Laurentian Highlands *see* Laurentian Mountains
15 P10 **Laurentian Mountains** *var.* Laurentian Highlands, *Fr.* Les Laurentides. *plateau* Newfoundland and Labrador/Québec, Canada
15 O12 **Laurentides** Québec, SE Canada
Laurentides, Les *see* Laurentian Mountains
107 M19 **Lauria** Basilicata, S Italy
194 I1 **Laurie Island** *island* Antarctica
21 T11 **Laurinburg** North Carolina, SE USA
30 M2 **Laurium** Michigan, N USA
Lauru *see* Choiseul
108 B9 **Lausanne** *It.* Losanna. Vaud, SW Switzerland
101 Q16 **Lausche** *Cz.* Luže. ▲ Czech Republic/Germany *see also* Luže
101 Q16 **Lausitzer Bergland** *var.* Lausitzer Gebirge, *Cz.* Gory Lużyckie, Lužické Hory, *Eng.* Lusatian Mountains. ▲▲ E Germany
Lausitzer Gebirge *see* Lausitzer Bergland
Lausitzer Neisse *see* Neisse
103 T12 **Lautaret, Col du** *pass* SE France
63 G15 **Lautaro** Araucanía, C Chile
101 F21 **Lauter** ≈ W Germany
108 I7 **Lauterach** Vorarlberg, NW Austria
101 I17 **Lauterbach** Hessen, C Germany
108 E9 **Lauterbrunnen** Bern, C Switzerland
169 U14 **Laut Kecil, Kepulauan** *island group* N Indonesia
187 X14 **Lautoka** Viti Levu, W Fiji
169 O8 **Laut, Pulau** *prev.* Laoet. *island* Borneo, C Indonesia
169 V14 **Laut, Pulau** *island* Kepulauan Natuna, W Indonesia
169 U13 **Laut, Selat** *strait* Borneo, C Indonesia
168 H8 **Laut Tawar, Danau** ◎ Sumatera, NW Indonesia
189 V14 **Lauvergne Island** *island* Chuuk, C Micronesia
98 M5 **Lauwers Meer** ◎ N Netherlands
98 M4 **Lauwersoog** Groningen, NE Netherlands
102 M14 **Lauzerte** Tarn-et-Garonne, S France
25 U13 **Lavaca Bay** *bay* Texas, SW USA
25 U12 **Lavaca River** ≈ Texas, SW USA
15 O12 **Laval** Québec, SE Canada
102 J6 **Laval** Mayenne, NW France
15 T6 **Laval** ≈ Québec, SE Canada
61 F19 **Lavalleja** ◈ *department* S Uruguay
15 O12 **Lavaltrie** Québec, SE Canada
186 M10 **Lavanggu** Rennell, S Solomon Islands
143 O14 **Lāvān, Jazīreh-ye** *island* S Iran
109 U8 **Lavant** ≈ S Austria
118 G5 **Lavassaare** *Ger.* Lawassaar. Pärnumaa, SW Estonia
104 L3 **La Vecilla de Curueño** Castilla-León, N Spain
45 N8 **La Vega** *var.* Concepción de la Vega. C Dominican Republic
La Vela *see* La Vela de Coro
54 J4 **La Vela de Coro** *var.* La Vela. Falcón, N Venezuela
103 N17 **Lavelanet** Ariège, S France
107 M17 **Lavello** Basilicata, S Italy
36 J8 **La Verkin** Utah, W USA
26 J8 **Laverne** Oklahoma, C USA
25 S12 **La Vernia** Texas, SW USA
93 K18 **Lavia** Länsi-Suomi, W Finland
14 I12 **Lavieille, Lake** ◎ Ontario, SE Canada
94 C12 **Lavik** Sogn og Fjordane, S Norway
La Vila Joíosa *see* Villajoyosa
33 U10 **Lavina** Montana, NW USA
194 H5 **Lavoisier Island** *island* Antarctica
23 U2 **Lavonia** Georgia, SE USA
103 R13 **la Voulte-sur-Rhône** Ardèche, E France
123 W5 **Lavrentiya** Chukotskiy Avtonomnyy Okrug, NE Russian Federation
115 H20 **Lávrio** *prev.* Lávrion. Attikí, C Greece
Lávrion *see* Lávrio
83 L22 **Lavumisa** *prev.* Gollel. SE Swaziland
149 T4 **Lawarai Pass** *pass* N Pakistan
Lawassaar *see* Lavassaare
141 P16 **Lawdar** SW Yemen
25 Q7 **Lawn** Texas, SW USA
195 Y4 **Law Promontory** *headland* Antarctica
77 O14 **Lawra** NW Ghana
185 E23 **Lawrence** Otago, South Island, NZ
31 P14 **Lawrence** Indiana, N USA
27 Q4 **Lawrence** Kansas, C USA
19 O10 **Lawrence** Massachusetts, NE USA
20 L5 **Lawrenceburg** Kentucky, S USA
20 I10 **Lawrenceburg** Tennessee, S USA
23 T3 **Lawrenceville** Georgia, SE USA
31 N15 **Lawrenceville** Illinois, N USA
21 V7 **Lawrenceville** Virginia, NE USA
27 S3 **Lawson** Missouri, C USA
26 L12 **Lawton** Oklahoma, C USA
140 I4 **Lawz, Jabal al** ▲ NW Saudi Arabia
95 L16 **Laxå** Örebro, C Sweden
127 T5 **Laya** ≈ NW Russian Federation
57 I19 **La Yarada** Tacna, SW Peru
141 S15 **Layjūn** C Yemen
141 Q9 **Laylā** *var.* Laila. Ar Riyāḍ, C Saudi Arabia
23 P4 **Lay Lake** ⊞ Alabama, S USA
45 P14 **Layou** Saint Vincent, Saint Vincent and the Grenadines
La Youne *see* El Ayoun
192 L5 **Laysan Island** *island* Hawaiian Islands, Hawaii, USA, C Pacific Ocean
36 L2 **Layton** Utah, W USA
34 L5 **Laytonville** California, N USA
172 H17 **Lazare, Pointe** *headland* Mahé, NE Seychelles
123 T12 **Lazarev** Khabarovskiy Kray, SE Russian Federation
112 L12 **Lazarevac** Serbia, C Serbia and Montenegro (Yugo.)
65 N22 **Lazarev Sea** *sea* Antarctica
40 M15 **Lázaro Cárdenas** Michoacán de Ocampo, SW Mexico
119 F15 **Lazdijai** Alytus, S Lithuania
107 H15 **Lazio** *anc.* Latium. ◈ *region* C Italy
111 A16 **Lázně Kynžvart** *Ger.* Bad Königswart. Karlovarský Kraj, W Czech Republic
Lazovsk *see* Sîngerei
167 R12 **Leach** Poŭthĭsăt, W Cambodia
27 X9 **Leachville** Arkansas, C USA
28 I9 **Lead** South Dakota, N USA
11 S16 **Leader** Saskatchewan, S Canada
19 S6 **Lead Mountain** ▲ Maine, NE USA
37 R5 **Leadville** Colorado, C USA
11 V12 **Leaf Rapids** Manitoba, C Canada
22 M7 **Leaf River** ≈ Mississippi, S USA
25 W11 **League City** Texas, SW USA

◆ Country ● Country Capital ◇ Dependent Territory ○ Dependent Territory Capital ◈ Administrative Region ✕ International Airport ▲ Mountain ▲▲ Mountain Range ✱ Volcano ≈ River ◎ Lake ⊞ Reservoir

92 K8 Leaibevuotna Nor. Olderfjord. Finnmark, N Norway
23 N7 Leakesville Mississippi, S USA
25 Q11 Leakey Texas, SW USA
Leal see Lihula
83 G15 Lealui Western, W Zambia
Leamhcán see Lucan
14 C18 Leamington Ontario, S Canada
Leamington/Leamington Spa see Royal Leamington Spa
Leammi see Lemmenjoki
25 S10 Leander Texas, SW USA
60 F13 Leandro N.Alem Misiones, NE Argentina
97 A20 Leane, Lough Ir. Loch Léin. ◎ SW Ireland
180 G8 Learmouth Western Australia
Leau see Zoutleeuw
L'Eau d'Heure see Plate Taille, Lac de la
190 D12 Leava Île Futuna, S Wallis and Futuna
Leavdnja see Lakselv
27 R3 Leavenworth Kansas, C USA
32 I8 Leavenworth Washington, NW USA
92 L8 Leavvajohka var. Levajok, Lœvvajok. Finnmark, N Norway
27 R4 Leawood Kansas, C USA
110 H6 Łeba Ger. Leba. Pomorskie, N Poland
110 I6 Łeba Ger. Leba. ≈ N Poland
101 D20 Lebach Saarland, SW Germany
Łeba, Jezioro see Łebsko, Jezioro
171 P8 Lebak Mindanao, S Philippines
31 O13 Lebanon Indiana, N USA
20 L6 Lebanon Kentucky, S USA
27 U6 Lebanon Missouri, C USA
19 N9 Lebanon New Hampshire, NE USA
32 G12 Lebanon Oregon, NW USA
18 H15 Lebanon Pennsylvania, NE USA
20 J8 Lebanon Tennessee, S USA
21 P7 Lebanon Virginia, NE USA
138 G6 Lebanon off. Republic of Lebanon, Ar. Al Lubnān, Fr. Liban. ◆ republic SW Asia
20 K6 Lebanon Junction Kentucky, S USA
Lebanon, Mount see Liban, Jebel
146 J10 Lebap Lebapskiy Velayat, NE Turkmenistan
Lebapskiy Velayat see Lebap Welaýaty
146 H11 Lebap Welaýaty Rus. Lebapskiy Velayat; prev. Rus. Chardzhevskaya Oblast', Turkm. Chärjew Oblasty. ◈ province E Turkmenistan
Lebasee see Łebsko, Jezioro
99 F17 Lebbeke Oost-Vlaanderen, NW Belgium
35 S14 Lebec California, W USA
Lebedin see Lebedyn
123 Q11 Lebedinyy Respublika Sakha (Yakutiya), NE Russian Federation
126 L6 Lebedyan' Lipetskaya Oblast', W Russian Federation
117 T4 Lebedyn Rus. Lebedin. Sums'ka Oblast', NE Ukraine
12 I12 Lebel-sur-Quévillon Québec, SE Canada
92 L8 Lebesby Finnmark, N Norway
102 M9 le Blanc Indre, C France
27 P5 Lebo Kansas, C USA
79 L15 Lebo Orientale, N Dem. Rep. Congo
110 H6 Lębork var. Lębórk, Ger. Lauenburg, Lauenburg in Pommern. Pomorskie, N Poland
103 O17 le Boulou Pyrénées-Orientales, S France
108 A9 Le Brassus Vaud, W Switzerland
104 J15 Lebrija Andalucía, S Spain
110 G6 Łebsko, Jezioro Ger. Lebasee; prev. Jezioro Łeba. ◎ N Poland
63 F14 Lebu Bío Bío, C Chile
Lebyazh'ye see Akku
104 F6 Leça da Palmeira Porto, N Portugal
103 U15 le Cannet Alpes-Maritimes, SE France
Le Cap see Cap-Haïtien
103 P2 le Cateau-Cambrésis Nord, N France
107 Q18 Lecce Puglia, SE Italy
106 D7 Lecco Lombardia, N Italy
29 V10 Le Center Minnesota, N USA
108 J7 Lech Vorarlberg, W Austria
101 K22 Lech ≈ Austria/Germany
115 D19 Lechainá var. Lehena, Lekhainá. Dytikí Ellás, S Greece
102 J11 le Château d'Oléron Charente-Maritime, W France
103 R3 le Chesne Ardennes, N France
103 R13 le Cheylard Ardèche, E France
108 K7 Lechtaler Alpen ▲ W Austria
100 H6 Leck Schleswig-Holstein, N Germany
14 L9 Lecointre, Lac ◎ Québec, SE Canada
22 H7 Lecompte Louisiana, S USA
103 Q9 le Creusot Saône-et-Loire, C France
Lecumberri see Lekunberri
110 P13 Łęczna Lubelskie, E Poland
110 J12 Łęczyca Ger. Lentschiza, Rus. Lenchitsa. Łódzkie, C Poland
100 F10 Leda ≈ NW Germany
109 Y9 Ledava ≈ NE Slovenia
99 F17 Lede Oost-Vlaanderen, NW Belgium
104 K6 Ledesma Castilla-León, N Spain
45 Q12 le Diamant SW Martinique
172 J16 Le Digue island Inner Islands, NE Seychelles
103 Q10 le Donjon Allier, C France
102 M10 le Dorat Haute-Vienne, C France
Ledo Salinarius see Lons-le-Saunier
11 Q14 Leduc Alberta, SW Canada
123 V7 Ledyanaya, Gora ▲ E Russian Federation
97 C21 Lee Ir. An Laoi. ≈ SW Ireland
29 U5 Leech Lake ◎ Minnesota, N USA
26 K10 Leedey Oklahoma, C USA
97 M17 Leeds N England, UK
23 P4 Leeds Alabama, S USA
29 O3 Leeds North Dakota, N USA
98 N6 Leek Groningen, NE Netherlands
99 K15 Leende Noord-Brabant, SE Netherlands
100 F10 Leer Niedersachsen, NW Germany
98 J13 Leerdam Zuid-Holland, C Netherlands
98 K12 Leersum Utrecht, C Netherlands
23 W11 Leesburg Florida, SE USA
21 V3 Leesburg Virginia, NE USA
27 R4 Lees Summit Missouri, C USA
22 G7 Leesville Louisiana, S USA
25 S12 Leesville Texas, SW USA
31 U13 Leesville Lake ⊠ Ohio, N USA
Leesville Lake see Smith Mountain Lake
183 P9 Leeton New South Wales, SE Australia
98 L6 Leeuwarden Fris. Ljouwert. Friesland, N Netherlands
180 I14 Leeuwin, Cape headland Western Australia
35 R8 Lee Vining California, W USA
45 V8 Leeward Islands island group E West Indies
Leeward Islands see Vent, Îles Sous le, W French Polynesia
Leeward Islands see Sotavento, Ilhas de, Cape Verde
79 G20 Léfini ≈ SE Congo
Léfka see Lefke
115 C17 Lefkáda prev. Levkás. Lefkáda, Iónioi Nísoi, Greece, C Mediterranean Sea
115 B17 Lefkáda It. Santa Maura; prev. Levkás, anc. Leucas. island Iónioi Nísoi, Greece, C Mediterranean Sea
115 H25 Lefká Óri ▲ Kríti, Greece, E Mediterranean Sea
115 B16 Lefkímmi var. Levkímmi. Kérkyra, Iónioi Nísoi, Greece, C Mediterranean Sea
Lefkoşa/Lefkosia see Nicosia
25 O2 Lefors Texas, SW USA
45 R12 le François E Martinique
180 L12 Lefroy, Lake salt lake Western Australia
Legaceaster see Chester
105 N8 Leganés Madrid, C Spain
171 P4 Legaspi off. Legaspi City. Luzon, N Philippines
Leghorn see Livorno
110 M11 Legionowo Mazowieckie, C Poland
99 K24 Léglise Luxembourg, SE Belgium
106 G8 Legnago Lombardia, NE Italy
106 D7 Legnano Veneto, NE Italy
111 F14 Legnica Ger. Liegnitz. Dolnośląskie, SW Poland
35 Q9 Le Grand California, W USA
103 Q15 le Grau-du-Roi Gard, S France
183 U3 Legume New South Wales, SE Australia
102 L4 le Havre Eng. Havre; prev. le Havre-de-Grâce. Seine-Maritime, N France
le Havre-de-Grâce see le Havre
Lehena see Lechainá
36 L3 Lehi Utah, W USA
18 I14 Lehighton Pennsylvania, NE USA
29 O6 Lehr North Dakota, N USA
38 A8 Lehua Island island Hawaiian Islands, Hawai'i, USA, C Pacific Ocean
149 S9 Leiah Punjab, NE Pakistan
109 W9 Leibnitz Steiermark, SE Austria
97 M19 Leicester Lat. Batae Coritanorum. C England, UK
97 M19 Leicestershire cultural region C England, UK
98 H11 Leiden prev. Leyden, anc. Lugdunum Batavorum. Zuid-Holland, W Netherlands
98 H11 Leiderdorp Zuid-Holland, W Netherlands
98 G11 Leidschendam Zuid-Holland, W Netherlands
99 D18 Leie Fr. Lys. ≈ Belgium/France
Leifear see Lifford
184 L4 Leigh Auckland, North Island, NZ
97 K17 Leigh NW England, UK
182 I5 Leigh Creek South Australia
23 O2 Leighton Alabama, S USA
97 M21 Leighton Buzzard E England, UK
Léim an Bhradáin see Leixlip
Léim an Mhadaidh see Limavady
Léime, Ceann see Loop Head, Ireland
Léime, Ceann see Slyne Head, Ireland
101 G20 Leimen Baden-Württemberg, SW Germany
100 I13 Leine ≈ NW Germany
101 J15 Leinefelde Thüringen, C Germany
Léin, Loch see Leane, Lough
97 D19 Leinster Ir. Cúige Laighean. cultural region E Ireland
97 F19 Leinster, Mount Ir. Stua Laighean. ▲ SE Ireland
119 F15 Leipalingis Alytus, S Lithuania
92 J12 Leipojärvi Norrbotten, N Sweden
31 R12 Leipsic Ohio, N USA
Leipsic see Leipzig
115 M20 Leipsoí island Dodekánisos, Greece, Aegean Sea
101 M15 Leipzig Pol. Lipsk; hist. Leipsic, anc. Lipsia. Sachsen, E Germany
101 M15 Leipzig Halle × Sachsen, E Germany
104 G9 Leiria anc. Collipo. Leiria, C Portugal
104 F9 Leiria ◈ district C Portugal
95 C15 Leirvik Hordaland, S Norway
118 E5 Leisi Ger. Laisberg. Saaremaa, W Estonia
104 J3 Leitariegos, Puerto de pass NW Spain
20 I6 Leitchfield Kentucky, S USA
109 Y5 Leitha Hung. Lajta. ≈ Austria/Hungary
Leitir Ceanainn see Letterkenny
Leitmeritz see Litoměřice
Leitomischl see Litomyšl
97 D16 Leitrim Ir. Liatroim. cultural region NW Ireland
115 F18 Leivádia prev. Levádhia. Stereá Ellás, C Greece
Leix see Laois
97 F18 Leixlip Eng. Salmon Leap, Ir. Léim an Bhradáin. E Ireland
64 N8 Leixões Porto, N Portugal
161 N12 Leiyang Hunan, S China
160 L16 Leizhou var. Haikang. Guangdong, S China
160 L16 Leizhou Bandao var. Luichow Peninsula. peninsula S China
98 H13 Lek ≈ SW Netherlands
114 I13 Lekánis ▲ NE Greece
172 H13 Le Kartala ▲ Grande Comore, NW Comoros
Le Kef see El Kef
79 G20 Lékéti, Monts de la ▲ S Congo
Lekhainá see Lechainá
114 H8 Lekhchevo Montana, NW Bulgaria
92 G11 Leknes Nordland, C Norway
79 E21 Le Kouilou ◈ province SW Congo
94 L13 Leksand Dalarna, C Sweden
126 H8 Leksozero, Ozero ◎ NW Russian Federation
105 Q3 Lekunberri var. Lecumberri. Navarra, N Spain
171 S11 Lelai, Tanjung headland Pulau Halmahera, N Indonesia
45 Q12 le Lamentin var. Lamentin. C Martinique
45 Q12 le Lamentin × (Fort-de-France) C Martinique
31 P6 Leland Michigan, N USA
22 J4 Leland Mississippi, S USA
95 J16 Lelång var. Lelången. ◎ S Sweden
Lelången see Lelång
Lel'chitsy see Lyel'chytsy
le Léman see Geneva, Lake
Leli see Tianlin
25 O3 Lelia Lake Texas, SW USA
113 I14 Lelija ▲ SE Bosnia and Herzegovina
108 C8 Le Locle Neuchâtel, W Switzerland
189 Y14 Lelu Kosrae, E Micronesia
Lelu see Lelu Island
189 Y14 Lelu Island var. Lelu. island Kosrae, E Micronesia
55 W9 Lelydorp Wanica, N Suriname
98 K9 Lelystad Flevoland, C Netherlands
63 K25 Le Maire, Estrecho de strait S Argentina
168 L10 Lemang Pulau Rangsang, W Indonesia
186 I7 Lemankoa Buka Island, NE PNG
Léman, Lac see Geneva, Lake
102 L6 le Mans Sarthe, NW France
29 S12 Le Mars Iowa, C USA
109 S3 Lembach im Mühlkreis Oberösterreich, N Austria
101 G23 Lemberg ▲ SW Germany
Lemberg see L'viv
Lemdiyya see Médéa
121 P3 Lemesós var. Limassol. SW Cyprus
100 H13 Lemgo Nordrhein-Westfalen, W Germany
33 P13 Lemhi Range ▲ Idaho, NW USA
9 S6 Lemieux Islands island group Nunavut, NE Canada
171 O11 Lemito Sulawesi, N Indonesia
92 L10 Lemmenjoki Lapp. Leammi. ≈ NE Finland
98 L7 Lemmer Fris. De Lemmer. Friesland, N Netherlands
28 L7 Lemmon South Dakota, N USA
36 M15 Lemmon, Mount ▲ Arizona, SW USA
Lemnos see Límnos
31 O14 Lemon, Lake ◎ Indiana, N USA
102 J5 le Mont St-Michel castle Manche, N France
35 Q11 Lemoore California, W USA
189 T13 Lemotol Bay bay Chuuk Islands, C Micronesia
45 Y5 le Moule var. Moule. Grande Terre, NE Guadeloupe
Lemovices see Limoges
Le Moyen-Ogooué see Moyen-Ogooué
12 M6 le Moyne, Lac ◎ Québec, E Canada
93 L18 Lempäälä Länsi-Suomi, W Finland
42 E7 Lempa, Río ≈ Central America
42 F7 Lempira prev. Gracias. ◈ department SW Honduras
Lemsalu see Limbaži
107 N17 Le Murge ▲ SE Italy
127 V6 Lemva ≈ NW Russian Federation
95 F21 Lemvig Ringkøbing, W Denmark
166 K8 Lemyethna Irrawaddy, SW Myanmar
30 K10 Lena Illinois, N USA
131 V4 Lena ≈ NE Russian Federation
173 N13 Lena Tablemount undersea feature S Indian Ocean
Lenchitsa see Łęczyca
59 N17 Lençóis Bahia, E Brazil
60 K9 Lençóis Paulista São Paulo, S Brazil
109 Y9 Lendava Hung. Lendva, Ger. Unterlimbach; prev. Dolnja Lendava. NE Slovenia
83 F20 Lendepas Hardap, SE Namibia
124 H9 Lendery Respublika Kareliya, NW Russian Federation
Lendum see Lens
Lendva see Lendava
27 R4 Lenexa Kansas, C USA
109 Q5 Lengau Oberösterreich, N Austria
145 Q17 Lenger Yuzhnyy Kazakhstan, S Kazakhstan
Lenghu see Lenghuzhen
159 O9 Lenghuzhen var. Lenghu. Qinghai, C China
159 T9 Lenglong Ling ▲ N China
108 D7 Lengnau Bern, W Switzerland
160 M12 Lengshuitan Hunan, S China
95 M20 Lenhovda Kronoberg, S Sweden
79 E20 Le Niari ◈ province SW Congo
Lenin see Akdepe, Turkmenistan
Lenin see Uzynkol', Kazakhstan
Leninabad see Khŭjand
Leninakan see Gyumri
Lenina, Pik see Lenin Peak
117 V12 Lenine Rus. Lenino. Respublika Krym, S Ukraine
Leningor see Leninogorsk
147 Q13 Leningrad Rus. Leningradskiy; prev. Mŭ'minobod, Rus. Muminabad. SW Tajikistan
Leningrad see Sankt-Peterburg
126 L13 Leningradskaya Krasnodarskiy Kray, SW Russian Federation
195 S16 Leningradskaya Russian research station Antarctica
124 H12 Leningradskaya Oblast' ◈ province NW Russian Federation
Leningradskiy see Leningrad
Lenino see Lenine, Ukraine
Lenino see Lyenina, Belarus
Leninobod see Khŭjand
145 X9 Leninogorsk Kaz. Leningor. Vostochnyy Kazakhstan, E Kazakhstan
127 T5 Leninogorsk Respublika Tatarstan, W Russian Federation
147 T12 Lenin Peak Rus. Pik Lenina, Taj. Qullai Lenin. ▲ Kyrgyzstan/Tajikistan
147 S8 Leninpol' Talasskaya Oblast', NW Kyrgyzstan
Lenin, Qullai see Lenin Peak
127 P11 Leninsk Volgogradskaya Oblast', SW Russian Federation
Leninsk see Akdepe, Turkmenistan
Leninsk see Asaka, Uzbekistan
Leninsk see Baykonyr, Kazakhstan
145 T8 Leninskiy Pavlodar, E Kazakhstan
122 I13 Leninsk-Kuznetskiy Kemerovskaya Oblast', S Russian Federation
125 P15 Leninskoye Kirovskaya Oblast', NW Russian Federation
Leninskoye see Uzynkol'
Leninsk-Turkmenski see Türkmenabat
Leninváros see Tiszaújváros
Lenkoran' see Länkäran
101 F15 Lenne ≈ W Germany
101 G16 Lennestadt Nordrhein-Westfalen, W Germany
29 R11 Lennox South Dakota, N USA
63 J25 Lennox, Isla Eng. Lennox Island. island S Chile
Lennox Island see Lennox, Isla
21 Q9 Lenoir North Carolina, SE USA
20 M9 Lenoir City Tennessee, S USA
108 C7 Le Noirmont Jura, NW Switzerland
14 L9 Lenôtre, Lac ◎ Québec, SE Canada
29 U15 Lenox Iowa, C USA
103 O2 Lens anc. Lendum, Lentium. Pas-de-Calais, N France
123 O11 Lensk Respublika Sakha (Yakutiya), NE Russian Federation
111 F24 Lenti Zala, SW Hungary
Lentia see Linz
93 N14 Lentiira Oulu, E Finland
107 L25 Lentini anc. Leontini. Sicilia, Italy, C Mediterranean Sea
Lentium see Lens
Lentschiza see Łęczyca
93 N15 Lentua ◎ E Finland
119 H14 Lentvaris Pol. Landwarów. Vilnius, SE Lithuania
108 F7 Lenzburg Aargau, N Switzerland
109 R5 Lenzing Oberösterreich, N Austria
77 P13 Léo SW Burkina
109 V7 Leoben Steiermark, C Austria
Leobschütz see Głubczyce
44 L9 Léogâne S Haiti
171 O11 Leok Sulawesi, N Indonesia
29 O7 Leola South Dakota, N USA
97 K20 Leominster W England, UK
19 N11 Leominster Massachusetts, NE USA
29 V16 Leon Iowa, C USA
40 M12 León var. León de los Aldamas. Guanajuato, C Mexico
42 I10 León León, NW Nicaragua
104 L4 León Castilla-León, NW Spain
42 I9 León ◈ department W Nicaragua
104 K4 León ◈ province Castilla-León, NW Spain
León see Cotopaxi
102 I15 Léon Landes, SW France
25 V9 Leona Texas, SW USA
180 K11 Leonara Western Australia
25 U5 Leonard Texas, SW USA
107 H15 Leonardo da Vinci prev. Fiumicino. × (Roma) Lazio, C Italy
21 X5 Leonardtown Maryland, NE USA
25 Q13 Leona River ≈ Texas, SW USA
41 Z11 Leona Vicario Quintana Roo, SE Mexico
101 H21 Leonberg Baden-Württemberg, SW Germany
62 M3 León, Cerro ▲ NW Paraguay
León de los Aldamas see León
109 T4 Leonding Oberösterreich, N Austria
107 I14 Leonessa Lazio, C Italy
107 K24 Leonforte Sicilia, Italy, C Mediterranean Sea
183 O13 Leongatha Victoria, SE Australia
115 F21 Leonídi Pelopónnisos, S Greece
104 J4 León, Montes de ▲ NW Spain
25 S8 Leon River ≈ Texas, SW USA
Leontini see Lentini
Léopold II, Lac see Mai-Ndombe, Lac
99 J17 Leopoldsburg Limburg, NE Belgium
Léopoldville see Kinshasa
26 I5 Leoti Kansas, C USA
116 M11 Leova Rus. Leovo. SW Moldova
Leovo see Leova
102 G8 le Palais Morbihan, NW France
27 X10 Lepanto Arkansas, C USA
169 N13 Lepar, Pulau island W Indonesia
104 I14 Lepe Andalucía, S Spain
Lepel' see Lyepyel'
83 I19 Lephephe Kweneng, SE Botswana
161 Q10 Leping Jiangxi, S China
Lépontiennes, Alpes/Lepontine, Alpi see Lepontine Alps
108 G10 Lepontine Alps Fr. Alpes Lépontiennes, It. Alpi Lepontine. ▲ Italy/Switzerland
79 G20 Le Pool ◈ province S Congo
173 O16 le Port NW Réunion
103 N1 le Portel Pas-de-Calais, N France
93 N17 Leppävirta Itä-Suomi, C Finland
45 Q11 le Prêcheur NW Martinique
Lepsi see Lepsy
145 V13 Lepsy Kaz. Lepsi. Almaty, SE Kazakhstan
145 V13 Lepsy Kaz. Lepsi. ≈ SE Kazakhstan
Le Puglie see Puglia
103 Q12 le Puy prev. le Puy-en-Velay, hist. Anicium, Podium Anicensis. Haute-Loire, C France
le Puy-en-Velay see le Puy
Le Raizet see le Raizet
45 X11 le Raizet var. Le Raizet. × (Pointe-à-Pitre) Grande Terre, C Guadeloupe
107 J24 Lercara Friddi Sicilia, Italy, C Mediterranean Sea
78 G12 Léré Mayo-Kébbi, SW Chad
Leribe see Hlotse
106 E10 Lerici Liguria, NW Italy
54 I14 Lérida Vaupés, SE Colombia
Lérida see Lleida
105 N5 Lerma Castilla-León, N Spain
40 M13 Lerma, Río ≈ C Mexico
115 F20 Lérna prehistoric site Pelopónnisos, S Greece
45 R11 le Robert E Martinique
115 M21 Léros island Dodekánisos, Greece, Aegean Sea
30 L13 Le Roy Illinois, N USA
27 Q6 Le Roy Kansas, C USA
29 W11 Le Roy Minnesota, N USA
18 E10 Le Roy New York, NE USA
Lerrnayin Gharabakh see Nagorno-Karabakh
95 J19 Lerum Västra Götaland, S Sweden
96 M2 Lerwick NE Scotland, UK
45 Y6 les Abymes var. Abymes. Grande Terre, C Guadeloupe
les Albères see Albères, Chaîne des
102 M4 les Andelys Eure, N France
45 Q12 les Anses-d'Arlets SW Martinique
105 U6 Les Borges Blanques var. Borjas Blancas. Cataluña, NE Spain
Lesbos see Lésvos
Les Cayes see Cayes
31 Q4 Les Cheneaux Islands island Michigan, N USA
103 T12 les Écrins ▲ E France
108 C10 Le Sépey Vaud, W Switzerland
15 T7 Les Escoumins Québec, SE Canada
Les Gonaïves see Gonaïves
Lesh/Leshi see Lezhë
160 H9 Leshan Sichuan, C China
108 D11 Les Haudères Valais, SW Switzerland
102 J9 les Herbiers Vendée, NW France
125 O8 Leshukonskoye Arkhangel'skaya Oblast', NW Russian Federation
Lesina see Hvar
107 M15 Lesina, Lago di ◎ SE Italy
114 K13 Lesítse ▲ NE Greece
94 G10 Lesja Oppland, S Norway
95 L15 Lesjöfors Värmland, C Sweden
111 O18 Lesko Podkarpackie, SE Poland
113 O15 Leskovac Serbia, SE Serbia and Montenegro (Yugo.)
113 M22 Leskovik var. Leskoviku. Korçë, S Albania
Leskoviku see Leskovik
33 P14 Leslie Idaho, NW USA
31 Q10 Leslie Michigan, N USA
Leśna/Lesnaya see Lyasnaya
102 F5 Lesneven Finistère, NW France
112 J11 Lešnica Serbia, W Serbia and Montenegro (Yugo.)
125 S13 Lesnoy Kirovskaya Oblast', NW Russian Federation
122 G10 Lesnoy Sverdlovskaya Oblast', C Russian Federation
122 K12 Lesosibirsk Krasnoyarskiy Kray, C Russian Federation
83 J23 Lesotho off. Kingdom of Lesotho; prev. Basutoland. ◆ monarchy S Africa
102 J12 Lesparre-Médoc Gironde, SW France
108 C8 Les Ponts-de-Martel Neuchâtel, W Switzerland
102 I9 les Sables-d'Olonne Vendée, NW France
103 P1 Lesquin × Nord, N France
109 S7 Lessach var. Lessachbach. ≈ E Austria
Lessachbach see Lessach
45 W11 les Saintes var. Îles des Saintes. island group S Guadeloupe
74 L5 Les Salines × (Annaba) NE Algeria
99 J22 Lesse ≈ SE Belgium
95 M21 Lessebo Kronoberg, S Sweden
194 M10 Lesser Antarctica var. West Antarctica. physical region Antarctica
45 P15 Lesser Antilles island group E West Indies
137 T10 Lesser Caucasus Rus. Malyy Kavkaz. ▲ SW Asia
Lesser Khingan Range see Xiao Hinggan Ling
11 P13 Lesser Slave Lake ◎ Alberta, W Canada
Lesser Sunda Islands see Nusa Tenggara
99 E19 Lessines Hainaut, SW Belgium
103 R16 les Stes-Maries-de-la-Mer Bouches-du-Rhône, SE France
14 G15 Lester B.Pearson var. Toronto. × (Toronto) Ontario, S Canada
29 U9 Lester Prairie Minnesota, N USA
93 L16 Lestijärvi Länsi-Suomi, W Finland
L'Estuaire see Estuaire
29 U9 Le Sueur Minnesota, N USA
108 B8 Les Verrières Neuchâtel, W Switzerland
115 L17 Lésvos anc. Lesbos. island E Greece
110 G12 Leszno Ger. Lissa. Wielkopolskie, C Poland
83 L20 Letaba Limpopo, NE South Africa
173 P17 le Tampon SW Réunion
97 O21 Letchworth E England, UK
111 G25 Letenye Zala, SW Hungary
11 Q17 Lethbridge Alberta, SW Canada
55 S11 Lethem S Guyana
83 H18 Letiahau ≈ W Botswana
54 J18 Leticia Amazonas, S Colombia
171 S16 Leti, Kepulauan island group E Indonesia
83 I18 Letlhakane Central, C Botswana
83 H20 Letlhakeng Kweneng, SE Botswana
114 J8 Letnitsa Lovech, N Bulgaria
103 N1 le Touquet-Paris-Plage Pas-de-Calais, N France
166 L8 Letpadan Pegu, SW Myanmar
166 K6 Letpan Arakan State, W Myanmar
102 M2 le Tréport Seine-Maritime, N France
166 M12 Letsôk-aw Kyun var. Letsutan Island; prev. Domel Island. island Mergui Archipelago, S Myanmar
Letsutan Island see Letsôk-aw Kyun
97 E14 Letterkenny Ir. Leitir Ceanainn. NW Ireland
Lettland see Latvia
116 M6 Letychiv Khmel'nyts'ka Oblast', W Ukraine
Lëtzebuerg see Luxembourg
116 H14 Leu Dolj, SW Romania
Leucas see Lefkáda
103 P17 Leucate Aude, S France
103 P17 Leucate, Étang de ◎ S France
108 E10 Leuk Valais, SW Switzerland
108 E10 Leukerbad Valais, SW Switzerland
Leusden see Leusden-Centrum
98 K11 Leusden-Centrum var. Leusden. Utrecht, C Netherlands
Leutensdorf see Litvínov
Leutschau see Levoča
99 H18 Leuven Fr. Louvain, Ger. Löwen. Vlaams Brabant, C Belgium
99 I20 Leuze Namur, C Belgium
Leuze see Leuze-en-Hainaut
99 E19 Leuze-en-Hainaut var. Leuze. Hainaut, SW Belgium
Léva see Levice
Levádhia see Leivádia
Levajok see Leavvajohka
36 L4 Levan Utah, W USA
93 E16 Levanger Nord-Trøndelag, C Norway
121 S12 Levantine Basin undersea feature E Mediterranean Sea
106 D10 Levanto Liguria, W Italy
107 H23 Levanzo, Isola di island Isole Egadi, S Italy
127 Q17 Levashi Respublika Dagestan, SW Russian Federation
24 M5 Levelland Texas, SW USA
39 P13 Levelock Alaska, USA
101 E16 Leverkusen Nordrhein-Westfalen, W Germany
111 J21 Levice Ger. Lewentz, Lewenz, Hung. Léva. Nitriansky Kraj, SW Slovakia
106 G6 Levico Terme Trentino-Alto Adige, N Italy
115 E20 Levídi Pelopónnisos, S Greece
103 P14 le Vigan Gard, S France
184 L13 Levin Manawatu-Wanganui, North Island, NZ
15 R10 Lévis var. Levis. Québec, SE Canada
21 P6 Levisa Fork ≈ Kentucky/Virginia, S USA
115 L21 Levítha island Kykládes, Greece, Aegean Sea

◆ Country ● Country Capital ◇ Dependent Territory ○ Dependent Territory Capital ◈ Administrative Region × International Airport ▲ Mountain ▲ Mountain Range ⩓ Volcano ≈ River ◎ Lake ⊠ Reservoir

18 L14 Levittown Long Island, New York, NE USA
18 J15 Levittown Pennsylvania, NE USA
Levkás see Lefkáda
Levkímmi see Lefkímmi
111 L19 Levoča Ger. Leutschau, Hung. Locse. Prešovský Kraj, E Slovakia
Lévrier, Baie du see Nouâdhibou, Dakhlet
103 N9 Levroux Indre, C France
114 J8 Levski Pleven, N Bulgaria
Levskigrad see Karlovo
126 L6 Lev Tolstoy Lipetskaya Oblast', W Russian Federation
187 X14 Levuka Ovalau, C Fiji
166 L6 Lewe Mandalay, C Myanmar
Lewentz/Lewenz see Levice
97 O23 Lewes SE England, UK
21 Z4 Lewes Delaware, NE USA
29 Q12 Lewis and Clark Lake ⊞ Nebraska/South Dakota, N USA
18 G14 Lewisburg Pennsylvania, NE USA
20 J10 Lewisburg Tennessee, S USA
21 S6 Lewisburg West Virginia, NE USA
96 F6 Lewis, Butt of headland NW Scotland, UK
96 F7 Lewis, Isle of island NW Scotland, UK
35 U4 Lewis, Mount ▲ Nevada, W USA
185 H16 Lewis Pass pass South Island, NZ
33 P7 Lewis Range ▲ Montana, NW USA
23 O3 Lewis Smith Lake ⊞ Alabama, S USA
32 M10 Lewiston Idaho, NW USA
19 P7 Lewiston Maine, NE USA
29 X10 Lewiston Minnesota, N USA
18 D9 Lewiston New York, NE USA
36 L1 Lewiston Utah, W USA
30 K13 Lewistown Illinois, N USA
33 T9 Lewistown Montana, NW USA
27 T14 Lewisville Arkansas, C USA
25 T6 Lewisville Texas, SW USA
25 T6 Lewisville, Lake ⊞ Texas, SW USA
Le Woleu-Ntem see Woleu-Ntem
23 U3 Lexington Georgia, SE USA
20 M5 Lexington Kentucky, S USA
22 L4 Lexington Mississippi, S USA
27 S4 Lexington Missouri, C USA
29 N16 Lexington Nebraska, C USA
20 S9 Lexington North Carolina, SE USA
27 N11 Lexington Oklahoma, C USA
21 R12 Lexington South Carolina, SE USA
20 G9 Lexington Tennessee, S USA
25 T10 Lexington Texas, SW USA
21 T6 Lexington Virginia, NE USA
21 X5 Lexington Park Maryland, NE USA
Leyden see Leiden
102 J14 Leyre ≈ SW France
171 Q5 Leyte island C Philippines
171 Q6 Leyte Gulf gulf E Philippines
111 O16 Leżajsk Podkarpackie, SE Poland
Lezha see Lezhë
113 K18 Lezhë var. Lezha; prev. Lesh, Leshi. Lezhë, NW Albania
113 K18 Lezhë ◈ district NW Albania
103 O16 Lézignan-Corbières Aude, S France
126 J7 L'gov Kurskaya Oblast', W Russian Federation
159 P15 Lhari Xizang Zizhiqu, W China
159 N16 Lhasa var. La-sa, Lassa. Xizang Zizhiqu, W China
159 O15 Lhasa He ≈ W China
158 K16 Lhazê var. Quxar. Xizang Zizhiqu, W China
158 K14 Lhazhong Xizang Zizhiqu, W China
168 H7 Lhoksukon Sumatera, W Indonesia
159 Q15 Lhorong var. Zito. Xizang Zizhiqu, W China
105 W6 L'Hospitalet de Llobregat var. Hospitalet. Cataluña, NE Spain
153 R11 Lhotse ▲ China/Nepal
159 N17 Lhozhag var. Garbo. Xizang Zizhiqu, W China
159 O16 Lhünzê var. Xingba. Xizang Zizhiqu, W China
159 N15 Lhünzhub var. Ganqu. Xizang Zizhiqu, W China
167 N8 Li Lamphun, NW Thailand
161 P12 Liancheng var. Lianfeng. Fujian, SE China
Liancheng see Guangnan, Yunnan, China
Liancheng see Qinglong, Guizhou, China
Lianfeng see Liancheng
160 K9 Liangping var. Liangshan. Chongqing Shi, C China
Liangshan see Liangping
Liangzhou see Wuwei
161 O9 Liangzi Hu ◎ C China
161 R12 Lianjiang Fujian, SE China
160 L15 Lianjiang Guangdong, S China
Lianjiang see Xingguo
161 O13 Lianping var. Yuanshan. Guangdong, S China
Lianshan see Huludao
Lian Xian see Lianzhou
160 M11 Lianyuan prev. Lantian. Hunan, S China
161 Q6 Lianyungang var. Xinpu. Jiangsu, E China
161 N13 Lianzhou var. Linxian; prev. Lian Xian. Guangdong, S China
Lianzhou see Hepu
Liao see Liaoning
161 P5 Liaocheng Shandong, E China
163 U13 Liaodong Bandao var. Liaotung Peninsula. peninsula NE China
163 T13 Liaodong Wan Eng. Gulf of Lantung, Gulf of Liaotung. gulf NE China
163 U11 Liao He ≈ NE China
163 U12 Liaoning var. Liao, Liaoning Sheng, Shengking; hist. Fengtien, Shenking. ◈ province NE China
Liaoning Sheng see Liaoning
Liaotung, Gulf of see Liaodong Wan
Liaotung Peninsula see Liaodong Bandao
163 V12 Liaoyang var. Liao-yang. Liaoning, NE China
163 V11 Liaoyuan var. Dongliao, Shuang-liao, Jap. Chengchiatun. Jilin, NE China
163 U12 Liaozhong Liaoning, NE China
Liaqatabad see Piplān
10 M10 Liard ≈ W Canada
Liard see Fort Liard
10 L10 Liard River British Columbia, W Canada
149 O15 Liāri Baluchistān, SW Pakistan
Liatroim see Leitrim
189 S6 Lib var. Ellep. island Ralik Chain, C Marshall Islands
Liban see Lebanon
138 H6 Liban, Jebel Ar. Jabal al Gharbt, Jabal Lubnān, Eng. Mount Lebanon. ▲ C Lebanon
Libau see Liepāja
33 N7 Libby Montana, NW USA
79 I16 Libenge Equateur, NW Dem. Rep. Congo
26 I7 Liberal Kansas, C USA
27 R7 Liberal Missouri, C USA
Liberalitas Julia see Évora
111 D15 Liberec Ger. Reichenberg. Liberecký Kraj, N Czech Republic
111 D15 Liberecký Kraj ◈ region N Czech Republic
42 K12 Liberia Guanacaste, NW Costa Rica
76 K17 Liberia off. Republic of Liberia. ◆ republic W Africa
61 D16 Libertad Corrientes, NE Argentina
61 E20 Libertad San José, S Uruguay
54 I7 Libertad Barinas, NW Venezuela
54 K6 Libertad Cojedes, N Venezuela
62 G12 Libertador off. Región del Libertador General Bernardo O'Higgins. ◈ region C Chile
Libertador General San Martín see Ciudad de Libertador General San Martín
20 L6 Liberty Kentucky, S USA
22 J7 Liberty Mississippi, S USA
27 R4 Liberty Missouri, C USA
18 J12 Liberty New York, NE USA
21 T9 Liberty North Carolina, SE USA
Libian Desert see Libyan Desert
99 J23 Libin Luxembourg, SE Belgium
160 K13 Libo var. Yuping. Guizhou, S China
Libohova see Libohovë
113 L23 Libohovë var. Libohova. Gjirokastër, S Albania
81 K18 Liboi North Eastern, E Kenya
102 K13 Libourne Gironde, SW France
99 K23 Libramont Luxembourg, SE Belgium
113 M20 Librazhd var. Librazhdi. Elbasan, E Albania
Librazhdi see Librazhd
79 C18 Libreville ● (Gabon) Estuaire, NW Gabon
75 P10 Libya off. Socialist People's Libyan Arab Jamahiriya, Ar. Al Jamāhīrīyah al 'Arabīyah al Lībīyah ash Sha'bīyah al Ishtirākīyah; prev. Libyan Arab Republic. ◆ Islamic state N Africa
75 T11 Libyan Desert var. Libian Desert, Ar. Aş Şahrā' al Lībīyah. desert N Africa
75 T8 Libyan Plateau var. Aḍ Ḍiffah. plateau Egypt/Libya
Lībīyah, Aş Şahrā' al see Libyan Desert
62 G12 Licantén Maule, C Chile
107 J25 Licata anc. Phintias. Sicilia, Italy, C Mediterranean Sea
137 P14 Lice Diyarbakır, SE Turkey
97 L19 Lichfield C England, UK
83 N14 Lichinga Niassa, N Mozambique
109 V3 Lichtenau Niederösterreich, N Austria
83 I21 Lichtenburg North-West, N South Africa
101 K18 Lichtenfels Bayern, SE Germany
98 O12 Lichtenvoorde Gelderland, E Netherlands
Lichtenwald see Sevnica
99 C17 Lichtervelde West-Vlaanderen, W Belgium
160 L9 Lichuan Hubei, C China
27 V7 Licking Missouri, C USA
20 M4 Licking River ≈ Kentucky, S USA
112 C11 Lički Osik Lika-Senj, C Croatia
Ličko-Senjska Županija see Lika-Senj
107 K19 Licosa, Punta headland S Italy
119 H16 Lida Rus. Lida. Hrodzyenskaya Voblasts', W Belarus
93 H17 Liden Västernorrland, C Sweden
29 R7 Lidgerwood North Dakota, N USA
Lidhorikíon see Lidoríki
95 K21 Lidhult Kronoberg, S Sweden
95 P16 Lidingö Stockholm, C Sweden
95 K17 Lidköping Västra Götaland, S Sweden
Lido di Iesolo see Lido di Jesolo
106 I8 Lido di Jesolo var. Lido di Iesolo. Veneto, NE Italy
107 H15 Lido di Ostia Lazio, C Italy
Lidokhorikion see Lidoríki
115 E18 Lidoríki prev. Lidhorikíon, Lidokhorikion. Stereá Ellás, C Greece
110 K9 Lidzbark Warmińsko-Mazurskie, NE Poland
110 L7 Lidzbark Warmiński Ger. Heilsberg. Warmińsko-Mazurskie, NE Poland,
109 U3 Liebenau Oberösterreich, N Austria
181 P7 Liebig, Mount ▲ Northern Territory, C Australia
109 V8 Lieboch Steiermark, SE Austria
108 I8 Liechtenstein off. Principality of Liechtenstein. ◆ principality C Europe
99 F18 Liedekerke Vlaams Brabant, C Belgium
99 K19 Liège Dut. Luik, Ger. Lüttich. Liège, E Belgium
99 K20 Liège Dut. Luik. ◈ province E Belgium
Liegnitz see Legnica
93 O16 Lieksa Itä-Suomi, E Finland
118 F10 Lielupe ≈ Latvia/Lithuania
118 G9 Lielvārde Ogre, C Latvia
167 U13 Liên Hương var. Tuy Phong. Binh Thuân, S Vietnam
Liên Nghia see Đưc Trong
109 P9 Lienz Tirol, W Austria
118 B10 Liepāja Ger. Libau. Liepāja, W Latvia
99 H17 Lier Fr. Lierre. Antwerpen, N Belgium
95 H15 Lierbyen Buskerud, S Norway
99 L21 Lierneux Liège, E Belgium
Lierre see Lier
101 D18 Lieser ≈ W Germany
109 U7 Liesing ≈ E Austria
108 E6 Liestal Basel-Land, N Switzerland
Lietuva see Lithuania
Lievenhof see Līvāni
103 O2 Liévin Pas-de-Calais, N France
14 M9 Lièvre, Rivière du ≈ Québec, SE Canada
109 T6 Liezen Steiermark, C Austria
97 E14 Lifford Ir. Leifear. NW Ireland
187 Q16 Lifou island Îles Loyauté, E New Caledonia
193 Y15 Lifuka island Ha'apai Group, C Tonga
171 P4 Ligao Luzon, N Philippines
Liger see Loire
42 H2 Lighthouse Reef reef E Belize
183 Q4 Lightning Ridge New South Wales, SE Australia
103 N9 Lignières Cher, C France
103 S5 Ligny-en-Barrois Meuse, NE France
83 P15 Ligonha ≈ NE Mozambique
31 P11 Ligonier Indiana, N USA
81 I25 Ligunga Ruvuma, S Tanzania
106 D9 Ligure, Appennino Eng. Ligurian Mountains. ▲ NW Italy
Ligure, Mar see Ligurian Sea
106 C9 Liguria ◈ region NW Italy
Ligurian Mountains see Ligure, Appennino
120 K6 Ligurian Sea Fr. Mer Ligurienne, It. Mar Ligure. sea N Mediterranean Sea
Ligurienne, Mer see Ligurian Sea
186 H5 Lihir Group island group NE PNG
38 B8 Līhu'e var. Lihue. Kaua'i, Hawai'i, USA, C Pacific Ocean
118 F5 Lihula Ger. Leal. Läänemaa, W Estonia
124 I2 Liinakhamari var. Linacmamari. Murmanskaya Oblast', NW Russian Federation
Liivi Laht see Riga, Gulf of
160 F11 Lijiang var. Dayan, Lijiang Naxizu Zizhixian. Yunnan, SW China
Lijiang Naxizu Zizhixian see Lijiang
112 C11 Lika-Senj off. Ličko-Senjska Županija. ◈ province W Croatia
79 N25 Likasi prev. Jadotville. Katanga, SE Dem. Rep. Congo
79 L16 Likati Orientale, N Dem. Rep. Congo
10 M15 Likely British Columbia, SW Canada
153 Y11 Likhapāni Assam, NE India
124 J16 Likhoslavl' Tverskaya Oblast', W Russian Federation
189 U5 Likiep Atoll atoll Ratak Chain, C Marshall Islands
95 D18 Liknes Vest-Agder, S Norway
79 H18 Likouala ≈ N Congo
79 H18 Likouala aux Herbes ≈ E Congo
190 B16 Liku E Niue
Likupang, Selat see Bangka, Selat
27 Y8 Lilbourn Missouri, C USA
103 X14 l'Île-Rousse Corse, France, C Mediterranean Sea
109 W5 Lilienfeld Niederösterreich, NE Austria
161 N11 Liling Hunan, S China
95 J18 Lilla Edet Västra Götaland, S Sweden
103 P1 Lille var. l'Isle, Dut. Rijssel, Flem. Ryssel; prev. Lisle, anc. Insula. Nord, N France
95 G24 Lillebælt var. Lille Bælt, Eng. Little Belt. strait S Denmark
102 L3 Lillebonne Seine-Maritime, N France
94 H12 Lillehammer Oppland, S Norway
103 O1 Lillers Pas-de-Calais, N France
95 F18 Lillesand Aust-Agder, S Norway
95 I15 Lillestrøm Akershus, S Norway
93 F18 Lillhärdal Jämtland, C Sweden
21 U10 Lillington North Carolina, SE USA
105 O9 Lillo Castilla-La Mancha, C Spain
10 M16 Lillooet British Columbia, SW Canada
83 M14 Lilongwe ● (Malawi) Central, W Malawi
83 M14 Lilongwe ✕ Central, W Malawi
83 M14 Lilongwe ≈ W Malawi
171 P7 Liloy Mindanao, S Philippines
Lilybaeum see Marsala
182 J7 Lilydale South Australia
183 P16 Lilydale Tasmania, SE Australia
113 J14 Lim ≈ Bosnia and Herzegovina/Serbia and Montenegro (Yugo.)
57 D15 Lima ● (Peru) Lima, W Peru
94 K13 Lima Dalarna, C Sweden
31 R12 Lima Ohio, NE USA
57 D14 Lima ◈ department W Peru
Lima see Jorge Chávez International
104 G5 Lima, Rio Sp. Limia ≈ Portugal/Spain see also Limia
111 L17 Limanowa Małopolskie, S Poland
168 M11 Limas Pulau Sebangka, W Indonesia
Limassol see Lemesós
97 F14 Limavady Ir. Léim an Mhadaidh. NW Northern Ireland, UK
63 J14 Limay Mahuida La Pampa, C Argentina
63 H15 Limay, Río ≈ W Argentina
101 N16 Limbach-Oberfrohna Sachsen, E Germany
81 F22 Limba Limba ≈ C Tanzania
107 C17 Limbara, Monte ▲ Sardegna, Italy, C Mediterranean Sea
118 G7 Limbaži Est. Lemsalu. Limbaži, N Latvia
44 M8 Limbé N Haiti
99 L19 Limbourg Liège, E Belgium
99 K17 Limburg ◈ province NE Belgium
99 L16 Limburg ◈ province SE Netherlands
101 F17 Limburg an der Lahn Hessen, W Germany
94 K13 Limedsforsen Dalarna, C Sweden
60 L9 Limeira São Paulo, S Brazil
97 C19 Limerick Ir. Luimneach. SW Ireland
97 C20 Limerick Ir. Luimneach. cultural region SW Ireland
19 S2 Limestone Maine, NE USA
25 U9 Limestone, Lake ◎ Texas, SW USA
39 P12 Lime Village Alaska, USA
95 F20 Limfjorden fjord N Denmark
95 J23 Limhamn Skåne, S Sweden
104 H5 Limia Port. Rio Lima ≈ Portugal/Spain see also Lima, Rio
93 L14 Liminka Oulu, C Finland
Limín Vathéos see Sámos
115 G17 Límni Évvoia, C Greece
115 J15 Límnos anc. Lemnos. island E Greece
102 M11 Limoges anc. Augustoritum Lemovicensium, Lemovices. Haute-Vienne, C France
37 U5 Limon Colorado, C USA
43 O13 Limón var. Puerto Limón. Limón, E Costa Rica
42 K4 Limón Colón, NE Honduras
43 N13 Limón off. Provincia de Limón. ◈ province E Costa Rica
106 A10 Limone Piemonte Piemonte, NE Italy
Limones see Valdéz
Limonum see Poitiers
103 N11 Limousin ◈ region C France
103 N16 Limoux Aude, S France
83 L19 Limpopo var. Crocodile. ≈ S Africa
83 J20 Limpopo prev. Northern Province, Northern Transvaal. ◈ province NE South Africa
160 K17 Limu Ling ▲ S China
113 M20 Lin var. Lini. Elbasan, E Albania
Linacmamari see Liinakhamari
62 G13 Linares Maule, C Chile
54 C13 Linares Nariño, SW Colombia
41 O9 Linares Nuevo León, NE Mexico
105 N12 Linares Andalucía, S Spain
107 G15 Linaro, Capo headland C Italy
106 D8 Linate ✕ (Milano) Lombardia, N Italy
167 T8 Lin Camh prev. Đưc Tho. Ha Tinh, N Vietnam
160 F13 Lincang Yunnan, SW China
Lincheng see Lingao
Linchuan see Fuzhou
61 B20 Lincoln Buenos Aires, E Argentina
185 H19 Lincoln Canterbury, South Island, NZ
97 N18 Lincoln anc. Lindum, Lindum Colonia. E England, UK
35 O6 Lincoln California, W USA
30 L13 Lincoln Illinois, N USA
26 M4 Lincoln Kansas, C USA
19 S5 Lincoln Maine, NE USA
27 T5 Lincoln Missouri, C USA
29 R16 Lincoln state capital Nebraska, C USA
32 F11 Lincoln City Oregon, NW USA
167 X10 Lincoln Island island E Paracel Islands
197 Q11 Lincoln Sea sea Arctic Ocean
97 N18 Lincolnshire cultural region E England, UK
21 R10 Lincolnton North Carolina, SE USA
25 V7 Lindale Texas, SW USA
101 I25 Lindau var. Lindau am Bodensee. Bayern, S Germany
Lindau am Bodensee see Lindau
123 P9 Linde ≈ NE Russian Federation
55 T9 Linden E Guyana
23 O6 Linden Alabama, S USA
20 H9 Linden Tennessee, S USA
25 X6 Linden Texas, SW USA
18 J16 Lindenwold New Jersey, NE USA
95 M15 Lindesberg Örebro, C Sweden
95 D18 Lindesnes headland S Norway
Líndhos see Líndos
81 K24 Lindi Lindi, SE Tanzania
81 J24 Lindi ◈ region SE Tanzania
79 N17 Lindi ≈ NE Dem. Rep. Congo
163 V7 Lindian Heilongjiang, NE China
185 E21 Lindis Pass pass South Island, NZ
83 J22 Lindley Free State, C South Africa
95 J19 Lindome Västra Götaland, S Sweden
163 S10 Lindong var. Bairin Zuoqi. Nei Mongol Zizhiqu, N China
115 O23 Líndos var. Líndhos. Ródos, Dodekánisos, Greece, Aegean Sea
14 I14 Lindsay Ontario, SE Canada
35 R11 Lindsay California, W USA
33 X8 Lindsay Montana, NW USA
27 N11 Lindsay Oklahoma, C USA
27 N5 Lindsborg Kansas, C USA
95 N21 Lindsdal Kalmar, S Sweden
Lindum/Lindum Colonia see Lincoln
191 W3 Line Islands island group E Kiribati
Linëvo see Linova
160 M5 Linfen var. Lin-fen. Shanxi, C China
155 F18 Linganamakki Reservoir ⊞ SW India
160 L17 Lingao var. Lincheng. Hainan, S China
171 N3 Lingayen Luzon, N Philippines
160 M6 Lingbao var. Guolüezhen. Henan, C China
94 N12 Lingbo Gävleborg, C Sweden
Lingeh see Bandar-e Langeh
100 E12 Lingen var. Lingen an der Ems. Niedersachsen, NW Germany
Lingen an der Ems see Lingen
168 M11 Lingga, Kepulauan island group W Indonesia
168 L11 Lingga, Pulau island Kepulauan Lingga, W Indonesia
14 J14 Lingham Lake ◎ Ontario, SE Canada
94 M13 Linghed Dalarna, C Sweden
33 Z15 Lingle Wyoming, C USA
18 G15 Linglestown Pennsylvania, NE USA
79 K18 Lingomo II Equateur, NW Dem. Rep. Congo
160 L15 Lingshan Guangxi Zhuangzu Zizhiqu, S China
160 L17 Lingshui var. Lingshui Lizu Zizhixian. Hainan, S China
Lingshui Lizu Zizhixian see Lingshui
155 G16 Lingsugūr Karnātaka, C India
107 L23 Linguaglossa Sicilia, Italy, C Mediterranean Sea
76 H10 Linguère N Senegal
159 W8 Lingwu Ningxia, N China
Lingxi Hunan, China see Yongshun
Lingxi Zhejiang, China see Cangnan
Lingxian/Ling Xian see Yanling
163 S12 Lingyuan Liaoning, NE China
163 U4 Linhai Heilongjiang, NE China
161 S10 Linhai var. Taizhou. Zhejiang, SE China
59 O20 Linhares Espírito Santo, SE Brazil
162 M13 Linhe Nei Mongol Zizhiqu, N China
Lini see Lin
139 S1 Līnik, Chiyā-ē ▲ N Iraq
95 M18 Linköping Östergötland, S Sweden
163 Y8 Linkou Heilongjiang, NE China
118 F11 Linkuva Šiauliai, N Lithuania
27 V5 Linn Missouri, C USA
25 S16 Linn Texas, SW USA
27 T2 Linneus Missouri, C USA
96 H10 Linnhe, Loch inlet W Scotland, UK
119 G19 Linova Rus. Linëvo. Brestskaya Voblasts', SW Belarus
161 O5 Linqing Shandong, E China
60 K8 Lins São Paulo, S Brazil
93 F17 Linsell Jämtland, C Sweden
160 J9 Linshui Sichuan, C China
44 K12 Linstead C Jamaica
159 U11 Lintan Gansu, N China
159 V11 Lintao Gansu, C China
15 S12 Lintère ≈ Québec, SE Canada
108 H8 Linth ≈ NW Switzerland
108 H8 Linthal Glarus, NE Switzerland
31 N15 Linton Indiana, N USA
29 N6 Linton North Dakota, N USA
163 R11 Linxi Nei Mongol Zizhiqu, N China
159 U11 Linxia var. Linxia Huizu Zizhizhou. Gansu, C China
Linxia Huizu Zizhizhou see Linxia
Linxian see Lianzhou
161 Q6 Linyi Shandong, S China
161 P4 Linyi Shandong, E China
160 M6 Linyi Shanxi, C China
109 T4 Linz anc. Lentia. Oberösterreich, N Austria
159 S8 Linze var. Shahepu. Gansu, N China
44 J13 Lionel Town C Jamaica
103 Q16 Lion, Golfe du Eng. Gulf of Lion, Gulf of Lions; anc. Sinus Gallicus. gulf S France
Lion, Gulf of/Lions, Gulf of see Lion, Golfe du
83 K16 Lions Den Mashonaland West, N Zimbabwe
14 F13 Lion's Head Ontario, S Canada
Lios Ceannúir, Bá see Liscannor Bay
Lios Mór see Lismore
Lios na gCearrbhach see Lisburn
Lios Tuathail see Listowel
79 G17 Liouesso La Sangha, N Congo
Liozno see Lyozna
171 O4 Lipa off. Lipa City. Luzon, N Philippines
25 S7 Lipan Texas, SW USA
Lipari Islands/Lipari, Isole see Eolie, Isole
107 L22 Lipari, Isola island Isole Eolie, S Italy
116 L8 Lipcani Rus. Lipkany. N Moldova
93 N17 Liperi Itä-Suomi, E Finland
126 L7 Lipetsk Lipetskaya Oblast', W Russian Federation
126 K6 Lipetskaya Oblast' ◈ province W Russian Federation
57 K22 Lipez, Cordillera de ▲ SW Bolivia
110 E10 Lipiany Ger. Lippehne. Zachodnio-pomorskie, W Poland
112 G9 Lipik Požega-Slavonija, NE Croatia
124 L12 Lipin Bor Vologodskaya Oblast', NW Russian Federation
160 L12 Liping var. Defeng. Guizhou, S China
Lipkany see Lipcani
119 H15 Lipnishki Rus. Lipnishki. Hrodzyenskaya Voblasts', W Belarus
110 J10 Lipno Kujawsko-pomorskie, C Poland
116 F11 Lipova Hung. Lippa. Arad, W Romania
Lipovets see Lypovets'
Lippa see Lipova
101 E14 Lippe ≈ W Germany
Lippehne see Lipiany
101 G14 Lippstadt Nordrhein-Westfalen, W Germany
25 P1 Lipscomb Texas, SW USA
Lipsia/Lipsk see Leipzig
Liptau-Sankt-Nikolaus/Liptószentmiklós see Liptovský Mikuláš
111 K19 Liptovský Mikuláš Ger. Liptau-Sankt-Nikolaus, Hung. Liptószentmiklós. Žilinský Kraj, N Slovakia
183 O13 Liptrap, Cape headland Victoria, SE Australia
160 L13 Lipu Guangxi Zhuangzu Zizhiqu, S China
141 X12 Liqbi S Oman
81 G17 Lira N Uganda
57 F15 Lircay Huancavelica, C Peru
107 J15 Liri ≈ C Italy
144 M8 Lisakovsk Kostanay, NW Kazakhstan
79 K17 Lisala Equateur, N Dem. Rep. Congo
104 F11 Lisboa Eng. Lisbon; anc. Felicitas Julia, Olisipo. ● (Portugal) Lisboa, W Portugal
104 F10 Lisboa ◈ Eng. Lisbon. district C Portugal
19 N7 Lisbon New Hampshire, NE USA
29 Q6 Lisbon North Dakota, N USA
Lisbon see Lisboa
19 Q8 Lisbon Falls Maine, NE USA
97 G15 Lisburn Ir. Lios na gCearrbhach. E Northern Ireland, UK
38 L6 Lisburne, Cape headland Alaska, USA
97 B19 Liscannor Bay Ir. Bá Lios Ceannúir. inlet W Ireland
113 Q19 Lisec ▲ E FYR Macedonia
160 F13 Lishe Jiang ≈ SW China
160 M4 Lishi Shanxi, C China
163 V10 Lishu Jilin, NE China
161 R10 Lishui Zhejiang, SE China
192 L5 Lisianski Island island Hawaiian Islands, Hawaii, USA, C Pacific Ocean
Lisichansk see Lysychans'k
102 L4 Lisieux anc. Noviomagus. Calvados, N France
126 L8 Liski prev. Georgiu-Dezh. Voronezhskaya Oblast', W Russian Federation
Lisle/l'Isle see Lille
103 N4 l'Isle-Adam Val-d'Oise, N France
103 R15 l'Isle-sur-la-Sorgue Vaucluse, SE France
15 S9 L'Islet Québec, SE Canada
182 M12 Lismore Victoria, SE Australia
97 D20 Lismore Ir. Lios Mór. S Ireland
Lissa see Vis, Croatia
Lissa see Leszno, Poland
98 H11 Lisse Zuid-Holland, W Netherlands
95 Q18 Lista peninsula S Norway
95 D18 Listafjorden fjord S Norway
195 R13 Lister, Mount ▲ Antarctica
126 M8 Listopadovka Voronezhskaya Oblast', W Russian Federation
14 F15 Listowel Ontario, S Canada
97 B20 Listowel Ir. Lios Tuathail. SW Ireland
160 L14 Litang Guangxi Zhuangzu Zizhiqu, S China
160 F9 Litang var. Gaocheng. Sichuan, C China
160 F10 Litang Qu ≈ C China
55 X12 Litani var. Itany. ≈ French Guiana/Suriname
138 G8 Līṭānī, Nahr el var. Nahr al Litant. ≈ C Lebanon
Litant, Nahr al see Līṭānī, Nahr el
Litauen see Lithuania
30 K14 Litchfield Illinois, N USA
29 U8 Litchfield Minnesota, N USA
36 K13 Litchfield Park Arizona, SW USA
183 S8 Lithgow New South Wales, SE Australia
115 I26 Líthino, Akrotírio headland Kríti, Greece, E Mediterranean Sea
118 D12 Lithuania off. Republic of Lithuania, Ger. Litauen, Lith. Lietuva, Pol. Litwa, Rus. Litva; prev. Lithuanian SSR, Rus. Litovskaya SSR. ◆ republic NE Europe
Lithuanian SSR see Lithuania
109 U11 Litija Ger. Littai. C Slovenia
18 H15 Lititz Pennsylvania, NE USA
115 F15 Litóchoro var. Litohoro, Litókhoron. Kentrikí Makedonía, N Greece
Litohoro/Litókhoron see Litóchoro

◆ Country ● Country Capital ◇ Dependent Territory ○ Dependent Territory Capital ◈ Administrative Region ✕ International Airport ▲ Mountain ▲ Mountain Range ⛰ Volcano ≈ River ◎ Lake ⊞ Reservoir

111 C15 **Litoměřice** *Ger.* Ústecký Kraj, NW Czech Republic
111 F17 **Litomyšl** *Ger.* Pardubický Kraj, C Czech Republic
111 G17 **Litovel** *Ger.* Littau. Olomoucký Kraj, E Czech Republic
123 S13 **Litovko** Khabarovskiy Kray, SE Russian Federation
Litovskaya SSR *see* Lithuania
Littai *see* Litija
Littau *see* Litovel
44 G1 **Little Abaco** *var.* Abaco Island. *island* N Bahamas
111 I21 **Little Alföld** *Ger.* Kleines Ungarisches Tiefland, *Hung.* Kisalföld, *Slvk.* Podunajská Rovina. *plain* Hungary/Slovakia
151 Q20 **Little Andaman** *island* Andaman Islands, India, NE Indian Ocean
26 M5 **Little Arkansas River** ≈ Kansas, C USA
184 L4 **Little Barrier Island** *island* N NZ
Little Belt *see* Lillebælt
38 M11 **Little Black River** ≈ Alaska, USA
27 O2 **Little Blue River** ≈ Kansas/Nebraska, C USA
44 D8 **Little Cayman** *island* E Cayman Islands
11 X11 **Little Churchill** ≈ Manitoba, C Canada
166 J10 **Little Coco Island** *island* SW Myanmar
36 L10 **Little Colorado River** ≈ Arizona, SW USA
14 E11 **Little Current** Manitoulin Island, Ontario, S Canada
12 E11 **Little Current** ≈ Ontario, S Canada
38 L8 **Little Diomede Island** *island* Alaska, USA
44 J4 **Little Exuma** *island* C Bahamas
29 U7 **Little Falls** Minnesota, N USA
18 J10 **Little Falls** New York, NE USA
24 M5 **Littlefield** Texas, SW USA
29 V3 **Littlefork** Minnesota, N USA
29 V3 **Little Fork River** ≈ Minnesota, N USA
11 N16 **Little Fort** British Columbia, SW Canada
11 Y14 **Little Grand Rapids** Manitoba, C Canada
97 N23 **Littlehampton** SE England, UK
35 T2 **Little Humboldt River** ≈ Nevada, W USA
44 K6 **Little Inagua** *var.* Inagua Islands. *island* S Bahamas
21 Q4 **Little Kanawha River** ≈ West Virginia, NE USA
83 F25 **Little Karoo** *plateau* S South Africa
39 O16 **Little Koniuji Island** *island* Shumagin Islands, Alaska, USA
44 H12 **Little London** W Jamaica
13 R10 **Little Mecatina** *Fr.* Rivière du Petit Mécatina. ≈ Newfoundland and Labrador/Québec, E Canada
96 F8 **Little Minch, The** *strait* NW Scotland, UK
27 T13 **Little Missouri River** ≈ Arkansas, USA
28 J7 **Little Missouri River** ≈ NW USA
28 J3 **Little Muddy River** ≈ North Dakota, N USA
151 Q22 **Little Nicobar** *island* Nicobar Islands, India, NE Indian Ocean
27 R6 **Little Osage River** ≈ Missouri, C USA
97 P20 **Little Ouse** ≈ E England, UK
149 V2 **Little Pamir** *Pash.* Pāmīr-e Khord, *Rus.* Malyy Pamir. ▲▲ Afghanistan/Tajikistan
21 U12 **Little Pee Dee River** ≈ North Carolina/South Carolina, SE USA
27 V10 **Little Red River** ≈ Arkansas, C USA
Little Rhody *see* Rhode Island
185 I19 **Little River** Canterbury, South Island, NZ
21 U12 **Little River** South Carolina, SE USA
27 Y9 **Little River** ≈ Arkansas/Missouri, C USA
27 R13 **Little River** ≈ Arkansas/Oklahoma, USA
23 T7 **Little River** ≈ Georgia, SE USA
22 H6 **Little River** ≈ Louisiana, S USA
25 T10 **Little River** ≈ Texas, SW USA
27 V12 **Little Rock** *state capital* Arkansas, C USA
31 N8 **Little Sable Point** *headland* Michigan, N USA
103 U11 **Little Saint Bernard Pass** *Fr.* Col du Petit St-Bernard, *It.* Colle di Piccolo San Bernardo. *pass* France/Italy
36 K7 **Little Salt Lake** ⊚ Utah, W USA
180 K8 **Little Sandy Desert** *desert* Western Australia
29 S13 **Little Sioux River** ≈ Iowa, C USA
38 E17 **Little Sitkin Island** *island* Aleutian Islands, Alaska, USA
11 O13 **Little Smoky** Alberta, W Canada
11 O14 **Little Smoky** ≈ Alberta, W Canada
37 P3 **Little Snake River** ≈ Colorado, C USA
64 A12 **Little Sound** *bay* Bermuda, NW Atlantic Ocean
37 T4 **Littleton** Colorado, C USA
19 N7 **Littleton** New Hampshire, NE USA
18 D11 **Little Valley** New York, NE USA
30 M15 **Little Wabash River** ≈ Illinois, N USA
14 D10 **Little White River** ≈ Ontario, S Canada
28 M12 **Little White River** ≈ South Dakota, N USA
25 R5 **Little Wichita River** ≈ Texas, SW USA
142 J4 **Little Zab** *Ar.* Nahraz Zāb aş Şaghīr, *Kurd.* Zē-i Kōya, *Per.* Rūdkhāneh-ye Zāb-e Kūchek. ≈ Iran/Iraq
79 D15 **Littoral** ◈ *province* W Cameroon
Littoria *see* Latina
Litva/Litwa *see* Lithuania
111 B15 **Litvínov** *Ger.* Ústecký Kraj, NW Czech Republic
116 M6 **Lityn** Vinnyts'ka Oblast', C Ukraine
Liu-chou/Liuchow *see* Liuzhou
163 W11 **Liuhe** Jilin, NE China
83 Q15 **Liúpo** Nampula, NE Mozambique
83 G14 **Liuwa Plain** *plain* W Zambia
160 L13 **Liuzhou** *var.* Liu-chou, Liuchow. Guangxi Zhuangzu Zizhiqu, S China
116 H8 **Livada** *Hung.* Sárköz. Satu Mare, NW Romania
115 J20 **Liváda, Akrotírio** *headland* Tínos, Kykládes, Greece, Aegean Sea
115 L21 **Livádi** *island* Kykládes, Greece, Aegean Sea
Livanátai *see* Livanátes
115 G18 **Livanátes** *prev.* Livanátai. Stereá Ellás, C Greece
118 I10 **Līvāni** *Ger.* Lievenhof. Preiļi, SE Latvia
65 E25 **Lively Island** *island* SE Falkland Islands
65 D25 **Lively Sound** *sound* SE Falkland Islands
39 R8 **Livengood** Alaska, USA
106 I7 **Livenza** ≈ NE Italy
35 O6 **Live Oak** California, W USA
23 U9 **Live Oak** Florida, SE USA
35 O9 **Livermore** California, W USA
20 I6 **Livermore** Kentucky, S USA
19 Q7 **Livermore Falls** Maine, NE USA
24 J10 **Livermore, Mount** ▲ Texas, SW USA
97 K17 **Liverpool** NW England, UK
183 S7 **Liverpool Range** ▲▲ New South Wales, SE Australia
96 J12 **Livingston** C Scotland, UK
23 N5 **Livingston** Alabama, S USA
35 P9 **Livingston** California, W USA
22 J8 **Livingston** Louisiana, S USA
33 S11 **Livingston** Montana, NW USA
20 L8 **Livingston** Tennessee, S USA
25 W9 **Livingston** Texas, SW USA
42 F4 **Livingston** Izabal, E Guatemala
83 I16 **Livingstone** *var.* Maramba. Southern, S Zambia
185 B22 **Livingstone Mountains** ▲▲ South Island, NZ
80 K13 **Livingstone Mountains** ▲▲ S Tanzania
82 N12 **Livingstonia** Northern, N Malawi
194 G4 **Livingston Island** *island* Antarctica
25 W9 **Livingston, Lake** ⊠ Texas, SW USA
112 F13 **Livno** Federacija Bosna I Hercegovina, SW Bosnia and Herzegovina
126 K7 **Livny** Orlovskaya Oblast', W Russian Federation
93 M14 **Livojoki** ≈ C Finland
31 R10 **Livonia** Michigan, N USA
106 E11 **Livorno** *Eng.* Leghorn. Toscana, C Italy
Livramento *see* Santana do Livramento
141 U8 **Līwā** *var.* Al Liwā'. *oasis region* S UAE
81 I24 **Liwale** Lindi, SE Tanzania
159 W9 **Liwangbu** Ningxia, N China
83 N15 **Liwonde** Southern, S Malawi
159 V11 **Lixian** *var.* Li Xian. Gansu, C China
160 H8 **Lixian** *var.* Li Xian, Zagunao. Sichuan, C China
Lixian Jiang *see* Black River
115 B18 **Lixoúri** *prev.* Lixoúrion. Kefallinía, Iónioi Nísoi, Greece, C Mediterranean Sea
Lixoúrion *see* Lixoúri
Lixus *see* Larache
Lizarra *see* Estella
33 U15 **Lizard Head Peak** ▲ Wyoming, C USA
97 H25 **Lizard Point** *headland* SW England, UK
112 L12 **Ljig** Serbia, C Serbia and Montenegro (Yugo.)
Ljouwert *see* Leeuwarden
Ljubelj *see* Loibl Pass
109 U11 **Ljubljana** *Ger.* Laibach, *It.* Lubiana; *anc.* Aemona, Emona. ● (Slovenia) C Slovenia
109 T11 **Ljubljana** ✕ C Slovenia
113 N17 **Ljuboten** ▲ S Serbia and Montenegro (Yugo.)
95 P19 **Ljugarn** Gotland, SE Sweden
84 G7 **Ljungan** ≈ N Sweden
93 F17 **Ljungan** ≈ C Sweden
95 K21 **Ljungby** Kronoberg, S Sweden
95 M17 **Ljungsbro** Östergötland, S Sweden
95 I18 **Ljungskile** Västra Götaland, S Sweden
94 M11 **Ljusdal** Gävleborg, C Sweden
94 M11 **Ljusnan** ≈ C Sweden
94 N12 **Ljusne** Gävleborg, C Sweden
95 P15 **Ljusterö** Stockholm, C Sweden
109 X9 **Ljutomer** *Ger.* Luttenberg. NE Slovenia
63 G15 **Llaima, Volcán** ▲ S Chile
105 X4 **Llançà** *var.* Llansá. Cataluña, NE Spain
97 J21 **Llandovery** C Wales, UK
97 J20 **Llandrindod Wells** E Wales, UK
97 J18 **Llandudno** N Wales, UK
97 I21 **Llanelli** *prev.* Llanelly. SW Wales, UK
Llanelly *see* Llanelli
104 M2 **Llanes** Asturias, N Spain
97 K19 **Llangollen** NE Wales, UK
25 R10 **Llano** Texas, SW USA
25 Q10 **Llano River** ≈ Texas, SW USA
54 I9 **Llanos** *physical region* Colombia/Venezuela
63 G16 **Llanquihue, Lago** ⊚ S Chile
Llansá *see* Llançà
105 U5 **Lleida** *Cast.* Lérida; *anc.* Ilerda. Cataluña, NE Spain
105 U5 **Lleida** *Cast.* Lérida ◈ *province* Cataluña, NE Spain
104 K12 **Llerena** Extremadura, W Spain
105 S9 **Llíria** País Valenciano, E Spain
105 W4 **Llivia** Cataluña, NE Spain
105 O3 **Llodio** País Vasco, N Spain
105 X5 **Lloret de Mar** Cataluña, NE Spain
Llorri *see* Tossal de l'Orri
10 L11 **Lloyd George, Mount** ▲ British Columbia, W Canada
11 R14 **Lloydminster** Alberta/Saskatchewan, SW Canada
36 L6 **Loa** Utah, W USA
169 S8 **Loagan Bunut** ⊚ East Malaysia
38 G12 **Loa, Mauna** ▲ Hawai'i, USA, C Pacific Ocean
Loanda *see* Luanda
79 J22 **Loange** ≈ S Dem. Rep. Congo
79 E21 **Loango** Le Kouilou, S Congo
106 B10 **Loano** Liguria, NW Italy
62 H4 **Loa, Río** ≈ N Chile
83 I20 **Lobatse** *var.* Lobatsi. Kgatleng, SE Botswana
Lobatsi *see* Lobatse
101 Q15 **Löbau** Sachsen, E Germany
79 H16 **Lobaye** ◈ *prefecture* SW Central African Republic
79 I16 **Lobaye** ≈ SW Central African Republic
99 G21 **Lobbes** Hainaut, S Belgium
61 D23 **Lobería** Buenos Aires, E Argentina
110 F8 **Łobez** *Ger.* Labes. Zachodnio-pomorskie, NW Poland
82 A13 **Lobito** Benguela, W Angola
Lobkovichi *see* Labkovichy
Lob Nor *see* Lop Nur
171 V13 **Lobo** Papua, E Indonesia
104 J11 **Lobón** Extremadura, W Spain
61 D20 **Lobos** Buenos Aires, E Argentina
40 E4 **Lobos, Cabo** *headland* NW Mexico
40 F6 **Lobos, Isla** *island* NW Mexico
Lobositz *see* Lovosice
Lobsens *see* Łobżenica
Loburi *see* Lop Buri
110 H9 **Łobżenica** *Ger.* Lobsens. Wielkopolskie, C Poland
108 G11 **Locarno** *Ger.* Luggarus. Ticino, S Switzerland
96 E9 **Lochboisdale** NW Scotland, UK
98 N11 **Lochem** Gelderland, E Netherlands
102 M8 **Loches** Indre-et-Loire, C France
Loch Garman *see* Wexford
96 H12 **Lochgilphead** W Scotland, UK
96 H7 **Lochinver** N Scotland, UK
96 F8 **Lochmaddy** NW Scotland, UK
96 J10 **Lochnagar** ▲ C Scotland, UK
99 E17 **Lochristi** Oost-Vlaanderen, NW Belgium
96 H9 **Lochy, Loch** ⊚ N Scotland, UK
182 G8 **Lock** South Australia
97 J14 **Lockerbie** S Scotland, UK
27 S13 **Lockesburg** Arkansas, C USA
183 P10 **Lockhart** New South Wales, SE Australia
25 S11 **Lockhart** Texas, SW USA
18 F13 **Lock Haven** Pennsylvania, NE USA
25 N4 **Lockney** Texas, SW USA
100 O12 **Löcknitz** ≈ NE Germany
18 E9 **Lockport** New York, NE USA
167 T13 **Lôc Ninh** Sông Be, S Vietnam
107 N23 **Locri** Calabria, SW Italy
Locse *see* Levoča
27 T2 **Locust Creek** ≈ Missouri, C USA
23 P3 **Locust Fork** ≈ Alabama, S USA
27 Q9 **Locust Grove** Oklahoma, C USA
94 E11 **Lodalskåpa** ▲ S Norway
183 N10 **Loddon River** ≈ Victoria, SE Australia
Lodensee *see* Klooga
103 P15 **Lodève** *anc.* Luteva. Hérault, S France
124 I12 **Lodeynoye Pole** Leningradskaya Oblast', NW Russian Federation
33 V11 **Lodge Grass** Montana, NW USA
28 J15 **Lodgepole Creek** ≈ Nebraska/Wyoming, C USA
149 T11 **Lodhrān** Punjab, E Pakistan
106 D8 **Lodi** Lombardia, NW Italy
35 O8 **Lodi** California, W USA
31 T12 **Lodi** Ohio, N USA
92 H10 **Lødingen** Nordland, C Norway
79 L20 **Lodja** Kasai Oriental, C Dem. Rep. Congo
37 O3 **Lodore, Canyon of** *canyon* Colorado, C USA
105 Q4 **Lodosa** Navarra, N Spain
81 H16 **Lodwar** Rift Valley, NW Kenya
110 K13 **Łódź** *Rus.* Lodz. Łódź, C Poland
110 J13 **Łódzkie** ◈ *province* C Poland
167 P8 **Loei** *var.* Loey, Muang Loei. Loei, C Thailand
98 I11 **Loenen** Utrecht, C Netherlands
167 R9 **Loeng Nok Tha** Yasothon, E Thailand
83 F24 **Loeriesfontein** Northern Cape, W South Africa
95 H20 **Læsø** *island* N Denmark
Loewoek *see* Luwuk
Loey *see* Loei
76 J16 **Lofa** ≈ N Liberia
109 P6 **Lofer** Salzburg, C Austria
92 F11 **Lofoten** *var.* Lofoten Islands. *island group* C Norway
Lofoten Islands *see* Lofoten
95 N18 **Loftahammar** Kalmar S Sweden
127 O10 **Log** Volgogradskaya Oblast', SW Russian Federation
77 S12 **Loga** Dosso, SW Niger
29 S14 **Logan** Iowa, C USA
26 K3 **Logan** Kansas, C USA
31 T14 **Logan** Ohio, N USA
36 L1 **Logan** Utah, W USA
21 P6 **Logan** West Virginia, NE USA
35 Y10 **Logandale** Nevada, W USA
19 O11 **Logan International** ✕ (Boston) Massachusetts, NE USA
11 N16 **Logan Lake** British Columbia, SW Canada
23 Q4 **Logan Martin Lake** ⊠ Alabama, S USA
10 G8 **Logan, Mount** ▲ Yukon Territory, W Canada
32 I7 **Logan, Mount** ▲ Washington, NW USA
33 P7 **Logan Pass** *pass* Montana, NW USA
31 O12 **Logansport** Indiana, N USA
22 F6 **Logansport** Louisiana, S USA
Logar *see* Lowgar
67 R11 **Loge** ≈ NW Angola
Logishin *see* Lahishyn
Log na Coille *see* Lugnaquillia Mountain
78 G11 **Logone** *var.* Logane. ≈ Cameroon/Chad
78 G13 **Logone-Occidental** *off.* Préfecture du Logone-Occidental. ◈ *prefecture* SW Chad
78 H13 **Logone Occidental** ≈ SW Chad
78 G13 **Logone-Oriental** *off.* Préfecture du Logone-Oriental. ◈ *prefecture* SW Chad
78 H13 **Logone Oriental** ≈ SW Chad
Logone Oriental *see* Pendé
L'Ogooué-Ivindo *see* Ogooué-Ivindo
L'Ogooué-Lolo *see* Ogooué-Lolo
L'Ogooué-Maritime *see* Ogooué-Maritime
Logoysk *see* Lahoysk
105 P4 **Logroño** *anc.* Vareia, *Lat.* Juliobriga. La Rioja, N Spain
104 L10 **Logrosán** Extremadura, W Spain
95 G20 **Løgstør** Nordjylland, N Denmark
95 H22 **Løgten** Århus, C Denmark
95 F24 **Løgumkloster** Sønderjylland, SW Denmark
Lögurinn *see* Lagarfljót
153 P15 **Lohārdaga** Jhārkhand, N India
152 H10 **Lohāru** Haryāna, N India
101 D15 **Lohausen** ✕ (Düsseldorf) Nordrhein-Westfalen, W Germany
189 O14 **Lohd** Pohnpei, E Micronesia
92 L12 **Lohiniva** Lappi, N Finland
Lohiszyn *see* Lahishyn
93 L20 **Lohja** *var.* Lojo. Etelä-Suomi, S Finland
169 V11 **Lohjanan** Borneo, C Indonesia
25 Q9 **Lohn** Texas, SW USA
100 G12 **Lohne** Niedersachsen, NW Germany
Lohr *see* Lohr am Main
101 I18 **Lohr am Main** *var.* Lohr. Bayern, C Germany
109 T10 **Loibl Pass** *Ger.* Loiblpass, *Slvn.* Ljubelj. *pass* Austria/Slovenia
167 N6 **Loi-Kaw** Kayah State, C Myanmar
93 K19 **Loimaa** Länsi-Suomi, W Finland
103 O6 **Loing** ≈ C France
167 R6 **Loi, Phou** ▲ N Laos
102 L7 **Loir** ≈ C France
103 Q11 **Loire** ◈ *department* E France
102 M7 **Loire** *var.* Liger. ≈ C France
102 I7 **Loire-Atlantique** ◈ *department* NW France
103 O7 **Loiret** ◈ *department* C France
102 M8 **Loir-et-Cher** ◈ *department* C France
101 L24 **Loisach** ≈ SE Germany
56 B9 **Loja** Loja, S Ecuador
104 M14 **Loja** Andalucía, S Spain
56 B9 **Loja** ◈ *province* S Ecuador
Lojo *see* Lohja
116 J4 **Lokachi** Volyns'ka Oblast', NW Ukraine
79 M20 **Lokandu** Maniema, C Dem. Rep. Congo
92 M11 **Lokan Tekojärvi** ⊚ NE Finland
137 Z11 **Lökbatan** *Rus.* Lokbatan. E Azerbaijan
99 F17 **Lokeren** Oost-Vlaanderen, NW Belgium
Lokhvitsa *see* Lokhvytsya
117 S4 **Lokhvytsya** *Rus.* Lokhvitsa. Poltavs'ka Oblast', NE Ukraine
81 H17 **Lokichar** Rift Valley, NW Kenya
81 G15 **Lokichokio** Rift Valley, NW Kenya
81 H15 **Lokitaung** Rift Valley, NW Kenya
92 M11 **Lokka** Lappi, N Finland
94 G8 **Løkken Verk** Sør-Trøndelag, S Norway
124 G16 **Loknya** Pskovskaya Oblast', W Russian Federation
77 V15 **Loko** Nassarawa, C Nigeria
77 U15 **Lokoja** Kogi, C Nigeria
81 H17 **Lokori** Rift Valley, W Kenya
77 R16 **Lokossa** S Benin
118 I3 **Loksa** *Ger.* Loxa. Harjumaa, NW Estonia
9 T7 **Loks Land** *island* Nunavut, NE Canada
80 C13 **Lol** ≈ S Sudan
76 K15 **Lola** Guinée-Forestière, SE Guinea
35 Q5 **Lola, Mount** ▲ California, W USA
81 H20 **Loliondo** Arusha, NE Tanzania
95 H25 **Lolland** *prev.* Laaland. *island* S Denmark
186 G6 **Lolobau Island** *island* E PNG
79 E16 **Lolodorf** Sud, SW Cameroon
114 G7 **Lom** *prev.* Lom-Palanka. Oblast Montana, NW Bulgaria
114 G7 **Lom** ≈ Montana, NW Bulgaria
79 M19 **Lomami** ≈ C Dem. Rep. Congo
57 F17 **Lomas** Arequipa, SW Peru
63 I23 **Lomas, Bahía** *bay* S Chile
61 D20 **Lomas de Zamora** Buenos Aires, E Argentina
61 D20 **Loma Verde** Buenos Aires, E Argentina
180 K4 **Lombadina** Western Australia
106 E6 **Lombardia** *Eng.* Lombardy. ◈ *region* N Italy
Lombardy *see* Lombardia
102 M15 **Lombez** Gers, S France
171 Q16 **Lomblen, Pulau** *island* Nusa Tenggara, S Indonesia
173 W7 **Lombok Basin** *undersea feature* E Indian Ocean
170 L16 **Lombok, Pulau** *island* Nusa Tenggara, C Indonesia
77 Q16 **Lomé** ● (Togo) S Togo
77 Q16 **Lomé** ✕ S Togo
79 L19 **Lomela** Kasai Oriental, C Dem. Rep. Congo
25 R9 **Lometa** Texas, SW USA
79 F16 **Lomié** Est, SE Cameroon
30 M8 **Lomira** Wisconsin, N USA
95 K23 **Lomma** Skåne, S Sweden
99 J16 **Lommel** Limburg, N Belgium
96 I11 **Lomond, Loch** ⊚ C Scotland, UK
197 R9 **Lomonosov Ridge** *var.* Harris Ridge, *Rus.* Khrebet Lomonsova. *undersea feature* Arctic Ocean
Lomonsova, Khrebet *see* Lomonosov Ridge
Lom-Palanka *see* Lom
Lomphat *see* Lumphăt
35 P14 **Lompoc** California, W USA
167 P9 **Lom Sak** *var.* Muang Lom Sak. Phetchabun, C Thailand
110 N9 **Łomża** *Rus.* Lomzha. Podlaskie, NE Poland
Lomzha *see* Łomża
155 D14 **Lonāvale** *prev.* Lonauli. Mahārāshtra, W India
63 G15 **Loncoche** Araucanía, C Chile
63 H14 **Loncopue** Neuquén, W Argentina
99 G17 **Londerzeel** Vlaams Brabant, C Belgium
Londinium *see* London
14 E16 **London** Ontario, S Canada
191 Y2 **London** Kiritimati, E Kiribati
97 O22 **London** *anc.* Augusta, *Lat.* Londinium. ● (UK) SE England, UK
21 N7 **London** Kentucky, S USA
31 S13 **London** Ohio, NE USA
25 Q10 **London** Texas, SW USA
97 O22 **London City** ✕ SE England, UK
97 E14 **Londonderry** *var.* Derry, *Ir.* Doire. NW Northern Ireland, UK
97 F14 **Londonderry** *cultural region* NW Northern Ireland, UK
180 M2 **Londonderry, Cape** *headland* Western Australia
63 H25 **Londonderry, Isla** *island* S Chile
43 O7 **Londres, Cayos** *reef* NE Nicaragua
60 I10 **Londrina** Paraná, S Brazil
27 N13 **Lone Grove** Oklahoma, C USA
14 E12 **Lonely Island** *island* Ontario, S Canada
35 T8 **Lone Mountain** ▲ Nevada, W USA
25 V6 **Lone Oak** Texas, SW USA
35 T11 **Lone Pine** California, W USA
Lone Star State *see* Texas
83 D14 **Longa** Cuando Cubango, C Angola
82 B12 **Longa** ≈ W Angola
83 E15 **Longa** ≈ SE Angola
Long'an *see* Pingwu
197 S4 **Longa, Proliv** *Eng.* Long Strait. *strait* NE Russian Federation
44 J13 **Long Bay** *bay* W Jamaica
21 V13 **Long Bay** *bay* North Carolina/South Carolina, E USA
35 T16 **Long Beach** California, W USA
22 M9 **Long Beach** Mississippi, S USA
18 L14 **Long Beach** Long Island, New York, NE USA
32 F9 **Long Beach** Washington, NW USA
18 K16 **Long Beach Island** *island* New Jersey, NE USA
65 M25 **Longbluff** *headland* SW Tristan da Cunha
23 U13 **Longboat Key** *island* Florida, SE USA
18 K15 **Long Branch** New Jersey, NE USA
44 J5 **Long Cay** *island* SE Bahamas
Longcheng *see* Xiaoxian
161 P14 **Longchuan** *var.* Laolong. Guangdong, S China
Longchuan *see* Nanhua
Longchuan Jiang *see* Shweli
32 K12 **Long Creek** Oregon, NW USA
159 W10 **Longde** Ningxia, N China
183 P16 **Longford** Tasmania, SE Australia
97 D17 **Longford** *Ir.* An Longfort. C Ireland
97 E17 **Longford** *Ir.* An Longfort. *cultural region* C Ireland
Longgang *see* Dazu
163 W11 **Longgang Shan** ▲▲ NE China
161 P1 **Longhua** Hebei, E China
169 U11 **Longiram** Borneo, C Indonesia
44 J4 **Long Island** *island* C Bahamas
12 H8 **Long Island** *island* Nunavut, C Canada
186 D7 **Long Island** *var.* Arop Island. *island* N PNG
18 L14 **Long Island** *island* New York, NE USA
Long Island *see* Bermuda
18 M14 **Long Island Sound** *sound* NE USA
160 K13 **Long Jiang** ≈ S China
163 U7 **Longjiang** Heilongjiang, NE China
163 Y10 **Longjing** *var.* Yanji. Jilin, NE China
161 R4 **Longkou** Shandong, E China
12 E11 **Longlac** Ontario, S Canada
19 S1 **Long Lake** ⊚ Maine, NE USA
31 O6 **Long Lake** ⊚ Michigan, N USA
31 R5 **Long Lake** ⊚ Michigan, N USA
29 N6 **Long Lake** ⊚ North Dakota, N USA
30 J4 **Long Lake** ⊠ Wisconsin, N USA
99 K23 **Longlier** Luxembourg, SE Belgium
160 I13 **Longlin** *var.* Longlin Gezu Zizhixian, Xinzhou. Guangxi Zhuangzu Zizhiqu, S China
37 T3 **Longmont** Colorado, C USA
29 N13 **Long Pine** Nebraska, C USA
Longping *see* Luodian
14 F17 **Long Point** *headland* Ontario, S Canada
14 K15 **Long Point** *headland* Ontario, SE Canada
184 P10 **Long Point** *headland* North Island, NZ
30 L2 **Long Point** *headland* Michigan, N USA
14 G17 **Long Point Bay** *lake bay* Ontario, S Canada
29 T7 **Long Prairie** Minnesota, N USA
Longquan *see* Fenggang
13 S11 **Long Range Mountains** *hill range* Newfoundland and Labrador, E Canada
65 H25 **Long Range Point** *headland* SE Saint Helena
181 V8 **Longreach** Queensland, E Australia
160 H7 **Longriba** Sichuan, C China
160 L10 **Longshan** *var.* Min'an. Hunan, S China
37 S3 **Longs Peak** ▲ Colorado, C USA
Long Strait *see* Longa, Proliv
102 K8 **Longué** Maine-et-Loire, NW France
13 P11 **Longue-Pointe** Québec, E Canada
103 S4 **Longuyon** Meurthe-et-Moselle, NE France
25 W7 **Longview** Texas, SW USA
32 G10 **Longview** Washington, NW USA
65 H25 **Longwood** C Saint Helena
25 P7 **Longworth** Texas, SW USA
103 S3 **Longwy** Meurthe-et-Moselle, NE France
159 V11 **Longxi** Gansu, C China
Longxian *see* Wengyuan
167 S14 **Long Xuyên** *var.* Longxuyen. An Giang, S Vietnam
161 Q13 **Longyan** Fujian, SE China
92 O3 **Longyearbyen** ○ (Svalbard) Spitsbergen, W Svalbard
160 J15 **Longzhou** Guangxi Zhuangzu Zizhiqu, S China
Longzhouping *see* Changyang
100 F12 **Löningen** Niedersachsen, NW Germany
27 V11 **Lonoke** Arkansas, C USA
95 L21 **Lönsboda** Skåne, S Sweden
103 S9 **Lons-le-Saunier** *anc.* Ledo Salinarius. Jura, E France
31 O15 **Loogootee** Indiana, N USA
31 Q9 **Looking Glass River** ≈ Michigan, N USA
21 X11 **Lookout, Cape** *headland* North Carolina, SE USA
39 O6 **Lookout Ridge** *ridge* Alaska, USA
181 N11 **Loongana** Western Australia
99 I14 **Loon op Zand** Noord-Brabant, S Netherlands
97 A19 **Loop Head** *Ir.* Ceann Léime. *headland* W Ireland
109 V4 **Loosdorf** Niederösterreich, NE Austria
158 G10 **Lop** Xinjiang Uygur Zizhiqu, NW China
112 J11 **Lopare** Republika Srpska, NE Bosnia and Herzegovina
Lopatichi *see* Lapatsichy
127 Q15 **Lopatin** Respublika Dagestan, SW Russian Federation
127 P7 **Lopatino** Penzenskaya Oblast', W Russian Federation
167 P10 **Lop Buri** *var.* Loburi. Lop Buri, C Thailand
25 R16 **Lopeno** Texas, SW USA
79 C18 **Lopez, Cap** *headland* W Gabon
98 I12 **Lopik** Utrecht, C Netherlands
Lop Nor *see* Lop Nur
158 M7 **Lop Nur** *var.* Lob Nor, Lop Nor, Lo-pu Po. *seasonal lake* NW China
Lopnur *see* Yuli
79 K17 **Lopori** ≈ NW Dem. Rep. Congo
98 O5 **Loppersum** Groningen, NE Netherlands
92 I8 **Lopphavet** *sound* N Norway
Lo-pu Po *see* Lop Nur
Lora *see* Lowrah
182 F3 **Lora Creek** *seasonal river* South Australia
104 K13 **Lora del Río** Andalucía, S Spain
148 M11 **Lora, Hāmūn-i** *wetland* SW Pakistan
31 T11 **Lorain** Ohio, N USA
25 O7 **Loraine** Texas, SW USA
31 R13 **Loramie, Lake** ⊠ Ohio, N USA
105 Q13 **Lorca** *Ar.* Lurka; *anc.* Eliocroca, *Lat.* Illur co. Murcia, S Spain
192 I10 **Lord Howe Island** *island* E Australia
Lord Howe Island *see* Ontong Java Atoll
175 O10 **Lord Howe Rise** *undersea feature* SW Pacific Ocean
192 J10 **Lord Howe Seamounts** *undersea feature* W Pacific Ocean
37 P15 **Lordsburg** New Mexico, SW USA
186 E5 **Lorengau** *var.* Lorungau. Manus Island, N PNG

◆ Country ● Country Capital ◇ Dependent Territory ○ Dependent Territory Capital ◈ Administrative Region ✕ International Airport ▲ Mountain ▲▲ Mountain Range Volcano ≈ River ⊚ Lake ⊠ Reservoir

25 N5 Lorenzo Texas, SW USA
142 K7 Lorestān off. Ostān-e Lorestān, var. Luristan. ◈ province W Iran
57 M17 Loreto Beni, N Bolivia
106 J12 Loreto Marche, C Italy
40 F8 Loreto Baja California Sur, W Mexico
40 M11 Loreto Zacatecas, C Mexico
56 E9 Loreto off. Departamento de Loreto. ◈ department NE Peru
81 K18 Lorian Swamp swamp E Kenya
54 E6 Lorica Córdoba, NW Colombia
102 G7 Lorient prev. l'Orient. Morbihan, NW France
111 K22 Lőrinci Heves, NE Hungary
14 G11 Loring Ontario, S Canada
33 V6 Loring Montana, NW USA
103 R13 Loriol-sur-Drôme Drôme, E France
21 U12 Loris South Carolina, SE USA
57 I18 Loriscota, Laguna ◎ S Peru
183 N13 Lorne Victoria, SE Australia
96 G11 Lorn, Firth of inlet W Scotland, UK
Loro Sae see East Timor
101 F24 Lörrach Baden-Württemberg, S Germany
103 T5 Lorraine ◈ region NE France
Lorungau see Lorengau
94 L11 Los Gävleborg, C Sweden
35 P14 Los Alamos California, W USA
37 S10 Los Alamos New Mexico, SW USA
42 F5 Los Amates Izabal, E Guatemala
35 S15 Los Angeles California, W USA
35 S15 Los Angeles ✕ California, W USA
63 G14 Los Ángeles Bío Bío, C Chile
35 T13 Los Angeles Aqueduct aqueduct California, W USA
Losanna see Lausanne
63 H20 Los Antiguos Santa Cruz, SW Argentina
189 Q16 Losap Atoll atoll C Micronesia
35 P10 Los Banos California, W USA
104 K16 Los Barrios Andalucía, S Spain
62 L5 Los Blancos Salta, N Argentina
42 L12 Los Chiles Alajuela, NW Costa Rica
105 O2 Los Corrales de Buelna Cantabria, N Spain
25 T17 Los Fresnos Texas, SW USA
35 N9 Los Gatos California, W USA
110 O11 Łosice Mazowieckie, E Poland
112 B11 Lošinj Ger. Lussin, It. Lussino. island W Croatia
Los Jardines see Ngetik Atoll
63 G15 Los Lagos Los Lagos, C Chile
63 F17 Los Lagos off. Región de los Lagos. ◈ region C Chile
Loslau see Wodzisław Śląski
64 N11 Los Llanos var. Los Llanos de Aridane. La Palma, Islas Canarias, Spain, NE Atlantic Ocean
Los Llanos de Aridane see Los Llanos
37 R11 Los Lunas New Mexico, SW USA
63 I16 Los Menucos Río Negro, C Argentina
40 H8 Los Mochis Sinaloa, C Mexico
35 N4 Los Molinos California, W USA
104 M9 Los Navalmorales Castilla-La Mancha, C Spain
25 S15 Los Olmos Creek ≈ Texas, SW USA
Losonc/Losontz see Lučenec
167 S5 Lô, Sông Chin. Panlong Jiang. ≈ China/Vietnam
44 B5 Los Palacios Pinar del Río, W Cuba
104 K14 Los Palacios y Villafranca Andalucía, S Spain
171 R16 Lospalos E East Timor
37 R12 Los Pinos Mountains ▲▲ New Mexico, SW USA
37 R11 Los Ranchos De Albuquerque New Mexico, SW USA
40 M14 Los Reyes Michoacán de Ocampo, SW Mexico
56 B7 Los Ríos ◈ province C Ecuador
64 O11 Los Rodeos ✕ (Santa Cruz de Tenerife) Tenerife, Islas Canarias, Spain, NE Atlantic Ocean
54 L4 Los Roques, Islas island group N Venezuela
43 S17 Los Santos Los Santos, S Panama
43 S17 Los Santos off. Provincia de Los Santos. ◈ province S Panama
Los Santos see Los Santos de Maimona
104 J12 Los Santos de Maimona var. Los Santos. Extremadura, W Spain
98 P10 Losser Overijssel, E Netherlands
96 J8 Lossiemouth NE Scotland, UK
61 B14 Los Tábanos Santa Fe, C Argentina
54 J4 Los Taques Falcón, N Venezuela
14 G11 Lost Channel Ontario, S Canada
54 L5 Los Teques Miranda, N Venezuela
35 Q12 Lost Hills California, W USA
36 I7 Lost Peak ▲ Utah, W USA
33 P11 Lost Trail Pass pass Montana, NW USA
186 G9 Losuia Kiriwina Island, SE PNG
62 G10 Los Vilos Coquimbo, C Chile
105 N10 Los Yébenes Castilla-La Mancha, C Spain
103 N13 Lot ◈ department S France
103 N13 Lot ≈ S France
63 F14 Lota Bío Bío, C Chile
81 G15 Lotagipi Swamp wetland Kenya/Sudan
102 K14 Lot-et-Garonne ◈ department SW France
83 K21 Lothair Mpumalanga, NE South Africa
33 R7 Lothair Montana, NW USA
79 L20 Loto Kasai Oriental, C Dem. Rep. Congo
192 H16 Lotofagā Upolu, SE Samoa
108 E10 Lötschbergtunnel tunnel Valais, SW Switzerland
25 T9 Lott Texas, SW USA
126 H3 Lotta var. Lutto. ≈ Finland/Russian Federation
184 Q7 Lottin Point headland North Island, NZ
Lötzen see Giżycko
Loualaba see Lualaba
167 P6 Louangnamtha var. Luong Nam Tha. Louang Namtha, N Laos
167 Q7 Louangphabang var. Louangphrabang, Luang Prabang. Louangphabang, N Laos
Louangphrabang see Louangphabang
194 H5 Loubet Coast physical region Antarctica
Loubomo see Dolisie
Louch see Loukhi
102 H6 Loudéac Côtes d'Armor, NW France
160 M11 Loudi Hunan, S China
79 F21 Loudima La Bouenza, S Congo
20 M9 Loudon Tennessee, S USA
31 T12 Loudonville Ohio, N USA
102 L8 Loudun Vienne, W France
102 K7 Loué Sarthe, NW France
76 G10 Louga NW Senegal
97 M19 Loughborough C England, UK
8 L4 Lougheed Island island Nunavut, N Canada
97 C18 Loughrea Ir. Baile Locha Riach. W Ireland
103 S9 Louhans Saône-et-Loire, C France
21 P5 Louisa Kentucky, S USA
21 V5 Louisa Virginia, NE USA
21 V9 Louisburg North Carolina, SE USA
25 U12 Louise Texas, SW USA
15 P11 Louiseville Québec, SE Canada
27 W3 Louisiana Missouri, C USA
22 G8 Louisiana off. State of Louisiana; also known as Creole State, Pelican State. ◈ state S USA
186 E5 Lou Island island N PNG
83 K19 Louis Trichardt Limpopo, NE South Africa
23 V4 Louisville Georgia, SE USA
30 M15 Louisville Illinois, N USA
20 K5 Louisville Kentucky, S USA
22 M4 Louisville Mississippi, S USA
29 S15 Louisville Nebraska, C USA
192 L11 Louisville Ridge undersea feature S Pacific Ocean
124 J6 Loukhi var. Louch. Respublika Kareliya, NW Russian Federation
79 H19 Loukoléla Cuvette, E Congo
104 G14 Loulé Faro, S Portugal
111 C16 Louny Ger. Laun. Ústecký kraj NW Czech Republic
29 O15 Loup City Nebraska, C USA
29 P15 Loup River ≈ Nebraska, C USA
15 S9 Loup, Rivière du ≈ Québec, SE Canada
12 K7 Loups Marins, Lacs des lakes Québec, NE Canada
102 K16 Lourdes Hautes-Pyrénées, S France
Lourenço Marques see Maputo
104 F11 Loures Lisboa, C Portugal
104 F10 Lourinhã Lisboa, C Portugal
115 C16 Loúros ≈ W Greece
104 G8 Lousã Coimbra, N Portugal
160 M10 Lou Shui ≈ C China
183 O5 Louth New South Wales, SE Australia
97 O18 Louth E England, UK
97 F17 Louth Ir. Lú. cultural region NE Ireland
115 H15 Loutrá Kentrikí Makedonía, N Greece
115 G19 Loutráki Pelopónnisos, S Greece
Louvain see Leuven
99 H19 Louvain-la Neuve Wallon Brabant, C Belgium
14 J8 Louvicourt Québec, SE Canada
102 M4 Louviers Eure, N France
30 K14 Lou Yaeger, Lake ▣ Illinois, N USA
93 J15 Lövånger Västerbotten, N Sweden
126 J14 Lovat' ≈ NW Russian Federation
113 J17 Lovćen ▲ S Serbia and Montenegro (Yugo.)
114 I8 Lovech Lovech, N Bulgaria
114 I9 Lovech ◈ province N Bulgaria
25 V9 Lovelady Texas, SW USA
37 T3 Loveland Colorado, C USA
33 U12 Lovell Wyoming, C USA
Lovello, Monte see Grosser Löffler
35 S4 Lovelock Nevada, W USA
106 E7 Lovere Lombardia, N Italy
30 L10 Loves Park Illinois, N USA
26 M2 Lovewell Reservoir ▣ Kansas, C USA
93 M19 Loviisa Swe. Lovisa. Etelä-Suomi, S Finland
37 V15 Loving New Mexico, SW USA
21 U6 Lovingston Virginia, NE USA
37 V14 Lovington New Mexico, SW USA
Lovisa see Loviisa
111 C15 Lovosice Ger. Lobositz. Ústecký Kraj, NW Czech Republic
124 K4 Lovozero Murmanskaya Oblast', NW Russian Federation
126 K4 Lovozero, Ozero ◎ NW Russian Federation
112 B9 Lovran It. Laurana. Primorje-Gorski Kotar, NW Croatia
116 E11 Lovrin Ger. Lowrin. Timiş, W Romania
82 E10 Lóvua Lunda Norte, NE Angola
82 G12 Lóvua Moxico, E Angola
65 D25 Low Bay bay East Falkland, Falkland Islands
9 P9 Low, Cape headland Nunavut, E Canada
33 N10 Lowell Idaho, NW USA
19 O10 Lowell Massachusetts, NE USA
Löwen see Leuven
Löwenberg in Schlesien see Lwówek Śląski
Lower Austria see Niederösterreich
Lower Bann see Bann
Lower California see Baja California
Lower Danube see Niederösterreich
185 L14 Lower Hutt Wellington, North Island, NZ
39 N11 Lower Kalskag Alaska, USA
35 O1 Lower Klamath Lake ◎ California, W USA
35 Q2 Lower Lake ◎ California/Nevada, W USA
97 E15 Lower Lough Erne ◎ SW Northern Ireland, UK
Lower Lusatia see Niederlausitz
Lower Normandy see Basse-Normandie, France
10 K9 Lower Post British Columbia, W Canada
29 T4 Lower Red Lake ◎ Minnesota, N USA
Lower Rhine see Neder Rijn
Lower Saxony see Niedersachsen
Lower Tunguska see Nizhnyaya Tunguska
97 Q19 Lowestoft E England, UK
149 Q5 Lowgar var. Logar. ◈ province E Afghanistan
182 H7 Low Hill South Australia
110 K12 Łowicz Łódzkie, C Poland
33 N13 Lowman Idaho, NW USA
149 P8 Lowrah var. Lora. ≈ SE Afghanistan
Lowrin see Lovrin
183 N17 Low Rocky Point headland Tasmania, SE Australia
18 I8 Lowville New York, NE USA
Loxa see Loksa
182 K9 Loxton South Australia
81 G21 Loya Tabora, C Tanzania
30 K6 Loyal Wisconsin, N USA
18 G13 Loyalsock Creek ≈ Pennsylvania, NE USA
35 Q5 Loyalton California, W USA
Lo-yang see Luoyang
187 Q16 Loyauté, Îles island group S New Caledonia
Loyev see Loyew
119 O20 Loyew Rus. Loyev. Homyel'skaya Voblasts', SE Belarus
125 S13 Loyno Kirovskaya Oblast', NW Russian Federation
103 P13 Lozère ◈ department S France
103 Q14 Lozère, Mont ▲ S France
112 J11 Loznica Serbia, W Serbia and Montenegro (Yugo.)
117 V7 Lozova Rus. Lozovaya. Kharkivs'ka Oblast', E Ukraine
Lozovaya see Lozova
105 N7 Lozoyuela Madrid, C Spain
Lœvvajok see Leavvajohka
Lu see Shandong, China
Lú see Louth, Ireland
82 F12 Luacano Moxico, E Angola
79 N21 Lualaba Fr. Loualaba. ≈ SE Dem. Rep. Congo
83 H14 Luampa Western, NW Zambia
83 H15 Luampa Kuta Western, W Zambia
161 P8 Lu'an Anhui, E China
104 K2 Luanco Asturias, N Spain
82 A11 Luanda var. Loanda, Port. São Paulo de Loanda. ● (Angola) Luanda, NW Angola
82 A11 Luanda ◈ province NW Angola
82 A11 Luanda ✕ Luanda, NW Angola
82 D12 Luando ≈ C Angola
Luang see Tapi, Mae Nam
83 G14 Luanginga var. Luanguinga. ≈ Angola/Zambia
167 N15 Luang, Khao ▲ SW Thailand
Luang Prabang see Louangphabang
167 P8 Luang Prabang Range Th. Thiukhaoluang Phrahang. ▲▲ Laos/Thailand
167 N16 Luang, Thale lagoon S Thailand
Luangua, Rio see Luangwa
82 E11 Luangue ≈ NE Angola
Luanguinga see Luanginga
83 K15 Luangwa var. Aruângua. Lusaka, C Zambia
83 K14 Luangwa var. Aruângua, Rio Luangua. ≈ Mozambique/Zambia
161 Q2 Luan He ≈ E China
190 G11 Luaniva, Île island E Wallis and Futuna
161 P2 Luanping var. Anjiangying. Hebei, E China
82 J13 Luanshya Copperbelt, C Zambia
62 K13 Luan Toro La Pampa, C Argentina
161 Q2 Luanxian var. Luan Xian. Hebei, E China
82 J12 Luapula ◈ province N Zambia
79 O25 Luapula ≈ Dem. Rep. Congo/Zambia
104 J2 Luarca Asturias, N Spain
169 R10 Luar, Danau ◎ Borneo, N Indonesia
79 L25 Luashi Katanga, S Dem. Rep. Congo
82 G12 Luau Port. Vila Teixeira de Sousa. Moxico, NE Angola
79 C16 Luba prev. San Carlos. Isla de Bioco, NW Equatorial Guinea
42 F4 Lubaantun ruins Toledo, S Belize
111 P16 Lubaczów var. Lúbaczów. Podkarpackie, SE Poland
Lubale see Lubalo
82 E11 Lubalo Lunda Norte, NE Angola
82 E11 Lubalo var. Lubale. ≈ Angola/Zaire
118 J9 Lubāna Madona, E Latvia
Lubānas Ezers see Lubāns
171 N4 Lubang Island island N Philippines
83 B15 Lubango Port. Sá da Bandeira. Huíla, SW Angola
118 J9 Lubāns var. Lubānas Ezers. ◎ E Latvia
79 M21 Lubao Kasai Oriental, C Dem. Rep. Congo
110 O13 Lubartów Ger. Qumälisch. Lubelskie, E Poland
100 G13 Lübbecke Nordrhein-Westfalen, NW Germany
100 O13 Lübben Brandenburg, E Germany
101 P14 Lübbenau Brandenburg, E Germany
25 N5 Lubbock Texas, SW USA
Lubcz see Lyubcha
19 U6 Lubec Maine, NE USA
100 K9 Lübeck Schleswig-Holstein, N Germany
100 K8 Lübecker Bucht bay N Germany
79 M21 Lubefu Kasai Oriental, C Dem. Rep. Congo
163 T10 Lubei var. Jarud Qi. Nei Mongol Zizhiqu, N China
111 O14 Lubelska, Wyżyna plateau SE Poland
111 O14 Lubelskie ◈ province E Poland
Lubembe see Luembe
Lüben see Lubin
144 H9 Lubenka Zapadnyy Kazakhstan, W Kazakhstan
79 P18 Lubero Nord Kivu, E Dem. Rep. Congo
79 L22 Lubi ≈ S Dem. Rep. Congo
Lubiana see Ljubljana
110 J11 Lubień Kujawski Kujawsko-pomorskie, C Poland
67 T11 Lubilandji ≈ S Dem. Rep. Congo
110 F13 Lubin Ger. Lüben. Dolnośląskie, SW Poland
111 O14 Lublin Rus. Lyublin. Lubelskie, E Poland
111 J15 Lubliniec Śląskie, S Poland
Lubnān, Jabal see Liban, Jebel
117 R5 Lubny Poltavs'ka Oblast', NE Ukraine
Luboml' see Lyuboml'
110 G11 Luboń Ger. Peterhof. Wielkolpolskie, C Poland
110 D12 Lubsko Ger. Sommerfeld. Lubuskie, W Poland
79 N24 Lubudi Katanga, SE Dem. Rep. Congo
168 L13 Lubuklinggau Sumatera, W Indonesia
79 N25 Lubumbashi prev. Élisabethville. Katanga, SE Dem. Rep. Congo
83 I14 Lubungu Central, C Zambia
110 E12 Lubuskie ◈ province W Poland
79 N18 Lubutu Maniema, E Dem. Rep. Congo
Luca see Lucca
82 C11 Lucala ≈ W Angola
14 E16 Lucan Ontario, S Canada
97 F18 Lucan Ir. Leamhcán. E Ireland
Lucanian Mountains see Lucano, Appennino
107 M18 Lucano, Appennino Eng. Lucanian Mountains. ▲▲ S Italy
82 F11 Lucapa var. Lukapa. Lunda Norte, NE Angola
29 V15 Lucas Iowa, C USA
61 C18 Lucas González Entre Ríos, E Argentina
65 C25 Lucas Point headland West Falkland, Falkland Islands
31 S15 Lucasville Ohio, N USA
106 F11 Lucca anc. Luca. Toscana, C Italy
44 H12 Lucea W Jamaica
97 H15 Luce Bay inlet SW Scotland, UK
22 M8 Lucedale Mississippi, S USA
171 O4 Lucena off. Lucena City. Luzon, N Philippines
104 M14 Lucena Andalucía, S Spain
105 S8 Lucena del Cid País Valenciano, E Spain
111 D15 Lučenec Ger. Losontz, Hung. Losonc. Banskobystrický Kraj, C Slovakia
Lucentum see Alicante
107 M16 Lucera Puglia, SE Italy
Lucerna/Lucerne see Luzern
Lucerne, Lake of see Vierwaldstätter See
40 J4 Lucero Chihuahua, N Mexico
123 S14 Luchegorsk Primorskiy Kray, SE Russian Federation
105 Q13 Luchena ≈ SE Spain
Lucheng see Kangding
82 N13 Lucheringo var. Luchulingo. ≈ N Mozambique
Luchesa see Luchosa
Luchin see Luchyn
118 N13 Luchosa Rus. Luchesa. ≈ N Belarus
Luchow see Hefei
100 K11 Lüchow Mecklenburg-Vorpommern, N Germany
Luchulingo see Lucheringo
119 N17 Luchyn Rus. Luchin. Homyel'skaya Voblasts', SE Belarus
55 U11 Lucie Rivier ≈ W Suriname
182 K11 Lucindale South Australia
83 A14 Lucira Namibe, SW Angola
Łuck see Luts'k
101 O14 Luckau Brandenburg, E Germany
100 N13 Luckenwalde Brandenburg, E Germany
14 E15 Lucknow Ontario,S Canada
152 L12 Lucknow var. Lakhnau. Uttar Pradesh, N India
102 J10 Luçon Vendée, NW France
44 I7 Lucrecia, Cabo headland E Cuba
82 F13 Lucusse Moxico, E Angola
Lüda see Dalian
114 M9 Luda Kamchiya ≈ E Bulgaria
Ludasch see Luduş
114 I10 Luda Yana ≈ C Bulgaria
112 F7 Ludbreg Varaždin, N Croatia
29 P7 Ludden North Dakota, N USA
101 F15 Lüdenscheid Nordrhein-Westfalen, W Germany
83 C21 Lüderitz prev. Angra Pequena. Karas, SW Namibia
152 H8 Ludhiāna Punjab, N India
31 O7 Ludington Michigan, N USA
97 K20 Ludlow W England, UK
35 W14 Ludlow California, W USA
28 J7 Ludlow South Dakota, N USA
18 M9 Ludlow Vermont, NE USA
114 L7 Ludogorie physical region NE Bulgaria
23 W6 Ludowici Georgia, SE USA
Ludsan see Ludza
116 I10 Luduş Ger. Ludasch, Hung. Marosludas. Mureş, C Romania
95 M14 Ludvika Dalarna, C Sweden
101 H21 Ludwigsburg Baden-Württemberg, SW Germany
100 O13 Ludwigsfelde Brandenburg, NE Germany
101 G20 Ludwigshafen var. Ludwigshafen am Rhein. Rheinland-Pfalz, W Germany
Ludwigshafen am Rhein see Ludwigshafen
101 L20 Ludwigskanal canal SE Germany
100 L10 Ludwigslust Mecklenburg-Vorpommern, N Germany
118 K10 Ludza Ger. Ludsan. Ludza, E Latvia
79 K21 Luebo Kasai Occidental, SW Dem. Rep. Congo
25 Q6 Lueders Texas, SW USA
79 N20 Lueki Maniema, C Dem. Rep. Congo
82 F10 Luembe var. Lubembe. ≈ Angola/Dem. Rep. Congo
82 E13 Luena var. Lwena, Port. Luso. Moxico, E Angola
79 M24 Luena Katanga, SE Dem. Rep. Congo
82 K12 Luena Northern, NE Zambia
82 F13 Luena ≈ E Angola
82 F16 Luengue ≈ SE Angola
67 V13 Luenha ≈ W Mozambique
83 G15 Lueti ≈ Angola/Zambia
160 J7 Lüeyang var. Hejiayan. Shaanxi, C China
161 P14 Lufeng Guangdong, S China
79 N24 Lufira ≈ SE Dem. Rep. Congo
79 N25 Lufira, Lac de Retenue de la var. Lac Tshangalele. ▣ SE Dem. Rep. Congo
25 W8 Lufkin Texas, SW USA
82 L11 Lufubu ≈ N Zambia
124 G14 Luga Leningradskaya Oblast', NW Russian Federation
126 G13 Luga ≈ NW Russian Federation
Luganer See see Lugano, Lago di
108 H11 Lugano Ger. Lauis. Ticino, S Switzerland
108 H12 Lugano, Lago di var. Ceresio, Ger. Luganer See. ◎ S Switzerland
Lugansk see Luhans'k
187 Q13 Luganville Espiritu Santo, C Vanuatu
Lugdunum see Lyon
Lugdunum Batavorum see Leiden
83 O15 Lugela Zambézia, NE Mozambique
83 O16 Lugela ≈ C Mozambique
82 P13 Lugenda, Rio ≈ N Mozambique
Luggarus see Locarno
Lugh Ganana see Luuq
97 G19 Lugnaquillia Mountain Ir. Log na Coille. ▲ E Ireland
106 H10 Lugo Emilia-Romagna, N Italy
104 I3 Lugo anc. Lugus Augusti. Galicia, NW Spain
104 I3 Lugo ◈ province Galicia, NW Spain
21 R12 Lugoff South Carolina, SE USA
116 F12 Lugoj Ger. Lugosch, Hung. Lugos. Timiş, W Romania
Lugos/Lugosch see Lugoj
Lugovoy/Lugovoye see Kulan
158 I13 Lugu Xizang Zizhiqu, W China
Lugus Augusti see Lugo
Luguvallium/Luguvallum see Carlisle
117 Y7 Luhans'k Rus. Lugansk; prev. Voroshilovgrad. Luhans'ka Oblast', E Ukraine
117 Y7 Luhans'k ✕ Luhans'ka Oblast', E Ukraine
117 X6 Luhans'ka Oblast' var. Luhans'k; prev. Voroshilovgrad, Rus. Voroshilovgradskaya Oblast'. ◈ province E Ukraine
161 Q7 Luhe Jiangsu, E China
171 S13 Luhu Pulau Seram, E Indonesia
Luhua see Heishui
160 G8 Luhuo var. Xindu, Tib. Zhaggo. Sichuan, C China
116 M3 Luhyny Zhytomyrs'ka Oblast', N Ukraine
83 G15 Lui ≈ W Zambia
83 G16 Luiana ≈ SE Angola
83 L15 Luia, Rio var. Ruya. ≈ Mozambique/Zimbabwe
Luichow Peninsula see Leizhou Bandao
Luik see Liège
82 C13 Luimbale Huambo, C Angola
Luimneach see Limerick
106 D6 Luino Lombardia, N Italy
82 E13 Luio ≈ E Angola
92 L11 Luiro ≈ NE Finland
79 N25 Luishia Katanga, SE Dem. Rep. Congo
59 M19 Luislândia do Oeste Minas Gerais, SE Brazil
40 K5 Luis L.León, Presa ▣ N Mexico
Luis Muñoz Marín see San Juan
195 N5 Luitpold Coast physical region Antarctica
79 K22 Luiza Kasai Occidental, S Dem. Rep. Congo
61 D20 Luján Buenos Aires, E Argentina
79 N24 Lukafu Katanga, SE Dem. Rep. Congo
Lukapa see Lucapa
112 I11 Lukavac Federacija Bosna I Hercegovina, NE Bosnia and Herzegovina
79 I20 Lukenie ≈ C Dem. Rep. Congo
79 H19 Lukolela Equateur, W Dem. Rep. Congo
119 M14 Lukoml'skaye, Vozyera Rus. Ozero Lukoml'skoye. ◎ N Belarus
Lukoml'skoye, Ozero see Lukoml'skaye, Vozyera
114 I8 Lukovit Lovech, N Bulgaria
110 O12 Łuków Ger. Bogendorf. Lubelskie, E Poland
127 O4 Lukoyanov Nizhegorodskaya Oblast', W Russian Federation
79 N22 Lukuga ≈ SE Dem. Rep. Congo
79 F21 Lukula Bas-Congo, SW Dem. Rep. Congo
83 G14 Lukulu Western, NW Zambia
189 R17 Lukunor Atoll atoll Mortlock Islands, C Micronesia
82 J12 Lukwesa Luapula, NE Zambia
93 K14 Luleå Norrbotten, N Sweden
92 J13 Luleälven ≈ N Sweden
136 C10 Lüleburgaz Kırklareli, NW Turkey
160 M4 Lüliang Shan ▲▲ C China
79 O21 Lulimba Maniema, E Dem. Rep. Congo
22 K9 Luling Louisiana, S USA
25 T11 Luling Texas, SW USA
79 I18 Lulonga ≈ NW Dem. Rep. Congo
79 K22 Lulua ≈ S Dem. Rep. Congo
Luluabourg see Kananga
192 L17 Luma Ta'ū, E American Samoa
169 S17 Lumajang Jawa, C Indonesia
158 G12 Lumajangdong Co ◎ W China
82 G13 Lumbala Kaquengue Moxico, E Angola
83 F14 Lumbala N'Guimbo var. Nguimbo, Port. Gago Coutinho, Vila Gago Coutinho. Moxico, E Angola
21 T11 Lumber River ≈ North Carolina/South Carolina, SE USA
Lumber State see Maine
22 L8 Lumberton Mississippi, S USA
21 U11 Lumberton North Carolina, SE USA
105 R4 Lumbier Navarra, N Spain
83 Q15 Lumbo Nampula, NE Mozambique
124 M4 Lumbovka Murmanskaya Oblast', NW Russian Federation
104 J7 Lumbrales Castilla-León, N Spain
153 W13 Lumding Assam, NE India
82 F12 Lumege var. Lumeje. Moxico, E Angola
Lumeje see Lumege
99 J17 Lummen Limburg, NE Belgium
93 J20 Lumparland Åland, SW Finland
167 T11 Lumphăt prev. Lomphat. Rôtânôkiri, NE Cambodia
11 U16 Lumsden Saskatchewan, S Canada
185 C23 Lumsden Southland, South Island, NZ
169 N14 Lumut, Tanjung headland Sumatera, W Indonesia
157 P4 Lün Töv, C Mongolia
116 I13 Lunca Corbului Argeş, S Romania
95 K23 Lund Skåne, S Sweden
35 X6 Lund Nevada, W USA
82 D11 Lunda Norte ◈ province NE Angola
82 E12 Lunda Sul ◈ province NE Angola
82 M13 Lundazi Eastern, NE Zambia
95 G16 Lunde Telemark, S Norway
Lundenburg see Břeclav
95 C17 Lundevatnet ◎ S Norway
Lundi see Runde
97 I23 Lundy island SW England, UK
100 J10 Lüneburg Niedersachsen, N Germany
100 J11 Lüneburger Heide heathland NW Germany
103 Q15 Lunel Hérault, S France
101 F14 Lünen Nordrhein-Westfalen, W Germany
13 P16 Lunenburg Nova Scotia, SE Canada
21 V7 Lunenburg Virginia, NE USA
103 T5 Lunéville Meurthe-et-Moselle, NE France
83 I14 Lunga ≈ C Zambia
Lunga, Isola see Dugi Otok
158 H12 Lungdo Xizang Zizhiqu, W China
158 I14 Lunggar Xizang Zizhiqu, W China
76 I15 Lungi ✕ (Freetown) W Sierra Leone
Lungkiang see Qiqihar
Lungleh see Lunglei
153 W15 Lunglei prev. Lungleh. Mizoram, NE India
158 L15 Lungsang Xizang Zizhiqu, W China
82 E13 Lungué-Bungo var. Lungwebungu. ≈ Angola/Zambia see also Lungwebungu
83 G14 Lungwebungu var. Lungué-Bungo. ≈ Angola/Zambia see also Lungué-Bungo
152 F12 Lūni Rājasthān, N India
152 F12 Lūni ≈ N India
Luninets see Luninyets
35 S7 Luning Nevada, W USA
Łuniniec see Luninyets
127 P6 Lunino Penzenskaya Oblast', W Russian Federation
119 J19 Luninyets Pol. Łuniniec, Rus. Luninets. Brestskaya Voblasts', SW Belarus

◆ Country ● Country Capital ◇ Dependent Territory ○ Dependent Territory Capital ◈ Administrative Region ✕ International Airport ▲ Mountain ▲▲ Mountain Range Volcano ≈ River ◎ Lake ▣ Reservoir

152 F10 **Lūnkaransar** Rājasthān, NW India
119 G17 **Lunna** Pol. Łunna, Rus. Lunna. Hrodzyenskaya Voblasts', W Belarus
76 I15 **Lunsar** W Sierra Leone
83 K14 **Lunsemfwa** ≈ C Zambia
158 J6 **Luntai** var. Bügür. Xinjiang Uygur Zizhiqu, NW China
98 K11 **Lunteren** Gelderland, C Netherlands
109 U5 **Lunz am See** Niederösterreich, C Austria
163 Y7 **Luobei** var. Fengxiang. Heilongjiang, NE China
Luocheng see Hui'an
160 J13 **Luodian** var. Longping. Guizhou, S China
160 M15 **Luoding** Guangdong, S China
160 M6 **Luo He** ≈ C China
160 L5 **Luo He** ≈ C China
161 N7 **Luohe** Henan, C China
Luolajarvi see Kuoloyarvi
Luong Nam Tha see Louangnamtha
160 L13 **Luoqing Jiang** ≈ S China
161 O8 **Luoshan** Henan, C China
161 O12 **Luoxiao Shan** ▲ S China
161 N6 **Luoyang** var. Honan, Lo-yang. Henan, C China
161 R12 **Luoyuan** var. Fengshan. Fujian, SE China
79 F21 **Luozi** Bas-Congo, W Dem. Rep. Congo
83 J17 **Lupane** Matabeleland North, W Zimbabwe
160 I12 **Lupanshui** prev. Shuicheng. Guizhou, S China
169 R10 **Lupar, Batang** ≈ East Malaysia
Lupatia see Altamura
116 G12 **Lupeni** Hung. Lupény. Hunedoara, SW Romania
Lupény see Lupeni
82 N13 **Lupiliche** Niassa, N Mozambique
83 E14 **Lupire** Cuando Cubango, E Angola
79 L22 **Luputa** Kasai Oriental, S Dem. Rep. Congo
121 P16 **Luqa** ✕ (Valletta) S Malta
159 U11 **Luqu** var. Ma'ai. Gansu, C China
45 U5 **Luquillo, Sierra de** ▲ E Puerto Rico
26 L4 **Luray** Kansas, C USA
21 U4 **Luray** Virginia, NE USA
103 T7 **Lure** Haute-Saône, E France
82 D11 **Luremo** Lunda Norte, NE Angola
97 F15 **Lurgan** Ir. An Lorgain. S Northern Ireland, UK
57 K18 **Luribay** La Paz, W Bolivia
Luring see Gêrzê
83 Q14 **Lúrio** Nampula, NE Mozambique
83 P14 **Lúrio, Rio** ≈ NE Mozambique
Luristan see Lorestān
Lurka see Lorca
83 J15 **Lusaka** ● (Zambia) Lusaka, SE Zambia
83 J15 **Lusaka** ◈ province C Zambia
83 J15 **Lusaka** ✕ Lusaka, C Zambia
79 L21 **Lusambo** Kasai Oriental, C Dem. Rep. Congo
186 F8 **Lusancay Islands and Reefs** island group SE PNG
79 I21 **Lusanga** Bandundu, SW Dem. Rep. Congo
79 N21 **Lusangi** Maniema, E Dem. Rep. Congo
Lusatian Mountains see Lausitzer Bergland
Lushar see Huangzhong
Lushnja see Lushnjë
113 K21 **Lushnjë** var. Lushnja. Fier, C Albania
81 J21 **Lushoto** Tanga, E Tanzania
102 L10 **Lusignan** Vienne, W France
33 Z15 **Lusk** Wyoming, C USA
Luso see Luena
102 L10 **Lussac-les-Châteaux** Vienne, W France
Lussin/Lussino see Lošinj
Lussinpiccolo see Mali Lošinj
108 I7 **Lustenau** Vorarlberg, W Austria
161 T14 **Lü Tao** var. Huoshao Dao, Lütao, Eng. Green Island. island SE Taiwan
Lūt, Baḩrat/Lut, Bahret see Dead Sea
22 K9 **Lutcher** Louisiana, S USA
143 T9 **Lūt, Dasht-e** var. Kavīr-e Lūt. desert E Iran
83 F14 **Lutembo** Moxico, E Angola
Lutetia/Lutetia Parisiorum see Paris
Luteva see Lodève
14 G15 **Luther Lake** ◎ Ontario, S Canada
186 K8 **Luti** Choiseul Island, NW Solomon Islands
Lūt, Kavīr-e see Lūt, Dasht-e
97 N21 **Luton** SE England, UK
97 N21 **Luton** ✕ (London) SE England, UK
108 B10 **Lutry** Vaud, SW Switzerland
8 K10 **Łutsel'ke** prev. Snowdrift. Northwest Territories, W Canada
29 Y4 **Lutsen** Minnesota, N USA
116 J4 **Luts'k** Pol. Łuck, Rus. Lutsk. Volyns'ka Oblast', NW Ukraine
Luttenberg see Ljutomer
Lüttich see Liège
83 G25 **Luttig** Western Cape, SW South Africa
Lutto see Lotta
82 E13 **Lutuai** Moxico, E Angola
117 Y7 **Lutuhyne** Luhans'ka Oblast', E Ukraine
171 V14 **Lutur, Pulau** island Kepulauan Aru, E Indonesia
23 V12 **Lutz** Florida, SE USA
Lutzow-Holm Bay see Lützow Holmbukta
195 V2 **Lützow Holmbukta** var. Lutzow-Holm Bay. bay Antarctica
81 L16 **Luuq** It. Lugh Ganana. Gedo, SW Somalia
92 M12 **Luusua** Lappi, NE Finland
23 Q6 **Luverne** Alabama, S USA
29 S11 **Luverne** Minnesota, N USA
79 O22 **Luvua** ≈ SE Dem. Rep. Congo
82 F13 **Luvuei** Moxico, E Angola
81 H24 **Luwego** ≈ S Tanzania
82 K12 **Luwingu** Northern, NE Zambia
171 P12 **Luwuk** prev. Loewoek. Sulawesi, C Indonesia
23 N3 **Luxapallila Creek** ≈ Alabama/Mississippi, S USA
99 M25 **Luxembourg** ● (Luxembourg) Luxembourg, S Luxembourg
99 M25 **Luxembourg** off. Grand Duchy of Luxembourg, var. Lëtzebuerg, Luxemburg. ◆ monarchy NW Europe
99 J23 **Luxembourg** ◈ province SE Belgium
99 L24 **Luxembourg** ◈ district S Luxembourg
31 N6 **Luxemburg** Wisconsin, N USA
Luxemburg see Luxembourg
103 U7 **Luxeuil-les-Bains** Haute-Saône, E France
160 E13 **Luxi** prev. Mangshi. Yunnan, SW China
82 E10 **Luxico** ≈ Angola/Dem. Rep. Congo
75 X10 **Luxor** Ar. Al Uqṣur. E Egypt
75 X10 **Luxor** ✕ C Egypt
160 M4 **Luya Shan** ▲ C China
102 J15 **Luy de Béarn** ≈ SW France
102 J15 **Luy de France** ≈ SW France
125 P12 **Luza** Kirovskaya Oblast', NW Russian Federation
127 Q12 **Luza** ≈ NW Russian Federation
104 I16 **Luz, Costa de la** coastal region SW Spain
111 K20 **Luže** var. Lausche. ▲ Czech Republic/Germany see also Lausche
108 F8 **Luzern** Fr. Lucerne, It. Lucerna. Luzern, C Switzerland
108 E8 **Luzern** Fr. Lucerne. ◈ canton C Switzerland
160 L13 **Luzhai** Guangxi Zhuangzu Zizhiqu, S China
118 K12 **Luzhki** Rus. Luzhki. Vitsyebskaya Voblasts', N Belarus
160 I10 **Luzhou** Sichuan, C China
Lužická Nisa see Neisse
Lužické Hory see Lausitzer Bergland
Lužnice see Lainsitz
171 O2 **Luzon** island N Philippines
171 N1 **Luzon Strait** strait Philippines/Taiwan
116 I5 **L'viv** Ger. Lemberg, Pol. Lwów, Rus. L'vov. L'vivs'ka Oblast', W Ukraine
L'viv see L'vivs'ka Oblast'
116 I4 **L'vivs'ka Oblast'** var. L'viv, Rus. L'vovskaya Oblast'. ◈ province NW Ukraine
L'vov see L'viv
L'vovskaya Oblast' see L'vivs'ka Oblast'
Lwena see Luena
Lwów see L'viv
110 F11 **Lwówek** Ger. Neustadt bei Pinne. Wielkolpolskie, C Poland
111 E14 **Lwówek Śląski** Ger. Löwenberg in Schlesien. Dolnośląskie, SW Poland
119 I18 **Lyakhavichy** Rus. Lyakhovichi. Brestskaya Voblasts', SW Belarus
Lyakhovichi see Lyakhavichy
185 B22 **Lyall, Mount** ▲ South Island, NZ
Lyallpur see Faisalābād
Lyangar see Langar
124 H11 **Lyaskelya** Respublika Kareliya, NW Russian Federation
119 I18 **Lyasnaya** Rus. Lesnaya. Brestskaya Voblasts', SW Belarus
119 F19 **Lyasnaya** Pol. Leśna, Rus. Lesnaya. ≈ SW Belarus
124 H15 **Lychkovo** Novgorodskaya Oblast', W Russian Federation
Lyck see Ełk
93 I15 **Lycksele** Västerbotten, N Sweden
18 G13 **Lycoming Creek** ≈ Pennsylvania, NE USA
Lycopolis see Asyūt
195 N3 **Lyddan Island** island Antarctica
83 K20 **Lydenburg** Mpumalanga, NE South Africa
119 L20 **Lyel'chytsy** Rus. Lel'chitsy. Homyel'skaya Voblasts', SE Belarus
119 P14 **Lyenina** Rus. Lenino. Mahilyowskaya Voblasts', E Belarus
118 L13 **Lyepyel'** Rus. Lepel'. Vitsyebskaya Voblasts', N Belarus
25 S17 **Lyford** Texas, SW USA
95 E17 **Lygna** ≈ S Norway
18 G14 **Lykens** Pennsylvania, NE USA
115 E21 **Lykódimo** ▲ S Greece
97 K24 **Lyme Bay** bay S England, UK
97 K24 **Lyme Regis** S England, UK
110 L7 **Łyna** Ger. Alle. ≈ N Poland
29 P12 **Lynch** Nebraska, C USA
20 J10 **Lynchburg** Tennessee, S USA
21 T6 **Lynchburg** Virginia, NE USA
21 T12 **Lynches River** ≈ South Carolina, SE USA
32 H6 **Lynden** Washington, NW USA
182 I5 **Lyndhurst** South Australia
27 Q5 **Lyndon** Kansas, C USA
19 N7 **Lyndonville** Vermont, NE USA
95 D18 **Lyngdal** Vest-Agder, S Norway
92 I9 **Lyngen** Lapp. Ivgovuotna. inlet Arctic Ocean
95 G17 **Lyngør** Aust-Agder, S Norway
92 I9 **Lyngseidet** Troms, N Norway
19 P11 **Lynn** Massachusetts, NE USA
Lynn see King's Lynn
23 R9 **Lynn Haven** Florida, SE USA
11 V11 **Lynn Lake** Manitoba, C Canada
Lynn Regis see King's Lynn
118 I13 **Lyntupy** Rus. Lyntupy. Vitsyebskaya Voblasts', NW Belarus
103 R11 **Lyon** Eng. Lyons; anc. Lugdunum. Rhône, E France
8 I6 **Lyon, Cape** headland Northwest Territories, NW Canada
18 K6 **Lyon Mountain** ▲ New York, NE USA
103 Q11 **Lyonnais, Monts du** ▲ C France
65 N25 **Lyon Point** headland SE Tristan da Cunha
182 E5 **Lyons** South Australia
37 T3 **Lyons** Colorado, C USA
23 V6 **Lyons** Georgia, SE USA
26 M5 **Lyons** Kansas, C USA
29 R14 **Lyons** Nebraska, C USA
18 G10 **Lyons** New York, NE USA
Lyons see Lyon
118 O13 **Lyozna** Rus. Liozno. Vitsyebskaya Voblasts', NE Belarus
117 S4 **Lypova Dolyna** Sums'ka Oblast', NE Ukraine
117 N6 **Lypovets'** Rus. Lipovets. Vinnyts'ka Oblast', C Ukraine
Lys see Leie
111 I18 **Lysá Hora** ▲ E Czech Republic
95 D16 **Lysefjorden** fjord S Norway
95 I18 **Lysekil** Västra Götaland, S Sweden
Lýsi see Akdoğan
33 V14 **Lysite** Wyoming, C USA
127 P3 **Lyskovo** Nizhegorodskaya Oblast', W Russian Federation
108 D8 **Lyss** Bern, W Switzerland
95 H22 **Lystrup** Århus, C Denmark
125 V14 **Lys'va** Permskaya Oblast', NW Russian Federation
117 P6 **Lysyanka** Cherkas'ka Oblast', C Ukraine
117 X6 **Lysychans'k** Rus. Lisichansk. Luhans'ka Oblast', E Ukraine
97 K17 **Lytham St Anne's** NW England, UK
185 I19 **Lyttelton** Canterbury, South Island, NZ
10 M17 **Lytton** British Columbia, SW Canada
119 L18 **Lyuban'** Rus. Lyuban'. Minskaya Voblasts', S Belarus
119 L18 **Lyubanskaye Vodaskhovishcha** ⊡ C Belarus
116 M5 **Lyubar** Zhytomyrs'ka Oblast', N Ukraine
Lyubashëvka see Lyubashivka
117 O8 **Lyubashivka** Rus. Lyubashëvka. Odes'ka Oblast', SW Ukraine
119 I16 **Lyubcha** Pol. Lubcz, Rus. Lyubcha. Hrodzyenskaya Voblasts', W Belarus
126 L4 **Lyubertsy** Moskovskaya Oblast', W Russian Federation
116 K2 **Lyubeshiv** Volyns'ka Oblast', NW Ukraine
124 M14 **Lyubim** Yaroslavskaya Oblast', NW Russian Federation
114 K11 **Lyubimets** Khaskovo, S Bulgaria
Lyublin see Lublin
116 I3 **Lyuboml'** Pol. Luboml. Volyns'ka Oblast', NW Ukraine
Lyubotin see Lyubotyn
117 U5 **Lyubotyn** Rus. Lyubotin. Kharkivs'ka Oblast', E Ukraine
126 I5 **Lyudinovo** Kaluzhskaya Oblast', W Russian Federation
127 T2 **Lyuk** Udmurtskaya Respublika, NW Russian Federation
114 M9 **Lyulyakovo** prev. Keremitlik. Burgas, E Bulgaria
119 I18 **Lyusina** Rus. Lyusino. Brestskaya Voblasts', SW Belarus
Lyusino see Lyusina

M

138 G9 **Ma'ād** Irbid, N Jordan
Ma'ai see Luqu
Maalahti see Malax
Maale see Male'
138 G13 **Ma'ān** Ma'ān, SW Jordan
138 H13 **Ma'ān** off. Muḩāfaẓat Ma'ān, var. Ma'an, Ma'ān. ◈ governorate S Jordan
93 M16 **Maaninka** Itä-Suomi, C Finland
162 K7 **Maanĭt** Bulgan, C Mongolia
162 M8 **Maanĭt** Töv, C Mongolia
93 N15 **Maanselkä** Oulu, C Finland
161 Q8 **Ma'anshan** Anhui, E China
188 F16 **Maap** island Caroline Islands, W Micronesia
118 H3 **Maardu** Ger. Maart. Harjumaa, NW Estonia
Ma'aret-en-Nu'man see Ma'arrat an Nu'mān
99 K16 **Maarheeze** Noord-Brabant, SE Netherlands
Maarianhamina see Mariehamn
138 I4 **Ma'arrat an Nu'mān** var. Ma'aret-en-Nu'man, Fr. Maarret enn Naamâne. Idlib, NW Syria
Maarret enn Naamâne see Ma'arrat an Nu'mān
98 I11 **Maarssen** Utrecht, C Netherlands
Maart see Maardu
99 L17 **Maas** Fr. Meuse. ≈ W Europe see also Meuse
99 M15 **Maasbree** Limburg, SE Netherlands
99 L17 **Maaseik** prev. Maeseyck. Limburg, NE Belgium
171 Q6 **Maasin** Leyte, C Philippines
99 L17 **Maasmechelen** Limburg, NE Belgium
98 G12 **Maassluis** Zuid-Holland, SW Netherlands
99 L18 **Maastricht** var. Maestricht; anc. Traietum ad Mosam, Traiectum Tungorum. Limburg, SE Netherlands
183 N18 **Maatsuyker Group** island group Tasmania, SE Australia
Maba see Qujiang
83 L20 **Mabalane** Gaza, S Mozambique
25 V7 **Mabank** Texas, SW USA
97 O18 **Mablethorpe** E England, UK
171 V12 **Maboi** Papua, E Indonesia
83 M19 **Mabote** Inhambane, S Mozambique
32 J10 **Mabton** Washington, NW USA
Mabuchi-gawa see Mabechi-gawa
83 H20 **Mabutsane** Southern, S Botswana
63 G19 **Macá, Cerro** ▲ S Chile
60 Q9 **Macaé** Rio de Janeiro, SE Brazil
82 N13 **Macaloge** Niassa, N Mozambique
Macan see Bonerate, Kepulauan
161 N15 **Macao** Chin. Aomen, Port. Macau. S China
104 H9 **Mação** Santarém, C Portugal
58 J11 **Macapá** state capital Amapá, N Brazil
43 S17 **Macaracas** Los Santos, S Panama
55 P6 **Macare, Caño** ≈ NE Venezuela
55 Q6 **Macareo, Caño** ≈ NE Venezuela
Macarsca see Makarska
MacArthur see Ormoc
182 L12 **Macarthur** Victoria, SE Australia
56 C7 **Macas** Morona Santiago, SE Ecuador
Macassar see Makassar
59 Q14 **Macau** Rio Grande do Norte, E Brazil
Macau see Macao
Macău see Makó, Hungary
65 E24 **Macbride Head** headland East Falkland, Falkland Islands
23 V9 **Macclenny** Florida, SE USA
97 L18 **Macclesfield** C England, UK
192 F6 **Macclesfield Bank** undersea feature N South China Sea
MacCluer Gulf see Berau, Teluk
181 N7 **Macdonald, Lake** salt lake Western Australia
181 Q7 **Macdonnell Ranges** ▲ Northern Territory, C Australia
96 K8 **Macduff** NE Scotland, UK
104 I6 **Macedo de Cavaleiros** Bragança, N Portugal
Macedonia Central see Kentrikí Makedonía
Macedonia East and Thrace see Anatolikí Makedonía kai Thráki
113 O19 **Macedonia, FYR** off. the Former Yugoslav Republic of Macedonia, var. Macedonia, Mac. Makedonija, abbrev. FYR Macedonia, FYROM. ◆ republic SE Europe
Macedonia West see Dytikí Makedonía
59 Q16 **Maceió** state capital Alagoas, E Brazil
76 K15 **Macenta** Guinée-Forestière, SE Guinea
106 J12 **Macerata** Marche, C Italy
11 S11 **MacFarlane** ≈ Saskatchewan, C Canada
182 H7 **Macfarlane, Lake** var. Lake Mcfarlane. ◎ South Australia
Macgillicuddy's Reeks Mountains see Macgillycuddy's Reeks
97 B21 **Macgillycuddy's Reeks** var. Macgillicuddy's Reeks Mountains, Ir. Na Cruacha Dubha. ▲ SW Ireland
11 X15 **MacGregor** Manitoba, S Canada
149 O10 **Mach** Baluchistān, SW Pakistan
56 C6 **Machachi** Pichincha, C Ecuador
83 M19 **Machaila** Gaza, S Mozambique
Machaire Fíolta see Magherafelt
Machaire Rátha see Maghera
81 I19 **Machakos** Eastern, S Kenya
56 B8 **Machala** El Oro, SW Ecuador
Machali see Madoi
83 J19 **Machaneng** Central, SE Botswana
83 M18 **Machanga** Sofala, E Mozambique
80 G13 **Machar Marshes** wetland SE Sudan
102 I8 **Machecoul** Loire-Atlantique, NW France
161 O9 **Macheng** Hubei, C China
155 J16 **Mācherla** Andhra Pradesh, C India
153 O11 **Machhapuchhre** ▲ C Nepal
19 T6 **Machias** Maine, NE USA
19 R3 **Machias River** ≈ Maine, NE USA
19 T6 **Machias River** ≈ Maine, NE USA
64 P5 **Machico** Madeira, Portugal, NE Atlantic Ocean
155 K16 **Machilīpatnam** var. Bandar Masulipatnam. Andhra Pradesh, E India
54 G5 **Machiques** Zulia, NW Venezuela
57 G15 **Machupicchu** Cusco, C Peru
83 M20 **Macia** var. Vila de Macia. Gaza, S Mozambique
Macías Nguema Biyogo see Bioco, Isla de
116 M13 **Măcin** Tulcea, SE Romania
183 T4 **Macintyre River** ≈ New South Wales/Queensland, SE Australia
181 Y7 **Mackay** Queensland, NE Australia
181 O7 **Mackay, Lake** salt lake Northern Territory/Western Australia
10 M13 **Mackenzie** British Columbia, W Canada
8 I9 **Mackenzie** ≈ Northwest Territories, NW Canada
195 Y6 **Mackenzie Bay** bay Antarctica
10 J1 **Mackenzie Bay** bay NW Canada
2 D9 **Mackenzie Delta** delta Northwest Territories, NW Canada
8 K3 **Mackenzie King Island** island Queen Elizabeth Islands, Northwest Territories, N Canada
8 H8 **Mackenzie Mountains** ▲ Northwest Territories, NW Canada
31 Q5 **Mackinac, Straits of** ◎ Michigan, N USA
194 K5 **Mackintosh, Cape** headland Antarctica
11 R15 **Macklin** Saskatchewan, S Canada
183 V6 **Macksville** New South Wales, SE Australia
183 V5 **Maclean** New South Wales, SE Australia
83 J24 **Maclear** Eastern Cape, SE South Africa
183 U6 **Macleay River** ≈ New South Wales, SE Australia
MacLeod see Fort Macleod
180 G9 **Macleod, Lake** ◎ Western Australia
10 I6 **Macmillan** ≈ Yukon Territory, NW Canada
30 J12 **Macomb** Illinois, N USA
107 B18 **Macomer** Sardegna, Italy, C Mediterranean Sea
82 Q13 **Macomia** Cabo Delgado, NE Mozambique
23 T5 **Macon** Georgia, SE USA
23 N4 **Macon** Mississippi, S USA
27 U3 **Macon** Missouri, C USA
103 R10 **Mâcon** anc. Matisco, Matisco Ædourum. Saône-et-Loire, C France
22 I6 **Macon, Bayou** ≈ Arkansas/Louisiana, SE USA
82 G13 **Macondo** Moxico, E Angola
83 M16 **Macossa** Manica, C Mozambique
11 T12 **Macoun Lake** ◎ Saskatchewan, C Canada
30 K14 **Macoupin Creek** ≈ Illinois, N USA
Macouria see Tonate
83 N18 **Macovane** Inhambane, SE Mozambique
183 N17 **Macquarie Harbour** inlet Tasmania, SE Australia
192 J13 **Macquarie Island** island NZ, SW Pacific Ocean
183 T8 **Macquarie, Lake** lagoon New South Wales, SE Australia
183 Q6 **Macquarie Marshes** wetland New South Wales, SE Australia
175 O13 **Macquarie Ridge** undersea feature SW Pacific Ocean
183 Q6 **Macquarie River** ≈ New South Wales, SE Australia
183 P17 **Macquarie River** ≈ Tasmania, SE Australia
195 V5 **Mac. Robertson Land** physical region Antarctica
97 C21 **Macroom** Ir. Maigh Chromtha. SW Ireland
42 G5 **Macuelizo** Santa Bárbara, NW Honduras
182 G2 **Macumba River** ≈ South Australia
57 I16 **Macusani** Puno, S Peru
56 E8 **Macusari, Río** ≈ N Peru
41 U15 **Macuspana** Tabasco, SE Mexico
138 G10 **Ma'dabā** var. Mādabā, Madeba; anc. Medeba. 'Al Āṣimah, NW Jordan
172 G2 **Madagascar** off. Democratic Republic of Madagascar, Malg. Madagasikara; prev. Malagasy Republic. ◆ republic W Indian Ocean
172 I5 **Madagascar** island W Indian Ocean
130 L17 **Madagascar Basin** undersea feature W Indian Ocean
130 L16 **Madagascar Plain** undersea feature W Indian Ocean
67 Y14 **Madagascar Plateau** var. Madagascar Ridge, Madagascar Rise, Rus. Madagaskarskiy Khrebet. undersea feature W Indian Ocean
Madagascar Ridge/Madagascar Rise see Madagascar Plateau
Madagasikara see Madagascar
Madagaskarskiy Khrebet see Madagascar Plateau
64 N2 **Madalena** Pico, Azores, Portugal, NE Atlantic Ocean
77 Y6 **Madama** Agadez, NE Niger
114 J12 **Madan** Smolyan, S Bulgaria
155 I19 **Madanapalle** Andhra Pradesh, E India
186 D7 **Madang** Madang, N PNG
186 C6 **Madang** ◈ province N PNG
146 G7 **Madaniyat** Rus. Madeniyet. Qoraqalpog'iston Respublikasi, W Uzbekistan
Madanīyīn see Médenine
77 U11 **Madaoua** Tahoua, SW Niger
Madaras see Vtáčnik
153 U15 **Madaripur** Dhaka, C Bangladesh
77 U12 **Madarounfa** Maradi, S Niger
Madarska see Hungary
Madau see Madaw
186 H9 **Madau Island** island SE PNG
146 B13 **Madaw** Rus. Madau. Balkan Welaýaty, W Turkmenistan
19 S1 **Madawaska** Maine, NE USA
14 J13 **Madawaska** ≈ Ontario, SE Canada
Madawaska Highlands see Haliburton Highlands
166 M4 **Madaya** Mandalay, C Myanmar
107 K17 **Maddaloni** Campania, S Italy
29 O3 **Maddock** North Dakota, N USA
99 I14 **Made** Noord-Brabant, S Netherlands
Madeba see Ma'dabā
64 L9 **Madeira** var. Ilha de Madeira. island Madeira, Portugal, NE Atlantic Ocean
Madeira, Ilha de see Madeira
64 O5 **Madeira Islands** Port. Região Autoónoma da Madeira. ◈ autonomous region Madeira, Portugal, NE Atlantic Ocean
64 L9 **Madeira Plain** undersea feature E Atlantic Ocean
64 L9 **Madeira Ridge** undersea feature E Atlantic Ocean
59 F14 **Madeira, Rio** Sp. Río Madera. ≈ Bolivia/Brazil see also Madera, Río
101 J25 **Mädelegabel** ▲ Austria/Germany
15 X6 **Madeleine** ≈ Québec, SE Canada
15 X5 **Madeleine, Cap de la** headland Québec, SE Canada
13 Q13 **Madeleine, Îles de la** Eng. Magdalen Islands. island group Québec, E Canada
29 U10 **Madelia** Minnesota, N USA
35 P3 **Madeline** California, W USA
30 K3 **Madeline Island** island Apostle Islands, Wisconsin, N USA
137 O15 **Maden** Elaziğ, SE Turkey
145 V12 **Madeniyet** Vostochnyy Kazakhstan, E Kazakhstan
Madeniyet see Madaniyat
40 H5 **Madera** Chihuahua, N Mexico
35 Q10 **Madera** California, W USA
56 L13 **Madera, Río** Port. Rio Madeira. ≈ Bolivia/Brazil see also Madeira, Rio
106 D6 **Madesimo** Lombardia, N Italy
141 O14 **Madhāb, Wādī** dry watercourse NW Yemen
153 R13 **Madhepura** prev. Madhipure. Bihār, NE India
Madhipure see Madhepura
153 Q13 **Madhubani** Bihār, N India
153 Q15 **Madhupur** Jhārkhand, NE India
154 I10 **Madhya Pradesh** prev. Central Provinces and Berar. ◈ state C India
57 K15 **Madidi, Río** ≈ W Bolivia
155 F20 **Madikeri** prev. Mercara. Karnātaka, W India
27 O13 **Madill** Oklahoma, C USA
79 G21 **Madimba** Bas-Congo, SW Dem. Rep. Congo
138 M4 **Ma'dīn** Ar Raqqah, C Syria
Madīnah, Minṭaqat al see Al Madīnah
76 M14 **Madinani** NW Ivory Coast
141 O17 **Madīnat ash Sha'b** prev. Al Ittiḥād. SW Yemen
138 K3 **Madīnat ath Thawrah** var. Ath Thawrah. Ar Raqqah, N Syria Asia
173 O6 **Madingley Rise** undersea feature W Indian Ocean
79 E21 **Madingo-Kayes** Le Kouilou, S Congo
79 F21 **Madingou** La Bouenza, S Congo
Madioen see Madiun
23 U8 **Madison** Florida, SE USA
23 T3 **Madison** Georgia, SE USA
31 P15 **Madison** Indiana, N USA
27 P6 **Madison** Kansas, C USA
19 Q6 **Madison** Maine, NE USA
29 S9 **Madison** Minnesota, N USA
22 K5 **Madison** Mississippi, S USA
29 Q14 **Madison** Nebraska, C USA
29 R10 **Madison** South Dakota, N USA
21 V5 **Madison** Virginia, NE USA
21 Q5 **Madison** West Virginia, NE USA
30 L9 **Madison** state capital Wisconsin, N USA
21 T6 **Madison Heights** Virginia, NE USA
20 I6 **Madisonville** Kentucky, S USA
20 M10 **Madisonville** Tennessee, S USA
25 V9 **Madisonville** Texas, SW USA
169 R16 **Madiun** prev. Madioen. Jawa, C Indonesia
Madjene see Majene
14 J14 **Madoc** Ontario, SE Canada
Madoera see Madura, Pulau
81 J18 **Mado Gashi** North Eastern, E Kenya
159 R11 **Madoi** var. Machali. Qinghai, C China
189 O13 **Madolenihmw** Pohnpei, E Micronesia
118 I9 **Madona** Ger. Modohn. Madona, E Latvia
107 J23 **Madonie** ▲ Sicilia, Italy, C Mediterranean Sea
141 Y11 **Madrakah, Ra's** headland E Oman
32 I12 **Madras** Oregon, NW USA
Madras see Chennai
57 H14 **Madre de Dios** off. Departamento de Madre de Dios. ◈ department E Peru
63 F22 **Madre de Dios, Isla** island S Chile
57 J14 **Madre de Dios, Río** ≈ Bolivia/Peru
25 T16 **Madre, Laguna** ◎ Texas, SW USA
41 Q9 **Madre, Laguna** lagoon NE Mexico
37 Q12 **Madre Mount** ▲ New Mexico, SW USA
105 N8 **Madrid** ● (Spain) Madrid, C Spain
29 V14 **Madrid** Iowa, C USA
105 N7 **Madrid** ◈ autonomous community C Spain
105 N10 **Madridejos** Castilla-La Mancha, C Spain
104 L7 **Madrigal de las Altas Torres** Castilla-León, N Spain
104 K10 **Madrigalejo** Extremadura, W Spain
34 L3 **Mad River** ≈ California, W USA
42 J8 **Madriz** ◈ department NW Nicaragua
104 K10 **Madroñera** Extremadura, W Spain
181 N12 **Madura** Western Australia
Madura see Madurai
155 H22 **Madurai** prev. Madura, Mathurai. Tamil Nādu, S India
169 S16 **Madura, Pulau** prev. Madoera. island C Indonesia
169 S16 **Madura, Selat** strait C Indonesia

◆ Country ● Country Capital ◇ Dependent Territory ○ Dependent Territory Capital ◈ Administrative Region ✕ International Airport ▲ Mountain ▲ Mountain Range ⩕ Volcano ≈ River ◎ Lake ⊡ Reservoir

127 *Q17* **Madzhalis** Respublika Dagestan, SW Russian Federation
114 *K12* **Madzharovo** Khaskovo, S Bulgaria
83 *M14* **Madzimoyo** Eastern, E Zambia
165 *O12* **Maebashi** *var.* Maebasi, Mayebashi. Gunma, Honshū, S Japan
Maebasi *see* Maebashi
167 *O6* **Mae Chan** Chiang Rai, NW Thailand
167 *N7* **Mae Hong Son** *var.* Maehongson, Muai To. Mae Hong Son, NW Thailand
Mae Nam Khong *see* Mekong
167 *Q7* **Mae Nam Nan** ∾ NW Thailand
167 *O10* **Mae Nam Tha Chin** ∾ W Thailand
167 *P7* **Mae Nam Yom** ∾ W Thailand
37 *O3* **Maeser** Utah, W USA
Maeseyck *see* Maaseik
167 *N9* **Mae Sot** *var.* Ban Mae Sot. Tak, W Thailand
Maestricht *see* Maastricht
167 *O7* **Mae Suai** *var.* Ban Mae Suai. Chiang Rai, NW Thailand
167 *O7* **Mae Tho, Doi** ▲ NW Thailand
172 *I4* **Maevatanana** Mahajanga, C Madagascar
187 *R13* **Maéwo** *prev.* Aurora. *island* C Vanuatu
171 *S11* **Mafa** Pulau Halmahera, E Indonesia
83 *I23* **Mafeteng** W Lesotho
99 *J21* **Maffe** Namur, SE Belgium
183 *P12* **Maffra** Victoria, SE Australia
81 *K23* **Mafia** *island* E Tanzania
81 *J23* **Mafia Channel** *sea waterway* E Tanzania
83 *I21* **Mafikeng** North-West, N South Africa
60 *J12* **Mafra** Santa Catarina, S Brazil
104 *F10* **Mafra** Lisboa, C Portugal
143 *Q17* **Mafraq** Abū Ẓaby, C UAE
Mafraq/Mafraq, Muḥāfaẓat al *see* Al Mafraq
123 *T10* **Magadan** Magadanskaya Oblast', E Russian Federation
123 *T9* **Magadanskaya Oblast'** ◈ *province* E Russian Federation
108 *G11* **Magadino** Ticino, S Switzerland
63 *G23* **Magallanes** *off.* Región de Magallanes y de la Antártica Chilena. ◈ *region* S Chile
Magallanes *see* Punta Arenas
Magallanes, Estrecho de *see* Magellan, Strait of
14 *I10* **Maganasipi, Lac** ◎ Québec, SE Canada
54 *F6* **Magangué** Bolívar, N Colombia
Magareva *see* Mangareva
77 *V12* **Magaria** Zinder, S Niger
186 *F10* **Magarida** Central, SW PNG
171 *O2* **Magat** ∾ Luzon, N Philippines
27 *T11* **Magazine Mountain** ▲ Arkansas, C USA
76 *I15* **Magburaka** C Sierra Leone
123 *Q13* **Magdagachi** Amurskaya Oblast', SE Russian Federation
62 *O12* **Magdalena** Buenos Aires, E Argentina
57 *M15* **Magdalena** Beni, N Bolivia
40 *F4* **Magdalena** Sonora, NW Mexico
37 *Q13* **Magdalena** New Mexico, SW USA
54 *F5* **Magdalena** *off.* Departamento del Magdalena. ◈ *province* N Colombia
40 *E9* **Magdalena, Bahía** *bay* W Mexico
63 *G19* **Magdalena, Isla** *island* Archipiélago de los Chonos, S Chile
40 *D8* **Magdalena, Isla** *island* W Mexico
47 *P6* **Magdalena, Río** ∾ C Colombia
40 *F4* **Magdalena, Río** ∾ NW Mexico
Magdalen Islands *see* Madeleine, Îles de la
100 *L13* **Magdeburg** Sachsen-Anhalt, C Germany
22 *L6* **Magee** Mississippi, S USA
169 *Q16* **Magelang** Jawa, C Indonesia
192 *K7* **Magellan Rise** *undersea feature* C Pacific Ocean
63 *H24* **Magellan, Strait of** *Sp.* Estrecho de Magallanes. *strait* Argentina/Chile
106 *D7* **Magenta** Lombardia, NW Italy
Magerøy *see* Magerøya
92 *K7* **Magerøya** *var.* Magerøy, *Lapp.* Máhkarávju. *island* N Norway
164 *C17* **Mage-shima** *island* Nansei-shotō, SW Japan
108 *G11* **Maggia** Ticino, S Switzerland
108 *G10* **Maggia** ∾ SW Switzerland
Maggiore, Lago *see* Maggiore, Lake
106 *C6* **Maggiore, Lake** *It.* Lago Maggiore. ◎ Italy/Switzerland
44 *I12* **Maggotty** W Jamaica
76 *I10* **Maghama** Gorgol, S Mauritania
97 *F14* **Maghera** *Ir.* Machaire Rátha. C Northern Ireland, UK
97 *F15* **Magherafelt** *Ir.* Machaire Fíolta. C Northern Ireland, UK
188 *H6* **Magicienne Bay** *bay* Saipan, S Northern Mariana Islands
105 *O13* **Magina** ▲ S Spain
81 *H24* **Magingo** Ruvuma, S Tanzania
112 *H11* **Maglaj** Federacija Bosna I Hercegovina, N Bosnia and Herzegovina
107 *Q19* **Maglie** Puglia, SE Italy
36 *L2* **Magna** Utah, W USA
Magnesia *see* Manisa
14 *G12* **Magnetawan** ∾ Ontario, S Canada
27 *T14* **Magnolia** Arkansas, C USA
22 *K7* **Magnolia** Mississippi, S USA
25 *V10* **Magnolia** Texas, SW USA
Magnolia State *see* Mississippi
95 *J15* **Magnor** Hedmark, S Norway
187 *Y14* **Mago** *prev.* Mango. *island* Lau Group, E Fiji
83 *L15* **Màgoé** Tete, NW Mozambique
15 *Q13* **Magog** Québec, SE Canada
83 *J15* **Magoye** Southern, S Zambia
41 *Q12* **Magozal** Veracruz-Llave, C Mexico
14 *B7* **Magpie** ∾ Ontario, S Canada
11 *Q17* **Magrath** Alberta, SW Canada
105 *R10* **Magro** ∾ E Spain
76 *I9* **Magta' Laḥjar** *var.* Magta Lahjar, Magta' Lahjar, Magtá Lahjar. Brakna, SW Mauritania
83 *L20* **Magude** Maputo, S Mozambique
77 *Y12* **Magumeri** Borno, NE Nigeria
189 *O14* **Magur Islands** *island group* Caroline Islands, C Micronesia
Magway *see* Magwe
166 *L6* **Magwe** *var.* Magway. Magwe, W Myanmar
166 *L6* **Magwe** *var.* Magway. ◈ *division* C Myanmar
Magyar-Becse *see* Bečej
Magyarkanizsa *see* Kanjiža
Magyarország *see* Hungary
Magyarzsombor *see* Zimbor
142 *J4* **Mahābād** *var.* Mehabad; *prev.* Sāūjbulāgh. Āžarbāyjān-e Bākhtarī, NW Iran
172 *H5* **Mahabo** Toliara, W Madagascar
Maha Chai *see* Samut Sakhon
155 *D14* **Mahād** Mahārāshtra, W India
81 *N17* **Mahadday Weyne** Shabeellaha Dhexe, C Somalia
79 *Q17* **Mahagi** Orientale, NE Dem. Rep. Congo
Mahāil *see* Muhāyil
172 *I4* **Mahajamba** *seasonal river* NW Madagascar
152 *G10* **Mahājan** Rājasthān, NW India
172 *I3* **Mahajanga** *var.* Majunga. Mahajanga, NW Madagascar
172 *I3* **Mahajanga** ◈ *province* W Madagascar
172 *I3* **Mahajanga** ✕ Mahajanga, NW Madagascar
169 *U10* **Mahakam, Sungai** *var.* Koetai, Kutai. ∾ Borneo, C Indonesia
83 *I19* **Mahalapye** *var.* Mahalatswe. Central, SE Botswana
Mahalatswe *see* Mahalapye
Mahalla el Kubra *see* El Mahalla el Kubra
171 *O13* **Mahalona** Sulawesi, C Indonesia
Mahameru *see* Semeru, Gunung
143 *S11* **Mahān** Kermān, E Iran
154 *N12* **Mahānadi** ∾ E India
172 *J5* **Mahanoro** Toamasina, E Madagascar
153 *P13* **Mahārājganj** Bihār, N India
154 *G13* **Mahārāshtra** ◈ *state* W India
172 *I4* **Mahavavy** *seasonal river* N Madagascar
155 *K24* **Mahaweli Ganga** ∾ C Sri Lanka
Mahbés *see* El Mahbas
155 *J15* **Mahbūbābād** Andhra Pradesh, E India
155 *H16* **Mahbūbnagar** Andhra Pradesh, C India
140 *M8* **Mahd adh Dhahab** Al Madīnah, W Saudi Arabia
55 *S9* **Mahdia** C Guyana
75 *N6* **Mahdia** *var.* Al Mahdīyah, Mehdia. NE Tunisia
155 *F20* **Mahe** *Fr.* Mahé; *prev.* Mayyali. Pondicherry, SW India
172 *I16* **Mahé** ✕ Mahé, NE Seychelles
172 *H16* **Mahé** *island* Inner Islands, NE Seychelles
173 *Y17* **Mahebourg** SE Mauritius
152 *L10* **Mahendranagar** Far Western, W Nepal
81 *I23* **Mahenge** Morogoro, SE Tanzania
185 *F22* **Maheno** Otago, South Island, NZ
154 *D9* **Mahesāna** Gujarāt, W India
154 *F11* **Maheshwar** Madhya Pradesh, C India
151 *F14* **Mahi** ∾ N India
184 *Q10* **Mahia Peninsula** *peninsula* North Island, NZ
119 *O16* **Mahilyow** *Rus.* Mogilëv. Mahilyowskaya Voblasts', E Belarus
119 *M16* **Mahilyowskaya Voblasts'** *prev. Rus.* Mogilëvskaya Oblast'. ◈ *province* E Belarus
191 *P7* **Mahina** Tahiti, W French Polynesia
185 *E23* **Mahinerangi, Lake** ◎ South Island, NZ
Máhkarávju *see* Magerøya
83 *L22* **Mahlabatini** KwaZulu/Natal, E South Africa
166 *L5* **Mahlaing** Mandalay, C Myanmar
109 *X8* **Mahldorf** Steiermark, SE Austria
Mahmūd-e 'Erāqī *see* Maḥmūd-e Rāqī
149 *R4* **Maḥmūd-e Rāqī** *var.* Mahmūd-e 'Erāqī. Kāpīsā, NE Afghanistan
Mahmudiya *see* Al Maḥmūdīyah
29 *S5* **Mahnomen** Minnesota, N USA
152 *K14* **Mahoba** Uttar Pradesh, N India
105 *Z9* **Mahón** *Cat.* Maó, *Eng.* Port Mahon; *anc.* Portus Magonis. Menorca, Spain, W Mediterranean Sea
18 *D14* **Mahoning Creek Lake** ⊞ Pennsylvania, NE USA
105 *Q10* **Mahora** Castilla-La Mancha, C Spain
Mähren *see* Moravia
Mährisch-Budwitz *see* Moravské Budějovice
Mährisch-Kromau *see* Moravský Krumlov
Mährisch-Neustadt *see* Uničov
Mährisch-Schönberg *see* Šumperk
Mährisch-Trübau *see* Moravská Třebová
Mährisch-Weisskirchen *see* Hranice
Māh-Shahr *see* Bandar-e Māhshahr
79 *N19* **Mahulu** Maniema, E Dem. Rep. Congo
154 *C12* **Mahuva** Gujarāt, W India
114 *N11* **Mahya Dağı** ▲ NW Turkey
105 *T6* **Maials** *var.* Mayals. Cataluña, NE Spain
191 *O2* **Maiana** *prev.* Hall Island. *atoll* Tungaru, W Kiribati
191 *S11* **Maiao** *var.* Tapuaemanu, Tubuai-Manu. *island* Îles du Vent, W French Polynesia
54 *H4* **Maicao** La Guajira, N Colombia
Mai Ceu/Mai Chio *see* Maych'ew
103 *U8* **Maîche** Doubs, E France
97 *N22* **Maidenhead** S England, UK
11 *S15* **Maidstone** Saskatchewan, S Canada
97 *P22* **Maidstone** SE England, UK
77 *Y13* **Maiduguri** Borno, NE Nigeria
108 *I8* **Maienfeld** Sankt Gallen, NE Switzerland
116 *J12* **Măieruş** *Hung.* Szászmagyarós. Braşov, C Romania
Maigh Chromtha *see* Macroom
Maigh Eo *see* Mayo
55 *N9* **Maigualida, Sierra** ▲▲ S Venezuela
154 *K9* **Maihar** Madhya Pradesh, C India
154 *K11* **Maikala Range** ▲▲ C India
67 *T10* **Maiko** ∾ W Dem. Rep. Congo
Mailand *see* Milano
152 *L11* **Mailāni** Uttar Pradesh, N India
149 *U10* **Māilsi** Punjab, E Pakistan
147 *R8* **Maimak** Talasskaya Oblast', NW Kyrgyzstan
Maimāna *see* Meymaneh
Maimansingh *see* Mymensingh
171 *V13* **Maimawa** Papua, E Indonesia
Maimuna *see* Al Maymūnah
101 *G18* **Main** ∾ C Germany
115 *F22* **Maïna** *ancient monument* Pelopónnisos, S Greece
115 *E20* **Maínalo** ▲▲ S Greece
101 *L22* **Mainburg** Bayern, SE Germany
Main Camp *see* Banana
14 *E12* **Main Channel** *lake channel* Ontario, S Canada
79 *I20* **Mai-Ndombe, Lac** *prev.* Lac Léopold II. ◎ W Dem. Rep. Congo
101 *K20* **Main-Donau-Kanal** *canal* SE Germany
19 *R6* **Maine** *off.* State of Maine; also known as Lumber State, Pine Tree State. ◈ *state* NE USA
102 *K6* **Maine** *cultural region* NW France
102 *J7* **Maine-et-Loire** ◈ *department* NW France
19 *Q9* **Maine, Gulf of** *gulf* NE USA
77 *X12* **Maïné-Soroa** Diffa, SE Niger
167 *N2* **Maingkwan** *var.* Mungkawn. Kachin State, N Myanmar
Main Island *see* Bermuda
Mainistir Fhear Maí *see* Fermoy
Mainistirna Búille *see* Boyle
Mainistir na Corann *see* Midleton
Mainistir na Féile *see* Abbeyfeale
96 *J5* **Mainland** *island* Orkney, N Scotland, UK
96 *L2* **Mainland** *island* Shetland, NE Scotland, UK
159 *P16* **Mainling** *var.* Tungdor. Xizang Zizhiqu, W China
152 *K12* **Mainpuri** Uttar Pradesh, N India
103 *N5* **Maintenon** Eure-et-Loir, C France
172 *H4* **Maintirano** Mahajanga, W Madagascar
93 *M15* **Mainua** Oulu, C Finland
101 *G18* **Mainz** *Fr.* Mayence. Rheinland-Pfalz, SW Germany
76 *I9* **Maio** *var.* Vila do Maio. Maio, S Cape Verde
76 *E10* **Maio** *var.* Mayo. *island* Ilhas de Sotavento, SE Cape Verde
62 *G12* **Maipo, Río** ∾ C Chile
62 *H12* **Maipo, Volcán** Ж W Argentina
61 *E22* **Maipú** Buenos Aires, E Argentina
62 *I11* **Maipú** Mendoza, E Argentina
62 *H11* **Maipú** Santiago, C Chile
54 *L5* **Maiquetía** Distrito Federal, N Venezuela
108 *I10* **Maira** *It.* Mera. ∾ Italy/Switzerland
106 *A9* **Maira** ∾ NW Italy
153 *V12* **Mairābari** Assam, NE India
44 *K7* **Maisí** Guantánamo, E Cuba
118 *H13* **Maišiagala** Vilnius, SE Lithuania
153 *V17* **Maiskhal Island** *island* SE Bangladesh
167 *N13* **Mai Sombun** Chumphon, SW Thailand
Maisur *see* Karnātaka, India
Maisur *see* Mysore, India
183 *T8* **Maitland** New South Wales, SE Australia
182 *I9* **Maitland** South Australia
14 *F15* **Maitland** ∾ Ontario, S Canada
195 *R1* **Maitri** *Indian research station* Antarctica
159 *N15* **Maizhokunggar** Xizang Zizhiqu, W China
43 *O10* **Maíz, Islas del** *var.* Corn Islands. *island group* SE Nicaragua
164 *J12* **Maizuru** Kyōto, Honshū, SW Japan
54 *F6* **Majagual** Sucre, N Colombia
41 *Z13* **Majahual** Quintana Roo, E Mexico
Majardah, Wādī *see* Medjerda, Oued/Mejerda
Mājeej *see* Mejit Island
171 *N13* **Majene** *prev.* Madjene. Sulawesi, C Indonesia
43 *V15* **Majé, Serranía de** ▲▲ E Panama
112 *I11* **Majevica** ▲▲ NE Bosnia and Herzegovina
81 *H15* **Majī** Southern, S Ethiopia
141 *X7* **Majis** NW Oman
Majorca *see* Mallorca
Mājro *see* Majuro Atoll
Majunga *see* Mahajanga
189 *Y3* **Majuro** ✕ Majuro Atoll, SE Marshall Islands
189 *Y2* **Majuro Atoll** *var.* Mājro. *atoll* Ratak Chain, SE Marshall Islands
189 *X2* **Majuro Lagoon** *lagoon* Majuro Atoll, SE Marshall Islands
76 *H11* **Maka** C Senegal
79 *F20* **Makabana** Le Niari, SW Congo
38 *D9* **Mākaha** *var.* Makaha. O'ahu, Hawai'i, USA, C Pacific Ocean
38 *B8* **Makahū'ena Point** *var.* Makahuena Point *headland* Kaua'i, Hawai'i, USA, C Pacific Ocean
38 *D9* **Makakilo City** O'ahu, Hawai'i, USA, C Pacific Ocean
83 *H18* **Makalamabedi** Central, C Botswana
Makale *see* Mek'elē
158 *K17* **Makalu** *Chin.* Makaru Shan. ▲ China/Nepal
81 *G23* **Makampi** Mbeya, S Tanzania
145 *X12* **Makanchi** *Kaz.* Maqanshy. Vostochnyy Kazakhstan, E Kazakhstan
42 *M8* **Makantaka** Región Autónoma Atlántico Norte, NE Nicaragua
190 *B16* **Makapu Point** *headland* W Niue
185 *C24* **Makarewa** Southland, South Island, NZ
117 *O4* **Makariv** Kyyivs'ka Oblast', N Ukraine
185 *D20* **Makarora** ∾ South Island, NZ
123 *T13* **Makarov** Ostrov Sakhalin, Sakhalinskaya Oblast', SE Russian Federation
197 *R9* **Makarov Basin** *undersea feature* Arctic Ocean
192 *I5* **Makarov Seamount** *undersea feature* W Pacific Ocean
113 *F15* **Makarska** *It.* Macarsca. Split-Dalmacija, SE Croatia
Makaru Shan *see* Makalu
125 *O15* **Makar'yev** Kostromskaya Oblast', NW Russian Federation
82 *L11* **Makasa** Northern, NE Zambia
Makasar *see* Makassar
Makasar, Selat *see* Makassar Straits
170 *M14* **Makassar** *var.* Macassar, Makasar; *prev.* Ujungpandang. Sulawesi, C Indonesia
192 *F7* **Makassar Straits** *Ind.* Selat Makasar. *strait* C Indonesia
144 *G12* **Makat** *Kaz.* Maqat. Atyrau, SW Kazakhstan
191 *T10* **Makatea** *island* Îles Tuamotu, C French Polynesia
139 *U7* **Makātū** E Iraq
172 *H6* **Makay** *var.* Massif du Makay. ▲▲ SW Madagascar
114 *J12* **Makaza** *pass* Bulgaria/Greece
Makedonija *see* Macedonia, FYR
190 *B16* **Makefu** W Niue
191 *V10* **Makemo** *atoll* Îles Tuamotu, C French Polynesia
76 *I15* **Makeni** C Sierra Leone
Makenzen *see* Orlyak
Makeyevka *see* Makiyivka
127 *Q16* **Makhachkala** *prev.* Petrovsk-Port. Respublika Dagestan, SW Russian Federation
144 *F11* **Makhambet** Atyrau, W Kazakhstan
Makharadze *see* Ozurget'i
139 *W13* **Makhfar Al Buṣayyah** S Iraq
139 *R4* **Makhmūr** N Iraq
138 *I11* **Makhrūq, Wadi al** *dry watercourse* E Jordan
139 *R4* **Makḥūl, Jabal** ▲ C Iraq
141 *R13* **Makhyah, Wādī** *dry watercourse* N Yemen
171 *V13* **Maki** Papua, E Indonesia
185 *G21* **Makikihi** Canterbury, South Island, NZ
191 *O2* **Makin** *prev.* Pitt Island. *atoll* Tungaru, W Kiribati
81 *I20* **Makindu** Eastern, S Kenya
145 *Q8* **Makinsk** Akmola, N Kazakhstan
187 *N10* **Makira** *off.* Makira Province. ◈ *province* SE Solomon Islands
Makira *see* San Cristobal
117 *X8* **Makiyivka** *Rus.* Makeyevka; *prev.* Dmitriyevsk. Donets'ka Oblast', E Ukraine
140 *L10* **Makkah** *Eng.* Mecca. Makkah, W Saudi Arabia
140 *M10* **Makkah** *var.* Minṭaqat Makkah. ◈ *province* W Saudi Arabia
13 *R7* **Makkovik** Newfoundland and Labrador, NE Canada
98 *K6* **Makkum** Friesland, N Netherlands
Mako *see* Makung
111 *M25* **Makó** *Rom.* Macău. Csongrád, SE Hungary
14 *G9* **Makobe Lake** ◎ Ontario, S Canada
79 *F18* **Makokou** Ogooué-Ivindo, NE Gabon
81 *G23* **Makongolosi** Mbeya, S Tanzania
81 *E19* **Makota** SW Uganda
79 *G18* **Makoua** Cuvette, C Congo
110 *M10* **Maków Mazowiecki** Mazowieckie, C Poland
111 *K17* **Maków Podhalański** Małopolskie, S Poland
143 *V14* **Makran** *cultural region* Iran/Pakistan
152 *G12* **Makrāna** Rājasthān, N India
143 *U15* **Makran Coast** *coastal region* SE Iran
119 *F20* **Makrany** *Rus.* Mokrany. Brestskaya Voblasts', SW Belarus
Makrinoros *see* Makrynóros
115 *H20* **Makrónisosi** *island* Kykládes, Greece, Aegean Sea
115 *D17* **Makrynóros** *var.* Makrinoros. ▲▲ C Greece
115 *G19* **Makryplági** ▲ C Greece
Maksamaa *see* Maxmo
124 *J15* **Maksatikha** *var.* Maksatha, Maksaticha. Tverskaya Oblast', W Russian Federation
154 *G10* **Maksi** Madhya Pradesh, C India
142 *I1* **Mākū** Āžarbāyjān-e Bākhtarī, NW Iran
153 *Y11* **Mākum** Assam, NE India
Makun *see* Makung
161 *R14* **Makung** *prev.* Mako, Makun. W Taiwan
164 *B16* **Makurazaki** Kagoshima, Kyūshū, SW Japan
77 *V15* **Makurdi** Benue, C Nigeria
38 *L17* **Makushin Volcano** Ж Unalaska Island, Alaska, USA
83 *K16* **Makwiro** Mashonaland West, N Zimbabwe
57 *D15* **Mala** Lima, W Peru
Mala *see* Mallow, Ireland
Mala *see* Malaita, Solomon Islands
93 *I14* **Malå** Västerbotten, N Sweden
190 *G12* **Mala'atoli** Île Uvea, E Wallis and Futuna
171 *P8* **Malabang** E Mindanao, S Phiippines
155 *E21* **Malabār Coast** *coast* SW India
79 *C16* **Malabo** *prev.* Santa Isabel. ● (Equatorial Guinea) Isla de Bioco, NW Equatorial Guinea
79 *C16* **Malabo** ✕ Isla de Bioco, N Equatorial Guinea
Malaca *see* Málaga
Malacca *see* Melaka
168 *I7* **Malacca, Strait of** *Ind.* Selat Malaka. *strait* Indonesia/Malaysia
Malacka *see* Malacky
111 *G20* **Malacky** *Hung.* Malacka. Bratislavský Kraj, W Slovakia
33 *R16* **Malad City** Idaho, NW USA
117 *Q4* **Mala Divytsya** Chernihivs'ka Oblast', N Ukraine
119 *J15* **Maladzyechna** *Pol.* Molodeczno, *Rus.* Molodechno. Minskaya Voblasts', C Belarus
190 *D12* **Malaee** Île Futuna, N Wallis and Futuna
37 *V15* **Malaga** New Mexico, SW USA
54 *G8* **Málaga** Santander, C Colombia
104 *M15* **Málaga** *anc.* Malaca. Andalucía, S Spain
104 *L15* **Málaga** ◈ *province* Andalucía, S Spain
104 *M15* **Málaga** ✕ Andalucía, S Spain
Malagasy Republic *see* Madagascar
105 *N10* **Malagón** Castilla-La Mancha, C Spain
97 *G18* **Malahide** *Ir.* Mullach Íde. E Ireland
187 *N9* **Malaita** *off.* Malaita Province. ◈ *province* N Solomon Islands
187 *N8* **Malaita** *var.* Mala. *island* N Solomon Islands
80 *F13* **Malakal** Upper Nile, S Sudan
112 *C10* **Mala Kapela** ▲▲ NW Croatia
25 *V7* **Malakoff** Texas, SW USA
Malakula *see* Malekula
149 *V7* **Malakwāl** *var.* Mālikwāla. Punjab, E Pakistan
186 *E7* **Malalamai** Madang, W PNG
GG *Q11* **Malamala** Sulawesi, C Indonesia
169 *S17* **Malang** Jawa, C Indonesia
83 *O14* **Malanga** Niassa, N Mozambique
Malange *see* Malanje
92 *I9* **Malangen** *sound* N Norway
82 *C11* **Malanje** *var.* Malange. Malanje, NW Angola
82 *C11* **Malanje** *var.* Malange. ◈ *province* N Angola
148 *M16* **Malān, Rās** *headland* SW Pakistan
77 *S13* **Malanville** NE Benin
Malapane *see* Ozimek
155 *F21* **Malappuram** Kerala, SW India
43 *T17* **Mala, Punta** *headland* S Panama
95 *N16* **Mälaren** ◎ C Sweden
62 *H13* **Malargüe** Mendoza, W Argentina
14 *J8* **Malartic** Québec, SE Canada
119 *F20* **Malaryta** *Pol.* Maloryta, *Rus.* Malorita. Brestskaya Voblasts', SW Belarus
63 *J19* **Malaspina** Chubut, SE Argentina
39 *U12* **Malaspina Glacier** *glacier* Alaska, USA
137 *N15* **Malatya** *anc.* Melitene. Malatya, SE Turkey
136 *M14* **Malatya** ◈ *province* C Turkey
117 *Q7* **Mala Vyska** *Rus.* Malaya Viska. Kirovohrads'ka Oblast', S Ukraine
83 *M14* **Malawi** *off.* Republic of Malaŵi; *prev.* Nyasaland, Nyasaland Protectorate. ◆ *republic* S Africa
Malawi, Lake *see* Nyasa, Lake
93 *J17* **Malax** *Fin.* Maalahti. Länsi-Suomi, W Finland
124 *H14* **Malaya Vishera** Novgorodskaya Oblast', W Russian Federation
Malaya Viska *see* Mala Vyska
171 *Q7* **Malaybalay** Mindanao, S Philippines
142 *L6* **Malāyer** *prev.* Daulatabad. Hamadān, W Iran
168 *J7* **Malay Peninsula** *peninsula* Malaysia/Thailand
168 *L7* **Malaysia** *var.* Federation of Malaysia; *prev.* the separate territories of Federation of Malaya, Sarawak and Sabah (North Borneo) and Singapore. ◆ *monarchy* SE Asia
137 *R14* **Malazgirt** Muş, E Turkey
15 *R8* **Malbaie** ∾ Québec, SE Canada
77 *T12* **Malbaza** Tahoua, S Niger
110 *J7* **Malbork** *Ger.* Marienburg, Marienburg in Westpreussen. Pomorskie, N Poland
100 *N9* **Malchin** Mecklenburg-Vorpommern, N Germany
100 *M9* **Malchiner See** ◎ NE Germany
99 *D16* **Maldegem** Oost-Vlaanderen, NW Belgium
98 *L13* **Malden** Gelderland, SE Netherlands
19 *O11* **Malden** Massachusetts, NE USA
27 *Y8* **Malden** Missouri, C USA
191 *X4* **Malden Island** *prev.* Independence Island. *atoll* E Kiribati
173 *Q6* **Maldives** *off.* Maldivian Divehi, Republic of Maldives. ◆ *republic* N Indian Ocean
Maldivian Divehi *see* Maldives
97 *P21* **Maldon** E England, UK
61 *G20* **Maldonado** Maldonado, S Uruguay
61 *G20* **Maldonado** ◈ *department* S Uruguay
41 *P17* **Maldonado, Punta** *headland* S Mexico
151 *K19* **Male'** *Div.* Maale ● (Maldives) Male' Atoll, C Maldives
106 *G6* **Malè** Trentino-Alto Adige, N Italy
76 *K13* **Maléa** *var.* Maléya. Haute-Guinée, NE Guinea
115 *G22* **Maléas, Akrotírio** *headland* S Greece
115 *L17* **Maléas, Akrotírio** *headland* Lésvos, E Greece
151 *K19* **Male' Atoll** *var.* Kaafu Atoll. *atoll* C Maldives
Malebo, Pool *see* Stanley Pool
154 *E12* **Mālegaon** Mahārāshtra, W India
81 *F15* **Malek** Jonglei, S Sudan
187 *Q13* **Malekula** *var.* Malakula; *prev.* Mallicolo. *island* W Vanuatu
189 *Y15* **Malem** Kosrae, E Micronesia
83 *O15* **Malema** Nampula, N Mozambique
79 *N23* **Malemba-Nkulu** Katanga, SE Dem. Rep. Congo
124 *K9* **Malen'ga** Respublika Kareliya, NW Russian Federation
95 *M20* **Målerås** Kalmar, S Sweden
103 *O6* **Malesherbes** Loiret, C France
115 *G18* **Malesína** Stereá Ellás, E Greece
Maléya *see* Maléa
127 *O15* **Malgobek** Chechenskaya Respublika, SW Russian Federation
105 *X5* **Malgrat de Mar** Cataluña, NE Spain
80 *C9* **Malha** Northern Darfur, W Sudan
139 *Q5* **Malḥāt** C Iraq
32 *K14* **Malheur Lake** ◎ Oregon, NW USA
32 *L14* **Malheur River** ∾ Oregon, NW USA
76 *I13* **Mali** Moyenne-Guinée, NW Guinea
77 *O9* **Mali** *off.* Republic of Mali, *Fr.* République du Mali; *prev.* French Sudan, Sudanese Republic. ◆ *republic* W Africa
171 *Q16* **Maliana** W East Timor
167 *O2* **Mali Hka** ∾ N Myanmar
Mali Idjoš *see* Mali Iđoš
112 *K8* **Mali Iđoš** *var.* Mali Idjoš, *Hung.* Kishegyes; *prev.* Krivaja. Serbia, N Serbia and Montenegro (Yugo.)
112 *K9* **Mali Kanal** *canal* N Serbia and Montenegro (Yugo.)
171 *P12* **Maliku** Sulawesi, N Indonesia
Malik, Wadi al *see* Milk, Wadi el
Mālikwāla *see* Malakwāl
167 *N11* **Mali Kyun** *var.* Tavoy Island. *island* Mergui Archipelago, S Myanmar
95 *M19* **Målilla** Kalmar, S Sweden
112 *B11* **Mali Lošinj** *It.* Lussinpiccolo. Primorje-Gorski Kotar, W Croatia
Malin *see* Malyn
171 *P7* **Malindang, Mount** ▲ Mindanao, S Philippines
81 *K20* **Malindi** Coast, SE Kenya
Malines *see* Mechelen
96 *E13* **Malin Head** *Ir.* Cionn Mhálanna. *headland* NW Ireland
171 *O11* **Malino, Gunung** ▲ Sulawesi, N Indonesia
113 *M21* **Maliq** *var.* Maliqi. Korçë, SE Albania
Maliqi *see* Maliq
171 *Q8* **Malita** Mindanao, S Philippines
154 *G12* **Malkāpur** Mahārāshtra, C India
136 *B10* **Malkara** Tekirdağ, NW Turkey
119 *J19* **Mal'kavichy** *Rus.* Mal'kovichi. Brestskaya Voblasts', SW Belarus
Malkiye *see* Al Mālikīyah
114 *L11* **Malko Sharkovo, Yazovir** ⊞ SE Bulgaria
114 *N11* **Malko Tŭrnovo** Burgas, E Bulgaria
Mal'kovichi *see* Mal'kavichy

183 R12 **Mallacoota** Victoria, SE Australia
96 G10 **Mallaig** N Scotland, UK
182 I9 **Mallala** South Australia
75 W9 **Mallawi** C Egypt
105 R5 **Mallén** Aragón, NE Spain
106 F5 **Malles Venosta** Ger. Mals im Vinschgau. Trentino-Alto Adige, N Italy
Mallicolo see Malekula
109 Q8 **Mallnitz** Salzburg, S Austria
105 W9 **Mallorca** Eng. Majorca; anc. Baleares Major. island Islas Baleares, Spain, W Mediterranean Sea
97 C20 **Mallow** Ir. Mala. SW Ireland
93 E15 **Malm** Nord-Trøndelag, C Norway
95 L19 **Malmbäck** Jönköping, S Sweden
92 J12 **Malmberget** Lapp. Malmivaara. Norrbotten, N Sweden
99 M20 **Malmédy** Liège, E Belgium
83 E25 **Malmesbury** Western Cape, SW South Africa
Malmivaara see Malmberget
95 N16 **Malmköping** Södermanland, C Sweden
95 K23 **Malmö** Skåne, S Sweden
95 K23 **Malmo** × Skåne, S Sweden
45 Q16 **Malmok** headland Bonaire, S Netherlands Antilles
95 M18 **Malmslätt** Östergötland, S Sweden
125 R16 **Malmyzh** Kirovskaya Oblast', NW Russian Federation
187 Q13 **Malo** island W Vanuatu
126 J7 **Maloarkhangel'sk** Orlovskaya Oblast', W Russian Federation
Maloelap see Maloelap Atoll
189 V6 **Maloelap Atoll** var. Maloelap. atoll E Marshall Islands
Maloenda see Malunda
108 I10 **Maloja** Graubünden, S Switzerland
82 L12 **Malole** Northern, NE Zambia
171 O3 **Malolos** Luzon, N Philippines
18 K6 **Malone** New York, NE USA
79 K25 **Malonga** Katanga, S Dem. Rep. Congo
111 L15 **Małopolska** plateau S Poland
111 K17 **Małopolskie** ◆ province S Poland
Malorita/Maloryta see Malaryta
124 K9 **Maloshuyka** Arkhangel'skaya Oblast', NW Russian Federation
114 G10 **Mal'ovitsa** ▲ W Bulgaria
145 V15 **Malovodnoye** Almaty, SE Kazakhstan
94 C10 **Måløy** Sogn og Fjordane, S Norway
126 K4 **Maloyaroslavets** Kaluzhskaya Oblast', W Russian Federation
122 G7 **Malozemel'skaya Tundra** physical region NW Russian Federation
104 J10 **Malpartida de Cáceres** Extremadura, W Spain
104 K9 **Malpartida de Plasencia** Extremadura, W Spain
106 C7 **Malpensa** × (Milano) Lombardia, N Italy
76 J6 **Malqteïr** desert N Mauritania
Mals im Vinschgau see Malles Venosta
118 J10 **Malta** Rēzekne, SE Latvia
33 V7 **Malta** Montana, NW USA
120 M11 **Malta** off. Republic of Malta. ◆ republic C Mediterranean Sea
109 R8 **Malta** var. Maltabach. ≈ S Austria
120 M11 **Malta** island Malta, C Mediterranean Sea
Maltabach see Malta
Malta, Canale di see Malta Channel
120 M11 **Malta Channel** It. Canale di Malta. strait Italy/Malta
83 D20 **Maltahöhe** Hardap, SW Namibia
97 N16 **Malton** N England, UK
171 R13 **Maluku** off. Propinsi Maluku, Dut. Molukken, Eng. Moluccas. ◆ province E Indonesia
171 R13 **Maluku** Dut. Molukken, Eng. Moluccas; prev. Spice Islands. island group E Indonesia
Maluku, Laut see Molucca Sea
171 R11 **Maluku Utara** off. Propinsi Maluku Utara. ◆ province E Indonesia
77 V13 **Malumfashi** Katsina, N Nigeria
171 N13 **Malunda** prev. Maloenda. Sulawesi, C Indonesia
94 K13 **Malung** Dalarna, C Sweden
94 K13 **Malungsfors** Dalarna, C Sweden
186 M8 **Maluu** var. Malu'u. Malaita, N Solomon Islands
155 D16 **Mālvan** Mahārāshtra, W India
Malventum see Benevento
27 U12 **Malvern** Arkansas, C USA
29 S15 **Malvern** Iowa, C USA
44 I13 **Malvern** ▲ W Jamaica
Malvinas, Islas see Falkland Islands
117 N4 **Malyn** Rus. Malin. Zhytomyrs'ka Oblast', N Ukraine
127 O11 **Malyye Derbety** Respublika Kalmykiya, SW Russian Federation
Malyy Kavkaz see Lesser Caucasus
123 Q6 **Malyy Lyakhovskiy, Ostrov** island NE Russian Federation
Malyy Pamir see Little Pamir
122 N5 **Malyy Taymyr, Ostrov** island Severnaya Zemlya, N Russian Federation
144 E10 **Malyy Uzen'** Kaz. Kishiözen. ≈ Kazakhstan/Russian Federation
122 L14 **Malyy Yenisey** var. Ka-Krem. ≈ S Russian Federation
127 S3 **Mamadysh** Respublika Tatarstan, W Russian Federation
117 N14 **Mamaia** Constanța, E Romania
187 W14 **Mamanuca Group** island group Yasawa Group, W Fiji
146 L13 **Mamash** Lebap Welaýaty, E Turkmenistan
79 O17 **Mambasa** Orientale, NE Dem. Rep. Congo
171 X13 **Mamberamo, Sungai** ≈ Papua, E Indonesia
79 G15 **Mambéré** ≈ SW Central African Republic
79 G15 **Mambéré-Kadéï** ◆ prefecture SW Central African Republic
Mambij see Manbij
79 H18 **Mambili** ≈ W Congo
83 N18 **Mambone** var. Nova Mambone. Inhambane, E Mozambique
171 O4 **Mamburao** Mindoro, N Philippines
172 I16 **Mamelles** island Inner Islands, NE Seychelles
99 M25 **Mamer** Luxembourg, SW Luxembourg
102 L6 **Mamers** Sarthe, NW France
79 D15 **Mamfe** Sud-Ouest, W Cameroon
145 P6 **Mamlyutka** Severnyy Kazakhstan, N Kazakhstan
36 M15 **Mammoth** Arizona, SW USA
33 S12 **Mammoth Hot Springs** Wyoming, C USA
Mamoedjoe see Mamuju
119 A14 **Mamonovo** Ger. Heiligenbeil. Kaliningradskaya Oblast', W Russian Federation
57 L14 **Mamoré, Rio** ≈ Bolivia/Brazil
76 I14 **Mamou** Moyenne-Guinée, W Guinea
22 H8 **Mamou** Louisiana, S USA
172 I14 **Mamoudzou** ○ (Mayotte) C Mayotte
172 I3 **Mampikony** Mahajanga, N Madagascar
77 P16 **Mampong** C Ghana
110 M7 **Mamry, Jezioro** Ger. Mauersee. ◎ NE Poland
171 N13 **Mamuju** prev. Mamoedjoe. Sulawesi, S Indonesia
83 F19 **Mamuno** Ghanzi, W Botswana
113 K19 **Mamuras** var. Mamurasi, Mamurras. Lezhë, C Albania
Mamurasi/Mamurras see Mamuras
76 L16 **Man** W Ivory Coast
55 X9 **Mana** NW French Guiana
56 A6 **Manabí** ◆ province W Ecuador
42 G4 **Manabique, Punta** var. Cabo Tres Puntas. headland E Guatemala
54 G11 **Manacacías, Río** ≈ C Colombia
58 F13 **Manacapuru** Amazonas, N Brazil
171 Q11 **Manado** prev. Menado. Sulawesi, C Indonesia
188 H5 **Managaha** island S Northern Mariana Islands
99 G20 **Manage** Hainaut, S Belgium
42 J10 **Managua** ● (Nicaragua) Managua, W Nicaragua
42 J10 **Managua** ◆ department W Nicaragua
42 J10 **Managua** × Managua, W Nicaragua
42 J10 **Managua, Lago de** var. Xolotlán. ◎ W Nicaragua
Manaḩ see Bilād Manaḩ
18 K16 **Manahawkin** New Jersey, NE USA
184 K11 **Manaia** Taranaki, North Island, NZ
172 J6 **Manakara** Fianarantsoa, SE Madagascar
152 J7 **Manāli** Himāchal Pradesh, NW India
131 U12 **Ma, Nam** Vtn. Sông Mã. ≈ Laos/Vietnam
Manama see Al Manāmah
186 D6 **Manam Island** island N PNG
67 Y13 **Mananara** ≈ SE Madagascar
182 M9 **Manangatang** Victoria, SE Australia
172 J6 **Mananjary** Fianarantsoa, SE Madagascar
76 L14 **Manankoro** Sikasso, SW Mali
76 J12 **Manantali, Lac de** ▣ W Mali
Manáos see Manaus
185 B23 **Manapouri** Southland, South Island, NZ
185 B23 **Manapouri, Lake** ◎ South Island, NZ
58 F13 **Manaquiri** Amazonas, NW Brazil
Manar see Mannar
158 K5 **Manas** Xinjiang Uygur Zizhiqu, NW China
153 U12 **Manās** var. Dangme Chu. ≈ Bhutan/India
147 R8 **Manas, Gora** ▲ Kyrgyzstan/Uzbekistan
158 K3 **Manas Hu** ◎ NW China
153 P10 **Manaslu** ▲ C Nepal
37 S8 **Manassa** Colorado, C USA
21 W4 **Manassas** Virginia, NE USA
45 T5 **Manatí** C Puerto Rico
171 R16 **Manatuto** N East Timor
186 E8 **Manau** Northern, S PNG
54 H4 **Manaure** La Guajira, N Colombia
58 F12 **Manaus** prev. Manáos. state capital Amazonas, NW Brazil
136 G17 **Manavgat** Antalya, SW Turkey
184 M13 **Manawatu** ≈ North Island, NZ
184 L11 **Manawatu-Wanganui** off. Manawatu-Wanganui Region. ◆ region North Island, NZ
171 R7 **Manay** Mindanao, S Philippines
138 K2 **Manbij** var. Mambij, Fr. Membidj. Ḩalab, N Syria
105 N13 **Mancha Real** Andalucía, S Spain
102 I4 **Manche** ◆ department N France
97 L17 **Manchester** Lat. Mancunium. NW England, UK
23 S5 **Manchester** Georgia, SE USA
29 Y13 **Manchester** Iowa, C USA
21 N7 **Manchester** Kentucky, S USA
19 O10 **Manchester** New Hampshire, NE USA
20 K10 **Manchester** Tennessee, S USA
18 M9 **Manchester** Vermont, NE USA
97 L18 **Manchester** × NW England, UK
149 P15 **Manchhar Lake** ◎ SE Pakistan
Man-chou-li see Manzhouli
131 X7 **Manchurian Plain** plain NE China
Máncio Lima see Japiim
Mancunium see Manchester
148 J15 **Mand** Baluchistān, SW Pakistan
Mand see Mand, Rūd-e
81 H25 **Manda** Iringa, SW Tanzania
172 H6 **Mandabe** Toliara, W Madagascar
162 I5 **Mandal** Hövsgöl, N Mongolia
162 L7 **Mandal** Töv, C Mongolia
95 E18 **Mandal** Vest-Agder, S Norway
166 L5 **Mandalay** Mandalay, C Myanmar
166 M6 **Mandalay** ◆ division C Myanmar
162 L9 **Mandalgovĭ** Dundgovĭ, C Mongolia
139 V7 **Mandalī** E Iraq
95 E18 **Mandalselva** ≈ S Norway
163 P11 **Mandalt** var. Sonid Zuoqi. Nei Mongol Zizhiqu, N China
28 M5 **Mandan** North Dakota, N USA
Mandargiri Hill see Mandār Hill
153 R14 **Mandār Hill** prev. Mandargiri Hill. Bihār, NE India
170 M13 **Mandar, Teluk** bay Sulawesi, C Indonesia
107 C19 **Mandas** Sardegna, Italy, C Mediterranean Sea
Mandasor see Mandsaur
81 L16 **Mandera** North Eastern, NE Kenya
33 V13 **Manderson** Wyoming, C USA
44 J12 **Mandeville** C Jamaica
22 K9 **Mandeville** Louisiana, S USA
152 I7 **Mandi** Himāchal Pradesh, NW India
76 K14 **Mandiana** Haute-Guinée, E Guinea
149 U10 **Mandi Būrewāla** var. Būrewāla. Punjab, E Pakistan
152 G9 **Mandi Dabwāli** Haryāna, NW India
Mandidzudzure see Chimanimani
83 M15 **Mandié** Manica, NW Mozambique
83 N14 **Mandimba** Niassa, N Mozambique
57 Q19 **Mandioré, Laguna** ◎ E Bolivia
154 J10 **Mandla** Madhya Pradesh, C India
83 M20 **Mandlakazi** var. Manjacaze. Gaza, S Mozambique
95 E24 **Mandø** var. Manø. island W Denmark
Mandoúdhion/Mandoudi see Mantoúdi
115 G19 **Mándra** Attikí, C Greece
172 I7 **Mandrare** ≈ S Madagascar
114 M10 **Mandra, Yazovir** salt lake SE Bulgaria
107 L23 **Mandrazzi, Portella** pass Sicilia, Italy, C Mediterranean Sea
172 J3 **Mandritsara** Mahajanga, N Madagascar
143 O13 **Mand, Rūd-e** var. Mand. ≈ S Iran
154 F9 **Mandsaur** prev. Mandasor. Madhya Pradesh, C India
154 F11 **Māndu** Madhya Pradesh, C India
169 W8 **Mandul, Pulau** island N Indonesia
83 G15 **Mandundu** Western, W Zambia
180 I13 **Mandurah** Western Australia
107 P18 **Manduria** Puglia, SE Italy
155 G20 **Mandya** Karnātaka, C India
77 P12 **Mané** C Burkina
106 E8 **Manerbio** Lombardia, NW Italy
Manevichi see Manevychi
116 K3 **Manevychi** Pol. Maniewicze, Rus. Manevichi. Volyns'ka Oblast', NW Ukraine
107 N16 **Manfredonia** Puglia, SE Italy
107 N16 **Manfredonia, Golfo di** gulf Adriatic Sea, N Mediterranean Sea
77 P13 **Manga** C Burkina
59 L16 **Mangabeiras, Chapada das** ▲ E Brazil
79 J20 **Mangai** Bandundu, W Dem. Rep. Congo
190 L17 **Mangaia** island group S Cook Islands
184 M9 **Mangakino** Waikato, North Island, NZ
116 M15 **Mangalia** anc. Callatis. Constanța, SE Romania
78 J11 **Mangalmé** Guéra, SE Chad
155 E19 **Mangalore** Karnātaka, W India
191 Y13 **Mangareva** var. Magareva. island Îles Tuamotu, SE French Polynesia
83 I23 **Mangaung** Free State, C South Africa
Mangaung see Bloemfontein
154 K9 **Mangawān** Madhya Pradesh, C India
184 M11 **Mangaweka** Manawatu-Wanganui, North Island, NZ
184 N11 **Mangaweka** ▲ North Island, NZ
79 P17 **Mangbwalu** Orientale, NE Dem. Rep. Congo
101 L24 **Mangfall** ≈ SE Germany
169 P13 **Manggar** Pulau Belitung, W Indonesia
166 M2 **Mangin Range** ▲ N Myanmar
139 R1 **Mangish** N Iraq
144 F15 **Mangistau** Kaz. Mangqystaū Oblysy; prev. Mangyshlaskaya. ◆ province SW Kazakhstan
Mangit see Mang'it
146 H8 **Mang'it** Rus. Mangit. Qoraqalpog'iston Respublikasi, W Uzbekistan
54 A13 **Manglares, Cabo** headland SW Colombia
149 V6 **Mangla Reservoir** ▣ NE Pakistan
159 N9 **Mangnai** var. Lao Mangnai. Qinghai, C China
Mango see Mago, Fiji
Mango see Sansanné-Mango, Togo
Mangoche see Mangochi
83 N14 **Mangochi** var. Mangoche; prev. Fort Johnston. Southern, SE Malawi
77 N14 **Mangodara** SW Burkina
172 H6 **Mangoky** ≈ W Madagascar
171 Q12 **Mangole, Pulau** island Kepulauan Sula, E Indonesia
184 J2 **Mangonui** Northland, North Island, NZ
Mangqystaū Oblysy see Mangistau
Mangqystaū Shyghanaghy see Mangyshlakskiy Zaliv
104 H7 **Mangualde** Viseu, N Portugal
61 H18 **Mangueira, Lagoa** ◎ S Brazil
77 X6 **Manguéni, Plateau du** ▲ NE Niger
163 T4 **Mangui** Nei Mongol Zizhiqu, N China
26 K11 **Mangum** Oklahoma, C USA
79 O18 **Manguredjipa** Nord Kivu, E Dem. Rep. Congo
83 L16 **Mangwendi** Mashonaland East, E Zimbabwe
144 F15 **Mangyshlak, Plato** plateau SW Kazakhstan
144 E14 **Mangyshlakskiy Zaliv** Kaz. Mangqystaū Shyghanaghy. gulf SW Kazakhstan
Mangyshlaskaya see Mangistau
162 I5 **Manhan** Hövsgöl, N Mongolia
27 O4 **Manhattan** Kansas, C USA
99 L21 **Manhay** Luxembourg, SE Belgium
83 L21 **Manhiça** prev. Vila de Manhiça. Maputo, S Mozambique
83 L21 **Manhoca** Maputo, S Mozambique
59 N20 **Manhuaçu** Minas Gerais, SE Brazil
143 R11 **Mānī** Kermān, C Iran
54 H10 **Maní** Casanare, C Colombia
83 M17 **Manica** var. Vila de Manica. Manica, W Mozambique
83 M17 **Manica** off. Província de Manica. ◆ province W Mozambique
83 L17 **Manicaland** ◆ province E Zimbabwe
15 U5 **Manic Deux, Réservoir** ▣ Québec, SE Canada
Manich see Manych
59 F14 **Manicoré** Amazonas, N Brazil
13 N11 **Manicouagan** Québec, SE Canada
13 N11 **Manicouagan** ≈ Québec, SE Canada
15 U6 **Manicouagan, Péninsule de** peninsula Québec, SE Canada
13 N11 **Manicouagan, Réservoir** ◎ Québec, E Canada
15 T4 **Manic Trois, Réservoir** ▣ Québec, SE Canada
79 M20 **Maniema** off. Région du Maniema. ◆ region E Dem. Rep. Congo
Maniewicze see Manevychi
160 F8 **Maniganggo** Sichuan, C China
11 Y15 **Manigotagan** Manitoba, S Canada
153 R13 **Manihāri** Bihār, N India
191 U9 **Manihi** island Îles Tuamotu, C French Polynesia
190 L13 **Manihiki** atoll N Cook Islands
175 U8 **Manihiki Plateau** undersea feature C Pacific Ocean
196 M14 **Maniitsoq** var. Manitsoq, Dan. Sukkertoppen. Kita, S Greenland
153 T15 **Manikganj** Dhaka, C Bangladesh
152 M14 **Mānikpur** Uttar Pradesh, N India
171 N4 **Manila** off. City of Manila. ● (Philippines) Luzon, N Philippines
27 Y9 **Manila** Arkansas, C USA
189 N16 **Manila Reef** reef W Micronesia
183 T6 **Manilla** New South Wales, SE Australia
192 P6 **Maniloa** island Tongatapu Group, S Tonga
123 U8 **Manily** Koryakskiy Avtonomnyy Okrug, E Russian Federation
171 V12 **Manim, Pulau** island E Indonesia
168 I11 **Maninjau, Danau** ◎ Sumatera, W Indonesia
153 W13 **Manipur** ◆ state NE India
153 X14 **Manipur Hills** hill range E India
136 C14 **Manisa** var. Manissa; prev. Saruhan, anc. Magnesia. Manisa, W Turkey
136 C13 **Manisa** var. Manissa. ◆ province W Turkey
Manissa see Manisa
31 O7 **Manistee** Michigan, N USA
31 P7 **Manistee River** ≈ Michigan, N USA
31 O4 **Manistique** Michigan, N USA
31 P4 **Manistique Lake** ◎ Michigan, N USA
11 W13 **Manitoba** ◆ province S Canada
11 X16 **Manitoba, Lake** ◎ Manitoba, S Canada
11 X17 **Manitou** Manitoba, S Canada
31 N2 **Manitou Island** island Michigan, N USA
14 H11 **Manitou Lake** ◎ Ontario, SE Canada
12 G15 **Manitoulin Island** island Ontario, S Canada
37 T5 **Manitou Springs** Colorado, C USA
14 G12 **Manitouwabing Lake** ◎ Ontario, S Canada
12 E12 **Manitouwadge** Ontario, S Canada
12 G15 **Manitowaning** Manitoulin Island, Ontario, S Canada
14 B7 **Manitowik Lake** ◎ Ontario, S Canada
31 N7 **Manitowoc** Wisconsin, N USA
Manitsoq see Maniitsoq
139 O7 **Mānī', Wādī al** dry watercourse W Iraq
12 J14 **Maniwaki** Québec, SE Canada
171 W13 **Maniwori** Papua, E Indonesia
54 E10 **Manizales** Caldas, W Colombia
112 F11 **Manjača** ▲ NW Bosnia and Herzegovina
Manjacaze see Mandlakazi
180 J14 **Manjimup** Western Australia
109 V4 **Mank** Niederösterreich, C Austria
79 I17 **Mankanza** Equateur, NW Dem. Rep. Congo
153 N12 **Mankāpur** Uttar Pradesh, N India
26 M3 **Mankato** Kansas, C USA
29 U10 **Mankato** Minnesota, N USA
117 O7 **Man'kivka** Cherkas'ka Oblast', C Ukraine
76 M15 **Mankono** C Ivory Coast
11 T17 **Mankota** Saskatchewan, S Canada
155 K23 **Mankulam** Northern Province, N Sri Lanka
39 Q9 **Manley Hot Springs** Alaska, USA
18 H10 **Manlius** New York, NE USA
105 W5 **Manlleu** Cataluña, NE Spain
29 V11 **Manly** Iowa, C USA
154 E13 **Manmād** Mahārāshtra, W India
182 J7 **Mannahill** South Australia
155 J23 **Mannar** var. Manar. Northern Province, NW Sri Lanka
155 I24 **Mannar, Gulf of** gulf India/Sri Lanka
155 J23 **Mannar Island** island N Sri Lanka
Mannersdorf see Mannersdorf am Leithagebirge
109 Y5 **Mannersdorf am Leithagebirge** var. Mannersdorf. Niederösterreich, E Austria
109 Y6 **Mannersdorf an der Rabnitz** Burgenland, E Austria
101 G20 **Mannheim** Baden-Württemberg, SW Germany
11 O12 **Manning** Alberta, W Canada
29 T14 **Manning** Iowa, C USA
28 K5 **Manning** North Dakota, N USA
21 S13 **Manning** South Carolina, SE USA
191 Y2 **Manning, Cape** headland Kiritimati, NE Kiribati
21 S3 **Mannington** West Virginia, NE USA
182 A1 **Mann Ranges** ▲ South Australia
107 C19 **Mannu** ≈ Sardegna, Italy, C Mediterranean Sea
11 R14 **Mannville** Alberta, SW Canada
76 J15 **Mano** ≈ Liberia/Sierra Leone
Manø see Mandø
39 O13 **Manokotak** Alaska, USA
171 V12 **Manokwari** Papua, E Indonesia
79 N22 **Manono** Shaba, SE Dem. Rep. Congo
25 T10 **Manor** Texas, SW USA
97 D16 **Manorhamilton** Ir. Cluainín. NW Ireland
103 S15 **Manosque** Alpes-de-Haute-Provence, SE France
12 L11 **Manouane, Lac** ◎ Québec, SE Canada
163 W12 **Manp'o** var. Manp'ojin. NW North Korea
Manp'ojin see Manp'o
191 T4 **Manra** prev. Sydney Island. atoll Phoenix Islands, C Kiribati
105 V5 **Manresa** Cataluña, NE Spain
152 H9 **Mānsa** Punjab, NW India
82 J12 **Mansa** prev. Fort Rosebery. Luapula, N Zambia
76 G12 **Mansa Konko** C Gambia
15 Q11 **Manseau** Québec, SE Canada
149 U5 **Mānsehra** North-West Frontier Province, NW Pakistan
9 Q9 **Mansel Island** island Nunavut, NE Canada
183 O12 **Mansfield** Victoria, SE Australia
97 M18 **Mansfield** C England, UK
27 S11 **Mansfield** Arkansas, C USA
22 G6 **Mansfield** Louisiana, S USA
19 O12 **Mansfield** Massachusetts, NE USA
31 T12 **Mansfield** Ohio, N USA
18 G12 **Mansfield** Pennsylvania, NE USA
18 M7 **Mansfield, Mount** ▲ Vermont, NE USA
59 M16 **Mansidão** Bahia, E Brazil
102 L11 **Mansle** Charente, W France
76 G12 **Mansôa** C Guinea-Bissau
47 V8 **Manso, Rio** ≈ C Brazil
Manşûra see El Manşûra
Mansurabad see Mehrān, Rūd-e
56 A6 **Manta** Manabí, W Ecuador
56 A6 **Manta, Bahía de** bay W Ecuador
57 F14 **Mantaro, Río** ≈ C Peru
35 O8 **Manteca** California, W USA
54 J7 **Mantecal** Apure, C Venezuela
31 N11 **Manteno** Illinois, N USA
21 Y9 **Manteo** Roanoke Island, North Carolina, SE USA
Mantes-Gassicourt see Mantes-la-Jolie
103 N5 **Mantes-la-Jolie** prev. Mantes-Gassicourt, Mantes-sur-Seine, anc. Medunta. Yvelines, N France
Mantes-sur-Seine see Mantes-la-Jolie
36 L5 **Manti** Utah, W USA
Mantinea see Mantíneia
115 F20 **Mantíneia** anc. Mantinea. site of ancient city Pelopónnisos, S Greece
59 M21 **Mantiqueira, Serra da** ▲ S Brazil
29 W10 **Mantorville** Minnesota, N USA
115 G17 **Mantoúdi** var. Mandoudi; prev. Mandoúdhion. Évvoia, C Greece
Mantoue see Mantova
106 F8 **Mantova** Eng. Mantua, Fr. Mantoue. Lombardia, NW Italy
93 M19 **Mäntsälä** Etelä-Suomi, S Finland
93 L17 **Mänttä** Länsi-Suomi, W Finland
Mantua see Mantova
125 O14 **Manturovo** Kostromskaya Oblast', NW Russian Federation
93 M18 **Mäntyharju** Ita-Suomi, SE Finland
92 M13 **Mäntyjärvi** Lappi, N Finland
190 L16 **Manuae** island S Cook Islands
191 Q10 **Manuae** atoll Îles Sous le Vent, W French Polynesia
192 L16 **Manua Islands** island group E American Samoa
40 L5 **Manuel Benavides** Chihuahua, N Mexico
61 D21 **Manuel J.Cobo** Buenos Aires, E Argentina
58 M12 **Manuel Luís, Recife** reef E Brazil
61 F15 **Manuel Viana** Rio Grande do Sul, S Brazil
59 I14 **Manuel Zinho** Pará, N Brazil
191 V11 **Manuhangi** atoll Îles Tuamotu, C French Polynesia
185 E22 **Manuherikia** ≈ South Island, NZ
171 P13 **Manui, Pulau** island N Indonesia
Manukau see Manurewa
184 L6 **Manukau Harbour** harbour North Island, NZ
191 Z2 **Manulu Lagoon** ◎ Kiritimati, E Kiribati
182 J7 **Manunda Creek** seasonal river South Australia
57 K15 **Manupari, Río** ≈ N Bolivia
184 L6 **Manurewa** var. Manukau. Auckland, North Island, NZ
57 K15 **Manurimi, Río** ≈ NW Bolivia
186 D5 **Manus** ◆ province N PNG
186 D5 **Manus Island** var. Great Admiralty Island. island N PNG
171 T16 **Manuwui** Pulau Babar, E Indonesia
29 Q3 **Manvel** North Dakota, N USA
33 Z14 **Manville** Wyoming, C USA
22 G6 **Many** Louisiana, S USA
81 H21 **Manyara, Lake** ◎ NE Tanzania
126 L12 **Manych** var. Manich. ≈ SW Russian Federation
127 N13 **Manych-Gudilo, Ozero** salt lake SW Russian Federation
83 H14 **Manyinga** North Western, NW Zambia
105 O11 **Manzanares** Castilla-La Mancha, C Spain
44 H7 **Manzanillo** Granma, E Cuba
40 K14 **Manzanillo** Colima, SW Mexico
40 K14 **Manzanillo, Bahía** bay SW Mexico
37 S11 **Manzano Mountains** ▲ New Mexico, SW USA
37 R12 **Manzano Peak** ▲ New Mexico, SW USA
163 R6 **Manzhouli** var. Man-chou-li. Nei Mongol Zizhiqu, N China
Manzil Bū Ruqaybah see Menzel Bourguiba
139 X9 **Manzilīyah** E Iraq
83 L21 **Manzini** prev. Bremersdorp. C Swaziland
83 L21 **Manzini** × (Mbabane) C Swaziland
78 G10 **Mao** Kanem, W Chad
45 N8 **Mao** NW Dominican Republic
Maó see Mahón
Maoemere see Maumere
159 W9 **Maojing** Gansu, N China
171 Y14 **Maoke, Pegunungan** Dut. Sneeuw-gebergte, Eng. Snow Mountains. ▲ Papua, E Indonesia
Maol Réidh, Caoc see Mweelrea
160 M15 **Maoming** Guangdong, S China
160 H8 **Maoxian** var. Mao Xian; prev. Fengyizhen. Sichuan, C China
83 L19 **Mapai** Gaza, SW Mozambique
158 H15 **Mapam Yumco** ◎ W China
83 I15 **Mapanza** Southern, S Zambia
54 J4 **Mapararí** Falcón, N Venezuela
41 U17 **Mapastepec** Chiapas, SE Mexico
169 V9 **Mapat, Pulau** island N Indonesia
171 Y15 **Mapi** Papua, E Indonesia
171 V11 **Mapia, Kepulauan** island group E Indonesia
40 L8 **Mapimí** Durango, C Mexico
83 N19 **Mapinhane** Inhambane, SE Mozambique
55 N7 **Mapire** Monagas, NE Venezuela
11 S17 **Maple Creek** Saskatchewan, S Canada
31 Q9 **Maple River** ≈ Michigan, N USA
29 P7 **Maple River** ≈ North Dakota/South Dakota, N USA
29 S13 **Mapleton** Iowa, C USA
29 U10 **Mapleton** Minnesota, N USA

◆ Country ● Country Capital ◇ Dependent Territory ○ Dependent Territory Capital ◆ Administrative Region × International Airport ▲ Mountain ▲ Mountain Range ⚠ Volcano ≈ River ◎ Lake ▣ Reservoir

29 R5 **Mapleton** North Dakota, N USA
32 F13 **Mapleton** Oregon, NW USA
36 L3 **Mapleton** Utah, W USA
192 K5 **Mapmaker Seamounts** undersea feature N Pacific Ocean
186 B6 **Maprik** East Sepik, NW PNG
83 L21 **Maputo** prev. Lourenço Marques. ● (Mozambique) Maputo, S Mozambique
83 L21 **Maputo** ◈ province S Mozambique
83 L21 **Maputo** × Maputo, S Mozambique
67 V14 **Maputo** ≈ S Mozambique
Maqanshy see Makanchi
Maqat see Makat
113 K19 **Maqë** ≈ NW Albania
113 M19 **Maqellarë** Dibër, C Albania
159 S12 **Maqên** var. Dawo; prev. Dawu. Qinghai, C China
159 S11 **Maqên Kangri** ▲ C China
159 U12 **Maqu** var. Nyinma. Gansu, C China
104 M9 **Maqueda** Castilla-La Mancha, C Spain
82 B9 **Maquela do Zombo** Uíge, NW Angola
63 I16 **Maquinchao** Río Negro, C Argentina
29 Z13 **Maquoketa** Iowa, C USA
29 Y13 **Maquoketa River** ≈ Iowa, C USA
14 F13 **Mar** Ontario, S Canada
95 F14 **Mår** ◎ S Norway
81 G19 **Mara** ◈ region N Tanzania
191 P8 **Maraa** Tahiti, W French Polynesia
58 D12 **Maraã** Amazonas, NW Brazil
191 O8 **Maraa, Pointe** headland Tahiti, W French Polynesia
59 K14 **Marabá** Pará, NE Brazil
54 H5 **Maracaibo** Zulia, NW Venezuela
Maracaibo, Gulf of see Venezuela, Golfo de
54 H5 **Maracaibo, Lago de** var. Lake Maracaibo. inlet NW Venezuela
Maracaibo, Lake see Maracaibo, Lago de
58 K10 **Maracá, Ilha de** island NE Brazil
59 H20 **Maracaju, Serra de** ▲▲ S Brazil
58 I11 **Maracanaquará, Planalto** ▲▲ NE Brazil
54 L5 **Maracay** Aragua, N Venezuela
Marada see Marādah
75 R9 **Marādah** var. Marada. N Libya
77 U12 **Maradi** Maradi, S Niger
77 U11 **Maradi** ◈ department S Niger
81 E21 **Maragarazi** var. Muragarazi. ≈ Burundi/Tanzania
Maragha see Marāgheh
142 J3 **Marāgheh** var. Maragha. Āżarbāyjān-e Khāvarī, NW Iran
141 P7 **Marāh** var. Marrāt. Ar Riyāḍ, C Saudi Arabia
55 N11 **Marahuaca, Cerro** ▲ S Venezuela
27 R5 **Marais des Cygnes River** ≈ Kansas/Missouri, C USA
58 L11 **Marajó, Baía de** bay N Brazil
59 K12 **Marajó, Ilha de** island N Brazil
191 O2 **Marakei** atoll Tungaru, W Kiribati
Marakesh see Marrakech
81 I18 **Maralal** Rift Valley, C Kenya
83 G21 **Maraleng** Kgalagadi, S Botswana
145 U8 **Maraldy, Ozero** ◎ NE Kazakhstan
182 C5 **Maralinga** South Australia
Máramarossziget see Sighetu Marmației
187 N9 **Maramasike** var. Small Malaita. island N Solomon Islands
Maramba see Livingstone
194 H3 **Marambio** Argentinian research station Antarctica
116 H9 **Maramureș** ◈ county NW Romania
36 L15 **Marana** Arizona, SW USA
105 P7 **Maranchón** Castilla-La Mancha, C Spain
142 J2 **Marand** var. Merend. Āżarbāyjān-e Khāvarī, NW Iran
Marandellas see Marondera
58 L13 **Maranhão** off. Estado do Maranhão. ◈ state E Brazil
104 H10 **Maranhão, Barragem do** ▣ C Portugal
149 O11 **Mārān, Koh-i** ▲ SW Pakistan
106 J7 **Marano, Laguna di** lagoon NE Italy
56 E9 **Marañón, Río** ≈ N Peru
102 J10 **Marans** Charente-Maritime, W France
83 M20 **Marão** Inhambane, S Mozambique
185 B23 **Mararoa** ≈ South Island, NZ
Maraș/Marash see Kahramanmaraș
107 M19 **Maratea** Basilicata, S Italy
104 G11 **Marateca** Setúbal, S Portugal
115 B20 **Marathiá, Akrotírio** headland Zákynthos, Iónioi Nísoi, Greece, C Mediterranean Sea
12 E12 **Marathon** Ontario, S Canada
23 Y17 **Marathon** Florida Keys, Florida, SE USA
24 L10 **Marathon** Texas, SW USA
Marathón see Marathónas
115 H19 **Marathónas** prev. Marathón. Attikí, C Greece
169 W9 **Maratua, Pulau** island N Indonesia
59 O18 **Maraú** Bahia, SE Brazil
143 R3 **Marāveh Tappeh** Golestān, N Iran
24 L11 **Maravillas Creek** ≈ Texas, SW USA
186 D8 **Marawaka** Eastern Highlands, C PNG
171 Q7 **Marawi** Mindanao, S Philippines
137 Y11 **Mārāzā** Rus. Maraza. E Azerbaijan
Marbat see Mirbāṭ
104 L16 **Marbella** Andalucía, S Spain
180 J7 **Marble Bar** Western Australia
36 L9 **Marble Canyon** canyon Arizona, SW USA
25 S10 **Marble Falls** Texas, SW USA
27 Y7 **Marble Hill** Missouri, C USA
33 T15 **Marbleton** Wyoming, C USA
Marburg see Maribor
Marburg see Marburg an der Lahn, Germany
101 H16 **Marburg an der Lahn** hist. Marburg. Hessen, W Germany
111 H23 **Marcal** ≈ W Hungary
42 G7 **Marcala** La Paz, SW Honduras
111 H24 **Marcali** Somogy, SW Hungary
83 A16 **Marca, Ponta da** headland SW Angola
59 I16 **Marcelândia** Mato Grosso, W Brazil
27 T3 **Marceline** Missouri, C USA
60 I13 **Marcelino Ramos** Rio Grande do Sul, S Brazil
55 Y12 **Marcel, Mont** ▲ S French Guiana
97 O19 **March** E England, UK
109 Z3 **March** var. Morava. ≈ C Europe see also Morava
106 I12 **Marche** Eng. Marches. ◈ region C Italy
103 N11 **Marche** cultural region C France
99 J21 **Marche-en-Famenne** Luxembourg, SE Belgium
104 K14 **Marchena** Andalucía, S Spain
57 B17 **Marchena, Isla** var. Bindloe Island. island Galapagos Islands, Ecuador, E Pacific Ocean
Marches see Marche
99 J20 **Marchin** Liège, E Belgium
181 S1 **Marchinbar Island** island Wessel Islands, Northern Territory, N Australia
62 L9 **Mar Chiquita, Laguna** ◎ C Argentina
103 Q10 **Marcigny** Saône-et-Loire, C France
23 W16 **Marco** Florida, SE USA
Marcodurum see Düren
59 O15 **Marcolândia** Pernambuco, E Brazil
106 I8 **Marco Polo** × (Venezia) Veneto, NE Italy
Marcq see Mark
116 M8 **Mărculești** Rus. Markulesty. N Moldova
29 S12 **Marcus** Iowa, C USA
39 S11 **Marcus Baker, Mount** ▲ Alaska, USA
192 I5 **Marcus Island** var. Minami Tori Shima. island E Japan
18 K8 **Marcy, Mount** ▲ New York, NE USA
149 T5 **Mardān** North-West Frontier Province, N Pakistan
63 N14 **Mar del Plata** Buenos Aires, E Argentina
137 Q16 **Mardin** Mardin, SE Turkey
137 Q16 **Mardin** ◈ province SE Turkey
137 Q16 **Mardin Dağları** ▲▲ SE Turkey
162 J9 **Mardzad** Övörhangay, C Mongolia
187 R17 **Maré** island Îles Loyauté, E New Caledonia
Marea Neagră see Black Sea
Mare de Déu del Toro see El Toro
181 W4 **Mareeba** Queensland, NE Australia
96 G8 **Maree, Loch** ◎ N Scotland, UK
Mareeq see Mereeg
Marek see Dupnitsa
76 J11 **Maréna** Kayes, W Mali
190 I2 **Marenanuka** atoll Tungaru, W Kiribati
29 X14 **Marengo** Iowa, C USA
102 J11 **Marennes** Charente-Maritime, W France
107 G23 **Marettimo, Isola** island Isole Egadi, S Italy
24 K10 **Marfa** Texas, SW USA
57 P17 **Marfil, Laguna** ◎ E Bolivia
Marganets see Marhanets'
25 Q4 **Margaret** Texas, SW USA
180 I14 **Margaret River** Western Australia
186 C7 **Margarima** Southern Highlands, W PNG
55 N4 **Margarita, Isla de** island N Venezuela
115 I25 **Margarítes** Kríti, Greece, E Mediterranean Sea
97 Q22 **Margate** prev. Mergate. SE England, UK
23 Z15 **Margate** Florida, SE USA
Margelan see Marg'ilon
103 P13 **Margeride, Montagnes de la** ▲ C France
Margherita see Jamaame
107 N16 **Margherita di Savoia** Puglia, SE Italy
Margherita, Lake see Ābaya Hāyk'
81 E18 **Margherita Peak** Fr. Pic Marguerite. ▲ Uganda/Dem. Rep. Congo
149 O4 **Marghī** Bāmīān, N Afghanistan
116 G9 **Marghita** Hung. Margitta. Bihor, NW Romania
Margilan see Marg'ilon
147 S10 **Marg'ilon** var. Margelan, Rus. Margilan. Farg'ona Viloyati, E Uzbekistan
116 K8 **Marginea** Suceava, NE Romania
Margitta see Marghita
148 K9 **Mārgow, Dasht-e** desert SW Afghanistan
99 L18 **Margraten** Limburg, SE Netherlands
10 M15 **Marguerite** British Columbia, SW Canada
15 V3 **Marguerite** ≈ Québec, SE Canada
194 I6 **Marguerite Bay** bay Antarctica
Marguerite, Pic see Margherita Peak
117 T9 **Marhanets'** Rus. Marganets. Dnipropetrovs'ka Oblast', E Ukraine
186 B9 **Mari** Western, SW PNG
191 R12 **Maria** island Îles Australes, SW French Polynesia
191 Y12 **Maria** atoll Groupe Actéon, SE French Polynesia
40 I12 **María Cleofas, Isla** island C Mexico
62 H4 **María Elena** var. Oficina María Elena. Antofagasta, N Chile
95 G21 **Mariager** Århus, C Denmark
61 C22 **María Ignacia** Buenos Aires, E Argentina
183 P17 **Maria Island** island Tasmania, SE Australia
40 H12 **María Madre, Isla** island C Mexico
40 I12 **María Magdalena, Isla** island C Mexico
192 H6 **Mariana Islands** island group Guam/Northern Mariana Islands
175 N3 **Mariana Trench** var. Challenger Deep. undersea feature W Pacific Ocean
153 X12 **Mariāni** Assam, NE India
27 X11 **Marianna** Arkansas, C USA
23 R8 **Marianna** Florida, SE USA
172 J16 **Marianne** island Inner Islands, NE Seychelles
95 M19 **Mariannelund** Jönköping, S Sweden
61 D15 **Mariano I.Loza** Corrientes, NE Argentina
Mariano Machado see Ganda
111 A16 **Mariánské Lázně** Ger. Marienbad. Karlovarský Kraj, W Czech Republic
Máriaradna see Radna
33 S7 **Marias River** ≈ Montana, NW USA
Maria-Theresiopel see Subotica
Máriatölgyes see Dubnica nad Váhom
184 H1 **Maria van Diemen, Cape** headland North Island, NZ
109 V5 **Mariazell** Steiermark, E Austria
141 P15 **Mar'ib** W Yemen
95 I25 **Maribo** Storstrøm, S Denmark
109 W9 **Maribor** Ger. Marburg. NE Slovenia
Marica see Maritsa
35 R13 **Maricopa** California, W USA
Maricourt see Kangiqsujuaq
81 D15 **Maridi** Western Equatoria, SW Sudan
194 M11 **Marie Byrd Land** physical region Antarctica
193 P14 **Marie Byrd Seamount** undersea feature N Amundsen Sea
45 X11 **Marie-Galante** var. Ceyre to the Caribs. island SE Guadeloupe
45 Y6 **Marie-Galante, Canal de** channel S Guadeloupe
93 J20 **Mariehamn** Fin. Maarianhamina. Åland, SW Finland
44 C4 **Mariel** La Habana, W Cuba
99 H22 **Mariembourg** Namur, S Belgium
Marienbad see Mariánské Lázně
Marienburg see Alūksne, Latvia
Marienburg see Malbork, Poland
Marienburg see Feldioara, Romania
Marienburg in Westpreussen see Malbork
Marienhausen see Viļaka
83 D20 **Mariental** Hardap, SW Namibia
18 D13 **Marienville** Pennsylvania, NE USA
Marienwerder see Kwidzyń
58 C12 **Marié, Rio** ≈ NW Brazil
95 K17 **Mariestad** Västra Götaland, S Sweden
23 S3 **Marietta** Georgia, SE USA
31 U14 **Marietta** Ohio, N USA
27 N13 **Marietta** Oklahoma, C USA
81 H18 **Marigat** Rift Valley, W Kenya
103 S16 **Marignane** Bouches-du-Rhône, SE France
Marignano see Melegnano
45 O11 **Marigot** NE Dominica
122 K12 **Mariinsk** Kemerovskaya Oblast', S Russian Federation
127 Q3 **Mariinskiy Posad** Respublika Mariy El, W Russian Federation
119 E14 **Marijampolė** prev. Kapsukas. Marijampolė, S Lithuania
Marijampolė ◈ province SW Lithuania
114 G12 **Marikostenovo** Blagoevgrad, SW Bulgaria
60 J9 **Marília** São Paulo, S Brazil
82 D11 **Marimba** Malanje, NW Angola
139 T1 **Mārī Mīlā** E Iraq
104 G4 **Marín** Galicia, NW Spain
35 N10 **Marina** California, W USA
Marina di Catanzaro see Catanzaro Marina
Mar'ina Gorka see Mar"ina Horka
119 L17 **Mar"ina Horka** Rus. Mar'ina Gorka. Minskaya Voblasts', C Belarus
171 O4 **Marinduque** island C Philippines
31 S9 **Marine City** Michigan, N USA
31 N6 **Marinette** Wisconsin, N USA
60 I10 **Maringá** Paraná, S Brazil
83 N16 **Maringuè** Sofala, C Mozambique
104 F9 **Marinha Grande** Leiria, C Portugal
107 I15 **Marino** Lazio, C Italy
59 A15 **Mário Lobão** Acre, W Brazil
23 O5 **Marion** Alabama, S USA
27 Y11 **Marion** Arkansas, C USA
30 L17 **Marion** Illinois, N USA
31 P13 **Marion** Indiana, N USA
29 X13 **Marion** Iowa, C USA
27 O5 **Marion** Kansas, C USA
20 H6 **Marion** Kentucky, S USA
21 P9 **Marion** North Carolina, SE USA
31 S12 **Marion** Ohio, N USA
21 T12 **Marion** South Carolina, SE USA
21 Q7 **Marion** Virginia, NE USA
27 O5 **Marion Lake** ▣ Kansas, C USA
21 S13 **Marion, Lake** ▣ South Carolina, SE USA
27 S8 **Marionville** Missouri, C USA
55 N7 **Maripa** Bolívar, E Venezuela
55 X11 **Maripasoula** W French Guiana
35 Q9 **Mariposa** California, W USA
61 G19 **Mariscala** Lavalleja, S Uruguay
62 M4 **Mariscal Estigarribia** Boquerón, NW Paraguay
56 C6 **Mariscal Sucre** var. Quito. × (Quito) Pichincha, C Ecuador
30 K16 **Marissa** Illinois, N USA
103 U14 **Maritime Alps** Fr. Alpes Maritimes, It. Alpi Marittime. ▲▲ France/Italy
Maritimes, Alpes see Maritime Alps
Maritime Territory see Primorskiy Kray
114 K11 **Maritsa** var. Marica, Gk. Évros, Turk. Meriç; anc. Hebrus. ≈ SW Europe see also Évros/Meriç
Maritsa see Simeonovgrad
Marittime, Alpi see Maritime Alps
Maritzburg see Pietermaritzburg
117 X9 **Mariupol'** prev. Zhdanov. Donets'ka Oblast', SE Ukraine
55 Q6 **Mariusa, Caño** ≈ NE Venezuela
142 J5 **Marīvān** prev. Dezh Shāhpūr. Kordestān, W Iran
127 R3 **Mariyets** Respublika Mariy El, W Russian Federation
Mariyskaya ASSR see Mariy El, Respublika
118 G4 **Märjamaa** Ger. Merjama. Raplamaa, NW Estonia
99 I15 **Mark** Fr. Marcq. ≈ Belgium/Netherlands
81 N17 **Marka** var. Merca. Shabeellaha Hoose, S Somalia
145 Z10 **Markakol', Ozero** Kaz. Marqaköl. ◎ E Kazakhstan
76 M12 **Markala** Ségou, W Mali
159 S15 **Markam** var. Gartog. Xizang Zizhiqu, W China
95 K21 **Markaryd** Kronoberg, S Sweden
142 L7 **Markazī** off. Ostān-e Markazī. ◈ province W Iran
14 F14 **Markdale** Ontario, S Canada
27 X10 **Marked Tree** Arkansas, C USA
98 N11 **Markelo** Overijssel, E Netherlands
98 J9 **Markermeer** ◎ C Netherlands
97 N20 **Market Harborough** C England, UK
97 N18 **Market Rasen** E England, UK
123 O10 **Markha** ≈ NE Russian Federation
12 H16 **Markham** Ontario, S Canada
25 V12 **Markham** Texas, SW USA
186 E7 **Markham** ≈ C PNG
195 Q11 **Markham, Mount** ▲ Antarctica
110 M11 **Marki** Mazowieckie, C Poland
158 F8 **Markit** Xinjiang Uygur Zizhiqu, NW China
117 Y5 **Markivka** Rus. Markovka. Luhans'ka Oblast', E Ukraine
35 Q7 **Markleeville** California, W USA
98 L8 **Marknesse** Flevoland, N Netherlands
79 H14 **Markounda** var. Marcounda. Ouham, NW Central African Republic
Markovka see Markivka
123 U7 **Markovo** Chukotskiy Avtonomnyy Okrug, NE Russian Federation
127 P8 **Marks** Saratovskaya Oblast', W Russian Federation
22 K2 **Marks** Mississippi, S USA
22 I7 **Marksville** Louisiana, S USA
101 I19 **Marktheidenfeld** Bayern, C Germany
101 J24 **Marktoberdorf** Bayern, S Germany
101 M18 **Marktredwitz** Bayern, E Germany
Markt-Übelbach see Übelbach
27 V3 **Mark Twain Lake** ▣ Missouri, C USA
Markulesty see Mărculești
101 E14 **Marl** Nordrhein-Westfalen, W Germany
182 E2 **Marla** South Australia
181 Y8 **Marlborough** Queensland, E Australia
97 M22 **Marlborough** S England, UK
185 I15 **Marlborough** off. Marlborough District. ◈ unitary authority South Island, NZ
103 P3 **Marle** Aisne, N France
31 S8 **Marlette** Michigan, N USA
25 T9 **Marlin** Texas, SW USA
21 R5 **Marlinton** West Virginia, NE USA
26 M12 **Marlow** Oklahoma, C USA
155 E17 **Marmagao** Goa, W India
Marmanda see Marmande
102 L13 **Marmande** anc. Marmanda. Lot-et-Garonne, SW France
136 C11 **Marmara** Balıkesir, NW Turkey
136 D11 **Marmara Denizi** Eng. Sea of Marmara. sea NW Turkey
114 N13 **Marmaraereğlisi** Tekirdağ, NW Turkey
Marmara, Sea of see Marmara Denizi
136 C16 **Marmaris** Muğla, SW Turkey
28 J6 **Marmarth** North Dakota, N USA
21 Q5 **Marmet** West Virginia, NE USA
106 H5 **Marmolada, Monte** ▲ N Italy
104 M13 **Marmolejo** Andalucía, S Spain
14 J14 **Marmora** Ontario, SE Canada
39 Q14 **Marmot Bay** bay Alaska, USA
103 Q4 **Marne** ◈ department N France
103 Q4 **Marne** ≈ N France
137 U10 **Marneuli** prev. Borchalo, Sarvani. S Georgia
78 I13 **Maro** Moyen-Chari, S Chad
54 L12 **Maroa** Amazonas, S Venezuela
172 J3 **Maroantsetra** Toamasina, NE Madagascar
191 W11 **Marokau** atoll Îles Tuamotu, C French Polynesia
172 J5 **Marolambo** Toamasina, E Madagascar
172 J2 **Maromokotro** ▲ N Madagascar
83 L16 **Marondera** prev. Marandellas. Mashonaland East, NE Zimbabwe
55 X9 **Maroni** Dut. Marowijne. ≈ French Guiana/Suriname
183 V2 **Maroochydore-Mooloolaba** Queensland, E Australia
171 N14 **Maros** Sulawesi, C Indonesia
116 H11 **Maros** var. Mureş, Mureşul, Ger. Marosch, Mieresch. ≈ Hungary/Romania see also Mureş
Marosch see Maros/Mureş
Maroshévíz see Toplița
Marosillye see Ilia
Marosludas see Luduș
Marosújvár/Marosújvárakna see Ocna Mureș
Marosvásárhely see Târgu Mureș
191 V14 **Marotiri** var. Îlots de Bass, Morotiri. island group Îles Australes, SW French Polynesia
78 G12 **Maroua** Extrême-Nord, N Cameroon
55 X12 **Marouini Rivier** ≈ SE Suriname
172 I3 **Marovoay** Mahajanga, NW Madagascar
55 W9 **Marowijne** ◈ district NE Suriname
Marowijne see Maroni
Marqaköl see Markakol', Ozero
193 P8 **Marquesas Fracture Zone** tectonic feature E Pacific Ocean
Marquesas Islands see Marquises, Îles
23 W17 **Marquesas Keys** island group Florida, SE USA
29 Y12 **Marquette** Iowa, C USA
31 N3 **Marquette** Michigan, N USA
103 N1 **Marquise** Pas-de-Calais, N France
191 X7 **Marquises, Îles** Eng. Marquesas Islands. island group N French Polynesia
183 Q6 **Marra Creek** ≈ New South Wales, SE Australia
80 B10 **Marra Hills** plateau W Sudan
80 B11 **Marra, Jebel** ▲ W Sudan
74 E7 **Marrakech** var. Marakesh, Eng. Marrakesh; prev. Morocco. W Morocco
Marrakesh see Marrakech
Marrāt see Marāh
183 N15 **Marrawah** Tasmania, SE Australia
182 I4 **Marree** South Australia
81 L17 **Marrehan** ▲ SW Somalia
83 N17 **Marromeu** Sofala, C Mozambique
104 J17 **Marroquí, Punta** headland SW Spain
183 N8 **Marrowie Creek** seasonal river New South Wales, SE Australia
83 O14 **Marrupa** Niassa, N Mozambique
182 D1 **Marryat** South Australia
75 Y10 **Marsa 'Alam** SE Egypt
75 R8 **Marsa al Burayqah** var. Al Burayqah. N Libya
81 J17 **Marsabit** Eastern, N Kenya
107 H23 **Marsala** anc. Lilybaeum. Sicilia, Italy, C Mediterranean Sea
121 P16 **Marsaxlokk Bay** bay SE Malta
65 G15 **Mars Bay** bay Ascension Island, C Atlantic Ocean
101 H15 **Marsberg** Nordrhein-Westfalen, W Germany
11 R15 **Marsden** Saskatchewan, S Canada
98 H7 **Marsdiep** strait NW Netherlands
103 R16 **Marseille** Eng. Marseilles; anc. Massilia. Bouches-du-Rhône, SE France
Marseille-Marignane see Provence
30 M11 **Marseilles** Illinois, N USA
Marseilles see Marseille
76 J16 **Marshall** W Liberia
39 N11 **Marshall** Alaska, USA
27 U9 **Marshall** Arkansas, C USA
31 N14 **Marshall** Illinois, N USA
31 Q10 **Marshall** Michigan, N USA
29 S9 **Marshall** Minnesota, N USA
27 T4 **Marshall** Missouri, C USA
21 O9 **Marshall** North Carolina, SE USA
25 X6 **Marshall** Texas, SW USA
189 S4 **Marshall Islands** off. Republic of the Marshall Islands. ◆ republic W Pacific Ocean
175 Q3 **Marshall Islands** island group W Pacific Ocean
192 K6 **Marshall Seamounts** undersea feature SW Pacific Ocean
29 W13 **Marshalltown** Iowa, C USA
19 P12 **Marshfield** Massachusetts, NE USA
27 T7 **Marshfield** Missouri, C USA
30 K6 **Marshfield** Wisconsin, N USA
44 H1 **Marsh Harbour** Great Abaco, W Bahamas
19 S3 **Mars Hill** Maine, NE USA
21 P9 **Mars Hill** North Carolina, SE USA
22 H10 **Marsh Island** island Louisiana, S USA
21 S11 **Marshville** North Carolina, SE USA
15 W5 **Marsoui** Québec, SE Canada
15 R8 **Mars, Rivière à** ≈ Québec, SE Canada
95 O15 **Märsta** Stockholm, C Sweden
95 H24 **Marstal** Fyn, C Denmark
95 I19 **Marstrand** Västra Götaland, S Sweden
25 U8 **Mart** Texas, SW USA
166 M9 **Martaban** var. Moktama. Mon State, S Myanmar
166 L9 **Martaban, Gulf of** gulf S Myanmar
107 Q19 **Martano** Puglia, SE Italy
Martapoera see Martapura
169 T13 **Martapura** prev. Martapoera. Borneo, C Indonesia
99 L23 **Martelange** Luxembourg, SE Belgium
114 L7 **Marten** Ruse, N Bulgaria
14 H10 **Marten River** Ontario, S Canada
11 T15 **Martensville** Saskatchewan, S Canada
Marteskirch see Târnăveni
Martes Tolosane see Martres-Tolosane
115 K25 **Mártha** Kríti, Greece, E Mediterranean Sea
183 Q6 **Marthaguy Creek** ≈ New South Wales, SE Australia
19 P13 **Martha's Vineyard** island Massachusetts, NE USA
108 C11 **Martigny** Valais, SW Switzerland
103 R16 **Martigues** Bouches-du-Rhône, SE France
111 J19 **Martin** Ger. Sankt Martin, Hung. Turócszentmárton; prev. Turčiansky Svätý Martin. Žilinský Kraj, N Slovakia
28 L11 **Martin** South Dakota, N USA
20 G8 **Martin** Tennessee, S USA
105 S7 **Martín** ≈ E Spain
107 P18 **Martina Franca** Puglia, SE Italy
185 M14 **Martinborough** Wellington, North Island, NZ
25 S11 **Martindale** Texas, SW USA
35 N8 **Martinez** California, W USA
23 V3 **Martinez** Georgia, SE USA
41 Q13 **Martínez de La Torre** Veracruz-Llave, E Mexico
45 Y12 **Martinique** ◇ French overseas department E West Indies
1 O15 **Martinique** island E West Indies
Martinique Channel see Martinique Passage
45 X12 **Martinique Passage** var. Dominica Channel, Martinique Channel. channel Dominica/Martinique
23 Q5 **Martin Lake** ▣ Alabama, S USA
115 G18 **Martíno** prev. Martínon. Stereá Ellás, C Greece
Martínon see Martíno
194 J11 **Martin Peninsula** peninsula Antarctica
39 S5 **Martin Point** headland Alaska, USA
109 V3 **Martinsberg** Niederösterreich, NE Austria
21 V3 **Martinsburg** West Virginia, NE USA
31 V13 **Martins Ferry** Ohio, N USA
Martinskirch see Târnăveni
31 O14 **Martinsville** Indiana, N USA
21 S8 **Martinsville** Virginia, NE USA
65 K16 **Martin Vaz, Ilhas** island group E Brazil
Martök see Martuk
184 M12 **Marton** Manawatu-Wanganui, North Island, NZ
105 N13 **Martos** Andalucía, S Spain
102 M16 **Martres-Tolosane** var. Martes Tolosane. Haute-Garonne, S France
92 M11 **Martti** Lappi, NE Finland
144 I9 **Martuk** Kaz. Martök. Aktyubinsk, NW Kazakhstan
137 U12 **Martuni** E Armenia
58 L11 **Marudá** Pará, E Brazil
169 V6 **Marudu, Teluk** bay East Malaysia
149 O8 **Ma'rūf** Kandahār, SE Afghanistan
164 H13 **Marugame** Kagawa, Shikoku, SW Japan
185 H16 **Maruia** ≈ South Island, NZ
98 M6 **Marum** Groningen, NE Netherlands
187 R13 **Marum, Mount** ▲ Ambrym, C Vanuatu
79 P23 **Marungu** ▲▲ SE Dem. Rep. Congo
191 Y12 **Marutea** atoll Groupe Actéon, C French Polynesia
143 O11 **Marv Dasht** var. Mervdasht. Fārs, S Iran
103 P13 **Marvejols** Lozère, S France
27 X12 **Marvell** Arkansas, C USA
36 L6 **Marvine, Mount** ▲ Utah, W USA
139 Q7 **Marwānīyah** C Iraq
152 F13 **Mārwār** var. Marwar Junction. Rājasthān, N India
Marwar Junction see Mārwār
11 R14 **Marwayne** Alberta, SW Canada
146 I14 **Mary** prev. Merv. Mary Welaýaty, S Turkmenistan
Mary see Mary Welaýaty
181 Z9 **Maryborough** Queensland, E Australia
182 M11 **Maryborough** Victoria, SE Australia
Maryborough see Port Laoise
83 G23 **Marydale** Northern Cape, W South Africa
117 W8 **Mar"yinka** Donets'ka Oblast', E Ukraine
Mary Island see Kanton
21 W4 **Maryland** off. State of Maryland; also known as America in Miniature, Cockade State, Free State, Old Line State. ◈ state NE USA
25 P7 **Maryneal** Texas, SW USA
97 J15 **Maryport** NW England, UK
13 U13 **Marystown** Newfoundland and Labrador, SE Canada
36 K6 **Marysvale** Utah, W USA
35 O6 **Marysville** California, W USA
27 O3 **Marysville** Kansas, C USA
31 S13 **Marysville** Michigan, N USA
31 S9 **Marysville** Ohio, N USA

◆ Country
● Country Capital
◇ Dependent Territory
○ Dependent Territory Capital
◈ Administrative Region
× International Airport
▲ Mountain
▲▲ Mountain Range
✻ Volcano
≈ River
◎ Lake
▣ Reservoir

32 H7 **Marysville** Washington, NW USA
27 R2 **Maryville** Missouri, C USA
21 N9 **Maryville** Tennessee, S USA
146 I15 **Mary Welayaty** *var.* Mary, *Rus.* Maryyskiy Velayat. ◆ *province* S Turkmenistan
Maryyskiy Velayat *see* Mary Welaýaty
Marzūq *see* Murzuq
42 J11 **Masachapa** *var.* Puerto Masachapa. Managua, W Nicaragua
81 G19 **Masai Mara National Reserve** *reserve* C Kenya
81 I21 **Masai Steppe** *grassland* NW Tanzania
81 F19 **Masaka** SW Uganda
169 T15 **Masalembo Besar, Pulau** *island* S Indonesia
137 Y13 **Masallı** *Rus.* Masally. S Azerbaijan
Masally *see* Masallı
171 N13 **Masamba** Sulawesi, C Indonesia
Masampo *see* Masan
163 Y16 **Masan** *prev.* Masampo. S South Korea
Masandam Peninsula *see* Musandam Peninsula
81 J25 **Masasi** Mtwara, SE Tanzania
Masawa *see* Massawa
42 J10 **Masaya** Masaya, W Nicaragua
42 J10 **Masaya** ◆ *department* W Nicaragua
171 P5 **Masbate** Masbate, N Philippines
171 P5 **Masbate** *island* C Philippines
74 I6 **Mascara** *var.* Mouaskar. NW Algeria
173 O7 **Mascarene Basin** *undersea feature* W Indian Ocean
173 O9 **Mascarene Islands** *island group* W Indian Ocean
173 N9 **Mascarene Plain** *undersea feature* W Indian Ocean
173 O7 **Mascarene Plateau** *undersea feature* W Indian Ocean
194 H5 **Mascart, Cape** *headland* Adelaide Island, Antarctica
62 J10 **Mascasín, Salinas de** *salt lake* C Argentina
40 K13 **Mascota** Jalisco, C Mexico
15 O12 **Mascouche** Québec, SE Canada
124 J9 **Masel'gskaya** Respublika Kareliya, NW Russian Federation
83 J23 **Maseru** ● (Lesotho) W Lesotho
83 J23 **Maseru** ✕ W Lesotho
Mashaba *see* Mashava
160 K14 **Mashan** *var.* Baishan. Guangxi Zhuangzu Zizhiqu, S China
83 K17 **Mashava** *prev.* Mashaba. Masvingo, SE Zimbabwe
143 U4 **Mashhad** *var.* Meshed. Khorāsān, NE Iran
165 S3 **Mashike** Hokkaidō, NE Japan
Mashīz *see* Bardsīr
149 N14 **Mashkai** ↝ SW Pakistan
143 X13 **Māshkel** *var.* Rūd-i Māshkel, Rūd-e Māshkīd. ↝ Iran/Pakistan
148 K12 **Māshkel, Hāmūn-i** *salt marsh* SW Pakistan
Māshkel, Rūd-i/Māshkīd, Rūd-e *see* Māshkel
83 K15 **Mashonaland Central** ◆ *province* N Zimbabwe
83 K16 **Mashonaland East** ◆ *province* NE Zimbabwe
83 J16 **Mashonaland West** ◆ *province* NW Zimbabwe
Mashtagi *see* Maştağa
141 S14 **Masīlah, Wādī al** *dry watercourse* SE Yemen
79 I21 **Masi-Manimba** Bandundu, SW Dem. Rep. Congo
81 F17 **Masindi** W Uganda
81 I19 **Masinga Reservoir** ⊠ S Kenya
Masīra *see* Maşīrah, Jazīrat
Masira, Gulf of *see* Maşīrah, Khalīj
141 Y10 **Maşīrah, Jazīrat** *var.* Masīra. *island* E Oman
141 Y10 **Maşīrah, Khalīj** *var.* Gulf of Masira. *bay* E Oman
Masis *see* Büyükağrı Dağı
79 O19 **Masisi** Nord Kivu, E Dem. Rep. Congo
Masjed-e Soleymān *see* Masjed Soleymān
142 L9 **Masjed Soleymān** *var.* Masjed-e Soleymān, Masjid-i Sulaiman. Khūzestān, SW Iran
Masjid-i Sulaiman *see* Masjed Soleymān
Maskat *see* Masqaţ
139 Q7 **Maskhān** C Iraq
141 X8 **Maskin** *var.* Miskin. NW Oman
97 B17 **Mask, Lough** *Ir.* Loch Measca. ⊘ W Ireland
114 N10 **Maslen Nos** *headland* E Bulgaria
172 K3 **Masoala, Tanjona** *headland* NE Madagascar
Masohi *see* Amahai
31 Q9 **Mason** Michigan, N USA
31 R14 **Mason** Ohio, N USA
25 Q10 **Mason** Texas, SW USA
21 P4 **Mason** West Virginia, NE USA
185 B25 **Mason Bay** *bay* Stewart Island, NZ
30 K13 **Mason City** Illinois, N USA
29 V12 **Mason City** Iowa, C USA
Mă, Sông *see* Ma, Nam
18 B16 **Masontown** Pennsylvania, NE USA
141 Y8 **Masqaţ** *var.* Maskat, *Eng.* Muscat. ● (Oman) NE Oman
106 E10 **Massa** Toscana, C Italy
18 M11 **Massachusetts** *off.* Commonwealth of Massachusetts; also known as Bay State, Old Bay State, Old Colony State. ◆ *state* NE USA
19 P11 **Massachusetts Bay** *bay* Massachusetts, NE USA
35 R2 **Massacre Lake** ⊘ Nevada, W USA
107 O18 **Massafra** Puglia, SE Italy
108 G11 **Massagno** Ticino, S Switzerland
78 G11 **Massaguet** Chari-Baguirmi, W Chad
Massakori *see* Massakory
78 G10 **Massakory** *var.* Massakori; *prev.* Dagana. Chari-Baguirmi, W Chad
78 H11 **Massalassef** Chari-Baguirmi, SW Chad
106 F13 **Massa Marittima** Toscana, C Italy
82 B11 **Massangano** Cuanza Norte, NW Angola
83 M18 **Massangena** Gaza, S Mozambique
80 J9 **Massawa** *var.* Masawa, *Amh.* Mits'iwa. E Eritrea
80 K9 **Massawa Channel** *channel* E Eritrea
18 J6 **Massena** New York, NE USA
78 H11 **Massenya** Chari-Baguirmi, SW Chad
10 I13 **Masset** Graham Island, British Columbia, SW Canada
102 L16 **Masseube** Gers, S France
14 E11 **Massey** Ontario, S Canada
103 P12 **Massiac** Cantal, C France
103 P12 **Massif Central** *plateau* C France
Massilia *see* Marseille
31 U12 **Massillon** Ohio, N USA
77 N12 **Massina** Ségou, W Mali
83 N19 **Massinga** Inhambane, SE Mozambique
83 L20 **Massingir** Gaza, SW Mozambique
195 Z10 **Masson Island** *island* Antarctica
Massoukou *see* Franceville
137 Z11 **Maştağa** *Rus.* Mashtagi, Mastaga. E Azerbaijan
Mastanli *see* Momchilgrad
184 M13 **Masterton** Wellington, North Island, NZ
18 M14 **Mastic** Long Island, New York, NE USA
149 O10 **Mastung** Baluchistān, SW Pakistan
119 J20 **Mastva** *Rus.* Mostva. ↝ SW Belarus
119 G17 **Masty** *Rus.* Mosty. Hrodzyenskaya Voblasts', W Belarus
164 F12 **Masuda** Shimane, Honshū, SW Japan
92 J11 **Masugnsbyn** Norrbotten, N Sweden
Masuku *see* Franceville
83 K17 **Masvingo** *prev.* Fort Victoria, Nyanda, Victoria. Masvingo, SE Zimbabwe
83 K18 **Masvingo** *prev.* Victoria. ◆ *province* SE Zimbabwe
138 H5 **Maşyāf** *Fr.* Misiaf. Ḩamāh, C Syria
Masyû Ko *see* Mashū-ko
110 E9 **Maszewo** Zachodnio-pomorskie, NW Poland
83 I17 **Matabeleland North** ◆ *province* W Zimbabwe
83 J18 **Matabeleland South** ◆ *province* S Zimbabwe
82 O13 **Mataca** Niassa, N Mozambique
14 G8 **Matachewan** Ontario, S Canada
79 F22 **Matadi** Bas-Congo, W Dem. Rep. Congo
25 O4 **Matador** Texas, SW USA
42 J9 **Matagalpa** Matagalpa, C Nicaragua
42 K9 **Matagalpa** ◆ *department* W Nicaragua
12 I12 **Matagami** Québec, S Canada
25 U13 **Matagorda** Texas, SW USA
25 U13 **Matagorda Bay** *inlet* Texas, SW USA
25 U14 **Matagorda Island** *island* Texas, SW USA
25 V13 **Matagorda Peninsula** *headland* Texas, SW USA
191 Q8 **Mataiea** Tahiti, W French Polynesia
191 T9 **Mataiva** *atoll* Îles Tuamotu, C French Polynesia
183 O7 **Matakana** New South Wales, SE Australia
184 N7 **Matakana Island** *island* NE NZ
83 C15 **Matala** Huíla, SW Angola
190 G12 **Matala'a Pointe** *headland* Île Uvea, N Wallis and Futuna
155 K25 **Matale** Central Province, C Sri Lanka
190 E12 **Matalesina, Pointe** *headland* Île Alofi, W Wallis and Futuna
76 I10 **Matam** NE Senegal
184 M8 **Matamata** Waikato, North Island, NZ
77 V12 **Matameye** Zinder, S Niger
40 L8 **Matamoros** Coahuila de Zaragoza, NE Mexico
41 P15 **Matamoros** *var.* Izúcar de Matamoros. Puebla, S Mexico
41 Q8 **Matamoros** Tamaulipas, C Mexico
75 S13 **Ma'ţan as Sārah** SE Libya
82 J12 **Matanda** Luapula, N Zambia
81 J24 **Matandu** ↝ S Tanzania
15 V6 **Matane** Québec, SE Canada
15 V6 **Matane** ↝ Québec, SE Canada
77 S12 **Matankari** Dosso, SW Niger
39 R11 **Matanuska River** ↝ Alaska, USA
54 G7 **Matanza** Santander, N Colombia
44 D4 **Matanzas** Matanzas, NW Cuba
15 V7 **Matapédia** ↝ Québec, SE Canada
15 V6 **Matapédia, Lac** ⊘ Québec, SE Canada
190 B17 **Mata Point** *headland* SE Niue
190 D12 **Matapu, Pointe** *headland* Île Futuna, W Wallis and Futuna
62 G12 **Mataquito, Río** ↝ C Chile
155 K26 **Matara** Southern Province, S Sri Lanka
115 D18 **Matarágka** *var.* Mataránga. Dytikí Ellás, C Greece
170 K16 **Mataram** Pulau Lombok, C Indonesia
Mataránga *see* Matarágka
181 Q3 **Mataranka** Northern Territory, N Australia
105 W6 **Mataró** *anc.* Illuro. Cataluña, E Spain
184 O8 **Matata** Bay of Plenty, North Island, NZ
192 K16 **Matātula, Cape** *headland* Tutuila, W American Samoa
185 D24 **Mataura** Southland, South Island, NZ
185 D24 **Mataura** ↝ South Island, NZ
Mata Uta *see* Matā'utu
190 G11 **Matā'utu** *var.* Mata Uta. ○ (Wallis and Futuna) Île Uvea, Wallis and Futuna
192 H16 **Matāutu** Upolu, C Samoa
190 G12 **Matā'utu, Baie de** *bay* Île Uvea, Wallis and Futuna
191 P7 **Mataval, Baie de** *bay* Tahiti, W French Polynesia
190 I16 **Matavera** Rarotonga, S Cook Islands
191 V16 **Mataveri** Easter Island, Chile, E Pacific Ocean
191 V17 **Mataveri** ✕ (Easter Island) Easter Island, Chile, E Pacific Ocean
184 P9 **Matawai** Gisborne, North Island, NZ
15 O10 **Matawin** ↝ Québec, SE Canada
145 V13 **Matay** Almaty, SE Kazakhstan
14 K8 **Matchi-Manitou, Lac** ⊘ Québec, SE Canada
41 O10 **Matehuala** San Luis Potosí, C Mexico
45 V13 **Matelot** Trinidad, Trinidad and Tobago
83 M15 **Matenge** Tete, NW Mozambique
107 O18 **Matera** Basilicata, S Italy
111 O21 **Mátészalka** Szabolcs-Szatmár-Bereg, E Hungary
93 H17 **Matfors** Västernorrland, C Sweden
102 K11 **Matha** Charente-Maritime, W France
(0) F15 **Mathematicians Seamounts** *undersea feature* E Pacific Ocean
21 X6 **Mathews** Virginia, NE USA
25 S14 **Mathis** Texas, SW USA
152 J11 **Mathura** *prev.* Muttra. Uttar Pradesh, N India
Mathurai *see* Madurai
171 R7 **Mati** Mindanao, S Philippines
Matianus *see* Orūmīyeh, Daryācheh-ye
Matiara *see* Matiāri
149 Q15 **Matiāri** *var.* Matiara. Sind, SE Pakistan
41 S16 **Matías Romero** Oaxaca, SE Mexico
43 O13 **Matina** Limón, E Costa Rica
14 D10 **Matinenda Lake** ⊘ Ontario, S Canada
19 R8 **Matinicus Island** *island* Maine, NE USA
Matisco/Matisco Ædourum *see* Mâcon
149 Q16 **Mātli** Sind, SE Pakistan
97 M18 **Matlock** C England, UK
59 F18 **Mato Grosso** *prev.* Vila Bela da Santissima Trindade. Mato Grosso, W Brazil
59 G17 **Mato Grosso** *off.* Estado de Mato Grosso; *prev.* Matto Grosso. ◆ *state* W Brazil
60 H8 **Mato Grosso do Sul** *off.* Estado de Mato Grosso do Sul. ◆ *state* S Brazil
59 I18 **Mato Grosso, Planalto de** *plateau* C Brazil
104 G6 **Matosinhos** *prev.* Matozinhos. Porto, NW Portugal
Matou *see* Pingguo
55 Z10 **Matoury** NE French Guiana
Matozinhos *see* Matosinhos
111 L21 **Mátra** ▲ N Hungary
141 Y8 **Maţraḩ** *var.* Mutrah. NE Oman
116 L12 **Mătraşeşti** Vrancea, E Romania
108 M8 **Matrei Am Brenner** Tirol, W Austria
109 P8 **Matrei in Osttirol** Tirol, W Austria
76 I15 **Matru** SW Sierra Leone
75 U7 **Maţrūḩ** *var.* Mersa Maţrūḩ; *anc.* Paraetonium. NW Egypt
165 U16 **Matsubara** *var.* Matubara. Kagoshima, Tokuno-shima, SW Japan
164 G12 **Matsue** *var.* Matsuye, Matue. Shimane, Honshū, SW Japan
165 Q6 **Matsumae** Hokkaidō, NE Japan
164 M12 **Matsumoto** *var.* Matumoto. Nagano, Honshū, S Japan
164 K14 **Matsusaka** *var.* Matsuzaka, Matusaka. Mie, Honshū, SW Japan
161 S12 **Matsu Tao** *Chin.* Mazu Dao. *island* NW Taiwan
Matsutō *see* Mattō
164 F14 **Matsuyama** *var.* Matuyama. Ehime, Shikoku, SW Japan
Matsuye *see* Matsue
Matsuzaka *see* Matsusaka
164 M14 **Matsuzaki** Shizuoka, Honshū, S Japan
14 F8 **Mattagami** ↝ Ontario, S Canada
14 F8 **Mattagami Lake** ⊘ Ontario, S Canada
62 K12 **Mattaldi** Córdoba, C Argentina
21 Y9 **Mattamuskeet, Lake** ⊘ North Carolina, SE USA
21 W6 **Mattaponi River** ↝ Virginia, NE USA
14 I11 **Mattawa** Ontario, SE Canada
14 I11 **Mattawa** ↝ Ontario, SE Canada
19 S5 **Mattawamkeag** Maine, NE USA
19 S4 **Mattawamkeag Lake** ⊘ Maine, NE USA
108 D11 **Matterhorn** *It.* Monte Cervino. ▲ Italy/Switzerland *see also* Cervino, Monte
35 W1 **Matterhorn** ▲ Nevada, W USA
32 L12 **Matterhorn** *var.* Sacajawea Peak. ▲ Oregon, NW USA
35 R8 **Matterhorn Peak** ▲ California, W USA
109 Y5 **Mattersburg** Burgenland, E Austria
108 E11 **Matter Vispa** ↝ S Switzerland
55 R7 **Matthews Ridge** N Guyana
44 K7 **Matthew Town** Great Inagua, S Bahamas
109 Q4 **Mattighofen** Oberösterreich, NW Austria
107 N16 **Mattinata** Puglia, SE Italy
141 T9 **Maţţī, Sabkhat** *salt flat* Saudi Arabia/UAE
18 M14 **Mattituck** Long Island, New York, NE USA
164 L11 **Mattō** *var.* Matsutō. Ishikawa, Honshū, SW Japan
Matto Grosso *see* Mato Grosso
30 M14 **Mattoon** Illinois, N USA
57 L16 **Mattos, Río** ↝ C Bolivia
Mattu *see* Metu
169 R9 **Matu** Sarawak, East Malaysia
57 E14 **Matucana** Lima, W Peru
Matudo *see* Matsudo
Matue *see* Matsue
187 Y15 **Matuku** *island* S Fiji
112 B9 **Matulji** Primorje-Gorski Kotar, NW Croatia
Matumoto *see* Matsumoto
55 P5 **Maturín** Monagas, NE Venezuela
Matusaka *see* Matsusaka
Matuura *see* Matsuura
Matuyama *see* Matsuyama
126 K11 **Matveyev Kurgan** Rostovskaya Oblast', SW Russian Federation
127 O8 **Matyshevo** Volgogradskaya Oblast', SW Russian Federation
153 O13 **Mau** *var.* Maunāth Bhanjan. Uttar Pradesh, N India
83 O14 **Maúa** Niassa, N Mozambique
102 M17 **Maubermé, Pic de** *var.* Tuc de Moubermé, *Sp.* Pico Mauberme; *prev.* Tuc de Maubermé. ▲ France/Spain *see also* Moubermé, Tuc de
Mauberme, Pico *see* Maubermé, Pic de/Moubermé, Tuc de
Maubermé, Tuc de *see* Maubermé, Pic de/Moubermé, Tuc de
103 Q2 **Maubeuge** Nord, N France
166 L8 **Maubin** Irrawaddy, SW Myanmar
152 L13 **Maudaha** Uttar Pradesh, N India
183 N9 **Maude** New South Wales, SE Australia
195 P3 **Maudheimvidda** *physical region* Antarctica
65 N22 **Maud Rise** *undersea feature* S Atlantic Ocean
109 Q4 **Mauerkirchen** Oberösterreich, NW Austria
Mauersee *see* Mamry, Jezioro
188 K2 **Maug Islands** *island group* N Northern Mariana Islands
103 Q15 **Mauguio** Hérault, S France
193 N5 **Maui** *island* Hawai'i, USA, C Pacific Ocean
190 M16 **Mauke** *atoll* S Cook Islands
62 G13 **Maule** *off.* Región del Maule. ◆ *region* C Chile
102 J9 **Mauléon** Deux-Sèvres, W France
102 J16 **Mauléon-Licharre** Pyrénées-Atlantiques, SW France
52 G13 **Maule, Río** ↝ C Chile
63 G17 **Maullín** Los Lagos, S Chile
Maulmain *see* Moulmein
31 R11 **Maumee** Ohio, N USA
31 Q12 **Maumee River** ↝ Indiana/Ohio, N USA
27 U11 **Maumelle** Arkansas, C USA
27 T11 **Maumelle, Lake** ⊠ Arkansas, C USA
171 O16 **Maumere** *prev.* Maoemere. Flores, S Indonesia
83 G17 **Maun** Ngamiland, C Botswana
Maunāth Bhanjan *see* Mau
Maunawai *see* Waimea
190 H16 **Maungaroa** ▲ Rarotonga, S Cook Islands
184 K3 **Maungatapere** Northland, North Island, NZ
184 K4 **Maungaturoto** Northland, North Island, NZ
191 R10 **Maupiti** *var.* Maurua. *island* Îles Sous le Vent, W French Polynesia
152 K14 **Mau Rānīpur** Uttar Pradesh, N India
22 K9 **Maurepas, Lake** ⊘ Louisiana, S USA
103 T16 **Maures** ▲ SE France
103 O12 **Mauriac** Cantal, C France
Maurice *see* Mauritius
65 J20 **Maurice Ewing Bank** *undersea feature* SW Atlantic Ocean
182 C4 **Maurice, Lake** *salt lake* South Australia
18 I17 **Maurice River** ↝ New Jersey, NE USA
25 Y10 **Mauriceville** Texas, SW USA
98 K12 **Maurik** Gelderland, C Netherlands
76 H8 **Mauritania** *off.* Islamic Republic of Mauritania, *Ar.* Mūrītānīyah. ◆ *republic* W Africa
173 W15 **Mauritius** *off.* Republic of Mauritius, *Fr.* Maurice. ◆ *republic* W Indian Ocean
130 M17 **Mauritius** *island* W Indian Ocean
173 N9 **Mauritius Trench** *undersea feature* W Indian Ocean
102 H6 **Mauron** Morbihan, NW France
103 N13 **Maurs** Cantal, C France
Maurua *see* Maupiti
Maury Mid-Ocean Channel *see* Maury Seachannel
64 L6 **Maury Seachannel** *var.* Maury Mid-Ocean Channel. *undersea feature* N Atlantic Ocean
30 K8 **Mauston** Wisconsin, N USA
109 R8 **Mauterndorf** Salzburg, NW Austria
109 T4 **Mauthausen** Oberösterreich, N Austria
109 Q9 **Mauthen** Kärnten, S Austria
83 F15 **Mavinga** Cuando Cubango, SE Angola
83 M17 **Mavita** Manica, W Mozambique
115 K22 **Mavrópetra, Akrotírio** *headland* Thíra, Kykládes, Greece, Aegean Sea
115 F16 **Mavrovoúni** ▲ C Greece
184 Q8 **Mawhai Point** *headland* North Island, NZ
166 L3 **Mawlaik** Sagaing, C Myanmar
Mawlamyine *see* Moulmein
141 N14 **Mawr, Wādī** *dry watercourse* NW Yemen
195 X5 **Mawson** *Australian research station* Antarctica
195 X5 **Mawson Coast** *physical region* Antarctica
28 M4 **Max** North Dakota, N USA
41 W12 **Maxcanú** Yucatán, SE Mexico
Maxesibebi *see* Mount Ayliff
109 Q5 **Maxglan** ✕ (Salzburg) Salzburg, W Austria
93 K16 **Maxmo** *Fin.* Maksamaa. Länsi-Suomi, W Finland
21 T11 **Maxton** North Carolina, SE USA
25 R8 **May** Texas, SW USA
186 B6 **May** ↝ NW PNG
123 R10 **Maya** ↝ E Russian Federation
151 Q19 **Māyābandar** Andaman and Nicobar Islands, India, E Indian Ocean
Mayadin *see* Al Mayādīn
44 L5 **Mayaguana** *island* SE Bahamas
44 L5 **Mayaguana Passage** *passage* SE Bahamas
45 S6 **Mayagüez** W Puerto Rico
45 R6 **Mayagüez, Bahía de** *bay* W Puerto Rico
Mayals *see* Maials
79 G20 **Mayama** Le Pool, SE Congo
37 V8 **Maya, Mesa De** ▲ Colorado, C USA
143 R4 **Mayamey** Semnān, N Iran
42 F3 **Maya Mountains** *Sp.* Montañas Mayas. ▲ Belize/Guatemala
44 I7 **Mayarí** Holguín, E Cuba
Mayas, Montañas *see* Maya Mountains
18 J17 **May, Cape** *headland* New Jersey, NE USA
80 J11 **Maych'ew** *var.* Mai Chio, *It.* Mai Ceu. Tigray, N Ethiopia
138 I2 **Maydān Ikbiz** Ḩalab, N Syria
149 Q5 **Maydān Shahr** Wardag, E Afghanistan
80 O12 **Maydh** Sanaag, N Somalia
Maydī *see* Mīdī
Mayebashi *see* Maebashi
Mayence *see* Mainz
102 K6 **Mayenne** Mayenne, NW France
102 J6 **Mayenne** ◆ *department* NW France
102 J7 **Mayenne** ↝ N France
36 K12 **Mayer** Arizona, SW USA
22 J4 **Mayersville** Mississippi, S USA
11 P14 **Mayerthorpe** Alberta, SW Canada
21 S12 **Mayesville** South Carolina, SE USA
185 G19 **Mayfield** Canterbury, South Island, NZ
33 N14 **Mayfield** Idaho, NW USA
20 G7 **Mayfield** Kentucky, S USA
36 L5 **Mayfield** Utah, W USA
162 K9 **Mayhan** Övörhangay, C Mongolia
37 T14 **Mayhill** New Mexico, SW USA
145 T9 **Maykain** *Kaz.* Mayqayyng. Pavlodar, NE Kazakhstan
126 L14 **Maykop** Respublika Adygeya, SW Russian Federation
Maylibash *see* Maylybas
Mayli-Say *see* Mayluu-Suu
147 T9 **Mayluu-Suu** *prev.* Mayli-Say, *Kir.* Mayly-Say. Dzhalal-Abadskaya Oblast', W Kyrgyzstan
144 L14 **Maylybas** *prev.* Maylibash. Kzylorda, S Kazakhstan
Mayly-Say *see* Mayluu-Suu
Maymana *see* Meymaneh
166 M5 **Maymyo** Mandalay, C Myanmar
123 V7 **Mayn** ↝ NE Russian Federation
127 Q5 **Mayna** Ul'yanovskaya Oblast', W Russian Federation
21 N8 **Maynardville** Tennessee, S USA
14 J13 **Maynooth** Ontario, SE Canada
10 I6 **Mayo** Yukon Territory, NW Canada
23 U9 **Mayo** Florida, SE USA
97 B16 **Mayo** *Ir.* Maigh Eo. *cultural region* W Ireland
Mayo *see* Maio
78 G12 **Mayo-Kébbi** *off.* Préfecture du Mayo-Kébbi, *var.* Mayo-Kébi. ◆ *prefecture* SW Chad
Mayo-Kébi *see* Mayo-Kébbi
79 F19 **Mayoko** Le Niari, SW Congo
171 P4 **Mayon Volcano** ☗ Luzon, N Philippines
61 A24 **Mayor Buratovich** Buenos Aires, E Argentina
104 L4 **Mayorga** Castilla-León, N Spain
184 N6 **Mayor Island** *island* NE NZ
Mayor Pablo Lagerenza *see* Capitán Pablo Lagerenza
173 I14 **Mayotte** ◇ *French territorial collectivity* E Africa
Mayoumba *see* Mayumba
44 J13 **May Pen** C Jamaica
Mayqayyng *see* Maykain
171 O1 **Mayraira Point** *headland* Luzon, N Philippines
109 N8 **Mayrhofen** Tirol, W Austria
186 A6 **May River** East Sepik, NW PNG
123 R13 **Mayskiy** Amurskaya Oblast', SE Russian Federation
127 O15 **Mayskiy** Kabardino-Balkarskaya Respublika, SW Russian Federation
145 U9 **Mayskoye** Pavlodar, NE Kazakhstan
18 J17 **Mays Landing** New Jersey, NE USA
21 N4 **Maysville** Kentucky, S USA
27 R2 **Maysville** Missouri, C USA
79 D20 **Mayumba** *var.* Mayoumba. Nyanga, S Gabon
31 S8 **Mayville** Michigan, N USA
18 C11 **Mayville** New York, NE USA
29 Q4 **Mayville** North Dakota, N USA
Mayyali *see* Mahe
Mayyit, Al Baḩr al *see* Dead Sea
83 J15 **Mazabuka** Southern, S Zambia
Mazaca *see* Kayseri
Mazagan *see* El-Jadida
32 J7 **Mazama** Washington, NW USA
103 O15 **Mazamet** Tarn, S France
143 O4 **Māzandarān** *off.* Ostān-e Māzandarān. ◆ *province* N Iran
156 F7 **Mazar** Xinjiang Uygur Zizhiqu, NW China
107 H24 **Mazara del Vallo** Sicilia, Italy, C Mediterranean Sea
149 O2 **Mazār-e Sharīf** *var.* Mazār-i Sharif. Balkh, N Afghanistan
Mazār-i Sharif *see* Mazār-e Sharīf
105 R13 **Mazarrón** Murcia, SE Spain
105 R14 **Mazarrón, Golfo de** *gulf* SE Spain
55 S9 **Mazaruni** ↝ N Guyana
42 B6 **Mazatenango** Suchitepéquez, SW Guatemala
40 I10 **Mazatlán** Sinaloa, C Mexico
36 L12 **Mazatzal Mountains** ▲ Arizona, SW USA
118 D10 **Mažeikiai** Telšiai, NW Lithuania
118 D7 **Mazirbe** Talsi, NW Latvia
40 G5 **Mazocahui** Sonora, NW Mexico
57 I18 **Mazocruz** Puno, S Peru
Mazoe, Rio *see* Mazowe
79 N21 **Mazomeno** Maniema, E Dem. Rep. Congo
159 Q6 **Mazong Shan** ▲ N China
83 L16 **Mazowe** *var.* Rio Mazoe. ↝ Mozambique/Zimbabwe
110 L11 **Mazowieckie** ◆ *province* C Poland
Mazra'a *see* Al Mazra'ah
138 G6 **Mazraat Kfar Debiâne** C Lebanon
118 H7 **Mazsalaca** *Est.* Väike-Salatsi, *Ger.* Salisburg. Valmiera, N Latvia
110 L9 **Mazury** *physical region* NE Poland
119 M20 **Mazyr** *Rus.* Mozyr'. Homyel'skaya Voblasts', SE Belarus
107 K25 **Mazzarino** Sicilia, Italy, C Mediterranean Sea
Mba *see* Ba
83 L21 **Mbabane** ● (Swaziland) NW Swaziland
Mbacké *see* Mbaké
77 N16 **Mbahiakro** E Ivory Coast
79 I16 **Mbaïki** *var.* M'Baïki. Lobaye, SW Central African Republic
79 F14 **Mbakaou, Lac de** ⊘ C Cameroon
76 G11 **Mbaké** *var.* Mbacké. W Senegal
82 L11 **Mbala** *prev.* Abercorn. Northern, NE Zambia
83 J18 **Mbalabala** *prev.* Balla Balla. Matabeleland South, SW Zimbabwe
81 G18 **Mbale** E Uganda
79 E16 **Mbalmayo** *var.* M'Balmayo. Centre, S Cameroon
81 H25 **Mbamba Bay** Ruvuma, S Tanzania
79 I18 **Mbandaka** *prev.* Coquilhatville. Equateur, NW Dem. Rep. Congo
82 B9 **M'Banza Congo** *var.* Mbanza Congo; *prev.* São Salvador, São Salvador do Congo. Zaire, NW Angola
79 G21 **Mbanza-Ngungu** Bas-Congo, W Dem. Rep. Congo
67 V11 **Mbarangandu** ↝ E Tanzania
81 E19 **Mbarara** SW Uganda
79 L15 **Mbari** ↝ SE Central African Republic
81 I24 **Mbarika Mountains** ▲ S Tanzania
83 J24 **Mbashe** ↝ S South Africa
Mbatiki *see* Batiki
78 F13 **Mbé** Nord, N Cameroon
81 J24 **Mbemkuru** *var.* Mbwemkuru. ↝ S Tanzania
Mbengga *see* Beqa
172 H13 **Mbéni** Grande Comore, NW Comoros
83 K18 **Mberengwa** Midlands, S Zimbabwe
81 G24 **Mbeya** Mbeya, SW Tanzania
81 G23 **Mbeya** ◆ *region* S Tanzania
79 E19 **Mbigou** Ngounié, C Gabon
Mbilua *see* Vella Lavella
79 F19 **Mbinda** Le Niari, SW Congo
79 D17 **Mbini** W Equatorial Guinea
Mbini *see* Uolo, Río
83 L18 **Mbizi** Masvingo, SE Zimbabwe
81 G23 **Mbogo** Mbeya, W Tanzania
79 N15 **Mboki** Haut-Mbomou, SE Central African Republic
79 G18 **Mbomo** Cuvette, NW Congo
79 L15 **Mbomou** ◆ *prefecture* SE Central African Republic
Mbomou/M'Bomu/Mbomu *see* Bomu
76 F11 **Mbour** W Senegal
76 I10 **Mbout** Gorgol, S Mauritania
79 J14 **Mbrès** *var.* Mbrés. Nana-Grébizi, C Central African Republic
79 L22 **Mbuji-Mayi** *prev.* Bakwanga. Kasai Oriental, S Dem. Rep. Congo
81 H21 **Mbulu** Arusha, N Tanzania
186 E5 **M'bunai** *var.* Bunai. Manus Island, N PNG
62 N8 **Mburucuyá** Corrientes, NE Argentina
Mbutha *see* Buca
Mbwemkuru *see* Mbemkuru
81 G21 **Mbwikwe** Singida, C Tanzania
13 O15 **McAdam** New Brunswick, SE Canada
25 O5 **McAdoo** Texas, SW USA
35 V2 **McAfee Peak** ▲ Nevada, W USA
27 P11 **McAlester** Oklahoma, C USA
25 S17 **McAllen** Texas, SW USA
21 S11 **McBee** South Carolina, SE USA
11 N14 **McBride** British Columbia, SW Canada
24 M9 **McCamey** Texas, SW USA
33 R15 **McCammon** Idaho, NW USA
35 X11 **McCarran** ✕ (Las Vegas) Nevada, W USA
39 T11 **McCarthy** Alaska, USA
30 M5 **McCaslin Mountain** *hill* Wisconsin, N USA
25 O2 **McClellan Creek** ↝ Texas, SW USA
21 T14 **McClellanville** South Carolina, SE USA
8 L6 **McClintock Channel** *channel* Nunavut, N Canada
195 R12 **McClintock, Mount** ▲ Antarctica

◆ COUNTRY ● COUNTRY CAPITAL ◇ DEPENDENT TERRITORY ○ DEPENDENT TERRITORY CAPITAL ◆ ADMINISTRATIVE REGION ✕ INTERNATIONAL AIRPORT ▲ MOUNTAIN ▲ MOUNTAIN RANGE ☗ VOLCANO ↝ RIVER ⊘ LAKE ⊠ RESERVOIR

35 N2 McCloud California, W USA
35 N3 McCloud River ≈ California, W USA
35 Q9 McClure, Lake ⊠ California, W USA
197 O8 McClure Strait *strait* Northwest Territories, N Canada
29 N4 McClusky North Dakota, N USA
21 T11 McColl South Carolina, SE USA
22 K7 McComb Mississippi, S USA
18 E16 McConnellsburg Pennsylvania, NE USA
31 T14 McConnelsville Ohio, N USA
28 M17 McCook Nebraska, C USA
21 P13 McCormick South Carolina, SE USA
11 W16 McCreary Manitoba, S Canada
27 W11 McCrory Arkansas, C USA
25 T10 McDade Texas, SW USA
23 O8 McDavid Florida, SE USA
35 T1 McDermitt Nevada, W USA
23 S4 McDonough Georgia, SE USA
36 L12 McDowell Mountains ⛰ Arizona, SW USA
20 H8 McEwen Tennessee, S USA
35 R12 McFarland California, W USA
McFarlane, Lake *see* Macfarlane, Lake
27 P12 McGee Creek Lake ⊠ Oklahoma, C USA
27 W13 McGehee Arkansas, C USA
35 X5 Mcgill Nevada, W USA
14 K11 McGillivray, Lac ◎ Québec, SE Canada
39 P10 Mcgrath Alaska, USA
25 T8 McGregor Texas, SW USA
33 O12 McGuire, Mount ▲ Idaho, NW USA
83 M14 Mchinji *prev.* Fort Manning. Central, W Malawi
28 M7 McIntosh South Dakota, N USA
9 S7 McKeand ≈ Baffin Island, Nunavut, NE Canada
191 R4 McKean Island *island* Phoenix Islands, C Kiribati
30 J13 McKee Creek ≈ Illinois, N USA
18 C15 Mckeesport Pennsylvania, NE USA
21 V7 McKenney Virginia, NE USA
20 G8 McKenzie Tennessee, S USA
185 B20 McKerrow, Lake ◎ South Island, NZ
39 Q10 McKinley, Mount *var.* Denali. ▲ Alaska, USA
39 R10 McKinley Park Alaska, USA
34 K3 McKinleyville California, W USA
25 U6 McKinney Texas, SW USA
26 I5 McKinney, Lake ◎ Kansas, C USA
28 M7 McLaughlin South Dakota, N USA
25 O2 McLean Texas, SW USA
30 M16 Mcleansboro Illinois, N USA
11 O13 McLennan Alberta, W Canada
14 L9 McLennan, Lac ◎ Québec, SE Canada
10 M13 McLeod Lake British Columbia, W Canada
27 N10 McLoud Oklahoma, C USA
32 G15 McLoughlin, Mount ▲ Oregon, NW USA
8 J4 M'Clure Strait *strait* NW Canada
37 U15 McMillan, Lake ⊠ New Mexico, SW USA
32 G11 McMinnville Oregon, NW USA
20 K9 McMinnville Tennessee, S USA
195 R13 McMurdo *US research station* Antarctica
24 H9 McNary Texas, SW USA
37 N13 Mcnary Arizona, SW USA
27 N5 McPherson Kansas, C USA
McPherson *see* Fort McPherson
23 U6 McRae Georgia, SE USA
29 P4 McVille North Dakota, N USA
83 J25 Mdantsane Eastern Cape, SE South Africa
167 T6 Me Ninh Binh, N Vietnam
26 J7 Meade Kansas, C USA
39 O5 Meade River ≈ Alaska, USA
35 Y11 Mead, Lake ⊠ Arizona/Nevada, W USA
24 M5 Meadow Texas, SW USA
11 S14 Meadow Lake Saskatchewan, C Canada
35 Y10 Meadow Valley Wash ≈ Nevada, W USA
22 J7 Meadville Mississippi, S USA
18 B12 Meadville Pennsylvania, NE USA
14 F14 Meaford Ontario, S Canada
Meáin, Inis *see* Inishmaan
104 G8 Mealhada Aveiro, N Portugal
13 R8 Mealy Mountains ⛰ Newfoundland and Labrador, E Canada
11 O10 Meander River Alberta, W Canada
32 E11 Meares, Cape *headland* Oregon, NW USA
47 V6 Mearim, Rio ≈ NE Brazil
Measca, Loch *see* Mask, Lough
97 F17 Meath *Ir.* An Mhí. *cultural region* E Ireland
11 T14 Meath Park Saskatchewan, S Canada
103 O5 Meaux Seine-et-Marne, N France
21 T9 Mebane North Carolina, SE USA
171 U12 Mebo, Gunung ▲ Papua, E Indonesia
94 I8 Mebonden Sør-Trøndelag, S Norway
82 A10 Mebridege ≈ NW Angola
35 W16 Mecca California, W USA
Mecca *see* Makkah
29 Y14 Mechanicsville Iowa, C USA
18 L10 Mechanicville New York, NE USA
99 H17 Mechelen *Eng.* Mechlin, *Fr.* Malines. Antwerpen, C Belgium
188 C8 Mecherchar *var.* Eil Malk. *island* Palau Islands, Palau
101 D17 Mechernich Nordrhein-Westfalen, W Germany
126 L12 Mechetinskaya Rostovskaya Oblast', SW Russian Federation
114 J11 Mechka ≈ S Bulgaria
Mechlin *see* Mechelen
61 D23 Mechongué Buenos Aires, E Argentina
115 L14 Mecidiye Edirne, NW Turkey
101 I24 Meckenbeuren Baden-Württemberg, S Germany
100 L8 Mecklenburger Bucht *bay* N Germany
100 M10 Mecklenburgische Seenplatte *wetland* NE Germany
100 L9 Mecklenburg-Vorpommern ◈ *state* NE Germany
83 Q15 Meconta Nampula, NE Mozambique
111 I25 Mecsek ⛰ SW Hungary
83 P14 Mecubúri ≈ N Mozambique
83 Q14 Mecúfi Cabo Delgado, NE Mozambique
82 O13 Mecula Niassa, N Mozambique
168 I8 Medan Sumatera, E Indonesia
61 A24 Médanos *var.* Medanos. Buenos Aires, E Argentina
61 C19 Médanos Entre Ríos, E Argentina
155 K24 Medawachchiya North Central Province, N Sri Lanka
106 C8 Mede Lombardia, N Italy
74 J5 Médéa *var.* El Mediyya, Lemdiyya. N Algeria
Medeba *see* Ma'dabā
54 E8 Medellín Antioquia, NW Colombia
100 H9 Medem ≈ NW Germany
98 J8 Medemblik Noord-Holland, NW Netherlands
75 N7 Médenine *var.* Madanīyīn. SE Tunisia
76 G9 Mederdra Trarza, SW Mauritania
Medeshamstede *see* Peterborough
42 F4 Medesto Mendez Izabal, NE Guatemala
19 O11 Medford Massachusetts, NE USA
27 N8 Medford Oklahoma, C USA
32 G15 Medford Oregon, NW USA
30 K6 Medford Wisconsin, N USA
39 P10 Medfra Alaska, USA
116 M14 Medgidia Constanța, SE Romania
Medgyes *see* Mediaș
43 O5 Media Luna, Arrecifes de la *reef* E Honduras
60 G11 Medianeira Paraná, S Brazil
29 Y15 Mediapolis Iowa, C USA
116 I11 Mediaș *Ger.* Mediasch, *Hung.* Medgyes. Sibiu, C Romania
41 S15 Medias Aguas Veracruz-Llave, SE Mexico
Mediasch *see* Mediaș
106 G10 Medicina Emilia-Romagna, C Italy
33 X16 Medicine Bow Wyoming, C USA
37 S2 Medicine Bow Mountains ⛰ Colorado/Wyoming, C USA
33 X16 Medicine Bow River ≈ Wyoming, C USA
11 R17 Medicine Hat Alberta, SW Canada
26 L7 Medicine Lodge Kansas, C USA
26 L7 Medicine Lodge River ≈ Kansas/Oklahoma, C USA
112 E7 Međimurje *off.* Međimurska Županija. ◈ *province* N Croatia
Međimurska Županija *see* Međimurje
54 G10 Medina Cundinamarca, C Colombia
18 E9 Medina New York, NE USA
29 O5 Medina North Dakota, N USA
31 T11 Medina Ohio, N USA
25 Q11 Medina Texas, SW USA
Medina *see* Al Madīnah
105 P6 Medinaceli Castilla-León, N Spain
104 L6 Medina del Campo Castilla-León, N Spain
104 L5 Medina de Ríoseco Castilla-León, N Spain
Médina Gonassé *see* Médina Gounas
76 H12 Médina Gounas *var.* Médina Gonassé. S Senegal
25 S12 Medina River ≈ Texas, SW USA
104 K16 Medina Sidonia Andalucía, S Spain
Medinat Israel *see* Israel
119 H14 Medininkai Vilnius, SE Lithuania
153 R16 Medinīpur West Bengal, NE India
Mediolanum *see* Saintes, France
Mediolanum *see* Milano, Italy
Mediomatrica *see* Metz
121 Q11 Mediterranean Ridge *undersea feature* C Mediterranean Sea
121 O16 Mediterranean Sea *Fr.* Mer Méditerranée. *sea* Africa/Asia/Europe
Méditerranée, Mer *see* Mediterranean Sea
79 N17 Medje Orientale, NE Dem. Rep. Congo
114 G7 Medkovets Montana, NW Bulgaria
93 J15 Medle Västerbotten, N Sweden
127 W7 Mednogorsk Orenburgskaya Oblast', W Russian Federation
123 W9 Mednyy, Ostrov *island* E Russian Federation
102 J12 Médoc *cultural region* SW France
159 Q16 Mêdog Xizang Zizhiqu, W China
28 J5 Medora North Dakota, N USA
79 E17 Médouneu Woleu-Ntem, N Gabon
106 I7 Meduna ≈ NE Italy
Medunta *see* Mantes-la-Jolie
Medveditsa *see* Medvedytsa
126 J16 Medveditsa *var.* Medvedica. ≈ W Russian Federation
127 O9 Medveditsa ≈ SW Russian Federation
112 E8 Medvednica ⛰ NE Croatia
125 R15 Medvedok Kirovskaya Oblast', NW Russian Federation
123 S6 Medvezh'i, Ostrova *island group* NE Russian Federation
124 J9 Medvezh'yegorsk Respublika Kareliya, NW Russian Federation
109 T11 Medvode *Ger.* Zwischenwässern. NW Slovenia
126 J4 Medyn' Kaluzhskaya Oblast', W Russian Federation
180 J10 Meekatharra Western Australia
37 Q4 Meeker Colorado, C USA
13 T12 Meelpaeg Lake ◎ Newfoundland and Labrador, E Canada
Meenen *see* Menen
101 M16 Meerane Sachsen, E Germany
101 D15 Meerbusch Nordrhein-Westfalen, W Germany
98 I12 Meerkerk Zuid-Holland, C Netherlands
99 L18 Meerssen *var.* Mersen. Limburg, SE Netherlands
152 J10 Meerut Uttar Pradesh, N India
33 U13 Meeteetse Wyoming, C USA
99 K17 Meeuwen Limburg, NE Belgium
81 J16 Mēga Oromo, C Ethiopia
81 J16 Mēga Escarpment *escarpment* S Ethiopia
Megála Kalívia *see* Megála Kalývia
115 E16 Megála Kalývia *var.* Megála Kalívia. Thessalía, C Greece
115 H14 Megáli Panagiá *var.* Megáli Panayía. Kentrikí Makedonía, N Greece
Megáli Panayía *see* Megáli Panagiá
Megáli Préspa, Límni *see* Prespa, Lake
114 K12 Megálo Livádi ▲ Bulgaria/Greece
115 E20 Megalópoli *prev.* Megalópolis. Pelopónnisos, S Greece
Megalópolis *see* Megalópoli
171 U12 Megamo Papua, E Indonesia
115 C18 Meganísi *island* Iónioi Nísoi, Greece, C Mediterranean Sea
Meganom, Mys *see* Mehanom, Mys
Mégantic *see* Lac-Mégantic
15 R12 Mégantic, Mont ▲ Québec, SE Canada
115 G19 Mégara Attikí, C Greece
25 R5 Megargel Texas, SW USA
98 K13 Megen Noord-Brabant, S Netherlands
153 U13 Meghālaya ◈ *state* NE India
153 U16 Meghna ≈ S Bangladesh
137 V14 Meghri *Rus.* Megri. SE Armenia
115 Q23 Megísti *var.* Kastellórizon. *island* SE Greece
Megri *see* Meghri
Mehabad *see* Mahābād
116 F13 Mehadia *Hung.* Mehádia. Caraș-Severin, SW Romania
92 L7 Mehamn Finnmark, N Norway
117 U13 Mehanom, Mys *Rus.* Mys Meganom. *headland* S Ukraine
149 P14 Mehar Sind, SE Pakistan
180 J8 Meharry, Mount ▲ Western Australia
Mehdia *see* Mahdia
116 G14 Mehedinți ◈ *county* SW Romania
153 S15 Meherpur Khulna, W Bangladesh
21 W8 Meherrin River ≈ North Carolina/Virginia, SE USA
Meheso *see* Mī'ēso
191 T11 Mehetia *island* Îles du Vent, W French Polynesia
118 K6 Mehikoorma Tartumaa, E Estonia
Me Hka *see* Nmai Hka
143 N5 Mehrabad × (Tehrān) Tehrān, N Iran
142 J7 Mehrān Īlām, W Iran
143 Q14 Mehrān, Rūd-e *prev.* Mansurabad. ≈ W Iran
143 Q9 Mehrīz Yazd, C Iran
149 R5 Mehtarlām *var.* Mehtar Lām, Meterlam, Methariam, Metharlam. Laghmān, E Afghanistan
103 N8 Mehun-sur-Yèvre Cher, C France
79 G14 Meiganga Adamaoua, NE Cameroon
160 H10 Meigu *var.* Bapu. Sichuan, C China
163 W11 Meihekou *var.* Hailong. Jilin, NE China
99 L15 Meijel Limburg, SE Netherlands
Meijiang *see* Ningdu
166 M5 Meiktila Mandalay, C Myanmar
Meilbhe, Loch *see* Melvin, Lough
108 G7 Meilen Zürich, N Switzerland
Meilu *see* Wuchuan
161 T12 Meinhua Yu *island* N Taiwan
101 J17 Meiningen Thüringen, C Germany
108 F9 Meiringen Bern, S Switzerland
Meishan *see* Jinzhai
101 O15 Meissen *var.* Meißen. Sachsen, E Germany
101 I15 Meissner ▲ C Germany
99 K25 Meix-devant-Virton Luxembourg, SE Belgium
Mei Xian *see* Meizhou
Meixing *see* Xinjin
161 P13 Meizhou *var.* Meixian, Mei Xian. Guangdong, S China
67 P2 Mejerda *var.* Oued Medjerda, Wādī Majardah. ≈ Algeria/Tunisia *see also* Medjerda, Oued
42 F7 Mejicanos San Salvador, C El Salvador
Méjico *see* Mexico
62 G5 Mejillones Antofagasta, N Chile
189 V5 Mejit Island *var.* Mājeej. *island* Ratak Chain, NE Marshall Islands
79 F17 Mékambo Ogooué-Ivindo, NE Gabon
80 J10 Mek'elē *var.* Makale. Tigray, N Ethiopia
74 I10 Mekerrhane, Sebkha *var.* Sebkha Meqerghane, Sebkra Mekerrhane. *salt flat* C Algeria
Mekerrhane, Sebkra *see* Mekerrhane, Sebkha
76 G10 Mékhé NW Senegal
146 G14 Mekhinli Ahal Welaýaty, C Turkmenistan
15 P9 Mékinac, Lac ◎ Québec, SE Canada
Meklong *see* Samut Songhram
74 G6 Meknès N Morocco
131 U12 Mekong *var.* Lan-ts'ang Chiang, *Cam.* Mékôngk, *Chin.* Lancang Jiang, *Lao.* Mènam Khong, *Th.* Mae Nam Khong, *Tib.* Dza Chu, *Vtn.* Sông Tiên Giang. ≈ SE Asia
Mékôngk *see* Mekong
167 T15 Mekong, Mouths of the *delta* S Vietnam
38 L12 Mekoryuk Nunivak Island, Alaska, USA
77 R14 Mékrou ≈ N Benin
168 K9 Melaka *var.* Malacca. Melaka, Peninsular Malaysia
168 L9 Melaka *var.* Malacca. ◈ *state* Peninsular Malaysia
Melaka, Selat *see* Malacca, Strait of
175 O6 Melanesia *island group* W Pacific Ocean
175 P5 Melanesian Basin *undersea feature* W Pacific Ocean
171 R9 Melanguane Pulau Karakelang, N Indonesia
169 R11 Melawi, Sungai ≈ Borneo, N Indonesia
183 N12 Melbourne *state capital* Victoria, SE Australia
27 V9 Melbourne Arkansas, C USA
23 Y12 Melbourne Florida, SE USA
29 W14 Melbourne Iowa, C USA
92 G10 Melbu Nordland, C Norway
Melchor de Mencos *see* Ciudad Melchor de Mencos
63 F19 Melchor, Isla *island* Archipiélago de los Chonos, S Chile
40 M9 Melchor Ocampo Zacatecas, C Mexico
14 C11 Meldrum Bay Manitoulin Island, Ontario, S Canada
Meleda *see* Mljet
106 D8 Melegnano *prev.* Marignano. Lombardia, N Italy
188 F9 Melekeok *var.* Melekeiok. Babeldaob, N Palau
112 L9 Melenci *Hung.* Melencze. Serbia, N Serbia and Montenegro (Yugo.)
Melencze *see* Melenci
127 N4 Melenki Vladimirskaya Oblast', W Russian Federation
127 V6 Meleuz Respublika Bashkortostan, W Russian Federation
12 L6 Mélèzes, Rivière aux ≈ Québec, C Canada
78 I11 Melfi Guéra, S Chad
107 M17 Melfi Basilicata, S Italy
11 U14 Melfort Saskatchewan, S Canada
104 H4 Melgaço Viana do Castelo, N Portugal
105 N4 Melgar de Fernamental Castilla-León, N Spain
74 L6 Melghir, Chott *var.* Chott Melrhir. *salt lake* E Algeria
94 H8 Melhus Sør-Trøndelag, S Norway
104 H3 Melide Galicia, NW Spain
Meligalá *see* Meligalás
115 E21 Meligalás *prev.* Meligalá. Pelopónnisos, S Greece
60 L12 Mel, Ilha do *island* S Brazil
120 E10 Melilla *anc.* Rusaddir, Russadir. Melilla, Spain, N Africa
71 N1 Melilla *enclave* Spain, N Africa
63 G18 Melimoyu, Monte ▲ S Chile
169 V11 Melintang, Danau ◎ Borneo, N Indonesia
117 U7 Melioratyvne Dnipropetrovs'ka Oblast', E Ukraine
62 G11 Melipilla Santiago, C Chile
115 I25 Mélissa, Akrotírio *headland* Kríti, Greece, E Mediterranean Sea
11 W17 Melita Manitoba, S Canada
Melita *see* Mljet
Melitene *see* Malatya
107 M23 Melito di Porto Salvo Calabria, SW Italy
117 U10 Melitopol' Zaporiz'ka Oblast', SE Ukraine
109 V4 Melk Niederösterreich, NE Austria
95 K15 Mellan-Fryken ◎ C Sweden
99 E17 Melle Oost-Vlaanderen, NW Belgium
100 G13 Melle Niedersachsen, NW Germany
95 J17 Mellerud Västra Götaland, S Sweden
102 K10 Melle-sur-Bretonne Deux-Sèvres, W France
29 P8 Mellette South Dakota, N USA
121 O15 Mellieha E Malta
80 B10 Mellit Northern Darfur, W Sudan
75 N7 Mellita × SE Tunisia
63 G21 Mellizo Sur, Cerro ▲ S Chile
100 G9 Mellum *island* NW Germany
83 L22 Melmoth KwaZulu/Natal, E South Africa
111 D16 Mělník *Ger.* Melnik. Středočeský Kraj, NW Czech Republic
122 J12 Mel'nikovo Tomskaya Oblast', C Russian Federation
61 G18 Melo Cerro Largo, NE Uruguay
Melodunum *see* Melun
Melrhir, Chott *see* Melghir, Chott
183 P7 Melrose New South Wales, SE Australia
182 I7 Melrose South Australia
29 T7 Melrose Minnesota, N USA
33 Q11 Melrose Montana, NW USA
37 V12 Melrose New Mexico, SW USA
108 I8 Mels Sankt Gallen, NE Switzerland
Melsetter *see* Chimanimani
33 V9 Melstone Montana, NW USA
101 I16 Melsungen Hessen, C Germany
92 L12 Meltaus Lappi, NW Finland
97 N19 Melton Mowbray C England, UK
82 Q13 Meluco Cabo Delgado, NE Mozambique
103 O5 Melun *anc.* Melodunum. Seine-et-Marne, N France
80 F12 Melut Upper Nile, SE Sudan
27 P5 Melvern Lake ⊠ Kansas, C USA
11 V16 Melville Saskatchewan, S Canada
Melville Bay/Melville Bugt *see* Qimusseriarsuaq
45 O11 Melville Hall × (Dominica) NE Dominica
181 O1 Melville Island *island* Northern Territory, N Australia
8 K5 Melville Island *island* Parry Islands, Northwest Territories, NW Canada
9 W9 Melville, Lake ◎ Newfoundland and Labrador, E Canada
9 O7 Melville Peninsula *peninsula* Nunavut, NE Canada
Melville Sound *see* Viscount Melville Sound
25 Q9 Melvin Texas, SW USA
97 D15 Melvin, Lough *Ir.* Loch Meilbhe. ◎ S Northern Ireland, UK/Ireland
169 S12 Memala Borneo, C Indonesia
113 L22 Memaliaj Gjirokastër, S Albania
83 Q14 Memba Nampula, NE Mozambique
83 Q14 Memba, Baia de *inlet* NE Mozambique
Membidj *see* Manbij
Memel *see* Neman, NE Europe
Memel *see* Klaipėda, Lithuania
101 J23 Memmingen Bayern, S Germany
27 U1 Memphis Missouri, C USA
20 E10 Memphis Tennessee, S USA
25 P3 Memphis Texas, SW USA
20 E10 Memphis × Tennessee, S USA
15 Q13 Memphrémagog, Lac *var.* Lake Memphremagog. ◎ Canada/USA *see also* Memphremagog, Lake
19 N6 Memphremagog, Lake *var.* Lac Memphrémagog. ◎ Canada/USA *see also* Memphrémagog, Lac
117 Q2 Mena Chernihivs'ka Oblast', NE Ukraine
27 S12 Mena Arkansas, C USA
Menaam *see* Menaldum
Menado *see* Manado
106 D6 Menaggio Lombardia, N Italy
29 T6 Menahga Minnesota, N USA
77 R10 Ménaka Goa, E Mali
98 K5 Menaldum *Fris.* Menaam. Friesland, N Netherlands
Mènam Khong *see* Mekong
74 E7 Menara × (Marrakech) C Morocco
25 Q9 Menard Texas, SW USA
193 Q12 Menard Fracture Zone *tectonic feature* E Pacific Ocean
30 M7 Menasha Wisconsin, N USA
Mencezi Garagum *see* Merkezi Garagumy
193 U9 Mendaña Fracture Zone *tectonic feature* E Pacific Ocean
169 S13 Mendawai, Sungai ≈ Borneo, C Indonesia
103 P13 Mende *anc.* Mimatum. Lozère, S France
81 J14 Mendebo ⛰ C Ethiopia
80 J9 Mendefera *prev.* Adi Ugri. S Eritrea
197 S7 Mendeleyev Ridge *undersea feature* Arctic Ocean
127 T3 Mendeleyevsk Respublika Tatarstan, W Russian Federation
101 F15 Menden Nordrhein-Westfalen, W Germany
22 L6 Mendenhall Mississippi, S USA
38 L13 Mendenhall, Cape *headland* Nunivak Island, Alaska, USA
41 P9 Méndez *var.* Villa de Méndez. Tamaulipas, C Mexico
80 H13 Mendī Oromo, C Ethiopia
186 C7 Mendi Southern Highlands, W PNG
97 K22 Mendip Hills *var.* Mendips. *hill range* S England, UK
Mendips *see* Mendip Hills
34 L6 Mendocino California, W USA
34 J3 Mendocino, Cape *headland* California, W USA
(0) B8 Mendocino Fracture Zone *tectonic feature* NE Pacific Ocean
35 P10 Mendota California, W USA
30 L11 Mendota Illinois, N USA
30 K8 Mendota, Lake ◎ Wisconsin, N USA
62 I11 Mendoza Mendoza, W Argentina
62 I12 Mendoza *off.* Provincia de Mendoza. ◈ *province* W Argentina
108 H12 Mendrisio Ticino, S Switzerland
168 L10 Mendung Pulau Mendol, W Indonesia
54 I5 Mene de Mauroa Falcón, NW Venezuela
54 I5 Mene Grande Zulia, NW Venezuela
136 B14 Menemen İzmir, W Turkey
99 C18 Menen *var.* Meenen, *Fr.* Menin. West-Vlaanderen, W Belgium
163 Q8 Menengiyn Tal *plain* E Mongolia
189 R9 Meneng Point *headland* SW Nauru
92 L10 Menesjärvi *Lapp.* Menešjávri. Lappi, N Finland
Menešjávri *see* Menesjärvi
107 I24 Menfi Sicilia, Italy, C Mediterranean Sea
161 P7 Mengcheng Anhui, E China
160 F15 Menghai Yunnan, SW China
160 F15 Mengla Yunnan, SW China
65 F24 Menguera Point *headland* East Falkland, Falkland Islands
160 M13 Mengzhu Ling ⛰ S China
160 H14 Mengzi Yunnan, SW China
Menin *see* Menen
182 L7 Menindee New South Wales, SE Australia
182 L7 Menindee Lake ◎ New South Wales, SE Australia
182 J10 Meningie South Australia
103 O5 Mennecy Essonne, N France
29 Q12 Menno South Dakota, N USA
114 H13 Menoíkio ⛰ NE Greece
31 N5 Menominee Michigan, N USA
30 M5 Menominee River ≈ Michigan/Wisconsin, N USA
30 M8 Menomonee Falls Wisconsin, N USA
30 I6 Menomonie Wisconsin, N USA
83 D14 Menongue *var.* Vila Serpa Pinto, *Port.* Serpa Pinto. Cuando Cubango, C Angola
120 H8 Menorca *Eng.* Minorca; *anc.* Balearis Minor. *island* Islas Baleares, Spain, W Mediterranean Sea
105 S13 Menor, Mar *lagoon* SE Spain
39 S10 Mentasta Lake ◎ Alaska, USA
39 S10 Mentasta Mountains ⛰ Alaska, USA
168 I13 Mentawai, Kepulauan *island group* W Indonesia
168 I12 Mentawai, Selat *strait* W Indonesia
168 M12 Mentok Pulau Bangka, W Indonesia
103 V15 Menton *It.* Mentone. Alpes-Maritimes, SE France
24 K8 Mentone Texas, SW USA
Mentone *see* Menton
31 U11 Mentor Ohio, N USA
169 U10 Menyapa, Gunung ▲ Borneo, N Indonesia
159 T9 Menyuan *var.* Menyuan Huizu Zizhixian. Qinghai, C China
Menyuan Huizu Zizhixian *see* Menyuan
74 M5 Menzel Bourguiba *var.* Manzil Bū Ruqaybah; *prev.* Ferryville. N Tunisia
136 M15 Menzelet Barajı ⊠ C Turkey
127 T4 Menzelinsk Respublika Tatarstan, W Russian Federation
180 K11 Menzies Western Australia
195 V6 Menzies, Mount ▲ Antarctica
40 J6 Meoqui Chihuahua, N Mexico
83 N14 Meponda Niassa, NE Mozambique
98 M8 Meppel Drenthe, NE Netherlands
100 E12 Meppen Niedersachsen, NW Germany
Meqerghane, Sebkha *see* Mekerrhane, Sebkha
105 T6 Mequinenza, Embalse de ⊠ NE Spain
30 M8 Mequon Wisconsin, N USA
Mera *see* Maira
182 D3 Meramangye, Lake *salt lake* South Australia
27 W5 Meramec River ≈ Missouri, C USA
Meran *see* Merano
168 K13 Merangin ≈ Sumatera, W Indonesia
106 G5 Merano *Ger.* Meran. Trentino-Alto Adige, N Italy
168 K8 Merapuh Lama Pahang, Peninsular Malaysia
106 D7 Merate Lombardia, N Italy
169 U13 Meratus, Pegunungan ⛰ Borneo, N Indonesia
171 Y16 Merauke, Sungai ≈ Papua, E Indonesia
182 L9 Merbein Victoria, SE Australia
99 F21 Merbes-le-Château Hainaut, S Belgium
Merca *see* Marka
54 C13 Mercaderes Cauca, SW Colombia
Mercara *see* Madikeri
35 P9 Merced California, W USA
61 C20 Mercedes Buenos Aires, E Argentina
61 D15 Mercedes Corrientes, NE Argentina
62 J11 Mercedes *prev.* Villa Mercedes. San Luis, C Argentina
61 D19 Mercedes Soriano, SW Uruguay
25 S17 Mercedes Texas, SW USA
35 R9 Merced Peak ▲ California, W USA
35 P9 Merced River ≈ California, W USA
18 B13 Mercer Pennsylvania, NE USA
99 G18 Merchtem Vlaams Brabant, C Belgium
15 O13 Mercier Québec, SE Canada
25 Q9 Mercury Texas, SW USA
184 M5 Mercury Islands *island group* N NZ
19 O9 Meredith New Hampshire, NE USA
65 B25 Meredith, Cape *var.* Cabo Belgrano *headland* West Falkland, Falkland Islands
37 V6 Meredith, Lake ◎ Colorado, C USA
25 N2 Meredith, Lake ⊠ Texas, SW USA
81 O16 Mereeg *var.* Mareeq, *It.* Meregh. Galguduud, E Somalia
117 V5 Merefa Kharkivs'ka Oblast', E Ukraine
Meregh *see* Mereeg
99 E17 Merelbeke Oost-Vlaanderen, NW Belgium
Merend *see* Marand

◆ Country ● Country Capital ◇ Dependent Territory ○ Dependent Territory Capital ◈ Administrative Region × International Airport ▲ Mountain ⛰ Mountain Range △ Volcano ≈ River ◎ Lake ⊠ Reservoir

167 T12 Mereuch Môndól Kiri, E Cambodia
Mergate see Margate
167 N12 Mergui Tenasserim, S Myanmar
166 M12 Mergui Archipelago island group S Myanmar
114 L12 Meriç Edirne, NW Turkey
114 L12 Meriç Bul. Maritsa, Gk. Évros; anc. Hebrus. ≈ SE Europe see also Évros/Maritsa
41 X12 Mérida Yucatán, SW Mexico
104 J11 Mérida anc. Augusta Emerita. Extremadura, W Spain
54 I6 Mérida Mérida, W Venezuela
54 H7 Mérida off. Estado Mérida. ◆ state W Venezuela
18 M13 Meriden Connecticut, NE USA
22 M5 Meridian Mississippi, S USA
25 S8 Meridian Texas, SW USA
102 J13 Mérignac Gironde, SW France
102 J13 Mérignac ✕ (Bordeaux) Gironde, SW France
93 J18 Merikarvia Länsi-Suomi, W Finland
183 R12 Merimbula New South Wales, SE Australia
182 L9 Meringur Victoria, SE Australia
Merín, Laguna see Mirim Lagoon
97 I19 Merioneth cultural region W Wales, UK
188 A11 Merir island Palau Islands, N Palau
188 B17 Merizo SW Guam
Merjama see Märjamaa
145 S16 Merke Zhambyl, S Kazakhstan
25 P7 Merkel Texas, SW USA
146 E12 Merkezi Garagumy var. Mencezi Garagum, Rus. Tsentral'nyye Nizmennyye Garagumy. desert C Turkmenistan
119 F15 Merkinė Alytus, S Lithuania
99 G16 Merksem Antwerpen, N Belgium
99 I15 Merksplas Antwerpen, N Belgium
Merkulovichi see Myerkulavichy
119 G15 Merkys ≈ S Lithuania
32 F15 Merlin Oregon, NW USA
61 C20 Merlo Buenos Aires, E Argentina
138 G8 Meron, Haré ▲ N Israel
74 K6 Merouane, Chott salt lake NE Algeria
80 F7 Merowe Northern, N Sudan
180 J12 Merredin Western Australia
97 I14 Merrick ▲ S Scotland, UK
32 H16 Merrill Oregon, NW USA
30 L5 Merrill Wisconsin, N USA
31 N11 Merrillville Indiana, N USA
19 O10 Merrimack River ≈ Massachusetts/New Hampshire, NE USA
28 L12 Merriman Nebraska, C USA
11 N17 Merritt British Columbia, SW Canada
23 Y12 Merritt Island Florida, SE USA
23 Y11 Merritt Island island Florida, SE USA
28 M12 Merritt Reservoir ▣ Nebraska, C USA
183 S7 Merriwa New South Wales, SE Australia
183 O8 Merriwagga New South Wales, SE Australia
22 G8 Merryville Louisiana, S USA
80 K9 Mersa Fatma E Eritrea
102 M7 Mer St-Aubin Loir-et-Cher, C France
Mersa Maṭrûḥ see Maṭrûḥ
99 M24 Mersch Luxembourg, C Luxembourg
101 M15 Merseburg Sachsen-Anhalt, C Germany
Mersen see Meerssen
97 K18 Mersey ≈ NW England, UK
136 J17 Mersin İçel, S Turkey
168 L9 Mersing Johor, Peninsular Malaysia
118 E8 Mērsrags Talsi, NW Latvia
152 G12 Merta var. Merta City. Rājasthān, N India
Merta City see Merta
152 F12 Merta Road Rājasthān, N India
97 J21 Merthyr Tydfil S Wales, UK
104 H13 Mértola Beja, S Portugal
144 G14 Mertvyy Kultuk, Sor salt flat SW Kazakhstan
195 V16 Mertz Glacier glacier Antarctica
99 M24 Mertzig Diekirch, C Luxembourg
25 O9 Mertzon Texas, SW USA
81 I18 Meru Eastern, C Kenya
103 N4 Méru Oise, N France
81 I20 Meru, Mount ▲ NE Tanzania
Merv see Mary
Mervdasht see Marv Dasht
136 K11 Merzifon Amasya, N Turkey
101 D20 Merzig Saarland, SW Germany
36 L14 Mesa Arizona, SW USA
29 V4 Mesabi Range ▲ Minnesota, N USA
54 H6 Mesa Bolívar Mérida, NW Venezuela
107 Q18 Mesagne Puglia, SE Italy
39 P12 Mesa Mountain ▲ Alaska, USA
115 J25 Mesará lowland Kríti, Greece, E Mediterranean Sea
37 S14 Mescalero New Mexico, SW USA
101 G15 Meschede Nordrhein-Westfalen, W Germany
137 Q12 Mescit Dağları ▲ NE Turkey
189 V13 Mesegon island Chuuk, C Micronesia
Meseritz see Międzyrzecz
54 F11 Mesetas Meta, C Colombia
Meshchera Lowland see Meshcherskaya Nizina
126 M4 Meshcherskaya Nizina Eng. Meshchera Lowland. basin W Russian Federation
126 J5 Meshchovsk Kaluzhskaya Oblast', W Russian Federation
125 R9 Meshchura Respublika Komi, NW Russian Federation
Meshed see Mashhad
Meshed-i-Sar see Bābolsar
80 E13 Meshra'er Req Warab, S Sudan
37 R15 Mesilla New Mexico, SW USA
108 H10 Mesocco Ger. Misox. Ticino, S Switzerland
115 D18 Mesolóngi prev. Mesolóngion. Dytikí Ellás, W Greece
Mesolóngion see Mesolóngi
14 E8 Mesomikenda Lake ◎ Ontario, S Canada
61 D15 Mesopotamia var. Mesopotamia Argentina. physical region NE Argentina
Mesopotamia Argentina see Mesopotamia
35 Y10 Mesquite Nevada, W USA
82 Q13 Messalo, Rio var. Mualo. ≈ NE Mozambique
Messana/Messene see Messina
99 L25 Messancy Luxembourg, SE Belgium
107 M23 Messina var. Messana, Messene; anc. Zancle. Sicilia, Italy, C Mediterranean Sea
Messina see Musina
Messina, Strait of see Messina, Stretto di
107 M23 Messina, Stretto di Eng. Strait of Messina. strait SW Italy
115 E21 Messíni Pelopónnisos, S Greece
115 E21 Messinía peninsula S Greece
115 E22 Messiniakós Kólpos gulf S Greece
122 J8 Messoyakha ≈ N Russian Federation
114 H11 Mesta Gk. Néstos, Turk. Kara Su. ≈ Bulgaria/Greece see also Néstos
Mestghanem see Mostaganem
137 R8 Mestia var. Mestiya. N Georgia
Mestiya see Mestia
115 K18 Mestón, Akrotírio headland Chíos, E Greece
106 H8 Mestre Veneto, NE Italy
59 M16 Mestre, Espigão ▲ E Brazil
169 N14 Mesuji ≈ Sumatera, W Indonesia
Mesule see Grosser Möseler
10 J10 Meszah Peak ▲ British Columbia, W Canada
54 G11 Meta off. Departamento del Meta. ◆ province C Colombia
15 Q8 Metabetchouane ≈ Québec, SE Canada
9 S7 Meta Incognita Peninsula peninsula Baffin Island, Nunavut, NE Canada
22 K9 Metairie Louisiana, S USA
32 M6 Metaline Falls Washington, NW USA
62 K6 Metán Salta, N Argentina
82 N13 Metangula Niassa, N Mozambique
42 E7 Metapán Santa Ana, NW El Salvador
54 K9 Meta, Río ≈ Colombia/Venezuela
106 I11 Metauro ≈ C Italy
80 H11 Metema Amhara, N Ethiopia
115 D15 Metéora religious building Thessalía, C Greece
65 O20 Meteor Rise undersea feature SW Indian Ocean
186 G5 Meteran New Hanover, NE PNG
Meterlam/Methariam/Metharlam see Mehtarlām
115 G20 Methanon peninsula S Greece
32 J6 Methow River ≈ Washington, NW USA
19 O10 Methuen Massachusetts, NE USA
185 G19 Methven Canterbury, South Island, NZ
Metis see Metz
113 G15 Metković Dubrovnik-Neretva, SE Croatia
39 Y14 Metlakatla Annette Island, Alaska, USA
109 V13 Metlika Ger. Möttling. SE Slovenia
109 T8 Metnitz Kärnten, S Austria
27 W12 Meto, Bayou ≈ Arkansas, C USA
168 M15 Metro Sumatera, W Indonesia
30 M17 Metropolis Illinois, N USA
Metropolitan see Santiago
35 N8 Metropolitan Oakland ✕ California, W USA
115 D15 Métsovo prev. Métsovon. Ípeiros, C Greece
Métsovon see Métsovo
23 V5 Metter Georgia, SE USA
99 H21 Mettet Namur, S Belgium
101 D20 Mettlach Saarland, SW Germany
Mettu see Metu
80 H13 Metu var. Mattu, Mettu. Oromo, C Ethiopia
169 T10 Metulang Borneo, N Indonesia
138 G8 Metulla Northern, N Israel
103 T4 Metz anc. Divodurum Mediomatricum, Mediomatrica, Metis. Moselle, NE France
101 H22 Metzingen Baden-Württemberg, S Germany
168 G8 Meulaboh Sumatera, W Indonesia
99 D18 Meulebeke West-Vlaanderen, W Belgium
103 U6 Meurthe ≈ NE France
103 S5 Meurthe-et-Moselle ◆ department NE France
103 S4 Meuse ◆ department NE France
84 F10 Meuse Dut. Maas. ≈ W Europe see also Maas
Mexcala, Río see Balsas, Río
25 U8 Mexia Texas, SW USA
58 K11 Mexiana, Ilha island NE Brazil
40 C1 Mexicali Baja California, NW Mexico
27 V4 Mexico Missouri, C USA
18 H9 Mexico New York, NE USA
40 L7 Mexico off. United Mexican States, var. Méjico, México, Sp. Estados Unidos Mexicanos. ◆ federal republic N Central America
41 O14 México var. Ciudad de México, Eng. Mexico City. ● (Mexico) México, C Mexico
41 O13 México ◆ state S Mexico
(0) J13 Mexico Basin var. Sigsbee Deep. undersea feature C Gulf of Mexico
Mexico City see México
México, Golfo de see Mexico, Gulf of
44 B4 Mexico, Gulf of Sp. Golfo de México. gulf W Atlantic Ocean
Meyadine see Al Mayādīn
39 Y14 Meyers Chuck Etolin Island, Alaska, USA
148 M3 Meymaneh var. Maimāna, Maymana. Fāryāb, NW Afghanistan
143 N7 Meymeh Eşfahān, C Iran
123 V7 Meynypil'gyno Chukotskiy Avtonomnyy Okrug, NE Russian Federation
108 A10 Meyrin Genève, SW Switzerland
166 L7 Mezaligon Irrawaddy, SW Myanmar
41 O15 Mezcala Guerrero, S Mexico
114 H8 Mezdra Vratsa, NW Bulgaria
103 P16 Mèze Hérault, S France
125 O6 Mezen' Arkhangel'skaya Oblast', NW Russian Federation
127 P8 Mezen' ≈ NW Russian Federation
Mezen, Bay of see Mezenskaya Guba
103 Q13 Mézenc, Mont ▲ C France
127 O8 Mezenskaya Guba var. Bay of Mezen. bay NW Russian Federation
Mezha see Myazha
122 H6 Mezhdusharskiy, Ostrov island Novaya Zemlya, N Russian Federation
Mezhëvo see Myezhava
127 W4 Mezhgor'ye Respublika Bashkortostan, W Russian Federation
Mezhgor'ye see Mizhhir"ya
117 V8 Mezhova Dnipropetrovs'ka Oblast', E Ukraine
10 J12 Meziadin Junction British Columbia, W Canada
111 G16 Mezileské Sedlo var. Przełęcz Międzyleska. pass Czech Republic/Poland
102 L14 Mézin Lot-et-Garonne, SW France
111 M24 Mezőberény Békés, SE Hungary
111 M25 Mezőhegyes Békés, SE Hungary
111 M25 Mezőkovácsháza Békés, SE Hungary
111 M21 Mezőkövesd Borsod-Abaúj-Zemplén, NE Hungary
Mezőtelegd see Tileagd
111 M23 Mezőtúr Jász-Nagykun-Szolnok, E Hungary
40 K10 Mezquital Durango, C Mexico
106 G6 Mezzolombardo Trentino-Alto Adige, N Italy
82 L13 Mfuwe Northern, N Zambia
121 O15 Mġarr Gozo, N Malta
126 H6 Mglin Bryanskaya Oblast', W Russian Federation
Mhálanna, Cionn see Malin Head
154 G10 Mhow Madhya Pradesh, C India
Miadzioł Nowy see Myadzyel
171 O6 Miagao Panay Island, C Philippines
41 R17 Miahuatlán var. Miahuatlán de Porfirio Díaz. Oaxaca, SE Mexico
Miahuatlán de Porfirio Díaz see Miahuatlán
104 K10 Miajadas Extremadura, W Spain
Miajlar see Myājlār
36 M14 Miami Arizona, SW USA
23 Z16 Miami Florida, SE USA
27 R8 Miami Oklahoma, C USA
25 O2 Miami Texas, SW USA
23 Z16 Miami ✕ Florida, SE USA
23 Z16 Miami Beach Florida, SE USA
23 Y15 Miami Canal canal Florida, SE USA
31 R14 Miamisburg Ohio, N USA
149 U10 Miān Channūn Punjab, E Pakistan
142 J4 Miāndowāb var. Mianduab, Miyāndoāb. Āžarbāyjān-e Bākhtarī, NW Iran
172 H5 Miandrivazo Toliara, C Madagascar
Mianduab see Miāndowāb
142 K3 Mīāneh var. Miyāneh. Āžarbāyjān-e Khāvarī, NW Iran
149 O16 Miāni Hōr lagoon S Pakistan
160 G10 Mianning Sichuan, C China
149 T7 Miānwāli Punjab, NE Pakistan
160 J7 Mianxian var. Mian Xian. Shaanxi, C China
160 I8 Mianyang Sichuan, C China
Mianyang see Xiantao
161 R3 Miaodao Qundao island group E China
161 S13 Miaoli N Taiwan
122 F11 Miass Chelyabinskaya Oblast', C Russian Federation
110 G8 Miastko Ger. Rummelsburg in Pommern. Pomorskie, N Poland
Miava see Myjava
11 O15 Mica Creek British Columbia, SW Canada
160 J7 Micang Shan ▲ C China
Mi Chai see Nong Khai
111 O19 Michalovce Ger. Grossmichel, Hung. Nagymihály. Košický Kraj, E Slovakia
99 M20 Michel, Baraque hill E Belgium
39 S5 Michelson, Mount ▲ Alaska, USA
45 P9 Miches E Dominican Republic
30 M4 Michigamme, Lake ◎ Michigan, N USA
30 M4 Michigamme Reservoir ▣ Michigan, N USA
31 N4 Michigamme River ≈ Michigan, N USA
31 O7 Michigan off. State of Michigan; also known as Great Lakes State, Lake State, Wolverine State. ◆ state N USA
31 O11 Michigan City Indiana, N USA
31 O8 Michigan, Lake ◎ N USA
31 P2 Michipicoten Bay lake bay Ontario, N Canada
14 A8 Michipicoten Island island Ontario, S Canada
14 B7 Michipicoten River Ontario, S Canada
Michurin see Tsarevo
126 M6 Michurinsk Tambovskaya Oblast', W Russian Federation
Mico, Punta/Mico, Punto see Monkey Point
42 L10 Mico, Río ≈ SE Nicaragua
45 T12 Micoud SE Saint Lucia
189 N16 Micronesia off. Federated States of Micronesia. ◆ federation W Pacific Ocean
175 P4 Micronesia island group W Pacific Ocean
169 O9 Midai, Pulau island Kepulauan Natuna, W Indonesia
Mid-Atlantic Cordillera see Mid-Atlantic Ridge
65 M17 Mid-Atlantic Ridge var. Mid-Atlantic Cordillera, Mid-Atlantic Rise, Mid-Atlantic Swell. undersea feature Atlantic Ocean
Mid-Atlantic Rise/Mid-Atlantic Swell see Mid-Atlantic Ridge
99 E15 Middelburg Zeeland, SW Netherlands
83 H24 Middelburg Eastern Cape, S South Africa
83 K21 Middelburg Mpumalanga, NE South Africa
95 G23 Middelfart Fyn, C Denmark
98 G13 Middelharnis Zuid-Holland, SW Netherlands
99 B16 Middelkerke West-Vlaanderen, W Belgium
98 I9 Middenbeemster Noord-Holland, C Netherlands
98 I8 Middenmeer Noord-Holland, NW Netherlands
35 Q2 Middle Alkali Lake ◎ California, W USA
193 S6 Middle America Trench undersea feature E Pacific Ocean
151 P19 Middle Andaman island Andaman Islands, India, NE Indian Ocean
Middle Atlas see Moyen Atlas
21 R3 Middlebourne West Virginia, NE USA
23 W9 Middleburg Florida, SE USA
Middleburg Island see 'Eua
Middle Caicos see Grand Caicos
25 N8 Middle Concho River ≈ Texas, SW USA
Middle Congo see Congo (Republic of)
39 R6 Middle Fork Chandalar River ≈ Alaska, USA
39 Q7 Middle Fork Koyukuk River ≈ Alaska, USA
33 O12 Middle Fork Salmon River ≈ Idaho, NW USA
11 T15 Middle Lake Saskatchewan, S Canada
28 L13 Middle Loup River ≈ Nebraska, C USA
185 E22 Middlemarch Otago, South Island, NZ
31 T15 Middleport Ohio, N USA
29 U14 Middle Raccoon River ≈ Iowa, C USA
29 R3 Middle River ≈ Minnesota, N USA
21 N8 Middlesboro Kentucky, S USA
97 M15 Middlesbrough N England, UK
42 G3 Middlesex Stann Creek, C Belize
97 N22 Middlesex cultural region SE England, UK
13 P15 Middleton Nova Scotia, SE Canada
20 F10 Middleton Tennessee, S USA
30 L9 Middleton Wisconsin, N USA
39 S13 Middleton Island island Alaska, USA
34 M7 Middletown California, W USA
21 Y2 Middletown Delaware, NE USA
18 K15 Middletown New Jersey, NE USA
18 K13 Middletown New York, NE USA
31 R14 Middletown Ohio, N USA
18 G15 Middletown Pennsylvania, NE USA
141 N14 Mīdī var. Maydī. NW Yemen
103 O16 Midi, Canal du canal S France
102 K17 Midi de Bigorre, Pic du ▲ S France
102 K17 Midi d'Ossau, Pic du ▲ SW France
173 R7 Mid-Indian Basin undersea feature N Indian Ocean
173 P7 Mid-Indian Ridge var. Central Indian Ridge. undersea feature C Indian Ocean
103 N14 Midi-Pyrénées ◆ region S France
25 N8 Midkiff Texas, SW USA
14 G13 Midland Ontario, S Canada
31 R8 Midland Michigan, N USA
28 M10 Midland South Dakota, N USA
24 M8 Midland Texas, SW USA
83 K17 Midlands ◆ province C Zimbabwe
97 D21 Midleton Ir. Mainistir na Corann. SW Ireland
25 T7 Midlothian Texas, SW USA
96 K12 Midlothian cultural region S Scotland, UK
172 I7 Midongy Fianarantsoa, S Madagascar
102 K15 Midou ≈ SW France
192 J6 Mid-Pacific Mountains var. Mid-Pacific Seamounts. undersea feature NW Pacific Ocean
Mid-Pacific Seamounts see Mid-Pacific Mountains
171 Q7 Midsayap Mindanao, S Philippines
36 L3 Midway Utah, W USA
192 L5 Midway Islands ◇ US territory C Pacific Ocean
33 X14 Midwest Wyoming, C USA
27 N10 Midwest City Oklahoma, C USA
152 M10 Mid Western ◆ zone W Nepal
98 P5 Midwolda Groningen, NE Netherlands
137 Q16 Midyat Mardin, SE Turkey
114 F8 Midzhur SCr. Midžor. ▲ Bulgaria/Serbia and Montenegro (Yugo.) see also Midžor
113 Q14 Midžor Bul. Midzhur. ▲ Bulgaria/Serbia and Montenegro (Yugo.) see also Midzhur
164 K14 Mie off. Mie-ken. ◆ prefecture Honshū, SW Japan
111 L16 Miechów Małopolskie, S Poland
110 F11 Międzychód Ger. Mitteldorf. Wielkopolskie, C Poland
Międzyleska, Przełęcz see Mezileské Sedlo
110 O12 Międzyrzec Podlaski Lubelskie, E Poland
110 E11 Międzyrzecz Ger. Meseritz. Lubelskie, W Poland
Mie-ken see Mie
102 L16 Miélan Gers, S France
111 N16 Mielec Podkarpackie, SE Poland
95 L21 Mien ◎ S Sweden
41 O8 Mier Tamaulipas, C Mexico
116 J11 Miercurea-Ciuc Ger. Szeklerburg, Hung. Csíkszereda. Harghita, C Romania
Mieresch see Maros/Mureş
Mieres del Camín see Mieres del Camino
104 K2 Mieres del Camino var. Mieres del Camín. Asturias, NW Spain
99 K15 Mierlo Noord-Brabant, SE Netherlands
41 O10 Mier y Noriega Nuevo León, NE Mexico
Mies see Stříbro
80 K13 Mī'ēso var. Meheso, Miesso. Oromo, C Ethiopia
Miesso see Mī'ēso
110 D10 Mieszkowice Ger. Bärwalde Neumark. Zachodnio-pomorskie, W Poland
18 G14 Mifflinburg Pennsylvania, NE USA
18 F14 Mifflintown Pennsylvania, NE USA
41 R15 Miguel Alemán, Presa ▣ SE Mexico
40 L9 Miguel Asua var. Miguel Auza. Zacatecas, C Mexico
Miguel Auza see Miguel Asua
43 S15 Miguel de la Borda var. Donoso. Colón, C Panama
41 N13 Miguel Hidalgo ✕ (Guadalajara) Jalisco, SW Mexico
40 H7 Miguel Hidalgo, Presa ▣ W Mexico
116 J14 Mihăileşti Giurgiu, S Romania
116 M14 Mihail Kogălniceanu var. Kogălniceanu; prev. Caramurat, Ferdinand. Constanţa, SE Romania
117 N14 Mihai Viteazu Constanţa, SE Romania
136 G12 Mihalıççık Eskişehir, NW Turkey
164 G13 Mihara Hiroshima, Honshū, SW Japan
165 N14 Mihara-yama ☒ Miyako-jima, SE Japan
105 S8 Mijares ≈ E Spain
98 I11 Mijdrecht Utrecht, C Netherlands
165 S4 Mikasa Hokkaidō, NE Japan
Mikashevichi see Mikashevichy
119 K19 Mikashevichy Pol. Mikaszewicze, Rus. Mikashevichi. Brestskaya Voblasts', SW Belarus
Mikaszewicze see Mikashevichy
126 L5 Mikhaylov Ryazanskaya Oblast', W Russian Federation
Mikhaylovgrad see Montana
195 Z8 Mikhaylov Island island Antarctica
145 T6 Mikhaylovka Pavlodar, N Kazakhstan
127 N9 Mikhaylovka Volgogradskaya Oblast', SW Russian Federation
Mikhaylovka see Mykhaylivka
81 K24 Mikindani Mtwara, SE Tanzania
93 N18 Mikkeli Swe. Sankt Michel. Itä-Suomi, E Finland
110 M8 Mikołajki Ger. Nikolaiken. Warmińsko-Mazurskie, NE Poland
Míkonos see Mýkonos
114 I9 Mikre Lovech, N Bulgaria
114 C13 Mikrí Préspa, Límni ◎ N Greece
127 P4 Mikulkin, Mys headland NW Russian Federation
81 I23 Mikumi Morogoro, SE Tanzania
125 R10 Mikun' Respublika Komi, NW Russian Federation
164 K13 Mikuni Fukui, Honshū, SW Japan
165 X13 Mikura-jima island E Japan
29 V7 Milaca Minnesota, N USA
62 J10 Milagro La Rioja, C Argentina
56 B7 Milagro Guayas, SW Ecuador
31 P4 Milakokia Lake ◎ Michigan, N USA
30 J1 Milan Illinois, N USA
31 R10 Milan Michigan, N USA
27 T2 Milan Missouri, C USA
37 Q11 Milan New Mexico, SW USA
20 G9 Milan Tennessee, S USA
Milan see Milano
95 F15 Miland Telemark, S Norway
83 N15 Milange Zambézia, NE Mozambique
106 D8 Milano Eng. Milan, Ger. Mailand; anc. Mediolanum. Lombardia, N Italy
25 U10 Milano Texas, SW USA
136 C15 Milas Muğla, SW Turkey
119 K21 Milashavichy Rus. Milashevichi. Homyel'skaya Voblasts', SE Belarus
Milashevichi see Milashavichy
119 I18 Milavidy Rus. Milovidy. Brestskaya Voblasts', SW Belarus
107 L23 Milazzo anc. Mylae. Sicilia, Italy, C Mediterranean Sea
29 R8 Milbank South Dakota, N USA
19 T7 Milbridge Maine, NE USA
100 L11 Milde ≈ C Germany
14 F14 Mildmay Ontario, S Canada
182 L9 Mildura Victoria, SE Australia
137 X12 Mil Düzü Rus. Mil'skaya Ravnina, Mil'skaya Step'. physical region C Azerbaijan
160 H13 Mile var. Miyang. Yunnan, SW China
Mile see Mili Atoll
181 Y10 Miles Queensland, E Australia
25 P8 Miles Texas, SW USA
33 X9 Miles City Montana, NW USA
11 U17 Milestone Saskatchewan, S Canada
107 N22 Mileto Calabria, SW Italy
107 K16 Miletto, Monte ▲ C Italy
18 M13 Milford Connecticut, NE USA
21 Y3 Milford var. Milford City. Delaware, NE USA
29 T11 Milford Iowa, C USA
19 S6 Milford Maine, NE USA
29 R16 Milford Nebraska, C USA
19 O10 Milford New Hampshire, NE USA
18 J13 Milford Pennsylvania, NE USA
25 T7 Milford Texas, SW USA
36 K6 Milford Utah, W USA
Milford see Milford Haven
Milford City see Milford
97 H21 Milford Haven prev. Milford. SW Wales, UK
27 O4 Milford Lake ▣ Kansas, C USA
185 B21 Milford Sound Southland, South Island, NZ
185 B21 Milford Sound inlet South Island, NZ
Milhau see Millau
Milḩ, Baḩr al see Razāzah, Buḩayrat ar
139 T10 Milḩ, Wādī al dry watercourse S Iraq
189 W8 Mili Atoll var. Mile. atoll Ratak Chain, SE Marshall Islands
110 H13 Milicz Dolnośląskie, SW Poland
107 L25 Militello in Val di Catania Sicilia, Italy, C Mediterranean Sea
123 V10 Mil'kovo Kamchatskaya Oblast', E Russian Federation
11 R17 Milk River Alberta, SW Canada
44 J13 Milk River ≈ C Jamaica
33 W7 Milk River ≈ Montana, NW USA
80 D9 Milk, Wadi el var. Wadi al Malik. ≈ C Sudan
99 L14 Mill Noord-Brabant, SE Netherlands
103 P14 Millau var. Milhau; anc. Æmilianum. Aveyron, S France
14 I14 Millbrook Ontario, SE Canada
23 U4 Milledgeville Georgia, SE USA
12 C12 Mille Lacs, Lac des ◎ Ontario, S Canada
29 V6 Mille Lacs Lake ◎ Minnesota, N USA
23 V4 Millen Georgia, SE USA
191 Y5 Millennium Island prev. Caroline Island, Thornton Island. atoll Line Islands, E Kiribati
29 O9 Miller South Dakota, N USA
30 K5 Miller Dam Flowage ◎ Wisconsin, N USA
39 U12 Miller, Mount ▲ Alaska, USA
126 L10 Millerovo Rostovskaya Oblast', SW Russian Federation
37 N17 Miller Peak ▲ Arizona, SW USA
31 T12 Millersburg Ohio, N USA
18 G15 Millersburg Pennsylvania, NE USA
185 D23 Millers Flat Otago, South Island, NZ
25 Q8 Millersview Texas, SW USA
106 B10 Millesimo Piemonte, NE Italy
12 C12 Milles Lacs, Lac des ◎ Ontario, SW Canada
25 Q13 Millett Texas, SW USA
103 N11 Millevaches, Plateau de plateau C France
182 K12 Millicent South Australia
98 M13 Millingen aan den Rijn Gelderland, SE Netherlands
20 E10 Millington Tennessee, S USA
19 R4 Millinocket Maine, NE USA
19 R4 Millinocket Lake ◎ Maine, NE USA
195 Z11 Mill Island island Antarctica
183 T3 Millmerran Queensland, E Australia
109 R9 Millstatt Kärnten, S Austria
97 B19 Milltown Malbay Ir. Sráid na Cathrach. W Ireland
18 J17 Millville New Jersey, NE USA
27 S13 Millwood Lake ▣ Arkansas, C USA
Milne Bank see Milne Seamounts
186 G10 Milne Bay ◆ province SE PNG
64 J8 Milne Seamounts var. Milne Bank. undersea feature N Atlantic Ocean
29 Q6 Milnor North Dakota, N USA
19 R5 Milo Maine, NE USA
115 I22 Mílos Mílos, Kykládes, Greece, Aegean Sea
115 I22 Mílos island Kykládes, Greece, Aegean Sea

◆ Country ● Country Capital ◇ Dependent Territory ○ Dependent Territory Capital ◆ Administrative Region ✕ International Airport ▲ Mountain ▲ Mountain Range ☒ Volcano ≈ River ◎ Lake ▣ Reservoir

110 H11 **Miłosław** Wielkolpolskie, C Poland
113 K19 **Milot** *var.* Miloti. Lezhë, C Albania
Miloti *see* Milot
117 Z5 **Milove** Luhans'ka Oblast', E Ukraine
Milovidy *see* Milavidy
182 L4 **Milparinka** New South Wales, SE Australia
35 N9 **Milpitas** California, W USA
Mil'skaya Ravnina/Mil'skaya Step' *see* Mil Düzü
14 G15 **Milton** Ontario, S Canada
185 E24 **Milton** Otago, South Island, NZ
21 Y4 **Milton** Delaware, NE USA
23 P8 **Milton** Florida, SE USA
18 G14 **Milton** Pennsylvania, NE USA
18 L7 **Milton** Vermont, NE USA
32 K11 **Milton-Freewater** Oregon, NW USA
97 N21 **Milton Keynes** SE England, UK
27 N3 **Miltonvale** Kansas, C USA
161 N10 **Miluo** Hunan, S China
30 M9 **Milwaukee** Wisconsin, N USA
Milyang *see* Miryang
Mimatum *see* Mende
37 Q15 **Mimbres Mountains** ▲▲ New Mexico, SW USA
182 D2 **Mimili** South Australia
102 J14 **Mimizan** Landes, SW France
Mimmaya *see* Minmaya
79 E19 **Mimongo** Ngounié, C Gabon
Min *see* Fujian
35 T7 **Mina** Nevada, W USA
143 S14 **Mīnāb** Hormozgān, SE Iran
Mînâ Baranîs *see* Berenice
149 R9 **Mīna Bāzār** Baluchistān, SW Pakistan
165 X17 **Minami-Iō-jima** *Eng.* San Augustine. *island* SE Japan
Min'an *see* Longshan
165 R5 **Minami-Kayabe** Hokkaidō, NE Japan
164 C17 **Minamitane** Kagoshima, Tanega-shima, SW Japan
Minami Tori Shima *see* Marcus Island
62 J4 **Mina Pirquitas** Jujuy, NW Argentina
173 O3 **Mīnā' Qābūs** NE Oman
61 F19 **Minas** Lavalleja, S Uruguay
13 P15 **Minas Basin** *bay* Nova Scotia, SE Canada
61 F17 **Minas de Corrales** Rivera, NE Uruguay
44 A5 **Minas de Matahambre** Pinar del Río, W Cuba
104 J13 **Minas de Ríotinto** Andalucía, S Spain
60 K7 **Minas Gerais** *off.* Estado de Minas Gerais. ◐ *state* E Brazil
42 E5 **Minas, Sierra de las** ▲▲ E Guatemala
41 T15 **Minatitlán** Veracruz-Llave, E Mexico
166 L6 **Minbu** Magwe, W Myanmar
149 V10 **Minchinābād** Punjab, E Pakistan
63 G17 **Minchinmávida, Volcán** ▲ S Chile
96 G7 **Minch, The** *var.* North Minch. *strait* NW Scotland, UK
106 F8 **Mincio** *anc.* Mincius. ≈ N Italy
Mincius *see* Mincio
26 M11 **Minco** Oklahoma, C USA
171 Q7 **Mindanao** *island* S Philippines
Mindanao Sea *see* Bohol Sea
101 J23 **Mindel** ≈ S Germany
101 J23 **Mindelheim** Bayern, S Germany
Mindello *see* Mindelo
76 C9 **Mindelo** *var.* Mindello; *prev.* Porto Grande. São Vicente, N Cape Verde
14 I13 **Minden** Ontario, SE Canada
100 H13 **Minden** *anc.* Minthun. Nordrhein-Westfalen, NW Germany
22 G5 **Minden** Louisiana, S USA
29 O16 **Minden** Nebraska, C USA
35 Q6 **Minden** Nevada, W USA
182 L8 **Mindona Lake** *seasonal lake* New South Wales, SE Australia
171 O4 **Mindoro** *island* N Philippines
171 N5 **Mindoro Strait** *strait* W Philippines
159 S9 **Mine** Gansu, N China
97 E21 **Mine Head** *Ir.* Mionn Ard. *headland* S Ireland
97 J23 **Minehead** SW England, UK
59 J19 **Mineiros** Goiás, C Brazil
25 V6 **Mineola** Texas, SW USA
25 S13 **Mineral** Texas, SW USA
127 N15 **Mineral'nyye Vody** Stavropol'skiy Kray, SW Russian Federation
30 K9 **Mineral Point** Wisconsin, N USA
25 S6 **Mineral Wells** Texas, SW USA
36 K6 **Minersville** Utah, W USA
31 U12 **Minerva** Ohio, N USA
107 N17 **Minervino Murge** Puglia, SE Italy
103 O16 **Minervois** *physical region* S France
158 I10 **Minfeng** *var.* Niya. Xinjiang Uygur Zizhiqu, NW China
79 O25 **Minga** Katanga, SE Dem. Rep. Congo
137 W11 **Mingäçevir** *Rus.* Mingechaur, Mingechevir. C Azerbaijan
137 W11 **Mingäçevir Su Anbarı** *Rus.* Mingechaurskoye Vodokhranilishche, Mingechevirskoye Vodokhranilishche. ▣ NW Azerbaijan
166 L8 **Mingaladon** ✖ (Yangon) Yangon, SW Myanmar
13 P11 **Mingan** Québec, E Canada
149 U5 **Mingāora** *var.* Mingora, Mongora. North-West Frontier Province, N Pakistan
146 K8 **Mingbuloq** *Rus.* Mynbulak. Navoiy Viloyati, N Uzbekistan
146 K9 **Mingbuloq Botig'l** *Rus.* Vpadina Mynbulak. *depression* N Uzbekistan
Mingechaur/Mingechevir *see* Mingäçevir
Mingechaurskoye Vodokhranilishche/Mingechevirskoye Vodokhranilishche *see* Mingäçevir Su Anbarı
161 Q7 **Mingguang** *prev.* Jiashan. Anhui, S China
166 L4 **Mingin** Sagaing, C Myanmar
105 Q10 **Minglanilla** Castilla-La Mancha, C Spain
31 V13 **Mingo Junction** Ohio, N USA
Mingora *see* Mingāora
163 V7 **Mingshui** Heilongjiang, NE China
Mingteke Daban *see* Mintaka Pass
83 Q14 **Minguri** Nampula, NE Mozambique
159 U10 **Minhe** *var.* Shangchuankou. Qinghai, C China
166 L6 **Minhla** Magwe, W Myanmar
167 S14 **Minh Lương** Kiên Giang, S Vietnam
104 G5 **Minho, Rio** *Sp.* Miño. ≈ Portugal/Spain *see also* Miño
104 G5 **Minho** *former province* N Portugal
155 C24 **Minicoy Island** *island* SW India
33 P15 **Minidoka** Idaho, NW USA
118 C11 **Minija** ≈ W Lithuania
180 G9 **Minilya** Western Australia
14 E8 **Minisinakwa Lake** ◎ Ontario, S Canada
45 T12 **Ministre Point** *headland* S Saint Lucia
11 V15 **Minitonas** Manitoba, S Canada
Minius *see* Miño
161 R12 **Min Jiang** ≈ SE China
160 H10 **Min Jiang** ≈ C China
182 H9 **Minlaton** South Australia
165 Q6 **Minmaya** *var.* Mimmaya. Aomori, Honshū, C Japan
77 U14 **Minna** Niger, C Nigeria
165 P16 **Minna-jima** *island* Sakishima-shotō, SW Japan
27 N4 **Minneapolis** Kansas, C USA
29 U9 **Minneapolis** Minnesota, N USA
29 V8 **Minneapolis-Saint Paul** ✖ Minnesota, N USA
11 W16 **Minnedosa** Manitoba, S Canada
26 J7 **Minneola** Kansas, C USA
29 S7 **Minnesota** *off.* State of Minnesota; also known as Gopher State, New England of the West, North Star State. ◐ *state* N USA
29 S9 **Minnesota River** ≈ Minnesota/South Dakota, N USA
29 V9 **Minnetonka** Minnesota, N USA
29 O3 **Minnewaukan** North Dakota, N USA
182 F7 **Minnipa** South Australia
104 H2 **Miño** Galicia, NW Spain
104 G5 **Miño** *var.* Mino, Minius, *Port.* Rio Minho. ≈ Portugal/Spain *see also* Minho, Rio
30 L4 **Minocqua** Wisconsin, N USA
30 L12 **Minonk** Illinois, N USA
Minorca *see* Menorca
28 M3 **Minot** North Dakota, N USA
159 U8 **Minqin** Gansu, N China
119 J16 **Minsk** ● (Belarus) Minskaya Voblasts', C Belarus
119 L16 **Minsk** ✖ Minskaya Voblasts', C Belarus
Minskaya Oblast' *see* Minskaya Voblasts'
119 K16 **Minskaya Voblasts'** *prev. Rus.* Minskaya Oblast'. ◐ *province* C Belarus
119 J16 **Minskaya Wzvyshsha** ▲▲ C Belarus
110 N12 **Mińsk Mazowiecki** *var.* Nowo-Minsk. Mazowieckie, C Poland
31 Q13 **Minster** Ohio, N USA
79 F15 **Minta** Centre, C Cameroon
149 W2 **Mintaka Pass** *Chin.* Mingteke Daban. *pass* China/Pakistan
115 D20 **Mínthi** ▲▲ S Greece
Minthun *see* Minden
13 O14 **Minto** New Brunswick, SE Canada
10 H6 **Minto** Yukon Territory, W Canada
39 R9 **Minto** Alaska, USA
29 Q3 **Minto** North Dakota, N USA
12 K6 **Minto, Lac** ◎ Québec, C Canada
195 R16 **Minto, Mount** ▲ Antarctica
11 U17 **Minton** Saskatchewan, S Canada
189 R15 **Minto Reef** *atoll* Caroline Islands, C Micronesia
37 R4 **Minturn** Colorado, C USA
107 J16 **Minturno** Lazio, C Italy
122 K13 **Minusinsk** Krasnoyarskiy Kray, S Russian Federation
108 G11 **Minusio** Ticino, S Switzerland
79 E17 **Minvoul** Woleu-Ntem, N Gabon
141 R13 **Minwakh** N Yemen
159 V11 **Minxian** *var.* Min Xian. Gansu, C China
Minya *see* El Minya
31 R6 **Mio** Michigan, N USA
Mionn Ard *see* Mine Head
158 L5 **Miquan** Xinjiang Uygur Zizhiqu, NW China
119 I17 **Mir** Hrodzyenskaya Voblasts', W Belarus
106 H8 **Mira** Veneto, NE Italy
104 G13 **Mira, Rio** ≈ S Portugal
12 K15 **Mirabel** *var.* Montreal. ✖ (Montréal) Québec, SE Canada
60 Q8 **Miracema** Rio de Janeiro, SE Brazil
54 G9 **Miraflores** Boyacá, C Colombia
40 G10 **Miraflores** Baja California Sur, W Mexico
44 L9 **Miragoâne** S Haiti
155 E16 **Miraj** Mahārāshtra, W India
61 E23 **Miramar** Buenos Aires, E Argentina
103 R15 **Miramas** Bouches-du-Rhône, SE France
102 K12 **Mirambeau** Charente-Maritime, W France
102 L13 **Miramont-de-Guyenne** Lot-et-Garonne, SW France
115 L25 **Mirampéllou Kólpos** *gulf* Krití, Greece, E Mediterranean Sea
158 L8 **Miran** Xinjiang Uygur Zizhiqu, NW China
54 M5 **Miranda** *off.* Estado Miranda. ◐ *state* N Venezuela
Miranda de Corvo *see* Miranda do Corvo
105 O3 **Miranda de Ebro** La Rioja, N Spain
104 G8 **Miranda do Corvo** *var.* Miranda de Corvo. Coimbra, N Portugal
104 J6 **Miranda do Douro** Bragança, N Portugal
102 L15 **Mirande** Gers, S France
104 I6 **Mirandela** Bragança, N Portugal
25 R15 **Mirando City** Texas, SW USA
106 G9 **Mirandola** Emilia-Romagna, N Italy
60 I8 **Mirandópolis** São Paulo, S Brazil
60 K8 **Mirassol** São Paulo, S Brazil
104 J3 **Miravalles** ▲ NW Spain
42 L12 **Miravalles, Volcán** ⛰ NW Costa Rica
141 W13 **Mirbāṭ** *var.* Marbat. S Oman
44 M9 **Mirebalais** C Haiti
103 T6 **Mirecourt** Vosges, NE France
103 N16 **Mirepoix** Ariège, S France
Mirgorod *see* Myrhorod
139 W10 **Mīr Ḥājī Khalīl** E Iraq
169 T8 **Miri** Sarawak, East Malaysia
77 W12 **Miria** Zinder, S Niger
182 F5 **Mirikata** South Australia
54 K4 **Mirimire** Falcón, N Venezuela
61 H18 **Mirim Lagoon** *var.* Lake Mirim, *Sp.* Laguna Merín. *lagoon* Brazil/Uruguay
Mirim, Lake *see* Mirim Lagoon
Mírina *see* Mýrina
172 H14 **Miringoni** Mohéli, S Comoros
143 W11 **Mīrjāveh** Sīstān va Balūchestān, SE Iran
195 Z9 **Mirny** *Russian research station* Antarctica
124 M10 **Mirnyy** Arkhangel'skaya Oblast', NW Russian Federation
123 O10 **Mirnyy** Respublika Sakha (Yakutiya), NE Russian Federation
Mironovka *see* Myronivka
110 F9 **Mirosławiec** Zachodnio-pomorskie, NW Poland
Mirovo *see* Vrattsa
100 N10 **Mirow** Mecklenburg-Vorpommern, N Germany
152 G6 **Mīrpur** Jammu and Kashmir, NW India
Mīrpur *see* New Mīrpur
149 P17 **Mīrpur Batoro** Sind, SE Pakistan
149 Q16 **Mīrpur Khās** Sind, SE Pakistan
149 P17 **Mīrpur Sakro** Sind, SE Pakistan
143 T14 **Mīr Shahdād** Hormozgān, S Iran
Mirtoan Sea *see* Mirtóo Pélagos
115 G21 **Mirtóo Pélagos** *Eng.* Mirtoan Sea; *anc.* Myrtoum Mare. *sea* S Greece
163 Z16 **Miryang** *var.* Milyang, *Jap.* Mitsuō. SE South Korea
Mirzachirla *see* Murzechirla
164 E14 **Misaki** Ehime, Shikoku, SW Japan
41 Q13 **Misantla** Veracruz-Llave, E Mexico
165 R7 **Misawa** Aomori, Honshū, C Japan
57 G14 **Mishagua, Río** ≈ C Peru
163 Z8 **Mishan** Heilongjiang, NE China
31 O11 **Mishawaka** Indiana, N USA
39 N6 **Misheguk Mountain** ▲ Alaska, USA
165 N14 **Mishima** *var.* Misima. Shizuoka, Honshū, S Japan
164 E12 **Mi-shima** *island* SW Japan
127 V4 **Mishkino** Respublika Bashkortostan, W Russian Federation
153 Y10 **Mishmi Hills** *hill range* NE India
161 N11 **Mi Shui** ≈ S China
Misiaf *see* Maşyāf
107 J23 **Misilmeri** Sicilia, Italy, C Mediterranean Sea
Misima *see* Mishima
Misión de Guana *see* Guana
60 F13 **Misiones** *off.* Provincia de Misiones. ◐ *province* NE Argentina
62 P8 **Misiones** *off.* Departamento de las Misiones. ◐ *department* S Paraguay
Misión San Fernando *see* San Fernando
Miskin *see* Maskin
Miskito Coast *see* La Mosquitia
43 O7 **Miskitos, Cayos** *island group* NE Nicaragua
111 M21 **Miskolc** Borsod-Abaúj-Zemplén, NE Hungary
171 T12 **Misool, Pulau** *island* Maluku, E Indonesia
Misox *see* Mesocco
29 Y3 **Misquah Hills** *hill range* Minnesota, N USA
75 P7 **Mişrātah** *var.* Misurata. NW Libya
14 C7 **Missanabie** Ontario, S Canada
58 E10 **Missão Catrimani** Roraima, N Brazil
14 D6 **Missinaibi** ≈ Ontario, S Canada
14 C7 **Missinaibi Lake** ◎ Ontario, S Canada
11 T13 **Missinipe** Saskatchewan, C Canada
28 M11 **Mission** South Dakota, N USA
25 S17 **Mission** Texas, SW USA
12 F10 **Missisa Lake** ◎ Ontario, C Canada
18 M6 **Missisquoi Bay** *lake bay* Canada/USA
14 C10 **Mississagi** ≈ Ontario, S Canada
14 G15 **Mississauga** Ontario, S Canada
31 P12 **Mississinewa Lake** ▣ Indiana, N USA
31 P12 **Mississinewa River** ≈ Indiana/Ohio, N USA
22 K4 **Mississippi** *off.* State of Mississippi; also known as Bayou State, Magnolia State. ◐ *state* SE USA
14 K13 **Mississippi** ≈ Ontario, SE Canada
22 M10 **Mississippi Delta** *delta* Louisiana, S USA
47 N1 **Mississippi Fan** *undersea feature* N Gulf of Mexico
14 L13 **Mississippi Lake** ◎ Ontario, SE Canada
(0) J11 **Mississippi River** ≈ C USA
22 M9 **Mississippi Sound** *sound* Alabama/Mississippi, S USA
33 P9 **Missoula** Montana, NW USA
27 T5 **Missouri** *off.* State of Missouri; also known as Bullion State, Show Me State. ◐ *state* C USA
25 V11 **Missouri City** Texas, SW USA
(0) J10 **Missouri River** ≈ C USA
15 Q6 **Mistassibi** ≈ Québec, SE Canada
15 P6 **Mistassini** Québec, SE Canada
15 P6 **Mistassini** ≈ Québec, SE Canada
12 J11 **Mistassini, Lac** ◎ Québec, SE Canada
109 Y3 **Mistelbach an der Zaya** Niederösterreich, NE Austria
107 L24 **Misterbianco** Sicilia, Italy, C Mediterranean Sea
95 N19 **Misterhult** Kalmar, S Sweden
57 H17 **Misti, Volcán** ▲ S Peru
Mistras *see* Mystrás
107 K23 **Mistretta** *anc.* Amestratus. Sicilia, Italy, C Mediterranean Sea
164 F12 **Misumi** Shimane, Honshū, SW Japan
Misurata *see* Mişrātah
83 O14 **Mitande** Niassa, N Mozambique
40 J13 **Mita, Punta de** *headland* C Mexico
55 W12 **Mitaraka, Massif du** ▲ NE South America
Mitau *see* Jelgava
181 X9 **Mitchell** Queensland, E Australia
14 E15 **Mitchell** Ontario, S Canada
28 I13 **Mitchell** Nebraska, C USA
32 J12 **Mitchell** Oregon, NW USA
29 P11 **Mitchell** South Dakota, N USA
23 P5 **Mitchell Lake** ▣ Alabama, S USA
31 P7 **Mitchell, Lake** ◎ Michigan, N USA
21 P9 **Mitchell, Mount** ▲ North Carolina, SE USA
181 V3 **Mitchell River** ≈ Queensland, NE Australia
97 D20 **Mitchelstown** *Ir.* Baile Mhistéala. SW Ireland
14 M9 **Mitchinamécus, Lac** ◎ Québec, SE Canada
Mitèmboni *see* Mitemele, Río
79 D17 **Mitemele, Río** *var.* Mitèmboni, Temboni, Utamboni. ≈ S Equatorial Guinea
149 S12 **Mithānkot** Punjab, E Pakistan
149 T7 **Mitha Tiwāna** Punjab, E Pakistan
149 R17 **Mithi** Sind, SE Pakistan
Míthimna *see* Míthymna
Mi Tho *see* My Tho
115 L16 **Míthymna** *var.* Míthimna. Lésvos, E Greece
190 L16 **Mitiaro** *island* S Cook Islands
Mitilíni *see* Mytilíni
15 U7 **Mitis** ≈ Québec, SE Canada
41 R16 **Mitla** Oaxaca, SE Mexico
165 P13 **Mito** Ibaraki, Honshū, S Japan
92 N2 **Mitra, Kapp** *headland* W Svalbard
184 M13 **Mitre** ▲ North Island, NZ
185 B21 **Mitre Peak** ▲ South Island, NZ
39 O15 **Mitrofania Island** *island* Alaska, USA
Mitrovica/Mitrowitz *see* Sremska Mitrovica, Serbia, Serbia and Montenegro (Yugo.)
Mitrovica/Mitrovicë *see* Kosovska Mitrovica, Serbia, Serbia and Montenegro (Yugo.)
172 H12 **Mitsamiouli** Grande Comore, NW Comoros
172 I3 **Mitsinjo** Mahajanga, NW Madagascar
Mits'iwa *see* Massawa
172 H13 **Mitsoudjé** Grande Comore, NW Comoros
Mitspe Ramon *see* Miẓpé Ramon
165 T5 **Mitsuishi** Hokkaidō, NE Japan
165 O11 **Mitsuke** *var.* Mituke. Niigata, Honshū, C Japan
Mitsuō *see* Miryang
164 C12 **Mitsushima** Nagasaki, Tsushima, SW Japan
100 G12 **Mittelandkanal** *canal* NW Germany
108 J7 **Mittelberg** Vorarlberg, NW Austria
Mitteldorf *see* Międzychód
Mittelstadt *see* Baia Sprie
Mitterburg *see* Pazin
109 P7 **Mittersill** Salzburg, NW Austria
101 N16 **Mittweida** Sachsen, E Germany
54 J13 **Mitú** Vaupés, SE Colombia
Mituke *see* Mitsuke
Mitumba, Chaîne des/Mitumba Range *see* Mitumba, Monts
79 O22 **Mitumba, Monts** *var.* Chaîne des Mitumba, Mitumba Range. ▲▲ E Dem. Rep. Congo
79 N23 **Mitwaba** Katanga, SE Dem. Rep. Congo
79 E18 **Mitzic** Woleu-Ntem, N Gabon
82 K11 **Miueru Wantipa, Lake** ◎ N Zambia
165 N14 **Miura** Kanagawa, Honshū, S Japan
165 Q10 **Miyagi** *off.* Miyagi-ken. ◐ *prefecture* Honshū, C Japan
138 M7 **Miyāh, Wādī al** *dry watercourse* E Syria
165 X13 **Miyake** Tōkyō, Miyako-jima, SE Japan
165 R8 **Miyako** Iwate, Honshū, C Japan
165 Q16 **Miyako-jima** *island* Sakishima-shotō, SW Japan
164 D16 **Miyakonojō** *var.* Miyakonzyô. Miyazaki, Kyūshū, SW Japan
Miyakonzyô *see* Miyakonojō
165 Q16 **Miyako-shotō** *island group* SW Japan
144 G11 **Miyaly** Atyrau, W Kazakhstan
Miyāndoāb *see* Mīāndowāb
Miyāneh *see* Mīāneh
Miyang *see* Mile
164 D16 **Miyazaki** Miyazaki, Kyūshū, SW Japan
164 D16 **Miyazaki** *off.* Miyazaki-ken. ◐ *prefecture* Kyūshū, SW Japan
164 J12 **Miyazu** Kyōto, Honshū, SW Japan
Miyory *see* Myory
164 G12 **Miyoshi** *var.* Miyosi. Hiroshima, Honshū, SW Japan
Miyosi *see* Miyoshi
Miza *see* Mizë
81 H14 **Mīzan Teferī** Southern, S Ethiopia
Mizda *see* Mizdah
75 O8 **Mizdah** *var.* Mizda. NW Libya
113 K20 **Mizë** *var.* Miza. Fier, W Albania
97 A22 **Mizen Head** *Ir.* Carn Uí Néid. *headland* SW Ireland
116 H7 **Mizhhir"ya** *Rus.* Mezhgor'ye. Zakarpats'ka Oblast', W Ukraine
160 L4 **Mizhi** Shaanxi, C China
116 K13 **Mizil** Prahova, SE Romania
114 H7 **Miziya** Vratsa, NW Bulgaria
153 W15 **Mizo Hills** *hill range* E India
153 W15 **Mizoram** ◐ *state* NE India
138 F12 **Miẓpé Ramon** *var.* Mitspe Ramon. Southern, S Israel
57 L19 **Mizque** Cochabamba, C Bolivia
57 M19 **Mizque, Río** ≈ C Bolivia
165 Q9 **Mizusawa** Iwate, Honshū, C Japan
95 M18 **Mjölby** Östergötland, S Sweden
95 G15 **Mjøndalen** Buskerud, S Norway
95 J19 **Mjörn** ◎ S Sweden
94 I13 **Mjøsa** *var.* Mjøsen. ◎ S Norway
Mjøsen *see* Mjøsa
81 G21 **Mkalama** Singida, C Tanzania
80 K13 **Mkata** ≈ C Tanzania
83 K14 **Mkushi** Central, C Zambia
83 L22 **Mkuze** KwaZulu/Natal, E South Africa
81 J22 **Mkwaja** Tanga, E Tanzania
111 D16 **Mladá Boleslav** *Ger.* Jungbunzlau. Středočeský Kraj, N Czech Republic
112 M12 **Mladenovac** Serbia, C Serbia and Montenegro (Yugo.)
114 L11 **Mladinovo** Khaskovo, S Bulgaria
113 O17 **Mlado Nagoričane** N FYR Macedonia
Mlanje *see* Mulanje
112 N12 **Mlava** ≈ E Serbia and Montenegro (Yugo.)
110 L9 **Mława** Mazowieckie, C Poland
113 G16 **Mljet** *It.* Meleda; *anc.* Melita. *island* S Croatia
116 K4 **Mlyniv** Rivnens'ka Oblast', NW Ukraine
83 I21 **Mmabatho** North-West, N South Africa
83 I19 **Mmashoro** Central, E Botswana
44 J7 **Moa** Holguín, E Cuba
76 J15 **Moa** ≈ Guinea/Sierra Leone
37 O6 **Moab** Utah, W USA
181 V1 **Moa Island** *island* Queensland, NE Australia
187 Y15 **Moala** *island* S Fiji
83 L21 **Moamba** Maputo, SW Mozambique
79 F19 **Moanda** *var.* Mouanda. Haut-Ogooué, SE Gabon
83 M15 **Moatize** Tete, NW Mozambique
79 P22 **Moba** Katanga, E Dem. Rep. Congo
Mobay *see* Montego Bay
79 K15 **Mobaye** Basse-Kotto, S Central African Republic
79 K15 **Mobayi-Mbongo** Equateur, NW Dem. Rep. Congo
25 P2 **Mobeetie** Texas, SW USA
27 U3 **Moberly** Missouri, C USA
23 N8 **Mobile** Alabama, S USA
23 N9 **Mobile Bay** *bay* Alabama, S USA
23 N8 **Mobile** ≈ Alabama, S USA
29 N8 **Mobridge** South Dakota, N USA
Mobutu Sese Seko, Lac *see* Albert, Lake
45 N8 **Moca** N Dominican Republic
Moçâmedes *see* Namibe
167 S6 **Môc Châu** Sơn La, N Vietnam
187 Z15 **Moce** *island* Lau Group, E Fiji
83 Q15 **Moçambique** Nampula, NE Mozambique
Mocha *see* Al Mukhā
193 T11 **Mocha Fracture Zone** *tectonic feature* SE Pacific Ocean
63 F14 **Mocha, Isla** *island* C Chile
56 C12 **Moche, Río** ≈ W Peru
167 S14 **Môc Hoa** Long An, S Vietnam
83 I20 **Mochudi** Kgatleng, SE Botswana
82 Q13 **Mocímboa da Praia** *var.* Vila de Mocímboa da Praia. Cabo Delgado, N Mozambique
94 L13 **Mockfjärd** Dalarna, C Sweden
21 R9 **Mocksville** North Carolina, SE USA
32 F8 **Moclips** Washington, NW USA
82 C13 **Môco** *var.* Morro de Môco. ▲ W Angola
54 D13 **Mocoa** Putumayo, SW Colombia
60 M8 **Mococa** São Paulo, S Brazil
Môco, Morro de *see* Môco
40 H8 **Mocorito** Sinaloa, C Mexico
40 J4 **Moctezuma** Chihuahua, N Mexico
41 N11 **Moctezuma** San Luis Potosí, C Mexico
40 G4 **Moctezuma** Sonora, NW Mexico
41 P12 **Moctezuma, Río** ≈ C Mexico
Mó, Cuan *see* Clew Bay
83 O16 **Mocuba** Zambézia, NE Mozambique
103 U12 **Modane** Savoie, E France
106 F9 **Modena** *anc.* Mutina. Emilia-Romagna, N Italy
36 I7 **Modena** Utah, W USA
35 O9 **Modesto** California, W USA
107 L25 **Modica** *anc.* Motyca. Sicilia, Italy, C Mediterranean Sea
83 J20 **Modimolle** *prev.* Nylstroom. Limpopo, NE South Africa
79 K17 **Modjamboli** Equateur, N Dem. Rep. Congo
109 X4 **Mödling** Niederösterreich, NE Austria
Modohn *see* Madona
163 N8 **Modot** Hentiy, C Mongolia
171 V14 **Modowi** Papua, E Indonesia
112 I12 **Modračko Jezero** ▣ NE Bosnia and Herzegovina
112 I10 **Modriča** Republika Srpska, N Bosnia and Herzegovina
183 O13 **Moe** Victoria, SE Australia
Moearatewe *see* Muaratewe
Moei, Mae Nam *see* Thaungyin
94 H13 **Moelv** Hedmark, S Norway
92 I10 **Moen** Troms, N Norway
Moen *see* Weno, Micronesia
Möen *see* Møn, Denmark
Moena *see* Muna, Pulau
36 M10 **Moenkopi Wash** ≈ Arizona, SW USA
185 F22 **Moeraki Point** *headland* South Island, NZ
99 F16 **Moerbeke** Oost-Vlaanderen, NW Belgium
99 H14 **Moerdijk** Noord-Brabant, S Netherlands
Moero, Lac *see* Mweru, Lake
101 D15 **Moers** *var.* Mörs.Nordrhein-Westfalen, W Germany
Moesi *see* Musi, Air
Moeskroen *see* Mouscron
96 J13 **Moffat** S Scotland, UK
185 C22 **Moffat Peak** ▲ South Island, NZ
152 H8 **Moga** Punjab, N India
79 N19 **Moga** Sud Kivu, E Dem. Rep. Congo
Mogadiscio/Mogadishu *see* Muqdisho
Mogador *see* Essaouira
104 J6 **Mogadouro** Bragança, N Portugal
167 N2 **Mogaung** Kachin State, N Myanmar
110 L13 **Mogielnica** Mazowieckie, C Poland
Mogilëv *see* Mahilyow
Mogilev-Podol'skiy *see* Mohyliv-Podil's'kyy
Mogilëvskaya Oblast' *see* Mahilyowskaya Voblasts'
110 I11 **Mogilno** Kujawsko-pomorskie, C Poland
60 L9 **Mogi-Mirim** *var.* Moji-Mirim. São Paulo, S Brazil
83 Q15 **Mogincual** Nampula, NE Mozambique
114 E13 **Moglenítsas** ≈ N Greece
106 H8 **Mogliano Veneto** Veneto, NE Italy
113 M21 **Moglicë** Korçë, SE Albania
123 O13 **Mogocha** Chitinskaya Oblast', S Russian Federation
122 J11 **Mogochin** Tomskaya Oblast', C Russian Federation
80 F13 **Mogogh** Jonglei, SE Sudan
171 U12 **Mogoi** Papua, E Indonesia
166 M4 **Mogok** Mandalay, C Myanmar
37 P14 **Mogollon Mountains** ▲▲ New Mexico, SW USA
36 M12 **Mogollon Rim** *cliff* Arizona, SW USA
61 E23 **Mogotes, Punta** *headland* E Argentina
42 J8 **Mogotón** ▲ NW Nicaragua
104 I14 **Moguer** Andalucía, S Spain
111 J26 **Mohács** Baranya, SW Hungary
185 C20 **Mohaka** ≈ North Island, NZ
28 M2 **Mohall** North Dakota, N USA
Moḩammadābād *see* Dargaz
74 F6 **Mohammedia** *prev.* Fédala. NW Morocco
74 F6 **Mohammed V** ✖ (Casablanca) W Morocco
Mohammerah *see* Khorramshahr
36 H10 **Mohave, Lake** ▣ Arizona/Nevada, W USA
36 I12 **Mohave Mountains** ▲▲ Arizona, SW USA
36 I15 **Mohawk Mountains** ▲▲ Arizona, SW USA
18 J10 **Mohawk River** ≈ New York, NE USA
163 T3 **Mohe** *var.* Xilinji. Heilongjiang, NE China
95 L20 **Moheda** Kronoberg, S Sweden
172 H13 **Mohéli** *var.* Mwali, Mohilla, Mohila, *Fr.* Moili. *island* S Comoros
152 I11 **Mohendergarh** Haryāna, N India
38 K12 **Mohican, Cape** *headland* Nunivak Island, Alaska, USA
Mohn *see* Muhu
101 G15 **Möhne** ≈ W Germany
101 G15 **Möhne-Stausee** ▣ W Germany
92 P2 **Mohn, Kapp** *headland* NW Svalbard
197 S14 **Mohns Ridge** *undersea feature* Greenland Sea/Norwegian Sea
57 I17 **Moho** Puno, SW Peru
Mohokare *see* Caledon
95 L17 **Moholm** Västra Götaland, S Sweden

◆ COUNTRY
● COUNTRY CAPITAL
◇ DEPENDENT TERRITORY
○ DEPENDENT TERRITORY CAPITAL
◐ ADMINISTRATIVE REGION
✖ INTERNATIONAL AIRPORT
▲ MOUNTAIN
▲▲ MOUNTAIN RANGE
⛰ VOLCANO
≈ RIVER
◎ LAKE
▣ RESERVOIR

36 J11 **Mohon Peak** ▲ Arizona, SW USA
81 J23 **Mohoro** Pwani, E Tanzania
Mohra *see* Moravice
Mohrungen *see* Morąg
116 M7 **Mohyliv-Podil's'kyy** *Rus.* Mogilev-Podol'skiy. Vinnyts'ka Oblast', C Ukraine
95 D17 **Moi** Rogaland, S Norway
116 K11 **Moinești** *Hung.* Mojnest. Bacău, E Romania
Móinteach Mílic *see* Mountmellick
14 J14 **Moira** ⩫ Ontario, SE Canada
92 G13 **Mo i Rana** Nordland, C Norway
153 X14 **Moirāng** Manipur, NE India
115 J25 **Moíres** Kríti, Greece, E Mediterranean Sea
118 H6 **Mõisaküla** *Ger.* Moiseküll. Viljandimaa, S Estonia
Moiseküll *see* Mõisaküla
15 W4 **Moisie** Québec, E Canada
15 W3 **Moisie** ⩫ Québec, SE Canada
102 M14 **Moissac** Tarn-et-Garonne, S France
78 I13 **Moïssala** Moyen-Chari, S Chad
55 O7 **Moitaco** Bolívar, E Venezuela
95 P15 **Möja** Stockholm, C Sweden
105 Q14 **Mojácar** Andalucía, S Spain
35 T13 **Mojave** California, W USA
35 V13 **Mojave Desert** *plain* California, W USA
35 V13 **Mojave River** ⩫ California, W USA
Moji-Mirim *see* Mogi-Mirim
113 K15 **Mojkovac** Montenegro, SW Serbia and Montenegro (Yugo.)
Mojnest *see* Moinești
Mōka *see* Mooka
153 Q13 **Mokāma** *prev.* Mokameh, Mukama. Bihār, N India
79 O25 **Mokambo** Katanga, SE Dem. Rep. Congo
Mokameh *see* Mokāma
38 D9 **Mōkapu Point** *var.* Mokapu Point *headland* O'ahu, Hawai'i, USA, C Pacific Ocean
184 L9 **Mokau** Waikato, North Island, NZ
184 L9 **Mokau** ⩫ North Island, NZ
35 P7 **Mokelumne River** ⩫ California, W USA
83 J23 **Mokhotlong** NE Lesotho
Mokil Atoll *see* Mwokil Atoll
95 N14 **Möklinta** Västmanland, C Sweden
184 L4 **Mokohinau Islands** *island group* N NZ
153 X12 **Mokokchūng** Nāgāland, NE India
78 F12 **Mokolo** Extrême-Nord, N Cameroon
83 J20 **Mokopane** *prev.* Potgietersrus. Limpopo, NE South Africa
185 D24 **Mokoreta** ⩫ South Island, NZ
163 X17 **Mokp'o** *Jap.* Moppo. SW South Korea
113 L16 **Mokra Gora** ▲ S Serbia and Montenegro (Yugo.)
Mokrany *see* Makrany
127 O5 **Moksha** ⩫ W Russian Federation
Moktama *see* Martaban
77 T14 **Mokwa** Niger, W Nigeria
99 J16 **Mol** *prev.* Moll. Antwerpen, N Belgium
107 O17 **Mola di Bari** Puglia, SE Italy
Molai *see* Moláoi
41 P13 **Molango** Hidalgo, C Mexico
115 F22 **Moláoi** *var.* Molai. Pelopónnisos, S Greece
41 Z12 **Molas del Norte, Punta** *var.* Punta Molas. *headland* SE Mexico
Molas, Punta *see* Molas del Norte, Punta
105 R11 **Molatón** ▲ C Spain
97 K18 **Mold** NE Wales, UK
Moldau *see* Moldova
Moldau *see* Vltava, Czech Republic
Moldavia *see* Moldova
Moldavian SSR/Moldavskaya SSR *see* Moldova
94 E9 **Molde** Møre og Romsdal, S Norway
Moldotau, Khrebet *see* Moldo-Too, Khrebet
147 V9 **Moldo-Too, Khrebet** *prev.* Khrebet Moldotau. ▲ C Kyrgyzstan
116 K9 **Moldova** ⩫ N Romania
116 K9 **Moldova** *Eng.* Moldavia, *Ger.* Moldau. *former province* NE Romania
116 L9 **Moldova** *off.* Republic of Moldova, *var.* Moldavia; *prev.* Moldavian SSR, *Rus.* Moldavskaya SSR. ◆ *republic* SE Europe
116 F13 **Moldova Nouă** *Ger.* Neumoldowa, *Hung.* Újmoldova. Caraș-Severin, SW Romania
116 F13 **Moldova Veche** *Ger.* Altmoldowa, *Hung.* Ómoldova. Caraș-Severin, SW Romania
Moldoveanul *see* Vârful Moldoveanu
83 I20 **Molepolole** Kweneng, SE Botswana
44 L8 **Môle-St-Nicolas** NW Haiti
118 H13 **Molėtai** Utena, E Lithuania
107 O17 **Molfetta** Puglia, SE Italy
171 P11 **Molibagu** Sulawesi, N Indonesia
62 G12 **Molina** Maule, C Chile
105 Q7 **Molina de Aragón** Castilla-La Mancha, C Spain
105 R13 **Molina de Segura** Murcia, SE Spain
30 J11 **Moline** Illinois, N USA
27 P7 **Moline** Kansas, C USA
79 P23 **Moliro** Katanga, SE Dem. Rep. Congo
107 K16 **Molise** ◆ *region* S Italy
95 K15 **Molkom** Värmland, C Sweden
Moll *see* Mol
109 Q9 **Möll** ⩫ S Austria
146 I14 **Mollanepes Adyndaky** *Rus.* Imeni Mollanepesa. Mary Welaýaty, S Turkmenistan
95 J22 **Mölle** Skåne, S Sweden
57 H18 **Mollendo** Arequipa, SW Peru
105 U5 **Mollerussa** Cataluña, NE Spain
108 H8 **Mollis** Glarus, NE Switzerland
95 J19 **Mölndal** Västra Götaland, S Sweden
95 J19 **Mölnlycke** Västra Götaland, S Sweden
117 U9 **Molochans'k** *Rus.* Molochansk. Zaporiz'ka Oblast', SE Ukraine
117 U10 **Molochna** *Rus.* Molochnaya. ⩫ S Ukraine
Molochnaya *see* Molochna
117 U10 **Molochnyy Lyman** *bay* N Black Sea
Molodechno/Molodeczno *see* Maladzyechna
195 V3 **Molodezhnaya** *Russian research station* Antarctica
126 J14 **Mologa** ⩫ NW Russian Federation
38 E9 **Moloka'i** *var.* Molokai. *island* Hawai'i, USA, C Pacific Ocean
175 X3 **Molokai Fracture Zone** *tectonic feature* NE Pacific Ocean
124 K15 **Molokovo** Tverskaya Oblast', W Russian Federation
127 Q14 **Moloma** ⩫ NW Russian Federation
183 R8 **Molong** New South Wales, SE Australia
83 H21 **Molopo** *seasonal river* Botswana/South Africa
115 F17 **Mólos** Stereá Elláda, C Greece
171 O11 **Molosipat** Sulawesi, N Indonesia
Molotov *see* Severodvinsk, Arkhangel'skaya Oblast'
Molotov *see* Perm'
79 G17 **Moloundou** Est, SE Cameroon
103 U5 **Molsheim** Bas-Rhin, NE France
11 X13 **Molson Lake** ◎ Manitoba, C Canada
Moluccas *see* Maluku
171 Q12 **Molucca Sea** *Ind.* Laut Maluku. *sea* E Indonesia
Molukken *see* Maluku
83 O15 **Molumbo** Zambézia, N Mozambique
171 T15 **Molu, Pulau** *island* Maluku, E Indonesia
83 P16 **Moma** Nampula, NE Mozambique
171 X14 **Momats** ⩫ Papua, E Indonesia
42 J11 **Mombacho, Volcán** ⩰ SW Nicaragua
81 K21 **Mombasa** Coast, SE Kenya
81 J21 **Mombasa** ✕ Coast, SE Kenya
Mombetsu *see* Monbetsu
114 J12 **Momchilgrad** *prev.* Mastanli. Kŭrdzhali, S Bulgaria
99 F23 **Momignies** Hainaut, S Belgium
54 E6 **Momil** Córdoba, NW Colombia
42 I10 **Momotombo, Volcán** ⩰ W Nicaragua
56 B5 **Mompiche, Ensenada de** *bay* NW Ecuador
79 K18 **Mompono** Equateur, NW Dem. Rep. Congo
54 F6 **Mompós** Bolívar, NW Colombia
95 J24 **Møn** *prev.* Möen. *island* SE Denmark
36 L4 **Mona** Utah, W USA
Mona, Canal de la *see* Mona Passage
96 E8 **Monach Islands** *island group* NW Scotland, UK
103 V14 **Monaco** *var.* Monaco-Ville; *anc.* Monoecus. ● (Monaco) S Monaco
103 V14 **Monaco** *off.* Principality of Monaco. ◆ *monarchy* W Europe
Monaco *see* München
Monaco Basin *see* Canary Basin
Monaco-Ville *see* Monaco
96 I9 **Monadhliath Mountains** ▲ N Scotland, UK
55 O6 **Monagas** *off.* Estado Monagas. ◆ *state* NE Venezuela
97 F16 **Monaghan** *Ir.* Muineachán. N Ireland
97 E16 **Monaghan** *Ir.* Muineachán. *cultural region* N Ireland
43 S16 **Monagrillo** Herrera, S Panama
24 L8 **Monahans** Texas, SW USA
45 Q9 **Mona, Isla** *island* W Puerto Rico
45 Q9 **Mona Passage** *Sp.* Canal de la Mona. *channel* Dominican Republic/Puerto Rico
43 O14 **Mona, Punta** *headland* E Costa Rica
155 K25 **Monaragala** Uva Province, SE Sri Lanka
33 S9 **Monarch** Montana, NW USA
10 H14 **Monarch Mountain** ▲ British Columbia, SW Canada
Monasterio *see* Monesterio
Monasterzyska *see* Monastyrys'ka
Monastir *see* Bitola
Monastyriska *see* Monastyrys'ka
117 O7 **Monastyryshche** Cherkas'ka Oblast', C Ukraine
116 J6 **Monastyrys'ka** *Pol.* Monasterzyska, *Rus.* Monastyriska. Ternopil's'ka Oblast', W Ukraine
79 E15 **Monatélé** Centre, SW Cameroon
165 U2 **Monbetsu** *var.* Mombetsu, Monbetu. Hokkaidō, NE Japan
Monbetu *see* Monbetsu
106 B8 **Moncalieri** Piemonte, NW Italy
104 G4 **Monção** Viana do Castelo, N Portugal
105 Q5 **Moncayo** ▲ N Spain
105 Q5 **Moncayo, Sierra del** ▲ N Spain
124 J4 **Monchegorsk** Murmanskaya Oblast', NW Russian Federation
101 D15 **Mönchengladbach** *prev.* München-Gladbach. Nordrhein-Westfalen, W Germany
104 F14 **Monchique** Faro, S Portugal
104 G14 **Monchique, Serra de** ▲ S Portugal
21 S14 **Moncks Corner** South Carolina, SE USA
41 N7 **Monclova** Coahuila de Zaragoza, NE Mexico
Moncorvo *see* Torre de Moncorvo
13 P14 **Moncton** New Brunswick, SE Canada
104 F8 **Mondego, Cabo** *headland* N Portugal
104 G8 **Mondego, Rio** ⩫ N Portugal
104 I2 **Mondoñedo** Galicia, NW Spain
99 N25 **Mondorf-les-Bains** Grevenmacher, SE Luxembourg
102 M7 **Mondoubleau** Loir-et-Cher, C France
30 J6 **Mondovi** Wisconsin, N USA
106 B9 **Mondovì** Piemonte, NW Italy
105 P3 **Mondragón** *var.* Arrasate. País Vasco, N Spain
107 J17 **Mondragone** Campania, S Italy
109 R5 **Mondsee** ◎ N Austria
115 G22 **Monemvasía** Pelopónnisos, S Greece
18 B15 **Monessen** Pennsylvania, NE USA
104 J12 **Monesterio** *var.* Monasterio. Extremadura, W Spain
14 L8 **Monet** Québec, SE Canada
27 S8 **Monett** Missouri, C USA
27 X9 **Monette** Arkansas, C USA
14 G11 **Monetville** Ontario, S Canada
106 J7 **Monfalcone** Friuli-Venezia Giulia, NE Italy
104 H10 **Monforte** Portalegre, C Portugal
104 I4 **Monforte de Lemos** Galicia, NW Spain
81 I24 **Monga** Lindi, SE Tanzania
79 L16 **Monga** Orientale, N Dem. Rep. Congo
81 F15 **Mongalla** Bahr el Gabel, S Sudan
153 U11 **Mongar** E Bhutan
167 U6 **Mong Cai** Quang Ninh, N Vietnam
180 I11 **Mongers Lake** *salt lake* Western Australia
186 K8 **Mongga** Kolombangara, NW Solomon Islands
167 O6 **Mōng Hpayak** Shan State, E Myanmar
Monghyr *see* Munger
106 B10 **Mongioie** ▲ NW Italy
167 N5 **Mōng Küng** Shan State, E Myanmar
Mongla *see* Mungla
188 C15 **Mongmong** C Guam
167 N6 **Mōng Nai** Shan State, E Myanmar
78 I11 **Mongo** Guéra, C Chad
76 I14 **Mongo** ⩫ N Sierra Leone
163 I8 **Mongolia** *Mong.* Mongol Uls. ◆ *republic* E Asia
131 V8 **Mongolia, Plateau of** *plateau* E Mongolia
Mongolküre *see* Zhaosu
Mongol Uls *see* Mongolia
79 E17 **Mongomo** E Equatorial Guinea
77 Y12 **Mongonu** *var.* Monguno. Borno, NE Nigeria
Mongora *see* Mingāora
78 K11 **Mongororo** Ouaddaï, SE Chad
Mongos, Chaîne des *see* Bongo, Massif des
79 I16 **Mongoumba** Lobaye, SW Central African Republic
Mongrove, Punta *see* Cayacal, Punta
83 G15 **Mongu** Western, W Zambia
76 I10 **Mônguel** Gorgol, SW Mauritania
Monguno *see* Mongonu
167 N4 **Mōng Yai** Shan State, E Myanmar
167 O5 **Mōng Yang** Shan State, E Myanmar
167 N3 **Mōng Yu** Shan State, E Myanmar
162 K8 **Mönhbulag** Övörhangay, C Mongolia
Mönh Sarĭdag *see* Munku-Sardyk, Gora
186 P9 **Moni** ⩫ S Papau New Guinea
115 I15 **Moní Megístis Lávras** *monastery* Kentrikí Makedonía, N Greece
115 F18 **Moní Osíou Loúkas** *monastery* Stereá Elláda, C Greece
54 F9 **Moniquirá** Boyacá, C Colombia
103 Q12 **Monistrol-sur-Loire** Haute-Loire, C France
35 V7 **Monitor Range** ▲ Nevada, W USA
115 I14 **Moní Vatopedíou** *monastery* Kentrikí Makedonía, N Greece
Monkchester *see* Newcastle upon Tyne
83 N14 **Monkey Bay** Southern, SE Malawi
43 N11 **Monkey Point** *var.* Punta Mico, Punte Mono, Punto Mico. *headland* SE Nicaragua
Monkey River *see* Monkey River Town
42 G3 **Monkey River Town** *var.* Monkey River. Toledo, SE Belize
14 M13 **Monkland** Ontario, SE Canada
79 J19 **Monkoto** Equateur, NW Dem. Rep. Congo
97 K21 **Monmouth** *Wel.* Trefynwy. SE Wales, UK
30 J12 **Monmouth** Illinois, N USA
32 F12 **Monmouth** Oregon, NW USA
97 K21 **Monmouth** *cultural region* SE Wales, UK
98 I10 **Monnickendam** Noord-Holland, C Netherlands
77 R15 **Mono** ⩫ C Togo
Monoecus *see* Monaco
35 R8 **Mono Lake** ◎ California, W USA
115 O23 **Monólithos** Ródos, Dodekánisos, Greece, Aegean Sea
19 Q12 **Monomoy Island** *island* Massachusetts, NE USA
31 O12 **Monon** Indiana, N USA
29 Y12 **Monona** Iowa, C USA
30 L9 **Monona** Wisconsin, N USA
18 B15 **Monongahela** Pennsylvania, NE USA
18 B16 **Monongahela River** ⩫ NE USA
107 P17 **Monopoli** Puglia, SE Italy
Mono, Punte *see* Monkey Point
111 K23 **Monor** Pest, C Hungary
Monostor *see* Beli Manastir
78 K8 **Monou** Borkou-Ennedi-Tibesti, NE Chad
105 S12 **Monovar** *Cat.* Monover País Valenciano, E Spain
Monover *see* Monovar
105 R7 **Monreal del Campo** Aragón, NE Spain
107 I23 **Monreale** Sicilia, Italy, C Mediterranean Sea
23 T3 **Monroe** Georgia, SE USA
29 W14 **Monroe** Iowa, C USA
22 I5 **Monroe** Louisiana, S USA
31 S10 **Monroe** Michigan, N USA
18 K13 **Monroe** New York, NE USA
21 S11 **Monroe** North Carolina, SE USA
36 L6 **Monroe** Utah, W USA
32 H7 **Monroe** Washington, NW USA
30 L9 **Monroe** Wisconsin, N USA
27 V3 **Monroe City** Missouri, C USA
31 O15 **Monroe Lake** ⊠ Indiana, N USA
23 O7 **Monroeville** Alabama, S USA
18 C15 **Monroeville** Pennsylvania, NE USA
76 J16 **Monrovia** ● (Liberia) W Liberia
76 J16 **Monrovia** ✕ W Liberia
105 T7 **Monroyo** Aragón, NE Spain
99 F20 **Mons** *Dut.* Bergen. Hainaut, S Belgium
104 I8 **Monsanto** Castelo Branco, C Portugal
106 H8 **Monselice** Veneto, NE Italy
166 M9 **Mon State** ◆ *state* S Myanmar
98 G12 **Monster** Zuid-Holland, W Netherlands
95 N20 **Mönsterås** Kalmar, S Sweden
101 F17 **Montabaur** Rheinland-Pfalz, W Germany
106 G8 **Montagnana** Veneto, NE Italy
35 N1 **Montague** California, W USA
25 S5 **Montague** Texas, SW USA
183 S11 **Montague Island** *island* New South Wales, SE Australia
39 S12 **Montague Island** *island* Alaska, USA
39 S13 **Montague Strait** *strait* N Gulf of Alaska
102 J8 **Montaigu** Vendée, NW France
Montaigu *see* Scherpenheuvel
105 S7 **Montalbán** Aragón, NE Spain
106 G13 **Montalcino** Toscana, C Italy
104 H5 **Montalegre** Vila Real, N Portugal
114 G8 **Montana** *prev.* Ferdinand, Mikhaylovgrad. Montana, NW Bulgaria
108 D10 **Montana** Valais, SW Switzerland
39 R11 **Montana** Alaska, USA
114 G8 **Montana** ◆ *province* NW Bulgaria
33 T9 **Montana** *off.* State of Montana; also known as Mountain State, Treasure State. ◆ *state* NW USA
104 J10 **Montánchez** Extremadura, W Spain
Montañita *see* La Montañita
15 Q8 **Mont-Apica** Québec, SE Canada
104 G10 **Montargil** Portalegre, C Portugal
104 G10 **Montargil, Barragem de** ⊠ C Portugal
103 O7 **Montargis** Loiret, C France
103 O4 **Montataire** Oise, N France
102 M14 **Montauban** Tarn-et-Garonne, S France
19 N14 **Montauk** Long Island, New York, NE USA
19 N14 **Montauk Point** *headland* Long Island, New York, NE USA
103 Q7 **Montbard** Côte d'Or, C France
103 U7 **Montbéliard** Doubs, E France
25 W11 **Mont Belvieu** Texas, SW USA
105 U6 **Montblanc** *var.* Montblanch. Cataluña, NE Spain
Montblanch *see* Montblanc
103 Q11 **Montbrison** Loire, E France
Montcalm, Lake *see* Dogai Coring
103 Q9 **Montceau-les-Mines** Saône-et-Loire, C France
103 U12 **Mont Cenis, Col du** *pass* E France
102 K15 **Mont-de-Marsan** Landes, SW France
103 O3 **Montdidier** Somme, N France
187 Q17 **Mont-Dore** Province Sud, S New Caledonia
20 K10 **Monteagle** Tennessee, S USA
57 M20 **Monteagudo** Chuquisaca, S Bolivia
41 R16 **Monte Albán** *ruins* Oaxaca, S Mexico
105 R11 **Montealegre del Castillo** Castilla-La Mancha, C Spain
59 N18 **Monte Azul** Minas Gerais, SE Brazil
14 M12 **Montebello** Québec, SE Canada
106 H7 **Montebelluna** Veneto, NE Italy
60 G13 **Montecarlo** Misiones, NE Argentina
61 D16 **Monte Caseros** Corrientes, NE Argentina
60 J13 **Monte Castelo** Santa Catarina, S Brazil
106 F11 **Montecatini Terme** Toscana, C Italy
42 H7 **Montecillos, Cordillera de** ▲ W Honduras
62 I12 **Monte Comén** Mendoza, W Argentina
44 M8 **Monte Cristi** *var.* San Fernando de Monte Cristi. NW Dominican Republic
58 C13 **Monte Cristo** Amazonas, W Brazil
107 E14 **Montecristo, Isola di** *island* Archipelago Toscano, C Italy
Monte Croce Carnico, Passo di *see* Plöcken Pass
58 J12 **Monte Dourado** Pará, NE Brazil
40 L11 **Monte Escobedo** Zacatecas, C Mexico
106 I13 **Montefalco** Umbria, C Italy
107 H14 **Montefiascone** Lazio, C Italy
105 N14 **Montefrío** Andalucía, S Spain
44 I11 **Montego Bay** *var.* Mobay. W Jamaica
Montego Bay *see* Sangster
104 J8 **Montehermoso** Extremadura, W Spain
104 F10 **Montejunto, Serra de** ▲ C Portugal
Monteleone di Calabria *see* Vibo Valentia
54 E7 **Montelíbano** Córdoba, NW Colombia
103 R13 **Montélimar** *anc.* Acunum Acusio, Montilium Adhemari. Drôme, E France
104 K15 **Montellano** Andalucía, S Spain
35 Y2 **Montello** Nevada, W USA
30 L8 **Montello** Wisconsin, N USA
63 J18 **Montemayor, Meseta de** *plain* SE Argentina
41 O9 **Montemorelos** Nuevo León, NE Mexico
104 G11 **Montemor-o-Novo** Évora, S Portugal
104 G8 **Montemor-o-Velho** *var.* Montemor-o-Vélho. Coimbra, N Portugal
104 H7 **Montemuro, Serra de** ▲ N Portugal
102 K12 **Montendre** Charente-Maritime, W France
61 I15 **Montenegro** Rio Grande do Sul, S Brazil
113 J16 **Montenegro** *Serb.* Crna Gora. ◆ *republic* SW Serbia and Montenegro (Yugo.)
62 G10 **Monte Patria** Coquimbo, N Chile
45 O9 **Monte Plata** E Dominican Republic
83 P14 **Montepuez** Cabo Delgado, N Mozambique
83 P14 **Montepuez** ⩫ N Mozambique
106 G13 **Montepulciano** Toscana, C Italy
62 L6 **Monte Quemado** Santiago del Estero, N Argentina
103 O6 **Montereau-Faut-Yonne** *anc.* Condate. Seine-St-Denis, N France
35 N11 **Monterey** California, W USA
20 L9 **Monterey** Tennessee, S USA
21 T5 **Monterey** Virginia, NE USA
Monterey *see* Monterrey
35 N10 **Monterey Bay** *bay* California, W USA
54 D6 **Montería** Córdoba, NW Colombia
57 N18 **Montero** Santa Cruz, C Bolivia
62 J7 **Monteros** Tucumán, C Argentina
104 I5 **Monterrei** Galicia, NW Spain
41 O8 **Monterrey** *var.* Monterey. Nuevo León, NE Mexico
32 F9 **Montesano** Washington, NW USA
107 M19 **Montesano sulla Marcellana** Campania, S Italy
107 N16 **Monte Sant' Angelo** Puglia, SE Italy
59 O16 **Monte Santo** Bahia, E Brazil
107 D18 **Monte Santu, Capo di** *headland* Sardegna, Italy, C Mediterranean Sea
59 M19 **Montes Claros** Minas Gerais, SE Brazil
107 K14 **Montesilvano Marina** Abruzzo, C Italy
23 P4 **Montevallo** Alabama, S USA
106 G12 **Montevarchi** Toscana, C Italy
29 S9 **Montevideo** Minnesota, N USA
61 F20 **Montevideo** ● (Uruguay) Montevideo, S Uruguay
37 S7 **Monte Vista** Colorado, C USA
23 T5 **Montezuma** Georgia, SE USA
29 W14 **Montezuma** Iowa, C USA
26 J6 **Montezuma** Kansas, C USA
103 U12 **Montgenèvre, Col de** *pass* France/Italy
97 K20 **Montgomery** E Wales, UK
23 Q5 **Montgomery** *state capital* Alabama, S USA
29 V9 **Montgomery** Minnesota, N USA
18 G13 **Montgomery** Pennsylvania, NE USA
21 Q5 **Montgomery** West Virginia, NE USA
97 K19 **Montgomery** *cultural region* E Wales, UK
Montgomery *see* Sāhīwāl
27 V4 **Montgomery City** Missouri, C USA
35 S8 **Montgomery Pass** *pass* Nevada, W USA
102 K12 **Montguyon** Charente-Maritime, W France
108 C10 **Monthey** Valais, SW Switzerland
27 V13 **Monticello** Arkansas, C USA
23 T4 **Monticello** Florida, SE USA
23 T8 **Monticello** Georgia, SE USA
30 M13 **Monticello** Illinois, N USA
31 O12 **Monticello** Indiana, N USA
29 Y13 **Monticello** Iowa, C USA
20 L7 **Monticello** Kentucky, S USA
29 V8 **Monticello** Minnesota, N USA
22 K7 **Monticello** Mississippi, S USA
27 V2 **Monticello** Missouri, C USA
18 J12 **Monticello** New York, NE USA
37 O7 **Monticello** Utah, W USA
106 F8 **Montichiari** Lombardia, N Italy
102 M12 **Montignac** Dordogne, SW France
99 G21 **Montignies-le-Tilleul** *var.* Montigny-le-Tilleul. Hainaut, S Belgium
14 J8 **Montigny, Lac de** ◎ Québec, SE Canada
103 S6 **Montigny-le-Roi** Haute-Marne, N France
Montigny-le-Tilleul *see* Montignies-le-Tilleul
43 R16 **Montijo** Veraguas, S Panama
104 F11 **Montijo** Setúbal, W Portugal
104 J11 **Montijo** Extremadura, W Spain
Montilium Adhemari *see* Montélimar
104 M13 **Montilla** Andalucía, S Spain
102 L3 **Montivilliers** Seine-Maritime, N France
15 U7 **Mont-Joli** Québec, SE Canada
14 M10 **Mont-Laurier** Québec, SE Canada
15 X5 **Mont-Louis** Québec, SE Canada
103 N17 **Mont-Louis** *var.* Mont Louis. Pyrénées-Orientales, S France
103 O10 **Montluçon** Allier, C France
15 R10 **Montmagny** Québec, SE Canada
103 S3 **Montmédy** Meuse, NE France
103 P5 **Montmirail** Marne, N France
15 R9 **Montmorency** ⩫ Québec, SE Canada
102 M10 **Montmorillon** Vienne, W France
107 J14 **Montorio al Vomano** Abruzzo, C Italy
104 M13 **Montoro** Andalucía, S Spain
33 S16 **Montpelier** Idaho, NW USA
29 P6 **Montpelier** North Dakota, N USA
18 M7 **Montpelier** *state capital* Vermont, NE USA
103 Q15 **Montpellier** Hérault, S France
102 L12 **Montpon-Ménestérol** Dordogne, SW France
12 K15 **Montréal** *Eng.* Montreal. Québec, SE Canada
14 G8 **Montreal** ⩫ Ontario, S Canada
14 C8 **Montreal** ⩫ Ontario, S Canada
Montreal *see* Mirabel
11 T14 **Montreal Lake** ◎ Saskatchewan, C Canada
14 B9 **Montreal River** Ontario, S Canada
103 N2 **Montreuil** Pas-de-Calais, N France
102 K8 **Montreuil-Bellay** Maine-et-Loire, NW France
108 C10 **Montreux** Vaud, SW Switzerland
108 B9 **Montricher** Vaud, W Switzerland
96 K10 **Montrose** E Scotland, UK
27 W14 **Montrose** Arkansas, C USA
37 Q6 **Montrose** Colorado, C USA
29 Y16 **Montrose** Iowa, C USA
18 H12 **Montrose** Pennsylvania, NE USA
21 X5 **Montross** Virginia, NE USA
15 O12 **Mont-St-Hilaire** Québec, SE Canada
103 S3 **Mont-St-Martin** Meurthe-et-Moselle, NE France
45 V10 **Montserrat** *var.* Emerald Isle. ◇ *UK dependent territory* E West Indies
105 V5 **Montserrat** ▲ NE Spain
104 M7 **Montuenga** Castilla-León, N Spain
99 M19 **Montzen** Liège, E Belgium
37 N8 **Monument Valley** *valley* Arizona/Utah, SW USA
166 L4 **Monywa** Sagaing, C Myanmar
106 D7 **Monza** Lombardia, N Italy
83 J15 **Monze** Southern, S Zambia
105 T5 **Monzón** Aragón, NE Spain
25 T9 **Moody** Texas, SW USA
98 L13 **Mook** Limburg, SE Netherlands
165 O12 **Mooka** *var.* Mōka. Tochigi, Honshū, S Japan
182 K3 **Moomba** South Australia
14 G13 **Moon** ⩫ Ontario, S Canada
Moon *see* Muhu
181 Y10 **Moonie** Queensland, E Australia
193 O5 **Moonless Mountains** *undersea feature* E Pacific Ocean
182 L13 **Moonlight Head** *headland* Victoria, SE Australia
Moon-Sund *see* Väinameri
182 H8 **Moonta** South Australia
Moor *see* Mór
180 I12 **Moora** Western Australia
98 H12 **Moordrecht** Zuid-Holland, C Netherlands
33 T9 **Moore** Montana, NW USA
27 N11 **Moore** Oklahoma, C USA
25 R12 **Moore** Texas, SW USA
191 S10 **Moorea** *island* Îles du Vent, W French Polynesia
21 U3 **Moorefield** West Virginia, NE USA
23 X14 **Moore Haven** Florida, SE USA
180 J11 **Moore, Lake** ◎ Western Australia
19 N7 **Moore Reservoir** ⊠ New Hampshire/Vermont, NE USA
44 G1 **Moores Island** *island* N Bahamas
21 R10 **Mooresville** North Carolina, SE USA
29 R5 **Moorhead** Minnesota, N USA
22 K4 **Moorhead** Mississippi, S USA
99 F18 **Moorsel** Oost-Vlaanderen, C Belgium
99 C18 **Moorslede** West-Vlaanderen, W Belgium
18 L8 **Moosalamoo, Mount** ▲ Vermont, NE USA
101 M22 **Moosburg an der Isar** Bayern, SE Germany
33 S14 **Moose** Wyoming, C USA
12 H11 **Moose** ⩫ Ontario, S Canada

12 H10 **Moose Factory** Ontario, S Canada
19 Q4 **Moosehead Lake** ◎ Maine, NE USA
11 U16 **Moose Jaw** Saskatchewan, S Canada
11 V14 **Moose Lake** Manitoba, C Canada
29 W6 **Moose Lake** Minnesota, N USA
19 P6 **Mooselookmeguntic Lake** ◎ Maine, NE USA
39 R12 **Moose Pass** Alaska, USA
19 P5 **Moose River** ≈ Maine, NE USA
18 J9 **Moose River** ≈ New York, NE USA
11 V16 **Moosomin** Saskatchewan, S Canada
12 H10 **Moosonee** Ontario, SE Canada
19 N12 **Moosup** Connecticut, NE USA
83 N16 **Mopeia** Zambézia, NE Mozambique
83 H18 **Mopipi** Central, C Botswana
Moppo *see* Mokp'o
77 N11 **Mopti** Mopti, C Mali
77 O11 **Mopti** ◆ *region* S Mali
57 H18 **Moquegua** Moquegua, SE Peru
57 H18 **Moquegua** *off.* Departamento de Moquegua. ◆ *department* S Peru
111 I23 **Mór** *Ger.* Moor. Fejér, C Hungary
78 G11 **Mora** Extrême-Nord, N Cameroon
104 G11 **Mora** Évora, S Portugal
105 N9 **Mora** Castilla-La Mancha, C Spain
94 L12 **Mora** Dalarna, C Sweden
29 V7 **Mora** Minnesota, N USA
37 T10 **Mora** New Mexico, SW USA
113 J17 **Morača** ≈ SW Serbia and Montenegro (Yugo.)
152 K10 **Morādābād** Uttar Pradesh, N India
105 U6 **Móra d'Ebre** *var.* Mora de Ebro. Cataluña, NE Spain
Mora de Ebro *see* Móra d'Ebre
105 S8 **Mora de Rubielos** Aragón, NE Spain
172 H4 **Morafenobe** Mahajanga, W Madagascar
110 K8 **Morąg** *Ger.* Mohrungen. Warmińsko-Mazurskie, NE Poland,
111 L25 **Mórahalom** Csongrád, S Hungary
105 N11 **Moral de Calatrava** Castilla-La Mancha, C Spain
63 G19 **Moraleda, Canal** *strait* SE Pacific Ocean
54 J3 **Morales** Bolívar, N Colombia
54 D12 **Morales** Cauca, SW Colombia
42 F5 **Morales** Izabal, E Guatemala
172 J5 **Moramanga** Toamasina, E Madagascar
27 Q6 **Moran** Kansas, C USA
25 Q7 **Moran** Texas, SW USA
181 X7 **Moranbah** Queensland, NE Australia
44 L13 **Morant Bay** E Jamaica
96 G10 **Morar, Loch** ◎ N Scotland, UK
Morata *see* Goodenough Island
105 Q12 **Moratalla** Murcia, SE Spain
108 C8 **Morat, Lac de** *Ger.* Murtensee. ◎ W Switzerland
84 I11 **Morava** *var.* March. ≈ C Europe *see also* March
Morava *see* Moravia, Czech Republic
Morava *see* Velika Morava, Serbia and Montenegro (Yugo.)
29 W15 **Moravia** Iowa, C USA
111 F18 **Moravia** *Cz.* Morava, *Ger.* Mähren. *cultural region* E Czech Republic
111 H17 **Moravice** *Ger.* Mohra. ≈ NE Czech Republic
118 E12 **Moravița** Timiș, SW Romania
111 G17 **Moravská Třebová** *Ger.* Mährisch-Trübau. Pardubický Kraj, C Czech Republic
111 E19 **Moravské Budějovice** *Ger.* Mährisch-Budwitz. Vysočina, C Czech Republic
111 H17 **Moravskoslezský Kraj** *prev.* Ostravský Kraj. ◆ *region* E Czech Republic
111 F19 **Moravský Krumlov** *Ger.* Mährisch-Kromau. Jihomoravský Kraj, SE Czech Republic
96 J8 **Moray** *cultural region* N Scotland, UK
96 J8 **Moray Firth** *inlet* N Scotland, UK
42 B10 **Morazán** ◆ *department* NE El Salvador
154 C10 **Morbi** Gujarāt, W India
102 G7 **Morbihan** ◆ *department* NW France
Mörbisch *see* Mörbisch am See
109 Y5 **Mörbisch am See** *var.* Mörbisch. Burgenland, E Austria
95 N21 **Mörbylånga** Kalmar, S Sweden
102 J14 **Morcenx** Landes, SW France
Morcheh Khort *see* Mūrcheh Khvort
163 T5 **Mordaga** Nei Mongol Zizhiqu, N China
11 X17 **Morden** Manitoba, S Canada
Mordovskaya ASSR/Mordvinia *see* Mordoviya, Respublika
127 N5 **Mordoviya, Respublika** *prev.* Mordovskaya ASSR, *Eng.* Mordovia, Mordvinia. ◆ *autonomous republic* W Russian Federation
126 M7 **Mordovo** Tambovskaya Oblast', W Russian Federation
Morea *see* Pelopónnisos
28 K8 **Moreau River** ≈ South Dakota, N USA
97 K16 **Morecambe** NW England, UK
97 K16 **Morecambe Bay** *inlet* NW England, UK
183 S4 **Moree** New South Wales, SE Australia
21 N5 **Morehead** Kentucky, S USA
21 X11 **Morehead City** North Carolina, SE USA
27 Y8 **Morehouse** Missouri, C USA
108 E10 **Mörel** Valais, SW Switzerland
54 D13 **Morelia** Caquetá, S Colombia
41 N14 **Morelia** Michoacán de Ocampo, S Mexico
105 T7 **Morella** País Valenciano, E Spain
40 I7 **Morelos** Chihuahua, N Mexico
41 O15 **Morelos** ◆ *state* S Mexico
154 H7 **Morena** Madhya Pradesh, C India
104 L12 **Morena, Sierra** ▲ S Spain
37 O14 **Morenci** Arizona, SW USA
31 R11 **Morenci** Michigan, N USA
116 J13 **Moreni** Dâmbovița, S Romania
94 D9 **Møre og Romsdal** ◆ *county* S Norway
10 I14 **Moresby Island** *island* Queen Charlotte Islands, British Columbia, SW Canada
183 W2 **Moreton Island** *island* Queensland, E Australia
103 O3 **Moreuil** Somme, N France
35 V7 **Morey Peak** ▲ Nevada, W USA
127 U4 **More-Yu** ≈ NW Russian Federation
103 T9 **Morez** Jura, E France
Mórfou *see* Güzelyurt
Morfou Bay/Mórfou, Kólpos *see* Güzelyurt Körfezi
182 J8 **Morgan** South Australia
23 S7 **Morgan** Georgia, SE USA
25 S8 **Morgan** Texas, SW USA
22 J10 **Morgan City** Louisiana, S USA
20 H6 **Morganfield** Kentucky, S USA
35 O10 **Morgan Hill** California, W USA
21 Q9 **Morganton** North Carolina, SE USA
20 J7 **Morgantown** Kentucky, S USA
21 S2 **Morgantown** West Virginia, NE USA
108 B10 **Morges** Vaud, SW Switzerland
148 M4 **Morghāb, Daryā-ye** *Rus.* Murgab, Murghab, *Turkm.* Murgap, Murgap Deryasy. ≈ Afghanistan/ Turkmenistan *see also* Murgap
96 I9 **Mor, Glen** *var.* Glen Albyn, Great Glen. *valley* N Scotland, UK
103 T5 **Morhange** Moselle, NE France
158 M5 **Mori** *var.* Mori Kazak Zizhixian. Xinjiang Uygur Zizhiqu, NW China
165 R5 **Mori** Hokkaidō, NE Japan
35 Y6 **Moriah, Mount** ▲ Nevada, W USA
37 S11 **Moriarty** New Mexico, SW USA
54 J12 **Morichal** Guaviare, E Colombia
Mori Kazak Zizhixian *see* Mori
Morin Dawa Daurzu Zizhiqi *see* Nirji
11 Q14 **Morinville** Alberta, SW Canada
165 R8 **Morioka** Iwate, Honshū, C Japan
183 T8 **Morisset** New South Wales, SE Australia
165 Q8 **Moriyoshi-yama** ▲ Honshū, C Japan
92 K13 **Morjärv** Norrbotten, N Sweden
127 R3 **Morki** Respublika Mariy El, W Russian Federation
123 N10 **Morkoka** ≈ NE Russian Federation
102 F5 **Morlaix** Finistère, NW France
95 M20 **Mörlunda** Kalmar, S Sweden
107 N19 **Mormanno** Calabria, SW Italy
36 L11 **Mormon Lake** ◎ Arizona, SW USA
35 Y10 **Mormon Peak** ▲ Nevada, W USA
Mormon State *see* Utah
45 Y5 **Morne-à-l'Eau** Grande Terre, N Guadeloupe
29 Y15 **Morning Sun** Iowa, C USA
193 S12 **Mornington Abyssal Plain** *undersea feature* SE Pacific Ocean
63 F22 **Mornington, Isla** *island* S Chile
181 T4 **Mornington Island** *island* Wellesley Islands, Queensland, N Australia
115 E18 **Mórnos** ≈ C Greece
149 P14 **Moro** Sind, SE Pakistan
32 I11 **Moro** Oregon, NW USA
186 E8 **Morobe** Morobe, C PNG
186 E8 **Morobe** ◆ *province* C PNG
31 N12 **Morocco** Indiana, N USA
74 E8 **Morocco** *off.* Kingdom of Morocco, *Ar.* Al Mamlakah. ◆ *monarchy* N Africa
Morocco *see* Marrakech
81 I22 **Morogoro** Morogoro, E Tanzania
81 H24 **Morogoro** ◆ *region* SE Tanzania
171 Q7 **Moro Gulf** *gulf* S Philippines
41 N13 **Moroleón** Guanajuato, C Mexico
172 H6 **Morombe** Toliara, W Madagascar
44 G5 **Morón** Ciego de Ávila, C Cuba
54 K5 **Morón** Carabobo, N Venezuela
Morón *see* Morón de la Frontera
163 N8 **Mörön** Hentiy, C Mongolia
162 I6 **Mörön** Hövsgöl, N Mongolia
56 D8 **Morona, Río** ≈ N Peru
56 C8 **Morona Santiago** ◆ *province* E Ecuador
172 H5 **Morondava** Toliara, W Madagascar
104 K14 **Morón de la Frontera** *var.* Morón. Andalucía, S Spain
172 G13 **Moroni** ● (Comoros) Grande Comore, NW Comoros
171 S10 **Morotai, Pulau** *island* Maluku, E Indonesia
Morotiri *see* Marotiri
81 H17 **Moroto** NE Uganda
Morozov *see* Bratan
126 M11 **Morozovsk** Rostovskaya Oblast', SW Russian Federation
97 L14 **Morpeth** N England, UK
Morphou *see* Güzelyurt
Morphou Bay *see* Güzelyurt Körfezi
28 I13 **Morrill** Nebraska, C USA
27 U11 **Morrilton** Arkansas, C USA
11 Q16 **Morrin** Alberta, SW Canada
184 M7 **Morrinsville** Waikato, North Island, NZ
11 X16 **Morris** Manitoba, S Canada
30 M11 **Morris** Illinois, N USA
29 S8 **Morris** Minnesota, N USA
14 M13 **Morrisburg** Ontario, SE Canada
197 R11 **Morris Jesup, Kap** *headland* N Greenland
182 B1 **Morris, Mount** ▲ South Australia
30 K10 **Morrison** Illinois, N USA
36 K13 **Morristown** Arizona, SW USA
18 J14 **Morristown** New Jersey, NE USA
21 O8 **Morristown** Tennessee, S USA
42 L11 **Morrito** Río San Juan, SW Nicaragua
35 P13 **Morro Bay** California, W USA
95 L22 **Mörrum** Blekinge, S Sweden
83 N16 **Morrumbala** Zambézia, NE Mozambique
83 N20 **Morrumbene** Inhambane, SE Mozambique
95 F21 **Mors** *island* NW Denmark
Mörs *see* Moers
25 N1 **Morse** Texas, SW USA
127 N6 **Morshansk** Tambovskaya Oblast', W Russian Federation
102 L5 **Mortagne-au-Perche** Orne, N France
102 J8 **Mortagne-sur-Sèvre** Vendée, NW France
104 G8 **Mortágua** Viseu, N Portugal
102 J5 **Mortain** Manche, N France
106 C8 **Mortara** Lombardia, N Italy
59 J17 **Mortes, Rio das** ≈ C Brazil
182 M12 **Mortlake** Victoria, SE Australia
Mortlock Group *see* Takuu Islands
189 Q17 **Mortlock Islands** *prev.* Nomoi Islands. *island group* C Micronesia
29 T9 **Morton** Minnesota, N USA
22 L5 **Morton** Mississippi, S USA
24 M5 **Morton** Texas, SW USA
32 H9 **Morton** Washington, NW USA
(0) D7 **Morton Seamount** *undersea feature* NE Pacific Ocean
45 U15 **Moruga** Trinidad, Trinidad and Tobago
183 P9 **Morundah** New South Wales, SE Australia
Moruroa *see* Mururoa
183 S11 **Moruya** New South Wales, SE Australia
103 Q8 **Morvan** *physical region* C France
185 G21 **Morven** Canterbury, South Island, NZ
183 O13 **Morwell** Victoria, SE Australia
127 N6 **Morzhovets, Ostrov** *island* NW Russian Federation
126 J4 **Mosal'sk** Kaluzhskaya Oblast', W Russian Federation
101 H20 **Mosbach** Baden-Württemberg, SW Germany
95 E18 **Mosby** Vest-Agder, S Norway
33 V9 **Mosby** Montana, NW USA
32 M9 **Moscow** Idaho, NW USA
20 F10 **Moscow** Tennessee, S USA
Moscow *see* Moskva
101 D19 **Mosel** *Fr.* Moselle. ≈ W Europe *see also* Moselle
103 T4 **Moselle** ◆ *department* NE France
103 T6 **Moselle** *Ger.* Mosel. ≈ W Europe *see also* Mosel
32 K9 **Moses Lake** ◎ Washington, NW USA
83 I18 **Mosetse** Central, E Botswana
92 H4 **Mosfellsbær** Sudhurland, SW Iceland
185 F23 **Mosgiel** Otago, South Island, NZ
126 M11 **Mosha** ≈ NW Russian Federation
81 I20 **Moshi** Kilimanjaro, NE Tanzania
110 G12 **Mosina** Wielkolpolskie, C Poland
30 L6 **Mosinee** Wisconsin, N USA
92 F13 **Mosjøen** Nordland, C Norway
123 S12 **Moskal'vo** Ostrov Sakhalin, Sakhalinskaya Oblast', SE Russian Federation
92 I13 **Moskosel** Norrbotten, N Sweden
126 K4 **Moskovskaya Oblast'** ◆ *province* W Russian Federation
Moskovskiy *see* Moskva
126 J3 **Moskva** *Eng.* Moscow. ● (Russian Federation) Gorod Moskva, W Russian Federation
147 Q14 **Moskva** *Rus.* Moskovskiy; *prev.* Chubek. SW Tajikistan
126 L4 **Moskva** ≈ W Russian Federation
83 I20 **Mosomane** Kgatleng, SE Botswana
Moson and Magyaróvár *see* Mosonmagyaróvár
111 H21 **Mosoni-Duna** *Ger.* Kleine Donau. ≈ NW Hungary
111 H21 **Mosonmagyaróvár** *Ger.* Wieselburg-Ungarisch-Altenburg; *prev.* Moson and Magyaróvár, *Ger.* Wieselburg and Ungarisch-Altenburg. Győr-Moson-Sopron, NW Hungary
Mospino *see* Mospyne
117 X8 **Mospyne** *Rus.* Mospino. Donets'ka Oblast', E Ukraine
54 B12 **Mosquera** Nariño, SW Colombia
37 U10 **Mosquero** New Mexico, SW USA
Mosquito Coast *see* La Mosquitia
31 U11 **Mosquito Creek Lake** ◎ Ohio, N USA
Mosquito Gulf *see* Mosquitos, Golfo de los
23 X11 **Mosquito Lagoon** *wetland* Florida, SE USA
43 N10 **Mosquito, Punta** *headland* E Nicaragua
43 W14 **Mosquito, Punta** *headland* NE Panama
43 Q15 **Mosquitos, Golfo de los** *Eng.* Mosquito Gulf. *gulf* N Panama
95 H16 **Moss** Østfold, S Norway
Mossâmedes *see* Namibe
22 G8 **Moss Bluff** Louisiana, S USA
185 C23 **Mossburn** Southland, South Island, NZ
83 G26 **Mosselbaai** *var.* Mosselbai, *Eng.* Mossel Bay. Western Cape, SW South Africa
Mosselbai/Mossel Bay *see* Mosselbaai
79 F20 **Mossendjo** Le Niari, SW Congo
183 N8 **Mossgiel** New South Wales, SE Australia
101 H22 **Mössingen** Baden-Württemberg, S Germany
181 W4 **Mossman** Queensland, NE Australia
59 P14 **Mossoró** Rio Grande do Norte, NE Brazil
23 N9 **Moss Point** Mississippi, S USA
183 S9 **Moss Vale** New South Wales, SE Australia
32 G9 **Mossyrock** Washington, NW USA
111 B15 **Most** *Ger.* Brüx. Ústecký Kraj, NW Czech Republic
121 P16 **Mosta** *var.* Musta. C Malta
74 I5 **Mostaganem** *var.* Mestghanem. NW Algeria
113 H14 **Mostar** Federacija Bosna I Hercegovina, S Bosnia and Herzegovina
61 J17 **Mostardas** Rio Grande do Sul, S Brazil
116 K14 **Mostiştea** ≈ S Romania
Mostva *see* Mastva
Mosty *see* Masty
116 H5 **Mostys'ka** L'vivs'ka Oblast', W Ukraine
Mosul *see* Al Mawşil
95 F15 **Møsvatnet** ◎ S Norway
80 J12 **Mot'a** Amhara, N Ethiopia
79 H16 **Motaba** ≈ N Congo
105 O10 **Mota del Cuervo** Castilla-La Mancha, C Spain
104 L5 **Mota del Marqués** Castilla-León, N Spain
42 F5 **Motagua, Río** ≈ Guatemala/Honduras
119 H19 **Motal'** Brestskaya Voblasts', SW Belarus
95 L17 **Motala** Östergötland, S Sweden
191 X7 **Motane** *var.* Mohotani. *island* Îles Marquises, NE French Polynesia
152 K13 **Moth** Uttar Pradesh, N India
Mother of Presidents/Mother of States *see* Virginia
96 I12 **Motherwell** C Scotland, UK
153 P12 **Motīhāri** Bihār, N India
105 Q10 **Motilla del Palancar** Castilla-La Mancha, C Spain
184 N7 **Motiti Island** *island* NE NZ
65 E25 **Motley Island** *island* SE Falkland Islands
83 J19 **Motloutse** ≈ E Botswana
41 V17 **Motozintla de Mendoza** Chiapas, SE Mexico
105 N15 **Motril** Andalucía, S Spain
116 G13 **Motru** Gorj, SW Romania
165 Q4 **Motsuta-misaki** *headland* Hokkaidō, NE Japan
28 L6 **Mott** North Dakota, N USA
Möttling *see* Metlika
107 O18 **Mottola** Puglia, SE Italy
184 P8 **Motu** ≈ North Island, NZ
185 I14 **Motueka** Tasman, South Island, NZ
185 I14 **Motueka** ≈ South Island, NZ
Motu Iti *see* Tupai
41 X12 **Motul** *var.* Motul de Felipe Carrillo Puerto. Yucatán, SE Mexico
Motul de Felipe Carrillo Puerto *see* Motul
191 U17 **Motu Nui** *island* Easter Island, Chile, E Pacific Ocean
191 Q10 **Motu One** *var.* Bellingshausen. *atoll* Îles Sous le Vent, W French Polynesia
190 I16 **Motutapu** *island* E Cook Islands
193 V15 **Motu Tapu** *island* Tongatapu Group, S Tonga
184 L5 **Motutapu Island** *island* N NZ
Motyca *see* Modica
Mouanda *see* Moanda
Mouaskar *see* Mascara
105 U3 **Moubermé, Tuc de** *Fr.* Pic de Maubermé, *Sp.* Pico Mauberme; *prev.* Tuc de Maubermé. ▲ France/Spain *see also* Maubermé, Pic de
45 N7 **Mouchoir Passage** *passage* SE Turks and Caicos Islands
76 I9 **Moudjéria** Tagant, SW Mauritania
108 C9 **Moudon** Vaud, W Switzerland
Mouhoun *see* Black Volta
79 E19 **Mouila** Ngounié, C Gabon
79 K14 **Mouka** Haute-Kotto, C Central African Republic
Moukden *see* Shenyang
183 N10 **Moulamein** New South Wales, SE Australia
Moulamein Creek *see* Billabong Creek
74 F6 **Moulay-Bousselham** NW Morocco
Moule *see* le Moule
80 M11 **Moulhoulé** N Djibouti
103 P9 **Moulins** Allier, C France
166 M9 **Moulmein** *var.* Maulmain, Mawlamyine. Mon State, S Myanmar
166 L8 **Moulmeingyun** Irrawaddy, SW Myanmar
74 G6 **Moulouya** *var.* Mulucha, Muluya, Mulwiya. *seasonal river* NE Morocco
23 O2 **Moulton** Alabama, S USA
29 W16 **Moulton** Iowa, C USA
25 T11 **Moulton** Texas, SW USA
23 T7 **Moultrie** Georgia, SE USA
21 S14 **Moultrie, Lake** ◎ South Carolina, SE USA
22 K3 **Mound Bayou** Mississippi, S USA
30 L17 **Mound City** Illinois, N USA
27 R6 **Mound City** Kansas, C USA
27 Q2 **Mound City** Missouri, C USA
29 N7 **Mound City** South Dakota, N USA
78 H13 **Moundou** Logone-Occidental, SW Chad
27 P10 **Mounds** Oklahoma, C USA
21 R2 **Moundsville** West Virginia, NE USA
167 Q12 **Moŭng Roessei** Bătdâmbâng, W Cambodia
Moun Hou *see* Black Volta
8 H8 **Mountain** ≈ Northwest Territories, NW Canada
37 S12 **Mountainair** New Mexico, SW USA
35 V1 **Mountain City** Nevada, W USA
21 Q8 **Mountain City** Tennessee, S USA
27 U7 **Mountain Grove** Missouri, C USA
27 U9 **Mountain Home** Arkansas, C USA
33 N15 **Mountain Home** Idaho, NW USA
25 Q11 **Mountain Home** Texas, SW USA
29 W4 **Mountain Iron** Minnesota, N USA
29 T10 **Mountain Lake** Minnesota, N USA
23 S3 **Mountain Park** Georgia, SE USA
35 W12 **Mountain Pass** *pass* California, W USA
27 T12 **Mountain Pine** Arkansas, C USA
39 Y14 **Mountain Point** Annette Island, Alaska, USA
Mountain State *see* Montana, USA
Mountain State *see* West Virginia, USA
27 V7 **Mountain View** Arkansas, C USA
38 H12 **Mountain View** Hawai'i, USA, C Pacific Ocean
27 V10 **Mountain View** Missouri, C USA
38 M11 **Mountain Village** Alaska, USA
21 R8 **Mount Airy** North Carolina, SE USA
83 K24 **Mount Ayliff** *Xh.* Maxesibebi. Eastern Cape, SE South Africa
29 U16 **Mount Ayr** Iowa, C USA
182 J9 **Mount Barker** South Australia
180 J14 **Mount Barker** Western Australia
183 P11 **Mount Beauty** Victoria, SE Australia
14 E16 **Mount Brydges** Ontario, S Canada
31 N16 **Mount Carmel** Illinois, N USA
30 K10 **Mount Carroll** Illinois, N USA
31 S9 **Mount Clemens** Michigan, N USA
185 E19 **Mount Cook** Canterbury, South Island, NZ
83 L16 **Mount Darwin** Mashonaland Central, NE Zimbabwe
19 S7 **Mount Desert Island** *island* Maine, NE USA
23 W11 **Mount Dora** Florida, SE USA
182 G5 **Mount Eba** South Australia
25 W8 **Mount Enterprise** Texas, SW USA
182 J4 **Mount Fitton** South Australia
83 J24 **Mount Fletcher** Eastern Cape, SE South Africa
14 F15 **Mount Forest** Ontario, S Canada
182 K12 **Mount Gambier** South Australia
181 W5 **Mount Garnet** Queensland, NE Australia
21 P6 **Mount Gay** West Virginia, NE USA
31 S12 **Mount Gilead** Ohio, N USA
186 C7 **Mount Hagen** Western Highlands, C PNG
18 J16 **Mount Holly** New Jersey, NE USA
21 R10 **Mount Holly** North Carolina, SE USA
27 T12 **Mount Ida** Arkansas, C USA
181 T6 **Mount Isa** Queensland, C Australia
21 U4 **Mount Jackson** Virginia, NE USA
18 D12 **Mount Jewett** Pennsylvania, NE USA
18 L13 **Mount Kisco** New York, NE USA
18 B15 **Mount Lebanon** Pennsylvania, NE USA
182 J8 **Mount Lofty Ranges** ▲ South Australia
180 J10 **Mount Magnet** Western Australia
184 N7 **Mount Maunganui** Bay of Plenty, North Island, NZ
97 E18 **Mountmellick** *Ir.* Móinteach Mílic. C Ireland
30 L10 **Mount Morris** Illinois, N USA
31 R9 **Mount Morris** Michigan, N USA
18 F10 **Mount Morris** New York, NE USA
18 B16 **Mount Morris** Pennsylvania, NE USA
30 K15 **Mount Olive** Illinois, N USA
21 V10 **Mount Olive** North Carolina, SE USA
21 N4 **Mount Olivet** Kentucky, S USA
29 Y15 **Mount Pleasant** Iowa, C USA
31 Q8 **Mount Pleasant** Michigan, N USA
18 C15 **Mount Pleasant** Pennsylvania, NE USA
21 T14 **Mount Pleasant** South Carolina, SE USA
20 I9 **Mount Pleasant** Tennessee, S USA
25 W6 **Mount Pleasant** Texas, SW USA
36 L4 **Mount Pleasant** Utah, W USA
63 N23 **Mount Pleasant** ✕ (Stanley) East Falkland, Falkland Islands
97 G25 **Mount's Bay** *inlet* SW England, UK
35 N2 **Mount Shasta** California, W USA
30 J13 **Mount Sterling** Illinois, N USA
21 N5 **Mount Sterling** Kentucky, S USA
18 E15 **Mount Union** Pennsylvania, NE USA
23 V6 **Mount Vernon** Georgia, SE USA
30 L16 **Mount Vernon** Illinois, N USA
20 M6 **Mount Vernon** Kentucky, S USA
27 S7 **Mount Vernon** Missouri, C USA
31 T13 **Mount Vernon** Ohio, N USA
32 K13 **Mount Vernon** Oregon, NW USA
25 W6 **Mount Vernon** Texas, SW USA
32 H7 **Mount Vernon** Washington, NW USA
20 L5 **Mount Washington** Kentucky, S USA
182 F8 **Mount Wedge** South Australia
30 L14 **Mount Zion** Illinois, N USA
181 Y9 **Moura** Queensland, NE Australia
58 F12 **Moura** Amazonas, NW Brazil
104 H12 **Moura** Beja, S Portugal
104 I12 **Mourão** Évora, S Portugal
76 L11 **Mourdiah** Koulikoro, W Mali
78 K7 **Mourdi, Dépression du** *desert lowland* Chad/Sudan
102 J16 **Mourenx** Pyrénées-Atlantiques, SW France
Mourgana *see* Mourgkána
115 C15 **Mourgkána** *var.* Mourgana. ▲ Albania/Greece
97 G16 **Mourne Mountains** *Ir.* Beanna Boirche. ▲ SE Northern Ireland, UK
115 I15 **Moúrtzeflos, Akrotírio** *headland* Límnos, E Greece
99 C19 **Mouscron** *Dut.* Moeskroen. Hainaut, W Belgium
Mouse River *see* Souris River
78 H10 **Moussoro** Kanem, W Chad
103 T11 **Moûtiers** Savoie, E France
172 J14 **Moutsamoudou** *var.* Mutsamudu. Anjouan, SE Comoros
74 K11 **Mouydir, Monts de** ▲ S Algeria
79 F20 **Mouyondzi** La Bouenza, S Congo
115 E16 **Mouzáki** *prev.* Mouzákion. Thessalía, C Greece
Mouzákion *see* Mouzáki
29 S13 **Moville** Iowa, C USA
82 E13 **Moxico** ◆ *province* E Angola
172 I14 **Moya** Anjouan, SE Comoros
40 L12 **Moyahua** Zacatecas, C Mexico
81 J16 **Moyalē** Oromo, C Ethiopia
76 I15 **Moyamba** W Sierra Leone
74 G7 **Moyen Atlas** *Eng.* Middle Atlas. ▲ N Morocco
78 H13 **Moyen-Chari** *off.* Préfecture du Moyen-Chari. ◆ *prefecture* S Chad
Moyen-Congo *see* Congo (Republic of)
83 J24 **Moyeni** *var.* Quthing. SW Lesotho
76 H13 **Moyenne-Guinée** ◆ *state* NW Guinea
79 D18 **Moyen-Ogooué** *off.* Province du Moyen-Ogooué, *var.* Le Moyen-Ogooué. ◆ *province* C Gabon
103 S4 **Moyeuvre-Grande** Moselle, NE France
33 N7 **Moyie Springs** Idaho, NW USA
146 G6 **Mo'ynoq** *Rus.* Muynak. Qoraqalpog'iston Respublikasi, NW Uzbekistan
81 F16 **Moyo** NW Uganda
56 D10 **Moyobamba** San Martín, NW Peru
78 H10 **Moyto** Chari-Baguirmi, W Chad
158 G9 **Moyu** *var.* Karakax. Xinjiang Uygur Zizhiqu, NW China
122 M9 **Moyyero** ≈ N Russian Federation
145 S15 **Moyynkum** *var.* Furmanovka, *Kaz.* Fūrmanov. Zhambyl, S Kazakhstan
145 Q15 **Moyynkum, Peski** *Kaz.* Moyynqum. *desert* S Kazakhstan
Moyynqum *see* Moyynkum, Peski
145 S12 **Moyynty** Karaganda, C Kazakhstan
145 S12 **Moyynty** ≈ C Kazakhstan
Mozambika, Lakandranon' i *see* Mozambique Channel
83 M18 **Mozambique** *off.* Republic of Mozambique; *prev.* People's Republic of Mozambique, Portuguese East Africa. ◆ *republic* S Africa
Mozambique Basin *see* Natal Basin
Mozambique, Canal de *see* Mozambique Channel
83 P17 **Mozambique Channel** *Fr.* Canal de Mozambique, *Mal.* Lakandranon' i Mozambika. *strait* W Indian Ocean
172 L11 **Mozambique Escarpment** *var.* Mozambique Scarp. *undersea feature* SW Indian Ocean
172 L10 **Mozambique Plateau** *var.* Mozambique Rise. *undersea feature* SW Indian Ocean
Mozambique Rise *see* Mozambique Plateau
Mozambique Scarp *see* Mozambique Escarpment
127 O15 **Mozdok** Respublika Severnaya Osetiya, SW Russian Federation

◆ COUNTRY ● COUNTRY CAPITAL ◇ DEPENDENT TERRITORY ○ DEPENDENT TERRITORY CAPITAL ◆ ADMINISTRATIVE REGION ✕ INTERNATIONAL AIRPORT ▲ MOUNTAIN ▲ MOUNTAIN RANGE ⊼ VOLCANO ≈ RIVER ◎ LAKE ⊡ RESERVOIR

57 K17 **Mozetenes, Serranías de** ▲ C Bolivia
126 J4 **Mozhaysk** Moskovskaya Oblast', W Russian Federation
127 T3 **Mozhga** Udmurtskaya Respublika, NW Russian Federation
Mozyr' *see* Mazyr
79 P22 **Mpala** Katanga, E Dem. Rep. Congo
79 G19 **Mpama** ≈ C Congo
81 E22 **Mpanda** Rukwa, W Tanzania
82 L11 **Mpande** Northern, NE Zambia
83 J18 **Mphoengs** Matabeleland South, SW Zimbabwe
81 F18 **Mpigi** S Uganda
82 L13 **Mpika** Northern, NE Zambia
83 J14 **Mpima** Central, C Zambia
82 J13 **Mpongwe** Copperbelt, C Zambia
82 K11 **Mporokoso** Northern, N Zambia
79 H20 **Mpouya** Plateaux, SE Congo
77 P16 **Mpraeso** C Ghana
82 L11 **Mpulungu** Northern, N Zambia
83 K21 **Mpumalanga** *prev.* Eastern Transvaal, *Afr.* Oos-Transvaal. ❖ *province* NE South Africa
83 D16 **Mpungu** Okavango, N Namibia
81 I22 **Mpwapwa** Dodoma, C Tanzania
Mqinvartsveri *see* Kazbek
110 M8 **Mrągowo** *Ger.* Sensburg. Warmińsko-Mazurskie, NE Poland
127 V6 **Mrakovo** Respublika Bashkortostan, W Russian Federation
172 I13 **Mramani** Anjouan, E Comoros
112 F12 **Mrkonjić Grad** Republika Srpska, W Bosnia and Herzegovina
110 H9 **Mrocza** Kujawsko-pomorskie, NW Poland
126 I14 **Msta** ≈ NW Russian Federation
Mtkvari *see* Kura
Mtoko *see* Mutoko
126 K6 **Mtsensk** Orlovskaya Oblast', W Russian Federation
81 K24 **Mtwara** Mtwara, SE Tanzania
81 J25 **Mtwara** ❖ *region* SE Tanzania
104 G14 **Mu** ▲ S Portugal
193 V15 **Mu'a** Tongatapu, S Tonga
Muai To *see* Mae Hong Son
83 P16 **Mualama** Zambézia, NE Mozambique
Mualo *see* Messalo, Rio
79 E22 **Muanda** Bas-Congo, SW Dem. Rep. Congo
Muang Chiang Rai *see* Chiang Rai
167 R6 **Muang Ham** Houaphan, N Laos
167 S8 **Muang Hinboun** Khammouan, C Laos
Muang Kalasin *see* Kalasin
Muang Khammouan *see* Thakhèk
167 S11 **Muang Không** Champasak, S Laos
167 S10 **Muang Khôngxédôn** *var.* Khong Sedone. Salavan, S Laos
Muang Khon Kaen *see* Khon Kaen
167 Q6 **Muang Khoua** Phôngsali, N Laos
Muang Krabi *see* Krabi
Muang Lampang *see* Lampang
Muang Lamphun *see* Lamphun
Muang Loei *see* Loei
Muang Lom Sak *see* Lom Sak
Muang Nakhon Sawan *see* Nakhon Sawan
167 Q6 **Muang Namo** Oudômxai, N Laos
Muang Nan *see* Nan
167 Q6 **Muang Ngoy** Louangphabang, N Laos
167 Q5 **Muang Ou Tai** Phôngsali, N Laos
Muang Pak Lay *see* Pak Lay
Muang Pakxan *see* Pakxan
167 T10 **Muang Pakxong** Champasak, S Laos
167 S9 **Muang Phalan** *var.* Muang Phalane. Savannakhét, S Laos
Muang Phalane *see* Muang Phalan
Muang Phan *see* Phan
Muang Phayao *see* Phayao
Muang Phichit *see* Phichit
167 T9 **Muang Phin** Savannakhét, S Laos
Muang Phitsanulok *see* Phitsanulok
Muang Phrae *see* Phrae
Muang Roi Et *see* Roi Et
Muang Sakon Nakhon *see* Sakon Nakhon
Muang Samut Prakan *see* Samut Prakan
167 P6 **Muang Sing** Louang Namtha, N Laos
Muang Ubon *see* Ubon Ratchathani
Muang Uthai Thani *see* Uthai Thani
167 P7 **Muang Vangviang** Viangchan, C Laos
Muang Xaignabouri *see* Xaignabouli
Muang Xay *see* Xai
167 S9 **Muang Xépôn** *var.* Sepone. Savannakhét, S Laos
168 K10 **Muar** *var.* Bandar Maharani. Johor, Peninsular Malaysia
168 I9 **Muara** Sumatera, W Indonesia
168 L13 **Muarabeliti** Sumatera, W Indonesia
168 K12 **Muarabungo** Sumatera, W Indonesia
168 L13 **Muaraenim** Sumatera, W Indonesia
169 T11 **Muarajuloi** Borneo, C Indonesia
169 U12 **Muarakaman** Borneo, C Indonesia
168 H12 **Muarasigep** Pulau Siberut, W Indonesia
168 L12 **Muaratembesi** Sumatera, W Indonesia
169 T12 **Muaratewe** *var.* Muaratewech; *prev.* Moearatewe. Borneo, C Indonesia
Muaratewech *see* Muaratewe
169 U10 **Muarawahau** Borneo, N Indonesia
138 G13 **Mubārak, Jabal** ▲ S Jordan
153 N13 **Mubārakpur** Uttar Pradesh, N India
Mubarek *see* Muborak
81 F18 **Mubende** SW Uganda
77 Y14 **Mubi** Adamawa, NE Nigeria
146 M12 **Muborak** *Rus.* Mubarek. Qashqadaryo Viloyati, S Uzbekistan
171 U12 **Mubrani** Papua, E Indonesia
67 U12 **Muchinga Escarpment** *escarpment* NE Zambia
127 N7 **Muchkapskiy** Tambovskaya Oblast', W Russian Federation
96 G10 **Muck** *island* W Scotland, UK
82 Q13 **Mucojo** Cabo Delgado, N Mozambique
82 F12 **Muconda** Lunda Sul, NE Angola
54 I10 **Muco, Río** ≈ E Colombia
83 O16 **Mucubela** Zambézia, NE Mozambique
42 J5 **Mucupina, Monte** ▲ N Honduras
136 J14 **Mucur** Kırşehir, C Turkey
143 U8 **Mūd** Khorāsān, E Iran
163 Y9 **Mudanjiang** *var.* Mu-tan-chiang. Heilongjiang, NE China
163 Y9 **Mudan Jiang** ≈ NE China
136 D11 **Mudanya** Bursa, NW Turkey
28 K8 **Mud Butte** South Dakota, N USA
155 G16 **Muddebihāl** Karnātaka, C India
27 P12 **Muddy Boggy Creek** ≈ Oklahoma, C USA
36 M6 **Muddy Creek** ≈ Utah, W USA
37 V7 **Muddy Creek Reservoir** ▣ Colorado, C USA
33 W15 **Muddy Gap** Wyoming, C USA
35 Y11 **Muddy Peak** ▲ Nevada, W USA
183 R7 **Mudgee** New South Wales, SE Australia
29 S3 **Mud Lake** ◎ Minnesota, N USA
29 P7 **Mud Lake Reservoir** ▣ South Dakota, N USA
167 N9 **Mudon** Mon State, S Myanmar
81 O14 **Mudug** *off.* Gobolka Mudug. ❖ *region* NE Somalia
81 O14 **Mudug** *var.* Mudugh. *plain* N Somalia
Mudugh *see* Mudug
83 Q15 **Muecate** Nampula, NE Mozambique
82 Q13 **Mueda** Cabo Delgado, NE Mozambique
42 L10 **Muelle de los Bueyes** Región Autónoma Atlántico Sur, SE Nicaragua
Muenchen *see* München
83 M14 **Muende** Tete, NW Mozambique
25 T5 **Muenster** Texas, SW USA
Muenster *see* Münster
43 O6 **Muerto, Cayo** *reef* NE Nicaragua
41 T17 **Muerto, Mar** *lagoon* SE Mexico
64 F11 **Muertos Trough** *undersea feature* N Caribbean Sea
83 H14 **Mufaya Kuta** Western, NW Zambia
82 J13 **Mufulira** Copperbelt, C Zambia
161 O10 **Mufu Shan** ▲ C China
Mugalzhar Taūlary *see* Mugodzhary, Gory
137 Y12 **Muğan Düzü** *Rus.* Muganskaya Ravnina, Muganskaya Step'. *physical region* S Azerbaijan
Muganskaya Ravnina/Muganskaya Step' *see* Muğan Düzü
106 K8 **Muggia** Friuli-Venezia Giulia, NE Italy
153 N14 **Mughal Sarāi** Uttar Pradesh, N India
Mughla *see* Muğla
141 W11 **Mughshin** *var.* Muqshin. S Oman
147 S12 **Mughsu** *Rus.* Muksu. ≈ C Tajikistan
164 H14 **Mugi** Tokushima, Shikoku, SW Japan
136 C16 **Muğla** *var.* Mughla. Muğla, SW Turkey
136 C16 **Muğla** *var.* Mughla. ❖ *province* SW Turkey
144 J11 **Mugodzhary, Gory** *Kaz.* Mugalzhar Taūlary. ▲ W Kazakhstan
83 O15 **Mugulama** Zambézia, NE Mozambique
139 U9 **Muḩammad** E Iraq
139 R8 **Muḩammadīyah** C Iraq
80 I6 **Muhammad Qol** Red Sea, NE Sudan
75 Y9 **Muhammad, Râs** *headland* E Egypt
Muhammerah *see* Khorramshahr
140 M12 **Muhāyil** *var.* Mahāil. 'Asīr, SW Saudi Arabia
139 O7 **Muḩaywīr** W Iraq
101 H21 **Mühlacker** Baden-Württemberg, SW Germany
Mühlbach *see* Sebeş
Mühldorf *see* Mühldorf am Inn
101 N23 **Mühldorf am Inn** *var.* Mühldorf. Bayern, SE Germany
101 J15 **Mühlhausen** *var.* Mühlhausen in Thüringen. Thüringen, C Germany
Mühlhausen in Thüringen *see* Mühlhausen
195 Q2 **Mühlig-Hofmann Mountains** ▲ Antarctica
93 L14 **Muhos** Oulu, C Finland
138 K6 **Muḩ, Sabkhat al** ◎ C Syria
118 E5 **Muhu** *Ger.* Mohn, Moon. *island* W Estonia
81 F19 **Muhutwe** Kagera, NW Tanzania
Muhu Väin *see* Väinameri
98 J10 **Muiden** Noord-Holland, C Netherlands
193 W15 **Mui Hopohoponga** *headland* Tongatapu, S Tonga
Muikamachi *see* Muika
Muinchille *see* Cootehill
Muineachán *see* Monaghan
97 F19 **Muine Bheag** *Eng.* Bagenalstown. SE Ireland
56 B5 **Muisne** Esmeraldas, NW Ecuador
83 P14 **Muite** Nampula, NE Mozambique
41 Z11 **Mujeres, Isla** *island* E Mexico
116 G7 **Mukacheve** *Hung.* Munkács, *Rus.* Mukachevo. Zakarpats'ka Oblast', W Ukraine
Mukachevo *see* Mukacheve
169 R9 **Mukah** Sarawak, East Malaysia
Mukalla *see* Al Mukallā
Mukama *see* Mokāma
Mukāshafa/Mukashshafah *see* Mukayshīfah
139 S6 **Mukayshīfah** *var.* Mukāshafa, Mukashshafah. N Iraq
167 R9 **Mukdahan** Mukdahan, E Thailand
Mukden *see* Shenyang
165 Y15 **Mukojima-rettō** *Eng.* Parry group. *island group* SE Japan
146 M14 **Mukry** Lebap Welaýaty, E Turkmenistan
Muksu *see* Mughsu
153 U14 **Muktagacha** *var.* Muktagachha. Dhaka, N Bangladesh
Muktagachha *see* Muktagacha
82 K13 **Mukuku** Central, C Zambia
82 K11 **Mukupa Kaoma** Northern, NE Zambia
81 I18 **Mukutan** Rift Valley, W Kenya
83 F16 **Mukwe** Caprivi, NE Namibia
105 R13 **Mula** Murcia, SE Spain
151 K20 **Mulaku Atoll** *var.* Meemu Atoll. *atoll* C Maldives
83 J15 **Mulalika** Lusaka, C Zambia
163 X8 **Mulan** Heilongjiang, NE China
83 N15 **Mulanje** *var.* Mlanje. Southern, S Malawi
40 H5 **Mulatos** Sonora, NW Mexico
23 P3 **Mulberry Fork** ≈ Alabama, S USA
39 P12 **Mulchatna River** ≈ Alaska, USA
125 W4 **Mul'da** Respublika Komi, NW Russian Federation
101 M14 **Mulde** ≈ E Germany
27 R10 **Muldrow** Oklahoma, C USA
40 E7 **Mulegé** Baja California Sur, W Mexico
108 I10 **Mulegns** Graubünden, S Switzerland
79 M21 **Mulenda** Kasai Oriental, C Dem. Rep. Congo
24 M4 **Muleshoe** Texas, SW USA
83 O15 **Mulevala** Zambézia, NE Mozambique
183 P5 **Mulgoa Creek** *seasonal river* New South Wales, SE Australia
105 O15 **Mulhacén** *var.* Cerro de Mulhacén. ▲ S Spain
Mulhacén, Cerro de *see* Mulhacén
Mülhausen *see* Mulhouse
101 E24 **Mülheim** Baden-Württemberg, SW Germany
101 E15 **Mülheim** *var.* Mulheim an der Ruhr. Nordrhein-Westfalen, W Germany
Mulheim an der Ruhr *see* Mülheim
103 U7 **Mulhouse** *Ger.* Mülhausen. Haut-Rhin, NE France
160 G11 **Muli** *var.* Qiaowa, Muli Zangzu Zizhixian. Sichuan, C China
171 X15 **Muli** *channel* Papua, E Indonesia
163 Y9 **Muling** Heilongjiang, NE China
Mullach Íde *see* Malahide
Mullaitivu *see* Mullaittivu
155 K23 **Mullaittivu** *var.* Mullaitivu. Northern Province, N Sri Lanka
33 N8 **Mullan** Idaho, NW USA
28 M13 **Mullen** Nebraska, C USA
183 Q6 **Mullengudgery** New South Wales, SE Australia
21 Q6 **Mullens** West Virginia, NE USA
Müller-gerbergte *see* Muller, Pegunungan
169 T10 **Muller, Pegunungan** *Dut.* Müller-gerbergte. ▲ Borneo, C Indonesia
31 Q5 **Mullett Lake** ◎ Michigan, N USA
18 J16 **Mullica River** ≈ New Jersey, NE USA
25 R8 **Mullin** Texas, SW USA
97 E17 **Mullingar** *Ir.* An Muileann gCearr. C Ireland
21 T12 **Mullins** South Carolina, SE USA
96 G11 **Mull, Isle of** *island* W Scotland, UK
127 R5 **Mullovka** Ul'yanovskaya Oblast', W Russian Federation
95 K19 **Mullsjö** Västra Götaland, S Sweden
183 V4 **Mullumbimby** New South Wales, SE Australia
83 H15 **Mulobezi** Western, SW Zambia
83 C15 **Mulondo** Huíla, SW Angola
83 G15 **Mulonga Plain** *plain* W Zambia
79 N23 **Mulongo** Katanga, SE Dem. Rep. Congo
149 T10 **Multān** Punjab, E Pakistan
93 L17 **Multia** Länsi-Suomi, W Finland
Mulucha *see* Moulouya
83 J14 **Mulungushi** Central, C Zambia
83 K14 **Mulungwe** Central, C Zambia
Muluya *see* Moulouya
27 N7 **Mulvane** Kansas, C USA
183 O10 **Mulwala** New South Wales, SE Australia
Mulwiya *see* Moulouya
182 K6 **Mulyungarie** South Australia
154 D13 **Mumbai** *prev.* Bombay. Mahārāshtra, W India
154 D13 **Mumbai** × Mahārāshtra, W India
83 D14 **Mumbué** Bié, C Angola
186 E8 **Mumeng** Morobe, C PNG
171 V12 **Mumi** Papua, E Indonesia
Muminabad/Mū'minobod *see* Leningrad
127 Q13 **Mumra** Astrakhanskaya Oblast', SW Russian Federation
41 X12 **Muna** Yucatán, SE Mexico
123 O9 **Muna** ≈ NE Russian Federation
152 C12 **Munābāo** Rājasthān, NW India
Munamägi *see* Suur Munamägi
171 O14 **Muna, Pulau** *prev.* Moena. *island* C Indonesia
101 L18 **Münchberg** Bayern, E Germany
101 L23 **München** *var.* Muenchen, *Eng.* Munich, *It.* Monaco. Bayern, SE Germany
München-Gladbach *see* Mönchengladbach
108 E6 **Münchenstein** Basel-Land, NW Switzerland
10 L10 **Muncho Lake** British Columbia, W Canada
31 P13 **Muncie** Indiana, N USA
18 G13 **Muncy** Pennsylvania, NE USA
11 Q14 **Mundare** Alberta, SW Canada
25 Q5 **Munday** Texas, SW USA
31 N10 **Mundelein** Illinois, N USA
101 I15 **Münden** Niedersachsen, C Germany
105 Q12 **Mundo** ≈ S Spain
82 B12 **Munenga** Cuanza Sul, NW Angola
105 P11 **Munera** Castilla-La Mancha, C Spain
20 E9 **Munford** Tennessee, S USA
20 K7 **Munfordville** Kentucky, S USA
182 D5 **Mungala** South Australia
83 M16 **Mungári** Manica, C Mozambique
79 O16 **Mungbere** Orientale, NE Dem. Rep. Congo
153 Q13 **Munger** *prev.* Monghyr. Bihār, NE India
182 I2 **Mungeranie** South Australia
Mu Nggava *see* Rennell
169 O10 **Mungguresak, Tanjung** *headland* Borneo, N Indonesia
Mungiki *see* Bellona
183 R4 **Mungindi** New South Wales, SE Australia
Mungkawn *see* Maingkwan
153 T16 **Mungla** *var.* Mongla. Khulna, S Bangladesh
82 C13 **Mungo** Huambo, W Angola
188 F16 **Munguuy Bay** *bay* Yap, W Micronesia
82 E13 **Munhango** Bié, C Angola
Munich *see* München
105 S7 **Muniesa** Aragón, NE Spain
31 O4 **Munising** Michigan, N USA
Munkács *see* Mukacheve
95 I17 **Munkedal** Västra Götaland, S Sweden
95 K15 **Munkfors** Värmland, C Sweden
122 M14 **Munku-Sardyk, Gora** *var.* Mönh Sarīdag. ▲ Mongolia/Russian Federation
99 E18 **Munkzwalm** Oost-Vlaanderen, NW Belgium
167 R10 **Mun, Mae Nam** ≈ E Thailand
153 U15 **Munshiganj** Dhaka, C Bangladesh
108 D8 **Münsingen** Bern, W Switzerland
103 U6 **Munster** Haut-Rhin, NE France
100 J11 **Munster** Niedersachsen, NW Germany
97 B20 **Munster** *Ir.* Cúige Mumhan. *cultural region* S Ireland
100 F13 **Münster** *var.* Muenster, Münster in Westfalen. Nordrhein-Westfalen, W Germany
108 F10 **Münster** Valais, S Switzerland
Münsterberg in Schlesien *see* Ziębice
Münster in Westfalen *see* Münster
100 E13 **Münsterland** *cultural region* NW Germany
100 F13 **Münster-Osnabruck** × Nordrhein-Westfalen, NW Germany
31 R4 **Munuscong Lake** ◎ Michigan, N USA
83 K17 **Munyati** ≈ C Zimbabwe
109 R3 **Münzkirchen** Oberösterreich, N Austria
92 K11 **Muodoslompolo** Norrbotten, N Sweden
92 M13 **Muojärvi** ◎ NE Finland
167 S6 **Mương Khên** Hoa Binh, N Vietnam
Muong Sai *see* Xai
167 Q7 **Muong Xiang Ngeun** *var.* Xieng Ngeun. Louangphabang, N Laos
92 K11 **Muonio** Lappi, N Finland
Muonioälv/Muoniojoki *see* Muonionjoki
92 K11 **Muonionjoki** *var.* Muoniojoki, *Swe.* Muonioälv. ≈ Finland/Sweden
83 N17 **Mupa** ≈ C Mozambique
83 E16 **Mupini** Okavango, NE Namibia
80 F8 **Muqaddam, Wadi** ≈ N Sudan
138 K9 **Muqāṭ** Al Mafraq, E Jordan
141 X7 **Muqaz** N Oman
81 N17 **Muqdisho** *Eng.* Mogadishu, *It.* Mogadiscio. ● (Somalia) Banaadir, S Somalia
81 N17 **Muqdisho** × Banaadir, E Somalia
Muqshin *see* Mughshin
109 T8 **Mur** *SCr.* Mura. ≈ C Europe
Mura *see* Mur
137 T14 **Muradiye** Van, E Turkey
Muragarazi *see* Maragarazi
165 O10 **Murakami** Niigata, Honshū, C Japan
63 G22 **Murallón, Cerro** ▲ S Argentina
81 E20 **Muramvya** C Burundi
81 I19 **Murang'a** *prev.* Fort Hall. Central, SW Kenya
81 H16 **Murangering** Rift Valley, NW Kenya
Murapara *see* Murupara
140 M5 **Murār, Bi'r al** *well* NW Saudi Arabia
125 Q13 **Murashi** Kirovskaya Oblast', NW Russian Federation
103 O12 **Murat** Cantal, C France
114 N12 **Muratlı** Tekirdağ, NW Turkey
137 R14 **Murat Nehri** *var.* Eastern Euphrates; *anc.* Arsanias. ≈ NE Turkey
107 D20 **Muravera** Sardegna, Italy, C Mediterranean Sea
165 P10 **Murayama** Yamagata, Honshū, C Japan
121 R13 **Muraysah, Ra's al** *headland* N Libya
104 I6 **Murça** Vila Real, N Portugal
80 Q11 **Murcanyo** Bari, NE Somalia
143 N8 **Mürcheh Khvort** *var.* Morcheh Khort. Eşfahān, C Iran
185 H15 **Murchison** Tasman, South Island, NZ
185 B22 **Murchison Mountains** ▲ South Island, NZ
180 I10 **Murchison River** ≈ Western Australia
105 R13 **Murcia** Murcia, SE Spain
105 Q13 **Murcia** ❖ *autonomous community* SE Spain
103 O13 **Mur-de-Barrez** Aveyron, S France
182 G8 **Murdinga** South Australia
28 M10 **Murdo** South Dakota, N USA
15 X6 **Murdochville** Québec, SE Canada
109 W9 **Mureck** Steiermark, SE Austria
114 M13 **Mürefte** Tekirdağ, NW Turkey
116 I10 **Mureş** ❖ *county* N Romania
84 J11 **Mureş** *var.* Maros, Mureşul, *Ger.* Marosch, Mieresch. ≈ Hungary/Romania *see also* Maros
Mureşul *see* Maros/Mureş
102 M16 **Muret** Haute-Garonne, S France
27 T13 **Murfreesboro** Arkansas, C USA
21 W8 **Murfreesboro** North Carolina, SE USA
20 J9 **Murfreesboro** Tennessee, S USA
Murgab *see* Morghāb, Daryā-ye/Murgap/Murghob
146 I14 **Murgap** *Rus.* Murgab. Mary Welaýaty, S Turkmenistan
146 J16 **Murgap** *var.* Murgap Deryasy, Murghab, *Pash.* Daryā-ye Morghāb, *Rus.* Murgab. ≈ Afghanistan/Turkmenistan *see also* Morghāb, Daryā-ye
Murgap Deryasy *see* Morghāb, Daryā-ye/Murgap
114 H9 **Murgash** ▲ W Bulgaria
Murghab *see* Morghāb, Daryā-ye/Murgap
147 U13 **Murghob** *Rus.* Murgab. SE Tajikistan
147 U13 **Murghob** *Rus.* Murgab. ≈ SE Tajikistan
181 Z10 **Murgon** Queensland, E Australia
190 I16 **Muri** Rarotonga, S Cook Islands
108 F7 **Muri** Aargau, W Switzerland
108 D8 **Muri** *var.* Muri bei Bern. Bern, W Switzerland
104 K3 **Murias de Paredes** Castilla-León, N Spain
Muri bei Bern *see* Muri
82 F11 **Muriege** Lunda Sul, NE Angola
189 P14 **Murilo Atoll** *atoll* Hall Islands, C Micronesia
Mūrītānīyah *see* Mauritania
100 N10 **Müritz** *var.* Müritzee. ◎ NE Germany
Müritzee *see* Müritz
100 L10 **Müritz-Elde-Kanal** *canal* N Germany
184 K6 **Muriwai Beach** Auckland, North Island, NZ
92 J13 **Murjek** Norrbotten, N Sweden
124 J3 **Murmansk** Murmanskaya Oblast', NW Russian Federation
124 I4 **Murmanskaya Oblast'** ❖ *province* NW Russian Federation
197 V14 **Murmansk Rise** *undersea feature* SW Barents Sea
124 J3 **Murmashi** Murmanskaya Oblast', NW Russian Federation
126 M5 **Murmino** Ryazanskaya Oblast', W Russian Federation
101 K24 **Murnau** Bayern, SE Germany
103 X16 **Muro, Capo di** *headland* Corse, France, C Mediterranean Sea
107 M18 **Muro Lucano** Basilicata, S Italy
127 N4 **Murom** Vladimirskaya Oblast', W Russian Federation
122 I11 **Muromtsevo** Omskaya Oblast', C Russian Federation
165 R5 **Muroran** Hokkaidō, NE Japan
104 G3 **Muros** Galicia, NW Spain
104 F3 **Muros e Noia, Ría de** *estuary* NW Spain
164 H15 **Muroto** Kōchi, Shikoku, SW Japan
164 H15 **Muroto-zaki** *headland* Shikoku, SW Japan
116 L7 **Murovani Kurylivtsi** Vinnyts'ka Oblast', C Ukraine
110 G11 **Murowana Goślina** Wielkolpolskie, C Poland
32 M14 **Murphy** Idaho, NW USA
21 N10 **Murphy** North Carolina, SE USA
35 P8 **Murphys** California, W USA
30 L17 **Murphysboro** Illinois, N USA
29 V15 **Murray** Iowa, C USA
20 H8 **Murray** Kentucky, S USA
182 J10 **Murray Bridge** South Australia
175 X2 **Murray Fracture Zone** *tectonic feature* NE Pacific Ocean
192 H11 **Murray, Lake** ◎ SW PNG
21 P12 **Murray, Lake** ▣ South Carolina, SE USA
10 K8 **Murray, Mount** ▲ Yukon Territory, NW Canada
Murray Range *see* Murray Ridge
173 O3 **Murray Ridge** *var.* Murray Range. *undersea feature* N Arabian Sea
183 N10 **Murray River** ≈ SE Australia
182 K10 **Murrayville** Victoria, SE Australia
149 U5 **Murree** Punjab, E Pakistan
101 I21 **Murrhardt** Baden-Württemberg, S Germany
183 O9 **Murrumbidgee River** ≈ New South Wales, SE Australia
83 P15 **Murrupula** Nampula, NE Mozambique
183 T7 **Murrurundi** New South Wales, SE Australia
109 X9 **Murska Sobota** *Ger.* Olsnitz. NE Slovenia
154 G12 **Murtajāpur** *prev.* Murtazapur. Mahārāshtra, C India
77 S16 **Murtala Muhammed** × (Lagos) Ogun, SW Nigeria
Murtazapur *see* Murtajāpur
108 C8 **Murten** Neuchâtel, W Switzerland
Murtensee *see* Morat, Lac de
182 L11 **Murtoa** Victoria, SE Australia
92 N13 **Murtovaara** Oulu, E Finland
Murua Island *see* Woodlark Island
155 D14 **Murud** Mahārāshtra, W India
184 O9 **Murupara** *var.* Murapara. Bay of Plenty, North Island, NZ
191 X12 **Mururoa** *var.* Moruroa. *atoll* Îles Tuamotu, SE French Polynesia
Murviedro *see* Sagunto
154 J9 **Murwāra** Madhya Pradesh, N India
183 V4 **Murwillumbah** New South Wales, SE Australia
146 H11 **Murzechirla** *prev.* Mirzachirla. Ahal Welaýaty, C Turkmenistan
Murzuk *see* Murzuq
75 O11 **Murzuq** *var.* Marzūq, Murzuk. SW Libya
Murzuq, Edeyin *see* Murzuq, Idhān
75 N11 **Murzuq, Ḩamādat** *plateau* W Libya
75 O11 **Murzuq, Idhān** *var.* Edeyin Murzuq. *desert* SW Libya
109 W6 **Mürzzuschlag** Steiermark, E Austria
137 Q14 **Muş** *var.* Mush. Muş, E Turkey
137 Q14 **Muş** *var.* Mush. ❖ *province* E Turkey
186 F9 **Musa** ≈ S PNG
118 G11 **Mūša** ≈ Latvia/Lithuania
75 X8 **Mûsa, Gebel** ▲ NE Egypt
Musaiyib *see* Al Musayyib
Musa Khel *see* Mūsā Khel Bazār
149 R9 **Mūsā Khel Bazār** *var.* Musa Khel. Baluchistān, SW Pakistan
114 H10 **Musala** ▲ W Bulgaria
168 H10 **Musala, Pulau** *island* W Indonesia
83 I15 **Musale** Southern, S Zambia
141 Y9 **Muşallā** NE Oman
141 W6 **Musandam Peninsula** *Ar.* Masandam Peninsula. *peninsula* N Oman
Musay'īd *see* Umm Sa'īd
Muscat *see* Masqaṭ
Muscat and Oman *see* Oman
29 Y14 **Muscatine** Iowa, C USA
Muscat Sīb Airport *see* Seeb
31 O15 **Muscatuck River** ≈ Indiana, N USA
30 K8 **Muscoda** Wisconsin, N USA
185 F19 **Musgrave, Mount** ▲ South Island, NZ
181 P9 **Musgrave Ranges** ▲ South Australia
Mush *see* Muş
138 H12 **Mushayyish, Qaşr al** *castle* Ma'ān, C Jordan
79 H20 **Mushie** Bandundu, W Dem. Rep. Congo
168 M13 **Musi, Air** *prev.* Moesi. ≈ Sumatera, W Indonesia
192 M4 **Musicians Seamounts** *undersea feature* N Pacific Ocean
54 D8 **Musinga, Alto** ▲ NW Colombia
29 T2 **Muskeg Bay** *lake bay* Minnesota, N USA
31 O8 **Muskegon** Michigan, N USA
31 O8 **Muskegon Heights** Michigan, N USA
31 P8 **Muskegon River** ≈ Michigan, N USA
31 T14 **Muskingum River** ≈ Ohio, N USA
95 P16 **Muskö** Stockholm, C Sweden
Muskogean *see* Tallahassee
27 Q10 **Muskogee** Oklahoma, C USA
14 H13 **Muskoka, Lake** ◎ Ontario, S Canada
80 H8 **Musmar** Red Sea, NE Sudan
83 K14 **Musofu** Central, C Zambia
81 G19 **Musoma** Mara, N Tanzania
82 L13 **Musoro** Central, C Zambia
186 F4 **Mussau Island** *island* NE PNG
98 P7 **Musselkanaal** Groningen, NE Netherlands
33 V9 **Musselshell River** ≈ Montana, NW USA
82 C12 **Mussende** Cuanza Sul, NW Angola
102 L12 **Mussidan** Dordogne, SW France
83 K19 **Musina** *prev.* Messina. Limpopo, NE South Africa
99 L25 **Musson** Luxembourg, SE Belgium
152 J9 **Mussoorie** Uttaranchal, N India
Musta *see* Mosta
152 M13 **Mustafābād** Uttar Pradesh, N India
136 D12 **Mustafakemalpaşa** Bursa, NW Turkey
Mustafa-Pasha *see* Svilengrad
81 M15 **Mustahīl** Somali, E Ethiopia

◆ COUNTRY ● COUNTRY CAPITAL ◇ DEPENDENT TERRITORY ○ DEPENDENT TERRITORY CAPITAL ❖ ADMINISTRATIVE REGION × INTERNATIONAL AIRPORT ▲ MOUNTAIN ▲ MOUNTAIN RANGE ⛰ VOLCANO ≈ RIVER ◎ LAKE ▣ RESERVOIR

24 M7 **Mustang Draw** *valley* Texas, SW USA
25 T14 **Mustang Island** *island* Texas, SW USA
Mustasaari *see* Korsholm
Mustér *see* Disentis
63 I19 **Musters, Lago** ◎ S Argentina
45 Y14 **Mustique** *island* C Saint Vincent and the Grenadines
118 I6 **Mustla** Viljandimaa, S Estonia
118 J4 **Mustvee** *Ger.* Tschorna. Jõgevamaa, E Estonia
42 L9 **Musún, Cerro** ▲ NE Nicaragua
183 T7 **Muswellbrook** New South Wales, SE Australia
111 M18 **Muszyna** Małopolskie, SE Poland
136 I17 **Mut** İçel, S Turkey
75 V10 **Mût** *var.* Mut. C Egypt
109 V9 **Muta** N Slovenia
190 B15 **Mutalau** N Niue
Mu-tan-chiang *see* Mudanjiang
82 I13 **Mutanda** North Western, NW Zambia
59 O17 **Mutá, Ponta do** *headland* E Brazil
83 L17 **Mutare** *var.* Mutari; *prev.* Umtali. Manicaland, E Zimbabwe
Mutari *see* Mutare
54 D8 **Mutatá** Antioquia, NW Colombia
Mutina *see* Modena
83 L16 **Mutoko** *prev.* Mtoko. Mashonaland East, NE Zimbabwe
81 J20 **Mutomo** Eastern, S Kenya
Mutrah *see* Maṭraḥ
79 M24 **Mutshatsha** Katanga, S Dem. Rep. Congo
165 R6 **Mutsu** *var.* Mutu. Aomori, Honshū, N Japan
165 R6 **Mutsu-wan** *bay* N Japan
108 E6 **Muttenz** Basel-Land, NW Switzerland
185 A26 **Muttonbird Islands** *island group* SW NZ
Mutu *see* Mutsu
83 O15 **Mutuáli** Nampula, N Mozambique
82 D13 **Mutumbo** Bié, C Angola
189 Y14 **Mutunte, Mount** *var.* Mount Buache. ▲ Kosrae, E Micronesia
155 K24 **Mutur** Eastern Province, E Sri Lanka
92 L13 **Muurola** Lappi, NW Finland
162 M14 **Mu Us Shadi** *var.* Ordos Desert, *prev.* Mu Us Shamo. *desert* N China
Mu Us Shamo *see* Mu Us Shadi
82 B11 **Muxima** Bengo, NW Angola
124 I8 **Muyezerskiy** Respublika Kareliya, NW Russian Federation
81 E20 **Muyinga** NE Burundi
42 K9 **Muy Muy** Matagalpa, C Nicaragua
Muynak *see* Mo'ynoq
79 N22 **Muyumba** Katanga, SE Dem. Rep. Congo
149 V5 **Muzaffarābād** Jammu and Kashmir, NE Pakistan
149 S10 **Muzaffargarh** Punjab, E Pakistan
152 J9 **Muzaffarnagar** Uttar Pradesh, N India
153 P13 **Muzaffarpur** Bihār, N India
158 H6 **Muzat He** ≈ W China
83 L15 **Muze** Tete, NW Mozambique
122 H8 **Muzhi** Yamalo-Nenetskiy Avtonomnyy Okrug, N Russian Federation
102 H7 **Muzillac** Morbihan, NW France
Muzkol, Khrebet *see* Muzqūl, Qatorkūhi
112 L9 **Mužlja** *Hung.* Felsőmuzslya; *prev.* Gornja Mužlja. Serbia, N Serbia and Montenegro (Yugo.)
54 F9 **Muzo** Boyacá, C Colombia
83 J15 **Muzoka** Southern, S Zambia
39 Y15 **Muzon, Cape** *headland* Dall Island, Alaska, USA
40 M6 **Múzquiz** Coahuila de Zaragoza, NE Mexico
147 U13 **Muzqūl, Qatorkūhi** *Rus.* Khrebet Muzkol. ▲▲ SE Tajikistan
158 G10 **Muztag** ▲ NW China
158 K10 **Muz Tag** ▲ W China
158 D8 **Muztagata** ▲ NW China
83 K17 **Mvuma** *prev.* Umvuma. Midlands, C Zimbabwe
82 L13 **Mwanya** Eastern, E Zambia
81 G20 **Mwanza** Mwanza, NW Tanzania
79 N23 **Mwanza** Katanga, SE Dem. Rep. Congo
81 F20 **Mwanza** ◈ *region* N Tanzania
82 M13 **Mwase Lundazi** Eastern, E Zambia
97 B17 **Mweelrea** *Ir.* Caoc Maol Réidh. ▲ W Ireland
79 K21 **Mweka** Kasai Occidental, C Dem. Rep. Congo
82 K12 **Mwenda** Luapula, N Zambia
79 L22 **Mwene-Ditu** Kasai Oriental, S Dem. Rep. Congo
83 L18 **Mwenezi** ≈ S Zimbabwe
79 O20 **Mwenga** Sud Kivu, E Dem. Rep. Congo
82 K11 **Mweru, Lake** *var.* Lac Moero. ◎ Dem. Rep. Congo/Zambia
82 H13 **Mwinilunga** North Western, NW Zambia
189 V16 **Mwokil Atoll** *var.* Mokil Atoll. *atoll* Caroline Islands, E Micronesia
Myadel' *see* Myadzyel
118 J13 **Myadzyel** *Pol.* Miadzioł Nowy, *Rus.* Myadel'. Minskaya Voblasts', N Belarus
152 C12 **Myājlār** *var.* Miajlar. Rājasthān, NW India
123 T9 **Myakit** Magadanskaya Oblast', E Russian Federation
23 W13 **Myakka River** ≈ Florida, SE USA
124 L14 **Myaksa** Vologodskaya Oblast', NW Russian Federation
183 U8 **Myall Lake** ◎ New South Wales, SE Australia
166 L7 **Myanaung** Irrawaddy, SW Myanmar
166 M4 **Myanmar** *off.* Union of Myanmar; *var.* Burma. ◆ *military dictatorship* SE Asia
166 K8 **Myaungmya** Irrawaddy, SW Myanmar
118 N11 **Myazha** *Rus.* Mezha. Vitsyebskaya Voblasts', NE Belarus
119 O18 **Myerkulavichy** *Rus.* Merkulovichi. Homyel'skaya Voblasts', SE Belarus
119 N14 **Myezhava** *Rus.* Mezhëvo. Vitsyebskaya Voblasts', NE Belarus
166 L5 **Myingyan** Mandalay, C Myanmar
167 N2 **Myitkyina** Kachin State, N Myanmar
166 M5 **Myittha** Mandalay, C Myanmar
111 H19 **Myjava** *Hung.* Miava. Trenčiansky Kraj, W Slovakia
Myjeldino *see* Myyëldino
117 U9 **Mykhaylivka** *Rus.* Mikhaylovka. Zaporiz'ka Oblast', SE Ukraine
95 A18 **Mykines** *Dan.* Myggenaes *Island* Faeroe Islands
116 I5 **Mykolayiv** L'vivs'ka Oblast', W Ukraine
117 Q10 **Mykolayiv** *Rus.* Nikolayev. Mykolayivs'ka Oblast', S Ukraine
117 Q10 **Mykolayiv** ✕ Mykolayivs'ka Oblast', S Ukraine
Mykolayiv *see* Mykolayivs'ka Oblast'
117 P9 **Mykolayivka** Odes'ka Oblast', SW Ukraine
117 S13 **Mykolayivka** Respublika Krym, S Ukraine
117 P9 **Mykolayivs'ka Oblast'** *var.* Mykolayiv, *Rus.* Nikolayevskaya Oblast'. ◈ *province* S Ukraine
115 J20 **Mýkonos** Mýkonos, Kykládes, Greece, Aegean Sea
115 K20 **Mýkonos** *var.* Míkonos. *island* Kykládes, Greece, Aegean Sea
125 R7 **Myla** Respublika Komi, NW Russian Federation
Mylae *see* Milazzo
93 M19 **Myllykoski** Etelä-Suomi, S Finland
Mymensing *see* Mymensingh
153 U14 **Mymensingh** *var.* Maimansingh, Mymensing; *prev.* Nasirābād. Dhaka, N Bangladesh
93 K19 **Mynämäki** Länsi-Suomi, W Finland
145 S14 **Mynaral** *Kaz.* Myngaral. Zhambyl, S Kazakhstan
Mynbulak *see* Mingbuloq
Mynbulak, Vpadina *see* Mingbuloq Botighi
Myngaral *see* Mynaral
166 K5 **Myohaung** Arakan State, W Myanmar
163 W13 **Myohyang-sanmaek** ▲▲ C North Korea
164 M11 **Myōkō-san** ▲ Honshū, S Japan
83 J15 **Myooye** Central, C Zambia
118 K12 **Myory** *prev.* Miyory. Vitsyebskaya Voblasts', N Belarus
92 J4 **Mýrdalsjökull** *glacier* S Iceland
92 G10 **Myre** Nordland, C Norway
117 S5 **Myrhorod** *Rus.* Mirgorod. Poltavs'ka Oblast', NE Ukraine
115 J15 **Mýrina** *var.* Mírina. Límnos, SE Greece
117 P5 **Myronivka** *Rus.* Mironovka. Kyyivs'ka Oblast', N Ukraine
21 U13 **Myrtle Beach** South Carolina, SE USA
32 F14 **Myrtle Creek** Oregon, NW USA
183 P11 **Myrtleford** Victoria, SE Australia
32 E14 **Myrtle Point** Oregon, NW USA
115 K25 **Mýrtos** Kríti, Greece, E Mediterranean Sea
Myrtoum Mare *see* Mirtóo Pélagos
93 G17 **Myrviken** Jämtland, C Sweden
95 I15 **Mysen** Østfold, S Norway
124 L15 **Myshkin** Yaroslavskaya Oblast', NW Russian Federation
111 K17 **Myślenice** Małopolskie, S Poland
110 D10 **Myślibórz** Zachodnio-pomorskie, NW Poland
155 G20 **Mysore** *var.* Maisur. Karnātaka, W India
Mysore *see* Karnātaka
115 F21 **Mystrás** *var.* Mistras. Pelopónnisos, S Greece
125 T12 **Mysy** Komi-Permyatskiy Avtonomnyy Okrug, NW Russian Federation
111 K15 **Myszków** Śląskie, S Poland
167 T14 **My Tho** *var.* Mi Tho. Tiên Giang, S Vietnam
Mytilene *see* Mytilíni
115 L17 **Mytilíni** *var.* Mitilíni; *anc.* Mytilene. Lésvos, E Greece
126 K3 **Mytishchi** Moskovskaya Oblast', W Russian Federation
37 N3 **Myton** Utah, W USA
92 K2 **Mývatn** ◎ C Iceland
125 T11 **Myyëldino** *var.* Myjeldino. Respublika Komi, NW Russian Federation
82 M13 **Mzimba** Northern, NW Malawi
82 M12 **Mzuzu** Northern, N Malawi

N

101 M19 **Naab** ≈ SE Germany
98 G12 **Naaldwijk** Zuid-Holland, W Netherlands
38 G12 **Nā'ālehu** *var.* Naalehu. Hawai'i, USA, C Pacific Ocean
93 K19 **Naantali** *Swe.* Nådendal. Länsi-Suomi, W Finland
98 J10 **Naarden** Noord-Holland, C Netherlands
109 U4 **Naarn** ≈ N Austria
97 F18 **Naas** *Ir.* An Nás, Nás na Ríogh. C Ireland
92 M9 **Näätämöjoki** *Lapp.* Njávdám. ≈ NE Finland
83 E23 **Nababeep** *var.* Nababiep. Northern Cape, W South Africa
Nababiep *see* Nababeep
Nabadwip *see* Navadwip
164 J14 **Nabari** Mie, Honshū, SW Japan
Nabatié *see* Nabatîyé
138 G8 **Nabatîyé** *var.* An Nabatîyah at Taḥtā, Nabatié, Nabatiyet et Tahta. SW Lebanon
Nabatiyet et Tahta *see* Nabatîyé
187 X14 **Nabavatu** Vanua Levu, N Fiji
190 I2 **Nabeina** *island* Tungaru, W Kiribati
127 T4 **Naberezhnyye Chelny** *prev.* Brezhnev. Respublika Tatarstan, W Russian Federation
39 T10 **Nabesna** Alaska, USA
39 T10 **Nabesna River** ≈ Alaska, USA
75 N5 **Nabeul** *var.* Nābul. NE Tunisia
152 I9 **Nābha** Punjab, NW India
171 W13 **Nabire** Papua, E Indonesia
141 O15 **Nabī Shu'ayb, Jabal an** ▲ W Yemen
138 F10 **Nablus** *var.* Nābulus, *Heb.* Shekhem; *anc.* Neapolis, *Bibl.* Shechem. N West Bank
187 X14 **Nabouwalu** Vanua Levu, N Fiji
Nābul *see* Nabeul
Nābulus *see* Nablus
187 Y13 **Nabuna** Vanua Levu, N Fiji
83 Q14 **Nacala** Nampula, NE Mozambique
42 H8 **Nacaome** Valle, S Honduras
Na Cealla Beaga *see* Killybegs
Na-ch'ii *see* Nagqu
164 J15 **Nachikatsuura** *var.* Nachi-Katsuura. Wakayama, Honshū, SE Japan
81 J24 **Nachingwea** Lindi, SE Tanzania
111 F16 **Náchod** Královéhradecký Kraj, N Czech Republic
Na Clocha Liatha *see* Greystones
40 G3 **Naco** Sonora, NW Mexico
25 X8 **Nacogdoches** Texas, SW USA
40 G4 **Nacozari de García** Sonora, NW Mexico
Nada *see* Danzhou
77 O14 **Nadawli** NW Ghana
104 I3 **Nadela** Galicia, NW Spain
Nådendal *see* Naantali
144 M7 **Nadezhdinka** *prev.* Nadezhdinskiy. Kostanay, N Kazakhstan
Nadezhdinskiy *see* Nadezhdinka
Nadgan *see* Nadqān, Qalamat
187 W14 **Nadi** *prev.* Nandi. Viti Levu, W Fiji
187 X14 **Nadi** *prev.* Nandi. ✕ Viti Levu, W Fiji
154 D10 **Nadiād** Gujarāt, W India
Nadikdik *see* Knox Atoll
116 E11 **Nădlac** *Ger.* Nadlak, *Hung.* Nagylak. Arad, W Romania
Nadlak *see* Nădlac
74 H6 **Nador** *prev.* Villa Nador. NE Morocco
141 S9 **Nadqān, Qalamat** *var.* Nadgan. *well* E Saudi Arabia
111 N22 **Nádudvar** Hajdú-Bihar, E Hungary
121 O15 **Nadur** Gozo, N Malta
187 X13 **Naduri** *prev.* Nanduri. Vanua Levu, N Fiji
116 I7 **Nadvirna** *Pol.* Nadwórna, *Rus.* Nadvornaya. Ivano-Frankivs'ka Oblast', W Ukraine
124 J8 **Nadvoitsy** Respublika Kareliya, NW Russian Federation
Nadvornaya/Nadwórna *see* Nadvirna
122 I9 **Nadym** Yamalo-Nenetskiy Avtonomnyy Okrug, N Russian Federation
122 I9 **Nadym** ≈ C Russian Federation
186 E7 **Nadzab** Morobe, C PNG
77 X13 **Nafada** Gombe, E Nigeria
108 H8 **Näfels** Glarus, NE Switzerland
115 E18 **Náfpaktos** *var.* Návpaktos. Dytikí Ellás, C Greece
115 F20 **Náfplio** *prev.* Návplion. Pelopónnisos, S Greece
139 U6 **Naft Khāneh** E Iraq
149 N13 **Nāg** Baluchistān, SW Pakistan
171 P4 **Naga** *off.* Naga City; *prev.* Nueva Caceres. Luzon, N Philippines
Nagaarzê *see* Nagarzê
12 F11 **Nagagami** ≈ Ontario, S Canada
164 F14 **Nagahama** Ehime, Shikoku, SW Japan
153 X12 **Nāga Hills** ▲▲ NE India
165 P10 **Nagai** Yamagata, Honshū, C Japan
Na Gaibhlte *see* Galty Mountains
39 N16 **Nagai Island** *island* Shumagin Islands, Alaska, USA
153 X12 **Nāgāland** ◈ *state* NE India
164 M11 **Nagano** Nagano, Honshū, S Japan
164 M12 **Nagano** *off.* Nagano-ken. ◈ *prefecture* Honshū, S Japan
165 N11 **Nagaoka** Niigata, Honshū, C Japan
153 W12 **Nagaon** *prev.* Nowgong. Assam, NE India
155 J21 **Nāgappattinam** *var.* Negapatam, Negapattinam. Tamil Nādu, SE India
Nagara Nayok *see* Nakhon Nayok
Nagara Panom *see* Nakhon Phanom
Nagara Pathom *see* Nakhon Pathom
Nagara Sridharmaraj *see* Nakhon Si Thammarat
Nagara Svarga *see* Nakhon Sawan
155 H16 **Nāgārjuna Sāgar** ▣ E India
42 I10 **Nagarote** León, SW Nicaragua
158 M16 **Nagarzê** *var.* Nagaarzê. Xizang Zizhiqu, W China
164 C14 **Nagasaki** Nagasaki, Kyūshū, SW Japan
164 C14 **Nagasaki** *off.* Nagasaki-ken. ◈ *prefecture* Kyūshū, SW Japan
Nagashima *see* Kii-Nagashima
164 E12 **Nagato** Yamaguchi, Honshū, SW Japan
152 F11 **Nāgaur** Rājasthān, NW India
154 F10 **Nāgda** Madhya Pradesh, C India
98 L8 **Nagele** Flevoland, N Netherlands
155 H24 **Nāgercoil** Tamil Nādu, SE India
153 X12 **Nāginimāra** Nāgāland, NE India
Na Gleannta *see* Glenties
165 T16 **Nago** Okinawa, Okinawa, SW Japan
154 K9 **Nāgod** Madhya Pradesh, C India
155 J26 **Nagoda** Southern Province, S Sri Lanka
101 G22 **Nagold** Baden-Württemberg, SW Germany
Nagorno-Karabakhskaya Avtonomnaya Oblast *see* Nagorno-Karabakh
123 Q12 **Nagornyy** Respublika Sakha (Yakutiya), NE Russian Federation
137 V12 **Nagorno-Karabakh** *var.* Nagorno-Karabakhskaya Avtonomnaya Oblast, *Arm.* Lerrnayin Gharabakh, *Az.* Dağliq Qarabağ, *Rus.* Nagornyy Karabakh. *former autonomous region* SW Azerbaijan
Nagornyy Karabakh *see* Nagorno-Karabakh
125 R13 **Nagorsk** Kirovskaya Oblast', NW Russian Federation
164 K13 **Nagoya** Aichi, Honshū, SW Japan
154 I12 **Nāgpur** Mahārāshtra, C India
156 K10 **Nagqu** *Chin.* Na-ch'ii; *prev.* Hei-ho. Xizang Zizhiqu, W China
152 J8 **Nāg Tibba Range** ▲▲ N India
45 O8 **Nagua** NE Dominican Republic
111 H25 **Nagyatád** Somogy, SW Hungary
Nagybánya *see* Baia Mare
Nagybecskerek *see* Zrenjanin
Nagydisznód *see* Cisnădie
Nagyenyed *see* Aiud
111 N21 **Nagykálló** Szabolcs-Szatmár-Bereg, E Hungary
111 G25 **Nagykanizsa** *Ger.* Grosskanizsa. Zala, SW Hungary
Nagykároly *see* Carei
111 K22 **Nagykáta** Pest, C Hungary
Nagykikinda *see* Kikinda
111 K23 **Nagykőrös** Pest, C Hungary
Nagy-Küküllő *see* Târnava Mare
Nagylak *see* Nădlac
Nagymihály *see* Michalovce
Nagyrőce *see* Revúca
Nagysomkút *see* Şomcuta Mare
Nagysurány *see* Šurany
Nagyszalonta *see* Salonta
Nagyszeben *see* Sibiu
Nagyszentmiklós *see* Sânnicolau Mare
Nagyszöllös *see* Vynohradiv
Nagyszombat *see* Trnava
Nagytapolcsány *see* Topoľčany
Nagyvárad *see* Oradea
165 S17 **Naha** Okinawa, Okinawa, SW Japan
152 J8 **Nāhan** Himāchal Pradesh, NW India
Nahang, Rūd-e *see* Nihing
Nahariya *see* Nahariyya
138 F8 **Nahariyya** *var.* Nahariya. Northern, N Israel
142 L6 **Nahāvand** *var.* Nehavend. Hamadān, W Iran
101 F19 **Nahe** ≈ SW Germany
Na h-Iarmhidhe *see* Westmeath
189 O13 **Nahnalaud** ▲ Pohnpei, E Micronesia
Nahoi, Cape *see* Cumberland, Cape
Nahtavárr *see* Nattavaara
63 H16 **Nahuel Huapi, Lago** ◎ W Argentina
23 W7 **Nahunta** Georgia, SE USA
40 J6 **Naica** Chihuahua, N Mexico
11 U15 **Naicam** Saskatchewan, S Canada
Naiman Qi *see* Daqin Tal
158 M4 **Naimin Bulak** *spring* NW China
13 P6 **Nain** Newfoundland and Labrador, NE Canada
143 P8 **Nā'īn** Eşfahān, C Iran
152 K10 **Naini Tāl** Uttaranchal, N India
154 J11 **Nainpur** Madhya Pradesh, C India
96 J8 **Nairn** N Scotland, UK
96 I8 **Nairn** *cultural region* NE Scotland, UK
81 I19 **Nairobi** ● (Kenya) Nairobi Area, S Kenya
81 I19 **Nairobi** ✕ Nairobi Area, S Kenya
82 P13 **Nairoto** Cabo Delgado, NE Mozambique
118 G3 **Naissaar** *island* N Estonia
Naissus *see* Niš
187 Z14 **Naitaba** *var.* Naitauba; *prev.* Naitamba. *island* Lau Group, E Fiji
Naitamba/Naitauba *see* Naitaba
81 I19 **Naivasha** Rift Valley, SW Kenya
81 H19 **Naivasha, Lake** ◎ SW Kenya
Najaf *see* An Najaf
143 N8 **Najafābād** *var.* Nejafabad. Eşfahān, C Iran
141 N7 **Najd** *var.* Nejd. *cultural region* C Saudi Arabia
105 O4 **Nájera** La Rioja, N Spain
105 P4 **Najerilla** ≈ N Spain
163 U7 **Naji** *var.* Arun Qi. Nei Mongol Zizhiqu, N China
152 J9 **Najībābād** Uttar Pradesh, N India
Najima *see* Fukuoka
163 Y11 **Najin** NE North Korea
139 T9 **Najm al Ḥassūn** C Iraq
141 O13 **Najrān** *var.* Abā as Su'ūd. Najrān, S Saudi Arabia
141 P12 **Najrān** *off.* Minṭaqat al Najrān. ◈ *province* S Saudi Arabia
165 T2 **Nakagawa** Hokkaidō, NE Japan
38 F9 **Nākālele Point** *var.* Nakalele Point *headland* Maui, Hawai'i, USA, C Pacific Ocean
164 D13 **Nakama** Fukuoka, Kyūshū, SW Japan
Nakambé *see* White Volta
Nakamti *see* Nek'emtē
164 F15 **Nakamura** Kōchi, Shikoku, SW Japan
186 H7 **Nakanai Mountains** ▲▲ New Britain, E PNG
164 H11 **Nakano-shima** *island* Oki-shotō, SW Japan
165 Q6 **Nakasato** Aomori, Honshū, C Japan
165 T5 **Nakasatsunai** Hokkaidō, NE Japan
165 W4 **Nakashibetsu** Hokkaidō, NE Japan
81 F18 **Nakasongola** C Uganda
165 T1 **Nakatonbetsu** Hokkaidō, NE Japan
164 L13 **Nakatsugawa** *var.* Nakatugawa. Gifu, Honshū, SW Japan
Nakatu *see* Nakatsu
Nakatugawa *see* Nakatsugawa
Naka-umi *see* Nakano-umi
Nakdong *see* Naktong-gang
Nakel *see* Nakło nad Notecią
80 J8 **Nakfa** N Eritrea
Nakhichevan' *see* Naxçıvan
123 S15 **Nakhodka** Primorskiy Kray, SE Russian Federation
122 J8 **Nakhodka** Yamalo-Nenetskiy Avtonomnyy Okrug, N Russian Federation
Nakhon Navok *see* Nakhon Nayok
167 P11 **Nakhon Nayok** *var.* Nagara Nayok, Nakhon Navok. C Thailand
167 O11 **Nakhon Pathom** *var.* Nagara Pathom, Nakorn Pathom. W Thailand
167 R8 **Nakhon Phanom** *var.* Nagara Panom. E Thailand
167 Q10 **Nakhon Ratchasima** *var.* Khorat, Korat. E Thailand
167 O9 **Nakhon Sawan** *var.* Muang Nakhon Sawan, Nagara Svarga. W Thailand
167 N15 **Nakhon Si Thammarat** *var.* Nagara Sridharmaraj, Nakhon Sithamnaraj. SW Thailand
Nakhon Sithamnaraj *see* Nakhon Si Thammarat
139 Y11 **Nakhrash** SE Iraq
10 I9 **Nakina** British Columbia, W Canada
110 H9 **Nakło nad Notecią** *Ger.* Nakel. Kujawsko-pomorskie, C Poland
39 P13 **Naknek** Alaska, USA
152 H8 **Nakodar** Punjab, NW India
82 M11 **Nakonde** Northern, NE Zambia
Nakorn Pathom *see* Nakhon Pathom
95 H24 **Nakskov** Storstrøm, SE Denmark
163 Y15 **Naktong-gang** *var.* Nakdong, *Jap.* Rakutō-kō. ≈ C South Korea
83 H18 **Nakuru** Rift Valley, SW Kenya
81 H19 **Nakuru, Lake** ◎ Rift Valley, C Kenya
11 O17 **Nakusp** British Columbia, SW Canada
149 N15 **Nāl** ≈ W Pakistan
162 M7 **Nalayh** Töv, C Mongolia
153 V12 **Nalbāri** Assam, NE India
63 G19 **Nalcayec, Isla** *island* Archipiélago de los Chonos, S Chile
127 N15 **Nal'chik** Kabardino-Balkarskaya Respublika, SW Russian Federation
155 I16 **Nalgonda** Andhra Pradesh, C India
153 S14 **Nalhāti** West Bengal, NE India
153 U14 **Nalitabari** Dhaka, N Bangladesh
155 I17 **Nallamala Hills** ▲▲ E India
136 G12 **Nallıhan** Ankara, NW Turkey
104 K2 **Nalón** ≈ NW Spain
167 N3 **Nalong** Kachin State, N Myanmar
75 N8 **Nālūt** NW Libya
171 T14 **Nama** Pulau Manawoka, E Indonesia
189 Q16 **Nama** *island* C Micronesia
83 O16 **Namacurra** Zambézia, NE Mozambique
188 F9 **Namai Bay** *bay* Babeldaob, N Palau
29 W2 **Namakan Lake** ◎ Canada/USA
143 O6 **Namak, Daryācheh-ye** *marsh* N Iran
143 T6 **Namak, Kavīr-e** *salt pan* NE Iran
167 O6 **Namaklwe** Shan State, E Myanmar
Namaksār, Kowl-e/Namakzār, Daryācheh-ye *see* Namakzar
148 J5 **Namakzar** *Pash.* Daryācheh-ye Namakzār, Kowl-e Namaksār. *marsh* Afghanistan/Iran
171 V15 **Namalau** Pulau Jursian, E Indonesia
81 I20 **Namanga** Rift Valley, S Kenya
147 S10 **Namangan** Namangan Viloyati, E Uzbekistan
Namanganskaya Oblast' *see* Namangan Viloyati
147 R10 **Namangan Viloyati** *Rus.* Namanganskaya Oblast'. ◈ *province* E Uzbekistan
83 Q14 **Namapa** Nampula, NE Mozambique
83 C21 **Namaqualand** *physical region* S Namibia
81 G18 **Namasagali** C Uganda
186 H6 **Namatanai** New Ireland, NE PNG
83 I14 **Nambala** Central, C Zambia
81 J23 **Nambanje** Lindi, SE Tanzania
83 G16 **Nambiya** Ngamiland, N Botswana
183 V2 **Nambour** Queensland, E Australia
183 V6 **Nambucca Heads** New South Wales, SE Australia
159 N15 **Nam Co** ◎ W China
167 R5 **Nam Cum** Lai Châu, N Vietnam
Namdik *see* Namorik Atoll
167 T6 **Nam Định** Nam Ha, N Vietnam
99 I20 **Namêche** Namur, SE Belgium
30 J4 **Namekagon Lake** ◎ Wisconsin, N USA
188 F10 **Namekakl Passage** *passage* Babeldaob, N Palau
Namen *see* Namur
83 P15 **Nametil** Nampula, NE Mozambique
163 X14 **Nam-gang** ≈ C North Korea
163 Y16 **Nam-gang** ≈ S South Korea
163 Y17 **Namhae-do** *Jap.* Nankai-tō. *island* S South Korea
Namhoi *see* Foshan
83 C19 **Namib Desert** *desert* W Namibia
83 A15 **Namibe** *Port.* Moçâmedes, Mossâmedes. Namibe, SW Angola
83 A15 **Namibe** ◈ *province* SE Angola
83 C18 **Namibia** *off.* Republic of Namibia, *var.* South West Africa, *Afr.* Suidwes-Afrika, *Ger.* Deutsch-Südwestafrika; *prev.* German Southwest Africa, South-West Africa. ◆ *republic* S Africa
65 O17 **Namibia Plain** *undersea feature* S Atlantic Ocean
165 Q11 **Namie** Fukushima, Honshū, C Japan
165 Q7 **Namioka** Aomori, Honshū, C Japan
40 I5 **Namiquipa** Chihuahua, N Mexico
159 P15 **Namjagbarwa Feng** ▲ W China
Namka *see* Doilungdêqên
171 R13 **Namlea** Pulau Buru, E Indonesia
158 L16 **Namling** Xizang Zizhiqu, W China
Namnetes *see* Nantes
167 R8 **Nam Ngum** ≈ C Laos
Namo *see* Namu Atoll
183 R5 **Namoi River** ≈ New South Wales, SE Australia
189 Q17 **Namoluk Atoll** *atoll* Mortlock Islands, C Micronesia
189 O15 **Namonuito Atoll** *atoll* Caroline Islands, C Micronesia
189 T9 **Namorik Atoll** *var.* Namdik. *atoll* Ralik Chain, S Marshall Islands
167 Q6 **Nam Ou** ≈ N Laos
32 M14 **Nampa** Idaho, NW USA
76 M11 **Nampala** Ségou, W Mali
163 W14 **Namp'o** SW North Korea
83 P15 **Nampula** Nampula, NE Mozambique
83 P15 **Nampula** *off.* Província de Nampula. ◈ *province* NE Mozambique
163 W13 **Namsan-ni** NW North Korea
Namslau *see* Namysłów
93 E15 **Namsos** Nord-Trøndelag, C Norway
93 F14 **Namsskogan** Nord-Trøndelag, C Norway
123 Q10 **Namsty** Respublika Sakha (Yakutiya), NE Russian Federation
167 O6 **Nam Teng** ≈ E Myanmar
167 P6 **Nam Tha** ≈ N Laos
167 N4 **Namtu** Shan State, E Myanmar
10 J15 **Namu** British Columbia, SW Canada
189 T7 **Namu Atoll** *var.* Namo. *atoll* Ralik Chain, C Marshall Islands
187 Y15 **Namuka-i-lau** *island* Lau Group, E Fiji
83 O15 **Namuli, Mont** ▲ NE Mozambique
83 P14 **Namuno** Cabo Delgado, N Mozambique
99 I20 **Namur** *Dut.* Namen. Namur, SE Belgium
99 H21 **Namur** *Dut.* Namen. ◈ *province* S Belgium
83 D17 **Namutoni** Kunene, N Namibia
163 Y16 **Namwŏn** *Jap.* Nangen. S South Korea
111 H14 **Namysłów** *Ger.* Namslau. Opolskie, S Poland
167 P7 **Nan** *var.* Muang Nan. Nan, NW Thailand
79 G15 **Nana** ≈ W Central African Republic
165 R5 **Nanae** Hokkaidō, NE Japan
79 I14 **Nana-Grébizi** ◈ *prefecture* N Central African Republic
10 L17 **Nanaimo** Vancouver Island, British Columbia, SW Canada
38 C9 **Nānākuli** *var.* Nanakuli. O'ahu, Hawai'i, USA, C Pacific Ocean
79 G15 **Nana-Mambéré** ◈ *prefecture* W Central African Republic
161 R13 **Nan'an** Fujian, SE China
183 U2 **Nanango** Queensland, E Australia
164 L11 **Nanao** Ishikawa, Honshū, SW Japan
161 Q14 **Nan'ao Dao** *island* S China
164 L10 **Nanatsu-shima** *island* SW Japan
56 F8 **Nanay, Río** ≈ NE Peru
160 J8 **Nanbu** Sichuan, C China
163 X7 **Nancha** Heilongjiang, NE China
161 P10 **Nanchang** *var.* Nan-ch'ang, Nanch'ang-hsien. Jiangxi, S China
Nanch'ang-hsien *see* Nanchang
161 P11 **Nancheng** *var.* Jianchang. Jiangxi, S China
Nan-ching *see* Nanjing
160 J9 **Nanchong** Sichuan, C China
160 J10 **Nanchuan** Chongqing Shi, C China
103 T5 **Nancy** Meurthe-et-Moselle, NE France

◆ Country ● Country Capital ◇ Dependent Territory ○ Dependent Territory Capital ◈ Administrative Region ✕ International Airport ▲ Mountain ▲▲ Mountain Range Volcano ≈ River ◎ Lake ▣ Reservoir

185 A22 **Nancy Sound** *sound* South Island, NZ
152 L9 **Nanda Devi** ▲ NW India
42 J11 **Nandaime** Granada, SW Nicaragua
160 K13 **Nandan** Guangxi Zhuangzu Zizhiqu, S China
155 H14 **Nānded** Mahārāshtra, C India
183 S5 **Nandewar Range** ▲ New South Wales, SE Australia
Nandi *see* Nadi
160 E13 **Nanding He** ⁓ China/Vietnam
Nándorhgy *see* Oţelu Roşu
154 E11 **Nandurbār** Mahārāshtra, W India
Nanduri *see* Naduri
155 I17 **Nandyāl** Andhra Pradesh, E India
161 P11 **Nanfeng** *var.* Qincheng. Jiangxi, S China
Nang *see* Nangxian
79 E15 **Nanga Eboko** Centre, C Cameroon
149 W4 **Nanga Parbat** ▲ India/Pakistan
169 R11 **Nangapinoh** Borneo, C Indonesia
149 R5 **Nangarhār** ◆ *province* E Afghanistan
169 S11 **Nangaserawai** *var.* Nangah Serawai. Borneo, C Indonesia
169 Q12 **Nangatayap** Borneo, C Indonesia
Nangen *see* Namwŏn
103 P5 **Nangis** Seine-et-Marne, N France
163 X13 **Nangnim-sanmaek** ▲ C North Korea
161 O4 **Nangong** Hebei, E China
159 Q14 **Nangqên** *var.* Xangda. Qinghai, C China
167 Q10 **Nang Rong** Buri Ram, E Thailand
159 O16 **Nangxian** *var.* Nang. Xizang Zizhiqu, W China
Nan Hai *see* South China Sea
160 L8 **Nan He** ⁓ C China
160 F12 **Nanhua** *var.* Longchuan. Yunnan, SW China
Naniwa *see* Ōsaka
155 G20 **Nanjangūd** Karnātaka, W India
161 Q8 **Nanjing** *var.* Nan-ching, Nanking; *prev.* Chianning, Chian-ning, Kiang-ning. Jiangsu, E China
Nankai-tō *see* Namhae-do
161 O12 **Nankang** *var.* Rongjiang. Jiangxi, S China
Nanking *see* Nanjing
161 N13 **Nan Ling** ▲ S China
160 L15 **Nanliu Jiang** ⁓ S China
189 P13 **Nan Madol** *ruins* Temwen Island, E Micronesia
160 K15 **Nanning** *var.* Nan-ning; *prev.* Yung-ning. Guangxi Zhuangzu Zizhiqu, S China
196 M15 **Nanortalik** Kitaa, S Greenland
Nanouki *see* Aranuka
160 H13 **Nanpan Jiang** ⁓ S China
152 M11 **Nānpāra** Uttar Pradesh, N India
161 Q12 **Nanping** *var.* Nan-p'ing; *prev.* Yenping. Fujian, SE China
Nanping *see* Jiuzhaigou
Nanpu *see* Pucheng
161 R12 **Nanri Dao** *island* SE China
165 S16 **Nansei-shotō** *Eng.* Ryukyu Islands. *island group* SW Japan
Nansei Syotō Trench *see* Ryukyu Trench
197 T10 **Nansen Basin** *undersea feature* Arctic Ocean
197 T10 **Nansen Cordillera** *var.* Arctic-Mid Oceanic Ridge, Nansen Ridge. *undersea feature* Arctic Ocean
Nansen Ridge *see* Nansen Cordillera
131 T9 **Nan Shan** ▲ C China
Nansha Qundao *see* Spratly Islands
12 K3 **Nantais, Lac** ⊚ Québec, NE Canada
103 N5 **Nanterre** Hauts-de-Seine, N France
102 I8 **Nantes** *Bret.* Naoned; *anc.* Condivincum, Namnetes. Loire-Atlantique, NW France
14 G17 **Nanticoke** Ontario, S Canada
18 H13 **Nanticoke** Pennsylvania, NE USA
21 Y4 **Nanticoke River** ⁓ Delaware/Maryland, NE USA
11 Q17 **Nanton** Alberta, SW Canada
161 S8 **Nantong** Jiangsu, E China
161 S13 **Nant'ou** W Taiwan
103 S10 **Nantua** Ain, E France
19 Q13 **Nantucket** Nantucket Island, Massachusetts, NE USA
19 Q13 **Nantucket Island** *island* Massachusetts, NE USA
19 Q13 **Nantucket Sound** *sound* Massachusetts, NE USA
82 P13 **Nantulo** Cabo Delgado, N Mozambique
189 O12 **Nanuh** Pohnpei, E Micronesia
190 D6 **Nanumaga** *var.* Nanumanga. *atoll* NW Tuvalu
Nanumanga *see* Nanumaga
190 D5 **Nanumea Atoll** *atoll* NW Tuvalu
59 O19 **Nanuque** Minas Gerais, SE Brazil
171 R10 **Nanusa, Kepulauan** *island group* N Indonesia
163 U4 **Nanweng He** ⁓ NE China
160 I10 **Nanxi** Sichuan, C China
161 N10 **Nanxian** *var.* Nan Xian, Nanzhou. Hunan, S China
161 N7 **Nanyang** *var.* Nan-yang. Henan, C China
161 P6 **Nanyang Hu** ⊚ E China
165 P10 **Nan'yō** Yamagata, Honshū, C Japan
81 I18 **Nanyuki** Central, C Kenya
160 M8 **Nanzhang** Hubei, C China
Nanzhou *see* Nanxian
105 T11 **Nao, Cabo de La** *headland* E Spain
12 M9 **Naococane, Lac** ⊚ Québec, E Canada
153 S14 **Naogaon** Rajshahi, NW Bangladesh
Naokot *see* Naukot
187 R13 **Naone** Maewo, C Vanuatu
Naoned *see* Nantes
115 E14 **Náousa** Kentrikí Makedonía, N Greece
35 N8 **Napa** California, W USA
39 O11 **Napaimiut** Alaska, USA
39 N12 **Napakiak** Alaska, USA
122 J7 **Napalkovo** Yamalo-Nenetskiy Avtonomnyy Okrug, N Russian Federation
12 I16 **Napanee** Ontario, SE Canada
39 N12 **Napaskiak** Alaska, USA
167 S5 **Na Phac** Cao Bāng, N Vietnam
184 O11 **Napier** Hawke's Bay, North Island, NZ
195 X3 **Napier Mountains** ▲ Antarctica
15 O13 **Napierville** Québec, SE Canada
23 W15 **Naples** Florida, SE USA
25 W5 **Naples** Texas, SW USA
Naples *see* Napoli
160 I14 **Napo** Guangxi Zhuangzu Zizhiqu, S China
56 C6 **Napo** ◆ *province* NE Ecuador
29 O6 **Napoleon** North Dakota, N USA
31 R11 **Napoleon** Ohio, N USA
Napoléon-Vendée *see* la Roche-sur-Yon
22 J9 **Napoleonville** Louisiana, S USA
107 K17 **Napoli** *Eng.* Naples, *Ger.* Neapel; *anc.* Neapolis. Campania, S Italy
107 J18 **Napoli, Golfo di** *gulf* S Italy
57 F7 **Napo, Río** ⁓ Ecuador/Peru
191 W9 **Napuka** *island* Îles Tuamotu, C French Polynesia
142 J3 **Naqadeh** Āžarbāyjān-e Bākhtarī, NW Iran
139 U6 **Naqnah** E Iraq
Nar *see* Nera
164 J14 **Nara** Nara, Honshū, SW Japan
76 L11 **Nara** Koulikoro, W Mali
164 J14 **Nara** *off.* Nara-ken. ◆ *prefecture* Honshū, SW Japan
149 R14 **Nāra Canal** *irrigation canal* S Pakistan
182 K11 **Naracoorte** South Australia
183 P8 **Naradhan** New South Wales, SE Australia
Naradhivas *see* Narathiwat
56 B8 **Naranjal** Guayas, W Ecuador
57 Q19 **Naranjos** Santa Cruz, E Bolivia
41 Q12 **Naranjos** Veracruz-Llave, E Mexico
159 Q6 **Naran Sebstein Bulag** *spring* NW China
143 X12 **Narānū** Sīstān va Balūchestān, SE Iran
164 B14 **Narao** Nagasaki, Nakadōri-jima, SW Japan
155 J16 **Narasaraopet** Andhra Pradesh, E India
158 J5 **Narat** Xinjiang Uygur Zizhiqu, W China
167 P17 **Narathiwat** *var.* Naradhivas. Narathiwat, SW Thailand
37 V10 **Nara Visa** New Mexico, SW USA
Nārāyāni *see* Gandak
Narbada *see* Narmada
Narbo Martius *see* Narbonne
103 P16 **Narbonne** *anc.* Narbo Martius. Aude, S France
Narborough Island *see* Fernandina, Isla
104 J2 **Narcea** ⁓ NW Spain
152 J9 **Narendranagar** Uttaranchal, N India
Nares Abyssal Plain *see* Nares Plain
64 G11 **Nares Plain** *var.* Nares Abyssal Plain. *undersea feature* NW Atlantic Ocean
197 P10 **Nares Strait** *Dan.* Nares Stræde. *strait* Canada/Greenland
Nares Stræde *see* Nares Strait
110 O9 **Narew** ⁓ E Poland
155 F17 **Nargund** Karnātaka, W India
83 D20 **Narib** Hardap, S Namibia
Narikrik *see* Knox Atoll
Narin Gol *see* Dong He
54 B13 **Nariño** *off.* Departamento de Nariño. ◆ *province* SW Colombia
165 P13 **Narita** Chiba, Honshū, S Japan
165 P13 **Narita** ✕ (Tōkyō) Chiba, Honshū, S Japan
Nariya *see* An Nu'ayrīyah
162 F5 **Nariyn Gol** ⁓ Mongolia/Russian Federation
152 J8 **Nārkanda** Himāchal Pradesh, NW India
92 L13 **Narkaus** Lappi, NW Finland
154 E11 **Narmada** *var.* Narbada. ⁓ C India
152 H11 **Narnaul** *var.* Nārnaul. Haryāna, N India
107 I14 **Narni** Umbria, C Italy
107 J24 **Naro** Sicilia, Italy, C Mediterranean Sea
Narodichi *see* Narodychi
127 V7 **Narodnaya, Gora** ▲ NW Russian Federation
117 N3 **Narodychi** *Rus.* Narodichi. Zhytomyrs'ka Oblast', N Ukraine
126 J4 **Naro-Fominsk** Moskovskaya Oblast', W Russian Federation
81 H19 **Narok** Rift Valley, SW Kenya
104 H2 **Narón** Galicia, NW Spain
183 S11 **Narooma** New South Wales, SE Australia
Narova *see* Narva
Narovlya *see* Narowlya
149 W8 **Nārowāl** Punjab, E Pakistan
119 N20 **Narowlya** *Rus.* Narovlya. Homyel'skaya Voblasts', SE Belarus
93 J17 **Närpes** *Fin.* Närpiö. Länsi-Suomi, W Finland
Närpiö *see* Närpes
183 S5 **Narrabri** New South Wales, SE Australia
183 P9 **Narrandera** New South Wales, SE Australia
183 Q4 **Narran Lake** ⊚ New South Wales, SE Australia
183 Q4 **Narran River** ⁓ New South Wales/Queensland, SE Australia
180 J13 **Narrogin** Western Australia
183 Q7 **Narromine** New South Wales, SE Australia
21 R6 **Narrows** Virginia, NE USA
196 M15 **Narsarsuaq** ✕ Kitaa, S Greenland
154 I10 **Narsimhapur** Madhya Pradesh, C India
Narsingdi *see* Narsinghdi
153 U15 **Narsinghdi** *var.* Narsingdi. Dhaka, C Bangladesh
154 H9 **Narsinghgarh** Madhya Pradesh, C India
163 Q11 **Nart** Nei Mongol Zizhiqu, N China
Nartës, Gjol i/Nartës, Laguna e *see* Nartës, Liqeni i
113 J22 **Nartës, Liqeni i** *var.* Gjol i Nartës, Laguna e Nartës. ⊚ SW Albania
115 F17 **Narthákí** ▲ C Greece
127 O15 **Nartkala** Kabardino-Balkarskaya Respublika, SW Russian Federation
118 K3 **Narva** Ida-Virumaa, NE Estonia
118 K4 **Narva** *prev.* Narova. ⁓ Estonia/Russian Federation
118 J3 **Narva Bay** *Est.* Narva Laht, *Ger.* Narwa-Bucht, *Rus.* Narvskiy Zaliv. *bay* Estonia/Russian Federation
Narva Laht *see* Narva Bay
126 F13 **Narva Reservoir** *Est.* Narva Veehoidla, *Rus.* Narvskoye Vodokhranilishche. ⊞ Estonia/Russian Federation
Narva Veehoidla *see* Narva Reservoir
92 H10 **Narvik** Nordland, C Norway
Narvskiy Zaliv *see* Narva Bay
Narvskoye Vodokhranilishche *see* Narva Reservoir
Narwa-Bucht *see* Narva Bay
152 I9 **Narwāna** Haryāna, NW India
125 R4 **Nar'yan-Mar** *prev.* Beloshchel'ye, Dzerzhinskiy. Nenetskiy Avtonomnyy Okrug, NW Russian Federation
122 J12 **Narym** Tomskaya Oblast', C Russian Federation
145 Y10 **Narymskiy Khrebet** *Kaz.* Naryn Zhotasy. ▲ E Kazakhstan
147 W9 **Naryn** Narynskaya Oblast', C Kyrgyzstan
147 U8 **Naryn** ⁓ Kyrgyzstan/Uzbekistan
145 W16 **Narynkol** *Kaz.* Naryngqol. Almaty, SE Kazakhstan
Naryn Oblasty *see* Narynskaya Oblast'
Narynqol *see* Narynkol
147 V9 **Narynskaya Oblast'** *Kir.* Naryn Oblasty. ◆ *province* C Kyrgyzstan
Naryn Zhotasy *see* Narymskiy Khrebet
126 J6 **Naryshkino** Orlovskaya Oblast', W Russian Federation
95 L14 **Nås** Dalarna, C Sweden
92 G13 **Nasafjellet** *Lapp.* Násávárre. ▲ C Norway
93 H16 **Nåsåker** Västernorrland, C Sweden
187 Y14 **Nasau** Koro, C Fiji
116 I9 **Năsăud** *Ger.* Nussdorf, *Hung.* Naszód. Bistriţa-Năsăud, N Romania
Násávárre *see* Nasafjellet
103 P13 **Nasbinals** Lozère, S France
Na Sceirí *see* Skerries
Nase *see* Naze
185 E22 **Naseby** Otago, South Island, NZ
143 R10 **Nāşerīyeh** Kermān, C Iran
25 X5 **Nash** Texas, SW USA
154 E13 **Nāshik** *prev.* Nāsik. Mahārāshtra, W India
56 E7 **Nashiño, Río** ⁓ Ecuador/Peru
29 W12 **Nashua** Iowa, C USA
33 W7 **Nashua** Montana, NW USA
19 O10 **Nashua** New Hampshire, NE USA
27 S13 **Nashville** Arkansas, C USA
23 U7 **Nashville** Georgia, SE USA
30 L16 **Nashville** Illinois, N USA
31 O14 **Nashville** Indiana, N USA
21 V9 **Nashville** North Carolina, SE USA
20 J8 **Nashville** *state capital* Tennessee, S USA
20 J9 **Nashville** ✕ Tennessee, S USA
64 H10 **Nashville Seamount** *undersea feature* NW Atlantic Ocean
112 H9 **Našice** Osijek-Baranja, E Croatia
110 M11 **Nasielsk** Mazowieckie, C Poland
93 K18 **Näsijärvi** ⊚ SW Finland
Nāsik *see* Nāshik
80 G13 **Nasir** Upper Nile, SE Sudan
149 Q12 **Nasīrābād** Baluchistān, SW Pakistan
148 K15 **Nasīrābād** Baluchistān, SW Pakistan
Nasīrābād *see* Mymensingh
Nasir, Buhayrat/Nâşir, Buheiret *see* Nasser, Lake
Nāsiri *see* Ahvāz
Nasiriya *see* An Nāşirīyah
Nás na Ríogh *see* Naas
107 L23 **Naso** Sicilia, Italy, C Mediterranean Sea
Nasratabad *see* Zābol
10 J11 **Nass** ⁓ British Columbia, SW Canada
77 V15 **Nassarawa** Nassarawa, C Nigeria
44 H2 **Nassau** ● (Bahamas) New Providence, N Bahamas
44 H2 **Nassau** ✕ New Providence, C Bahamas
190 J13 **Nassau** *island* N Cook Islands
23 W8 **Nassau Sound** *sound* Florida, SE USA
108 L7 **Nassereith** Tirol, W Austria
95 L19 **Nässjö** Jönköping, S Sweden
99 K22 **Nassogne** Luxembourg, SE Belgium
12 J6 **Nastapoka Islands** *island group* Nunavut, C Canada
93 M19 **Nastola** Etelä-Suomi, S Finland
171 O4 **Nasugbu** Luzon, N Philippines
94 N11 **Näsviken** Gävleborg, C Sweden
Naszód *see* Năsăud
83 I17 **Nata** Central, NE Botswana
54 E11 **Natagaima** Tolima, C Colombia
59 Q14 **Natal** Rio Grande do Norte, E Brazil
168 I11 **Natal** Sumatera, N Indonesia
Natal *see* KwaZulu/Natal
173 L10 **Natal Basin** *var.* Mozambique Basin. *undersea feature* W Indian Ocean
25 R12 **Natalia** Texas, SW USA
67 W15 **Natal Valley** *undersea feature* SW Indian Ocean
Natanya *see* Netanya
143 O7 **Naţanz** Eşfahān, C Iran
13 Q11 **Natashquan** Québec, E Canada
13 Q10 **Natashquan** ⁓ Newfoundland and Labrador/Québec, E Canada
22 J7 **Natchez** Mississippi, S USA
22 G6 **Natchitoches** Louisiana, S USA
108 E10 **Naters** Valais, S Switzerland
Nathanya *see* Netanya
92 O3 **Nathorst Land** *physical region* W Svalbard
Nathula *see* Nacula
186 E9 **National Capital District** ◆ *province* S PNG
35 U17 **National City** California, W USA
184 M10 **National Park** Manawatu-Wanganui, North Island, NZ
77 R14 **Natitingou** NW Benin
40 B5 **Natividad, Isla** *island* W Mexico
165 Q10 **Natori** Miyagi, Honshū, C Japan
18 C14 **Natrona Heights** Pennsylvania, NE USA
81 H20 **Natron, Lake** ⊚ Kenya/Tanzania
Natsrat *see* Nazerat
166 L7 **Nattalin** Pegu, C Myanmar
92 J12 **Nattavaara** *Lapp.* Nahtavárr. Norrbotten, N Sweden
109 S3 **Natternbach** Oberösterreich, N Austria
95 M22 **Nättraby** Blekinge, S Sweden
169 P10 **Natuna Besar, Pulau** *island* Kepulauan Natuna, W Indonesia
169 O9 **Natuna Islands** *see* Natuna, Kepulauan
169 O9 **Natuna, Kepulauan** *var.* Natuna Islands. *island group* W Indonesia
169 N9 **Natuna, Laut** *sea* W Indonesia
21 N6 **Natural Bridge** *tourist site* Kentucky, C USA
173 V11 **Naturaliste Fracture Zone** *tectonic feature* E Indian Ocean
174 J10 **Naturaliste Plateau** *undersea feature* E Indian Ocean
Nau *see* Nov
103 O14 **Naucelle** Aveyron, S France
83 D20 **Nauchas** Hardap, C Namibia
108 K9 **Nauders** Tirol, W Austria
Naugard *see* Nowogard
118 F12 **Naujamiestis** Panevėžys, C Lithuania
118 E10 **Naujoji Akmenė** Šiauliai, NW Lithuania
149 R16 **Naukot** *var.* Naokot. Sind, SE Pakistan
101 L16 **Naumburg** *var.* Naumburg an der Saale. Sachsen-Anhalt, C Germany
Naumburg am Queis *see* Nowogrodziec
Naumburg an der Saale *see* Naumburg
191 W15 **Naunau** *ancient monument* Easter Island, Chile, E Pacific Ocean
138 G10 **Nā'ūr** 'Al Āşimah, W Jordan
189 Q8 **Nauru** *off.* Republic of Nauru; *prev.* Pleasant Island. ◆ *republic* W Pacific Ocean
175 P5 **Nauru** *island* W Pacific Ocean
189 Q9 **Nauru International** ✕ S Nauru
Nausari *see* Navsāri
19 Q12 **Nauset Beach** *beach* Massachusetts, NE USA
Naushahra *see* Nowshera
149 P14 **Naushahro Fīroz** Sind, SE Pakistan
Naushara *see* Nowshera
187 X14 **Nausori** Viti Levu, W Fiji
56 F9 **Nauta** Loreto, N Peru
153 O12 **Nautanwa** Uttar Pradesh, N India
41 R13 **Nautla** Veracruz-Llave, E Mexico
Nauzad *see* Now Zād
41 N6 **Nava** Coahuila de Zaragoza, NE Mexico
Navabad *see* Navobod
104 L6 **Nava del Rey** Castilla-León, N Spain
153 S15 **Navadwīp** *prev.* Nabadwip. West Bengal, NE India
104 M9 **Navahermosa** Castilla-La Mancha, C Spain
119 I16 **Navahrudak** *Pol.* Nowogródek, *Rus.* Novogrudok. Hrodzyenskaya Voblasts', W Belarus
119 I16 **Navahrudskaye Wzvyshsha** ▲ W Belarus
36 M8 **Navajo Mount** ▲ Utah, W USA
37 Q9 **Navajo Reservoir** ⊞ New Mexico, SW USA
104 K9 **Navalmoral de la Mata** Extremadura, W Spain
104 K10 **Navalvillar de Pelea** Extremadura, W Spain
97 F17 **Navan** *Ir.* An Uaimh. E Ireland
Navanagar *see* Jāmnagar
118 L12 **Navapolatsk** *Rus.* Novopolotsk. Vitsyebskaya Voblasts', N Belarus
149 P6 **Nāvar, Dasht-e** *Pash.* Dasht-i-Nawar. *desert* C Afghanistan
123 W6 **Navarin, Mys** *headland* NE Russian Federation
63 I25 **Navarino, Isla** *island* S Chile
105 Q4 **Navarra** *Eng./Fr.* Navarre. ◆ *autonomous community* N Spain
Navarre *see* Navarra
105 P4 **Navarrete** La Rioja, N Spain
61 C20 **Navarro** Buenos Aires, E Argentina
105 O12 **Navas de San Juan** Andalucía, S Spain
25 V10 **Navasota** Texas, SW USA
25 U9 **Navasota River** ⁓ Texas, SW USA
44 I9 **Navassa Island** ◇ *US unincorporated territory* C West Indies
119 L19 **Navasyolki** *Rus.* Novosëlki. Homyel'skaya Voblasts', SE Belarus
119 H17 **Navayel'nya** *Pol.* Nowojelnia, *Rus.* Novoyel'nya. Hrodzyenskaya Voblasts', W Belarus
171 Y13 **Naver** Papua, E Indonesia
118 H5 **Navesti** ⁓ C Estonia
104 J2 **Navia** Asturias, N Spain
104 J2 **Navia** ⁓ NW Spain
59 I21 **Naviraí** Mato Grosso do Sul, SW Brazil
126 I6 **Navlya** Bryanskaya Oblast', W Russian Federation
187 X13 **Navoalevu** Vanua Levu, N Fiji
147 R12 **Navobod** *Rus.* Navabad, Novabad. C Tajikistan
147 P13 **Navobod** *Rus.* Navabad. W Tajikistan
Navoi *see* Navoiy
146 M11 **Navoiy** *Rus.* Navoi. Navoiy Viloyati, C Uzbekistan
Navoiyskaya Oblast' *see* Navoiy Viloyati
40 G7 **Navojoa** Sonora, NW Mexico
Navolat *see* Navolato
42 H9 **Navolato** *var.* Navolat. Sinaloa, C Mexico
187 Q13 **Navonda** Ambae, C Vanuatu
Návpaktos *see* Náfpaktos
Návplion *see* Náfplio
77 P14 **Navrongo** N Ghana
154 D12 **Navsāri** *var.* Nausari. Gujarāt, W India
187 X15 **Navua** Viti Levu, W Fiji
138 H8 **Nawá** Dar'ā, S Syria
Nawabashah *see* Nawābshāh
153 S14 **Nawabganj** Rajshahi, NW Bangladesh
153 S14 **Nawābganj** Uttar Pradesh, N India
149 Q15 **Nawābshāh** *var.* Nawabashah. Sind, S Pakistan
153 P14 **Nawāda** Bihār, N India
152 H11 **Nawalgarh** Rājasthān, N India
Nawāl, Sabkhat an *see* Noual, Sebkhet en
Nawar, Dasht-i- *see* Nāvar, Dasht-e
167 N4 **Nawnghkio** *var.* Nawngkio. Shan State, C Myanmar
Nawngkio *see* Nawnghkio
146 K8 **Navoiy Viloyati** *Rus.* Navoiyskaya Oblast'. ◆ *province* N Uzbekistan
137 U13 **Naxçıvan** *Rus.* Nakhichevan'. SW Azerbaijan
160 I10 **Naxi** Sichuan, C China
115 K21 **Náxos** *var.* Naxos. Náxos, Kykládes, Greece, Aegean Sea
115 K21 **Náxos** *island* Kykládes, Greece, Aegean Sea
40 J11 **Nayarit** ◆ *state* C Mexico
187 Y14 **Nayau** *island* Lau Group, E Fiji
143 S8 **Nāy Band** Yazd, E Iran
165 T2 **Nayoro** Hokkaidō, NE Japan
104 F9 **Nazaré** *var.* Nazare. Leiria, C Portugal
24 M4 **Nazareth** Texas, SW USA
Nazareth *see* Nazerat
173 O8 **Nazareth Bank** *undersea feature* W Indian Ocean
40 K9 **Nazas** Durango, C Mexico
57 F16 **Nazca** Ica, S Peru
(0) L17 **Nazca Plate** *tectonic feature*
193 U9 **Nazca Ridge** *undersea feature* E Pacific Ocean
165 V15 **Naze** *var.* Nase. Kagoshima, Amami-ōshima, SW Japan
138 G9 **Nazerat** *var.* Natsrat, *Ar.* En Nazira, *Eng.* Nazareth. Northern, N Israel
137 R14 **Nazik Gölü** ⊚ E Turkey
136 C15 **Nazilli** Aydın, SW Turkey
137 P14 **Nazimiye** Tunceli, E Turkey
Nazinon *see* Red Volta
10 L15 **Nazko** British Columbia, SW Canada
127 O16 **Nazran'** Ingushskaya Respublika, SW Russian Federation
80 J13 **Nazrēt** *var.* Adama, Hadama. Oromo, C Ethiopia
Nazwāh *see* Nizwá
82 J13 **Nchanga** Copperbelt, C Zambia
82 J11 **Nchelenge** Luapula, N Zambia
Ncheu *see* Ntcheu
Ndaghamcha, Sebkra de *see* Te-n-Dghâmcha, Sebkhet
81 G21 **Ndala** Tabora, C Tanzania
82 B11 **N'Dalatando** *Port.* Salazar, Vila Salazar. Cuanza Norte, NW Angola
77 S14 **Ndali** C Benin
81 E18 **Ndeke** SW Uganda
78 J13 **Ndélé** Bamingui-Bangoran, N Central African Republic
79 E19 **Ndendé** Ngounié, S Gabon
79 E20 **Ndindi** Nyanga, S Gabon
78 G11 **Ndjamena** *var.* N'Djamena; *prev.* Fort-Lamy. ● (Chad) Chari-Baguirmi, W Chad
78 G11 **Ndjamena** ✕ Chari-Baguirmi, W Chad
79 D18 **Ndjolé** Moyen-Ogooué, W Gabon
82 J13 **Ndola** Copperbelt, C Zambia
Ndrhamcha, Sebkha de *see* Te-n-Dghâmcha, Sebkhet
79 L15 **Ndu** Orientale, N Dem. Rep. Congo
81 H21 **Nduguti** Singida, C Tanzania
186 M9 **Nduindui** Guadalcanal, C Solomon Islands
Nduke *see* Kolombangara
115 F16 **Néa Anchiálos** *var.* Nea Anhialos, Néa Ankhíalos. Thessalía, C Greece
Nea Anhialos/Néa Ankhíalos *see* Néa Anchiálos
115 H18 **Néa Artáki** Évvoia, C Greece
97 F15 **Neagh, Lough** ⊚ E Northern Ireland, UK
32 F7 **Neah Bay** Washington, NW USA
115 J22 **Nea Kaméni** *island* Kykládes, Greece, Aegean Sea
181 O8 **Neale, Lake** ⊚ Northern Territory, C Australia
182 G2 **Neales River** *seasonal river* South Australia
115 G14 **Néa Moudanía** *var.* Néa Moudhaniá. Kentrikí Makedonía, N Greece
Néa Moudhaniá *see* Néa Moudanía
116 K10 **Neamţ** ◆ *county* NE Romania
Neapel *see* Napoli
115 D14 **Neápoli** *prev.* Neápolis. Dytikí Makedonía, N Greece
115 K25 **Neápoli** Kríti, Greece, E Mediterranean Sea
115 G22 **Neápoli** Pelopónnisos, S Greece
Neapolis *see* Napoli, Italy
Neapolis *see* Nablus, West Bank
Neápolis *see* Neápoli, Greece
38 D16 **Near Islands** *island group* Aleutian Islands, Alaska, USA
97 J21 **Neath** S Wales, UK
114 H13 **Néa Zíchni** *var.* Néa Zíkhni; *prev.* Néa Zíkhna. Kentrikí Makedonía, NE Greece
Néa Zíkhna/Néa Zíkhni *see* Néa Zíchni
42 C5 **Nebaj** Quiché, W Guatemala
77 P13 **Nebbou** S Burkina
Nebitdag *see* Balkanabat
54 M13 **Neblina, Pico da** ▲ NW Brazil
124 I13 **Nebolchi** Novgorodskaya Oblast', W Russian Federation
36 L4 **Nebo, Mount** ▲ Utah, W USA
28 L14 **Nebraska** *off.* State of Nebraska; also known as Blackwater State, Cornhusker State, Tree Planters State. ◆ *state* C USA
29 S16 **Nebraska City** Nebraska, C USA
107 K23 **Nebrodi, Monti** *var.* Monti Caronie. ▲ Sicilia, Italy, C Mediterranean Sea
10 L14 **Nechako** ⁓ British Columbia, SW Canada
29 Q2 **Neche** North Dakota, N USA
25 V8 **Neches** Texas, SW USA
25 W8 **Neches River** ⁓ Texas, SW USA
101 H20 **Neckar** ⁓ SW Germany
101 H20 **Neckarsulm** Baden-Württemberg, SW Germany
192 L5 **Necker Island** *island* C British Virgin Islands
175 U3 **Necker Ridge** *undersea feature* N Pacific Ocean
61 D23 **Necochea** Buenos Aires, E Argentina
104 H2 **Neda** Galicia, NW Spain
115 E20 **Nédas** ⁓ S Greece
25 Y11 **Nederland** Texas, SW USA
Nederland *see* Netherlands
98 K12 **Neder Rijn** *Eng.* Lower Rhine. ⁓ C Netherlands
99 L16 **Nederweert** Limburg, SE Netherlands
95 G16 **Nedre Tokke** ⊚ S Norway
Nedrigaylov *see* Nedryhayliv
117 S3 **Nedryhayliv** *Rus.* Nedrigaylov. Sums'ka Oblast', NE Ukraine
98 O11 **Neede** Gelderland, E Netherlands
33 T13 **Needle Mountain** ▲ Wyoming, C USA
35 Y14 **Needles** California, W USA
97 M24 **Needles, The** *rocks* Isle of Wight, S England, UK
62 O7 **Ñeembucú** *off.* Departamento de Ñeembucú. ◆ *department* SW Paraguay
30 M7 **Neenah** Wisconsin, N USA
11 W16 **Neepawa** Manitoba, S Canada
99 K16 **Neerpelt** Limburg, NE Belgium
74 M6 **Nefta** ✕ W Tunisia
126 L15 **Neftegorsk** Krasnodarskiy Kray, SW Russian Federation
127 U3 **Neftekamsk** Respublika Bashkortostan, W Russian Federation
127 O14 **Neftekumsk** Stavropol'skiy Kray, SW Russian Federation
Neftezavodsk *see* Seýdi
82 C10 **Negage** *var.* N'Gage. Uíge, NW Angola
Negapatam/Negapattinam *see* Nāgappattinam
169 T17 **Negara** Bali, Indonesia
169 T13 **Negara** Borneo, C Indonesia
Negara Brunei Darussalam *see* Brunei
31 N4 **Negaunee** Michigan, N USA
81 J15 **Negēlē** *var.* Negelli, *It.* Neghelli. Oromo, C Ethiopia
Negelli *see* Negēlē
Negeri Pahang Darul Makmur *see* Pahang
Negeri Selangor Darul Ehsan *see* Selangor
168 K9 **Negeri Sembilan** *var.* Negri Sembilan. ◆ *state* Peninsular Malaysia
92 P3 **Negerpynten** *headland* S Svalbard
Negev *see* HaNegev
Neghelli *see* Negēlē
116 I12 **Negoiu** *var.* Negoiul. ▲ S Romania
Negoiul *see* Negoiu
82 P13 **Negomane** *var.* Negomano. Cabo Delgado, N Mozambique
Negomano *see* Negomane
155 J25 **Negombo** Western Province, SW Sri Lanka
Negoreloye *see* Nyeharelaye
112 P12 **Negotin** Serbia, E Serbia and Montenegro (Yugo.)
113 P19 **Negotino** C FYR Macedonia
56 A10 **Negra, Punta** *headland* NW Peru
104 G3 **Negreira** Galicia, NW Spain
116 L10 **Negreşti** Vaslui, E Romania
Negreşti *see* Negreşti-Oaş
116 H8 **Negreşti-Oaş** *Hung.* Avasfelsőfalu; *prev.* Negreşti. Satu Mare, NE Romania
44 H12 **Negril** W Jamaica
Negri Sembilan *see* Negeri Sembilan
63 K15 **Negro, Río** ⁓ E Argentina
62 N7 **Negro, Río** ⁓ NE Argentina
57 N17 **Negro, Río** ⁓ E Bolivia
62 O5 **Negro, Río** ⁓ C Paraguay
48 F6 **Negro, Río** ⁓ N South America

◆ Country ● Country Capital ◇ Dependent Territory ○ Dependent Territory Capital ◆ Administrative Region ✕ International Airport ▲ Mountain ▲ Mountain Range ⁓ River ⊚ Lake ⊞ Reservoir
Volcano

61 E18 **Negro, Río** ≈ Brazil/Uruguay
Negro, Río see Sico Tinto, Río, Honduras
Negro, Río see Chixoy, Río, Guatemala/Mexico
171 P6 **Negros** island C Philippines
116 M15 **Negru Vodă** Constanța, SE Romania
13 P13 **Neguac** New Brunswick, SE Canada
14 B7 **Negwazu, Lake** ◎ Ontario, S Canada
Négyfalu see Săcele
32 F10 **Nehalem** Oregon, NW USA
32 F10 **Nehalem River** ≈ Oregon, NW USA
Nehavend see Nahāvand
143 V9 **Nehbandān** Khorāsān, E Iran
163 V6 **Nehe** Heilongjiang, NE China
193 Y14 **Neiafu** 'Uta Vava'u, N Tonga
45 N9 **Neiba** var. Neyba. SW Dominican Republic
Néid, Carn Uí see Mizen Head
92 M9 **Neiden** Finnmark, N Norway
Neidín see Kenmare
Néifinn see Nephin
103 S10 **Neige, Crêt de la** ▲ E France
173 O16 **Neiges, Piton des** ▲ C Réunion
15 R9 **Neiges, Rivière des** ≈ Québec, SE Canada
160 I10 **Neijiang** Sichuan, C China
30 K6 **Neillsville** Wisconsin, N USA
Nei Monggol Zizhiqu/Nei Mongol see Nei Mongol Zizhiqu
163 Q10 **Nei Mongol Gaoyuan** plateau NE China
163 O12 **Nei Mongol Zizhiqu** var. Nei Mongol, Eng. Inner Mongolia, Inner Mongolian Autonomous Region; prev. Nei Monggol Zizhiqu. ◈ autonomous region N China
161 O4 **Neiqiu** Hebei, E China
Neiriz see Neyrīz
101 Q16 **Neisse** Cz. Lužická Nisa, Ger. Lausitzer Neisse, Pol. Nisa, Nysa Łużycka. ≈ C Europe
Neisse see Nysa
54 E11 **Neiva** Huila, S Colombia
160 M7 **Neixiang** Henan, C China
Nejafabad see Najafābād
11 V9 **Nejanilini Lake** ◎ Manitoba, C Canada
Nejd see Najd
80 I13 **Nek'emtē** var. Lakemti, Nakamti. Oromo, C Ethiopia
126 M9 **Nekhayevskiy** Volgogradskaya Oblast', SW Russian Federation
30 K7 **Nekoosa** Wisconsin, N USA
Neksø see Nexø
115 C16 **Nekyomanteío** ancient monument Ípeiros, W Greece
104 H7 **Nelas** Viseu, N Portugal
124 H16 **Nelidovo** Tverskaya Oblast', W Russian Federation
29 P13 **Neligh** Nebraska, C USA
123 R11 **Nel'kan** Khabarovskiy Kray, E Russian Federation
92 M10 **Nellim** var. Nellimö, Lapp. Njellim. Lappi, N Finland
Nellimö see Nellim
155 J18 **Nellore** Andhra Pradesh, E India
123 T14 **Nel'ma** Khabarovskiy Kray, SE Russian Federation
61 B17 **Nelson** Santa Fe, C Argentina
11 O17 **Nelson** British Columbia, SW Canada
185 I14 **Nelson** Nelson, South Island, NZ
97 L17 **Nelson** NW England, UK
29 P17 **Nelson** Nebraska, C USA
185 J14 **Nelson** ◈ unitary authority South Island, NZ
11 X12 **Nelson** ≈ Manitoba, C Canada
183 U8 **Nelson Bay** New South Wales, SE Australia
182 K13 **Nelson, Cape** headland Victoria, SE Australia
63 G23 **Nelson, Estrecho** strait SE Pacific Ocean
11 W12 **Nelson House** Manitoba, C Canada
30 J4 **Nelson Lake** ◎ Wisconsin, N USA
31 T14 **Nelsonville** Ohio, N USA
27 S2 **Nelsoon River** ≈ Iowa/Missouri, C USA
83 K21 **Nelspruit** Mpumalanga, NE South Africa
76 L10 **Néma** Hodh ech Chargui, SE Mauritania
118 D13 **Neman** Ger. Ragnit. Kaliningradskaya Oblast', W Russian Federation
84 I9 **Neman** Bel. Nyoman, Ger. Memel, Lith. Nemunas, Pol. Niemen, Rus. Neman. ≈ NE Europe
Nemausus see Nîmes
115 F19 **Neméa** Pelopónnisos, S Greece
Německý Brod see Havlíčkův Brod
14 D7 **Nemegosenda** ≈ Ontario, S Canada
14 D8 **Nemegosenda Lake** ◎ Ontario, S Canada
119 H14 **Nemencinė** Vilnius, SE Lithuania
Nemetocenna see Arras
Nemirov see Nemyriv
103 O6 **Nemours** Seine-et-Marne, N France
Nemunas see Neman
165 W4 **Nemuro** Hokkaidō, NE Japan
165 W4 **Nemuro-hantō** peninsula Hokkaidō, NE Japan
165 W3 **Nemuro-kaikyō** strait Japan/Russian Federation
165 W4 **Nemuro-wan** bay N Japan
116 H5 **Nemyriv** Rus. Nemirov. L'vivs'ka Oblast', NW Ukraine
117 N7 **Nemyriv** Rus. Nemirov. Vinnyts'ka Oblast', C Ukraine
97 D19 **Nenagh** Ir. An tAonach. C Ireland
39 R9 **Nenana** Alaska, USA
39 R9 **Nenana River** ≈ Alaska, USA
187 P10 **Nendö** var. Swallow Island. island Santa Cruz Islands, E Solomon Islands
97 O19 **Nene** ≈ E England, UK
125 R4 **Nenetskiy Avtonomnyy Okrug** ◈ autonomous district NW Russian Federation
191 W11 **Nengonengo** atoll Îles Tuamotu, C French Polynesia
163 U6 **Nen Jiang** var. Nonni. ≈ NE China
163 V6 **Nenjiang** Heilongjiang, NE China
189 P16 **Neoch** atoll Caroline Islands, C Micronesia
115 D18 **Neochóri** Dytikí Ellás, C Greece
27 Q7 **Neodesha** Kansas, C USA
29 S14 **Neola** Iowa, C USA
115 M19 **Néon Karlovási** var. Néon Karlovásion. Sámos, Dodekánisos, Greece, Aegean Sea
Néon Karlovásion see Néon Karlovási
115 E16 **Néon Monastíri** Thessalía, C Greece
27 R8 **Neosho** Missouri, C USA
27 Q7 **Neosho River** ≈ Kansas/Oklahoma, C USA
123 N12 **Nepa** ≈ C Russian Federation
153 N10 **Nepal** off. Kingdom of Nepal. ◆ monarchy S Asia
152 M11 **Nepalganj** Mid Western, SW Nepal
14 L13 **Nepean** Ontario, SE Canada
36 L4 **Nephi** Utah, W USA
97 B16 **Nephin** Ir. Néifinn. ▲ W Ireland
67 T9 **Nepoko** ≈ NE Dem. Rep. Congo
18 K15 **Neptune** New Jersey, NE USA
182 G10 **Neptune Islands** island group South Australia
107 I14 **Nera** anc. Nar. ≈ C Italy
102 L14 **Nérac** Lot-et-Garonne, SW France
111 D16 **Neratovice** Ger. Neratowitz. Středočeský Kraj, C Czech Republic
Neratowitz see Neratovice
123 O13 **Nercha** ≈ S Russian Federation
123 O13 **Nerchinsk** Chitinskaya Oblast', S Russian Federation
123 P14 **Nerchinskiy Zavod** Chitinskaya Oblast', S Russian Federation
124 M15 **Nerekhta** Kostromskaya Oblast', NW Russian Federation
118 H10 **Nereta** Aizkraukle, S Latvia
106 K13 **Nereto** Abruzzo, C Italy
113 H15 **Neretva** ≈ Bosnia and Herzegovina/Croatia
115 C17 **Nerikós** ruins Lefkáda, Iónioi Nísoi, Greece, C Mediterranean Sea
83 F15 **Neriquinha** Cuando Cubango, SE Angola
118 I13 **Neris** Bel. Viliya, Pol. Wilia; prev. Pol. Wilja. ≈ Belarus/Lithuania
Neris see Viliya
105 N15 **Nerja** Andalucía, S Spain
126 L16 **Nerl'** ≈ W Russian Federation
105 P12 **Nerpio** Castilla-La Mancha, C Spain
104 J13 **Nerva** Andalucía, S Spain
98 L4 **Nes** Friesland, N Netherlands
94 G13 **Nesbyen** Buskerud, S Norway
92 L2 **Neskaupstadhur** Austurland, E Iceland
92 F13 **Nesna** Nordland, C Norway
26 K5 **Ness City** Kansas, C USA
Nesselsdorf see Kopřivnice
108 H7 **Nesslau** Sankt Gallen, NE Switzerland
96 I9 **Ness, Loch** ◎ N Scotland, UK
Nesterov see Zhovkva
114 I12 **Néstos** Bul. Mesta, Turk. Kara Su. ≈ Bulgaria/Greece see also Mesta
95 C14 **Nesttun** Hordaland, S Norway
Nesvizh see Nyasvizh
138 F9 **Netanya** var. Natanya, Nathanya. Central, C Israel
98 I9 **Netherlands** off. Kingdom of the Netherlands, var. Holland, Dut. Koninkrijk der Nederlanden, Nederland. ◆ monarchy NW Europe
45 S9 **Netherlands Antilles** prev. Dutch West Indies. ◇ Dutch autonomous region S Caribbean Sea
Netherlands East Indies see Indonesia
Netherlands Guiana see Suriname
Netherlands New Guinea see Papua
116 L4 **Netishyn** Khmel'nyts'ka Oblast', W Ukraine
138 E11 **Netivot** Southern, S Israel
107 O21 **Neto** ≈ S Italy
9 Q6 **Nettilling Lake** ◎ Baffin Island, Nunavut, N Canada
29 V3 **Nett Lake** ◎ Minnesota, N USA
107 I16 **Nettuno** Lazio, C Italy
Netum see Noto
41 U16 **Netzahualcóyotl, Presa** ⊡ SE Mexico
Netze see Noteć
Neu Amerika see Puławy
Neubetsche see Novi Bečej
Neubidschow see Nový Bydžov
Neubistritz see Nová Bystřice
100 N9 **Neubrandenburg** Mecklenburg-Vorpommern, NE Germany
101 K22 **Neuburg an der Donau** Bayern, S Germany
108 C8 **Neuchâtel** Ger. Neuenburg. Neuchâtel, W Switzerland
108 C8 **Neuchâtel** Ger. Neuenburg. ◈ canton W Switzerland
108 C8 **Neuchâtel, Lac de** Ger. Neuenburger See. ◎ W Switzerland
Neudorf see Spišská Nová Ves
100 L10 **Neue Elde** canal N Germany
Neuenburg see Neuchâtel
Neuenburg an der Elbe see Nymburk
Neuenburger See see Neuchâtel, Lac de
108 F7 **Neuenhof** Aargau, N Switzerland
100 H11 **Neuenland** ✕ (Bremen) Bremen, NW Germany
Neuenstadt see La Neuveville
101 C18 **Neuerburg** Rheinland-Pfalz, W Germany
99 K24 **Neufchâteau** Luxembourg, SE Belgium
103 S6 **Neufchâteau** Vosges, NE France
102 M3 **Neufchâtel-en-Bray** Seine-Maritime, N France
109 S3 **Neufelden** Oberösterreich, N Austria
Neugradisk see Nova Gradiška
Neuhaus see Jindřichův Hradec
Neuhäusel see Nové Zámky
108 G6 **Neuhausen** var. Neuhausen am Rheinfall. Schaffhausen, N Switzerland
Neuhausen am Rheinfall see Neuhausen
101 I17 **Neuhof** Hessen, C Germany
Neuhof see Zgierz
Neukuhren see Pionerskiy
Neu-Langenburg see Tukuyu
109 W4 **Neulengbach** Niederösterreich, NE Austria
113 G15 **Neum** Federacija Bosna I Hercegovina, S Bosnia and Herzegovina
Neumark see Nowy Targ, Nowy Sącz, Poland
Neumark see Nowe Miasto Lubawskie, Toruń, Poland
Neumarkt see Neumarkt im Hausruckkreis, Oberösterreich, Austria
Neumarkt see Neumarkt am Wallersee, Salzburg, Austria
Neumarkt see Środa Śląska, Wrocław, Poland
Neumarkt see Târgu Secuiesc, Covasna, Romania
Neumarkt see Târgu Mureș, Mureș, Romania
109 Q5 **Neumarkt am Wallersee** var. Neumarkt. Salzburg, NW Austria
109 R4 **Neumarkt im Hausruckkreis** var. Neumarkt. Oberösterreich, N Austria
101 L20 **Neumarkt in der Oberpfalz** Bayern, SE Germany
Neumarktl see Tržič
Neumoldowa see Moldova Nouă
100 J8 **Neumünster** Schleswig-Holstein, N Germany
109 X5 **Neunkirchen** var. Neunkirchen am Steinfeld. Niederösterreich, E Austria
101 E20 **Neunkirchen** Saarland, SW Germany
Neunkirchen am Steinfeld see Neunkirchen
Neuoderberg see Bohumín
63 I15 **Neuquén** Neuquén, SE Argentina
63 H14 **Neuquén** off. Provincia de Neuquén. ◈ province W Argentina
63 H14 **Neuquén, Río** ≈ W Argentina
Neurode see Nowa Ruda
100 N11 **Neuruppin** Brandenburg, NE Germany
Neusalz an der Oder see Nowa Sól
Neu Sandec/Neusandez see Małopolskie
101 K22 **Neusäss** Bayern, S Germany
Neusatz see Novi Sad
Neuschliss see Gherla
21 N8 **Neuse River** ≈ North Carolina, SE USA
109 Z5 **Neusiedl am See** Burgenland, E Austria
111 G22 **Neusiedler See** Hung. Fertő. ◎ Austria/Hungary
Neusohl see Banská Bystrica
101 D15 **Neuss** anc. Novaesium, Novesium. Nordrhein-Westfalen, W Germany
Neuss see Nyon
Neustadt see Neustadt an der Aisch, Bayern, Germany
Neustadt see Neustadt bei Coburg, Bayern, Germany
Neustadt see Prudnik, Opole, Poland
Neustadt see Baia Mare, Maramureș, Romania
100 I12 **Neustadt am Rübenberge** Niedersachsen, N Germany
101 J19 **Neustadt an der Aisch** var. Neustadt. Bayern, C Germany
Neustadt an der Haardt see Neustadt an der Weinstrasse
101 F20 **Neustadt an der Weinstrasse** prev. Neustadt an der Haardt, hist. Niewenstat, anc. Nova Civitas. Rheinland-Pfalz, SW Germany
101 K18 **Neustadt bei Coburg** var. Neustadt. Bayern, C Germany
Neustadt bei Pinne see Lwówek
Neustadt in Oberschlesien see Prudnik
Neustadtl see Novo mesto
Neustadtl in Mähren see Nové Město na Moravě
Neustettin see Szczecinek
108 M8 **Neustift im Stubaital** var. Stubaital. Tirol, W Austria
100 N10 **Neustrelitz** Mecklenburg-Vorpommern, NE Germany
Neutitschein see Nový Jičín
Neutra see Nitra
101 J22 **Neu-Ulm** Bayern, S Germany
Neuveville see La Neuveville
103 N12 **Neuvic** Corrèze, C France
Neuwarp see Nowe Warpno
100 G9 **Neuwerk** island NW Germany
101 E17 **Neuwied** Rheinland-Pfalz, W Germany
Neuzen see Terneuzen
126 H12 **Neva** ≈ NW Russian Federation
29 V14 **Nevada** Iowa, C USA
27 R6 **Nevada** Missouri, C USA
35 R5 **Nevada** off. State of Nevada; also known as Battle Born State, Sagebrush State, Silver State. ◈ state W USA
35 P6 **Nevada City** California, W USA
124 G16 **Nevel'** Pskovskaya Oblast', W Russian Federation
123 T14 **Nevel'sk** Ostrov Sakhalin, Sakhalinskaya Oblast', SE Russian Federation
123 Q13 **Never** Amurskaya Oblast', SE Russian Federation
127 Q6 **Neverkino** Penzenskaya Oblast', W Russian Federation
103 P9 **Nevers** anc. Noviodunum. Nièvre, C France
18 J12 **Neversink River** ≈ New York, NE USA
183 Q6 **Nevertire** New South Wales, SE Australia
113 H15 **Nevesinje** Republika Srpska, S Bosnia and Herzegovina
118 G12 **Nevėžis** ≈ C Lithuania
126 M14 **Nevinnomyssk** Stavropol'skiy Kray, SW Russian Federation
45 W10 **Nevis** island Saint Kitts and Nevis
Nevoso, Monte see Veliki Snežnik
Nevrokop see Gotse Delchev
136 J14 **Nevşehir** var. Nevshehr. Nevşehir, C Turkey
136 J14 **Nevşehir** var. Nevshehr. ◈ province C Turkey
Nevshehr see Nevşehir
122 G10 **Nev'yansk** Sverdlovskaya Oblast', C Russian Federation
81 J25 **Newala** Mtwara, SE Tanzania
31 P16 **New Albany** Indiana, N USA
22 M2 **New Albany** Mississippi, S USA
29 Y11 **New Albin** Iowa, C USA
55 U8 **New Amsterdam** E Guyana
183 Q4 **New Angledool** New South Wales, SE Australia
21 Y2 **Newark** Delaware, NE USA
18 K14 **Newark** New Jersey, NE USA
18 G10 **Newark** New York, NE USA
31 T13 **Newark** Ohio, N USA
Newark see Newark-on-Trent
35 W5 **Newark Lake** ◎ Nevada, W USA
97 N18 **Newark-on-Trent** var. Newark. C England, UK
22 M7 **New Augusta** Mississippi, S USA
19 P12 **New Bedford** Massachusetts, NE USA
32 G11 **Newberg** Oregon, NW USA
21 X10 **New Bern** North Carolina, SE USA
20 F8 **Newbern** Tennessee, S USA
31 P4 **Newberry** Michigan, N USA
21 Q12 **Newberry** South Carolina, SE USA
18 F15 **New Bloomfield** Pennsylvania, NE USA
25 X5 **New Boston** Texas, SW USA
25 S11 **New Braunfels** Texas, SW USA
31 Q13 **New Bremen** Ohio, N USA
97 F18 **Newbridge** Ir. An Droichead Nua. C Ireland
18 B14 **New Brighton** Pennsylvania, NE USA
18 M12 **New Britain** Connecticut, NE USA
186 G7 **New Britain** island E PNG
192 I8 **New Britain Trench** undersea feature W Pacific Ocean
18 J15 **New Brunswick** New Jersey, NE USA
15 V8 **New Brunswick** Fr. Nouveau-Brunswick. ◈ province SE Canada
18 K13 **Newburgh** New York, NE USA
97 M22 **Newbury** S England, UK
19 P10 **Newburyport** Massachusetts, NE USA
77 T14 **New Bussa** Niger, W Nigeria
187 O17 **New Caledonia** var. Kanaky, Fr. Nouvelle-Calédonie. ◇ French overseas territory SW Pacific Ocean
187 O15 **New Caledonia** island SW Pacific Ocean
175 O10 **New Caledonia Basin** undersea feature W Pacific Ocean
183 T8 **Newcastle** New South Wales, SE Australia
13 O14 **Newcastle** New Brunswick, SE Canada
14 I15 **Newcastle** Ontario, SE Canada
97 C20 **Newcastle** Ir. An Caisleán Nua. SW Ireland
83 K22 **Newcastle** KwaZulu/Natal, E South Africa
97 G16 **Newcastle** Ir. An Caisleán Nua. SE Northern Ireland, UK
31 P13 **New Castle** Indiana, N USA
20 L5 **New Castle** Kentucky, S USA
27 N11 **Newcastle** Oklahoma, C USA
18 B13 **New Castle** Pennsylvania, NE USA
25 R6 **Newcastle** Texas, SW USA
36 J7 **Newcastle** Utah, W USA
21 S6 **New Castle** Virginia, NE USA
33 Z13 **Newcastle** Wyoming, C USA
45 W10 **Newcastle** ✕ Nevis, Saint Kitts and Nevis
97 L14 **Newcastle** ✕ NE England, UK
Newcastle see Newcastle upon Tyne
97 L18 **Newcastle-under-Lyme** C England, UK
97 M14 **Newcastle upon Tyne** var. Newcastle; hist. Monkchester, Lat. Pons Aelii. NE England, UK
181 Q4 **Newcastle Waters** Northern Territory, N Australia
Newchwang see Yingkou
18 K13 **New City** New York, NE USA
31 U13 **Newcomerstown** Ohio, N USA
18 G15 **New Cumberland** Pennsylvania, NE USA
21 R1 **New Cumberland** West Virginia, NE USA
152 I10 **New Delhi** ● (India) Delhi, N India
11 O17 **New Denver** British Columbia, SW Canada
28 J9 **Newell** South Dakota, N USA
21 Q13 **New Ellenton** South Carolina, SE USA
22 J6 **Newellton** Louisiana, S USA
28 K6 **New England** North Dakota, N USA
19 P8 **New England** cultural region NE USA
New England of the West see Minnesota
183 U5 **New England Range** ▲ New South Wales, SE Australia
64 G9 **New England Seamounts** var. Bermuda-New England Seamount Arc. undersea feature W Atlantic Ocean
38 M14 **Newenham, Cape** headland Alaska, USA
138 F11 **Newé Zohar** Southern, E Israel
18 D9 **Newfane** New York, NE USA
97 M23 **New Forest** physical region S England, UK
13 T12 **Newfoundland** Fr. Terre-Neuve. island Newfoundland and Labrador, SE Canada
13 R9 **Newfoundland and Labrador** Fr. Terre Neuve. ◈ province E Canada
65 J8 **Newfoundland Basin** undersea feature NW Atlantic Ocean
64 I8 **Newfoundland Ridge** undersea feature NW Atlantic Ocean
64 J8 **Newfoundland Seamounts** undersea feature N Sargasso Sea
18 G16 **New Freedom** Pennsylvania, NE USA
186 K9 **New Georgia** island New Georgia Islands, NW Solomon Islands
186 K8 **New Georgia Islands** island group NW Solomon Islands
186 L8 **New Georgia Sound** var. The Slot. sound E Solomon Sea
30 L9 **New Glarus** Wisconsin, N USA
13 Q15 **New Glasgow** Nova Scotia, SE Canada
New Goa see Panaji
186 A6 **New Guinea** Dut. Nieuw Guinea, Ind. Irian. island Indonesia/PNG
192 H8 **New Guinea Trench** undersea feature SW Pacific Ocean
32 I6 **Newhalem** Washington, NW USA
39 P13 **Newhalen** Alaska, USA
29 X13 **Newhall** Iowa, C USA
14 F16 **New Hamburg** Ontario, S Canada
19 N9 **New Hampshire** off. State of New Hampshire; also known as The Granite State. ◈ state NE USA
29 W12 **New Hampton** Iowa, C USA
186 G5 **New Hanover** island NE PNG
18 M13 **New Haven** Connecticut, NE USA
31 Q12 **New Haven** Indiana, N USA
27 W5 **New Haven** Missouri, C USA
97 P23 **Newhaven** SE England, UK
10 K13 **New Hazelton** British Columbia, SW Canada
New Hebrides see Vanuatu
175 P9 **New Hebrides Trench** undersea feature N Coral Sea
18 H15 **New Holland** Pennsylvania, NE USA
22 I9 **New Iberia** Louisiana, S USA
186 G5 **New Ireland** ◈ province NE PNG
186 G5 **New Ireland** island NE PNG
65 A24 **New Island** island W Falkland Islands
18 J15 **New Jersey** off. State of New Jersey; also known as The Garden State. ◈ state NE USA
18 C14 **New Kensington** Pennsylvania, NE USA
21 W6 **New Kent** Virginia, NE USA
27 O8 **Newkirk** Oklahoma, C USA
21 Q9 **Newland** North Carolina, SE USA
28 L6 **New Leipzig** North Dakota, N USA
14 H9 **New Liskeard** Ontario, S Canada
22 G7 **Newllano** Louisiana, S USA
19 N13 **New London** Connecticut, NE USA
29 Y15 **New London** Iowa, C USA
29 T8 **New London** Minnesota, N USA
27 V3 **New London** Missouri, C USA
30 M7 **New London** Wisconsin, N USA
27 Y8 **New Madrid** Missouri, C USA
180 J8 **Newman** Western Australia
194 M13 **Newman Island** island Antarctica
14 H15 **Newmarket** Ontario, S Canada
97 P20 **Newmarket** E England, UK
19 P10 **Newmarket** New Hampshire, NE USA
21 U4 **New Market** Virginia, NE USA
21 R2 **New Martinsville** West Virginia, NE USA
31 U14 **New Matamoras** Ohio, N USA
32 M12 **New Meadows** Idaho, NW USA
26 R12 **New Mexico** off. State of New Mexico; also known as Land of Enchantment, Sunshine State. ◈ state SW USA
149 V6 **New Mirpur** var. Mīrpur. Sind, SE Pakistan
151 T17 **New Moore Island** island E India
23 S4 **Newnan** Georgia, SE USA
183 P17 **New Norfolk** Tasmania, SE Australia
22 K9 **New Orleans** Louisiana, S USA
22 K9 **New Orleans** ✕ Louisiana, S USA
18 K12 **New Paltz** New York, NE USA
31 U12 **New Philadelphia** Ohio, N USA
184 K10 **New Plymouth** Taranaki, North Island, NZ
97 M24 **Newport** S England, UK
97 K22 **Newport** SE Wales, UK
27 W10 **Newport** Arkansas, C USA
31 N13 **Newport** Indiana, N USA
22 M3 **Newport** Kentucky, S USA
31 W9 **Newport** Minnesota, N USA
32 F12 **Newport** Oregon, NW USA
34 O13 **Newport** Rhode Island, NE USA
23 O9 **Newport** Tennessee, S USA
21 N6 **Newport** Vermont, NE USA
34 M7 **Newport** Washington, NW USA
23 X7 **Newport News** Virginia, NE USA
99 N20 **Newport Pagnell** SE England, UK
25 U12 **New Port Richey** Florida, SE USA
31 V9 **New Prague** Minnesota, N USA
46 H3 **New Providence** island N Bahamas
99 H24 **Newquay** SW England, UK
99 I20 **New Quay** SW Wales, UK
31 V10 **New Richland** Minnesota, N USA
13 X7 **New-Richmond** Québec, SE Canada
31 R15 **New Richmond** Ohio, N USA
32 I5 **New Richmond** Wisconsin, N USA
44 G1 **New River** ≈ N Belize
57 T12 **New River** ≈ SE Guyana
23 R6 **New River** ≈ West Virginia, NE USA
44 G1 **New River Lagoon** ◎ N Belize
24 J8 **New Roads** Louisiana, S USA
20 L14 **New Rochelle** New York, NE USA
31 O4 **New Rockford** North Dakota, N USA
97 P23 **New Romney** SE England, UK
97 F20 **New Ross** Ir. Ros Mhic Thriúin. SE Ireland
97 F16 **Newry** Ir. An tIúr. SE Northern Ireland, UK
28 M5 **New Salem** North Dakota, N USA
New Sarum see Salisbury
29 W14 **New Sharon** Iowa, C USA
New Siberian Islands see Novosibirskiye Ostrova
23 X11 **New Smyrna Beach** Florida, SE USA
183 O7 **New South Wales** ◈ state SE Australia
39 O13 **New Stuyahok** Alaska, USA
21 N8 **New Tazewell** Tennessee, SE USA
38 M12 **Newtok** Alaska, USA
23 S7 **Newton** Georgia, SE USA
29 W14 **Newton** Iowa, C USA
27 N6 **Newton** Kansas, C USA
19 O11 **Newton** Massachusetts, NE USA
22 M5 **Newton** Mississippi, S USA
18 J14 **Newton** New Jersey, NE USA
21 R9 **Newton** North Carolina, SE USA
25 Y9 **Newton** Texas, SW USA
97 J24 **Newton Abbot** SW England, UK
96 K13 **Newton St Boswells** SE Scotland, UK
97 I14 **Newton Stewart** S Scotland, UK
92 O2 **Newtontoppen** ▲ C Svalbard
28 K3 **New Town** North Dakota, N USA
97 J20 **Newtown** E Wales, UK
97 G15 **Newtownabbey** Ir. Baile na Mainistreach. E Northern Ireland, UK
97 G15 **Newtownards** Ir. Baile Nua na hArda. SE Northern Ireland, UK
29 U10 **New Ulm** Minnesota, N USA
28 K10 **New Underwood** South Dakota, N USA
25 V10 **New Waverly** Texas, SW USA
18 K14 **New York** New York, NE USA
18 G10 **New York** ◈ state NE USA
35 X13 **New York Mountains** ▲ California, W USA
184 K12 **New Zealand** abbrev. NZ. ◆ commonwealth republic SW Pacific Ocean
95 M24 **Nexø** var. Neksø. Bornholm, E Denmark
125 O15 **Neya** Kostromskaya Oblast', NW Russian Federation
Neyba see Neiba
143 Q12 **Neyrīz** var. Neiriz, Niriz. Fārs, S Iran
143 T4 **Neyshābūr** var. Nishapur. Khorāsān, NE Iran
155 J21 **Neyveli** Tamil Nādu, SE India
Nezhin see Nizhyn
33 N10 **Nezperce** Idaho, NW USA
22 H8 **Nezpique, Bayou** ≈ Louisiana, S USA
77 Y13 **Ngadda** ≈ NE Nigeria
N'Gage see Negage
185 G16 **Ngahere** West Coast, South Island, NZ
77 Z12 **Ngala** Borno, NE Nigeria
83 G17 **Ngamiland** ◈ district N Botswana
158 K16 **Ngamring** Xizang Zizhiqu, W China
81 K19 **Ngangerabeli Plain** plain SE Kenya
158 I14 **Ngangla Ringco** ◎ W China
158 G13 **Nganglong Kangri** ▲ W China
158 K15 **Ngangzê Co** ◎ W China
79 F14 **Ngaoundéré** var. N'Gaoundéré. Adamaoua, N Cameroon
81 E20 **Ngara** Kagera, NW Tanzania
188 F8 **Ngardmau Bay** bay Babeldaob, N Palau

◆ Country ● Country Capital ◇ Dependent Territory ○ Dependent Territory Capital ◈ Administrative Region ✕ International Airport ▲ Mountain ▲ Mountain Range ⩲ Volcano ≈ River ◎ Lake ⊡ Reservoir

188 F7 **Ngaregur** *island* Palau Islands, N Palau
Ngarrab *see* Gyaca
184 L7 **Ngaruawahia** Waikato, North Island, NZ
184 N11 **Ngaruroro** ≈ North Island, NZ
190 I16 **Ngatangiia** Rarotonga, S Cook Islands
184 M6 **Ngatea** Waikato, North Island, NZ
166 L8 **Ngathainggyaung** Irrawaddy, SW Myanmar
Ngatik *see* Ngetik Atoll
Ngau *see* Gau
188 C7 **Ngcheangel** *var.* Kayangel Islands. *island* Palau Islands, N Palau
188 E10 **Ngchemiangel** Babeldaob, N Palau
188 C8 **Ngeaur** *var.* Angaur. *island* Palau Islands, S Palau
188 E10 **Ngerkeai** Babeldaob, N Palau
188 F9 **Ngermechau** Babeldaob, N Palau
188 C8 **Ngeruktabel** *prev.* Urukthapel. *island* Palau Islands, S Palau
188 F8 **Ngetbong** Babeldaob, N Palau
189 T17 **Ngetik Atoll** *var.* Ngatik; *prev.* Los Jardines. *atoll* Caroline Islands, E Micronesia
188 E10 **Ngetkip** Babeldaob, N Palau
Nggamea *see* Qamea
83 C16 **N'Giva** *var.* Ondjiva, *Port.* Vila Pereira de Eça. Cunene, S Angola
79 G20 **Ngo** Plateaux, SE Congo
167 S7 **Ngoc Lac** Thanh Hoa, N Vietnam
79 G17 **Ngoko** ≈ Cameroon/Congo
81 H19 **Ngorengore** Rift Valley, SW Kenya
159 Q11 **Ngoring Hu** ◎ C China
Ngorolaka *see* Banifing
81 H20 **Ngorongoro Crater** *crater* N Tanzania
79 D19 **Ngounié** *off.* Province de la Ngounié, *var.* La Ngounié. ◈ *province* S Gabon
79 D19 **Ngounié** ≈ Congo/Gabon
78 H10 **Ngoura** *var.* NGoura. Chari-Baguirmi, W Chad
78 G10 **Ngouri** *var.* NGouri; *prev.* Fort-Millot. Lac, W Chad
77 Y10 **Ngourti** Diffa, E Niger
77 Y11 **Nguigmi** *var.* N'Guigmi. Diffa, SE Niger
Nguimbo *see* Lumbala N'Guimbo
188 F15 **Ngulu Atoll** *atoll* Caroline Islands, W Micronesia
187 R14 **Nguna** *island* C Vanuatu
N'Gunza *see* Sumbe
169 U17 **Ngurah Rai** ✕ (Bali) Bali, S Indonesia
77 W12 **Nguru** Yobe, NE Nigeria
Ngwaketze *see* Southern
83 I16 **Ngweze** ≈ S Zambia
83 M17 **Nhamatanda** Sofala, C Mozambique
58 G12 **Nhamundá, Rio** *var.* Jamundá, Yamundá. ≈ N Brazil
60 J7 **Nhandeara** São Paulo, S Brazil
N'Harea *see* Nharêa
82 D12 **Nharêa** *var.* N'Harea, Nhareia. Bié, W Angola
Nhareia *see* Nharêa
167 V12 **Nha Trang** Khanh Hoa, S Vietnam
182 L11 **Nhill** Victoria, SE Australia
83 L22 **Nhlangano** *prev.* Goedgegun. SW Swaziland
181 S1 **Nhulunbuy** Northern Territory, N Australia
77 N10 **Niafounké** Tombouctou, W Mali
31 N5 **Niagara** Wisconsin, N USA
14 H16 **Niagara** ≈ Ontario, S Canada
14 G15 **Niagara Escarpment** *hill range* Ontario, S Canada
14 H16 **Niagara Falls** Ontario, S Canada
18 D9 **Niagara Falls** New York, NE USA
17 S7 **Niagara Falls** *waterfall* Canada/USA
76 K12 **Niagassola** *var.* Nyagassola. Haute-Guinée, NE Guinea
77 R12 **Niamey** ● (Niger) Niamey, SW Niger
77 R12 **Niamey** ✕ Niamey, SW Niger
77 R14 **Niamtougou** N Togo
79 O16 **Niangara** Orientale, NE Dem. Rep. Congo
77 O10 **Niangay, Lac** ◎ E Mali
77 N14 **Niangoloko** SW Burkina
27 U6 **Niangua River** ≈ Missouri, C USA
79 O17 **Nia-Nia** Orientale, NE Dem. Rep. Congo
19 N13 **Niantic** Connecticut, NE USA
163 U7 **Nianzishan** Heilongjiang, NE China
168 H10 **Nias, Pulau** *island* W Indonesia
82 O13 **Niassa** *off.* Província do Niassa. ◈ *province* N Mozambique
191 U10 **Niau** *island* Îles Tuamotu, C French Polynesia
95 G20 **Nibe** Nordjylland, N Denmark
189 Q8 **Nibok** N Nauru
118 C10 **Nīca** Liepāja, W Latvia
Nicaea *see* Nice
42 J9 **Nicaragua** *off.* Republic of Nicaragua. ◆ *republic* Central America
42 K11 **Nicaragua, Lago de** *var.* Cocibolca, Gran Lago, *Eng.* Lake Nicaragua. ◎ S Nicaragua
Nicaragua, Lake *see* Nicaragua, Lago de
64 D11 **Nicaraguan Rise** *undersea feature* NW Caribbean Sea
Nicaria *see* Ikaría
107 N21 **Nicastro** Calabria, SW Italy
103 V15 **Nice** *It.* Nizza; *anc.* Nicaea. Alpes-Maritimes, SE France
Nice *see* Côte d'Azur
Nicephorium *see* Ar Raqqah
12 M9 **Nichicun, Lac** ◎ Québec, E Canada
164 D16 **Nichinan** *var.* Nitinan. Miyazaki, Kyūshū, SW Japan
44 E4 **Nicholas Channel** *channel* N Cuba
Nicholas II Land *see* Severnaya Zemlya
149 U2 **Nicholas Range** *Pash.* Selseleh-ye Kūh-e Vākhān, *Taj.* Qatorkŭhi Vakhon. ▲ Afghanistan/Tajikistan
20 M6 **Nicholasville** Kentucky, S USA
44 G2 **Nicholls Town** Andros Island, NW Bahamas
21 U12 **Nichols** South Carolina, SE USA
55 U9 **Nickerie** ◈ *district* NW Suriname
55 V9 **Nickerie Rivier** ≈ NW Suriname
151 P22 **Nicobar Islands** *island group* India, E Indian Ocean
116 L9 **Nicolae Bălcescu** Botoşani, NE Romania
15 P11 **Nicolet** Québec, SE Canada
15 Q12 **Nicolet** ≈ Québec, SE Canada
31 Q4 **Nicolet, Lake** ◎ Michigan, N USA
29 U10 **Nicollet** Minnesota, N USA
61 F19 **Nico Pérez** Florida, S Uruguay
Nicopolis *see* Nikopol, Bulgaria
Nicopolis *see* Nikópoli, Greece
121 P2 **Nicosia** *Gk.* Lefkosía, *Turk.* Lefkoşa. ● (Cyprus) C Cyprus
107 K24 **Nicosia** Sicilia, Italy, C Mediterranean Sea
107 N22 **Nicotera** Calabria, SW Italy
42 K13 **Nicoya** Guanacaste, W Costa Rica
42 L14 **Nicoya, Golfo de** *gulf* W Costa Rica
42 L14 **Nicoya, Península de** *peninsula* NW Costa Rica
Nictheroy *see* Niterói
118 B12 **Nida** *Ger.* Nidden. Klaipėda, SW Lithuania
111 L15 **Nida** ≈ S Poland
Nidaros *see* Trondheim
108 D8 **Nidau** Bern, W Switzerland
101 H17 **Nidda** ≈ W Germany
Nidden *see* Nida
95 F17 **Nidelva** ≈ S Norway
110 L9 **Nidzica** *Ger.* Niedenburg. Warmińsko-Mazurskie, NE Poland,
100 H6 **Niebüll** Schleswig-Holstein, N Germany
Niedenburg *see* Nidzica
99 N25 **Niederanven** Luxembourg, C Luxembourg
103 V4 **Niederbronn-les-Bains** Bas-Rhin, NE France
Niederdonau *see* Niederösterreich
109 S7 **Niedere Tauern** ▲ C Austria
101 P14 **Niederlausitz** *Eng.* Lower Lusatia, *Lus.* Donja Łužyca. *physical region* E Germany
109 U5 **Niederösterreich** *off.* Land Niederösterreich, *Eng.* Lower Austria, *Ger.* Niederdonau; *prev.* Lower Danube. ◈ *state* NE Austria
100 G12 **Niedersachsen** *Eng.* Lower Saxony, *Fr.* Basse-Saxe. ◈ *state* NW Germany
79 D17 **Niefang** *var.* Sevilla de Niefang. NW Equatorial Guinea
83 G23 **Niekerkshoop** Northern Cape, W South Africa
99 G17 **Niel** Antwerpen, N Belgium
Niélé *see* Niellé
76 M14 **Niellé** *var.* Niélé. N Ivory Coast
79 O22 **Niemba** Katanga, E Dem. Rep. Congo
111 G15 **Niemcza** *Ger.* Nimptsch. Dolnośląskie, SW Poland
Niemen *see* Neman
92 J13 **Niemisel** Norrbotten, N Sweden
111 H15 **Niemodlin** *Ger.* Falkenberg. Opolskie, S Poland
76 M13 **Niéna** Sikasso, SW Mali
100 H12 **Nienburg** Niedersachsen, N Germany
100 N13 **Nieplitz** ≈ NE Germany
111 L16 **Niepołomice** Małopolskie, S Poland
101 D14 **Niers** ≈ Germany/Netherlands
101 Q15 **Niesky** *Lus.* Niska. Sachsen, E Germany
Nieśwież *see* Nyasvizh
Nieuport *see* Nieuwpoort
98 O8 **Nieuw-Amsterdam** Drenthe, NE Netherlands
55 W9 **Nieuw Amsterdam** Commewijne, NE Suriname
99 M14 **Nieuw-Bergen** Limburg, SE Netherlands
98 O7 **Nieuw-Buinen** Drenthe, NE Netherlands
98 J12 **Nieuwegein** Utrecht, C Netherlands
98 P6 **Nieuwe Pekela** Groningen, NE Netherlands
98 P5 **Nieuweschans** Groningen, NE Netherlands
Nieuw Guinea *see* New Guinea
98 I11 **Nieuwkoop** Zuid-Holland, C Netherlands
98 M9 **Nieuwleusen** Overijssel, S Netherlands
98 J11 **Nieuw-Loosdrecht** Utrecht, C Netherlands
55 U9 **Nieuw Nickerie** Nickerie, NW Suriname
98 P5 **Nieuwolda** Groningen, NE Netherlands
99 B17 **Nieuwpoort** *var.* Nieuport. West-Vlaanderen, W Belgium
99 G14 **Nieuw-Vossemeer** Noord-Brabant, S Netherlands
98 P7 **Nieuw-Weerdinge** Drenthe, NE Netherlands
40 L10 **Nieves** Zacatecas, C Mexico
64 O11 **Nieves, Pico de las** ▲ Gran Canaria, Islas Canarias, Spain, NE Atlantic Ocean
103 P8 **Nièvre** ◈ *department* C France
Niewenstat *see* Neustadt an der Weinstrasse
136 J15 **Niğde** Niğde, C Turkey
136 J15 **Niğde** ◈ *province* C Turkey
83 J21 **Nigel** Gauteng, NE South Africa
77 V10 **Niger** *off.* Republic of Niger. ◆ *republic* W Africa
77 T14 **Niger** ◈ *state* C Nigeria
67 P8 **Niger** ≈ W Africa
Niger Cone *see* Niger Fan
67 P9 **Niger Delta** *delta* S Nigeria
67 P9 **Niger Fan** *var.* Niger Cone. *undersea feature* E Atlantic Ocean
77 T13 **Nigeria** *off.* Federal Republic of Nigeria. ◆ *federal republic* W Africa
77 T17 **Niger, Mouths of the** *delta* S Nigeria
185 C24 **Nightcaps** Southland, South Island, NZ
14 F7 **Night Hawk Lake** ◎ Ontario, S Canada
65 M19 **Nightingale Island** *island* S Tristan da Cunha, S Atlantic Ocean
38 M12 **Nightmute** Alaska, USA
114 G13 **Nigrita** Kentrikí Makedonía, NE Greece
148 J15 **Nihing** *Per.* Rūd-e Nahang. ≈ Iran/Pakistan
191 V10 **Nihiru** *atoll* Îles Tuamotu, C French Polynesia
Nihommatsu *see* Nihonmatsu
Nihon *see* Japan
165 P11 **Nihonmatsu** *var.* Nihommatsu, Nihonmatu. Fukushima, Honshū, C Japan
Nihonmatu *see* Nihonmatsu
62 I12 **Nihuil, Embalse del** ◎ W Argentina
165 O10 **Niigata** Niigata, Honshū, C Japan
165 O11 **Niigata** *off.* Niigata-ken. ◈ *prefecture* Honshū, C Japan
165 G14 **Niihama** Ehime, Shikoku, SW Japan
38 A8 **Niʻihau** *var.* Niihau. *island* Hawaiʻi, USA, C Pacific Ocean
165 X12 **Nii-jima** *island* E Japan
165 H12 **Niimi** Okayama, Honshū, SW Japan
165 O10 **Niitsu** *var.* Niitu. Niigata, Honshū, C Japan
Niitu *see* Niitsu
105 P15 **Níjar** Andalucía, S Spain
98 K11 **Nijkerk** Gelderland, C Netherlands
99 H16 **Nijlen** Antwerpen, N Belgium
98 L13 **Nijmegen** *Ger.* Nimwegen; *anc.* Noviomagus. Gelderland, SE Netherlands
98 N10 **Nijverdal** Overijssel, E Netherlands
190 G16 **Nikao** Rarotonga, S Cook Islands
Nikaria *see* Ikaría
124 I2 **Nikel'** Murmanskaya Oblast', NW Russian Federation
171 Q17 **Nikiniki** Timor, S Indonesia
131 Q15 **Nikitin Seamount** *undersea feature* E Indian Ocean
77 S14 **Nikki** E Benin
Niklasmarkt *see* Gheorgheni
39 P10 **Nikolai** Alaska, USA
Nikolaiken *see* Mikołajki
Nikolainkaupunki *see* Länsi-Suomi
Nikolayev *see* Mykolayiv
Nikolayevka *see* Zhetigen
127 P9 **Nikolayevsk** Volgogradskaya Oblast', SW Russian Federation
Nikolayevskaya Oblast' *see* Mykolayivs'ka Oblast'
123 S12 **Nikolayevsk-na-Amure** Khabarovskiy Kray, SE Russian Federation
127 P6 **Nikol'sk** Penzenskaya Oblast', W Russian Federation
125 O13 **Nikol'sk** Vologodskaya Oblast', NW Russian Federation
Nikol'sk *see* Ussuriysk
38 K17 **Nikolski** Umnak Island, Alaska, USA
Nikol'skiy *see* Satpayev
127 V7 **Nikol'skoye** Orenburgskaya Oblast', W Russian Federation
Nikol'sk-Ussuriyskiy *see* Ussuriysk
114 J7 **Nikopol** *anc.* Nicopolis. Pleven, N Bulgaria
117 S9 **Nikopol'** Dnipropetrovs'ka Oblast', SE Ukraine
115 C17 **Nikópoli** *anc.* Nicopolis. *site of ancient city* Ípeiros, W Greece
136 M12 **Niksar** Tokat, N Turkey
143 V14 **Nīkshahr** Sīstān va Balūchestān, SE Iran
113 J16 **Nikšić** Montenegro, SW Serbia and Montenegro (Yugo.)
191 R4 **Nikumaroro** *prev.* Gardner Island, Kemins Island. *atoll* Phoenix Islands, C Kiribati
191 P3 **Nikunau** *var.* Nukunau; *prev.* Byron Island. *atoll* Tungaru, W Kiribati
155 G21 **Nilambūr** Kerala, SW India
35 X16 **Niland** California, W USA
67 T3 **Nile** *Ar.* Nahr an Nīl. ≈ N Africa
80 G8 **Nile** *former province* NW Uganda
75 W7 **Nile Delta** *delta* N Egypt
67 T3 **Nile Fan** *undersea feature* E Mediterranean Sea
31 O11 **Niles** Michigan, N USA
31 V11 **Niles** Ohio, N USA
155 F20 **Nīleswaram** Kerala, SW India
14 K10 **Nilgaut, Lac** ◎ Québec, SE Canada
158 I5 **Nilka** Xinjiang Uygur Zizhiqu, NW China
Nīl, Nahr an *see* Nile
93 N16 **Nilsiä** Itä-Suomi, C Finland
154 F9 **Nimach** Madhya Pradesh, C India
152 G14 **Nimbāhera** Rājasthān, N India
76 L15 **Nimba, Monts** *var.* Nimba Mountains. ▲ W Africa
Nimba Mountains *see* Nimba, Monts
Nimburg *see* Nymburk
103 Q15 **Nîmes** *anc.* Nemausus, Nismes. Gard, S France
152 H11 **Nīm ka Thāna** Rājasthān, N India
183 R11 **Nimmitabel** New South Wales, SE Australia
Nimptsch *see* Niemcza
195 R11 **Nimrod Glacier** *glacier* Antarctica
Nimroze *see* Nīmrūz
148 K8 **Nīmrūz** *var.* Nimroze; *prev.* Chakhānsūr. ◈ *province* SW Afghanistan
81 F16 **Nimule** Eastern Equatoria, S Sudan
Nimwegen *see* Nijmegen
155 C23 **Nine Degree Channel** *channel* India/Maldives
18 G9 **Ninemile Point** *headland* New York, NE USA
173 S8 **Ninetyeast Ridge** *undersea feature* E Indian Ocean
183 P13 **Ninety Mile Beach** *beach* Victoria, SE Australia
184 I2 **Ninety Mile Beach** *beach* North Island, NZ
21 P12 **Ninety Six** South Carolina, SE USA
163 Y9 **Ning'an** Heilongjiang, NE China
161 S9 **Ningbo** *var.* Ning-po, Yin-hsien; *prev.* Ninghsien. Zhejiang, SE China
161 U12 **Ningde** Fujian, SE China
161 P12 **Ningdu** *var.* Meijiang. Jiangxi, S China
Ning'er *see* Pu'er
186 A7 **Ningerum** Western, SW PNG
161 R9 **Ningguo** Anhui, E China
161 S9 **Ninghai** Zhejiang, SE China
Ning-hsia *see* Ningxia
Ninghsien *see* Ningbo
160 J15 **Ningming** *var.* Chengzhong. Guangxi Zhuangzu Zizhiqu, S China
160 H11 **Ningnan** *var.* Pisha. Sichuan, C China
Ning-po *see* Ningbo
Ningsia/Ningsia Hui/Ningsia Hui Autonomous Region *see* Ningxia
160 J5 **Ningxia** *off.* Ningxia Huizu Zizhiqu, *var.* Ning-hsia, Ningsia, *Eng.* Ningsia Hui, Ningsia Hui Autonomous Region. ◈ *autonomous region* N China
159 X10 **Ningxian** Gansu, N China
167 T7 **Ninh Binh** Ninh Binh, N Vietnam
167 V12 **Ninh Hoa** Khanh Hoa, S Vietnam
186 C4 **Ninigo Group** *island group* N PNG
39 Q12 **Ninilchik** Alaska, USA
27 N7 **Ninnescah River** ≈ Kansas, C USA
195 U16 **Ninnis Glacier** *glacier* Antarctica
165 R8 **Ninohe** Iwate, Honshū, C Japan
99 F18 **Ninove** Oost-Vlaanderen, C Belgium
171 O4 **Ninoy Aquino** ✕ (Manila) Luzon, N Philippines
Nio *see* Íos
29 F12 **Niobrara** Nebraska, C USA
28 M12 **Niobrara River** ≈ Nebraska/Wyoming, C USA
79 I20 **Nioki** Bandundu, W Dem. Rep. Congo
76 M11 **Niono** Ségou, C Mali
76 K11 **Nioro** *var.* Nioro du Sahel. Kayes, W Mali
76 G11 **Nioro du Rip** SW Senegal
Nioro du Sahel *see* Nioro
102 K10 **Niort** Deux-Sèvres, W France
172 H14 **Nioumachoua** Mohéli, S Comoros
186 C7 **Nipa** Southern Highlands, W PNG
11 U14 **Nipawin** Saskatchewan, S Canada
12 D12 **Nipigon** Ontario, S Canada
12 D11 **Nipigon, Lake** ◎ Ontario, S Canada
11 S13 **Nipin** ≈ Saskatchewan, C Canada
14 G11 **Nipissing, Lake** ◎ Ontario, S Canada
35 P13 **Nipomo** California, W USA
Nippon *see* Japan
138 K6 **Niqniqīyah, Jabal an** ▲ C Syria
62 I9 **Niquivil** San Juan, W Argentina
171 Y13 **Nirabotong** Papua, E Indonesia
Niriz *see* Neyrīz
163 U7 **Nirji** *var.* Morin Dawa Daurzu Zizhiqu. Nei Mongol Zizhiqu, N China
155 I14 **Nirmal** Andhra Pradesh, C India
153 Q13 **Nirmāli** Bihār, NE India
113 O14 **Niš** *Eng.* Nish, *Ger.* Nisch; *anc.* Naissus. Serbia, SE Serbia and Montenegro (Yugo.)
104 H9 **Nisa** Portalegre, C Portugal
Nisa *see* Neisse
141 P4 **Nişab** Al Ḩudūd ash Shamālīyah, N Saudi Arabia
141 Q15 **Nişāb** *var.* Anşāb. SW Yemen
113 P14 **Nišava** *Bul.* Nishava. ≈ Bulgaria/Serbia and Montenegro (Yugo.) *see also* Nishava
107 K25 **Niscemi** Sicilia, Italy, C Mediterranean Sea
Nisch/Nish *see* Niš
165 R4 **Niseko** Hokkaidō, NE Japan
Nishapur *see* Neyshābūr
114 G9 **Nishava** *var.* Nišava. ≈ Bulgaria/Serbia and Montenegro (Yugo.) *see also* Nišava
118 L11 **Nishcha** *Rus.* Nishcha. ≈ N Belarus
165 C17 **Nishinoomote** Kagoshima, Tanega-shima, SW Japan
165 X15 **Nishino-shima** *Eng.* Rosario. *island* Ogasawara-shotō, SE Japan
165 I13 **Nishiwaki** *var.* Nisiwaki. Hyōgo, Honshū, SW Japan
141 U14 **Nishtūn** SE Yemen
Nisiros *see* Nísyros
Nisiwaki *see* Nishiwaki
Niska *see* Niesky
113 O14 **Niška Banja** Serbia, SE Serbia and Montenegro (Yugo.)
12 D6 **Niskibi** ≈ Ontario, C Canada
111 O15 **Nisko** Podkarpackie, SE Poland
10 H7 **Nisling** ≈ Yukon Territory, W Canada
99 H22 **Nismes** Namur, S Belgium
Nismes *see* Nîmes
116 M10 **Nisporeni** *Rus.* Nisporeny. W Moldova
Nisporeny *see* Nisporeni
95 K20 **Nissan** ≈ S Sweden
Nissan Islands *see* Green Islands
95 F16 **Nisser** ◎ S Norway
95 E21 **Nissum Bredning** *inlet* NW Denmark
29 U6 **Nisswa** Minnesota, N USA
Nistru *see* Dniester
115 M22 **Nísyros** *var.* Nisiros. *island* Dodekánisos, Greece, Aegean Sea
118 H8 **Nītaure** Cēsis, C Latvia
60 P10 **Niterói** *prev.* Nictheroy. Rio de Janeiro, SE Brazil
14 F16 **Nith** ≈ Ontario, S Canada
96 J13 **Nith** ≈ S Scotland, UK
Nitinan *see* Nichinan
111 I21 **Nitra** *Ger.* Neutra, *Hung.* Nyitra. Nitriansky Kraj, SW Slovakia
111 I20 **Nitra** *Ger.* Neutra, *Hung.* Nyitra. ≈ W Slovakia
111 I21 **Nitriansky Kraj** ◈ *region* SW Slovakia
21 Q5 **Nitro** West Virginia, NE USA
95 H14 **Nittedal** Akershus, S Norway
Niuatobutabu *see* Niuatoputapu
193 X13 **Niuatoputapu** *var.* Niuatobutabu; *prev.* Keppel Island. *island* N Tonga
193 U15 **Niu'Aunofa** *headland* Tongatapu, S Tonga
Niuchwang *see* Yingkou
190 B16 **Niue** ◇ *self-governing territory in free association with NZ* S Pacific Ocean
190 F10 **Niulakita** *var.* Nurakita. *atoll* S Tuvalu
190 E6 **Niutao** *atoll* NW Tuvalu
93 L15 **Nivala** Oulu, C Finland
102 I15 **Nive** ≈ SW France
99 G19 **Nivelles** Wallon Brabant, C Belgium
103 P8 **Nivernais** *cultural region* C France
15 N8 **Niverville, Lac** ◎ Québec, SE Canada
27 T7 **Nixa** Missouri, C USA
35 R5 **Nixon** Nevada, W USA
25 S12 **Nixon** Texas, SW USA
Niya *see* Minfeng
Niyazov *see* Nyýazow
155 H14 **Nizāmābād** Andhra Pradesh, C India
155 H15 **Nizām Sāgar** ◎ C India
127 N16 **Nizhegorodskaya Oblast'** ◈ *province* W Russian Federation
Nizhnegorskiy *see* Nyzhn'ohirs'kyy
127 S4 **Nizhnekamsk** Respublika Tatarstan, W Russian Federation
127 U3 **Nizhnekamskoye Vodokhranilishche** ▣ W Russian Federation
123 S14 **Nizhneleninskoye** Yevreyskaya Avtonomnaya Oblast', SE Russian Federation
122 L13 **Nizhneudinsk** Irkutskaya Oblast', S Russian Federation
122 I10 **Nizhnevartovsk** Khanty-Mansiyskiy Avtonomnyy Okrug, C Russian Federation
123 Q7 **Nizhneyansk** Respublika Sakha (Yakutiya), NE Russian Federation
127 Q11 **Nizhniy Baskunchak** Astrakhanskaya Oblast', SW Russian Federation
127 O6 **Nizhniy Lomov** Penzenskaya Oblast', W Russian Federation
127 P3 **Nizhniy Novgorod** *prev.* Gor'kiy. Nizhegorodskaya Oblast', W Russian Federation
125 T8 **Nizhniy Odes** Respublika Komi, NW Russian Federation
Nizhniy Pyandzh *see* Panji Poyon
122 G10 **Nizhniy Tagil** Sverdlovskaya Oblast', C Russian Federation
125 T9 **Nizhnyaya-Omra** Respublika Komi, NW Russian Federation
125 P5 **Nizhnyaya Pesha** Nenetskiy Avtonomnyy Okrug, NW Russian Federation
117 Q3 **Nizhyn** *Rus.* Nezhin. Chernihivs'ka Oblast', NE Ukraine
136 M17 **Nizip** Gaziantep, S Turkey
141 X8 **Nizwá** *var.* Nazwāh. NE Oman
Nizza *see* Nice
106 C9 **Nizza Monferrato** Piemonte, NE Italy
Njávdám *see* Näätämöjoki
Njellim *see* Nellim
81 H24 **Njombe** Iringa, S Tanzania
81 G23 **Njombe** ≈ C Tanzania
92 I10 **Njunis** ▲ N Norway
93 H17 **Njurunda** Västernorrland, C Sweden
94 N11 **Njutånger** Gävleborg, C Sweden
79 D14 **Nkambe** Nord-Ouest, NW Cameroon
Nkata Bay *see* Nkhata Bay
79 F21 **Nkayi** *prev.* Jacob. La Bouenza, S Congo
83 J17 **Nkayi** Matabeleland North, W Zimbabwe
82 N13 **Nkhata Bay** *var.* Nkata Bay. Northern, N Malawi
81 E22 **Nkonde** Kigoma, N Tanzania
79 D15 **Nkongsamba** *var.* N'Kongsamba. Littoral, W Cameroon
83 E16 **Nkurenkuru** Okavango, N Namibia
77 Q15 **Nkwanta** E Ghana
167 O2 **Nmai Hka** *var.* Me Hka. ≈ N Myanmar
Noardwâlde *see* Noordwolde
39 N7 **Noatak** Alaska, USA
39 N7 **Noatak River** ≈ Alaska, USA
Nobeji *see* Noheji
164 E15 **Nobeoka** Miyazaki, Kyūshū, SW Japan
27 N11 **Noble** Oklahoma, C USA
31 P13 **Noblesville** Indiana, N USA
165 R5 **Noboribetsu** *var.* Noboribetu. Hokkaidō, NE Japan
Noboribetu *see* Noboribetsu
59 H18 **Nobres** Mato Grosso, W Brazil
107 N21 **Nocera Terinese** Calabria, S Italy
41 Q16 **Nochixtlán** *var.* Asunción Nochixtlán. Oaxaca, SE Mexico
25 S5 **Nocona** Texas, SW USA
63 K21 **Nodales, Bahía de los** *bay* S Argentina
27 Q2 **Nodaway River** ≈ Iowa/Missouri, C USA
27 R8 **Noel** Missouri, C USA
95 C17 **Nærbø** Rogaland, S Norway
95 I24 **Næstved** Storstrøm, SE Denmark
40 H3 **Nogales** Chihuahua, NW Mexico
40 F3 **Nogales** Sonora, NW Mexico
36 M17 **Nogales** Arizona, SW USA
Nogal Valley *see* Dooxo Nugaaleed
102 K15 **Nogaro** Gers, S France
110 J7 **Nogat** ≈ N Poland
164 D12 **Nōgata** Fukuoka, Kyūshū, SW Japan
127 P15 **Nogayskaya Step'** *steppe* SW Russian Federation
102 M6 **Nogent-le-Rotrou** Eure-et-Loir, C France
103 O4 **Nogent-sur-Oise** Oise, N France
103 P6 **Nogent-sur-Seine** Aube, N France
122 L10 **Noginsk** Evenkiyskiy Avtonomnyy Okrug, N Russian Federation
126 L3 **Noginsk** Moskovskaya Oblast', W Russian Federation
123 T12 **Nogliki** Ostrov Sakhalin, Sakhalinskaya Oblast', SE Russian Federation
164 K12 **Nōgōhaku-san** ▲ Honshū, SW Japan
162 D5 **Nogoonnuur** Bayan-Ölgiy, NW Mongolia
61 C18 **Nogoyá** Entre Ríos, E Argentina
111 K21 **Nógrád** *off.* Nógrád Megye. ◈ *county* N Hungary
105 U5 **Noguera Pallaresa** ≈ NE Spain
105 U4 **Noguera Ribagorçana** ≈ NE Spain
101 E19 **Nohfelden** Saarland, SW Germany
38 A8 **Nohili Point** *headland* Kauaʻi, Hawaiʻi, USA, C Pacific Ocean
104 G3 **Noia** Galicia, NW Spain
103 N16 **Noire, Montagne** ▲ S France
15 P12 **Noire, Rivière** ≈ Québec, SE Canada
14 J10 **Noire, Rivière** ≈ Québec, SE Canada
Noire, Rivière *see* Black River
102 G6 **Noires, Montagnes** ▲ NW France
102 H8 **Noirmoutier-en-l'Île** Vendée, NW France
102 H8 **Noirmoutier, Île de** *island* NW France
187 Q10 **Noka** Nendö, E Solomon Islands
83 G17 **Nokaneng** Ngamiland, NW Botswana
93 L18 **Nokia** Länsi-Suomi, W Finland
148 K11 **Nok Kundi** Baluchistān, SW Pakistan
30 L14 **Nokomis** Illinois, N USA
30 K5 **Nokomis, Lake** ▣ Wisconsin, N USA
78 G9 **Nokou** Kanem, W Chad
187 Q12 **Nokuku** Espiritu Santo, W Vanuatu
95 J18 **Nol** Västra Götaland, S Sweden
79 H16 **Nola** Sangha-Mbaéré, SW Central African Republic
25 P7 **Nolan** Texas, SW USA
125 R15 **Nolinsk** Kirovskaya Oblast', NW Russian Federation
95 B19 **Nólsoy** *Dan.* Nolsø *Island* Faeroe Islands
186 B7 **Nomad** Western, SW Papau New Guinea
164 B16 **Noma-zaki** *headland* Kyūshū, SW Japan
40 K10 **Nombre de Dios** Durango, C Mexico
42 I5 **Nombre de Dios, Cordillera** ▲ N Honduras
38 M9 **Nome** Alaska, USA
29 Q6 **Nome** North Dakota, N USA
38 M9 **Nome, Cape** *headland* Alaska, USA
Nōmi-jima *see* Nishi-Nōmi-jima
14 M11 **Nominingue, Lac** ◎ Québec, SE Canada
Nomoi Islands *see* Mortlock Islands
164 B16 **Nomo-zaki** *headland* Kyūshū, SW Japan
193 X15 **Nomuka** *island* Nomuka Group, C Tonga
193 X15 **Nomuka Group** *island group* W Tonga
189 Q15 **Nomwin Atoll** *atoll* Hall Islands, C Micronesia
8 L10 **Nonacho Lake** ◎ Northwest Territories, NW Canada
Nondaburi *see* Nonthaburi
39 P12 **Nondalton** Alaska, USA
163 V10 **Nong'an** Jilin, NE China
167 P10 **Nong Bua Khok** Nakhon Ratchasima, C Thailand
167 Q9 **Nong Bua Lamphu** Udon Thani, E Thailand
167 R7 **Nông Hèt** Xiangkhoang, N Laos
Nongkaya *see* Nong Khai
167 Q8 **Nong Khai** *var.* Mi Chai, Nongkaya. Nong Khai, E Thailand
167 N14 **Nong Met** Surat Thani, SW Thailand
83 L22 **Nongoma** KwaZulu/Natal, E South Africa
167 P9 **Nong Phai** Phetchabun, C Thailand
153 U13 **Nongstoin** Meghālaya, NE India
83 C19 **Nonidas** Erongo, N Namibia
Nonni *see* Nen Jiang
40 I7 **Nonoava** Chihuahua, N Mexico

◆ Country ◇ Dependent Territory ◈ Administrative Region ▲ Mountain ▲ Mountain Range ⛰ Volcano ◎ Lake
● Country Capital ◇ Dependent Territory Capital ✕ International Airport ≈ River ▣ Reservoir

191 O3 **Nonouti** prev. Sydenham Island. atoll Tungaru, W Kiribati
167 O11 **Nonthaburi** var. Nondaburi, Nontha Buri. Nonthaburi, C Thailand
102 L11 **Nontron** Dordogne, SW France
181 P1 **Noonamah** Northern Territory, N Australia
28 K2 **Noonan** North Dakota, N USA
99 E14 **Noord-Beveland** var. North Beveland. island SW Netherlands
99 J14 **Noord-Brabant** Eng. North Brabant. ◈ province S Netherlands
98 H7 **Noorder Haaks** spit NW Netherlands
98 H9 **Noord-Holland** Eng. North Holland. ◈ province NW Netherlands
Noordhollandsch Kanaal see Noordhollands Kanaal
98 H8 **Noordhollands Kanaal** var. Noordhollandsch Kanaal. canal NW Netherlands
Noord-Kaap see Northern Cape
98 L8 **Noordoostpolder** island N Netherlands
45 P16 **Noordpunt** headland Curaçao, C Netherlands Antilles
98 I8 **Noord-Scharwoude** Noord-Holland, NW Netherlands
Noordwes see North-West
98 G11 **Noordwijk aan Zee** Zuid-Holland, W Netherlands
98 H11 **Noordwijkerhout** Zuid-Holland, W Netherlands
98 M7 **Noordwolde** Fris. Noardwâlde. Friesland, N Netherlands
Noordzee see North Sea
98 H10 **Noordzee-Kanaal** canal NW Netherlands
93 K18 **Noormarkku** Swe. Norrmark. Länsi-Suomi, W Finland
39 N8 **Noorvik** Alaska, USA
10 J17 **Nootka Sound** inlet British Columbia, W Canada
82 A9 **Nóqui** Zaire, NW Angola
95 L15 **Nora** Örebro, C Sweden
147 Q13 **Norak** Rus. Nurek. W Tajikistan
13 I13 **Noranda** Quebec, SE Canada
29 W12 **Nora Springs** Iowa, C USA
95 M14 **Norberg** Västmanland, C Sweden
14 K13 **Norcan Lake** ◎ Ontario, SE Canada
197 R12 **Nord** Avannaarsua, N Greenland
78 F13 **Nord** Eng. North. ◈ province N Cameroon
103 P2 **Nord** ◈ department N France
92 P1 **Nordaustlandet** island NE Svalbard
95 G24 **Nordborg** Ger. Nordburg. Sønderjylland, SW Denmark
Nordburg see Nordborg
95 F23 **Nordby** Ribe, W Denmark
11 P15 **Nordegg** Alberta, SW Canada
100 E9 **Norden** Niedersachsen, NW Germany
100 G10 **Nordenham** Niedersachsen, NW Germany
122 M6 **Nordenshel'da, Arkhipelag** island group N Russian Federation
92 O3 **Nordenskiold Land** physical region W Svalbard
100 E9 **Norderney** island NW Germany
100 J9 **Norderstedt** Schleswig-Holstein, N Germany
94 C11 **Nordfjord** physical region S Norway
94 D11 **Nordfjord** fjord S Norway
94 D11 **Nordfjordeid** Sogn og Fjordane, S Norway
92 G11 **Nordfold** Nordland, C Norway
Nordfriesische Inseln see North Frisian Islands
100 H7 **Nordfriesland** cultural region N Germany
101 K15 **Nordhausen** Thüringen, C Germany
25 T13 **Nordheim** Texas, SW USA
94 C13 **Nordhordland** physical region S Norway
100 E12 **Nordhorn** Niedersachsen, NW Germany
92 I1 **Nordhurfjördhur** Vestfirdhir, NW Iceland
92 J1 **Nordhurland Eystra** ◈ region N Iceland
92 I2 **Nordhurland Vestra** ◈ region N Iceland
172 H16 **Nord, Île du** island Inner Islands, NE Seychelles
95 F20 **Nordjylland** off. Nordjyllands Amt. ◈ county N Denmark
92 K7 **Nordkapp** Eng. North Cape. headland N Norway
92 O1 **Nordkapp** headland N Svalbard
92 L7 **Nordkinn** headland N Norway
79 N19 **Nord Kivu** off. Région du Nord Kivu. ◈ region E Dem. Rep. Congo
92 G12 **Nordland** ◈ county C Norway
101 J21 **Nördlingen** Bayern, S Germany
93 I16 **Nordmaling** Västerbotten, N Sweden
95 K15 **Nordmark** Värmland, C Sweden
Nord, Mer du see North Sea
94 F8 **Nordmøre** physical region S Norway
100 I8 **Nord-Ostee-Kanal** canal N Germany
(0) J3 **Nordostrundingen** headland NE Greenland
79 D14 **Nord-Ouest** Eng. North-West. ◈ province NW Cameroon
Nord-Ouest, Territoires du see Northwest Territories
103 N2 **Nord-Pas-de-Calais** ◈ region N France
101 F19 **Nordpfälzer Bergland** ⛰ W Germany
Nord, Pointe see Fatua, Pointe
187 P16 **Nord, Province** ◈ province C New Caledonia
101 D14 **Nordrhein-Westfalen** Eng. North Rhine-Westphalia, Fr. Rhénanie du Nord-Westphalie. ◈ state W Germany
Nordsee/Nordsjøen/Nordsøen see North Sea
100 H7 **Nordstrand** island N Germany
93 E15 **Nord-Trøndelag** ◈ county C Norway
97 E19 **Nore** Ir. An Fheoir. ≈ S Ireland
29 Q14 **Norfolk** Nebraska, C USA
21 X7 **Norfolk** Virginia, NE USA
97 P19 **Norfolk** cultural region E England, UK
192 K10 **Norfolk Island** ◇ Australian external territory SW Pacific Ocean
175 P9 **Norfolk Ridge** undersea feature W Pacific Ocean
27 U8 **Norfork Lake** ⊞ Arkansas/Missouri, C USA
98 N6 **Norg** Drenthe, NE Netherlands
Norge see Norway
95 D14 **Norheimsund** Hordaland, S Norway
25 S16 **Norias** Texas, SW USA
164 L12 **Norikura-dake** ▲ Honshū, S Japan
122 K8 **Noril'sk** Taymyrskiy (Dolgano-Nenetskiy) Avtonomnyy Okrug, N Russian Federation
14 I13 **Norland** Ontario, SE Canada
21 V8 **Norlina** North Carolina, SE USA
30 L13 **Normal** Illinois, N USA
27 N11 **Norman** Oklahoma, C USA
Norman see Tulita
186 G9 **Normanby Island** island SE PNG
Normandes, Îles see Channel Islands
58 G9 **Normandia** Roraima, N Brazil
102 L5 **Normandie** Eng. Normandy. cultural region N France
102 J5 **Normandie, Collines de** hill range NW France
Normandy see Normandie
25 V9 **Normangee** Texas, SW USA
21 Q10 **Norman, Lake** ⊞ North Carolina, SE USA
44 K13 **Norman Manley** × (Kingston) E Jamaica
181 U5 **Norman River** ≈ Queensland, NE Australia
181 U4 **Normanton** Queensland, NE Australia
8 I8 **Norman Wells** Northwest Territories, NW Canada
12 H12 **Normétal** Québec, S Canada
11 V15 **Norquay** Saskatchewan, S Canada
94 N11 **Norra Dellen** ◎ C Sweden
93 G15 **Norråker** Jämtland, C Sweden
94 N12 **Norrala** Gävleborg, C Sweden
Norra Ny see Stöllet
92 G13 **Norra Storfjället** ▲ N Sweden
92 I13 **Norrbotten** ◈ county N Sweden
95 G23 **Nørre Aaby** var. Nørre Åby. Fyn, C Denmark
Nørre Åby see Nørre Aaby
95 I24 **Nørre Alslev** Storstrøm, SE Denmark
95 E23 **Nørre Nebel** Ribe, W Denmark
95 G20 **Nørresundby** Nordjylland, N Denmark
21 N8 **Norris Lake** ⊞ Tennessee, S USA
18 I15 **Norristown** Pennsylvania, NE USA
95 N17 **Norrköping** Östergötland, S Sweden
Norrmark see Noormarkku
94 N13 **Norrsundet** Gävleborg, C Sweden
95 P15 **Norrtälje** Stockholm, C Sweden
180 L12 **Norseman** Western Australia
93 I14 **Norsjö** Västerbotten, N Sweden
95 G16 **Norsjø** ◎ S Norway
123 R13 **Norsk** Amurskaya Oblast', SE Russian Federation
Norske Havet see Norwegian Sea
187 Q13 **Norsup** Malekula, C Vanuatu
191 V15 **Norte, Cabo** headland Easter Island, Chile, E Pacific Ocean
54 F7 **Norte de Santander** off. Departamento de Norte de Santander. ◈ province N Colombia
61 E21 **Norte, Punta** headland E Argentina
21 R13 **North** South Carolina, SE USA
North see Nord
18 L10 **North Adams** Massachusetts, NE USA
113 L17 **North Albanian Alps** Alb. Bjeshkët e Namuna, SCr. Prokletije. ⛰ Albania/Serbia and Montenegro (Yugo.)
97 M15 **Northallerton** N England, UK
180 J12 **Northam** Western Australia
83 J20 **Northam** Northern, N South Africa
1 **North America** continent
1 N12 **North American Basin** undersea feature W Sargasso Sea
(0) C5 **North American Plate** tectonic feature
18 M11 **North Amherst** Massachusetts, NE USA
97 N20 **Northampton** C England, UK
97 M20 **Northamptonshire** cultural region C England, UK
151 P18 **North Andaman** island Andaman Islands, India, NE Indian Ocean
65 D25 **North Arm** East Falkland, Falkland Islands
21 Q13 **North Augusta** South Carolina, SE USA
173 W8 **North Australian Basin** Fr. Bassin Nord de l' Australie. undersea feature E Indian Ocean
31 R11 **North Baltimore** Ohio, N USA
11 T15 **North Battleford** Saskatchewan, S Canada
14 H11 **North Bay** Ontario, S Canada
12 H6 **North Belcher Islands** island group Belcher Islands, Nunavut, C Canada
29 R15 **North Bend** Nebraska, C USA
32 E14 **North Bend** Oregon, NW USA
96 K12 **North Berwick** SE Scotland, UK
North Beveland see Noord-Beveland
North Borneo see Sabah
183 P5 **North Bourke** New South Wales, SE Australia
North Brabant see Noord-Brabant
182 F2 **North Branch Neales** seasonal river South Australia
44 M6 **North Caicos** island NW Turks and Caicos Islands
26 L10 **North Canadian River** ≈ Oklahoma, C USA
31 U12 **North Canton** Ohio, N USA
13 R13 **North, Cape** headland Cape Breton Island, Nova Scotia, SE Canada
184 I1 **North Cape** headland North Island, NZ
186 G5 **North Cape** headland New Ireland, NE PNG
North Cape see Nordkapp
18 J17 **North Cape May** New Jersey, NE USA
12 C9 **North Caribou Lake** ◎ Ontario, C Canada
21 U10 **North Carolina** off. State of North Carolina; also known as Old North State, Tar Heel State, Turpentine State. ◈ state SE USA
North Celebes see Sulawesi Utara
155 J24 **North Central Province** ◈ province N Sri Lanka
31 S4 **North Channel** lake channel Canada/USA
97 G14 **North Channel** strait Northern Ireland/Scotland, UK
21 S14 **North Charleston** South Carolina, SE USA
31 N10 **North Chicago** Illinois, N USA
195 Y10 **Northcliffe Glacier** glacier Antarctica
31 Q14 **North College Hill** Ohio, N USA
25 O8 **North Concho River** ≈ Texas, SW USA
19 O8 **North Conway** New Hampshire, NE USA
27 V14 **North Crossett** Arkansas, C USA
28 L4 **North Dakota** off. State of North Dakota; also known as Flickertail State, Peace Garden State, Sioux State. ◈ state N USA
North Devon Island see Devon Island
97 O22 **North Downs** hill range SE England, UK
18 C11 **North East** Pennsylvania, NE USA
83 I18 **North East** ◈ district NE Botswana
65 G15 **North East Bay** bay Ascension Island, C Atlantic Ocean
38 L10 **Northeast Cape** headland Saint Lawrence Island, Alaska, USA
81 J17 **North Eastern** ◈ province Kenya
North East Frontier Agency/North East Frontier Agency of Assam see Arunāchal Pradesh
65 E25 **North East Island** island E Falkland Islands
189 V11 **Northeast Island** island Chuuk, C Micronesia
44 L12 **North East Point** headland E Jamaica
44 L6 **Northeast Point** headland Great Inagua, S Bahamas
44 K5 **Northeast Point** headland Acklins Island, SE Bahamas
191 Z2 **Northeast Point** headland Kiritimati, E Kiribati
44 H2 **Northeast Providence Channel** channel N Bahamas
101 J14 **Northeim** Niedersachsen, C Germany
29 X14 **North English** Iowa, C USA
138 G8 **Northern** ◈ district N Israel
82 M12 **Northern** ◈ region N Malawi
186 F8 **Northern** ◈ province S PNG
80 D7 **Northern** ◈ state N Sudan
82 K12 **Northern** ◈ province NE Zambia
80 B13 **Northern Bahr el Ghazal** ◈ state SW Sudan
Northern Border Region see Al Ḥudūd ash Shamālīyah
83 F24 **Northern Cape** off. Northern Cape Province, Afr. Noord-Kaap. ◈ province W South Africa
190 K14 **Northern Cook Islands** island group N Cook Islands
80 B8 **Northern Darfur** ◈ state NW Sudan
Northern Dvina see Severnaya Dvina
97 F14 **Northern Ireland** var. The Six Counties. political division UK
80 D9 **Northern Kordofan** ◈ state C Sudan
187 Z14 **Northern Lau Group** island group Lau Group, NE Fiji
188 K3 **Northern Mariana Islands** ◇ US commonwealth territory W Pacific Ocean
155 J23 **Northern Province** ◈ province N Sri Lanka
Northern Province see Limpopo
Northern Rhodesia see Zambia
Northern Sporades see Vóreioi Sporádes
182 D1 **Northern Territory** ◈ territory N Australia
Northern Transvaal see Limpopo
Northern Ural Hills see Severnyye Uvaly
84 I9 **North European Plain** plain N Europe
27 V2 **North Fabius River** ≈ Missouri, C USA
65 D24 **North Falkland Sound** sound N Falkland Islands
29 V9 **Northfield** Minnesota, N USA
19 O9 **Northfield** New Hampshire, NE USA
175 Q8 **North Fiji Basin** undersea feature N Coral Sea
97 Q22 **North Foreland** headland SE England, UK
35 P6 **North Fork American River** ≈ California, W USA
39 R7 **North Fork Chandalar River** ≈ Alaska, USA
28 K7 **North Fork Grand River** ≈ North Dakota/South Dakota, N USA
21 O6 **North Fork Kentucky River** ≈ Kentucky, S USA
39 Q7 **North Fork Koyukuk River** ≈ Alaska, USA
39 Q10 **North Fork Kuskokwim River** ≈ Alaska, USA
26 K11 **North Fork Red River** ≈ Oklahoma/Texas, SW USA
26 K3 **North Fork Solomon River** ≈ Kansas, C USA
23 W14 **North Fort Myers** Florida, SE USA
31 P5 **North Fox Island** island Michigan, N USA
100 G6 **North Frisian Islands** var. Nordfriesische Inseln. island group N Germany
197 N9 **North Geomagnetic Pole** pole Arctic Ocean
18 M13 **North Haven** Connecticut, NE USA
184 J5 **North Head** headland North Island, NZ
18 L6 **North Hero** Vermont, NE USA
35 O7 **North Highlands** California, W USA
North Holland see Noord-Holland
81 I16 **North Horr** Eastern, N Kenya
151 K21 **North Huvadhu Atoll** var. Gaafu Alifu Atoll. atoll S Maldives
65 A24 **North Island** island W Falkland Islands
184 N9 **North Island** island N NZ
21 U14 **North Island** island South Carolina, SE USA
31 O11 **North Judson** Indiana, N USA
North Kazakhstan see Severnyy Kazakhstan
31 V10 **North Kingsville** Ohio, N USA
163 Y13 **North Korea** off. Democratic People's Republic of Korea, Kor. Chosŏn-minjujuŭi-inmin-kanghwaguk. ◆ republic E Asia
153 X11 **North Lakhimpur** Assam, NE India
184 J3 **Northland** off. Northland Region. ◈ region North Island, NZ
192 K11 **Northland Plateau** undersea feature S Pacific Ocean
35 X11 **North Las Vegas** Nevada, W USA
31 O11 **North Liberty** Indiana, N USA
29 X14 **North Liberty** Iowa, C USA
27 V12 **North Little Rock** Arkansas, C USA
28 M13 **North Loup River** ≈ Nebraska, C USA
151 K18 **North Maalhosmadulu Atoll** var. North Malosmadulu Atoll, Raa Atoll. atoll N Maldives
31 U10 **North Madison** Ohio, N USA
31 P12 **North Manchester** Indiana, N USA
31 P6 **North Manitou Island** island Michigan, N USA
29 U10 **North Mankato** Minnesota, N USA
23 Z15 **North Miami** Florida, SE USA
151 K18 **North Miladummadulu Atoll** atoll N Maldives
North Minch see Minch, The
23 W15 **North Naples** Florida, SE USA
175 P8 **North New Hebrides Trench** undersea feature N Coral Sea
23 Y15 **North New River Canal** ≈ Florida, SE USA
151 K20 **North Nilandhe Atoll** var. Faafu Atoll. atoll C Maldives
36 L2 **North Ogden** Utah, W USA
North Ossetia see Severnaya Osetiya-Alaniya, Respublika
35 S10 **North Palisade** ▲ California, W USA
189 U11 **North Pass** passage Chuuk Islands, C Micronesia
28 M15 **North Platte** Nebraska, C USA
33 X17 **North Platte River** ≈ C USA
65 G14 **North Point** headland Ascension Island, C Atlantic Ocean
172 I16 **North Point** headland Mahé, NE Seychelles
31 S6 **North Point** headland Michigan, N USA
31 R5 **North Point** headland Michigan, N USA
39 S9 **North Pole** Alaska, USA
197 R9 **North Pole** pole Arctic Ocean
23 O4 **Northport** Alabama, S USA
23 W14 **North Port** Florida, SE USA
32 L6 **Northport** Washington, NW USA
32 L12 **North Powder** Oregon, NW USA
29 U13 **North Raccoon River** ≈ Iowa, C USA
North Rhine-Westphalia see Nordrhein-Westfalen
97 M16 **North Riding** cultural region N England, UK
96 G5 **North Rona** island NW Scotland, UK
96 K4 **North Ronaldsay** island NE Scotland, UK
36 L2 **North Salt Lake** Utah, W USA
11 P15 **North Saskatchewan** ≈ Alberta/Saskatchewan, S Canada
35 X5 **North Schell Peak** ▲ Nevada, W USA
North Scotia Ridge see South Georgia Ridge
86 D10 **North Sea** Dan. Nordsøen, Dut. Noordzee, Fr. Mer du Nord, Ger. Nordsee, Nor. Nordsjøen; prev. German Ocean, Lat. Mare Germanicum. sea NW Europe
35 T6 **North Shoshone Peak** ▲ Nevada, W USA
North Siberian Lowland/North Siberian Plain see Severo-Sibirskaya Nizmennost'
29 R13 **North Sioux City** South Dakota, N USA
96 K4 **North Sound, The** sound N Scotland, UK
183 T4 **North Star** New South Wales, SE Australia
North Star State see Minnesota
183 V3 **North Stradbroke Island** island Queensland, E Australia
North Sulawesi see Sulawesi Utara
North Sumatra see Sumatera Utara
14 D17 **North Sydenham** ≈ Ontario, S Canada
18 H9 **North Syracuse** New York, NE USA
184 K9 **North Taranaki Bight** gulf North Island, NZ
12 H9 **North Twin Island** island Nunavut, C Canada
96 E8 **North Uist** island NW Scotland, UK
97 L14 **Northumberland** cultural region N England, UK
181 Y7 **Northumberland Isles** island group Queensland, NE Australia
13 Q14 **Northumberland Strait** strait SE Canada
32 G14 **North Umpqua River** ≈ Oregon, NW USA
45 Q13 **North Union** Saint Vincent, Saint Vincent and the Grenadines
10 L17 **North Vancouver** British Columbia, SW Canada
18 K9 **Northville** New York, NE USA
97 Q19 **North Walsham** E England, UK
39 T10 **Northway** Alaska, USA
83 G21 **North-West** off. North-West Province, Afr. Noordwes. ◈ province N South Africa
North-West see Nord-Ouest
64 I6 **Northwest Atlantic Mid-Ocean Canyon** undersea feature N Atlantic Ocean
180 G8 **North West Cape** headland Western Australia
38 J9 **Northwest Cape** headland Saint Lawrence Island, Alaska, USA
82 H13 **North Western** ◈ province W Zambia
155 J24 **North Western Province** ◈ province W Sri Lanka
149 U4 **North-West Frontier Province** ◈ province NW Pakistan
96 H8 **North West Highlands** ⛰ N Scotland, UK
192 J4 **Northwest Pacific Basin** undersea feature NW Pacific Ocean
191 Y2 **Northwest Point** headland Kiritimati, E Kiribati
44 G1 **Northwest Providence Channel** channel N Bahamas
13 Q8 **North West River** Newfoundland and Labrador, E Canada
8 J9 **Northwest Territories** Fr. Territoires du Nord-Ouest. ◈ territory NW Canada
97 K18 **Northwich** C England, UK
25 Q5 **North Wichita River** ≈ Texas, SW USA
18 J17 **North Wildwood** New Jersey, NE USA
21 R9 **North Wilkesboro** North Carolina, SE USA
19 P8 **North Windham** Maine, NE USA
197 Q6 **Northwind Plain** undersea feature Arctic Ocean
29 V11 **Northwood** Iowa, C USA
29 Q4 **Northwood** North Dakota, N USA
97 M15 **North York Moors** moorland N England, UK
25 V9 **North Zulch** Texas, SW USA
26 K2 **Norton** Kansas, C USA
31 S13 **Norton** Ohio, N USA
21 P7 **Norton** Virginia, NE USA
39 N9 **Norton Bay** bay Alaska, USA
Norton de Matos see Balombo
31 O9 **Norton Shores** Michigan, N USA
38 M10 **Norton Sound** inlet Alaska, USA
27 Q3 **Nortonville** Kansas, C USA
102 I8 **Nort-sur-Erdre** Loire-Atlantique, NW France
195 N2 **Norvegia, Cape** headland Antarctica
18 L13 **Norwalk** Connecticut, NE USA
29 V14 **Norwalk** Iowa, C USA
31 S11 **Norwalk** Ohio, N USA
19 P7 **Norway** Maine, NE USA
31 N5 **Norway** Michigan, N USA
93 E17 **Norway** off. Kingdom of Norway, Nor. Norge. ◆ monarchy N Europe
11 X13 **Norway House** Manitoba, C Canada
197 R16 **Norwegian Basin** undersea feature NW Norwegian Sea
84 D6 **Norwegian Sea** Nor. Norske Havet. sea NE Atlantic Ocean
197 S17 **Norwegian Trench** undersea feature NE North Sea
14 F16 **Norwich** Ontario, S Canada
97 Q19 **Norwich** E England, UK
19 N13 **Norwich** Connecticut, NE USA
18 I11 **Norwich** New York, NE USA
29 U9 **Norwood** Minnesota, N USA
31 Q15 **Norwood** Ohio, N USA
14 H11 **Nosbonsing, Lake** ◎ Ontario, S Canada
Nösen see Bistriţa
165 T1 **Noshappu-misaki** headland Hokkaidō, NE Japan
165 P7 **Noshiro** var. Nosiro; prev. Noshirominato. Akita, Honshū, C Japan
Noshirominato/Nosiro see Noshiro
117 Q3 **Nosivka** Rus. Nosovka. Chernihivs'ka Oblast', NE Ukraine
67 T14 **Nosop** var. Nossob, Nossop. ≈ Botswana/Namibia
125 S4 **Nosovaya** Nenetskiy Avtonomnyy Okrug, NW Russian Federation
Nosovka see Nosivka
143 V11 **Noṣratābād** Sīstān va Balūchestān, E Iran
95 J18 **Nossebro** Västra Götaland, S Sweden
96 K6 **Noss Head** headland N Scotland, UK
Nossi-Bé see Be, Nosy
83 E20 **Nossob** ≈ E Namibia
Nossob/Nossop see Nosop
172 J2 **Nosy Be** × Antsirañana, N Madagascar
172 J6 **Nosy Varika** Fianarantsoa, SE Madagascar
14 L10 **Notawassi** ≈ Québec, SE Canada
14 M9 **Notawassi, Lac** ◎ Québec, SE Canada
36 J5 **Notch Peak** ▲ Utah, W USA
110 G10 **Noteć** Ger. Netze. ≈ NW Poland
Nóties Sporádes see Dodekánisos
115 J22 **Nótion Aigaíon** Eng. Aegean South. ◈ region E Greece
115 H18 **Nótios Evvoïkós Kólpos** gulf E Greece
115 B16 **Nótio Stenó Kérkyras** strait W Greece
107 L25 **Noto** anc. Netum. Sicilia, Italy, C Mediterranean Sea
164 M10 **Noto** Ishikawa, Honshū, SW Japan
95 G15 **Notodden** Telemark, S Norway
107 L25 **Noto, Golfo di** gulf Sicilia, Italy, C Mediterranean Sea
164 L10 **Noto-hantō** peninsula Honshū, SW Japan
164 L11 **Noto-jima** island SW Japan
13 T11 **Notre Dame Bay** bay Newfoundland and Labrador, E Canada
15 P6 **Notre-Dame-de-Lorette** Québec, SE Canada
14 L11 **Notre-Dame-de-Pontmain** Québec, SE Canada
15 T8 **Notre-Dame-du-Lac** Québec, SE Canada
15 Q6 **Notre-Dame-du-Rosaire** Québec, SE Canada
15 U8 **Notre-Dame, Monts** ⛰ Québec, S Canada
77 R16 **Notsé** S Togo
14 G14 **Nottawasaga** ≈ Ontario, S Canada
14 G14 **Nottawasaga Bay** lake bay Ontario, S Canada
12 I11 **Nottaway** ≈ Québec, SE Canada
23 S1 **Nottely Lake** ⊞ Georgia, SE USA
95 H16 **Nøtterøy** island S Norway
97 M19 **Nottingham** C England, UK
9 E14 **Nottingham Island** island Nunavut, NE Canada
97 P8 **Nottinghamshire** cultural region C England, UK
21 V7 **Nottoway** Virginia, NE USA
21 V7 **Nottoway River** ≈ Virginia, NE USA
76 G7 **Nouâdhibou** prev. Port-Étienne. Dakhlet Nouâdhibou, W Mauritania
76 G7 **Nouâdhibou** × Dakhlet Nouâdhibou, W Mauritania
76 F7 **Nouâdhibou, Dakhlet** prev. Baie du Lévrier. bay W Mauritania
76 F7 **Nouâdhibou, Râs** prev. Cap Blanc. headland NW Mauritania
76 G9 **Nouakchott** ● (Mauritania) Nouakchott District, SW Mauritania
76 G9 **Nouakchott** × Trarza, SW Mauritania
120 J11 **Noual, Sebkhet en** var. Sabkhat an Nawāl. salt flat C Tunisia
76 G8 **Nouâmghâr** var. Nouamrhar. Dakhlet Nouâdhibou, W Mauritania
Nouamrhar see Nouâmghâr
Nouă Sulița see Novoselytsya
187 Q17 **Nouméa** ○ (New Caledonia) Province Sud, S New Caledonia
79 E15 **Noun** ≈ C Cameroon
77 N12 **Nouna** W Burkina
83 H24 **Noupoort** Northern Cape, C South Africa
Nouveau-Brunswick see New Brunswick
Nouveau-Comptoir see Wemindji
15 T4 **Nouvel, Lacs** ◎ Québec, SE Canada
15 W7 **Nouvelle** Québec, SE Canada
15 W7 **Nouvelle** ≈ Québec, SE Canada
Nouvelle-Calédonie see New Caledonia
Nouvelle Écosse see Nova Scotia
103 R3 **Nouzonville** Ardennes, N France
147 Q11 **Nov** Rus. Nau. NW Tajikistan
59 I21 **Nova Alvorada** Mato Grosso do Sul, SW Brazil
Novabad see Navobod
111 D19 **Nová Bystřice** Ger. Neubistritz. Jihočeský Kraj, S Czech Republic
116 H13 **Novaci** Gorj, SW Romania
Nova Civitas see Neustadt an der Weinstrasse

◆ Country ● Country Capital ◇ Dependent Territory ○ Dependent Territory Capital ◈ Administrative Region × International Airport ▲ Mountain ⛰ Mountain Range ⊼ Volcano ≈ River ◎ Lake ⊞ Reservoir

Novaesium see Neuss
60 H10 **Nova Esperança** Paraná, S Brazil
106 H11 **Novafeltria** Marche, C Italy
60 Q9 **Nova Friburgo** Rio de Janeiro, SE Brazil
82 D12 **Nova Gaia** var. Cambundi-Catembo. Malanje, NE Angola
109 S12 **Nova Gorica** W Slovenia
112 G10 **Nova Gradiška** Ger. Neugradisk, Hung. Újgradiska. Brod-Posavina, NE Croatia
60 K7 **Nova Granada** São Paulo, S Brazil
60 O10 **Nova Iguaçu** Rio de Janeiro, SE Brazil
117 S10 **Nova Kakhovka** Rus. Novaya Kakhovka. Khersons'ka Oblast', SE Ukraine
Nová Karvinná see Karviná
Nova Lamego see Gabú
Nova Lisboa see Huambo
112 C11 **Novalja** Lika-Senj, W Croatia
119 M14 **Novalukoml'** Rus. Novolukoml'. Vitsyebskaya Voblasts', N Belarus
Nova Mambone see Mambone
83 P16 **Nova Nabúri** Zambézia, NE Mozambique
117 Q9 **Nova Odesa** var. Novaya Odessa. Mykolayivs'ka Oblast', S Ukraine
60 H10 **Nova Olímpia** Paraná, S Brazil
61 I15 **Nova Prata** Rio Grande do Sul, S Brazil
14 H12 **Novar** Ontario, S Canada
106 C7 **Novara** anc. Novaria. Piemonte, NW Italy
Novaria see Novara
117 P7 **Novarkanels'k** Kirovohrads'ka Oblast', C Ukraine
13 P15 **Nova Scotia** Fr. Nouvelle Écosse. ◆ province SE Canada
(0) M9 **Nova Scotia** physical region SE Canada
34 M8 **Novato** California, W USA
192 M7 **Nova Trough** undersea feature W Pacific Ocean
116 L7 **Nova Ushtsya** Khmel'nyts'ka Oblast', W Ukraine
83 M17 **Nova Vanduzi** Manica, C Mozambique
117 U5 **Nova Vodolaha** Rus. Novaya Vodolaga. Kharkivs'ka Oblast', E Ukraine
123 O12 **Novaya Chara** Chitinskaya Oblast', S Russian Federation
122 M12 **Novaya Igirma** Irkutskaya Oblast', C Russian Federation
Novaya Kakhovka see Nova Kakhovka
144 E10 **Novaya Kazanka** Zapadnyy Kazakhstan, W Kazakhstan
124 I12 **Novaya Ladoga** Leningradskaya Oblast', NW Russian Federation
127 R5 **Novaya Malykla** Ul'yanovskaya Oblast', W Russian Federation
Novaya Odessa see Nova Odesa
123 Q5 **Novaya Sibir', Ostrov** island Novosibirskiye Ostrova, NE Russian Federation
Novaya Vodolaga see Nova Vodolaha
119 P17 **Novaya Yel'nya** Rus. Novaya Yel'nya. Mahilyowskaya Voblasts', E Belarus
122 I6 **Novaya Zemlya** island group N Russian Federation
Novaya Zemlya Trough see East Novaya Zemlya Trough
114 K10 **Nova Zagora** Sliven, C Bulgaria
105 S12 **Novelda** País Valenciano, E Spain
111 H19 **Nové Mesto nad Váhom** Ger. Waagneustadtl, Hung. Vágújhely. Trenčiansky Kraj, W Slovakia
111 F17 **Nové Město na Moravě** Ger. Neustadtl in Mähren. Vysočina, C Czech Republic
Novesium see Neuss
111 I21 **Nové Zámky** Ger. Neuhäusel, Hung. Érsekújvár. Nitriansky Kraj, SW Slovakia
Novgorod see Velikiy Novgorod
Novgorod-Severskiy see Novhorod-Sivers'kyy
122 C7 **Novgorodskaya Oblast'** ◆ province W Russian Federation
117 R8 **Novhorodka** Kirovohrads'ka Oblast', C Ukraine
117 R2 **Novhorod-Sivers'kyy** Rus. Novgorod-Severskiy. Chernihivs'ka Oblast', NE Ukraine
31 R10 **Novi** Michigan, N USA
Novi see Novi Vinodolski
112 L9 **Novi Bečej** prev. Új-Becse, Vološinovo, Ger. Neubetsche, Hung. Törökbecse. Serbia, N Serbia and Montenegro (Yugo.)
25 Q8 **Novice** Texas, SW USA
112 A9 **Novigrad** Istra, NW Croatia
Novi Grad see Bosanski Novi
114 G9 **Novi Iskŭr** Sofiya-Grad, W Bulgaria
106 C9 **Novi Ligure** Piemonte, NW Italy
99 L22 **Noville** Luxembourg, SE Belgium
194 I10 **Noville Peninsula** peninsula Thurston Island, Antarctica
Noviodunum see Soissons, Aisne, France
Noviodunum see Nevers, Nièvre, France
Noviodunum see Nyon, Vaud, Switzerland
Noviomagus see Lisieux, France
Noviomagus see Nijmegen, Netherlands
114 M8 **Novi Pazar** Shumen, NE Bulgaria
113 M15 **Novi Pazar** Turk. Yenipazar. Serbia, S Serbia and Montenegro (Yugo.)
112 K10 **Novi Sad** Ger. Neusatz, Hung. Újvidék. Serbia, N Serbia and Montenegro (Yugo.)
117 T6 **Novi Sanzhary** Poltavs'ka Oblast', C Ukraine
112 H12 **Novi Travnik** prev. Pučarevo. Federacija Bosna I Hercegovina, C Bosnia and Herzegovina
112 B10 **Novi Vinodolski** var. Novi. Primorje-Gorski Kotar, NW Croatia
58 F12 **Novo Airão** Amazonas, N Brazil
127 N14 **Novoaleksandrovsk** Stavropol'skiy Kray, SW Russian Federation
Novoalekseyevka see Khobda
127 N9 **Novoanninskiy** Volgogradskaya Oblast', SW Russian Federation
58 F13 **Novo Aripuanã** Amazonas, N Brazil
117 Y6 **Novoaydar** Luhans'ka Oblast', E Ukraine
117 X9 **Novoazovs'k** Rus. Novoazovsk. Donets'ka Oblast', E Ukraine
123 R14 **Novobureyskiy** Amurskaya Oblast', SE Russian Federation
127 Q3 **Novocheboksarsk** Chuvashskaya Respublika, W Russian Federation
127 R5 **Novocheremshansk** Ul'yanovskaya Oblast', W Russian Federation
126 L12 **Novocherkassk** Rostovskaya Oblast', SW Russian Federation
127 R6 **Novodevich'ye** Samarskaya Oblast', W Russian Federation
124 M8 **Novodvinsk** Arkhangel'skaya Oblast', NW Russian Federation
Novograd-Volynskiy see Novohrad-Volyns'kyy
Novogrudok see Navahrudak
61 I15 **Novo Hamburgo** Rio Grande do Sul, S Brazil
59 H16 **Novo Horizonte** Mato Grosso, W Brazil
60 K8 **Novo Horizonte** São Paulo, S Brazil
116 M4 **Novohrad-Volyns'kyy** Rus. Novograd-Volynskiy. Zhytomyrs'ka Oblast', N Ukraine
145 O7 **Novoishimskiy** prev. Kuybyshevskiy. Severnyy Kazakhstan, N Kazakhstan
144 L14 **Novokazalinsk** see Ayteke Bi
126 M8 **Novokhopersk** Voronezhskaya Oblast', W Russian Federation
127 R6 **Novokuybyshevsk** Samarskaya Oblast', W Russian Federation
122 J13 **Novokuznetsk** prev. Stalinsk. Kemerovskaya Oblast', S Russian Federation
195 R1 **Novolazarevskaya** Russian research station Antarctica
Novolukoml' see Novalukoml'
109 V12 **Novo mesto** Ger. Rudolfswert; prev. Ger. Neustadtl. SE Slovenia
126 K15 **Novomikhaylovskiy** Krasnodarskiy Kray, SW Russian Federation
112 L8 **Novo Miloševo** Serbia, N Serbia and Montenegro (Yugo.)
Novomirgorod see Novomyrhorod
126 L5 **Novomoskovsk** Tul'skaya Oblast', W Russian Federation
117 U7 **Novomoskovs'k** Rus. Novomoskovsk. Dnipropetrovs'ka Oblast', E Ukraine
117 V8 **Novomykolayivka** Zaporiz'ka Oblast', SE Ukraine
117 Q7 **Novomyrhorod** Rus. Novomirgorod. Kirovohrads'ka Oblast', S Ukraine
127 N8 **Novonikolayevskiy** Volgogradskaya Oblast', SW Russian Federation
127 P10 **Novonikol'skoye** Volgogradskaya Oblast', SW Russian Federation
127 X7 **Novoorsk** Orenburgskaya Oblast', W Russian Federation
126 M13 **Novopokrovskaya** Krasnodarskiy Kray, SW Russian Federation
Novopolotsk see Navapolatsk
117 Y5 **Novopskov** Luhans'ka Oblast', E Ukraine
Novoradomsk see Radomsko
Novo Redondo see Sumbe
127 R8 **Novorepnoye** Saratovskaya Oblast', W Russian Federation
126 K14 **Novorossiysk** Krasnodarskiy Kray, SW Russian Federation
Novorossiyskiy/Novorossiyskoye see Akzhar
124 F15 **Novorzhev** Pskovskaya Oblast', W Russian Federation
Novoselitsa see Novoselytsya
117 S12 **Novoselivs'ke** Respublika Krym, S Ukraine
Novosëlki see Navasyolki
114 G6 **Novo Selo** Vidin, NW Bulgaria
113 M14 **Novo Selo** Serbia, C Serbia and Montenegro (Yugo.)
116 K8 **Novoselytsya** Rom. Nouă Sulița, Rus. Novoselitsa. Chernivets'ka Oblast', W Ukraine
127 U7 **Novosergiyevka** Orenburgskaya Oblast', W Russian Federation
126 L11 **Novoshakhtinsk** Rostovskaya Oblast', SW Russian Federation
122 J12 **Novosibirsk** Novosibirskaya Oblast', C Russian Federation
122 J12 **Novosibirskaya Oblast'** ◆ province C Russian Federation
122 M4 **Novosibirskiye Ostrova** Eng. New Siberian Islands. island group N Russian Federation
126 K6 **Novosil'** Orlovskaya Oblast', W Russian Federation
124 G16 **Novosokol'niki** Pskovskaya Oblast', W Russian Federation
127 Q6 **Novospasskoye** Ul'yanovskaya Oblast', W Russian Federation
127 X8 **Novotroitsk** Orenburgskaya Oblast', W Russian Federation
Novotroitskoye see Brlik, Kazakhstan
Novotroitskoye see Novotroyits'ke, Ukraine
117 T11 **Novotroyits'ke** Rus. Novotroitskoye. Khersons'ka Oblast', S Ukraine
Novoukrainka see Novoukrayinka
117 Q8 **Novoukrayinka** Rus. Novoukrainka. Kirovohrads'ka Oblast', C Ukraine
127 Q5 **Novoul'yanovsk** Ul'yanovskaya Oblast', W Russian Federation
127 W8 **Novouralets** Orenburgskaya Oblast', W Russian Federation
122 G10 **Novoural'ske** Chelyabinskaya Oblast', S Russian Federation
Novo-Urgench see Urganch
116 I4 **Novovolyns'k** Rus. Novovolynsk. Volyns'ka Oblast', NW Ukraine
117 S9 **Novovorontsovka** Khersons'ka Oblast', S Ukraine
147 Y7 **Novovoznesenovka** Issyk-Kul'skaya Oblast', E Kyrgyzstan
125 R14 **Novovyatsk** Kirovskaya Oblast', NW Russian Federation
Novoyel'nya see Navayel'nya
124 I7 **Novoye Yushozero** Respublika Kareliya, NW Russian Federation
117 O6 **Novozhyvotiv** Vinnyts'ka Oblast', C Ukraine
126 H6 **Novozybkov** Bryanskaya Oblast', W Russian Federation
112 F9 **Novska** Sisak-Moslavina, NE Croatia
Nový Bohumín see Bohumín
111 D15 **Nový Bor** Ger. Haida; prev. Bor u České Lípy, Hajda. Liberecký Kraj, N Czech Republic
111 E16 **Nový Bydžov** Ger. Neubidschow. Královéhradecký Kraj, N Czech Republic
119 G18 **Novy Dvor** Rus. Novyy Dvor. Hrodzyenskaya Voblasts', W Belarus
111 I17 **Nový Jičín** Ger. Neutitschein. Moravskoslezský Kraj, E Czech Republic
118 K12 **Novy Pahost** Rus. Novyy Pogost. Vitsyebskaya Voblasts', NW Belarus
Novyy Bug see Novyy Buh
117 R9 **Novyy Buh** Rus. Novyy Bug. Mykolayivs'ka Oblast', S Ukraine
117 Q4 **Novyy Bykiv** Chernihivs'ka Oblast', N Ukraine
Novyy Dvor see Novy Dvor
Novyye Aneny see Anenii Noi
127 P7 **Novyye Burasy** Saratovskaya Oblast', W Russian Federation
Novyy Margilan see Farg'ona
126 K8 **Novyy Oskol** Belgorodskaya Oblast', W Russian Federation
Novyy Pogost see Novy Pahost
127 R2 **Novyy Tor"yal** Respublika Mariy El, W Russian Federation
123 N12 **Novyy Uoyan** Respublika Buryatiya, S Russian Federation
122 J9 **Novyy Urengoy** Yamalo-Nenetskiy Avtonomnyy Okrug, N Russian Federation
Novyy Uzen' see Zhanaozen
111 N16 **Nowa Dęba** Podkarpackie, SE Poland
111 G15 **Nowa Ruda** Ger. Neurode. Dolnośląskie, SW Poland
110 F12 **Nowa Sól** var. Nowasól, Ger. Neusalz an der Oder. Lubuskie, W Poland
27 Q8 **Nowata** Oklahoma, C USA
142 M6 **Nowbarān** Markazī, W Iran
110 J8 **Nowe** Kujawsko-pomorskie, C Poland
110 K9 **Nowe Miasto Lubawskie** Ger. Neumark. Warmińsko-Mazurskie, NE Poland
110 L13 **Nowe Miasto nad Pilicą** Mazowieckie, C Poland
110 D8 **Nowe Warpno** Ger. Neuwarp. Zachodnio-pomorskie, NW Poland
Nowgong see Nagaon
110 E8 **Nowogard** var. Nowógard, Ger. Naugard. Zachodnio-pomorskie, NW Poland
110 N9 **Nowogród** Podlaskie, NE Poland
Nowogródek see Navahrudak
111 E14 **Nowogrodziec** Ger. Naumburg am Queis. Dolnośląskie, SW Poland
Nowojelnia see Navayel'nya
Nowo-Minsk see Mińsk Mazowiecki
33 V13 **Nowood River** ≈ Wyoming, C USA
Nowo-Święciany see Švenčionėliai
183 S10 **Nowra-Bomaderry** New South Wales, SE Australia
149 T5 **Nowshera** var. Naushahra, Naushara. North-West Frontier Province, NE Pakistan
110 J7 **Nowy Dwór Gdański** Ger. Tiegenhof. Pomorskie, N Poland
110 L11 **Nowy Dwór Mazowiecki** Mazowieckie, C Poland
111 M17 **Nowy Sącz** Ger. Neu Sandec. Małopolskie, S Poland
111 L18 **Nowy Targ** Ger. Neumark. Małopolskie, S Poland
110 F11 **Nowy Tomyśl** var. Nowy Tomysl. Wielkolpolskie, C Poland
148 M7 **Now Zād** var. Nauzad. Helmand, S Afghanistan
23 N4 **Noxubee River** ≈ Alabama/Mississippi, S USA
122 I10 **Noyabr'sk** Yamalo-Nenetskiy Avtonomnyy Okrug, N Russian Federation
102 L8 **Noyant** Maine-et-Loire, NW France
39 X14 **Noyes Island** island Alexander Archipelago, Alaska, USA
103 O3 **Noyon** Oise, N France
102 I7 **Nozay** Loire-Atlantique, NW France
82 L12 **Nsando** Northern, NE Zambia
83 N16 **Nsanje** Southern, S Malawi
77 Q17 **Nsawam** SE Ghana
79 E16 **Nsimalen** ✕ Centre, C Cameroon
82 K12 **Nsombo** Northern, NE Zambia
82 H13 **Ntambu** North Western, NW Zambia
83 N14 **Ntcheu** var. Ncheu. Central, S Malawi
79 D17 **Ntem** prev. Campo, Kampo. ≈ Cameroon/Equatorial Guinea
83 I14 **Ntemwa** North Western, NW Zambia
Ntlenyana, Mount see Thabana Ntlenyana
79 I19 **Ntomba, Lac** var. Lac Tumba. ⊚ NW Dem. Rep. Congo
81 E19 **Ntungamo** SW Uganda
81 E18 **Ntusi** SW Uganda
83 H18 **Ntwetwe Pan** salt lake NE Botswana
93 M15 **Nuasjärvi** ⊚ C Finland
80 F11 **Nuba Mountains** ▲ C Sudan
68 I9 **Nubian Desert** desert NE Sudan
116 G10 **Nucet** Hung. Diófás. Bihor, W Romania
Nu Chiang see Salween
145 U9 **Nuclear Testing Ground** nuclear site Pavlodar, E Kazakhstan
56 E9 **Nucuray, Río** ≈ N Peru
25 R14 **Nueces River** ≈ Texas, SW USA
11 V9 **Nueltin Lake** ⊚ Manitoba/Nunavut, C Canada
99 K15 **Nuenen** Noord-Brabant, S Netherlands
62 G6 **Nuestra Señora, Bahía** bay N Chile
61 D14 **Nuestra Señora Rosario de Caa Catí** Corrientes, NE Argentina
54 J9 **Nueva Antioquia** Vichada, E Colombia
Nueva Caceres see Naga
41 C7 **Nueva Ciudad Guerrera** Tamaulipas, C Mexico
55 N4 **Nueva Esparta** off. Estado Nueva Esparta. ◆ state NE Venezuela
44 C5 **Nueva Gerona** Isla de la Juventud, S Cuba
42 H8 **Nueva Guadalupe** San Miguel, E El Salvador
42 M11 **Nueva Guinea** Región Autónoma Atlántico Sur, SE Nicaragua
61 D19 **Nueva Helvecia** Colonia, SW Uruguay
63 J25 **Nueva, Isla** island S Chile
40 M14 **Nueva Italia** Michoacán de Ocampo, SW Mexico
56 D5 **Nueva Loja** var. Lago Agrio. Sucumbíos, NE Ecuador
42 F6 **Nueva Ocotepeque** prev. Ocotepeque. Ocotepeque, W Honduras
61 D19 **Nueva Palmira** Colonia, SW Uruguay
41 N6 **Nueva Rosita** Coahuila de Zaragoza, NE Mexico
42 E7 **Nueva San Salvador** prev. Santa Tecla. La Libertad, SW El Salvador
42 J8 **Nueva Segovia** ◆ department NW Nicaragua
Nueva Tabarca see Plana, Isla
Nueva Villa de Padilla see Nuevo Padilla
61 B21 **Nueve de Julio** Buenos Aires, E Argentina
44 H6 **Nuevitas** Camagüey, E Cuba
61 D18 **Nuevo Berlín** Río Negro, W Uruguay
40 I4 **Nuevo Casas Grandes** Chihuahua, N Mexico
43 T14 **Nuevo Chagres** Colón, C Panama
41 W15 **Nuevo Coahuila** Campeche, E Mexico
63 K17 **Nuevo, Golfo** gulf S Argentina
41 O7 **Nuevo Laredo** Tamaulipas, NE Mexico
41 N8 **Nuevo León** ◆ state NE Mexico
41 P10 **Nuevo Padilla** var. Nueva Villa de Padilla. Tamaulipas, C Mexico
56 E6 **Nuevo Rocafuerte** Orellana, E Ecuador
162 G6 **Nuga** Dzavhan, W Mongolia
80 O13 **Nugaal** off. Gobolka Nugaal. ◆ region N Somalia
185 E24 **Nugget Point** headland South Island, NZ
186 J5 **Nuguria Islands** island group E PNG
184 P10 **Nuhaka** Hawke's Bay, North Island, NZ
138 M10 **Nuhaydayn, Wādī an** dry watercourse W Iraq
190 E7 **Nui Atoll** atoll W Tuvalu
Nu Jiang see Salween
Nûk see Nuuk
182 G7 **Nukey Bluff** hill South Australia
Nukha see Şäki
123 T9 **Nukh Yablonevyy, Gora** ▲ E Russian Federation
186 K7 **Nukiki** Choiseul Island, NW Solomon Islands
186 B6 **Nuku** Sandaun, NW PNG
193 W15 **Nuku** island Tongatapu Group, NE Tonga
193 U15 **Nuku'alofa** Tongatapu, S Tonga
193 Y16 **Nuku'alofa** ● (Tonga) Tongatapu, S Tonga
190 G12 **Nukuatea** island N Wallis and Futuna
190 F7 **Nukufetau Atoll** atoll C Tuvalu
190 G12 **Nukuhifala** island E Wallis and Futuna
191 W7 **Nuku Hiva** island Îles Marquises, NE French Polynesia
193 O8 **Nuku Hiva Island** island Îles Marquises, N French Polynesia
190 F9 **Nukulaelae Atoll** var. Nukulailai. atoll E Tuvalu
Nukulailai see Nukulaelae Atoll
190 G11 **Nukuloa** island N Wallis and Futuna
186 L6 **Nukumanu Islands** prev. Tasman Group. island group NE PNG
Nukunau see Nikunau
190 J9 **Nukunonu Atoll** island C Tokelau
190 J9 **Nukunonu Village** Nukunonu Atoll, C Tokelau
189 S18 **Nukuoro Atoll** atoll Caroline Islands, S Micronesia
146 H8 **Nukus** Qoraqalpog'iston Respublikasi, W Uzbekistan
190 G11 **Nukutapu** island N Wallis and Futuna
39 O9 **Nulato** Alaska, USA
39 O10 **Nulato Hills** ▲ Alaska, USA
105 T9 **Nules** País Valenciano, E Spain
Nuling see Sultan Kudarat
182 C6 **Nullarbor** South Australia
180 M11 **Nullarbor Plain** plateau South Australia/Western Australia
163 S12 **Nulu'erhu Shan** ▲ N China
77 X14 **Numan** Adamawa, E Nigeria
165 S3 **Numata** Hokkaidō, NE Japan
81 C15 **Numatinna** ≈ W Sudan
95 F14 **Numedalen** valley S Norway
95 G14 **Numedalslågen** var. Laagen. ≈ S Norway
93 L19 **Nummela** Etelä-Suomi, S Finland
183 O11 **Numurkah** Victoria, SE Australia
196 L16 **Nunap Isua** var. Uummannarsuaq, Dan. Kap Farvel, Eng. Cape Farewell. headland S Greenland
9 N8 **Nunavut** ◆ Territory N Canada
54 H9 **Nunchia** Casanare, C Colombia
97 M20 **Nuneaton** C England, UK
153 W14 **Nungba** Manipur, NE India
38 L12 **Nunivak Island** island Alaska, USA
152 I5 **Nun Kun** ▲ NW India
98 L10 **Nunspeet** Gelderland, E Netherlands
107 C18 **Nuoro** Sardegna, Italy, C Mediterranean Sea
75 R12 **Nuqayy, Jabal** hill range S Libya
54 C9 **Nuquí** Chocó, W Colombia
143 O4 **Nūr** Māzandarān, N Iran
145 Q9 **Nura** ≈ N Kazakhstan
143 N11 **Nūrābād** Fārs, C Iran
Nurakita see Niulakita
Nurata see Nurota
Nuratau, Khrebet see Nurota Tizmasi
136 L17 **Nur Dağları** ▲ S Turkey
Nurek see Norak
Nuremberg see Nürnberg
136 M15 **Nurhak** Kahramanmaraş, S Turkey
182 J9 **Nuriootpa** South Australia
127 S5 **Nurlat** Respublika Tatarstan, W Russian Federation
93 N15 **Nurmes** Itä-Suomi, E Finland
101 K20 **Nürnberg** Eng. Nuremberg. Bayern, S Germany
101 K20 **Nürnberg** ✕ Bayern, SE Germany
146 M10 **Nurota** Rus. Nurata. Navoiy Viloyati, C Uzbekistan
147 N10 **Nurota Tizmasi** Rus. Khrebet Nuratau. ▲ C Uzbekistan
149 T8 **Nūrpur** Punjab, E Pakistan
183 P6 **Nurri, Mount** hill New South Wales, SE Australia
25 T13 **Nursery** Texas, SW USA
171 O16 **Nusa Tenggara** Eng. Lesser Sunda Islands. island group East Timor/ Indonesia
169 V17 **Nusa Tenggara Barat** off. Propinsi Nusa Tenggara Barat, Eng. West Nusa Tenggara. ◆ province S Indonesia
171 O16 **Nusa Tenggara Timur** off. Propinsi Nusa Tenggara Timur, Eng. East Nusa Tenggara. ◆ province S Indonesia
171 U14 **Nusawulan** Papua, E Indonesia
137 Q16 **Nusaybin** var. Nisibin. Manisa, SE Turkey
39 O14 **Nushagak Bay** bay Alaska, USA
39 O13 **Nushagak Peninsula** headland Alaska, USA
39 O13 **Nushagak River** ≈ Alaska, USA
160 E11 **Nu Shan** ▲ SW China
149 N11 **Nushki** Baluchistān, SW Pakistan
Nussdorf see Năsăud
112 J9 **Nuštar** Vukovar-Srijem, E Croatia
99 L18 **Nuth** Limburg, SE Netherlands
100 N13 **Nuthe** ≈ NE Germany
Nutmeg State see Connecticut
39 T10 **Nutzotin Mountains** ▲ Alaska, USA
64 I5 **Nuuk** var. Nûk, Dan. Godthaab, Godthåb. ○ (Greenland). Kitaa, SW Greenland
92 L13 **Nuupas** Lappi, NW Finland
191 O7 **Nuupere, Pointe** headland Moorea, W French Polynesia
191 O7 **Nuuroa, Pointe** headland Tahiti, W French Polynesia
Nüürst see Baga Nuur
Nuwara see Nuwara Eliya
155 K25 **Nuwara Eliya** var. Nuwara. Central Province, S Sri Lanka
182 E7 **Nuyts Archipelago** island group South Australia
83 F17 **Nxaunxau** Ngamiland, NW Botswana
39 N12 **Nyac** Alaska, USA
122 H9 **Nyagan'** Khanty-Mansiyskiy Avtonomnyy Okrug, N Russian Federation
Nyagassola see Niagassola
Nyagquka see Yajiang
81 I18 **Nyahururu** Central, W Kenya
182 M10 **Nyah West** Victoria, SE Australia
158 M15 **Nyainqêntanglha Feng** ▲ W China
159 N15 **Nyainqêntanglha Shan** ▲ W China
80 B11 **Nyala** Southern Darfur, W Sudan
83 M16 **Nyamapanda** Mashonaland East, NE Zimbabwe
81 H25 **Nyamtumbo** Ruvuma, S Tanzania
Nyanda see Masvingo
124 M11 **Nyandoma** Arkhangel'skaya Oblast', NW Russian Federation
83 M16 **Nyanga** prev. Inyanga. Manicaland, E Zimbabwe
79 D20 **Nyanga** off. Province de la Nyanga, var. La Nyanga. ◆ province SW Gabon
79 E20 **Nyanga** ≈ Congo/Gabon
81 F20 **Nyantakara** Kagera, NW Tanzania
81 G19 **Nyanza** ◆ province W Kenya
81 E21 **Nyanza-Lac** S Burundi
68 J14 **Nyasa, Lake** var. Lake Malawi; prev. Lago Nyassa. ⊚ E Africa
Nyasaland/Nyasaland Protectorate see Malawi
Nyassa, Lago see Nyasa, Lake
119 J17 **Nyasvizh** Pol. Nieśwież, Rus. Nesvizh. Minskaya Voblasts', C Belarus
166 M8 **Nyaunglebin** Pegu, SW Myanmar
166 M5 **Nyaung-u** Magwe, C Myanmar
95 H24 **Nyborg** Fyn, C Denmark
95 N21 **Nybro** Kalmar, S Sweden
119 J16 **Nyeharelaye** Rus. Negoreloye. Minskaya Voblasts', C Belarus
195 W3 **Nye Mountains** ▲ Antarctica
81 I19 **Nyeri** Central, C Kenya
118 M11 **Nyeshcharda, Vozyera** ⊚ N Belarus
92 O2 **Ny-Friesland** physical region N Svalbard
95 L14 **Nyhammar** Dalarna, C Sweden
160 F7 **Nyikog Qu** ≈ C China
158 L14 **Nyima** Xizang Zizhiqu, W China
83 L14 **Nyimba** Eastern, E Zambia
159 P16 **Nyingchi** var. Pula. Xizang Zizhiqu, W China
Nyinma see Maqu
111 O21 **Nyírbátor** Szabolcs-Szatmár-Bereg, E Hungary
111 N21 **Nyíregyháza** Szabolcs-Szatmár-Bereg, NE Hungary
Nyiro see Ewaso Ng'iro
Nyitra see Nitra
Nyitrabánya see Handlová
93 K16 **Nykarleby** Fin. Uusikaarlepyy. Länsi-Suomi, W Finland
95 I25 **Nykøbing** Storstrøm, SE Denmark
95 I22 **Nykøbing** Vestsjælland, C Denmark
95 F21 **Nykøbing** Viborg, NW Denmark
95 N17 **Nyköping** Södermanland, S Sweden
95 L15 **Nykroppa** Värmland, C Sweden
Nylstroom see Modimolle
183 P7 **Nymagee** New South Wales, SE Australia
183 V5 **Nymboida** New South Wales, SE Australia
183 U5 **Nymboida River** ≈ New South Wales, SE Australia
111 D16 **Nymburk** var. Neuenburg an der Elbe, Ger. Nimburg. Středočeský Kraj, C Czech Republic
95 O16 **Nynäshamn** Stockholm, C Sweden
183 Q6 **Nyngan** New South Wales, SE Australia
Nyoman see Neman
108 A10 **Nyon** Ger. Neuss; anc. Noviodunum. Vaud, SW Switzerland
79 D16 **Nyong** ≈ SW Cameroon
103 S14 **Nyons** Drôme, E France
79 D14 **Nyos, Lac** Eng. Lake Nyos. ⊚ NW Cameroon
Nyos, Lake see Nyos, Lac
125 U11 **Nyrob** var. Nyrov. Permskaya Oblast', NW Russian Federation
Nyrov see Nyrob
111 H15 **Nysa** Ger. Neisse. Opolskie, S Poland
Nysa Łużycka see Neisse
Nyslott see Savonlinna
32 M13 **Nyssa** Oregon, NW USA
Nystad see Uusikaupunki
95 I25 **Nysted** Storstrøm, SE Denmark
125 U14 **Nytva** Permskaya Oblast', NW Russian Federation
165 P8 **Nyūdō-zaki** headland Honshū, C Japan
125 P9 **Nyukhcha** Arkhangel'skaya Oblast', NW Russian Federation
126 H8 **Nyuk, Ozero** var. Ozero Njuk. ⊚ NW Russian Federation
125 O12 **Nyuksenitsa** var. Njuksenica. Vologodskaya Oblast', NW Russian Federation
79 O22 **Nyunzu** Katanga, SE Dem. Rep. Congo
123 O10 **Nyurba** Respublika Sakha (Yakutiya), NE Russian Federation
123 O11 **Nyuya** Respublika Sakha (Yakutiya), NE Russian Federation

◆ Country ● Country Capital ◇ Dependent Territory ○ Dependent Territory Capital ◆ Administrative Region ✕ International Airport ▲ Mountain ▲ Mountain Range Volcano ≈ River ⊚ Lake ⊠ Reservoir

146 K12 Nyýazow Rus. Niyazov. Lebap Welaýaty, NE Turkmenistan
117 T10 Nyzhni Sirohozy Khersons'ka Oblast', S Ukraine
117 U12 Nyzhn'ohirs'kyy Rus. Nizhnegorskiy. Respublika Krym, S Ukraine
81 G21 Nzega Tabora, C Tanzania
76 K15 Nzérékoré Guinée-Forestière, SE Guinea
82 A10 N'Zeto prev. Ambrizete. Zaire, NW Angola
79 M24 Nzilo, Lac prev. Lac Delcommune. ◎ SE Dem. Rep. Congo

O

29 O11 Oacoma South Dakota, N USA
29 N9 Oahe Dam dam South Dakota, N USA
28 M9 Oahe, Lake ⊠ North Dakota/South Dakota, N USA
38 C9 O'ahu var. Oahu island Hawai'i, USA, C Pacific Ocean
165 V4 O-Akan-dake ▲ Hokkaidō, NE Japan
182 K8 Oakbank South Australia
19 P13 Oak Bluffs Martha's Vineyard, New York, NE USA
36 K4 Oak City Utah, W USA
37 R3 Oak Creek Colorado, C USA
35 P8 Oakdale California, W USA
22 H8 Oakdale Louisiana, S USA
29 P7 Oakes North Dakota, N USA
22 J4 Oak Grove Louisiana, S USA
97 N19 Oakham C England, UK
32 H7 Oak Harbor Washington, NW USA
21 R5 Oak Hill West Virginia, NE USA
35 N8 Oakland California, W USA
29 T15 Oakland Iowa, C USA
19 Q7 Oakland Maine, NE USA
21 T3 Oakland Maryland, NE USA
29 R14 Oakland Nebraska, C USA
31 N11 Oak Lawn Illinois, N USA
33 P16 Oakley Idaho, NW USA
26 I4 Oakley Kansas, C USA
31 N10 Oak Park Illinois, N USA
11 X16 Oak Point Manitoba, S Canada
32 G13 Oakridge Oregon, NW USA
20 M9 Oak Ridge Tennessee, S USA
184 K10 Oakura Taranaki, North Island, NZ
22 L7 Oak Vale Mississippi, S USA
14 G16 Oakville Ontario, S Canada
25 V8 Oakwood Texas, SW USA
185 F22 Oamaru Otago, South Island, NZ
96 F13 Oa, Mull of headland W Scotland, UK
171 O11 Oan Sulawesi, N Indonesia
185 J17 Oaro Canterbury, South Island, NZ
35 X2 Oasis Nevada, W USA
195 S15 Oates Land physical region Antarctica
183 P17 Oatlands Tasmania, SE Australia
36 I11 Oatman Arizona, SW USA
41 R16 Oaxaca var. Oaxaca de Juárez; prev. Antequera. Oaxaca, SE Mexico
41 Q16 Oaxaca ◈ state SE Mexico
Oaxaca de Juárez see Oaxaca
122 I19 Ob' ∽ C Russian Federation
14 G9 Obabika Lake ◎ Ontario, S Canada
Obagan see Ubagan
118 M12 Obal' Rus. Obol'. Vitsyebskaya Voblasts', N Belarus
79 E16 Obala Centre, SW Cameroon
14 C6 Oba Lake ◎ Ontario, S Canada
164 J12 Obama Fukui, Honshū, SW Japan
96 H11 Oban W Scotland, UK
Oban see Halfmoon Bay
Obando see Puerto Inírida
104 I4 O Barco var. El Barco, El Barco de Valdeorras, O Barco de Valdeorras. Galicia, NW Spain
O Barco de Valdeorras see O Barco
Obbia see Hobyo
93 J16 Obbola Västerbotten, N Sweden
Obbrovazzo see Obrovac
Obchuga see Abchuha
Obdorsk see Salekhard
Óbecse see Bečej
118 I11 Obeliai Panevėžys, NE Lithuania
60 F13 Oberá Misiones, NE Argentina
108 E8 Oberburg Bern, W Switzerland
109 Q9 Oberdrauburg Salzburg, S Austria
Oberglogau see Głogówek
109 W4 Ober Grafendorf Niederösterreich, NE Austria
101 E15 Oberhausen Nordrhein-Westfalen, W Germany
Oberhollabrunn see Tulln
Oberlaibach see Vrhnika
101 Q15 Oberlausitz Lus. Hornja Łužica. physical region E Germany
26 J2 Oberlin Kansas, C USA
22 H8 Oberlin Louisiana, S USA
31 T11 Oberlin Ohio, N USA
103 U5 Obernai Bas-Rhin, NE France
109 R4 Obernberg-am-Inn Oberösterreich, N Austria
Oberndorf see Oberndorf am Neckar
101 G23 Oberndorf am Neckar var. Oberndorf. Baden-Württemberg, SW Germany
109 Q5 Oberndorf bei Salzburg Salzburg, W Austria
Oberneustadtl see Kysucké Nové Mesto
183 S8 Oberon New South Wales, SE Australia
109 Q4 Oberösterreich off. Land Oberösterreich, Eng. Upper Austria. ◈ state NW Austria
Oberpahlen see Põltsamaa
101 M19 Oberpfälzer Wald ⛰ SE Germany
109 Y6 Oberpullendorf Burgenland, E Austria
Oberradkersburg see Gornja Radgona
101 G18 Oberursel Hessen, W Germany
109 Q8 Obervellach Salzburg, S Austria
109 X7 Oberwart Burgenland, SE Austria
Oberwischau see Vişeu de Sus
109 T7 Oberwölz var. Oberwölz-Stadt. Steiermark, SE Austria
Oberwölz-Stadt see Oberwölz
31 S13 Obetz Ohio, N USA
Ob', Gulf of see Obskaya Guba
54 G8 Obia Santander, C Colombia
58 H12 Óbidos Pará, NE Brazil
104 F10 Óbidos Leiria, C Portugal
Obidovichi see Abidavichy
147 Q13 Obigarm W Tajikistan
165 T2 Obihiro Hokkaidō, NE Japan
Obi-Khingou see Khingov
147 P13 Obikiik SW Tajikistan
113 N16 Obilić Serbia, S Serbia and Montenegro (Yugo.)
127 O12 Obil'noye Respublika Kalmykiya, SW Russian Federation
20 F8 Obion Tennessee, S USA
20 F8 Obion River ∽ Tennessee, S USA
171 S12 Obi, Pulau island Maluku, E Indonesia
165 S2 Obira Hokkaidō, NE Japan
127 N11 Oblivskaya Rostovskaya Oblast', SW Russian Federation
123 R14 Obluch'ye Yevreyskaya Avtonomnaya Oblast', SE Russian Federation
126 K4 Obninsk Kaluzhskaya Oblast', W Russian Federation
114 J8 Obnova Pleven, N Bulgaria
79 N15 Obo Haut-Mbomou, E Central African Republic
159 T9 Obo Qinghai, C China
80 M11 Obock E Djibouti
Obol' see Obal'
Obolyanka see Abalyanka
171 V13 Obome Papua, E Indonesia
110 G11 Oborniki Wielkolpolskie, C Poland
79 G19 Obouya Cuvette, C Congo
126 J8 Oboyan' Kurskaya Oblast', W Russian Federation
124 M9 Obozerskiy Arkhangel'skaya Oblast', NW Russian Federation
112 L11 Obrenovac Serbia, N Serbia and Montenegro (Yugo.)
112 D12 Obrovac It. Obbrovazzo. Zadar, SW Croatia
Obrovo see Abrova
35 Q3 Observation Peak ▲ California, W USA
122 J8 Obskaya Guba Eng. Gulf of Ob'. gulf N Russian Federation
173 N13 Ob' Tablemount undersea feature S Indian Ocean
173 T10 Ob' Trench undersea feature E Indian Ocean
77 P16 Obuasi S Ghana
117 P5 Obukhiv Rus. Obukhov. Kyyivs'ka Oblast', N Ukraine
Obukhov see Obukhiv
127 U14 Obva ∽ NW Russian Federation
117 V10 Obytichna Kosa spit SE Ukraine
117 V10 Obytichna Zatoka gulf SE Ukraine
105 O3 Oca ∽ N Spain
23 W10 Ocala Florida, SE USA
40 M7 Ocampo Coahuila de Zaragoza, NE Mexico
54 G7 Ocaña Norte de Santander, N Colombia
105 N9 Ocaña Castilla-La Mancha, C Spain
106 N4 O Carballiño Cast. Carballiño Galicia, NW Spain
37 T9 Ocate New Mexico, SW USA
Ocavango see Okavango
54 D14 Occidental, Cordillera ⛰ W Colombia
57 D14 Occidental, Cordillera ⛰ W S America
21 Q6 Oceana West Virginia, NE USA
21 Z4 Ocean City Maryland, NE USA
18 J17 Ocean City New Jersey, NE USA
10 K15 Ocean Falls British Columbia, SW Canada
Ocean Island see Kure Atoll
Ocean Island see Banaba
64 J9 Oceanographer Fracture Zone tectonic feature NW Atlantic Ocean
35 U17 Oceanside California, W USA
22 M9 Ocean Springs Mississippi, S USA
Ocean State see Rhode Island
25 O9 O C Fisher Lake ⊠ Texas, SW USA
117 Q10 Ochakiv Rus. Ochakov. Mykolayivs'ka Oblast', S Ukraine
Ochakov see Ochakiv
Ochamchira see Och'amch'ire
137 Q9 Och'amch'ire Rus. Ochamchira. W Georgia
Ochansk see Okhansk
125 T15 Ocher Permskaya Oblast', NW Russian Federation
115 I19 Óchi ▲ Évvoia, C Greece
165 W4 Ochiishi-misaki headland Hokkaidō, NE Japan
23 S9 Ochlockonee River ∽ Florida/Georgia, SE USA
44 K12 Ocho Rios C Jamaica
Ochrida see Ohrid
Ochrida, Lake see Ohrid, Lake
101 J19 Ochsenfurt Bayern, C Germany
23 U7 Ocilla Georgia, SE USA
94 N13 Ockelbo Gävleborg, C Sweden
Ocker see Oker
95 I19 Öckerö Västra Götaland, S Sweden
23 U6 Ocmulgee River ∽ Georgia, SE USA
116 H11 Ocna Mureş Hung. Marosújvár; prev. Ocna Mureşului; prev. Hung. Marosújvárakna. Alba, C Romania
Ocna Mureşului see Ocna Mureş
116 H11 Ocna Sibiului Ger. Salzburg, Hung. Vizakna. Sibiu, C Romania
116 H13 Ocnele Mari prev. Vioara. Vâlcea, S Romania
116 L7 Ocniţa Rus. Oknitsa. N Moldova
23 U4 Oconee, Lake ⊠ Georgia, SE USA
23 U5 Oconee River ∽ Georgia, SE USA
30 M9 Oconomowoc Wisconsin, N USA
30 M6 Oconto Wisconsin, N USA
30 M6 Oconto Falls Wisconsin, N USA
30 M6 Oconto River ∽ Wisconsin, N USA
104 I3 O Corgo Galicia, NW Spain
41 V16 Ocosingo Chiapas, SE Mexico
42 J8 Ocotal Nueva Segovia, NW Nicaragua
42 F6 Ocotepeque ◈ department W Honduras
Ocotepeque see Nueva Ocotepeque
40 L13 Ocotlán Jalisco, SW Mexico
41 R16 Ocotlán var. Ocotlán de Morelos. Oaxaca, SE Mexico
Ocotlán de Morelos see Ocotlán
41 U16 Ocozocuautla Chiapas, SE Mexico
21 Y10 Ocracoke Island island North Carolina, SE USA
102 I3 Octeville Manche, N France
October Revolution Island see Oktyabr'skoy Revolyutsii, Ostrov
43 R17 Ocú Herrera, S Panama
83 Q14 Ocua Cabo Delgado, NE Mozambique
Ocumare see Ocumare del Tuy
54 M5 Ocumare del Tuy var. Ocumare. Miranda, N Venezuela
77 P17 Oda SE Ghana
165 G12 Ōda var. Oda. Shimane, Honshū, SW Japan
92 K3 Ódáðahraun lava flow C Iceland
165 Q7 Ōdate Akita, Honshū, C Japan
165 N14 Odawara Kanagawa, Honshū, S Japan
95 D14 Odda Hordaland, S Norway
95 G22 Odder Århus, C Denmark
Oddur see Xuddur
29 T13 Odebolt Iowa, C USA
104 H14 Odeleite Faro, S Portugal
25 Q4 Odell Texas, SW USA
25 T14 Odem Texas, SW USA
104 F13 Odemira Beja, S Portugal
136 C14 Ödemiş İzmir, SW Turkey
Ödenburg see Sopron
83 I22 Odendaalsrus Free State, C South Africa
Odenpäh see Otepää
95 H23 Odense Fyn, C Denmark
101 H19 Odenwald ⛰ W Germany
84 H10 Oder Cz./Pol. Odra. ∽ C Europe
Oderberg see Bohumín
100 P11 Oderbruch wetland Germany/Poland
Oderhaff see Szczeciński, Zalew
100 O11 Oder-Havel-Kanal canal NE Germany
Oderhellen see Odorheiu Secuiesc
100 P13 Oder-Spree-Kanal canal NE Germany
Odertal see Zdzieszowice
106 I7 Oderzo Veneto, NE Italy
117 P10 Odesa Rus. Odessa. Odes'ka Oblast', SW Ukraine
Odesa see Odes'ka Oblast'
95 L18 Ödeshög Östergötland, S Sweden
117 O9 Odes'ka Oblast' var. Odesa, Rus. Odesskaya Oblast'. ◈ province SW Ukraine
24 M8 Odessa Texas, SW USA
32 K8 Odessa Washington, NW USA
Odessa see Odesa
Odesskaya Oblast' see Odes'ka Oblast'
122 H12 Odesskoye Omskaya Oblast', C Russian Federation
Odessus see Varna
102 F6 Odet ∽ NW France
104 I14 Odiel ∽ SW Spain
76 L14 Odienné NW Ivory Coast
171 O4 Odiongan Tablas Island, C Philippines
116 L12 Odobeşti Vrancea, E Romania
110 H13 Odolanów Ger. Adelnau. Wielkopolskie, C Poland
167 R13 Ŏdôngk Kâmpóng Spoe, S Cambodia
25 N6 O'Donnell Texas, SW USA
98 O7 Odoorn Drenthe, NE Netherlands
Odorhei see Odorheiu Secuiesc
116 J11 Odorheiu Secuiesc Ger. Oderhellen, Hung. Vámosudvarhely; prev. Odorhei; Ger. Hofmarkt. Harghita, C Romania
Odra see Oder
112 J9 Odžaci Ger. Hodschag, Hung. Hodság. Serbia, NW Serbia and Montenegro (Yugo.)
59 N14 Oeiras Piauí, E Brazil
104 F11 Oeiras Lisboa, C Portugal
101 G14 Oelde Nordrhein-Westfalen, W Germany
28 J11 Oelrichs South Dakota, N USA
Oels/Oels in Schlesien see Oleśnica
101 M17 Oelsnitz Sachsen, E Germany
29 X12 Oelwein Iowa, C USA
Oeniadae see Oiniádes
191 N17 Oeno Island atoll Pitcairn Islands, C Pacific Ocean
Oesel see Saaremaa
108 L7 Oetz var. Ötz. Tirol, W Austria
137 P11 Of Trabzon, NE Turkey
30 K15 O'Fallon Illinois, N USA
27 W4 O'Fallon Missouri, C USA
107 N16 Ofanto ∽ S Italy
97 D18 Offaly Ir. Ua Uíbh Fhailí; prev. King's County. cultural region C Ireland
101 H18 Offenbach var. Offenbach am Main. Hessen, W Germany
Offenbach am Main see Offenbach
101 F22 Offenburg Baden-Württemberg, SW Germany
182 C2 Officer Creek seasonal river South Australia
Oficina María Elena see María Elena
Oficina Pedro de Valdivia see Pedro de Valdivia
115 K22 Ofidoússa island Kykládes, Greece, Aegean Sea
Ofiral see Sharm el Sheikh
92 H10 Ofotfjorden fjord N Norway
192 L16 Ofu island Manua Islands, E American Samoa
165 R9 Ōfunato Iwate, Honshū, C Japan
165 P8 Oga Akita, Honshū, C Japan
Ogaadeen see Ogadēn
165 Q9 Ogachi Akita, Honshū, C Japan
165 P9 Ogachi-tōge pass Honshū, C Japan
81 N14 Ogadēn Som. Ogaadeen. plateau Ethiopia/Somalia
165 P8 Oga-hantō peninsula Honshū, C Japan
165 K13 Ōgaki Gifu, Honshū, SW Japan
28 L15 Ogallala Nebraska, C USA
168 M14 Ogan, Air ∽ Sumatera, W Indonesia
165 Y15 Ogasawara-shotō Eng. Bonin Islands. island group SE Japan
14 J9 Ogascanane, Lac ◎ Québec, SE Canada
165 R7 Ogawara-ko ◎ Honshū, C Japan
77 T15 Ogbomosho var. Ogmoboso. Oyo, W Nigeria
Ogbomoso see Ogbomosho
29 U13 Ogden Iowa, C USA
36 L2 Ogden Utah, W USA
18 I6 Ogdensburg New York, NE USA
23 W5 Ogeechee River ∽ Georgia, SE USA
Oger see Ogre
146 F6 Og'iyon Sho'rxogi wetland NW Uzbekistan
165 N10 Ogi Niigata, Sado, C Japan
10 H5 Ogilvie Yukon Territory, NW Canada
10 H4 Ogilvie ∽ Yukon Territory, NW Canada
10 H5 Ogilvie Mountains ⛰ Yukon Territory, NW Canada
Oginskiy Kanal see Ahinski Kanal
146 B10 Oglanly Balkan Welaýaty, W Turkmenistan
23 T5 Oglethorpe Georgia, SE USA
23 T2 Oglethorpe, Mount ▲ Georgia, SE USA
106 F7 Oglio anc. Ollius. ∽ N Italy
103 T8 Ognon ∽ E France
123 R13 Ogodzha Amurskaya Oblast', S Russian Federation
77 W16 Ogoja Cross River, S Nigeria
12 C10 Ogoki ∽ Ontario, S Canada
12 D11 Ogoki Lake ◎ Ontario, C Canada
162 K10 Ögöömör Ömnögovĭ, S Mongolia
79 F19 Ogooué ∽ Congo/Gabon
79 E18 Ogooué-Ivindo off. Province de l'Ogooué-Ivindo, var. L'Ogooué-Ivindo. ◈ province N Gabon
79 E19 Ogooué-Lolo off. Province de l'Ogooué-Lolo, var. L'Ogooué-Lolo. ◈ province C Gabon
79 C19 Ogooué-Maritime off. Province de l'Ogooué-Maritime, var. L'Ogooué-Maritime. ◈ province W Gabon
165 D14 Ogōri Fukuoka, Kyūshū, SW Japan
114 H7 Ogosta ∽ NW Bulgaria
112 Q9 Ogražden Bul. Ograzhden. ⛰ Bulgaria/FYR Macedonia see also Ograzhden
114 G12 Ograzhden Mac. Ogražden. ⛰ Bulgaria/FYR Macedonia see also Ogražden
118 G9 Ogre Ger. Oger. Ogre, C Latvia
118 H9 Ogre ∽ C Latvia
112 C10 Ogulin Karlovac, NW Croatia
77 S16 Ogun ◈ state SW Nigeria
Ogurdzhaly, Ostrov see Ogurjaly Adasy
146 A12 Ogurjaly Adasy Rus. Ogurdzhaly, Ostrov. island W Turkmenistan
77 U16 Ogwashi-Uku Delta, S Nigeria
185 B23 Ohai Southland, South Island, NZ
147 Q10 Ohangaron Rus. Akhangaran. Toshkent Viloyati, E Uzbekistan
147 Q10 Ohangaron Rus. Akhangaran. ∽ E Uzbekistan
83 C16 Ohangwena ◈ district N Namibia
30 M10 O'Hare ✕ (Chicago) Illinois, N USA
165 R6 Ōhata Aomori, Honshū, C Japan
184 L13 Ohau Manawatu-Wanganui, North Island, NZ
185 E20 Ohau, Lake ◎ South Island, NZ
Ohcejohka see Utsjoki
99 J20 Ohey Namur, SE Belgium
191 X15 O'Higgins, Cabo headland Easter Island, Chile, E Pacific Ocean
O'Higgins, Lago see San Martín, Lago
31 S12 Ohio off. State of Ohio; also known as The Buckeye State. ◈ state N USA
(0) L10 Ohio River ∽ N USA
Ohlau see Oława
101 H16 Ohm ∽ C Germany
193 W16 Ohonua 'Eua, E Tonga
23 V5 Ohoopee River ∽ Georgia, SE USA
100 L12 Ohre Ger. Eger. ∽ Czech Republic/Germany
Ohri see Ohrid
113 M20 Ohrid Turk. Ochrida, Ohri. SW FYR Macedonia
113 M20 Ohrid, Lake var. Lake Ochrida, Alb. Liqeni i Ohrit, Mac. Ohridsko Ezero. ◎ Albania/FYR Macedonia
Ohridsko Ezero/Ohrit, Liqeni i see Ohrid, Lake
184 L9 Ohura Manawatu-Wanganui, North Island, NZ
58 J9 Oiapoque Amapá, E Brazil
58 J10 Oiapoque, Rio var. Fleuve l'Oyapok, Oyapock. ∽ Brazil/French Guiana see also Oyapok, Fleuve l'
15 O9 Oies, Île aux island Québec, SE Canada
92 L13 Oijärvi Oulu, C Finland
92 L12 Oikarainen Lappi, N Finland
188 F10 Oikuul Babeldaob, N Palau
18 C13 Oil City Pennsylvania, NE USA
18 C12 Oil Creek ∽ Pennsylvania, NE USA
35 R13 Oildale California, W USA
Oileán Ciarral see Castleisland
Oil Islands see Chagos Archipelago
115 D18 Oiniádes anc. Oeniadae. site of ancient city Dytikí Ellás, W Greece
115 L18 Oinoússes island E Greece
Oirr, Inis see Inisheer
99 J15 Oirschot Noord-Brabant, S Netherlands
103 N4 Oise ◈ department N France
103 P3 Oise ∽ N France
99 J14 Oisterwijk Noord-Brabant, S Netherlands
45 O14 Oistins S Barbados
165 E4 Ōita Ōita, Kyūshū, SW Japan
165 D14 Ōita off. Ōita-ken. ◈ prefecture Kyūshū, SW Japan
115 E17 Oíti ▲ C Greece
165 S4 Oiwake Hokkaidō, NE Japan
35 R14 Ojai California, W USA
94 K13 Öje Dalarna, C Sweden
93 J14 Öjebyn Norrbotten, N Sweden
165 B13 Ojika-jima island SW Japan
40 K5 Ojinaga Chihuahua, N Mexico
40 M11 Ojo Caliente var. Ojocaliente. Zacatecas, C Mexico
40 D6 Ojo de Liebre, Laguna var. Laguna Scammon, Scammon Lagoon. lagoon W Mexico
62 I7 Ojos del Salado, Cerro ▲ W Argentina
105 R7 Ojos Negros Aragón, NE Spain
40 M12 Ojuelos de Jalisco Aguascalientes, C Mexico
127 N4 Oka ∽ W Russian Federation
83 D19 Okahandja Otjozondjupa, C Namibia
184 L9 Okahukura Manawatu-Wanganui, North Island, NZ
184 J3 Okaihau Northland, North Island, NZ
83 D18 Okakarara Otjozondjupa, N Namibia
13 P5 Okak Islands island group Newfoundland and Labrador, E Canada
10 M17 Okanagan ∽ British Columbia, SW Canada
11 N17 Okanagan Lake ◎ British Columbia, SW Canada
Ókanizsa see Kanjiža
83 C16 Okankolo Otjikoto, N Namibia
32 K6 Okanogan River ∽ Washington, NW USA
83 D18 Okaputa Otjozondjupa, N Namibia
149 V9 Okāra Punjab, E Pakistan
26 M10 Okarche Oklahoma, C USA
Okarem see Ekerem
189 X14 Okat Harbor harbour Kosrae, E Micronesia
22 M5 Okatibbee Creek ∽ Mississippi, S USA
83 C17 Okaukuejo Kunene, N Namibia
Okavanggo see Cubango/Okavango
83 E17 Okavango ◈ district NW Namibia
83 G17 Okavango var. Cubango, Kavango, Kavengo, Kubango, Okavanggo, Port. Ocavango. ∽ S Africa see also Cubango
83 G17 Okavango Delta wetland N Botswana
164 M12 Okaya Nagano, Honshū, S Japan
164 H13 Okayama Okayama, Honshū, SW Japan
164 H13 Okayama off. Okayama-ken. ◈ prefecture Honshū, SW Japan
164 L14 Okazaki Aichi, Honshū, C Japan
110 M12 Okęcie ✕ (Warszawa) Mazowieckie, C Poland
23 Y13 Okeechobee Florida, SE USA
23 Y14 Okeechobee, Lake ◎ Florida, SE USA
26 M9 Okeene Oklahoma, C USA
23 V8 Okefenokee Swamp wetland Georgia, SE USA
97 J24 Okehampton SW England, UK
27 P10 Okemah Oklahoma, C USA
77 U16 Okene Kogi, S Nigeria
100 K13 Oker var. Ocker. ∽ NW Germany
101 J14 Oker-Stausee ◎ C Germany
123 T12 Okha Ostrov Sakhalin, Sakhalinskaya Oblast', SE Russian Federation
125 U15 Okhansk var. Ochansk. Permskaya Oblast', NW Russian Federation
123 S10 Okhotsk Khabarovskiy Kray, E Russian Federation
192 J2 Okhotsk, Sea of sea NW Pacific Ocean
117 T4 Okhtyrka Rus. Akhtyrka. Sums'ka Oblast', NE Ukraine
83 E23 Okiep Northern Cape, W South Africa
Oki-guntō see Oki-shotō
164 H11 Oki-kaikyō strait SW Japan
165 P16 Okinawa Okinawa, SW Japan
165 S16 Okinawa off. Okinawa-ken. ◈ prefecture Okinawa, SW Japan
165 S16 Okinawa island SW Japan
165 U16 Okinoerabu-jima island Nansei-shotō, SW Japan
164 F15 Okino-shima island SW Japan
164 H11 Oki-shotō var. Oki-guntō. island group SW Japan
77 T16 Okitipupa Ondo, SW Nigeria
166 L8 Okkan Pegu, SW Myanmar
27 N10 Oklahoma off. State of Oklahoma; also known as The Sooner State. ◈ state C USA
27 N11 Oklahoma City state capital Oklahoma, C USA
25 Q4 Oklaunion Texas, SW USA
23 W10 Oklawaha River ∽ Florida, SE USA
27 P10 Okmulgee Oklahoma, C USA
Oknitsa see Ocniţa
22 M3 Okolona Mississippi, S USA
165 U2 Okoppe Hokkaidō, NE Japan
11 Q16 Okotoks Alberta, SW Canada
80 H6 Oko, Wadi ∽ NE Sudan
79 G19 Okoyo Cuvette, W Congo
77 S15 Okpara ∽ Benin/Nigeria
92 J8 Øksfjord Finnmark, N Norway
125 R4 Oksino Nenetskiy Avtonomnyy Okrug, NW Russian Federation
92 G13 Oksskolten ▲ C Norway
Oksu see Oqsu
144 M8 Oktaybr'skiy Kostanay, N Kazakhstan
186 B7 Ok Tedi Western, W PNG
Oktemberyan see Armavir
166 M7 Oktwin Pegu, C Myanmar
127 R6 Oktyabr'sk Samarskaya Oblast', W Russian Federation
Oktyabr'sk see Kandyagash
125 N12 Oktyabr'skiy Arkhangel'skaya Oblast', NW Russian Federation
122 E10 Oktyabr'skiy Kamchatskaya Oblast', E Russian Federation
127 T5 Oktyabr'skiy Respublika Bashkortostan, W Russian Federation
127 O11 Oktyabr'skiy Volgogradskaya Oblast', SW Russian Federation
Oktyabr'skiy see Aktsyabrski
127 V7 Oktyabr'skoye Orenburgskaya Oblast', W Russian Federation
122 M5 Oktyabr'skoy Revolyutsii, Ostrov Eng. October Revolution Island. island Severnaya Zemlya, N Russian Federation
164 C15 Ōkuchi var. Ōkuti. Kagoshima, Kyūshū, SW Japan
Okulovka see Uglovka
165 Q4 Okushiri-tō var. Okusiri Tô. island NE Japan
Okusiri Tô see Okushiri-tō
77 S15 Okuta Kwara, W Nigeria
Ōkuti see Ōkuchi
83 F19 Okwa var. Chapman's. ∽ Botswana/Namibia
123 T10 Ola Magadanskaya Oblast', E Russian Federation
27 T11 Ola Arkansas, C USA
Ola see Ala
35 T11 Olacha Peak ▲ California, W USA
92 J1 Ólafsfjördhur Nordhurland Eystra, N Iceland
92 H3 Ólafsvík Vesturland, W Iceland
Oláhbrettye see Bretea-Română
Oláhszentgyörgy see Sângeorz-Băi
Oláh-Toplicza see Toplița
35 T11 Olancha California, W USA
42 J5 Olanchito Yoro, C Honduras
42 J6 Olancho ◈ department E Honduras
95 O20 Öland island S Sweden
95 O19 Ölands norra udde headland S Sweden
95 N22 Ölands södra udde headland S Sweden
182 K7 Olary South Australia
27 R4 Olathe Kansas, C USA
61 C22 Olavarría Buenos Aires, E Argentina
92 O2 Olav V Land physical region C Svalbard
111 H14 Oława Ger. Ohlau. Dolnośląskie, SW Poland
107 D17 Olbia prev. Terranova Pausania. Sardegna, Italy, C Mediterranean Sea
44 G5 Old Bahama Channel channel Bahamas/Cuba
Old Bay State/Old Colony State see Massachusetts
10 H2 Old Crow Yukon Territory, NW Canada
Old Dominion see Virginia
Oldeberkeap see Oldeberkoop
98 M7 Oldeberkoop Fris. Oldeberkeap. Friesland, N Netherlands
98 L10 Oldebroek Gelderland, E Netherlands
98 L8 Oldemarkt Overijssel, N Netherlands
94 E11 Olden Sogn og Fjordane, C Norway
100 G10 Oldenburg Niedersachsen, NW Germany
100 K8 Oldenburg var. Oldenburg in Holstein. Schleswig-Holstein, N Germany
Oldenburg in Holstein see Oldenburg
98 P10 Oldenzaal Overijssel, E Netherlands
Olderfjord see Leaibevuotna
18 J8 Old Forge New York, NE USA
Old Goa see Goa
97 L17 Oldham NW England, UK
39 Q14 Old Harbor Kodiak Island, Alaska, USA
44 J13 Old Harbour C Jamaica

◆ Country ● Country Capital ◇ Dependent Territory ○ Dependent Territory Capital ◈ Administrative Region ✕ International Airport ▲ Mountain ⛰ Mountain Range ⚠ Volcano ∽ River ◎ Lake ⊠ Reservoir

97 C22 **Old Head of Kinsale** *Ir.* An Seancheann. *headland* SW Ireland
20 J8 **Old Hickory Lake** ▣ Tennessee, S USA
Old Line State *see* Maryland
Old North State *see* North Carolina
81 I17 **Ol Doinyo Lengeyo** ▲ C Kenya
11 Q16 **Olds** Alberta, SW Canada
19 O7 **Old Speck Mountain** ▲ Maine, NE USA
19 S6 **Old Town** Maine, NE USA
11 T17 **Old Wives Lake** ◎ Saskatchewan, S Canada
162 J7 **Öldziyt** Arhangay, C Mongolia
163 N10 **Öldziyt** Dornogovĭ, SE Mongolia
188 H6 **Oleai** *var.* San Jose. Saipan, S Northern Mariana Islands
18 E11 **Olean** New York, NE USA
110 O7 **Olecko** *Ger.* Treuburg. Warmińsko-Mazurskie, NE Poland
106 C7 **Oleggio** Piemonte, NE Italy
123 P11 **Olëkma** Amurskaya Oblast', SE Russian Federation
123 P12 **Olëkma** ↝ C Russian Federation
123 P11 **Olëkminsk** Respublika Sakha (Yakutiya), NE Russian Federation
117 W7 **Oleksandrivka** Donets'ka Oblast', E Ukraine
117 R7 **Oleksandrivka** *Rus.* Aleksandrovka. Kirovohrads'ka Oblast', C Ukraine
117 Q9 **Oleksandrivka** Mykolayivs'ka Oblast', S Ukraine
117 S7 **Oleksandriya** *Rus.* Aleksandriya. Kirovohrads'ka Oblast', C Ukraine
93 B20 **Ølen** Hordaland, S Norway
124 J4 **Olenegorsk** Murmanskaya Oblast', NW Russian Federation
123 N9 **Olenëk** Respublika Sakha (Yakutiya), NE Russian Federation
123 N9 **Olenëk** ↝ NE Russian Federation
123 O7 **Olenëkskiy Zaliv** *bay* N Russian Federation
124 K6 **Olenitsa** Murmanskaya Oblast', NW Russian Federation
102 I11 **Oléron, Île d'** *island* W France
111 H14 **Oleśnica** *Ger.* Oels, Oels in Schlesien. Dolnośląskie, SW Poland
111 I15 **Olesno** *Ger.* Rosenberg. Opolskie, S Poland
116 M3 **Olevs'k** *Rus.* Olevsk. Zhytomyrs'ka Oblast', N Ukraine
123 S15 **Ol'ga** Primorskiy Kray, SE Russian Federation
Olga, Mount *see* Kata Tjuta
92 P2 **Olgastretet** *strait* E Svalbard
162 D5 **Ölgiy** Bayan-Ölgiy, W Mongolia
95 F23 **Ølgod** Ribe, W Denmark
104 H14 **Olhão** Faro, S Portugal
93 L14 **Olhava** Oulu, C Finland
112 B12 **Olib** *It.* Ulbo. *island* W Croatia
83 B16 **Olifa** Kunene, NW Namibia
83 E20 **Olifants** *var.* Elephant River. ↝ E Namibia
83 E25 **Olifants** *var.* Elefantes. ↝ SW South Africa
83 G22 **Olifantshoek** Northern Cape, N South Africa
188 L15 **Olimarao Atoll** *atoll* Caroline Islands, C Micronesia
Ólimbos *see* Ólympos
Olimpo *see* Fuerte Olimpo
59 Q15 **Olinda** Pernambuco, E Brazil
Olinthos *see* Ólynthos
83 I20 **Oliphants Drift** Kgatleng, SE Botswana
Olisipo *see* Lisboa
Olita *see* Alytus
105 Q4 **Olite** Navarra, N Spain
62 K10 **Oliva** Córdoba, C Argentina
105 T11 **Oliva** País Valenciano, E Spain
104 I12 **Oliva de la Frontera** Extremadura, W Spain
Olivares *see* Olivares de Júcar
62 H9 **Olivares, Cerro de** ▲ N Chile
105 P9 **Olivares de Júcar** *var.* Olivares. Castilla-La Mancha, C Spain
22 L1 **Olive Branch** Mississippi, S USA
21 O5 **Olive Hill** Kentucky, S USA
35 O6 **Olivehurst** California, W USA
104 G7 **Oliveira de Azeméis** Aveiro, N Portugal
104 I11 **Olivenza** Extremadura, W Spain
11 N17 **Oliver** British Columbia, SW Canada
103 N7 **Olivet** Loiret, C France
29 Q12 **Olivet** South Dakota, N USA
29 T9 **Olivia** Minnesota, N USA
185 C20 **Olivine Range** ▲ South Island, NZ
108 H10 **Olivone** Ticino, S Switzerland
Ölkeyek *see* Ul'kayak
127 O9 **Ol'khovka** Volgogradskaya Oblast', SW Russian Federation
111 K16 **Olkusz** Małopolskie, S Poland
22 I6 **Olla** Louisiana, S USA
62 I4 **Ollagüe, Volcán** *var.* Oyahue, Volcán Oyahue. ▲ N Chile
189 U13 **Ollan** *island* Chuuk, C Micronesia
188 F7 **Ollei** Babeldaob, N Palau
Ollius *see* Oglio
108 C10 **Ollon** Vaud, W Switzerland
147 Q10 **Olmaliq** *Rus.* Almalyk. Toshkent Viloyati, E Uzbekistan
104 M6 **Olmedo** Castilla-León, N Spain
56 B10 **Olmos** Lambayeque, W Peru
Olmütz *see* Olomouc
30 M15 **Olney** Illinois, N USA
25 R5 **Olney** Texas, SW USA
95 L22 **Olofström** Blekinge, S Sweden
187 N9 **Olomburi** Malaita, N Solomon Islands
111 H17 **Olomouc** *Ger.* Olmütz, *Pol.* Ołomuniec. Olomoucký Kraj, E Czech Republic
111 H18 **Olomoucký Kraj** ◈ region E Czech Republic
Ołomuniec *see* Olomouc
122 D7 **Olonets** Respublika Kareliya, NW Russian Federation
171 N3 **Olongapo** *off.* Olongapo City. Luzon, N Philippines
102 J16 **Oloron-Ste-Marie** Pyrénées-Atlantiques, SW France
192 L16 **Olosega** *island* Manua Islands, E American Samoa
105 W4 **Olot** Cataluña, NE Spain
146 K12 **Olot** *Rus.* Alat. Buxoro Viloyati, C Uzbekistan
112 I12 **Olovo** Federacija Bosna I Hercegovina, E Bosnia and Herzegovina
123 O14 **Olovyannaya** Chitinskaya Oblast', S Russian Federation
123 T7 **Oloy** ↝ NE Russian Federation
101 F16 **Olpe** Nordrhein-Westfalen, W Germany
109 N8 **Olperer** ▲ SW Austria
Olshanka *see* Vil'shanka
Ol'shany *see* Al'shany
Olsnitz *see* Murska Sobota
98 M10 **Olst** Overijssel, E Netherlands
110 L8 **Olsztyn** *Ger.* Allenstein. Warmińsko-Mazurskie, NE Poland.
110 L8 **Olsztynek** *Ger.* Hohenstein in Ostpreussen. Warmińsko-Mazurskie, NE Poland,
116 I14 **Olt** ◈ *county* SW Romania
116 I14 **Olt** *var.* Oltul, *Ger.* Alt. ↝ S Romania
108 E7 **Olten** Solothurn, NW Switzerland
116 K14 **Oltenița** *prev. Eng.* Oltenitsa, *anc.* Constantiola. Călărași, SE Romania
Oltenitsa *see* Oltenița
116 H14 **Olteț** ↝ S Romania
24 M4 **Olton** Texas, SW USA
137 R12 **Oltu** Erzurum, NE Turkey
Oltul *see* Olt
146 G7 **Oltynko'l** Qoraqalpog'iston Respublikasi, NW Uzbekistan
161 S15 **Oluan Pi** *Eng.* Cape Olwanpi. *headland* S Taiwan
Ólubló *see* Stará Ľubovňa
137 R11 **Olur** Erzurum, NE Turkey
104 L15 **Olvera** Andalucía, S Spain
Ol'viopol' *see* Pervomays'k
Olwanpi, Cape *see* Oluan Pi
32 G9 **Olympia** *state capital* Washington, NW USA
115 D20 **Olympía** Dytikí Ellás, S Greece
182 H5 **Olympic Dam** South Australia
32 F7 **Olympic Mountains** ▲ Washington, NW USA
121 O3 **Ólympos** *var.* Troodos, *Eng.* Mount Olympus. ▲ C Cyprus
115 F15 **Ólympos** *var.* Ólimbos, *Eng.* Mount Olympus. ▲ N Greece
115 L17 **Ólympos** ▲ Lésvos, E Greece
16 C5 **Olympus, Mount** ▲ Washington, NW USA
Olympus, Mount *see* Ólympos
115 G14 **Ólynthos** *var.* Olinthos; *anc.* Olynthus. *site of ancient city* Kentrikí Makedonía, N Greece
Olynthus *see* Ólynthos
117 Q3 **Olyshivka** Chernihivs'ka Oblast', N Ukraine
123 W8 **Olyutorskiy, Mys** *headland* E Russian Federation
123 V8 **Olyutorskiy Zaliv** *bay* E Russian Federation
186 M10 **Om** ↝ W PNG
131 S6 **Om'** ↝ N Russian Federation
158 I13 **Oma** Xizang Zizhiqu, W China
165 R6 **Ōma** Aomori, Honshū, C Japan
127 P6 **Oma** ↝ NW Russian Federation
164 M12 **Ōmachi** *var.* Ōmati. Nagano,Honshū, S Japan
165 Q8 **Ōmagari** Akita, Honshū, C Japan
97 E15 **Omagh** *Ir.* An Ómaigh. W Northern Ireland, UK
29 S15 **Omaha** Nebraska, C USA
83 E19 **Omaheke** ◈ *district* W Namibia
141 W10 **Oman** *off.* Sultanate of Oman, *Ar.* Salṭanat 'Umān; *prev.* Muscat and Oman. ◆ *monarchy* SW Asia
131 O10 **Oman Basin** *var.* Bassin d'Oman. *undersea feature* N Indian Ocean
Oman, Bassin d' *see* Oman Basin
131 N10 **Oman, Gulf of** *Ar.* Khalīj 'Umān. *gulf* N Arabian Sea
184 J3 **Omapere** Northland, North Island, NZ
185 E20 **Omarama** Canterbury, South Island, NZ
112 F11 **Omarska** Republika Srpska, NW Bosnia and Herzegovina
83 C18 **Omaruru** Erongo, NW Namibia
83 C19 **Omaruru** ↝ W Namibia
83 E17 **Omatako** ↝ NE Namibia
Ōmati *see* Ōmachi
83 E18 **Omawewozonyanda** Omaheke, E Namibia
165 R6 **Ōma-zaki** *headland* Honshū, C Japan
Ombai *see* Alor, Pulau
83 C16 **Ombalantu** Omusati, N Namibia
79 H15 **Ombella-Mpoko** ◈ *prefecture* S Central African Republic
Ombetsu *see* Onbetsu
83 B17 **Ombombo** Kunene, NW Namibia
79 D19 **Omboué** Ogooué-Maritime, W Gabon
106 G13 **Ombrone** ↝ C Italy
80 F9 **Omdurman** *var.* Umm Durmān. Khartoum, C Sudan
165 N13 **Ōme** Tōkyō, Honshū, S Japan
106 C6 **Omegna** Piemonte, NE Italy
183 P12 **Omeo** Victoria, SE Australia
138 F11 **'Omer** Southern, C Israel
41 P16 **Ometepec** Guerrero, S Mexico
42 K11 **Ometepe, Isla de** *island* S Nicaragua
Om Hajer *see* Om Hajer
80 I10 **Om Hajer** *var.* Om Hager. SW Eritrea
165 J13 **Ōmi-Hachiman** *var.* Ōmihachiman. Shiga, Honshū, SW Japan
10 L12 **Omineca Mountains** ▲ British Columbia, W Canada
113 F14 **Omiš** *It.* Almissa. Split-Dalmacija, S Croatia
112 B10 **Omišalj** Primorje-Gorski Kotar, NW Croatia
83 D19 **Omitara** Khomas, C Namibia
41 O16 **Omitlán, Río** ↝ S Mexico
39 X14 **Ommaney, Cape** *headland* Baranof Island, Alaska, USA
98 N9 **Ommen** Overijssel, E Netherlands
162 K11 **Ömnögovĭ** ◈ *province* S Mongolia
191 X7 **Omoa** Fatu Hira, NE French Polynesia
Omo Botego *see* Omo Wenz
Ómoldova *see* Moldova Veche
123 T7 **Omolon** Chukotskiy Avtonomnyy Okrug, NE Russian Federation
123 T7 **Omolon** ↝ NE Russian Federation
123 Q8 **Omoloy** ↝ NE Russian Federation
165 P8 **Omono-gawa** ↝ Honshū, C Japan
81 I14 **Omo Wenz** *var.* Omo Botego. ↝ Ethiopia/Kenya
122 H12 **Omsk** Omskaya Oblast', C Russian Federation
122 H11 **Omskaya Oblast'** ◈ *province* C Russian Federation
165 U2 **Ōmu** Hokkaidō, NE Japan
110 M9 **Omulew** ↝ NE Poland
116 J12 **Omul, Vârful** *prev.* Vîrful Omu. ▲ C Romania
83 D16 **Omundaungilo** Ohangwena, N Namibia
164 C14 **Ōmura** Nagasaki, Kyūshū, SW Japan
83 B17 **Omusati** ◈ *district* N Namibia
164 C14 **Ōmuta** Fukuoka, Kyūshū, SW Japan
125 S14 **Omutninsk** Kirovskaya Oblast', NW Russian Federation
Omu, Vîrful *see* Omul, Vârful
29 V7 **Onamia** Minnesota, N USA
21 Y5 **Onancock** Virginia, NE USA
14 E10 **Onaping Lake** ◎ Ontario, S Canada
30 M12 **Onarga** Illinois, N USA
15 R6 **Onatchiway, Lac** ◎ Québec, SE Canada
29 S14 **Onawa** Iowa, C USA
165 U5 **Onbetsu** *var.* Ombetsu. Hokkaidō, NE Japan
83 B16 **Oncócua** Cunene, SW Angola
105 S9 **Onda** País Valenciano, E Spain
111 N18 **Ondava** ↝ NE Slovakia
Ondjiva *see* N'Giva
77 T16 **Ondo** Ondo, SW Nigeria
77 T16 **Ondo** ◈ *state* SW Nigeria
163 N8 **Öndörhaan** *var.* Undur Khan; *prev.* Tsetsen Khan. Hentiy, E Mongolia
83 D18 **Ondundazongonda** Otjozondjupa, N Namibia
151 K21 **One and Half Degree Channel** *channel* S Maldives
187 Z15 **Oneata** *island* Lau Group, E Fiji
124 L9 **Onega** Arkhangel'skaya Oblast', NW Russian Federation
122 E7 **Onega** ↝ NW Russian Federation
Onega Bay *see* Onezhskaya Guba
Onega, Lake *see* Onezhskoye Ozero
18 I10 **Oneida** New York, NE USA
20 M8 **Oneida** Tennessee, S USA
18 H9 **Oneida Lake** ◎ New York, NE USA
29 P13 **O'Neill** Nebraska, C USA
123 V12 **Onekotan, Ostrov** *island* Kuril'skiye Ostrova, SE Russian Federation
23 P3 **Oneonta** Alabama, S USA
18 J11 **Oneonta** New York, NE USA
190 I16 **Oneroa** *island* S Cook Islands
116 K11 **Onești** *Hung.* Onyest; *prev.* Gheorghe Gheorghiu-Dej. Bacău, E Romania
193 V15 **Onevai** *island* Tongatapu Group, S Tonga
108 A11 **Onex** Genève, SW Switzerland
126 K8 **Onezhskaya Guba** *Eng.* Onega Bay. *bay* NW Russian Federation
122 D7 **Onezhskoye Ozero** *Eng.* Lake Onega. ◎ NW Russian Federation
83 C16 **Ongandjera** Omusati, N Namibia
184 N12 **Ongaonga** Hawke's Bay, North Island, NZ
162 K9 **Ongi** Dundgovĭ, C Mongolia
162 J8 **Ongi** Övörhangay, C Mongolia
163 W14 **Ongjin** SW North Korea
155 J17 **Ongole** Andhra Pradesh, E India
162 K8 **Ongon** Övörhangay, C Mongolia
Ongtüstik Qazaqstan Oblysy *see* Yuzhnyy Kazakhstan
99 I21 **Onhaye** Namur, S Belgium
166 M8 **Onhne** Pegu, SW Myanmar
137 S9 **Oni** N Georgia
29 N9 **Onida** South Dakota, N USA
164 F15 **Onigajō-yama** ▲ Shikoku, SW Japan
172 H7 **Onilahy** ↝ S Madagascar
77 U16 **Onitsha** Anambra, S Nigeria
164 I13 **Ono** Hyōgo, Honshū, SW Japan
187 K15 **Ono** *island* SW Fiji
164 K12 **Ōno** Fukui, Honshū, SW Japan
164 E13 **Onoda** Yamaguchi, Honshū, SW Japan
187 Z16 **Ono-i-lau** *island* SE Fiji
164 D13 **Ōnojō** *var.* Ōnozyô. Fukuoka, Kyūshū, SW Japan
Onomiti *see* Onomichi
163 O7 **Onon Gol** ↝ N Mongolia
Ononte *see* Orontes
55 N6 **Onoto** Anzoátegui, NE Venezuela
191 O3 **Onotoa** *prev.* Clerk Island. *atoll* Tungaru, W Kiribati
Ōnozyô *see* Ōnojō
95 I19 **Onsala** Halland, S Sweden
83 E23 **Onseepkans** Northern Cape, W South Africa
104 F4 **Ons, Illa de** *island* NW Spain
180 H7 **Onslow** Western Australia
21 W11 **Onslow Bay** *bay* North Carolina, E USA
98 P6 **Onstwedde** Groningen, NE Netherlands
164 C16 **On-take** ▲ Kyūshū, SW Japan
35 T15 **Ontario** California, W USA
32 M13 **Ontario** Oregon, NW USA
12 D10 **Ontario** ◈ *province* S Canada
9 P14 **Ontario, Lake** ◎ Canada/USA
(0) L9 **Ontario Peninsula** *peninsula* Canada/USA
Onteniente *see* Ontinyent
105 S11 **Ontinyent** *var.* Onteniente. País Valenciano, E Spain
93 N15 **Ontojärvi** ◎ E Finland
30 L3 **Ontonagon** Michigan, N USA
30 L3 **Ontonagon River** ↝ Michigan, N USA
186 M7 **Ontong Java Atoll** *prev.* Lord Howe Island. *atoll* N Solomon Islands
175 N5 **Ontong Java Rise** *undersea feature* W Pacific Ocean
Onuba *see* Huelva
55 W9 **Onverwacht** Para, N Suriname
Onyest *see* Onești
182 J7 **Oodla Wirra** South Australia
182 F2 **Oodnadatta** South Australia
182 C5 **Ooldea** South Australia
27 Q8 **Oologah Lake** ▣ Oklahoma, C USA
Oos-Kaap *see* Eastern Cape
Oos-Londen *see* East London
99 E17 **Oostakker** Oost-Vlaanderen, NW Belgium
99 D15 **Oostburg** Zeeland, SW Netherlands
98 K9 **Oostelijk-Flevoland** *polder* C Netherlands
99 B16 **Oostende** *Eng.* Ostend, *Fr.* Ostende. West-Vlaanderen, NW Belgium
99 B16 **Oostende** ✕ West-Vlaanderen, NW Belgium
98 L12 **Oosterbeek** Gelderland, SE Netherlands
99 I14 **Oosterhout** Noord-Brabant, S Netherlands
98 O5 **Oostermoers Vaart** *var.* Hunze. ↝ NE Netherlands
99 F14 **Oosterschelde** *Eng.* Eastern Scheldt. *inlet* SW Netherlands
99 E14 **Oosterscheldedam** *dam* SW Netherlands
98 M7 **Oosterwolde** *Fris.* Easterwâlde. Friesland, N Netherlands
98 I9 **Oosthuizen** Noord-Holland, NW Netherlands
99 H16 **Oostmalle** Antwerpen, N Belgium
Oos-Transvaal *see* Mpumalanga
99 E15 **Oost-Souburg** Zeeland, SW Netherlands
99 E17 **Oost-Vlaanderen** *Eng.* East Flanders. ◈ *province* NW Belgium
98 J5 **Oost-Vlieland** Friesland, N Netherlands
98 F12 **Oostvoorne** Zuid-Holland, SW Netherlands
Ootacamund *see* Udagamandalam
98 O10 **Ootmarsum** Overijssel, E Netherlands
10 K14 **Ootsa Lake** ▣ British Columbia, SW Canada
114 L8 **Opaka** Tŭrgovishte, N Bulgaria
79 M18 **Opala** Orientale, C Dem. Rep. Congo
125 Q13 **Oparino** Kirovskaya Oblast', NW Russian Federation
14 H8 **Opasatica, Lac** ◎ Québec, SE Canada
112 B9 **Opatija** *It.* Abbazia. Primorje-Gorski Kotar, NW Croatia
111 N15 **Opatów** Świętokrzyskie, C Poland
111 I17 **Opava** *Ger.* Troppau. Moravskoslezský Kraj, E Czech Republic
111 H16 **Opava** *Ger.* Oppa. ↝ NE Czech Republic
Ópazova *see* Stara Pazova
Ópécska *see* Pecica
14 E8 **Opeepeesway Lake** ◎ Ontario, S Canada
23 R5 **Opelika** Alabama, S USA
22 I8 **Opelousas** Louisiana, S USA
186 G6 **Open Bay** *bay* New Britain, E PNG
14 I12 **Opeongo Lake** ◎ Ontario, SE Canada
99 K17 **Opglabbeek** Limburg, NE Belgium
33 W6 **Opheim** Montana, NW USA
39 P10 **Ophir** Alaska, USA
Ophiusa *see* Formentera
79 N18 **Opienge** Orientale, E Dem. Rep. Congo
185 G20 **Opihi** ↝ South Island, NZ
12 J9 **Opinaca** ↝ Québec, C Canada
12 J10 **Opinaca, Réservoir** ▣ Québec, E Canada
117 T5 **Opishnya** *Rus.* Oposhnya. Poltavs'ka Oblast', NE Ukraine
98 I8 **Opmeer** Noord-Holland, NW Netherlands
77 V17 **Opobo** Akwa Ibom, S Nigeria
124 F16 **Opochka** Pskovskaya Oblast', W Russian Federation
110 L13 **Opoczno** Łodzkie, C Poland
111 I15 **Opole** *Ger.* Oppeln. Opolskie, S Poland
111 H15 **Opolskie** ◈ *province* S Poland
Opornyy *see* Borankul
104 G4 **O Porriño** *var.* Porriño. Galicia, NW Spain
Oporto *see* Porto
Oposhnya *see* Opishnya
184 P8 **Opotiki** Bay of Plenty, North Island, NZ
23 Q7 **Opp** Alabama, S USA
Oppa *see* Opava
94 G9 **Oppdal** Sør-Trøndelag, S Norway
Oppeln *see* Opole
107 N23 **Oppido Mamertina** Calabria, SW Italy
Oppidum Ubiorum *see* Köln
94 F12 **Oppland** ◈ *county* S Norway
118 J12 **Opsa** *Rus.* Opsa. Vitsyebskaya Voblasts', NW Belarus
26 I8 **Optima Lake** ▣ Oklahoma, C USA
184 J11 **Opunake** Taranaki, North Island, NZ
191 N6 **Opunohu, Baie d'** *bay* Moorea, W French Polynesia
83 B17 **Opuwo** Kunene, NW Namibia
146 H6 **Oqqal'a** *var.* Akkala, *Rus.* Karakala. Qoraqalpog'iston Respublikasi, NW Uzbekistan
147 V13 **Oqsu** *Rus.* Oksu. ↝ SE Tajikistan
147 P14 **Oqtogh, Qatorkŭhi** *Rus.* Khrebet Aktau. ▲ SW Tajikistan
146 M11 **Oqtosh** *Rus.* Aktash. Samarqand Viloyati, C Uzbekistan
147 N11 **Oqtov Tizmasi** *Rus.* Khrebet Aktau. ▲ C Uzbekistan
30 J12 **Oquawka** Illinois, N USA
144 J10 **Or'** *Kaz.* Or. ↝ Kazakhstan/Russian Federation
36 M15 **Oracle** Arizona, SW USA
147 N13 **O'radaryo** *Rus.* Uradar'ya. ↝ S Uzbekistan
116 F9 **Oradea** *prev.* Oradea Mare, *Ger.* Grosswardein, *Hung.* Nagyvárad. Bihor, NW Romania
Oradea Mare *see* Oradea
113 M17 **Orahovac** *Alb.* Rahovec. Serbia, S Serbia and Montenegro (Yugo.)
112 H9 **Orahovica** Virovitica-Podravina, NE Croatia
152 K13 **Orai** Uttar Pradesh, N India
92 K12 **Orajärvi** Lappi, NW Finland
Or Akiva *see* Or 'Aqiva
Oral *see* Ural'sk
74 I5 **Oran** *var.* Ouahran, Wahran. NW Algeria
183 R8 **Orange** New South Wales, SE Australia
103 R14 **Orange** *anc.* Arausio. Vaucluse, SE France
25 Y10 **Orange** Texas, SW USA
21 V5 **Orange** Virginia, NE USA
21 R13 **Orangeburg** South Carolina, SE USA
58 J9 **Orange, Cabo** *headland* NE Brazil
29 S12 **Orange City** Iowa, C USA
Orange Cone *see* Orange Fan
172 J10 **Orange Fan** *var.* Orange Cone. *undersea feature* SW Indian Ocean
Orange Free State *see* Free State
25 S14 **Orange Grove** Texas, SW USA
18 K13 **Orange Lake** New York, NE USA
23 V10 **Orange Lake** ◎ Florida, SE USA
Orange Mouth/Orangemund *see* Oranjemund
23 W9 **Orange Park** Florida, SE USA
83 E23 **Orange River** *Afr.* Oranjerivier. ↝ S Africa
14 G15 **Orangeville** Ontario, S Canada
36 M5 **Orangeville** Utah, W USA
42 G1 **Orange Walk** Orange Walk, N Belize
42 F1 **Orange Walk** ◈ *district* NW Belize
100 N11 **Oranienburg** Brandenburg, NE Germany
98 O7 **Oranjekanaal** *canal* NE Netherlands
83 D23 **Oranjemund** *var.* Orangemund; *prev.* Orange Mouth. Karas, SW Namibia
Oranjerivier *see* Orange River
45 N16 **Oranjestad** ○ (Aruba) W Aruba
Oranje Vrystaat *see* Free State
Orany *see* Varėna
83 H18 **Orapa** Central, C Botswana
138 F9 **Or 'Aqiva** *var.* Or Akiva. Haifa, W Israel
112 I10 **Orašje** Federacija Bosna I Hercegovina, N Bosnia and Herzegovina
116 G11 **Orăștie** *Ger.* Broos, *Hung.* Szászváros. Hunedoara, W Romania
Orașul Stalin *see* Brașov
111 K18 **Orava** *Hung.* Árva, *Pol.* Orawa. ↝ N Slovakia
Oravainen *see* Oravais
93 K16 **Oravais** *Fin.* Oravainen. Länsi-Suomi, W Finland
Oravicabánya *see* Oravița
116 F13 **Oravița** *Ger.* Orawitza, *Hung.* Oravicabánya. Caraș-Severin, SW Romania
Orawa *see* Orava
185 B24 **Orawia** Southland, South Island, NZ
Orawitza *see* Oravița
103 P16 **Orb** ↝ S France
106 C9 **Orba** ↝ NW Italy
158 H12 **Orba Co** ◎ W China
108 B9 **Orbe** Vaud, W Switzerland
107 G14 **Orbetello** Toscana, C Italy
104 K3 **Orbigo** ↝ NW Spain
183 Q12 **Orbost** Victoria, SE Australia
95 O14 **Örbyhus** Uppsala, C Sweden
194 I1 **Orcadas** *Argentinian research station* South Orkney Islands, Antarctica
105 P12 **Orcera** Andalucía, S Spain
33 P9 **Orchard Homes** Montana, NW USA
37 P5 **Orchard Mesa** Colorado, C USA
18 D10 **Orchard Park** New York, NE USA
Orchid Island *see* Lan Yü
115 G18 **Orchómenos** *var.* Orhomenos, Orkhómenos; *prev.* Skripón, *anc.* Orchomenus. Stereá Ellás, C Greece
Orchomenus *see* Orchómenos
106 B7 **Orco** ↝ NW Italy
103 R8 **Or, Côte d'** *physical region* C France
29 O14 **Ord** Nebraska, C USA
Ordat' *see* Ordats'
119 O15 **Ordats'** *Rus.* Ordat'. Mahilyowskaya Voblasts', E Belarus
36 K8 **Orderville** Utah, W USA
104 H2 **Ordes** Galicia, NW Spain
35 V14 **Ord Mountain** ▲ California, W USA
163 N14 **Ordos** *prev.* Dongsheng. Nei Mongol Zizhiqu, N China
Ordos Desert *see* Mu Us Shadi
188 B16 **Ordot** C Guam
137 N11 **Ordu** *anc.* Cotyora. Ordu, N Turkey
136 M11 **Ordu** ◈ *province* N Turkey
137 V14 **Ordubad** SW Azerbaijan
105 O3 **Orduña** País Vasco, N Spain
37 U6 **Ordway** Colorado, C USA
117 T9 **Ordzhonikidze** Dnipropetrovs'ka Oblast', E Ukraine
Ordzhonikidze *see* Denisovka, Kazakhstan
Ordzhonikidze *see* Vladikavkaz, Russian Federation
Ordzhonikidze *see* Yenakiyeve, Ukraine
Ordzhonikidzeabad *see* Kofarnihon
55 U9 **Orealla** E Guyana
113 G15 **Orebić** *It.* Sabbioncello. Dubrovnik-Neretva, S Croatia
95 M16 **Örebro** Örebro, C Sweden
95 L16 **Örebro** ◈ *county* C Sweden
25 W6 **Ore City** Texas, SW USA
30 L10 **Oregon** Illinois, N USA
27 Q2 **Oregon** Missouri, C USA
31 R11 **Oregon** Ohio, N USA
32 H13 **Oregon** *off.* State of Oregon; also known as Beaver State, Sunset State, Valentine State, Webfoot State. ◈ *state* NW USA
32 G11 **Oregon City** Oregon, NW USA
95 P14 **Öregrund** Uppsala, C Sweden
Orekhov *see* Orikhiv
126 L3 **Orekhovo-Zuyevo** Moskovskaya Oblast', W Russian Federation
Orekhovsk *see* Arekhawsk
Orel *see* Oril'
126 J6 **Orël** Orlovskaya Oblast', W Russian Federation
56 E11 **Orellana** Loreto, N Peru
56 E6 **Orellana** ◈ *province* NE Ecuador
104 L11 **Orellana, Embalse de** ▣ W Spain
36 L3 **Orem** Utah, W USA
Ore Mountains *see* Erzgebirge/Krušné Hory
127 V7 **Orenburg** *prev.* Chkalov. Orenburgskaya Oblast', W Russian Federation
127 V7 **Orenburg** ✕ Orenburgskaya Oblast', W Russian Federation
127 T7 **Orenburgskaya Oblast'** ◈ *province* W Russian Federation
Orense *see* Ourense
188 C8 **Oreor** *var.* Koror. *island* N Palau
Oreor *see* Koror
185 B24 **Orepuki** Southland, South Island, NZ
114 L12 **Orestiáda** *prev.* Orestiás. Anatolikí Makedonía kai Thráki, NE Greece
Orestiás *see* Orestiáda
Öresund/Øresund *see* Sound, The
185 C23 **Oreti** ↝ South Island, NZ
184 L5 **Orewa** Auckland, North Island, NZ
65 A25 **Orford, Cape** *headland* West Falkland, Falkland Islands
44 B5 **Órganos, Sierra de los** ▲ W Cuba
37 R15 **Organ Peak** ▲ New Mexico, SW USA
105 N9 **Orgaz** Castilla-La Mancha, C Spain
Orgeyev *see* Orhei
162 I6 **Orgil** Hövsgöl, C Mongolia
105 O15 **Orgiva** *var.* Orjiva. Andalucía, S Spain
162 I9 **Örgön** Bayanhongor, C Mongolia
117 N9 **Orhei** *var.* Orheiu, *Rus.* Orgeyev. N Moldova
Orheiu *see* Orhei
105 R3 **Orhi** *var.* Orhy, Pico de Orhy, Pic d'Orhy. ▲ France/Spain *see also* Orhy
Orhomenos *see* Orchómenos
162 K6 **Orhon** ◈ *province* N Mongolia
162 L6 **Orhon Gol** ↝ N Mongolia
102 J16 **Orhy** *var.* Orhi, Pico de Orhy, Pic d'Orhy. ▲ France/Spain *see also* Orhi
Orhy, Pic d'/Orhy, Pico de *see* Orhi/Orhy
34 L2 **Orick** California, W USA
32 L6 **Orient** Washington, NW USA
48 D6 **Oriental, Cordillera** ▲ Bolivia/Peru
48 D6 **Oriental, Cordillera** ▲ C Colombia
57 H16 **Oriental, Cordillera** ▲ C Peru
63 M15 **Oriente** Buenos Aires, E Argentina

◆ Country • Country Capital ◇ Dependent Territory ○ Dependent Territory Capital ◈ Administrative Region ✕ International Airport ▲ Mountain ▲ Mountain Range ⨯ Volcano ↝ River ◎ Lake ▣ Reservoir

105 R12 **Orihuela** País Valenciano, E Spain
117 V9 **Orikhiv** Rus. Orekhov. Zaporiz'ka Oblast', SE Ukraine
113 K22 **Orikum** var. Orikumi. Vlorë, SW Albania
Orikumi see Orikum
117 V6 **Oril'** Rus. Orel. ≈ E Ukraine
14 H14 **Orillia** Ontario, S Canada
93 M19 **Orimattila** Etelä-Suomi, S Finland
33 Y15 **Orin** Wyoming, C USA
47 R4 **Orinoco, Río** ≈ Colombia/Venezuela
186 C9 **Oriomo** Western, SW PNG
30 K11 **Orion** Illinois, N USA
29 Q5 **Oriska** North Dakota, N USA
153 P17 **Orissa** ◈ state NE India
Orissaar see Orissaare
118 E5 **Orissaare** Ger. Orissaar. Saaremaa, W Estonia
107 B19 **Oristano** Sardegna, Italy, C Mediterranean Sea
107 A19 **Oristano, Golfo di** gulf Sardegna, Italy, C Mediterranean Sea
54 D13 **Orito** Putumayo, SW Colombia
93 L18 **Orivesi** Häme, SW Finland
93 N17 **Orivesi** ◎ Länsi-Suomi, SE Finland
58 H12 **Oriximiná** Pará, NE Brazil
41 Q14 **Orizaba** Veracruz-Llave, E Mexico
41 Q14 **Orizaba, Volcán Pico de** var. Citlaltépetl. ▲ S Mexico
95 I16 **Ørje** Østfold, S Norway
113 I16 **Orjen** ⛰ Bosnia and Herzegovina/Serbia and Montenegro (Yugo.)
Orjiva see Orgiva
94 G8 **Orkanger** Sør-Trøndelag, S Norway
94 G8 **Orkdalen** valley S Norway
95 K22 **Örkelljunga** Skåne, S Sweden
Orkhaniye see Botevgrad
Orkhómenos see Orchómenos
94 H9 **Orkla** ≈ S Norway
Orkney see Orkney Islands
65 J22 **Orkney Deep** undersea feature Scotia Sea/Weddell Sea
96 J4 **Orkney Islands** var. Orkney, Orkneys. island group N Scotland, UK
Orkneys see Orkney Islands
24 K8 **Orla** Texas, SW USA
35 N5 **Orland** California, W USA
23 X11 **Orlando** Florida, SE USA
23 X12 **Orlando** ✕ Florida, SE USA
107 K23 **Orlando, Capo d'** headland Sicilia, Italy, C Mediterranean Sea
Orlau see Orlová
103 N6 **Orléanais** cultural region C France
34 L2 **Orleans** California, W USA
19 Q12 **Orleans** Massachusetts, NE USA
103 N7 **Orléans** anc. Aurelianum. Loiret, C France
15 R10 **Orléans, Île d'** island Québec, SE Canada
Orléansville see Chlef
111 F16 **Orlice** Ger. Adler. ≈ NE Czech Republic
122 L13 **Orlik** Respublika Buryatiya, S Russian Federation
125 Q14 **Orlov** prev. Khalturin. Kirovskaya Oblast', NW Russian Federation
111 I17 **Orlová** Ger. Orlau, Pol. Orłowa. Moravskoslezský Kraj, E Czech Republic
Orlov, Mys see Orlovskiy, Mys
126 I6 **Orlovskaya Oblast'** ◈ province W Russian Federation
126 M5 **Orlovskiy, Mys** var. Mys Orlov. headland NW Russian Federation
Orłowa see Orlová
103 O5 **Orly** ✕ (Paris) Essonne, N France
119 G16 **Orlya** Rus. Orlya. Hrodzyenskaya Voblasts', W Belarus
114 M7 **Orlyak** prev. Makenzen, Trubchular, Rom. Trupcilar. Dobrich, NE Bulgaria
148 L16 **Ormāra** Baluchistān, SW Pakistan
171 P5 **Ormoc** off. Ormoc City, var. MacArthur. Leyte, C Philippines
23 X10 **Ormond Beach** Florida, SE USA
109 X10 **Ormož** Ger. Friedau. NE Slovenia
14 J13 **Ormsby** Ontario, SE Canada
97 K17 **Ormskirk** NW England, UK
Ormsö see Vormsi
15 N13 **Ormstown** Québec, SE Canada
Ormuz, Strait of see Hormuz, Strait of
103 T8 **Ornans** Doubs, E France
102 K5 **Orne** ◈ department N France
102 K5 **Orne** ≈ N France
92 G12 **Ørnes** Nordland, C Norway
110 L7 **Orneta** Warmińsko-Mazurskie, NE Poland
95 P16 **Ornö** Stockholm, C Sweden
37 Q3 **Orno Peak** ▲ Colorado, C USA
93 I16 **Örnsköldsvik** Västernorrland, C Sweden
163 X13 **Oro** E North Korea
45 T6 **Orocovis** C Puerto Rico
54 H10 **Orocué** Casanare, E Colombia
77 N13 **Orodara** SW Burkina
105 S4 **Oroel, Peña de** ▲ N Spain
33 N10 **Orofino** Idaho, NW USA
162 I9 **Orog Nuur** ◎ S Mongolia
35 U14 **Oro Grande** California, W USA
37 S15 **Orogrande** New Mexico, SW USA
191 Q7 **Orohena, Mont** ⩚ Tahiti, W French Polynesia
Orolaunum see Arlon
Orol Dengizi see Aral Sea
189 S15 **Oroluk Atoll** atoll Caroline Islands, C Micronesia
81 J13 **Oromo** ◈ region C Ethiopia
13 O15 **Oromocto** New Brunswick, SE Canada
191 S4 **Orona** prev. Hull Island. atoll Phoenix Islands, C Kiribati
191 V17 **Orongo** ancient monument Easter Island, Chile, E Pacific Ocean
138 I3 **Orontes** var. Ononte, Ar. Nahr el Aassi, Nahr al 'Āṣī. ≈ SW Asia
104 L9 **Oropesa** Castilla-La Mancha, C Spain
105 T8 **Oropesa** País Valenciano, E Spain
Oropeza see Cochabamba
Oroqen Zizhiqi see Alihe
171 P7 **Oroquieta** var. Oroquieta City. Mindanao, S Philippines
40 J8 **Oro, Río del** ≈ C Mexico
59 O14 **Orós, Açude** ⊡ E Brazil
107 D18 **Orosei, Golfo di** gulf Tyrrhenian Sea, C Mediterranean Sea
111 M24 **Orosháza** Békés, SE Hungary
Orosirá Rodhópis see Rhodope Mountains
111 I22 **Oroszlány** Komárom-Esztergom, W Hungary
188 B16 **Orote Peninsula** peninsula W Guam
123 T9 **Orotukan** Magadanskaya Oblast', E Russian Federation
35 O5 **Oroville** California, W USA
32 K6 **Oroville** Washington, NW USA
35 O5 **Oroville, Lake** ⊡ California, W USA
(0) G15 **Orozco Fracture Zone** tectonic feature E Pacific Ocean
64 I7 **Orphan Knoll** undersea feature NW Atlantic Ocean
29 V3 **Orr** Minnesota, N USA
95 M21 **Orrefors** Kalmar, S Sweden
182 I7 **Orroroo** South Australia
31 T12 **Orrville** Ohio, N USA
94 L12 **Orsa** Dalarna, C Sweden
Orschowa see Orşova
Orschütz see Orzyc
119 O14 **Orsha** Rus. Orsha. Vitsyebskaya Voblasts', NE Belarus
127 Q2 **Orshanka** Respublika Mariy El, W Russian Federation
108 C11 **Orsières** Valais, SW Switzerland
127 X8 **Orsk** Orenburgskaya Oblast', W Russian Federation
116 F13 **Orşova** Ger. Orschowa, Hung. Orsova. Mehedinţi, SW Romania
94 D10 **Ørsta** Møre og Romsdal, S Norway
95 O15 **Örsundsbro** Uppsala, C Sweden
136 D16 **Ortaca** Muğla, SW Turkey
107 M16 **Orta Nova** Puglia, SE Italy
136 I17 **Orta Toroslar** ⛰ S Turkey
54 E11 **Ortega** Tolima, W Colombia
104 H1 **Ortegal, Cabo** headland NW Spain
Ortelsburg see Szczytno
102 J15 **Orthez** Pyrénées-Atlantiques, SW France
57 K14 **Orthon, Río** ≈ N Bolivia
60 J10 **Ortigueira** Paraná, S Brazil
104 H1 **Ortigueira** Galicia, NW Spain
106 H5 **Ortisei** Ger. Sankt-Ulrich. Trentino-Alto Adige, N Italy
40 F6 **Ortiz** Sonora, NW Mexico
54 L5 **Ortiz** Guárico, N Venezuela
Ortler see Ortles
106 F5 **Ortles** Ger. Ortler. ▲ N Italy
107 K14 **Ortona** Abruzzo, C Italy
29 R8 **Ortonville** Minnesota, N USA
147 W8 **Orto-Tokoy** Issyk-Kul'skaya Oblast', NE Kyrgyzstan
93 I15 **Örträsk** Västerbotten, N Sweden
100 J12 **Örtze** ≈ NW Germany
Oruba see Aruba
142 I3 **Orūmīyeh** var. Rizaiyeh, Urmia, Urmiyeh; prev. Reẓā'īyeh. Āzarbāyjān-e Bākhtarī, NW Iran
142 J3 **Orūmīyeh, Daryācheh-ye** var. Matianus, Sha Hi, Urumi Yeh, Eng. Lake Urmia; prev. Daryācheh-ye Reẓā'īyeh. ◎ NW Iran
57 K19 **Oruro** Oruro, W Bolivia
57 J19 **Oruro** ◈ department W Bolivia
95 I18 **Orust** island S Sweden
Orūzgān/Orūzgān see Urūzgān
106 H13 **Orvieto** anc. Velsuna. Umbria, C Italy
194 K7 **Orville Coast** physical region Antarctica
114 H7 **Oryakhovo** Vratsa, NW Bulgaria
Oryokko see Yalu
117 R5 **Orzhytsya** Poltavs'ka Oblast', C Ukraine
110 M9 **Orzyc** Ger. Orschütz. ≈ NE Poland
110 N8 **Orzysz** Ger. Arys. Warmińsko-Mazurskie, NE Poland
94 I10 **Os** Hedmark, S Norway
125 U15 **Osa** Permskaya Oblast', NW Russian Federation
29 W11 **Osage** Iowa, C USA
27 U5 **Osage Beach** Missouri, C USA
27 P5 **Osage City** Kansas, C USA
27 U7 **Osage Fork River** ≈ Missouri, C USA
27 U5 **Osage River** ≈ Missouri, C USA
164 J13 **Ōsaka** hist. Naniwa. Ōsaka, Honshū, SW Japan
164 I13 **Ōsaka** off. Ōsaka-fu, var. Ōsaka Hu. ◈ urban prefecture Honshū, SW Japan
Ōsaka-fu/Ōsaka Hu see Ōsaka
145 R10 **Osakarovka** Karaganda, C Kazakhstan
29 T7 **Osakis** Minnesota, N USA
43 N16 **Osa, Península de** peninsula S Costa Rica
60 M10 **Osasco** São Paulo, S Brazil
27 R5 **Osawatomie** Kansas, C USA
26 L3 **Osborne** Kansas, C USA
173 S8 **Osborn Plateau** undersea feature E Indian Ocean
95 L21 **Osby** Skåne, S Sweden
Osca see Huesca
92 N2 **Oscar II Land** physical region W Svalbard
27 Y10 **Osceola** Arkansas, C USA
29 V15 **Osceola** Iowa, C USA
27 S6 **Osceola** Missouri, C USA
29 Q15 **Osceola** Nebraska, C USA
101 N15 **Oschatz** Sachsen, E Germany
100 K13 **Oschersleben** Sachsen-Anhalt, C Germany
31 R7 **Oscoda** Michigan, N USA
Ösel see Saaremaa
94 H6 **Osen** Sør-Trøndelag, S Norway
94 I12 **Osensjøen** ◎ S Norway
164 A14 **Ōse-zaki** headland Fukue-jima, SW Japan
147 T10 **Osh** Oshskaya Oblast', SW Kyrgyzstan
83 C16 **Oshakati** Oshana, N Namibia
83 C16 **Oshana** ◈ district N Namibia
14 H15 **Oshawa** Ontario, SE Canada
165 R10 **Oshika-hantō** peninsula Honshū, C Japan
83 C16 **Oshikango** Ohangwena, N Namibia
Oshikoto see Otjikoto
165 P5 **Ō-shima** island NE Japan
165 N14 **Ō-shima** island S Japan
165 Q5 **Oshima-hantō** ⛰ Hokkaidō, NE Japan
83 D17 **Oshivelo** Otjikoto, N Namibia
28 K14 **Oshkosh** Nebraska, C USA
30 M7 **Oshkosh** Wisconsin, N USA
Oshmyany see Ashmyany
Osh Oblasty see Oshskaya Oblast'
77 T16 **Oshogbo** var. Osogbo. Osun, W Nigeria
147 T11 **Oshskaya Oblast'** Kir. Osh Oblasty. ◈ province SW Kyrgyzstan
Oshun see Osun
79 J20 **Oshwe** Bandundu, C Dem. Rep. Congo
Osiek see Osijek
112 I9 **Osijek** prev. Osiek, Osjek, Ger. Esseg, Hung. Eszék. Osijek-Baranja, E Croatia
112 I9 **Osijek-Baranja** off. Osječko-Baranjska Županija. ◈ province E Croatia
106 J12 **Osimo** Marche, C Italy
122 M12 **Osinovka** Irkutskaya Oblast', C Russian Federation
Osintorf see Asintorf
112 N11 **Osipaonica** Serbia, NE Serbia and Montenegro (Yugo.)
Osipenko see Berdyans'k
Osipovichi see Asipovichy
Osječko-Baranjska Županija see Osijek-Baranja
Osjek see Osijek
29 W15 **Oskaloosa** Iowa, C USA
27 Q4 **Oskaloosa** Kansas, C USA
95 N20 **Oskarshamn** Kalmar, S Sweden
95 J21 **Oskarström** Halland, S Sweden
14 M8 **Oskélanéo** Québec, SE Canada
Öskemen see Ust'-Kamenogorsk
Oskil see Oskol
117 W5 **Oskol** Ukr. Oskil. ≈ Russian Federation/Ukraine
93 D20 **Oslo** prev. Christiania, Kristiania. ● (Norway) Oslo, S Norway
93 D20 **Oslo** ◈ county S Norway
93 D21 **Oslofjorden** fjord S Norway
155 G15 **Osmānābād** Mahārāshtra, C India
136 J11 **Osmancık** Çorum, N Turkey
136 L16 **Osmaniye** Osmaniye, S Turkey
136 L16 **Osmaniye** ◈ province S Turkey
95 O16 **Ösmo** Stockholm, C Sweden
118 E3 **Osmussaar** island W Estonia
100 G13 **Osnabrück** Niedersachsen, NW Germany
110 D11 **Ośno Lubuskie** Ger. Drossen. Lubuskie, W Poland
Osogbo see Oshogbo
113 P19 **Osogov Mountains** var. Osogovske Planine, Osogovski Planina, Mac. Osogovski Planini. ⛰ Bulgaria/FYR Macedonia
Osogovske Planine/Osogovski Planina/Osogovski Planini see Osogov Mountains
165 R6 **Osore-yama** ▲ Honshū, C Japan
Oşorhei see Târgu Mureş
61 J16 **Osório** Rio Grande do Sul, S Brazil
63 G16 **Osorno** Los Lagos, C Chile
104 M4 **Osorno** Castilla-León, N Spain
11 N17 **Osoyoos** British Columbia, SW Canada
95 C14 **Osøyro** Hordaland, S Norway
54 J6 **Ospino** Portuguesa, N Venezuela
98 K13 **Oss** Noord-Brabant, S Netherlands
104 H11 **Ossa** ▲ S Portugal
115 F15 **Óssa** ⛰ C Greece
23 X6 **Ossabaw Island** island Georgia, SE USA
23 X6 **Ossabaw Sound** sound Georgia, SE USA
183 O16 **Ossa, Mount** ▲ Tasmania, SE Australia
104 H11 **Ossa, Serra d'** ⛰ SE Portugal
77 U16 **Osse** ≈ S Nigeria
30 J6 **Osseo** Wisconsin, N USA
109 S9 **Ossiacher See** ◎ S Austria
18 K13 **Ossining** New York, NE USA
123 V9 **Ossora** Koryakskiy Avtonomnyy Okrug, E Russian Federation
124 I15 **Ostashkov** Tverskaya Oblast', W Russian Federation
100 H9 **Oste** ≈ NW Germany
Ostee see Baltic Sea
Ostend/Ostende see Oostende
117 P3 **Oster** Chernihivs'ka Oblast', N Ukraine
95 O14 **Österbybruk** Uppsala, C Sweden
95 M19 **Österbymo** Östergotland, S Sweden
94 K12 **Österdalälven** ≈ C Sweden
94 I12 **Østerdalen** valley S Norway
95 L18 **Östergötland** ◈ county S Sweden
100 H10 **Osterholz-Scharmbeck** Niedersachsen, NW Germany
Östermark see Teuva
Östermyra see Seinäjoki
Osterode/Osterode in Ostpreussen see Ostróda
94 J11 **Østrehogna** prev. Härjåhågnen Swe. Härjahågnen, Härjehågna. ▲ Norway/Sweden
101 J14 **Osterode am Harz** Niedersachsen, C Germany
94 C13 **Osterøy** island S Norway
Österreich see Austria
93 G16 **Östersund** Jämtland, C Sweden
95 N14 **Östervåla** Västmanland, C Sweden
101 H22 **Ostfildern** Baden-Württemberg, SW Germany
95 H16 **Østfold** ◈ county S Norway
100 E9 **Ostfriesische Inseln** Eng. East Frisian Islands. island group NW Germany
100 F10 **Ostfriesland** historical region NW Germany
95 P14 **Östhammar** Uppsala, C Sweden
Ostia Aterni see Pescara
106 G8 **Ostiglia** Lombardia, N Italy
95 J14 **Östmark** Värmland, C Sweden
95 K22 **Östra Ringsjön** ◎ S Sweden
111 I17 **Ostrava** Moravskoslezský Kraj, E Czech Republic
Ostravský Kraj see Moravskoslezský Kraj
110 K8 **Ostróda** Ger. Osterode, Osterode in Ostpreussen. Warmińsko-Mazurskie, NE Poland
Ostrog/Ostróg see Ostroh
126 L8 **Ostrogozhsk** Voronezhskaya Oblast', W Russian Federation
116 L4 **Ostroh** Pol. Ostróg, Rus. Ostrog. Rivnens'ka Oblast', NW Ukraine
110 N9 **Ostrołęka** Ger. Wiesenhof, Rus. Ostrolenka. Mazowieckie, C Poland
111 A16 **Ostrov** Ger. Schlackenwerth. Karlovarský Kraj, W Czech Republic
124 F15 **Ostrov** Latv. Austrava. Pskovskaya Oblast', W Russian Federation
Ostrovets see Ostrowiec Świętokrzyski
113 M21 **Ostrovicës, Mali i** ▲ SE Albania
165 Z2 **Ostrov Iturup** island NE Russian Federation
124 M4 **Ostrovnoy** Murmanskaya Oblast', NW Russian Federation
114 L7 **Ostrovo** prev. Golema Ada. Razgrad, N Bulgaria
125 N15 **Ostrovskoye** Kostromskaya Oblast', NW Russian Federation
Ostrów see Ostrów Wielkopolski
Ostrowiec see Ostrowiec Świętokrzyski
111 M14 **Ostrowiec Świętokrzyski** var. Ostrowiec, Rus. Ostrovets. Świętokrzyskie, C Poland
110 P13 **Ostrów Lubelski** Lubelskie, E Poland
110 N10 **Ostrów Mazowiecka** var. Ostrów Mazowiecki. Mazowieckie, C Poland
Ostrów Mazowiecki see Ostrów Mazowiecka
Ostrowo see Ostrów Wielkopolski
110 H13 **Ostrów Wielkopolski** var. Ostrów, Ger. Ostrowo. Wielkopolskie, C Poland
Ostryna see Astryna
110 I13 **Ostrzeszów** Wielkopolskie, C Poland
107 P18 **Ostuni** Puglia, SE Italy
Ostyako-Voguls'k see Khanty-Mansiysk
Osum see Osumit, Lumi i
114 I9 **Osŭm** ≈ N Bulgaria
164 C17 **Ōsumi-hantō** ⛰ Kyūshū, SW Japan
164 C17 **Ōsumi-kaikyō** strait SW Japan
113 L22 **Osumit, Lumi i** var. Osum. ≈ SE Albania
77 T16 **Osun** var. Oshun. ◈ state SW Nigeria
104 L14 **Osuna** Andalucía, S Spain
60 J8 **Osvaldo Cruz** São Paulo, S Brazil
Osveya see Asvyeya
18 J7 **Oswegatchie River** ≈ New York, NE USA
27 Q7 **Oswego** Kansas, C USA
18 H9 **Oswego** New York, NE USA
97 K19 **Oswestry** W England, UK
111 J16 **Oświęcim** Ger. Auschwitz. Małopolskie, S Poland
185 E22 **Otago** off. Otago Region. ◈ region South Island, NZ
185 F23 **Otago Peninsula** peninsula South Island, NZ
165 F13 **Ōtake** Hiroshima, Honshū, SW Japan
184 L13 **Otaki** Wellington, North Island, NZ
93 M15 **Otanmäki** Oulu, C Finland
145 T15 **Otar** Zhambyl, SE Kazakhstan
165 R4 **Otaru** Hokkaidō, NE Japan
185 C24 **Otatara** Southland, South Island, NZ
185 C24 **Otautau** Southland, South Island, NZ
93 M18 **Otava** Isä-Suomi, E Finland
111 B18 **Otava** Ger. Wottawa. ≈ SW Czech Republic
56 C6 **Otavalo** Imbabura, N Ecuador
83 D17 **Otavi** Otjozondjupa, N Namibia
165 P12 **Ōtawara** Tochigi, Honshū, S Japan
83 B16 **Otchinjau** Cunene, SW Angola
116 F12 **Oţelu Roşu** Ger. Ferdinandsberg, Hung. Nándorhgy. Caras-Severin, SW Romania
185 E21 **Otematata** Canterbury, South Island, NZ
118 I6 **Otepää** Ger. Odenpäh. Valgamaa, SE Estonia
32 K9 **Othello** Washington, NW USA
115 A15 **Othonoí** island Iónioi Nísoi, Greece, C Mediterranean Sea
Othris see Óthrys
115 F17 **Óthrys** var. Othris. ⛰ C Greece
77 Q14 **Oti** ≈ N Togo
40 K10 **Otinapa** Durango, C Mexico
185 G17 **Otira** West Coast, South Island, NZ
37 V3 **Otis** Colorado, C USA
12 L10 **Otish, Monts** ⛰ Québec, E Canada
83 C17 **Otjikondo** Kunene, N Namibia
83 C17 **Otjikoto** var. Oshikoto. ◈ district N Namibia
83 E18 **Otjinene** Omaheke, NE Namibia
83 D18 **Otjiwarongo** Otjozondjupa, N Namibia
83 D18 **Otjosondu** var. Otjosundu. Otjozondjupa, C Namibia
Otjosundu see Otjosondu
83 D18 **Otjozondjupa** ◈ district C Namibia
112 C11 **Otočac** Lika-Senj, W Croatia
Otog Qi see Ulan
112 J10 **Otok** Vukovar-Srijem, E Croatia
116 K14 **Otopeni** ✕ (Bucureşti) Bucureşti, S Romania
184 L8 **Otorohanga** Waikato, North Island, NZ
12 D9 **Otoskwin** ≈ Ontario, C Canada
165 G14 **Ōtoyo** Kōchi, Shikoku, SW Japan
95 E16 **Otra** ≈ S Norway
107 R19 **Otranto** Puglia, SE Italy
Otranto, Canale d' see Otranto, Strait of
107 Q18 **Otranto, Strait of** It. Canale d'Otranto. strait Albania/Italy
111 H18 **Otrokovice** Ger. Otrokowitz. Zlínský Kraj, E Czech Republic
Otrokowitz see Otrokovice
31 P10 **Otsego** Michigan, N USA
31 Q6 **Otsego Lake** ◎ Michigan, N USA
18 I11 **Otselic River** ≈ New York, NE USA
164 J14 **Ōtsu** var. Ôtu. Shiga, Honshū, SW Japan
94 G11 **Otta** Oppland, S Norway
189 U13 **Otta** island Chuuk, C Micronesia
94 F11 **Otta** ≈ S Norway
189 U13 **Otta Pass** passage Chuuk Islands, C Micronesia
95 J22 **Ottarp** Skåne, S Sweden
14 L12 **Ottawa** ● (Canada) Ontario, SE Canada
30 L11 **Ottawa** Illinois, N USA
27 Q5 **Ottawa** Kansas, C USA
31 R12 **Ottawa** Ohio, N USA
14 L12 **Ottawa** var. Uplands. ✕ Ontario, SE Canada
14 M12 **Ottawa** Fr. Outaouais. ≈ Ontario/Québec, SE Canada
12 I4 **Ottawa Islands** island group Nunavut, C Canada
18 L8 **Otter Creek** ≈ Vermont, NE USA
36 L6 **Otter Creek Reservoir** ⊡ Utah, W USA
98 L11 **Otterlo** Gelderland, E Netherlands
94 D9 **Otterøya** island S Norway
29 S6 **Otter Tail Lake** ◎ Minnesota, N USA
29 R7 **Otter Tail River** ≈ Minnesota, C USA
95 H23 **Otterup** Fyn, C Denmark
99 H19 **Ottignies** Wallon Brabant, C Belgium
101 L23 **Ottobrunn** Bayern, SE Germany
29 X15 **Ottumwa** Iowa, C USA
Ôtu see Ōtsu
83 B16 **Otuazuma** Kunene, NW Namibia
Otuki see Ōtsuki
77 V16 **Oturkpo** Benue, S Nigeria
193 Y15 **Otu Tolu Group** island group SE Tonga
182 M13 **Otway, Cape** headland Victoria, SE Australia
63 H24 **Otway, Seno** inlet S Chile
Ötz see Oetz
108 L8 **Ötztaler Ache** ≈ W Austria
108 L9 **Ötztaler Alpen** It. Alpi Venoste. ⛰ SW Austria
27 T12 **Ouachita, Lake** ⊡ Arkansas, C USA
27 R11 **Ouachita Mountains** ⛰ Arkansas/Oklahoma, C USA
27 U13 **Ouachita River** ≈ Arkansas/Louisiana, C USA
Ouadaï see Ouaddaï
76 J7 **Ouadâne** var. Ouadane. Adrar, C Mauritania
78 K13 **Ouadda** Haute-Kotto, N Central African Republic
78 J10 **Ouaddaï** off. Préfecture du Ouaddaï, var. Ouadaï, Wadai. ◈ prefecture SE Chad
77 P13 **Ouagadougou** var. Wagadugu. ● (Burkina) C Burkina
77 P13 **Ouagadougou** ✕ C Burkina
77 O12 **Ouahigouya** NW Burkina
Ouahran see Oran
79 J14 **Ouaka** ◈ prefecture C Central African Republic
79 J15 **Ouaka** ≈ S Central African Republic
Oualam see Ouallam
76 M9 **Oualâta** var. Oualata. Hodh ech Chargui, SE Mauritania
77 R11 **Ouallam** var. Oualam. Tillabéri, W Niger
172 H14 **Ouanani** Mohéli, S Comoros
55 Z10 **Ouanary** E French Guiana
78 L13 **Ouanda Djallé** Vakaga, NE Central African Republic
79 N14 **Ouando** Haut-Mbomou, SE Central African Republic
79 L15 **Ouango** Mbomou, S Central African Republic
77 N14 **Ouangolodougou** var. Wangolodougou. N Ivory Coast
172 I13 **Ouani** Anjouan, SE Comoros
79 M15 **Ouara** ≈ E Central African Republic
76 K7 **Ouarâne** desert C Mauritania
15 O11 **Ouareau** ≈ Québec, SE Canada
74 K7 **Ouargla** var. Wargla. NE Algeria
74 F8 **Ouarzazate** S Morocco
77 Q11 **Ouatagouna** Gao, E Mali
74 G6 **Ouazzane** var. Ouezzane, Ar. Wazan, Wazzan. N Morocco
Oubangui see Ubangi
Oubangui-Chari see Central African Republic
Oubari, Edeyen d' see Awbārī, Idhān
98 G13 **Oud-Beijerland** Zuid-Holland, SW Netherlands
98 F13 **Ouddorp** Zuid-Holland, SW Netherlands
77 P9 **Oudeïka** oasis C Mali
98 G13 **Oude Maas** ≈ SW Netherlands
99 E18 **Oudenaarde** Fr. Audenarde. Oost-Vlaanderen, SW Belgium
99 H14 **Oudenbosch** Noord-Brabant, S Netherlands
98 P6 **Oude Pekela** Groningen, NE Netherlands
Ouderkerk see Ouderkerk aan den Amstel
98 I10 **Ouderkerk aan den Amstel** var. Ouderkerk. Noord-Holland, C Netherlands
98 I6 **Oudeschild** Noord-Holland, NW Netherlands
99 G14 **Oude-Tonge** Zuid-Holland, SW Netherlands
98 I12 **Oudewater** Utrecht, C Netherlands
Oudjda see Oujda
98 L5 **Oudkerk** Friesland, N Netherlands
102 J7 **Oudon** ≈ NW France
98 I9 **Oudorp** Noord-Holland, NW Netherlands
83 G25 **Oudtshoorn** Western Cape, SW South Africa
99 I16 **Oud-Turnhout** Antwerpen, N Belgium
74 F7 **Oued-Zem** C Morocco
187 P16 **Ouégoa** Province Nord, C New Caledonia
76 L13 **Ouéléssébougou** var. Ouolossébougou. Koulikoro, SW Mali
77 N16 **Ouellé** E Ivory Coast
77 R16 **Ouémé** ≈ C Benin
77 O13 **Ouessa** S Burkina
102 D5 **Ouessant, Île d'** Eng. Ushant. island NW France
79 H17 **Ouésso** La Sangha, NW Congo
79 D15 **Ouest** Eng. West. ◈ province W Cameroon
190 G11 **Ouest, Baie de l'** bay Îles Wallis, Wallis and Futuna
15 Y7 **Ouest, Pointe de l'** headland Québec, SE Canada
Ouezzane see Ouazzane
99 K20 **Ouffet** Liège, E Belgium
79 H14 **Ouham** ◈ prefecture NW Central African Republic
78 I13 **Ouham** ≈ Central African Republic/Chad
79 G14 **Ouham-Pendé** ◈ prefecture W Central African Republic
77 R16 **Ouidah** Eng. Whydah, Wida. S Benin
74 H6 **Oujda** Ar. Oudjda, Ujda. NE Morocco
76 I7 **Oujeft** Adrar, C Mauritania
93 L15 **Oulainen** Oulu, C Finland
Ould Yanja see Ould Yenjé
76 J10 **Ould Yenjé** var. Ould Yanja. Guidimaka, S Mauritania
93 L14 **Oulu** Swe. Uleåborg. Oulu, C Finland
93 M14 **Oulu** Swe. Uleåborg. ◈ province N Finland
93 L15 **Oulujärvi** Swe. Uleträsk. ◎ C Finland
93 M14 **Oulujoki** Swe. Uleälv. ≈ C Finland
93 L14 **Oulunsalo** Oulu, C Finland
106 A8 **Oulx** Piemonte, NE Italy
78 J9 **Oum-Chalouba** Borkou-Ennedi-Tibesti, NE Chad
76 M16 **Oumé** C Ivory Coast
74 F7 **Oum er Rbia** ≈ C Morocco
78 J10 **Oum-Hadjer** Batha, E Chad
92 K10 **Ounasjoki** ≈ N Finland
78 J7 **Ounianga Kébir** Borkou-Ennedi-Tibesti, N Chad
Ouolossébougou see Ouéléssébougou
Oup see Auob
99 K19 **Oupeye** Liège, E Belgium
99 N21 **Our** ≈ NW Europe
37 Q7 **Ouray** Colorado, C USA
103 R7 **Ource** ≈ C France
104 G9 **Ourém** Santarém, C Portugal
104 H4 **Ourense** Cast. Orense; Lat. Aurium. Galicia, NW Spain
104 I4 **Ourense** Cast. Orense ◈ province Galicia, NW Spain
59 O15 **Ouricuri** Pernambuco, E Brazil
60 J9 **Ourinhos** São Paulo, S Brazil
104 G13 **Ourique** Beja, S Portugal
59 M20 **Ouro Preto** Minas Gerais, NE Brazil
Ours, Grand Lac de l' see Great Bear Lake
99 K20 **Ourthe** ≈ E Belgium
165 Q9 **Ōu-sanmyaku** ⛰ Honshū, C Japan
97 M17 **Ouse** ≈ N England, UK
Ouse see Great Ouse
102 H7 **Oust** ≈ NW France
Outaouais see Ottawa
15 T4 **Outardes Quatre, Réservoir** ⊡ Québec, SE Canada
15 T5 **Outardes, Rivière aux** ≈ Québec, SE Canada
96 E8 **Outer Hebrides** var. Western Isles. island group NW Scotland, UK
30 K3 **Outer Island** island Apostle Islands, Wisconsin, N USA
35 S16 **Outer Santa Barbara Passage** passage California, SW USA
104 G3 **Outes** Galicia, NW Spain
83 C18 **Outjo** Kunene, N Namibia
11 T16 **Outlook** Saskatchewan, S Canada
93 N16 **Outokumpu** Itä-Suomi, E Finland
96 M2 **Out Skerries** island group NE Scotland, UK
187 Q16 **Ouvéa** island Îles Loyauté, NE New Caledonia
103 S14 **Ouvèze** ≈ SE France
182 L9 **Ouyen** Victoria, SE Australia
39 Q14 **Ouzinkie** Kodiak Island, Alaska, USA
137 O13 **Ovacık** Tunceli, E Turkey
106 C9 **Ovada** Piemonte, NE Italy

◆ Country ● Country Capital ◇ Dependent Territory ○ Dependent Territory Capital ◈ Administrative Region ✕ International Airport ▲ Mountain ⛰ Mountain Range ⩚ Volcano ≈ River ◎ Lake ⊡ Reservoir

187 X14 **Ovalau** *island* C Fiji
62 G9 **Ovalle** Coquimbo, N Chile
83 C17 **Ovamboland** *physical region* N Namibia
54 L10 **Ovana, Cerro** ▲ S Venezuela
104 G7 **Ovar** Aveiro, N Portugal
114 L10 **Ovcharitsa, Yazovir** ⊠ SE Bulgaria
54 E6 **Ovejas** Sucre, NW Colombia
101 E16 **Overath** Nordrhein-Westfalen, W Germany
98 F13 **Overflakkee** *island* SW Netherlands
99 H19 **Overijse** Vlaams Brabant, C Belgium
98 N10 **Overijssel** ◆ *province* E Netherlands
98 M9 **Overijssels Kanaal** *canal* E Netherlands
92 K13 **Överkalix** Norrbotten, N Sweden
27 R4 **Overland Park** Kansas, C USA
99 L14 **Overloon** Noord-Brabant, SE Netherlands
99 K16 **Overpelt** Limburg, NE Belgium
35 Y10 **Overton** Nevada, W USA
25 W7 **Overton** Texas, SW USA
92 K13 **Övertorneå** Norrbotten, N Sweden
95 N18 **Överum** Kalmar, S Sweden
92 G13 **Överuman** ◎ N Sweden
117 P11 **Ovidiopol'** Odes'ka Oblast', SW Ukraine
116 M14 **Ovidiu** Constanţa, SE Romania
45 N10 **Oviedo** SW Dominican Republic
104 K2 **Oviedo** *anc.* Asturias. Asturias, NW Spain
104 K2 **Oviedo** ✕ Asturias, N Spain
Ovilava *see* Wels
118 D7 **Ovišī** Ventspils, W Latvia
146 K10 **Ovminzatov-Tog'lari** *Rus.* Gory Auminzatau. ▲▲ N Uzbekistan
162 H6 **Övögdiy** Dzavhan, C Mongolia
163 P10 **Ovoot** Sühbaatar, SE Mongolia
157 O4 **Övörhangay** ◆ *province* C Mongolia
94 E12 **Øvre Årdal** Sogn og Fjordane, S Norway
95 K15 **Övre Fryken** ◎ C Sweden
92 J11 **Övre Soppero** *Lapp.* Badje-Sohppar. Norrbotten, N Sweden
117 N3 **Ovruch** Zhytomyrs'ka Oblast', N Ukraine
162 J8 **Övt** Övörhangay, C Mongolia
185 E24 **Owaka** Otago, South Island, NZ
79 H18 **Owando** *prev.* Fort-Rousset. Cuvette, C Congo
164 J14 **Owase** Mie, Honshū, SW Japan
27 P9 **Owasso** Oklahoma, C USA
29 V10 **Owatonna** Minnesota, N USA
173 O4 **Owen Fracture Zone** *tectonic feature* W Arabian Sea
185 H15 **Owen, Mount** ▲ South Island, NZ
185 H15 **Owen River** Tasman, South Island, NZ
44 D8 **Owen Roberts** ✕ Grand Cayman, Cayman Islands
20 I6 **Owensboro** Kentucky, S USA
35 T11 **Owens Lake** *salt flat* California, W USA
14 F14 **Owen Sound** Ontario, S Canada
14 F13 **Owen Sound** ◎ Ontario, S Canada
35 T10 **Owens River** ≈ California, W USA
186 F9 **Owen Stanley Range** ▲▲ S PNG
27 V5 **Owensville** Missouri, C USA
20 M4 **Owenton** Kentucky, S USA
77 U17 **Owerri** Imo, S Nigeria
184 M10 **Owhango** Manawatu-Wanganui, North Island, NZ
21 N5 **Owingsville** Kentucky, S USA
77 T16 **Owo** Ondo, SW Nigeria
31 R9 **Owosso** Michigan, N USA
35 V1 **Owyhee** Nevada, W USA
32 L14 **Owyhee, Lake** ◎ Oregon, NW USA
32 L15 **Owyhee River** ≈ Idaho/Oregon, NW USA
92 K1 **Öxarfjördhur** *var.* Axarfjördhur. *fjord* N Iceland
94 K12 **Oxberg** Dalarna, C Sweden
11 V17 **Oxbow** Saskatchewan, S Canada
95 O17 **Oxelösund** Södermanland, S Sweden
185 H18 **Oxford** Canterbury, South Island, NZ
97 M21 **Oxford** *Lat.* Oxonia. S England, UK
23 Q3 **Oxford** Alabama, S USA
22 L2 **Oxford** Mississippi, S USA
29 N16 **Oxford** Nebraska, C USA
18 I11 **Oxford** New York, NE USA
21 U8 **Oxford** North Carolina, SE USA
31 Q14 **Oxford** Ohio, N USA
18 H16 **Oxford** Pennsylvania, NE USA
11 X12 **Oxford House** Manitoba, C Canada
29 Y13 **Oxford Junction** Iowa, C USA
11 X12 **Oxford Lake** ◎ Manitoba, C Canada
97 M21 **Oxfordshire** *cultural region* S England, UK
Oxia *see* Oxyá
41 X12 **Oxkutzcab** Yucatán, SE Mexico
35 R15 **Oxnard** California, W USA
Oxonia *see* Oxford
14 I12 **Oxtongue** ≈ Ontario, SE Canada
Oxus *see* Amu Darya
115 E15 **Oxyá** *var.* Oxia. ▲ C Greece
164 L11 **Oyabe** Toyama, Honshū, SW Japan
Oyahue/Oyahue, Volcán *see* Ollagüe, Volcán
165 O12 **Oyama** Tochigi, Honshū, S Japan
47 U5 **Oyapock** ≈ E French Guiana
Oyapock *see* Oiapoque, Rio
55 Z10 **Oyapok, Baie de L'** *bay* Brazil/French Guiana
55 Z11 **Oyapok, Fleuve l'** *var.* Oyapock, Rio Oiapoque. ≈ Brazil/French Guiana *see also* Oiapoque, Rio
79 E17 **Oyem** Woleu-Ntem, N Gabon
11 R16 **Oyen** Alberta, SW Canada
95 I15 **Øyeren** ◎ S Norway
162 G6 **Oygon** Dzavhan, N Mongolia
96 I7 **Oykel** ≈ N Scotland, UK
123 R9 **Oymyakon** Respublika Sakha (Yakutiya), NE Russian Federation
79 H19 **Oyo** Cuvette, C Congo
77 S15 **Oyo** Oyo, W Nigeria
77 S15 **Oyo** ◆ *state* SW Nigeria
56 D13 **Oyón** Lima, C Peru
103 S10 **Oyonnax** Ain, E France
146 L10 **Oyoqig'itma** *Rus.* Ayakagytma. Buxoro Viloyati, C Uzbekistan
146 M9 **Oyoqquduq** *Rus.* Ayakkuduk. Navoiy Viloyati, N Uzbekistan
32 F9 **Oysterville** Washington, NW USA
95 D14 **Øystese** Hordaland, S Norway
147 U10 **Oy-Tal** Oshskaya Oblast', SW Kyrgyzstan
147 T10 **Oy-Tal** ≈ SW Kyrgyzstan
145 S16 **Oytal** Zhambyl, S Kazakhstan
Oyyl *see* Uil
Ozarichi *see* Azarychy
23 R7 **Ozark** Alabama, S USA
27 S10 **Ozark** Arkansas, C USA
27 T8 **Ozark** Missouri, C USA
27 T8 **Ozark Plateau** *plain* Arkansas/Missouri, C USA
27 T6 **Ozarks, Lake of the** ⊠ Missouri, C USA
192 L10 **Ozbourn Seamount** *undersea feature* W Pacific Ocean
111 L20 **Ózd** Borsod-Abaúj-Zemplén, NE Hungary
112 D11 **Ozeblin** ▲ C Croatia
123 V11 **Ozernovskiy** Kamchatskaya Oblast', E Russian Federation
144 M7 **Ozërnoye** *var.* Ozërnyy. Kostanay, N Kazakhstan
124 I15 **Ozërnyy** Tverskaya Oblast', W Russian Federation
Ozërnyy *see* Ozërnoye
115 D18 **Ozerós, Límni** ◎ W Greece
122 F11 **Ozërsk** Chelyabinskaya Oblast', C Russian Federation
119 D14 **Ozersk** *prev.* Darkehnen, *Ger.* Angerapp. Kaliningradskaya Oblast', W Russian Federation
126 L4 **Ozery** Moskovskaya Oblast', W Russian Federation
Özgön *see* Uzgen
107 C17 **Ozieri** Sardegna, Italy, C Mediterranean Sea
111 I15 **Ozimek** *Ger.* Malapane. Opolskie, S Poland
127 R8 **Ozinki** Saratovskaya Oblast', W Russian Federation
Oziya *see* Ojiya
25 O10 **Ozona** Texas, SW USA
Ozorkov *see* Ozorków
110 J12 **Ozorków** *Rus.* Ozorkov. Łódź, C Poland
164 F14 **Ōzu** Ehime, Shikoku, SW Japan
137 R10 **Ozurget'i** *prev.* Makharadze. W Georgia

P

99 J17 **Paal** Limburg, NE Belgium
196 M14 **Paamiut** *var.* Pâmiut, *Dan.* Frederikshåb. Kitaa, S Greenland
167 N8 **Pa-an** Karen State, S Myanmar
101 L22 **Paar** ≈ SE Germany
83 E26 **Paarl** Western Cape, SW South Africa
93 L15 **Paavola** Oulu, C Finland
96 E8 **Pabbay** *island* NW Scotland, UK
153 T15 **Pabna** Rajshahi, W Bangladesh
109 U4 **Pabneukirchen** Oberösterreich, N Austria
118 H13 **Pabradė** *Pol.* Podbrodzie. Vilnius, SE Lithuania
56 L13 **Pacahuaras,** ≈ N Bolivia
Pacaraima, Sierra/Pacaraim, Serra *see* Pakaraima Mountains
56 B11 **Pacasmayo** La Libertad, W Peru
42 D6 **Pacaya, Volcán de** ⛰ S Guatemala
115 K23 **Pachía** *island* Kykládes, Greece, Aegean Sea
107 L26 **Pachino** Sicilia, Italy, C Mediterranean Sea
56 F12 **Pachitea, Río** ≈ C Peru
154 I11 **Pachmarhi** Madhya Pradesh, C India
121 P3 **Páchna** *var.* Pakhna. SW Cyprus
115 H25 **Páchnes** ▲ Kríti, Greece, E Mediterranean Sea
54 F9 **Pacho** Cundinamarca, C Colombia
154 F12 **Pāchora** Mahārāshtra, C India
41 P13 **Pachuca** *var.* Pachuca de Soto. Hidalgo, C Mexico
Pachuca de Soto *see* Pachuca
27 W5 **Pacific** Missouri, C USA
192 L14 **Pacific-Antarctic Ridge** *undersea feature* S Pacific Ocean
32 F8 **Pacific Beach** Washington, NW USA
35 N10 **Pacific Grove** California, W USA
29 S15 **Pacific Junction** Iowa, C USA
198-199 **Pacific Ocean** *ocean*
131 Z10 **Pacific Plate** *tectonic feature*
113 J15 **Pačir** ▲ SW Serbia and Montenegro (Yugo.)
182 L5 **Packsaddle** New South Wales, SE Australia
32 H9 **Packwood** Washington, NW USA
Padalung *see* Phatthalung
168 J12 **Padang** Sumatera, W Indonesia
168 L9 **Padang Endau** Pahang, Peninsular Malaysia
Padangpandjang *see* Padangpanjang
168 I11 **Padangpanjang** *prev.* Padangpandjang. Sumatera, W Indonesia
168 I10 **Padangsidempuan** *prev.* Padangsidimpoean. Sumatera, W Indonesia
Padangsidimpoean *see* Padangsidempuan
124 I9 **Padany** Respublika Kareliya, NW Russian Federation
93 M18 **Padasjoki** Etelä-Suomi, S Finland
57 M22 **Padcaya** Tarija, S Bolivia
101 H14 **Paderborn** Nordrhein-Westfalen, NW Germany
Padeşul/Padeş, Vîrful *see* Padeş, Vârful
116 F12 **Padeş, Vârful** *var.* Padeşul; *prev.* Vîrful Padeş. ▲ W Romania
112 L10 **Padinska Skela** Serbia, N Serbia and Montenegro (Yugo.)
Padma *see* Brahmaputra
153 S14 **Padma** *var.* Ganges. ≈ Bangladesh/India *see also* Ganges
106 H8 **Padova** *Eng.* Padua; *anc.* Patavium. Veneto, NE Italy
82 A10 **Padrão, Ponta do** *headland* NW Angola
25 T16 **Padre Island** *island* Texas, SW USA
104 G3 **Padrón** Galicia, NW Spain
118 K13 **Padsvillye** *Rus.* Podsvil'ye. Vitsyebskaya Voblasts', N Belarus
182 K11 **Padthaway** South Australia
Padua *see* Padova
20 G7 **Paducah** Kentucky, S USA
25 P4 **Paducah** Texas, SW USA
105 N15 **Padul** Andalucía, S Spain
191 P8 **Paea** Tahiti, W French Polynesia
185 L14 **Paekakariki** Wellington, North Island, NZ
163 X11 **Paektu-san** *var.* Baitou Shan. ▲ China/North Korea
163 V15 **Paengnyŏng-do** *island* NW South Korea
184 M7 **Paeroa** Waikato, North Island, NZ
54 D12 **Páez** Cauca, SW Colombia
121 O3 **Páfos** *var.* Paphos. W Cyprus
121 O3 **Páfos** ✕ SW Cyprus
83 L19 **Pafúri** Gaza, SW Mozambique
112 C12 **Pag** *It.* Pago. Lika-Senj, W Croatia
112 B11 **Pag** *It.* Pago. *island* Zadar, SW Croatia
171 P7 **Pagadian** Mindanao, S Philippines
168 J13 **Pagai Selatan, Pulau** *island* Kepulauan Mentawai, W Indonesia
168 J13 **Pagai Utara, Pulau** *island* Kepulauan Mentawai, W Indonesia
188 K4 **Pagan** *island* C Northern Mariana Islands
115 G16 **Pagasitikós Kólpos** *gulf* E Greece
36 L8 **Page** Arizona, SW USA
29 Q5 **Page** North Dakota, N USA
118 D13 **Pagėgiai** *Ger.* Pogegen. Tauragė, SW Lithuania
21 S11 **Pageland** South Carolina, SE USA
81 G16 **Pager** ≈ NE Uganda
149 Q5 **Paghmān** Kābul, E Afghanistan
Pago *see* Pag
188 C16 **Pago Bay** *bay* E Guam, W Pacific Ocean
115 M20 **Pagóndas** *var.* Pagóndhas. Sámos, Dodekánisos, Greece, Aegean Sea
Pagóndhas *see* Pagóndas
192 J16 **Pago Pago** ○ (American Samoa) Tutuila, W American Samoa
37 R8 **Pagosa Springs** Colorado, C USA
38 H12 **Pāhala** *var.* Pahala. Hawai'i, USA, C Pacific Ocean
168 K8 **Pahang** *off.* Negeri Pahang Darul Makmur. ◆ *state* Peninsular Malaysia
Pahang *see* Pahang, Sungai
168 L8 **Pahang, Sungai** *var.* Pahang, Sungei Pahang. ≈ Peninsular Malaysia
149 S8 **Pahārpur** North-West Frontier Province, NW Pakistan
185 B24 **Pahia Point** *headland* South Island, NZ
184 M13 **Pahiatua** Manawatu-Wanganui, North Island, NZ
38 H12 **Pāhoa** *var.* Pahoa. Hawai'i, USA, C Pacific Ocean
23 Y14 **Pahokee** Florida, SE USA
35 X9 **Pahranagat Range** ▲▲ Nevada, W USA
35 W11 **Pahrump** Nevada, W USA
Pahsien *see* Chongqing
35 V9 **Pahute Mesa** ▲▲ Nevada, W USA
167 N7 **Pai** Mae Hong Son, NW Thailand
38 F10 **Pā'ia** *var.* Paia. Maui, Hawai'i, USA, C Pacific Ocean
Pai-ch'eng *see* Baicheng
118 H4 **Paide** *Ger.* Weissenstein. Järvamaa, N Estonia
97 J24 **Paignton** SW England, UK
184 K3 **Paihia** Northland, North Island, NZ
93 M18 **Päijänne** ◎ S Finland
114 F13 **Páïko** ▲▲ N Greece
57 M17 **Paila, Río** ≈ C Bolivia
167 Q12 **Pailin** Bătdâmbâng, W Cambodia
54 F6 **Pailitas** Cesar, N Colombia
38 F9 **Pailolo Channel** *channel* Hawai'i, USA, C Pacific Ocean
93 K19 **Paimio** *Swe.* Pemar. Länsi-Suomi, W Finland
165 O16 **Paimi-saki** *var.* Yaeme-saki. *headland* Iriomote-jima, SW Japan
102 G5 **Paimpol** Côtes d'Armor, NW France
168 J12 **Painan** Sumatera, W Indonesia
63 G23 **Paine, Cerro** ▲ S Chile
31 U11 **Painesville** Ohio, N USA
31 S14 **Paint Creek** ≈ Ohio, N USA
36 L10 **Painted Desert** *desert* Arizona, SW USA
Paint Hills *see* Wemindji
30 M4 **Paint River** ≈ Michigan, N USA
25 P8 **Paint Rock** Texas, SW USA
21 O6 **Paintsville** Kentucky, S USA
Paisance *see* Piacenza
96 I12 **Paisley** W Scotland, UK
32 I15 **Paisley** Oregon, NW USA
105 R10 **País Valenciano** *var.* Valencia, *Cat.* València; *anc.* Valentia. ◆ *autonomous community* NE Spain
105 O3 **País Vasco** *Basq.* Euskadi, *Eng.* The Basque Country, *Sp.* Provincias Vascongadas. ◆ *autonomous community* N Spain
56 A9 **Paita** Piura, NW Peru
169 V6 **Paitan, Teluk** *bay* Sabah, East Malaysia
104 H7 **Paiva, Rio** ≈ N Portugal
92 K12 **Pajala** Norrbotten, N Sweden
104 K3 **Pajares, Puerto de** *pass* NW Spain
54 G9 **Pajárito** Boyacá, C Colombia
54 G4 **Pajaro** La Guajira, S Colombia
Pakanbaru *see* Pekanbaru
55 Q10 **Pakaraima Mountains** *var.* Serra Pacaraim, Sierra Pacaraima. ▲▲ N South America
167 P10 **Pak Chong** Nakhon Ratchasima, C Thailand
123 V8 **Pakhachi** Koryakskiy Avtonomnyy Okrug, E Russian Federation
Pakhna *see* Páchna
189 U16 **Pakin Atoll** *atoll* Caroline Islands, E Micronesia
149 Q12 **Pakistan** *off.* Islamic Republic of Pakistan, *var.* Islami Jamhuriya e Pakistan. ◆ *republic* S Asia
Pakistan, Islami Jamhuriya e *see* Pakistan
167 P8 **Pak Lay** *var.* Muang Pak Lay. Xaignabouli, C Laos
Paknam *see* Samut Prakan
166 L5 **Pakokku** Magwe, C Myanmar
110 I10 **Pakość** *Ger.* Pakosch. Kujawski-pomorskie, C Poland
Pakosch *see* Pakość
149 V10 **Pākpattan** Punjab, E Pakistan
167 O15 **Pak Phanang** *var.* Ban Pak Phanang. Nakhon Si Thammarat, SW Thailand
112 G9 **Pakrac** *Hung.* Pakrácz. Požega-Slavonija, NE Croatia
Pakrácz *see* Pakrac
118 F11 **Pakruojis** Šiauliai, N Lithuania
111 J24 **Paks** Tolna, S Hungary
Pak Sane *see* Pakxan
Paksé *see* Pakxé
167 Q10 **Pak Thong Chai** Nakhon Ratchasima, C Thailand
149 R6 **Paktīā** ◆ *province* SE Afghanistan
149 Q7 **Paktīkā** ◆ *province* SE Afghanistan
171 N12 **Pakuli** Sulawesi, C Indonesia
81 F17 **Pakwach** NW Uganda
167 R8 **Pakxan** *var.* Muang Pakxan, Pak Sane. Bolikhamxai, C Laos
167 S10 **Pakxé** *var.* Paksé. Champasak, S Laos
78 G12 **Pala** Mayo-Kébbi, SW Chad
61 A17 **Palacios** Santa Fe, C Argentina
25 V13 **Palacios** Texas, SW USA
105 X5 **Palafrugell** Cataluña, NE Spain
107 L24 **Palagonia** Sicilia, Italy, C Mediterranean Sea
113 E17 **Palagruža** *It.* Pelagosa. *island* SW Croatia
115 G20 **Palaiá Epídavros** Pelopónnisos, S Greece
121 P3 **Palaichóri** *var.* Palekhori. C Cyprus
115 H25 **Palaiochóra** Kríti, Greece, E Mediterranean Sea
115 A15 **Palaiolastrítsa** *religious building* Kérkyra, Iónioi Nísoi, Greece, C Mediterranean Sea
115 J19 **Palaiópoli** Ándros, Kykládes, Greece, Aegean Sea
103 N5 **Palaiseau** Essonne, N France
Palakkad *see* Pālghāt
154 N11 **Pāla Laharha** Orissa, E India
83 G19 **Palamakoloi** Ghanzi, C Botswana
115 E16 **Palamás** Thessalía, C Greece
105 X5 **Palamós** Cataluña, NE Spain
118 J5 **Palamuse** *Ger.* Sankt-Bartholomäi. Jõgevamaa, E Estonia
183 Q14 **Palana** Tasmania, SE Australia
123 U9 **Palana** Koryakskiy Avtonomnyy Okrug, E Russian Federation
118 C11 **Palanga** *Ger.* Polangen. Klaipėda, NW Lithuania
143 V10 **Palangān, Kūh-e** ▲▲ E Iran
Palangkaraja *see* Palangkaraya
169 T12 **Palangkaraya** *prev.* Palangkaraja. Borneo, C Indonesia
155 H22 **Palani** Tamil Nādu, SE India
Palanka *see* Bačka Palanka
154 D9 **Pālanpur** Gujarāt, W India
Palantia *see* Palencia
83 I19 **Palapye** Central, SE Botswana
155 J19 **Pālār** ≈ SE India
104 H3 **Palas de Rei** Galicia, NW Spain
123 T9 **Palatka** Magadanskaya Oblast', E Russian Federation
23 W10 **Palatka** Florida, SE USA
188 B9 **Palau** *var.* Belau. ◆ *republic* W Pacific Ocean
131 Y14 **Palau Islands** *var.* Palau. *island group* N Palau
192 G16 **Palauli Bay** *bay* Savai'i, Samoa, C Pacific Ocean
167 N11 **Palaw** Tenasserim, S Myanmar
170 M6 **Palawan** *island* W Philippines
171 N6 **Palawan Passage** *passage* W Philippines
192 E7 **Palawan Trough** *undersea feature* S South China Sea
155 H23 **Pālayankottai** Tamil Nādu, SE India
107 L25 **Palazzolo Acreide** *anc.* Acrae. Sicilia, Italy, C Mediterranean Sea
118 G3 **Paldiski** *prev.* Baltiski, *Eng.* Baltic Port, *Ger.* Baltischport. Harjumaa, NW Estonia
112 I13 **Pale** Republika Srpska, E Bosnia and Herzegovina
Palekhori *see* Palaichóri
168 L13 **Palembang** Sumatera, W Indonesia
63 G18 **Palena** Los Lagos, S Chile
63 G18 **Palena, Río** ≈ S Chile
104 M5 **Palencia** *anc.* Palantia, Pallantia. Castilla-León, NW Spain
104 M3 **Palencia** ◆ *province* Castilla-León, N Spain
35 X15 **Palen Dry Lake** ◎ California, W USA
41 V15 **Palenque** Chiapas, SE Mexico
41 V15 **Palenque** *var.* Ruinas de Palenque. *ruins* Chiapas, SE Mexico
45 O9 **Palenque, Punta** *headland* S Dominican Republic
Palenque, Ruinas de *see* Palenque
Palerme *see* Palermo
107 I23 **Palermo** *Fr.* Palerme; *anc.* Panhormus, Panormus. Sicilia, Italy, C Mediterranean Sea
25 V8 **Palestine** Texas, SW USA
25 V7 **Palestine, Lake** ⊠ Texas, SW USA
107 I15 **Palestrina** Lazio, C Italy
166 K5 **Paletwa** Chin State, W Myanmar
155 G21 **Pālghāt** *var.* Palakkad; *prev.* Fulicat. Kerala, SW India
152 F13 **Pāli** Rājasthān, N India
167 N16 **Palian** Trang, SW Thailand
189 O12 **Palikir** ● (Micronesia) Pohnpei, E Micronesia
Palimé *see* Kpalimé
107 L19 **Palinuro, Capo** *headland* S Italy
115 H15 **Palioúri, Akrotírio** *var.* Akra Kanestron. *headland* N Greece
33 R14 **Palisades Reservoir** ⊠ Idaho, NW USA
99 J23 **Paliseul** Luxembourg, SE Belgium
154 C11 **Pālitāna** Gujarāt, W India
118 F4 **Palivere** Läänemaa, W Estonia
41 V14 **Palizada** Campeche, SE Mexico
93 L18 **Pälkäne** Länsi-Suomi, W Finland
155 J22 **Palk Strait** *strait* India/Sri Lanka
155 J23 **Pallai** Northern Province, NW Sri Lanka
Pallantia *see* Palencia
106 C6 **Pallanza** Piemonte, NE Italy
127 Q9 **Pallasovka** Volgogradskaya Oblast', SW Russian Federation
Pallene/Pallíni *see* Kassándra
185 L15 **Palliser Bay** *bay* North Island, NZ
185 L15 **Palliser, Cape** *headland* North Island, NZ
191 U9 **Palliser, Îles** *island group* Îles Tuamotu, C French Polynesia
105 X9 **Palma** *var.* Palma de Mallorca. Mallorca, Spain, W Mediterranean Sea
105 X9 **Palma** ✕ Mallorca, Spain, W Mediterranean Sea
82 Q12 **Palma** Cabo Delgado, N Mozambique
105 X10 **Palma, Badia de** *bay* Mallorca, Spain, W Mediterranean Sea
104 L13 **Palma del Río** Andalucía, S Spain
Palma de Mallorca *see* Palma
107 J25 **Palma di Montechiaro** Sicilia, Italy, C Mediterranean Sea
106 J7 **Palmanova** Friuli-Venezia Giulia, NE Italy
54 J7 **Palmarito** Apure, C Venezuela
43 N15 **Palmar Sur** Puntarenas, SE Costa Rica
60 I12 **Palmas** Paraná, S Brazil
59 K16 **Palmas** *var.* Palmas do Tocantins. Tocantins, C Brazil
76 L18 **Palmas, Cape** *Fr.* Cap des Palmes. *headland* SW Ivory Coast
Palmas do Tocantins *see* Palmas
54 D11 **Palmaseca** ✕ (Cali) Valle del Cauca, SW Colombia
107 B21 **Palmas, Golfo di** *gulf* Sardegna, Italy, C Mediterranean Sea
44 I7 **Palma Soriano** Santiago de Cuba, E Cuba
23 Y12 **Palm Bay** Florida, SE USA
35 T14 **Palmdale** California, W USA
61 H14 **Palmeira das Missões** Rio Grande do Sul, S Brazil
82 A11 **Palmeirinhas, Ponta das** *headland* NW Angola
39 R11 **Palmer** Alaska, USA
19 N11 **Palmer** Massachusetts, NE USA
25 U7 **Palmer** Texas, SW USA
194 H4 **Palmer** *US research station* Antarctica
15 R11 **Palmer** ≈ Québec, SE Canada
37 T5 **Palmer Lake** Colorado, C USA
194 J6 **Palmer Land** *physical region* Antarctica
14 F15 **Palmerston** Ontario, SE Canada
185 F22 **Palmerston** Otago, South Island, NZ
190 K15 **Palmerston** *island* S Cook Islands
Palmerston *see* Darwin
184 M12 **Palmerston North** Manawatu-Wanganui, North Island, NZ
Palmés, Cap des *see* Palmas, Cape
23 V13 **Palmetto** Florida, SE USA
Palmetto State *see* South Carolina
107 M22 **Palmi** Calabria, SW Italy
54 D11 **Palmira** Valle del Cauca, W Colombia
56 F8 **Palmira, Río** ≈ N Peru
61 D19 **Palmitas** Soriano, SW Uruguay
Palmnicken *see* Yantarnyy
35 V15 **Palm Springs** California, W USA
27 V2 **Palmyra** Missouri, C USA
18 G10 **Palmyra** New York, NE USA
18 G15 **Palmyra** Pennsylvania, NE USA
21 V5 **Palmyra** Virginia, NE USA
Palmyra *see* Tudmur
192 L7 **Palmyra Atoll** ◇ *US privately owned unincorporated territory* C Pacific Ocean
154 P12 **Palmyras Point** *headland* E India
35 N9 **Palo Alto** California, W USA
25 O1 **Palo Duro Creek** ≈ Texas, SW USA
Paloe *see* Palu
Paloe *see* Denpasar, Bali, C Indonesia
168 L9 **Paloh** Johor, Peninsular Malaysia
80 F12 **Paloich** Upper Nile, SE Sudan
40 I3 **Palomas** Chihuahua, N Mexico
107 I15 **Palombara Sabina** Lazio, C Italy
105 S13 **Palos, Cabo de** *headland* SE Spain
104 I14 **Palos de la Frontera** Andalucía, S Spain
60 G11 **Palotina** Paraná, S Brazil
32 M9 **Palouse** Washington, NW USA
32 L9 **Palouse River** ≈ Washington, NW USA
35 Y16 **Palo Verde** California, USA
57 E16 **Palpa** Ica, W Peru
95 M16 **Pålsboda** Örebro, C Sweden
93 M15 **Paltamo** Oulu, C Finland
171 N12 **Palu** *prev.* Paloe. Sulawesi, C Indonesia
137 P14 **Palu** Elazığ, E Turkey
152 I11 **Palwal** Haryāna, N India
123 U6 **Palyavaam** ≈ NE Russia
77 Q13 **Pama** SE Burkina
172 J14 **Pamandzi** ✕ (Mamoudzou) Petite-Terre, E Mayotte
Pamangkat *see* Pemangkat
143 R11 **Pā Mazār** Kermān, C Iran
83 N19 **Pambarra** Inhambane, SE Mozambique
171 X12 **Pamdai** Papua, E Indonesia
103 N16 **Pamiers** Ariège, S France
147 T14 **Pamir** *var.* Daryā-ye Pāmīr, *Taj.* Dar"yoi Pomir. ≈ Afghanistan/Tajikistan *see also* Pāmīr, Daryā-ye
Pamir/Pāmīr, Daryā-ye *see* Pamirs
149 U1 **Pāmīr, Daryā-ye** *var.* Pamir, *Taj.* Dar"yoi Pomir. ≈ Afghanistan/Tajikistan *see also* Pamir
Pāmīr-e Khord *see* Little Pamir
131 Q8 **Pamirs** *Pash.* Daryā-ye Pāmīr, *Rus.* Pamir. ▲▲ C Asia
Pâmiut *see* Paamiut
21 X10 **Pamlico River** ≈ North Carolina, SE USA
21 Y10 **Pamlico Sound** *sound* North Carolina, SE USA
25 O2 **Pampa** Texas, SW USA
Pampa Aullagas, Lago *see* Poopó, Lago
61 B21 **Pampa Húmeda** *grassland* E Argentina
56 A10 **Pampa las Salinas** *salt lake* NW Peru
57 F15 **Pampas** Huancavelica, C Peru
62 K13 **Pampas** *plain* C Argentina
55 O4 **Pampatar** Nueva Esparta, NE Venezuela
Pampeluna *see* Pamplona
104 H8 **Pampilhosa da Serra** *var.* Pampilhosa de Serra. Coimbra, N Portugal
173 Y15 **Pamplemousses** N Mauritius
54 G7 **Pamplona** Norte de Santander, N Colombia
105 Q3 **Pamplona** *Basq.* Iruña; *prev.* Pampeluna, *anc.* Pompaelo. Navarra, N Spain
114 I11 **Pamporovo** *prev.* Vasil Kolarov. Smolyan, S Bulgaria
136 D15 **Pamukkale** Denizli, W Turkey
21 W5 **Pamunkey River** ≈ Virginia, NE USA
152 K5 **Pamzal** Jammu and Kashmir, NW India
30 L14 **Pana** Illinois, N USA
41 Y11 **Panabá** Yucatán, SE Mexico
35 Y8 **Panaca** Nevada, W USA
115 E19 **Panachaikó** ▲▲ S Greece
14 F11 **Panache Lake** ◎ Ontario, S Canada
114 I10 **Panagyurishte** Pazardzhik, C Bulgaria
168 M16 **Panaitan, Pulau** *island* S Indonesia
115 D18 **Panaitolikó** ▲▲ C Greece
155 E17 **Panaji** *var.* Pangim, Panjim, New Goa. Goa, W India
43 T14 **Panama** *off.* Republic of Panama. ◆ *republic* Central America
43 T15 **Panamá** *var.* Ciudad de Panamá, *Eng.* Panama City. ● (Panama) Panamá, C Panama
43 U14 **Panamá** *off.* Provincia de Panamá. ◆ *province* E Panama
43 U15 **Panamá, Bahía de** *bay* N Gulf of Panama
193 T7 **Panama Basin** *undersea feature* E Pacific Ocean
43 T15 **Panama Canal** *canal* E Panama
23 R9 **Panama City** Florida, SE USA
43 T14 **Panama City** ✕ Panamá, C Panama
Panama City *see* Panamá
23 Q9 **Panama City Beach** Florida, SE USA
43 T17 **Panamá, Golfo de** *var.* Gulf of Panama. *gulf* S Panama
Panama, Gulf of *see* Panamá, Golfo de
Panama, Isthmus of *see* Panamá, Istmo de
43 T15 **Panamá, Istmo de** *Eng.* Isthmus of Panama; *prev.* Isthmus of Darien. *isthmus* E Panama
35 U11 **Panamint Range** ▲▲ California, W USA
107 L22 **Panarea, Isola** *island* Isole Eolie, S Italy

◆ Country ● Country Capital ◇ Dependent Territory ○ Dependent Territory Capital ◆ Administrative Region ✕ International Airport ▲ Mountain ▲▲ Mountain Range ⛰ Volcano ≈ River ◎ Lake ⊠ Reservoir

106 G9 **Panaro** ≈ N Italy
171 P6 **Panay Gulf** *gulf* C Philippines
171 P5 **Panay Island** *island* C Philippines
35 W7 **Pancake Range** ⛰ Nevada, W USA
112 M11 **Pančevo** *Ger.* Pantschowa, *Hung.* Pancsova. Serbia, N Serbia and Montenegro (Yugo.)
113 M15 **Pančićev Vrh** ▲ SW Serbia and Montenegro (Yugo.)
116 L12 **Panciu** Vrancea, E Romania
116 F10 **Pâncota** *Hung.* Pankota; *prev.* Pîncota. Arad, W Romania
Pancsova *see* Pančevo
83 N20 **Panda** Inhambane, SE Mozambique
171 X12 **Pandaidori, Kepulauan** *island group* E Indonesia
25 N11 **Pandale** Texas, SW USA
169 P12 **Pandang Tikar, Pulau** *island* N Indonesia
61 F20 **Pan de Azúcar** Maldonado, S Uruguay
118 H11 **Pandėlys** Panevėžys, NE Lithuania
155 F15 **Pandharpur** Mahārāshtra, W India
182 J1 **Pandie Pandie** South Australia
171 O12 **Pandiri** Sulawesi, C Indonesia
61 F20 **Pando** Canelones, S Uruguay
57 J14 **Pando** ◈ *department* N Bolivia
192 K9 **Pandora Bank** *undersea feature* W Pacific Ocean
95 G20 **Pandrup** Nordjylland, N Denmark
153 V12 **Pandu** Assam, NE India
79 J15 **Pandu** Equateur, NW Dem. Rep. Congo
Paneas *see* Bāniyās
59 F15 **Panelas** Mato Grosso, W Brazil
118 G12 **Panevėžys** Panevėžys, C Lithuania
118 G11 **Panevėžys** ◈ *province* NE Lithuania
Panfilov *see* Zharkent
127 N9 **Panfilovo** Volgogradskaya Oblast', SW Russian Federation
79 N17 **Panga** Orientale, N Dem. Rep. Congo
193 Y15 **Pangai** Lifuka, C Tonga
114 H13 **Pangaío** ⛰ N Greece
79 G20 **Pangala** Le Pool, S Congo
81 J22 **Pangani** Tanga, E Tanzania
81 I21 **Pangani** ≈ NE Tanzania
186 K8 **Panggoe** Choiseul Island, NW Solomon Islands
79 N20 **Pangi** Maniema, E Dem. Rep. Congo
Pangim *see* Panaji
168 H8 **Pangkalanbrandan** Sumatera, W Indonesia
Pangkalanbun *see* Pangkalanbuun
169 R13 **Pangkalanbuun** *var.* Pangkalanbun. Borneo, C Indonesia
169 N12 **Pangkalpinang** Pulau Bangka, W Indonesia
11 U17 **Pangman** Saskatchewan, S Canada
Pang-Nga *see* Phang-Nga
9 S6 **Pangnirtung** Baffin Island, Nunavut, NE Canada
152 K6 **Pangong Tso** *var.* Bangong Co. ◎ China/India *see also* Bangong Co
36 K7 **Panguitch** Utah, W USA
186 J7 **Panguna** Bougainville Island, NE PNG
171 N8 **Pangutaran Group** *island group* Sulu Archipelago, SW Philippines
25 N2 **Panhandle** Texas, SW USA
Panhormus *see* Palermo
171 W14 **Paniai, Danau** ◎ Papua, E Indonesia
79 L21 **Pania-Mutombo** Kasai Oriental, C Dem. Rep. Congo
Panicherevo *see* Dolno Panicherevo
187 P16 **Panié, Mont** ▲ C New Caledonia
152 I10 **Pānīpat** Haryāna, N India
147 Q14 **Panj** *Rus.* Pyandzh; *prev.* Kirovabad. SW Tajikistan
147 P15 **Panj** *Rus.* Pyandzh. ≈ Afghanistan/Tajikistan
149 O5 **Panjāb** Bāmīān, C Afghanistan
147 O12 **Panjakent** *Rus.* Pendzhikent. W Tajikistan
148 L14 **Panjgūr** Baluchistān, SW Pakistan
Panjim *see* Panaji
163 U12 **Panjin** Liaoning, NE China
147 P14 **Panji Poyon** *Rus.* Nizhniy Pyandzh. SW Tajikistan
149 Q4 **Panjshīr** ≈ E Afghanistan
Pankota *see* Pâncota
77 W14 **Pankshin** Plateau, C Nigeria
163 Y10 **Pan Ling** ⛰ N China
Panlong Jiang *see* Lô, Sông
154 J9 **Panna** Madhya Pradesh, C India
99 M16 **Panningen** Limburg, SE Netherlands
149 R13 **Pāno Āqil** Sind, SE Pakistan
121 P3 **Páno Léfkara** S Cyprus
121 O3 **Páno Panagiá** *var.* Pano Panayia. W Cyprus
Pano Panayia *see* Páno Panagiá
Panopolis *see* Akhmîm
29 U14 **Panora** Iowa, C USA
60 I8 **Panorama** São Paulo, S Brazil
115 I24 **Pánormos** Kríti, Greece, E Mediterranean Sea
Panormus *see* Palermo
163 W11 **Panshi** Jilin, NE China
59 H19 **Pantanal** *var.* Pantanalmato-Grossense. *swamp* SW Brazil
Pantanalmato-Grossense *see* Pantanal
61 H16 **Pântano Grande** Rio Grande do Sul, S Brazil
171 Q16 **Pantar, Pulau** *island* Kepulauan Alor, S Indonesia
21 X9 **Pantego** North Carolina, SE USA
107 G25 **Pantelleria** *anc.* Cossyra, Cosyra. Sicilia, Italy, C Mediterranean Sea
107 G25 **Pantelleria, Isola di** *island* SW Italy
Pante Macassar/Pante Makassar *see* Pante Makasar
171 Q16 **Pante Makasar** *var.* Pante Macassar, Pante Makassar. W East Timor
152 K10 **Pantnagar** Uttaranchal, N India
115 A15 **Pantokrátoras** ▲ Kérkyra, Iónioi Nísoi, Greece, C Mediterranean Sea
Pantschowa *see* Pančevo
41 P11 **Pánuco** Veracruz-Llave, E Mexico
41 P11 **Pánuco, Río** ≈ C Mexico
160 I12 **Panxian** Guizhou, S China
168 I10 **Panyabungan** Sumatera, N Indonesia
77 W14 **Panyam** Plateau, C Nigeria
157 N13 **Panzhihua** *prev.* Dukou, Tu-k'ou. Sichuan, C China
79 I22 **Panzi** Bandundu, SW Dem. Rep. Congo
42 E5 **Panzós** Alta Verapaz, E Guatemala
Pao-chi/Paoki *see* Baoji
Pao-king *see* Shaoyang
107 N20 **Paola** Calabria, SW Italy
121 P16 **Paola** E Malta
27 R5 **Paola** Kansas, C USA
31 O15 **Paoli** Indiana, N USA
187 R14 **Paonangisu** Éfaté, C Vanuatu
171 S13 **Paoni** *var.* Pauni. Pulau Seram, E Indonesia
37 Q5 **Paonia** Colorado, C USA
191 O7 **Paopao** Moorea, W French Polynesia
Pao-shan *see* Baoshan
Pao-ting *see* Baoding
Pao-t'ou/Paotow *see* Baotou
79 H14 **Paoua** Ouham-Pendé, W Central African Republic
Pap *see* Pop
111 H23 **Pápa** Veszprém, W Hungary
42 J12 **Papagayo, Golfo de** *gulf* NW Costa Rica
38 H11 **Pāpā'ikou** *var.* Papaikou. Hawai'i, USA, C Pacific Ocean
41 R15 **Papaloapan, Río** ≈ S Mexico
184 L6 **Papakura** Auckland, North Island, NZ
41 Q13 **Papantla** *var.* Papantla de Olarte. Veracruz-Llave, E Mexico
Papantla de Olarte *see* Papantla
191 P8 **Papara** Tahiti, W French Polynesia
184 K4 **Paparoa** Northland, North Island, NZ
185 G16 **Paparoa Range** ⛰ South Island, NZ
115 K20 **Pápas, Akrotirio** *headland* Ikaría, Dodekánisos, Greece, Aegean Sea
96 L2 **Papa Stour** *island* NE Scotland, UK
184 L6 **Papatoetoe** Auckland, North Island, NZ
185 E25 **Papatowai** Otago, South Island, NZ
96 K4 **Papa Westray** *island* NE Scotland, UK
191 T10 **Papeete** ○ (French Polynesia) Tahiti, W French Polynesia
100 F11 **Papenburg** Niedersachsen, NW Germany
98 H13 **Papendrecht** Zuid-Holland, SW Netherlands
191 Q7 **Papenoo** Tahiti, W French Polynesia
191 Q7 **Papenoo Rivière** ≈ Tahiti, W French Polynesia
191 N7 **Papetoai** Moorea, W French Polynesia
92 L3 **Papey** *island* E Iceland
Paphos *see* Páfos
40 H5 **Papigochic, Río** ≈ NW Mexico
118 E10 **Papilė** Šiauliai, NW Lithuania
29 S15 **Papillion** Nebraska, C USA
15 T5 **Papinachois** ≈ Québec, SE Canada
171 X13 **Papua** *var.* Irian Barat, West Irian, West New Guinea, West Papua ; *prev.* Dutch New Guinea, Irian Jaya, Netherlands New Guinea. ◈ *province* E Indonesia
186 C9 **Papua, Gulf of** *gulf* S PNG
186 C8 **Papua New Guinea** *off.* Independent State of Papua New Guinea; *prev.* Territory of Papua and New Guinea, *abbrev.* PNG. ◆ *commonwealth republic* NW Melanesia
192 H8 **Papua Plateau** *undersea feature* N Coral Sea
112 G9 **Papuk** ⛰ NE Croatia
167 N8 **Papun** Karen State, S Myanmar
42 L14 **Paquera** Puntarenas, W Costa Rica
55 V9 **Para** ◈ *district* N Suriname
58 I13 **Pará** *off.* Estado do Pará. ◈ *state* NE Brazil
Pará *see* Belém
180 I8 **Paraburdoo** Western Australia
57 E16 **Paracas, Península de** *peninsula* W Peru
59 L19 **Paracatu** Minas Gerais, NE Brazil
192 E6 **Paracel Islands** ◇ *disputed territory* SE Asia
182 I6 **Parachilna** South Australia
149 R6 **Pārachinār** North-West Frontier Province, NW Pakistan
112 N13 **Paraćin** Serbia, C Serbia and Montenegro (Yugo.)
14 K8 **Paradis** Québec, SE Canada
39 N11 **Paradise** *var.* Paradise Hill. Alaska, USA
35 O5 **Paradise** California, W USA
35 X11 **Paradise** Nevada, W USA
Paradise Hill *see* Paradise
37 R11 **Paradise Hills** New Mexico, SW USA
Paradise of the Pacific *see* Hawaii
36 L13 **Paradise Valley** Arizona, SW USA
35 T2 **Paradise Valley** Nevada, W USA
115 O22 **Paradisi** ✕ (Ródos) Ródos, Dodekánisos, Greece, Aegean Sea
154 P12 **Pārādwīp** Orissa, E India
Paraetonium *see* Maṭrūḥ
117 R4 **Parafiyivka** Chernihivs'ka Oblast', N Ukraine
36 K7 **Paragonah** Utah, W USA
27 X9 **Paragould** Arkansas, C USA
47 X8 **Paraguaçu** *var.* Paraguassú. ≈ E Brazil
60 J9 **Paraguaçu Paulista** São Paulo, S Brazil
54 H4 **Paraguaipoa** Zulia, NW Venezuela
62 O6 **Paraguarí** Paraguarí, S Paraguay
62 O7 **Paraguarí** *off.* Departamento de Paraguarí. ◈ *department* S Paraguay
55 O8 **Paragua, Río** ≈ SE Venezuela
57 O16 **Paraguá, Río** ≈ NE Bolivia
Paraguassú *see* Paraguaçu
62 N5 **Paraguay** ◆ *republic* C South America
47 U10 **Paraguay** *var.* Río Paraguay. ≈ C South America
Parahiba/Parahyba *see* Paraíba
59 P15 **Paraíba** *off.* Estado da Paraíba; *prev.* Parahiba, Parahyba. ◈ *state* E Brazil
Paraíba *see* João Pessoa
60 P9 **Paraíba do Sul, Rio** ≈ SE Brazil
Parainen *see* Pargas
43 N14 **Paraíso** Cartago, C Costa Rica
41 U14 **Paraíso** Tabasco, SE Mexico
57 O17 **Paraiso, Río** ≈ E Bolivia
Parajd *see* Praid
77 S14 **Parakou** C Benin
121 Q2 **Paralimni** E Cyprus
115 G18 **Paralímni, Límni** ◎ C Greece
55 W8 **Paramaribo** ● (Suriname) Paramaribo, N Suriname
55 W9 **Paramaribo** ◈ *district* N Suriname
55 W9 **Paramaribo** ✕ Paramaribo, N Suriname
Paramithiá *see* Paramythiá
56 C13 **Paramonga** Lima, W Peru
123 V12 **Paramushir, Ostrov** *island* SE Russian Federation
115 C16 **Paramythiá** *var.* Paramithiá. Ípeiros, W Greece
62 M10 **Paraná** Entre Ríos, E Argentina
60 H11 **Paraná** *off.* Estado do Paraná. ◈ *state* S Brazil
47 U11 **Paraná** *var.* Alto Paraná. ≈ C South America
60 K12 **Paranaguá** Paraná, S Brazil
59 J20 **Paranaíba, Rio** ≈ E Brazil
61 C19 **Paraná Ibicuy, Río** ≈ E Argentina
59 H15 **Paranaíta** Mato Grosso, W Brazil
60 H9 **Paranapanema, Rio** ≈ S Brazil
60 K11 **Paranapiacaba, Serra do** ⛰ S Brazil
60 H9 **Paranavaí** Paraná, S Brazil
143 N5 **Parandak** Markazī, W Iran
114 I12 **Paranéstio** Anatolikí Makedonía kai Thráki, NE Greece
191 W11 **Paraoa** *atoll* Îles Tuamotu, C French Polynesia
184 L13 **Paraparaumu** Wellington, North Island, NZ
57 N20 **Parapetí, Río** ≈ SE Bolivia
54 L10 **Paraque, Cerro** ▲ W Venezuela
154 I11 **Parasiya** Madhya Pradesh, C India
115 M23 **Paraspóri, Akrotírio** *headland* Kárpathos, SE Greece
60 O10 **Parati** Rio de Janeiro, SE Brazil
59 K14 **Parauapebas** Pará, N Brazil
103 Q10 **Paray-le-Monial** Saône-et-Loire, C France
Parbatsar *see* Parvatsar
154 G13 **Parbhani** Mahārāshtra, C India
100 L10 **Parchim** Mecklenburg-Vorpommern, N Germany
Parchwitz *see* Prochowice
110 P13 **Parczew** Lubelskie, E Poland
60 L8 **Pardo, Rio** ≈ S Brazil
111 E16 **Pardubice** *Ger.* Pardubitz. Pardubický Kraj, C Czech Republic
111 E17 **Pardubický Kraj** ◈ region C Czech Republic
Pardubitz *see* Pardubice
119 F16 **Parechcha** *Pol.* Porzecze, *Rus.* Porech'ye. Hrodzyenskaya Voblasts', W Belarus
59 F17 **Parecis, Chapada dos** *var.* Serra dos Parecis. ⛰ W Brazil
Parecis, Serra dos *see* Parecis, Chapada dos
104 M4 **Paredes de Nava** Castilla-León, N Spain
189 U12 **Parem** *island* Chuuk, C Micronesia
189 O12 **Parem Island** *island* E Micronesia
184 I1 **Parengarenga Harbour** *inlet* North Island, NZ
15 N8 **Parent** Québec, SE Canada
102 J14 **Parentis-en-Born** Landes, SW France
Parenzo *see* Poreč
185 G20 **Pareora** Canterbury, South Island, NZ
171 N14 **Parepare** Sulawesi, C Indonesia
115 B16 **Párga** Ípeiros, W Greece
93 K20 **Pargas** *Swe.* Parainen. Länsi-Suomi, W Finland
64 O5 **Pargo, Ponta do** *headland* Madeira, Portugal, NE Atlantic Ocean
Paria, Golfo de *see* Paria, Gulf of
55 N6 **Pariaguán** Anzoátegui, NE Venezuela
45 X17 **Paria, Gulf of** *var.* Golfo de Paria. *gulf* Trinidad and Tobago/Venezuela
57 I15 **Pariamanu, Río** ≈ E Peru
36 L8 **Paria River** ≈ Utah, W USA
Parichi *see* Parychy
40 M14 **Paricutín, Volcán** ✱ C Mexico
43 P16 **Parida, Isla** *island* SW Panama
55 T8 **Parika** NE Guyana
93 O18 **Parikkala** Etelä-Suomi, S Finland
58 E10 **Parima, Serra** *var.* Sierra Parima. ⛰ Brazil/Venezuela *see also* Parima, Sierra
55 N11 **Parima, Sierra** *var.* Serra Parima. ⛰ Brazil/Venezuela *see also* Parima, Serra
57 F17 **Parinacochas, Laguna** ◎ SW Peru
56 A9 **Pariñas, Punta** *headland* NW Peru
58 H12 **Parintins** Amazonas, N Brazil
103 O5 **Paris** *anc.* Lutetia, Lutetia Parisiorum, Parisii. ● (France) Paris, N France
191 Y2 **Paris** Kiritimati, E Kiribati
27 S11 **Paris** Arkansas, C USA
33 S16 **Paris** Idaho, NW USA
31 N14 **Paris** Illinois, N USA
20 M5 **Paris** Kentucky, S USA
27 V3 **Paris** Missouri, C USA
20 H8 **Paris** Tennessee, S USA
25 V5 **Paris** Texas, SW USA
Parisii *see* Paris
43 S16 **Parita** Herrera, S Panama
43 S16 **Parita, Bahía de** *bay* S Panama
Parkan/Párkány *see* Štúrovo
93 K18 **Parkano** Länsi-Suomi, W Finland
27 N6 **Park City** Kansas, C USA
36 L3 **Park City** Utah, W USA
36 I12 **Parker** Arizona, SW USA
23 R9 **Parker** Florida, SE USA
29 R11 **Parker** South Dakota, N USA
35 Z14 **Parker Dam** California, W USA
29 W13 **Parkersburg** Iowa, C USA
21 Q3 **Parkersburg** West Virginia, NE USA
29 T7 **Parkers Prairie** Minnesota, N USA
171 P8 **Parker Volcano** ✱ Mindanao, S Philippines
181 W13 **Parkes** New South Wales, SE Australia
30 K4 **Park Falls** Wisconsin, N USA
Parkhar *see* Farkhor
14 E16 **Parkhill** Ontario, S Canada
29 T5 **Park Rapids** Minnesota, N USA
29 Q3 **Park River** North Dakota, N USA
29 Q11 **Parkston** South Dakota, N USA
10 L17 **Parksville** Vancouver Island, British Columbia, SW Canada
37 S3 **Parkview Mountain** ▲ Colorado, C USA
105 N8 **Parla** Madrid, C Spain
29 S8 **Parle, Lac qui** ▣ Minnesota, N USA
115 F20 **Parlía Tyroú** Pelopónnisos, S Greece
155 G14 **Parli Vaijnāth** Mahārāshtra, C India
106 F9 **Parma** Emilia-Romagna, N Italy
31 T11 **Parma** Ohio, N USA
Parnahyba *see* Parnaíba
58 N13 **Parnaíba** *var.* Parnahyba. Piauí, E Brazil
65 J14 **Parnaíba Ridge** *undersea feature* C Atlantic Ocean
58 N13 **Parnaíba, Rio** ≈ NE Brazil
115 F18 **Parnassós** ⛰ C Greece
185 J17 **Parnassus** Canterbury, South Island, NZ
182 H10 **Parndana** South Australia
115 H19 **Párnitha** ⛰ C Greece
115 F21 **Párnon** ⛰ S Greece
118 G5 **Pärnu** *Ger.* Pernau, *Latv.* Pērnava; *prev. Rus.* Pernov. Pärnumaa, SW Estonia
118 G6 **Pärnu** *var.* Parnu Jõgi, *Ger.* Pernau. ≈ SW Estonia
118 G5 **Pärnu-Jaagupi** *Ger.* Sankt-Jakobi. Pärnumaa, SW Estonia
Parnu Jõgi *see* Pärnu
118 G5 **Pärnu Laht** *Ger.* Pernauer Bucht. *bay* SW Estonia
118 F5 **Pärnumaa** *off.* Pärnu Maakond. ◈ *province* SW Estonia
153 T11 **Paro** W Bhutan
153 T11 **Paro** ✕ (Thimphu) W Bhutan
185 G17 **Paroa** West Coast, South Island, NZ
163 X14 **P'aro-ho** *var.* Hwach'ŏn-chŏsuji. ◎ N South Korea
183 N6 **Paroo River** *seasonal river* New South Wales/ Queensland, SE Australia
Paropamisus Range *see* Sefīdkūh, Selseleh-ye
115 J21 **Páros** Páros, Kykládes, Greece, Aegean Sea
115 J21 **Páros** *island* Kykládes, Greece, Aegean Sea
36 K7 **Parowan** Utah, W USA
103 U13 **Parpaillon** ⛰ SE France
108 I9 **Parpan** Graubünden, S Switzerland
62 G13 **Parral** Maule, C Chile
Parral *see* Hidalgo del Parral
183 T9 **Parramatta** New South Wales, SE Australia
21 Y6 **Parramore Island** *island* Virginia, NE USA
40 M8 **Parras** *var.* Parras de la Fuente. Coahuila de Zaragoza, NE Mexico
Parras de la Fuente *see* Parras
42 M14 **Parrita** Puntarenas, S Costa Rica
8 L5 **Parry Channel** *channel* N Canada
14 G13 **Parry Island** *island* Ontario, S Canada
8 M4 **Parry Islands** *island group* Nunavut, NW Canada
14 G12 **Parry Sound** Ontario, S Canada
110 F7 **Parsęta** *Ger.* Persante. ≈ NW Poland
28 L3 **Parshall** North Dakota, N USA
27 Q7 **Parsons** Kansas, C USA
20 H9 **Parsons** Tennessee, S USA
21 T3 **Parsons** West Virginia, NE USA
Parsonstown *see* Birr
100 P11 **Parsteiner See** ◎ NE Germany
107 I24 **Partanna** Sicilia, Italy, C Mediterranean Sea
108 J8 **Partenen** Graubünden, E Switzerland
102 K9 **Parthenay** Deux-Sèvres, W France
95 J19 **Partille** Västra Götaland, S Sweden
107 I23 **Partinico** Sicilia, Italy, C Mediterranean Sea
111 I20 **Partizánske** *prev.* Šimonovany; *Hung.* Simony. Trenčiansky Kraj, W Slovakia
58 H11 **Paru de Oeste, Rio** ≈ N Brazil
182 K9 **Paruna** South Australia
58 I11 **Paru, Rio** ≈ N Brazil
Parvān *see* Parwān
155 M14 **Pārvatipuram** Andhra Pradesh, E India
152 G12 **Parvatsar** *prev.* Parbatsar. Rājasthān, N India
149 Q5 **Parwān** *Per.* Parvān. ◈ *province* E Afghanistan
158 I15 **Paryang** Xizang Zizhiqu, W China
119 M18 **Parychy** *Rus.* Parichi. Homyel'skaya Voblasts', SE Belarus
83 J21 **Parys** Free State, C South Africa
35 T15 **Pasadena** California, W USA
25 W11 **Pasadena** Texas, SW USA
56 B8 **Pasaje** El Oro, SW Ecuador
137 T9 **P'asanauri** N Georgia
168 I13 **Pasapuat** Pulau Pagai Utara, W Indonesia
167 N7 **Pasawng** Kayah State, C Myanmar
114 L13 **Paşayiğit** Edirne, NW Turkey
23 N9 **Pascagoula** Mississippi, S USA
22 M8 **Pascagoula River** ≈ Mississippi, S USA
116 F12 **Paşcani** *Hung.* Páskán. Iaşi, NE Romania
109 T4 **Pasching** Oberösterreich, N Austria
32 K10 **Pasco** Washington, NW USA
56 E13 **Pasco** *off.* Departamento de Pasco. ◈ *department* C Peru
191 N11 **Pascua, Isla de** *var.* Rapa Nui, *Eng.* Easter Island. *island* E Pacific Ocean
63 G21 **Pascua, Río** ≈ S Chile
103 N1 **Pas-de-Calais** ◈ *department* N France
100 P10 **Pasewalk** Mecklenburg-Vorpommern, NE Germany
11 T10 **Pasfield Lake** ◎ Saskatchewan, C Canada
Pa-shih Hai-hsia *see* Bashi Channel
Pashkeni *see* Bolyarovo
Pashmakli *see* Smolyan
153 X10 **Pāsighāt** Arunāchel Pradesh, NE India
137 Q12 **Pasinler** Erzurum, NE Turkey
Pasi Oloy, Qatorkŭhi *see* Zaalayskiy Khrebet
42 E3 **Pasión, Río de la** ≈ N Guatemala
168 J12 **Pasirganting** Sumatera, W Indonesia
Pasirpangarayan *see* Bagansiapiapi
168 K6 **Pasir Puteh** *var.* Pasir Putih. Kelantan, Peninsular Malaysia
169 R9 **Pasir, Tanjung** *headland* East Malaysia
95 N20 **Påskallavik** Kalmar, S Sweden
Páskán *see* Paşcani
Paskevicha, Zaliv *see* Tushchybas, Zaliv
110 K7 **Pasłęk** *Ger.* Preußisch Holland. Warmińsko-Mazurskie, NE Poland
110 K7 **Pasłęka** *Ger.* Passarge. ≈ N Poland
148 K16 **Pasni** Baluchistān, SW Pakistan
63 I18 **Paso de Indios** Chubut, S Argentina
54 L7 **Paso del Caballo** Guárico, N Venezuela
61 E15 **Paso de los Libres** Corrientes, NE Argentina
61 E18 **Paso de los Toros** Tacuarembó, C Uruguay
35 P12 **Paso Robles** California, W USA
15 Y7 **Paspébiac** Québec, SE Canada
11 U14 **Pasquia Hills** ⛰ Saskatchewan, S Canada
149 W7 **Pasrūr** Punjab, E Pakistan
30 M1 **Passage Island** *island* Michigan, N USA
65 B24 **Passage Islands** *island group* W Falkland Islands
8 K5 **Passage Point** *headland* Banks Island, Northwest Territories, NW Canada
Passarge *see* Pasłęka
115 C15 **Passarón** *ancient monument* Ípeiros, W Greece
Passarowitz *see* Požarevac
101 O22 **Passau** Bayern, SE Germany
22 M9 **Pass Christian** Mississippi, S USA
107 L26 **Passero, Capo** *headland* Sicilia, Italy, C Mediterranean Sea
171 P5 **Passi** Panay Island, C Philippines
61 H14 **Passo Fundo** Rio Grande do Sul, S Brazil
60 H13 **Passo Fundo, Barragem de** ▣ S Brazil
61 H15 **Passo Real, Barragem de** ▣ S Brazil
59 L20 **Passos** Minas Gerais, NE Brazil
167 X10 **Passu Keah** *island* S Paracel Islands
118 J13 **Pastavy** *Pol.* Postawy, *Rus.* Postavy. Vitsyebskaya Voblasts', NW Belarus
56 D7 **Pastaza** ◈ *province* E Ecuador
56 D9 **Pastaza, Río** ≈ Ecuador/Peru
61 A21 **Pasteur** Buenos Aires, E Argentina
15 V3 **Pasteur** ≈ Québec, SE Canada
147 Q12 **Pastigav** *Rus.* Pastigov. W Tajikistan
Pastigov *see* Pastigav
54 C13 **Pasto** Nariño, SW Colombia
38 M10 **Pastol Bay** *bay* Alaska, USA
37 O8 **Pastora Peak** ▲ Arizona, SW USA
105 O8 **Pastrana** Castilla-La Mancha, C Spain
169 S16 **Pasuruan** *prev.* Pasoeroean. Jawa, C Indonesia
118 F11 **Pasvalys** Panevėžys, N Lithuania
111 K21 **Pásztó** Nógrád, N Hungary
189 U12 **Pata** *var.* Patta. *atoll* Chuuk Islands, C Micronesia
36 M16 **Patagonia** Arizona, SW USA
63 H20 **Patagonia** *physical region* Argentina/Chile
Patalung *see* Phatthalung
154 D9 **Pātan** Gujarāt, W India
154 J10 **Pātan** Madhya Pradesh, C India
171 S11 **Patani** Pulau Halmahera, E Indonesia
Patani *see* Pattani
15 V7 **Patapédia Est** ≈ Québec, SE Canada
116 K13 **Pătârlagele** *prev.* Pătîriagele. Buzău, SE Romania
Patavium *see* Padova
182 I5 **Patawarta Hill** ▲ South Australia
182 L10 **Patchewollock** Victoria, SE Australia
184 K11 **Patea** Taranaki, North Island, NZ
184 K11 **Patea** ≈ North Island, NZ
77 U15 **Pategi** Kwara, C Nigeria
81 K20 **Pate Island** *var.* Patta Island. *island* SE Kenya
105 S10 **Paterna** País Valenciano, E Spain
109 R9 **Paternion** *Slvn.* Špatrjan. Kärnten, S Austria
107 L24 **Paternò** *anc.* Hybla, Hybla Major. Sicilia, Italy, C Mediterranean Sea
32 J7 **Pateros** Washington, NW USA
18 J14 **Paterson** New Jersey, NE USA
32 J10 **Paterson** Washington, NW USA
185 C25 **Paterson Inlet** *inlet* Stewart Island, NZ
98 N6 **Paterswolde** Drenthe, NE Netherlands
152 H7 **Pathānkot** Himāchal Pradesh, N India
Pathein *see* Bassein
33 W15 **Pathfinder Reservoir** ▣ Wyoming, C USA
167 O11 **Pathum Thani** *var.* Patumdhani, Prathum Thani. Pathum Thani, C Thailand
54 C12 **Patía** *var.* El Bordo. Cauca, SW Colombia
152 I9 **Patiāla** *var.* Puttiala. Punjab, NW India
54 B12 **Patía, Río** ≈ SW Colombia
188 D15 **Pati Point** *headland* NE Guam
Pătîriagele *see* Pătârlagele
56 C13 **Pativilca** Lima, W Peru
166 M1 **Pātkai Bum** *var.* Patkai Range. ⛰ Myanmar/India
Patkai Range *see* Pātkai Bum
115 L20 **Pátmos** Pátmos, Dodekánisos, Greece, Aegean Sea
115 L20 **Pátmos** *island* Dodekánisos, Greece, Aegean Sea
153 P13 **Patna** *var.* Azimabad. Bihār, N India
154 M12 **Patnāgarh** Orissa, E India
171 O5 **Patnongon** Panay Island, C Philippines
137 S13 **Patnos** Ağrı, E Turkey
60 H12 **Pato Branco** Paraná, S Brazil
31 O16 **Patoka Lake** ◎ Indiana, N USA
92 L9 **Patoniva** *Lapp.* Buoddobohki. Lappi, N Finland
113 K21 **Patos** *var.* Patosi. Fier, SW Albania
Patos *see* Patos de Minas
59 K19 **Patos de Minas** *var.* Patos. Minas Gerais, NE Brazil
Patosi *see* Patos
61 I17 **Patos, Lagoa dos** *lagoon* S Brazil
62 J9 **Patquía** La Rioja, C Argentina
115 E19 **Pátra** *Eng.* Patras; *prev.* Pátrai. Dytikí Ellás, S Greece
Pátrai/Patras *see* Pátra
115 D18 **Patraïkós Kólpos** *gulf* S Greece
92 G2 **Patreksfjördhur** Vestfirdhir, W Iceland
24 M7 **Patricia** Texas, SW USA
63 F21 **Patricio Lynch, Isla** *island* S Chile
Patta *see* Pata
Patta Island *see* Pate Island
167 O16 **Pattani** *var.* Patani. Pattani, SW Thailand
167 P12 **Pattaya** Chon Buri, S Thailand
19 S4 **Patten** Maine, NE USA
35 O9 **Patterson** California, W USA
22 J10 **Patterson** Louisiana, S USA
35 R7 **Patterson, Mount** ▲ California, W USA
31 P4 **Patterson, Point** *headland* Michigan, N USA
107 L23 **Patti** Sicilia, Italy, C Mediterranean Sea
107 L23 **Patti, Golfo di** *gulf* Sicilia, Italy, C Mediterranean Sea
93 L14 **Pattijoki** Oulu, W Finland
193 Q4 **Patton Escarpment** *undersea feature* E Pacific Ocean
27 S2 **Pattonsburg** Missouri, C USA
(0) D6 **Patton Seamount** *undersea feature* NE Pacific Ocean
10 J12 **Pattullo, Mount** ▲ British Columbia, W Canada
Patuakhali *see* Patukhali
42 M5 **Patuca, Río** ≈ E Honduras
153 U16 **Patukhali** *var.* Patuakhali. Khulna, S Bangladesh
Patumdhani *see* Pathum Thani
40 M14 **Pátzcuaro** Michoacán de Ocampo, SW Mexico
42 C6 **Patzicía** Chimaltenango, S Guatemala
102 K16 **Pau** Pyrénées-Atlantiques, SW France
102 J12 **Pauillac** Gironde, SW France
166 L5 **Pauk** Magwe, W Myanmar
8 I6 **Paulatuk** Northwest Territories, NW Canada
42 K5 **Paulayá, Río** ≈ NE Honduras

22 M6 **Paulding** Mississippi, S USA
31 Q12 **Paulding** Ohio, N USA
29 S12 **Paullina** Iowa, C USA
59 P15 **Paulo Afonso** Bahia, E Brazil
38 M16 **Pauloff Harbor** var. Pavlor Harbour. Sanak Island, Alaska, USA
27 N12 **Pauls Valley** Oklahoma, C USA
166 L7 **Paungde** Pegu, C Myanmar
Pauni see Paoni
152 K9 **Pauri** Uttaranchal, N India
Pautalia see Kyustendil
142 J5 **Pāveh** Kermānshāh, NW Iran
126 L5 **Pavelets** Ryazanskaya Oblast', W Russian Federation
106 D8 **Pavia** anc. Ticinum. Lombardia, N Italy
118 C9 **Pāvilosta** Liepāja, W Latvia
125 P14 **Pavino** Kostromskaya Oblast', NW Russian Federation
114 J8 **Pavlikeni** Veliko Tŭrnovo, N Bulgaria
145 T8 **Pavlodar** Pavlodar, NE Kazakhstan
145 S9 **Pavlodar** off. Pavlodarskaya Oblast', Kaz. Pavlodar Oblysy. ◆ province NE Kazakhstan
Pavlodar Oblysy/Pavlodarskaya Oblast' see Pavlodar
Pavlograd see Pavlohrad
117 U7 **Pavlohrad** Rus. Pavlograd. Dnipropetrovs'ka Oblast', E Ukraine
Pavlor Harbour see Pauloff Harbor
145 R9 **Pavlovka** Akmola, C Kazakhstan
127 V4 **Pavlovka** Respublika Bashkortostan, W Russian Federation
127 Q7 **Pavlovka** Ul'yanovskaya Oblast', W Russian Federation
127 N3 **Pavlovo** Nizhegorodskaya Oblast', W Russian Federation
126 L9 **Pavlovsk** Voronezhskaya Oblast', W Russian Federation
126 L13 **Pavlovskaya** Krasnodarskiy Kray, SW Russian Federation
117 S7 **Pavlysh** Kirovohrads'ka Oblast', C Ukraine
106 F10 **Pavullo nel Frignano** Emilia-Romagna, C Italy
27 P8 **Pawhuska** Oklahoma, C USA
21 U13 **Pawleys Island** South Carolina, SE USA
167 N6 **Pawn** ≈ C Myanmar
30 K14 **Pawnee** Illinois, N USA
27 O9 **Pawnee** Oklahoma, C USA
37 U2 **Pawnee Buttes** ▲ Colorado, C USA
29 S17 **Pawnee City** Nebraska, C USA
26 K5 **Pawnee River** ≈ Kansas, C USA
31 O10 **Paw Paw** Michigan, N USA
31 O10 **Paw Paw Lake** Michigan, N USA
19 O12 **Pawtucket** Rhode Island, NE USA
Pax Augusta see Badajoz
115 I25 **Paximádia** island SE Greece
Pax Julia see Beja
115 B16 **Paxoí** island Iónioi Nísoi, Greece, C Mediterranean Sea
39 S10 **Paxson** Alaska, USA
147 O11 **Paxtakor** Jizzax Viloyati, C Uzbekistan
30 M13 **Paxton** Illinois, N USA
124 J11 **Pay** Respublika Kareliya, NW Russian Federation
166 M8 **Payagyi** Pegu, SW Myanmar
108 C9 **Payerne** Ger. Peterlingen. Vaud, W Switzerland
32 M13 **Payette** Idaho, NW USA
32 M13 **Payette** ≈ Idaho, NW USA
127 V2 **Pay-Khoy, Khrebet** ▲▲ NW Russian Federation
Payne see Kangirsuk
12 K4 **Payne, Lac** ◎ Québec, NE Canada
29 T8 **Paynesville** Minnesota, N USA
169 S8 **Payong, Tanjung** headland East Malaysia
Payo Obispo see Chetumal
61 D18 **Paysandú** Paysandú, W Uruguay
61 D17 **Paysandú** ◆ department W Uruguay
102 I7 **Pays de la Loire** ◆ region NW France
36 L12 **Payson** Arizona, SW USA
36 L4 **Payson** Utah, W USA
127 W4 **Payyer, Gora** ▲ NW Russian Federation
Payzawat see Jiashi
137 Q11 **Pazar** Rize, NE Turkey
136 F10 **Pazarbaşı Burnu** headland NW Turkey
136 M16 **Pazarcık** Kahramanmaraş, S Turkey
114 I10 **Pazardzhik** prev. Tatar Pazardzhik.Pazardzhik, C Bulgaria
114 H11 **Pazardzhik** ◆ province C Bulgaria
54 H9 **Paz de Ariporo** Casanare, E Colombia
112 A10 **Pazin** Ger. Mitterburg, It. Pisino. Istra, NW Croatia
42 D7 **Paz, Río** ≈ El Salvador/Guatemala
113 O18 **Pčinja** ≈ N FYR Macedonia
193 V15 **Pea** Tongatapu, S Tonga
27 O6 **Peabody** Kansas, C USA
11 O12 **Peace** ≈ Alberta/British Columbia, W Canada
Peace Garden State see North Dakota
11 Q10 **Peace Point** Alberta, C Canada
11 O12 **Peace River** Alberta, W Canada
23 W13 **Peace River** ≈ Florida, SE USA
11 N17 **Peachland** British Columbia, SW Canada
36 J10 **Peach Springs** Arizona, SW USA
Peach State see Georgia
23 S4 **Peachtree City** Georgia, SE USA
189 Y13 **Peacock Point** point SE Wake Island
97 M18 **Peak District** physical region C England, UK
183 Q7 **Peak Hill** New South Wales, SE Australia
65 G15 **Peak, The** ▲ C Ascension Island
105 O13 **Peal de Becerro** Andalucía, S Spain
189 X11 **Peale Island** island N Wake Island
37 O6 **Peale, Mount** ▲ Utah, W USA
39 O4 **Peard Bay** bay Alaska, USA
23 Q7 **Pea River** ≈ Alabama/Florida, S USA
25 W11 **Pearland** Texas, SW USA
38 D9 **Pearl City** O'ahu, Hawai'i, USA, C Pacific Ocean
38 D9 **Pearl Harbor** inlet O'ahu, Hawai'i, USA, C Pacific Ocean
Pearl Islands see Perlas, Archipiélago de las
Pearl Lagoon see Perlas, Laguna de
22 M5 **Pearl River** ≈ Louisiana /Mississippi, S USA
25 Q13 **Pearsall** Texas, SW USA
23 U7 **Pearson** Georgia, SE USA
25 P4 **Pease River** ≈ Texas, SW USA
12 F7 **Peawanuk** Ontario, C Canada
83 P16 **Pebane** Zambézia, NE Mozambique
65 C23 **Pebble Island** island N Falkland Islands
65 C23 **Pebble Island Settlement** Pebble Island, N Falkland Islands
113 L16 **Peć** Alb. Pejë, Turk. Ipek. Serbia, S Serbia and Montenegro (Yugo.)
25 R8 **Pecan Bayou** ≈ Texas, SW USA
22 H10 **Pecan Island** Louisiana, S USA
60 L12 **Peças, Ilha das** island S Brazil
30 L10 **Pecatonica River** ≈ Illinois/Wisconsin, N USA
108 G10 **Peccia** Ticino, S Switzerland
Pechenegi see Pechenihy
Pechenezhskoye Vodokhranilishche see Pecheniz'ke Vodoskhovyshche
124 I2 **Pechenga** Fin. Petsamo. Murmanskaya Oblast', NW Russian Federation
117 V5 **Pechenihy** Rus. Pechenegi. Kharkivs'ka Oblast', E Ukraine
117 V5 **Pecheniz'ke Vodoskhovyshche** Rus. Pechenezhskoye Vodokhranilishche. ▣ E Ukraine
125 U7 **Pechora** Respublika Komi, NW Russian Federation
127 R6 **Pechora** ≈ NW Russian Federation
Pechora Bay see Pechorskaya Guba
Pechora Sea see Pechorskoye More
127 S3 **Pechorskaya Guba** Eng. Pechora Bay. bay NW Russian Federation
122 H7 **Pechorskoye More** Eng. Pechora Sea. sea NW Russian Federation
116 E11 **Pecica** Ger. Petschka, Hung. Ópécska. Arad, W Romania
24 K8 **Pecos** Texas, SW USA
25 N11 **Pecos River** ≈ New Mexico/Texas, SW USA
111 I25 **Pécs** Ger. Fünfkirchen; Lat. Sopianae. Baranya, SW Hungary
43 T17 **Pedasí** Los Santos, S Panama
Pedde see Pedja
183 O17 **Pedder, Lake** ◎ Tasmania, SE Australia
44 M10 **Pedernales** SW Dominican Republic
55 Q5 **Pedernales** Delta Amacuro, NE Venezuela
25 R10 **Pedernales River** ≈ Texas, SW USA
62 H6 **Pedernales, Salar de** salt lake N Chile
Pedhoulas see Pedoulás
55 X11 **Pédima** var. Malavate. SW French Guiana
182 F1 **Pedirka** South Australia
171 S11 **Pediwang** Pulau Halmahera, E Indonesia
118 I5 **Pedja** var. Pedja Jõgi, Ger. Pedde. ≈ E Estonia
Pedja Jõgi see Pedja
121 O3 **Pedoulás** var. Pedhoulas. W Cyprus
59 N18 **Pedra Azul** Minas Gerais, NE Brazil
104 I3 **Pedrafita, Porto de** var. Puerto de Piedrafita. pass NW Spain
76 E9 **Pedra Lume** Sal, NE Cape Verde
43 P16 **Pedregal** Chiriquí, W Panama
54 J4 **Pedregal** Falcón, N Venezuela
40 L9 **Pedriceña** Durango, C Mexico
60 L11 **Pedro Barros** São Paulo, S Brazil
39 Q13 **Pedro Bay** Alaska, USA
62 H4 **Pedro de Valdivia** var. Oficina Pedro de Valdivia. Antofagasta, N Chile
62 P4 **Pedro Juan Caballero** Amambay, E Paraguay
63 L15 **Pedro Luro** Buenos Aires, E Argentina
105 O10 **Pedro Muñoz** Castilla-La Mancha, C Spain
155 J22 **Pedro, Point** headland NW Sri Lanka
182 K9 **Peebinga** South Australia
96 J13 **Peebles** SE Scotland, UK
31 S15 **Peebles** Ohio, N USA
96 J12 **Peebles** cultural region SE Scotland, UK
18 K13 **Peekskill** New York, NE USA
97 I16 **Peel** W Isle of Man
8 G7 **Peel** ≈ Northwest Territories/Yukon Territory, NW Canada
8 K5 **Peel Point** headland Victoria Island, Northwest Territories, NW Canada
8 M5 **Peel Sound** passage Nunavut, N Canada
100 N9 **Peene** ≈ NE Germany
99 K17 **Peer** Limburg, NE Belgium
14 H14 **Pefferlaw** Ontario, S Canada
185 I18 **Pegasus Bay** bay South Island, NZ
121 O3 **Pégeia** var. Peyia. SW Cyprus
109 V7 **Peggau** Steiermark, SE Austria
101 L19 **Pegnitz** Bayern, SE Germany
101 L19 **Pegnitz** ≈ SE Germany
105 T11 **Pego** País Valenciano, E Spain
166 L8 **Pegu** var. Bago. Pegu, SW Myanmar
166 L7 **Pegu** ◆ division S Myanmar
189 N13 **Pehleng** Pohnpei, E Micronesia
114 M12 **Pehlivanköy** Kırklareli, NW Turkey
77 R14 **Péhonko** C Benin
61 B21 **Pehuajó** Buenos Aires, E Argentina
Pei-ching see Beijing/Beijing Shi
100 J13 **Peine** Niedersachsen, C Germany
Pei-p'ing see Beijing/Beijing Shi
Peipsi Järv/Peipus-See see Peipus, Lake
118 J5 **Peipus, Lake** Est. Peipsi Järv, Ger. Peipus-See, Rus. Chudskoye Ozero. ◎ Estonia/Russian Federation
115 H19 **Peiraías** prev. Piraiévs, Eng. Piraeus. Attikí, C Greece
Peisern see Pyzdry
60 I8 **Peixe, Rio do** ≈ S Brazil
59 I16 **Peixoto de Azevedo** Mato Grosso, W Brazil
168 O11 **Pejantan, Pulau** island W Indonesia
Pejë see Peć
112 N11 **Pek** ≈ E Serbia and Montenegro (Yugo.)
167 R7 **Pèk** var. Xieng Khouang; prev. Xiangkhoang. Xiangkhoang, N Laos
169 Q16 **Pekalongan** Jawa, C Indonesia
168 K11 **Pekanbaru** var. Pakanbaru. Sumatera, W Indonesia
30 L12 **Pekin** Illinois, N USA
Peking see Beijing/Beijing Shi
Pelabohan Kelang/Pelabuhan Kelang see Pelabuhan Klang
168 J9 **Pelabuhan Klang** var. Kuala Pelabohan Kelang, Pelabohan Kelang, Pelabuhan Kelang, Port Klang, Port Swettenham. Selangor, Peninsular Malaysia
120 L11 **Pelagie, Isole** island group SW Italy
Pelagosa see Palagruža
22 L5 **Pelahatchie** Mississippi, S USA
169 T14 **Pelaihari** var. Pleihari. Borneo, C Indonesia
103 U14 **Pelat, Mont** ▲ SE France
116 F12 **Peleaga, Vârful** prev. Vîrful Peleaga. ▲ W Romania
Peleaga, Vîrful see Peleaga, Vârful
123 O11 **Peleduy** Respublika Sakha (Yakutiya), NE Russian Federation
14 C18 **Pelee Island** island Ontario, S Canada
45 Q11 **Pelée, Montagne** Ѫ N Martinique
14 D18 **Pelee, Point** headland Ontario, S Canada
171 P12 **Pelei** Pulau Peleng, N Indonesia
Peleliu see Beliliou
171 P12 **Peleng, Pulau** island Kepulauan Banggai, N Indonesia
23 T7 **Pelham** Georgia, SE USA
111 E18 **Pelhřimov** Ger. Pilgram. Vysočina, C Czech Republic
39 W13 **Pelican** Chichagof Island, Alaska, USA
191 Z3 **Pelican Lagoon** ◎ Kiritimati, E Kiribati
29 U6 **Pelican Lake** ◎ Minnesota, N USA
29 V3 **Pelican Lake** ◎ Minnesota, N USA
30 L5 **Pelican Lake** ◎ Wisconsin, N USA
44 G1 **Pelican Point** Grand Bahama Island, N Bahamas
83 B19 **Pelican Point** headland W Namibia
29 S6 **Pelican Rapids** Minnesota, N USA
Pelican State see Louisiana
11 U13 **Pelikan Narrows** Saskatchewan, C Canada
115 L18 **Pelinaío** ▲ Chíos, E Greece
Pelinnaeum see Pelinnaío
115 E16 **Pelinnaío** anc. Pelinnaeum. ruins Thessalía, C Greece
113 N20 **Pelister** ▲ SW FYR Macedonia
113 G15 **Pelješac** peninsula S Croatia
92 M12 **Pelkosenniemi** Lappi, NE Finland
29 W15 **Pella** Iowa, C USA
114 F13 **Pélla** site of ancient city Kentrikí Makedonía, N Greece
23 Q3 **Pell City** Alabama, S USA
61 A22 **Pellegrini** Buenos Aires, E Argentina
92 K12 **Pello** Lappi, NW Finland
100 G7 **Pellworm** island N Germany
10 H6 **Pelly** ≈ Yukon Territory, NW Canada
9 N7 **Pelly Bay** Nunavut, N Canada
10 I8 **Pelly Mountains** ▲▲ Yukon Territory, W Canada
Pélmonostor see Beli Manastir
37 P13 **Pelona Mountain** ▲ New Mexico, SW USA
Peloponnese/Peloponnesus see Pelopónnisos
115 E20 **Pelopónnisos** Eng. Peloponnese. ◆ region S Greece
115 E20 **Pelopónnisos** var. Morea, Eng. Peloponnese; anc. Peloponnesus. peninsula S Greece
107 L23 **Peloritani, Monti** anc. Pelorus and Neptunius. ▲▲ Sicilia, Italy, C Mediterranean Sea
107 M22 **Peloro, Capo** var. Punta del Faro. headland S Italy
Pelorus and Neptunius see Peloritani, Monti
61 H17 **Pelotas** Rio Grande do Sul, S Brazil
61 I14 **Pelotas, Rio** ≈ S Brazil
92 K10 **Peltovuoma** Lapp. Bealdovuopmi. Lappi, N Finland
19 R4 **Pemadumcook Lake** ◎ Maine, NE USA
169 Q16 **Pemalang** Jawa, C Indonesia
169 P10 **Pemangkat** var. Pamangkat. Borneo, C Indonesia
Pemar see Paimio
168 I9 **Pematangsiantar** Sumatera, W Indonesia
83 Q14 **Pemba** prev. Port Amelia, Porto Amélia. Cabo Delgado, NE Mozambique
81 J22 **Pemba** ◆ region E Tanzania
81 K21 **Pemba** island E Tanzania
83 Q14 **Pemba, Baia de** inlet NE Mozambique
81 J21 **Pemba Channel** channel E Tanzania
180 J14 **Pemberton** Western Australia
10 M16 **Pemberton** British Columbia, SW Canada
29 Q2 **Pembina** North Dakota, N USA
29 Q2 **Pembina** ≈ Canada/USA
11 P15 **Pembina** ≈ Alberta, SW Canada
171 X16 **Pembre** Papua, E Indonesia
14 K12 **Pembroke** Ontario, SE Canada
97 H21 **Pembroke** SW Wales, UK
23 W6 **Pembroke** Georgia, SE USA
21 U11 **Pembroke** North Carolina, SE USA
21 R7 **Pembroke** Virginia, NE USA
97 H21 **Pembroke** cultural region SW Wales, UK
Pembuang, Sungai see Seruyan, Sungai
43 S15 **Peña Blanca, Cerro** ▲ C Panama
104 K8 **Peña de Francia, Sierra de la** ▲▲ W Spain
104 G6 **Penafiel** var. Peñafiel. Porto, N Portugal
105 N6 **Peñafiel** Castilla-León, N Spain
105 S8 **Peñagolosa** ▲ E Spain
105 N7 **Peñalara, Pico de** ▲ C Spain
171 X16 **Penambo, Banjaran** var. Banjaran Tama Abu, Penambo Range. ▲▲ Indonesia/Malaysia
Penambo Range see Penambo, Banjaran
41 O10 **Peña Nevada, Cerro** ▲ C Mexico
Penang see Pinang, Pulau, Peninsular Malaysia
Penang see Pinang
Penang see George Town
60 J8 **Penápolis** São Paulo, S Brazil
104 L7 **Peñaranda de Bracamonte** Castilla-León, N Spain
105 S8 **Peñarroya** ▲ E Spain
104 L12 **Peñarroya-Pueblonuevo** Andalucía, S Spain
97 K22 **Penarth** S Wales, UK
104 K1 **Peñas, Cabo de** headland N Spain
63 F20 **Penas, Golfo de** gulf S Chile
Pen-ch'i see Benxi
79 H14 **Pendé** var. Logone Oriental. ≈ Central African Republic/Chad
76 I14 **Pendembu** E Sierra Leone
29 R13 **Pender** Nebraska, C USA
Penderma see Bandırma
32 K11 **Pendleton** Oregon, NW USA
32 M7 **Pend Oreille, Lake** ◎ Idaho, NW USA
32 M7 **Pend Oreille River** ≈ Idaho/Washington, NW USA
Pendzhikent see Panjakent
Peneius see Pineiós
104 G8 **Penela** Coimbra, N Portugal
14 G13 **Penetanguishene** Ontario, S Canada
151 H15 **Penganga** ≈ C India
161 T12 **P'engchia Yu** island N Taiwan
79 M21 **Penge** Kasai Oriental, C Dem. Rep. Congo
Penghu Archipelago/P'enghu Ch'üntao/Penghu Islands see P'enghu Liehtao
161 R14 **P'enghu Liehtao** var. P'enghu Ch'üntao, Penghu Islands, Eng. Penghu Archipelago, Pescadores, Jap. Hoko-guntō, Hoko-shotō. island group W Taiwan
Penghu Shuidao/P'enghu Shuitao see Pescadores Channel
161 R4 **Penglai** var. Dengzhou. Shandong, E China
Peng-pu see Bengbu
Penhsihu see Benxi
Penibético, Sistema see Béticos, Sistemas
104 F10 **Peniche** Leiria, W Portugal
169 U17 **Penida, Nusa** island S Indonesia
Peninsular State see Florida
105 T8 **Peñíscola** País Valenciano, E Spain
40 M13 **Pénjamo** Guanajuato, C Mexico
Penki see Benxi
102 F7 **Penmarch, Pointe de** headland NW France
107 L15 **Penna, Punta della** headland C Italy
107 K14 **Penne** Abruzzo, C Italy
Penner see Penneru
155 J18 **Penneru** var. Penner. ≈ C India
182 I10 **Penneshaw** South Australia
18 C14 **Penn Hills** Pennsylvania, NE USA
Penninae, Alpes/Pennine, Alpi see Pennine Alps
108 D11 **Pennine Alps** Fr. Alpes Pennines, It. Alpi Pennine; Lat. Alpes Penninae. ▲▲ Italy/Switzerland
Pennine Chain see Pennines
97 L15 **Pennines** var. Pennine Chain. ▲▲ N England, UK
Pennines, Alpes see Pennine Alps
21 O8 **Pennington Gap** Virginia, NE USA
18 I16 **Penns Grove** New Jersey, NE USA
18 I16 **Pennsville** New Jersey, NE USA
18 E14 **Pennsylvania** off. Commonwealth of Pennsylvania; also known as The Keystone State. ◆ state NE USA
18 G10 **Penn Yan** New York, NE USA
124 H16 **Peno** Tverskaya Oblast', W Russian Federation
19 R7 **Penobscot Bay** bay Maine, NE USA
19 S5 **Penobscot River** ≈ Maine, NE USA
182 K12 **Penola** South Australia
40 K9 **Peñón Blanco** Durango, C Mexico
182 E7 **Penong** South Australia
43 S16 **Penonomé** Coclé, C Panama
190 L13 **Penrhyn** atoll N Cook Islands
192 M9 **Penrhyn Basin** undersea feature C Pacific Ocean
183 S9 **Penrith** New South Wales, SE Australia
97 K15 **Penrith** NW England, UK
23 O9 **Pensacola** Florida, SE USA
23 O9 **Pensacola Bay** bay Florida, SE USA
195 N7 **Pensacola Mountains** ▲▲ Antarctica
182 L12 **Penshurst** Victoria, SE Australia
187 R13 **Pentecost** Fr. Pentecôte. island C Vanuatu
15 V4 **Pentecôte** ≈ Québec, SE Canada
Pentecôte see Pentecost
15 V4 **Pentecôte, Lac** ◎ Québec, SE Canada
8 H15 **Penticton** British Columbia, SW Canada
96 J6 **Pentland Firth** strait N Scotland, UK
96 J12 **Pentland Hills** hill range S Scotland, UK
171 Q12 **Penu** Pulau Taliabu, E Indonesia
155 H18 **Penukonda** Andhra Pradesh, E India
166 L7 **Penwegon** Pegu, C Myanmar
24 M8 **Penwell** Texas, SW USA
97 J21 **Pen y Fan** ▲ SE Wales, UK
97 L16 **Pen-y-ghent** ▲ N England, UK
127 O6 **Penza** Penzenskaya Oblast', W Russian Federation
97 G25 **Penzance** SW England, UK
127 N6 **Penzenskaya Oblast'** ◆ province W Russian Federation
123 U7 **Penzhina** ≈ E Russian Federation
123 U9 **Penzhinskaya Guba** bay E Russian Federation
Penzig see Pieńsk
36 K13 **Peoria** Arizona, SW USA
30 L12 **Peoria** Illinois, N USA
30 L12 **Peoria Heights** Illinois, N USA
31 N11 **Peotone** Illinois, N USA
18 J11 **Pepacton Reservoir** ▣ New York, NE USA
76 I15 **Pepel** W Sierra Leone
30 I6 **Pepin, Lake** ▣ Minnesota/Wisconsin, N USA
99 L20 **Pepinster** Liège, E Belgium
113 L20 **Peqin** var. Peqini. Elbasan, C Albania
Peqini see Peqin
40 D7 **Pequeña, Punta** headland W Mexico
168 J8 **Perak** ◆ state Peninsular Malaysia
105 R7 **Perales del Alfambra** Aragón, NE Spain
115 C15 **Pérama** var. Perama. Ípeiros, W Greece
92 M13 **Perä-Posio** Lappi, NE Finland
15 Z6 **Percé** Québec, SE Canada
15 Z6 **Percé, Rocher** island Québec, S Canada
102 L5 **Perche, Collines de** ▲ N France
109 X4 **Perchtoldsdorf** Niederösterreich, NE Austria
180 L6 **Percival Lakes** lakes Western Australia
105 T3 **Perdido, Monte** ▲ NE Spain
23 O8 **Perdido River** ≈ Alabama/Florida, S USA
Perece Vela Basin see West Mariana Basin
116 G7 **Perechyn** Zakarpats'ka Oblast', W Ukraine
54 E10 **Pereira** Risaralda, W Colombia
60 I7 **Pereira Barreto** São Paulo, S Brazil
59 G15 **Pereirinha** Pará, N Brazil
127 N10 **Perelazovskiy** Volgogradskaya Oblast', SW Russian Federation
127 S7 **Perelyub** Saratovskaya Oblast', W Russian Federation
31 P7 **Pere Marquette River** ≈ Michigan, N USA
Peremyshl see Przemyśl
116 I5 **Peremyshlyany** L'vivs'ka Oblast', W Ukraine
Pereshchepino see Pereshchepyne
116 L9 **Pereshchepyne** Rus. Pereshchepino. Dnipropetrovs'ka Oblast', E Ukraine
126 L16 **Pereslavl'-Zalesskiy** Yaroslavskaya Oblast', W Russian Federation
117 Y7 **Pereval's'k** Luhans'ka Oblast', E Ukraine
127 U7 **Perevolotskiy** Orenburgskaya Oblast', W Russian Federation
Pereyaslav-Khmel'nitskiy see Pereyaslav-Khmel'nyts'kyy
117 Q5 **Pereyaslav-Khmel'nyts'kyy** Rus. Pereyaslav-Khmel'nitskiy. Kyyivs'ka Oblast', N Ukraine
109 U4 **Perg** Oberösterreich, N Austria
61 B19 **Pergamino** Buenos Aires, E Argentina
106 G6 **Pergine Valsugana** Ger. Persen. Trentino-Alto Adige, N Italy
29 S6 **Perham** Minnesota, N USA
93 L16 **Perho** Länsi-Suomi, W Finland
116 E11 **Periam** Ger. Perjamosch, Hung. Perjámos. Timiș, W Romania
15 Q6 **Péribonca** ≈ Québec, SE Canada
12 L11 **Péribonca, Lac** ◎ Québec, SE Canada
15 Q6 **Péribonca, Petite Rivière** ≈ Québec, SE Canada
15 Q7 **Péribonka** Québec, SE Canada
40 I9 **Pericos** Sinaloa, C Mexico
169 Q10 **Perigi** Borneo, C Indonesia
102 L12 **Périgueux** anc. Vesuna. Dordogne, SW France
54 G5 **Perijá, Serranía de** ▲▲ Columbia/Venezuela
115 H17 **Peristéra** island Vóreioi Sporádes, Greece
63 H20 **Perito Moreno** Santa Cruz, S Argentina
155 G22 **Periyāl** var. Periyār. ≈ SW India
Periyār see Periyāl
155 G23 **Periyār Lake** ◎ S India
Perjámos/Perjamosch see Periam
27 O9 **Perkins** Oklahoma, C USA
116 L7 **Perkivtsi** Chernivets'ka Oblast', W Ukraine
43 U15 **Perlas, Archipiélago de las** Eng. Pearl Islands. island group SE Panama
43 O10 **Perlas, Cayos de** reef SE Nicaragua
43 N9 **Perlas, Laguna de** Eng. Pearl Lagoon. lagoon E Nicaragua
43 N10 **Perlas, Punta de** headland E Nicaragua
100 L11 **Perleberg** Brandenburg, N Germany
Perlepe see Prilep
168 I6 **Perlis** ◆ state Peninsular Malaysia
125 U14 **Perm'** prev. Molotov. Permskaya Oblast', NW Russian Federation
113 M22 **Përmet** var. Përmeti, Prëmet. Gjirokastër, S Albania
Përmeti see Përmet
125 U15 **Permskaya Oblast'** ◆ province NW Russian Federation
59 P15 **Pernambuco** off. Estado de Pernambuco. ◆ state E Brazil
Pernambuco see Recife
Pernambuco Abyssal Plain see Pernambuco Plain
47 Y6 **Pernambuco Plain** var. Pernambuco Abyssal Plain. undersea feature E Atlantic Ocean
65 K15 **Pernambuco Seamounts** undersea feature C Atlantic Ocean
182 H6 **Pernatty Lagoon** salt lake South Australia
Pernau see Pärnu
Pernauer Bucht see Pärnu Laht
Pērnava see Pärnu
114 G9 **Pernik** prev. Dimitrovo. Pernik, W Bulgaria
114 G10 **Pernik** ◆ province W Bulgaria
93 K20 **Perniö** Swe. Bjärnå. Länsi-Suomi, W Finland
109 X5 **Pernitz** Niederösterreich, E Austria
Pernov see Pärnu
103 O3 **Péronne** Somme, N France
14 L8 **Péronne, Lac** ◎ Québec, SE Canada
106 A8 **Perosa Argentina** Piemonte, NE Italy
41 Q14 **Perote** Veracruz-Llave, E Mexico
Pérouse see Perugia
191 W15 **Pérouse, Bahía de la** bay Easter Island, Chile, E Pacific Ocean
Perovsk see Kyzylorda
103 O17 **Perpignan** Pyrénées-Orientales, S France
113 M20 **Përrenjas** var. Përrenjasi, Prenjas, Prenjasi. Elbasan, E Albania
Përrenjasi see Përrenjas
92 O2 **Perriertoppen** ▲ C Svalbard
25 S6 **Perrin** Texas, SW USA
23 Y16 **Perrine** Florida, SE USA
37 S12 **Perro, Laguna del** ◎ New Mexico, SW USA
102 G5 **Perros-Guirec** Côtes d'Armor, NW France
23 T9 **Perry** Florida, SE USA
23 T5 **Perry** Georgia, SE USA
29 U14 **Perry** Iowa, C USA
18 E10 **Perry** New York, NE USA
27 N9 **Perry** Oklahoma, C USA
27 Q3 **Perry Lake** ▣ Kansas, C USA
31 R11 **Perrysburg** Ohio, N USA
25 O1 **Perryton** Texas, SW USA
39 O15 **Perryville** Alaska, USA
27 U11 **Perryville** Arkansas, C USA
27 Y6 **Perryville** Missouri, C USA
Persante see Parsęta
Persen see Pergine Valsugana
Pershay see Pyarshai
117 V7 **Pershotravens'k** Dnipropetrovs'ka Oblast', E Ukraine
117 W9 **Pershotravneve** Donets'ka Oblast', E Ukraine
Persia see Iran
141 T5 **Persian Gulf** var. The Gulf Ar. Khalīj al 'Arabī, Per. Khalīj-e Fars. gulf SW Asia
Persis see Fārs
95 K22 **Perstorp** Skåne, S Sweden
137 O14 **Pertek** Tunceli, C Turkey
183 P16 **Perth** Tasmania, SE Australia

◆ Country ● Country Capital ◇ Dependent Territory ○ Dependent Territory Capital ◆ Administrative Region ✕ International Airport ▲ Mountain ▲▲ Mountain Range Ѫ Volcano ≈ River ◎ Lake ▣ Reservoir

180 I13 **Perth** state capital Western Australia
14 L13 **Perth** Ontario, SE Canada
96 J11 **Perth** C Scotland, UK
180 I12 **Perth** × Western Australia
96 J10 **Perth** cultural region C Scotland, UK
173 V10 **Perth Basin** undersea feature SE Indian Ocean
103 S15 **Pertuis** Vaucluse, SE France
103 Y16 **Pertusato, Capo** headland Corse, France, C Mediterranean Sea
30 L11 **Peru** Illinois, N USA
31 P12 **Peru** Indiana, N USA
57 E13 **Peru** off. Republic of Peru. ◆ republic W South America
Peru see Beru
193 T9 **Peru Basin** undersea feature E Pacific Ocean
193 U8 **Peru-Chile Trench** undersea feature E Pacific Ocean
112 F13 **Perućko Jezero** ◎ S Croatia
106 H13 **Perugia** Fr. Pérouse; anc. Perusia. Umbria, C Italy
Perugia, Lake of see Trasimeno, Lago
61 D15 **Perugorría** Corrientes, NE Argentina
60 M11 **Peruíbe** São Paulo, S Brazil
155 B21 **Perumalpār** reef India, N Indian Ocean
Perusia see Perugia
99 D20 **Péruwelz** Hainaut, SW Belgium
137 R15 **Pervari** Siirt, SE Turkey
127 O4 **Pervomaysk** Nizhegorodskaya Oblast', W Russian Federation
117 X7 **Pervomays'k** Luhans'ka Oblast', E Ukraine
117 P8 **Pervomays'k** prev. Ol'viopol'. Mykolayivs'ka Oblast', S Ukraine
117 S12 **Pervomays'ke** Respublika Krym, S Ukraine
125 R14 **Pervomayskiy** Kirovskaya Oblast', NW Russian Federation
127 V7 **Pervomayskiy** Orenburgskaya Oblast', W Russian Federation
126 M6 **Pervomayskiy** Tambovskaya Oblast', W Russian Federation
117 V6 **Pervomays'kyy** Kharkivs'ka Oblast', E Ukraine
122 F10 **Pervoural'sk** Sverdlovskaya Oblast', C Russian Federation
123 V11 **Pervyy Kuril'skiy Proliv** strait E Russian Federation
99 I19 **Perwez** Wallon Brabant, C Belgium
106 I11 **Pesaro** anc. Pisaurum. Marche, C Italy
35 N9 **Pescadero** California, W USA
Pescadores see P'enghu Liehtao
161 S14 **Pescadores Channel** var. Penghu Shuidao, P'enghu Shuitao. channel W Taiwan
107 K14 **Pescara** anc. Aternum, Ostia Aterni. Abruzzo, C Italy
107 K15 **Pescara** ≈ C Italy
106 F11 **Pescia** Toscana, C Italy
108 C8 **Peseux** Neuchâtel, W Switzerland
127 P6 **Pesha** ≈ NW Russian Federation
149 T5 **Peshāwar** North-West Frontier Province, N Pakistan
149 T6 **Peshāwar** × North-West Frontier Province, N Pakistan
113 M19 **Peshkopi** var. Peshkopia, Peshkopija. Dibër, NE Albania
Peshkopia/Peshkopija see Peshkopi
114 I11 **Peshtera** Pazardzhik, C Bulgaria
31 N6 **Peshtigo** Wisconsin, N USA
31 N6 **Peshtigo River** ≈ Wisconsin, N USA
Peski see Pyeski
Peski Taskuduk see Tosquduq Qumlari
125 S13 **Peskovka** Kirovskaya Oblast', NW Russian Federation
103 S8 **Pesmes** Haute-Saône, E France
104 H6 **Peso da Régua** var. Pêso da Regua. Vila Real, N Portugal
40 F5 **Pesqueira** Sonora, NW Mexico
102 J13 **Pessac** Gironde, SW France
111 J23 **Pest** off. Pest Megye. ◈ county C Hungary
124 J14 **Pestovo** Novgorodskaya Oblast', W Russian Federation
40 M15 **Petacalco, Bahía** bay W Mexico
Petach-Tikva/Petah Tiqva see Petah Tiqwa
138 F10 **Petah Tiqwa** var. Petach-Tikva, Petah Tiqva, Petakh Tikva.Tel Aviv, C Israel
Petakh Tikva see Petah Tiqwa
93 L17 **Petäjävesi** Länsi-Suomi, W Finland
22 M7 **Petal** Mississippi, S USA
115 I19 **Petalioí** island C Greece
115 H19 **Petalión, Kólpos** gulf E Greece
115 J19 **Pétalo** ▲ Ándros, Kykládes, Greece, Aegean Sea
34 M8 **Petaluma** California, W USA
99 L25 **Pétange** Luxembourg, SW Luxembourg
54 M5 **Petare** Miranda, N Venezuela
41 N16 **Petatlán** Guerrero, S Mexico
83 L14 **Petauke** Eastern, E Zambia
14 J12 **Petawawa** Ontario, SE Canada
14 J11 **Petawawa** ≈ Ontario, SE Canada
Petchaburi see Phetchaburi
42 D2 **Petén** off. Departamento del Petén. ◈ department N Guatemala
42 D2 **Petén Itzá, Lago** var. Lago de Flores. ◎ N Guatemala
30 K7 **Petenwell Lake** ▣ Wisconsin, N USA
14 D6 **Peterbell** Ontario, S Canada
182 I7 **Peterborough** South Australia
14 I14 **Peterborough** Ontario, SE Canada
97 N20 **Peterborough** prev. Medeshamstede. E England, UK
19 N10 **Peterborough** New Hampshire, NE USA
96 L8 **Peterhead** NE Scotland, UK
Peterhof see Luboń
193 Q14 **Peter I Island** ◇ Norwegian dependency Antarctica
194 H9 **Peter I Island** var. Peter I øy. island Antarctica
Peter I øy see Peter I Island
97 M14 **Peterlee** N England, UK
Peterlingen see Payerne
197 P14 **Petermann Bjerg** ▲ C Greenland
11 S12 **Peter Pond Lake** ◎ Saskatchewan, C Canada
39 X13 **Petersburg** Mytkof Island, Alaska, USA
30 K13 **Petersburg** Illinois, N USA
31 N16 **Petersburg** Indiana, N USA
29 Q3 **Petersburg** North Dakota, N USA
25 N5 **Petersburg** Texas, SW USA
21 V7 **Petersburg** Virginia, NE USA
21 T4 **Petersburg** West Virginia, NE USA
100 H12 **Petershagen** Nordrhein-Westfalen, NW Germany
55 S9 **Peters Mine** var. Peter's Mine. N Guyana
107 O21 **Petilia Policastro** Calabria, SW Italy
44 M9 **Pétionville** S Haiti
45 X6 **Petit-Bourg** Basse Terre, C Guadeloupe
15 Y5 **Petit-Cap** Québec, SE Canada
45 Y6 **Petit Cul-de-Sac Marin** bay C Guadeloupe
44 M9 **Petite-Rivière-de-l'Artibonite** C Haiti
173 X16 **Petite Rivière Noire, Piton de la** ▲ C Mauritius
15 R9 **Petite-Rivière-St-François** Québec, SE Canada
44 L9 **Petit-Goâve** S Haiti
Petitjean see Sidi-Kacem
13 N10 **Petit Lac Manicouagan** ◎ Québec, E Canada
19 T7 **Petit Manan Point** headland Maine, NE USA
Petit Mécatina, Rivière du see Little Mecatina
11 N10 **Petitot** ≈ Alberta/British Columbia, W Canada
45 S12 **Petit Piton** ▲ SW Saint Lucia
Petit-Popo see Aného
Petit St-Bernard, Col du see Little Saint Bernard Pass
13 O8 **Petitsikapau Lake** ◎ Newfoundland and Labrador, E Canada
92 L11 **Petkula** Lappi, N Finland
41 X12 **Peto** Yucatán, SE Mexico
62 G10 **Petorca** Valparaíso, C Chile
31 Q5 **Petoskey** Michigan, N USA
138 G14 **Petra** archaeological site Ma'ān, W Jordan
Petra see Wādī Mūsā
115 F14 **Pétras, Sténa** pass N Greece
123 S16 **Petra Velikogo, Zaliv** bay SE Russian Federation
Petrel see Petrer
14 K15 **Petre, Point** headland Ontario, SE Canada
105 S12 **Petrer** var. Petrel. País Valenciano, E Spain
125 U11 **Petretsovo** Permskaya Oblast', NW Russian Federation
114 G12 **Petrich** Blagoevgrad, SW Bulgaria
187 P15 **Petrie, Récif** reef N New Caledonia
37 N11 **Petrified Forest** prehistoric site Arizona, SW USA
Petrikau see Piotrków Trybunalski
Petrikov see Pyetrykaw
116 H12 **Petrila** Hung. Petrilla. Hunedoara, W Romania
Petrilla see Petrila
112 E9 **Petrinja** Sisak-Moslavina, C Croatia
Petroaleksandrovsk see Türtkŭl
Petrőcz see Bački Petrovac
124 G12 **Petrodvorets** Fin. Pietarhovi. Leningradskaya Oblast', NW Russian Federation
Petrograd see Sankt-Peterburg
Petrokov see Piotrków Trybunalski
54 G6 **Petrólea** Norte de Santander, NE Colombia
14 D16 **Petrolia** Ontario, S Canada
25 S4 **Petrolia** Texas, SW USA
59 O15 **Petrolina** Pernambuco, E Brazil
45 T6 **Petrona, Punta** headland C Puerto Rico
Petropavl see Petropavlovsk
117 V7 **Petropavlivka** Dnipropetrovs'ka Oblast', E Ukraine
145 P6 **Petropavlovsk** Kaz. Petropavl. Severnyy Kazakhstan, N Kazakhstan
123 V11 **Petropavlovsk-Kamchatskiy** Kamchatskaya Oblast', E Russian Federation
60 P9 **Petrópolis** Rio de Janeiro, SE Brazil
116 H12 **Petroşani** var. Petroşeni, Ger. Petroschen, Hung. Petrozsény. Hunedoara, W Romania
Petroschen/Petroşeni see Petroşani
Petroskoi see Petrozavodsk
Petrovac/Petrovácz see Bački Petrovac
113 J17 **Petrovac na Moru** Montenegro, SW Serbia and Montenegro (Yugo.)
117 S8 **Petrove** Kirovohrads'ka Oblast', C Ukraine
113 O18 **Petrovec** C FYR Macedonia
Petrovgrad see Zrenjanin
127 P7 **Petrovsk** Saratovskaya Oblast', W Russian Federation
124 J9 **Petrovskiy Yam** Respublika Kareliya, NW Russian Federation
Petrovsk-Port see Makhachkala
127 P9 **Petrov Val** Volgogradskaya Oblast', SW Russian Federation
124 J11 **Petrozavodsk** Fin. Petroskoi. Respublika Kareliya, NW Russian Federation
Petrozsény see Petroşani
83 D20 **Petrusdal** Hardap, C Namibia
117 T7 **Petrykivka** Dnipropetrovs'ka Oblast', E Ukraine
Petsamo see Pechenga
Petschka see Pecica
Pettau see Ptuj
109 S5 **Pettenbach** Oberösterreich, C Austria
25 S13 **Pettus** Texas, SW USA
122 G12 **Petukhovo** Kurganskaya Oblast', C Russian Federation
Petuna see Songyuan
109 R4 **Peuerbach** Oberösterreich, N Austria
62 G12 **Peumo** Libertador, C Chile
123 T6 **Pevek** Chukotskiy Avtonomnyy Okrug, NE Russian Federation
27 X5 **Pevely** Missouri, C USA
Peyia see Pégeia
102 J15 **Peyrehorade** Landes, SW France
126 J14 **Peza** ≈ NW Russian Federation
103 P16 **Pézenas** Hérault, S France
111 H20 **Pezinok** Ger. Bösing, Hung. Bazin. Bratislavský Kraj, W Slovakia
101 L22 **Pfaffenhofen an der Ilm** Bayern, SE Germany
108 G7 **Pfäffikon** Schwyz, C Switzerland
101 F20 **Pfälzer Wald** hill range W Germany
101 N22 **Pfarrkirchen** Bayern, SE Germany
101 G21 **Pforzheim** Baden-Württemberg, SW Germany
101 H24 **Pfullendorf** Baden-Württemberg, S Germany
108 K8 **Pfunds** Tirol, W Austria
101 G19 **Pfungstadt** Hessen, W Germany
83 L20 **Phalaborwa** Limpopo, NE South Africa
152 E11 **Phalodi** Rājasthān, NW India
152 E12 **Phalsund** Rājasthān, NW India
155 E15 **Phaltan** Mahārāshtra, W India
167 O7 **Phan** var. Muang Phan. Chiang Rai, NW Thailand
167 O14 **Phangan, Ko** island SW Thailand
166 M15 **Phang-Nga** var. Pang-Nga, Phangnga. Phangnga, SW Thailand
Phan Rang/Phanrang see Phan Rang-Thap Cham
167 V13 **Phan Rang-Thap Cham** var. Phanrang, Phan Rang, Phan Rang Thap Cham. Ninh Thuận, S Vietnam
167 U13 **Phan Ri** Binh Thuận, S Vietnam
167 u13 **Phan Thiêt** Binh Thuận, S Vietnam
Pharnacia see Giresun
25 S17 **Pharr** Texas, SW USA
Pharus see Hvar
167 N16 **Phatthalung** var. Padalung, Patalung. Phatthalung, SW Thailand
167 O7 **Phayao** var. Muang Phayao. Phayao, NW Thailand
11 U10 **Phelps Lake** ◎ Saskatchewan, C Canada
21 X9 **Phelps Lake** ◎ North Carolina, SE USA
23 R5 **Phenix City** Alabama, S USA
167 T8 **Pheo** Quang Binh, C Vietnam
Phet Buri see Phetchaburi
167 O11 **Phetchaburi** var. Bejraburi, Petchaburi, Phet Buri. Phetchaburi, SW Thailand
167 O9 **Phichit** var. Bichitra, Muang Phichit, Pichit. Phichit, C Thailand
22 M5 **Philadelphia** Mississippi, S USA
18 I7 **Philadelphia** New York, NE USA
18 I16 **Philadelphia** Pennsylvania, NE USA
18 I16 **Philadelphia** × Pennsylvania, NE USA
Philadelphia see 'Ammān
28 L10 **Philip** South Dakota, N USA
99 H22 **Philippeville** Namur, S Belgium
Philippeville see Skikda
21 S3 **Philippi** West Virginia, NE USA
Philippi see Fílippoi
195 Y9 **Philippi Glacier** glacier Antarctica
192 G6 **Philippine Basin** undersea feature W Pacific Ocean
131 X12 **Philippine Plate** tectonic feature
171 O5 **Philippines** off. Republic of the Philippines. ◆ republic SE Asia
133 P13 **Philippines** island group W Pacific Ocean
171 P3 **Philippine Sea** sea W Pacific Ocean
192 F6 **Philippine Trench** undersea feature W Philippine Sea
83 H23 **Philippolis** Free State, C South Africa
Philippopolis see Plovdiv, Bulgaria
Philippopolis see Shahbā', Syria
45 V9 **Philipsburg** Sint Maarten, N Netherlands Antilles
33 P10 **Philipsburg** Montana, NW USA
39 R6 **Philip Smith Mountains** ▲ Alaska, USA
152 H8 **Phillaur** Punjab, N India
183 N13 **Phillip Island** island Victoria, SE Australia
25 N2 **Phillips** Texas, SW USA
30 K5 **Phillips** Wisconsin, N USA
26 K3 **Phillipsburg** Kansas, C USA
18 I14 **Phillipsburg** New Jersey, NE USA
21 S7 **Philpott Lake** ▣ Virginia, NE USA
Phintias see Licata
167 P9 **Phitsanulok** var. Bisnulok, Muang Phitsanulok, Pitsanulok. Phitsanulok, C Thailand
Phlórina see Flórina
Phnom Penh see Phnum Penh
167 S13 **Phnum Penh** var. Phnom Penh. ● (Cambodia) Phnum Penh, S Cambodia
167 S11 **Phnum Tbêng Meanchey** Preăh Vihéar, N Cambodia
36 K13 **Phoenix** state capital Arizona, SW USA
Phoenix Island see Rawaki
191 R3 **Phoenix Islands** island group C Kiribati
18 I15 **Phoenixville** Pennsylvania, NE USA
83 K22 **Phofung** var. Mont-aux-Sources. ▲ N Lesotho
167 Q10 **Phon** Khon Kaen, E Thailand
167 Q5 **Phôngsali** var. Phong Saly. Phôngsali, N Laos
Phong Saly see Phôngsali
167 Q8 **Phônhông** C Laos
167 R5 **Phô Rang** Lao Cai, N Vietnam
Phort Láirge, Cuan see Waterford Harbour
167 N10 **Phra Chedi Sam Ong** Kanchanaburi, W Thailand
167 O8 **Phrae** var. Muang Phrae, Prae. Phrae, NW Thailand
Phra Nakhon Si Ayutthaya see Ayutthaya
167 M14 **Phra Thong, Ko** island SW Thailand
Phu Cương see Thu Dâu Một
166 M15 **Phuket** var. Bhuket, Puket, Mal. Ujung Salang; prev. Junkseylon, Salang. Phuket, SW Thailand
166 M15 **Phuket** × Phuket, SW Thailand
166 M15 **Phuket, Ko** island SW Thailand
154 N12 **Phulabāni** prev. Phulbani. Orissa, E India
Phulbani see Phulabāni
167 U9 **Phú Lôc** Th,a Thiên-Huê, C Vietnam
167 S13 **Phumĭ Banam** Prey Vêng, S Cambodia
167 R13 **Phumĭ Chŏâm** Kâmpóng Spœ, SW Cambodia
167 T11 **Phumĭ Kalêng** Stœng Trêng, NE Cambodia
167 S12 **Phumĭ Kâmpóng Trâbêk** prev. Phum Kompong Trabek. Kâmpóng Thum, C Cambodia
167 Q11 **Phumĭ Koŭk Kduŏch** Bătdâmbâng, NW Cambodia
167 T11 **Phumĭ Labăng** Rôtânôkiri, NE Cambodia
167 S11 **Phumĭ Mlu Prey** Preăh Vihéar, N Cambodia
167 R11 **Phumĭ Moŭng** Siĕmréab, NW Cambodia
167 Q12 **Phumĭ Prâmaôy** Poŭthĭsăt, W Cambodia
167 Q13 **Phumĭ Samĭt** Kaôh Kông, SW Cambodia
167 R11 **Phumĭ Sâmraông** prev. Phum Samrong. Siĕmréab, NW Cambodia
167 S12 **Phumĭ Siĕmbok** Stœng Trêng, N Cambodia
167 S11 **Phumĭ Thalabârĭvăt** Stœng Trêng, N Cambodia
167 R13 **Phumĭ Veal Renh** Kâmpôt, SW Cambodia
167 P13 **Phumĭ Yeay Sên** Kaôh Kông, SW Cambodia
Phum Kompong Trabek see Phumĭ Kâmpóng Trâbêk
Phum Samrong see Phumĭ Sâmraông
167 V11 **Phu My** Binh Đinh, C Vietnam
167 S14 **Phung Hiêp** Cân Thơ, S Vietnam
153 T12 **Phuntsholing** SW Bhutan
167 R15 **Phước Long** Minh Hai, S Vietnam
167 R14 **Phu Quốc, Đao** var. Phu Quoc Island. island S Vietnam
Phu Quoc Island see Phu Quốc, Đao
167 S6 **Phu Tho** Vinh Phu, N Vietnam
Phu Vinh see Tra Vinh
189 T13 **Piaanu Pass** passage Chuuk Islands, C Micronesia
106 E8 **Piacenza** Fr. Paisance; anc. Placentia. Emilia-Romagna, N Italy
107 K14 **Pianella** Abruzzo, C Italy
107 M15 **Pianosa, Isola** island Archipelago Toscano, C Italy
171 U13 **Piar** Papua, E Indonesia
45 U14 **Piarco** var. Port of Spain. × (Port-of-Spain) Trinidad, Trinidad and Tobago
110 M12 **Piaseczno** Mazowieckie, C Poland
116 I15 **Piatra** Teleorman, S Romania
116 L10 **Piatra-Neamţ** Hung. Karácsonkő. Neamţ, NE Romania
Piauhy see Piauí
59 N15 **Piauí** off. Estado do Piauí; prev. Piauhy. ◈ state E Brazil
106 I7 **Piave** ≈ NE Italy
107 K24 **Piazza Armerina** var. Chiazza. Sicilia, Italy, C Mediterranean Sea
81 G14 **Pibor** Amh. Pībor Wenz. ≈ Ethiopia/Sudan
81 G14 **Pibor Post** Jonglei, SE Sudan
Pībor Wenz see Pibor
Pibrans see Příbram
36 K11 **Picacho Butte** ▲ Arizona, SW USA
40 D4 **Picachos, Cerro** ▲ NW Mexico
103 O4 **Picardie** Eng. Picardy. ◈ region N France
Picardy see Picardie
22 L8 **Picayune** Mississippi, S USA
Piccolo San Bernardo, Colle di see Little Saint Bernard Pass
62 K5 **Pichanal** Salta, N Argentina
147 P12 **Pichandar** W Tajikistan
27 R8 **Picher** Oklahoma, C USA
62 G12 **Pichilemu** Libertador, C Chile
40 F9 **Pichilingue** Baja California Sur, W Mexico
56 B6 **Pichincha** ◈ province N Ecuador
56 C6 **Pichincha** ▲ N Ecuador
Pichit see Phichit
41 U15 **Pichucalco** Chiapas, SE Mexico
22 L5 **Pickens** Mississippi, S USA
21 O11 **Pickens** South Carolina, SE USA
14 G11 **Pickerel** ≈ Ontario, S Canada
14 H15 **Pickering** Ontario, S Canada
97 N16 **Pickering** N England, UK
31 S13 **Pickerington** Ohio, N USA
12 C10 **Pickle Lake** Ontario, C Canada
29 P12 **Pickstown** South Dakota, N USA
25 V6 **Pickton** Texas, SW USA
23 N1 **Pickwick Lake** ▣ S USA
64 N2 **Pico** var. Ilha do Pico. island Azores, Portugal, NE Atlantic Ocean
63 J19 **Pico de Salamanca** Chubut, SE Argentina
1 P9 **Pico Fracture Zone** tectonic feature NW Atlantic Ocean
Pico, Ilha do see Pico
59 O14 **Picos** Piauí, E Brazil
63 I20 **Pico Truncado** Santa Cruz, SE Argentina
183 S9 **Picton** New South Wales, SE Australia
14 K15 **Picton** Ontario, SE Canada
185 K14 **Picton** Marlborough, South Island, NZ
63 H15 **Picún Leufú, Arroyo** ≈ SW Argentina
Pidálion see Gkréko, Akrotíri
155 K25 **Pidurutalagala** ▲ S Sri Lanka
116 K6 **Pidvolochys'k** Ternopil's'ka Oblast', W Ukraine
107 K16 **Piedimonte Matese** Campania, S Italy
27 X7 **Piedmont** Missouri, C USA
21 P11 **Piedmont** South Carolina, SE USA
17 S12 **Piedmont** escarpment E USA
Piedmont see Piemonte
31 U13 **Piedmont Lake** ▣ Ohio, N USA
104 M11 **Piedrabuena** Castilla-La Mancha, C Spain
Piedrafita, Puerto de see Pedrafita, Porto de
104 L8 **Piedrahita** Castilla-León, N Spain
41 N6 **Piedras Negras** var. Ciudad Porfirio Díaz. Coahuila de Zaragoza, NE Mexico
61 E21 **Piedras, Punta** headland E Argentina
57 I14 **Piedras, Río de las** ≈ E Peru
111 J16 **Piekary Śląskie** Śląskie, S Poland
93 M17 **Pieksämäki** Isä-Suomi, E Finland
109 V5 **Pielach** ≈ NE Austria
93 M16 **Pielavesi** Itä-Suomi, C Finland
93 M16 **Pielavesi** ◎ C Finland
93 N16 **Pielinen** var. Pielisjärvi. ◎ E Finland
Pielisjärvi see Pielinen
106 A8 **Piemonte** Eng. Piedmont. ◈ region NW Italy
111 L18 **Pieniny** ▲ Poland/Slovakia
111 E14 **Pieńsk** Ger. Penzig. Dolnośląskie, SW Poland
29 Q13 **Pierce** Nebraska, C USA
11 R14 **Pierceland** Saskatchewan, C Canada
115 E14 **Piéria** ▲ N Greece
29 N10 **Pierre** state capital South Dakota, N USA
102 K16 **Pierrefitte-Nestalas** Hautes-Pyrénées, S France
103 R14 **Pierrelatte** Drôme, E France
15 P11 **Pierreville** Québec, SE Canada
15 O7 **Pierriche** ≈ Québec, SE Canada
111 H20 **Piešt'any** Ger. Pistyan, Hung. Pöstyén. Trnavský, W Slovakia
109 X5 **Piesting** ≈ E Austria
Pietarhovi see Petrodvorets
Pietari see Sankt-Peterburg
Pietarsaari see Jakobstad
83 K23 **Pietermaritzburg** var. Maritzburg. KwaZulu/Natal, E South Africa
Pietersburg see Polokwane
107 K24 **Pietraperzia** Sicilia, Italy, C Mediterranean Sea
107 N22 **Pietra Spada, Passo della** pass SW Italy
83 K22 **Piet Retief** Mpumalanga, E South Africa
116 I9 **Pietrosul, Vârful** prev. Vîrful Pietrosu. ▲ N Romania
116 J10 **Pietrosul, Vârful** prev. Vîrful Pietrosu. ▲ N Romania
Pietrosu, Vîrful see Pietrosul, Vârful
106 I6 **Pieve di Cadore** Veneto, NE Italy
14 C18 **Pigeon Bay** lake bay Ontario, S Canada
27 X8 **Piggott** Arkansas, C USA
83 L21 **Piggs Peak** NW Swaziland
Pigs, Bay of see Cochinos, Bahía de
61 A23 **Pigüé** Buenos Aires, E Argentina
41 O12 **Piguícas** ▲ C Mexico
193 W15 **Piha Passage** passage S Tonga
Pihkva Järv see Pskov, Lake
93 N18 **Pihlajavesi** ◎ SE Finland
93 J18 **Pihlava** Länsi-Suomi, W Finland
93 L16 **Pihtipudas** Länsi-Suomi, W Finland
40 L14 **Pihuamo** Jalisco, SW Mexico
189 U11 **Piis Moen** var. Pis. atoll Chuuk Islands, C Micronesia
41 U17 **Pijijiapán** Chiapas, SE Mexico
98 G12 **Pijnacker** Zuid-Holland, W Netherlands
42 H5 **Pijol, Pico** ▲ NW Honduras
Pikaar see Bikar Atoll
124 I13 **Pikalevo** Leningradskaya Oblast', NW Russian Federation
188 M15 **Pikelot** island Caroline Islands, C Micronesia
30 M5 **Pike River** ≈ Wisconsin, N USA
37 T5 **Pikes Peak** ▲ Colorado, C USA
21 P6 **Pikeville** Kentucky, S USA
20 L9 **Pikeville** Tennessee, S USA
Pikinni see Bikini Atoll
79 H18 **Pikounda** La Sangha, C Congo
110 G9 **Piła** Ger. Schneidemühl. Wielkopolskie, C Poland
62 N6 **Pilagá, Riacho** ≈ NE Argentina
61 D20 **Pilar** Buenos Aires, E Argentina
62 N7 **Pilar** var. Villa del Pilar. Ñeembucú, S Paraguay
62 N6 **Pilcomayo, Río** ≈ C South America
147 R12 **Pildon** Rus. Pil'don. C Tajikistan
Piles see Pylés
Pilgram see Pelhřimov
152 L10 **Pīlībhīt** Uttar Pradesh, N India
110 M13 **Pilica** ≈ C Poland
115 G16 **Pílio** ▲ C Greece
111 J22 **Pilisvörösvár** Pest, N Hungary
65 G15 **Pillar Bay** bay Ascension Island, C Atlantic Ocean
183 P17 **Pillar, Cape** headland Tasmania, SE Australia
Pillau see Baltiysk
183 R5 **Pilliga** New South Wales, SE Australia
44 H8 **Pilón** Granma, E Cuba
Pilos see Pýlos
11 W17 **Pilot Mound** Manitoba, S Canada
21 S8 **Pilot Mountain** North Carolina, SE USA
39 O14 **Pilot Point** Alaska, USA
25 T5 **Pilot Point** Texas, SW USA
32 K11 **Pilot Rock** Oregon, NW USA
38 M11 **Pilot Station** Alaska, USA
Pilsen see Plzeň
111 K18 **Pilsko** ▲ N Slovakia
Pilten see Piltene
118 D8 **Piltene** Ger. Pilten. Ventspils, W Latvia
111 M16 **Pilzno** Podkarpackie, SE Poland
Pilzno see Plzeň
37 N14 **Pima** Arizona, SW USA
58 H13 **Pimenta** Pará, N Brazil
59 F16 **Pimenta Bueno** Rondônia, W Brazil
56 B11 **Pimentel** Lambayeque, W Peru
105 S6 **Pina** Aragón, NE Spain
119 I20 **Pina** Rus. Pina. ≈ SW Belarus
40 E2 **Pinacate, Sierra del** ▲ NW Mexico
63 H22 **Pináculo, Cerro** ▲ S Argentina
191 X11 **Pinaki** atoll Îles Tuamotu, E French Polynesia
37 N15 **Pinaleno Mountains** ▲ Arizona, SW USA
171 P4 **Pinamalayan** Mindoro, N Philippines
169 Q10 **Pinang** Borneo, C Indonesia
168 J7 **Pinang** var. Penang. ◈ state Peninsular Malaysia
Pinang see Pinang, Pulau, Peninsular Malaysia
Pinang see George Town
168 J7 **Pinang, Pulau** var. Penang, Pinang; prev. Prince of Wales Island. island Peninsular Malaysia
44 B5 **Pinar del Río** Pinar del Río, W Cuba
114 N11 **Pınarhisar** Kırklareli, NW Turkey
171 O3 **Pinatubo, Mount** ☒ Luzon, N Philippines
11 Y16 **Pinawa** Manitoba, S Canada
11 Q17 **Pincher Creek** Alberta, SW Canada
30 L16 **Pinckneyville** Illinois, N USA
Pincota see Pâncota
111 L15 **Pińczów** Świętokrzyskie, C Poland
149 U7 **Pind Dādan Khān** Punjab, E Pakistan
Píndhos/Píndhos Óros see Píndos
149 V8 **Pindi Bhattiān** Punjab, E Pakistan
149 U6 **Pindi Gheb** Punjab, E Pakistan
115 D15 **Píndos** var. Píndhos Óros, Eng. Pindus Mountains; prev. Píndhos. ▲ C Greece
Pindus Mountains see Píndos
18 J16 **Pine Barrens** physical region New Jersey, NE USA
27 V12 **Pine Bluff** Arkansas, C USA
23 X11 **Pine Castle** Florida, SE USA
29 V7 **Pine City** Minnesota, N USA
181 P2 **Pine Creek** Northern Territory, N Australia
35 V4 **Pine Creek** ≈ Nevada, W USA
18 F13 **Pine Creek** ≈ Pennsylvania, NE USA
27 Q13 **Pine Creek Lake** ▣ Oklahoma, C USA
33 T15 **Pinedale** Wyoming, C USA
11 X15 **Pine Dock** Manitoba, S Canada
11 Y16 **Pine Falls** Manitoba, S Canada
35 R10 **Pine Flat Lake** ▣ California, W USA
125 N8 **Pinega** Arkhangel'skaya Oblast', NW Russian Federation
127 N8 **Pinega** ≈ NW Russian Federation
15 N12 **Pine Hill** Québec, SE Canada

◆ COUNTRY ● COUNTRY CAPITAL ◇ DEPENDENT TERRITORY ○ DEPENDENT TERRITORY CAPITAL ◈ ADMINISTRATIVE REGION × INTERNATIONAL AIRPORT ▲ MOUNTAIN ▲ MOUNTAIN RANGE ☒ VOLCANO ≈ RIVER ◎ LAKE ▣ RESERVOIR

11 T12 **Pinehouse Lake** ◎ Saskatchewan, C Canada
21 T10 **Pinehurst** North Carolina, SE USA
115 D19 **Pineiós** ≈ S Greece
115 E16 **Pineiós** *var.* Piniós; *anc.* Peneius. ≈ C Greece
29 W10 **Pine Island** Minnesota, N USA
23 V15 **Pine Island** *island* Florida, SE USA
194 K10 **Pine Island Glacier** *glacier* Antarctica
25 X9 **Pineland** Texas, SW USA
23 V13 **Pinellas Park** Florida, SE USA
10 M13 **Pine Pass** *pass* British Columbia, W Canada
8 J10 **Pine Point** Northwest Territories, W Canada
28 K12 **Pine Ridge** South Dakota, N USA
29 U6 **Pine River** Minnesota, N USA
31 Q8 **Pine River** ≈ Michigan, N USA
30 M4 **Pine River** ≈ Wisconsin, N USA
106 A8 **Pinerolo** Piemonte, NE Italy
25 W6 **Pines, Lake O' the** ⊞ Texas, SW USA
Pines, The Isle of the *see* Juventud, Isla de la
Pine Tree State *see* Maine
21 N7 **Pineville** Kentucky, S USA
22 H7 **Pineville** Louisiana, S USA
27 R8 **Pineville** Missouri, C USA
21 R10 **Pineville** North Carolina, SE USA
21 Q6 **Pineville** West Virginia, NE USA
33 V8 **Piney Buttes** *physical region* Montana, NW USA
160 H14 **Pingbian** *var.* Pingbian Miaozu Zizhixian, Yuping. Yunnan, SW China
Pingbian Miaozu Zizhixian *see* Pingbian
157 S9 **Pingdingshan** Henan, C China
161 R4 **Pingdu** Shandong, E China
189 W16 **Pingelap Atoll** *atoll* Caroline Islands, E Micronesia
160 K14 **Pingguo** *var.* Matou. Guangxi Zhuangzu Zizhiqu, S China
161 Q13 **Pinghe** *var.* Xiaoxi. Fujian, SE China
P'ing-hsiang *see* Pingxiang
161 N10 **Pingjiang** Hunan, S China
Pingkiang *see* Harbin
160 L8 **Pingli** Shaanxi, C China
159 W10 **Pingliang** *var.* Kongtong, P'ing-liang. Gansu, C China
159 W8 **Pingluo** Ningxia, N China
Pingma *see* Tiandong
167 O7 **Ping, Mae Nam** ≈ W Thailand
161 Q1 **Pingquan** Hebei, E China
29 P5 **Pingree** North Dakota, N USA
163 W9 **Pingshan** Jilin, NE China
Pingsiang *see* Pingxiang
161 S14 **P'ingtung** *Jap.* Heitō. S Taiwan
160 I8 **Pingwu** *var.* Long'an. Sichuan, C China
160 J15 **Pingxiang** Guangxi Zhuangzu Zizhiqu, S China
161 O11 **Pingxiang** *var.* P'ing-hsiang; *prev.* Pingsiang. Jiangxi, S China
161 S11 **Pingyang** *var.* Kunyang. Zhejiang, SE China
161 P5 **Pingyi** Shandong, E China
161 P5 **Pingyin** Shandong, E China
60 H13 **Pinhalzinho** Santa Catarina, S Brazil
60 I12 **Pinhão** Paraná, S Brazil
61 H17 **Pinheiro Machado** Rio Grande do Sul, S Brazil
104 I7 **Pinhel** Guarda, N Portugal
Piniós *see* Pineiós
168 I11 **Pini, Pulau** *island* Kepulauan Batu, W Indonesia
109 Y7 **Pinka** ≈ SE Austria
109 X7 **Pinkafeld** Burgenland, SE Austria
Pinkiang *see* Harbin
10 M12 **Pink Mountain** British Columbia, W Canada
166 M3 **Pinlebu** Sagaing, N Myanmar
38 J12 **Pinnacle Island** *island* Alaska, USA
180 I12 **Pinnacles, The** *tourist site* Western Australia
182 K10 **Pinnaroo** South Australia
Pinne *see* Pniewy
100 I9 **Pinneberg** Schleswig-Holstein, N Germany
115 I15 **Pínnes, Akrotírio** *headland* N Greece
Pinos, Isla de *see* Juventud, Isla de la
35 R14 **Pinos, Mount** ▲ California, W USA
105 R12 **Pinoso** País Valenciano, E Spain
105 N14 **Pinos-Puente** Andalucía, S Spain
41 Q17 **Pinotepa Nacional** *var.* Santiago Pinotepa Nacional. Oaxaca, SE Mexico
114 F13 **Pínovo** ▲ N Greece
187 R17 **Pins, Île des** *var.* Kunyé. *island* E New Caledonia
119 I20 **Pinsk** *Pol.* Pińsk. Brestskaya Voblasts', SW Belarus
14 D18 **Pins, Pointe aux** *headland* Ontario, S Canada
57 B16 **Pinta, Isla** *var.* Abingdon. *island* Galapagos Islands, Ecuador, E Pacific Ocean
125 Q12 **Pinyug** Kirovskaya Oblast', NW Russian Federation
57 B17 **Pinzón, Isla** *var.* Duncan Island. *island* Galapagos Islands, Ecuador, E Pacific Ocean
35 Y8 **Pioche** Nevada, W USA
106 F13 **Piombino** Toscana, C Italy
(0) C9 **Pioneer Fracture Zone** *tectonic feature* NE Pacific Ocean
122 L5 **Pioner, Ostrov** *island* Severnaya Zemlya, N Russian Federation
118 A13 **Pionerskiy** *Ger.* Neukuhren. Kaliningradskaya Oblast', W Russian Federation
110 N13 **Pionki** Mazowieckie, C Poland
184 L9 **Piopio** Waikato, North Island, NZ
110 K13 **Piotrków Trybunalski** *Ger.* Petrikau, *Rus.* Petrokov. Łodzkie, C Poland
152 F12 **Pīpār Road** Rājasthān, N India
115 I16 **Pipéri** *island* Vóreioi Sporádes, Greece, Aegean Sea
29 S10 **Pipestone** Minnesota, N USA
12 C9 **Pipestone** ≈ Ontario, C Canada
61 E21 **Pipinas** Buenos Aires, E Argentina
149 T7 **Piplān** *prev.* Liaqatabad. Punjab, E Pakistan
15 R5 **Pipmuacan, Réservoir** ⊞ Québec, SE Canada
Piqan *see* Shanshan
31 R13 **Piqua** Ohio, N USA
105 P5 **Piqueras, Puerto de** *pass* N Spain
60 H11 **Piquiri, Rio** ≈ S Brazil
60 L9 **Piracicaba** São Paulo, S Brazil
Piraeus/Piraiévs *see* Peiraías
60 K10 **Piraju** São Paulo, S Brazil
60 K9 **Pirajuí** São Paulo, S Brazil
63 G21 **Pirámide, Cerro** ▲ S Chile
Piramiva *see* Pyramíva
109 R13 **Piran** *It.* Pirano. SW Slovenia
62 N6 **Pirané** Formosa, N Argentina
59 J18 **Piranhas** Goiás, S Brazil
Pirano *see* Piran
142 I4 **Pīrānshahr** Āzarbāyjān-e Bākhtarī, NW Iran
59 M19 **Pirapora** Minas Gerais, NE Brazil
60 I9 **Pirapòzinho** São Paulo, S Brazil
61 G19 **Piraraja** Lavalleja, S Uruguay
60 L9 **Pirassununga** São Paulo, S Brazil
45 V6 **Pirata, Monte** ▲ E Puerto Rico
60 I13 **Piratuba** Santa Catarina, S Brazil
114 I9 **Pirdop** *prev.* Srednogorie. Sofiya, W Bulgaria
191 P7 **Pirea** Tahiti, W French Polynesia
59 K18 **Pirenópolis** Goiás, S Brazil
153 S13 **Pirganj** Rajshahi, NW Bangladesh
Pirgi *see* Pyrgí
Pírgos *see* Pýrgos
61 F20 **Piriápolis** Maldonado, S Uruguay
114 G11 **Pirin** ▲ SW Bulgaria
Pirineos *see* Pyrenees
58 N13 **Piripiri** Piauí, E Brazil
118 H4 **Pirita** *var.* Pirita Jõgi. ≈ NW Estonia
Pirita Jõgi *see* Pirita
54 J6 **Píritu** Portuguesa, N Venezuela
93 L18 **Pirkkala** Länsi-Suomi, W Finland
101 F20 **Pirmasens** Rheinland-Pfalz, SW Germany
101 P16 **Pirna** Sachsen, E Germany
Piroe *see* Piru
113 Q15 **Pirot** Serbia, SE Serbia and Montenegro (Yugo.)
152 H6 **Pīr Panjāl Range** ▲ NE India
43 W16 **Pirre, Cerro** ▲ SE Panama
137 Y11 **Pirsaat** *Rus.* Pirsagat. ≈ E Azerbaijan
Pirsagat *see* Pirsaat
143 V11 **Pīr Shūrān, Selseleh-ye** ▲ SE Iran
92 M12 **Pirttikoski** Lappi, N Finland
Pirttikylä *see* Pörtom
171 R13 **Piru** *prev.* Piroe. Pulau Seram, E Indonesia
Piryatin *see* Pyryatyn
Pis *see* Piis Moen
106 F11 **Pisa** *var.* Pisae. Toscana, C Italy
Pisae *see* Pisa
189 V12 **Pisar** *atoll* Chuuk Islands, C Micronesia
Pisaurum *see* Pesaro
14 M10 **Piscatosine, Lac** ◎ Québec, SE Canada
109 W7 **Pischeldorf** Steiermark, SE Austria
Pischk *see* Simeria
107 L19 **Pisciotta** Campania, S Italy
57 E16 **Pisco** Ica, SW Peru
116 G9 **Pișcolt** *Hung.* Piskolt. Satu Mare, NW Romania
57 E16 **Pisco, Río** ≈ E Peru
111 C18 **Písek** Budějovický Kraj, S Czech Republic
31 R14 **Pisgah** Ohio, N USA
Pisha *see* Ningnan
158 F9 **Pishan** *var.* Guma. Xinjiang Uygur Zizhiqu, NW China
117 N8 **Pishchanka** Vinnyts'ka Oblast', C Ukraine
113 K21 **Pishë** Fier, SW Albania
143 X14 **Pīshīn** Sīstān va Balūchestān, SE Iran
149 O9 **Pishīn** North-West Frontier Province, NW Pakistan
149 N11 **Pishin Lora** *var.* Psein Lora, *Pash.* Pseyn Bowr. ≈ SW Pakistan
Pishma *see* Pizhma
Pishpek *see* Bishkek
171 O14 **Pising** Pulau Kabaena, C Indonesia
Pisino *see* Pazin
Piski *see* Simeria
Piskolt *see* Pișcolt
147 Q9 **Piskom** *Rus.* Pskem. ≈ E Uzbekistan
Piskom Tizmasi *see* Pskemskiy Khrebet
35 P13 **Pismo Beach** California, W USA
77 P12 **Pissila** C Burkina
62 H8 **Pissis, Monte** ▲ N Argentina
41 X12 **Piste** Yucatán, E Mexico
107 O18 **Pisticci** Basilicata, S Italy
106 F11 **Pistoia** *anc.* Pistoria, Pistoriæ. Toscana, C Italy
32 E15 **Pistol River** Oregon, NW USA
Pistoria/Pistoriæ *see* Pistoia
15 U5 **Pistuacanis** ≈ Québec, SE Canada
Pistyan *see* Piešt'any
104 M5 **Pisuerga** ≈ N Spain
110 N8 **Pisz** *Ger.* Johannisburg. Warmińsko-Mazurskie, NE Poland
76 I13 **Pita** Moyenne-Guinée, NW Guinea
54 D12 **Pitalito** Huila, S Colombia
60 I11 **Pitanga** Paraná, S Brazil
182 M9 **Pitarpunga Lake** *salt lake* New South Wales, SE Australia
193 P10 **Pitcairn Island** *island* S Pitcairn Islands
193 P10 **Pitcairn Islands** ◇ *UK dependent territory* C Pacific Ocean
93 J14 **Piteå** Norrbotten, N Sweden
92 I13 **Piteälven** ≈ N Sweden
116 I13 **Pitești** Argeș, S Romania
Pithagorio *see* Pythagóreio
180 I12 **Pithara** Western Australia
103 N6 **Pithiviers** Loiret, C France
152 L9 **Pithorāgarh** Uttaranchal, N India
188 B16 **Piti** W Guam
106 G13 **Pitigliano** Toscana, C Italy
40 F3 **Pitiquito** Sonora, NW Mexico
Pitkäranta *see* Pitkyaranta
38 M11 **Pitkas Point** Alaska, USA
124 H11 **Pitkyaranta** *Fin.* Pitkäranta. Respublika Kareliya, NW Russian Federation
96 J10 **Pitlochry** C Scotland, UK
18 I16 **Pitman** New Jersey, NE USA
146 I9 **Pitnak** *Rus.* Druzhba. Xorazm Viloyati, W Uzbekistan
112 G8 **Pitomača** Virovitica-Podravina, NE Croatia
35 O2 **Pit River** ≈ California, W USA
63 G15 **Pitrufquén** Araucanía, S Chile
Pitsanulok *see* Phitsanulok
Pitschen *see* Byczyna
Pitsunda *see* Bichvint'a
109 X6 **Pitten** ≈ E Austria
10 J14 **Pitt Island** *island* British Columbia, W Canada
Pitt Island *see* Makin
22 M3 **Pittsboro** Mississippi, S USA
21 T9 **Pittsboro** North Carolina, SE USA
27 R7 **Pittsburg** Kansas, C USA
25 W6 **Pittsburg** Texas, SW USA
18 B14 **Pittsburgh** Pennsylvania, NE USA
30 J14 **Pittsfield** Illinois, N USA
19 R6 **Pittsfield** Maine, NE USA
18 L11 **Pittsfield** Massachusetts, NE USA
183 U3 **Pittsworth** Queensland, E Australia
62 I8 **Pituil** La Rioja, NW Argentina
56 A10 **Piura** Piura, NW Peru
56 A9 **Piura** *off.* Departamento de Piura. ◈ *department* NW Peru
35 S13 **Piute Peak** ▲ California, W USA
113 J15 **Piva** ≈ SW Serbia and Montenegro (Yugo.)
117 V5 **Pivdenne** Kharkivs'ka Oblast', E Ukraine
117 P8 **Pivdennyy Buh** *Rus.* Yuzhnyy Bug. ≈ S Ukraine
54 F5 **Pivijay** Magdalena, N Colombia
109 T13 **Pivka** *prev.* Šent Peter, *Ger.* Sankt Peter, *It.* San Pietro del Carso. SW Slovenia
117 U13 **Pivnichno-Kryms'kyy Kanal** *canal* S Ukraine
113 J15 **Pivsko Jezero** ⊞ SW Serbia and Montenegro (Yugo.)
111 M18 **Piwniczna** Małopolskie, S Poland
35 R12 **Pixley** California, W USA
127 Q15 **Pizhma** *var.* Pishma. ≈ NW Russian Federation
13 U13 **Placentia** Newfoundland and Labrador, SE Canada
Placentia *see* Piacenza
13 U13 **Placentia Bay** *inlet* Newfoundland and Labrador, SE Canada
171 P5 **Placer** Masbate, N Philippines
35 P7 **Placerville** California, W USA
44 F5 **Placetas** Villa Clara, C Cuba
113 Q18 **Plačkovica** ▲ E FYR Macedonia
36 L2 **Plain City** Utah, W USA
22 G4 **Plain Dealing** Louisiana, S USA
31 O14 **Plainfield** Indiana, N USA
18 K14 **Plainfield** New Jersey, NE USA
33 O8 **Plains** Montana, NW USA
24 L6 **Plains** Texas, SW USA
29 X10 **Plainview** Minnesota, N USA
29 Q13 **Plainview** Nebraska, C USA
25 N4 **Plainview** Texas, SW USA
26 K4 **Plainville** Kansas, C USA
115 L25 **Pláka, Akrotírio** *headland* Kríti, Greece, E Mediterranean Sea
115 J15 **Pláka, Akrotírio** *headland* Límnos, E Greece
113 N19 **Plakenska Planina** ▲ SW FYR Macedonia
44 K5 **Plana Cays** *islets* SE Bahamas
105 S12 **Plana, Isla** *var.* Nueva Tabarca. *island* E Spain
59 L18 **Planaltina** Goiás, S Brazil
83 O14 **Planalto Moçambicano** *plateau* N Mozambique
112 N10 **Plandište** Serbia, NE Serbia and Montenegro (Yugo.)
100 N13 **Plane** ≈ NE Germany
54 E6 **Planeta Rica** Córdoba, NW Colombia
29 P11 **Plankinton** South Dakota, N USA
30 M11 **Plano** Illinois, N USA
25 U6 **Plano** Texas, SW USA
23 W12 **Plant City** Florida, SE USA
22 J9 **Plaquemine** Louisiana, S USA
104 K9 **Plasencia** Extremadura, W Spain
112 P7 **Plaska** Podlaskie, NE Poland
114 C10 **Plaški** Karlovac, C Croatia
113 N19 **Plasnica** SW FYR Macedonia
13 N14 **Plaster Rock** New Brunswick, SE Canada
107 J24 **Platani** *anc.* Halycus. ≈ Sicilia, Italy, C Mediterranean Sea
115 G17 **Plataniá** Thessalía, C Greece
115 G24 **Plátanos** Kríti, Greece, E Mediterranean Sea
65 H18 **Plata, Río de la** *var.* River Plate. *estuary* Argentina/Uruguay
77 V15 **Plateau** ◈ *state* C Nigeria
79 G19 **Plateaux** *var.* Région des Plateaux. ◈ *province* C Congo
92 P1 **Platen, Kapp** *headland* NE Svalbard
Plate, River *see* Plata, Río de la
99 G22 **Plate Taille, Lac de la** *var.* L'Eau d'Heure. ◎ SE Belgium
Plathe *see* Płoty
39 N13 **Platinum** Alaska, USA
54 F5 **Plato** Magdalena, N Colombia
29 O11 **Platte** South Dakota, N USA
27 R3 **Platte City** Missouri, C USA
Plattensee *see* Balaton
27 R3 **Platte River** ≈ Iowa/Missouri, USA
29 Q15 **Platte River** ≈ Nebraska, C USA
37 T3 **Platteville** Colorado, C USA
30 K9 **Platteville** Wisconsin, N USA
101 N21 **Plattling** Bayern, SE Germany
27 R3 **Plattsburg** Missouri, C USA
18 L6 **Plattsburgh** New York, NE USA
29 S15 **Plattsmouth** Nebraska, C USA
101 M17 **Plauen** *var.* Plauen im Vogtland. Sachsen, E Germany
Plauen im Vogtland *see* Plauen
100 M10 **Plauer See** ◎ NE Germany
113 L16 **Plav** Montenegro, SW Serbia and Montenegro (Yugo.)
118 I10 **Pļaviņas** *Ger.* Stockmannshof. Aizkraukle, S Latvia
126 K5 **Plavsk** Tul'skaya Oblast', W Russian Federation
41 Z12 **Playa del Carmen** Quintana Roo, E Mexico
40 J12 **Playa Los Corchos** Nayarit, SW Mexico
37 P16 **Playas Lake** ◎ New Mexico, SW USA
41 S15 **Playa Vicenté** Veracruz-Llave, SE Mexico
167 U11 **Plây Cu** *var.* Pleiku. Gia Lai, C Vietnam
28 L3 **Plaza** North Dakota, N USA
63 I15 **Plaza Huincul** Neuquén, C Argentina
36 L3 **Pleasant Grove** Utah, W USA
29 V14 **Pleasant Hill** Iowa, C USA
27 R4 **Pleasant Hill** Missouri, C USA
Pleasant Island *see* Nauru
36 K13 **Pleasant, Lake** ⊞ Arizona, SW USA
19 P8 **Pleasant Mountain** ▲ Maine, NE USA
27 R5 **Pleasanton** Kansas, C USA
25 R12 **Pleasanton** Texas, SW USA
185 G20 **Pleasant Point** Canterbury, South Island, NZ
19 R5 **Pleasant River** ≈ Maine, NE USA
18 J17 **Pleasantville** New Jersey, NE USA
103 N12 **Pléaux** Cantal, C France
111 B19 **Plechý** *Ger.* Plöckenstein. ▲ Austria/Czech Republic
Plebeo *see* Plibo
Pleihari *see* Pelaihari
Pleiku *see* Plây Cu
101 M16 **Pleisse** ≈ E Germany
Plencia *see* Plentzia
184 O7 **Plenty, Bay of** *bay* North Island, NZ
33 Y6 **Plentywood** Montana, NW USA
105 O2 **Plentzia** *var.* Plencia. País Vasco, N Spain
102 H5 **Plérin** Côtes d'Armor, NW France
124 M10 **Plesetsk** Arkhangel'skaya Oblast', NW Russian Federation
Pleshchenitsy *see* Plyeshchanitsy
Pleskau *see* Pskov
Pleskauer See *see* Pskov, Lake
Pleskava *see* Pskov
112 E8 **Pleso International** ✕ (Zagreb) Zagreb, NW Croatia
Pless *see* Pszczyna
15 Q11 **Plessisville** Québec, SE Canada
110 H12 **Pleszew** Wielkopolskie, C Poland
12 L10 **Plétipi, Lac** ◎ Québec, SE Canada
101 F15 **Plettenberg** Nordrhein-Westfalen, W Germany
114 I8 **Pleven** *prev.* Plevna. Pleven, N Bulgaria
114 I8 **Pleven** ◈ *province* N Bulgaria
Plevlja/Plevlje *see* Pljevlja
Plevna *see* Pleven
Plezzo *see* Bovec
Pliberk *see* Bleiburg
76 L17 **Plibo** *var.* Pleebo. SE Liberia
121 R11 **Pliny Trench** *undersea feature* C Mediterranean Sea
118 K13 **Plisa** *Rus.* Plissa. Vitsyebskaya Voblasts', N Belarus
Plissa *see* Plisa
112 D11 **Plitvica Selo** Lika-Senj, W Croatia
112 D11 **Plješevica** ▲ C Croatia
113 K14 **Pljevlja** *prev.* Plevlja, Plevlje. Montenegro, N Serbia and Montenegro (Yugo.)
Ploça *see* Ploçë
Plocce *see* Ploče
113 G15 **Ploče** *It.* Plocce; *prev.* Kardeljevo. Dubrovnik-Neretva, SE Croatia
113 K22 **Ploçë** *var.* Ploça. Vlorë, SW Albania
110 K11 **Płock** *Ger.* Plozk. Mazowieckie, C Poland
109 Q10 **Plöcken Pass** *Ger.* Plöckenpass, *It.* Passo di Monte Croce Carnico. *pass* SW Austria
Plöckenstein *see* Plechý
99 B19 **Ploegsteert** Hainaut, W Belgium
102 H6 **Ploërmel** Morbihan, NW France
Ploeşti *see* Ploiești
116 K13 **Ploiești** *prev.* Ploești. Prahova, SE Romania
115 L17 **Plomári** *prev.* Plomárion. Lésvos, E Greece
Plomárion *see* Plomári
103 O12 **Plomb du Cantal** ▲ C France
183 V6 **Plomer, Point** *headland* New South Wales, SE Australia
100 J8 **Plön** Schleswig-Holstein, N Germany
110 L11 **Płońsk** Mazowieckie, C Poland
119 J20 **Plotnitsa** *Rus.* Plotnitsa. Brestskaya Voblasts', SW Belarus
110 E8 **Płoty** *Ger.* Plathe. Zachodnio-pomorskie, NW Poland
102 G7 **Plouay** Morbihan, NW France
111 D15 **Ploučnice** *Ger.* Polzen. ≈ NE Czech Republic
114 I10 **Plovdiv** *prev.* Eumolpias, *anc.* Evmolpia, Philippopolis, *Lat.* Trimontium. Plovdiv, C Bulgaria *24.47*
116 J11 **Plovdiv** ◈ *province* C Bulgaria
30 L6 **Plover** Wisconsin, N USA
Plozk *see* Płock
27 U11 **Plumerville** Arkansas, C USA
19 P10 **Plum Island** *island* Massachusetts, NE USA
32 M9 **Plummer** Idaho, NW USA
83 J18 **Plumtree** Matabeleland South, SW Zimbabwe
118 D11 **Plungė** Telšiai, W Lithuania
113 J15 **Plužine** Montenegro, SW Serbia and Montenegro (Yugo.)
119 K14 **Plyeshchanitsy** *Rus.* Pleshchenitsy. Minskaya Voblasts', N Belarus
45 V10 **Plymouth** ○ (Montserrat) SW Montserrat
97 I24 **Plymouth** SW England, UK
31 O11 **Plymouth** Indiana, N USA
19 P12 **Plymouth** Massachusetts, NE USA
19 N8 **Plymouth** New Hampshire, NE USA
21 X9 **Plymouth** North Carolina, SE USA
30 M8 **Plymouth** Wisconsin, N USA
97 J20 **Plynlimon** ▲ C Wales, UK
124 G14 **Plyussa** Pskovskaya Oblast', W Russian Federation
111 B17 **Plzeň** *Ger.* Pilsen, *Pol.* Pilzno. Plzeňský Kraj, W Czech Republic
111 B17 **Plzeňský Kraj** ◈ *region* W Czech Republic
110 F11 **Pniewy** *Ger.* Pinne. Wielkolpolskie, C Poland
106 D8 **Po** ≈ N Italy
77 P13 **Pô** S Burkina
42 M13 **Poás, Volcán** ⚲ NW Costa Rica
77 S16 **Pobè** S Benin
123 S8 **Pobeda, Gora** ▲ NE Russian Federation
Pobeda Peak *see* Pobedy, Pik/Tomür Feng
147 Z7 **Pobedy, Pik** *var.* Pobeda Peak, *Chin.* Tomür Feng. ▲ China/Kyrgyzstan *see also* Tomür Feng
110 H11 **Pobiedziska** *Ger.* Pudewitz. Wielkolpolskie, C Poland
Po, Bocche del *see* Po, Foci del
27 W9 **Pocahontas** Arkansas, C USA
29 U12 **Pocahontas** Iowa, C USA
33 Q15 **Pocatello** Idaho, NW USA
167 S13 **Pochentong** ✕ (Phnum Penh) Phnum Penh, S Cambodia
126 I6 **Pochep** Bryanskaya Oblast', W Russian Federation
126 H4 **Pochinok** Smolenskaya Oblast', W Russian Federation
41 R17 **Pochutla** *var.* San Pedro Pochutla. Oaxaca, SE Mexico
62 I6 **Pocitos, Salar** *var.* Salar Quirón. *salt lake* NW Argentina
101 O22 **Pocking** Bayern, SE Germany
186 I10 **Pocklington Reef** *reef* SE PNG
59 P15 **Poço da Cruz, Açude** ⊞ E Brazil
27 R11 **Pocola** Oklahoma, C USA
21 Y5 **Pocomoke City** Maryland, NE USA
59 L21 **Poços de Caldas** Minas Gerais, NE Brazil
124 H14 **Podberez'ye** Novgorodskaya Oblast', NW Russian Federation
Podbrodzie *see* Pabradė
125 U8 **Podcher'ye** Respublika Komi, NW Russian Federation
111 E16 **Poděbrady** *Ger.* Podiebrad. Středočeský Kraj, C Czech Republic
126 L9 **Podgorenskiy** Voronezhskaya Oblast', W Russian Federation
113 J17 **Podgorica** *prev.* Titograd. Montenegro, SW Serbia and Montenegro (Yugo.)
113 K17 **Podgorica** ✕ Montenegro, SW Serbia and Montenegro (Yugo.)
122 L12 **Podgornyy** Krasnoyarskiy Kray, C Russian Federation
109 T13 **Podgrad** SW Slovenia
Podiebrad *see* Poděbrady
116 M5 **Podil's'ka Vysochina** *plateau* W Ukraine
Podium Anicensis *see* le Puy
122 L11 **Podkamennaya Tunguska** *Eng.* Stony Tunguska. ≈ C Russian Federation
113 N17 **Podkarpackie** ◈ *province* SE Poland
Pod Klošter *see* Arnoldstein
110 O9 **Podlaskie** ◈ *province* NE Poland
127 Q8 **Podlesnoye** Saratovskaya Oblast', W Russian Federation
126 K4 **Podol'sk** Moskovskaya Oblast', W Russian Federation
76 H10 **Podor** N Senegal
125 P12 **Podosinovets** Kirovskaya Oblast', NW Russian Federation
124 I12 **Podporozh'ye** Leningradskaya Oblast', NW Russian Federation
Podravska Slatina *see* Slatina, Croatia
112 J13 **Podromanlja** Republika Srpska, SE Bosnia & Herzegovina
Podsvil'ye *see* Padsvillye
116 L9 **Podu Iloaiei** *prev.* Podul Iloaiei. Iași, NE Romania
113 N15 **Podujevo** Serbia, S Serbia and Montenegro (Yugo.)
Podul Iloaiei *see* Podu Iloaiei
Podunajská Rovina *see* Little Alföld
124 M12 **Podyuga** Arkhangel'skaya Oblast', NW Russian Federation
56 A9 **Poechos, Embalse** ◎ NW Peru
55 W10 **Poeketi** Sipaliwini, E Suriname
100 L8 **Poel** *island* N Germany
83 M20 **Poelela, Lagoa** ◎ S Mozambique
Poerwodadi *see* Purwodadi
Poetovio *see* Ptuj
83 E23 **Pofadder** Northern Cape, W South Africa
106 I9 **Po, Foci del** *var.* Bocche del Po. ≈ NE Italy
116 E12 **Pogăniș** ≈ W Romania
Pogegen *see* Pagėgiai
106 G12 **Poggibonsi** Toscana, C Italy
107 I14 **Poggio Mirteto** Lazio, C Italy
109 V4 **Pöggstall** Niederösterreich, N Austria
116 L13 **Pogoanele** Buzău, SE Romania
Pogónion *see* Delvináki
113 M21 **Pogradec** *var.* Pogradeci. Korçë, SE Albania
Pogradeci *see* Pogradec
123 S15 **Pogranichnyy** Primorskiy Kray, SE Russian Federation
38 M16 **Pogromni Volcano** ▲ Unimak Island, Alaska, USA
163 Z15 **P'ohang** *Jap.* Hokō. E South Korea
15 T9 **Pohénégamook, Lac** ◎ Québec, SE Canada
93 L20 **Pohja** *Swe.* Pojo. Etelä-Suomi, SW Finland
Pohjanlahti *see* Bothnia, Gulf of
189 U16 **Pohnpei** ◈ *state* E Micronesia
189 O12 **Pohnpei** ✕ Pohnpei, E Micronesia
189 O12 **Pohnpei** *prev.* Ponape Ascension Island. *island* E Micronesia
111 F19 **Pohořelice** *Ger.* Pohrlitz. Jihomoravský Kraj, SE Czech Republic
109 V10 **Pohorje** *Ger.* Bacher. ▲ N Slovenia
117 N6 **Pohrebyshche** Vinnyts'ka Oblast', C Ukraine
Pohrlitz *see* Pohořelice
161 P9 **Po Hu** ⊞ E China
116 G15 **Poiana Mare** Dolj, S Romania
Poictiers *see* Poitiers
127 N6 **Poim** Penzenskaya Oblast', W Russian Federation
159 N15 **Poindo** Xizang Zizhiqu, W China
195 Y13 **Poinsett, Cape** *headland* Antarctica
29 R9 **Poinsett, Lake** ◎ South Dakota, N USA
22 I10 **Point Au Fer Island** *island* Louisiana, S USA
39 X14 **Point Baker** Prince of Wales Island, Alaska, USA
25 U13 **Point Comfort** Texas, SW USA
Point de Galle *see* Galle
44 K10 **Pointe à Gravois** *headland* SW Haiti
22 L10 **Pointe a la Hache** Louisiana, S USA
45 Y6 **Pointe-à-Pitre** Grande Terre, C Guadeloupe
15 U7 **Pointe-au-Père** Québec, SE Canada
15 V5 **Pointe-aux-Anglais** Québec, SE Canada
45 T10 **Pointe du Cap** *headland* N Saint Lucia
79 E21 **Pointe-Noire** Le Kouilou, S Congo
45 X6 **Pointe Noire** Basse Terre, W Guadeloupe
79 E21 **Pointe-Noire** ✕ Le Kouilou, S Congo
45 U15 **Point Fortin** Trinidad, Trinidad and Tobago
38 M6 **Point Hope** Alaska, USA
39 N5 **Point Lay** Alaska, USA
18 B16 **Point Marion** Pennsylvania, NE USA
18 K16 **Point Pleasant** New Jersey, NE USA
21 P4 **Point Pleasant** West Virginia, NE USA
45 R14 **Point Salines** ✕ (St.George's) SW Grenada
102 L9 **Poitiers** *prev.* Poictiers, *anc.* Limonum. Vienne, W France
102 K9 **Poitou** *cultural region* W France
102 K10 **Poitou-Charentes** ◈ *region* W France
103 N3 **Poix-de-Picardie** Somme, N France
Pojo *see* Pohja
37 S10 **Pojoaque** New Mexico, SW USA
152 E11 **Pokaran** Rājasthān, NW India
183 R4 **Pokataroo** New South Wales, SE Australia
119 P18 **Pokats'** *Rus.* Pokot'. ≈ SE Belarus
29 V5 **Pokegama Lake** ◎ Minnesota, N USA
184 L6 **Pokeno** Waikato, North Island, NZ
153 O11 **Pokhara** Western, C Nepal

◆ COUNTRY ● COUNTRY CAPITAL ◇ DEPENDENT TERRITORY ○ DEPENDENT TERRITORY CAPITAL ◈ ADMINISTRATIVE REGION ✕ INTERNATIONAL AIRPORT ▲ MOUNTAIN ▲ MOUNTAIN RANGE ⚲ VOLCANO ≈ RIVER ◎ LAKE ⊞ RESERVOIR

127 T6 **Pokhvistnevo** Samarskaya Oblast', W Russian Federation
55 W10 **Pokigron** Sipaliwini, C Suriname
92 L10 **Pokka** *Lapp.* Bohkká. Lappi, N Finland
79 N16 **Poko** Orientale, NE Dem. Rep. Congo
Pokot' *see* Pokats'
Po-ko-to Shan *see* Bogda Shan
147 S7 **Pokrovka** Talasskaya Oblast', NW Kyrgyzstan
Pokrovka *see* Kyzyl-Suu
117 V8 **Pokrovs'ke** *Rus.* Pokrovskoye. Dnipropetrovs'ka Oblast', E Ukraine
Pokrovskoye *see* Pokrovs'ke
Pola *see* Pula
37 N10 **Polacca** Arizona, SW USA
104 L2 **Pola de Laviana** Asturias, N Spain
104 K2 **Pola de Lena** Asturias, N Spain
104 L2 **Pola de Siero** Asturias, N Spain
191 Y3 **Poland** Kiritimati, E Kiribati
110 H12 **Poland** *off.* Republic of Poland, *var.* Polish Republic, *Pol.* Polska, Rzeczpospolita Polska; *prev. Pol.* Polska Rzeczpospolita Ludowa, Polish People's Republic. ◆ *republic* C Europe
Polangen *see* Palanga
110 G7 **Polanów** *Ger.* Pollnow. Zachodnio-pomorskie, NW Poland
136 H13 **Polatlı** Ankara, C Turkey
118 L12 **Polatsk** *Rus.* Polotsk. Vitsyebskaya Voblasts', N Belarus
110 F8 **Połczyn-Zdrój** *Ger.* Bad Polzin. Zachodnio-pomorskie, NW Poland
Polekhatum *see* Pulhatyn
149 Q3 **Pol-e Khomrī** *var.* Pul-i-Khumri. Baghlān, NE Afghanistan
197 S10 **Pole Plain** *undersea feature* Arctic Ocean
143 P5 **Pol-e Safid** *var.* Pol-e-Sefid, Pul-i-Sefid. Māzandarān, N Iran
Pol-e-Sefid *see* Pol-e Safid
118 B13 **Polessk** *Ger.* Labiau. Kaliningradskaya Oblast', W Russian Federation
Polesskoye *see* Polis'ke
171 N13 **Polewali** Sulawesi, C Indonesia
114 G11 **Polezhan** ▲ SW Bulgaria
78 F13 **Poli** Nord, N Cameroon
Poli *see* Pólis
107 M19 **Policastro, Golfo di** *gulf* S Italy
110 D8 **Police** *Ger.* Politz. Zachodniopomorskie, NW Poland
172 I17 **Police, Pointe** *headland* Mahé, NE Seychelles
115 L17 **Polichnítos** *var.* Polihnitos, Políkhnitos. Lésvos, E Greece
Poligiros *see* Polýgyros
107 P17 **Polignano a Mare** Puglia, SE Italy
103 S9 **Poligny** Jura, E France
Polihnitos *see* Polichnítos
Polikastro/Políkastron *see* Polýkastro
Políkhnitos *see* Polichnítos
114 K8 **Polikrayshte** Veliko Tŭrnovo, N Bulgaria
171 O3 **Polillo Islands** *island group* N Philippines
109 Q9 **Polinik** ▲ SW Austria
121 O2 **Pólis** *var.* Poli. W Cyprus
Polish People's Republic *see* Poland
Polish Republic *see* Poland
117 O3 **Polis'ke** *Rus.* Polesskoye. Kyyivs'ka Oblast', N Ukraine
107 N22 **Polistena** Calabria, SW Italy
Politz *see* Police
Políyiros *see* Polýgyros
29 V14 **Polk City** Iowa, C USA
110 F13 **Polkowice** *Ger.* Heerwegen. Dolnośląskie, SW Poland
155 G22 **Pollāchi** Tamil Nādu, SE India
109 W7 **Pöllau** Steiermark, SE Austria
189 T13 **Polle** *atoll* Chuuk Islands, C Micronesia
Pollnow *see* Polanów
29 N7 **Pollock** South Dakota, N USA
92 L8 **Polmak** Finnmark, N Norway
30 L10 **Polo** Illinois, N USA
193 V15 **Poloa** *island* Tongatapu Group, N Tonga
42 E5 **Polochic, Río** ≈ C Guatemala
Pologi *see* Polohy
117 V9 **Polohy** *Rus.* Pologi. Zaporiz'ka Oblast', SE Ukraine
83 K20 **Polokwane** *prev.* Pietersburg. Limpopo, NE South Africa
14 M10 **Polonais, Lac des** ⊗ Québec, SE Canada
61 G20 **Polonio, Cabo** *headland* E Uruguay
155 K24 **Polonnaruwa** North Central Province, C Sri Lanka
116 L5 **Polonne** *Rus.* Polonnoye. Khmel'nyts'ka Oblast', NW Ukraine
Polonnoye *see* Polonne
Polotsk *see* Polatsk
109 T7 **Pöls** *var.* Pölsbach. ≈ E Austria
Pölsbach *see* Pöls
Polska/Polska, Rzeczpospolita/Polska Rzeczpospolita Ludowa *see* Poland
114 L10 **Polski Gradets** Stara Zagora, C Bulgaria
114 K8 **Polsko Kosovo** Ruse, N Bulgaria
33 P8 **Polson** Montana, NW USA
117 T6 **Poltava** Poltavs'ka Oblast', NE Ukraine
Poltava *see* Poltavs'ka Oblast'
117 R5 **Poltavs'ka Oblast'** *var.* Poltava, *Rus.* Poltavskaya Oblast'. ◈ *province* NE Ukraine
Poltavskaya Oblast' *see* Poltavs'ka Oblast'
Poltoratsk *see* Aşgabat
118 I5 **Põltsamaa** *Ger.* Oberpahlen. Jõgevamaa, E Estonia
118 I4 **Põltsamaa** *var.* Põltsamaa Jõgi. ≈ C Estonia
Põltsamaa Jõgi *see* Põltsamaa
122 I8 **Poluy** ≈ N Russian Federation
118 J6 **Põlva** *Ger.* Pölwe. Põlvamaa, SE Estonia
93 N16 **Polvijärvi** Itä-Suomi, E Finland
Pölwe *see* Põlva
115 I22 **Polýaigos** *island* Kykládes, Greece, Aegean Sea
115 I22 **Polyaígou Folégandrou, Stenó** *strait* Kykládes, Greece, Aegean Sea
124 J3 **Polyarnyy** Murmanskaya Oblast', NW Russian Federation
127 W5 **Polyarnyy Ural** ▲ NW Russian Federation
115 G14 **Polýgyros** *var.* Poligiros, Políyiros. Kentrikí Makedonía, N Greece
114 F13 **Polýkastro** *var.* Polikastro; *prev.* Políkastron. Kentrikí Makedonía, N Greece
193 O9 **Polynesia** *island group* C Pacific Ocean
115 J15 **Polýochni** *site of ancient city* Límnos, E Greece
41 Y13 **Polyuc** Quintana Roo, E Mexico
109 V10 **Polzela** C Slovenia
Polzen *see* Ploučnice
56 D12 **Pomabamba** Ancash, C Peru
185 D23 **Pomahaka** ≈ South Island, NZ
106 F12 **Pomarance** Toscana, C Italy
104 G9 **Pombal** Leiria, C Portugal
76 D9 **Pombas** Santo Antão, NW Cape Verde
83 N19 **Pomene** Inhambane, SE Mozambique
110 G8 **Pomerania** *cultural region* Germany/Poland
110 D7 **Pomeranian Bay** *Ger.* Pommersche Bucht, *Pol.* Zatoka Pomorska. *bay* Germany/Poland
31 T15 **Pomeroy** Ohio, N USA
32 L10 **Pomeroy** Washington, NW USA
117 Q8 **Pomichna** Kirovohrads'ka Oblast', C Ukraine
186 H7 **Pomio** New Britain, E PNG
Pomir, Dar"yoi *see* Pamir/Pāmīr, Daryā-ye
27 T6 **Pomme de Terre Lake** ⊠ Missouri, C USA
29 S8 **Pomme de Terre River** ≈ Minnesota, N USA
Pommersche Bucht *see* Pomeranian Bay
35 T15 **Pomona** California, W USA
114 N9 **Pomorie** Burgas, E Bulgaria
Pomorska, Zatoka *see* Pomeranian Bay
110 H8 **Pomorskie** ◈ *province* N Poland
127 Q4 **Pomorskiy Proliv** *strait* NW Russian Federation
125 T10 **Pomozdino** Respublika Komi, NW Russian Federation
Pompaelo *see* Pamplona
23 Z15 **Pompano Beach** Florida, SE USA
107 K18 **Pompei** Campania, S Italy
33 V10 **Pompeys Pillar** Montana, NW USA
Ponape Ascension Island *see* Pohnpei
29 R13 **Ponca** Nebraska, C USA
27 O8 **Ponca City** Oklahoma, C USA
45 T6 **Ponce** C Puerto Rico
23 X10 **Ponce de Leon Inlet** *inlet* Florida, SE USA
22 K8 **Ponchatoula** Louisiana, S USA
26 M8 **Pond Creek** Oklahoma, C USA
155 J20 **Pondicherry** *var.* Puduchcheri, *Fr.* Pondichéry. Pondicherry, SE India
151 I20 **Pondicherry** *var.* Puduchcheri, *Fr.* Pondichéry. ◈ *union territory* India
Pondichéry *see* Pondicherry
197 N11 **Pond Inlet** Baffin Island, Nunavut, NE Canada
187 P16 **Ponérihouen** Province Nord, C New Caledonia
104 J4 **Ponferrada** Castilla-León, NW Spain
184 N13 **Pongaroa** Manawatu-Wanganui, North Island, NZ
167 Q12 **Pong Nam Ron** Chantaburi, S Thailand
81 C14 **Pongo** ≈ S Sudan
152 I7 **Pong Reservoir** ⊠ N India
111 N14 **Poniatowa** Lubelskie, E Poland
167 R12 **Pônley** Kâmpóng Chhnăng, C Cambodia
155 I20 **Ponnaiyār** ≈ SE India
11 Q15 **Ponoka** Alberta, SW Canada
127 U6 **Ponomarevka** Orenburgskaya Oblast', W Russian Federation
169 Q17 **Ponorogo** Jawa, C Indonesia
124 M5 **Ponoy** Murmanskaya Oblast', NW Russian Federation
122 F6 **Ponoy** ≈ NW Russian Federation
102 K11 **Pons** Charente-Maritime, W France
Pons *see* Ponts
Pons Aelii *see* Newcastle upon Tyne
Pons Vetus *see* Pontevedra
99 G20 **Pont-à-Celles** Hainaut, S Belgium
102 K16 **Pontacq** Pyrénées-Atlantiques, SW France
64 P3 **Ponta Delgada** São Miguel, Azores, Portugal, NE Atlantic Ocean
64 P3 **Ponta Delgado** ✕ São Miguel, Azores, Portugal, NE Atlantic Ocean
64 N2 **Ponta do Pico** ▲ Pico, Azores, Portugal, NE Atlantic Ocean
60 J11 **Ponta Grossa** Paraná, S Brazil
103 S5 **Pont-à-Mousson** Meurthe-et-Moselle, NE France
103 T9 **Pontarlier** Doubs, E France
106 G11 **Pontassieve** Toscana, C Italy
102 L4 **Pont-Audemer** Eure, N France
22 K9 **Pontchartrain, Lake** ⊗ Louisiana, S USA
102 I8 **Pontchâteau** Loire-Atlantique, NW France
103 R10 **Pont-de-Vaux** Ain, E France
104 G4 **Ponteareas** Galicia, NW Spain
106 J6 **Pontebba** Friuli-Venezia Giulia, NE Italy
104 G4 **Ponte Caldelas** Galicia, NW Spain
107 J16 **Pontecorvo** Lazio, C Italy
104 G5 **Ponte da Barca** Viana do Castelo, N Portugal
104 G5 **Ponte de Lima** Viana do Castelo, N Portugal
106 F11 **Pontedera** Toscana, C Italy
104 H10 **Ponte de Sor** Portalegre, C Portugal
104 H2 **Pontedeume** Galicia, NW Spain
106 F6 **Ponte di Legno** Lombardia, N Italy
11 T17 **Ponteix** Saskatchewan, S Canada
59 N20 **Ponte Nova** Minas Gerais, NE Brazil
59 G18 **Pontes e Lacerda** Mato Grosso, W Brazil
104 G4 **Pontevedra** *anc.* Pons Vetus. Galicia, NW Spain
104 G3 **Pontevedra** ◈ *province* Galicia, NW Spain
104 G4 **Pontevedra, Ría de** *estuary* NW Spain
30 M12 **Pontiac** Illinois, N USA
31 R9 **Pontiac** Michigan, N USA
169 P11 **Pontianak** Borneo, C Indonesia
107 I16 **Pontino, Agro** *plain* C Italy
Pontisarae *see* Pontoise
102 H6 **Pontivy** Morbihan, NW France
102 F6 **Pont-l'Abbé** Finistère, NW France
103 N4 **Pontoise** *anc.* Briva Isarae, Cergy-Pontoise, Pontisarae. Val-d'Oise, N France
11 W13 **Ponton** Manitoba, C Canada
102 J5 **Pontorson** Manche, N France
22 M2 **Pontotoc** Mississippi, S USA
25 R9 **Pontotoc** Texas, SW USA
106 E10 **Pontremoli** Toscana, C Italy
108 J10 **Pontresina** Graubünden, S Switzerland
105 U5 **Ponts** *var.* Pons. Cataluña, NE Spain
103 R14 **Pont-St-Esprit** Gard, S France
97 K21 **Pontypool** *Wel.* Pontypŵl. SE Wales, UK
97 J22 **Pontypridd** S Wales, UK
Pontypŵl *see* Pontypool
43 R17 **Ponuga** Veraguas, SE Panama
184 L6 **Ponui Island** *island* N NZ
119 K14 **Ponya** *Rus.* Ponya. ≈ N Belarus
107 I17 **Ponziane, Isole** *island* C Italy
182 F7 **Poochera** South Australia
97 L24 **Poole** S England, UK
25 S6 **Poolville** Texas, SW USA
Poona *see* Pune
182 M8 **Pooncarie** New South Wales, SE Australia
183 N6 **Poopelloe Lake** *seasonal lake* New South Wales, SE Australia
57 K19 **Poopó** Oruro, C Bolivia
57 K19 **Poopó, Lago** *var.* Lago Pampa Aullagas. ⊗ W Bolivia
184 L3 **Poor Knights Islands** *island* N NZ
39 P10 **Poorman** Alaska, USA
182 E3 **Pootnoura** South Australia
147 R10 **Pop** *Rus.* Pap. Namangan Viloyati, E Uzbekistan
117 X7 **Popasna** *Rus.* Popasnaya. Luhans'ka Oblast', E Ukraine
Popasnaya *see* Popasna
54 D12 **Popayán** Cauca, SW Colombia
99 B18 **Poperinge** West-Vlaanderen, W Belgium
123 N7 **Popigay** Taymyrskiy (Dolgano-Nenetskiy) Avtonomnyy Okrug, N Russian Federation
123 N7 **Popigay** ≈ N Russian Federation
117 O5 **Popil'nya** Zhytomyrs'ka Oblast', N Ukraine
182 K8 **Popiltah Lake** *seasonal lake* New South Wales, SE Australia
33 X7 **Poplar** Montana, NW USA
11 Y14 **Poplar** ≈ Manitoba, C Canada
27 X8 **Poplar Bluff** Missouri, C USA
33 X6 **Poplar River** ≈ Montana, NW USA
41 P14 **Popocatépetl** ※ S Mexico
79 H21 **Popokabaka** Bandundu, SW Dem. Rep. Congo
107 J15 **Popoli** Abruzzo, C Italy
186 F9 **Popondetta** Northern, S PNG
112 F9 **Popovača** Sisak-Moslavina, NE Croatia
114 J10 **Popovitsa** Tŭrgovishte, C Bulgaria
114 L8 **Popovo** Tŭrgovishte, N Bulgaria
Popovo *see* Iskra
Popper *see* Poprad
30 M5 **Popple River** ≈ Wisconsin, N USA
111 L19 **Poprad** *Ger.* Deutschendorf, *Hung.* Poprád. Prešovský Kraj, E Slovakia
111 L18 **Poprad** *Ger.* Popper, *Hung.* Poprád. ≈ Poland/Slovakia
111 L19 **Poprad-Tatry** ✕ (Poprad) Prešovský Kraj, E Slovakia
21 X7 **Poquoson** Virginia, NE USA
149 O15 **Porāli** ≈ SW Pakistan
184 N12 **Porangahau** Hawke's Bay, North Island, NZ
59 K17 **Porangatu** Goiás, C Brazil
119 G18 **Porazava** *Pol.* Porozow, *Rus.* Porozovo. Hrodzyenskaya Voblasts', W Belarus
154 A11 **Porbandar** Gujarāt, W India
10 I13 **Porcher Island** *island* British Columbia, SW Canada
104 M13 **Porcuna** Andalucía, S Spain
14 F7 **Porcupine** Ontario, S Canada
64 M6 **Porcupine Bank** *undersea feature* N Atlantic Ocean
11 V15 **Porcupine Hills** ▲ Manitoba/Saskatchewan, S Canada
30 L3 **Porcupine Mountains** *hill range* Michigan, N USA
64 M7 **Porcupine Plain** *undersea feature* E Atlantic Ocean
8 G7 **Porcupine River** ≈ Canada/USA
106 I7 **Pordenone** *anc.* Portenau. Friuli-Venezia Giulia, NE Italy
54 H9 **Pore** Casanare, E Colombia
112 A9 **Poreč** *It.* Parenzo. Istra, NW Croatia
60 I9 **Porecatu** Paraná, M15S Brazil
Porech'ye *see* Parechcha
127 P4 **Poretskoye** Chuvashskaya Respublika, W Russian Federation
77 Q13 **Porga** N Benin
186 B7 **Porgera** Enga, W PNG
93 K18 **Pori** *Swe.* Björneborg. Länsi-Suomi, W Finland
185 L14 **Porirua** Wellington, North Island, NZ
92 I12 **Porjus** *Lapp.* Bårjås. Norrbotten, N Sweden
124 G14 **Porkhov** Pskovskaya Oblast', W Russian Federation
55 O4 **Porlamar** Nueva Esparta, NE Venezuela
102 I8 **Pornic** Loire-Atlantique, NW France
186 B7 **Poroma** Southern Highlands, W PNG
123 T13 **Poronaysk** Ostrov Sakhalin, Sakhalinskaya Oblast', SE Russian Federation
115 G20 **Póros** Póros, S Greece
115 C19 **Póros** Kefallinía, Iónioi Nísoi, Greece, C Mediterranean Sea
115 G20 **Póros** *island* S Greece
81 G24 **Poroto Mountains** ▲ SW Tanzania
112 B10 **Porozina** Primorje-Gorski Kotar, NW Croatia
Porozovo/Porozow *see* Porazava
195 X15 **Porpoise Bay** *bay* Antarctica
65 G15 **Porpoise Point** *headland* NE Ascension Island
65 C25 **Porpoise Point** *headland* East Falkland, Falkland Islands
108 C6 **Porrentruy** Jura, NW Switzerland
106 F10 **Porretta Terme** Emilia-Romagna, C Italy
Porriño *see* O Porriño
92 L7 **Porsangerfjorden** *Lapp.* Porsáŋgguvuotna. *fjord* N Norway
92 K8 **Porsangerhalvøya** *peninsula* N Norway
Porsáŋgguvuotna *see* Porsangerfjorden
95 G16 **Porsgrunn** Telemark, S Norway
136 E13 **Porsuk Çayı** ≈ C Turkey
Porsy *see* Boldumsaz
57 N18 **Portachuelo** Santa Cruz, C Bolivia
182 I9 **Port Adelaide** South Australia
97 F15 **Portadown** *Ir.* Port An Dúnáin. S Northern Ireland, UK
31 P10 **Portage** Michigan, N USA
18 D15 **Portage** Pennsylvania, NE USA
30 K8 **Portage** Wisconsin, N USA
30 M3 **Portage Lake** ⊗ Michigan, N USA
11 X16 **Portage la Prairie** Manitoba, S Canada
31 R11 **Portage River** ≈ Ohio, N USA
27 Y8 **Portageville** Missouri, C USA
28 L2 **Portal** North Dakota, N USA
10 L17 **Port Alberni** Vancouver Island, British Columbia, SW Canada
14 E15 **Port Albert** Ontario, S Canada
104 I10 **Portalegre** *anc.* Ammaia, Amoea. Portalegre, E Portugal
104 H10 **Portalegre** ◈ *district* C Portugal
37 V12 **Portales** New Mexico, SW USA
39 X14 **Port Alexander** Baranof Island, Alaska, USA
83 I25 **Port Alfred** Eastern Cape, S South Africa
10 J16 **Port Alice** Vancouver Island, British Columbia, SW Canada
22 J8 **Port Allen** Louisiana, S USA
Port Amelia *see* Pemba
Port An Dúnáin *see* Portadown
32 G7 **Port Angeles** Washington, NW USA
44 L12 **Port Antonio** NE Jamaica
115 D16 **Pórta Panagiá** *religious building* Thessalía, C Greece
25 T14 **Port Aransas** Texas, SW USA
97 E18 **Portarlington** *Ir.* Cúil an tSúdaire. C Ireland
183 P17 **Port Arthur** Tasmania, SE Australia
25 Y11 **Port Arthur** Texas, SW USA
96 G12 **Port Askaig** W Scotland, UK
182 I7 **Port Augusta** South Australia
44 M9 **Port-au-Prince** ● (Haiti) C Haiti
44 M9 **Port-au-Prince** ✕ E Haiti
22 I8 **Port Barre** Louisiana, S USA
151 Q19 **Port Blair** Andaman and Nicobar Islands, SE India
25 X12 **Port Bolivar** Texas, SW USA
105 X4 **Portbou** Cataluña, NE Spain
77 N17 **Port Bouet** ✕ (Abidjan) SE Ivory Coast
182 I8 **Port Broughton** South Australia
14 F17 **Port Burwell** Ontario, S Canada
12 G17 **Port Burwell** Québec, NE Canada
182 M13 **Port Campbell** Victoria, SE Australia
15 V4 **Port-Cartier** Québec, SE Canada
185 F23 **Port Chalmers** Otago, South Island, NZ
23 W14 **Port Charlotte** Florida, SE USA
38 L9 **Port Clarence** Alaska, USA
10 I13 **Port Clements** Graham Island, British Columbia, SW Canada
31 S11 **Port Clinton** Ohio, N USA
14 H17 **Port Colborne** Ontario, S Canada
15 Y7 **Port-Daniel** Québec, SE Canada
Port Darwin *see* Darwin
183 O17 **Port Davey** *headland* Tasmania, SE Australia
44 K8 **Port-de-Paix** NW Haiti
181 W4 **Port Douglas** Queensland, NE Australia
10 J13 **Port Edward** British Columbia, SW Canada
83 K24 **Port Edward** KwaZulu/Natal, SE South Africa
58 J12 **Portel** Pará, NE Brazil
104 H12 **Portel** Évora, S Portugal
14 E14 **Port Elgin** Ontario, S Canada
45 Y14 **Port Elizabeth** Bequia, Saint Vincent and the Grenadines
83 I26 **Port Elizabeth** Eastern Cape, S South Africa
96 G13 **Port Ellen** W Scotland, UK
Portenau *see* Pordenone
97 H16 **Port Erin** SW Isle of Man
45 Q13 **Porter Point** *headland* Saint Vincent, Saint Vincent and the Grenadines
185 G18 **Porters Pass** *pass* South Island, NZ
83 E25 **Porterville** Western Cape, SW South Africa
35 R12 **Porterville** California, W USA
Port-Étienne *see* Nouâdhibou
182 L13 **Port Fairy** Victoria, SE Australia
184 M4 **Port Fitzroy** Great Barrier Island, Auckland, NE NZ
Port Florence *see* Kisumu
Port-Francqui *see* Ilebo
79 C18 **Port-Gentil** Ogooué-Maritime, W Gabon
182 I7 **Port Germein** South Australia
22 J6 **Port Gibson** Mississippi, S USA
39 Q13 **Port Graham** Alaska, USA
77 U17 **Port Harcourt** Rivers, S Nigeria
10 J16 **Port Hardy** Vancouver Island, British Columbia, SW Canada
Port Harrison *see* Inukjuak
13 R14 **Port Hawkesbury** Cape Breton Island, Nova Scotia, SE Canada
180 I6 **Port Hedland** Western Australia
39 O15 **Port Heiden** Alaska, USA
97 I19 **Porthmadog** *var.* Portmadoc. NW Wales, UK
14 I15 **Port Hope** Ontario, SE Canada
13 S9 **Port Hope Simpson** Newfoundland and Labrador, E Canada
65 C24 **Port Howard Settlement** West Falkland, Falkland Islands
31 T9 **Port Huron** Michigan, N USA
107 K17 **Portici** Campania, S Italy
137 Y13 **Port-Il'ic** *Rus.* Port Il'ich. SE Azerbaijan
Port Il'ich *see* Port-Il'ic
104 G14 **Portimão** *var.* Vila Nova de Portimão. Faro, S Portugal
25 T17 **Port Isabel** Texas, SW USA
18 J13 **Port Jervis** New York, NE USA
55 S7 **Port Kaituma** NW Guyana
126 K12 **Port-Katon** Rostovskaya Oblast', SW Russian Federation
183 S9 **Port Kembla** New South Wales, SE Australia
182 F8 **Port Kenny** South Australia
Port Klang *see* Pelabuhan Klang
Port Láirge *see* Waterford
183 S8 **Portland** New South Wales, SE Australia
182 L13 **Portland** Victoria, SE Australia
184 K4 **Portland** Northland, North Island, NZ
31 Q13 **Portland** Indiana, N USA
19 P8 **Portland** Maine, NE USA
31 Q9 **Portland** Michigan, N USA
29 Q4 **Portland** North Dakota, N USA
32 G11 **Portland** Oregon, NW USA
20 J8 **Portland** Tennessee, S USA
25 T14 **Portland** Texas, SW USA
32 G11 **Portland** ✕ Oregon, NW USA
182 L13 **Portland Bay** *bay* Victoria, SE Australia
44 K13 **Portland Bight** *bay* S Jamaica
97 L24 **Portland Bill** *var.* Bill of Portland. *headland* S England, UK
Portland, Bill of *see* Portland Bill
183 P15 **Portland, Cape** *headland* Tasmania, SE Australia
10 J12 **Portland Inlet** *inlet* British Columbia, W Canada
184 P11 **Portland Island** *island* E NZ
65 F15 **Portland Point** *headland* SW Ascension Island
44 J13 **Portland Point** *headland* C Jamaica
103 P16 **Port-la-Nouvelle** Aude, S France
Portlaoighise *see* Port Laoise
97 E18 **Port Laoise** *var.* Portlaoise, *Ir.* Portlaoighise; *prev.* Maryborough. C Ireland
25 U13 **Port Lavaca** Texas, SW USA
182 G9 **Port Lincoln** South Australia
39 Q14 **Port Lions** Kodiak Island, Alaska, USA
76 I15 **Port Loko** W Sierra Leone
65 E24 **Port Louis** East Falkland, Falkland Islands
45 Y5 **Port-Louis** Grande Terre, N Guadeloupe
173 X16 **Port Louis** ● (Mauritius) NW Mauritius
Port Louis *see* Scarborough
Port-Lyautey *see* Kénitra
182 K12 **Port MacDonnell** South Australia
183 U7 **Port Macquarie** New South Wales, SE Australia
Portmadoc *see* Porthmadog
Port Mahon *see* Mahón
44 K12 **Port Maria** C Jamaica
10 K16 **Port McNeill** Vancouver Island, British Columbia, SW Canada
13 P11 **Port-Menier** Île d'Anticosti, Québec, E Canada
39 N15 **Port Moller** Alaska, USA
44 L13 **Port Morant** E Jamaica
44 K13 **Portmore** C Jamaica
186 D9 **Port Moresby** ● (PNG) Central/National Capital District, SW PNG
Port Natal *see* Durban
25 Y11 **Port Neches** Texas, SW USA
182 G9 **Port Neill** South Australia
15 S6 **Portneuf** ≈ Québec, SE Canada
15 R6 **Portneuf, Lac** ⊗ Québec, SE Canada
83 D23 **Port Nolloth** Northern Cape, W South Africa
18 J17 **Port Norris** New Jersey, NE USA
Port-Nouveau-Québec *see* Kangiqsualujjuaq
104 G6 **Porto** *Eng.* Oporto; *anc.* Portus Cale. Porto, NW Portugal
104 G6 **Porto** *var.* Pôrto. ◈ *district* N Portugal
104 G6 **Porto** ✕ Porto, W Portugal
61 I16 **Porto Alegre** *var.* Pôrto Alegre. *state capital* Rio Grande do Sul, S Brazil
Porto Alexandre *see* Tombua
82 B12 **Porto Amboim** Cuanza Sul, NW Angola
Porto Amélia *see* Pemba
Porto Bello *see* Portobelo
43 T14 **Portobelo** *var.* Porto Bello, Puerto Bello. Colón, N Panama
60 G10 **Pôrto Camargo** Paraná, S Brazil
25 U13 **Port O'Connor** Texas, SW USA
Pôrto de Mós *see* Porto de Moz
58 J12 **Porto de Moz** *var.* Pôrto de Mós. Pará, NE Brazil
64 O5 **Porto do Moniz** Madeira, Portugal, NE Atlantic Ocean
59 H16 **Porto dos Gaúchos** Mato Grosso, W Brazil
Porto Edda *see* Sarandë
107 J24 **Porto Empedocle** Sicilia, Italy, C Mediterranean Sea
59 H20 **Porto Esperança** Mato Grosso do Sul, SW Brazil
106 E13 **Portoferraio** Toscana, C Italy
96 G6 **Port of Ness** NW Scotland, UK
45 U14 **Port-of-Spain** ● (Trinidad and Tobago) Trinidad, Trinidad and Tobago
Port of Spain *see* Piarco
103 X15 **Porto, Golfe de** *gulf* Corse, France, C Mediterranean Sea
Porto Grande *see* Mindelo
106 I7 **Portogruaro** Veneto, NE Italy
35 P5 **Portola** California, W USA
187 Q13 **Port-Olry** Espiritu Santo, C Vanuatu
93 J17 **Pörtom** *Fin.* Pirttikylä. Länsi-Suomi, W Finland
Port Omna *see* Portumna
59 G21 **Porto Murtinho** Mato Grosso do Sul, SW Brazil
59 K16 **Porto Nacional** Tocantins, C Brazil
77 S16 **Porto-Novo** ● (Benin) S Benin
23 X10 **Port Orange** Florida, SE USA
32 G8 **Port Orchard** Washington, NW USA
Porto Re *see* Kraljevica
32 E15 **Port Orford** Oregon, NW USA
Porto Rico *see* Puerto Rico
106 J13 **Porto San Giorgio** Marche, C Italy
107 F14 **Porto San Stefano** Toscana, C Italy
64 P5 **Porto Santo** *var.* Vila Baleira. Porto Santo, Madeira, Portugal, NE Atlantic Ocean
64 Q5 **Porto Santo** ✕ Porto Santo, Madeira, Portugal, NE Atlantic Ocean
64 P5 **Porto Santo** *var.* Ilha do Porto Santo. *island* Madeira, Portugal, NE Atlantic Ocean
60 H9 **Porto São José** Paraná, S Brazil
59 O19 **Porto Seguro** Bahia, E Brazil
107 B17 **Porto Torres** Sardegna, Italy, C Mediterranean Sea
59 J23 **Porto União** Santa Catarina, S Brazil
103 Y16 **Porto-Vecchio** Corse, France, C Mediterranean Sea
59 E15 **Porto Velho** *var.* Velho. *state capital* Rondônia, W Brazil
56 A6 **Portoviejo** *var.* Puertoviejo. Manabí, W Ecuador
185 B26 **Port Pegasus** *bay* Stewart Island, NZ

◆ Country ● Country Capital ◇ Dependent Territory ○ Dependent Territory Capital ◈ Administrative Region ✕ International Airport ▲ Mountain ▲ Mountain Range ※ Volcano ≈ River ⊗ Lake ⊠ Reservoir

14 H15 **Port Perry** Ontario, SE Canada
183 N12 **Port Phillip Bay** harbour Victoria, SE Australia
182 I8 **Port Pirie** South Australia
96 G9 **Portree** N Scotland, UK
Port Rex see East London
Port Rois see Portrush
44 K13 **Port Royal** E Jamaica
21 R15 **Port Royal** South Carolina, SE USA
21 R15 **Port Royal Sound** inlet South Carolina, SE USA
97 F14 **Portrush** Ir. Port Rois. N Northern Ireland, UK
75 W7 **Port Said** Ar. Būr Sa'īd. N Egypt
23 R9 **Port Saint Joe** Florida, SE USA
23 Y11 **Port Saint John** Florida, SE USA
83 K24 **Port St.Johns** Eastern Cape, SE South Africa
103 R16 **Port-St-Louis-du-Rhône** Bouches-du-Rhône, SE France
44 K10 **Port Salut** SW Haiti
65 E24 **Port Salvador** inlet East Falkland, Falkland Islands
65 D24 **Port San Carlos** East Falkland, Falkland Islands
13 S10 **Port Saunders** Newfoundland and Labrador, SE Canada
83 K24 **Port Shepstone** KwaZulu/Natal, E South Africa
45 O11 **Portsmouth** var. Grand-Anse. NW Dominica
97 N24 **Portsmouth** S England, UK
19 P10 **Portsmouth** New Hampshire, NE USA
31 S15 **Portsmouth** Ohio, N USA
21 X7 **Portsmouth** Virginia, NE USA
14 E17 **Port Stanley** Ontario, S Canada
65 B25 **Port Stephens** inlet West Falkland, Falkland Islands
65 B25 **Port Stephens Settlement** West Falkland, Falkland Islands
97 F14 **Portstewart** Ir. Port Stíobhaird. N Northern Ireland, UK
Port Stíobhaird see Portstewart
80 I7 **Port Sudan** Red Sea, NE Sudan
22 L10 **Port Sulphur** Louisiana, S USA
Port Swettenham see Klang/Pelabuhan Klang
97 J22 **Port Talbot** S Wales, UK
92 L11 **Porttipahdan Tekojärvi** ⊚ N Finland
32 G7 **Port Townsend** Washington, NW USA
104 H9 **Portugal** off. Republic of Portugal. ◆ republic SW Europe
105 O2 **Portugalete** País Vasco, N Spain
54 J6 **Portuguesa** off. Estado Portuguesa. ◈ state N Venezuela
Portuguese East Africa see Mozambique
Portuguese Guinea see Guinea-Bissau
Portuguese Timor see East Timor
Portuguese West Africa see Angola
97 D18 **Portumna** Ir. Port Omna. W Ireland
Portus Cale see Porto
Portus Magnus see Almería
Portus Magonis see Mahón
103 P17 **Port-Vendres** var. Port Vendres. Pyrénées-Orientales, S France
182 H9 **Port Victoria** South Australia
187 Q14 **Port-Vila** var. Vila. ● (Vanuatu) Éfaté, C Vanuatu
182 I9 **Port Wakefield** South Australia
31 N8 **Port Washington** Wisconsin, N USA
57 J14 **Porvenir** Pando, NW Bolivia
63 I24 **Porvenir** Magallanes, S Chile
61 D18 **Porvenir** Paysandú, W Uruguay
93 M19 **Porvoo** Swe. Borgå. Etelä-Suomi, S Finland
Porzecze see Parechcha
104 M10 **Porzuna** Castilla-La Mancha, C Spain
61 E14 **Posadas** Misiones, NE Argentina
104 L13 **Posadas** Andalucía, S Spain
Poschega see Požega
108 J11 **Poschiavino** ≈ Italy/Switzerland
108 J10 **Poschiavo** Ger. Puschlav. Graubünden, S Switzerland
112 D12 **Posedarje** Zadar, SW Croatia
Posen see Poznań
126 L14 **Poshekhon'ye** Yaroslavskaya Oblast', W Russian Federation
92 M13 **Posio** Lappi, NE Finland
Poskam see Zepu
Posnania see Poznań
171 O12 **Poso** Sulawesi, C Indonesia
171 O12 **Poso, Danau** ⊚ Sulawesi, C Indonesia
137 R10 **Posof** Ardahan, NE Turkey
25 R6 **Possum Kingdom Lake** ⊠ Texas, SW USA
25 N6 **Post** Texas, SW USA
Postavy/Postawy see Pastavy
12 I7 **Poste-de-la-Baleine** Québec, NE Canada
99 M17 **Posterholt** Limburg, SE Netherlands
83 G22 **Postmasburg** Northern Cape, N South Africa
Pôsto Diuarum see Campo de Diauarum
59 I16 **Pôsto Jacaré** Mato Grosso, W Brazil
109 T12 **Postojna** Ger. Adelsberg, It. Postumia. SW Slovenia
Postumia see Postojna
29 X12 **Postville** Iowa, C USA
Pöstyén see Piešt'any
113 G14 **Posušje** Federacija Bosna I Herzegovina, SE Bosnia & Herzegovina
171 O16 **Pota** Flores, C Indonesia
115 G23 **Potamós** Antikýthira, S Greece
55 S9 **Potaru River** ≈ C Guyana
83 I21 **Potchefstroom** North-West, N South Africa
27 R11 **Poteau** Oklahoma, C USA
25 R12 **Poteet** Texas, SW USA
115 G14 **Poteídaia** site of ancient city Kentrikí Makedonía, N Greece
Potentia see Potenza
107 M18 **Potenza** anc. Potentia. Basilicata, S Italy
185 A24 **Poteriteri, Lake** ⊚ South Island, NZ
104 M2 **Potes** Cantabria, N Spain
Potgietersrus see Mokopane
25 S12 **Poth** Texas, SW USA
32 J9 **Potholes Reservoir** ⊠ Washington, NW USA
137 Q9 **P'ot'i** W Georgia
77 X13 **Potiskum** Yobe, NE Nigeria
Potkozarje see Ivanjska
32 M9 **Potlatch** Idaho, NW USA
33 N9 **Pot Mountain** ▲ Idaho, NW USA
113 H14 **Potoci** Federacija Bosna I Hercegovina, SE Bosnia & Herzegovina
21 V3 **Potomac River** ≈ NE USA
27 W6 **Potosi** Missouri, C USA
57 L20 **Potosí** Potosí, S Bolivia
42 H9 **Potosí** Chinandega, NW Nicaragua
57 K21 **Potosí** ◈ department SW Bolivia
62 H7 **Potrerillos** Atacama, N Chile
42 H5 **Potrerillos** Cortés, NW Honduras
62 H8 **Potro, Cerro del** ▲ N Chile
100 N12 **Potsdam** Brandenburg, NE Germany
18 J7 **Potsdam** New York, NE USA
109 X5 **Pottendorf** Niederösterreich, E Austria
109 X5 **Pottenstein** Niederösterreich, E Austria
18 I15 **Pottstown** Pennsylvania, NE USA
18 H14 **Pottsville** Pennsylvania, NE USA
155 L25 **Pottuvil** Eastern Province, SE Sri Lanka
149 U6 **Potwar Plateau** plateau NE Pakistan
102 J7 **Pouancé** Maine-et-Loire, W France
15 R6 **Poulin de Courval, Lac** ⊚ Québec, SE Canada
18 L9 **Poultney** Vermont, NE USA
187 O16 **Poum** Province Nord, W New Caledonia
59 L21 **Pouso Alegre** Minas Gerais, NE Brazil
192 I16 **Poutasi** Upolu, SE Samoa
167 R12 **Poŭthĭsăt** prev. Pursat. Poŭthĭsăt, W Cambodia
167 R12 **Poŭthĭsăt, Stœng** prev. Pursat. ≈ W Cambodia
102 J9 **Pouzauges** Vendée, NW France
Po, Valle del see Po Valley
106 F8 **Po Valley** It. Valle del Po. valley N Italy
111 I19 **Považská Bystrica** Ger. Waagbistritz, Hung. Vágbeszterce. Trenčiansky Kraj, W Slovakia
124 I10 **Povenets** Respublika Kareliya, NW Russian Federation
184 Q9 **Poverty Bay** inlet North Island, NZ
112 K12 **Povlen** ▲ W Serbia and Montenegro (Yugo.)
104 G6 **Póvoa de Varzim** Porto, NW Portugal
127 N8 **Povorino** Voronezhskaya Oblast', W Russian Federation
Povungnituk see Puvirnituq
12 J3 **Povungnituk, Rivière de** ≈ Québec, NE Canada
14 H11 **Powassan** Ontario, S Canada
35 U17 **Poway** California, W USA
33 W14 **Powder River** Wyoming, C USA
33 Y10 **Powder River** ≈ Montana/Wyoming, NW USA
32 L12 **Powder River** ≈ Oregon, NW USA
33 W13 **Powder River Pass** pass Wyoming, C USA
33 U12 **Powell** Wyoming, C USA
65 I22 **Powell Basin** undersea feature NW Weddell Sea
36 M8 **Powell, Lake** ⊚ Utah, W USA
37 R4 **Powell, Mount** ▲ Colorado, C USA
10 L17 **Powell River** British Columbia, SW Canada
31 N5 **Powers** Michigan, N USA
28 K2 **Powers Lake** North Dakota, N USA
21 V6 **Powhatan** Virginia, NE USA
31 V13 **Powhatan Point** Ohio, N USA
97 J20 **Powys** cultural region E Wales, UK
187 P17 **Poya** Province Nord, C New Caledonia
161 P10 **Poyang Hu** ⊚ S China
30 L7 **Poygan, Lake** ⊚ Wisconsin, N USA
109 Y2 **Poysdorf** Niederösterreich, NE Austria
112 N11 **Požarevac** Ger. Passarowitz. Serbia, NE Serbia and Montenegro (Yugo.)
41 Q13 **Poza Rica** var. Poza Rica de Hidalgo. Veracruz-Llave, E Mexico
Poza Rica de Hidalgo see Poza Rica
112 L13 **Požega** Prev. Slavonska Požega; Ger. Poschega, Hung. Pozsega. Požega-Slavonija, NE Croatia
112 H9 **Požega-Slavonija** off. Požeško-Slavonska Županija. ◈ province NE Croatia
125 U13 **Pozhva** Komi-Permyatskiy Avtonomnyy Okrug, NW Russian Federation
110 G11 **Poznań** Ger. Posen, Posnania. Wielkolpolskie, C Poland
105 O13 **Pozo Alcón** Andalucía, S Spain
62 H3 **Pozo Almonte** Tarapacá, N Chile
104 L12 **Pozoblanco** Andalucía, S Spain
105 Q11 **Pozo Cañada** Castilla-La Mancha, C Spain
62 N5 **Pozo Colorado** Presidente Hayes, C Paraguay
63 J20 **Pozos, Punta** headland S Argentina
Pozsega see Požega
Pozsony see Bratislava
55 N5 **Pozuelos** Anzoátegui, NE Venezuela
107 L26 **Pozzallo** Sicilia, Italy, C Mediterranean Sea
107 K17 **Pozzuoli** anc. Puteoli. Campania, S Italy
77 P17 **Pra** ≈ S Ghana
111 C19 **Prachatice** Ger. Prachatitz. Jihočeský Kraj, S Czech Republic
Prachatitz see Prachatice
167 P11 **Prachin Buri** var. Prachinburi. Prachin Buri, C Thailand
Prachuab Girikhand see Prachuap Khiri Khan
167 O12 **Prachuap Khiri Khan** var. Prachuab Girikhand. Prachuap Khiri Khan, SW Thailand
111 H16 **Praděd** Ger. Altvater. ▲ NE Czech Republic
54 D11 **Pradera** Valle del Cauca, SW Colombia
103 O17 **Prades** Pyrénées-Orientales, S France
59 O19 **Prado** Bahia, SE Brazil
54 E11 **Prado** Tolima, C Colombia
Prado del Ganso see Goose Green
Prae see Phrae
Prag/Praga/Prague see Praha
27 O10 **Prague** Oklahoma, C USA
111 D16 **Praha** Eng. Prague, Ger. Prag, Pol. Praga. ● (Czech Republic) Středočeský Kraj, NW Czech Republic
116 J13 **Prahova** ◈ county SE Romania
116 J13 **Prahova** ≈ S Romania
76 E10 **Praia** ● (Cape Verde) Santiago, S Cape Verde
83 M21 **Praia do Bilene** Gaza, S Mozambique
83 M20 **Praia do Xai-Xai** Gaza, S Mozambique
116 J10 **Praid** Hung. Parajd. Harghita, C Romania
26 J3 **Prairie Dog Creek** ≈ Kansas/Nebraska, C USA
30 J9 **Prairie du Chien** Wisconsin, N USA
27 S9 **Prairie Grove** Arkansas, C USA
31 P10 **Prairie River** ≈ Michigan, N USA
Prairie State see Illinois
25 V11 **Prairie View** Texas, SW USA
167 Q10 **Prakhon Chai** Buri Ram, E Thailand
109 R4 **Pram** ≈ N Austria
109 S4 **Prambachkirchen** Oberösterreich, N Austria
118 H2 **Prangli** island N Estonia
154 J13 **Prānhita** ≈ C India
172 I15 **Praslin** island Inner Islands, NE Seychelles
115 O23 **Prasonísi, Akrotírio** headland Ródos, Dodekánisos, Greece, Aegean Sea
111 I14 **Praszka** Opolskie, S Poland
119 M18 **Pratasy** Rus. Protasy. Homyel'skaya Voblasts', SE Belarus
167 Q10 **Prathai** Nakhon Ratchasima, E Thailand
Prathet Thai see Thailand
Prathum Thani see Pathum Thani
63 F21 **Prat, Isla** island S Chile
106 G11 **Prato** Toscana, C Italy
103 O17 **Prats-de-Mollo-la-Preste** Pyrénées-Orientales, S France
26 L6 **Pratt** Kansas, C USA
108 E6 **Pratteln** Basel-Land, NW Switzerland
193 O2 **Pratt Seamount** undersea feature N Pacific Ocean
23 P5 **Prattville** Alabama, S USA
Praust see Pruszcz Gdański
114 M7 **Pravda** prev. Dogrular. Silistra, NE Bulgaria
119 B14 **Pravdinsk** Ger. Friedland. Kaliningradskaya Oblast', W Russian Federation
104 K2 **Pravia** Asturias, N Spain
118 L12 **Prazaroki** Rus. Prozoroki. Vitsyebskaya Voblasts', N Belarus
Prázsmár see Prejmer
167 S11 **Preăh Vihéar** Preăh Vihéar, N Cambodia
116 J12 **Predeal** Hung. Predeál. Braşov, C Romania
109 S8 **Predlitz** Steiermark, SE Austria
11 V15 **Preeceville** Saskatchewan, S Canada
Preenkuln see Priekule
102 K6 **Pré-en-Pail** Mayenne, NW France
109 T4 **Pregarten** Oberösterreich, N Austria
54 H7 **Pregonero** Táchira, NW Venezuela
118 J10 **Preiļi** Ger. Preli. Preiļi, SE Latvia
116 J12 **Prejmer** Ger. Tartlau, Hung. Prázsmár. Braşov, S Romania
113 J16 **Prekornica** ▲▲ SW Serbia and Montenegro (Yugo.)
Preli see Preiļi
Prëmet see Përmet
100 M12 **Premnitz** Brandenburg, NE Germany
25 S15 **Premont** Texas, SW USA
113 H14 **Prenj** ▲▲ S Bosnia and Herzegovina
Prenjas/Prenjasi see Përrenjas
22 L7 **Prentiss** Mississippi, S USA
Preny see Prienai
100 O10 **Prenzlau** Brandenburg, NE Germany
123 N11 **Preobrazhenka** Irkutskaya Oblast', C Russian Federation
166 J9 **Preparis Island** island SW Myanmar
Prerau see Přerov
111 H18 **Přerov** Ger. Prerau. Olomoucký Kraj, E Czech Republic
Preschau see Prešov
14 M14 **Prescott** Ontario, SE Canada
36 K12 **Prescott** Arizona, SW USA
27 T13 **Prescott** Arkansas, C USA
32 L10 **Prescott** Washington, NW USA
30 H6 **Prescott** Wisconsin, N USA
185 A24 **Preservation Inlet** inlet South Island, NZ
112 O7 **Preševo** Serbia, SE Serbia and Montenegro (Yugo.)
29 N10 **Presho** South Dakota, N USA
58 M13 **Presidente Dutra** Maranhão, E Brazil
60 I8 **Presidente Epitácio** São Paulo, S Brazil
62 N5 **Presidente Hayes** off. Departamento de Presidente Hayes. ◈ department C Paraguay
60 I9 **Presidente Prudente** São Paulo, S Brazil
Presidente Stroessner see Ciudad del Este
Presidente Vargas see Itabira
60 I8 **Presidente Venceslau** São Paulo, S Brazil
193 O10 **President Thiers Seamount** undersea feature C Pacific Ocean
24 J11 **Presidio** Texas, SW USA
Preslav see Veliki Preslav
111 M19 **Prešov** var. Preschau, Ger. Eperies, Hung. Eperjes. Prešovský Kraj, E Slovakia
111 M19 **Prešovský Kraj** ◈ region E Slovakia
113 N20 **Prespa, Lake** Alb. Liqen i Prespës, Gk. Límni Megáli Préspa, Limni Prespa, Mac. Prespansko Ezero, Serb. Prespansko Jezero. ⊚ SE Europe
Prespa, Limni/Prespansko Ezero/Prespansko Jezero/Prespës, Liqen i see Prespa, Lake
19 S2 **Presque Isle** Maine, NE USA
18 B11 **Presque Isle** headland Pennsylvania, NE USA
Pressburg see Bratislava
77 P17 **Prestea** SW Ghana
111 B17 **Přeštice** Ger. Pschestitz. Plzeňský Kraj, W Czech Republic
97 K17 **Preston** NW England, UK
23 S6 **Preston** Georgia, SE USA
33 R16 **Preston** Idaho, NW USA
29 Z13 **Preston** Iowa, C USA
29 X11 **Preston** Minnesota, N USA
21 O6 **Prestonsburg** Kentucky, S USA
96 I13 **Prestwick** W Scotland, UK
83 I21 **Pretoria** var. Epitoli, Tshwane. ● (South Africa-administrative capital) Gauteng, NE South Africa
Pretoria-Witwatersrand-Vereeniging see Gauteng
Pretusha see Pretushë
113 M21 **Pretushë** var. Pretusha. Korçë, SE Albania
Preussisch Eylau see Bagrationovsk
Preussisch-Stargard see Starogard Gdański
Preußisch Holland see Pasłęk
115 C17 **Préveza** Ípeiros, W Greece
37 V3 **Prewitt Reservoir** ⊠ Colorado, C USA
167 S13 **Prey Vêng** Prey Vêng, S Cambodia
144 M12 **Priaral'skiye Karakumy, Peski** desert SW Kazakhstan
123 P14 **Priargunsk** Chitinskaya Oblast', S Russian Federation
38 K14 **Pribilof Islands** island group Alaska, USA
113 K14 **Priboj** Serbia, W Serbia and Montenegro (Yugo.)
111 C17 **Příbram** Ger. Pibrans. Středočeský Kraj, W Czech Republic
36 M4 **Price** Utah, W USA
37 N5 **Price River** ≈ Utah, W USA
23 N8 **Prichard** Alabama, S USA
25 R8 **Priddy** Texas, SW USA
105 P8 **Priego** Castilla-La Mancha, C Spain
104 M14 **Priego de Córdoba** Andalucía, S Spain
118 C10 **Priekule** Ger. Preenkuln. Liepāja, SW Latvia
118 C12 **Priekulė** Ger. Prökuls. Klaipėda, W Lithuania
119 F14 **Prienai** Pol. Preny. Kaunas, S Lithuania
83 G23 **Prieska** Northern Cape, C South Africa
32 M7 **Priest Lake** ⊚ Idaho, NW USA
32 M7 **Priest River** Idaho, NW USA
104 M3 **Prieta, Peña** ▲ N Spain
40 J10 **Prieto, Cerro** ▲ C Mexico
111 J19 **Prievidza** var. Priewitz, Ger. Priwitz, Hung. Privigye. Trenčiansky Kraj, C Slovakia
Priewitz see Prievidza
112 F10 **Prijedor** Republika Srpska, NW Bosnia & Herzegovina
113 K14 **Prijepolje** Serbia, W Serbia and Montenegro (Yugo.)
Prikaspiyskaya Nizmennost' see Caspian Depression
113 O19 **Prilep** Turk. Perlepe. S FYR Macedonia
108 B9 **Prilly** Vaud, SW Switzerland
Priluki see Pryluky
62 L10 **Primero, Río** ≈ C Argentina
29 S12 **Primghar** Iowa, C USA
112 B9 **Primorje-Gorski Kotar** off. Primorsko-Goranska Županija. ◈ province NW Croatia
118 A13 **Primorsk** Ger. Fischhausen. Kaliningradskaya Oblast', W Russian Federation
124 G12 **Primorsk** Fin. Koivisto. Leningradskaya Oblast', NW Russian Federation
Primorsk/Primorskoye see Prymors'k
123 S14 **Primorskiy Kray** prev. Eng. Maritime Territory. ◈ territory SE Russian Federation
114 N10 **Primorsko** prev. Keupriya. Burgas, E Bulgaria
126 K13 **Primorsko-Akhtarsk** Krasnodarskiy Kray, SW Russian Federation
117 U13 **Primors'kyy** Respublika Krym, S Ukraine
113 D14 **Primošten** Šibenik-Knin, S Croatia
11 R13 **Primrose Lake** ⊚ Saskatchewan, C Canada
11 T14 **Prince Albert** Saskatchewan, S Canada
83 G25 **Prince Albert** Western Cape, SW South Africa
8 J5 **Prince Albert Peninsula** peninsula Victoria Island, Northwest Territories, NW Canada
8 J6 **Prince Albert Sound** inlet Northwest Territories, N Canada
8 J5 **Prince Alfred, Cape** headland Northwest Territories, NW Canada
9 P6 **Prince Charles Island** island Nunavut, NE Canada
195 W6 **Prince Charles Mountains** ▲▲ Antarctica
Prince-Édouard, Île-du see Prince Edward Island
172 M13 **Prince Edward Fracture Zone** tectonic feature SW Indian Ocean
13 P14 **Prince Edward Island** Fr. Île-du Prince-Édouard. ◈ province SE Canada
13 Q14 **Prince Edward Island** Fr. Île-du Prince-Édouard. island SE Canada
173 M12 **Prince Edward Islands** island group S South Africa
21 X4 **Prince Frederick** Maryland, NE USA
10 M14 **Prince George** British Columbia, SW Canada
21 W6 **Prince George** Virginia, NE USA
8 L3 **Prince Gustaf Adolf Sea** sea Nunavut, N Canada
197 Q3 **Prince of Wales, Cape** headland Alaska, USA
9 N3 **Prince of Wales Icefield** ice feature Nunavut, N Canada
181 V1 **Prince of Wales Island** island Queensland, E Australia
8 L5 **Prince of Wales Island** island Queen Elizabeth Islands, Nunavut, NW Canada
39 Y14 **Prince of Wales Island** island Alexander Archipelago, Alaska, USA
Prince of Wales Island see Pinang, Pulau
8 J5 **Prince of Wales Strait** strait Northwest Territories, N Canada
8 K4 **Prince Patrick Island** island Parry Islands, Northwest Territories, NW Canada
9 N5 **Prince Regent Inlet** channel Nunavut, N Canada
10 J13 **Prince Rupert** British Columbia, SW Canada
Prince's Island see Príncipe
21 Y5 **Princess Anne** Maryland, NE USA
195 R1 **Princess Astrid Kyst** physical region Antarctica
181 W2 **Princess Charlotte Bay** bay Queensland, NE Australia
195 W7 **Princess Elizabeth Land** physical region Antarctica
10 J14 **Princess Royal Island** island British Columbia, SW Canada
45 U15 **Princes Town** Trinidad, Trinidad and Tobago
11 N17 **Princeton** British Columbia, SW Canada
30 L11 **Princeton** Illinois, N USA
31 N16 **Princeton** Indiana, N USA
29 Z14 **Princeton** Iowa, C USA
20 H7 **Princeton** Kentucky, S USA
29 V8 **Princeton** Minnesota, N USA
27 S1 **Princeton** Missouri, C USA
18 J15 **Princeton** New Jersey, NE USA
21 R6 **Princeton** West Virginia, NE USA
39 S12 **Prince William Sound** inlet Alaska, USA
67 P9 **Príncipe** var. Príncipe Island, Eng. Prince's Island. island N Sao Tome and Principe
Príncipe Island see Príncipe
32 I13 **Prineville** Oregon, NW USA
28 J11 **Pringle** South Dakota, N USA
25 N1 **Pringle** Texas, SW USA
99 H14 **Prinsenbeek** Noord-Brabant, S Netherlands
98 L6 **Prinses Margriet Kanaal** canal N Netherlands
195 T2 **Prinsesse Ragnhild Kyst** physical region Antarctica
195 U2 **Prins Harald Kyst** physical region Antarctica
92 N2 **Prins Karls Forland** island W Svalbard
43 N8 **Prinzapolka** Región Autónoma Atlántico Norte, NE Nicaragua
42 L8 **Prinzapolka, Río** ≈ NE Nicaragua
122 H9 **Priob'ye** Khanty-Mansiyskiy Avtonomnyy Okrug, N Russian Federation
104 H1 **Prior, Cabo** headland NW Spain
29 V9 **Prior Lake** Minnesota, N USA
124 H11 **Priozersk** Fin. Käkisalmi. Leningradskaya Oblast', NW Russian Federation
119 J20 **Pripet** Bel. Prypyats', Ukr. Pryp"yat'. ≈ Belarus/Ukraine
119 J20 **Pripet Marshes** wetland Belarus/Ukraine
Prishtinë see Priština
126 J8 **Pristen'** Kurskaya Oblast', W Russian Federation
113 N16 **Priština** Alb. Prishtinë. Serbia, S Serbia and Montenegro (Yugo.)
100 M10 **Pritzwalk** Brandenburg, NE Germany
103 R13 **Privas** Ardèche, E France
107 I16 **Priverno** Lazio, C Italy
Privigye see Prievidza
112 C12 **Privlaka** Zadar, SW Croatia
124 M15 **Privolzhsk** Ivanovskaya Oblast', NW Russian Federation
127 P7 **Privolzhskaya Vozvyshennost'** var. Volga Uplands. ▲▲ W Russian Federation
127 P8 **Privolzhskoye** Saratovskaya Oblast', W Russian Federation
Priwitz see Prievidza
127 N13 **Priyutnoye** Respublika Kalmykiya, SW Russian Federation
113 M17 **Prizren** Alb. Prizreni. Serbia, S Serbia and Montenegro (Yugo.)
Prizreni see Prizren
107 I24 **Prizzi** Sicilia, Italy, C Mediterranean Sea
113 P18 **Probištip** NE FYR Macedonia
169 S16 **Probolinggo** Jawa, C Indonesia
Probstberg see Wyszków
111 F14 **Prochowice** Ger. Parchwitz. Dolnośląskie, SW Poland
29 W5 **Proctor** Minnesota, N USA
25 R8 **Proctor** Texas, SW USA
25 R8 **Proctor Lake** ⊠ Texas, SW USA
155 I18 **Proddatūr** Andhra Pradesh, E India
104 H9 **Proença-a-Nova** Castelo Branco, C Portugal
95 I24 **Præstø** Storstrøm, SE Denmark
99 I21 **Profondeville** Namur, SE Belgium
41 W11 **Progreso** Yucatán, SE Mexico
123 R14 **Progress** Amurskaya Oblast', SE Russian Federation
127 O15 **Prokhladnyy** Kabardino-Balkarskaya Respublika, SW Russian Federation
Prokletije see North Albanian Alps
Prökuls see Priekulė
113 O15 **Prokuplje** Serbia, SE Serbia and Montenegro (Yugo.)
124 H14 **Proletariy** Novgorodskaya Oblast', W Russian Federation
126 M12 **Proletarsk** Rostovskaya Oblast', SW Russian Federation
126 J8 **Proletarskiy** Belgorodskaya Oblast', W Russian Federation
166 L7 **Prome** var. Pyè. Pegu, C Myanmar
60 J8 **Promissão** São Paulo, S Brazil
60 J8 **Promissão, Represa de** ⊠ S Brazil
125 V4 **Promyshlennyy** Respublika Komi, NW Russian Federation
119 O16 **Pronya** Rus. Pronya. ≈ E Belarus
10 M11 **Prophet River** British Columbia, W Canada
30 K11 **Prophetstown** Illinois, N USA
59 P16 **Propriá** Sergipe, E Brazil
103 X16 **Propriano** Corse, France, C Mediterranean Sea
Prościejów see Prostějov
Proskurov see Khmel 'nyts'kyy
114 H12 **Prosotsáni** Anatolikí Makedonía kai Thráki, NE Greece
171 Q7 **Prosperidad** Mindanao, S Philippines
32 J10 **Prosser** Washington, NW USA
Prossnitz see Prostějov
111 G18 **Prostějov** Ger. Prossnitz, Pol. Prościejów. Olomoucký Kraj, E Czech Republic
117 V8 **Prosyana** Dnipropetrovs'ka Oblast', E Ukraine
111 L16 **Proszowice** Małopolskie, S Poland
Protasy see Pratasy
172 J11 **Protea Seamount** undersea feature SW Indian Ocean
115 D21 **Próti** island S Greece
114 N8 **Provadiya** Varna, E Bulgaria
103 S15 **Provence** prev. Marseille-Marignane. ✖ (Marseille) Bouches-du-Rhône, SE France
103 T14 **Provence** cultural region SE France
103 T14 **Provence-Alpes-Côte d'Azur** ◈ region SE France
20 H6 **Providence** Kentucky, S USA
19 N12 **Providence** state capital Rhode Island, NE USA
36 L1 **Providence** Utah, W USA
Providence see Fort Providence
67 X10 **Providence Atoll** var. Providence. atoll S Seychelles
14 D12 **Providence Bay** Manitoulin Island, Ontario, S Canada
23 R6 **Providence Canyon** valley Alabama/Georgia, S USA
22 I5 **Providence, Lake** ⊚ Louisiana, S USA
35 X13 **Providence Mountains** ▲▲ California, W USA
44 L6 **Providenciales** island W Turks and Caicos Islands
19 Q12 **Provincetown** Massachusetts, NE USA
103 P5 **Provins** Seine-et-Marne, N France
36 L3 **Provo** Utah, W USA
11 R15 **Provost** Alberta, SW Canada
112 G13 **Prozor** Federacija Bosna I Hercegovina, SW Bosnia & Herzegovina
Prozoroki see Prazaroki
60 I11 **Prudentópolis** Paraná, S Brazil
39 R5 **Prudhoe Bay** Alaska, USA
39 R4 **Prudhoe Bay** bay Alaska, USA
111 H16 **Prudnik** Ger. Neustadt, Neustadt in Oberschlesien. Opolskie, S Poland

119 J16 **Prudy** *Rus.* Prudy. Minskaya Voblasts', C Belarus
101 D18 **Prüm** Rheinland-Pfalz, W Germany
101 D18 **Prüm** ≈ W Germany
Prusa *see* Bursa
110 J7 **Pruszcz Gdański** *Ger.* Praust. Pomorskie, N Poland
110 M12 **Pruszków** *Ger.* Kaltdorf. Mazowieckie, C Poland
116 K8 **Prut** *Ger.* Pruth. ≈ E Europe
Pruth *see* Prut
108 L8 **Prutz** Tirol, W Austria
Prużana *see* Pruzhany
119 G19 **Pruzhany** *Pol.* Prużana. Brestskaya Voblasts', SW Belarus
124 I11 **Pryazha** Respublika Kareliya, NW Russian Federation
117 U10 **Pryazovs'ke** Zaporiz'ka Oblast', SE Ukraine
Prychornomors'ka Nyzovyna *see* Black Sea Lowland
Prydniprovs'ka Nyzovyna/Prydnyaprows kaya Nizina *see* Dnieper Lowland
195 Y7 **Prydz Bay** *bay* Antarctica
117 R4 **Pryluky** *Rus.* Priluki. Chernihivs'ka Oblast', NE Ukraine
117 V10 **Prymors'k** *Rus.* Primorsk; *prev.* Primorskoye. Zaporiz'ka Oblast', SE Ukraine
27 Q9 **Pryor** Oklahoma, C USA
33 U11 **Pryor Creek** ≈ Montana, NW USA
Pryp"yat'/Prypyats' *see* Pripet
110 M10 **Przasnysz** Mazowieckie, C Poland
111 K14 **Przedbórz** Łodzkie, S Poland
111 P17 **Przemyśl** *Rus.* Peremyshl. Podkarpackie, SE Poland
111 O16 **Przeworsk** Podkarpackie, SE Poland
Przheval'sk *see* Karakol
110 L13 **Przysucha** Mazowieckie, SE Poland
115 H18 **Psachná** *var.* Psahna, Psakhná. Évvoia, C Greece
Psahna/Psakhná *see* Psachná
115 K18 **Psará** *island* E Greece
115 I16 **Psathoúra** *island* Vóreioi Sporádes, Greece, Aegean Sea
Pschestitz *see* Přeštice
Psein Lora *see* Pishin Lora
117 S5 **Psël** ≈ Russian Federation/Ukraine
115 M21 **Psérimos** *island* Dodekánisos, Greece, Aegean Sea
Pseyn Bowr *see* Pishin Lora
Pskem *see* Piskom
147 R8 **Pskemskiy Khrebet** *Uzb.* Piskom Tizmasi. ▲ Kyrgyzstan/Uzbekistan
124 F14 **Pskov** *Ger.* Pleskau, *Latv.* Pleskava. Pskovskaya Oblast', W Russian Federation
118 K6 **Pskov, Lake** *Est.* Pihkva Järv, *Ger.* Pleskauer See, *Rus.* Pskovskoye Ozero. ◎ Estonia/Russian Federation
124 F15 **Pskovskaya Oblast'** ◆ *province* W Russian Federation
Pskovskoye Ozero *see* Pskov, Lake
112 G9 **Psunj** ▲ NE Croatia
111 J17 **Pszczyna** *Ger.* Pless. Śląskie, S Poland
Ptačnik/Ptacsnik *see* Vtáčnik
115 D17 **Ptéri** ▲ C Greece
Ptich' *see* Ptsich
115 E14 **Ptolemaïda** *prev.* Ptolemaïs. Dytikí Makedonía, N Greece
Ptolemaïs *see* Ptolemaïda, Greece
Ptolemaïs *see* 'Akko, Israel
119 M19 **Ptsich** *Rus.* Ptich'. Homyel'skaya Voblasts', SE Belarus
119 M18 **Ptsich** *Rus.* Ptich'. ≈ SE Belarus
109 X10 **Ptuj** *Ger.* Pettau; *anc.* Poetovio. NE Slovenia
61 A23 **Puán** Buenos Aires, E Argentina
192 H15 **Pu'apu'a** Savai'i, C Samoa
192 G15 **Puava, Cape** *headland* Savai'i, NW Samoa
56 F12 **Pucallpa** Ucayali, C Peru
57 J17 **Pucarani** La Paz, NW Bolivia
Pučarevo *see* Novi Travnik
157 U12 **Pucheng** *var.* Nanpu. Fujian, SE China
160 L6 **Pucheng** Shaanxi, C China
125 N16 **Puchezh** Ivanovskaya Oblast', W Russian Federation
111 I19 **Púchov** *Hung.* Puhó. Trenčiansky Kraj, W Slovakia
116 J13 **Pucioasa** Dâmbovița, S Romania
110 I6 **Puck** Pomorskie, N Poland
30 L8 **Puckaway Lake** ◎ Wisconsin, N USA
63 G15 **Pucón** Araucanía, S Chile
93 M14 **Pudasjärvi** Oulu, C Finland
148 L8 **Pūdeh Tal, Shelleh-ye** ≈ SW Afghanistan
127 S1 **Pudem** Udmurtskaya Respublika, NW Russian Federation
Pudewitz *see* Pobiedziska
124 K11 **Pudozh** Respublika Kareliya, NW Russian Federation
97 M17 **Pudsey** N England, UK
Puduchcheri *see* Pondicherry
151 H21 **Pudukkottai** Tamil Nādu, SE India
171 Z13 **Pue** Papua, E Indonesia
41 P14 **Puebla** *var.* Puebla de Zaragoza. Puebla, S Mexico
41 P15 **Puebla** ◆ *state* S Mexico
104 L11 **Puebla de Alcocer** Extremadura, W Spain
Puebla de Don Fabrique *see* Puebla de Don Fadrique
105 P13 **Puebla de Don Fadrique** *var.* Puebla de Don Fabrique. Andalucía, S Spain
104 J11 **Puebla de la Calzada** Extremadura, W Spain
104 J5 **Puebla de Sanabria** Castilla-León, N Spain
104 I4 **Puebla de Trives** *see* A Pobla de Trives
Puebla de Zaragoza *see* Puebla
37 T6 **Pueblo** Colorado, C USA
37 N10 **Pueblo Colorado Wash** *valley* Arizona, SW USA
61 C16 **Pueblo Libertador** Corrientes, NE Argentina
40 J10 **Pueblo Nuevo** Durango, C Mexico
42 J8 **Pueblo Nuevo** Estelí, NW Nicaragua
54 J3 **Pueblo Nuevo** Falcón, N Venezuela
42 B6 **Pueblo Nuevo Tiquisate** *var.* Tiquisate. Escuintla, SW Guatemala
41 Q11 **Pueblo Viejo, Laguna de** *lagoon* E Mexico
63 J14 **Puelches** La Pampa, C Argentina
104 L14 **Puente-Genil** Andalucía, S Spain
105 Q3 **Puente la Reina** *Bas.* Gares. Navarra, N Spain
104 L12 **Puente Nuevo, Embalse de** ▣ S Spain
57 D14 **Puente Piedra** Lima, W Peru
160 F14 **Pu'er** *var.* Ning'er. Yunnan, SW China
45 V6 **Puerca, Punta** *headland* E Puerto Rico
37 R12 **Puerco, Rio** ≈ New Mexico, SW USA
57 J17 **Puerto Acosta** La Paz, W Bolivia
63 G19 **Puerto Aisén** Aisén, S Chile
41 R17 **Puerto Ángel** Oaxaca, SE Mexico
Puerto Argentino *see* Stanley
41 T17 **Puerto Arista** Chiapas, SE Mexico
43 O16 **Puerto Armuelles** Chiriquí, SW Panama
Puerto Arrecife *see* Arrecife
54 D14 **Puerto Asís** Putumayo, SW Colombia
54 L9 **Puerto Ayacucho** Amazonas, SW Venezuela
57 C18 **Puerto Ayora** Galapagos Islands, Ecuador, E Pacific Ocean
57 C18 **Puerto Baquerizo Moreno** *var.* Baquerizo Moreno. Galapagos Islands, Ecuador, E Pacific Ocean
42 G4 **Puerto Barrios** Izabal, E Guatemala
Puerto Bello *see* Portobelo
54 F8 **Puerto Berrío** Antioquia, C Colombia
54 F9 **Puerto Boyaca** Boyacá, C Colombia
54 K4 **Puerto Cabello** Carabobo, N Venezuela
43 N7 **Puerto Cabezas** *var.* Bilwi. Región Autónoma Atlántico Norte, NE Nicaragua
54 L9 **Puerto Carreño** Vichada, E Colombia
54 E4 **Puerto Colombia** Atlántico, N Colombia
42 H4 **Puerto Cortés** Cortés, NW Honduras
54 J4 **Puerto Cumarebo** Falcón, N Venezuela
Puerto de Cabras *see* Puerto del Rosario
55 Q5 **Puerto de Hierro** Sucre, NE Venezuela
64 O11 **Puerto de la Cruz** Tenerife, Islas Canarias, Spain, NE Atlantic Ocean
64 Q11 **Puerto del Rosario** *var.* Puerto de Cabras. Fuerteventura, Islas Canarias, Spain, NE Atlantic Ocean
63 J20 **Puerto Deseado** Santa Cruz, SE Argentina
40 F8 **Puerto Escondido** Baja California Sur, W Mexico
41 R17 **Puerto Escondido** Oaxaca, SE Mexico
60 G12 **Puerto Esperanza** Misiones, NE Argentina
56 D6 **Puerto Francisco de Orellana** *var.* Coca. Orellana, N Ecuador
54 H10 **Puerto Gaitán** Meta, C Colombia
Puerto Gallegos *see* Río Gallegos
60 G12 **Puerto Iguazú** Misiones, NE Argentina
56 F12 **Puerto Inca** Huánuco, N Peru
54 L11 **Puerto Inírida** *var.* Obando. Guainía, E Colombia
42 K13 **Puerto Jesús** Guanacaste, NW Costa Rica
41 Z11 **Puerto Juárez** Quintana Roo, SE Mexico
55 N5 **Puerto La Cruz** Anzoátegui, NE Venezuela
54 E14 **Puerto Leguízamo** Putumayo, S Colombia
43 N5 **Puerto Lempira** Gracias a Dios, E Honduras
Puerto Libertad *see* La Libertad
54 I11 **Puerto Limón** Meta, E Colombia
54 D13 **Puerto Limón** Putumayo, SW Colombia
Puerto Limón *see* Limón
105 N11 **Puertollano** Castilla-La Mancha, C Spain
63 K17 **Puerto Lobos** Chubut, SE Argentina
54 I3 **Puerto López** La Guajira, N Colombia
105 Q14 **Puerto Lumbreras** Murcia, SE Spain
41 V17 **Puerto Madero** Chiapas, SE Mexico
63 K17 **Puerto Madryn** Chubut, S Argentina
Puerto Magdalena *see* Bahía Magdalena
57 J15 **Puerto Maldonado** Madre de Dios, E Peru
Puerto Masachapa *see* Masachapa
Puerto México *see* Coatzacoalcos
63 G17 **Puerto Montt** Los Lagos, C Chile
41 Z12 **Puerto Morelos** Quintana Roo, SE Mexico
54 L10 **Puerto Nariño** Vichada, E Colombia
63 H23 **Puerto Natales** Magallanes, S Chile
43 X15 **Puerto Obaldía** San Blas, NE Panama
44 H6 **Puerto Padre** Las Tunas, E Cuba
54 L9 **Puerto Páez** Apure, C Venezuela
40 E3 **Puerto Peñasco** Sonora, NW Mexico
55 N5 **Puerto Píritu** Anzoátegui, NE Venezuela
45 N8 **Puerto Plata** *var.* San Felipe de Puerto Plata. N Dominican Republic
45 N8 **Puerto Plata** ✈ N Dominican Republic
Puerto Presidente Stroessner *see* Ciudad del Este
171 N6 **Puerto Princesa** *off.* Puerto Princesa City. Palawan, W Philippines
Puerto Princesa City *see* Puerto Princesa
Puerto Príncipe *see* Camagüey
Puerto Quellón *see* Quellón
60 F13 **Puerto Rico** Misiones, NE Argentina
57 K14 **Puerto Rico** Pando, N Bolivia
54 E12 **Puerto Rico** Caquetá, S Colombia
45 U5 **Puerto Rico** *off.* Commonwealth of Puerto Rico; *prev.* Porto Rico. ◇ *US commonwealth territory* C West Indies
64 F11 **Puerto Rico** *island* C West Indies
64 G11 **Puerto Rico Trench** *undersea feature* NE Caribbean Sea
54 I8 **Puerto Rondón** Arauca, E Colombia
Puerto San José *see* San José
63 J21 **Puerto San Julián** *var.* San Julián. Santa Cruz, SE Argentina
63 I22 **Puerto Santa Cruz** *var.* Santa Cruz. Santa Cruz, SE Argentina
Puerto Sauce *see* Juan L.Lacaze
57 Q20 **Puerto Suárez** Santa Cruz, E Bolivia
54 D13 **Puerto Umbría** Putumayo, SW Colombia
40 J13 **Puerto Vallarta** Jalisco, SW Mexico
63 G16 **Puerto Varas** Los Lagos, C Chile
42 M13 **Puerto Viejo** Heredia, NE Costa Rica
Puertoviejo *see* Portoviejo
57 B18 **Puerto Villamil** *var.* Villamil. Galapagos Islands, Ecuador, E Pacific Ocean
54 F8 **Puerto Wilches** Santander, N Colombia
63 H20 **Pueyrredón, Lago** *var.* Lago Cochrane. ◎ S Argentina
127 R7 **Pugachëv** Saratovskaya Oblast', W Russian Federation
127 T3 **Pugachëvo** Udmurtskaya Respublika, NW Russian Federation
32 H8 **Puget Sound** *sound* Washington, NW USA
107 O17 **Puglia** *var.* Le Puglie, *Eng.* Apulia. ◆ *region* SE Italy
107 N17 **Puglia, Canosa di** *anc.* Canusium. Puglia, SE Italy
118 I6 **Puhja** *Ger.* Kawelecht. Tartumaa, SE Estonia
Puhó *see* Púchov
105 V4 **Puigcerdà** Cataluña, NE Spain
Puigmal *see* Puigmal d'Err
103 N17 **Puigmal d'Err** *var.* Puigmal. ▲ S France
76 I16 **Pujehun** S Sierra Leone
Puka *see* Pukë
185 E20 **Pukaki, Lake** ◎ South Island, NZ
38 F10 **Pukalani** Maui, Hawai'i, USA, C Pacific Ocean
190 J13 **Pukapuka** *atoll* N Cook Islands
191 X9 **Pukapuka** *atoll* Îles Tuamotu, E French Polynesia
Pukari Neem *see* Purekkari Neem
191 X11 **Pukarua** *var.* Pukaruha. *atoll* Îles Tuamotu, E French Polynesia
Pukaruha *see* Pukarua
14 A7 **Pukaskwa** ≈ Ontario, S Canada
11 V12 **Pukatawagan** Manitoba, C Canada
191 X16 **Pukatikei, Maunga** ⅄ Easter Island, Chile, E Pacific Ocean
182 C1 **Pukatja** *var.* Ernabella. South Australia
163 Y12 **Pukch'ŏng** E North Korea
113 L18 **Pukë** *var.* Puka. Shkodër, N Albania
184 L6 **Pukekohe** Auckland, North Island, NZ
184 L7 **Pukemiro** Waikato, North Island, NZ
190 D12 **Puke, Mont** ▲ Île Futuna, W Wallis and Futuna
Puket *see* Phuket
185 C20 **Puketeraki Range** ▲ South Island, NZ
184 N13 **Puketoi Range** ▲ North Island, NZ
185 F21 **Pukeuri Junction** Otago, South Island, NZ
119 L16 **Pukhavichy** *Rus.* Pukhovichi. Minskaya Voblasts', C Belarus
Pukhovichi *see* Pukhavichy
124 M10 **Puksoozero** Arkhangel'skaya Oblast', NW Russian Federation
112 A10 **Pula** *It.* Pola; *prev.* Pulj. Istra, NW Croatia
Pula *see* Nyingchi
163 U14 **Pulandian** *var.* Xinjin. Liaoning, NE China
163 T14 **Pulandian Wan** *bay* NE China
189 O15 **Pulap Atoll** *atoll* Caroline Islands, C Micronesia
18 H9 **Pulaski** New York, NE USA
20 I10 **Pulaski** Tennessee, S USA
21 R7 **Pulaski** Virginia, NE USA
171 Y14 **Pulau, Sungai** ≈ Papua, E Indonesia
110 N13 **Puławy** *Ger.* Neu Amerika. Lubelskie, E Poland
146 I16 **Pulhatyn** *Rus.* Polekhatum; *prev.* Pul'-I-Khatum. Ahal Welaýaty, S Turkmenistan
101 E16 **Pulheim** Nordrhein-Westfalen, W Germany
Pulicat *see* Pālghāt
155 J19 **Pulicat Lake** *lagoon* SE India
Pul'-I-Khatum *see* Pulhatyn
Pul-i-Khumri *see* Pol-e Khomrī
Pul-i-Sefid *see* Pol-e Safīd
Pulj *see* Pula
109 W2 **Pulkau** ≈ NE Austria
93 L15 **Pulkkila** Oulu, C Finland
122 C7 **Pul'kovo** ✈ (Sankt-Peterburg) Leningradskaya Oblast', NW Russian Federation
32 M9 **Pullman** Washington, NW USA
108 B10 **Pully** Vaud, SW Switzerland
40 F7 **Púlpita, Punta** *headland* W Mexico
110 M10 **Pułtusk** Mazowieckie, C Poland
158 H10 **Pulu** Xinjiang Uygur Zizhiqu, W China
137 P13 **Pülümür** Tunceli, E Turkey
189 N16 **Pulusuk** *island* Caroline Islands, C Micronesia
189 N16 **Puluwat Atoll** *atoll* Caroline Islands, C Micronesia
25 N11 **Pumpville** Texas, SW USA
191 P7 **Punaauia** *var.* Hakapehi. Tahiti, W French Polynesia
56 B8 **Puná, Isla** *island* SW Ecuador
185 G16 **Punakaiki** West Coast, South Island, NZ
153 T11 **Punakha** C Bhutan
57 L18 **Punata** Cochabamba, C Bolivia
155 E14 **Pune** *prev.* Poona. Mahārāshtra, W India
83 M17 **Pungoè, Rio** *var.* Púnguè, Pungwe. ≈ C Mozambique
21 X10 **Pungo River** ≈ North Carolina, SE USA
Púnguè/Pungwe *see* Pungoè, Rio
79 N19 **Punia** Maniema, E Dem. Rep. Congo
62 H8 **Punilla, Sierra de la** ▲ W Argentina
161 P14 **Puning** Guangdong, S China
62 G10 **Punitaqui** Coquimbo, C Chile
152 H8 **Punjab** ◆ *state* NW India
149 T9 **Punjab** *prev.* West Punjab, Western Punjab. ◆ *province* E Pakistan
131 Q9 **Punjab Plains** *plain* N India
93 O17 **Punkaharju** *var.* Punkasalmi. Isä-Suomi, E Finland
Punkasalmi *see* Punkaharju
57 I17 **Puno** Puno, SE Peru
57 H17 **Puno** *off.* Departamento de Puno. ◆ *department* S Peru
61 B24 **Punta Alta** Buenos Aires, E Argentina
63 H24 **Punta Arenas** *prev.* Magallanes. Magallanes, S Chile
45 T6 **Punta, Cerro de** ▲ C Puerto Rico
43 T15 **Punta Chame** Panamá, C Panama
57 G17 **Punta Colorada** Arequipa, SW Peru
40 F9 **Punta Coyote** Baja California Sur, W Mexico
62 G8 **Punta de Díaz** Atacama, N Chile
61 G20 **Punta del Este** Maldonado, S Uruguay
63 K17 **Punta Delgada** Chubut, SE Argentina
55 O5 **Punta de Mata** Monagas, NE Venezuela
55 O4 **Punta de Piedras** Nueva Esparta, NE Venezuela
42 F4 **Punta Gorda** Toledo, SE Belize
43 N11 **Punta Gorda** Región Autónoma Atlántico Sur, SE Nicaragua
23 W14 **Punta Gorda** Florida, SE USA
42 M11 **Punta Gorda, Río** ≈ SE Nicaragua
62 H6 **Punta Negra, Salar de** *salt lake* N Chile
40 D5 **Punta Prieta** Baja California, NW Mexico
42 L13 **Puntarenas** Puntarenas, W Costa Rica
42 L13 **Puntarenas** *off.* Provincia de Puntarenas. ◆ *province* W Costa Rica
54 J4 **Punto Fijo** Falcón, N Venezuela
105 S4 **Puntón de Guara** ▲ N Spain
18 D14 **Punxsutawney** Pennsylvania, NE USA
93 M14 **Puolanka** Oulu, C Finland
57 J17 **Pupuya, Nevado** ▲ W Bolivia
Puqi *see* Chibi
57 F16 **Puquio** Ayacucho, S Peru
122 J9 **Pur** ≈ N Russian Federation
186 D7 **Purari** ≈ S PNG
27 N11 **Purcell** Oklahoma, C USA
11 O16 **Purcell Mountains** ▲ British Columbia, SW Canada
105 P14 **Purchena** Andalucía, S Spain
27 S8 **Purdy** Missouri, C USA
118 I2 **Purekkari Neem** *prev.* Pukari Neem. *headland* N Estonia
37 U7 **Purgatoire River** ≈ Colorado, C USA
Purgstall *see* Purgstall an der Erlauf
109 V5 **Purgstall an der Erlauf** *var.* Purgstall. Niederösterreich, NE Austria
154 O13 **Puri** *var.* Jagannath. Orissa, E India
Puriramya *see* Buriram
109 X4 **Purkersdorf** Niederösterreich, NE Austria
98 I9 **Purmerend** Noord-Holland, C Netherlands
151 G16 **Pūrna** ≈ C India
Purnea *see* Pūrnia
153 R13 **Pūrnia** *prev.* Purnea. Bihār, NE India
Pursat *see* Poŭthĭsăt, Poŭthĭsăt, W Cambodia
Pursat *see* Poŭthĭsăt, Stœng, W Cambodia
Purulia *see* Puruliya
150 L13 **Puruliya** *prev.* Purulia. West Bengal, NE India
47 G7 **Purus, Rio** *Sp.* Río Purús. ≈ Brazil/Peru
186 C9 **Purutu Island** *island* SW PNG
93 N17 **Puruvesi** ◎ SE Finland
22 L7 **Purvis** Mississippi, S USA
114 J11 **Pŭrvomay** *prev.* Borisovgrad. Plovdiv, C Bulgaria
169 R16 **Purwodadi** *prev.* Poerwodadi. Jawa, C Indonesia
169 P16 **Purwokerto** *prev.* Poerwokerto. Jawa, C Indonesia
169 P16 **Purworejo** *prev.* Poerworedjo. Jawa, C Indonesia
20 H8 **Puryear** Tennessee, S USA
154 H13 **Pusad** Mahārāshtra, C India
163 Z16 **Pusan** *off.* Pusan-gwangyŏksi, *var.* Busan, *Jap.* Fusan. SE South Korea
168 H7 **Pusatgajo, Pegunungan** ▲ Sumatera, NW Indonesia
Puschlav *see* Poschiavo
Pushkin *see* Tsarskoye Selo
127 Q8 **Pushkino** Saratovskaya Oblast', W Russian Federation
Pushkino *see* Biläsuvar
111 M22 **Püspökladány** Hajdú-Bihar, E Hungary
118 J3 **Püssi** *Ger.* Isenhof. Ida-Virumaa, NE Estonia
116 I5 **Pustomyty** L'vivs'ka Oblast', W Ukraine
124 F16 **Pustoshka** Pskovskaya Oblast', W Russian Federation
Pusztakalán *see* Călan
167 N1 **Putao** *prev.* Fort Hertz. Kachin State, N Myanmar
184 M8 **Putaruru** Waikato, North Island, NZ
Puteoli *see* Pozzuoli
161 R12 **Putian** Fujian, SE China
107 O17 **Putignano** Puglia, SE Italy
Puting *see* De'an
Putivl' *see* Putyvl'
41 Q16 **Putla** *var.* Putla de Guerrero. Oaxaca, SE Mexico
Putla de Guerrero *see* Putla
19 N12 **Putnam** Connecticut, NE USA
25 Q7 **Putnam** Texas, SW USA
18 M10 **Putney** Vermont, NE USA
111 L20 **Putnok** Borsod-Abaúj-Zemplén, NE Hungary
Putorana, Gory/Putorana Mountains *see* Putorana, Plato
122 L8 **Putorana, Plato** *var.* Gory Putorana, *Eng.* Putorana Mountains. ▲ N Russian Federation
168 K9 **Putrajaya** ● (Malaysia), Kuala Lumpur, Peninsular Malaysia
62 H2 **Putre** Tarapacá, N Chile
155 J24 **Puttalam** North Western Province, W Sri Lanka
155 J24 **Puttalam Lagoon** *lagoon* W Sri Lanka
99 H17 **Putte** Antwerpen, C Belgium
94 E10 **Puttegga** ▲ S Norway
98 K11 **Putten** Gelderland, C Netherlands
100 K7 **Puttgarden** Schleswig-Holstein, N Germany
Puttiala *see* Patiāla
101 D20 **Püttlingen** Saarland, SW Germany
54 D14 **Putumayo** *off.* Intendencia del Putumayo. ◆ *province* S Colombia
48 E7 **Putumayo, Río** *var.* Rio Içá. ≈ NW South America *see also* Içá, Rio
169 P11 **Putus, Tanjung** *headland* Borneo, N Indonesia
116 J8 **Putyla** Chernivets'ka Oblast', W Ukraine
117 S3 **Putyvl'** *Rus.* Putivl'. Sums'ka Oblast', NE Ukraine
93 M18 **Puula** ◎ SE Finland
93 N18 **Puumala** Isä-Suomi, E Finland
118 I5 **Puurmani** *Ger.* Talkhof. Jõgevamaa, E Estonia
99 G17 **Puurs** Antwerpen, N Belgium
38 P10 **Pu'u 'Ula'ula** *var.* Red Hill. ▲ Maui, Hawai'i, USA, C Pacific Ocean
38 A8 **Pu'uwai** *var.* Puuwai. Ni'ihau, Hawai'i, USA, C Pacific Ocean
12 J4 **Puvirnituq** *prev.* Povungnituk. Québec, NE Canada
32 H8 **Puyallup** Washington, NW USA
161 O5 **Puyang** Henan, C China
161 R9 **Puyang Jiang** *var.* Tsien Tang. ≈ SE China
103 O11 **Puy-de-Dôme** ◆ *department* C France
103 N15 **Puylaurens** Tarn, S France
102 M13 **Puy-l'Evêque** Lot, S France
103 N17 **Puymorens, Col de** *pass* S France
56 C7 **Puyo** Pastaza, C Ecuador
185 A24 **Puysegur Point** *headland* South Island, NZ
148 J8 **Pūzak, Hāmūn-e** *Pash.* Hāmūn-i-Puzak. ◎ SW Afghanistan
Puzak, Hāmūn-i- *see* Pūzak, Hāmūn-e
81 J23 **Pwani** *Eng.* Coast. ◆ *region* E Tanzania
79 O23 **Pweto** Katanga, SE Dem. Rep. Congo
97 I19 **Pwllheli** NW Wales, UK
189 O14 **Pwok** Pohnpei, E Micronesia
122 I9 **Pyakupur** ≈ N Russian Federation
124 M6 **Pyalitsa** Murmanskaya Oblast', NW Russian Federation
124 K10 **Pyal'ma** Respublika Kareliya, NW Russian Federation
Pyandzh *see* Panj
126 I6 **Pyaozero, Ozero** ◎ NW Russian Federation
166 L9 **Pyapon** Irrawaddy, SW Myanmar
119 J15 **Pyarshai** *Rus.* Pershay. Minskaya Voblasts', C Belarus
122 K8 **Pyasina** ≈ N Russian Federation
114 I10 **Pyasŭchnik, Yazovir** ▣ C Bulgaria
Pyatikhatki *see* P"yatykhatky
117 S7 **P"yatykhatky** *Rus.* Pyatikhatki. Dnipropetrovs'ka Oblast', E Ukraine
166 M6 **Pyawbwe** Mandalay, C Myanmar
127 T3 **Pychas** Udmurtskaya Respublika, NW Russian Federation
Pyè *see* Prome
166 K6 **Pyechin** Chin State, W Myanmar
119 G17 **Pyeski** *Rus.* Peski. Hrodzyenskaya Voblasts', W Belarus
119 L19 **Pyetrykaw** *Rus.* Petrikov. Homyel'skaya Voblasts', SE Belarus
93 M16 **Pyhäjärvi** ◎ C Finland
93 O17 **Pyhäjärvi** ◎ SE Finland
93 L15 **Pyhäjoki** Oulu, W Finland
93 L15 **Pyhäjoki** ≈ W Finland
93 M15 **Pyhäntä** Oulu, C Finland
93 M16 **Pyhäsalmi** Oulu, C Finland
93 O17 **Pyhäselkä** ◎ SE Finland
93 M19 **Pyhtää** *Swe.* Pyttis. Etelä-Suomi, S Finland
166 M6 **Pyinmana** Mandalay, C Myanmar
115 N24 **Pylés** *var.* Piles. Kárpathos, SE Greece
115 D21 **Pýlos** *var.* Pilos. Pelopónnisos, S Greece
18 B12 **Pymatuning Reservoir** ▣ Ohio/Pennsylvania, NE USA
163 X15 **P'yŏngt'aek** NW South Korea
163 V14 **P'yŏngyang** *var.* P'yŏngyang-si, *Eng.* Pyongyang. ● (North Korea) SW North Korea
P'yŏngyang-si *see* P'yŏngyang
35 Q4 **Pyramid Lake** ◎ Nevada, W USA
37 P15 **Pyramid Mountains** ▲ New Mexico, SW USA
37 R5 **Pyramid Peak** ▲ Colorado, C USA
115 D17 **Pyramíva** *var.* Piramiva. ▲ C Greece
Pyrenaei Montes *see* Pyrenees
86 B12 **Pyrenees** *Fr.* Pyrénées, *Sp.* Pirineos; *anc.* Pyrenaei Montes. ▲ SW Europe
102 J16 **Pyrénées-Atlantiques** ◆ *department* SW France
103 N17 **Pyrénées-Orientales** ◆ *department* S France
115 L19 **Pyrgí** *var.* Pirgi. Chíos, E Greece
115 D20 **Pýrgos** *var.* Pírgos. Dytikí Ellás, S Greece
Pyritz *see* Pyrzyce
115 E19 **Pýrros** ≈ S Greece
117 R4 **Pyryatyn** *Rus.* Piryatin. Poltavs'ka Oblast', NE Ukraine
110 D9 **Pyrzyce** *Ger.* Pyritz. Zachodnio-pomorskie, NW Poland
124 F15 **Pytalovo** *Latv.* Abrene; *prev.* Jaunlatgale. Pskovskaya Oblast', W Russian Federation
115 M20 **Pythagóreio** *var.* Pithagorio. Sámos, Dodekánisos, Greece, Aegean Sea
14 L11 **Pythonga, Lac** ◎ Québec, SE Canada
Pyttis *see* Pyhtää
166 M7 **Pyu** Pegu, C Myanmar
166 M8 **Pyuntaza** Pegu, SW Myanmar
153 N11 **Pyuthan** Mid Western, W Nepal
110 H12 **Pyzdry** *Ger.* Peisern. Wielkopolskie, C Poland

Q

138 H13 **Qā' al Jafr** ◎ S Jordan
197 O11 **Qaanaaq** *var.* Qânâq, *Dan.* Thule. Avannaarsua, N Greenland
138 G7 **Qabb Eliâs** E Lebanon
Qabil *see* Al Qābil
Qabırrı *see* Iori
Qābis *see* Gabès
Qābis, Khalīj *see* Gabès, Golfe de
Qabqa *see* Gonghe
141 S14 **Qabr Hūd** C Yemen
Qacentina *see* Constantine
148 L4 **Qādes** Bādghīs, NW Afghanistan
139 T11 **Qādisīyah** S Iraq
143 O4 **Qa'emshahr** *prev.* 'Alīābad, Shāhī. Māzandarān, N Iran
143 U7 **Qā'en** *var.* Qain, Qāyen. Khorāsān, E Iran
141 U13 **Qafa** *spring/well* SW Oman
Qafşah *see* Gafsa
163 Q12 **Qagan Nur** *var.* Xulun Hobot Qagan, Zhengxiangbai Qi. Nei Mongol Zizhiqu, N China
163 V9 **Qagan Nur** ◎ NE China
163 Q11 **Qagan Nur** ◎ N China
Qagan Us *see* Dulan

◆ Country ● Country Capital ◇ Dependent Territory ○ Dependent Territory Capital ◆ Administrative Region ✈ International Airport ▲ Mountain ▲ Mountain Range ⅄ Volcano ≈ River ◎ Lake ▣ Reservoir

158 H13 Qagcaka Xizang Zizhiqu, W China
Qagcheng see Xiangcheng
Qahremānshahr see Kermānshāh
159 Q10 Qaidam He ≈ C China
156 L8 Qaidam Pendi basin C China
Qain see Qā'en
Qala Āhangarān see Chaghcharān
139 U3 Qaļā Diza var. Qal 'at Dīzah. NE Iraq
Qal'ah Sālih see Qal'at Şāliḥ
147 R13 Qal'aikhum Rus. Kalaikhum. S Tajikistan
Qala Nau see Qal'eh-ye Now
141 V17 Qalansīyah Suquṭrā, W Yemen
Qala Panja see Qal'eh-ye Panjeh
Qala Shāhar see Qal'eh Shahr
Qalāt see Kalāt
139 W9 Qal'at Aḥmad E Iraq
141 N11 Qal'at Bīshah 'Asīr, SW Saudi Arabia
138 H4 Qal'at Burzay Ḥamāh, W Syria
Qal 'at Dīzah see Qaļā Diza
139 W9 Qal'at Ḥusayh E Iraq
139 V10 Qal'at Majnūnah S Iraq
139 X11 Qal'at Şāliḥ var. Qal'ah Sālih. E Iraq
139 V10 Qal'at Sukkar SE Iraq
Qalba Zhotasy see Kalbinskiy Khrebet
143 Q12 Qal'eh Biābān Fārs, S Iran
149 N4 Qal'eh Shahr Pash. Qala Shāhar. Sar-e Pol, N Afghanistan
148 L4 Qal'eh-ye Now var. Qala Nau. Bādghīs, NW Afghanistan
149 T2 Qal'eh-ye Panjeh var. Qala Panja. Badakhshān, NE Afghanistan
Qamar Bay see Qamar, Ghubbat al
141 U14 Qamar, Ghubbat al Eng. Qamar Bay. bay Oman/Yemen
141 V13 Qamar, Jabal al ▲ SW Oman
147 N12 Qamashi Qashqadaryo Viloyati, S Uzbekistan
Qambar see Kambar
159 R14 Qamdo Xizang Zizhiqu, W China
75 R7 Qamīnis NE Libya
Qamishly see Al Qāmishlī
Qânâq see Qaanaaq
Qandahār see Kandahār
80 Q11 Qandala Bari, NE Somalia
Qandyaghash see Kandyagash
138 L2 Qanṭārī Ar Raqqah, N Syria
Qapiciğ Dağı see Qazangödağ
158 H5 Qapqal var. Qapqal Xibe Zizhixian. Xinjiang Uygur Zizhiqu, NW China
Qapqal Xibe Zizhixian see Qapqal
Qapshagay Böyeni see Kapchagayskoye Vodokhranilishche
Qapugtang see Zadoi
196 M15 Qaqortoq Dan. Julianehåb. Kitaa, S Greenland
75 U8 Qâra var. Qārah. NW Egypt
139 T4 Qara Anjīr N Iraq
Qarabāgh see Qarah Bāgh
Qaraböget see Karaboget
Qarabulaq see Karabulak
Qarabutaq see Karabutak
Qaraghandy/Qaraghandy Oblysy see Karaganda
Qaraghayly see Karagayly
139 U4 Qara Gol NE Iraq
Qārah see Qâra
148 J4 Qarah Bāgh var. Qarabāgh. Herāt, NW Afghanistan
138 G7 Qaraoun, Lac de var. Buḥayrat al Qir'awn. ◎ S Lebanon
Qaraoy see Karaoy
Qaraqoyyn see Karakoyyn, Ozero
Qara Qum see Garagum
Qarasū see Karasu
Qaratal see Karatal
Qarataū see Karatau, Khrebet, Kazakhstan
Qarataū see Karatau, Zhambyl, Kazakhstan
Qaraton see Karaton
80 P13 Qardho var. Kardh, It. Gardo. Bari, N Somalia
142 M6 Qareh Chāy ≈ N Iran
142 K2 Qareh Sū ≈ NW Iran
Qariateïne see Al Qaryatayn
Qarkilik see Ruoqiang
147 O13 Qarluq Rus. Karluk. Surxondaryo Viloyati, S Uzbekistan
147 U12 Qarokŭl Rus. Karakul'. E Tajikistan
147 T12 Qarokŭl Rus. Ozero Karakul'. ◎ E Tajikistan
Qarqan see Qiemo
158 K9 Qarqan He ≈ NW China
Qarqannah, Juzur see Kerkenah, Îles de
Qarqaraly see Karkaralinsk
149 O1 Qarqīn Jowzjān, N Afghanistan
Qars see Kars
Qarsaqbay see Karsakpay
146 M12 Qarshi Rus. Karshi; prev. Bek-Budi. Qashqadaryo Viloyati, S Uzbekistan
146 L12 Qarshi Cho'li Rus. Karshinskaya Step. grassland S Uzbekistan
146 M13 Qarshi Kanali Rus. Karshinskiy Kanal. canal Turkmenistan/Uzbekistan
Qaryatayn see Al Qaryatayn
146 M12 Qashqadaryo Viloyati Rus. Kashkadar'inskaya Oblast'. ◐ province S Uzbekistan
Qasigianguit see Qasigiannguit
197 N13 Qasigiannguit var. Qasigianguit, Dan. Christianshåb. Kitaa, C Greenland
Qaşim, Minṭaqat see Al Qaşīm
139 P8 Qaşr 'Amīj C Iraq
139 R9 Qaşr Darwīshāh C Iraq
142 J6 Qaşr-e Shīrīn Kermānshāh, W Iran
75 V10 Qasr Farâfra W Egypt
Qassim see Al Qaşīm
141 O16 Qa'tabah SW Yemen
138 H7 Qaṭanā var. Katana. Dimashq, S Syria
143 N15 Qatar off. State of Qatar, Ar. Dawlat Qaṭar. ◆ monarchy SW Asia
Qatrana see Al Qaṭrānah
143 Q12 Qaṭrūyeh Fārs, S Iran
Qattara Depression/Qaṭṭārah, Munkhafaḍ al see Qaṭṭâra, Monkhafad el
75 U8 Qaṭṭâra, Monkhafad el var. Munkhafaḍ al Qaṭṭārah, Eng. Qattara Depression. desert NW Egypt
Qaṭṭīnah, Buḥayrat see Ḥimş, Buḥayrat
Qaydār see Qeydār
Qāyen see Qā'en
147 Q11 Qayroqqum Rus. Kayrakkum. NW Tajikistan
147 Q10 Qayroqqum, Obanbori Rus. Kayrakkumskoye Vodokhranilishche. ⊞ NW Tajikistan
137 V13 Qazangödağ Rus. Gora Kapydzhik, Turk. Qapiciğ Dağı. ▲ SW Azerbaijan
139 U7 Qazānīyah var. Dhū Shaykh. E Iraq
Qazaqstan/Qazaqstan Respublikasy see Kazakhstan
137 T9 Qazbegi Rus. Kazbegi. NE Georgia
149 P15 Qāzi Aḥmad var. Kazi Ahmad. Sind, SE Pakistan
137 Y12 Qazimämmäd Rus. Kazi Magomed. SE Azerbaijan
Qazris see Cáceres
142 M4 Qazvīn var. Kazvin. Qazvīn, N Iran
142 M5 Qazvīn ◐ province N Iran
187 Z13 Qelelevu Lagoon lagoon NE Fiji
75 X10 Qena var. Qinā; anc. Caene, Caenepolis. E Egypt
113 L23 Qeparo Vlorë, S Albania
Qeqertarssuaq see Qeqertarsuaq
197 N13 Qeqertarsuaq var. Qeqertarssuaq, Dan. Godhavn. Kitaa, S Greenland
196 M13 Qeqertarsuaq island W Greenland
197 N13 Qeqertarsuup Tunua Dan. Disko Bugt. inlet W Greenland
Qerveh see Qorveh
143 S14 Qeshm Hormozgān, S Iran
143 R14 Qeshm var. Jazīreh-ye Qeshm, Qeshm Island. island S Iran
Qeshm Island/Qeshm, Jazīreh-ye see Qeshm
142 L4 Qeydār var. Qaydār. Zanjān, NW Iran
142 K5 Qezel Owzan, Rūd-e var. Ki Zil Uzen, Qi Zil Uzun. ≈ NW Iran
Qian see Guizhou
161 Q2 Qian'an Hebei, E China
Qian Gorlo/Qian Gorlos/Qian Gorlos Mongolzu Zizhixian/Qianguozhen see Qianguo
163 V9 Qianguo var. Qian Gorlo, Qian Gorlos, Qian Gorlos Mongolzu Zizhixian, Qianguozhen. Jilin, NE China
161 N9 Qianjiang Hubei, C China
160 K10 Qianjiang Sichuan, C China
160 L14 Qian Jiang ≈ S China
160 G9 Qianning var. Gartar. Sichuan, C China
163 U13 Qian Shan ⛰ NE China
160 H10 Qianwei var. Yujin. Sichuan, C China
160 J11 Qianxi Guizhou, S China
Qiaotou see Datong
159 Q7 Qiaowan Gansu, N China
Qibilī see Kebili
158 K9 Qiemo var. Qarqan. Xinjiang Uygur Zizhiqu, NW China
160 J10 Qijiang var. Gunan. Chongqing Shi, C China
159 N5 Qijiaojing Xinjiang Uygur Zizhiqu, NW China
Qike see Xunke
149 P9 Qila Saifullāh Baluchistān, SW Pakistan
159 S9 Qilian var. Babao. Qinghai, C China
159 N8 Qilian Shan var. Kilien Mountains. ⛰ N China
197 O11 Qimusseriarsuaq Dan. Melville Bugt, Eng. Melville Bay. bay NW Greenland
Qinā see Qena
159 W11 Qin'an Gansu, C China
Qincheng see Nanfeng
Qing see Qinghai
163 W7 Qing'an Heilongjiang, NE China
161 R5 Qingdao var. Ching-Tao, Ch'ing-tao, Tsingtao, Tsintao, Ger. Tsingtau. Shandong, E China
163 V8 Qinggang Heilongjiang, NE China
Qinggil see Qinghe
159 P11 Qinghai var. Chinghai, Koko Nor, Qing, Qinghai Sheng, Tsinghai. ◐ province C China
159 S10 Qinghai Hu var. Ch'ing Hai, Tsing Hai, Mong. Koko Nor. ◎ C China
Qinghai Sheng see Qinghai
158 M3 Qinghe var. Qinggil. Xinjiang Uygur Zizhiqu, NW China
160 L4 Qingjian Shaanxi, C China
160 L9 Qing Jiang ≈ C China
Qingjiang see Huai'an
Qingkou see Ganyu
160 I12 Qinglong var. Liancheng. Guizhou, S China
161 Q2 Qinglong Hebei, E China
Qingshan see Wudalianchi
159 R12 Qingshuihe Qinghai, C China
159 X10 Qingyang var. Xifeng. Gansu, C China
Qingyang see Jinjiang
161 N14 Qingyuan Guangdong, S China
163 V11 Qingyuan var. Qingyuan Manzu Zizhixian. Liaoning, NE China
Qingyuan Manzu Zizhixian see Qingyuan
158 L13 Qingzang Gaoyuan var. Xizang Gaoyuan, Eng. Plateau of Tibet. plateau W China
161 Q4 Qingzhou prev. Yidu. Shandong, E China
157 R9 Qin He ≈ C China
161 Q2 Qinhuangdao Hebei, E China
160 K7 Qin Ling ⛰ C China
Qin Xian see Qinxian
161 N5 Qinxian var. Qin Xian. Shanxi, C China
161 N6 Qinyang Henan, C China
160 K15 Qinzhou Guangxi Zhuangzu Zizhiqu, S China
Qiong see Hainan
160 L17 Qionghai prev. Jiaji. Hainan, S China
160 H9 Qionglai Sichuan, C China
160 H8 Qionglai Shan ⛰ C China
Qiongxi see Hongyuan
160 L17 Qiongzhou Haixia var. Hainan Strait. strait S China
163 U7 Qiqihar var. Ch'i-ch'i-ha-erh, Tsitsihar; prev. Lungkiang. Heilongjiang, NE China
143 P12 Qīr Fārs, S Iran
158 H10 Qira Xinjiang Uygur Zizhiqu, NW China
Qir'awn, Buḥayrat al see Qaraoun, Lac de
138 F11 Qiryat Gat var. Kiryat Gat. Southern, C Israel
138 G8 Qiryat Shemona Northern, N Israel
Qishlaq see Garmsär
141 U14 Qishn SE Yemen
138 G9 Qishon, Naḥal ≈ N Israel
Qita Ghazzah see Gaza Strip
156 K5 Qitai Xinjiang Uygur Zizhiqu, NW China
163 Y8 Qitaihe Heilongjiang, NE China
141 W12 Qitbīt, Wādī dry watercourse S Oman
161 O5 Qixian var. Qi Xian, Zhaoge. Henan, C China
Qīzān see Jīzān
Qizil Orda see Kyzylorda
Qizil Qum/Qizilqum see Kyzyl Kum
147 V14 Qizilrabot Rus. Kyzylrabot. SE Tajikistan
146 J10 Qizilravot Rus. Kyzylrabat. Buxoro Viloyati, C Uzbekistan
Qi Zil Uzun see Qezel Owzan, Rūd-e
139 S4 Qizil Yār N Iraq
Qoghaly see Kugaly
Qogir Feng see K2
143 N6 Qom var. Kum, Qum. Qom, N Iran
143 N6 Qom ◐ province N Iran
Qomisheh see Shahreẓā
Qomolangma Feng see Everest, Mount
142 M7 Qom, Rūd-e ≈ C Iran
Qomsheh see Shahreẓā
Qomul see Hami
Qondūz see Kunduz
146 G7 Qo'ng'irot Rus. Kungrad. Qoraqalpog'iston Respublikasi, NW Uzbekistan
Qongyrat see Konyrat
Qoqek see Tacheng
147 R10 Qo'qon var. Khokand, Rus. Kokand. Farg'ona Viloyati, E Uzbekistan
Qorabowur Kirlari see Karabaur', Uval
Qoradaryo see Karadar'ya
146 G6 Qorajar Rus. Karadzhar. Qoraqalpog'iston Respublikasi, NW Uzbekistan
146 K12 Qorako'l Rus. Karakul'. Buxoro Viloyati, C Uzbekistan
146 H7 Qorao'zak Rus. Karauzyak. Qoraqalpog'iston Respublikasi, NW Uzbekistan
146 E5 Qoraqalpog'iston Rus. Karakalpakya. Qoraqalpog'iston Respublikasi, NW Uzbekistan
146 G7 Qoraqalpog'iston Respublikasi Rus. Respublika Karakalpakstan. ◐ autonomous republic NW Uzbekistan
Qorgazhyn see Kurgal'dzhino
138 H6 Qornet es Saouda ▲ NE Lebanon
146 L12 Qorovulbozor Rus. Karaulbazar. Buxoro Viloyati, C Uzbekistan
142 K5 Qorveh var. Qerveh, Qurveh. Kordestān, W Iran
147 N11 Qo'shrabot Rus. Kushrabat. Samarqand Viloyati, C Uzbekistan
Qosshaghyl see Koschagyl
Qostanay/Qostanay Oblysy see Kostanay
143 P12 Qoṭbābād Fārs, S Iran
143 R13 Qoṭbābād Hormozgān, S Iran
138 H6 Qoubaïyât var. Al Qubayyāt. N Lebanon
Qoussantîna see Constantine
158 K16 Qowowuyag see Cho Oyu
147 O11 Qo'ytosh Rus. Koytash. Jizzax Viloyati, C Uzbekistan
146 G7 Qozonketkan Rus. Kazanketken. Qoraqalpog'iston Respublikasi, W Uzbekistan
146 H6 Qozoqdaryo Rus. Kazakdar'ya. Qoraqalpog'iston Respublikasi, NW Uzbekistan
19 N11 Quabbin Reservoir ⊞ Massachusetts, NE USA
100 F12 Quakenbrück Niedersachsen, NW Germany
18 I15 Quakertown Pennsylvania, NE USA
182 M10 Quambatook Victoria, SE Australia
25 Q4 Quanah Texas, SW USA
167 V10 Quang Ngai var. Quangngai, Quang Nghia. Quang Ngai, C Vietnam
Quang Nghia see Quang Ngai
167 T9 Quang Tri Quang Tri, C Vietnam
Quanjiang see Suichuan
Quan Long see Ca Mau
152 L4 Quanshuigou China/India
161 R13 Quanzhou var. Ch'uan-chou, Tsinkiang; prev. Chin-chiang. Fujian, SE China
160 M12 Quanzhou Guangxi Zhuangzu Zizhiqu, S China
11 V16 Qu'Appelle ≈ Saskatchewan, S Canada
12 M3 Quaqtaq prev. Koartac. Québec, NE Canada
61 E16 Quaraí Rio Grande do Sul, S Brazil
59 H24 Quaraí, Rio Sp. Río Cuareim. ≈ Brazil/Uruguay see also Cuareim, Río
171 N13 Quarles, Pegunungan ⛰ Sulawesi, C Indonesia
Quarnero see Kvarner
107 C20 Quartu Sant' Elena Sardegna, Italy, C Mediterranean Sea
29 X13 Quasqueton Iowa, C USA
173 X16 Quatre Bornes W Mauritius
172 I17 Quatre Bornes Mahé, NE Seychelles
137 X10 Quba Rus. Kuba. N Azerbaijan
Qubba see Ba'qūbah
143 T3 Qūchān var. Kuchan. Khorāsān, NE Iran
183 R10 Queanbeyan New South Wales, SE Australia
15 Q10 Québec var. Quebec. Québec, SE Canada
14 K10 Québec var. Quebec. ◐ province SE Canada
61 D17 Quebracho Paysandú, W Uruguay
101 K14 Quedlinburg Sachsen-Anhalt, C Germany
138 H10 Queen Alia ✕ ('Ammān) 'Al 'Ammān, C Jordan
10 L16 Queen Bess, Mount ▲ British Columbia, SW Canada
10 I14 Queen Charlotte British Columbia, SW Canada
65 B24 Queen Charlotte Bay bay West Falkland, Falkland Islands
10 H14 Queen Charlotte Islands Fr. Îles de la Reine-Charlotte. island group British Columbia, SW Canada
10 I15 Queen Charlotte Sound sea area British Columbia, W Canada
10 J16 Queen Charlotte Strait strait British Columbia, W Canada
27 U1 Queen City Missouri, C USA
25 X5 Queen City Texas, SW USA
8 L3 Queen Elizabeth Islands Fr. Îles de la Reine-Élisabeth. island group Nunavut, N Canada
195 Y10 Queen Mary Coast physical region Antarctica
65 N24 Queen Mary's Peak ▲ C Tristan da Cunha
196 M8 Queen Maud Gulf gulf Arctic Ocean
195 P11 Queen Maud Mountains ⛰ Antarctica
Queen's County see Laois
181 U7 Queensland ◐ state N Australia
192 I9 Queensland Plateau undersea feature N Coral Sea
183 O16 Queenstown Tasmania, SE Australia
185 C22 Queenstown Otago, South Island, NZ
83 I24 Queenstown Eastern Cape, S South Africa
Queenstown see Cobh
32 F8 Queets Washington, NW USA
61 D18 Queguay Grande, Río ≈ W Uruguay
59 O16 Queimadas Bahia, E Brazil
82 D11 Quela Malanje, NW Angola
83 O16 Quelimane var. Kilimane, Kilmain, Quilimane. Zambézia, NE Mozambique
63 G18 Quellón var. Puerto Quellón. Los Lagos, S Chile
Quelpart see Cheju-do
37 P12 Quemado New Mexico, SW USA
25 O12 Quemado Texas, SW USA
44 K7 Quemado, Punta de headland E Cuba
Quemoy see Chinmen Tao
62 K13 Quemú Quemú La Pampa, E Argentina
155 E17 Quepem Goa, W India
42 M14 Quepos Puntarenas, S Costa Rica
Que Que see Kwekwe
61 D23 Quequén Buenos Aires, E Argentina
61 D23 Quequén Grande, Río ≈ E Argentina
61 C23 Quequén Salado, Río ≈ E Argentina
Quera see Chur
41 N13 Querétaro Querétaro de Arteaga, C Mexico
40 F4 Querobabi Sonora, NW Mexico
42 M13 Quesada var. Ciudad Quesada, San Carlos. Alajuela, N Costa Rica
105 O13 Quesada Andalucía, S Spain
161 O7 Queshan Henan, C China
10 M15 Quesnel British Columbia, SW Canada
37 S9 Questa New Mexico, SW USA
102 H7 Questembert Morbihan, NW France
57 K22 Quetena, Río ≈ SW Bolivia
149 O10 Quetta Baluchistān, SW Pakistan
Quetzalcoalco see Coatzacoalcos
Quetzaltenango see Quezaltenango
56 E6 Quevedo Los Ríos, C Ecuador
42 B6 Quezaltenango var. Quetzaltenango. Quezaltenango, W Guatemala
42 A2 Quezaltenango off. Departamento de Quezaltenango, var. Quetzaltenango. ◐ department SW Guatemala
42 E6 Quezaltepeque Chiquimula, SE Guatemala
170 M6 Quezon Palawan, W Philippines
161 P5 Qufu Shandong, E China
82 B12 Quibala Cuanza Sul, NW Angola
82 B11 Quibaxe var. Quibaxi. Cuanza Norte, NW Angola
Quibaxi see Quibaxe
54 D9 Quibdó Chocó, W Colombia
102 G7 Quiberon Morbihan, NW France
102 G7 Quiberon, Baie de bay NW France
54 J5 Quíbor Lara, N Venezuela
42 C4 Quiché off. Departamento del Quiché. ◐ department W Guatemala
99 E21 Quiévrain Hainaut, S Belgium
40 I9 Quila Sinaloa, C Mexico
83 B14 Quilengues Huíla, SW Angola
Quilimane see Quelimane
57 G15 Quillabamba Cusco, C Peru
57 L18 Quillacollo Cochabamba, C Bolivia
62 H4 Quillagua Antofagasta, N Chile
103 N17 Quillan Aude, S France
11 U15 Quill Lakes ◎ Saskatchewan, S Canada
62 G11 Quillota Valparaíso, C Chile
155 G23 Quilon var. Kolam, Kollam. Kerala, SW India
181 V9 Quilpie Queensland, C Australia
149 O4 Quil-Qala Bāmīān, N Afghanistan
62 L7 Quimilí Santiago del Estero, C Argentina
57 O19 Quimome Santa Cruz, E Bolivia
102 F6 Quimper anc. Quimper Corentin. Finistère, NW France
Quimper Corentin see Quimper
102 G7 Quimperlé Finistère, NW France
32 F8 Quinault Washington, NW USA
32 F8 Quinault River ≈ Washington, NW USA
35 P5 Quincy California, W USA
23 S8 Quincy Florida, SE USA
30 I13 Quincy Illinois, N USA
19 O11 Quincy Massachusetts, NE USA
32 J9 Quincy Washington, NW USA
54 E10 Quindío off. Departamento del Quindío. ◐ province C Colombia
54 E10 Quindío, Nevado del ▲ C Colombia
62 J10 Quines San Luis, C Argentina
39 N13 Quinhagak Alaska, USA
76 G13 Quinhámel W Guinea-Bissau
Qui Nhon/Quinhon see Quy Nhơn
Quinindé see Rosa Zárate
25 U6 Quinlan Texas, SW USA
61 H17 Quinta Rio Grande do Sul, S Brazil
105 O10 Quintanar de la Orden Castilla-La Mancha, C Spain
41 X13 Quintana Roo ◐ state SE Mexico
105 S6 Quinto Aragón, NE Spain
108 G10 Quinto Ticino, S Switzerland
27 Q11 Quinton Oklahoma, C USA
62 K12 Quinto, Río ≈ C Argentina
82 A10 Quinzau Zaire, NW Angola
14 H8 Quinze, Lac des ◎ Québec, SE Canada
83 B15 Quipungo Huíla, C Angola
62 G13 Quirihue Bío Bío, C Chile
82 D12 Quirima Malanje, NW Angola
183 T6 Quirindi New South Wales, SE Australia
55 P5 Quiriquire Monagas, NE Venezuela
14 D10 Quirke Lake ◎ Ontario, S Canada
61 B21 Quiroga Buenos Aires, E Argentina
104 I4 Quiroga Galicia, NW Spain
Quiróm, Salar see Pocitos, Salar
56 B9 Quiroz, Río ≈ NW Peru
82 Q13 Quissanga Cabo Delgado, NE Mozambique
83 M20 Quissico Inhambane, S Mozambique
25 O4 Quitaque Texas, SW USA
82 Q13 Quiterajo Cabo Delgado, NE Mozambique
23 T6 Quitman Georgia, SE USA
22 M6 Quitman Mississippi, S USA
25 V6 Quitman Texas, SW USA
56 C6 Quito ● (Ecuador) Pichincha, N Ecuador
Quito see Mariscal Sucre
58 P13 Quixadá Ceará, E Brazil
83 Q15 Quixaxe Nampula, NE Mozambique
160 J9 Qu Jiang ≈ C China
161 R10 Qu Jiang ≈ SE China
161 N13 Qujiang var. Maba. Guangdong, S China
160 H12 Qujing Yunnan, SW China
Qulan see Kulan
163 T8 Qulin Gol prev. Chaor He. ≈ N China
146 L10 Quljuqtov-Tog'lari Rus. Gory Kul'dzhuktau. ⛰ C Uzbekistan
Qulsary see Kul'sary
Qulyndy Zhazyghy see Kulunda Steppe
Qum see Qom
Qumälisch see Lubartów
159 P11 Qumar He ≈ C China
159 Q12 Qumarlêb var. Yuegaitan. Qinghai, C China
Qumisheh see Shahreẓā
147 O14 Qumqo'rg'on Rus. Kumkurgan. Surxondaryo Viloyati, S Uzbekistan
Qunaytirah/Qunayṭirah, Muḥāfaẓat al/Qunaytra see Al Qunayṭirah
189 V12 Quoi island Chuuk, C Micronesia
9 N8 Quoich ≈ Nunavut, NE Canada
83 E26 Quoin Point headland SW South Africa
182 I7 Quorn South Australia
Qurein see Al Kuwayt
147 P14 Qŭrghonteppa Rus. Kurgan-Tyube. SW Tajikistan
Qurlurtuuq see Kugluktuk
Qurveh see Qorveh
Qusair see Quseir
137 X10 Qusar Rus. Kusary. NE Azerbaijan
Quşayr see Al Quşayr
75 Y10 Quseir var. Al Quşayr, Qusair. E Egypt
142 I2 Qūshchī Āžarbāyjān-e Bākhtarī, N Iran
Qusmuryn see Kushmurun, Kostanay, Kazakhstan
Qusmuryn see Kushmurun, Ozero, Kazakhstan
Quṭayfah/Qutayfe/Quteife see Al Quṭayfah
Quthing see Moyeni
147 S10 Quvasoy Rus. Kuvasay. Farg'ona Viloyati, E Uzbekistan
Quwair see Guwêr
Quxar see Lhazê
Qu Xian see Quzhou
159 N16 Qüxü var. Xoi. Xizang Zizhiqu, W China
Quyang see Jingzhou, Hunan
167 V13 Quy Chanh Ninh Thuận, S Vietnam
167 V11 Quy Nhơn var. Quinhon, Qui Nhon. Bình Định, C Vietnam
161 R10 Quzhou var. Qu Xian. Zhejiang, SE China
Qyteti Stalin see Kuçovë
Qyzylorda/Qyzylorda Oblysy see Kyzylorda
Qyzyltū see Kishkenekol'
Qyzylzhar see Kyzylzhar

R

109 R4 Raab Oberösterreich, N Austria
109 X8 Raab Hung. Rába. ≈ Austria/Hungary see also Rába
Raab see Győr
109 V2 Raabs an der Thaya Niederösterreich, E Austria
93 L14 Raahe Swe. Brahestad. Oulu, W Finland
98 M10 Raalte Overijssel, E Netherlands
99 I14 Raamsdonksveer Noord-Brabant, S Netherlands
92 L12 Raanujärvi Lappi, NW Finland
96 G9 Raasay island NW Scotland, UK
118 H3 Raasiku Ger. Rasik. Harjumaa, NW Estonia
112 B11 Rab It. Arbe. Primorje-Gorski Kotar, NW Croatia
112 B11 Rab It. Arbe. island NW Croatia
171 N16 Raba Sumbawa, S Indonesia
111 G22 Rába Ger. Raab. ≈ Austria/Hungary see also Raab
112 A10 Rabac Istra, NW Croatia
104 I2 Rábade Galicia, NW Spain
80 F10 Rabak White Nile, C Sudan
186 G9 Rabaraba Milne Bay, SE PNG
102 K16 Rabastens-de-Bigorre Hautes-Pyrénées, S France
121 O16 Rabat W Malta
74 F6 Rabat var. al Dar al Baida. ● (Morocco) NW Morocco
Rabat see Victoria
186 H6 Rabaul New Britain, E PNG
Rabbah Ammon/Rabbath Ammon see 'Ammān
28 K8 Rabbit Creek ≈ South Dakota, N USA
14 H10 Rabbit Lake ◎ Ontario, S Canada
187 Y14 Rabi prev. Rambi. island N Fiji
140 K9 Rābigh Makkah, W Saudi Arabia
42 D5 Rabinal Baja Verapaz, C Guatemala
168 G9 Rabi, Pulau island NW Indonesia, East Indies
111 L17 Rabka Małopolskie, S Poland
155 F16 Rabkavi Karnātaka, W India
Râbniţa see Rîbniţa
109 Y6 Rabnitz ≈ E Austria
124 J7 Rabocheostrovsk Respublika Kareliya, NW Russian Federation
23 U1 Rabun Bald ▲ Georgia, SE USA
75 S11 Rabyānah SE Libya
75 S11 Rabyānah, Ramlat var. Rebiana Sand Sea, Şaḥrā' Rabyānah. desert SE Libya
Rabyānah, Şaḥrā' see Rabyānah, Ramlat
116 L11 Răcăciuni Bacău, E Romania
Racaka see Riwoqê
107 J24 Racalmuto Sicilia, Italy, C Mediterranean Sea
116 J14 Răcari Dâmboviţa, SE Romania
Răcari see Durankulak
116 F13 Răcăşdia Hung. Rakasd. Caraş-Severin, SW Romania
106 B9 Racconigi Piemonte, NE Italy
31 T15 Raccoon Creek ≈ Ohio, N USA
13 V13 Race, Cape headland Newfoundland and Labrador, E Canada
22 K10 Raceland Louisiana, S USA
19 Q12 Race Point headland Massachusetts, NE USA
167 S14 Rach Gia Kiên Giang, S Vietnam
167 S14 Rach Gia, Vinh bay S Vietnam
76 J8 Rachid Tagant, C Mauritania

110 L10 **Raciąż** Mazowieckie, C Poland
111 I16 **Racibórz** *Ger.* Ratibor. Śląskie, S Poland
31 N9 **Racine** Wisconsin, N USA
14 D7 **Racine Lake** ◎ Ontario, S Canada
111 J23 **Ráckeve** Pest, C Hungary
Rácz-Becse *see* Bečej
141 O15 **Radā'** *var.* Ridā'. W Yemen
113 O15 **Radan** ▲ SE Serbia and Montenegro (Yugo.)
63 J19 **Rada Tilly** Chubut, SE Argentina
116 K8 **Rădăuţi** *Ger.* Radautz, *Hung.* Rádóc. Suceava, N Romania
116 L8 **Rădăuţi-Prut** Botoşani, NE Romania
Radautz *see* Rădăuţi
Radbusa *see* Radbuza
111 A17 **Radbuza** *Ger.* Radbusa. ⤳ SE Czech Republic
20 K6 **Radcliff** Kentucky, S USA
139 O2 **Radd, Wādī ar** *dry watercourse* N Syria
95 H16 **Råde** Østfold, S Norway
109 V11 **Radeče** *Ger.* Ratschach. C Slovenia
Radein *see* Radenci
116 J4 **Radekhiv** *Pol.* Radziechów, *Rus.* Radekhov. L'vivs'ka Oblast', W Ukraine
Radekhov *see* Radekhiv
109 X9 **Radenci** *Ger.* Radein; *prev.* Radinci. NE Slovenia
109 S9 **Radenthein** Kärnten, S Austria
21 R7 **Radford** Virginia, NE USA
154 C9 **Rādhanpur** Gujarāt, W India
Radinci *see* Radenci
127 Q6 **Radishchevo** Ul'yanovskaya Oblast', W Russian Federation
12 I9 **Radisson** Québec, E Canada
11 P16 **Radium Hot Springs** British Columbia, SW Canada
116 F11 **Radna** *Hung.* Máriaradna. Arad, W Romania
114 K10 **Radnevo** Stara Zagora, C Bulgaria
97 J20 **Radnor** *cultural region* E Wales, UK
Radnót *see* Iernut
Rádóc *see* Rădăuţi
101 H24 **Radolfzell am Bodensee** Baden-Württemberg, S Germany
110 M13 **Radom** Mazowieckie, C Poland
116 I14 **Radomireşti** Olt, S Romania
111 K14 **Radomsko** *Rus.* Novoradomsk. Łodzkie, C Poland
117 N4 **Radomyshl'** Zhytomyrs'ka Oblast', N Ukraine
113 P19 **Radoviš** *prev.* Radovište. E FYR Macedonia
Radovište *see* Radoviš
94 B13 **Radøy** *island* S Norway
109 R7 **Radstadt** Salzburg, NW Austria
182 E8 **Radstock, Cape** *headland* South Australia
119 G15 **Radun'** *Rus.* Radun'. Hrodzyenskaya Voblasts', W Belarus
126 M3 **Raduzhnyy** Vladimirskaya Oblast', W Russian Federation
118 F11 **Radviliškis** Šiauliai, N Lithuania
11 U17 **Radville** Saskatchewan, S Canada
140 K7 **Raḍwá, Jabal** ▲ W Saudi Arabia
111 P16 **Radymno** Podkarpackie, SE Poland
116 J5 **Radyvyliv** Rivnens'ka Oblast', NW Ukraine
Radziechów *see* Radekhiv
110 I11 **Radziejów** Kujawsko-pomorskie, C Poland
110 O12 **Radzyń Podlaski** Lubelskie, E Poland
8 J7 **Rae** ⤳ Nunavut, NW Canada
152 M13 **Rāe Bareli** Uttar Pradesh, N India
Rae-Edzo *see* Edzo
21 T11 **Raeford** North Carolina, SE USA
99 M19 **Raeren** Liège, E Belgium
9 N7 **Rae Strait** *strait* Nunavut, N Canada
184 L11 **Raetihi** Manawatu-Wanganui, North Island, NZ
191 U13 **Raevavae** *var.* Raivavae. *island* Îles Australes, SW French Polynesia
Rafa *see* Rafah
62 M10 **Rafaela** Santa Fe, E Argentina
138 E11 **Rafah** *var.* Rafa, Rafaḥ, *Heb.* Rafiah, Raphiah. SW Gaza Strip
79 L15 **Rafaï** Mbomou, SE Central African Republic
141 O4 **Rafḥah** Al Ḥudūd ash Shamālīyah, N Saudi Arabia
Rafiah *see* Rafah
143 R10 **Rafsanjān** Kermān, C Iran
80 B13 **Raga** Western Bahr el Ghazal, SW Sudan
19 S8 **Ragged Island** *island* Maine, NE USA
44 I5 **Ragged Island Range** *island group* S Bahamas
184 L7 **Raglan** Waikato, North Island, NZ
22 G8 **Ragley** Louisiana, S USA
Ragnit *see* Neman
107 K25 **Ragusa** Sicilia, Italy, C Mediterranean Sea
Ragusa *see* Dubrovnik
Ragusavecchia *see* Cavtat
171 P14 **Raha** Pulau Muna, C Indonesia
119 N17 **Rahachow** *Rus.* Rogachëv. Homyel'skaya Voblasts', SE Belarus
67 U6 **Rahad** *var.* Nahr ar Rahad. ⤳ W Sudan
Rahad, Nahr ar *see* Rahad
Rahaeng *see* Tak
138 F11 **Rahat** Southern, C Israel
140 L8 **Rahaṭ, Ḩarrat** *lavaflow* W Saudi Arabia
149 S12 **Rahīmyār Khān** Punjab, SE Pakistan
95 I14 **Råholt** Akershus, S Norway
Rahovec *see* Orahovac
191 S10 **Raiatea** *island* Îles Sous le Vent, W French Polynesia
155 H16 **Rāichūr** Karnātaka, C India
Raidestos *see* Tekirdağ
153 S13 **Rāiganj** West Bengal, NE India
154 M11 **Raigarh** Chhattīsgarh, C India
183 O16 **Railton** Tasmania, SE Australia
36 L8 **Rainbow Bridge** *natural arch* Utah, W USA
23 Q3 **Rainbow City** Alabama, S USA
11 N11 **Rainbow Lake** Alberta, W Canada
21 R5 **Rainelle** West Virginia, NE USA
32 G10 **Rainier** Oregon, NW USA
32 H9 **Rainier, Mount** 🌋 Washington, NW USA
23 Q2 **Rainsville** Alabama, S USA
12 B11 **Rainy Lake** ◎ Canada/USA
12 A11 **Rainy River** Ontario, C Canada
Raippaluoto *see* Replot
154 K12 **Raipur** Chhattīsgarh, C India
154 H10 **Raisen** Madhya Pradesh, C India
15 N13 **Raisin** ⤳ Ontario, SE Canada
31 R11 **Raisin, River** ⤳ Michigan, N USA
Raivavae *see* Raevavae
149 W9 **Rāiwind** Punjab, E Pakistan
171 T12 **Raja Ampat, Kepulauan** *island group* E Indonesia
155 L16 **Rājahmundry** Andhra Pradesh, E India
155 I18 **Rājampet** Andhra Pradesh, E India
Rajang *see* Rajang, Batang
169 S9 **Rajang, Batang** *var.* Rajang. ⤳ East Malaysia
149 S11 **Rājanpur** Punjab, E Pakistan
155 H23 **Rājapālaiyam** Tamil Nādu, SE India
152 E12 **Rājasthān** ◈ *state* NW India
153 T15 **Rajbari** Dhaka, C Bangladesh
153 R12 **Rajbiraj** Eastern, E Nepal
154 G9 **Rājgarh** Madhya Pradesh, C India
152 H10 **Rājgarh** Rājasthān, NW India
153 P14 **Rājgīr** Bihār, N India
110 O8 **Rajgród** Podlaskie, NE Poland
154 L12 **Rājim** Chhattīsgarh, C India
112 C11 **Rajinac, Mali** ▲ W Croatia
154 B10 **Rājkot** Gujarāt, W India
153 R14 **Rājmahal** Jhārkhand, NE India
153 Q14 **Rājmahal Hills** *hill range* N India
154 K12 **Rāj Nāndgaon** Chhattīsgarh, C India
152 I8 **Rājpura** Punjab, NW India
153 S14 **Rajshahi** *prev.* Rampur Boalia. Rajshahi, W Bangladesh
153 S13 **Rajshahi** ◈ *division* NW Bangladesh
190 K13 **Rakahanga** *atoll* N Cook Islands
185 H19 **Rakaia** Canterbury, South Island, NZ
185 G19 **Rakaia** ⤳ South Island, NZ
152 H3 **Rakaposhi** ▲ N India
Rakasd *see* Răcăşdia
169 N15 **Rakata, Pulau** *var.* Pulau Krakatau. *island* S Indonesia
141 U10 **Rakbah, Qalamat ar** *well* SE Saudi Arabia
Rakhine State *see* Arakan State
116 I8 **Rakhiv** Zakarpats'ka Oblast', W Ukraine
141 V13 **Rakhyūt** SW Oman
192 K9 **Rakiraki** Viti Levu, W Fiji
Rakka *see* Ar Raqqah
118 I4 **Rakke** Lääne-Virumaa, NE Estonia
95 I16 **Rakkestad** Østfold, S Norway
110 F12 **Rakoniewice** *Ger.* Rakwitz. Wielkolpolskie, C Poland
Rakonitz *see* Rakovník
83 H18 **Rakops** Central, C Botswana
111 C16 **Rakovník** *Ger.* Rakonitz. Středočeský Kraj, W Czech Republic
114 J10 **Rakovski** Plovdiv, C Bulgaria
Rakutō-kō *see* Naktong-gang
118 I3 **Rakvere** *Ger.* Wesenberg. Lääne-Virumaa, N Estonia
Rakwitz *see* Rakoniewice
22 L6 **Raleigh** Mississippi, S USA
21 U9 **Raleigh** *state capital* North Carolina, SE USA
21 Y11 **Raleigh Bay** *bay* North Carolina, SE USA
21 U9 **Raleigh-Durham** ✕ North Carolina, SE USA
189 S6 **Ralik Chain** *island group* Ralik Chain, W Marshall Islands
25 N5 **Ralls** Texas, SW USA
18 G13 **Ralston** Pennsylvania, NE USA
141 O16 **Ramādah** W Yemen
Ramadi *see* Ar Ramādī
105 N2 **Ramales de la Victoria** Cantabria, N Spain
138 F10 **Ramallah** C West Bank
61 C19 **Ramallo** Buenos Aires, E Argentina
155 H20 **Rāmanagaram** Karnātaka, E India
155 I23 **Rāmanāthapuram** Tamil Nādu, SE India
154 N12 **Rāmapur** Orissa, E India
155 I14 **Rāmāreddi** *var.* Kāmāreddi, Kamareddy. Andhra Pradesh, C India
138 F10 **Ramat Gan** Tel Aviv, W Israel
103 T6 **Rambervillers** Vosges, NE France
Rambi *see* Rabi
103 N5 **Rambouillet** Yvelines, N France
186 E5 **Rambutyo Island** *island* N PNG
153 Q12 **Ramechhap** Central, C Nepal
183 R12 **Rame Head** *headland* Victoria, SE Australia
126 L4 **Ramenskoye** Moskovskaya Oblast', W Russian Federation
124 J15 **Rameshki** Tverskaya Oblast', W Russian Federation
153 P14 **Rāmgarh** Jhārkhand, N India
152 D11 **Rāmgarh** Rājasthān, NW India
142 M9 **Rāmhormoz** *var.* Ram Hormuz, Ramuz. Khūzestān, SW Iran
Ram Hormuz *see* Rāmhormoz
Ram, Jebel *see* Ramm, Jabal
138 F10 **Ramla** *var.* Ramle, Ramleh, *Ar.* Er Ramle. Central, C Israel
Ramle/Ramleh *see* Ramla
138 F14 **Ramm, Jabal** *var.* Jebel Ram. ▲ SW Jordan
152 K10 **Rāmnagar** Uttaranchal, N India
95 N15 **Ramnäs** Västmanland, C Sweden
Râmnicul-Sărat *see* Râmnicu Sărat
116 L12 **Râmnicu Sărat** *prev.* Râmnicul-Sărat, Rîmnicu-Sărat. Buzău, E Romania
116 I13 **Râmnicu Vâlcea** *prev.* Rîmnicu Vîlcea. Vâlcea, C Romania
Ramokgwebana *see* Ramokgwebane
83 J18 **Ramokgwebane** *var.* Ramokgwebana. Central, NE Botswana
126 L7 **Ramon'** Voronezhskaya Oblast', W Russian Federation
35 V17 **Ramona** California, W USA
56 A10 **Ramón, Laguna** ◎ NW Peru
14 G7 **Ramore** Ontario, S Canada
40 M11 **Ramos** San Luis Potosí, C Mexico
41 N8 **Ramos Arizpe** Coahuila de Zaragoza, NE Mexico
40 J9 **Ramos, Río de** ⤳ C Mexico
83 I21 **Ramotswa** South East, S Botswana
39 R8 **Rampart** Alaska, USA
8 H8 **Ramparts** ⤳ Northwest Territories, NW Canada
152 K10 **Rāmpur** Uttar Pradesh, N India
154 F9 **Rāmpura** Madhya Pradesh, C India
Rampur Boalia *see* Rajshahi
166 K6 **Ramree Island** *island* W Myanmar
141 W6 **Rams** *var.* Ar Rams. Ra's al Khaymah, NE UAE
143 N4 **Rāmsar** *prev.* Sakhtsar. Māzandarān, N Iran
93 H16 **Ramsele** Västernorrland, N Sweden
21 T9 **Ramseur** North Carolina, SE USA
97 I16 **Ramsey** NE Isle of Man
97 I16 **Ramsey Bay** *bay* NE Isle of Man
14 E9 **Ramsey Lake** ◎ Ontario, S Canada
97 Q22 **Ramsgate** SE England, UK
94 M10 **Ramsjö** Gävleborg, C Sweden
154 I12 **Rāmtek** Mahārāshtra, C India
Ramtha *see* Ar Ramthā
Ramuz *see* Rāmhormoz
118 G12 **Ramygala** Panevėžys, C Lithuania
152 H14 **Rāna Pratāp Sāgar** ◎ N India
169 V7 **Ranau** Sabah, East Malaysia
168 L14 **Ranau, Danau** ◎ Sumatera, W Indonesia
62 H12 **Rancagua** Libertador, C Chile
99 G22 **Rance** Hainaut, S Belgium
102 H6 **Rance** ⤳ NW France
60 J9 **Rancharia** São Paulo, S Brazil
153 P15 **Rānchi** Jhārkhand, N India
61 D21 **Ranchos** Buenos Aires, E Argentina
37 S9 **Ranchos De Taos** New Mexico, SW USA
63 G16 **Ranco, Lago** ◎ C Chile
95 C16 **Randaberg** Rogaland, S Norway
29 U7 **Randall** Minnesota, N USA
107 L23 **Randazzo** Sicilia, Italy, C Mediterranean Sea
95 G21 **Randers** Århus, C Denmark
92 I12 **Randijaure** ◎ N Sweden
21 T9 **Randleman** North Carolina, SE USA
19 O11 **Randolph** Massachusetts, NE USA
29 Q13 **Randolph** Nebraska, C USA
36 M1 **Randolph** Utah, W USA
100 P9 **Randow** ⤳ NE Germany
95 H14 **Randsfjorden** ◎ S Norway
92 K13 **Råneå** Norrbotten, N Sweden
92 G12 **Ranelva** ⤳ C Norway
93 F15 **Ranemsletta** Nord-Trøndelag, C Norway
76 H10 **Ranérou** C Senegal
Råneš *see* Ringvassøya
185 E22 **Ranfurly** Otago, South Island, NZ
167 P17 **Rangae** Narathiwat, SW Thailand
153 V16 **Rangamati** Chittagong, SE Bangladesh
184 I2 **Rangaunu Bay** *bay* North Island, NZ
19 P6 **Rangeley** Maine, NE USA
37 O4 **Rangely** Colorado, C USA
25 R7 **Ranger** Texas, SW USA
14 C9 **Ranger Lake** Ontario, S Canada
14 C9 **Ranger Lake** ◎ Ontario, S Canada
153 V12 **Rangia** Assam, NE India
185 I18 **Rangiora** Canterbury, South Island, NZ
191 T9 **Rangiroa** *atoll* Îles Tuamotu, W French Polynesia
184 N9 **Rangitaiki** ⤳ North Island, NZ
185 F19 **Rangitata** ⤳ South Island, NZ
184 M12 **Rangitikei** ⤳ North Island, NZ
184 L6 **Rangitoto Island** *island* N NZ
Rangkasbitoeng *see* Rangkasbitung
169 N16 **Rangkasbitung** *prev.* Rangkasbitoeng. Jawa, SW Indonesia
167 P9 **Rang, Khao** ▲ C Thailand
147 V13 **Rangkŭl** *Rus.* Rangkul'. SE Tajikistan
Rangkul' *see* Rangkŭl
Rangoon *see* Yangon
153 T13 **Rangpur** Rajshahi, N Bangladesh
155 F18 **Rānibennur** Karnātaka, W India
153 R15 **Rāniganj** West Bengal, NE India
149 Q13 **Rānīpur** Sind, SE Pakistan
Rāniyah *see* Rānya
25 N9 **Rankin** Texas, SW USA
9 O9 **Rankin Inlet** Nunavut, C Canada
183 P8 **Rankins Springs** New South Wales, SE Australia
Rankovićevo *see* Kraljevo
108 I7 **Rankweil** Vorarlberg, W Austria
Rann *see* Brežice
127 T8 **Ranneye** Orenburgskaya Oblast', W Russian Federation
96 I10 **Rannoch, Loch** ◎ C Scotland, UK
191 U17 **Rano Kau** *var.* Rano Kao. *crater* Easter Island, Chile, E Pacific Ocean
167 N14 **Ranong** Ranong, SW Thailand
186 J8 **Ranongga** *var.* Ghanongga. *island* NW Solomon Islands
191 W16 **Rano Raraku** *ancient monument* Easter Island, Chile, E Pacific Ocean
171 V12 **Ransiki** Papua, E Indonesia
92 K12 **Rantajärvi** Norrbotten, N Sweden
93 N17 **Rantasalmi** Isä-Suomi, SE Finland
169 U13 **Rantau** Borneo, C Indonesia
168 L10 **Rantau, Pulau** *var.* Pulau Tebingtinggi. *island* W Indonesia
171 N13 **Rantepao** Sulawesi, C Indonesia
30 M13 **Rantoul** Illinois, N USA
93 L15 **Rantsila** Oulu, C Finland
92 L13 **Ranua** Lappi, NW Finland
139 T3 **Rānya** *var.* Rāniyah. NE Iraq
157 X3 **Raohe** Heilongjiang, NE China
74 H9 **Raoui, Erg er** *desert* W Algeria
193 O10 **Rapa** *island* Îles Australes, S French Polynesia
191 V14 **Rapa Iti** *island* Îles Australes, SW French Polynesia
106 D10 **Rapallo** Liguria, NW Italy
Rapa Nui *see* Pascua, Isla de
Raphiah *see* Rafah
21 V5 **Rapidan River** ⤳ Virginia, NE USA
28 J10 **Rapid City** South Dakota, N USA
15 P8 **Rapide-Blanc** Québec, SE Canada
14 I8 **Rapide-Deux** Québec, SE Canada
118 K6 **Räpina** *Ger.* Rappin. Põlvamaa, SE Estonia
118 G4 **Rapla** *Ger.* Rappel. Raplamaa, NW Estonia
118 G4 **Raplamaa** *off.* Rapla Maakond. ◈ *province* NW Estonia
21 X6 **Rappahonnock River** ⤳ Virginia, NE USA
Rappel *see* Rapla
108 G7 **Rapperswil** Sankt Gallen, NE Switzerland
Rappin *see* Räpina
153 N12 **Rāpti** ⤳ N India
57 K16 **Rapulo, Río** ⤳ E Bolivia
Raqqah/Raqqah, Muḥāfaẓat al *see* Ar Raqqah
18 J8 **Raquette Lake** ◎ New York, NE USA
18 J6 **Raquette River** ⤳ New York, NE USA
191 V10 **Raraka** *atoll* Îles Tuamotu, C French Polynesia
191 V10 **Raroia** *atoll* Îles Tuamotu, C French Polynesia
190 H15 **Rarotonga** ✕ Rarotonga, S Cook Islands, C Pacific Ocean
190 H16 **Rarotonga** *island* S Cook Islands, C Pacific Ocean
147 P12 **Rarz** W Tajikistan
Ras al 'Ain *see* Ra's al 'Ayn
139 N2 **Ra's al 'Ayn** *var.* Ras al 'Ain. Al Ḥasakah, N Syria
138 H3 **Ra's al Basīṭ** Al Lādhiqīyah, W Syria
Ra's al-Hafgī *see* Ra's al Khafjī
141 R5 **Ra's al Khafjī** *var.* Ra's al-Hafgī. Ash Sharqīyah, NE Saudi Arabia
Ras al-Khaimah/Ras al Khaimah *see* Ra's al Khaymah
143 R15 **Ra's al Khaymah** *var.* Ras al Khaimah. Ra's al Khaymah, NE UAE
143 R15 **Ra's al Khaymah** *var.* Ras al-Khaimah. ✕ Ra's al Khaymah, NE UAE
138 G13 **Ra's an Naqb** Ma'ān, S Jordan
61 B26 **Rasa, Punta** *headland* E Argentina
171 V12 **Rasawi** Papua, E Indonesia
Râşcani *see* Rîşcani
80 J10 **Ras Dashen Terara** ▲ N Ethiopia
151 K19 **Rasdu Atoll** *atoll* C Maldives
118 E12 **Raseiniai** Kaunas, C Lithuania
75 X8 **Râs Ghârib** E Egypt
162 D6 **Rashaant** Bayan-Ölgiy, W Mongolia
162 L10 **Rashaant** Dundgovĭ, C Mongolia
162 J6 **Rashaant** Hövsgöl, N Mongolia
139 Y11 **Rashīd** E Iraq
75 V7 **Rashîd** *Eng.* Rosetta. N Egypt
142 M3 **Rasht** *var.* Resht. Gīlān, NW Iran
139 S2 **Rashwān** N Iraq
Rasik *see* Raasiku
113 M15 **Raška** Serbia, C Serbia and Montenegro (Yugo.)
119 P15 **Rasna** *Rus.* Ryasna. Mahilyowskaya Voblasts', E Belarus
116 J12 **Râşnov** *prev.* Rîşno, Rozsnyó, *Hung.* Barcarozsnyó. Braşov, C Romania
118 L11 **Rasony** *Rus.* Rossony. Vitsyebskaya Voblasts', N Belarus
Ra's Shamrah *see* Ugarit
127 N7 **Rasskazovo** Tambovskaya Oblast', W Russian Federation
119 O16 **Rasta** ⤳ E Belarus
Rastadt *see* Rastatt
Rastâne *see* Ar Rastān
141 S6 **Ras Tannūrah** *Eng.* Ras Tanura. Ash Sharqīyah, NE Saudi Arabia
Ras Tanura *see* Ra's Tannūrah
101 G21 **Rastatt** *var.* Rastadt. Baden-Württemberg, SW Germany
Rastenburg *see* Kętrzyn
149 V7 **Rasūlnagar** Punjab, E Pakistan
189 U6 **Ratak Chain** *island group* Ratak Chain, E Marshall Islands
119 K15 **Ratamka** *Rus.* Ratomka. Minskaya Voblasts', C Belarus
93 G17 **Rätan** Jämtland, C Sweden
152 G11 **Ratangarh** Rājasthān, NW India
Rat Buri *see* Ratchaburi
167 O11 **Ratchaburi** *var.* Rat Buri. Ratchaburi, W Thailand
29 W15 **Rathbun Lake** ▣ Iowa, C USA
Ráth Caola *see* Rathkeale
166 K5 **Rathedaung** Arakan State, W Myanmar
100 M12 **Rathenow** Brandenburg, NE Germany
97 C19 **Rathkeale** *Ir.* Ráth Caola. SW Ireland
96 F13 **Rathlin Island** *Ir.* Reachlainn. *island* N Northern Ireland, UK
97 C20 **Ráthluirc** *Ir.* An Ráth. SW Ireland
Ratibor *see* Racibórz
Ratisbon/Ratisbona/ Ratisbonne *see* Regensburg
Rätische Alpen *see* Rhaetian Alps
38 E17 **Rat Island** *island* Aleutian Islands, Alaska, USA
38 E17 **Rat Islands** *island group* Aleutian Islands, Alaska, USA
154 F10 **Ratlām** *prev.* Rutlam. Madhya Pradesh, C India
155 D15 **Ratnāgiri** Mahārāshtra, W India
155 K26 **Ratnapura** Sabaragamuwa Province, S Sri Lanka
116 J2 **Ratne** *Rus.* Ratno. Volyns'ka Oblast', NW Ukraine
Ratno *see* Ratne
Ratomka *see* Ratamka
37 U8 **Raton** New Mexico, SW USA
139 O7 **Ratqah, Wādī ar** *dry watercourse* W Iraq
Ratschach *see* Radeče
167 O16 **Rattaphum** Songkhla, SW Thailand
26 L6 **Rattlesnake Creek** ⤳ Kansas, C USA
94 L13 **Rättvik** Dalarna, C Sweden
100 K9 **Ratzeburg** Mecklenburg-Vorpommern, N Germany
100 K9 **Ratzeburger See** ◎ N Germany
10 J10 **Ratz, Mount** ▲ British Columbia, SW Canada
61 D22 **Rauch** Buenos Aires, E Argentina
41 U16 **Raudales** Chiapas, SE Mexico
Raudhatain *see* Ar Rawḍatayn
Raudnitz an der Elbe *see* Roudnice nad Labem
92 K1 **Raufarhöfn** Nordhurland Eystra, NE Iceland
94 H13 **Raufoss** Oppland, S Norway
Raukawa *see* Cook Strait
184 Q8 **Raukumara** ▲ North Island, NZ
192 K11 **Raukumara Plain** *undersea feature* N Coral Sea
184 P8 **Raukumara Range** ⛰ North Island, NZ
154 N11 **Rāulakela** *var.* Raurkela; *prev.* Rourkela. Orissa, E. India
95 F15 **Rauland** Telemark, S Norway
93 J19 **Rauma** *Swe.* Raumo. Länsi-Suomi, W Finland
94 F10 **Rauma** ⤳ S Norway
Raumo *see* Rauma
118 H8 **Rauna** Cēsis, C Latvia
169 T17 **Raung, Gunung** ▲ Jawa, S Indonesia
Raurkela *see* Rāulakela
95 J22 **Raus** Skåne, S Sweden
165 W3 **Rausu** Hokkaidō, NE Japan
165 W3 **Rausu-dake** ▲ Hokkaidō, NE Japan
93 M17 **Rautalampi** Itä-Suomi, C Finland
93 N16 **Rautavaara** Itä-Suomi, C Finland
116 M9 **Răutel** ⤳ C Moldova
93 O18 **Rautjärvi** Etelä-Suomi, S Finland
Rautu *see* Sosnovo
191 V11 **Ravahere** *atoll* Îles Tuamotu, C French Polynesia
107 J25 **Ravanusa** Sicilia, Italy, C Mediterranean Sea
143 S9 **Rāvar** Kermān, C Iran
147 Q11 **Ravat** Batkenskaya Oblast', SW Kyrgyzstan
18 K11 **Ravena** New York, NE USA
106 H10 **Ravenna** Emilia-Romagna, N Italy
29 O15 **Ravenna** Nebraska, C USA
31 U11 **Ravenna** Ohio, N USA
101 I24 **Ravensburg** Baden-Württemberg, S Germany
181 W4 **Ravenshoe** Queensland, NE Australia
180 K13 **Ravensthorpe** Western Australia
21 Q4 **Ravenswood** West Virginia, NE USA
149 U9 **Rāvi** ⤳ India/Pakistan
112 C9 **Ravna Gora** Primorje-Gorski Kotar, NW Croatia
109 U10 **Ravne na Koroškem** *Ger.* Gutenstein. N Slovenia
139 P6 **Rāwah** W Iraq
191 T4 **Rawaki** *prev.* Phoenix Island. *atoll* Phoenix Islands, C Kiribati
149 U6 **Rāwalpindi** Punjab, NE Pakistan
110 L13 **Rawa Mazowiecka** Łódzkie, C Poland
139 T2 **Rawāndiz** *var.* Rawandoz, Rawāndūz. N Iraq
Rawandoz/Rawāndūz *see* Rawāndiz
171 U12 **Rawas** Papua, E Indonesia
139 O4 **Rawḍah** ◎ E Syria
110 G13 **Rawicz** *Ger.* Rawitsch. Wielkopolskie, C Poland
Rawitsch *see* Rawicz
180 M11 **Rawlinna** Western Australia
33 W16 **Rawlins** Wyoming, C USA
63 K17 **Rawson** Chubut, SE Argentina
159 R16 **Rawu** Xizang Zizhiqu, W China
153 P12 **Raxaul** Bihār, N India
28 K3 **Ray** North Dakota, N USA
169 S11 **Raya, Bukit** ▲ Borneo, C Indonesia
155 I18 **Rāyachoti** Andhra Pradesh, E India
Rāyadrug *see* Rāyagarha
155 M14 **Rāyagarha** *prev.* Rāyadrug. Orissa, E India
138 H7 **Rayak** *var.* Rayaq, Riyāq. E Lebanon
Rayaq *see* Rayak
139 T2 **Rāyat** E Iraq
169 N12 **Raya, Tanjung** *headland* Pulau Bangka, W Indonesia
13 R13 **Ray, Cape** *headland* Newfoundland and Labrador, E Canada
123 Q13 **Raychikhinsk** Amurskaya Oblast', SE Russian Federation
127 U5 **Rayevskiy** Respublika Bashkortostan, W Russian Federation
11 Q17 **Raymond** Alberta, SW Canada
22 K6 **Raymond** Mississippi, S USA
32 F9 **Raymond** Washington, NW USA
183 T8 **Raymond Terrace** New South Wales, SE Australia
25 T17 **Raymondville** Texas, SW USA
11 U16 **Raymore** Saskatchewan, S Canada
39 Q8 **Ray Mountains** ⛰ Alaska, USA
22 H9 **Rayne** Louisiana, S USA
41 O12 **Rayón** San Luis Potosí, C Mexico
40 G4 **Rayón** Sonora, NW Mexico
167 P12 **Rayong** Rayong, S Thailand
25 T5 **Ray Roberts, Lake** ◎ Texas, SW USA
18 E15 **Raystown Lake** ▣ Pennsylvania, NE USA
141 V13 **Raysūt** SW Oman
27 R4 **Raytown** Missouri, C USA
22 I5 **Rayville** Louisiana, S USA
142 L5 **Razan** Hamadān, W Iran
139 S9 **Razāzah, Buḥayrat ar** *var.* Baḥr al Milḥ. ◎ C Iraq
114 L9 **Razboyna** ▲ E Bulgaria
Razdan *see* Hrazdan
Razdolnoye *see* Rozdol'ne
Razelm, Lacul *see* Razim, Lacul
139 U2 **Razga** E Iraq
114 L8 **Razgrad** Razgrad, N Bulgaria
114 L8 **Razgrad** ◈ *province* N Bulgaria
117 N13 **Razim, Lacul** *prev.* Lacul Razelm. *lagoon* NW Black Sea
114 G11 **Razlog** Blagoevgrad, SW Bulgaria
118 K10 **Rāznas Ezers** ◎ SE Latvia
102 E6 **Raz, Pointe du** *headland* NW France
Reachlainn *see* Rathlin Island
Reachrainn *see* Lambay Island
97 N22 **Reading** S England, UK
18 H15 **Reading** Pennsylvania, NE USA
48 C7 **Real, Cordillera** ⛰ C Ecuador
62 K12 **Realicó** La Pampa, C Argentina
25 R15 **Realitos** Texas, SW USA
108 G9 **Realp** Uri, C Switzerland
167 Q12 **Reăng Kesei** Bătdâmbâng, W Cambodia
191 Y11 **Reao** *atoll* Îles Tuamotu, E French Polynesia
Reate *see* Rieti
180 L11 **Rebecca, Lake** ◎ Western Australia
Rebiana Sand Sea *see* Rabyānah, Ramlat
124 H8 **Reboly** Respublika Kareliya, NW Russian Federation
165 S1 **Rebun** Rebun-tō, NE Japan
165 S1 **Rebun-tō** *island* NE Japan
106 J12 **Recanati** Marche, C Italy
Rechitsa *see* Rechytsa
109 Y7 **Rechnitz** Burgenland, SE Austria
119 J20 **Rechytsa** *Rus.* Rechitsa. Brestskaya Voblasts', SW Belarus
119 O19 **Rechytsa** *Rus.* Rechitsa. Homyel'skaya Voblasts', SE Belarus
59 Q15 **Recife** *prev.* Pernambuco. *state capital* Pernambuco, E Brazil
83 I26 **Recife, Cape** *Afr.* Kaap Recife. *headland* S South Africa
Recife, Kaap *see* Recife, Cape
172 I16 **Récifs, Îles aux** *island* Inner Islands, NE Seychelles
101 E14 **Recklinghausen** Nordrhein-Westfalen, W Germany
100 M8 **Recknitz** ⤳ NE Germany
99 K23 **Recogne** Luxembourg, SE Belgium
61 C15 **Reconquista** Santa Fe, C Argentina
195 O6 **Recovery Glacier** *glacier* Antarctica
59 G15 **Recreio** Mato Grosso, W Brazil
27 X9 **Rector** Arkansas, C USA
110 E9 **Recz** *Ger.* Reetz Neumark. Zachodnio-pomorskie, NW Poland
99 L24 **Redange** *var.* Redange-sur-Attert. Diekirch, W Luxembourg

◆ Country ● Country Capital ◇ Dependent Territory ○ Dependent Territory Capital ◈ Administrative Region ✕ International Airport ▲ Mountain ⛰ Mountain Range 🌋 Volcano ⤳ River ◎ Lake ▣ Reservoir

Redange-sur-Attert see Redange
18 C13 **Redbank Creek** ≈ Pennsylvania, NE USA
13 S9 **Red Bay** Quebec, E Canada
23 N2 **Red Bay** Alabama, S USA
35 N4 **Red Bluff** California, W USA
24 J8 **Red Bluff Reservoir** ◎ New Mexico/Texas, SW USA
30 K16 **Red Bud** Illinois, N USA
30 J5 **Red Cedar River** ≈ Wisconsin, N USA
11 R17 **Redcliff** Alberta, SW Canada
83 K17 **Redcliff** Midlands, C Zimbabwe
182 L9 **Red Cliffs** Victoria, SE Australia
29 P17 **Red Cloud** Nebraska, C USA
22 L8 **Red Creek** ≈ Mississippi, S USA
11 P15 **Red Deer** Alberta, SW Canada
11 Q16 **Red Deer** ≈ Alberta, SW Canada
39 O11 **Red Devil** Alaska, USA
35 N3 **Redding** California, W USA
97 L20 **Redditch** W England, UK
29 P9 **Redfield** South Dakota, N USA
24 J12 **Redford** Texas, SW USA
45 V13 **Redhead** Trinidad, Trinidad and Tobago
182 I8 **Red Hill** South Australia
Red Hill see Pu'u 'Ula'ula
26 K7 **Red Hills** hill range Kansas, C USA
13 T12 **Red Indian Lake** ◎ Newfoundland and Labrador, E Canada
124 J16 **Redkino** Tverskaya Oblast', W Russian Federation
12 A10 **Red Lake** Ontario, C Canada
36 I10 **Red Lake** salt flat Arizona, SW USA
29 S4 **Red Lake Falls** Minnesota, N USA
29 R4 **Red Lake River** ≈ Minnesota, N USA
35 U15 **Redlands** California, W USA
18 G16 **Red Lion** Pennsylvania, NE USA
33 U11 **Red Lodge** Montana, NW USA
32 H13 **Redmond** Oregon, NW USA
36 L5 **Redmond** Utah, W USA
32 H8 **Redmond** Washington, NW USA
Rednitz see Regnitz
29 T15 **Red Oak** Iowa, C USA
18 K12 **Red Oaks Mill** New York, NE USA
102 I7 **Redon** Ille-et-Vilaine, NW France
45 W10 **Redonda** island SW Antigua and Barbuda
104 G4 **Redondela** Galicia, NW Spain
104 H11 **Redondo** Évora, S Portugal
39 Q12 **Redoubt Volcano** ▲ Alaska, USA
11 Y16 **Red River** ≈ Canada/USA
131 U12 **Red River** var. Yuan, Chin. Yuan Jiang, Vtn. Sông Hông Hà. ≈ China/Vietnam
25 W4 **Red River** ≈ S USA
22 H7 **Red River** ≈ Louisiana, S USA
30 M6 **Red River** ≈ Wisconsin, N USA
Red Rock, Lake see Red Rock Reservoir
29 W14 **Red Rock Reservoir** var. Lake Red Rock. ⊡ Iowa, C USA
80 H7 **Red Sea** ◈ state NE Sudan
75 Y9 **Red Sea** anc. Sinus Arabicus. sea Africa/Asia
21 T11 **Red Springs** North Carolina, SE USA
8 I9 **Redstone** ≈ Northwest Territories, NW Canada
11 V17 **Redvers** Saskatchewan, S Canada
77 P13 **Red Volta** var. Nazinon, Fr. Volta Rouge. ≈ Burkina/Ghana
11 Q14 **Redwater** Alberta, SW Canada
28 M16 **Red Willow Creek** ≈ Nebraska, C USA
29 W9 **Red Wing** Minnesota, N USA
35 N9 **Redwood City** California, W USA
29 T9 **Redwood Falls** Minnesota, N USA
31 P7 **Reed City** Michigan, N USA
28 K6 **Reeder** North Dakota, N USA
35 R11 **Reedley** California, W USA
33 T11 **Reedpoint** Montana, NW USA
30 K8 **Reedsburg** Wisconsin, N USA
32 E13 **Reedsport** Oregon, NW USA
187 Q9 **Reef Islands** island group Santa Cruz Islands, E Solomon Islands
185 H16 **Reefton** West Coast, South Island, NZ
20 F8 **Reelfoot Lake** ◎ Tennessee, S USA
97 D17 **Ree, Lough** Ir. Loch Rí. ◎ C Ireland
Reengus see Rīngas
35 U4 **Reese River** ≈ Nevada, W USA
98 M8 **Reest** ≈ E Netherlands
Reetz Neumark see Recz
Reevhtse see Rossvatnet
137 N13 **Refahiye** Erzincan, C Turkey
23 N4 **Reform** Alabama, S USA
95 K20 **Reftele** Jönköping, S Sweden
25 T14 **Refugio** Texas, SW USA
110 E8 **Rega** ≈ NW Poland
Regar see Tursunzoda
101 O21 **Regen** Bayern, SE Germany
101 M20 **Regen** ≈ SE Germany
101 M21 **Regensburg** Eng. Ratisbon, Fr. Ratisbonne; hist. Ratisbona, anc. Castra Regina, Reginum. Bayern, SE Germany
101 M21 **Regenstauf** Bayern, SE Germany
74 I10 **Reggane** C Algeria
98 N9 **Regge** ≈ E Netherlands
Reggio see Reggio nell' Emilia
Reggio Calabria see Reggio di Calabria
107 M23 **Reggio di Calabria** var. Reggio Calabria, Gk. Rhegion; anc. Regium, Rhegium. Calabria, SW Italy
Reggio Emilia see Reggio nell' Emilia
106 F9 **Reggio nell' Emilia** var. Reggio Emilia, abbrev. Reggio; anc. Regium Lepidum. Emilia-Romagna, N Italy
116 I10 **Reghin** Ger. Sächsisch-Reen, Hung. Szászrégen; prev. Reghinul Săsesc, Ger. Sächsisch-Regen. Mureș, C Romania
Reghinul Săsesc see Reghin
11 U16 **Regina** Saskatchewan, S Canada
11 U16 **Regina** × Saskatchewan, S Canada
55 Z10 **Régina** E French Guiana
11 U16 **Regina Beach** Saskatchewan, S Canada
Reginum see Regensburg
Registan see Rīgestān
60 L11 **Registro** São Paulo, S Brazil
Regium see Reggio di Calabria
Regium Lepidum see Reggio nell' Emilia
101 K19 **Regnitz** var. Rednitz. ≈ SE Germany
40 K10 **Regocijo** Durango, W Mexico
104 H12 **Reguengos de Monsaraz** Évora, S Portugal
101 M18 **Rehau** Bayern, E Germany
83 D19 **Rehoboth** Hardap, C Namibia
Rehoboth/Rehovoth see Reḥovot
21 Z4 **Rehoboth Beach** Delaware, NE USA
138 F10 **Reḥovot** var. Rehoboth, Rekhovot, Rehovoth. Central, C Israel
81 J20 **Rei** spring/well S Kenya
Reichenau see Rychnov nad Kněžnou, Czech Republic
Reichenau see Bogatynia, Poland
101 M17 **Reichenbach** var. Reichenbach im Vogtland. Sachsen, E Germany
Reichenbach see Dzierżoniów
Reichenbach im Vogtland see Reichenbach
Reichenberg see Liberec
181 O11 **Reid** Western Australia
23 V6 **Reidsville** Georgia, SE USA
21 T8 **Reidsville** North Carolina, SE USA
Reifnitz see Ribnica
97 O22 **Reigate** SE England, UK
Reikjavik see Reykjavík
102 I10 **Ré, Île de** island W France
37 N15 **Reiley Peak** ▲ Arizona, SW USA
103 Q4 **Reims** Eng. Rheims; anc. Durocortorum, Remi. Marne, N France
63 G23 **Reina Adelaida, Archipiélago** island group S Chile
45 O16 **Reina Beatrix** × (Oranjestad) C Aruba
108 F7 **Reinach** Aargau, W Switzerland
108 E6 **Reinach** Basel-Land, NW Switzerland
64 O11 **Reina Sofía** × (Tenerife) Tenerife, Islas Canarias, Spain, NE Atlantic Ocean
29 W13 **Reinbeck** Iowa, C USA
100 J10 **Reinbek** Schleswig-Holstein, N Germany
11 U12 **Reindeer** ≈ Saskatchewan, C Canada
11 U11 **Reindeer Lake** ◎ Manitoba/Saskatchewan, C Canada
Reine-Charlotte, Îles de la see Queen Charlotte Islands
Reine-Élisabeth, Îles de la see Queen Elizabeth Islands
94 F13 **Reineskarvet** ▲ S Norway
184 H1 **Reinga, Cape** headland North Island, NZ
105 N3 **Reinosa** Cantabria, N Spain
109 R8 **Reisseck** ▲ S Austria
21 W3 **Reisterstown** Maryland, NE USA
Reisui see Yŏsu
98 N5 **Reitdiep** ≈ NE Netherlands
191 V10 **Reitoru** atoll Îles Tuamotu, C French Polynesia
95 M17 **Rejmyre** Östergötland, S Sweden
Reka see Rijeka
Reka Ili see Ile/Ili He
95 N16 **Rekarne** Västmanland, C Sweden 16.04
Rekhovot see Reḥovot
8 K9 **Reliance** Northwest Territories, C Canada
33 U16 **Reliance** Wyoming, C USA
74 I5 **Relizane** var. Ghelîzâne, Ghilizane. NW Algeria
182 I7 **Remarkable, Mount** ▲ South Australia
54 E8 **Remedios** Antioquia, N Colombia
43 Q16 **Remedios** Veraguas, W Panama
42 D8 **Remedios, Punta** headland SW El Salvador
Remi see Reims
99 N25 **Remich** Grevenmacher, SE Luxembourg
99 J19 **Remicourt** Liège, E Belgium
14 H8 **Rémigny, Lac** ◎ Québec, SE Canada
55 Z10 **Rémire** NE French Guiana
127 N13 **Remontnoye** Rostovskaya Oblast', SW Russian Federation
171 U14 **Remoon** Pulau Kur, E Indonesia
99 L20 **Remouchamps** Liège, E Belgium
103 R15 **Remoulins** Gard, S France
173 X16 **Rempart, Mont du** var. Mount Rempart. hill W Mauritius
101 E15 **Remscheid** Nordrhein-Westfalen, W Germany
29 S12 **Remsen** Iowa, C USA
94 I12 **Rena** Hedmark, S Norway
94 I11 **Renåa** ≈ S Norway
Renaix see Ronse
118 H7 **Rencēni** Valmiera, N Latvia
118 D9 **Renda** Kuldīga, W Latvia
107 N20 **Rende** Calabria, SW Italy
99 K21 **Rendeux** Luxembourg, SE Belgium
Rendina see Rentína
30 L16 **Rend Lake** ⊡ Illinois, N USA
186 K9 **Rendova** island New Georgia Islands, NW Solomon Islands
100 I8 **Rendsburg** Schleswig-Holstein, N Germany
108 B9 **Renens** Vaud, SW Switzerland
14 K12 **Renfrew** Ontario, SE Canada
96 I12 **Renfrew** cultural region SW Scotland, UK
168 L11 **Rengat** Sumatera, W Indonesia
153 W12 **Rengma Hills** ▲▲ NE India
62 H12 **Rengo** Libertador, C Chile
116 M12 **Reni** Odes'ka Oblast', SW Ukraine
80 F11 **Renk** Upper Nile, E Sudan
93 L19 **Renko** Etelä-Suomi, S Finland
98 L12 **Renkum** Gelderland, SE Netherlands
182 K9 **Renmark** South Australia
186 L10 **Rennell** var. Mu Nggava. island S Solomon Islands
181 Q4 **Renner Springs Roadhouse** Northern Territory, N Australia
102 I6 **Rennes** Bret. Roazon; anc. Condate. Ille-et-Vilaine, NW France
195 S16 **Rennick Glacier** glacier Antarctica
11 Y16 **Rennie** Manitoba, S Canada
35 Q5 **Reno** Nevada, W USA
106 H10 **Reno** ≈ N Italy
35 Q5 **Reno-Cannon** × Nevada, W USA
83 F24 **Renoster** ≈ SW South Africa
15 T5 **Renouard, Lac** ◎ Québec, SE Canada
18 F13 **Renovo** Pennsylvania, NE USA
161 O3 **Renqiu** Hebei, E China
160 I9 **Renshou** Sichuan, C China
31 N12 **Rensselaer** Indiana, N USA
18 L11 **Rensselaer** New York, NE USA
105 Q2 **Rentería** Basq. Errenteria. País Vasco, N Spain
115 E17 **Rentína** var. Rendina. Thessalía, C Greece
29 T9 **Renville** Minnesota, N USA
77 O13 **Réo** W Burkina
15 O12 **Repentigny** Québec, SE Canada
146 K13 **Repetek** Lebap Welaýaty, E Turkmenistan
93 J16 **Replot** Fin. Raippaluoto. island W Finland
Reppen see Rzepin
Reps see Rupea
27 T7 **Republic** Missouri, C USA
32 K7 **Republic** Washington, NW USA
27 N3 **Republican River** ≈ Kansas/Nebraska, C USA
9 O7 **Repulse Bay** Northwest Territories, N Canada
56 F9 **Requena** Loreto, NE Peru
105 R10 **Requena** País Valenciano, E Spain
103 O14 **Réquista** Aveyron, S France
136 M12 **Reşadiye** Tokat, N Turkey
Reschenpass see Resia, Passo di
Reschitza see Reşiţa
113 N20 **Resen** Turk. Resne. SW FYR Macedonia
60 J11 **Reserva** Paraná, S Brazil
11 V15 **Reserve** Saskatchewan, S Canada
37 P13 **Reserve** New Mexico, SW USA
Reshetilovka see Reshetylivka
117 S6 **Reshetylivka** Rus. Reshetilovka. Poltavs'ka Oblast', NE Ukraine
Resht see Rasht
106 F5 **Resia, Passo di** Ger. Reschenpass. pass Austria/Italy
Resicabánya see Reşiţa
62 N7 **Resistencia** Chaco, NE Argentina
116 F12 **Reşiţa** Ger. Reschitza, Hung. Resicabánya. Caraş-Severin, W Romania
Resne see Resen
8 K4 **Resolute** var. Qausuittuq. Nunavut, N Canada
Resolution see Fort Resolution
9 T7 **Resolution Island** island Nunavut, NE Canada
185 A23 **Resolution Island** island SW NZ
15 W7 **Restigouche** Québec, SE Canada
11 W17 **Reston** Manitoba, S Canada
14 H11 **Restoule Lake** ◎ Ontario, S Canada
54 F10 **Restrepo** Meta, C Colombia
42 B6 **Retalhuleu** Retalhuleu, SW Guatemala
42 A1 **Retalhuleu** off. Departamento de Retalhuleu. ◈ department SW Guatemala
97 N18 **Retford** C England, UK
103 Q3 **Rethel** Ardennes, N France
Rethimno/Réthimnon see Réthymno
115 I25 **Réthymno** var. Rethimno; prev. Réthimnon. Kríti, Greece, E Mediterranean Sea
Retiche, Alpi see Rhaetian Alps
99 J16 **Retie** Antwerpen, N Belgium
111 J21 **Rétság** Nógrád, N Hungary
109 W2 **Retz** Niederösterreich, NE Austria
173 N15 **Réunion** off. La Réunion. ◇ French overseas department W Indian Ocean
130 L17 **Réunion** island W Indian Ocean
105 U6 **Reus** Cataluña, E Spain
99 J15 **Reusel** Noord-Brabant, S Netherlands
108 F7 **Reuss** ≈ NW Switzerland
Reuţel see Ciuhuru
101 H22 **Reutlingen** Baden-Württemberg, S Germany
108 L7 **Reutte** Tirol, W Austria
99 M16 **Reuver** Limburg, SE Netherlands
28 K7 **Reva** South Dakota, N USA
Reval/Revel' see Tallinn
124 J4 **Revda** Murmanskaya Oblast', NW Russian Federation
122 F6 **Revda** Sverdlovskaya Oblast', C Russian Federation
103 N16 **Revel** Haute-Garonne, S France
11 O16 **Revelstoke** British Columbia, SW Canada
43 N13 **Reventazón, Río** ≈ E Costa Rica
106 G9 **Revere** Lombardia, N Italy
39 Y14 **Revillagigedo Island** island Alexander Archipelago, Alaska, USA
103 R3 **Revin** Ardennes, N France
92 O3 **Revnosa** headland C Svalbard
Revolyutsii, Pik see Revolyutsiya, Qullai
147 T13 **Revolyutsiya, Qullai** Rus. Pik Revolyutsii. ▲ SE Tajikistan
111 L19 **Revúca** Ger. Grossrauschenbach, Hung. Nagyrőce. Banskobystrický Kraj, C Slovakia
154 K9 **Rewa** Madhya Pradesh, C India
152 I11 **Rewāri** Haryāna, N India
33 R14 **Rexburg** Idaho, NW USA
78 G13 **Rey Bouba** Nord, NE Cameroon
92 L3 **Reydharfjördhur** Austurland, E Iceland
57 K16 **Reyes** Beni, NW Bolivia
34 L8 **Reyes, Point** headland California, W USA
54 B12 **Reyes, Punta** headland SW Colombia
136 L17 **Reyhanlı** Hatay, S Turkey
43 U16 **Rey, Isla del** island Archipiélago de las Perlas, SE Panama
92 H2 **Reykhólar** Vestfirdhir, W Iceland
92 K2 **Reykjahlídh** Nordhurland Eystra, NE Iceland
92 I4 **Reykjanes** ◈ region SW Iceland
197 O16 **Reykjanes Basin** var. Irminger Basin. undersea feature N Atlantic Ocean
197 N17 **Reykjanes Ridge** undersea feature N Atlantic Ocean
92 H4 **Reykjavík** var. Reikjavik. ● (Iceland) Höfudhborgarsvaedhi, W Iceland
18 D13 **Reynoldsville** Pennsylvania, NE USA
41 P8 **Reynosa** Tamaulipas, C Mexico
Reẓā'īyeh see Orūmīyeh
Reẓā'īyeh, Daryācheh-ye see Orūmīyeh, Daryācheh-ye
102 I8 **Rezé** Loire-Atlantique, NW France
118 K10 **Rēzekne** Ger. Rositten; prev. Rus. Rezhitsa. Rēzekne, SE Latvia
Rezhitsa see Rēzekne
117 N9 **Rezina** NE Moldova
114 N11 **Rezovo** Turk. Rezve. Burgas, E Bulgaria
114 N11 **Rezovska Reka** Turk. Rezve Deresi. ≈ Bulgaria/Turkey see also Rezve Deresi
Rezve see Rezovo
114 N11 **Rezve Deresi** Bul. Rezovska Reka. ≈ Bulgaria/Turkey see also Rezovska Reka
Rhadames see Ghadāmis
Rhaedestus see Tekirdağ
108 J10 **Rhaetian Alps** Fr. Alpes Rhétiques, Ger. Rätische Alpen, It. Alpi Retiche. ▲▲ C Europe
108 I9 **Rhätikon** ▲▲ C Europe
101 G14 **Rheda-Wiedenbrück** Nordrhein-Westfalen, W Germany
98 M12 **Rheden** Gelderland, E Netherlands
Rhegion/Rhegium see Reggio di Calabria
Rheims see Reims
Rhein see Rhine
101 E17 **Rheinbach** Nordrhein-Westfalen, W Germany
100 F13 **Rheine** var. Rheine in Westfalen. Nordrhein-Westfalen, NW Germany
Rheine in Westfalen see Rheine
Rheinfeld see Rheinfelden
101 F24 **Rheinfelden** Baden-Württemberg, S Germany
108 E6 **Rheinfelden** var. Rheinfeld. Aargau, N Switzerland
101 E17 **Rheinisches Schiefergebirge** var. Rhine State Uplands, Eng. Rhenish Slate Mountains. ▲▲ W Germany
101 D18 **Rheinland-Pfalz** Eng. Rhineland-Palatinate, Fr. Rhénanie-Palatinat. ◈ state W Germany
101 G18 **Rhein/Main** × (Frankfurt am Main) Hessen, W Germany
Rhénanie du Nord-Westphalie see Nordrhein-Westfalen
Rhénanie-Palatinat see Rheinland-Pfalz
98 K12 **Rhenen** Utrecht, C Netherlands
Rhenish Slate Mountains see Rheinisches Schiefergebirge
Rhétiques, Alpes see Rhaetian Alps
100 N10 **Rhin** ≈ NE Germany
Rhin see Rhine
84 F10 **Rhine** Dut. Rijn, Fr. Rhin, Ger. Rhein. ≈ W Europe
30 L5 **Rhinelander** Wisconsin, N USA
Rhineland-Palatinate see Rheinland-Pfalz
Rhine State Uplands see Rheinisches Schiefergebirge
100 N11 **Rhinkanal** canal NE Germany
81 F17 **Rhino Camp** NW Uganda
74 D7 **Rhir, Cap** headland W Morocco
106 D7 **Rho** Lombardia, N Italy
19 N12 **Rhode Island** off. State of Rhode Island and Providence Plantations; also known as Little Rhody, Ocean State. ◈ state NE USA
19 O13 **Rhode Island** island Rhode Island, NE USA
19 O13 **Rhode Island Sound** sound Maine/Rhode Island, NE USA
Rhodes see Ródos
Rhode-Saint-Genèse see Sint-Genesius-Rode
84 L14 **Rhodes Basin** undersea feature E Mediterranean Sea
Rhodesia see Zimbabwe
114 I12 **Rhodope Mountains** var. Rodhópi Óri, Bul. Rhodope Planina, Rodopi, Gk. Orosirá Rodhópis, Turk. Dospad Dagh. ▲▲ Bulgaria/Greece
Rhodope Planina see Rhodope Mountains
Rhodos see Ródos
101 I18 **Rhön** ▲▲ C Germany
103 Q10 **Rhône** ◈ department E France
86 C12 **Rhône** ≈ France/Switzerland
103 R12 **Rhône-Alpes** ◈ region E France
98 G13 **Rhoon** Zuid-Holland, SW Netherlands
96 G9 **Rhum** var. Rum. island W Scotland, UK
Rhuthun see Ruthin
97 J18 **Rhyl** NE Wales, UK
59 K18 **Rialma** Goiás, S Brazil
104 L3 **Riaño** Castilla-León, N Spain
105 O9 **Riansáres** ≈ C Spain
152 H6 **Riāsi** Jammu and Kashmir, NW India
168 K10 **Riau** off. Propinsi Riau. ◈ province W Indonesia
Riau Archipelago see Riau, Kepulauan
168 M11 **Riau, Kepulauan** var. Riau Archipelago, Dut. Riouw-Archipel. island group W Indonesia
105 O6 **Riaza** Castilla-León, N Spain
105 N6 **Riaza** ≈ N Spain
81 K17 **Riba** spring/well NE Kenya
104 H4 **Ribadavia** Galicia, NW Spain
104 J2 **Ribadeo** Galicia, NW Spain
104 L2 **Ribadesella** Asturias, N Spain
104 G10 **Ribatejo** former province C Portugal
83 P15 **Ribáuè** Nampula, N Mozambique
97 K17 **Ribble** ≈ NW England, UK
95 F23 **Ribe** Ribe, W Denmark
95 F23 **Ribe** off. Ribe Amt, var. Ripen. ◈ county W Denmark
104 G3 **Ribeira** Galicia, NW Spain
64 O5 **Ribeira Brava** Madeira, Portugal, NE Atlantic Ocean
64 P3 **Ribeira Grande** São Miguel, Azores, Portugal, NE Atlantic Ocean
60 L8 **Ribeirão Preto** São Paulo, S Brazil
60 L11 **Ribeira, Rio** ≈ S Brazil
107 I24 **Ribera** Sicilia, Italy, C Mediterranean Sea
57 L14 **Riberalta** Beni, N Bolivia
105 W4 **Ribes de Freser** Cataluña, NE Spain
30 L6 **Rib Mountain** ▲ Wisconsin, N USA
109 U12 **Ribnica** Ger. Reifnitz. S Slovenia
117 N9 **Rîbniţa** var. Râbniţa, Rus. Rybnitsa. NE Moldova
100 M8 **Ribnitz-Damgarten** Mecklenburg-Vorpommern, NE Germany
111 D16 **Říčany** Ger. Ritschan. Středočeský Kraj, W Czech Republic
29 U7 **Rice** Minnesota, N USA
30 J5 **Rice Lake** Wisconsin, N USA
14 I15 **Rice Lake** ◎ Ontario, SE Canada
14 E8 **Rice Lake** ◎ Ontario, S Canada
23 V3 **Richard B.Russell Lake** ⊡ Georgia, SE USA
25 U6 **Richardson** Texas, SW USA
11 R11 **Richardson** ≈ Alberta, C Canada
10 I3 **Richardson Mountains** ▲▲ Yukon Territory, NW Canada
185 C21 **Richardson Mountains** ▲▲ South Island, NZ
42 F3 **Richardson Peak** ▲ SE Belize
76 G10 **Richard Toll** N Senegal
28 L5 **Richardton** North Dakota, N USA
14 F13 **Rich, Cape** headland Ontario, S Canada
102 L8 **Richelieu** Indre-et-Loire, C France
33 P15 **Richfield** Idaho, NW USA
36 K5 **Richfield** Utah, W USA
18 J10 **Richfield Springs** New York, NE USA
18 M6 **Richford** Vermont, NE USA
27 R6 **Rich Hill** Missouri, C USA
13 P14 **Richibucto** New Brunswick, SE Canada
108 G8 **Richisau** Glarus, NE Switzerland
23 S6 **Richland** Georgia, SE USA
27 U6 **Richland** Missouri, C USA
25 U8 **Richland** Texas, SW USA
32 K10 **Richland** Washington, NW USA
30 K8 **Richland Center** Wisconsin, N USA
21 W11 **Richlands** North Carolina, SE USA
21 Q7 **Richlands** Virginia, NE USA
25 R9 **Richland Springs** Texas, SW USA
183 S8 **Richmond** New South Wales, SE Australia
10 L17 **Richmond** British Columbia, SW Canada
14 L13 **Richmond** Ontario, SE Canada
15 Q12 **Richmond** Québec, SE Canada
185 I14 **Richmond** Tasman, South Island, NZ
35 N8 **Richmond** California, W USA
31 Q14 **Richmond** Indiana, N USA
20 M6 **Richmond** Kentucky, S USA
27 S4 **Richmond** Missouri, C USA
25 V11 **Richmond** Texas, SW USA
36 L1 **Richmond** Utah, W USA
21 W6 **Richmond** state capital Virginia, NE USA
14 H15 **Richmond Hill** Ontario, S Canada
185 J15 **Richmond Range** ▲ South Island, NZ
27 S12 **Rich Mountain** ▲ Arkansas, C USA
31 S13 **Richwood** Ohio, N USA
21 R5 **Richwood** West Virginia, NE USA
104 K5 **Ricobayo, Embalse de** ⊡ NW Spain
Ricomagus see Riom
Ridā' see Radā'
98 H13 **Ridderkerk** Zuid-Holland, SW Netherlands
33 N16 **Riddle** Idaho, NW USA
32 F14 **Riddle** Oregon, NW USA
14 L13 **Rideau** ≈ Ontario, SE Canada
35 T12 **Ridgecrest** California, W USA
18 L13 **Ridgefield** Connecticut, NE USA
22 K5 **Ridgeland** Mississippi, S USA
21 R15 **Ridgeland** South Carolina, SE USA
20 F8 **Ridgely** Tennessee, S USA
14 D17 **Ridgetown** Ontario, S Canada
Ridgeway see Ridgway
21 R12 **Ridgeway** South Carolina, SE USA
18 D13 **Ridgway** var. Ridgeway. Pennsylvania, NE USA
11 W16 **Riding Mountain** ▲▲ Manitoba, S Canada
Ried see Ried im Innkreis
109 R4 **Ried im Innkreis** var. Ried. Oberösterreich, NW Austria
109 X8 **Riegersburg** Steiermark, SE Austria
108 E6 **Riehen** Basel-Stadt, NW Switzerland
92 J9 **Riehppegáisá** var. Rieppe. ▲ N Norway
99 K18 **Riemst** Limburg, NE Belgium
Rieppe see Riehppegáisá
101 O15 **Riesa** Sachsen, E Germany
63 H24 **Riesco, Isla** island S Chile
107 K25 **Riesi** Sicilia, Italy, C Mediterranean Sea
83 F25 **Riet** ≈ SW South Africa
83 I23 **Riet** ≈ SW South Africa
118 D11 **Rietavas** Telšiai, W Lithuania
83 F19 **Rietfontein** Omaheke, E Namibia
107 I14 **Rieti** anc. Reate. Lazio, C Italy
84 D14 **Rif** var. Er Rif, Er Riff, Riff. ▲▲ N Morocco
Riff see Rif
37 Q4 **Rifle** Colorado, C USA
31 R7 **Rifle River** ≈ Michigan, N USA
81 H18 **Rift Valley** ◈ province Kenya
Rift Valley see Great Rift Valley
118 F9 **Riga** Eng. Riga. ● (Latvia) Riga, C Latvia
Rigaer Bucht see Riga, Gulf of
118 F6 **Riga, Gulf of** Est. Liivi Laht, Ger. Rigaer Bucht, Latv. Rīgas Jūras Līcis, Rus. Rizhskiy Zaliv; prev. Est. Riia Laht. gulf Estonia/Latvia
143 U12 **Rīgān** Kermān, SE Iran
Rīgas Jūras Līcis see Riga, Gulf of
15 N12 **Rigaud** ≈ Ontario/Québec, SE Canada
33 R14 **Rigby** Idaho, NW USA
148 M10 **Rīgestān** var. Registan. desert region S Afghanistan
32 M11 **Riggins** Idaho, NW USA
13 R8 **Rigolet** Newfoundland and Labrador, NE Canada
78 G9 **Rig-Rig** Kanem, W Chad
118 F4 **Riguldi** Läänemaa, W Estonia
Riia Laht see Riga, Gulf of
93 L19 **Riihimäki** Etelä-Suomi, S Finland
195 O2 **Riiser-Larsen Ice Shelf** ice shelf Antarctica
195 U2 **Riiser-Larsen Peninsula** peninsula Antarctica
65 P22 **Riiser-Larsen Sea** sea Antarctica
40 D2 **Riíto** Sonora, NW Mexico
112 B9 **Rijeka** Ger. Sankt Veit am Flaum, It. Fiume, Slvn. Reka; anc. Tarsatica. Primorje-Gorski Kotar, NW Croatia
99 I14 **Rijen** Noord-Brabant, S Netherlands
99 H15 **Rijkevorsel** Antwerpen, N Belgium
Rijn see Rhine
98 G11 **Rijnsburg** Zuid-Holland, W Netherlands
Rijssel see Lille
98 N10 **Rijssen** Overijssel, E Netherlands
98 G12 **Rijswijk** Eng. Ryswick. Zuid-Holland, W Netherlands
92 I10 **Riksgränsen** Norrbotten, N Sweden
165 U4 **Rikubetsu** Hokkaidō, NE Japan
165 R9 **Rikuzen-Takata** Iwate, Honshū, C Japan
27 O4 **Riley** Kansas, C USA
99 I17 **Rillaar** Vlaams Brabant, C Belgium
Rí, Loch see Ree, Lough
114 G11 **Rilska Reka** ≈ W Bulgaria
77 T12 **Rima** ≈ N Nigeria
141 N7 **Rimah, Wādī ar** var. Wādī ar Rummah. dry watercourse C Saudi Arabia
Rimaszombat see Rimavská Sobota

◆ Country ● Country Capital ◇ Dependent Territory ○ Dependent Territory Capital ◈ Administrative Region × International Airport ▲ Mountain ▲▲ Mountain Range Volcano ≈ River ◎ Lake ⊡ Reservoir

191 R12 **Rimatara** island Îles Australes, SW French Polynesia
111 L20 **Rimavská Sobota** Ger. Gross-Steffelsdorf, Hung. Rimaszombat. Banskobystrický Kraj, C Slovakia
11 Q15 **Rimbey** Alberta, SW Canada
95 P15 **Rimbo** Stockholm, C Sweden
95 M18 **Rimforsa** Östergötland, S Sweden
106 I11 **Rimini** anc. Ariminum. Emilia-Romagna, N Italy
Rîmnicu-Sărat see Râmnicu Sărat
Rîmnicu Vîlcea see Râmnicu Vâlcea
149 Y3 **Rimo Muztāgh** ▲▲ India/Pakistan
15 U7 **Rimouski** Québec, SE Canada
158 M16 **Rinbung** Xizang Zizhiqu, W China
162 I5 **Rinchinlhümbe** Hövsgöl, N Mongolia
62 I5 **Rincón, Cerro** ▲ N Chile
104 M15 **Rincón de la Victoria** Andalucía, S Spain
Rincón del Bonete, Lago Artificial de see Río Negro, Embalse del
105 Q4 **Rincón de Soto** La Rioja, N Spain
94 G8 **Rindal** Møre og Romsdal, S Norway
115 J20 **Ríneia** island Kykládes, Greece, Aegean Sea
152 H11 **Rīngas** prev. Reengus, Rīngus. Rājasthān, N India
95 H24 **Ringe** Fyn, C Denmark
94 H11 **Ringebu** Oppland, S Norway
Ringen see Rõngu
186 K8 **Ringgi** Kolombangara, NW Solomon Islands
23 R1 **Ringgold** Georgia, SE USA
22 G5 **Ringgold** Louisiana, S USA
25 S5 **Ringgold** Texas, SW USA
95 E22 **Ringkøbing** Ringkøbing, W Denmark
95 E21 **Ringkøbing** off. Ringkøbing Amt. ◈ county W Denmark
95 E22 **Ringkøbing Fjord** fjord W Denmark
33 S10 **Ringling** Montana, NW USA
27 N13 **Ringling** Oklahoma, C USA
94 H13 **Ringsaker** Hedmark, S Norway
95 I23 **Ringsted** Vestsjælland, E Denmark
Ringus see Rīngas
92 I9 **Ringvassøya** Lapp. Ráneš. island N Norway
18 K13 **Ringwood** New Jersey, NE USA
Rinn Duáin see Hook Head
100 H13 **Rinteln** Niedersachsen, NW Germany
Rio see Rio de Janeiro
115 E18 **Río** Dytikí Ellás, S Greece
56 C7 **Riobamba** Chimborazo, C Ecuador
60 P9 **Rio Bonito** Rio de Janeiro, SE Brazil
59 C16 **Rio Branco** state capital Acre, W Brazil
61 H18 **Río Branco** Cerro Largo, NE Uruguay
Rio Branco, Território de see Roraima
41 P8 **Río Bravo** Tamaulipas, C Mexico
63 G16 **Río Bueno** Los Lagos, C Chile
55 P5 **Río Caribe** Sucre, NE Venezuela
54 M5 **Río Chico** Miranda, N Venezuela
63 H18 **Río Cisnes** Aisén, S Chile
60 L9 **Rio Claro** São Paulo, S Brazil
45 V14 **Rio Claro** Trinidad, Trinidad and Tobago
54 J5 **Río Claro** Lara, N Venezuela
63 K15 **Río Colorado** Río Negro, E Argentina
62 K11 **Río Cuarto** Córdoba, C Argentina
60 P10 **Rio de Janeiro** var. Rio. state capital Rio de Janeiro, SE Brazil
60 P9 **Rio de Janeiro** off. Estado do Rio de Janeiro. ◈ state SE Brazil
43 R17 **Río de Jesús** Veraguas, S Panama
34 K3 **Rio Dell** California, W USA
60 K13 **Rio do Sul** Santa Catarina, S Brazil
63 I23 **Río Gallegos** var. Gallegos, Puerto Gallegos. Santa Cruz, S Argentina
61 I18 **Rio Grande** var. São Pedro do Rio Grande do Sul. Rio Grande do Sul, S Brazil
24 I9 **Rio Grande** ≈ Texas, SW USA
63 J24 **Río Grande** Tierra del Fuego, S Argentina
40 L10 **Río Grande** Zacatecas, C Mexico
42 J9 **Río Grande** León, NW Nicaragua
45 V5 **Río Grande** E Puerto Rico
25 R17 **Rio Grande City** Texas, SW USA
59 P14 **Rio Grande do Norte** off. Estado do Rio Grande do Norte. ◈ state E Brazil
61 G15 **Rio Grande do Sul** off. Estado do Rio Grande do Sul. ◈ state S Brazil
65 M17 **Rio Grande Fracture Zone** tectonic feature C Atlantic Ocean
65 J18 **Rio Grande Gap** undersea feature S Atlantic Ocean
Rio Grande Plateau see Rio Grande Rise
65 J18 **Rio Grande Rise** var. Rio Grande Plateau. undersea feature SW Atlantic Ocean
54 G4 **Ríohacha** La Guajira, N Colombia
43 S16 **Río Hato** Coclé, C Panama
25 T17 **Rio Hondo** Texas, SW USA
56 D10 **Rioja** San Martín, N Peru
41 Y11 **Río Lagartos** Yucatán, SE Mexico
103 P11 **Riom** anc. Ricomagus. Puy-de-Dôme, C France
104 F10 **Rio Maior** Santarém, C Portugal
103 O12 **Riom-ès-Montagnes** Cantal, C France
60 J12 **Rio Negro** Paraná, S Brazil
63 I15 **Río Negro** off. Provincia de Río Negro. ◈ province C Argentina
61 D18 **Río Negro** ◈ department W Uruguay
47 V12 **Río Negro, Embalse del** var. Lago Artificial de Rincón del Bonete. ⊟ C Uruguay
107 M17 **Rionero in Vulture** Basilicata, S Italy
137 S9 **Rioni** ≈ W Georgia
105 P12 **Riópar** Castilla-La Mancha, C Spain
61 H16 **Rio Pardo** Rio Grande do Sul, S Brazil
37 R11 **Rio Rancho Estates** New Mexico, SW USA
42 L11 **Río San Juan** ◈ department S Nicaragua
54 E9 **Ríosucio** Caldas, W Colombia
54 C7 **Ríosucio** Chocó, NW Colombia
62 K10 **Río Tercero** Córdoba, C Argentina
54 J5 **Río Tocuyo** Lara, N Venezuela
Riouw-Archipel see Riau, Kepulauan
59 J19 **Rio Verde** Goiás, C Brazil
41 O12 **Río Verde** var. Rioverde. San Luis Potosí, C Mexico
35 O8 **Rio Vista** California, W USA
112 M11 **Ripanj** Serbia, N Serbia and Montenegro (Yugo.)
106 J13 **Ripatransone** Marche, C Italy
Ripen see Ribe
22 M2 **Ripley** Mississippi, S USA
31 R15 **Ripley** Ohio, N USA
20 F9 **Ripley** Tennessee, S USA
21 Q4 **Ripley** West Virginia, NE USA
105 W4 **Ripoll** Cataluña, NE Spain
97 M16 **Ripon** N England, UK
30 M7 **Ripon** Wisconsin, N USA
107 L24 **Riposto** Sicilia, Italy, C Mediterranean Sea
99 L14 **Rips** Noord-Brabant, SE Netherlands
54 D9 **Risaralda** off. Departamento de Risaralda. ◈ province C Colombia
116 L8 **Rîşcani** var. Râşcani, Rus. Ryshkany. NW Moldova
152 J9 **Rishikesh** Uttaranchal, N India
165 S1 **Rishiri-tō** var. Risiri Tô. island NE Japan
165 S1 **Rishiri-yama** ⩘ Rishiri-tō, NE Japan
25 R7 **Rising Star** Texas, SW USA
31 Q15 **Rising Sun** Indiana, N USA
Risiri Tô see Rishiri-tō
102 L4 **Risle** ≈ N France
Rîşno see Râşnov
27 V13 **Rison** Arkansas, C USA
95 G17 **Risør** Aust-Agder, S Norway
92 H10 **Risøyhamn** Nordland, C Norway
101 I23 **Riss** ≈ S Germany
118 G4 **Risti** Ger. Kreuz. Läänemaa, W Estonia
15 V8 **Ristigouche** ≈ Québec, SE Canada
93 N18 **Ristiina** Isä-Suomi, E Finland
93 N14 **Ristijärvi** Oulu, C Finland
188 C14 **Ritidian Point** headland N Guam
Ritschan see Říčany
35 R9 **Ritter, Mount** ▲ California, W USA
31 T12 **Rittman** Ohio, N USA
32 L9 **Ritzville** Washington, NW USA
Riva see Riva del Garda
61 A21 **Rivadavia** Buenos Aires, E Argentina
108 F7 **Riva del Garda** var. Riva Trentino-Alto Adige, N Italy
106 B8 **Rivarolo Canavese** Piemonte, W Italy
42 K11 **Rivas** Rivas, SW Nicaragua
42 J11 **Rivas** ◈ department SW Nicaragua
103 R11 **Rive-de-Gier** Loire, E France
61 A22 **Rivera** Buenos Aires, E Argentina
61 F16 **Rivera** Rivera, NE Uruguay
61 F17 **Rivera** ◈ department NE Uruguay
35 P9 **Riverbank** California, W USA
76 K17 **River Cess** SW Liberia
28 M4 **Riverdale** North Dakota, N USA
30 I6 **River Falls** Wisconsin, N USA
11 T16 **Riverhurst** Saskatchewan, S Canada
183 O10 **Riverina** physical region New South Wales, SE Australia
80 G8 **River Nile** ◈ state NE Sudan
63 F19 **Rivero, Isla** island Archipiélago de los Chonos, S Chile
11 W16 **Rivers** Manitoba, S Canada
77 U17 **Rivers** ◈ state S Nigeria
185 D23 **Riversdale** Southland, South Island, NZ
83 F26 **Riversdale** Western Cape, SW South Africa
35 U15 **Riverside** California, W USA
25 W9 **Riverside** Texas, SW USA
37 U3 **Riverside Reservoir** ⊟ Colorado, C USA
10 K15 **Rivers Inlet** British Columbia, SW Canada
10 K15 **Rivers Inlet** inlet British Columbia, SW Canada
11 X15 **Riverton** Manitoba, S Canada
185 C24 **Riverton** Southland, South Island, NZ
30 L13 **Riverton** Illinois, N USA
36 L3 **Riverton** Utah, W USA
33 V15 **Riverton** Wyoming, C USA
14 G10 **River Valley** Ontario, S Canada
13 P14 **Riverview** New Brunswick, SE Canada
103 O17 **Rivesaltes** Pyrénées-Orientales, S France
36 H11 **Riviera** Arizona, SW USA
25 S15 **Riviera** Texas, SW USA
23 Z14 **Riviera Beach** Florida, SE USA
15 Q10 **Rivière-à-Pierre** Québec, SE Canada
15 T9 **Rivière-Bleue** Québec, SE Canada
15 T8 **Rivière-du-Loup** Québec, SE Canada
173 Y15 **Rivière du Rempart** NE Mauritius
45 R12 **Rivière-Pilote** S Martinique
173 O17 **Rivière St-Etienne, Point de la** headland SW Réunion
13 S10 **Rivière-St-Paul** Québec, E Canada
Rivière Sèche see Bel Air
116 K4 **Rivne** Pol. Równe, Rus. Rovno. Rivnens'ka Oblast', NW Ukraine
Rivne see Rivnens'ka Oblast'
116 K3 **Rivnens'ka Oblast'** var. Rivne, Rus. Rovenskaya Oblast'. ◈ province NW Ukraine
106 B8 **Rivoli** Piemonte, NW Italy
159 Q14 **Riwoqê** var. Racaka. Xizang Zizhiqu, W China
99 H19 **Rixensart** Wallon Brabant, C Belgium
Riyadh/Riyāḑ, Minţaqat ar see Ar Riyāḑ
Riyāq see Rayak
Rizaiyeh see Orūmīyeh
137 P11 **Rize** Rize, NE Turkey
137 P11 **Rize** prev. Çoruh. ◈ province NE Turkey
161 R5 **Rizhao** Shandong, E China
Rizhskiy Zaliv see Riga, Gulf of
Rizokarpaso/Rizokárpason see Dipkarpaz
107 O21 **Rizzuto, Capo** headland S Italy
95 F15 **Rjukan** Telemark, S Norway
95 D16 **Rjuven** ▲▲ S Norway
76 H9 **Rkîz** Trarza, W Mauritania
95 H14 **Roa** Oppland, S Norway
105 N5 **Roa** Castilla-León, N Spain
45 T9 **Road Town** ○ (British Virgin Islands) Tortola, C British Virgin Islands
96 F6 **Roag, Loch** inlet NW Scotland, UK
37 O5 **Roan Cliffs** cliff Colorado/Utah, W USA
21 P9 **Roan High Knob** var. Roan Mountain. ▲ North Carolina/Tennessee, SE USA
Roan Mountain see Roan High Knob
103 Q10 **Roanne** anc. Rodunma. Loire, E France
23 R4 **Roanoke** Alabama, S USA
21 S7 **Roanoke** Virginia, NE USA
21 Z9 **Roanoke Island** island North Carolina, SE USA
21 W8 **Roanoke Rapids** North Carolina, SE USA
21 X9 **Roanoke River** ≈ North Carolina/Virginia, SE USA
37 O4 **Roan Plateau** plain Utah, W USA
37 R5 **Roaring Fork River** ≈ Colorado, C USA
25 O5 **Roaring Springs** Texas, SW USA
42 J4 **Roatán** var. Coxen Hole, Coxin Hole. Islas de la Bahía, N Honduras
42 I4 **Roatán, Isla de** island Islas de la Bahía, N Honduras
Roat Kampuchea see Cambodia
Roazon see Rennes
143 T7 **Robāţ-e Chāh Gonbad** Yazd, E Iran
143 R7 **Robāţ-e Khān** Yazd, C Iran
143 T7 **Robāţ-e Khvosh Āb** Yazd, E Iran
143 R8 **Robāţ-e Posht-e Bādām** Yazd, NE Iran
143 Q8 **Robāţ-e Rizāb** Yazd, C Iran
175 S8 **Robbie Ridge** undersea feature W Pacific Ocean
21 T10 **Robbins** North Carolina, SE USA
183 N15 **Robbins Island** island Tasmania, SE Australia
21 N10 **Robbinsville** North Carolina, SE USA
182 J12 **Robe** South Australia
21 W9 **Robersonville** North Carolina, SE USA
25 P8 **Robert Lee** Texas, SW USA
35 V5 **Roberts Creek Mountain** ▲ Nevada, W USA
93 J15 **Robertsfors** Västerbotten, N Sweden
27 R11 **Robert S.Kerr Reservoir** ⊟ Oklahoma, C USA
38 L12 **Roberts Mountain** ▲ Nunivak Island, Alaska, USA
83 F26 **Robertson** Western Cape, SW South Africa
194 H4 **Robertson Island** island Antarctica
76 J16 **Robertsport** W Liberia
182 J8 **Robertstown** South Australia
Robert Williams see Caála
15 P7 **Roberval** Québec, SE Canada
31 N15 **Robinson** Illinois, N USA
193 U11 **Róbinson Crusoe, Isla** island Islas Juan Fernández, Chile, E Pacific Ocean
180 J9 **Robinson Range** ▲▲ Western Austral
182 M9 **Robinvale** Victoria, SE Australia
105 P11 **Robledo** Castilla-La Mancha, C Spain
54 G5 **Robles** var. La Paz, Robles La Paz. Cesar, N Colombia
Robles La Paz see Robles
11 V15 **Roblin** Manitoba, S Canada
11 S17 **Robsart** Saskatchewan, S Canada
11 N15 **Robson, Mount** ▲ British Columbia, SW Canada
25 T14 **Robstown** Texas, SW USA
25 P6 **Roby** Texas, SW USA
104 E11 **Roca, Cabo da** headland C Portugal
Rocadas see Xangongo
41 S14 **Roca Partida, Punta** headland C Mexico
47 X6 **Rocas, Atol das** island E Brazil
107 L18 **Roccadaspide** var. Rocca d'Aspide. Campania, S Italy
107 K15 **Roccaraso** Abruzzo, C Italy
106 H10 **Rocca San Casciano** Emilia-Romagna, C Italy
106 G13 **Roccastrada** Toscana, C Italy
61 G20 **Rocha** Rocha, E Uruguay
61 G19 **Rocha** ◈ department E Uruguay
97 L17 **Rochdale** NW England, UK
102 L11 **Rochechouart** Haute-Vienne, C France
99 J22 **Rochefort** Namur, SE Belgium
102 J11 **Rochefort** var. Rochefort sur Mer. Charente-Maritime, W France
Rochefort sur Mer see Rochefort
125 N10 **Rochegda** Arkhangel'skaya Oblast', NW Russian Federation
30 L10 **Rochelle** Illinois, N USA
25 Q9 **Rochelle** Texas, SW USA
15 V3 **Rochers Ouest, Rivière aux** ≈ Québec, SE Canada
97 O22 **Rochester** anc. Durobrivae. SE England, UK
31 O12 **Rochester** Indiana, N USA
29 W10 **Rochester** Minnesota, N USA
19 O9 **Rochester** New Hampshire, NE USA
18 F9 **Rochester** New York, NE USA
25 P5 **Rochester** Texas, SW USA
31 S9 **Rochester Hills** Michigan, N USA
Rocheuses, Montagnes/Rockies see Rocky Mountains
64 M6 **Rockall** island UK, N Atlantic Ocean
64 L6 **Rockall Bank** undersea feature N Atlantic Ocean
84 B8 **Rockall Rise** undersea feature N Atlantic Ocean
84 C9 **Rockall Trough** undersea feature N Atlantic Ocean
35 U2 **Rock Creek** ≈ Nevada, W USA
25 T10 **Rockdale** Texas, SW USA
195 N12 **Rockefeller Plateau** plateau Antarctica
30 K11 **Rock Falls** Illinois, N USA
23 Q5 **Rockford** Alabama, S USA
30 L10 **Rockford** Illinois, N USA
12 Q12 **Rock Forest** Québec, SE Canada
11 T17 **Rockglen** Saskatchewan, S Canada
181 Y8 **Rockhampton** Queensland, E Australia
21 R11 **Rock Hill** South Carolina, SE USA
180 I13 **Rockingham** Western Australia
21 T11 **Rockingham** North Carolina, SE USA
30 J11 **Rock Island** Illinois, N USA
25 U12 **Rock Island** Texas, SW USA
14 C10 **Rock Lake** Ontario, S Canada
29 O2 **Rock Lake** North Dakota, N USA
14 I12 **Rock Lake** ◎ Ontario, SE Canada
14 M12 **Rockland** Ontario, SE Canada
19 R7 **Rockland** Maine, NE USA
182 L11 **Rocklands Reservoir** ⊟ Victoria, SE Australia
35 O7 **Rocklin** California, W USA
23 R3 **Rockmart** Georgia, SE USA
31 N16 **Rockport** Indiana, N USA
27 Q1 **Rock Port** Missouri, C USA
25 T14 **Rockport** Texas, SW USA
32 I7 **Rockport** Washington, NW USA
29 S11 **Rock Rapids** Iowa, C USA
30 K11 **Rock River** ≈ Illinois/Wisconsin, N USA
44 I3 **Rock Sound** Eleuthera Island, C Bahamas
33 U17 **Rock Springs** Wyoming, C USA
25 P11 **Rocksprings** Texas, SW USA
55 T9 **Rockstone** C Guyana
29 S12 **Rock Valley** Iowa, C USA
31 N14 **Rockville** Indiana, N USA
21 W3 **Rockville** Maryland, NE USA
25 U6 **Rockwall** Texas, SW USA
29 U13 **Rockwell City** Iowa, C USA
31 S10 **Rockwood** Michigan, N USA
20 M9 **Rockwood** Tennessee, S USA
25 Q8 **Rockwood** Texas, SW USA
37 U6 **Rocky Ford** Colorado, C USA
14 D9 **Rocky Island Lake** ◎ Ontario, S Canada
21 V9 **Rocky Mount** North Carolina, SE USA
21 S7 **Rocky Mount** Virginia, NE USA
33 Q8 **Rocky Mountain** ▲ Montana, NW USA
11 P15 **Rocky Mountain House** Alberta, SW Canada
37 T3 **Rocky Mountain National Park** national park Colorado, C USA
2 E12 **Rocky Mountains** var. Rockies, Fr. Montagnes Rocheuses. ▲▲ Canada/USA
42 H1 **Rocky Point** headland NE Belize
83 A17 **Rocky Point** headland NW Namibia
95 F14 **Rødberg** Buskerud, S Norway
95 I25 **Rødby** Storstrøm, SE Denmark
95 I25 **Rødbyhavn** Storstrøm, SE Denmark
13 T10 **Roddickton** Newfoundland and Labrador, SE Canada
95 F23 **Rødding** Sønderjylland, SW Denmark
95 M22 **Rödeby** Blekinge, S Sweden
98 N6 **Roden** Drenthe, NE Netherlands
62 H9 **Rodeo** San Juan, W Argentina
103 O14 **Rodez** anc. Segodunum. Aveyron, S France
Rodholívos see Rodolívos
Rodhópi Óri see Rhodope Mountains
Ródhos/Rodi see Ródos
107 N15 **Rodi Garganico** Puglia, SE Italy
101 N20 **Roding** Bayern, SE Germany
113 J19 **Rodinit, Kepi i** headland W Albania
116 I9 **Rodnei, Munţii** ▲▲ N Romania
184 L4 **Rodney, Cape** headland North Island, NZ
38 L9 **Rodney, Cape** headland Alaska, USA
124 M16 **Rodniki** Ivanovskaya Oblast', W Russian Federation
119 Q16 **Rodnya** Rus. Rodnya. Mahilyowskaya Voblasts', E Belarus
Rodó see José Enrique Rodó
114 H13 **Rodolívos** var. Rodholívos. Kentrikí Makedonía, NE Greece
Rodopi see Rhodope Mountains
115 O22 **Ródos** var. Ródhos, Eng. Rhodes, It. Rodi. Ródos, Dodekánisos, Greece, Aegean Sea
115 O22 **Ródos** var. Ródhos, Eng. Rhodes, It. Rodi; anc. Rhodos. island Dodekánisos, Greece, Aegean Sea
Rodosto see Tekirdağ
59 A14 **Rodrigues** Amazonas, W Brazil
173 P8 **Rodrigues** var. Rodriquez. island E Mauritius
Rodriquez see Rodrigues
Rodunma see Roanne
180 I7 **Roebourne** Western Australia
83 J20 **Roedtan** Limpopo, NE South Africa
98 H11 **Roelofarendsveen** Zuid-Holland, W Netherlands
Roepat see Rupat, Pulau
Roer see Rur
99 M16 **Roermond** Limburg, SE Netherlands
99 C18 **Roeselare** Fr. Roulers; prev. Rousselaere. West-Vlaanderen, W Belgium
9 P8 **Roes Welcome Sound** strait Nunavut, N Canada
Roeteng see Ruteng
Rofreit see Rovereto
Rogachëv see Rahachow
57 L15 **Rogagua, Laguna** ◎ NW Bolivia
95 C16 **Rogaland** ◈ county S Norway
25 Y9 **Roganville** Texas, SW USA
109 W11 **Rogaška Slatina** Ger. Rohitsch-Sauerbrunn; prev. Rogatec-Slatina. E Slovenia
Rogatec-Slatina see Rogaška Slatina
112 J13 **Rogatica** Republica Srpska, SE Bosnia & Herzegovina
Rogatin see Rohatyn
93 F17 **Rogen** ◎ C Sweden
27 S9 **Rogers** Arkansas, C USA
29 P5 **Rogers** North Dakota, N USA
25 T9 **Rogers** Texas, SW USA
31 R5 **Rogers City** Michigan, N USA
Roger Simpson Island see Abemama
35 T14 **Rogers Lake** salt flat California, W USA
21 Q8 **Rogers, Mount** ▲ Virginia, NE USA
33 O16 **Rogerson** Idaho, NW USA
11 O16 **Rogers Pass** pass British Columbia, SW Canada
21 O8 **Rogersville** Tennessee, S USA
99 L16 **Roggel** Limburg, SE Netherlands
Roggeveen see Roggewein, Cabo
193 R10 **Roggeveen Basin** undersea feature E Pacific Ocean
191 X16 **Roggewein, Cabo** var. Roggeveen. headland Easter Island, Chile, E Pacific Ocean
103 Y13 **Rogliano** Corse, France, C Mediterranean Sea
107 N21 **Rogliano** Calabria, SW Italy
92 G12 **Rognan** Nordland, C Norway
100 K10 **Rögnitz** ≈ N Germany
Rogozhina/Rogozhinë see Rrogozhinë
110 G10 **Rogoźno** Wielkopolskie, C Poland
32 E15 **Rogue River** ≈ Oregon, NW USA
116 I6 **Rohatyn** Rus. Rogatin. Ivano-Frankivs'ka Oblast', W Ukraine
189 O14 **Rohi** Pohnpei, E Micronesia
Rohitsch-Sauerbrunn see Rogaška Slatina
149 Q13 **Rohri** Sind, SE Pakistan
152 I10 **Rohtak** Haryāna, N India
Roi Ed see Roi Et
167 R9 **Roi Et** var. Muang Roi Et, Roi Ed. Roi Et, E Thailand
191 U9 **Roi Georges, Îles du** island group Îles Tuamotu, C French Polynesia
153 Y10 **Roing** Arunāchal Pradesh, NE India
118 E7 **Roja** Talsi, NW Latvia
61 B20 **Rojas** Buenos Aires, E Argentina
149 R12 **Rojhān** Punjab, E Pakistan
41 Q12 **Rojo, Cabo** headland C Mexico
45 Q10 **Rojo, Cabo** headland W Puerto Rico
168 K10 **Rokan Kiri, Sungai** ≈ Sumatera, W Indonesia
Rokha see Rokhah
149 R4 **Rokhah** var. Rokha. Kāpīsā, E Afghanistan
118 I11 **Rokiškis** Panevėžys, NE Lithuania
165 R7 **Rokkasho** Aomori, Honshū, C Japan
111 B17 **Rokycany** Ger. Rokytzan. Plzeňský Kraj, NW Czech Republic
117 P6 **Rokytne** Kyyivs'ka Oblast', N Ukraine
116 L3 **Rokytne** Rivnens'ka Oblast', NW Ukraine
Rokytzan see Rokycany
158 L11 **Rola Co** ◎ W China
29 V13 **Roland** Iowa, C USA
95 D15 **Røldal** Hordaland, S Norway
98 O7 **Rolde** Drenthe, NE Netherlands
29 O2 **Rolette** North Dakota, N USA
27 V6 **Rolla** Missouri, C USA
29 O2 **Rolla** North Dakota, N USA
108 A10 **Rolle** Vaud, W Switzerland
181 X8 **Rolleston** Queensland, E Australia
185 H19 **Rolleston** Canterbury, South Island, NZ
185 G18 **Rolleston Range** ▲▲ South Island, NZ
14 H8 **Rollet** Québec, SE Canada
22 J4 **Rolling Fork** Mississippi, S USA
20 L6 **Rolling Fork** ≈ Kentucky, S USA
14 J11 **Rolphton** Ontario, SE Canada
Röm see Rømø
181 X10 **Roma** Queensland, E Australia
107 I15 **Roma** Eng. Rome. ● (Italy) Lazio, C Italy
95 P19 **Roma** Gotland, SE Sweden
21 T14 **Romain, Cape** headland South Carolina, SE USA
13 P11 **Romaine** ≈ Newfoundland and Labrador/Québec, E Canada
25 R17 **Roma Los Saenz** Texas, SW USA
114 H8 **Roman** Vratsa, NW Bulgaria
116 L10 **Roman** Hung. Románvásár. Neamţ, NE Romania
64 M13 **Romanche Fracture Zone** tectonic feature E Atlantic Ocean
61 C15 **Romang** Santa Fe, C Argentina
171 R15 **Romang, Pulau** var. Pulau Roma. island Kepulauan Damar, E Indonesia
171 R15 **Romang, Selat** strait Nusa Tenggara, S Indonesia
116 J11 **Romania** Bul. Rumŭniya, Ger. Rumänien, Hung. Románia, Rom. România, SCr. Rumunjska, Ukr. Rumuniya; prev. Republica Socialistă România, Roumania, Rumania, Socialist Republic of Romania, Rom. Romînia. ◆ republic SE Europe
117 T14 **Roman-Kash** ▲ S Ukraine
23 W16 **Romano, Cape** headland Florida, SE USA
44 G5 **Romano, Cayo** island C Cuba
123 O13 **Romanovka** Respublika Buryatiya, S Russian Federation
127 N8 **Romanovka** Saratovskaya Oblast', W Russian Federation
108 I6 **Romanshorn** Thurgau, NE Switzerland
103 R12 **Romans-sur-Isère** Drôme, E France
189 U12 **Romanum** island Chuuk, C Micronesia
Románvásár see Roman
39 S5 **Romanzof Mountains** ▲▲ Alaska, USA
Roma, Pulau see Romang, Pulau
103 S4 **Rombas** Moselle, NE France
23 R2 **Rome** Georgia, SE USA
18 I9 **Rome** New York, NE USA
Rome see Roma
31 S9 **Romeo** Michigan, N USA
Römerstadt see Rýmařov
Rometan see Romiton
103 P5 **Romilly-sur-Seine** Aube, N France
Romînia see Romania
146 L11 **Romiton** Rus. Rometan. Buxoro Viloyati, C Uzbekistan
21 U3 **Romney** West Virginia, NE USA
117 S4 **Romny** Sums'ka Oblast', NE Ukraine
95 E24 **Rømø** Ger. Röm. island SW Denmark
117 S5 **Romodan** Poltavs'ka Oblast', NE Ukraine
127 P5 **Romodanovo** Respublika Mordoviya, W Russian Federation
Romorantin see Romorantin-Lanthenay
103 N8 **Romorantin-Lanthenay** var. Romorantin. Loir-et-Cher, C France
94 F9 **Romsdal** physical region S Norway
94 F10 **Romsdalen** valley S Norway
94 E9 **Romsdalsfjorden** fjord S Norway
33 P8 **Ronan** Montana, NW USA
59 M14 **Roncador** Maranhão, E Brazil
186 M7 **Roncador Reef** reef N Solomon Islands
59 J17 **Roncador, Serra do** ▲▲ C Brazil
21 S6 **Ronceverte** West Virginia, NE USA
107 H14 **Ronciglione** Lazio, C Italy
104 L15 **Ronda** Andalucía, S Spain
94 G11 **Rondane** ▲▲ S Norway
104 L15 **Ronda, Serranía de** ▲▲ S Spain
95 H22 **Rønde** Århus, C Denmark
Rŏndik see Rongrik Atoll
59 E16 **Rondônia** off. Estado de Rondônia; prev. Território de Rondônia. ◈ state W Brazil
59 I18 **Rondonópolis** Mato Grosso, W Brazil
94 G11 **Rondslottet** ▲ S Norway
95 P20 **Ronehamn** Gotland, SE Sweden
160 L13 **Rong'an** var. Chang'an, Rongan. Guangxi Zhuangzu Zizhiqu, S China
Rongcheng see Jianli
189 R4 **Rongelap Atoll** var. Rŏnļap. atoll Ralik Chain, NW Marshall Islands
Rongerik see Rongrik Atoll
160 K12 **Rongjiang** var. Guzhou. Guizhou, S China
160 L13 **Rong Jiang** ≈ S China
Rongjiang see Nankang
Rong, Kas see Rŭng, Kaôh
167 P8 **Rong Kwang** Phrae, NW Thailand
189 T4 **Rongrik Atoll** var. Rŏndik, Rongerik. atoll Ralik Chain, N Marshall Islands

◆ Country ● Country Capital ◇ Dependent Territory ○ Dependent Territory Capital ◈ Administrative Region ✈ International Airport ▲ Mountain ▲▲ Mountain Range ⩘ Volcano ≈ River ◎ Lake ⊟ Reservoir

189 *X2* **Rongrong** *island* SE Marshall Islands
160 *L13* **Rongshui** *var.* Rongshui Miaozu Zizhixian. Guangxi Zhuangzu Zizhiqu, S China
Rongshui Miaozu Zizhixian *see* Rongshui
118 *I6* **Rõngu** *Ger.* Ringen. Tartumaa, SE Estonia
Rongwo *see* Tongren
160 *L15* **Rongxian** *var.* Rong Xian. Guangxi Zhuangzu Zizhiqu, S China
Rongzhag *see* Danba
Roniu *see* Ronui, Mont
189 *N13* **Ronkiti** Pohnpei, E Micronesia
Rōnḷap *see* Rongelap Atoll
95 *L24* **Rønne** Bornholm, E Denmark
95 *M22* **Ronneby** Blekinge, S Sweden
194 *J7* **Ronne Entrance** *inlet* Antarctica
194 *L6* **Ronne Ice Shelf** *ice shelf* Antarctica
99 *E19* **Ronse** *Fr.* Renaix. Oost-Vlaanderen, SW Belgium
191 *R8* **Ronui, Mont** *var.* Roniu. ⛰ Tahiti, W French Polynesia
30 *K14* **Roodhouse** Illinois, N USA
83 *C19* **Rooibank** Erongo, W Namibia
65 *N24* **Rookery Point** *headland* NE Tristan da Cunha
171 *V13* **Roon, Pulau** *island* E Indonesia
173 *V7* **Roo Rise** *undersea feature* E Indian Ocean
152 *J9* **Roorkee** Uttaranchal, N India
99 *H15* **Roosendaal** Noord-Brabant, S Netherlands
25 *P10* **Roosevelt** Texas, SW USA
37 *N3* **Roosevelt** Utah, W USA
47 *T8* **Roosevelt** ≈ W Brazil
195 *O13* **Roosevelt Island** *island* Antarctica
10 *L10* **Roosevelt, Mount** ▲ British Columbia, W Canada
11 *P17* **Roosville** British Columbia, SW Canada
29 *X10* **Root River** ≈ Minnesota, N USA
111 *N16* **Ropczyce** Podkarpackie, SE Poland
181 *Q3* **Roper Bar** Northern Territory, N Australia
24 *M5* **Ropesville** Texas, SW USA
102 *K14* **Roquefort** Landes, SW France
61 *C21* **Roque Pérez** Buenos Aires, E Argentina
58 *E10* **Roraima** *off.* Estado de Roraima; *prev.* Território de Rio Branco, Território de Roraima. ◐ *state* N Brazil
58 *F9* **Roraima, Mount** ▲ N South America
Ro Ro Reef *see* Malolo Barrier Reef
94 *I9* **Røros** Sør-Trøndelag, S Norway
108 *I7* **Rorschach** Sankt Gallen, NE Switzerland
93 *E14* **Rørvik** Nord-Trøndelag, C Norway
119 *G17* **Ros'** *Rus.* Ross'. Hrodzyenskaya Voblasts', W Belarus
119 *G17* **Ros'** *Rus.* Ross'. ≈ W Belarus
117 *O6* **Ros'** ≈ N Ukraine
44 *K7* **Rosa, Lake** ◎ Great Inagua, S Bahamas
32 *M9* **Rosalia** Washington, NW USA
191 *W15* **Rosalia, Punta** *headland* Easter Island, Chile, E Pacific Ocean
45 *P12* **Rosalie** E Dominica
35 *T14* **Rosamond** California, W USA
35 *S14* **Rosamond Lake** *salt flat* California, W USA
61 *B18* **Rosario** Santa Fe, C Argentina
40 *J11* **Rosario** Sinaloa, C Mexico
40 *G6* **Rosario** Sonora, NW Mexico
62 *O6* **Rosario** San Pedro, C Paraguay
61 *E20* **Rosario** Colonia, SW Uruguay
54 *H5* **Rosario** Zulia, NW Venezuela
Rosario *see* Rosarito
40 *B4* **Rosario, Bahía del** *bay* NW Mexico
62 *K6* **Rosario de la Frontera** Salta, N Argentina
61 *C18* **Rosario del Tala** Entre Ríos, E Argentina
61 *F16* **Rosário do Sul** Rio Grande do Sul, S Brazil
59 *H18* **Rosário Oeste** Mato Grosso, W Brazil
40 *E7* **Rosarito** Baja California, NW Mexico
40 *B1* **Rosarito** *var.* Rosario. Baja California, NW Mexico
40 *E7* **Rosarito** Baja California Sur, W Mexico
104 *L9* **Rosarito, Embalse del** ▣ W Spain
107 *N22* **Rosarno** Calabria, SW Italy
56 *B5* **Rosa Zárate** *var.* Quinindé. Esmeraldas, SW Ecuador
Roscianum *see* Rossano
29 *O8* **Roscoe** South Dakota, N USA
25 *P7* **Roscoe** Texas, SW USA
102 *F5* **Roscoff** Finistère, NW France
Ros Comáin *see* Roscommon
97 *C17* **Roscommon** *Ir.* Ros Comáin. C Ireland
31 *Q7* **Roscommon** Michigan, N USA
97 *C17* **Roscommon** *Ir.* Ros Comáin. *cultural region* C Ireland
Ros. Cré *see* Roscrea
97 *D19* **Roscrea** *Ir.* Ros. Cré. C Ireland
45 *X12* **Roseau** *prev.* Charlotte Town. ● (Dominica) SW Dominica
29 *S2* **Roseau** Minnesota, N USA
173 *Y16* **Rose Belle** SE Mauritius
183 *O16* **Rosebery** Tasmania, SE Australia
21 *U11* **Roseboro** North Carolina, SE USA
25 *T9* **Rosebud** Texas, SW USA
33 *W10* **Rosebud Creek** ≈ Montana, NW USA
32 *F14* **Roseburg** Oregon, NW USA
22 *J3* **Rosedale** Mississippi, S USA
99 *H21* **Rosée** Namur, S Belgium
55 *U8* **Rose Hall** E Guyana
173 *X16* **Rose Hill** W Mauritius
80 *H12* **Roseires, Reservoir** *var.* Lake Rusayris. ▣ E Sudan
Rosenau *see* Rožnov pod Radhoštěm, Czech Republic
Rosenau *see* Rožňava, Slovakia
25 *V11* **Rosenberg** Texas, SW USA
Rosenberg *see* Olesno, Poland
Rosenberg *see* Ružomberok, Slovakia
100 *I10* **Rosengarten** Niedersachsen, N Germany
101 *M24* **Rosenheim** Bayern, S Germany
Rosenhof *see* Zilupe
105 *X4* **Roses** Cataluña, NE Spain
105 *X4* **Roses, Golf de** *gulf* NE Spain
107 *K14* **Roseto degli Abruzzi** Abruzzo, C Italy
11 *S16* **Rosetown** Saskatchewan, S Canada
Rosetta *see* Rashîd
35 *O7* **Roseville** California, W USA
30 *J12* **Roseville** Illinois, N USA
29 *V8* **Roseville** Minnesota, N USA
29 *R7* **Rosholt** South Dakota, N USA
106 *F12* **Rosignano Marittimo** Toscana, C Italy
116 *I14* **Roşiori de Vede** Teleorman, S Romania
114 *K8* **Rositsa** ≈ N Bulgaria
Rositten *see* Rēzekne
95 *J23* **Roskilde** Roskilde, E Denmark
95 *I23* **Roskilde** *off.* Roskilde Amt. ◐ *county* E Denmark
Ros Láir *see* Rosslare
126 *H5* **Roslavl'** Smolenskaya Oblast', W Russian Federation
32 *I8* **Roslyn** Washington, NW USA
99 *K14* **Rosmalen** Noord-Brabant, S Netherlands
Ros Mhic Thriúin *see* New Ross
113 *P19* **Rosoman** C FYR Macedonia
102 *F6* **Rosporden** Finistère, NW France
185 *F17* **Ross** West Coast, South Island, NZ
10 *J7* **Ross** ≈ Yukon Territory, W Canada
Ross' *see* Ros'
96 *H8* **Ross and Cromarty** *cultural region* N Scotland, UK
107 *O20* **Rossano** *anc.* Roscianum. Calabria, SW Italy
22 *L5* **Ross Barnett Reservoir** ▣ Mississippi, S USA
11 *W16* **Rossburn** Manitoba, S Canada
14 *H13* **Rosseau** Ontario, S Canada
14 *H13* **Rosseau, Lake** ◎ Ontario, S Canada
186 *I10* **Rossel Island** *prev.* Yela Island. *island* SE PNG
195 *P12* **Ross Ice Shelf** *ice shelf* Antarctica
13 *P16* **Rossignol, Lake** ◎ Nova Scotia, SE Canada
83 *C19* **Rössing** Erongo, W Namibia
195 *Q14* **Ross Island** *island* Antarctica
Rossitten *see* Rybachiy
Rossiyskaya Federatsiya *see* Russian Federation
11 *N17* **Rossland** British Columbia, SW Canada
97 *F20* **Rosslare** *Ir.* Ros Láir. SE Ireland
97 *F20* **Rosslare Harbour** Wexford, SE Ireland
101 *M14* **Rosslau** Sachsen-Anhalt, E Germany
76 *G10* **Rosso** Trarza, SW Mauritania
103 *X14* **Rosso, Cap** *headland* Corse, France, C Mediterranean Sea
93 *H16* **Rossön** Jämtland, C Sweden
97 *K21* **Ross-on-Wye** W England, UK
Rossony *see* Rasony
126 *L9* **Rossosh'** Voronezhskaya Oblast', W Russian Federation
181 *Q7* **Ross River** Northern Territory, N Australia
10 *J7* **Ross River** Yukon Territory, W Canada
205 *O15* **Ross Sea** *sea* Antarctica
92 *G13* **Røssvatnet** *Lapp.* Reevhtse. ◎ C Norway
23 *R1* **Rossville** Georgia, SE USA
Rostak *see* Ar Rustāq
143 *P14* **Rostāq** Hormozgān, S Iran
117 *N5* **Rostavytsya** ≈ N Ukraine
11 *T15* **Rosthern** Saskatchewan, S Canada
100 *M8* **Rostock** Mecklenburg-Vorpommern, NE Germany
126 *L16* **Rostov** Yaroslavskaya Oblast', W Russian Federation
Rostov *see* Rostov-na-Donu
126 *L12* **Rostov-na-Donu** *var.* Rostov, *Eng.* Rostov-on-Don. Rostovskaya Oblast', SW Russian Federation
Rostov-on-Don *see* Rostov-na-Donu
126 *L10* **Rostovskaya Oblast'** ◐ *province* SW Russian Federation
93 *J14* **Rosvik** Norrbotten, N Sweden
23 *S3* **Roswell** Georgia, SE USA
37 *U14* **Roswell** New Mexico, SW USA
94 *K12* **Rot** Dalarna, C Sweden
101 *I23* **Rot** ≈ S Germany
104 *J15* **Rota** Andalucía, S Spain
188 *K9* **Rota** *island* S Northern Mariana Islands
25 *P6* **Rotan** Texas, SW USA
Rotcher Island *see* Tamana
100 *I11* **Rotenburg** Niedersachsen, NW Germany
Rotenburg *see* Rotenburg an der Fulda
101 *I16* **Rotenburg an der Fulda** *var.* Rotenburg. Thüringen, C Germany
101 *L18* **Roter Main** ≈ E Germany
101 *K20* **Roth** Bayern, SE Germany
101 *G16* **Rothaargebirge** ▲▲ W Germany
Rothenburg *see* Rothenburg ob der Tauber
101 *J20* **Rothenburg ob der Tauber** *var.* Rothenburg. Bayern, S Germany
194 *H6* **Rothera** *UK research station* Antarctica
185 *I17* **Rotherham** Canterbury, South Island, NZ
97 *M17* **Rotherham** N England, UK
96 *H12* **Rothesay** W Scotland, UK
108 *E7* **Rothrist** Aargau, N Switzerland
194 *H6* **Rothschild Island** *island* Antarctica
171 *P17* **Roti, Pulau** *island* S Indonesia
183 *O8* **Roto** New South Wales, SE Australia
184 *N8* **Rotoiti, Lake** ◎ North Island, NZ
Rotomagus *see* Rouen
107 *N19* **Rotondella** Basilicata, S Italy
103 *X15* **Rotondo, Monte** ▲ Corse, France, C Mediterranean Sea
185 *I15* **Rotoroa, Lake** ◎ South Island, NZ
184 *N8* **Rotorua** Bay of Plenty, North Island, NZ
184 *N8* **Rotorua, Lake** ◎ North Island, NZ
101 *N22* **Rott** ≈ SE Germany
108 *F10* **Rotten** ≈ S Switzerland
109 *T6* **Rottenmann** Steiermark, E Austria
98 *H12* **Rotterdam** Zuid-Holland, SW Netherlands
18 *K10* **Rotterdam** New York, NE USA
95 *M21* **Rottnen** ◎ S Sweden
98 *N4* **Rottumeroog** *island* Waddeneilanden, NE Netherlands
98 *N4* **Rottumerplaat** *island* Waddeneilanden, NE Netherlands
101 *G23* **Rottweil** Baden-Württemberg, S Germany
191 *O7* **Rotui, Mont** ⛰ Moorea, W French Polynesia
103 *P1* **Roubaix** Nord, N France
111 *C15* **Roudnice nad Labem** *Ger.* Raudnitz an der Elbe. Ústecký Kraj, NW Czech Republic
102 *M4* **Rouen** *anc.* Rotomagus. Seine-Maritime, N France
171 *X13* **Rouffaer Reserves** *reserve* Papua, E Indonesia
15 *N10* **Rouge, Rivière** ≈ Québec, SE Canada
20 *J6* **Rough River** ≈ Kentucky, S USA
20 *J6* **Rough River Lake** ▣ Kentucky, S USA
Rouhaïbé *see* Ar Ruḩaybah
102 *K11* **Rouillac** Charente, W France
Roulers *see* Roeselare
Roumania *see* Romania
173 *Y15* **Round Island** *var.* Île Ronde. *island* NE Mauritius
14 *J12* **Round Lake** ◎ Ontario, SE Canada
35 *U7* **Round Mountain** Nevada, W USA
25 *R10* **Round Mountain** Texas, SW USA
183 *U5* **Round Mountain** ▲ New South Wales, SE Australia
25 *S10* **Round Rock** Texas, SW USA
33 *U10* **Roundup** Montana, NW USA
55 *Y10* **Roura** NE French Guiana
Rourkela *see* Rāulakela
96 *J4* **Rousay** *island* N Scotland, UK
Rousselaere *see* Roeselare
103 *O17* **Roussillon** *cultural region* S France
15 *V7* **Routhierville** Québec, SE Canada
99 *K25* **Rouvroy** Luxembourg, SE Belgium
14 *I7* **Rouyn-Noranda** Québec, SE Canada
Rouyuanchengzi *see* Huachi
92 *L12* **Rovaniemi** Lappi, N Finland
106 *E7* **Rovato** Lombardia, N Italy
125 *N11* **Rovdino** Arkhangel'skaya Oblast', NW Russian Federation
Roven'ki *see* Roven'ky
117 *Y8* **Roven'ky** *var.* Roven'ki. Luhans'ka Oblast', E Ukraine
Rovenskaya Oblast' *see* Rivnens'ka Oblast'
Rovenskaya Sloboda *see* Rovyenskaya Slabada
106 *G7* **Rovereto** *Ger.* Rofreit. Trentino-Alto Adige, N Italy
167 *S12* **Rôviĕng Tbong** Preăh Vihéar, N Cambodia
Rovigno *see* Rovinj
106 *H8* **Rovigo** Veneto, NE Italy
112 *A10* **Rovinj** *It.* Rovigno. Istra, NW Croatia
54 *E10* **Rovira** Tolima, C Colombia
Rovno *see* Rivne
127 *P9* **Rovnoye** Saratovskaya Oblast', W Russian Federation
82 *Q12* **Rovuma, Rio** *var.* Ruvuma. ≈ Mozambique/Tanzania *see also* Ruvuma
119 *O19* **Rovyenskaya Slabada** *Rus.* Rovenskaya Sloboda. Homyel'skaya Voblasts', SE Belarus
183 *R5* **Rowena** New South Wales, SE Australia
21 *T11* **Rowland** North Carolina, SE USA
9 *P5* **Rowley** ≈ Baffin Island, Nunavut, NE Canada
9 *P6* **Rowley Island** *island* Nunavut, NE Canada
173 *W8* **Rowley Shoals** *reef* NW Australia
171 *O4* **Roxas** Mindoro, N Philippines
171 *P5* **Roxas City** Panay Island, C Philippines
21 *U8* **Roxboro** North Carolina, SE USA
185 *D23* **Roxburgh** Otago, South Island, NZ
96 *K13* **Roxburgh** *cultural region* SE Scotland, UK
182 *H5* **Roxby Downs** South Australia
95 *M17* **Roxen** ◎ S Sweden
25 *V5* **Roxton** Texas, SW USA
15 *P12* **Roxton-Sud** Québec, SE Canada
33 *U8* **Roy** Montana, NW USA
37 *U10* **Roy** New Mexico, SW USA
97 *E17* **Royal Canal** *Ir.* An Chanáil Ríoga. *canal* C Ireland
30 *L1* **Royale, Isle** *island* Michigan, N USA
37 *S6* **Royal Gorge** *valley* Colorado, C USA
97 *M20* **Royal Leamington Spa** *var.* Leamington, Leamington Spa. C England, UK
97 *O23* **Royal Tunbridge Wells** *var.* Tunbridge Wells. SE England, UK
24 *L9* **Royalty** Texas, SW USA
102 *J11* **Royan** Charente-Maritime, W France
65 *B24* **Roy Cove Settlement** West Falkland, Falkland Islands
103 *O3* **Roye** Somme, N France
95 *H15* **Røyken** Buskerud, S Norway
93 *F14* **Røyrvik** Nord-Trøndelag, C Norway
25 *U6* **Royse City** Texas, SW USA
97 *O21* **Royston** E England, UK
23 *U2* **Royston** Georgia, SE USA
114 *L10* **Roza** *prev.* Gyulovo. Yambol, E Bulgaria
113 *L16* **Rožaje** Montenegro, SW Serbia and Montenegro (Yugo.)
110 *M10* **Różan** Mazowieckie, C Poland
117 *O10* **Rozdil'na** Odes'ka Oblast', SW Ukraine
117 *S12* **Rozdol'ne** *Rus.* Razdolnoye. Respublika Krym, S Ukraine
145 *Q9* **Rozhdestvenka** Akmola, C Kazakhstan
116 *I6* **Rozhnyativ** Ivano-Frankivs'ka Oblast', W Ukraine
116 *J3* **Rozhyshche** Volyns'ka Oblast', NW Ukraine
Roznau am Radhost *see* Rožnov pod Radhoštěm
111 *L19* **Rožňava** *Ger.* Rosenau, *Hung.* Rozsnyó. Košický Kraj, E Slovakia
116 *K10* **Roznov** Neamţ, NE Romania
111 *I18* **Rožnov pod Radhoštěm** *Ger.* Rosenau, Roznau am Radhost. Zlínský Kraj, E Czech Republic
Rózsahegy *see* Ružomberok
Rozsnyó *see* Râşnov, Romania
Rozsnyó *see* Rožňava, Slovakia
113 *K18* **Rranxë** Shkodër, NW Albania
113 *L18* **Rrëshen** *var.* Rresheni, Rrshen. Lezhë, C Albania
Rresheni *see* Rrëshen
Rrogozhina *see* Rrogozhinë
113 *K20* **Rrogozhinë** *var.* Rogozhina, Rogozhinë, Rrogozhina. Tiranë, W Albania
Rrshen *see* Rrëshen
112 *O13* **Rtanj** ▲ E Serbia and Montenegro (Yugo.)
127 *O7* **Rtishchevo** Saratovskaya Oblast', W Russian Federation
184 *N12* **Ruahine Range** *var.* Ruarine. ▲▲ North Island, NZ
185 *L14* **Ruamahanga** ≈ North Island, NZ
Ruanda *see* Rwanda
184 *M10* **Ruapehu, Mount** ▲ North Island, NZ
185 *C25* **Ruapuke Island** *island* SW NZ
Ruarine *see* Ruahine Range
184 *O9* **Ruatahuna** Bay of Plenty, North Island, NZ
184 *Q8* **Ruatoria** Gisborne, North Island, NZ
184 *K4* **Ruawai** Northland, North Island, NZ
15 *N8* **Ruban** ≈ Québec, SE Canada
81 *I22* **Rubeho Mountains** ▲▲ C Tanzania
165 *U3* **Rubeshibe** Hokkaidō, NE Japan
Rubezhnoye *see* Rubizhne
113 *L18* **Rubik** Lezhë, C Albania
54 *H7* **Rubio** Táchira, W Venezuela
117 *X6* **Rubizhne** *Rus.* Rubezhnoye. Luhans'ka Oblast', E Ukraine
81 *F20* **Rubondo Island** *island* N Tanzania
122 *I13* **Rubtsovsk** Altayskiy Kray, S Russian Federation
39 *P9* **Ruby** Alaska, USA
35 *W3* **Ruby Dome** ▲ Nevada, W USA
35 *W4* **Ruby Lake** ◎ Nevada, W USA
35 *W4* **Ruby Mountains** ▲▲ Nevada, W USA
33 *Q12* **Ruby Range** ▲▲ Montana, NW USA
118 *C10* **Rucava** Liepāja, SW Latvia
Rūdān *see* Dehbārez
Rudelstadt *see* Ciechanowiec
Rudensk *see* Rudzyensk
119 *G14* **Rūdiškės** Vilnius, S Lithuania
95 *H24* **Rudkøbing** Fyn, C Denmark
145 *V14* **Rudnichnyy** *Kaz.* Rūdnīchnyy. Almaty, SE Kazakhstan
125 *S13* **Rudnichnyy** Kirovskaya Oblast', NW Russian Federation
114 *N9* **Rudnik** Varna, E Bulgaria
Rudny *see* Rudnyy
126 *H4* **Rudnya** Smolenskaya Oblast', W Russian Federation
127 *O8* **Rudnya** Volgogradskaya Oblast', SW Russian Federation
144 *M7* **Rudnyy** *var.* Rudny. Kostanay, N Kazakhstan
122 *K3* **Rudol'fa, Ostrov** *island* Zemlya Frantsa-Iosifa, NW Russian Federation
Rudolf, Lake *see* Turkana, Lake
Rudolfswert *see* Novo mesto
101 *L17* **Rudolstadt** Thüringen, C Germany
31 *Q4* **Rudyard** Michigan, N USA
33 *S7* **Rudyard** Montana, NW USA
119 *K16* **Rudzyensk** *Rus.* Rudensk. Minskaya Voblasts', C Belarus
104 *L6* **Rueda** Castilla-León, N Spain
114 *F10* **Ruen** ▲ Bulgaria/FYR Macedonia
80 *G10* **Rufa'a** Gezira, C Sudan
102 *L10* **Ruffec** Charente, W France
21 *R14* **Ruffin** South Carolina, SE USA
81 *J23* **Rufiji** ≈ E Tanzania
61 *A20* **Rufino** Santa Fe, C Argentina
76 *F11* **Rufisque** W Senegal
83 *K14* **Rufunsa** Lusaka, C Zambia
118 *J9* **Rugāji** Balvi, E Latvia
161 *R7* **Rugao** Jiangsu, E China
97 *M20* **Rugby** C England, UK
29 *N3* **Rugby** North Dakota, N USA
100 *N7* **Rügen** *headland* NE Germany
Ruhaybeh *see* Ar Ruḩaybah
81 *E19* **Ruhengeri** NW Rwanda
Ruhja *see* Rūjiena
100 *M10* **Ruhner Berg** *hill* N Germany
118 *F7* **Ruhnu** *var.* Ruhnu Saar, *Swe.* Runö. *island* SW Estonia
Ruhnu Saar *see* Ruhnu
101 *G15* **Ruhr** ≈ W Germany
91 *W5* **Ruhr Valley** *industrial region* W Germany
161 *S11* **Rui'an** *var.* Rui an. Zhejiang, SE China
161 *P10* **Ruichang** Jiangxi, S China
24 *J11* **Ruidosa** Texas, SW USA
37 *S14* **Ruidoso** New Mexico, SW USA
161 *P12* **Ruijin** Jiangxi, S China
160 *D13* **Ruili** Yunnan, SW China
98 *N8* **Ruinen** Drenthe, NE Netherlands
99 *D17* **Ruiselede** West-Vlaanderen, W Belgium
64 *P5* **Ruivo de Santana, Pico** ▲ Madeira, Portugal, NE Atlantic Ocean
40 *J12* **Ruiz** Nayarit, SW Mexico
54 *E10* **Ruiz, Nevado del** ⛰ W Colombia
138 *J9* **Rujaylah, Ḩarrat ar** *salt lake* N Jordan
Rujen *see* Rūjiena
118 *H7* **Rūjiena** *Est.* Ruhja, *Ger.* Rujen. Valmiera, N Latvia
79 *I18* **Ruki** ≈ W Dem. Rep. Congo
81 *E22* **Rukwa** ◐ *region* SW Tanzania
81 *F23* **Rukwa, Lake** ◎ SE Tanzania
25 *P6* **Rule** Texas, SW USA
22 *K3* **Ruleville** Mississippi, S USA
Rum *see* Rhum
112 *K10* **Ruma** Serbia, N Serbia and Montenegro (Yugo.)
Rumadiya *see* Ar Ramādī
141 *Q7* **Rumāḩ** Ar Riyāḑ, C Saudi Arabia
Rumaitha *see* Ar Rumaythah
Rumania/Rumänien *see* Romania
Rumänisch-Sankt-Georgen *see* Sângeorz-Băi
139 *Y13* **Rumaylah** SE Iraq
139 *P2* **Rumaylah, Wādī** *dry watercourse* NE Syria
171 *U13* **Rumbati** Papua, E Indonesia
81 *E14* **Rumbek** El Buhayrat, S Sudan
Rumburg *see* Rumburk
111 *D14* **Rumburk** *Ger.* Rumburg. Ústecký Kraj, NW Czech Republic
44 *J4* **Rum Cay** *island* C Bahamas
99 *M26* **Rumelange** Luxembourg, S Luxembourg
99 *D20* **Rumes** Hainaut, SW Belgium
19 *P7* **Rumford** Maine, NE USA
110 *I6* **Rumia** Pomorskie, N Poland
113 *J17* **Rumija** ▲▲ SW Serbia and Montenegro (Yugo.)
103 *T11* **Rumilly** Haute-Savoie, E France
139 *O6* **Rūmiyah** W Iraq
Rummah, Wādī ar *see* Rimah, Wādī ar
Rummelsburg in Pommern *see* Miastko
165 *S3* **Rumoi** Hokkaidō, NE Japan
82 *M12* **Rumphi** *var.* Rumpi. Northern, N Malawi
Rumpi *see* Rumphi
29 *V7* **Rum River** ≈ Minnesota, N USA
188 *F16* **Rumung** *island* Caroline Islands, W Micronesia
Rumuniya/Rumŭniya/Rumunjska *see* Romania
185 *G16* **Runanga** West Coast, South Island, NZ
184 *P7* **Runaway, Cape** *headland* North Island, NZ
97 *K18* **Runcorn** C England, UK
118 *K10* **Rundāni** Ludza, E Latvia
83 *L18* **Runde** *var.* Lundi. ≈ SE Zimbabwe
83 *E16* **Rundu** *var.* Runtu. Okavango, NE Namibia
93 *I16* **Rundvik** Västerbotten, N Sweden
81 *G20* **Runere** Mwanza, N Tanzania
25 *S13* **Runge** Texas, SW USA
167 *Q13* **Rŭng, Kaôh** *prev.* Kas Rong. *island* SW Cambodia
79 *O16* **Rungu** Orientale, NE Dem. Rep. Congo
81 *F23* **Rungwa** Rukwa, W Tanzania
81 *G22* **Rungwa** Singida, C Tanzania
94 *M13* **Runn** ◎ C Sweden
24 *M4* **Running Water Draw** *valley* New Mexico/Texas, SW USA
Runö *see* Ruhnu
Runtu *see* Rundu
189 *V12* **Ruo** *island* Caroline Islands, C Micronesia
158 *L9* **Ruoqiang** *var.* Jo-ch'iang, *Uigh.* Charkhlik, Charkhliq, Qarkilik. Xinjiang Uygur Zizhiqu, NW China
159 *S7* **Ruo Shui** ≈ N China
92 *L8* **Ruostekfielbmá** *var.* Rustefjelbma Finnmark, N Norway
93 *L18* **Ruovesi** Länsi-Suomi, W Finland
112 *B9* **Rupa** Primorje-Gorski Kotar, NW Croatia
182 *M11* **Rupanyup** Victoria, SE Australia
168 *K9* **Rupat, Pulau** *prev.* Roepat. *island* W Indonesia
168 *K10* **Rupat, Selat** *strait* Sumatera, W Indonesia
116 *J11* **Rupea** *Ger.* Reps, *Hung.* Kőhalom; *prev.* Cohalm. Braşov, C Romania
99 *G17* **Rupel** ≈ N Belgium
Rupella *see* la Rochelle
33 *P15* **Rupert** Idaho, NW USA
21 *R5* **Rupert** West Virginia, NE USA
Rupert House *see* Fort Rupert
12 *J10* **Rupert, Rivière de** ≈ Québec, C Canada
194 *M13* **Ruppert Coast** *physical region* Antarctica
100 *N11* **Ruppiner Kanal** *canal* NE Germany
55 *S11* **Rupununi River** ≈ S Guyana
101 *D16* **Rur** *Dut.* Roer. ≈ Germany/Netherlands
58 *H13* **Rurópolis Presidente Medici** Pará, N Brazil
191 *S12* **Rurutu** *island* Îles Australes, SW French Polynesia
Rusaddir *see* Melilla
83 *L17* **Rusape** Manicaland, E Zimbabwe
Rusayris, Lake *see* Roseires, Reservoir
Ruschuk/Rusçuk *see* Ruse
114 *K7* **Ruse** *var.* Ruschuk, Rustchuk, *Turk.* Rusçuk. Ruse, N Bulgaria
114 *L7* **Ruse** ◐ *province* N Bulgaria
109 *W10* **Ruše** NE Slovenia
114 *K7* **Rusenski Lom** ≈ N Bulgaria
97 *G17* **Rush** *Ir.* An Ros. E Ireland
161 *S4* **Rushan** *var.* Xiacun. Shandong, E China
Rushan *see* Rŭshon
Rushanskiy Khrebet *see* Rushon, Qatorkŭhi
29 *V7* **Rush City** Minnesota, N USA
37 *V5* **Rush Creek** ≈ Colorado, C USA
29 *X10* **Rushford** Minnesota, N USA
154 *N13* **Rushikulya** ≈ E India
14 *D8* **Rush Lake** ◎ Ontario, S Canada
30 *M7* **Rush Lake** ◎ Wisconsin, N USA
28 *J10* **Rushmore, Mount** ▲ South Dakota, N USA
147 *S13* **Rŭshon** *Rus.* Rushan. S Tajikistan
147 *S14* **Rushon, Qatorkŭhi** *Rus.* Rushanskiy Khrebet. ▲▲ SE Tajikistan
26 *M12* **Rush Springs** Oklahoma, C USA
45 *V15* **Rushville** Trinidad, Trinidad and Tobago
30 *J13* **Rushville** Illinois, N USA
28 *K12* **Rushville** Nebraska, C USA
183 *O11* **Rushworth** Victoria, SE Australia
25 *W8* **Rusk** Texas, SW USA
93 *I14* **Rusksele** Västerbotten, N Sweden
118 *C12* **Rusnė** Klaipėda, W Lithuania
114 *M10* **Rusokastrenska Reka** ≈ E Bulgaria
Russadir *see* Melilla
109 *X3* **Russbach** ≈ NE Austria
11 *V16* **Russell** Manitoba, S Canada
184 *K2* **Russell** Northland, North Island, NZ
26 *L4* **Russell** Kansas, C USA
21 *O4* **Russell** Kentucky, S USA
20 *L7* **Russell Springs** Kentucky, S USA
23 *O2* **Russellville** Alabama, S USA
27 *T11* **Russellville** Arkansas, C USA
20 *J7* **Russellville** Kentucky, S USA
101 *G18* **Rüsselsheim** Hessen, W Germany
Russenes *see* Olderfjord
Russia *see* Russian Federation
Russian America *see* Alaska
122 *J11* **Russian Federation** *off.* Russian Federation, *var.* Russia, *Latv.* Krievija, *Rus.* Rossiyskaya Federatsiya. ◆ *republic* Asia/Europe
39 *N11* **Russian Mission** Alaska, USA
34 *M7* **Russian River** ≈ California, W USA
194 *L13* **Russkaya** *Russian research station* Antarctica
122 *J5* **Russkaya Gavan'** Novaya Zemlya, Arkhangel'skaya Oblast', N Russian Federation
122 *J5* **Russkiy, Ostrov** *island* N Russian Federation
109 *Y5* **Rust** Burgenland, E Austria
Rustaq *see* Ar Rustāq
137 *U10* **Rust'avi** SE Georgia
21 *T7* **Rustburg** Virginia, NE USA
Rustchuk *see* Ruse
Rustefjelbma *see* Ruostekfjelbmá
83 *I21* **Rustenburg** North-West, N South Africa
22 *H5* **Ruston** Louisiana, S USA
81 *E21* **Rutana** SE Burundi
62 *I4* **Rutana, Volcán** ▲ N Chile
Rutanzige, Lake *see* Edward, Lake
Rutba *see* Ar Ruţbah
104 *M14* **Rute** Andalucía, S Spain
171 *N16* **Ruteng** *prev.* Roeteng. Flores, C Indonesia
194 *L8* **Rutford Ice Stream** *ice feature* Antarctica
35 *X6* **Ruth** Nevada, W USA
101 *G15* **Rüthen** Nordrhein-Westfalen, W Germany
14 *D17* **Rutherford** Ontario, S Canada
21 *Q10* **Rutherfordton** North Carolina, SE USA
97 *J18* **Ruthin** *Wel.* Rhuthun. NE Wales, UK
108 *G7* **Rüti** Zürich, N Switzerland
Rutlam *see* Ratlām
18 *M9* **Rutland** Vermont, NE USA

◆ Country
● Country Capital
◇ Dependent Territory
○ Dependent Territory Capital
◐ Administrative Region
✕ International Airport
▲ Mountain
▲▲ Mountain Range
⛰ Volcano
≈ River
◎ Lake
▣ Reservoir

97 N19 **Rutland** *cultural region* C England, UK
21 N8 **Rutledge** Tennessee, S USA
158 G12 **Rutög** *var.* Rutog, Rutok. Xizang Zizhiqu, W China
Rutok *see* Rutög
79 P19 **Rutshuru** Nord Kivu, E Dem. Rep. Congo
98 L8 **Rutten** Flevoland, N Netherlands
127 Q17 **Rutul** Respublika Dagestan, SW Russian Federation
93 L14 **Ruukki** Oulu, C Finland
98 N11 **Ruurlo** Gelderland, E Netherlands
143 S15 **Ru'ūs al Jibāl** *headland* Oman/UAE
138 I7 **Ru'ūs aṭ Ṭiwāl, Jabal** ▲ W Syria
81 H23 **Ruvuma** ◆ *region* SE Tanzania
81 I25 **Ruvuma** *var.* Rio Rovuma. ≈ Mozambique/Tanzania *see also* Rovuma, Rio
Ruwais *see* Ar Ruways
138 L9 **Ruwayshid, Wadi ar** *dry watercourse* NE Jordan
141 Z10 **Ruways, Ra's ar** *headland* E Oman
79 P18 **Ruwenzori** ▲ Uganda/Dem. Rep. Congo
141 Y8 **Ruwi** NE Oman
114 F9 **Ruy** ▲ Bulgaria/Serbia and Montenegro (Yugo.)
Ruya *see* Luia, Rio
81 E20 **Ruyigi** E Burundi
127 P5 **Ruzayevka** Respublika Mordoviya, W Russian Federation
119 G18 **Ruzhany** *Rus.* Ruzhany. Brestskaya Voblasts', SW Belarus
114 I10 **Rŭzhevo Konare** *var.* Rŭzhevo Konare. Plovdiv, C Bulgaria
Ruzhin *see* Ruzhyn
114 G7 **Ruzhintsi** Vidin, NW Bulgaria
161 N6 **Ruzhou** Henan, C China
117 N5 **Ruzhyn** *Rus.* Ruzhin. Zhytomyrs'ka Oblast', N Ukraine
111 K19 **Ružomberok** *Ger.* Rosenberg, *Hung.* Rózsahegy. Žilinský Kraj, N Slovakia
111 C16 **Ruzyně** ✈ (Praha) Praha, C Czech Republic
81 D19 **Rwanda** *off.* Rwandese Republic; *prev.* Ruanda. ◆ *republic* C Africa
Rwandese Republic *see* Rwanda
95 G22 **Ry** Århus, C Denmark
Ryasna *see* Rasna
126 L5 **Ryazan'** Ryazanskaya Oblast', W Russian Federation
126 L5 **Ryazanskaya Oblast'** ◆ *province* W Russian Federation
126 M6 **Ryazhsk** Ryazanskaya Oblast', W Russian Federation
118 B13 **Rybachiy** *Ger.* Rossitten. Kaliningradskaya Oblast', W Russian Federation
126 J2 **Rybachiy, Poluostrov** *peninsula* NW Russian Federation
Rybach'ye *see* Balykchy
126 L15 **Rybinsk** *prev.* Andropov. Yaroslavskaya Oblast', W Russian Federation
126 K14 **Rybinskoye Vodokhranilishche** *Eng.* Rybinsk Reservoir, Rybinsk Sea. ⊠ W Russian Federation
Rybinsk Reservoir/Rybinsk Sea *see* Rybinskoye Vodokhranilishche
111 I16 **Rybnik** Śląskie, S Poland
Rybnitsa *see* Rîbniţa
111 F16 **Rychnov nad Kněžnou** *Ger.* Reichenau. Královéhradecký Kraj, N Czech Republic
110 I12 **Rychwał** Wielkolpolskie, C Poland
11 O13 **Rycroft** Alberta, W Canada
95 L21 **Ryd** Kronoberg, S Sweden
95 L20 **Rydaholm** Jönköping, S Sweden
194 I8 **Rydberg Peninsula** *peninsula* Antarctica
97 P23 **Rye** SE England, UK
33 T10 **Ryegate** Montana, NW USA
35 S3 **Rye Patch Reservoir** ⊠ Nevada, W USA
95 D15 **Ryfylke** *physical region* S Norway
95 H16 **Rygge** Østfold, S Norway
110 N13 **Ryki** Lubelskie, E Poland
Rykovo *see* Yenakiyeve
126 I7 **Ryl'sk** Kurskaya Oblast', W Russian Federation
183 S8 **Rylstone** New South Wales, SE Australia
111 H17 **Rýmařov** *Ger.* Römerstadt. Moravskoslezský Kraj, E Czech Republic
144 E11 **Ryn-Peski** *desert* W Kazakhstan
165 N10 **Ryōtsu** *var.* Ryôtu. Niigata, Sado, C Japan
Ryôtu *see* Ryōtsu
110 K10 **Rypin** Kujawsko-pomorskie, C Poland
Ryshkany *see* Rîşcani
Ryssel *see* Lille
Ryswick *see* Rijswijk
95 M24 **Rytterknægten** *hill* E Denmark
192 G5 **Ryukyu Trench** *var.* Nansei Syotō Trench. *undersea feature* S East China Sea
110 D11 **Rzepin** *Ger.* Reppen. Lubuskie, W Poland
111 N16 **Rzeszów** Podkarpackie, SE Poland
124 I16 **Rzhev** Tverskaya Oblast', W Russian Federation
Rzhishchev *see* Rzhyshchiv
117 P5 **Rzhyshchiv** *Rus.* Rzhishchev. Kyyivs'ka Oblast', N Ukraine

S

138 E11 **Sa'ad** Southern, W Israel
109 P7 **Saalach** ≈ W Austria
101 L14 **Saale** ≈ C Germany
101 L17 **Saalfeld** *var.* Saalfeld an der Saale. Thüringen, C Germany
Saalfeld *see* Zalewo
Saalfeld an der Saale *see* Saalfeld
108 C8 **Saane** ≈ W Switzerland
101 D19 **Saar** *Fr.* Sarre. ≈ France/Germany
101 E20 **Saarbrücken** *Fr.* Sarrebruck. Saarland, SW Germany
Saarburg *see* Sarrebourg
Saare *see* Saaremaa
118 D6 **Sääre** *var.* Sjar. Saaremaa, W Estonia
118 D5 **Saaremaa** *off.* Saare Maakond. ◆ *province* W Estonia
118 E6 **Saaremaa** *Ger.* Oesel, Ösel; *prev.* Saare. *island* W Estonia
92 L12 **Saarenkylä** Lappi, N Finland
Saargemund *see* Sarreguemines
93 L17 **Saarijärvi** Länsi-Suomi, W Finland
Saar in Mähren *see* Žďár nad Sázavou
92 M10 **Saariselkä** *Lapp.* Suoločielgi. Lappi, N Finland
92 L10 **Saariselkä** *hill range* NE Finland
101 D20 **Saarland** *Fr.* Sarre. ◆ *state* SW Germany
Saarlautern *see* Saarlouis
101 D20 **Saarlouis** *prev.* Saarlautern. Saarland, SW Germany
108 E11 **Saaser Vispa** ≈ S Switzerland
137 X12 **Saatlı** *Rus.* Saatly. C Azerbaijan
Saatly *see* Saatlı
Saaz *see* Žatec
45 V9 **Saba** *island* N Netherlands Antilles
138 J7 **Sab' Ābār** *var.* Sab'a Biyar, Sa'b Bi'ār. Ḥimṣ, C Syria
Sab'a Biyar *see* Sab' Ābār
112 K11 **Šabac** Serbia, W Serbia and Montenegro (Yugo.)
105 W5 **Sabadell** Cataluña, E Spain
164 K12 **Sabae** Fukui, Honshū, SW Japan
169 V7 **Sabah** *prev.* British North Borneo, North Borneo. ◆ *state* East Malaysia
168 J8 **Sabak** *var.* Sabak Bernam. Selangor, Peninsular Malaysia
Sabak Bernam *see* Sabak
38 D16 **Sabak, Cape** *headland* Agattu Island, Alaska, USA
81 J20 **Sabaki** ≈ S Kenya
142 L2 **Sabalān, Kuhhā-ye** ▲ NW Iran
154 H7 **Sabalgarh** Madhya Pradesh, C India
44 E4 **Sabana, Archipiélago de** *island group* C Cuba
42 H7 **Sabanagrande** *var.* Sabana Grande. Francisco Morazán, S Honduras
54 E5 **Sabanalarga** Atlántico, N Colombia
41 W14 **Sabancuy** Campeche, SE Mexico
45 N8 **Sabaneta** NW Dominican Republic
54 J4 **Sabaneta** Falcón, N Venezuela
188 H4 **Sabaneta, Puntan** *prev.* Ushi Point. *headland* Saipan, S Northern Mariana Islands
171 X14 **Sabang** Papua, E Indonesia
116 L10 **Săbăoani** Neamţ, NE Romania
155 J26 **Sabaragamuwa Province** ◆ *province* C Sri Lanka
Sabaria *see* Szombathely
154 D10 **Sābarmati** ≈ NW India
171 S10 **Sabatai** Pulau Morotai, E Indonesia
141 Q15 **Sab'atayn, Ramlat as** *desert* C Yemen
107 I16 **Sabaudia** Lazio, C Italy
57 J19 **Sabaya** Oruro, S Bolivia
Sa'b Bi'ār *see* Sab' Ābār
Sabbioncello *see* Orebić
148 I8 **Sāberī, Hāmūn-e** *var.* Daryācheh-ye Hāmūn, Daryācheh-ye Sīstān. ◎ Afghanistan/Iran *see also* Sīstān, Daryācheh-ye
27 P2 **Sabetha** Kansas, C USA
75 P10 **Sabhā** C Libya
67 V13 **Sabi** *var.* Rio Save. ≈ Mozambique/Zimbabwe *see also* Save, Rio
118 E8 **Sabile** *Ger.* Zabeln. Talsi, NW Latvia
31 R14 **Sabina** Ohio, N USA
40 I3 **Sabinal** Chihuahua, N Mexico
25 Q12 **Sabinal** Texas, SW USA
25 Q11 **Sabinal River** ≈ Texas, SW USA
105 S4 **Sabiñánigo** Aragón, NE Spain
41 N6 **Sabinas** Coahuila de Zaragoza, NE Mexico
41 O8 **Sabinas Hidalgo** Nuevo León, NE Mexico
41 N6 **Sabinas, Río** ≈ NE Mexico
22 F9 **Sabine Lake** ◎ Louisiana/Texas, S USA
92 O3 **Sabine Land** *physical region* C Svalbard
25 W7 **Sabine River** ≈ Louisiana/Texas, SW USA
137 X12 **Sabirabad** C Azerbaijan
Sabkha *see* As Sabkhah
171 O4 **Sablayan** Mindoro, N Philippines
13 P16 **Sable, Cape** *headland* Newfoundland and Labrador, SE Canada
23 X17 **Sable, Cape** *headland* Florida, SE USA
13 R16 **Sable Island** *island* Nova Scotia, SE Canada
14 L11 **Sables, Lac des** ◎ Québec, SE Canada
14 E10 **Sables, Rivière aux** ≈ Ontario, S Canada
102 K7 **Sable-sur-Sarthe** Sarthe, NW France
127 U7 **Sablya, Gora** ▲ NW Russian Federation
77 U14 **Sabon Birnin Gwari** Kaduna, C Nigeria
77 V11 **Sabon Kafi** Zinder, C Niger
104 I6 **Sabor, Rio** ≈ N Portugal
14 J8 **Sabourin, Lac** ◎ Québec, SE Canada
102 J14 **Sabres** Landes, SW France
195 X13 **Sabrina Coast** *physical region* Antarctica
140 M11 **Sabt al Ulayā** 'Asīr, SW Saudi Arabia
104 I8 **Sabugal** Guarda, N Portugal
29 Z13 **Sabula** Iowa, C USA
141 N13 **Ṣabyā** Jīzān, SW Saudi Arabia
Sabzawar *see* Sabzevār
Sabzawaran *see* Sabzvārān
143 S4 **Sabzevār** *var.* Sabzawar. Khorāsān, NE Iran
143 T12 **Sabzvārān** *var.* Sabzawaran; *prev.* Jiroft. Kermān, SE Iran
Sacajawea Peak *see* Matterhorn
82 C9 **Sacandica** Uíge, NW Angola
42 A2 **Sacatepéquez** *off.* Departamento de Sacatepéquez. ◆ *department* S Guatemala
104 F11 **Sacavém** Lisboa, W Portugal
29 T13 **Sac City** Iowa, C USA
105 P8 **Sacedón** Castilla-La Mancha, C Spain
116 J12 **Săcele** *Ger.* Vierdörfer, *Hung.* Négyfalu; *prev. Ger.* Sieben Dörfer, *Hung.* Hétfalu. Braşov, C Romania
12 C8 **Sachigo** Ontario, C Canada
12 C7 **Sachigo** ≈ Ontario, C Canada
12 C8 **Sachigo Lake** ◎ Ontario, C Canada
163 Y16 **Sach'ŏn** *Jap.* Sansenhō; *prev.* Samch'ŏnpŏ. S South Korea
101 O15 **Sachsen** *Eng.* Saxony, *Fr.* Saxe. ◆ *state* E Germany
101 K14 **Sachsen-Anhalt** *Eng.* Saxony-Anhalt. ◆ *state* C Germany
109 R9 **Sachsenburg** Salzburg, S Austria
Sachsenfeld *see* Žalec
8 I5 **Sachs Harbour** Banks Island, Northwest Territories, N Canada
Sächsisch-Reen/Sächsisch-Regen *see* Reghin
18 H8 **Sackets Harbor** New York, NE USA
13 P14 **Sackville** New Brunswick, SE Canada
19 P9 **Saco** Maine, NE USA
19 P8 **Saco River** ≈ Maine/New Hampshire, NE USA
35 O7 **Sacramento** *state capital* California, W USA
37 T14 **Sacramento Mountains** ▲ New Mexico, SW USA
35 N6 **Sacramento River** ≈ California, W USA
35 N5 **Sacramento Valley** *valley* California, W USA
36 I10 **Sacramento Wash** *valley* Arizona, SW USA
105 N15 **Sacratif, Cabo** *headland* S Spain
116 F9 **Săcueni** *prev.* Săcuieni, *Hung.* Székelyhid. Bihor, W Romania
Săcuieni *see* Săcueni
105 R4 **Sádaba** Aragón, NE Spain
Sá da Bandeira *see* Lubango
138 I6 **Ṣadad** Ḥimṣ, W Syria
141 O13 **Ṣa'dah** NW Yemen
167 O16 **Sadao** Songkhla, SW Thailand
142 L8 **Sadd-e Dez, Daryācheh-ye** ◎ W Iran
19 S3 **Saddleback Mountain** *hill* Maine, NE USA
19 P6 **Saddleback Mountain** ▲ Maine, NE USA
167 S14 **Sa Đec** Đông Thap, S Vietnam
141 W13 **Sadḥ** S Oman
76 J11 **Sadiola** Kayes, W Mali
149 R12 **Sādiqābād** Punjab, E Pakistan
153 Y10 **Sadiya** Assam, NE India
139 W9 **Sa'diyah, Hawr as** ◎ E Iraq
165 N9 **Sado** *var.* Sadoga-shima. *island* C Japan
Sadoga-shima *see* Sado
104 F12 **Sado, Rio** ≈ S Portugal
114 I8 **Sadovets** Pleven, N Bulgaria
127 O11 **Sadovoye** Respublika Kalmykiya, SW Russian Federation
105 W9 **Sa Dragonera** *var.* Isla Dragonera. *island* Islas Baleares, Spain, W Mediterranean Sea
95 H20 **Sæby** Nordjylland, N Denmark
105 P9 **Saelices** Castilla-La Mancha, C Spain
Saena Julia *see* Siena
Saetabicula *see* Alzira
114 O12 **Safaalan** Tekirdağ, NW Turkey
Safad *see* Ẕefat
Ṣafāqis *see* Sfax
192 I16 **Safata Bay** *bay* Upolo, Samoa, C Pacific Ocean
Safed *see* Ẕefat
Safed, Āb-i- *see* Sefīd, Darya-ye
139 X11 **Ṣaffāf, Ḥawr aṣ** *wetland* S Iraq
95 J16 **Säffle** Värmland, C Sweden
37 N15 **Safford** Arizona, SW USA
74 E7 **Safi** W Morocco
143 V9 **Safīdābeh** Khorāsān, E Iran
142 M4 **Safīd, Rūd-e** ≈ NW Iran
126 I4 **Safonovo** Smolenskaya Oblast', W Russian Federation
136 H11 **Safranbolu** Karabük, N Turkey
139 Y13 **Safwān** SE Iraq
158 J16 **Saga** *var.* Gya'gya. Xizang Zizhiqu, W China
164 C14 **Saga** Saga, Kyūshū, SW Japan
164 C13 **Saga** *off.* Saga-ken. ◆ *prefecture* Kyūshū, SW Japan
165 P10 **Sagae** Yamagata, Honshū, C Japan
166 L3 **Sagaing** Sagaing, C Myanmar
166 L5 **Sagaing** ◆ *division* N Myanmar
165 N13 **Sagamihara** Kanagawa, Honshū, S Japan
165 N14 **Sagami-nada** *inlet* SW Japan
Sagan *see* Żagań
29 Y3 **Saganaga Lake** ◎ Minnesota, N USA
155 F18 **Sāgar** Karnātaka, W India
154 I9 **Sāgar** *prev.* Saugor. Madhya Pradesh, C India
15 S8 **Sagard** Québec, SE Canada
Sagarmatha *see* Everest, Mount
Sagebrush State *see* Nevada
143 V11 **Sāghand** Yazd, C Iran
19 N14 **Sag Harbor** Long Island, New York, NE USA
Saghez *see* Saqqez
31 R8 **Saginaw** Michigan, N USA
31 R8 **Saginaw Bay** *lake bay* Michigan, N USA
144 H11 **Sagiz** Atyrau, W Kazakhstan
64 H6 **Saglek Bank** *undersea feature* W Labrador Sea
13 P5 **Saglek Bay** *bay* SW Labrador Sea
Saglouc/Sagluk *see* Salluit
103 X15 **Sagonne, Golfe de** *gulf* Corse, France, C Mediterranean Sea
105 P13 **Sagra** ▲ S Spain
104 F14 **Sagres** Faro, S Portugal
37 S7 **Saguache** Colorado, C USA
44 J7 **Sagua de Tánamo** Holguín, E Cuba
44 E5 **Sagua la Grande** Villa Clara, C Cuba
15 R7 **Saguenay** ≈ Québec, SE Canada
74 C9 **Saguia al Hamra** *var.* As Saqia al Hamra. ≈ N Western Sahara
Sagunt/Saguntum *see* Sagunto
105 S9 **Sagunto** *Cat.* Sagunt, *Ar.* Murbiedro; *anc.* Saguntum. País Valenciano, E Spain
138 H10 **Saḥāb** 'Ammān, NW Jordan
54 E6 **Sahagún** Córdoba, NW Colombia
104 L4 **Sahagún** Castilla-León, N Spain
141 X8 **Saḥam** N Oman
68 F9 **Sahara** *desert* Libya/Algeria
75 U9 **Sahara el Gharbîya** *var.* Aṣ Ṣaḥrā' al Gharbīyah, *Eng.* Western Desert. *desert* C Egypt
75 X9 **Sahara el Sharqîya** *var.* Aṣ Ṣaḥrā' ash Sharqīyah, *Eng.* Arabian Desert, Eastern Desert. *desert* E Egypt
Saharan Atlas *see* Atlas Saharien
152 J9 **Sahāranpur** Uttar Pradesh, N India
64 L10 **Saharan Seamounts** *var.* Saharian Seamounts. *undersea feature* E Atlantic Ocean
153 Q13 **Saharsa** Bihār, NE India
67 O7 **Sahel** *physical region* C Africa
153 R14 **Sāhibganj** Jhārkhand, NE India
139 Q7 **Sāhilīyah** C Iraq
138 H4 **Sāḥilīyah, Jibāl as** ▲ NW Syria
114 M13 **Şahin** Tekirdağ, NW Turkey
149 U8 **Sāhīwāl** Punjab, E Pakistan
149 U9 **Sāhīwāl** *prev.* Montgomery. Punjab, E Pakistan
141 W11 **Ṣaḥmah, Ramlat as** *desert* C Oman
139 T13 **Ṣaḥrā' al Ḥijārah** *desert* S Iraq
40 H5 **Sahuaripa** Sonora, NW Mexico
36 M16 **Sahuarita** Arizona, SW USA
40 L13 **Sahuayo** *var.* Sahuayo de José María Morelos; *prev.* Sahuayo de Díaz, Sahuayo de Porfirio Díaz. Michoacán de Ocampo, SW Mexico
Sahuayo de Díaz/Sahuayo de José María Morelos/Sahuayo de Porfirio Díaz *see* Sahuayo
173 W8 **Sahul Shelf** *undersea feature* N Timor Sea
167 P17 **Sai Buri** Pattani, SW Thailand
74 I6 **Saïda** NW Algeria
138 G7 **Saïda** *var.* Ṣaydā, Sayida; *anc.* Sidon. W Lebanon
Sa'īdābād *see* Sīrjān
80 B13 **Sa'id Bundas** Western Bahr el Ghazal, SW Sudan
186 E7 **Saidor** Madang, N PNG
153 S13 **Saidpur** *var.* Syedpur. Rajshahi, NW Bangladesh
108 C7 **Saignelégier** Jura, NW Switzerland
164 H11 **Saigō** Shimane, Dōgo, SW Japan
Saigon *see* Hô Chi Minh
163 P11 **Saihan Tal** *var.* Sonid Youqi. Nei Mongol Zizhiqu, N China
162 I12 **Saihan Toroi** Nei Mongol Zizhiqu, N China
Sai Hun *see* Syr Darya
92 M11 **Saija** Lappi, NE Finland
164 G14 **Saijō** Ehime, Shikoku, SW Japan
164 E15 **Saiki** Ōita, Kyūshū, SW Japan
93 N18 **Saimaa** ◎ SE Finland
93 N18 **Saimaa Canal** *Fin.* Saimaan Kanava, *Rus.* Saymenskiy Kanal. *canal* Finland/Russia
Saimaan Kanava *see* Saimaa Canal
40 L10 **Saín Alto** Zacatecas, C Mexico
96 L12 **St Abb's Head** *headland* SE Scotland, UK
11 Y16 **St.Adolphe** Manitoba, S Canada
103 O15 **St-Affrique** Aveyron, S France
15 Q10 **St-Agapit** Québec, SE Canada
97 O21 **St Albans** *anc.* Verulamium. E England, UK
18 L6 **Saint Albans** Vermont, NE USA
21 Q5 **Saint Albans** West Virginia, NE USA
St Alban's Head *see* St.Aldhelm's Head
11 Q14 **St.Albert** Alberta, SW Canada
99 M24 **St. Aldhelm's Head** *var.* St.Alban's Head. *headland* S England, UK
15 S8 **St-Alexandre** Québec, SE Canada
15 O11 **St-Alexis-des-Monts** Québec, SE Canada
103 P2 **St-Amand-les-Eaux** Nord, N France
103 O9 **St-Amand-Montrond** *var.* St-Amand-Mont-Rond. Cher, C France
15 Q7 **St-Ambroise** Québec, SE Canada
173 P16 **St-André** NE Réunion
14 M12 **St-André-Avellin** Québec, SE Canada
102 K12 **St-André-de-Cubzac** Gironde, SW France
96 K11 **St Andrews** E Scotland, UK
23 Q9 **Saint Andrews Bay** *bay* Florida, SE USA
23 W7 **Saint Andrew Sound** *sound* Georgia, SE USA
Saint Anna Trough *see* Svyataya Anna Trough
44 J11 **St.Ann's Bay** C Jamaica
13 T10 **St.Anthony** Newfoundland and Labrador, SE Canada
33 R13 **Saint Anthony** Idaho, NW USA
182 M11 **Saint Arnaud** Victoria, SE Australia
185 I15 **St.Arnaud Range** ▲ South Island, NZ
15 T8 **St-Arsène** Québec, SE Canada
13 R10 **St-Augustin** Québec, E Canada
23 X9 **Saint Augustine** Florida, SE USA
97 H24 **St Austell** SW England, UK
103 T4 **St-Avold** Moselle, NE France
103 N17 **St-Barthélemy** ▲ S France
102 L17 **St-Béat** Haute-Garonne, S France
97 I15 **St Bees Head** *headland* NW England, UK
173 P16 **St-Benoit** E Réunion
103 T13 **St-Bonnet** Hautes-Alpes, SE France
St.Botolph's Town *see* Boston
97 G21 **St Brides Bay** *inlet* SW Wales, UK
102 H5 **St-Brieuc** Côtes d'Armor, NW France
102 H5 **St-Brieuc, Baie de** *bay* NW France
102 L7 **St-Calais** Sarthe, NW France
15 Q10 **St-Casimir** Québec, SE Canada
14 H16 **St.Catharines** Ontario, S Canada
45 S14 **St.Catherine, Mount** ▲ N Grenada
64 C11 **St Catherine Point** *headland* E Bermuda
23 X6 **Saint Catherines Island** *island* Georgia, SE USA
97 M24 **St Catherine's Point** *headland* S England, UK
103 N13 **St-Céré** Lot, S France
108 A10 **St.Cergue** Vaud, W Switzerland
103 R11 **St-Chamond** Loire, E France
33 S16 **Saint Charles** Idaho, NW USA
27 X4 **Saint Charles** Missouri, C USA
103 P13 **St-Chély-d'Apcher** Lozère, S France
Saint Christopher-Nevis *see* Saint Kitts and Nevis
31 S9 **Saint Clair** Michigan, N USA
14 D17 **St.Clair** ≈ Canada/USA
183 O17 **St.Clair, Lake** ◎ Tasmania, SE Australia
14 C17 **St.Clair, Lake** *var.* Lac à L'eau Claire. ◎ Canada/USA
31 S10 **Saint Clair Shores** Michigan, N USA
103 S10 **St-Claude** *anc.* Condate. Jura, E France
45 X6 **St-Claude** Basse Terre, SW Guadeloupe
23 X12 **Saint Cloud** Florida, E USA
29 U8 **Saint Cloud** Minnesota, N USA
45 T9 **Saint Croix** *island* S Virgin Islands (US)
30 J4 **Saint Croix Flowage** ⊠ Wisconsin, N USA
19 T5 **Saint Croix River** ≈ Canada/USA
29 W7 **Saint Croix River** ≈ Minnesota/Wisconsin, N USA
45 S14 **St.David's** SE Grenada
97 H21 **St David's** SW Wales, UK
97 G21 **St David's Head** *headland* SW Wales, UK
64 C12 **St David's Island** *island* E Bermuda
173 O16 **St-Denis** ○ (Réunion) NW Réunion
103 U6 **St-Dié** Vosges, NE France
103 R5 **St-Dizier** *anc.* Desiderii Fanum. Haute-Marne, N France
15 N11 **St-Donat** Québec, SE Canada
15 N11 **Ste-Adèle** Québec, SE Canada
15 N11 **Ste-Agathe-des-Monts** Québec, SE Canada
172 I16 **Sainte Anne** *island* Inner Islands, NE Seychelles
11 Y16 **Ste.Anne** Manitoba, S Canada
45 R12 **Ste-Anne** Grande Terre, E Guadeloupe
45 Y6 **Ste-Anne** SE Martinique
15 Q10 **Ste-Anne** ≈ Québec, SE Canada
15 W6 **Ste-Anne-des-Monts** Québec, SE Canada
14 M10 **Ste-Anne-du-Lac** Québec, SE Canada
15 U4 **Ste-Anne, Lac** ◎ Québec, SE Canada
15 S10 **Ste-Apolline** Québec, SE Canada
15 U7 **Ste-Blandine** Québec, SE Canada
15 R10 **Ste-Claire** Québec, SE Canada
15 Q10 **Ste-Croix** Québec, SE Canada
108 B8 **Ste-Croix** Vaud, SW Switzerland
103 P14 **Ste-Énimie** Lozère, S France
27 Y6 **Sainte Genevieve** Missouri, C USA
103 S12 **St-Egrève** Isère, E France
39 T12 **Saint Elias, Cape** *headland* Kayak Island, Alaska, USA
39 U11 **Saint Elias, Mount** ▲ Alaska, USA
10 G8 **Saint Elias Mountains** ▲ Canada/USA
55 Y10 **St-Élie** N French Guiana
103 O10 **St-Eloy-les-Mines** Puy-de-Dôme, C France
15 R7 **Ste-Marguerite** ≈ Québec, SE Canada
15 S7 **Ste-Marguerite-Nord-Est** ≈ Québec, SE Canada
15 V4 **Ste-Marguerite, Pointe** *headland* Québec, SE Canada
15 R10 **Ste-Marie** Québec, SE Canada
45 Q11 **Ste-Marie** NE Martinique
173 P16 **Ste-Marie** NE Réunion
103 U6 **Ste-Marie-aux-Mines** Haut-Rhin, NE France
12 J14 **Ste-Marie, Lac** ⊠ Quebec, S Canada
172 K4 **Sainte Marie, Nosy** *island* E Madagascar
102 L8 **Ste-Maure-de-Touraine** Indre-et-Loire, C France
103 R4 **Ste-Menehould** Marne, NE France
Ste-Perpétue *see* Ste-Perpétue-de-l'Islet
15 S9 **Ste-Perpétue-de-l'Islet** *var.* Ste-Perpétue. Québec, SE Canada
45 X11 **Ste-Rose** Basse Terre, N Guadeloupe
173 P16 **Ste-Rose** E Réunion
11 W15 **Ste.Rose du Lac** Manitoba, S Canada
102 J11 **Saintes** *anc.* Mediolanum. Charente-Maritime, W France
45 X7 **Saintes, Canal des** *channel* SW Guadeloupe
Saintes, Îles des *see* les Saintes
173 P16 **Ste-Suzanne** N Réunion
15 P10 **Ste-Thècle** Québec, SE Canada
103 Q12 **St-Étienne** Loire, E France
102 M4 **St-Étienne-du-Rouvray** Seine-Maritime, N France
Saint Eustatius *see* Sint Eustatius
14 M11 **Ste-Véronique** Québec, SE Canada
15 T7 **St-Fabien** Québec, SE Canada
15 P7 **St-Félicien** Québec, SE Canada
15 O11 **St-Félix-de-Valois** Québec, SE Canada
103 Y14 **St-Florent** Corse, France, C Mediterranean Sea
103 Y14 **St-Florent, Golfe de** *gulf* Corse, France, C Mediterranean Sea
103 P6 **St-Florentin** Yonne, C France
103 N9 **St-Florent-sur-Cher** Cher, C France
103 P12 **St-Flour** Cantal, C France
26 H2 **Saint Francis** Kansas, C USA
83 H26 **St.Francis, Cape** *headland* S South Africa
27 X10 **Saint Francis River** ≈ Arkansas/Missouri, C USA
22 J8 **Saint Francisville** Louisiana, S USA
15 Q12 **St-François** ≈ Québec, SE Canada
45 Y6 **St-François** Grande Terre, E Guadeloupe
15 R11 **St-François, Lac** ◎ Québec, SE Canada
27 X7 **Saint Francois Mountains** ▲ Missouri, C USA
St-Gall/Saint Gall/St.Gallen *see* Sankt Gallen
102 L16 **St-Gaudens** Haute-Garonne, S France
15 R12 **St-Gédéon** Québec, SE Canada
181 X10 **Saint George** Queensland, E Australia
64 B12 **St George** N Bermuda
38 K15 **Saint George** Saint George Island, Alaska, USA
21 S14 **Saint George** South Carolina, SE USA
36 J8 **Saint George** Utah, W USA
13 R12 **St.George, Cape** *headland* Newfoundland and Labrador, E Canada
186 I6 **St.George, Cape** *headland* New Ireland, NE PNG
38 J15 **Saint George Island** *island* Pribilof Islands, Alaska, USA
23 S10 **Saint George Island** *island* Florida, SE USA
99 J19 **Saint-Georges** Liège, E Belgium
15 R11 **St-Georges** Québec, SE Canada
55 Z11 **St-Georges** E French Guiana
45 R14 **St.George's** ● (Grenada) SW Grenada
13 R12 **St.George's Bay** *inlet* Newfoundland and Labrador, E Canada
97 G21 **Saint George's Channel** *channel* Ireland/Wales, UK
186 H6 **St.George's Channel** *channel* NE PNG
64 B11 **St George's Island** *island* E Bermuda
99 I21 **Saint-Gérard** Namur, S Belgium
Saint-Germain *see* St-Germain-en-Laye
15 P12 **St-Germain-de-Grantham** Québec, SE Canada
103 N5 **St-Germain-en-Laye** *var.* St-Germain. Yvelines, N France
102 H8 **St-Gildas, Pointe du** *headland* NW France
103 R15 **St-Gilles** Gard, S France
102 I9 **St-Gilles-Croix-de-Vie** Vendée, NW France
173 O16 **St-Gilles-les-Bains** W Réunion
102 M16 **St-Girons** Ariège, S France
Saint Gotthard *see* Szentgotthárd
108 G9 **St.Gotthard Tunnel** *tunnel* Ticino, S Switzerland
97 H22 **St Govan's Head** *headland* SW Wales, UK
34 M7 **Saint Helena** California, W USA
65 F24 **Saint Helena** ◇ *UK dependent territory* C Atlantic Ocean
67 O12 **Saint Helena** *island* C Atlantic Ocean
83 E25 **St.Helena Bay** *bay* SW South Africa
65 M16 **Saint Helena Fracture Zone** *tectonic feature* C Atlantic Ocean
34 M7 **Saint Helena, Mount** ▲ California, W USA
21 S15 **Saint Helena Sound** *inlet* South Carolina, SE USA

◆ Country ● Country Capital ◇ Dependent Territory ○ Dependent Territory Capital ◆ Administrative Region ✈ International Airport ▲ Mountain ▲ Mountain Range ▲ Volcano ≈ River ◎ Lake ⊠ Reservoir

31 Q7 **Saint Helen, Lake** ⊚ Michigan, N USA
183 Q16 **Saint Helens** Tasmania, SE Australia
97 K18 **St Helens** NW England, UK
32 G10 **Saint Helens** Oregon, NW USA
32 H10 **Saint Helens, Mount** ж Washington, NW USA
97 L26 **St Helier** ○ (Jersey) S Jersey, Channel Islands
15 S9 **St-Hilarion** Québec, SE Canada
99 K22 **Saint-Hubert** Luxembourg, SE Belgium
15 T8 **St-Hubert** Québec, SE Canada
15 P12 **St-Hyacinthe** Québec, SE Canada
St.Iago de la Vega *see* Spanish Town
31 Q4 **Saint Ignace** Michigan, N USA
15 O10 **St-Ignace-du-Lac** Québec, SE Canada
12 D12 **St.Ignace Island** *island* Ontario, S Canada
108 C7 **St.Imier** Bern, W Switzerland
97 G25 **St Ives** SW England, UK
29 U10 **Saint James** Minnesota, N USA
10 I15 **St.James, Cape** *headland* Graham Island, British Columbia, SW Canada
15 O13 **St-Jean** *var.* St-Jean-sur-Richelieu. Québec, SE Canada
55 X9 **St-Jean** NW French Guiana
15 R8 **St-Jean** ≈ Québec, SE Canada
Saint-Jean-d'Acre *see* 'Akko
102 K11 **St-Jean-d'Angély** Charente-Maritime, W France
103 N7 **St-Jean-de-Braye** Loiret, C France
102 I16 **St-Jean-de-Luz** Pyrénées-Atlantiques, SW France
103 T12 **St-Jean-de-Maurienne** Savoie, E France
102 I9 **St-Jean-de-Monts** Vendée, NW France
103 Q14 **St-Jean-du-Gard** Gard, S France
15 Q7 **St-Jean, Lac** ⊚ Québec, SE Canada
102 I16 **St-Jean-Pied-de-Port** Pyrénées-Atlantiques, SW France
15 S9 **St-Jean-Port-Joli** Québec, SE Canada
St-Jean-sur-Richelieu *see* St-Jean
15 N12 **St-Jérôme** Québec, SE Canada
25 T5 **Saint Jo** Texas, SW USA
13 O15 **St.John** New Brunswick, SE Canada
26 L6 **Saint John** Kansas, C USA
76 K16 **Saint John** ≈ C Liberia
45 T9 **Saint John** *island* C Virgin Islands (US)
22 I6 **Saint John, Lake** ⊚ Louisiana, S USA
19 Q2 **Saint John** *Fr.* Saint-John. ≈ Canada/USA
45 W10 **St John's** ● (Antigua and Barbuda) Antigua, Antigua and Barbuda
13 V12 **St.John's** Newfoundland and Labrador, E Canada
37 O12 **Saint Johns** Arizona, SW USA
31 Q9 **Saint Johns** Michigan, N USA
13 V12 **St.John's** × Newfoundland and Labrador, E Canada
23 X11 **Saint Johns River** ≈ Florida, SE USA
45 N12 **St.Joseph** W Dominica
173 P17 **St-Joseph** S Réunion
22 J6 **Saint Joseph** Louisiana, S USA
31 O10 **Saint Joseph** Michigan, N USA
27 R3 **Saint Joseph** Missouri, C USA
20 I10 **Saint Joseph** Tennessee, S USA
22 R9 **Saint Joseph Bay** *bay* Florida, SE USA
15 R11 **St-Joseph-de-Beauce** Québec, SE Canada
12 C10 **St.Joseph, Lake** ⊚ Ontario, C Canada
31 Q11 **Saint Joseph River** ≈ N USA
14 C11 **Saint Joseph's Island** *island* Ontario, S Canada
15 N11 **St-Jovite** Québec, SE Canada
121 P16 **St Julian's** N Malta
St-Julien *see* St-Julien-en-Genevois
103 T10 **St-Julien-en-Genevois** *var.* St-Julien. Haute-Savoie, E France
102 M11 **St-Junien** Haute-Vienne, C France
103 Q11 **St-Just-St-Rambert** Loire, E France
96 D8 **St Kilda** *island* NW Scotland, UK
45 V10 **Saint Kitts** *island* Saint Kitts and Nevis
45 U10 **Saint Kitts and Nevis** *off.* Federation of Saint Christopher and Nevis, *var.* Saint Christopher-Nevis. ◆ *commonwealth republic* E West Indies
11 X16 **St.Laurent** Manitoba, S Canada
St-Laurent *see* St-Laurent-du-Maroni
55 X9 **St-Laurent-du-Maroni** *var.* St-Laurent. NW French Guiana
St-Laurent, Fleuve *see* St.Lawrence
102 J12 **St-Laurent-Médoc** Gironde, SW France
13 N12 **St.Lawrence** *Fr.* Fleuve St-Laurent. ≈ Canada/USA
13 Q12 **St.Lawrence, Gulf of** *gulf* NW Atlantic Ocean
38 K10 **Saint Lawrence Island** *island* Alaska, USA
14 M14 **Saint Lawrence River** ≈ Canada/USA
99 L25 **Saint-Léger** Luxembourg, SE Belgium
13 N14 **St.Léonard** New Brunswick, SE Canada
15 P11 **St-Léonard** Québec, SE Canada
173 O17 **St-Leu** W Réunion
102 J4 **St-Lô** *anc.* Briovera, Laudus. Manche, N France
11 T15 **St.Louis** Saskatchewan, S Canada
103 V7 **St-Louis** Haut-Rhin, NE France
173 O17 **St-Louis** S Réunion
76 G10 **Saint Louis** NW Senegal
27 X4 **Saint Louis** Missouri, C USA
29 W5 **Saint Louis River** ≈ Minnesota, N USA
103 T7 **St-Loup-sur-Semouse** Haute-Saône, E France
15 O12 **St-Luc** Québec, SE Canada
83 L22 **St.Lucia** KwaZulu/Natal, E South Africa
45 X13 **Saint Lucia** ◆ *commonwealth republic* SE West Indies
47 S3 **Saint Lucia** *island* SE West Indies
83 L22 **St.Lucia, Cape** *headland* E South Africa
45 Y13 **Saint Lucia Channel** *channel* Martinique/Saint Lucia
23 Y14 **Saint Lucie Canal** *canal* Florida, SE USA
23 Z13 **Saint Lucie Inlet** *inlet* Florida, SE USA
96 L2 **St Magnus Bay** *bay* N Scotland, UK
102 K10 **St-Maixent-l'École** Deux-Sèvres, W France
11 Y16 **St.Malo** Manitoba, S Canada
102 I5 **St-Malo** Ille-et-Vilaine, NW France
102 H4 **St-Malo, Golfe de** *gulf* NW France
44 L9 **St-Marc** C Haiti
44 L9 **St-Marc, Canal de** *channel* W Haiti
55 Y12 **Saint-Marcel, Mont** ▲ S French Guiana
103 S12 **St-Marcellin-le-Mollard** Isère, E France
96 K5 **St Margaret's Hope** NE Scotland, UK
32 M9 **Saint Maries** Idaho, NW USA
23 T9 **Saint Marks** Florida, SE USA
108 D11 **St.Martin** Valais, SW Switzerland
Saint Martin *see* Sint Maarten
31 O5 **Saint Martin Island** *island* Michigan, N USA
22 I9 **Saint Martinville** Louisiana, S USA
185 E20 **St.Mary, Mount** ▲ South Island, NZ
186 E8 **St.Mary, Mount** ▲ S PNG
182 I6 **Saint Mary Peak** ▲ South Australia
183 Q16 **Saint Marys** Tasmania, SE Australia
14 E16 **St.Marys** Ontario, S Canada
38 M11 **Saint Marys** Alaska, USA
23 W8 **Saint Marys** Georgia, SE USA
27 P4 **Saint Marys** Kansas, C USA
31 Q4 **Saint Marys** Ohio, N USA
21 R3 **Saint Marys** West Virginia, NE USA
23 W8 **Saint Marys River** ≈ Florida/Georgia, SE USA
31 Q4 **Saint Marys River** ≈ Michigan, N USA
102 D6 **St-Mathieu, Pointe** *headland* NW France
38 J12 **Saint Matthew Island** *island* Alaska, USA
21 R13 **Saint Matthews** South Carolina, SE USA
St.Matthew's Island *see* Zadetkyi Kyun
186 G4 **St.Matthias Group** *island group* NE PNG
108 C11 **St.Maurice** Valais, SW Switzerland
15 P9 **St-Maurice** ≈ Québec, SE Canada
102 J13 **St-Médard-en-Jalles** Gironde, SW France
39 N10 **Saint Michael** Alaska, USA
St.Michel *see* Mikkeli
15 N10 **St-Michel-des-Saints** Québec, SE Canada
103 S5 **St-Mihiel** Meuse, NE France
108 J10 **St.Moritz** *Ger.* Sankt Moritz, *Rmsch.* San Murezzan. Graubünden, SE Switzerland
102 H8 **St-Nazaire** Loire-Atlantique, NW France
Saint Nicholas *see* São Nicolau
Saint-Nicolas *see* Sint-Niklaas
103 N1 **St-Omer** Pas-de-Calais, N France
102 J11 **Saintonge** *cultural region* W France
15 S9 **St-Pacôme** Québec, SE Canada
15 S10 **St-Pamphile** Québec, SE Canada
15 S9 **St-Pascal** Québec, SE Canada
14 J11 **St-Patrice, Lac** ⊚ Québec, SE Canada
11 R14 **St.Paul** Alberta, SW Canada
173 O16 **St-Paul** NW Réunion
38 K14 **Saint Paul** Saint Paul Island, Alaska, USA
29 V8 **Saint Paul** *state capital* Minnesota, N USA
29 P15 **Saint Paul** Nebraska, C USA
21 P7 **Saint Paul** Virginia, NE USA
77 Q17 **Saint Paul, Cape** *headland* S Ghana
103 O17 **St-Paul-de-Fenouillet** Pyrénées-Orientales, S France
65 K14 **Saint Paul Fracture Zone** *tectonic feature* E Atlantic Ocean
38 J14 **Saint Paul Island** *island* Pribilof Islands, Alaska, USA
102 J15 **St-Paul-les-Dax** Landes, SW France
21 U11 **Saint Pauls** North Carolina, SE USA
Saint Paul's Bay *see* San Pawl il-Bahar
191 R16 **St Paul's Point** *headland* Pitcairn Island, Pitcairn Islands
29 U10 **Saint Peter** Minnesota, N USA
97 L26 **St Peter Port** ○ (Guernsey) C Guernsey, Channel Islands
23 V13 **Saint Petersburg** Florida, SE USA
Saint Petersburg *see* Sankt-Peterburg
23 V13 **Saint Petersburg Beach** Florida, SE USA
173 P17 **St-Philippe** SE Réunion
45 Q11 **St-Pierre** NW Martinique
173 O17 **St-Pierre** SW Réunion
13 S13 **St-Pierre and Miquelon** *Fr.* Îles St-Pierre et Miquelon. ◇ *French territorial collectivity* NE North America
15 P11 **St-Pierre, Lac** ⊚ Québec, SE Canada
102 F5 **St-Pol-de-Léon** Finistère, NW France
103 O2 **St-Pol-sur-Ternoise** Pas-de-Calais, N France
St. Pons *see* St-Pons-de-Thomières
103 O16 **St-Pons-de-Thomières** *var.* St.Pons. Hérault, S France
103 P10 **St-Pourçain-sur-Sioule** Allier, C France
15 S11 **St-Prosper** Québec, SE Canada
103 P3 **St-Quentin** Aisne, N France
15 R10 **St-Raphaël** Québec, SE Canada
103 U15 **St-Raphaël** Var, SE France
15 Q10 **St-Raymond** Québec, SE Canada
33 O9 **Saint Regis** Montana, NW USA
18 J7 **Saint Regis River** ≈ New York, NE USA
103 R15 **St-Rémy-de-Provence** Bouches-du-Rhône, SE France
15 V6 **St-René-de-Matane** Québec, SE Canada
102 M9 **St-Savin** Vienne, W France
15 S8 **St-Siméon** Québec, SE Canada
23 X7 **Saint Simons Island** *island* Georgia, SE USA
191 Y2 **Saint Stanislas Bay** *bay* Kiritimati, E Kiribati
13 O15 **St.Stephen** New Brunswick, SE Canada
39 X12 **Saint Terese** Alaska, USA
14 E17 **St.Thomas** Ontario, S Canada
29 Q2 **Saint Thomas** North Dakota, N USA
45 T9 **Saint Thomas** *island* W Virgin Islands (US)
Saint Thomas *see* São Tomé, Sao Tome and Principe
Saint Thomas *see* Charlotte Amalie, Virgin Islands (US)
15 P10 **St-Tite** Québec, SE Canada
Saint-Trond *see* Sint-Truiden
103 U16 **St-Tropez** Var, SE France
Saint Ubes *see* Setúbal
102 L3 **St-Valéry-en-Caux** Seine-Maritime, N France
103 Q9 **St-Vallier** Saône-et-Loire, C France
106 B7 **St-Vincent** Valle d'Aosta, NW Italy
45 Q14 **Saint Vincent** *island* N Saint Vincent and the Grenadines
Saint Vincent *see* São Vicente
45 W14 **Saint Vincent and the Grenadines** ◆ *commonwealth republic* SE West Indies
Saint Vincent, Cape *see* São Vicente, Cabo de
102 I15 **St-Vincent-de-Tyrosse** Landes, SW France
182 I9 **Saint Vincent, Gulf** *gulf* South Australia
23 R10 **Saint Vincent Island** *island* Florida, SE USA
45 T12 **Saint Vincent Passage** *passage* Saint Lucia/Saint Vincent and the Grenadines
183 N18 **Saint Vincent, Point** *headland* Tasmania, SE Australia
Saint-Vith *see* Sankt-Vith
11 S14 **St.Walburg** Saskatchewan, S Canada
St Wolfgangsee *see* Wolfgangsee
102 M11 **St-Yrieix-la-Perche** Haute-Vienne, C France
Saint Yves *see* Setúbal
15 Y5 **St-Yvon** Québec, SE Canada
188 H5 **Saipan** *island* ● (Northern Mariana Islands) S Northern Mariana Islands
188 H6 **Saipan Channel** *channel* S Northern Mariana Islands
188 H6 **Saipan International Airport** × Saipan, S Northern Mariana Islands
74 G6 **Sais** × (Fès) C Morocco
Saishū *see* Cheju
Saishū *see* Cheju-do
102 J16 **Saison** ≈ SW France
169 R10 **Sai, Sungai** ≈ Borneo, N Indonesia
165 N13 **Saitama** *off.* Saitama-ken. ◈ *prefecture* Honshū, S Japan
Saiyid Abid *see* Sayyid 'Abīd
57 J19 **Sajama, Nevado** ▲ W Bolivia
141 V13 **Sājir, Ras** *headland* S Oman
111 M20 **Sajószentpéter** Borsod-Abaúj-Zemplén, NE Hungary
83 F24 **Sak** ≈ SW South Africa
81 J18 **Saka** Coast, E Kenya
167 P11 **Sa Kaeo** Prachin Buri, C Thailand
164 J14 **Sakai** Ōsaka, Honshū, SW Japan
164 H14 **Sakaide** Kagawa, Shikoku, SW Japan
164 H12 **Sakaiminato** Tottori, Honshū, SW Japan
140 M3 **Sakākah** Al Jawf, NW Saudi Arabia
28 L4 **Sakakawea, Lake** ⊡ North Dakota, N USA
12 J9 **Sakami, Lac** ⊚ Québec, C Canada
79 O26 **Sakania** Katanga, SE Dem. Rep. Congo
146 K12 **Sakar** Lebap Welaýaty, E Turkmenistan
172 H7 **Sakaraha** Toliara, SW Madagascar
146 I14 **Sakarçäge** *var.* Sakarchäge, *Rus.* Sakar-Chaga. Mary Welaýaty, C Turkmenistan
Sakar-Chaga/Sakarchäge *see* Sakarçäge
Sak'art'velo *see* Georgia
136 F11 **Sakarya** ◈ *province* NW Turkey
136 F12 **Sakarya Nehri** ≈ NW Turkey
150 K13 **Sakasaul'skiy** *var.* Saksaul'skoye *Kaz.* Sekseūil. Kyzylorda, S Kazakhstan
Saksaul'skoye *see* Sakasaul'skiy
165 P9 **Sakata** Yamagata, Honshū, C Japan
123 P9 **Sakha (Yakutiya), Respublika** *var.* Respublika Yakutiya, Yakutiya, *Eng.* Yakutia. ◈ *autonomous republic* NE Russian Federation
Sakhalin *see* Sakhalin, Ostrov
192 I3 **Sakhalin, Ostrov** *var.* Sakhalin. *island* SE Russian Federation
123 U12 **Sakhalinskaya Oblast'** ◈ *province* SE Russian Federation
123 T12 **Sakhalinskiy Zaliv** *gulf* E Russian Federation
Sakhnovshchina *see* Sakhnovshchyna
117 U6 **Sakhnovshchyna** *Rus.* Sakhnovshchina. Kharkivs'ka Oblast', E Ukraine
Sakhon Nakhon *see* Sakon Nakhon
Sakhtsar *see* Rāmsar
Saki *see* Saky
137 W10 **Şäki** *Rus.* Sheki; *prev.* Nukha. NW Azerbaijan
118 E13 **Šakiai** *Ger.* Schaken. Marijampolė, S Lithuania
165 O16 **Sakishima-shotō** *var.* Sakisima Syotô. *island group* SW Japan
Sakiz *see* Saqqez
Sakiz-Adasi *see* Chíos
155 F19 **Sakleshpur** Karnātaka, E India
167 S9 **Sakon Nakhon** *var.* Muang Sakon Nakhon, Sakhon Nakhon. Sakon Nakhon, E Thailand
149 P15 **Sakrand** Sind, SE Pakistan
83 F24 **Sak River** *Afr.* Sakrivier. Northern Cape, W South Africa
Sakrivier *see* Sak River
Saksaul'skiy *see* Saksaul'skoye
144 K13 **Saksaul'skoye** *prev.* Saksaul'skiy, *Kaz.* Sekseūil. Kzylorda, S Kazakhstan
95 I25 **Sakskøbing** Storstrøm, SE Denmark
165 N12 **Saku** Nagano, Honshū, S Japan
117 S13 **Saky** *Rus.* Saki. Respublika Krym, S Ukraine
76 E9 **Sal** *island* Ilhas de Barlavento, NE Cape Verde
127 N12 **Sal** ≈ SW Russian Federation
111 I21 **Sal'a** *Hung.* Sellye, Vágsellye. Nitriansky Kraj, SW Slovakia
95 N15 **Sala** Västmanland, C Sweden
15 N13 **Salaberry-de-Valleyfield** *var.* Valleyfield. Québec, SE Canada
118 G7 **Salacgrīva** *Est.* Salatsi. Limbaži, N Latvia
107 M18 **Sala Consilina** Campania, S Italy
40 C2 **Salada, Laguna** ⊚ NW Mexico
61 D14 **Saladas** Corrientes, NE Argentina
61 C21 **Saladillo** Buenos Aires, E Argentina
61 B16 **Saladillo, Río** ≈ C Argentina
25 T9 **Salado** Texas, SW USA
63 J16 **Salado, Arroyo** ≈ SE Argentina
37 Q12 **Salado, Rio** ≈ New Mexico, SW USA
61 D21 **Salado, Río** ≈ E Argentina
62 J12 **Salado, Río** ≈ C Argentina
41 N7 **Salado, Río** ≈ NE Mexico
143 N6 **Salafchegān** *var.* Sarafjagān. Qom, N Iran
77 Q15 **Salaga** C Ghana
192 G5 **Sala'ilua** Savai'i, W Samoa
116 G9 **Sălaj** ◈ *county* NW Romania
83 H20 **Salajwe** Kweneng, SE Botswana
78 H9 **Salal** Kanem, W Chad
80 I6 **Salala** Red Sea, NE Sudan
141 V13 **Şalālah** SW Oman
42 D5 **Salamá** Baja Verapaz, C Guatemala
42 J6 **Salamá** Olancho, C Honduras
62 G16 **Salamanca** Coquimbo, C Chile
41 N13 **Salamanca** Guanajuato, C Mexico
104 K7 **Salamanca** *anc.* Helmantica, Salmantica. Castilla-León, NW Spain
18 D11 **Salamanca** New York, NE USA
104 J7 **Salamanca** ◈ *province* Castilla-León, W Spain
63 J19 **Salamanca, Pampa de** *plain* S Argentina
78 J12 **Salamat** *off.* Préfecture du Salamat. ◈ *prefecture* SE Chad
78 I12 **Salamat, Bahr** ≈ S Chad
54 F5 **Salamina** Magdalena, N Colombia
115 G19 **Salamína** *var.* Salamís. Salamína, C Greece
115 G19 **Salamína** *island* C Greece
Salamís *see* Salamína
138 I5 **Salamīyah** *var.* As Salamīyah. Ḩamāh, W Syria
31 P12 **Salamonie Lake** ⊡ Indiana, N USA
31 P12 **Salamonie River** ≈ Indiana, N USA
Salang *see* Phuket
192 I16 **Salani** Upolu, SE Samoa
118 C11 **Salantai** Klaipėda, NW Lithuania
104 K2 **Salas** Asturias, N Spain
105 O5 **Salas de los Infantes** Castilla-León, N Spain
102 M16 **Salat** ≈ S France
189 V13 **Salat** *island* Chuuk, C Micronesia
169 Q16 **Salatiga** Jawa, C Indonesia
189 V13 **Salat Pass** *passage* W Pacific Ocean
Salatsi *see* Salacgrīva
167 T10 **Salavan** *var.* Saravan, Saravane. Salavan, S Laos
127 V6 **Salavat** Respublika Bashkortostan, W Russian Federation
56 C12 **Salaverry** La Libertad, N Peru
171 T12 **Salawati, Pulau** *island* E Indonesia
193 R10 **Sala y Gomez** *island* Chile, E Pacific Ocean
Sala y Gomez Fracture Zone *see* Sala y Gomez Ridge
193 S10 **Sala y Gomez Ridge** *var.* Sala y Gomez Fracture Zone. *tectonic feature* SE Pacific Ocean
61 A22 **Salazar** Buenos Aires, E Argentina
54 G7 **Salazar** Norte de Santander, N Colombia
Salazar *see* N'Dalatando
173 P16 **Salazie** C Réunion
103 N8 **Salbris** Loir-et-Cher, C France
57 G15 **Salcantay, Nevado** ▲ C Peru
45 O8 **Salcedo** N Dominican Republic
39 S9 **Salcha River** ≈ Alaska, USA
119 H15 **Šalčininkai** Vilnius, SE Lithuania
Saldae *see* Béjaïa
54 E11 **Saldaña** Tolima, C Colombia
104 M4 **Saldaña** Castilla-León, N Spain
83 E25 **Saldanha** Western Cape, SW South Africa
Salduba *see* Zaragoza
61 B23 **Saldungaray** Buenos Aires, E Argentina
118 D9 **Saldus** *Ger.* Frauenburg. Saldus, W Latvia
183 P13 **Sale** Victoria, SE Australia
74 F6 **Salé** NW Morocco
74 F6 **Salé** × (Rabat) W Morocco
Salehābād *see* Andīmeshk
170 M16 **Saleh, Teluk** *bay* Nusa Tenggara, S Indonesia
122 H8 **Salekhard** *prev.* Obdorsk. Yamalo-Nenetskiy Avtonomnyy Okrug, N Russian Federation
192 H16 **Sālelologa** Savai'i, C Samoa
155 H21 **Salem** Tamil Nādu, SE India
27 V9 **Salem** Arkansas, C USA
30 L15 **Salem** Illinois, N USA
31 P15 **Salem** Indiana, N USA
19 P11 **Salem** Massachusetts, NE USA
27 V6 **Salem** Missouri, C USA
18 I16 **Salem** New Jersey, NE USA
31 U12 **Salem** Ohio, N USA
32 G12 **Salem** *state capital* Oregon, NW USA
29 Q11 **Salem** South Dakota, N USA
36 L4 **Salem** Utah, W USA
21 S7 **Salem** Virginia, NE USA
21 R3 **Salem** West Virginia, NE USA
107 H23 **Salemi** Sicilia, Italy, C Mediterranean Sea
Salemy *see* As Sālimī
94 K12 **Sälen** Dalarna, C Sweden
107 Q18 **Salentina, Campi** Puglia, SE Italy
107 Q18 **Salentina, Penisola** *peninsula* SE Italy
107 L18 **Salerno** *anc.* Salernum. Campania, S Italy
107 L18 **Salerno, Golfo di** *Eng.* Gulf of Salerno. *gulf* S Italy
Salerno, Gulf of *see* Salerno, Golfo di
Salernum *see* Salerno
97 K17 **Salford** NW England, UK
Salgir *see* Salhyr
111 K21 **Salgótarján** Nógrád, N Hungary
59 O15 **Salgueiro** Pernambuco, E Brazil
94 C13 **Salhus** Hordaland, S Norway
117 T12 **Salhyr** *Rus.* Salgir. ≈ S Ukraine
171 Q9 **Salibabu, Pulau** *island* N Indonesia
37 S6 **Salida** Colorado, C USA
102 J15 **Salies-de-Béarn** Pyrénées-Atlantiques, SW France
136 C14 **Salihli** Manisa, W Turkey
119 K18 **Salihorsk** *Rus.* Soligorsk. Minskaya Voblasts', S Belarus
119 K18 **Salihorskaye Vodaskhovishcha** ⊡ C Belarus
83 N14 **Salima** Central, C Malawi
166 L5 **Salin** Magwe, W Myanmar
27 N4 **Salina** Kansas, C USA
36 L5 **Salina** Utah, W USA
41 S17 **Salina Cruz** Oaxaca, SE Mexico
107 L22 **Salina, Isola** *island* Isole Eolie, S Italy
44 J5 **Salina Point** *headland* Acklins Island, SE Bahamas
56 A7 **Salinas** Guayas, W Ecuador
40 M11 **Salinas** *var.* Salinas de Hidalgo. San Luis Potosí, C Mexico
45 T6 **Salinas** C Puerto Rico
35 O10 **Salinas** California, W USA
Salinas, Cabo de *see* Salines, Cap de ses
Salinas de Hidalgo *see* Salinas
82 A13 **Salinas, Ponta das** *headland* W Angola
45 O10 **Salinas, Punta** *headland* S Dominican Republic
Salinas, Río *see* Chixoy, Río
35 O11 **Salinas River** ≈ California, W USA
22 H6 **Saline Lake** ⊚ Louisiana, S USA
25 R17 **Salineno** Texas, SW USA
27 V14 **Saline River** ≈ Arkansas, C USA
30 M17 **Saline River** ≈ Illinois, N USA
105 X10 **Salines, Cap de ses** *var.* Cabo de Salinas. *headland* Mallorca, Spain, W Mediterranean Sea
Salisburg *see* Mazsalaca
45 O12 **Salisbury** *var.* Baroui. W Dominica
97 M23 **Salisbury** *var.* New Sarum. S England, UK
21 Y4 **Salisbury** Maryland, NE USA
27 T3 **Salisbury** Missouri, C USA
21 S9 **Salisbury** North Carolina, SE USA
Salisbury *see* Harare
9 Q7 **Salisbury Island** *island* Nunavut, NE Canada
Salisbury, Lake *see* Bisina, Lake
97 L23 **Salisbury Plain** *plain* S England, UK
21 R14 **Salkehatchie River** ≈ South Carolina, SE USA
138 I9 **Şalkhad** As Suwaydā', SW Syria
92 M12 **Salla** Lappi, NE Finland
Sállan *see* Sørøya
103 U11 **Sallanches** Haute-Savoie, E France
105 V5 **Sallent** Cataluña, NE Spain
61 A22 **Salliqueló** Buenos Aires, E Argentina
27 R10 **Sallisaw** Oklahoma, C USA
80 I7 **Sallom** Red Sea, NE Sudan
12 J2 **Salluit** *prev.* Saglouc, Sagluk. Québec, NE Canada
Sallūm, Khalīj as *see* Salûm, Gulf of
13 S11 **Sally's Cove** Newfoundland and Labrador, E Canada
139 W9 **Salmān Bin 'Arāzah** E Iraq
Salmantica *see* Salamanca
142 I2 **Salmās** *prev.* Dilman, Shāpūr. Āžarbāyjān-e Bākhtarī, NW Iran
124 I11 **Salmi** Respublika Kareliya, NW Russian Federation
33 P12 **Salmon** Idaho, NW USA
11 N16 **Salmon Arm** British Columbia, SW Canada
192 L5 **Salmon Bank** *undersea feature* N Pacific Ocean
Salmon Leap *see* Leixlip
34 L2 **Salmon Mountains** ▲ California, W USA
14 J15 **Salmon Point** *headland* Ontario, SE Canada
33 N11 **Salmon River** ≈ Idaho, NW USA
18 K6 **Salmon River** ≈ New York, NE USA
33 N12 **Salmon River Mountains** ▲ Idaho, NW USA
18 I9 **Salmon River Reservoir** ⊡ New York, NE USA
93 K19 **Salo** Länsi-Suomi, W Finland
106 F7 **Salò** Lombardia, N Italy
Salona/Salonae *see* Solin
103 S15 **Salon-de-Provence** Bouches-du-Rhône, SE France
Salonica/Salonika *see* Thessaloníki
115 I14 **Salonikós, Akrotírio** *headland* Thásos, E Greece
116 F10 **Salonta** *Hung.* Nagyszalonta. Bihor, W Romania
104 I9 **Salor** ≈ W Spain
105 U6 **Salou** Cataluña, NE Spain
76 H11 **Saloum** ≈ C Senegal
42 H4 **Sal, Punta** *headland* NW Honduras
92 N3 **Salpynten** *headland* W Svalbard
138 I3 **Salqīn** Idlib, W Syria
93 F14 **Salsbruket** Nord-Trøndelag, C Norway
126 M13 **Sal'sk** Rostovskaya Oblast', SW Russian Federation
107 K25 **Salso** ≈ Sicilia, Italy, C Mediterranean Sea
107 J25 **Salso** ≈ Sicilia, Italy, C Mediterranean Sea
106 E9 **Salsomaggiore Terme** Emilia-Romagna, N Italy
Salt *see* As Salt
62 J6 **Salta** Salta, NW Argentina
62 K6 **Salta** *off.* Provincia de Salta. ◈ *province* N Argentina
97 I24 **Saltash** SW England, UK
24 I8 **Salt Basin** *basin* Texas, SW USA
11 V16 **Saltcoats** Saskatchewan, S Canada
30 L13 **Salt Creek** ≈ Illinois, N USA
24 J9 **Salt Draw** ≈ Texas, SW USA
97 F21 **Saltee Islands** *island group* SE Ireland
92 G12 **Saltfjorden** *inlet* C Norway
24 I8 **Salt Flat** Texas, SW USA
27 N8 **Salt Fork Arkansas River** ≈ Oklahoma, C USA
31 T13 **Salt Fork Lake** ⊡ Ohio, N USA
26 J11 **Salt Fork Red River** ≈ Oklahoma/Texas, C USA
95 J23 **Saltholm** *island* E Denmark
41 N8 **Saltillo** Coahuila de Zaragoza, NE Mexico
182 L5 **Salt Lake** *salt lake* New South Wales, SE Australia
37 V15 **Salt Lake** ⊚ New Mexico, SW USA
36 K2 **Salt Lake City** *state capital* Utah, W USA
61 C20 **Salto** Buenos Aires, E Argentina
61 D17 **Salto** Salto, N Uruguay
61 E17 **Salto** ◈ *department* N Uruguay
107 I14 **Salto** ≈ C Italy
62 Q6 **Salto del Guairá** Canindeyú, E Paraguay
61 D17 **Salto Grande, Embalse de** *var.* Lago de Salto Grande. ⊡ Argentina/Uruguay
Salto Grande, Lago de *see* Salto Grande, Embalse de
35 W16 **Salton Sea** ⊚ California, W USA
60 I12 **Salto Santiago, Represa de** ⊡ S Brazil
149 U7 **Salt Range** ▲ E Pakistan
36 M13 **Salt River** ≈ Arizona, SW USA
20 L5 **Salt River** ≈ Kentucky, S USA
27 V3 **Salt River** ≈ Missouri, C USA
95 F17 **Saltrød** Aust-Agder, S Norway
95 P16 **Saltsjöbaden** Stockholm, C Sweden
92 G12 **Saltstraumen** Nordland, C Norway
21 Q7 **Saltville** Virginia, NE USA
Saluces/Saluciae *see* Saluzzo
21 Q12 **Saluda** South Carolina, SE USA
21 X6 **Saluda** Virginia, NE USA
21 Q12 **Saluda River** ≈ South Carolina, SE USA
75 T7 **Salûm** *var.* As Sallūm. NW Egypt
152 F14 **Sālumbar** Rājasthān, N India
75 T7 **Salûm, Gulf of** *Ar.* Khalīj as Sallūm. *gulf* Egypt/Libya
171 O11 **Salumpaga** Sulawesi, N Indonesia

155 M14 **Sālūr** Andhra Pradesh, E India
55 Y9 **Salut, Îles du** *island group* N French Guiana
106 A9 **Saluzzo** *Fr.* Saluces; *anc.* Saluciae. Piemonte, NW Italy
63 F23 **Salvación, Bahía** *bay* S Chile
59 P17 **Salvador** *prev.* São Salvador. Bahia, E Brazil
65 E24 **Salvador** East Falkland, Falkland Islands
22 K10 **Salvador, Lake** ◎ Louisiana, S USA
Salvaleón de Higüey *see* Higüey
104 F10 **Salvaterra de Magos** Santarém, C Portugal
41 N13 **Salvatierra** Guanajuato, C Mexico
105 P3 **Salvatierra** *Basq.* Agurain. País Vasco, N Spain
Salwa/Salwah *see* As Salwā
166 M7 **Salween** *Bur.* Thanlwin, *Chin.* Nu Chiang, Nu Jiang. ≈ SE Asia
137 Y12 **Salyan** *Rus.* Sal'yany. SE Azerbaijan
153 N11 **Salyan** *var.* Sallyana. Mid Western, W Nepal
Sal'yany *see* Salyan
21 O6 **Salyersville** Kentucky, S USA
109 V6 **Salza** ≈ E Austria
109 Q7 **Salzach** ≈ Austria/Germany
109 Q6 **Salzburg** *anc.* Juvavum. Salzburg, N Austria
109 O8 **Salzburg** *off.* Land Salzburg. ◈ *state* C Austria
Salzburg *see* Ocna Sibiului
Salzburg Alps *see* Salzburger Kalkalpen
109 Q7 **Salzburger Kalkalpen** *Eng.* Salzburg Alps. ▲▲ C Austria
100 J13 **Salzgitter** *prev.* Watenstedt-Salzgitter. Niedersachsen, C Germany
101 G14 **Salzkotten** Nordrhein-Westfalen, W Germany
100 K11 **Salzwedel** Sachsen-Anhalt, N Germany
152 D11 **Sām** Rājasthān, NW India
Šamac *see* Bosanski Šamac
54 G9 **Samacá** Boyacá, C Colombia
40 I7 **Samachique** Chihuahua, N Mexico
141 Y8 **Şamad** NE Oman
Sama de Langreo *see* Sama
Samaden *see* Samedan
57 M19 **Samaipata** Santa Cruz, C Bolivia
167 T10 **Samakhixai** *var.* Attapu, Attopeu. Attapu, S Laos
Samakov *see* Samokov
42 B6 **Samalá, Río** ≈ SW Guatemala
40 J3 **Samalayuca** Chihuahua, N Mexico
155 L16 **Sāmalkot** Andhra Pradesh, E India
45 P8 **Samaná** *var.* Santa Bárbara de Samaná. E Dominican Republic
45 P8 **Samaná, Bahía de** *bay* E Dominican Republic
44 K4 **Samana Cay** *island* SE Bahamas
136 K17 **Samandaği** Hatay, S Turkey
149 P3 **Samangān** ◈ *province* N Afghanistan
Samangān *see* Āybak
165 T5 **Samani** Hokkaidō, NE Japan
54 C13 **Samaniego** Nariño, SW Colombia
171 Q5 **Samar** *island* C Philippines
127 S6 **Samara** *prev.* Kuybyshev. Samarskaya Oblast', W Russian Federation
127 S6 **Samara** ✕ Samarskaya Oblast', W Russian Federation
127 T7 **Samara** ≈ W Russian Federation
117 V7 **Samara** ≈ E Ukraine
186 G10 **Samarai** Milne Bay, SE PNG
Samarang *see* Semarang
138 G9 **Samarian Hills** *hill range* N Israel
54 L9 **Samariapo** Amazonas, C Venezuela
169 V11 **Samarinda** Borneo, C Indonesia
Samarkand *see* Samarqand
Samarkandskaya Oblast' *see* Samarqand Viloyati
Samarkandski/Samarkandskoye *see* Temirtau
Samarobriva *see* Amiens
147 N11 **Samarqand** *Rus.* Samarkand. Samarqand Viloyati, C Uzbekistan
146 M11 **Samarqand Viloyati** *Rus.* Samarkandskaya Oblast'. ◈ *province* C Uzbekistan
139 S6 **Sāmarrā'** C Iraq
127 R7 **Samarskaya Oblast'** *prev.* Kuybyshevskaya Oblast'. ◈ *province* W Russian Federation
153 Q13 **Samastīpur** Bihār, N India
76 L14 **Samatiguila** NW Ivory Coast
119 Q17 **Samatsevichy** *Rus.* Samotevichi. Mahilyowskaya Voblasts', E Belarus
Samawa *see* As Samāwah
137 Y11 **Şamaxı** *Rus.* Shemakha. E Azerbaijan
152 H6 **Samba** Jammu and Kashmir, NW India
79 K18 **Samba** Equateur, NW Dem. Rep. Congo
79 N21 **Samba** Maniema, E Dem. Rep. Congo
169 W10 **Sambaliung, Pegunungan** ▲▲ Borneo, N Indonesia
154 M11 **Sambalpur** Orissa, E India
67 X12 **Sambao** ≈ W Madagascar
169 Q10 **Sambas, Sungai** ≈ Borneo, N Indonesia
172 K2 **Sambava** Antsiraňana, NE Madagascar
152 J10 **Sambhal** Uttar Pradesh, N India
152 H12 **Sāmbhar Salt Lake** ◎ N India
107 N21 **Sambiase** Calabria, SW Italy
116 H5 **Sambir** *Rus.* Sambor. L'vivs'ka Oblast', NW Ukraine
82 C13 **Sambo** Huambo, C Angola
Sambor *see* Sambir
61 E21 **Samborombón, Bahía** *bay* NE Argentina
99 H20 **Sambre** ≈ Belgium/France
43 V16 **Sambú, Río** ≈ SE Panama
163 Z14 **Samch'ŏk** *Jap.* Sanchoku. NE South Korea
Samch'ŏnpŏ *see* Sach'ŏn
81 I21 **Same** Kilimanjaro, NE Tanzania
108 J10 **Samedan** *Ger.* Samaden. Graubünden, S Switzerland
84 K12 **Samfya** Luapula, N Zambia
141 W13 **Samḥān, Jabal** ▲ SW Oman
115 C18 **Sámi** Kefallinía, Iónioi Nísoi, Greece, C Mediterranean Sea
56 F10 **Samiria, Río** ≈ N Peru
Samirum *see* Semīrom
137 V11 **Şämkir** *Rus.* Shamkhor. NW Azerbaijan
167 S7 **Sam, Nam** *Vtn.* Sông Chu. ≈ Laos/Vietnam
Samnān *see* Semnān
Sam Neua *see* Xam Nua
75 P10 **Samnū** C Libya
192 H15 **Samoa** *off.* Independent State of Samoa, *var.* Sāmoa; *prev.* Western Samoa ◆ *monarchy* W Polynesia
192 L9 **Sāmoa** *island group* American /Samoa
175 T9 **Samoa Basin** *undersea feature* W Pacific Ocean
Sāmoa-i-Sisifo *see* Samoa
112 D8 **Samobor** Zagreb, N Croatia
114 H10 **Samokov** *var.* Samakov. Sofiya, W Bulgaria
111 H21 **Šamorín** *Ger.* Sommerein, *Hung.* Somorja. Trnavský Kraj, W Slovakia
115 M19 **Sámos** *prev.* Limín Vathéos. Sámos, Dodekánisos, Greece, Aegean Sea
115 M20 **Sámos** *island* Dodekánisos, Greece, Aegean Sea
Samosch *see* Szamos
168 I9 **Samosir, Pulau** *island* W Indonesia
Samotevichi *see* Samatsevichy
Samothrace *see* Samothráki
115 K14 **Samothráki** Samothráki, NE Greece
115 J14 **Samothráki** *anc.* Samothrace. *island* NE Greece
115 A15 **Samothráki** *island* Iónioi Nísoi, Greece, C Mediterranean Sea
Samotschin *see* Szamocin
Sampê *see* Xiangcheng
169 S13 **Sampit** Borneo, C Indonesia
169 S12 **Sampit, Sungai** ≈ Borneo, N Indonesia
Sampoku *see* Sanpoku
186 H7 **Sampun** New Britain, E PNG
79 N24 **Sampwe** Katanga, SE Dem. Rep. Congo
25 X8 **Sam Rayburn Reservoir** ⊞ Texas, SW USA
167 Q6 **Sam Sao, Phou** ▲▲ Laos/Thailand
95 H22 **Samsø** *island* E Denmark
95 H23 **Samsø Bælt** *channel* E Denmark
167 T7 **Sầm Sơn** Thanh Hoa, N Vietnam
136 L11 **Samsun** *anc.* Amisus. Samsun, N Turkey
136 K11 **Samsun** ◈ *province* N Turkey
137 R9 **Samtredia** W Georgia
59 E15 **Samuel, Represa de** ⊞ W Brazil
167 O14 **Samui, Ko** *island* SW Thailand
Samundari *see* Samundri
149 U9 **Samundri** *var.* Samundari. Punjab, E Pakistan
137 X10 **Samur** ≈ Azerbaijan/Russian Federation
137 Y11 **Samur-Abşeron Kanalı** *Rus.* Samur-Apsheronskiy Kanal. *canal* E Azerbaijan
Samur-Apsheronskiy Kanal *see* Samur-Abşeron Kanalı
167 O11 **Samut Prakan** *var.* Muang Samut Prakan, Paknam. Samut Prakan, C Thailand
167 O11 **Samut Sakhon** *var.* Maha Chai, Samut Sakorn, Tha Chin. Samut Sakhon, C Thailand
Samut Sakorn *see* Samut Sakhon
167 O11 **Samut Songhram** *prev.* Meklong. Samut Songkhram, SW Thailand
77 N12 **San** Ségou, C Mali
111 O15 **San** ≈ SE Poland
141 O15 **Şan'ā'** *Eng.* Sana. ● (Yemen) W Yemen
112 F11 **Sana** ≈ NW Bosnia and Herzegovina
80 O12 **Sanaag** *off.* Gobolka Sanaag. ◈ *region* N Somalia
114 J8 **Sanadinovo** Pleven, N Bulgaria
195 P1 **Sanae** *South African research station* Antarctica
139 Y10 **Sanāf, Hawr as** ◎ S Iraq
79 E15 **Sanaga** ≈ C Cameroon
54 D12 **San Agustín** Huila, SW Colombia
171 R8 **San Agustin, Cape** *headland* Mindanao, S Philippines
37 Q13 **San Agustin, Plains of** *plain* New Mexico, SW USA
38 M16 **Sanak Islands** *island group* Aleutian Islands, Alaska, USA
193 U10 **San Ambrosio, Isla** *Eng.* San Ambrosio Island. *island* W Chile
San Ambrosio Island *see* San Ambrosio, Isla
171 Q12 **Sanana** Pulau Sanana, E Indonesia
171 Q12 **Sanana, Pulau** *island* Maluku, E Indonesia
142 K5 **Sanandaj** *prev.* Sinneh. Kordestān, W Iran
35 P8 **San Andreas** California, W USA
2 C13 **San Andreas Fault** *fault* W USA
54 G8 **San Andrés** Santander, C Colombia
61 C20 **San Andrés de Giles** Buenos Aires, E Argentina
37 R14 **San Andres Mountains** ▲▲ New Mexico, SW USA
41 S15 **San Andrés Tuxtla** *var.* Tuxtla. Veracruz-Llave, E Mexico
25 P8 **San Angelo** Texas, SW USA
107 A20 **San Antioco, Isola di** *island* W Italy
42 F4 **San Antonio** Toledo, S Belize
62 G11 **San Antonio** Valparaíso, C Chile
188 H6 **San Antonio** Saipan, S Northern Mariana Islands
37 R13 **San Antonio** New Mexico, SW USA
25 R12 **San Antonio** Texas, SW USA
54 M11 **San Antonio** Amazonas, S Venezuela
54 I7 **San Antonio** Barinas, C Venezuela
55 O5 **San Antonio** Monagas, NE Venezuela
25 S12 **San Antonio** ✕ Texas, SW USA
San Antonio *see* San Antonio del Táchira
San Antonio Abad *see* Sant Antoni de Portmany
25 U13 **San Antonio Bay** *inlet* Texas, SW USA
61 E22 **San Antonio, Cabo** *headland* E Argentina
44 A5 **San Antonio, Cabo de** *headland* W Cuba
105 T11 **San Antonio, Cabo de** *headland* E Spain
54 H7 **San Antonio de Caparo** Táchira, W Venezuela
62 J5 **San Antonio de los Cobres** Salta, NE Argentina
54 H7 **San Antonio del Táchira** *var.* San Antonio. Táchira, W Venezuela
35 T15 **San Antonio, Mount** ▲ California, W USA
63 K16 **San Antonio Oeste** Río Negro, E Argentina
25 T13 **San Antonio River** ≈ Texas, SW USA
54 J5 **Sanare** Lara, N Venezuela
103 T16 **Sanary-sur-Mer** Var, SE France
25 X8 **San Augustine** Texas, SW USA
141 T13 **Sanāw** *var.* Sanaw. NE Yemen
41 O11 **San Bartolo** San Luis Potosí, C Mexico
107 L16 **San Bartolomeo in Galdo** Campania, S Italy
106 K13 **San Benedetto del Tronto** Marche, C Italy
42 E3 **San Benito** Petén, N Guatemala
25 T17 **San Benito** Texas, SW USA
54 E6 **San Benito Abad** Sucre, N Colombia
35 P11 **San Benito Mountain** ▲ California, W USA
35 O10 **San Benito River** ≈ California, W USA
108 H10 **San Bernardino** Graubünden, S Switzerland
35 U15 **San Bernardino** California, W USA
62 H11 **San Bernardo** Santiago, C Chile
40 J8 **San Bernardo** Durango, C Mexico
164 G12 **Sanbe-san** ▲ Kyūshū, SW Japan
40 J12 **San Blas** Nayarit, C Mexico
40 H8 **San Blas** Sinaloa, C Mexico
43 V14 **San Blas** *off.* Comarca de San Blas. ◈ *special territory* NE Panama
43 U14 **San Blas, Archipiélago de** *island group* NE Panama
23 Q10 **San Blas, Cape** *headland* Florida, SE USA
43 V14 **San Blas, Cordillera de** ▲▲ NE Panama
62 J8 **San Blas de los Sauces** Catamarca, NW Argentina
106 G8 **San Bonifacio** Veneto, NE Italy
29 S12 **Sanborn** Iowa, C USA
40 M7 **San Buenaventura** Coahuila de Zaragoza, NE Mexico
105 S5 **San Caprasio** ▲ N Spain
62 G13 **San Carlos** Bío Bío, C Chile
40 E9 **San Carlos** Baja California Sur, W Mexico
41 N5 **San Carlos** Coahuila de Zaragoza, NE Mexico
San Carlos, Estrecho de *see* Falkland Sound
41 P9 **San Carlos** Tamaulipas, C Mexico
42 L12 **San Carlos** Río San Juan, S Nicaragua
43 T16 **San Carlos** Panamá, C Panama
171 N3 **San Carlos** *off.* San Carlos City. Luzon, N Philippines
36 M14 **San Carlos** Arizona, SW USA
61 G20 **San Carlos** Maldonado, S Uruguay
54 K5 **San Carlos** Cojedes, N Venezuela
San Carlos *see* Quesada, Costa Rica
San Carlos *see* Luba, Equatorial Guinea
61 B17 **San Carlos Centro** Santa Fe, C Argentina
171 P6 **San Carlos City** Negros, C Philippines
San Carlos de Ancud *see* Ancud
63 H16 **San Carlos de Bariloche** Río Negro, SW Argentina
61 B21 **San Carlos de Bolívar** Buenos Aires, E Argentina
54 H6 **San Carlos del Zulia** Zulia, W Venezuela
54 L12 **San Carlos de Río Negro** Amazonas, S Venezuela
San Carlos, Estrecho de *see* Falkland Sound
36 M14 **San Carlos Reservoir** ⊞ Arizona, SW USA
42 M12 **San Carlos, Río** ≈ N Costa Rica
65 D24 **San Carlos Settlement** East Falkland, Falkland Islands
61 C23 **San Cayetano** Buenos Aires, E Argentina
103 O8 **Sancerre** Cher, C France
158 G7 **Sanchakou** Xinjiang Uygur Zizhiqu, NW China
Sanchoku *see* Samch'ŏk
41 O12 **San Ciro** San Luis Potosí, C Mexico
105 P10 **San Clemente** Castilla-La Mancha, C Spain
35 T16 **San Clemente** California, W USA
61 E21 **San Clemente del Tuyú** Buenos Aires, E Argentina
35 S17 **San Clemente Island** *island* Channel Islands, California, W USA
103 O9 **Sancoins** Cher, C France
187 N10 **San Cristobal** *var.* Makira. *island* SE Solomon Islands
61 B16 **San Cristóbal** Santa Fe, C Argentina
44 B4 **San Cristóbal** Pinar del Río, W Cuba
45 O9 **San Cristóbal** *var.* Benemérita de San Cristóbal. S Dominican Republic
54 H7 **San Cristóbal** Táchira, W Venezuela
San Cristóbal *see* San Cristóbal de Las Casas
41 U16 **San Cristóbal de Las Casas** *var.* San Cristóbal. Chiapas, SE Mexico
187 N10 **San Cristóbal, Isla** *var.* Chatham Island. *island* Galapagos Islands, Ecuador, E Pacific Ocean
42 D5 **San Cristóbal Verapaz** Alta Verapaz, C Guatemala
44 F6 **Sancti Spíritus** Sancti Spíritus, C Cuba
103 O11 **Sancy, Puy de** ▲ C France
95 D15 **Sand** Rogaland, S Norway
169 W7 **Sandakan** Sabah, East Malaysia
182 K9 **Sandalwood** South Australia
Sandalwood Island *see* Sumba, Pulau
94 D11 **Sandane** Sogn og Fjordane, S Norway
114 G12 **Sandanski** *prev.* Sveti Vrach. Blagoevgrad, SW Bulgaria
76 J11 **Sandaré** Kayes, W Mali
95 J19 **Sandared** Västra Götaland, S Sweden
94 N12 **Sandarne** Gävleborg, C Sweden
186 B5 **Sandaun** *prev.* West Sepik. ◈ *province* NW PNG
96 K4 **Sanday** *island* NE Scotland, UK
31 P15 **Sand Creek** ≈ Indiana, N USA
95 H15 **Sande** Vestfold, S Norway
95 H16 **Sandefjord** Vestfold, S Norway
77 O15 **Sandégué** E Ivory Coast
77 P14 **Sandema** N Ghana
37 O11 **Sanders** Arizona, SW USA
24 M11 **Sanderson** Texas, SW USA
23 U4 **Sandersville** Georgia, SE USA
92 H4 **Sandgerdhi** Sudhurland, SW Iceland
28 K14 **Sand Hills** ▲▲ Nebraska, C USA
25 S14 **Sandia** Texas, SW USA
35 T17 **San Diego** California, W USA
25 S14 **San Diego** Texas, SW USA
136 F14 **Sandıklı** Afyon, W Turkey
152 L12 **Sandīla** Uttar Pradesh, N India
121 N15 **San Dimitri, Ras** *var.* San Dimitri Point. *headland* Gozo, NW Malta
168 J13 **Sanding, Selat** *strait* W Indonesia
30 J3 **Sand Island** *island* Apostle Islands, Wisconsin, N USA
95 C16 **Sandnes** Rogaland, S Norway
92 F13 **Sandnessjøen** Nordland, C Norway
79 L24 **Sandoa** Katanga, S Dem. Rep. Congo
111 N15 **Sandomierz** *Rus.* Sandomir. Świętokrzyskie, C Poland
Sandomir *see* Sandomierz
54 C13 **Sandoná** Nariño, SW Colombia
106 I7 **San Donà di Piave** Veneto, NE Italy
124 K14 **Sandovo** Tverskaya Oblast', W Russian Federation
166 K7 **Sandoway** Arakan State, W Myanmar
97 M24 **Sandown** S England, UK
95 B19 **Sandoy** *Dan.* Sandø *Island* Faeroe Islands
39 N16 **Sand Point** Popof Island, Alaska, USA
65 N24 **Sand Point** *headland* E Tristan da Cunha
31 R7 **Sand Point** *headland* Michigan, N USA
32 M7 **Sandpoint** Idaho, NW USA
93 H14 **Sandsele** Västerbotten, N Sweden
10 I14 **Sandspit** Moresby Island, British Columbia, SW Canada
27 P9 **Sand Springs** Oklahoma, C USA
29 W7 **Sandstone** Minnesota, N USA
36 K15 **Sand Tank Mountains** ▲▲ Arizona, SW USA
31 S8 **Sandusky** Michigan, N USA
31 S11 **Sandusky** Ohio, N USA
31 S12 **Sandusky River** ≈ Ohio, N USA
83 D22 **Sandverhaar** Karas, S Namibia
95 L24 **Sandvig** Bornholm, E Denmark
95 H15 **Sandvika** Akershus, S Norway
94 N13 **Sandviken** Gävleborg, C Sweden
30 M11 **Sandwich** Illinois, N USA
Sandwich Island *see* Éfaté
Sandwich Islands *see* Hawaiian Islands
153 V16 **Sandwip Island** *island* SE Bangladesh
11 U12 **Sandy Bay** Saskatchewan, C Canada
183 N16 **Sandy Cape** *headland* Tasmania, SE Australia
36 L3 **Sandy City** Utah, W USA
31 U12 **Sandy Creek** ≈ Ohio, N USA
21 O5 **Sandy Hook** Kentucky, S USA
18 K15 **Sandy Hook** *headland* New Jersey, NE USA
Sandykachi/Sandykgachy *see* Sandykgaçy
146 J15 **Sandykgaçy** *var.* Sandykgachy, *Rus.* Sandykachi. Mary Welaýaty, S Turkmenistan
146 L13 **Sandykly Gumy** *Rus.* Peski Sandykly. *desert* E Turkmenistan
Sandykly, Peski *see* Sandykly Gumy
11 Q13 **Sandy Lake** Alberta, W Canada
12 B8 **Sandy Lake** Ontario, C Canada
12 B8 **Sandy Lake** ◎ Ontario, C Canada
23 S3 **Sandy Springs** Georgia, SE USA
24 H8 **San Elizario** Texas, SW USA
99 L25 **Sanem** Luxembourg, SW Luxembourg
42 K5 **San Esteban** Olancho, C Honduras
105 O6 **San Esteban de Gormaz** Castilla-León, N Spain
40 E5 **San Esteban, Isla** *island* NW Mexico
San Eugenio/San Eugenio del Cuareim *see* Artigas
62 H11 **San Felipe** *var.* San Felipe de Aconcagua. Valparaíso, C Chile
40 D3 **San Felipe** Baja California, NW Mexico
40 N12 **San Felipe** Guanajuato, C Mexico
54 K5 **San Felipe** Yaracuy, NW Venezuela
44 B5 **San Felipe, Cayos de** *island group* W Cuba
San Felipe de Aconcagua *see* San Felipe
San Felipe de Puerto Plata *see* Puerto Plata
37 R11 **San Felipe Pueblo** New Mexico, SW USA
San Feliú de Guixols *see* Sant Feliu de Guíxols
193 T10 **San Félix, Isla** *Eng.* San Felix Island. *island* W Chile
San Felix Island *see* San Félix, Isla
54 L11 **San Fernanado de Atabapo** Amazonas, S Venezuela
40 C4 **San Fernando** *var.* Misión San Fernando. Baja California, NW Mexico
41 P9 **San Fernando** Tamaulipas, C Mexico
171 N2 **San Fernando** Luzon, N Philippines
171 O3 **San Fernando** Luzon, N Philippines
104 J16 **San Fernando** *prev.* Isla de León. Andalucía, S Spain
45 U14 **San Fernando** Trinidad, Trinidad and Tobago
35 S15 **San Fernando** California, W USA
54 L7 **San Fernando** *var.* San Fernando de Apure. Apure, C Venezuela
San Fernando de Apure *see* San Fernando
62 L8 **San Fernando del Valle de Catamarca** *var.* Catamarca. Catamarca, NW Argentina
San Fernando de Monte Cristi *see* Monte Cristi
41 P9 **San Fernando, Río** ≈ C Mexico
23 X11 **Sanford** Florida, SE USA
19 P9 **Sanford** Maine, NE USA
21 T10 **Sanford** North Carolina, SE USA
25 N2 **Sanford** Texas, SW USA
39 T10 **Sanford, Mount** ▲ Alaska, USA
42 G8 **San Francisco** *var.* Gotera, San Francisco Gotera. Morazán, E El Salvador
43 R16 **San Francisco** Veraguas, C Panama
171 N2 **San Francisco** *var.* Aurora. Luzon, N Philippines
35 L8 **San Francisco** California, W USA
54 H5 **San Francisco** Zulia, NW Venezuela
34 M8 **San Francisco** ✕ California, W USA
35 N9 **San Francisco Bay** *bay* California, W USA
61 C24 **San Francisco de Bellocq** Buenos Aires, E Argentina
40 I6 **San Francisco de Borja** Chihuahua, N Mexico
42 J6 **San Francisco de la Paz** Olancho, C Honduras
40 J7 **San Francisco del Oro** Chihuahua, N Mexico
40 M12 **San Francisco del Rincón** Jalisco, SW Mexico
45 O8 **San Francisco de Macorís** C Dominican Republic
San Francisco de Satipo *see* Satipo
San Francisco Gotera *see* San Francisco
San Francisco Telixtlahuaca *see* Telixtlahuaca
107 K23 **San Fratello** Sicilia, Italy, C Mediterranean Sea
San Fructuoso *see* Tacuarembó
82 C12 **Sanga** Cuanza Sul, NW Angola
56 C5 **San Gabriel** Carchi, N Ecuador
159 S15 **Sa'ngain** Xizang Zizhiqu, W China
154 E13 **Sangamner** Mahārāshtra, W India
152 H12 **Sāngāner** Rājasthān, N India
Sangan, Koh-i- *see* Sangān, Kūh-e
149 N6 **Sangān, Kūh-e** *Pash.* Koh-i-Sangan. ▲ C Afghanistan
123 P10 **Sangar** Respublika Sakha (Yakutiya), NE Russian Federation
169 V11 **Sangasanga** Borneo, C Indonesia
103 N1 **Sangatte** Pas-de-Calais, N France
107 B19 **San Gavino Monreale** Sardegna, Italy, C Mediterranean Sea
57 D16 **Sangayan, Isla** *island* W Peru
30 L14 **Sangchris Lake** ⊞ Illinois, N USA
171 N16 **Sangeang, Pulau** *island* S Indonesia
116 I10 **Sângeorgiu de Pădure** *prev.* Erdăt-Sângeorz, Sîngeorgiu de Pădure, *Hung.* Erdőszentgyörgy. Mureş, C Romania
116 I9 **Sângeorz-Băi** *var.* Singeroz Băi, *Ger.* Rumänisch-Sankt-Georgen, *Hung.* Oláhszentgyőrgy; *prev.* Sîngeorz-Băi. Bistriţa-Năsăud, N Romania
35 R10 **Sanger** California, W USA
25 T5 **Sanger** Texas, SW USA
Sângerei *see* Sîngerei
101 L15 **Sangerhausen** Sachsen-Anhalt, C Germany
45 S6 **San Germán** W Puerto Rico
San Germano *see* Cassino
161 N2 **Sanggan He** ≈ E China
169 Q11 **Sanggau** Borneo, C Indonesia
79 H16 **Sangha** ≈ Central African Republic/Congo
79 G16 **Sangha-Mbaéré** ◈ *prefecture* SW Central African Republic
149 Q15 **Sānghar** Sind, SE Pakistan
115 F22 **Sangiás** ▲ S Greece
Sangihe, Kepulauan *see* Sangir, Kepulauan
171 Q9 **Sangihe, Pulau** *var.* Sangir. *island* N Indonesia
54 G8 **San Gil** Santander, C Colombia
106 F12 **San Gimignano** Toscana, C Italy
148 M8 **Sangin** *var.* Sangīn. Helmand, S Afghanistan
107 O21 **San Giovanni in Fiore** Calabria, SW Italy
107 M16 **San Giovanni Rotondo** Puglia, SE Italy
106 G12 **San Giovanni Valdarno** Toscana, C Italy
Sangir *see* Sangihe, Pulau
171 Q10 **Sangir, Kepulauan** *var.* Kepulauan Sangihe. *island group* N Indonesia
162 K9 **Sangiyn Dalay** Dundgovĭ, C Mongolia
162 H9 **Sangiyn Dalay** Govĭ-Altay, C Mongolia
162 K11 **Sangiyn Dalay** Ömnögovĭ, S Mongolia
162 K8 **Sangiyn Dalay** Övörhangay, C Mongolia
163 Y15 **Sangju** *Jap.* Shōshū. C South Korea
167 R11 **Sangkha** Surin, E Thailand
169 W10 **Sangkulirang** Borneo, N Indonesia
169 W10 **Sangkulirang, Teluk** *bay* Borneo, N Indonesia
155 E16 **Sāngli** Mahārāshtra, W India
79 E16 **Sangmélima** Sud, S Cameroon
35 V15 **San Gorgonio Mountain** ▲ California, W USA
37 T8 **Sangre de Cristo Mountains** ▲▲ Colorado /New Mexico, C USA
61 A20 **San Gregorio** Santa Fe, C Argentina
61 F18 **San Gregorio de Polanco** Tacuarembó, C Uruguay
45 V14 **Sangre Grande** Trinidad, Trinidad and Tobago
159 N16 **Sangri** Xizang Zizhiqu, W China
152 H9 **Sangrūr** Punjab, NW India
44 I11 **Sangster** *off.* Sir Donald Sangster International Airport, *var.* Montego Bay. ✕ (Montego Bay) W Jamaica
59 G17 **Sangue, Rio do** ≈ W Brazil
105 R4 **Sangüesa** Navarra, N Spain
61 C16 **San Gustavo** Entre Ríos, E Argentina
Sangyuan *see* Wuqiao
40 C6 **San Hipólito, Punta** *headland* W Mexico
23 W15 **Sanibel** Sanibel Island, Florida, SE USA
23 V15 **Sanibel Island** *island* Florida, SE USA
60 F13 **San Ignacio** Misiones, NE Argentina
42 F2 **San Ignacio** *prev.* Cayo, El Cayo. Cayo, W Belize
57 L16 **San Ignacio** Beni, N Bolivia
57 O18 **San Ignacio** Santa Cruz, E Bolivia
42 M14 **San Ignacio** *var.* San Ignacio de Acosta. San José, W Costa Rica
40 E6 **San Ignacio** Baja California Sur, W Mexico
40 J10 **San Ignacio** Sinaloa, W Mexico
56 B9 **San Ignacio** Cajamarca, N Peru
San Ignacio de Acosta *see* San Ignacio
40 D7 **San Ignacio, Laguna** *lagoon* W Mexico
12 I6 **Sanikiluaq** Belcher Islands, Nunavut, C Canada
171 O3 **San Ildefonso Peninsula** *peninsula* Luzon, N Philippines
Saniquillie *see* Sanniquellie
61 D20 **San Isidro** Buenos Aires, E Argentina
43 N14 **San Isidro** *var.* San Isidro de El General. San José, SE Costa Rica
San Isidro de El General *see* San Isidro
54 E5 **San Jacinto** Bolívar, N Colombia
35 U16 **San Jacinto** California, W USA
35 V15 **San Jacinto Peak** ▲ California, W USA
61 F14 **San Javier** Misiones, NE Argentina
61 C16 **San Javier** Santa Fe, C Argentina
105 S13 **San Javier** Murcia, SE Spain
61 D18 **San Javier** Río Negro, W Uruguay
61 C16 **San Javier, Río** ≈ C Argentina
160 L12 **Sanjiang** *var.* Guyi, Sanjiang Dongzu Zizhixian. Guangxi Zhuangzu Zizhiqu, S China
Sanjiang *see* Jinping, Guizhou
Sanjiang Dongzu Zizhixian *see* Sanjiang
Sanjiaocheng *see* Haiyan
165 N11 **Sanjō** *var.* Sanzyô. Niigata, Honshū, C Japan
57 M15 **San Joaquín** Beni, N Bolivia
55 O6 **San Joaquín** Anzoátegui, NE Venezuela
35 O9 **San Joaquin River** ≈ California, W USA
35 P10 **San Joaquin Valley** *valley* California, W USA
61 A18 **San Jorge** Santa Fe, C Argentina

◆ Country ● Country Capital ◇ Dependent Territory ○ Dependent Territory Capital ◈ Administrative Region ✕ International Airport ▲ Mountain ▲▲ Mountain Range ▼ Volcano ≈ River ◎ Lake ⊞ Reservoir

40 *D3* **San Jorge, Bahía de** *bay* NW Mexico
San Jorge, Isla de *see* Weddell Island
63 *J19* **San Jorge, Golfo** *var.* Gulf of San Jorge. *gulf* S Argentina
San Jorge, Gulf of *see* San Jorge, Golfo
188 *K8* **San Jose** Tinian, S Northern Mariana Islands
35 *N9* **San Jose** California, W USA
61 *F14* **San José** Misiones, NE Argentina
57 *P19* **San José** *var.* San José de Chiquitos. Santa Cruz, E Bolivia
42 *M14* **San José** ● (Costa Rica) San José, C Costa Rica
42 *C7* **San José** *var.* Puerto San José. Escuintla, S Guatemala
40 *G6* **San José** Sonora, NW Mexico
105 *U11* **San José** Eivissa, Spain, W Mediterranean Sea
54 *H5* **San José** Zulia, NW Venezuela
42 *M14* **San José** *off.* Provincia de San José. ◆ *province* W Costa Rica
61 *E19* **San José** ◆ *department* S Uruguay
42 *M13* **San José** ✕ Alajuela, C Costa Rica
San José *see* San José del Guaviare, Colombia
San José *see* San José de Mayo, S Uruguay
171 *O3* **San Jose City** Luzon, N Philippines
San José de Cúcuta *see* Cúcuta
61 *D16* **San José de Feliciano** Entre Ríos, E Argentina
55 *O6* **San José de Guanipa** *var.* El Tigrito. Anzoátegui, NE Venezuela
62 *I9* **San José de Jáchal** San Juan, W Argentina
40 *G10* **San José del Cabo** Baja California Sur, W Mexico
54 *G12* **San José del Guaviare** *var.* San José. Guaviare, S Colombia
61 *E20* **San José de Mayo** *var.* San José. San José, S Uruguay
54 *I10* **San José de Ocuné** Vichada, E Colombia
41 *O9* **San José de Raíces** Nuevo León, NE Mexico
63 *K17* **San José, Golfo** *gulf* E Argentina
40 *F9* **San José, Isla** *island* W Mexico
43 *U16* **San José, Isla** *island* SE Panama
25 *U14* **San Jose Island** *island* Texas, SW USA
62 *I10* **San Juan** San Juan, W Argentina
45 *N9* **San Juan** *var.* San Juan de la Maguana. C Dominican Republic
57 *E17* **San Juan** Ica, S Peru
45 *U5* **San Juan** ○ (Puerto Rico) NE Puerto Rico
62 *H10* **San Juan** *off.* Provincia de San Juan. ◆ *province* W Argentina
45 *U5* **San Juan** *var.* Luis Muñoz Marin. ✕ NE Puerto Rico
San Juan *see* San Juan de los Morros
62 *O7* **San Juan Bautista** Misiones, S Paraguay
35 *O10* **San Juan Bautista** California, W USA
San Juan Bautista *see* Villahermosa
San Juan Bautista Cuicatlán *see* Cuicatlán
San Juan Bautista Tuxtepec *see* Tuxtepec
79 *C17* **San Juan, Cabo** *headland* S Equatorial Guinea
105 *S12* **San Juan de Alicante** País Valenciano, E Spain
54 *H7* **San Juan de Colón** Táchira, NW Venezuela
40 *L9* **San Juan de Guadalupe** Durango, C Mexico
San Juan de la Maguana *see* San Juan
54 *G4* **San Juan del Cesar** La Guajira, N Colombia
40 *L15* **San Juan de Lima, Punta** *headland* SW Mexico
42 *I8* **San Juan de Limay** Estelí, NW Nicaragua
43 *N12* **San Juan del Norte** *var.* Greytown. Río San Juan, SE Nicaragua
54 *K4* **San Juan de los Cayos** Falcón, N Venezuela
40 *M12* **San Juan de los Lagos** Jalisco, C Mexico
54 *L5* **San Juan de los Morros** *var.* San Juan. Guárico, N Venezuela
40 *K9* **San Juan del Río** Durango, C Mexico
41 *O13* **San Juan del Río** Querétaro de Arteaga, C Mexico
42 *J11* **San Juan del Sur** Rivas, SW Nicaragua
54 *M9* **San Juan de Manapiare** Amazonas, S Venezuela
40 *E7* **San Juanico** Baja California Sur, W Mexico
40 *D7* **San Juanico, Punta** *headland* W Mexico
32 *G6* **San Juan Islands** *island group* Washington, NW USA
40 *I6* **San Juanito** Chihuahua, N Mexico
40 *I12* **San Juanito, Isla** *island* C Mexico
37 *R8* **San Juan Mountains** ▲ Colorado, C USA
54 *E5* **San Juan Nepomuceno** Bolívar, NW Colombia
44 *E5* **San Juan, Pico** ▲ C Cuba
191 *W15* **San Juan, Punta** *headland* Easter Island, Chile, E Pacific Ocean
42 *M12* **San Juan, Río** ∾ Costa Rica/Nicaragua
41 *S15* **San Juan, Río** ∾ SE Mexico
37 *O8* **San Juan River** ∾ Colorado/Utah, W USA
San Julián *see* Puerto San Julián
61 *B17* **San Justo** Santa Fe, C Argentina
109 *W5* **Sankt Aegyd-am-Neuwalde** Niederösterreich, E Austria
109 *U9* **Sankt Andrä** *Slvn.* Šent Andraž. Kärnten, S Austria
Sankt Andrä *see* Szentendre
Sankt Anna *see* Sântana
108 *K8* **Sankt Anton-am-Arlberg** Vorarlberg, W Austria
101 *E16* **Sankt Augustin** Nordrhein-Westfalen, W Germany
Sankt-Bartholomäi *see* Palamuse
101 *F24* **Sankt Blasien** Baden-Württemberg, SW Germany
109 *R3* **Sankt Florian am Inn** Oberösterreich, N Austria
108 *I7* **Sankt Gallen** *var.* St.Gallen, *Eng.* Saint Gall, *Fr.* St-Gall. Sankt Gallen, NE Switzerland
108 *H8* **Sankt Gallen** *var.* St.Gallen, Eng, Saint Gall, *Fr.* St-Gall. ◆ *canton* NE Switzerland
108 *J8* **Sankt Gallenkirch** Vorarlberg, W Austria
109 *Q5* **Sankt Georgen** Salzburg, N Austria
Sankt Georgen *see* Đurđevac, Croatia
Sankt-Georgen *see* Sfântu Gheorghe, Romania
109 *R6* **Sankt Gilgen** Salzburg, NW Austria
Sankt Gotthard *see* Szentgotthárd
101 *E20* **Sankt Ingbert** Saarland, SW Germany
Sankt-Jakobi *see* Viru-Jaagupi, Lääne-Virumaa, Estonia
Sankt-Jakobi *see* Pärnu-Jaagupi, Pärnumaa, Estonia
Sankt Johann *see* Sankt Johann in Tirol
109 *T7* **Sankt Johann am Tauern** Steiermark, E Austria
109 *Q7* **Sankt Johann im Pongau** Salzburg, NW Austria
109 *P6* **Sankt Johann in Tirol** *var.* Sankt Johann. Tirol, W Austria
Sankt-Johannis *see* Järva-Jaani
108 *L8* **Sankt Leonhard** Tirol, W Austria
Sankt Margarethen *see* Sankt Margarethen im Burgenland
109 *Y5* **Sankt Margarethen im Burgenland** *var.* Sankt Margarethen. Burgenland, E Austria
Sankt Martin *see* Martin
109 *X8* **Sankt Martin an der Raab** Burgenland, SE Austria
109 *U7* **Sankt Michael in Obersteiermark** Steiermark, SE Austria
Sankt Michel *see* Mikkeli
Sankt Moritz *see* St.Moritz
108 *E11* **Sankt Niklaus** Valais, S Switzerland
109 *S7* **Sankt Nikolai** *var.* Sankt Nikolai im Sölktal. Steiermark, SE Austria
Sankt Nikolai im Sölktal *see* Sankt Nikolai
109 *U9* **Sankt Paul** *var.* Sankt Paul im Lavanttal. Kärnten, S Austria
Sankt Paul im Lavanttal *see* Sankt Paul
Sankt Peter *see* Pivka
109 *W9* **Sankt Peter am Ottersbach** Steiermark, SE Austria
124 *J13* **Sankt-Peterburg** *prev.* Leningrad, Petrograd, *Eng.* Saint Petersburg, *Fin.* Pietari. Leningradskaya Oblast', NW Russian Federation
100 *H8* **Sankt Peter-Ording** Schleswig-Holstein, N Germany
109 *V4* **Sankt Pölten** Niederösterreich, N Austria
109 *W7* **Sankt Ruprecht** *var.* Sankt Ruprecht an der Raab. Steiermark, SE Austria
Sankt Ruprecht an der Raab *see* Sankt Ruprecht
Sankt-Ulrich *see* Ortisei
109 *T4* **Sankt Valentin** Niederösterreich, C Austria
Sankt Veit am Flaum *see* Rijeka
109 *T9* **Sankt Veit an der Glan** *Slvn.* Šent Vid. Kärnten, S Austria
99 *M21* **Sankt-Vith** *var.* Saint-Vith. Liège, E Belgium
101 *E20* **Sankt Wendel** Saarland, SW Germany
109 *R6* **Sankt Wolfgang** Salzburg, NW Austria
79 *K21* **Sankuru** ∾ C Dem. Rep. Congo
40 *D8* **San Lázaro, Cabo** *headland* W Mexico
137 *O16* **Şanlıurfa** *prev.* Sanli Urfa, Urfa, *anc.* Edessa. Şanlıurfa, S Turkey
137 *O16* **Şanlıurfa** *prev.* Urfa. ◆ *province* SE Turkey
137 *O16* **Şanlıurfa Yaylası** *plateau* SE Turkey
61 *B18* **San Lorenzo** Santa Fe, C Argentina
57 *M21* **San Lorenzo** Tarija, S Bolivia
56 *C5* **San Lorenzo** Esmeraldas, N Ecuador
42 *H8* **San Lorenzo** Valle, S Honduras
56 *A6* **San Lorenzo, Cabo** *headland* W Ecuador
105 *N8* **San Lorenzo de El Escorial** *var.* El Escorial. Madrid, C Spain
40 *E5* **San Lorenzo, Isla** *island* NW Mexico
57 *C14* **San Lorenzo, Isla** *island* W Peru
63 *G20* **San Lorenzo, Monte** ▲ S Argentina
40 *I9* **San Lorenzo, Río** ∾ C Mexico
104 *J15* **Sanlúcar de Barrameda** Andalucía, S Spain
104 *J14* **Sanlúcar la Mayor** Andalucía, S Spain
40 *F11* **San Lucas** Baja California Sur, NW Mexico
40 *E6* **San Lucas** *var.* Cabo San Lucas. Baja California Sur, W Mexico
40 *G11* **San Lucas, Cabo** *var.* San Lucas Cape. *headland* W Mexico
San Lucas Cape *see* San Lucas, Cabo
62 *J11* **San Luis** San Luis, C Argentina
42 *E4* **San Luis** Petén, NE Guatemala
40 *D2* **San Luis** *var.* San Luis Río Colorado. Sonora, NW Mexico
42 *M7* **San Luis** Región Autónoma Atlántico Norte, NE Nicaragua
36 *H15* **San Luis** Arizona, SW USA
37 *T8* **San Luis** Colorado, C USA
54 *J4* **San Luis** Falcón, N Venezuela
62 *J11* **San Luis** *off.* Provincia de San Luis. ◆ *province* C Argentina
41 *N12* **San Luis de la Paz** Guanajuato, C Mexico
40 *K8* **San Luis del Cordero** Durango, C Mexico
40 *D4* **San Luis, Isla** *island* NW Mexico
42 *E6* **San Luis Jilotepeque** Jalapa, SE Guatemala
57 *M16* **San Luis, Laguna de** ◎ NW Bolivia
35 *P13* **San Luis Obispo** California, W USA
37 *R7* **San Luis Peak** ▲ Colorado, C USA
41 *N11* **San Luis Potosí** San Luis Potosí, C Mexico
41 *N11* **San Luis Potosí** ◆ *state* C Mexico
35 *O10* **San Luis Reservoir** ⊡ California, W USA
San Luis Río Colorado *see* San Luis
37 *S8* **San Luis Valley** *basin* Colorado, C USA
107 *C19* **Sanluri** Sardegna, Italy, C Mediterranean Sea
61 *D23* **San Manuel** Buenos Aires, E Argentina
36 *M15* **San Manuel** Arizona, SW USA
106 *F11* **San Marcello Pistoiese** Toscana, C Italy
107 *N20* **San Marco Argentano** Calabria, SW Italy
54 *E6* **San Marcos** Sucre, N Colombia
42 *M14* **San Marcos** San José, C Costa Rica
42 *B5* **San Marcos** San Marcos, W Guatemala
42 *F6* **San Marcos** Ocotepeque, SW Honduras
41 *O16* **San Marcos** Guerrero, S Mexico
25 *S11* **San Marcos** Texas, SW USA
42 *A5* **San Marcos** *off.* Departamento de San Marcos. ◆ *department* W Guatemala
San Marcos de Arica *see* Arica
40 *E6* **San Marcos, Isla** *island* W Mexico
106 *H11* **San Marino** ● (San Marino) C San Marino
106 *I11* **San Marino** *off.* Republic of San Marino. ◆ *republic* S Europe
62 *I11* **San Martín** Mendoza, C Argentina
54 *F11* **San Martín** Meta, C Colombia
56 *D11* **San Martín** *off.* Departamento de San Martín. ◆ *department* C Peru
194 *I5* **San Martín** *Argentinian research station* Antarctica
63 *H16* **San Martín de los Andes** Neuquén, W Argentina
104 *M8* **San Martín de Valdeiglesias** Madrid, C Spain
63 *G21* **San Martín, Lago** *var.* Lago O'Higgins. ◎ S Argentina
106 *H6* **San Martino di Castrozza** Trentino-Alto Adige, N Italy
57 *N16* **San Martín, Río** ∾ N Bolivia
San Martín Texmelucan *see* Texmelucan
35 *N9* **San Mateo** California, W USA
55 *O6* **San Mateo** Anzoátegui, NE Venezuela
42 *B4* **San Mateo Ixtatán** Huehuetenango, W Guatemala
57 *Q18* **San Matías** Santa Cruz, E Bolivia
63 *K16* **San Matías, Golfo** *var.* Gulf of San Matías. *gulf* E Argentina
San Matías, Gulf of *see* San Matías
15 *O8* **Sanmaur** Québec, SE Canada
161 *T10* **Sanmen Wan** *bay* E China
160 *M6* **Sanmenxia** *var.* Shan Xian. Henan, C China
Sânmiclăuş Mare *see* Sânnicolau Mare
61 *D14* **San Miguel** Corrientes, NE Argentina
57 *L16* **San Miguel** Beni, N Bolivia
42 *G8* **San Miguel** San Miguel, SE El Salvador
40 *L6* **San Miguel** Coahuila de Zaragoza, N Mexico
40 *J9* **San Miguel** *var.* San Miguel de Cruces. Durango, C Mexico
43 *U16* **San Miguel** Panamá, SE Panama
35 *P12* **San Miguel** California, W USA
42 *B9* **San Miguel** ◆ *department* E El Salvador
41 *N13* **San Miguel de Allende** Guanajuato, C Mexico
San Miguel de Cruces *see* San Miguel
San Miguel de Ibarra *see* Ibarra
61 *D21* **San Miguel del Monte** Buenos Aires, E Argentina
62 *J7* **San Miguel de Tucumán** *var.* Tucumán. Tucumán, N Argentina
43 *V16* **San Miguel, Golfo de** *gulf* S Panama
35 *P15* **San Miguel Island** *island* California, W USA
42 *L11* **San Miguelito** Río San Juan, S Nicaragua
43 *T15* **San Miguelito** Panamá, C Panama
57 *N18* **San Miguel, Río** ∾ E Bolivia
56 *D6* **San Miguel, Río** ∾ Colombia/Ecuador
40 *I7* **San Miguel, Río** ∾ N Mexico
42 *G8* **San Miguel, Volcán de** ⚠ SE El Salvador
161 *Q12* **Sanming** Fujian, SE China
106 *F11* **San Miniato** Toscana, C Italy
San Murezzan *see* St.Moritz
Sannār *see* Sennar
107 *M15* **Sannicandro Garganico** Puglia, SE Italy
40 *H6* **San Nicolás** Sonora, NW Mexico
61 *C19* **San Nicolás de los Arroyos** Buenos Aires, E Argentina
35 *R16* **San Nicolas Island** *island* Channel Islands, California, W USA
Sânnicolaul-Mare *see* Sânnicolau Mare
116 *E11* **Sânnicolau Mare** *var.* Sânnicolaul-Mare, *Hung.* Nagyszentmiklós; *prev.* Sânmiclăuş Mare, Sînnicolau Mare. Timiş, W Romania
123 *Q6* **Sannikova, Proliv** *strait* NE Russian Federation
76 *K16* **Sanniquellie** *var.* Saniquillie. NE Liberia
165 *R7* **Sannohe** Aomori, Honshū, C Japan
Sanntaler Alpen *see* Kamnikško-Savinjske Alpe
111 *O17* **Sanok** Podkarpackie, SE Poland
54 *E5* **San Onofre** Sucre, NW Colombia
57 *K21* **San Pablo** Potosí, S Bolivia
171 *O4* **San Pablo** *off.* San Pablo City. Luzon, N Philippines
San Pablo Balleza *see* Balleza
35 *N8* **San Pablo Bay** *bay* California, W USA
40 *C6* **San Pablo, Punta** *headland* W Mexico
43 *R16* **San Pablo, Río** ∾ C Panama
171 *P4* **San Pascual** Burias Island, C Philippines
121 *Q16* **San Pawl il-Bahar** *Eng.* Saint Paul's Bay. E Malta
61 *C19* **San Pedro** Buenos Aires, E Argentina
62 *K5* **San Pedro** Jujuy, N Argentina
60 *G13* **San Pedro** Misiones, NE Argentina
42 *H1* **San Pedro** Corozal, NE Belize
40 *L8* **San Pedro** *var.* San Pedro de las Colonias. Coahuila de Zaragoza, NE Mexico
62 *O5* **San Pedro** San Pedro, SE Paraguay
62 *O6* **San Pedro** *off.* Departamento de San Pedro. ◆ *department* C Paraguay
77 *N16* **San Pedro** ✕ (Yamoussoukro) C Ivory Coast
44 *G6* **San Pedro** ∾ C Cuba
San Pedro *see* San Pedro del Pinatar
76 *M17* **San-Pédro** S Ivory Coast
42 *D5* **San Pedro Carchá** Alta Verapaz, C Guatemala
35 *S16* **San Pedro Channel** *channel* California, W USA
62 *I5* **San Pedro de Atacama** Antofagasta, N Chile
San Pedro de Durazno *see* Durazno
40 *G5* **San Pedro de la Cueva** Sonora, NW Mexico
San Pedro de las Colonias *see* San Pedro
56 *B11* **San Pedro de Lloc** La Libertad, NW Peru
105 *S13* **San Pedro del Pinatar** *var.* San Pedro. Murcia, SE Spain
45 *P9* **San Pedro de Macorís** SE Dominican Republic
40 *C3* **San Pedro Mártir, Sierra** ▲ NW Mexico
San Pedro Pochutla *see* Pochutla
42 *D2* **San Pedro, Río** ∾ Guatemala/Mexico
40 *K10* **San Pedro, Río** ∾ C Mexico
104 *J10* **San Pedro, Sierra de** ▲ W Spain
42 *G5* **San Pedro Sula** Cortés, NW Honduras
San Pedro Tapanatepec *see* Tapanatepec
62 *I4* **San Pedro, Volcán** ▲ N Chile
106 *E7* **San Pellegrino Terme** Lombardia, N Italy
25 *T16* **San Perlita** Texas, SW USA
San Pietro *see* Supetar
San Pietro del Carso *see* Pivka
107 *A20* **San Pietro, Isola di** *island* W Italy
32 *K7* **Sanpoil River** ∾ Washington, NW USA
165 *C9* **Sanpoku** *var.* Sampoku. Niigata, Honshū, C Japan
40 *C3* **San Quintín** Baja California, NW Mexico
40 *B3* **San Quintín, Bahía de** *bay* NW Mexico
40 *B3* **San Quintín, Cabo** *headland* NW Mexico
62 *I12* **San Rafael** Mendoza, W Argentina
41 *N9* **San Rafael** Nuevo León, NE Mexico
34 *M8* **San Rafael** California, W USA
37 *Q11* **San Rafael** New Mexico, SW USA
54 *H4* **San Rafael** *var.* El Moján. Zulia, NW Venezuela
42 *J8* **San Rafael del Norte** Jinotega, NW Nicaragua
42 *J10* **San Rafael del Sur** Managua, SW Nicaragua
36 *M5* **San Rafael Knob** ▲ Utah, W USA
35 *Q14* **San Rafael Mountains** ▲ California, W USA
42 *M13* **San Ramón** Alajuela, C Costa Rica
57 *E14* **San Ramón** Junín, C Peru
61 *F19* **San Ramón** Canelones, S Uruguay
62 *K5* **San Ramón de la Nueva Orán** Salta, N Argentina
57 *O16* **San Ramón, Río** ∾ E Bolivia
106 *B11* **San Remo** Liguria, NW Italy
54 *J3* **San Román, Cabo** *headland* NW Venezuela
61 *C15* **San Roque** Corrientes, NE Argentina
188 *I4* **San Roque** Saipan, S Northern Mariana Islands
104 *K15* **San Roque** Andalucía, S Spain
25 *R9* **San Saba** Texas, SW USA
25 *Q9* **San Saba River** ∾ Texas, SW USA
61 *D17* **San Salvador** Entre Ríos, E Argentina
42 *F7* **San Salvador** ● (El Salvador) San Salvador, SW El Salvador
42 *A10* **San Salvador** ◆ *department* C El Salvador
42 *F8* **San Salvador** ✕ La Paz, S El Salvador
44 *K4* **San Salvador** *prev.* Watlings Island. *island* E Bahamas
62 *J5* **San Salvador de Jujuy** *var.* Jujuy. Jujuy, N Argentina
42 *F7* **San Salvador, Volcán de** ⚠ C El Salvador
77 *Q14* **Sansanne-Mango** *var.* Mango. N Togo
45 *S5* **San Sebastián** W Puerto Rico
63 *J24* **San Sebastián, Bahía** *bay* S Argentina
Sansenhō *see* Sach'ŏn
106 *H12* **Sansepolcro** Toscana, C Italy
107 *M16* **San Severo** Puglia, SE Italy
112 *F11* **Sanski Most** Federacija Bosna I Hercegovina, NW Bosnia & Herzegovina
171 *W12* **Sansundi** Papua, E Indonesia
104 *K11* **Santa Amalia** Extremadura, W Spain
60 *F13* **Santa Ana** Misiones, NE Argentina
57 *L16* **Santa Ana** Beni, N Bolivia
42 *E7* **Santa Ana** Santa Ana, NW El Salvador
40 *F4* **Santa Ana** Sonora, NW Mexico
35 *T16* **Santa Ana** California, W USA
55 *N6* **Santa Ana** Nueva Esparta, NE Venezuela
42 *A9* **Santa Ana** ◆ *department* NW El Salvador
Santa Ana de Coro *see* Coro
42 *E7* **Santa Ana, Volcán de** *var.* La Matepec. ⚠ W El Salvador
40 *J7* **Santa Barbara** Chihuahua, N Mexico
35 *Q14* **Santa Barbara** California, W USA
42 *G6* **Santa Bárbara** Santa Bárbara, W Honduras
54 *L11* **Santa Bárbara** Amazonas, S Venezuela
54 *I7* **Santa Bárbara** Barinas, W Venezuela
42 *F5* **Santa Bárbara** ◆ *department* NW Honduras
Santa Bárbara *see* Iscuandé
35 *Q15* **Santa Barbara Channel** *channel* California, W USA
Santa Bárbara de Samaná *see* Samaná
35 *R16* **Santa Barbara Island** *island* Channel Islands, California, W USA
54 *E5* **Santa Catalina** Bolívar, N Colombia
43 *R15* **Santa Catalina** Bocas del Toro, W Panama
35 *T17* **Santa Catalina, Gulf of** *gulf* California, W USA
40 *F8* **Santa Catalina, Isla** *island* W Mexico
35 *S16* **Santa Catalina Island** *island* Channel Islands, California, W USA
41 *N8* **Santa Catarina** Nuevo León, NE Mexico
60 *H13* **Santa Catarina** *off.* Estado de Santa Catarina. ◆ *state* S Brazil
Santa Catarina de Tepehuanes *see* Tepehuanes
60 *L13* **Santa Catarina, Ilha de** *island* S Brazil
45 *Q16* **Santa Catherina** Curaçao, C Netherlands Antilles
44 *E5* **Santa Clara** Villa Clara, C Cuba
35 *N9* **Santa Clara** California, W USA
36 *J8* **Santa Clara** Utah, W USA
Santa Clara *see* Santa Clara de Olimar
61 *F18* **Santa Clara de Olimar** *var.* Santa Clara. Cerro Largo, NE Uruguay
61 *A17* **Santa Clara de Saguier** Santa Fe, C Argentina
Santa Coloma *see* Santa Coloma de Gramenet
105 *X5* **Santa Coloma de Farners** *var.* Santa Coloma de Farnés. Cataluña, NE Spain
Santa Coloma de Farnés *see* Santa Coloma de Farners
105 *W6* **Santa Coloma de Gramanet** *var.* Santa Coloma. Cataluña, NE Spain
104 *G2* **Santa Comba** Galicia, NW Spain
Santa Comba *see* Uaco Cungo
104 *H8* **Santa Comba Dão** Viseu, N Portugal
82 *C10* **Santa Cruz** Uíge, NW Angola
57 *N19* **Santa Cruz** *var.* Santa Cruz de la Sierra. Santa Cruz, C Bolivia
62 *G12* **Santa Cruz** Libertador, C Chile
42 *K13* **Santa Cruz** Guanacaste, W Costa Rica
44 *I12* **Santa Cruz** W Jamaica
64 *P6* **Santa Cruz** Madeira, Portugal, NE Atlantic Ocean
35 *N10* **Santa Cruz** California, W USA
63 *H20* **Santa Cruz** *off.* Provincia de Santa Cruz. ◆ *province* S Argentina
57 *O18* **Santa Cruz** ◆ *department* E Bolivia
Santa Cruz *see* Viru-Viru
Santa Cruz *see* Puerto Santa Cruz
Santa Cruz Barillas *see* Barillas
59 *O18* **Santa Cruz Cabrália** Bahia, E Brazil
Santa Cruz de El Seibo *see* El Seibo
64 *N11* **Santa Cruz de la Palma** La Palma, Islas Canarias, Spain, NE Atlantic Ocean
Santa Cruz de la Sierra *see* Santa Cruz
105 *O9* **Santa Cruz de la Zarza** Castilla-La Mancha, C Spain
42 *C5* **Santa Cruz del Quiché** Quiché, W Guatemala
105 *N8* **Santa Cruz del Retamar** Castilla-La Mancha, C Spain
Santa Cruz del Seibo *see* El Seibo
44 *G7* **Santa Cruz del Sur** Camagüey, C Cuba
105 *O11* **Santa Cruz de Mudela** Castilla-La Mancha, C Spain
64 *Q11* **Santa Cruz de Tenerife** Tenerife, Islas Canarias, Spain, NE Atlantic Ocean
64 *P11* **Santa Cruz de Tenerife** ◆ *province* Islas Canarias, Spain, NE Atlantic Ocean
60 *K9* **Santa Cruz do Rio Pardo** São Paulo, S Brazil
61 *H15* **Santa Cruz do Sul** Rio Grande do Sul, S Brazil
57 *C17* **Santa Cruz, Isla** *var.* Indefatigable Island, Isla Chávez. *island* Galapagos Islands, Ecuador, E Pacific Ocean
40 *F8* **Santa Cruz, Isla** *island* W Mexico
35 *Q15* **Santa Cruz Island** *island* California, W USA
187 *Q10* **Santa Cruz Islands** *island group* E Solomon Islands
63 *I22* **Santa Cruz, Río** ∾ S Argentina
36 *L15* **Santa Cruz River** ∾ Arizona, SW USA
61 *C17* **Santa Elena** Entre Ríos, E Argentina
42 *F2* **Santa Elena** Cayo, W Belize
25 *R16* **Santa Elena** Texas, SW USA
56 *A7* **Santa Elena, Bahía de** *bay* W Ecuador
55 *R10* **Santa Elena de Uairén** Bolívar, E Venezuela
42 *K12* **Santa Elena, Península** *peninsula* NW Costa Rica
56 *A7* **Santa Elena, Punta** *headland* W Ecuador
104 *L11* **Santa Eufemia** Andalucía, S Spain
107 *N21* **Santa Eufemia, Golfo di** *gulf* S Italy
105 *S4* **Santa Eulalia de Gállego** Aragón, NE Spain
105 *V11* **Santa Eulalia del Río** Eivissa, Spain, W Mediterranean Sea
61 *B17* **Santa Fe** Santa Fe, C Argentina
105 *N14* **Santa Fe** Andalucía, S Spain
37 *S10* **Santa Fe** *state capital* New Mexico, SW USA
61 *B15* **Santa Fe** *off.* Provincia de Santa Fe. ◆ *province* C Argentina
Santa Fe *see* Bogotá
44 *C6* **Santa Fé** *var.* La Fe. Isla de la Juventud, W Cuba
43 *R16* **Santa Fé** Veraguas, C Panama
Santa Fe de Bogotá *see* Bogotá
60 *J7* **Santa Fé do Sul** São Paulo, S Brazil
57 *B18* **Santa Fe, Isla** *var.* Barrington Island. *island* Galapagos Islands, Ecuador, E Pacific Ocean
23 *V9* **Santa Fe River** ∾ Florida, SE USA
59 *M15* **Santa Filomena** Piauí, E Brazil
40 *G10* **Santa Genoveva** ▲ W Mexico
153 *S14* **Santahar** Rajshahi, NW Bangladesh
60 *G11* **Santa Helena** Paraná, S Brazil
54 *J5* **Santa Inés** Lara, N Venezuela
63 *G24* **Santa Inés, Isla** *island* S Chile
62 *J13* **Santa Isabel** La Pampa, C Argentina
43 *U14* **Santa Isabel** Colón, N Panama
186 *L8* **Santa Isabel** *var.* Bughotu. *island* N Solomon Islands
Santa Isabel *see* Malabo
58 *D11* **Santa Isabel do Rio Negro** Amazonas, NW Brazil
61 *C15* **Santa Lucia** Corrientes, NE Argentina
57 *I17* **Santa Lucía** Puno, S Peru
61 *F20* **Santa Lucía** *var.* Santa Lucia. Canelones, S Uruguay
42 *B6* **Santa Lucía Cotzumalguapa** Escuintla, SW Guatemala
107 *L23* **Santa Lucia del Mela** Sicilia, Italy, C Mediterranean Sea
35 *O11* **Santa Lucia Range** ▲ California, W USA
40 *D9* **Santa Margarita, Isla** *island* W Mexico
61 *G15* **Santa Maria** Rio Grande do Sul, S Brazil
35 *P13* **Santa Maria** California, W USA
64 *Q4* **Santa Maria** ✕ Santa Maria, Azores, Portugal, NE Atlantic Ocean
64 *P3* **Santa Maria** *island* Azores, Portugal, NE Atlantic Ocean
Santa Maria *see* Gaua.
62 *J7* **Santa María** Catamarca, N Argentina
Santa María Asunción Tlaxiaco *see* Tlaxiaco
40 *G9* **Santa María, Bahía** *bay* W Mexico
83 *L21* **Santa Maria, Cabo de** *headland* S Mozambique
104 *G15* **Santa Maria, Cabo de** *headland* S Portugal
44 *J4* **Santa Maria, Cape** *headland* Long Island, C Bahamas
107 *J17* **Santa Maria Capua Vetere** Campania, S Italy
59 *M17* **Santa Maria da Vitória** Bahia, E Brazil

◆ Country ● Country Capital ◇ Dependent Territory ○ Dependent Territory Capital ◆ Administrative Region ✕ International Airport ▲ Mountain ▲ Mountain Range ⚠ Volcano ∾ River ◎ Lake ⊡ Reservoir

55 N9 **Santa Maria de Erebato** Bolívar, SE Venezuela
104 G7 **Santa Maria da Feira** Aveiro, N Portugal
55 N6 **Santa María de Ipire** Guárico, C Venezuela
Santa Maria del Buen Aire *see* Buenos Aires
40 J8 **Santa María del Oro** Durango, C Mexico
41 N12 **Santa María del Río** San Luis Potosí, C Mexico
Santa Maria di Castellabate *see* Castellabate
107 Q20 **Santa Maria di Leuca, Capo** *headland* SE Italy
108 K10 **Santa Maria-im-Münstertal** Graubünden, SE Switzerland
57 B18 **Santa María, Isla** *var.* Isla Floreana, Charles Island. *island* Galapagos Islands, Ecuador, E Pacific Ocean
40 J3 **Santa María, Laguna de** ◎ N Mexico
61 G16 **Santa Maria, Rio** ⁓ S Brazil
43 R16 **Santa María, Río** ⁓ C Panama
36 J12 **Santa Maria River** ⁓ Arizona, SW USA
107 G15 **Santa Marinella** Lazio, C Italy
54 F4 **Santa Marta** Magdalena, N Colombia
104 J11 **Santa Marta** Extremadura, W Spain
Santa Maura *see* Lefkáda
35 S15 **Santa Monica** California, W USA
116 F10 **Sântana** *Ger.* Sankt Anna, *Hung.* Újszentanna; *prev.* Sintana. Arad, W Romania
61 F16 **Santana, Coxilha de** *hill range* S Brazil
61 H16 **Santana da Boa Vista** Rio Grande do Sul, S Brazil
61 F16 **Santana do Livramento** *prev.* Livramento. Rio Grande do Sul, S Brazil
105 N2 **Santander** Cantabria, N Spain
54 F8 **Santander** *off.* Departamento de Santander. ◈ *province* C Colombia
Santander Jiménez *see* Jiménez
Sant'Andrea *see* Svetac
107 B20 **Sant'Antioco** Sardegna, Italy, C Mediterranean Sea
105 V11 **Sant Antoni de Portmany** *Cas.* San Antonio Abad. Eivissa, Spain, W Mediterranean Sea
104 J13 **Santa Olalla del Cala** Andalucía, S Spain
35 R15 **Santa Paula** California, W USA
36 L4 **Santaquin** Utah, W USA
58 I12 **Santarém** Pará, N Brazil
104 G10 **Santarém** *anc.* Scalabis. Santarém, W Portugal
104 G10 **Santarém** ◈ *district* C Portugal
44 F4 **Santaren Channel** *channel* W Bahamas
54 K10 **Santa Rita** Vichada, E Colombia
188 B16 **Santa Rita** SW Guam
42 H5 **Santa Rita** Cortés, NW Honduras
40 E9 **Santa Rita** Baja California Sur, W Mexico
54 H5 **Santa Rita** Zulia, NW Venezuela
59 I19 **Santa Rita de Araguaia** Goiás, S Brazil
Santa Rita de Cassia *see* Cássia
61 D14 **Santa Rosa** Corrientes, NE Argentina
62 K13 **Santa Rosa** La Pampa, C Argentina
61 G14 **Santa Rosa** Rio Grande do Sul, S Brazil
58 E10 **Santa Rosa** Roraima, N Brazil
56 B8 **Santa Rosa** El Oro, SW Ecuador
57 I16 **Santa Rosa** Puno, S Peru
34 M7 **Santa Rosa** California, W USA
37 U11 **Santa Rosa** New Mexico, SW USA
55 O6 **Santa Rosa** Anzoátegui, NE Venezuela
42 A3 **Santa Rosa** *off.* Departamento de Santa Rosa. ◈ *department* SE Guatemala
Santa Rosa *see* Santa Rosa de Copán
63 J15 **Santa Rosa, Bajo de** *basin* E Argentina
42 F6 **Santa Rosa de Copán** *var.* Santa Rosa. Copán, W Honduras
54 E8 **Santa Rosa de Osos** Antioquia, C Colombia
35 Q15 **Santa Rosa Island** *island* California, W USA
23 O9 **Santa Rosa Island** *island* Florida, SE USA
40 E6 **Santa Rosalía** Baja California Sur, W Mexico
54 K6 **Santa Rosalía** Portuguesa, NW Venezuela
188 C15 **Santa Rosa, Mount** ▲ NE Guam
35 V16 **Santa Rosa Mountains** ▲ California, W USA
35 T2 **Santa Rosa Range** ▲ Nevada, W USA
62 M8 **Santa Sylvina** Chaco, N Argentina
Santa Tecla *see* Nueva San Salvador
61 B19 **Santa Teresa** Santa Fe, C Argentina
59 O20 **Santa Teresa** Espírito Santo, SE Brazil
107 M23 **Santa Teresa di Riva** Sicilia, Italy, C Mediterranean Sea
61 E21 **Santa Teresita** Buenos Aires, E Argentina
61 H19 **Santa Vitória do Palmar** Rio Grande do Sul, S Brazil
35 Q14 **Santa Ynez River** ⁓ California, W USA
Sant Carles de la Rápida *see* Sant Carles de la Ràpita
105 U7 **Sant Carles de la Ràpita** *var.* Sant Carles de la Rápida. Cataluña, NE Spain
105 W5 **Sant Celoni** Cataluña, NE Spain
35 U17 **Santee** California, W USA
21 T13 **Santee River** ⁓ South Carolina, SE USA
40 K15 **San Telmo, Punta** *headland* SW Mexico
107 O17 **Santeramo in Colle** Puglia, SE Italy
105 X5 **Sant Feliu de Guíxols** *var.* San Feliú de Guixols. Cataluña, NE Spain
105 W6 **Sant Feliu de Llobregat** Cataluña, NE Spain
106 C7 **Santhià** Piemonte, NE Italy
61 F15 **Santiago** Rio Grande do Sul, S Brazil
62 H11 **Santiago** *var.* Gran Santiago. ● (Chile) Santiago, C Chile
45 N8 **Santiago** *var.* Santiago de los Caballeros. N Dominican Republic
40 G10 **Santiago** Baja California Sur, W Mexico
41 O8 **Santiago** Nuevo León, NE Mexico
43 R16 **Santiago** Veraguas, S Panama
57 E16 **Santiago** Ica, SW Peru
104 G3 **Santiago** *var.* Santiago de Compostela, *Eng.* Compostella; *anc.* Campus Stellae. Galicia, NW Spain
62 H11 **Santiago** *off.* Región Metropolitana de Santiago, *var.* Metropolitan. ◈ *region* C Chile
62 H11 **Santiago** ✕ Santiago, C Chile
104 G3 **Santiago** ✕ Galicia, NW Spain
76 D10 **Santiago** *var.* São Tiago. *island* Ilhas de Sotavento, S Cape Verde
Santiago *see* Santiago de Cuba, Cuba
Santiago *see* Grande de Santiago, Río, Mexico
42 B6 **Santiago Atitlán** Sololá, SW Guatemala
43 Q16 **Santiago, Cerro** ▲ W Panama
Santiago de Compostela *see* Santiago
44 I8 **Santiago de Cuba** *var.* Santiago. Santiago de Cuba, E Cuba
Santiago de Guayaquil *see* Guayaquil
62 K8 **Santiago del Estero** Santiago del Estero, C Argentina
61 A15 **Santiago del Estero** *off.* Provincia de Santiago del Estero. ◈ *province* N Argentina
40 I8 **Santiago de los Caballeros** Sinaloa, W Mexico
Santiago de los Caballeros *see* Santiago, Dominican Republic
Santiago de los Caballeros *see* Guatemala, Guatemala
42 F8 **Santiago de María** Usulután, SE El Salvador
104 F12 **Santiago do Cacém** Setúbal, S Portugal
40 J12 **Santiago Ixcuintla** Nayarit, C Mexico
Santiago Jamiltepec *see* Jamiltepec
24 L11 **Santiago Mountains** ▲ Texas, SW USA
40 J9 **Santiago Papasquiaro** Durango, C Mexico
Santiago Pinotepa Nacional *see* Pinotepa Nacional
56 C8 **Santiago, Río** ⁓ N Peru
40 M10 **San Tiburcio** Zacatecas, C Mexico
105 N2 **Santillana** Cantabria, N Spain
54 I5 **San Timoteo** Zulia, NW Venezuela
Santi Quaranta *see* Sarandë
Santissima Trinidad *see* Chilung
105 O12 **Santisteban del Puerto** Andalucía, S Spain
105 U7 **Sant Jordi, Golf de** *gulf* NE Spain
105 T8 **Sant Mateu** País Valenciano, E Spain
25 S7 **Santo** Texas, SW USA
Santo *see* Espiritu Santo
60 M10 **Santo Amaro, Ilha de** *island* SE Brazil
61 G14 **Santo Ângelo** Rio Grande do Sul, S Brazil
76 C9 **Santo Antão** *island* Ilhas de Barlavento, N Cape Verde
60 J10 **Santo Antônio da Platina** Paraná, S Brazil
58 C13 **Santo Antônio do Içá** Amazonas, N Brazil
57 Q18 **Santo Corazón, Río** ⁓ E Bolivia
44 E5 **Santo Domingo** Villa Clara, C Cuba
45 O9 **Santo Domingo** *prev.* Ciudad Trujillo. ● (Dominican Republic) SE Dominican Republic
40 E8 **Santo Domingo** Baja California Sur, W Mexico
40 M10 **Santo Domingo** San Luis Potosí, C Mexico
42 L10 **Santo Domingo** Chontales, S Nicaragua
105 P4 **Santo Domingo de la Calzada** La Rioja, N Spain
56 B6 **Santo Domingo de los Colorados** Pichincha, NW Ecuador
Santo Domingo Tehuantepec *see* Tehuantepec
55 O6 **San Tomé** Anzoátegui, NE Venezuela
San Tomé de Guayana *see* Ciudad Guayana
105 R13 **Santomera** Murcia, SE Spain
105 O2 **Santoña** Cantabria, N Spain
Santorin/Santoríni *see* Thíra
60 M10 **Santos** São Paulo, S Brazil
65 J17 **Santos Plateau** *undersea feature* SW Atlantic Ocean
104 G6 **Santo Tirso** Porto, N Portugal
40 B2 **Santo Tomás** Baja California, NW Mexico
42 L10 **Santo Tomás** Chontales, S Nicaragua
42 G5 **Santo Tomás de Castilla** Izabal, E Guatemala
40 B2 **Santo Tomás, Punta** *headland* NW Mexico
57 H16 **Santo Tomás, Río** ⁓ C Peru
57 B18 **Santo Tomás, Volcán** ⛰ Galapagos Islands, Ecuador, E Pacific Ocean
61 F14 **Santo Tomé** Corrientes, NE Argentina
Santo Tomé de Guayana *see* Ciudad Guayana
98 H10 **Santpoort** Noord-Holland, W Netherlands
Santurce *see* Santurtzi
105 O2 **Santurtzi** *var.* Santurce, Santurzi. País Vasco, N Spain
Santurzi *see* Santurtzi
63 G20 **San Valentín, Cerro** ▲ S Chile
42 F8 **San Vicente** San Vicente, C El Salvador
40 C2 **San Vicente** Baja California, NW Mexico
188 H6 **San Vicente** Saipan, S Northern Mariana Islands
42 B9 **San Vicente** ◈ *department* E El Salvador
104 I10 **San Vicente de Alcántara** Extremadura, W Spain
105 N2 **San Vicente de Barakaldo** *var.* Baracaldo. País Vasco, N Spain
57 E15 **San Vicente de Cañete** *var.* Cañete. Lima, W Peru
104 M2 **San Vicente de la Barquera** Cantabria, N Spain
54 E12 **San Vicente del Caguán** Caquetá, S Colombia
42 F8 **San Vicente, Volcán de** ⛰ C El Salvador
43 O15 **San Vito** Puntarenas, SE Costa Rica
106 I7 **San Vito al Tagliamento** Friuli-Venezia Giulia, NE Italy
107 H23 **San Vito, Capo** *headland* Sicilia, Italy, C Mediterranean Sea
107 P18 **San Vito dei Normanni** Puglia, SE Italy
160 L17 **Sanya** *var.* Ya Xian. Hainan, S China
83 J16 **Sanyati** ⁓ N Zimbabwe
25 Q16 **San Ygnacio** Texas, SW USA
160 L6 **Sanyuan** Shaanxi, C China
123 P11 **Sanyyakhtakh** Respublika Sakha (Yakutiya), NE Russian Federation
146 J15 **S.A.Nyýazow Adyndaky** *Rus.* Imeni S.A.Niyazova. Mary Welaýaty, S Turkmenistan
82 C10 **Sanza Pombo** Uíge, NW Angola
Sanzyô *see* Sanjō
104 G14 **São Bartolomeu de Messines** Faro, S Portugal
60 M10 **São Bernardo do Campo** São Paulo, S Brazil
61 F15 **São Borja** Rio Grande do Sul, S Brazil
104 H14 **São Brás de Alportel** Faro, S Portugal
60 M10 **São Caetano do Sul** São Paulo, S Brazil
60 L9 **São Carlos** São Paulo, S Brazil
59 P16 **São Cristóvão** Sergipe, E Brazil
61 F15 **São Francisco de Assis** Rio Grande do Sul, S Brazil
58 K13 **São Félix** Pará, NE Brazil
São Félix *see* São Félix do Araguaia
59 J16 **São Félix do Araguaia** *var.* São Félix. Mato Grosso, W Brazil
59 J14 **São Félix do Xingu** Pará, NE Brazil
60 Q9 **São Fidélis** Rio de Janeiro, SE Brazil
76 D10 **São Filipe** Fogo, S Cape Verde
60 K12 **São Francisco do Sul** Santa Catarina, S Brazil
60 K12 **São Francisco, Ilha de** *island* S Brazil
59 P16 **São Francisco, Rio** ⁓ E Brazil
61 G16 **São Gabriel** Rio Grande do Sul, S Brazil
60 P10 **São Gonçalo** Rio de Janeiro, SE Brazil
81 H23 **Sao Hill** Iringa, S Tanzania
60 R9 **São João da Barra** Rio de Janeiro, SE Brazil
104 G7 **São João da Madeira** Aveiro, N Portugal
58 M12 **São João de Cortes** Maranhão, E Brazil
59 M21 **São João del Rei** Minas Gerais, NE Brazil
59 N15 **São João do Piauí** Piauí, E Brazil
59 N14 **São João dos Patos** Maranhão, E Brazil
58 C11 **São Joaquim** Amazonas, NW Brazil
61 J14 **São Joaquim** Santa Catarina, S Brazil
60 L7 **São Joaquim da Barra** São Paulo, S Brazil
64 N2 **São Jorge** *island* Azores, Portugal, NE Atlantic Ocean
61 K14 **São José** Santa Catarina, S Brazil
60 M8 **São José do Rio Pardo** São Paulo, S Brazil
60 K8 **São José do Rio Preto** São Paulo, S Brazil
60 N10 **São Jose dos Campos** São Paulo, S Brazil
61 I17 **São Lourenço do Sul** Rio Grande do Sul, S Brazil
58 F11 **São Luís** Roraima, N Brazil
58 M12 **São Luís** *state capital* Maranhão, NE Brazil
58 M12 **São Luís, Ilha de** *island* NE Brazil
61 F14 **São Luiz Gonzaga** Rio Grande do Sul, S Brazil
104 I10 **São Mamede** ▲ C Portugal
São Mandol *see* São Manuel, Rio
47 U8 **São Manuel** ⁓ C Brazil
59 H15 **São Manuel, Rio** *var.* São Mandol, Teles Pirés. ⁓ C Brazil
58 C11 **São Marcelino** Amazonas, NW Brazil
58 N12 **São Marcos, Baía de** *bay* N Brazil
59 O20 **São Mateus** Espírito Santo, SE Brazil
60 J12 **São Mateus do Sul** Paraná, S Brazil
64 P3 **São Miguel** *island* Azores, Portugal, NE Atlantic Ocean
60 G13 **São Miguel d'Oeste** Santa Catarina, S Brazil
45 P9 **Saona, Isla** *island* SE Dominican Republic
172 H12 **Saondzou** ▲ Grande Comore, NW Comoros
103 R10 **Saône** ⁓ E France
103 Q9 **Saône-et-Loire** ◈ *department* C France
76 D9 **São Nicolau** *Eng.* Saint Nicholas. *island* Ilhas de Barlavento, N Cape Verde
60 M10 **São Paulo** *state capital* São Paulo, S Brazil
60 K9 **São Paulo** *off.* Estado de São Paulo. ◈ *state* S Brazil
São Paulo de Loanda *see* Luanda
São Pedro do Rio Grande do Sul *see* Rio Grande
104 H7 **São Pedro do Sul** Viseu, N Portugal
64 K13 **São Pedro e São Paulo** *undersea feature* C Atlantic Ocean
59 M14 **São Raimundo das Mangabeiras** Maranhão, E Brazil
59 Q14 **São Roque, Cabo de** *headland* E Brazil
São Salvador/São Salvador do Congo *see* M'Banza Congo, Angola
São Salvador *see* Salvador, Brazil
60 N10 **São Sebastião, Ilha de** *island* S Brazil
83 N19 **São Sebastião, Ponta** *headland* C Mozambique
104 F13 **São Teotónio** Beja, S Portugal
São Tiago *see* Santiago
79 B18 **São Tomé** ● (Sao Tome and Principe) São Tomé, S Sao Tome and Principe
79 B18 **São Tomé** ✕ São Tomé, S Sao Tome and Principe
79 B18 **São Tomé** *Eng.* Saint Thomas. *island* S Sao Tome and Principe
79 B17 **Sao Tome and Principe** *off.* Democratic Republic of Sao Tome and Principe. ◆ *republic* E Atlantic Ocean
74 H9 **Saoura, Oued** ⁓ NW Algeria
60 M10 **São Vicente** *Eng.* Saint Vincent. São Paulo, S Brazil
64 O5 **São Vicente** Madeira, Portugal, NE Atlantic Ocean
76 C9 **São Vicente** *Eng.* Saint Vincent. *island* Ilhas de Barlavento, N Cape Verde
São Vicente, Cabo de *see* São Vicente, Cabo de
104 F14 **São Vicente, Cabo de** *Eng.* Cape Saint Vincent, *Port.* Cabo de São Vicente. *headland* S Portugal
Sápai *see* Sápes
Sapaleri, Cerro *see* Zapaleri, Cerro
Saparoea *see* Saparua
171 S13 **Saparua** *prev.* Saparoea. C Indonesia
168 L11 **Sapat** Sumatera, W Indonesia
77 U17 **Sapele** Delta, S Nigeria
23 X7 **Sapelo Island** *island* Georgia, SE USA
23 X7 **Sapelo Sound** *sound* Georgia, SE USA
114 K13 **Sápes** *var.* Sápai. Anatolikí Makedonía kai Thráki, NE Greece
115 D22 **Sapiéntza** *island* S Greece
Sapir *see* Sappir
61 I15 **Sapiranga** Rio Grande do Sul, S Brazil
114 K13 **Sápka** ▲ NE Greece
56 D11 **Saposoa** San Martín, N Peru
119 F16 **Sapotskino** *Pol.* Sopockinie, *Rus.* Sopotskin. Hrodzyenskaya Voblasts', W Belarus
77 P13 **Sapoui** *var.* Sapouy. S Burkina
Sapouy *see* Sapoui
138 F12 **Sappir** *var.* Sapir. Southern, S Israel
165 S4 **Sapporo** Hokkaidō, NE Japan
107 M19 **Sapri** Campania, S Italy
169 T16 **Sapudi, Pulau** *island* S Indonesia
27 P9 **Sapulpa** Oklahoma, C USA
142 J4 **Saqqez** *var.* Saghez, Sakiz, Saqqiz. Kordestān, NW Iran
Saqqiz *see* Saqqez
139 U8 **Sarābādī** E Iraq
167 P10 **Sara Buri** *var.* Saraburi. Saraburi, C Thailand
24 K9 **Saragosa** Texas, SW USA
Saragossa *see* Zaragoza
Saragt *see* Sarahs
56 B8 **Saraguro** Loja, S Ecuador
146 I15 **Sarahs** *var.* Saragt, *Rus.* Serakhs. Ahal Welaýaty, S Turkmenistan
126 M6 **Sarai** Ryazanskaya Oblast', W Russian Federation
Sarāi *see* Sarāy
154 M12 **Saraipāli** Chhattīsgarh, C India
149 T9 **Sarāi Sidhu** Punjab, E Pakistan
93 M15 **Säräisniemi** Oulu, C Finland
113 I14 **Sarajevo** ● (Bosnia and Herzegovina) Federacija Bosna I Hercegovina, SE Bosnia and Herzegovina
112 I13 **Sarajevo** ✕ Federacija Bosna I Hercegovina, C Bosnia and Herzegovina
143 V4 **Sarakhs** Khorāsān, NE Iran
115 H17 **Sarakíniko, Akrotírio** *headland* Évvoia, C Greece
115 I18 **Sarakinó** *island* Vóreioi Sporádes, Greece, Aegean Sea
127 V7 **Saraktash** Orenburgskaya Oblast', W Russian Federation
30 L15 **Sara, Lake** ▣ Illinois, N USA
23 N8 **Saraland** Alabama, S USA
55 V9 **Saramacca** ◈ *district* N Suriname
55 V10 **Saramacca Rivier** ⁓ C Suriname
166 M2 **Saramati** ▲ N Myanmar
145 R10 **Saran'** *Kaz.* Saran. Karaganda, C Kazakhstan
18 K7 **Saranac Lake** New York, NE USA
18 K7 **Saranac River** ⁓ New York, NE USA
Saranda *see* Sarandë
113 L23 **Sarandë** *var.* Saranda, *It.* Porto Edda; *prev.* Santi Quaranta. Vlorë, S Albania
61 H14 **Sarandi** Rio Grande do Sul, S Brazil
61 F19 **Sarandí del Yí** Durazno, C Uruguay
61 F19 **Sarandí Grande** Florida, S Uruguay
171 Q8 **Sarangani Islands** *island group* S Philippines
127 P5 **Saransk** Respublika Mordoviya, W Russian Federation
115 C14 **Sarantáporos** ⁓ N Greece
114 H9 **Sarantsi** Sofiya, W Bulgaria
127 T3 **Sarapul** Udmurtskaya Respublika, NW Russian Federation
Sarāqeb *see* Sarāqib
138 I3 **Sarāqib** *Fr.* Sarāqeb. Idlib, N Syria
54 J5 **Sarare** Lara, N Venezuela
55 O10 **Sarariña** Amazonas, S Venezuela
143 S10 **Sar Ashk** Kermān, C Iran
23 V13 **Sarasota** Florida, SE USA
117 O11 **Sarata** Odes'ka Oblast', SW Ukraine
116 I10 **Sărăţel** *Hung.* Szeretfalva. Bistriţa-Năsăud, N Romania
25 X10 **Saratoga** Texas, SW USA
18 K10 **Saratoga Springs** New York, NE USA
127 P8 **Saratov** Saratovskaya Oblast', W Russian Federation
127 P8 **Saratovskaya Oblast'** ◈ *province* W Russian Federation
127 Q7 **Saratovskoye Vodokhranilishche** ▣ W Russian Federation
Saravan/Saravane *see* Salavan
169 S9 **Sarawak** ◈ *state* East Malaysia
Sarawak *see* Kuching
139 U6 **Sarāy** *var.* Sarāi. E Iraq
136 D10 **Saray** Tekirdağ, NW Turkey
76 J12 **Saraya** SE Senegal
143 W14 **Sarbāz** Sīstān va Balūchestān, SE Iran
143 U8 **Sarbīsheh** Khorāsān, E Iran
111 J24 **Sárbogárd** Fejér, C Hungary
Şarcad *see* Sarkad
27 S7 **Sarcoxie** Missouri, C USA
152 L11 **Sārda** *Nep.* Kali. ⁓ India/Nepal
152 G10 **Sardārshahr** Rājasthān, NW India
107 C18 **Sardegna** *Eng.* Sardinia. ◈ *region* Italy, C Mediterranean Sea
107 A18 **Sardegna** *Eng.* Sardinia. *island* Italy, C Mediterranean Sea
42 K13 **Sardinal** Guanacaste, NW Costa Rica
54 G7 **Sardinata** Norte de Santander, N Colombia
Sardinia *see* Sardegna
120 K8 **Sardinia-Corsica Trough** *undersea feature* Tyrrhenian Sea, C Mediterranean Sea
22 L2 **Sardis** Mississippi, S USA
22 L2 **Sardis Lake** ▣ Mississippi, S USA
27 P12 **Sardis Lake** ▣ Oklahoma, C USA
92 H12 **Sarek** ▲ N Sweden
149 N3 **Sar-e Pol** *var.* Sar-i-Pul. Sar-e Pol, N Afghanistan
149 O3 **Sar-e Pol** ◈ *province* N Afghanistan
Sar-e Pol *see* Sar-e Pol-e Żahāb
142 J6 **Sar-e Pol-e Żahāb** *var.* Sar-e Pol, Sar-i Pul. Kermānshāh, W Iran
147 T13 **Sarez, Kŭli** *Rus.* Sarezskoye Ozero. ◎ SE Tajikistan
Sarezskoye Ozero *see* Sarez, Kŭli
64 G10 **Sargasso Sea** *sea* W Atlantic Ocean
149 U8 **Sargodha** Punjab, NE Pakistan
78 I13 **Sarh** *prev.* Fort-Archambault. Moyen-Chari, S Chad
143 P4 **Sārī** *var.* Sari, Sāri. Māzandarān, N Iran
115 N23 **Saría** *island* SE Greece
Sariasiya *see* Sariosiyo
40 F3 **Saric** Sonora, NW Mexico
188 K6 **Sarigan** *island* C Northern Mariana Islands
136 D14 **Sarıgöl** Manisa, SW Turkey
139 T6 **Sārihah** E Iraq
137 R12 **Sarıkamış** Kars, NE Turkey
169 R9 **Sarikei** Sarawak, East Malaysia
147 U12 **Sarikol Range** *Rus.* Sarykol'skiy Khrebet. ▲ China/Tajikistan
181 Y7 **Sarina** Queensland, NE Australia
Sarine *see* La Sarine
105 S5 **Sariñena** Aragón, NE Spain
147 O13 **Sariosiyo** *Rus.* Sariasiya. Surxondaryo Viloyati, S Uzbekistan
Sar-i-Pul *see* Sar-e Pol, Afghanistan
Sar-i Pul *see* Sar-e Pol-e Żahāb, Iran
Sariqamish Kŭli *see* Sarygamyş Köli
149 V1 **Sarī Qūl** *Rus.* Ozero Zurkul', *Taj.* Zŭrkŭl. ◎ Afghanistan/Tajikistan *see also* Zŭrkŭl
75 Q12 **Sarīr Tibistī** *var.* Serir Tibesti. *desert* S Libya
25 S15 **Sarita** Texas, SW USA
163 W14 **Sariwŏn** SW North Korea
114 P12 **Sarıyer** İstanbul, NW Turkey
97 L26 **Sark** *Fr.* Sercq. *island* Channel Islands
111 N24 **Sarkad** *Rom.* Şarcad. Békés, SE Hungary
145 W14 **Sarkand** Almaty, SW Kazakhstan
Sarkani *see* Krasnogorskoye
152 D11 **Sarkāri Tala** Rājasthān, NW India
136 G15 **Şarkikaraağaç** *var.* Şarki Karaağaç. Isparta, SW Turkey
136 L13 **Şarkışla** Sivas, C Turkey
136 C11 **Şarköy** Tekirdağ, NW Turkey
Sarköz *see* Livada
Sarlat *see* Sarlat-la-Canéda
102 M13 **Sarlat-la-Canéda** *var.* Sarlat. Dordogne, SW France
109 S3 **Sarleinsbach** Oberösterreich, N Austria
171 Y12 **Sarmi** Papua, E Indonesia
63 I19 **Sarmiento** Chubut, S Argentina
63 H25 **Sarmiento, Monte** ▲ S Chile
94 J11 **Särna** Dalarna, C Sweden
108 F8 **Sarnen** Obwalden, C Switzerland
108 F9 **Sarner See** ◎ C Switzerland
14 D16 **Sarnia** Ontario, S Canada
116 L3 **Sarny** Rivnens'ka Oblast', NW Ukraine
171 O13 **Saroako** Sulawesi, C Indonesia
118 L13 **Sarochyna** *Rus.* Sorochino. Vitsyebskaya Voblasts', N Belarus
168 L12 **Sarolangun** Sumatera, W Indonesia
165 U3 **Saroma** Hokkaidō, NE Japan
165 V3 **Saroma-ko** ◎ Hokkaidō, NE Japan
Saronic Gulf *see* Saronikós Kólpos
115 H20 **Saronikós Kólpos** *Eng.* Saronic Gulf. *gulf* S Greece
106 D7 **Saronno** Lombardia, N Italy
136 B11 **Saros Körfezi** *gulf* NW Turkey
111 N20 **Sárospatak** Borsod-Abaúj-Zemplén, NE Hungary
127 O4 **Sarov** *prev.* Sarova. Respublika Mordoviya, SW Russian Federation
Sarova *see* Sarov
127 P12 **Sarpa** Respublika Kalmykiya, SW Russian Federation
127 P12 **Sarpa, Ozero** ◎ SW Russian Federation
113 M18 **Šar Planina** ▲ FYR Macedonia/Serbia and Montenegro (Yugo.)
95 I16 **Sarpsborg** Østfold, S Norway
139 U5 **Sarqalā** N Iraq
103 U4 **Sarralbe** Moselle, NE France
Sarre *see* Saar, France/Germany
Sarre *see* Saarland, Germany
103 U5 **Sarrebourg** *Ger.* Saarburg. Moselle, NE France
Sarrebruck *see* Saarbrücken
103 U4 **Sarreguemines** *prev.* Saargemund. Moselle, NE France
104 I3 **Sarria** Galicia, NW Spain
105 S8 **Sarrión** Aragón, NE Spain
42 F4 **Sarstoon** *Sp.* Río Sarstún. ⁓ Belize/Guatemala
Sarstún, Río *see* Sarstoon
123 Q9 **Sartang** ⁓ NE Russian Federation
103 X16 **Sartène** Corse, France, C Mediterranean Sea
102 K7 **Sarthe** ◈ *department* NW France
102 K7 **Sarthe** ⁓ N France
115 H15 **Sárti** Kentrikí Makedonía, N Greece
Sartu *see* Daqing
165 T1 **Sarufutsu** Hokkaidō, NE Japan
Saruhan *see* Manisa
152 G9 **Sarūpsar** Rājasthān, NW India
137 U13 **Şärur** *prev.* Il'ichevsk. SW Azerbaijan
Sarvani *see* Marneuli
111 G23 **Sárvár** Vas, W Hungary
143 P11 **Sarvestān** Fārs, S Iran
171 W12 **Sarwon** Papua, E Indonesia
Saryagach *see* Saryagash
145 P17 **Saryagash** *var.* Saryagach, *Kaz.* Saryaghash. Yuzhnyy Kazakhstan, S Kazakhstan
Saryaghash *see* Saryagash
Saryarqa *see* Kazakhskiy Melkosopochnik
147 W8 **Sary-Bulak** Narynskaya Oblast', C Kyrgyzstan
147 U10 **Sary-Bulak** Oshskaya Oblast', SW Kyrgyzstan
117 S14 **Sarych, Mys** *headland* S Ukraine
147 Z7 **Sary-Dzhaz** *var.* Aksu He. ⁓ China/Kyrgyzstan *see also* Aksu He
146 F8 **Sarygamyş Köli** *Rus.* Sarykamyshkoye Ozero, *Uzb.* Sariqamish Kŭli. *salt lake* Kazakhstan/Uzbekistan
144 G13 **Sarykamys** *Kaz.* Saryqamys. Mangistau, SW Kazakhstan
Sarykamyshkoye Ozero *see* Sarygamyş Köli
145 N7 **Sarykol'** *prev.* Uritskiy. Kostanay, N Kazakhstan
Sarykol'skiy Khrebet *see* Sarikol Range
144 M10 **Sarykopa, Ozero** ◎ C Kazakhstan
145 V15 **Saryozek** *Kaz.* Saryözek. Almaty, SE Kazakhstan
Saryqamys *see* Sarykamys
145 S13 **Saryshagan** *Kaz.* Saryshahan. Karaganda, SE Kazakhstan
Saryshahan *see* Saryshagan
145 O13 **Sarysu** ⁓ S Kazakhstan
147 T11 **Sary-Tash** Oshskaya Oblast', SW Kyrgyzstan
145 T12 **Saryterek** Karaganda, C Kazakhstan
Saryyazynskoye Vodokhranilischche *see* Saryýazy Suw Howdany
146 J15 **Saryýazy Suw Howdany** *Rus.* Saryyazynskoye Vodokhranilische. ▣ S Turkmenistan
145 T14 **Saryyesik-Atyrau, Peski** *desert* E Kazakhstan
106 E10 **Sarzana** Liguria, NW Italy
188 B17 **Sasalaguan, Mount** ▲ S Guam
153 O14 **Sasarām** Bihār, N India
186 M8 **Sasari, Mount** ▲ Santa Isabel, N Solomon Islands

◆ Country ● Country Capital ◇ Dependent Territory ○ Dependent Territory Capital ◈ Administrative Region ✕ International Airport ▲ Mountain ▲ Mountain Range ⛰ Volcano ⁓ River ◎ Lake ▣ Reservoir

164 C13 **Sasebo** Nagasaki, Kyūshū, SW Japan
14 I9 **Saseginaga, Lac** ◎ Québec, SE Canada
Saseno *see* Sazan
11 R13 **Saskatchewan** ◆ *province* SW Canada
11 U14 **Saskatchewan** ≈ Manitoba/Saskatchewan, C Canada
11 T15 **Saskatoon** Saskatchewan, S Canada
11 T15 **Saskatoon** × Saskatchewan, S Canada
123 N7 **Saskylakh** Respublika Sakha (Yakutiya), NE Russian Federation
42 L7 **Saslaya, Cerro** ▲ N Nicaragua
38 G17 **Sasmik, Cape** *headland* Tanaga Island, Alaska, USA
119 N19 **Sasnovy Bor** *Rus.* Sosnovyy Bor. Homyel'skaya Voblasts', SE Belarus
127 N5 **Sasovo** Ryazanskaya Oblast', W Russian Federation
25 S12 **Saspamco** Texas, SW USA
109 W9 **Sass** *var.* Sassbach. ≈ SE Austria
76 M17 **Sassandra** S Ivory Coast
76 M17 **Sassandra** *var.* Ibo, Sassandra Fleuve. ≈ S Ivory Coast
Sassandra Fleuve *see* Sassandra
107 B17 **Sassari** Sardegna, Italy, C Mediterranean Sea
Sassbach *see* Sass
98 H11 **Sassenheim** Zuid-Holland, W Netherlands
Sassmacken *see* Valdemārpils
100 O7 **Sassnitz** Mecklenburg-Vorpommern, NE Germany
99 E16 **Sas van Gent** Zeeland, SW Netherlands
145 W12 **Sasykkol', Ozero** ◎ E Kazakhstan
117 O12 **Sasyk Kunduk, Ozero** ◎ SW Ukraine
76 J12 **Satadougou** Kayes, SW Mali
105 V11 **Sa Talaiassa** ▲ Eivissa, Spain, W Mediterranean Sea
164 C17 **Sata-misaki** *headland* Kyūshū, SW Japan
26 I7 **Satanta** Kansas, C USA
155 E15 **Sātāra** Mahārāshtra, W India
192 G15 **Sātaua** Savai'i, NW Samoa
188 M16 **Satawal** *island* Caroline Islands, C Micronesia
189 R17 **Satawan Atoll** *atoll* Mortlock Islands, C Micronesia
23 Y12 **Satellite Beach** Florida, SE USA
95 M14 **Säter** Dalarna, C Sweden
Sathmar *see* Satu Mare
23 V7 **Satilla River** ≈ Georgia, SE USA
57 F14 **Satipo** *var.* San Francisco de Satipo. Junín, C Peru
122 F11 **Satka** Chelyabinskaya Oblast', C Russian Federation
153 T16 **Satkhira** Khulna, SW Bangladesh
146 J13 **Şatlyk** *Rus.* Shatlyk. Mary Welaýaty, C Turkmenistan
154 K9 **Satna** *prev.* Sutna. Madhya Pradesh, C India
103 R11 **Satolas** × (Lyon) Rhône, E France
111 N20 **Sátoraljaújhely** Borsod-Abaúj-Zemplén, NE Hungary
145 O12 **Satpayev** *prev.* Nikol'skiy. Karaganda, C Kazakhstan
154 G11 **Sātpura Range** ▲ C India
167 P12 **Sattahip** *var.* Ban Sattahip, Ban Sattahipp. Chon Buri, S Thailand
92 L11 **Sattanen** Lappi, NE Finland
Satul *see* Satun
116 H9 **Satulung** *Hung.* Kővárhosszúfalu. Maramureş, N Romania
Satul-Vechi *see* Staro Selo
116 G8 **Satu Mare** *Ger.* Sathmar, *Hung.* Szatmárrnémeti. Satu Mare, NW Romania
116 G8 **Satu Mare** ◆ *county* NW Romania
167 N16 **Satun** *var.* Satul, Setul. Satun, SW Thailand
192 G16 **Satupaiteau** Savai'i, W Samoa
Sau *see* Sava
14 F14 **Sauble** ≈ Ontario, S Canada
14 F13 **Sauble Beach** Ontario, S Canada
61 C16 **Sauce** Corrientes, NE Argentina
Sauce *see* Juan L.Lacaze
36 K15 **Sauceda Mountains** ▲ Arizona, SW USA
61 C17 **Sauce de Luna** Entre Ríos, E Argentina
63 L15 **Sauce Grande, Río** ≈ E Argentina
40 K6 **Saucillo** Chihuahua, N Mexico
95 D15 **Sauda** Rogaland, S Norway
145 Q16 **Saudakent** *Kaz.* Saūdakent; *prev.* Baykadam *Kaz.* Bayqadam. Zhambyl, S Kazakhstan
92 J2 **Saudhárkrókur** Nordhurland Vestra, N Iceland
141 P9 **Saudi Arabia** *off.* Kingdom of Saudi Arabia, *Ar.* Al 'Arabīyah as Su'ūdīyah, Al Mamlakah al 'Arabīyah as Su'ūdīyah. ◆ *monarchy* SW Asia
101 D19 **Sauer** *var.* Sûre. ≈ NW Europe *see also* Sûre
101 F15 **Sauerland** *forest* W Germany
14 F14 **Saugeen** ≈ Ontario, S Canada
18 K12 **Saugerties** New York, NE USA
Saugor *see* Sāgar
10 K15 **Saugstad, Mount** ▲ British Columbia, SW Canada
Sāūjbulāgh *see* Mahābād
102 J11 **Saujon** Charente-Maritime, W France
29 T7 **Sauk Centre** Minnesota, N USA
30 L8 **Sauk City** Wisconsin, N USA
29 U7 **Sauk Rapids** Minnesota, N USA
55 Y11 **Saül** C French Guiana
103 O7 **Sauldre** ≈ C France
101 I23 **Saulgau** Baden-Württemberg, SW Germany
103 Q8 **Saulieu** Côte d'Or, C France
118 G8 **Saulkrasti** Rīga, C Latvia
15 S6 **Sault-aux-Cochons, Rivière du** ≈ Québec, SE Canada
31 Q4 **Sault Sainte Marie** Michigan, N USA
12 F14 **Sault Ste.Marie** Ontario, S Canada
145 P7 **Saumalkol'** *prev.* Volodarskoye. Severnyy Kazakhstan, N Kazakhstan
190 E13 **Sauma, Pointe** *headland* Île Alofi, W Wallis and Futuna
171 T16 **Saumlaki** *var.* Saumlakki. Pulau Yamdena, E Indonesia
Saumlakki *see* Saumlaki
15 R12 **Saumon, Rivière au** ≈ Québec, SE Canada
102 K8 **Saumur** Maine-et-Loire, NW France
185 F23 **Saunders, Cape** *headland* South Island, NZ
195 N13 **Saunders Coast** *physical region* Antarctica
65 B23 **Saunders Island** *island* NW Falkland Islands
65 C24 **Saunders Island** Settlement Saunders Island, NW Falkland Islands
82 F11 **Saurimo** *Port.* Henrique de Carvalho, Vila Henrique de Carvalho. Lunda Sul, NE Angola
55 S11 **Sauriwaunawa** S Guyana
82 D12 **Sautar** Malanje, NW Angola
45 S13 **Sauteurs** N Grenada
102 K13 **Sauveterre-de-Guyenne** Gironde, SW France
119 O14 **Sava** *Rus.* Sava. Mahilyowskaya Voblasts', E Belarus
84 H11 **Sava** *Eng.* Save, *Ger.* Sau, *Hung.* Száva. ≈ SE Europe
42 J5 **Savá** Colón, N Honduras
33 Y8 **Savage** Montana, NW USA
183 N16 **Savage River** Tasmania, SE Australia
77 R15 **Savalou** S Benin
30 K10 **Savanna** Illinois, N USA
23 X6 **Savannah** Georgia, SE USA
27 R2 **Savannah** Missouri, C USA
20 H10 **Savannah** Tennessee, S USA
21 O12 **Savannah River** ≈ Georgia/South Carolina, SE USA
Savannakhét *see* Khanthabouli
44 H12 **Savanna-La-Mar** W Jamaica
12 B10 **Savant Lake** ◎ Ontario, S Canada
155 F17 **Savanūr** Karnātaka, W India
93 J16 **Sävar** Västerbotten, N Sweden
Savaria *see* Szombathely
154 C11 **Sāvarkundla** *var.* Kundla. Gujarāt, W India
116 F11 **Săvârşin** *Hung.* Soborsin; *prev.* Săvirşin. Arad, W Romania
136 C13 **Savaştepe** Balıkesir, W Turkey
147 P11 **Savat** *Rus.* Sawot. Sirdaryo Viloyati, E Uzbekistan
Sávdijári *see* Skaulo
83 N18 **Save** Inhambane, E Mozambique
102 L16 **Save** ≈ S France
83 L17 **Save** *var.* Sabi. ≈ Mozambique/Zimbabwe *see also* Sabi
Save *see* Sava
77 R15 **Savè** SE Benin
142 M6 **Sāveh** Markazī, W Iran
116 L8 **Săveni** Botoşani, NE Romania
103 N16 **Saverdun** Ariège, S France
103 U5 **Saverne** *var.* Zabern; *anc.* Tres Tabernae. Bas-Rhin, NE France
Savichi *see* Savichy
119 O21 **Savichy** *Rus.* Savichi. Homyel'skaya Voblasts', SE Belarus
106 B9 **Savigliano** Piemonte, NW Italy
Savigsivik *see* Savissivik
Savinichi *see* Savinichy
119 Q16 **Savinichy** *Rus.* Savinichi. Mahilyowskaya Voblasts', E Belarus
109 U10 **Savinja** ≈ C Slovenia
Savinski *see* Savinskiy
106 H11 **Savio** ≈ C Italy
Săvirşin *see* Săvârşin
197 O11 **Savissivik** *var.* Savigsivik. Avannaarsua, S Greenland
93 N18 **Savitaipale** Etelä-Suomi, S Finland
113 J15 **Šavnik** Montenegro, SW Serbia and Montenegro (Yugo.)
108 I9 **Savognin** Graubünden, S Switzerland
103 T12 **Savoie** ◆ *department* E France
106 C10 **Savona** Liguria, NW Italy
93 N17 **Savonlinna** *Swe.* Nyslott. Itä-Suomi, SE Finland
93 N17 **Savonranta** Itä-Suomi, SE Finland
38 K10 **Savoonga** Saint Lawrence Island, Alaska, USA
30 M13 **Savoy** Illinois, N USA
117 O8 **Savran'** Odes'ka Oblast', SW Ukraine
137 R11 **Şavşat** Artvin, NE Turkey
95 L19 **Sävsjö** Jönköping, S Sweden
Savu, Kepulauan *see* Sawu, Kepulauan
92 M11 **Savukoski** Lappi, NE Finland
Savu, Pulau *see* Sawu, Pulau
187 Y14 **Savusavu** Vanua Levu, N Fiji
171 O17 **Savu Sea** *Ind.* Laut Sawu. *sea* S Indonesia
83 H17 **Savute** Chobe, N Botswana
139 N7 **Şawāb 'Uqlat** *well* W Iraq
138 M7 **Sawāb, Wādī as** *dry watercourse* W Iraq
152 H13 **Sawāi Mādhopur** Rājasthān, N India**Sawakin** *see* Suakin
167 R8 **Sawang Daen Din** Sakon Nakhon, E Thailand
167 O8 **Sawankhalok** *var.* Swankalok. Sukhothai, NW Thailand
165 P13 **Sawara** Chiba, Honshū, S Japan
37 R5 **Sawatch Range** ▲ Colorado, C USA
141 N12 **Sawdā', Jabal** ▲ SW Saudi Arabia
75 P9 **Sawdā', Jabal as** ▲ C Libya
Sawdirī *see* Sodiri
97 F14 **Sawel Mountain** ▲ C Northern Ireland, UK
Sawhāj *see* Sohāg
77 O15 **Sawla** N Ghana
Sawot *see* Savat
141 X12 **Şawqirah** *var.* Suqrah. S Oman
141 X12 **Şawqirah, Dawḩat** *var.* Ghubbat Sawqirah, Sukra Bay, Suqrah Bay. *bay* S Oman
Sawqirah, Ghubbat *see* Şawqirah, Dawḩat
183 V5 **Sawtell** New South Wales, SE Australia
138 K7 **Şawt, Wādī aş** *dry watercourse* S Syria
171 O17 **Sawu, Kepulauan** *var.* Kepulauan Savu. *island group* S Indonesia
Sawu, Laut *see* Savu Sea
171 O17 **Sawu, Pulau** *var.* Pulau Savu. *island* Kepulauan Sawu, S Indonesia
105 S12 **Sax** País Valenciano, E Spain
Saxe *see* Sachsen
108 C11 **Saxon** Valais, SW Switzerland
Saxony *see* Sachsen
Saxony-Anhalt *see* Sachsen-Anhalt
77 R12 **Say** Niamey, SW Niger
15 V7 **Sayabec** Québec, SE Canada
Sayaboury *see* Xaignabouli
145 U12 **Sayak** *Kaz.* Sayaq. Karaganda, E Kazakhstan
57 D14 **Sayán** Lima, W Peru
131 T6 **Sayanskiy Khrebet** ▲ S Russian Federation
Sayaq *see* Sayak
146 K13 **Saýat** *Rus.* Sayat. Lebap Welaýaty, E Turkmenistan
42 D3 **Sayaxché** Petén, N Guatemala
Şaydā/Sayida *see* Saïda
141 T15 **Sayḩūt** E Yemen
29 U14 **Saylorville Lake** ◎ Iowa, C USA
Saymenskiy Kanal *see* Saimaa Canal
163 N10 **Saynshand** Dornogovĭ, SE Mongolia
162 J11 **Saynshand** Ömnögovĭ, S Mongolia
162 F7 **Sayn-Ust** Govĭ-Altay, W Mongolia
Say-Ötesh *see* Say-Utës
138 J7 **Şayqal, Bahr** ◎ S Syria
Sayrab *see* Sayrob
158 H4 **Sayram Hu** ◎ NW China
26 K11 **Sayre** Oklahoma, C USA
18 H12 **Sayre** Pennsylvania, NE USA
18 K15 **Sayreville** New Jersey, NE USA
147 N13 **Sayrob** *Rus.* Sayrab. Surxondaryo Viloyati, S Uzbekistan
40 L13 **Sayula** Jalisco, SW Mexico
141 R14 **Say'ūn** *var.* Saywūn. C Yemen
144 G14 **Say-Utës** *Kaz.* Say-Ötesh. Mangistau, SW Kazakhstan
10 K16 **Sayward** Vancouver Island, British Columbia, SW Canada
Saywūn *see* Say 'ūn
Sayyāl *see* As Sayyāl
139 U8 **Sayyid 'Abīd** *var.* Saiyid Abid. E Iraq
113 J22 **Sazan** *var.* Ishulli i Sazanit, *It.* Saseno. *island* SW Albania
Sazanit, Ishulli i *see* Sazan
Sazau/Sazawa *see* Sázava
111 E17 **Sázava** *var.* Sazau, *Ger.* Sazawa. ≈ C Czech Republic
124 J14 **Sazonovo** Vologodskaya Oblast', NW Russian Federation
102 G6 **Scaër** Finistère, NW France
97 J15 **Scafell Pike** ▲ NW England, UK
Scalabis *see* Santarém
96 M2 **Scalloway** N Scotland, UK
38 M11 **Scammon Bay** Alaska, USA
Scammon Lagoon/Scammon, Laguna *see* Ojo de Liebre, Laguna
84 F7 **Scandinavia** *geophysical region* NW Europe
Scania *see* Skåne
96 K5 **Scapa Flow** *sea basin* N Scotland, UK
107 K26 **Scaramia, Capo** *headland* Sicilia, Italy, C Mediterranean Sea
14 H15 **Scarborough** Ontario, SE Canada
45 Z16 **Scarborough** *prev.* Port Louis. Tobago, Trinidad and Tobago
97 N16 **Scarborough** N England, UK
185 I17 **Scargill** Canterbury, South Island, NZ
96 E7 **Scarp** *island* NW Scotland, UK
Scarpanto *see* Kárpathos
Scarpanto Strait *see* Karpathou, Stenó
107 G25 **Scauri** Sicilia, Italy, C Mediterranean Sea
Scealg, Bá na *see* Ballinskelligs Bay
Scebeli *see* Shebeli
100 K10 **Schaale** ≈ N Germany
100 K9 **Schaalsee** ◎ N Germany
99 G18 **Schaerbeek** Brussels, C Belgium
108 G6 **Schaffhausen** *Fr.* Schaffhouse. Schaffhausen, N Switzerland
108 G6 **Schaffhausen** *Fr.* Schaffhouse. ◆ *canton* N Switzerland
Schaffhouse *see* Schaffhausen
98 I8 **Schagen** Noord-Holland, NW Netherlands
Schaken *see* Šakiai
98 M10 **Schalkhaar** Overijssel, E Netherlands
109 R3 **Schärding** Oberösterreich, N Austria
100 G9 **Scharhörn** *island* NW Germany
Schässburg *see* Sighişoara
Schaulen *see* Šiauliai
30 M10 **Schaumburg** Illinois, N USA
Schebschi Mountains *see* Shebshi Mountains
98 P6 **Scheemda** Groningen, NE Netherlands
100 I10 **Scheessel** Niedersachsen, NW Germany
13 N8 **Schefferville** Québec, E Canada
Schelde *see* Scheldt
99 D18 **Scheldt** *Dut.* Schelde, *Fr.* Escaut. ≈ W Europe
35 X5 **Schell Creek Range** ▲ Nevada, W USA
18 K10 **Schenectady** New York, NE USA
99 I17 **Scherpenheuvel** *Fr.* Montaigu. Vlaams Brabant, C Belgium
98 K11 **Scherpenzeel** Gelderland, C Netherlands
25 S12 **Schertz** Texas, SW USA
98 G11 **Scheveningen** Zuid-Holland, W Netherlands
98 G12 **Schiedam** Zuid-Holland, SW Netherlands
99 M24 **Schieren** Diekirch, NE Luxembourg
98 M4 **Schiermonnikoog** *Fris.* Skiermûntseach. Friesland, N Netherlands
98 M4 **Schiermonnikoog** *Fris.* Skiermûntseach. *island* Waddeneilanden, N Netherlands
99 K14 **Schijndel** Noord-Brabant, S Netherlands
Schil *see* Jiu
99 H16 **Schilde** Antwerpen, N Belgium
Schillen *see* Zhilino
103 V5 **Schiltigheim** Bas-Rhin, NE France
106 G7 **Schio** Veneto, NE Italy
98 H10 **Schiphol** × (Amsterdam) Noord-Holland, C Netherlands
Schippenbeil *see* Sępopol
Schiria *see* Şiria
Schivelbein *see* Świdwin
115 D22 **Schíza** *island* S Greece
175 U3 **Schjetman Reef** *reef* Antarctica
Schlackenwerth *see* Ostrov
109 R7 **Schladming** Steiermark, SE Austria
Schlan *see* Slaný
Schlanders *see* Silandro
100 I7 **Schlei** *inlet* N Germany
101 D17 **Schleiden** Nordrhein-Westfalen, W Germany
Schlelau *see* Szydłowiec
100 I7 **Schleswig** Schleswig-Holstein, N Germany
29 T13 **Schleswig** Iowa, C USA
100 H8 **Schleswig-Holstein** ◆ *state* N Germany
Schlettstadt *see* Sélestat
108 F7 **Schlieren** Zürich, N Switzerland
Schlochau *see* Człuchów
Schloppe *see* Człopa
101 I18 **Schlüchtern** Hessen, C Germany
101 J17 **Schmalkalden** Thüringen, C Germany
109 W2 **Schmida** ≈ NE Austria
65 F19 **Schmidt-Ott Seamount** *var.* Schmitt-Ott Seamount, Schmitt-Ott Tablemount. *undersea feature* SW Indian Ocean
Schmiegel *see* Śmigiel
Schmitt-Ott Seamount/Schmitt-Ott Tablemount *see* Schmidt-Ott Seamount
15 V3 **Schmon** ≈ Québec, SE Canada
101 M18 **Schneeberg** ▲ W Germany
Schneeberg *see* Veliki Snežnik
Schnee-Eifel *see* Schneifel
Schneekoppe *see* Sněžka
Schneidemühl *see* Piła
101 D18 **Schneifel** *var.* Schnee-Eifel. *plateau* W Germany
Schnelle Körös/Schnelle Kreisch *see* Crişul Repede
100 I11 **Schneverdingen** *var.* Schneverdingen (Wümme). Niedersachsen, NW Germany
Schneverdingen (Wümme) *see* Schneverdingen
Schoden *see* Skuodas
18 K10 **Schoharie** New York, NE USA
18 K11 **Schoharie Creek** ≈ New York, NE USA
115 J21 **Schoinoússa** *island* Kykládes, Greece, Aegean Sea
100 L13 **Schönebeck** Sachsen-Anhalt, C Germany
Schöneck *see* Skarszewy
100 O12 **Schönefeld** × (Berlin) Berlin, NE Germany
101 K24 **Schongau** Bayern, S Germany
100 K13 **Schöningen** Niedersachsen, C Germany
Schönlanke *see* Trzcianka
Schönsee *see* Kowalewo Pomorskie
31 P10 **Schoolcraft** Michigan, N USA
98 O8 **Schoonebeek** Drenthe, NE Netherlands
98 I12 **Schoonhoven** Zuid-Holland, C Netherlands
98 H8 **Schoorl** Noord-Holland, NW Netherlands
Schooten *see* Schoten
101 F24 **Schopfheim** Baden-Württemberg, SW Germany
101 I21 **Schorndorf** Baden-Württemberg, S Germany
100 F10 **Schortens** Niedersachsen, NW Germany
99 H16 **Schoten** *var.* Schooten. Antwerpen, N Belgium
183 Q17 **Schouten Island** *island* Tasmania, SE Australia
186 C5 **Schouten Islands** *island group* NW PNG
98 E13 **Schouwen** *island* SW Netherlands
45 Q12 **Schœlcher** W Martinique
Schreiberhau *see* Szklarska Poręba
109 U2 **Schrems** Niederösterreich, E Austria
101 L22 **Schrobenhausen** Bayern, SE Germany
18 L8 **Schroon Lake** ◎ New York, NE USA
108 J8 **Schruns** Vorarlberg, W Austria
Schubin *see* Szubin
25 U11 **Schulenburg** Texas, SW USA
Schuls *see* Scuol
108 E8 **Schüpfheim** Luzern, C Switzerland
35 S6 **Schurz** Nevada, W USA
101 I24 **Schussen** ≈ S Germany
Schüttenhofen *see* Sušice
29 R15 **Schuyler** Nebraska, C USA
18 L10 **Schuylerville** New York, NE USA
101 K20 **Schwabach** Bayern, SE Germany
Schwabenalb *see* Schwäbische Alb
101 I23 **Schwäbische Alb** *var.* Schwabenalb, *Eng.* Swabian Jura. ▲ S Germany
101 I22 **Schwäbisch Gmünd** *var.* Gmünd. Baden-Württemberg, SW Germany
101 I21 **Schwäbisch Hall** *var.* Hall. Baden-Württemberg, SW Germany
101 H16 **Schwalm** ≈ C Germany
109 V9 **Schwanberg** Steiermark, SE Austria
108 H8 **Schwanden** Glarus, E Switzerland
101 M20 **Schwandorf** Bayern, SE Germany
109 S5 **Schwanenstadt** Oberösterreich, NW Austria
169 S11 **Schwaner, Pegunungan** ▲ Borneo, N Indonesia
109 W5 **Schwarza** ≈ E Austria
109 P9 **Schwarzach** ≈ S Austria
101 M20 **Schwarzach** *Cz.* Černice. ≈ Czech Republic/Germany
Schwarzach *see* Schwarzach im Pongau, Austria
Schwarzach *see* Svratka, Czech Republic
109 Q7 **Schwarzach im Pongau** *var.* Schwarzach. Salzburg, NW Austria
Schwarzawa *see* Svratka
101 N14 **Schwarze Elster** ≈ E Germany
Schwarze Körös *see* Crişul Negru
108 D9 **Schwarzenburg** Bern, W Switzerland
83 D21 **Schwarzrand** ▲ S Namibia
101 G23 **Schwarzwald** *Eng.* Black Forest. ▲ SW Germany
Schwarzwasser *see* Wda
39 P7 **Schwatka Mountains** ▲ Alaska, USA
109 N7 **Schwaz** Tirol, W Austria
109 Y4 **Schwechat** Niederösterreich, NE Austria
109 Y4 **Schwechat** × (Wien) Wien, E Austria
100 P11 **Schwedt** Brandenburg, NE Germany
101 D19 **Schweich** Rheinland-Pfalz, SW Germany
Schweidnitz *see* Świdnica
101 J18 **Schweinfurt** Bayern, SE Germany
Schweiz *see* Switzerland
100 L9 **Schwerin** Mecklenburg-Vorpommern, N Germany
Schwerin *see* Skwierzyna
100 L9 **Schweriner See** ◎ N Germany
Schwertberg *see* Świecie
101 F15 **Schwerte** Nordrhein-Westfalen, W Germany
Schwiebus *see* Świebodzin
100 P13 **Schwielochsee** ◎ NE Germany
Schwihau *see* Švihov
Schwiz *see* Schwyz
108 G8 **Schwyz** *var.* Schwiz. Schwyz, C Switzerland
108 G8 **Schwyz** *var.* Schwiz. ◆ *canton* C Switzerland
14 J11 **Schyan** ≈ Québec, SE Canada
Schyl *see* Jiu
107 I24 **Sciacca** Sicilia, Italy, C Mediterranean Sea
Sciasciamana *see* Shashemenē
107 L26 **Scicli** Sicilia, Italy, C Mediterranean Sea
97 F25 **Scilly, Isles of** *island group* SW England, UK
111 H17 **Ścinawa** *Ger.* Steinau an der Elbe. Dolnośląskie, SW Poland
Scio *see* Chíos
31 S14 **Scioto River** ≈ Ohio, N USA
36 L5 **Scipio** Utah, W USA
33 X6 **Scobey** Montana, NW USA
183 T7 **Scone** New South Wales, SE Australia
Scoresby Sound/Scoresbysund *see* Ittoqqortoormiit
Scoresby Sund *see* Kangertittivaq
Scorno, Punta dello *see* Caprara, Punta
34 K3 **Scotia** California, W USA
47 Y14 **Scotia Plate** *tectonic feature*
47 V15 **Scotia Ridge** *undersea feature* S Atlantic Ocean
194 H2 **Scotia Sea** *sea* SW Atlantic Ocean
29 Q12 **Scotland** South Dakota, N USA
25 R5 **Scotland** Texas, SW USA
96 H11 **Scotland** *national region* UK
21 W8 **Scotland Neck** North Carolina, SE USA
195 R13 **Scott Base** *NZ research station* Antarctica
10 J16 **Scott, Cape** *headland* Vancouver Island, British Columbia, SW Canada
26 I5 **Scott City** Kansas, C USA
27 Y7 **Scott City** Missouri, C USA
195 R14 **Scott Coast** *physical region* Antarctica
18 C15 **Scottdale** Pennsylvania, NE USA
195 Y11 **Scott Glacier** *glacier* Antarctica
195 Q17 **Scott Island** *island* Antarctica
26 L11 **Scott, Mount** ▲ Oklahoma, USA
32 G15 **Scott, Mount** ▲ Oregon, NW USA
34 M1 **Scott River** ≈ California, W USA
28 I13 **Scottsbluff** Nebraska, C USA
23 Q2 **Scottsboro** Alabama, S USA
31 P15 **Scottsburg** Indiana, N USA
183 P16 **Scottsdale** Tasmania, SE Australia
36 L13 **Scottsdale** Arizona, SW USA
45 O12 **Scotts Head Village** *var.* Cachacrou. S Dominica
192 L14 **Scott Shoal** *undersea feature* S Pacific Ocean
20 K7 **Scottsville** Kentucky, S USA
29 U14 **Scranton** Iowa, C USA
18 I13 **Scranton** Pennsylvania, NE USA
186 B6 **Screw** ≈ NW PNG
29 R14 **Scribner** Nebraska, C USA
Scrobesbyrig' *see* Shrewsbury
14 I14 **Scugog** ≈ Ontario, SE Canada
14 I14 **Scugog, Lake** ◎ Ontario, SE Canada
97 N17 **Scunthorpe** E England, UK
108 K9 **Scuol** *Ger.* Schuls. Graubünden, E Switzerland
Scupi *see* Skopje
Scutari *see* Shkodër
113 K17 **Scutari, Lake** *Alb.* Liqeni i Shkodrës, *SCr.* Skadarsko Jezero. ◎ Albania/Serbia and Montenegro (Yugo.)
Scyros *see* Skýros
Scythopolis *see* Bet She'an
25 U13 **Seadrift** Texas, SW USA
21 Y4 **Seaford** *var.* Seaford City. Delaware, NE USA
Seaford City *see* Seaford
14 E15 **Seaforth** Ontario, S Canada
24 M6 **Seagraves** Texas, SW USA
11 X9 **Seal** ≈ Manitoba, C Canada
182 M10 **Sea Lake** Victoria, SE Australia
83 G26 **Seal, Cape** *headland* S South Africa
65 D26 **Sea Lion Islands** *island group* SE Falkland Islands
19 S8 **Seal Island** *island* Maine, NE USA
25 V11 **Sealy** Texas, SW USA
35 X12 **Searchlight** Nevada, W USA
27 V11 **Searcy** Arkansas, C USA
19 R7 **Searsport** Maine, NE USA
35 N10 **Seaside** California, W USA
32 F10 **Seaside** Oregon, NW USA
18 K16 **Seaside Heights** New Jersey, NE USA
32 H8 **Seattle** Washington, NW USA
32 H9 **Seattle-Tacoma** × Washington, NW USA
185 J16 **Seaward Kaikoura Range** ▲ South Island, NZ
42 J9 **Sébaco** Matagalpa, W Nicaragua
19 P8 **Sebago Lake** ◎ Maine, NE USA
169 S13 **Sebangan, Teluk** *bay* Borneo, C Indonesia
169 S13 **Sebanganu, Teluk** *bay* Borneo, C Indonesia
Sebaste/Sebastia *see* Sivas
23 Y12 **Sebastian** Florida, SE USA
40 C5 **Sebastían Vizcaíno, Bahía** *bay* NW Mexico
19 R6 **Sebasticook Lake** ◎ Maine, NE USA
34 M7 **Sebastopol** California, W USA
Sebastopol *see* Sevastopol'
169 W8 **Sebatik, Pulau** *island* N Indonesia
19 R5 **Sebec Lake** ◎ Maine, NE USA
76 K12 **Sébékoro** Kayes, W Mali
Sebenico *see* Šibenik
40 G6 **Seberi, Cerro** ▲ NW Mexico
116 H11 **Sebeş** *Ger.* Mühlbach, *Hung.* Szászsebes; *prev.* Sebeşu Săsesc. Alba, W Romania
Sebes-Körös *see* Crişul Repede
Sebeşu Săsesc *see* Sebeş
31 R8 **Sebewaing** Michigan, N USA
124 F16 **Sebezh** Pskovskaya Oblast', W Russian Federation
137 N12 **Şebinkarahisar** Giresun, N Turkey
116 F11 **Sebiş** *Hung.* Borossebes. Arad, W Romania
Sebkra Azz el Matti *see* Azzel Matti, Sebkha
19 Q4 **Seboomook Lake** ◎ Maine, NE USA
74 G6 **Sebou** *var.* Sebu. ≈ N Morocco
20 I6 **Sebree** Kentucky, S USA
23 X13 **Sebring** Florida, SE USA
Sebta *see* Ceuta
Sebu *see* Sebou
169 U13 **Sebuku, Pulau** *island* N Indonesia
169 W8 **Sebuku, Teluk** *bay* Borneo, N Indonesia
106 F10 **Secchia** ≈ N Italy
10 L17 **Sechelt** British Columbia, SW Canada
56 C12 **Sechin, Río** ≈ W Peru
56 A10 **Sechura, Bahía de** *bay* NW Peru
185 A22 **Secretary Island** *island* SW NZ
155 I15 **Secunderābād** *var.* Sikandarabad. Andhra Pradesh, C India
57 L17 **Sécure, Río** ≈ C Bolivia
118 D10 **Seda** Telšiai, NW Lithuania
27 T5 **Sedalia** Missouri, C USA
103 R3 **Sedan** Ardennes, N France
27 P7 **Sedan** Kansas, C USA
105 N3 **Sedano** Castilla-León, N Spain
104 H10 **Seda, Ribeira de** *stream* C Portugal
185 K15 **Seddon** Marlborough, South Island, NZ
185 H15 **Seddonville** West Coast, South Island, NZ
143 U7 **Sedeh** Khorāsān, E Iran
122 I11 **Sedel'nikovo** Omskaya Oblast', C Russian Federation0
138 E11 **Sederot** Southern, S Israel
65 B23 **Sedge Island** *island* NW Falkland Islands
76 G12 **Sédhiou** SW Senegal
11 U16 **Sedley** Saskatchewan, S Canada
Sedlez *see* Siedlce
117 Q2 **Sedniv** Chernihivs'ka Oblast', N Ukraine
36 L11 **Sedona** Arizona, SW USA
Sedunum *see* Sion
118 F12 **Šeduva** Šiauliai, N Lithuania
141 Y8 **Seeb** *var.* Muscat Sīb Airport. × (Masqaţ) NE Oman
Seeb *see* As Sīb

◆ COUNTRY ◇ DEPENDENT TERRITORY ◆ ADMINISTRATIVE REGION ▲ MOUNTAIN ▲ VOLCANO ◎ LAKE
● COUNTRY CAPITAL ○ DEPENDENT TERRITORY CAPITAL × INTERNATIONAL AIRPORT ▲ MOUNTAIN RANGE ≈ RIVER ◎ RESERVOIR

108 M7 **Seefeld-in-Tirol** Tirol, W Austria
83 E22 **Seeheim Noord** Karas, S Namibia
Seeland *see* Sjælland
195 N9 **Seelig, Mount** ▲ Antarctica
Seeonee *see* Seoni
162 E6 **Seer** Hovd, W Mongolia
102 L5 **Sées** Orne, N France
101 J14 **Seesen** Niedersachsen, C Germany
Seesker Höhe *see* Szeska Góra
100 J10 **Seevetal** Niedersachsen, N Germany
109 V6 **Seewiesen** Steiermark, E Austria
136 J13 **Şefaatli** *var.* Kızılkoca. Yozgat, C Turkey
149 N3 **Sefīd, Darya-ye** *Pash.* Āb-i-Safed. ≈ N Afghanistan
148 K5 **Sefīd Kūh, Selseleh-ye** *Eng.* Paropamisus Range. ▲ W Afghanistan
74 G6 **Sefrou** N Morocco
185 E19 **Sefton, Mount** ▲ South Island, NZ
171 S13 **Segaf, Kepulauan** *island group* E Indonesia
169 W7 **Segama, Sungai** ≈ East Malaysia
168 L9 **Segamat** Johor, Peninsular Malaysia
77 S13 **Ségbana** NE Benin
Segestica *see* Sisak
Segesvár *see* Sighişoara
171 T12 **Seget** Papua, E Indonesia
Segewold *see* Sigulda
124 J9 **Segezha** Respublika Kareliya, NW Russian Federation
Seghedin *see* Szeged
Segna *see* Senj
107 I16 **Segni** Lazio, C Italy
Segodunum *see* Rodez
105 S9 **Segorbe** País Valenciano, E Spain
76 M12 **Ségou** *var.* Segu. Ségou, C Mali
76 M12 **Ségou** ◆ *region* SW Mali
54 E8 **Segovia** Antioquia, N Colombia
105 N7 **Segovia** Castilla-León, C Spain
104 M6 **Segovia** ◆ *province* Castilla-León, N Spain
Segoviao Wangkí *see* Coco, Río
126 J9 **Segozero, Ozero** ◎ NW Russian Federation
105 U5 **Segre** ≈ NE Spain
102 J7 **Segré** Maine-et-Loire, NW France
Segu *see* Ségou
38 I17 **Seguam Island** *island* Aleutian Islands, Alaska, USA
38 I17 **Seguam Pass** *strait* Aleutian Islands, Alaska, USA
77 Y7 **Séguédine** Agadez, NE Niger
76 M15 **Séguéla** W Ivory Coast
25 S11 **Seguin** Texas, SW USA
38 E17 **Segula Island** *island* Aleutian Islands, Alaska, USA
62 K10 **Segundo, Río** ≈ C Argentina
105 Q12 **Segura** ≈ S Spain
105 P13 **Sierra de Segura** ▲ S Spain
83 G18 **Sehithwa** Ngamiland, N Botswana
154 H10 **Sehore** Madhya Pradesh, C India
186 G9 **Sehulea** Normanby Island, S PNG
149 P15 **Sehwān** Sind, SE Pakistan
109 V8 **Seiersberg** Steiermark, SE Austria
26 L9 **Seiling** Oklahoma, C USA
103 S9 **Seille** ≈ E France
99 J20 **Seilles** Namur, SE Belgium
93 K17 **Seinäjoki** *Swe.* Östermyra. Länsi-Suomi, W Finland
12 B12 **Seine** ≈ Ontario, S Canada
102 M4 **Seine** ≈ N France
102 K4 **Seine, Baie de la** *bay* N France
Seine, Banc de la *see* Seine Seamount
103 O5 **Seine-et-Marne** ◆ *department* N France
102 L3 **Seine-Maritime** ◆ *department* N France
84 B14 **Seine Plain** *undersea feature* E Atlantic Ocean
84 B15 **Seine Seamount** *var.* Banc de la Seine. *undersea feature* E Atlantic Ocean
102 E6 **Sein, Île de** *island* NW France
171 Y14 **Seinma** Papua, E Indonesia
Seisbierrum *see* Sexbierum
109 U5 **Seitenstetten Markt** Niederösterreich, C Austria
Seiyu *see* Chŏnju
95 H22 **Sejerø** *island* E Denmark
110 P7 **Sejny** Podlaskie, NE Poland
81 G20 **Seke** Shinyanga, N Tanzania
164 L13 **Seki** Gifu, Honshū, SW Japan
161 U12 **Sekibi-sho** *island* China/Japan/Taiwan
165 U3 **Sekihoku-tōge** *pass* Hokkaidō, NE Japan
Sekondi *see* Sekondi-Takoradi
77 P17 **Sekondi-Takoradi** *var.* Sekondi. S Ghana
80 J11 **Sek'ot'a** Amhara, N Ethiopia
Sekseūil *see* Saksaul'skiy
32 I9 **Selah** Washington, NW USA
168 J8 **Selangor** *var.* Negeri Selangor Darul Ehsan. ◆ *state* Peninsular Malaysia
Selânik *see* Thessaloníki
168 K10 **Selapanjang** Pulau Rantau, W Indonesia
167 R10 **Selaphum** Roi Et, E Thailand
171 T16 **Selaru, Pulau** *island* Kepulauan Tanimbar, E Indonesia
171 U13 **Selassi** Papua, E Indonesia
168 J7 **Selatan, Selat** *strait* Peninsular Malaysia
39 N8 **Selawik** Alaska, USA
39 N8 **Selawik Lake** ◎ Alaska, USA
171 N14 **Selayar, Selat** *strait* Sulawesi, C Indonesia
95 C14 **Selbjørnsfjorden** *fjord* S Norway
94 H8 **Selbusjøen** ◎ S Norway
97 M17 **Selby** N England, UK
29 N8 **Selby** South Dakota, N USA
21 Z4 **Selbyville** Delaware, NE USA
136 B15 **Selçuk** *var.* Akıncılar. İzmir, SW Turkey
39 Q13 **Seldovia** Alaska, USA
107 M18 **Sele** *anc.* Silarius. ≈ S Italy
83 J19 **Selebi-Phikwe** Central, E Botswana
42 B5 **Selegua, Río** ≈ W Guatemala
131 X7 **Selemdzha** ≈ SE Russian Federation
131 U7 **Selenga** *Mong.* Selenge Mörön. ≈ Mongolia/Russian Federation
162 K6 **Selenge** Bulgan, N Mongolia
162 J6 **Selenge** Hövsgöl, N Mongolia
79 I19 **Selenge** Bandundu, W Dem. Rep. Congo
162 L6 **Selenge** ◆ *province* N Mongolia
Selenge Mörön *see* Selenga
123 N14 **Selenginsk** Respublika Buryatiya, S Russian Federation
Selenica *see* Selenicë
113 K22 **Selenicë** *var.* Selenica. Vlorë, SW Albania
123 Q8 **Selennyakh** ≈ NE Russian Federation
100 J8 **Selenter See** ◎ N Germany
Sele Sound *see* Soela Väin
103 U6 **Sélestat** *Ger.* Schlettstadt. Bas-Rhin, NE France
Selety *see* Sileti
Seleucia *see* Silifke
92 I4 **Selfoss** Sudhurland, SW Iceland
28 M7 **Selfridge** North Dakota, N USA
76 I15 **Seli** ≈ N Sierra Leone
76 I11 **Sélibabi** *var.* Sélibaby. Guidimaka, S Mauritania
Sélibaby *see* Sélibabi
Selidovka/Selidovo *see* Selydove
126 I15 **Seliger, Ozero** ◎ W Russian Federation
36 J11 **Seligman** Arizona, SW USA
27 S8 **Seligman** Missouri, C USA
80 E6 **Selima Oasis** *oasis* N Sudan
76 L13 **Sélingué, Lac de** ⊠ S Mali
Selinoús *see* Kréstena
18 G14 **Selinsgrove** Pennsylvania, NE USA
Selishche *see* Syelishcha
124 I16 **Selizharovo** Tverskaya Oblast', W Russian Federation
94 C10 **Selje** Sogn og Fjordane, S Norway
11 X16 **Selkirk** Manitoba, S Canada
96 K13 **Selkirk** SE Scotland, UK
96 K13 **Selkirk** *cultural region* SE Scotland, UK
11 O16 **Selkirk Mountains** ▲ British Columbia, SW Canada
193 T11 **Selkirk Rise** *undersea feature* SE Pacific Ocean
115 F21 **Sellasía** Pelopónnisos, S Greece
44 M9 **Selle, Pic de la** *var.* La Selle. ▲ SE Haiti
102 M8 **Selles-sur-Cher** Loir-et-Cher, C France
36 K16 **Sells** Arizona, SW USA
Sellye *see* Sal'a
23 P5 **Selma** Alabama, S USA
35 Q11 **Selma** California, W USA
20 G10 **Selmer** Tennessee, S USA
173 N17 **Sel, Pointe au** *headland* W Réunion
Selseleh-ye Kūh-e Vākhān *see* Nicholas Range
127 S2 **Selty** Udmurtskaya Respublika, NW Russian Federation
Selukwe *see* Shurugwi
62 L9 **Selva** Santiago del Estero, N Argentina
11 T9 **Selwyn Lake** ◎ Northwest Territories/Saskatchewan, C Canada
10 K6 **Selwyn Mountains** ▲ Yukon Territory, NW Canada
181 T6 **Selwyn Range** ▲ Queensland, C Australia
117 W8 **Selydove** *var.* Selidovka, *Rus.* Selidovo. Donets'ka Oblast', SE Ukraine
Selzaete *see* Zelzate
Seman *see* Semanit, Lumi i
168 M15 **Semangka, Teluk** *bay* Sumatera, SW Indonesia
113 D22 **Semanit, Lumi i** *var.* Seman. ≈ W Albania
169 Q16 **Semarang** *var.* Samarang. Jawa, C Indonesia
169 Q10 **Sematan** Sarawak, East Malaysia
171 P17 **Semau, Pulau** *island* S Indonesia
169 V8 **Sembakung, Sungai** ≈ Borneo, N Indonesia
79 G17 **Sembé** La Sangha, NW Congo
169 S13 **Sembulu, Danau** ◎ Borneo, N Indonesia
Semendria *see* Smederevo
117 R1 **Semenivka** Chernihivs'ka Oblast', N Ukraine
117 S6 **Semenivka** *Rus.* Semenovka. Poltavs'ka Oblast', NE Ukraine
127 O3 **Semenov** Nizhegorodskaya Oblast', W Russian Federation
Semenovka *see* Semenivka
169 S17 **Semeru, Gunung** *var.* Mahameru. ▲ Jawa, S Indonesia
Semey *see* Semipalatinsk
Semezhevo *see* Syemyezhava
126 L7 **Semiluki** Voronezhskaya Oblast', W Russian Federation
33 W16 **Seminoe Reservoir** ⊠ Wyoming, C USA
27 O11 **Seminole** Oklahoma, C USA
24 M6 **Seminole** Texas, SW USA
23 S8 **Seminole, Lake** ⊠ Florida/Georgia, SE USA
Semiozernoye *see* Auliyekol'
145 V9 **Semipalatinsk** *Kaz.* Semey. Vostochnyy Kazakhstan, E Kazakhstan
143 O9 **Semīrom** *var.* Samirum. Eşfahān, C Iran
38 F17 **Semisopochnoi Island** *island* Aleutian Islands, Alaska, USA
169 R11 **Semitau** Borneo, C Indonesia
81 E18 **Semliki** ≈ Uganda/Dem. Rep. Congo
143 P5 **Semnān** *var.* Samnān. Semnān, N Iran
143 Q5 **Semnān** *off.* Ostān-e Semnān. ◆ *province* N Iran
99 K24 **Semois** ≈ SE Belgium
108 E8 **Sempacher See** ◎ C Switzerland
Sena *see* Vila de Sena
30 L12 **Senachwine Lake** ◎ Illinois, N USA
59 O14 **Senador Pompeu** Ceará, E Brazil
Sena Gallica *see* Senigallia
59 C15 **Sena Madureira** Acre, W Brazil
155 L25 **Senanayake Samudra** ◎ E Sri Lanka
83 G15 **Senanga** Western, SW Zambia
27 Y9 **Senath** Missouri, C USA
22 L2 **Senatobia** Mississippi, S USA
164 C16 **Sendai** Kagoshima, Kyūshū, SW Japan
165 Q10 **Sendai** Miyagi, Honshū, C Japan
165 Q11 **Sendai-wan** *bay* E Japan
101 J23 **Senden** Bayern, S Germany
154 F11 **Sendhwa** Madhya Pradesh, C India
111 H21 **Senec** *Ger.* Wartberg, *Hung.* Szenc; *prev.* Szempcz. Bratislavský Kraj, W Slovakia
27 P3 **Seneca** Kansas, C USA
27 R8 **Seneca** Missouri, C USA
32 K13 **Seneca** Oregon, NW USA
21 O11 **Seneca** South Carolina, SE USA
18 G11 **Seneca Lake** ◎ New York, NE USA
31 U13 **Senecaville Lake** ⊠ Ohio, N USA
76 G11 **Senegal** *off.* Republic of Senegal, *Fr.* Sénégal. ◆ *republic* W Africa
76 H9 **Senegal** *Fr.* Sénégal. ≈ W Africa
31 O4 **Seney Marsh** *wetland* Michigan, N USA
101 P14 **Senftenberg** Brandenburg, E Germany
82 L11 **Senga Hill** Northern, NE Zambia
158 G13 **Sênggê Zangbo** ≈ W China
171 Z13 **Senggi** Papua, E Indonesia
127 R5 **Sengiley** Ul'yanovskaya Oblast', W Russian Federation
63 I19 **Senguerr, Río** ≈ S Argentina
83 J16 **Sengwa** ≈ C Zimbabwe
Senia *see* Senj
111 H19 **Senica** *Ger.* Senitz, *Hung.* Szenice. Trnavský Kraj, W Slovakia
Seniça *see* Sjenica
106 J11 **Senigallia** *anc.* Sena Gallica. Marche, C Italy
136 F15 **Senirkent** Isparta, SW Turkey
Senitz *see* Senica
112 C10 **Senj** *Ger.* Zengg, *It.* Segna; *anc.* Senia. Lika-Senj, NW Croatia
163 O10 **Senj** Dornogovĭ, SE Mongolia
92 H9 **Senja** *prev.* Senjen. *island* N Norway
Senjen *see* Senja
161 U12 **Senkaku-shotō** *island group* SW Japan
137 R12 **Şenkaya** Erzurum, NE Turkey
83 I16 **Senkobo** Southern, S Zambia
103 O4 **Senlis** Oise, N France
167 T12 **Senmonorom** Môndól Kiri, E Cambodia
80 G10 **Sennar** *var.* Sannār. Sinnar, C Sudan
Senno *see* Syanno
Senones *see* Sens
109 W11 **Senovo** E Slovenia
103 P6 **Sens** *anc.* Agendicum, Senones. Yonne, C France
Sensburg *see* Mrągowo
167 S11 **Sên, Stœng** ≈ C Cambodia
42 F7 **Sensuntepeque** Cabañas, NE El Salvador
112 L8 **Senta** *Hung.* Zenta. Serbia, N Serbia and Montenegro (Yugo.)
Šent Andraž *see* Sankt Andrä
171 Y13 **Sentani, Danau** ◎ Papua, E Indonesia
28 J5 **Sentinel Butte** ▲ North Dakota, N USA
10 M13 **Sentinel Peak** ▲ British Columbia, W Canada
59 N16 **Sento Sé** Bahia, E Brazil
Šent Peter *see* Pivka
Šent Vid *see* Sankt Veit an der Glan
Seo de Urgel *see* La See d'Urgel
154 I7 **Seondha** Madhya Pradesh, C India
154 J11 **Seoni** *prev.* Seeonee. Madhya Pradesh, C India
Seoul *see* Sŏul
184 I13 **Separation Point** *headland* South Island, NZ
169 V10 **Sepasu** Borneo, N Indonesia
186 B6 **Sepik** ≈ Indonesia/PNG
Sepone *see* Muang Xépôn
110 M7 **Sępopol** *Ger.* Schippenbeil. Warmińsko-Mazurskie, NE Poland,
116 F10 **Şepreuş** *Hung.* Seprős. Arad, W Romania
Seprős *see* Şepreuş
Şepşi-Sângeorz/Sepsiszentgyőrgy *see* Sfântu Gheorghe
15 W4 **Sept-Îles** Québec, SE Canada
105 N6 **Sepúlveda** Castilla-León, N Spain
104 K8 **Sequeros** Castilla-León, N Spain
104 L5 **Sequillo** ≈ NW Spain
32 G7 **Sequim** Washington, NW USA
35 S11 **Sequoia National Park** *national park* California, W USA
137 Q14 **Şerafettin Dağları** ▲ E Turkey
127 N10 **Serafimovich** Volgogradskaya Oblast', SW Russian Federation
171 Q10 **Serai** Sulawesi, N Indonesia
99 K19 **Seraing** Liège, E Belgium
Sêraitang *see* Baima
Serajgonj *see* Shirajganj Ghat
Serakhs *see* Sarahs
171 W13 **Serami** Papua, E Indonesia
Seram, Laut *see* Ceram Sea
Serampore/Serampur *see* Shrīrāmpur
171 S13 **Seram, Pulau** *var.* Serang, *Eng.* Ceram. *island* Maluku, E Indonesia
169 N15 **Serang** Jawa, C Indonesia
Serang *see* Seram, Pulau
169 P9 **Serasan, Pulau** *island* Kepulauan Natuna, W Indonesia
169 P9 **Serasan, Selat** *strait* Indonesia/Malaysia
112 M12 **Serbia** *Ger.* Serbien, *Serb.* Srbija. ◆ *republic* Serbia and Montenegro (Yugo.)
112 M13 **Serbia and Montenegro (Yugo.)** *off.* Federal Republic of Serbia and Montenegro (Yugo.), *SCr.* Jugoslavija, Savezna Republika Jugoslavija. ◆ *federal republic* SE Europe
Serbien *see* Serbia
Serca *see* Sark
146 D12 **Serdar** *prev.* *Rus.* Gyzylarbat, Kizyl-Arvat. Balkan Welaýaty, W Turkmenistan
Serdica *see* Sofiya
127 O7 **Serdobsk** Penzenskaya Oblast', W Russian Federation
145 X9 **Serebryansk** Vostochnyy Kazakhstan, E Kazakhstan
123 Q12 **Serebryanyy Bor** Respublika Sakha (Yakutiya), NE Russian Federation
111 H20 **Sered'** *Hung.* Szered. Trnavský Kraj, SW Slovakia
117 S1 **Seredyna-Buda** Sums'ka Oblast', NE Ukraine
118 E13 **Seredžius** Tauragė, C Lithuania
136 I14 **Şereflikoçhisar** Ankara, C Turkey
106 D7 **Seregno** Lombardia, N Italy
103 P7 **Serein** ≈ C France
168 K9 **Seremban** Negeri Sembilan, Peninsular Malaysia
81 H20 **Serengeti Plain** *plain* N Tanzania
82 K13 **Serenje** Central, E Zambia
Seres *see* Sérres
116 J5 **Seret** ≈ W Ukraine
Seret/Sereth *see* Siret
115 I21 **Serfopoúla** *island* Kykládes, Greece, Aegean Sea
127 P4 **Sergach** Nizhegorodskaya Oblast', W Russian Federation
29 S13 **Sergeant Bluff** Iowa, C USA
163 P7 **Sergelen** Dornod, NE Mongolia
163 O9 **Sergelen** Sühbaatar, E Mongolia
168 H8 **Sergeulangit, Pegunungan** ▲ Sumatera, NW Indonesia
122 L5 **Sergeya Kirova, Ostrova** *island* N Russian Federation
Sergeyevichi *see* Syarhyeyevichy
145 O7 **Sergeyevka** Severnyy Kazakhstan, N Kazakhstan
Sergiopol *see* Ayagoz
59 P16 **Sergipe** *off.* Estado de Sergipe. ◆ *state* E Brazil
126 L3 **Sergiyev Posad** Moskovskaya Oblast', W Russian Federation
126 K5 **Sergozero, Ozero** ◎ NW Russian Federation
46 J17 **Serhetabat** *prev.* *Rus.* Gushgy, Kushka. Mary Welaýaty, S Turkmenistan
169 Q10 **Serian** Sarawak, East Malaysia
169 O15 **Seribu, Kepulauan** *island group* S Indonesia
115 I21 **Sérifos** *anc.* Seriphos. *island* Kykládes, Greece, Aegean Sea
115 I21 **Sérifou, Stenó** *strait* SE Greece
136 F16 **Serik** Antalya, SW Turkey
106 E7 **Serio** ≈ N Italy
Seriphos *see* Sérifos
Serir Tibesti *see* Sarīr Tibisti
Sêrkog *see* Sêrtar
127 S5 **Sernovodsk** Samarskaya Oblast', W Russian Federation
127 R2 **Sernur** Respublika Mariy El, W Russian Federation
110 M11 **Serock** Mazowieckie, C Poland
61 B18 **Serodino** Santa Fe, C Argentina
Seroei *see* Serui
105 P14 **Serón** Andalucía, S Spain
99 E14 **Serooskerke** Zeeland, SW Netherlands
105 T6 **Seròs** Cataluña, NE Spain
122 G10 **Serov** Sverdlovskaya Oblast', C Russian Federation
83 I19 **Serowe** Central, SE Botswana
104 H13 **Serpa** Beja, S Portugal
Serpa Pinto *see* Menongue
182 A4 **Serpentine Lakes** *salt lake* South Australia
45 T15 **Serpent's Mouth, The** *Sp.* Boca de la Serpiente. *strait* Trinidad and Tobago/Venezuela
Serpiente, Boca de la *see* Serpent's Mouth, The
126 K4 **Serpukhov** Moskovskaya Oblast', W Russian Federation
60 K13 **Serra do Mar** ▲ S Brazil
Sérrai *see* Sérres
107 N22 **Serra San Bruno** Calabria, SW Italy
103 S14 **Serres** Hautes-Alpes, SE France
114 H13 **Sérres** *var.* Seres; *prev.* Sérrai. Kentrikí Makedonía, NE Greece
62 J9 **Serrezuela** Córdoba, C Argentina
59 O16 **Serrinha** Bahia, E Brazil
59 M19 **Serro** *var.* Sêrro. Minas Gerais, NE Brazil
Sêrro *see* Serro
Sert *see* Siirt
Sertá *see* Sertã
104 H9 **Sertã** *var.* Sertá. Castelo Branco, C Portugal
60 L8 **Sertãozinho** São Paulo, S Brazil
160 F7 **Sêrtar** *var.* Sêrkog. Sichuan, C China
171 W13 **Serui** *prev.* Seroei. Papua, E Indonesia
83 J19 **Serule** Central, E Botswana
169 S12 **Seruyan, Sungai** *var.* Sungai Pembuang. ≈ Borneo, N Indonesia
115 E14 **Sérvia** Dytikí Makedonía, N Greece
160 E7 **Sêrxü** *var.* Jugar. Sichuan, C China
123 R13 **Seryshevo** Amurskaya Oblast', SE Russian Federation
Sesana *see* Sežana
169 V8 **Sesayap, Sungai** ≈ Borneo, N Indonesia
Sesdlets *see* Siedlce
79 N17 **Sese** Orientale, N Dem. Rep. Congo
81 F18 **Sese Islands** *island group* S Uganda
83 H16 **Sesheke** *var.* Sesheko. Western, SE Zambia
Sesheko *see* Sesheke
106 C8 **Sesia** *anc.* Sessites. ≈ NW Italy
104 F11 **Sesimbra** Setúbal, S Portugal
115 N22 **Sesklió** *island* Dodekánisos, Greece, Aegean Sea
30 L16 **Sesser** Illinois, N USA
Sessites *see* Sesia
106 G11 **Sesto Fiorentino** Toscana, C Italy
106 E7 **Sesto San Giovanni** Lombardia, N Italy
106 A8 **Sestriere** Piemonte, NE Italy
106 D10 **Sestri Levante** Liguria, NW Italy
107 C20 **Sestu** Sardegna, Italy, C Mediterranean Sea
112 E8 **Sesvete** Zagreb, N Croatia
118 G12 **Šeta** Kaunas, C Lithuania
Setabis *see* Xátiva
165 Q4 **Setana** Hokkaidō, NE Japan
103 Q16 **Sète** *prev.* Cette. Hérault, S France
58 J11 **Sete Ilhas** Amapá, NE Brazil
59 L20 **Sete Lagoas** Minas Gerais, NE Brazil
60 G10 **Sete Quedas, Ilha das** *island* S Brazil
92 I10 **Setermoen** Troms, N Norway
95 E17 **Setesdal** *valley* S Norway
43 W16 **Setetule, Cerro** ▲ SE Panama
21 Q5 **Seth** West Virginia, NE USA
Setia *see* Sezze
74 K5 **Sétif** *var.* Stif. N Algeria
164 L13 **Seto** Aichi, Honshū, SW Japan
164 G13 **Seto-naikai** *Eng.* Inland Sea. *sea* S Japan
165 V16 **Setouchi** *var.* Setoushi. Kagoshima, Amami-Ō-shima, SW Japan
74 F6 **Settat** W Morocco
79 D20 **Setté Cama** Ogooué-Maritime, SW Gabon
11 W13 **Setting Lake** ◎ Manitoba, C Canada
97 L16 **Settle** N England, UK
189 Y12 **Settlement** E Wake Island
104 F11 **Setúbal** *Eng.* Saint Ubes, Saint Yves. Setúbal, W Portugal
104 F11 **Setúbal** ◆ *district* S Portugal
104 F12 **Setúbal, Baía de** *bay* W Portugal
Setul *see* Satun
12 B10 **Seul, Lac** ◎ Ontario, S Canada
103 R8 **Seurre** Côte d'Or, C France
137 U11 **Sevan** C Armenia
137 V12 **Sevana Lich** *Eng.* Lake Sevan, *Rus.* Ozero Sevan. ◎ E Armenia
Sevan, Lake/Sevan, Ozero *see* Sevana Lich
77 N11 **Sévaré** Mopti, C Mali
117 S14 **Sevastopol'** *Eng.* Sebastopol. Respublika Krym, S Ukraine
25 R14 **Seven Sisters** Texas, SW USA
10 K13 **Seven Sisters Peaks** ▲ British Columbia, SW Canada
99 M15 **Sevenum** Limburg, SE Netherlands
103 P14 **Séverac-le-Château** Aveyron, S France
14 H13 **Severn** ≈ Ontario, S Canada
97 L21 **Severn** *Wel.* Hafren. ≈ England/Wales, UK
127 O11 **Severnaya Dvina** *var.* Northern Dvina. ≈ NW Russian Federation
127 N16 **Severnaya Osetiya-Alaniya, Respublika** *Eng.* North Ossetia; *prev.* Respublika Severnaya Osetiya, Severo-Osetinskaya SSR. ◆ *autonomous republic* SW Russian Federation
Severnaya Osetiya, Respublika *see* Severnaya Osetiya-Alaniya Respublika
122 M5 **Severnaya Zemlya** *var.* Nicholas II Land. *island group* N Russian Federation
127 T5 **Severnoye** Orenburgskaya Oblast', W Russian Federation
35 S3 **Severn Troughs Range** ▲ Nevada, W USA
125 W3 **Severnyy** Respublika Komi, NW Russian Federation
144 I13 **Severnyy Chink Ustyurta** ▲ W Kazakhstan
127 Q13 **Severnyye Uvaly** *var.* Northern Ural Hills. *hill range* NW Russian Federation
145 O6 **Severnyy Kazakhstan** *off.* Severo-Kazakhstanskaya Oblast', *var.* North Kazakhstan, *Kaz.* Soltūstik Qazaqstan Oblysy. ◆ *province* N Kazakhstan
127 V9 **Severnyy Ural** ▲ NW Russian Federation
Severo-Alichurskiy Khrebet *see* Alichuri Shimolí, Qatorkŭhi
123 N12 **Severobaykal'sk** Respublika Buryatiya, S Russian Federation
Severodonetsk *see* Syeverodonets'k
124 M8 **Severodvinsk** *prev.* Molotov, Sudostroy. Arkhangel'skaya Oblast', NW Russian Federation
Severo-Kazakhstanskaya Oblast' *see* Severnyy Kazakhstan
123 U11 **Severo-Kuril'sk** Sakhalinskaya Oblast', SE Russian Federation
124 J3 **Severomorsk** Murmanskaya Oblast', NW Russian Federation
Severo-Osetinskaya SSR *see* Severnaya Osetiya-Alaniya, Respublika
122 M7 **Severo-Sibirskaya Nizmennost'** *var.* North Siberian Plain, *Eng.* North Siberian Lowland. *lowlands* N Russian Federation
122 G10 **Severoural'sk** Sverdlovskaya Oblast', C Russian Federation
122 L11 **Severo-Yeniseyskiy** Krasnoyarskiy Kray, C Russian Federation
122 J12 **Seversk** Tomskaya Oblast', C Russian Federation
126 M11 **Severskiy Donets** *Ukr.* Sivers'kyy Donets'. ≈ Russian Federation/Ukraine *see also* Sivers'kyy Donets'
92 M9 **Sevettijärvi** Lappi, N Finland
36 M5 **Sevier Bridge Reservoir** ⊠ Utah, W USA
36 J4 **Sevier Desert** *plain* Utah, W USA
36 J5 **Sevier Lake** ◎ Utah, W USA
21 N9 **Sevierville** Tennessee, S USA
104 J14 **Sevilla** *Eng.* Seville; *anc.* Hispalis. Andalucía, SW Spain
104 J13 **Sevilla** ◆ *province* Andalucía, SW Spain
Sevilla de Niefang *see* Niefang
43 O16 **Sevilla, Isla** *island* SW Panama
Seville *see* Sevilla
114 J9 **Sevlievo** Gabrovo, N Bulgaria
Sevluš/Sevlyush *see* Vynohradiv
109 V11 **Sevnica** *Ger.* Lichtenwald. E Slovenia
126 I7 **Sevsk** Bryanskaya Oblast', W Russian Federation
76 J15 **Sewa** ≈ E Sierra Leone
39 R12 **Seward** Alaska, USA
29 R15 **Seward** Nebraska, C USA
10 G8 **Seward Glacier** *glacier* Yukon Territory, W Canada
197 Q3 **Seward Peninsula** *peninsula* Alaska, USA
Seward's Folly *see* Alaska
62 H12 **Sewell** Libertador, C Chile
98 K5 **Sexbierum** *Fris.* Seisbierrum. Friesland, N Netherlands
11 O13 **Sexsmith** Alberta, W Canada
41 W13 **Seybaplaya** Campeche, SE Mexico
173 N6 **Seychelles** *off.* Republic of Seychelles. ◆ *republic* W Indian Ocean
67 Z9 **Seychelles** *island group* NE Seychelles
173 N6 **Seychelles Bank** *var.* Le Banc des Seychelles. *undersea feature* W Indian Ocean
Seychelles, Le Banc des *see* Seychelles Bank
172 H17 **Seychellois, Morne** ▲ Mahé, NE Seychelles
92 L2 **Seydhisfjördhur** Austurland, E Iceland
146 J12 **Seýdi** *Rus.* Seydi; *prev.* Neftezavodsk. Lebap Welaýaty, E Turkmenistan
136 G16 **Seydişehir** Konya, SW Turkey
136 J13 **Seyfe Gölü** ◎ C Turkey
Seyhan *see* Adana
136 K16 **Seyhan Barajı** ⊠ S Turkey
136 K17 **Seyhan Nehri** ≈ S Turkey
136 F13 **Seyitgazi** Eskişehir, W Turkey
126 J7 **Seym** ≈ W Russian Federation
117 S3 **Seym** ≈ N Ukraine
123 T9 **Seymchan** Magadanskaya Oblast', E Russian Federation
114 N12 **Seymen** Tekirdağ, NW Turkey
183 O11 **Seymour** Victoria, SE Australia
83 I25 **Seymour** Eastern Cape, S South Africa
29 W16 **Seymour** Iowa, C USA
27 U7 **Seymour** Missouri, C USA
25 Q5 **Seymour** Texas, SW USA
114 M12 **Şeytan Deresi** ≈ NW Turkey
109 S12 **Sežana** *It.* Sesana. SW Slovenia
103 P5 **Sézanne** Marne, N France
107 I16 **Sezze** *anc.* Setia. Lazio, C Italy
115 H25 **Sfákia** Kríti, Greece, E Mediterranean Sea
115 D21 **Sfaktiría** *island* S Greece
116 J11 **Sfântu Gheorghe** *Ger.* Sankt-Georgen, *Hung.* Sepsiszentgyőrgy; *prev.* Şepşi-Sângeorz, Sfîntu Gheorghe. Covasna, C Romania
117 N13 **Sfântu Gheorghe, Braţul** *var.* Gheorghe Braţul. ≈ E Romania
75 N6 **Sfax** *Ar.* Şafāqis. E Tunisia
75 N6 **Sfax** ✕ E Tunisia
Sfîntu Gheorghe *see* Sfântu Gheorghe
98 H13 **'s-Gravendeel** Zuid-Holland, SW Netherlands
98 F11 **'s-Gravenhage** *var.* Den Haag, *Eng.* The Hague, *Fr.* La Haye. ● (Netherlands-seat of government) Zuid-Holland, W Netherlands
98 G12 **'s-Gravenzande** Zuid-Holland, W Netherlands
Shaan/Shaanxi Sheng *see* Shaanxi

◆ Country ◇ Dependent Territory ◆ Administrative Region ▲ Mountain ⚲ Volcano ◎ Lake
● Country Capital ○ Dependent Territory Capital ✕ International Airport ▲ Mountain Range ≈ River ⊠ Reservoir

159 X11 **Shaanxi** *var.* Shaan, Shaanxi Sheng, Shan-hsi, Shenshi, Shensi. ◆ *province* C China
Shaartuz *see* Shahrtuz
Shabani *see* Zvishavane
81 N17 **Shabeellaha Dhexe** *off.* Gobolka Shabeellaha Dhexe. ◆ *region* E Somalia
81 L17 **Shabeellaha Hoose** *off.* Gobolka Shabeellaha Hoose. ◆ *region* S Somalia
Shabeelle, Webi *see* Shebeli
114 O7 **Shabla** Dobrich, NE Bulgaria
114 O7 **Shabla, Nos** *headland* NE Bulgaria
13 N9 **Shabogama Lake** ⊚ Newfoundland and Labrador, E Canada
79 N20 **Shabunda** Sud Kivu, E Dem. Rep. Congo
141 Q15 **Shabwah** C Yemen
158 F8 **Shache** *var.* Yarkant. Xinjiang Uygur Zizhiqu, NW China
Shacheng *see* Huailai
195 R12 **Shackleton Coast** *physical region* Antarctica
195 Z10 **Shackleton Ice Shelf** *ice shelf* Antarctica
Shaddādī *see* Ash Shadādah
28 K7 **Shadehill Reservoir** ⊠ South Dakota, N USA
122 G11 **Shadrinsk** Kurganskaya Oblast', C Russian Federation
31 O12 **Shafer, Lake** ⊠ Indiana, N USA
35 R13 **Shafter** California, W USA
24 J11 **Shafter** Texas, SW USA
97 L23 **Shaftesbury** S England, UK
185 F22 **Shag** ∼ South Island, NZ
145 V9 **Shagan** ∼ E Kazakhstan
39 O11 **Shageluk** Alaska, USA
122 K14 **Shagonar** Respublika Tyva, S Russian Federation
185 F22 **Shag Point** *headland* South Island, NZ
144 J12 **Shagyray, Plato** *plain* SW Kazakhstan
Shahābād *see* Eslāmābād
168 K9 **Shah Alam** Selangor, Peninsular Malaysia
117 O12 **Shahany, Ozero** ⊚ SW Ukraine
138 H9 **Shahbā'** *anc.* Philippopolis. As Suwaydā', S Syria
Shahbān *see* Ad Dayr
149 P17 **Shāhbandar** Sind, SE Pakistan
149 P13 **Shāhdād Kot** Sind, SW Pakistan
143 T10 **Shahdād, Namakzār-e** *salt pan* E Iran
149 Q15 **Shāhdādpur** Sind, SE Pakistan
154 K10 **Shahdol** Madhya Pradesh, C India
161 N7 **Sha He** ∼ C China
Shahepu *see* Linze
153 N13 **Shāhganj** Uttar Pradesh, N India
152 C11 **Shāhgarh** Rājasthān, NW India
Sha Hi *see* Orūmīyeh, Daryācheh-ye, Iran
Shāhī *see* Qā'emshahr, Māzandarān, Iran
139 Q6 **Shāhimah** *var.* Shahma. C Iraq
Shahjahanabad *see* Delhi
152 L11 **Shāhjahānpur** Uttar Pradesh, N India
Shahma *see* Shāhimah
149 U7 **Shāhpur** Punjab, E Pakistan
Shāhpur *see* Shāhpur Chākar
152 G13 **Shāhpura** Rājasthān, N India
149 Q15 **Shāhpur Chākar** *var.* Shāhpur. Sind, SE Pakistan
148 M5 **Shahrak** Ghowr, C Afghanistan
143 Q11 **Shahr-e Bābak** Kermān, C Iran
143 N8 **Shahr-e Kord** *var.* Shahr Kord. Chahār Maḩall va Bakhtīārī, C Iran
143 O9 **Shahreẕā** *var.* Qomisheh, Qumisheh, Shahriza; *prev.* Qomsheh. Eşfahān, C Iran
147 N12 **Shahrisabz** *Rus.* Shakhrisabz. Qashqadaryo Viloyati, S Uzbekistan
147 P11 **Shahriston** *Rus.* Shakhristan. NW Tajikistan
Shahriza *see* Shahreẕā
Shahr-i-Zabul *see* Zābol
Shahr Kord *see* Shahr-e Kord
147 P14 **Shahrtuz** *Rus.* Shaartuz. SW Tajikistan
143 Q4 **Shāhrūd** *prev.* Emāmrūd, Emāmshahr. Semnān, N Iran
Shahsavār/Shahsawar *see* Tonekābon
Shaidara *see* Step' Nardara
Shaikh Ābid *see* Shaykh 'Ābid
Shaikh Fāris *see* Shaykh Fāris
Shaikh Najm *see* Shaykh Najm
138 K5 **Sha'īr, Jabal** ▲ C Syria
154 G10 **Shājāpur** Madhya Pradesh, C India
80 J8 **Shakal, Ras** *headland* NE Sudan
83 G17 **Shakawe** Ngamiland, N Botswana
Shakhdarinskiy Khrebet *see* Shokhdara, Qatorkŭhi
Shakhrikhan *see* Sharixon
Shakhrisabz *see* Shahrisabz
Shakhristan *see* Shahriston
117 X8 **Shakhtars'k** *Rus.* Shakhtërsk. Donets'ka Oblast', SE Ukraine
Shakhtërsk *see* Shakhtars'k
145 R10 **Shakhtinsk** Karaganda, C Kazakhstan
126 L11 **Shakhty** Rostovskaya Oblast', SW Russian Federation
127 P2 **Shakhun'ya** Nizhegorodskaya Oblast', W Russian Federation
77 S15 **Shaki** Oyo, W Nigeria
81 J15 **Shakīso** Oromo, C Ethiopia
117 X8 **Shakmars'k** Donets'ka Oblast', E Ukraine
29 V9 **Shakopee** Minnesota, N USA
165 R3 **Shakotan-misaki** *headland* Hokkaidō, NE Japan
39 N9 **Shaktoolik** Alaska, USA
81 J14 **Shala Hāyk'** ⊚ C Ethiopia
124 M10 **Shalakusha** Arkhangel'skaya Oblast', NW Russian Federation
145 U8 **Shalday** Pavlodar, NE Kazakhstan
127 P16 **Shali** Chechenskaya Respublika, SW Russian Federation
141 W12 **Shalīm** *var.* Shelim. S Oman
Shaliuhe *see* Gangca
144 K12 **Shalkar** *var.* Chelkar. Aktyubinsk, W Kazakhstan
144 F9 **Shalkar, Ozero** *prev.* Chelkar, Ozero. ⊚ W Kazakhstan
21 V12 **Shallotte** North Carolina, SE USA
25 N5 **Shallowater** Texas, SW USA
124 K11 **Shal'skiy** Respublika Kareliya, NW Russian Federation
160 F9 **Shaluli Shan** ▲ C China
81 F22 **Shama** ∼ C Tanzania
11 Z11 **Shamattawa** Manitoba, C Canada
12 F8 **Shamattawa** ∼ Ontario, C Canada
Shām, Bādiyat ash *see* Syrian Desert
Shamiya *see* Ash Shāmīyah
141 X8 **Shām, Jabal ash** *var.* Jebel Sham. ▲ NW Oman
Sham, Jebel *see* Shām, Jabal ash
Shamkhor *see* Şämkir
18 G14 **Shamokin** Pennsylvania, NE USA
25 P2 **Shamrock** Texas, SW USA
Sha'nabī, Jabal ash *see* Chambi, Jebel
139 Y12 **Shanāwah** E Iraq
Shancheng *see* Taining
159 T8 **Shandan** Gansu, N China
Shandī *see* Shendi
161 Q5 **Shandong** *var.* Lu, Shandong Sheng, Shantung. ◆ *province* E China
161 R4 **Shandong Bandao** *var.* Shantung Peninsula. *peninsula* E China
Shandong Peninsula *see* Shandong Bandao
Shandong Sheng *see* Shandong
139 U8 **Shandrūkh** E Iraq
83 J17 **Shangani** ∼ W Zimbabwe
161 O15 **Shangchuan Dao** *island* S China
Shangchuankou *see* Minhe
163 P12 **Shangdu** Nei Mongol Zizhiqu, N China
161 O11 **Shanggao** *var.* Aoyang. Jiangxi, S China
161 S8 **Shanghai** *var.* Shang-hai. Shanghai Shi, E China
Shanghai *see* Shanghai Shi
161 S8 **Shanghai Shi** *var.* Hu, Shanghai. ◆ *municipality* E China
161 P13 **Shanghang** Fujian, SE China
160 K14 **Shanglin** *var.* Dafeng. Guangxi Zhuangzu Zizhiqu, S China
83 G15 **Shangombo** Western, W Zambia
Shangpai *see* Feixi
161 O6 **Shangqiu** *var.* Zhuji. Henan, C China
161 Q10 **Shangrao** Jiangxi, S China
161 S9 **Shangyu** *var.* Baiguan. Zhejiang, SE China
163 X9 **Shangzhi** Heilongjiang, NE China
160 L7 **Shangzhou** *var.* Shang Xian. Shaanxi, C China
163 W9 **Shanhetun** Heilongjiang, NE China
Shan-hsi *see* Shaanxi, China
Shan-hsi *see* Shanxi, China
159 O6 **Shankou** Xinjiang Uygur Zizhiqu, W China
184 M13 **Shannon** Manawatu-Wanganui, North Island, NZ
97 B19 **Shannon** ✕ W Ireland
97 C17 **Shannon** *Ir.* An tSionainn. ∼ W Ireland
167 N6 **Shan Plateau** *plateau* E Myanmar
158 M6 **Shanshan** *var.* Piqan. Xinjiang Uygur Zizhiqu, NW China
Shansi *see* Shanxi
167 N5 **Shan State** ◆ *state* E Myanmar
Shantar Islands *see* Shantarskiye Ostrova
123 S12 **Shantarskiye Ostrova** *Eng.* Shantar Islands. *island group* E Russian Federation
161 Q14 **Shantou** *var.* Shan-t'ou, Swatow. Guangdong, S China
Shantung *see* Shandong
Shantung Peninsula *see* Shandong Bandao
163 O14 **Shanxi** *var.* Jin, Shan-hsi, Shansi, Shanxi Sheng. ◆ *province* C China
Shan Xian *see* Sanmenxia
161 P6 **Shanxian** *var.* Shan Xian. Shandong, E China
Shanxi Sheng *see* Shanxi
160 L7 **Shanyang** Shaanxi, C China
161 N13 **Shanyin** *var.* Daiyue. Shanxi, China
161 O13 **Shaoguan** *var.* Shao-kuan, *Cant.* Kukong; *prev.* Ch'u-chiang. Guangdong, S China
Shao-kuan *see* Shaoguan
161 Q11 **Shaowu** Fujian, SE China
161 S9 **Shaoxing** Zhejiang, SE China
160 M12 **Shaoyang** *var.* Tangdukou. Hunan, S China
160 M11 **Shaoyang** *var.* Baoqing, Shao-yang; *prev.* Pao-king. Hunan, S China
96 K5 **Shapinsay** *island* NE Scotland, UK
127 S4 **Shapkina** ∼ NW Russian Federation
Shāpūr *see* Salmās
158 M4 **Shaqiuhe** Xinjiang Uygur Zizhiqu, W China
139 T2 **Shaqlāwa** *var.* Shaqlāwah. E Iraq
Shaqlāwah *see* Shaqlāwa
138 I8 **Shaqqā** As Suwaydā', S Syria
141 P7 **Shaqrā'** Ar Riyāḑ, C Saudi Arabia
Shaqrā *see* Shuqrah
145 W10 **Shar** *var.* Charsk. Vostochnyy Kazakhstan, E Kazakhstan
149 O6 **Sharan** Urūzgān, SE Afghanistan
Sharaqpur *see* Sharqpur
Sharbaqty *see* Shcherbakty
141 X12 **Sharbatāt** S Oman
141 X12 **Sharbithāt, Ras** *var.* Ra's Sharbatāt. *headland* S Oman
14 K14 **Sharbot Lake** Ontario, SE Canada
145 P17 **Shardara** *var.* Chardara. Yuzhnyy Kazakhstan, S Kazakhstan
Shardara Dalasy *see* Step' Nardara
162 F8 **Sharga** Govĭ-Altay, W Mongolia
162 H6 **Sharga** Hövsgöl, N Mongolia
116 M7 **Sharhorod** Vinnyts'ka Oblast', C Ukraine
162 K10 **Sharhulsan** Ömnögovĭ, S Mongolia
165 V3 **Shari** Hokkaidō, NE Japan
Shari *see* Chari
139 T6 **Shārī, Buḩayrat** ⊚ C Iraq
147 S10 **Sharixon** *Rus.* Shakhrikhan. Andijon Viloyati, E Uzbekistan
Sharjah *see* Ash Shāriqah
118 K12 **Sharkawshchyna** *var.* Sharkowshchyna, *Pol.* Szarkowszczyzna, *Rus.* Sharkovshchina. Vitsyebskaya Voblasts', NW Belarus
180 G9 **Shark Bay** *bay* Western Australia
141 Y9 **Sharkh** E Oman
Sharkovshchina/Sharkowshchyna *see* Sharkawshchyna
127 U6 **Sharlyk** Orenburgskaya Oblast', W Russian Federation
Sharm ash Shaykh *see* Sharm el Sheikh
75 Y9 **Sharm el Sheikh** *var.* Ofiral, Sharm ash Shaykh. E Egypt
18 B13 **Sharon** Pennsylvania, NE USA
26 H4 **Sharon Springs** Kansas, C USA
31 Q14 **Sharonville** Ohio, N USA
Sharourah *see* Sharūrah
29 O10 **Sharpe, Lake** ⊠ South Dakota, N USA
Sharqī, Al Jabal ash/Sharqi, Jebel esh *see* Anti-Lebanon
Sharqiyah, Al Minţaqah ash *see* Ash Sharqīyah
138 I6 **Sharqīyat an Nabk, Jabal** ▲ W Syria
149 W8 **Sharqpur** *var.* Sharaqpur. Punjab, E Pakistan
141 Q13 **Sharūrah** *var.* Sharourah. Najrān, S Saudi Arabia
125 O14 **Shar'ya** Kostromskaya Oblast', NW Russian Federation
145 V15 **Sharyn** *var.* Charyn. ∼ SE Kazakhstan
Sharyn *see* Charyn
83 J18 **Shashe** Central, NE Botswana
83 J18 **Shashe** *var.* Shashi. ∼ Botswana/Zimbabwe
81 J14 **Shashemenē** *var.* Shashemenne, Shashhamana, *It.* Sciasciamana. Oromo, C Ethiopia
Shashemenne/Shashhamana *see* Shashemenē
Shashi *see* Shashe
Shashi/Sha-shih/Shasi *see* Jingzhou, Hubei
35 N3 **Shasta Lake** ⊠ California, W USA
35 N2 **Shasta, Mount** ▲ California, W USA
127 O4 **Shatki** Nizhegorodskaya Oblast', W Russian Federation
Shatlyk *see* Şatlyk
Shatra *see* Ash Shaţrah
119 K17 **Shatsk** *Rus.* Shatsk. Minskaya Voblasts', C Belarus
127 N5 **Shatsk** Ryazanskaya Oblast', W Russian Federation
26 J9 **Shattuck** Oklahoma, C USA
145 P16 **Shaul'der** Yuzhnyy Kazakhstan, S Kazakhstan
11 S17 **Shaunavon** Saskatchewan, S Canada
Shavat *see* Shovot
158 K4 **Shawan** Xinjiang Uygur Zizhiqu, NW China
14 G12 **Shawanaga** Ontario, S Canada
30 M6 **Shawano** Wisconsin, N USA
30 M6 **Shawano Lake** ⊚ Wisconsin, N USA
15 P10 **Shawinigan** *prev.* Shawinigan Falls. Québec, SE Canada
Shawinigan Falls *see* Shawinigan
15 P10 **Shawinigan-Sud** Québec, SE Canada
138 J5 **Shawmarīyah, Jabal ash** ▲ C Syria
27 O11 **Shawnee** Oklahoma, C USA
14 K12 **Shawville** Québec, SE Canada
145 Q16 **Shayan** *var.* Chayan. Yuzhnyy Kazakhstan, S Kazakhstan
Shaykh *see* Ash Shakk
139 W9 **Shaykh 'Ābid** *var.* Shaikh Ābid. E Iraq
139 Y10 **Shaykh Fāris** *var.* Shaikh Fāris. E Iraq
139 T7 **Shaykh Ḩātim** E Iraq
Shaykh, Jabal ash *see* Hermon, Mount
139 X10 **Shaykh Najm** *var.* Shaikh Najm. E Iraq
139 W9 **Shaykh Sa'd** E Iraq
147 T14 **Shazud** SE Tajikistan
119 N18 **Shchadryn** *Rus.* Shchedrin. Homyel'skaya Voblasts', SE Belarus
119 H18 **Shchara** ∼ SW Belarus
Shchedrin *see* Shchadryn
Shcheglovsk *see* Kemerovo
126 K5 **Shchëkino** Tul'skaya Oblast', W Russian Federation
125 S7 **Shchel'yayur** Respublika Komi, NW Russian Federation
145 U8 **Shcherbakty** *Kaz.* Sharbaqty. Pavlodar, E Kazakhstan
126 K7 **Shchigry** Kurskaya Oblast', W Russian Federation
Shchitkovichi *see* Shchytkavichy
117 Q2 **Shchors** Chernihivs'ka Oblast', N Ukraine
117 T8 **Shchors'k** Dnipropetrovs'ka Oblast', E Ukraine
Shchuchin *see* Shchuchyn
145 Q7 **Shchuchinsk** *prev.* Shchuchye. Akmola, N Kazakhstan
Shchuchye *see* Shchuchinsk
119 G16 **Shchuchyn** *Pol.* Szczuczyn Nowogródzki, *Rus.* Shchuchin. Hrodzyenskaya Voblasts', W Belarus
119 K17 **Shchytkavichy** *Rus.* Shchitkovichi. Minskaya Voblasts', C Belarus
122 J13 **Shebalino** Respublika Altay, S Russian Federation
126 J9 **Shebekino** Belgorodskaya Oblast', W Russian Federation
Shebelë Wenz, Wabē *see* Shebeli
81 L14 **Shebeli** *Amh.* Wabē Shebelē Wenz, *It.* Scebeli, *Som.* Webi Shabeelle. ∼ Ethiopia/Somalia
113 M20 **Shebenikut, Maja e** ▲ E Albania
149 N2 **Sheberghān** *var.* Shibarghān, Shiberghan, Shiberghān. Jowzjān, N Afghanistan
144 F14 **Shebir** Mangistau, SW Kazakhstan
31 N8 **Sheboygan** Wisconsin, N USA
77 X15 **Shebshi Mountains** *var.* Schebschi Mountains. ▲ E Nigeria
Shechem *see* Nablus
Shedadi *see* Ash Shadādah
13 P14 **Shediac** New Brunswick, SE Canada
126 L15 **Shedok** Krasnodarskiy Kray, SW Russian Federation
80 N12 **Sheekh** Woqooyi Galbeed, N Somalia
38 M11 **Sheenjek River** ∼ Alaska, USA
96 D13 **Sheep Haven** *Ir.* Cuan na gCaorach. *inlet* N Ireland
35 X10 **Sheep Range** ▲ Nevada, W USA
98 M13 **'s-Heerenberg** Gelderland, E Netherlands
97 P22 **Sheerness** SE England, UK
13 Q15 **Sheet Harbour** Nova Scotia, SE Canada
185 H18 **Sheffield** Canterbury, South Island, NZ
97 M18 **Sheffield** N England, UK
23 O2 **Sheffield** Alabama, S USA
29 V12 **Sheffield** Iowa, C USA
25 N10 **Sheffield** Texas, SW USA
63 H22 **Shehuen, Río** ∼ S Argentina
Shekhem *see* Nablus
149 V8 **Shekhūpura** Punjab, NE Pakistan
Sheki *see* Şäki
124 L14 **Sheksna** Vologodskaya Oblast', NW Russian Federation
123 T5 **Shelagskiy, Mys** *headland* NE Russian Federation
27 V3 **Shelbina** Missouri, C USA
13 F16 **Shelburne** Nova Scotia, SE Canada
14 G14 **Shelburne** Ontario, S Canada
33 R7 **Shelby** Montana, NW USA
21 Q10 **Shelby** North Carolina, SE USA
31 S12 **Shelby** Ohio, N USA
30 L14 **Shelbyville** Illinois, N USA
31 P14 **Shelbyville** Indiana, N USA
20 L5 **Shelbyville** Kentucky, S USA
27 V2 **Shelbyville** Missouri, C USA
20 J10 **Shelbyville** Tennessee, S USA
25 X8 **Shelbyville** Texas, SW USA
30 L14 **Shelbyville, Lake** ⊠ Illinois, N USA
29 S12 **Sheldon** Iowa, C USA
38 M11 **Sheldons Point** Alaska, USA
Shelekhov Gulf *see* Shelikhova, Zaliv
123 U9 **Shelikhova, Zaliv** *Eng.* Shelekhov Gulf. *gulf* E Russian Federation
39 P14 **Shelikof Strait** *strait* Alaska, USA
Shelim *see* Shalīm
11 T14 **Shellbrook** Saskatchewan, S Canada
28 L3 **Shell Creek** ∼ North Dakota, N USA
Shellif *see* Chelif, Oued
22 I10 **Shell Keys** *island group* Louisiana, S USA
30 I4 **Shell Lake** Wisconsin, N USA
29 W12 **Shell Rock** Iowa, C USA
185 C26 **Shelter Point** *headland* Stewart Island, NZ
18 L13 **Shelton** Connecticut, NE USA
32 G8 **Shelton** Washington, NW USA
Shemakha *see* Şamaxı
145 W9 **Shemonaikha** Vostochnyy Kazakhstan, E Kazakhstan
127 Q4 **Shemursha** Chuvashskaya Respublika, W Russian Federation
38 D16 **Shemya Island** *island* Aleutian Islands, Alaska, USA
29 T16 **Shenandoah** Iowa, C USA
21 U4 **Shenandoah** Virginia, NE USA
21 U4 **Shenandoah Mountains** *ridge* West Virginia, NE USA
21 V3 **Shenandoah River** ∼ West Virginia, NE USA
77 W15 **Shendam** Plateau, C Nigeria
80 G8 **Shendi** *var.* Shandī. River Nile, NE Sudan
76 I15 **Shenge** SW Sierra Leone
146 L10 **Shengeldi** *Rus.* Chingildi. Navoiy Viloyati, N Uzbekistan
145 U15 **Shengel'dy** Almaty, SE Kazakhstan
113 K18 **Shëngjin** *var.* Shëngjini. Lezhë, NW Albania
Shëngjini *see* Shëngjin
Shengking *see* Liaoning
Sheng Xian/Shengxian *see* Shengzhou
161 S9 **Shengzhou** *var.* Shengxian, Sheng Xian. Zhejiang, SE China
Shenking *see* Liaoning
125 N11 **Shenkursk** Arkhangel'skaya Oblast', NW Russian Federation
160 L3 **Shenmu** Shaanxi, C China
113 L19 **Shën Noj i Madh** ▲ C Albania
160 L8 **Shennong Ding** *var.* Dashennongjia. ▲ C China
Shenshi/Shensi *see* Shaanxi
163 V12 **Shenyang** *Chin.* Shen-yang, *Eng.* Moukden, Mukden; *prev.* Fengtien. Liaoning, NE China
161 O15 **Shenzhen** Guangdong, S China
154 G8 **Sheopur** Madhya Pradesh, C India
116 L5 **Shepetivka** *Rus.* Shepetovka. Khmel'nyts'ka Oblast', NW Ukraine
Shepetovka *see* Shepetivka
25 W10 **Shepherd** Texas, SW USA
187 R14 **Shepherd Islands** *island group* C Vanuatu
20 K5 **Shepherdsville** Kentucky, S USA
183 O11 **Shepparton** Victoria, SE Australia
97 P22 **Sheppey, Isle of** *island* SE England, UK
Sherabad *see* Sherobod
9 O4 **Sherard, Cape** *headland* Nunavut, N Canada
97 L23 **Sherborne** S England, UK
76 H16 **Sherbro Island** *island* SW Sierra Leone
15 Q12 **Sherbrooke** Québec, SE Canada
29 T11 **Sherburn** Minnesota, N USA
78 H6 **Sherda** Borkou-Ennedi-Tibesti, N Chad
80 G7 **Shereik** River Nile, N Sudan
126 K3 **Sheremet'yevo** ✕ (Moskva) Moskovskaya Oblast', W Russian Federation
153 P14 **Shergāti** Bihār, N India
27 U12 **Sheridan** Arkansas, C USA
33 W12 **Sheridan** Wyoming, C USA
182 G8 **Sheringa** South Australia
25 U5 **Sherman** Texas, SW USA
194 J10 **Sherman Island** *island* Antarctica
19 S4 **Sherman Mills** Maine, NE USA
29 O15 **Sherman Reservoir** ⊠ Nebraska, C USA
147 N14 **Sherobod** *Rus.* Sherabad. Surxondaryo Viloyati, S Uzbekistan
147 O13 **Sherobod** *Rus.* Sherabad. ∼ S Uzbekistan
153 T14 **Sherpur** Dhaka, N Bangladesh
37 T4 **Sherrelwood** Colorado, C USA
99 J14 **'s-Hertogenbosch** *Fr.* Bois-le-Duc, *Ger.* Herzogenbusch. Noord-Brabant, S Netherlands
28 M2 **Sherwood** North Dakota, N USA
11 Q14 **Sherwood Park** Alberta, SW Canada
56 F13 **Sheshea, Río** ∼ E Peru
143 T5 **Sheshtamad** Khorāsān, NE Iran
29 S10 **Shetek, Lake** ⊚ Minnesota, N USA
96 M2 **Shetland Islands** *island group* NE Scotland, UK
144 F14 **Shetpe** Mangistau, SW Kazakhstan
154 C11 **Shetrunji** ∼ W India
Shevchenko *see* Aktau
117 W5 **Shevchenkove** Kharkivs'ka Oblast', E Ukraine
81 H14 **Shewa Gīmīra** Southern, S Ethiopia
161 Q9 **Shexian** *var.* Huicheng, She Xian. Anhui, E China
161 R6 **Sheyang** *prev.* Hede. Jiangsu, E China
29 O4 **Sheyenne** North Dakota, N USA
29 P4 **Sheyenne River** ∼ North Dakota, N USA
96 G7 **Shiant Islands** *island group* NW Scotland, UK
123 U12 **Shiashkotan, Ostrov** *island* Kuril'skiye Ostrova, SE Russian Federation
31 R9 **Shiawassee River** ∼ Michigan, N USA
141 R14 **Shibām** C Yemen
Shibarghān *see* Sheberghān
165 O10 **Shibata** *var.* Sibata. Niigata, Honshū, C Japan
Shiberghan/Shiberghān *see* Sheberghān
Shibh Jazīrat Sīnā' *see* Sinai
Shibīn al Kawm *see* Shibīn el Kôm
75 W8 **Shibīn el Kôm** *var.* Shibīn al Kawm. N Egypt
143 O13 **Shīb, Kūh-e** ▲ S Iran
12 D8 **Shibogama Lake** ⊚ Ontario, C Canada
Shibotsu-jima *see* Zelënyy, Ostrov
164 B16 **Shibushi** Kagoshima, Kyūshū, SW Japan
189 U13 **Shichiyo Islands** *island group* Chuuk, C Micronesia
Shickshock Mountains *see* Chic-Chocs, Monts
145 S8 **Shiderti** *var.* Shiderty. Pavlodar, NE Kazakhstan
145 S9 **Shiderti** ∼ N Kazakhstan
Shiderty *see* Shiderti
96 G10 **Shiel, Loch** ⊚ N Scotland, UK
164 J13 **Shiga** *off.* Shiga-ken, *var.* Siga. ◆ *prefecture* Honshū, SW Japan
Shigatse *see* Xigazê
141 U13 **Shiḩan** *oasis* NE Yemen
Shih-chia-chuang/Shihmen *see* Shijiazhuang
158 K4 **Shihezi** Xinjiang Uygur Zizhiqu, NW China
Shiichi *see* Shyichy
113 K19 **Shijak** *var.* Shijaku. Durrës, W Albania
Shijaku *see* Shijak
161 O4 **Shijiazhuang** *var.* Shih-chia-chuang; *prev.* Shihmen. Hebei, E China
165 R5 **Shikabe** Hokkaidō, NE Japan
149 Q13 **Shikārpur** Sind, S Pakistan
127 Q7 **Shikhany** Saratovskaya Oblast', W Russian Federation
189 V12 **Shiki Islands** *island group* Chuuk, C Micronesia
164 G14 **Shikoku** *var.* Sikoku. *island* SW Japan
192 H5 **Shikoku Basin** *var.* Sikoku Basin. *undersea feature* N Philippine Sea
164 G14 **Shikoku-sanchi** ▲ Shikoku, SW Japan
165 X4 **Shikotan, Ostrov** *Jap.* Shikotan-tō. *island* NE Russian Federation
Shikotan-tō *see* Shikotan, Ostrov
165 R4 **Shikotsu-ko** *var.* Sikotu Ko. ⊚ Hokkaidō, NE Japan
81 N15 **Shilabo** Somali, E Ethiopia
127 X7 **Shil'da** Orenburgskaya Oblast', W Russian Federation
139 V3 **Shīler, Āw-e** ∼ E Iraq
153 S12 **Shiliguri** *prev.* Siliguri. West Bengal, NE India
Shiliu *see* Changjiang
131 V7 **Shilka** ∼ S Russian Federation
18 H15 **Shillington** Pennsylvania, NE USA
153 V13 **Shillong** Meghālaya, NE India
126 M5 **Shilovo** Ryazanskaya Oblast', W Russian Federation
164 C14 **Shimabara** *var.* Simabara. Nagasaki, Kyūshū, SW Japan
164 C14 **Shimabara-wan** *bay* SW Japan
164 F12 **Shimane** *off.* Shimane-ken, *var.* Simane. ◆ *prefecture* Honshū, SW Japan
164 G11 **Shimane-hantō** *peninsula* Honshū, SW Japan
123 Q13 **Shimanovsk** Amurskaya Oblast', SE Russian Federation
Shimbir Berris *see* Shimbiris
80 O12 **Shimbiris** *var.* Shimbir Berris. ▲ N Somalia
165 T4 **Shimizu** Hokkaidō, NE Japan
164 M14 **Shimizu** *var.* Simizu. Shizuoka, Honshū, S Japan
152 I8 **Shimla** *prev.* Simla. Himāchal Pradesh, N India
Shimminato *see* Shinminato
165 N14 **Shimoda** *var.* Simoda. Shizuoka, Honshū, S Japan
165 O13 **Shimodate** *var.* Simodate. Ibaraki, Honshū, S Japan
155 F18 **Shimoga** Karnātaka, W India
164 C15 **Shimo-jima** *island* SW Japan
164 B15 **Shimo-Koshiki-jima** *island* SW Japan
81 J21 **Shimoni** Coast, S Kenya
164 D13 **Shimonoseki** *var.* Simonoseki; *hist.* Akamagaseki, Bakan. Yamaguchi, Honshū, SW Japan
124 G14 **Shimsk** Novgorodskaya Oblast', NW Russian Federation
141 W7 **Shināş** N Oman
148 J6 **Shīndand** Farāh, W Afghanistan
Shinei *see* Hsinying
25 T12 **Shiner** Texas, SW USA
167 N1 **Shingbwiyang** Kachin State, N Myanmar
145 W11 **Shingozha** Vostochnyy Kazakhstan, E Kazakhstan
164 J15 **Shingū** *var.* Singû. Wakayama, Honshū, SW Japan
14 F8 **Shining Tree** Ontario, S Canada
165 P9 **Shinjō** *var.* Sinzyô. Yamagata, Honshū, C Japan
96 I7 **Shin, Loch** ⊚ N Scotland, UK
21 S3 **Shinnston** West Virginia, NE USA
138 I6 **Shinshār** *Fr.* Chinnchâr. Ḩimş, W Syria
Shinshū *see* Chinju
165 T4 **Shintoku** Hokkaidō, NE Japan
81 G20 **Shinyanga** Shinyanga, NW Tanzania
81 G20 **Shinyanga** ◆ *region* N Tanzania
165 Q10 **Shiogama** *var.* Siogama. Miyagi, Honshū, C Japan
164 M12 **Shiojiri** *var.* Sioziri. Nagano, Honshū, S Japan
164 I15 **Shiono-misaki** *headland* Honshū, SW Japan
165 Q12 **Shioya-zaki** *headland* Honshū, C Japan
114 J9 **Shipchenski Prokhod** *pass* C Bulgaria
160 G14 **Shiping** Yunnan, SW China
13 P13 **Shippagan** *var.* Shippegan. New Brunswick, SE Canada
Shippegan *see* Shippagan
18 F15 **Shippensburg** Pennsylvania, NE USA
37 O9 **Ship Rock** ▲ New Mexico, SW USA
37 P9 **Shiprock** New Mexico, SW USA
15 R6 **Shipshaw** ∼ Québec, SE Canada
123 V10 **Shipunskiy, Mys** *headland* E Russian Federation
160 K7 **Shiquan** Shaanxi, C China
122 K13 **Shira** Respublika Khakasiya, S Russian Federation
153 T14 **Shirajganj Ghat** *var.* Serajgonj, Sirajganj. Rajshahi, C Bangladesh
165 P12 **Shirakawa** *var.* Sirakawa. Fukushima, Honshū, C Japan
164 M13 **Shirane-san** ▲ Honshū, S Japan
165 U14 **Shiranuka** Hokkaidō, NE Japan
195 N12 **Shirase Coast** *physical region* Antarctica
165 U3 **Shirataki** Hokkaidō, NE Japan
143 O11 **Shīrāz** *var.* Shīrāz. Fārs, S Iran
83 N15 **Shire** *var.* Chire. ∼ Malawi/Mozambique
162 G7 **Shiree** Dzavhan, W Mongolia

◆ Country ● Country Capital ◇ Dependent Territory ○ Dependent Territory Capital ◆ Administrative Region ✕ International Airport ▲ Mountain ▲ Mountain Range ⛰ Volcano ∼ River ⊚ Lake ⊠ Reservoir

163 O9 **Shireet** Sühbaatar, SE Mongolia
165 W3 **Shiretoko-hantō** headland Hokkaidō, NE Japan
165 W3 **Shiretoko-misaki** headland Hokkaidō, NE Japan
127 N5 **Shiringushi** Respublika Mordoviya, W Russian Federation
148 M3 **Shīrīn Tagāb** Fāryāb, N Afghanistan
149 N2 **Shīrīn Tagāb** ≈ N Afghanistan
165 R6 **Shiriya-zaki** headland Honshū, C Japan
144 I12 **Shirkala, Gryada** plain W Kazakhstan
165 P10 **Shiroishi** var. Siroisi. Miyagi, Honshū, C Japan
Shirokoye see Shyroke
165 O10 **Shirone** var. Sirone. Niigata, Honshū, C Japan
164 L12 **Shirotori** Gifu, Honshū, SW Japan
197 T1 **Shirshov Ridge** undersea feature W Bering Sea
Shirshütür/Shirshyutyur, Peski see Şirşütür Gumy
143 T3 **Shīrvān** var. Shirwān. Khorāsān, NE Iran
Shirwa, Lake see Chilwa, Lake
Shirwān see Shīrvān
159 N5 **Shisanjianfang** Xinjiang Uygur Zizhiqu, W China
38 M16 **Shishaldin Volcano** ▲ Unimak Island, Alaska, USA
Shishchitsy see Shyshchytsy
38 M8 **Shishmaref** Alaska, USA
Shisur see Ash Shişar
164 L13 **Shitara** Aichi, Honshū, SW Japan
152 D12 **Shiv** Rājasthān, NW India
151 E15 **Shivāji Sāgar** prev. Konya Reservoir ⊠ W India
154 H8 **Shivpuri** Madhya Pradesh, C India
36 J9 **Shivwits Plateau** plain Arizona, SW USA
Shiwālik Range see Siwalik Range
160 M8 **Shiyan** Hubei, C China
Shizilu see Junan
160 H13 **Shizong** var. Danfeng. Yunnan, SW China
165 R10 **Shizugawa** Miyagi, Honshū, NE Japan
159 W8 **Shizuishan** var. Dawukou. Ningxia, N China
165 T5 **Shizunai** Hokkaidō, NE Japan
165 M14 **Shizuoka** var. Sizuoka. Shizuoka, Honshū, S Japan
164 M13 **Shizuoka** off. Shizuoka-ken, var. Sizuoka. ◆ prefecture Honshū, S Japan
Shklov see Shklow
119 N15 **Shklow** Rus. Shklov. Mahilyowskaya Voblasts', E Belarus
113 K18 **Shkodër** var. Shkodra, It. Scutari, SCr. Skadar. Shkodër, NW Albania
113 K17 **Shkodër** ◆ district NW Albania
Shkodra see Shkodër
Shkodrës, Liqeni i see Scutari, Lake
Shkumbi/Shkumbin see Shkumbinit, Lumi i
113 L20 **Shkumbinit, Lumi i** var. Shkumbî, Shkumbin. ≈ C Albania
Shligigh, Cuan see Sligo Bay
122 L4 **Shmidta, Ostrov** island Severnaya Zemlya, N Russian Federation
183 S10 **Shoalhaven River** ≈ New South Wales, SE Australia
11 W16 **Shoal Lake** Manitoba, S Canada
31 O15 **Shoals** Indiana, N USA
164 I13 **Shōdo-shima** island SW Japan
Shōka see Changhua
122 M5 **Shokal'skogo, Proliv** strait N Russian Federation
147 T14 **Shokhdara, Qatorkŭhi** Rus. Shakhdarinskiy Khrebet. ▲ SE Tajikistan
145 P17 **Sholakkorgan** var. Chulakkurgan. Yuzhnyy Kazakhstan, S Kazakhstan
145 N9 **Sholaksay** Kostanay, N Kazakhstan
Sholāpur see Solāpur
Sholdaneshty see Şoldăneşti
Shoqpar see Chokpar
155 G21 **Shoranūr** Kerala, SW India
155 G16 **Shorāpur** Karnātaka, C India
30 M11 **Shorewood** Illinois, N USA
Shorkazakhly, Solonchak see Kazakhlyshor, Solonchak
145 Q9 **Shortandy** Akmola, C Kazakhstan
Shortepa/Shor Tepe see Shūr Tappeh
186 J7 **Shortland Island** var. Alu. island NW Solomon Islands
Shosambetsu see Shosanbetsu
165 S2 **Shosanbetsu** var. Shosambetsu. Hokkaidō, NE Japan
33 O15 **Shoshone** Idaho, NW USA
35 T6 **Shoshone Mountains** ▲ Nevada, W USA
33 U12 **Shoshone River** ≈ Wyoming, C USA
83 I19 **Shoshong** Central, SE Botswana
33 V14 **Shoshoni** Wyoming, C USA
Shōshū see Sangju
117 S2 **Shostka** Sums'ka Oblast', NE Ukraine
185 C21 **Shotover** ≈ South Island, NZ
146 H9 **Shovot** Rus. Shavat. Xorazm Viloyati, W Uzbekistan
37 N12 **Show Low** Arizona, SW USA
Show Me State see Missouri
125 O4 **Shoyna** Nenetskiy Avtonomnyy Okrug, NW Russian Federation
124 M11 **Shozhma** Arkhangel'skaya Oblast', NW Russian Federation
117 Q7 **Shpola** Cherkas'ka Oblast', N Ukraine
Shqipëria/Shqipërisë, Republika e see Albania
22 G5 **Shreveport** Louisiana, S USA
97 K19 **Shrewsbury** hist. Scrobesbyrig'. W England, UK
152 D11 **Shri Mohangarh** prev. Sri Mohangorh. Rājasthān, NW India
153 S16 **Shrīrāmpur** prev. Serampore, Serampur. West Bengal, NE India
97 K19 **Shropshire** cultural region W England, UK
145 S16 **Shu** Kaz. Shū. Zhambyl, SE Kazakhstan
Shū see Chu
160 G13 **Shuangbai** var. Tuodian. Yunnan, SW China
163 W9 **Shuangcheng** Heilongjiang, NE China
Shuangcheng see Zherong
160 E14 **Shuangjiang** var. Weiyuan. Yunnan, SW China
Shuangjiang see Jiangkou
163 U10 **Shuangliao** var. Zhengjiatun. Jilin, NE China
Shuang-liao see Liaoyuan
163 Y7 **Shuangyashan** var. Shuang-ya-shan. Heilongjiang, NE China
Shu'aymiah see Shu'aymīyah
141 W12 **Shu'aymīyah** var. Shu'aymiah. S Oman
144 I10 **Shubarkuduk** Kaz. Shubarqudyq. Aktyubinsk, W Kazakhstan
Shubarqudyq see Shubarkuduk
145 N12 **Shubar-Tengiz, Ozero** ◎ C Kazakhstan
39 S5 **Shublik Mountains** ▲ Alaska, USA
Shubrā al Khaymah see Shubrâ el Kheima
121 U13 **Shubrâ el Kheima** var. Shubrā al Khaymah. N Egypt
158 E8 **Shufu** Xinjiang Uygur Zizhiqu, NW China
147 S14 **Shughnon, Qatorkŭhi** Rus. Shugnanskiy Khrebet. ▲ SE Tajikistan
Shugnanskiy Khrebet see Shughnon, Qatorkŭhi
161 Q6 **Shu He** ≈ E China
Shuiding see Huocheng
Shuidong see Dianbai
Shuiji see Laixi
Shū-Ile Taūlary see Chu-Iliyskiye Gory
Shuiluocheng see Zhuanglang
149 T10 **Shujāābād** Punjab, E Pakistan
163 W9 **Shulan** Jilin, NE China
158 E8 **Shule** Xinjiang Uygur Zizhiqu, NW China
Shuleh see Shule He
159 Q8 **Shule He** var. Shuleh, Sulo. ≈ C China
30 K9 **Shullsburg** Wisconsin, N USA
39 N16 **Shumagin Islands** island group Alaska, USA
146 G7 **Shumanay** Qoraqalpog'iston Respublikasi, W Uzbekistan
114 M8 **Shumen** Shumen, NE Bulgaria
114 M8 **Shumen** ◆ province NE Bulgaria
127 P4 **Shumerlya** Chuvashskaya Respublika, W Russian Federation
122 G11 **Shumikha** Kurganskaya Oblast', C Russian Federation
118 M12 **Shumilina** Rus. Shumilino. Vitsyebskaya Voblasts', NE Belarus
Shumilino see Shumilina
123 V11 **Shumshu, Ostrov** island SE Russian Federation
116 K5 **Shums'k** Ternopil's'ka Oblast', W Ukraine
39 O7 **Shungnak** Alaska, USA
Shunsen see Ch'unch'ŏn
Shuoxian see Shuozhou
161 N3 **Shuozhou** var. Shuoxian. Shanxi, C China
141 P16 **Shuqrah** var. Shaqrā. SW Yemen
Shurab see Shŭrob
147 R11 **Shŭrob** Rus. Shurab. NW Tajikistan
143 T10 **Shūr, Rūd-e** ≈ E Iran
149 O2 **Shūr Tappeh** var. Shortepa, Shor Tepe. Balkh, N Afghanistan
83 K17 **Shurugwi** prev. Selukwe. Midlands, C Zimbabwe
142 L8 **Shūsh** anc. Susa, Bibl. Shushan. Khūzestān, SW Iran
Shushan see Shūsh
142 L9 **Shūshtar** var. Shustar, Shushter. Khūzestān, SW Iran
Shushter/Shustar see Shūshtar
141 T9 **Shuţfah, Qalamat** well E Saudi Arabia
139 V9 **Shuwayjah, Hawr ash** var. Hawr as Suwayqiyah. ◎ E Iraq
124 M16 **Shuya** Ivanovskaya Oblast', W Russian Federation
39 Q14 **Shuyak Island** island Alaska, USA
166 M4 **Shwebo** Sagaing, C Myanmar
166 L7 **Shwedaung** Pegu, W Myanmar
166 M7 **Shwegyin** Pegu, SW Myanmar
167 N4 **Shweli** Chin. Longchuan Jiang. ≈ Myanmar/China
166 M6 **Shwemyo** Mandalay, C Myanmar
Shyghys Qazagastan Oblysy see Vostochnyy Kazakhstan
Shyghys Qongyrat see Shygys Konyrat
145 T12 **Shygys Konyrat** var. Vostochno-Kounradskiy, Kaz. Shyghys Qongyrat. Karaganda, C Kazakhstan
119 M19 **Shychy** Rus. Shichi. Homyel'skaya Voblasts', SE Belarus
145 Q17 **Shymkent** prev. Chimkent. Yuzhnyy Kazakhstan, S Kazakhstan
Shyngghyrlaū see Chingirlau
152 J5 **Shyok** Jammu and Kashmir, NW India
117 S9 **Shyroke** Rus. Shirokoye. Dnipropetrovs'ka Oblast', E Ukraine
117 O9 **Shyryayeve** Odes'ka Oblast', SW Ukraine
117 S5 **Shyshaky** Poltavs'ka Oblast', C Ukraine
119 K17 **Shyshchytsy** Rus. Shishchitsy. Minskaya Voblasts', C Belarus
149 Y3 **Siachen Muztāgh** ▲ NE Pakistan
Siadehan see Tākestān
148 M13 **Siāhān Range** ▲ W Pakistan
142 I1 **Siāh Chashmeh** Āžarbāyjān-e Bākhtarī, N Iran
149 W7 **Siālkot** Punjab, NE Pakistan
186 E7 **Sialum** Morobe, C PNG
Siam see Thailand
Siam, Gulf of see Thailand, Gulf of
Sian see Xi'an
Siang see Brahmaputra
Siangtan see Xiangtan
169 N8 **Siantan, Pulau** island Kepulauan Anambas, W Indonesia
54 H11 **Siare, Río** ≈ C Colombia
171 R6 **Siargao Island** island S Philippines
186 F7 **Siassi** Umboi Island, C PNG
115 D14 **Siátista** Dytikí Makedonía, N Greece
166 K4 **Siatlai** Chin State, W Myanmar
171 P6 **Siaton** Negros, C Philippines
171 P6 **Siaton Point** headland Negros, C Philippines
118 F11 **Šiauliai** Ger. Schaulen. Šiauliai, N Lithuania
118 E11 **Šiauliai** ◆ province N Lithuania
171 Q10 **Siau, Pulau** island N Indonesia
83 J15 **Siavonga** Southern, SE Zambia
Siazan' see Siyäzän
Sibah see As Sībah
107 N20 **Sibari** Calabria, S Italy
Sibata see Shibata
127 X6 **Sibay** Respublika Bashkortostan, W Russian Federation
93 M19 **Sibbo** Fin. Sipoo. Etelä-Suomi, S Finland
112 D13 **Šibenik** It. Sebenico. Šibenik-Knin, S Croatia
Šibenik see Šibenik-Knin
112 E13 **Šibenik-Knin** off. Šibenska Županija. var. Šibenik. ◆ province S Croatia
Šibenska Županija see Šibenik-Knin
Siberia see Sibir'
Siberoet see Siberut, Pulau
168 H12 **Siberut, Pulau** prev. Siberoet. island Kepulauan Mentawai, W Indonesia
168 I12 **Siberut, Selat** strait W Indonesia
Sibetu see Shibetsu
149 P11 **Sibi** Baluchistān, SW Pakistan
186 B9 **Sibidiri** Western, SW PNG
123 N10 **Sibir'** var. Siberia. physical region NE Russian Federation
122 J13 **Sibirskiy** Altayskiy Kray, S Russian Federation
79 F20 **Sibiti** La Lékoumou, S Congo
81 G21 **Sibiti** ≈ C Tanzania
116 I12 **Sibiu** Ger. Hermannstadt, Hung. Nagyszeben. Sibiu, C Romania
116 I11 **Sibiu** ◆ county C Romania
29 S11 **Sibley** Iowa, C USA
169 R9 **Sibu** Sarawak, East Malaysia
Sibukawa see Shibukawa
42 G2 **Sibun** ≈ E Belize
79 I15 **Sibut** prev. Fort-Sibut. Kémo, S Central African Republic
171 P4 **Sibuyan Island** island C Philippines
171 P4 **Sibuyan Sea** sea C Philippines
189 U1 **Sibylla Island** island N Marshall Islands
11 N16 **Sicamous** British Columbia, SW Canada
Sichelburger Gebirge see Gorjanci/Žumberačko Gorje
167 N14 **Sichon** var. Ban Sichon, Si Chon. Nakhon Si Thammarat, SW Thailand
160 H9 **Sichuan** var. Chuan, Sichuan Sheng, Ssu-ch'uan, Szechuan, Szechwan. ◆ province C China
160 I9 **Sichuan Pendi** basin C China
Sichuan Sheng see Sichuan
103 S16 **Sicie, Cap** headland SE France
107 J24 **Sicilia** Eng. Sicily; anc. Trinacria. ◆ region Italy, C Mediterranean Sea
107 M24 **Sicilia** Eng. Sicily; anc. Trinacria. island Italy, C Mediterranean Sea
Sicilian Channel see Sicily, Strait of
Sicily see Sicilia
107 H24 **Sicily, Strait of** var. Sicilian Channel. strait C Mediterranean Sea
42 K5 **Sico Tinto, Río** var. Río Negro. ≈ NE Honduras
57 H16 **Sicuani** Cusco, S Peru
112 J10 **Šid** Serbia, NW Serbia and Montenegro (Yugo.)
115 A15 **Sidári** Kérkyra, Iónioi Nísoi, Greece, C Mediterranean Sea
169 Q11 **Sidas** Borneo, C Indonesia
98 O5 **Siddeburen** Groningen, NE Netherlands
154 D9 **Siddhapur** prev. Siddhpur, Sidhpur. Gujarāt, W India
Siddhpur see Siddhapur
155 I15 **Siddipet** Andhra Pradesh, C India
77 N14 **Sidéradougou** SW Burkina
107 N23 **Siderno** Calabria, SW Italy
Siders see Sierre
154 L9 **Sidhi** Madhya Pradesh, C India
Sidhirókastron see Sidirókastro
Sidhpur see Siddhapur
Sīdī al Hānī', Sabkhat see Sidi el Hani, Sebkhet de
75 U7 **Sidi Barrâni** NW Egypt
74 I6 **Sidi Bel Abbès** var. Sidi bel Abbès, Sidi-Bel-Abbès. NW Algeria
74 E7 **Sidi-Bennour** W Morocco
74 M6 **Sidi Bouzid** var. Gammouda, Sīdī Bu Zayd. C Tunisia
74 D8 **Sidi-Ifni** SW Morocco
74 G6 **Sidi-Kacem** prev. Petitjean. N Morocco
114 G12 **Sidirókastro** prev. Sidhirókastron. Kentrikí Makedonía, NE Greece
194 L12 **Sidley, Mount** ▲ Antarctica
29 S16 **Sidney** Iowa, C USA
33 Y7 **Sidney** Montana, NW USA
28 J15 **Sidney** Nebraska, C USA
18 I11 **Sidney** New York, NE USA
31 R13 **Sidney** Ohio, N USA
23 T2 **Sidney Lanier, Lake** ⊠ Georgia, SE USA
Sidon see Saïda
122 J9 **Sidorovsk** Yamalo-Nenetskiy Avtonomnyy Okrug, N Russian Federation
Sidra/Sidra, Gulf of see Surt, Khalīj, N Libya
Sidra see Surt, N Libya
Sīdī Bu Zayd see Sidi Bouzid
Siebenbürgen see Transylvania
Sieben Dörfer see Săcele
110 O12 **Siedlce** Ger. Sedlez, Rus. Sesdlets. Mazowieckie, C Poland
101 E16 **Sieg** ≈ W Germany
101 F16 **Siegen** Nordrhein-Westfalen, W Germany
109 X4 **Sieghartskirchen** Niederösterreich, E Austria
110 O11 **Siemiatycze** Podlaskie, NE Poland
167 T11 **Siĕmpang** Stœ̆ng Trêng, NE Cambodia
167 R11 **Siĕmréab** prev. Siemreap. Siĕmréab, NW Cambodia
Siemreap see Siĕmréab
106 G12 **Siena** Fr. Sienne; anc. Saena Julia. Toscana, C Italy
Sienne see Siena
92 K12 **Sieppijärvi** Lappi, NW Finland
110 J13 **Sieradz** Sieradz, C Poland
110 K10 **Sierpc** Mazowieckie, C Poland
24 I9 **Sierra Blanca** Texas, SW USA
37 S14 **Sierra Blanca Peak** ▲ New Mexico, SW USA
35 P5 **Sierra City** California, W USA
63 I16 **Sierra Colorada** Río Negro, S Argentina
62 I13 **Sierra del Nevado** ▲ W Argentina
63 J16 **Sierra Grande** Río Negro, S Argentina
76 G15 **Sierra Leone** off. Republic of Sierra Leone. ◆ republic W Africa
64 M13 **Sierra Leone Basin** undersea feature E Atlantic Ocean
66 K8 **Sierra Leone Fracture Zone** tectonic feature E Atlantic Ocean
Sierra Leone Ridge see Sierra Leone Rise
64 L13 **Sierra Leone Rise** var. Sierra Leone Ridge, Sierra Leone Schwelle. undersea feature E Atlantic Ocean
Sierra Leone Schwelle see Sierra Leone Rise
41 U17 **Sierra Madre** var. Sierra de Soconusco. ▲ Guatemala/Mexico
37 R2 **Sierra Madre** ▲ Colorado/Wyoming, C USA
(0) H15 **Sierra Madre del Sur** ▲ S Mexico
(0) G13 **Sierra Madre Occidental** var. Western Sierra Madre. ▲ C Mexico
(0) H13 **Sierra Madre Oriental** var. Eastern Sierra Madre. ▲ C Mexico
44 H8 **Sierra Maestra** ▲ E Cuba
40 L7 **Sierra Mojada** Coahuila de Zaragoza, NE Mexico
105 O14 **Sierra Nevada** ▲ S Spain
35 P6 **Sierra Nevada** ▲ W USA
54 F4 **Sierra Nevada de Santa Marta** ▲ NE Colombia
42 K5 **Sierra Río Tinto** ▲ NE Honduras
24 J10 **Sierra Vieja** ▲ Texas, SW USA
37 N16 **Sierra Vista** Arizona, SW USA
108 D10 **Sierre** Ger. Siders. Valais, SW Switzerland
36 L16 **Sierrita Mountains** ▲ Arizona, SW USA
Siete Moai see Ahu Akivi
76 M15 **Sifié** W Ivory Coast
115 I21 **Sífnos** anc. Siphnos. island Kykládes, Greece, Aegean Sea
115 I21 **Sífnou, Stenó** strait SE Greece
Siga see Shiga
103 P16 **Sigean** Aude, S France
Sighet see Sighetu Marmaţiei
Sighetul Marmaţiei see Sighetu Marmaţiei
116 I8 **Sighetu Marmaţiei** var. Sighet, Sighetul Marmaţiei, Hung. Máramarossziget. Maramureş, N Romania
116 I11 **Sighişoara** Ger. Schässburg, Hung. Segesvár. Mureş, C Romania
168 G7 **Sigli** Sumatera, W Indonesia
92 J1 **Siglufjördhur** Nordhurland Vestra, N Iceland
101 H23 **Sigmaringen** Baden-Württemberg, S Germany
101 N20 **Signalberg** ▲ SE Germany
36 I13 **Signal Peak** ▲ Arizona, SW USA
Signan see Xi'an
194 H1 **Signy** UK research station South Orkney Islands, Antarctica
29 X15 **Sigourney** Iowa, C USA
115 K17 **Sígri, Akrotírio** headland Lésvos, E Greece
Sigsbee Deep see Mexico Basin
47 N2 **Sigsbee Escarpment** undersea feature N Gulf of Mexico
56 C8 **Sigsig** Azuay, S Ecuador
95 O15 **Sigtuna** Stockholm, C Sweden
42 H6 **Siguatepeque** Comayagua, W Honduras
105 P7 **Sigüenza** Castilla-La Mancha, C Spain
105 R4 **Sigües** Aragón, NE Spain
76 K13 **Siguiri** Haute-Guinée, NE Guinea
118 G8 **Sigulda** Ger. Segewold. Rīga, C Latvia
Sihanoukville see Kâmpóng Saôm
108 G8 **Sihlsee** ◎ NW Switzerland
93 K18 **Siikainen** Länsi-Suomi, W Finland
93 M16 **Siilinjärvi** Itä-Suomi, C Finland
137 R15 **Siirt** var. Sert; anc. Tigranocerta. Siirt, SE Turkey
137 R15 **Siirt** var. Sert. ◆ province SE Turkey
187 N8 **Sikaiana** var. Stewert Islands. island group W Solomon Islands
Sikandarabad see Secunderābād
152 J11 **Sikandra Rao** Uttar Pradesh, N India
10 M11 **Sikanni Chief** British Columbia, W Canada
10 M11 **Sikanni Chief** ≈ British Columbia, W Canada
152 H11 **Sīkar** Rājasthān, N India
76 M13 **Sikasso** Sikasso, S Mali
76 L13 **Sikasso** ◆ region SW Mali
167 N3 **Sikaw** Kachin State, C Myanmar
83 H14 **Sikelenge** Western, W Zambia
27 Y7 **Sikeston** Missouri, C USA
93 J14 **Sikfors** Norrbotten, N Sweden
123 T14 **Sikhote-Alin', Khrebet** ▲ SE Russian Federation
Siking see Xi'an
115 J22 **Síkinos** island Kykládes, Greece, Aegean Sea
153 S11 **Sikkim** Tib. Denjong. ◆ state N India
111 I26 **Siklós** Baranya, SW Hungary
Sikoku see Shikoku
Sikoku Basin see Shikoku Basin
83 G14 **Sikongo** Western, W Zambia
Sikotu Ko see Shikotsu-ko
Sikouri/Sikoúrion see Sykoúri
123 P8 **Siktyakh** Respublika Sakha (Yakutiya), NE Russian Federation
118 D12 **Šilalė** Tauragė, W Lithuania
106 G5 **Silandro** Ger. Schlanders. Trentino-Alto Adige, N Italy
41 N12 **Silao** Guanajuato, C Mexico
Silarius see Sele
153 W14 **Silchar** Assam, NE India
108 G9 **Silenen** Uri, C Switzerland
21 T9 **Siler City** North Carolina, SE USA
33 U11 **Silesia** Montana, NW USA
110 F13 **Silesia** physical region SW Poland
74 K12 **Silet** S Algeria
145 R8 **Sileti** var. Selety. ≈ N Kazakhstan
Siletitengiz see Siletiteniz, Ozero
145 R7 **Siletiteniz, Ozero** Kaz. Siletitengiz. ◎ N Kazakhstan
172 H16 **Silhouette** island Inner Islands, SE Seychelles
136 I17 **Silifke** anc. Seleucia. İçel, S Turkey
Siliguri see Shiliguri
156 J10 **Siling Co** ◎ W China
Silinhot see Xilinhot
192 G15 **Silisili** ▲ Savai'i, C Samoa
114 M6 **Silistra** var. Silistria; anc. Durostorum. Silistra, NE Bulgaria
116 M7 **Silistra** ◆ province NE Bulgaria
Silistria see Silistra
136 D10 **Silivri** İstanbul, NW Turkey
94 L13 **Siljan** ◎ C Sweden
95 G22 **Silkeborg** Århus, C Denmark
108 M8 **Sill** ≈ W Austria
105 S10 **Silla** País Valenciano, E Spain
62 H3 **Sillajguay, Cordillera** ▲ N Chile
118 K3 **Sillamäe** Ger. Sillamäggi. Ida-Virumaa, NE Estonia
Sillamäggi see Sillamäe
Sillein see Žilina
109 P9 **Sillian** Tirol, W Austria
112 B10 **Šilo** Primorje-Gorski Kotar, NW Croatia
27 R9 **Siloam Springs** Arkansas, C USA
25 X10 **Silsbee** Texas, SW USA
143 W15 **Sīlūp, Rūd-e** ≈ SE Iran
118 C12 **Šilutė** Ger. Heydekrug. Klaipėda, W Lithuania
137 Q15 **Silvan** Dıyarbakır, SE Turkey
108 J10 **Silvaplana** Graubünden, S Switzerland
Silva Porto see Kuito
58 M12 **Silva, Recife do** reef E Brazil
154 D12 **Silvassa** Dādra and Nagar Haveli, W India
29 X4 **Silver Bay** Minnesota, N USA
37 P15 **Silver City** New Mexico, SW USA
18 D10 **Silver Creek** New York, NE USA
37 N12 **Silver Creek** ≈ Arizona, SW USA
27 P4 **Silver Lake** Kansas, C USA
32 I14 **Silver Lake** Oregon, NW USA
35 T9 **Silver Peak Range** ▲ Nevada, W USA
21 W3 **Silver Spring** Maryland, NE USA
Silver State see Nevada
Silver State see Colorado
37 Q7 **Silverton** Colorado, C USA
18 K16 **Silverton** New Jersey, NE USA
32 G11 **Silverton** Oregon, NW USA
25 N4 **Silverton** Texas, SW USA
104 G14 **Silves** Faro, S Portugal
54 D12 **Silvia** Cauca, SW Colombia
108 J9 **Silvrettagruppe** ▲ Austria/Switzerland
Sily-Vajdej see Vulcan
108 L7 **Silz** Tirol, W Austria
172 I13 **Sima** Anjouan, SE Comoros
Simabara see Shimabara
Simada see Shimada
83 H15 **Simakando** Western, W Zambia
Simane see Shimane
119 L20 **Simanichy** Rus. Simonichi. Homyel'skaya Voblasts', SE Belarus
160 F14 **Simao** Yunnan, SW China
152 J12 **Simara** Central, C Nepal
14 I8 **Simard, Lac** ◎ Québec, SE Canada
136 D13 **Simav** Kütahya, W Turkey
136 D13 **Simav Çayı** ≈ NW Turkey
79 L18 **Simba** Orientale, N Dem. Rep. Congo
186 C7 **Simbai** Madang, N PNG
Simbirsk see Ul'yanovsk
14 F17 **Simcoe** Ontario, S Canada
14 H14 **Simcoe, Lake** ◎ Ontario, S Canada
80 J11 **Sīmēn** ▲ N Ethiopia
114 K11 **Simeonovgrad** prev. Maritsa. Khaskovo, S Bulgaria
116 G11 **Simeria** Ger. Pischk, Hung. Piski. Hunedoara, W Romania
107 L24 **Simeto** ≈ Sicilia, Italy, C Mediterranean Sea
168 G9 **Simeulue, Pulau** island NW Indonesia
117 T13 **Simferopol'** Respublika Krym, S Ukraine
117 T13 **Simferopol'** ✈ Respublika Krym, S Ukraine
Simi see Sými
152 M9 **Simikot** Far Western, NW Nepal
54 F7 **Simití** Bolívar, N Colombia
114 G11 **Simitla** Blagoevgrad, SW Bulgaria
35 S15 **Simi Valley** California, W USA
Simizu see Shimizu
Simla see Shimla
Şimlăul Silvaniei/Şimleul Silvaniei see Şimleu Silvaniei
116 G9 **Şimleu Silvaniei** Hung. Szilágysomlyó; prev. Şimlăul Silvaniei, Şimleul Silvaniei. Sălaj, NW Romania
Simmer see Simmerbach
101 E19 **Simmerbach** var. Simmer. ≈ W Germany
101 F18 **Simmern** Rheinland-Pfalz, W Germany
22 I7 **Simmesport** Louisiana, S USA
119 F14 **Simnas** Alytus, S Lithuania
92 L13 **Simo** Lappi, NW Finland
Simoda see Shimoda
Simodate see Shimodate
92 M13 **Simojärvi** ◎ N Finland
92 L13 **Simojoki** ≈ NW Finland
41 U15 **Simojovel** var. Simojovel de Allende. Chiapas, SE Mexico
Simojovel de Allende see Simojovel
56 B7 **Simon Bolivar** var. Guayaquil. ✈ (Quayaquil) Guayas, W Ecuador
54 L5 **Simon Bolívar** ✈ (Caracas) Distrito Federal, N Venezuela
Simonichi see Simanichy
14 M12 **Simon, Lac** ◎ Québec, SE Canada
Simonoseki see Shimonoseki
Šimonovany see Partizánske
Simonstad see Simon's Town
83 E26 **Simon's Town** var. Simonstad. Western Cape, SW South Africa
Simony see Partizánske
Simotuma see Shimotsuma
Simpeln see Simplon
99 M18 **Simpelveld** Limburg, SE Netherlands
108 E11 **Simplon** var. Simpeln. Valais, SW Switzerland
108 E11 **Simplon Pass** pass S Switzerland
106 C6 **Simplon Tunnel** tunnel Italy/Switzerland
Simpson see Fort Simpson
182 G1 **Simpson Desert** desert Northern Territory/South Australia
10 J9 **Simpson Peak** ▲ British Columbia, W Canada
9 N7 **Simpson Peninsula** peninsula Nunavut, NE Canada
21 P11 **Simpsonville** South Carolina, SE USA
95 L23 **Simrishamn** Skåne, S Sweden
123 U13 **Simushir, Ostrov** island Kuril'skiye Ostrova, SE Russia
Sinā'/Sinai Peninsula see Sinai
168 G9 **Sinabang** Sumatera, W Indonesia
81 N15 **Sina Dhaqa** Galguduud, C Somalia
75 X8 **Sinai** var. Sinai Peninsula, Ar. Shibh Jazīrat Sīnā', Sīnā'. physical region NE Egypt
116 J12 **Sinaia** Prahova, SE Romania
188 B16 **Sinajana** C Guam
40 H8 **Sinaloa** ◆ state C Mexico
54 H4 **Sinamaica** Zulia, NW Venezuela
163 X14 **Sinan-ni** SE North Korea
Sinano Gawa see Shinano-gawa
Sīnāwan see Sīnāwin
75 N8 **Sīnāwin** var. Sīnāwan. NW Libya
83 J16 **Sinazongwe** Southern, S Zambia
166 L6 **Sinbaungwe** Magwe, W Myanmar
166 L5 **Sinbyugyun** Magwe, W Myanmar
54 E6 **Since** Sucre, NW Colombia
54 E6 **Sincelejo** Sucre, N Colombia
166 J5 **Sinchaingbyin** var. Zullapara. Arakan State, W Myanmar
23 U4 **Sinclair, Lake** ⊠ Georgia, SE USA
10 M14 **Sinclair Mills** British Columbia, SW Canada
149 Q14 **Sind** var. Sindh. ◆ province SE Pakistan
154 I8 **Sind** ≈ N India
95 H19 **Sindal** Nordjylland, N Denmark
171 P7 **Sindañgan** Mindanao, S Philippines
79 D19 **Sindara** Ngounié, W Gabon
152 E13 **Sindari** prev. Sindri. Rājasthān, N India
114 N8 **Sindel** Varna, E Bulgaria
101 H22 **Sindelfingen** Baden-Württemberg, SW Germany
155 G16 **Sindgi** Karnātaka, C India
Sindh see Sind
118 G5 **Sindi** Ger. Zintenhof. Pärnumaa, SW Estonia

◆ COUNTRY ● COUNTRY CAPITAL ◇ DEPENDENT TERRITORY ○ DEPENDENT TERRITORY CAPITAL ◆ ADMINISTRATIVE REGION ✈ INTERNATIONAL AIRPORT ▲ MOUNTAIN ▲ MOUNTAIN RANGE ▲ VOLCANO ≈ RIVER ◎ LAKE ⊠ RESERVOIR

136 C13 **Sındırgı** Balıkesir, W Turkey
77 N14 **Sindou** SW Burkina
Sindri see Sindari
149 T9 **Sind Sāgar Doāb** desert E Pakistan
126 M11 **Sinegorskiy** Rostovskaya Oblast', SW Russian Federation
123 S9 **Sinegor'ye** Magadanskaya Oblast', E Russian Federation
114 O12 **Sinekli** İstanbul, NW Turkey
104 F12 **Sines** Setúbal, S Portugal
104 F12 **Sines, Cabo de** headland S Portugal
92 L12 **Sinettä** Lappi, NW Finland
186 H6 **Sinewit, Mount** ▲ New Britain, C PNG
80 G11 **Singa** var. Sinja, Sinjah. Sinnar, E Sudan
78 J12 **Singako** Moyen-Chari, S Chad
Singan see Xi'an
168 K10 **Singapore** ● (Singapore) S Singapore
168 L10 **Singapore** off. Republic of Singapore. ◆ republic SE Asia
168 L10 **Singapore Strait** var. Strait of Singapore, Mal. Selat Singapura. strait Indonesia/Singapore
Singapore, Strait of/Singapura, Selat see Singapore Strait
169 U17 **Singaraja** Bali, C Indonesia
Singatoka see Sigatoka
167 O10 **Sing Buri** var. Singhaburi. Sing Buri, C Thailand
101 H24 **Singen** Baden-Württemberg, S Germany
Singeorgiu de Pădure see Sângeorgiu de Pădure
Singeorz-Băi/Singeroz Băi see Sângeorz-Băi
116 M9 **Singerei** var. Sângerei; prev. Lazovsk. N Moldova
Singhaburi see Sing Buri
81 H21 **Singida** Singida, C Tanzania
81 G22 **Singida** ◈ region C Tanzania
Singidunum see Beograd
166 M2 **Singkaling Hkamti** Sagaing, N Myanmar
171 N14 **Singkang** Sulawesi, C Indonesia
168 J11 **Singkarak, Danau** ◎ Sumatera, W Indonesia
169 N10 **Singkawang** Borneo, C Indonesia
168 M11 **Singkep, Pulau** island Kepulauan Lingga, W Indonesia
168 H9 **Singkilbaru** Sumatera, W Indonesia
183 T7 **Singleton** New South Wales, SE Australia
Singora see Songkhla
Singû see Shingū
Sining see Xining
107 D17 **Siniscola** Sardegna, Italy, C Mediterranean Sea
113 F14 **Sinj** Split-Dalmacija, SE Croatia
Sinja/Sinjah see Singa
Sinjajevina see Sinjavina
139 P3 **Sinjār** NW Iraq
139 P2 **Sinjār, Jabal** ▲ N Iraq
113 K15 **Sinjavina** var. Sinjajevina. ▲ SW Serbia and Montenegro (Yugo.)
80 I7 **Sinkat** Red Sea, NE Sudan
Sinkiang/Sinkiang Uighur Autonomous Region see Xinjiang Uygur Zizhiqu
Sinmartin see Târnăveni
163 V13 **Sinmi-do** island NW North Korea
Sinminato see Shinminato
101 I18 **Sinn** ≈ C Germany
Sinnamarie see Sinnamary
55 Y9 **Sinnamary** var. Sinnamarie. N French Guiana
Sinn'anyô see Shinnanyō
80 G11 **Sinnar** ◈ state E Sudan
Sinneh see Sanandaj
18 E13 **Sinnemahoning Creek** ≈ Pennsylvania, NE USA
Sinnicolau Mare see Sânnicolau Mare
Sino/Sinoe see Greenville
Sinoe, Lacul see Sinoie, Lacul
Sinoia see Chinhoyi
117 N14 **Sinoie, Lacul** prev. Lacul Sinoe. lagoon SE Romania
59 H16 **Sinop** Mato Grosso, W Brazil
136 K10 **Sinop** anc. Sinope. Sinop, N Turkey
136 J10 **Sinop** ◈ province N Turkey
136 K10 **Sinop Burnu** headland N Turkey
Sinope see Sinop
163 Y12 **Sinp'o** E North Korea
101 H20 **Sinsheim** Baden-Württemberg, SW Germany
Sinsiro see Shinshiro
Sintana see Sântana
169 R11 **Sintang** Borneo, C Indonesia
99 F14 **Sint Annaland** Zeeland, SW Netherlands
98 L5 **Sint Annaparochie** Friesland, N Netherlands
45 V9 **Sint Eustatius** Eng. Saint Eustatius. island N Netherlands Antilles
99 G19 **Sint-Genesius-Rode** Fr. Rhode-Saint-Genèse. Vlaams Brabant, C Belgium
99 F16 **Sint-Gillis-Waas** Oost-Vlaanderen, N Belgium
99 H17 **Sint-Katelijne-Waver** Antwerpen, C Belgium
99 E18 **Sint-Lievens-Houtem** Oost-Vlaanderen, NW Belgium
45 V9 **Sint Maarten** Eng. Saint Martin. island N Netherlands Antilles
99 F14 **Sint Maartensdijk** Zeeland, SW Netherlands
99 L19 **Sint-Martens-Voeren** Fr. Fouron-Saint-Martin. Limburg, NE Belgium
99 J14 **Sint-Michielsgestel** Noord-Brabant, S Netherlands
Sînt-Miclăuş see Gheorgheni
45 O16 **Sint Nicholaas** S Aruba
99 F16 **Sint-Niklaas** Fr. Saint-Nicolas. Oost-Vlaanderen, N Belgium
99 K14 **Sint-Oedenrode** Noord-Brabant, S Netherlands
25 T14 **Sinton** Texas, SW USA
99 G14 **Sint Philipsland** Zeeland, SW Netherlands
99 G19 **Sint-Pieters-Leeuw** Vlaams Brabant, C Belgium
104 E11 **Sintra** prev. Cintra. Lisboa, W Portugal
99 J18 **Sint-Truiden** Fr. Saint-Trond. Limburg, NE Belgium
99 H14 **Sint Willebrord** Noord-Brabant, S Netherlands
163 V13 **Sinŭiju** W North Korea
80 P13 **Sinujiif** Nugaal, NE Somalia
Sinus Aelaniticus see Aqaba, Gulf of
Sinus Gallicus see Lion, Golfe du
Sinyang see Xinyang
Sinyavka see Sinyawka
119 I18 **Sinyawka** Rus. Sinyavka. Minskaya Voblasts', SW Belarus
Sinying see Hsinying
Sinyukha see Synyukha
Sinzi-ko see Shinji-ko
Sinzyô see Shinjō
111 I24 **Sió** ≈ W Hungary
171 O7 **Siocon** Mindanao, S Philippines
111 I24 **Siófok** Somogy, C Hungary
Siogama see Shiogama
83 G15 **Sioma** Western, SW Zambia
108 D11 **Sion** Ger. Sitten; anc. Sedunum. Valais, SW Switzerland
103 O11 **Sioule** ≈ C France
29 S12 **Sioux Center** Iowa, C USA
29 R13 **Sioux City** Iowa, C USA
29 R11 **Sioux Falls** South Dakota, N USA
12 B11 **Sioux Lookout** Ontario, S Canada
29 T12 **Sioux Rapids** Iowa, C USA
Sioux State see North Dakota
Sioziri see Shiojiri
171 P6 **Sipalay** Negros, C Philippines
55 V11 **Sipaliwini** ◈ district S Suriname
45 U15 **Siparia** Trinidad, Trinidad and Tobago
Siphnos see Sífnos
163 V11 **Siping** var. Ssu-p'ing, Szeping; prev. Ssu-p'ing-chieh. Jilin, NE China
11 X12 **Sipiwesk** Manitoba, C Canada
11 W13 **Sipiwesk Lake** ◎ Manitoba, C Canada
195 O11 **Siple Coast** physical region Antarctica
194 K12 **Siple Island** island Antarctica
194 K13 **Siple, Mount** ▲ Siple Island, Antarctica
Sipoo see Sibbo
112 G12 **Šipovo** Republika Srpska, W Bosnia and Herzegovina
23 O4 **Sipsey River** ≈ Alabama, S USA
168 I13 **Sipura, Pulau** island W Indonesia
(0) G16 **Siqueiros Fracture Zone** tectonic feature E Pacific Ocean
42 L10 **Siquia, Río** ≈ SE Nicaragua
43 N13 **Siquirres** Limón, E Costa Rica
54 J5 **Siquisique** Lara, N Venezuela
155 G19 **Sīra** Karnātaka, W India
95 D16 **Sira** ≈ S Norway
167 P12 **Siracha** var. Ban Si Racha, Si Racha. Chon Buri, S Thailand
107 L25 **Siracusa** Eng. Syracuse. Sicilia, Italy, C Mediterranean Sea
Sirajganj see Shirajganj Ghat
Sirakawa see Shirakawa
11 N14 **Sir Alexander, Mount** ▲ British Columbia, W Canada
137 O12 **Şiran** Gümüşhane, NE Turkey
77 Q12 **Sirba** ≈ E Burkina
143 O17 **Şīr Banī Yās** island W UAE
95 D17 **Sirdalsvannet** ◎ S Norway
Sir Darya/Sirdaryo see Syr Darya
147 P10 **Sirdaryo** Sirdaryo Viloyati, E Uzbekistan
147 O11 **Sirdaryo Viloyati** Rus. Syrdar'inskaya Oblast'. ◈ province E Uzbekistan
Sir Donald Sangster International Airport see Sangster
181 S3 **Sir Edward Pellew Group** island group Northern Territory, NE Australia
116 K8 **Siret** Ger. Sereth, Hung. Szeret. Suceava, N Romania
116 K8 **Siret** var. Siretul, Ger. Sereth, Rus. Seret, Ukr. Siret. ≈ Romania/Ukraine
Siretul see Siret
140 K3 **Sirḥān, Wādī as** dry watercourse Jordan/Saudi Arabia
152 I8 **Sirhind** Punjab, N India
116 F11 **Şiria** Ger. Schiria. Arad, W Romania
Siria see Syria
143 S14 **Sīrīk** Hormozgān, SE Iran
167 P8 **Sirikit Reservoir** ⊠ N Thailand
58 K12 **Sirituba, Ilha** island NE Brazil
143 R11 **Sīrjān** prev. Sa'īdābād. Kermān, S Iran
182 H9 **Sir Joseph Banks Group** island group South Australia
92 K11 **Sirkka** Lappi, N Finland
Sirna see Sýrna
137 R16 **Şırnak** Şırnak, SE Turkey
137 S16 **Şırnak** ◈ province SE Turkey
Siroisi see Shiroishi
155 J14 **Sironcha** Mahārāshtra, C India
Sirone see Shirone
Síros see Sýros
Sirotino see Sirotsina
118 M12 **Sirotsina** Rus. Sirotino. Vitsyebskaya Voblasts', N Belarus
152 H9 **Sirsa** Haryāna, NW India
173 Y17 **Sir Seewoosagur Ramgoolam** × (Port Louis) SE Mauritius
155 E18 **Sirsi** Karnātaka, W India
146 K12 **Şirşütür Gumy** var. Shirshütür, Rus. Peski Shirshyutyur. desert E Turkmenistan
Sirte see Surt
182 A2 **Sir Thomas, Mount** ▲ South Australia
Sirti, Gulf of see Surt, Khalīj
142 J5 **Sīrvān, Rūdkhāneh-ye** var. Nahr Diyālá, Sirwan. ≈ Iran/Iraq see also Diyālá, Nahr
118 H13 **Širvintos** Vilnius, SE Lithuania
Sirwan see Diyālá, Nahr/Sīrvān, Rūdkhāneh-ye
11 N15 **Sir Wilfrid Laurier, Mount** ▲ British Columbia, SW Canada
14 M10 **Sir-Wilfrid, Mont** ▲ Québec, SE Canada
Sisačko-Moslavačka Županija see Sisak-Moslavina
112 E9 **Sisak** var. Siscia, Ger. Sissek, Hung. Sziszek; anc. Segestica. Sisak-Moslavina, C Croatia
167 R10 **Si Sa Ket** var. Sisaket, Sri Saket. Si Sa Ket, E Thailand
112 E9 **Sisak-Moslavina** off. Sisačko-Moslavačka Županija. ◈ province C Croatia
167 O8 **Si Satchanala** Sukhothai, NW Thailand
Siscia see Sisak
83 G22 **Sishen** Northern Cape, NW South Africa
137 V13 **Sisian** SE Armenia
197 N13 **Sisimiut** var. Holsteinborg, Holsteinsborg, Holstenborg, Holstensborg. Kitaa, S Greenland
30 M1 **Siskiwit Bay** lake bay Michigan, N USA
34 L1 **Siskiyou Mountains** ▲ California/Oregon, W USA
167 Q11 **Sisŏphŏn** Bătdâmbâng, NW Cambodia
108 E7 **Sissach** Basel-Land, NW Switzerland
186 B5 **Sissano** Sandaun, NW PNG
Sissek see Sisak
29 R7 **Sisseton** South Dakota, N USA
143 W9 **Sīstān, Daryācheh-ye** var. Daryācheh-ye Hāmūn, Hāmūn-e Şāberī. ◎ Afghanistan/Iran see also Şāberī, Hāmūn-e
143 V12 **Sīstān va Balūchestān** off. Ostān-e Sīstān va Balūchestān, var. Balūchestān va Sīstān. ◈ province SE Iran
103 T14 **Sisteron** Alpes-de-Haute-Provence, SE France
32 H13 **Sisters** Oregon, NW USA
65 G15 **Sisters Peak** ▲ N Ascension Island
21 R3 **Sistersville** West Virginia, NE USA
Sistova see Svishtov
Sitakund see Sitakunda
153 V16 **Sitakunda** var. Sitakund. Chittagong, SE Bangladesh
153 P12 **Sītāmarhi** Bihār, N India
152 L11 **Sītāpur** Uttar Pradesh, N India
Sitaș Cristuru see Cristuru Secuiesc
115 L25 **Siteía** var. Sitía. Kríti, Greece, E Mediterranean Sea
105 V6 **Sitges** Cataluña, NE Spain
115 H15 **Sithonía** peninsula NE Greece
Sitía see Siteía
54 F4 **Sitionuevo** Magdalena, N Colombia
39 X13 **Sitka** Baranof Island, Alaska, USA
39 Q15 **Sitkinak Island** island Trinity Islands, Alaska, USA
166 M7 **Sittang** var. Sittoung. ≈ S Myanmar
99 L17 **Sittard** Limburg, SE Netherlands
Sitten see Sion
108 H7 **Sitter** ≈ NW Switzerland
109 U10 **Sittersdorf** Kärnten, S Austria
Sittoung see Sittang
166 K6 **Sittwe** var. Akyab. Arakan State, W Myanmar
42 L8 **Siuna** Región Autónoma Atlántico Norte, NE Nicaragua
153 R15 **Siuri** West Bengal, NE India
Siut see Asyût
123 Q13 **Sivaki** Amurskaya Oblast', SE Russian Federation
136 M13 **Sivas** anc. Sebastia, Sebaste. Sivas, C Turkey
136 M13 **Sivas** ◈ province C Turkey
137 O15 **Siverek** Şanlıurfa, S Turkey
117 X6 **Sivers'k** Donets'ka Oblast', E Ukraine
124 G13 **Siverskiy** Leningradskaya Oblast', NW Russian Federation
117 X6 **Sivers'kyy Donets'** Rus. Severskiy Donets. ≈ Russian Federation/Ukraine see also Severskiy Donets
125 W5 **Sivomaskinskiy** Respublika Komi, NW Russian Federation
136 G13 **Sivrihisar** Eskişehir, W Turkey
99 F22 **Sivry** Hainaut, S Belgium
123 V9 **Sivuchiy, Mys** headland E Russian Federation
75 U9 **Siwa** var. Sīwah. NW Egypt
Sīwah see Siwa
152 J9 **Siwalik Range** var. Shiwālik Range. ▲ India/Nepal
153 O13 **Siwān** Bihār, N India
43 O14 **Sixaola, Río** ≈ Costa Rica/Panama
Six Counties, The see Northern Ireland
103 T16 **Six-Fours-les-Plages** Var, SE France
161 Q7 **Sixian** var. Si Xian. Anhui, E China
22 J9 **Six Mile Lake** ◎ Louisiana, S USA
139 V3 **Siyāh Gūz** E Iraq
155 L25 **Siyambalanduwa** Uva Province, SE Sri Lanka
137 Y10 **Siyäzän** Rus. Siazan'. NE Azerbaijan
Sizebolu see Sozopol
Sizuoka see Shizuoka
Sjar see Sääre
113 L15 **Sjenica** Turk. Seniça. Serbia, SW Serbia and Montenegro (Yugo.)
94 G11 **Sjoa** ≈ S Norway
95 K23 **Sjöbo** Skåne, S Sweden
95 I24 **Sjælland** Eng. Zealand, Ger. Seeland. island E Denmark
94 E9 **Sjøholt** Møre og Romsdal, S Norway
92 O1 **Sjuøyane** island group N Svalbard
Skadar see Shkodër
Skadarsko Jezero see Scutari, Lake
117 R11 **Skadovs'k** Khersons'ka Oblast', S Ukraine
92 I2 **Skagaströnd** prev. Höfdhakaupstadhur. Nordhurland Vestra, N Iceland
95 H19 **Skagen** Nordjylland, N Denmark
Skagerak see Skagerrak
95 L16 **Skagern** ◎ C Sweden
197 T17 **Skagerrak** var. Skagerak. channel N Europe
94 G12 **Skaget** ▲ S Norway
32 H7 **Skagit River** ≈ Washington, NW USA
39 W12 **Skagway** Alaska, USA
92 K8 **Skáidi** Finnmark, N Norway
115 F21 **Skála** Pelopónnisos, S Greece
116 K6 **Skalat** Pol. Skałat. Ternopil's'ka Oblast', W Ukraine
95 J22 **Skälderviken** inlet Denmark/Sweden
124 J3 **Skalistyy** Murmanskaya Oblast', NW Russian Federation
92 I12 **Skalka** ◎ N Sweden
114 I12 **Skalotí** Anatolikí Makedonía kai Thráki, NE Greece
95 G22 **Skanderborg** Århus, C Denmark
95 K22 **Skåne** Eng. Scania. ◈ county S Sweden
75 N6 **Skanès** × (Sousse) E Tunisia
95 C15 **Skånevik** Hordaland, S Norway
95 M18 **Skänninge** Östergötland, S Sweden
95 J23 **Skanör med Falsterbo** Skåne, S Sweden
115 H17 **Skantzoúra** island Vóreioi Sporádes, Greece, Aegean Sea
95 K18 **Skara** Västra Götaland, S Sweden
95 M17 **Skärblacka** Östergötland, S Sweden
95 I18 **Skärhamn** Västra Götaland, S Sweden
95 I14 **Skarnes** Hedmark, S Norway
119 M21 **Skarodnaye** Rus. Skorodnoye. Homyel'skaya Voblasts', SE Belarus
110 I8 **Skarszewy** Ger. Schöneck. Pomorskie, NW Poland
111 M14 **Skarżysko-Kamienna** Świętokrzyskie, C Poland
95 K16 **Skattkärr** Värmland, C Sweden
118 D12 **Skaudvilė** Tauragė, SW Lithuania
92 J12 **Skaulo** Lapp. Sávdijári. Norrbotten, N Sweden
111 K17 **Skawina** Małopolskie, S Poland
10 K12 **Skeena** ≈ British Columbia, SW Canada
10 I11 **Skeena Mountains** ▲ British Columbia, W Canada
97 O18 **Skegness** E England, UK
92 J4 **Skeidharársandur** coast S Iceland
93 J15 **Skellefteå** Västerbotten, N Sweden
93 I14 **Skellefteälven** ≈ N Sweden
93 J15 **Skelleftehamn** Västerbotten, N Sweden
25 O2 **Skellytown** Texas, SW USA
95 J19 **Skene** Västra Götaland, S Sweden
97 G17 **Skerries** Ir. Na Sceirí. E Ireland
95 H15 **Ski** Akershus, S Norway
115 G17 **Skíathos** Skíathos, Vóreioi Sporádes, Greece, Aegean Sea
115 G17 **Skíathos** island Vóreioi Sporádes, Greece, Aegean Sea
27 P9 **Skiatook** Oklahoma, C USA
27 P9 **Skiatook Lake** ⊠ Oklahoma, C USA
97 B22 **Skibbereen** Ir. An Sciobairín. SW Ireland
92 I9 **Skibotn** Troms, N Norway
119 F16 **Skidal'** Rus. Skidel'. Hrodzyenskaya Voblasts', W Belarus
97 K15 **Skiddaw** ▲ NW England, UK
Skidel' see Skidal'
25 T14 **Skidmore** Texas, SW USA
95 G16 **Skien** Telemark, S Norway
Skiermûntseach see Schiermonnikoog
110 L12 **Skierniewice** Łodzkie, C Poland
74 L5 **Skikda** prev. Philippeville. NE Algeria
30 M16 **Skillet Fork** ≈ Illinois, N USA
95 L19 **Skillingaryd** Jönköping, S Sweden
115 B19 **Skinári, Akrotírio** headland Zákynthos, Iónioi Nísoi, Greece, C Mediterranean Sea
95 M15 **Skinnskatteberg** Västmanland, C Sweden
182 M12 **Skipton** Victoria, SE Australia
97 L16 **Skipton** N England, UK
Skiropoula see Skyropoúla
Skíros see Skýros
95 F21 **Skive** Viborg, NW Denmark
94 F11 **Skjåk** Oppland, S Norway
92 K2 **Skjálfandafljót** ≈ C Iceland
95 F22 **Skjern** Ringkøbing, W Denmark
95 F22 **Skjern Å** var. Skjern Aa. ≈ W Denmark
Skjern Aa see Skjern Å
92 G12 **Skjerstad** Nordland, C Norway
92 J8 **Skjervøy** Troms, N Norway
92 I10 **Skjold** Troms, N Norway
111 I17 **Skoczów** Śląskie, S Poland
95 I24 **Skælskør** Vestsjælland, E Denmark
109 T11 **Škofja Loka** Ger. Bischoflack. NW Slovenia
94 N12 **Skog** Gävleborg, C Sweden
95 K16 **Skoghall** Värmland, C Sweden
31 N10 **Skokie** Illinois, N USA
116 H6 **Skole** L'vivs'ka Oblast', W Ukraine
115 D19 **Skóllis** ▲ S Greece
167 S13 **Skon** Kâmpóng Cham, C Cambodia
115 H17 **Skópelos** Skópelos, Vóreioi Sporádes, Greece, Aegean Sea
115 H17 **Skópelos** island Vóreioi Sporádes, Greece, Aegean Sea
126 L5 **Skopin** Ryazanskaya Oblast', W Russian Federation
113 N18 **Skopje** var. Üsküb, Turk. Üsküp; prev. Skoplje, anc. Scupi. ● (FYR Macedonia) N FYR Macedonia
113 O18 **Skopje** × N FYR Macedonia
Skoplje see Skopje
110 I8 **Skórcz** Ger. Skurz. Pomorskie, N Poland
Skorodnoye see Skarodnaye
93 H16 **Skorped** Västernorrland, C Sweden
95 G21 **Skørping** Nordjylland, N Denmark
95 K18 **Skövde** Västra Götaland, S Sweden
123 Q13 **Skovorodino** Amurskaya Oblast', SE Russian Federation
19 Q6 **Skowhegan** Maine, NE USA
11 W15 **Skownan** Manitoba, S Canada
94 H13 **Skreia** Oppland, S Norway
Skripón see Orchómenos
118 H9 **Skrīveri** Aizkraukle, S Latvia
118 J11 **Skrudaliena** Daugvapils, SE Latvia
118 D9 **Skrunda** Kuldīga, W Latvia
95 C16 **Skudeneshavn** Rogaland, S Norway
83 L20 **Skukuza** Mpumalanga, NE South Africa
97 B22 **Skull** Ir. An Scoil. SW Ireland
22 L3 **Skuna River** ≈ Mississippi, S USA
29 X15 **Skunk River** ≈ Iowa, C USA
118 C10 **Skuodas** Ger. Schoden, Pol. Szkudy. Klaipėda, NW Lithuania
95 K23 **Skurup** Skåne, S Sweden
Skurz see Skórcz
114 H8 **Skŭt** ≈ NW Bulgaria
94 O13 **Skutskär** Uppsala, C Sweden
95 B19 **Skúvoy** Dan. Skuø Island Faeroe Islands
Skvira see Skvyra
117 O5 **Skvyra** Rus. Skvira. Kyyivs'ka Oblast', N Ukraine
39 Q11 **Skwentna** Alaska, USA
110 E11 **Skwierzyna** Ger. Schwerin. Lubuskie, W Poland
36 K13 **Sky Harbour** × (Phoenix) Arizona, SW USA
96 G9 **Skye, Isle of** island NW Scotland, UK
32 I8 **Skykomish** Washington, NW USA
Skylge see Terschelling
63 F19 **Skyring, Peninsula** peninsula S Chile
63 H24 **Skyring, Seno** inlet S Chile
115 H17 **Skyropoúla** var. Skiropoula. island Vóreioi Sporádes, Greece, Aegean Sea
115 I17 **Skýros** var. Skíros. Skýros, Vóreioi Sporádes, Greece, Aegean Sea
115 I17 **Skýros** var. Skíros; anc. Scyros. island Vóreioi Sporádes, Greece, Aegean Sea
118 J12 **Slabodka** Rus. Slobodka. Vitsyebskaya Voblasts', NW Belarus
95 I23 **Slagelse** Vestsjælland, E Denmark
93 I14 **Slagnäs** Norrbotten, N Sweden
39 T10 **Slana** Alaska, USA
97 F20 **Slaney** Ir. An tSláine. ≈ SE Ireland
116 J13 **Slănic** Prahova, SE Romania
116 K11 **Slănic Moldova** Bacău, E Romania
113 H16 **Slano** Dubrovnik-Neretva, SE Croatia
124 F13 **Slantsy** Leningradskaya Oblast', NW Russian Federation
111 C16 **Slaný** Ger. Schlan. Střední Čechy, NW Czech Republic
111 I16 **Śląskie** ◈ province S Poland
12 C10 **Slate Falls** Ontario, S Canada
27 T4 **Slater** Missouri, C USA
112 H9 **Slatina** Hung. Szlatina prev. Podravska Slatina. Virovitica-Podravina, NE Croatia
116 I14 **Slatina** Olt, S Romania
25 N5 **Slaton** Texas, SW USA
95 H14 **Slattum** Akershus, S Norway
11 R10 **Slave** ≈ Alberta/Northwest Territories, C Canada
68 E11 **Slave Coast** coastal region W Africa
11 P13 **Slave Lake** Alberta, SW Canada
122 I13 **Slavgorod** Altayskiy Kray, S Russian Federation
Slavgorod see Slawharad
Slavonia see Slavonija
112 G9 **Slavonija** Eng. Slavonia, Ger. Slawonien, Hung. Szlavonia, Szlavonország. cultural region NE Croatia
Slavonska Požega see Požega,
112 H10 **Slavonski Brod** Ger. Brod, Hung. Bród; prev. Brod, Brod na Savi. Brod-Posavina, NE Croatia
116 L4 **Slavuta** Khmel'nyts'ka Oblast', NW Ukraine
117 P2 **Slavutych** Chernihivs'ka Oblast', N Ukraine
123 R15 **Slavyanka** Primorskiy Kray, SE Russian Federation
114 J8 **Slavyanovo** Pleven, N Bulgaria
Slavyansk see Slov"yans'k
126 K14 **Slavyansk-na-Kubani** Krasnodarskiy Kray, SW Russian Federation
119 N20 **Slavyechna** Rus. Slovechna. ≈ Belarus/Ukraine
119 O16 **Slawharad** Rus. Slavgorod. Mahilyowskaya Voblasts', E Belarus
110 G7 **Sławno** Zachodnio-pomorskie, NW Poland
Slawonien see Slavonija
29 S10 **Slayton** Minnesota, N USA
97 N18 **Sleaford** E England, UK
97 A20 **Slea Head** Ir. Ceann Sléibhe. headland SW Ireland
96 G9 **Sleat, Sound of** strait NW Scotland, UK
Sledyuki see Slyedzyuki
12 I5 **Sleeper Islands** island group Nunavut, C Canada
31 O6 **Sleeping Bear Point** headland Michigan, N USA
29 T10 **Sleepy Eye** Minnesota, N USA
39 O11 **Sleetmute** Alaska, USA
Sléibhe, Ceann see Slea Head
Slēmānī see As Sulaymānīyah
195 O5 **Slessor Glacier** glacier Antarctica
22 L9 **Slidell** Louisiana, S USA
18 K12 **Slide Mountain** ▲ New York, NE USA
98 I13 **Sliedrecht** Zuid-Holland, C Netherlands
121 P16 **Sliema** N Malta
97 G16 **Slieve Donard** ▲ SE Northern Ireland, UK
Sligeach see Sligo
97 D16 **Sligo** Ir. Sligeach. NW Ireland
97 C16 **Sligo** Ir. Sligeach. cultural region NW Ireland
97 C15 **Sligo Bay** Ir. Cuan Shligigh. inlet NW Ireland
18 B13 **Slippery Rock** Pennsylvania, NE USA
95 P19 **Slite** Gotland, SE Sweden
114 L9 **Sliven** var. Slivno. Sliven, C Bulgaria
114 L10 **Sliven** ◈ province C Bulgaria
114 G9 **Slivnitsa** Sofiya, W Bulgaria
Slivno see Sliven
114 L7 **Slivo Pole** Ruse, N Bulgaria
29 S13 **Sloan** Iowa, C USA
35 X12 **Sloan** Nevada, W USA
Slobodka see Slabodka
125 R14 **Slobodskoy** Kirovskaya Oblast', NW Russian Federation
Slobodzeya see Slobozia
117 O10 **Slobozia** Rus. Slobodzeya. E Moldova
116 L14 **Slobozia** Ialomița, SE Romania
98 O5 **Slochteren** Groningen, NE Netherlands
119 H17 **Slonim** Pol. Słonim, Rus. Slonim. Hrodzyenskaya Voblasts', W Belarus
98 K7 **Sloter Meer** ◎ N Netherlands
Slot, The see New Georgia Sound
97 N22 **Slough** S England, UK
111 J20 **Slovakia** off. Slovenská Republika, Ger. Slowakei, Hung. Szlovákia, Slvk. Slovensko. ◆ republic C Europe
Slovak Ore Mountains see Slovenské rudohorie
Slovechna see Slavyechna
109 S12 **Slovenia** off. Republic of Slovenia, Ger. Slowenien, Slvn. Slovenija. ◆ republic SE Europe
Slovenija see Slovenia
109 V10 **Slovenj Gradec** Ger. Windischgraz. N Slovenia
109 W10 **Slovenska Bistrica** Ger. Windischfeistritz. NE Slovenia
Slovenská Republika see Slovakia
109 W10 **Slovenske Konjice** E Slovenia
111 K20 **Slovenské rudohorie** Eng. Slovak Ore Mountains, Ger. Slowakisches Erzgebirge, Ungarisches Erzgebirge. ▲ C Slovakia
Slovensko see Slovakia
117 Y7 **Slov"yanoserbs'k** Luhans'ka Oblast', E Ukraine
117 W6 **Slov"yans'k** Rus. Slavyansk. Donets'ka Oblast', E Ukraine
Slowakei see Slovakia
Slowakisches Erzgebirge see Slovenské rudohorie
Slowenien see Slovenia
110 D11 **Słubice** Ger. Frankfurt. Lubuskie, W Poland
119 K19 **Sluch** Rus. Sluch'. ≈ C Belarus
116 L4 **Sluch** ≈ NW Ukraine
99 D16 **Sluis** Zeeland, SW Netherlands
112 D10 **Slunj** Hung. Szluin. Karlovac, C Croatia
110 I11 **Słupca** Wielkolpolskie, C Poland
110 G6 **Słupia** Ger. Stolpe. ≈ NW Poland
110 G6 **Słupsk** Ger. Stolp. Pomorskie, N Poland
119 K18 **Slutsk** Rus. Slutsk. Minskaya Voblasts', S Belarus
119 O16 **Slyedzyuki** Rus. Sledyuki. Mahilyowskaya Voblasts', E Belarus
97 A17 **Slyne Head** Ir. Ceann Léime. headland W Ireland
27 U14 **Smackover** Arkansas, C USA
95 L20 **Småland** cultural region S Sweden
95 K20 **Smålandsstenar** Jönköping, S Sweden
Small Malaita see Maramasike
13 O8 **Smallwood Reservoir** ⊠ Newfoundland and Labrador, S Canada
119 N14 **Smalyany** Rus. Smolyany. Vitsyebskaya Voblasts', NE Belarus
119 L15 **Smalyavichy** Rus. Smolevichi. Minskaya Voblasts', C Belarus
74 C9 **Smara** var. Es Semara. N Western Sahara
119 I14 **Smarhon'** Pol. Smorgonie, Rus. Smorgon'. Hrodzyenskaya Voblasts', W Belarus
112 M11 **Smederevo** Ger. Semendria. Serbia, N Serbia and Montenegro (Yugo.)
112 M12 **Smederevska Palanka** Serbia, C Serbia and Montenegro (Yugo.)
95 M14 **Smedjebacken** Dalarna, C Sweden
116 L13 **Smeeni** Buzău, SE Romania
Smela see Smila
107 D16 **Smeralda, Costa** cultural region Sardegna, Italy, C Mediterranean Sea

◆ COUNTRY ◇ DEPENDENT TERRITORY ◈ ADMINISTRATIVE REGION ▲ MOUNTAIN ▲ VOLCANO ◎ LAKE
● COUNTRY CAPITAL ○ DEPENDENT TERRITORY CAPITAL × INTERNATIONAL AIRPORT ▲ MOUNTAIN RANGE ≈ RIVER ⊠ RESERVOIR

111 J22 **Śmigiel** *Ger.* Schmiegel. Wielkolpolskie, C Poland
117 Q6 **Smila** *Rus.* Smela. Cherkas'ka Oblast', C Ukraine
98 N7 **Smilde** Drenthe, NE Netherlands
11 S16 **Smiley** Saskatchewan, S Canada
25 T12 **Smiley** Texas, SW USA
Smilten *see* Smiltene
118 I8 **Smiltene** *Ger.* Smilten. Valka, N Latvia
123 T13 **Smirnykh** Ostrov Sakhalin, Sakhalinskaya Oblast', SE Russian Federation
11 Q13 **Smith** Alberta, W Canada
39 P4 **Smith Bay** *bay* Alaska, USA
12 I3 **Smith, Cape** *headland* Québec, NE Canada
26 L3 **Smith Center** Kansas, C USA
10 K13 **Smithers** British Columbia, SW Canada
21 V10 **Smithfield** North Carolina, SE USA
36 L1 **Smithfield** Utah, W USA
21 X7 **Smithfield** Virginia, NE USA
12 I3 **Smith Island** *island* Nunavut, C Canada
Smith Island *see* Sumisu-jima
20 H7 **Smithland** Kentucky, S USA
21 T7 **Smith Mountain Lake** *var.* Leesville Lake. ▣ Virginia, NE USA
34 L1 **Smith River** California, W USA
33 R9 **Smith River** ≈ Montana, NW USA
14 L13 **Smiths Falls** Ontario, SE Canada
33 N13 **Smiths Ferry** Idaho, NW USA
20 K7 **Smiths Grove** Kentucky, S USA
183 N15 **Smithton** Tasmania, SE Australia
18 L14 **Smithtown** Long Island, New York, NE USA
20 K9 **Smithville** Tennessee, S USA
25 T11 **Smithville** Texas, SW USA
Šmohor *see* Hermagor
35 Q4 **Smoke Creek Desert** *desert* Nevada, W USA
11 O14 **Smoky** ≈ Alberta, W Canada
182 E7 **Smoky Bay** South Australia
183 V6 **Smoky Cape** *headland* New South Wales, SE Australia
26 L4 **Smoky Hill River** ≈ Kansas, C USA
26 L4 **Smoky Hills** *hill range* Kansas, C USA
11 Q14 **Smoky Lake** Alberta, SW Canada
94 E8 **Smøla** *island* W Norway
126 H4 **Smolensk** Smolenskaya Oblast', W Russian Federation
126 H4 **Smolenskaya Oblast'** ◈ *province* W Russian Federation
Smolensk-Moscow Upland *see* Smolensko-Moskovskaya Vozvyshennost'
126 J3 **Smolensko-Moskovskaya Vozvyshennost'** *var.* Smolensk-Moscow Upland. ▲▲ W Russian Federation
Smolevichi *see* Smalyavichy
115 C15 **Smolikás** ▲ W Greece
114 I12 **Smolyan** *prev.* Pashmakli. Smolyan, S Bulgaria
114 I12 **Smolyan** ◈ *province* S Bulgaria
Smolyany *see* Smalyany
33 S15 **Smoot** Wyoming, C USA
12 G12 **Smooth Rock Falls** Ontario, S Canada
Smorgon'/Smorgonie *see* Smarhon'
95 K23 **Smygehamn** Skåne, S Sweden
194 I7 **Smyley Island** *island* Antarctica
21 Y3 **Smyrna** Delaware, NE USA
23 S3 **Smyrna** Georgia, SE USA
20 J9 **Smyrna** Tennessee, S USA
Smyrna *see* İzmir
97 I16 **Snaefell** ▲ C Isle of Man
92 H3 **Snaefellsjökull** ▲ W Iceland
10 J4 **Snake** ≈ Yukon Territory, NW Canada
29 O8 **Snake Creek** ≈ South Dakota, N USA
183 P13 **Snake Island** *island* Victoria, SE Australia
35 Y6 **Snake Range** ▲▲ Nevada, W USA
32 K10 **Snake River** ≈ NW USA
29 V6 **Snake River** ≈ Minnesota, N USA
28 L12 **Snake River** ≈ Nebraska, C USA
33 Q14 **Snake River Plain** *plain* Idaho, NW USA
93 F15 **Snåsa** Nord-Trøndelag, C Norway
21 O8 **Sneedville** Tennessee, S USA
98 K6 **Sneek** Friesland, N Netherlands
Sneeuw-gebergte *see* Maoke, Pegunungan
95 F22 **Snejbjerg** Ringkøbing, C Denmark
122 G11 **Snezhinsk** Chelyabinskaya Oblast', W Russian Federation
124 J3 **Snezhnogorsk** Murmanskaya Oblast', NW Russian Federation
122 K9 **Snezhnogorsk** Taymyrskiy (Dolgano-Nenetskiy) Avtonomnyy Okrug, N Russian Federation
Snezhnoye *see* Snizhne
111 G15 **Sněžka** *Ger.* Schneekoppe, *Pol.* Śnieżka. ▲ Czech Republic/Poland
110 N8 **Śniardwy, Jezioro** *Ger.* Spirdingsee. ◎ NE Poland
Sniečkus *see* Visaginas
Śnieżka *see* Sněžka
117 R10 **Snihurivka** Mykolayivs'ka Oblast', S Ukraine
116 I5 **Snilov** ✈ (L'viv) L'vivs'ka Oblast', W Ukraine
111 O19 **Snina** *Hung.* Szinna. Prešovský Kraj, E Slovakia
117 Y8 **Snizhne** *Rus.* Snezhnoye. Donets'ka Oblast', SE Ukraine
92 J3 **Snækollur** ▲ C Iceland
94 G10 **Snøhetta** *var.* Snohetta. ▲ S Norway
92 G12 **Snøtinden** ▲ C Norway
97 I18 **Snowdon** ▲ NW Wales, UK
97 I18 **Snowdonia** ▲▲ NW Wales, UK
8 K10 **Snowdrift** ≈ Northwest Territories, NW Canada
Snowdrift *see* Łutselk'e
37 N12 **Snowflake** Arizona, SW USA
21 Y5 **Snow Hill** Maryland, NE USA
21 W10 **Snow Hill** North Carolina, SE USA
194 H3 **Snowhill Island** *island* Antarctica
11 V13 **Snow Lake** Manitoba, C Canada
37 R5 **Snowmass Mountain** ▲ Colorado, C USA
18 M10 **Snow, Mount** ▲ Vermont, NE USA
34 M5 **Snow Mountain** ▲ California, W USA
Snow Mountains *see* Maoke, Pegunungan
33 N7 **Snowshoe Peak** ▲ Montana, NW USA
182 I8 **Snowtown** South Australia
36 K1 **Snowville** Utah, W USA
35 X3 **Snow Water Lake** ◎ Nevada, W USA
183 Q11 **Snowy Mountains** ▲▲ New South Wales/Victoria, SE Australia
183 Q12 **Snowy River** ≈ New South Wales/Victoria, SE Australia
44 K5 **Snug Corner** Acklins Island, SE Bahamas
167 T13 **Snuŏl** Krâchéh, E Cambodia
116 J7 **Snyatyn** *Rus.* Snyatyn. Ivano-Frankivs'ka Oblast', W Ukraine
26 L12 **Snyder** Oklahoma, C USA
25 O6 **Snyder** Texas, SW USA
172 H3 **Soalala** Mahajanga, W Madagascar
172 J4 **Soanierana-Ivongo** Toamasina, E Madagascar
171 R11 **Soasiu** *var.* Tidore. Pulau Tidore, E Indonesia
54 G8 **Soatá** Boyacá, C Colombia
172 I5 **Soavinandriana** Antananarivo, C Madagascar
77 V13 **Soba** Kaduna, C Nigeria
163 Y16 **Sobaek-sanmaek** ▲▲ S South Korea
80 F13 **Sobat** ≈ E Sudan
171 Z14 **Sobger, Sungai** ≈ Papua, E Indonesia
171 V13 **Sobiei** Papua, E Indonesia
126 M3 **Sobinka** Vladimirskaya Oblast', W Russian Federation
127 S7 **Sobolevo** Orenburgskaya Oblast', W Russian Federation
Soborsin *see* Săvârşin
164 D15 **Sobo-san** ▲ Kyūshū, SW Japan
111 G14 **Sobótka** Dolnośląskie, SW Poland
59 O15 **Sobradinho** Bahia, E Brazil
Sobradinho, Barragem de *see* Sobradinho, Represa de
59 O16 **Sobradinho, Represa de** *var.* Barragem de Sobradinho. ▣ E Brazil
58 O13 **Sobral** Ceará, E Brazil
105 T4 **Sobrarbe** *physical region* NE Spain
109 R10 **Soča** *It.* Isonzo. ≈ Italy/Slovenia
110 L11 **Sochaczew** Mazowieckie, C Poland
126 L15 **Sochi** Krasnodarskiy Kray, SW Russian Federation
114 G13 **Sochós** *var.* Sohos, Sokhós. Kentrikí Makedonía, N Greece
191 R11 **Société, Archipel de la** *var.* Archipel de Tahiti, Îles de la Société, *Eng.* Society Islands. *island group* W French Polynesia
Société, Îles de la/Society Islands *see* Société, Archipel de la
21 T11 **Society Hill** South Carolina, SE USA
175 W9 **Society Ridge** *undersea feature* C Pacific Ocean
62 I5 **Socompa, Volcán** ▲ N Chile
Soconusco, Sierra de *see* Sierra Madre
54 G8 **Socorro** Santander, C Colombia
37 R13 **Socorro** New Mexico, SW USA
Socotra *see* Suquṭrā
167 S14 **Soc Trăng** *var.* Khanh Hung. Soc Trăng, S Vietnam
105 P10 **Socuéllamos** Castilla-La Mancha, C Spain
35 W13 **Soda Lake** *salt flat* California, W USA
92 L11 **Sodankylä** Lappi, N Finland
Sodari *see* Sodiri
33 R15 **Soda Springs** Idaho, NW USA
Soddo/Soddu *see* Sodo
20 L10 **Soddy Daisy** Tennessee, S USA
95 N14 **Söderfors** Uppsala, C Sweden
94 N12 **Söderhamn** Gävleborg, C Sweden
95 N17 **Söderköping** Östergötland, S Sweden
95 N17 **Södermanland** ◈ *county* C Sweden
95 O16 **Södertälje** Stockholm, C Sweden
80 D10 **Sodiri** *var.* Sawdirī, Sodari. Northern Kordofan, C Sudan
81 I14 **Sodo** *var.* Soddo, Soddu. Southern, S Ethiopia
94 N11 **Södra Dellen** ◎ C Sweden
95 M19 **Södra Vi** Kalmar, S Sweden
18 G9 **Sodus Point** *headland* New York, NE USA
171 Q17 **Soe** *prev.* Soë. Timor, C Indonesia
169 N15 **Soekarno-Hatta** ✈ (Jakarta) Jawa, S Indonesia
Soëla-Sund *see* Soela Väin
118 E5 **Soela Väin** *prev. Eng.* Sele Sound, *Ger.* Dagden-Sund, Soëla-Sund. *strait* W Estonia
Soemba *see* Sumba, Pulau
Soembawa *see* Sumbawa
Soemenep *see* Sumenep
Soengaipenoeh *see* Sungaipenuh
Soerabaja *see* Surabaya
101 G14 **Soest** Nordrhein-Westfalen, W Germany
98 J11 **Soest** Utrecht, C Netherlands
100 F11 **Soeste** ≈ NW Germany
98 J11 **Soesterberg** Utrecht, C Netherlands
115 E16 **Sofádes** *var.* Sofádhes. Thessalía, C Greece
Sofádhes *see* Sofádes
83 N18 **Sofala** Sofala, C Mozambique
83 N17 **Sofala** ◈ *province* C Mozambique
83 N18 **Sofala, Baia de** *bay* E Mozambique
172 J3 **Sofia** *seasonal river* NW Madagascar
Sofia *see* Sofiya
115 G19 **Sofikó** Pelopónnisos, S Greece
Sofi-Kurgan *see* Sopu-Korgon
114 G10 **Sofiya** *var.* Sophia, *Eng.* Sofia; *Lat.* Serdica. ● (Bulgaria) Sofiya-Grad, W Bulgaria
114 G9 **Sofiya** ✈ Sofiya-Grad, W Bulgaria
114 H9 **Sofiya** ◈ *province* W Bulgaria
114 G9 **Sofiya-Grad** ◈ *municipality* W Bulgaria
Sofiyevka *see* Sofiyivka
117 S8 **Sofiyivka** *Rus.* Sofiyevka. Dnipropetrovs'ka Oblast', E Ukraine
123 R13 **Sofiysk** Khabarovskiy Kray, SE Russian Federation
123 S12 **Sofiysk** Khabarovskiy Kray, SE Russian Federation
124 I6 **Sofporog** Respublika Kareliya, NW Russian Federation
165 Y14 **Sōfu-gan** *island* Izu-shotō, SE Japan
156 K10 **Sog** Xizang Zizhiqu, W China
54 G9 **Sogamoso** Boyacá, C Colombia
136 I11 **Soğanlı Çayı** ≈ N Turkey
94 E12 **Sogn** *physical region* S Norway
94 E12 **Sogndal** *see* Sogndalsfjøra.
94 E12 **Sogndalsfjøra** *var.* Sogndal. Sogn og Fjordane, S Norway
95 E18 **Søgne** Vest-Agder, S Norway
94 D12 **Sognefjorden** *fjord* NE North Sea
94 C12 **Sogn Og Fjordane** ◈ *county* S Norway
162 I11 **Sogo Nur** ◎ N China
159 T12 **Sogruma** Qinghai, W China
163 X17 **Sŏgwip'o** S South Korea
75 X10 **Sohâg** *var.* Sawhāj, Suliag. C Egypt
Sohar *see* Şuḩār
64 H9 **Sohm Plain** *undersea feature* NW Atlantic Ocean
100 H7 **Soholmer Au** ≈ N Germany
Sohos *see* Sochós
Sohrau *see* Żory
99 F20 **Soignies** Hainaut, SW Belgium
159 R15 **Soila** Xizang Zizhiqu, W China
103 P4 **Soissons** *anc.* Augusta Suessionum, Noviodunum. Aisne, N France
164 H13 **Sōja** Okayama, Honshū, SW Japan
152 F13 **Sojat** Rājasthān, N India
163 W13 **Sŏjosŏn-man** *inlet* W North Korea
116 I4 **Sokal'** *Rus.* Sokal. L'vivs'ka Oblast', NW Ukraine
163 Y14 **Sokch'o** N South Korea
136 B15 **Söke** Aydın, SW Turkey
189 N12 **Sokehs Island** *island* E Micronesia
79 M24 **Sokele** Katanga, SE Dem. Rep. Congo
147 R11 **Sokh** *Uzb.* Sŭkh. ≈ Kyrgyzstan/Uzbekistan
Sokh *see* So'x
Sokhós *see* Sochós
137 Q8 **Sokhumi** *Rus.* Sukhumi. NW Georgia
113 O14 **Sokobanja** Serbia, E Serbia and Montenegro (Yugo.)
77 R15 **Sokodé** C Togo
123 T10 **Sokol** Magadanskaya Oblast', E Russian Federation
124 M13 **Sokol** Vologodskaya Oblast', NW Russian Federation
110 P9 **Sokółka** Podlaskie, NE Poland
76 M11 **Sokolo** Ségou, W Mali
111 A16 **Sokolov** *Ger.* Falkenau an der Eger; *prev.* Falknov nad Ohří. Karlovarský Kraj, W Czech Republic
111 O16 **Sokołów Małopolski** Podkarpackie, SE Poland
110 O11 **Sokołów Podlaski** Mazowieckie, E Poland
76 G11 **Sokone** W Senegal
77 T12 **Sokoto** Sokoto, NW Nigeria
77 T12 **Sokoto** ◈ *state* NW Nigeria
77 S12 **Sokoto** ≈ NW Nigeria
Sokotra *see* Suquṭrā
147 U7 **Sokuluk** Chuyskaya Oblast', N Kyrgyzstan
116 L7 **Sokyryany** Chernivets'ka Oblast', W Ukraine
95 C16 **Sola** Rogaland, S Norway
187 R12 **Sola** Vanua Lava, N Vanuatu
95 C17 **Sola** ✈ (Stavanger) Rogaland, S Norway
81 H18 **Solai** Rift Valley, W Kenya
152 I8 **Solan** Himāchal Pradesh, N India
185 A25 **Solander Island** *island* SW NZ
Solano *see* Bahía Solano
155 F15 **Solāpur** *var.* Sholāpur. Mahārāshtra, W India
93 H16 **Solberg** Västernorrland, C Sweden
116 K9 **Solca** *Ger.* Solka. Suceava, N Romania
105 O16 **Sol, Costa del** *coastal region* S Spain
106 F5 **Solda** *Ger.* Sulden. Trentino-Alto Adige, N Italy
117 N9 **Şoldăneşti** *Rus.* Sholdaneshty. N Moldova
Soldau *see* Wkra
108 L8 **Sölden** Tirol, W Austria
27 P3 **Soldier Creek** ≈ Kansas, C USA
39 R12 **Soldotna** Alaska, USA
110 I10 **Solec Kujawski** Kujawsko-pomorskie, C Poland
61 B16 **Soledad** Santa Fe, C Argentina
55 E4 **Soledad** Atlántico, N Colombia
35 O11 **Soledad** California, W USA
55 O7 **Soledad** Anzoátegui, NE Venezuela
Soledad *see* East Falkland
Soledad, Isla *see* East Falkland
61 H15 **Soledade** Rio Grande do Sul, S Brazil
103 Y15 **Solenzara** Corse, France, C Mediterranean Sea
Soleure *see* Solothurn
94 C12 **Solheim** Hordaland, S Norway
127 N14 **Soligalich** Kostromskaya Oblast', NW Russian Federation
Soligorsk *see* Salihorsk
97 L20 **Solihull** C England, UK
125 U13 **Solikamsk** Permskaya Oblast', NW Russian Federation
127 V8 **Sol'-Iletsk** Orenburgskaya Oblast', W Russian Federation
57 G17 **Solimana, Nevado** ▲ S Peru
58 E13 **Solimões, Rio** ≈ C Brazil
113 E14 **Solin** *It.* Salona; *anc.* Salonae. Split-Dalmacija, S Croatia
101 E15 **Solingen** Nordrhein-Westfalen, W Germany
Solka *see* Solca
93 H16 **Sollefteå** Västernorrland, C Sweden
95 O15 **Sollentuna** Stockholm, C Sweden
94 L13 **Sollerön** Dalarna, C Sweden
101 I14 **Solling** *hill range* C Germany
95 O16 **Solna** Stockholm, C Sweden
126 K3 **Solnechnogorsk** Moskovskaya Oblast', W Russian Federation
123 R10 **Solnechnyy** Khabarovskiy Kray, SE Russian Federation
122 K13 **Solnechnyy** Krasnoyarskiy Kray, C Russian Federation
123 S13 **Solnechnyy** Respublika Sakha (Yakutiya), NE Russian Federation
107 L17 **Solofra** Campania, S Italy
168 J11 **Solok** Sumatera, W Indonesia
42 C6 **Sololá** Sololá, W Guatemala
42 A2 **Sololá** *off.* Departamento de Sololá. ◈ *department* SW Guatemala
81 J16 **Sololo** Eastern, N Kenya
42 C4 **Soloma** Huehuetenango, W Guatemala
38 M9 **Solomon** Alaska, USA
27 N4 **Solomon** Kansas, C USA
187 N9 **Solomon Islands** *prev.* British Solomon Islands Protectorate. ◆ *commonwealth republic* W Pacific Ocean
186 L7 **Solomon Islands** *island group* PNG/Solomon Islands
26 M3 **Solomon River** ≈ Kansas, C USA
186 H8 **Solomon Sea** *sea* W Pacific Ocean
31 U11 **Solon** Ohio, N USA
117 T8 **Solone** Dnipropetrovs'ka Oblast', E Ukraine
171 P16 **Solor, Kepulauan** *island group* S Indonesia
126 M4 **Solotcha** Ryazanskaya Oblast', W Russian Federation
108 D7 **Solothurn** *Fr.* Soleure. Solothurn, NW Switzerland
108 D7 **Solothurn** *Fr.* Soleure. ◈ *canton* NW Switzerland
126 J7 **Solovetskiye Ostrova** *island group* NW Russian Federation
105 V5 **Solsona** Cataluña, NE Spain
113 E14 **Šolta** *It.* Solta. *island* S Croatia
Solṭānābād *see* Kāshmar
142 L4 **Solṭānīyeh** Zanjān, NW Iran
100 I11 **Soltau** Niedersachsen, NW Germany
124 G14 **Sol'tsy** Novgorodskaya Oblast', W Russian Federation
Soltüstik Qazaqstan Oblysy *see* Severnyy Kazakhstan
Solun *see* Thessaloníki
113 O19 **Solunska Glava** ▲ C FYR Macedonia
95 L22 **Sölvesborg** Blekinge, S Sweden
97 J15 **Solway Firth** *inlet* England/Scotland, UK
82 I13 **Solwezi** North Western, NW Zambia
165 Q11 **Sōma** Fukushima, Honshū, C Japan
136 C13 **Soma** Manisa, W Turkey
81 M14 **Somali** ◈ *region* E Ethiopia
81 O15 **Somalia** *off.* Somali Democratic Republic, *Som.* Jamuuriyada Demuqraadiga Soomaaliyeed, Soomaaliya; *prev.* Italian Somaliland, Somaliland Protectorate. ◆ *republic* E Africa
173 N6 **Somali Basin** *undersea feature* W Indian Ocean
67 Y8 **Somali Plain** *undersea feature* W Indian Ocean
112 J8 **Sombor** *Hung.* Zombor. Serbia, NW Serbia and Montenegro (Yugo.)
99 H20 **Sombreffe** Namur, S Belgium
40 L10 **Sombrerete** Zacatecas, C Mexico
45 V8 **Sombrero** *island* N Anguilla
151 Q21 **Sombrero Channel** *channel* Nicobar Islands, India
116 H9 **Şomcuta Mare** *Hung.* Nagysomkút; *prev.* Somcuţa Mare. Maramureş, N Romania
167 R9 **Somdet** Kalasin, E Thailand
99 L15 **Someren** Noord-Brabant, SE Netherlands
93 L19 **Somero** Länsi-Suomi, W Finland
33 P7 **Somers** Montana, NW USA
64 A12 **Somerset** *var.* Somerset Village. W Bermuda
37 Q5 **Somerset** Colorado, C USA
20 M7 **Somerset** Kentucky, S USA
19 O12 **Somerset** Massachusetts, NE USA
97 K23 **Somerset** *cultural region* SW England, UK
Somerset East *see* Somerset-Oos
64 A12 **Somerset Island** *island* W Bermuda
197 N9 **Somerset Island** *island* Queen Elizabeth Islands, Nunavut, NW Canada
Somerset Nile *see* Victoria Nile
83 I25 **Somerset-Oos** *Eng.* Somerset East. Eastern Cape, S South Africa
83 E26 **Somerset-Wes** *Eng.* Somerset West. Western Cape, SW South Africa
Somerset West *see* Somerset-Wes
Somers Islands *see* Bermuda
18 J17 **Somers Point** New Jersey, NE USA
19 P9 **Somersworth** New Hampshire, NE USA
36 H15 **Somerton** Arizona, SW USA
18 J14 **Somerville** New Jersey, NE USA
20 F10 **Somerville** Tennessee, S USA
25 U10 **Somerville** Texas, SW USA
25 T10 **Somerville Lake** ▣ Texas, SW USA
Someş/Somesch/Someşul *see* Szamos
103 N2 **Somme** ◈ *department* N France
103 N2 **Somme** ≈ N France
95 L18 **Sommen** Jönköping, S Sweden
95 M18 **Sommen** ◎ S Sweden
101 K16 **Sömmerda** Thüringen, C Germany
Sommerein *see* Šamorín
Sommerfeld *see* Lubsko
55 Y11 **Sommet Tabulaire** *var.* Mont Itoupé. ▲ S French Guiana
111 H25 **Somogy** *off.* Somogy Megye. ◈ *county* SW Hungary
Somorja *see* Šamorín
105 N7 **Somosierra, Puerto de** *pass* N Spain
187 Y14 **Somosomo** Taveuni, N Fiji
42 I9 **Somotillo** Chinandega, NW Nicaragua
42 I8 **Somoto** Madriz, NW Nicaragua
110 I11 **Sompolno** Wielkolpolskie, C Poland
105 S3 **Somport** *var.* Puerto de Somport, *Fr.* Col du Somport; *anc.* Summus Portus. *pass* France/Spain *see also* Somport, Col du
102 J17 **Somport, Col du** *var.* Puerto de Somport, *Sp.* Somport; *anc.* Summus Portus. *pass* France/Spain *see also* Somport
Somport, Puerto de *see* Somport/Somport, Col du
99 K15 **Son** Noord-Brabant, S Netherlands
95 H15 **Son** Akershus, S Norway
154 L9 **Son** *var.* Sone. ≈ C India
43 R16 **Soná** Veraguas, W Panama
Sonag *see* Zêkog
154 M12 **Sonapur** *prev.* Sonepur. Orissa, E India
95 G24 **Sønderborg** *Ger.* Sonderburg. Sønderjylland, SW Denmark
Sonderburg *see* Sønderborg
95 F24 **Sønderjylland** *off.* Sønderjyllands Amt. ◈ *county* SW Denmark
101 K15 **Sondershausen** Thüringen, C Germany
Søndre Strømfjord *see* Kangerlussuaq
106 E6 **Sondrio** Lombardia, N Italy
Sone *see* Son
Sonepur *see* Sonapur
57 K22 **Sonequera** ▲ S Bolivia
167 V12 **Sông Câu** Phu Yên, C Vietnam
167 R15 **Sông Đốc** Minh Hai, S Vietnam
81 H25 **Songea** Ruvuma, S Tanzania
163 X10 **Songhua Hu** ◎ NE China
163 Y7 **Songhua Jiang** *var.* Sungari. ≈ NE China
161 S8 **Songjiang** Shanghai Shi, E China
Sŏngjin *see* Kimch'aek
167 O16 **Songkhla** *var.* Songkla, *Mal.* Singora. Songkhla, SW Thailand
Songkla *see* Songkhla
163 T13 **Song Ling** ▲▲ NE China
163 W14 **Songnim** SW North Korea
82 B10 **Songo** Uíge, NW Angola
83 M15 **Songo** Tete, NW Mozambique
79 F21 **Songololo** Bas-Congo, SW Dem. Rep. Congo
160 H7 **Songpan** *var.* Jin'an, *Tib.* Sungpu. Sichuan, C China
163 Y17 **Sŏngsan** S South Korea
161 R11 **Songxi** Fujian, SE China
160 M6 **Songxian** *var.* Song Xian. Henan, C China
161 R10 **Songyang** *var.* Xiping. Zhejiang, SE China
163 V9 **Songyuan** *var.* Fu-yü, Petuna; *prev.* Fuyu. Jilin, NE China
Sonid Youqi *see* Saihan Tal
Sonid Zuoqi *see* Mandalt
152 I10 **Sonīpat** Haryāna, N India
93 M15 **Sonkajärvi** Itä-Suomi, C Finland
167 R6 **Sơn La** Sơn La, N Vietnam
149 O16 **Sonmiāni** Baluchistān, S Pakistan
149 O16 **Sonmiāni Bay** *bay* S Pakistan
101 K18 **Sonneberg** Thüringen, C Germany
101 N24 **Sonntagshorn** ▲ Austria/Germany
Sonoita *see* Sonoyta
40 E3 **Sonoita, Rio** *var.* Río Sonoyta. ≈ Mexico/USA
35 N7 **Sonoma** California, W USA
35 T3 **Sonoma Peak** ▲ Nevada, W USA
35 P8 **Sonora** California, W USA
25 O10 **Sonora** Texas, SW USA
40 F5 **Sonora** ◈ *state* NW Mexico
35 X17 **Sonoran Desert** *var.* Desierto de Altar. *desert* Mexico/USA *see also* Altar, Desierto de
40 G5 **Sonora, Río** ≈ NW Mexico
40 E2 **Sonoyta** *var.* Sonoita. Sonora, NW Mexico
Sonoyta, Río *see* Sonoita, Rio
142 K6 **Sonqor** *var.* Sunqur. Kermānshāh, W Iran
105 N9 **Sonseca** *var.* Sonseca con Casalgordo. Castilla-La Mancha, C Spain
Sonseca con Casalgordo *see* Sonseca
54 E9 **Sonsón** Antioquia, W Colombia
42 E7 **Sonsonate** Sonsonate, W El Salvador
42 A9 **Sonsonate** ◈ *department* SW El Salvador
188 A10 **Sonsorol Islands** *island group* S Palau
112 J9 **Sonta** *Hung.* Szond; *prev.* Szonta. Serbia, NW Serbia and Montenegro (Yugo.)
167 S6 **Sơn Tây** *var.* Sontay. Ha Tây, N Vietnam
101 J25 **Sonthofen** Bayern, S Germany
Soochow *see* Suzhou
Soomaaliya/Soomaaliyeed, Jamuuriyada Demuqraadiga *see* Somalia
Soome Laht *see* Finland, Gulf of
Sooner State *see* Oklahoma
23 V5 **Soperton** Georgia, SE USA
167 S6 **Sop Hao** Houaphan, N Laos
Sophia *see* Sofiya
171 S10 **Sopi** Pulau Morotai, E Indonesia
Sopianae *see* Pécs
171 U13 **Sopinusa** Papua, E Indonesia
81 B14 **Sopo** ≈ W Sudan
Sopockinie/Sopotskin *see* Sapotskino
114 I9 **Sopot** Plovdiv, C Bulgaria
110 I7 **Sopot** *Ger.* Zoppot. Pomorskie, N Poland
167 O8 **Sop Prap** *var.* Ban Sop Prap. Lampang, NW Thailand
111 G22 **Sopron** *Ger.* Ödenburg. Győr-Moson-Sopron, NW Hungary
147 U11 **Sopu-Korgon** *var.* Sofi-Kurgan. Oshskaya Oblast', SW Kyrgyzstan
152 H5 **Sopur** Jammu and Kashmir, NW India
107 J15 **Sora** Lazio, C Italy
154 N13 **Sorada** Orissa, E India
93 H17 **Söråker** Västernorrland, C Sweden
57 J17 **Sorata** La Paz, W Bolivia
Sorau/Sorau in der Niederlausitz *see* Żary
105 Q14 **Sorbas** Andalucía, S Spain
Sord/Sórd Choluim Chille *see* Swords
15 O11 **Sorel** Québec, SE Canada
183 P17 **Sorell** Tasmania, SE Australia
183 O17 **Sorell, Lake** ◎ Tasmania, SE Australia
106 E8 **Soresina** Lombardia, N Italy
95 D14 **Sørfjorden** *fjord* S Norway
94 N11 **Sörforsa** Gävleborg, C Sweden
103 R14 **Sorgues** Vaucluse, SE France
136 K13 **Sorgun** Yozgat, C Turkey
105 P5 **Soria** Castilla-León, N Spain
105 P6 **Soria** ◈ *province* Castilla-León, N Spain
61 D19 **Soriano** Soriano, SW Uruguay
61 D19 **Soriano** ◈ *department* SW Uruguay
92 O4 **Sørkapp** *headland* SW Svalbard
143 T5 **Sorkh, Kūh-e** ▲▲ NE Iran
Soro *see* Ghazal, Bahr el
95 I23 **Sorø** Vestsjælland, E Denmark
116 M8 **Soroca** *Rus.* Soroki. N Moldova
60 L10 **Sorocaba** São Paulo, S Brazil
Sorochino *see* Sarochyna
127 T7 **Sorochinsk** Orenburgskaya Oblast', W Russian Federation
Soroki *see* Soroca
188 H15 **Sorol** *atoll* Caroline Islands, W Micronesia
171 T12 **Sorong** Papua, E Indonesia
81 G17 **Soroti** C Uganda
Sørøy *see* Sørøya
92 J8 **Sørøya** *var.* Sørøy, *Lapp.* Sállan. *island* N Norway
104 G11 **Sorraia, Rio** ≈ C Portugal
92 I10 **Sørreisa** Troms, N Norway
107 K18 **Sorrento** *anc.* Surrentum. Campania, S Italy
104 H10 **Sor, Ribeira de** *stream* C Portugal
195 T3 **Sør Rondane Mountains** ▲▲ Antarctica
93 H14 **Sorsele** Västerbotten, N Sweden
107 B17 **Sorso** Sardegna, Italy, C Mediterranean Sea
171 P4 **Sorsogon** Luzon, N Philippines
105 U4 **Sort** Cataluña, NE Spain
124 H11 **Sortavala** Respublika Kareliya, NW Russian Federation
107 L25 **Sortino** Sicilia, Italy, C Mediterranean Sea
92 G10 **Sortland** Nordland, C Norway
94 G9 **Sør-Trøndelag** ◈ *county* S Norway
95 I15 **Sørumsand** Akershus, S Norway
118 D6 **Sõrve Säär** *headland* SW Estonia
95 K22 **Sösdala** Skåne, S Sweden
105 R4 **Sos del Rey Católico** Aragón, NE Spain
93 F15 **Sösjöfjällen** ▲ C Sweden
126 K7 **Sosna** ≈ W Russian Federation
62 H12 **Sosneado, Cerro** ▲ W Argentina
125 S9 **Sosnogorsk** Respublika Komi, NW Russian Federation
124 J8 **Sosnovets** Respublika Kareliya, NW Russian Federation
Sosnovets *see* Sosnowiec
127 Q3 **Sosnovka** Chuvashskaya Respublika, W Russian Federation
125 S16 **Sosnovka** Kirovskaya Oblast', NW Russian Federation
126 M6 **Sosnovka** Murmanskaya Oblast', NW Russian Federation
126 M6 **Sosnovka** Tambovskaya Oblast', W Russian Federation

◆ Country ● Country Capital ◇ Dependent Territory ○ Dependent Territory Capital ◈ Administrative Region ✈ International Airport ▲ Mountain ▲▲ Mountain Range ⋇ Volcano ≈ River ◎ Lake ▣ Reservoir

124 H12 **Sosnovo** Fin. Rautu. Leningradskaya Oblast', NW Russian Federation
Sosnovyy Bor see Sasnovy Bor
111 J16 **Sosnowiec** Ger. Sosnowitz, Rus. Sosnovets. Śląskie, S Poland
Sosnowitz see Sosnowiec
117 R2 **Sosnytsya** Chernihivs'ka Oblast', N Ukraine
109 V10 **Šoštanj** N Slovenia
122 G10 **Sos'va** Sverdlovskaya Oblast', C Russian Federation
54 D12 **Sotará, Volcán** ⛰ S Colombia
76 D10 **Sotavento, Ilhas de** var. Leeward Islands. island group S Cape Verde
93 N15 **Sotkamo** Oulu, C Finland
109 W11 **Sotla** ≈ E Slovenia
41 P10 **Soto la Marina** Tamaulipas, C Mexico
41 P10 **Soto la Marina, Río** ≈ C Mexico
95 B14 **Sotra** island S Norway
41 X12 **Sotuta** Yucatán, SE Mexico
79 F17 **Souanké** La Sangha, NW Congo
76 M17 **Soubré** S Ivory Coast
115 H24 **Soúda** var. Soúdha, Eng. Suda. Kríti, Greece, E Mediterranean Sea
Soúdha see Soúda
Soueida see As Suwaydā'
114 L12 **Souflí** prev. Souflíon. Anatolikí Makedonía kai Thráki, NE Greece
Souflíon see Souflí
45 S11 **Soufrière** W Saint Lucia
45 X6 **Soufrière** ⛰ Basse Terre, S Guadeloupe
102 M13 **Souillac** Lot, S France
173 Y17 **Souillac** S Mauritius
74 M5 **Souk Ahras** NE Algeria
74 E6 **Souk-el-Arba-Rharb** var. Souk el Arba du Rharb, Souk-el-Arba-du-Rharb, Souk-el-Arba-el-Rhab. NW Morocco
Soukhné see As Sukhnah
163 X14 **Sŏul** off. Sŏul-t'ŭkpyŏlsi, Eng. Seoul, Jap. Keijō; prev. Kyŏngsŏng. ● (South Korea) NW South Korea
102 J11 **Soulac-sur-Mer** Gironde, SW France
99 L19 **Soumagne** Liège, E Belgium
18 M14 **Sound Beach** Long Island, New York, NE USA
95 J22 **Sound, The** Dan. Øresund, Swe. Öresund. strait Denmark/Sweden
115 H20 **Soúnio, Akrotírio** headland C Greece
138 F8 **Soûr** var. Şūr; anc. Tyre. SW Lebanon
Sources, Mont-aux- see Phofung
104 G8 **Soure** Coimbra, N Portugal
11 W17 **Souris** Manitoba, S Canada
13 Q14 **Souris** Prince Edward Island, SE Canada
28 L2 **Souris River** var. Mouse River. ≈ Canada/USA
25 X10 **Sour Lake** Texas, SW USA
115 F17 **Sourpi** Thessalía, C Greece
104 H11 **Sousel** Portalegre, C Portugal
75 N6 **Sousse** var. Sūsah. NE Tunisia
14 H11 **South** ≈ Ontario, S Canada
South see Sud
83 G23 **South Africa** off. Republic of South Africa, Afr. Suid-Afrika. ◆ republic S Africa
48-49 **South America** continent
2 J17 **South American Plate** tectonic feature
97 M23 **Southampton** hist. Hamwih, Lat. Clausentum. S England, UK
19 N14 **Southampton** Long Island, New York, NE USA
9 P8 **Southampton Island** island Nunavut, NE Canada
151 P20 **South Andaman** island Andaman Islands, India, NE Indian Ocean
13 Q6 **South Aulatsivik Island** island Newfoundland and Labrador, E Canada
182 E4 **South Australia** ❖ state S Australia
South Australian Abyssal Plain see South Australian Plain
192 G11 **South Australian Basin** undersea feature SW Indian Ocean
173 X12 **South Australian Plain** var. South Australian Abyssal Plain. undersea feature SE Indian Ocean
37 R13 **South Baldy** ▲ New Mexico, SW USA
23 Y14 **South Bay** Florida, SE USA
14 E12 **South Baymouth** Manitoulin Island, Ontario, S Canada
30 L10 **South Beloit** Illinois, N USA
31 O11 **South Bend** Indiana, N USA
25 R6 **South Bend** Texas, SW USA
32 F9 **South Bend** Washington, NW USA
South Beveland see Zuid-Beveland
South Borneo see Kalimantan Selatan
21 U7 **South Boston** Virginia, NE USA
182 F2 **South Branch Neales** seasonal river South Australia
21 U3 **South Branch Potomac River** ≈ West Virginia, NE USA
185 H19 **Southbridge** Canterbury, South Island, NZ
19 N12 **Southbridge** Massachusetts, NE USA
183 P17 **South Bruny Island** island Tasmania, SE Australia
18 L7 **South Burlington** Vermont, NE USA
44 M6 **South Caicos** island S Turks and Caicos Islands
South Cape see Ka Lae
23 V3 **South Carolina** off. State of South Carolina; also known as The Palmetto State. ❖ state SE USA
South Carpathians see Carpaţii Meridionali
South Celebes see Sulawesi Selatan
21 Q5 **South Charleston** West Virginia, NE USA
192 D7 **South China Basin** undersea feature SE South China Sea
169 R8 **South China Sea** Chin. Nan Hai, Ind. Laut Cina Selatan, Vtn. Biên Đông. sea SE Asia
33 Z10 **South Dakota** off. State of South Dakota; also known as The Coyote State, Sunshine State. ❖ state N USA
23 X10 **South Daytona** Florida, SE USA
37 R10 **South Domingo Pueblo** New Mexico, SW USA
97 N23 **South Downs** hill range SE England, UK
83 I21 **South East** ❖ district SE Botswana
65 H15 **South East Bay** bay Ascension Island, C Atlantic Ocean
183 O17 **South East Cape** headland Tasmania, SE Australia
38 K10 **Southeast Cape** headland Saint Lawrence Island, Alaska, USA
South-East Celebes see Sulawesi Tenggara
192 G12 **Southeast Indian Ridge** undersea feature Indian Ocean/Pacific Ocean
Southeast Island see Tagula Island
193 P13 **Southeast Pacific Basin** var. Belling Hausen Mulde. undersea feature SE Pacific Ocean
65 H15 **South East Point** headland SE Ascension Island
183 O14 **South East Point** headland Victoria, S Australia
191 Z3 **South East Point** headland Kiritimati, NE Kiribati
44 L5 **Southeast Point** headland Mayaguana, SE Bahamas
South-East Sulawesi see Sulawesi Tenggara
11 U12 **Southend** Saskatchewan, C Canada
97 P22 **Southend-on-Sea** E England, UK
83 H20 **Southern** var. Bangwaketse, Ngwaketze. ❖ district SE Botswana
81 I15 **Southern** ❖ region S Ethiopia
138 E13 **Southern** ❖ district S Israel
83 N15 **Southern** ❖ region S Malawi
83 I15 **Southern** ❖ province S Zambia
185 E19 **Southern Alps** ▲ South Island, NZ
190 K15 **Southern Cook Islands** island group S Cook Islands
180 K12 **Southern Cross** Western Australia
80 A12 **Southern Darfur** ❖ state W Sudan
186 B7 **Southern Highlands** ❖ province W PNG
11 V11 **Southern Indian Lake** ◎ Manitoba, C Canada
80 E11 **Southern Kordofan** ❖ state C Sudan
187 Z15 **Southern Lau Group** island group Lau Group, SE Fiji
173 S13 **Southern Ocean** ocean
21 T10 **Southern Pines** North Carolina, SE USA
155 J26 **Southern Province** ❖ province S Sri Lanka
96 I13 **Southern Uplands** ▲ S Scotland, UK
Southern Urals see Yuzhnyy Ural
183 P16 **South Esk River** ≈ Tasmania, SE Australia
11 U16 **Southey** Saskatchewan, S Canada
27 V2 **South Fabius River** ≈ Missouri, C USA
31 S10 **Southfield** Michigan, N USA
192 K10 **South Fiji Basin** undersea feature S Pacific Ocean
97 Q22 **South Foreland** headland SE England, UK
35 P7 **South Fork American River** ≈ California, W USA
28 K7 **South Fork Grand River** ≈ South Dakota, N USA
35 T12 **South Fork Kern River** ≈ California, W USA
39 Q7 **South Fork Koyukuk River** ≈ Alaska, USA
39 Q11 **South Fork Kuskokwim River** ≈ Alaska, USA
26 H2 **South Fork Republican River** ≈ C USA
26 L3 **South Fork Solomon River** ≈ Kansas, C USA
31 P5 **South Fox Island** island Michigan, N USA
20 G8 **South Fulton** Tennessee, S USA
195 U10 **South Geomagnetic Pole** pole Antarctica
65 J20 **South Georgia** island South Georgia and the South Sandwich Islands, SW Atlantic Ocean
65 K21 **South Georgia and the South Sandwich Islands** ◇ UK dependent territory SW Atlantic Ocean
47 Y14 **South Georgia Ridge** var. North Scotia Ridge. undersea feature SW Atlantic Ocean
181 Q1 **South Goulburn Island** island Northern Territory, N Australia
153 U16 **South Hatia Island** island SE Bangladesh
31 O10 **South Haven** Michigan, N USA
21 V7 **South Hill** Virginia, NE USA
South Holland see Zuid-Holland
21 P8 **South Holston Lake** ▣ Tennessee/Virginia, S USA
175 N1 **South Honshu Ridge** undersea feature W Pacific Ocean
26 M6 **South Hutchinson** Kansas, C USA
151 K21 **South Huvadhu Atoll** var. Gaafu Dhaalu Atoll. atoll S Maldives
173 U14 **South Indian Basin** undersea feature Indian Ocean/Pacific Ocean
11 W11 **South Indian Lake** Manitoba, C Canada
81 I17 **South Island** island NW Kenya
185 C20 **South Island** island S NZ
65 B23 **South Jason** island Jason Islands, NW Falkland Islands
South Kalimantan see Kalimantan Selatan
South Kazakhstan see Yuzhnyy Kazakhstan
163 X15 **South Korea** off. Republic of Korea, Kor. Taehan Min'guk. ◆ republic E Asia
35 Q6 **South Lake Tahoe** California, W USA
25 N6 **Southland** Texas, SW USA
185 B23 **Southland** off. Southland Region. ❖ region South Island, NZ
29 N15 **South Loup River** ≈ Nebraska, C USA
151 K19 **South Maalhosmadulu Atoll** var. Baa Atoll. atoll N Maldives
14 E15 **South Maitland** ≈ Ontario, S Canada
192 E8 **South Makassar Basin** undersea feature E Java Sea
31 O6 **South Manitou Island** island Michigan, N USA
151 K18 **South Miladummadulu Atoll** atoll N Maldives
21 X8 **South Mills** North Carolina, SE USA
8 H9 **South Nahanni** ≈ Northwest Territories, NW Canada
39 P13 **South Naknek** Alaska, USA
14 M13 **South Nation** ≈ Ontario, SE Canada
44 F9 **South Negril Point** headland W Jamaica
151 K20 **South Nilandhe Atoll** var. Dhaalu Atoll. atoll C Maldives
36 L2 **South Ogden** Utah, W USA
18 M14 **Southold** Long Island, New York, NE USA
194 H1 **South Orkney Islands** island group Antarctica
137 S9 **South Ossetia** former autonomous region SW Georgia
South Pacific Basin see Southwest Pacific Basin
19 P7 **South Paris** Maine, NE USA
33 U15 **South Pass** pass Wyoming, C USA
189 U13 **South Pass** passage Chuuk Islands, C Micronesia
20 K10 **South Pittsburg** Tennessee, S USA
28 K15 **South Platte River** ≈ Colorado/Nebraska, C USA
31 T16 **South Point** Ohio, N USA
65 G15 **South Point** headland S Ascension Island
31 R6 **South Point** headland Michigan, N USA
South Point see Ka Lae
195 P9 **South Pole** pole Antarctica
183 P17 **Southport** Tasmania, SE Australia
97 K17 **Southport** NW England, UK
21 V12 **Southport** North Carolina, SE USA
19 P8 **South Portland** Maine, NE USA
14 H12 **South River** Ontario, S Canada
21 U11 **South River** ≈ North Carolina, SE USA
96 K5 **South Ronaldsay** island NE Scotland, UK
36 L2 **South Salt Lake** Utah, W USA
65 L21 **South Sandwich Islands** island group SE South Georgia and South Sandwich Islands
65 K21 **South Sandwich Trench** undersea feature SW Atlantic Ocean
11 S16 **South Saskatchewan** ≈ Alberta/Saskatchewan, S Canada
65 I21 **South Scotia Ridge** undersea feature S Scotia Sea
11 V10 **South Seal** ≈ Manitoba, C Canada
194 G4 **South Shetland Islands** island group Antarctica
65 H22 **South Shetland Trough** undersea feature Atlantic Ocean/Pacific Ocean
97 M14 **South Shields** NE England, UK
29 R13 **South Sioux City** Nebraska, C USA
192 J9 **South Solomon Trench** undersea feature W Pacific Ocean
183 V3 **South Stradbroke Island** island Queensland, E Australia
South Sulawesi see Sulawesi Selatan
South Sumatra see Sumatera Selatan
184 K11 **South Taranaki Bight** bight SE Tasman Sea
South Tasmania Plateau see Tasman Plateau
36 M15 **South Tucson** Arizona, SW USA
12 H9 **South Twin Island** island Nunavut, C Canada
96 E9 **South Uist** island NW Scotland, UK
South-West see Sud-Ouest
South-West Africa/South West Africa see Namibia
65 F15 **South West Bay** bay Ascension Island, C Atlantic Ocean
183 N18 **South West Cape** headland Tasmania, SE Australia
185 B26 **South West Cape** headland Stewart Island, NZ
38 J10 **Southwest Cape** headland Saint Lawrence Island, Alaska, USA
Southwest Indian Ocean Ridge see Southwest Indian Ridge
173 N11 **Southwest Indian Ridge** var. Southwest Indian Ocean Ridge. undersea feature SW Indian Ocean
192 L10 **Southwest Pacific Basin** var. South Pacific Basin. undersea feature SE Pacific Ocean
44 H2 **Southwest Point** headland Great Abaco, N Bahamas
191 X3 **South West Point** headland Kiritimati, NE Kiribati
65 G25 **South West Point** headland SW Saint Helena
25 P5 **South Wichita River** ≈ Texas, SW USA
97 Q20 **Southwold** E England, UK
19 Q12 **South Yarmouth** Massachusetts, NE USA
116 J10 **Sovata** Hung. Szováta. Mureş, C Romania
107 N22 **Soverato** Calabria, SW Italy
Sovetabad see Ghafurov
126 C2 **Sovetsk** Ger. Tilsit. Kaliningradskaya Oblast', W Russian Federation
125 Q15 **Sovetsk** Kirovskaya Oblast', NW Russian Federation
127 N10 **Sovetskaya** Rostovskaya Oblast', SW Russian Federation
Sovetskoye see Ketchenery
146 I15 **Sovet"yab** prev. Sovet"yap. Ahal Welaýaty, S Turkmenistan
Sovet"yap see Sovet"yab
117 U12 **Sovyets'kyy** Respublika Krym, S Ukraine
83 I18 **Sowa** var. Sua. Central, NE Botswana
Sowa Pan see Sua Pan
83 J21 **Soweto** Gauteng, NE South Africa
147 R11 **So'x** Rus. Sokh. Farg'ona Viloyati, E Uzbekistan
Sōya-kaikyō see La Perouse Strait
165 T1 **Sōya-misaki** headland Hokkaidō, NE Japan
127 N7 **Soyana** ≈ NW Russian Federation
146 A8 **Soye, Mys** var. Mys Suz. headland NW Turkmenistan
82 A10 **Soyo** Zaire, NW Angola
80 J10 **Soyra** ▲ C Eritrea
Sozaq see Suzak
119 P16 **Sozh** Rus. Sozh. ≈ NE Europe
114 N10 **Sozopol** prev. Sizebolu anc. Apollonia. Burgas, E Bulgaria
172 J15 **Sœurs, Les** island group Inner Islands, W Seychelles
99 L20 **Spa** Liège, E Belgium
194 I7 **Spaatz Island** island Antarctica
144 M14 **Space Launching Centre** space station Kzylorda, S Kazakhstan
105 O7 **Spain** off. Kingdom of Spain, Sp. España; anc. Hispania, Iberia, Lat. Hispana. ◆ monarchy SW Europe
Spalato see Split
97 O19 **Spalding** E England, UK
14 D11 **Spanish** Ontario, S Canada
36 L3 **Spanish Fork** Utah, W USA
64 B12 **Spanish Point** headland C Bermuda
14 E9 **Spanish River** ≈ Ontario, S Canada
44 K13 **Spanish Town** hist. St.Iago de la Vega. C Jamaica
115 H24 **Spánta, Akrotírio** headland Kríti, Greece, E Mediterranean Sea
35 Q5 **Sparks** Nevada, W USA
Sparnacum see Épernay
95 N16 **Sparreholm** Södermanland, C Sweden
23 U4 **Sparta** Georgia, SE USA
30 K16 **Sparta** Illinois, N USA
31 P9 **Sparta** Michigan, N USA
21 R8 **Sparta** North Carolina, SE USA
20 L9 **Sparta** Tennessee, S USA
30 J7 **Sparta** Wisconsin, N USA
Sparta see Spárti
21 Q11 **Spartanburg** South Carolina, SE USA
115 F21 **Spárti** Eng. Sparta. Pelopónnisos, S Greece
107 B21 **Spartivento, Capo** headland Sardegna, Italy, C Mediterranean Sea
11 P17 **Sparwood** British Columbia, SW Canada
126 I4 **Spas-Demensk** Kaluzhskaya Oblast', W Russian Federation
126 M4 **Spas-Klepiki** Ryazanskaya Oblast', W Russian Federation
Spasovo see Kulen Vakuf
123 R15 **Spassk-Dal'niy** Primorskiy Kray, SE Russian Federation
126 M5 **Spassk-Ryazanskiy** Ryazanskaya Oblast', W Russian Federation
115 H19 **Spáta** Attikí, C Greece
121 Q11 **Spátha, Akrotírio** headland Kríti, Greece, E Mediterranean Sea
Špatrjan see Paternion
28 I9 **Spearfish** South Dakota, N USA
25 O1 **Spearman** Texas, SW USA
65 C25 **Speedwell Island** island S Falkland Islands
65 C25 **Speedwell Island Settlement** S Falkland Islands
65 G25 **Speery Island** island S Saint Helena
45 N14 **Speightstown** NW Barbados
106 I13 **Spello** Umbria, C Italy
39 R12 **Spenard** Alaska, USA
Spence Bay see Taloyoak
31 O14 **Spencer** Indiana, N USA
29 T12 **Spencer** Iowa, C USA
29 P12 **Spencer** Nebraska, C USA
21 S9 **Spencer** North Carolina, SE USA
20 L9 **Spencer** Tennessee, S USA
21 Q4 **Spencer** West Virginia, NE USA
30 K6 **Spencer** Wisconsin, N USA
182 G10 **Spencer, Cape** headland South Australia
39 V13 **Spencer, Cape** headland Alaska, USA
182 H9 **Spencer Gulf** gulf South Australia
18 F9 **Spencerport** New York, NE USA
31 Q12 **Spencerville** Ohio, N USA
115 E17 **Spercheiáda** var. Sperhiada, Sperkhiás. Stereá Ellás, C Greece
115 E17 **Spercheiós** ≈ C Greece
Sperhiada see Spercheiáda
95 G14 **Sperillen** ◎ S Norway
Sperkhiás see Spercheiáda
101 I18 **Spessart** hill range C Germany
Spétsai see Spétses
115 G21 **Spétses** prev. Spétsai. Spétses, S Greece
115 G21 **Spétses** island S Greece
96 J8 **Spey** ≈ NE Scotland, UK
101 G20 **Speyer** Eng. Spires; anc. Civitas Nemetum, Spira. Rheinland-Pfalz, SW Germany
101 G20 **Speyerbach** ≈ W Germany
107 N20 **Spezzano Albanese** Calabria, SW Italy
Spice Islands see Maluku
100 F9 **Spiekeroog** island NW Germany
109 W9 **Spielfeld** Steiermark, SE Austria
65 N21 **Spiess Seamount** undersea feature S Atlantic Ocean
108 E9 **Spiez** Bern, W Switzerland
98 G13 **Spijkenisse** Zuid-Holland, SW Netherlands
39 T6 **Spike Mountain** ▲ Alaska, USA
115 I25 **Spíli** Kríti, Greece, E Mediterranean Sea
108 D10 **Spillgerten** ▲ W Switzerland
118 F9 **Spilva** ✈ (Rīga) Rīga, C Latvia
107 N17 **Spinazzola** Puglia, SE Italy
149 O9 **Spīn Būldak** Kandahār, S Afghanistan
Spira see Speyer
Spirdingsee see Śniardwy, Jezioro
Spires see Speyer
29 T11 **Spirit Lake** Iowa, C USA
29 T11 **Spirit Lake** ◎ Iowa, C USA
11 N13 **Spirit River** Alberta, W Canada
11 S14 **Spiritwood** Saskatchewan, S Canada
27 R11 **Spiro** Oklahoma, C USA
111 L19 **Spišská Nová Ves** Ger. Neudorf, Zipser Neudorf, Hung. Igló. Košický Kraj, E Slovakia
137 T11 **Spitak** NW Armenia
92 O2 **Spitsbergen** island NW Svalbard
Spittal see Spittal an der Drau
109 R9 **Spittal an der Drau** var. Spittal. Kärnten, S Austria
109 V3 **Spitz** Niederösterreich, NE Austria
94 D9 **Spjelkavik** Møre og Romsdal, S Norway
25 W10 **Splendora** Texas, SW USA
113 E14 **Split** It. Spalato. Split-Dalmacija, S Croatia
113 E14 **Split** ✈ Split-Dalmacija, S Croatia
113 E14 **Split-Dalmacija** off. Splitsko-Dalmatinska Županija. ❖ province S Croatia
11 X12 **Split Lake** ◎ Manitoba, C Canada
Splitsko-Dalmatinska Županija see Split-Dalmacija
108 H10 **Splügen** Graubünden, S Switzerland
Spodnji Dravograd see Dravograd
25 P12 **Spofford** Texas, SW USA
118 J11 **Špoģi** Daugavpils, SE Latvia
32 L8 **Spokane** Washington, NW USA
32 L8 **Spokane River** ≈ Washington, NW USA
106 I13 **Spoleto** Umbria, C Italy
30 J4 **Spooner** Wisconsin, N USA
30 K12 **Spoon River** ≈ Illinois, N USA
21 W5 **Spotsylvania** Virginia, NE USA
32 L8 **Sprague** Washington, NW USA
170 J5 **Spratly Island** island SW Spratly Islands
192 E6 **Spratly Islands** Chin. Nansha Qundao. ◇ disputed territory SE Asia
32 J12 **Spray** Oregon, NW USA
112 I11 **Spreča** ≈ N Bosnia and Herzegovina
100 P13 **Spree** ≈ E Germany
100 P13 **Spreewald** wetland NE Germany
101 P14 **Spremberg** Brandenburg, E Germany
25 W11 **Spring** Texas, SW USA
31 Q10 **Spring Arbor** Michigan, N USA
83 E23 **Springbok** Northern Cape, W South Africa
18 I15 **Spring City** Pennsylvania, NE USA
20 L9 **Spring City** Tennessee, S USA
36 L4 **Spring City** Utah, W USA
35 W3 **Spring Creek** Nevada, W USA
27 S9 **Springdale** Arkansas, C USA
31 Q14 **Springdale** Ohio, N USA
100 I13 **Springe** Niedersachsen, N Germany
37 U9 **Springer** New Mexico, SW USA
37 W7 **Springfield** Colorado, C USA
23 W5 **Springfield** Georgia, SE USA
30 K14 **Springfield** state capital Illinois, N USA
20 L6 **Springfield** Kentucky, S USA
18 M12 **Springfield** Massachusetts, NE USA
29 T10 **Springfield** Minnesota, N USA
27 T7 **Springfield** Missouri, C USA
31 R13 **Springfield** Ohio, N USA
32 G13 **Springfield** Oregon, NW USA
29 Q12 **Springfield** South Dakota, N USA
20 J8 **Springfield** Tennessee, S USA
18 M9 **Springfield** Vermont, NE USA
30 K14 **Springfield, Lake** ◎ Illinois, N USA
55 T8 **Spring Garden** NE Guyana
30 K8 **Spring Green** Wisconsin, N USA
29 X11 **Spring Grove** Minnesota, N USA
22 G4 **Springhill** Louisiana, S USA
23 V12 **Spring Hill** Florida, SE USA
27 R4 **Spring Hill** Kansas, C USA
13 P15 **Springhill** Nova Scotia, SE Canada
20 I9 **Spring Hill** Tennessee, S USA
21 U10 **Spring Lake** North Carolina, SE USA
24 M4 **Springlake** Texas, SW USA
35 W11 **Spring Mountains** ▲ Nevada, W USA
65 B24 **Spring Point** West Falkland, Falkland Islands
27 W9 **Spring River** ≈ Arkansas/Missouri, C USA
27 S7 **Spring River** ≈ Missouri/Oklahoma, C USA
83 J21 **Springs** Gauteng, NE South Africa
185 H16 **Springs Junction** West Coast, South Island, NZ
181 X8 **Springsure** Queensland, E Australia
29 W11 **Spring Valley** Minnesota, N USA
18 K13 **Spring Valley** New York, NE USA
29 N12 **Springview** Nebraska, C USA
18 D11 **Springville** New York, NE USA
36 L3 **Springville** Utah, W USA
Sprottau see Szprotawa
15 V4 **Sproule, Pointe** headland Québec, SE Canada
11 Q14 **Spruce Grove** Alberta, SW Canada
21 T4 **Spruce Knob** ▲ West Virginia, NE USA
35 X3 **Spruce Mountain** ▲ Nevada, W USA
21 P9 **Spruce Pine** North Carolina, SE USA
98 G13 **Spui** ≈ SW Netherlands
107 O19 **Spulico, Capo** headland S Italy
25 O5 **Spur** Texas, SW USA
97 O17 **Spurn Head** headland E England, UK
99 H20 **Spy** Namur, S Belgium
95 I15 **Spydeberg** Østfold, S Norway
185 J17 **Spy Glass Point** headland South Island, NZ
10 L17 **Squamish** British Columbia, SW Canada
19 O8 **Squam Lake** ◎ New Hampshire, NE USA
19 S2 **Squa Pan Mountain** ▲ Maine, NE USA
39 N16 **Squaw Harbor** Unga Island, Alaska, USA
14 E11 **Squaw Island** island Ontario, S Canada
107 O22 **Squillace, Golfo di** gulf S Italy
107 Q18 **Squinzano** Puglia, SE Italy
Sráid na Cathrach see Milltown Malbay
167 S11 **Srâlau** Stœng Trêng, N Cambodia
Srath an Urláir see Stranorlar
112 G10 **Srbac** Republika Srpska, N Bosnia & Herzegovina
Srbinje see Foča
Srbija see Serbia
Srbobran see Donji Vakuf
112 K9 **Srbobran** var. Bácsszenttamás, Hung. Szenttamás. Serbia, N Serbia and Montenegro (Yugo.)
167 R13 **Srê Âmběl** Kaôh Kông, SW Cambodia
112 K13 **Srebrenica** Republika Srpska, E Bosnia & Herzegovina
112 I11 **Srebrenik** Federacija Bosna I Hercegovina, E Bosnia & Herzegovina
114 M10 **Sredets** prev. Grudovo. Burgas, E Bulgaria
114 K10 **Sredets** prev. Syulemeshlii. Stara Zagora, C Bulgaria
114 M10 **Sredetska Reka** ≈ SE Bulgaria
123 U9 **Sredinnyy Khrebet** ▲ E Russian Federation
114 N7 **Sredishte** Rom. Beibunar; prev. Knyazhevo. Dobrich, NE Bulgaria
114 I10 **Sredna Gora** ▲ C Bulgaria
123 R7 **Srednekolymsk** Respublika Sakha (Yakutiya), NE Russian Federation
126 K7 **Srednerusskaya Vozvyshennost'** Eng. Central Russian Upland. ▲ W Russian Federation
122 L9 **Srednesibirskoye Ploskogor'ye** var. Central Siberian Uplands, Eng. Central Siberian Plateau. ▲ N Russian Federation
127 V13 **Sredniy Ural** ▲ NW Russian Federation
167 T12 **Srê Khtŭm** Môndól Kiri, E Cambodia
111 G12 **Śrem** Wielkolpolskie, C Poland
112 K10 **Sremska Mitrovica** prev. Mitrovica, Ger. Mitrowitz. Serbia, NW Serbia and Montenegro (Yugo.)
167 R11 **Srêng, Stœng** ≈ NW Cambodia
167 R11 **Srê Noy** Siĕmréab, NW Cambodia
Srepok, Sông see Srêpôk, Tônle
167 T12 **Srêpôk, Tônle** var. Sông Srepok. ≈ Cambodia/Vietnam
123 P13 **Sretensk** Chitinskaya Oblast', S Russian Federation
169 R10 **Sri Aman** Sarawak, East Malaysia
117 R4 **Sribne** Chernihivs'ka Oblast', N Ukraine
155 I25 **Sri Jayawardanapura** var. Sri Jayawardenepura; prev. Kotte. Western Province, W Sri Lanka
155 M14 **Srīkākulam** Andhra Pradesh, E India
155 I25 **Sri Lanka** off. Democratic Socialist Republic of Sri Lanka; prev. Ceylon. ◆ republic S Asia
130 F14 **Sri Lanka** island S Asia
153 V14 **Srimangal** Chittagong, E Bangladesh
Sri Mohangorh see Shri Mohangarh
152 H5 **Srīnagar** Jammu and Kashmir, N India
167 N10 **Srinagarind Reservoir** ◎ W Thailand
155 F19 **Sringeri** Karnātaka, W India
155 K25 **Sri Pada** Eng. Adam's Peak. ▲ S Sri Lanka
Sri Saket see Si Sa Ket
111 G14 **Środa Śląska** Ger. Neumarkt. Dolnośląskie, SW Poland
110 H12 **Środa Wielkopolska** Wielkolpolskie, C Poland
Srpska Kostajnica see Bosanska Kostajnica
113 G14 **Srpska, Republika** ❖ republic Bosnia & Herzegovina
Srpski Brod see Bosanski Brod
Ssu-ch'uan see Sichuan
Ssu-p'ing/Ssu-p'ing-chieh see Siping
Stablo see Stavelot
99 G15 **Stabroek** Antwerpen, N Belgium
Stackeln see Strenči
96 I5 **Stack Skerry** island N Scotland, UK
100 I9 **Stade** Niedersachsen, NW Germany

94 C10 **Stadlandet** *peninsula* S Norway
109 R5 **Stadl-Paura** Oberösterreich, NW Austria
119 L20 **Stadolichy** *Rus.* Stodolichi. Homyel'skaya Voblasts', SE Belarus
98 P7 **Stadskanaal** Groningen, NE Netherlands
101 H16 **Stadtallendorf** Hessen, C Germany
101 K23 **Stadtbergen** Bayern, S Germany
108 G7 **Stäfa** Zürich, NE Switzerland
95 K23 **Staffanstorp** Skåne, S Sweden
101 K18 **Staffelstein** Bayern, C Germany
97 L19 **Stafford** C England, UK
26 L6 **Stafford** Kansas, C USA
21 W4 **Stafford** Virginia, NE USA
97 L19 **Staffordshire** *cultural region* C England, UK
19 N12 **Stafford Springs** Connecticut, NE USA
115 H14 **Stágira** Kentrikí Makedonía, N Greece
118 G7 **Staicele** Limbaži, N Latvia
Ştaierdorf-Anina *see* Anina
109 V8 **Stainz** Steiermark, SE Austria
Stájerlakanina *see* Anina
117 Y7 **Stakhanov** Luhans'ka Oblast', E Ukraine
108 E11 **Stalden** Valais, SW Switzerland
Stalin *see* Varna
Stalinabad *see* Dushanbe
Stalingrad *see* Volgograd
Staliniri *see* Ts'khinvali
Stalino *see* Donets'k
Stalinobod *see* Dushanbe
Stalinov Štít *see* Gerlachovský štít
Stalinsk *see* Novokuznetsk
Stalinskaya Oblast' *see* Donets'ka Oblast'
Stalinski Zaliv *see* Varnenski Zaliv
Stalin, Yazovir *see* Iskŭr, Yazovir
8 K2 **Stallworthy, Cape** *headland* Nunavut, N Canada
111 N15 **Stalowa Wola** Podkarpackie, SE Poland
114 I11 **Stamboliyski** Plovdiv, C Bulgaria
114 J8 **Stamboliyski, Yazovir** ⊠ N Bulgaria
97 N19 **Stamford** E England, UK
18 L14 **Stamford** Connecticut, NE USA
25 P6 **Stamford** Texas, SW USA
25 Q6 **Stamford, Lake** ⊠ Texas, SW USA
108 I10 **Stampa** Graubünden, SE Switzerland
Stampalia *see* Astypálaia
27 T14 **Stamps** Arkansas, C USA
92 G11 **Stamsund** Nordland, C Norway
27 R2 **Stanberry** Missouri, C USA
195 O3 **Stancomb-Wills Glacier** *glacier* Antarctica
83 K21 **Standerton** Mpumalanga, E South Africa
31 R7 **Standish** Michigan, N USA
20 M6 **Stanford** Kentucky, S USA
33 S9 **Stanford** Montana, NW USA
95 P19 **Stånga** Gotland, SE Sweden
94 I13 **Stange** Hedmark, S Norway
83 L23 **Stanger** KwaZulu/Natal, E South Africa
Stanimaka *see* Asenovgrad
Stanislau *see* Ivano-Frankivs'k
35 P8 **Stanislaus River** ≈ California, W USA
Stanislav *see* Ivano-Frankivs'k
Stanislavskaya Oblast' *see* Ivano-Frankivs'ka Oblast'
Stanisławów *see* Ivano-Frankivs'k
Stanke Dimitrov *see* Dupnitsa
183 O15 **Stanley** Tasmania, SE Australia
65 E24 **Stanley** *var.* Port Stanley, Puerto Argentino ○ (Falkland Islands) East Falkland, Falkland Islands
33 O13 **Stanley** Idaho, NW USA
28 L3 **Stanley** North Dakota, N USA
21 U4 **Stanley** Virginia, NE USA
30 J6 **Stanley** Wisconsin, N USA
79 G21 **Stanley Pool** *var.* Pool Malebo. ◎ Congo/Dem. Rep. Congo
155 H20 **Stanley Reservoir** ⊠ S India
Stanleyville *see* Kisangani
42 G3 **Stann Creek** ◈ *district* SE Belize
Stann Creek *see* Dangriga
123 Q12 **Stanovoy Khrebet** ▲ SE Russian Federation
108 F8 **Stans** Unterwalden, C Switzerland
97 O21 **Stansted** ✕ (London) Essex, E England, UK
183 U4 **Stanthorpe** Queensland, E Australia
21 N6 **Stanton** Kentucky, S USA
31 Q8 **Stanton** Michigan, N USA
29 Q14 **Stanton** Nebraska, C USA
28 L5 **Stanton** North Dakota, N USA
25 N7 **Stanton** Texas, SW USA
32 H7 **Stanwood** Washington, NW USA
117 Y7 **Stanychno-Luhans'ke** Luhans'ka Oblast', E Ukraine
108 K7 **Stanzach** Tirol, W Austria
98 M9 **Staphorst** Overijssel, E Netherlands
14 D18 **Staples** Ontario, S Canada
29 T6 **Staples** Minnesota, N USA
28 M14 **Stapleton** Nebraska, C USA
25 S8 **Star** Texas, SW USA
111 M14 **Starachowice** Świętokrzyskie, C Poland
Stara Kanjiža *see* Kanjiža
111 M18 **Stará Ľubovňa** *Ger.* Altlublau, *Hung.* Prešovský Kraj, E Slovakia
112 L10 **Stara Pazova** *Ger.* Altpasua, *Hung.* Ópazova. Serbia, N Serbia and Montenegro (Yugo.)
Stara Planina *see* Balkan Mountains
114 L9 **Stara Reka** ≈ C Bulgaria
116 M5 **Stara Synyava** Khmel'nyts'ka Oblast', W Ukraine
116 I2 **Stara Vyzhivka** Volyns'ka Oblast', NW Ukraine
Staraya Belitsa *see* Staraya Byelitsa
119 M14 **Staraya Byelitsa** *Rus.* Staraya Belitsa. Vitsyebskaya Voblasts', NE Belarus
127 R5 **Staraya Mayna** Ul'yanovskaya Oblast', W Russian Federation
119 O18 **Staraya Rudnya** *Rus.* Staraya Rudnya. Homyel'skaya Voblasts', SE Belarus
124 H14 **Staraya Russa** Novgorodskaya Oblast', W Russian Federation
114 K10 **Stara Zagora** *Lat.* Augusta Trajana. Stara Zagora, C Bulgaria
116 K10 **Stara Zagora** ◈ *province* C Bulgaria
29 S8 **Starbuck** Minnesota, N USA
191 W4 **Starbuck Island** *prev.* Volunteer Island. *island* E Kiribati
27 V13 **Star City** Arkansas, C USA
112 F13 **Staretina** ▲ W Bosnia and Herzegovina
Stargard in Pommern *see* Stargard Szczeciński
110 E9 **Stargard Szczeciński** *Ger.* Stargard in Pommern. Zachodnio-pomorskie, NW Poland
187 N10 **Star Harbour** *harbour* San Cristobal, SE Solomon Islands
Stari Bečej *see* Bečej
113 F15 **Stari Grad** *It.* Cittavecchia. Split-Dalmacija, S Croatia
124 J16 **Staritsa** Tverskaya Oblast', W Russian Federation
23 V9 **Starke** Florida, SE USA
22 M4 **Starkville** Mississippi, S USA
186 B7 **Star Mountains** *Ind.* Pegunungan Sterren. ▲ Indonesia/PNG
101 L23 **Starnberg** Bayern, SE Germany
101 L24 **Starnberger See** ◎ SE Germany
Starobel'sk *see* Starobil's'k
117 X8 **Starobesheve** Donets'ka Oblast', E Ukraine
117 Y6 **Starobil's'k** *Rus.* Starobel'sk. Luhans'ka Oblast', E Ukraine
Starobin *see* Starobyn
119 K18 **Starobyn** *Rus.* Starobin. Minskaya Voblasts', S Belarus
126 H6 **Starodub** Bryanskaya Oblast', W Russian Federation
110 I8 **Starogard Gdański** *Ger.* Preussisch-Stargard. Pomorskie, N Poland
145 P16 **Staroikan** Yuzhnyy Kazakhstan, S Kazakhstan
Starokonstantinov *see* Starokostyantyniv
116 L5 **Starokostyantyniv** *Rus.* Starokonstantinov. Khmel'nyts'ka Oblast', NW Ukraine
126 K12 **Starominskaya** Krasnodarskiy Kray, SW Russian Federation
114 L7 **Staro Selo** *Rom.* Satul-Vechi; *prev.* Star-Smil. Silistra, NE Bulgaria
126 K12 **Staroshcherbinovskaya** Krasnodarskiy Kray, SW Russian Federation
127 V6 **Starosubkhangulovo** Respublika Bashkortostan, W Russian Federation
35 S4 **Star Peak** ▲ Nevada, W USA
Star-Smil *see* Staro Selo
97 J25 **Start Point** *headland* SW England, UK
Startsy *see* Kirawsk
Starum *see* Stavoren
119 L18 **Staryya Darohi** *Rus.* Staryye Dorogi. Minskaya Voblasts', S Belarus
Staryye Dorogi *see* Staryya Darohi
127 T2 **Staryye Zyattsy** Udmurtskaya Respublika, NW Russian Federation
117 U13 **Staryy Krym** Respublika Krym, S Ukraine
126 K8 **Staryy Oskol** Belgorodskaya Oblast', W Russian Federation
116 H6 **Staryy Sambir** L'vivs'ka Oblast', W Ukraine
101 L14 **Stassfurt** *var.* Staßfurt. Sachsen-Anhalt, C Germany
111 M15 **Staszów** Świętokrzyskie, C Poland
29 W13 **State Center** Iowa, C USA
18 E14 **State College** Pennsylvania, NE USA
18 K15 **Staten Island** *island* New York, NE USA
Staten Island *see* Estados, Isla de los
23 U8 **Statenville** Georgia, SE USA
23 W5 **Statesboro** Georgia, SE USA
States, The *see* United States of America
21 R9 **Statesville** North Carolina, SE USA
95 G16 **Stathelle** Telemark, S Norway
30 K15 **Staunton** Illinois, N USA
21 T5 **Staunton** Virginia, NE USA
95 C16 **Stavanger** Rogaland, S Norway
99 L21 **Stavelot** *Dut.* Stablo. Liège, E Belgium
95 G16 **Stavern** Vestfold, S Norway
Stavers Island *see* Vostok Island
98 J7 **Stavoren** *Fris.* Starum. Friesland, N Netherlands
126 M14 **Stavropol'** *prev.* Voroshilovsk. Stavropol'skiy Kray, SW Russian Federation
Stavropol' *see* Tol'yatti
126 M14 **Stavropol'skaya Vozvyshennost'** ▲ SW Russian Federation
126 M14 **Stavropol'skiy Kray** ◈ *territory* SW Russian Federation
115 H14 **Stavrós** Kentrikí Makedonía, N Greece
115 J24 **Stavrós, Akrotírio** *headland* Kríti, Greece, E Mediterranean Sea
115 K21 **Stavrós, Akrotírio** *headland* Náxos, Kykládes, Greece, Aegean Sea
114 I12 **Stavroúpoli** *prev.* Stavroúpolis. Anatolikí Makedonía kai Thráki, NE Greece
Stavroúpolis *see* Stavroúpoli
117 O6 **Stavyshche** Kyyivs'ka Oblast', N Ukraine
182 M11 **Stawell** Victoria, SE Australia
110 N9 **Stawiski** Podlaskie, NE Poland
14 G14 **Stayner** Ontario, S Canada
37 R3 **Steamboat Springs** Colorado, C USA
20 M8 **Stearns** Kentucky, S USA
39 N10 **Stebbins** Alaska, USA
108 K7 **Steeg** Tirol, W Austria
27 Y9 **Steele** Missouri, C USA
29 N5 **Steele** North Dakota, N USA
194 J5 **Steele Island** *island* Antarctica
30 K16 **Steeleville** Illinois, N USA
27 W6 **Steelville** Missouri, C USA
99 G14 **Steenbergen** Noord-Brabant, S Netherlands
Steenkool *see* Bintuni
11 O10 **Steen River** Alberta, W Canada
98 M8 **Steenwijk** Overijssel, N Netherlands
65 A23 **Steeple Jason** *island* Jason Islands, NW Falkland Islands
174 J8 **Steep Point** *headland* Western Australia
116 L9 **Ştefăneşti** Botoşani, NE Romania
Stefanie, Lake *see* Ch'ew Bahir
8 L5 **Stefansson Island** *island* Nunavut, N Canada
117 O10 **Ştefan Vodă** *Rus.* Suvorovo. SE Moldova
63 H18 **Steffen, Cerro** ▲ S Chile
108 D9 **Steffisburg** Bern, C Switzerland
95 J24 **Stege** Storstrøm, SE Denmark
116 G10 **Ştei** *Hung.* Vaskohsziklás. Bihor, W Romania
Steier *see* Steyr
Steierdorf/Steierdorf-Anina *see* Anina
109 T7 **Steiermark** *off.* Land Steiermark, *Eng.* Styria. ◈ *state* C Austria
101 J19 **Steigerwald** *hill range* C Germany
99 L17 **Stein** Limburg, SE Netherlands
Stein *see* Stein an der Donau, Austria
Stein *see* Kamnik, Slovenia
108 M8 **Steinach** Tirol, W Austria
Steinamanger *see* Szombathely
109 W3 **Stein an der Donau** *var.* Stein. Niederösterreich, NE Austria
Steinau an der Elbe *see* Ścinawa
11 Y16 **Steinbach** Manitoba, S Canada
Steiner Alpen *see* Kamniško-Savinjske Alpe
99 L24 **Steinfort** Luxembourg, W Luxembourg
100 H12 **Steinhuder Meer** ◎ NW Germany
93 E15 **Steinkjer** Nord-Trøndelag, C Norway
Stejarul *see* Karapelit
99 F16 **Stekene** Oost-Vlaanderen, NW Belgium
83 E26 **Stellenbosch** Western Cape, SW South Africa
98 F13 **Stellendam** Zuid-Holland, SW Netherlands
39 T12 **Steller, Mount** ▲ Alaska, USA
103 Y14 **Stello, Monte** ▲ Corse, France, C Mediterranean Sea
106 F5 **Stelvio, Passo dello** *pass* Italy/Switzerland
103 R3 **Stenay** Meuse, NE France
100 L12 **Stendal** Sachsen-Anhalt, C Germany
118 E8 **Stende** Talsi, NW Latvia
182 H10 **Stenhouse Bay** South Australia
95 J23 **Stenløse** Frederiksborg, E Denmark
95 L19 **Stensjön** Jönköping, S Sweden
95 K18 **Stenstorp** Västra Götaland, S Sweden
95 I18 **Stenungsund** Västra Götaland, S Sweden
Stepanakert *see* Xankändi
137 T11 **Step'anavan** N Armenia
100 K9 **Stepenitz** ≈ N Germany
29 O10 **Stephan** South Dakota, N USA
29 R3 **Stephen** Minnesota, N USA
27 T14 **Stephens** Arkansas, C USA
184 J13 **Stephens, Cape** *headland* D'Urville Island, Marlborough, SW NZ
21 V3 **Stephens City** Virginia, NE USA
182 L6 **Stephens Creek** New South Wales, SE Australia
184 K13 **Stephens Island** *island* C NZ
31 N5 **Stephenson** Michigan, N USA
13 S12 **Stephenville** Newfoundland and Labrador, SE Canada
25 S7 **Stephenville** Texas, SW USA
145 P17 **Step' Nardara** *Kaz.* Shardara Dalasy; *prev.* Shaidara. *grassland* S Kazakhstan
145 R8 **Stepnogorsk** Akmola, C Kazakhstan
127 O15 **Stepnoye** Stavropol'skiy Kray, SW Russian Federation
145 Q8 **Stepnyak** Akmola, N Kazakhstan
192 J17 **Steps Point** *headland* Tutuila, W American Samoa
115 F17 **Stereá Ellás** *Eng.* Greece Central. ◈ *region* C Greece
83 J24 **Sterkspruit** Eastern Cape, SE South Africa
127 U6 **Sterlibashevo** Respublika Bashkortostan, W Russian Federation
39 R12 **Sterling** Alaska, USA
37 V3 **Sterling** Colorado, C USA
30 K11 **Sterling** Illinois, N USA
26 M5 **Sterling** Kansas, C USA
25 O8 **Sterling City** Texas, SW USA
31 S9 **Sterling Heights** Michigan, N USA
21 W3 **Sterling Park** Virginia, NE USA
37 V2 **Sterling Reservoir** ⊠ Colorado, C USA
22 I5 **Sterlington** Louisiana, S USA
127 U6 **Sterlitamak** Respublika Bashkortostan, W Russian Federation
Sternberg *see* Šternberk
111 H17 **Šternberk** *Ger.* Sternberg. Olomoucký Kraj, E Czech Republic
141 V17 **Stēroh** Suquṭrā, S Yemen
110 G11 **Stęszew** Wielkolpolskie, C Poland
Stettin *see* Szczecin
Stettiner Haff *see* Szczeciński, Zalew
11 Q15 **Stettler** Alberta, SW Canada
31 V13 **Steubenville** Ohio, N USA
97 O21 **Stevenage** E England, UK
23 Q1 **Stevenson** Alabama, S USA
32 H11 **Stevenson** Washington, NW USA
182 E1 **Stevenson Creek** *seasonal river* South Australia
39 Q13 **Stevenson Entrance** *strait* Alaska, USA
30 L6 **Stevens Point** Wisconsin, N USA
39 R8 **Stevens Village** Alaska, USA
33 P10 **Stevensville** Montana, NW USA
93 E25 **Stevns Klint** *headland* E Denmark
10 J12 **Stewart** British Columbia, W Canada
10 J6 **Stewart** ≈ Yukon Territory, NW Canada
10 I6 **Stewart Crossing** Yukon Territory, NW Canada
63 H25 **Stewart, Isla** *island* S Chile
185 B25 **Stewart Island** *island* S NZ
181 W6 **Stewart, Mount** ▲ Queensland, E Australia
10 H6 **Stewart River** Yukon Territory, NW Canada
27 R3 **Stewartsville** Missouri, C USA
11 S16 **Stewart Valley** Saskatchewan, S Canada
29 W10 **Stewartville** Minnesota, N USA
Steyerlak-Anina *see* Anina
109 T5 **Steyr** *var.* Steier. Oberösterreich, N Austria
109 T5 **Steyr** ≈ NW Austria
29 P11 **Stickney** South Dakota, N USA
98 L5 **Stiens** Friesland, N Netherlands
Stif *see* Sétif
27 Q11 **Stigler** Oklahoma, C USA
107 N18 **Stigliano** Basilicata, S Italy
95 N17 **Stigtomta** Södermanland, C Sweden
10 I11 **Stikine** ≈ British Columbia, W Canada
Stilida/Stilís *see* Stylída
95 G22 **Stilling** Århus, C Denmark
29 W8 **Stillwater** Minnesota, N USA
27 O9 **Stillwater** Oklahoma, C USA
35 S5 **Stillwater Range** ▲ Nevada, W USA
18 I8 **Stillwater Reservoir** ⊠ New York, NE USA
107 O22 **Stilo, Punta** *headland* S Italy
27 R10 **Stilwell** Oklahoma, C USA
113 N17 **Štimlje** Serbia, S Serbia and Montenegro (Yugo.)
25 N1 **Stinnett** Texas, SW USA
113 P18 **Štip** E FYR Macedonia
Stira *see* Stýra
96 J12 **Stirling** C Scotland, UK
96 I12 **Stirling** *cultural region* C Scotland, UK
180 J14 **Stirling Range** ▲ Western Australia
93 E16 **Stjørdalshalsen** Nord-Trøndelag, C Norway
Stochód *see* Stokhid
101 H24 **Stockach** Baden-Württemberg, S Germany
25 S12 **Stockdale** Texas, SW USA
109 X3 **Stockerau** Niederösterreich, NE Austria
93 H20 **Stockholm** ● (Sweden) Stockholm, C Sweden
95 O15 **Stockholm** ◈ *county* C Sweden
Stockmannshof *see* Pļaviņas
97 L18 **Stockport** NW England, UK
65 K15 **Stocks Seamount** *undersea feature* C Atlantic Ocean
35 O8 **Stockton** California, W USA
26 L3 **Stockton** Kansas, C USA
27 S6 **Stockton** Missouri, C USA
30 K3 **Stockton Island** *island* Apostle Islands, Wisconsin, N USA
27 S7 **Stockton Lake** ⊠ Missouri, C USA
97 M15 **Stockton-on-Tees** *var.* Stockton on Tees. N England, UK
24 M10 **Stockton Plateau** *plain* Texas, SW USA
28 M16 **Stockville** Nebraska, C USA
93 H17 **Stöde** Västernorrland, C Sweden
Stodolichi *see* Stadolichy
167 S11 **Stœng Trêng** *prev.* Stung Treng. Stœng Trêng, NE Cambodia
113 M19 **Stogovo Karaorman** ▲ W FYR Macedonia
Stoke *see* Stoke-on-Trent
97 L19 **Stoke-on-Trent** *var.* Stoke. C England, UK
182 M15 **Stokes Point** *headland* Tasmania, SE Australia
116 J2 **Stokhid** *Pol.* Stochód, *Rus.* Stokhod. ≈ NW Ukraine
Stokhod *see* Stokhid
92 I4 **Stokkseyri** Sudhurland, SW Iceland
92 G10 **Stokmarknes** Nordland, C Norway
Stol *see* Veliki Krš
113 H15 **Stolac** Federacija Bosna I Hercegovina, S Bosnia and Herzegovina
Stolbce *see* Stowbtsy
101 D16 **Stolberg** *var.* Stolberg im Rheinland. Nordrhein-Westfalen, W Germany
Stolberg im Rheinland *see* Stolberg
123 P6 **Stolbovoy, Ostrov** *island* NE Russian Federation
Stolbtsy *see* Stowbtsy
119 J20 **Stolin** *Rus.* Stolin. Brestskaya Voblasts', SW Belarus
95 K14 **Stöllet** *var.* Norra Ny. Värmland, C Sweden
Stolp *see* Słupsk
Stolpe *see* Słupia
Stolpmünde *see* Ustka
115 F15 **Stómio** Thessalía, C Greece
14 J11 **Stonecliffe** Ontario, SE Canada
96 L10 **Stonehaven** NE Scotland, UK
97 M23 **Stonehenge** *ancient monument* Wiltshire, S England, UK
23 T3 **Stone Mountain** ▲ Georgia, SE USA
11 X16 **Stonewall** Manitoba, S Canada
21 S3 **Stonewood** West Virginia, NE USA
14 D17 **Stoney Point** Ontario, S Canada
92 H10 **Stonglandseidet** Troms, N Norway
65 N25 **Stonybeach Bay** *bay* Tristan da Cunha, SE Atlantic Ocean
35 N5 **Stony Creek** ≈ California, W USA
65 N25 **Stonyhill Point** *headland* S Tristan da Cunha
14 I14 **Stony Lake** ◎ Ontario, SE Canada
11 Q14 **Stony Plain** Alberta, SW Canada
21 R9 **Stony Point** North Carolina, SE USA
18 G8 **Stony Point** *headland* New York, NE USA
11 T10 **Stony Rapids** Saskatchewan, C Canada
39 P11 **Stony River** Alaska, USA
Stony Tunguska *see* Podkamennaya Tunguska
12 G10 **Stooping** ≈ Ontario, C Canada
100 I9 **Stör** ≈ N Germany
95 M15 **Storå** Örebro, S Sweden
95 J16 **Stora Gla** ◎ C Sweden
95 I16 **Stora Le** *Nor.* Store Le. ◎ Norway/Sweden
92 I12 **Stora Lulevatten** ◎ N Sweden
92 H13 **Storavan** ◎ N Sweden
93 I20 **Storby** Åland, SW Finland
94 E10 **Stordalen** Møre og Romsdal, S Norway
Storebelt *see* Storebælt
95 H23 **Storebælt** *var.* Store Bælt, *Eng.* Great Belt, Storebelt. *channel* Baltic Sea/Kattegat
95 M19 **Storebro** Kalmar, S Sweden
95 J24 **Store Heddinge** Storstrøm, SE Denmark
Store Le *see* Stora Le
93 E16 **Støren** Sør-Trøndelag, S Norway
92 O4 **Storfjorden** *fjord* S Norway
95 L15 **Storfors** Värmland, C Sweden
92 G13 **Storforshei** Nordland, C Norway
Storhammer *see* Hamar
100 L10 **Störkanal** *canal* N Germany
93 F16 **Storlien** Jämtland, C Sweden
183 P17 **Storm Bay** *inlet* Tasmania, SE Australia
29 T12 **Storm Lake** Iowa, C USA
29 S13 **Storm Lake** ◎ Iowa, C USA
96 G7 **Stornoway** NW Scotland, UK
Storojineţ *see* Storozhynets'
92 P1 **Storøya** *island* NE Svalbard
125 S10 **Storozhevsk** Respublika Komi, NW Russian Federation
Storozhinets *see* Storozhynets'
116 K8 **Storozhynets'** *Ger.* Storozynetz, *Rom.* Storojineţ, *Rus.* Storozhinets. Chernivets'ka Oblast', W Ukraine
Storozynetz *see* Storozhynets'
92 H11 **Storriten** ▲ C Norway
19 N12 **Storrs** Connecticut, NE USA
94 I11 **Storsjøen** ◎ S Norway
94 N13 **Storsjön** ◎ C Sweden
93 F16 **Storsjön** ◎ C Sweden
92 J9 **Storslett** Troms, N Norway
94 H11 **Storsølnkletten** ▲ S Norway
92 I9 **Storsteinnes** Troms, N Norway
95 I24 **Storstrøm** *off.* Storstrøms Amt. ◈ *county* SE Denmark
93 J14 **Storsund** Norrbotten, N Sweden
94 J9 **Storsylen** *Swe.* Sylarna. ▲ Norway/Sweden
92 H11 **Stortoppen** ▲ N Sweden
93 H14 **Storuman** Västerbotten, N Sweden
93 H14 **Storuman** ◎ N Sweden
94 N13 **Storvik** Gävleborg, C Sweden
95 O14 **Storvreta** Uppsala, C Sweden
29 V13 **Story City** Iowa, C USA
11 V17 **Stoughton** Saskatchewan, S Canada
19 O11 **Stoughton** Massachusetts, NE USA
30 L9 **Stoughton** Wisconsin, N USA
97 L23 **Stour** ≈ E England, UK
97 P21 **Stour** ≈ S England, UK
27 T5 **Stover** Missouri, C USA
95 G21 **Støvring** Nordjylland, N Denmark
119 J17 **Stowbtsy** *Pol.* Stolbce, *Rus.* Stolbtsy. Minskaya Voblasts', C Belarus
25 X11 **Stowell** Texas, SW USA
97 P20 **Stowmarket** E England, UK
114 N8 **Stozher** Dobrich, NE Bulgaria
97 E14 **Strabane** *Ir.* An Srath Bán. W Northern Ireland, UK
121 S11 **Strabo Trench** *undersea feature* C Mediterranean Sea
27 T7 **Strafford** Missouri, C USA
183 N17 **Strahan** Tasmania, SE Australia
111 C18 **Strakonice** *Ger.* Strakonitz. Jihočeský Kraj, S Czech Republic
Strakonitz *see* Strakonice
100 N8 **Stralsund** Mecklenburg-Vorpommern, NE Germany
99 L16 **Stramproy** Limburg, SE Netherlands
83 E26 **Strand** Western Cape, SW South Africa
94 E10 **Stranda** Møre og Romsdal, S Norway
97 G15 **Strangford Lough** *Ir.* Loch Cuan. *inlet* E Northern Ireland, UK
95 N16 **Strängnäs** Södermanland, C Sweden
97 E14 **Stranorlar** *Ir.* Srath an Urláir. NW Ireland
97 H14 **Stranraer** S Scotland, UK
11 U16 **Strasbourg** Saskatchewan, S Canada
103 V5 **Strasbourg** *Ger.* Strassburg; *anc.* Argentoratum. Bas-Rhin, NE France
37 U4 **Strasburg** Colorado, C USA
29 N7 **Strasburg** North Dakota, N USA
31 U12 **Strasburg** Ohio, N USA
21 U3 **Strasburg** Virginia, NE USA
117 N10 **Strășeni** *var.* Strasheny. C Moldova
Strasheny *see* Strășeni
109 T8 **Strassburg** Kärnten, S Austria
Strassburg *see* Strasbourg, France
Strassburg *see* Aiud, Romania
99 M25 **Strassen** Luxembourg, S Luxembourg
109 R5 **Strasswalchen** Salzburg, C Austria
14 F16 **Stratford** Ontario, S Canada
184 K10 **Stratford** Taranaki, North Island, NZ
35 Q11 **Stratford** California, W USA
29 V13 **Stratford** Iowa, C USA
27 O12 **Stratford** Oklahoma, C USA
25 N1 **Stratford** Texas, SW USA
30 K6 **Stratford** Wisconsin, N USA
Stratford *see* Stratford-upon-Avon
97 M20 **Stratford-upon-Avon** *var.* Stratford. C England, UK
183 O17 **Strathgordon** Tasmania, SE Australia
11 Q16 **Strathmore** Alberta, SW Canada
35 R11 **Strathmore** California, W USA
14 E16 **Strathroy** Ontario, S Canada
96 I6 **Strathy Point** *headland* N Scotland, UK
37 W4 **Stratton** Colorado, C USA
19 P6 **Stratton** Maine, NE USA
18 M10 **Stratton Mountain** ▲ Vermont, NE USA
101 N21 **Straubing** Bayern, SE Germany
100 O12 **Strausberg** Brandenburg, E Germany
32 K13 **Strawberry Mountain** ▲ Oregon, NW USA
29 X12 **Strawberry Point** Iowa, C USA
36 M3 **Strawberry Reservoir** ⊠ Utah, W USA
36 M4 **Strawberry River** ≈ Utah, W USA
25 R7 **Strawn** Texas, SW USA
113 P17 **Straža** ▲ Bulgaria/FYR Macedonia
111 I19 **Strážov** *Hung.* Sztrazsó. ▲ NW Slovakia
182 F7 **Streaky Bay** South Australia
182 E7 **Streaky Bay** *bay* South Australia
30 L12 **Streator** Illinois, N USA
Streckenbach *see* Świdnik
111 C17 **Středočeský kraj** ◈ *region* C Czech Republic
Strednogorie *see* Pirdop
29 O6 **Streeter** North Dakota, N USA
25 U8 **Streetman** Texas, SW USA
116 G13 **Strehaia** Mehedinți, SW Romania
Strehlen *see* Strzelin
114 I10 **Strelcha** Pazardzhik, C Bulgaria
122 L12 **Strelka** Krasnoyarskiy Kray, C Russian Federation
126 L6 **Strel'na** ≈ NW Russian Federation
118 H7 **Strenči** *Ger.* Stackeln. Valka, N Latvia
108 K8 **Strengen** Tirol, W Austria
106 C6 **Stresa** Piemonte, NE Italy
Streshin *see* Streshyn
119 N18 **Streshyn** *Rus.* Streshin. Homyel'skaya Voblasts', SE Belarus
95 B18 **Streymoy** *Dan.* Strømø *Island* Faeroe Islands
95 G23 **Strib** Fyn, C Denmark
111 A17 **Stříbro** *Ger.* Mies. Plzeňský Kraj, W Czech Republic
186 B7 **Strickland** ≈ SW PNG
Striegau *see* Strzegom
Strigonium *see* Esztergom
98 H13 **Strijen** Zuid-Holland, SW Netherlands
63 H21 **Strobel, Lago** ◎ S Argentina
61 B25 **Stroeder** Buenos Aires, E Argentina
115 C20 **Strofádes** *island* Iónioi Nísoi, Greece, C Mediterranean Sea
Strofilia *see* Strofyliá
115 G17 **Strofyliá** *var.* Strofilia. Évvoia, C Greece
100 O10 **Strom** ≈ NE Germany
107 L22 **Stromboli** ⩕ Isola Stromboli, SW Italy
107 L22 **Stromboli, Isola** *island* Isole Eolie, S Italy
96 H9 **Stromeferry** N Scotland, UK
96 J5 **Stromness** N Scotland, UK
94 N11 **Strömsbruk** Gävleborg, C Sweden
29 Q15 **Stromsburg** Nebraska, C USA
95 K21 **Strömsnäsbruk** Kronoberg, S Sweden
95 I17 **Strömstad** Västra Götaland, S Sweden
93 G16 **Strömsund** Jämtland, C Sweden
93 G15 **Ströms Vattudal** *valley* N Sweden
27 V14 **Strong** Arkansas, C USA
Strongilí *see* Strongylí
107 O21 **Strongoli** Calabria, SW Italy
31 T11 **Strongsville** Ohio, N USA
115 Q23 **Strongylí** *var.* Strongilí. *island* SE Greece
96 K5 **Stronsay** *island* NE Scotland, UK
97 L21 **Stroud** C England, UK
27 O10 **Stroud** Oklahoma, C USA
18 I14 **Stroudsburg** Pennsylvania, NE USA
95 F21 **Struer** Ringkøbing, W Denmark
113 M20 **Struga** SW FYR Macedonia
Strugi-Kranyse *see* Strugi-Krasnyye
124 G14 **Strugi-Krasnyye** *var.* Strugi-Kranyse. Pskovskaya Oblast', W Russian Federation
114 G11 **Struma** *Gk.* Strymónas. ≈ Bulgaria/Greece *see also* Strymónas
97 G21 **Strumble Head** *headland* SW Wales, UK
113 Q19 **Strumeshnitsa** *Mac.* Strumica. ≈ Bulgaria/FYR Macedonia
113 Q19 **Strumica** E FYR Macedonia
Strumica *see* Strumeshnitsa

◆ Country ◇ Dependent Territory ◈ Administrative Region ▲ Mountain ⩕ Volcano ◎ Lake
● Country Capital ○ Dependent Territory Capital ✕ International Airport ▲ Mountain Range ≈ River ⊠ Reservoir

114 *G11* **Strumyani** Blagoevgrad, SW Bulgaria
31 *V12* **Struthers** Ohio, N USA
114 *I10* **Stryama** ≈ C Bulgaria
114 *G13* **Strymónas** ***Bul.*** Struma. ≈ Bulgaria/Greece ***see also*** Struma
115 *H14* **Strymonikós Kólpos** *gulf* N Greece
116 *I6* **Stryy** L'vivs'ka Oblast', NW Ukraine
116 *H6* **Stryy** ≈ W Ukraine
111 *F14* **Strzegom** ***Ger.*** Striegau. Wałbrzych, SW Poland
110 *E10* **Strzelce Krajeńskie** ***Ger.*** Friedeberg Neumark. Lubuskie, W Poland
111 *I15* **Strzelce Opolskie** ***Ger.*** Gross Strehlitz. Opolskie, S Poland
182 *K3* **Strzelecki Creek** *seasonal river* South Australia
182 *J3* **Strzelecki Desert** *desert* South Australia
111 *G15* **Strzelin** ***Ger.*** Strehlen. Dolnośląskie, SW Poland
110 *I11* **Strzelno** Kujawsko-pomorskie, C Poland
111 *N17* **Strzyżów** Podkarpackie, SE Poland
Stua Laighean *see* Leinster, Mount
23 *Y13* **Stuart** Florida, SE USA
29 *U14* **Stuart** Iowa, C USA
29 *O13* **Stuart** Nebraska, C USA
21 *S8* **Stuart** Virginia, NE USA
10 *L13* **Stuart** ≈ British Columbia, SW Canada
39 *N10* **Stuart Island** *island* Alaska, USA
10 *L13* **Stuart Lake** ◎ British Columbia, SW Canada
185 *B22* **Stuart Mountains** ⛰ South Island, NZ
182 *F3* **Stuart Range** *hill range* South Australia
Stubaital *see* Neustift im Stubaital
95 *I24* **Stubbekøbing** Storstrøm, SE Denmark
45 *P14* **Stubbs** Saint Vincent, Saint Vincent and the Grenadines
109 *V6* **Stübming** ≈ E Austria
114 *J11* **Studen Kladenets, Yazovir** ⊠ S Bulgaria
185 *G21* **Studholme** Canterbury, South Island, NZ
Stuhlweissenberg *see* Székesfehérvár
Stuhm *see* Sztum
12 *C7* **Stull Lake** ◎ Ontario, C Canada
Stung Treng *see* Stŏeng Trêng
126 *L4* **Stupino** Moskovskaya Oblast', W Russian Federation
27 *U4* **Sturgeon** Missouri, C USA
14 *G10* **Sturgeon** ≈ Ontario, S Canada
31 *N6* **Sturgeon Bay** Wisconsin, N USA
14 *G11* **Sturgeon Falls** Ontario, S Canada
12 *C11* **Sturgeon Lake** ◎ Ontario, S Canada
30 *M3* **Sturgeon River** ≈ Michigan, N USA
20 *H6* **Sturgis** Kentucky, S USA
31 *P11* **Sturgis** Michigan, N USA
28 *J9* **Sturgis** South Dakota, N USA
112 *D10* **Šturlić** Federacija Bosna I Hercegovina, NW Bosnia and Herzegovina
111 *J22* **Štúrovo** ***Hung.*** Párkány; ***prev.*** Parkan. Nitriansky Kraj, W Slovakia
182 *L4* **Sturt, Mount** *hill* New South Wales, SE Australia
181 *P4* **Sturt Plain** *plain* Northern Territory, N Australia
181 *T9* **Sturt Stony Desert** *desert* South Australia
83 *J25* **Stutterheim** Eastern Cape, S South Africa
101 *H21* **Stuttgart** Baden-Württemberg, SW Germany
27 *W12* **Stuttgart** Arkansas, C USA
92 *H2* **Stykkishólmur** Vesturland, W Iceland
115 *F17* **Stylída** ***var.*** Stilida, Stilís. Stereá Ellás, C Greece
116 *K2* **Styr** ***Rus.*** Styr'. ≈ Belarus/Ukraine
115 *I19* **Stýra** ***var.*** Stira. Évvoia, C Greece
Styria *see* Steiermark
Su *see* Jiangsu
Sua *see* Sowa
171 *Q17* **Suai** W East Timor
54 *G9* **Suaita** Santander, C Colombia
80 *I7* **Suakin** ***var.*** Sawakin. Red Sea, NE Sudan
161 *T13* **Suao** ***Jap.*** Suō. N Taiwan
Suao *see* Suau
83 *I18* **Sua Pan** ***var.*** Sowa Pan. *salt lake* NE Botswana
40 *G6* **Suaqui Grande** Sonora, NW Mexico
61 *A16* **Suardi** Santa Fe, C Argentina
54 *D11* **Suárez** Cauca, SW Colombia
186 *G10* **Suau** ***var.*** Suao. Suaul Island, SE PNG
118 *G12* **Subačius** Panevėžys, NE Lithuania
168 *K9* **Subang** ***prev.*** Soebang. Jawa, C Indonesia
169 *O16* **Subang** ✕ (Kuala Lumpur) Pahang, Peninsular Malaysia
131 *S10* **Subansiri** ≈ NE India
118 *I11* **Subate** Daugvapils, SE Latvia
139 *N5* **Subaykhān** Dayr az Zawr, E Syria
Subei/Subei Mongolzu Zizhixian *see* Dangchengwan
169 *P9* **Subi Besar, Pulau** *island* Kepulauan Natuna, W Indonesia
Subiyah *see* Aş Şubayhīyah
26 *I7* **Sublette** Kansas, C USA
112 *K8* **Subotica** ***Ger.*** Maria-Theresiopel, ***Hung.*** Szabadka. Serbia, N Serbia and Montenegro (Yugo.)
116 *K9* **Suceava** ***Ger.*** Suczawa, ***Hung.*** Szucsava. Suceava, NE Romania
116 *J9* **Suceava** ◈ *county* NE Romania
116 *K9* **Suceava** ***Ger.*** Suczawa. ≈ N Romania
112 *E12* **Sučevići** Zadar, SW Croatia
111 *K17* **Sucha Beskidzka** Małopolskie, S Poland
111 *M14* **Suchedniów** Świętokrzyskie, C Poland
42 *A2* **Suchitepéquez** ***off.*** Departamento de Suchitepéquez. ◈ *department* SW Guatemala
Su-chou *see* Suzhou
Suchow *see* Suzhou, Jiangsu, China
Suchow *see* Xuzhou, Jiangsu, China
97 *D17* **Suck** ≈ C Ireland
Sucker State *see* Illinois
186 *F9* **Suckling, Mount** ▲ S PNG
57 *L19* **Sucre** ***hist.*** Chuquisaca, La Plata. ● (Bolivia-legal capital) Chuquisaca, S Bolivia
54 *E6* **Sucre** Santander, N Colombia
56 *A7* **Sucre** Manabí, W Ecuador
54 *E6* **Sucre** ***off.*** Departamento de Sucre. ◈ *province* N Colombia
55 *O5* **Sucre** ***off.*** Estado Sucre. ◈ *state* NE Venezuela
56 *D6* **Sucumbíos** ◈ *province* NE Ecuador
113 *G15* **Sućuraj** Split-Dalmacija, S Croatia
58 *K10* **Sucuriju** Amapá, NE Brazil
Suczawa *see* Suceava
79 *E16* **Sud** ***Eng.*** South. ◈ *province* S Cameroon
126 *K13* **Suda** ≈ NW Russian Federation
Suda *see* Soúda
117 *U13* **Sudak** Respublika Krym, S Ukraine
24 *M4* **Sudan** Texas, SW USA
80 *C10* **Sudan** ***off.*** Republic of Sudan, ***Ar.*** Jumhuriyat as-Sudan; ***prev.*** Anglo-Egyptian ***Sudan.*** ◆ *republic* N Africa
Sudanese Republic *see* Mali
Sudan, Jumhuriyat as- *see* Sudan
14 *F10* **Sudbury** Ontario, S Canada
97 *P20* **Sudbury** E England, UK
Sud, Canal de *see* Gonâve, Canal de la
80 *E13* **Sudd** *swamp region* S Sudan
100 *K10* **Sude** ≈ N Germany
Sudest Island *see* Tagula Island
111 *E15* **Sudeten** ***var.*** Sudetes, Sudetic Mountains, ***Cz./Pol.*** Sudety. ⛰ Czech Republic/Poland
Sudetes/ Sudetic Mountains/ Sudety *see* Sudeten
92 *G1* **Sudhureyri** Vestfirdhir, NW Iceland
92 *J4* **Sudhurland** ◈ *region* S Iceland
95 *B19* **Sudhuroy** ***Dan.*** Suderø *Island* Faeroe Islands
124 *M15* **Sudislavl'** Kostromskaya Oblast', NW Russian Federation
Südkarpaten *see* Carpații Meridionali
79 *N20* **Sud Kivu** ***off.*** Région Sud Kivu. ◈ *region* E Dem. Rep. Congo
Südliche Morava *see* Južna Morava
100 *E12* **Süd-Nord-Kanal** *canal* NW Germany
126 *M3* **Sudogda** Vladimirskaya Oblast', W Russian Federation
Sudostroy *see* Severodvinsk
79 *C15* **Sud-Ouest** ***Eng.*** South-West. ◈ *province* W Cameroon
173 *X17* **Sud Ouest, Pointe** *headland* SW Mauritius
187 *P17* **Sud, Province** ◈ *province* S New Caledonia
126 *J8* **Sudzha** Kurskaya Oblast', W Russian Federation
81 *D15* **Sue** ≈ S Sudan
105 *S10* **Sueca** País Valenciano, E Spain
114 *I10* **Sŭedinenie** Plovdiv, C Bulgaria
Suero *see* Alzira
75 *X8* **Suez** ***Ar.*** As Suways, El Suweis. NE Egypt
75 *W7* **Suez Canal** ***Ar.*** Qanāt as Suways. *canal* NE Egypt
75 *X8* **Suez, Gulf of** ***Ar.*** Khalīj as Suways. *gulf* NE Egypt
11 *R17* **Suffield** Alberta, SW Canada
21 *X7* **Suffolk** Virginia, NE USA
97 *P20* **Suffolk** *cultural region* E England, UK
142 *J2* **Şūfīān** Āžarbāyjān-e Khāvarī, N Iran
31 *N12* **Sugar Creek** ≈ Illinois, N USA
30 *L13* **Sugar Creek** ≈ Illinois, N USA
31 *R3* **Sugar Island** *island* Michigan, N USA
25 *V11* **Sugar Land** Texas, SW USA
19 *P6* **Sugarloaf Mountain** ▲ Maine, NE USA
65 *G24* **Sugar Loaf Point** *headland* N Saint Helena
136 *G16* **Suğla Gölü** ◎ SW Turkey
123 *T8* **Sugoy** ≈ E Russian Federation
158 *F7* **Sugun** Xinjiang Uygur Zizhiqu, W China
147 *U11* **Sugut, Gora** ▲ SW Kyrgyzstan
169 *V6* **Sugut, Sungai** ≈ East Malaysia
159 *O9* **Suhai Hu** ◎ C China
162 *K14* **Suhait** Nei Mongol Zizhiqu, N China
141 *X7* **Şuḩār** ***var.*** Sohar. N Oman
162 *L6* **Sühbaatar** Selenge, N Mongolia
163 *P9* **Sühbaatar** ◈ *province* E Mongolia
101 *K17* **Suhl** Thüringen, C Germany
108 *F7* **Suhr** Aargau, N Switzerland
Sui'an *see* Zhangpu
161 *O12* **Suichuan** ***var.*** Quanjiang. Jiangxi, S China
Suid-Afrika *see* South Africa
160 *L4* **Suide** Shaanxi, C China
Suidwes-Afrika *see* Namibia
163 *Y9* **Suifenhe** Heilongjiang, NE China
Suigen *see* Suwŏn
163 *W8* **Suihua** Heilongjiang, NE China
Súilí, Loch *see* Swilly, Lough
161 *Q6* **Suining** Jiangsu, E China
160 *I9* **Suining** Sichuan, C China
103 *Q4* **Suippes** Marne, N France
97 *E20* **Suir** ***Ir.*** An tSiúir. ≈ S Ireland
165 *J13* **Suita** Ōsaka, Honshū, SW Japan
160 *L16* **Suixi** Guangdong, S China
Sui Xian *see* Suizhou
163 *T13* **Suizhong** Liaoning, NE China
161 *N8* **Suizhou** ***prev.*** Sui Xian. Hubei, C China
149 *P17* **Sujāwal** Sind, SE Pakistan
169 *O16* **Sukabumi** ***prev.*** Soekaboemi. Jawa, C Indonesia
169 *Q12* **Sukadana, Teluk** *bay* Borneo, W Indonesia
165 *P11* **Sukagawa** Fukushima, Honshū, C Japan
Sukarnapura *see* Jayapura
Sukarno, Puntjak *see* Jaya, Puncak
Sŭkh *see* Sokh
114 *N8* **Sukha Reka** ≈ NE Bulgaria
126 *J5* **Sukhinichi** Kaluzhskaya Oblast', W Russian Federation
Sukhne *see* As Sukhnah
131 *Q4* **Sukhona** ***var.*** Tot'ma. ≈ NW Russian Federation
167 *O8* **Sukhothai** ***var.*** Sukotai. Sukhothai, W Thailand
Sukhumi *see* Sokhumi
Sukkertoppen *see* Maniitsoq
149 *Q13* **Sukkur** Sind, SE Pakistan
Sukotai *see* Sukhothai
Sukra Bay *see* Şawqirah, Dawḩat
125 *V15* **Suksun** Permskaya Oblast', NW Russian Federation
165 *F15* **Sukumo** Kōchi, Shikoku, SW Japan
94 *B12* **Sula** *island* S Norway
127 *Q5* **Sula** ≈ NW Russian Federation
117 *R5* **Sula** ≈ N Ukraine
42 *H6* **Sulaco, Río** ≈ NW Honduras
Sulaimaniya *see* As Sulaymānīyah
149 *S10* **Sulaimān Range** ⛰ C Pakistan
127 *Q16* **Sulak** Respublika Dagestan, SW Russian Federation
127 *Q16* **Sulak** ≈ SW Russian Federation
171 *Q13* **Sula, Kepulauan** *island group* C Indonesia
136 *I12* **Sulakyurt** ***var.*** Konur. Kırıkkale, N Turkey
171 *P17* **Sulamu** Timor, S Indonesia
96 *F5* **Sula Sgeir** *island* NW Scotland, UK
171 *N13* **Sulawesi** ***Eng.*** Celebes. *island* C Indonesia
Sulawesi, Laut *see* Celebes Sea
171 *N14* **Sulawesi Selatan** ***off.*** Propinsi Sulawesi Selatan, ***Eng.*** South Celebes, South Sulawesi. ◈ *province* C Indonesia
171 *P12* **Sulawesi Tengah** ***off.*** Propinsi Sulawesi Tengah, ***Eng.*** Central Celebes, Central Sulawesi. ◈ *province* N Indonesia
171 *O14* **Sulawesi Tenggara** ***off.*** Propinsi Sulawesi Tenggara, ***Eng.*** South-East Celebes, South-East Sulawesi. ◈ *province* C Indonesia
171 *P11* **Sulawesi Utara** ***off.*** Propinsi Sulawesi Utara, ***Eng.*** North Celebes, North Sulawesi. ◈ *province* N Indonesia
139 *T5* **Sulaymān Beg** N Iraq
95 *D15* **Suldalsvatnet** ◎ S Norway
Sulden *see* Solda
110 *E12* **Sulechów** ***Ger.*** Züllichau. Lubuskie, W Poland
110 *E11* **Sulęcin** Lubuskie, W Poland
77 *U14* **Suleja** Niger, C Nigeria
111 *K14* **Sulejów** Łodzkie, S Poland
96 *I5* **Sule Skerry** *island* N Scotland, UK
Suliag *see* Sohâg
76 *J16* **Sulima** S Sierra Leone
117 *O13* **Sulina** Tulcea, SE Romania
117 *N13* **Sulina Brațul** ≈ SE Romania
100 *H12* **Sulingen** Niedersachsen, NW Germany
Sulisjielmmá *see* Sulitjelma
92 *H12* **Suliskongen** ▲ C Norway
92 *H12* **Sulitjelma** ***Lapp.*** Sulisjielmmá. Nordland, C Norway
56 *A9* **Sullana** Piura, NW Peru
23 *N3* **Sulligent** Alabama, S USA
30 *M14* **Sullivan** Illinois, N USA
31 *N15* **Sullivan** Indiana, N USA
27 *W5* **Sullivan** Missouri, C USA
Sullivan Island *see* Lanbi Kyun
96 *M1* **Sullom Voe** NE Scotland, UK
103 *O7* **Sully-sur-Loire** Loiret, C France
Sulmo *see* Sulmona
107 *K15* **Sulmona** ***anc.*** Sulmo. Abruzzo, C Italy
Sulo *see* Shule He
114 *M11* **Süloğlu** Edirne, NW Turkey
22 *G9* **Sulphur** Louisiana, S USA
27 *O12* **Sulphur** Oklahoma, C USA
28 *K9* **Sulphur Creek** ≈ South Dakota, N USA
24 *M5* **Sulphur Draw** ≈ Texas, SW USA
25 *W5* **Sulphur River** ≈ Arkansas/Texas, SW USA
25 *V6* **Sulphur Springs** Texas, SW USA
24 *M6* **Sulphur Springs Draw** ≈ Texas, SW USA
14 *D8* **Sultan** Ontario, S Canada
Sultānābād *see* Arāk
Sultan Alonto, Lake *see* Lanao, Lake
136 *G15* **Sultan Dağları** ⛰ C Turkey
114 *N13* **Sultanköy** Tekirdağ, NW Turkey
171 *Q7* **Sultan Kudarat** ***var.*** Nuling. Mindanao, S Philippines
152 *M13* **Sultānpur** Uttar Pradesh, N India
171 *O9* **Sulu Archipelago** *island group* SW Philippines
192 *F7* **Sulu Basin** *undersea feature* SE South China Sea
Sülüktü *see* Sulyukta
Sulu, Laut *see* Sulu Sea
169 *X6* **Sulu Sea** ***Ind.*** Laut Sulu. *sea* SW Philippines
145 *O15* **Sulutobe** ***Kaz.*** Sulūtöbe. Kzylorda, S Kazakhstan
147 *Q11* **Sulyukta** ***Kir.*** Sülüktü. Batkenskaya Oblast', SW Kyrgyzstan
Sulz *see* Sulz am Neckar
101 *G22* **Sulz am Neckar** ***var.*** Sulz. Baden-Württemberg, SW Germany
101 *L20* **Sulzbach-Rosenberg** Bayern, SE Germany
195 *N13* **Sulzberger Bay** *bay* Antarctica
Sumail *see* Summēl
113 *F15* **Sumartin** Split-Dalmacija, S Croatia
32 *H6* **Sumas** Washington, NW USA
168 *J10* **Sumatera** ***Eng.*** Sumatra. *island* W Indonesia
168 *J12* **Sumatera Barat** ***off.*** Propinsi Sumatera Barat, ***Eng.*** West Sumatra. ◈ *province* W Indonesia
168 *L13* **Sumatera Selatan** ***off.*** Propinsi Sumatera Selatan, ***Eng.*** South Sumatra. ◈ *province* W Indonesia
168 *H10* **Sumatera Utara** ***off.*** Propinsi Sumatera Utara, ***Eng.*** North Sumatra. ◈ *province* W Indonesia
Sumatra *see* Sumatera
Šumava *see* Bohemian Forest
Sumayl *see* Summēl
139 *U7* **Sumayr al Muḩammad** E Iraq
171 *N17* **Sumba, Pulau** ***Eng.*** Sandalwood Island; ***prev.*** Soemba. *island* Nusa Tenggara, C Indonesia
146 *D12* **Sumbar** ≈ W Turkmenistan
192 *E9* **Sumbawa** ***prev.*** Soembawa. *island* Nusa Tenggara, C Indonesia
170 *L16* **Sumbawabesar** Sumbawa, S Indonesia
81 *F23* **Sumbawanga** Rukwa, W Tanzania
82 *B12* **Sumbe** ***prev.*** N'Gunza, ***Port.*** Novo Redondo. Cuanza Sul, W Angola
96 *M3* **Sumburgh Head** *headland* NE Scotland, UK
111 *H23* **Sümeg** Veszprém, W Hungary
80 *C12* **Sumeih** Southern Darfur, S Sudan
169 *T16* **Sumenep** ***prev.*** Soemenep. Pulau Madura, C Indonesia
Sumgait *see* Sumqayıt, Azerbaijan
Sumgait *see* Sumqayıtçay, Azerbaijan
165 *Y14* **Sumisu-jima** ***Eng.*** Smith Island. *island* SE Japan
139 *Q2* **Summēl** ***var.*** Sumail, Sumayl. N Iraq
31 *O5* **Summer Island** *island* Michigan, N USA
32 *H15* **Summer Lake** ◎ Oregon, NW USA
11 *N17* **Summerland** British Columbia, SW Canada
13 *P14* **Summerside** Prince Edward Island, SE Canada
21 *R5* **Summersville** West Virginia, NE USA
21 *R5* **Summersville Lake** ⊠ West Virginia, NE USA
21 *S13* **Summerton** South Carolina, SE USA
23 *R2* **Summerville** Georgia, SE USA
21 *S14* **Summerville** South Carolina, SE USA
39 *R10* **Summit** Alaska, USA
35 *V6* **Summit Mountain** ▲ Nevada, W USA
37 *R8* **Summit Peak** ▲ Colorado, C USA
Summus Portus *see* Somport, Col du
29 *X12* **Sumner** Iowa, C USA
22 *K3* **Sumner** Mississippi, S USA
185 *H17* **Sumner, Lake** ◎ South Island, NZ
37 *U12* **Sumner, Lake** ⊠ New Mexico, SW USA
111 *G17* **Šumperk** ***Ger.*** Mährisch-Schönberg. Olomoucký Kraj, E Czech Republic
42 *F7* **Sumpul, Río** ≈ El Salvador/Honduras
137 *Z11* **Sumqayıt** ***Rus.*** Sumgait. E Azerbaijan
137 *Y11* **Sumqayıtçay** ***Rus.*** Sumgait. ≈ E Azerbaijan
147 *R9* **Sumsar** Dzhalal-Abadskaya Oblast', W Kyrgyzstan
117 *S3* **Sums'ka Oblast'** ***var.*** Sumy, ***Rus.*** Sumskaya Oblast'. ◈ *province* NE Ukraine
Sumskaya Oblast' *see* Sums'ka Oblast'
124 *J8* **Sumskiy Posad** Respublika Kareliya, NW Russian Federation
21 *S12* **Sumter** South Carolina, SE USA
117 *T3* **Sumy** Sums'ka Oblast', NE Ukraine
Sumy *see* Sums'ka Oblast'
159 *Q15* **Sumzom** Xizang Zizhiqu, W China
125 *R15* **Suna** Kirovskaya Oblast', NW Russian Federation
126 *I10* **Suna** ≈ NW Russian Federation
165 *S3* **Sunagawa** Hokkaidō, NE Japan
153 *V13* **Sunamganj** Chittagong, NE Bangladesh
163 *W14* **Sunan** ✕ (P'yŏngyang) SW North Korea
Sunan/Sunan Yugurzu Zizhixian *see* Hongwansi
19 *N9* **Sunapee Lake** ◎ New Hampshire, NE USA
139 *P4* **Sunaysilah** *salt marsh* N Iraq
20 *M8* **Sunbright** Tennessee, S USA
33 *R6* **Sunburst** Montana, NW USA
183 *N12* **Sunbury** Victoria, SE Australia
21 *X8* **Sunbury** North Carolina, SE USA
18 *G14* **Sunbury** Pennsylvania, NE USA
61 *A17* **Sunchales** Santa Fe, C Argentina
163 *W13* **Sunch'ŏn** SW North Korea
163 *Y16* **Sunch'ŏn** ***Jap.*** Junten. S South Korea
36 *K13* **Sun City** Arizona, SW USA
19 *O9* **Suncook** New Hampshire, NE USA
161 *P5* **Suncun** ***prev.*** Xinwen. Shandong, E China
Sunda Islands *see* Greater Sunda Islands
33 *Z12* **Sundance** Wyoming, C USA
153 *T17* **Sundarbans** *wetland* Bangladesh/India
154 *M11* **Sundargarh** Orissa, E India
131 *U15* **Sunda Shelf** *undersea feature* S South China Sea
Sunda Trench *see* Java Trench
131 *U17* **Sunda Trough** *undersea feature* E Indian Ocean
95 *O16* **Sundbyberg** Stockholm, C Sweden
97 *M14* **Sunderland** ***var.*** Wearmouth. NE England, UK
101 *F15* **Sundern** Nordrhein-Westfalen, W Germany
136 *F12* **Sündiken Dağları** ⛰ C Turkey
24 *M5* **Sundown** Texas, SW USA
11 *P16* **Sundre** Alberta, SW Canada
14 *H12* **Sundridge** Ontario, S Canada
93 *H17* **Sundsvall** Västernorrland, C Sweden
26 *H4* **Sunflower, Mount** ▲ Kansas, C USA
Sunflower State *see* Kansas
169 *N14* **Sungaibuntu** Sumatera, SW Indonesia
168 *K12* **Sungaidareh** Sumatera, W Indonesia
167 *P17* **Sungai Kolok** ***var.*** Sungai Ko-Lok. Narathiwat, SW Thailand
168 *K12* **Sungaipenuh** ***prev.*** Soengaipenoeh. Sumatera, W Indonesia
169 *P11* **Sungaipinyuh** Borneo, C Indonesia
Sungari *see* Songhua Jiang
Sungaria *see* Dzungaria
Sungei Pahang *see* Pahang, Sungai
167 *O8* **Sung Men** Phrae, NW Thailand
83 *M15* **Sungo** Tete, NW Mozambique
Sungpu *see* Songpan
168 *M13* **Sungsang** Sumatera, W Indonesia
114 *M9* **Sungurlare** Burgas, E Bulgaria
136 *J12* **Sungurlu** Çorum, N Turkey
112 *F9* **Sunja** Sisak-Moslavina, C Croatia
153 *Q12* **Sun Koshi** ≈ E Nepal
94 *F9* **Sunndalen** *valley* S Norway
94 *F9* **Sunndalsøra** Møre og Romsdal, S Norway
95 *K15* **Sunne** Värmland, C Sweden
95 *O15* **Sunnersta** Uppsala, C Sweden
94 *C11* **Sunnfjord** *physical region* S Norway
95 *C15* **Sunnhordland** *physical region* S Norway
94 *D10* **Sunnmøre** *physical region* S Norway
37 *N4* **Sunnyside** Utah, W USA
32 *J10* **Sunnyside** Washington, NW USA
35 *N9* **Sunnyvale** California, W USA
30 *L8* **Sun Prairie** Wisconsin, N USA
Sunqur *see* Sonqor
25 *N1* **Sunray** Texas, SW USA
22 *I8* **Sunset** Louisiana, S USA
25 *S5* **Sunset** Texas, SW USA
Sunset State *see* Oregon
181 *Z10* **Sunshine Coast** *cultural region* Queensland, E Australia
Sunshine State *see* Florida, USA
Sunshine State *see* New Mexico, USA
Sunshine State *see* South Dakota, USA
123 *O10* **Suntar** Respublika Sakha (Yakutiya), NE Russian Federation
39 *R10* **Suntrana** Alaska, USA
148 *J15* **Suntsar** Baluchistān, SW Pakistan
163 *W15* **Sunwi-do** *island* SW North Korea
163 *W6* **Sunwu** Heilongjiang, NE China
77 *O16* **Sunyani** W Ghana
Suō *see* Suao
93 *M17* **Suolahti** Länsi-Suomi, W Finland
Suoločielgi *see* Saariselkä
Suomenlahti *see* Finland, Gulf of
Suomen Tasavalta/Suomi *see* Finland
93 *N14* **Suomussalmi** Oulu, E Finland
165 *E13* **Suō-nada** *sea* SW Japan
93 *M17* **Suonenjoki** Itä-Suomi, C Finland
167 *S13* **Suŏng** Kâmpóng Cham, C Cambodia
124 *I10* **Suoyarvi** Respublika Kareliya, NW Russian Federation
Supanburi *see* Suphan Buri
57 *D14* **Supe** Lima, W Peru
15 *V7* **Supérieur, Lac** ◎ Québec, SE Canada
Supérieur, Lac *see* Superior, Lake
36 *M14* **Superior** Arizona, SW USA
33 *O9* **Superior** Montana, NW USA
29 *P17* **Superior** Nebraska, C USA
30 *I3* **Superior** Wisconsin, N USA
41 *S17* **Superior, Laguna** *lagoon* S Mexico
31 *N2* **Superior, Lake** ***Fr.*** Lac Supérieur. ◎ Canada/USA
36 *L13* **Superstition Mountains** ⛰ Arizona, SW USA
113 *F14* **Supetar** ***It.*** San Pietro. Split-Dalmacija, S Croatia
167 *O10* **Suphan Buri** ***var.*** Supanburi. Suphan Buri, W Thailand
171 *V12* **Supiori, Pulau** *island* E Indonesia
188 *K2* **Supply Reef** *reef* N Northern Mariana Islands
195 *O7* **Support Force Glacier** *glacier* Antarctica
137 *R10* **Sup'sa** ***var.*** Supsa. ≈ W Georgia
Sūq 'Abs *see* 'Abs
139 *W12* **Sūq ash Shuyūkh** SE Iraq
138 *H4* **Şuqaylibīyah** Ḩamāh, W Syria
161 *Q6* **Suqian** Jiangsu, E China
Suqrah *see* Şawqirah
Suqrah Bay *see* Şawqirah, Dawḩat
141 *V16* **Suquṭrā** ***var.*** Sokotra, ***Eng.*** Socotra. *island* SE Yemen
141 *Z8* **Şūr** NE Oman
Şūr *see* Soûr
127 *P5* **Sura** Penzenskaya Oblast', W Russian Federation
127 *P4* **Sura** ≈ W Russian Federation
149 *N12* **Sūrāb** Baluchistān, SW Pakistan
Surabaja *see* Surabaya
192 *E8* **Surabaya** ***prev.*** Soerabaja, Surabaja. Jawa, C Indonesia
95 *N15* **Surahammar** Västmanland, C Sweden
169 *Q16* **Surakarta** ***Eng.*** Solo; ***prev.*** Soerakarta. Jawa, S Indonesia
Surakhany *see* Suraxanı
137 *S10* **Surami** C Georgia
143 *X13* **Sūrān** Sīstān va Balūchestān, SE Iran
111 *I21* **Šurany** ***Hung.*** Nagysurány. Nitriansky Kraj, SW Slovakia
154 *D12* **Sūrat** Gujarāt, W India
Suratdhani *see* Surat Thani
152 *G9* **Sūratgarh** Rājasthān, NW India
167 *N14* **Surat Thani** ***var.*** Suratdhani. Surat Thani, SW Thailand
119 *Q16* **Suraw** ***Rus.*** Surov. ≈ E Belarus
137 *Z11* **Suraxanı** ***Rus.*** Surakhany. E Azerbaijan
141 *Y11* **Surayr** E Oman
138 *K2* **Suraysāt** Ḩalab, N Syria
118 *O12* **Surazh** ***Rus.*** Surazh. Vitsyebskaya Voblasts', NE Belarus
126 *H6* **Surazh** Bryanskaya Oblast', W Russian Federation
191 *V17* **Sur, Cabo** *headland* Easter Island, Chile, E Pacific Ocean
112 *L11* **Surčin** Serbia, N Serbia and Montenegro (Yugo.)
116 *H9* **Surduc** ***Hung.*** Szurduk. Sălaj, NW Romania
113 *P16* **Surdulica** Serbia, SE Serbia and Montenegro (Yugo.)
99 *L24* **Sûre** ***var.*** Sauer. ≈ W Europe ***see also*** Sauer
154 *C10* **Surendranagar** Gujarāt, W India
18 *K16* **Surf City** New Jersey, NE USA
183 *V3* **Surfers Paradise** Queensland, E Australia
21 *U13* **Surfside Beach** South Carolina, SE USA
102 *J10* **Surgères** Charente-Maritime, W France
122 *H10* **Surgut** Khanty-Mansiyskiy Avtonomnyy Okrug, C Russian Federation
122 *K10* **Surgutikha** Krasnoyarskiy Kray, N Russian Federation
98 *M6* **Surhuisterveen** Friesland, N Netherlands
105 *V5* **Súria** Cataluña, NE Spain
143 *P10* **Sūrīān** Fārs, S Iran
155 *J15* **Suriāpet** Andhra Pradesh, C India
171 *Q6* **Surigao** Mindanao, S Philippines
167 *R10* **Surin** Surin, E Thailand
55 *U11* **Suriname** ***off.*** Republic of Suriname, ***var.*** Surinam; ***prev.*** Dutch Guiana, Netherlands Guiana. ◆ *republic* N South America
Sūrīya/Sūrīyah, Al-Jumhūrīyah al-'Arabīyah as - *see* Syria
Surkhab, Darya-i- *see* Kahmard, Daryā-ye
Surkhandar'inskaya Oblast' *see* Surxondaryo Viloyati
Surkhandar'ya *see* Surxondaryo
Surkhet *see* Birendranagar
147 *R12* **Surkhob** ≈ C Tajikistan
137 *P11* **Sürmene** Trabzon, NE Turkey
Surov *see* Suraw
127 *N11* **Surovikino** Volgogradskaya Oblast', SW Russian Federation
35 *N11* **Sur, Point** *headland* California, W USA
187 *N15* **Surprise, Île** *island* N New Caledonia
61 *E22* **Sur, Punta** *headland* E Argentina
Surrentum *see* Sorrento
28 *M3* **Surrey** North Dakota, N USA
97 *O22* **Surrey** *cultural region* SE England, UK
21 *X7* **Surry** Virginia, NE USA
108 *F8* **Sursee** Luzern, W Switzerland
127 *P6* **Sursk** Penzenskaya Oblast', W Russian Federation
127 *P5* **Surskoye** Ul'yanovskaya Oblast', W Russian Federation
75 *P8* **Surt** ***var.*** Sidra, Sirte. N Libya
95 *I19* **Surte** Västra Götaland, S Sweden
75 *Q8* **Surt, Khalīj** ***Eng.*** Gulf of Sidra, Gulf of Sirti, Sidra. *gulf* N Libya
92 *I5* **Surtsey** *island* S Iceland
137 *N17* **Suruç** Şanlıurfa, S Turkey
168 *L13* **Surulangun** Sumatera, W Indonesia
147 *P13* **Surxondaryo** ***Rus.*** Surkhandar'ya. ≈ Tajikistan/Uzbekistan
147 *N13* **Surxondaryo Viloyati** ***Rus.*** Surkhandar'inskaya Oblast'. ◈ *province* S Uzbekistan
Süs *see* Susch
106 *A8* **Susa** Piemonte, NE Italy
165 *E12* **Susa** Yamaguchi, Honshū, SW Japan
Susa *see* Shūsh
113 *E16* **Sušac** ***It.*** Cazza. *island* SW Croatia
Sūsah *see* Sousse
165 *G14* **Susaki** Kōchi, Shikoku, SW Japan
165 *I15* **Susami** Wakayama, Honshū, SW Japan
142 *K9* **Sūsangerd** ***var.*** Susangird. Khūzestān, SW Iran
Susangird *see* Sūsangerd
35 *P4* **Susanville** California, W USA
108 *J9* **Susch** ***var.*** Süs. Graubünden, SE Switzerland
137 *N12* **Suşehri** Sivas, N Turkey
Susiana *see* Khūzestān
111 *B18* **Sušice** ***Ger.*** Schüttenhofen. Plzeňský Kraj, W Czech Republic
39 *R11* **Susitna** Alaska, USA
39 *R11* **Susitna River** ≈ Alaska, USA
127 *Q3* **Suslonger** Respublika Mariy El, W Russian Federation
105 *N14* **Suspiro del Moro, Puerto del** *pass* S Spain

◆ COUNTRY
● COUNTRY CAPITAL
◇ DEPENDENT TERRITORY
○ DEPENDENT TERRITORY CAPITAL
◈ ADMINISTRATIVE REGION
✕ INTERNATIONAL AIRPORT
▲ MOUNTAIN
⛰ MOUNTAIN RANGE
Ж VOLCANO
≈ RIVER
◎ LAKE
⊠ RESERVOIR

18 *H16* **Susquehanna River** ≈ New York/Pennsylvania, NE USA
13 *O15* **Sussex** New Brunswick, SE Canada
18 *J13* **Sussex** New Jersey, NE USA
21 *W7* **Sussex** Virginia, NE USA
97 *O23* **Sussex** *cultural region* S England, UK
183 *S10* **Sussex Inlet** New South Wales, SE Australia
99 *L17* **Susteren** Limburg, SE Netherlands
10 *K12* **Sustut Peak** ▲ British Columbia, W Canada
123 *S9* **Susuman** Magadanskaya Oblast', E Russian Federation
188 *H6* **Susupe** Saipan, S Northern Mariana Islands
136 *D12* **Susurluk** Balıkesir, NW Turkey
114 *M13* **Susuzmüsellim** Tekirdağ, NW Turkey
136 *F15* **Sütçüler** İsparta, SW Turkey
116 *L13* **Şuţeşti** Brăila, SE Romania
83 *F25* **Sutherland** Western Cape, SW South Africa
28 *L15* **Sutherland** Nebraska, C USA
96 *I7* **Sutherland** *cultural region* N Scotland, UK
185 *B21* **Sutherland Falls** *waterfall* South Island, NZ
32 *F14* **Sutherlin** Oregon, NW USA
149 *V10* **Sutlej** ≈ India/Pakistan
Sutna *see* Satna
35 *P7* **Sutter Creek** California, W USA
39 *R11* **Sutton** Alaska, USA
29 *Q16* **Sutton** Nebraska, C USA
21 *R4* **Sutton** West Virginia, NE USA
12 *F8* **Sutton** ≈ Ontario, C Canada
97 *M19* **Sutton Coldfield** C England, UK
21 *R4* **Sutton Lake** ▣ West Virginia, NE USA
15 *P13* **Sutton, Monts** *hill range* Québec, SE Canada
12 *F8* **Sutton Ridges** ⛰ Ontario, C Canada
165 *Q4* **Suttsu** Hokkaidō, NE Japan
39 *P15* **Sutwik Island** *island* Alaska, USA
162 *K7* **Süüj** Bulgan, C Mongolia
118 *H5* **Suure-Jaani** *Ger.* Gross-Sankt-Johannis. Viljandimaa, S Estonia
118 *J7* **Suur Munamägi** *var.* Munamägi, *Ger.* Eier-Berg. ▲ SE Estonia
118 *F5* **Suur Väin** *Ger.* Grosser Sund. *strait* W Estonia
147 *U8* **Suusamyr** Chuyskaya Oblast', C Kyrgyzstan
187 *X14* **Suva** ● (Fiji) Viti Levu, W Fiji
187 *X15* **Suva** × Viti Levu, C Fiji
113 *N18* **Suva Gora** ⛰ W FYR Macedonia
118 *H11* **Suvainiškis** Panevėžys, NE Lithuania
Suvalkai/Suvalki *see* Suwałki
113 *P15* **Suva Planina** ⛰ SE Serbia and Montenegro (Yugo.)
113 *M17* **Suva Reka** Serbia, S Serbia and Montenegro (Yugo.)
126 *K5* **Suvorov** Tul'skaya Oblast', W Russian Federation
117 *N12* **Suvorove** Odes'ka Oblast', SW Ukraine
Suvorovo *see* Ştefan Vodă
Suwaik *see* As Suwayq
Suwaira *see* Aş Şuwayrah
110 *O7* **Suwałki** *Lith.* Suvalkai, *Rus.* Suvalki. Podlaskie, NE Poland
167 *R10* **Suwannaphum** Roi Et, E Thailand
23 *V8* **Suwannee River** ≈ Florida/Georgia, SE USA
Şuwār *see* Aş Şuwār
190 *K14* **Suwarrow** *atoll* N Cook Islands
Suwaydá/Suwaydā', Muḩāfaẓat as *see* As Suwaydā'
143 *R16* **Suwaydān** *var.* Sweiham. Abū Ẓaby, E UAE
Suwayqiyah, Hawr as *see* Shuwayjah, Hawr ash
Suways, Khalīj as *see* Suez, Gulf of
Suways, Qanāt as *see* Suez Canal
Suweida *see* As Suwaydā'
Suweon *see* Suwŏn
163 *X15* **Suwŏn** *var.* Suweon, *Jap.* Suigen. NW South Korea
Su Xian *see* Suzhou
143 *R14* **Sūzā** Hormozgān, S Iran
145 *P15* **Suzak** *Kaz.* Sozaq. Yuzhnyy Kazakhstan, S Kazakhstan
Suzaka *see* Suzuka
126 *M3* **Suzdal'** Vladimirskaya Oblast', W Russian Federation
161 *P7* **Suzhou** *var.* Su Xian. Anhui, E China
161 *R8* **Suzhou** *var.* Soochow, Suchou, Suchow; *prev.* Wuhsien. Jiangsu, E China
Suzhou *see* Jiuquan
163 *V12* **Suzi He** ≈ NE China
Suz, Mys *see* Soye, Mys
165 *M10* **Suzu** Ishikawa, Honshū, SW Japan
165 *K14* **Suzuka** Mie, Honshū, SW Japan
165 *N12* **Suzuka** *var.* Suzaka. Nagano, Honshū, S Japan
165 *M10* **Suzu-misaki** *headland* Honshū, SW Japan
Svågälv *see* Svågan
94 *M10* **Svågan** *var.* Svågälv. ≈ C Sweden
Svalava/Svaljava *see* Svalyava
92 *O2* **Svalbard** ◇ *Norwegian dependency* Arctic Ocean
92 *J2* **Svalbardhseyri** Nordhurland Eystra, N Iceland
95 *K22* **Svalöv** Skåne, S Sweden
116 *H7* **Svalyava** *Cz.* Svalava, Svaljava, *Hung.* Szolyva. Zakarpats'ka Oblast', W Ukraine
92 *O2* **Svanbergfjellet** ▲ C Svalbard
95 *M24* **Svaneke** Bornholm, E Denmark
95 *L22* **Svängsta** Blekinge, S Sweden
95 *J16* **Svanskog** Värmland, C Sweden
95 *L16* **Svartå** Örebro, C Sweden
95 *L15* **Svartälven** ≈ C Sweden
92 *G12* **Svartisen** *glacier* C Norway
117 *X6* **Svatove** *Rus.* Svatovo. Luhans'ka Oblast', E Ukraine
Svatovo *see* Svatove
Sväty Kríž nad Hronom *see* Žiar nad Hronom
167 *Q11* **Svay Chék, Stœng** ≈ Cambodia/Thailand
167 *S13* **Svay Riĕng** Svay Riĕng, S Cambodia
92 *O3* **Sveagruva** Spitsbergen, W Svalbard
95 *K23* **Svedala** Skåne, S Sweden
118 *H12* **Svėdesai** Utena, NE Lithuania
93 *G18* **Sveg** Jämtland, C Sweden
118 *C12* **Švėkšna** Klaipėda, W Lithuania
94 *C11* **Svelgen** Sogn og Fjordane, S Norway
95 *H15* **Svelvik** Vestfold, S Norway
118 *I13* **Švenčionėliai** *Pol.* Nowo-Święciany. Vilnius, SE Lithuania
118 *I13* **Švenčionys** *Pol.* Swięciany. Vilnius, SE Lithuania
95 *H24* **Svendborg** Fyn, C Denmark
95 *K19* **Svenljunga** Västra Götaland, S Sweden
92 *P2* **Svenskøya** *island* E Svalbard
93 *G17* **Svenstavik** Jämtland, C Sweden
95 *G20* **Svenstrup** Nordjylland, N Denmark
118 *H12* **Šventoji** ≈ C Lithuania
117 *Z8* **Sverdlovs'k** *Rus.* Sverdlovsk; *prev.* Imeni Sverdlova Rudnik. Luhans'ka Oblast', E Ukraine
Sverdlovsk *see* Yekaterinburg
127 *W2* **Sverdlovskaya Oblast'** ◈ *province* C Russian Federation
8 *M3* **Sverdrup Islands** *island group* Nunavut, N Canada
122 *K6* **Sverdrup, Ostrov** *island* N Russian Federation
Sverige *see* Sweden
113 *D15* **Svetac** *prev.* Sveti Andrea, *It.* Sant'Andrea. *island* SW Croatia
Sveti Andrea *see* Svetac
Sveti Nikola *see* Sveti Nikole
113 *O18* **Sveti Nikole** *prev.* Sveti Nikola. C FYR Macedonia
Sveti Vrach *see* Sandanski
123 *T14* **Svetlaya** Primorskiy Kray, SE Russian Federation
126 *B2* **Svetlogorsk** Kaliningradskaya Oblast', W Russian Federation
122 *K9* **Svetlogorsk** Krasnoyarskiy Kray, N Russian Federation
Svetlogorsk *see* Svyetlahorsk
127 *N14* **Svetlograd** Stavropol'skiy Kray, SW Russian Federation
Svetlovodsk *see* Svitlovods'k
119 *A14* **Svetlyy** *Ger.* Zimmerbude. Kaliningradskaya Oblast', W Russian Federation
127 *Y8* **Svetlyy** Orenburgskaya Oblast', W Russian Federation
127 *P8* **Svetlyy** Saratovskaya Oblast', SW Russian Federation
124 *G11* **Svetogorsk** *Fin.* Enso. Leningradskaya Oblast', NW Russian Federation
Svetozarevo *see* Jagodina
111 *B18* **Švihov** *Ger.* Schwihau. Plzeňský Kraj, W Czech Republic
112 *E13* **Svilaja** ⛰ SE Croatia
112 *N12* **Svilajnac** Serbia, C Serbia and Montenegro (Yugo.)
114 *L11* **Svilengrad** *prev.* Mustafa-Pasha. Khaskovo, S Bulgaria
Svinecea Mare, Munte *see* Svinecea Mare, Vârful
116 *F13* **Svinecea Mare, Vârful** *var.* Munte Svinecea Mare. ▲ SW Romania
95 *B18* **Svínoy** *Dan.* Svinø *Island* Faeroe Islands
147 *N14* **Svintsovyy Rudnik** *Turkm.* Swintsowyy Rudnik. Lebap Welaýaty, E Turkmenistan
118 *I13* **Svir** *Rus.* Svir'. Minskaya Voblasts', NW Belarus
126 *I12* **Svir'** *canal* NW Russian Federation
Svir', Ozero *see* Svir, Vozyera
119 *I14* **Svir, Vozyera** *Rus.* Ozero Svir'. ◎ C Belarus
114 *J7* **Svishtov** *prev.* Sistova. Veliko Tŭrnovo, N Bulgaria
119 *F18* **Svislach** *Pol.* Świsłocz, *Rus.* Svisloch'. Hrodzyenskaya Voblasts', W Belarus
119 *M17* **Svislach** *Rus.* Svisloch'. Mahilyowskaya Voblasts', E Belarus
119 *L17* **Svislach** *Rus.* Svisloch'. ≈ E Belarus
Svisloch' *see* Svislach
111 *F17* **Svitavy** *Ger.* Zwittau. Pardubický Kraj, C Czech Republic
117 *S6* **Svitlovods'k** *Rus.* Svetlovodsk. Kirovohrads'ka Oblast', C Ukraine
Svizzera *see* Switzerland
123 *Q13* **Svobodnyy** Amurskaya Oblast', SE Russian Federation
114 *G9* **Svoge** Sofiya, W Bulgaria
92 *G11* **Svolvær** Nordland, C Norway
111 *F18* **Svratka** *Ger.* Schwarzach, Schwarzawa. ≈ SE Czech Republic
113 *P14* **Svrljig** Serbia, E Serbia and Montenegro (Yugo.)
197 *U10* **Svyataya Anna Trough** *var.* Saint Anna Trough. *undersea feature* N Kara Sea
126 *M4* **Svyatoy Nos, Mys** *headland* NW Russian Federation
119 *N18* **Svyetlahorsk** *Rus.* Svetlogorsk. Homyel'skaya Voblasts', SE Belarus
Swabian Jura *see* Schwäbische Alb
97 *P19* **Swaffham** E England, UK
23 *V5* **Swainsboro** Georgia, SE USA
83 *C19* **Swakop** ≈ W Namibia
83 *C19* **Swakopmund** Erongo, W Namibia
97 *M15* **Swale** ≈ N England, UK
Swallow Island *see* Nendö
99 *M16* **Swalmen** Limburg, SE Netherlands
12 *G8* **Swan** ≈ Ontario, C Canada
97 *L24* **Swanage** S England, UK
182 *M10* **Swan Hill** Victoria, SE Australia
11 *P13* **Swan Hills** Alberta, W Canada
65 *D24* **Swan Island** *island* C Falkland Islands
Swankalok *see* Sawankhalok
29 *U10* **Swan Lake** ◎ Minnesota, N USA
21 *Y10* **Swanquarter** North Carolina, SE USA
182 *J9* **Swan Reach** South Australia
11 *V15* **Swan River** Manitoba, S Canada
183 *P17* **Swansea** Tasmania, SE Australia
97 *J22* **Swansea** *Wel.* Abertawe. S Wales, UK
21 *R13* **Swansea** South Carolina, SE USA
19 *S7* **Swans Island** *island* Maine, NE USA
28 *L17* **Swanson Lake** ▣ Nebraska, C USA
31 *R11* **Swanton** Ohio, N USA
110 *G11* **Swarzędz** Poznań, C Poland
Swatow *see* Shantou
83 *L22* **Swaziland** *off.* Kingdom of Swaziland. ◆ *monarchy* S Africa
93 *G18* **Sweden** *off.* Kingdom of Sweden, *Swe.* Sverige. ◆ *monarchy* N Europe
Swedru *see* Agona Swedru
25 *V12* **Sweeny** Texas, SW USA
33 *R6* **Sweetgrass** Montana, NW USA
32 *G12* **Sweet Home** Oregon, NW USA
25 *T12* **Sweet Home** Texas, SW USA
27 *T4* **Sweet Springs** Missouri, C USA
20 *M10* **Sweetwater** Tennessee, S USA
25 *P7* **Sweetwater** Texas, SW USA
33 *V15* **Sweetwater River** ≈ Wyoming, C USA
Sweiham *see* Suwaydān
83 *F26* **Swellendam** Western Cape, SW South Africa
111 *G15* **Świdnica** *Ger.* Schweidnitz. Wałbrzych, SW Poland
111 *O14* **Świdnik** *Ger.* Streckenbach. Lubelskie, E Poland
110 *F8* **Świdwin** *Ger.* Schivelbein. Zachodnio-pomorskie, NW Poland
111 *F15* **Świebodzice** *Ger.* Freiburg in Schlesien, Swiebodzice. Wałbrzych, SW Poland
110 *E11* **Świebodzin** *Ger.* Schwiebus. Lubuskie, W Poland
Swięciany *see* Švenčionys
110 *I9* **Świecie** *Ger.* Schwertberg. Kujawsko-pomorskie, N Poland
111 *L15* **Świętokrzyskie** ◈ *province* C Poland
11 *T16* **Swift Current** Saskatchewan, S Canada
98 *K9* **Swifterbant** Flevoland, C Netherlands
183 *Q12* **Swifts Creek** Victoria, SE Australia
96 *E13* **Swilly, Lough** *Ir.* Loch Súilí. *inlet* N Ireland
97 *M22* **Swindon** S England, UK
Swinemünde *see* Świnoujście
110 *D8* **Świnoujście** *Ger.* Swinemünde. Zachodnio-pomorskie, NW Poland
Swintsowyy Rudnik *see* Svintsovyy Rudnik
Świsłocz *see* Svislach
Swiss Confederation *see* Switzerland
108 *E9* **Switzerland** *off.* Swiss Confederation, *Fr.* La Suisse, *Ger.* Schweiz, *It.* Svizzera; *anc.* Helvetia. ◆ *federal republic* C Europe
97 *F17* **Swords** *Ir.* Sord, Sórd Choluim Chille. E Ireland
18 *H13* **Swoyersville** Pennsylvania, NE USA
126 *I10* **Syamozero, Ozero** ◎ NW Russian Federation
124 *M13* **Syamzha** Vologodskaya Oblast', NW Russian Federation
118 *N13* **Syanno** *Rus.* Senno. Vitsyebskaya Voblasts', NE Belarus
119 *K16* **Syarhyeyevichy** *Rus.* Sergeyevichi. Minskaya Voblasts', C Belarus
124 *I12* **Syas'stroy** Leningradskaya Oblast', NW Russian Federation
Sycaminum *see* Ḩefa
30 *M10* **Sycamore** Illinois, N USA
126 *J3* **Sychëvka** Smolenskaya Oblast', W Russian Federation
111 *H14* **Syców** *Ger.* Gross Wartenberg. Dolnośląskie, SW Poland
14 *E17* **Sydenham** ≈ Ontario, S Canada
Sydenham Island *see* Nonouti
183 *T9* **Sydney** *state capital* New South Wales, SE Australia
13 *R14* **Sydney** Cape Breton Island, Nova Scotia, SE Canada
Sydney Island *see* Manra
13 *R14* **Sydney Mines** Cape Breton Island, Nova Scotia, SE Canada
Syedpur *see* Saidpur
119 *K18* **Syelishcha** *Rus.* Selishche. Minskaya Voblasts', C Belarus
119 *J18* **Syemyezhava** *Rus.* Semezhevo. Minskaya Voblasts', C Belarus
Syene *see* Aswân
117 *X6* **Syeverodonets'k** *Rus.* Severodonetsk. Luhans'ka Oblast', E Ukraine
161 *T6* **Sÿiao Shan** *island* SE China
100 *H11* **Syke** Niedersachsen, NW Germany
94 *D10* **Sykkylven** Møre og Romsdal, S Norway
115 *F15* **Sykoúri** *var.* Sikouri; *prev.* Sikoúrion. Thessalía, C Greece
125 *R11* **Syktyvkar** *prev.* Ust'-Sysol'sk. Respublika Komi, NW Russian Federation
23 *Q4* **Sylacauga** Alabama, S USA
Sylarna *see* Storsylen
153 *V14* **Sylhet** Chittagong, NE Bangladesh
100 *G6* **Sylt** *island* NW Germany
21 *O10* **Sylva** North Carolina, SE USA
127 *V15* **Sylva** ≈ NW Russian Federation
23 *W5* **Sylvania** Georgia, SE USA
31 *R11* **Sylvania** Ohio, N USA
11 *Q15* **Sylvan Lake** Alberta, SW Canada
33 *T13* **Sylvan Pass** *pass* Wyoming, C USA
23 *T7* **Sylvester** Georgia, SE USA
25 *P6* **Sylvester** Texas, SW USA
10 *L11* **Sylvia, Mount** ▲ British Columbia, W Canada
122 *K11* **Sym** ≈ C Russian Federation
115 *N22* **Sými** *var.* Simi. *island* Dodekánisos, Greece, Aegean Sea
117 *U8* **Synel'nykove** Dnipropetrovs'ka Oblast', E Ukraine
125 *U6* **Synya** Respublika Komi, NW Russian Federation
117 *P7* **Synyukha** *Rus.* Sinyukha. ≈ S Ukraine
Syôbara *see* Shōbara
195 *V2* **Syowa** *Japanese research station* Antarctica
26 *H6* **Syracuse** Kansas, C USA
29 *S16* **Syracuse** Nebraska, C USA
18 *H10* **Syracuse** New York, NE USA
Syracuse *see* Siracusa
Syrdar'inskaya Oblast' *see* Sirdaryo Viloyati
Syrdariya *see* Syr Darya
144 *L14* **Syr Darya** *var.* Sai Hun, Sir Darya, Syrdarya, *Kaz.* Syrdariya, *Rus.* Syrdar'ya, *Uzb.* Sirdaryo; *anc.* Jaxartes. ≈ C Asia
138 *J6* **Syria** *off.* Syrian Arab Republic, *var.* Siria, Syrie, *Ar.* Al-Jumhūrīyah al-'Arabīyah as-Sūrīyah, Sūrīya. ◆ *republic* SW Asia
138 *L9* **Syrian Desert** *Ar.* Al Hamad, Bādiyat ash Shām. *desert* SW Asia
Syrie *see* Syria
115 *L22* **Sýrna** *var.* Sirna. *island* Kykládes, Greece, Aegean Sea
115 *I20* **Sýros** *var.* Síros. *island* Kykládes, Greece, Aegean Sea
93 *M18* **Sysmä** Etelä-Suomi, S Finland
127 *R12* **Sysola** ≈ NW Russian Federation
Syulemeshlii *see* Sredets
127 *S2* **Syumsi** Udmurtskaya Respublika, NW Russian Federation
114 *K10* **Syuyutliyka** ≈ C Bulgaria
Syvash, Zaliv *see* Syvash, Zatoka
117 *U12* **Syvash, Zatoka** *Rus.* Zaliv Syvash. *inlet* S Ukraine
127 *Q6* **Syzran'** Samarskaya Oblast', W Russian Federation
Szabadka *see* Subotica
111 *N21* **Szabolcs-Szatmár-Bereg** *off.* Szabolcs-Szatmár-Bereg Megye. ◈ *county* E Hungary
110 *G10* **Szamocin** *Ger.* Samotschin. Wielkolpolskie, C Poland
116 *H8* **Szamos** *var.* Someş, Someşul, *Ger.* Samosch, Somesch. ≈ Hungary/Romania
Szamosújvár *see* Gherla
110 *G11* **Szamotuły** Poznań, C Poland
Szarkowszczyzna *see* Sharkawshchyna
111 *M24* **Szarvas** Békés, SE Hungary
Szászmagyarós *see* Măieruş
Szászrégen *see* Reghin
Szászsebes *see* Sebeş
Szászváros *see* Orăştie
Szatmárrnémeti *see* Satu Mare
Száva *see* Sava
111 *P15* **Szczebrzeszyn** Lubelskie, E Poland
110 *D9* **Szczecin** *Eng./Ger.* Stettin. Zachodnio-pomorskie, NW Poland
110 *G8* **Szczecinek** *Ger.* Neustettin. Zachodnio-pomorskie, NW Poland
110 *D8* **Szczeciński, Zalew** *var.* Stettiner Haff, *Ger.* Oderhaff. *bay* Germany/Poland
111 *K15* **Szczekociny** Śląskie, S Poland
110 *N8* **Szczuczyn** Podlaskie, NE Poland
Szczuczyn Nowogródzki *see* Shchuchyn
110 *M8* **Szczytno** *Ger.* Ortelsburg. Warmińsko-Mazurskie, NE Poland,
Szechuan/Szechwan *see* Sichuan
111 *K21* **Szécsény** Nógrád, N Hungary
111 *L25* **Szeged** *Ger.* Szegedin, *Rom.* Seghedin. Csongrád, SE Hungary
Szegedin *see* Szeged
111 *N23* **Szeghalom** Békés, SE Hungary
Székelyhid *see* Săcueni
Székelykeresztúr *see* Cristuru Secuiesc
111 *I23* **Székesfehérvár** *Ger.* Stuhlweissenberg; *anc.* Alba Regia. Fejér, W Hungary
Szeklerburg *see* Miercurea-Ciuc
Szekler Neumarkt *see* Târgu Secuiesc
111 *J25* **Szekszárd** Tolna, S Hungary
Szempcz/Szenc *see* Senec
Szenice *see* Senica
Szentágota *see* Agnita
111 *J22* **Szentendre** *Ger.* Sankt Andrä. Pest, N Hungary
111 *L24* **Szentes** Csongrád, SE Hungary
111 *F23* **Szentgotthárd** *Eng.* Saint Gotthard, *Ger.* Sankt Gotthard. Vas, W Hungary
Szentgyörgy *see* Đurđevac
Szenttamás *see* Srbobran
Széphely *see* Jebel
Szeping *see* Siping
Szered *see* Sered'
111 *N21* **Szerencs** Borsod-Abaúj-Zemplén, NE Hungary
Szeret *see* Siret
Szeretfalva *see* Sărăţel
110 *N7* **Szeska Góra** *var.* Szeskie Wygórza, *Ger.* Seesker Höhe. *hill* NE Poland
Szeskie Wygórza *see* Szeska Góra
111 *H25* **Szigetvár** Baranya, SW Hungary
Szilágşomlyó *see* Şimleu Silvaniei
Szinna *see* Snina
Sziszek *see* Sisak
Szitás-Keresztúr *see* Cristuru Secuiesc
111 *E15* **Szklarska Poręba** *Ger.* Schreiberhau. Dolnośląskie, SW Poland
Szkudy *see* Skuodas
Szlatina *see* Slatina, Croatia
Szlavonia/Szlavonország *see* Slavonija
Szlovákia *see* Slovakia
Szluin *see* Slunj
111 *L23* **Szolnok** Jász-Nagykun-Szolnok, C Hungary
Szolyva *see* Svalyava
111 *G23* **Szombathely** *Ger.* Steinamanger; *anc.* Sabaria, Savaria. Vas, W Hungary
Szond/Szonta *see* Sonta
Szováta *see* Sovata
110 *F13* **Szprotawa** *Ger.* Sprottau. Lubuskie, W Poland
Sztálinváros *see* Dunaújváros
Sztrazsó *see* Strážov
110 *J8* **Sztum** *Ger.* Stuhm. Pomorskie, N Poland
110 *H10* **Szubin** *Ger.* Schubin. Kujawsko-pomorskie, W Poland
Szucsava *see* Suceava
Szurduk *see* Surduc
111 *M14* **Szydłowiec** *Ger.* Schlelau. Mazowieckie, C Poland

T

Taalintehdas *see* Dalsbruk
171 *O4* **Taal, Lake** ◎ Luzon, NW Philippines
95 *J23* **Taastrup** *var.* Tåstrup. København, E Denmark
111 *I24* **Tab** Somogy, W Hungary
171 *P4* **Tabaco** Luzon, N Philippines
186 *G4* **Tabalo** Mussau Island, NE PNG
104 *K5* **Tábara** Castilla-León, N Spain
186 *H5* **Tabar Islands** *island group* NE PNG
Tabariya, Bahrat *see* Tiberias, Lake
143 *S7* **Ţabas** *var.* Golshan. Yazd, C Iran
43 *P15* **Tabasará, Serranía de** ⛰ W Panama
41 *U15* **Tabasco** ◈ *state* SE Mexico
Tabasco *see* Grijalva, Río
127 *Q2* **Tabashino** Respublika Mariy El, W Russian Federation
58 *B13* **Tabatinga** Amazonas, N Brazil
74 *G9* **Tabelbala** W Algeria
11 *Q17* **Taber** Alberta, SW Canada
171 *V15* **Taberfane** Pulau Trangan, E Indonesia
95 *L19* **Taberg** Jönköping, S Sweden
191 *O3* **Tabiteuea** *prev.* Drummond Island. *atoll* Tungaru, W Kiribati
171 *O5* **Tablas Island** *island* C Philippines
184 *Q10* **Table Cape** *headland* North Island, NZ
13 *S13* **Table Mountain** ▲ Newfoundland and Labrador, E Canada
173 *P17* **Table, Pointe de la** *headland* SE Réunion
27 *S8* **Table Rock Lake** ▣ Arkansas/Missouri, C USA
36 *K14* **Table Top** ▲ Arizona, SW USA
186 *D8* **Tabletop, Mount** ▲ C PNG
123 *R7* **Tabor** Respublika Sakha (Yakutiya), NE Russian Federation
29 *S15* **Tabor** Iowa, C USA
111 *D18* **Tábor** Jihočeský Kraj, S Czech Republic
81 *F21* **Tabora** Tabora, W Tanzania
81 *F21* **Tabora** ◈ *region* C Tanzania
21 *U12* **Tabor City** North Carolina, SE USA
147 *Q10* **Taboshar** NW Tajikistan
76 *L18* **Tabou** *var.* Tabu. S Ivory Coast
142 *J2* **Tabrīz** *var.* Tebriz; *anc.* Tauris. Āẕarbāyjān-e Khāvarī, NW Iran
Tabu *see* Tabou
191 *W1* **Tabuaeran** *prev.* Fanning Island. *atoll* Line Islands, E Kiribati
171 *O2* **Tabuk** Luzon, N Philippines
140 *J4* **Tabūk** Tabūk, NW Saudi Arabia
140 *J5* **Tabūk** *off.* Minţaqat Tabūk. ◈ *province* NW Saudi Arabia
187 *Q13* **Tabwemasana, Mount** ▲ Espiritu Santo, W Vanuatu
95 *O15* **Täby** Stockholm, C Sweden
41 *N14* **Tacámbaro** Michoacán de Ocampo, SW Mexico
42 *A5* **Tacaná, Volcán** ☒ Guatemala/Mexico
43 *X16* **Tacarcuna, Cerro** ▲ SE Panama
Tachau *see* Tachov
158 *J3* **Tacheng** *var.* Qoqek. Xinjiang Uygur Zizhiqu, NW China
54 *H7* **Táchira** *off.* Estado Táchira. ◈ *state* W Venezuela
161 *T13* **Tachoshui** N Taiwan
111 *A17* **Tachov** *Ger.* Tachau. Plzeňský Kraj, W Czech Republic
171 *Q5* **Tacloban** *off.* Tacloban City. Leyte, C Philippines
57 *I19* **Tacna** Tacna, SE Peru
57 *H18* **Tacna** *off.* Departamento de Tacna. ◈ *department* S Peru
32 *H8* **Tacoma** Washington, NW USA
18 *L11* **Taconic Range** ⛰ NE USA
62 *L6* **Taco Pozo** Formosa, N Argentina
57 *M20* **Tacsara, Cordillera de** ⛰ S Bolivia
61 *F17* **Tacuarembó** *prev.* San Fructuoso. Tacuarembó, C Uruguay
61 *E18* **Tacuarembó** ◈ *department* C Uruguay
61 *F17* **Tacuarembó, Río** ≈ C Uruguay
83 *I14* **Taculi** North Western, NW Zambia
171 *Q8* **Tacurong** Mindanao, S Philippines
77 *V8* **Tadek** ≈ NW Niger
74 *J9* **Tademaït, Plateau du** *plateau* C Algeria
187 *R17* **Tadine** Province des Îles Loyauté, E New Caledonia
80 *L11* **Tadjoura** E Djibouti
80 *M11* **Tadjoura, Golfe de** *Eng.* Gulf of Tajura. *inlet* E Djibouti
Tadmor/Tadmur *see* Tudmur
11 *W10* **Tadoule Lake** ◎ Manitoba, C Canada
15 *S8* **Tadoussac** Québec, SE Canada
155 *H18* **Tādpatri** Andhra Pradesh, E India
Tadzhikabad *see* Tojikobod
Tadzhikistan *see* Tajikistan
163 *Y14* **T'aebaek-sanmaek** ⛰ E South Korea
163 *V15* **Taechŏng-do** *island* NW South Korea
163 *X13* **Taedong-gang** ≈ C North Korea
163 *Y16* **Taegu** *off.* Taegu-gwangyŏksi, *var.* Daegu, *Jap.* Taikyū. SE South Korea
Taehan-haehyŏp *see* Korea Strait
Taehan Min'guk *see* South Korea
163 *Y15* **Taejŏn** *off.* Taejŏn-gwangyŏksi, *Jap.* Taiden. C South Korea
193 *Z13* **Tafahi** *island* N Tonga
105 *Q4* **Tafalla** Navarra, N Spain
75 *M12* **Tafassâsset, Oued** ≈ SE Algeria
77 *W7* **Tafassâsset, Ténéré du** *desert* N Niger
55 *U11* **Tafelberg** ▲ S Suriname
97 *J21* **Taff** ≈ SE Wales, UK
Tafila/Ţafīlah, Muḩāfaẓat aţ *see* Aţ Ţafīlah
77 *N15* **Tafiré** N Ivory Coast
142 *M6* **Tafresh** Markazī, W Iran
143 *Q9* **Taft** Yazd, C Iran
35 *R13* **Taft** California, W USA
25 *T14* **Taft** Texas, SW USA
143 *W12* **Taftān, Kūh-e** ▲ SE Iran
35 *R13* **Taft Heights** California, W USA
189 *Y14* **Tafunsak** Kosrae, E Micronesia
192 *G16* **Tāga** Savai'i, SW Samoa
149 *O6* **Tagāb** Kāpīsā, E Afghanistan
39 *O8* **Tagagawik River** ≈ Alaska, USA
165 *Q10* **Tagajō** *var.* Tagazyô. Miyagi, Honshū, C Japan
126 *K12* **Taganrog** Rostovskaya Oblast', SW Russian Federation
126 *K12* **Taganrog, Gulf of** *Rus.* Taganrogskiy Zaliv, *Ukr.* Tahanroz'ka Zatoka. *gulf* Russian Federation/Ukraine
Taganrogskiy Zaliv *see* Taganrog, Gulf of
76 *J8* **Tagant** ◈ *region* C Mauritania
148 *M14* **Tagas** Baluchistān, SW Pakistan
171 *O4* **Tagaytay** Luzon, N Philippines
Tagazyô *see* Tagajō
171 *P6* **Tagbilaran** *var.* Tagbilaran City. Bohol, C Philippines
106 *B10* **Taggia** Liguria, NW Italy
77 *V9* **Taghouaji, Massif de** ▲ C Niger
107 *J15* **Tagliacozzo** Lazio, C Italy
106 *J7* **Tagliamento** ≈ NE Italy
149 *N3* **Tagow Bāy** *var.* Bai. Sar-e Pol, N Afghanistan
146 *H9* **Tagta** *var.* Tahta, *Rus.* Takhta. Daşoguz Welaýaty, N Turkmenistan
146 *J16* **Tagtabazar** *Rus.* Takhtabazar. Mary Welaýaty, S Turkmenistan
59 *L17* **Taguatinga** Tocantins, C Brazil
186 *I10* **Tagula** Tagula Island, SE PNG
186 *I11* **Tagula Island** *prev.* Southeast Island, Sudest Island. *island* SE PNG
171 *Q7* **Tagum** Mindanao, S Philippines
54 *C7* **Tagún, Cerro** *elevation* Colombia/Panama
105 *P7* **Tagus** *Port.* Rio Tejo, *Sp.* Río Tajo. ≈ Portugal/Spain
64 *M9* **Tagus Plain** *undersea feature* E Atlantic Ocean
191 *S10* **Tahaa** *island* Îles Sous le Vent, W French Polynesia
191 *U10* **Tahanea** *atoll* Îles Tuamotu, C French Polynesia
Tahanroz'ka Zatoka *see* Taganrog, Gulf of
74 *K12* **Tahat** ▲ SE Algeria
163 *U4* **Tahe** Heilongjiang, NE China
162 *G9* **Tahilt** Govĭ-Altay, W Mongolia
191 *T10* **Tahiti** *island* Îles du Vent, W French Polynesia
Tahiti, Archipel de *see* Société, Archipel de la
118 *E4* **Tahkuna nina** *headland* W Estonia
148 *K12* **Tāhlāb** ≈ W Pakistan
148 *K12* **Tāhlāb, Dasht-i** *desert* SW Pakistan
27 *R10* **Tahlequah** Oklahoma, C USA
35 *Q6* **Tahoe City** California, W USA
35 *P6* **Tahoe, Lake** ◎ California/Nevada, W USA
Tahoena *see* Tahuna
25 *N6* **Tahoka** Texas, SW USA
32 *F8* **Taholah** Washington, NW USA
77 *T11* **Tahoua** Tahoua, W Niger
77 *T11* **Tahoua** ◈ *department* W Niger
31 *P3* **Tahquamenon Falls** *waterfall* Michigan, N USA
31 *P4* **Tahquamenon River** ≈ Michigan, N USA
139 *V10* **Taḩrīr** S Iraq
10 *K17* **Tahsis** Vancouver Island, British Columbia, SW Canada
Tahta *see* Tagta
75 *W9* **Ţahta** C Egypt
136 *L15* **Tahtalı Dağları** ⛰ C Turkey
57 *I14* **Tahuamanu, Río** ≈ Bolivia/Peru
56 *F13* **Tahuanía, Río** ≈ E Peru
191 *X7* **Tahuata** *island* Îles Marquises, NE French Polynesia
171 *Q10* **Tahuna** *prev.* Tahoena. Pulau Sangihe, N Indonesia
76 *L17* **Taï** SW Ivory Coast
161 *P5* **Tai'an** Shandong, E China
191 *R8* **Taiarapu, Presqu'île de** *peninsula* Tahiti, W French Polynesia
Taibad *see* Tāybād

◆ Country
● Country Capital
◇ Dependent Territory
○ Dependent Territory Capital
◈ Administrative Region
× International Airport
▲ Mountain
⛰ Mountain Range
☒ Volcano
≈ River
◎ Lake
▣ Reservoir

160 K7 Taibai Shan ▲ C China
105 Q12 Taibilla, Sierra de ▲ S Spain
Taibus Qi see Baochang
Taichū see T'aichung
161 S13 T'aichung Jap. Taichū; prev. Taiwan. C Taiwan
Taiden see Taejŏn
185 E23 Taieri ≈ South Island, NZ
115 E21 Taïgetos ▲ S Greece
161 N4 Taihang Shan ▲ C China
184 M11 Taihape Manawatu-Wanganui, North Island, NZ
161 O7 Taihe Anhui, E China
161 O12 Taihe var. Chengjiang. Jiangxi, S China
Taihoku see T'aipei
161 R8 Tai Hu ◎ E China
161 P9 Taihu Anhui, E China
159 O9 Taikang var. Dorbod, Dorbod Mongolzu Zizhixian. Heilongjiang, NE China
161 O6 Taikang Henan, C China
165 T5 Taiki Hokkaidō, NE Japan
166 L8 Taikkyi Yangon, SW Myanmar
Taikyū see Taegu
163 U8 Tailai Heilongjiang, NE China
168 I12 Taileleo Pulau Siberut, W Indonesia
182 J10 Tailem Bend South Australia
96 I8 Tain N Scotland, UK
161 S14 T'ainan Jap. Tainan; prev. Dainan. S Taiwan
115 E22 Taínaro, Akrotírio headland S Greece
161 Q11 Taining var. Shancheng. Fujian, SE China
191 W7 Taiohae prev. Madisonville. Nuku Hiva, NE French Polynesia
161 T13 T'aipei Jap. Taihoku; prev. Daihoku. ● (Taiwan) N Taiwan
168 J7 Taiping Perak, Peninsular Malaysia
163 S8 Taiping Ling ▲ NE China
165 Q4 Taisei Hokkaidō, NE Japan
165 G12 Taisha Shimane, Honshū, SW Japan
109 R4 Taiskirchen Oberösterreich, NW Austria
63 F20 Taitao, Peninsula de peninsula S Chile
Taitō see T'aitung
161 T14 T'aitung Jap. Taitō. S Taiwan
92 M13 Taivalkoski Oulu, E Finland
93 K19 Taivassalo Länsi-Suomi, W Finland
161 T14 Taiwan off. Republic of China, var. Formosa, Formo'sa. ◆ republic E Asia
192 F5 Taiwan var. Formosa. island E Asia
Taiwan see T'aichung
T'aiwan Haihsia/Taiwan Haixia see Taiwan Strait
Taiwan Shan see Chungyang Shanmo
161 R13 Taiwan Strait var. Formosa Strait, Chin. T'aiwan Haihsia, Taiwan Haixia. strait China/Taiwan
161 N4 Taiyuan prev. T'ai-yuan, T'ai-yüan, Yangku. Shanxi, C China
161 R7 Taizhou Jiangsu, E China
161 S10 Taizhou var. Jiaojiang; prev. Haimen. Zhejiang, SE China
Taizhou see Linhai
141 O16 Ta'izz SW Yemen
141 O16 Ta'izz × SW Yemen
75 P12 Tajarhī SW Libya
147 P13 Tajikistan off. Republic of Tajikistan, Rus. Tadzhikistan, Taj. Jumhurii Tojikiston; prev. Tajik S.S.R. ◆ republic C Asia
Tajik S.S.R see Tajikistan
165 O11 Tajima Fukushima, Honshū, C Japan
Tajoe see Tayu
Tajo, Río see Tagus
42 B5 Tajumulco, Volcán ✺ W Guatemala
105 P7 Tajuña ≈ C Spain
Tajura, Gulf of see Tadjoura, Golfe de
167 O9 Tak var. Raheng. Tak, W Thailand
189 U4 Taka Atoll var. Tōke. atoll Ratak Chain, N Marshall Islands
165 P12 Takahagi Ibaraki, Honshū, S Japan
165 H13 Takahashi var. Takahasi. Okayama, Honshū, SW Japan
Takahasi see Takahashi
189 P12 Takaieu Island island E Micronesia
184 I13 Takaka Tasman, South Island, NZ
170 M14 Takalar Sulawesi, C Indonesia
165 H13 Takamatsu var. Takamatu. Kagawa, Shikoku, SW Japan
Takamatu see Takamatsu
165 D14 Takamori Kumamoto, Kyūshū, SW Japan
165 D16 Takanabe Miyazaki, Kyūshū, SW Japan
170 M16 Takan, Gunung ▲ Pulau Sumba, S Indonesia
165 Q7 Takanosu Akita, Honshū, C Japan
Takao see Kaohsiung
165 L11 Takaoka Toyama, Honshū, SW Japan
184 N12 Takapau Hawke's Bay, North Island, NZ
191 U9 Takapoto atoll Îles Tuamotu, C French Polynesia
184 L5 Takapuna Auckland, North Island, NZ
165 J13 Takarazuka Hyōgo, Honshū, SW Japan
191 U9 Takaroa atoll Îles Tuamotu, C French Polynesia
165 N12 Takasaki Gunma, Honshū, S Japan
164 L12 Takayama Gifu, Honshū, SW Japan
164 K12 Takefu var. Takehu. Fukui, Honshū, SW Japan
Takehu see Takefu
164 C14 Takeo Saga, Kyūshū, SW Japan
Takeo see Takêv
164 C17 Take-shima island Nansei-shotō, SW Japan
142 M5 Tākestān var. Takistan; prev. Siadehan. Qazvin, N Iran
164 D14 Taketa Ōita, Kyūshū, SW Japan
167 R13 Takêv prev. Takeo. Takêv, S Cambodia
167 O10 Tak Fah Nakhon Sawan, C Thailand
139 T13 Takhādīd well S Iraq
149 R3 Takhār ◈ province NE Afghanistan
Takhiatash see Taxiatosh
167 S13 Ta Khmau Kândal, S Cambodia
Takhta see Tagta
Takhtabazar see Tagtabazar
145 O8 Takhtabrod Severnyy Kazakhstan, N Kazakhstan
Takhtakupyr see Taxtako'pir
142 M8 Takht-e Shāh, Kūh-e ▲ C Iran
77 V12 Takiéta Zinder, S Niger
8 J8 Takijuq Lake ◎ Nunavut, NW Canada
165 S3 Takikawa Hokkaidō, NE Japan
165 U3 Takinoue Hokkaidō, NE Japan
Takistan see Tākestān
185 B23 Takitimu Mountains ▲ South Island, NZ
Takkaze see Tekezē
165 R7 Takko Aomori, Honshū, C Japan
10 L13 Takla Lake ◎ British Columbia, SW Canada
Takla Makan Desert see Taklimakan Shamo
158 H9 Taklimakan Shamo Eng. Takla Makan Desert. desert NW China
167 T12 Takôk Môndól Kiri, E Cambodia
39 P10 Takotna Alaska, USA
Takow see Kaohsiung
123 O12 Taksimo Respublika Buryatiya, S Russian Federation
164 C13 Taku Saga, Kyūshū, SW Japan
10 I10 Taku ≈ British Columbia, W Canada
166 M15 Takua Pa var. Ban Takua Pa. Phangnga, SW Thailand
77 W16 Takum Taraba, E Nigeria
191 V10 Takume atoll Îles Tuamotu, C French Polynesia
190 L16 Takutea island S Cook Islands
186 K6 Takuu Islands prev. Mortlock Group. island group NE PNG
119 L18 Tal' Rus. Tal'. Minskaya Voblasts', S Belarus
40 L13 Tala Jalisco, C Mexico
61 F19 Tala Canelones, S Uruguay
Talabriga see Aveiro, Portugal
Talabriga see Talavera de la Reina, Spain
119 N14 Talachyn Rus. Tolochin. Vitsyebskaya Voblasts', NE Belarus
149 U7 Talagang Punjab, E Pakistan
155 J23 Talaimannar Northern Province, NW Sri Lanka
117 R3 Talalayivka Chernihivs'ka Oblast', N Ukraine
43 O15 Talamanca, Cordillera de ▲ S Costa Rica
56 A9 Talara Piura, NW Peru
104 L11 Talarrubias Extremadura, W Spain
147 S8 Talas Talasskaya Oblast', NW Kyrgyzstan
147 S8 Talas ≈ NW Kyrgyzstan
186 G7 Talasea New Britain, E PNG
Talas Oblasty see Talasskaya Oblast'
147 S8 Talasskaya Oblast' Kir. Talas Oblasty. ◈ province NW Kyrgyzstan
147 S8 Talasskiy Alatau, Khrebet ▲ Kazakhstan/Kyrgyzstan
77 U12 Talata Mafara Zamfara, NW Nigeria
171 R9 Talaud, Kepulauan island group E Indonesia
104 M9 Talavera de la Reina anc. Caesarobriga, Talabriga. Castilla-La Mancha, C Spain
104 J11 Talavera la Real Extremadura, W Spain
186 F7 Talawe, Mount ▲ New Britain, C PNG
23 S5 Talbotton Georgia, SE USA
183 R7 Talbragar River ≈ New South Wales, SE Australia
62 G13 Talca Maule, C Chile
62 F13 Talcahuano Bío Bío, C Chile
154 N12 Tālcher Orissa, E India
25 W5 Talco Texas, SW USA
145 V14 Taldykorgan Kaz. Taldyqorghan; prev. Taldy-Kurgan. Almaty, SE Kazakhstan
Taldy-Kurgan/Taldyqorghan see Taldykorgan
147 Y7 Taldy-Suu Issyk-Kul'skaya Oblast', E Kyrgyzstan
147 U10 Taldy-Suu Oshskaya Oblast', SW Kyrgyzstan
Tal-e Khosravī see Yāsūj
193 Y15 Taleki Tonga island Otu Tolu Group, C Tonga
193 Y15 Taleki Vavu'u island Otu Tolu Group, C Tonga
102 J13 Talence Gironde, SW France
145 U16 Talgar Kaz. Talghar. Almaty, SE Kazakhstan
Talghar see Talgar
171 Q12 Taliabu, Pulau island Kepulauan Sula, C Indonesia
115 L22 Taliarós, Akrotírio headland Astypálaia, Kykládes, Greece, Aegean Sea
Ta-lien see Dalian
27 Q12 Talihina Oklahoma, C USA
Talimardzhan see Tollimarjon
Talin see T'alin
137 T12 T'alin Rus. Talin; prev. Verin T'alin. W Armenia
81 E15 Tali Post Bahr el Gabel, S Sudan
Taliq-an see Tāloqān
Taliş Dağları see Talish Mountains
142 L2 Talish Mountains Az. Taliş Dağları, Per. Kūhhā-ye Ţavālesh, Rus. Talyshskiye Gory. ▲ Azerbaijan/Iran
170 M16 Taliwang Sumbawa, C Indonesia
119 L17 Tal'ka Rus. Tal'ka. Minskaya Voblasts', C Belarus
39 R11 Talkeetna Alaska, USA
39 R11 Talkeetna Mountains ▲ Alaska, USA
Talkhof see Puurmani
92 H2 Tálknafjördhur Vestfirdhir, W Iceland
139 Q3 Tall 'Abţah N Iraq
138 M2 Tall Abyaḑ var. Tell Abiad. Ar Raqqah, N Syria
23 Q4 Talladega Alabama, S USA
139 Q2 Tall 'Afar N Iraq
23 S8 Tallahassee prev. Muskogean. state capital Florida, SE USA
22 L2 Tallahatchie River ≈ Mississippi, S USA
Tall al Abyaḑ see At Tall al Abyaḑ
139 W12 Tall al Laḩm S Iraq
183 P11 Tallangatta Victoria, SE Australia
23 R4 Tallapoosa River ≈ Alabama/Georgia, S USA
103 T13 Tallard Hautes-Alpes, SE France
139 Q3 Tall ash Sha'īr N Iraq
23 O5 Tallassee Alabama, S USA
139 R4 Tall 'Azbah NW Iraq
138 I5 Tall Bīsah Ḩimş, W Syria
139 R3 Tall Ḩassūnah N Iraq
139 Q2 Tall Ḩuqnah var. Tell Huqnah. N Iraq
Tallin see Tallinn
118 G3 Tallinn Ger. Reval, Rus. Tallin; prev. Revel. ● (Estonia) Harjumaa, NW Estonia
118 H3 Tallinn × Harjumaa, NW Estonia
138 H5 Tall Kalakh var. Tell Kalakh. Ḩimş, C Syria
139 R2 Tall Kayf NW Iraq
Tall Kūchak see Tall Kūshik
139 P2 Tall Kūshik var. Tall Kūchak. Al Ḩasakah, E Syria
31 U12 Tallmadge Ohio, N USA
22 J5 Tallulah Louisiana, S USA
139 Q2 Tall 'Uwaynāt NW Iraq
139 Q2 Tall Zāhir N Iraq
122 J13 Tal'menka Altayskiy Kray, S Russian Federation
117 P7 Tal'ne Rus. Tal'noye. Cherkas'ka Oblast', C Ukraine
Tal'noye see Tal'ne
80 E12 Talodi Southern Kordofan, C Sudan
188 B16 Talofofo SE Guam
188 B16 Talofofo Bay bay SE Guam
26 L9 Taloga Oklahoma, C USA
123 T10 Talon Magadanskaya Oblast', E Russian Federation
14 H11 Talon, Lake ◎ Ontario, S Canada
149 R2 Tāloqān var. Taliq-an. Takhār, NE Afghanistan
126 M8 Talovaya Voronezhskaya Oblast', W Russian Federation
9 N6 Taloyoak prev. Spence Bay. Nunavut, N Canada
25 Q8 Talpa Texas, SW USA
40 K13 Talpa de Allende Jalisco, C Mexico
23 S9 Talquin, Lake ▣ Florida, SE USA
Talsen see Talsi
162 H9 Talshand Govĭ-Altay, C Mongolia
118 E8 Talsi Ger. Talsen. Talsi, NW Latvia
143 V11 Tal Sīah Sīstān va Balūchestān, SE Iran
62 G6 Taltal Antofagasta, N Chile
8 K10 Taltson ≈ Northwest Territories, NW Canada
168 K11 Taluk Sumatera, W Indonesia
92 J8 Talvik Finnmark, N Norway
182 M7 Talyawalka Creek ≈ New South Wales, SE Australia
Talyshskiye Gory see Talish Mountains
29 W14 Tama Iowa, C USA
Tama Abu, Banjaran see Penambo, Banjaran
169 U9 Tamabo, Banjaran ▲ East Malaysia
190 B16 Tamakautoga SW Niue
127 N7 Tamala Penzenskaya Oblast', W Russian Federation
77 P15 Tamale C Ghana
191 P3 Tamana prev. Rotcher Island. atoll Tungaru, W Kiribati
74 K12 Tamanrasset var. Tamenghest. S Algeria
74 J13 Tamanrasset wadi Algeria/Mali
166 M2 Tamanthi Sagaing, N Myanmar
97 I24 Tamar ≈ SW England, UK
Tamar see Tudmur
54 H9 Támara Casanare, C Colombia
54 F7 Tamar, Alto de ▲ C Colombia
173 X16 Tamarin E Mauritius
105 T5 Tamarite de Litera var. Tararite de Llitera. Aragón, NE Spain
111 I24 Tamási Tolna, S Hungary
Tamatave see Toamasina
41 O9 Tamaulipas ◈ state C Mexico
41 P10 Tamaulipas, Sierra de ▲ C Mexico
56 F12 Tamaya, Río ≈ E Peru
40 I9 Tamazula Durango, C Mexico
40 L14 Tamazula Jalisco, C Mexico
Tamazulápam see Tamazulapán
41 Q15 Tamazulapán var. Tamazulápam. Oaxaca, SE Mexico
41 P12 Tamazunchale San Luis Potosí, C Mexico
76 H11 Tambacounda SE Senegal
83 M16 Tambara Manica, C Mozambique
77 T13 Tambawel Sokoto, NW Nigeria
186 M9 Tambea Guadalcanal, C Solomon Islands
169 N10 Tambelan, Kepulauan island group W Indonesia
57 E15 Tambo de Mora Ica, W Peru
170 L16 Tambora, Gunung ✺ Sumbawa, S Indonesia
61 E17 Tambores Paysandú, W Uruguay
57 F14 Tambo, Río ≈ C Peru
56 F7 Tamboryacu, Río ≈ N Peru
126 M7 Tambov Tambovskaya Oblast', W Russian Federation
126 L6 Tambovskaya Oblast' ◈ province W Russian Federation
104 H3 Tambre ≈ NW Spain
169 V7 Tambunan Sabah, East Malaysia
81 C15 Tambura Western Equatoria, SW Sudan
Tamchaket see Tâmchekket
76 J9 Tâmchekket var. Tamchaket. Hodh el Gharbi, S Mauritania
167 T7 Tam Điêp Ninh Binh, N Vietnam
Tamdybulak see Tomdibuloq
54 H8 Tame Arauca, C Colombia
104 H6 Tâmega, Rio Sp. Río Támega. ≈ Portugal/Spain
115 H20 Tamélos, Akrotírio headland Kéa, Kykládes, Greece, Aegean Sea
Tamenghest see Tamanrasset
77 V8 Tamgak, Adrar ▲ C Niger
76 I13 Tamgue ▲ NW Guinea
41 Q12 Tamiahua Veracruz-Llave, E Mexico
41 Q12 Tamiahua, Laguna de lagoon E Mexico
23 Y16 Tamiami Canal canal Florida, SE USA
188 F17 Tamil Harbor harbour Yap, W Micronesia
155 H21 Tamil Nādu prev. Madras. ◈ state SE India
99 H20 Tamines Namur, S Belgium
116 E12 Tamiš Ger. Temesch, Hung. Temes, SCr. Tamiš. ≈ Romania/Serbia and Montenegro (Yugo.)
167 U10 Tam Ky Quang Nam-Đa Nẵng, C Vietnam
Tammerfors see Tampere
Tammisaari see Ekenäs
95 N14 Tämnaren ◎ C Sweden
191 Q7 Tamotoe, Passe passage Tahiti, W French Polynesia
23 V12 Tampa Florida, SE USA
23 V12 Tampa × Florida, SE USA
23 V13 Tampa Bay bay Florida, SE USA
93 L18 Tampere Swe. Tammerfors. Länsi-Suomi, W Finland
41 Q11 Tampico Tamaulipas, C Mexico
171 P14 Tampo Pulau Muna, C Indonesia
167 V11 Tam Quan Binh Đinh, C Vietnam
162 J13 Tamsag Muchang Nei Mongol Zizhiqu, N China
Tamsal see Tamsalu
118 I4 Tamsalu Ger. Tamsal. Lääne-Virumaa, NE Estonia
109 S8 Tamsweg Salzburg, SW Austria
166 L3 Tamu Sagaing, N Myanmar
41 P12 Tamuín San Luis Potosí, C Mexico
188 C15 Tamuning NW Guam
183 T6 Tamworth New South Wales, SE Australia
97 M19 Tamworth C England, UK
81 K19 Tana ≈ SE Kenya
Tana see Deatnu/Tenojoki
164 I15 Tanabe Wakayama, Honshū, SW Japan
92 L8 Tana Bru Finnmark, N Norway
39 T10 Tanacross Alaska, USA
92 L7 Tanafjorden Lapp. Deanuvuotna. fjord N Norway
38 G17 Tanaga Island island Aleutian Islands, Alaska, USA
38 G17 Tanaga Volcano ▲ Tanaga Island, Alaska, USA
107 M18 Tanagro ≈ S Italy
80 H11 T'ana Hāyk' Eng. Lake Tana. ◎ NW Ethiopia
168 H11 Tanahbela, Pulau island Kepulauan Batu, W Indonesia
171 H15 Tanahjampea, Pulau island W Indonesia
168 H11 Tanahmasa, Pulau island Kepulauan Batu, W Indonesia
Tanais see Don
152 L10 Tanakpur Uttaranchal, N India
Tana, Lake see T'ana Hāyk'
181 P5 Tanami Desert desert Northern Territory, N Australia
167 T14 Tân An Long An, S Vietnam
39 Q9 Tanana Alaska, USA
Tananarive see Antananarivo
39 Q9 Tanana River ≈ Alaska, USA
95 C15 Tananger Rogaland, S Norway
188 H5 Tanapag Saipan, S Northern Mariana Islands
188 H5 Tanapag, Puetton bay Saipan, S Northern Mariana Islands
106 C9 Tanaro ≈ N Italy
163 Y12 Tanch'ŏn E North Korea
40 M14 Tancítaro, Cerro ✺ C Mexico
153 N12 Tānda Uttar Pradesh, N India
77 O15 Tanda E Ivory Coast
116 L14 Ţăndărei Ialomiţa, SE Romania
63 N14 Tandil Buenos Aires, E Argentina
78 H12 Tandjilé off. Préfecture du Tandjilé. ◈ prefecture SW Chad
Tandjoeng see Tanjung
Tandjoengpandan see Tanjungpandan
Tandjoengpinang see Tanjungpinang
Tandjoengredeb see Tanjungredeb
149 Q16 Tando Allāhyār Sind, SE Pakistan
149 Q17 Tando Bāgo Sind, SE Pakistan
149 Q16 Tando Muhammad Khān Sind, SE Pakistan
182 L7 Tandou Lake seasonal lake New South Wales, SE Australia
94 L11 Tandsjöborg Gävleborg, C Sweden
155 H15 Tāndūr Andhra Pradesh, C India
164 C17 Tanega-shima island Nansei-shotō, SW Japan
165 R7 Taneichi Iwate, Honshū, C Japan
Tanen Taunggyi see Tane Range
167 N8 Tane Range Bur. Tanen Taunggyi. ▲ W Thailand
111 P15 Tanew ≈ SE Poland
21 W2 Taneytown Maryland, NE USA
74 H12 Tanezrouft desert Algeria/Mali
138 L7 Ţanf, Jabal aţ ▲ SE Syria
81 J21 Tanga Tanga, E Tanzania
81 I22 Tanga ◈ region E Tanzania
153 T14 Tangail Dhaka, C Bangladesh
186 I5 Tanga Islands island group NE PNG
155 K26 Tangalla Southern Province, S Sri Lanka
Tanganyika and Zanzibar see Tanzania
68 I13 Tanganyika, Lake ◎ E Africa
56 E7 Tangarana, Río ≈ N Peru
Tangdukou see Shaoyang
191 V16 Tangaroa, Maunga ✺ Easter Island, Chile, E Pacific Ocean
74 G5 Tanger var. Tangiers, Tangier, Fr./Ger. Tangerk, Sp. Tánger; anc. Tingis. NW Morocco
169 N15 Tangerang Jawa, C Indonesia
Tangerk see Tanger
100 M12 Tangermünde Sachsen-Anhalt, C Germany
159 O12 Tanggulashan var. Togton Heyan; var. Tuotuoheyan. Qinghai, C China
156 K10 Tanggula Shan var. Dangla, Tangla Range. ▲ W China
159 N13 Tanggula Shan ▲ W China
156 K10 Tanggula Shankou Tib. Dang La. pass W China
161 N7 Tanghe Henan, C China
149 T5 Tāngi North-West Frontier Province, NW Pakistan
Tangier see Tanger
21 Y5 Tangier Island island Virginia, NE USA
Tangiers see Tanger
22 K8 Tangipahoa River ≈ Louisiana, S USA
Tangla Range see Tanggula Shan
164 J12 Tango-hantō peninsula Honshū, SW Japan
156 I10 Tangra Yumco var. Tangro Tso. ◎ W China
Tangro Tso see Tangra Yumco
157 T7 Tangshan var. T'ang-shan. Hebei, E China
77 R14 Tanguiéta NW Benin
163 X7 Tangwang He ≈ NE China
163 X7 Tangyuan Heilongjiang, NE China
92 M11 Tanhua Lappi, N Finland
171 U16 Tanimbar, Kepulauan island group Maluku, E Indonesia
Tanintharyi see Tenasserim
139 U4 Tānjarō ≈ E Iraq
131 T15 Tanjong Piai headland Peninsular Malaysia
Tanjore see Thanjāvūr
169 U12 Tanjung prev. Tandjoeng. Borneo, C Indonesia
169 W9 Tanjungbatu Borneo, N Indonesia
Tanjungkarang see Bandarlampung
169 N13 Tanjungpandan prev. Tandjoengpandan. Pulau Belitung, W Indonesia
168 M10 Tanjungpinang prev. Tandjoengpinang. Pulau Bintan, W Indonesia
169 V9 Tanjungredeb var. Tanjungredep; prev. Tandjoengredeb. Borneo, C Indonesia
Tanjungredep see Tanjungredeb
149 S8 Tānk North-West Frontier Province, NW Pakistan
187 S15 Tanna island S Vanuatu
93 F17 Tännäs Jämtland, C Sweden
Tannenhof see Krynica
108 K7 Tannheim Tirol, W Austria
Tannu-Tuva see Tyva, Respublika
171 Q12 Tano Pulau Taliabu, E Indonesia
77 O17 Tano ≈ S Ghana
152 D10 Tanot Rājasthān, NW India
77 V11 Tanout Zinder, C Niger
41 P12 Tanquián San Luis Potosí, C Mexico
77 R13 Tansarga E Burkina
167 T13 Tan Son Nhat × (Hô Chi Minh) Tây Ninh, S Vietnam
75 V8 Tanta var. Tantā, Tantâ. N Egypt
74 D9 Tan-Tan SW Morocco
41 P12 Tantoyuca Veracruz-Llave, E Mexico
152 J12 Tāntpur Uttar Pradesh, N India
Tan-tung see Dandong
38 M12 Tanunak Alaska, USA
166 L5 Ta-nyaung Magwe, W Myanmar
167 S5 Tân Yên Tuyên Quang, N Vietnam
81 F22 Tanzania off. United Republic of Tanzania, Swa. Jamhuri ya Muungano wa Tanzania; prev. German East Africa, Tanganyika and Zanzibar. ◆ republic E Africa
Tanzania, Jamhuri ya Muungano wa see Tanzania
Taoan/Tao'an see Taonan
163 T8 Tao'er He ≈ NE China
159 U11 Tao He ≈ C China
163 U9 Taonan var. Taoan, Tao'an. Jilin, NE China
T'aon-an see Baicheng
Taongi see Bokaak Atoll
107 M23 Taormina anc. Tauromenium. Sicilia, Italy, C Mediterranean Sea
37 S9 Taos New Mexico, SW USA
Taoudenit see Taoudenni
77 O6 Taoudenni var. Taoudenit. Tombouctou, N Mali
74 G6 Taounate N Morocco
161 S13 T'aoyüan Jap. Tōen. N Taiwan
118 I3 Tapa Ger. Taps. Lääne-Virumaa, NE Estonia
41 V17 Tapachula Chiapas, SE Mexico
Tapaiu see Gvardeysk
59 H14 Tapajós, Rio var. Tapajóz. ≈ NW Brazil
Tapajóz see Tapajós, Rio
61 C21 Tapalqué var. Tapalquén. Buenos Aires, E Argentina
Tapalquén see Tapalqué
Tapanahoni see Tapanahony Rivier
55 W11 Tapanahony Rivier var. Tapanahoni. ≈ E Suriname
41 T16 Tapanatepec var. San Pedro Tapanatepec. Oaxaca, SE Mexico
185 D23 Tapanui Otago, South Island, NZ
59 C14 Tapauá Amazonas, N Brazil
47 R7 Tapauá, Rio ≈ W Brazil
185 I14 Tapawera Tasman, South Island, NZ
61 I16 Tapes Rio Grande do Sul, S Brazil
76 K16 Tapeta C Liberia
154 H11 Tāpi prev. Tāpti. ≈ W India
104 J2 Tapia de Casariego Asturias, N Spain
56 F10 Tapiche, Río ≈ N Peru
167 N15 Tapi, Mae Nam var. Luang. ≈ SW Thailand
186 E8 Tapini Central, S PNG
Tapirapecó, Serra see Tapirapecó, Sierra
55 N13 Tapirapecó, Sierra Port. Serra Tapirapecó. ▲ Brazil/Venezuela
77 R13 Tapoa ≈ Benin/Niger
188 H5 Tapochau, Mount ▲ Saipan, S Northern Mariana Islands
111 H24 Tapolca Veszprém, W Hungary
21 X5 Tappahannock Virginia, NE USA
31 U13 Tappan Lake ▣ Ohio, N USA
165 Q6 Tappi-zaki headland Honshū, C Japan
Taps see Tapa
Tāpti see Tāpi
185 J16 Tapuaenuku ▲ South Island, NZ
171 N8 Tapul Group island group Sulu Archipelago, SW Philippines
58 E11 Tapurucuará var. Tapuruquara. Amazonas, NW Brazil
Tapuruquara see Tapurucuará
192 J17 Taputapu, Cape headland Tutuila, W American Samoa
141 W13 Ţāqah S Oman
139 T3 Taqtaq N Iraq
61 J15 Taquara Rio Grande do Sul, S Brazil
59 H19 Taquari, Rio ≈ C Brazil
60 L8 Taquaritinga São Paulo, S Brazil
122 I11 Tara Omskaya Oblast', C Russian Federation
83 I16 Tara Southern, S Zambia
113 J15 Tara ≈ SW Serbia and Montenegro (Yugo.)
112 K13 Tara ▲ W Serbia and Montenegro (Yugo.)
77 W15 Taraba ◈ state E Nigeria
77 X15 Taraba ≈ E Nigeria
75 O7 Tarābulus var. Ţarābulus al Gharb, Eng. Tripoli. ● (Libya) NW Libya
75 O7 Tarābulus × NW Libya
Tarābulus/Ţarābulus ash Shām see Tripoli
Ţarābulus al Gharb see Ţarābulus
105 O7 Taracena Castilla-La Mancha, C Spain
117 N12 Taraclia Rus. Tarakilya. S Moldova
139 V10 Tarād al Kahf SE Iraq
183 R10 Tarago New South Wales, SE Australia
169 V8 Tarakan Borneo, C Indonesia
169 V9 Tarakan, Pulau island N Indonesia
Tarakilya see Taraclia
165 P16 Tarama-jima island Sakishima-shotō, SW Japan
184 K10 Taranaki off. Taranaki Region. ◈ region North Island, NZ
184 K10 Taranaki, Mount var. Egmont. ▲ North Island, NZ
105 O9 Tarancón Castilla-La Mancha, C Spain
188 M15 Tarang Reef reef C Micronesia
96 E7 Taransay island NW Scotland, UK
107 P18 Taranto var. Tarentum. Puglia, SE Italy
107 O19 Taranto, Golfo di Eng. Gulf of Taranto. gulf S Italy
Taranto, Gulf of see Taranto, Golfo di
62 G3 Tarapacá off. Región de Tarapacá. ◈ region N Chile
187 N9 Tarapaina Maramasike Island, N Solomon Islands
56 D10 Tarapoto San Martín, N Peru
138 M6 Ţaraq an Na'jah hill range E Syria
138 M6 Ţaraq Sidāwī hill range E Syria
103 Q11 Tarare Rhône, E France
Tararite de Llitera see Tamarite de Litera
184 M13 Tararua Range ▲ North Island, NZ
151 Q22 Tarāsa Dwīp island Nicobar Islands, India, NE Indian Ocean
103 Q15 Tarascon Bouches-du-Rhône, SE France
102 M17 Tarascon-sur-Ariège Ariège, S France
117 P6 Tarashcha Kyyivs'ka Oblast', N Ukraine
57 L18 Tarata Cochabamba, C Bolivia
57 I18 Tarata Tacna, SW Peru
190 H2 Taratai atoll Tungaru, W Kiribati
59 B15 Tarauacá Acre, W Brazil
59 B15 Tarauacá, Rio ≈ NW Brazil
191 Q8 Taravao Tahiti, W French Polynesia
191 R8 Taravao, Baie de bay Tahiti, W French Polynesia
191 Q8 Taravao, Isthme de isthmus Tahiti, W French Polynesia
103 X16 Taravo ≈ Corse, France, C Mediterranean Sea
190 J3 Tarawa × Tarawa, W Kiribati
190 H2 Tarawa atoll Tungaru, W Kiribati
184 N10 Tarawera Hawke's Bay, North Island, NZ
184 N8 Tarawera, Lake ◎ North Island, NZ
184 N8 Tarawera, Mount ▲ North Island, NZ
105 S8 Tarayuela ▲ N Spain

◆ Country ◇ Dependent Territory ◈ Administrative Region ▲ Mountain ✺ Volcano ◎ Lake
● Country Capital ○ Dependent Territory Capital × International Airport ▲ Mountain Range ≈ River ▣ Reservoir

151 R16 **Taraz** *prev.* Aulie Ata, Auliye-Ata, Dzhambul, Zhambyl. Zhambyl, S Kazakhstan.
105 Q5 **Tarazona** Aragón, NE Spain
105 Q10 **Tarazona de la Mancha** Castilla-La Mancha, C Spain
145 X12 **Tarbagatay, Khrebet** ▲ China/Kazakhstan
96 J8 **Tarbat Ness** *headland* N Scotland, UK
149 U5 **Tarbela Reservoir** ⊠ N Pakistan
96 H12 **Tarbert** W Scotland, UK
96 F7 **Tarbert** Western Isles, NW Scotland, UK
102 K16 **Tarbes** *anc.* Bigorra. Hautes-Pyrénées, S France
21 W9 **Tarboro** North Carolina, SE USA
Tarca *see* Torysa
106 J6 **Tarcento** Friuli-Venezia Giulia, NE Italy
182 F5 **Tarcoola** South Australia
105 S5 **Tardienta** Aragón, NE Spain
102 L11 **Tardoire** ≈ W France
183 U7 **Taree** New South Wales, SE Australia
92 K12 **Tärendö** *Lapp.* Deargget. Norrbotten, N Sweden
Tarentum *see* Taranto
74 C9 **Tarfaya** SW Morocco
116 J13 **Târgovişte** *prev.* Tîrgovişte. Dâmboviţa, S Romania
116 M12 **Târgu Bujor** *prev.* Tîrgu Bujor. Galaţi, E Romania
116 H13 **Târgu Cărbuneşti** *prev.* Tîrgu. Gorj, SW Romania
116 L9 **Târgu Frumos** *prev.* Tîrgu Frumos. Iaşi, NE Romania
116 H13 **Targu Jui** *prev.* Tîrgu Jiu. Gorj, W Romania
116 H9 **Târgu Lăpuş** *prev.* Tîrgu Lăpuş. Maramureş, N Romania
Târgul-Neamţ *see* Târgu-Neamţ
Târgul-Săcuiesc *see* Târgu Secuiesc
116 I10 **Târgu Mureş** *prev.* Oşorhei, Tîrgu Mures, *Ger.* Neumarkt, *Hung.* Marosvásárhely. Mureş, C Romania
116 K9 **Târgu-Neamţ** *var.* Târgul-Neamţ; *prev.* Tîrgu-Neamţ. Neamţ, NE Romania
116 K11 **Târgu Ocna** *Hung.* Aknavásár; *prev.* Tîrgu Ocna. Bacău, E Romania
116 K11 **Târgu Secuiesc** *Ger.* Neumarkt, Szekler Neumarkt, *Hung.* Kezdivásárhely; *prev.* Chezdi-Oşorheiu, Târgul-Săcuiesc, Tîrgu Secuiesc. Covasna, E Romania
145 X10 **Targyn** Vostochnyy Kazakhstan, E Kazakhstan
Tar Heel State *see* North Carolina
186 C7 **Tari** Southern Highlands, W PNG
143 P17 **Ţarif** Abū Ẓaby, C UAE
104 K16 **Tarifa** Andalucía, S Spain
84 C14 **Tarifa, Punta de** *headland* SW Spain
57 M21 **Tarija** Tarija, S Bolivia
57 M21 **Tarija** ◈ *department* S Bolivia
141 R14 **Tarīm** C Yemen
Tarim Basin *see* Tarim Pendi
81 G19 **Tarime** Mara, N Tanzania
131 S8 **Tarim He** ≈ NW China
159 H8 **Tarim Pendi** *Eng.* Tarim Basin. *basin* NW China
149 N7 **Tarin Kowt** *var.* Terinkot. Urūzgān, C Afghanistan
171 O12 **Taripa** Sulawesi, C Indonesia
117 Q12 **Tarkhankut, Mys** *headland* S Ukraine
27 Q1 **Tarkio** Missouri, C USA
122 J9 **Tarko-Sale** Yamalo-Nenetskiy Avtonomnyy Okrug, N Russian Federation
77 P17 **Tarkwa** S Ghana
171 O3 **Tarlac** Luzon, N Philippines
95 F22 **Tarm** Ringkøbing, W Denmark
57 E14 **Tarma** Junín, C Peru
103 N15 **Tarn** ◈ *department* S France
102 M15 **Tarn** ≈ S France
111 L22 **Tarna** ≈ C Hungary
92 G13 **Tärnaby** Västerbotten, N Sweden
149 P8 **Tarnak Rūd** ≈ SE Afghanistan
116 J11 **Târnava Mare** *Ger.* Grosse Kokel, *Hung.* Nagy-Küküllő; *prev.* Tîrnava Mare. ≈ S Romania
116 I11 **Târnava Mică** *Ger.* Kleine Kokel, *Hung.* Kis-Küküllo; *prev.* Tîrnava Mică. ≈ C Romania
116 I11 **Târnăveni** *Ger.* Marteskirch, Martinskirch, *Hung.* Dicsőszentmárton; *prev.* Sînmartin, Tîrnăveni. Mureş, C Romania
102 L14 **Tarn-et-Garonne** ◈ *department* S France
111 P18 **Tarnica** ▲ SE Poland
111 N15 **Tarnobrzeg** Podkarpackie, SE Poland
125 N12 **Tarnogskiy Gorodok** Vologodskaya Oblast', NW Russian Federation
Tarnopol *see* Ternopil'
111 M16 **Tarnów** Małopolskie, SE Poland
Tarnowice/Tarnowitz *see* Tarnowskie Góry
111 J16 **Tarnowskie Góry** *var.* Tarnowice, Tarnowskie Gory, *Ger.* Tarnowitz. Śląskie, S Poland
95 N14 **Tärnsjö** Västmanland, C Sweden
106 E9 **Taro** ≈ NW Italy
186 I6 **Taron** New Ireland, NE PNG
74 E8 **Taroudannt** *var.* Taroudant. SW Morocco
Taroudant *see* Taroudannt
23 V12 **Tarpon, Lake** ◎ Florida, SE USA
23 V12 **Tarpon Springs** Florida, SE USA
107 G14 **Tarquinia** *anc.* Tarquinii; *hist.* Corneto. Lazio, C Italy
Tarquinii *see* Tarquinia
Tarraco *see* Tarragona
76 D10 **Tarrafal** Santiago, S Cape Verde
105 V6 **Tarragona** *anc.* Tarraco. Cataluña, E Spain
105 T7 **Tarragona** ◈ *province* Cataluña, NE Spain
183 O17 **Tarraleah** Tasmania, SE Australia
23 P3 **Tarrant City** Alabama, S USA
185 D21 **Tarras** Otago, South Island, NZ
Tarrasa *see* Terrassa
105 U5 **Tàrrega** *var.* Tarrega. Cataluña, NE Spain
21 W9 **Tar River** ≈ North Carolina, SE USA
Tarsatica *see* Rijeka
136 J17 **Tarsus** İçel, S Turkey
62 K4 **Tartagal** Salta, N Argentina
137 V12 **Tärtär** *Rus.* Terter. ≈ SW Azerbaijan
102 J15 **Tartas** Landes, SW France
139 Q6 **Tartasah** C Iraq
Tartlau *see* Prejmer
Tartous/Tartouss *see* Ţarţūs
118 J5 **Tartu** *Ger.* Dorpat; *prev. Rus.* Yurev, Yur'yev. Tartumaa, SE Estonia
118 I5 **Tartumaa** *off.* Tartu Maakond. ◈ *province* E Estonia
138 H5 **Ţarţūs** *Fr.* Tartouss; *anc.* Tortosa. Tarţūs, W Syria
138 H5 **Ţarţūs** *off.* Muḥāfaẓat Ţarţūs, *var.* Tartous, Tartus. ◈ *governorate* W Syria
164 C16 **Tarumizu** Kagoshima, Kyūshū, SW Japan
126 K4 **Tarusa** Kaluzhskaya Oblast', W Russian Federation
117 N11 **Tarutyne** Odes'ka Oblast', SW Ukraine
162 I7 **Tarvagatyn Nuruu** ▲ N Mongolia
106 J6 **Tarvisio** Friuli-Venezia Giulia, NE Italy
Tarvisium *see* Treviso
57 O16 **Tarvo, Río** ≈ E Bolivia
14 G8 **Tarzwell** Ontario, S Canada
40 K5 **Tasajera, Sierra de la** ▲ N Mexico
145 S13 **Tasaral** Karaganda, C Kazakhstan
Tasböget *see* Tasbuget
145 N15 **Tasbuget** *Kaz.* Tasböget. Kzylorda, S Kazakhstan
108 E11 **Tasch** Valais, SW Switzerland
Tasek Kenyir *see* Kenyir, Tasik
122 J14 **Tashanta** Respublika Altay, S Russian Federation
Tashauz *see* Daşoguz
Tashi Chho Dzong *see* Thimphu
153 U11 **Tashigang** E Bhutan
137 T11 **Tashir** *prev.* Kalinino. N Armenia
143 Q11 **Ţashk, Daryācheh-ye** ◎ C Iran
Tashkent *see* Toshkent
Tashkentskaya Oblast' *see* Toshkent Viloyati
Tashkepri *see* Daşköpri
Tash-Kömür *see* Tash-Kumyr
147 S9 **Tash-Kumyr** *Kir.* Tash-Kömür. Dzhalal-Abadskaya Oblast', W Kyrgyzstan
127 T7 **Tashla** Orenburgskaya Oblast', W Russian Federation
Tashqurghan *see* Kholm
122 J13 **Tashtagol** Kemerovskaya Oblast', S Russian Federation
95 H24 **Tåsinge** *island* C Denmark
12 M5 **Tasiujaq** Québec, E Canada
77 W11 **Tasker** Zinder, C Niger
145 W12 **Taskesken** Vostochnyy Kazakhstan, E Kazakhstan
136 J10 **Taşköprü** Kastamonu, N Turkey
Taskuduk, Peski *see* Goshquduq Qum
186 G5 **Taskul** New Ireland, NE PNG
137 S13 **Taşlıçay** Ağrı, E Turkey
185 H14 **Tasman** *off.* Tasman District. ◈ *unitary authority* South Island, NZ
192 J12 **Tasman Basin** *var.* East Australian Basin. *undersea feature* S Tasman Sea
185 I14 **Tasman Bay** *inlet* South Island, NZ
192 I13 **Tasman Fracture Zone** *tectonic feature* S Indian Ocean
185 E19 **Tasman Glacier** *glacier* South Island, NZ
Tasman Group *see* Nukumanu Islands
183 N15 **Tasmania** *prev.* Van Diemen's Land. ◈ *state* SE Australia
183 Q16 **Tasmania** *island* SE Australia
185 H14 **Tasman Mountains** ▲ South Island, NZ
183 P17 **Tasman Peninsula** *peninsula* Tasmania, SE Australia
192 I11 **Tasman Plain** *undersea feature* W Tasman Sea
192 I12 **Tasman Plateau** *var.* South Tasmania Plateau. *undersea feature* SW Tasman Sea
192 I11 **Tasman Sea** *sea* SW Pacific Ocean
116 G9 **Tăşnad** *Ger.* Trestenberg, Trestendorf, *Hung.* Tasnád. Satu Mare, NW Romania
136 L11 **Taşova** Amasya, N Turkey
77 T10 **Tassara** Tahoua, W Niger
12 K4 **Tassialouc, Lac** ◎ Québec, C Canada
Tassili du Hoggar *see* Tassili ta-n-Ahaggar
74 L11 **Tassili-n-Ajjer** *plateau* E Algeria
74 K14 **Tassili ta-n-Ahaggar** *var.* Tassili du Hoggar. *plateau* S Algeria
59 M15 **Tasso Fragoso** Maranhão, E Brazil
Tåstrup *see* Taastrup
145 O9 **Tasty-Taldy** Akmola, C Kazakhstan
143 W10 **Tāsūkī** Sīstān va Balūchestān, SE Iran
111 I22 **Tata** *Ger.* Totis. Komárom-Esztergom, NW Hungary
74 E8 **Tata** SW Morocco
Tataaihoa, Pointe *see* Vénus, Pointe
111 I22 **Tatabánya** Komárom-Esztergom, NW Hungary
191 X10 **Tatakoto** *atoll* Îles Tuamotu, E French Polynesia
75 N7 **Tataouine** *var.* Taţāwīn. SE Tunisia
55 O5 **Tataracual, Cerro** ▲ NE Venezuela
117 O12 **Tatarbunary** Odes'ka Oblast', SW Ukraine
119 M17 **Tatarka** *Rus.* Tatarka. Mahilyowskaya Voblasts', E Belarus
Tatar Pazardzhik *see* Pazardzhik
122 I12 **Tatarsk** Novosibirskaya Oblast', C Russian Federation
Tatarskaya ASSR *see* Tatarstan, Respublika
123 T13 **Tatarskiy Proliv** *Eng.* Tatar Strait. *strait* SE Russian Federation
127 R4 **Tatarstan, Respublika** *prev.* Tatarskaya ASSR. ◈ *autonomous republic* W Russian Federation
Tatar Strait *see* Tatarskiy Proliv
Taţāwīn *see* Tataouine
171 N12 **Tate** Sulawesi, N Indonesia
141 N11 **Tathlīth** 'Asīr, S Saudi Arabia
141 O11 **Tathlīth, Wādī** *dry watercourse* S Saudi Arabia
183 R11 **Tathra** New South Wales, SE Australia
127 P8 **Tatishchevo** Saratovskaya Oblast', W Russian Federation
39 S12 **Tatitlek** Alaska, USA
10 L15 **Tatla Lake** British Columbia, SW Canada
121 Q2 **Tatlısu** *Gk.* Akanthoú. N Cyprus
11 Z10 **Tatnam, Cape** *headland* Manitoba, C Canada
Tatra/Tátra *see* Tatra Mountains
111 K18 **Tatra Mountains** *Ger.* Tatra, *Hung.* Tátra, *Pol./Slvk.* Tatry. ▲ Poland/Slovakia
Tatry *see* Tatra Mountains
164 I13 **Tatsuno** *var.* Tatuno. Hyōgo, Honshū, SW Japan
145 S16 **Tatti** *var.* Tatty. Zhambyl, S Kazakhstan
Tatty *see* Tatti
60 L10 **Tatuí** São Paulo, S Brazil
37 V14 **Tatum** New Mexico, SW USA
25 X7 **Tatum** Texas, SW USA
Ta-t'ung/Tatung *see* Datong
Tatuno *see* Tatsuno
137 R14 **Tatvan** Bitlis, SE Turkey
95 C16 **Tau** Rogaland, S Norway
192 L17 **Ta'ū** *var.* Tau. *island* Manua Islands, E American Samoa
193 W15 **Tau** *island* Tongatapu Group, N Tonga
59 O14 **Tauá** Ceará, E Brazil
60 N10 **Taubaté** São Paulo, S Brazil
101 I19 **Tauber** ≈ SW Germany
101 I19 **Tauberbiscofsheim** Baden-Württemberg, C Germany
144 E14 **Tauchik** *Kaz.* Taūshyq. Mangistau, SW Kazakhstan
191 W10 **Tauere** *atoll* Îles Tuamotu, C French Polynesia
101 H17 **Taufstein** ▲ C Germany
190 I17 **Taukoka** *island* SE Cook Islands
145 T15 **Taukum, Peski** *desert* SE Kazakhstan
184 L10 **Taumarunui** Manawatu-Wanganui, North Island, NZ
59 A15 **Taumaturgo** Acre, W Brazil
27 X6 **Taum Sauk Mountain** ▲ Missouri, C USA
83 H22 **Taung** North-West, N South Africa
166 L6 **Taungdwingyi** Magwe, C Myanmar
166 M6 **Taunggyi** Shan State, C Myanmar
166 L5 **Taungtha** Mandalay, C Myanmar
166 K7 **Taungup** Arakan State, W Myanmar
149 S9 **Taunsa** Punjab, E Pakistan
97 K23 **Taunton** SW England, UK
19 O12 **Taunton** Massachusetts, NE USA
101 F18 **Taunus** ▲ W Germany
101 G18 **Taunusstein** Hessen, W Germany
184 N9 **Taupo** Waikato, North Island, NZ
184 M9 **Taupo, Lake** ◎ North Island, NZ
109 R8 **Taurach** *var.* Taurachbach. ≈ E Austria
Taurachbach *see* Taurach
118 D12 **Tauragė** *Ger.* Tauroggen. Tauragė, SW Lithuania
118 D13 **Tauragė** ◈ *province* SW Lithuania
54 G10 **Tauramena** Casanare, C Colombia
184 N7 **Tauranga** Bay of Plenty, North Island, NZ
15 O10 **Taureau, Réservoir** ⊠ Québec, SE Canada
107 N22 **Taurianova** Calabria, SW Italy
Tauris *see* Tabrīz
184 I2 **Tauroa Point** *headland* North Island, NZ
Tauroggen *see* Tauragė
Tauromenium *see* Taormina
Taurus Mountains *see* Toros Dağları
Taus *see* Domažlice
Taūshyq *see* Tauchik
105 R5 **Tauste** Aragón, NE Spain
191 V16 **Tautara, Motu** *island* Easter Island, Chile, E Pacific Ocean
191 R8 **Tautira** Tahiti, W French Polynesia
Tauz *see* Tovuz
Ţavālesh, Kūhhā-ye *see* Talish Mountains
136 D15 **Tavas** Denizli, SW Turkey
Tavastehus *see* Hämeenlinna
Tavau *see* Davos
122 G10 **Tavda** Sverdlovskaya Oblast', C Russian Federation
122 G10 **Tavda** ≈ C Russian Federation
105 T11 **Tavernes de la Valldigna** País Valenciano, E Spain
81 J20 **Taveta** Coast, S Kenya
187 Y14 **Taveuni** *island* N Fiji
147 R13 **Tavildara** *Rus.* Tavil'dara, Tovil'-Dora. C Tajikistan
162 L8 **Tavin** Dundgovĭ, C Mongolia
104 H14 **Tavira** Faro, S Portugal
97 I24 **Tavistock** SW England, UK
167 N10 **Tavoy** *var.* Dawei. Tenasserim, S Myanmar
Tavoy Island *see* Mali Kyun
115 E16 **Tavropoú, Techníti Límni** ⊠ C Greece
136 E13 **Tavşanlı** Kütahya, NW Turkey
187 X14 **Tavua** Viti Levu, W Fiji
97 J23 **Taw** ≈ SW England, UK
185 L14 **Tawa** Wellington, North Island, NZ
25 V6 **Tawakoni, Lake** ⊠ Texas, SW USA
153 V11 **Tawang** Arunāchal Pradesh, NE India
169 R17 **Tawang, Teluk** *bay* Jawa, S Indonesia
31 R7 **Tawas Bay** ◎ Michigan, N USA
31 R7 **Tawas City** Michigan, N USA
169 V8 **Tawau** Sabah, East Malaysia
141 U10 **Ţawīl, Qalamat aţ** *well* SE Saudi Arabia
171 N9 **Tawitawi** *island* SW Philippines
Ţawkar *see* Tokar
Tāwūq *see* Dāqūq
Tawzar *see* Tozeur
41 O15 **Taxco** *var.* Taxco de Alarcón. Guerrero, S Mexico
Taxco de Alarcón *see* Taxco
146 H8 **Taxiatosh** *Rus.* Takhiatash. Qoraqalpog'iston Respublikasi, W Uzbekistan
158 D9 **Taxkorgan** *var.* Taxkorgan Tajik Zizhixian. Xinjiang Uygur Zizhiqu, NW China
Taxkorgan Tajik *see* Taxkorgan
146 H7 **Taxtako'pir** *Rus.* Takhtakupyr. Qoraqalpog'iston Respublikasi, NW Uzbekistan
96 J10 **Tay** ≈ C Scotland, UK
143 V6 **Tāybād** *var.* Taibad, Tāyybād, Tayyebāt. Khorāsān, NE Iran
Taybert at Turkz *see* Ţayyibat at Turkī
124 J3 **Taybola** Murmanskaya Oblast', NW Russian Federation
81 M16 **Tayeeglow** Bakool, C Somalia
96 K11 **Tay, Firth of** *inlet* E Scotland, UK
122 J12 **Tayga** Kemerovskaya Oblast', S Russian Federation
162 G8 **Taygan** Govĭ-Altay, C Mongolia
123 T9 **Taygonos, Mys** *headland* E Russian Federation
96 I11 **Tay, Loch** ◎ C Scotland, UK
11 N12 **Taylor** British Columbia, W Canada
29 O14 **Taylor** Nebraska, C USA
18 I13 **Taylor** Pennsylvania, NE USA
25 T10 **Taylor** Texas, SW USA
37 Q11 **Taylor, Mount** ▲ New Mexico, SW USA
37 R5 **Taylor Park Reservoir** ⊠ Colorado, C USA
37 R6 **Taylor River** ≈ Colorado, C USA
21 P11 **Taylors** South Carolina, SE USA
20 L5 **Taylorsville** Kentucky, S USA
21 R6 **Taylorsville** North Carolina, SE USA
30 L14 **Taylorville** Illinois, N USA
140 K5 **Taymā'** Tabūk, NW Saudi Arabia
122 M10 **Taymura** ≈ C Russian Federation
123 O7 **Taymylyr** Respublika Sakha (Yakutiya), NE Russian Federation
122 L7 **Taymyr, Ozero** ◎ N Russian Federation
122 M6 **Taymyr, Poluostrov** *peninsula* N Russian Federation
122 L8 **Taymyrskiy (Dolgano-Nenetskiy) Avtonomnyy Okrug** *var.* Taymyrskiy Avtonomnyy Okrug. ◈ *autonomous district* N Russian Federation
167 S13 **Tây Ninh** Tây Ninh, S Vietnam
122 L12 **Tayshet** Irkutskaya Oblast', S Russian Federation
171 N5 **Taytay** Palawan, W Philippines
169 Q16 **Tayu** *prev.* Tajoe. Jawa, C Indonesia
Tāyybād/Tayyebāt *see* Tāybād
138 L5 **Ţayyibah** *var.* At Taybé. Ḥimş, C Syria
138 I4 **Ţayyibat at Turkī** *var.* Taybert at Turkz. Ḥamāh, W Syria
145 P7 **Tayynsha** *prev.* Krasnoarmeysk. Severnyy Kazakhstan, N Kazakhstan
122 J10 **Taz** ≈ N Russian Federation
74 G6 **Taza** NE Morocco
139 T4 **Tāza Khurmātū** E Iraq
165 Q8 **Tazawa-ko** ◎ Honshū, C Japan
Taz, Bay of *see* Tazovskaya Guba
21 N8 **Tazewell** Tennessee, S USA
21 Q7 **Tazewell** Virginia, NE USA
75 S11 **Tāzirbū** SE Libya
39 S11 **Tazlina Lake** ◎ Alaska, USA
122 J8 **Tazovskiy** Yamalo-Nenetskiy Avtonomnyy Okrug, N Russian Federation
137 U10 **T'bilisi** *Eng.* Tiflis. ● (Georgia) SE Georgia
137 T10 **T'bilisi** ✕ S Georgia
79 E14 **Tchabal Mbabo** ▲ NW Cameroon
Tchad *see* Chad
Tchad, Lac *see* Chad, Lake
77 S15 **Tchaourou** E Benin
79 E20 **Tchibanga** Nyanga, S Gabon
Tchien *see* Zwedru
77 Z6 **Tchigaï, Plateau du** ▲ NE Niger
77 V9 **Tchighozérine** Agadez, C Niger
77 T10 **Tchin-Tabaradene** Tahoua, W Niger
78 G13 **Tcholliré** Nord, NE Cameroon
Tchongking *see* Chongqing
22 K4 **Tchula** Mississippi, S USA
110 I7 **Tczew** *Ger.* Dirschau. Pomorskie, N Poland
116 I10 **Teaca** *Ger.* Tekendorf, *Hung.* Teke; *prev. Ger.* Tekendorf. Bistriţa-Năsăud, N Romania
40 J11 **Teacapán** Sinaloa, C Mexico
190 A10 **Teafuafou** *island* Funafuti Atoll, C Tuvalu
25 U8 **Teague** Texas, SW USA
191 R9 **Teahupoo** Tahiti, W French Polynesia
190 H15 **Te Aiti Point** *headland* Rarotonga, S Cook Islands
65 D24 **Teal Inlet** East Falkland, Falkland Islands
185 B22 **Te Anau** Southland, South Island, NZ
185 B22 **Te Anau, Lake** ◎ South Island, NZ
41 U15 **Teapa** Tabasco, SE Mexico
184 Q7 **Te Araroa** Gisborne, North Island, NZ
184 M7 **Te Aroha** Waikato, North Island, NZ
Teate *see* Chieti
190 A9 **Te Ava Fuagea** *channel* Funafuti Atoll, SE Tuvalu
190 B8 **Te Ava I Te Lape** *channel* Funafuti Atoll, SE Tuvalu
190 B9 **Te Ava Pua Pua** *channel* Funafuti Atoll, SE Tuvalu
184 M8 **Te Awamutu** Waikato, North Island, NZ
171 X12 **Teba** Papua, E Indonesia
104 L15 **Teba** Andalucía, S Spain
126 M15 **Teberda** Karachayevo-Cherkesskaya Respublika, SW Russian Federation
74 M6 **Tébessa** NE Algeria
62 O7 **Tebicuary, Río** ≈ S Paraguay
168 L13 **Tebingtinggi** Sumatera, W Indonesia
168 I8 **Tebingtinggi** Sumatera, N Indonesia
Tebingtinggi, Pulau *see* Rantau, Pulau
Tebriz *see* Tabrīz
137 U9 **Tebulos Mt'a** *Rus.* Gora Tebulosmta. ▲ Georgia/Russian Federation
Tebulosmta, Gora *see* Tebulos Mt'a
41 Q14 **Tecamachalco** Puebla, S Mexico
40 B1 **Tecate** Baja California, NW Mexico
136 M13 **Tecer Dağları** ▲ C Turkey
103 O17 **Tech** ≈ S France
77 P16 **Techiman** W Ghana
117 N15 **Techirghiol** Constanţa, SE Romania
74 A12 **Techla** *var.* Techlé. SW Western Sahara
Techlé *see* Techla
63 H18 **Tecka, Sierra de** ▲ SW Argentina
Teckendorf *see* Teaca
40 K13 **Tecolotlán** Jalisco, SW Mexico
40 K14 **Tecomán** Colima, SW Mexico
35 V12 **Tecopa** California, W USA
40 G5 **Tecoripa** Sonora, NW Mexico
41 N16 **Tecpan** *var.* Tecpan de Galeana. Guerrero, S Mexico
Tecpan de Galeana *see* Tecpan
40 J11 **Tecuala** Nayarit, C Mexico
116 L12 **Tecuci** Galaţi, E Romania
31 R10 **Tecumseh** Michigan, N USA
29 S16 **Tecumseh** Nebraska, C USA
27 O11 **Tecumseh** Oklahoma, C USA
Tedzhen *see* Harīrūd/Tejen
146 H15 **Tedzhenstroy** *Turkm.* Tejenstroy. Ahal Welaýaty, S Turkmenistan
162 I7 **Teel** Arhangay, C Mongolia
97 L15 **Tees** ≈ N England, UK
14 E15 **Teeswater** Ontario, S Canada
190 A10 **Tefala** *island* Funafuti Atoll, C Tuvalu
58 D13 **Tefé** Amazonas, N Brazil
74 K11 **Tefedest** ▲ S Algeria
136 E16 **Tefenni** Burdur, SW Turkey
58 D13 **Tefé, Rio** ≈ NW Brazil
169 P16 **Tegal** Jawa, C Indonesia
100 O12 **Tegel** ✕ (Berlin) Berlin, NE Germany
99 M15 **Tegelen** Limburg, SE Netherlands
101 L24 **Tegernsee** ◎ SE Germany
107 M18 **Teggiano** Campania, S Italy
77 U14 **Tegina** Niger, C Nigeria
42 I7 **Tegucigalpa** ● (Honduras) Francisco Morazán, SW Honduras
42 H7 **Tegucigalpa** ✕ Central District, C Honduras
Tegucigalpa *see* Central District, Honduras
Tegucigalpa *see* Francisco Morazán, Honduras
77 U9 **Teguidda-n-Tessoumt** Agadez, C Niger
64 Q11 **Teguise** Lanzarote, Islas Canarias, Spain, NE Atlantic Ocean
122 K12 **Tegul'det** Tomskaya Oblast', C Russian Federation
35 S13 **Tehachapi** California, W USA
35 S13 **Tehachapi Mountains** ▲ California, W USA
Tehama *see* Tihāmah
Teheran *see* Tehrān
77 O14 **Téhini** NE Ivory Coast
143 N5 **Tehrān** *var.* Teheran. ● (Iran) Tehrān, N Iran
143 N6 **Tehrān** *off.* Ostān-e Tehrān, *var.* Tehran. ◈ *province* N Iran
152 K9 **Tehri** Uttaranchal, N India
Tehri *see* Tikamgarh
41 Q15 **Tehuacán** Puebla, S Mexico
41 S17 **Tehuantepec** *var.* Santo Domingo Tehuantepec. Oaxaca, SE Mexico
41 S17 **Tehuantepec, Golfo de** *var.* Gulf of Tehuantepec. *gulf* S Mexico
Tehuantepec, Gulf of *see* Tehuantepec, Golfo de
Tehuantepec, Isthmus of *see* Tehuantepec, Istmo de
41 T16 **Tehuantepec, Istmo de** *var.* Isthmus of Tehuantepec. *isthmus* SE Mexico
(0) I16 **Tehuantepec Ridge** *undersea feature* E Pacific Ocean
41 S16 **Tehuantepec, Río** ≈ SE Mexico
191 W10 **Tehuata** *atoll* Îles Tuamotu, C French Polynesia
64 O11 **Teide, Pico de** ▲ Gran Canaria, Islas Canarias, Spain, NE Atlantic Ocean
97 I21 **Teifi** ≈ SW Wales, UK
80 B9 **Teiga Plateau** *plateau* W Sudan
97 J24 **Teignmouth** SW England, UK
Teisen *see* Chech'ŏn
116 H1 **Teiuş** *Ger.* Dreikirchen, *Hung.* Tövis. Alba, C Romania
169 U17 **Tejakula** Bali, C Indonesia
146 H14 **Tejen** *Rus.* Tedzhen. Ahal Welaýaty, S Turkmenistan
146 I15 **Tejen** *Per.* Harīrūd, *Rus.* Tedzhen. ≈ Afghanistan/Iran *see also* Harīrūd
Tejenstroy *see* Tedzhenstroy
35 S14 **Tejon Pass** *pass* California, W USA
Tejo, Rio *see* Tagus
41 O14 **Tejupilco** *var.* Tejupilco de Hidalgo. México, S Mexico
Tejupilco de Hidalgo *see* Tejupilco
184 P7 **Te Kaha** Bay of Plenty, North Island, NZ
29 S14 **Tekamah** Nebraska, C USA
184 I1 **Te Kao** Northland, North Island, NZ
185 F20 **Tekapo** ≈ South Island, NZ
185 F19 **Tekapo, Lake** ◎ South Island, NZ
184 P9 **Te Karaka** Gisborne, North Island, NZ
184 L7 **Te Kauwhata** Waikato, North Island, NZ
41 X12 **Tekax** *var.* Tekax de Álvaro Obregón. Yucatán, SE Mexico
Tekax de Álvaro Obregón *see* Tekax
Teke/Tekendorf *see* Teaca
136 A14 **Teke Burnu** *headland* W Turkey
114 M12 **Teke Deresi** ≈ NW Turkey
146 D10 **Tekedzhik, Gory** *hill range* NW Turkmenistan
145 V14 **Tekeli** Almaty, SE Kazakhstan
145 R7 **Teke, Ozero** ◎ N Kazakhstan
158 I5 **Tekes** Xinjiang Uygur Zizhiqu, NW China
145 W16 **Tekes** Almaty, SE Kazakhstan
Tekes *see* Tekes He
158 H5 **Tekes He** *Rus.* Tekes. ≈ China/Kazakhstan
80 I10 **Tekezē** *var.* Takkaze. ≈ Eritrea/Ethiopia
Tekhtin *see* Tsyakhtsin
136 C10 **Tekirdağ** *It.* Rodosto; *anc.* Bisanthe, Raidestos, Rhaedestus. Tekirdağ, NW Turkey
136 C10 **Tekirdağ** ◈ *province* NW Turkey
155 N14 **Tekkali** Andhra Pradesh, E India
115 K15 **Tekke Burnu** *Turk.* İlyasbaba Burnu. *headland* NW Turkey
137 Q13 **Tekman** Erzurum, NE Turkey
32 M9 **Tekoa** Washington, NW USA
190 H16 **Te Kou** ▲ Rarotonga, S Cook Islands
Tekrit *see* Tikrīt
171 P12 **Teku** Sulawesi, N Indonesia
184 L9 **Te Kuiti** Waikato, North Island, NZ
42 H4 **Tela** Atlántida, NW Honduras
138 F12 **Telalim** Southern, S Israel
Telanaipura *see* Jambi
137 U10 **T'elavi** E Georgia
138 F10 **Tel Aviv** ◈ *district* W Israel
Tel Aviv-Jaffa *see* Tel Aviv-Yafo
138 F10 **Tel Aviv-Yafo** *var.* Tel Aviv-Jaffa. Tel Aviv, C Israel
138 F10 **Tel Aviv-Yafo** ✕ Tel Aviv, C Israel
111 E18 **Telč** *Ger.* Teltsch. Vysočina, C Czech Republic
186 B6 **Telefomin** Sandaun, NW PNG
10 J10 **Telegraph Creek** British Columbia, W Canada
190 B10 **Telele** *island* Funafuti Atoll, C Tuvalu
60 J11 **Telêmaco Borba** Paraná, S Brazil
95 E15 **Telemark** ◈ *county* S Norway
62 J13 **Telén** La Pampa, C Argentina
Teleneshty *see* Teleneşti
116 M9 **Teleneşti** *Rus.* Teleneshty. C Moldova
104 J4 **Teleno, El** ▲ NW Spain
116 I15 **Teleorman** ◈ *county* S Romania
116 I14 **Teleorman** ≈ S Romania
25 V5 **Telephone** Texas, SW USA
35 U11 **Telescope Peak** ▲ California, W USA
Teles Pirés *see* São Manuel, Rio
97 L19 **Telford** C England, UK
108 L7 **Telfs** Tirol, W Austria
42 I9 **Telica** León, NW Nicaragua
42 J6 **Telica, Río** ≈ C Honduras
76 I13 **Télimélé** Guinée-Maritime, W Guinea
43 O14 **Telire, Río** ≈ Costa Rica/Panama
114 I8 **Telish** *prev.* Azizie. Pleven, N Bulgaria
41 R16 **Telixtlahuaca** *var.* San Francisco Telixtlahuaca. Oaxaca, SE Mexico
10 K13 **Telkwa** British Columbia, SW Canada
25 P4 **Tell** Texas, SW USA
Tell Abiad *see* Tall Abyaḍ
Tell Abiad/Tell Abyad *see* At Tall al Abyaḍ
31 O16 **Tell City** Indiana, N USA
38 M9 **Teller** Alaska, USA
Tell Huqnah *see* Tall Ḥuqnah
155 F20 **Tellicherry** *var.* Thalassery. Kerala, SW India
20 M10 **Tellico Plains** Tennessee, S USA
Tell Kalakh *see* Tall Kalakh
Tell Mardīkh *see* Ebla
54 E11 **Tello** Huila, C Colombia
Tell Shedadi *see* Ash Shadādah
37 Q7 **Telluride** Colorado, C USA
Tel'man/Tel'mansk *see* Gubadag
117 X9 **Tel'manove** Donets'ka Oblast', E Ukraine
162 H6 **Telmen Nuur** ◎ NW Mongolia
Teloekbetoeng *see* Bandarlampung
41 O15 **Teloloapan** Guerrero, S Mexico
Telo Martius *see* Toulon
127 V8 **Telposiz, Gora** ▲ NW Russian Federation
Telschen *see* Telšiai
63 J17 **Telsen** Chubut, S Argentina
118 D11 **Telšiai** *Ger.* Telschen. Telšiai, NW Lithuania
118 D11 **Telšiai** ◈ *province* NW Lithuania
Teltsch *see* Telč
Telukbetung *see* Bandarlampung
168 H10 **Telukdalam** Pulau Nias, W Indonesia
14 H9 **Temagami** Ontario, S Canada
14 G9 **Temagami, Lake** ◎ Ontario, S Canada

◆ Country ● Country Capital ◇ Dependent Territory ○ Dependent Territory Capital ◈ Administrative Region ✕ International Airport ▲ Mountain ▲ Mountain Range ⩕ Volcano ≈ River ◎ Lake ⊠ Reservoir

190 H16 **Te Manga** ▲ Rarotonga, S Cook Islands
191 W12 **Tematangi** *atoll* Îles Tuamotu, S French Polynesia
41 X11 **Temax** Yucatán, SE Mexico
171 E14 **Tembagapura** Papua, E Indonesia
131 U5 **Tembenchi** ≈ N Russian Federation
55 P6 **Temblador** Monagas, NE Venezuela
105 N9 **Tembleque** Castilla-La Mancha, C Spain
Temboni *see* Mitemele, Río
35 U16 **Temecula** California, W USA
168 K7 **Temengor, Tasik** ◎ Peninsular Malaysia
112 L9 **Temerin** Serbia, N Serbia and Montenegro (Yugo.)
Temes/Temesch *see* Tamiš
Temeschburg/Temeschwar *see* Timişoara
Temes-Kubin *see* Kovin
Temesvár/Temeswar *see* Timişoara
Teminaboean *see* Teminabuan
171 U12 **Teminabuan** *prev.* Teminaboean. Papua, E Indonesia
145 P17 **Temirlanovka** Yuzhnyy Kazakhstan, S Kazakhstan
145 R10 **Temirtau** *prev.* Samarkandski, Samarkandskoye. Karaganda, C Kazakhstan
14 H10 **Témiscaming** Québec, SE Canada
Témiscamingue, Lac *see* Timiskaming, Lake
15 T8 **Témiscouata, Lac** ◎ Québec, SE Canada
127 N5 **Temnikov** Respublika Mordoviya, W Russian Federation
191 Y13 **Temoe** *island* Îles Gambier, E French Polynesia
183 Q9 **Temora** New South Wales, SE Australia
40 H7 **Témoris** Chihuahua, W Mexico
40 I5 **Temósachic** Chihuahua, N Mexico
187 Q10 **Temotu** *off.* Temotu Province. ◆ *province* E Solomon Islands
36 L14 **Tempe** Arizona, SW USA
Tempelburg *see* Czaplinek
107 C17 **Tempio Pausania** Sardegna, Italy, C Mediterranean Sea
42 K12 **Tempisque, Río** ≈ NW Costa Rica
25 T9 **Temple** Texas, SW USA
100 O12 **Templehof** ✕ (Berlin) Berlin, NE Germany
97 D19 **Templemore** *Ir.* An Teampall Mór. C Ireland
100 O11 **Templin** Brandenburg, NE Germany
41 P12 **Tempoal** *var.* Tempoal de Sánchez. Veracruz-Llave, E Mexico
Tempoal de Sánchez *see* Tempoal
41 P13 **Tempoal, Río** ≈ C Mexico
83 E14 **Tempué** Moxico, C Angola
126 J14 **Temryuk** Krasnodarskiy Kray, SW Russian Federation
99 G17 **Temse** Oost-Vlaanderen, N Belgium
63 F15 **Temuco** Araucanía, C Chile
185 G20 **Temuka** Canterbury, South Island, NZ
189 P13 **Temwen Island** *island* E Micronesia
56 C6 **Tena** Napo, C Ecuador
41 W13 **Tenabo** Campeche, E Mexico
Tenaghau *see* Aola
25 X7 **Tenaha** Texas, SW USA
39 X13 **Tenake** Chichagof Island, Alaska, USA
155 K16 **Tenāli** Andhra Pradesh, E India
Tenan *see* Ch'ŏnan
41 O14 **Tenancingo** *var.* Tenencingo de Degollado. México, S Mexico
191 X12 **Tenararo** *island* Groupe Actéon, SE French Polynesia
167 N12 **Tenasserim** Tenasserim, S Myanmar
167 N11 **Tenasserim** *var.* Tanintharyi. ◆ *division* S Myanmar
98 O5 **Ten Boer** Groningen, NE Netherlands
97 I21 **Tenby** SW Wales, UK
80 K11 **Tendaho** Afar, NE Ethiopia
103 V14 **Tende** Alpes Maritimes, SE France
151 Q20 **Ten Degree Channel** *strait* Andaman and Nicobar Islands, India, E Indian Ocean
80 F11 **Tendelti** White Nile, E Sudan
76 G8 **Te-n-Dghâmcha, Sebkhet** *var.* Sebkha de Ndrhamcha, Sebkra de Ndaghamcha. *salt lake* W Mauritania
165 P10 **Tendō** Yamagata, Honshū, C Japan
74 H7 **Tendrara** NE Morocco
117 Q11 **Tendrivs'ka Kosa** *spit* S Ukraine
117 Q11 **Tendrivs'ka Zatoka** *gulf* S Ukraine
Tenencingo de Degollado *see* Tenancingo
77 N11 **Ténenkou** Mopti, C Mali
77 W9 **Ténéré** *physical region* C Niger
77 W9 **Ténére, Erg du** *desert* C Niger
64 O11 **Tenerife** *island* Islas Canarias, Spain, NE Atlantic Ocean
74 J5 **Ténès** NW Algeria
170 M15 **Tengah, Kepulauan** *island group* C Indonesia
169 V11 **Tenggarong** Borneo, C Indonesia
162 J15 **Tengger Shamo** *desert* N China
168 L8 **Tenggul, Pulau** *island* Peninsular Malaysia
Tengiz Köl *see* Tengiz, Ozero
145 P9 **Tengiz, Ozero** *Kaz.* Tengiz Köl. *salt lake* C Kazakhstan
76 M14 **Tengréla** *var.* Tingréla. N Ivory Coast
160 M14 **Tengxian** *var.* Teng Xian. Guangxi Zhuangzu Zizhiqu, S China
194 H2 **Teniente Rodolfo Marsh** *Chilean research station* South Shetland Islands, Antarctica
32 G9 **Tenino** Washington, NW USA
112 I9 **Tenja** Osijek-Baranja, E Croatia
188 B16 **Tenjo, Mount** ▲ W Guam
155 H23 **Tenkāsi** Tamil Nādu, SE India
79 N24 **Tenke** Katanga, SE Dem. Rep. Congo
Tenke *see* Tinca
123 Q7 **Tenkeli** Respublika Sakha (Yakutiya), NE Russian Federation
27 R10 **Tenkiller Ferry Lake** ▣ Oklahoma, C USA
77 Q13 **Tenkodogo** S Burkina
181 Q5 **Tennant Creek** Northern Territory, C Australia
20 G9 **Tennessee** *off.* State of Tennessee; also known as The Volunteer State. ◆ *state* SE USA
37 R5 **Tennessee Pass** *pass* Colorado, C USA
20 H10 **Tennessee River** ≈ S USA
23 N2 **Tennessee Tombigbee Waterway** *canal* Alabama/Mississippi, S USA
99 K22 **Tenneville** Luxembourg, SE Belgium
92 M11 **Tenniöjoki** ≈ NE Finland
92 L9 **Tenojoki** *Lapp.* Deatnu, *Nor.* Tana. ≈ Finland/Norway *see also* Deatnu
169 U7 **Tenom** Sabah, East Malaysia
Tenos *see* Tínos
41 V15 **Tenosique** *var.* Tenosique de Pino Suárez. Tabasco, SE Mexico
Tenosique de Pino Suárez *see* Tenosique
22 I6 **Tensas River** ≈ Louisiana, S USA
23 O8 **Tensaw River** ≈ Alabama, S USA
74 E7 **Tensift** *seasonal river* W Morocco
171 O12 **Tentena** *var.* Tenteno. Sulawesi, C Indonesia
Tenteno *see* Tentena
183 U4 **Tenterfield** New South Wales, SE Australia
23 X16 **Ten Thousand Islands** *island group* Florida, SE USA
60 H9 **Teodoro Sampaio** São Paulo, S Brazil
59 N19 **Teófilo Otoni** *var.* Theophilo Ottoni. Minas Gerais, NE Brazil
116 K5 **Teofipol'** Khmel'nyts'ka Oblast', W Ukraine
191 Q8 **Teohatu** Tahiti, W French Polynesia
41 P14 **Teotihuacán** *ruins* México, S Mexico
Teotilán *see* Teotitlán del Camino
41 Q15 **Teotitlán del Camino** *var.* Teotilán. Oaxaca, S Mexico
190 G12 **Tepa** Île Uvea, E Wallis and Futuna
191 P8 **Tepaee, Récif** *reef* Tahiti, W French Polynesia
40 L14 **Tepalcatepec** Michoacán de Ocampo, SW Mexico
190 A16 **Tepa Point** *headland* SW Niue
40 L13 **Tepatitlán** *var.* Tepatitlán de Morelos. Jalisco, SW Mexico
Tepatitlán de Morelos *see* Tepatitlán
40 J9 **Tepehuanes** *var.* Santa Catarina de Tepehuanes. Durango, C Mexico
Tepelena *see* Tepelenë
113 L22 **Tepelenë** *var.* Tepelena, *It.* Tepeleni. Gjirokastër, S Albania
Tepeleni *see* Tepelenë
40 K12 **Tepic** Nayarit, C Mexico
111 C15 **Teplice** *Ger.* Teplitz; *prev.* Teplice-Šanov, Teplitz-Schönau. Ústecký Kraj, NW Czech Republic
Teplice-Šanov/Teplitz/Teplitz-Schönau *see* Teplice
117 O7 **Teplyk** Vinnyts'ka Oblast', C Ukraine
123 R10 **Teplyy Klyuch** Respublika Sakha (Yakutiya), NE Russian Federation
40 E5 **Tepoca, Cabo** *headland* NW Mexico
191 W9 **Tepoto** *island* Îles du Désappointement, C French Polynesia
92 L11 **Tepsa** Lappi, N Finland
190 B8 **Tepuka** *atoll* Funafuti Atoll, C Tuvalu
184 N7 **Te Puke** Bay of Plenty, North Island, NZ
40 L13 **Tequila** Jalisco, SW Mexico
41 O13 **Tequisquiapan** Querétaro de Arteaga, C Mexico
104 J5 **Tera** ≈ NW Spain
77 Q12 **Téra** Tillabéri, W Niger
191 V1 **Teraina** *prev.* Washington Island. *atoll* Line Islands, E Kiribati
81 F15 **Terakeka** Bahr el Gabel, S Sudan
107 J14 **Teramo** *anc.* Interamna. Abruzzo, C Italy
98 P7 **Ter Apel** Groningen, NE Netherlands
104 H11 **Tera, Ribeira de** ≈ S Portugal
185 K14 **Terawhiti, Cape** *headland* North Island, NZ
98 N12 **Terborg** Gelderland, E Netherlands
137 P13 **Tercan** Erzincan, NE Turkey
64 O2 **Terceira** ✕ Terceira, Azores, Portugal, NE Atlantic Ocean
64 O2 **Terceira** *var.* Ilha Terceira. *island* Azores, Portugal, NE Atlantic Ocean
Terceira, Ilha *see* Terceira
116 K6 **Terebovlya** Ternopil's'ka Oblast', W Ukraine
127 O15 **Terek** ≈ SW Russian Federation
Terekhovka *see* Tsyerakhowka
147 R9 **Terek-Say** Dzhalal-Abadskaya Oblast', W Kyrgyzstan
145 Z10 **Terekty** *prev.* Alekseevka, Alekseyevka. Vostochnyy Kazakhstan, E Kazakhstan
168 L7 **Terengganu** *var.* Trengganu. ◆ *state* Peninsular Malaysia
127 X7 **Terensay** Orenburgskaya Oblast', W Russian Federation
58 N13 **Teresina** *var.* Therezina. *state capital* Piauí, NE Brazil
60 P9 **Teresópolis** Rio de Janeiro, SE Brazil
110 P12 **Terespol** Lubelskie, E Poland
191 V16 **Terevaka, Maunga** ⛰ Easter Island, Chile, E Pacific Ocean
103 P3 **Tergnier** Aisne, N France
43 O14 **Teribe, Río** ≈ NW Panama
124 K3 **Teriberka** Murmanskaya Oblast', NW Russian Federation
Terijoki *see* Zelenogorsk
Terinkot *see* Tarīn Kowt
145 O10 **Terisakkan** *Kaz.* Terisaqqan. ≈ C Kazakhstan
Terisaqqan *see* Terisakkan
24 K12 **Terlingua** Texas, SW USA
24 K11 **Terlingua Creek** ≈ Texas, SW USA
62 K7 **Termas de Río Hondo** Santiago del Estero, N Argentina
136 M11 **Terme** Samsun, N Turkey
Termez *see* Termiz
Termia *see* Kýthnos
107 J23 **Termini Imerese** *anc.* Thermae Himerenses. Sicilia, Italy, C Mediterranean Sea
41 V14 **Términos, Laguna de** *lagoon* SE Mexico
77 X10 **Termit-Kaoboul** Zinder, C Niger
147 O14 **Termiz** *Rus.* Termez. Surxondaryo Viloyati, S Uzbekistan
107 L15 **Termoli** Molise, C Italy
Termonde *see* Dendermonde
98 P5 **Termunten** Groningen, NE Netherlands
171 R11 **Ternate** Pulau Ternate, E Indonesia
109 T5 **Ternberg** Oberösterreich, N Austria
99 E15 **Terneuzen** *var.* Neuzen. Zeeland, SW Netherlands
123 T14 **Terney** Primorskiy Kray, SE Russian Federation
107 I14 **Terni** *anc.* Interamna Nahars. Umbria, C Italy
109 X6 **Ternitz** Niederösterreich, E Austria
117 V7 **Ternivka** Dnipropetrovs'ka Oblast', E Ukraine
116 K6 **Ternopil'** *Pol.* Tarnopol, *Rus.* Ternopol'. Ternopil's'ka Oblast', W Ukraine
Ternopil' *see* Ternopil's'ka Oblast'
116 I6 **Ternopil's'ka Oblast'** *var.* Ternopil', *Rus.* Ternopol'skaya Oblast'. ◆ *province* NW Ukraine
Ternopol' *see* Ternopil'
Ternopol'skaya Oblast' *see* Ternopil's'ka Oblast'
123 U13 **Terpeniya, Mys** *headland* Ostrov Sakhalin, SE Russian Federation
Térraba, Río *see* Grande de Térraba, Río
10 J13 **Terrace** British Columbia, W Canada
12 D12 **Terrace Bay** Ontario, S Canada
107 I16 **Terracina** Lazio, C Italy
93 F14 **Terråk** Troms, N Norway
26 M13 **Terral** Oklahoma C USA
107 B19 **Terralba** Sardegna, Italy, C Mediterranean Sea
Terranova di Sicilia *see* Gela
Terranova Pausania *see* Olbia
105 W5 **Terrassa** *Cast.* Tarrasa. Cataluña, E Spain
15 O12 **Terrebonne** Québec, SE Canada
22 J11 **Terrebonne Bay** *bay* Louisiana, SE USA
31 N14 **Terre Haute** Indiana, N USA
25 U6 **Terrell** Texas, SW USA
Terre Neuve *see* Newfoundland and Labrador
33 Q14 **Terreton** Idaho, NW USA
103 T7 **Territoire-de-Belfort** ◆ *department* E France
33 X9 **Terry** Montana, NW USA
28 I9 **Terry Peak** ▲ South Dakota, N USA
136 H14 **Tersakan Gölü** ◎ C Turkey
98 J4 **Terschelling** *Fris.* Skylge. *island* Waddeneilanden, N Netherlands
78 H10 **Tersef** Chari-Baguirmi, C Chad
147 X8 **Terskey Ala-Too, Khrebet** ⛰ Kazakhstan/Kyrgyzstan
Terter *see* Tärtär
105 R8 **Teruel** *anc.* Turba. Aragón, E Spain
105 R7 **Teruel** ◆ *province* Aragón, E Spain
114 M7 **Tervel** *prev.* Kurtbunar, *Rom.* Curtbunar. Dobrich, NE Bulgaria
93 M16 **Tervo** Itä-Suomi, C Finland
92 L13 **Tervola** Lappi, NW Finland
Tervueren *see* Tervuren
99 H18 **Tervuren** *var.* Tervueren. Vlaams Brabant, C Belgium
112 H11 **Tešanj** Federacija Bosna I Hercegovina, N Bosnia and Herzegovina
Teschen *see* Cieszyn
83 M19 **Tesenane** Inhambane, S Mozambique
80 I9 **Teseney** *var.* Tessenei. W Eritrea
39 P5 **Teshekpuk Lake** ◎ Alaska, USA
162 K6 **Teshig** Bulgan, N Mongolia
165 T2 **Teshio** Hokkaidō, NE Japan
165 T2 **Teshio-sanchi** ⛰ Hokkaidō, NE Japan
Těšín *see* Cieszyn
Tesio Gawa *see* Teshio-gawa
Tesiyn Gol *see* Tes-Khem
131 T7 **Tes-Khem** *var.* Tesiyn Gol. ≈ Mongolia/Russian Federation
112 H11 **Teslić** Republika Srpska, N Bosnia and Herzegovina
10 I9 **Teslin** Yukon Territory, W Canada
10 I8 **Teslin** ≈ British Columbia/Yukon Territory, W Canada
77 Q8 **Tessalit** Kidal, NE Mali
77 V12 **Tessaoua** Maradi, S Niger
99 J17 **Tessenderlo** Limburg, NE Belgium
Tessenei *see* Teseney
14 L7 **Tessier, Lac** ◎ Québec, SE Canada
Tessin *see* Ticino
97 M23 **Test** ≈ S England, UK
Testama *see* Tõstamaa
55 P4 **Testigos, Islas los** *island group* N Venezuela
37 S10 **Tesuque** New Mexico, SW USA
103 O17 **Têt** *var.* Tet. ≈ S France
54 G5 **Tetas, Cerro de las** ▲ NW Venezuela
83 M15 **Tete** Tete, NW Mozambique
83 M15 **Tete** *off.* Província de Tete. ◆ *province* NW Mozambique
11 N15 **Tête Jaune Cache** British Columbia, SW Canada
184 O8 **Te Teko** Bay of Plenty, North Island, NZ
186 K9 **Tetepare** *island* New Georgia Islands, NW Solomon Islands
Teterev *see* Teteriv
116 M5 **Teteriv** *Rus.* Teterev. ≈ N Ukraine
100 M9 **Teterow** Mecklenburg-Vorpommern, NE Germany
114 I9 **Teteven** Lovech, N Bulgaria
191 T10 **Tetiaroa** *atoll* Îles du Vent, W French Polynesia
105 P14 **Tetica de Bacares** ▲ S Spain
Tetiyev *see* Tetiyiv
117 O6 **Tetiyiv** *Rus.* Tetiyev. Kyyivs'ka Oblast', N Ukraine
39 T10 **Tetlin** Alaska, USA
33 R8 **Teton River** ≈ Montana, NW USA
74 G5 **Tétouan** *var.* Tetouan, Tetuán. N Morocco
Tetova/Tetovë *see* Tetovo
114 L7 **Tetovo** Razgrad, N Bulgaria
113 N18 **Tetovo** *Alb.* Tetova, Tetovë, *Turk.* Kalkandelen. NW FYR Macedonia
115 E20 **Tetrázio** ⛰ S Greece
Tetschen *see* Děčín
Tetuán *see* Tétouan
191 Q8 **Tetufera, Mont** ▲ Tahiti, W French Polynesia
127 R4 **Tetyushi** Respublika Tatarstan, W Russian Federation
108 I7 **Teufen** Sankt Gallen, NE Switzerland
40 L12 **Teul** *var.* Teul de Gonzáles Ortega. Zacatecas, C Mexico
107 B21 **Teulada** Sardegna, Italy, C Mediterranean Sea
Teul de Gonzáles Ortega *see* Teul
11 X16 **Teulon** Manitoba, S Canada
42 I7 **Teupasenti** El Paraíso, S Honduras
165 S2 **Teuri-tō** *island* NE Japan
100 G13 **Teutoburger Wald** *Eng.* Teutoburg Forest. *hill range* NW Germany
Teutoburg Forest *see* Teutoburger Wald
93 K17 **Teuva** *Swe.* Östermark. Länsi-Suomi, W Finland
107 H15 **Tevere** *Eng.* Tiber. ≈ C Italy
138 G9 **Teverya** *var.* Tiberias, Tverya. Northern, N Israel
96 K13 **Teviot** ≈ SE Scotland, UK
Tevli *see* Tewli
122 H11 **Tevriz** Omskaya Oblast', C Russian Federation
185 B24 **Te Waewae Bay** *bay* South Island, NZ
97 L21 **Tewkesbury** C England, UK
119 F19 **Tewli** *Rus.* Tevli. Brestskaya Voblasts', SW Belarus
159 U12 **Têwo** *var.* Dêngkagoin. Gansu, C China
25 U12 **Texana, Lake** ◎ Texas, SW USA
27 S14 **Texarkana** Arkansas, C USA
25 X5 **Texarkana** Texas, SW USA
25 N9 **Texas** *off.* State of Texas; also known as The Lone Star State. ◆ *state* S USA
25 W12 **Texas City** Texas, SW USA
41 P14 **Texcoco** México, C Mexico
98 I6 **Texel** *island* Waddeneilanden, NW Netherlands
26 H8 **Texhoma** Oklahoma, C USA
25 N1 **Texhoma** Texas, SW USA
37 W12 **Texico** New Mexico, SW USA
24 L1 **Texline** Texas, SW USA
41 P14 **Texmelucan** *var.* San Martín Texmelucan. Puebla, S Mexico
27 O13 **Texoma, Lake** ▣ Oklahoma/Texas, C USA
25 N9 **Texon** Texas, SW USA
83 J23 **Teyateyaneng** NW Lesotho
124 M16 **Teykovo** Ivanovskaya Oblast', W Russian Federation
126 M16 **Teza** ≈ W Russian Federation
41 Q13 **Teziutlán** Puebla, S Mexico
153 V12 **Tezpur** Assam, NE India
9 N10 **Tha-Anne** ≈ Nunavut, NE Canada
83 K23 **Thabana Ntlenyana** *var.* Thabantshonyana, Mount Ntlenyana. ▲ E Lesotho
Thabantshonyana *see* Thabana Ntlenyana
83 J23 **Thaba Putsoa** ▲ C Lesotho
167 Q8 **Tha Bo** Nong Khai, E Thailand
103 T12 **Thabor, Pic du** ▲ E France
Tha Chin *see* Samut Sakhon
166 M7 **Thagaya** Pegu, C Myanmar
Thai, Ao *see* Thailand, Gulf of
167 T6 **Thai Binh** Thai Binh, N Vietnam
167 S7 **Thai Hoa** Nghê An, N Vietnam
167 P9 **Thailand** *off.* Kingdom of Thailand, *Th.* Prathet Thai; *prev.* Siam. ◆ *monarchy* SE Asia
167 P13 **Thailand, Gulf of** *var.* Gulf of Siam, *Th.* Ao Thai, *Vtn.* Vinh Thai Lan. *gulf* SE Asia
Thai Lan, Vinh *see* Thailand, Gulf of
167 T6 **Thai Nguyên** Bäc Thai, N Vietnam
167 S8 **Thakhèk** *prev.* Muang Khammouan. Khammouan, C Laos
153 S13 **Thakurgaon** Rajshahi, NW Bangladesh
149 S6 **Thal** North-West Frontier Province, NW Pakistan
166 M15 **Thalang** Phuket, SW Thailand
Thalassery *see* Tellicherry
167 Q10 **Thalat Khae** Nakhon Ratchasima, C Thailand
109 Q5 **Thalgau** Salzburg, NW Austria
108 G7 **Thalwil** Zürich, NW Switzerland
83 I20 **Thamaga** Kweneng, SE Botswana
Thamarid *see* Thamarīt
141 V13 **Thamarīt** *var.* Thamarid, Thumrayt. SW Oman
141 P16 **Thamar, Jabal** ▲ SW Yemen
184 M6 **Thames** Waikato, North Island, NZ
14 D17 **Thames** ≈ Ontario, S Canada
97 O22 **Thames** ≈ S England, UK
184 M6 **Thames, Firth of** *gulf* North Island, NZ
14 D17 **Thamesville** Ontario, S Canada
141 S13 **Thamūd** N Yemen
167 N9 **Thanbyuzayat** Mon State, S Myanmar
152 I9 **Thānesar** Haryāna, NW India
167 T7 **Thanh Hoa** Thanh Hoa, N Vietnam
Thanintari Taungdan *see* Bilauktaung Range
155 I21 **Thanjāvūr** *prev.* Tanjore. Tamil Nādu, SE India
Thanlwin *see* Salween
103 U7 **Thann** Haut-Rhin, NE France
167 O16 **Tha Nong Phrom** Phatthalung, SW Thailand
167 N13 **Thap Sakae** *var.* Thap Sakau. Prachuap Khiri Khan, SW Thailand
Thap Sakau *see* Thap Sakae
98 L10 **'t Harde** Gelderland, E Netherlands
152 D11 **Thar Desert** *var.* Great Indian Desert, Indian Desert. *desert* India/Pakistan
181 V10 **Thargomindah** Queensland, C Australia
150 D11 **Thar Pārkar** *desert* SE Pakistan
139 S7 **Tharthār al Furāt, Qanāt ath** *canal* C Iraq
139 R7 **Tharthār, Buḩayrat ath** ◎ C Iraq
139 R5 **Tharthār, Wādī ath** *dry watercourse* N Iraq
167 N13 **Tha Sae** Chumphon, SW Thailand
167 N15 **Tha Sala** Nakhon Si Thammarat, SW Thailand
114 I13 **Thásos** Thásos, E Greece
115 I14 **Thásos** *island* E Greece
37 N14 **Thatcher** Arizona, SW USA
167 T5 **Thât Khê** *var.* Trâng Dinh. Lang Son, N Vietnam
166 M8 **Thaton** Mon State, S Myanmar
167 S9 **That Phanom** Nakhon Phanom, E Thailand
167 R10 **Tha Tum** Surin, E Thailand
103 P16 **Thau, Bassin de** *var.* Étang de Thau. ◎ S France
Thau, Étang de *see* Thau, Bassin de
166 L3 **Thaungdut** Sagaing, N Myanmar
167 O8 **Thaungyin** *Th.* Mae Nam Moei. ≈ Myanmar/Thailand
167 R8 **Tha Uthen** Nakhon Phanom, E Thailand
109 W2 **Thaya** *var.* Dyje. ≈ Austria/Czech Republic *see also* Dyje
27 V8 **Thayer** Missouri, C USA
166 L6 **Thayetmyo** Magwe, C Myanmar
33 S15 **Thayne** Wyoming, C USA
166 M5 **Thazi** Mandalay, C Myanmar
Thebes *see* Thíva
44 L5 **The Carlton** *var.* Abraham Bay. Mayaguana, SE Bahamas
45 O14 **The Crane** *var.* Crane. S Barbados
32 I11 **The Dalles** Oregon, NW USA
28 M14 **Thedford** Nebraska, C USA
The Hague *see* 's-Gravenhage
Theiss *see* Tisa/Tisza
8 M9 **Thelon** ≈ Northwest Territories/Nunavut, N Canada
11 V15 **Theodore** Saskatchewan, S Canada
23 N8 **Theodore** Alabama, S USA
36 L13 **Theodore Roosevelt Lake** ▣ Arizona, SW USA
Theodosia *see* Feodosiya
Theophilo Ottoni *see* Teófilo Otoni
11 V13 **The Pas** Manitoba, C Canada
31 T14 **The Plains** Ohio, N USA
Thera *see* Thíra
172 H17 **Thérèse, Île** *island* Inner Islands, NE Seychelles
Therezina *see* Teresina
115 L20 **Therma** Ikaría, Dodekánisos, Greece, Aegean Sea
Thermae Himerenses *see* Termini Imerese
Thermae Pannonicae *see* Baden
Thermaic Gulf/Thermaicus Sinus *see* Thermaïkós Kólpos
121 Q8 **Thermaïkós Kólpos** *Eng.* Thermaic Gulf; *anc.* Thermaicus Sinus. *gulf* N Greece
Thermiá *see* Kýthnos
115 L17 **Thermís** Lésvos, E Greece
115 E18 **Thérmo** Dytikí Ellás, C Greece
33 V14 **Thermopolis** Wyoming, C USA
183 P10 **The Rock** New South Wales, SE Australia
195 O5 **Theron Mountains** ⛰ Antarctica
115 G18 **Thespiés** Stereá Ellás, C Greece
115 E16 **Thessalía** *Eng.* Thessaly. ◆ *region* C Greece
14 C10 **Thessalon** Ontario, S Canada
115 G14 **Thessaloníki** *Eng.* Salonica, Salonika, *SCr.* Solun, *Turk.* Selânik. Kentrikí Makedonía, N Greece
115 G14 **Thessaloníki** ✕ Kentrikí Makedonía, N Greece
Thessaly *see* Thessalía
84 B12 **Theta Gap** *undersea feature* E Atlantic Ocean
97 P20 **Thetford** E England, UK
15 R11 **Thetford-Mines** Québec, SE Canada
113 K17 **Theth** *var.* Thethi. Shkodër, N Albania
Thethi *see* Theth
99 L20 **Theux** Liège, E Belgium
45 V9 **The Valley** O (Anguilla) E Anguilla
27 N10 **The Village** Oklahoma, C USA
25 W10 **The Woodlands** Texas, SW USA
Thiamis *see* Thýamis
Thian Shan *see* Tien Shan
22 J9 **Thibodaux** Louisiana, S USA
29 S3 **Thief Lake** ◎ Minnesota, N USA
29 S3 **Thief River** ≈ Minnesota, N USA
29 S3 **Thief River Falls** Minnesota, N USA
Thièle *see* La Thielle
32 G14 **Thielsen, Mount** ▲ Oregon, NW USA
Thielt *see* Tielt
106 G7 **Thiene** Veneto, NE Italy
Thienen *see* Tienen
103 P11 **Thiers** Puy-de-Dôme, C France
76 F11 **Thiès** W Senegal
81 I19 **Thika** Central, S Kenya
Thikombia *see* Cikobia
151 K18 **Thiladhunmathi Atoll** *var.* Tiladummati Atoll. *atoll* N Maldives
Thimbu *see* Thimphu
153 T11 **Thimphu** *var.* Thimbu; *prev.* Tashi Chho Dzong. ● (Bhutan) W Bhutan
92 H2 **Thingeyri** Vestfirdhir, NW Iceland
92 I3 **Thingvellir** Sudhurland, SW Iceland
187 Q17 **Thio** Province Sud, C New Caledonia
103 T4 **Thionville** *Ger.* Diedenhofen. Moselle, NE France
115 K22 **Thíra** Thíra, Kykládes, Greece, Aegean Sea
115 K22 **Thíra** *prev.* Santorin, Santoríni, *anc.* Thera. *island* Kykládes, Greece, Aegean Sea
115 J22 **Thirasía** *island* Kykládes, Greece, Aegean Sea
97 M16 **Thirsk** N England, UK
14 F12 **Thirty Thousand Islands** *island group* Ontario, S Canada
Thiruvanathapuram *see* Trivandrum
95 F20 **Thisted** Viborg, NW Denmark
Thistil Fjord *see* Thistilfjördhur
92 L1 **Thistilfjördhur** *var.* Thistil Fjord. *fjord* NE Iceland
182 G9 **Thistle Island** *island* South Australia
Thithia *see* Cicia
Thiukhaoluang Phrahang *see* Luang Prabang Range
115 G18 **Thíva** *Eng.* Thebes; *prev.* Thívai. Stereá Ellás, C Greece
Thívai *see* Thíva
102 M12 **Thiviers** Dordogne, SW France
92 J4 **Thjórsá** ≈ C Iceland
9 N10 **Thlewiaza** ≈ Nunavut, NE Canada
8 L10 **Thoa** ≈ Northwest Territories, NW Canada
99 G14 **Tholen** Zeeland, SW Netherlands
99 F14 **Tholen** *island* SW Netherlands
26 L10 **Thomas** Oklahoma, C USA
21 T3 **Thomas** West Virginia, NE USA
27 U3 **Thomas Hill Reservoir** ▣ Missouri, C USA
23 S5 **Thomaston** Georgia, SE USA
19 R7 **Thomaston** Maine, NE USA
25 T12 **Thomaston** Texas, SW USA
23 O6 **Thomasville** Alabama, S USA
23 T8 **Thomasville** Georgia, SE USA
21 S9 **Thomasville** North Carolina, SE USA
35 N5 **Thomes Creek** ≈ California, W USA
11 W12 **Thompson** Manitoba, C Canada
29 R4 **Thompson** North Dakota, N USA
(0) F8 **Thompson** ≈ Alberta/British Columbia, SW Canada
33 O8 **Thompson Falls** Montana, NW USA
29 Q10 **Thompson, Lake** ◎ South Dakota, N USA
34 M3 **Thompson Peak** ▲ California, W USA
27 S2 **Thompson River** ≈ Missouri, C USA
185 A22 **Thompson Sound** *sound* South Island, NZ
8 J5 **Thomsen** ≈ Banks Island, Northwest Territories, NW Canada
23 V4 **Thomson** Georgia, SE USA
103 T10 **Thonon-les-Bains** Haute-Savoie, E France
103 O15 **Thoré** *var.* Thore. ≈ S France
37 P11 **Thoreau** New Mexico, SW USA
Thorenburg *see* Turda
92 J3 **Thórisvatn** ◎ C Iceland
92 P4 **Thor, Kapp** *headland* S Svalbard
92 I4 **Thorlákshöfn** Sudhurland, SW Iceland
Thorn *see* Toruń
25 T10 **Thorndale** Texas, SW USA
14 H10 **Thorne** Ontario, S Canada
97 J14 **Thornhill** S Scotland, UK
25 U8 **Thornton** Texas, SW USA
Thornton Island *see* Millennium Island
14 H16 **Thorold** Ontario, S Canada
32 I9 **Thorp** Washington, NW USA
195 S3 **Thorshavnheiane** *physical region* Antarctica
92 L1 **Thórshöfn** Nordhurland Eystra, NE Iceland
Thospitis *see* Van Gölü
167 S14 **Thôt Nôt** Cân Thơ, S Vietnam
102 K8 **Thouars** Deux-Sèvres, W France
153 X14 **Thoubal** Manipur, NE India
102 K9 **Thouet** ≈ W France
Thoune *see* Thun
18 H7 **Thousand Islands** *island* Canada/USA
35 S15 **Thousand Oaks** California, W USA
114 L12 **Thrace** *cultural region* SE Europe
114 J13 **Thracian Sea** *Gk.* Thrakikó Pélagos; *anc.* Thracium Mare. *sea* Greece/Turkey
Thracium Mare/Thrakikó Pélagos *see* Thracian Sea
Thrá Lí, Bá *see* Tralee Bay
33 R11 **Three Forks** Montana, NW USA

◆ Country ● Country Capital ◇ Dependent Territory ○ Dependent Territory Capital ◆ Administrative Region ✕ International Airport ▲ Mountain ⛰ Mountain Range ⛰ Volcano ≈ River ◎ Lake ▣ Reservoir

160 M8 Three Gorges Dam *dam* Hubei, C China
11 Q16 Three Hills Alberta, SW Canada
183 N15 Three Hummock Island *island* Tasmania, SE Australia
184 H1 Three Kings Islands *island group* N NZ
175 P10 Three Kings Rise *undersea feature* W Pacific Ocean
77 O18 Three Points, Cape *headland* S Ghana
31 P10 Three Rivers Michigan, N USA
25 S13 Three Rivers Texas, SW USA
83 G24 Three Sisters Northern Cape, SW South Africa
32 H13 Three Sisters ▲ Oregon, NW USA
187 N10 Three Sisters Islands *island group* SE Solomon Islands
Thrissur *see* Trichūr
25 Q6 Throckmorton Texas, SW USA
180 M10 Throssell, Lake *salt lake* Western Australia
115 K25 Thryptís ▲ Kríti, Greece, E Mediterranean Sea
167 T13 Thu Dâu Môt *var.* Phu Cương. Sông Be, S Vietnam
167 S6 Thu Do ✈ (Ha Nôi) Ha Nôi, N Vietnam
99 G21 Thuin Hainaut, S Belgium
149 Q12 Thul Sind, SE Pakistan
Thule *see* Qaanaaq
83 J18 Thuli *var.* Tuli. ≈ S Zimbabwe
Thumrayt *see* Thamarīt
108 D9 Thun *Fr.* Thoune. Bern, W Switzerland
12 C12 Thunder Bay Ontario, S Canada
30 M1 Thunder Bay *lake bay* S Canada
31 R6 Thunder Bay *lake bay* Michigan, N USA
31 R6 Thunder Bay River ≈ Michigan, N USA
27 N11 Thunderbird, Lake ⊠ Oklahoma, C USA
28 L8 Thunder Butte Creek ≈ South Dakota, N USA
108 E9 Thuner See ⊚ C Switzerland
167 N15 Thung Song *var.* Cha Mai. Nakhon Si Thammarat, SW Thailand
108 H7 Thur ≈ N Switzerland
108 G6 Thurgau *Fr.* Thurgovie. ◆ *canton* NE Switzerland
Thurgovie *see* Thurgau
Thuringe *see* Thüringen
108 J7 Thüringen Vorarlberg, W Austria
101 J17 Thüringen *Eng.* Thuringia, *Fr.* Thuringe. ◆ *state* C Germany
101 J17 Thüringer Wald *Eng.* Thuringian Forest. ▲ C Germany
Thuringia *see* Thüringen
Thuringian Forest *see* Thüringer Wald
97 D19 Thurles *Ir.* Durlas. S Ireland
21 W2 Thurmont Maryland, NE USA
Thurø *see* Thurø By
95 H24 Thurø By *var.* Thurø. Fyn, C Denmark
14 M12 Thurso Québec, SE Canada
96 J6 Thurso N Scotland, UK
194 I10 Thurston Island *island* Antarctica
108 I9 Thusis Graubünden, S Switzerland
115 C15 Thýamis *var.* Thiamis. ≈ W Greece
95 E21 Thyborøn *var.* Tyborøn. Ringkøbing, W Denmark
195 U3 Thyer Glacier *glacier* Antarctica
115 L20 Thýmaina *island* Dodekánisos, Greece, Aegean Sea
83 N15 Thyolo *var.* Cholo. Southern, S Malawi
183 U6 Tia New South Wales, SE Australia
54 H5 Tía Juana Zulia, NW Venezuela
Tiancheng *see* Chongyang
160 J14 Tiandong *var.* Pingma. Guangxi Zhuangzu Zizhiqu, S China
161 O3 Tianjin *var.* Tientsin. Tianjin Shi, E China
Tianjin *see* Tianjin Shi
161 P3 Tianjin Shi *var.* Jin, Tianjin, T'ien-ching, Tientsin. ◆ *municipality* E China
159 S10 Tianjun *var.* Xinyuan. Qinghai, C China
160 J13 Tianlin *var.* Leli. Guangxi Zhuangzu Zizhiqu, S China
Tian Shan *see* Tien Shan
159 W11 Tianshui Gansu, C China
150 I7 Tianshuihai Xinjiang Uygur Zizhiqu, W China
161 S10 Tiantai Zhejiang, SE China
160 J14 Tianyang *var.* Tianzhou. Guangxi Zhuangzu Zizhiqu, S China
Tianzhou *see* Tianyang
159 U9 Tianzhu *var.* Huazangsi, Tianzhu Zangzu Zizhixian. Gansu, C China
Tianzhu Zangzu Zizhixian *see* Tianzhu
191 Q7 Tiarei Tahiti, W French Polynesia
74 J6 Tiaret *var.* Tihert. NW Algeria
77 N17 Tiassalé S Ivory Coast
192 I16 Ti'avea Upolu, SE Samoa
Tiba *see* Chiba
60 J11 Tibagi *var.* Tibají. Paraná, S Brazil
60 J10 Tibagi, Rio *var.* Rio Tibají. ≈ S Brazil
Tibají *see* Tibagi
Tibají, Rio *see* Tibagi, Rio
139 Q9 Tibal, Wādī *dry watercourse* S Iraq
54 G9 Tibaná Boyacá, C Colombia
79 F14 Tibati Adamaoua, N Cameroon
76 K15 Tibé, Pic de ▲ SE Guinea
Tiber *see* Tevere, Italy
Tiber *see* Tivoli, Italy
Tiberias *see* Teverya
138 G8 Tiberias, Lake *var.* Chinnereth, Sea of Bahr Tabariya, Sea of Galilee, *Ar.* Bahrat Tabariya, *Heb.* Yam Kinneret. ⊚ N Israel
67 Q5 Tibesti *var.* Tibesti Massif, *Ar.* Tibistī. ▲ N Africa
Tibesti Massif *see* Tibesti
Tibetan Autonomous Region *see* Xizang Zizhiqu
Tibet, Plateau of *see* Qingzang Gaoyuan
Tibistī *see* Tibesti
14 K7 Tiblemont, Lac ⊚ Québec, SE Canada
139 X9 Ţīb, Nahr aţ ≈ S Iraq
Tibnī *see* At Tibnī
182 L4 Tibooburra New South Wales, SE Australia
95 L18 Tibro Västra Götaland, S Sweden
40 E5 Tiburón, Isla *var.* Isla del Tiburón. *island* NW Mexico
Tiburón, Isla del *see* Tiburón, Isla
23 W14 Tice Florida, SE USA
Tichau *see* Tychy
114 L8 Ticha, Yazovir ⊠ NE Bulgaria
76 K9 Tichit *var.* Tichitt. Tagant, C Mauritania
Tichitt *see* Tichit
108 G11 Ticino *Fr./Ger.* Tessin. ◆ *canton* S Switzerland
106 D8 Ticino ≈ Italy/Switzerland
108 H11 Ticino *Ger.* Tessin. ≈ SW Switzerland
Ticinum *see* Pavia
41 X12 Ticul Yucatán, SE Mexico
95 K18 Tidaholm Västra Götaland, S Sweden
Tidjikdja *see* Tidjikja
76 J8 Tidjikja *var.* Tidjikdja; *prev.* Fort-Cappolani. Tagant, C Mauritania
Tidore *see* Soasiu
171 R11 Tidore, Pulau *island* E Indonesia
Tîdra, Île *see* Et Tidra
77 N16 Tiébissou *var.* Tiebissou. C Ivory Coast
Tiefa *see* Diaobingshan
108 I9 Tiefencastel Graubünden, S Switzerland
Tiegenhof *see* Nowy Dwór Gdański
T'ieh-ling *see* Tieling
98 K13 Tiel Gelderland, C Netherlands
163 W7 Tieli Heilongjiang, NE China
163 V11 Tieling *var.* T'ieh-ling. Liaoning, NE China
152 L4 Tielongtan China/India
99 D17 Tielt *var.* Thielt. West-Vlaanderen, W Belgium
T'ien-ching *see* Tianjin Shi
99 I18 Tienen *var.* Thienen, *Fr.* Tirlemont. Vlaams Brabant, C Belgium
Tiên Giang, Sông *see* Mekong
147 X9 Tien Shan *Chin.* Thian Shan, Tian Shan, T'ien Shan, *Rus.* Tyan'-Shan'. ▲ C Asia
Tientsin *see* Tianjin
Tientsin *see* Tianjin Shi
167 U6 Tiên Yên Quang Ninh, N Vietnam
95 O14 Tierp Uppsala, C Sweden
62 H7 Tierra Amarilla Atacama, N Chile
37 R9 Tierra Amarilla New Mexico, SW USA
41 R15 Tierra Blanca Veracruz-Llave, E Mexico
41 O16 Tierra Colorada Guerrero, S Mexico
63 J17 Tierra Colorada, Bajo de la *basin* SE Argentina
63 I25 Tierra del Fuego *off.* Provincia de la Tierra del Fuego. ◆ *province* S Argentina
63 J24 Tierra del Fuego *island* Argentina/Chile
54 D7 Tierralta Córdoba, NW Colombia
104 K9 Tiétar ≈ W Spain
60 L10 Tietê São Paulo, S Brazil
60 J8 Tietê, Rio ≈ S Brazil
32 I9 Tieton Washington, NW USA
32 J6 Tiffany Mountain ▲ Washington, NW USA
31 S12 Tiffin Ohio, N USA
31 Q11 Tiffin River ≈ Ohio, N USA
Tiflis *see* T'bilisi
23 U7 Tifton Georgia, SE USA
171 R13 Tifu Pulau Buru, E Indonesia
38 L17 Tigalda Island *island* Aleutian Islands, Alaska, USA
115 I15 Tigáni, Akrotírio *headland* Límnos, E Greece
169 V6 Tiga Tarok Sabah, East Malaysia
117 O10 Tighina *Rus.* Bendery; *prev.* Bender. E Moldova
145 X9 Tigiretskiy Khrebet ▲ E Kazakhstan
79 F14 Tignère Adamaoua, N Cameroon
13 P14 Tignish Prince Edward Island, SE Canada
Tigranocerta *see* Siirt
80 I11 Tigray ◆ *province* N Ethiopia
41 O11 Tigre, Cerro del ▲ C Mexico
56 F8 Tigre, Río ≈ N Peru
139 X10 Tigris *Ar.* Dijlah, *Turk.* Dicle. ≈ Iraq/Turkey
76 G9 Tiguent Trarza, SW Mauritania
74 M10 Tiguentourine E Algeria
77 V10 Tiguidit, Falaise de *ridge* C Niger
141 N13 Tihāmah *var.* Tehama. *plain* Saudi Arabia/Yemen
Tihert *see* Tiaret
Ti-hua/Tihwa *see* Ürümqi
41 Q13 Tihuatlán Veracruz-Llave, E Mexico
40 B1 Tijuana Baja California, NW Mexico
42 E2 Tikal Petén, N Guatemala
154 I9 Tīkamgarh *prev.* Tehri. Madhya Pradesh, C India
158 L7 Tikanlik Xinjiang Uygur Zizhiqu, NW China
77 P12 Tikaré N Burkina
39 O12 Tikchik Lakes *lakes* Alaska, USA
191 T9 Tikehau *atoll* Îles Tuamotu, C French Polynesia
191 V9 Tikei *island* Îles Tuamotu, C French Polynesia
126 L13 Tikhoretsk Krasnodarskiy Kray, SW Russian Federation
124 I13 Tikhvin Leningradskaya Oblast', NW Russian Federation
193 P9 Tiki Basin *undersea feature* S Pacific Ocean
76 K13 Tikinsso ≈ NE Guinea
184 Q8 Tikitiki Gisborne, North Island, NZ
79 D16 Tiko Sud-Ouest, SW Cameroon
187 R11 Tikopia *island*, E Soloman Islands
139 S6 Tikrīt *var.* Tekrit. N Iraq
124 I8 Tiksha Respublika Kareliya, NW Russian Federation
126 I6 Tikshozero, Ozero ⊚ NW Russian Federation
123 P7 Tiksi Respublika Sakha (Yakutiya), NE Russian Federation
42 A6 Tilapa San Marcos, SW Guatemala
42 L13 Tilarán Guanacaste, NW Costa Rica
99 J14 Tilburg Noord-Brabant, S Netherlands
14 D17 Tilbury Ontario, S Canada
182 K4 Tilcha South Australia
Tilcha Creek *see* Callabonna Creek
29 Q14 Tilden Nebraska, C USA
25 R13 Tilden Texas, SW USA
14 H10 Tilden Lake Ontario, S Canada
116 G9 Tileagd *Hung.* Mezőtelegd. Bihor, W Romania
77 Q8 Tilemsi, Vallée de ≈ C Mali
123 V8 Tilichiki Koryakskiy Avtonomnyy Okrug, E Russian Federation
Tiligul *see* Tilihul
Tiligul'skiy Liman *see* Tilihul's'kyy Lyman
117 P9 Tilihul *Rus.* Tiligul. ≈ SW Ukraine
117 P10 Tilihul's'kyy Lyman *Rus.* Tiligul'skiy Liman. ⊚ S Ukraine
Tilimsen *see* Tlemcen
Tilio Martius *see* Toulon
77 R11 Tillabéri *var.* Tillabéry. Tillabéri, W Niger
77 R11 Tillabéri ◆ *department* SW Niger
Tillabéry *see* Tillabéri
32 F11 Tillamook Oregon, NW USA
32 E11 Tillamook Bay *inlet* Oregon, NW USA
151 Q22 Tillanchāng Dwīp *island* Nicobar Islands, India, NE Indian Ocean
95 N15 Tillberga Västmanland, C Sweden
Tillenberg *see* Dyleń
21 S10 Tillery, Lake ⊠ North Carolina, SE USA
77 T10 Tillia Tahoua, W Niger
23 N8 Tillmans Corner Alabama, S USA
14 F17 Tillsonburg Ontario, S Canada
115 N22 Tílos *island* Dodekánisos, Greece, Aegean Sea
183 N5 Tilpa New South Wales, SE Australia
Tilsit *see* Sovetsk
31 N13 Tilton Illinois, N USA
126 K7 Tim Kurskaya Oblast', W Russian Federation
54 D12 Timaná Huila, S Colombia
Timan Ridge *see* Timanskiy Kryazh
127 Q6 Timanskiy Kryazh *Eng.* Timan Ridge. *ridge* NW Russian Federation
185 G20 Timaru Canterbury, South Island, NZ
127 S6 Timashevo Samarskaya Oblast', W Russian Federation
126 K13 Timashevsk Krasnodarskiy Kray, SW Russian Federation
Timbaki/Timbákion *see* Tympáki
22 K10 Timbalier Bay *bay* Louisiana, S USA
22 K11 Timbalier Island *island* Louisiana, S USA
76 L10 Timbedgha *var.* Timbédra. Hodh ech Chargui, SE Mauritania
Timbédra *see* Timbedgha
32 G10 Timber Oregon, NW USA
181 O3 Timber Creek Northern Territory, N Australia
28 M8 Timber Lake South Dakota, N USA
54 D12 Timbío Cauca, SW Colombia
54 C12 Timbiquí Cauca, SW Colombia
83 O17 Timbue, Ponta *headland* C Mozambique
Timbuktu *see* Tombouctou
169 W8 Timbun Mata, Pulau *island* E Malaysia
77 P8 Timétrine *var.* Ti-n-Kâr. *oasis* C Mali
Timfi *see* Týmfi
Timfristos *see* Tymfristós
77 V9 Tîmia Agadez, C Niger
171 X14 Timika Papua, E Indonesia
74 I9 Timimoun C Algeria
Timiris, Cap *see* Timirist, Râs
76 F8 Timirist, Râs *var.* Cap Timiris. *headland* NW Mauritania
145 O7 Timiryazevo Severnyy Kazakhstan, N Kazakhstan
116 E11 Timiş ◆ *county* SW Romania
14 H9 Timiskaming, Lake *Fr.* Lac Témiscamingue. ⊚ Ontario/Québec, SE Canada
116 E11 Timişoara *Ger.* Temeschwar, Temeswar, *Hung.* Temesvár; *prev.* Temeschburg. Timiş, W Romania
116 E11 Timişoara ✈ Timiş, W Romania
Timkovichi *see* Tsimkavichy
77 U8 Ti-m-Meghsoï ≈ NW Niger
100 K8 Timmendorfer Strand Schleswig-Holstein, N Germany
14 F7 Timmins Ontario, S Canada
21 S12 Timmonsville South Carolina, SE USA
30 K5 Timms Hill ▲ Wisconsin, N USA
112 P12 Timok ≈ E Serbia and Montenegro (Yugo.)
58 N13 Timon Maranhão, E Brazil
171 Q16 Timor *island* East Timor/Indonesia
171 Q17 Timor Sea *sea* E Indian Ocean
Timor Timur *see* East Timor
Timor Trench *see* Timor Trough
192 G8 Timor Trough *var.* Timor Trench. *undersea feature* NE Timor Sea
61 A21 Timote Buenos Aires, E Argentina
54 I6 Timotes Mérida, NW Venezuela
25 X8 Timpson Texas, SW USA
123 Q11 Timpton ≈ NE Russian Federation
93 H17 Timrå Västernorrland, C Sweden
20 J10 Tims Ford Lake ⊠ Tennessee, S USA
168 L7 Timur, Banjaran ▲ Peninsular Malaysia
171 Q8 Tinaca Point *headland* Mindanao, S Philippines
54 K5 Tinaco Cojedes, N Venezuela
64 Q11 Tinajo Lanzarote, Islas Canarias, Spain, NE Atlantic Ocean
187 P10 Tinakula *island* Santa Cruz Islands, E Solomon Islands
54 K5 Tinaquillo Cojedes, N Venezuela
116 F10 Tinca *Hung.* Tenke. Bihor, W Romania
155 J20 Tindivanam Tamil Nādu, SE India
74 E9 Tindouf W Algeria
74 E9 Tindouf, Sebkha de *salt lake* W Algeria
104 J2 Tineo Asturias, N Spain
77 R9 Ti-n-Essako Kidal, E Mali
183 T5 Tingha New South Wales, SE Australia
Tingis *see* Tanger
Tinglett *see* Tinglev
95 F24 Tinglev *Ger.* Tinglett. Sønderjylland, SW Denmark
56 E12 Tingo María Huánuco, C Peru
Tingréla *see* Tengréla
158 K16 Tingri *var.* Xêgar. Xizang Zizhiqu, W China
95 M21 Tingsryd Kronoberg, S Sweden
95 P19 Tingstäde Gotland, SE Sweden
62 H12 Tinguiririca, Volcán ▲ C Chile
94 F9 Tingvoll Møre og Romsdal, S Norway
188 K8 Tinian *island* S Northern Mariana Islands
Ti-n-Kâr *see* Timétrine
Tinnevelly *see* Tirunelveli
95 G15 Tinnoset Telemark, S Norway
95 F15 Tinnsjø ⊚ S Norway
Tino *see* Chino
115 J20 Tínos Tínos, Kykládes, Greece, Aegean Sea
115 J20 Tínos *anc.* Tenos. *island* Kykládes, Greece, Aegean Sea
153 R14 Tinpahar Jhārkhand, NE India
153 X11 Tinsukia Assam, NE India
76 K10 Tintâne Hodh el Gharbi, S Mauritania
62 L7 Tintina Santiago del Estero, N Argentina
182 K10 Tintinara South Australia
104 I14 Tinto ≈ SW Spain
77 S8 Ti-n-Zaouâtene Kidal, NE Mali
Tiobraid Árann *see* Tipperary
28 K3 Tioga North Dakota, N USA
18 G12 Tioga Pennsylvania, NE USA
25 T5 Tioga Texas, SW USA
35 Q8 Tioga Pass *pass* California, W USA
18 G12 Tioga River ≈ New York/Pennsylvania, NE USA
Tioman Island *see* Tioman, Pulau
168 M9 Tioman, Pulau *var.* Tioman Island. *island* Peninsular Malaysia
18 C12 Tionesta Pennsylvania, NE USA
18 D12 Tionesta Creek ≈ Pennsylvania, NE USA
168 J13 Tiop Pulau Pagai Selatan, W Indonesia
77 O12 Tiou NW Burkina
18 H11 Tioughnioga River ≈ New York, NE USA
74 J5 Tipasa *var.* Tipaza. N Algeria
Tipaza *see* Tipasa
42 J10 Tipitapa Managua, W Nicaragua
31 R13 Tipp City Ohio, N USA
31 O12 Tippecanoe River ≈ Indiana, N USA
97 D20 Tipperary *Ir.* Tiobraid Árann. S Ireland
97 D19 Tipperary *Ir.* Tiobraid Árann. *cultural region* S Ireland
35 R12 Tipton California, W USA
31 P13 Tipton Indiana, N USA
29 Y14 Tipton Iowa, C USA
27 U5 Tipton Missouri, C USA
36 I10 Tipton, Mount ▲ Arizona, SW USA
20 F8 Tiptonville Tennessee, S USA
12 E12 Tip Top Mountain ▲ Ontario, S Canada
155 G19 Tiptūr Karnātaka, W India
Tiquisate *see* Pueblo Nuevo Tiquisate
58 L13 Tiracambu, Serra do ▲ E Brazil
Tirana *see* Tiranë
113 K19 Tirana Rinas ✈ Durrës, W Albania
113 L20 Tiranë *var.* Tirana. ● (Albania) Tiranë, C Albania
113 K20 Tiranë ◆ *district* W Albania
140 I5 Tirān, Jazīrat *island* Egypt/Saudi Arabia
106 F6 Tirano Lombardia, N Italy
182 I2 Tirari Desert *desert* South Australia
117 O10 Tiraspol *Rus.* Tiraspol'. E Moldova
184 M8 Tirau Waikato, North Island, NZ
136 C14 Tire İzmir, SW Turkey
137 O11 Tirebolu Giresun, N Turkey
96 F11 Tiree *island* W Scotland, UK
Tirgovişte *see* Târgovişte
Tirgu *see* Târgu Cărbuneşti
Tirgu Bujor *see* Târgu Bujor
Tirgu Frumos *see* Târgu Frumos
Tirgu Jiu *see* Targu Jui
Tirgu Lăpuş *see* Târgu Lăpuş
Tirgu Mures *see* Târgu Mureş
Tirgu-Neamţ *see* Târgu-Neamţ
Tirgu Ocna *see* Târgu Ocna
Tirgu Secuiesc *see* Târgu Secuiesc
149 T3 Tirich Mīr ▲ NW Pakistan
76 J5 Tiris Zemmour ◆ *region* N Mauritania
Tirlemont *see* Tienen
127 W5 Tirlyanskiy Respublika Bashkortostan, W Russian Federation
Tirnava Mare *see* Târnava Mare
Tirnava Mică *see* Târnava Mică
Tirnăveni *see* Târnăveni
Tírnavos *see* Týrnavos
Tirnovo *see* Veliko Tŭrnovo
154 J11 Tirodi Madhya Pradesh, C India
108 K8 Tirol *off.* Land Tirol, *var.* Tyrol, *It.* Tirolo. ◆ *state* W Austria
Tirolo *see* Tirol
Tirreno, Mare *see* Tyrrhenian Sea
107 B19 Tirso ≈ Sardegna, Italy, C Mediterranean Sea
95 H22 Tirstrup ✈ (Århus) Århus, C Denmark
155 I21 Tiruchchirāppalli *prev.* Trichinopoly. Tamil Nādu, SE India
155 H23 Tirunelveli *var.* Tinnevelly. Tamil Nādu, SE India
155 J19 Tirupati Andhra Pradesh, E India
155 I20 Tiruppattūr Tamil Nādu, SE India
155 H21 Tiruppūr Tamil Nādu, SW India
155 I20 Tiruvannāmalai Tamil Nādu, SE India
112 L10 Tisa *Ger.* Theiss, *Hung.* Tisza, *Rus.* Tissa, *Ukr.* Tysa. ≈ SE Europe *see also* Tisza
Tischnowitz *see* Tišnov
11 U14 Tisdale Saskatchewan, S Canada
27 O13 Tishomingo Oklahoma, C USA
95 M17 Tisnaren ⊚ S Sweden
111 F18 Tišnov *Ger.* Tischnowitz. Jihomoravský Kraj, SE Czech Republic
Tissa *see* Tisa/Tisza
74 J6 Tissemsilt N Algeria
153 S12 Tista ≈ NE India
112 L8 Tisza *Ger.* Theiss, *Rom./Slvn./SCr.* Tisa, *Rus.* Tissa, *Ukr.* Tysa. ≈ SE Europe *see also* Tisa
111 L23 Tiszaföldvár Jász-Nagykun-Szolnok, E Hungary
111 M22 Tiszafüred Jász-Nagykun-Szolnok, E Hungary
111 L23 Tiszakécske Bács-Kiskun, C Hungary
111 M21 Tiszaújváros *prev.* Leninváros. Borsod-Abaúj-Zemplén, NE Hungary
111 N21 Tiszavasvári Szabolcs-Szatmár-Bereg, NE Hungary
Titibu *see* Chichibu
57 I17 Titicaca, Lake ⊚ Bolivia/Peru
190 H17 Titikaveka Rarotonga, S Cook Islands
154 M13 Titilāgarh Orissa, E India
168 K8 Titiwangsa, Banjaran ▲ Peninsular Malaysia
Titograd *see* Podgorica
Titose *see* Chitose
Titova Mitrovica *see* Kosovska Mitrovica
Titovo Užice *see* Užice
113 M18 Titov Vrv ▲ NW FYR Macedonia
94 F7 Titran Sør-Trøndelag, S Norway
31 Q8 Tittabawassee River ≈ Michigan, N USA
116 J13 Titu Dâmboviţa, S Romania
79 M16 Titule Orientale, N Dem. Rep. Congo
23 X11 Titusville Florida, SE USA
18 C12 Titusville Pennsylvania, NE USA
76 G11 Tivaouane W Senegal
113 I17 Tivat Montenegro, SW Serbia and Montenegro (Yugo.)
14 E14 Tiverton Ontario, S Canada
97 J23 Tiverton SW England, UK
19 O12 Tiverton Rhode Island, NE USA
107 I15 Tivoli *anc.* Tiber. Lazio, C Italy
25 U13 Tivoli Texas, SW USA
141 Z8 Ţīwī NE Oman
Tiworo *see* Tioro, Selat
41 Y11 Tizimín Yucatán, SE Mexico
74 K5 Tizi Ouzou *var.* Tizi-Ouzou. N Algeria
74 D8 Tiznit SW Morocco
113 I14 Tjentište Republika Srpska, SE Bosnia and Herzegovina
Tjepoe/Tjepu *see* Cepu
98 L7 Tjeukemeer ⊚ N Netherlands
Tjiamis *see* Ciamis
Tjiandjoer *see* Cianjur
Tjilatjap *see* Cilacap
Tjiledoeg *see* Ciledug
95 F23 Tjæreborg Ribe, W Denmark
95 I18 Tjörn *island* S Sweden
92 O3 Tjuvfjorden *fjord* S Svalbard
Tkvarcheli *see* Tqvarch'eli
40 L8 Tlahualilo Durango, N Mexico
41 P14 Tlalnepantla México, C Mexico
41 Q13 Tlapacoyán Veracruz-Llave, E Mexico
41 P16 Tlapa de Comonfort Guerrero, S Mexico
40 L13 Tlaquepaque Jalisco, C Mexico
Tlascala *see* Tlaxcala
41 P14 Tlaxcala *var.* Tlascala, Tlaxcala de Xicohténcatl. Tlaxcala, C Mexico
41 P14 Tlaxcala ◆ *state* S Mexico
Tlaxcala de Xicohténcatl *see* Tlaxcala
41 P14 Tlaxco *var.* Tlaxco de Morelos. Tlaxcala, S Mexico
Tlaxco de Morelos *see* Tlaxco
41 Q16 Tlaxiaco *var.* Santa María Asunción Tlaxiaco. Oaxaca, S Mexico
74 I6 Tlemcen *var.* Tilimsen, Tlemsen. NW Algeria
Tlemsen *see* Tlemcen
138 L4 Tlété Ouâte Rharbi, Jebel ▲ N Syria
116 J7 Tlumach Ivano-Frankivs'ka Oblast', W Ukraine
127 P17 Tlyarata Respublika Dagestan, SW Russian Federation
116 K10 Toaca, Vârful *prev.* Virful Toaca. ▲ NE Romania
Toaca, Virful *see* Toaca, Vârful
187 R13 Toak Ambrym, C Vanuatu
172 J4 Toamasina *var.* Tamatave. Toamasina, E Madagascar
172 J4 Toamasina ◆ *province* E Madagascar
172 J4 Toamasina ✈ Toamasina, E Madagascar
21 X6 Toano Virginia, NE USA
191 U10 Toau *atoll* Îles Tuamotu, C French Polynesia
45 T6 Toa Vaca, Embalse ⊠ C Puerto Rico
62 K13 Toay La Pampa, C Argentina
159 R14 Toba Xizang Zizhiqu, W China
164 K14 Toba Mie, Honshū, SW Japan
168 I9 Toba, Danau ⊚ Sumatera, W Indonesia
45 Y16 Tobago *island* NE Trinidad and Tobago
149 Q9 Toba Kākar Range ▲ NW Pakistan
105 Q12 Tobarra Castilla-La Mancha, C Spain
149 U9 Toba Tek Singh Punjab, E Pakistan
171 R11 Tobelo Pulau Halmahera, E Indonesia
14 E12 Tobermory Ontario, S Canada
96 G10 Tobermory W Scotland, UK
165 S4 Tōbetsu Hokkaidō, NE Japan
180 M6 Tobin Lake ⊚ Western Australia
11 U14 Tobin Lake ⊚ Saskatchewan, C Canada
35 T4 Tobin, Mount ▲ Nevada, W USA
165 O9 Tobi-shima *island* C Japan
169 N13 Toboali Pulau Bangka, W Indonesia
144 M8 Tobol *Kaz.* Tobyl. Kostanay, N Kazakhstan
144 L8 Tobol *Kaz.* Tobyl. ≈ Kazakhstan/Russian Federation
122 H11 Tobol'sk Tyumenskaya Oblast', C Russian Federation
Tobruch/Tobruk *see* Ţubruq
125 R3 Tobseda Nenetskiy Avtonomnyy Okrug, NW Russian Federation
Tobyl *see* Tobol
127 Q6 Tobysh ≈ NW Russian Federation
54 F10 Tocaima Cundinamarca, C Colombia
59 K16 Tocantins *off.* Estado do Tocantins. ◆ *state* C Brazil
59 K15 Tocantins, Rio ≈ N Brazil
23 T2 Toccoa Georgia, SE USA
165 O12 Tochigi *off.* Tochigi-ken, *var.* Totigi. ◆ *prefecture* Honshū, S Japan
165 O11 Tochio *var.* Totio. Niigata, Honshū, C Japan
95 I15 Töcksfors Värmland, C Sweden
42 J5 Tocoa Colón, N Honduras
62 H4 Tocopilla Antofagasta, N Chile
62 I4 Tocorpuri, Cerro de ▲ Bolivia/Chile
183 O10 Tocumwal New South Wales, SE Australia
54 K4 Tocuyo de La Costa Falcón, NW Venezuela
152 H13 Toda Rāisingh Rājasthān, N India
106 H13 Todi Umbria, C Italy
108 G9 Tödi ▲ NE Switzerland
171 T12 Todlo Papua, E Indonesia
165 S9 Todoga-saki *headland* Honshū, C Japan
59 P17 Todos os Santos, Baía de *bay* E Brazil
40 F10 Todos Santos Baja California Sur, W Mexico
40 B2 Todos Santos, Bahía de *bay* NW Mexico
Toeban *see* Tuban
Toekang Besi Eilanden *see* Tukangbesi, Kepulauan
Tōen *see* T'aoyüan
185 D25 Toetoes Bay *bay* South Island, NZ
11 Q14 Tofield Alberta, SW Canada
10 K17 Tofino Vancouver Island, British Columbia, SW Canada
189 X17 Tofol Kosrae, E Micronesia
95 J20 Tofta Halland, S Sweden
95 H15 Tofte Buskerud, S Norway
95 F24 Toftlund Sønderjylland, SW Denmark
193 X15 Tofua *island* Ha'apai Group, C Tonga
187 Q12 Toga *island* Torres Islands, N Vanuatu
80 N13 Togdheer *off.* Gobolka Togdheer. ◆ *region* NW Somalia
Toghyzaq *see* Toguzak
164 L11 Togi Ishikawa, Honshū, SW Japan
39 N13 Togiak Alaska, USA
171 O11 Togian, Kepulauan *island group* C Indonesia
77 Q15 Togo *off.* Togolese Republic; *prev.* French Togoland. ◆ *republic* W Africa
162 F8 Tögrög Govĭ-Altay, SW Mongolia
162 E7 Tögrög Hovd, W Mongolia
159 N12 Togton He *var.* Tuotuo He. ≈ C China
Togton Heyan *see* Tanggulashan
144 L7 Toguzak *Kaz.* Toghyzaq. ≈ Kazakhstan/Russian Federation
37 P10 Tohatchi New Mexico, SW USA
191 O7 Tohiea, Mont ▲ Moorea, W French Polynesia
93 O17 Tohmajärvi Itä-Suomi, E Finland
137 N14 Tohma Çayı ≈ C Turkey
93 L16 Toholampi Länsi-Suomi, W Finland
162 M10 Töhöm Dornogovĭ, SE Mongolia
23 X12 Tohopekaliga, Lake ⊚ Florida, SE USA
164 M14 Toi Shizuoka, Honshū, S Japan
190 B15 Toi N Niue
93 L19 Toijala Länsi-Suomi, W Finland

◆ Country ● Country Capital ◇ Dependent Territory ○ Dependent Territory Capital ◆ Administrative Region ✈ International Airport ▲ Mountain ▲ Mountain Range Volcano ≈ River ⊚ Lake ⊠ Reservoir

171 P12 **Toima** Sulawesi, N Indonesia
164 D17 **Toi-misaki** *headland* Kyūshū, SW Japan
171 Q17 **Toineke** Timor, S Indonesia
Toirc, Inis *see* Inishturk
35 U6 **Toiyabe Range** ▲▲ Nevada, W USA
Tojikiston, Jumhurii *see* Tajikistan
147 R12 **Tojikobod** *Rus.* Tadzhikabad. C Tajikistan
164 G12 **Tōjō** Hiroshima, Honshū, SW Japan
39 T10 **Tok** Alaska, USA
164 K13 **Tōkai** Aichi, Honshū, SW Japan
111 N21 **Tokaj** Borsod-Abaúj-Zemplén, NE Hungary
165 N11 **Tōkamachi** Niigata, Honshū, C Japan
185 D25 **Tokanui** Southland, South Island, NZ
80 I7 **Tokar** *var.* Ṭawkar. Red Sea, NE Sudan
136 L12 **Tokat** Tokat, N Turkey
136 L12 **Tokat** ◈ *province* N Turkey
Tokati Gawa *see* Tokachi-gawa
163 X15 **Tŏkchŏk-gundo** *island group* NW South Korea
Tŏke *see* Taka Atoll
190 J9 **Tokelau** ◇ *NZ overseas territory* W Polynesia
Tőketerebes *see* Trebišov
Tokhtamyshbek *see* Tŭkhtamish
24 M6 **Tokio** Texas, SW USA
Tokio *see* Tōkyō
189 W11 **Toki Point** *point* NW Wake Island
Tokkuztara *see* Gongliu
147 V7 **Tokmak** *Kir.* Tokmok. Chuyskaya Oblast', N Kyrgyzstan
117 V9 **Tokmak** *var.* Velykyy Tokmak. Zaporiz'ka Oblast', SE Ukraine
Tokmok *see* Tokmak
184 Q8 **Tokomaru Bay** Gisborne, North Island, NZ
165 V3 **Tokoro** Hokkaidō, NE Japan
184 M8 **Tokoroa** Waikato, North Island, NZ
76 K14 **Tokounou** Haute-Guinée, C Guinea
38 M12 **Toksook Bay** Alaska, USA
Toksu *see* Xinhe
Toksum *see* Toksun
158 L6 **Toksun** *var.* Toksum. Xinjiang Uygur Zizhiqu, NW China
147 T8 **Toktogul** Talasskaya Oblast', NW Kyrgyzstan
147 T9 **Toktogul'skoye Vodokhranilishche** ▣ W Kyrgyzstan
Toktomush *see* Tŭkhtamish
193 Y14 **Toku** *island* Vava'u Group, N Tonga
165 U16 **Tokunoshima** Kagoshima, Tokuno-shima, SW Japan
165 U16 **Tokuno-shima** *island* Nansei-shotō, SW Japan
164 I14 **Tokushima** *var.* Tokusima. Tokushima, Shikoku, SW Japan
164 H14 **Tokushima** *off.* Tokushima-ken, *var.* Tokusima. ◈ *prefecture* Shikoku, SW Japan
Tokusima *see* Tokushima
164 E13 **Tokuyama** Yamaguchi, Honshū, SW Japan
165 N13 **Tōkyō** *var.* Tokio. ● (Japan) Tōkyō, Honshū, S Japan
165 O13 **Tōkyō** *off.* Tōkyō-to. ◈ *capital district* Honshū, S Japan
145 T12 **Tokyrau** ≈ C Kazakhstan
149 O3 **Tokzār** *Pash.* Tukzār. Sar-e Pol, N Afghanistan
145 X13 **Tokzhaylau** *prev.* Dzerzhinskoye. Almaty, E Kazakhstan
189 U12 **Tol** *atoll* Chuuk Islands, C Micronesia
184 Q9 **Tolaga Bay** Gisborne, North Island, NZ
172 I7 **Tôlañaro** *prev.* Faradofay, Fort-Dauphin. Toliara, SE Madagascar
162 D6 **Tolbo** Bayan-Ölgiy, W Mongolia
Tolbukhin *see* Dobrich
60 L11 **Toledo** Paraná, S Brazil
54 G8 **Toledo** Norte de Santander, N Colombia
105 N9 **Toledo** *anc.* Toletum. Castilla-La Mancha, C Spain
30 M14 **Toledo** Illinois, N USA
29 W13 **Toledo** Iowa, C USA
31 R11 **Toledo** Ohio, N USA
32 F12 **Toledo** Oregon, NW USA
32 G9 **Toledo** Washington, NW USA
42 F3 **Toledo** ◈ *district* S Belize
104 M9 **Toledo** ◈ *province* Castilla-La Mancha, C Spain
25 Y7 **Toledo Bend Reservoir** ▣ Louisiana/Texas, SW USA
104 M10 **Toledo, Montes de** ▲▲ C Spain
106 J12 **Tolentino** Marche, C Italy
Toletum *see* Toledo
94 H10 **Tolga** Hedmark, S Norway
158 J3 **Toli** Xinjiang Uygur Zizhiqu, NW China
172 H7 **Toliara** *var.* Toliary; *prev.* Tuléar. Toliara, SW Madagascar
172 H7 **Toliara** ◈ *province* SW Madagascar
Toliary *see* Toliara
54 D11 **Tolima** *off.* Departamento del Tolima. ◈ *province* C Colombia
171 N11 **Tolitoli** Sulawesi, C Indonesia
95 K22 **Tollarp** Skåne, S Sweden
100 N9 **Tollense** ≈ NE Germany
100 N10 **Tollensesee** ◎ NE Germany
36 K13 **Tolleson** Arizona, SW USA
146 M13 **Tollimarjon** *Rus.* Talimardzhan. Qashqadaryo Viloyati, S Uzbekistan
Tolmein *see* Tolmin
106 J6 **Tolmezzo** Friuli-Venezia Giulia, NE Italy
109 S11 **Tolmin** *Ger.* Tolmein, *It.* Tolmino. W Slovenia
Tolmino *see* Tolmin
111 J25 **Tolna** *Ger.* Tolnau. Tolna, S Hungary
111 I24 **Tolna** *off.* Tolna Megye. ◈ *county* SW Hungary
Tolnau *see* Tolna
79 I20 **Tolo** Bandundu, W Dem. Rep. Congo
Tolochin *see* Talachyn
190 D12 **Toloke** Île Futuna, W Wallis and Futuna
30 M13 **Tolono** Illinois, N USA
105 Q3 **Tolosa** País Vasco, N Spain
Tolosa *see* Toulouse
171 O13 **Tolo, Teluk** *bay* Sulawesi, C Indonesia
39 R9 **Tolovana River** ≈ Alaska, USA
123 U10 **Tolstoy, Mys** *headland* E Russian Federation
63 G15 **Toltén** Araucanía, C Chile
63 G15 **Toltén, Río** ≈ S Chile
54 E6 **Tolú** Sucre, NW Colombia
41 O14 **Toluca** *var.* Toluca de Lerdo. México, S Mexico
Toluca de Lerdo *see* Toluca
41 O14 **Toluca, Nevado de** ⚹ C Mexico
127 R6 **Tol'yatti** *prev.* Stavropol'. Samarskaya Oblast', W Russian Federation
77 O12 **Toma** NW Burkina
30 K7 **Tomah** Wisconsin, N USA
30 L5 **Tomahawk** Wisconsin, N USA
117 T8 **Tomakivka** Dnipropetrovs'ka Oblast', E Ukraine
165 S4 **Tomakomai** Hokkaidō, NE Japan
165 S2 **Tomamae** Hokkaidō, NE Japan
104 G9 **Tomar** Santarém, W Portugal
123 T13 **Tomari** Ostrov Sakhalin, Sakhalinskaya Oblast', SE Russian Federation
115 C16 **Tómaros** ▲ W Greece
Tomaschow *see* Tomaszów Lubelski, Poland
Tomaschow *see* Tomaszów Mazowiecki, Poland
61 E16 **Tomás Gomensoro** Artigas, N Uruguay
117 N7 **Tomashpil'** Vinnyts'ka Oblast', C Ukraine
Tomaszów *see* Tomaszów Mazowiecki
111 P15 **Tomaszów Lubelski** *Ger.* Tomaschow. Lubelskie, E Poland
Tomaszów Mazowiecka *see* Tomaszów Mazowiecki
110 L13 **Tomaszów Mazowiecki** *var.* Tomaszów Mazowiecka; *prev.* Tomaszów, *Ger.* Tomaschow. Łodzkie, C Poland
40 J13 **Tomatlán** Jalisco, C Mexico
81 F15 **Tombe** Jonglei, S Sudan
23 N4 **Tombigbee River** ≈ Alabama/Mississippi, S USA
82 A10 **Tomboco** Zaire, NW Angola
77 O10 **Tombouctou** *Eng.* Timbuktu. Tombouctou, N Mali
77 N9 **Tombouctou** ◈ *region* W Mali
37 N16 **Tombstone** Arizona, SW USA
83 A15 **Tombua** *Port.* Porto Alexandre. Namibe, SW Angola
83 J19 **Tom Burke** Limpopo, NE South Africa
146 L9 **Tomdibuloq** *Rus.* Tamdybulak. Navoiy Viloyati, N Uzbekistan
146 L9 **Tomditow-Tog'lari** ▲▲ N Uzbekistan
62 G13 **Tomé** Bío Bío, C Chile
58 L12 **Tomé-Açu** Pará, NE Brazil
95 L23 **Tomelilla** Skåne, S Sweden
105 O10 **Tomelloso** Castilla-La Mancha, C Spain
14 H10 **Tomiko Lake** ◎ Ontario, S Canada
77 N12 **Tominian** Ségou, C Mali
171 N12 **Tomini, Gulf of** *var.* Teluk Tomini; *prev.* Teluk Gorontalo. *bay* Sulawesi, C Indonesia
Tomini, Teluk *see* Tomini, Gulf of
165 Q11 **Tomioka** Fukushima, Honshū, C Japan
113 G14 **Tomislavgrad** Federacija Bosna I Hercegovina, SW Bosnia and Herzegovina
181 O9 **Tomkinson Ranges** ▲▲ South Australia/Western Australia
123 Q11 **Tommot** Respublika Sakha (Yakutiya), NE Russian Federation
171 Q11 **Tomohon** Sulawesi, N Indonesia
54 K9 **Tomo, Río** ≈ E Colombia
113 L21 **Tomorrit, Mali i** ▲ S Albania
11 S17 **Tompkins** Saskatchewan, S Canada
20 K8 **Tompkinsville** Kentucky, S USA
171 N11 **Tompo** Sulawesi, N Indonesia
180 I8 **Tom Price** Western Australia
122 J12 **Tomsk** Tomskaya Oblast', C Russian Federation
122 I11 **Tomskaya Oblast'** ◈ *province* C Russian Federation
18 K16 **Toms River** New Jersey, NE USA
Tom Steed Lake *see* Tom Steed Reservoir
26 L12 **Tom Steed Reservoir** *var.* Tom Steed Lake. ▣ Oklahoma, C USA
171 U13 **Tomu** Papua, E Indonesia
158 H6 **Tomür Feng** *var.* Pobeda Peak, *Rus.* Pik Pobedy. ▲ China/Kyrgyzstan *see also* Pobedy, Pik
189 N13 **Tomworoahlang** Pohnpei, E Micronesia
41 U17 **Tonalá** Chiapas, SE Mexico
106 F6 **Tonale, Passo del** *pass* N Italy
164 I11 **Tonami** Toyama, Honshū, SW Japan
58 C12 **Tonantins** Amazonas, W Brazil
32 K6 **Tonasket** Washington, NW USA
55 Y9 **Tonate** *var.* Macouria. N French Guiana
18 D10 **Tonawanda** New York, NE USA
171 Q11 **Tondano** Sulawesi, C Indonesia
104 H7 **Tondela** Viseu, N Portugal
95 F24 **Tønder** *Ger.* Tondern. Sønderjylland, SW Denmark
Tondern *see* Tønder
143 N4 **Tonekābon** *var.* Shahsawar, Tonkābon; *prev.* Shahsavār. Māzandarān, N Iran
Tonezh *see* Tonyezh
193 Y14 **Tonga** *off.* Kingdom of Tonga, *var.* Friendly Islands. ◆ *monarchy* SW Pacific Ocean
175 R9 **Tonga** *island group* SW Pacific Ocean
83 K23 **Tongaat** KwaZulu/Natal, E South Africa
161 Q13 **Tong'an** *var.* Datong, Tong an. Fujian, SE China
27 Q4 **Tonganoxie** Kansas, C USA
39 Y13 **Tongass National Forest** *reserve* Alaska, USA
193 Y16 **Tongatapu** ✕ Tongatapu, S Tonga
193 Y16 **Tongatapu** *island* Tongatapu Group, S Tonga
193 Y16 **Tongatapu Group** *island group* S Tonga
175 S9 **Tonga Trench** *undersea feature* S Pacific Ocean
161 N8 **Tongbai Shan** ▲▲ C China
161 P8 **Tongcheng** Anhui, E China
160 L6 **Tongchuan** Shaanxi, C China
160 L12 **Tongdao** *var.* Tongdao Dongzu Zizhixian; *prev.* Shuangjiang. Hunan, S China
159 T11 **Tongde** *var.* Gabasumdo. Qinghai, C China
99 K19 **Tongeren** *Fr.* Tongres. Limburg, NE Belgium
163 Y14 **Tonghae** NE South Korea
160 G13 **Tonghai** *var.* Xiushan. Yunnan, SW China
163 X8 **Tonghe** Heilongjiang, NE China
163 W11 **Tonghua** Jilin, NE China
163 Z6 **Tongjiang** Heilongjiang, NE China
163 Y13 **Tongjosŏn-man** *prev.* Broughton Bay. *bay* E North Korea
163 V7 **Tongken He** ≈ NE China
167 T7 **Tongking, Gulf of** *Chin.* Beibu Wan, *Vtn.* Vinh Bắc Bộ. *gulf* China/Vietnam
163 U10 **Tongliao** Nei Mongol Zizhiqu, N China
161 Q9 **Tongling** Anhui, E China
161 R9 **Tonglu** Zhejiang, SE China
187 R14 **Tongoa** *island* Shepherd Islands, S Vanuatu
62 G9 **Tongoy** Coquimbo, C Chile
160 L11 **Tongren** Guizhou, S China
159 T11 **Tongren** *var.* Rongwo. Qinghai, C China
Tongres *see* Tongeren
153 U11 **Tongsa** *var.* Tongsa Dzong. C Bhutan
Tongsa Dzong *see* Tongsa
Tongshan *see* Xuzhou
Tongshi *see* Wuzhishan
159 P12 **Tongtian He** ≈ C China
96 I6 **Tongue** N Scotland, UK
44 H3 **Tongue of the Ocean** *strait* C Bahamas
33 X10 **Tongue River** ≈ Montana, NW USA
33 W11 **Tongue River Reservoir** ▣ Montana, NW USA
159 V11 **Tongwei** Gansu, C China
159 W9 **Tongxin** Ningxia, N China
163 U9 **Tongyu** *var.* Kaitong. Jilin, NE China
160 J11 **Tongzi** Guizhou, S China
40 G5 **Tónichi** Sonora, NW Mexico
81 D14 **Tonj** Warab, SW Sudan
152 H13 **Tonk** Rājasthān, N India
Tonkābon *see* Tonekābon
27 N8 **Tonkawa** Oklahoma, C USA
167 Q12 **Tônlé Sap** *Eng.* Great Lake. ◎ W Cambodia
102 L14 **Tonneins** Lot-et-Garonne, SW France
103 Q7 **Tonnerre** Yonne, C France
Tonoas *see* Dublon
35 U8 **Tonopah** Nevada, W USA
164 H13 **Tonoshō** Okayama, Shōdo-shima, SW Japan
43 S17 **Tonosí** Los Santos, S Panama
95 H16 **Tønsberg** Vestfold, S Norway
39 T11 **Tonsina** Alaska, USA
95 D17 **Tonstad** Vest-Agder, S Norway
193 X15 **Tonumea** *island* Nomuka Group, W Tonga
137 O11 **Tonya** Trabzon, NE Turkey
119 K20 **Tonyezh** *Rus.* Tonezh. Homyel'skaya Voblasts', SE Belarus
36 L3 **Tooele** Utah, W USA
122 L13 **Toora-Khem** Respublika Tyva, S Russian Federation
183 O5 **Toorale East** New South Wales, SE Australia
83 H25 **Toorberg** ▲ S South Africa
118 G5 **Tootsi** Pärnumaa, SW Estonia
183 U3 **Toowoomba** Queensland, E Australia
27 Q4 **Topeka** *state capital* Kansas, C USA
111 M18 **Topla** *Hung.* Toplya. ≈ NE Slovakia
122 J12 **Topki** Kemerovskaya Oblast', S Russian Federation
Toplicza *see* Toplița
116 J10 **Toplița** *Ger.* Töplitz, *Hung.* Maroshévíz; *prev.* Toplița Română, *Hung.* Oláh-Toplicza, Toplicza. Harghita, C Romania
Toplița Română/Töplitz *see* Toplița
Toplya *see* Topla
111 I20 **Topoľčany** *Hung.* Nagytapolcsány. Nitriansky Kraj, SW Slovakia
40 G8 **Topolobampo** Sinaloa, C Mexico
116 I13 **Topoloveni** Argeș, S Romania
114 L11 **Topolovgrad** *prev.* Kavakli. Khaskovo, S Bulgaria
Topolya *see* Bačka Topola
126 I6 **Topozero, Ozero** ◎ NW Russian Federation
32 J10 **Toppenish** Washington, NW USA
181 P4 **Top Springs Roadhouse** Northern Territory, N Australia
189 U11 **Tora** *island* Chuuk, C Micronesia
Toraigh *see* Tory Island
189 U11 **Tora Island Pass** *passage* Chuuk Islands, C Micronesia
143 U5 **Torbat-e Ḩeydarīyeh** *var.* Turbat-i-Haidari. Khorāsān, NE Iran
143 V5 **Torbat-e Jām** *var.* Turbat-i-Jam. Khorāsān, NE Iran
39 Q11 **Torbert, Mount** ▲ Alaska, USA
31 P6 **Torch Lake** ◎ Michigan, N USA
Törcsvár *see* Bran
Torda *see* Turda
104 L6 **Tordesillas** Castilla-León, N Spain
92 K13 **Töre** Norrbotten, N Sweden
95 L17 **Töreboda** Västra Götaland, S Sweden
95 J21 **Torekov** Skåne, S Sweden
92 O3 **Torell Land** *physical region* SW Svalbard
117 Y8 **Torez** Donets'ka Oblast', SE Ukraine
101 N14 **Torgau** Sachsen, E Germany
Torgay Üstirti *see* Turgayskaya Stolovaya Strana
Torghay *see* Turgay
95 N22 **Torhamn** Blekinge, S Sweden
99 C17 **Torhout** West-Vlaanderen, W Belgium
106 B8 **Torino** *Eng.* Turin. Piemonte, NW Italy
165 U15 **Tori-shima** *island* Izu-shotō, SE Japan
81 F16 **Torit** Eastern Equatoria, S Sudan
186 H6 **Toriu** New Britain, E PNG
148 M4 **Torkestān, Selseleh-ye Band-e** *var.* Bandi-i Turkistan. ▲▲ NW Afghanistan
104 L7 **Tormes** ≈ W Spain
Tornacum *see* Tournai
Torneå *see* Tornio
92 K12 **Torneälven** *var.* Torniojoki, *Fin.* Tornionjoki. ≈ Finland/Sweden
92 I11 **Torneträsk** ◎ N Sweden
13 O4 **Torngat Mountains** ▲▲ Newfoundland and Labrador, NE Canada
24 H8 **Tornillo** Texas, SW USA
92 K13 **Tornio** *Swe.* Torneå. Lappi, NW Finland
Torniojoki/Tornionjoki *see* Torneälven
61 B23 **Tornquist** Buenos Aires, E Argentina
104 L6 **Toro** Castilla-León, N Spain
62 H9 **Toro, Cerro del** ▲ N Chile
77 R12 **Torodi** Tillabéri, SW Niger
Törökbecse *see* Novi Bečej
186 J7 **Torokina** Bougainville Island, NE PNG
111 L23 **Törökszentmiklós** Jász-Nagykun-Szolnok, E Hungary
42 G7 **Torola, Río** ≈ El Salvador/Honduras
Toronaíos, Kólpos *see* Kassándras, Kólpos
14 H15 **Toronto** Ontario, S Canada
31 V12 **Toronto** Ohio, N USA
Toronto *see* Lester B.Pearson
27 P6 **Toronto Lake** ▣ Kansas, C USA
35 V16 **Toro Peak** ▲ California, W USA
124 H16 **Toropets** Tverskaya Oblast', W Russian Federation
81 G18 **Tororo** E Uganda
136 H16 **Toros Dağları** *Eng.* Taurus Mountains. ▲▲ S Turkey
183 N13 **Torquay** Victoria, SE Australia
97 J24 **Torquay** SW England, UK
104 M5 **Torquemada** Castilla-León, N Spain
35 S16 **Torrance** California, W USA
104 G12 **Torrão** Setúbal, S Portugal
104 H8 **Torre, Alto da** ▲ C Portugal
107 K18 **Torre Annunziata** Campania, S Italy
105 T8 **Torreblanca** País Valenciano, E Spain
104 L15 **Torrecilla** ▲ S Spain
105 P4 **Torrecilla en Cameros** La Rioja, N Spain
105 N13 **Torredelcampo** Andalucía, S Spain
107 K17 **Torre del Greco** Campania, S Italy
104 I6 **Torre de Moncorvo** *var.* Moncorvo, Tôrre de Moncorvo. Bragança, N Portugal
104 J9 **Torrejoncillo** Extremadura, W Spain
105 O8 **Torrejón de Ardoz** Madrid, C Spain
105 N7 **Torrelaguna** Madrid, C Spain
105 N2 **Torrelavega** Cantabria, N Spain
107 M16 **Torremaggiore** Puglia, SE Italy
104 M15 **Torremolinos** Andalucía, S Spain
182 I6 **Torrens, Lake** *salt lake* South Australia
105 S10 **Torrent** *Cas.* Torrente *var.* Torrent de l'Horta. País Valenciano, E Spain
Torrent de l'Horta/Torrente *see* Torrent
40 L8 **Torreón** Coahuila de Zaragoza, NE Mexico
105 R13 **Torre Pacheco** Murcia, SE Spain
106 A8 **Torre Pellice** Piemonte, NE Italy
105 O13 **Torreperogil** Andalucía, S Spain
61 J15 **Torres** Rio Grande do Sul, S Brazil
Torrès, Îles *see* Torres Islands
187 Q11 **Torres Islands** *Fr.* Îles Torrès. *island group* N Vanuatu
104 G9 **Torres Novas** Santarém, C Portugal
181 V1 **Torres Strait** *strait* Australia/PNG
104 F10 **Torres Vedras** Lisboa, C Portugal
105 S13 **Torrevieja** País Valenciano, E Spain
186 B6 **Torricelli Mountains** ▲▲ NW PNG
96 G8 **Torridon, Loch** *inlet* NW Scotland, UK
106 D9 **Torriglia** Liguria, NW Italy
104 M9 **Torrijos** Castilla-La Mancha, C Spain
18 L12 **Torrington** Connecticut, NE USA
33 Z15 **Torrington** Wyoming, C USA
94 P16 **Torröjen** *see* Torrön
Torrön *prev.* Torröjen. ◎ C Sweden
105 N15 **Torrox** Andalucía, S Spain
94 N13 **Torsåker** Gävleborg, C Sweden
95 N21 **Torsås** Kalmar, S Sweden
95 J14 **Torsby** Värmland, C Sweden
95 N16 **Torshälla** Södermanland, C Sweden
95 B19 **Tórshavn** *Dan.* Thorshavn. *Dependent territory capital* Faeroe Islands
Torshiz *see* Kāshmar
146 I9 **To'rtkok'l** *Rus.* Turtkul'; *prev.* Petroaleksandrovsk. Qoraqalpog'iston Respublikasi, W Uzbekistan
45 T9 **Tortola** *island* C British Virgin Islands
106 D9 **Tortona** *anc.* Dertona. Piemonte, NW Italy
107 L23 **Tortorici** Sicilia, Italy
105 U7 **Tortosa** *anc.* Dertosa. Cataluña, E Spain
Tortosa *see* Ṭarṭūs
105 U7 **Tortosa, Cap** *headland* E Spain
44 L8 **Tortue, Île de la** *var.* Tortuga Island. *island* N Haiti
55 Y10 **Tortue, Montagne** ▲ C French Guiana
Tortuga, Isla *see* La Tortuga, Isla
Tortuga Island *see* Tortue, Île de la
54 C11 **Tortugas, Golfo** *gulf* W Colombia
45 T5 **Tortuguero, Laguna** *lagoon* N Puerto Rico
137 Q12 **Tortum** Erzurum, NE Turkey
Torugart, Pereval *see* Turugart Shankou
137 O12 **Torul** Gümüşhane, NE Turkey
110 J10 **Toruń** *Ger.* Thorn. Toruń, Kujawsko-pomorskie, C Poland
95 K20 **Torup** Halland, S Sweden
118 I6 **Tõrva** *Ger.* Törwa. Valgamaa, S Estonia
Törwa *see* Tõrva
96 D13 **Tory Island** *Ir.* Toraigh. *island* NW Ireland
111 N19 **Torysa** *Hung.* Tarca. ≈ NE Slovakia
Törzburg *see* Bran
124 J16 **Torzhok** Tverskaya Oblast', W Russian Federation
164 F15 **Tosa-Shimizu** *var.* Tosasimizu. Kōchi, Shikoku, SW Japan
Tosasimizu *see* Tosa-Shimizu
164 G15 **Tosa-wan** *bay* SW Japan
83 H21 **Tosca** North-West, N South Africa
106 F12 **Toscana** *Eng.* Tuscany. ◈ *region* C Italy
107 E14 **Toscano, Archipelago** *Eng.* Tuscan Archipelago. *island group* C Italy
106 G10 **Tosco-Emiliano, Appennino** *Eng.* Tuscan-Emilian Mountains. ▲▲ C Italy
Tōsei *see* Tungshih
165 N15 **To-shima** *island* Izu-shotō, SE Japan
147 Q9 **Toshkent** *Eng./Rus.* Tashkent. ● (Uzbekistan) Toshkent Viloyati, E Uzbekistan
147 Q9 **Toshkent** ✕ Toshkent Viloyati, E Uzbekistan
147 P9 **Toshkent Viloyati** *Rus.* Tashkentskaya Oblast'. ◈ *province* E Uzbekistan
124 H13 **Tosno** Leningradskaya Oblast', NW Russian Federation
159 Q10 **Toson Hu** ◎ C China
162 H6 **Tosontsengel** Dzavhan, NW Mongolia
146 I8 **Tosquduq Qumlari** *Rus.* Peski Taskuduk. *desert* W Uzbekistan
105 U4 **Tossal de l'Orri** *var.* Llorri. ▲ NE Spain
61 A15 **Tostado** Santa Fe, C Argentina
118 F6 **Tõstamaa** *Ger.* Testama. Pärnumaa, SW Estonia
100 I10 **Tostedt** Niedersachsen, NW Germany
136 J11 **Tosya** Kastamonu, N Turkey
95 F15 **Totak** ◎ S Norway
105 R13 **Totana** Murcia, SE Spain
94 H13 **Toten** *physical region* S Norway
83 G18 **Toteng** Ngamiland, C Botswana
102 M3 **Tôtes** Seine-Maritime, N France
Totigi *see* Tochigi
Totio *see* Tochio
Totis *see* Tata
189 U13 **Totiw** *island* Chuuk, C Micronesia
125 N13 **Tot'ma** *var.* Totma. Vologodskaya Oblast', NW Russian Federation
Tot'ma *see* Sukhona
55 V9 **Totness** Coronie, N Suriname
42 C5 **Totonicapán** Totonicapán, W Guatemala
42 A2 **Totonicapán** *off.* Departamento de Totonicapán. ◈ *department* W Guatemala
61 B18 **Totoras** Santa Fe, C Argentina
187 Y15 **Totoya** *island* S Fiji
183 Q7 **Tottenham** New South Wales, SE Australia
164 I12 **Tottori** Tottori, Honshū, SW Japan
164 H12 **Tottori** *off.* Tottori-ken. ◈ *prefecture* Honshū, SW Japan
76 I6 **Touâjîl** Tiris Zemmour, N Mauritania
76 L15 **Touba** W Ivory Coast
76 G11 **Touba** W Senegal
74 E7 **Toubkal, Jbel** ▲ W Morocco
32 K10 **Touchet** Washington, NW USA
103 P7 **Toucy** Yonne, C France
77 O12 **Tougan** W Burkina
74 L7 **Touggourt** NE Algeria
77 Q12 **Tougouri** N Burkina
76 J13 **Tougué** Moyenne-Guinée, NW Guinea
76 K12 **Toukoto** Kayes, W Mali
103 S5 **Toul** Meurthe-et-Moselle, NE France
76 L16 **Toulépleu** *var.* Toulobli. W Ivory Coast
161 S14 **Touliu** C Taiwan
15 U3 **Toulnustouc** ≈ Québec, SE Canada
Toulobli *see* Toulépleu
103 T16 **Toulon** *anc.* Telo Martius, Tilio Martius. Var, SE France
30 K12 **Toulon** Illinois, N USA
102 M15 **Toulouse** *anc.* Tolosa. Haute-Garonne, S France
102 M15 **Toulouse** ✕ Haute-Garonne, S France
77 N16 **Toumodi** C Ivory Coast
74 G9 **Tounassine, Hamada** *hill range* W Algeria
166 M7 **Toungoo** Pegu, C Myanmar
102 L8 **Touraine** *cultural region* C France
Tourane *see* Đà Nẵng
103 P1 **Tourcoing** Nord, N France
104 F2 **Touriñán, Cabo** *headland* NW Spain
76 J6 **Tourine** Tiris Zemmour, N Mauritania
102 J3 **Tourlaville** Manche, N France
99 D19 **Tournai** *var.* Tournay, *Dut.* Doornik; *anc.* Tornacum. Hainaut, SW Belgium
102 L16 **Tournay** Hautes-Pyrénées, S France
Tournay *see* Tournai
103 R12 **Tournon** Ardèche, E France
103 R9 **Tournus** Saône-et-Loire, C France
59 Q14 **Touros** Rio Grande do Norte, E Brazil
102 L8 **Tours** *anc.* Caesarodunum, Turoni. Indre-et-Loire, C France
183 Q17 **Tourville, Cape** *headland* Tasmania, SE Australia
162 L8 **Töv** ◈ *province* C Mongolia
54 H7 **Tovar** Mérida, NW Venezuela
126 L5 **Tovarkovskiy** Tul'skaya Oblast', W Russian Federation
Tovil'-Dora *see* Tavildara
Tövis *see* Teiuș
137 V11 **Tovuz** *Rus.* Tauz. W Azerbaijan
165 R7 **Towada** Aomori, Honshū, C Japan
184 K3 **Towai** Northland, North Island, NZ
18 H12 **Towanda** Pennsylvania, NE USA
29 W4 **Tower** Minnesota, N USA
171 N12 **Towera** Sulawesi, N Indonesia
Tower Island *see* Genovesa, Isla
180 M13 **Tower Peak** ▲ Western Australia
35 U11 **Towne Pass** *pass* California, W USA
29 N3 **Towner** North Dakota, N USA
33 R10 **Townsend** Montana, NW USA
181 X6 **Townsville** Queensland, NE Australia
Towoeti Meer *see* Towuti, Danau
148 K4 **Towraghoudī** Herāt, NW Afghanistan
21 X3 **Towson** Maryland, NE USA
171 O13 **Towuti, Danau** *Dut.* Towoeti Meer. ◎ Sulawesi, C Indonesia
Toxkan He *see* Ak-say
24 K9 **Toyah** Texas, SW USA
165 R4 **Tōya-ko** ◎ Hokkaidō, NE Japan
164 L11 **Toyama** Toyama, Honshū, SW Japan
164 L11 **Toyama** *off.* Toyama-ken. ◈ *prefecture* Honshū, SW Japan
164 L11 **Toyama-wan** *bay* W Japan
164 H15 **Tōyo** Kōchi, Shikoku, SW Japan
Toyohara *see* Yuzhno-Sakhalinsk
164 L14 **Toyohashi** *var.* Toyohasi. Aichi, Honshū, SW Japan
Toyohasi *see* Toyohashi
164 L14 **Toyokawa** Aichi, Honshū, SW Japan
164 I14 **Toyooka** Hyōgo, Honshū, SW Japan
164 L13 **Toyota** Aichi, Honshū, SW Japan
165 T1 **Toyotomi** Hokkaidō, NE Japan
Toytepa *see* To'ytepa
147 Q10 **To'ytepa** *Rus.* Toytepa. Toshkent Viloyati, E Uzbekistan
74 M6 **Tozeur** *var.* Tawzar. W Tunisia
39 Q8 **Tozi, Mount** ▲ Alaska, USA
137 Q9 **Tqvarch'eli** *Rus.* Tkvarcheli. NW Georgia
Trablous *see* Tripoli
137 O11 **Trabzon** *Eng.* Trebizond; *anc.* Trapezus. Trabzon, NE Turkey
137 O11 **Trabzon** *Eng.* Trebizond. ◈ *province* NE Turkey
13 P13 **Tracadie** New Brunswick, SE Canada
Trachenberg *see* Żmigród
15 O11 **Tracy** Québec, SE Canada
35 O8 **Tracy** California, W USA
29 S10 **Tracy** Minnesota, N USA
20 K10 **Tracy City** Tennessee, S USA
106 D7 **Tradate** Lombardia, N Italy
84 F6 **Traena Bank** *undersea feature* E Norwegian Sea
29 W13 **Traer** Iowa, C USA
104 J16 **Trafalgar, Cabo de** *headland* SW Spain
Traiectum ad Mosam/Traiectum Tungorum *see* Maastricht
Tráigh Mhór *see* Tramore
11 O17 **Trail** British Columbia, SW Canada
58 B11 **Traíra, Serra do** ▲▲ NW Brazil
109 V5 **Traisen** Niederösterreich, NE Austria
109 W4 **Traisen** ≈ NE Austria
109 X4 **Traiskirchen** Niederösterreich, NE Austria
Trajani Portus *see* Civitavecchia
Trajectum ad Rhenum *see* Utrecht
119 H14 **Trakai** *Ger.* Traken, *Pol.* Troki. Vilnius, SE Lithuania
Traken *see* Trakai
97 B20 **Tralee** *Ir.* Trá Lí. SW Ireland
97 A20 **Tralee Bay** *Ir.* Bá Thrá Lí. *bay* SW Ireland
Trá Li *see* Tralee
Trälleborg *see* Trelleborg
Tralles *see* Aydın
61 J16 **Tramandaí** Rio Grande do Sul, S Brazil
108 C7 **Tramelan** Bern, W Switzerland
Trá Mhór *see* Tramore
97 E20 **Tramore** *Ir.* Tráigh Mhór, Trá Mhór. S Ireland
95 L18 **Tranås** Jönköping, S Sweden

◆ Country ● Country Capital ◇ Dependent Territory ○ Dependent Territory Capital ◈ Administrative Region ✕ International Airport ▲ Mountain ▲▲ Mountain Range ⚹ Volcano ≈ River ◎ Lake ▣ Reservoir

62 *J7* **Trancas** Tucumán, N Argentina
104 *I7* **Trancoso** Guarda, N Portugal
95 *H22* **Tranebjerg** Århus, C Denmark
95 *K19* **Tranemo** Västra Götaland, S Sweden
167 *N16* **Trang** Trang, S Thailand
171 *V15* **Trangan, Pulau** *island* Kepulauan Aru, E Indonesia
Trâng Dinh *see* Thât Khê
183 *Q7* **Trangie** New South Wales, SE Australia
94 *K12* **Trängslet** Dalarna, C Sweden
107 *N16* **Trani** Puglia, SE Italy
61 *F17* **Tranqueras** Rivera, NE Uruguay
63 *G17* **Tranqui, Isla** *island* S Chile
39 *V6* **Trans-Alaska pipeline** *oil pipeline* Alaska, USA
195 *Q10* **Transantarctic Mountains** ▲ Antarctica
Transcarpathian Oblast *see* Zakarpats'ka Oblast'
Transilvania *see* Transylvania
Transilvaniei, Alpi *see* Carpații Meridionali
Transjordan *see* Jordan
172 *L11* **Transkei Basin** *undersea feature* SW Indian Ocean
117 *O10* **Transnistria** *cultural region* E Moldova
122 *E9* **Trans-Siberian Railway** *Railroad* Russian Federation
Transsylvanische Alpen/Transylvanian Alps *see* Carpații Meridionali
94 *K12* **Transtrand** Dalarna, C Sweden
116 *G10* **Transylvania** *Eng.* Ardeal, Transilvania, *Ger.* Siebenbürgen, *Hung.* Erdély. *cultural region* NW Romania
167 *S14* **Tra Ôn** Vinh Long, S Vietnam
107 *H23* **Trapani** *anc.* Drepanum. Sicilia, Italy, C Mediterranean Sea
167 *S12* **Trâpeăng Vêng** Kâmpóng Thum, C Cambodia
Trapezus *see* Trabzon
114 *L9* **Trapoklovo** Sliven, C Bulgaria
183 *P13* **Traralgon** Victoria, SE Australia
76 *H9* **Trarza** ◈ *region* SW Mauritania
Trasimenischersee *see* Trasimeno, Lago
106 *H12* **Trasimeno, Lago** *Eng.* Lake of Perugia, *Ger.* Trasimenischersee. ◎ C Italy
95 *J20* **Träslövsläge** Halland, S Sweden
Trás-os-Montes *see* Cucumbi
104 *I6* **Trás-os-Montes e Alto Douro** *former province* N Portugal
167 *Q12* **Trat** *var.* Bang Phra. Trat, S Thailand
Trá Tholl, Inis *see* Inishtrahull
Traù *see* Trogir
109 *T4* **Traun** Oberösterreich, N Austria
109 *S5* **Traun** ⁓ N Austria
Traun, Lake *see* Traunsee
101 *N23* **Traunreut** Bayern, SE Germany
109 *S5* **Traunsee** *var.* Gmundner See, *Eng.* Lake Traun. ◎ N Austria
Trautenau *see* Trutnov
21 *P11* **Travelers Rest** South Carolina, SE USA
182 *L8* **Travellers Lake** *seasonal lake* New South Wales, SE Australia
31 *P6* **Traverse City** Michigan, N USA
29 *R7* **Traverse, Lake** ◎ Minnesota/South Dakota, N USA
185 *I16* **Travers, Mount** ▲ South Island, NZ
11 *P17* **Travers Reservoir** ⊠ Alberta, SW Canada
167 *T14* **Tra Vinh** *var.* Phu Vinh. Tra Vinh, S Vietnam
25 *S10* **Travis, Lake** ⊠ Texas, SW USA
112 *H12* **Travnik** Federacija Bosna I Hercegovina, C Bosnia and Herzegovina
109 *V11* **Trbovlje** *Ger.* Trifail. C Slovenia
23 *V13* **Treasure Island** Florida, SE USA
Treasure State *see* Montana
186 *I8* **Treasury Islands** *island group* NW Solomon Islands
106 *D9* **Trebbia** *anc.* Trebia. ⁓ NW Italy
100 *N8* **Trebel** ⁓ NE Germany
103 *O16* **Trèbes** Aude, S France
Trebia *see* Trebbia
111 *F18* **Třebíč** *Ger.* Trebitsch. Vysočina, S Czech Republic
113 *I16* **Trebinje** Republika Srpska, S Bosnia and Herzegovina
111 *N20* **Trebišov** *Hung.* Tőketerebes. Košický Kraj, E Slovakia
Trebitsch *see* Třebíč
Trebizond *see* Trabzon
ZaporizhzhyaŚląskie, S Poland
Trebišnica *see* Trebišnjica
113 *H16* **Trebišnjica** *var.* Trebišnica. ⁓ S Bosnia and Herzegovina
111 *N20* **Trebišov** *Hung.* Tőketerebes. Košický Kraj, E Slovakia
Trebitsch *see* Třebíč
Trebizond *see* Trabzon
Trebnitz *see* Trzebnica
109 *V12* **Trebnje** SE Slovenia
111 *D19* **Třeboň** *Ger.* Wittingau. Jihočeský Kraj, S Czech Republic
104 *J15* **Trebujena** Andalucía, S Spain
100 *I7* **Treene** ⁓ N Germany
Tree Planters State *see* Nebraska
109 *S9* **Treffen** Kärnten, S Austria
Trefynwy *see* Monmouth
102 *G5* **Tréguier** Côtes d'Armor, NW France
61 *G18* **Treinta y Tres** Treinta y Tres, E Uruguay
61 *F18* **Treinta y Tres** ◈ *department* E Uruguay
122 *F11* **Trëkhgornyy** Chelyabinskaya, C Russian Federation
114 *F9* **Treklyanska Reka** ⁓ W Bulgaria
102 *K8* **Trélazé** Maine-et-Loire, NW France
63 *K17* **Trelew** Chubut, SE Argentina
95 *K23* **Trelleborg** *var.* Trälleborg. Skåne, S Sweden
113 *P15* **Trem** ▲ SE Serbia and Montenegro (Yugo.)
15 *N11* **Tremblant, Mont** ▲ Québec, SE Canada
99 *H17* **Tremelo** Vlaams Brabant, C Belgium
107 *M15* **Tremiti, Isole** *island group* SE Italy
30 *K12* **Tremont** Illinois, N USA
36 *L1* **Tremonton** Utah, W USA
105 *U4* **Tremp** Cataluña, NE Spain
30 *J7* **Trempealeau** Wisconsin, N USA
15 *P8* **Trenche** ⁓ Québec, SE Canada
15 *O7* **Trenche, Lac** ◎ Québec, SE Canada
111 *I20* **Trenčiansky Kraj** ◈ *region* W Slovakia
111 *I19* **Trenčín** *Ger.* Trentschin, *Hung.* Trencsén. Trenčiansky Kraj, W Slovakia
Trencsén *see* Trenčín
Trengganu *see* Terengganu
61 *A21* **Trenque Lauquen** Buenos Aires, E Argentina
14 *J14* **Trent** ⁓ Ontario, SE Canada
97 *N18* **Trent** ⁓ C England, UK
Trent *see* Trento
106 *F5* **Trentino-Alto Adige** *prev.* Venezia Tridentina. ◈ *region* N Italy
106 *G6* **Trento** *Eng.* Trent, *Ger.* Trient; anc.Tridentum. Trentino-Alto Adige, N Italy
14 *J15* **Trenton** Ontario, SE Canada
23 *V10* **Trenton** Florida, SE USA
23 *R1* **Trenton** Georgia, SE USA
31 *S10* **Trenton** Michigan, N USA
27 *S2* **Trenton** Missouri, C USA
28 *M17* **Trenton** Nebraska, C USA
18 *J15* **Trenton** *state capital* New Jersey, NE USA
21 *W10* **Trenton** North Carolina, SE USA
20 *G9* **Trenton** Tennessee, S USA
36 *L1* **Trenton** Utah, W USA
Trentschin *see* Trenčín
Treptow an der Rega *see* Trzebiatów
61 *C23* **Tres Arroyos** Buenos Aires, E Argentina
61 *J15* **Três Cachoeiras** Rio Grande do Sul, S Brazil
106 *E7* **Trescore Balneario** Lombardia, N Italy
41 *V17* **Tres Cruces, Cerro** ▲ SE Mexico
57 *K18* **Tres Cruces, Cordillera** ▲ W Bolivia
113 *N18* **Treska** ⁓ NW FYR Macedonia
113 *I14* **Treskavica** ▲ SE Bosnia and Herzegovina
59 *J20* **Três Lagoas** Mato Grosso do Sul, SW Brazil
40 *H12* **Tres Marías, Islas** *island group* C Mexico
59 *M19* **Três Marias, Represa** ⊠ SE Brazil
63 *F20* **Tres Montes, Península** *headland* S Chile
105 *O3* **Trespaderne** Castilla-León, N Spain
60 *G13* **Três Passos** Rio Grande do Sul, S Brazil
61 *A23* **Tres Picos, Cerro** ▲ E Argentina
63 *G17* **Tres Picos, Cerro** ▲ SW Argentina
60 *I12* **Três Pinheiros** Paraná, S Brazil
59 *M21* **Três Pontas** Minas Gerais, SE Brazil
Tres Puntas, Cabo *see* Manabique, Punta
60 *P9* **Três Rios** Rio de Janeiro, SE Brazil
Tres Tabernae *see* Saverne
Trestenberg/Trestendorf *see* Tășnad
41 *R15* **Tres Valles** Veracruz-Llave, SE Mexico
94 *H12* **Tretten** Oppland, S Norway
Treuburg *see* Olecko
101 *K21* **Treuchtlingen** Bayern, S Germany
100 *N13* **Treuenbrietzen** Brandenburg, E Germany
95 *F16* **Treungen** Telemark, S Norway
63 *H17* **Trevelín** Chubut, SW Argentina
Treves/Trèves *see* Trier
106 *I13* **Trevi** Umbria, C Italy
106 *E7* **Treviglio** Lombardia, N Italy
104 *J4* **Trevinca, Peña** ▲ NW Spain
105 *P3* **Treviño** Castilla-León, N Spain
106 *I7* **Treviso** *anc.* Tarvisium. Veneto, NE Italy
97 *G24* **Trevose Head** *headland* SW England, UK
Trg *see* Feldkirchen in Kärnten
183 *P17* **Triabunna** Tasmania, SE Australia
21 *W4* **Triangle** Virginia, NE USA
83 *L18* **Triangle** Masvingo, SE Zimbabwe
115 *L23* **Tría Nisía** *island* Kykládes, Greece, Aegean Sea
Triberg *see* Triberg im Schwarzwald
101 *G23* **Triberg im Schwarzwald** *var.* Triberg. Baden-Württemberg, SW Germany
153 *P11* **Tribhuvan** ✕ (Kathmandu) Central, C Nepal
54 *C9* **Tribugá, Golfo de** *gulf* W Colombia
181 *W4* **Tribulation, Cape** *headland* Queensland, NE Australia
108 *M8* **Tribulaun** ▲ SW Austria
11 *U17* **Tribune** Saskatchewan, S Canada
26 *H5* **Tribune** Kansas, C USA
107 *N18* **Tricarico** Basilicata, S Italy
107 *Q19* **Tricase** Puglia, SE Italy
Trichinopoly *see* Tiruchchirāppalli
115 *D18* **Trichonída, Límni** ◎ C Greece
155 *G22* **Trichūr** *var.* Thrissur. Kerala, SW India
Tricorno *see* Triglav
183 *O8* **Trida** New South Wales, SE Australia
35 *S1* **Trident Peak** ▲ Nevada, W USA
Tridentum/Trient *see* Trento
109 *T6* **Trieben** Steiermark, SE Austria
101 *D19* **Trier** *Eng.* Treves, *Fr.* Trèves; *anc.* Augusta Treverorum. Rheinland-Pfalz, SW Germany
106 *K7* **Trieste** *Slvn.* Trst. Friuli-Venezia Giulia, NE Italy
Trieste, Golfo di/Triest, Golf von *see* Trieste, Gulf of
106 *J8* **Trieste, Gulf of** *Cro.* Tršćanski Zaljev, *Ger.* Golf von Triest, *It.* Golfo di Trieste, *Slvn.* Tržaški Zaliv. *gulf* S Europe
109 *W4* **Triesting** ⁓ W Austria
Trifail *see* Trbovlje
116 *L9* **Trifești** Iași, NE Romania
109 *S10* **Triglav** *It.* Tricorno. ▲ NW Slovenia
104 *I14* **Trigueros** Andalucía, S Spain
115 *E16* **Tríkala** *prev.* Trikkala. Thessalía, C Greece
115 *E17* **Trikeriótis** ⁓ C Greece
Trikkala *see* Tríkala
Trikomo/Tríkomon *see* İskele
97 *F17* **Trim** *Ir.* Baile Átha Troim. E Ireland
108 *E7* **Trimbach** Solothurn, NW Switzerland
109 *Q5* **Trimmelkam** Oberösterreich, N Austria
29 *U11* **Trimont** Minnesota, N USA
Trimontium *see* Plovdiv
Trinacria *see* Sicilia
155 *K24* **Trincomalee** *var.* Trinkomali. Eastern Province, NE Sri Lanka
65 *K16* **Trindade, Ilha da** *island* Brazil, W Atlantic Ocean
47 *Y9* **Trindade Spur** *undersea feature* SW Atlantic Ocean
111 *J17* **Třinec** *Ger.* Trzynietz. Moravskoslezský Kraj, E Czech Republic
57 *M16* **Trinidad** Beni, N Bolivia
54 *H9* **Trinidad** Casanare, E Colombia
44 *E6* **Trinidad** Sancti Spíritus, C Cuba
37 *U8* **Trinidad** Colorado, C USA
61 *E19* **Trinidad** Flores, S Uruguay
45 *Y17* **Trinidad** *island* C Trinidad and Tobago
Trinidad *see* Jose Abad Santos
45 *Y16* **Trinidad and Tobago** *off.* Republic of Trinidad and Tobago. ◆ *republic* SE West Indies
63 *F22* **Trinidad, Golfo** *gulf* S Chile
61 *B24* **Trinidad, Isla** *island* E Argentina
107 *N16* **Trinitapoli** Puglia, SE Italy
55 *X10* **Trinité, Montagnes de la** ▲ C French Guiana
25 *W9* **Trinity** Texas, SW USA
13 *U12* **Trinity Bay** *inlet* Newfoundland and Labrador, E Canada
39 *P15* **Trinity Islands** *island group* Alaska, USA
35 *N2* **Trinity Mountains** ▲ California, W USA
35 *S4* **Trinity Peak** ▲ Nevada, W USA
35 *S5* **Trinity Range** ▲ Nevada, W USA
35 *N2* **Trinity River** ⁓ California, W USA
25 *V8* **Trinity River** ⁓ Texas, SW USA
Trinkomali *see* Trincomalee
173 *Y15* **Triolet** NW Mauritius
107 *O20* **Trionto, Capo** *headland* S Italy
115 *J16* **Tripití, Akrotírio** *headland* Ágios Efstrátios, E Greece
138 *G6* **Tripoli** *var.* Tarābulus, Ţarābulus ash Shām, Trâblous; *anc.* Tripolis. N Lebanon
29 *X12* **Tripoli** Iowa, C USA
Tripoli *see* Ţarābulus
115 *F20* **Trípoli** *prev.* Trípolis. Pelopónnisos, S Greece
Tripolis *see* Tripoli, Lebanon
Trípolis *see* Trípoli, Greece
29 *Q12* **Tripp** South Dakota, N USA
153 *V15* **Tripura** *var.* Hill Tippera. ◈ *state* NE India
108 *K8* **Trisanna** ⁓ W Austria
100 *H8* **Trischen** *island* NW Germany
65 *M24* **Tristan da Cunha** ◇ *dependency of Saint Helena* SE Atlantic Ocean
67 *P15* **Tristan da Cunha** *island* SE Atlantic Ocean
65 *L18* **Tristan da Cunha Fracture Zone** *tectonic feature* S Atlantic Ocean
167 *S14* **Tri Tôn** An Giang, S Vietnam
167 *W10* **Triton Island** *island* S Paracel Islands
155 *G24* **Trivandrum** *var.* Thiruvanathapuram. Kerala, SW India
111 *H20* **Trnava** *Ger.* Tyrnau, *Hung.* Nagyszombat. Trnavský Kraj, W Slovakia
111 *H20* **Trnavský Kraj** ◈ *region* W Slovakia
Trnovo *see* Veliko Tŭrnovo
Trobriand Island *see* Kiriwina Island
Trobriand Islands *see* Kiriwina Islands
11 *Q16* **Trochu** Alberta, SW Canada
109 *U7* **Trofaiach** Steiermark, SE Austria
93 *F14* **Trofors** Troms, N Norway
113 *E14* **Trogir** *It.* Traù. Split-Dalmacija, S Croatia
112 *F13* **Troglav** ▲ Bosnia and Herzegovina/Croatia
107 *M16* **Troia** Puglia, SE Italy
107 *K24* **Troina** Sicilia, Italy, C Mediterranean Sea
173 *O16* **Trois-Bassins** W Réunion
101 *E17* **Troisdorf** Nordrhein-Westfalen, W Germany
74 *H5* **Trois Fourches, Cap des** *headland* NE Morocco
15 *T8* **Trois-Pistoles** Québec, SE Canada
99 *L21* **Trois-Ponts** Liège, E Belgium
15 *P11* **Trois-Rivières** Québec, SE Canada
55 *Y12* **Trois Sauts** S French Guiana
99 *M22* **Troisvierges** Diekirch, N Luxembourg
122 *F11* **Troitsk** Chelyabinskaya Oblast', S Russian Federation
125 *T9* **Troitsko-Pechorsk** Respublika Komi, NW Russian Federation
127 *V7* **Troitskoye** Orenburgskaya Oblast', W Russian Federation
Troki *see* Trakai
94 *F9* **Trolla** ▲ S Norway
95 *J18* **Trollhättan** Västra Götaland, S Sweden
94 *G9* **Trollheimen** ▲ S Norway
94 *E9* **Trolltindan** ▲ S Norway
58 *H11* **Trombetas, Rio** ⁓ NE Brazil
130 *L16* **Tromelin, Île** *island* N Réunion
92 *I9* **Troms** ◈ *county* N Norway
92 *I9* **Tromsø** *Fin.* Tromssa. Troms, N Norway
84 *F5* **Tromsøflaket** *undersea feature* W Barents Sea
Tromssa *see* Tromsø
94 *H10* **Tron** ▲ S Norway
35 *U12* **Trona** California, W USA
63 *G16* **Tronador, Cerro** ▲ S Chile
94 *H8* **Trondheim** *Ger.* Drontheim; *prev.* Nidaros, Trondhjem. Sør-Trøndelag, S Norway
94 *H7* **Trondheimsfjorden** *fjord* S Norway
Trondhjem *see* Trondheim
107 *J14* **Tronto** ⁓ C Italy
Troodos *see* Ólympos
121 *P3* **Troódos** *var.* Troodos Mountains. ▲ C Cyprus
Troodos Mountains *see* Troódos
96 *I13* **Troon** W Scotland, UK
107 *M22* **Tropea** Calabria, SW Italy
36 *L7* **Tropic** Utah, W USA
64 *L10* **Tropic Seamount** *var.* Banc du Tropique. *undersea feature* E Atlantic Ocean
Tropique, Banc du *see* Tropic Seamount
Tropoja *see* Tropojë
113 *L17* **Tropojë** *var.* Tropoja. Kukës, N Albania
Troppau *see* Opava
95 *O16* **Trosa** Södermanland, C Sweden
118 *H12* **Troškūnai** Utena, E Lithuania
101 *G23* **Trossingen** Baden-Württemberg, SW Germany
117 *T4* **Trostyanets'** *Rus.* Trostyanets. Sums'ka Oblast', NE Ukraine
117 *N7* **Trostyanets'** *Rus.* Trostyanets. Vinnyts'ka Oblast', C Ukraine
116 *L11* **Trotuş** ⁓ E Romania
44 *M8* **Trou-du-Nord** N Haiti
25 *W7* **Troup** Texas, SW USA
8 *I10* **Trout** ⁓ Northwest Territories, NW Canada
33 *N8* **Trout Creek** Montana, NW USA
32 *H10* **Trout Lake** Washington, NW USA
12 *B9* **Trout Lake** ◎ Ontario, S Canada
33 *T12* **Trout Peak** ▲ Wyoming, C USA
102 *L4* **Trouville** Calvados, N France
97 *L22* **Trowbridge** S England, UK
23 *Q6* **Troy** Alabama, S USA
27 *Q3* **Troy** Kansas, C USA
27 *W4* **Troy** Missouri, C USA
18 *L10* **Troy** New York, NE USA
21 *S10* **Troy** North Carolina, SE USA
31 *R13* **Troy** Ohio, N USA
25 *T9* **Troy** Texas, SW USA
114 *I9* **Troyan** Lovech, N Bulgaria
114 *I9* **Troyanski Prokhod** *pass* N Bulgaria
145 *N6* **Troyebratskiy** Severnyy Kazakhstan, N Kazakhstan
103 *Q6* **Troyes** *anc.* Augustobona Tricassium. Aube, N France
117 *X5* **Troyits'ke** Luhans'ka Oblast', E Ukraine
35 *W7* **Troy Peak** ▲ Nevada, W USA
113 *G15* **Trpanj** Dubrovnik-Neretva, S Croatia
Tršćanski Zaljev *see* Trieste, Gulf of
Trst *see* Trieste
113 *N14* **Trstenik** Serbia, C Serbia and Montenegro (Yugo.)
126 *I6* **Trubchevsk** Bryanskaya Oblast', W Russian Federation
Trubchular *see* Orlyak
37 *S10* **Truchas Peak** ▲ New Mexico, SW USA
143 *P16* **Trucial Coast** *physical region* C UAE
Trucial States *see* United Arab Emirates
35 *Q6* **Truckee** California, W USA
35 *R5* **Truckee River** ⁓ Nevada, W USA
127 *Q13* **Trudfront** Astrakhanskaya Oblast', SW Russian Federation
14 *I9* **Truite, Lac à la** ◎ Québec, SE Canada
42 *K4* **Trujillo** Colón, NE Honduras
56 *C12* **Trujillo** La Libertad, NW Peru
104 *K10* **Trujillo** Extremadura, W Spain
54 *I6* **Trujillo** Trujillo, NW Venezuela
54 *I6* **Trujillo** *off.* Estado Trujillo. ◈ *state* W Venezuela
Truk *see* Chuuk
Truk Islands *see* Chuuk Islands
29 *U10* **Truman** Minnesota, N USA
27 *X10* **Trumann** Arkansas, C USA
36 *J9* **Trumbull, Mount** ▲ Arizona, SW USA
114 *F9* **Trŭn** Pernik, W Bulgaria
183 *Q8* **Trundle** New South Wales, SE Australia
131 *U13* **Trung Phân** *physical region* S Vietnam
Trupcilar *see* Orlyak
13 *Q15* **Truro** Nova Scotia, SE Canada
97 *H25* **Truro** SW England, UK
25 *P5* **Truscott** Texas, SW USA
116 *K9* **Trușeşti** Botoșani, NE Romania
116 *H6* **Truskavets'** L'vivs'ka Oblast', W Ukraine
95 *H22* **Trustrup** Århus, C Denmark
10 *M11* **Trutch** British Columbia, W Canada
37 *Q14* **Truth Or Consequences** New Mexico, SW USA
111 *F15* **Trutnov** *Ger.* Trautenau. Královéhradecký Kraj, NE Czech Republic
103 *P13* **Truyère** ⁓ C France
114 *K9* **Tryavna** Lovech, N Bulgaria
28 *M14* **Tryon** Nebraska, C USA
94 *I11* **Trysilelva** ⁓ S Norway
112 *D10* **Tržac** Federacija Bosna I Hercegovina, NW Bosnia and Herzegovina
Tržaški Zaliv *see* Trieste, Gulf of
110 *G10* **Trzcianka** *Ger.* Schönlanke. Piła, Wielkopolskie, C Poland
110 *E7* **Trzebiatów** *Ger.* Treptow an der Rega. Zachodnio-pomorskie, NW Poland
111 *G14* **Trzebnica** *Ger.* Trebnitz. Dolnośląskie, SW Poland
109 *T10* **Tržič** *Ger.* Neumarktl. NW Slovenia
Trzynietz *see* Třinec
Tsabong *see* Tshabong
162 *G7* **Tsagaanchuluut** Dzavhan, C Mongolia
163 *P7* **Tsagaanders** Dornod, NE Mongolia
163 *S8* **Tsagaannuur** Dornod, E Mongolia
162 *G8* **Tsagaan-Olom** Govĭ-Altay, C Mongolia
162 *J8* **Tsagaan-Ovoo** Övörhangay, C Mongolia
162 *D5* **Tsagaantüngi** Bayan-Ölgiy, NW Mongolia
127 *P12* **Tsagan Aman** Respublika Kalmykiya, SW Russian Federation
23 *V11* **Tsala Apopka Lake** ◎ Florida, SE USA
Tsamkong *see* Zhanjiang
Tsangpo *see* Brahmaputra
162 *L9* **Tsant** Dundgovĭ, C Mongolia
83 *G17* **Tsao** Ngamiland, NW Botswana
172 *I4* **Tsaratanana** Mahajanga, C Madagascar
114 *N10* **Tsarevo** *prev.* Michurin. Burgas, E Bulgaria
Tsarigrad *see* İstanbul
Tsaritsyn *see* Volgograd
124 *G13* **Tsarskoye Selo** *prev.* Pushkin. Leningradskaya Oblast', NW Russian Federation
117 *T7* **Tsarychanka** Dnipropetrovs'ka Oblast', E Ukraine
83 *H21* **Tsatsu** Southern, S Botswana
81 *J20* **Tsavo** Coast, S Kenya
83 *E21* **Tsawisis** Karas, S Namibia
Tschakathurn *see* Čakovec
Tschaslau *see* Čáslav
Tschenstochau *see* Częstochowa
Tschernembl *see* Črnomelj
28 *K6* **Tschida, Lake** ⊠ North Dakota, N USA
Tschorna *see* Mustvee
83 *I17* **Tsebanana** Central, NE Botswana
Tsefat *see* Ẕefat
162 *G8* **Tseel** Govĭ-Altay, SW Mongolia
126 *M13* **Tselina** Rostovskaya Oblast', SW Russian Federation
Tselinograd *see* Astana
Tselinogradskaya Oblast' *see* Akmola
162 *J6* **Tsengel** Hövsgöl, N Mongolia
162 *E7* **Tsenher** Hovd, W Mongolia
Tsentral'nyye Nizmennyye Garagumy *see* Merkezi Garagumy
83 *E21* **Tses** Karas, S Namibia
Tseshevlya *see* Tsyeshawlya
162 *E7* **Tsetsegnuur** Hovd, W Mongolia
Tsetsen Khan *see* Öndörhaan
162 *J7* **Tsetserleg** Arhangay, C Mongolia
77 *R16* **Tsévié** S Togo
83 *G21* **Tshabong** *var.* Tsabong. Kgalagadi, SW Botswana
83 *G20* **Tshane** Kgalagadi, SW Botswana
Tshangalele, Lac *see* Lufira, Lac de Retenue de la
83 *H17* **Tshauxaba** Central, C Botswana
79 *F21* **Tshela** Bas-Congo, W Dem. Rep. Congo
79 *K22* **Tshibala** Kasai Occidental, S Dem. Rep. Congo
79 *J22* **Tshikapa** Kasai Occidental, SW Dem. Rep. Congo
79 *L22* **Tshilenge** Kasai Oriental, S Dem. Rep. Congo
79 *L24* **Tshimbalanga** Katanga, S Dem. Rep. Congo
79 *L22* **Tshimbulu** Kasai Occidental, S Dem. Rep. Congo
Tshiumbe *see* Chiumbe
79 *M21* **Tshofa** Kasai Oriental, C Dem. Rep. Congo
79 *K18* **Tshuapa** ⁓ C Dem. Rep. Congo
Tshwane *see* Pretoria
114 *G7* **Tsibritsa** ⁓ NW Bulgaria
Tsien Tang *see* Puyang Jiang
114 *I12* **Tsigansko Gradishte** ▲ Bulgaria/Greece
8 *H7* **Tsiigehtchic** *prev.* Arctic Red River. Northwest Territories, NW Canada
127 *Q7* **Tsil'ma** ⁓ NW Russian Federation
119 *J17* **Tsimkavichy** *Rus.* Timkovichi. Minskaya Voblasts', C Belarus
126 *M11* **Tsimlyansk** Rostovskaya Oblast', SW Russian Federation
127 *N11* **Tsimlyanskoye Vodokhranilishche** *var.* Tsimlyansk Vodoskhovshche, *Eng.* Tsimlyansk Reservoir ⊠ SW Russian Federation
Tsimlyansk Reservoir *see* Tsimlyanskoye Vodokhranilishche
Tsimlyansk Vodoskhovshche *see* Tsimlyanskoye Vodokhranilishche
Tsinan *see* Jinan
Tsing Hai *see* Qinghai Hu, China
Tsinghai *see* Qinghai, China
Tsingtao/Tsingtau *see* Qingdao
Tsingyuan *see* Baoding
Tsinkiang *see* Quanzhou
Tsintao *see* Qingdao
83 *D17* **Tsintsabis** Otjikoto, N Namibia
172 *H8* **Tsiombe** *var.* Tsihombe. Toliara, S Madagascar
123 *O13* **Tsipa** ⁓ S Russian Federation
172 *H5* **Tsiribihina** ⁓ W Madagascar
172 *I5* **Tsiroanomandidy** Antananarivo, C Madagascar
189 *U13* **Tsis** *island* Chuuk, C Micronesia
Tsitsihar *see* Qiqihar
127 *Q3* **Tsivil'sk** Chuvashskaya Respublika, W Russian Federation
137 *T9* **Ts'khinvali** *prev.* Staliniri. C Georgia
119 *J19* **Tsna** ⁓ SW Belarus
126 *I15* **Tsna** *var.* Zna. ⁓ W Russian Federation
162 *K11* **Tsoohor** Ömnögovĭ, S Mongolia
164 *K14* **Tsu** *var.* Tu. Mie, Honshū, SW Japan
165 *O10* **Tsubame** *var.* Tubame. Niigata, Honshū, C Japan
165 *V3* **Tsubetsu** Hokkaidō, NE Japan
165 *O13* **Tsuchiura** *var.* Tutiura. Ibaraki, Honshū, S Japan
165 *Q6* **Tsugaru-kaikyō** *strait* N Japan
164 *E14* **Tsukumi** *var.* Tukumi. Ōita, Kyūshū, SW Japan
162 *E5* **Tsul-Ulaan** Bayan-Ölgiy, W Mongolia
83 *D17* **Tsumeb** Otjikoto, N Namibia
83 *F17* **Tsumkwe** Otjozondjupa, NE Namibia
164 *D15* **Tsuno** Miyazaki, Kyūshū, SW Japan
164 *D12* **Tsuno-shima** *island* SW Japan
164 *K12* **Tsuruga** *var.* Turuga. Fukui, Honshū, SW Japan
164 *H12* **Tsurugi-san** ▲ Shikoku, SW Japan
165 *P9* **Tsuruoka** *var.* Turuoka. Yamagata, Honshū, C Japan
164 *C12* **Tsushima** *var.* Tsushima-tō, Tusima. *island group* SW Japan
Tsushima-tō *see* Tsushima
164 *H12* **Tsuyama** *var.* Tuyama. Okayama, Honshū, SW Japan
83 *G19* **Tswaane** Ghanzi, W Botswana
119 *N16* **Tsyakhtsin** *Rus.* Tekhtin. Mahilyowskaya Voblasts', E Belarus
119 *P19* **Tsyerakhowka** *Rus.* Terekhovka. Homyel'skaya Voblasts', SE Belarus
119 *I17* **Tsyeshawlya** *Rus.* Cheshevlya, Tseshevlya. Brestskaya Voblasts', SW Belarus
Tsyurupinsk *see* Tsyurupyns'k
117 *R10* **Tsyurupyns'k** *Rus.* Tsyurupinsk. Khersons'ka Oblast', S Ukraine
Tu *see* Tsu
186 *C7* **Tua** ⁓ C PNG
Tuaim *see* Tuam
184 *L6* **Tuakau** Waikato, North Island, NZ
97 *C17* **Tuam** *Ir.* Tuaim. W Ireland
185 *K14* **Tuamarina** Marlborough, South Island, NZ
Tuamotu, Archipel des *see* Tuamotu, Îles
193 *Q9* **Tuamotu Fracture Zone** *tectonic feature* E Pacific Ocean
191 *W9* **Tuamotu, Îles** *var.* Archipel des Tuamotu, Dangerous Archipelago, Tuamotu Islands. *island group* N French Polynesia
Tuamotu Islands *see* Tuamotu, Îles
175 *X10* **Tuamotu Ridge** *undersea feature* C Pacific Ocean
167 *R5* **Tuân Giao** Lai Châu, N Vietnam
171 *O2* **Tuao** Luzon, N Philippines
190 *B15* **Tuapa** NW Niue
43 *N7* **Tuapí** Región Autónoma Atlántico Norte, NE Nicaragua
126 *K15* **Tuapse** Krasnodarskiy Kray, SW Russian Federation
169 *U6* **Tuaran** Sabah, East Malaysia
104 *I6* **Tua, Rio** ⁓ N Portugal
192 *H15* **Tuasivi** Savai'i, C Samoa
185 *B24* **Tuatapere** Southland, South Island, NZ
36 *M9* **Tuba City** Arizona, SW USA
138 *H11* **Ţūbah, Qaşr aţ** *castle* Ma'ān, C Jordan
Tubame *see* Tsubame
169 *R16* **Tuban** *prev.* Toeban. Jawa, C Indonesia
141 *O16* **Tuban, Wādī** *dry watercourse* SW Yemen
61 *K14* **Tubarão** Santa Catarina, S Brazil
98 *O10* **Tubbergen** Overijssel, E Netherlands
Tubeke *see* Tubize
101 *H22* **Tübingen** *var.* Tuebingen. Baden-Württemberg, SW Germany
127 *W6* **Tubinskiy** Respublika Bashkortostan, W Russian Federation
99 *G19* **Tubize** *Dut.* Tubeke. Wallon Brabant, C Belgium
76 *J16* **Tubmanburg** NW Liberia
75 *T7* **Ţubruq** *Eng.* Tobruk, *It.* Tobruch. NE Libya
191 *T13* **Tubuai** *island* Îles Australes, SW French Polynesia
Tubuai, Îles/Tubuai Islands *see* Australes, Îles
40 *F3* **Tubutama** Sonora, NW Mexico
54 *K4* **Tucacas** Falcón, N Venezuela
59 *P16* **Tucano** Bahia, E Brazil
57 *P19* **Tucavaca, Río** ⁓ E Bolivia
110 *H8* **Tuchola** Kujawsko-pomorskie, C Poland
111 *M17* **Tuchów** Małopolskie, SE Poland
23 *S3* **Tucker** Georgia, SE USA
27 *W10* **Tuckerman** Arkansas, C USA
64 *B12* **Tucker's Town** E Bermuda
Tuckum *see* Tukums
36 *M15* **Tucson** Arizona, SW USA
62 *J7* **Tucumán** *off.* Provincia de Tucumán. ◈ *province* N Argentina
Tucumán *see* San Miguel de Tucumán
37 *V11* **Tucumcari** New Mexico, SW USA
58 *H13* **Tucunaré** Pará, N Brazil
55 *Q6* **Tucupita** Delta Amacuro, NE Venezuela

◆ Country ● Country Capital ◇ Dependent Territory ○ Dependent Territory Capital ◈ Administrative Region ✕ International Airport ▲ Mountain ▲ Mountain Range ⁂ Volcano ⁓ River ◎ Lake ⊠ Reservoir

58 K13 **Tucuruí, Represa de** ⊠ NE Brazil
110 F9 **Tuczno** Zachodnio-pomorskie, NW Poland
Tuddo *see* Tudu
105 Q5 **Tudela** *Basq.* Tutera; *anc.* Tutela. Navarra, N Spain
104 M6 **Tudela de Duero** Castilla-León, N Spain
138 K6 **Tudmur** *var.* Tadmur, Tamar, *Gk.* Palmyra; *Bibl.* Tadmor. Ḩimş, C Syria
118 J4 **Tudu** *Ger.* Tuddo. Lääne-Virumaa, NE Estonia
Tuebingen *see* Tübingen
122 J14 **Tuekta** Respublika Altay, S Russian Federation
104 I5 **Tuela, Rio** ≈ N Portugal
153 X12 **Tuensang** Nāgāland, NE India
136 L15 **Tufanbeyli** Adana, C Turkey
Tüffer *see* Laško
186 F9 **Tufi** Northern, S PNG
193 O3 **Tufts Plain** *undersea feature* N Pacific Ocean
Tugalan *see* Kolkhozobod
67 V14 **Tugela** ≈ SE South Africa
21 P6 **Tug Fork** ≈ S USA
39 P15 **Tugidak Island** *island* Trinity Islands, Alaska, USA
171 O2 **Tuguegarao** Luzon, N Philippines
123 S12 **Tugur** Khabarovskiy Kray, SE Russian Federation
161 P4 **Tuhai He** ≈ E China
104 G4 **Tui** Galicia, NW Spain
77 O13 **Tui** *var.* Grand Balé. ≈ W Burkina
57 J16 **Tuichi, Río** ≈ W Bolivia
64 Q11 **Tuineje** Fuerteventura, Islas Canarias, Spain, NE Atlantic Ocean
43 X16 **Tuira, Río** ≈ SE Panama
Tuisarkan *see* Tūysarkān
Tujiabu *see* Yongxiu
127 W5 **Tukan** Respublika Bashkortostan, W Russian Federation
171 P14 **Tukangbesi, Kepulauan** *Dut.* Toekang Besi Eilanden. *island group* C Indonesia
147 V13 **Tŭkhtamish** *Rus.* Toktomush, *prev.* Tokhtamyshbek. SE Tajikistan
184 O12 **Tukituki** ≈ North Island, NZ
Tu-k'ou *see* Panzhihua
121 P12 **Tūkrah** NE Libya
8 H6 **Tuktoyaktuk** Northwest Territories, NW Canada
168 I9 **Tuktuk** Pulau Samosir, W Indonesia
Tukumi *see* Tsukumi
118 E9 **Tukums** *Ger.* Tuckum. Tukums, W Latvia
81 G24 **Tukuyu** *prev.* Neu-Langenburg. Mbeya, S Tanzania
Tukzār *see* Tokzār
41 O13 **Tula** *var.* Tula de Allende. Hidalgo, C Mexico
41 O11 **Tula** Tamaulipas, C Mexico
126 K5 **Tula** Tul'skaya Oblast', W Russian Federation
Tulach Mhór *see* Tullamore
Tula de Allende *see* Tula
159 N10 **Tulage Ar Gol** ≈ W China
186 M9 **Tulaghi** *var.* Tulagi. Florida Islands, C Solomon Islands
Tulagi *see* Tulaghi
41 P13 **Tulancingo** Hidalgo, C Mexico
35 R11 **Tulare** California, W USA
29 P9 **Tulare** South Dakota, N USA
35 Q12 **Tulare Lake Bed** *salt flat* California, W USA
37 S14 **Tularosa** New Mexico, SW USA
37 P13 **Tularosa Mountains** ▲ New Mexico, SW USA
37 S15 **Tularosa Valley** *basin* New Mexico, SW USA
83 E25 **Tulbagh** Western Cape, SW South Africa
56 C5 **Tulcán** Carchi, N Ecuador
117 N13 **Tulcea** Tulcea, E Romania
117 N13 **Tulcea** ◆ *county* SE Romania
Tul'chin *see* Tul'chyn
117 N7 **Tul'chyn** *Rus.* Tul'chin. Vinnyts'ka Oblast', C Ukraine
Tuléar *see* Toliara
35 O1 **Tulelake** California, W USA
116 J10 **Tulgheş** *Hung.* Gyergyótölgyes. Harghita, C Romania
Tul'govichi *see* Tul'havichy
119 N20 **Tul'havichy** *Rus.* Tul'govichi. Homyel'skaya Voblasts', SE Belarus
Tuli *see* Thuli
25 N4 **Tulia** Texas, SW USA
8 I9 **Tulita** *prev.* Fort Norman, Norman. Northwest Territories, NW Canada
20 J10 **Tullahoma** Tennessee, S USA
183 N12 **Tullamarine** ✕ (Melbourne) Victoria, SE Australia
183 Q7 **Tullamore** New South Wales, SE Australia
97 E18 **Tullamore** *Ir.* Tulach Mhór. C Ireland
103 N12 **Tulle** *anc.* Tutela. Corrèze, C France
109 X3 **Tulln** *var.* Oberhollabrunn. Niederösterreich, NE Austria
109 W4 **Tulln** ≈ NE Austria
22 H6 **Tullos** Louisiana, S USA
97 F19 **Tullow** *Ir.* An Tullach. SE Ireland
181 W5 **Tully** Queensland, NE Australia
126 J3 **Tuloma** ≈ NW Russian Federation
114 K10 **Tulovo** Stara Zagora, C Bulgaria
27 P9 **Tulsa** Oklahoma, C USA
153 N11 **Tulsipur** Mid Western, W Nepal
126 K6 **Tul'skaya Oblast'** ◆ *province* W Russian Federation
126 L14 **Tul'skiy** Respublika Adygeya, SW Russian Federation
186 E5 **Tulu** Manus Island, N PNG
54 D10 **Tuluá** Valle del Cauca, W Colombia
116 M12 **Tulucești** Galați, E Romania
39 N12 **Tuluksak** Alaska, USA
41 Z12 **Tulum, Ruinas de** *ruins* Quintana Roo, SE Mexico
122 M13 **Tulun** Irkutskaya Oblast', S Russian Federation
169 R17 **Tulungagung** *prev.* Toeloengagoeng. Jawa, C Indonesia
186 J6 **Tulun Islands** *var.* Kilinailau Islands; *prev.* Carteret Islands. *island group* NE PNG
126 M4 **Tuma** Ryazanskaya Oblast', W Russian Federation
54 B12 **Tumaco** Nariño, SW Colombia
54 B12 **Tumaco, Bahía de** *bay* SW Colombia
Tuman-gang *see* Tumen
42 L8 **Tuma, Río** ≈ N Nicaragua
95 O16 **Tumba** Stockholm, C Sweden
Tumba, Lac *see* Ntomba, Lac
169 S12 **Tumbangsenamang** Borneo, C Indonesia
183 Q10 **Tumbarumba** New South Wales, SE Australia
56 A8 **Tumbes** Tumbes, NW Peru
56 A9 **Tumbes** *off.* Departamento de Tumbes. ◆ *department* NW Peru
19 P5 **Tumbledown Mountain** ▲ Maine, NE USA
11 N13 **Tumbler Ridge** British Columbia, W Canada
167 Q12 **Tumbŏt, Phnum** ▲ W Cambodia
182 G9 **Tumby Bay** South Australia
163 Y10 **Tumen** Jilin, NE China
163 Y11 **Tumen** *Chin.* Tumen Jiang, *Kor.* Tuman-gang, *Rus.* Tumyn'tszyan. ≈ E Asia
Tumen Jiang *see* Tumen
55 Q8 **Tumeremo** Bolívar, E Venezuela
155 G19 **Tumkūr** Karnātaka, W India
96 I10 **Tummel** ≈ C Scotland, UK
188 B15 **Tumon Bay** *bay* W Guam
77 P14 **Tumu** NW Ghana
58 I10 **Tumuc Humac Mountains** *var.* Serra Tumucumaque. ▲ N South America
Tumucumaque, Serra *see* Tumuc Humac Mountains
183 Q10 **Tumut** New South Wales, SE Australia
Tumyn'tszyan *see* Tumen
Tün *see* Ferdows
45 U14 **Tunapuna** Trinidad, Trinidad and Tobago
60 K11 **Tunas** Paraná, S Brazil
Tunbridge Wells *see* Royal Tunbridge Wells
114 L11 **Tunca Nehri** *Bul.* Tundzha. ≈ Bulgaria/Turkey ***see also*** Tundzha
137 O14 **Tunceli** *var.* Kalan. Tunceli, E Turkey
137 O14 **Tunceli** ◆ *province* C Turkey
152 J12 **Tūndla** Uttar Pradesh, N India
81 I25 **Tunduru** Ruvuma, S Tanzania
114 L10 **Tundzha** *Turk.* Tunca Nehri. ≈ Bulgaria/Turkey ***see also*** Tunca Nehri
155 H17 **Tungabhadra** ≈ S India
155 F17 **Tungabhadra Reservoir** ⊠ S India
191 P2 **Tungaru** *prev.* Gilbert Islands. *island group* W Kiribati
171 P7 **Tungawan** Mindanao, S Philippines
Tungdor *see* Mainling
T'ung-shan *see* Xuzhou
161 Q16 **Tungsha Tao** *Chin.* Dongsha Qundao, *Eng.* Pratas Island. *island* S Taiwan
161 S13 **Tungshih** *Jap.* Tōsei. N Taiwan
8 H9 **Tungsten** Northwest Territories, W Canada
Tung-t'ing Hu *see* Dongting Hu
56 A13 **Tungurahua** ◆ *province* C Ecuador
95 F14 **Tunhovdfjorden** ⊠ S Norway
22 K2 **Tunica** Mississippi, S USA
75 N5 **Tunis** *var.* Tūnis. ● (Tunisia) NE Tunisia
75 N5 **Tunis, Golfe de** *Ar.* Khalīj Tūnis. *gulf* NE Tunisia
75 N6 **Tunisia** *off.* Republic of Tunisia, *Ar.* Al Jumhūrīyah at Tūnisīyah, *Fr.* République Tunisienne. ◆ *republic* N Africa
Tūnisīyah, Al Jumhūrīyah at *see* Tunisia
Tūnis, Khalīj *see* Tunis, Golfe de
54 G9 **Tunja** Boyacá, C Colombia
93 F14 **Tunnsjøen** *Lapp.* Dātnejaevrie. ⊚ C Norway
39 N12 **Tuntutuliak** Alaska, USA
147 U8 **Tunuk** Chuyskaya Oblast', C Kyrgyzstan
13 Q6 **Tunungayualok Island** *island* Newfoundland and Labrador, E Canada
62 H11 **Tunuyán** Mendoza, W Argentina
197 P14 **Tunu** ◆ *province* E Greenland
62 I11 **Tunuyán, Río** ≈ W Argentina
Tunxi *see* Huangshan
Tuodian *see* Shuangbai
Tuoji *see* Zhongba
35 P9 **Tuolumne River** ≈ California, W USA
Tương Buong *see* Tương Đương
167 R7 **Tương Đương** *var.* Tuong Buong. Nghê An, N Vietnam
160 I13 **Tuoniang Jiang** ≈ S China
Tuotuo He *see* Togton He
Tuotuoheyan *see* Tanggulashan
Tüp *see* Tyup
60 J9 **Tupã** São Paulo, S Brazil
191 S10 **Tupai** *var.* Motu Iti. *atoll* Îles Sous le Vent, W French Polynesia
61 G15 **Tupanciretã** Rio Grande do Sul, S Brazil
22 M2 **Tupelo** Mississippi, S USA
59 K18 **Tupiraçaba** Goiás, S Brazil
57 L21 **Tupiza** Potosí, S Bolivia
11 N13 **Tupper** British Columbia, W Canada
18 J8 **Tupper Lake** ⊚ New York, NE USA
146 J10 **Tuproqqal'a** *Rus.* Turpakkla. Xorazm Viloyati, W Uzbekistan
62 H11 **Tupungato, Volcán** ▲ W Argentina
163 T9 **Tuquan** Nei Mongol Zizhiqu, N China
54 C13 **Túquerres** Nariño, SW Colombia
153 U13 **Tura** Meghālaya, NE India
122 M10 **Tura** Evenkiyskiy Avtonomnyy Okrug, N Russian Federation
122 G10 **Tura** ≈ C Russian Federation
140 M10 **Turabah** Makkah, W Saudi Arabia
55 O8 **Turagua, Cerro** ▲ C Venezuela
184 L12 **Turakina** Manawatu-Wanganui, North Island, NZ
185 K15 **Turakirae Head** *headland* North Island, NZ
186 B8 **Turama** ≈ S PNG
122 K13 **Turan** Respublika Tyva, S Russian Federation
184 M10 **Turangi** Waikato, North Island, NZ
146 F11 **Turan Lowland** *var.* Turan Plain, *Kaz.* Turan Oypaty, *Rus.* Turanskaya Nizmennost', *Turk.* Turan Pesligi, *Uzb.* Turon Pasttekisligi. *plain* C Asia
Turan Oypaty/Turan Pesligi/Turan Plain/Turanskaya Nizmennost' *see* Turan Lowland
138 K7 **Ţurāq al 'Ilab** *hill range* S Syria
119 K20 **Turaw** *Rus.* Turov. Homyel'skaya Voblasts', SE Belarus
140 L2 **Ţurayf** Al Ḩudūd ash Shamālīyah, NW Saudi Arabia
Turba *see* Teruel
54 E5 **Turbaco** Bolívar, N Colombia
148 K15 **Turbat** Baluchistān, SW Pakistan
Turbat-i-Haidari *see* Torbat-e Ḩeydarīyeh
Turbat-i-Jam *see* Torbat-e Jām
54 D7 **Turbo** Antioquia, NW Colombia
Turčianský Svätý Martin *see* Martin
116 H10 **Turda** *Ger.* Thorenburg, *Hung.* Torda. Cluj, NW Romania
142 M7 **Ţureh** Markazī, W Iran
191 X12 **Tureia** *atoll* Îles Tuamotu, SE French Polynesia
110 I12 **Turek** Wielkopolskie, C Poland
93 L19 **Turenki** Etelä-Suomi, S Finland
Turfan *see* Turpan
145 R8 **Turgay** *Kaz.* Torghay. Akmola, W Kazakhstan
145 N10 **Turgay** *Kaz.* Torgay. ≈ C Kazakhstan
144 M8 **Turgayskaya Stolovaya Strana** *Kaz.* Torgay Üstirti. *plateau* Kazakhstan/Russian Federation
Turgel *see* Türi
114 L8 **Türgovishte** *prev.* Eski Dzhumaya. Türgovishte, N Bulgaria
114 L8 **Türgovishte** ◆ *province* N Bulgaria
136 C14 **Turgutlu** Manisa, W Turkey
136 L12 **Turhal** Tokat, N Turkey
118 H4 **Türi** *Ger.* Turgel. Järvamaa, N Estonia
105 S9 **Turia** ≈ E Spain
58 M12 **Turiaçu** Maranhão, E Brazil
Turin *see* Torino
116 I3 **Turiys'k** Volyns'ka Oblast', NW Ukraine
Turja *see* Tur"ya
116 H6 **Turka** L'vivs'ka Oblast', W Ukraine
81 H16 **Turkana, Lake** *var.* Lake Rudolf. ⊚ N Kenya
145 P16 **Turkestan** *Kaz.* Türkistan. Yuzhnyy Kazakhstan, S Kazakhstan
147 Q12 **Turkestan Range** *Rus.* Turkestanskiy Khrebet. ▲ C Asia
Turkestanskiy Khrebet *see* Turkestan Range
111 M23 **Túrkeve** Jász-Nagykun-Szolnok, E Hungary
25 O4 **Turkey** Texas, SW USA
136 H14 **Turkey** *off.* Republic of Turkey, *Turk.* Türkiye Cumhuriyeti. ◆ *republic* SW Asia
181 N4 **Turkey Creek** Western Australia
26 M9 **Turkey Creek** ≈ Oklahoma, C USA
37 T9 **Turkey Mountains** ▲ New Mexico, SW USA
29 X11 **Turkey River** ≈ Iowa, C USA
127 N7 **Turki** Saratovskaya Oblast', W Russian Federation
121 O1 **Turkish Republic of Northern Cyprus** ◇ *disputed territory* Cyprus
Türkistan *see* Turkestan
Türkistan, Bandi-i *see* Torkestān, Selseleh-ye Band-e
Türkiye Cumhuriyeti *see* Turkey
146 K12 **Türkmenabat** *prev. Rus.* Chardzhev, Chardzhou, Chardzhui, Lenin-Turkmenski, *Turkm.* Chärjew. Lebap Welaýaty, E Turkmenistan
146 A11 **Türkmen Aylagy** *Rus.* Turkmenskiy Zaliv. *lake gulf* W Turkmenistan
Turkmenbashi *see* Türkmenbaşy
146 A10 **Türkmenbaşy** *Rus.* Turkmenbashi; *prev.* Krasnovodsk. Balkan Welaýaty, W Turkmenistan
146 A10 **Türkmenbaşy Aylagy** *prev. Rus.* Krasnovodskiy Zaliv, *Turkm.* Krasnowodsk Aylagy. *lake gulf* W Turkmenistan
146 J14 **Türkmengala** *Rus.* Turkmen-kala; *prev.* Turkmen-Kala. Mary Welaýaty, S Turkmenistan
146 G13 **Turkmenistan** *off.* Turkmenistan; *prev.* Turkmenskaya Soviet Socialist Republic. ◆ *republic* C Asia
Turkmen-kala/Turkmen-Kala *see* Türkmengala
Turkmenskaya Soviet Socialist Republic *see* Turkmenistan
Turkmenskiy Zaliv *see* Türkmen Aylagy
136 L16 **Türkoğlu** Kahramanmaraş, S Turkey
44 L6 **Turks and Caicos Islands** ◇ *UK dependent territory* N West Indies
64 G10 **Turks and Caicos Islands** *island group* N West Indies
45 N6 **Turks Islands** *island group* SE Turks and Caicos Islands
93 K19 **Turku** *Swe.* Åbo. Länsi-Suomi, W Finland
81 H17 **Turkwel** *seasonal river* NW Kenya
27 P9 **Turley** Oklahoma, C USA
35 P9 **Turlock** California, W USA
118 I12 **Turmantas** Utena, NE Lithuania
54 L5 **Turmero** Aragua, N Venezuela
Turmberg *see* Wieżyca
184 N13 **Turnagain, Cape** *headland* North Island, NZ
Turnau *see* Turnov
42 H2 **Turneffe Islands** *island group* E Belize
18 M11 **Turners Falls** Massachusetts, NE USA
11 P16 **Turner Valley** Alberta, SW Canada
99 I16 **Turnhout** Antwerpen, N Belgium
109 V5 **Turnitz** Niederösterreich, E Austria
11 S12 **Turnor Lake** ⊚ Saskatchewan, C Canada
111 E15 **Turnov** *Ger.* Turnau. Liberecký Kraj, N Czech Republic
Tŭrnovo *see* Veliko Tŭrnovo
116 I15 **Turnu Măgurele** *var.* Turnu-Măgurele. Teleorman, S Romania
Turnu Severin *see* Drobeta-Turnu Severin
Turócszentmárton *see* Martin
Turoni *see* Tours
Turon Pasttekisligi *see* Turan Lowland
Turov *see* Turaw
Turpakkla *see* Tuproqqal'a
158 M6 **Turpan** *var.* Turfan. Xinjiang Uygur Zizhiqu, NW China
Turpan Depression *see* Turpan Pendi
158 M6 **Turpan Pendi** *Eng.* Turpan Depression. *depression* NW China
158 M5 **Turpan Zhan** Xinjiang Uygur Zizhiqu, W China
Turpentine State *see* North Carolina
44 F8 **Turquino, Pico** ▲ E Cuba
27 Y10 **Turrell** Arkansas, C USA
43 N14 **Turrialba** Cartago, E Costa Rica
96 K8 **Turriff** NE Scotland, UK
139 V7 **Tursāq** E Iraq
Turshiz *see* Kāshmar
Tursunzade *see* Tursunzoda
147 P13 **Tursunzoda** *Rus.* Tursunzade; *prev.* Regar. W Tajikistan
162 J4 **Turt** Hövsgöl, N Mongolia
Turtkul' *see* To'rtko'l
29 O9 **Turtle Creek** ≈ South Dakota, N USA
30 K4 **Turtle Flambeau Flowage** ⊠ Wisconsin, N USA
11 S14 **Turtleford** Saskatchewan, S Canada
28 M4 **Turtle Lake** North Dakota, N USA
92 K12 **Turtola** Lappi, NW Finland
122 M10 **Turu** ≈ N Russian Federation
Turuga *see* Tsuruga
147 V10 **Turugart Pass** *pass* China/Kyrgyzstan
158 E7 **Turugart Shankou** *var.* Pereval Torugart. *pass* China/Kyrgyzstan
122 K9 **Turukhan** ≈ N Russian Federation
122 K9 **Turukhansk** Krasnoyarskiy Kray, N Russian Federation
139 N3 **Ţurumbah** *well* NE Syria
Turuoka *see* Tsuruoka
144 H14 **Turush** Mangistau, SW Kazakhstan
60 K7 **Turvo, Rio** ≈ S Brazil
116 J2 **Tur"ya** *Pol.* Turja, *Rus.* Tur'ya. ≈ NW Ukraine
23 O4 **Tuscaloosa** Alabama, S USA
23 O4 **Tuscaloosa, Lake** ⊚ Alabama, S USA
Tuscan Archipelago *see* Toscano, Archipelago
Tuscan-Emilian Mountains *see* Tosco-Emiliano, Appennino
Tuscany *see* Toscana
35 V2 **Tuscarora** Nevada, W USA
18 F15 **Tuscarora Mountain** *ridge* Pennsylvania, NE USA
30 M14 **Tuscola** Illinois, N USA
25 P7 **Tuscola** Texas, SW USA
23 O2 **Tuscumbia** Alabama, S USA
92 O4 **Tusenøyane** *island group* S Svalbard
144 K13 **Tushchybas, Zaliv** *prev.* Zaliv Paskevicha. *lake gulf* SW Kazakhstan
171 Y15 **Tusirah** Papua, E Indonesia
23 Q5 **Tuskegee** Alabama, S USA
94 E8 **Tustna** *island* S Norway
39 R12 **Tustumena Lake** ⊚ Alaska, USA
110 K13 **Tuszyn** Łodzkie, C Poland
137 S13 **Tutak** Ağrı, E Turkey
185 C20 **Tutamoe Range** ▲ North Island, NZ
Tutasev *see* Tutayev
124 L15 **Tutayev** *var.* Tutasev. Yaroslavskaya Oblast', W Russian Federation
Tutela *see* Tulle, France
Tutela *see* Tudela, Spain
Tutera *see* Tudela
155 H23 **Tuticorin** Tamil Nādu, SE India
113 L15 **Tutin** Serbia, S Serbia and Montenegro (Yugo.)
184 O10 **Tutira** Hawke's Bay, North Island, NZ
Tutiura *see* Tsuchiura
122 K10 **Tutonchany** Evenkiyskiy Avtonomnyy Okrug, N Russian Federation
114 L6 **Tutrakan** Silistra, NE Bulgaria
29 N5 **Tuttle** North Dakota, N USA
26 M11 **Tuttle** Oklahoma, C USA
27 O3 **Tuttle Creek Lake** ⊠ Kansas, C USA
101 H23 **Tuttlingen** Baden-Württemberg, S Germany
171 R16 **Tutuala** W East Timor
192 K17 **Tutuila** *island* W American Samoa
83 I18 **Tutume** Central, E Botswana
39 N7 **Tututalak Mountain** ▲ Alaska, USA
22 K3 **Tutwiler** Mississippi, S USA
162 L8 **Tuul Gol** ≈ N Mongolia
93 O16 **Tuupovaara** Itä-Suomi, E Finland
Tuva *see* Tyva, Respublika
190 E7 **Tuvalu** *prev.* Ellice Islands. ◆ *commonwealth republic* SW Pacific Ocean
Tuvana-i-Tholo *see* Tuvana-i-Colo
Tuvinskaya ASSR *see* Tyva, Respublika
Tuvutha *see* Tuvuca
141 P9 **Tuwayq, Jabal** ▲ C Saudi Arabia
138 H13 **Ţuwayyil ash Shihāq** *desert* S Jordan
11 U16 **Tuxford** Saskatchewan, S Canada
167 U12 **Tu Xoay** Đắc Lắc, S Vietnam
40 L14 **Tuxpan** Jalisco, C Mexico
40 J12 **Tuxpan** Nayarit, C Mexico
41 Q12 **Tuxpán** *var.* Tuxpán de Rodríguez Cano. Veracruz-Llave, E Mexico
Tuxpán de Rodríguez Cano *see* Tuxpán
41 R15 **Tuxtepec** *var.* San Juan Bautista Tuxtepec. Oaxaca, S Mexico
41 U16 **Tuxtla** *var.* Tuxtla Gutiérrez. Chiapas, SE Mexico
Tuxtla *see* San Andrés Tuxtla
Tuxtla Gutiérrez *see* Tuxtla
Tuyama *see* Tsuyama
167 T5 **Tuyên Quang** Tuyên Quang, N Vietnam
167 U13 **Tuy Hoa** Binh Thuân, S Vietnam
167 V12 **Tuy Hoa** Phu Yên, S Vietnam
127 U5 **Tuymazy** Respublika Bashkortostan, W Russian Federation
142 L6 **Tūysarkān** *var.* Tuisarkan, Tuyserkān. Hamadān, W Iran
Tuyserkān *see* Tūysarkān
145 W16 **Tuyuk** *Kaz.* Tuyyq. Almaty, SE Kazakhstan
Tuyyq *see* Tuyuk
136 I14 **Tuz Gölü** ⊚ C Turkey
125 Q15 **Tuzha** Kirovskaya Oblast', NW Russian Federation
113 K17 **Tuzi** Montenegro, SW Serbia and Montenegro (Yugo.)
139 T5 **Tūz Khurmātū** N Iraq
112 I11 **Tuzla** Federacija Bosna I Hercegovina, NE Bosnia and Herzegovina
117 N15 **Tuzla** Constanța, SE Romania
137 T12 **Tuzluca** Iğdır, NE Turkey
95 J20 **Tvååker** Halland, S Sweden
95 F17 **Tvedestrand** Aust-Agder, S Norway
124 J16 **Tver'** *prev.* Kalinin. Tverskaya Oblast', W Russian Federation
Tverya *see* Teverya
124 I15 **Tverskaya Oblast'** ◆ *province* W Russian Federation
126 I15 **Tvertsa** ≈ W Russian Federation
110 H13 **Twardogóra** *Ger.* Festenberg. Dolnośląskie, SW Poland
14 J14 **Tweed** Ontario, SE Canada
96 K13 **Tweed** ≈ England/Scotland, UK
98 O7 **Tweede-Exloërmond** Drenthe, NE Netherlands
183 V3 **Tweed Heads** New South Wales, SE Australia
98 M11 **Twello** Gelderland, E Netherlands
35 W15 **Twentynine Palms** California, W USA
25 P9 **Twin Buttes Reservoir** ⊠ Texas, SW USA
33 O15 **Twin Falls** Idaho, NW USA
39 N13 **Twin Hills** Alaska, USA
11 O11 **Twin Lakes** Alberta, W Canada
33 O12 **Twin Peaks** ▲ Idaho, NW USA
185 I14 **Twins, The** ▲ South Island, NZ
29 S5 **Twin Valley** Minnesota, N USA
100 G11 **Twistringen** Niedersachsen, NW Germany
185 E20 **Twizel** Canterbury, South Island, NZ
29 X5 **Two Harbors** Minnesota, N USA
11 R14 **Two Hills** Alberta, SW Canada
31 N7 **Two Rivers** Wisconsin, N USA
116 H8 **Tyachiv** Zakarpats'ka Oblast', W Ukraine
Tyan'-Shan' *see* Tien Shan
166 L3 **Tyao** ≈ Myanmar/India
117 R6 **Tyas'myn** ≈ N Ukraine
23 X6 **Tybee Island** Georgia, SE USA
Tyborøn *see* Thyborøn
111 J16 **Tychy** *Ger.* Tichau. Śląskie, S Poland
111 O16 **Tyczyn** Podkarpackie, SE Poland
94 I8 **Tydal** Sør-Trøndelag, S Norway
115 H24 **Tyflós** ≈ Kríti, Greece, E Mediterranean Sea
21 S3 **Tygart Lake** ⊠ West Virginia, NE USA
123 Q13 **Tygda** Amurskaya Oblast', SE Russian Federation
21 Q11 **Tyger River** ≈ South Carolina, SE USA
32 I11 **Tygh Valley** Oregon, NW USA
94 F12 **Tyin** ⊚ S Norway
29 S10 **Tyler** Minnesota, N USA
25 W7 **Tyler** Texas, SW USA
25 W7 **Tyler, Lake** ⊠ Texas, SW USA
22 K7 **Tylertown** Mississippi, S USA
22 K7 **Tylihuls'kyy Lyman** ⊚ SW Ukraine
Tylos *see* Bahrain
115 C15 **Týmfi** *var.* Timfi. ▲ W Greece
115 E17 **Tymfristós** *var.* Timfristos. ▲ C Greece
115 J25 **Tympáki** *var.* Timbaki; *prev.* Timbákion. Kríti, Greece, E Mediterranean Sea
123 Q12 **Tynda** Amurskaya Oblast', SE Russian Federation
29 Q12 **Tyndall** South Dakota, N USA
97 L14 **Tyne** ≈ N England, UK
97 M14 **Tynemouth** NE England, UK
97 L14 **Tyneside** *cultural region* NE England, UK
94 H10 **Tynset** Hedmark, S Norway
39 Q12 **Tyonek** Alaska, USA
Tyôsi *see* Chōshi
Tyras *see* Dniester, Moldova/Ukraine
Tyras *see* Bilhorod-Dnistrovs'kyy, Ukraine
Tyre *see* Soûr
95 G14 **Tyrifjorden** ⊚ S Norway
95 K22 **Tyringe** Skåne, S Sweden
123 R13 **Tyrma** Khabarovskiy Kray, SE Russian Federation
Tyrnau *see* Trnava
115 F15 **Týrnavos** *var.* Tírnavos. Thessalía, C Greece
127 N16 **Tyrnyauz** Kabardino-Balkarskaya Respublika, SW Russian Federation
Tyrol *see* Tirol
18 E14 **Tyrone** Pennsylvania, NE USA
97 E15 **Tyrone** *cultural region* W Northern Ireland, UK
93 F19 **Tyrsil** Hedmark, S Norway
182 M10 **Tyrrell, Lake** *salt lake* Victoria, SE Australia
84 H14 **Tyrrhenian Basin** *undersea feature* Tyrrhenian Sea, C Mediterranean Sea
120 L8 **Tyrrhenian Sea** *It.* Mare Tirreno. *sea* N Mediterranean Sea
Tysa *see* Tisa/Tisza
116 J7 **Tysmenytsya** Ivano-Frankivs'ka Oblast', W Ukraine
95 C14 **Tysnesøya** *island* S Norway
95 C14 **Tysse** Hordaland, S Norway
95 D14 **Tyssedal** Hordaland, S Norway
95 O17 **Tystberga** Södermanland, C Sweden
118 E12 **Tytuvėnai** Šiauliai, C Lithuania
144 D14 **Tyub-Karagan, Mys** *headland* SW Kazakhstan
147 V8 **Tyugel'-Say** Narynskaya Oblast', C Kyrgyzstan
122 H11 **Tyukalinsk** Omskaya Oblast', C Russian Federation
127 V7 **Tyul'gan** Orenburgskaya Oblast', W Russian Federation
122 G11 **Tyumen'** Tyumenskaya Oblast', C Russian Federation
122 H11 **Tyumenskaya Oblast'** ◆ *province* C Russian Federation
147 Y7 **Tyup** *Kir.* Tüp. Issyk-Kul'skaya Oblast', NE Kyrgyzstan
122 L14 **Tyva, Respublika** *prev.* Tannu-Tuva, Tuva, Tuvinskaya ASSR. ◆ *autonomous republic* C Russian Federation
117 N7 **Tyvriv** Vinnyts'ka Oblast', C Ukraine
97 J21 **Tywi** ≈ S Wales, UK
97 I19 **Tywyn** W Wales, UK
83 K20 **Tzaneen** Limpopo, NE South Africa
Tzekung *see* Zigong
41 X12 **Tzucacab** Yucatán, SE Mexico

U

82 B12 **Uaco Cungo** *var.* Waku Kungo, *Port.* Santa Comba. Cuanza Sul, C Angola
UAE *see* United Arab Emirates
191 X7 **Ua Huka** *island* Îles Marquises, NE French Polynesia
58 E10 **Uaiacás** Roraima, N Brazil
Uamba *see* Wamba
Uanle Uen *see* Wanlaweyn
191 W7 **Ua Pu** *island* Îles Marquises, NE French Polynesia
81 L17 **Uar Garas** *spring/well* SW Somalia
58 G12 **Uatumã, Rio** ≈ C Brazil
Ua Uíbh Fhailí *see* Offaly
58 C11 **Uaupés, Rio** *var.* Río Vaupés. ≈ Brazil/Colombia ***see also*** Vaupés, Río
145 X9 **Uba** ≈ E Kazakhstan
145 N6 **Ubagan** *Kaz.* Obagan. ≈ Kazakhstan/Russian Federation
186 G7 **Ubai** New Britain, E PNG
79 J15 **Ubangi** *Fr.* Oubangui. ≈ C Africa
Ubangi-Shari *see* Central African Republic
116 M3 **Ubarts'** *Ukr.* Ubort'. ≈ Belarus/Ukraine ***see also*** Ubort'
54 F9 **Ubaté** Cundinamarca, C Colombia
60 N10 **Ubatuba** São Paulo, S Brazil
149 R12 **Ubauro** Sind, SE Pakistan
171 Q6 **Ubay** Bohol, C Philippines
103 U14 **Ubaye** ≈ SE France
Ubayid, Wadi al *see* Ubayyiḑ, Wādī al
139 N8 **Ubaylah** W Iraq
139 O10 **Ubayyiḑ, Wādī al** *var.* Wadi al Ubayid. *dry watercourse* SW Iraq
98 L13 **Ubbergen** Gelderland, E Netherlands
164 E13 **Ube** Yamaguchi, Honshū, SW Japan
105 O13 **Úbeda** Andalucía, S Spain
109 V7 **Übelbach** *var.* Markt-Übelbach. Steiermark, SE Austria
59 L20 **Uberaba** Minas Gerais, SE Brazil
57 Q19 **Uberaba, Laguna** ⊚ E Bolivia
59 K19 **Uberlândia** Minas Gerais, SE Brazil
101 H24 **Überlingen** Baden-Württemberg, S Germany
77 U16 **Ubiaja** Edo, S Nigeria
104 K3 **Ubiña, Peña** ▲ NW Spain
57 H17 **Ubinas, Volcán** ▲ S Peru
Ubol Rajadhani/Ubol Ratchathani *see* Ubon Ratchathani
167 P9 **Ubolratna Reservoir** ⊠ C Thailand

167 *S10* **Ubon Ratchathani** *var.* Muang Ubon, Ubol Rajadhani, Ubol Ratchathani, Udon Ratchathani. Ubon Ratchathani, E Thailand
119 *L20* **Ubort'** *Bel.* Ubarts'. ≈ Belarus/Ukraine **see also** Ubarts'
104 *K15* **Ubrique** Andalucía, S Spain
Ubsu-Nur, Ozero *see* Uvs Nuur
79 *M18* **Ubundu** Orientale, C Dem. Rep. Congo
146 *J13* **Uçajy** *var.* Üchajy, *Rus.* Uch-Adzhi. Mary Welaýaty, C Turkmenistan
137 *X11* **Ucar** *Rus.* Udzhary. C Azerbaijan
56 *G13* **Ucayali** *off.* Departamento de Ucayali. ◈ *department* E Peru
56 *F10* **Ucayali, Río** ≈ C Peru
Uccle *see* Ukkel
Uch-Adzhi/Üchajy *see* Üçajy
127 *X4* **Uchaly** Respublika Bashkortostan, W Russian Federation
145 *W13* **Ucharal** *Kaz.* Üsharal. Almaty, E Kazakhstan
164 *C17* **Uchinoura** Kagoshima, Kyūshū, SW Japan
165 *R5* **Uchiura-wan** *bay* NW Pacific Ocean
Uchkuduk *see* Uchquduq
Uchkurghan *see* Uchqo'rg'on
146 *K8* **Uchquduq** *Rus.* Uchkuduk. Navoiy Viloyati, N Uzbekistan
147 *S9* **Uchqo'rg'on** *Rus.* Uchkurghan. Namangan Viloyati, E Uzbekistan
Uchsay *see* Uchsoy
146 *G6* **Uchsoy** *Rus.* Uchsay. Qoraqalpog'iston Respublikasi, NW Uzbekistan
Uchtagan Gumy/ Uchtagan, Peski *see* Uçtagan Gumy
123 *R11* **Uchur** ≈ E Russian Federation
100 *O10* **Uckermark** *cultural region* E Germany
10 *K17* **Ucluelet** Vancouver Island, British Columbia, SW Canada
146 *D10* **Uçtagan Gumy** *var.* Uchtagan Gumy, *Rus.* Peski Uchtagan. *desert* NW Turkmenistan
122 *M13* **Uda** ≈ S Russian Federation
123 *R12* **Uda** ≈ E Russian Federation
123 *N6* **Udachnyy** Respublika Sakha (Yakutiya), NE Russian Federation
155 *G21* **Udagamandalam** *var.* Udhagamandalam; *prev.* Ootacamund. Tamil Nādu, SW India
152 *F14* **Udaipur** *prev.* Oodeypore. Rājasthān, N India
Udayadhani *see* Uthai Thani
143 *N16* **'Udayd, Khawr al** *var.* Khor al Udeid. *inlet* Qatar/Saudi Arabia
112 *D11* **Udbina** Lika-Senj, W Croatia
95 *I18* **Uddevalla** Västra Götaland, S Sweden
Uddjaur *see* Uddjaure
92 *H13* **Uddjaure** *var.* Uddjaur. ◎ N Sweden
Udeid, Khor al *see* 'Udayd, Khawr al
99 *K14* **Uden** Noord-Brabant, SE Netherlands
Uden *see* Udenhout
99 *J14* **Udenhout** *var.* Uden. Noord-Brabant, S Netherlands
155 *H14* **Udgīr** Mahārāshtra, C India
Udhagamandalam *see* Udagamandalam
152 *H6* **Udhampur** Jammu and Kashmir, NW India
139 *X14* **'Udhaybah, 'Uqlat al** *well* S Iraq
106 *J7* **Udine** *anc.* Utina. Friuli-Venezia Giulia, NE Italy
175 *T14* **Udintsev Fracture Zone** *tectonic feature* S Pacific Ocean
Udipi *see* Udupi
Udmurtia *see* Udmurtskaya Respublika
127 *S2* **Udmurtskaya Respublika** *Eng.* Udmurtia. ◈ *autonomous republic* NW Russian Federation
124 *J15* **Udomlya** Tverskaya Oblast', W Russian Federation
Udon Ratchathani *see* Ubon Ratchathani
167 *Q8* **Udon Thani** *var.* Ban Mak Khaeng, Udorndhani. Udon Thani, N Thailand
Udorndhani *see* Udon Thani
189 *U12* **Udot** *atoll* Chuuk Islands, C Micronesia
123 *S12* **Udskaya Guba** *bay* E Russian Federation
155 *E19* **Udupi** *var.* Udipi. Karnātaka, SW India
Udzhary *see* Ucar
100 *O9* **Uecker** ≈ NE Germany
100 *P9* **Ueckermünde** Mecklenburg-Vorpommern, NE Germany
164 *M12* **Ueda** *var.* Uyeda. Nagano, Honshū, S Japan
79 *L16* **Uele** *var.* Welle. ≈ NE Dem. Rep. Congo
Uele (upper course) *see* Uolo, Río, Equatorial Guinea/Gabon
Uele (upper course) *see* Kibali, Dem. Rep. Congo
123 *W5* **Uelen** Chukotskiy Avtonomnyy Okrug, NE Russian Federation
100 *J11* **Uelzen** Niedersachsen, N Germany
164 *J14* **Ueno** Mie, Honshū, SW Japan
127 *V4* **Ufa** Respublika Bashkortostan, W Russian Federation
127 *V4* **Ufa** ≈ W Russian Federation
Ufra *see* Kenar
83 *C18* **Ugab** ≈ C Namibia
118 *D8* **Ugāle** Ventspils, NW Latvia
81 *F17* **Uganda** *off.* Republic of Uganda. ◆ *republic* E Africa
138 *G4* **Ugarit** *Ar.* Ra's Shamrah. *site of ancient city* Al Lādhiqīyah, NW Syria
39 *O14* **Ugashik** Alaska, USA
107 *Q19* **Ugento** Puglia, SE Italy
105 *O15* **Ugíjar** Andalucía, S Spain
103 *T11* **Ugine** Savoie, E France
123 *R13* **Uglegorsk** Amurskaya Oblast', SE Russian Federation
125 *V13* **Ugleural'sk** Permskaya Oblast', S Russian Federation
124 *L15* **Uglich** Yaroslavskaya Oblast', W Russian Federation
124 *I14* **Uglovka** *var.* Okulovka. Novgorodskaya Oblast', W Russian Federation
126 *I4* **Ugra** ≈ W Russian Federation
147 *V9* **Ugyut** Narynskaya Oblast', C Kyrgyzstan
111 *H19* **Uherské Hradiště** *Ger.* Ungarisch-Hradisch. Zilinský kraj, E Czech Republic
111 *H19* **Uherský Brod** *Ger.* Ungarisch-Brod. Zilinský kraj, E Czech Republic
111 *B17* **Úhlava** *Ger.* Angel. ≈ W Czech Republic
Uhorshchyna *see* Hungary
31 *T13* **Uhrichsville** Ohio, N USA
Uhuru Peak *see* Kilimanjaro
96 *G8* **Uig** N Scotland, UK
82 *B10* **Uíge** *Port.* Carmona, Vila Marechal Carmona. Uíge, NW Angola
82 *B10* **Uíge** ◈ *province* N Angola
193 *Y15* **Uiha** *island* Ha'apai Group, C Tonga
189 *U13* **Uijec** *island* Chuuk, C Micronesia
163 *X14* **Ŭijŏngbu** *Jap.* Giseifu. NW South Korea
144 *H10* **Uil** *Kaz.* Oyyl. Aktyubinsk, W Kazakhstan
144 *H10* **Uil** *Kaz.* Oyyl. ≈ W Kazakhstan
36 *M3* **Uinta Mountains** ⛰ Utah, W USA
83 *C18* **Uis** Erongo, NW Namibia
83 *I25* **Uitenhage** Eastern Cape, S South Africa
98 *H9* **Uitgeest** Noord-Holland, W Netherlands
98 *I11* **Uithoorn** Noord-Holland, C Netherlands
98 *O4* **Uithuizen** Groningen, NE Netherlands
98 *O4* **Uithuizermeeden** Groningen, NE Netherlands
189 *R6* **Ujae Atoll** *var.* Wūjae. *atoll* Ralik Chain, W Marshall Islands
Ujain *see* Ujjain
111 *I16* **Ujazd** Opolskie, S Poland
Új-Becse *see* Novi Bečej
Ujda *see* Oujda
189 *N5* **Ujelang Atoll** *var.* Wujlān. *atoll* Ralik Chain, W Marshall Islands
111 *N21* **Újfehértó** Szabolcs-Szatmár-Bereg, E Hungary
Újgradiska *see* Nova Gradiška
164 *J13* **Uji** *var.* Uzi. Kyōto, Honshū, SW Japan
81 *E21* **Ujiji** Kigoma, W Tanzania
154 *G10* **Ujjain** *prev.* Ujain. Madhya Pradesh, C India
Újlak *see* Ilok
'Ujmān *see* 'Ajmān
Újmoldova *see* Moldova Nouă
Újszentanna *see* Sântana
Ujungpandang *see* Makassar
Ujung Salang *see* Phuket
Újvidék *see* Novi Sad
154 *E11* **Ukāi Reservoir** ⊡ W India
81 *G19* **Ukara Island** *island* N Tanzania
'Ukash, Wādī *see* 'Akāsh, Wādī
81 *F19* **Ukerewe Island** *island* N Tanzania
139 *S9* **Ukhayḍhīr** C Iraq
153 *X13* **Ukhrul** Manipur, NE India
125 *S9* **Ukhta** Respublika Komi, NW Russian Federation
34 *L6* **Ukiah** California, W USA
32 *K12* **Ukiah** Oregon, NW USA
99 *G18* **Ukkel** *Fr.* Uccle. Brussels, C Belgium
118 *G13* **Ukmergė** *Pol.* Wiłkomierz. Vilnius, C Lithuania
Ukraina *see* Ukraine
116 *L6* **Ukraine** *off.* Ukraine, *Rus.* Ukraina, *Ukr.* Ukrayina; *prev.* Ukrainian Soviet Socialist Republic, Ukrainskaya S.S.R. ◆ *republic* SE Europe
Ukrainskay S.S.R/ Ukrayina *see* Ukraine
82 *B13* **Uku** Cuanza Sul, NW Angola
164 *B13* **Uku-jima** *island* Gotō-rettō, SW Japan
83 *F20* **Ukwi** Kgalagadi, SW Botswana
118 *M13* **Ula** *Rus.* Ulla. Vitsyebskaya Voblasts', N Belarus
136 *C16* **Ula** Muğla, SW Turkey
118 *M13* **Ula** *Rus.* Ulla. ≈ N Belarus
162 *L7* **Ulaanbaatar** *Eng.* Ulan Bator; *prev.* Urga. ● (Mongolia) Töv, C Mongolia
163 *N8* **Ulaan-Ereg** Hentiy, E Mongolia
162 *E5* **Ulaangom** Uvs, NW Mongolia
162 *E7* **Ulaantolgoy** Hovd, W Mongolia
162 *I8* **Ulaan-Uul** Bayanhongor, C Mongolia
163 *O10* **Ulaan-Uul** Dornogovĭ, SE Mongolia
162 *M14* **Ulan** *var.* Otog Qi. Nei Mongol Zizhiqu, N China
159 *R10* **Ulan** *var.* Xireg; *prev.* Xiligou. Qinghai, C China
Ulan Bator *see* Ulaanbaatar
162 *L13* **Ulan Buh Shamo** *desert* N China
Ulanhad *see* Chifeng
163 *T8* **Ulanhot** Nei Mongol Zizhiqu, N China
127 *Q14* **Ulan Khol** Respublika Kalmykiya, SW Russian Federation
162 *M13* **Ulansuhai Nur** ◎ N China
123 *N14* **Ulan-Ude** *prev.* Verkhneudinsk. Respublika Buryatiya, S Russian Federation
159 *N12* **Ulan Ul Hu** ◎ C China
187 *N9* **Ulawa Island** *island* SE Solomon Islands
138 *J7* **'Ulayyānīyah, Bi'r al** *var.* Al Hilbeh. *well* S Syria
123 *S12* **Ul'banskiy Zaliv** *strait* E Russian Federation
Ulbo *see* Olib
113 *J18* **Ulcinj** Montenegro, SW Serbia and Montenegro (Yugo.)
163 *O7* **Uldz** Hentiy, NE Mongolia
Uleåborg *see* Oulu
Uleälv *see* Oulujoki
95 *G16* **Ulefoss** Telemark, S Norway
Uleträsk *see* Oulujärvi
113 *L19* **Ulëz** *var.* Ulëza. Dibër, C Albania
Ulëza *see* Ulëz
95 *F22* **Ulfborg** Ringkøbing, W Denmark
98 *N13* **Ulft** Gelderland, E Netherlands
162 *G7* **Uliastay** *prev.* Jibhalanta. Dzavhan, W Mongolia
188 *F8* **Ulimang** Babeldaob, N Palau
67 *T10* **Ulindi** ≈ W Dem. Rep. Congo
188 *H14* **Ulithi Atoll** *atoll* Caroline Islands, W Micronesia
112 *N10* **Uljma** Serbia, NE Serbia and Montenegro (Yugo.)
144 *L11* **Ul'kayak** *Kaz.* Ölkeyek. ≈ C Kazakhstan
145 *Q7* **Ul'ken-Karoy, Ozero** ◎ N Kazakhstan
Ülkenözen *see* Bol'shoy Uzen'
Ülkenqobda *see* Bol'shaya Khobda
104 *G3* **Ulla** ≈ NW Spain
Ulla *see* Ula
183 *S10* **Ulladulla** New South Wales, SE Australia
153 *T14* **Ullapara** Rajshahi, W Bangladesh
96 *H7* **Ullapool** N Scotland, UK
95 *J20* **Ullared** Halland, S Sweden
105 *T7* **Ulldecona** Cataluña, NE Spain
92 *I9* **Ullsfjorden** *fjord* N Norway
97 *K15* **Ullswater** ◎ NW England, UK
101 *I22* **Ulm** Baden-Württemberg, S Germany
33 *R8* **Ulm** Montana, NW USA
183 *V5* **Ulmarra** New South Wales, SE Australia
116 *K13* **Ulmeni** Buzău, C Romania
116 *K14* **Ulmeni** Călărași, S Romania
42 *L7* **Ulmukhuás** Región Autónoma Atlántico Norte, NE Nicaragua
188 *C8* **Ulong** *var.* Aulong. *island* Palau Islands, N Palau
83 *N14* **Ulonguè** *var.* Ulongwé. Tete, NW Mozambique
Ulongwé *see* Ulonguè
95 *K19* **Ulricehamn** Västra Götaland, S Sweden
98 *N5* **Ulrum** Groningen, NE Netherlands
163 *Z16* **Ulsan** *Jap.* Urusan. SE South Korea
94 *D10* **Ulsteinvik** Møre og Romsdal, S Norway
97 *D15* **Ulster** ◈ *province* Northern Ireland, UK/Ireland
171 *Q10* **Ulu** Pulau Siau, N Indonesia
123 *Q11* **Ulu** Respublika Sakha (Yakutiya), NE Russian Federation
42 *H5* **Ulúa, Río** ≈ NW Honduras
136 *D12* **Ulubat Gölü** ◎ NW Turkey
136 *E12* **Uludağ** ▲ NW Turkey
158 *D7* **Ulugqat** Xinjiang Uygur Zizhiqu, W China
136 *J16* **Ulukışla** Niğde, S Turkey
189 *O15* **Ulul** *island* Caroline Islands, C Micronesia
83 *L22* **Ulundi** KwaZulu/Natal, E South Africa
158 *M3* **Ulungur He** ≈ NW China
158 *K2* **Ulungur Hu** ◎ NW China
181 *P8* **Uluru** *var.* Ayers Rock. *rocky outcrop* Northern Territory, C Australia
97 *K16* **Ulverston** NW England, UK
183 *O16* **Ulverstone** Tasmania, SE Australia
94 *D13* **Ulvik** Hordaland, S Norway
93 *J18* **Ulvila** Länsi-Suomi, W Finland
117 *O8* **Ulyanivka** *Rus.* Ul'yanovka. Kirovohrads'ka Oblast', C Ukraine
Ul'yanovka *see* Ulyanivka
127 *Q5* **Ul'yanovsk** *prev.* Simbirsk. Ul'yanovskaya Oblast', W Russian Federation
127 *Q5* **Ul'yanovskaya Oblast'** ◈ *province* W Russian Federation
145 *S10* **Ul'yanovskiy** Karaganda, C Kazakhstan
Ul'yanovskiy Kanal *see* Ul'yanow Kanali
146 *M13* **Ul'yanow Kanali** *Rus.* Ul'yanovskiy Kanal. *canal* Turkmenistan/Uzbekistan
Ulyshylanshyq *see* Uly-Zhylanshyk
26 *H6* **Ulysses** Kansas, C USA
145 *O12* **Ulytau, Gory** ⛰ C Kazakhstan
145 *N11* **Uly-Zhylanshyk** *Kaz.* Ulyshylanshyq. ≈ C Kazakhstan
112 *A9* **Umag** *It.* Umago. Istra, NW Croatia
Umago *see* Umag
189 *V13* **Uman** *atoll* Chuuk Islands, C Micronesia
117 *O7* **Uman'** *Rus.* Uman. Cherkas'ka Oblast', C Ukraine
41 *W12* **Umán** Yucatán, SE Mexico
Umanak/Umanaq *see* Uummannaq
'Umān, Khalīj *see* Oman, Gulf of
'Umān, Salṭanat *see* Oman
154 *K10* **Umaria** Madhya Pradesh, C India
149 *R16* **Umar Kot** Sind, SE Pakistan
188 *B17* **Umatac** SW Guam
188 *A17* **Umatac Bay** *bay* SW Guam
139 *S6* **Umayqah** C Iraq
124 *J5* **Umba** Murmanskaya Oblast', NW Russian Federation
138 *I8* **Umbāshī, Khirbat al** *ruins* As Suwaydā', S Syria
80 *A12* **Umbelasha** ≈ W Sudan
106 *H12* **Umbertide** Umbria, C Italy
61 *B17* **Umberto** *var.* Humberto. Santa Fe, C Argentina
186 *E7* **Umboi Island** *var.* Rooke Island. *island* C PNG
126 *J4* **Umbozero, Ozero** ◎ NW Russian Federation
106 *H13* **Umbria** ◈ *region* C Italy
Umbrian-Machigian Mountains *see* Umbro-Marchigiano, Appennino
106 *I12* **Umbro-Marchigiano, Appennino** *Eng.* Umbrian-Machigian Mountains. ⛰ C Italy
93 *J16* **Umeå** Västerbotten, N Sweden
93 *H14* **Umeälven** ≈ N Sweden
39 *Q5* **Umiat** Alaska, USA
83 *K23* **Umlazi** KwaZulu/Natal, E South Africa
139 *X10* **Umm al Baqar, Hawr** *var.* Birkat ad Dawaymah. *spring* S Iraq
141 *U12* **Umm al Ḥayt, Wādī** *var.* Wādī Amilḥayt. *seasonal river* SW Oman
Umm al Qaiwain *see* Umm al Qaywayn
143 *R15* **Umm al Qaywayn** *var.* Umm al Qaiwain. Umm al Qaywayn, NE UAE
139 *Q5* **Umm al Ṭūz** C Iraq
138 *J3* **Umm 'Āmūd** Ḥalab, N Syria
141 *Y10* **Umm ar Ruṣāṣ** *var.* Umm Ruṣayṣ. W Oman
141 *X9* **Ummas Samīn** *salt flat* C Oman
141 *V9* **Umm az Zumūl** *oasis* E Saudi Arabia
80 *A9* **Umm Buru** Western Darfur, W Sudan
80 *A12* **Umm Dafag** Southern Darfur, W Sudan
Umm Durmān *see* Omdurman
138 *F9* **Umm el Fahm** Haifa, N Israel
80 *F9* **Umm Inderab** Northern Kordofan, C Sudan
80 *C10* **Umm Keddada** Northern Darfur, W Sudan
140 *J7* **Umm Lajj** Tabūk, W Saudi Arabia
138 *L10* **Umm Maḥfur** ≈ N Jordan
139 *Y13* **Umm Qaṣr** SE Iraq
Umm Ruṣayṣ *see* Umm ar Ruṣāṣ
80 *F11* **Umm Ruwaba** *var.* Umm Ruwābah, Um Ruwāba. Northern Kordofan, C Sudan
Umm Ruwābah *see* Umm Ruwaba
143 *N16* **Umm Sa'īd** *var.* Musay'īd. S Qatar
138 *K10* **Umm Ṭuways, Wādī** *dry watercourse* N Jordan
38 *J17* **Umnak Island** *island* Aleutian Islands, Alaska, USA
32 *F13* **Umpqua River** ≈ Oregon, NW USA
82 *D13* **Umpulo** Bié, C Angola
154 *I12* **Umred** Mahārāshtra, C India
139 *Y10* **Umr Sawān, Hawr** ◎ S Iraq
Um Ruwāba *see* Umm Ruwaba
Umtali *see* Mutare
83 *J24* **Umtata** Eastern Cape, SE South Africa
77 *V17* **Umuahia** Abia, SW Nigeria
60 *H10* **Umuarama** Paraná, S Brazil
Umvuma *see* Mvuma
83 *K18* **Umzingwani** ≈ S Zimbabwe
112 *D11* **Una** ≈ Bosnia and Herzegovina/Croatia
112 *E12* **Unac** ≈ W Bosnia and Herzegovina
23 *T6* **Unadilla** Georgia, SE USA
18 *I10* **Unadilla River** ≈ New York, NE USA
59 *L18* **Unaí** Minas Gerais, SE Brazil
39 *N10* **Unalakleet** Alaska, USA
38 *K17* **Unalaska Island** *island* Aleutian Islands, Alaska, USA
185 *I16* **Una, Mount** ▲ South Island, NZ
82 *N13* **Unango** Niassa, N Mozambique
Unao *see* Unnão
92 *L12* **Unari** Lappi, N Finland
141 *O6* **'Unayzah** *var.* Anaiza. Al Qaṣīm, C Saudi Arabia
138 *L10* **'Unayzah, Jabal** ▲ Jordan/Saudi Arabia
Unci *see* Almería
57 *K19* **Uncía** Potosí, C Bolivia
37 *Q7* **Uncompahgre Peak** ▲ Colorado, C USA
37 *P6* **Uncompahgre Plateau** *plain* Colorado, C USA
95 *L17* **Unden** ◎ S Sweden
28 *M4* **Underwood** North Dakota, N USA
171 *T13* **Undur** Pulau Seram, E Indonesia
Undur Khan *see* Öndörhaan
126 *H6* **Unecha** Bryanskaya Oblast', W Russian Federation
39 *N16* **Unga** Unga Island, Alaska, USA
Ungaria *see* Hungary
183 *P8* **Ungarie** New South Wales, SE Australia
Ungarisch-Brod *see* Uherský Brod
Ungarisches Erzgebirge *see* Slovenské rudohorie
Ungarisch-Hradisch *see* Uherské Hradiště
Ungarn *see* Hungary
12 *M4* **Ungava Bay** *bay* Québec, E Canada
12 *J2* **Ungava, Péninsule d'** *peninsula* Québec, SE Canada
Ungeny *see* Ungheni
116 *M9* **Ungheni** *Rus.* Ungeny. W Moldova
Unguja *see* Zanzibar
146 *G10* **Üngüz Angyrsyndaky Garagum** *Rus.* Zaungukskiye Garagumy. *desert* N Turkmenistan
146 *H11* **Unguz, Solonchakovyye Vpadiny** *salt marsh* C Turkmenistan
Ungvár *see* Uzhhorod
60 *I12* **União da Vitória** Paraná, S Brazil
111 *G17* **Uničov** *Ger.* Mährisch-Neustadt. Olomoucký Kraj, E Czech Republic
110 *J12* **Uniejów** Łódzkie, C Poland
112 *A11* **Unije** *island* W Croatia
38 *L16* **Unimak Island** *island* Aleutian Islands, Alaska, USA
38 *L16* **Unimak Pass** *strait* Aleutian Islands, Alaska, USA
27 *W5* **Union** Missouri, C USA
32 *L12* **Union** Oregon, NW USA
21 *Q11* **Union** South Carolina, SE USA
21 *R6* **Union** West Virginia, NE USA
62 *J12* **Unión** San Luis, C Argentina
61 *B25* **Unión, Bahía** *bay* E Argentina
31 *Q13* **Union City** Indiana, N USA
31 *Q10* **Union City** Michigan, N USA
18 *C12* **Union City** Pennsylvania, NE USA
20 *G8* **Union City** Tennessee, S USA
32 *G14* **Union Creek** Oregon, NW USA
83 *G25* **Uniondale** Western Cape, SW South Africa
40 *K13* **Unión de Tula** Jalisco, SW Mexico
30 *M9* **Union Grove** Wisconsin, N USA
45 *Y15* **Union Island** *island* S Saint Vincent and the Grenadines
46 *K5* **Union Reefs** *reef* SW Mexico
(0) *D7* **Union Seamount** *undersea feature* NE Pacific Ocean
23 *Q6* **Union Springs** Alabama, S USA
20 *H6* **Uniontown** Kentucky, S USA
18 *C16* **Uniontown** Pennsylvania, NE USA
27 *T1* **Unionville** Missouri, C USA
141 *V8* **United Arab Emirates** *Ar.* Al Imārāt al 'Arabīyah al Muttaḥidah, *abbrev.* UAE; *prev.* Trucial States. ◆ *federation* SW Asia
United Arab Republic *see* Egypt
97 *H14* **United Kingdom** *off.* UK of Great Britain and Northern Ireland, *abbrev.* UK. ◆ *monarchy* NW Europe
United Mexican States *see* Mexico
United Provinces *see* Uttar Pradesh
16 *L10* **United States of America** *off.* United States of America, *var.* America, The States, *abbrev.* U.S., USA. ◆ *federal republic*
124 *J10* **Unitsa** Respublika Kareliya, NW Russian Federation
11 *S15* **Unity** Saskatchewan, S Canada
Unity State *see* Wahda
105 *Q8* **Universales, Montes** ⛰ C Spain
27 *X4* **University City** Missouri, C USA
187 *Q13* **Unmet** Malekula, C Vanuatu
101 *F15* **Unna** Nordrhein-Westfalen, W Germany
152 *L12* **Unnão** *prev.* Unao. Uttar Pradesh, N India
187 *R15* **Unpongkor** Erromango, S Vauautu
Unruhstadt *see* Kargowa
96 *M1* **Unst** *island* NE Scotland, UK
101 *K16* **Unstrut** ≈ C Germany
Unterdrauburg *see* Dravograd
Unterlimbach *see* Lendava
101 *L23* **Unterschleissheim** Bayern, SE Germany
101 *H24* **Untersee** ◎ Germany/Switzerland
100 *O10* **Unterueckersee** ◎ NE Germany
108 *F9* **Unterwalden** ◈ *canton* C Switzerland
55 *N12* **Unturán, Sierra de** ⛰ Brazil/Venezuela
159 *N11* **Unuli Horog** Qinghai, W China
136 *M11* **Ünye** Ordu, W Turkey
Unza *see* Unzha
127 *O14* **Unzha** *var.* Unza. ≈ NW Russian Federation
79 *E17* **Uolo, Río** *var.* Eyo (lower course), Mbini, Uele (upper course), Woleu; *prev.* Benito. ≈ Equatorial Guinea/Gabon
55 *Q10* **Uonán** Bolívar, SE Venezuela
161 *T12* **Uotsuri-shima** *island* China/Japan/Taiwan
165 *M11* **Uozu** Toyama, Honshū, SW Japan
42 *L12* **Upala** Alajuela, NW Costa Rica
55 *P7* **Upata** Bolívar, E Venezuela
79 *M23* **Upemba, Lac** ◎ SE Dem. Rep. Congo
197 *O12* **Upernavik** *var.* Upernivik. Kitaa, C Greenland
Upernivik *see* Upernavik
83 *F22* **Upington** Northern Cape, W South Africa
Uplands *see* Ottawa
192 *I16* **Upolu** *island* SE Samoa
38 *G11* **'Upolu Point** *var.* Upolu Point *headland* Hawai'i, USA, C Pacific Ocean
Upper Austria *see* Oberösterreich
Upper Bann *see* Bann
14 *M13* **Upper Canada Village** *tourist site* Ontario, SE Canada
18 *I16* **Upper Darby** Pennsylvania, NE USA
28 *L2* **Upper Des Lacs Lake** ⊡ North Dakota, N USA
185 *L14* **Upper Hutt** Wellington, North Island, NZ
29 *X11* **Upper Iowa River** ≈ Iowa, C USA
32 *H15* **Upper Klamath Lake** ◎ Oregon, NW USA
34 *M6* **Upper Lake** California, W USA
35 *Q1* **Upper Lake** ◎ California, W USA
10 *K9* **Upper Liard** Yukon Territory, W Canada
97 *E16* **Upper Lough Erne** ◎ SW Northern Ireland, UK
80 *F12* **Upper Nile** ◈ *state* E Sudan
29 *T3* **Upper Red Lake** ◎ Minnesota, N USA
31 *S12* **Upper Sandusky** Ohio, N USA
Upper Volta *see* Burkina
95 *O15* **Upplandsväsby** *var.* Upplands Väsby. Stockholm, C Sweden
95 *O15* **Uppsala** Uppsala, C Sweden
95 *O14* **Uppsala** ◈ *county* C Sweden
38 *J12* **Upright Cape** *headland* Saint Matthew Island, Alaska, USA
20 *K6* **Upton** Kentucky, S USA
33 *Y13* **Upton** Wyoming, C USA
141 *N7* **'Uqlat aṣ Ṣuqūr** Al Qaṣīm, W Saudi Arabia
Uqturpan *see* Wushi
54 *C7* **Urabá, Golfo de** *gulf* NW Colombia
Uracas *see* Farallon de Pajaros
Uradar'ya *see* O'radaryo
Urad Qianqi *see* Xishanzui
165 *U5* **Urahoro** Hokkaidō, NE Japan
165 *T5* **Urakawa** Hokkaidō, NE Japan
127 *X6* **Ural** *Kaz.* Zayyq. ≈ Kazakhstan/Russian Federation
183 *T6* **Uralla** New South Wales, SE Australia
Ural Mountains *see* Ural'skiye Gory
144 *F8* **Ural'sk** *Kaz.* Oral. Zapadnyy Kazakhstan, NW Kazakhstan
Ural'skaya Oblast' *see* Zapadnyy Kazakhstan
127 *W5* **Ural'skiye Gory** *var.* Ural'skiy Khrebet, *Eng.* Ural Mountains. ⛰ Kazakhstan/Russian Federation
Ural'skiy Khrebet *see* Ural'skiye Gory
138 *I3* **Urām aṣ Ṣughrá** Ḥalab, N Syria
183 *P10* **Urana** New South Wales, SE Australia
11 *S10* **Uranium City** Saskatchewan, C Canada
58 *F10* **Uraricoera** Roraima, N Brazil
47 *S5* **Uraricoera, Rio** ≈ N Brazil
Ura-Tyube *see* Üroteppa
165 *O13* **Urawa** Saitama, Honshū, S Japan
122 *H10* **Uray** Khanty-Mansiyskiy Avtonomnyy Okrug, C Russian Federation
141 *R7* **'Uray'irah** Ash Sharqīyah, E Saudi Arabia
30 *M13* **Urbana** Illinois, N USA
31 *R13* **Urbana** Ohio, N USA
29 *V14* **Urbandale** Iowa, C USA
106 *I11* **Urbania** Marche, C Italy
106 *I11* **Urbino** Marche, C Italy
57 *H16* **Urcos** Cusco, S Peru
144 *D10* **Urda** Zapadnyy Kazakhstan, W Kazakhstan
105 *N10* **Urda** Castilla-La Mancha, C Spain
162 *E7* **Urdgol** Hovd, W Mongolia
Urdunn *see* Jordan
145 *X12* **Urdzhar** *Kaz.* Ürzhar. Vostochnyy Kazakhstan, E Kazakhstan
97 *L16* **Ure** ≈ N England, UK
119 *K18* **Urechcha** *Rus.* Urech'ye. Minskaya Voblasts', S Belarus
Urech'ye *see* Urechcha
127 *P2* **Uren'** Nizhegorodskaya Oblast', W Russian Federation
122 *J9* **Urengoy** Yamalo-Nenetskiy Avtonomnyy Okrug, N Russian Federation
184 *K10* **Urenui** Taranaki, North Island, NZ
187 *Q12* **Ureparapara** *island* Banks Islands, N Vanuatu
40 *G5* **Ures** Sonora, NW Mexico
Urfa *see* Şanlıurfa
Urga *see* Ulaanbaatar
146 *H9* **Urganch** *Rus.* Urgench; *prev.* Novo-Urgench. Xorazm Viloyati, W Uzbekistan
Urgench *see* Urganch
136 *J14* **Ürgüp** Nevşehir, C Turkey
147 *O12* **Urgut** Samarqand Viloyati, C Uzbekistan
158 *K3* **Urho** Xinjiang Uygur Zizhiqu, W China
152 *G5* **Uri** Jammu and Kashmir, NW India
108 *G9* **Uri** ◈ *canton* C Switzerland
54 *F11* **Uribe** Meta, C Colombia
54 *H4* **Uribia** La Guajira, N Colombia
116 *G12* **Uricani** *Hung.* Hobicaurikány. Hunedoara, SW Romania
57 *M21* **Uriondo** Tarija, S Bolivia
40 *I7* **Urique** Chihuahua, N Mexico
40 *I7* **Urique, Río** ≈ N Mexico
56 *E9* **Uritiyacu, Río** ≈ N Peru
Uritskiy *see* Sarykol'
98 *K8* **Urk** Flevoland, N Netherlands
136 *B14* **Urla** İzmir, W Turkey
116 *K13* **Urlați** Prahova, SE Romania
127 *V4* **Urman** Respublika Bashkortostan, W Russian Federation
147 *P12* **Urmetan** W Tajikistan
Urmia *see* Orūmīyeh
Urmia, Lake *see* Orūmīyeh, Daryācheh-ye
Urmiyeh *see* Orūmīyeh
113 *N17* **Uroševac** *Alb.* Ferizaj. Serbia, S Serbia and Montenegro (Yugo.)
147 *P11* **Üroteppa** *Rus.* Ura-Tyube. NW Tajikistan
54 *D8* **Urrao** Antioquia, W Colombia
Ursat'yevskaya *see* Xovos
162 *I11* **Urt** Ömnögovĭ, S Mongolia
127 *X7* **Urtazym** Orenburgskaya Oblast', W Russian Federation
59 *K18* **Uruaçu** Goiás, C Brazil
40 *M14* **Uruapan** *var.* Uruapan del Progreso. Michoacán de Ocampo, SW Mexico
Uruapan del Progreso *see* Uruapan
57 *G15* **Urubamba, Cordillera** ⛰ C Peru
57 *G14* **Urubamba, Río** ≈ C Peru
58 *G12* **Urucará** Amazonas, N Brazil
61 *E16* **Uruguaiana** Rio Grande do Sul, S Brazil
Uruguai, Rio *see* Uruguay
61 *E18* **Uruguay** *off.* Oriental Republic of Uruguay; *prev.* La Banda Oriental. ◆ *republic* E South America
61 *E15* **Uruguay** *var.* Rio Uruguai, Río Uruguay. ≈ E South America
Uruguay, Río *see* Uruguay
Urumchi *see* Ürümqi
158 *L5* **Ürümqi** *var.* Tihwa, Urumchi, Urumqi, Urumtsi, Wu-lu-k'o-mu-shi, Wu-lu-mu-ch'i; *prev.* Ti-hua. *autonomous region capital* Xinjiang Uygur Zizhiqu, NW China
Urumtsi *see* Ürümqi
Urundi *see* Burundi
183 *V6* **Urunga** New South Wales, SE Australia
188 *C15* **Uruno Point** *headland* NW Guam

◆ Country ● Country Capital ◇ Dependent Territory ○ Dependent Territory Capital ◈ Administrative Region ✈ International Airport ▲ Mountain ⛰ Mountain Range Volcano ≈ River ◎ Lake ⊡ Reservoir

123 U13 **Urup, Ostrov** *island* Kuril'skiye Ostrova, SE Russian Federation
141 P11 **'Urūq al Mawārid** *desert* S Saudi Arabia
Urusan *see* Ulsan
127 T5 **Urussu** Respublika Tatarstan, W Russian Federation
184 K10 **Uruti** Taranaki, North Island, NZ
57 K19 **Uru Uru, Lago** ◎ W Bolivia
55 P9 **Uruyén** Bolívar, SE Venezuela
149 O7 **Ūrūzgān** *var.* Oruzgān, Orūzgān. Urūzgān, C Afghanistan
149 N6 **Urūzgān** *Per.* Orūzgān. ◆ *province* C Afghanistan
165 T3 **Uryū-gawa** ↝ Hokkaidō, NE Japan
165 T2 **Uryū-ko** ◎ Hokkaidō, NE Japan
127 N8 **Uryupinsk** Volgogradskaya Oblast', SW Russian Federation
Ürzhar *see* Urdzhar
125 R16 **Urzhum** Kirovskaya Oblast', NW Russian Federation
116 K13 **Urziceni** Ialomiţa, SE Romania
U.S./USA *see* United States of America
164 E14 **Usa** Ōita, Kyūshū, SW Japan
119 L16 **Usa** *Rus.* Usa. ↝ C Belarus
127 T6 **Usa** ↝ NW Russian Federation
136 E14 **Uşak** *prev.* Ushak. Uşak, W Turkey
136 D14 **Uşak** *var.* Ushak. ◆ *province* W Turkey
83 C19 **Usakos** Erongo, W Namibia
81 J21 **Usambara Mountains** ▲ NE Tanzania
81 G23 **Usangu Flats** *wetland* SW Tanzania
65 D24 **Usborne, Mount** ▲ East Falkland, Falkland Islands
100 O8 **Usedom** *island* NE Germany
99 M24 **Useldange** Diekirch, C Luxembourg
118 L12 **Ushacha** *Rus.* Ushacha. Vitsyebskaya Voblasts', N Belarus
Ushachi *see* Ushacha
118 L13 **Ushacha** *Rus.* Ushachi. Vitsyebskaya Voblasts', N Belarus
Ushak *see* Uşak
122 L4 **Ushakova, Ostrov** *island* Severnaya Zemlya, N Russian Federation
Ushant *see* Ouessant, Île d'
Üsharal *see* Ucharal
164 B15 **Ushibuka** *var.* Usibuka. Kumamoto, Shimo-jima, SW Japan
Ushi Point *see* Sabaneta, Puntan
145 V14 **Ushtobe** *Kaz.* Üshtöbe. Almaty, SE Kazakhstan
63 I25 **Ushuaia** Tierra del Fuego, S Argentina
39 R10 **Usibelli** Alaska, USA
Usibuka *see* Ushibuka
186 D7 **Usino** Madang, N PNG
125 U6 **Usinsk** Respublika Komi, NW Russian Federation
97 K22 **Usk** *Wel.* Wysg. ↝ SE Wales, UK
Uskočke Planine/ Uskokengebirge *see* Gorjanci/Žumberačko Gorje
Uskoplje *see* Gornji Vakuf
Üsküb *see* Skopje
114 M11 **Üsküpdere** Kırklareli, NW Turkey
126 L7 **Usman'** Lipetskaya Oblast', W Russian Federation
118 D8 **Usmas Ezers** ◎ NW Latvia
125 U13 **Usol'ye** Permskaya Oblast', NW Russian Federation
41 T16 **Uspanapa, Río** ↝ SE Mexico
145 R11 **Uspenskiy** Karaganda, C Kazakhstan
103 O11 **Ussel** Corrèze, C France
163 Z6 **Ussuri** *var.* Usuri, Wusuri, *Chin.* Wusuli Jiang. ↝ China/Russian Federation
123 S15 **Ussuriysk** *prev.* Nikol'sk, Nikol'sk-Ussuriyskiy, Voroshilov. Primorskiy Kray, SE Russian Federation
136 J10 **Usta Burnu** *headland* N Turkey
149 P13 **Usta Muhammad** Baluchistān, SW Pakistan
123 V11 **Ust'-Bol'sheretsk** Kamchatskaya Oblast', E Russian Federation
127 N9 **Ust'-Buzulukskaya** Volgogradskaya Oblast', SW Russian Federation
111 C16 **Ústecký Kraj** ◆ *region* NW Czech Republic
108 G7 **Uster** Zürich, NE Switzerland
107 I22 **Ustica, Isola d'** *island* S Italy
122 M11 **Ust'-Ilimsk** Irkutskaya Oblast', C Russian Federation
111 C15 **Ústí nad Labem** *Ger.* Aussig. Ústecký Kraj, NW Czech Republic
111 F17 **Ústí nad Orlicí** *Ger.* Wildenschwert. Pardubický Kraj, E Czech Republic
Ustinov *see* Izhevsk
113 J14 **Ustiprača** Republika Srpska, SE Bosnia and Herzegovina
122 H11 **Ust'-Ishim** Omskaya Oblast', C Russian Federation
110 G6 **Ustka** *Ger.* Stolpmünde. Pomorskie, N Poland
123 V9 **Ust'-Kamchatsk** Kamchatskaya Oblast', E Russian Federation
145 X9 **Ust'-Kamenogorsk** *Kaz.* Öskemen. Vostochnyy Kazakhstan, E Kazakhstan
123 T10 **Ust'-Khayryuzovo** Koryakskiy Avtonomnyy Okrug, E Russian Federation
122 I14 **Ust'-Koksa** Respublika Altay, S Russian Federation
125 S11 **Ust'-Kulom** Respublika Komi, NW Russian Federation
123 Q8 **Ust'-Kuyga** Respublika Sakha (Yakutiya), NE Russian Federation
126 L14 **Ust'-Labinsk** Krasnodarskiy Kray, SW Russian Federation
123 R10 **Ust'-Maya** Respublika Sakha (Yakutiya), NE Russian Federation
123 R9 **Ust'-Nera** Respublika Sakha (Yakutiya), NE Russian Federation
123 P12 **Ust'-Nyukzha** Amurskaya Oblast', S Russian Federation
123 O7 **Ust'-Olenëk** Respublika Sakha (Yakutiya), NE Russian Federation
123 T9 **Ust'-Omchug** Magadanskaya Oblast', E Russian Federation
122 M13 **Ust'-Ordynskiy** Ust'-Ordynskiy Buryatskiy Avtonomnyy Okrug, S Russian Federation
122 M13 **Ust'-Ordynskiy Buryatskiy Avtonomnyy Okrug** ◆ *autonomous district* S Russian Federation
125 N8 **Ust'-Pinega** Arkhangel'skaya Oblast', NW Russian Federation
122 K8 **Ust'-Port** Taymyrskiy (Dolgano-Nenetskiy) Avtonomnyy Okrug, N Russian Federation
114 L11 **Ustrem** *prev.* Vakav. Yambol, E Bulgaria
111 O18 **Ustrzyki Dolne** Podkarpackie, SE Poland
Ust'-Sysol'sk *see* Syktyvkar
125 R7 **Ust'-Tsil'ma** Respublika Komi, NW Russian Federation
Ust Urt *see* Ustyurt Plateau
127 O11 **Ust'ya** ↝ NW Russian Federation
123 V10 **Ust'yevoye** *prev.* Kirovskiy. Kamchatskaya Oblast', E Russian Federation
117 R8 **Ustynivka** Kirovohrads'ka Oblast', C Ukraine
144 H15 **Ustyurt Plateau** *var.* Ust Urt, *Uzb.* Ustyurt Platosi. *plateau* Kazakhstan/Uzbekistan
Ustyurt Platosi *see* Ustyurt Plateau
124 K14 **Ustyuzhna** Vologodskaya Oblast', NW Russian Federation
158 J4 **Usu** Xinjiang Uygur Zizhiqu, NW China
171 O13 **Usu** Sulawesi, C Indonesia
164 E14 **Usuki** Ōita, Kyūshū, SW Japan
42 G8 **Usulután** Usulután, SE El Salvador
42 B9 **Usulután** ◆ *department* SE El Salvador
41 W16 **Usumacinta, Río** ↝ Guatemala/Mexico
Usumbura *see* Bujumbura
Usuri *see* Ussuri
171 W14 **Uta** Papua, E Indonesia
36 K5 **Utah** *off.* State of Utah; also known as Beehive State, Mormon State. ◆ *state* W USA
36 L3 **Utah Lake** ◎ Utah, W USA
Utaidhani *see* Uthai Thani
93 M14 **Utajärvi** Oulu, C Finland
Utamboni *see* Mitemele, Río
Utaradit *see* Uttaradit
165 T3 **Utashinai** *var.* Utasinai. Hokkaidō, NE Japan
Utasinai *see* Utashinai
193 Y14 **'Uta Vava'u** *island* Vava'u Group, N Tonga
37 V9 **Ute Creek** ↝ New Mexico, SW USA
118 H12 **Utena** Utena, E Lithuania
118 H12 **Utena** ◆ *province* E Lithuania
37 V10 **Ute Reservoir** ⊠ New Mexico, SW USA
167 O10 **Uthai Thani** *var.* Muang Uthai Thani, Udayadhani, Utaidhani. Uthai Thani, W Thailand
149 O15 **Uthal** Baluchistān, SW Pakistan
18 I10 **Utica** New York, NE USA
105 R10 **Utiel** País Valenciano, E Spain
11 O13 **Utikuma Lake** ◎ Alberta, W Canada
42 I4 **Utila, Isla de** *island* Islas de la Bahía, N Honduras
Utina *see* Udine
59 O17 **Utinga** Bahia, E Brazil
Utirik *see* Utrik Atoll
95 M22 **Utlängan** *island* S Sweden
117 U11 **Utlyuts'kyy Lyman** *bay* S Ukraine
95 P16 **Utö** Stockholm, C Sweden
25 Q12 **Utopia** Texas, SW USA
98 J11 **Utrecht** *Lat.* Trajectum ad Rhenum. Utrecht, C Netherlands
83 K22 **Utrecht** KwaZulu/Natal, E South Africa
98 I11 **Utrecht** ◆ *province* C Netherlands
104 K14 **Utrera** Andalucía, S Spain
189 V4 **Utrik Atoll** *var.* Utirik, Utrōk, Utrōnk. *atoll* Ratak Chain, N Marshall Islands
Utrōk/Utrōnk *see* Utrik Atoll
95 B16 **Utsira** *island* SW Norway
92 L8 **Utsjoki** *var.* Ohcejohka. Lappi, N Finland
165 O12 **Utsunomiya** *var.* Utunomiya. Tochigi, Honshū, S Japan
127 P13 **Utta** Respublika Kalmykiya, SW Russian Federation
167 O8 **Uttaradit** *var.* Utaradit. Uttaradit, N Thailand
152 J8 **Uttaranchal** ◆ *state* N India
152 J9 **Uttarkāshi** Uttaranchal, N India
152 K11 **Uttar Pradesh** *prev.* United Provinces, United Provinces of Agra and Oudh. ◆ *state* N India
45 T5 **Utuado** C Puerto Rico
158 K3 **Utubulak** Xinjiang Uygur Zizhiqu, W China
39 N5 **Utukok River** ↝ Alaska, USA
Utunomiya *see* Utsunomiya
187 P10 **Utupua** *island* Santa Cruz Islands, E Solomon Islands
144 G9 **Utva** ↝ NW Kazakhstan
189 Y15 **Utwe** Kosrae, E Micronesia
189 X15 **Utwe Harbor** *harbour* Kosrae, E Micronesia
162 J7 **Uubulan** Arhangay, C Mongolia
118 G6 **Uulu** Pärnumaa, SW Estonia
197 N13 **Uummannaq** *var.* Umanak, Umanaq. Kitaa, C Greenland
Uummannarsuaq *see* Nunap Isua
162 E4 **Üüreg Nuur** ◎ NW Mongolia
Uusikaarlepyy *see* Nykarleby
93 J19 **Uusikaupunki** *Swe.* Nystad. Länsi-Suomi, W Finland
127 S2 **Uva** Udmurtskaya Respublika, NW Russian Federation
113 L14 **Uvac** ↝ W Serbia and Montenegro (Yugo.)
25 Q12 **Uvalde** Texas, SW USA
155 K25 **Uva Province** ◆ *province* SE Sri Lanka
119 O18 **Uvaravichy** *Rus.* Uvarovichi. Homyel'skaya Voblasts', SE Belarus
54 J11 **Uvá, Río** ↝ E Colombia
Uvarovichi *see* Uvaravichy
127 N7 **Uvarovo** Tambovskaya Oblast', W Russian Federation
122 H10 **Uvat** Tyumenskaya Oblast', C Russian Federation
190 G12 **Uvea, Île** *island* N Wallis and Futuna
81 E21 **Uvinza** Kigoma, W Tanzania
79 O20 **Uvira** Sud Kivu, E Dem. Rep. Congo
162 E5 **Uvs** ◆ *province* NW Mongolia
162 F5 **Uvs Nuur** *var.* Ozero Ubsu-Nur. ◎ Mongolia/Russian Federation
164 F14 **Uwa** Ehime, Shikoku, SW Japan
164 F14 **Uwajima** *var.* Uwazima. Ehime, Shikoku, SW Japan
80 B5 **'Uwaynāt, Jabal al** *var.* Jebel Uweinat. ▲ Libya/Sudan
Uwazima *see* Uwajima
Uweinat, Jebel *see* 'Uwaynāt, Jabal al
14 H14 **Uxbridge** Ontario, S Canada
Uxellodunum *see* Issoudun
Uxin Qi *see* Dabqig
41 X12 **Uxmal, Ruinas** *ruins* Yucatán, SE Mexico
131 Q5 **Uy** ↝ Kazakhstan/Russian Federation
144 K15 **Uyaly** Kzylorda, S Kazakhstan
123 R8 **Uyandina** ↝ NE Russian Federation
122 L12 **Uyar** Krasnoyarskiy Kray, S Russian Federation
162 L10 **Üydzen** Ömnögovi, S Mongolia
Uyeda *see* Ueda
122 K5 **Uyedineniya, Ostrov** *island* N Russian Federation
77 V17 **Uyo** Akwa Ibom, S Nigeria
162 D8 **Üyönch** Hovd, W Mongolia
145 Q15 **Uyuk** Zhambyl, S Kazakhstan
141 V13 **'Uyūn** SW Oman
57 K20 **Uyuni** Potosí, W Bolivia
57 J20 **Uyuni, Salar de** *wetland* SW Bolivia
146 I9 **Uzbekistan** *off.* Republic of Uzbekistan. ◆ *republic* C Asia
158 D8 **Uzbel Shankou** *Rus.* Pereval Kyzyl-Dzhiik. *pass* China/Tajikistan
146 B11 **Uzboý** *prev. Rus.* Imeni 26 Bakinskikh Komissarov, *Turkm.* 26 Baku Komissarlary Adyndaky. Balkan Welaýaty, W Turkmenistan
119 J17 **Uzda** *Rus.* Uzda. Minskaya Voblasts', C Belarus
103 N12 **Uzerche** Corrèze, C France
103 R14 **Uzès** Gard, S France
147 T10 **Uzgen** *Kir.* Özgön. Oshskaya Oblast', SW Kyrgyzstan
117 O3 **Uzh** ↝ N Ukraine
Uzhgorod *see* Uzhhorod
116 G7 **Uzhhorod** *Rus.* Uzhgorod; *prev.* Ungvár. Zakarpats'ka Oblast', W Ukraine
Uzi *see* Uji
112 K13 **Užice** *prev.* Titovo Užice. Serbia, W Serbia and Montenegro (Yugo.)
Uzin *see* Uzyn
126 L5 **Uzlovaya** Tul'skaya Oblast', W Russian Federation
108 H7 **Uznach** Sankt Gallen, NE Switzerland
145 U16 **Uzunagach** Almaty, SE Kazakhstan
136 B10 **Uzunköprü** Edirne, NW Turkey
118 D11 **Užventis** Šiauliai, C Lithuania
117 P5 **Uzyn** *Rus.* Uzin. Kyyivs'ka Oblast', N Ukraine
145 N7 **Uzynkol'** *prev.* Lenin, Leninskoye. Kostanay, N Kazakhstan

V

Vääksy *see* Asikkala
83 H23 **Vaal** ↝ C South Africa
93 M14 **Vaala** Oulu, C Finland
93 N19 **Vaalimaa** Etelä-Suomi, S Finland
99 M19 **Vaals** Limburg, SE Netherlands
93 J16 **Vaasa** *Swe.* Vasa; *prev.* Nikolainkaupunki. Vaasa, W Finland
98 L10 **Vaassen** Gelderland, E Netherlands
118 G11 **Vabalninkas** Panevėžys, NE Lithuania
Vabkent *see* Vobkent
111 J22 **Vác** *Ger.* Waitzen. Pest, N Hungary
61 I14 **Vacaria** Rio Grande do Sul, S Brazil
35 N7 **Vacaville** California, W USA
103 R15 **Vaccarès, Étang de** ◎ SE France
44 L10 **Vache, Île à** *island* SW Haiti
173 Y16 **Vacoas** W Mauritius
32 G10 **Vader** Washington, NW USA
94 D12 **Vadheim** Sogn og Fjordane, S Norway
154 D11 **Vadodara** *prev.* Baroda. Gujarāt, W India
92 M8 **Vadsø** *Fin.* Vesisaari. Finnmark, N Norway
95 L17 **Vadstena** Östergötland, S Sweden
108 I8 **Vaduz** ● (Liechtenstein) W Liechtenstein
Vág *see* Váh
127 N12 **Vaga** ↝ NW Russian Federation
94 G11 **Vågåmo** Oppland, S Norway
112 D12 **Vaganski Vrh** ▲ W Croatia
95 A19 **Vágar** *Dan.* Vågø. *Island* Faeroe Islands
Vágbeszterce *see* Považská Bystrica
95 L19 **Vaggeryd** Jönköping, S Sweden
95 O16 **Vagnhärad** Södermanland, C Sweden
104 G7 **Vagos** Aveiro, N Portugal
Vágsellye *see* Sal'a
92 H10 **Vågsfjorden** *fjord* N Norway
94 C10 **Vågsøy** *island* S Norway
Vágújhely *see* Nové Mesto nad Váhom
111 I21 **Váh** *Ger.* Waag, *Hung.* Vág. ↝ W Slovakia
93 K16 **Vähäkyrö** Länsi-Suomi, W Finland
191 X11 **Vahitahi** *atoll* Îles Tuamotu, E French Polynesia
Váhtjer *see* Gällivare
Vaidei *see* Vulcan
22 L4 **Vaiden** Mississippi, S USA
155 I23 **Vaigai** ↝ SE India
191 V16 **Vaihu** Easter Island, Chile, E Pacific Ocean
118 I6 **Väike Emajõgi** ↝ S Estonia
118 I4 **Väike-Maarja** *Ger.* Klein-Marien. Lääne-Virumaa, NE Estonia
Väike-Salatsi *see* Mazsalaca
37 R4 **Vail** Colorado, C USA
193 V15 **Vaina** Tongatapu, S Tonga
118 E5 **Väinameri** *prev.* Muhu Väin, *Ger.* Moon-Sund. *sea* E Baltic Sea
93 N18 **Vainikkala** Etelä-Suomi, SE Finland
118 D10 **Vaiņode** Liepāja, SW Latvia
155 H23 **Vaippār** ↝ SE India
191 W11 **Vairaatea** *atoll* Îles Tuamotu, C French Polynesia
191 R8 **Vairao** Tahiti, W French Polynesia
103 R14 **Vaison-la-Romaine** Vaucluse, SE France
190 G11 **Vaitupu** Île Uvea, E Wallis and Futuna
190 F7 **Vaitupu** *atoll* C Tuvalu
Vajdahunyad *see* Hunedoara
Vajdej *see* Vulcan
78 K12 **Vakaga** ◆ *prefecture* NE Central African Republic
114 H10 **Vakarel** Sofiya, W Bulgaria
Vakav *see* Ustrem
137 O11 **Vakfıkebir** Trabzon, NE Turkey
122 J10 **Vakh** ↝ C Russian Federation
Vakhon, Qatorkŭhi *see* Nicholas Range
147 P14 **Vakhsh** SW Tajikistan
147 Q12 **Vakhsh** ↝ SW Tajikistan
127 P1 **Vakhtan** Nizhegorodskaya Oblast', W Russian Federation
94 C13 **Vaksdal** Hordaland, S Norway
127 O8 **Vashka** ↝ NW Russian Federation
Valachia *see* Wallachia
108 D11 **Valais** *Ger.* Wallis. ◆ *canton* SW Switzerland
113 M21 **Valamarës, Mali i** ▲ SE Albania
127 S2 **Valamaz** Udmurtskaya Respublika, NW Russian Federation
113 Q19 **Valandovo** SE FYR Macedonia
111 I18 **Valašské Meziříčí** *Ger.* Wallachisch-Meseritsch, *Pol.* Wałeckie Międzyrzecze. Zlínský Kraj, E Czech Republic
115 I17 **Valáxa** *island* Vóreioi Sporádes, Greece, Aegean Sea
95 K16 **Vålberg** Värmland, C Sweden
116 H12 **Vâlcea** *prev.* Vîlcea. ◆ *county* SW Romania
63 J16 **Valcheta** Río Negro, E Argentina
15 P12 **Valcourt** Québec, SE Canada
Valdai Hills *see* Valdayskaya Vozvyshennost'
104 M3 **Valdavia** ↝ N Spain
124 I15 **Valday** Novgorodskaya Oblast', W Russian Federation
126 I15 **Valdayskaya Vozvyshennost'** *var.* Valdai Hills. *hill range* W Russian Federation
104 L9 **Valdecañas, Embalse de** ⊠ W Spain
118 E8 **Valdemārpils** *Ger.* Sassmacken. Talsi, NW Latvia
95 N18 **Valdemarsvik** Östergötland, S Sweden
105 N8 **Valdemoro** Madrid, C Spain
105 O11 **Valdepeñas** Castilla-La Mancha, C Spain
104 L5 **Valderaduey** ↝ NE Spain
104 L5 **Valderas** Castilla-León, N Spain
105 T7 **Valderrobres** *var.* Vall-de-roures. Aragón, NE Spain
63 K17 **Valdés, Península** *peninsula* SE Argentina
39 S11 **Valdez** Alaska, USA
56 C5 **Valdéz** *var.* Limones. Esmeraldas, NW Ecuador
Valdia *see* Weldiya
103 U11 **Val d'Isère** Savoie, E France
63 G15 **Valdivia** Los Lagos, C Chile
Valdivia Bank *see* Valdivia Seamount
65 P17 **Valdivia Seamount** *var.* Valdivia Bank. *undersea feature* E Atlantic Ocean
103 N4 **Val-d'Oise** ◆ *department* N France
14 J8 **Val-d'Or** Québec, SE Canada
23 U8 **Valdosta** Georgia, SE USA
94 G13 **Valdres** *physical region* S Norway
32 L13 **Vale** Oregon, NW USA
116 F9 **Valea lui Mihai** *Hung.* Érmihályfalva. Bihor, NW Romania
11 N15 **Valemount** British Columbia, SW Canada
59 O17 **Valença** Bahia, E Brazil
104 F4 **Valença do Minho** Viana do Castelo, N Portugal
59 N14 **Valença do Piauí** Piauí, E Brazil
103 N8 **Valençay** Indre, C France
103 R13 **Valence** *anc.* Valentia, Valentia Julia, Ventia. Drôme, E France
105 S10 **Valencia** País Valenciano, E Spain
54 K5 **Valencia** Carabobo, N Venezuela
105 R10 **Valencia** *Cat.* València. ◆ *province* País Valenciano, E Spain
105 S10 **Valencia** ✕ Valencia, E Spain
Valencia/Valencia *see* País Valenciano
104 I10 **Valencia de Alcántara** Extremadura, W Spain
104 L4 **Valencia de Don Juan** Castilla-León, N Spain
105 U9 **Valencia, Golfo de** *var.* Gulf of Valencia. *gulf* E Spain
Valencia, Gulf of *see* Valencia, Golfo de
97 A21 **Valencia Island** *Ir.* Dairbhre. *island* SW Ireland
103 P2 **Valenciennes** Nord, N France
116 K13 **Vălenii de Munte** Prahova, SE Romania
Valentia *see* Valence, France
Valentia *see* País Valenciano
Valentia Julia *see* Valence
103 T8 **Valentigney** Doubs, E France
28 M12 **Valentine** Nebraska, C USA
24 J10 **Valentine** Texas, SW USA
Valentine State *see* Oregon
106 C8 **Valenza** Piemonte, NW Italy
94 I13 **Våler** Hedmark, S Norway
54 I6 **Valera** Trujillo, NW Venezuela
192 M11 **Valerie Guyot** *undersea feature* S Pacific Ocean
Valetta *see* Valletta
118 I7 **Valga** *Ger.* Walk, *Latv.* Valka. Valgamaa, S Estonia
118 I7 **Valgamaa** *off.* Valga Maakond. ◆ *province* S Estonia
43 Q15 **Valiente, Península** *peninsula* NW Panama
103 X16 **Valinco, Golfe de** *gulf* Corse, France, C Mediterranean Sea
112 L12 **Valjevo** Serbia, W Serbia and Montenegro (Yugo.)
Valjok *see* Válljohka
118 I7 **Valka** *Ger.* Walk. Valka, N Latvia
Valka *see* Valga
93 L18 **Valkeakoski** Länsi-Suomi, W Finland
93 M19 **Valkeala** Etelä-Suomi, S Finland
99 L18 **Valkenburg** Limburg, SE Netherlands
99 K15 **Valkenswaard** Noord-Brabant, S Netherlands
119 G15 **Valkininkai** Alytus, S Lithuania
117 U5 **Valky** Kharkivs'ka Oblast', E Ukraine
41 Y12 **Valladolid** Yucatán, SE Mexico
104 M5 **Valladolid** Castilla-León, NW Spain
104 L5 **Valladolid** ◆ *province* Castilla-León, N Spain
103 U15 **Vallauris** Alpes-Maritimes, SE France
Vall-de-roures *see* Valderrobres
105 S9 **Vall d'Uxó** País Valenciano, E Spain
95 E16 **Valle** Aust-Agder, S Norway
105 N2 **Valle** Cantabria, N Spain
42 H8 **Valle** ◆ *department* S Honduras
105 N8 **Vallecas** Madrid, C Spain
37 Q8 **Vallecito Reservoir** ⊠ Colorado, C USA
106 A7 **Valle d'Aosta** ◆ *region* NW Italy
41 O14 **Valle de Bravo** México, S Mexico
55 N5 **Valle de Guanape** Anzoátegui, N Venezuela
54 M6 **Valle de La Pascua** Guárico, N Venezuela
54 B11 **Valle del Cauca** *off.* Departamento del Valle del Cauca. ◆ *province* W Colombia
41 N13 **Valle de Santiago** Guanajuato, C Mexico
40 J7 **Valle de Zaragoza** Chihuahua, N Mexico
54 G5 **Valledupar** Cesar, N Colombia
76 G10 **Vallée de Ferlo** ↝ NW Senegal
57 M19 **Vallegrande** Santa Cruz, C Bolivia
41 P8 **Valle Hermoso** Tamaulipas, C Mexico
35 N8 **Vallejo** California, W USA
62 G8 **Vallenar** Atacama, N Chile
95 O15 **Vallentuna** Stockholm, C Sweden
121 P16 **Valletta** *prev.* Valetta. ● (Malta) E Malta
27 N6 **Valley Center** Kansas, C USA
29 Q5 **Valley City** North Dakota, N USA
32 I15 **Valley Falls** Oregon, NW USA
Valleyfield *see* Salaberry-de-Valleyfield
21 S4 **Valley Head** West Virginia, NE USA
25 T8 **Valley Mills** Texas, SW USA
75 W10 **Valley of the Kings** *ancient monument* E Egypt
29 R11 **Valley Springs** South Dakota, N USA
20 K5 **Valley Station** Kentucky, S USA
11 O13 **Valleyview** Alberta, W Canada
25 T5 **Valley View** Texas, SW USA
61 C21 **Vallimanca, Arroyo** ↝ E Argentina
92 L9 **Válljohka** *var.* Valjok. Finnmark, N Norway
107 M19 **Vallo della Lucania** Campania, S Italy
108 B9 **Vallorbe** Vaud, W Switzerland
105 V6 **Valls** Cataluña, NE Spain
94 N11 **Vallsta** Gävleborg, C Sweden
94 N12 **Vallvik** Gävleborg, C Sweden
11 T17 **Val Marie** Saskatchewan, S Canada
118 H7 **Valmiera** *Est.* Volmari, *Ger.* Wolmar. Valmiera, N Latvia
105 N3 **Valnera** ▲ N Spain
102 J3 **Valognes** Manche, N France
Valona *see* Vlorë
Valona Bay *see* Vlorës, Gjiri i
104 G6 **Valongo** *var.* Valongo de Gaia. Porto, N Portugal
Valongo de Gaia *see* Valongo
104 M5 **Valoria la Buena** Castilla-León, N Spain
119 J15 **Valozhyn** *Pol.* Wołożyn, *Rus.* Volozhin. Minskaya Voblasts', C Belarus
104 I5 **Valpaços** Vila Real, N Portugal
23 P8 **Valparaiso** Florida, SE USA
31 N11 **Valparaiso** Indiana, N USA
62 G11 **Valparaíso** Valparaíso, C Chile
40 L11 **Valparaíso** Zacatecas, C Mexico
62 G11 **Valparaíso** *off.* Región de Valparaíso. ◆ *region* C Chile
Valpo *see* Valpovo
112 I9 **Valpovo** *Hung.* Valpó. Osijek-Baranja, E Croatia
103 R14 **Valréas** Vaucluse, SE France
Vals *see* Vals-Platz
154 D12 **Valsād** *prev.* Bulsar. Gujarāt, W India
Valsbaai *see* False Bay
171 T12 **Valse Pisang, Kepulauan** *island group* E Indonesia
108 H9 **Vals-Platz** *var.* Vals. Graubünden, S Switzerland
171 X16 **Vals, Tanjung** *headland* Papua, SE Indonesia
93 N15 **Valtimo** Itä-Suomi, E Finland
115 D17 **Váltou** ▲ C Greece
127 O12 **Valuyevka** Rostovskaya Oblast', SW Russian Federation
126 K9 **Valuyki** Belgorodskaya Oblast', W Russian Federation
36 L2 **Val Verda** Utah, W USA
64 N12 **Valverde** Hierro, Islas Canarias, Spain, NE Atlantic Ocean
104 I13 **Valverde del Camino** Andalucía, S Spain
95 G23 **Vamdrup** Vejle, C Denmark
94 L12 **Våmhus** Dalarna, C Sweden
93 K18 **Vammala** Länsi-Suomi, W Finland
Vámosudvarhely *see* Odorheiu Secuiesc
137 S14 **Van** Van, E Turkey
25 V7 **Van** Texas, SW USA
137 T14 **Van** ◆ *province* E Turkey
137 T11 **Vanadzor** *prev.* Kirovakan. N Armenia
25 U5 **Van Alstyne** Texas, SW USA
33 W10 **Vananda** Montana, NW USA
116 I11 **Vânători** *Hung.* Héjjasfalva; *prev.* Vînători. Mureş, C Romania
191 W12 **Vanavana** *atoll* Îles Tuamotu, SE French Polynesia
Vana-Vändra *see* Vändra
122 M11 **Vanavara** Evenkiyskiy Avtonomnyy Okrug, C Russian Federation
15 Q8 **Van Bruyssel** Québec, SE Canada
27 R10 **Van Buren** Arkansas, C USA
19 S1 **Van Buren** Maine, NE USA
27 W7 **Van Buren** Missouri, C USA
19 T5 **Vanceboro** Maine, NE USA
21 W10 **Vanceboro** North Carolina, SE USA
21 O4 **Vanceburg** Kentucky, S USA
Vanch *see* Vanj
10 L17 **Vancouver** British Columbia, SW Canada
32 G11 **Vancouver** Washington, NW USA
10 L17 **Vancouver** ✕ British Columbia, SW Canada
10 K16 **Vancouver Island** *island* British Columbia, SW Canada
Vanda *see* Vantaa
171 X13 **Van Daalen** ↝ Papua, E Indonesia
30 L15 **Vandalia** Illinois, N USA
27 V3 **Vandalia** Missouri, C USA
31 R13 **Vandalia** Ohio, N USA
25 U13 **Vanderbilt** Texas, SW USA
31 Q10 **Vandercook Lake** Michigan, N USA
10 L14 **Vanderhoof** British Columbia, SW Canada
18 K8 **Vanderwhacker Mountain** ▲ New York, NE USA
181 P1 **Van Diemen Gulf** *gulf* Northern Territory, N Australia
Van Diemen's Land *see* Tasmania
118 H5 **Vändra** *Ger.* Fennern; *prev.* Vana-Vändra. Pärnumaa, SW Estonia
Vandsburg *see* Więcbork
34 L4 **Van Duzen River** ↝ California, W USA
118 F13 **Vandžiogala** Kaunas, C Lithuania
41 N10 **Vanegas** San Luis Potosí, C Mexico
Vaner, Lake *see* Vänern
95 K17 **Vänern** *Eng.* Lake Vaner; *prev.* Lake Vener. ◎ S Sweden
95 J18 **Vänersborg** Västra Götaland, S Sweden
94 F12 **Vang** Oppland, S Norway
172 I7 **Vangaindrano** Fianarantsoa, SE Madagascar
137 S14 **Van Gölü** *Eng.* Lake Van; *anc.* Thospitis. *salt lake* E Turkey
186 L9 **Vangunu** *island* New Georgia Islands, NW Solomon Islands
24 J9 **Van Horn** Texas, SW USA
187 Q11 **Vanikolo** *var.* Vanikoro. *island* Santa Cruz Islands, E Solomon Islands
Vanikoro *see* Vanikolo
186 A5 **Vanimo** Sandaun, NW PNG
123 T13 **Vanino** Khabarovskiy Kray, SE Russian Federation
155 G19 **Vānīvilāsa Sāgara** ◎ SW India
147 S13 **Vanj** *Rus.* Vanch. S Tajikistan
116 G14 **Vânju Mare** *prev.* Vînju Mare. Mehedinţi, SW Romania
15 N12 **Vankleek Hill** Ontario, SE Canada
Van, Lake *see* Van Gölü
93 I16 **Vännäs** Västerbotten, N Sweden
93 I15 **Vännäsby** Västerbotten, N Sweden
102 H7 **Vannes** *anc.* Dariorigum. Morbihan, NW France
92 I8 **Vannøya** *island* N Norway
103 T12 **Vanoise, Massif de la** ▲ E France
83 E24 **Vanrhynsdorp** Western Cape, SW South Africa
21 P7 **Vansant** Virginia, NE USA
94 L13 **Vansbro** Dalarna, C Sweden
95 D18 **Vanse** Vest-Agder, S Norway
9 P7 **Vansittart Island** *island* Nunavut, NE Canada
93 M20 **Vantaa** *Swe.* Vanda. Etelä-Suomi, S Finland

93 L19 **Vantaa** × (Helsinki) Etelä-Suomi, S Finland
32 J9 **Vantage** Washington, NW USA
187 Z14 **Vanua Balavu** prev. Vanua Mbalavu. island Lau Group, E Fiji
187 R12 **Vanua Lava** island Banks Islands, N Vanuatu
187 Y13 **Vanua Levu** island N Fiji
Vanua Mbalavu see Vanua Balavu
187 R12 **Vanuatu** off. Republic of Vanuatu; prev. New Hebrides. ◆ republic SW Pacific Ocean
175 P8 **Vanuatu** island group SW Pacific Ocean
31 Q12 **Van Wert** Ohio, N USA
187 Q17 **Vao** Province Sud, S New Caledonia
Vapincum see Gap
117 N7 **Vapnyarka** Vinnyts'ka Oblast', C Ukraine
103 T15 **Var** ◈ department SE France
103 U14 **Var** ≈ SE France
95 J18 **Vara** Västra Götaland, S Sweden
Varadinska Županija see Varaždin
118 J10 **Varakļani** Madona, C Latvia
106 C7 **Varallo** Piemonte, NE Italy
143 O5 **Varāmīn** var. Veramin. Tehrān, N Iran
153 N14 **Vārānasi** prev. Banaras, Benares, hist. Kasi. Uttar Pradesh, N India
125 T3 **Varandey** Nenetskiy Avtonomnyy Okrug, NW Russian Federation
92 M8 **Varangerbotn** Finnmark, N Norway
92 M8 **Varangerfjorden** Lapp. Várjjatvuotna. fjord N Norway
92 M8 **Varangerhalvøya** Lapp. Várnjárga. peninsula N Norway
Varannó see Vranov nad Topľou
107 M15 **Varano, Lago di** ◎ SE Italy
118 J13 **Varapayeva** Rus. Voropayevo. Vitsyebskaya Voblasts', NW Belarus
Varasd see Varaždin
112 E7 **Varaždin** Ger. Warasdin, Hung. Varasd. Varaždin, N Croatia
112 E7 **Varaždin** off. Varadinska Županija. ◈ province N Croatia
106 C10 **Varazze** Liguria, NW Italy
95 J20 **Varberg** Halland, S Sweden
Vardak see Wardag
113 Q19 **Vardar** Gk. Axiós. ≈ FYR Macedonia/Greece see also Axiós
95 F23 **Varde** Ribe, W Denmark
137 V12 **Vardenis** E Armenia
92 N8 **Vardø** Fin. Vuoreija. Finnmark, N Norway
115 E18 **Vardoúsia** ▲▲ C Greece
Vareia see Logroño
100 G10 **Varel** Niedersachsen, NW Germany
119 G15 **Varėna** Pol. Orany. Alytus, S Lithuania
15 O12 **Varennes** Québec, SE Canada
103 P10 **Varennes-sur-Allier** Allier, C France
112 I12 **Vareš** Federacija Bosna I Hercegovina, E Bosnia and Herzegovina
106 D7 **Varese** Lombardia, N Italy
116 J12 **Vârful Moldoveanu** var. Moldoveanul; prev. Virful Moldoveanu. ▲ C Romania
Varganzi see Warganza
95 J18 **Vårgårda** Västra Götaland, S Sweden
95 J18 **Vargön** Västra Götaland, S Sweden
95 C17 **Varhaug** Rogaland, S Norway
Várjjatvuotna see Varangerfjorden
93 N17 **Varkaus** Itä-Suomi, C Finland
92 J2 **Varmahlidh** Nordhurland Vestra, N Iceland
95 J15 **Värmland** ◈ county C Sweden
95 K16 **Värmlandsnäs** peninsula S Sweden
114 N8 **Varna** prev. Stalin, anc. Odessus. Varna, E Bulgaria
114 N8 **Varna** × Varna, E Bulgaria
114 N8 **Varna** ◈ province E Bulgaria
95 L20 **Värnamo** Jönköping, S Sweden
114 N8 **Varnenski Zaliv** prev. Stalinski Zaliv. bay E Bulgaria
114 N8 **Varnensko Ezero** estuary E Bulgaria
118 D11 **Varniai** Telšiai, W Lithuania
Várnjárga see Varangerhalvøya
Varnoús see Baba
111 D14 **Varnsdorf** Ger. Warnsdorf. Ústecký Kraj, N Czech Republic
111 I23 **Várpalota** Veszprém, W Hungary
Varshava see Warszawa
118 K6 **Värska** Põlvamaa, SE Estonia
98 N12 **Varsseveld** Gelderland, E Netherlands
115 D19 **Vartholomió** prev. Vartholomión. Dytikí Ellás, S Greece
Vartholomión see Vartholomió
137 Q14 **Varto** Muş, E Turkey
95 K18 **Vartofta** Västra Götaland, S Sweden
93 O17 **Värtsilä** Itä-Suomi, E Finland
Värtsilä see Vyartsilya
117 R4 **Varva** Chernihivs'ka Oblast', NE Ukraine
59 H18 **Várzea Grande** Mato Grosso, SW Brazil
106 D9 **Varzi** Lombardia, N Italy
Varzimanor Ayni see Ayní
126 K5 **Varzuga** ≈ NW Russian Federation
103 P8 **Varzy** Nièvre, C France
111 G23 **Vas** off. Vas Megye. ◈ county W Hungary
Vasa see Vaasa
190 A9 **Vasafua** island Funafuti Atoll, C Tuvalu
111 O21 **Vásárosnamény** Szabolcs-Szatmár-Bereg, E Hungary
104 H13 **Vascão, Ribeira de** ≈ S Portugal
116 G10 **Vaşcău** Hung. Vaskoh. Bihor, NE Romania
Vascongadas, Provincias see País Vasco
Vashess Bay see Vaskess Bay
Vāsht see Khāsh
Vasilevichi see Vasilyevichy
115 G14 **Vasiliká** Kentrikí Makedonía, NE Greece
115 C18 **Vasilikí** Lefkáda, Iónioi Nísoi, Greece, C Mediterranean Sea
115 K25 **Vasilikí** Kríti, Greece, E Mediterranean Sea
119 G16 **Vasilishki** Pol. Wasiliszki, Rus. Vasilishki. Hrodzyenskaya Voblasts', W Belarus
Vasil Kolarov see Pamporovo
Vasil'kov see Vasyl'kiv
119 N19 **Vasilyevichy** Rus. Vasilevichi. Homyel'skaya Voblasts', SE Belarus
191 Y3 **Vaskess Bay** var. Vashess Bay. bay Kiritimati, E Kiribati
Vaskoh see Vaşcău
Vaskohsziklás see Ştei
116 M10 **Vaslui** Vaslui, C Romania
116 L11 **Vaslui** ◈ county NE Romania
31 R8 **Vassar** Michigan, N USA
95 E15 **Vassdalsegga** ▲ S Norway
60 P9 **Vassouras** Rio de Janeiro, SE Brazil
95 N15 **Västerås** Västmanland, C Sweden
93 G15 **Västerbotten** ◈ county N Sweden
94 K12 **Västerdalälven** ≈ C Sweden
95 O16 **Västerhaninge** Stockholm, C Sweden
94 M10 **Västernorrland** ◈ county C Sweden
95 N19 **Västervik** Kalmar, S Sweden
95 M15 **Västmanand** ◈ county C Sweden
107 L15 **Vasto** anc. Histonium. Abruzzo, C Italy
95 J19 **Västra Götaland** ◈ county S Sweden
95 J16 **Västra Silen** ◎ S Sweden
111 G23 **Vasvár** Ger. Eisenburg. Vas, W Hungary
117 U9 **Vasylivka** Zaporiz'ka Oblast', SE Ukraine
117 O5 **Vasyl'kiv** Rus. Vasil'kov. Kyyivs'ka Oblast', N Ukraine
122 I11 **Vasyugan** ≈ C Russian Federation
103 N8 **Vatan** Indre, C France
Vaté see Efate
107 G15 **Vatican City** off. Vatican City State. ◆ papal state S Europe
107 M22 **Vaticano, Capo** headland S Italy
92 K3 **Vatnajökull** glacier SE Iceland
95 P15 **Vätö** Stockholm, C Sweden
187 Z16 **Vatoa** island Lau Group, SE Fiji
172 J5 **Vatomandry** Toamasina, E Madagascar
116 J9 **Vatra Dornei** Ger. Dorna Watra. Suceava, NE Romania
116 J9 **Vatra Moldoviței** Suceava, NE Romania
Vatter, Lake see Vättern
95 L18 **Vättern** Eng. Lake Vatter; prev. Lake Vetter. ◎ S Sweden
187 X5 **Vatulele** island SW Fiji
117 P7 **Vatutine** Cherkas'ka Oblast', C Ukraine
187 W15 **Vatu Vara** island Lau Group, E Fiji
103 R14 **Vaucluse** ◈ department SE France
103 S5 **Vaucouleurs** Meuse, NE France
108 B9 **Vaud** Ger. Waadt. ◈ canton SW Switzerland
15 N12 **Vaudreuil** Québec, SE Canada
37 T12 **Vaughn** New Mexico, SW USA
54 I14 **Vaupés** off. Comisaría del Vaupés. ◈ province SE Colombia
54 I13 **Vaupés, Río** var. Rio Uaupés. ≈ Brazil/Colombia see also Uaupés, Rio
103 Q15 **Vauvert** Gard, S France
11 R17 **Vauxhall** Alberta, SW Canada
99 K23 **Vaux-sur-Sûre** Luxembourg, SE Belgium
172 J4 **Vavatenina** Toamasina, E Madagascar
193 Y14 **Vava'u Group** island group N Tonga
76 M16 **Vavoua** W Ivory Coast
127 S2 **Vavozh** Udmurtskaya Respublika, NW Russian Federation
155 K23 **Vavuniya** Northern Province, N Sri Lanka
119 G17 **Vawkavysk** Pol. Wołkowysk, Rus. Volkovysk. Hrodzyenskaya Voblasts', W Belarus
119 F17 **Vawkavyskaye Wzvyshsha** Rus. Volkovyskiye Vysoty. hill range W Belarus
95 P15 **Vaxholm** Stockholm, C Sweden
95 L21 **Växjö** var. Vexiö. Kronoberg, S Sweden
127 T1 **Vaygach, Ostrov** island NW Russian Federation
137 V13 **Vayk'** prev. Azizbekov. SE Armenia
Vazáš see Vittangi
125 P8 **Vazhgort** prev. Chasovo. Respublika Komi, NW Russian Federation
45 V10 **V.C.Bird** × (St John's) Antigua, Antigua and Barbuda
95 C16 **Veavågen** Rogaland, S Norway
29 Q7 **Veblen** South Dakota, N USA
98 N9 **Vecht** Ger. Vechte. ≈ Germany/Netherlands see also Vechte
100 G12 **Vechta** Niedersachsen, NW Germany
100 E12 **Vechte** Dut. Vecht. ≈ Germany/Netherlands see also Vecht
118 I8 **Vecpiebalga** Cēsis, C Latvia
118 G9 **Vecumnieki** Bauska, C Latvia
Vedāvati see Hagari
95 J20 **Veddige** Halland, S Sweden
116 J15 **Vedea** ≈ S Romania
127 P16 **Vedeno** Chechenskaya Respublika, SW Russian Federation
98 O6 **Veendam** Groningen, NE Netherlands
98 K12 **Veenendaal** Utrecht, C Netherlands
99 E14 **Veere** Zeeland, SW Netherlands
24 M2 **Vega** Texas, SW USA
92 E13 **Vega** island C Norway
45 T5 **Vega Baja** C Puerto Rico
38 D17 **Vega Point** headland Kiska Island, Alaska, USA
95 F17 **Vegår** ◎ S Norway
99 K14 **Veghel** Noord-Brabant, S Netherlands
Veglia see Krk
114 E13 **Vegorítis, Límni** ◎ N Greece
11 Q14 **Vegreville** Alberta, SW Canada
95 K21 **Veinge** Halland, S Sweden
61 B21 **Veinticinco de Mayo** var. 25 de Mayo. Buenos Aires, E Argentina
63 I14 **Veinticinco de Mayo** La Pampa, C Argentina
119 F15 **Veisiejai** Alytus, S Lithuania
95 F23 **Vejen** Ribe, W Denmark
104 K16 **Vejer de la Frontera** Andalucía, S Spain
95 G23 **Vejle** Vejle, C Denmark
95 F23 **Vejle** off. Vejle Amt. ◈ county C Denmark
114 M7 **Vekilski** Shumen, NE Bulgaria
54 G3 **Vela, Cabo de la** headland NE Colombia
Vela Goa see Goa
113 F15 **Vela Luka** Dubrovnik-Neretva, S Croatia
61 G19 **Velázquez** Rocha, E Uruguay
101 E15 **Velbert** Nordrhein-Westfalen, W Germany
109 S9 **Velden** Kärnten, S Austria
Veldes see Bled
99 K15 **Veldhoven** Noord-Brabant, S Netherlands
112 C11 **Velebit** ▲▲ C Croatia
114 N11 **Veleka** ≈ SE Bulgaria
109 V10 **Velenje** Ger. Wöllan. N Slovenia
190 E12 **Vele, Pointe** headland Île Futuna, S Wallis and Futuna
113 O18 **Veles** Turk. Köprülü. C FYR Macedonia
113 M20 **Velešta** SW FYR Macedonia
115 F16 **Velestíno** prev. Velestínon. Thessalía, C Greece
Velestínon see Velestíno
Velevshchina see Vyelyewshchyna
54 F9 **Vélez** Santander, C Colombia
105 Q13 **Vélez Blanco** Andalucía, S Spain
104 M17 **Vélez de la Gomera, Peñon de** island group S Spain
105 N15 **Vélez-Málaga** Andalucía, S Spain
105 Q13 **Vélez Rubio** Andalucía, S Spain
Velha Goa see Goa
Velho see Porto Velho
112 E8 **Velika Gorica** Zagreb, N Croatia
112 C9 **Velika Kapela** ▲▲ NW Croatia
Velika Kikinda see Kikinda
112 D10 **Velika Kladuša** Federacija Bosna I Hercegovina, NW Bosnia and Herzegovina
112 N11 **Velika Morava** var. Glavn'a Morava, Morava, Ger. Grosse Morava. ≈ C Serbia and Montenegro (Yugo.)
112 N12 **Velika Plana** Serbia, C Serbia and Montenegro (Yugo.)
109 U10 **Velika Raduha** ▲ N Slovenia
123 V7 **Velikaya** ≈ NE Russian Federation
126 F15 **Velikaya** ≈ W Russian Federation
Velikaya Berestovitsa see Vyalikaya Byerastavitsa
Velikaya Lepetikha see Velyka Lepetykha
Veliki Bečkerek see Zrenjanin
112 P12 **Veliki Krš** var. Stol. ▲ E Serbia and Montenegro (Yugo.)
114 L8 **Veliki Preslav** prev. Preslav. Shumen, NE Bulgaria
112 B9 **Veliki Risnjak** ▲ NW Croatia
109 T13 **Veliki Snežnik** Ger. Schneeberg, It. Monte Nevoso. ▲ SW Slovenia
112 J13 **Veliki Stolac** ▲ E Bosnia and Herzegovina
Velikiy Bor see Vyaliki Bor
124 G16 **Velikiye Luki** Pskovskaya Oblast', W Russian Federation
124 H14 **Velikiy Novgorod** prev. Novgorod. Novgorodskaya Oblast', W Russian Federation
125 P12 **Velikiy Ustyug** Vologodskaya Oblast', NW Russian Federation
112 N11 **Veliko Gradište** Serbia, NE Serbia and Montenegro (Yugo.)
155 I18 **Velikonda Range** ▲▲ SE India
114 K9 **Veliko Tŭrnovo** prev. Tirnovo, Trnovo, Tŭrnovo. Veliko Tŭrnovo, N Bulgaria
114 K8 **Veliko Tŭrnovo** ◈ province N Bulgaria
Velikovec see Völkermarkt
125 R5 **Velikovisochnoye** Nenetskiy Avtonomnyy Okrug, NW Russian Federation
76 H12 **Vélingara** C Senegal
76 H11 **Vélingara** S Senegal
114 H11 **Velingrad** Pazardzhik, C Bulgaria
126 H3 **Velizh** Smolenskaya Oblast', W Russian Federation
111 F16 **Velká Deštná** var. Deštná, Grosskoppe, Ger. Deschnaer Koppe. ▲ NE Czech Republic
111 F18 **Velké Meziříčí** Ger. Grossmeseritsch. Vysočina, C Czech Republic
92 N1 **Velkomstpynten** headland NW Svalbard
111 K21 **Veľký Krtíš** Banskobystrický Kraj, C Slovakia
186 J8 **Vella Lavella** var. Mbilua. island New Georgia Islands, NW Solomon Islands
107 I15 **Velletri** Lazio, C Italy
95 K23 **Vellinge** Skåne, S Sweden
155 I19 **Vellore** Tamil Nādu, SE India
Velobriga see Viana do Castelo
115 G21 **Velopoúla** island S Greece
98 M12 **Velp** Gelderland, SE Netherlands
Velsen see Velsen-Noord
98 H9 **Velsen-Noord** var. Velsen. Noord-Holland, W Netherlands
125 N12 **Vel'sk** var. Velsk. Arkhangel'skaya Oblast', NW Russian Federation
Velsuna see Orvieto
98 K10 **Veluwemeer** lake channel C Netherlands
28 M3 **Velva** North Dakota, N USA
115 E14 **Velvendós** var. Velvendos. Dytikí Makedonía, N Greece
117 S5 **Velyka Bahachka** Poltavs'ka Oblast', C Ukraine
117 S9 **Velyka Lepetykha** Rus. Velikaya Lepetikha. Khersons'ka Oblast', S Ukraine
117 O10 **Velyka Mykhaylivka** Odes'ka Oblast', SW Ukraine
117 W8 **Velyka Novosilka** Donets'ka Oblast', E Ukraine
117 S9 **Velyka Oleksandrivka** Khersons'ka Oblast', S Ukraine
117 T4 **Velyka Pysanivka** Sums'ka Oblast', NE Ukraine
116 G6 **Velykyy Bereznyy** Zakarpats'ka Oblast', W Ukraine
117 W4 **Velykyy Burluk** Kharkivs'ka Oblast', E Ukraine
Velykyy Tokmak see Tokmak
173 P7 **Vema Fracture Zone** tectonic feature W Indian Ocean
65 P18 **Vema Seamount** undersea feature SW Indian Ocean
93 F17 **Vemdalen** Jämtland, C Sweden
95 N19 **Vena** Kalmar, S Sweden
41 N11 **Venado** San Luis Potosí, C Mexico
62 L11 **Venado Tuerto** Entre Ríos, E Argentina
61 A19 **Venado Tuerto** Santa Fe, C Argentina
107 K16 **Venafro** Molise, C Italy
55 Q9 **Venamo, Cerro** ▲ E Venezuela
106 B8 **Venaria** Piemonte, NW Italy
103 U15 **Vence** Alpes-Maritimes, SE France
104 H5 **Venda Nova** Vila Real, N Portugal
104 G11 **Vendas Novas** Évora, S Portugal
102 J9 **Vendée** ◈ department NW France
103 Q6 **Vendeuvre-sur-Barse** Aube, NE France
102 M7 **Vendôme** Loir-et-Cher, C France
Venedig see Venezia
Vener, Lake see Vänern
106 I8 **Veneta, Laguna** lagoon NE Italy
Venetia see Venezia
39 S7 **Venetie** Alaska, USA
106 H8 **Veneto** var. Venezia Euganea. ◈ region NE Italy
114 M7 **Venets** Shumen, NE Bulgaria
126 L5 **Venev** Tul'skaya Oblast', W Russian Federation
106 I8 **Venezia** Eng. Venice, Fr. Venise, Ger. Venedig; anc. Venetia. Veneto, NE Italy
Venezia Euganea see Veneto
Venezia, Golfo di see Venice, Gulf of
Venezia Tridentina see Trentino-Alto Adige
54 K8 **Venezuela** off. Republic of Venezuela; prev. Estados Unidos de Venezuela, United States of Venezuela. ◆ republic N South America
Venezuela, Cordillera de see Costa, Cordillera de la
54 I4 **Venezuela, Golfo de** Eng. Gulf of Maracaibo, Gulf of Venezuela. gulf NW Venezuela
Venezuela, Gulf of see Venezuela, Golfo de
64 F11 **Venezuelan Basin** undersea feature E Caribbean Sea
155 D16 **Vengurla** Mahārāshtra, W India
39 O15 **Veniaminof, Mount** ▲ Alaska, USA
23 V14 **Venice** Florida, SE USA
22 L10 **Venice** Louisiana, S USA
Venice see Venezia
106 J8 **Venice, Gulf of** It. Golfo di Venezia, Slvn. Beneški Zaliv. gulf N Adriatic Sea
Venise see Venezia
94 K13 **Venjan** Dalarna, C Sweden
94 K13 **Venjansjön** ◎ C Sweden
155 J18 **Venkatagiri** Andhra Pradesh, E India
99 M15 **Venlo** prev. Venloo. Limburg, SE Netherlands
Venloo see Venlo
95 E18 **Vennesla** Vest-Agder, S Norway
107 M17 **Venosa** anc. Venusia. Basilicata, S Italy
Venoste, Alpi see Ötztaler Alpen
Venraij see Venray
99 M14 **Venray** var. Venraij. Limburg, SE Netherlands
118 C8 **Venta** Ger. Windau. ≈ Latvia/Lithuania
Venta Belgarum see Winchester
40 G9 **Ventana, Punta Arena de la** var. Punta de la Ventana. headland W Mexico
Ventana, Punta de la see Ventana, Punta Arena de la
61 B23 **Ventana, Sierra de la** hill range E Argentina
Ventia see Valence
191 S11 **Vent, Îles du** var. Windward Islands. island group Archipel de la Société, W French Polynesia
191 R10 **Vent, Îles Sous le** var. Leeward Islands. island group Archipel de la Société, W French Polynesia
106 B11 **Ventimiglia** Liguria, NW Italy
97 M24 **Ventnor** S England, UK
18 J17 **Ventnor City** New Jersey, NE USA
103 S14 **Ventoux, Mont** ▲ SE France
118 C8 **Ventspils** Ger. Windau. Ventspils, NW Latvia
54 M10 **Ventuari, Río** ≈ S Venezuela
35 R15 **Ventura** California, W USA
182 F8 **Venus Bay** South Australia
Venusia see Venosa
191 P7 **Vénus, Pointe** var. Pointe Tataaihoa. headland Tahiti, W French Polynesia
41 V16 **Venustiano Carranza** Chiapas, SE Mexico
41 N7 **Venustiano Carranza, Presa** ⊡ NE Mexico
61 B15 **Vera** Santa Fe, C Argentina
105 Q14 **Vera** Andalucía, S Spain
63 K18 **Vera, Bahía** bay E Argentina
41 R14 **Veracruz** var. Veracruz Llave. Veracruz-Llave, E Mexico
41 Q13 **Veracruz-Llave** var. Veracruz. ◈ state E Mexico
43 Q16 **Veraguas** off. Provincia de Veraguas. ◈ province W Panama
Veramin see Varāmīn
154 B12 **Verāval** Gujarāt, W India
106 C6 **Verbania** Piemonte, NW Italy
107 N20 **Verbicaro** Calabria, SW Italy
108 D11 **Verbier** Valais, SW Switzerland
Vercellae see Vercelli
106 C8 **Vercelli** anc. Vercellae. Piemonte, NW Italy
103 S13 **Vercors** physical region E France
Verdal see Verdalsøra
93 E16 **Verdalsøra** var. Verdal. Nord-Trøndelag, C Norway
Verde, Cabo see Cape Verde
44 J5 **Verde, Cape** headland Long Island, C Bahamas
104 M2 **Verde, Costa** coastal region N Spain
Verde Grande, Río/Verde Grande y de Belem, Río see Verde, Río
100 H11 **Verden** Niedersachsen, NW Germany
57 J19 **Verde, Río** ≈ SE Brazil
57 P16 **Verde, Río** ≈ Bolivia/Brazil
40 M12 **Verde, Río** var. Río Verde Grande, Río Verde Grande y de Belem. ≈ C Mexico
41 Q16 **Verde, Río** ≈ SE Mexico
36 L13 **Verde River** ≈ Arizona, SW USA
Verdhikoúsa/Verdhikoússa see Verdikoússa
27 Q8 **Verdigris River** ≈ Kansas/Oklahoma, C USA
115 E15 **Verdikoússa** var. Verdhikoúsa, Verdhikoússa. Thessalía, C Greece
103 S15 **Verdon** ≈ SE France
15 O12 **Verdun** Québec, SE Canada
103 S4 **Verdun** var. Verdun-sur-Meuse; anc. Verodunum. Meuse, NE France
Verdun-sur-Meuse see Verdun
83 J21 **Vereeniging** Gauteng, NE South Africa
Veremeyki see Vyeramyeyki
125 T14 **Vereshchagino** Permskaya Oblast', NW Russian Federation
76 G14 **Verga, Cap** headland W Guinea
61 G18 **Vergara** Treinta y Tres, E Uruguay
108 G11 **Vergeletto** Ticino, S Switzerland
18 L8 **Vergennes** Vermont, NE USA
Veria see Véroia
104 I5 **Verín** Galicia, NW Spain
Verin T'alin see T'alin
118 K6 **Veriora** Põlvamaa, SE Estonia
117 T7 **Verkhivtseve** Dnipropetrovs'ka Oblast', E Ukraine
127 W3 **Verkhniye Kigi** Respublika Bashkortostan, W Russian Federation
Verkhnedvinsk see Vyerkhnyadzvinsk
122 K10 **Verkhneimbatsk** Krasnoyarskiy Kray, N Russian Federation
124 I3 **Verkhnetulomskiy** Murmanskaya Oblast', NW Russian Federation
126 I3 **Verkhnetulomskoye Vodokhranilishche** ⊡ NW Russian Federation
Verkhneudinsk see Ulan-Ude
123 P10 **Verkhnevilyuysk** Respublika Sakha (Yakutiya), NE Russian Federation
127 W5 **Verkhniy Avzyan** Respublika Bashkortostan, W Russian Federation
127 Q11 **Verkhniy Baskunchak** Astrakhanskaya Oblast', SW Russian Federation
117 T9 **Verkhniy Rohachyk** Khersons'ka Oblast', S Ukraine
123 Q11 **Verkhnyaya Amga** Respublika Sakha (Yakutiya), NE Russian Federation
125 V6 **Verkhnyaya Inta** Respublika Komi, NW Russian Federation
125 O10 **Verkhnyaya Toyma** Arkhangel'skaya Oblast', NW Russian Federation
126 K6 **Verkhov'ye** Orlovskaya Oblast', W Russian Federation
116 I8 **Verkhovyna** Ivano-Frankivs'ka Oblast', W Ukraine
123 P8 **Verkhoyanskiy Khrebet** ▲▲ NE Russian Federation
117 T7 **Verkhn'odniprovs'k** Dnipropetrovs'ka Oblast', E Ukraine
101 G14 **Verl** Nordrhein-Westfalen, NW Germany
92 N1 **Verlegenhuken** headland N Svalbard
82 A9 **Vermelha, Ponta** headland NW Angola
103 P7 **Vermenton** Yonne, C France
11 R14 **Vermilion** Alberta, SW Canada
31 T11 **Vermilion** Ohio, N USA
22 I10 **Vermilion Bay** bay Louisiana, S USA
29 V4 **Vermilion Lake** ◎ Minnesota, N USA
14 F9 **Vermilion River** ≈ Ontario, S Canada
30 L12 **Vermilion River** ≈ Illinois, N USA
29 R12 **Vermillion** South Dakota, N USA
29 R12 **Vermillion River** ≈ South Dakota, N USA
15 O9 **Vermillon, Rivière** ≈ Québec, SE Canada
115 E14 **Vérmio** ▲▲ N Greece
18 L8 **Vermont** off. State of Vermont; also known as The Green Mountain State. ◈ state NE USA
113 K16 **Vermosh** var. Vermoshi. Shkodër, N Albania
Vermoshi see Vermosh
37 O3 **Vernal** Utah, W USA
14 G11 **Verner** Ontario, S Canada
102 M5 **Verneuil-sur-Avre** Eure, N France
114 D13 **Vérno** ▲ N Greece
11 N17 **Vernon** British Columbia, SW Canada
102 M4 **Vernon** Eure, N France
23 N3 **Vernon** Alabama, S USA
31 P15 **Vernon** Indiana, N USA
25 Q4 **Vernon** Texas, SW USA
32 G10 **Vernonia** Oregon, NW USA
14 G12 **Vernon, Lake** ◎ Ontario, S Canada
22 G7 **Vernon Lake** ⊡ Louisiana, S USA
23 Y13 **Vero Beach** Florida, SE USA
Verőcze see Virovitica
Verodunum see Verdun
115 E14 **Véroia** var. Veria, Vérroia, Turk. Karaferiye. Kentrikí Makedonía, N Greece
106 E8 **Verolanuova** Lombardia, N Italy
14 K14 **Verona** Ontario, SE Canada
106 G8 **Verona** Veneto, NE Italy
29 P6 **Verona** North Dakota, N USA
30 L9 **Verona** Wisconsin, N USA
61 E20 **Verónica** Buenos Aires, E Argentina
22 J9 **Verret, Lake** ◎ Louisiana, S USA
Vérroia see Véroia
103 N5 **Versailles** Yvelines, N France
31 P15 **Versailles** Indiana, N USA
20 M5 **Versailles** Kentucky, S USA
27 U5 **Versailles** Missouri, C USA
31 Q13 **Versailles** Ohio, N USA
Versecz see Vršac
108 A10 **Versoix** Genève, SW Switzerland
15 Z6 **Verte, Pointe** headland Québec, SE Canada
111 I22 **Vértes** ▲▲ NW Hungary
44 G6 **Vertientes** Camagüey, C Cuba
114 G13 **Vertískos** ▲▲ N Greece
102 I8 **Vertou** Loire-Atlantique, NW France
Verulamium see St Albans
99 L19 **Verviers** Liège, E Belgium
103 Y14 **Vescovato** Corse, France, C Mediterranean Sea
99 L20 **Vesdre** ≈ E Belgium
117 U10 **Vesele** Rus. Veseloye. Zaporiz'ka Oblast', S Ukraine
111 D18 **Veselí nad Lužnicí** var. Weseli an der Lainsitz, Ger. Frohenbruck. Jihočeský Kraj, S Czech Republic
114 M9 **Veselinovo** Shumen, E Bulgaria
126 L12 **Veselovskoye Vodokhranilishche** ⊡ SW Russian Federation
Veseloye see Vesele
117 Q9 **Veselynove** Mykolayivs'ka Oblast', S Ukraine
Veseya see Vyasyeya
126 M10 **Veshenskaya** Rostovskaya Oblast', SW Russian Federation
127 Q5 **Veshkayma** Ul'yanovskaya Oblast', W Russian Federation
Vesisaari see Vadsø
Vesontio see Besançon
103 T7 **Vesoul** anc. Vesulium, Vesulum. Haute-Saône, E France
95 J20 **Vessigebro** Halland, S Sweden
95 D17 **Vest-Agder** ◈ county S Norway
23 P4 **Vestavia Hills** Alabama, S USA
84 F6 **Vesterålen** island NW Norway
92 G10 **Vesterålen** island group N Norway
87 V3 **Vestervig** Viborg, NW Denmark
92 H2 **Vestfirdhir** ◈ region NW Iceland
92 G11 **Vestfjorden** fjord C Norway
95 G16 **Vestfold** ◈ county S Norway
95 B18 **Vestmanna** Dan. Vestmanhavn Faeroe Islands
92 I4 **Vestmannaeyjar** Sudhurland, S Iceland
94 E9 **Vestnes** Møre og Romsdal, S Norway
95 I23 **Vestsjælland** off. Vestsjællands Amt. ◈ county E Denmark
92 H3 **Vesturland** ◈ region W Iceland
92 G11 **Vestvågøya** island C Norway
Vesulium/Vesulum see Vesoul
Vesuna see Périgueux
107 K17 **Vesuvio** Eng. Vesuvius. ⛰ S Italy
Vesuvius see Vesuvio
124 K14 **Ves'yegonsk** Tverskaya Oblast', W Russian Federation
111 I23 **Veszprém** Ger. Veszprim. Veszprém, W Hungary
111 H23 **Veszprém** off. Veszprém Megye. ◈ county W Hungary
Veszprim see Veszprém
Vetka see Vyetka
95 M19 **Vetlanda** Jönköping, S Sweden
127 P1 **Vetluga** Nizhegorodskaya Oblast', W Russian Federation
127 P14 **Vetluga** ≈ NW Russian Federation
125 O14 **Vetluzhskiy** Kostromskaya Oblast', NW Russian Federation
127 P2 **Vetluzhskiy** Nizhegorodskaya Oblast', W Russian Federation
107 H14 **Vetralla** Lazio, C Italy
114 M9 **Vetren** prev. Zhitarovo. Burgas, E Bulgaria
114 M8 **Vetrino** Varna, E Bulgaria
Vetrino see Vyetryna
122 L7 **Vetrovaya, Gora** ▲ N Russian Federation
Vetter, Lake see Vättern

◆ Country ● Country Capital ◇ Dependent Territory ○ Dependent Territory Capital ◈ Administrative Region × International Airport ▲ Mountain ▲▲ Mountain Range ⛰ Volcano ≈ River ◎ Lake ⊡ Reservoir

106 J13 **Vettore, Monte** ▲ C Italy
99 A17 **Veurne** *var.* Furnes. West-Vlaanderen, W Belgium
31 Q15 **Vevay** Indiana, N USA
108 C10 **Vevey** *Ger.* Vivis; *anc.* Vibiscum. Vaud, SW Switzerland
Vexiö *see* Växjö
103 S13 **Veynes** Hautes-Alpes, SE France
103 N11 **Vézère** ∽ W France
114 I9 **Vezhen** ▲ C Bulgaria
136 K11 **Vezirköprü** Samsun, N Turkey
57 J18 **Viacha** La Paz, W Bolivia
27 R10 **Vian** Oklahoma, C USA
Viana de Castelo *see* Viana do Castelo
104 H12 **Viana do Alentejo** Évora, S Portugal
104 I4 **Viana do Bolo** Galicia, NW Spain
104 G5 **Viana do Castelo** *var.* Viana de Castelo; *anc.* Velobriga. Viana do Castelo, NW Portugal
104 G5 **Viana do Castelo** *var.* Viana de Castelo. ◈ *district* N Portugal
98 J12 **Vianen** Zuid-Holland, C Netherlands
167 Q8 **Viangchan** *Eng./Fr.* Vientiane. ● (Laos) C Laos
167 P6 **Viangphoukha** *var.* Vieng Pou Kha. Louang Namtha, N Laos
104 K13 **Viar** ∽ SW Spain
106 E11 **Viareggio** Toscana, C Italy
103 O14 **Viaur** ∽ S France
Vibiscum *see* Vevey
95 G21 **Viborg** Viborg, NW Denmark
29 R12 **Viborg** South Dakota, N USA
95 F21 **Viborg** *off.* Viborg Amt. ◈ *county* NW Denmark
107 N22 **Vibo Valentia** *prev.* Monteleone di Calabria; *anc.* Hipponium. Calabria, SW Italy
105 W5 **Vic** *var.* Vich; *anc.* Ausa, Vicus Ausonensis. Cataluña, NE Spain
102 K16 **Vic-en-Bigorre** Hautes-Pyrénées, S France
40 K10 **Vicente Guerrero** Durango, C Mexico
41 P10 **Vicente Guerrero, Presa** *var.* Presa de las Adjuntas. ▣ NE Mexico
Vicentia *see* Vicenza
106 G8 **Vicenza** *anc.* Vicentia. Veneto, NE Italy
Vich *see* Vic
54 J10 **Vichada** *off.* Comisaría del Vichada. ◈ *province* E Colombia
54 K10 **Vichada, Río** ∽ E Colombia
61 G17 **Vichadero** Rivera, NE Uruguay
Vichegda *see* Vychegda
124 M16 **Vichuga** Ivanovskaya Oblast', W Russian Federation
103 P10 **Vichy** Allier, C France
26 K9 **Vici** Oklahoma, C USA
31 P10 **Vicksburg** Michigan, N USA
22 J5 **Vicksburg** Mississippi, S USA
103 O12 **Vic-sur-Cère** Cantal, C France
29 X14 **Victor** Iowa, C USA
59 I21 **Víctor** Mato Grosso do Sul, SW Brazil
182 I10 **Victor Harbor** South Australia
61 C18 **Victoria** Entre Ríos, E Argentina
10 L17 **Victoria** Vancouver Island, British Columbia, SW Canada
45 R14 **Victoria** NW Grenada
42 H6 **Victoria** Yoro, NW Honduras
121 O15 **Victoria** *var.* Rabat. Gozo, NW Malta
116 I12 **Victoria** *Ger.* Viktoriastadt. Braşov, C Romania
172 H17 **Victoria** ● (Seychelles) Mahé, SW Seychelles
25 U13 **Victoria** Texas, SW USA
183 N12 **Victoria** ◈ *state* SE Australia
174 K7 **Victoria** ∽ Western Australia
Victoria *see* Labuan, East Malaysia
Victoria *see* Masvingo, Zimbabwe
Victoria Bank *see* Vitória Seamount
11 Y15 **Victoria Beach** Manitoba, S Canada
Victoria de Durango *see* Durango
Victoria de las Tunas *see* Las Tunas
83 I16 **Victoria Falls** Matabeleland North, W Zimbabwe
83 I16 **Victoria Falls** ✈ Matabeleland North, W Zimbabwe
83 I16 **Victoria Falls** *waterfall* Zambia/Zimbabwe
Victoria Falls *see* Iguaçu, Salto do
63 F19 **Victoria, Isla** *island* Archipiélago de los Chonos, S Chile
8 K6 **Victoria Island** *island* Northwest Territories/Nunavut, NW Canada
182 L8 **Victoria, Lake** ◎ New South Wales, SE Australia
68 I12 **Victoria, Lake** *var.* Victoria Nyanza. ◎ E Africa
195 S13 **Victoria Land** *physical region* Antarctica
166 L5 **Victoria, Mount** ▲ W Myanmar
187 X14 **Victoria, Mount** ▲ Viti Levu, W Fiji
186 E9 **Victoria, Mount** ▲ S PNG
81 F17 **Victoria Nile** *var.* Somerset Nile. ∽ C Uganda
Victoria Nyanza *see* Victoria, Lake
42 G3 **Victoria Peak** ▲ SE Belize
185 H16 **Victoria Range** ▲▲ South Island, NZ
181 O3 **Victoria River** ∽ Northern Territory, N Australia
181 P3 **Victoria River Roadhouse** Northern Territory, N Australia
15 Q11 **Victoriaville** Québec, SE Canada
Victoria-Wes *see* Victoria West
83 G24 **Victoria West** *Afr.* Victoria-Wes. Northern Cape, W South Africa
62 J13 **Victorica** La Pampa, C Argentina
195 T3 **Victor, Mount** ▲ Antarctica
35 U14 **Victorville** California, W USA
62 G9 **Vicuña** Coquimbo, N Chile
62 K11 **Vicuña Mackenna** Córdoba, C Argentina
Vicus Ausonensis *see* Vic
Vicus Elbii *see* Viterbo
33 X7 **Vida** Montana, NW USA
23 V6 **Vidalia** Georgia, SE USA
22 J7 **Vidalia** Louisiana, S USA
95 F22 **Videbæk** Ringkøbing, C Denmark
60 I13 **Videira** Santa Catarina, S Brazil
116 J14 **Videle** Teleorman, S Romania
Videm-Krško *see* Krško
Vídeň *see* Wien
104 H12 **Vidigueira** Beja, S Portugal
114 J9 **Vidima** ∽ N Bulgaria
114 G7 **Vidin** *anc.* Bononia. Vidin, NW Bulgaria
114 F8 **Vidin** ◈ *province* NW Bulgaria
154 H10 **Vidisha** Madhya Pradesh, C India
25 Y10 **Vidor** Texas, SW USA
95 L20 **Vidöstern** ◎ S Sweden
92 J13 **Vidsel** Norrbotten, N Sweden
118 H9 **Vidzemes Augstiene** ▲ C Latvia
118 J12 **Vidzy** *Rus.* Vidzy. Vitsyebskaya Voblasts', NW Belarus
63 L16 **Viedma** Río Negro, E Argentina
63 H22 **Viedma, Lago** ◎ S Argentina
45 O11 **Vieille Case** *var.* Itassi. N Dominica
104 M2 **Vieja, Peña** ▲ N Spain
40 E4 **Viejo, Cerro** ▲ NW Mexico
56 B9 **Viejo, Cerro** ▲ N Peru
118 E10 **Viekšniai** Telšiai, NW Lithuania
105 U3 **Vielha** *var.* Viella. Cataluña, NE Spain
Viella *see* Vielha
99 L21 **Vielsalm** Luxembourg, E Belgium
Vieng Pou Kha *see* Viangphoukha
23 T6 **Vienna** Georgia, SE USA
30 L17 **Vienna** Illinois, N USA
27 V5 **Vienna** Missouri, C USA
21 Q3 **Vienna** West Virginia, NE USA
Vienna *see* Wien, Austria
Vienna *see* Vienne, France
103 R11 **Vienne** *anc.* Vienna. Isère, E France
102 L10 **Vienne** ◈ *department* W France
102 L9 **Vienne** ∽ W France
Vientiane *see* Viangchan
Vientos, Paso de los *see* Windward Passage
45 V6 **Vieques** *var.* Isabel Segunda. E Puerto Rico
45 V6 **Vieques, Isla de** *island* E Puerto Rico
45 V6 **Vieques, Pasaje de** *passage* E Puerto Rico
45 V5 **Vieques, Sonda de** *sound* E Puerto Rico
Vierdörfer *see* Săcele
93 M15 **Vieremä** Itä-Suomi, C Finland
99 M14 **Vierlingsbeek** Noord-Brabant, SE Netherlands
101 G20 **Viernheim** Hessen, W Germany
101 D15 **Viersen** Nordrhein-Westfalen, W Germany
108 G8 **Vierwaldstätter See** *Eng.* Lake of Lucerne. ◎ C Switzerland
103 N8 **Vierzon** Cher, C France
40 L8 **Viesca** Coahuila de Zaragoza, NE Mexico
118 H10 **Viesīte** *Ger.* Eckengraf. Jēkabpils, S Latvia
107 N15 **Vieste** Puglia, SE Italy
167 T8 **Vietnam** *off.* Socialist Republic of Vietnam, *Vtn.* Công Hoa Xa Hôi Chu Nghia Viêt Nam. ◆ *republic* SE Asia
167 S5 **Viêt Quang** Ha Giang, N Vietnam
Vietri *see* Viêt Tri
167 S6 **Viêt Tri** *var.* Vietri. Vinh Phu, N Vietnam
30 L4 **Vieux Desert, Lac** ◎ Michigan/Wisconsin, N USA
45 Y13 **Vieux Fort** S Saint Lucia
45 X6 **Vieux-Habitants** Basse Terre, SW Guadeloupe
119 G14 **Vievis** Vilnius, S Lithuania
171 N2 **Vigan** Luzon, N Philippines
106 D8 **Vigevano** Lombardia, N Italy
107 N18 **Viggiano** Basilicata, S Italy
58 L12 **Vigia** Pará, NE Brazil
41 Y12 **Vigía Chico** Quintana Roo, SE Mexico
Vigie *see* George FL Charles
102 K17 **Vignemale** *var.* Pic de Vignemale. ▲ France/Spain
Vignemale, Pic de *see* Vignemale
106 G10 **Vignola** Emilia-Romagna, C Italy
104 G4 **Vigo** Galicia, NW Spain
104 G4 **Vigo, Ría de** *estuary* NW Spain
94 D9 **Vigra** *island* S Norway
95 C17 **Vigrestad** Rogaland, S Norway
93 L15 **Vihanti** Oulu, C Finland
149 U10 **Vihāri** Punjab, E Pakistan
102 K8 **Vihiers** Maine-et-Loire, NW France
111 O19 **Vihorlat** ▲ E Slovakia
93 L19 **Vihti** Etelä-Suomi, S Finland
Viipuri *see* Vyborg
93 M16 **Viitasaari** Länsi-Suomi, W Finland
118 K3 **Viivikonna** Ida-Virumaa, NE Estonia
155 K16 **Vijayawāda** *prev.* Bezwada. Andhra Pradesh, SE India
Vijosa/Vijosë *see* Aóos, Albania/Greece
Vijosa/Vijosë *see* Vjosës, Lumi i, Albania/Greece
Vik *see* Vikøyri
92 J4 **Vík** Sudhurland, S Iceland
94 L13 **Vika** Dalarna, C Sweden
92 L12 **Vikajärvi** Lappi, N Finland
94 L13 **Vikarbyn** Dalarna, C Sweden
95 J22 **Viken** Skåne, S Sweden
95 L17 **Viken** ◎ C Sweden
95 G15 **Vikersund** Buskerud, S Norway
114 G11 **Vikhren** ▲ SW Bulgaria
11 R15 **Viking** Alberta, SW Canada
84 E7 **Viking Bank** *undersea feature* N North Sea
95 M14 **Vikmanshyttan** Dalarna, C Sweden
94 D12 **Vikøyri** *var.* Vik. Sogn og Fjordane, S Norway
93 H17 **Viksjö** Västernorrland, C Sweden
Viktoriastadt *see* Victoria
Vila *see* Port-Vila
Vila Arriaga *see* Bibala
Vila Artur de Paiva *see* Cubango
Vila Bela da Santissima Trindade *see* Mato Grosso
58 B12 **Vila Bittencourt** Amazonas, NW Brazil
Vila da Ponte *see* Cubango
64 O2 **Vila da Praia da Vitória** Terceira, Azores, Portugal, NE Atlantic Ocean
Vila de Aljustrel *see* Cangamba
Vila de Almoster *see* Chiange
Vila de João Belo *see* Xai-Xai
Vila de Macia *see* Macia
Vila de Manhiça *see* Manhiça
Vila de Manica *see* Manica
Vila de Mocímboa da Praia *see* Mocímboa da Praia
83 N16 **Vila de Sena** *var.* Sena. Sofala, C Mozambique
104 F14 **Vila do Bispo** Faro, S Portugal
104 G6 **Vila do Conde** Porto, NW Portugal
Vila do Maio *see* Maio
64 P3 **Vila do Porto** Santa Maria, Azores, Portugal, NE Atlantic Ocean
83 K15 **Vila do Zumbo** *prev.* Vila do Zumbo, Zumbo. Tete, NW Mozambique
Vila do Zumbu *see* Vila do Zumbo
104 I6 **Vila Flor** *var.* Vila Flôr. Bragança, N Portugal
105 V6 **Vilafranca del Penedès** *var.* Villafranca del Panadés. Cataluña, NE Spain
104 F10 **Vila Franca de Xira** *var.* Vilafranca de Xira. Lisboa, C Portugal
Vila Gago Coutinho *see* Lumbala N'Guimbo
104 G3 **Vilagarcía de Arousa** *var.* Villagarcía de Arosa. Galicia, NW Spain
Vila General Machado *see* Camacupa
Vila Henrique de Carvalho *see* Saurimo
102 I7 **Vilaine** ∽ NW France
Vila João de Almeida *see* Chibia
118 K8 **Viļaka** *Ger.* Marienhausen. Balvi, NE Latvia
104 I2 **Vilalba** Galicia, NW Spain
Vila Marechal Carmona *see* Uíge
Vila Mariano Machado *see* Ganda
172 G3 **Vilanandro, Tanjona** *headland* W Madagascar
Vilanculos *see* Vilankulo
118 J10 **Viļāni** Rēzekne, E Latvia
83 N19 **Vilankulo** *var.* Vilanculos. Inhambane, E Mozambique
Vila Norton de Matos *see* Balombo
104 G6 **Vila Nova de Famalicão** *var.* Vila Nova de Famalicao. Braga, N Portugal
104 I6 **Vila Nova de Foz Côa** *var.* Vila Nova de Fozcôa. Guarda, N Portugal
104 F6 **Vila Nova de Gaia** Porto, NW Portugal
Vila Nova de Portimão *see* Portimão
105 V6 **Vilanova i La Geltrú** Cataluña, NE Spain
Vila Pereira de Eça *see* N'Giva
104 H6 **Vila Pouca de Aguiar** Vila Real, N Portugal
104 H6 **Vila Real** *var.* Vila Rial. Vila Real, N Portugal
104 H6 **Vila Real** ◈ *district* N Portugal
105 T9 **Vila-real de los Infantes** *var.* Villarreal. País Valenciano, E Spain
104 H14 **Vila Real de Santo António** Faro, S Portugal
104 J7 **Vilar Formoso** Guarda, N Portugal
Vila Rial *see* Vila Real
59 J15 **Vila Rica** Mato Grosso, W Brazil
Vila Robert Williams *see* Caála
Vila Salazar *see* N'Dalatando
Vila Serpa Pinto *see* Menongue
Vila Teixeira da Silva *see* Bailundo
Vila Teixeira de Sousa *see* Luau
104 H9 **Vila Velha de Ródão** Castelo Branco, C Portugal
104 G5 **Vila Verde** Braga, N Portugal
104 H11 **Vila Viçosa** Évora, S Portugal
57 G15 **Vilcabamba, Cordillera de** ▲▲ C Peru
Vîlcea *see* Vâlcea
122 J4 **Vil'cheka, Zemlya** *Eng.* Wilczek Land. *island* Zemlya Frantsa-Iosifa, NW Russian Federation
95 F22 **Vildbjerg** Ringkøbing, C Denmark
Vileyka *see* Vilyeyka
93 H15 **Vilhelmina** Västerbotten, N Sweden
59 F17 **Vilhena** Rondônia, W Brazil
115 G19 **Vília** Attikí, C Greece
Viliya *see* Viliya
119 I14 **Viliya** *Lith.* Neris, *Rus.* Viliya. ∽ W Belarus
Viliya *see* Neris
118 H5 **Viljandi** *Ger.* Fellin. Viljandimaa, S Estonia
118 H5 **Viljandimaa** *off.* Viljandi Maakond. ◈ *province* SW Estonia
119 E14 **Vilkaviškis** *Pol.* Wyłkowyszki. Marijampolė, SW Lithuania
118 F13 **Vilkija** Kaunas, C Lithuania
197 V9 **Vil'kitskogo, Proliv** *strait* N Russian Federation
Vilkovo *see* Vylkove
57 L21 **Villa Abecia** Chuquisaca, S Bolivia
41 N5 **Villa Acuña** *var.* Ciudad Acuña. Coahuila de Zaragoza, NE Mexico
40 J4 **Villa Ahumada** Chihuahua, N Mexico
45 O9 **Villa Altagracia** C Dominican Republic
56 L13 **Villa Bella** Beni, N Bolivia
104 J3 **Villablino** Castilla-León, N Spain
54 K6 **Villa Bruzual** Portuguesa, N Venezuela
105 O9 **Villacañas** Castilla-La Mancha, C Spain
105 O12 **Villacarrillo** Andalucía, S Spain
104 M7 **Villacastín** Castilla-León, N Spain
Villa Cecilia *see* Ciudad Madero
109 S9 **Villach** *Slvn.* Beljak. Kärnten, S Austria
107 B20 **Villacidro** Sardegna, Italy, C Mediterranean Sea
Villa Concepción *see* Concepción
104 L4 **Villada** Castilla-León, N Spain
40 M10 **Villa de Cos** Zacatecas, C Mexico
54 L5 **Villa de Cura** *var.* Cura. Aragua, N Venezuela
Villa del Nevoso *see* Ilirska Bistrica
Villa del Pilar *see* Pilar
104 M13 **Villa del Río** Andalucía, S Spain
Villa de Méndez *see* Méndez
42 H6 **Villa de San Antonio** Comayagua, W Honduras
105 N4 **Villadiego** Castilla-León, N Spain
105 T8 **Villafames** País Valenciano, E Spain
41 U16 **Villa Flores** Chiapas, SE Mexico
104 J3 **Villafranca del Bierzo** Castilla-León, N Spain
105 S8 **Villafranca del Cid** País Valenciano, E Spain
104 J11 **Villafranca de los Barros** Extremadura, W Spain
105 N10 **Villafranca de los Caballeros** Castilla-La Mancha, C Spain
Villafranca del Panadés *see* Vilafranca del Penedès
106 F8 **Villafranca di Verona** Veneto, NE Italy
107 J23 **Villafrati** Sicilia, Italy, C Mediterranean Sea
Villagarcía de Arosa *see* Vilagarcía de Arousa
41 O9 **Villagrán** Tamaulipas, C Mexico
61 C17 **Villaguay** Entre Ríos, E Argentina
62 O5 **Villa Hayes** Presidente Hayes, S Paraguay
41 U15 **Villahermosa** *prev.* San Juan Bautista. Tabasco, SE Mexico
105 O11 **Villahermosa** Castilla-La Mancha, C Spain
64 O11 **Villahermoso** Gomera, Islas Canarias, Spain, NE Atlantic Ocean
Villa Hidalgo *see* Hidalgo
105 T12 **Villajoyosa** *Cat.* La Vila Joíosa. País Valenciano, E Spain
Villa Juárez *see* Juárez
Villalba *see* Collado Villalba
41 N8 **Villaldama** Nuevo León, NE Mexico
104 L5 **Villalón de Campos** Castilla-León, N Spain
61 A25 **Villalonga** Buenos Aires, E Argentina
104 L5 **Villalpando** Castilla-León, N Spain
40 K9 **Villa Madero** *var.* Francisco I.Madero. Durango, C Mexico
41 O9 **Villa Mainero** Tamaulipas, C Mexico
Villamaña *see* Villamañán
104 L4 **Villamañán** *var.* Villamaña. Castilla-León, N Spain
62 L10 **Villa María** Córdoba, C Argentina
61 C17 **Villa María Grande** Entre Ríos, E Argentina
57 K21 **Villa Martín** Potosí, SW Bolivia
104 K15 **Villamartín** Andalucía, S Spain
62 J8 **Villa Mazán** La Rioja, NW Argentina
Villa Mercedes *see* Mercedes
Villamil *see* Puerto Villamil
Villa Nador *see* Nador
54 G5 **Villanueva** La Guajira, N Colombia
42 H5 **Villanueva** Cortés, NW Honduras
40 L11 **Villanueva** Zacatecas, C Mexico
42 I9 **Villa Nueva** Chinandega, NW Nicaragua
37 T11 **Villanueva** New Mexico, SW USA
104 M12 **Villanueva de Córdoba** Andalucía, S Spain
105 O12 **Villanueva del Arzobispo** Andalucía, S Spain
104 K11 **Villanueva de la Serena** Extremadura, W Spain
104 L5 **Villanueva del Campo** Castilla-León, N Spain
105 O11 **Villanueva de los Infantes** Castilla-La Mancha, C Spain
61 C14 **Villa Ocampo** Santa Fe, C Argentina
40 J8 **Villa Ocampo** Durango, C Mexico
40 J7 **Villa Orestes Pereyra** Durango, C Mexico
105 N3 **Villarcayo** Castilla-León, N Spain
104 L5 **Villardefrades** Castilla-León, N Spain
105 S9 **Villar del Arzobispo** País Valenciano, E Spain
105 Q6 **Villaroya de la Sierra** Aragón, NE Spain
Villarreal *see* Vila-real de los Infantes
62 P6 **Villarrica** Guairá, SE Paraguay
63 G15 **Villarrica, Volcán** ✱ S Chile
105 P10 **Villarrobledo** Castilla-La Mancha, C Spain
105 N10 **Villarrubia de los Ojos** Castilla-La Mancha, C Spain
18 J17 **Villas** New Jersey, NE USA
105 O3 **Villasana de Mena** Castilla-León, N Spain
107 M23 **Villa San Giovanni** Calabria, S Italy
61 D18 **Villa San José** Entre Ríos, E Argentina
Villa Sanjurjo *see* Al-Hoceïma
105 P6 **Villasayas** Castilla-León, N Spain
107 C20 **Villasimius** Sardegna, Italy, C Mediterranean Sea
41 N6 **Villa Unión** Coahuila de Zaragoza, NE Mexico
40 K10 **Villa Unión** Durango, C Mexico
40 J10 **Villa Unión** Sinaloa, C Mexico
62 K12 **Villa Valeria** Córdoba, C Argentina
105 N8 **Villaverde** Madrid, C Spain
54 F10 **Villavicencio** Meta, C Colombia
104 L2 **Villaviciosa** Asturias, N Spain
104 L12 **Villaviciosa de Córdoba** Andalucía, S Spain
57 L22 **Villazón** Potosí, S Bolivia
14 J8 **Villebon, Lac** ◎ Québec, SE Canada
Ville de Kinshasa *see* Kinshasa
102 J5 **Villedieu-les-Poêles** Manche, N France
Villefranche *see* Villefranche-sur-Saône
103 N16 **Villefranche-de-Lauragais** Haute-Garonne, S France
103 N14 **Villefranche-de-Rouergue** Aveyron, S France
103 R10 **Villefranche-sur-Saône** *var.* Villefranche. Rhône, E France
14 H9 **Ville-Marie** Québec, SE Canada
102 M15 **Villemur-sur-Tarn** Haute-Garonne, S France
105 S11 **Villena** País Valenciano, E Spain
Villeneuve-d'Agen *see* Villeneuve-sur-Lot
102 L13 **Villeneuve-sur-Lot** *var.* Villeneuve-d'Agen; *hist.* Gajac. Lot-et-Garonne, SW France
103 P6 **Villeneuve-sur-Yonne** Yonne, C France
22 H8 **Ville Platte** Louisiana, S USA
103 R11 **Villeurbanne** Rhône, E France
101 G23 **Villingen-Schwenningen** Baden-Württemberg, S Germany
29 T15 **Villisca** Iowa, C USA
Villmanstrand *see* Lappeenranta
Vilna *see* Vilnius
119 H14 **Vilnius** *Pol.* Wilno, *Ger.* Wilna; *prev. Rus.* Vilna. ● (Lithuania) Vilnius, SE Lithuania
119 H15 **Vilnius** ◈ *province* SE Lithuania
119 H14 **Vilnius** ✈ Vilnius, SE Lithuania
117 S7 **Vil'nohirs'k** Dnipropetrovs'ka Oblast', E Ukraine
117 U8 **Vil'nyans'k** Zaporiz'ka Oblast', SE Ukraine
93 L17 **Vilppula** Länsi-Suomi, W Finland
101 M20 **Vils** ∽ SE Germany
118 C5 **Vilsandi Saar** *island* W Estonia
117 P8 **Vil'shanka** *Rus.* Olshanka. Kirovohrads'ka Oblast', C Ukraine
101 O22 **Vilshofen** Bayern, SE Germany
155 J20 **Viluppuram** Tamil Nādu, SE India
113 J16 **Vilusi** Montenegro, SW Serbia and Montenegro (Yugo.)
99 G18 **Vilvoorde** *Fr.* Vilvorde. Vlaams Brabant, C Belgium
Vilvorde *see* Vilvoorde
119 J14 **Vilyeyka** *Pol.* Wilejka, *Rus.* Vileyka. Minskaya Voblasts', NW Belarus
123 V11 **Vilyuchinsk** Kamchatskaya, Oblast', E Russian Federation
123 P10 **Vilyuy** ∽ NE Russian Federation
123 P10 **Vilyuysk** Respublika Sakha (Yakutiya), NE Russian Federation
123 N10 **Vilyuyskoye Vodokhranilishche** ▣ NE Russian Federation
104 G2 **Vimianzo** Galicia, NW Spain
95 M19 **Vimmerby** Kalmar, S Sweden
102 L5 **Vimoutiers** Orne, N France
93 L16 **Vimpeli** Länsi-Suomi, W Finland
79 G14 **Vina** ∽ Cameroon/Chad
62 G11 **Viña del Mar** Valparaíso, C Chile
19 R8 **Vinalhaven Island** *island* Maine, NE USA
105 T8 **Vinaròs** País Valenciano, E Spain
Vînători *see* Vânători
31 N15 **Vincennes** Indiana, N USA
195 Y12 **Vincennes Bay** *bay* Antarctica
25 O7 **Vincent** Texas, SW USA
95 H24 **Vindeby** Fyn, C Denmark
93 I15 **Vindeln** Västerbotten, N Sweden
95 F21 **Vinderup** Ringkøbing, C Denmark
Vindhya Mountains *see* Vindhya Range
153 N14 **Vindhya Range** *var.* Vindhya Mountains. ▲▲ N India
Vindobona *see* Wien
20 K6 **Vine Grove** Kentucky, S USA
18 J17 **Vineland** New Jersey, NE USA
116 E11 **Vinga** Arad, W Romania
95 M16 **Vingåker** Södermanland, C Sweden
167 S8 **Vinh** Nghê An, N Vietnam
104 I5 **Vinhais** Bragança, N Portugal
167 T9 **Vinh Linh** Quang Tri, C Vietnam
Vinh Loi *see* Bac Liêu
167 S14 **Vinh Long** *var.* Vinhlong. Vinh Long, S Vietnam
113 Q18 **Vinica** NE FYR Macedonia
109 V13 **Vinica** SE Slovenia
114 G8 **Vinishte** Montana, NW Bulgaria
27 Q8 **Vinita** Oklahoma, C USA
Vînju Mare *see* Vânju Mare
98 I11 **Vinkeveen** Utrecht, C Netherlands
116 L6 **Vin'kivtsi** Khmel'nyts'ka Oblast', W Ukraine
112 I10 **Vinkovci** *Ger.* Winkowitz, *Hung.* Vinkovcze. Vukovar-Srijem, E Croatia
Vinkovcze *see* Vinkovci
Vinnitsa *see* Vinnytsya
Vinnitskaya Oblast'/Vinnytsya *see* Vinnyts'ka Oblast'
116 M7 **Vinnyts'ka Oblast'** *var.* Vinnytsya, *Rus.* Vinnitskaya Oblast'. ◈ *province* C Ukraine
117 N6 **Vinnytsya** *Rus.* Vinnitsa. Vinnyts'ka Oblast', C Ukraine
117 N6 **Vinnytsya** ✈ Vinnyts'ka Oblast', N Ukraine
Vinogradov *see* Vynohradiv
194 L8 **Vinson Massif** ▲ Antarctica
94 G11 **Vinstra** Oppland, S Norway
116 K12 **Vintilă Vodă** Buzău, SE Romania
29 X13 **Vinton** Iowa, C USA
22 F9 **Vinton** Louisiana, S USA
155 J17 **Vinukonda** Andhra Pradesh, E India
Vioara *see* Ocnele Mari
83 E23 **Vioolsdrif** Northern Cape, SW South Africa
109 S12 **Vipava** ∽ SW Slovenia
82 M13 **Viphya Mountains** ▲▲ C Malawi
171 Q4 **Virac** Catanduanes Island, N Philippines
124 K8 **Virandozero** Respublika Kareliya, NW Russian Federation
137 P16 **Viranşehir** Şanlıurfa, SE Turkey
154 D13 **Virār** Mahārāshtra, W India
11 W16 **Virden** Manitoba, S Canada
30 K14 **Virden** Illinois, N USA
Virdois *see* Virrat
102 J5 **Vire** Calvados, N France
102 J4 **Vire** ∽ N France
83 A15 **Virei** Namibe, SW Angola
Virful Moldoveanu *see* Vârful Moldoveanu
35 R5 **Virginia Peak** ▲ Nevada, W USA
45 U9 **Virgin Gorda** *island* C British Virgin Islands
83 I22 **Virginia** Free State, C South Africa
30 K13 **Virginia** Illinois, N USA
29 W4 **Virginia** Minnesota, N USA
21 T6 **Virginia** *off.* Commonwealth of Virginia; also known as Mother of Presidents, Mother of States, Old Dominion. ◈ *state* NE USA
21 Y7 **Virginia Beach** Virginia, NE USA
33 R11 **Virginia City** Montana, NW USA
35 Q6 **Virginia City** Nevada, W USA
14 H8 **Virginiatown** Ontario, S Canada
Virgin Islands *see* British Virgin Islands
45 T9 **Virgin Islands (US)** *var.* Virgin Islands of the United States; *prev.* Danish West Indies. ◇ *US unincorporated territory* E West Indies
45 T9 **Virgin Passage** *passage* Puerto Rico/Virgin Islands (US)
35 Y10 **Virgin River** ∽ Nevada/Utah, W USA
Virihaur *see* Virihaure
92 H12 **Virihaure** *var.* Virihaur. ◎ N Sweden
167 T11 **Virôchey** Rôtânôkiri, NE Cambodia
93 N19 **Virolahti** Etelä-Suomi, S Finland
30 J8 **Viroqua** Wisconsin, N USA
112 G8 **Virovitica** *Ger.* Virovititz, *Hung.* Verőcze; *prev. Ger.* Werowitz. Virovitica-Podravina, NE Croatia
112 G8 **Virovitica-Podravina** *off.* Virovitičko-Podravska Županija. ◈ *province* NE Croatia
Virovititz *see* Virovitica
113 J17 **Virpazar** Montenegro, SW Serbia and Montenegro (Yugo.)
93 L17 **Virrat** *Swe.* Virdois. Länsi-Suomi, SW Finland
95 M20 **Virserum** Kalmar, S Sweden
99 K25 **Virton** Luxembourg, SE Belgium
118 F5 **Virtsu** *Ger.* Werder. Läänemaa, W Estonia
56 C12 **Virú** La Libertad, C Peru
Virudhunagar *see* Virudunagar
155 H23 **Virudunagar** *var.* Virudhunagar. Tamil Nādu, SE India
118 I3 **Viru-Jaagupi** *Ger.* Sankt-Jakobi. Lääne-Virumaa, NE Estonia
57 N19 **Viru-Viru** *var.* Santa Cruz. ✈ (Santa Cruz) Santa Cruz, C Bolivia
113 E15 **Vis** *It.* Lissa; *anc.* Issa. *island* S Croatia
Vis *see* Fish
118 I12 **Visaginas** *prev.* Sniečkus. Utena, E Lithuania
155 M15 **Visākhapatnam** Andhra Pradesh, SE India
35 R11 **Visalia** California, W USA
Višau *see* Vişeu
95 P19 **Visby** *Ger.* Wisby. Gotland, SE Sweden
197 N9 **Viscount Melville Sound** *prev.* Melville Sound. *sound* Northwest Territories/Nunavut, N Canada
99 L19 **Visé** Liège, E Belgium
112 K13 **Višegrad** Republika Srpska, E Bosnia and Herzegovina
58 L12 **Viseu** Pará, NE Brazil
104 H7 **Viseu** *prev.* Vizeu. Viseu, N Portugal

◆ Country ● Country Capital ◇ Dependent Territory ○ Dependent Territory Capital ◈ Administrative Region ✈ International Airport ▲ Mountain ▲▲ Mountain Range ✱ Volcano ∽ River ◎ Lake ▣ Reservoir

104 H7 **Viseu** *var.* Vizeu. ◈ *district* N Portugal
116 I8 **Vişeu** *Hung.* Visó; *prev.* Vişău. ≈ NW Romania
116 I8 **Vişeu de Sus** *var.* Vişeul de Sus, *Ger.* Oberwischau, *Hung.* Felsővisó. Maramureş, N Romania
Vişeul de Sus *see* Vişeu de Sus
127 R10 **Vishera** ≈ NW Russian Federation
95 J19 **Viskafors** Västra Götaland, S Sweden
95 J20 **Viskan** ≈ S Sweden
95 L21 **Vislanda** Kronoberg, S Sweden
Vislinskiy Zaliv *see* Vistula Lagoon
Visó *see* Vişeu
112 H13 **Visoko** Federacija Bosna I Hercegovina, C Bosnia and Herzegovina
106 A9 **Viso, Monte** ▲ NW Italy
108 E10 **Visp** Valais, SW Switzerland
108 E10 **Vispa** ≈ S Switzerland
95 M21 **Vissefjärda** Kalmar, S Sweden
100 I11 **Visselhövede** Niedersachsen, NW Germany
95 G23 **Vissenbjerg** Fyn, C Denmark
35 U17 **Vista** California, W USA
58 C11 **Vista Alegre** Amazonas, NW Brazil
114 J13 **Vistonída, Límni** ◎ NE Greece
92 K12 **Visttasjohka** ≈ N Sweden
Vistula *see* Wisła
119 A14 **Vistula Lagoon** *Ger.* Frisches Haff, *Pol.* Zalew Wiślany, *Rus.* Vislinskiy Zaliv. *lagoon* Poland/Russian Federation
114 I8 **Vit** ≈ NW Bulgaria
Vitebsk *see* Vitsyebsk
Vitebskaya Oblast' *see* Vitsyebskaya Voblasts'
107 H14 **Viterbo** *anc.* Vicus Elbii. Lazio, C Italy
112 H12 **Vitez** Federacija Bosna I Hercegovina, C Bosnia and Herzegovina
167 S14 **Vi Thanh** Cân Thơ, S Vietnam
Viti *see* Fiji
186 E7 **Vitiaz Strait** *strait* NE PNG
104 J7 **Vitigudino** Castilla-León, N Spain
187 W15 **Viti Levu** *island* W Fiji
123 O11 **Vitim** ≈ C Russian Federation
123 O12 **Vitimskiy** Irkutskaya Oblast', C Russian Federation
109 V2 **Vitis** Niederösterreich, N Austria
Vitoria *see* Vitoria-Gasteiz
59 O20 **Vitória** Espírito Santo, SE Brazil
Vitoria Bank *see* Vitória Seamount
59 N18 **Vitória da Conquista** Bahia, E Brazil
105 P3 **Vitoria-Gasteiz** *var.* Vitoria, *Eng.* Vittoria. País Vasco, N Spain
65 J16 **Vitória Seamount** *var.* Victoria Bank, Vitoria Bank. *undersea feature* C Atlantic Ocean
112 F13 **Vitorog** ▲ SW Bosnia and Herzegovina
102 J6 **Vitré** Ille-et-Vilaine, NW France
103 R5 **Vitry-le-François** Marne, N France
114 D13 **Vítsoi** ▲ N Greece
118 N13 **Vitsyebsk** *Rus.* Vitebsk. Vitsyebskaya Voblasts', NE Belarus
118 K13 **Vitsyebskaya Voblasts'** *prev. Rus.* Vitebskaya Oblast'. ◈ *province* N Belarus
92 J11 **Vittangi** *Lapp.* Vazáš. Norrbotten, N Sweden
103 R8 **Vitteaux** Côte d'Or, C France
103 S6 **Vittel** Vosges, NE France
95 N15 **Vittinge** Västmanland, C Sweden
107 K25 **Vittoria** Sicilia, Italy, C Mediterranean Sea
Vittoria *see* Vitoria-Gasteiz
106 I7 **Vittorio Veneto** Veneto, NE Italy
175 Q9 **Vitu Levu** *island* W Fiji
192 L6 **Vityaz Seamount** *undersea feature* C Pacific Ocean
175 Q7 **Vityaz Trench** *undersea feature* W Pacific Ocean
108 G8 **Vitznau** Luzern, W Switzerland
104 I1 **Viveiro** Galicia, NW Spain
105 S9 **Viver** País Valenciano, E Spain
103 Q13 **Viverais, Monts du** ▲▲ C France
122 L9 **Vivi** ≈ N Russian Federation
22 F4 **Vivian** Louisiana, S USA
29 N10 **Vivian** South Dakota, N USA
103 R13 **Viviers** Ardèche, E France
Vivis *see* Vevey
83 K19 **Vivo** Limpopo, NE South Africa
102 L10 **Vivonne** Vienne, W France
Vizakna *see* Ocna Sibiului
105 O2 **Vizcaya** *Basq.* Bizkaia. ◈ *province* País Vasco, N Spain
Vizcaya, Golfo de *see* Biscay, Bay of
136 C10 **Vize** Kırklareli, NW Turkey
122 K4 **Vize, Ostrov** *island* Severnaya Zemlya, N Russian Federation
Vizeu *see* Viseu
155 M15 **Vizianagaram** *var.* Vizianagram. Andhra Pradesh, E India
Vizianagram *see* Vizianagaram
103 S12 **Vizille** Isère, E France
125 R11 **Vizinga** Respublika Komi, NW Russian Federation
116 M13 **Viziru** Brăila, SE Romania
113 K21 **Vjosës, Lumi i** *var.* Vijosa, Vijosë, *Gk.* Aóos. ≈ Albania/Greece *see also* Aóos
99 H18 **Vlaams Brabant** ◈ *province* C Belgium
Vlaanderen *see* Flanders
98 G12 **Vlaardingen** Zuid-Holland, SW Netherlands
116 F10 **Vlădeasa, Vârful** *prev.* Vîrful Vlădeasa. ▲ NW Romania
Vlădeasa, Vîrful *see* Vlădeasa, Vârful
113 P16 **Vladičin Han** Serbia, SE Serbia and Montenegro (Yugo.)
127 O16 **Vladikavkaz** *prev.* Dzaudzhikau, Ordzhonikidze. Respublika Severnaya Osetiya, SW Russian Federation
126 M3 **Vladimir** Vladimirskaya Oblast', W Russian Federation
144 M7 **Vladimirovka** Kostanay, N Kazakhstan
Vladimirovka *see* Yuzhno-Sakhalinsk
126 L3 **Vladimirskaya Oblast'** ◈ *province* W Russian Federation
126 I3 **Vladimirskiy Tupik** Smolenskaya Oblast', W Russian Federation
Vladimir-Volynskiy *see* Volodymyr-Volyns'kyy
123 Q7 **Vladivostok** Primorskiy Kray, SE Russian Federation
117 U13 **Vladyslavivka** Respublika Krym, S Ukraine
98 P6 **Vlagtwedde** Groningen, NE Netherlands
Vlajna *see* Kukavica
112 J12 **Vlasenica** Republika Srpska, E Bosnia and Herzegovina
112 G12 **Vlašić** ▲ C Bosnia and Herzegovina
111 D17 **Vlašim** *Ger.* Wlaschim. Středočeský Kraj, C Czech Republic
113 P15 **Vlasotince** Serbia, SE Serbia and Montenegro (Yugo.)
123 Q7 **Vlasovo** Respublika Sakha (Yakutiya), NE Russian Federation
98 I11 **Vleuten** Utrecht, C Netherlands
98 I5 **Vlieland** *Fris.* Flylân. *island* Waddeneilanden, N Netherlands
98 I5 **Vliestroom** *strait* NW Netherlands
99 J14 **Vlijmen** Noord-Brabant, S Netherlands
99 E15 **Vlissingen** *Eng.* Flushing, *Fr.* Flessingue. Zeeland, SW Netherlands
Vlodava *see* Włodawa
Vlonë/Vlora *see* Vlorë
113 K22 **Vlorë** *prev.* Vlonë, *It.* Valona, Vlora. Vlorë, SW Albania
113 K22 **Vlorë** ◈ *district* SW Albania
113 K22 **Vlorës, Gjiri i** *var.* Valona Bay. *bay* SW Albania
Vlotslavsk *see* Włocławek
111 C16 **Vltava** *Ger.* Moldau. ≈ W Czech Republic
126 K3 **Vnukovo** ✕ (Moskva) Gorod Moskva, W Russian Federation
146 L11 **Vobkent** *Rus.* Vabkent. Buxoro Viloyati, C Uzbekistan
25 Q9 **Voca** Texas, SW USA
109 R5 **Vöcklabruck** Oberösterreich, NW Austria
112 D13 **Vodice** Šibenik-Knin, S Croatia
126 K10 **Vodlozero, Ozero** ◎ NW Russian Federation
112 A10 **Vodnjan** *It.* Dignano d'Istria. Istra, NW Croatia
125 S9 **Vodnyy** Respublika Komi, NW Russian Federation
95 G20 **Vodskov** Nordjylland, N Denmark
92 H4 **Vogar** Sudhurland, SW Iceland
Vogelkop *see* Doberai, Jazirah
77 X15 **Vogel Peak** *prev.* Dim lang. ▲ E Nigeria
101 H17 **Vogelsberg** ▲▲ C Germany
106 D8 **Voghera** Lombardia, N Italy
112 I13 **Vogošća** Federacija Bosna I Hercegovina, SE Bosnia and Herzegovina
101 M17 **Vogtland** *historical region* E Germany
127 V12 **Vogul'skiy Kamen', Gora** ▲ NW Russian Federation
187 P16 **Voh** Province Nord, C New Caledonia
Vohémar *see* Iharaña
172 H8 **Vohimena, Tanjona** *Fr.* Cap Sainte Marie. *headland* S Madagascar
172 J6 **Vohipeno** Fianarantsoa, SE Madagascar
118 H5 **Võhma** *Ger.* Wöchma. Viljandimaa, S Estonia
81 J20 **Voi** Coast, S Kenya
76 K15 **Voinjama** N Liberia
103 S12 **Voiron** Isère, E France
109 V8 **Voitsberg** Steiermark, SE Austria
95 F24 **Vojens** *Ger.* Woyens. Sønderjylland, SW Denmark
112 K9 **Vojvodina** *Ger.* Wojwodina. *Region* N Serbia and Montenegro (Yugo.)
15 S6 **Volant** ≈ Québec, SE Canada
Volaterrae *see* Volterra
43 P15 **Volcán** *var.* Hato del Volcán. Chiriquí, W Panama
Volchansk *see* Vovchans'k
Volchya *see* Vovcha
94 D10 **Volda** Møre og Romsdal, S Norway
98 J9 **Volendam** Noord-Holland, C Netherlands
124 L15 **Volga** Yaroslavskaya Oblast', W Russian Federation
29 R10 **Volga** South Dakota, N USA
122 C11 **Volga** ≈ NW Russian Federation
Volga-Baltic Waterway *see* Volgo-Baltiyskiy Kanal
Volga Hills/Volga Uplands *see* Privolzhskaya Vozvyshennost'
126 L13 **Volgo-Baltiyskiy Kanal** *Eng.* Volga-Baltic Waterway. *canal* NW Russian Federation
126 M12 **Volgodonsk** Rostovskaya Oblast', SW Russian Federation
127 O10 **Volgograd** *prev.* Stalingrad, Tsaritsyn. Volgogradskaya Oblast', SW Russian Federation
127 N9 **Volgogradskaya Oblast'** ◈ *province* SW Russian Federation
127 P10 **Volgogradskoye Vodokhranilishche** ▣ SW Russian Federation
101 J19 **Volkach** Bayern, C Germany
109 U9 **Völkermarkt** *Slvn.* Velikovec. Kärnten, S Austria
124 I12 **Volkhov** Leningradskaya Oblast', NW Russian Federation
101 D20 **Völklingen** Saarland, SW Germany
Volkovysk *see* Vawkavysk
Volkovyskiye Vysoty *see* Vawkavyskaye Wzvyshsha
83 K22 **Volksrust** Mpumalanga, E South Africa
98 L8 **Vollenhove** Overijssel, N Netherlands
119 L16 **Volma** *Rus.* Volma. ≈ C Belarus
Volmari *see* Valmiera
117 W9 **Volnovakha** Donets'ka Oblast', SE Ukraine
116 K6 **Volochys'k** Khmel'nyts'ka Oblast', W Ukraine
117 O6 **Volodarka** Kyyivs'ka Oblast', N Ukraine
117 W9 **Volodars'ke** Donets'ka Oblast', E Ukraine
127 R13 **Volodarskiy** Astrakhanskaya Oblast', SW Russian Federation
Volodarskoye *see* Saumalkol'
117 N8 **Volodars'k-Volyns'kyy** Zhytomyrs'ka Oblast', N Ukraine
116 K3 **Volodymerets'** Rivnens'ka Oblast', NW Ukraine
116 I3 **Volodymyr-Volyns'kyy** *Pol.* Włodzimierz, *Rus.* Vladimir-Volynskiy. Volyns'ka Oblast', NW Ukraine
124 L14 **Vologda** Vologodskaya Oblast', W Russian Federation
124 L12 **Vologodskaya Oblast'** ◈ *province* NW Russian Federation
126 K3 **Volokolamsk** Moskovskaya Oblast', W Russian Federation
126 K9 **Volokonovka** Belgorodskaya Oblast', W Russian Federation
115 G16 **Vólos** Thessalía, C Greece
124 M11 **Voloshka** Arkhangel'skaya Oblast', NW Russian Federation
Vološinovo *see* Novi Bečej
116 H7 **Volovets'** Zakarpats'ka Oblast', W Ukraine
114 K7 **Volovo** Ruse, N Bulgaria
Volozhin *see* Valozhyn
127 Q7 **Vol'sk** Saratovskaya Oblast', W Russian Federation
77 Q17 **Volta** ≈ SE Ghana
Volta Blanche *see* White Volta
77 P16 **Volta, Lake** ▣ SE Ghana
Volta Noire *see* Black Volta
60 O9 **Volta Redonda** Rio de Janeiro, SE Brazil
Volta Rouge *see* Red Volta
106 F12 **Volterra** *anc.* Volaterrae. Toscana, C Italy
107 K17 **Volturno** ≈ S Italy
113 I15 **Volujak** ▲▲ SW Serbia and Montenegro (Yugo.)
Volunteer Island *see* Starbuck Island
65 F24 **Volunteer Point** *headland* East Falkland, Falkland Islands
Volunteer State *see* Tennessee
114 H13 **Vólvi, Límni** ◎ N Greece
Volyn *see* Volyns'ka Oblast'
116 I3 **Volyns'ka Oblast'** *var.* Volyn, *Rus.* Volynskaya Oblast'. ◈ *province* NW Ukraine
Volynskaya Oblast' *see* Volyns'ka Oblast'
127 Q3 **Volzhsk** Respublika Mariy El, W Russian Federation
127 O10 **Volzhskiy** Volgogradskaya Oblast', SW Russian Federation
172 I7 **Vondrozo** Fianarantsoa, SE Madagascar
114 K9 **Voneshta Voda** Veliko Tŭrnovo, N Bulgaria
39 P10 **Von Frank Mountain** ▲ Alaska, USA
115 C17 **Vónitsa** Dytikí Ellás, W Greece
118 J6 **Võnnu** *Ger.* Wendau. Tartumaa, SE Estonia
98 G12 **Voorburg** Zuid-Holland, W Netherlands
98 H11 **Voorschoten** Zuid-Holland, W Netherlands
98 M11 **Voorst** Gelderland, E Netherlands
98 K11 **Voorthuizen** Gelderland, C Netherlands
92 L2 **Vopnafjördhur** Austurland, E Iceland
92 L2 **Vopnafjördhur** *bay* E Iceland
Vora *see* Vorë
119 H15 **Voranava** *Pol.* Werenów, *Rus.* Voronovo. Hrodzyenskaya Voblasts', W Belarus
108 I8 **Vorarlberg** *off.* Land Vorarlberg. ◈ *state* W Austria
109 X7 **Vorau** Steiermark, E Austria
98 N11 **Vorden** Gelderland, E Netherlands
108 H9 **Vorderrhein** ≈ SE Switzerland
92 J2 **Vordhufell** ▲ N Iceland
95 I24 **Vordingborg** Storstrøm, SE Denmark
113 K19 **Vorë** *var.* Vora. Tiranë, W Albania
115 H17 **Vóreioi Sporádes** *var.* Vórioi Sporádhes, *Eng.* Northern Sporades. *island group* E Greece
115 J17 **Vóreion Aigaíon** *Eng.* Aegean North. ◈ *region* SE Greece
115 G18 **Voreiós Evvoïkós Kólpos** *gulf* E Greece
197 S16 **Voring Plateau** *undersea feature* N Norwegian Sea
Vórioi Sporádhes *see* Vóreioi Sporádes
125 W4 **Vorkuta** Respublika Komi, NW Russian Federation
95 I14 **Vorma** ≈ S Norway
118 E4 **Vormsi** *var.* Vormsi Saar, *Ger.* Worms, *Swed.* Ormsö. *island* W Estonia
Vormsi Saar *see* Vormsi
127 N7 **Vorona** ≈ W Russian Federation
126 L7 **Voronezh** Voronezhskaya Oblast', W Russian Federation
126 L7 **Voronezh** ≈ W Russian Federation
126 K8 **Voronezhskaya Oblast'** ◈ *province* W Russian Federation
Voronovitsya *see* Voronovytsya
Voronovo *see* Voranava
117 N6 **Voronovytsya** *Rus.* Voronovitsya. Vinnyts'ka Oblast', C Ukraine
122 K7 **Vorontsovo** Taymyrskiy (Dolgano-Nenetskiy) Avtonomnyy Okrug, N Russian Federation
126 K3 **Voron'ya** ≈ NW Russian Federation
Voropayevo *see* Varapayeva
Voroshilov *see* Ussuriysk
Voroshilovgrad *see* Luhans'k, Ukraine
Voroshilovgrad *see* Luhans'ka Oblast', Ukraine
Voroshilovgradskaya Oblast' *see* Luhans'ka Oblast'
Voroshilovsk *see* Stavropol', Russian Federation
Voroshilovsk *see* Alchevs'k, Ukraine
137 V13 **Vorotan** *Az.* Bärgušad. ≈ Armenia/Azerbaijan
127 P3 **Vorotynets** Nizhegorodskaya Oblast', W Russian Federation
117 S3 **Vorozhba** Sums'ka Oblast', NE Ukraine
117 T5 **Vorskla** ≈ Russian Federation/Ukraine
99 I17 **Vorst** Antwerpen, N Belgium
83 G21 **Vorstershoop** North-West, N South Africa
118 H6 **Võrtsjärv** *Ger.* Wirz-See. ◎ SE Estonia
118 J7 **Võru** *Ger.* Werro. Võrumaa, SE Estonia
147 R11 **Vorukh** N Tajikistan
118 J7 **Võrumaa** *off.* Võru Maakond. ◈ *province* SE Estonia
83 G24 **Vosburg** Northern Cape, W South Africa
147 Q14 **Vose'** *Rus.* Vose; *prev.* Aral. SW Tajikistan
103 S6 **Vosges** ◈ *department* NE France
103 U6 **Vosges** ▲▲ NE France
126 L4 **Voskresensk** Moskovskaya Oblast', W Russian Federation
127 P2 **Voskresenskoye** Nizhegorodskaya Oblast', W Russian Federation
127 V6 **Voskresenskoye** Respublika Bashkortostan, W Russian Federation
124 K13 **Voskresenskoye** Vologodskaya Oblast', NW Russian Federation
94 D13 **Voss** Hordaland, S Norway
94 D13 **Voss** *physical region* S Norway
99 I16 **Vosselaar** Antwerpen, N Belgium
94 D13 **Vosso** ≈ S Norway
Vostochno-Kazakhstanskaya Oblast' *see* Shygys Konyrat
145 T12 **Vostochno-Kounradskiy** *Kaz.* Shyghys Qongyrat. Zhezkazgan, C Kazakhstan
123 S5 **Vostochno-Sibirskoye More** *Eng.* East Siberian Sea. *sea* Arctic Ocean
145 X10 **Vostochnyy Kazakhstan** *off.* Vostochno-Kazakhstanskaya Oblast', *var.* East Kazakhstan, *Kaz.* Shyghys Qazagastan Oblysy. ◈ *province* E Kazakhstan
Vostochnyy Sayan *see* Eastern Sayans
Vostock Island *see* Vostok Island
195 U10 **Vostok** *Russian research station* Antarctica
191 X5 **Vostok Island** *var.* Vostock Island; *prev.* Stavers Island. *island* Line Islands, SE Kiribati
127 T2 **Votkinsk** Udmurtskaya Respublika, NW Russian Federation
127 U15 **Votkinskoye Vodokhranilishche** *var.* Votkinsk Reservoir. ▣ NW Russian Federation
Votkinsk Reservoir *see* Votkinskoye Vodokhranilishche
60 J7 **Votuporanga** São Paulo, S Brazil
104 H7 **Vouga, Rio** ≈ N Portugal
115 E14 **Voúrinos** ▲ N Greece
115 G24 **Voúxa, Akrotírio** *headland* Kríti, Greece, E Mediterranean Sea
103 R4 **Vouziers** Ardennes, N France
117 V7 **Vovcha** *Rus.* Volchya. ≈ E Ukraine
117 V4 **Vovchans'k** *Rus.* Volchansk. Kharkivs'ka Oblast', E Ukraine
103 N6 **Voves** Eure-et-Loir, C France
79 M14 **Vovodo** ≈ S Central African Republic
94 M12 **Voxna** Gävleborg, C Sweden
94 L11 **Voxnan** ≈ C Sweden
114 F7 **Voynishka Reka** ≈ NW Bulgaria
125 T9 **Voyvozh** Respublika Komi, NW Russian Federation
124 M12 **Vozhega** Vologodskaya Oblast', NW Russian Federation
126 L12 **Vozhe, Ozero** ◎ NW Russian Federation
117 Q9 **Voznesens'k** *Rus.* Voznesensk. Mykolayivs'ka Oblast', S Ukraine
124 J12 **Voznesen'ye** Leningradskaya Oblast', NW Russian Federation
144 J14 **Vozrozhdeniya, Ostrov** *Uzb.* Wozrojdeniye Oroli. *island* Kazakhstan/Uzbekistan
Vpadina Mynbulak *see* Mingbuloq Botig'l
95 G20 **Vrå** *var.* Vraa. Nordjylland, N Denmark
Vraa *see* Vrå
114 H9 **Vrachesh** Sofiya, NW Bulgaria
115 C19 **Vrachíonas** ▲ Zákynthos, Iónioi Nísoi, Greece, C Mediterranean Sea
117 P8 **Vradiyivka** Mykolayivs'ka Oblast', S Ukraine
113 G14 **Vran** ▲ SW Bosnia and Herzegovina
116 K12 **Vrancea** ◈ *county* E Romania
147 T14 **Vrang** SE Tajikistan
123 T4 **Vrangelya, Ostrov** *Eng.* Wrangel Island. *island* NE Russian Federation
112 H13 **Vranica** ▲ C Bosnia and Herzegovina
113 O16 **Vranje** Serbia, SE Serbia and Montenegro (Yugo.)
Vranov *see* Vranov nad Topl'ou
111 N19 **Vranov nad Topl'ou** *var.* Vranov, *Hung.* Varannó. Prešovský Kraj, E Slovakia
114 H8 **Vratsa** Vratsa, NW Bulgaria
114 H8 **Vratsa** ◈ *province* NW Bulgaria
114 F10 **Vrattsa** *prev.* Mirovo. Kyustendil, W Bulgaria
112 G11 **Vrbanja** ≈ NW Bosnia and Herzegovina
112 K9 **Vrbas** Serbia, NW Serbia and Montenegro (Yugo.)
112 G13 **Vrbas** ≈ N Bosnia and Herzegovina
112 E8 **Vrbovec** Zagreb, N Croatia
112 C9 **Vrbovsko** Primorje-Gorski Kotar, NW Croatia
111 E15 **Vrchlabí** *Ger.* Hohenelbe. Královéhradecký Kraj, NE Czech Republic
83 J22 **Vrede** Free State, E South Africa
100 E13 **Vreden** Nordrhein-Westfalen, NW Germany
83 E25 **Vredenburg** Western Cape, SW South Africa
99 I23 **Vresse-sur-Semois** Namur, SE Belgium
95 L16 **Vretstorp** Örebro, C Sweden
113 G15 **Vrgorac** *prev.* Vrhgorac. Split-Dalmacija, SE Croatia
Vrhgorac *see* Vrgorac
109 T12 **Vrhnika** *Ger.* Oberlaibach. W Slovenia
155 I21 **Vriddhāchalam** Tamil Nādu, SE India
98 N6 **Vries** Drenthe, NE Netherlands
98 O10 **Vriezenveen** Overijssel, E Netherlands
95 L20 **Vrigstad** Jönköping, S Sweden
108 H9 **Vrin** Graubünden, S Switzerland
112 E13 **Vrlika** Split-Dalmacija, S Croatia
113 M14 **Vrnjačka Banja** Serbia, C Serbia and Montenegro (Yugo.)
Vrondádhes/Vrondados *see* Vrontádos
115 L18 **Vrontádos** *var.* Vrondados; *prev.* Vrondádhes. Chíos, E Greece
98 N9 **Vroomshoop** Overijssel, E Netherlands
112 N10 **Vršac** *Ger.* Werschetz, *Hung.* Versecz. Serbia, NE Serbia and Montenegro (Yugo.)
112 M10 **Vršački Kanal** *canal* N Serbia and Montenegro (Yugo.)
83 H21 **Vryburg** North-West, N South Africa
83 K22 **Vryheid** KwaZulu/Natal, E South Africa
111 I18 **Vsetín** *Ger.* Wsetin. Zlínský Kraj, E Czech Republic
111 J20 **Vtáčnik** *Hung.* Madaras, Ptacsnik; *prev.* Ptačnik. ▲ W Slovakia
Vuadil' *see* Wodil
Vuanggava *see* Vuaqava
114 I11 **Vŭcha** ≈ SW Bulgaria
113 N16 **Vučitrn** Serbia, S Serbia and Montenegro (Yugo.)
99 J14 **Vught** Noord-Brabant, S Netherlands
117 W8 **Vuhledar** Donets'ka Oblast', E Ukraine
112 I9 **Vuka** ≈ E Croatia
113 K17 **Vukël** *var.* Vukli. Shkodër, N Albania
Vukli *see* Vukël
112 J9 **Vukovar** *Hung.* Vukovár. Vukovar-Srijem, E Croatia
112 I10 **Vukovar-Srijem** *off.* Vukovarsko-Srijemska Županija. ◈ *province* E Croatia
125 U8 **Vuktyl** Respublika Komi, NW Russian Federation
11 Q17 **Vulcan** Alberta, SW Canada
116 G12 **Vulcan** *Ger.* Wulkan, *Hung.* Zsilyvajdevulkán; *prev.* Crivadia Vulcanului, Vaidei, *Hung.* Sily-Vajdej, Vajdej. Hunedoara, W Romania
116 M12 **Vulcănești** *Rus.* Vulkaneshty. S Moldova
107 L22 **Vulcano, Isola** *island* Isole Eolie, S Italy
114 G7 **Vŭlchedrŭm** Montana, NW Bulgaria
114 N8 **Vŭlchidol** *prev.* Kurt-Dere. Varna, NE Bulgaria
Vulkaneshty *see* Vulcănești
123 V11 **Vulkannyy** Kamchatskaya Oblast', E Russian Federation
36 J13 **Vulture Mountains** ▲▲ Arizona, SW USA
167 T14 **Vung Tau** *prev. Fr.* Cape Saint Jacques, Cap Saint-Jacques. Ba Ria-Vung Tau, S Vietnam
187 X15 **Vunisea** Kadavu, SE Fiji
Vuohčču *see* Vuotso
93 N15 **Vuokatti** Oulu, C Finland
93 M15 **Vuolijoki** Oulu, C Finland
Vuolleriebme *see* Vuollerim
92 J13 **Vuollerim** *Lapp.* Vuolleriebme. Norrbotten, N Sweden
Vuoreija *see* Vardø
92 L10 **Vuotso** *Lapp.* Vuohčču. Lappi, N Finland
114 J11 **Vŭrbitsa** *prev.* Filevo. Khaskovo, S Bulgaria
114 J12 **Vŭrbitsa** ≈ S Bulgaria
127 Q4 **Vurnary** Chuvashskaya Respublika, W Russian Federation
114 G8 **Vŭrshets** Montana, NW Bulgaria
119 F17 **Vyalikaya Byerastavitsa** *Pol.* Brzostowica Wielka, *Rus.* Bol'shaya Berëstovitsa; *prev.* Velikaya Berestovitsa. Hrodzyenskaya Voblasts', SW Belarus
119 N20 **Vyaliki Bor** *Rus.* Velikiy Bor. Homyel'skaya Voblasts', SE Belarus
119 J18 **Vyaliki Rozhan** *Rus.* Bol'shoy Rozhan. Minskaya Voblasts', S Belarus
124 H10 **Vyartsilya** *Fin.* Värtsilä. Respublika Kareliya, NW Russian Federation
119 K17 **Vyasyeya** *Rus.* Veseya. Minskaya Voblasts', C Belarus
127 R15 **Vyatka** ≈ NW Russian Federation
Vyatka *see* Kirov
125 S16 **Vyatskiye Polyany** Kirovskaya Oblast', NW Russian Federation
123 S14 **Vyazemskiy** Khabarovskiy Kray, SE Russian Federation
126 I4 **Vyaz'ma** Smolenskaya Oblast', W Russian Federation
127 N3 **Vyazniki** Vladimirskaya Oblast', W Russian Federation
127 O8 **Vyazovka** Volgogradskaya Oblast', SW Russian Federation
119 J14 **Vyazyn'** *Rus.* Vyazyn'. Minskaya Voblasts', NW Belarus
124 G11 **Vyborg** *Fin.* Viipuri. Leningradskaya Oblast', NW Russian Federation
127 P11 **Vychegda** *var.* Vichegda. ≈ NW Russian Federation
119 L14 **Vyelyewshchyna** *Rus.* Velevshchina. Vitsyebskaya Voblasts', N Belarus
119 P16 **Vyeramyeyki** *Rus.* Veremeyki. Mahilyowskaya Voblasts', E Belarus
118 K11 **Vyerkhnyadzvinsk** *Rus.* Verkhnedvinsk. Vitsyebskaya Voblasts', N Belarus
119 P18 **Vyetka** *Rus.* Vetka. Homyel'skaya Voblasts', SE Belarus
118 L12 **Vyetryna** *Rus.* Vetrino. Vitsyebskaya Voblasts', N Belarus
Vygonovskoye, Ozero *see* Vyhanashchanskaye, Vozyera
126 J9 **Vygozero, Ozero** ◎ NW Russian Federation
Vyhanashchanskaye Vozyera *see* Vyhanawskaye, Vozyera
119 I18 **Vyhanawskaye, Vozyera** *var.* Vyhanashchanskaye Vozyera, *Rus.* Ozero Vygonovskoye. ◎ SW Belarus
127 N4 **Vyksa** Nizhegorodskaya Oblast', W Russian Federation
117 O12 **Vylkove** *Rus.* Vilkovo. Odes'ka Oblast', SW Ukraine
127 R9 **Vym'** ≈ NW Russian Federation
116 H8 **Vynohradiv** *Cz.* Sevluš, *Hung.* Nagyszöllös, *Rus.* Vinogradov; *prev.* Sevlyush. Zakarpats'ka Oblast', W Ukraine
124 G13 **Vyritsa** Leningradskaya Oblast', NW Russian Federation
97 J19 **Vyrnwy** *Wel.* Afon Efyrnwy. ≈ E Wales, UK
145 X9 **Vysheivanovskiy Belak, Gora** ▲ E Kazakhstan
117 P4 **Vyshhorod** Kyyivs'ka Oblast', N Ukraine
124 I15 **Vyshniy Volochek** Tverskaya Oblast', W Russian Federation
111 G18 **Vyškov** *Ger.* Wischau. Jihomoravský Kraj, SE Czech Republic
111 F17 **Vysoké Mýto** *Ger.* Hohenmauth. Pardubický Kraj, C Czech Republic
117 S9 **Vysokopillya** Khersons'ka Oblast', S Ukraine
126 K3 **Vysokovsk** Moskovskaya Oblast', W Russian Federation
124 K12 **Vytegra** Vologodskaya Oblast', NW Russian Federation
116 J8 **Vyzhnytsya** Chernivets'ka Oblast', W Ukraine

W

77 O14 **Wa** NW Ghana
Waadt *see* Vaud
Waag *see* Váh
Waagbistritz *see* Považská Bystrica
Waagneustadtl *see* Nové Mesto nad Váhom
81 M16 **Waajid** Gedo, SW Somalia
98 L13 **Waal** ≈ S Netherlands
187 O16 **Waala** Province Nord, W New Caledonia
99 I14 **Waalwijk** Noord-Brabant, S Netherlands
99 E16 **Waarschoot** Oost-Vlaanderen, NW Belgium
186 C7 **Wabag** Enga, W PNG
15 N7 **Wabano** ≈ Québec, SE Canada
11 P11 **Wabasca** ≈ Alberta, SW Canada
31 P12 **Wabash** Indiana, N USA
29 X9 **Wabasha** Minnesota, N USA
31 N13 **Wabash River** ≈ N USA
14 C7 **Wabatongushi Lake** ◎ Ontario, S Canada
81 L15 **Wabē Gestro Wenz** ≈ SE Ethiopia
14 B9 **Wabos** Ontario, S Canada
11 W13 **Wabowden** Manitoba, C Canada
110 J9 **Wąbrzeźno** Kujawsko-pomorskie, N Poland
21 U12 **Waccamaw River** ≈ South Carolina, SE USA
23 U11 **Waccasassa Bay** *bay* Florida, SE USA
99 F16 **Wachtebeke** Oost-Vlaanderen, NW Belgium
25 T8 **Waco** Texas, SW USA
26 M3 **Waconda Lake** *var.* Great Elder Reservoir. ▣ Kansas, C USA
Wadai *see* Ouaddaï
Wad Al-Hajarah *see* Guadalajara
164 I12 **Wadayama** Hyōgo, Honshū, SW Japan
80 D10 **Wad Banda** Western Kordofan, C Sudan
75 P9 **Waddān** NW Libya
98 J4 **Waddeneilanden** *Eng.* West Frisian Islands. *island group* N Netherlands
98 J6 **Waddenzee** *var.* Wadden Zee. *sea* SE North Sea

◆ COUNTRY ● COUNTRY CAPITAL ◇ DEPENDENT TERRITORY ○ DEPENDENT TERRITORY CAPITAL ◈ ADMINISTRATIVE REGION ✕ INTERNATIONAL AIRPORT ▲ MOUNTAIN ▲▲ MOUNTAIN RANGE ⛰ VOLCANO ≈ RIVER ◎ LAKE ▣ RESERVOIR

10 L16 **Waddington, Mount** ▲ British Columbia, SW Canada
98 H12 **Waddinxveen** Zuid-Holland, C Netherlands
11 U15 **Wadena** Saskatchewan, S Canada
29 T6 **Wadena** Minnesota, N USA
108 G7 **Wädenswil** Zürich, N Switzerland
21 S11 **Wadesboro** North Carolina, SE USA
155 G16 **Wādi** Karnātaka, C India
138 G10 **Wādī as Sīr** *var.* Wadi es Sir. 'Al 'Ammān, NW Jordan
Wadi es Sir *see* Wādī as Sīr
80 F5 **Wadi Halfa** *var.* Wādī Ḥalfā'. Northern, N Sudan
138 G13 **Wādī Mūsā** *var.* Petra. Ma'ān, S Jordan
23 V4 **Wadley** Georgia, SE USA
Wad Madanī *see* Wad Medani
80 G10 **Wad Medani** *var.* Wad Madanī. Gezira, C Sudan
80 F10 **Wad Nimr** White Nile, C Sudan
165 U16 **Wadomari** Kagoshima, Okinoerabu-jima, SW Japan
111 K17 **Wadowice** Małopolskie, S Poland
35 R5 **Wadsworth** Nevada, W USA
31 T12 **Wadsworth** Ohio, N USA
25 T11 **Waelder** Texas, SW USA
Waereghem *see* Waregem
163 U13 **Wafangdian** *var.* Fuxian, Fu Xian. Liaoning, NE China
171 R13 **Waflia** Pulau Buru, E Indonesia
Wagadugu *see* Ouagadougou
98 K12 **Wageningen** Gelderland, SE Netherlands
55 V9 **Wageningen** Nickerie, NW Suriname
9 O8 **Wager Bay** *inlet* Nunavut, N Canada
183 P10 **Wagga Wagga** New South Wales, SE Australia
180 J13 **Wagin** Western Australia
108 H8 **Wägitaler See** ◎ SW Switzerland
29 P12 **Wagner** South Dakota, N USA
27 Q9 **Wagoner** Oklahoma, C USA
37 U10 **Wagon Mound** New Mexico, SW USA
32 J14 **Wagontire** Oregon, NW USA
110 H10 **Wągrowiec** Wielkopolskie, NW Poland
149 U6 **Wāh** Punjab, NE Pakistan
171 S13 **Wahai** Pulau Seram, E Indonesia
169 V10 **Wahau, Sungai** ↝ Borneo, C Indonesia
Wahaybah, Ramlat Al *see* Wahībah, Ramlat Āl
80 D13 **Wahda** *var.* Unity State. ◆ *state* S Sudan
38 D9 **Wahiawā** *var.* Wahiawa. O'ahu, Hawai'i, USA, C Pacific Ocean
Wahībah, Ramlat Ahl *see* Wahībah, Ramlat Āl
141 Y9 **Wahībah, Ramlat Āl** *var.* Ramlat Ahl Wahibah, Ramlat Al Wahaybah, *Eng.* Wahibah Sands. *desert* N Oman
Wahibah Sands *see* Wahībah, Ramlat Āl
101 E16 **Wahn** × (Köln) Nordrhein-Westfalen, W Germany
29 R15 **Wahoo** Nebraska, C USA
29 R6 **Wahpeton** North Dakota, N USA
Wahran *see* Oran
36 J6 **Wah Wah Mountains** ▲ Utah, W USA
38 D9 **Waialua** O'ahu, Hawai'i, USA, C Pacific Ocean
38 D9 **Wai'anae** *var.* Waianae. O'ahu, Hawai'i, USA, C Pacific Ocean
184 Q8 **Waiapu** ↝ North Island, NZ
185 I17 **Waiau** Canterbury, South Island, NZ
185 I17 **Waiau** ↝ South Island, NZ
185 B23 **Waiau** ↝ South Island, NZ
101 H21 **Waiblingen** Baden-Württemberg, S Germany
Waidhofen *see* Waidhofen an der Ybbs, Niederösterreich, Austria
Waidhofen *see* Waidhofen an der Thaya, Niederösterreich, Austria
109 V2 **Waidhofen an der Thaya** *var.* Waidhofen. Niederösterreich, NE Austria
109 U5 **Waidhofen an der Ybbs** *var.* Waidhofen. Niederösterreich, E Austria
171 T11 **Waigeo, Pulau** *island* Maluku, E Indonesia
184 L5 **Waiheke Island** *island* N NZ
184 M7 **Waihi** Waikato, North Island, NZ
185 C20 **Waihou** ↝ North Island, NZ
Waikaboebak *see* Waikabubak
170 M17 **Waikabubak** *prev.* Waikaboebak. Pulau Sumba, C Indonesia
185 D23 **Waikaia** ↝ South Island, NZ
185 D23 **Waikaka** Southland, South Island, NZ
184 L13 **Waikanae** Wellington, North Island, NZ
184 M7 **Waikare, Lake** ◎ North Island, NZ
184 O9 **Waikaremoana, Lake** ◎ North Island, NZ
185 I17 **Waikari** Canterbury, South Island, NZ
184 L8 **Waikato** *off.* Waikato Region. ◆ *region* North Island, NZ
184 M8 **Waikato** ↝ North Island, NZ
182 J9 **Waikerie** South Australia
185 F23 **Waikouaiti** Otago, South Island, NZ
38 H11 **Wailea** Hawai'i, USA, C Pacific Ocean
38 F10 **Wailuku** Maui, Hawai'i, USA, C Pacific Ocean
185 H18 **Waimakariri** ↝ South Island, NZ
38 D9 **Waimānalo Beach** *var.* Waimanalo Beach. O'ahu, Hawai'i, USA, C Pacific Ocean
185 G15 **Waimangaroa** West Coast, South Island, NZ
185 G21 **Waimate** Canterbury, South Island, NZ
38 G11 **Waimea** *var.* Kamuela. Hawai'i, USA, C Pacific Ocean
38 D9 **Waimea** *var.* Maunawai. O'ahu, Hawai'i, USA, C Pacific Ocean
38 B8 **Waimea** Kaua'i, Hawai'i, USA, C Pacific Ocean
99 M20 **Waimes** Liège, E Belgium
154 J11 **Wainganga** *var.* Wain River. ↝ C India
Waingapoe *see* Waingapu
171 N17 **Waingapu** *prev.* Waingapoe. Pulau Sumba, C Indonesia
55 S7 **Waini** ↝ N Guyana
55 S7 **Waini Point** *headland* NW Guyana
Wain River *see* Wainganga
11 R15 **Wainwright** Alberta, SW Canada
39 O5 **Wainwright** Alaska, USA
184 K4 **Waiotira** Northland, North Island, NZ
184 M11 **Waiouru** Manawatu-Wanganui, North Island, NZ
171 W14 **Waipa** Papua, E Indonesia
184 L8 **Waipa** ↝ North Island, NZ
184 P9 **Waipaoa** ↝ North Island, NZ
185 D25 **Waipapa Point** *headland* South Island, NZ
185 I18 **Waipara** Canterbury, South Island, NZ
184 N12 **Waipawa** Hawke's Bay, North Island, NZ
184 K4 **Waipu** Northland, North Island, NZ
184 N12 **Waipukurau** Hawke's Bay, North Island, NZ
171 U14 **Wair** Pulau Kai Besar, E Indonesia
Wairakai *see* Wairakei
184 N9 **Wairakei** *var.* Wairakai. Waikato, North Island, NZ
185 M14 **Wairarapa, Lake** ◎ North Island, NZ
185 J15 **Wairau** ↝ South Island, NZ
184 P10 **Wairoa** Hawke's Bay, North Island, NZ
184 P10 **Wairoa** ↝ North Island, NZ
184 J4 **Wairoa** ↝ North Island, NZ
184 N9 **Waitahanui** Waikato, North Island, NZ
184 M6 **Waitakaruru** Waikato, North Island, NZ
185 F21 **Waitaki** ↝ South Island, NZ
184 K10 **Waitara** Taranaki, North Island, NZ
184 M7 **Waitoa** Waikato, North Island, NZ
184 L8 **Waitomo Caves** Waikato, North Island, NZ
184 L11 **Waitotara** Taranaki, North Island, NZ
184 L11 **Waitotara** ↝ North Island, NZ
32 L10 **Waitsburg** Washington, NW USA
Waitzen *see* Vác
184 L6 **Waiuku** Auckland, North Island, NZ
164 L10 **Wajima** *var.* Wazima. Ishikawa, Honshū, SW Japan
81 K17 **Wajir** North Eastern, NE Kenya
81 I14 **Waka** Southern, SW Ethiopia
79 J17 **Waka** Equateur, NW Dem. Rep. Congo
14 D9 **Wakami Lake** ◎ Ontario, S Canada
164 I12 **Wakasa** Tottori, Honshū, SW Japan
164 J12 **Wakasa-wan** *bay* C Japan
185 C22 **Wakatipu, Lake** ◎ South Island, NZ
11 T15 **Wakaw** Saskatchewan, S Canada
164 I14 **Wakayama** Wakayama, Honshū, SW Japan
164 I15 **Wakayama** *off.* Wakayama-ken. ◆ *prefecture* Honshū, SW Japan
26 K4 **Wa Keeney** Kansas, C USA
185 I14 **Wakefield** Tasman, South Island, NZ
97 M17 **Wakefield** N England, UK
27 O4 **Wakefield** Kansas, C USA
30 L4 **Wakefield** Michigan, N USA
21 U9 **Wake Forest** North Carolina, SE USA
Wakeham Bay *see* Kangiqsujuaq
189 Y11 **Wake Island** ◇ *US unincorporated territory* NW Pacific Ocean
189 Y12 **Wake Island** × NW Pacific Ocean
189 Y12 **Wake Island** *atoll* NW Pacific Ocean
189 X12 **Wake Lagoon** *lagoon* Wake Island, NW Pacific Ocean
166 L8 **Wakema** Irrawaddy, SW Myanmar
Wakhan *see* Khandūd
164 H14 **Waki** Tokushima, Shikoku, SW Japan
165 T1 **Wakkanai** Hokkaidō, NE Japan
83 K22 **Wakkerstroom** Mpumalanga, E South Africa
14 C10 **Wakomata Lake** ◎ Ontario, S Canada
183 N10 **Wakool** New South Wales, SE Australia
Wakra *see* Al Wakrah
Waku Kungo *see* Uaco Cungo
186 J7 **Wakunai** Bougainville Island, NE PNG
Walachei/Walachia *see* Wallachia
155 K26 **Walawe Ganga** ↝ S Sri Lanka
111 F15 **Wałbrzych** *Ger.* Waldenburg, Waldenburg in Schlesien. Dolnośląskie, SW Poland
183 T6 **Walcha** New South Wales, SE Australia
101 K24 **Walchensee** ◎ SE Germany
99 D14 **Walcheren** *island* SW Netherlands
29 Z14 **Walcott** Iowa, C USA
33 W16 **Walcott** Wyoming, C USA
99 G21 **Walcourt** Namur, S Belgium
110 G9 **Wałcz** *Ger.* Deutsch Krone. Zachodnio-pomorskie, NW Poland
108 H7 **Wald** Zürich, N Switzerland
109 U3 **Waldaist** ↝ N Austria
180 I9 **Waldburg Range** ▲ Western Australia
37 R3 **Walden** Colorado, C USA
18 K13 **Walden** New York, NE USA
Waldenburg/Waldenburg in Schlesien *see* Wałbrzych
11 T15 **Waldheim** Saskatchewan, S Canada
Waldia *see* Weldiya
101 M23 **Waldkraiburg** Bayern, SE Germany
27 T14 **Waldo** Arkansas, C USA
23 V9 **Waldo** Florida, SE USA
19 R7 **Waldoboro** Maine, NE USA
21 W4 **Waldorf** Maryland, NE USA
32 F12 **Waldport** Oregon, NW USA
27 S11 **Waldron** Arkansas, C USA
195 Y13 **Waldron, Cape** *headland* Antarctica
101 F24 **Waldshut-Tiengen** Baden-Württemberg, S Germany
171 P12 **Walea, Selat** *strait* Sulawesi, C Indonesia
Wałeckie Międzyrzecze *see* Valašské Meziříčí
108 H8 **Walensee** ◎ NW Switzerland
38 L8 **Wales** Alaska, USA
97 J20 **Wales** *Wel.* Cymru. *national region* UK
9 O7 **Wales Island** *island* Nunavut, NE Canada
77 P14 **Walewale** N Ghana
99 M24 **Walferdange** Luxembourg, C Luxembourg
183 Q5 **Walgett** New South Wales, SE Australia
194 K10 **Walgreen Coast** *physical region* Antarctica
29 Q2 **Walhalla** North Dakota, N USA
21 O11 **Walhalla** South Carolina, SE USA
79 O19 **Walikale** Nord Kivu, E Dem. Rep. Congo
Walk *see* Valga, Estonia
Walk *see* Valka, Latvia
29 U5 **Walker** Minnesota, N USA
15 V4 **Walker, Lac** ◎ Québec, SE Canada
35 S7 **Walker Lake** ◎ Nevada, W USA
35 R6 **Walker River** ↝ Nevada, W USA
28 K10 **Wall** South Dakota, N USA
173 U9 **Wallaby Plateau** *undersea feature* E Indian Ocean
33 N8 **Wallace** Idaho, NW USA
21 V11 **Wallace** North Carolina, SE USA
14 D17 **Wallaceburg** Ontario, S Canada
22 F5 **Wallace Lake** ▣ Louisiana, S USA
11 P13 **Wallace Mountain** ▲ Alberta, W Canada
116 J14 **Wallachia** *var.* Walachia, *Ger.* Walachei, *Rom.* Valachia. *cultural region* S Romania
Wallachisch-Meseritsch *see* Valašské Meziříčí
183 U4 **Wallangarra** New South Wales, SE Australia
182 I8 **Wallaroo** South Australia
32 L10 **Walla Walla** Washington, NW USA
45 V9 **Wallblake** × (The Valley) C Anguilla
101 H19 **Walldürn** Baden-Württemberg, SW Germany
100 F12 **Wallenhorst** Niedersachsen, NW Germany
Wallenthal *see* Hațeg
109 S4 **Wallern** Oberösterreich, N Austria
Wallern *see* Wallern im Burgenland
109 Z5 **Wallern im Burgenland** *var.* Wallern. Burgenland, E Austria
18 M9 **Wallingford** Vermont, NE USA
25 V11 **Wallis** Texas, SW USA
Wallis *see* Valais
192 K9 **Wallis and Futuna** *Fr.* Territoire de Wallis et Futuna. ◇ *French overseas territory* C Pacific Ocean
108 G7 **Wallisellen** Zürich, N Switzerland
190 H11 **Wallis, Îles** *island group* N Wallis and Futuna
99 H19 **Wallon Brabant** ◆ *province* C Belgium
31 Q5 **Walloon Lake** ◎ Michigan, N USA
32 K10 **Wallula** Washington, NW USA
32 K10 **Wallula, Lake** ◎ Washington, NW USA
21 S8 **Walnut Cove** North Carolina, SE USA
35 N8 **Walnut Creek** California, W USA
26 K5 **Walnut Creek** ↝ Kansas, C USA
27 W9 **Walnut Ridge** Arkansas, C USA
25 S7 **Walnut Springs** Texas, SW USA
182 L10 **Walpeup** Victoria, SE Australia
187 R17 **Walpole, Île** *island* SE New Caledonia
39 N13 **Walrus Islands** *island group* Alaska, USA
97 L19 **Walsall** C England, UK
37 T7 **Walsenburg** Colorado, C USA
11 S17 **Walsh** Alberta, SW Canada
37 W7 **Walsh** Colorado, C USA
100 I11 **Walsrode** Niedersachsen, NW Germany
Waltenberg *see* Zalău
21 R14 **Walterboro** South Carolina, SE USA
Walter F. George Lake *see* Walter F. George Reservoir
23 R6 **Walter F. George Reservoir** *var.* Walter F. George Lake. ▣ Alabama/Georgia, SE USA
26 M12 **Walters** Oklahoma, C USA
101 J16 **Waltershausen** Thüringen, C Germany
173 N10 **Walters Shoal** *var.* Walters Shoals. *reef* S Madagascar
Walters Shoals *see* Walters Shoal
22 M3 **Walthall** Mississippi, S USA
20 M4 **Walton** Kentucky, S USA
18 J11 **Walton** New York, NE USA
79 O20 **Walungu** Sud Kivu, E Dem. Rep. Congo
Walvisbaai *see* Walvis Bay
83 C19 **Walvis Bay** *Afr.* Walvisbaai. Erongo, NW Namibia
83 B19 **Walvis Bay** *bay* NW Namibia
Walvish Ridge *see* Walvis Ridge
65 O17 **Walvis Ridge** *var.* Walvish Ridge. *undersea feature* E Atlantic Ocean
171 X16 **Wamal** Papua, E Indonesia
171 U15 **Wamar, Pulau** *island* Kepulauan Aru, E Indonesia
77 V15 **Wamba** Nassarawa, C Nigeria
79 O17 **Wamba** Orientale, NE Dem. Rep. Congo
79 H22 **Wamba** *var.* Uamba. ↝ Angola/Dem. Rep. Congo
27 P4 **Wamego** Kansas, C USA
18 I10 **Wampsville** New York, NE USA
42 K6 **Wampú, Río** ↝ E Honduras
171 X16 **Wan** Papua, E Indonesia
Wan *see* Anhui
183 N4 **Wanaaring** New South Wales, SE Australia
185 D21 **Wanaka** Otago, South Island, NZ
185 D20 **Wanaka, Lake** ◎ South Island, NZ
171 W14 **Wanapiri** Papua, E Indonesia
14 F9 **Wanapitei** ↝ Ontario, S Canada
14 F10 **Wanapitei Lake** ◎ Ontario, S Canada
18 K14 **Wanaque** New Jersey, NE USA
171 U12 **Wanau** Papua, E Indonesia
185 F22 **Wanbrow, Cape** *headland* South Island, NZ
Wanchuan *see* Zhangjiakou
171 W13 **Wandai** *var.* Komeyo. Papua, E Indonesia
163 Z8 **Wanda Shan** ▲ NE China
197 R11 **Wandel Sea** *sea* Arctic Ocean
160 D13 **Wanding** *var.* Wandingzhen. Yunnan, SW China
Wandingzhen *see* Wanding
99 H20 **Wanfercée-Baulet** Hainaut, S Belgium
184 L12 **Wanganui** Manawatu-Wanganui, North Island, NZ
184 L11 **Wanganui** ↝ North Island, NZ
183 P11 **Wangaratta** Victoria, SE Australia
160 J8 **Wangcang** *var.* Hongjiang; *prev.* Fengjiaba. Sichuan, C China
Wangda *see* Zogang
101 I24 **Wangen im Allgäu** Baden-Württemberg, S Germany
Wangerin *see* Węgorzyno
100 F9 **Wangerooge** *island* NW Germany
171 W13 **Wanggar** Papua, E Indonesia
160 J13 **Wangmo** *var.* Fuxing. Guizhou, S China
Wangolodougou *see* Ouangolodougou
161 S9 **Wangpan Yang** *sea* E China
163 Y10 **Wangqing** Jilin, NE China
167 P8 **Wang Saphung** Loei, C Thailand
167 O6 **Wan Hsa-la** Shan State, E Myanmar
55 W9 **Wanica** ◆ *district* N Suriname
79 M18 **Wanie-Rukula** Orientale, C Dem. Rep. Congo
Wankie *see* Hwange
Wanki, Río *see* Coco, Río
81 N17 **Wanlaweyn** *var.* Wanle Weyn, *It.* Uanle Uen. Shabeellaha Hoose, SW Somalia
Wanle Weyn *see* Wanlaweyn
180 I12 **Wanneroo** Western Australia
160 L17 **Wanning** Hainan, S China
167 Q8 **Wanon Niwat** Sakon Nakhon, E Thailand
155 H16 **Wanparti** Andhra Pradesh, C India
Wansen *see* Wiązów
160 L11 **Wanshan** Guizhou, S China
99 M14 **Wanssum** Limburg, SE Netherlands
184 N12 **Wanstead** Hawke's Bay, North Island, NZ
Wanxian *see* Wanzhou
188 F16 **Wanyaan** Yap, Micronesia
160 K8 **Wanyuan** Sichuan, C China
161 O11 **Wanzai** *var.* Kangle. Jiangxi, S China
99 J20 **Wanze** Liège, E Belgium
160 K9 **Wanzhou** *var.* Wanxian. Chongqing Shi, C China
31 R12 **Wapakoneta** Ohio, N USA
12 D7 **Wapaseese** ↝ Ontario, C Canada
32 I10 **Wapato** Washington, NW USA
29 Y15 **Wapello** Iowa, C USA
11 N13 **Wapiti** ↝ Alberta/British Columbia, SW Canada
27 X7 **Wappapello Lake** ▣ Missouri, C USA
18 K13 **Wappingers Falls** New York, NE USA
29 X13 **Wapsipinicon River** ↝ Iowa, C USA
14 L9 **Wapus** ↝ Québec, SE Canada
160 H7 **Waqên** Sichuan, C China
21 Q7 **War** West Virginia, NE USA
80 D13 **Warab** Warab, SW Sudan
81 D14 **Warab** ◆ *state* SW Sudan
155 J15 **Warangal** Andhra Pradesh, C India
Waraşdin *see* Varaždin
183 O16 **Waratah** Tasmania, SE Australia
183 O14 **Waratah Bay** *bay* Victoria, SE Australia
101 H15 **Warburg** Nordrhein-Westfalen, W Germany
182 I1 **Warburton Creek** *seasonal river* South Australia
180 M9 **Warburton** Western Australia
99 M20 **Warche** ↝ E Belgium
149 P5 **Wardag** *var.* Wardak, *Per.* Vardak. ◆ *province* E Afghanistan
Wardak *see* Wardag
32 K9 **Warden** Washington, NW USA
154 I12 **Wardha** Mahārāshtra, W India
121 N15 **Wardija, Ras il-** *var.* Wardija Point. *headland* Gozo, NW Malta
139 P3 **Wardīyah** N Iraq
185 E19 **Ward, Mount** ▲ South Island, NZ
10 L11 **Ware** British Columbia, W Canada
99 D18 **Waregem** *var.* Waereghem. West-Vlaanderen, W Belgium
99 J19 **Waremme** Liège, E Belgium
100 N10 **Waren** Mecklenburg-Vorpommern, NE Germany
171 W13 **Waren** Papua, E Indonesia
101 F14 **Warendorf** Nordrhein-Westfalen, W Germany
21 P12 **Ware Shoals** South Carolina, SE USA
98 N4 **Warffum** Groningen, NE Netherlands
81 O15 **Wargalo** Mudug, E Somalia
146 M12 **Warganza** *Rus.* Varganzi. Qashqadaryo Viloyati, S Uzbekistan
Wargla *see* Ouargla
183 T4 **Warialda** New South Wales, SE Australia
154 F13 **Wāri Godri** Mahārāshtra, C India
167 R10 **Warin Chamrap** Ubon Ratchathani, E Thailand
25 R11 **Waring** Texas, SW USA
39 O6 **Waring Mountains** ▲ Alaska, USA
110 M12 **Warka** Mazowieckie, E Poland
184 L5 **Warkworth** Auckland, North Island, NZ
171 U12 **Warmandi** Papua, E Indonesia
83 E22 **Warmbad** Karas, S Namibia
98 H8 **Warmenhuizen** Noord-Holland, NW Netherlands
110 L8 **Warmińsko-Mazurskie** ◆ *province* NW Poland
97 L22 **Warminster** S England, UK
18 I15 **Warminster** Pennsylvania, NE USA
35 V8 **Warm Springs** Nevada, W USA
32 H12 **Warm Springs** Oregon, NW USA
21 S5 **Warm Springs** Virginia, NE USA
100 M8 **Warnemünde** Mecklenburg-Vorpommern, NE Germany
27 Q10 **Warner** Oklahoma, C USA
35 Q2 **Warner Mountains** ▲ California, W USA
23 T5 **Warner Robins** Georgia, SE USA
57 N18 **Warnes** Santa Cruz, C Bolivia
100 M9 **Warnow** ↝ NE Germany
Warnsdorf *see* Varnsdorf
98 M11 **Warnsveld** Gelderland, E Netherlands
154 I13 **Warora** Mahārāshtra, C India
182 L11 **Warracknabeal** Victoria, SE Australia
183 O13 **Warragul** Victoria, SE Australia
183 O4 **Warrego River** *seasonal river* New South Wales/Queensland, E Australia
183 Q6 **Warren** New South Wales, SE Australia
11 X16 **Warren** Manitoba, S Canada
27 V14 **Warren** Arkansas, C USA
31 S10 **Warren** Michigan, N USA
25 R3 **Warren** Minnesota, N USA
31 U11 **Warren** Ohio, N USA
18 D12 **Warren** Pennsylvania, NE USA
25 X10 **Warren** Texas, SW USA
97 G16 **Warrenpoint** *Ir.* An Pointe. SE Northern Ireland, UK
27 S4 **Warrensburg** Missouri, C USA
83 H22 **Warrenton** Northern Cape, N South Africa
23 U4 **Warrenton** Georgia, SE USA
27 W4 **Warrenton** Missouri, C USA
21 V8 **Warrenton** North Carolina, SE USA
21 V4 **Warrenton** Virginia, NE USA
77 U17 **Warri** Delta, S Nigeria
97 L18 **Warrington** C England, UK
23 O9 **Warrington** Florida, SE USA
23 P3 **Warrior** Alabama, S USA
182 L13 **Warrnambool** Victoria, SE Australia
29 T2 **Warroad** Minnesota, N USA
183 S6 **Warrumbungle Range** ▲ New South Wales, SE Australia
154 J12 **Wārsa** Mahārāshtra, C India
31 P11 **Warsaw** Indiana, N USA
20 L4 **Warsaw** Kentucky, S USA
27 T5 **Warsaw** Missouri, C USA
18 E10 **Warsaw** New York, NE USA
21 V10 **Warsaw** North Carolina, SE USA
21 X5 **Warsaw** Virginia, NE USA
Warsaw/Warschau *see* Warszawa
81 N17 **Warshiikh** Shabeellaha Dhexe, C Somalia
101 G15 **Warstein** Nordrhein-Westfalen, W Germany
110 M11 **Warszawa** *Eng.* Warsaw, *Ger.* Warschau, *Rus.* Varshava. ● (Poland) Mazowieckie, C Poland
110 J13 **Warta** Sieradz, C Poland
110 D11 **Warta** *Ger.* Warthe. ↝ W Poland
Wartberg *see* Senec
20 M9 **Wartburg** Tennessee, S USA
108 J7 **Warth** Vorarlberg, NW Austria
Warthe *see* Warta
169 U12 **Waru** Borneo, C Indonesia
171 T13 **Waru** Pulau Seram, E Indonesia
139 N6 **Wa'r, Wādī al** *dry watercourse* E Syria
183 U3 **Warwick** Queensland, E Australia
15 Q11 **Warwick** Québec, SE Canada
97 M20 **Warwick** C England, UK
18 K13 **Warwick** New York, NE USA
29 P4 **Warwick** North Dakota, N USA
19 O12 **Warwick** Rhode Island, NE USA
97 L20 **Warwickshire** *cultural region* C England, UK
14 G14 **Wasaga Beach** Ontario, S Canada
77 U13 **Wasagu** Kebbi, NW Nigeria
36 M2 **Wasatch Range** ▲ W USA
35 R12 **Wasco** California, W USA
29 V10 **Waseca** Minnesota, N USA
14 H13 **Washago** Ontario, S Canada
19 S2 **Washburn** Maine, NE USA
28 M5 **Washburn** North Dakota, N USA
30 K3 **Washburn** Wisconsin, N USA
31 S14 **Washburn Hill** *hill* Ohio, N USA
154 H13 **Wāshīm** Mahārāshtra, C India
97 M14 **Washington** NE England, UK
23 U3 **Washington** Georgia, SE USA
30 L12 **Washington** Illinois, N USA
31 N15 **Washington** Indiana, N USA
29 X15 **Washington** Iowa, C USA
27 O3 **Washington** Kansas, C USA
27 W5 **Washington** Missouri, C USA
21 X9 **Washington** North Carolina, SE USA
18 B15 **Washington** Pennsylvania, NE USA
25 V10 **Washington** Texas, SW USA
36 J8 **Washington** Utah, W USA
21 V4 **Washington** Virginia, NE USA
32 I9 **Washington** *off.* State of Washington; also known as Chinook State, Evergreen State. ◆ *state* NW USA
Washington *see* Washington Court House
31 S14 **Washington Court House** *var.* Washington. Ohio, NE USA
21 W4 **Washington DC** ● (USA) District of Columbia, NE USA
31 O5 **Washington Island** *island* Wisconsin, N USA
Washington Island *see* Teraina
19 O7 **Washington, Mount** ▲ New Hampshire, NE USA
26 M11 **Washita River** ↝ Oklahoma/Texas, C USA
97 O18 **Wash, The** *inlet* E England, UK
32 L9 **Washtucna** Washington, NW USA
Wasiliszki *see* Vasilishki
110 P9 **Wasilków** Podlaskie, NE Poland
39 R11 **Wasilla** Alaska, USA
55 U9 **Wasjabo** Sipaliwini, NW Suriname
11 X11 **Waskaiowaka Lake** ◎ Manitoba, C Canada
11 T14 **Waskesiu Lake** Saskatchewan, C Canada
25 X7 **Waskom** Texas, SW USA
110 G13 **Wąsosz** Dolnośląskie, SW Poland
42 M6 **Waspam** *var.* Waspán. Región Autónoma Atlántico Norte, NE Nicaragua
Waspán *see* Waspam
165 T3 **Wassamu** Hokkaidō, NE Japan
108 G9 **Wassen** Uri, C Switzerland
98 G11 **Wassenaar** Zuid-Holland, W Netherlands
99 N24 **Wasserbillig** Grevenmacher, E Luxembourg
Wasserburg *see* Wasserburg am Inn
101 M23 **Wasserburg am Inn** *var.* Wasserburg. Bayern, SE Germany
101 I17 **Wasserkuppe** ▲ C Germany
103 R5 **Wassy** Haute-Marne, N France
171 N14 **Watampone** *var.* Bone. Sulawesi, C Indonesia
171 R13 **Watawa** Pulau Buru, E Indonesia
Watenstedt-Salzgitter *see* Salzgitter
18 M13 **Waterbury** Connecticut, NE USA
21 R11 **Wateree Lake** ▣ South Carolina, SE USA
21 R12 **Wateree River** ↝ South Carolina, SE USA
97 E20 **Waterford** *Ir.* Port Láirge. S Ireland
31 S9 **Waterford** Michigan, N USA
97 E20 **Waterford** *Ir.* Port Láirge. *cultural region* S Ireland
97 E21 **Waterford Harbour** *Ir.* Cuan Phort Láirge. *inlet* S Ireland
98 G12 **Wateringen** Zuid-Holland, W Netherlands
99 G19 **Waterloo** Wallon Brabant, C Belgium
14 F16 **Waterloo** Ontario, S Canada
15 P12 **Waterloo** Québec, SE Canada
30 K16 **Waterloo** Illinois, N USA
29 X13 **Waterloo** Iowa, C USA
18 G10 **Waterloo** New York, NE USA
30 L4 **Watersmeet** Michigan, N USA
23 V9 **Watertown** Florida, SE USA
18 I8 **Watertown** New York, NE USA
29 R9 **Watertown** South Dakota, N USA
30 M8 **Watertown** Wisconsin, N USA
22 L3 **Water Valley** Mississippi, S USA
27 O3 **Waterville** Kansas, C USA
17 V6 **Waterville** Maine, NE USA
29 V10 **Waterville** Minnesota, N USA
18 I10 **Waterville** New York, NE USA
14 E16 **Watford** Ontario, S Canada
97 N21 **Watford** SE England, UK
28 K4 **Watford City** North Dakota, N USA
141 X12 **Wāṭif** S Oman
18 G11 **Watkins Glen** New York, NE USA
Watlings Island *see* San Salvador
171 U15 **Watnil** Pulau Kai Kecil, E Indonesia
26 M10 **Watonga** Oklahoma, C USA
11 T16 **Watrous** Saskatchewan, S Canada
37 T10 **Watrous** New Mexico, SW USA
79 P16 **Watsa** Orientale, NE Dem. Rep. Congo
31 N12 **Watseka** Illinois, N USA
79 J19 **Watsikengo** Equateur, C Dem. Rep. Congo
182 C5 **Watson** South Australia
11 U15 **Watson** Saskatchewan, S Canada
195 O10 **Watson Escarpment** ▲ Antarctica
10 K9 **Watson Lake** Yukon Territory, W Canada
35 N10 **Watsonville** California, W USA
167 Q8 **Wattay** × (Viangchan) Viangchan, C Laos

109 N7 **Wattens** Tirol, W Austria
20 M9 **Watts Bar Lake** ⊠ Tennessee, S USA
108 H7 **Wattwil** Sankt Gallen, NE Switzerland
171 T14 **Watubela, Kepulauan** island group E Indonesia
101 N24 **Watzmann** ▲ SE Germany
186 E8 **Wau** Morobe, C PNG
81 D14 **Wau** var. Wāw. Western Bahr el Ghazal, S Sudan
29 Q8 **Waubay** South Dakota, N USA
29 Q8 **Waubay Lake** ◎ South Dakota, N USA
183 U7 **Wauchope** New South Wales, SE Australia
23 W13 **Wauchula** Florida, SE USA
30 M10 **Wauconda** Illinois, N USA
182 J7 **Waukaringa** South Australia
31 N10 **Waukegan** Illinois, N USA
30 M9 **Waukesha** Wisconsin, N USA
29 X11 **Waukon** Iowa, C USA
30 L8 **Waunakee** Wisconsin, N USA
30 L7 **Waupaca** Wisconsin, N USA
30 M8 **Waupun** Wisconsin, N USA
26 M13 **Wauconda** Oklahoma, C USA
26 M12 **Waurika Lake** ⊠ Oklahoma, C USA
30 L6 **Wausau** Wisconsin, N USA
31 R11 **Wauseon** Ohio, N USA
30 L7 **Wautoma** Wisconsin, N USA
30 M9 **Wauwatosa** Wisconsin, N USA
22 L9 **Waveland** Mississippi, S USA
97 Q20 **Waveney** ≈ E England, UK
184 L11 **Waverley** Taranaki, North Island, NZ
29 W12 **Waverly** Iowa, C USA
27 T4 **Waverly** Missouri, C USA
29 R15 **Waverly** Nebraska, C USA
18 G12 **Waverly** New York, NE USA
20 H8 **Waverly** Tennessee, S USA
21 W7 **Waverly** Virginia, NE USA
99 H19 **Wavre** Wallon Brabant, C Belgium
166 M8 **Waw** Pegu, SW Myanmar
Wāw see Wau
14 B7 **Wawa** Ontario, S Canada
77 T14 **Wawa** Niger, W Nigeria
75 Q11 **Wāw al Kabīr** S Libya
43 N7 **Wawa, Río** var. Rio Huahua. ≈ NE Nicaragua
186 B8 **Wawoi** ≈ SW PNG
25 T7 **Waxahachie** Texas, SW USA
158 L9 **Waxxari** Xinjiang Uygur Zizhiqu, NW China
23 V7 **Waycross** Georgia, SE USA
180 K10 **Way, Lake** ◎ Western Australia
31 P9 **Wayland** Michigan, N USA
29 R13 **Wayne** Nebraska, C USA
18 K14 **Wayne** New Jersey, NE USA
21 P5 **Wayne** West Virginia, NE USA
23 V4 **Waynesboro** Georgia, SE USA
22 M7 **Waynesboro** Mississippi, S USA
20 H10 **Waynesboro** Tennessee, S USA
21 U5 **Waynesboro** Virginia, NE USA
18 B16 **Waynesburg** Pennsylvania, NE USA
27 U6 **Waynesville** Missouri, C USA
21 O10 **Waynesville** North Carolina, SE USA
26 L8 **Waynoka** Oklahoma, C USA
Wazan see Ouazzane
Wazima see Wajima
149 V7 **Wazīrābād** Punjab, NE Pakistan
Wazzan see Ouazzane
110 I8 **Wda** var. Czarna Woda, Ger. Schwarzwasser. ≈ N Poland
187 Q16 **Wé** Province des Îles Loyauté, E New Caledonia
97 O23 **Weald, The** lowlands SE England, UK
186 A9 **Weam** Western, SW PNG
97 L15 **Wear** ≈ N England, UK
Wearmouth see Sunderland
26 L10 **Weatherford** Oklahoma, C USA
25 S6 **Weatherford** Texas, SW USA
34 M3 **Weaverville** California, W USA
27 R7 **Webb City** Missouri, C USA
192 G8 **Weber Basin** undersea feature S Ceram Sea
Webfoot State see Oregon
18 F9 **Webster** New York, NE USA
29 Q8 **Webster** South Dakota, N USA
29 V13 **Webster City** Iowa, C USA
27 X5 **Webster Groves** Missouri, C USA
21 S4 **Webster Springs** var. Addison. West Virginia, NE USA
171 S11 **Weda, Teluk** bay Pulau Halmahera, E Indonesia
65 B25 **Weddell Island** var. Isla San José. Island W Falkland Islands
65 K22 **Weddell Plain** undersea feature SW Atlantic Ocean
65 K23 **Weddell Sea** sea SW Atlantic Ocean
65 B25 **Weddell Settlement** Weddell Island, W Falkland Islands
182 M11 **Wedderburn** Victoria, SE Australia
100 I9 **Wedel** Schleswig-Holstein, N Germany
92 N3 **Wedel Jarlsberg Land** physical region SW Svalbard
100 I12 **Wedemark** Niedersachsen, NW Germany
10 M17 **Wedge Mountain** ▲ British Columbia, SW Canada
23 R4 **Wedowee** Alabama, S USA
171 U15 **Weduar** Pulau Kai Besar, E Indonesia
35 N2 **Weed** California, W USA
15 Q12 **Weedon Centre** Québec, SE Canada
18 E13 **Weedville** Pennsylvania, NE USA
100 F10 **Weener** Niedersachsen, NW Germany
29 S16 **Weeping Water** Nebraska, C USA
99 L16 **Weert** Limburg, SE Netherlands
98 I10 **Weesp** Noord-Holland, C Netherlands
183 S5 **Wee Waa** New South Wales, SE Australia
110 N7 **Węgorzewo** Ger. Angerburg. Warmińsko-Mazurskie, NE Poland
110 E9 **Węgorzyno** Ger. Wangerin. Zachodnio-pomorskie, NW Poland
110 N11 **Węgrów** Ger. Bingerau. Mazowieckie, E Poland
98 N5 **Wehe-Den Hoorn** Groningen, NE Netherlands
98 M12 **Wehl** Gelderland, E Netherlands
Wehlau see Znamensk
168 F7 **Weh, Pulau** island NW Indonesia
Wei see Weifang
161 P1 **Weichang** prev. Zhuizishan. Hebei, E China
Weichsel see Wisła
101 M16 **Weida** Thüringen, C Germany
Weiden see Weiden in der Oberpfalz
101 M19 **Weiden in der Oberpfalz** var. Weiden. Bayern, SE Germany
161 Q4 **Weifang** var. Wei, Wei-fang; prev. Weihsien. Shandong, E China
161 S4 **Weihai** Shandong, E China
160 K6 **Wei He** ≈ C China
Weihsien see Weifang
101 G17 **Weilburg** Hessen, W Germany
101 K24 **Weilheim in Oberbayern** Bayern, SE Germany
183 P4 **Weilmoringle** New South Wales, SE Australia
101 L16 **Weimar** Thüringen, C Germany
25 U11 **Weimar** Texas, SW USA
160 L6 **Weinan** Shaanxi, C China
108 H6 **Weinfelden** Thurgau, NE Switzerland
101 I24 **Weingarten** Baden-Württemberg, S Germany
101 G20 **Weinheim** Baden-Württemberg, SW Germany
160 H11 **Weining** var. Weining Yizu Huizu Miaozu Zizhixian. Guizhou, S China
Weining Yizu Huizu Miaozu Zizhixian see Weining
181 V2 **Weipa** Queensland, NE Australia
11 Y11 **Weir River** Manitoba, C Canada
21 R1 **Weirton** West Virginia, NE USA
32 M13 **Weiser** Idaho, NW USA
160 F12 **Weishan** Yunnan, SW China
161 P6 **Weishan Hu** ◎ E China
101 M15 **Weisse Elster** Eng. White Elster. ≈ Czech Republic/Germany
Weisse Körös/Weisse Kreisch see Crişul Alb
108 L7 **Weissenbach am Lech** Tirol, W Austria
101 K21 **Weissenburg in Bayern** Bayern, SE Germany
Weissenburg see Wissembourg, France
Weissenburg see Alba Iulia, Romania
101 M15 **Weissenfels** var. Weißenfels. Sachsen-Anhalt, C Germany
109 R9 **Weissensee** ◎ S Austria
Weissenstein see Paide
108 E11 **Weisshorn** var. Flüela Wisshorn. ▲ SW Switzerland
Weisskirchen see Bela Crkva
23 R3 **Weiss Lake** ⊠ Alabama, S USA
101 Q14 **Weisswasser** Lus. Běla Woda. Sachsen, E Germany
99 M22 **Weiswampach** Diekirch, N Luxembourg
109 U2 **Weitra** Niederösterreich, N Austria
161 O4 **Weixian** var. Wei Xian. Hebei, E China
159 V11 **Weiyuan** Gansu, C China
Weiyuan see Shuangjiang
160 F14 **Weiyuan Jiang** ≈ SW China
109 W7 **Weiz** Steiermark, SE Austria
Weizhou see Wenchuan
160 K16 **Weizhou Dao** island S China
110 I6 **Wejherowo** Pomorskie, NW Poland
27 Q8 **Welch** Oklahoma, C USA
24 M6 **Welch** Texas, SW USA
21 Q6 **Welch** West Virginia, NE USA
45 O14 **Welchman Hall** C Barbados
80 J11 **Weldiya** var. Waldia, It. Valdia. Amhara, N Ethiopia
21 W8 **Weldon** North Carolina, SE USA
25 V9 **Weldon** Texas, SW USA
99 M19 **Welkenraedt** Liège, E Belgium
193 O2 **Welker Seamount** undersea feature N Pacific Ocean
83 I22 **Welkom** Free State, C South Africa
14 H16 **Welland** Ontario, S Canada
14 G16 **Welland** ≈ Ontario, S Canada
97 O19 **Welland** ≈ C England, UK
14 H17 **Welland Canal** canal Ontario, S Canada
155 K25 **Wellawaya** Uva Province, SE Sri Lanka
Welle see Uele
181 T4 **Wellesley Islands** island group Queensland, N Australia
99 J22 **Wellin** Luxembourg, SE Belgium
97 N20 **Wellingborough** C England, UK
183 R7 **Wellington** New South Wales, SE Australia
14 J15 **Wellington** Ontario, SE Canada
185 L14 **Wellington** ● (NZ) Wellington, North Island, NZ
83 E26 **Wellington** Western Cape, SW South Africa
37 T2 **Wellington** Colorado, C USA
27 N7 **Wellington** Kansas, C USA
35 R7 **Wellington** Nevada, W USA
31 T11 **Wellington** Ohio, N USA
25 P3 **Wellington** Texas, SW USA
36 M4 **Wellington** Utah, W USA
185 M14 **Wellington** off. Wellington Region. ◈ region North Island, NZ
185 L14 **Wellington** × Wellington, North Island, NZ
Wellington see Wellington, Isla
63 F22 **Wellington, Isla** var. Wellington. island S Chile
183 P12 **Wellington, Lake** ◎ Victoria, SE Australia
29 X14 **Wellman** Iowa, C USA
24 M6 **Wellman** Texas, SW USA
97 K22 **Wells** SW England, UK
29 V11 **Wells** Minnesota, N USA
35 X2 **Wells** Nevada, W USA
25 W8 **Wells** Texas, SW USA
18 F12 **Wellsboro** Pennsylvania, NE USA
21 R1 **Wellsburg** West Virginia, NE USA
184 K4 **Wellsford** Auckland, North Island, NZ
180 L9 **Wells, Lake** ◎ Western Australia
181 N4 **Wells, Mount** ▲ Western Australia
97 P18 **Wells-next-the-Sea** E England, UK
31 T15 **Wellston** Ohio, N USA
27 O10 **Wellston** Oklahoma, C USA
18 E11 **Wellsville** New York, NE USA
31 V12 **Wellsville** Ohio, N USA
36 L1 **Wellsville** Utah, W USA
36 I14 **Wellton** Arizona, SW USA
109 S4 **Wels** anc. Ovilava. Oberösterreich, N Austria
99 K15 **Welschap** × (Eindhoven) Noord-Brabant, S Netherlands
100 P10 **Welse** ≈ NE Germany
22 H9 **Welsh** Louisiana, S USA
97 K19 **Welshpool** Wel. Y Trallwng. E Wales, UK
97 O21 **Welwyn Garden City** SE England, UK
79 K18 **Wema** Equateur, NW Dem. Rep. Congo
81 G21 **Wembere** ≈ C Tanzania
11 N13 **Wembley** Alberta, W Canada
12 I9 **Wemindji** prev. Nouveau-Comptoir, Paint Hills. Québec, C Canada
99 G18 **Wemmel** Vlaams Brabant, C Belgium
32 J8 **Wenatchee** Washington, NW USA
160 M17 **Wenchang** Hainan, S China
161 R11 **Wencheng** var. Daxue. Zhejiang, SE China
77 P16 **Wenchi** W Ghana
Wen-chou/Wenchow see Wenzhou
160 H8 **Wenchuan** var. Weizhou. Sichuan, C China
Wendau see Võnnu
Wenden see Cēsis
161 S4 **Wendeng** Shandong, E China
81 J14 **Wendo** Southern, S Ethiopia
36 J2 **Wendover** Utah, W USA
14 D9 **Wenebegon** ≈ Ontario, S Canada
14 D8 **Wenebegon Lake** ◎ Ontario, S Canada
108 E9 **Wengen** Bern, W Switzerland
161 O13 **Wengyuan** var. Longxian. Guangdong, S China
189 P15 **Weno** prev. Moen. Chuuk, C Micronesia
189 V12 **Weno** prev. Moen. atoll Chuuk Islands, C Micronesia
158 N13 **Wenquan** Qinghai, C China
159 H4 **Wenquan** var. Arixang. Xinjiang Uygur Zizhiqu, NW China
Wenquan see Yingshan
160 H14 **Wenshan** var. Kaihua. Yunnan, SW China
158 H6 **Wensu** Xinjiang Uygur Zizhiqu, W China
182 L8 **Wentworth** New South Wales, SE Australia
27 W4 **Wentzville** Missouri, C USA
159 V12 **Wenxian** var. Wen Xian. Gansu, C China
161 S10 **Wenzhou** var. Wen-chou, Wenchow. Zhejiang, SE China
34 L4 **Weott** California, W USA
99 I20 **Wépion** Namur, SE Belgium
100 O11 **Werbellinsee** ◎ NE Germany
99 L21 **Werbomont** Liège, E Belgium
83 G20 **Werda** Kgalagadi, S Botswana
Werder see Virtsu
81 N14 **Werder** Somali, E Ethiopia
Werenów see Voranava
171 U13 **Weri** Papua, E Indonesia
98 I13 **Werkendam** Noord-Brabant, S Netherlands
101 M20 **Wernberg-Köblitz** Bayern, SE Germany
101 J18 **Werneck** Bayern, C Germany
101 K14 **Wernigerode** Sachsen-Anhalt, C Germany
Werowitz see Virovitica
101 J16 **Werra** ≈ C Germany
183 N12 **Werribee** Victoria, SE Australia
183 T6 **Werris Creek** New South Wales, SE Australia
Werro see Võru
Werschetz see Vršac
101 K23 **Wertach** ≈ S Germany
101 I19 **Wertheim** Baden-Württemberg, SW Germany
98 J8 **Wervershoof** Noord-Holland, NW Netherlands
Wervicq see Wervik
99 C18 **Wervik** var. Wervicq, Werwick. West-Vlaanderen, W Belgium
Werwick see Wervik
101 D14 **Wesel** Nordrhein-Westfalen, W Germany
Weseli an der Lainsitz see Veselí nad Lužnicí
Wesenberg see Rakvere
100 H12 **Weser** ≈ NW Germany
Wes-Kaap see Western Cape
25 S17 **Weslaco** Texas, SW USA
14 J13 **Weslemkoon Lake** ◎ Ontario, SE Canada
181 R1 **Wessel Islands** island group Northern Territory, N Australia
29 P9 **Wessington** South Dakota, N USA
29 P10 **Wessington Springs** South Dakota, N USA
25 T8 **West** Texas, SW USA
West see Ouest
30 M9 **West Allis** Wisconsin, N USA
182 E8 **Westall, Point** headland South Australia
West Antarctica see Lesser Antarctica
14 G11 **West Arm** Ontario, S Canada
West Azerbaijan see Āzarbāyjān-e Gharbī
138 F10 **West Bank** disputed region SW Asia
11 N17 **Westbank** British Columbia, SW Canada
14 E11 **West Bay** Manitoulin Island, Ontario, S Canada
22 L11 **West Bay** bay Louisiana, S USA
30 M8 **West Bend** Wisconsin, N USA
153 R16 **West Bengal** ◈ state NE India
West Borneo see Kalimantan Barat
29 Y14 **West Branch** Iowa, C USA
31 R7 **West Branch** Michigan, N USA
18 F13 **West Branch Susquehanna River** ≈ Pennsylvania, NE USA
97 L20 **West Bromwich** C England, UK
19 P8 **Westbrook** Maine, NE USA
29 T10 **Westbrook** Minnesota, N USA
29 Y15 **West Burlington** Iowa, C USA
96 L2 **West Burra** island NE Scotland, UK
30 J8 **Westby** Wisconsin, N USA
44 L6 **West Caicos** island W Turks and Caicos Islands
185 A24 **West Cape** headland South Island, NZ
174 L4 **West Caroline Basin** undersea feature SW Pacific Ocean
18 I16 **West Chester** Pennsylvania, NE USA
185 E18 **West Coast** off. West Coast Region. ◈ region South Island, NZ
25 V12 **West Columbia** Texas, SW USA
29 W10 **West Concord** Minnesota, N USA
29 V14 **West Des Moines** Iowa, C USA
37 Q6 **West Elk Peak** ▲ Colorado, C USA
44 F1 **West End** Grand Bahama Island, N Bahamas
44 F1 **West End Point** headland Grand Bahama Island, N Bahamas
98 O7 **Westerbork** Drenthe, NE Netherlands
98 N3 **Westereems** strait Germany/Netherlands
98 O9 **Westerhaar-Vriezenveensewijk** Overijssel, E Netherlands
100 G6 **Westerland** Schleswig-Holstein, N Germany
99 I17 **Westerlo** Antwerpen, N Belgium
19 N13 **Westerly** Rhode Island, NE USA
81 G18 **Western** ◈ province W Kenya
153 N11 **Western** ◈ zone C Nepal
186 A8 **Western** ◈ province SW PNG
186 J8 **Western** off. Western Province. ◈ province NW Solomon Islands
83 G15 **Western** ◈ province SW Zambia
180 K8 **Western Australia** ◈ state W Australia
80 A13 **Western Bahr el Ghazal** ◈ state SW Sudan
Western Bug see Bug
83 F25 **Western Cape** off. Western Cape Province, Afr. Wes-Kaap. ◈ province SW South Africa
80 A11 **Western Darfur** ◈ state W Sudan
Western Desert see Sahara el Gharbîya
118 G9 **Western Dvina** Bel. Dzvina, Ger. Düna, Latv. Daugava, Rus. Zapadnaya Dvina. ≈ W Europe
81 D15 **Western Equatoria** ◈ state SW Sudan
155 E16 **Western Ghats** ▲ SW India
186 C7 **Western Highlands** ◈ province C PNG
Western Isles see Outer Hebrides
80 C12 **Western Kordofan** ◈ state C Sudan
21 T3 **Westernport** Maryland, NE USA
155 J26 **Western Province** ◈ province SW Sri Lanka
74 B10 **Western Sahara** ◇ disputed territory N Africa
Western Samoa see Samoa
Western Sayans see Zapadnyy Sayan
Western Scheldt see Westerschelde
Western Sierra Madre see Madre Occidental, Sierra
99 E15 **Westerschelde** Eng. Western Scheldt; prev. Honte. inlet S North Sea
31 S13 **Westerville** Ohio, N USA
101 F17 **Westerwald** ▲ W Germany
65 C25 **West Falkland** var. Gran Malvina, Isla Gran Malvina. island W Falkland Islands
29 R5 **West Fargo** North Dakota, N USA
188 M15 **West Fayu Atoll** atoll Caroline Islands, C Micronesia
18 C11 **Westfield** New York, NE USA
30 L7 **Westfield** Wisconsin, N USA
West Flanders see West-Vlaanderen
27 S10 **West Fork** Arkansas, C USA
29 P16 **West Fork Big Blue River** ≈ Nebraska, C USA
29 U12 **West Fork Des Moines River** ≈ Iowa/Minnesota, C USA
25 S5 **West Fork Trinity River** ≈ Texas, SW USA
30 L16 **West Frankfort** Illinois, N USA
98 I8 **West-Friesland** physical region NW Netherlands
West Frisian Islands see Waddeneilanden
19 T5 **West Grand Lake** ◎ Maine, NE USA
18 M12 **West Hartford** Connecticut, NE USA
18 M13 **West Haven** Connecticut, NE USA
27 X12 **West Helena** Arkansas, C USA
28 M2 **Westhope** North Dakota, N USA
195 Y8 **West Ice Shelf** ice shelf Antarctica
47 R2 **West Indies** island group SE North America
West Irian see Papua
West Java see Jawa Barat
36 L3 **West Jordan** Utah, W USA
West Kalimantan see Kalimantan Barat
99 D14 **Westkapelle** Zeeland, SW Netherlands
31 O13 **West Lafayette** Indiana, N USA
31 T13 **West Lafayette** Ohio, N USA
West Lake see Kagera
29 Y14 **West Liberty** Iowa, C USA
21 O5 **West Liberty** Kentucky, S USA
Westliche Morava see Zapadna Morava
10 J13 **Westlock** Alberta, SW Canada
14 E17 **West Lorne** Ontario, S Canada
96 J12 **West Lothian** cultural region S Scotland, UK
99 H16 **Westmalle** Antwerpen, N Belgium
192 G6 **West Mariana Basin** var. Perece Vela Basin. undersea feature W Pacific Ocean
97 E17 **Westmeath** Ir. An Iarmhí, Na h-Iarmhidhe. cultural region C Ireland
27 Y11 **West Memphis** Arkansas, C USA
21 W2 **Westminster** Maryland, NE USA
21 O11 **Westminster** South Carolina, SE USA
22 I5 **West Monroe** Louisiana, S USA
18 D15 **Westmont** Pennsylvania, NE USA
27 O3 **Westmoreland** Kansas, C USA
35 W17 **Westmorland** California, W USA
186 E6 **West New Britain** ◈ province E PNG
West New Guinea see Papua
83 K18 **West Nicholson** Matabeleland South, S Zimbabwe
29 T14 **West Nishnabotna River** ≈ Iowa, C USA
175 P11 **West Norfolk Ridge** undersea feature W Pacific Ocean
25 P12 **West Nueces River** ≈ Texas, SW USA
West Nusa Tenggara see Nusa Tenggara Barat
29 T11 **West Okoboji Lake** ◎ Iowa, C USA
33 R16 **Weston** Idaho, NW USA
21 R4 **Weston** West Virginia, NE USA
97 J22 **Weston-super-Mare** SW England, UK
23 Z14 **West Palm Beach** Florida, SE USA
West Papua see Papua
188 E9 **West Passage** passage Babeldaob, N Palau
23 O9 **West Pensacola** Florida, SE USA
27 V8 **West Plains** Missouri, C USA
35 P7 **West Point** California, W USA
23 R5 **West Point** Georgia, SE USA
22 M3 **West Point** Mississippi, S USA
29 R14 **West Point** Nebraska, C USA
21 X6 **West Point** Virginia, NE USA
182 G10 **West Point** headland South Australia
65 B24 **Westpoint Island Settlement** Westpoint Island, NW Falkland Islands
23 R4 **West Point Lake** ⊠ Alabama/Georgia, SE USA
97 B16 **Westport** Ir. Cathair na Mart. W Ireland
185 G15 **Westport** West Coast, South Island, NZ
32 F10 **Westport** Oregon, NW USA
32 F9 **Westport** Washington, NW USA
31 S15 **West Portsmouth** Ohio, N USA
West Punjab see Punjab
11 V14 **Westray** Manitoba, C Canada
96 J4 **Westray** island NE Scotland, UK
14 F9 **Westree** Ontario, S Canada
97 L16 **West Riding** cultural region N England, UK
West River see Xi Jiang
30 J7 **West Salem** Wisconsin, N USA
65 H21 **West Scotia Ridge** undersea feature W Scotia Sea
West Sepik see Sandaun
173 N4 **West Sheba Ridge** undersea feature W Indian Ocean
West Siberian Plain see Zapadno-Sibirskaya Ravnina
31 S11 **West Sister Island** island Ohio, N USA
West-Skylge see West-Terschelling
West Sumatra see Sumatera Barat
98 J5 **West-Terschelling** Fris. West-Skylge. Friesland, N Netherlands
64 J7 **West Thulean Rise** undersea feature N Atlantic Ocean
29 X12 **West Union** Iowa, C USA
31 R15 **West Union** Ohio, N USA
21 R3 **West Union** West Virginia, NE USA
31 N13 **Westville** Illinois, N USA
21 R3 **West Virginia** off. State of West Virginia; also known as The Mountain State. ◈ state NE USA
99 A17 **West-Vlaanderen** Eng. West Flanders. ◈ province W Belgium
35 R7 **West Walker River** ≈ California/Nevada, W USA
35 P4 **Westwood** California, W USA
183 P9 **West Wyalong** New South Wales, SE Australia
171 Q16 **Wetar, Pulau** island Kepulauan Damar, E Indonesia
171 R16 **Wetar, Selat** var. Wetar Strait. strait Nusa Tenggara, S Indonesia
Wetar Strait see Wetar, Selat
11 Q15 **Wetaskiwin** Alberta, SW Canada
81 K21 **Wete** Pemba, E Tanzania
166 M4 **Wetlet** Sagaing, C Myanmar
37 T6 **Wet Mountains** ▲ Colorado, C USA
101 E15 **Wetter** Nordrhein-Westfalen, W Germany
101 H17 **Wetter** ≈ W Germany
99 F17 **Wetteren** Oost-Vlaanderen, NW Belgium
108 F7 **Wettingen** Aargau, N Switzerland
27 P11 **Wetumka** Oklahoma, C USA
23 Q5 **Wetumpka** Alabama, S USA
108 G7 **Wetzikon** Zürich, N Switzerland
101 G17 **Wetzlar** Hessen, W Germany
99 C18 **Wevelgem** West-Vlaanderen, W Belgium
38 M6 **Wevok** var. Wewuk. Alaska, USA
23 R9 **Wewahitchka** Florida, SE USA
186 C6 **Wewak** East Sepik, NW PNG
27 O11 **Wewoka** Oklahoma, C USA
Wewuk see Wevok
97 F20 **Wexford** Ir. Loch Garman. SE Ireland
97 F20 **Wexford** Ir. Loch Garman. cultural region SE Ireland
30 L7 **Weyauwega** Wisconsin, N USA
11 U17 **Weyburn** Saskatchewan, S Canada
Weyer see Weyer Markt
109 U5 **Weyer Markt** var. Weyer. Oberösterreich, N Austria
100 H11 **Weyhe** Niedersachsen, NW Germany
97 L24 **Weymouth** S England, UK
19 P11 **Weymouth** Massachusetts, NE USA
99 H18 **Wezembeek-Oppem** Vlaams Brabant, C Belgium
98 M9 **Wezep** Gelderland, E Netherlands
184 M9 **Whakamaru** Waikato, North Island, NZ
184 O8 **Whakatane** Bay of Plenty, North Island, NZ
184 O8 **Whakatane** ≈ North Island, NZ
9 O9 **Whale Cove** Nunavut, C Canada
96 M2 **Whalsay** island NE Scotland, UK
184 L11 **Whangaehu** ≈ North Island, NZ
184 M6 **Whangamata** Waikato, North Island, NZ
184 Q9 **Whangara** Gisborne, North Island, NZ
184 K3 **Whangarei** Northland, North Island, NZ
184 K3 **Whangaruru Harbour** inlet North Island, NZ
25 V12 **Wharton** Texas, SW USA
173 U8 **Wharton Basin** var. West Australian Basin. undersea feature E Indian Ocean
185 E18 **Whataroa** West Coast, South Island, NZ
8 K10 **Wha Ti** prev. Lac La Martre. Northwest Territories, W Canada
184 K6 **Whatipu** Auckland, North Island, NZ
33 Y16 **Wheatland** Wyoming, C USA
14 D18 **Wheatley** Ontario, S Canada
30 M10 **Wheaton** Illinois, N USA
29 R7 **Wheaton** Minnesota, N USA
37 T4 **Wheat Ridge** Colorado, C USA
25 P2 **Wheeler** Texas, SW USA
23 O2 **Wheeler Lake** ⊠ Alabama, S USA
35 Y6 **Wheeler Peak** ▲ Nevada, W USA
37 T9 **Wheeler Peak** ▲ New Mexico, SW USA
31 S15 **Wheelersburg** Ohio, N USA
21 R2 **Wheeling** West Virginia, NE USA
97 L16 **Whernside** ▲ N England, UK
182 F9 **Whidbey, Point** headland South Australia
180 I7 **Whim Creek** Western Australia
10 L17 **Whistler** British Columbia, SW Canada
21 W8 **Whitakers** North Carolina, SE USA
14 H15 **Whitby** Ontario, S Canada
97 N15 **Whitby** N England, UK
10 G6 **White** ≈ Yukon Territory, W Canada
13 T11 **White Bay** bay Newfoundland and Labrador, E Canada
20 I8 **White Bluff** Tennessee, S USA
28 J6 **White Butte** ▲ North Dakota, N USA
19 R5 **White Cap Mountain** ▲ Maine, NE USA
22 J9 **White Castle** Louisiana, S USA
182 M5 **White Cliffs** New South Wales, SE Australia
31 P8 **White Cloud** Michigan, N USA
11 P14 **Whitecourt** Alberta, SW Canada
25 O2 **White Deer** Texas, SW USA
White Elster see Weisse Elster
24 M5 **Whiteface** Texas, SW USA
18 K7 **Whiteface Mountain** ▲ New York, NE USA
29 W5 **Whiteface Reservoir** ⊠ Minnesota, N USA
33 O7 **Whitefish** Montana, NW USA
31 N9 **Whitefish Bay** Wisconsin, N USA
31 Q3 **Whitefish Bay** lake bay Canada/USA
14 E11 **Whitefish Falls** Ontario, S Canada
14 B7 **Whitefish Lake** ◎ Ontario, S Canada
29 U6 **Whitefish Lake** ◎ Minnesota, C USA
31 Q3 **Whitefish Point** headland Michigan, N USA

◆ Country ● Country Capital ◇ Dependent Territory ○ Dependent Territory Capital ◈ Administrative Region × International Airport ▲ Mountain ▲ Mountain Range ⅄ Volcano ≈ River ◎ Lake ⊠ Reservoir

31 O4 **Whitefish River** ≈ Michigan, N USA
25 O4 **Whiteflat** Texas, SW USA
27 V12 **White Hall** Arkansas, C USA
30 K14 **White Hall** Illinois, N USA
31 O8 **Whitehall** Michigan, N USA
18 L9 **Whitehall** New York, NE USA
31 S13 **Whitehall** Ohio, N USA
30 J7 **Whitehall** Wisconsin, N USA
97 J15 **Whitehaven** NW England, UK
10 I8 **Whitehorse** *territory capital* Yukon Territory, W Canada
184 O7 **White Island** *island* NE NZ
14 K13 **White Lake** ◎ Ontario, SE Canada
22 H10 **White Lake** ◎ Louisiana, S USA
186 G7 **Whiteman Range** ⛰ New Britain, E PNG
183 Q15 **Whitemark** Tasmania, SE Australia
35 S9 **White Mountains** ⛰ California/Nevada, W USA
19 N7 **White Mountains** ⛰ Maine/New Hampshire, NE USA
80 F11 **White Nile** ◈ *state* C Sudan
67 U7 **White Nile** *var.* Bahr el Jebel. ≈ S Sudan
81 E14 **White Nile** *Ar.* Al Baḥr al Abyaḍ, An Nīl al Abyaḍ, Bahr el Jebel. ≈ SE Sudan
25 W5 **White Oak Creek** ≈ Texas, SW USA
10 H9 **White Pass** *pass* Canada/USA
32 I9 **White Pass** *pass* Washington, NW USA
21 O9 **White Pine** Tennessee, S USA
18 K14 **White Plains** New York, NE USA
25 O5 **White River** ≈ Texas, SW USA
28 M11 **White River** South Dakota, N USA
27 W12 **White River** ≈ Arkansas, SE USA
37 P3 **White River** ≈ Colorado/Utah, C USA
31 N15 **White River** ≈ Indiana, N USA
31 O8 **White River** ≈ Michigan, N USA
28 K11 **White River** ≈ South Dakota, N USA
18 M8 **White River** ≈ Vermont, NE USA
37 N13 **Whiteriver** Arizona, SW USA
25 O5 **White River Lake** ▣ Texas, SW USA
32 H11 **White Salmon** Washington, NW USA
18 I10 **Whitesboro** New York, NE USA
25 T5 **Whitesboro** Texas, SW USA
21 O7 **Whitesburg** Kentucky, S USA
White Sea *see* Beloye More
White Sea-Baltic Canal/White Sea Canal *see* Belomorsko-Baltiyskiy Kanal
63 I25 **Whiteside, Canal** *channel* S Chile
33 S10 **White Sulphur Springs** Montana, NW USA
21 R6 **White Sulphur Springs** West Virginia, NE USA
20 J6 **Whitesville** Kentucky, S USA
32 I10 **White Swan** Washington, NW USA
21 U12 **Whiteville** North Carolina, SE USA
20 F10 **Whiteville** Tennessee, S USA
77 Q13 **White Volta** *var.* Nakambé, *Fr.* Volta Blanche. ≈ Burkina/Ghana
30 M9 **Whitewater** Wisconsin, N USA
37 P14 **Whitewater Baldy** ▲ New Mexico, SW USA
23 X17 **Whitewater Bay** *bay* Florida, SE USA
31 Q14 **Whitewater River** ≈ Indiana/Ohio, N USA
11 V16 **Whitewood** Saskatchewan, S Canada
28 J9 **Whitewood** South Dakota, N USA
25 U5 **Whitewright** Texas, SW USA
97 I15 **Whithorn** S Scotland, UK
184 M6 **Whitianga** Waikato, North Island, NZ
19 N11 **Whitinsville** Massachusetts, NE USA
20 M8 **Whitley City** Kentucky, S USA
21 Q11 **Whitmire** South Carolina, SE USA
31 R10 **Whitmore Lake** Michigan, N USA
195 N9 **Whitmore Mountains** ⛰ Antarctica
14 I12 **Whitney** Ontario, SE Canada
25 T8 **Whitney** Texas, SW USA
25 S8 **Whitney, Lake** ▣ Texas, SW USA
35 S11 **Whitney, Mount** ▲ California, W USA
181 Y6 **Whitsunday Group** *island group* Queensland, E Australia
25 S6 **Whitt** Texas, SW USA
29 U12 **Whittemore** Iowa, C USA
39 R12 **Whittier** Alaska, USA
35 T15 **Whittier** California, W USA
83 I25 **Whittlesea** Eastern Cape, S South Africa
20 K10 **Whitwell** Tennessee, S USA
8 L10 **Wholdaia Lake** ◎ Northwest Territories, NW Canada
182 H7 **Whyalla** South Australia
Whydah *see* Ouidah
14 F13 **Wiarton** Ontario, S Canada
171 O13 **Wiau** Sulawesi, C Indonesia
111 H15 **Wiązów** *Ger.* Wansen. Dolnośląskie, SW Poland
33 Y8 **Wibaux** Montana, NW USA
27 N6 **Wichita** Kansas, C USA
25 R5 **Wichita Falls** Texas, SW USA
26 L11 **Wichita Mountains** ⛰ Oklahoma, C USA
25 R5 **Wichita River** ≈ Texas, SW USA
96 K5 **Wick** N Scotland, UK
36 K13 **Wickenburg** Arizona, SW USA
24 L8 **Wickett** Texas, SW USA
180 I7 **Wickham** Western Australia
182 M14 **Wickham, Cape** *headland* Tasmania, SE Australia
20 G7 **Wickliffe** Kentucky, S USA
97 G19 **Wicklow** *Ir.* Cill Mhantáin. E Ireland
97 F19 **Wicklow** *Ir.* Cill Mhantáin. *cultural region* E Ireland
97 G19 **Wicklow Head** *Ir.* Ceann Chill Mhantáin. *headland* E Ireland
97 F18 **Wicklow Mountains** *Ir.* Sléibhte Chill Mhantáin. ⛰ E Ireland
14 H10 **Wicksteed Lake** ◎ Ontario, S Canada
Wida *see* Ouidah
65 G15 **Wideawake Airfield** × (Georgetown) SW Ascension Island
97 K18 **Widnes** C England, UK
110 H9 **Więcbork** *Ger.* Vandsburg. Kujawsko-pomorskie, C Poland
101 E17 **Wied** ≈ W Germany
101 F16 **Wiehl** Nordrhein-Westfalen, W Germany
111 L17 **Wieliczka** Małopolskie, S Poland
110 G12 **Wielkopolskie** ◈ *province* C Poland
111 J14 **Wieluń** Sieradz, C Poland
109 X4 **Wien** *Eng.* Vienna, *Hung.* Bécs, *Slvk.* Vídeň, *Slvn.* Dunaj; *anc.* Vindobona. ● (Austria) Wien, NE Austria
109 X4 **Wien** *off.* Land Wien, *Eng.* Vienna. ◈ *state* NE Austria
109 X5 **Wiener Neustadt** Niederösterreich, E Austria
110 G7 **Wieprza** *Ger.* Wipper. ≈ NW Poland
98 O10 **Wierden** Overijssel, E Netherlands
98 I7 **Wieringerwerf** Noord-Holland, NW Netherlands
Wieruschow *see* Wieruszów
111 I14 **Wieruszów** *Ger.* Wieruschow. Łódzkie, C Poland
109 V9 **Wies** Steiermark, SE Austria
Wiesbachhorn *see* Grosses Wiesbachhorn
101 G18 **Wiesbaden** Hessen, W Germany
Wieselburg and Ungarisch-Altenburg/Wieselburg-Ungarisch-Altenburg *see* Mosonmagyaróvár
Wiesenhof *see* Ostrołęka
101 G20 **Wiesloch** Baden-Württemberg, SW Germany
100 F10 **Wiesmoor** Niedersachsen, NW Germany
110 I7 **Wieżyca** *Ger.* Turmberg. *hill* Pomorskie, N Poland
97 L17 **Wigan** NW England, UK
37 U3 **Wiggins** Colorado, C USA
22 M8 **Wiggins** Mississippi, S USA
Wigorna Ceaster *see* Worcester
97 I14 **Wigtown** S Scotland, UK
97 H14 **Wigtown** *cultural region* SW Scotland, UK
97 I15 **Wigtown Bay** *bay* SW Scotland, UK
98 L13 **Wijchen** Gelderland, SE Netherlands
92 N1 **Wijdefjorden** *fjord* NW Svalbard
98 M10 **Wijhe** Overijssel, E Netherlands
98 J12 **Wijk bij Duurstede** Utrecht, C Netherlands
98 J13 **Wijk en Aalburg** Noord-Brabant, S Netherlands
99 H16 **Wijnegem** Antwerpen, N Belgium
14 E11 **Wikwemikong** Manitoulin Island, Ontario, S Canada
108 H7 **Wil** Sankt Gallen, NE Switzerland
29 R16 **Wilber** Nebraska, C USA
32 K8 **Wilbur** Washington, NW USA
27 Q11 **Wilburton** Oklahoma, C USA
182 M6 **Wilcannia** New South Wales, SE Australia
18 D12 **Wilcox** Pennsylvania, NE USA
Wilczek Land *see* Vil'cheka, Zemlya
109 U6 **Wildalpen** Steiermark, E Austria
31 O13 **Wildcat Creek** ≈ Indiana, N USA
108 L9 **Wilde Kreuzspitze** *It.* Picco di Croce. ▲ Austria/Italy
Wildenschwert *see* Ústí nad Orlicí
98 O6 **Wildervank** Groningen, NE Netherlands
100 G11 **Wildeshausen** Niedersachsen, NW Germany
108 D10 **Wildhorn** ▲ SW Switzerland
11 R17 **Wild Horse** Alberta, SW Canada
27 N12 **Wildhorse Creek** ≈ Oklahoma, C USA
28 L14 **Wild Horse Hill** ▲ Nebraska, C USA
109 W8 **Wildon** Steiermark, SE Austria
24 M2 **Wildorado** Texas, SW USA
25 R6 **Wild Rice River** ≈ Minnesota/North Dakota, N USA
Wilejka *see* Vilyeyka
195 Y9 **Wilhelm II Coast** *physical region* Antarctica
195 X9 **Wilhelm II Land** *physical region* Antarctica
55 U11 **Wilhelmina Gebergte** ⛰ C Suriname
18 B13 **Wilhelm, Lake** ▣ Pennsylvania, NE USA
92 O2 **Wilhelmøya** *island* C Svalbard
Wilhelm-Pieck-Stadt *see* Guben
109 V4 **Wilhelmsburg** Niederösterreich, E Austria
100 G10 **Wilhelmshaven** Niedersachsen, NW Germany
Wilia/Wilja *see* Neris
18 H13 **Wilkes Barre** Pennsylvania, NE USA
21 R9 **Wilkesboro** North Carolina, SE USA
195 W15 **Wilkes Coast** *physical region* Antarctica
189 W12 **Wilkes Island** *island* N Wake Island
195 X12 **Wilkes Land** *physical region* Antarctica
11 S15 **Wilkie** Saskatchewan, S Canada
194 I6 **Wilkins Ice Shelf** *ice shelf* Antarctica
182 D4 **Wilkinsons Lakes** *salt lake* South Australia
Wiłkomierz *see* Ukmergė
182 K11 **Willalooka** South Australia
32 G11 **Willamette River** ≈ Oregon, NW USA
183 O8 **Willandra Billabong Creek** *seasonal river* New South Wales, SE Australia
32 F9 **Willapa Bay** *inlet* Washington, NW USA
27 T7 **Willard** Missouri, C USA
37 S12 **Willard** New Mexico, SW USA
31 S12 **Willard** Ohio, N USA
36 L1 **Willard** Utah, W USA
186 G6 **Willaumez Peninsula** *headland* New Britain, E PNG
37 N15 **Willcox** Arizona, SW USA
37 N16 **Willcox Playa** *salt flat* Arizona, SW USA
99 G17 **Willebroek** Antwerpen, C Belgium
45 P16 **Willemstad** ○ (Netherlands Antilles) Curaçao, Netherlands Antilles
99 G14 **Willemstad** Noord-Brabant, S Netherlands
11 S11 **William** ≈ Saskatchewan, C Canada
23 O6 **William "Bill" Dannelly Reservoir** ▣ Alabama, S USA
182 G3 **William Creek** South Australia
181 T15 **William, Mount** ▲ South Australia
36 K11 **Williams** Arizona, SW USA
29 X14 **Williamsburg** Iowa, C USA
20 M8 **Williamsburg** Kentucky, S USA
31 R15 **Williamsburg** Ohio, N USA
21 X6 **Williamsburg** Virginia, NE USA
10 M15 **Williams Lake** British Columbia, SW Canada
21 P6 **Williamson** West Virginia, NE USA
31 N13 **Williamsport** Indiana, N USA
18 G13 **Williamsport** Pennsylvania, NE USA
21 W9 **Williamston** North Carolina, SE USA
21 P11 **Williamston** South Carolina, SE USA
20 M4 **Williamstown** Kentucky, S USA
18 L10 **Williamstown** Massachusetts, NE USA
18 J16 **Willingboro** New Jersey, NE USA
11 Q14 **Willingdon** Alberta, SW Canada
25 W10 **Willis** Texas, SW USA
108 F8 **Willisau** Luzern, W Switzerland
83 F24 **Williston** Northern Cape, W South Africa
23 V10 **Williston** Florida, SE USA
28 J3 **Williston** North Dakota, N USA
21 Q13 **Williston** South Carolina, SE USA
10 L12 **Williston Lake** ▣ British Columbia, W Canada
34 L5 **Willits** California, W USA
29 T8 **Willmar** Minnesota, N USA
10 K11 **Will, Mount** ▲ British Columbia, W Canada
31 T11 **Willoughby** Ohio, N USA
11 U17 **Willow Bunch** Saskatchewan, S Canada
32 J11 **Willow Creek** ≈ Oregon, NW USA
39 R11 **Willow Lake** Alaska, USA
8 I9 **Willowlake** ≈ Northwest Territories, NW Canada
83 H25 **Willowmore** Eastern Cape, S South Africa
30 L5 **Willow Reservoir** ▣ Wisconsin, N USA
35 N5 **Willows** California, W USA
27 V7 **Willow Springs** Missouri, C USA
182 I7 **Wilmington** South Australia
21 Y2 **Wilmington** Delaware, NE USA
21 V12 **Wilmington** North Carolina, SE USA
31 R14 **Wilmington** Ohio, N USA
20 M6 **Wilmore** Kentucky, S USA
29 R8 **Wilmot** South Dakota, N USA
Wilna/Wilno *see* Vilnius
101 G16 **Wilnsdorf** Nordrhein-Westfalen, W Germany
99 G16 **Wilrijk** Antwerpen, N Belgium
100 I10 **Wilseder Berg** *hill* NW Germany
67 Z12 **Wilshaw Ridge** *undersea feature* W Indian Ocean
21 V9 **Wilson** North Carolina, SE USA
25 N5 **Wilson** Texas, SW USA
182 A7 **Wilson Bluff** *headland* South Australia/Western Australia
35 Y7 **Wilson Creek Range** ⛰ Nevada, W USA
23 O1 **Wilson Lake** ▣ Alabama, S USA
26 M4 **Wilson Lake** ▣ Kansas, C USA
37 P7 **Wilson, Mount** ▲ Colorado, C USA
183 P13 **Wilsons Promontory** *peninsula* Victoria, SE Australia
29 Y14 **Wilton** Iowa, C USA
19 P7 **Wilton** Maine, NE USA
28 M5 **Wilton** North Dakota, N USA
97 L22 **Wiltshire** *cultural region* S England, UK
99 M23 **Wiltz** Diekirch, NW Luxembourg
180 K9 **Wiluna** Western Australia
99 M23 **Wilwerwiltz** Diekirch, NE Luxembourg
29 P5 **Wimbledon** North Dakota, N USA
42 K7 **Wina** *var.* Güina. Jinotega, N Nicaragua
31 O12 **Winamac** Indiana, N USA
81 G19 **Winam Gulf** *var.* Kavirondo Gulf. *gulf* SW Kenya
83 I22 **Winburg** Free State, C South Africa
19 N10 **Winchendon** Massachusetts, NE USA
14 M13 **Winchester** Ontario, SE Canada
97 M23 **Winchester** *hist.* Wintanceaster, *Lat.* Venta Belgarum. S England, UK
32 M10 **Winchester** Idaho, NW USA
30 J14 **Winchester** Illinois, N USA
31 Q13 **Winchester** Indiana, N USA
20 M5 **Winchester** Kentucky, S USA
18 M10 **Winchester** New Hampshire, NE USA
20 K10 **Winchester** Tennessee, S USA
21 V3 **Winchester** Virginia, NE USA
99 L22 **Wincrange** Diekirch, NW Luxembourg
10 I5 **Wind** ≈ Yukon Territory, NW Canada
183 S8 **Windamere, Lake** ◎ New South Wales, SE Australia
Windau *see* Ventspils, Latvia
Windau *see* Venta, Latvia/Lithuania
18 D15 **Windber** Pennsylvania, NE USA
23 T3 **Winder** Georgia, SE USA
97 K15 **Windermere** NW England, UK
14 C7 **Windermere Lake** ◎ Ontario, S Canada
31 U11 **Windham** Ohio, N USA
83 D19 **Windhoek** *Ger.* Windhuk. ● (Namibia) Khomas, C Namibia
83 D20 **Windhoek** × Khomas, C Namibia
Windhuk *see* Windhoek
15 O8 **Windigo** Québec, SE Canada
15 O8 **Windigo** ≈ Québec, SE Canada
Windischfeistritz *see* Slovenska Bistrica
109 T6 **Windischgarsten** Oberösterreich, W Austria
Windischgraz *see* Slovenj Gradec
37 T16 **Wind Mountain** ▲ New Mexico, SW USA
29 T10 **Windom** Minnesota, N USA
37 Q7 **Windom Peak** ▲ Colorado, C USA
181 U9 **Windorah** Queensland, C Australia
37 O10 **Window Rock** Arizona, SW USA
31 N9 **Wind Point** *headland* Wisconsin, N USA
33 U14 **Wind River** ≈ Wyoming, C USA
13 P15 **Windsor** Nova Scotia, SE Canada
14 C17 **Windsor** Ontario, S Canada
15 Q12 **Windsor** Québec, SE Canada
97 N22 **Windsor** S England, UK
37 T3 **Windsor** Colorado, C USA
18 M12 **Windsor** Connecticut, NE USA
27 T5 **Windsor** Missouri, C USA
21 X9 **Windsor** North Carolina, SE USA
18 M12 **Windsor Locks** Connecticut, NE USA
25 R5 **Windthorst** Texas, SW USA
45 Z14 **Windward Islands** *island group* E West Indies
Windward Islands *see* Vent, Îles du, Archipel de la Société, French Polynesia
Windward Islands *see* Barlavento, Ilhas de, Cape Verde
44 K8 **Windward Passage** *Sp.* Paso de los Vientos. *channel* Cuba/Haiti
55 T9 **Wineperu** C Guyana
23 O3 **Winfield** Alabama, S USA
29 Y15 **Winfield** Iowa, C USA
27 O7 **Winfield** Kansas, C USA
25 W6 **Winfield** Texas, SW USA
21 Q4 **Winfield** West Virginia, NE USA
29 N5 **Wing** North Dakota, N USA
183 U7 **Wingham** New South Wales, SE Australia
12 G16 **Wingham** Ontario, S Canada
33 T8 **Winifred** Montana, NW USA
12 E8 **Winisk** ≈ Ontario, S Canada
12 E9 **Winisk Lake** ◎ Ontario, C Canada
24 L8 **Wink** Texas, SW USA
36 M14 **Winkelman** Arizona, SW USA
11 X17 **Winkler** Manitoba, S Canada
109 Q9 **Winklern** Tirol, W Austria
Winkowitz *see* Vinkovci
32 G9 **Winlock** Washington, NW USA
77 P17 **Winneba** SE Ghana
29 U11 **Winnebago** Minnesota, N USA
29 R13 **Winnebago** Nebraska, C USA
30 M7 **Winnebago, Lake** ◎ Wisconsin, N USA
30 M7 **Winneconne** Wisconsin, N USA
35 T3 **Winnemucca** Nevada, W USA
35 R4 **Winnemucca Lake** ◎ Nevada, W USA
101 H21 **Winnenden** Baden-Württemberg, SW Germany
29 N11 **Winner** South Dakota, N USA
33 U9 **Winnett** Montana, NW USA
14 I9 **Winneway** Québec, SE Canada
22 H6 **Winnfield** Louisiana, S USA
29 U4 **Winnibigoshish, Lake** ◎ Minnesota, N USA
25 X11 **Winnie** Texas, SW USA
11 Y16 **Winnipeg** Manitoba, S Canada
11 X16 **Winnipeg** × Manitoba, S Canada
(C) J8 **Winnipeg** ≈ Manitoba, S Canada
11 X16 **Winnipeg Beach** Manitoba, S Canada
11 W14 **Winnipeg, Lake** ◎ Manitoba, C Canada
11 W15 **Winnipegosis** Manitoba, S Canada
11 W15 **Winnipegosis, Lake** ◎ Manitoba, C Canada
19 O8 **Winnipesaukee, Lake** ◎ New Hampshire, NE USA
22 I6 **Winnsboro** Louisiana, S USA
21 R12 **Winnsboro** South Carolina, SE USA
25 W6 **Winnsboro** Texas, SW USA
29 X10 **Winona** Minnesota, N USA
22 L4 **Winona** Mississippi, S USA
27 W7 **Winona** Missouri, C USA
25 W7 **Winona** Texas, SW USA
18 M7 **Winooski River** ≈ Vermont, NE USA
98 P6 **Winschoten** Groningen, NE Netherlands
100 J10 **Winsen** Niedersachsen, N Germany
36 M11 **Winslow** Arizona, SW USA
19 Q7 **Winslow** Maine, NE USA
18 M12 **Winsted** Connecticut, NE USA
32 F14 **Winston** Oregon, NW USA
21 S9 **Winston Salem** North Carolina, SE USA
98 N5 **Winsum** Groningen, NE Netherlands
Wintanceaster *see* Winchester
23 W11 **Winter Garden** Florida, SE USA
10 J16 **Winter Harbour** Vancouver Island, British Columbia, SW Canada
23 W12 **Winter Haven** Florida, SE USA
23 X11 **Winter Park** Florida, SE USA
25 P8 **Winters** Texas, SW USA
29 U15 **Winterset** Iowa, C USA
98 O12 **Winterswijk** Gelderland, E Netherlands
108 G6 **Winterthur** Zürich, NE Switzerland
29 U9 **Winthrop** Minnesota, N USA
32 J7 **Winthrop** Washington, NW USA
181 V7 **Winton** Queensland, E Australia
185 C24 **Winton** Southland, South Island, NZ
21 X8 **Winton** North Carolina, SE USA
101 K15 **Wipper** ≈ C Germany
101 K14 **Wipper** ≈ C Germany
Wipper *see* Wieprza
182 G6 **Wirraminna** South Australia
182 F4 **Wirrida** South Australia
182 F7 **Wirrulla** South Australia
Wirsitz *see* Wyrzysk
Wirz-See *see* Võrtsjärv
97 O19 **Wisbech** E England, UK
Wisby *see* Visby
19 Q8 **Wiscasset** Maine, NE USA
Wischau *see* Vyškov
30 J5 **Wisconsin** *off.* State of Wisconsin; also known as The Badger State. ◈ *state* N USA
30 L8 **Wisconsin Dells** Wisconsin, N USA
30 L8 **Wisconsin, Lake** ▣ Wisconsin, N USA
30 L7 **Wisconsin Rapids** Wisconsin, N USA
30 L7 **Wisconsin River** ≈ Wisconsin, N USA
33 P11 **Wisdom** Montana, NW USA
21 P7 **Wise** Virginia, NE USA
39 Q7 **Wiseman** Alaska, USA
96 J12 **Wishaw** W Scotland, UK
29 O6 **Wishek** North Dakota, N USA
32 I11 **Wishram** Washington, NW USA
111 J17 **Wisła** Śląskie, S Poland
110 K11 **Wisła** *Eng.* Vistula, *Ger.* Weichsel. ≈ C Poland
Wiślany, Zalew *see* Vistula Lagoon
111 M16 **Wisłoka** ≈ SE Poland
100 L9 **Wismar** Mecklenburg-Vorpommern, N Germany
29 R14 **Wisner** Nebraska, C USA
103 V4 **Wissembourg** *var.* Weissenburg. Bas-Rhin, NE France
30 J6 **Wissota, Lake** ▣ Wisconsin, N USA
97 O18 **Witham** ≈ E England, UK
97 O17 **Withernsea** E England, UK
37 Q13 **Withington, Mount** ▲ New Mexico, SW USA
23 U8 **Withlacoochee River** ≈ Florida/Georgia, SE USA
110 H11 **Witkowo** Wielkopolskie, C Poland
97 M21 **Witney** S England, UK
101 E15 **Witten** Nordrhein-Westfalen, W Germany
101 N14 **Wittenberg** Sachsen-Anhalt, E Germany
30 L6 **Wittenberg** Wisconsin, N USA
100 L11 **Wittenberge** Brandenburg, N Germany
103 U7 **Wittenheim** Haut-Rhin, NE France
180 I7 **Wittenoom** Western Australia
Wittingau *see* Třeboň
100 K12 **Wittingen** Niedersachsen, C Germany
101 E18 **Wittlich** Rheinland-Pfalz, SW Germany
100 F9 **Wittmund** Niedersachsen, NW Germany
100 M10 **Wittstock** Brandenburg, NE Germany
186 F6 **Witu Islands** *island group* E PNG
110 O7 **Wiżajny** Podlaskie, NE Poland
55 W10 **W.J. van Blommesteinmeer** ▣ E Suriname
110 L11 **Wkra** *Ger.* Soldau. ≈ C Poland
110 I6 **Władysławowo** Pomorskie, N Poland
Wlaschim *see* Vlašim
111 E14 **Wleń** *Ger.* Lähn. Dolnośląskie, SW Poland
110 J11 **Włocławek** *Ger./Rus.* Vlotslavsk. Kujawsko-pomorskie, C Poland
110 P13 **Włodawa** *Rus.* Vlodava. Lubelskie, SE Poland
Włodzimierz *see* Volodymyr-Volyns'kyy
111 K15 **Włoszczowa** Świętokrzyskie, C Poland
83 C19 **Wlotzkasbaken** Erongo, W Namibia
15 R12 **Woburn** Québec, SE Canada
19 O11 **Woburn** Massachusetts, NE USA
Wocheiner Feistritz *see* Bohinjska Bistrica
Wöchma *see* Võhma
147 S11 **Wodil** *var.* Vuadil'. Farg'ona Viloyati, E Uzbekistan
181 V14 **Wodonga** Victoria, SE Australia
111 I17 **Wodzisław Śląski** *Ger.* Loslau. Śląskie, S Poland
98 I11 **Woerden** Zuid-Holland, C Netherlands
98 I8 **Wognum** Noord-Holland, NW Netherlands
Wohlau *see* Wołów
108 F7 **Wohlen** Aargau, NW Switzerland
195 R2 **Wohlthat Mountains** ⛰ Antarctica
Wojerecy *see* Hoyerswerda
Wōjjā *see* Wotje Atoll
Wojwodina *see* Vojvodina
171 V15 **Wokam, Pulau** *island* Kepulauan Aru, E Indonesia
97 N22 **Woking** SE England, UK
Woldenberg Neumark *see* Dobiegniew
188 K15 **Woleai Atoll** *atoll* Caroline Islands, W Micronesia
Woleu *see* Uolo, Río
79 E17 **Woleu-Ntem** *off.* Province du Woleu-Ntem, *var.* Le Woleu-Ntem. ◈ *province* W Gabon
32 F15 **Wolf Creek** Oregon, NW USA
26 K9 **Wolf Creek** ≈ Oklahoma/Texas, SW USA
37 R7 **Wolf Creek Pass** *pass* Colorado, C USA
19 O9 **Wolfeboro** New Hampshire, NE USA
25 U5 **Wolfe City** Texas, SW USA
14 L15 **Wolfe Island** *island* Ontario, SE Canada
101 M14 **Wolfen** Sachsen-Anhalt, E Germany
100 J13 **Wolfenbüttel** Niedersachsen, C Germany
109 T4 **Wolfern** Oberösterreich, N Austria
109 Q6 **Wolfgangsee** *var.* Abersee, St Wolfgangsee. ◎ N Austria
39 P9 **Wolf Mountain** ▲ Alaska, USA
33 X7 **Wolf Point** Montana, NW USA
22 L8 **Wolf River** ≈ Mississippi, S USA
30 M7 **Wolf River** ≈ Wisconsin, N USA
109 U9 **Wolfsberg** Kärnten, SE Austria
100 K12 **Wolfsburg** Niedersachsen, N Germany
57 B17 **Wolf, Volcán** ☼ Galapagos Islands, Ecuador, E Pacific Ocean
100 O8 **Wolgast** Mecklenburg-Vorpommern, NE Germany
108 F8 **Wolhusen** Luzern, W Switzerland
110 D8 **Wolin** *Ger.* Wollin. Zachodnio-pomorskie, NW Poland
109 Y3 **Wolkersdorf** Niederösterreich, NE Austria
Wołkowysk *see* Vawkavysk
Wöllan *see* Velenje
8 J6 **Wollaston, Cape** *headland* Victoria Island, Northwest Territories, NW Canada
63 J25 **Wollaston, Isla** *island* S Chile
11 U11 **Wollaston Lake** Saskatchewan, C Canada
11 T10 **Wollaston Lake** ◎ Saskatchewan, C Canada
8 J6 **Wollaston Peninsula** *peninsula* Victoria Island, Northwest Territories/ Nunavut, NW Canada
Wollin *see* Wolin
183 S9 **Wollongong** New South Wales, SE Australia
Wolmar *see* Valmiera
100 L13 **Wolmirstedt** Sachsen-Anhalt, C Germany
110 M11 **Wołomin** Mazowieckie, C Poland
110 G3 **Wołów** *Ger.* Wohlau. Dolnośląskie, SW Poland
Wołożyn *see* Valozhyn
14 G11 **Wolseley Bay** Ontario, S Canada
29 P10 **Wolsey** South Dakota, N USA
110 F12 **Wolsztyn** Wielkopolskie, W Poland
98 M7 **Wolvega** *Fris.* Wolvegea. Friesland, N Netherlands
Wolvegea *see* Wolvega
97 K19 **Wolverhampton** C England, UK
Wolverine State *see* Michigan
99 G18 **Wolvertem** Vlaams Brabant, C Belgium
99 H16 **Wommelgem** Antwerpen, N Belgium
186 D7 **Wonenara** *var.* Wonerara. Eastern Highlands, C PNG
Wonerara *see* Wonenara
Wongalara Lake *see* Wongalarroo Lake
183 N6 **Wongalarroo Lake** *var.* Wongalara Lake. *seasonal lake* New South Wales, SE Australia
163 Y15 **Wŏnju** *Jap.* Genshū. N South Korea
10 M12 **Wonowon** British Columbia, W Canada
163 X13 **Wŏnsan** SE North Korea
183 O13 **Wonthaggi** Victoria, SE Australia
23 N2 **Woodall Mountain** ▲ Mississippi, S USA
23 W7 **Woodbine** Georgia, SE USA
29 S14 **Woodbine** Iowa, C USA
18 J17 **Woodbine** New Jersey, NE USA
21 W4 **Woodbridge** Virginia, NE USA
183 V4 **Woodburn** New South Wales, SE Australia
32 G11 **Woodburn** Oregon, NW USA
20 K9 **Woodbury** Tennessee, S USA
183 V5 **Wooded Bluff** *headland* New South Wales, SE Australia
183 V3 **Woodenbong** New South Wales, SE Australia
35 R11 **Woodlake** California, W USA
35 N7 **Woodland** California, W USA
19 T5 **Woodland** Maine, NE USA

◆ Country
● Country Capital
◇ Dependent Territory
○ Dependent Territory Capital
◈ Administrative Region
× International Airport
▲ Mountain
⛰ Mountain Range
☼ Volcano
≈ River
◎ Lake
▣ Reservoir

32 G10 **Woodland** Washington, NW USA
37 T5 **Woodland Park** Colorado, C USA
186 I9 **Woodlark Island** *var.* Murua Island. *island* SE PNG
Woodle Island *see* Kuria
11 T17 **Wood Mountain** ⛰ Saskatchewan, S Canada
30 K15 **Wood River** Illinois, N USA
29 P16 **Wood River** Nebraska, C USA
39 R9 **Wood River** ≈ Alaska, USA
39 O13 **Wood River Lakes** *lakes* Alaska, USA
182 C1 **Woodroffe, Mount** ▲ South Australia
21 P11 **Woodruff** South Carolina, SE USA
30 K4 **Woodruff** Wisconsin, N USA
25 T14 **Woodsboro** Texas, SW USA
31 U13 **Woodsfield** Ohio, N USA
181 P4 **Woods, Lake** ◎ Northern Territory, N Australia
11 Z16 **Woods, Lake of the** *Fr.* Lac des Bois. ◎ Canada/USA
25 Q6 **Woodson** Texas, SW USA
13 N14 **Woodstock** New Brunswick, SE Canada
14 F16 **Woodstock** Ontario, S Canada
30 M10 **Woodstock** Illinois, N USA
18 M9 **Woodstock** Vermont, NE USA
21 U4 **Woodstock** Virginia, NE USA
19 N8 **Woodsville** New Hampshire, NE USA
184 M12 **Woodville** Manawatu-Wanganui, North Island, NZ
22 J7 **Woodville** Mississippi, S USA
25 X9 **Woodville** Texas, SW USA
26 K9 **Woodward** Oklahoma, C USA
29 O5 **Woodworth** North Dakota, N USA
171 W12 **Wool** Papua, E Indonesia
183 V5 **Woolgoolga** New South Wales, E Australia
182 H6 **Woomera** South Australia
19 O12 **Woonsocket** Rhode Island, NE USA
29 P10 **Woonsocket** South Dakota, N USA
31 T12 **Wooster** Ohio, N USA
80 L12 **Woqooyi Galbeed** *off.* Gobolka Woqooyi Galbeed. ◈ *region* NW Somalia
108 E8 **Worb** Bern, C Switzerland
83 F26 **Worcester** Western Cape, SW South Africa
97 L20 **Worcester** *hist.* Wigorna Ceaster. W England, UK
19 N11 **Worcester** Massachusetts, NE USA
97 L20 **Worcestershire** *cultural region* C England, UK
32 H16 **Worden** Oregon, NW USA
109 O6 **Wörgl** Tirol, W Austria
171 V15 **Workai, Pulau** *island* Kepulauan Aru, E Indonesia
97 J15 **Workington** NW England, UK
98 K7 **Workum** Friesland, N Netherlands
33 V13 **Worland** Wyoming, C USA
Wormatia *see* Worms
99 N25 **Wormeldange** Grevenmacher, E Luxembourg
98 I9 **Wormer** Noord-Holland, C Netherlands
101 G19 **Worms** *anc.* Augusta Vangionum, Borbetomagus, Wormatia. Rheinland-Pfalz, SW Germany
Worms *see* Vormsi
101 K21 **Wörnitz** ≈ S Germany
101 G21 **Wörth am Rhein** Rheinland-Pfalz, SW Germany
25 U8 **Wortham** Texas, SW USA
109 S9 **Wörther See** ◎ S Austria
97 O23 **Worthing** SE England, UK
29 S11 **Worthington** Minnesota, N USA
31 S13 **Worthington** Ohio, N USA
35 W8 **Worthington Peak** ▲ Nevada, W USA
171 Y13 **Wosi** Papua, E Indonesia
171 V13 **Wosimi** Papua, E Indonesia
189 R5 **Wotho Atoll** *var.* Wōtto. *atoll* Ralik Chain, W Marshall Islands
189 V5 **Wotje Atoll** *var.* Wōjjā. *atoll* Ratak Chain, E Marshall Islands
Wotoe *see* Wotu
Wottawa *see* Otava
Wōtto *see* Wotho Atoll
171 O13 **Wotu** *prev.* Wotoe. Sulawesi, C Indonesia
98 K11 **Woudenberg** Utrecht, C Netherlands
98 I13 **Woudrichem** Noord-Brabant, S Netherlands
43 N8 **Wounta** *var.* Huaunta. Región Autónoma Atlántico Norte, NE Nicaragua
171 P14 **Wowoni, Pulau** *island* C Indonesia
81 J17 **Woyamdero Plain** *plain* E Kenya
Woyens *see* Vojens
Wozrojdeniye Oroli *see* Vozrozhdeniya, Ostrov
Wrangel Island *see* Vrangelya, Ostrov
39 Y13 **Wrangell** Wrangell Island, Alaska, USA
38 C15 **Wrangell, Cape** *headland* Attu Island, Alaska, USA
39 S11 **Wrangell, Mount** ▲ Alaska, USA
39 T11 **Wrangell Mountains** ⛰ Alaska, USA
197 S7 **Wrangel Plain** *undersea feature* Arctic Ocean
96 H6 **Wrath, Cape** *headland* N Scotland, UK
37 W3 **Wray** Colorado, C USA
44 K13 **Wreck Point** *headland* C Jamaica
83 C23 **Wreck Point** *headland* W South Africa
23 V4 **Wrens** Georgia, SE USA
97 K18 **Wrexham** NE Wales, UK
27 R13 **Wright City** Oklahoma, C USA
194 J12 **Wright Island** *island* Antarctica
13 N9 **Wright, Mont** ▲ Québec, E Canada
25 X5 **Wright Patman Lake** ⊠ Texas, SW USA
36 M16 **Wrightson, Mount** ▲ Arizona, SW USA
23 U5 **Wrightsville** Georgia, SE USA
21 W12 **Wrightsville Beach** North Carolina, SE USA
35 T15 **Wrightwood** California, W USA
8 H9 **Wrigley** Northwest Territories, W Canada
111 G14 **Wrocław** *Eng./Ger.* Breslau. Dolnośląskie, SW Poland
110 F10 **Wronki** *Ger.* Fronicken. Wielkopolskie, NW Poland
110 H11 **Września** Wielkolpolskie, C Poland
110 F12 **Wschowa** Lubuskie, W Poland
Wsetin *see* Vsetín
161 O5 **Wu'an** Hebei, E China
180 I12 **Wubin** Western Australia
163 W9 **Wuchang** Heilongjiang, NE China
Wuchang *see* Wuhan
Wu-chou/Wuchow *see* Wuzhou
160 M16 **Wuchuan** *var.* Meilu. Guangdong, S China
160 K10 **Wuchuan** *var.* Duru, Gelaozu Miaozu Zizhixian. Guizhou, S China
163 O13 **Wuchuan** Nei Mongol Zizhiqu, N China
163 V6 **Wudalianchi** Heilongjiang, NE China
163 V6 **Wudalianchi** *prev.* Dedu, Qingshan. Heilongjiang, NE China
159 O11 **Wudaoliang** Qinghai, C China
141 Q13 **Wuday'ah** *spring/well* S Saudi Arabia
77 V13 **Wudil** Kano, N Nigeria
160 G12 **Wuding** *var.* Jincheng. Yunnan, SW China
182 G8 **Wudinna** South Australia
157 P10 **Wudu** Gansu, C China
160 L9 **Wufeng** Hubei, C China
161 O11 **Wugong Shan** ⛰ S China
157 P7 **Wuhai** *var.* Haibowan. Nei Mongol Zizhiqu, N China
161 O9 **Wuhan** *var.* Han-kou, Han-k'ou, Hanyang, Wuchang, Wu-han; *prev.* Hankow. Hubei, C China
161 Q7 **Wuhe** Anhui, E China
Wuhsi/Wu-hsi *see* Wuxi
Wuhsien *see* Suzhou
161 Q8 **Wuhu** *var.* Wu-na-mu. Anhui, E China
Wujae *see* Ujae Atoll
160 K11 **Wu Jiang** ≈ C China
Wujlān *see* Ujelang Atoll
77 W15 **Wukari** Taraba, E Nigeria
160 H11 **Wulian Feng** ⛰ SW China
160 F13 **Wuliang Shan** ⛰ SW China
160 K11 **Wuling Shan** ⛰ S China
109 Y5 **Wulka** ≈ E Austria
Wulkan *see* Vulcan
109 T3 **Wullowitz** Oberösterreich, N Austria
Wu-lu-k'o-mu-shi/Wu-lu-mu-ch'i *see* Ürümqi
79 D14 **Wum** Nord-Ouest, NE Cameroon
160 H12 **Wumeng Shan** ⛰ SW China
160 K14 **Wuming** Guangxi Zhuangzu Zizhiqu, S China
100 I10 **Wümme** ≈ NW Germany
Wu-na-mu *see* Wuhu
171 X13 **Wunen** Papua, E Indonesia
12 D9 **Wunnummin Lake** ◎ Ontario, C Canada
80 D13 **Wun Rog** Warab, S Sudan
101 M18 **Wunsiedel** Bayern, E Germany
100 I12 **Wunstorf** Niedersachsen, NW Germany
166 M3 **Wuntho** Sagaing, N Myanmar
101 F15 **Wupper** ≈ W Germany
101 E15 **Wuppertal** *prev.* Barmen-Elberfeld. Nordrhein-Westfalen, W Germany
160 K5 **Wuqi** Shaanxi, C China
161 P4 **Wuqiao** *var.* Sangyuan. Hebei, E China
101 L23 **Würm** ≈ SE Germany
77 T12 **Wurno** Sokoto, NW Nigeria
101 I19 **Würzburg** Bayern, SW Germany
101 N15 **Wurzen** Sachsen, E Germany
160 L9 **Wu Shan** ⛰ C China
158 G7 **Wushi** *var.* Uqturpan. Xinjiang Uygur Zizhiqu, NW China
Wusih *see* Wuxi
65 N18 **Wüst Seamount** *undersea feature* S Atlantic Ocean
Wusuli Jiang/Wusuri *see* Ussuri
161 N3 **Wutai Shan** *var.* Beitai Ding. ▲ C China
160 H10 **Wutongqiao** Sichuan, C China
159 P6 **Wutongwozi Quan** *spring* NW China
99 H15 **Wuustwezel** Antwerpen, N Belgium
186 B4 **Wuvulu Island** *island* NW PNG
159 U9 **Wuwei** *var.* Liangzhou. Gansu, C China
161 R8 **Wuxi** *var.* Wuhsi, Wu-hsi, Wusih. Jiangsu, E China
Wuxing *see* Huzhou
160 L14 **Wuxuan** Guangxi Zhuangzu Zizhiqu, S China
Wuyang *see* Zhenyuan
160 K11 **Wuyang He** ≈ S China
163 X6 **Wuyiling** Heilongjiang, NE China
157 T12 **Wuyi Shan** ⛰ SE China
161 Q11 **Wuyishan** *prev.* Chong'an. Fujian, SE China
162 M13 **Wuyuan** Nei Mongol Zizhiqu, N China
160 L17 **Wuzhi Shan** ▲ S China
160 L17 **Wuzhishan** *prev.* Tongshi. Hainan, S China
159 W8 **Wuzhong** Ningxia, N China
160 M14 **Wuzhou** *var.* Wu-chou, Wuchow. Guangxi Zhuangzu Zizhiqu, S China
18 H12 **Wyalusing** Pennsylvania, NE USA
182 M10 **Wycheproof** Victoria, SE Australia
97 K21 **Wye** *Wel.* Gwy. ≈ England/Wales, UK
Wyłkowyszki *see* Vilkaviškis
97 P19 **Wymondham** E England, UK
29 R17 **Wymore** Nebraska, C USA
182 E5 **Wynbring** South Australia
181 N3 **Wyndham** Western Australia
29 R6 **Wyndmere** North Dakota, N USA
27 X11 **Wynne** Arkansas, C USA
27 N12 **Wynnewood** Oklahoma, C USA
183 O15 **Wynyard** Tasmania, SE Australia
11 U15 **Wynyard** Saskatchewan, S Canada
33 V11 **Wyola** Montana, NW USA
182 A4 **Wyola Lake** *salt lake* South Australia
31 P9 **Wyoming** Michigan, N USA
33 V14 **Wyoming** *off.* State of Wyoming; also known as The Equality State. ◈ *state* C USA
33 S15 **Wyoming Range** ⛰ Wyoming, C USA
183 T8 **Wyong** New South Wales, SE Australia
110 G9 **Wyrzysk** *Ger.* Wirsitz. Wielkopolskie, C Poland
Wysg *see* Usk
110 O10 **Wysokie Mazowieckie** Łomża, E Poland
110 M11 **Wyszków** *Ger.* Probstberg. Mazowieckie, C Poland
110 L11 **Wyszogród** Mazowieckie, C Poland
21 R7 **Wytheville** Virginia, NE USA

X

80 Q12 **Xaafuun** *It.* Hafun. Bari, NE Somalia
80 Q12 **Xaafuun, Raas** *var.* Ras Hafun. *headland* NE Somalia
Xàbia *see* Jávea
42 C4 **Xaclbal, Río** *var.* Xalbal. ≈ Guatemala/Mexico
137 Y10 **Xaçmaz** *Rus.* Khachmas. N Azerbaijan
80 O12 **Xadeed** *var.* Haded. *physical region* N Somalia
159 O14 **Xagquka** Xizang Zizhiqu, W China
167 Q6 **Xai** *var.* Muang Xay, Muong Sai. Oudômxai, N Laos
158 F10 **Xaidulla** Xinjiang Uygur Zizhiqu, W China
167 Q7 **Xaignabouli** *prev.* Muang Xaignabouri, *Fr.* Sayaboury. Xaignabouli, N Laos
167 R7 **Xai Lai Leng, Phou** ▲ Laos/Vietnam
158 L15 **Xainza** Xizang Zizhiqu, W China
158 L16 **Xaitongmoin** Xizang Zizhiqu, W China
83 M20 **Xai-Xai** *prev.* João Belo, Vila de João *Bel.* Gaza, S Mozambique
Xalbal *see* Xaclbal, Río
80 P13 **Xalin** Nugaal, N Somalia
146 H7 **Xalqobod** *Rus.* Khalkabad. Qoraqalpog'iston Respublikasi, W Uzbekistan
167 R6 **Xam Nua** *var.* Sam Neua. Houaphan, N Laos
82 D11 **Xá-Muteba** *Port.* Cinco de Outubro. Lunda Norte, NE Angola
Xangda *see* Nangqên
83 C16 **Xangongo** *Port.* Rocadas. Cunene, SW Angola
137 W12 **Xankändi** *Rus.* Khankendi; *prev.* Stepanakert. SW Azerbaijan
137 V11 **Xanlar** *Rus.* Khanlar. NW Azerbaijan
114 J13 **Xánthi** Anatolikí Makedonía kai Thráki, NE Greece
60 H13 **Xanxerê** Santa Catarina, S Brazil
81 O15 **Xarardheere** Mudug, E Somalia
137 Z11 **Xärä Zirä Adası** *Rus.* Ostrov Bulla. *island* E Azerbaijan
162 K13 **Xar Burd** *prev.* Bayan Nuru. Nei Mongol Zizhiqu, N China
163 T11 **Xar Moron** ≈ NE China
Xarra *see* Xarrë
113 L23 **Xarrë** *var.* Xarra. Vlorë, S Albania
82 D12 **Xassengue** Lunda Sul, NW Angola
105 S11 **Xàtiva** *var.* Jativa; *anc.* Setabis. País Valenciano, E Spain
Xauen *see* Chefchaouen
60 K10 **Xavantes, Represa de** *var.* Represa de Chavantes. ⊠ S Brazil
158 I7 **Xayar** Xinjiang Uygur Zizhiqu, W China
Xäzär Dänizi *see* Caspian Sea
167 S8 **Xé Bangfai** ≈ C Laos
167 T9 **Xé Banghiang** *var.* Bang Hieng. ≈ S Laos
Xégar *see* Tingri
31 R14 **Xenia** Ohio, N USA
Xeres *see* Jeréz de la Frontera
115 E15 **Xeriás** ≈ C Greece
115 G17 **Xeró** ▲ Évvoia, C Greece
83 H18 **Xhumo** Central, C Botswana
161 N15 **Xiachuan Dao** *island* S China
Xiacun *see* Rushan
Xiaguan *see* Dali
159 U11 **Xiahe** *var.* Labrang. Gansu, C China
161 Q13 **Xiamen** *var.* Hsia-men; *prev.* Amoy. Fujian, SE China
160 L6 **Xi'an** *var.* Changan, Sian, Signan, Siking, Singan, Xian. Shaanxi, C China
160 L10 **Xianfeng** *var.* Gaoleshan. Hubei, C China
Xiang *see* Hunan
161 N7 **Xiangcheng** Henan, C China
160 F10 **Xiangcheng** *var.* Sampê, *Tib.* Qagcheng. Sichuan, C China
160 M8 **Xiangfan** *var.* Xiangyang. Hubei, C China
161 N10 **Xiang Jiang** ≈ S China
Xiangkhoang *see* Pèk
167 Q7 **Xiangkhoang, Plateau de** *var.* Plain of Jars. *plateau* N Laos
161 N11 **Xiangtan** *var.* Hsiang-t'an, Siangtan. Hunan, S China
161 N11 **Xiangxiang** Hunan, S China
Xiangyang *see* Xiangfan
161 S10 **Xianju** Zhejiang, SE China
Xianshui *see* Dawu
160 F8 **Xianshui He** ≈ C China
161 N9 **Xiantao** *var.* Mianyang. Hubei, C China
161 R10 **Xianxia Ling** ⛰ SE China
160 K6 **Xianyang** Shaanxi, C China
158 L5 **Xiaocaohu** Xinjiang Uygur Zizhiqu, W China
161 O9 **Xiaogan** Hubei, C China
Xiaogang *see* Dongxiang
163 W6 **Xiao Hinggan Ling** *Eng.* Lesser Khingan Range. ⛰ NE China
160 M6 **Xiao Shan** ⛰ C China
160 M12 **Xiao Shui** ≈ S China
Xiaoxi *see* Pinghe
161 P6 **Xiaoxian** *var.* Longcheng, Xiao Xian. Anhui, E China
160 G11 **Xichang** Sichuan, C China
41 P11 **Xicoténcatl** Tamaulipas, C Mexico
Xieng Khouang *see* Pèk
Xieng Ngeun *see* Muong Xiang Ngeun
160 J11 **Xifeng** *var.* Yongjing. Guizhou, S China
Xifeng *see* Qingyang
Xigang *see* Helan
158 L16 **Xigazê** *var.* Jih-k'a-tse, Shigatse, Xigaze. Xizang Zizhiqu, W China
160 I8 **Xi He** ≈ C China
159 W11 **Xihe** *var.* Hanyuan. Gansu, C China
Xihuachi *see* Heshui
159 W10 **Xiji** Ningxia, N China
160 M14 **Xi Jiang** *var.* Hsi Chiang, *Eng.* West River. ≈ S China
159 Q7 **Xijian Quan** *spring* NW China
160 K15 **Xijin Shuiku** ⊠ S China
Xilaganí *see* Xylaganí
Xiligou *see* Ulan
160 I13 **Xilin** *var.* Bada. Guangxi Zhuangzu Zizhiqu, S China
163 Q10 **Xilinhot** *var.* Silinhot. Nei Mongol Zizhiqu, N China
Xilinji *see* Mohe
Xilokastro *see* Xylókastro
Xin *see* Xinjiang Uygur Zizhiqu
161 R10 **Xin'anjiang Shuiku** ⊠ SE China
Xin'anzhen *see* Xinyi
Xin Barag Youqi *see* Altan Emel
Xin Barag Zuoqi *see* Amgalang
163 W12 **Xinbin** *var.* Xinbin Manzu Zizhixian. Liaoning, NE China
Xinbin Manzu Zizhixian *see* Xinbin
161 O7 **Xincai** Henan, C China
Xincheng *see* Zhaojue
Xindu *see* Luhuo
161 O13 **Xinfeng** *var.* Jiading. Jiangxi, S China
161 O14 **Xinfengjiang Shuiku** ⊠ S China
Xingba *see* Lhünzê
163 T13 **Xingcheng** Liaoning, NE China
82 E11 **Xinge** Lunda Norte, NE Angola
161 P12 **Xingguo** *var.* Lianjiang. Jiangxi, S China
159 S11 **Xinghai** *var.* Ziketan. Qinghai, C China
161 R7 **Xinghua** Jiangsu, E China
Xingkai Hu *see* Khanka, Lake
161 P13 **Xingning** Guangdong, S China
160 I13 **Xingren** Guizhou, S China
161 O4 **Xingtai** Hebei, E China
59 J14 **Xingu, Rio** ≈ C Brazil
159 P6 **Xingxingxia** Xinjiang Uygur Zizhiqu, NW China
160 I13 **Xingyi** Guizhou, S China
158 I6 **Xinhe** *var.* Toksu. Xinjiang Uygur Zizhiqu, NW China
161 Q10 **Xin Hot** *var.* Abag Qi. Nei Mongol Zizhiqu, N China
Xinhua *see* Funing
163 T12 **Xinhui** *var.* Aohan Qi. Nei Mongol Zizhiqu, N China
159 T10 **Xining** *var.* Hsining, Hsi-ning, Sining. *province capital* Qinghai, C China
161 O4 **Xinji** *prev.* Shulu. Hebei, E China
161 P10 **Xinjian** Jiangxi, S China
Xinjiang *see* Xinjiang Uygur Zizhiqu
162 D8 **Xinjiang Uygur Zizhiqu** *var.* Sinkiang, Sinkiang Uighur Autonomous Region, Xin, Xinjiang. ◈ *autonomous region* NW China
160 H9 **Xinjin** *var.* Meixing, *Tib.* Zainlha. Sichuan, C China
Xinjin *see* Pulandian
Xinjing *see* Jingxi
163 U12 **Xinmin** Liaoning, NE China
160 M12 **Xinning** *var.* Jinshi. Hunan, S China
Xinpu *see* Lianyungang
Xinshan *see* Anyuan
161 P5 **Xintai** Shandong, E China
Xinwen *see* Suncun
Xin Xian *see* Xinzhou
161 N6 **Xinxiang** Henan, C China
161 O8 **Xinyang** *var.* Hsin-yang, Sinyang. Henan, C China
161 Q6 **Xinyi** *var.* Xin'anzhen. Jiangsu, E China
161 Q6 **Xinyi He** ≈ E China
161 O11 **Xinyu** Jiangxi, S China
158 I5 **Xinyuan** *var.* Künes. Xinjiang Uygur Zizhiqu, NW China
Xinyuan *see* Tianjun
161 N3 **Xinzhou** *var.* Xin Xian. Shanxi, C China
Xinzhou *see* Longlin
104 H4 **Xinzo de Limia** Galicia, NW Spain
Xions *see* Książ Wielkopolski
161 O7 **Xiping** Henan, C China
Xiping *see* Songyang
159 T11 **Xiqing Shan** ⛰ C China
59 N16 **Xique-Xique** Bahia, E Brazil
Xireg *see* Ulan
115 E14 **Xirovoúni** ▲ N Greece
162 M13 **Xishanzui** *var.* Urad Qianqi. Nei Mongol Zizhiqu, N China
160 J11 **Xishui** Guizhou, S China
Xi Ujimqin Qi *see* Bayan Ul
160 K11 **Xiushan** *var.* Zhonghe. Chongqing Shi, C China
Xiushan *see* Tonghai
161 O10 **Xiu Shui** ≈ S China
146 H9 **Xiva** *Rus.* Khiva. Xorazm Viloyati, W Uzbekistan
158 J16 **Xixabangma Feng** ▲ W China
160 M7 **Xixia** Henan, C China
Xixón *see* Gijón
Xixona *see* Jijona
Xizang *see* Xizang Zizhiqu
Xizang Gaoyuan *see* Qingzang Gaoyuan
160 E9 **Xizang Zizhiqu** *var.* Thibet, Tibetan Autonomous Region, Xizang, *Eng.* Tibet. ◈ *autonomous region* W China
163 U14 **Xizhong Dao** *island* N China
Xoi *see* Qüxü
146 H8 **Xo'jayli** *Rus.* Khodzheyli. Qoraqalpog'iston Respublikasi, W Uzbekistan
Xolotlán *see* Managua, Lago de
146 I9 **Xonqa** *Rus.* Khanka. Xorazm Viloyati, W Uzbekistan
146 H9 **Xorazm Viloyati** *Rus.* Khorezmskaya Oblast'. ◈ *province* W Uzbekistan
159 N9 **Xorkol** Xinjiang Uygur Zizhiqu, NW China
147 P11 **Xovos** *var.* Ursat'yevskaya, *Rus.* Khavast. Sirdaryo Viloyati, E Uzbekistan
41 X14 **Xpujil** Quintana Roo, E Mexico
161 Q8 **Xuancheng** *var.* Xuanzhou. Anhui, E China
167 T9 **Xuân Đuc** Quang Binh, C Vietnam
160 L9 **Xuan'en** *var.* Zhushan. Hubei, C China
160 K8 **Xuanhan** Sichuan, C China
161 O2 **Xuanhua** Hebei, E China
161 P4 **Xuanhui He** ≈ E China
Xuanzhou *see* Xuancheng
161 N7 **Xuchang** Henan, C China
137 X10 **Xudat** *Rus.* Khudat. NE Azerbaijan
81 M16 **Xuddur** *var.* Hudur, *It.* Oddur. Bakool, SW Somalia
80 O13 **Xudun** Nugaal, N Somalia
160 L11 **Xuefeng Shan** ⛰ S China
Xulun Hobot Qagan *see* Qagan Nur
42 F2 **Xunantunich** *ruins* Cayo, W Belize
163 W6 **Xun He** ≈ NE China
160 L7 **Xun He** ≈ C China
160 L14 **Xun Jiang** ≈ S China
163 W5 **Xunke** *var.* Qike. Heilongjiang, NE China
161 P13 **Xunwu** *var.* Changning. Jiangxi, S China
161 O3 **Xushui** Hebei, E China
160 L16 **Xuwen** Guangdong, S China
160 I11 **Xuyong** *var.* Yongning. Sichuan, C China
161 P6 **Xuzhou** *var.* Hsu-chou, Suchow, Tongshan; *prev.* T'ung-shan. Jiangsu, E China
114 K13 **Xylaganí** *var.* Xilaganí. Anatolikí Makedonía kai Thráki, NE Greece
115 F19 **Xylókastro** *var.* Xilokastro. Pelopónnisos, S Greece

Y

160 H9 **Ya'an** *var.* Yaan. Sichuan, C China
182 L10 **Yaapeet** Victoria, SE Australia
79 D15 **Yabassi** Littoral, W Cameroon
81 J15 **Yabēlo** Oromo, C Ethiopia
114 H9 **Yablanitsa** Lovech Oblast, W Bulgaria
43 N7 **Yablis** Región Autónoma Atlántico Norte, NE Nicaragua
123 O14 **Yablonovyy Khrebet** ⛰ S Russian Federation
162 J14 **Yabrai Shan** ⛰ NE China
45 U6 **Yabucoa** E Puerto Rico
160 J11 **Yachi He** ≈ S China
32 H10 **Yacolt** Washington, NW USA
54 M10 **Yacuaray** Amazonas, S Venezuela
57 M22 **Yacuiba** Tarija, S Bolivia
57 K16 **Yacuma, Río** ≈ C Bolivia
155 H16 **Yādgīr** Karnātaka, C India
21 R8 **Yadkin River** ≈ North Carolina, SE USA
21 R9 **Yadkinville** North Carolina, SE USA
127 P3 **Yadrin** Chuvashskaya Respublika, W Russian Federation
165 O16 **Yaeyama-shotō** *var.* Yaegama-shotō. *island group* SW Japan
75 O8 **Yafran** NW Libya
165 S2 **Yagashiri-tō** *island* NE Japan
65 H21 **Yaghan Basin** *undersea feature* SE Pacific Ocean
123 S9 **Yagodnoye** Magadanskaya Oblast', E Russian Federation
Yagotin *see* Yahotyn
78 G12 **Yagoua** Extrême-Nord, NE Cameroon
159 Q11 **Yagradagzê Shan** ▲ C China
Yaguachi *see* Yaguachi Nuevo
56 B7 **Yaguachi Nuevo** *var.* Yaguachi. Guayas, W Ecuador
Yaguarón, Río *see* Jaguarão, Rio
117 Q11 **Yahorlyts'kyy Lyman** *bay* S Ukraine
117 Q5 **Yahotyn** *Rus.* Yagotin. Kyyivs'ka Oblast', N Ukraine
40 L12 **Yahualica** Jalisco, SW Mexico
79 L17 **Yahuma** Orientale, N Dem. Rep. Congo
136 K15 **Yahyalı** Kayseri, C Turkey
167 N15 **Yai, Khao** ▲ SW Thailand
164 M14 **Yaizu** Shizuoka, Honshū, S Japan
160 G9 **Yajiang** *var.* Hekou, *Tib.* Nyagquka. Sichuan, C China
119 O14 **Yakawlyevichi** *Rus.* Yakovlevichi. Vitsyebskaya Voblasts', NE Belarus
163 S6 **Yakeshi** Nei Mongol Zizhiqu, N China
32 I9 **Yakima** Washington, NW USA
32 J10 **Yakima River** ≈ Washington, NW USA
114 G7 **Yakimovo** Montana, NW Bulgaria
Yakkabag *see* Yakkabog'
147 N12 **Yakkabog'** *Rus.* Yakkabag. Qashqadaryo Viloyati, S Uzbekistan
148 L12 **Yakmach** Baluchistān, SW Pakistan
77 O12 **Yako** W Burkina
39 W13 **Yakobi Island** *island* Alexander Archipelago, Alaska, USA
79 K16 **Yakoma** Equateur, N Dem. Rep. Congo
114 H11 **Yakoruda** Blagoevgrad, SW Bulgaria
Yakovlevichi *see* Yakawlyevichi
127 T2 **Yakshur-Bod'ya** Udmurtskaya Respublika, NW Russian Federation
165 Q5 **Yakumo** Hokkaidō, NE Japan
164 B17 **Yaku-shima** *island* Nansei-shotō, SW Japan
39 V12 **Yakutat** Alaska, USA
39 U12 **Yakutat Bay** *inlet* Alaska, USA
Yakutia/Yakutiya/Yakutiya, Respublika *see* Sakha (Yakutiya), Respublika
123 Q10 **Yakutsk** Respublika Sakha (Yakutiya), NE Russian Federation
167 O17 **Yala** Yala, SW Thailand
182 D6 **Yalata** South Australia
31 S9 **Yale** Michigan, N USA
180 I11 **Yalgoo** Western Australia
114 O12 **Yalıköy** İstanbul, NW Turkey
79 L14 **Yalinga** Haute-Kotto, C Central African Republic
119 M17 **Yalizava** *Rus.* Yelizovo. Mahilyowskaya Voblasts', E Belarus
44 L13 **Yallahs Hill** ▲ E Jamaica
22 L3 **Yalobusha River** ≈ Mississippi, S USA
79 H15 **Yaloké** Ombella-Mpoko, W Central African Republic
160 E7 **Yalong Jiang** ≈ C China
136 E11 **Yalova** Yalova, NW Turkey
136 E11 **Yalova** ◈ *province* NW Turkey
Yaloveny *see* Ialoveni
Yalpug *see* Ialpug
Yalpug, Ozero *see* Yalpuh, Ozero
117 N12 **Yalpuh, Ozero** *Rus.* Ozero Yalpug. ◎ SW Ukraine
117 T14 **Yalta** Respublika Krym, S Ukraine
163 W12 **Yalu** *Chin.* Yalu Jiang, *Jap.* Oryokko, *Kor.* Amnok-kang. ≈ China/North Korea
Yalu Jiang *see* Yalu
136 F14 **Yalvaç** Isparta, SW Turkey
165 R9 **Yamada** Iwate, Honshū, C Japan
165 D14 **Yamaga** Kumamoto, Kyūshū, SW Japan
165 P10 **Yamagata** Yamagata, Honshū, C Japan
165 P9 **Yamagata** *off.* Yamagata-ken. ◈ *prefecture* Honshū, C Japan
164 C16 **Yamagawa** Kagoshima, Kyūshū, SW Japan
164 E13 **Yamaguchi** *var.* Yamaguti. Yamaguchi, Honshū, SW Japan
164 E13 **Yamaguchi** *off.* Yamaguchi-ken, *var.* Yamaguti. ◈ *prefecture* Honshū, SW Japan
Yamaguti *see* Yamaguchi
123 X5 **Yamalo-Nenetskiy Avtonomnyy Okrug** ◈ *autonomous district* N Russian Federation
122 J7 **Yamal, Poluostrov** *peninsula* N Russian Federation
165 N13 **Yamanashi** *off.* Yamanashi-ken, *var.* Yamanasi. ◈ *prefecture* Honshū, S Japan
Yamanasi *see* Yamanashi
Yamaniyah, Al Jumhūrīyah al *see* Yemen
127 W5 **Yamantau** ▲ W Russian Federation
Yamasaki *see* Yamazaki
15 P12 **Yamaska** ≈ Québec, SE Canada
192 G4 **Yamato Ridge** *undersea feature* S Sea of Japan
164 I13 **Yamazaki** *var.* Yamasaki. Hyōgo, Honshū, SW Japan
183 V5 **Yamba** New South Wales, SE Australia
81 D16 **Yambio** *var.* Yambiyo. Western Equatoria, S Sudan
Yambiyo *see* Yambio
114 L10 **Yambol** *Turk.* Yanboli. Yambol, E Bulgaria
114 M11 **Yambol** ◈ *province* E Bulgaria
79 M17 **Yambuya** Orientale, N Dem. Rep. Congo
171 T15 **Yamdena, Pulau** *prev.* Jamdena. *island* Kepulauan Tanimbar, E Indonesia
165 O14 **Yame** Fukuoka, Kyūshū, SW Japan
166 M6 **Yamethin** Mandalay, C Myanmar
186 C6 **Yaminbot** East Sepik, NW PNG
181 U9 **Yamma Yamma, Lake** ◎ Queensland, C Australia
76 M16 **Yamoussoukro** ● (Ivory Coast) C Ivory Coast
37 P3 **Yampa River** ≈ Colorado, C USA
117 S2 **Yampil'** Sums'ka Oblast', NE Ukraine
116 M8 **Yampil'** Vinnyts'ka Oblast', C Ukraine
123 T9 **Yamsk** Magadanskaya Oblast', E Russian Federation
152 J8 **Yamuna** *prev.* Jumna. ≈ N India
152 I9 **Yamunānagar** Haryāna, N India
Yamundá *see* Nhamundá, Rio
145 U8 **Yamyshevo** Pavlodar, NE Kazakhstan
159 N16 **Yamzho Yumco** ◎ W China
123 Q8 **Yana** ≈ NE Russian Federation
186 H9 **Yanaba Island** *island* SE PNG
155 L16 **Yanam** *var.* Yanaon. Pondicherry, E India
160 L5 **Yan'an** *var.* Yanan. Shaanxi, C China
Yanaon *see* Yanam
127 U3 **Yanaul** Respublika Bashkortostan, W Russian Federation
118 O12 **Yanavichy** *Rus.* Yanovichi. Vitsyebskaya Voblasts', NE Belarus
Yanboli *see* Yambol
140 K8 **Yanbu' al Baḩr** Al Madīnah, W Saudi Arabia
21 T8 **Yanceyville** North Carolina, SE USA
161 R7 **Yancheng** Jiangsu, E China
159 W8 **Yanchi** Ningxia, N China
160 L5 **Yanchuan** Shaanxi, C China
183 O10 **Yanco Creek** *seasonal river* New South Wales, SE Australia
183 O6 **Yanda Creek** *seasonal river* New South Wales, SE Australia

◆ Country ● Country Capital ◇ Dependent Territory ○ Dependent Territory Capital ◈ Administrative Region × International Airport ▲ Mountain ⛰ Mountain Range ⚘ Volcano ≈ River ◎ Lake ⊠ Reservoir

182 K4 **Yandama Creek** seasonal river New South Wales/South Australia
161 S11 **Yandang Shan** ▲ SE China
Yandua see Yadua
159 O6 **Yandun** Xinjiang Uygur Zizhiqu, W China
76 L13 **Yanfolila** Sikasso, SW Mali
79 M18 **Yangambi** Orientale, N Dem. Rep. Congo
158 M15 **Yangbajain** Xizang Zizhiqu, W China
Yangchow see Yangzhou
160 M15 **Yangchun** Guangdong, S China
161 N2 **Yanggao** Shanxi, C China
Yanggeta see Yaqeta
Yangiabad see Yangiobod
Yangibazar see Dzhany-Bazar, Kyrgyzstan
Yangi-Bazar see Kofarnihon, Tajikistan
Yangiklshak see Yangiqishloq
146 M13 **Yangi-Nishon** Rus. Yang-Nishan. Qashqadaryo Viloyati, S Uzbekistan
147 Q9 **Yangiobod** Rus. Yangiabad. Toshkent Viloyati, E Uzbekistan
147 O10 **Yangiqishloq** Rus. Yangiklshak. Jizzax Viloyati, C Uzbekistan
147 P11 **Yangiyer** Sirdaryo Viloyati, E Uzbekistan
147 P9 **Yangiyoʻl** Rus. Yangiyul'. Toshkent Viloyati, E Uzbekistan
160 M15 **Yangjiang** Guangdong, S China
Yangku see Taiyuan
Yang-Nishan see Yangi-Nishon
166 L8 **Yangon** Eng. Rangoon. ● (Myanmar) Yangon, S Myanmar
166 M8 **Yangon** Eng. Rangoon. ◈ division SW Myanmar
160 K17 **Yangpu Gang** harbour Hainan, S China
161 N4 **Yangquan** Shanxi, C China
161 N13 **Yangshan** Guangdong, S China
167 U12 **Yang Sin, Chu** ▲ S Vietnam
Yangtze see Chang Jiang/Jinsha Jiang
Yangtze Kiang see Chang Jiang
161 R7 **Yangzhou** var. Yangchow. Jiangsu, E China
160 L5 **Yan He** ≈ C China
163 Y10 **Yanji** Jilin, NE China
Yanji see Longjing
Yanjing see Yanyuan
29 Q12 **Yankton** South Dakota, N USA
161 O12 **Yanling** prev. Lingxian, Ling Xian. Hunan, S China
Yannina see Ioánnina
123 Q7 **Yano-Indigirskaya Nizmennost'** plain NE Russian Federation
Yanovichi see Yanavichy
155 K24 **Yan Oya** ≈ N Sri Lanka
158 K6 **Yanqi** var. Yanqi Huizu Zizhixian. Xinjiang Uygur Zizhiqu, NW China
Yanqi Huizu Zizhixian see Yanqi
161 Q10 **Yanshan** var. Hekou. Jiangxi, S China
160 H14 **Yanshan** var. Jiangna. Yunnan, SW China
161 P2 **Yan Shan** ▲ E China
163 X8 **Yanshou** Heilongjiang, NE China
123 Q7 **Yanskiy Zaliv** bay N Russian Federation
183 O4 **Yantabulla** New South Wales, SE Australia
161 R4 **Yantai** var. Yan-t'ai; prev. Chefoo, Chih-fu. Shandong, E China
118 A13 **Yantarnyy** Ger. Palmnicken. Kaliningradskaya Oblast', W Russian Federation
114 J9 **Yantra** Gabrovo, N Bulgaria
114 K9 **Yantra** ≈ N Bulgaria
160 G11 **Yanyuan** var. Yanjing. Sichuan, C China
161 P5 **Yanzhou** Shandong, E China
79 E16 **Yaoundé** var. Yaunde. ● (Cameroon) Centre, S Cameroon
188 I14 **Yap** ◈ state W Micronesia
188 F16 **Yap** island Caroline Islands, W Micronesia
57 M18 **Yapacani, Rio** ≈ C Bolivia
171 W14 **Yapa Kopra** Papua, E Indonesia
Yapan see Yapen, Selat
Yapanskoye More see East Sea/Japan, Sea of
77 P15 **Yapei** N Ghana
12 M10 **Yapeitso, Mont** ▲ Québec, E Canada
171 W12 **Yapen, Pulau** prev. Japen. island E Indonesia
171 W12 **Yapen, Selat** var. Yapan. strait Papua, E Indonesia
61 E15 **Yapeyú** Corrientes, NE Argentina
136 I11 **Yapraklı** Çankırı, N Turkey
174 M3 **Yap Trench** var. Yap Trough. undersea feature SE Philippine Sea
Yap Trough see Yap Trench
Yapurá see Caquetá, Río, Brazil/Colombia
Yapurá see Japurá, Rio, Brazil/Colombia
197 I12 **Yaqaga** island N Fiji
197 H12 **Yaqeta** prev. Yanggeta. island Yasawa Group, NW Fiji
40 G6 **Yaqui** Sonora, NW Mexico
32 E12 **Yaquina Bay** bay Oregon, NW USA
40 G6 **Yaqui, Río** ≈ NW Mexico
54 K5 **Yaracuy** off. Estado Yaracuy. ◈ state NW Venezuela
Yaradzhi see Yarajy
146 E13 **Yarajy** Rus. Yaradzhi. Ahal Welaýaty, C Turkmenistan
125 Q15 **Yaransk** Kirovskaya Oblast', NW Russian Federation
136 F17 **Yardımcı Burnu** headland SW Turkey
97 Q19 **Yare** ≈ E England, UK
125 S9 **Yarega** Respublika Komi, NW Russian Federation
116 I7 **Yaremcha** Ivano-Frankivs'ka Oblast', W Ukraine
189 Q9 **Yaren** SW Nauru
125 Q10 **Yarensk** Arkhangel'skaya Oblast', NW Russian Federation
155 F16 **Yargatti** Karnātaka, W India
164 M12 **Yariga-take** ▲ Honshū, S Japan
141 O15 **Yarīm** W Yemen
54 F14 **Yarí, Río** ≈ SW Colombia
54 K5 **Yaritagua** Yaracuy, N Venezuela
Yarkand see Yarkant He
Yarkant see Shache
158 E9 **Yarkant He** var. Yarkand. ≈ NW China
149 U3 **Yarkhūn** ≈ NW Pakistan
Yarlung Zangbo Jiang see Brahmaputra
116 L6 **Yarmolyntsi** Khmel'nyts'ka Oblast', W Ukraine
13 O16 **Yarmouth** Nova Scotia, SE Canada
Yarmouth see Great Yarmouth
Yaroslav see Jarosław
124 L15 **Yaroslavl'** Yaroslavskaya Oblast', W Russian Federation
124 K14 **Yaroslavskaya Oblast'** ◈ province W Russian Federation
123 N11 **Yaroslavskiy** Respublika Sakha (Yakutiya), NE Russian Federation
183 P13 **Yarram** Victoria, SE Australia
183 O11 **Yarrawonga** Victoria, SE Australia
182 L4 **Yarriarraburra Swamp** wetland New South Wales, SE Australia
122 I8 **Yar-Sale** Yamalo-Nenetskiy Avtonomnyy Okrug, N Russian Federation
122 K11 **Yartsevo** Krasnoyarskiy Kray, C Russian Federation
126 I4 **Yartsevo** Smolenskaya Oblast', W Russian Federation
54 E8 **Yarumal** Antioquia, NW Colombia
187 W14 **Yasawa Group** island group NW Fiji
77 V12 **Yashi** Katsina, N Nigeria
77 S14 **Yashikera** Kwara, W Nigeria
147 T14 **Yashilkŭl** Rus. Ozero Yashil'kul'. ◎ SE Tajikistan
Yashil'kul', Ozero see Yashilkŭl
165 P9 **Yashima** Akita, Honshū, C Japan
127 P13 **Yashkul'** Respublika Kalmykiya, SW Russian Federation
146 F13 **Yashlyk** Ahal Welaýaty, C Turkmenistan
Yasinovataya see Yasynuvata
114 N10 **Yasna Polyana** Burgas, SE Bulgaria
167 R10 **Yasothon** Yasothon, E Thailand
183 R10 **Yass** New South Wales, SE Australia
Yassy see Iaşi
164 H12 **Yasugi** Shimane, Honshū, SW Japan
143 N10 **Yāsūj** var. Yesuj; prev. Tal-e Khosravī. Kohgīlūyeh va Būyer Aḩmad, C Iran
136 M11 **Yasun Burnu** headland N Turkey
117 X8 **Yasynuvata** Rus. Yasinovataya. Donets'ka Oblast', SE Ukraine
136 C15 **Yatağan** Muğla, SW Turkey
165 Q7 **Yatate-tōge** pass Honshū, C Japan
187 Q17 **Yaté** Province Sud, S New Caledonia
27 P6 **Yates Center** Kansas, C USA
185 B21 **Yates Point** headland South Island, NZ
9 N9 **Yathkyed Lake** ◎ Nunavut, NE Canada
171 T16 **Yatoke** Pulau Babar, E Indonesia
79 M18 **Yatolema** Orientale, N Dem. Rep. Congo
164 C15 **Yatsushiro** var. Yatusiro. Kumamoto, Kyūshū, SW Japan
164 C15 **Yatsushiro-kai** bay SW Japan
138 F11 **Yatta** var. Yuta. S West Bank
81 J20 **Yatta Plateau** plateau SE Kenya
Yatusiro see Yatsushiro
57 F17 **Yauca, Río** ≈ SW Peru
45 S6 **Yauco** W Puerto Rico
Yaunde see Yaoundé
Yavan see Yovon
Yavarí see Javari, Rio
56 G9 **Yavari Mirim, Río** ≈ NE Peru
40 G7 **Yavaros** Sonora, NW Mexico
154 I13 **Yavatmāl** Mahārāshtra, C India
54 M9 **Yaví, Cerro** ▲ C Venezuela
43 W16 **Yaviza** Darién, SE Panama
138 F10 **Yavne** Central, W Israel
116 H5 **Yavoriv** Pol. Jaworów, Rus. Yavorov. L'vivs'ka Oblast', NW Ukraine
Yavorov see Yavoriv
164 F14 **Yawatahama** Ehime, Shikoku, SW Japan
Ya Xian see Sanya
136 L17 **Yayladaği** Hatay, S Turkey
125 V13 **Yayva** Permskaya Oblast', NW Russian Federation
127 V12 **Yayva** ≈ NW Russian Federation
143 Q9 **Yazd** var. Yezd. Yazd, C Iran
143 Q8 **Yazd** off. Ostān-e Yazd, var. Yezd. ◈ province C Iran
Yazgulemskiy Khrebet see Yazgulom, Qatorkŭhi
147 S13 **Yazgulom, Qatorkŭhi** Rus. Yazgulemskiy Khrebet. ▲ S Tajikistan
22 K5 **Yazoo City** Mississippi, S USA
22 K3 **Yazoo River** ≈ Mississippi, S USA
127 Q5 **Yazykovo** Ul'yanovskaya Oblast', W Russian Federation
109 U4 **Ybbs** Niederösterreich, NE Austria
109 U4 **Ybbs** ≈ C Austria
95 G22 **Yding Skovhøj** hill C Denmark
115 G26 **Ýdra** var. Ídhra, Idra. Ýdra, S Greece
115 G21 **Ýdra** var. Ídhra. island S Greece
115 G20 **Ýdras, Kólpos** strait S Greece
167 N10 **Ye** Mon State, S Myanmar
183 O12 **Yea** Victoria, SE Australia
Yebaishou see Jianping
78 I5 **Yebbi-Bou** Borkou-Ennedi-Tibesti, N Chad
158 F9 **Yecheng** var. Kargilik. Xinjiang Uygur Zizhiqu, NW China
105 R11 **Yecla** Murcia, SE Spain
40 H6 **Yécora** Sonora, NW Mexico
Yedintsy see Edineţ
124 J13 **Yefimovskiy** Leningradskaya Oblast', NW Russian Federation
126 K6 **Yefremov** Tul'skaya Oblast', W Russian Federation
Yêgainnyin see Henan
137 U12 **Yeghegis** Rus. Yekhegis. ≈ C Armenia
145 T10 **Yegindybulak** Kaz. Egindibulaq. Karaganda, C Kazakhstan
126 L4 **Yegor'yevsk** Moskovskaya Oblast', W Russian Federation
Yehuda, Haré see Judaean Hills
81 E15 **Yei** ≈ S Sudan
161 P8 **Yeji** var. Yejiaji. Anhui, E China
Yejiaji see Yeji
122 G10 **Yekaterinburg** prev. Sverdlovsk. Sverdlovskaya Oblast', C Russian Federation
Yekaterinodar see Krasnodar
Yekaterinoslav see Dnipropetrovs'k
123 R13 **Yekaterinoslavka** Amurskaya Oblast', SE Russian Federation
127 O7 **Yekaterinovka** Saratovskaya Oblast', W Russian Federation
76 K16 **Yekepa** NE Liberia
127 T3 **Yelabuga** Respublika Tatarstan, W Russian Federation
Yela Island see Rossel Island
127 O8 **Yelan'** Volgogradskaya Oblast', SW Russian Federation
117 Q9 **Yelanets'** Rus. Yelanets. Mykolayivs'ka Oblast', S Ukraine
126 L7 **Yelets** Lipetskaya Oblast', W Russian Federation
125 W4 **Yeletskiy** Respublika Komi, NW Russian Federation
76 J11 **Yélimané** Kayes, W Mali
Yelisavetpol see Gäncä
Yelizavetgrad see Kirovohrad
123 T12 **Yelizavety, Mys** headland SE Russian Federation
Yelizovo see Yalizava
127 S5 **Yelkhovka** Samarskaya Oblast', W Russian Federation
96 M1 **Yell** island NE Scotland, UK
155 E17 **Yellāpur** Karnātaka, W India
11 U17 **Yellow Grass** Saskatchewan, S Canada
Yellowhammer State see Alabama
11 O15 **Yellowhead Pass** pass Alberta/British Columbia, SW Canada
8 K10 **Yellowknife** territory capital Northwest Territories, W Canada
8 K9 **Yellowknife** ≈ Northwest Territories, NW Canada
23 P8 **Yellow River** ≈ Alabama/Florida, S USA
30 I4 **Yellow River** ≈ Wisconsin, N USA
30 J6 **Yellow River** ≈ Wisconsin, N USA
30 K7 **Yellow River** ≈ Wisconsin, N USA
Yellow River see Huang He
157 V8 **Yellow Sea** Chin. Huang Hai, Kor. Hwang-Hae. sea E Asia
33 S13 **Yellowstone Lake** ◎ Wyoming, C USA
33 T13 **Yellowstone National Park** national park Wyoming, NW USA
33 Y8 **Yellowstone River** ≈ Montana/Wyoming, NW USA
96 L1 **Yell Sound** strait N Scotland, UK
27 U9 **Yellville** Arkansas, C USA
122 K10 **Yeloguy** ≈ C Russian Federation
Yëloten see Ýolöten
119 M20 **Yel'sk** Rus. Yel'sk. Homyel'skaya Voblasts', SE Belarus
77 T13 **Yelwa** Kebbi, W Nigeria
21 R15 **Yemassee** South Carolina, SE USA
141 O15 **Yemen** off. Republic of Yemen, Ar. Al Jumhūrīyah al Yamanīyah, Al Yaman. ◆ republic SW Asia
116 M4 **Yemil'chyne** Zhytomyrs'ka Oblast', N Ukraine
124 M10 **Yemtsa** Arkhangel'skaya Oblast', NW Russian Federation
126 M10 **Yemtsa** ≈ NW Russian Federation
125 R10 **Yemva** prev. Zheleznodorozhnyy. Respublika Komi, NW Russian Federation
77 U17 **Yenagoa** Bayelsa, S Nigeria
117 X7 **Yenakiyeve** Rus. Yenakiyevo; prev. Ordzhonikidze, Rykovo. Donets'ka Oblast', E Ukraine
Yenakiyevo see Yenakiyeve
166 L6 **Yenangyaung** Magwe, W Myanmar
167 S5 **Yên Bai** Yên Bai, N Vietnam
183 P9 **Yenda** New South Wales, SE Australia
77 Q14 **Yendi** NE Ghana
Yêndum see Zhag'yab
158 E8 **Yengisar** Xinjiang Uygur Zizhiqu, NW China
121 R1 **Yenierenköy** var. Yialousa, Gk. Agialoúsa. NE Cyprus
Yenipazar see Novi Pazar
136 E12 **Yenişehir** Bursa, NW Turkey
Yenisei Bay see Yeniseyskiy Zaliv
122 K12 **Yeniseysk** Krasnoyarskiy Kray, C Russian Federation
197 W10 **Yeniseyskiy Zaliv** var. Yenisei Bay. bay N Russian Federation
127 Q12 **Yenotayevka** Astrakhanskaya Oblast', SW Russian Federation
126 L4 **Yenozero, Ozero** ◎ NW Russian Federation
Yenping see Nanping
39 Q11 **Yentna** ≈ Alaska, USA
180 M10 **Yeo, Lake** salt lake Western Australia
183 R7 **Yeoval** New South Wales, SE Australia
97 K23 **Yeovil** SW England, UK
40 H6 **Yepachic** Chihuahua, N Mexico
181 Y8 **Yeppoon** Queensland, E Australia
126 M5 **Yerakhtur** Ryazanskaya Oblast', W Russian Federation
Yeraliyev see Kuryk
146 F12 **Yerbent** Ahal Welaýaty, C Turkmenistan
123 N11 **Yerbogachen** Irkutskaya Oblast', C Russian Federation
137 T12 **Yerevan** Eng. Erivan. ● (Armenia) C Armenia
137 U12 **Yerevan** ✕ C Armenia
145 R9 **Yereymentau** var. Jermentau, Yermentau, Kaz. Ereymentaū. Akmola, C Kazakhstan
127 O12 **Yergeni** hill range SW Russian Federation
Yeriho see Jericho
35 R6 **Yerington** Nevada, W USA
136 J13 **Yerköy** Yozgat, C Turkey
114 L13 **Yerlisu** Edirne, NW Turkey
Yermak see Aksu
145 R9 **Yermentau** Kaz. Ereymentaū, Jermentau. Akmola, C Kazakhstan
145 R9 **Yermentau, Gory** ▲ C Kazakhstan
125 R5 **Yermitsa** Respublika Komi, NW Russian Federation
35 V14 **Yermo** California, W USA
123 P13 **Yerofey Pavlovich** Amurskaya Oblast', SE Russian Federation
99 F15 **Yerseke** Zeeland, SW Netherlands
127 Q8 **Yershov** Saratovskaya Oblast', W Russian Federation
125 P9 **Yërtom** Respublika Komi, NW Russian Federation
56 D13 **Yerupaja, Nevado** ▲ C Peru
Yerushalayim see Jerusalem
105 R4 **Yesa, Embalse de** ⊞ NE Spain
144 F9 **Yesensay** Zapadnyy Kazakhstan, NW Kazakhstan
145 V15 **Yesik** Kaz. Esik; prev. Issyk. Almaty, SE Kazakhstan
145 O8 **Yesil'** Kaz. Esil. Akmola, C Kazakhstan
136 K15 **Yeşilhisar** Kayseri, C Turkey
136 L11 **Yeşilırmak** anc. Iris. ≈ N Turkey
37 U12 **Yeso** New Mexico, SW USA
Yeso see Hokkaidō
127 N15 **Yessentuki** Stavropol'skiy Kray, SW Russian Federation
122 M9 **Yessey** Evenkiyskiy Avtonomnyy Okrug, N Russian Federation
105 P12 **Yeste** Castilla-La Mancha, C Spain
Yesuj see Yāsūj
183 T4 **Yetman** New South Wales, SE Australia
76 L4 **Yetti** physical region N Mauritania
166 M4 **Ye-u** Sagaing, C Myanmar
102 H9 **Yeu, Île d'** island NW France
Yevlakh see Yevlax
137 W11 **Yevlax** Rus. Yevlakh. C Azerbaijan
117 S13 **Yevpatoriya** Respublika Krym, S Ukraine
126 K12 **Yeya** ≈ SW Russian Federation
158 I10 **Yeyik** Xinjiang Uygur Zizhiqu, W China
126 K12 **Yeysk** Krasnodarskiy Kray, SW Russian Federation
Yezd see Yazd
Yezerishche see Yezyaryshcha
Yezhou see Jianshi
Yezo see Hokkaidō
118 N11 **Yezyaryshcha** Rus. Yezerishche. Vitsyebskaya Voblasts', NE Belarus
Yialí see Gyalí
Yialousa see Yenierenköy
163 V7 **Yi'an** Heilongjiang, NE China
Yiannitsá see Giannitsá
160 I10 **Yibin** Sichuan, C China
158 K13 **Yibug Caka** ◎ W China
160 M9 **Yichang** Hubei, C China
160 L5 **Yichuan** Shaanxi, C China
157 W3 **Yichun** Heilongjiang, NE China
163 X6 **Yichun** var. I-ch'un. Heilongjiang, NE China
161 O11 **Yichun** Jiangxi, S China
160 M9 **Yidu** prev. Zhicheng. Hubei, C China
Yidu see Qingzhou
188 C15 **Yigo** NE Guam
161 Q5 **Yi He** ≈ E China
163 X8 **Yilan** Heilongjiang, NE China
136 C9 **Yıldız Dağları** ▲ NW Turkey
136 L13 **Yıldızeli** Sivas, N Turkey
163 U4 **Yilehuli Shan** ▲ NE China
163 S7 **Yimin He** ≈ NE China
159 W8 **Yinchuan** var. Yinch'uan, Yin-ch'uan, Yinchwan. Ningxia, N China
Yinchwan see Yinchuan
Yindu He see Indus
161 N14 **Yingde** Guangdong, S China
161 O7 **Ying He** ≈ C China
163 U13 **Yingkou** var. Ying-k'ou, Yingkow; prev. Newchwang, Niuchwang. Liaoning, NE China
Yingkow see Yingkou
161 P9 **Yingshan** var. Wenquan. Hubei, C China
Yingshan see Guangshui
161 Q10 **Yingtan** Jiangxi, S China
Yin-hsien see Ningbo
158 H5 **Yining** var. I-ning, Uigh. Gulja, Kuldja. Xinjiang Uygur Zizhiqu, NW China
160 K11 **Yinjiang** var. Yinjiang Tujiazu Miaozu Zizhixian. Guizhou, S China
Yinjiang Tujiazu Miaozu Zizhixian see Yinjiang
166 L4 **Yinmabin** Sagaing, C Myanmar
163 N13 **Yin Shan** ▲ N China
Yin-tu Ho see Indus
159 P15 **Yi'ong Zangbo** ≈ W China
Yioúra see Gyáros
81 I14 **Yirga 'Alem** It. Irgalem. Southern, S Ethiopia
61 E19 **Yí, Río** ≈ C Uruguay
81 E14 **Yirol** El Buhayrat, S Sudan
163 S8 **Yirshi** var. Yirxie. Nei Mongol Zizhiqu, N China
Yirxie see Yirshi
161 Q5 **Yishui** Shandong, E China
Yisrael/Yisra'el see Israel
Yíthion see Gýtheio
Yitiaoshan see Jingtai
163 W10 **Yitong** var. Yitong Manzu Zizhixian. Jilin, NE China
Yitong Manzu Zizhixian see Yitong
159 P5 **Yiwu** var. Aratürük. Xinjiang Uygur Zizhiqu, NW China
163 U12 **Yiwulü Shan** ▲ N China
163 T12 **Yixian** var. Yizhou. Liaoning, NE China
161 N10 **Yiyang** Hunan, S China
161 Q10 **Yiyang** Jiangxi, S China
161 N13 **Yizhang** Hunan, S China
Yizhou see Yixian
93 K19 **Yläne** Länsi-Suomi, W Finland
93 L14 **Yli-Ii** Oulu, C Finland
93 L14 **Ylikiiminki** Oulu, C Finland
92 N13 **Yli-Kitka** ◎ NE Finland
93 K17 **Ylistaro** Länsi-Suomi, W Finland
92 K13 **Ylitornio** Lappi, NW Finland
93 L15 **Ylivieska** Oulu, W Finland
93 L18 **Ylöjärvi** Länsi-Suomi, W Finland
95 N17 **Yngaren** ◎ C Sweden
25 T12 **Yoakum** Texas, SW USA
77 X13 **Yobe** ◈ state NE Nigeria
165 R3 **Yobetsu-dake** ▲ Hokkaidō, NE Japan
80 L11 **Yoboki** C Djibouti
22 M4 **Yockanookany River** ≈ Mississippi, S USA
22 L2 **Yocona River** ≈ Mississippi, S USA
171 Y15 **Yodom** Papua, E Indonesia
169 Q16 **Yogyakarta** prev. Djokjakarta, Jogjakarta, Jokyakarta. Jawa, C Indonesia
169 P17 **Yogyakarta** off. Daerah Istimewa Yogyakarta, var. Djokjakarta, Jogjakarta, Jokyakarta. ◈ autonomous district S Indonesia
165 Q3 **Yoichi** Hokkaidō, NE Japan
42 G6 **Yojoa, Lago de** ◎ NW Honduras
79 G16 **Yokadouma** Est, SE Cameroon
Yokaichi see Yōkaichi
164 K13 **Yokkaichi** var. Yokkaiti. Mie, Honshū, SW Japan
Yokkaiti see Yokkaichi
79 E15 **Yoko** Centre, C Cameroon
165 V15 **Yokoate-jima** island Nansei-shotō, SW Japan
165 R6 **Yokohama** Aomori, Honshū, C Japan
165 O14 **Yokosuka** Kanagawa, Honshū, S Japan
164 G12 **Yokota** Shimane, Honshū, SW Japan
165 Q9 **Yokote** Akita, Honshū, C Japan
77 Y14 **Yola** Adamawa, E Nigeria
79 L19 **Yolombo** Equateur, C Dem. Rep. Congo
146 J14 **Ýolöten** Rus. Yëloten, prev. Iolotan'. Mary Welaýaty, S Turkmenistan
165 Y15 **Yome-jima** island Ogasawara-shotō, SE Japan
76 K16 **Yomou** Guinée-Forestière, SE Guinea
171 Y15 **Yomuka** Papua, E Indonesia
188 C16 **Yona** E Guam
164 H12 **Yonago** Tottori, Honshū, SW Japan
165 N16 **Yonaguni** Okinawa, SW Japan
165 N16 **Yonaguni-jima** island Nansei-shotō, SW Japan
165 T16 **Yonaha-dake** ▲ Okinawa, SW Japan
163 X14 **Yonan** SW North Korea
165 P10 **Yonezawa** Yamagata, Honshū, C Japan
161 Q12 **Yong'an** var. Yongan. Fujian, SE China
Yong'an see Fengjie
159 T9 **Yongchang** Gansu, N China
161 P7 **Yongcheng** Henan, C China
163 Z15 **Yŏngch'ŏn** Jap. Eisen. SE South Korea
160 J10 **Yongchuan** Chongqing Shi, C China
159 U10 **Yongdeng** Gansu, C China
Yongding see Yongren
131 W9 **Yongding He** ≈ E China
161 P11 **Yongfeng** var. Enjiang. Jiangxi, S China
158 L5 **Yongfengqu** Xinjiang Uygur Zizhiqu, W China
160 L13 **Yongfu** Guangxi Zhuangzu Zizhiqu, S China 24.57
163 X13 **Yŏnghŭng** E North Korea
159 U10 **Yongjing** Gansu, C China
Yongjing see Xifeng
163 Y15 **Yŏngju** Jap. Eishū. C South Korea
Yongning see Xuyong
160 E12 **Yongping** Yunnan, SW China
160 G12 **Yongren** var. Yongding. Yunnan, SW China
160 L10 **Yongshun** var. Lingxi. Hunan, S China
161 P10 **Yongxiu** var. Tujiabu. Jiangxi, S China
160 M12 **Yongzhou** Hunan, S China
18 K14 **Yonkers** New York, NE USA
103 Q7 **Yonne** ◈ department C France
103 P6 **Yonne** ≈ C France
54 H9 **Yopal** var. El Yopal. Casanare, C Colombia
158 E8 **Yopurga** var. Yukuriawat. Xinjiang Uygur Zizhiqu, NW China
147 S11 **Yordon** var. Iordan, Rus. Jardan. Farg'ona Viloyati, E Uzbekistan
180 J12 **York** Western Australia
97 M16 **York** anc. Eboracum, Eburacum. N England, UK
23 N5 **York** Alabama, S USA
29 Q15 **York** Nebraska, C USA
18 G16 **York** Pennsylvania, NE USA
21 R11 **York** South Carolina, SE USA
14 J13 **York** ≈ Ontario, SE Canada
15 X6 **York** ≈ Québec, SE Canada
181 V1 **York, Cape** headland Queensland, NE Australia
182 I9 **Yorke Peninsula** peninsula South Australia
182 I9 **Yorketown** South Australia
19 P9 **York Harbor** Maine, NE USA
21 X6 **York River** ≈ Virginia, NE USA
97 M16 **Yorkshire** cultural region N England, UK
97 L16 **Yorkshire Dales** physical region N England, UK
11 V16 **Yorkton** Saskatchewan, S Canada
25 T12 **Yorktown** Texas, SW USA
21 X6 **Yorktown** Virginia, NE USA
30 M11 **Yorkville** Illinois, N USA
42 J5 **Yoro** Yoro, C Honduras
42 H5 **Yoro** ◈ department N Honduras
165 T16 **Yoron-jima** island Nansei-shotō, SW Japan
77 N13 **Yorosso** Sikasso, S Mali
35 R8 **Yosemite National Park** national park California, W USA
127 Q3 **Yoshkar-Ola** Respublika Mariy El, W Russian Federation
Yosino Gawa see Yoshino-gawa
Yösönbulag see Altay
171 Y16 **Yos Sudarso, Pulau** var. Pulau Dolak, Pulau Kolepom; prev. Jos Sudarso. island E Indonesia
163 Y17 **Yŏsu** Jap. Reisui. S South Korea
165 R4 **Yotei-zan** ▲ Hokkaidō, NE Japan
97 D21 **Youghal** Ir. Eochaill. S Ireland
97 D21 **Youghal Bay** Ir. Cuan Eochaille. inlet S Ireland
18 C15 **Youghiogheny River** ≈ Pennsylvania, NE USA
160 K14 **You Jiang** ≈ S China
183 Q9 **Young** New South Wales, SE Australia
11 T15 **Young** Saskatchewan, S Canada
61 E18 **Young** Río Negro, W Uruguay
182 G5 **Younghusband, Lake** salt lake South Australia
182 J10 **Younghusband Peninsula** peninsula South Australia
184 Q10 **Young Nicks Head** headland North Island, NZ
185 D20 **Young Range** ▲ South Island, NZ
191 Q15 **Young's Rock** island Pitcairn Island, Pitcairn Islands
11 R16 **Youngstown** Alberta, SW Canada
31 V12 **Youngstown** Ohio, N USA
159 N9 **Youshashan** Qinghai, C China
Youth, Isle of see Juventud, Isla de la
77 N11 **Youvarou** Mopti, C Mali
160 K10 **Youyang** var. Zhongduo. Chongqing Shi, C China
163 Y7 **Youyi** Heilongjiang, NE China
147 P13 **Yovon** Rus. Yavan. SW Tajikistan
136 J13 **Yozgat** Yozgat, C Turkey
136 K13 **Yozgat** ◈ province C Turkey
62 O6 **Ypacaraí** var. Ypacaray. Central, S Paraguay
Ypacaray see Ypacaraí
62 P5 **Ypané, Río** ≈ C Paraguay
Ypres see Ieper
114 I13 **Ypsário** var. Ipsario. ▲ Thásos, E Greece
31 R10 **Ypsilanti** Michigan, N USA
34 M1 **Yreka** California, W USA
Yrendagüé see General Eugenio A. Garay
186 G5 **Ysabel Channel** channel N PNG
14 K8 **Yser, Lac** ◎ Québec, SE Canada
147 Y8 **Yshtyk** Issyk-Kul'skaya Oblast', E Kyrgyzstan
Yssel see IJssel
103 Q12 **Yssingeaux** Haute-Loire, C France
95 K23 **Ystad** Skåne, S Sweden
Ysyk-Köl see Balykchy, Kyrgyzstan
Ysyk-Köl see Issyk-Kul', Ozero, Kyrgyzstan
Ysyk-Köl Oblasty see Issyk-Kul'skaya Oblast'
96 L8 **Ythan** ≈ NE Scotland, UK
Y Trallwng see Welshpool
94 C13 **Ytre Arna** Hordaland, S Norway
94 B12 **Ytre Sula** island S Norway
93 G17 **Ytterhogdal** Jämtland, C Sweden
Yu see Henan
Yuan Jiang see Red River
161 S13 **Yüanlin** Jap. Inrin. C Taiwan
161 N3 **Yuanping** Shanxi, C China
Yuanquan see Anxi
Yuanshan see Lianping
161 O11 **Yuan Shui** ≈ S China
35 O6 **Yuba City** California, W USA
35 O6 **Yuba River** ≈ California, W USA
80 H13 **Yubdo** Oromo, C Ethiopia
165 U3 **Yūbetsu** Hokkaidō, NE Japan
Yūbetsu-gawa see Yabetsu-gawa
126 L3 **Yubileynyy** Moskovskaya Oblast', SW Russian Federation
41 X12 **Yucatán** ◈ state SE Mexico
47 O3 **Yucatan Basin** var. Yucatan Deep. undersea feature N Caribbean Sea
Yucatán, Canal de see Yucatan Channel
41 Y10 **Yucatan Channel** Sp. Canal de Yucatán. channel Cuba/Mexico
Yucatan Deep see Yucatan Basin
Yucatan Peninsula see Yucatán, Península de
41 X13 **Yucatán, Península de** Eng. Yucatan Peninsula. peninsula Guatemala/Mexico
36 I11 **Yucca** Arizona, SW USA
35 V15 **Yucca Valley** California, W USA
161 P4 **Yucheng** Shandong, E China
Yuci see Jinzhong
131 X5 **Yudoma** ≈ E Russian Federation
161 P12 **Yudu** var. Gongjiang. Jiangxi, C China
Yue see Guangdong
Yuecheng see Yuexi
160 M12 **Yuecheng Ling** ▲ S China
Yuegaitan see Qumarlêb
181 P7 **Yuendumu** Northern Territory, N Australia
160 H10 **Yuexi** var. Yuecheng. Sichuan, C China

◆ Country ● Country Capital ◇ Dependent Territory ○ Dependent Territory Capital ◈ Administrative Region ✕ International Airport ▲ Mountain ▲ Mountain Range ⩕ Volcano ≈ River ◎ Lake ⊞ Reservoir

161 *N10* **Yueyang** Hunan, S China
125 *U14* **Yug** Permskaya Oblast', NW Russian Federation
127 *P13* **Yug** ≈ NW Russian Federation
123 *R10* **Yugorenok** Respublika Sakha (Yakutiya), NE Russian Federation
122 *H9* **Yugorsk** Khanty-Mansiyskiy Avtonomnyy Okrug, C Russian Federation
122 *H7* **Yugorskiy Poluostrov** *peninsula* NW Russian Federation
Yugoslavia *see* Serbia and Montenegro (Yugo.)
146 *K14* **Yugo-Vostochnyye Garagumy** *prev.* Yugo-Vostochnyye Karakumy. *desert* E Turkmenistan
Yugo-Vostochnyye Karakumy *see* Yugo-Vostochnyye Garagumy
Yuhu *see* Eryuan
161 *S10* **Yuhuan Dao** *island* SE China
160 *L14* **Yu Jiang** ≈ S China
Yujin *see* Qianwei
123 *S7* **Yukagirskoye Ploskogor'ye** *plateau* NE Russian Federation
118 *L11* **Yukhavichy** *Rus.* Yukhovichi. Vitsyebskaya Voblasts', N Belarus
126 *J4* **Yukhnov** Kaluzhskaya Oblast', W Russian Federation
Yukhovichi *see* Yukhavichy
79 *J20* **Yuki** *var.* Yuki Kengunda. Bandundu, W Dem. Rep. Congo
Yuki Kengunda *see* Yuki
26 *M10* **Yukon** Oklahoma, C USA
(0) *F4* **Yukon** ≈ Canada/USA
Yukon *see* Yukon Territory
39 *S7* **Yukon Flats** *salt flat* Alaska, USA
10 *I5* **Yukon Territory** *var.* Yukon, *Fr.* Territoire du Yukon. ◈ *territory* NW Canada
137 *T16* **Yüksekova** Hakkâri, SE Turkey
123 *N10* **Yukta** Evenkiyskiy Avtonomnyy Okrug, C Russian Federation
165 *O13* **Yukuhashi** *var.* Yukuhasi. Fukuoka, Kyūshū, SW Japan
Yukuhasi *see* Yukuhashi
Yukuriawat *see* Yopurga
127 *O9* **Yula** ≈ NW Russian Federation
181 *P8* **Yulara** Northern Territory, N Australia
127 *W6* **Yuldybayevo** Respublika Bashkortostan, W Russian Federation
23 *W8* **Yulee** Florida, SE USA
158 *K7* **Yuli** *var.* Lopnur. Xinjiang Uygur Zizhiqu, NW China
161 *T14* **Yüli** C Taiwan
160 *L15* **Yulin** Guangxi Zhuangzu Zizhiqu, S China
160 *L4* **Yulin** Shaanxi, C China
161 *T14* **Yüli Shan** ▲ E Taiwan
160 *F11* **Yulong Xueshan** ▲ SW China
36 *H14* **Yuma** Arizona, SW USA
37 *W3* **Yuma** Colorado, C USA
54 *K5* **Yumare** Yaracuy, N Venezuela
63 *G14* **Yumbel** Bío Bío, C Chile
79 *N19* **Yumbi** Maniema, E Dem. Rep. Congo
159 *R8* **Yumen** *var.* Laojunmiao, Yümen. Gansu, N China
159 *Q7* **Yumenzhen** Gansu, N China
158 *J3* **Yumin** Xinjiang Uygur Zizhiqu, NW China
Yun *see* Yunnan
136 *G14* **Yunak** Konya, W Turkey
45 *O8* **Yuna, Río** ≈ E Dominican Republic
38 *I17* **Yunaska Island** *island* Aleutian Islands, Alaska, USA
160 *M6* **Yuncheng** Shanxi, C China
161 *N14* **Yunfu** Guangdong, S China
57 *L18* **Yungas** *physical region* E Bolivia
Yungki *see* Jilin
Yung-ning *see* Nanning
160 *I12* **Yungui Gaoyuan** *plateau* SW China
Yunjinghong *see* Jinghong
160 *M15* **Yunkai Dashan** ▲▲ S China
Yunki *see* Jilin
160 *E11* **Yun Ling** ▲▲ SW China
161 *N9* **Yunmeng** Hubei, C China
157 *N14* **Yunnan** *var.* Yun, Yunnan Sheng, Yünnan, Yun-nan. ◈ *province* SW China
Yunnan *see* Kunming
Yunnan Sheng *see* Yunnan
165 *P15* **Yunomae** Kumamoto, Kyūshū, SW Japan
161 *N8* **Yun Shui** ≈ C China
182 *J7* **Yunta** South Australia
161 *Q14* **Yunxiao** Fujian, SE China
160 *K9* **Yunyang** Sichuan, C China
193 *S9* **Yupanqui Basin** *undersea feature* E Pacific Ocean
Yuping Guizhou, China *see* Libo
Yuping Yunnan, China *see* Pingbian
Yuratishki *see* Yuratsishki
119 *I15* **Yuratsishki** *Pol.* Juraciszki, *Rus.* Yuratishki. Hrodzyenskaya Voblasts', W Belarus
Yurev *see* Tartu
122 *J12* **Yurga** Kemerovskaya Oblast', S Russian Federation
56 *E10* **Yurimaguas** Loreto, N Peru
127 *P3* **Yurino** Respublika Mariy El, W Russian Federation
41 *N13* **Yuriria** Guanajuato, C Mexico
125 *T13* **Yurla** Komi-Permyatskiy Avtonomnyy Okrug, NW Russian Federation
Yuruá, Río *see* Juruá, Rio
114 *M13* **Yürük** Tekirdağ, NW Turkey
158 *G10* **Yurungkax He** ≈ W China
125 *Q14* **Yur'ya** *var.* Jarja. Kirovskaya Oblast', NW Russian Federation
Yur'yev *see* Tartu
125 *N16* **Yur'yevets** Ivanovskaya Oblast', W Russian Federation
126 *M3* **Yur'yev-Pol'skiy** Vladimirskaya Oblast', W Russian Federation
117 *V7* **Yur"yivka** Dnipropetrovs'ka Oblast', E Ukraine
42 *I7* **Yuscarán** El Paraíso, S Honduras
161 *P12* **Yu Shan** ▲ S China
159 *R13* **Yushu** *var.* Gyêgu. Qinghai, C China
127 *P12* **Yusta** Respublika Kalmykiya, SW Russian Federation
124 *I10* **Yustozero** Respublika Kareliya, NW Russian Federation
137 *Q11* **Yusufeli** Artvin, NE Turkey
164 *F14* **Yusuhara** Kōchi, Shikoku, SW Japan
125 *T14* **Yus'va** Permskaya Oblast', NW Russian Federation
Yuta *see* Yatta
161 *P2* **Yutian** Hebei, E China
158 *H10* **Yutian** *var.* Keriya. Xinjiang Uygur Zizhiqu, NW China
62 *K5* **Yuto** Jujuy, NW Argentina
62 *P7* **Yuty** Caazapá, S Paraguay
160 *G13* **Yuxi** Yunnan, SW China
161 *O2* **Yuxian** *prev.* Yu Xian. Hebei, E China
165 *Q9* **Yuzawa** Akita, Honshū, C Japan
125 *N16* **Yuzha** Ivanovskaya Oblast', W Russian Federation
Yuzhno-Alichurskiy Khrebet *see* Alichuri Janubí, Qatorkŭhi
Yuzhno-Kazakhstanskaya Oblast' *see* Yuzhnyy Kazakhstan
123 *T13* **Yuzhno-Sakhalinsk** *Jap.* Toyohara; *prev.* Vladimirovka. Ostrov Sakhalin, Sakhalinskaya Oblast', SE Russian Federation
127 *P14* **Yuzhno-Sukhokumsk** Respublika Dagestan, SW Russian Federation
145 *Z10* **Yuzhnyy Altay, Khrebet** ▲▲ E Kazakhstan
Yuzhnyy Bug *see* Pivdennyy Buh
145 *O15* **Yuzhnyy Kazakhstan** *off.* Yuzhno-Kazakhstanskaya Oblast', *Eng.* South Kazakhstan, *Kaz.* Ongtüstik Qazaqstan Oblysy; *prev.* Chimkentskaya Oblast'. ◈ *province* S Kazakhstan
123 *U10* **Yuzhnyy, Mys** *headland* E Russian Federation
127 *W6* **Yuzhnyy Ural** *var.* Southern Urals. ▲▲ W Russian Federation
159 *V10* **Yuzhong** Gansu, C China
Yuzhou *see* Chongqing
103 *N5* **Yvelines** ◈ *department* N France
108 *B9* **Yverdon** *var.* Yverdon-les-Bains, *Ger.* Iferten; *anc.* Eborodunum. Vaud, W Switzerland
Yverdon-les-Bains *see* Yverdon
102 *M3* **Yvetot** Seine-Maritime, N France
146 *H8* **Ýylanly** *Rus.* Il'yaly. Daşoguz Welaýaty, N Turkmenistan

Z

147 *T12* **Zaalayskiy Khrebet** *Taj.* Qatorkŭhi Pasi Oloy. ▲▲ Kyrgyzstan/Tajikistan
Zaamin *see* Zomin
Zaandam *see* Zaanstad
98 *I10* **Zaanstad** *prev.* Zaandam. Noord-Holland, C Netherlands
Zabadani *see* Az Zabdānī
119 *L18* **Zabalatstsye** *Rus.* Zabolot'ye. Homyel'skaya Voblasts', SE Belarus
112 *L9* **Žabalj** *Ger.* Josefsdorf, *Hung.* Zsablya; *prev.* Józseffalva;. Serbia, N Serbia and Montenegro (Yugo.)
Zāb aş Şaghīr, Nahraz *see* Little Zab
123 *P14* **Zabaykal'sk** Chitinskaya Oblast', S Russian Federation
Zāb-e Kūchek, Rūdkhāneh-ye *see* Little Zab
Zabeln *see* Sabile
Zabéré *see* Zabré
Zabern *see* Saverne
141 *N16* **Zabīd** W Yemen
141 *O16* **Zabīd, Wādī** *dry watercourse* SW Yemen
Žabinka *see* Zhabinka
Ząbkowice *see* Ząbkowice Śląskie
111 *G15* **Ząbkowice Śląskie** *var.* Ząbkowice, *Ger.* Frankenstein, Frankenstein in Schlesien. Dolnośląskie, SW Poland
110 *P10* **Zabłudów** Podlaskie, NE Poland
112 *D8* **Zabok** Krapina-Zagorje, N Croatia
143 *W9* **Zābol** *var.* Shahr-i-Zabul, Zabul; *prev.* Nasratabad. Sīstān va Balūchestān, E Iran
Zābol *see* Zābul
143 *W13* **Zāboli** Sīstān va Balūchestān, SE Iran
Zabolot'ye *see* Zabalatstsye
77 *Q13* **Zabré** *var.* Zabéré. S Burkina
111 *G17* **Zábřeh** *Ger.* Hohenstadt. Olomoucký Kraj, E Czech Republic
111 *J16* **Zabrze** *Ger.* Hindenburg, Hindenburg in Oberschlesien. Śląskie, S Poland
149 *O7* **Zābul** *Per.* Zābol. ◈ *province* SE Afghanistan
Zabul *see* Zābol
42 *E6* **Zacapa** Zacapa, E Guatemala
42 *A3* **Zacapa** *off.* Departamento de Zacapa. ◈ *department* E Guatemala
40 *M14* **Zacapú** Michoacán de Ocampo, SW Mexico
41 *V14* **Zacatal** Campeche, SE Mexico
40 *M11* **Zacatecas** Zacatecas, C Mexico
40 *L10* **Zacatecas** ◈ *state* C Mexico
42 *F8* **Zacatecoluca** La Paz, S El Salvador
41 *P15* **Zacatepec** Morelos, S Mexico
41 *Q13* **Zacatlán** Puebla, S Mexico
144 *F8* **Zachagansk** Zapadnyy Kazakhstan, NW Kazakhstan
115 *D20* **Zacháro** *var.* Zaharo, Zakháro. Dytikí Ellás, S Greece
22 *J8* **Zachary** Louisiana, S USA
117 *U6* **Zachepylivka** Kharkivs'ka Oblast', E Ukraine
Zachist'ye *see* Zachystsye
110 *E9* **Zachodnio-pomorskie** ◈ *province* NW Poland
119 *L14* **Zachystsye** *Rus.* Zachist'ye. Minskaya Voblasts', NW Belarus
40 *L13* **Zacoalco** *var.* Zacoalco de Torres. Jalisco, SW Mexico
Zacoalco de Torres *see* Zacoalco
41 *P13* **Zacualtipán** Hidalgo, C Mexico
112 *C12* **Zadar** *It.* Zara; *anc.* Iader. Zadar, W Croatia
112 *C12* **Zadar** *off.* Zadarsko-Kninska Županija *prev.* Zadar-Knin. ◈ *province* SW Croatia
Zadar-Knin *see* Zadar
166 *M14* **Zadetkyi Kyun** *var.* St. Matthew's Island. *island* Mergui Archipelago, S Myanmar
67 *Q9* **Zadié** *var.* Djadié. ≈ NE Gabon
159 *Q13* **Zadoi** *var.* Qapugtang. Qinghai, C China
126 *L7* **Zadonsk** Lipetskaya Oblast', W Russian Federation
75 *X8* **Za'farâna** E Egypt
149 *W7* **Zafarwāl** Punjab, E Pakistan
121 *Q1* **Zafer Burnu** *var.* Cape Andreas, Cape Apostolas Andreas, *Gk.* Akrotíri Apostólou Andréa. *headland* NE Cyprus
107 *J23* **Zafferano, Capo** *headland* Sicilia, Italy, C Mediterranean Sea
114 *M7* **Zafirovo** Silistra, NE Bulgaria
115 *L23* **Zaforá** *island* Kykládes, Greece, Aegean Sea
104 *J12* **Zafra** Extremadura, W Spain
110 *E13* **Żagań** *var.* Zagań, Żegań, *Ger.* Sagan. Lubuskie, W Poland
118 *F10* **Žagarė** *Pol.* Żagory. Šiauliai, N Lithuania
75 *W7* **Zagazig** *var.* Az Zaqāzīq. N Egypt
74 *M5* **Zaghouan** *var.* Zaghwān. NE Tunisia
Zaghwān *see* Zaghouan
115 *G16* **Zagorá** Thessalía, C Greece
Zagorod'ye *see* Zaharoddzye
Żagory *see* Žagarė
Zágráb *see* Zagreb
112 *E8* **Zagreb** *Ger.* Agram, *Hung.* Zágráb. ● (Croatia) Zagreb, N Croatia
112 *E8* **Zagreb** *prev.* Grad Zagreb. ◈ *province* NC Croatia
142 *L7* **Zāgros, Kūhhā-ye** *Eng.* Zagros Mountains. ▲▲ W Iran
Zagros Mountains *see* Zāgros, Kūhhā-ye
112 *O12* **Žagubica** Serbia, E Serbia and Montenegro (Yugo.)
Zagunao *see* Lixian
111 *L22* **Zagyva** ≈ N Hungary
Zaharo *see* Zacháro
119 *G19* **Zaharoddzye** *Rus.* Zagorod'ye. *physical region* SW Belarus
143 *W11* **Zāhedān** *var.* Zahidan; *prev.* Duzdab. Sīstān va Balūchestān, SE Iran
Zahidan *see* Zāhedān
Zaḩlah *see* Zahlé
138 *H7* **Zahlé** *var.* Zaḩlah. C Lebanon
146 *J14* **Zähmet** *Rus.* Zakhmet. Mary Welaýaty, C Turkmenistan
111 *O20* **Záhony** Szabolcs-Szatmár-Bereg, NE Hungary
141 *N13* **Ẓahrān** 'Asīr, S Saudi Arabia
139 *R12* **Ẓahrat al Baṭn** *hill range* S Iraq
120 *H11* **Zahrez Chergui** *var.* Zahrez Chergüi. *marsh* N Algeria
Zainlha *see* Xinjin
127 *S4* **Zainsk** Respublika Tatarstan, W Russian Federation
82 *A10* **Zaire** *prev.* Congo. ◈ *province* NW Angola
Zaire *see* Congo (Democratic Republic of)
Zaire *see* Congo (river)
112 *P13* **Zaječar** Serbia, E Serbia and Montenegro (Yugo.)
83 *L18* **Zaka** Masvingo, E Zimbabwe
122 *M14* **Zakamensk** Respublika Buryatiya, S Russian Federation
116 *G7* **Zakarpats'ka Oblast'** *Eng.* Transcarpathian Oblast, *Rus.* Zakarpatskaya Oblast'. ◈ *province* W Ukraine
Zakarpatskaya Oblast' *see* Zakarpats'ka Oblast'
Zakataly *see* Zaqatala
Zakháro *see* Zacháro
Zakhidnyy Buh/Zakhodni Buh *see* Bug
Zakhmet *see* Zähmet
139 *Q1* **Zākhō** *var.* Zākhū. N Iraq
Zākhū *see* Zākhō
Zákinthos *see* Zákynthos
111 *L18* **Zakopane** Małopolskie, S Poland
78 *J12* **Zakouma** Salamat, S Chad
115 *L25* **Zákros** Kríti, Greece, E Mediterranean Sea
115 *C19* **Zákynthos** *var.* Zákinthos. Zákynthos, W Greece
115 *C20* **Zákynthos** *var.* Zákinthos, *It.* Zante. *island* Iónioi Nísoi, Greece, C Mediterranean Sea
115 *C19* **Zakýnthou, Porthmós** *strait* SW Greece
111 *G24* **Zala** *off.* Zala Megye. ◈ *county* W Hungary
111 *G24* **Zala** ≈ W Hungary
138 *M4* **Zalābiyah** Dayr az Zawr, C Syria
111 *G24* **Zalaegerszeg** Zala, W Hungary
104 *K11* **Zalamea de la Serena** Extremadura, W Spain
104 *J13* **Zalamea la Real** Andalucía, S Spain
163 *U7* **Zalantun** *var.* Butha Qi. Nei Mongol Zizhiqu, N China
111 *G23* **Zalaszentgrót** Zala, SW Hungary
Zalatna *see* Zlatna
116 *G9* **Zalău** *Ger.* Waltenberg, *Hung.* Zilah; *prev. Ger.* Zillenmarkt. Sălaj, NW Romania
109 *V10* **Žalec** *Ger.* Sachsenfeld. C Slovenia
117 *S9* **Zalenodol's'k** Dnipropetrovs'ka Oblast', E Ukraine
110 *K8* **Zalewo** *Ger.* Saalfeld. Warmińsko-Mazurskie, NE Poland
141 *N9* **Ẓalim** Makkah, W Saudi Arabia
80 *A11* **Zalingei** *var.* Zalinje. Western Darfur, W Sudan
Zalinje *see* Zalingei
116 *K7* **Zalishchyky** Ternopil's'ka Oblast', W Ukraine
Zallah *see* Zillah
98 *J13* **Zaltbommel** Gelderland, C Netherlands
124 *H15* **Zaluch'ye** Novgorodskaya Oblast', NW Russian Federation
Zamak *see* Zamakh
141 *Q14* **Zamakh** *var.* Zamak. N Yemen
136 *K15* **Zamantı Irmağı** ≈ C Turkey
Zambesi/Zambeze *see* Zambezi
83 *G14* **Zambezi** North Western, W Zambia
83 *K15* **Zambezi** *var.* Zambesi, *Port.* Zambeze. ≈ S Africa
83 *O15* **Zambézia** *off.* Província da Zambézia. ◈ *province* C Mozambique
83 *I14* **Zambia** *off.* Republic of Zambia; *prev.* Northern Rhodesia. ◆ *republic* S Africa
171 *O8* **Zamboanga** *off.* Zamboanga City. Mindanao, S Philippines
54 *E5* **Zambrano** Bolívar, N Colombia
110 *N10* **Zambrów** Łomża, E Poland
83 *L14* **Zambué** Tete, NW Mozambique
77 *T13* **Zamfara** ≈ NW Nigeria
Zamkog *see* Zamtang
56 *C9* **Zamora** Zamora Chinchipe, S Ecuador
104 *K6* **Zamora** Castilla-León, NW Spain
104 *K5* **Zamora** ◈ *province* Castilla-León, NW Spain
Zamora *see* Barinas
56 *A13* **Zamora Chinchipe** ◈ *province* S Ecuador
40 *M13* **Zamora de Hidalgo** Michoacán de Ocampo, SW Mexico
111 *P15* **Zamość** *Rus.* Zamoste. Lubelskie, E Poland
Zamoste *see* Zamość
160 *G7* **Zamtang** *var.* Zarkog; *prev.* Gamba. Sichuan, C China
75 *O8* **Zamzam, Wādī** *dry watercourse* NW Libya
79 *F20* **Zanaga** La Lékoumou, S Congo
41 *T16* **Zanatepec** Oaxaca, SE Mexico
105 *P9* **Záncara** ≈ C Spain
Zancle *see* Messina
158 *G14* **Zanda** Xizang Zizhiqu, W China
98 *H10* **Zandvoort** Noord-Holland, W Netherlands
39 *P8* **Zane Hills** *hill range* Alaska, USA
31 *T13* **Zanesville** Ohio, N USA
Zanga *see* Hrazdan
142 *L4* **Zanjān** *var.* Zenjan, Zinjan. Zanjān, NW Iran
142 *L4* **Zanjān** *off.* Ostān-e Zanjān, *var.* Zenjan, Zinjan. ◈ *province* NW Iran
Zante *see* Zákynthos
81 *J22* **Zanzibar** Zanzibar, E Tanzania
81 *J22* **Zanzibar** ◈ *region* E Tanzania
81 *J22* **Zanzibar** *Swa.* Unguja. *island* E Tanzania
81 *J22* **Zanzibar Channel** *channel* E Tanzania
165 *P10* **Zaō-san** ▲ Honshū, C Japan
161 *N8* **Zaoyang** Hubei, C China
124 *J2* **Zaozërsk** Murmanskaya Oblast', NW Russian Federation
161 *Q6* **Zaozhuang** Shandong, E China
28 *L4* **Zap** North Dakota, N USA
112 *L13* **Zapadna Morava** *Ger.* Westliche Morava. ≈ C Serbia and Montenegro (Yugo.)
124 *H16* **Zapadnaya Dvina** Tverskaya Oblast', W Russian Federation
Zapadnaya Dvina *see* Western Dvina
122 *I9* **Zapadno-Sibirskaya Ravnina** *Eng.* West Siberian Plain. *plain* C Russian Federation
Zapadnyy Bug *see* Bug
144 *E9* **Zapadnyy Kazakhstan** *off.* Zapadno-Kazakhstanskaya Oblast', *Eng.* West Kazakhstan, *Kaz.* Batys Qazaqstan Oblysy; *prev.* Ural'skaya Oblast'. ◈ *province* NW Kazakhstan
122 *K13* **Zapadnyy Sayan** *Eng.* Western Sayans. ▲▲ S Russian Federation
63 *H15* **Zapala** Neuquén, W Argentina
62 *I4* **Zapaleri, Cerro** *var.* Cerro Sapaleri. ▲ N Chile
25 *Q16* **Zapata** Texas, SW USA
44 *D5* **Zapata, Península de** *peninsula* W Cuba
61 *G19* **Zapicán** Lavalleja, S Uruguay
65 *J19* **Zapiola Ridge** *undersea feature* SW Atlantic Ocean
65 *L19* **Zapiola Seamount** *undersea feature* S Atlantic Ocean
124 *I2* **Zapolyarnyy** Murmanskaya Oblast', NW Russian Federation
117 *U8* **Zaporizhzhya** *Rus.* Zaporozh'ye; *prev.* Aleksandrovsk. Zaporiz'ka Oblast', SE Ukraine
Zaporizhzhya *see* Zaporiz'ka Oblast'
117 *U9* **Zaporiz'ka Oblast'** *var.* Zaporizhzhya, *Rus.* Zaporozhskaya Oblast'. ◈ *province* SE Ukraine
Zaporozhskaya Oblast' *see* Zaporiz'ka Oblast'
Zaporozh'ye *see* Zaporizhzhya
40 *L14* **Zapotiltic** Jalisco, SW Mexico
158 *G13* **Zapug** Xizang Zizhiqu, W China
137 *V10* **Zaqatala** *Rus.* Zakataly. NW Azerbaijan
159 *P13* **Zaqên** Qinghai, W China
159 *Q13* **Za Qu** ≈ C China
136 *M13* **Zara** Sivas, C Turkey
Zara *see* Zadar
Zarafshan *see* Zarafshon
147 *P12* **Zarafshon** *Rus.* Zeravshan. W Tajikistan
146 *L9* **Zarafshon** *Rus.* Zarafshan. Navoiy Viloyati, N Uzbekistan
Zarafshon *see* Zeravshan
147 *O12* **Zarafshon, Qatorkŭhi** *Rus.* Zeravshanskiy Khrebet, *Uzb.* Zarafshon Tizmasi. ▲▲ Tajikistan/Uzbekistan
Zarafshon Tizmasi *see* Zarafshon, Qatorkŭhi
54 *E7* **Zaragoza** Antioquia, N Colombia
40 *I5* **Zaragoza** Chihuahua, N Mexico
41 *N6* **Zaragoza** Coahuila de Zaragoza, NE Mexico
41 *O10* **Zaragoza** Nuevo León, NE Mexico
105 *R5* **Zaragoza** *Eng.* Saragossa; *anc.* Caesaraugusta, Salduba. Aragón, NE Spain
105 *R6* **Zaragoza** ◈ *province* Aragón, NE Spain
105 *R5* **Zaragoza** ✕ Aragón, NE Spain
143 *S10* **Zarand** Kermān, C Iran
148 *J9* **Zaranj** Nīmrūz, SW Afghanistan
118 *I11* **Zarasai** Utena, E Lithuania
62 *N12* **Zárate** *prev.* General José F.Uriburu. Buenos Aires, E Argentina
105 *Q2* **Zarautz** *var.* Zarauz. País Vasco, N Spain
Zarauz *see* Zarautz
Zaravecchia *see* Biograd na Moru
Zarāyīn *see* Zarēn
126 *L4* **Zaraysk** Moskovskaya Oblast', W Russian Federation
55 *N6* **Zaraza** Guárico, N Venezuela
Zarbdar *see* Zarbdor
147 *P11* **Zarbdor** *Rus.* Zarbdar. Jizzax Viloyati, C Uzbekistan
142 *M8* **Zard Kūh** ▲ SW Iran
124 *I5* **Zarechensk** Murmanskaya Oblast', NW Russian Federation
127 *P6* **Zarechnyy** Penzenskaya Oblast', W Russian Federation
149 *Q7* **Zareh Sharan** Paktīkā, E Afghanistan
39 *Y14* **Zarembo Island** *island* Alexander Archipelago, Alaska, USA
139 *V4* **Zarēn** *var.* Zarāyīn. E Iraq
149 *Q7* **Zarghūn Shahr** *var.* Katawaz. Paktīkā, SE Afghanistan
77 *V13* **Zaria** Kaduna, C Nigeria
116 *K2* **Zarichne** Rivnens'ka Oblast', NW Ukraine
122 *J13* **Zarinsk** Altayskiy Kray, S Russian Federation
116 *J12* **Zărneşti** *Hung.* Zernest. Braşov, C Romania
115 *J25* **Zarós** Kríti, Greece, E Mediterranean Sea
100 *O9* **Zarow** ≈ NE Germany
Zarqa/Zarqā', Muḩāfaẓat az *see* Az Zarqā'
120 *G10* **Záruby** ▲ W Slovakia
56 *B8* **Zaruma** El Oro, SW Ecuador
110 *E13* **Żary** *Ger.* Sorau, Sorau in der Niederlausitz. Lubuskie, W Poland
54 *D10* **Zarzal** Valle del Cauca, W Colombia
42 *I7* **Zarzalar, Cerro** ▲ S Honduras
152 *I5* **Zāskār** ≈ NE India
152 *I5* **Zāskār Range** ▲▲ NE India
119 *K15* **Zaslawye** Minskaya Voblasts', C Belarus
116 *K7* **Zastavna** Chernivets'ka Oblast', W Ukraine
111 *B16* **Žatec** *Ger.* Saaz. Ústecký Kraj, NW Czech Republic
Zaumgarten *see* Chrzanów
Zaunguzskiye Garagumy *see* Üngüz Angyrsyndaky Garagum
25 *X9* **Zavalla** Texas, SW USA
99 *H18* **Zaventem** Vlaams Brabant, C Belgium
99 *H18* **Zaventem** ✕ (Brussel/Bruxelles) Vlaams Brabant, C Belgium
Zavertse *see* Zawiercie
114 *L7* **Zavet** Razgrad, NE Bulgaria
127 *O12* **Zavetnoye** Rostovskaya Oblast', SW Russian Federation
156 *M3* **Zavhan Gol** ≈ W Mongolia
112 *H12* **Zavidovići** Federacija Bosna I Hercegovina, N Bosnia and Herzegovina
123 *R13* **Zavitinsk** Amurskaya Oblast', SE Russian Federation
Zawia *see* Az Zāwiyah
111 *K15* **Zawiercie** *Rus.* Zavertse. Śląskie, S Poland
75 *P11* **Zawīlah** *var.* Zuwaylah, *It.* Zueila. C Libya
138 *I4* **Zāwīyah, Jabal az** ▲ NW Syria
109 *Y3* **Zaya** ≈ NE Austria
166 *M8* **Zayatkyi** Pegu, C Myanmar
145 *Y11* **Zaysan** Vostochnyy Kazakhstan, E Kazakhstan
Zaysan Köl *see* Zaysan, Ozero
145 *Y11* **Zaysan, Ozero** *Kaz.* Zaysan Köl. ◎ E Kazakhstan
159 *R16* **Zayü** *var.* Gyigang. Xizang Zizhiqu, W China
Zayyq *see* Ural
44 *F6* **Zaza** ≈ C Cuba
116 *K5* **Zbarazh** Ternopil's'ka Oblast', W Ukraine
116 *J5* **Zboriv** Ternopil's'ka Oblast', W Ukraine
111 *F18* **Zbraslav** Jihomoravský Kraj, SE Czech Republic
116 *K6* **Zbruch** ≈ W Ukraine
Žďár *see* Žďár nad Sázavou
111 *F17* **Žďár nad Sázavou** *Ger.* Saar in Mähren; *prev.* Žďár. Vysočina, C Czech Republic
116 *K4* **Zdolbuniv** *Pol.* Zdołbunów, *Rus.* Zdolbunov. Rivnens'ka Oblast', NW Ukraine
Zdolbunov/Zdołbunów *see* Zdolbuniv
110 *J13* **Zduńska Wola** Sieradz, C Poland
117 *O4* **Zdvizh** ≈ N Ukraine
Zdzięciół *see* Dzyatlava
111 *I16* **Zdzieszowice** *Ger.* Odertal. Opolskie, S Poland
Zealand *see* Sjælland
188 *K6* **Zealandia Bank** *undersea feature* C Pacific Ocean
63 *H20* **Zeballos, Monte** ▲ S Argentina
83 *K20* **Zebediela** Limpopo, NE South Africa
113 *L18* **Zebë, Mal** *var.* Mali i Zebës. ▲ NE Albania
Zebës, Mali i *see* Zebë, Mal
21 *V9* **Zebulon** North Carolina, SE USA
112 *K8* **Žednik** *Hung.* Bácsjózseffalva. Serbia, N Serbia and Montenegro (Yugo.)
99 *C15* **Zeebrugge** West-Vlaanderen, NW Belgium
183 *N16* **Zeehan** Tasmania, SE Australia
99 *L14* **Zeeland** Noord-Brabant, SE Netherlands
29 *N7* **Zeeland** North Dakota, N USA
99 *E14* **Zeeland** ◈ *province* SW Netherlands
83 *I21* **Zeerust** North-West, N South Africa
98 *K10* **Zeewolde** Flevoland, C Netherlands
138 *G8* **Ẕefat** *var.* Safed, Tsefat, *Ar.* Safad. Northern, N Israel
Żegań *see* Żagań
Zehden *see* Cedynia
100 *O11* **Zehdenick** Brandenburg, NE Germany
Zē-i Bādīnān *see* Great Zab
Zeiden *see* Codlea
146 *M14* **Zeidskoye Vodokhranilishche** ▣ E Turkmenistan
Zē-i Kōya *see* Little Zab
181 *P7* **Zeil, Mount** ▲ Northern Territory, C Australia
98 *J12* **Zeist** Utrecht, C Netherlands
101 *M16* **Zeitz** Sachsen-Anhalt, E Germany
159 *T11* **Zêkog** *var.* Sonag. Qinghai, C China
Zelaya Norte *see* Atlántico Norte, Región Autónoma
Zelaya Sur *see* Atlántico Sur, Región Autónoma
99 *F17* **Zele** Oost-Vlaanderen, NW Belgium
110 *N12* **Żelechów** Lubelskie, E Poland
113 *H14* **Zelena Glava** ▲ SE Bosnia and Herzegovina
113 *I14* **Zelengora** ▲▲ S Bosnia and Herzegovina
124 *I5* **Zelenoborskiy** Murmanskaya Oblast', NW Russian Federation
127 *R3* **Zelenodol'sk** Respublika Tatarstan, W Russian Federation
122 *L12* **Zelenogorsk** Krasnoyarskiy Kray, C Russian Federation
124 *G12* **Zelenogorsk** *Fin.* Terijoki. Leningradskaya Oblast', NW Russian Federation
126 *K3* **Zelenograd** Moskovskaya Oblast', W Russian Federation
118 *B13* **Zelenogradsk** *Ger.* Cranz, Kranz. Kaliningradskaya Oblast', W Russian Federation
127 *O15* **Zelenokumsk** Stavropol'skiy Kray, SW Russian Federation
165 *X4* **Zelënyy, Ostrov** *var.* Shibotsu-jima. *island* NE Russian Federation
Železna Kapela *see* Eisenkappel
Železna Vrata *see* Demir Kapija
112 *L11* **Železniki** Serbia, N Serbia and Montenegro (Yugo.)
98 *N12* **Zelhem** Gelderland, E Netherlands
113 *N18* **Želino** NW FYR Macedonia
113 *M14* **Željin** ▲ C Serbia and Montenegro (Yugo.)
101 *K17* **Zella-Mehlis** Thüringen, C Germany
109 *P7* **Zell am See** *var.* Zell-am-See. Salzburg, S Austria
109 *N7* **Zell am Ziller** Tirol, W Austria
Zelle *see* Celle
109 *W2* **Zellerndorf** Niederösterreich, NE Austria
109 *U7* **Zeltweg** Steiermark, S Austria
119 *G17* **Zel'va** *Pol.* Zelwa. Hrodzyenskaya Voblasts', W Belarus
118 *H13* **Želva** Vilnius, C Lithuania
Zelwa *see* Zel'va
99 *E16* **Zelzate** *var.* Selzaete. Oost-Vlaanderen, NW Belgium
118 *E11* **Žemaičių Aukštumas** *physical region* W Lithuania
118 *C12* **Žemaičių Naumiestis** Klaipėda, SW Lithuania
Zembin *see* Zyembin
127 *N6* **Zemetchino** Penzenskaya Oblast', W Russian Federation
79 *M15* **Zémio** Haut-Mbomou, E Central African Republic
41 *R16* **Zempoaltepec, Cerro** ▲ SE Mexico
99 *G17* **Zemst** Vlaams Brabant, C Belgium
112 *L11* **Zemun** Serbia, N Serbia and Montenegro (Yugo.)
Zendajan *see* Zendeh Jan
148 *J5* **Zendeh Jan** *var.* Zendajan, Zindajān. Herāt, NW Afghanistan
Zengg *see* Senj
112 *H12* **Zenica** Federacija Bosna I Hercegovina, C Bosnia and Herzegovina
Zenjan *see* Zanjān
Zen'kov *see* Zin'kiv
Zenshū *see* Chŏnju
Zenta *see* Senta
Zentûzi *see* Zentsūji
82 *B11* **Zenza do Itombe** Cuanza Norte, NW Angola
112 *H12* **Žepče** Federacija Bosna I Hercegovina, N Bosnia and Herzegovina

◆ Country ● Country Capital ◇ Dependent Territory ○ Dependent Territory Capital ◈ Administrative Region ✕ International Airport ▲ Mountain ▲▲ Mountain Range Volcano ≈ River ◎ Lake ▣ Reservoir

23 W12 **Zephyrhills** Florida, SE USA
192 L9 **Zephyr Reef** *reef* Pacific Ocean
158 F9 **Zepu** *var.* Poskam. Xinjiang Uygur Zizhiqu, NW China
147 Q12 **Zeravshan** *Taj./Uzb.* Zarafshon. ⁓ Tajikistan/Uzbekistan
Zeravshan *see* Zarafshon
Zeravshanskiy Khrebet *see* Zarafshon, Qatorkŭhi
101 M14 **Zerbst** Sachsen-Anhalt, E Germany
145 P8 **Zerenda** Akmola, N Kazakhstan
110 H12 **Żerków** Wielkopolskie, C Poland
108 E11 **Zermatt** Valais, SW Switzerland
Zernest *see* Zărnești
108 J9 **Zernez** Graubünden, SE Switzerland
126 L12 **Zernograd** Rostovskaya Oblast', SW Russian Federation
Zestafoni *see* Zestap'oni
137 S9 **Zestap'oni** *Rus.* Zestafoni. C Georgia
98 H12 **Zestienhoven** ✕ (Rotterdam) Zuid-Holland, SW Netherlands
113 J16 **Zeta** ⁓ SW Serbia and Montenegro (Yugo.)
8 L6 **Zeta Lake** ◎ Victoria Island, Nunavut, N Canada
98 L12 **Zetten** Gelderland, SE Netherlands
101 M17 **Zeulenroda** Thüringen, C Germany
100 H10 **Zeven** Niedersachsen, NW Germany
98 M12 **Zevenaar** Gelderland, SE Netherlands
99 H14 **Zevenbergen** Noord-Brabant, S Netherlands
131 X6 **Zeya** ⁓ SE Russian Federation
Zeya Reservoir *see* Zeyskoye Vodokhranilishche
143 T11 **Zeynalābād** Kermān, C Iran
123 R12 **Zeyskoye Vodokhranilishche** *Eng.* Zeya Reservoir. ▣ SE Russian Federation
104 H8 **Zêzere, Rio** ⁓ C Portugal
Zgerzh *see* Zgierz
138 H6 **Zgharta** N Lebanon
110 K12 **Zgierz** *Ger.* Neuhof, *Rus.* Zgerzh. Łódź, C Poland
111 E14 **Zgorzelec** *Ger.* Görlitz. Dolnośląskie, SW Poland
158 J15 **Zhabdün** Xizang Zizhiqu, W China
119 F19 **Zhabinka** *Pol.* Żabinka, *Rus.* Zhabinka. Brestskaya Voblasts', SW Belarus
Zhaggo *see* Luhuo
159 R15 **Zhag'yab** *var.* Yêndum. Xizang Zizhiqu, W China
144 L9 **Zhailma** *Kaz.* Zhayylma. Kostanay, N Kazakhstan
145 V16 **Zhalanash** Almaty, SE Kazakhstan
Zhalashash *see* Dzhalagash
145 S7 **Zhalauly, Ozero** ◎ NE Kazakhstan
144 E9 **Zhalpaktal** *prev.* Furmanovo. Zapadnyy Kazakhstan, W Kazakhstan
119 G16 **Zhaludok** *Rus.* Zheludok. Hrodzyenskaya Voblasts', W Belarus
Zhaman-Akkol', Ozero *see* Akkol', Ozero
Zhambyl *see* Taraz
145 Q14 **Zhambyl** *off.* Zhambylskaya Oblast', *Kaz.* Zhambyl Oblysy; *prev.* Dzhambulskaya Oblast'. ◆ *province* S Kazakhstan
Zhambyl Oblysy/Zhambylskaya Oblast' *see* Zhambyl
Zhamo *see* Bomi
145 S12 **Zhamshy** ⁓ C Kazakhstan
144 M15 **Zhanadar'ya** Kzylorda, S Kazakhstan
145 O15 **Zhanakorgan** *Kaz.* Zhangaqorghan. Kzylorda, S Kazakhstan
159 N16 **Zhanang** *var.* Chatang. Xizang Zizhiqu, W China
145 T12 **Zhanaortalyk** Karaganda, C Kazakhstan
144 F15 **Zhanaozen** *Kaz.* Zhangaözen, *prev.* Novyy Uzen'. Mangistau, W Kazakhstan
145 Q16 **Zhanatas** Zhambyl, S Kazakhstan
Zhangaözen *see* Zhanaozen
Zhangaqazaly *see* Ayteke Bi
Zhangaqorghan *see* Zhanakorgan
161 O2 **Zhangbei** Hebei, E China
Zhangdian *see* Zibo
Zhanggu *see* Danba
163 X9 **Zhangguangcai Ling** ▲ NE China
145 W10 **Zhangiztobe** Vostochnyy Kazakhstan, E Kazakhstan
159 W11 **Zhangjiachuan** Gansu, N China
160 L10 **Zhangjiajie** *var.* Dayong. Hunan, S China
161 O2 **Zhangjiakou** *var.* Changkiakow, Zhang-chia-k'ou, *Eng.* Kalgan; *prev.* Wanchuan. Hebei, E China
161 Q13 **Zhangping** Fujian, SE China
161 Q13 **Zhangpu** *var.* Sui'an. Fujian, SE China
163 U11 **Zhangwu** Liaoning, NE China
159 S8 **Zhangye** *var.* Ganzhou. Gansu, N China
161 Q13 **Zhangzhou** Fujian, SE China
163 W6 **Zhan He** ⁓ NE China
Zhanibek/Zhänibek *see* Dzhanibek
160 L16 **Zhanjiang** *var.* Chanchiang, Chan-chiang, *Cant.* Tsamkong, *Fr.* Fort-Bayard. Guangdong, S China
Zhansügirov *see* Dzhansugurov
163 V8 **Zhaodong** Heilongjiang, NE China
Zhaoge *see* Qixian
160 H11 **Zhaojue** *var.* Xincheng. Sichuan, C China
161 N14 **Zhaoqing** Guangdong, S China
Zhaoren *see* Changwu
158 H5 **Zhaosu** *var.* Mongolküre. Xinjiang Uygur Zizhiqu, NW China
160 H11 **Zhaotong** Yunnan, SW China
163 V9 **Zhaoyuan** Heilongjiang, NE China
163 V9 **Zhaozhou** Heilongjiang, NE China
145 X13 **Zharbulak** Vostochnyy Kazakhstan, E Kazakhstan
158 J15 **Zhari Namco** ◎ W China
144 I12 **Zharkamys** *Kaz.* Zharqamys. Aktyubinsk, W Kazakhstan
145 W15 **Zharkent** *prev.* Panfilov. Almaty, SE Kazakhstan
124 H17 **Zharkovskiy** Tverskaya Oblast', W Russian Federation
145 W11 **Zharma** Vostochnyy Kazakhstan, E Kazakhstan
144 F14 **Zharmysh** Mangistau, SW Kazakhstan
Zharqamys *see* Zharkamys
118 L13 **Zhary** *Rus.* Zhary. Vitsyebskaya Voblasts', N Belarus
Zhaslyk *see* Jasliq
158 J14 **Zhaxi Co** ◎ W China
Zhayylma *see* Zhailma
Zhdanov *see* Beyläqan, Azerbaijan
Zhdanov *see* Mariupol', Ukraine
Zhe *see* Zhejiang
161 R10 **Zhejiang** *var.* Che-chiang, Chekiang, Zhe, Zhejiang Sheng. ◆ *province* SE China
Zhejiang Sheng *see* Zhejiang
145 S7 **Zhelezinka** Pavlodar, N Kazakhstan
119 C14 **Zheleznodorozhnyy** *Ger.* Gerdauen. Kaliningradskaya Oblast', W Russian Federation
Zheleznodorozhnyy *see* Yemva
122 K12 **Zheleznogorsk** Krasnoyarskiy Kray, C Russian Federation
126 J7 **Zheleznogorsk** Kurskaya Oblast', W Russian Federation
127 N15 **Zheleznovodsk** Stavropol'skiy Kray, SW Russian Federation
Zhëltyye Vody *see* Zhovti Vody
Zheludok *see* Zhaludok
Zhem *see* Emba
160 K7 **Zhenba** Shaanxi, C China
160 I13 **Zhenfeng** Guizhou, S China
Zhengjiatun *see* Shuangliao
159 X10 **Zhengning** Gansu, N China
Zhengxiangbai Qi *see* Qagan Nur
161 N6 **Zhengzhou** *var.* Ch'eng-chou, Chengchow; *prev.* Chenghsien. Henan, C China
161 R8 **Zhenjiang** *var.* Chenkiang. Jiangsu, E China
163 U9 **Zhenlai** Jilin, NE China
160 I11 **Zhenxiong** Yunnan, SW China
160 K11 **Zhenyuan** *var.* Wuyang. Guizhou, S China
161 R11 **Zherong** *var.* Shuangcheng. Fujian, SE China
145 U15 **Zhetigen** *prev.* Nikolayevka Almaty, SE Kazakhstan
Zhetiqara *see* Zhitikara
144 F15 **Zhetybay** Mangistau, SW Kazakhstan
145 P17 **Zhetysay** *var.* Dzhetysay. Yuzhnyy Kazakhstan
160 M11 **Zhexi Shuiku** ▣ C China
145 Q12 **Zhezdy** Karaganda, C Kazakhstan
145 O12 **Zhezkazgan** *Kaz.* Zhezqazghan; *prev.* Dzhezkazgan. Karaganda, C Kazakhstan
Zhezqazghan *see* Zhezkazgan
Zhicheng *see* Yidu
Zhidachov *see* Zhydachiv
159 Q12 **Zhidoi** *var.* Gyaijêpozhanggê. Qinghai, C China
122 M13 **Zhigalovo** Irkutskaya Oblast', S Russian Federation
127 R6 **Zhigulevsk** Samarskaya Oblast', W Russian Federation
118 D13 **Zhilino** *Ger.* Schillen. Kaliningradskaya Oblast', W Russian Federation
Zhiloy, Ostrov *see* Çiloy Adası
127 O8 **Zhirnovsk** Volgogradskaya Oblast', SW Russian Federation
Zhitarovo *see* Vetren
144 L8 **Zhitikara** *Kaz.* Zhetiqara. *prev.* Dzhetygara, NW Kazakhstan
Zhitkovichi *see* Zhytkavichy
127 P10 **Zhitkur** Volgogradskaya Oblast', SW Russian Federation
Zhitomir *see* Zhytomyr
Zhitomirskaya Oblast' *see* Zhytomyrs'ka Oblast'
126 J5 **Zhizdra** Kaluzhskaya Oblast', W Russian Federation
119 N18 **Zhlobin** Homyel'skaya Voblasts', SE Belarus
Zhmerinka *see* Zhmerynka
115 M7 **Zhmerynka** *Rus.* Zhmerinka. Vinnyts'ka Oblast', C Ukraine
149 R9 **Zhob** *var.* Fort Sandeman. Baluchistān, SW Pakistan
149 F8 **Zhob** ⁓ C Pakistan
Zhodino *see* Zhodzina
119 L15 **Zhodzina** *Rus.* Zhodino. Minskaya Voblasts', C Belarus
123 Q5 **Zhokhova, Ostrov** *island* Novosibirskiye Ostrova, NE Russian Federation
Zholkev/Zholkva *see* Zhovkva
Zholsaly *see* Dzhusaly
Zhondor *see* Jondor
158 L15 **Zhongba** *var.* Tuoji. Xizang Zizhiqu, W China
160 F11 **Zhongdian** Yunnan, SW China
Zhongduo *see* Youyang
Zhonghe *see* Xiushan
Zhonghua Renmin Gongheguo *see* China
159 V9 **Zhongning** Ningxia, N China
Zhongping *see* Huize
161 N15 **Zhongshan** Guangdong, S China
195 X7 **Zhongshan** *Chinese research station* Antarctica
160 M6 **Zhongtiao Shan** ▲ C China
159 V9 **Zhongwei** Ningxia, N China
160 K9 **Zhongxian** *var.* Zhong Xian, Zhongzhou. Chongqing Shi, C China
161 N9 **Zhongxiang** Hubei, C China
Zhongzhou *see* Zhongxian
161 O7 **Zhoukou** *var.* Zhoukouzhen. Henan, C China
Zhoukouzhen *see* Zhoukou
161 S9 **Zhoushan** Zhejiang, S China
161 S9 **Zhoushan Qundao** *Eng.* Zhoushan Islands. *island group* SE China
116 I5 **Zhovkva** *Pol.* Żółkiew, *Rus.* Zholkev, Zholkva; *prev.* Nesterov. L'vivs'ka Oblast', NW Ukraine
117 S7 **Zhovti Vody** *Rus.* Zhëltyye Vody. Dnipropetrovs'ka Oblast', E Ukraine
117 Q10 **Zhovtneve** *Rus.* Zhovtnevoye. Mykolayivs'ka Oblast', S Ukraine
Zhovtnevoye *see* Zhovtneve
114 K9 **Zhrebchevo, Yazovir** ▣ C Bulgaria
163 V13 **Zhuanghe** Liaoning, NE China
159 W11 **Zhuanglang** *var.* Shuiluocheng. Gansu, C China
145 P15 **Zhuantobe** *Kaz.* Zhūantöbe. Yuzhnyy Kazakhstan, S Kazakhstan
161 Q5 **Zhucheng** Shandong, E China
159 V12 **Zhugqu** Gansu, C China
161 N15 **Zhuhai** Guangdong, S China
Zhuizishan *see* Weichang
Zhuji *see* Shangqiu
126 I5 **Zhukovka** Bryanskaya Oblast', W Russian Federation
161 N7 **Zhumadian** Henan, C China
161 O3 **Zhuozhou** *prev.* Zhuo Xian. Hebei, E China
162 L14 **Zhuozi Shan** ▲ N China
Zhuravichi *see* Zhuravichy
119 O17 **Zhuravichy** *Rus.* Zhuravichi. Homyel'skaya Voblasts', SE Belarus
145 Q8 **Zhuravlevka** Akmola, N Kazakhstan
117 Q4 **Zhurivka** Kyyivs'ka Oblast', N Ukraine
144 J11 **Zhuryn** Aktyubinsk, W Kazakhstan
145 T15 **Zhusandala, Step'** *grassland* SE Kazakhstan
160 L8 **Zhushan** Hubei, C China
Zhushan *see* Xuan'en
Zhuyang *see* Dazhu
161 N11 **Zhuzhou** Hunan, S China
116 I6 **Zhydachiv** *Pol.* Żydaczów, *Rus.* Zhidachov. L'vivs'ka Oblast', NW Ukraine
144 G9 **Zhympity** *prev.* Dzhambeyty. Zapadnyy Kazakhstan, W Kazakhstan
119 K19 **Zhytkavichy** *Rus.* Zhitkovichi. Homyel'skaya Voblasts', SE Belarus
117 N4 **Zhytomyr** *Rus.* Zhitomir. Zhytomyrs'ka Oblast', NW Ukraine
Zhytomyr *see* Zhytomyrs'ka Oblast'
116 M4 **Zhytomyrs'ka Oblast'** *var.* Zhytomyr, *Rus.* Zhitomirskaya Oblast'. ◆ *province* N Ukraine
153 U15 **Zia** ✕ (Dhaka) Dhaka, C Bangladesh
111 J20 **Žiar nad Hronom** *var.* Svätý Kríž nad Hronom, *Ger.* Heiligenkreuz, *Hung.* Garamszentkereszt. Banskobystrický Kraj, C Slovakia
161 Q4 **Zibo** *var.* Zhangdian. Shandong, E China
160 L4 **Zichang** *prev.* Wayaobu. Shaanxi, C China
Zichenau *see* Ciechanów
111 G15 **Ziębice** *Ger.* Münsterberg in Schlesien. Dolnośląskie, SW Poland
Ziebingen *see* Cybinka
Ziegenhais *see* Głuchołazy
110 E12 **Zielona Góra** *Ger.* Grünberg, Grünberg in Schlesien, Grüneberg. Lubuskie, W Poland
99 F14 **Zierikzee** Zeeland, SW Netherlands
160 I10 **Zigong** *var.* Tzekung. Sichuan, C China
76 G12 **Ziguinchor** SW Senegal
41 N16 **Zihuatanejo** Guerrero, S Mexico
Ziketan *see* Xinghai
Zilah *see* Zalău
127 W7 **Zilair** Respublika Bashkortostan, W Russian Federation
136 L12 **Zile** Tokat, N Turkey
111 J18 **Žilina** *Ger.* Sillein, *Hung.* Zsolna. Žilinský Kraj, N Slovakia
111 J19 **Žilinský Kraj** ◆ *region* N Slovakia
75 Q9 **Zillah** *var.* Zallah. C Libya
Zillenmarkt *see* Zalău
109 N7 **Ziller** ⁓ W Austria
Zillertal Alps *see* Zillertaler Alpen
109 N8 **Zillertaler Alpen** *Eng.* Zillertal Alps, *It.* Alpi Aurine. ▲ Austria/Italy
118 K10 **Zilupe** *Ger.* Rosenhof. Ludza, E Latvia
41 O13 **Zimapán** Hidalgo, C Mexico
83 I16 **Zimba** Southern, S Zambia
83 J17 **Zimbabwe** *off.* Republic of Zimbabwe; *prev.* Rhodesia. ◆ *republic* S Africa
116 H10 **Zimbor** *Hung.* Magyarzsombor. Sălaj, NW Romania
Zimmerbude *see* Svetlyy
116 J15 **Zimnicea** Teleorman, S Romania
114 L9 **Zimnitsa** Yambol, E Bulgaria
127 N12 **Zimovniki** Rostovskaya Oblast', SW Russian Federation
Zindajān *see* Zendeh Jan
77 V12 **Zinder** Zinder, S Niger
77 W11 **Zinder** ◆ *department* S Niger
77 P12 **Ziniaré** C Burkina
Zinjan *see* Zanjān
141 P16 **Zinjibār** SW Yemen
117 T4 **Zin'kiv** *var.* Zen'kov. Poltavs'ka Oblast', NE Ukraine
Zinov'yevsk *see* Kirovohrad
Zintenhof *see* Sindi
31 N10 **Zion** Illinois, N USA
54 F10 **Zipaquirá** Cundinamarca, C Colombia
Zipser Neudorf *see* Spišská Nová Ves
111 H23 **Zirc** Veszprém, W Hungary
113 D14 **Žirje** *It.* Zuri. *island* S Croatia
Zirknitz *see* Cerknica
108 M7 **Zirl** Tirol, W Austria
101 K20 **Zirndorf** Bayern, SE Germany
160 M11 **Zi Shui** ⁓ C China
109 Y3 **Zistersdorf** Niederösterreich, NE Austria
41 O14 **Zitácuaro** Michoacán de Ocampo, SW Mexico
Zito *see* Lhorong
101 Q16 **Zittau** Sachsen, E Germany
112 I12 **Živinice** Federacija Bosna I Hercegovina, E Bosnia and Herzegovina
Ziwa Magharibi *see* Kagera
81 J14 **Ziway Hāyk'** ◎ C Ethiopia
161 N12 **Zixing** Hunan, S China
127 W7 **Ziyanchurino** Orenburgskaya Oblast', W Russian Federation
160 K8 **Ziyang** Shaanxi, C China
Zizhixian *see* Taxkorgan
111 I20 **Zlaté Moravce** *Hung.* Aranyosmarót. Nitriansky Kraj, SW Slovakia
112 K13 **Zlatibor** ▲ W Serbia and Montenegro (Yugo.)
114 L9 **Zlati Voyvoda** Sliven, E Bulgaria
116 G11 **Zlatna** *Ger.* Kleinschlatten, *Hung.* Zalatna; *prev. Ger.* Goldmarkt. Alba, C Romania
114 I8 **Zlatna Panega** Lovech, N Bulgaria
114 N8 **Zlatni Pyasŭtsi** Dobrich, NE Bulgaria
122 F11 **Zlatoust** Chelyabinskaya Oblast', C Russian Federation
111 M19 **Zlatý Stôl** *Ger.* Goldener Tisch, *Hung.* Aranyosasztal. ▲ C Slovakia
113 P18 **Zletovo** NE FYR Macedonia
111 H18 **Zlín** *prev.* Gottwaldov. Zlínský Kraj, SE Czech Republic
113 H19 **Zlínský Kraj** ◆ *region* E Czech Republic
75 O7 **Zlīṭan** W Libya
110 F9 **Złocieniec** *Ger.* Falkenburg in Pommern. Zachodnio-pomorskie, NW Poland
110 J13 **Złoczew** Sieradz, S Poland
Złoczów *see* Zolochiv
111 F14 **Złotoryja** *Ger.* Goldberg. Dolnośląskie, W Poland
110 G9 **Złotów** Wielkopolskie, NW Poland
110 G13 **Żmigród** *Ger.* Trachenberg. Dolnośląskie, SW Poland
126 J6 **Zmiyevka** Orlovskaya Oblast', W Russian Federation
117 V5 **Zmiyiv** Kharkivs'ka Oblast', E Ukraine
Zna *see* Tsna
Znaim *see* Znojmo
126 M7 **Znamenka** Tambovskaya Oblast', W Russian Federation
Znamenka *see* Znam"yanka
127 P11 **Znamensk** Astrakhanskaya Oblast', SW Russian Federation
119 C14 **Znamensk** *Ger.* Wehlau. Kaliningradskaya Oblast', W Russian Federation
117 R7 **Znam"yanka** *Rus.* Znamenka. Kirovohrads'ka Oblast', C Ukraine
110 H10 **Żnin** Kujawsko-pomorskie, C Poland
111 F19 **Znojmo** *Ger.* Znaim. Jihomoravský Kraj, S Czech Republic
79 N16 **Zobia** Orientale, N Dem. Rep. Congo
83 N15 **Zóbuè** Tete, NW Mozambique
98 G12 **Zoetermeer** Zuid-Holland, W Netherlands
108 E7 **Zofingen** Aargau, N Switzerland
159 R15 **Zogang** *var.* Wangda. Xizang Zizhiqu, W China
106 E7 **Zogno** Lombardia, N Italy
142 M10 **Zohreh, Rūd-e** ⁓ SW Iran
160 H7 **Zoigê** *var.* Dagcagoin. Sichuan, C China
Żółkiew *see* Zhovkva
108 D8 **Zollikofen** Bern, W Switzerland
Zolochev *see* Zolochiv
117 U4 **Zolochiv** *Rus.* Zolochev. Kharkivs'ka Oblast', E Ukraine
116 J5 **Zolochiv** *Pol.* Złoczów, *Rus.* Zolochev. L'vivs'ka Oblast', W Ukraine
117 X7 **Zolote** *Rus.* Zolotoye. Luhans'ka Oblast', E Ukraine
117 Q6 **Zolotonosha** Cherkas'ka Oblast', C Ukraine
Zolotoye *see* Zolote
Zólyom *see* Zvolen
83 N15 **Zomba** Southern, S Malawi
Zombor *see* Sombor
99 D17 **Zomergem** Oost-Vlaanderen, NW Belgium
147 P11 **Zomin** *Rus.* Zaamin. Jizzax Viloyati, C Uzbekistan
79 I15 **Zongo** Equateur, N Dem. Rep. Congo
136 G10 **Zonguldak** Zonguldak, NW Turkey
136 H10 **Zonguldak** ◆ *province* NW Turkey
99 K17 **Zonhoven** Limburg, NE Belgium
142 I2 **Zonūz** Āẕarbāyjān-e Khāvarī, NW Iran
103 Y16 **Zonza** Corse, France, C Mediterranean Sea
Zoppot *see* Sopot
Zorgho *see* Zorgo
77 Q13 **Zorgo** *var.* Zorgho. C Burkina
104 K10 **Zorita** Extremadura, W Spain
147 U14 **Zorkŭl** *Rus.* Ozero Zorkul'. ◎ SE Tajikistan
Zorkul', Ozero *see* Zorkŭl
56 A8 **Zorritos** Tumbes, N Peru
111 J16 **Żory** *var.* Zory, *Ger.* Sohrau. Śląskie, S Poland
76 K15 **Zorzor** N Liberia
99 E18 **Zottegem** Oost-Vlaanderen, NW Belgium
77 R15 **Zou** ⁓ S Benin
78 H6 **Zouar** Borkou-Ennedi-Tibesti, N Chad
76 J6 **Zouérat** *var.* Zouérate, Zouîrât. Tiris Zemmour, N Mauritania
Zouérate *see* Zouérat
Zoug *see* Zug
Zouîrât *see* Zouérat
76 M16 **Zoukougbeu** C Ivory Coast
98 M5 **Zoutkamp** Groningen, NE Netherlands
99 J18 **Zoutleeuw** *Fr.* Léau. Vlaams Brabant, C Belgium
112 L9 **Zrenjanin** *prev.* Petrovgrad, Veliki Bečkerek, *Ger.* Grossbetschkerek, *Hung.* Nagybecskerek. Serbia, N Serbia and Montenegro (Yugo.)
112 E10 **Zrinska Gora** ▲ C Croatia
Zsablya *see* Žabalj
101 N16 **Zschopau** ⁓ E Germany
Zsebely *see* Jebel
Zsibó *see* Jibou
Zsil/Zsily *see* Jiu
Zsilyvajdevulkán *see* Vulcan
Zsolna *see* Žilina
Zsombolya *see* Jimbolia
Zsupanya *see* Županja
55 N7 **Zuata** Anzoátegui, NE Venezuela
105 N14 **Zubia** Andalucía, S Spain
65 P16 **Zubov Seamount** *undersea feature* E Atlantic Ocean
124 I16 **Zubtsov** Tverskaya Oblast', W Russian Federation
108 M8 **Zuckerhütl** ▲ SW Austria
Zueila *see* Zawilah
76 M16 **Zuénoula** C Ivory Coast
105 S5 **Zuera** Aragón, NE Spain
141 V13 **Ẓufār** *Eng.* Dhofar. *physical region* SW Oman
108 G8 **Zug** *Fr.* Zoug. Zug, C Switzerland
108 G8 **Zug** *Fr.* Zoug. ◆ *canton* C Switzerland
137 R9 **Zugdidi** W Georgia
108 G8 **Zuger See** ◎ NW Switzerland
101 K25 **Zugspitze** ▲ S Germany
99 E15 **Zuid-Beveland** *var.* South Beveland. *island* SW Netherlands
98 K10 **Zuidelijk-Flevoland** *polder* C Netherlands
Zuider Zee *see* IJsselmeer
98 G12 **Zuid-Holland** *Eng.* South Holland. ◆ *province* W Netherlands
98 N5 **Zuidhorn** Groningen, NE Netherlands
98 O6 **Zuidlaardermeer** ◎ NE Netherlands
98 O6 **Zuidlaren** Drenthe, NE Netherlands
99 K14 **Zuid-Willemsvaart Kanaal** *canal* S Netherlands
98 N8 **Zuidwolde** Drenthe, NE Netherlands
Zuitai/Zuitaizi *see* Kangxian
105 O14 **Zújar** Andalucía, S Spain
104 L11 **Zújar** ⁓ W Spain
104 L11 **Zújar, Embalse del** ▣ W Spain
80 I9 **Zula** E Eritrea
54 G6 **Zulia** *off.* Estado Zulia. ◆ *state* NW Venezuela
Zullapara *see* Sinchaingbyin
Züllichau *see* Sulechów
105 F3 **Zumárraga** País Vasco, N Spain
112 D8 **Žumberačko Gorje** *var.* Gorjanči, Uskocke Planine, Žumberak, *Ger.* Uskokengebirge; *prev.* Sichelburger Gebirge. ▲ Croatia/Slovenia *see also* Gorjanci
Žumberak *see* Gorjanci/Žumberačko Gorje
194 K7 **Zumberge Coast** *coastal feature* Antarctica
Zumbo *see* Vila do Zumbo
29 W10 **Zumbro Falls** Minnesota, N USA
29 W10 **Zumbro River** ⁓ Minnesota, N USA
29 W10 **Zumbrota** Minnesota, N USA
99 H15 **Zundert** Noord-Brabant, S Netherlands
Zungaria *see* Dzungaria
77 U14 **Zungeru** Niger, C Nigeria
161 P2 **Zunhua** Hebei, E China
37 O11 **Zuni** New Mexico, SW USA
37 P11 **Zuni Mountains** ▲ New Mexico, SW USA
160 J11 **Zunyi** Guizhou, S China
160 J15 **Zuo Jiang** ⁓ China/Vietnam
108 J9 **Zuoz** Graubünden, SE Switzerland
112 I10 **Županja** *Hung.* Zsupanya. Vukovar-Srijem, E Croatia
113 M17 **Žur** Serbia, S Serbia and Montenegro (Yugo.)
127 T2 **Zura** Udmurtskaya Respublika, NW Russian Federation
139 V8 **Zurbāṭīyah** E Iraq
Zuri *see* Žirje
108 F7 **Zürich** *Eng./Fr.* Zurich, *It.* Zurigo. Zürich, N Switzerland
108 G6 **Zürich** *Eng./Fr.* Zurich. ◆ *canton* N Switzerland
Zurich, Lake *see* Zürichsee
108 G7 **Zürichsee** *Eng.* Lake Zurich. ◎ NE Switzerland
Zurigo *see* Zürich
149 V1 **Zūrkūl** *Pash.* Sarī Qūl, *Rus.* Ozero Zurkul'. ◎ Afghanistan/Tajikistan *see also* Sarī Qūl
Zurkul', Ozero *see* Sarī Qūl/Zūrkūl
110 K10 **Żuromin** Mazowieckie, N Poland
108 J8 **Zürs** Vorarlberg, W Austria
77 T13 **Zuru** Kebbi, W Nigeria
108 F6 **Zurzach** Aargau, N Switzerland
101 J22 **Zusam** ⁓ S Germany
98 M11 **Zutphen** Gelderland, E Netherlands
75 N7 **Zuwārah** NW Libya
Zuwaylah *see* Zawilah
125 R14 **Zuyevka** Kirovskaya Oblast', NW Russian Federation
161 N10 **Zuzhou** Hunan, S China
Zvenigorodka *see* Zvenyhorodka
117 P6 **Zvenyhorodka** *Rus.* Zvenigorodka. Cherkas'ka Oblast', C Ukraine
123 N12 **Zvezdnyy** Irkutskaya Oblast', C Russian Federation
125 U14 **Zvëzdnyy** Permskaya Oblast', NW Russian Federation
83 K18 **Zvishavane** *prev.* Shabani. Matabeleland South, S Zimbabwe
111 J20 **Zvolen** *Ger.* Altsohl, *Hung.* Zólyom. Banskobystrický Kraj, C Slovakia
112 J12 **Zvornik** E Bosnia and Herzegovina
98 M5 **Zwaagwesteinde** *Fris.* De Westerein. Friesland, N Netherlands
98 H10 **Zwanenburg** Noord-Holland, C Netherlands
98 L8 **Zwarte Meer** ◎ N Netherlands
98 M9 **Zwarte Water** ⁓ N Netherlands
98 M8 **Zwartsluis** Overijssel, E Netherlands
76 L17 **Zwedru** *var.* Tchien. E Liberia
98 O8 **Zweeloo** Drenthe, NE Netherlands
101 E20 **Zweibrücken** *Fr.* Deux-Ponts; *Lat.* Bipontium. Rheinland-Pfalz, SW Germany
108 D9 **Zweisimmen** Fribourg, W Switzerland
101 M15 **Zwenkau** Sachsen, E Germany
109 V3 **Zwettl** Wien, NE Austria
109 T3 **Zwettl an der Rodl** Oberösterreich, N Austria
99 D18 **Zwevegem** West-Vlaanderen, W Belgium
101 M17 **Zwickau** Sachsen, E Germany
101 O21 **Zwiesel** Bayern, SE Germany
98 H13 **Zwijndrecht** Zuid-Holland, SW Netherlands
101 N16 **Zwikauer Mulde** ⁓ E Germany
Zwischenwässern *see* Medvode
Zwittau *see* Svitavy
110 N13 **Zwoleń** Mazowieckie, SE Poland
98 M9 **Zwolle** Overijssel, E Netherlands
22 G6 **Zwolle** Louisiana, S USA
110 K12 **Żychlin** Łódzkie, C Poland
Żydaczów *see* Zhydachiv
119 L14 **Zyembin** *Rus.* Zembin. Minskaya Voblasts', C Belarus
Zyôetu *see* Jōetsu
110 L12 **Żyrardów** Mazowieckie, C Poland
123 S8 **Zyryanka** Respublika Sakha (Yakutiya), NE Russian Federation
145 Y9 **Zyryanovsk** Vostochnyy Kazakhstan, E Kazakhstan
111 J17 **Żywiec** *Ger.* Bäckermühle Schulzenmühle. Śląskie, S Poland

◆ Country ● Country Capital ◇ Dependent Territory ○ Dependent Territory Capital ◆ Administrative Region ✕ International Airport ▲ Mountain ▲ Mountain Range ✕ Volcano ⁓ River ◎ Lake ▣ Reservoir

Picture Credits

Dorling Kindersley would like to express their thanks to the following individuals, companies, and institutions for their help in preparing this atlas.

Earth Resource Mapping Ltd., Egham, Surrey
Brian Groombridge, World Conservation Monitoring Centre, Cambridge
The British Library, London
British Library of Political and Economic Science, London
The British Museum, London
The City Business Library, London
King's College, London
National Meteorological Library and Archive, Bracknell
The Printed Word, London
The Royal Geographical Society, London
University of London Library
Paul Beardmore
Philip Boyes
Hayley Crockford
Alistair Dougal
Reg Grant
Louise Keane
Zoe Livesley
Laura Porter
Jeff Eidenshink
Chris Hornby
Rachelle Smith
Ray Pinchard
Robert Meisner
Fiona Strawbridge

Every effort has been made to trace the copyright holders and we apologize in advance for any unintentional omissions. We would be pleased to insert the appropriate acknowledgment in any subsequent edition of this publication.

Adams Picture Library: 86CLA; **G Andrews:** 186CR; **Ardea London Ltd:** K Ghana 150C; M Iljima 132TC; R Waller 148TR; Art Directors **Aspect Picture Library:** P Carmichael 160TR; 131CR(below); G Tompkinson 190TRB; **Axiom:** C Bradley 148CA, 158CA; J Holmes xivCRA, xxivBCR, xxviiCRB, 150TCR, 165C(below), 166TL, J Morris 75TL, 77CRB, J Spaull 134BL; **Bridgeman Art Library, London / New York:** Collection of the Earl of Pembroke, Wilton House xxBC; **The J. Allan Cash Photolibrary:** xlBR, xliiCLA, xlivCL, 10BC, 60CL, 69CLB, 70CL, 72CLB, 75BR, 76BC, 87BL, 109BR, 138BCL, 141TL, 154CR, 178BR, 181TR; **Bruce Coleman Ltd:** 86BC, 98CL, 100TC; S Alden 192BC(below); Atlantide xxviTCR, 138BR; E Bjurstrom 141BR; S Bond 96CRB; T Buchholz xvCL, 92TR, 123TCL; J Burton xxiiiC; J Cancalosi 181TRB; B J Coates xxvBL, 192CL; B Coleman 63TL; B & C Colhoun 2TR, 36CB; A Compost xxiiiCBR; Dr S Coyne 45TL; G Cubitt xviTCL, 169BR, 178TR, 184TR; P Davey xxviiCLB, 121TL(below); N Devore 189CBL; S J Doylee xxiiCRR; H Flygare xviiCRA; M P L Fogden 17C(above) ; Jeff Foott Productions xxiiiCRB, 11CRA; M Freeman 91BRA; P van Gaalen 86TR; G Gualco 140C; B Henderson 194CR; Dr C Henneghien 69C; HPH Photography, H Van den Berg 69CR; C Hughes 69BCL; C James xxxixTC; J Johnson 39CR, 197TR; J Jurka 91CA; S C Kaufman 28C; S J Krasemann 33TR; H Lange 10TRB, 68CA; C Lockwood 32BC; L C Marigo xxiiBC, xxviiCLA, 49CRA, 59BR; M McCoy 187TR; D Meredith 3CR; J Murray xvCR, 179BR; Orion Press 165CR(above); Orion Services & Trading Co. Inc. 164CR; C Ott 17BL; Dr E Pott 9TR, 40CL, 87C, 93TL, 194CLB; F Prenzel 186BC, 193BC; M Read 42BR, 43CRB; H Reinhard xxiiCR, xxviiTR, 194BR; L Lee Rue III 151BCL; J Shaw xixTL; K N Swenson 194BC; P Terry 115CR; N Tomalin 54BCL; P Ward 78TC; S Widstrand 57TR; K Wothe 91C, 173TCL; J T Wright 127BR; **Colorific:** Black Star / L Mulvehil 156CL; Black Star / R Rogers 57BR; Black Star / J Rupp 161BCR; Camera Tres / C. Meyer 59BRA; R Caputo / Matrix 78CL; J. Hill 117CLB; M Koene 55TR; G Satterley xliiCLAR; M Yamashita 156BL, 167CR(above); **Comstock:** 108CRB; Corbis UK Ltd: 170TR, 170BL; **D Cousens:** 147 CRA; **Sue Cunningham Photographic:** 51CR; S Alden 192BC(below) **James Davis Travel Photography:** xxxviTCB, xxxviTR, xxxviCL, 13CA, 19BC, 49TLB, 56BCR, 57CLA, 61BCL, 93BC, 94TC, 102TR, 120CB, 158BC, 179CRA, 191BR; **G Dunnet:** 124CA; **Environmental Picture Library:** Chris Westwood 126C; **Eye Ubiquitous:** xlCA; L. Fordyce 12CLA; L Johnstone 6CRA, 28BLA, 30CB; S. Miller xxiCA; M Southern 73BLA; **Chris Fairclough Colour Library:** xliBR; **Ffotograff:** N. Tapsell 158CL **FLPA -Images of nature:** 123TR; **Geoscience Features:** xviBCR, xviBR, 102CL, 108BC, 122BR; Solar Film 64TC; **gettyone stone**: 131BC, 133BR, 164CR(above); G Johnson 130BL; R Passmore 120TR; D Austen 187CL; G Allison 186CL; L Ulrich 17TL; M Vines 17BL; R Wells 193BL; **Robert Harding Picture Library:** xviiTC, xxivCR, xxxC, xxxvTC, 2TLB, 3CA, 15CRB, 15CR, 37BC, 38CRA, 50BL, 95BR, 99CR, 114CR, 122BL, 131CLA, 142CB, 143TL, 147TR, 168TR, 168CA, 166BR; P G. Adam 13TCB; D Atchison-Jones 70BLA; J Bayne 72BCL; B Schuster 80CR; C Bowman 50BR, 53CA, 62CL, 70CRL; C Campbell xxiBC; G Corrigan 159CRB, 161CRB; P Craven xxxvBL; R Cundy 69BR; Delu 79BC; A Durand 111BR; Financial Times 142BR; R Frerck 51BL; T Gervis 3BCL, 7CR; I Griffiths xxxCL, 77TL; T Hall 166CRA; D Harney 142CA; S Harris xliiiBCL; G Hellier xvCRB, 135BL; F Jackson 137BCR; Jacobs xxxviiTL; P Koch 139TR; F Joseph Land 122TR; Y Marcoux 9BR; S Massif xvBC; A Mills 88CLB; L Murray 114TR; R Rainford xlivBL; G Renner 74CB, 194C; C Rennie 48CL, 116BR; R Richardson 118CL; P Van Riel 48BR; E Rooney 124TR; Sassoon xxivCL, 148CLB; P Scholey 176TR; M Short 137TL; E Simanor xxviiCR; V Southwell 139CR; J Strachan 42TR, 111BL, 132BCR; C Tokeley 131CLA; A C Waltham 161C; T Waltham xviiBL, xxiiCLLL, 138CRB; Westlight 37CR; N Wheeler 139BL; A Williams xxxviiiBR, xlTR; A Woolfitt 95BRA; Paul Harris: 168TC; **Hutchison Library:** 131CR (above) 6BL; P. Collomb 137CR; C. Dodwell 130TR; S Errington 70BCL; P. Hellyer 142BC; J. Horner xxxiTC; R. Ian Lloyd 134CRA; N. Durrell McKenna xxviBCR; J.Nowell 135CLB, 143TC; A Zvoznikov xxiiCL; **Image Bank:** 87BR; J Banagan 190BCA; A Becker xxivBCL; M Khansa 121CR, M Isy-Schwart 193CR(above), 191CL; Khansa K Forest 163TR; Lomeo xxivTCR; T Madison 170TL(below); C Molyneux xxiiCRRR; C Navajas xviiiTR; Ocean Images Inc. 192CLB; J van Os xviiTCR; S Proehl 6CL; T Rakke xixTC, 64CL; M Reitz 196CA; M Romanelli 166CL(below); G A Rossi 151BCR, 176BLA; B Roussel 109TL; S Satushek xviiBCR; Stock Photos / J M Spielman xxivTRL; **Images Colour Library:** xxiiCLL, xxxixTR, xliCR, xliiiBL, 3BR, 19BR, 37TL, 44TL, 62TC, 91BR, 102CLB, 103CR, 150CL, 180CA; 164BC, 165TL; **Impact Photos:** J & G Andrews 186BL; C. Bluntzer 156BR; Cosmos / G. Buthaud 65BC; S Franklin 126BL; A. le Garsmeur 131C; A Indge xxviiTC; C Jones xxxiCB, 70BL; V. Nemirousky 137BR; J Nicholl 76TCR; C. Penn 187C(below); G Sweeney xviiBR, 196CB, 196TR, J & G Andrews 186TR; **JVZ Picture Library:** T Nilson 135TC; **Frank Lane Picture Agency:** xxiTCR, xxiiiBL, 93TR; A Christiansen 58CRA; J Holmes xivBL; S. McCutcheon 3C; Silvestris 173TCR; D Smith xxiiBCL; W Wisniewsli 195BR; **Leeds Castle Foundation:** xxxviiBC; **Magnum:** Abbas 83CR, 136CA; S Franklin 134CRB; D Hurn 4BCL; P. Jones-Griffiths 191BL; H Kubota xviBCL, 156CLB; F Maver xviBL; S McCurry 73CL, 133BCR; G. Rodger 74TR; C Steele Perkins 72BL; **Mountain Camera / John Cleare:** 153TR; C Monteath 153CR; **Nature Photographers:** E.A. Janes 112CL; **Natural Science Photos:** M Andera 110C; **Network Photographers Ltd.:** C Sappa / Rapho 119BL; **N.H.P.A.:** N. J. Dennis xxiiiCL; D Heuchlin xxiiiCLA; S Krasemann 15BL, 25BR, 38TC; K Schafer 49CB; R Tidman 160CLB; D Tomlinson 145CR; M Wendler 48TR; **Nottingham Trent University:** T Waltham xivCL, xvBR; **Novosti:** 144BLA; **Oxford Scientific Films:** D Allan xxiiTR; H R Bardarson xviiiBC; D Bown xxiiiCBLL; M Brown 140BL; M Colbeck 147CAR; W Faidley 3TL; L Gould xxiiiTRB; D Guravich xxiiiTR; P Hammerschmidy / Okapia 87CLA; M Hill 57TL, 195TR; C Menteath ; J Netherton 2CRB; S Osolinski 82CA; R Packwood 72CA; M Pitts 179TC; N Rosing xxiiiCBL, 9TR, 197BR; D Simonson 57C; Survival Anglia / C Catton 137TR; R Toms xxiiiBR; K Wothe xxiBL, xviiCLA; **Panos Pictures:** B Aris 133C; P Barker xxivBR; T Bolstao 153BR; N Cooper 82CB, 153TC; J-L Dugast 166C(below), 167BR; J Hartley 73CA, 90CL; J Holmes 149BC; J Morris 76CLB; M Rose 146TR; D Sansoni 155CL; C Stowers 163TL; **Edward Parker:** 49TL, 49CLB; **Pictor International:** xivBR, xvBRA, xixTCL, xxCL, 3CLA, 17BR, 20TR, 20CRB, 23BCA, 23CL, 26CB, 27BC, 30CA, 33TRB, 34BC, 34BR, 34CR, 38CB, 38CL, 43CL, 63BR, 65TC, 82CL, 83CLB, 99BR, 107CLA, 166TR, 171CL(above), 180CLB, 185TL; **Pictures Colour Library:** xxiBCL, xxiiBR, xxviBCL, 6BR, 15TR, 8TR, 16CL(above), 19TL, 20BL, 24C, 24CLA, 27TR, 32TRB, 36BC, 41CA, 43CRA, 68BL, 90TCB, 94BL, 99BL, 106CA, 107CLB, 107CR, 107BR, 117BL, 164BC, 192BL, K Forest 165TL(below); **Planet Earth Pictures:** 193CR(below); D Barrett 148CB, 184CA; R Coomber 16BL; G Douwma 172BR; E Edmonds 173BR; J Lythgoe 196BL; A Mounter 172CR; M Potts 6CA; P Scoones xxTR; J Walencik 110TR; J Waters 53BCL; **Popperfoto:** Reuters / J Drake xxxiiCLA; **Rex Features:** 165CR; Antelope xxxiiCLB; M Friedel xxiCR; I McIlgorm xxxCBR; J Shelley xxxCR; Sipa Press xxxCR; Sipa Press / Alix xxxCBL; Sipa Press / Chamussy 176BL; **Robert Harding Picture Library:** C. Tokeley 131TL; J Strachan 132BL; Franz Joseph Land 122TR; Franz Joseph Land 364/7088 123BL, 169C(above), 170C(above), 168CL, Tony Waltham 186CR(below), Y Marcoux 9BR; **Russia & Republics Photolibrary:** M Wadlow 118CR, 119CL, 124BC, 124CL, 125TL, 125BR, 126TCR; **Science Photo Library:** Earth Satellite Corporation xixTRB, xxxiCR, 49BCL; F Gohier xiCR; J Heseltine xviTCB; K Kent xvBLA; P Menzell xvBL; N.A.S.A. xBC; D Parker xivBC; University of Cambridge Collection Air Pictures 87CLB; RJ Wainscoat / P Arnold, Inc. xiBC; D Weintraub xiBL; **South American Pictures:** 57BL, 62TR; R Francis 52BL; Guyana Space Centre 50TR; T Morrison 49CRB, 49BL, 50CR, 52TR, 54TR, 60BL, 61C; **Southampton Oceanography:** xviiiBL; **Sovofoto / Eastfoto:** xxxiiCBR; **Spectrum Colour Library:** 50BC, 160BC; J King 145BR; **Frank Spooner Pictures:** Gamma-Liason/Vogel 131CL(above); 26CRB; E. Baitel xxxiiBC; Bernstein xxxiCL; Contrast 112CR; Diard / Photo News 113CL; Liaison / C. Hires xxxiiTCB; Liaison / Nickelsberg xxxiiTR; Marleen 113TL; Novosti 116CA; P. Piel xxxCA; N Quidu 135CL; H Stucke 188CLB, 190CA; Torrengo / Figaro 78BR; A Zamur 113BL; **Still Pictures:** C Caldicott 77TC; A Crump 189CL; M & C Denis-Huot xxiiBL, 78CR, 81BL; M Edwards xxiCRL, 53BL, 64CR, 69BLA, 155BR; J Frebet 53CLB; H Giradet 53TC; E Parker 52CL; M Gunther 121BC; **Tony Stone Images:** xxviTR, 4CA, 7BL, 7CL, 13CRB, 39BR, 58C, 97BC, 101BR, 106TR, 109CL, 109CRB, 164CLB, 165C,180CB, 181BR, 188BC, 192TR; G Allison 18TR, 31CRB, 187CRB; D Armand 14TCB; D Austen 180TR, 186CL, 187CL; J Beatty 74CL; O Benn xxviBR; K Biggs xxiTL; R Bradbury 44BR; R A Butcher xxviTL; J Callahan xxviiCRA; P Chesley 185BCL, 188C; W Clay 30BL, 31CRA; J Cornish 96BL, 107TL; C Condina 41CB; T Craddock xxivTR; P Degginger 36CLB; Demetrio 5BR; N DeVore xxivBC; A Diesendruck 60BR; S Egan 87CRA, 96BR; R Elliot xxiiBCR; S Elmore 19C; J Garrett 73CR; S Grandadam 14BR; R Grosskopf 28BL; D Hanson 104BC; C Harvey 69TL; G Hellier 110BL, 165CR; S Huber 103CRB; D Hughs xxxiBR; A Husmo 91TR; G Irvine 31BC; J Jangoux 58CL; D Johnston xviiTR; A Kehr 113C; R Koskas xviTR; J Lamb 96CRA; J Lawrence 75CRA; L Lefkowitz 7CA; M Lewis 45CLA; S Mayman 55BR; Murray & Associates 45CR; G Norways 104CA; N Parfitt xxviiCL, 68TCR, 81TL; R Passmore 121TR; N Press xviBCA; E Pritchard 88CA, 90CLR; T Raymond 21BL, 29TR; L Resnick 74BR; M Rogers 80BR; A Sacks 28TCB; C Saule 90CR; S Schulhof xxivTC; P Seaward 34CL; M Segal 32BL; V Shenai 152CL; R Sherman 26CL; H Sitton 136CR; R Smith xxvBLA, 56C; S Studd 108CLA; H Strand 49BR, 63TR; P Tweedie 177CR; L Ulrich 17BL; M Vines 17TC; A B Wadham 60CR; J Warden 63CLB; R Wells 23CRA, 193BL; G Yeowell 34BL; **Telegraph Colour Library:** 61CRB, 61TCR, 157TL; R Antrobus xxxixBR; J Sims 26BR; **Topham Picturepoint:** xxxiCBL, 162BR, 168TR, 168BC; **Travel Ink:** A Cowin 88TR; **Trip:** 140BR, 144CA, 155CRA; B Ashe 159TR; D Cole 190BCL, 190CR; D Davis 89BL; I Deineko xxxiTR; J Dennis 22BL; Dinodia 154CL; Eye Ubiquitous / L Fordyce 2CLB; A Gasson 149CR; W Jacobs 43TL, 54BL, 177BC, 178CLA, 185BCR, 186BL; P Kingsbury 112C; K Knight 177BR; V Kolpakov 147BL; T Noorits 87TL, 119BR, 146CL; R Power 41TR; N Ray 166BL, 168TC; C Rennie 116CLB; V Sidoropolev 145TR; E Smith 183BC, 183TL; **Woodfin Camp & Associates:** 92BLR; **World Pictures:** xvCRA, xviiCRA, 9CRB, 22CL, 23BC, 24BL, 35BL, 40TR, 51TR, 71BR, 80TCR, 82TR, 83BL, 86BCR, 96TC, 98BL, 100CR, 101CR, 103BC, 105TC, 157BL, 161BCL, 162CLB, 172CLB, 172BC, 179BL, 182CB, 183C, 184CL, 185CR; 121BR, 121TT; **Zefa Picture Library:** xviBLR, xviiBCL, xviiiCL, 3CL, 8BC, 8CT, 9CR, 13BC, 14TC, 16TR, 21TL, 22CRB, 25BL, 32TCR, 36BCR, 59BCL, 65TCL, 69CLA, 79TL, 81BR, 87CRB, 92C, 98C, 99TL, 100BL, 107TR, 118CRB, 120BL; 122C(below), 124CLA, 164BR, 183TR; Anatol 113BR; Barone 114BL; Brandenburg 5C; A J Brown 44TR; H J Clauss 55CLB; Damm 71BC; Evert 92BL; W Felger 3BL; J Fields 189CRA; R Frerck 4BL; G Heil 56BR; K Heibig 115BR; Heilman 28BC; Hunter 8C; Kitchen 10TR, 8CL, 8BL, 9TR; Dr H Kramarz 7BLA, 123CR(below); Mehlio 155BL; J F Raga 24TR; Rossenbach 105BR; Streichan 89TL; T Stewart 13TR, 19CR; Sunak 54BR, 162TR; D H Teuffen 95TL; B Zaunders 40BC. **Additional Photography:** Geoff Dann; Rob Reichenfeld; H Taylor; Jerry Young.